Headquarters USA

A Directory of Contact Information for Headquarters and Other Central Offices of Major Businesses & Organizations in the United States and in Canada

2018

40th EDITION

Volume 1:
Alphabetical by Organization Name

Mailing Addresses, Telephone Numbers, Toll-Free Phone Numbers, Fax Numbers, and World Wide Web Addresses for:

- Associations, Foundations, and Similar Organizations
- Businesses, Industries, and Professions of All Types
- Colleges, Universities, Vocational & Technical Schools, and Other Educational Institutions
- Electronic Resources, including Internet Companies, Organizations, and Web Sites
- Embassies, Consulates, and UN Missions & Agencies
- Government Agencies & Offices at All Levels — City, County, State, Federal
- Libraries, Museums & Galleries, Zoos & Botanical Gardens, Performing Arts Organizations & Facilities, and Other Cultural Institutions
- Media Newspapers, Magazines, Newsletters; and Radio & Television Companies, Networks, Stations and Syndicators
- Research Centers & Organizations, including Scientific, Public Policy, and Market Research
- Professional Sports Teams, Other Sports Organizations, and Sports Facilities

and also including an Area/Zip Code Guide Covering more than 12,000 US Cities and Towns, as well as Area Code Tables in State & Numerical Order; and a detailed Index to Classified Headings under which listings are organized in the Directory's Classified Section.

Omnigraphics

Omnigraphics

Pearline Jaikumar, *Editor*
Karthikeyan Ponnambalam, *Research Manager*

* * *

ISBN 978-0-7808-1604-6

ISSN 1531-2909

Printed in the United States of America

Omnigraphics
615 Griswold, Ste. 901, Detroit, MI 48226
Phone Orders: 800-234-1340 • Fax Orders: 800-875-1340
Mail Orders: P.O. Box 8002 • Aston, PA 19014-8002
www.omnigraphics.com

Table of Contents

Volume 1:
Alphabetical by Organization Name

Volume 2:
Classified by Subject

How To Use This Directory

Headquarters USA lists headquarters and other central offices for the largest and most important businesses, organizations, agencies, and institutions in the United States. Listings also are included for top Canadian businesses and organizations.

The 2018 edition of *Headquarters USA* contains 129,516 listings, presented by name and by subject. Individual listings in both the Alphabetical and Classified sections present each company or organization name along with its full address and telephone number. Most listings also include fax numbers (49,890) and web sites (123,512), and 55,667 listings include toll-free telephone numbers. Trading symbols and corresponding stock exchanges are provided for 2,849 publicly traded companies.

Research and Verification a Year-Round Effort

Headquarters USA is compiled by a team of experienced editorial personnel who research the information to be published in the directory on a year-round basis. Data are verified as accurate by direct contact with the companies and organizations listed, and this effort is also carried out continuously.

Preparation of *Headquarters USA* includes not only the addition of completely new types of information but also the re-evaluation of listing criteria for some of the existing categories of information. This may result in changes in the number of listings published for certain categories—for instance, some very large subject categories may be reduced in size to allow for the introduction of completely new categories of information; a relatively small subject category may be expanded to provide more significant companies in that area; or, in some cases, new, more specific categories may be developed from larger, existing categories that are more general in nature.

What's Included in *Headquarters USA?*

Headquarters USA provides detailed, accurate contact information for a wide range of US and Canadian **businesses, professions, and organizations,** including:

- agricultural establishments
- associations & organizations
- Better Business Bureaus
- colleges & universities
- consulates & embassies
- building & construction industries
- chambers of commerce
- convention centers
- cultural organizations
- financial institutions
- foundations
- government offices
- internet resources
- libraries
- manufacturing companies
- media & communications
- military bases
- mining companies
- political organizations
- research centers
- retail sales
- service industries
- sports teams
- transportation and utilities
- United Nations missions
- wholesalers & distributors
- world trade centers

Criteria for Listing

For the most part, criteria employed in selecting listings for *Headquarters USA* parallel the ranking systems used by the industries represented. A variety of resources are used in gathering rankings data, including "top lists" compiled by associations as well as those found in business magazines and other published sources.

Most ranking schemes are based on annual sales, and this is reflected in the selection of data for *Headquarters USA*. However, other criteria are employed as well. For example, hospitals are selected on the basis of the number of beds available, law firms are selected according to the number of attorneys in the firm, newspapers are chosen by circulation, and so on.

It should be noted that some companies are listed even if they don't meet the listing criterion established for that particular type of business. Examples of this include some companies that are involved in new technologies, companies that are publicly traded on major US stock exchanges, and subsidiaries or divisions of certain large companies, provided that the parent company meets the criterion.

Special Features

- a United States map denoting **time zones**;
- **area code** tables that provide up-to-date lists of all valid US telephone area codes in state and area code order;
- tables of **abbreviations** — one that lists the standard abbreviations used throughout *Headquarters USA* and another providing two-letter state and Canadian province abbreviations;

- a **Classified Headings Table** that lists all of the subject categories under which listings appear in the Classified Section;
- an **Area Code and Zip Code Guide** listing area codes and zip codes for the more than 12,000 US cities in which the companies and organizations listed in *Headquarters USA* are located. Information is presented in alphabetical order by city name, with the area code(s) and zip code(s) provided for each city; and
- an **Index to Classified Headings** that identifies all of the subject headings under which listings are organized in the Classified Section of *Headquarters USA*. The index also includes "See" and "See also" references to help guide users to appropriate subject categories. The number given with each index citation refers to the page on which a particular subject category begins.

How Do I Find What I'm Looking For?

The overall arrangement of *Headquarters USA* is much like that found in a local telephone directory and is just as easy to use. Listings are organized in two main sections: an **Alphabetical Section** and a **Classified Section**. As the names suggest, the Alphabetical Section presents listings alphabetically, by company or organization name, and the Classified Section presents the same information in a classified subject arrangement according to business or organization type. For the most part, listings appear at least once in both sections of the directory.

Listings in the Classified Section are organized according to organization type or, for businesses, a company's primary business activity. At least one classified listing is provided for each company or organization included in *Headquarters USA*, but very large companies that conduct business in a variety of areas may be listed more than once so that the company is represented in all appropriate subject categories.

Some of the subject headings in the Classified Section also include information about listing criteria, other explanatory comments, or notes regarding a special arrangement of listings (i.e., while listings generally appear in alphabetical order within each classified subject category, some information is grouped by state or city name within a particular subject, with listings then alphabetized within this framework).

- **Alphabetizing *in Headquarters USA***

Alphabetizing throughout *Headquarters USA* is on a word-by-word, rather than letter-by-letter, basis. No distinction is made between upper and lower case letters, and articles, conjunctions, and most prepositions are ignored for sorting purposes. Names that begin with symbols or numerals rather than letters file first. Symbols that may accompany numerals (e.g., a pound sign [#] or dollar sign [$]) are ignored for alphabetical sorting.

The following example illustrates these alphabetizing rules:

1 on 1 Computing
$1 Sunglasses Ltd
3M Co
All Weather Vacuuming
C & S Inc
Calido Hotels
Cambridge Fire Insurance
Damon Corp
DAS Co
Data Generation Inc
La Quinta Motor Inns
Laacke Co

- **Classification Codes**

The subject headings under which listings appear in the Classified Section are numbered sequentially, and these numbered headings are duplicated in the Classified Headings Table that precedes the Classified Section. The numbers are also used as "classification codes" that appear in the "Class" column to the right of listings in the Alphabetical Section. Users of the Alphabetical Section can quickly determine a company's principal business activity by simply matching the "Class" number for a particular listing to the corresponding subject heading number. (This "linking" mechanism is illustrated in the sample pages and accompanying explanatory comments presented just inside the back cover of this directory.)

Some listings in the Classified Section are organized under a second level of subheadings within a broader category named in a heading. In situations where there are two levels of headings, two levels of classification codes are given as well. For instance, if a heading numbered as 200 is followed by a series of subheadings, the first subheading would be numbered 200-1, the second would be 200-2, and so on. Headings that have been created *only* to provide a reference to another heading category (i.e., "See" references) are not numbered.

Content of Individual Listings

Each listing in *Headquarters USA* consists of the formal name of the company, organization, institution, or government office; street or other mailing address; city, state, and zip code; and telephone number (with area code). Fax numbers also are provided for most listings, and, where available, toll-free numbers are given as well. Most listings also include web sites. Trading symbols and corresponding stock exchanges are provided for Public companies.

- **Company and Organization Names**

  As a general rule, complete official names are given for companies and organizations listed in *Headquarters USA*. In the case of listings for companies that are clearly named after individuals, information usually is presented both by the person's first name *and* by the last name. For example, Matthew Bender & Co Inc would be listed that way and as Bender Matthew & Co Inc; LL Bean Inc would also be listed as Bean LL Inc; and so on. However, listings in the people categories (such as US Senators, Representatives, Delegates) are always presented with the last name first—e.g., Leahy Patrick, but not Patrick Leahy. Companies that are well known by an acronym or initialism—for example, IBM—usually are listed both by acronym and by full name (i.e., "IBM" and "International Business Machines Corp").

- **Addresses**

  Addresses provided in this directory usually are street addresses, unless mail cannot be accepted at a particular location, in which case a post office box or other mailing address is provided. All listings also include the city, state (or province, if Canadian), and zip code (five-digit for US listings, six-digit for Canadian listings).

- **Telephone Numbers**

  Phone numbers listed in *Headquarters USA* are for the main switchboard of a company or organization. Area codes are included with all telephone numbers listed.

- **Fax Numbers**

  Most fax listings provided in *Headquarters USA* represent a company's direct facsimile number. In instances where this is not the case, an asterisk appears next to the fax number and a brief explanatory note is inserted below the name/address data (example: **Fax:* Cust Svc indicates that the fax number given is for the company's Customer Service department).

  Since fax area codes are almost always the same as the telephone area code, the area code given with the phone number is not repeated with the fax number. However, if the area code for the fax number is *different* from the telephone area code, an asterisk appears to the right of the fax number, indicating that the correct area code is provided below the company name and address.

- **Toll-Free Telephone Numbers**

  Toll-free numbers are listed below the company or organization's name and address. If the number given is intended for a specific use (e.g., for orders, technical support, customer service, sales, etc.), a notation is included to that effect.

- **Web Sites**

  Web sites are provided for 123,512 listings in this edition. The "http://" that begins most web site addresses is ***not*** included with that information here.

- **Stock Exchange Information**

  Trading symbols and corresponding stock exchanges are given as bulleted items under the individual listings for publicly traded companies in both the Alphabetical and Classified sections of the book.

Comments Welcome

The editors and staff of *Headquarters USA* are committed to maintaining the highest degree of accuracy possible, and our efforts to provide the most up-to-date information available are ongoing. Comments from readers concerning this publication, including suggestions for additions and improvements, are welcome. Please send to:

> Editor — *Headquarters USA*
> Omnigraphics
> 615 Griswold, Ste. 901
> Detroit, MI 48226
> editorial@omnigraphics.com

TIME ZONES MAP

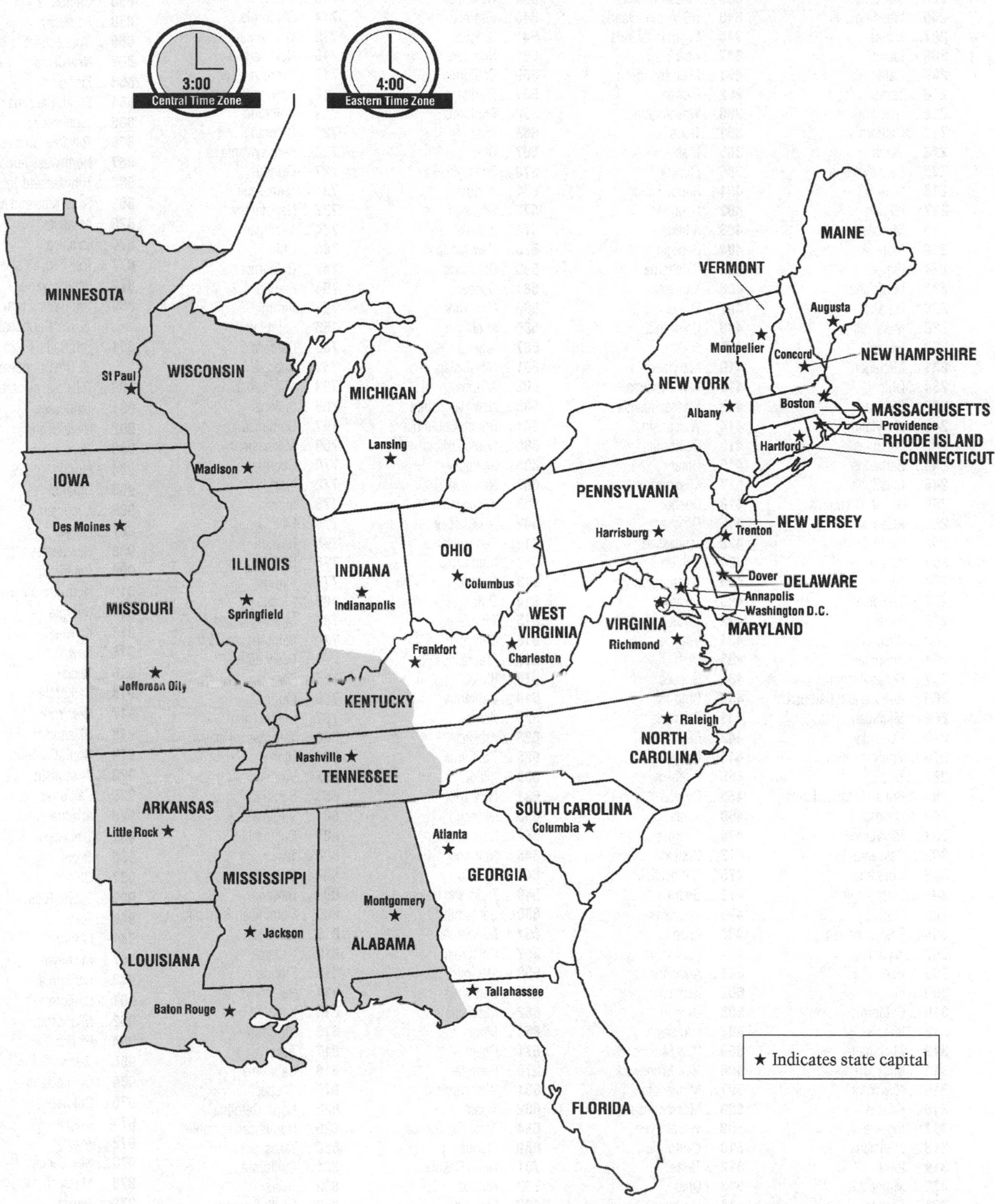

3:00
Central Time Zone
4:00
Eastern Time Zone
MINNESOTA
St Paul
WISCONSIN
Madison
IOWA
Des Moines
ILLINOIS
Springfield
MISSOURI
Jefferson City
MICHIGAN
Lansing
INDIANA
Indianapolis
OHIO
Columbus
KENTUCKY
Frankfort
TENNESSEE
Nashville
ARKANSAS
Little Rock
MISSISSIPPI
Jackson
LOUISIANA
Baton Rouge
ALABAMA
Montgomery
GEORGIA
Atlanta
FLORIDA
Tallahassee
SOUTH CAROLINA
Columbia
NORTH CAROLINA
Raleigh
VIRGINIA
Richmond
WEST VIRGINIA
Charleston
PENNSYLVANIA
Harrisburg
NEW YORK
Albany
MAINE
Augusta
VERMONT
Montpelier
NEW HAMPSHIRE
Concord
MASSACHUSETTS
Boston
RHODE ISLAND
Providence
CONNECTICUT
Hartford
NEW JERSEY
Trenton
DELAWARE
Dover
MARYLAND
Annapolis
Washington D.C.
★ Indicates state capital

Area Codes in Numerical Order

201 ... New Jersey
202 ... District of Columbia
203 ... Connecticut
204 ... Manitoba
205 ... Alabama
206 ... Washington
207 ... Maine
208 ... Idaho
209 ... California
210 ... Texas
212 ... New York
213 ... California
214 ... Texas
215 ... Pennsylvania
216 ... Ohio
217 ... Illinois
218 ... Minnesota
219 ... Indiana
224 ... Illinois
225 ... Louisiana
226 ... Ontario
228 ... Mississippi
229 ... Georgia
231 ... Michigan
234 ... Ohio
239 ... Florida
240 ... Maryland
242 ... Bahamas
246 ... Barbados
248 ... Michigan
250 ... British Columbia
251 ... Alabama
252 ... North Carolina
253 ... Washington
254 ... Texas
256 ... Alabama
260 ... Indiana
262 ... Wisconsin
264 ... Anguilla
267 ... Pennsylvania
268 ... Antigua and Barbuda
269 ... Michigan
270 ... Kentucky
276 ... Virginia
281 ... Texas
284 ... British Virgin Islands
289 ... Ontario
301 ... Maryland
302 ... Delaware
303 ... Colorado
304 ... West Virginia
305 ... Florida
306 ... Saskatchewan
307 ... Wyoming
308 ... Nebraska
309 ... Illinois
310 ... California
312 ... Illinois
313 ... Michigan
314 ... Missouri
315 ... New York
316 ... Kansas
317 ... Indiana
318 ... Louisiana
319 ... Iowa
320 ... Minnesota
321 ... Florida
323 ... California
325 ... Texas
330 ... Ohio
331 ... Illinois
334 ... Alabama
336 ... North Carolina
337 ... Louisiana
339 ... Massachusetts
340 ... US Virgin Islands
345 ... Cayman Islands
347 ... New York
351 ... Massachusetts
352 ... Florida
360 ... Washington
361 ... Texas
385 ... Utah
386 ... Florida
401 ... Rhode Island
402 ... Nebraska
403 ... Alberta
404 ... Georgia
405 ... Oklahoma
406 ... Montana
407 ... Florida
408 ... California
409 ... Texas
410 ... Maryland
412 ... Pennsylvania
413 ... Massachusetts
414 ... Wisconsin
415 ... California
416 ... Ontario
417 ... Missouri
418 ... Quebec
419 ... Ohio
423 ... Tennessee
424 ... California
425 ... Washington
430 ... Texas
432 ... Texas
434 ... Virginia
435 ... Utah
438 ... Quebec
440 ... Ohio
441 ... Bermuda
442 ... California
443 ... Maryland
450 ... Quebec
458 ... Oregon
469 ... Texas
470 ... Georgia
473 ... Grenada
475 ... Connecticut
478 ... Georgia
479 ... Arkansas
480 ... Arizona
484 ... Pennyslvania
501 ... Arkansas
502 ... Kentucky
503 ... Oregon
504 ... Louisiana
505 ... New Mexico
506 ... New Brunswick
507 ... Minnesota
508 ... Massachusetts
509 ... Washington
510 ... California
512 ... Texas
513 ... Ohio
514 ... Quebec
515 ... Iowa
516 ... New York
517 ... Michigan
518 ... New York
519 ... Ontario
520 ... Arizona
530 ... California
534 ... Wisconsin
540 ... Virginia
541 ... Oregon
551 ... New Jersey
559 ... California
561 ... Florida
562 ... California
563 ... Iowa
567 ... Ohio
570 ... Pennsylvania
571 ... Virginia
573 ... Missouri
574 ... Indiana
575 ... New Mexico
580 ... Oklahoma
581 ... Quebec
585 ... New York
586 ... Michigan
587 ... Alberta
601 ... Mississippi
602 ... Arizona
603 ... New Hampshire
604 ... British Columbia
605 ... South Dakota
606 ... Kentucky
607 ... New York
608 ... Wisconsin
609 ... New Jersey
610 ... Pennsylvania
612 ... Minnesota
613 ... Ontario
614 ... Ohio
615 ... Tennessee
616 ... Michigan
617 ... Massachusetts
618 ... Illinois
619 ... California
620 ... Kansas
623 ... Arizona
626 ... California
630 ... Illinois
631 ... New York
636 ... Missouri
641 ... Iowa
646 ... New York
647 ... Ontario
649 ... Turks and Caicos
650 ... California
651 ... Minnesota
657 ... California
660 ... Missouri
661 ... California
662 ... Mississippi
664 ... Montserrat
671 ... Guam
678 ... Georgia
681 ... West Virginia
682 ... Texas
684 ... American Samoa
689 ... Florida
701 ... North Dakota
702 ... Nevada
703 ... Virginia
704 ... North Carolina
705 ... Ontario
706 ... Georgia
707 ... California
708 ... Illinois
709 ... Newfoundland
712 ... Iowa
713 ... Texas
714 ... California
715 ... Wisconsin
716 ... New York
717 ... Pennsylvania
718 ... New York
719 ... Colorado
720 ... Colorado
724 ... Pennsylvania
727 ... Florida
731 ... Tennessee
732 ... New Jersey
734 ... Michigan
740 ... Ohio
747 ... California
754 ... Florida
757 ... Virginia
758 ... Saint Lucia
760 ... California
762 ... Georgia
763 ... Minnesota
765 ... Indiana
767 ... Dominica
769 ... Mississippi
770 ... Georgia
772 ... Florida
773 ... Illinois
774 ... Massachusetts
775 ... Nevada
778 ... British Columbia
779 ... Illinois
780 ... Alberta
781 ... Massachusetts
784 ... Saint Vincent & the Grenadines
785 ... Kansas
786 ... Florida
787 ... Puerto Rico
800 ... Toll-free; all states
801 ... Utah
802 ... Vermont
803 ... South Carolina
804 ... Virginia
805 ... California
806 ... Texas
807 ... Ontario
808 ... Hawaii
809 ... Dominican Republic
810 ... Michigan
812 ... Indiana
813 ... Florida
814 ... Pennsylvania
815 ... Illinois
816 ... Missouri
817 ... Texas
818 ... California
819 ... Quebec
828 ... North Carolina
829 ... Dominican Republic
830 ... Texas
831 ... California
832 ... Texas
843 ... South Carolina
845 ... New York
847 ... Illinois
848 ... New Jersey
850 ... Florida
855 ... Toll-free; all states
856 ... New Jersey
857 ... Massachusetts
858 ... California
859 ... Kentucky
860 ... Connecticut
862 ... New Jersey
863 ... Florida
864 ... South Carolina
865 ... Tennessee
866 ... Toll-free; all states
867 ... NorthWest Territories
868 ... Trinidad and Tobago
869 ... Saint Kitts and Nevis
870 ... Arkansas
876 ... Jamaica
877 ... Toll-free; all states
878 ... Pennsylvania
880 ... Toll Calls: From Canada & The Caribbean
881 ... Toll Calls: From Canada & The Caribbean
888 ... Toll-free; all states
901 ... Tennessee
902 ... Nova Scotia
903 ... Texas
904 ... Florida
905 ... Ontario
906 ... Michigan
907 ... Alaska
908 ... New Jersey
909 ... California
910 ... North Carolina
912 ... Georgia
913 ... Kansas
914 ... New York
915 ... Texas
916 ... California
917 ... New York
918 ... Oklahoma
919 ... North Carolina
920 ... Wisconsin
925 ... California
928 ... Arizona
931 ... Tennessee
936 ... Texas
937 ... Ohio
939 ... Puerto Rico
940 ... Texas
941 ... Florida
947 ... Michigan
949 ... California
951 ... California
952 ... Minnesota
954 ... Florida
956 ... Texas
959 ... Connecticut
970 ... Colorado
971 ... Oregon
972 ... Texas
973 ... New Jersey
978 ... Massachusetts
979 ... Texas
980 ... North Carolina
985 ... Louisiana
989 ... Michigan

Area Codes in State Order

Alabama
205 Birmingham & Tuscaloosa
251 Southwest
256 North & East Central
334 South

Alaska
907 All locations

American Samoa
684 All locations

Arizona
480 East of Phoenix including Tempe & Scottsdale
520 Southeast
602 Phoenix
623 West of Phoenix including Glendale
928 Most of State except South Central & Southeast areas

Arkansas
479 West Central & Northwest
501 Little Rock & surrounding areas
870 East & South

California
209 Central
213 Los Angeles
310 Long Beach/West
323 Los Angeles
408 West Central
415 San Francisco
424 Long Beach/West
442 Southeast except San Diego Area
510 Oakland
530 North
559 Central
562 Long Beach
619 San Diego & surrounding area (except North)
626 Pasadena/East
650 South of San Francisco
657 Northern Orange County
661 Bakersfield & Northern La County
707 Northwest
714 Northern Orange County
747 Burbank & Glendale Area
760 Southeast except San Diego Area
805 South
818 Burbank & Glendale Area
831 West Central
858 San Diego/North
909 San Bernardino & surrounding area
916 Sacramento & surrounding area
925 East of Oakland
949 Southern Orange County
951 Riverside & surrounding area (except North)

Canada
204 All locations in Manitoba
226 Southern Ontario
250 Outside Vancouver Area including Vancouver Island
289 North of Toronto
306 All locations in Saskatchewan
403 Southern Alberta
416 Toronto
418 Eastern Quebec
438 Montreal Metro Area
450 Outside Montreal Metro Area
506 All locations in New Brunswick
514 Montreal Metro Area
519 Southern Ontario
581 Eastern Quebec
587 All locations in Alberta
604 Vancouver Area
613 Northeast of Toronto
647 Toronto
705 Eastern Ontario
709 All locations in Newfoundland
778 Vancouver Area
780 Central & Northern Alberta
807 Western Ontario
819 Western Quebec
867 All locations in Yukon & Northwest Territories
902 All locations in Nova Scotia & Prince Edward Island
905 North of Toronto

Caribbean, Bahamas & Bermuda
242 Bahamas
246 Barbados
264 Anguilla
268 Antigua & Barbuda
284 British Virgin Islands
340 US Virgin Islands
345 Cayman Islands
441 Bermuda
473 Grenada
649 Turks & Caicos
664 Montserrat
758 Saint Lucia
767 Dominica
784 Saint Vincent & Grenadines
787 Puerto Rico
809 Dominican Republic
829 Dominican Republic
868 Trinidad & Tobago
869 Saint Kitts & Nevis
876 Jamaica
939 Puerto Rico

Colorado
303 Denver
719 South & East
720 Denver
970 West & North

Connecticut
203 Southwest
475 Southwest
860 Except Southwest
959 Except Southwest

Delaware
302 All locations

District of Columbia
202 All locations

Florida
239 Southwest (Lee, Collier & part of Monroe Counties)
305 Southeast
321 Central & East Central
352 Gainesville, Ocala & surrounding areas
386 Northeast except Jacksonville, St. Augustine & surrounding areas
407 Central
561 Palm Beach County
689 Central & East Central
727 Saint Petersburg/Clearwater
754 Fort Lauderdale & surrounding area
772 Martin, St. Lucie, Indian River & part of Brevard Counties
786 Southeast
813 Tampa
850 Northwest
863 South Central
904 Jacksonville, St. Augustine & surrounding areas
941 Southwest (Sarasota, Char Lotte & Manatee Counties)
954 Fort Lauderdale & surrounding area

Georgia
229 Southwest
404 Atlanta
470 Atlanta & surrounding area
478 Central
678 Atlanta Area
706 North except Atlanta Area
762 North except Atlanta Area
770 Atlanta suburbs
912 Southeast

Guam
671 All locations

Hawaii
808 All locations

Idaho
208 All locations

Illinois
217 Central
224 Suburban Chicago
309 West
312 Chicago
331 Northeast
618 South
630 Northeast
708 Northeast
773 Chicago (outside central commercial area)
779 North
815 North
847 Suburban Chicago

Indiana
219 North West
260 Northeast
317 Indianapolis Metro Area
574 North Central
765 Central except Indianapolis Metro Area
812 South

Iowa
319 East Central
515 Central including Des Moines & Ames
563 East
641 South central & East Central
712 West

Kansas
316 Wichita & surrounding area
620 South except Wichita & surrounding area
785 North except Kansas City
913 Kansas City

Kentucky
270 West & Central
502 North including Louisville
606 East
859 North Central

Louisiana
225 East Central
318 North & West
337 West Central & Southwest
504 New Orleans Area
985 Southeast except New Orleans Area

Maine
207 All locations

Maryland
240 West
301 West
410 East
443 East

Massachusetts
339 Outside Metro Boston
351 North
413 West
508 Southeast
617 Boston Metro Area
774 Southeast
781 Outside Metro Boston
857 Boston Metro Area
978 North

Michigan
231 Northwest
248 East (Oakland County)
269 Southwest
313 Detroit & inner suburbs
517 South Central
586 East (Macomb County)
616 West/Southwest
734 West of Detroit
810 East (except Oakland & Macomb Counties)
906 North
947 East (Oakland County)
989 Central

Minnesota
218 North
320 Central except Minneapolis/Saint Paul Metro Area
507 South
612 Minneapolis
651 Saint Paul & East Central
763 Suburbs North & Northwest of Minneapolis
952 Suburbs South & Southwest of Minneapolis

Mississippi
228 Gulfport/Biloxi & surrounding area
601 South except Gulfport/Biloxi & surrounding area
662 North
769 South except Gulfport/Biloxi & surrounding area

Missouri
314 Saint Louis
417 Southwest
573 East except Saint Louis Metro Area
636 East (outside Saint Louis)
660 North except Kansas City & Saint Joseph
816 Kansas City & Saint Joseph

Montana
406 All locations

Nebraska
308 West
402 East

Nevada
702 Las Vegas Area
775 All locations except Las Vegas

New Hampshire
603 All locations

New Jersey
201 Northeast
551 Northeast
609 Southeast
732 East Central
848 East Central
856 Southwest
862 Northwest
908 West Central
973 Northwest

Area Codes in State Order (continued)

New Mexico
505 Northwest
575 Entire State except Northwest

New York
212 New York City
315 North Central
347 New York City
516 Nassau County
518 Northeast
585 West-Central
607 South Central
631 Suffolk County
646 New York City
716 West
718 New York City
845 North & West of Westchester County
914 Westchester County
917 New York City

North Carolina
252 East
336 Greensboro & Winston-Salem areas
704 Southwest
828 West
910 South Central
919 North Central
980 Southwest

North Dakota
701 All locations

Ohio
216 Cleveland Metro Area
234 Northeast except Cleveland
330 Northeast except Cleveland
419 Northwest
440 North Central except Cleveland Metro Area
513 Southwest
567 Northwest
614 Columbus Area
740 East & Central except Columbus Area
937 Southwest except Cincinnati Area

Oklahoma
405 Central
580 South & West
918 Northeast

Oregon
458 Outside Portland Area
503 Portland Area
541 Outside Portland Area
971 Portland Area

Pennsylvania
215 Philadelphia
267 Philadelphia
412 Pittsburgh Metro Area
484 Southeast
570 Northeast
610 Southeast
717 Southeast
724 Outside Pittsburgh Metro Area
814 West
878 Pittsburgh & surrounding area

Rhode Island
401 All locations

South Carolina
803 Central
843 East
864 Northwest

South Dakota
605 All locations

Tennessee
423 Northeast & Southeast
615 North Central
731 West except Shelby, Fayette & Tipton Counties
865 Knoxville & surrounding area
901 Southwest (Shelby, Fayette & Tipton Counties)
931 Nashville & North Central

Texas
210 San Antonio Metro Area
214 Dallas
254 North Central
281 Houston
325 Central
361 Corpus Christi & surrounding Area
409 East of Houston Area
430 Northeast
432 West Central
469 Dallas
512 Austin & surrounding area
682 Fort Worth Metro Area & Arlington
713 Houston
806 Northwest
817 Fort Worth Metro Area & Arlington
830 South Central
832 Houston
903 Northeast
915 West (including El Paso)
936 North of Houston Area
940 North
956 South
972 Dallas
979 West of Houston Area

Toll Calls: From Canada & The Caribbean
880
881

Toll-Free; All States
800
844
855
866
877
888

Utah
385 Salt Lake City, Ogden & Provo Metro areas
435 All locations except Salt Lake City/Ogden/Provo Metro areas
801 Salt Lake City, Ogden & Provo Metro areas

Vermont
802 All locations

Virginia
276 Southwest
434 South & Central
540 North
571 Northeast
703 Northeast
757 Norfolk & surrounding area
804 East

Washington
206 Seattle Area
253 Tacoma Area
360 West except Seattle, Tacoma & Everett areas
425 East of Seattle between Everett & Kent
509 East

West Virginia
304 All locations
681 All locations

Wisconsin
262 Southeast except Milwaukee
414 Milwaukee
534 North
608 Southwest
715 North
920 Southeast except Milwaukee & surrounding area (South)

Wyoming
307 All locations

Alphabetical Section

Listings in this section are presented in alphabetical order by company or organization name. Alphabetizing is on a word-by-word rather than letter-by-letter basis.

For a detailed explanation of the scope and arrangement of listings, please refer to "How to Use This Directory" at the beginning of this book.Page elements and listing formats are illustrated on the sample pages with accompanying explanatory notes found just inside the back cover.

SYMBOLS & NUMERALS

				Phone	Fax	Class
1 Biotechnology PO Box 758 *TF:* 800-951-4246 ■ *Web:* www.1biotechnology.com	Oneco	FL	34264	941-355-8451	351-0026	415
1 EDI Source Inc 31875 Solon Rd Ste 2 *Web:* www.1edisource.com	Solon	OH	44139	440-519-7800		179
1 Stop Design Shop Inc 30 RB Sixth Rd *Web:* www.1stopdesign.com	Woburn	MA	01801	781-938-3866		344
1 to 1 Printers LLC 15031 Woodham Dr Ste 370 *Web:* www.1to1printers.com	Houston	TX	77073	281-821-4400		627
10 Degrees South 4183 Roswell Rd NE *Web:* www.10degreessouth.com	Atlanta	GA	30342	404-705-8870		671
100 Fountain Spa at the Pillar & Post Inn 48 John St PO Box 48 *TF:* 888-669-5566 ■ *Web:* www.vintage-hotels.com	Niagara-on-the-Lake	ON	L0S1J0	905-468-2123	468-3551	707
100.3 Jack FM 4131 N Central Expy Ste 1000 *Web:* jackontheweb.cbslocal.com	Dallas	TX	75204	214-525-7000		645-44
100.5 The Wolf 1856 S Glenstone Ave *Web:* 1005thewolf.iheart.com	Springfield	MO	65804	417-890-5555		645-157
100.7 Star 651 Holiday Dr Foster Plz 5 *Web:* starpittsburgh.cbslocal.com	Pittsburgh	PA	15220	412-920-9400	920-9449	645-125
100.7 WLEV 2158 Ave C Ste 100 *TF:* 800-772-8336 ■ *Web:* www.wlevradio.com	Bethlehem	PA	18017	610-266-7600		645
100.7 WMMS 6200 Oak Tree Blvd S 4th Fl *Web:* www.wmms.com	Cleveland	OH	44131	216-520-2600		645-38
101 Livestock Market Inc 4400 Hwy 101 *Web:* www.101livestock.com	Aromas	CA	95004	831-726-3303		446
101 Pipe & Casing Inc 30101 Agoura Ct Ste 201 *Web:* www.101pipe.com	Agoura Hills	CA	91301	818-707-9101		492
101.5 Lite FM 20450 NW Second Ave *Fax Area Code:* 305 ■ *TF:* 877-790-1015 ■ *Web:* www.litemiami.com	Miami	FL	33169	877-790-1015	521-1414*	645-99
101.7 The Beach 60 Garden Ct Ste 300 *TF:* 800-365-8630 ■ *Web:* www.1017thebeach.com	Monterey	CA	93940	831-658-5200	658-5299	645-103
101.9 The Rocket FM 125 Corporate Terr *Web:* www.myhotsprings.com	Hot Springs	AR	71913	501-525-9700		645-74
1010data Inc 750 Third Ave 4th Fl *Web:* www.1010data.com	New York	NY	10017	212-405-1010		180
102.5 The Game 1824 Murfreesboro Rd *TF:* 800-657-6910 ■ *Web:* www.thegamenashville.com	Nashville	TN	37217	615-399-1029	361-9873	645-108
102.7 The Vibe 3811 Rogers Ave *Web:* www.1027thevibe.com	Fort Smith	AR	72903	479-452-0681	452-0873	645-61
102.7Jack FM 711 W 40th St *TF:* 888-410-1027 ■ *Web:* 1027jackfm.iheart.com	Baltimore	MD	21211	410-366-7600		645-16
102.9 The Whale 869 Blue Hills Ave *Web:* www.1029thewhale.com	Bloomfield	CT	06002	860-243-1115	286-8257	645
103.5 KISS FM 233 N Michigan Ave Ste 2800 *Web:* 1035kissfm.iheart.com	Chicago	IL	60601	312-540-2000		645-36
103.7 Kiss FM 11800 W Grange Ave *Web:* www.1037kissfm.com	Hales Corners	WI	53130	414-529-1250		645
103.7 Tha Beat 208 N Thomas *Web:* kbtt.fm	Shreveport	LA	71107	318-222-3122	320-0102	645-151
103.7 The Beat 83 E Shaw Ave Ste 150 *Web:* thebeat1037.iheart.com	Fresno	CA	93710	559-230-4300	243-4301	645-64
103.9 Bob FM 1601 E 57th Ave *Web:* www.1039bobfm.com	Spokane	WA	99223	509-448-1000	448-7015	645-154
103.9 The Bear WRBR 237 W Edison Rd *Web:* www.wrbr.com	Mishawaka	IN	46545	574-258-5483		645
104.1 Jack FM 625 Second Ave S *Web:* 1041jackfm.cbslocal.com	Minneapolis	MN	55402	612-370-0611		645-101
104.5 Radio Latina 2403 Hoover Ave *Web:* wp.1045radiolatina.com	National City	CA	91950	619-336-7800	420-1092	645
104.7 FM Praize Power 1350 WLOU 2001 W Broadway *Web:* www.wlouonline.com	Louisville	KY	40203	502-776-1240		645-93
104.7 Kiss FM 4686 E Van Buren St Ste 300 *TF:* 844-289-7234	Phoenix	AZ	85008	602-374-6000		645-123
105.1 The Bounce 1 Radio Plaza *Web:* www.detroitsports1051.com	Ferndale	MI	48220	248-414-5600	542-8800	645
105.5 WERC-FM 600 Beacon Pkwy W Ste 400 *Web:* wercfm.iheart.com	Birmingham	AL	35209	205-439-9600	439-8390	645-20
105.7 man up ! 2-B PAI Pk *Web:* 1057manup.iheart.com	Greensboro	NC	27409	336-822-2000		645
105.9 KGBX 1856 S Glenstone Ave *TF:* 800-445-1059 ■ *Web:* kgbx.iheart.com	Springfield	MO	65804	417-890-5555		645-157
105.9 The X 200 Fleet St 4th Fl *Web:* 1059thex.iheart.com	Pittsburgh	PA	15220	412-937-1441	937-0323	645-125
106.1 KISS FM 14001 N Dallas Pkwy Ste 300 *Web:* www.1061kissfm.com	Dallas	TX	75240	214-866-8000	866-8008	645-44
106.1 Kiss Fm Seattle 645 Elliott Ave W Ste 400 *TF:* 888-343-1061 ■ *Web:* kissfmseattle.iheart.com	Seattle	WA	98119	206-494-2000		645-150
106.3 WORD 25 Garlington Rd *Web:* www.1063word.com	Greenville	SC	29615	864-271-9200		645-68
106.5 The Beat 3245 Basie Rd *Web:* 1065thebeat.iheart.com	Richmond	VA	23228	804-474-0000		645-134
106.7 lite FM 32 Ave of the Americas 2nd Fl *TF:* 800-222-1067 ■ *Web:* www.1067litefm.com	New York	NY	10013	212-377-7900		645-111
106.7 The Eagle 13333 SW 68th Pkwy Ste 310 *TF:* 844-289-7234 ■ *Web:* 1067theeagle.iheart.com	Tigard	OR	97223	503-323-6400		645-128
106.9 Play 612 S Fourth St *Web:* www.1069play.com	Louisville	KY	40202	502-589-4800	589-1377	645-93
1060 at the Genesee Grande 1060 E Genesee St *Web:* www.1060restaurant.com	Syracuse	NY	13210	315-476-9000		671
107.1 The Monkey 9471 Three Rivers Rd Ste A *TF:* 800-782-7987 ■ *Web:* www.1071themonkey.net	Gulfport	MS	39503	228-388-1071		645-69
107.3 BBT 300 Arboretum Pl Ste 590 *Web:* www.1073bbt.com	Richmond	VA	23236	804-327-9902	327-9911	645-134
107.3 Jack FM 11700 Central Pkwy *Web:* 1073jack.iheart.com	Jacksonville	FL	32224	904-636-0507		645-79
107.5 Kiss Fm 2141 Grand Ave *Web:* 1075kissfm.iheart.com	Des Moines	IA	50312	515-245-8854	245-8902	645-48
107.5 WGCI FM 233 N Michigan Ave Ste 2800 *Web:* wgci.iheart.com	Chicago	IL	60601	312-540-2000		645-36
107.9 Nash Icon 821 Pineville Rd *Web:* www.1079nashicon.com	Chattanooga	TN	37405	423-756-6141		645-34
107.9 The Bear 4270 Byrd Dr *Web:* 1079thebear.iheart.com	Loveland	CO	80538	970-461-2560		645
107.9 The Link 1 Julian Price Pl *TF:* 844-258-8477 ■ *Web:* www.1079thelink.com	Charlotte	NC	28208	704-570-1079		645-33
1075 KZL 192 E Lewis St *TF:* 800-682-1075 ■ *Web:* www.1075kzl.com	Greensboro	NC	27406	336-274-8042	274-1629	645
10C Technologies Inc 14285 Midway Rd Ste 125 *Web:* www.10ctech.com	Addison	TX	75001	972-385-2486		253
10G LLC 100 Morey Dr *Web:* www.10g.com	Woodridge	IL	60517	630-754-2400		407
#1 Cochran 4520 William Penn Hwy *Web:* cochran.com	Monroeville	PA	15146	412-373-3333		57
1&1 Internet Inc 701 Lee Rd Ste 300 *Fax Area Code:* 610 ■ *TF:* 877-461-2631 ■ *Web:* www.1and1.com	Chesterbrook	PA	19087	877-461-2631	560-1501*	690
11 X 17 Inc 2034 N *TF:* 800-521-2788 ■ *Web:* www.11x17.com	Jacksonville	TX	75766	903-541-0100		627
110 Technologies LLC 27 Technology Way Millyard Technology Park *Web:* 110technology.com	Nashua	NH	03060	603-886-2800		196
1105 Media Inc 9201 Oakdale Ave Ste 101 *Web:* www.1105media.com	Chatsworth	CA	91311	818-814-5200	734-1522	637-9
111 Chop House 111 Shrewsbury St *Web:* www.111chophouse.com	Worcester	MA	01604	508-799-4111		671
1185 Design Inc 941Emerson St *Web:* www.1185design.com	Palo Alto	CA	94301	650-325-4804		344
1-2-1 Marketing Services Group Inc 20195 S Diamond Lake Rd Ste 700 *Web:* www.121msg.com	Rogers	MN	55374	763-428-8123		195
1-2-3 Payroll & HR Services Inc PO Box 96 *Web:* www.1-2-3payroll.com	Holtsville	NY	11742	631-654-1811		734
123Greetingscom Inc 1674 Broadway Ste 403 *Web:* www.123greetings.com	New York	NY	10019	212-246-0044		130
12th Armored Div Memorial Museum 1289 N Second St *Web:* www.12tharmoredmuseum.com	Abilene	TX	79601	325-677-6515		520
13 Coins 125 Boren Ave N *Web:* www.13coins.com	Seattle	WA	98109	206-682-2513		671
1310 News 2001 Thurston Dr *Web:* www.1310news.com	Ottawa	ON	K1G6C9	613-736-2001		645-117
1394 Trade Assn 23117 39th Ave SE *Web:* www.1394ta.org	Bothell	WA	98021	425-870-6574	320-3897	48-9
13D Research (USVI) LLC 6115 Estate Smith Bay PO Box 2 Ste 333 *Web:* www.13d.com	St Thomas	VI	00802	340-775-3330		401

Company / Address	City	State	Zip	Phone	Fax	Class
1440 KEYS 2117 Leopard St	Corpus Christi	TX	78408	361-883-3516	882-9767	645-43
Web: www.1440keys.com						
1470 WMBD 1211 SW Fifth Ave Ste 750	Portland	OR	97204	309-637-3700		645-121
Web: www.1470wmbd.com						
14th Street Playhouse						
1280 Peachtree St NE	Atlanta	GA	30309	404-733-4738		572
15 Ria 1515 Rhode Island Ave NW	Washington	DC	20005	202-742-0015	332-8436	671
Web: www.15ria.com						
1515 On Market 1515 Market St	Denver	CO	80202	303-571-0011		671
Web: www.1515restaurant.com						
15625 Ft Bend Ltd 15625 SW Fwy	Sugar Land	TX	77478	281-207-1500		57
160 Over 90						
510 Wallnut St 19th Fl	Philadelphia	PA	19106	215-732-3200		4
Web: www.160over90.com						
1620 SAVOY 1620 Market St	Little Rock	AR	72211	501-221-1620		671
17 Hundred 90 Restaurant						
307 E President St	Savannah	GA	31401	912-236-7122		671
Web: www.17hundred90.com						
1703 Restaurant						
1703 Robin Hood Rd	Winston-Salem	NC	27104	336-725-5767		671
Web: www.localedge.com						
1789 Restaurant 1226 36th St NW	Washington	DC	20007	202-965-1789	337-1541	671
Web: www.1789restaurant.com						
1797 Ezekiel Harris House						
560 Reynolds St	Augusta	GA	30904	706-722-8454		50-3
Web: www.augustamuseum.org/harrishouse.php						
180 Business Solutions						
1000 W Wilshire Blvd Ste 203	Oklahoma City	OK	73116	405-840-4180		193
Web: 180business.com						
180 Medical Inc						
5324 W Reno Ste A	Oklahoma City	OK	73127	405-702-7700		475
Web: www.180medical.com						
1-800 Postcards Inc 121 Varick St	New York	NY	10013	800-767-8227		627
TF: 800-767-8227 ■ *Web:* www.1800postcards.com						
1-800-Flowers.com Inc						
1 Old Country Rd Ste 500	Carle Place	NY	11514	516-237-6000		292
NASDAQ: FLWS ■ *TF:* 800-356-9377 ■ *Web:* ww30.1800flowers.com						
1-800-Got-Junk						
887 Great Northern Way	Vancouver	BC	V5T4T5	800-468-5865		310
TF: 800-468-5865 ■ *Web:* www.1800gotjunk.com						
1-800-Water Damage 1167 Mercer St	Seattle	WA	98109	206-381-3041		310
TF: 800-928-3732 ■ *Web:* www.1800waterdamage.com						
180s Inc 700 S Caroline St	Baltimore	MD	21231	410-534-6320	534-6321	155-9
TF: 877-725-4386 ■ *Web:* www.180s.com						
1859 Historic Hotels Ltd PO Box 59	Galveston	TX	77553	409-763-8536		379
Web: www.1859historichotels.com						
1859 Jail Marshal's Home & Museum						
217 N Main St	Independence	MO	64050	816-252-1892		50-3
Web: www.jchs.org/jail/museum.html						
1881 Custer County Courthouse Museum						
411 Mt Rushmore Rd PO Box 826	Custer	SD	57730	605-673-2443	673-2443	520
TF: 800-226-6398 ■ *Web:* www.1881courthousemuseum.com						
1886 Crescent Hotel & Spa						
75 Prospect Ave	Eureka Springs	AR	72632	479-253-9766		379
TF: 877-342-9766 ■ *Web:* www.crescent-hotel.com						
1888 Mills LLC						
1520 Kensington Rd Ste 115	Oak Brook	IL	60523	800-346-3660		746
TF: 800-346-3660 ■ *Web:* www.1888mills.com						
1928 Jewelry Co 3000 W Empire Ave	Burbank	CA	91504	818-841-1928		408
TF: 800-227-1928 ■ *Web:* www.1928.com						
1932 & 1980 Lake Placid Winter Olympic Museum						
Olympic Ctr 2634 Main St	Lake Placid	NY	12946	518-523-1655	523-9275	522
TF: 800-462-6236 ■ *Web:* www.orda.org						
1938 Media 1 Astor Pl Ph Ste J	New York	NY	10003	917-407-7600		7
Web: 1938media.com						
195 Lumber Company Killeen Ltd						
3032 S Ft Hood St	Killeen	TX	76542	254-634-2188		690
Web: www.195lumberco.com						
1Cloud 25 Lowell St Ste 407	Manchester	NH	03101	603-296-0760		225
Web: 1cloudbusiness.com						
1K Studios LLC						
3400 W Olive Ave Ste 300	Burbank	CA	91505	818-531-3800		344
Web: weareonek.com						
1MAGE Software Inc						
384 Inverness Pkwy Ste 206	Englewood	CO	80112	800-844-1468	796-0587*	178-1
**Fax Area Code: 303* ■ *TF:* 800-844-1468 ■ *Web:* www.1mage.com						
1Mart Corp						
570 El Camino Real Ste 150	Redwood City	CA	94063	650-363-7700		459
Web: americangene.com						
1secureaudit LLC 1600 Tysons Blvd Fl 8	Mc Lean	VA	22102	424-220-8940		194
TF: 800-321-0706 ■ *Web:* www.1secureaudit.com						
1st Advantage Federal Credit Union						
110 Cybernetics Way	Yorktown	VA	23693	757-877-2444		219
Web: 1stadvantage.org						
1st Bank 201 N Wilbur PO Box 347	Broadus	MT	59317	406-436-2611		70
Web: www.our1stbank.com						
1st Bank & Trust of Broken Bow						
710 S Park Dr	Broken Bow	OK	74728	580-584-9123		70
Web: 1stbankandtrust.com						
1st Choice Facilities Services Corp						
1941 Whitfield Park Loop	Sarasota	FL	34243	866-241-0070		186
TF: 866-241-0070						
1st Colonial Bancorp Inc						
1040 Haddon Ave	Collingswood	NJ	08108	856-858-1100	858-9255	70
OTC: FCOB ■ *TF:* 800-500-1044 ■ *Web:* www.1stcolonial.com						
1st Constitution Bancorp						
2650 Rt 130 & Dey Rd	Cranbury	NJ	08512	609-655-4500	655-5653	360-2
NASDAQ: FCCY ■ *Web:* www.1stconstitution.com						
1st Discount Brokerage Inc						
8927 Hypoluxo Rd Ste A-5	Lake Worth	FL	33467	561-515-3200	515-3201	690
TF: 888-642-2811 ■ *Web:* www.1db.com						
1st Interstate Motel						
20 SE Wyoming Blvd	Casper	WY	82609	307-234-9125		379
1st Mechanical						
1295 Bluegrass Lakes Pkwy	Alpharetta	GA	30004	770-346-0792		610
TF: 888-346-0792 ■ *Web:* www.1stmech.com						
1st Midamerica Credit Union						
731 E Bethalto Dr	Bethalto	IL	62010	618-258-3168		219
Web: 1stmidamerica.org						
1st NRG Corp 10184 Park Meadows Dr	Lone Tree	CO	80124	720-484-5706		536
Web: 1stnrg-corp.com						
1st Source Bank 100 N Michigan St	South Bend	IN	46601	574-235-2254		70
TF: 800-513-2360 ■ *Web:* www.1stsource.com						
1st Summit Bancorp 125 Donald Ln	Johnstown	PA	15904	814-262-4000		70
Web: 1stsummit.com						
1st United Door Technologies Inc						
7255 S Kyrene Ste 104	Tempe	AZ	85283	480-705-6632		236
Web: www.firstudt.com						
1stMovement LLC, The						
751 N Fair Oaks Ave Ste 101	Pasadena	CA	91103	626-689-4993		7
Web: www.the1stmovement.com						
1-Stop Translation USA LLC						
3700 Wilshire Blvd Ste 630	Los Angeles	CA	90010	213-480-0011		317
TF: 800-969-6853 ■ *Web:* www.1stopasia.com						
1stWEST Financial Corp						
1536 Cole Blvd Ste 333	Lakewood	CO	80401	866-670-3443		466
TF: 866-670-3443 ■ *Web:* www.1stwest.com						
2 Checkoutcom Inc 1785 O'Brien Rd	Columbus	OH	43228	614-921-2450		459
TF: 877-294-0273 ■ *Web:* www.2checkout.com						
2 Places At 1 Time Inc						
270 Peachtree St 20th Fl	Atlanta	GA	30303	877-275-2237	800-7888*	463
**Fax Area Code: 404* ■ *TF:* 877-275-2237 ■ *Web:* www.2placesat1time.com						
2020 Companies LLC						
3575 Lone Star Cir Ste 200	Fort Worth	TX	76177	817-490-0100		195
Web: www.2020companies.com						
2020 Exhibits Inc						
10550 S Sam Huston Pkwy W	Houston	TX	77071	713-354-0900		196
TF: 800-856-6659 ■ *Web:* www.2020exhibits.com						
2030 Inc 607 Cerrillos Rd	Santa Fe	NM	87505	505-988-5309		463
Web: www.architecture2030.org						
20k Group 714 Worthshire St	Houston	TX	77008	713-224-1877	583-5549	393
Web: www.20kgroup.com						
211 Clover Lane 211 Clover Ln	Louisville	KY	40207	502-896-9570		671
Web: 211clover.com						
212 Market Restaurant						
212 Market St	Chattanooga	TN	37402	423-265-1212	267-6757	671
Web: www.212market.com						
215 Holding Co 215 S 11th St	Minneapolis	MN	55403	612-332-4732		360-2
Web: ffmbank.com						
215 McCann 215 Leidesdorff St	San Francisco	CA	94111	415-262-3500		7
Web: 215mccann.com						
219 Design						
67 E Evelyn Ave Ste 11	Mountain View	CA	94041	650-969-4219		261
Web: www.219design.com						
219 Restaurant 219 King St	Alexandria	VA	22314	703-549-1141	549-0035	671
Web: www.219restaurant.com						
21c Museum Hotel 700 W Main St	Louisville	KY	40202	502-217-6300	578-6601*	379
**Fax Area Code: 513* ■ *Web:* www.21cmuseumhotels.com						
21st Amendment Inc						
1158 W 86th St	Indianapolis	IN	46260	317-846-1678		443
Web: www.21stamendment.com						
21st Century Christian Inc						
PO Box 40526	Nashville	TN	37204	615-383-3842		96
TF: 800-251-2477 ■ *Web:* www.21stcc.com						
21st Century Systems Inc 6825 Pine St	Omaha	NE	68106	402-505-7881		177
Web: www.21csi.com						
21st Mortgage Corp						
620 Market St Ste 100	Knoxville	TN	37902	865-523-2120		509
TF: 800-955-0021 ■ *Web:* www.21stmortgage.com						
22 Bowen's 22 Bowen's Wharf	Newport	RI	02840	401-841-8884		671
Web: www.22bowens.com						
22 Squared						
1170 Peachtree St NE 14th Fl	Atlanta	GA	30309	404-347-8700		4
TF: 800-561-3357 ■ *Web:* www.22squared.com						
220 Marketing 3405 Kenyon St Ste 501	San Diego	CA	92110	877-220-6584		195
TF: 877-220-6584 ■ *Web:* www.220marketing.com						
24 Asset Management Corp						
13155 SW 42nd St Ste 200	Miami	FL	33175	855-414-2424		393
TF: 855-414-2424 ■ *Web:* www.24asset.com						
24 Hour Co 6521 Arlington Blvd	Falls Church	VA	22042	703-533-7209		344
Web: www.24hrco.com						
240 Union 240 Union Blvd	Lakewood	CO	80228	303-989-3562	989-3565	671
Web: www.240union.com						
24eight LLC 711 Third Ave 11th Fl	New York	NY	10017	212-888-2248	888-7448	647
24hourtek LLC 268 Bush St	San Francisco	CA	94104	415-294-4449		175
TF: 855-378-0787 ■ *Web:* www.24hourtek.com						
2600 Magazine PO Box 752	Middle Island	NY	11953	631-751-2600	474-2677	457-7
Web: www.2600.com						
262 With Donna						
11762 marco beach dr	Jacksonville	FL	32224	904-551-0732		138
Web: breastcancermarathon.com						
284 Partners LLC						
339 E Liberty Ste 340	Ann Arbor	MI	48104	734-369-8723		463
Web: www.284partners.com						
29 Prime Inc 2967 Michelson Dr Ste G467	Irvine	CA	92612	949-777-6616		5
2Advanced Studios LLC						
32 Journey Ste 200	Aliso Viejo	CA	92656	949-521-7000		7
Web: www.2advanced.com						
2B Productions Inc						
1674 Broadway Ste 902	New York	NY	10019	212-765-8202		4
Web: www.2binc.com						
2b Technologies Inc						
2100 Central Ave Ste 105	Boulder	CO	80301	303-273-0559		743
Web: www.twobtech.com						
2GIG Technologies Inc						
2961 W Maple Loop Dr Ste 300	Lehi	UT	84043	801-221-9162		693
Web: www.2gig.com						
2H Offshore Inc						
15990 N Barkers Landing Ste 200	Houston	TX	77079	281-258-2000		256
Web: www.2hoffshore.com						
2Is Inc 75 West St	Walpole	MA	02081	508-850-7520	850-7521	256
Web: www.2is-inc.com						
2KDirect Inc						
3000 Broad St Ste 115	San Luis Obispo	CA	93401	805-597-5000		387
Web: www.ipromote.com						
2lemetry Inc 1321 15th St Ste 200	Denver	CO	80202	720-606-2646		224
Web: 2lemetry.com						

				Phone	Fax	Class
2nd Swing Inc 13031 Ridgedale Dr *Web:* www.2ndswing.com	Minnetonka	MN	55305	952-546-1906		711
2nd Wind Exercise Equipment Inc 7585 Equitable Dr *Web:* www.2ndwindexercise.com	Eden Prairie	MN	55344	952-544-5249	544-5053	711
2ndEdison Inc 11 El Gavilan Rd *Web:* www.2ndedison.com	Orinda	CA	94563	925-253-1002		196
2plus2 Partners Inc 5980 Horton St Ste 105 *TF:* 800-377-4911 ■ *Web:* www.2plus2.com	Emeryville	CA	94608	510-652-7700		177
3 Amigos 1657 St Catherine W *Web:* www.3amigosrestaurant.com	Montreal	QC	H3H1L7	514-939-3329		671
3 Arts Entertainment Inc 9460 Wilshire Blvd *Web:* 3arts.com	Beverly Hills	CA	90212	310-888-3200		708
3 Ball Entertainment 3650 Redondo Beach Ave *Web:* 3ballentertainment.com	Redondo Beach	CA	90278	424-236-7500		514
3 Doors Down Cafe 1429 SE 37th St *Web:* www.3doorsdowncafe.com	Portland	OR	97214	503-236-6886		671
3 e Consulting Services 6 Dickinson Dr Ste 111 *TF:* 800-626-6049 ■ *Web:* 3econsultingservices.com	Chadds Ford	PA	19317	610-358-5950		196
3 Kings Environmental Inc 1311 SE Grace Ave *Web:* www.3kingsenvironmental.com	Battle Ground	WA	98604	360-666-5464		194
3 KMTV News Now 10714 Mockingbird Dr *Web:* www.kmtv.com	Omaha	NE	68127	402-592-3333	592-9434	741-94
3 Media Web Solutions Inc 7 Felton St Ste 280 *Web:* www.3mediaweb.com	Hudson	MA	01749	508-845-8900		195
3 Sixty Manufacturing 158 Martinvale Ln	San Jose	CA	95119	408-365-0360		767
3 Strikes Inc 1905 Elizabeth Ave *Web:* www.3strikes.com	Rahway	NJ	07065	732-382-3020		344
3 U Technologies 11681 Leonidas Horton Rd *Web:* www.3utech.com	Conroe	TX	77304	936-441-3043		256
30 Dps 118 N Tejon St 304 *Web:* www.30dps.com	Colorado Springs	CO	80903	719-380-9996		180
300 Feet Out 1035 Folsom St *Web:* www.300feetout.com	San Francisco	CA	94103	415-551-2377		344
300 North Capital LLC 300 N Lake Ave Ste 210	Pasadena	CA	91101	626-449-8500		401
3030 Ocean 3030 Holiday Dr *Web:* www.3030ocean.com	Fort Lauderdale	FL	33316	954-765-3030		671
31 Inc 100 Enterprise Dr *Web:* www.31inc.com	Newcomerstown	OH	43832	740-498-8324		754
32 Automotive 610 W Main St	Batavia	OH	45103	513-732-2124		57
32 Degrees Capital 650 635-8th Ave S W *Web:* www.32degrees.ca	Calgary	AB	T2P3M3	403-695-1069		528
32 East 32 E Atlantic Ave *Web:* www.32east.com	Delray Beach	FL	33444	561-276-7868		671
320 Guest Ranch Inc 205 Buffalo Horn Creek Rd *TF:* 800-243-0320 ■ *Web:* www.320ranch.com	Gallatin Gateway	MT	59730	406-995-4283		239
33Across Inc 229 W 28th St 12th Fl *TF:* 888-297-4094 ■ *Web:* www.33across.com	New York	NY	10001	888-297-4094		387
33rd Co Inc 1800 Wooddale Dr Ste 100 *Web:* www.33rdcompany.com	Woodbury	MN	55125	651-777-5500	777-5501	652
33rd Street Bistro 3301 Folsom Blvd *Web:* www.33rdstreetbistro.com	Sacramento	CA	95816	916-455-2233		671
352-MEDIA 133 SW 130th Way Ste D *Web:* www.352inc.com	Newberry	FL	32669	352-374-9657		196
356th Fighter Group 4919 Mt Pleasant Rd	North Canton	OH	44720	330-494-7418		671
360 Bc Group Inc 25562 Gloriosa Dr *Web:* 360-biz.com	Mission Viejo	CA	92691	949-916-9120		195
360 Cloud Solutions LLC 14350 N 87th St Ste 165 *Web:* www.360cloudsolutions.com	Scottsdale	AZ	85260	480-295-3420		196
360 Electrical LLC 1935 E Vine Ste 360 *Web:* www.360electrical.com	Murray	UT	84121	801-364-4900		815
360 Imaging Inc 120 Fredette St *TF:* 800-239-9702 ■ *Web:* www.360imaging.com	Gardner	MA	01440	978-632-7100		92
360 Media Ventures 30 Danforth St *Web:* aura360.com	Portland	ME	04101	207-699-2360		195
360 Press Solutions 2009 Windy Terr *Web:* www.360presssolutions.com	Cedar Park	TX	78613	512-381-2360		194
360 Services Inc 12623 Newburgh Rd	Livonia	MI	48150	734-591-9360		225
360 Solutions LLC 2114 Austin Ave *TF:* 800-374-2879 ■ *Web:* www.360solutions.com	Waco	TX	76701	254-755-7000		194
360 Systems Inc 3281 Grande Vista Dr *Web:* 360systems.com	Newbury Park	CA	91320	818-991-0360		246
360 Technologies Inc 15401 Debba Dr *TF:* 888-883-0360 ■ *Web:* www.360tech.com	Austin	TX	78734	512-266-7360		463
360 Trading Networks Inc 521 Fifth Ave 38th Fl *Web:* www.360t.com	New York	NY	10175	212-776-2900		690
3660 on the Rise 3660 Waialae Ave *Web:* 3660ontherise.com	Honolulu	HI	96816	808-737-1177	735-6105	671
39 Rue De Jean 39 John St *Web:* www.holycityhospitality.com	Charleston	SC	29403	843-722-8881	722-8835	671
390th Memorial Museum 6000 E Valencia Rd *TF:* 800-639-4992 ■ *Web:* 390th.org	Tucson	AZ	85706	520-574-0287	574-3030	520
3balls.com 319 Manley St Ste 1 *TF:* 888-289-0300 ■ *Web:* www.3balls.com	West Bridgewater	MA	02379	888-289-0300		711
3C Consulting Corp 850 W Jackson Blvd *Web:* www.3ccomp.com	Chicago	IL	60607	312-226-8118		260
3CLogic Inc 9201 Corporate Blvd Ste 470 *Web:* www.3clogic.com	Rockville	MD	20850	240-454-6347		177
3D Biomatrix Inc 1600 Huron Pkwy Bldg 520 2nd Fl	Ann Arbor	MI	48109	734-272-4688		668
3D Exhibits Inc 2900 Lively Blvd *TF:* 800-471-9617 ■ *Web:* www.3dexhibits.com	Elk Grove Village	IL	60007	847-250-9000	860-8165	232
3D Instruments LP 2900 E White Star Ave *Web:* www.3dinstruments.com	Anaheim	CA	92806	714-399-9200		201
3-D International 1825 Smelter Ave	Black Eagle	MT	59414	406-453-6561		671
3D Internet 633 W Fifth St US Bank Twr 28th Fl *TF:* 800-442-5299 ■ *Web:* www.3dinternet.com/index.php	Los Angeles	CA	90071	800-442-5299		5
3D Lacrosse LLC 1301 S Jason St Unit K *Web:* www.3dlacrosse.com	Denver	CO	80223	303-346-2888		713
3D Medical Manufacturing Inc 1006 W 15th St *Web:* www.3dmedicalmfg.com	Riviera Beach	FL	33404	561-842-7175		228
3D Research Corp 360D Quality Cir Ste 450	Huntsville	AL	35806	256-705-5410		261
3D Systems Inc 333 Three D Systems Cir *TF:* 800-793-3669 ■ *Web:* www.3dsystems.com	Rock Hill	SC	29730	803-326-3900		178-8
3D2B Inc 80-02 Kew Gardens Rd Ste 903 *TF:* 800-395-7707 ■ *Web:* www.3d2b.com	Kew Gardens	NY	11415	718-709-0900		5
3Dlabs Inc Ltd 1901 McCarthy Blvd *TF:* 800-464-3348 ■ *Web:* www.3dlabs.com	Milpitas	CA	95035	408-530-4700		625
3E Company Inc 3207 Grey Hawk Ct *Web:* www.3ecompany.com	Carlsbad	CA	92010	760-602-8700		196
3e Marketing Communications 3933 N Ventura Dr *TF:* 800-882-1844 ■ *Web:* www.3elitho.com	Arlington Heights	IL	60004	847-398-8677		627
3esi-Enersight Inc 227 - 11th Ave SW Ste 400 *Web:* 3esi-enersight.com	Calgary	AB	T2R1R9	403-270-3270	270-3343	539
3G Tech Inc 6910 Hayvenhurst Ave Unit 100 *TF:* 800-943-9511 ■ *Web:* www.gggtech.com	Van Nuys	CA	91406	818-510-4709	510-4716	386
3Gtms Inc 8 Progress Dr *TF:* 800-677-3110 ■ *Web:* www.3gtms.com	Shelton	CT	06484	203-567-4610		180
3H Group Inc 505 Riverfront Parkaway *Web:* www.3hgrouphotels.com	Chattanooga	TN	37402	423-499-0497		463
3i People Inc 5755 N Point Pkwy Ste 9 *TF:* 800-686-1363 ■ *Web:* www.3ipeople.com	Alpharetta	GA	30022	404-636-2397		624
3LK Construction LLC 18401 Weaver St *Web:* www.3lkconstruction.com	Detroit	MI	48228	313-493-9101		186
3M Austin Plant 11705 Research Blvd *Fax Area Code: 800 ■ *Web:* www.3m.com	Austin	TX	78759	512-984-2711	245-0329*	253
3M Canada Co 300 Tartan Dr *Fax Area Code: 800 ■ *TF:* 888-364-3577 ■ *Web:* 3m.com/intl/ca	London	ON	N5V4M9	888-364-3577	479-4453*	732
3M Co 3M Ctr Bldg 225-3S-06 *NYSE:* MMM ■ *Fax: Mail Rm ■ *TF:* 800-364-3577 ■ *Web:* www.3m.com	Saint Paul	MN	55144	651-733-1110	733-9973*	185
3M Digital Signage 600 Ericksen Ave NE Ste 200 *Web:* www.3mdigitalsignage.com	Bainbridge Island	WA	98110	206-855-2000	855-4930	614
3M Electronic Handling & Protection Div 6801 River Place Blvd *TF:* 800-328-1368 ■ *Web:* 3m.com	Austin	TX	78726	800-328-1368		253
3M ESPE Dental Products Div 3M Ctr *Fax Area Code: 651 ■ *TF:* 800-634-2249 ■ *Web:* 3m.com	Saint Paul	MN	55144	888-364-3577	733-2481*	228
3M Interconnect Solutions Div 6801 River Place Blvd *TF:* 800-225-5373 ■ *Web:* www.3m.com	Austin	TX	78726	512-984-1800		253
3M Telecommunications Div 6801 River Place Blvd *TF:* 800-426-8688 ■ *Web:* 3m.com	Austin	TX	78726	800-426-8688	626-0329	248
3M Touch Systems 501 Griffin Brook Dr *TF:* 866-407-6666 ■ *Web:* www.3m.com	Methuen	MA	01844	978-659-9000		173-1
3M Unitek 2724 Peck Rd *TF:* 800-634-5300 ■ *Web:* www.3m.com	Monrovia	CA	91016	800-634-5300		228
3marketeers Advertising Inc 785 The Almeda *TF:* 800-908-5395 ■ *Web:* www.3marketeers.com	San Jose	CA	95126	408-293-3233	293-2433	4
3P Partners 5B Park Ln *Web:* www.3ppartnersdls.com	Hilton Head Island	SC	29928	843-842-2585		463
3Play Media Inc 125 Cambridge Park Dr *Web:* www.3playmedia.com	Cambridge	MA	02140	617-764-5189		514
3plus Logistics Co 20250 S Alameda St *Web:* e3pl.com	Rancho Dominguez	CA	90221	310-667-5160		194
3PS Inc 1300 Arrow Point Dr *Web:* www.3psinc.com	Cedar Park	TX	78613	512-610-5200		201
3Q Digital Inc 1710 S Amphlett Blvd Ste 320 *Web:* 3qdigital.com	San Mateo	CA	94002	650-539-4124		5
3rd Alternative Inc 145 Merritts Rd *TF:* 800-628-7070 ■ *Web:* www.3rdalternative.net	Farmingdale	NY	11735	516-753-1515		396
3rd Federal Bank 3 Penns Trail *Web:* www.3rdfedbank.com	Newtown	PA	18940	215-579-4600	579-2381	70
3s Global Business Solutions 7923 Nita Ave *Web:* www.3sgbs.com	Canoga Park	CA	91304	818-453-4403		180
3S Services LLC 2535 Loop 517 PO Box 248 *Web:* 3sservices.com	Carrizo Springs	TX	78834	830-876-4155		538
3sharp LLC 18300 Redmond Way Ste 210 *Web:* www.3sharp.com	Redmond	WA	98052	425-882-1032		180
3tech Corp 2828 W Parker Rd Ste B101 *Web:* www.3tech.com	Plano	TX	75075	972-490-4443		180

Name / Address	City	State	ZIP	Phone	Fax	Class
3-V Biosciences Inc 1050 Hamilton Ct *Web:* www.3vbio.com	Menlo Park	CA	94025	650-561-8600		231
4 Bells Restaurant 1610 Harmon Pl. *Web:* 4bells.com	Minneapolis	MN	55403	612-904-1163		671
4 Consulting Inc 1221 Abrams Rd *Web:* www.4ci-usa.com	Richardson	TX	75081	214-698-8633		177
4 County Electric Power Association 5265 S Frontage Rd *Web:* www.4county.org	Columbus	MS	39701	662-327-8900	327-8790	245
4 Guys Inc 230 Industrial Pk Rd *TF:* 800-400-8017 ■ *Web:* www.4guysfire.com	Meyersdale	PA	15552	814-634-8373	634-0076	59
4 Sight Inc 135 Fifth Ave *Web:* www.4sightinc.com	New York	NY	10010	212-253-0525		186
4 Wheel Parts 20315 96 Ave. **Fax Area Code:* 604 ■ *TF:* 855-554-2402 ■ *Web:* www.4wheelparts.com	Langley	BC	V1M0E4	778-726-2787	882-0680*	755
40 Steak & Seafood 1401 Interchange Ave	Bismarck	ND	58501	701-255-4040		671
401 K Advisors LLC 1000 Skokie Blvd Ste 500 *Web:* 401kadvisorschicago.com	Wilmette	IL	60091	847-256-4300		251
40-Up Tackle Co 16 Union Ave PO Box 442 *Web:* www.40uptackleco.com	Westfield	MA	01086	413-562-0385		208
411 Local Search Corp Inc 1200 Eglinton Ave E Ste 300 N York *TF:* 866-411-4411 ■ *Web:* www.411.ca	Toronto	ON	M3C1H9	416-849-1432		387
415 Productions Inc 2507 Bryant St *Web:* www.415.com	San Francisco	CA	94110	415-642-4200		809
419 West 3865 Electric Rd *Web:* 419-west.com	Roanoke	VA	24018	540-776-0419		671
42 Inc 2150 Allston Way Ste 300 *Web:* www.42inc.com	Berkeley	CA	94704	510-548-7948		180
45 Allen Plaza Development LLC 45 Ivan Allen Jr Blvd. *Web:* www.watlantadowntown.com	Atlanta	GA	30308	404-582-5800		378
45 Bistro 123 E Broughton St. *Web:* www.marshallhouse.com	Savannah	GA	31401	912-234-3111		671
456 Fish 456 Granby St *Web:* www.456fish.com	Norfolk	VA	23507	757-625-4444		671
45th Infantry Div Museum 2145 NE 36th St *Web:* www.45thdivisionmuseum.com	Oklahoma City	OK	73111	405-424-5313		520
48 Degrees North 6327 Seaview Ave NW *Web:* www.48north.com	Seattle	WA	98107	206-789-7350	789-6392	457-4
480 Biomedical Inc 480 Arsenal St *Web:* www.480biomedical.com	Watertown	MA	02472	617-393-4600		475
495 Productions Holdings LLC 9560 Wilshire Blvd 5th Fl *Web:* www.495productions.com	Beverly Hills	CA	90212	310-273-6700	247-1111	514
4C Foods Corp 580 Fountain Ave *TF:* 800-297-9227 ■ *Web:* www.4c.com	Brooklyn	NY	11208	718-272-4242	272-2899	296-40
4checks.com 8245 N Union Blvd *TF:* 800-995-9925 ■ *Web:* www.4checks.com	Colorado Springs	CO	80920	800-995-9925		142
4comm Inc 40 Burt Dr Ste 4 *Web:* 4commny.com	Deer Park	NY	11729	631-254-1000		224
4D Inc 3031 Tisch Way Ste 900 *TF:* 800-785-3303 ■ *Web:* www.4d.com	San Jose	CA	95128	408-557-4600	261-9879	178-1
4D Pharmacy Management Systems Inc 2520 Industrial Row Dr *Web:* www.4dpharmacy.com	Troy	MI	48084	248-540-8066		237
4-D Properties 2870 N Swan Rd	Tucson	AZ	85712	520-325-9600		652
4D Technology Corp 3280 E Hemisphere Loop Ste 146 *Web:* www.4dtechnology.com	Tucson	AZ	85706	520-294-5600		544
4g Unwired Inc 325 Fifth Ave Ste 100 *Web:* www.4gunwired.com	Indialantic	FL	32903	321-726-4183		256
4L Communications Inc 1555 Regent Ave W. *Web:* www.4lcommunications.com	Winnipeg	MB	R2C4J2	204-336-0606		736
4Life Research 9850 S 300 W *TF Sales:* 888-454-3374 ■ *Web:* www.4life.com	Sandy	UT	84070	801-256-3102	562-3611	366
4-M Precision Stamping Inc 4000 Technology Park Blvd *Web:* www.4mprecision.com	Auburn	NY	13021	315-252-8415		488
4Mads 834 Bush St Ste A *Web:* 4mads.com	San Francisco	CA	94108	415-795-3686		5
4over Inc 5900 San Fernando Rd *TF:* 877-782-2737 ■ *Web:* www.4over.com	Glendale	CA	91202	877-782-2737		627
4P Therapeutics LLC 680 Engineering Dr Ste 150 **Fax Area Code:* 866 ■ *Web:* www.4ptherapeutics.com	Peachtree Corners	GA	30092	770-263-1900	381-2103*	743
4patientcare 100 Oceangate Ste 1200 *Web:* 4patientcare.com	Long Beach	CA	90802	562 861-1800		196
4Refuel Canada Ltd 9440-202 St Ste 215 *Web:* 4refuel.com	Langley	BC	V1M4A6	604-513-0386		539
4Rivers Equipment 3763 Monarch St. *TF:* 800-490-6162 ■ *Web:* 4riversequipment.com	Frederick	CO	80516	303-833-5900		358
4Sight Group LLC 4001 Kennett Pk Ste 134-233 *TF:* 800-490-2131 ■ *Web:* www.4SightGroup.com	Wilmington	DE	19807	800-490-2131		180
4-Star Trailers Inc 10000 NW Tenth St *TF:* 800-848-3095 ■ *Web:* www.4startrailers.com	Oklahoma City	OK	73127	405-324-7827		779
4th Source Inc 2502 N Rocky Point Dr Ste 960 *TF:* 855-875-4700 ■ *Web:* www.4thsource.com	Tampa	FL	33607	855-875-4700		177
5 Alarm Fire & Safety Equipment LLC 350 Austin Cir *TF:* 800-615-6789 ■ *Web:* www.5alarm.com	Delafield	WI	53018	262-646-5911		693
5 Metacom Inc 10401 N Meridian St Ste 100 *Web:* www.5metacom.com	Indianapolis	IN	46290	317-580-7540	580-7550	7
5 Seasons Brewing Co 5600 Roswell Rd. *Web:* www.5seasonsbrewing.com	Sandy Springs	GA	30342	404-255-5911		671
5 Star Equine Products Inc 4589 Hwy 71 S *TF:* 800-533-3377 ■ *Web:* www.5starequineproducts.com	Hatfield	AR	71945	870-389-6328		711
5 Star Sports Calendar LLC 3340 N College Ave *Web:* www.fivestarsports.com	Fayetteville	AR	72703	479-444-8428		4
5.11 Inc 4300 Spyres Way *TF:* 866-451-1726 ■ *Web:* www.511tactical.com	Modesto	CA	95356	209-527-4511	527-1511	157-5
50 Forks 3601 W Sunflower Ave. *Web:* www.artinstitutes.edu	Santa Ana	CA	92704	714-338-1325		671
50 Yard Line Steakhouse 2549 Loop 289 S *Web:* 50-yardline.com	Lubbock	TX	79423	806-745-3991		671
500 Festival Inc 500 Festival Bldg 21 Virginia Ave Ste 500 *TF:* 800-638-4296 ■ *Web:* www.500festival.com	Indianapolis	IN	46204	317-927-3378		720
500 West Hotel 500 W Broadway *Web:* www.500westhotelsd.com	San Diego	CA	92101	619-234-5252		379
50000 Feet Inc 1700 W Irving Park Rd Ste 110 *Web:* www.50000feet.com	Chicago	IL	60613	773-529-6760		226
518 Prints LLC 1548 Burden Lake Rd Ste 4 *Web:* www.fiveoneeightprints.com	Averill Park	NY	12018	518-674-5346		627
518 West 518 W Jones St.	Raleigh	NC	27603	919-829-2518		671
5280 Solutions Inc 8740 Lucent Blvd Ste 400 *Web:* www.5280solutions.com	Highlands Ranch	CO	80129	303-696-5280		225
529 Wellington 529 Wellington Crescent. *Web:* 529wellington.ca	Winnipeg	MB	R3M0B9	204-487-8325		671
530medialab 115 W Fourth St Ste C1 *Web:* 530medialab.com	Long Beach	CA	90802	562-624-5888		344
54th Street Grill 18700 E 38th Terr *Web:* www.54thstreetgrill.com	Independence	MO	64057	816-795-7077		671
555 East 555 E Ocean Blvd. *Web:* www.555east.com	Long Beach	CA	90802	562-437-0626		671
55KRC 8044 Montgomery Rd Ste 650 *Web:* www.55krc.com	Cincinnati	OH	45236	513-686-8314		645-37
57th Street Antique Row 875 57th St. *Web:* 57thstreetantiquerow.com	Sacramento	CA	95819	916-451-3110		460
5J Oilfield Services LLC 4090 N Hwy 79 *Web:* www.5joilfield.net	Palestine	TX	75801	903-723-0253		536
5th Avenue Theatre Association 1308 Fifth Ave. *TF:* 800-838-3006 ■ *Web:* www.5thavenue.org	Seattle	WA	98101	206-625-1900		749
5th Business 5100 Orbitor Dr Ste 100 *TF:* 866-875-2220 ■ *Web:* www.5thbusiness.com	Mississauga	ON	L4W4Z4	905-275-2220		195
5th Wheel Training Institute 536 Brazeau Blvd *Web:* www.5thwheeltraining.com	New Liskeard	ON	P0J1P0	705-647-7202		507
5W Public Relations LLC 1166 Ave of the Americas 4th Fl *Web:* www.5wpr.com	New York	NY	10036	212-999-5585		636
600 WREC 2650 Thousand Oaks Blvd Ste 4100 *TF:* 800-474-9732 ■ *Web:* 600wrec.iheart.com	Memphis	TN	38118	901-259-1300		645-98
610 Magnolia 610 Magnolia Ave. *Web:* www.610magnolia.com	Louisville	KY	40208	502-636-0783		671
614 Media Group Inc 458 E Main St *TF:* 800-613-6131 ■ *Web:* www.614mediagroup.com	Columbus	OH	43215	614-488-4400		5
63 Ranch PO Box 979 *TF:* 888-395-5151 ■ *Web:* 63ranch.com	Livingston	MT	59047	888-395-5151		239
66 Diner 1405 Central Ave NE. *Web:* www.66diner.com	Albuquerque	NM	87106	505-247-1421		671
66 Federal Credit Union PO Box 1358 *TF:* 800-897-6991 ■ *Web:* www.truitycu.org	Bartlesville	OK	74005	918-336-7662		219
680 Partners LLC 600 Madison Ave 11th Fl *Web:* www.680partners.com	New York	NY	10022	212-931-5311	931-5310	260
6D Global Technologies Inc 17 State St Ste 2550 *Web:* www.6dglobal.com	New York	NY	10004	646-681-4900		787
6k Systems Inc 44084 Riverside Pkwy Ste 340 *TF:* 800-373-2804 ■ *Web:* www.6ksystems.com	Leesburg	VA	20176	703-724-1320		177
6s Marketing 1120 Hamilton St. *TF:* 888-642-6765 ■ *Web:* www.6smarketing.com	Vancouver	BC	V6B2S2	604-642-6765		195
6th Street Consulting 250 N Harbor Dr Ste 321 *Web:* www.6sc.com	Redondo Beach	CA	90277	310-694-3844		196
7 Cedars Casino 170756 Hwy 101 *Web:* www.7cedarsresort.com	Sequim	WA	98382	360-683-7777		452
7 D Ranch 7D Ranch PO Box 100 *TF:* 888-587-9885 ■ *Web:* www.7dranch.com	Cody	WY	82414	307-587-9885	587-9885	239
7 Layers Inc 15 Musick *Web:* www.7layers.com	Irvine	CA	92618	949-716-6512		261
7 Medical Systems LLC 651 Nicollet Mall Ste 501 *Web:* www.7medical.com	Minneapolis	MN	55402	612-230-7700		177
7 Stars Test Only 7905 Balboa Ave Ste D *Web:* 7starstestonly.com	San Diego	CA	92111	858-278-8737		62
700 WLW 8044 Montgomery Rd Ste 650 *Web:* www.700wlw.com	Cincinnati	OH	45236	513-686-8300		645-37
701 Restaurant 701 Pennsylvania Ave NW *Web:* www.701restaurant.com	Washington	DC	20004	202-393-0701		671
71 Sainte Peter 71 N San Pedro St. *TF:* 800-825-0012 ■ *Web:* www.71saintpeter.com	San Jose	CA	95110	408-971-8523	938-3440	671

Name / Address	City	State	Zip	Phone	Fax	Class
710 Book Store 819 S Illinois Ave *Web:* www.seventen.com	Carbondale	IL	62901	618-549-7304		95
717 Parking Services Inc 1523 N Franklin St *Web:* 717parking.com	Tampa	FL	33602	813-228-7722		562
74 State LLC 74 State St *Web:* www.74state.com	Albany	NY	12207	518-434-7410		707
75 Chestnut 75 Chestnut St *Web:* www.75chestnut.com	Boston	MA	02108	617-227-2175		671
790 WAEB 1541 Alta Dr Sunburst Office Bldg Fl 4 *Web:* www.790waeb.com	Whitehall	PA	18052	610-434-1742		645
7clans Paradise Casino 7500 Hwy 177 *Web:* www.okparadisecasino.com	Red Rock	OK	74651	580-723-4005		132
7-Eleven Inc 1722 Routh Ste 100 *TF:* 800-255-0711 ■ *Web:* www.7-eleven.com	Dallas	TX	75221	800-255-0711		204
7-sigma Inc 2843 26th Ave S *TF:* 888-722-8396 ■ *Web:* www.7-sigma.com	Minneapolis	MN	55406	612-722-5358		608
7strategy LLC 117 N Cooper St *TF:* 888-231-3062 ■ *Web:* www.7strategy.com	Olathe	KS	66061	913-638-2130		180
7Summits LLC 1110 Old World Third St Ste 500 *TF:* 866-705-6372 ■ *Web:* www.7summitsinc.com	Milwaukee	WI	53203	866-705-6372		195
7thOnline Inc 24 W 40th St 11th Fl *TF:* 800-775-7571 ■ *Web:* www.7thonline.com	New York	NY	10018	212-997-1717		224
802 Creative Partners Inc 768 S Main St PO Box 54 *Web:* www.802creative.com	Bethel	VT	05032	802-234-9755		7
804 Technology LLC 5381 Hwy N Ste 201 *Web:* 804technology.com	Cottleville	MO	63004	636-928-0330		261
82 Queen 82 Queen St *Web:* www.82queen.com	Charleston	SC	29401	843-723-7591		671
84 Lumber Co 1019 Rt 519 *TF:* 800-664-1984 ■ *Web:* www.84lumber.com	Eighty Four	PA	15330	724-228-8820		191-3
87AM Holdings LLC 233 Broadway 13th Fl *Web:* www.87am.com	New York	NY	10279	646-626-5555		195
889 Global Solutions 2501 Brookwood Rd *Web:* www.889globalsolutions.com	Columbus	OH	43209	614-235-8889		787
89 Degrees Inc 25 Mall Rd *Web:* www.89degrees.com	Burlington	MA	01803	781-221-5400		194
89 North Inc 1 Mill St Unit 285 *Web:* www.89north.com	Burlington	VT	05401	802-881-0302		261
89.1 WBOI 3204 Clairmont Ct *TF General:* 800-471-9264 ■ *Web:* wboi.org	Fort Wayne	IN	46808	260-452-1189		645-63
89.9 The Wave 90 Lovett Lake Ct *Web:* 899thewave.fm	Halifax	NS	B3S0H6	902-422-1651		645-70
8fold LLC 58 Mackenzie Rd *Web:* www.8foldworks.com	Morristown	NJ	07960	973-300-0070		195
8th Air Force Museum 88 Shreveport Rd *TF:* 800-827-1000 ■ *Web:* barksdaleglobalpowermuseum.com	Bossier City	LA	71110	318-752-0055		520
8x8 Inc 810 W Maude Ave *NASDAQ: EGHT* ■ *TF:* 888-898-8733 ■ *Web:* www.8x8.com	Sunnyvale	CA	94085	408-727-1885	980-0432	696
9 Bangkok Restaurant 571 Central Ave *Web:* 9bangkok.info	Saint Petersburg	FL	33701	727-894-5990	826-6164	671
9 Story Entertainment Inc 23 Fraser Ave *Web:* www.9story.com	Toronto	ON	M6K1Y7	416-530-9900		514
911 Restoration Enterprises Inc 7721 Densmore Ave *TF:* 888-243-6653 ■ *Web:* www.911restoration.com	Van Nuys	CA	91406	310-421-2014		667
919 Marketing Company Inc 102 Avent Ferry Rd *TF:* 800-284-4522 ■ *Web:* www.919marketing.com	Holly Springs	NC	27540	919-557-7890		195
92.1 The Beat 1003 Norfolk Sq *Web:* thebeatva.iheart.com	Norfolk	VA	23502	757-466-0009		645-112
92.3 FM KGON 0700 SW Bancroft St *TF:* 800-222-9236 ■ *Web:* www.kgon.com	Portland	OR	97239	503-223-1441	223-6909	645-128
92.5 FM WVNN 1717 Hwy 72 E *TF:* 866-494-9866 ■ *Web:* www.wvnn.com	Athens	AL	35611	256-830-8300	232-6842	645
92.5 WESC-FM 101 N Main St Ste 1000, 10th Fl *TF:* 800-248-0863 ■ *Web:* wescfm.iheart.com	Greenville	SC	29601	800-248-0863		645-68
92.9 BOB FM 4590 E 29th St Ste 711 *Web:* www.929bobfm.com	Tulsa	OK	74114	918-743-7814		645-168
92.9 The Game 1201 Peachtree St Ste 800 *Web:* atlanta.cbslocal.com/station/92-9-the-game	Atlanta	GA	30361	404-898-8900	898-8916	645-10
92nd St Young Men's & Young Women's Hebrew Assn 1395 Lexington Ave *TF:* 800-385-1689 ■ *Web:* www.92y.org	New York	NY	10128	212-415-5500	415-5788	48-20
93.1 FM WZAK 2510 St Clair Ave NE *Web:* wzakcleveland.hellobeautiful.com	Cleveland	OH	44114	216-579-1111	771-4164	645-38
93.1 The Mountain 2880 Meade Ave Ste B-250 *TF:* 844-289-7234 ■ *Web:* 931theparty.iheart.com	Las Vegas	NV	89102	702-238-7300	732-4890	645-88
93.3 The Beat 11700 Central Pkwy *Web:* wjbt.iheart.com	Jacksonville	FL	32224	904-636-0507		645-79
93.9 The beat 6810 N Shadeland Ave *Web:* www.939thebeat.com	Indianapolis	IN	46220	317-842-9550	921-1996	645-77
93.9 The Beat Honolulu 650 Iwilei Rd Ste 400 *TF:* 844-289-7234 ■ *Web:* 939jamz.iheart.com	Honolulu	HI	96817	808-550-9200	550-9288	645-73
930 AM The Answer 9601 McAllister Fwy Ste 1200 *TF:* 866-308-8867 ■ *Web:* 930amtheanswer.com	San Antonio	TX	78216	210-344-8481		645-143
937 The beat 2000 W Loop S Ste 300 *Web:* 937thebeathouston.com	Houston	TX	77027	713-212-8000		645-75
94 HJY 75 Oxford St Ste 301 *TF:* 844-289-7234 ■ *Web:* 94hjy.iheart.com	Providence	RI	02905	401-224-1994		645-129
94.1 The Beat 245 Alfred St *Web:* 941thebeat.iheart.com	Savannah	GA	31408	912-964-7794	964-9414	645-148
94.3 The Drive 177 Lombard Ave *TF:* 800-782-0175 ■ *Web:* www.943thedrive.ca	Winnipeg	MB	R3B0W5	204-944-1031	989-5291	645-177
94.5 KTI Country 720 E Capitol Dr *Web:* www.wtmj.com/kticountry	Milwaukee	WI	53212	414-332-9611	967-5266	645-100
94th Aero Squadron Restaurants 16320 Raymer St *Web:* www.94thvannuys.com/94thvannuys	Van Nuys	CA	91406	818-994-7437		670
95.7 Hallelujah FM 2650 Thousand Oaks Blvd Ste 4100 *TF:* 844-885-9425 ■ *Web:* hallelujahfm.iheart.com	Memphis	TN	38118	901-259-1300	761-1358	645-98
96.1 KISS 200 Fleet St *Web:* 961kiss.iheart.com	Pittsburgh	PA	15220	412-937-1441	937-0323	645-125
96.1 KWS 1111 Virginia St E *Web:* www.961thewolf.com	Charleston	WV	25301	304-342-8131		645-32
96.1 The Fox 505 University Ave *TF:* 844-289-1894 ■ *Web:* 961thefox.iheart.com	Grand Forks	ND	58203	701-775-0575	746-1410	645-65
96.5 FM KISS Country 600 Old Marion Rd NE *TF:* 800-258-0096 ■ *Web:* 965kisscountry.iheart.com	Cedar Rapids	IA	52402	319-395-0530		645-29
96.5 KISS-FM 6200 Oak Tree Blvd S 4th Fl *Web:* www.kisscleveland.com	Independence	OH	44131	216-520-2600		645
96.5 KVKI 6341 Westport Ave *TF:* 800-487-1840 ■ *Web:* www.965kvki.com	Shreveport	LA	71129	318-688-1130	687-8574	645-151
96.5 The Mill fm 500 Commercial St *Web:* 965themill.com	Manchester	NH	03101	603-669-5777	669-4641	645-97
96.7 Steve FM 316 Greystone Blvd *Web:* 967stevefm.iheart.com	Columbia	SC	29210	803-343-1100		645-40
96.7fm 125 Corporate Terr *Web:* www.myhotsprings.com	Hot Springs	AR	71913	501-525-9700		645-74
97.1 the Eagle 14001 N Dallas Pkwy Ste 300 *Web:* www.kegl.com	Dallas	TX	75240	214-866-8000		645-44
97.1 THE WAVE 1666 Blairs Pond Rd **Fax Area Code:* 302 ■ *Web:* www.971thewave.com	Milford	DE	19963	410-912-9710	422-3069*	645
97.3 Kiss FM 245 Alfred St *TF:* 800-543-3548 ■ *Web:* 973kissfm.iheart.com	Savannah	GA	31408	912-964-7794		645-148
97.3 NOW Milwaukee 12100 W Howard Ave *Web:* 973now.iheart.com	Greenfield	WI	53228	414-545-8900	327-3200	645
97.9 CPR Rock 9471 Three Rivers Rd Ste A *Web:* www.979cprrocks.com	Gulfport	MS	39503	228-388-2001		645-69
97.9 WIBB 7080 Industrial Hwy *Web:* wibb.iheart.com	Macon	GA	31216	478-781-1063		645-95
98 Rock 5345 Madison Ave *Web:* www.krxq.net	Sacramento	CA	95841	916-334-7777		645-140
98 Rock 59 Windermere Blvd *Web:* www.my98rock.com	Charleston	SC	29407	843-769-4799		645-31
98 TXT 3900 11th Ave S *Web:* 98txt.iheart.com	Tuscaloosa	AL	35401	205-344-4589		645-170
98.1 Fm KMBZ 7000 Squibb Rd *Web:* www.kmbz.com	Mission	KS	66202	913-744-3600		645
98.1 KDD 7755 Freedom Ave *Web:* wkdd.iheart.com	North Canton	OH	44720	330-836-4700		645
98.1 KHAK 425 Second St SE 4th Fl *Web:* www.khak.com	Cedar Rapids	IA	52401	319-365-9431		645-29
98.1 The Bull 2601 Nicholasville Rd *Web:* wbul.iheart.com	Lexington	KY	40503	859-422-1000		645-89
98.5 KFOX 201 Third St Ste 1200 *TF:* 877-410-5369 ■ *Web:* www.kfox.com	San Francisco	CA	94103	877-410-5369		645-146
98.7 The Gater 3071 Continental Dr *Web:* gaterrocks.iheart.com	West Palm Beach	FL	33407	561-616-6600	616-6677	645-173
98.7 WNNS 1510 N Third St *Web:* www.wnns.com	Riverton	IL	62705	217-629-5483	629-7952	645-155
98.9 The Bear WBYR 2915 Maples Rd *Web:* www.989thebear.com	Fort Wayne	IN	46816	260-447-5511	471-5224	645-63
98.9 The Vibe (WKIM-FM) 5629 Murray Rd *Web:* www.989thevibe.com	Memphis	TN	38119	901-682-1106		645-98
98.9 The Wolf 300 Arboretum Pl Ste 590 *Web:* www.989wolf.com	Richmond	VA	23236	804-327-9902		645-134
99 Cents Only Stores 4000 Union Pacific Ave *TF:* 888-582-5999 ■ *Web:* www.99only.com	Commerce	CA	90023	323-980-8145		791
99.3/105.7 Kiss FM 2809 Emerywood Pkwy Ste 300 *Web:* kissrichmond.com	Richmond	VA	23294	804-672-9299		645-134
99.5 Magic FM 500 Fourth St NW 5th Fl *Web:* www.995magicfm.com	Albuquerque	NM	87102	505-767-6700		645-4
99.5 The River 1203 Troy-Schenectady Rd **Fax Area Code:* 210 ■ *TF:* 844-289-7234 ■ *Web:* 995theriver.iheart.com	Latham	NY	12110	518-452-4800	832-3149*	645
99.5 WMAG 2-B PAI Pk *TF:* 800-876-0995 ■ *Web:* 995wmag.iheart.com	Greensboro	NC	27409	336-822-2000		645
99.9 KEZ 4686 E Van Buren St *Web:* kez999.iheart.com	Phoenix	AZ	85008	602-374-6000		645-123
99.9 KISS COUNTRY 13 Summerlin Rd *Web:* 99kisscountry.iheart.com	Asheville	NC	28806	828-257-2700		645-9
99-7 THE MIX 3055 S Fourth St *Web:* www.997kissfm.com	Springfield	IL	62703	217-528-3033	528-5348	645-155
9Dots Management Corp 1100 E Hector St Ste 245	Conshohocken	PA	19428	610-684-6220		178-10
9summer LLC 7 Research Dr *Web:* www.9summer.com	Woodbridge	CT	06525	203-397-0500		4
@Com Technology LLC 1353 Pine St Ste E *Web:* www.atcomtechnology.com	Walnut Creek	CA	94596	480-624-2500		396
@Comm Corp 150 Dow St *TF:* 800-641-5400 ■ *Web:* www.atcomm.com	Manchester	NH	03101	650-375-8188		178-7
@Law Magazine 8159 E 41st St *Web:* www.nals.org	Tulsa	OK	74145	918-582-5188	582-5907	457-15
@radical.media 435 Hudson St 6th Fl *Web:* www.radicalmedia.com	New York	NY	10014	212-462-1500		514

Company	City	State	ZIP	Phone	Fax	Class
&Barr 600 E Washington St *Web:* andbarr.co	Orlando	FL	32801	407-849-0100		4

A

Company	City	State	ZIP	Phone	Fax	Class
A & A Express Inc PO Box 707 *TF:* 800-658-3549 ■ *Web:* www.aaexpressinc.com	Brandon	SD	57005	605-582-2402	582-7300	780
A & A Global Industries Inc 17 Stenersen Ln *TF:* 800-638-6000 ■ *Web:* aaglobal.com	Cockeysville	MD	21030	410-252-1020		483
A & A Home Health Services 1240 Blalock Rd	Houston	TX	77055	713-783-8803		363
A & A Industrial Piping Inc 6 Gardner Rd *Web:* www.a-agroup.com	Fairfield	NJ	07004	973-882-2622		610
A & A Industries Inc 320 Jubilee Dr *Web:* www.aandaindustries.com	Peabody	MA	01960	978-977-9660		91
A & A Maintenance Enterprise Inc 965 Midland Ave *TF:* 800-280-0601 ■ *Web:* www.aamaintenance.com	Yonkers	NY	10704	914-969-0009		192
A & A Mechanical Inc 1111 Ulrich Ave *Web:* aamechanical.com	Louisville	KY	40219	502-968-0164		35
A & A Pharmachem Inc 4-77 Auriga Dr *Web:* www.aapharmachem.com	Ottawa	ON	K2E7Z7	613-228-2600		231
A & a Printing Inc 320 Queen Anne Ave N *TF:* 800-745-9565 ■ *Web:* aaprinting.com	Seattle	WA	98109	206-285-1700		627
A & A Safety Inc 1126 Ferris Rd *Web:* www.aasafetyinc.com	Amelia	OH	45102	513-943-6100		8
A & A Stepping Stone Mfg Inc 10291 Ophir Rd *Web:* www.aasteppingstone.com	Newcastle	CA	95658	530-885-7481		183
A & B Aerospace Inc 612 Ayon Ave *Web:* abaerospace.com	Azusa	CA	91702	626-334-2976	334-6539	21
A & B Aluminum & Brass Foundry 11165 Denton Dr *TF:* 800-743-4995 ■ *Web:* www.abfoundryonline.com	Dallas	TX	75229	972-247-3579	247-4981	492
A & B Brush Manufacturing Corp 1150 Three Ranch Rd *Web:* abbrush.com	Duarte	CA	91010	626-303-8856	303-1207	103
A & B Freight Line Inc 4805 Sandy Hollow Rd *TF:* 800-231-2235 ■ *Web:* www.aandbfreight.com	Rockford	IL	61125	815-874-4700		314
A & B Lobster House 700 Front St *Web:* www.aandblobsterhouse.com	Key West	FL	33040	305-294-5880		671
A & B Mechanical Contractors Inc 272 West 3620 South *Web:* abmechanicalcontractors.com	Salt Lake City	UT	84115	801-263-1700		189-10
A & B Pipe & Supply Inc 6500 NW 37th Ave	Miami	FL	33147	305-691-5000		612
A & B Properties Inc 822 Bishop St *Web:* www.abprop.com	Honolulu	HI	96813	808-525-6676	525-8447	653
A & D Constructors Inc 707 Schrader Dr *Web:* www.adconstructors.com	Evansville	IN	47712	812-428-3708		492
A & d Technical Supply Company Inc 4320 S 89th St *TF:* 800-228-2753 ■ *Web:* www.adtechsupply.com	Omaha	NE	68127	402-592-4950		113
A & D Technology Inc 4622 Runway Blvd *Web:* www.aanddtech.com	Ann Arbor	MI	48108	734-973-1111		407
A & E Construction Co 152 Garrett Rd *Web:* www.aeconstruction.com	Upper Darby	PA	19082	610-449-3152	449-6325	186
A & E Manufacturing Company Inc 2110 Hartel St *Web:* www.ae-mfg.com	Levittown	PA	19057	215-943-9460		697
A & E Stores Inc 1000 Huyler St *Web:* www.aestores.com	Teterboro	NJ	07608	201-393-0600	393-0233	157-6
A & E Testing 1514 Rochester St *Web:* www.shawndra.com	Lima	NY	14485	585-624-4500		743
A & E Tire Inc 3855 E 52nd Ave *Web:* www.aetire.com	Denver	CO	80216	303-308-6900		755
A & H Sportswear Company Inc 16 N Franklin St Ste 22	Pen Argyl	PA	18072	610-863-4136		155-17
A & J Mfg Co 14831 Franklin Ave *Web:* www.aj-racks.com	Tustin	CA	92780	714-544-9570	544-4215	254
A & J Washroom Accessories Inc 509 Temple Hill Rd *Web:* www.ajwashroom.com	New Windsor	NY	12553	845-562-3332		361
A & K Development Company Inc 410 Chambers St *Web:* www.akdco.net	Eugene	OR	97402	541-686-0012		298
A & K Railroad Materials Inc 1505 S Redwood Rd **Fax:* Sales ■ *TF Sales:* 800-453-8812 ■ *Web:* www.akrailroad.com	Salt Lake City	UT	84104	801-974-5484	972-2041*	770
A & L Handles Inc 244 Shoemaker Rd *Web:* www.alhandles.com	Pottstown	PA	19464	610-323-1516		499
A & L Metal Processing 1920 George St	Sandusky	OH	44870	419-627-0022		481
A & M Aviation Inc 130 S Clow International Pkwy Ste B *TF:* 800-548-1978 ■ *Web:* www.aandmaviation.com	Bolingbrook	IL	60490	630-759-1555		63
A & M Business Interior Services 1300 Washington Ave N *Web:* www.ambis.com	Minneapolis	MN	55411	612-627-1700		320
A & M Dental Laboratories Inc 425 S Santa Fe St *TF:* 800-487-8051 ■ *Web:* www.aandmdental.com	Santa Ana	CA	92705	714-547-8051		415
A & M Printing 3589 Nevada St *TF:* 800-826-8260 ■ *Web:* www.anmprinting.com	Pleasanton	CA	94566	925-484-3690		627
A & M Tool & Die Company Inc 64 Mill St *Web:* www.am-tool.com	Southbridge	MA	01550	508-764-3241		757
A & N Associates Inc 6716 Alexander Bell Dr Ste 118 *Web:* www.anassoc.com	Columbia	MD	21046	410-872-0050		261
A & N Trailer Parts 6028 S 118th E Ave *TF:* 800-272-1898 ■ *Web:* www.antrailerparts.com	Tulsa	OK	74146	918-461-8404		120
A & R Mechanical Contractors Inc 11244 E 55th Pl *Web:* www.aandrmechanical.com	Tulsa	OK	74146	918-250-6500		610
A & S Building Systems LP 1880 Hwy 116 *Web:* www.a-s.com	Caryville	TN	37714	865-426-2141		106
A & S Services Group LLC 310 N Zarfoss Dr *TF:* 800-227-6782 ■ *Web:* askinard.com	York	PA	17404	717-759-3017		311
A & T Chevrolet Inc 801 Bethlehem Pk	Sellersville	PA	18960	215-257-8022		57
A & W Oil Company Inc 1101 N Liberty St *Web:* www.awoil.com	Waynesboro	GA	30830	706-554-2121		579
A & W Products Company Inc 14 Gardner St *Web:* www.awproducts.com	Port Jervis	NY	12771	845-856-5156		534
A & W Sheet Metal Inc 602 Blazier St	West Monroe	LA	71292	318-387-9489		697
A & Z Hayward Co 655 Waterman Ave *TF:* 800-556-7462 ■ *Web:* www.azhayward.com	East Providence	RI	02914	401-438-0550	438-6970	408
A & Z Pharmaceutical Inc 180 Oser Ave Ste 300 *Web:* www.azpharmaceutical.com	Hauppauge	NY	11788	631-952-3800	952-3900	231
A & Z Pharmaceutical LLC 2275 Swallow Hill Rd Bldg 1200 *Web:* www.azpharm.com	Pittsburgh	PA	15220	412-279-8000		231
A + I 16 W 22nd St Fl 11 *Web:* www.aplusi.com	New York	NY	10010	212-460-9500		2
A 1 Auto Recyclers 7804 S Hwy 79 *TF:* 800-456-0715 ■ *Web:* www.a1autorecyclers.com	Rapid City	SD	57701	605-348-8442		54
A 1 Nethosting 265 Mar Vista Dr *Web:* a1nethosting.com	Vista	CA	92083	760-758-4007		396
A 1 Termite & Pest Control Inc 2686 Morganton Blvd SW *TF:* 800-532-7378 ■ *Web:* www.a1termitepc.com	Lenoir	NC	28645	828-758-4312		577
A 2000 Network Solutions 237 Goolsby Blvd *TF:* 800-553-2447 ■ *Web:* a2000ns.com	Deerfield Beach	FL	33442	954-480-8430		180
A A Blueprint Company Inc 2757 Gilchrist Rd *TF:* 800-821-3700 ■ *Web:* aablueprint.com	Akron	OH	44305	330-794-8803		781
A A Office Equipment & Furniture 2140 American Ave *Web:* www.aaoffice.com	Hayward	CA	94545	510-782-6110		321
A Alfred Taubman Ctr for State & Local Government Harvard Univ John F Kennedy School of Government 79 JFK St *Web:* www.hks.harvard.edu/centers/taubman	Cambridge	MA	02138	617-495-2199	496-1722	634
A All Languages Ltd 421 Bloor St E Ste 306 *TF:* 800-567-8100 ■ *Web:* www.alllanguages.com	Toronto	ON	M4W3T1	416-975-5000		317
A B C Awning & Venetian Blind Corp 858 Saint Andrews Blvd *Web:* www.abcfence.net	Charleston	SC	29407	843-766-6311		362
A B C Doors 5100 S Willow *Web:* www.abcdoors.com	Houston	TX	77035	713-729-9700		236
A B S Advanced Business Solutions 600 S John Redditt Dr	Lufkin	TX	75904	936-639-4744		693
A b Salon Interiors Inc 14220 66th St N Ste E *Web:* www.absalonequipment.com	Clearwater	FL	33764	727-531-5405		77
A Bales Security Agency Inc 9700 Dr Martin Luther King Jr St N Ste 200 *Web:* www.balessecurity.com	Saint Petersburg	FL	33702	727-592-9101		693
A Better Chance Inc 253 W 35th St 6th Fl *TF:* 800-562-7865 ■ *Web:* www.abetterchance.org	New York	NY	10001	646-346-1310		48-11
A Better Image Printing 4310 Garrett Rd *Web:* www.abetterimageprinting.com	Durham	NC	27707	919-967-0319		627
A Better Solution Inc 4303 Cedar Lake Cv *Web:* www.abs-consulting.com	Conley	GA	30288	770-252-1500		693
A Betterway Rent-a-car Inc 1110 Northchase Pkwy SE *TF:* 800-527-0700 ■ *Web:* www.budgetatl.com	Marietta	GA	30067	770-240-3305		126
A Ble Advocates for Basic Legal Equality Inc 525 Jefferson Ave *Web:* www.lawolaw.org	Toledo	OH	43604	419-255-0814		428
A Bommarito Wines Inc 2827 S Brentwood Blvd *Web:* www.abommaritowines.com	Saint Louis	MO	63144	314-961-8996		80-3
A Bright Idea LLC 210 Archer St *Web:* www.abrightideaonline.com	Bel Air	MD	21014	410-836-7180		4
A C e International Company Inc 85 Independence Dr *TF:* 800-223-4685 ■ *Web:* www.aceintl.com	Taunton	MA	02780	508-884-9600		194
A C I Media 2485 S Marion Ave *Web:* www.acimedia.com	Lake City	FL	32025	386-758-2266		809
A C Nelson Rv World 11818 L St *TF:* 888-655-2332 ■ *Web:* www.acnrv.com	Omaha	NE	68137	402-333-1122	333-1054	57
A C Tool Supply 5456 E Mcdowell Rd Ste 123 *Web:* www.aikencolon.com	Mesa	AZ	85215	480-968-6698		544
A Caring Exprnce Hm Healthcare 21 Douglas Ave *TF:* 800-564-3520 ■ *Web:* www.acaringexperience.com	Providence	RI	02908	401-453-4545		393

Phone Fax Class

A Colonial Moving & Storage Co
17 Mercer St. . . . . Hackensack NJ 07601 201-343-5777 343-1934 519
TF: 877-549-7783 ■ *Web:* www.colonialmoving.com

A Contemporary Theatre (ACT)
700 Union St Kreielsheimer Pl . . . . . Seattle WA 98101 206-292-7660 292-7670 572
TF: 888-584-4849 ■ *Web:* www.acttheatre.org

A D I Services 210 Commerce Cir. . . . . Kearneysville WV 25430 304-870-4384 770
Web: www.adiservices.com

A D Morgan Corp, The 716 N Renellie Dr . . . . . Tampa FL 33609 813-832-3033 831-9860 186
Web: www.admorgan.com

A D Singleton & Company CPA Inc
441 S Escondido Blvd . . . . . Escondido CA 92025 760-747-4605 2
Web: adscpa.com

A D Vision Inc
5750 Bintliff Dr Ste 210 . . . . . Houston TX 77036 713-341-7100 525

A Daigger & Company Inc
620 Lakeview Pkwy. . . . . Vernon Hills IL 60061 847-816-5060 320-7200* 603
**Fax Area Code:* 800 ■ *TF:* 800-621-7193 ■ *Web:* www.daigger.com

A Diamond Production Inc
2150 Cesar Chavez St. . . . . San Francisco CA 94124 415-920-6800 321
Web: www.thefutonshop.com

A Duchini Inc 2550 McKinley Ave . . . . . Erie PA 16503 814-456-7027 183
TF: 800-937-7317 ■ *Web:* www.duchini.com

A Duda & Sons Inc 1200 Duda Trail . . . . . Oviedo FL 32765 407-365-2111 365-2147 10-11
Web: www.duda.com

A Duie Pyle Inc
650 Westtown Rd PO Box 564 . . . . . West Chester PA 19381 610-696-5800 449
TF: 800-523-5020 ■ *Web:* www.aduiepyle.com

A E C Group Inc, The
1735 Fifth Ave. . . . . McKeesport PA 15132 412-678-1440 189-4
Web: www.aecgroup.com

A E Data Integration Inc
933 N Kenmore St Ste 318 . . . . . Arlington VA 22201 703-075-2095 809
Web: www.aediinc.com

A e Graphics Inc
4075 N 124th St Ste A . . . . . Brookfield WI 53005 262-781-7744 113
Web: aegraphics.com

A Epstein & Sons International Inc
600 W Fulton St . . . . . Chicago IL 60661 312-454-9100 454-9100 261
Web: www.epsteinglobal.com

A F A Industries 140 E Pond Dr . . . . . Romeo MI 48065 586-752-2900 326
TF: 800-753-5237 ■ *Web:* www.afaindustries.com

A F K Corp 300 Pacific St . . . . . Ripon WI 54971 920-748-2265 492
Web: www.afkfoundry.com

A Few of My Favorite Things
108 N Sixth St . . . . . Wyoming IL 61491 309-695-9966 292
Web: afewofmyfavoritethingsflowershop.com

A Finkl & Sons Co
2011 N Southport Ave. . . . . Chicago IL 60614 773-975-2510 348-5347 723
TF: 800-343-2562 ■ *Web:* www.finkl.com

A Fish Called Avalon 700 Ocean Dr. . . . . Miami Beach FL 33139 305-532-1727 671
Web: www.afishcalledavalon.com

A G Adjustments Ltd
740 Walt Whitman Rd. . . . . Melville NY 11747 631-425-8800 160
Web: www.agaltd.com

A G Equipment Company Inc
3401 W Albany . . . . . Broken Arrow OK 74012 918-250-7386 172
Web: www.agequipmentcompany.com

A G H Industries Inc
7420 Whitehall St . . . . . Richland Hills TX 76118 817-284-1742 22
Web: www.aghindustries.com

A G Miller Company Inc
53 Batavia St. . . . . Springfield MA 01109 413-732-9297 734-1236 192
Web: www.agmiller.com

A G Wassenaar Inc
2180 S Ivanhoe St Ste 5 . . . . . Denver CO 80222 303-759-8100 196

A Glimmer of Hope
3600 N Capital of Texas Hwy Bldg B
Bldg B Ste 330 . . . . . Austin TX 78746 512-328-9944 328-8872 305
Web: glimmer.org

A Graziano Inc 71 Adams St . . . . . Braintree MA 02184 781-843-7300 182
Web: www.grazianoconcrete.com

A H Belo Corp
508 Young St PO Box 224866 . . . . . Dallas TX 75202 214-977-8200 977-8201 580
NYSE: AHC ■ *TF:* 800-230-1074 ■ *Web:* www.ahbelo.com

A H Lundberg Associates Inc
13201 Bel Red Rd. . . . . Bellevue WA 98005 425-283-5070 261
Web: lundbergllc.com

A H Stock Manufacturing Corp
8402 Center Rd. . . . . Newton WI 53063 920-726-4211 567
Web: www.ahstockmfg.com

A Homecrest Outdoor Living LLC
1250 Homecrest Ave. . . . . Wadena MN 56482 218-631-1000 319-4
TF: 800-225-3570 ■ *Web:* www.homecrest.com

a i Solutions Inc
4500 Forbes Blvd Ste 300 . . . . . Lanham MD 20706 301-306-1756 306-1754 194
Web: www.ai-solutions.com

A J Blosenski Inc
1600 Chestnut Tree Rd . . . . . Honey Brook PA 19344 610-942-2707 638
TF: 800-343-6583 ■ *Web:* www.ajblosenski.com

A J Clarke Real Estate Corp
1035 River Rd. . . . . New Milford NJ 07646 201-836-7464 652

A J Johns Inc 3225 Anniston Rd . . . . . Jacksonville FL 32246 904-641-2055 641-2102 189-11
Web: www.ajjohns.com

A J Martini Inc 5 Lowell Ave . . . . . Winchester MA 01890 781-569-6900 186

A J Sackett & Sons Co, The
1701 S Highland Ave . . . . . Baltimore MD 21224 410-276-4466 480
TF: 800-274-4466 ■ *Web:* www.ajsackett.com

A Jewish Voice for Peace Inc
1611 Telegraph Ave Ste 550 . . . . . Oakland CA 94612 510-465-1777 615
Web: jewishvoiceforpeace.org

A L H Group Inc
880 Industrial Way . . . . . San Luis Obispo CA 93401 805-541-8739 177
Web: alh.alh-group.com

A L Schutzman Company Inc
N21 W23560 Ridge View Pkwy W . . . . . Waukesha WI 53188 262-832-8200 805
Web: www.alschutzman.com

A La Carte Event Pavilion Ltd
4050 Dana Shores Dr . . . . . Tampa FL 33634 813-831-5390 379

A La Lucia 315 Madison St . . . . . Alexandria VA 22314 703-836-5123 671
Web: www.alalucia.com

A La Lucie 159 N Limestone St . . . . . Lexington KY 40507 859-252-5277 225-5027 671
Web: www.alalucie.com

A Larry Ross Communications Inc
4300 Marsh Ridge Rd Ste 114 . . . . . Carrollton TX 75010 972-267-1111 636
Web: www.alarryross.com

A Lava & Son Co 4800 S Kilbourn Ave . . . . . Chicago IL 60632 773-254-2800 320
TF: 800-777-5282 ■ *Web:* www.alavason.com

A M C Colorgrafix Inc 2085 Peck Rd . . . . . El Monte CA 91733 626-575-1788 592
TF: 800-421-8703 ■ *Web:* www.amc-color.com

A M Solutions 100 Interstate Blvd . . . . . Edgerton WI 53534 608-884-3452 5
Web: www.amsolutionswi.com

A Matter of Fax 105 Harrison Ave. . . . . Harrison NJ 07029 973-482-3700 179
TF: 800-433-3329 ■ *Web:* www.amatteroffax.com

A Media Web & Graphic Design
2200 Adeline St Ste 320 . . . . . Oakland CA 94607 510-763-5442 344
TF: 800-708-1790 ■ *Web:* www.amedianysf.com

A Meyers & Sons Corp 325 W 38th St . . . . . New York NY 10018 212-279-6632 594

A Morton Thomas & Associates Inc
800 King Farm Blvd 4th Fl . . . . . Rockville MD 20850 301-881-2545 186
Web: www.amtengineering.com

A N Culbertson & Company Inc
1 Boars Head Pointe Ste 101 . . . . . Charlottesville VA 22903 434-972-7766 401
TF: 800-541-1419 ■ *Web:* www.anculbertson.com

A New Path 2527 Doubletree Rd . . . . . Spring Valley CA 91978 619-670-1184 787
Web: anewpathsite.org

A Noble Grille 380 Knollwood St. . . . . Winston-Salem NC 27103 336-777-8477 671
Web: roosterskitchen.com

A Nonini Winery Inc 2640 N Dickenson . . . . . Fresno CA 93723 559-275-1936 50-7
TF: 800-561-3357 ■ *Web:* www.noniniwinery.com

A Nose For Clothes
14271 SW 120th St Ste 102 . . . . . Miami FL 33186 305-253-8631 157-6
Web: www.anoseforclothes.com

A One Staffing LLC
3639 New Getwell Rd Ste 1 . . . . . Memphis TN 38118 901-367-5757 260
TF: 800-561-3357 ■ *Web:* www.aonestaffing.com

A P F Travel Inc 1721 Garvey Ave Fl 2 . . . . . Alhambra CA 91803 626-282-9988 775
TF: 800-888-9168 ■ *Web:* www.apftravel.com

A p Machine & Tool Inc
1301 Elm St . . . . . Terre Haute IN 47807 812-232-4939 697
Web: apmachineandtool.com

A Partner in Technology
105 Dresden Ave. . . . . Gardiner ME 04345 207-582-0888 180
TF: 877-582-0888 ■ *Web:* www.apitechnology.com

A Pavillion Agency Inc
15 E 40 St Ste 400 . . . . . New York NY 10016 212-889-6609 260
Web: pavillionagency.com

A Plus Arts Academy
270 S Napoleon Ave . . . . . Columbus OH 43213 614-338-0767 463
Web: aplusarts.com

A Plus Benefits Inc 395 W 600 N. . . . . Lindon UT 84042 801-443-1090 390
TF: 800-748-5102 ■ *Web:* www.aplusbenefits.com

A Plus Designs Inc & Outfitters Plus Outlet Store
56988 635th St. . . . . Atlantic IA 50022 712-243-4379 687
Web: www.aplusdesignsinc.com

A Plus Family Care
4538 Callaghan Rd . . . . . San Antonio TX 78228 210-342-2819 363

A Plus International Inc
5138 Eucalyptus Ave. . . . . Chino CA 91710 909-591-5168 591-0359 475
TF: 800-762-1123 ■ *Web:* www.aplusgroup.net

A Plus Letter Service Inc
200 Syracuse Ct . . . . . Lakewood NJ 08701 732-905-2010 5
Web: www.aplusletter.com

A r C Informatique Inc
1770 Ifuc Mitis . . . . . Chicoutimi QC G7K1H4 418-545-9224 180
Web: www.arcinformatique.com

A R Mays Construction Inc
6900 E Indian School Rd Ste 200 . . . . . Scottsdale AZ 85251 480-850-6900 186
Web: www.armays.com

A Rifkin Co 1400 Sans Souci Pkwy . . . . . Wilkes-Barre PA 18706 570-825-9551 825-5282 67
TF Cust Svc: 800-458-7300 ■ *Web:* www.arifkin.com

A Ruiz Construction Company & Associates Inc
1601 Cortland Ave . . . . . San Francisco CA 94110 415-647-4010 186
Web: www.aruizconstruction.com

A S E Industries Inc 23850 Pinewood . . . . . Warren MI 48091 586-754-7480 207
Web: www.aseind.com

A Schulman Inc 3550 W Market St . . . . . Akron OH 44333 330-666-3751 668-7204 605-2
NASDAQ: SHLM ■ *TF:* 800-547-3746 ■ *Web:* www.aschulman.com

A Star Electric Co
200 Seegers Ave . . . . . Elk Grove Village IL 60007 847-439-4122 625
Web: www.astareg.com

A Stucki Co 2600 Neville Rd . . . . . Pittsburgh PA 15225 412-771-7300 771-7308 650
TF: 888-266-6630 ■ *Web:* www.stucki.com

A T Klemens & Son Inc
814 12th St N . . . . . Great Falls MT 59401 406-452-9541 610
Web: www.atklemens.com

A T R Sales Inc 41 Talbot Rd . . . . . Northborough MA 01532 508-393-8529 711
Web: www.atrsales.com

A T Secure Net 2001 Columbus St . . . . . Bakersfield CA 93305 661-872-4807 225
Web: atsecure.net

A Taste of New York Inc 10 Roberta Ln. . . . . Syosset NY 11791 516-677-0239 742
Web: www.tasteofny.com

A Tavola 2148 W Chicago Ave . . . . . Chicago IL 60622 773-276-7567 671
Web: atavolachi.com

A Teichert & Son Inc
3500 American River Dr . . . . . Sacramento CA 95864 916-484-3011 182
TF: 800-283-0222 ■ *Web:* www.teichert.com

A Tenenbaum Company Inc
4500 W Bethany Rd . . . . . North Little Rock AR 72117 501-945-0881 945-3865 686
Web: www.trg.net

A to B Realty 1975 Hamilton Ave Ste 9 . . . . . San Jose CA 95125 408-626-4800 626-9384 652
Web: www.atobrealty.com

A to Z Logos 3947 Catamarca Dr . . . . . San Diego CA 92124 858-715-4775 475
Web: a2zlogos.espwebsite.com

A Total Tan 1400 Teal Rd Ste 4. . . . . Lafayette IN 47905 765-474-1514 226
Web: atotaltan.net

	City	State	Zip	Phone	Fax	Class
A Touch of Garlic Restaurant						
427 White St	Springfield	MA	01108	413-736-7868		671
A Very Private Eye Inc						
3936 S Semoran Blvd Ste 487	Orlando	FL	32822	407-273-6646	687-8880*	400
*Fax Area Code: 866 ■ Web: www.averyprivateeye.com						
A W North Carolina Inc						
4112 Old Oxford Hwy	Durham	NC	27712	919-479-6400		247
Web: www.aw-nc.com						
A Web That Works						
2733 Concession Rd 7	Bowmanville	ON	L1C3K6	905-263-2666	263-8989	4
TF: 800-579-9253 ■ Web: www.awebthatworks.com						
A William Roberts Jr & Assoc Inc						
234 Seven Farms Dr Ste 210	Charleston	SC	29492	843-722-8414		768
Web: scheduledepo.com						
A Worldwide Golf Co 75 Brainard Rd	Hartford	CT	06114	860-522-6829		711
Web: www.golferswarehouse.com						
A Y R Consulting Group						
3708 Rodale Way Ste 200	Dallas	TX	75287	972-820-8400		194
Web: ayrconsulting.com						
A Yankee Line 370 W First St	Boston	MA	02127	617-268-8890	268-6960	107
TF: 800-942-8890 ■ Web: www.yankeeline.us						
A Zahner Sheet Metal Company Inc						
1400 E Ninth St	Kansas City	MO	64106	816-474-8882	474-7994	189-12
TF: 800-467-3125 ■ Web: www.azahner.com						
A Zerega's Sons Inc PO Box 241	Fair Lawn	NJ	07410	201-797-1400	797-0148	296-31
Web: www.zerega.com						
A'Gaci LLC						
12460 Network Blvd Ste 106	San Antonio	TX	78249	866-265-3036		157-6
TF: 866-265-3036 ■ Web: www.agacistore.com						
A'viands LLC						
1751 County Rd B W Ste 300	Roseville	MN	55113	651-631-0940		299
Web: www.aviands.com						
A+ School Apparel 401 Knoss Ave	Star City	AR	71667	800-227-3215	628-9020*	155-19
*Fax Area Code: 888 ■ TF: 800-227-3215 ■ Web: www.schoolapparel.com						
A. Carlisle & Company of Nevada Inc						
1080 Bible Way	Reno	NV	89502	775-323-5163		627
Web: www.acarlisleprinting.com						
A. J. Edmond Co 1530 W 16th St	Long Beach	CA	90813	562-437-1802		108
TF: 800-836-5355 ■ Web: ajedmondco.com						
A. M. Ortega Construction Inc						
10125 Ch Rd	Lakeside	CA	92040	619-390-1988	390-1941	189-4
TF: 800-909-1988 ■ Web: www.amortega.com						
A. Smith & Company Productions Inc						
9911 W Pico Blvd Ste 128	Los Angeles	CA	90035	310-432-4800		738
Web: www.asmithco.com						
A. Smith Bowman Distillery						
1 Bowman Dr	Fredericksburg	VA	22408	540-373-4555		80-1
Web: www.asmithbowman.com						
A.B. Data Ltd 600 A B Data Dr	Milwaukee	WI	53217	414-961-6400		260
Web: abdata.com						
A.C. Coy Co 395 Valley Brook Rd	Canonsburg	PA	15317	724-820-1820		261
TF: 800-784-5773 ■ Web: www.accoy.com						
A.C. Schultes of Maryland Inc						
16289 Sussex Hwy	Bridgeville	DE	19933	410-841-6710		393
Web: www.acschultes.com						
A.C. White Transfer & Storage Co Inc						
1775 Founders Pkwy	Alpharetta	GA	30009	770-325-9100		685
Web: www.atlantamovingcorp.com						
A.D. Susman & Associates Inc						
3033 Chimney Rock Rd Ste 690	Houston	TX	77056	713-668-7998		260
Web: www.adsusman.com						
A.D.D. Marketing Inc						
6600 Lexington Ave	Los Angeles	CA	90038	323-790-0500		195
Web: www.addmarketing.com						
A.E. Litho Offset Printers Inc						
450 Broad St	Beverly	NJ	08010	609-239-0700		627
Web: aelitho.com						
A.G. Ferrari Foods 2000 N Loop Rd	Alameda	CA	94502	510-346-2100	351-2672	345
TF: 877-878-2783 ■ Web: www.agferrari.com						
A.J. Antunes & Co 180 Kehoe Blvd	Carol Stream	IL	60188	630-784-1000		253
Web: www.ajantunes.com						
A.J. Catagnus Inc 1299 W James St	Norristown	PA	19401	610-277-2727		660
Web: www.ajcatagnus.com						
A.J. O'Neal & Associates Inc						
109 Falkenburg Rd N	Tampa	FL	33619	813-654-4199		260
Web: www.ajoneal.com						
A.O.W. Associates Inc 30 Essex St	Albany	NY	12206	518-482-3400		186
Web: aowassoc.com						
A.R. Sandri Inc 400 Chapman St	Greenfield	MA	01301	413-772-2121		579
TF: 800-628-1900 ■ Web: www.sandri.com						
A.r.e. Inc PO Box 1100	Massillon	OH	44648	330-481-1333	730-4545	516
Web: www.4are.com						
A.R.M. Solutions Inc PO Box 2929	Camarillo	CA	93011	888-772-6468		160
TF: 888-772-6468 ■ Web: www.armsolutions.com						
A.S.G. Staffing Inc						
231 W Grand Ave Ste 102	Bensenville	IL	60106	630-787-6150		193
TF: 800-264-1170 ■ Web: www.asgstaffing.com						
A.T. Still University of Health Sciences						
800 W Jefferson St	Kirksville	MO	63501	660-626-2121		162
TF: 866-626-2878 ■ Web: www.atsu.edu						
A/G (Assemblies of God)						
1445 N Boonville Ave	Springfield	MO	65802	417-862-2781		48-20
TF: 800-641-4310 ■ Web: www.ag.org						
A-1 Action Nursing Care Inc						
3508 Greencastle Rd	Burtonsville	MD	20866	301-890-7575		363
Web: a1actionnursingcare.com						
A-1 Contract Staffing Inc						
3829 Coconut Palm Dr	Tampa	FL	33619	813-620-1661		631
TF: 800-966-5562 ■ Web: www.a1hr.com						
A-1 Crane Services Ltd						
1148 Sta Main	Grande Prairie	AB	T8V4B5	780-532-8212		393
Web: ncsg.com						
A-1 Creative Packaging Corp						
400 Industrial Blvd	Palmyra	WI	53156	262-495-2151		88
Web: creativeplastics.com						
A-1 Hospitality LLC						
7809 W Quinault Ave	Kennewick	WA	99336	509-783-2164		377
Web: www.hotelsa1.com						
A-1 Jays Machinery 2228 Oakland Rd	San Jose	CA	95131	408-262-1845		454
Web: www.a1jays.com						
A-1 Production Inc						
5809 E Leighty Rd	Kendallville	IN	46755	260-347-0960	347-4727	621
Web: www.a1production.com						
A1 Roof Trusses Ltd Co						
4451 Saint Lucie Blvd	Fort Pierce	FL	34946	772-409-1010		194
Web: www.a1truss.com						
A1 Staffing & Recruiting Agency Inc						
7407 NW 23rd St	Bethany	OK	73008	405-787-7600		260
TF: 800-233-1261 ■ Web: www.a1staffingok.com						
A1 Teletronics Inc						
2550 118th Ave N 00	Saint Petersburg	FL	33716	727-576-5001		246
Web: www.a1teletronics.com						
A-1 Tool Corp 1425 Armitage Ave	Melrose Park	IL	60160	708-345-5000		697
Web: www.a1toolco.com						
A123 Systems Inc 200 W St	Waltham	MA	02451	617-778-5700	924-8910	74
TF: 800-224-7654 ■ Web: www.a123systems.com						
A2 Inc 245 W 29th St Ste 1601	New York	NY	10001	212-807-8772		187
Web: www.a2inc.com						
A2F-Consulting LLC						
4915 St Elmo Ave Ste 205	Bethesda	MD	20814	301-907-9400		463
Web: www.a2f-c.com						
A2LA (American Association for Laboratory Accreditation)						
5301 Buckeystown Pike Ste 350	Frederick	MD	21704	301-644-3248	662-2974	49-19
TF: 800-321-2211 ■ Web: www.a2la.org						
A2mg Inc 8601 E US Hwy 40	Kansas City	MO	64129	816-874-4500	241-6521	697
A2Z Field Services LLC						
7450 Industrial Pkwy Ste 105	Plain City	OH	43064	614-873-0211		365
TF: 800-713-2001 ■ Web: www.a2zfieldservices.com						
A2z Global LLC 6981 N Park Dr	Pennsauken	NJ	08109	856-910-0300		768
Web: a2zglobal.com						
A2Z Science & Nature Store						
57 King St	NorthHampton	MA	01060	413-586-1611		761
Web: a2zscience.com						
A3 Communications Inc						
1038 Kinley Rd Bldg B	Irmo	SC	29063	803-744-5000		196
Web: a3communications.com						
A-588 & A-572 Steel Co, The						
133 Sebago Lake Dr	Sewickley	PA	15143	412-366-1980		492
Web: www.a588a572steel.com						
AA (Alcoholics Anonymous)						
475 Riverside Dr 11th Fl	New York	NY	10115	212-870-3400	870-3003	48-21
TF: 800-437-3584 ■ Web: www.aa.org						
AA Consulting Inc 9 Locust St	Douglas	MA	01516	774-280-9036		463
Web: www.aa-consulting-inc.com						
AA Importing Co Inc 7700 Hall St	Saint Louis	MO	63147	314-383-8800	383-2608	361
TF Cust Svc: 800-325-0602 ■ Web: www.aaimporting.com						
A&A Machine & Fabrication LLC						
3101 Texas Ave	La Marque	TX	77568	409-938-4274		454
Web: www.aagroup.com						
A&A Merchandising Ltd						
3250 Lakeshore Blvd W	Toronto	ON	M8V1M1	416-503-3343		636
Web: www.aamerch.com						
Aa Temps Inc 7002 Little River Tpke	Annandale	VA	22003	703-642-9050		5
TF: 800-901-8367 ■ Web: www.ardelle.com						
AA Wheel & Truck Supply Inc						
717 E 16th Ave	Kansas City	MO	64116	816-221-9556	221-9558	61
Web: www.aawheel.com						
AAA (American Academy of Audiology)						
11730 Plaza America Dr Ste 300	Reston	VA	20190	703-790-8466	790-8631	49-8
TF: 800-222-2336 ■ Web: www.audiology.org						
AAA (American Angus Assn)						
3201 Frederick Ave	Saint Joseph	MO	64506	816-383-5100	233-9703	48-2
TF: 800-821-5478 ■ Web: www.angus.org						
AAA (American Anthropological Assn)						
2200 Wilson Blvd Ste 600	Arlington	VA	22201	703-528-1902	528-3546	49-5
Web: www.americananthro.org						
AAA (American Arbitration Assn Inc)						
1633 Broadway 10th Fl	New York	NY	10019	212-716-5800		41
TF: 800-778-7879 ■ Web: www.adr.org						
AAA (American Automobile Assn Inc)						
1000 AAA Dr	Heathrow	FL	32746	407-444-4240	444-4247	48-23
Web: www.aaa.com						
AAA (American Ambulance Assn)						
8400 Westpark Dr Fl 2	McLean	VA	22102	703-610-9018		49-21
TF: 800-523-4447 ■ Web: www.the-aaa.org						
AAA (Appraisers Assn of America)						
386 Pk Ave S Ste 2000	New York	NY	10016	212-889-5404	889-5503	49-12
Web: appraisersassociation.org						
AAA Aircraft Supply LLC 68 Shaker Rd	Enfield	CT	06082	860-749-5192		57
Web: aaa-aircraft.com						
AAA Akron 111 W Center St	Akron	OH	44308	330-762-0631	762-5965	53
Web: www.aaa.com						
AAA Alarm Systems Ltd						
180 Nature Pkwy	Winnipeg	MB	R3P0X7	204-949-0078		693
TF: 866-949-0078 ■ Web: www.aaasecure.ca/aaa						
AAA Allied Group Inc						
15 W Central Pkwy	Cincinnati	OH	45202	513-762-3100		53
TF: 800-543-2345 ■ Web: ohiovalley.aaa.com						
AAA Carolinas 6600 AAA Dr	Charlotte	NC	28212	704-569-3600	285-6176	53
TF: 800-477-4222 ■ Web: locator.carolinas.aaa.com						
AAA Chicago Motor Club						
975 Meridian Lake Dr	Aurora	IL	60504	866-968-7222	499-8200*	53
*Fax Area Code: 630 ■ TF: 866-968-7222 ■ Web: www.aaa.com						
AAA Club Alliance Inc						
7150 W Central Ave	Toledo	OH	43617	419-843-1200		53
TF: 800-222-4357 ■ Web: www.nwohio.aaa.com						
AAA Collections Inc						
3500 S First Avenue Cir	Sioux Falls	SD	57105	605-339-1333		160
TF: 800-611-7371 ■ Web: www.aaa-coll.com						
AAA Colorado 4100 E Arkansas Ave	Denver	CO	80222	303-753-8800		53
TF: 866-625-3601 ■ Web: www.colorado.aaa.com						
Aaa Concrete Products Corp						
1224 E Broad Ave	Albany	GA	31705	229-436-4626		182
Web: www.aaaconcrete.biz						
AAA Cooper Transportation						
1751 Kinsey Rd	Dothan	AL	36303	334-793-2284		780
TF: 800-633-7571 ■ Web: www.aaacooper.com						

Name / Address	City	State	Zip	Phone	Fax	Class
AAA Digital Imaging Inc						
5706 New Peachtree Rd	Chamblee	GA	30341	770-451-7861		174
Web: www.aaadi.com						
AAA East Central 5900 Baum Blvd	Pittsburgh	PA	15206	412-365-7196		53
Web: www.aaa.com						
AAA East Penn 1020 W Hamilton St	Allentown	PA	18101	800-222-4357		53
TF: 800-222-4357 ■ *Web:* www.aaa.com						
AAA Environmental Inc						
2036 Chesnee Hwy	Spartanburg	SC	29303	864-582-1222	454-0442*	667
**Fax Area Code:* 314 ■ *TF:* 888-296-3803 ■ *Web:* www.aaaenvironmental.com						
AAA Financial Corp						
9600 W Sample Rd	Coral Springs	FL	33065	954-344-2530		509
Web: www.aaafinancial.com						
Aaa Flag & Banner Manufacturing Co						
8955 National Blvd	Los Angeles	CA	90034	800-266-4222	836-7253*	287
**Fax Area Code:* 310 ■ *TF:* 800-266-4222 ■ *Web:* www.aaaflag.com						
AAA Glass & Mirror Co 3300 McCart	Fort Worth	TX	76110	817-924-4444		362
Web: www.aaa-glass.com						
AAA Hawaii						
1130 N Nimitz Hwy Ste A-170	Honolulu	HI	96817	808-593-2221		53
TF: 800-736-2886 ■ *Web:* hawaii.aaa.com/home.html						
AAA Hoosier Motor Club						
3750 Guion Rd	Indianapolis	IN	46222	317-923-1500	923-5991*	53
**Fax:* Cust Svc ■ *Web:* www.aaa.com						
AAA Hudson Valley 618 Delaware Ave	Albany	NY	12209	518-426-1000	426-1595	53
Web: www.aaa.com						
AAA Mailing Services Inc						
5224 Hwy 50 W	Jefferson City	MO	65109	573-893-7679		627
TF: 800-463-3339 ■ *Web:* www.aaamailing.com						
AAA Massillon Auto Club						
1972 Wales Rd NE	Massillon	OH	44646	330-833-1084		53
TF: 800-222-4357 ■ *Web:* www.aaa.com						
AAA Merrimack Valley						
49 OrchaRd Hill Rd	North Andover	MA	01845	978-681-9200		53
TF: 800-594-7992 ■ *Web:* www.aaa.com						
AAA Michigan 1 Auto Club Dr	Dearborn	MI	48126	800-222-6424		53
TF: 800-222-6424 ■ *Web:* www.aaa.com						
AAA Minneapolis						
5400 Auto Club Way	Minneapolis	MN	55416	952-927-2600	927-2559	53
Web: www.aaa.com						
AAA Minnesota/Iowa						
600 W Travelers Trl	Burnsville	MN	55337	952-707-4500		53
TF: 800-222-1333 ■ *Web:* www.aaa.com/ppinternational/international.html						
AAA Missouri 12901 N Forty Dr	Saint Louis	MO	63141	314-523-7350		53
TF: 800-222-4357 ■ *Web:* aaa.com						
AAA MountainWest 2100 11th Ave	Helena	MT	59601	406-447-8100	442-5671	53
TF: 800-332-6119 ■ *Web:* www.aaa.com						
Aaa Moving & Storage Inc						
747 E Ship Creek Ave	Anchorage	AK	99501	888-927-3330	276-1986*	780
**Fax Area Code:* 907 ■ *TF:* 888-995-3331 ■ *Web:* www.alliedalaska.com						
AAA Nebraska 815 N 98th St	Omaha	NE	68114	402-390-1000		53
TF: 800-222-6327 ■ *Web:* www.aaa.com/ppinternational/international.html						
AAA North Penn 1035 N Washington Ave	Scranton	PA	18509	570-348-2511	348-2563	53
TF: 800-222-4357 ■ *Web:* www.aaa.com						
AAA Northampton County						
3914 Hecktown Rd	Easton	PA	18045	610-258-2371		53
Web: www.aaa.com						
AAA Northern New England						
68 Marginal Way	Portland	ME	04104	207-780-6800	780-6986	53
TF: 800-222-4357 ■ *Web:* www.northernnewengland.aaa.com						
AAA Northway 112 Railroad St	Schenectady	NY	12305	518-374-4696		53
TF: 866-222-7283 ■ *Web:* aaa.com						
AAA Ohio Auto Club						
90 E Wilson Bridge Rd	Worthington	OH	43085	614-431-7901		53
TF: 888-222-6446 ■ *Web:* ohio.aaa.com						
AAA Oklahoma 2121 E 15th St	Tulsa	OK	74104	918-748-1000	748-1111	53
TF: 800-222-2582 ■ *Web:* www.ok.aaa.com						
AAA Properties 331 Wall St	Chico	CA	95928	530-895-3500		379
Web: aaapropertieschico.com						
AAA Reading-Berks 920 Van Reed Rd	Wyomissing	PA	19610	610-374-4531		53
Web: www.aaa.com						
AAA Refrigeration Service Inc						
1804 Nereid Ave	Bronx	NY	10466	718-324-2231		610
Web: www.aaarefrig.com						
AAA Schuylkill County						
340 S Centre St	Pottsville	PA	17901	570-622-4991		53
Web: www.aaa.com						
AAA Shelby County 920 Wapakoneta Ave	Sidney	OH	45365	937-492-3167		53
Web: www.aaa.com						
AAA South Jersey 700 Laurel Oak Rd	Voorhees	NJ	08043	856-783-4222		53
TF: 800-222-4357 ■ *Web:* www.aaa.com						
AAA Southern New England						
110 Royal Little Dr	Providence	RI	02904	401-868-2000		53
TF: 800-222-7448 ■ *Web:* www.aaa.com						
AAA Southern Pennsylvania						
2840 Eastern Blvd	York	PA	17402	717-600-8700		53
TF: 800-222-1469 ■ *Web:* www.aaa.com						
Aaa Standard Services Inc 4117 S Ave	Toledo	OH	43615	419-535-0274		104
Web: www.aaastandardservices.com						
AAA Susquehanna Valley 1001 Market St	Sunbury	PA	17801	570-286-4507		53
Web: www.aaa.com						
AAA Tidewater Virginia						
5366 Virginia Beach Blvd	Virginia Beach	VA	23462	757-233-3800	233-3896	53
Web: www.aaa.com						
AAA Utica & Central New York						
409 Court St	Utica	NY	13502	800-222-4357		53
TF: 800-222-4357 ■ *Web:* www.aaa.com						
AAA Western & Central New York						
100 International Dr	Williamsville	NY	14221	716-633-9860	633-4439	53
TF: 800-836-2582 ■ *Web:* westerncentralny.aaa.com						
AAA Wisconsin 8401 Excelsior Dr	Madison	WI	53717	608-828-2495		53
TF: 800-236-1300 ■ *Web:* newsroom.aaa.com						
AAAA (American Assn of Adv Agencies)						
1065 Ave of the Americas 16th Fl	New York	NY	10018	212-682-2500	682-8391	49-18
TF: 800-537-4180 ■ *Web:* www.aaaa.org						
AAAA (Army Aviation Assn of America)						
593 Main St	Monroe	CT	06468	203-268-2450	268-5870	48-19
Web: www.quad-a.org						
AAAA Benefits						
11020 David Taylor Dr Ste 305	Charlotte	NC	28262	704-594-6270		138
Web: www.aaaabenefits.com						
AAAAI (American Academy of Allergy Asthma & Immunology)						
555 E Wells St Ste 1100	Milwaukee	WI	53202	414-272-6071	272-6070	49-8
TF: 800-654-2452 ■ *Web:* www.aaaai.org						
AAAASF (American Assn for Accreditation of Ambulatory Surgery Facilities Inc)						
5101 Washington St Ste 2F PO Box 9500	Gurnee	IL	60031	847-775-1985		48-1
TF: 888-545-5222 ■ *Web:* www.aaaasf.org						
AAACCVB (Annapolis & Anne Arundel County Conference & Visitors Bureau)						
26 W St	Annapolis	MD	21401	410-280-0445	263-9591	206
TF: 888-302-2852 ■ *Web:* www.visitannapolis.org						
AAACE (American Assn for Adult & Continuing Education)						
1827 Powers Ferry Rd Bldg 14 Ste 100	Atlanta	GA	30339	678-271-4319		49-5
Web: www.aaace.org						
AAAE (American Assn of Airport Executives)						
601 Madison St Ste 400	Alexandria	VA	22314	703-824-0500	820-1395	49-21
TF: 800-609-7374 ■ *Web:* www.aaae.org						
AAAHC (Accreditation Assn for Ambulatory Health Care)						
5250 Old OrchaRd Rd Ste 200	Skokie	IL	60077	847-853-6060	853-9028	48-1
Web: www.aaahc.org						
AAAI (Association for the Advancement of Artificial Intelligence)						
445 Burgess Dr Ste 100	Menlo Park	CA	94025	650-328-3123	321-4457	48-9
TF: 800-548-4664 ■ *Web:* www.aaai.org						
AAAOM (American Assn of Acupunture & Oriental Medicine)						
PO Box 162340	Sacramento	CA	95816	916-443-4770		48-17
TF: 866-455-7999 ■ *Web:* www.aaaomonline.org						
AAAP (American Academy of Addiction Psychiatry)						
400 Massasoit Ave 2nd Fl Ste 307	East Providence	RI	02914	401-524-3076	272-0922	49-15
TF: 800-263-6317 ■ *Web:* www.aaap.org						
AAAS (American Assn for the Advancement of Science)						
1200 New York Ave NW	Washington	DC	20005	202-326-6400	682-0816	49-19
Web: www.aaas.org						
AAB (American Association of Bioanalysts)						
906 Olive St Ste 1200	Saint Louis	MO	63101	314-241-1445	241-1449	49-8
TF: 800-457-3332 ■ *Web:* www.aab.org						
Aabaco Plastics Inc						
9520 Midwest Ave	Garfield Heights	OH	44125	216-663-9494	663-9475*	66
**Fax:* Sales ■ *Web:* www.aabacoplastics.com						
AABBA (Anchorage Alaska Bed & Breakfast Assn)						
PO Box 242623	Anchorage	AK	99524	907-272-5909		376
TF: 888-584-5147 ■ *Web:* www.anchorage-bnb.com						
Aabbitt Adhesives Inc 2403 N Oakley	Chicago	IL	60647	800-222-2488		3
TF: 800-222-2488 ■ *Web:* www.aabbitt.com						
AABBN (Alexandria & Arlington Bed & Breakfast Networks)						
4938 Hampden Ln Ste 164	Bethesda	MD	20814	703-549-3415	517-9179*	376
**Fax Area Code:* 202 ■ *TF:* 888-549-3415 ■ *Web:* www.aabbn.com						
AABC (American Amateur Baseball Congress)						
100 W Broadway	Farmington	NM	87401	505-327-3120		48-22
Web: www.aabc.us						
AABC (Association for Biblical Higher Education)						
5850 T G Lee Blvd Ste 130	Orlando	FL	32822	407-207-0808		48-1
TF: 800-525-1611 ■ *Web:* www.abhc.org						
AABP (American Association of Bovine Practitioners)						
1130 E Main St Ste 302	Ashland	OH	44805	419-496-0685	496-0697	48-2
Web: www.aabp.org						
AABR (Association for the Advancement of the Blind & Retarded)						
1508 College Pt Blvd	College Point	NY	11356	718-321-3800		48-17
Web: www.aabr.org						
AAC (Arlington Arts Ctr)						
3550 Wilson Blvd	Arlington	VA	22201	703-248-6800	248-6849	50-2
Web: www.arlingtonartscenter.org						
AAC (American Adoption Congress)						
PO Box 42730	Washington	DC	20015	202-483-3399		48-6
TF: 800-735-2929 ■ *Web:* www.americanadoptioncongress.org						
AAC (American Actuator Corp)						
89 Selleck St	Stamford	CT	06902	203-324-6334		456
Web: www.americanactuator.com						
AAC Contracting Inc 175 Humboldt St	Rochester	NY	14610	585-527-8000		607
Web: www.aac-contracting.com						
AACA (Antique Automobile Club of America)						
501 W Governor Rd PO Box 417	Hershey	PA	17033	717-534-1910	534-9101	48-18
TF: 800-211-4371 ■ *Web:* www.aaca.org						
Aaca Parts & Supplies						
3227 Military Pkwy Ste 244	Mesquite	TX	75149	972-223-8484		35
TF: 800-280-5986 ■ *Web:* www.aacapartsandsupplies.com						
AACAP (American Academy of Child & Adolescent Psychiatry)						
3615 Wisconsin Ave NW	Washington	DC	20016	202-966-7300	966-2891	49-15
TF: 800-333-7636 ■ *Web:* www.aacap.org						
AACC (Asset Acceptance Capital Corp)						
28405 Van Dyke Ave	Warren	MI	48093	586-939-9600		160
NASDAQ: AACC ■ *TF:* 800-545-9931 ■ *Web:* www.assetacceptance.com						
AACC (American Assn for Clinical Chemistry Inc)						
1850 K St NW Ste 625	Washington	DC	20006	202-857-0717	887-5093	49-19
TF Cust Svc: 800-892-1400 ■ *Web:* www.aacc.org						
AACC (American Assn of Cereal Chemists Inc)						
3340 Pilot Knob Rd	Saint Paul	MN	55121	651-454-7250	454-0766	49-6
TF: 800-328-7560 ■ *Web:* www.aaccnet.org/default.aspx						
AACC (American Association of Community Colleges)						
1 Dupont Cir NW Ste 410	Washington	DC	20036	202-728-0200	833-2467	49-5
Web: www.aacc.nche.edu						
A-account Plumbing & Drain Cleaning LLC						
5128 S Eastern Ave	Oklahoma City	OK	73129	405-672-5754		610
AACD (American Academy of Cosmetic Dentistry)						
402 W Wilson St	Madison	WI	53703	608-222-8583	222-9540	49-8
TF: 800-543-9220 ■ *Web:* www.aacd.com						
AACE (American Association of Clinical Endocrinologists)						
245 Riverside Ave Ste 2000	Jacksonville	FL	32202	904-353-7878	353-8185	49-8
TF: 800-435-7352 ■ *Web:* www.aace.com						
AACE (Association for the Advancement of Computing in Education)						
PO Box 1545	Chesapeake	VA	23327	757-366-5606	997-8760*	49-5
**Fax Area Code:* 703 ■ *TF:* 800-352-5397 ■ *Web:* www.aace.org						
AACE International - Assn for the Advancement of Cost Engineering						
1265 Suncrest Towne Centre Dr Ste 100	Morgantown	WV	26505	304-296-8444	291-5728	49-1
Web: www.aacei.org						
AACI (American Assn of Crop Insurers)						
1 Massachusetts Ave NW Ste 800	Washington	DC	20001	202-789-4100	408-7763	49-9
Web: www.cropinsurers.com						

Phone | Fax | Class

AACN (American Assn of Colleges of Nursing)
1 Dupont Cir NW Ste 530 Washington DC 20036 202-463-6930 785-8320 49-5
Web: www.aacn.nche.edu

AACN (American Assn of Critical-Care Nurses)
101 Columbia Aliso Viejo CA 92656 949-362-2000 362-2020 49-8
TF: 800-809-2273 ■ *Web:* www.aacn.org

AACOM (American Assn of Colleges of Osteopathic Medicine)
5550 Friendship Blvd Ste 310 Chevy Chase MD 20815 301-968-4100 968-4101 49-8
TF: 800-356-7836 ■ *Web:* www.aacom.org

Aacom Inc 201 Stuyvesant Ave Lyndhurst NJ 07071 201-438-2244 196
TF: 800-273-3719 ■ *Web:* www.aacomnj.com

AACPDM (American Academy for Cerebral Palsy & Developmental Medicine)
555 E Wells St Ste 1100 Milwaukee WI 53202 414-918-3014 276-2146 48-17
TF: 800-274-2237 ■ *Web:* www.aacpdm.org

AACPM (American Assn of Colleges of Podiatric Medicine)
15850 Crabbs Branch Way Ste 320 Rockville MD 20855 301-948-9760 948-1928 49-8
Web: www.aacpm.org

AACR (American Assn for Cancer Research)
615 Chestnut St 17th Fl Philadelphia PA 19106 215-440-9300 49-8
TF: 866-423-3965 ■ *Web:* www.aacr.org

AACRAO (American Assn of Collegiate Registrars & Admissions Officers)
1 Dupont Cir NW Ste 520 Washington DC 20036 202-293-9161 872-8857 49-5
TF: 800-222-4922 ■ *Web:* www.aacrao.org

AACS (American Academy of Cosmetic Surgery)
225 W Wacker Dr Ste 650 Chicago IL 60606 312-981-6760 981-6787 49-8
Web: www.cosmeticsurgery.org

AACSB International - Assn to Advance Collegiate Schools of Business
777 S Harbour Island Blvd Ste 750 Tampa FL 33602 813-769-6500 769-6559 48-11
TF: 800-227-5558 ■ *Web:* www.aacsb.edu

AACTE (American Assn of Colleges for Teacher Education)
1307 New York Ave NW Ste 300 Washington DC 20005 202-293-2450 457-8095 49-5
Web: www.aacte.org

AAC&U (Association of American Colleges & Universities)
1818 R St NW Washington DC 20009 202-387-3760 265-9532 49-5
Web: www.aacu.org

AAD (American Academy of Dermatology)
930 E Woodfield Rd Schaumburg IL 60173 847-330-0230 330-0050 49-8
TF: 800-868-2472 ■ *Web:* www.aad.org

AADEP (American Academy of Disability Evaluating Physicians)
223 W Jackson Blvd Ste 1104 Chicago IL 60606 312-663-1171 663-1175 49-8
TF: 800-456-6095 ■ *Web:* www.iaime.org

Aadfw Inc 1350 Westpark Way Euless TX 76040 817-540-0153 192
Web: www.aadfwinc.com

AADGP (American Academy of Dental Group Practice)
2525 E Arizona Biltmore Cir Ste 127 Phoenix AZ 85016 602-381-1185 381-1093 49-8
TF: 800-475-2098 ■ *Web:* www.aadgp.org

AADL (Ann Arbor District Library)
343 S Fifth Ave Ann Arbor MI 48104 734-327-4200 327-8309 434-3
TF: 800-230-4085 ■ *Web:* www.aadl.org

AADMM (American Assn of Daily Money Managers)
174 Crestview Dr Bellefonte PA 16823 877-326-5991 355-2452* 49-2
**Fax Area Code:* 814 ■ *TF:* 877-326-5991 ■ *Web:* www.aadmm.com

AADP (American Association of Drugless Practitioners)
2200 Market St Ste 803 Galveston TX 77550 409-621-2600 48-17
TF: 888-764-2237 ■ *Web:* www.aadp.net

AAE (American Assn of Endodontists)
211 E Chicago Ave Ste 1100 Chicago IL 60611 312-266-7255 266-9867 49-8
TF: 800-872-3636 ■ *Web:* www.aae.org

AAE Systems Inc 642 N Pastoria Ave Sunnyvale CA 94085 408-732-1710 180
Web: www.aaesys.com

AAEA (American Agricultural Economics Assn)
555 E Wells St Ste 1100 Milwaukee WI 53202 414-918-3190 48-2
Web: www.aaea.org

AAEI (American Association of Exporters & Importers)
1050 17th St NW Ste 810 Washington DC 20036 202-857-8009 857-7843 49-18
Web: www.aaei.org

AAEP (American Assn of Equine Practitioners)
4075 Iron Works Pkwy Lexington KY 40511 859-233-0147 233-1968 48-3
TF: 800-443-0177 ■ *Web:* www.aaep.org

AAES (American Assn of Engineering Societies)
1620 'I' St NW Ste 210 Washington DC 20006 202-296-2237 296-1151 49-19
TF Orders: 888-400-2237 ■ *Web:* www.aaes.org

AAF (American Adv Federation)
1101 Vermont Ave NW Ste 500 Washington DC 20005 202-898-0089 898-0159 49-18
TF: 800-999-2231 ■ *Web:* www.aaf.org

AAF International Corp
10300 Ormsby Pk Pl Ste 600 Louisville KY 40223 502-637-0011 223-6500* 18
**Fax Area Code:* 888 ■ *TF:* 888-223-2003 ■ *Web:* www.aafintl.com

AAFA (American Apparel & Footwear Assn)
740 sixth St NW 3rd and 4th Fl Washington DC 22209 202-853-9080 522-6741* 49-4
**Fax Area Code:* 703 ■ *TF:* 800-520-2262 ■ *Web:* www.aafaglobal.org

AAFA (Asthma & Allergy Foundation of America)
8201 Corporate Dr Ste 1000 Landover MD 20785 202-466-7643 466-8940 48-17
TF: 800-727-8462 ■ *Web:* www.aafa.org

AAFCS (American Assn of Family & Consumer Sciences)
400 N Columbus St Ste 202 Alexandria VA 22314 703-706-4600 706-4663 49-5
TF: 800-424-8080 ■ *Web:* www.aafcs.org

AAFD (American Assn of Franchisees & Dealers)
PO Box 10158 Palm Desert CA 92255 619-209-3775 855-1988* 49-18
**Fax Area Code:* 866 ■ *TF:* 800-733-9858 ■ *Web:* www.aafd.org

Aafedt, Forde, Gray, Monson & Hager PA
150 S Fifth St Ste 2600 Minneapolis MN 55402 612-339-8965 428
Web: www.aafedt.com

AAFP (American Academy of Family Physicians)
11400 Tomahawk Creek Pkwy Leawood KS 66211 913-906-6000 906-6075 49-8
TF: 800-274-2237 ■ *Web:* www.aafp.org

AAFPRS (American Academy of Facial Plastic & Reconstructive Surgery)
310 S Henry St Alexandria VA 22314 703-299-9291 299-8898 49-8
Web: aafprs.org

AAG (Association of American Geographers)
1710 16th St NW Washington DC 20009 202-234-1450 234-2744 49-19
TF: 800-696-7353 ■ *Web:* www.aag.org

AAGL (American Assn of Gynecological Laparoscopists)
6757 Katella Ave Cypress CA 90630 714-503-6200 503-6201 49-8
TF: 800-554-2245 ■ *Web:* www.aagl.org

AAGP (American Assn for Geriatric Psychiatry)
7910 Woodmont Ave Ste 1050 Bethesda MD 20814 301-654-7850 654-4137 49-15
Web: www.aagponline.org

AAHA (American Animal Hospital Assn)
12575 W Bayaud Ave Lakewood CO 80228 303-986-2800 986-1700 48-3
TF: 800-252-2242 ■ *Web:* www.aaha.org/default.aspx

AAHCP (American Academy of Home Care Physicians)
PO Box 1037 Edgewood MD 21040 410-676-7966 676-7980 49-8
Web: aahcm.org

AAH-PERD (American Alliance for Health Physical Education Recreation & Dance)
1900 Assn Dr Reston VA 20191 703-476-3400 476-9527 48-22
TF: 800-213-7193 ■ *Web:* shapeamerica.org

AAHPM (American Academy of Hospice & Palliative Medicine)
4700 West Lake Ave Glenview IL 60025 847-375-4712 49-8
Web: www.aahpm.org

AAI (Africa-America Institute)
420 Lexington Ave Ste 1706 New York NY 10170 212-949-5666 682-6174 48-14
Web: www.aaionline.org

AAI (American Assn of Immunologists)
9650 Rockville Pike Bethesda MD 20814 301-634-7178 634-7887 49-8
Web: www.aai.org

AAI (American Athletic Inc)
200 American Ave Jefferson IA 50129 800-247-3978 346
TF: 800-247-3978 ■ *Web:* www.americanathletic.com

AAI (Arab American Institute)
1600 K St NW Ste 601 Washington DC 20006 202-429-9210 429-9214 48-8
Web: www.aaiusa.org

AAI Corp 124 Industry Ln Hunt Valley MD 21030 410-666-1400 529
TF: 800-655-2616 ■ *Web:* textronsystems.com/company-overview/rebrand

AAIA (Association on American Indian Affairs)
966 Hungerford Dr Ste 12-B Rockville MD 20850 240-314-7155 314-7159 457-17
Web: www.indian-affairs.org

AAIA (Automotive Aftermarket Industry Assn)
7101 Wisconsin Ave Bethesda MD 20814 301-654-6664 654-3299 49-21
TF: 800-936-8906 ■ *Web:* autocare.org

AAIDD (American Assn on Intellectual & Developmental Disabilities)
444 N Capitol St NW Ste 846 Washington DC 20001 202-387-1968 387-2193 48-17
TF: 800-424-3688 ■ *Web:* www.aaidd.org

AAIHDS (American Assn of Integrated Healthcare Delivery Systems Inc)
4435 Waterfront Dr Ste 101 Glen Allen VA 23060 804-747-5823 747-5316 49-8
TF: 888-491-8833 ■ *Web:* www.aaihds.org

AAII (American Assn of Individual Investors)
625 N Michigan Ave Ste 1900 Chicago IL 60611 312-280-0170 280-9883 49-2
TF: 800-428-2244 ■ *Web:* www.aaii.com

AAIM Employers' Association LLC
1600 S Brentwood Ste 400 St. Louis MO 63144 314-968-3600 764
TF: 800-877-0209 ■ *Web:* www.aaimea.org

AAIP (Association of American Indian Physicians)
1225 Sovereign Row Ste 103 Oklahoma City OK 73108 405-946-7072 946-7651 49-8
Web: www.aaip.org

Aaipharma Services Corp
2320 Scientific Park Dr Wilmington NC 28405 910-254-7000 238
Web: www.alcaminow.com/redirect

AAIS (American Assn of Insurance Services)
1745 S Naperville Rd Wheaton IL 60189 630-681 8347 681-8356 49-9
TF: 800-564-2247 ■ *Web:* www.aaisonline.com

AAJ (American Assn for Justice)
777 Sixth St NW Ste 200 Washington DC 20001 202-965-3500 49-10
TF: 800-424-2725 ■ *Web:* www.justice.org

AAJ Technologies
6301 NW Fifth Way Ste 1700 Fort Lauderdale FL 33309 954-689-3984 180
TF: 800-443-5210 ■ *Web:* www.aajtech.com

Aakron Rule Corp 8 Indianola Ave Akron NY 14001 716-542-5483 534
Web: www.aakronline.com

Aaladin Industries Inc
32584 477th Ave Elk Point SD 57025 605-356-3325 454
Web: www.aaladin.com

AALAS (American Association for Laboratory Animal Science)
9190 Crestwyn Hills Dr Memphis TN 38125 901-754-8620 753-0046 49-19
Web: www.aalas.org

Aalborg Instruments & Controls
20 Corporate Dr Orangeburg NY 10962 800-866-3837 201
TF: 800-866-3837 ■ *Web:* www.aalborg.com

AALDEF (Asian American Legal Defense & Education Fund)
99 Hudson St 12th Fl New York NY 10013 212-966-5932 966-4303 48-8
TF: 800-966-5946 ■ *Web:* www.aaldef.org

AALE (American Academy for Liberal Education)
1200 G St NW Ste 883 Washington DC 20005 202-434-8971 452-8620 48-1
Web: www.aale.org

Aalfs Mfg Co 1005 Fourth St Sioux City IA 51101 712-252-1877 252-5205 155-11
Web: aalfs.com

AALL (American Assn of Law Libraries)
53 W Jackson Blvd Ste 940 Chicago IL 60604 312-939-4764 431-1097 49-11
TF: 800-285-2221 ■ *Web:* www.aallnet.org

AALS (Association of American Law Schools)
1201 Connecticut Ave NW Ste 800 Washington DC 20036 202-296-8851 296-8869 49-5
Web: www.aals.org

AALU (Association for Advanced Life Underwriting)
11921 Freedom Dr Ste 1100 Heston VA 20190 703-641-9400 641-9885 49-9
TF: 888-275-0092 ■ *Web:* www.aalu.org

AAM (American Assn of Museums)
1575 Eye St NW Ste 400 Washington DC 20005 202-289-1818 289-6578 48-4
TF: 866-226-2150 ■ *Web:* www.aam-us.org

AAMA (American Amusement Machine Assn)
450 E Higgins Rd Ste 201 Elk Grove Village IL 60007 847-290-9088 290-9121 48-23
Web: www.coin-op.org

AAMA (Asia America MultiTechnology Assn)
1270 Oakmead Pkwy Sunnyvale CA 94085 408-736-2554 49-13
Web: www.aamasv.com

AAMA (American Academy of Medical Acupuncture)
1970 E Grand Ave Ste 330 El Segundo CA 90245 310-364-0193 48-17
Web: www.medicalacupuncture.org

AAMA (American Architectural Manufacturers Assn)
1827 Walden Office Sq Ste 550 Schaumburg IL 60173 847-303-5664 303-5774 49-3
Web: www.aamanet.org

AAMA (American Assn of Medical Assistants)
20 N Wacker Dr Ste 1575 Chicago IL 60606 312-899-1500 899-1259 49-8
TF: 800-228-2262 ■ *Web:* www.aama-ntl.org

AAMC (Association of American Medical Colleges)
2450 N St NW Washington DC 20037 202-828-0400 828-1125 49-5
TF: 800-273-8255 ■ *Web:* www.aamc.org

Name / Address	Phone	Fax	Class
A-American Self Storage Management Co Inc 11560 Tennessee Ave.....................Los Angeles CA 90064 *TF:* 888-333-6479 ■ *Web:* www.aamericanselfstorage.com	310-914-4022	914-4042	803-3
AAMFT (American Assn for Marriage & Family Therapy) 112 S Alfred St.......................... Alexandria VA 22314 *Web:* www.aamft.org	703-838-9808	838-9805	48-6
AAMGA (American Assn of Managing General Agents) 610 Freedom Business Ctr Ste 110 .... King of Prussia PA 19406 *Web:* www.aamga.org	610-992-0022	992-0021	49-9
AAMI (Association for the Advancement of Medical Instrumentation) 4301 N Fairfax Dr Ste 301 .... Arlington VA 22203 *TF:* 800-332-2264 ■ *Web:* www.aami.org	703-525-4890	276-0793	49-8
AAMRO (American Assn of Medical Review Officers) PO Box 12873 .... Research Triangle Park NC 27709 *TF:* 800-489-1839 ■ *Web:* www.aamro.com	919-489-5407	490-1010	49-8
AAMSE (American Assn of Medical Society Executives) 1000 Westgate Dr Ste 252 ....St. Paul MN 55114 *Web:* www.aamse.org	651-288-3432	290-2266	49-8
AAMVA (American Assn of Motor Vehicle Administrators) 4301 Wilson Blvd Ste 400 .... Arlington VA 22203 *TF:* 800-221-9253 ■ *Web:* www.aamva.org	703-522-4200	522-1553	49-7
AAN (Association of Alternative Newsweeklies) 115615th St NW.......................Washington DC 20005 *TF:* 866-415-0704 ■ *Web:* www.altweeklies.com	202-289-8484	289-2004	49-14
AAN (American Academy of Neurology) 1080 Montreal Ave...................... Saint Paul MN 55116 *TF:* 800-879-1960 ■ *Web:* www.aan.com	651-695-1940	695-2791	49-8
AANA (Arthroscopy Assn of North America) 9400 W Higgins Rd Ste 200................ Rosemont IL 60018 *TF:* 877-924-0305 ■ *Web:* www.aana.org	847-292-2262	292-2268	49-8
AaNA (Alaska Nurses Assn) 3701 E Tudor Rd Ste 208 ....Anchorage AK 99507 *Web:* www.aknurse.org	907-274-0827	272-0292	533
AANA (American Assn of Nurse Anesthetists) 222 S Prospect Ave.......................... Park Ridge IL 60068 *TF:* 855-526-2262 ■ *Web:* www.aana.com	847-692-7050	692-6968	49-8
AANAPAC (American Association of Nurse Anesthetists PAC) 222 S Prospect Ave...........................Park Ridge IL 60068 *TF:* 855-526-2262 ■ *Web:* aana.com	847-692-7050	692-6968	615
AANEM (American Assn of Neuromuscular & Electrodiagnostic Medicine) 2621 Superior Dr NW......................Rochester MN 55901 *TF:* 844-347-3277 ■ *Web:* www.aanem.org	507-288-0100	288-1225	49-8
Aangan Classic Indian & Napalese Cuisine 3500 Walnut St...........................Harrisburg PA 17109 *Web:* www.aanganonline.com	717-909-7777		671
Aaniiih Nakoda College 269 Blackfeet Ave............................Harlem MT 59526 *Web:* www.ancollege.edu	406-353-2607		165
AANN (American Assn of Neuroscience Nurses) 4700 West Lake Ave........................ Glenview IL 60025 *TF:* 888-557-2266 ■ *Web:* www.aann.org	847-375-4733	375-6430	49-8
AANP (American Academy of Nurse Practitioners) PO Box 12846 .... Austin TX 78711 *TF:* 800-981-2491 ■ *Web:* www.aanp.org	512-442-4262	442-6469	49-8
AANP (American Assn of Naturopathic Physicians) 818 18th St Ste 250 .... Washington DC 20006 *TF:* 866-538-2267 ■ *Web:* www.naturopathic.org	202-237-8150	237-8152	48-17
AANS (American Assn of Neurological Surgeons) 5550 Meadowbrook Dr...............Rolling Meadows IL 60008 *TF:* 888-566-2267 ■ *Web:* www.aans.org	847-378-0500	378-0600	49-8
AAO (American Academy of Optometry) 6110 Executive Blvd Ste 506 .... Rockville MD 20852 *Web:* www.aaopt.org	301-984-1441	984-4737	49-8
AAO (American Assn of Orthodontists) 401 N Lindbergh Blvd........................ Saint Louis MO 63141 *TF:* 800-424-2841 ■ *Web:* www.mylifemysmile.org	314-993-1700		49-8
AAO-HNS (American Academy of Otolaryngology-Head & Neck Surgery) 1650 Diagonal Rd.......................... Alexandria VA 22314 *TF:* 877-722-6467 ■ *Web:* www.entnet.org	703-836-4444	683-5100	49-8
AAOMS (American Assn of Oral & Maxillofacial Surgeons) 9700 W Bryn Mawr Ave .... Rosemont IL 60018 *TF:* 800-822-6637 ■ *Web:* www.aaoms.org	847-678-6200	678-6286	49-8
AAON Inc 2425 S Yukon Ave....................... Tulsa OK 74107 *NASDAQ: AAON* ■ *Web:* www.aaon.com	918-583-2266	583-6094	14
AAOP (American Academy of Orthotists & Prosthetists) 1331 H St NW Ste 501 ....Washington DC 20005 *Web:* www.oandp.org	202-380-3663	380-3447	49-8
AAOS (American Academy of Orthopaedic Surgeons) 6300 N River Rd............................ Rosemont IL 60018 *TF:* 800-346-2267 ■ *Web:* www.aaos.org	847-823-7186	823-8125	49-8
AAP (American Academy of Pediatrics) 141 NW Pt Blvd ....Elk Grove Village IL 60007 *TF:* 800-433-9016 ■ *Web:* www.aap.org	847-434-4000	434-8000	49-8
AAP (American Academy of Periodontology) 737 N Michigan Ave Ste 800 ....Chicago IL 60611 *TF:* 800-282-4867 ■ *Web:* www.perio.org	312-787-5518	787-3670	49-8
AAP (Association of American Publishers Inc) 71 Fifth Ave..............................New York NY 10003 *TF:* 866-271-4968 ■ *Web:* www.publishers.org	212-255-0200	255-7007	49-16
AAPA (American Academy of Physician Assistants) 2318 Mill Rd Ste 1300...................... Alexandria VA 22314 *Web:* www.aapa.org	703-836-2272	684-1924	615
AAPA (American Academy of Physician Assistants) 950 N Washington St .... Alexandria VA 22314 *TF:* 800-692-2326 ■ *Web:* www.aapa.org	703-836-2272	684-1924	49-8
AAPA (American Assn of Port Authorities) 1010 Duke St .... Alexandria VA 22314 *Web:* www.aapa-ports.org	703-684-5700	684-6321	49-21
AAPAR (American Association for Physical Activity & Recreation) 1900 Assn Dr.............................. Reston VA 20191 *TF:* 800-213-7193 ■ *Web:* shapeamerica.org/aapar	703-476-3400	476-9527	48-23
AAPB (Association for Applied Psychophysiology & Biofeedback) 10200 W 44th Ave Ste 304............... Wheat Ridge CO 80033 *TF:* 800-477-8892 ■ *Web:* www.aapb.org	303-422-8436	422-8894	49-8
AAPC (American Association of Political Consultants) 8400 W pk Dr 2nd Fl .... McLean VA 22102 *Web:* www.theaapc.org	703-245-8020		48-7
AAPCC (American Assn of Poison Control Centers) 3201 New Mexico Ave Ste 310.............Washington DC 20016 *TF:* 800-222-1222 ■ *Web:* www.aapcc.org	800-222-1222		49-8
Aapco Automotive Warehouse 2997 E La Palma Ave .... Anaheim CA 92806	714-630-5600	666-2913	61
AAPCO Southeast Inc 506 Webb Rd ....Concord NC 28025 *TF:* 800-654-7721 ■ *Web:* www.aapcogroup.com	704-784-2690		186
AAPD (American Academy of Pediatric Dentistry) 211 E Chicago Ave Ste 1600 ....Chicago IL 60611 *TF:* 800-974-3084 ■ *Web:* www.aapd.org	312-337-2169	337-6329	49-8
AAPG (American Association of Petroleum Geologists) 1444 S Boulder Ave PO Box 979 .... Tulsa OK 74119 *TF:* 800-364-2274 ■ *Web:* www.aapg.org	918-584-2555	560-2665	48-12
AAPG Explorer Magazine 1444 S Boulder Ave .... Tulsa OK 74119 *TF:* 800-364-2274 ■ *Web:* www.aapg.org	918-584-2555	560-2636	457-21
AAPL (American Academy of Psychiatry & the Law) 1 Regency Dr PO Box 30 ....Bloomfield CT 06002 *TF:* 800-331-1389 ■ *Web:* www.aapl.org	860-242-5450	286-0787	49-15
AAPL (American Assn of Professional Landmen) 4100 Fossil Creek Blvd......................Fort Worth TX 76137 *TF:* 888-566-2275 ■ *Web:* www.landman.org	817-847-7700	847-7704	48-12
AAPM (American Academy of Pain Management) 13947 Mono Way Ste A ....Sonora CA 95370 *TF:* 888-519-9901 ■ *Web:* www.aapainmanage.org	209-533-9744	533-9750	49-8
AAPM&R (American Academy of Physical Medicine & Rehabilitation) 9700 W Bryn Mawr Ave Ste 200.............. Rosemont IL 60018 *Web:* www.aapmr.org	847-737-6000		49-8
AAPPO (American Association of Preferred Provider Organizations) 974 Breckenridge Ln Ste 162..................Louisville KY 40202 *Web:* nasho.org	502 403-1122	403-1129	49-8
AAPS (American Assn of Pharmaceutical Scientists) 2107 Wilson Blvd Ste 700 .... Arlington VA 22201 *TF:* 877-998-2277 ■ *Web:* www.aaps.org	703-243-2800	243-9650	49-19
AAPS (American Association of Physician Specialists Inc) 5550 W Executive Dr Ste 400.................. Tampa FL 33609 *TF:* 800-232-3188 ■ *Web:* www.aapsus.org	813-433-2277	830-6599	49-8
AAPT (American Assn of Physics Teachers) 1 Physics Ellipse .... College Park MD 20740 *TF:* 800-446-8923 ■ *Web:* www.aapt.org	301-209-3311	209-0845	49-5
AAR (American Academy of Religion) 825 Houston Mill Rd NE Ste 300 .... Atlanta GA 30329 *Web:* www.aarweb.org	404-727-3049	727-7959	48-20
AAR 1100 N Wood Dale Rd ....Wood Dale IL 60191 *TF:* 800-422-2213 ■ *Web:* www.aarcorp.com	630-227-2000		770
AAR (Alliance for Aging Research) 750 17th St NW Ste 1100................Washington DC 20006 **Fax Area Code:* 770 ■ *TF:* 866-840-6283 ■ *Web:* www.agingresearch.org	202-293-2856	234-5030*	48-17
AAR (Association of American Railroads) 425 Third St SW........................Washington DC 20024 *TF:* 800-533-6644 ■ *Web:* www.aar.org	202-639-2100	639-2286	49-21
AAR Aircraft Component Services 747 Zeckendorf Blvd...................... Garden City NY 11530 *TF:* 800-422-2213 ■ *Web:* www.aarcorp.com	516-222-9000	222-0987	24
AAR Aircraft Services 6611 S Meridian Ave .... Oklahoma City OK 73159 *TF:* 800-422-2213 ■ *Web:* www.aarcorp.com	630-227-2000		24
AAR Aircraft Turbine Ctr 1100 N Wood Dale Rd 1 AAR Pl.............Wood Dale IL 60191 *TF General:* 800-422-2213 ■ *Web:* www.aarcorp.com	630-227 2000		770
AAR Cargo Systems 2870 Cargo Cir ....Memphis TN 38118 *Web:* www.aarcorp.com	919-705-2400	705-2499	22
AAR Composites 14201 Myerlake Cir......... Clearwater FL 33760 *TF:* 800-422-2213 ■ *Web:* aarcorp.com	727-539-8585	539-0316	22
AAR Corp 1100 N Wood Dale Rd 1 AAR Pl ....Wood Dale IL 60191 *NYSE: AIR* ■ *TF:* 800-422-2213 ■ *Web:* www.aarcorp.com	630-227-2000	227-2019	21
AAR Defense Systems & Logistics 1100 N Wood Dale Rd ....Wood Dale IL 60191 *TF:* 877-227-9200 ■ *Web:* aarcorp.com	630-227-2000		770
AAR Landing Gear Services 9371 NW 100th St .... Miami FL 33178 *TF:* 800-422-2213 ■ *Web:* www.aarcorp.com	305-887-4027		24
AARC (American Assn for Respiratory Care) 9425 N MacArthur Blvd Ste 100...................Irving TX 75063 *TF:* 800-272-3900 ■ *Web:* www.aarc.org	972-243-2272	484-2720	49-8
Aarch Caster & Equipment 314 Axminister Dr........................... Fenton MO 63026 *TF:* 888-349-0220 ■ *Web:* www.aarchcaster.com	636-349-0220		351
Aarcher 910 Commerce Rd................... Annapolis MD 21401 *TF:* 800-517-8408 ■ *Web:* www.aarcherinc.com	410-897-9100		192
AARDA (American Autoimmune Related Disease Assn) 22100 Gratiot Ave.......................... Eastpointe MI 48021 *TF:* 800-598-4668 ■ *Web:* www.aarda.org	586-776-3900	776-3903	48-17
Aareas Interactive 1120 Finch Ave W.........................North York ON M3J3H7 *Web:* www.aareas.com	416-661-2244		809
AArete LLC 1 S Dearborn Ste 2100 ....Chicago IL 60603	312-212-4282		463
Aarhuskarlshamn USA Inc 131 Marsh St ....Newark NJ 07114 *Web:* www.aak.com	973-741-5049		296-30
Aaron & Company Inc PO Box 8310 ....Piscataway NJ 08855 *TF:* 800-734-4822 ■ *Web:* www.aaronco.com	732-752-8200		612
Aaron Bell International Inc 9101 E Kenyon Ave Ste 2300...................Denver CO 80237 *Web:* www.aaron-bell.com	720-200-0470		401
Aaron Bros Inc 8001 Ridgepoint Dr Ste 500.......................Irving TX 75063 *Web:* www.aaronbrothers.com	214-492-6200		45
Aaron Carlson Corp 1505 Central Ave NE......................Minneapolis MN 55413 *Web:* www.aaroncarlson.com	612-789-8885		499
Aaron Diamond AIDS Research Ctr 455 First Ave 7th Fl ....New York NY 10016 *TF:* 800-782-2737 ■ *Web:* www.adarc.org	212-448-5000	725-1126	668
Aaron M Priest Literary Agency 200 W 41st St 21st Fl........................New York NY 10036 *Web:* aaronpriest.com	212-818-0344	573-9417	444

Name / Address	City	State	Zip	Phone	Fax	Class
Aaron Riechert Carpol & Riffle APC 900 Veterans Blvd Ste 600 *Web:* www.arcr.com	Redwood City	CA	94063	650-368-4662		41
Aaron Thomas Company Inc 7421 Chapman Ave. *TF:* 800-394-4776 ■ *Web:* www.packaging.com	Garden Grove	CA	92841	714-894-4468		88
AaronEquipment Company Inc 735 E Green St *TF:* 800-492-2766 ■ *Web:* www.aaronequipment.com	Bensenville	IL	60106	630-350-2200	350-9047	385
Aarons Grant & Habif LLC 3500 Piedmont Rd Ste 500 *Web:* www.aghllc.com	Atlanta	GA	30305	404-233-5486		2
AARP 601 E St NW *TF:* 888-687-2277 ■ *Web:* www.aarp.org	Washington	DC	20049	202-434-2277		48-6
AARP Grandparent Information Ctr 601 E St NW *TF:* 888-687-2277 ■ *Web:* aarp.org/relationships/grandparenting	Washington	DC	20049	202-434-3525	434-6474	48-6
AARP Health Care Options PO Box 1017 *TF:* 800-523-5800 ■ *Web:* www.aarphealthcare.com	Montgomeryville	PA	18936	800-523-5800		391-3
AARP Motoring Plan 601 E St NW *TF:* 800-555-1121 ■ *Web:* www.aarproadside.com	Washington	DC	20049	800-555-1121		53
AARP Public Policy Institute 601 E St NW *TF:* 888-687-2277 ■ *Web:* aarp.org/research/ppi	Washington	DC	20049	202-434-2277		634
AARP the Magazine 601 E St NW *TF:* 888-687-2277 ■ *Web:* www.aarp.org	Washington	DC	20049	202-434-3525		457-10
Aarrowcast Inc 2900 E Richmond St *TF:* 800-392-2266 ■ *Web:* www.aarrowcast.com	Shawano	WI	54166	715-526-3600	526-9758	307
AARTS (Association of Advanced Rabbinical & Talmudic Schools) 11 Broadway	New York	NY	10004	212-363-1991		49-5
AAS (American Assn of Suicidology) 5221 Wisconsin Ave NW 2nd Fl *Web:* www.suicidology.org	Washington	DC	20015	202-237-2280	237-2282	48-17
AAS (Association for Asian Studies) 825 Victors Way Ste 310 *TF:* 800-316-2739 ■ *Web:* www.asian-studies.org	Ann Arbor	MI	48108	734-665-2490	665-3801	48-11
AAS (American Antiquarian Society) 185 Salisbury St *Web:* www.americanantiquarian.org	Worcester	MA	01609	508-755-5221	753-3311	48-4
AAS (American Astronomical Society) 2000 Florida Ave NW Ste 400 *Web:* www.aas.org	Washington	DC	20009	202-328-2010	234-2560	49-19
AASA (American Assn of School Administrators) 801 N Quincy St Ste 700 *TF:* 800-771-1162 ■ *Web:* www.aasa.org	Arlington	VA	22203	703-528-0700	841-1543	49-5
AASC (Applied Aerospace Structures Corp) 3437 S Airport Way PO Box 6189 *Web:* www.aascworld.com	Stockton	CA	95206	209-982-0160	983-3375	504
AASCU (American Assn of State Colleges & Universities) 1307 New York Ave NW 5th Fl *TF:* 800-558-3417 ■ *Web:* www.aascu.org	Washington	DC	20005	202-293-7070	296-5819	49-5
Aasgard Summit Management Services Inc 4017 13th Ave W *Web:* aasgardsummit.net	Seattle	WA	98119	206-284-0475		193
AASHTO (American Assn of State Highway & Transportation Officials) 444 N Capitol St NW Ste 249 *Web:* www.transportation.org	Washington	DC	20001	202-624-5800	624-5806	49-7
AASL (American Assn of School Librarians) 50 E Huron St *TF:* 800-545-2433 ■ *Web:* www.ala.org/aasl	Chicago	IL	60611	312-280-4386	664-7459	49-11
AASLD (American Association for the Study of Liver Diseases) 1001 N Fairfax St Ste 400 *Web:* www.aasld.org	Alexandria	VA	22314	703-299-9766	299-9622	49-8
AASLH (American Assn for State & Local History) 1717 Church St *Web:* www.aaslh.org	Nashville	TN	37203	615-320-3203	327-9013	48-4
AASM (American Academy of Sleep Medicine) 2510 N Frontage Rd Ste 920 *Web:* www.aasmnet.org	Darien	IL	60561	708-492-0930	492-0943	48-17
Aasys Group 11301 N US Hwy 301 Ste 106 *TF:* 800-852-7091 ■ *Web:* www.aasysgroup.com	Thonotosassa	FL	33592	813-246-4757		180
AATB (American Association of Tissue Banks) 8200 Greensboro Dr Ste 320 *TF:* 800-767-7643 ■ *Web:* www.aatb.org	McLean	VA	22101	703-827-9582	356-2198	49-8
AATBS (Association for Advanced Training in the Behavioral Sciences) 5126 Ralston St *TF:* 800-472-1931 ■ *Web:* aatbs.com	Ventura	CA	93003	805-676-3030	676-3033	49-5
AATCC (American Assn of Textile Chemists & Colorists) 1 Davis Dr PO Box 12215 *Web:* www.aatcc.org	Research Triangle Park	NC	27709	919-549-8141	549-8933	49-13
AATF (American Assn of Teachers of French) 302 N Granite St *Web:* www.frenchteachers.org	Marion	IL	62959	618-453-5731		49-5
AATG (American Assn of Teachers of German) 112 Haddontowne Ct Ste 104 *TF:* 800-835-6770 ■ *Web:* www.aatg.org	Cherry Hill	NJ	08034	856-795-5553	795-9398	49-5
AATH (Association for Applied & Therapeutic Humor) 65 Enterprise **Fax Area Code:* 949 ■ *TF:* 888-747-2284 ■ *Web:* www.aath.org	Aliso Viejo	CA	92656	815-708-6587	715-6931*	48-17
AATS (American Assn for Thoracic Surgery) 900 Cummings Ctr Ste 221-U *TF:* 800-424-5249 ■ *Web:* www.aats.org	Beverly	MA	01915	978-927-8330	522-8469	49-8
AATSP (American Assn of Teachers of Spanish & Portuguese) 900 Ladd Rd *Web:* www.aatsp.org	Walled Lake	MI	48390	248-960-2180	960-9570	49-5
AAU (Amateur Athletic Union of the US) 1910 Hotel Plaza Blvd *TF:* 800-228-4872 ■ *Web:* www.aausports.org	Lake Buena Vista	FL	32830	407-934-7200	934-7242	48-22
AAU (Association of American Universities) 1200 New York Ave NW Ste 550 *Web:* www.aau.edu	Washington	DC	20005	202-408-7500	408-8184	49-5
AAUP (American Assn of University Professors) 1133 Nineteenth St Ste 200 *TF:* 800-424-2973 ■ *Web:* www.aaup.org	Washington	DC	20036	202-737-5900	737-5526	49-5
AAUW (American Assn of University Women) 1111 16th St NW *TF:* 800-326-2289 ■ *Web:* www.aauw.org	Washington	DC	20036	202-785-7700	872-1425	49-5
AAUW Outlook Magazine 1111 16th St NW *TF:* 800-326-2289 ■ *Web:* www.aauw.org	Washington	DC	20036	202-785-7700	872-1425	457-10
Aava Whistler Hotel Ltd 4005 Whistler Way *TF:* 800-663-5644 ■ *Web:* www.aavawhistlerhotel.com	Whistler	BC	V0N1B4	604-932-2522		378
Aavid Thermalloy LLC 70 Commercial St Ste 200 *TF:* 855-322-2843 ■ *Web:* www.aavid.com	Concord	NH	03301	603-224-9988	223-1790	253
AAVIN Equity Partners LP 1245 First Ave SE Ste 630 *Web:* www.aavin.com	Cedar Rapids	IA	52402	319-247-1072		792
Aavispro LLC 113 Amberwood Ct *TF:* 800-881-5101 ■ *Web:* www.aavispro.com	Bethel Park	PA	15102	412-833-5444		261
AAVSO (American Assn of Variable Star Observers) 49 Bay State Rd *TF:* 888-802-7827 ■ *Web:* www.aavso.org	Cambridge	MA	02138	617-354-0484	354-0665	49-19
Aaxon Laundry Systems 6100 N Powerline Rd *TF:* 800-826-1012 ■ *Web:* www.aaxon.com	Ft. Lauderdale	FL	33309	954-772-7100		111
AAyuja Inc 35453B Dumbarton Ct *TF:* 800-422-6237 ■ *Web:* www.aayuja.com	Newark	CA	94560	415-658-6070		5
AB (AllianceBernstein Holding LP) 1345 Ave of the Americas *NYSE: AB* ■ **Fax:* Hum Res ■ *TF Cust Svc:* 800-221-5672 ■ *Web:* www.abglobal.com/home.htm	New York	NY	10105	212-486-5800	969-2293*	401
AB Carter Inc 4801 York Hwy *TF:* 800-288-4101 ■ *Web:* www.abcarter.com	Gastonia	NC	28052	704-865-1201		744
AB Controls Inc 15530 Rockfield Blvd Ste B2 *Web:* www.abcontrols.com	Irvine	CA	92618	949-341-0977		177
Ab Ovo Inc 2320-H Walsh Ave *TF:* 866-549-0782 ■ *Web:* www.abovoinc.com	Santa Clara	CA	95051	408-567-9090		196
A&B Precision Metals Inc 13715 Mt Anderson St *Web:* www.abprecisionmetals.com	Reno	NV	89506	775-323-2546		567
A&B Printing & Mailing 2908 S Highland Dr Ste B *TF:* 800-882-1844 ■ *Web:* www.abprint.com	Las Vegas	NV	89109	702-731-5888		627
A&B Process Systems Corp 201 S Wisconsin Ave *TF:* 888-258-2789 ■ *Web:* www.abprocess.com	Stratford	WI	54484	715-687-4332		492
AB Staffing Solutions LLC 3451 Mercy Rd *TF:* 888-515-3900 ■ *Web:* www.abstaffing.com	Gilbert	AZ	85297	480-345-6668		631
AB Watley Direct Inc 50 Broad St Ste 1614 **Fax Area Code:* 212	New York	NY	10004	646-753-9301	202-5204*	690
A&B Wiper Supply Inc 11350 Norcom Rd *TF:* 800-333-7247 ■ *Web:* www.bestrags.com	Philadelphia	PA	19154	215-482-6100	482-6190	508
AB Young Cos Inc 15305 Stony Creek Way *TF:* 800-886-7001 ■ *Web:* www.abyoung.com	Noblesville	IN	46060	317-565-5000		612
ABA (American Bicycle Assn) 1645 W Sunrise Blvd *TF:* 866-650-4867 ■ *Web:* www.usabmx.com	Gilbert	AZ	85233	480-961-1903	961-1842	48-22
ABA (American Burn Assn) 625 N Michigan Ave Ste 2550 *Web:* www.ameriburn.org	Chicago	IL	60611	312-642-9260	642-9130	49-8
ABA (American Bankers Assn) 1120 Connecticut Ave NW *TF Cust Svc:* 800-226-5377 ■ *Web:* www.aba.com	Washington	DC	20036	202-663-5000		49-2
ABA (American Baptist Assn) 4605 N State Line Ave *TF:* 800-264-2482 ■ *Web:* www.abaptist.org	Texarkana	TX	75503	903-792-2783	792-8128	48-20
ABA (American Bar Assn) 321 N Clark St *TF:* 800-285-2221 ■ *Web:* www.americanbar.org	Chicago	IL	60654	312-988-5000		49-10
ABA (American Booksellers Assn) 200 White Plains Rd Ste 600 *TF:* 800-637-0037 ■ *Web:* www.bookweb.org	Tarrytown	NY	10591	914-591-2665	591-2720	49-18
ABA Commission on Domestic Violence 321 N Clark St 9th Fl **Fax Area Code:* 202 ■ *TF:* 800-799-7233 ■ *Web:* www.americanbar.org/groups/domestic_violence.html	Chicago	IL	60654	312-988-5000	662-1594*	49-10
ABA Commission on Law & Aging (COLA) 1050 Connecticut Ave NW Ste 400 *Web:* www.americanbar.org/groups/law_aging.html	Washington	DC	20036	202-662-1000	662-8698	49-10
ABA Marketing Network 1120 Connecticut Ave NW *TF:* 800-226-5377 ■ *Web:* www.aba.com/marketingnetwork	Washington	DC	20036	202-663-5000	828-5053	49-2
Ababa Bolt 1466 - 1 Pioneer Way	El Cajon	CA	92020	619-440-1781		350
Abacrombie Inn 58 W Biddle St	Baltimore	MD	21201	410-244-8413		671
Abacus *Kent Rathbun* 4511 McKinney Ave	Dallas	TX	75205	214-559-3111	559-3113	671
Abacus Automation Inc 264 Shields Dr *Web:* abacusautomation.com	Bennington	VT	05201	802-442-3662		194
Abacus Business Solutions Inc 15301 Roosevelt Blvd Ste 303	Clearwater	FL	33760	727-524-0177	524-0188	180
Abacus Corp 610 Gusryan St *TF:* 800-230-0043 ■ *Web:* www.abacuscorporation.com	Baltimore	MD	21224	410-633-1900		631
Abacus Group LLC 14 Penn Plaza *Web:* www.abacusgrpllc.com	New York	NY	10122	212-812-8444		193
Abacus Group LLC, The 2541 Lafayette Plaza Dr	Albany	GA	31707	229-436-6032		390
Abacus Planning Group Inc 2500 Devine St *Web:* www.abacusplanninggroup.com	Columbia	SC	29205	803-933-0054		194
Abacus Private Equity Brookfield Pl - TD-Canada Trust Tower 161 Bay St Ste 2430 *Web:* www.abacuspe.com	Toronto	ON	M5J2S1	416-861-8711	861-9979	528
ABACUS Project Management Inc 3030 N Central Ave Ste 1207 *Web:* www.abacuspm.com	Phoenix	AZ	85012	602-265-6870		194
Abacus Software Inc 3413 Roger B Chaffee Memorial Blvd SE *Web:* www.abacuspub.com	Grand Rapids	MI	49546	616-241-3404		178-6

Phone | Fax | Class

Abacus Technology Corp
5454 Wisconsin Ave Ste 1100 . . . Chevy Chase MD 20815 301-907-8500 180
TF: 800-225-2135 ■ *Web:* www.abacustech.com

Abad Foam Inc 6560 Caballero Blvd . . . Buena Park CA 90620 714-994-2223 601
Web: www.abadfoam.com

Abalon Precision Mfg Corp 1040 Home St. . . . Bronx NY 10459 718-589-5682 589-0300 697
TF: 800-888-2225

Abalonetti Seafood Trattoria
57 Fisherman's Wharf . . . Monterey CA 93940 831-373-1851 373-2058 671
Web: www.restauranteur.com/abalonetti

Abanaki Corp 17387 Munn Rd . . . Chagrin Falls OH 44023 440-543-7400 537
Web: www.abanaki.com

ABAPAC (American Bankers Assn PAC)
1120 Connecticut Ave NW . . . Washington DC 20036 800-226-5377 663-7544* 615
**Fax Area Code:* 202 ■ *TF:* 800-226-5377 ■ *Web:* www.aba.com/default.htm

ABA-PGT Inc 10 Gear Dr PO Box 8270 . . . Manchester CT 06040 860-649-4591 643-7619 757
TF: 800-890-9000 ■ *Web:* www.abapgt.com

Abarca Health LLC
650 ave munoz rivera . . . San juan PR 00918 787-523-1212 363
Web: www.abarcahealth.com

Abaris Inc
1255 Treat Blvd Ste 140 . . . Walnut Creek CA 94597 949-333-3500 177
Web: www.abaris-inc.com

Abaris Training Resources Inc
5401 Longley Ln Ste 49 . . . Reno NV 89511 775-827-6568 507
Web: www.abaris.com

ABARTA Oil & Gas Company Inc
200 Alpha Dr . . . Pittsburgh PA 15238 412-963-6443 536
TF: 800-428-0981 ■ *Web:* www.abartaenergy.com

Abatement Technologies
605 Satellite Blvd Ste 300 . . . Suwanee GA 30024 678-889-4200 358-2394* 37
**Fax Area Code:* 800 ■ *TF:* 800-634-9091 ■ *Web:* www.abatement.com

Abatix Corp 2400 Skyline Dr Ste 400 . . . Mesquite TX 75149 214-381-0322 388-0443 385
TF: 800-426-3983 ■ *Web:* www.abatix.com

Abaxis Inc 3240 Whipple Rd . . . Union City CA 94587 510-675-6500 441-6150 419
NASDAQ: ABAX ■ *TF:* 800-822-2947 ■ *Web:* www.abaxis.com

Abb Enterprise Inc 1010 E 18th St . . . Los Angeles CA 90021 213-748-7480 627
Web: www.abblabels.com

ABB Flexible Automation Inc
12040 Regency Pkwy . . . Cary NC 27518 919-856-2360 735
Web: www.abb.com

Abba 89 Old Colony Way . . . Orleans MA 02653 508-255-8144 671
Web: www.abbarestaurant.com

Abba Staffing & Consulting Services
2350 Airport Fwy Ste 130 . . . Bedford TX 76022 817-354-2800 260
Web: www.abbastaffing.com

Abba Technologies Inc
1501 San Pedro Dr NE . . . Albuquerque NM 87110 505-889-3337 889-3338 194
TF: 888-222-2832 ■ *Web:* www.abbatech.com

Abbacore LLC
7803 Cambridge Dr . . . Prairie Village KS 66208 913-908-4654 631
Web: www.abbacore.com

Abbco Inc 2401 American Ln . . . Elkgrove Vlg IL 60007 630-595-7115 595-6431 455
TF: 866-986-6546 ■ *Web:* www.abbcoinc.net

Abbe Museum 26 Mt Desert St . . . Bar Harbor ME 04609 207-288-3519 288-8979 520
Web: www.abbemuseum.org

Abbeville Chamber of Commerce
107 Ct Sq . . . Abbeville SC 29620 864-366-4600 139
Web: www.visitabbevillesc.com

Abbeville County
21 Old Calhoun Falls Rd . . . Abbeville SC 29620 864-366-5312 338
TF: 800-922-6081 ■ *Web:* www.abbevillecountysc.com/sheriff.aspx

Abbeville County School District 60
400 Greenville St . . . Abbeville SC 29620 864-366-5427 685
Web: www.acsd.k12.sc.us

Abbey Delray 2000 Lowson Blvd . . . Delray Beach FL 33445 561-454-2000 672
TF: 888-791-9363 ■ *Web:* lifespacecommunities.com

Abbey Party Rents 411 Allan St . . . Daly City CA 94014 415-715-6900 292
Web: www.abbeyrentssf.com

Abbey Resort & Fontana Spa
269 Fontana Blvd . . . Fontana WI 53125 262-275-9000 669
TF: 800-709-1323 ■ *Web:* www.theabbeyresort.com

Abbey Travel Ltd
522 N Washington St . . . Naperville IL 60563 630-420-0400 772
Web: www.wehrlitravel.com

Abbey, Weitzenberg, Warren & Emery PC
100 Stony Point Rd Ste 200 . . . Santa Rosa CA 95401 707-542-5050 428
TF: 800-973-1177 ■ *Web:* www.abbeylaw.com

Abbeys 145 Zane St . . . Wheeling WV 26003 304-233-0729 671

Abbi Agency Inc, The 1385 Haskell St . . . Reno NV 89509 775-323-2977 636
Web: theabbiagency.com

Abbi Home Care Inc 6453 SW Blvd . . . Benbrook TX 76132 817-377-0889 377-0890 363
TF: 877-383-2224 ■ *Web:* abbihomecare.com

Abbington Distinctive Banquets
3S002 IL Rt 53 . . . Glen Ellyn IL 60137 630-942-8600 671
Web: www.abbingtonbanquets.com

Abbot & Abbot Box Corp
37-11 Tenth St . . . Long Island NY 11101 888-525-7186 392-8439* 200
**Fax Area Code:* 718 ■ *TF:* 888-525-7186 ■ *Web:* www.abbotbox.com

Abbot Construction 3408 First Ave S . . . Seattle WA 98134 206-467-8500 447-1885 186
Web: www.jrabbott.com

Abbotsford Chamber of Commerce
32900 S Fraser Way Ste 207 . . . Abbotsford BC V2S5A1 604-859-9651 850-6880 137
Web: www.abbotsfordchamber.com

Abbotsford Virtual School
33952 Pine St . . . Abbotsford BC V2S2P3 604-859-9803 685
Web: avs.sd34.bc.ca

Abbott 625 Cleveland Ave . . . Columbus OH 43215 614-624-7485 296-10
TF PR: 800-227-5767 ■ *Web:* abbottnutrition.com

Abbott 26531 Ynez Rd . . . Temecula CA 92591 800-227-9902 111
TF: 800-227-9902 ■ *Web:* www.abbottvascular.com

Abbott Ambulance Inc
2500 Abbott Pl . . . Saint Louis MO 63143 314-768-1000 30
TF: 888-974-7035 ■ *Web:* www.abbottems.org

Abbott Ball Company Inc
19 Railroad Pl . . . West Hartford CT 06133 860-236-5901 492
Web: www.abbottball.com

Abbott Company Ltd 345 E Flower St . . . Phoenix AZ 85012 602-224-9092 2
Web: acoabbott.com

Abbott Diagnostics 675 N Field Dr . . . Lake Forest IL 60045 224-667-6100 231
TF: 800-387-8378 ■ *Web:* www.corelaboratory.abbott/us/en/home

Abbott Greg (R) PO Box 12428 . . . Austin TX 78711 512-463-2000 463-5571 343
Web: gov.texas.gov

Abbott Interfast Corp 190 Abbott Dr . . . Wheeling IL 60090 847-459-6200 459-4076 621
TF: 800-877-0789 ■ *Web:* www.abbott-interfast.com

Abbott Laboratories Fund
100 Abbott Pk Rd . . . Abbott Park IL 60064 224-667-6100 304
NYSE: ABT ■ *Web:* abbott.com

Abbott Laboratories Pharmaceutical Products Div
100 Research Dr Bioresearch Ctr . . . Worcester MA 01605 224-667-6100 582
TF: 866-427-8477 ■ *Web:* www.abbott.com

Abbott Nicholson PC
300 River Pl Ste 3000 . . . Detroit MI 48207 313-566-2500 466
TF: 800-900-4250 ■ *Web:* www.abbottnicholson.com

Abbott Northwestern Hospital
800 E 28th St . . . Minneapolis MN 55407 612-863-4000 374-3
TF: 800-582-5175 ■ *Web:* www.allinahealth.org

Abbott Printing Company Inc
110 Atlantic Dr . . . Maitland FL 32751 407-831-2999 627
Web: www.abbottcg.com

Abbott Smith 11697 W Grand Ave . . . Northlake IL 60164 708-223-1194 260

Abbott Stringham & Lynch
1550 Leigh Ave . . . San Jose CA 95125 408-377-8700 2
Web: www.aslcpa.com

Abbott Terrace Health Ctr
135 South Rd . . . Farmington CT 06032 203-755-4870 371
TF: 800-369-6220 ■ *Web:* athenahealthcare.com

Abbott's Meat Inc 3623 Blackington Ave . . . Flint MI 48532 810-232-7128 473
TF: 800-678-1962 ■ *Web:* www.abbottsmeat.com

Abbozzo Gallery
401 Richmond Stt W Ste 128 . . . Toronto ON M5V3A8 416-260-2220 42
TF: 866-844-4481 ■ *Web:* www.abbozzogallery.com

ABBTECH Professional Resources Inc
45625 Willow Pond Plaza . . . Sterling VA 20164 703-450-5252 344
Web: www.abbtech.com

AbbVie Pharmaceutical Contract Manufacturing
1401 Sheridan Rd . . . North Chicago IL 60064 847-938-8524 938-0659 584
TF: 888-299-7416

Abbyland Foods Inc
502 E Linden St PO Box 69 . . . Abbotsford WI 54405 715-223-6386 223-6388 473
TF: 800-732-5483 ■ *Web:* www.abbyland.com

ABBYY Language Services
880 N McCarthy Blvd . . . Milpitas CA 95035 856-782-8106 393
Web: abbyy-ls.com

ABC (America's Blood Centers)
725 15th St NW Ste 700 . . . Washington DC 20005 202-393-5725 393-1282 49-8
TF: 888-872-5663 ■ *Web:* www.americasblood.org

ABC (American Business Conference)
1828 L St NW Ste 908 . . . Washington DC 20036 202-822-9300 467-4070 49-12
Web: www.americanbusinessconference.org

ABC (ArcBest) 3801 Old Greenwood Rd . . . Fort Smith AR 72903 800-610-5544 785-6124* 780
NASDAQ: ARCB ■ **Fax Area Code:* 479 ■ *TF:* 800-610-5544 ■ *Web:* arcb.com

ABC (Associated Builders & Contractors Inc)
4250 Fairfax Dr . . . Arlington VA 22203 703-812-2000 812-8235 49-3
TF: 877-889-5627 ■ *Web:* www.abc.org

ABC (Audit Bureau of Circulations)
48 W Seegers Rd . . . Arlington Heights IL 60005 224-366-6939 605-0483* 49-18
**Fax Area Code:* 847 ■ *TF:* 800-759-6397 ■ *Web:* www.auditedmedia.com

ABC American Bio-clinical
2730 N Main St Ste 101 . . . Los Angeles CA 90031 800-262-1688 418
TF: 800-262-1688 ■ *Web:* www.abclab.com

ABC Appliance Inc
1 Silverdome Industrial Pk . . . Pontiac MI 48343 800-981-3866 35
TF: 800-981-3866 ■ *Web:* www.abcwarehouse.com

ABC Billing Solutions
13200 Strickland Rd Ste 114-336 . . . Raleigh NC 27612 919-870-5939 870-5939 393
Web: www.abcbillingsolutions.com

ABC Columbia 5807 Shakespeare Rd . . . Columbia SC 29223 803-754-7525 741-33
Web: abccolumbia.com

ABC Compounding Company Inc & Acme Wholesale
6970 Jonesboro Rd . . . Morrow GA 30260 770-968-9222 968-7281 151
TF: 800-795-9222 ■ *Web:* www.abccompounding.com

ABC Electric Corp 2425 46th St . . . Astoria NY 11103 718-956-0000 112
Web: www.abcelectriccorp.com

Abc Fence Systems Inc
963 Industrial Park Dr . . . Chipley FL 32428 850-638-8876 200
Web: www.abcfencesystems.com

ABC Fine Wines & Spirits
8989 S Orange Ave . . . Orlando FL 32824 407-851-0000 443
Web: abcfws.com

ABC Global Services
6400 Shafer Ct Ste 310 . . . Rosemont IL 60018 800-722-5179 771
TF: 800-722-5179 ■ *Web:* www.abccst.com

ABC Home & Commercial Services
9475 Hwy 290 E . . . Austin TX 78724 512-837-9500 577
TF: 800-427-7142 ■ *Web:* www.abchomeandcommercial.com

ABC Home Medical Supply Inc
15 E Uwchlan Ave Ste 430 . . . Exton PA 19341 866-897-8588 475
TF: 866-897-8588 ■ *Web:* www.abc-med.com

ABC Inc 7 Lincoln Sq . . . New York NY 10023 212-456-7777 739
Web: www.abc.go.com

ABC Industrie PO Box 77 . . . Warsaw IN 46581 574-267-5166 267-2045 370
TF: 800-426-0921 ■ *Web:* www.abc-industries.net

ABC Metals Inc 500 W Clinton St . . . Logansport IN 46947 800-238-8470 753-6110* 492
**Fax Area Code:* 574 ■ *TF:* 800-238-8470 ■ *Web:* www.abcmetals.com

ABC NewsOne 47 W 66th St . . . New York NY 10023 212-456-2700 742
Web: abcnews.extremereach.com/pg/ntaxnji=/abcnewsone

A-B-C Packaging Machine Corp
811 Live Oak St . . . Tarpon Springs FL 34689 727-937-5144 938-1239 547
TF: 800-237-5975 ■ *Web:* www.abcpackaging.com

ABC Polymers Inc
5682 E Ponce De Leon Ave . . . Stone Mountain GA 30083 770-938-8336 603
Web: www.abcpolymers.com

ABC Professional Tree Services Inc
201 Flint Ridge Rd . . . Webster TX 77598 281-280-1100 776
Web: www.abctree.com

Name / Address	City	State	ZIP	Phone	Fax	Class
Abc Quality Consulting Services						
1115 Grand Cyn	Brea	CA	92821	714-256-0223		196
Web: abcquality.com						
ABC Seamless 3001 Fiechtner Dr	Fargo	ND	58103	701-293-5952		191-4
TF: 800-732-6577 ■ *Web:* www.abcseamless.com						
ABC Security Service Inc						
1840 Embarcadero	Oakland	CA	94606	510-436-0666		693
ABC Supply Company Inc 1 ABC Pkwy	Beloit	WI	53511	608-362-7777		191-4
TF: 888-492-1047 ■ *Web:* www.abcsupply.com						
ABC Testing Inc						
95 First St PO Box 868	Bridgewater	MA	02324	508-697-6068		418
Web: www.abcndt.com						
ABC Window Company Inc						
621 S Bon View Ave	Ontario	CA	91761	909-391-6491		329
ABC21 WPTA 3401 Butler Rd	Fort Wayne	IN	46808	260-483-0584	483-2568	741-51
Web: www.21alive.com						
ABCA (American Baseball Coaches Assn)						
108 S University Ave Ste 3	Mount Pleasant	MI	48858	989-775-3300		48-22
Web: www.abca.org						
ABC-Amega Inc 1100 Main St	Buffalo	NY	14209	716-885-4444	878-2872	160
Web: www.abc-amega.com						
ABC-CLIO Inc 130 Cremona Dr	Goleta	CA	93117	805-968-1911	685-9685	637-2
TF: 800-368-6868 ■ *Web:* www.abc-clio.com						
Abcm Corp 1320 Fourth St NE PO Box 436	Hampton	IA	50441	641-456-5636	456-2320	450
Web: www.abcmcorp.com						
Abco Automation Inc						
6202 Technology Dr	Browns Summit	NC	27214	336-375-6400		201
Web: www.goabco.com						
Abco Cleaning Products 6800 NW 36th Ave	Miami	FL	33147	305-694-2226	694-0451	508
TF: 888-694-2226 ■ *Web:* www.abcoproducts.com						
Abco Distribution Inc						
6282 Proprietors Rd	Worthington	OH	43085	800-821-9435		628
TF: 800-821-9435 ■ *Web:* www.printingbyabco.com						
Abco Inc 1621 Wall St	Dallas	TX	75215	214-565-1191	428-8996	86
TF: 800-969-2226 ■ *Web:* abcodigital.com						
Abco Laboratories Inc						
2450 S Watney Way	Fairfield	CA	94533	707-432-2200	432-2240	296-37
TF: 800-678-2226 ■ *Web:* www.abcolabs.com						
Abco Office Furniture						
4121 Rushton St	Florence	AL	35630	256-767-4100	760-1247	319-1
TF: 800-336-0070 ■ *Web:* www.abcofurniture.com						
Abco Refrigeration Supply Corp						
49-70 31st St	Long Island	NY	11101	718-937-9000		665
ABCT (Association for Behavioral & Cognitive Therapies)						
305 Seventh Ave 16th Fl	New York	NY	10001	212-647-1890	647-1865	49-15
TF: 800-685-2228 ■ *Web:* www.abct.org/home						
Abdo Eick & Meyers LLP 5201 Eden Ave	Edina	MN	55436	952-835-9090		734
Web: www.aemcpas.com						
Abe & Louie's 793 Boylston St	Boston	MA	02116	617-536-6300		671
Web: www.abeandlouies.com						
ABeam Consulting (USA) Ltd						
8445 Freeport Pkwy 4th Fl	Irving	TX	75063	972-929-3130		194
Web: www.abeam.com						
Abec Inc 3998 Schelden Cir	Bethlehem	PA	18017	610 861-4666	861-2636	298
Web: www.abec.com						
Abe-El Produce 42143 Rd 120	Orosi	CA	93647	559-528-3030		10-11
Abel Automatics Inc 165 Aviador St	Camarillo	CA	93010	805-484-8789	482-0701	710
TF: 866-511-7444 ■ *Web:* www.abelreels.com						
Abel Reel, The 165 Aviador St	Camarillo	CA	93010	805-484-8789	482-0701	756
TF: 866-511-7444 ■ *Web:* www.abelreels.com						
Abell Corp 2500 Sterlington Rd	Monroe	LA	71203	318-345-2600		280
Abeln, Magy, Underberg & Associates						
1907 E Wayzata Blvd Ste 120	Wayzata	MN	55391	952-404-5085		260
Web: www.abelnmagy.com						
ABELSoft Inc 3310 S Service Rd	Burlington	ON	L7N3M6	800-267-2235		463
TF: 800-267-2235 ■ *Web:* www.abelsoft.com						
Abelson Herron Halpern LLP						
333 S Grand Ave Ste 1550	Los Angeles	CA	90071	213-402-1900		428
Web: www.abelsonherron.com						
Abelson-Taylor Inc 33 W Monroe St	Chicago	IL	60603	312-894-5500		4
Web: abelsontaylor.com						
Abengoa Bioenergy Corp						
16150 Main Cir Dr Ste 300	Chesterfield	MO	63017	636-728-0508	728-1148	144
Web: www.abengoabioenergy.com						
ABEO Group, The						
212 S Tryon St Ste 1750	Charlotte	NC	28281	704-790-5200		47
Web: www.theabeogroup.com						
Abercrombie & Fitch Co						
6301 Fitch Pass	New Albany	OH	43054	614-283-6500		157-4
NYSE: ANF ■ *TF:* 800-732-0330 ■ *Web:* www.abercrombie.com						
Abercrombie Oil Company Inc						
PO Box 1422	Danville	VA	24543	434-792-8022		579
Aberdare Ventures						
1 Embarcadero Ctr Ste 4000	San Francisco	CA	94111	415-392-7442	392-4264	792
Web: www.aberdare.com						
Aberdeen 123 S Lincoln St	Aberdeen	SD	57401	605-626-7025		21
Web: www.aberdeen.sd.us						
Aberdeen & Rockfish Railroad Co						
101 E Main St	Aberdeen	NC	28315	910-944-2341	944-9738	648
TF: 800-849-8985 ■ *Web:* www.aberdeen-rockfish.com						
Aberdeen Alliance Church of The Christian & Missionary Alliance, The						
1106 S Roosevelt St	Aberdeen	SD	57401	605-225-9724		48-20
Aberdeen American News						
124 S Second St	Aberdeen	SD	57402	605-225-4100		532-2
TF: 800-925-4100 ■ *Web:* www.aberdeennews.com/mld/americannews						
Aberdeen Area Chamber of Commerce						
516 S Main St	Aberdeen	SD	57401	605-225-2860	225-2437	139
TF: 800-874-9038 ■ *Web:* www.aberdeen-chamber.com						
Aberdeen Asset Management Inc						
1735 Market St 32nd Fl	Philadelphia	PA	19103	215-405-5700		401
Web: www.aberdeen-asset.com						
Aberdeen Barn						
5805 Northampton Blvd	Virginia Beach	VA	23455	757-464-1580		671
Web: www.aberdeenbarn.com						
Aberdeen Barn 1601 Richmond Rd	Williamsburg	VA	23185	757-229-6661		671
TF: 800-899-9841 ■ *Web:* www.aberdeen-barn.com						
Aberdeen Chrysler Center Inc						
901 Auto Plaza Dr	Aberdeen	SD	57401	605-225-1656		57
Web: www.aberdeenchrysler.com						
Aberdeen Convention & Visitors Bureau						
10 Railroad Ave SW PO Box 78	Aberdeen	SD	57401	605-225-2414	225-3573	206
TF: 800-645-3851 ■ *Web:* www.visitaberdeensd.com						
Aberdeen Group Inc 451 D St Ste 710	Boston	MA	02210	617-854-5200		466
TF: 800-577-7891 ■ *Web:* www.aberdeen.com						
Aberdeen Hospital 835 E River Rd	New Glasgow	NS	B2H3S6	902-752-7600	755-2356	374-2
TF: 800-611-6345 ■ *Web:* www.aberdeenhealthfoundation.com						
Aberdeen LLC						
9130 Norwalk Blvd	Santa Fe Springs	CA	90670	562-699-6998	695-5570*	173-2
**Fax:* Sales ■ *TF:* 800-500-9526 ■ *Web:* www.aberdeeninc.com						
Aberdeen School District 5						
216 N G St	Aberdeen	WA	98520	360-538-2000		685
Web: www.asd5.org						
Aberfoyle Metal Treaters Ltd						
18 Kerr Cres	Guelph	ON	N0B2J0	519-763-1120	763-1121	484
Web: www.aberfoyle-mt.com						
ABET Inc 415 N Charles St Ste 1050	Baltimore	MD	21201	410-347-7700	625-2238	48-1
TF: 800-621-7440 ■ *Web:* www.abet.org						
ABF Farm Services Inc						
7761 W Undine Rd	Stockton	CA	95206	209-462-0208		10-4
ABFB Corp 128 Main St	Lyndonville	VT	05851	802-626-5339		345
Web: www.whitesmarket.com						
ABG Communications 3810 Wabash Dr	Mira Loma	CA	91752	951-361-7100		627
TF: 888-685-7100 ■ *Web:* www.abgraphics.com						
ABG Sundal Collier Inc						
850 Third Ave Ste 9-C	New York	NY	10022	212-605-3800		690
Web: www.abgsc.com						
Abha Architects Inc						
1621 N Lincoln St	Wilmington	DE	19806	302-658-6426		261
Web: abha.com						
Abhasa Waikiki Spa at the Royal Hawaiian Hotel						
2259 Kalakaua Ave	Honolulu	HI	96815	808-922-8200		707
Web: www.abhasa.com						
Abhe & Svoboda Inc 18100 Dairy Ln	Jordan	MN	55352	952-447-6025		186
TF: 800-678-5664 ■ *Web:* www.abheonline.com						
ABHES (Accrediting Bureau of Health Education Schools)						
7777 Leesburg Pike Ste 314 N	Falls Church	VA	22043	703-917-9503	917-4109	48-1
TF: 800-228-9290 ■ *Web:* www.abhes.org						
ABI (Advanced Biotechnologies Inc)						
9108 Guilford Rd	Columbia	MD	21046	410-792-9779	497-9773*	231
**Fax Area Code:* 301 ■ *TF:* 800-426-0764 ■ *Web:* www.abionline.com						
ABI (Atkinson-Baker Inc)						
500 N Brand Blvd 3rd Fl	Glendale	CA	91203	818-551-7300		445
TF: 800-288-3376 ■ *Web:* www.depo.com						
ABI (American Biltrite Inc Tape Products Div)						
105 Whittendale Dr	Moorestown	NJ	08057	856-778-0700	224-6325*	732
**Fax Area Code:* 888 ■ *TF:* 888-224-6325 ■ *Web:* www.abitape.com						
ABI (American Bankruptcy Institute)						
66 Canal Ctr Plaza Ste 600	Alexandria	VA	22314	703-739-0800	739-1060	49-10
Web: www.abi.org						
ABIA (Austin-Bergstrom International Airport)						
3600 Presidential Blvd	Austin	TX	78719	512-530-2242		27
Web: www.ci.austin.tx.us						
Abidance Consulting Corp						
5680 Hwy 6 Ste 311	Missouri City	TX	77459	713-253-8820		463
Web: www.abidanceconsulting.com						
Abide International Inc 561 First St W	Sonoma	CA	95476	707-935-1577		186
Web: www.abideinternational.com						
Abiding Faith Free Lutheran Church						
433 Crestview Ave	Ortonville	MN	56278	320-839-3949		48-20
Web: aflc.org						
Abidon Leasing						
5301 E State St Ste 215	Rockford	IL	61108	815-226-8700		51
Abigal Press Inc 9735 133rd Ave	Ozone Park	NY	11417	718-641-5350		627
Web: abigal.com						
Abila Inc 7901 Jones Branch Dr	Mclean	VA	22102	703-506-7000		177
Web: www.abila.com/lp/avectra						
Abilene Aero 2850 Airport Blvd	Abilene	TX	79602	325-677-2601		63
Web: www.abileneaero.com						
Abilene Ag Service & Supply Inc						
303 S 14th St	Abilene	TX	79602	325-677-4371		276
Abilene Ballet Theatre						
1265 N Second St	Abilene	TX	79601	325-675-0303		573-1
Web: www.abileneballettheatre.org						
Abilene Chamber of Commerce						
174 Cypress St Ste 200	Abilene	TX	79601	325-677-7241		139
Web: www.abilenechamber.com						
Abilene Christian University Brown Library (ACU)						
760 Library Ct	Abilene	TX	79699	325-674-2000		434-6
TF: 800-460-6228 ■ *Web:* www.acu.edu/academics/library						
Abilene City Hall 555 Walnut St	Abilene	TX	79601	325-676-6200	676-6229	337
TF: 800-727-7704 ■ *Web:* www.abilenetx.com						
Abilene Civic Ctr 1100 N Sixth St	Abilene	TX	79601	325-676-6211	676-6343	572
Web: www.abilenetx.com						
Abilene Community Theatre (ACT)						
809 Barrow	Abilene	TX	79605	325-673-6271		572
Web: www.abilenecommunitytheatre.org						
Abilene Convention & Visitors Bureau						
1101 N First St	Abilene	TX	79601	325-676-2556	676-1630	206
TF: 800-727-7704 ■ *Web:* www.abilenevisitors.com						
Abilene Convention & Visitors Bureau						
201 NW Second St	Abilene	KS	67410	785-263-2231	263-4125	206
TF: 800-569-5915 ■ *Web:* www.abilenecityhall.com						
Abilene Machine Inc PO Box 129	Abilene	KS	67410	785-655-9455	655-3838	274
TF: 800-255-0337 ■ *Web:* www.abilenemachine.com						
Abilene Philharmonic Orchestra						
401 Cypress St Ste 520	Abilene	TX	79601	325-677-6710		573-3
TF: 800-460-0610 ■ *Web:* www.abilenephilharmonic.org						
Abilene Public Library 202 Cedar St	Abilene	TX	79601	325-677-2474	676-6024	434-3
Web: www.abilenetx.com						
Abilene Regional Airport						
2933 Airport Blvd	Abilene	TX	79602	325-676-6367	676-6317	27
Web: www.abilenetx.com/airport						
Abilene Regional Medical Ctr						
6250 S Hwy 83-84	Abilene	TX	79606	325-428-1000	795-2113	374-3
TF: 800-888-2504 ■ *Web:* www.abileneregional.com						

Name / Address	City	State	Zip	Phone	Fax	Class
Abilene Reporter-News 101 Cypress St *Fax: Edit ■ TF: 866-604-2020 ■ Web: www.reporternews.com	Abilene	TX	79601	325-673-4271	670-5242*	532-2
Abilene Seafood Tavern 1882 S Clack St	Abilene	TX	79605	325-695-1770		671
Abilene State Park 150 Pk Rd 32 Web: tpwd.texas.gov/state-parks/abilene	Tuscola	TX	79562	325-572-3204		565
Abilene Zoological Gardens 2070 Zoo Ln Nelson Pk TF: 800-899-9841 ■ Web: www.abilenetx.com	Abilene	TX	79602	325-676-6085	676-6084	823
Ability Building Center Inc 1911 14th St NW TF: 800-543-7709 ■ Web: www.abcinc.org	Rochester	MN	55903	507-281-6262		627
Ability Center of Greater Toledo Inc 5605 Monroe St TF: 866-885-5733 ■ Web: www.abilitycenter.org	Sylvania	OH	43560	419-885-5733		672
Ability Engineering Technology inc 16140 S Vincennes Ave Web: www.abilityengineering.com	South Holland	IL	60473	708-331-0025		454
Ability Janitorial Services Ltd 884 Churchill Ave S	Ottawa	ON	K1Z5H2	613-722-3566		104
Ability Metal Co 1355 Greenleaf Ave Web: abilitymetal.com	Elk Grove Village	IL	60007	847-437-7040		492
ABIM (American Board of Internal Medicine) 510 Walnut St Ste 1700 TF: 800-441-2246 ■ Web: www.abim.org	Philadelphia	PA	19106	215-446-3500	446-3590	48-1
AbiMar Foods, Inc 5425 N First St Web: www.abimarfoods.com	Abilene	TX	79603	325-691-5425	691-5471	296-9
Abingdon Capital Management LLC 1650 Tysons Blvd Ste 1575 Web: www.abingdoncapital.com	Mclean	VA	22102	703-269-3400		401
Abingdon Convention & Visitors Bureau 335 Cummings St TF: 800-435-3440 ■ Web: visitabingdonvirginia.com	Abingdon	VA	24210	276-676-2282		206
Abington Memorial Hospital 1200 Old York Rd Web: abingtonhealth.org	Abington	PA	19001	215-481-2000		374-3
ABIOMED Inc 22 Cherry Hill Dr NASDAQ: ABMD ■ TF: 800-422-8666 ■ Web: www.abiomed.com	Danvers	MA	01923	978-777-5410	777-8411	250
Abipa Canada Inc 3700 Ave des Grandes Tourelles TF: 877-963-6888 ■ Web: www.abipa.com	Boisbraind	QC	J7H0A1	450-963-6888	963-8881	21
Abita Brewing Co 21084 Hwy 36 TF: 800-737-2311 ■ Web: www.abita.com	Covington	LA	70433	985-893-3143	898-3546	102
Abita Trace Animal Clinic 69142 Hwy 59 Ste E TF: 800-640-3274 ■ Web: www.medi-vet.com	Mandeville	LA	70471	985-892-5656		794
Abitec Corp Inc PO Box 569 TF Sales: 800-555-1255 ■ Web: www.abiteccorp.com	Columbus	OH	43215	614-429-6464	299-8279	296-29
Abitibi Geophysique Ltd 1740 ch Sullivan 1400 Web: www.ageophysics.com	Val-d'or	QC	J9P7H1	819-874-8800		192
AbitibiBowater Inc 1155 Metcalfe St Ste 800 Web: www.rcsolutofp.com	Montreal	QC	H3B5H2	514-875-2160		557
ABKCO Music & Records Inc 85 Fifth Ave Ste 11 Web: www.abkco.com	New York	NY	10003	212-399-0300		657
ABL (American Beverage Licensees) 5101 River Rd Ste 108 Web: www.ablusa.org	Bethesda	MD	20816	301-656-1494	656-7539	49-6
ABL Employment 777 Guelph Line Ste 212 Web: www.ablemployment.com	Burlington	ON	L7R3N2	905-631-7050		260
ABL Lights Inc 660 Golf Club Blvd Web: abllights.com	Mosinee	WI	54455	715-693-1530		362
Ablaze Wireless 4010 Moorpark Ave Ste 201 Web: www.ablazewireless.com	San Jose	CA	95117	408-615-0888		179
Able 2 Products Company Inc PO Box 543 TF: 800-641-4098 ■ Web: www.able2products.com	Cassville	MO	65625	417-847-4791	847-2222	438
Able Aerospace Services Inc 7706 E Velocity Way Web: www.ableengineering.com	Mesa	AZ	85212	602-304-1227		21
Able Die Casting Corp 3907 Wesley Terr Web: www.ablediecasting.com	Schiller Park	IL	60176	847-678-1991		358
Able Distributing Company Inc 2727 W Growers Ave Web: www.abledistributing.com	Phoenix	AZ	85053	602-993-0957		612
Able Electric Service 2626 Electronic Ln Web: ableelectricservice.com	Dallas	TX	75220	214-350-5721		362
Able Global Partners LLC 641 Lexington Ave 15th Fl Web: www.ableglobalps.com	New York	NY	10022	212-581-7011		691
Able Infosat Communications Inc 5906 Broadway St Web: www.able-usa.com	Pearland	TX	77581	281-485-8800		45
ABLE Innovations LLC 1100 Lakeway Dr Ste 200 TF: 800-347-5447 ■ Web: www.ableinnovations.com	Bellingham	WA	98229	360-714-1390		768
Able Management Solutions Inc 470 Olde Worthington Rd	Westerville	OH	43082	614-868-1144		47
Able Manufacturing & Assembly LLC 1000 Schifferdecker Web: www.ablemfg.com	Joplin	MO	64801	417-623-3060		480
Able Plumbing Inc 2336 Bob Boozer Dr	Omaha	NE	68130	402-334-8887		610
Able Service Contractors Inc 13505 Dulles Technology Dr Ste 2 Web: www.ableservice.com	Herndon	VA	20171	571-323-2990		104
Able Services 868 Folsom St TF: 800-461-9577 ■ Web: www.ableserve.com	San Francisco	CA	94107	415-546-6534		256
Able Steel Equipment Co Inc 50-02 23rd St TF: 800-428-8722 ■ Web: www.ablesteelequipment.com	Long Island	NY	11101	718-361-9240	937-5742	286
Able Steel Fabricators Inc 4150 E Quartz Cir TF: 800-478-3864 ■ Web: www.ablesteel.com	Mesa	AZ	85215	480-830-2253		480
Able Wire Edm Inc 440 W Atlas St TF: 800-660-1946 ■ Web: www.ableedm.com	Brea	CA	92821	714-255-1967		757
AbleSys Corp 20954 Corsair Blvd Web: www.ablesys.com	Hayward	CA	94545	510-265-1883		177
ABM Equipment & Supply LLC 333 Second St NE Web: www.abm-highway.com	Hopkins	MN	55343	952-938-5451	938-0159	61
ABM Industries 600 Harrison St Ste 600 Web: locations.abm.com	San Francisco	CA	94107	415-351-4428		152
ABM Industries Inc 8020 W Doe Ste C Web: www.abm.com	Visalia	SC	93291	559-651-1612		721
ABMA (American Boiler Manufacturers Assn) 8221 Old Courthouse Rd Ste 207 TF: 800-227-1966 ■ Web: www.abma.com	Vienna	VA	22182	703-356-7172		49-13
ABMC (American Bio Medica Corp) 122 Smith Rd OTC: ABMC ■ TF General: 800-227-1243 ■ Web: www.abmc.com	Kinderhook	NY	12106	518-758-8158	758-8172	85
ABMC (Advocate BroMenn Medical Ctr) 1304 Franklin Ave Web: www.advocatehealth.com/bromenn/default.cfm?id=1	Normal	IL	61761	309-454-1400		374-3
Abmech Inc 976 Forest Ave TF: 800-686-3626 ■ Web: www.abmechinc.com	West Homestead	PA	15120	412-462-7440		667
ABMP (Associated Bodywork & Massage Professionals) 25188 Genesee Trl Rd Ste 200 *Fax Area Code: 800 ■ TF: 800-458-2267 ■ Web: www.abmp.com	Golden	CO	80401	303-674-8478	667-8260*	48-17
ABMS (American Board of Medical Specialties) 353 N Clark St Ste 1400 Web: www.abms.org	Chicago	IL	60654	312-436-2600		48-1
Abna Engineering Inc 4140 Lindell Blvd Web: abnacorp.com	Saint Louis	MO	63108	314-454-0222		256
ABOL Software Inc 413 Creekstone Ridge TF: 800-713-7278 ■ Web: www.iabol.com	Woodstock	GA	30188	678-494-3172		174
Abonmarche Consultants Inc 361 First St Web: www.abonmarche.com	Manistee	MI	49660	231-723-1198		256
Aboriginal People's Television Network Inc 339 Portage Ave Web: www.aptn.ca	Winnipeg	MB	R3B2C3	204-947-9331		116
Aboundi Inc 4 Bud Way Unit 10 Web: www.aboundi.com	Nashua	NH	03063	603-889-8188		225
About Face Productions Inc 956 s bartlett rd Web: www.aboutfaceproductions.biz	Bartlett	IL	60103	630-540-2444		260
ABOUT-Consulting LLC 330 Kennett Pike Ste 205	Chadds Ford	PA	19317	610-388-9455		256
Above All Advertising Inc 9080 Activity Rd Ste A TF: 866-552-2683 ■ Web: www.abovealladvertising.net	San Diego	CA	92126	858-549-2226	777-3537	8
Above Security Inc 955 Michele-Bohec Blvd Ste 244 TF: 866-430-8166 ■ Web: www.abovesecurity.com	Blainville	QC	J7C5J6	450-430-8166		364
ABRA (American Buckskin Registry Assn Inc) 1141 Hartnell Ave TF: 800-458-4283 ■ Web: www.americanbuckskin.org	Redding	CA	96002	530-223-1420		48-3
Abraham & London Ltd 7 Old Sherman Tpke Ste 108 Web: www.abrahamlondon.com	Danbury	CT	06810	203-798-7537		260
Abraham Baldwin Agricultural College 2802 Moore Hwy ABAC 3 *Fax: Admissions ■ TF: 800-733-3653 ■ Web: www.abac.edu	Tifton	GA	31793	229-391-5001	391-4931*	162
Abraham Lincoln Birthplace National Historic Site 2995 Lincoln Farm Rd Web: www.nps.gov	Hodgenville	KY	42748	270-358-3137	358-3874	564
Abraham Lincoln Capital Airport 1200 Capital Airport Dr TF: 800-943-5436 ■ Web: www.flyspi.com	Springfield	IL	62707	217-788-1060	788-8056	27
Abraham Lincoln Presidential Library & Museum 112 N Sixth St TF: 800-610-2094 ■ Web: www.alplm.org	Springfield	IL	62701	217-557-6250		434-2
Abraham Lincoln Tourism Bureau of Logan County 1555 Fifth St Web: tourlogancounty.com	Lincoln	IL	62656	217-732-8687		206
Abraham Ralph (Rep R - LA) 417 Cannon HOB Web: abraham.house.gov	Washington	DC	20515	202-225-8490	225-5639	342-2
Abraham Watkins Nichols Sorrels Agosto & Friend 800 Commerce St Web: abrahamwatkins.com	Houston	TX	77002	713-222-7211		428
Abrahamson Uiterwyk & Barnes 2639 Mccormick Dr Web: www.theinjurylawyers.com	Clearwater	FL	33759	727-725-9411		428
Abrakadoodle Inc 46030 Manekin Pl Ste 110 Web: www.abrakadoodle.com	Sterling	VA	20166	703-860-6570		310
Abram S. Hewitt State Forest c/o Wawayanda State Pk 885 Warwick Tpke Web: www.njparksandforests.org/parks/abram.html	Hewitt	NJ	07421	973-853-4462		565
Abrams & Jossel Consulting Inc 39 S Lasalle St Ste 1410 Web: www.ajworkout.com	Chicago	IL	60603	312-629-8585		463
Abrams Airborne Manufacturing Inc 3735 N Romero Rd TF: 800-955-4465 ■ Web: www.abrams.com	Tucson	AZ	85705	520-887-1727	293-8807	697
Abrams Artists Agency 750 N San Vicente Blvd E tower 11th Fl Web: www.abramsartists.com	Los Angeles	CA	90069	310-859-0625		708
Abrams Construction Inc 7 Kent St Ste 2 Web: www.abrams-properties.com	Brookline	MA	02445	617-566-9090	566-9098	186
Abrams Consulting Group Inc 3020 Wchester Ave Ste 307 Web: www.abramsconsulting.com	Purchase	NY	10577	914-696-5100		194

Phone | Fax | Class

Abrams Foster Nole & Williams PA
West Quadrangle 2 Hamill Rd Ste 241 ... Baltimore MD 21210 410-433-6830 2
Web: www.afnw.com

Abrams Hebrew Academy
31 W College Ave ... Yardley PA 19067 215-493-1800 685
Web: abramsonline.org

Abrams Planetarium
Michigan State University ... East Lansing MI 48824 517-355-4676 598
Web: www.pa.msu.edu/abrams

Abrasive Technology Inc
8400 Green Meadows Dr ... Lewis Center OH 43035 740-548-4100 1
Web: www.abrasive-tech.com

Abrasive-Form Inc 454 Scott Dr ... Bloomingdale IL 60108 630-893-7800 893-6313 757
Web: www.abrasive-form.com

Abraxas Energy Consulting LLC
811 Palm St ... San Luis Obispo CA 93401 805-547-2050 261
Web: www.abraxasenergy.com

Abraxas Petroleum Corp
18803 Meisner Dr ... San Antonio TX 78258 210-490-4788 490-8816* 536
NASDAQ: AXAS ■ **Fax:* Acctg ■ *TF:* 800-732-0330 ■ *Web:* www.abraxaspetroleum.com

Abreo 515 E State St ... Rockford IL 61104 815-968-9463 671
Web: www.abreorockford.com

Abresist Corp PO Box 38 ... Urbana IN 46990 260-774-3327 183
TF: 800-348-0717 ■ *Web:* www.abresist.com

Abric (North America) Inc
220 Barren Springs Dr Ste 1 ... Houston TX 77090 281-569-7100 326
Web: www.abric.com

Abrisa Industrial Glass Inc
200 S Hallock Dr ... Santa Paula CA 93060 805-525-4902 329
Web: abrisatechnologies.com

Abrisa Technologies
200 S Hallock Dr ... Santa Paula CA 93060 877-622-7472 525-8604* 332
**Fax Area Code:* 805 ■ *TF:* 877-622-7472 ■ *Web:* www.abrisatechnologies.com

A-Brite Plating Company Inc
3000 W 121st St ... Cleveland OH 44111 216-252-2995 481
Web: www.abriteplating.com

ABRY Partners LLC
888 Boylston ÿSte. 1600 ... Boston MA 02199 617-859-2959 859-8797 405
TF: 800-777-3674 ■ *Web:* www.abry.com

ABS (American Bureau of Shipping)
16855 Northchase Dr ... Houston TX 77060 281-877-5800 877-5803 49-21
Web: www.eagle.org

ABS (American Bonanza Society)
1922 Midfield Rd ... Wichita KS 67206 316-945-1700 945-1710 48-18
Web: www.bonanza.org

ABS by Allan Schwartz
1231 Long Beach Ave ... Los Angeles CA 90021 213-895-4400 157-6
Web: www.absstyle.com

ABS Capital Partners
400 E Pratt St Ste 910 ... Baltimore MD 21202 410-246-5600 246-5606 792
Web: www.abscapital.com

ABS Corp 7031 N 16th St ... Omaha NE 68112 402-453-6970 584
TF: 800-359-2345 ■ *Web:* www.abs-corporation.com

ABS Direct Inc 4724 Enterprise Way ... Modesto CA 95356 209-545-6090 317
Web: www.absdirectinc.com

ABS Global Inc 1525 River Rd ... DeForest WI 53532 608-846-3721 846-6442 11-2
TF Cust Svc: 800-356-5331 ■ *Web:* www.absglobal.com

ABS Group of Cos Inc
Abs Plaza 16855 Northchase Dr ... Houston TX 77060 281-673-2800 194
Web: www.abs-group.com

ABS Ventures 950 Winter St Ste 2600 ... Waltham MA 02451 781-250-0400 792
Web: www.absventures.com

Absaroka Ranch PO Box 929 ... Dubois WY 82513 307-455-2275 455-2275 239
TF: 800-545-0019 ■ *Web:* www.absarokaranch.com

Abscope Environmental Inc
7086 Commercial Dr ... Canastota NY 13032 315-697-8437 667
TF: 800-273-5318 ■ *Web:* www.abscope.com

Absecon Lighthouse
31 S Rhode Island Ave ... Atlantic City NJ 08401 609-449-1360 449-1919 50-3
Web: www.abseconlighthouse.org

Absher Construction Company Inc
1001 Shaw Rd ... Puyallup WA 98372 253-845-9544 841-0925 186
TF: 800-474-0711 ■ *Web:* absherco.com

Absinthe Brasserie & Bar
398 Hayes St ... San Francisco CA 94102 415-551-1590 671
Web: www.absinthe.com

ABSMC (Alta Bates Summit Medical Ctr)
2450 Ashby Ave ... Berkeley CA 94705 510-204-4444 374-3
TF: 800-994-6610 ■ *Web:* www.altabatessummit.org

Abso-Clean Industries Inc
199 Wales Ave ... Tonawanda NY 14150 716-693-2111 151

Absocold Corp PO Box 1545 ... Richmond IN 47375 765-935-7501 935-3450 610
TF: 800-843-3714 ■ *Web:* www.absocold.com

ABSOFT Corp
2111 Cass Lake Rd Ste 102 ... Keego Harbor MI 48309 248-220-1190 220-1194 177
Web: absoft.com

Absolut Aire Inc
5496 N Riverview Dr ... Kalamazoo MI 49004 269-382-1875 382-5291 14
TF: 800-804-4000 ■ *Web:* www.absolutaire.com

AbsolutData Technologies Inc
1851 Harbor Bay Pkwy Ste 125 ... Alameda CA 94502 510-748-9922 466
Web: www.absolutdata.com

Absolute Analysis Inc
2393 Teller Rd Ste 109 ... Newbury Park CA 91320 805-376-6048 407
Web: www.absoluteanalysis.com

Absolute Consulting Inc
7552 Navarre Pkwy Unit 63 ... Navarre FL 32566 850-939-8965 260
Web: www.absoluteconsulting.com

Absolute Electronics Inc
W137 N8589 Landover Ct ... Menomonee Falls WI 53051 262-250-1151 203
Web: www.absoluteelectronics.net

Absolute Energy LLC
1372 State Line Rd ... St. Ansgar IA 50472 641-326-2220 539
TF: 800-571-7171 ■ *Web:* www.absenergy.org

Absolute Exhibits Inc
1382 Valencia Ave Ste H ... Tustin CA 92780 714-685-2800 184
TF: 800-543-5484 ■ *Web:* www.absoluteexhibits.com

Absolute Investment Advisers LLC
18 Shipyard Dr Ste 3C ... Hingham MA 02043 781-740-1904 401
Web: www.absoluteadvisers.com

Absolute Machine Tools Inc
7420 Industrial Pkwy ... Lorain OH 44053 440-960-6911 358
TF: 800-852-7825 ■ *Web:* www.absolutemachine.com

Absolute Magic Computers/Internet
PO Box 672 ... San Juan Capistrano CA 92693 714-899-8154 196
Web: www.absolutemagic.com

Absolute Media Inc 1150 Summer St ... Stamford CT 06905 203-327-9090 7
TF: 800-877-8893 ■ *Web:* www.absolutemediainc.com

Absolute Mfg
20350 71St Ave NE Unit C ... Arlington WA 98223 360-435-1116 454
Web: www.absolutemanufacturing.com

Absolute Standards Inc 44 Rossotto Dr ... Hamden CT 06514 203-281-2917 743
TF: 800-368-1131 ■ *Web:* www.absolutestandards.com

Absolute Technologies Inc
4890 E La Palma Ave ... Anaheim CA 92807 714-692-6570 463
Web: www.absolutetechnologies.com

Absopure Water Co 8845 General Dr ... Plymouth MI 48170 800-422-7678 805
TF: 800-422-7678 ■ *Web:* www.absopure.com

ABT (American Ballet Theatre)
890 Broadway 3rd Fl ... New York NY 10003 212-477-3030 254-5938 573-1
Web: www.abt.org

Abt Assoc Inc 55 Wheeler St ... Cambridge MA 02138 617-492-7100 492-5219 466
Web: www.abtassociates.com

ABT Inc 259 Murdock Rd ... Troutman NC 28166 704-528-9806 492
TF: 800-438-6057 ■ *Web:* www.abtdrains.com

ABT Internet Inc 175 E Shore Rd ... Great Neck NY 11023 516-829-5484 829-2955 398
TF: 800-367-3414 ■ *Web:* www.abt.net

ABTA (American Brain Tumor Assn)
2720 River Rd ... Des Plaines IL 60018 847-827-9910 827-9918 48-17
TF: 800-886-2282 ■ *Web:* www.abta.org

Abtech
17300 SW Upper Boones Ferry Rd Ste 110 ... Portland OR 97224 503-924-1090 177
Web: www.abtech-pdx.com

Abtex Corp 89 Main St PO Box 188 ... Dresden NY 14441 315-536-7403 586
Web: www.abtex.com

Abuelo's Mexican Food Embassy
3501 W 45th Ave ... Amarillo TX 79109 806-354-8294 671
Web: www.abuelos.com

Abuelo's Mexican Food Embassy
1041 IH- 20 W ... Arlington TX 76017 817-468-2622 671
Web: www.abuelos.com

Abundant Life Christian Academy
1494 Banks Rd ... Margate FL 33063 954-979-2665 148
TF: 800-948-6291 ■ *Web:* www.alcapro.com

Abundant Life Tabernacle Upci
591 Broadway ... Kingston NY 12401 845-338-9883 48-20

Abundant Love Church Inc
2615 New Haven Ave ... Fort Wayne IN 46803 260-420-5683 48-20
Web: abundantlove.faithweb.com

ABWA (American Business Women's Assn)
11050 Roe Ave Ste 200 ... Overland Park KS 66211 800-228-0007 660-0101* 49-12
**Fax Area Code:* 913 ■ *TF:* 800-228-0007 ■ *Web:* www.abwa.org

ABX Air Inc 145 Hunter Dr ... Wilmington OH 45177 937-382-5591 12
TF: 800-736-3973 ■ *Web:* www.abxair.com

Abx Engineering 880 Hinckley Rd ... Burlingame CA 94010 650-552-2322 256
TF: 800-366-4588 ■ *Web:* www.abxengineering.com

ABYC (American Boat & Yacht Council Inc)
613 Third St Ste 10 ... Annapolis MD 21403 410-990-4460 990-4466 49-21
TF: 800-678-4333 ■ *Web:* www.abycinc.org

AC & T Company Inc
11535 Hopewell Rd ... Hagerstown MD 21740 301-582-2700 316
TF: 800-458-3835 ■ *Web:* www.acandt.com

AC Central Reservations Inc
201 Tilton Rd London Sq Mall Ste 17B ... Northfield NJ 08225 609-383-8880 383-8616 376
TF: 888-227-6667 ■ *Web:* www.acrooms.com

AC Corp 301 Creek Ridge Rd ... Greensboro NC 27406 336-273-4472 765-0416 189-10
TF: 800-422-7378 ■ *Web:* www.accorporation.com

AC Dellovade Inc 108 Cavasina Dr ... Canonsburg PA 15317 724-873-8190 873-8187 189-12
Web: www.acdellovade.com

AC Doctor LLC
2151 W Hillsboro Blvd Ste 400 ... Deerfield Beach FL 33442 866-264-1479 791
TF: 866-264-1479 ■ *Web:* www.acdoctor.com

AC Electric Co
2921 Hangar Way PO Box 81977 ... Bakersfield CA 93308 661-410-0000 410-0400 189-4
Web: www.a-celectric.com

AC Gilbert's Discovery Village
116 Marion St NE ... Salem OR 97301 503-371-3631 316-3485 521
Web: www.acgilbert.org

AC Group Inc 118 Lyndsey Dr ... Montgomery TX 77316 281-413-5572 194
Web: www.acgroup.org

AC Horn & Co 1269 Majesty Dr ... Dallas TX 75247 214-630-3311 697
TF: 800-657-6155 ■ *Web:* www.achornmfg.com

AC Lordi Corp
75 Valley Stream Pkwy Ste 201 ... Malvern PA 19355 610-738-0100 194
Web: www.aclordi.com

AC Miller Concrete Products Inc
31 E Bridge St ... Spring City PA 19475 610-948-4600 948-9750 183
Web: www.acmiller.com

AC Moore Arts & Crafts Inc
130 AC Moore Dr ... Berlin NJ 08009 888-226-6673 45
NASDAQ: ACMR ■ *TF:* 888-226-6673 ■ *Web:* www.acmoore.com

AC Nutrition 158 N Main St ... Winters TX 79567 325-754-4546 754-4546 447
TF: 800-588-3333 ■ *Web:* www.acnutrition.com

AC Products Co
4299 S Apple Creek Rd ... Apple Creek OH 44606 330-698-1105 362
Web: www.acproducts.com

AC Square Inc
1050 Shell Blvd Ste 8179 ... Foster City CA 94404 650-293-2730 194

ACA (Agriculture Council of America)
11020 King St Ste 205 ... Overland Park KS 66210 913-491-1895 491-6502 48-2
TF: 800-753-9073 ■ *Web:* www.agday.org

ACA (NCADD) 217 Broadway Ste 712 ... New York NY 10007 800-527-5344 48-17
TF: 800-622-2255 ■ *Web:* www.ncadd.org

ACA (Auto Club of America Corp)
9411 N Georgia St ... Oklahoma City OK 73120 405-751-4430 751-4462 53
TF: 800-411-2007 ■ *Web:* www.autoclubofamerica.com

Name / Address	City	State	ZIP	Phone	Fax	Class
ACA (American Camp Assn) 5000 State Rd 67 N *TF:* 800-428-2267 ■ *Web:* www.acacamps.org	Martinsville	IN	46151	765-342-8456	342-2065	48-23
ACA (American Canoe Assn) 503 Sophia St Ste 100 **Fax Area Code:* 888 ■ *TF:* 888-229-3792 ■ *Web:* www.americancanoe.org	Fredericksburg	VA	22401	540-907-4460	229-3792*	48-22
ACA (American Chiropractic Assn) 1701 Clarendon Blvd 2nd Fl *TF:* 800-986-4636 ■ *Web:* www.acatoday.org	Arlington	VA	22209	703-276-8800	243-2593	49-8
ACA (American Composers Alliance Inc) 802 W 190th St Ste 1B *Web:* www.composers.com	New York	NY	10040	212-925-0458		48-4
ACA (American Correctional Assn) 206 N Washington St Ste 200 *TF:* 800-222-5646 ■ *Web:* www.aca.org	Alexandria	VA	22314	703-224-0000		49-7
ACA (American Counseling Assn) 5999 Stevenson Ave *TF:* 800-347-6647 ■ *Web:* www.counseling.org	Alexandria	VA	22304	703-823-9800	823-0252	49-15
ACA (American AgCredit) PO Box 1120 *TF:* 800-800-4865 ■ *Web:* www.agloan.com	Santa Rosa	CA	95402	707-545-1200		216
ACA Associates Inc 545 Fifth Ave Ste 1009 *Web:* www.aca-assoc.com	New York	NY	10017	212-808-4424		463
ACA Galleries 529 W 20th St 5th Fl *TF:* 800-965-4827 ■ *Web:* www.acagalleries.com	New York	NY	10011	212-206-8080	206-8498	42
ACA International - Assn of Credit & Collection Professionals 4040 W 70th St PO Box 390106 *Web:* www.acainternational.org	Minneapolis	MN	55439	952-926-6547	926-1624	49-2
ACAA (American Coal Ash Assn) 15200 E Girard Ave Ste 3050 *Web:* www.acaa-usa.org	Aurora	CO	80014	720-870-7897	870-7889	48-12
ACAAI (American College of Allergy Asthma & Immunology) 85 W Algonquin Rd Ste 550 *Web:* www.acaai.org	Arlington Heights	IL	60005	847-427-1200	427-1294	49-8
Acacia 2637 Lawrenceville Rd *Web:* www.acacianj.com	Lawrenceville	NJ	08648	609-895-9885		671
Acacia Capital Corp 101 S Ellsworth Ave Ste 300 *Web:* www.acacia-capital.com	San Mateo	CA	94401	650-372-6400		217
Acacia Home & Garden Inc 101 McLin Creek Rd N PO Box 426 *TF:* 800-626-1114 ■ *Web:* www.acaciahomeandgarden.com	Conover	NC	28613	828-465-1700	465-4205	319-2
Acacia Mid-Town 2601 W Cary St *Web:* www.acaciarestaurant.com	Richmond	VA	23220	804-562-0138		671
Acacia Research Corp 520 Newport Center Dr 12th Fl *NASDAQ: ACTG* ■ *Web:* www.acaciaresearch.com	Newport Beach	CA	92660	949-480-8300	480-8301	405
Academe Magazine 1133 19th St NW Ste 200 *TF:* 800-424-2973 ■ *Web:* www.aaup.org	Washington	DC	20036	202-737-5900	737-5526	457-8
Academic Apparel 20644 Superior St *TF:* 800-626-5000 ■ *Web:* www.academicapparel.com	Chatsworth	CA	91311	818-886-0697	886-0743	155-14
Academic Approach LLC, The 342 W Armitage Ave *Web:* www.academicapproach.com	Chicago	IL	60614	773-348-8914		242
Academic Keys LLC 1066 Storrs Rd Ste D *Web:* www.academickeys.com	Storrs	CT	06268	860-429-0218		194
Academica Corp 6340 Sunset Dr *Web:* www.academica.org	Miami	FL	33143	305-669-2906		623
Academie Ste Cecile International School (ASCIS) 925 Cousineau Rd *Web:* academiestececile.ca	Windsor	ON	N9G1V8	519-969-1291	969-7953	622
Academy Bus LLC 111 Paterson Ave *TF:* 800-442-7272 ■ *Web:* www.academybus.com	Hoboken	NJ	07030	201-420-7000	420-8087	760
Academy Capital Management 500 N Vly Mills Dr Ste 200 *Web:* www.academycapitalmgmt.com	Waco	TX	76710	254-751-0555		528
Academy Fire Protection Inc 42 Broadway 2nd Fl *TF:* 800-773-4736 ■ *Web:* www.academyfire.com	Lynbrook	NY	11563	800-773-4736		393
Academy for Educational Development (AED) 1825 Connecticut Ave NW Ste 800 *Web:* www.fhi360.org	Washington	DC	20009	202-884-8000	884-8400	48-11
Academy for Guided Imagery Inc 30765 Coast Hwy *Web:* www.acadgi.com	Malibu	CA	90265	424-242-6369		766
Academy Hotel Colorado Springs, The 8110 N Academy Blvd *TF:* 800-766-8524 ■ *Web:* www.theacademyhotel.com	Colorado Springs	CO	80920	719-598-5770	598-5965	379
Academy Leadership LLC 10120 Vly Forge Cir *Web:* www.academyleadership.com	King Of Prussia	PA	19406	610-783-0630		194
Academy of Art University 79 New Montgomery St *TF:* 800-544-2787 ■ *Web:* www.academyart.edu	San Francisco	CA	94105	415-274-2200	618-6287	166
Academy of Court Reporting Columbus 150 E Gay St *TF:* 866-865-8067 ■ *Web:* www.miamijacobs.edu	Columbus	OH	43215	614-221-7770		800
Academy of General Dentistry (AGD) 211 E Chicago Ave Ste 900 *TF:* 888-243-3368 ■ *Web:* www.agd.org	Chicago	IL	60611	312-440-4300	440-0559	49-8
Academy of Managed Care Pharmacy (AMCP) 100 N Pitt St Ste 400 *TF:* 800-827-2627 ■ *Web:* www.amcp.org	Alexandria	VA	22314	703-683-8416	683-8417	49-8
Academy of Management (AOM) 235 Elm Rd PO Box 3020 *TF:* 800-633-4931 ■ *Web:* aom.org	Briarcliff Manor	NY	10510	914-923-2607	923-2615	49-12
Academy of Model Aeronautics (AMA) 5161 E Memorial Dr *TF:* 800-435-9262 ■ *Web:* www.modelaircraft.org	Muncie	IN	47302	765-287-1256	289-4248	48-18
Academy of Motion Picture Arts & Sciences 8949 Wilshire Blvd *TF:* 800-697-8799 ■ *Web:* www.oscars.org	Beverly Hills	CA	90211	310-247-3000	859-9619	48-4
Academy of Motion Picture Arts & Sciences Herrick Library 333 S La Cienega Blvd *Web:* www.oscars.org	Beverly Hills	CA	90211	310-247-3020		434-4
Academy of Music 1500 Walnut St *Web:* www.kimmelcenter.org	Philadelphia	PA	19102	215-790-5800		572
Academy of Nail Skin & Hair Inc 928 Broadwater Ave Ste C *Web:* academyofnailandskin.com	Billings	MT	59101	406-252-3232		166
Academy of Natural Sciences Museum 1900 Benjamin Franklin Pkwy *TF:* 800-652-4143 ■ *Web:* www.ansp.org	Philadelphia	PA	19103	215-299-1000	299-1028	520
Academy of Natural Sciences of Drexel University 1900 Benjamin Franklin Pkwy *TF:* 800-652-4143 ■ *Web:* www.ansp.org	Philadelphia	PA	19103	215-299-1000	299-1079	668
Academy of Notre Dame De Namur 560 Sproul Rd *Web:* www.ndapa.org	Villanova	PA	19085	610-687-0650		685
Academy of Osseointegration 85 W Algonquin Rd Ste 550 *TF:* 800-656-7736 ■ *Web:* www.osseo.org	Arlington Heights	IL	60005	847-439-1919	439-1569	49-8
Academy of Political Science 475 Riverside Dr Ste 1274 *Web:* www.psqonline.org	New York	NY	10115	212-870-2500	870-2202	48-11
Academy of Students of Pharmacy American Pharmacists Assn 1100 15th St NW Ste 400 *TF:* 800-237-2742 ■ *Web:* www.pharmacist.com	Washington	DC	20005	202-628-4410	783-2351	49-8
Academy of Television Arts & Sciences 5220 Lankershim Blvd *Web:* emmys.com	North Hollywood	CA	91601	818-754-2800		49-14
Academy of Vocal Arts (AVA) 1920 Spruce St *TF:* 800-356-7372 ■ *Web:* www.avaopera.org	Philadelphia	PA	19103	215-735-1685	732-2189	573-2
Academy Packing Company Inc 2881 Wyoming St *Web:* academypackingcompany.com	Dearborn	MI	48120	313-841-4900		473
Academy Solutions Group LLC 6700 Alexander Bell Dr Ste 195 *TF:* 800-574-0896 ■ *Web:* www.asg-llc.com	Columbia	MD	21046	410-290-0871		261
Academy Sports & Outdoors 1800 N Mason Rd *TF:* 888-922-2336 ■ *Web:* www.academy.com	Katy	TX	77449	281-646-5200		711
AcademyHealth 1801 K St NW Ste 701 *Web:* www.academyhealth.org	Washington	DC	20006	202-292-6700	292-6800	49-8
AcademyOne Inc 601 Willowbrook Ln *Web:* www.academyone.com	West Chester	PA	19382	610-436-5680		177
Acadia 1303 NE Fremont St *Web:* www.acadiapdx.com	Portland	OR	97212	503-249-5001		671
Acadia 3000 Kavanaugh Blvd Ste 202 *Web:* www.acadiahillcrest.com	Little Rock	AR	72205	501-603-9630		671
Acadia Divinity College 38 Highland Ave *TF:* 866-875-8975 ■ *Web:* www.acadiadiv.ca	Wolfville	NS	B4P2R6	902-585-2210		167-3
Acadia Enviromental Technology 48 Free St *Web:* www.acadiaenvironmental.com	Portland	ME	04101	207-780-1230		194
Acadia Inn 98 Eden St *TF:* 800-638-3636 ■ *Web:* www.acadiainn.com	Bar Harbor	ME	04609	207-288-3500		379
Acadia National Park 20 McFarland Hill Dr *Web:* www.nps.gov	Bar Harbor	ME	04609	207-288-3338	288-8813	564
Acadia National Park Tours 53 Main St *Web:* www.nationalparktours.com	Bar Harbor	ME	04609	207-288-0300		760
Acadia Parish Library 1125 N Parkerson Ave *Web:* www.acadia.lib.la.us	Crowley	LA	70526	337-788-1880	788-3759	434-3
ACADIA Pharmaceuticals Inc 3911 Sorrento Valley Blvd *NASDAQ: ACAD* ■ *TF:* 800-901-5231 ■ *Web:* www.acadia-pharm.com	San Diego	CA	92121	858-558-2871	558-2872	85
Acadia Polymers Inc 5251 Concourse Dr	Roanoke	VA	24019	540-265-2700		60
Acadia Realty Trust 1311 Mamaroneck Ave Ste 260 *NYSE: AKR* ■ *Web:* www.acadiarealty.com	White Plains	NY	10605	914-288-8100		655
Acadia University 15 University Ave *TF:* 877-585-1121 ■ *Web:* www2.acadiau.ca	Wolfville	NS	B4P2R6	902-542-2201		785
Acadian Ambulance Service Inc PO Box 98000 **Fax Area Code:* 337 ■ *TF:* 800-259-3333 ■ *Web:* www.acadian.com	Lafayette	LA	70509	800-259-3333	291-2211*	30
Acadian Asset Management Inc 260 Franklin St *TF:* 800-946-0166 ■ *Web:* www.acadian-asset.com	Boston	MA	02110	617-850-3500		401
Acadian Contractors Inc 17102 W La Hwy 330 *TF:* 800-800-1101 ■ *Web:* www.acadiancontractors.com	Abbeville	LA	70510	337-893-6397		538
Acadiana Center for the Arts 101 W Vermilion St *Web:* www.acadianacenterforthearts.org	Lafayette	LA	70501	337-233-7060	233-7062	50-2
Acadiana Computer Systems Inc 324 Dulles Dr *TF:* 800-925-5947 ■ *Web:* www.acsmd.com	Lafayette	LA	70506	337-981-2494		180
Acadiana Legal Service Corp 1020 Surrey St *Web:* www.la-law.org	Lafayette	LA	70501	337-237-4320		428
Acadiana Symphony Orchestra 412 Travis St *TF:* 800-826-4919 ■ *Web:* www.acadianasymphony.org	Lafayette	LA	70503	337-232-4277	237-4712	573-3
Acai Solutions LLC 1285 Ave Of Americas 35th Fl *Web:* www.acaisolutions.com	New York	NY	10019	212-554-4460		194
Acalanes Union High School Dist 1212 Pleasant Hill Rd *Web:* www.acalanes.k12.ca.us	Lafayette	CA	94549	925-280-3900	932-2336	685
ACAOM (Accreditation Commission for Acupuncture & Oriental Medicine) 8941 Aztec Dr *Web:* www.acaom.org	Eden Prairie	MN	55347	952-212-2434	657-7068	48-1
ACA-PAC (American Chiropractic Assn PAC) 1701 Clarendon Blvd *TF:* 800-986-4636 ■ *Web:* www.acatoday.org	Arlington	VA	22209	703-276-8800	243-2593	615
ACAWSO (Adult Children of Alcoholics World Service Organization Inc) PO Box 3216 *TF:* 800-422-4453 ■ *Web:* www.adultchildren.org	Torrance	CA	90510	562-595-7831		48-21

	Phone	Fax	Class
ACB (American Council of the Blind) 1155 15th St NW Ste 1004 Washington DC 20005 *TF:* 800-424-8666 ■ *Web:* www.acb.org	202-467-5081	467-5085	48-17
ACB (American Council of the Blind) 2200 Wilson Blvd Ste 650 Arlington VA 22201 **Fax Area Code:* 703 ■ *TF:* 800-424-8666 ■ *Web:* www.acb.org	202-467-5081	465-5085*	48-11
ACB (America's Community Bankers) 1120 Connecticut Ave NW Washington DC 20036 *TF:* 800-226-5377 ■ *Web:* www.aba.com	800-226-5377		49-2
ACB American Inc 4351 Winston Ave. Covington KY 41015	859-261-8745		160
ACB Insurance Inc 7715 Loma Ct Ste E Fishers IN 46038 *Web:* acb-insurance.com	317-915-8601		390
ACB Solutions 551 W Dimond Blvd. Anchorage AK 99515 *TF:* 866-261-4225 ■ *Web:* www.acbsolutions.net	907-267-4200		180
Acbel Polytech Inc 251 Dominion Dr Ste 103 Morrisville NC 27560 *Web:* www.acbel.com	919-388-4316		396
ACBL (American Contract Bridge League) 6575 Windchase Blvd. Horn Lake MS 38637 *TF Sales:* 800-264-2743 ■ *Web:* www.acbl.org	662-253-3100	253-3187	48-18
ACBSP (Association of Collegiate Business Schools & Programs) 11520 W 119th St. Overland Park KS 66213 *Web:* www.acbsp.org	913-339-9356	339-6226	48-1
ACC (Alice Chamber of Commerce) 612 E Main St PO Box 1609 Alice TX 78333 *Web:* www.alicetxchamber.org	361-664-3454	664-2291	139
ACC (Alpena Community College) 665 Johnson St Alpena MI 49707 *TF:* 888-468-6222 ■ *Web:* discover.alpenacc.edu	989-356-9021		162
ACC (American College of Cardiology) 2400 N St NW. Washington DC 20037 *TF Cust Svc:* 800-253-4636 ■ *Web:* www.acc.org	202-375-6000	375-7000	49-8
ACC (Association of Corporate Counsel) 1025 Connecticut Ave NW Ste 200. Washington DC 20036 *TF:* 877-647-3411 ■ *Web:* www.acc.com	202-293-4103	293-4701	49-10
ACC (Austin Community College) 5930 Middle Fiskville Rd Austin TX 78752 **Fax:* Admissions ■ *TF:* 877-442-3522 ■ *Web:* www.austincc.edu	512-223-7000	223-7665*	162
ACC Environmental Consultants Inc 7977 Capwell Dr Ste 100 Oakland CA 94621 *Web:* www.accenv.com	510-638-8400		194
ACC Recycling Corp 1190 20th St N. Saint Petersburg FL 33713	727-892-9216		660
Acc Technical Services Inc 106 Dwight Park Cir. Syracuse NY 13209 *TF:* 855-484-4500 ■ *Web:* www.acctek.com	315-484-4500		463
ACCA (Air Conditioning Contractors of America) 2800 S Shirlington Rd Ste 300. Arlington VA 22206 *TF:* 800-786-4452 ■ *Web:* www.acca.org	703-575-4477	575-8107	49-3
ACCC (Association of Community Cancer Centers) 11600 Nebel St Ste 201 Rockville MD 20852 *Web:* www.accc-cancer.org	301-984-9496	770-1949	49-8
ACCCE (American Coalition for Clean Coal Electricity) 1152 15th St NW Ste 400. Washington DC 20005 *Web:* americaspower.org	202-459-4800		48-12
ACC&CE (Association of Consulting Chemists & Chemical Engineers) 514 Corrigan Way. Cary NJ 27519 *Web:* www.chemconsult.org	908-500-9333		49-19
ACCCI (American Coke & Coal Chemicals Institute) 25 Massachusetts AveNW Ste 800 Washington DC 20001 *Web:* www.accci.org	202-452-7198	463-6573	48-12
ACCE (American Chamber of Commerce Executives) 4875 Eisenhower Ave Ste 250 Alexandria VA 22304 *TF:* 800-394-2223 ■ *Web:* www.acce.org	703-998-0072	212-9512	49-12
ACCE (American Council for Construction Education) 1717 N Loop 1604 E Ste 320 San Antonio TX 78232 *Web:* www.acce-hq.org	210-495-6161	495-6168	48-1
Accede Mold & Tool Company Inc 1125 Lexington Ave Rochester NY 14606 *TF:* 888-236-2427 ■ *Web:* www.accedemold.com	585-254-6490		697
Accel Aviation Accessories LLC 11900 Lacy Ln Fort Myers FL 33966 *TF:* 888-686-4880 ■ *Web:* www.accelaviation.com	239-275-8202	275-7311	359
Accel Partners 428 University Ave Palo Alto CA 94301 *Web:* www.accel.com	650-614-4800		792
Accel Plastics 4146 B Pl NW Auburn WA 98001 *Web:* www.accelplastics.com	253-854-0034		596
Accelerant Sales Group LLC 39 E Hanover Ave Ste C3 Morris Plains NJ 07950 *Web:* www.accelerantsales.com	973-331-0600		195
Accelerated Genetics E 10890 Penny Ln Baraboo WI 53913 *TF:* 800-451-9275 ■ *Web:* www.accelgen.com	608-356-8357	356-4387	11-2
Accelerated Technology Laboratories Inc 496 Holly Grove School Rd West End NC 27376 *Web:* www.atlab.com	910-673-8165		177
Accelero Health Partners LLC 117 VIP Dr Ste 320. Wexford PA 15090 *Web:* www.acceleroheolth.com	724-799-8210		194
Acceleron Pharma Inc 128 Sidney St Cambridge MA 02139 *Web:* www.acceleronpharma.com	617-649-9200		231
Acceleros 11900 Metric Blvd Ste J-163. Austin TX 78758 *Web:* www.acceleros.com	512-736-8385		41
Acceles Inc 13771 N Fountain Hills Blvd Ste 114-115 Fountain Hills AZ 85268 *TF:* 877-260-6725 ■ *Web:* www.acceles.com	877-260-6725	260-6725	196
Acceleware Ltd 435 10 Ave SE. Calgary AB T2G0W3 *TF:* 800-829-4444 ■ *Web:* www.acceleware.com	403-249-9099		177
Accelian LLC 1222 Earnestine St. Mc Lean VA 22101 *TF:* 888-543-0051 ■ *Web:* www.accelianllc.com	703-543-1616		809
Accelon Capital 2470 El Camino Real Ste 210 Palo Alto CA 94306 *Web:* www.acceloncapital.com	650-213-8353		691
Accelrys Inc 10188 Telesis Ct Ste 100 San Diego CA 92121 *NASDAQ:* ACCL ■ *TF:* 888-249-2284 ■ *Web:* www.accelrys.com	858-799-5000	799-5100	178-5
Accent 7171 Mercy Rd Ste 200 Omaha NE 68106 *TF:* 800-397-7243 ■ *Web:* www.onlineaccent.com	402-397-9920		393

	Phone	Fax	Class
Accent Computer Solutions Inc 8438 Red Oak St. Rancho Cucamonga CA 91730 *TF:* 800-481-4369 ■ *Web:* www.accentonit.com	909-204-4801		463
Accent Controls Inc 400 NW Platte Valley Dr Riverside MO 64150 *Web:* www.accentcontrols.com	816-483-6330		256
Accent Health 60 E 42nd St Ste 1543 New York NY 10165 *TF:* 800-235-4930 ■ *Web:* www.accenthealth.com	800-235-4930		740
Accent Imaging Inc 8121 Brownleigh Dr. Raleigh NC 27617 *Web:* www.accentimaging.com	919-782-3332		344
Accent Information Systems Inc 585 Sunbury Rd Delaware OH 43015 *TF:* 800-589-7379 ■ *Web:* www.accentservices.com	740-548-7378		196
Accent Inns Ltd 3233 Maple St. Victoria BC V8X4Y9 *TF:* 800-663-0298 ■ *Web:* www.accentinns.com	250-475-7500		707
Accent Inns Vancouver Airport 10551 St Edwards Dr Richmond BC V6X3L8 *TF:* 800-663-0298 ■ *Web:* www.accentinns.com	604-273-3311	273-9522	379
Accent Inns Vancouver-Burnaby 3777 Henning Dr Burnaby BC V5C6N5 *TF:* 800-663-0298 ■ *Web:* www.accentinns.com/burnaby/hotel-amenities	604-473-5000	473-5095	379
Accent Marble & Granite Inc 21609 N 12th Ave Ste 800 Phoenix AZ 85027 *Web:* accentmarblegranite.com	623-582-1501		191-1
Accent Office Interiors Inc 2108 Gilliam Ln # 3 Tallahassee FL 32308 *Web:* www.accentoffice.com	850-386-5201		393
Accent on Arrangements Inc 615 Baronne St Ste 303 New Orleans LA 70113 *TF:* 800-672-6124 ■ *Web:* www.accent-dmc.com	504-524-1227		149
Accent on Cincinnati 915 W Eigth St Cincinnati OH 45203 *Web:* www.accentcinti.com	513-721-8687		184
Accent Packaging Inc 10131 FM 2920 Rd Tomball TX 77375 *Web:* www.accentwire.com	281-251-3700		492
Accent Plastics Inc 1925 Elise Cir Corona CA 92879 *Web:* www.accentplastics.com	951-273-7777		608
Accent Plumbing Inc 21101 Fm 685. Pflugerville TX 78660	512-251-2819		189-10
Accentia BioPharmaceuticals Inc 324 S Hyde Pk Ave Ste 350 Tampa FL 33606 *OTC:* ABPI	813-864-2554	258-6912	582
Accenture Inc 5450 Explorer Dr Ste 400 Mississauga ON L4W5M1 *Web:* www.accenture.com	416-641-5000		194
Acceptance Insurance Cos Inc 300 W Broadway Ste 1600 Council Bluffs IA 51503 *Web:* www.aicins.com	712-329-3600		391-4
Access 1188 E Arques Ave Sunnyvale CA 94085 *Web:* www.access-company.com	408-400-3000	400-1500	178-12
Access America 673 Emory Valley Rd Oak Ridge TN 37830 *TF:* 800-860-2140 ■ *Web:* www.accessam.com	865-482-2140	482-2306	736
Access America 2805 N Parham Rd. Richmond VA 23294 *TF:* 800-284-8300 ■ *Web:* www.allianztravelinsurance.com	800-284-8300		391-7
Access Bio Inc 65 Clyde Rd Ste A Somerset NJ 08873 *Web:* www.accessbio.net	732-873-4040		415
Access Business Group 7575 Fulton St E Ada MI 49355 *TF Cust Svc:* 800-879-2732 ■ *Web:* www.accessbusinessgroup.com	800-879-2732		449
Access Cable Television Inc 302 Enterprise Dr Somerset KY 42501 *Web:* www.accesshsd.net	606-677-2444		116
Access College Foundation 7300 Newport Ave Ste 500 Norfolk VA 23505 *Web:* www.accesscollege.org	757-962-6113		242
Access Communications Co-operative Ltd 2250 Park St. Regina SK S4N7K7 *TF:* 866-211-6334 ■ *Web:* www.myaccess.ca	306-569-2225		116
Access Computers Inc 538 W Main St Lebanon OH 45036 *Web:* www.accesscomputersus.com	513-932-5454		175
Access Credit Management Inc 11225 Huron Ln Ste 222 Little Rock AR 72211 *Web:* arcollectors.com	501-664-2922		160
Access Direct Systems Inc 91 Executive Blvd Farmingdale NY 11735 *Web:* accessdirect.com	631-420-0770	420-1647	5
Access Energy Co-op 1800 W Washington St. Mount Pleasant IA 52641 *TF:* 866-242-4232 ■ *Web:* www.accessenergycoop.com	319-385-1577	385-6873	245
Access Financial Resources Inc 3621 NW 63rd Ste A1 Oklahoma City OK 73116 *Web:* afradvice.com	405-848-9826		690
Access Highway Inc 96 Carleton Ave Central Islip NY 11722	631-232-9119		194
Access Industries Inc 730 Fifth Ave New York NY 10019 *Web:* www.accessindustries.com	212-247-6400		360-3
Access Innovations Inc 4725 Indian School Rd NE Ste 100. Albuquerque NM 87110 *TF:* 800-926-8328 ■ *Web:* www.accessinn.com	505-265-3591	256-1080	177
Access Intelligence LLC 4 Choke Cherry Rd 2nd Fl Rockville MD 20850 *TF:* 800-777-5006 ■ *Web:* www.accessintel.com	301-354-2000		637-9
Access International Group Inc 248 Columbia Tpk Florham Park NJ 07932 *Web:* www.accessig.com	973-360-0750		178-10
Access Magazine 444 N Michigan Ave Ste 3400 Chicago IL 60611 *TF:* 800-243-2342 ■ *Web:* adha.org/publications	312-440-8900	467-1806	457-16
Access Management Group 1100 Northmeadow Pkwy Ste 114 Roswell GA 30076 *Web:* www.accessmgt.com	770-777-6890		391-4
Access National Corp 1800 Robert Fulton Dr Ste 310. Reston VA 20191 *NASDAQ:* ANCX ■ *TF:* 800-931-0370 ■ *Web:* www.accessnationalbank.com	703-871-2100	766-3386	360-2
Access Optics LLC 2201 N Maple Ave Broken Arrow OK 74012 *Web:* www.accessoptics.com	918-294-1234		544
Access Point Inc 1100 Crescent Green Cary NC 27518 *TF:* 877-419-4274 ■ *Web:* www.accesspointinc.com	919-851-4838		736

Name / Address	City	State	ZIP	Phone	Fax	Class
Access Property Management						
4 Walter E Foran Blvd Ste 311	Flemington	NJ	08822	908-806-2600		652
Web: www.accesspm.com						
Access Securities Inc						
30 Buxton Farm Rd	Stamford	CT	06905	203-322-3377		690
Web: www.accesssecurities.com						
Access Softek Inc						
727 Allston Way Ste C	Berkeley	CA	94710	510-848-0606		177
Web: www.accessoftek.com						
Access Specialties International LLC						
15230 Carrousel Way	Rosemount	MN	55068	651-453-1283		174
TF: 800-332-1013 ■ *Web:* www.access-specialties.com						
Access To Media 432 Front St	Chicopee	MA	01013	866-612-0034		7
TF: 866-612-0034 ■ *Web:* www.accesstomedia.com						
Access US 712 N Second St Ste 300	Saint Louis	MO	63102	314-655-7700	655-7701	398
TF: 800-638-6373 ■ *Web:* accessus.net						
Access Worldwide Inc						
5192 Southridge Pkwy Ste 112	Atlanta	GA	30349	404-675-0633		5
TF: 877-564-8581 ■ *Web:* www.accessworldwide.net						
AccessAlpha Worldwide LLC						
630 Davis St Ste 201	Evanston	IL	60201	847-475-6000		428
Web: www.accessalpha.com						
AccessESP LLC						
3656 Westchase Dr Ste 421	Houston	TX	77042	713-589-2599		539
Web: www.accessesp.com						
AccessIT Group Inc						
2000 Valley Forge Cir Ste 106	King Of Prussia	PA	19406	610-783-5200		180
Web: www.accessitgroup.com						
Accesso LLC						
1025 Greenwood Blvd Ste 500	Lake Mary	FL	32746	407-333-7311		387
Web: www.accesso.com						
Accesso Partners LLC						
1140 E Hallandale Beach Blvd	Hallandale Beach	FL	33009	954-454-4665		205
TF: 800-421-3403 ■ *Web:* www.accessopartners.com						
Accessorie Air Compressor Systems Inc						
1858 N Case St	Orange	CA	92865	714-634-2292		172
Web: accessorieair.com						
Accessory Export LLC 4105 Indus Way	Riverside	CA	92503	951-687-1140		736
Web: www.empirecase.com						
AccessPoint LLC						
28800 Orchard Lake Rd	Farmington Hills	MI	48334	866-513-3861		734
TF: 866-513-3861 ■ *Web:* www.accesspointhr.com						
ACCET (Accrediting Council for Continuing Education & Training)						
1722 N St NW	Washington	DC	20036	202-955-1113	955-1118	48-1
TF: 800-515-6218 ■ *Web:* www.accet.org						
ACCF (American Council for Capital Formation)						
1001 Connecticut Ave NW Ste 620	Washington	DC	20036	202-293-5811	785-8165	49-2
Web: www.accf.org						
Accident Fund Co						
232 S Capitol Ave PO Box 40790	Lansing	MI	48901	517-342-4200		391-4
TF Mktg: 888-276-0327 ■ *Web:* www.accidentfund.com						
Accion Labs US Inc						
1121 Boyce Rd Ste 1400	Pittsburgh	PA	15241	412-979-8111		631
Web: accionlabs.com						
Accipiter Radar Technologies Inc						
576 Hwy 20 W	Fonthill	ON	L0S1C0	905-228-6888		256
Web: www.accipiterradar.com						
Acclaim Print & Copy Centers Inc						
6345 Scarlett Ct	Dublin	CA	94568	925-829-7750		113
Web: www.acclaimprint.com						
Acclaim Systems Inc						
110 E Pennsylvania Blvd	Feasterville	PA	19053	215-354-1420		177
Web: www.acclaimsystems.com						
Acclinet Corp 490 S Stark Hwy	Weare	NH	03281	603-529-4220		396
Web: www.acclinet.com						
Acclivus Corp 14520 Midway Rd	Dallas	TX	75244	972-628-2500	386-6720	194
Web: www.acclivus.com						
ACCO Engineered Systems						
6265 San Fernando Rd	Glendale	CA	91201	818-244-6571		189-10
TF Cust Svc: 800-998-2226 ■ *Web:* www.accoair.com						
Acco Material Handling Solutions						
76 Acco Dr	York	PA	17402	800-967-7333	715-8897	190
TF: 800-967-7333 ■ *Web:* www.accolifting.com						
Accokeek Foundation 3400 Bryan Pt Rd	Accokeek	MD	20607	301-283-2113		520
TF: 800-217-4273 ■ *Web:* www.accokeekfoundation.org						
Accomack County						
23296 Courthouse Ave Ste 203	Accomac	VA	23301	757-787-5700	787-2468	338
TF: 800-552-5019 ■ *Web:* www.co.accomack.va.us						
Accomack County Public Schools						
PO Box 330	Accomac	VA	23301	757-787-5754	787-2951	449
Web: www.accomack.k12.va.us						
Accommodations Plus Inc						
1200 Rt 109	Lindenhurst	NY	11757	516-798-4444		376
TF: 800-345-8082 ■ *Web:* www.apihotels.com						
Accompass 1052 Yonge St	Toronto	ON	M4W2L1	416-969-8588		463
TF: 866-969-8588 ■ *Web:* www.accompass.com						
Accord Carton 6155 W 115th St	Alsip	IL	60803	800-648-6780		45
TF: 800-648-6780 ■ *Web:* accordcarton.com						
Accord Creditor Services LLC						
PO Box 10005	Newnan	GA	30271	800-373-0760		393
TF: 800-373-0760 ■ *Web:* www.accordcreditorservices.com						
Accord Financial Corp						
Ste 1803 77 Bloor St W	Toronto	ON	M5S1M2	416-961-0007		403
Web: www.accordfinancial.com						
Accord Hum Res Inc						
210 Pk Ave Ste 1200	Oklahoma City	OK	73102	405-232-9888		631
Accord Industries 4001 Forsyth Rd	Winter Park	FL	32792	407-671-6989	679-2297	183
TF General: 800-876-6989 ■ *Web:* www.universal100.com						
Accordant Company LLC						
365 S St Ste 100	Morristown	NJ	07960	973-887-8900		179
TF: 800-363-1002 ■ *Web:* www.accordantco.com						
Account Control Systems Inc						
148 Veterans Dr Ste 4	Northvale	NJ	07647	800-482-8026		160
TF: 800-482-8026 ■ *Web:* accountcontrolsystems.com						
Accountants in Transition Inc						
10509 Vista Sorrento Pkwy Ste 300	San Diego	CA	92121	858-404-9900		2
Web: calltsg.com						
Accounting Career Consultants						
1001 Craig Rd Ste 391	Saint Louis	MO	63146	314-569-9898		2
Web: www.careeradvancers.com						
Accounting Principals						
10151 Deerwood Park Blvd Ste 400	Jacksonville	FL	32256	800-981-3849		721
TF: 800-981-3849 ■ *Web:* www.accountingprincipals.com						
Accounting Software Inc						
9125 39th Ave SW Ste 150	Lakewood	WA	98499	253-952-6040		179
Web: www.acctsoft.com						
Accounts Management Center Inc						
1976 E Grand Ave	Hot Springs	AR	71901	501-623-5594		160
Accounts Payable Chexs Inc						
1829 Ranchlands Blvd NW	Calgary	AB	T3G2A7	403-247-8913		2
TF: 888-437-0624 ■ *Web:* www.apchexs.com						
Accoutrements 10915 47th Ave W	Mukilteo	WA	98275	425-349-3838	349-5188	328
TF: 800-886-2221 ■ *Web:* www.accoutrements.com						
ACCP (American College of Clinical Pharmacy)						
13000 W 87th St Pkwy	Lenexa	KS	66215	913-492-3311	492-0088	49-8
Web: www.accp.com						
ACCP (American College of Chest Physicians)						
3300 Dundee Rd	Northbrook	IL	60062	847-498-1400	498-5460	49-8
TF: 800-343-2227 ■ *Web:* www.chestnet.org						
Accra Manufacturing Inc						
17703 15th Ave SE	Bothell	WA	98012	425-424-1000		454
Web: www.accramfg.com						
Accram Inc 2901 W Clarendon Ave	Phoenix	AZ	85017	800-786-0288		175
TF: 800-786-0288 ■ *Web:* www.accram.com						
Accratronics Seals Corp						
2211 Kenmere Ave	Burbank	CA	91504	818-843-1500	841-2117	326
TF: 800-800-1828 ■ *Web:* www.accratronics.com						
Accreditation Assn for Ambulatory Health Care (AAAHC)						
5250 Old OrchaRd Rd Ste 200	Skokie	IL	60077	847-853-6060	853-9028	48-1
Web: www.aaahc.org						
Accreditation Commission for Acupuncture & Oriental Medicine (ACAOM)						
8941 Aztec Dr	Eden Prairie	MN	55347	952-212-2434	657-7068	48-1
Web: www.acaom.org						
Accreditation Council for Graduate Medical Education (ACGME)						
515 N State St Ste 2000	Chicago	IL	60610	312-755-5000	755-7498	48-1
Web: www.acgme.org						
Accreditation Council for Pharmacy Education						
20 N Clark St Ste 2500	Chicago	IL	60603	312-664-3575	228-2631*	48-1
**Fax Area Code:* 866 ■ *Web:* www.acpe-accredit.org						
Accreditation Review Commission on Education for the Physician Assistant Inc (ARC-PA)						
12000 Findley Rd Ste 240	Duluth	GA	30097	770-476-1224	476-1738	48-1
Web: www.arc-pa.org						
Accredited Surety & Casualty Company Inc						
4798 New Broad St Ste 200	Orlando	FL	32814	407-629-2131		390
Web: www.accredited-inc.com						
Accrediting Bureau of Health Education Schools (ABHES)						
7777 Leesburg Pike Ste 314 N	Falls Church	VA	22043	703-917-9503	917-4109	48-1
TF: 800-228-9290 ■ *Web:* www.abhes.org						
Accrediting Commission of Career Schools & Colleges of Technology (ACCSCT)						
2101 Wilson Blvd Ste 302	Arlington	VA	22201	703-247-4212	247-4533	48-1
TF: 800-842-0229 ■ *Web:* www.accsc.org						
Accrediting Council for Continuing Education & Training (ACCET)						
1722 N St NW	Washington	DC	20036	202-955-1113	955-1118	48-1
TF: 800-515-6218 ■ *Web:* www.accet.org						
Accrediting Council for Independent Colleges & Schools (ACICS)						
750 First St NE Ste 980	Washington	DC	20002	202-336-6780	842-2593	48-1
TF: 800-258-3826 ■ *Web:* www.acics.org						
Accrediting Council on Education in Journalism & Mass Communications (ACEJMC)						
University of Kansas, The						
1435 Jayhawk Blvd	Lawrence	KS	66045	785-864-2700	864-5006	48-1
Web: www2.ku.edu						
Accredo Health Group Inc						
1640 Century Ctr Pkwy	Memphis	TN	38134	901-385-3600		587
TF: 877-222-7336 ■ *Web:* www.accredo.com						
Accrete Construction LLC						
801 Valley Ave NW	Puyallup	WA	98371	253-922-3399		186
Web: www.bpci.net						
Accretive Solutions Inc						
1 S Wacker Dr Ste 950	Chicago	IL	60606	312-994-4600	994-4638	266
Web: www.accretivesolutions.com						
Accretive Technologies Inc						
330 Research Ct Ste 250	Norcross	GA	30092	678-328-2440	246-9186*	225
**Fax Area Code:* 770 ■ *Web:* www.accretive.com						
Accro Tool Inc						
401 Hunt Valley Dr	New Kensington	PA	15068	724-339-3560		567
Web: www.accrotool.net						
ACCS Enterprises Inc						
539 Sawgrass Corporate Pkwy	Sunrise	FL	33325	954-472-3300		608
Web: www.headsuponline.com						
Accs Inc 260 Oakhurst St	Altamonte Springs	FL	32701	407-767-5557		180
Web: www.accs.net						
ACCSCT (Accrediting Commission of Career Schools & Colleges of Technology)						
2101 Wilson Blvd Ste 302	Arlington	VA	22201	703-247-4212	247-4533	48-1
TF: 800-842-0229 ■ *Web:* www.accsc.org						
Accsense Inc 460 Ward Dr Ste E-2	Santa Barbara	CA	93111	805-681-3500		693
Web: accsense.com						
ACCT (Association of Community College Trustees)						
1101 17th St NW Ste 300	Washington	DC	20036	202-775-4667	223-1297	49-5
TF: 866-895-2228 ■ *Web:* www.acct.org						
Accton Technology Corp						
1200 Crossman Ave Ste 130	Sunnyvale	CA	94089	408-747-0994	747-0982	176
Web: www.accton.com						
Accu Fire Fabrication Inc						
8 Progress Dr	Morrisville	PA	19067	215-428-2400		595
Web: www.accu-fire.com/index.php						
Accu Personnel Inc						
911 Kings Hwy N	Cherry Hill	NJ	08034	856-482-2222		260
Web: www.accustaffing.com						
Accu Reference Medical Lab						
1901 E Linden Ave Unit 4	Linden	NJ	07036	908-474-1004		415
TF: 800-756-7236 ■ *Web:* www.accureference.com						
Accu Therm Inc PO Box 249	Monroe City	MO	63456	573-735-1060	735-1066	386
TF: 888-925-4332 ■ *Web:* www.accutherm.com						
ACCU Translations 3 Mays Crescent	Waterdown	ON	L0R2H4	905-639-0323		317
Web: www.accutranslation.com						

				Phone	Fax	Class
ACCU-BREAK Pharmaceuticals Inc 1000 S Pine Island Rd Ste 430 *Web:* www.accubreakpharmaceuticals.com	Plantation	FL	33324	954-236-7351		231
Accubuilt Inc 2550 Central Pt Pkwy *Web:* www.accubuilt.com	Lima	OH	45804	419-222-1501		516
AccuCode Inc 6886 S Yosemite St Ste 100 *TF:* 866-705-9879 ■ *Web:* www.accucode.com	Centennial	CO	80112	303-639-6111		177
Accucom Consulting Inc 250 Post Rd E *Web:* www.accucomci.com	Westport	CT	06880	203-221-1212	221-1946	194
ACCUCOM Technical Services Inc 660 N Glenville *Web:* www.accucom.com	Richardson	TX	75081	972-238-7502		179
AccuConference 6300 Ridglea Pl Ste 318 *TF:* 800-977-4607 ■ *Web:* www.accuconference.com	Ft Worth	TX	76116	800-977-4607		317
AccuData Holdings Inc 5220 Summerlin Commons Blvd Ste 200 *Web:* www.accudata.com	Fort Myers	FL	33907	239-425-4400		387
Accuduct Manufacturing Inc 316 Ellingson Rd *Web:* www.accuduct.com	Algona	WA	98001	253-939-7741		697
Accudyn Products Inc 2400 Yoder Dr *Web:* www.accudyn.com	Erie	PA	16506	814-833-7615		608
Accudynamics LLC 240 Kenneth Welch Dr *Web:* www.accudynamics.com	Lakeville	MA	02347	508-946-4545		454
Accu-Fab Inc 801 Beacon Lake Dr *Web:* www.accufabnc.com	Raleigh	NC	27610	919-212-6400		697
Accufax PO Box 35563 **Fax Area Code:* 866 ■ *TF:* 800-256-8898 ■ *Web:* www.accufax-us.com	Tulsa	OK	74153	800-256-8898	936-3027*	635
Accugenix Inc 223 Lake Dr *TF:* 877-274-8371 ■ *Web:* criver.com/products-services	Newark	DE	19702	302-292-8888		418
Accuimage LLC 2807 Biloxi Ave *Web:* www.accuimagellc.com	Nashville	TN	37204	615-242-7226		317
Accu-Label Inc 2021 Research Dr *TF:* 888-482-5223 ■ *Web:* www.acculabel.com	Fort Wayne	IN	46808	260-482-5223		627
Acculease Construction Equipment Inc 63 Clifton St *Web:* www.acculease.com	Farmingdale	NY	11735	631-577-0101		690
Acculink 1055 Greenville Blvd SW *TF:* 800-948-4110 ■ *Web:* www.acculink.com	Greenville	NC	27834	252-321-5805		627
Acculynk Inc 3225 Cumberland Blvd SE Ste 550 *Web:* www.acculynk.com	Atlanta	GA	30339	678-894-7010		387
Accuma Corp 133 Fanjoy Rd *Web:* www.accuma.com/accumaUsa/index.asp?arg=1&lang=eng	Statesville	NC	28625	704-873-1488		596
Accume Partners LLC 341 New Albany Rd *Web:* www.accumepartners.com	Moorestown	NJ	08057	856-914-9500		734
Accumedic Computer Systems Inc 11 Grace Ave Ste 401 *TF:* 800-765-9300 ■ *Web:* www.accumedic.com	Great Neck	NY	11021	516-466-6800		177
Accumedscript LLP 1601 Bethel Rd Ste 210 *Web:* www.accumedscript.com	Columbus	OH	43220	614-804-5656		177
Accumulators Inc 1175 Brittmoore Rd *Web:* www.accumulators.com	Houston	TX	77043	713-465-0202		537
Accumyn LLC 1415 Congress St Ste 200 *Web:* www.accumyn.com	Houston	TX	77002	713-800-2550		194
Accupac Inc 1501 Industrial Blvd *Web:* www.accupac.com	Mainland	PA	19451	215-256-7000		583
AccuPay Payroll Inc 50 S Penn St Ste A5 *Web:* www.accupay.net	Hatboro	PA	19040	267-803-1213		2
Accuplace 1800 NW 69th Ave Ste 102 *Web:* www.accuplace.com	Plantation	FL	33313	954-791-1500		547
Accuplan Benefits Services 515 East 4500 South Ste G200 **Fax Area Code:* 877 ■ *TF:* 800-454-2649 ■ *Web:* www.accuplan.net	Salt Lake City	UT	84107	801-266-9900	890-0929*	49-2
Accuprint Inc 2414 Palumbo Dr *Web:* www.accuprint.us	Lexington	KY	40509	859-268-8844		627
Accupro Trademark Services LLP 401 W Georgia St Ste 702 *Web:* accuprotm.com	Vancouver	BC	V6B5A1	604-661-9292		196
Accura Engineering 3342 International Park Dr SE *TF:* 800-295-9595 ■ *Web:* www.accuraengineering.com	Atlanta	GA	30316	404-241-8722		225
Accura Technics LLC 310 Marlboro St *Web:* www.accuratechnics.com	Keene	NH	03431	603-355-2727		454
Accuracy in Media Inc (AIM) 4350 EW Hwy Ste 555 *TF:* 800-787-4567 ■ *Web:* www.aim.org	Bethesda	MD	20814	202-364-4401	364-4098	49-14
Accurate Air Engineering Inc 16207 Carmennita Rd *TF:* 800-438-5577 ■ *Web:* www.accurateair.com	Cerritos	CA	90703	562-484-6370	484-6371	385
Accurate Alloys Inc 5455 Irwindale Ave *TF:* 800-842-2222 ■ *Web:* www.accuratealloys.com	Irwindale	CA	91706	626-338-4012	337-8393	492
Accurate Biometrics Inc 4849 N Milwaukee Ave Ste 101 *TF:* 866-361-9944 ■ *Web:* www.accuratebiometrics.com	Chicago	IL	60630	773-685-5699		400
Accurate Boring Co 17420 Malyn Blvd *Web:* www.accurateboring.com	Fraser	MI	48026	586-294-7555	294-2530	455
Accurate Box Company Inc 86 Fifth Ave *TF:* 800-220-7981 ■ *Web:* www.accuratebox.com	Paterson	NJ	07524	973-345-2000		100
Accurate Bushing Company Inc 443 N Ave *TF Sales:* 800-932-0076 ■ *Web:* www.smithbearing.com	Garwood	NJ	07027	908-789-1121	789-9429	75
Accurate Chemical & Scientific Corp 300 Shames Dr *TF:* 800-645-6264 ■ *Web:* www.accuratechemical.com	Westbury	NY	11590	516-333-2221	997-4948	231
Accurate Color & Compounding Inc 1666 Dearborn Ave *Web:* www.accurate-color.com	Aurora	IL	60505	630-978-1227		596
Accurate Computer Technology Inc 17821 Sky Park Cir Ste J *Web:* www.accuratecomputer.com	Irvine	CA	92614	949-261-6677		177
Accurate Controls 326 Blackburn St *Web:* www.accuratecontrols.com	Ripon	WI	54971	920-748-6603		693
Accurate Diagnostic Labs Inc 3000 Hadley Rd *TF:* 800-899-4237 ■ *Web:* www.adlabs.net	South Plainfield	NJ	07080	732-839-3300		415
Accurate Dial & Nameplate Inc 329 Mira Loma Ave **Fax Area Code:* 818 ■ *TF:* 800-400-4455 ■ *Web:* www.accuratedial.com	Glendale	CA	91204	323-245-9181	243-6793*	413
Accurate Dispersions Inc 192 W 155th St *Web:* www.accurate-dispersions.com	South Holland	IL	60478	708-333-1337		550
Accurate Elastomer Products Inc 1112 Swenson Blvd *Web:* www.accurateelastomer.com	Elgin	TX	78621	512-285-4585		596
Accurate Energetics Systems LLC 5891 Hwy 230 W *Web:* www.aesys.biz	McEwen	TN	37101	931-729-4207		268
Accurate Flannel Bag Co 468 Totowa Ave	Paterson	NJ	07522	929-356-6791		349
Accurate Heating & Cooling 3001 River Rd *Web:* accuratehvac.com	Chillicothe	OH	45601	740-775-5005		610
Accurate Insurance Inc 416 First St *Web:* accurateinsinc.com	Glenwood	IA	51534	712-527-9106		390
Accurate Machine LLC 5124 Trademark Dr *Web:* www.accuratemachine.cc	Raleigh	NC	27610	919-212-0266		454
Accurate Mailing Services Inc 401 Madison St Ste 1	Reidsville	NC	27320	336-361-3151		5
Accurate Mailings Inc 215 O'Neill Ave *TF:* 800-732-3290 ■ *Web:* www.accuratemailings.com	Belmont	CA	94002	650-508-8885		5
Accurate Metal Fabricating 1657 N Kostner Ave *Web:* www.accuratemetalfab.com	Chicago	IL	60639	773-235-0400		295
Accurate Partitions Corp 8000 Joliet Rd PO Box 287 *TF:* 800-933-4525 ■ *Web:* www.accuratepartitions.com	McCook	IL	60525	708-442-6800	442-7439	609
Accurate Perforating Co 3636 S Kedzie Ave *TF:* 800-621-0273 ■ *Web:* www.accurateperforating.com	Chicago	IL	60632	773-254-3232	254-9453	488
Accurate Plumbing 7595 Fishel Dr S *Web:* www.accurateplumbinginc.com	Dublin	OH	43016	614-526-0131		610
Accurate Printing Inc 2380 Research Ct Ste 100 *TF:* 800-463-3339 ■ *Web:* www.accurateprinting.com	Woodbridge	VA	22192	703-494-0707		113
Accurate Staffing Consultants Inc 804 First Ave S *TF:* 800-264-1170 ■ *Web:* www.accuratestaffing.com	Conover	NC	28613	828-466-1018		260
Accurate Surgical & Scientific Instruments Corp 300 Shames Dr *TF:* 800-645-3569 ■ *Web:* www.accuratesurgical.com	Westbury	NY	11590	516-333-2570	997-4948	476
Accurate Technologies Inc 47199 Cartier Dr *Web:* www.accuratetechnologies.com	Wixom	MI	48393	248-848-9200		153
Accuray Inc 1310 Chesapeake Terr *NASDAQ: ARAY* ■ *TF:* 888-522-3740 ■ *Web:* www.accuray.com	Sunnyvale	CA	94089	408-716-4600	716-4601	476
Accu-Read Inc PO Box 18277 *Web:* accureadinc.com	Spokane	WA	99228	509-670-5894		463
Accurecord Inc 200 Broadhollow Rd Ste 308 *Web:* www.accurecord.com	Melville	NY	11747	631-243-6400		2
Accuride Corp 7140 Office Cir *NYSE: ACW* ■ *TF Cust Svc:* 800-823-8332 ■ *Web:* www.accuridecorp.com	Evansville	IN	47715	812-962-5000		60
Accuride International Inc 12311 Shoemaker Ave *Web:* www.accuride.com	Santa Fe Springs	CA	90670	562-903-0200	903-0208	487
Accuristix 2844 Bristol Cir *TF:* 866-356-6830 ■ *Web:* www.accuristix.com	Oakville	ON	L6H6G4	905-829-9927		360-2
Accuscreen Systems 1038 Main St *Web:* www.accuscreensystems.com	Baton Rouge	LA	70802	225-343-8378		196
Accu-Sort Systems Inc 511 School House Rd *TF:* 800-227-2633 ■ *Web:* www.datalogic.com	Telford	PA	18969	215-723-0981	721-5551	173-7
Accusource Inc 1240 E Ontario Ave Ste 102-140 *TF:* 888-649-6272 ■ *Web:* www.accusource-online.com	Corona	CA	92881	951-734-8882		743
AccuSpec Electronics LLC 8140 Hawthorne Dr *Web:* accuspecelectronic.com	Erie	PA	16509	814-464-2000		253
AccuSport Inc 4310 Enterprise Dr Ste C *Web:* www.accusport.com	Winston-Salem	NC	27106	336-759-3300		639
Accu-Tec Inc 1735 W Burnett St *TF:* 800-463-3339 ■ *Web:* www.accu-tec.com	Louisville	KY	40210	502-339-7511		88
Accutech Films Inc 620 Hardin St *Web:* www.accutechfilms.com	Coldwater	OH	45828	419-678-8700		600
AccuTech LLC 2641 La Mirada Dr *TF:* 800-749-9910 ■ *Web:* www.accutech-llc.com	Vista	CA	92081	760-599-6555		476
Accutemp Engineering Inc 108 School St *Web:* www.accutemp-eng.com	Watertown	MA	02472	617-926-1221		256
Accutemp Products Inc 8415 N Clinton Pk *Web:* accutemp.net	Fort Wayne	IN	46825	260-493-0415		406
Accutest Laboratories 2235 Rt 130 Bldg B *Web:* www.accutest.com	Dayton	NJ	08810	732-329-0200	329-3499	743
Accu-time Systems Inc 420 Somers Rd *TF:* 800-355-4648 ■ *Web:* www.accu-time.com	Ellington	CT	06029	860-870-5000	872-1511	56
Accutrack Medical Billing 15703 Freeman Ave	Lawndale	CA	90260	310-679-2141		2
Accutrans Inc 2740 Indiana Ave *Web:* accutransinc.com	Kenner	LA	70062	504-469-0500		610
Accutrend Data Corp 7860 E Berry Pl *Web:* www.newbusinessreporter.com	Greenwood Village	CO	80111	303-488-0011		5
AccuTrex Products Inc 112 Southpointe Blvd *Web:* www.accutrex.com	Canonsburg	PA	15317	724-746-4300		599

Name / Address	City	State	Zip	Phone	Fax	Class
Accutron Inc 1733 Parkside Ln *TF:* 800-531-2221 ■ *Web:* www.accutron-inc.com	Phoenix	AZ	85027	623-780-2020		228
Accuturn Corp 6510 Box Springs Blvd Ste A *TF:* 800-557-1449 ■ *Web:* www.accuturninc.com	Riverside	CA	92507	951-656-6621		454
Accuvia Consulting Inc 19636 Club House Rd Ste 120 *Web:* www.accuvia.com	Gaithersburg	MD	20886	301-944-1220		396
Accuvoice Inc 343 Wainwright Dr	Northbrook	IL	60062	847-559-7272		194
AccuWeather Inc 385 Science Pk Rd *TF Sales:* 800-566-6606 ■ *Web:* www.accuweather.com	State College	PA	16803	814-235-8650	238-1339	530
Accuzip 3216 El Camino Real *TF:* 800-233-0555 ■ *Web:* www.accuzip.com	Atascadero	CA	93422	805-461-7300		177
ACD (American College of Dentists) 839J Quince Orchard Blvd Ste J *Web:* www.acd.org	Gaithersburg	MD	20878	301-977-3223	977-3330	49-8
ACD Systems International Inc 129-1335 Bear Mtn Pkwy *Web:* www.acdsee.com	Victoria	BC	V9B6T9	250-419-6700	419-6742	178-8
ACDA (American Choral Directors Assn) 545 Couch Dr *Web:* www.acda.org	Oklahoma City	OK	73102	405-232-8161	232-8162	48-4
ACDI/VOCA 50 F St NW Ste 1075 *TF:* 800-929-8622 ■ *Web:* www.acdivoca.org	Washington	DC	20001	202-638-4661		48-5
ACDS (Association for Children with Down Syndrome Inc) 4 Fern Pl *TF:* 800-342-9871 ■ *Web:* www.acds.org	Plainview	NY	11803	516-933-4700	933-9524	48-17
ACE (American Council on Exercise) 4851 Paramount Dr *TF:* 800-825-3636 ■ *Web:* www.acefitness.org	San Diego	CA	92123	858-576-6500	576-6564	48-17
ACE (Altamont Commuter Express) 949 E Ch St *TF:* 800-411-7245 ■ *Web:* www.acerail.com	Stockton	CA	95202	800-411-7245		468
ACE (American Council on Education) 1 Dupont Cir NW Ste 800 *Web:* www.acenet.edu	Washington	DC	20036	202-939-9300	833-4760	49-5
Ace Asphalt & Paving Co 115 S Averill Ave *TF:* 800-592-5329 ■ *Web:* aceasphaltpaving.com	Flint	MI	48506	810-238-1737	238-4326	188-4
ACE Bakery Ltd 1 Hafis Rd *Web:* www.acebakery.com	Toronto	ON	M6M2V6	416-241-3600		297-8
Ace Bolt & Screw Co 200 Brooklyn Ave	San Antonio	TX	78215	210-226-0244		351
ACE Cash Express 1231 Greenway Dr Ste 600 *TF:* 800-817-5106 ■ *Web:* www.acecashexpress.com	Irving	TX	75038	972-550-5000		141
Ace Charter High School 1929 N Stone Ave *Web:* www.acehs.org	Tucson	AZ	85705	520-628-8316		138
Ace Clearwater Enterprises 19015 Magellan Dr *Web:* www.aceclearwater.com	Torrance	CA	90502	310 538 5380	323-2137	22
Ace Doran Hauling & Rigging Company Inc 1601 Blue Rock St *TF:* 800 829-0929 ■ *Web:* www.acedoran.com	Cincinnati	OH	45223	513-681-7900		780
ACE Duraflo Pipe Restoration Inc 3122 W Alpine Ave *Web:* www.restoremypipes.com	Santa Ana	CA	92704	714-564-7600		610
Ace Endico Corp 00 International Blvd *Web:* www.aceendico.com	Brewster	NY	10509	845-940-1501	940-1516	68
Ace Forms of Kansas Inc 2900 N Rotary Terr **Fax Area Code:* 620 ■ *TF:* 800-223-9287 ■ *Web:* www.aceforms.com	Pittsburg	KS	66762	800-223-9287	232-1111*	110
Ace Glass Inc 1430 NW Blvd PO Box 688 **Fax Area Code:* 800 ■ *TF:* 800-223-4524 ■ *Web:* www.aceglass.com	Vineland	NJ	08360	856-692-3333	543-6752*	333
Ace Golf Inc 820 S Kings Ave *TF:* 800-388-8255 ■ *Web:* www.ace-golf.com	Brandon	FL	33511	813-651-4653		354
Ace Group Inc, The 149 W 27th St	New York	NY	10001	212-255-7846		626
Ace Hardware Corp 2200 Kensington Ct *TF:* 800-832-5660 ■ *Web:* www.acehardware.com	Oak Brook	IL	60523	630-990-6600		364
Ace Hotel & Swim Club 701 E Palm Canyon Dr *TF:* 800-747-3279 ■ *Web:* www.acehotel.com	Palm Springs	CA	92264	504-900-1180		377
Ace ImageWear 4120 Truman Rd *TF:* 800-366-0564 ■ *Web:* www.aceimagewear.com	Kansas City	MO	64127	816-231-5737	231-3550	442
Ace Industries Inc 6295 McDonough Dr *Web:* www.aceindustries.com	Norcross	GA	30093	770-441-0898		358
Ace Irrigation & Manufacturing Co 4740 E 39th St *Web:* www.acenebraska.com	Kearney	NE	68847	308-237-5173		697
Ace Mailing Corp 2757 16th St *Web:* www.acemailingsf.com	San Francisco	CA	94103	415-863-4223		225
Ace Mart - Downtown San Antonio 1220 S St Mary's *TF:* 888-898-8079 ■ *Web:* acemart.com	San Antonio	TX	78210	210-224-0082	224-1629	114
Ace Medical Inc 94-910 Moloalo St *TF:* 866-678-3601 ■ *Web:* www.acemedicalinc.com	Waipahu	HI	96797	808-678-3600		475
Ace Parking Management Inc 645 Ash St *TF General:* 855-223-7275 ■ *Web:* www.aceparking.com	San Diego	CA	92101	619-233-6624	233-0741	562
Ace Payroll Services Inc 1860 Walt Whitman Rd Ste 600 *Web:* www.acepayroll.com	Melville	NY	11747	516-420-9500		2
Ace Personnel (AP) 5909 Woodson Rd *Web:* www.acepersonnel.com	Mission	KS	66202	913-384-1100		721
Ace Precision Machining Corp 977 Blue Ribbon Cir N *Web:* www.aceprecision.com	Oconomowoc	WI	53066	262-252-4003		454
Ace Products Management G 12801 W Silver Spring Rd *TF:* 800-294-9007 ■ *Web:* www.brandedproducts.com	Butler	WI	53007	262-754-1289		463
Ace Pump and Supply 6013 Johnson St *Web:* acepumpandsupply.com	Hollywood	FL	33024	954-981-7424		641
Ace Pump Corp PO Box 13187 *Web:* www.acepumps.com	Memphis	TN	38113	901-948-8514	774-6147	641
Ace Ranking 211 Sutter St Ste 400 *Web:* www.acerankings.com	San Francisco	CA	94108	415-536-3929		195
ACE Recovery Inc 450 Blackbrook Rd *Web:* www.acerecovery.com	Painesville	OH	44077	440-856-7000		160
Ace Relocation Systems Inc 5608 Eastgate Dr *TF:* 800-453-0964 ■ *Web:* www.acerelocation.com	San Diego	CA	92121	858-677-5500	677-5587	780
ACE Rent A Car 4529 W 96th St *TF:* 866-551-8267 ■ *Web:* www.acerentacar.com	Indianapolis	IN	46241	317-248-5686		126
Ace Reprographic Service Inc 74 E 30th St *Web:* www.acereprographics.com	Paterson	NJ	07514	973-684-5945		627
Ace Sign Systems Inc 3621 W Royerton Rd *TF:* 800-607-6010 ■ *Web:* www.acesign.com	Muncie	IN	47304	765-288-1000		701
Ace Speedway 3401 Altamahaw Race Track Rd *Web:* www.acespeedway.com	Altamahaw	NC	27244	336-585-1200	585-1209	515
Ace Technologies Inc 2375 Zanker Rd Ste 250 *Web:* www.acetechnologies.com	San Jose	CA	95131	408-521-1139		177
Ace Tool Co 7337 Bryan Dairy Rd *TF:* 800-777-5910 ■ *Web:* www.acetoolco.com	Largo	FL	33777	727-544-4331	544-6211	61
Ace Transfer Co 1017 Hometown St *Web:* www.acetransco.com	Springfield	OH	45504	937-398-1103		687
Ace Tube Bending 14 Journey *TF:* 800-252-7087 ■ *Web:* www.acetubebending.com	Aliso Viejo	CA	92656	949-362-2220		595
Ace Weekly 185 Jefferson *Web:* www.aceweekly.com	Lexington	KY	40508	859-225-4889		532-5
Ace Wire & Cable Co Inc 7201 51st Ave *TF:* 800-225-2354 ■ *Web:* www.acewireco.com	Woodside	NY	11377	718-458-9200	335-6340	813
Ace World Wide Moving 1900 E College Ave *TF:* 800-558-3980 ■ *Web:* www.aceworldwide.com	Cudahy	WI	53110	414-764-1000	764-1650	519
Ace-Atlas Corp 5214 Flushing Ave *Web:* www.ace-atlas.com	Maspeth	NY	11378	718-497-3003		610
ACEC (Allamakee-Clayton Electric Co-op) 229 Hwy 51 PO Box 715 *TF:* 888-788-1551 ■ *Web:* www.acrec.com	Postville	IA	52162	563-864-7611	864-7820	245
ACEC (American Council of Engineering Cos) 1015 15th St NW 8th Fl *TF:* 800-338-1391 ■ *Web:* www.acec.org	Washington	DC	20005	202-347-7474	898-0068	49-19
Aceco 4419 Federal Way *TF:* 800-359-7012 ■ *Web:* www.aceco.com	Boise	ID	83716	208-343-7712		350
ACEEE (American Council for an Energy-Efficient Economy) 529 14th St NW Ste 600 *Web:* www.aceee.org	Washington	DC	20045	202-507-4000	429-2248	48-7
ACEI (Association for Childhood Education International) 1101 16th St NW Ste 300 **Fax Area Code:* 301 ■ *TF:* 800-423-3563 ■ *Web:* www.acei.org	Washington	DC	20036	202-372-9986	570-2212*	49-5
ACEJMC (Accrediting Council on Education in Journalism & Mass Communications) *University of Kansas, The* 1435 Jayhawk Blvd *Web:* www2.ku.edu	Lawrence	KS	66045	785-864-2700	864-5006	48-1
Acentech Inc 33 Moulton St *Web:* www.acentech.com	Cambridge	MA	02138	617-499-8000		463
Acento Advertising Inc 2001 Whilshire Blvd Ste 600 *Web:* www.acento.com	Santa Monica	CA	90403	310-943-8300		4
ACEP (American College of Emergency Physicians) 1125 Executive Cir PO Box 619911 *TF:* 800-798-1822 ■ *Web:* www.acep.org	Dallas	TX	75261	972-550-0911	580-2816	49-8
Acer America Corp 333 W San Carlos St Ste 1500 **Fax: Sales* ■ *TF:* 866-695-2237 ■ *Web:* www.accr.com	San Jose	CA	95110	408-533-7700	533-4574*	173-2
Acer Group 2320 E Valencia Dr *TF:* 800-248-9602 ■ *Web:* acergroup.com	Fullerton	CA	92831	714-632-9701		358
ACerS (American Ceramic Society) 600 N Cleveland Ave # 210 *TF:* 866-721-3322 ■ *Web:* www.ceramics.org	Westerville	OH	43082	614-890-4700	899-6109	48-4
ACES (American College of Eye Surgeons/American Board of Eye Surgery) 334 E Lake Rd Ste 135 *TF:* 800-223-2233 ■ *Web:* www.aces-abes.org	Palm Harbor	FL	34685	727-366-1487	836-9783	49-8
ACES 4140 W 99th St *Web:* www.acespower.com	Carmel	IN	46032	317-344-7000		463
ACES Systems 10737 Lexington Dr *Web:* www.acessystems.com	Knoxville	TN	37932	865-671-2003		256
Ace-Tex Enterprises 7601 Central St *TF:* 800-444-3800 ■ *Web:* www.ace-tex.com	Detroit	MI	48210	313-834-4000	834-0260	442
ACF (Association of Consulting Foresters of America) 312 Montgomery St Ste 208 *TF:* 888-540-8733 ■ *Web:* www.acf-foresters.org	Alexandria	VA	22314	703-548-0990	548-6395	48-2
ACF (American Culinary Federation Inc) 180 Ctr Pl Way *TF:* 800-624-9458 ■ *Web:* www.acfchefs.org	Saint Augustine	FL	32095	904-824-4468	825-4758	49-6
ACF (Administration for Children & Families) 370 L'Enfant Promenade SW *Web:* www.acf.hhs.gov	Washington	DC	20447	202-401-9215	401-5450	340-10
ACF Components & Fasteners Inc 31012 Huntwood Ave *TF Cust Svc:* 800-227-2901 ■ *Web:* www.acfcom.com	Hayward	CA	94544	510-487-2100	471-7018	246
ACFA (Alameda County Fair Assn) 4501 Pleasanton Ave *TF:* 800-874-9253 ■ *Web:* www.alamedacountyfair.com	Pleasanton	CA	94566	925-426-7600	426-7599	642
ACFAS (American College of Foot & Ankle Surgeons) 8725 W Higgins Rd Ste 555 *TF:* 800-421-2237 ■ *Web:* www.acfas.org	Chicago	IL	60631	773-693-9300	693-9304	49-8
ACFC (American Coalition for Fathers & Children) 1718 M St NW Ste 1187 *TF:* 800-978-3237 ■ *Web:* www.acfc.org	Washington	DC	20036	800-978-3237		48-6
ACFC (Atlantic Coast Bank) 505 Haines Ave *NASDAQ: ACFC* ■ *TF:* 800-342-2824 ■ *Web:* www.atlanticcoastbank.net	Waycross	GA	31501	912-283-4711		360-2
ACFE (Association of Certified Fraud Examiners) 716 W Ave *TF:* 800-245-3321 ■ *Web:* www.acfe.com	Austin	TX	78701	512-478-9000	478-9297	49-1

	Phone	Fax	Class
ACFEI (American College of Forensic Examiners International) 2750 E Sunshine St .... Springfield MO 65804 *TF:* 800-423-9737 ■ *Web:* www.acfei.com	417-881-3818	881-4702	49-8
ACG (American College of Gastroenterology) 6400 Goldsboro Rd Ste 450 .... Bethesda MD 20817 *Web:* gi.org	301-263-9000	263-9025	49-8
ACG (American Cotton Growers Textile Div) PO Box 2827 .... Lubbock TX 79408 *TF:* 800-333-8011 ■ *Web:* pcca.com/services/denim	806-763-8011	762-7400	745-1
ACG (Association for Corporate Growth) 125 S Wacker Dr Ste 3100 .... Chicago IL 60606 *TF:* 877-358-2220 ■ *Web:* www.acg.org	312-957-4260		49-12
ACG Advisory Services Inc 1640 Huguenot Rd .... Midlothian VA 23113 *TF:* 800-231-6409 ■ *Web:* www.acgworldwide.com	804-323-1886		528
Acg Inc 7007 Corporate Way .... Dayton OH 45459 *TF:* 800-890-5023 ■ *Web:* www.acgcbs.com	937-433-8122		180
ACG Research 1780 E Tradewind Ct .... Gilbert AZ 85234 *Web:* acgcc.com	408-200-0967		466
ACG Systems Inc 133 Defense Hwy Ste 206 .... Annapolis MD 21401 *Web:* www.acgsys.com	410-224-0224		647
Acg Tech Systems Inc 6 Rock Island .... Ardmore OK 73401 *Web:* www.acgsystem.com	580-222-4467		396
ACGIH (American Conference of Governmental Industrial Hygienists) 1330 Kemper Meadows Dr .... Cincinnati OH 45240 *Web:* www.acgih.org	513-742-2020	742-3355	49-7
ACGME (Accreditation Council for Graduate Medical Education) 515 N State St Ste 2000 .... Chicago IL 60610 *Web:* www.acgme.org	312-755-5000	755-7498	48-1
ACH (Alliance Community Hospital) 200 E State St .... Alliance OH 44601 *Web:* www.achosp.org	330-596-6000		374-3
ACH Foam Technologies LLC 5250 Sherman St .... Denver CO 80216 *TF:* 800-525-8697 ■ *Web:* www.achfoam.com	303-297-3844		601
ACH Food Cos Inc 7171 Goodlet Farms Pkwy .... Cordova TN 38016 *TF:* 800-691-1106 ■ *Web:* www.achfood.com	901-381-3000	381-2968	296-30
ACH Payment Solutions Inc 6919 Treymore Ct .... Sarasota FL 34243 *Web:* www.achpaymentsolutions.com	941-360-8859		225
ACHA (American College Health Assn) 1362 Mellon Rd Ste 180 .... Hanover MD 21076 *Web:* www.acha.org	410-859-1500	859-1510	49-8
Achaogen Inc 7000 Shoreline Ct Ste 371 .... South San Francisco CA 94080 *Web:* www.achaogen.com	650-266-1120		743
ACHE (Association for Continuing Higher Education) 1700 Asp Ave .... Norman OK 73072 *TF:* 800-807-2243 ■ *Web:* www.acheinc.org	800-807-2243		49-5
ACHE (American Migraine Foundation) 19 Mantua Rd .... Mount Royal NJ 08061 *Web:* americanmigrainefoundation.org	856-423-0043	423-0082	48-17
ACHE (American College of Healthcare Executives) 1 N Franklin St Ste 1700 .... Chicago IL 60606 *Web:* www.ache.org	312-424-2800	424-0023	49-8
A-Check America Inc 1501 Research Park Dr .... Riverside CA 92507 *TF:* 877-345-2021 ■ *Web:* www.acheckglobal.com	951-750-1501		260
Achieva Inc 197 Funder Dr PO Box 729 .... Mocksville NC 27028 *TF:* 800-788-7213 ■ *Web:* www.achievaweb.com	336-751-7104		319-3
Achieve IT Solutions Inc 640 Belle Terre Rd Bldg B .... Port Jefferson NY 11777 *TF:* 800-225-3813 ■ *Web:* www.achieveits.com	631-543-3200		177
Achieve LLC 233 McCrea St Ste 200 .... Indianapolis IN 46225 *Web:* www.achieveagency.com	317-637-3000		195
AchieveGlobal Inc 8875 Hidden River Pkwy Ste 400 .... Tampa FL 33637 *TF:* 800-566-0630 ■ *Web:* www.achieve.com.tr/en/training.asp	813-631-5517	631-5796	765
Achievement Incentives & Meetings 64 River Rd .... East Hanover NJ 07936 *TF:* 800-454-1424 ■ *Web:* www.aimtrav.com	973-386-9500		194
Achilles USA Inc 1407 80th St SW .... Everett WA 98203 *Web:* www.achillesusa.com	425-353-7000		600
Achillion Pharmaceuticals Inc 300 George St Rm 202 .... New Haven CT 06511 *Web:* www.achillion.com	203-624-7000		583
achoo! ALLERGY & AIR Products Inc 3411 Pierce Dr Ste 100 .... Atlanta GA 30341 *Web:* www.achooallergy.com	770-455-9999		690
ACI (Arkansas Correctional Industries) 6841 W 13th St .... Pine Bluff AR 71602 *TF:* 877-635-7213 ■ *Web:* www.acicatalog.com	870-730-0385	850-8440	630
ACI (Axis Communications Inc) 100 Apollo Dr .... Chelmsford MA 01824 *TF:* 800-444-2947 ■ *Web:* www.axis.com	978-614-2000	614-2100	176
ACI (Atlantic Corporate Interiors Inc) 7001 Muirkirk Meadows Dr Ste A .... Beltsville MD 20705 *Web:* www.aciinc.com	301-931-3600	931-3601	321
ACI (American Concrete Institute International) 38800 Country Club Dr PO Box 9094 ..... Farmington Hills MI 48331 *Web:* www.concrete.org	248-848-3700	848-3701	49-3
ACI (ACI) 500 W 57th St .... New York NY 10019 **Fax Area Code:* 646 ■ *TF:* 800-724-4444 ■ *Web:* www.acirehab.org	212-293-3000	565-3404*	726
ACI (American Consumer Industries Inc) 1105 N Market St Ste 1150 .... Wilmington DE 19801 *Web:* www.aciinc.net	303-495-2665		787
ACI (New Mexico Assn of Commerce & Industry) 2201 Buena Vista Dr SE Ste 410 Ste 410 ...... Albuquerque NM 87106 *Web:* www.nmaci.org	505-842-0644	842-0734	140
ACI Communications 5115 Douglas Fir Rd Ste A .... Calabasas CA 91302 *Web:* www.acicommunications.com	818-223-3600	223-3609	225
ACI Consulting Corp 155 N Riverview Dr .... Anaheim Hills CA 92808 *Web:* www.aciconsulting.com	714-282-0378		180
ACI Controls Inc 295 Main St .... West Seneca NY 14224 *Web:* www.aci-controls.com	716-675-9450		358
Aci Event Group 652 Hayes St .... San Francisco CA 94102 *Web:* www.acieventgroup.com	415-553-7880		195
ACI Merchant Services Inc 136 E Watson Ave Ste 204 .... Langhorne PA 19047 *Web:* acimerchant.com	215-741-6970		225
ACI Worldwide Inc 6060 Coventry Dr .... Elkhorn NE 68022 *NASDAQ: ACIW* ■ *Web:* aciworldwide.com	402-390-7600		178-10
ACI Worldwide Inc 3520 Kraft Rd Ste 300 .... Naples FL 34105 *TF:* 877-276-5554 ■ *Web:* www.aciworldwide.com	972-599-5600		178-1
Acic Fine Chemicals Inc 81 St Claire Blvd .... Brantford ON N3S7X6 *TF:* 800-265-6727 ■ *Web:* www.acic.com	519-751-3668	751-1378	479
ACICS (Accrediting Council for Independent Colleges & Schools) 750 First St NE Ste 980 .... Washington DC 20002 *TF:* 800-258-3826 ■ *Web:* www.acics.org	202-336-6780	842-2593	48-1
Acid Piping Technology Inc 2890 Arnold Tenbrook Rd .... Arnold MO 63010 *Web:* www.acidpiping.com	636-296-4668		492
Acier Picard Inc 3000 Rue De L' Etchemin .... Levis QC G6W7X6 *TF:* 888-834-0646 ■ *Web:* www.acierpicard.com	418-834-8300		492
ACIL (American Council of Independent Laboratories) 1875 I St NW Ste 500 .... Washington DC 20006 *TF:* 800-368-1131 ■ *Web:* www.acil.org	202-887-5872	887-0021	49-19
ACI-NA (Airports Council International of North America) 1775 K St NW Ste 500 .... Washington DC 20006 *Web:* www.aci-na.org	202-293-8500	331-1362	49-21
ACIPCO (American Cast Iron Pipe Co) 1501 31st Ave N .... Birmingham AL 35207 *TF:* 800-442-2347 ■ *Web:* www.american-usa.com	205-325-7701		307
ACIST Medical Systems Inc 7905 Fuller Rd .... Eden Prairie MN 55344 *TF:* 888-667-6648 ■ *Web:* www.acist.com	952-941-3507		476
ACK Controls Inc 2600 Happy Valley Rd .... Glasgow KY 42141	270-678-6200		57
Acker & Sons Inc 10516 Summit Ave .... Kensington MD 20895 *Web:* ackerandsonsinc.com	301-897-0700		610
Acker Merrall & Condit Company Inc 160 W 72nd St .... New York NY 10023 *Web:* www.ackerwines.com	212-787-1700		443
Ackerman McQueen Inc (AM) 1601 NW Expy Ste 1100 .... Oklahoma City OK 73118 *TF:* 800-438-7325 ■ *Web:* www.am.com	405-843-7777	848-8034	4
Ackerman Oil Company Inc 2060 S Lube Way .... Jasper IN 47546 *Web:* www.ackoil.com	812-482-6666		541
Ackermann Public Relations & Marketing 1111 Northshore Dr Ste N-400 .... Knoxville TN 37919 *TF General:* 877-325-9453 ■ *Web:* www.ackermannpr.com	865-584-0550	588-3009	636
Ackerman-practicon Inc 801 E Charleston Rd .... Palo Alto CA 94303 *Web:* www.apcts.com	650-965-1000		256
Ackley Lake State Park 4600 Giant Springs Rd .... Great Falls MT 59405 *Web:* www.fwp.mt.gov	406-454-5840		565
Ackman-Ziff Real estate Group LLC 711 Third Ave 11th Fl .... New York NY 10017 *Web:* www.ackmanziff.com	212-697-3333		652
Ackroo Inc 62 Steacie Dr Ste 201 .... Ottawa ON K2K2A9 *TF:* 888-405-0066 ■ *Web:* ackroo.com	613-599-2396		317
ACL (Atlantic Container Line) 50 Cardinal Dr .... Westfield NJ 07090 *TF:* 800-225-1235 ■ *Web:* www.aclcargo.com	908-518-5300	518-7321	313
ACL Distribution Inc 4722 Danvers Dr .... Grand Rapids MI 49512 *Web:* www.aclperformance.com.au	616-956-1300		75
ACLI (American Council of Life Insurers) 101 Constitution Ave NW Ste 700 W .... Washington DC 20001 *Web:* www.acli.com	202-624-2000		49-9
ACLU (American Civil Liberties Union) 125 Broad St 18th Fl .... New York NY 10004 *TF:* 877-867-1025 ■ *Web:* www.aclu.org	212-549-2500	549-2580	48-8
ACM (Association of Children's Museums) 2711 Jefferson Davis Hwy Ste 600 .... Arlington VA 22202 *Web:* www.childrensmuseums.org	703-224-3100		48-4
ACM (Association for Computing Machinery) 2 Penn Plaza Ste 701 .... New York NY 10121 *TF:* 800-342-6626 ■ *Web:* www.acm.org	212-626-0500	944-1318	48-9
ACM Capital Partners LLC 2103 Coral Way Ste 604 .... Miami FL 33145 *Web:* www.acmcapitalpartners.com	305-960-8851		194
Acm Chemistries Inc 3190 Reps Miller Rd Ste 100 .... Norcross GA 30071 *Web:* acmchem.com	770-417-3490		183
ACM Medical Laboratory Inc 160 Elmgrove Pk .... Rochester NY 14624 *Web:* www.acmlab.com	585-247-3500		415
ACMA (American Composites Manufacturers Assn) 3033 Wilson Blvd Ste 420 .... Arlington VA 22201 *Web:* www.acmanet.org	703-525-0743	525-0743	49-13
ACMA Computers Inc 1565 Reliance Way .... Fremont CA 94539 *TF Sales:* 800-786-6888 ■ *Web:* www.acma.com	510-257-6800	257-6801	173-2
ACMAT Corp 233 Main St .... New Britain CT 06051 *OTC: ACMT* ■ *Web:* www.acmatcorp.com	860-229-9000		391-5
ACMC (Ashtabula County Medical Ctr) 2420 Lake Ave .... Ashtabula OH 44004 *TF:* 800-722-3330 ■ *Web:* www.acmchealth.org	440-997-2262	997-6644	374-3
ACMC (Affiliated Community Medical Centers) 101 Willmar Ave SW .... Willmar MN 56201 *TF:* 888-225-6580 ■ *Web:* www.acmc.com	320-231-5000		374-3
ACMC (Advocate Condell Medical Ctr) 801 S Milwaukee Ave .... Libertyville IL 60048 *Web:* www.advocatehealth.com/condell	847-362-2900	362-1721	374-3
ACMCM (American College of Managed Care Medicine) 4435 Waterfront Dr Ste 101 .... Glen Allen VA 23060 *TF:* 888-491-8833 ■ *Web:* www.acmcm.org	804-527-1905	747-5316	49-8

Name / Address	City	State	Zip	Phone	Fax	Class
ACME (Association for Couples in Marriage Enrichment) PO Box 21374	Winston-Salem	NC	27120	800-634-8325		48-6
TF: 800-634-8325 ■ *Web:* www.bettermarriages.org						
Acme Aerospace Inc 528 W 21st St	Tempe	AZ	85282	480-894-6864		21
Web: www.acme-aero.com						
Acme Architectural Products Inc 251 Lombardy St	Brooklyn	NY	11222	718-384-7800		480
Web: www.acmesalesgroup.com						
Acme Block & Brick Inc 248 Dayton Spur Rd	Crossville	TN	38555	931-484-8435		183
Web: www.acmeblockandbrick.com						
Acme Brick 3024 Acme Brick Plaza	Fort Worth	TX	76109	817-332-4101	390-2404	150
Web: brick.com						
ACME Business Consulting LLC 249 NW Park Ave	Portland	OR	97209	503-232-1416		196
TF: 800-927-2363 ■ *Web:* www.acmebusinessconsulting.com						
Acme Communications Inc 2101 E Fourth St Ste 202	Santa Ana	CA	92705	714-245-9499		738
PINK: ACME ■ *Web:* www.acmecommunications.com						
Acme Construction Company Inc 7695 Bond St	Cleveland	OH	44139	440-232-7474	232-7477	188-8
TF: 800-686-5077 ■ *Web:* www.acmerrinc.com						
Acme Corrugated Box Company Inc 2700 Turnpike Dr	Hatboro	PA	19040	215-245-4500		100
Web: acmebox.com						
ACME Cosmetic Components 80 Seaview Dr	Secaucus	NJ	07094	718-335-3000	335-3037	488
Web: www.acmcpano.com						
Acme Cryogenics Inc 2801 Mitchell Ave	Allentown	PA	18103	610-966-4488		454
TF: 800-422-2790 ■ *Web:* www.acmecryo.com						
Acme Distribution Centers Inc 18101 E Colfax Ave	Aurora	CO	80011	303-340-2100	340-2424	803-1
TF: 800-444-3614 ■ *Web:* www.acmedistribution.com						
Acme Dynamics Inc 3608 Sydney Rd PO Box 1780	Plant City	FL	33566	813-752-3137	752-4580	641
TF: 800 622-9355 ■ *Web:* www.acmedynamics.com						
Acme Electric N85 W12545 Westbrook Crossing	Menomonee Falls	WI	53051	910-738-1121		386
TF: 800-334-5214 ■ *Web:* www.hubbell-acmeelectric.com						
Acme Engineering & Manufacturing Corp PO Box 978	Muskogee	OK	74402	918-682-7791	682-0134	18
TF: 800-382-2263 ■ *Web:* www.acmefan.com						
Acme Farms Inc 1024 S King St	Seattle	WA	98104	206-323-4300		297-10
Acme Felt Works Co 6500 Stanford Ave	Los Angeles	CA	90001	323-752-3778		745-6
Acme Food Sales Inc 5940 First Ave S	Seattle	WA	98108	206-762-5150		297-8
TF: 800-777-2263 ■ *Web:* www.acmefood.com						
Acme Gear Company Inc 130 W Forest Ave	Englewood	NJ	07631	201-568-2245		709
Web: www.acmegear.com						
Acme Holding Co 24200 Marmon Ave	Warren	MI	48089	586-759-3332	759-3334	1
TF: 800-873-7957 ■ *Web:* www.acmeabrasive.com						
Acme Industrial Co 441 Maple Ave	Carpentersville	IL	60110	847-428-3911	428-1820	493
TF: 800-323-5582 ■ *Web:* www.acmeindustrial.com						
Acme Industries Inc 1325 Pratt Blvd	Elk Grove Village	IL	60007	847-296-3346	296-8622	454
Web: www.acmeind.com						
Acme Machell 2000 Airport Rd	Waukesha	WI	53187	262-521-2870	521-2894	677
Web: www.acmemachell.com						
Acme Manufacturing Co 4240 N Atlantic Blvd	Auburn Hills	MI	48326	248-393-7300		455
Web: www.acmemfg.com						
Acme Manufacturing Co 7601 State Rd	Philadelphia	PA	19136	215-268-1700		097
Acme Markets Inc 75 Valley Stream Pkwy	Malvern	PA	19355	610-889-4000		345
TF: 877-932-7948 ■ *Web:* www.acmemarkets.com						
Acme Merchandise and Apparel Inc 46 Blackburn Ctr Ste 47	Gloucester	MA	01930	978-282-4800		195
Web: www.acmeapparel.com						
Acme Metals & Steel Supply Inc 14930 S San Pedro St	Gardena	CA	90248	310-329-2263		492
Web: www.acmemetalsonline.com						
Acme Oyster House 724 Iberville St	New Orleans	LA	70130	225-906-2372		671
Web: www.acmeoyster.com						
Acme Paper & Supply Company Inc 8229 Sandy Ct PO Box 422	Savage	MD	20763	410-792-2333	792-2137	548
TF: 800-462-5812 ■ *Web:* www.acmepaper.com						
Acme Pizza & Bakery Equipment Inc 7039 E Slauson Blvd	Commerce	CA	90040	323-722-7900	726-4700	298
Web: www.acmepbe.com						
ACME Portable Machines Inc 1330 Mtn View Cir	Azusa	CA	91702	626-610-1888	610-1881	173-2
Web: www.acmeportable.com						
Acme Press Inc 2312 Stanwell Dr	Concord	CA	94520	925-682-1111		41
Web: www.calitho.com						
Acme Rolling Steel Door Corp 1099 Linden Ave	Ridgefield	NJ	07657	201-943-7070		234
Web: www.acmedoor.com						
Acme Sample Books Inc 2410 Schirra Pl	High Point	NC	27263	336-883-4187	883-4565	86
Web: www.acmesample.com						
Acme Smoked Fish Corp 30 Gem St	Brooklyn	NY	11222	718-383-8585		296-13
Web: www.acmesmokedfish.com						
Acme Spirally Wound Paper Products Inc 4810 W 139th St PO Box 35320	Cleveland	OH	44135	216-267-2950	267-0239	125
TF: 800-274-2797 ■ *Web:* www.acmespiral.com						
Acme Truck Line Inc 200 Westbank Expy PO Box 183	Gretna	LA	70053	504-368-2510	345-2263*	780
**Fax Area Code:* 888 ■ *TF:* 800-825-6246 ■ *Web:* www.acmetruck.com						
Acme United Corp 60 Round Hill Rd	Fairfield	CT	06824	203-254-6060		476
NYSE: ACU ■ *TF:* 800-835-2263 ■ *Web:* www.acmeunited.com						
Acme Wire Products Co 7 Broadway Ave	Mystic	CT	06355	860-572-0511		449
TF: 800-723-7015 ■ *Web:* www.acmewire.com						
Acme Worldwide Enterprises Inc 1710 Randolph Ct SE	Albuquerque	NM	87106	505-243-0400		256
Web: www.acme-worldwide.com						
Acme-McCrary Corp 159 N St PO Box 1287	Asheboro	NC	27204	336-625-2161	629-2263	155-10
Web: www.acme-mccrary.com						
Acme-Monaco Corp 75 Winchell Dr	New Britain	CT	06052	860-224-1349		492
TF: 800-523-5474 ■ *Web:* www.acmemonaco.com						
ACMH (Armstrong County Memorial Hospital) 1 Nolte Dr	Kittanning	PA	16201	724-543-8500	543-8704	374-3
Web: www.acmh.org						
ACMI (The Art And Creative Materials Institute Inc) 99 Derby St Ste 200	Hingham	MA	02043	781-293-4100	294-0808	48-18
Web: www.acminet.org						
ACN 1100 Ave des Canadiens-de-Montreal Ste 450	Montreal	QC	H3B2S2	514-390-8666		224
Web: acncanada.ca						
ACNM (American College of Nurse-Midwives) 8403 Colesville Rd Ste 1550	Silver Spring	MD	20910	240-485-1800	485-1818	49-8
TF: 800-468-3571 ■ *Web:* www.midwife.org						
Aco Polymer Products Inc 9470 Pinecore Dr	Mentor	OH	44060	440-639-7230	639-7235	608
TF: 800-543-4764 ■ *Web:* acousa.com						
ACOEM (American College of Occupational & Environmental Medicine) 25 NW Pt Blvd Ste 700	Elk Grove Village	IL	60007	847-818-1800	818-9266	49-8
Web: www.acoem.org						
ACOFP (American College of Osteopathic Family Physicians) 330 E Algonquin Rd Ste 1	Arlington Heights	IL	60005	847-952-5100	228-9755	49-8
TF: 800-323-0794 ■ *Web:* www.acofp.org						
ACOG (American College of Obstetricians & Gynecologists) 409 12th St SW PO Box 96920	Washington	DC	20090	202-863-1648		49-8
Web: acog.org						
ACOM Solutions Inc 2850 E 29th St	Long Beach	CA	90806	562-424-7899	424-8662	178-1
TF: 800-347-3638 ■ *Web:* www.acom.com						
Acoma Business Enterprise I 40 Exit 102	Acoma	NM	87034	505-552-7800		377
Web: www.skycity.com						
Acor Orthopaedic Inc 18530 S Miles Pkwy	Cleveland	OH	44128	216-662-4500	662-4547	301
TF: 800-237-2267 ■ *Web:* www.acor.com						
ACORD (Association for Co-op Operations Research & Development) 1 Blue Hill Plaza PO Box 1529	Pearl River	NY	10965	845-620-1700	620-3600	49-9
TF: 800-444-3341 ■ *Web:* www.acord.org						
Acorda Therapeutics Inc 420 Saw Mill River RD	Ardsley	NY	10502	914-347-4300	347-4560	85
NASDAQ: ACOR ■ *Web:* www.acorda.com						
Acorn Consulting 803 Curtis St	Menlo Park	CA	94025	650-329-8923		194
Acorn Deck House Co 852 Main St	Acton	MA	01720	978-263-6800		106
TF: 800-727-3325 ■ *Web:* www.deckhouse.com						
Acorn Design and Manufacturing 24 Terry Ln	Lebanon	PA	17042	717-964-1111		393
TF: 800-600-0134 ■ *Web:* acorndisplay.com						
Acorn Energy Inc 3903 Centerville Rd	Wilmington	DE	19807	302-656-1708		787
Web: www.acornenergy.com						
Acorn Engineering Co 15125 Proctor Ave PO Box 3527	City of Industry	CA	91744	626-336-4561	961-2200	609
TF: 800-488-8999 ■ *Web:* www.acorneng.com						
Acorn Environmental Consultants Inc 8040 Stevens Ave S Ste	Minneapolis	MN	55420	952-888-4901		196
Web: www.acornenvironmental.com						
Acorn Gencon Plastics Inc 15125 Proctor Ave	City of Industry	CA	91746	626-968-6681	855-4860	386
TF: 800-782-7706 ■ *Web:* www.whitehallmfg.com						
Acorn Industrial Inc 7311 Acc Blvd	Raleigh	NC	27617	919-256-6500		610
Acorn Manufacturing Company Inc 457 School St	Mansfield	MA	02048	800-835-0121		350
TF: 800 835 0121 ■ *Web:* www.acornmfg.com						
Acorn Petroleum Inc 529 Sahwatch St	Colorado Springs	CO	80903	719-634-8874		581
Web: www.acornpetroleuminc.com						
Acorn Press Inc 500 E Oregon Rd	Lancaster	PA	17606	717-569-3264	569-3403	627
Web: www.acornpress.com						
Acorn Technology 23103 Miles Rd	Cleveland	OH	44128	216-663-1244		729
Web: www.acorntechnology.com						
Acorn Wire & Iron Works Inc 2035 S Racine Ave	Chicago	IL	60608	773-585-0600	585-2403	279
TF: 800-552-2676 ■ *Web:* www.acornwire.com						
Acotel Interactive Inc 80 Pine St 29th Fl	New York	NY	10005	212-400-1212		736
Web: www.flycell.com						
Acousti Engineering Company of Florida Inc 4656 34th St SW	Orlando	FL	32811	407-425-3467	425-5108	189-9
TF: 800-434-3467 ■ *Web:* www.acousti.com						
Acoustic Neuroma Assn (ANA) 600 Peachtree Pkwy Ste 108	Cumming	GA	30041	770-205-8211	205-0239	48-17
TF: 877-200-8211 ■ *Web:* www.anausa.org						
Acoustic Sounds Inc 1500 S Ninth St	Salina	KS	67401	785-825-8609	825-0156	463
TF: 888-926-2564 ■ *Web:* store.acousticsounds.com						
Acoustical Society of America (ASA) 1305 Walt Whitman Rd Ste 300	Melville	NY	11747	516-576-2360	576-2377	49-19
TF: 800-828-8840 ■ *Web:* www.acousticalsociety.org						
Acoustics by Design Inc 124 Fulton St E Ste 200	Grand Rapids	MI	49503	616-241-5810		256
Web: www.acousticsbydesign.com						
ACP (American College of Physicians) 190 N Independence Mall W	Philadelphia	PA	19106	215-351-2400	351-2594	49-8
TF: 800-523-1546 ■ *Web:* www.acponline.org						
ACP (Associated Collegiate Press) 2221 University Ave SE Ste 121	Minneapolis	MN	55414	612-625-8335	626-0720	48-11
Web: www.studentpress.org						
ACP (Associated Church Press The) 924 Woodcrest Way	Oviedo	FL	32765	407-341-6615	386-3236	49-16
Web: www.theacp.org						
ACPA (American College Personnel Assn) 1 Dupont Cir NW Ste 300	Washington	DC	20036	202-835-2272	296-3286	49-5
TF: 800-228-5424 ■ *Web:* www.myacpa.org						
ACPA (American Concrete Pavement Assn) 5420 Old OrchaRd Rd Ste A-100	Skokie	IL	60077	847-966-2272	966-9970	49-3
TF: 800-281-7899 ■ *Web:* www.acpa.org						

	Phone	Fax	Class
ACPA (American Chronic Pain Assn) PO Box 850 .... Rocklin CA 95677 *Fax Area Code: 916 ■ TF: 800-533-3231 ■ Web: theacpa.org	800-533-3231	652-8190*	48-17
ACPE (American College of Physician Executives) 400 N Ashley Dr Ste 400 .... Tampa FL 33602 TF: 800-562-8088 ■ Web: www.physicianleaders.org	813-287-2000	287-8993	49-8
ACPE (Association for Clinical Pastoral Education) 1549 Clairmont Rd Ste 103 .... Decatur GA 30033 Web: www.acpe.edu	404-320-1472		48-1
ACPHS (Albany College of Pharmacy) 106 New Scotland Ave .... Albany NY 12208 *Fax: Admissions ■ TF General: 888-203-8010 ■ Web: www.acphs.edu	518-694-7221	694-7322*	166
ACPM (American College of Preventive Medicine) 455 Massachusetts Ave NW .... Washington DC 20001 Web: www.acpm.org	202-466-2044	466-2662	49-8
Acqua Fine Foods 671 The Queensway .... Toronto ON M8Y1K8 Web: www.acqua.ca	416-368-7171		671
Acqua Hotel 555 Redwood Hwy........ Mill Valley CA 94941 TF: 888-662-9555 ■ Web: www.marinhotels.com	415-380-0400	380-9696	379
Acqualina 17875 Collins Ave........ Sunny Isles Beach FL 33160 TF: 877-312-9742 ■ Web: www.acqualinaresort.com	305-918-8000	918-8100	379
Acquavella Galleries Inc 18 E 79th St .... New York NY 10075 Web: www.acquavellagalleries.com	212-734-6300	794-9394	42
Acquerello 1722 Sacramento St........ San Francisco CA 94109 Web: www.acquerello.com	415-567-5432	567-6432	671
Acquest International 909 Third Ave 27th Fl........ New York NY 10022 Web: www.acquestinternational.com	212-719-1500		194
Acquidata Inc 6800 Gulfport Blvd S Ste 201-205........ St Petersburg FL 33707 TF: 800-748-1277 ■ Web: www.acquidata.com	860-910-4747		177
Acquire Media Corp 3 Becker Farm Rd Ste 401 .... Roseland NJ 07068 Web: www.acquiremedia.com	973-422-0800		387
Acquireo.com 14584 Baseline Ave Ste 300142........ Fontana CA 92336 Web: www.acquireo.com	909-266-0840		366
Acquisitions Northwest Inc 210 SW Morrison Ste 600 .... Portland OR 97204 Web: www.acquisitionsnw.com	503-225-0479		401
Acquizition.biz Inc 1100 Rene-Levesque Blvd W 24th Fl........ Montreal QC H3B4X9 TF: 866-499-0334 ■ Web: www.acquizition.biz	514-499-0334		387
ACR (Applied Computer Research Inc) PO Box 41730 .... Phoenix AZ 85080 Web: www.itmarketintelligence.com	602-885-5311		637-11
ACR (American College of Radiology) 1892 Preston White Dr........ Reston VA 20191 TF: 800-227-5463 ■ Web: www.acr.org	703-648-8900		49-8
ACR (American College of Rheumatology) 2200 Lake Blvd NE .... Atlanta GA 30319 Web: www.rheumatology.org	404-633-3777	633-1870	49-8
ACR Aircraft Component Repair Inc 25058 Anza Dr .... Valencia CA 91355 Web: www.acr.aero	661-295-6677	295-6679	20
ACR Electronics Inc 5757 Ravenswood Rd .... Fort Lauderdale FL 33312 TF: 800-432-0227 ■ Web: www.acrartex.com	954-981-3333	983-5087	678
ACR Group Inc 3200 Wilcrest Dr Ste 440........ Houston TX 77042 Web: www.acrgroup.com	713-780-8532	780-4067	612
ACR Supply Company Inc 4040 S Alston Ave .... Durham NC 27713 TF: 800-442-4044 ■ Web: www.acrsupply.com	919-765-8081		111
Acraloc Corp 113 Flint Rd........ Oak Ridge TN 37830 TF: 800-275-8777 ■ Web: www.acraloc.com	865-483-1368	483-3500	547
Acranet 521 W Maxwell Ave........ Spokane WA 99201 TF: 800-304-1249 ■ Web: www.acranet.com	800-304-1249		180
ACRC (Atlantic City Racing Course) 4501 Black Horse Pk .... Mays Landing NJ 08330 Web: acracecourse.com	609-641-2190		642
Acres Enterprises Inc 610 W Liberty St........ Wauconda IL 60084 Web: www.acresgroup.com	847-526-4554		776
Acrilex Inc 230 Culver Ave........ Jersey City NJ 07305 Web: www.acrilex.com	201-333-1500		596
Acrion Technologies Inc 7777 Exchange St Ste 5 .... Cleveland OH 44125 Web: www.acrion.com	216-659-5566		261
ACRL (Association of College & Research Libraries) 50 E Huron St........ Chicago IL 60611 TF: 800-545-2433 ■ Web: www.ala.org/acrl/aboutacrl	312-280-2519	280-2520	49-11
Acro Automation Systems Inc 2900 W Green Tree Rd .... Milwaukee WI 53209 TF: 800-352-4511 ■ Web: www.acro.com	414-352-4540	352-1609	811
Acro Industries Inc 554 Colfax St .... Rochester NY 14606 Web: www.acroind.com	585-254-3661	254-0415	454
Acro Labels Inc 2530 Wyandotte Rd .... Willow Grove PA 19090 TF: 800-355-2235 ■ Web: www.acrolabels.com	215-657-5366	657-3325	413
Acro Media Inc 2303 Leckie Rd Ste 103........ Kelowna BC V1X6Y5 TF: 877-763-8844 ■ Web: acromediainc.com	250-763-8884	763-6936	809
Acroamatics Inc 5385 Holli Ste 105 .... Santa Barbara CA 93111 TF: 800-533-5667 ■ Web: www.acroamatics.com	805-967-9909		225
AcrobatAnt LLC 1336 E 15th St........ Tulsa OK 74120 TF: 800-984-7239 ■ Web: www.acrobatant.us	918-938-7901		195
Acromag Inc 30765 S Wixom Rd........ Wixom MI 48393 TF: 877-295-7092 ■ Web: www.acromag.com	248-624-1541	624-9234	625
Acromil Corp 18421 Railroad St........ City of Industry CA 91748 Web: www.acromil.com	626-964-2522	810-6100	22
Acropolis Computers Inc 915 Whitelaw Ave........ Wood River IL 62095 TF: 800-851-4452 ■ Web: www.acropolistech.com	618-254-8733		175
Acropolis Family Restaurant 708 Elmwood Ave........ Buffalo NY 14222 Web: www.acropolisopa.com	716-886-2977		671
Acropolis Restaurant 416 N Eugene St........ Greensboro NC 27401	336-273-3306		671
Acropolis, The 2213 Hamilton Pl Blvd .... Chattanooga TN 37421 Web: www.acropolisgrill.com	423-899-5341		671
Acroprint Time Recorder Co 5640 Departure Dr .... Raleigh NC 27616 TF: 800-334-7190 ■ Web: acroprint.com	919-872-5800	850-0720	534
Acrow Corp of America 181 New Rd Ste 202........ Parsippany NJ 07054 Web: www.acrowusa.com	973-244-0080		480
Acrowood Corp 4425 S Third Ave PO Box 1028 .... Everett WA 98203 TF: 800-359-7012 ■ Web: www.acrowood.com	425-258-3555	252-7622	821
ACRP (Association of Clinical Research Professionals) 999 Canal Center Plaza Ste 800........ Alexandria VA 22314 TF: 888-508-5731 ■ Web: www.acrpnet.org	703-254-8100	254-8101	49-8
ACRS (Associated Communications & Research Services Inc) 817 NE 63rd St........ Oklahoma City OK 73105	405-843-9966		196
ACRT Inc 1333 Home Ave........ Akron OH 44310 TF: 800-622-2562 ■ Web: www.acrtinc.com	330-945-7500	945-7200	193
Acry Fab Inc 584 Progress Way........ Sun Prairie WI 53590 Web: vollrath.com	608-837-0045		608
Acrylic Design Assoc 6050 Nathan Ln N........ Plymouth MN 55442 TF: 800-445-2167 ■ Web: www.acrylicdesign.com	763-559-8395	559-2589	233
Acrylic Plastic Products Company Inc 4815 Hwy 80 W .... Jackson MS 39209 TF: 800-331-8819 ■ Web: acrylic1plasticproducts.com	601-922-2651		608
Acryline USA Inc 2015 Becancour .... Lyster QC G0S1V0 TF: 800-567-0920 ■ Web: www.acryline.ca	800-567-0920		350
ACS (American Cancer Society) 250 William St NW........ Atlanta GA 30303 TF: 800-227-2345 ■ Web: www.cancer.org	404-320-3333		48-17
ACS (American Chemical Society) 1155 16th St NW .... Washington DC 20036 TF: 800-227-5558 ■ Web: www.acs.org	202-872-4600	872-4615	49-19
ACS (American College of Surgeons) 633 N St Clair St........ Chicago IL 60611 TF: 800-621-4111 ■ Web: www.facs.org	312-202-5000	202-5001	49-8
ACS (American Cetacean Society) 745 W Paseo Del Mar........ San Pedro CA 90731 Web: www.acsonline.org	310-548-6279		48-3
ACS (American Cybersystems Inc) 2400 Meadowbrook Pkwy........ Duluth GA 30096 *Fax Area Code: 877 ■ Web: www.acsicorp.com	770-493-5588	270-6248*	194
ACS Assoc Inc 2145 Edge Hill Rd........ Huntingdon Valley PA 19006	215-784-0661		194
ACS Development Corporation Inc 16148 Sand Canyon Ave........ Irvine CA 92618 Web: www.acsirvine.com	949-263-1920		186
ACS Group 1100 E Woodfield Rd Ste 588........ Schaumburg IL 60173 Web: www.acscorporate.com/aec	847-273-7700	273-7804	14
ACS Group, The 2900 S 160th St .... New Berlin WI 53151 TF: 800-423-3183 ■ Web: www.acscorporate.com	262-641-8600		14
ACS Industries Inc 1 New England Way........ Lincoln RI 02865 TF: 866-783-4838 ■ Web: www.acsindustries.com	401-769-4700	333-6088	688
ACS Manufacturing Inc 1601 Commerce Blvd........ Denison TX 75020 Web: www.acsmanufacturing.com	903-462-2001		192
ACS of Texas 16622 Sperry Gardens Dr........ Houston TX 77095 TF: 800-245-8503 ■ Web: www.acsoftexas.com	832-593-9990		35
ACSA (Association of Collegiate Schools of Architecture) 1735 New York Ave NW 3rd Fl........ Washington DC 20006 TF: 877-426-6323 ■ Web: www.acsa-arch.org	202-785-2324	628-0448	49-5
Acsel Corp 2876 Guardian Ln .... Virginia Beach VA 23452 Web: acsel.org	757-463-5240		2
ACSH (American Council on Science & Health) 110 E 42nd St Ste 1300 .... New York NY 10017 TF: 866-905-2694 ■ Web: www.acsh.org	212-362-7044	362-4919	49-19
ACSI (Association of Christian Schools International) 731 Chapel Hills Dr .... Colorado Springs CO 80920 TF Cust Svc: 800-367-0798 ■ Web: www.acsi.org	719-528-6906		49-5
Acsion Industries Inc PO Box 429........ Pinawa MB R0E1L0 Web: www.acsion.com	204-753-2255		317
Acsis Inc 9 E Stow Rd........ Marlton NJ 08053 Web: www.acsisinc.com	856-673-3000		180
ACSM (American College of Sports Medicine) 401 W Michigan St PO Box 1440........ Indianapolis IN 46202 Web: www.acsm.org	317-637-9200	634-7817	49-8
Acstar Insurance Co 233 Main St .... New Britain CT 06051 TF: 800-331-6053 ■ Web: www.acstarins.com	860-224-2000		391-5
AcSys Biometrics Corp 1100 Burloak Dr Ste 703 .... Burlington ON L7L6B2 Web: www.acsysbiometrics.com	905-331-7337	634-1101	84
Acsys Inc 111 Anza Blvd Ste 400........ Burlingame CA 94010	650-579-1111	579-1927	260
ACT (Association of Civilian Technicians) 12620 Lake Ridge Dr .... Woodbridge VA 22192 TF: 800-729-3277 ■ Web: www.actnat.com	703-494-4845	494-0961	48-19
ACT (A Contemporary Theatre) 700 Union St Kreielsheimer Pl .... Seattle WA 98101 TF: 888-584-4849 ■ Web: www.acttheatre.org	206-292-7660	292-7670	572
ACT (Abilene Community Theatre) 809 Barrow .... Abilene TX 79605 Web: www.abilenecommunitytheatre.org	325-673-6271		572
ACT (American Conservatory Theater) 30 Grant Ave 6th Fl........ San Francisco CA 94108 Web: www.act-sf.org	415-834-3200	749-2291	573-4
ACT Clean Technologies Inc 5412 Bolsa Ave Ste A .... Huntington Beach CA 92649 Web: www.actcleantech.com	714-373-1984		539
ACT Inc 500 ACT Dr PO Box 168 .... Iowa City IA 52243 Web: www.act.org	319-337-1000	337-1735	244
ACT Litigation Services Inc 27200 Tourney Rd Ste 450........ Valencia CA 91355 Web: discoverready.com	661-284-6401		396
ACT TeleConferencing Inc 1526 Cole Blvd Ste 300 .... Lakewood CO 80401	303-233-3500	238-0096	736

Company / Address	City	State	ZIP	Phone	Fax	Class
Act Too Consulting Inc 917 W Inyokern Rd Ste C *Web:* www.acttooconsulting.com	Ridgecrest	CA	93555	760-301-5566		463
ACT UP 12 Wooster St *TF:* 800-272-3900 ■ *Web:* www.actupny.org	New York	NY	10013	212-966-4873		48-8
ACT Video Productions Inc 3640 S Cedar St Ste G *Web:* www.actvp.com	Tacoma	WA	98409	253-926-2440	926-1130	514
Act2 Retirement Consulting LLC 5120 Watchwood Path *TF:* 866-992-9256 ■ *Web:* www.act2retirement.com	Columbia	MD	21044	866-992-9256		463
Acta Inc 2790 Skypark Dr Ste 310 *Web:* www.actainc.com	Torrance	CA	90505	310-530-1008		261
Actavis Elizabeth LLC 200 Elmora Ave	Elizabeth	NJ	07202	908-527-9100		583
ACTE (Association for Career & Technical Education) 1410 King St *TF:* 800-826-9972 ■ *Web:* www.acteonline.org	Alexandria	VA	22314	703-683-3111	683-7424	49-5
ACTE (Association of Corporate Travel Executives) 515 King St Ste 440 *Web:* www.acte.org	Alexandria	VA	22314	703-683-5322	683-2720	48-23
ACTEC (American College of Trust & Estate Counsel) 901 15th St NW Ste 525 *Web:* www.actec.org	Washington	DC	20005	202-684-8460	684-8459	49-10
Actega Wit Inc 125 Technology Dr *Web:* www.actega.com/wit	Lincolnton	NC	28092	704-735-8282		388
Actel Corp 2061 Stierlin Ct *TF:* 800-262-1060 ■ *Web:* www.microsemi.com	Mountain View	CA	94043	650-318-4200	318-4600	696
Actelis Networks Inc 6150 Stevenson Blvd *Web:* www.actelis.com	Fremont	CA	94538	510-545-1045		729
ACTEON North America Inc 124 Gaither Dr Ste 140 *TF:* 800-289-6367 ■ *Web:* www.acteongroup.com	Mount Laurel	NJ	08054	856-222-9988		228
Acterra Group Inc Corporate Centre 200 200 35th St *Web:* www.acterragroup.com	Marion	IA	52302	319-377-6357		61
ACTFL (American Council on the Teaching of Foreign Languages) 1001 N Fairfax St Ste 200 *TF:* 844-685-4373 ■ *Web:* www.actfl.org	Alexandria	VA	22314	703-894-2900	894-2905	49-5
ActForex Inc 110 Wall St 7th Fl *Web:* www.actforex.com	New York	NY	10005	212-425-7111		225
ActiFi Inc 3030 Harbor Ln Ste 216 *Web:* www.actifi.com	Plymouth	MN	55447	763-550-0223		225
Actify LLC 7635 Interactive Way Ste 200 *TF:* 800-467-0830 ■ *Web:* www.actifywireless.com	Indianapolis	IN	46278	800-467-0830		246
Actimis Pharmaceuticals Inc 10835 Rd To The Cure Ste 200 *Web:* www.actimis.com	San Diego	CA	92121	858-458-1890		743
Actinix Inc 1800 Green Hills Rd Ste 105 *Web:* www.actinix.com	Scotts Valley	CA	95066	831-440-9388		419
Actinobac Biomed Inc 15 Pelham Rd *Web:* www.actinobac.com	Kendall Park	NJ	08824	732-371-2694		231
Actinver Securities Inc 5075 Wheimer Rd Galleria Financial Tower Ste 650 *Web:* www.actinversecurities.com	Houston	TX	77056	713-885-9843		690
Action Against Hunger 247 W 37th St 10th Fl *TF:* 877-777-1420 ■ *Web:* www.actionagainsthunger.org	New York	NY	10018	212-967-7800	967-5480	48-5
Action Air Conditioning & Htg 3506 Ave S	Galveston	TX	77550	409-765-8026		610
Action Aircraft Lp 10570 Olympic Dr *TF:* 800-909-7616 ■ *Web:* www.actionaircraft.com	Dallas	TX	75220	214-351-1284		21
Action Bolt & Tool Co (WURTH) 701 Boutwell Rd Ste A-1 **Fax Area Code:* 561 ■ *TF:* 800-423-0700 ■ *Web:* www.actionboltandtool.com	Lake Worth	FL	33461	800-423-0700	845-0255*	351
Action Box Co Inc 6207 N Houston Rosslyn Rd *Web:* www.actionboxinc.com	Houston	TX	77091	713-869-7701	869-2086	100
Action Capital Corp 230 Peachtree St Ste 910 *TF:* 800-525-7767 ■ *Web:* www.actioncapital.com	Atlanta	GA	30343	404-524-3181	577-4880	272
Action Carrier Inc 1720 S Southeastern Ave Ste 220	Sioux Falls	SD	57103	605-335-5500		780
Action Co 1425 N Tennessee St *TF Sales:* 800-937-3700 ■ *Web:* www.actioncompany.com	McKinney	TX	75069	972-542-8700	562-7300	431
Action Craft 830 NE 24th Ln *Web:* www.actioncraft.com	Cape Coral	FL	33909	239-574-7800	574-7805	90
Action Fabricating Inc 1244 Hawk St *Web:* www.actionfabricating.com	Detroit Lakes	MN	56501	218-847-4034		697
Action Facilities Management Inc 115 Malone Dr *Web:* www.actionfacilities.com	Morgantown	WV	26501	304-599-6850		256
Action Fasteners 265 Edinburgh Dr *TF:* 800-561-7019 ■ *Web:* www.actionfasteners.com	Moncton	NB	E1E2K9	506-857-8950		351
Action Floor Systems LLC 4781 N US Hwy 51 *TF:* 800-746-3512 ■ *Web:* www.actionfloors.com	Mercer	WI	54547	715-476-3512		290
Action Inc 1308 Church St *Web:* action-mechanical.com	Barling	AR	72923	479-452-5723		189-10
Action Lead Solutions 2232 N Clybourn Ave Ste 300 *Web:* actionleadsolutions.com	Chicago	IL	60614	773-661-1570		195
Action Learning Systems Inc 135 S Rosemead Blvd *Web:* www.actionlearningsystems.com	Pasadena	CA	91107	626-744-5344		194
Action Lift Inc 1 Memco Dr *TF:* 800-294-5438 ■ *Web:* actionliftinc.com	Pittston	PA	18640	570-655-2100		358
Action Machined Products Inc 1355 Bangor St *Web:* www.actionmachined.com	Copiague	NY	11726	631-842-2333		488
Action Mailing Corp 3165 W Heartland Dr *TF:* 866-990-9001 ■ *Web:* action-mailing.com	Liberty	MO	64068	816-415-9000		5
Action Maintenance Systems Inc 251 251 E Empire St *TF:* 800-985-9569 ■ *Web:* actionmaintenance.net	San Jose	CA	95112	408-287-8000		104
Action Manufacturing Co 100 E Erie Ave *TF:* 800-499-7455 ■ *Web:* www.action-mfg.com	Philadelphia	PA	19134	215-739-6400		268
ACTION On-Line Inc 4 S Central Ave Ste 1 *Web:* actionol.com	Saint Louis	MO	63105	314-726-4994		637-9
Action Packaging 6995 Southbelt Dr SE *TF:* 800-463-3339 ■ *Web:* www.actionpackaging.com	Caledonia	MI	49316	616-871-5200		100
Action Pact Inc 7709 W Lisbon Ave *Web:* www.actionpact.com	Milwaukee	WI	53222	414-258-3649		463
Action Pest Control Inc 2301 S Green River Rd *TF:* 800-467-5530 ■ *Web:* www.actionpest.com	Evansville	IN	47715	812-477-5546		577
Action Plumbing Supply Co 5411 NW 15th St *Web:* www.actionsupply.com	Margate	FL	33063	954-971-7782		612
Action Reporter Media *Wisconsin Media* N6637 Rolling Meadows Dr *Web:* www.fdlreporter.com	Dallas	TX	75267	920-922-4600		532-2
Action Sales & Metal Company Inc 1625 E Pacific Coast Hwy *Web:* actionsalesmetal.com	Wilmington	CA	90744	310-549-5666		723
Action Screen Print Inc 30w260 Butterfield Rd Unit 203 *TF:* 800-661-5892 ■ *Web:* actionscreen.com	Warrenville	IL	60555	630-393-1990		687
Action Security Inc 243 E Fifth Ave *TF:* 800-478-3785 ■ *Web:* actionsecurity.com	Anchorage	AK	99501	907-279-7050		693
Action Sports Systems Inc 617 Carbon City Rd PO Box 1442 *TF:* 800-631-1091 ■ *Web:* www.actionsportsuniforms.com	Morganton	NC	28655	828-584-8000		155-19
Action Stainless & Alloys Inc 1505 Halsey Way *TF:* 800-749-2523 ■ *Web:* www.actionstainless.com	Carrollton	TX	75007	972-466-1500		492
Action SuperAbrasive Products Inc 945 Greenbriar Pkwy *Web:* www.actionsuper.com	Brimfield	OH	44240	330-673-7333		295
Action Supply Inc 1413 Old Stagecoach Rd *Web:* www.actionsupplyco.com	Ocean View	NJ	08230	609-390-0663		182
Action Tire 2405 Weaver Way *Web:* www.actiontireco.com	Doraville	GA	30340	770-263-9695	448-3888	57
Action Travel Center Inc 5900 Harper Rd *TF:* 800-391-1167 ■ *Web:* www.actiontvl.com	Solon	OH	44139	440-248-4949		775
Action Water Sports 4155 32nd Ave *TF:* 800-394-3227 ■ *Web:* www.actionwater.com	Hudsonville	MI	49426	616-896-3100		711
ActionCOACH 5781 S Ft Apache Rd *TF:* 888-483-2828 ■ *Web:* www.actioncoach.com	Las Vegas	NV	89148	702-795-3188	795-3183	765
ActioNet Inc 2600 Park Tower Dr Ste 1000 *Web:* www.actionet.com	Vienna	VA	22180	703-204-0090		624
Actionlink LLC 4100 Embassy Pkwy *TF:* 888-737-8757 ■ *Web:* www.actionlink.com	Akron	OH	44333	888-737-8757		196
ActionTec Electronics Inc 760 N Mary Ave *TF Tech Supp:* 888-436-0657 ■ *Web:* www.actiontec.com	Sunnyvale	CA	94085	408-752-7700	541-9003	173-3
Activar Inc 7808 Creekridge Cir *Web:* www.activar.com	Minneapolis	MN	55439	952-944-3533		360-2
Activation Laboratories Ltd 1336 Sandhill Dr *TF:* 888-228-5227 ■ *Web:* www.actlabs.com	Ancaster	ON	L9G4V5	905-648-9611		743
Active Aero Group 2068 E St **Fax:* Hum Res ■ *TF Cust Svc:* 800-872-5387 ■ *Web:* www.activeaero.com	Belleville	MI	48111	734-547-7200	547-7222*	13
Active Captive Management 16485 Laguna Canyon Rd Ste 200 *TF:* 800-921-0155 ■ *Web:* www.activecaptive.com	Irvine	CA	92618	949-727-0155		2
Active Concepts Inc 107 Technology Dr Ste 506 *Web:* activeconceptsllc.com	Lincolnton	NC	28092	704-276-7100		317
Active Day/Senior Care Inc 400 Redland Ct Ste 114 *TF:* 877-435-3372 ■ *Web:* www.seniorcarectrs.com	Owings Mills	MD	21117	866-724-9599		451
Active Environmental Technologies Inc 203 Pine St *Web:* www.active-env.com	Mount Holly	NJ	08060	609-702-1500		194
Active Fire Sprinkler Corp 63 Flushing Ave	Brooklyn	NY	11205	718-834-8300		189-13
Active Imagination Inc 1434 W Alabama St *Web:* www.aimagination.com	Houston	TX	77006	713-528-6100		344
Active Network 10182 Telesis Ct Ste 100 *TF:* 888-543-7223 ■ *Web:* www.activenetwork.com	San Diego	CA	92121	858-964-3800	551-7619	7
Active Parenting Publishers 1955 Vaughn Rd Ste 108 *TF:* 800-825-0060 ■ *Web:* www.activeparenting.com	Kennesaw	GA	30144	770-429-0565	429-0334	513
Active Plumbing Supply Co 216 Richmond St *Web:* www.activeplumbing.com	Painesville	OH	44077	440-352-4411		612
Active Power Inc 2128 W Breaker Ln BldgBk12 *NASDAQ:* ACPW ■ *Web:* www.activepower.com	Austin	TX	78758	512-836-6464	836-4511	767
Active Professionals Inc 9647b Folsom Blvd *Web:* activeprofessionalconferences.com	Sacramento	CA	95827	916-361-0931		734
Active Recycling Company Inc 2000 W Slauson Ave *Web:* www.activelosangeles.com	Los Angeles	CA	90047	323-295-7774		660
Active Staffing Services 41 W 33rd St 3rd Fl *Web:* www.activestaffing.com	New York	NY	10001	212-244-6444		260
Activeforevercom 10799 N 90th St *TF:* 800-377-8033 ■ *Web:* www.activeforever.com	Scottsdale	AZ	85260	480-459-3202		321

	Phone	Fax	Class
activePDF Inc 27405 Puerta Real Ste 100 ... Mission Viejo CA 92691 *TF:* 866-468-6733 ■ *Web:* www.activepdf.com	949-582-9002	582-9004	178-12
ActiveStrategy Inc 620 W Germantown Pk ... Plymouth Meeting PA 19462	484-690-0700		225
Activeworlds Inc 95 Parker St ... Newburyport MA 01950 *Web:* www.activeworlds.com	978-499-0222	499-0221	178-7
Activision Inc 3100 Ocean Pk Blvd ... Santa Monica CA 90405 *TF:* 800-509-5586 ■ *Web:* www.activision.com	310-255-2000		178-6
Activo Inc 161 Alden Rd Unit 6 ... Markham ON L3R3W7 *Web:* www.activo.ca	905-752-1900		180
Acton Institute for the Study of Religion & Liberty 161 Ottawa Ave NW Ste 301 ... Grand Rapids MI 49503 *TF:* 800-345-2286 ■ *Web:* www.acton.org	616-454-3080	454-9454	634
ACTON Marketing LLC 3401 NW 39th St ... Lincoln NE 68524 *Web:* www.acton.com	402-470-2909		195
Acton Technologies Inc 100 Thompson St ... Pittston PA 18640 *Web:* www.actontech.com	570-654-0612		605-2
Actor's Theatre of Charlotte 650 E Stonewall St ... Charlotte NC 28202 *Web:* www.atcharlotte.org	704-342-2251		572
Actors Theatre of Louisville 316 W Main St ... Louisville KY 40202 *TF:* 800-428-5849 ■ *Web:* www.actorstheatre.org	502-584-1205	561-3300	749
Actors' Equity Assn 1560 Broadway ... New York NY 10036 *TF:* 866-270-4232 ■ *Web:* www.actorsequity.org	212-869-8530	719-9815	414
Actron Manufacturing Inc 1841 Railroad St ... Corona CA 92880 *Web:* www.actronmfginc.com	951-371-0885		22
Actron Steel Inc 2866 Cass Rd ... Traverse City MI 49685	231-947-3981		198
Actsoft Inc 8910 N Dale Mabry Hwy ... Tampa FL 33614 *TF:* 888-732-6638 ■ *Web:* www.actsoft.com	813-936-2331	936-7541	177
Actuarial Management Resources Inc 4964 University Pkwy ... Winston-Salem NC 27106 *Web:* www.actmanre.com	336-759-0008		463
Actuarial Research Corp 6928 Little River Tpke Ste E ... Annandale VA 22003 *Web:* www.aresearch.com	703-941-7400		196
Actuarial Systems Corp 15840 Monte St Ste 108 ... Sylmar CA 91342 *TF:* 800-950-2082 ■ *Web:* www.asc-net.com	800-950-2082		390
Actuate Corp 2207 Bridgepointe Pkwy Ste 500 ... San Mateo CA 94404 *NASDAQ: OTEX* ■ *TF Sales:* 800-914-2259 ■ *Web:* www.actuate.com	650-645-3000		178-1
ACU (Abilene Christian University Brown Library) 760 Library Ct ... Abilene TX 79699 *TF:* 800-460-6228 ■ *Web:* www.acu.edu/academics/library	325-674-2000		434-6
ACU (American Conservative Union, The) 1331 H St NW Ste 500 ... Washington DC 20005 *Web:* www.conservative.org	202-347-9388		48-7
ACU Serve Corp 2020 Front St Ste 205 ... Cuyahoga Fls OH 44221 *TF:* 800-887-8965 ■ *Web:* acuservecorp.com	330-923-5258		2
ACUHO-I (Association of College & University Housing Officers International) 941 Chatham Ln Ste 318 ... Columbus OH 43221 *Web:* www.acuho-i.org	614-292-0099	292-3205	49-5
ACUI (Association of College Unions International) 120 W Seventh St 1 City Ctr Ste 200 ... Bloomington IN 47404 *TF:* 800-228-5424 ■ *Web:* www.acui.org	812-245-2284	245-6710	49-5
Acuity Audio Visual 11301 Industrial Rd ... Manassas VA 20109 *TF:* 800-771-8330 ■ *Web:* www.acuityav.com	703-361-6080		196
Acuity Brands Inc 1170 Peachtree St NE Ste 2400 ... Atlanta GA 30309 *NYSE: AYI* ■ *Web:* www.acuitybrands.com	404-853-1400		360-3
Acuity Inc 11710 Plaza America Dr Ste 100 ... Herndon VA 20170 *Web:* www.myacuity.com	703-766-0977		196
Acuity Insurance 2800 S Taylor Dr ... Sheboygan WI 53081 *TF:* 800-467-8725 ■ *Web:* www.acuity.com	920-458-9131	458-1618	391-4
Aculabs Inc 2 Kennedy Blvd ... East Brunswick NJ 08816 *Web:* www.aculabs.com	732-777-2588		415
Acumen Business Connections Inc 1999 N Amidon Ave Ste 230 ... Wichita KS 67203 *TF:* 800-864-4644 ■ *Web:* acumenprocessing.com	316-265-4477		251
Acumen Capital Finance Partners Ltd 404 Sixth Ave SW Ste 700 ... Calgary AB T2P0R9 *TF:* 888-422-8636 ■ *Web:* www.acumencapital.com	403-571-0300		401
Acumen Enterprises Inc 1504 Falcon ... Desoto TX 75115 *Web:* acumen-enterprises.com	972-572-0701		261
Acumen Fiscal Agent LLC 4542 E Inverness Ave Ste 210 ... Mesa AZ 85206 *Web:* www.acumenfiscalagent.com	480-497-0343		734
Acumen Learning LLC 226 N Orem Blvd ... Orem UT 84057 *Web:* acumenlearning.com	801-224-5444		765
Acumen Solutions Inc 1660 International Dr Ste 500 ... McLean VA 22102 *Web:* www.acumensolutions.com	703-600-4000	600-4001	180
Acumenex Com 2201 Brant St ... Burlington ON L7P3N8 *TF:* 877-788-5028 ■ *Web:* www.acumenex.com	877-788-5028		396
Acumentra Health Inc 2020 SW Fourth Ave Ste 520 ... Portland OR 97201	503-279-0100	279-0190	194
Acumera Inc 3112 Windsor Rd Ste A-130 ... Austin TX 78703 *Web:* www.acumera.net	512-687-7400		624
Acumeter Laboratories 2976 Cleveland Ave N ... St Paul MN 55113 *Web:* www.acumeter.com	651-765-9686		821
Acupac Packaging Inc 55 Ramapo Valley Rd ... Mahwah NJ 07430 *Web:* www.acupac.com	201-529-3434		557
Acupay System LLC 30 Broad St 46th Fl ... New York NY 10004 *Web:* www.acupay.com	212-422-1222		401
ACuPowder International LLC 901 Lehigh Ave ... Union NJ 07083 *TF:* 800-232-3198 ■ *Web:* www.acupowder.com	908-851-4500		492
Acupuncture & Massage College 10506 N Kendall Dr ... Miami FL 33176 **Fax:* Admissions ■ *Web:* www.amcollege.edu	305-595-9500	595-2622*	800
Acura Medical Systems Inc 8990 Cotter St ... Lewis Center OH 43035 *Web:* acuramed.com	614-781-0600		57
Acura Neon 1801 N Willow Ave ... Broken Arrow OK 74012 *Web:* www.anisigns.com	918-252-2258		57
Acura of Bellevue 13424 NE 20th St ... Bellevue WA 98005 *Web:* www.acuraofbellevue.com	425-644-3000		57
Acuren Group Inc 7450 - 18th St ... Edmonton AB T6P1N8 *TF:* 800-663-9729 ■ *Web:* www.acuren.com	780-440-2131		787
Acushnet holdings Corp 333 Bridge St ... Fairhaven MA 02719 **Fax:* Hum Res ■ *TF:* 800-225-8500 ■ *Web:* www.acushnetcompany.com	508-979-2000	979-3927*	710
Acusis LLC 4 Smithfield St ... Pittsburgh PA 15222 *Web:* www.acusis.com	412-209-1300	209-1299	478
Acusphere Inc 99 Hayden Ave Ste 385 ... Lexington MA 02421 *OTC: ACUS* ■ **Fax Area Code:* 978 ■ *Web:* www.acusphere.com	617-648-8800	863-9993*	85
AcuSport Corp 1 Hunter Pl ... Bellefontaine OH 43311 **Fax:* Sales ■ *TF:* 800-543-3150 ■ *Web:* www.acusport.com	937-593-7010	592-5625*	710
ACUTA (Association for Communications Technology Professionals in Higher Education) 152 W Zandale Dr Ste 200 ... Lexington KY 40503 *Web:* www.acuta.org	859-278-3338	278-3268	49-5
Acutec Precision Machining Inc 16891 State Hwy 198 ... Saegertown PA 16433 *Web:* www.acutecprecision.com	814-763-3214		454
AcuTech Group Inc 1919 Gallows Rd Ste 900 ... Vienna VA 22182 *Web:* www.acutech-consulting.com	703-676-3180		194
Acutrack Inc 350 Sonic Ave ... Livermore CA 94551 *Web:* www.acutrack.com	925-579-5000		514
Acutronic USA Inc 700 Waterfront Dr ... Pittsburgh PA 15222 *Web:* www.acutronic.com	412-926-1200		529
Acutus Medical Inc 2210 Faraday Ave Ste 100 ... Carlsbad CA 92008 *Web:* www.acutusmedical.com	442-232-6080		743
ACW Management Corp 2527 Echester Dr ... High Point NC 27265 *Web:* www.acleanerworld.com	336-841-4188	841-4117	426
Acxiom Corp 601 E Third St ... Little Rock AR 72201 *NASDAQ: ACXM* ■ *TF:* 888-322-9466 ■ *Web:* www.acxiom.com	501-342-7799		5
Acxius Strategic Consulting LLC 500 Campus Dr Ste 300 ... Morganville NJ 07751 *TF:* 800-860-2255 ■ *Web:* www.acxius.com	732-972-7970		180
ACY (Atlantic City International Airport) 101 Atlantic City International Airport Ste 106 ... Egg Harbor Township NJ 08234 *Web:* www.sjta.com	609-645-7895		27
Ad Art Co 3260 E 26th St ... Los Angeles CA 90058 *TF:* 800-266-7522 ■ *Web:* www.adartco.com	323-981-8941	980-0515	701
Ad Astra Information Systems LLC 6900 W 80th St Ste 300 ... Overland Park KS 66204 *Web:* www.aais.com	913-652-4100		177
Ad Cetera Inc 15570 Quorum Dr ... Addison TX 75001 *Web:* www.adceterainc.com	972-387-5577		7
Ad Display Sign Systems Inc 27255 Katy Fwy ... Katy TX 77494 *Web:* addisplaysigns.com	281-392-2828	392-7446	701
A&D Environmental Services Inc 2718 Uwharrie Rd ... Archdale NC 27261 *TF:* 800-434-7750 ■ *Web:* www.adenviro.com	336-434-7750		63
AD Huesing Corp 527 37th Ave ... Rock Island IL 61201 *Web:* www.huesing.com	309-788-5652		805
AD Makepeace Company Inc 158 Tihonet Rd ... Wareham MA 02571 *Web:* www.admakepeace.com	508-295-1000		315-1
Ad Partners Inc 4631 Woodland Corporate Blvd Ste 109 ... Tampa FL 33614 *Web:* adpartnersagency.com	813-418-4645		4
AD Potts & Assoc Inc 11524 Jefferson Ave ... Newport News VA 23601	757-595-4610		727
Ad Results Media 320 Westcott St Ste 101 ... Houston TX 77055 *Web:* www.adresultsinc.com	713-783-1800		7
Ad Solutions Group Inc 1200 Harger Rd Ste 203 ... Oak Brook IL 60523 *Web:* www.adsgroup.net	630-574-4545		177
AD Sutton & Sons Inc 20 W 33rd St ... New York NY 10001 *Web:* adsutton.com	212-695-7070	947-6253	430
ad2 Inc 1990 E Grand Ave Ste 200 ... El Segundo CA 90245 *Web:* www.ad2.com	310-356-7500		5
ADA (American Dental Assn) 211 E Chicago Ave ... Chicago IL 60611 *TF:* 800-621-8099 ■ *Web:* www.ada.org	312-440-2500		49-8
ADA (American Diabetes Assn) 1701 N Beauregard St ... Alexandria VA 22311 *TF:* 800-232-3472 ■ *Web:* www.diabetes.org	703-549-1500		48-17
ADA (Americans for Democratic Action) 1625 K St NW Ste 210 ... Washington DC 20006 *TF:* 855-712-8441 ■ *Web:* www.adaction.org	202-785-5980	785-5969	48-7
Ada Area Chamber of Commerce 209 W Main St ... Ada OK 74820 *Web:* www.adachamber.com	580-332-2506		139
Ada Business Computers 1003 N Mississippi Ave ... Ada OK 74820 *Web:* www.adacomp.com	580-436-2803		177
Ada Community Library 10664 W Victory Rd ... Boise ID 83709 *Web:* www.adalib.org	208-362-0181		31
Ada Evening News Corp PO Box 489 ... Ada OK 74821 *Web:* theadanews.com	580-310-7500	332-8734	637-8
Ada Metal Products Inc 7120 Capitol Dr ... Lincolnwood IL 60712 *TF:* 800-419-1931 ■ *Web:* www.adametal.com	847-673-1190	673-4860	489
ADA Station Communication Inc 1079 Livingston Rd ... Crossville TN 38555 *Web:* www.adastation.com	931-707-5389		179

Name / Address	City	State	ZIP	Phone	Fax	Class
ADA Technologies Inc 8100 Shaffer Pkwy Ste 130 *Web:* www.adatech.com	Littleton	CO	80127	303-792-5615		668
ADAA (Art Dealers Assn of America) 205 Lexington Ave Ste 901 **Fax Area Code: 646* ■ *TF:* 800-272-8258 ■ *Web:* www.artdealers.org	New York	NY	10016	212-488-5550	688-6809*	48-4
ADAA (Anxiety Disorders Assn of America) 8730 Georgia Ave Ste 600 *TF:* 800-922-8947 ■ *Web:* www.adaa.org	Silver Spring	MD	20910	240-485-1001	485-1035	48-17
ADAA (American Dental Assistants Assn) 140 N Bloomingdale Rd *TF:* 877-874-3785 ■ *Web:* www.adaausa.org	Bloomingdale	IL	60108	312-541-1550		49-8
Adacel Technologies Ltd 9677 Tradeport Dr *Web:* www.adacelinc.com	Orlando	FL	32827	407-581-1560	581-1581	178-10
ADA-ES Inc 9135 S Ridgeline Blvd Ste 200 *NASDAQ: ADES* ■ *TF:* 888-822-8617 ■ *Web:* www.adaes.com	Highlands Ranch	CO	80129	303-734-1727		145
Adair County 424 Public Sq *Web:* www.columbia-adaircounty.com	Columbia	KY	42728	270-384-4703		338
Adair County 400 Public Sq *TF:* 800-247-4023 ■ *Web:* www.adaircountyiowa.org/contact-us	Greenfield	IA	50849	641-743-2546	743-2565	338
Adair County 106 W Washington St *Web:* adaircountymissouri.com	Kirksville	MO	63501	660-665-3350		338
Adair County PO Box 31 *Web:* adair.oklahoma.usassessor.com	Stilwell	OK	74960	918-696-2012	696-6729	338
Adair County Board of Education 1204 Greensburg St *Web:* adair.k12.ky.us	Columbia	KY	42728	270-384-2476		685
Adair Printing Technologies 7850 Second St *TF:* 800-637-5025 ■ *Web:* adairgraphic.com	Dexter	MI	48130	734-426-2822	426-4360	626
Adair State Park Hwy 51 & Hwy 59 *Web:* www.oklahomacampers.com	Stilwell	OK	74960	918-696-6613		565
Adalet 4801 W 150th St **Fax: Sales* ■ *Web:* www.adalet.com	Cleveland	OH	44135	216-267-9000	267-1681*	816
Adam Broderick Salon & Spa 89 Danbury Rd *TF:* 800-438-3834 ■ *Web:* www.adambroderick.com	Ridgefield	CT	06877	203-431-3994		77
Adam Matthews Inc 2104 Plantside Dr *Web:* www.adammatthews.com	Louisville	KY	40299	502-499-2253		345
Adam Moore Law Firm, The 3773 Cherry Creek N Dr ste 575 *Web:* www.adammoorelaw.com	Denver	CO	80209	303-228-2171		428
Adam Ross Cut Stone Co 1003 Broadway *Web:* www.adamrosscutstone.com	Albany	NY	12204	518-463-6674		724
Adam's European Contracting Inc 589 Johnson Ave *TF:* 800-364-2059 ■ *Web:* www.adamseuro.com	Brooklyn	NY	11237	718-417-9000		251
Adam's Mark Hotels & Resorts 120 Church St *Web:* www.adamsmark.com	Buffalo	NY	14202	716-845-5100		379
Adam's Rib 1210 State St *Web:* adams-rib-smoke-house.com	Salem	OR	97301	503-362-2194		671
Adamo Construction Inc 11980 Woodside Ave Ste 5 *TF:* 800-554-6364 ■ *Web:* www.adamoconstruction.com	Lakeside	CA	92040	619-390-6706		186
Adams & Associates of Nevada Inc 10395 Double R Blvd *Web:* www.adamsaai.com	Reno	NV	89521	775-348-0900		195
Adams & Brooks Inc 1915 S Hoover St *TF Orders:* 800-999-9808 ■ *Web:* www.adams-brooks.com	Los Angeles	CA	90007	213-749-3226	746-7614	296-8
Adams & Clark Inc 1720 W Fourth Ave *Web:* adamsandclark.com	Spokane	WA	99201	509-747-4600		727
Adams & Garth Staffing 2119 Berkmar Dr *TF:* 800-452-7391 ■ *Web:* adamsandgarth.com	Charlottesville	VA	22901	434-974-7878		260
Adams & Knight Inc 80 Avon Meadow Ln *Web:* www.adamsknight.com	Avon	CT	06001	860-676-2300		4
Adams & Longino Advertising Inc 605 Lynndale Ct Ste F *Web:* www.adamsadv.com	Greenville	NC	27858	252-355-5566		7
Adams & Smith Inc 1380 W Ctr St *Web:* www.adamsandsmith.com	Lindon	UT	84042	801-785-6900	785-6400	189-14
Adams & Westlake Ltd 940 N Michigan St *Web:* www.adlake.com	Elkhart	IN	46514	574-264-1141		650
Adams Addressing Assoc Inc 39 Faranella Dr *TF:* 800-631-6245 ■ *Web:* www.adamsdms.com	East Hanover	NJ	07936	973-887-3409		195
Adams Air & Hydraulics Inc 7209 E Adamo Dr *TF:* 800-282-4165 ■ *Web:* www.adamsair.com	Tampa	FL	33619	813-626-4128		358
Adams Alma (Rep D - NC) 222 Cannon HOB *Web:* adams.house.gov	Washington	DC	20515	202-225-1510	225-1512	342-2
Adams Arms Inc 612 Florida Ave *Web:* www.adamsarms.net	Palm Harbor	FL	34683	727-853-0550		807
Adams Auto Corp 501 NE Colbern Rd	Lees Summit	MO	64086	816-358-7600		57
Adams Avenue Business Assn 4649 Hawley Blvd *Web:* www.adamsavenuebusiness.com	San Diego	CA	92116	619-282-7329	282-8751	460
Adams Building Contractors 3300 Yukon Dr *Web:* www.adamsbc.com	Jackson	MI	49201	517-748-9099		186
Adams Capital Management Inc 500 Blackburn Ave *Web:* www.acm.com	Sewickley	PA	15143	412-749-9454	749-9459	792
Adams Cattle LLC 327 S First Ave *Web:* www.adamslandandcattle.com	Broken Bow	NE	68822	308-872-6494		446
Adams Co 8040 Chavenelle Rd *Web:* www.theadamscompany.com	Dubuque	IA	52002	563-583-3591	583-8048	620
Adams Communication & Engineering Technology Inc 11637 Terr Dr Ste 201 *Web:* www.adamscomm.com	Waldorf	MD	20602	301-861-5000		256
Adams Construction Co 523 Rutherford Ave NE *TF:* 800-237-6060 ■ *Web:* www.adamspaving.com	Roanoke	VA	24016	540-982-2366	982-2942	188-4
Adams County 500 Ninth St *Web:* www.adamscountyia.com	Corning	IA	50841	641-322-3240	322-4647	338
Adams County 201 Industrial Ave PO Box 48 *Web:* www.co.adams.id.us	Council	ID	83612	208-253-6125	253-6127	338
Adams County 313 W Jefferson St *Web:* www.co.adams.in.us	Decatur	IN	46733	260-724-5300	724-5313	338
Adams County PO Box 95 *Web:* www.adamscounty.org	Hastings	NE	68901	402-461-7107	461-7185	338
Adams County 314 State St PO Box 1008 *Web:* www.adamscountyms.net	Natchez	MS	39120	601-442-2431		338
Adams County 507 Vermont St *Web:* www.co.adams.il.us	Quincy	IL	62301	217-277-2150	277-2155	338
Adams County 210 W Broadway *Web:* www.co.adams.wa.us	Ritzville	WA	99169	509-659-3257	659-0118	338
Adams County 110 W Main St *TF:* 800-840-5711 ■ *Web:* adamscountyoh.gov	West Union	OH	45693	937-544-2011		338
Adams County Public Library 140 Baltimore St *TF:* 800-548-3240 ■ *Web:* www.adamslibrary.org	Gettysburg	PA	17325	717-334-5716	334-7992	434-3
Adams County Travel & Visitors Bureau 509 E Main St *TF:* 877-232-6764 ■ *Web:* www.adamscountytravel.org	West Union	OH	45693	937-544-5639		139
Adams County Winery 251 Peach Tree Rd *TF:* 877-601-7936 ■ *Web:* www.adamscountywinery.com	Orrtanna	PA	17353	717-334-4631		50-7
Adams Electric & Plumbing LLC 606 N Main St *Web:* adamsep.com	Pratt	KS	67124	620-672-7279		610
Adams Electric Co-op 700 Eastwood St PO Box 247 *TF:* 800 232 4707 ■ *Web:* www.adamselectric.coop	Camp Point	IL	62320	217 593 7701	593-7120	245
Adams Electric Co-op Inc 1338 Biglerville Rd PO Box 1055 *TF:* 888-232-6732 ■ *Web:* www.adamsec.coop	Gettysburg	PA	17325	717-334-2171		245
Adams Elevator Equipment Co 6310 W Howard St *TF:* 800-929-9247 ■ *Web:* www.adamselevator.com	Niles	IL	60714	847-581-2900	581-2949	678
Adams Express Co 500 E Pratt St Ste 1300 *NYSE: ADX* ■ *TF:* 800-638-2479 ■ *Web:* www.adamsexpress.com	Baltimore	MD	21202	410-752-5900		405
Adams Extract & Spice LLC 3217 Johnston Rd *Web:* www.adamsextract.com	Gonzales	TX	78629	830-672-1850		297-8
Adams Golf 2801 E Plano Pkwy	Plano	TX	75074	972-673-9000		710
Adams Group Inc, The 925 Gervais St *Web:* www.adamsgroup.com	Columbia	SC	29201	803-765-1223		195
Adams Harkness Techventures 60 State St	Boston	MA	02109	617-788-1670		792
Adams Homestead & Nature Preserve 272 Westshore Dr *Web:* gfp.sd.gov	McCook Lake	SD	57049	605-232-0873		565
Adams Jhonson & Duncan 3128 Colby Ave *Web:* adamslawyers.com	Everett	WA	98201	425-339-8556		428
Adams Keegan Inc 6750 Poplar Ave Ste 400 *TF:* 800-621-1308 ■ *Web:* www.adamskeegan.com	Memphis	TN	38119	800-621-1308		631
Adams Lake State Park c/o Shawnee State Pk 4404 State Rt 125 *Web:* parks.ohiodnr.gov/adamslake	Portsmouth	OH	45663	740-858-6652		565
Adams Manufacturing Corp 109 W Park Rd *Web:* www.adamsmfg.com	Portersville	PA	16051	724-368-8837		596
Adams McClure LP 1245 S Inca St *Web:* www.adamsmcclure.com	Denver	CO	80223	303-777-1984		627
Adams Mfg Company Inc 9790 Midwest Ave *Web:* www.adamsmanufacturing.com	Cleveland	OH	44125	216-587-6801	587-6807	37
Adams Museum 54 Sherman St *TF:* 800-335-0275 ■ *Web:* deadwoodhistory.org	Deadwood	SD	57732	605-578-1714		520
Adams National Historical Park 135 Adams St *Web:* www.nps.gov	Quincy	MA	02169	617-773-1177		564
Adams Oceanfront Resort 4 Read St *TF:* 800-448-8080 ■ *Web:* www.adamsoceanfront.com	Dewey Beach	DE	19971	302-227-3030		379
Adams Outdoor Adv Co 911 SW Adams St *TF:* 800-843-5843 ■ *Web:* www.adamsoutdoor.com	Peoria	IL	61602	309-692-2482	692-8452	8
Adams Products Co 5701 McCrimmon Pkwy PO Box 189 *TF:* 800-672-3131 ■ *Web:* www.adamsproducts.com	Morrisville	NC	27560	919-467-2218	469 0509	183
Adams Rehmann & Heggan Assoc 850 S White Horse Pk *Web:* arh-us.com	Hammonton	NJ	08037	609-561-0482		261
Adams Remco Inc PO Box 3968 *TF:* 800-627-2113 ■ *Web:* www.adamsremco.com	South Bend	IN	46619	574-288-2113		112
Adams Resources & Energy Inc 17 S Briar Hollow Ln Ste 100 *NYSE: AE* ■ *Web:* www.adamsresources.com	Houston	TX	77027	713-881-3600		536
Adams Resources Inc 17 S Briar Hollow Ln *TF:* 800-577-8853 ■ *Web:* www.adamsresources.com	Houston	TX	77001	713-881-3600		579
Adams Rite Aerospace 4141 N Palm St *Web:* www.ar-aero.com	Fullerton	CA	92835	714-278-6500		22
Adams Rite Manufacturing Co 10027 S 51st St Ste 102 *TF:* 800-872-3267 ■ *Web:* www.adamsrite.com	Phoenix	AZ	85044	909-632-2300		350
Adams Rural Electric Co-op Inc 4800 SR 125 *TF:* 800-283-1846 ■ *Web:* www.adamsrec.com	West Union	OH	45693	937-544-2305		245
Adams State College 208 Edgemont Blvd *TF:* 800-824-6494 ■ *Web:* www.adams.edu	Alamosa	CO	81102	719-587-7712	587-7522	166
Adams Street Partners LLC 1 N Wacker Dr Ste 2200 *Web:* www.adamsstreetpartners.com	Chicago	IL	60606	312-553-7890		792
Adams Unlimited 80 Broad St Ste 3202 *TF:* 800-582-6208 ■ *Web:* adams-pr.com	New York	NY	10004	212-956-5900		195

Company	City	State	Zip	Phone	Fax	Class
Adams USA Inc 610 S Jefferson Ave *TF:* 800-426-9784 ■ *Web:* www.adamsusa.com	Cookeville	TN	38501	800-426-9784		710
Adams Youth Services Ctr 1933 E Bridge St *TF:* 800-772-1213 ■ *Web:* colorado.gov	Brighton	CO	80601	303-659-4450	637-0471	412
Adamsahern Sign Solutions Inc 30 Arbor St Ste 3 *Web:* www.adamsahern.com	Hartford	CT	06106	860-523-8835		701
Adams-Burch Inc 1901 Stanford Ct *TF Cust Svc:* 800-347-8093 ■ *Web:* www.adams-burch.com	Landover	MD	20785	301-276-2000		300
Adams-Columbia Electric Co-op 401 E Lake St *TF:* 800-831-8629 ■ *Web:* acecwi.com	Friendship	WI	53934	608-339-3346	339-7756	245
AdamsGabbert 9200 Indian Creek Pkwy Ste 205 *Web:* www.adamsgabbert.com	Overland Park	KS	66210	913-735-4390		463
Adamson Analytical Laboratories Inc 200 Crouse Dr *Web:* www.adamsonlab.com	Corona	CA	92879	951-549-9657	549-9659	743
Adamson Associates Architects 401 Wellington St W 3rd Fl *Web:* www.adamson-associates.com	Toronto	ON	M5V1E7	416-967-1500		123
Adamson Global Technology Corp 13101 N Eron Church Rd **Fax Area Code:* 804 ■ *TF:* 800-525-7703 ■ *Web:* www.adamsontank.com	Chester	VA	23836	800-525-7703	796-2037*	91
Adamson Industries Corp 45 Research Dr *Web:* www.adamsonindustries.com	Haverhill	MA	01832	978-681-0370		295
Adamson Motors Inc 4800 Hwy 52 N *Web:* adamsonmotors.com	Rochester	MN	55901	507-289-4004		57
Adamy Valuation Advisors 50 Louis St NW Ste 405 *Web:* www.adamyvaluation.com	Grand Rapids	MI	49503	616-284-3700		734
ADAPT Corp 1733 Woodside Rd Ste 220 *Web:* www.adaptsoft.com	Redwood City	CA	94061	650-306-2400		261
Adapt Plastics Inc 7949 Forest Hills Rd *Web:* adaptplastics.com	Loves Park	IL	61111	815-633-9263		608
Adapt Software Applications 959 S Coast Dr Ste 100 *Web:* www.adaptcrm.com	Costa Mesa	CA	92626	714-389-1584		177
Adaptek Systems Inc 14224 Plank St *Web:* www.adapteksystems.com	Fort Wayne	IN	46818	260-637-8660		194
Adaption Technologies Ventures Ltd 1009 Pruitt Rd *Web:* adpt-tech.com	Spring	TX	77380	281-465-3320		668
Adaptiva 3005 112th Ave NE Ste 250 *Web:* www.adaptiva.com	Bellevue	WA	98004	425-823-4500		196
Adaptive Driving Access Inc 3430 E Sam Houston Pkwy S *TF:* 800-488-0359 ■ *Web:* www.adaptivedriving.com	Pasadena	TX	77505	281-487-1969		62
Adaptive Equipment Inc 2512 NE First Blvd Ste 700 *Web:* www.adaptivequipment.com	Gainesville	FL	32609	352-372-7821		180
Adaptive Flight Inc 885 Franklin Rd Ste 330	Marietta	GA	30067	770-951-8755		256
Adaptive Micro Systems Inc 7840 N 86th St *TF:* 800-558-4187 ■ *Web:* www.adaptivedisplays.com	Milwaukee	WI	53224	414-357-2020	357-2029	178-7
Adaptive Networks Inc 123 Highland Ave *TF:* 800-244-4462 ■ *Web:* www.adaptivenetworks.com	Needham	MA	02494	781-444-4170		387
Adaptive Switch Laboratories Inc 125 Spur 191 Ste C *Web:* www.asl-inc.com	Spicewood	TX	78669	830-798-0005		250
adaptiveARC Inc PO Box 5568 *Web:* www.adaptivearc.com	Oceanside	CA	92052	215-676-7876		192
adaQuest Inc 14450 NE 29th Pl Ste Ste 220 *Web:* www.adaquest.com	Bellevue	WA	98007	425-284-7800		194
Adasia Communications Inc 400 Sylvan Ave Ste 200 *Web:* www.adasia-us.com	Englewood Cliffs	NJ	07632	201-608-0388		4
ADB (American Drill Bushings Co) 5740 Hunt Rd *TF:* 800-423-4425 ■ *Web:* www.americandrillbushing.com	Valdosta	GA	31606	229-253-8928	253-8929	493
ADB Consulting & CRO Inc 8569 Pines Blvd Ste 215 *TF:* 800-511-0184 ■ *Web:* www.adbccro.com	Pembroke Pines	FL	33024	954-517-1970		196
ADC (American-Arab Anti Discrimination Committee) 1990 M St NW Ste 610 *TF:* 800-253-3931 ■ *Web:* www.adc.org	Washington	DC	20036	202-244-2990	244-3196	48-8
Adc Information Technologies Inc 950 Michigan Ave *Web:* www.ibswebsite.com	Columbus	OH	43215	614-240-5999		180
AdCare Health Systems Inc 1145 Hembree Rd *NYSE:* ADK ■ *Web:* www.adcarehealth.com	Roswell	GA	30076	678-869-5116		363
AdCare Hospital of Worcester 107 Lincoln St *TF:* 800-252-6465 ■ *Web:* www.adcare.com	Worcester	MA	01605	508-799-9000		726
Adcetera Design Studio Inc 3000 Louisiana St *Web:* www.adcetera.com	Houston	TX	77006	713-522-8006		344
Adchem Corp 1852 County Rd 58 *TF:* 800-424-9300 ■ *Web:* www.adchem.com	Riverhead	NY	11901	631-727-6000	727-6010	732
AdChem Manufacturing Technologies Inc 369 Progress Dr *Web:* www.acmtct.com	Manchester	CT	06042	860-645-0592		370
ADCI of Delaware LLC 5550 Friendship Blvd Ste 340 *Web:* www.adcit.com	Chevy Chase	MD	20815	301-951-4423		387
Adco Advertising Agency 1302 W Pioneer Pkwy Ste 100 *TF:* 800-322-0160 ■ *Web:* www.adcoagency.com	Peoria	IL	61615	309-692-7880		7
Adco Circuits 2868 Bond St *Web:* www.adcocircuits.com	Rochester Hills	MI	48309	248-853-6620	853-6698	253
ADCO Companies LTD 3657 Pine Ln *Web:* www.adcoboiler.com	Bessemer	AL	35022	205-428-2326		612
Adco Container Co 9959 Canoga Ave *TF:* 800-497-9764 ■ *Web:* www.adcocontainer.com	Chatsworth	CA	91311	818-998-2565		362
Adco Global Inc 100 Tri State International Ste 135 *Web:* www.adcoglobal.com	Lincolnshire	IL	60069	847-282-3485	282-3481	3
Adco Inc 1909 W Oakridge *TF:* 800-821-7556 ■ *Web:* www.adco-inc.com	Albany	GA	31707	800-821-7556		151
Adco Industries 11333 Pagemill Rd *TF:* 800-527-4609 ■ *Web:* www.adcoindustries.com	Dallas	TX	75243	214-217-7800	217-7810	43
Adco Landscaping 1532 W Olympic Blvd *Web:* www.adcoservices.com	Montebello	CA	90640	323-725-2581		776
Adco Litho Line Inc 2700 W Roosevelt Rd	Broadview	IL	60155	708-345-8200		9
Adco Manufacturing Inc 2170 Academy Ave *TF:* 888-608-5946 ■ *Web:* www.adcomfg.com	Sanger	CA	93657	559-875-5563	875-7665	385
Adco Products Inc 4401 Page Ave *Web:* www.adcocorp.com	Michigan Center	MI	49254	517-764-0334		3
Adcole Corp 669 Forest St *TF:* 800-858-5802 ■ *Web:* www.adcole.com	Marlborough	MA	01752	508-485-9100	481-6142	472
Adcolor Inc 950 Brookstown Ave *Web:* www.adcolornc.com	Winston-Salem	NC	27101	336-778-7390		344
Adcomm Inc 89 Leuning St *Web:* adcomminc.com	South Hackensack	NJ	07606	201-342-6349		767
Adconion Media Group Ltd 901 Marshall St Ste 200 *Web:* amobee.com	Redwood City	CA	94063	650-353-4399		514
Adcor Industries Inc 234 S Haven St *Web:* www.adcorindustries.com	Baltimore	MD	21224	410-327-3083		454
Adcotron EMS Inc 12 Ch St Marine Industrial Pk *TF:* 800-331-8923 ■ *Web:* www.adcotron.com	Boston	MA	02210	617-598-3000	598-3001	695
Adcraft Products Company Inc 1230 S Sherman St *Web:* www.adcraftproducts.com	Anaheim	CA	92805	714-776-1230		627
ADD Inc 311 Summer St	Boston	MA	02210	617-234-3100	661-7118	261
Add Rob Litho LLC 11 W Passaic St *Web:* www.addroblitho.com	Rochelle Park	NJ	07662	201-556-0700		708
Add Staff Inc 2118 Hollow Brook Dr *TF:* 800-332-6682 ■ *Web:* www.addstaffinc.com	Colorado Springs	CO	80918	719-528-8888		260
Add3 LLC 500 E Pk St 2nd Fl *Web:* www.add3.com	Seattle	WA	98122	206-568-3772		195
ADDA (American Design Drafting Assn) 105 E Main St *Web:* www.adda.org	Newbern	TN	38059	731-627-0802	627-9321	48-4
ADDCO LLC 240 Arlington Ave E *TF:* 800-616-4408 ■ *Web:* www.addco.com	Saint Paul	MN	55117	651-488-8600		700
Adden Furniture Inc 710 Chelmsford St *TF:* 800-625-3876 ■ *Web:* www.addenfurniture.com	Lowell	MA	01851	978-454-7848	453-1449	319-3
AdDent Inc 43 Miry Brook Rd *Web:* www.addent.com	Danbury	CT	06810	203-778-0200		228
Addictive Mobility Inc 72 Fraser Ave Ste 201 *Web:* addictivemobility.com	Toronto	ON	M6K3J7	416-535-0706		224
Addington Oil Corp 2154 US Hwy 23 N Ste 102 *TF:* 800-999-2328 ■ *Web:* www.addingtonoil.com	Weber City	VA	24290	276-386-3961		324
Addis Red Sea 544 Tremont St *Web:* www.addisredsea.com	Boston	MA	02116	617-426-8727		671
Addison Biological Laboratory Inc 507 N Cleveland Ave *TF:* 800-331-2530 ■ *Web:* www.addisonlabs.com	Fayette	MO	65248	660-248-2215	248-2554	584
Addison Capital Partners 319 Clematis St Ste 211 *Web:* www.addisoncapitalpartners.com	West Palm Beach	FL	33401	561-835-4041		401
Addison Chamber of Commerce & Industry 777 W Army Trial Blvd Ste D *Web:* www.addisonchamber.org	Addison	IL	60101	630-543-4300	543-4355	139
Addison Clark Management LLC 10 Wright St Ste 100 *Web:* www.leask.com	Westport	CT	06880	203-222-4000		807
Addison County 93 Ct St *Web:* www.addisoncounty.com	Middlebury	VT	05753	802-388-7951	388-8066	338
Addison County Chamber of Commerce 93 Ct St *Web:* www.addisoncounty.com	Middlebury	VT	05753	802-388-7951	388-8066	139
Addison House Interiors Inc 5201 NW 77th Ave Ste 400 *TF:* 800-426-2988 ■ *Web:* www.addisonhouse.com	Doral	FL	33166	305-640-2400		321
Addison Precision Manufacturing 500 Avis St *Web:* www.addisonprec.com	Rochester	NY	14615	585-254-1386		454
Addison Public Library 4 Friendship Plaza *Web:* www.addisonlibrary.org	Addison	IL	60101	630-543-3617		434-3
Addison The Grand Del Mar 5200 Grand Del Mar Way *Web:* www.addisondelmar.com	San Diego	CA	92130	858-314-1900		671
Addison Whitney Inc 11525 N Community House Rd Ste 350 *Web:* addisonwhitney.com	Charlotte	NC	28277	704-347-5700		463
Addison's An American Grill 709 Cherry St *Web:* www.addisonsgrill.com	Columbia	MO	65201	573-256-1995		671
Addison, The 2 E Camino Real *Web:* www.theaddison.com	Boca Raton	FL	33432	561-372-0568		671
Addmaster Corp 225 Huntington Dr *TF:* 800-786-5528 ■ *Web:* www.addmaster.com	Monrovia	CA	91016	626-358-2395	358-2784	173-6
Addonics Technologies Inc 1918 Junction Ave *Web:* www.addonics.com	San Jose	CA	95131	408-573-8580		174

	Phone	Fax	Class
Adducent Technology Inc PO Box 1057 ... Rohnert Park CA 94928 *TF:* 800-648-0656 ■ *Web:* www.adducenttechnology.com	800-648-0656		529
Addus HealthCare Inc 2401 S Plum Grove Rd ... Palatine IL 60067 *NASDAQ: ADUS* ■ *TF:* 888-233-8746 ■ *Web:* www.addus.com	847-303-5300		353
Addvantage Group LLC, The 126 E Wing St Ste 132 ... Arlington Heights IL 60004 *Web:* www.theaddvantagegroup.com	847-392-9576		463
ADDvantage Technologies Group Inc 1221 E Houston ... Broken Arrow OK 74012 *NASDAQ: AEY* ■ *Web:* www.addvantagetechnologies.com	918-251-9121		246
Addwater2 Inc 383 First St W ... Sonoma CA 95476 *Web:* addwater2.com	707-938-1223		4
Addx Corp 4900 Seminary Rd Ste 570 ... Alexandria VA 22311 *Web:* www.addxcorp.com	703-933-7637		194
Addy's Dutch Cafe & Restaurant 17 E Coffee St ... Greenville SC 29601 *TF:* 800-257-3529 ■ *Web:* www.addysdutchcafe.com	864-232-2339		671
ADEA (American Dental Education Assn) 1400 K St NW Ste 1100 ... Washington DC 20005 *TF:* 800-353-2237 ■ *Web:* www.adea.org	202-289-7201	289-7204	49-5
ADEC (Association for Death Education & Counseling) 111 Deer Lake Rd Ste 100 ... Deerfield IL 60015 *Web:* www.adec.org	847-509-0403	480-9282	49-8
A-dec Inc 2601 Crestview Dr ... Newberg OR 97132 *TF Cust Svc:* 800-547-1883 ■ *Web:* a-dec.com/en	503-538-7478	538-0276	228
Adec Industries 2700 Industrial Pkwy ... Elkhart IN 46516 *TF:* 866-730-3111 ■ *Web:* www.adecinc.com	574-295-3167		88
ADEC Solutions USA 10 Monument St ... Deposit NY 13754 *Web:* www.adecsolutions-usa.com	607-467-4600		225
Adecco Inc 175 Broad Hollow Rd ... Melville NY 11747 *TF General:* 800-978-3729 ■ *Web:* www.adeccousa.com	631-844-7650		721
Adega 33 Elm St ... Toronto ON M5G1H1 *Web:* www.adegarestaurante.ca	416-977-4338		671
Adega Grill 130 Ferry St ... Newark NJ 07105 *Web:* www.adegagrill.com	973-589-8830		671
Adel Wiggins Group of Transdigm Inc 5000 Triggs St ... Los Angeles CA 90022 *Web:* www.adelwiggins.com	323-269-9181		567
Adelaide Environmental Health Associates 1511 Route 22 ... Brewster NY 10509 *Web:* adelaidellc.com	845-278-7710		463
Adelberg Rudow 7 Saint Paul St Ste 600 ... Baltimore MD 21202 *Web:* www.adelbergrudow.com	410-539-5195		428
Adell Plastics Inc 4530 Annapolis Rd ... Baltimore MD 21227 *TF:* 800-638-5218 ■ *Web:* www.adellplas.com	410-789-7780		745-2
Adelman Travel Group 6080 N Port Washington Rd ... Milwaukee WI 53217 *TF Cust Svc:* 800-248-5562 ■ *Web:* www.adelmantravel.com	414-352-7600	352-3900	771
Adelphi Consulting Group Inc 8209 SW Cirrus Dr ... Beaverton OR 97008 *TF:* 800-698-1942 ■ *Web:* adelphigroup.net	503-641-3501		196
Adelphi University PO Box 701 ... Garden City NY 11530 **Fax:* Admissions ■ *TF:* 800-233-5744 ■ *Web:* www.adelphi.edu	516-877-3050	877-3039*	166
Manhattan Ctr 75 Varick St 2nd Fl ... New York NY 10013 *TF:* 800-233-5744 ■ *Web:* www.adelphi.edu	212-965-8340	431-5161	166
Adelphia Steel Equipment Co 7372 State Rd ... Philadelphia PA 19136 *TF:* 800-865-8211 ■ *Web:* www.adelphiafurniture.com	215-333-6300	331-6090	319-1
Adelphoi Village Inc 1119 Village Way ... Latrobe PA 15650 *Web:* www.adelphoivillage.org	724-520-1111	520-1878	303
Adelsberger Donna & Associates 2782 Jenkintown Rd ... Glenside PA 19038 *Web:* dlalawyers.com	215-576-8690		428
Adelt Mechanical Ltd 2640 Argentia Rd ... Mississauga ON L5N6C5 *Web:* www.adeltmechanical.com	905-812-7900		664
Adena Regional Medical Ctr 272 Hospital Rd ... Chillicothe OH 45601 *TF:* 800-582-7277 ■ *Web:* www.adena.org	740-779-7500		374-3
Adept Consulting Services Inc 408 W Main St ... Lansdale PA 19446 *Web:* www.adeptusa.com	215-855-3610		196
Adept Corp 4601 N Susquehanna Trial ... York PA 17406 *TF:* 800-451-2254 ■ *Web:* adeptcorp.com	717-266-3606		358
Adept Fasteners Inc 28709 Industry Dr ... Valencia CA 91355 *Web:* www.adeptfasteners.com	661-257-6600		621
ADEPT Technologies LLC 2865 Wall Triana Hwy ... Huntsville AL 35824 *Web:* www.adept-technologies.com	256-851-2932		21
Adept Technology Inc 5960 Inglewood Dr ... Pleasanton CA 94588 *NASDAQ: ADEP* ■ *TF:* 800-292-3378 ■ *Web:* www.adept.com	925-245-3400	960-0452	386
Adera Development Corp 1055 Dunsmuir St Ste 2200 Four Bentall Centre PO BOX 49214 ... Vancouver BC V7X1K8 *Web:* www.adera.com	604-684-8277		627
Aderans Hair Goods Inc 9135 Independence Ave ... Chatsworth CA 91311 *TF Sales:* 877-413-5225 ■ *Web:* www.simplicityhair.com	877-413-5225		348
Aderholt Robert (Rep R - AL) 235 Cannon House Office Bldg ... Washington DC 20515 *Web:* aderholt.house.gov	202-225-4876		342-2
Ades & Gish Nurseries 2222 N Twin Oaks Valley Rd ... San Marcos CA 92069 *Web:* www.agnurseries.com	760-410-0400	410-0433	369
ADESA Inc 13085 Hamilton Crossing Blvd ... Carmel IN 46032 *TF:* 800-923-3725 ■ *Web:* www.adesa.com	317-815-1100	249-4600	51
ADEX Corp 1035 Windward Ridge Pkwy Ste 500 ... Alpharetta GA 30005 *TF:* 800-451-9899 ■ *Web:* www.adextelecom.com	678-393-7900		224
AD-EX International Inc 1301 Glendale-Milford Rd ... Cincinnati OH 45215 *TF:* 800-742-2913 ■ *Web:* www.adex-intl.com	513-771-2339		195
Adex Media Inc 883 N Shoreline Blvd Ste A200 ... Mountain View CA 94943 *Web:* www.adex.com	650-967-3040	967-3185	195
Adexa Inc 5933 W Century Blvd 12th Fl ... Los Angeles CA 90045 *TF:* 888-300-7692 ■ *Web:* www.adexa.com	310-642-2100	338-9878	178-1
ADF Engineering Inc 228 Byers Rd Ste 202 ... Miamisburg OH 45342 *Web:* www.adfengineering.com	937-847-2700		256
Adfirmative LLC 11416 Hollister Dr Ste ... Austin TX 78739 **Fax Area Code:* 714 ■ *TF:* 866-966-9968 ■ *Web:* adfirmative.com	866-966-9968	908-1628*	195
Adflex Corp 300 Ormond St ... Rochester NY 14605 *TF:* 800-807-0795 ■ *Web:* www.adflexcorp.com	585-454-2950		781
ADFLOW Networks Inc 3170 Harvester Rd Ste 102 ... Burlington ON L7N3W8 *Web:* adflownetworks.com	905-333-0200		7
ADG (Art Directors Guild) 11969 Ventura Blvd Ste 200 ... Studio City CA 91604 *Web:* www.adg.org	818-762-9995	762-9997	48-4
ADG Promotional Products 2300 Main St ... Hugo MN 55038 *TF:* 800-852-5208 ■ *Web:* www.adgpromo.com	800-852-5208	886-6790	9
ADGA (American Dairy Goat Assn) 209 W Main St PO Box 865 ... Spindale NC 28160 *TF:* 800-306-8937 ■ *Web:* www.adga.org	828-286-3801	287-0476	48-2
Adguide Publications Inc 3109 W 50 St Ste 121 ... Minneapolis MN 55410 *Web:* www.collegerecruiter.com	952-848-2211		260
ADH Health Products Inc 215 N Rt 303 ... Congers NY 10920 *Web:* www.adhhealth.com	845-268-0027	268-2988	231
ADHA (American Dental Hygienists' Assn) 444 N Michigan Ave Ste 3400 ... Chicago IL 60611 *TF:* 800-243-2342 ■ *Web:* www.adha.org	312-440-8900	467-1806	49-8
Higher Education Dept 423 Main St Ste 400 ... Little Rock AR 72201 *Web:* www.adhe.edu	501-371-2000		339-4
Adherent Technologies Inc 11208 Cochiti SE ... Albuquerque NM 87123 *Web:* www.adherent-tech.com	505-346-1688		668
Adhesive & Sealant Council Inc (ASC) 7101 Wisconsin Ave Ste 990 ... Bethesda MD 20814 *Web:* www.ascouncil.org	301-986-9700	986-9795	49-13
Adhesive Applications Inc 41 O'Neill St ... EastHampton MA 01027	413-527-7120	527-7249	732
Adhesive Packaging Specialties Inc 103 Foster St ... Peabody MA 01960 *TF:* 800-222-1117 ■ *Web:* www.adhesivepackaging.com	978-531-3300	532-8901	548
Adhesive Systems Inc 14410 Woodrow Wilson ... Detroit MI 48238 *Web:* dchem.com/adhesive-systems	313-865-4448		3
Adhesives Research Inc 400 Seaks Run Rd PO Box 100 ... Glen Rock PA 17327 *TF:* 800-445-6240 ■ *Web:* www.adhesivesresearch.com	717-235-7979	235-8320	3
AdHub LLC, The 146 Alexander St ... Rochester NY 14607 *TF:* 866-712-2986 ■ *Web:* www.adhub.com	585-442-2585		393
Adi American Distributors Inc 2 Emery Ave ... Randolph NJ 07869 *TF:* 800-877-0510 ■ *Web:* www.americandistr.com	973-328-1181	328-2302	246
ADI Meetings & Events 4801 S Lakeshore Dr Ste 108 ... Tempe AZ 85282 *Web:* www.adimeetings.com	480-350-9090		384
ADI Technologies Inc 1487 Chain Bridge Rd Ste 204 ... Mclean VA 22101 *Web:* www.aditechnologies.com	703-734-9626		463
Adial Pharmaceuticals 204 E High St ... Charlottesville VA 22902 *Web:* www.adialpharma.com	434-422-9800		668
Adicio Inc 1 Carlsbad Research Ctr 2382 Faraday Ave Ste 350 ... Carlsbad CA 92008 *Web:* www.adicio.com	760-602-9502		177
Adidas Printing Inc 264 Salem St ... Medford MA 02155 *Web:* adidasprinting.com	781-391-8850		627
Adiligy LLC 845 Third Ave 6th Fl ... New York NY 10022 *Web:* www.adiligy.com	646-290-5288		194
Adinch Inc 2670 Leavenworth St Ste E ... San Francisco CA 94133	415-800-4475		5
Adino Inc 360 W Alden Ct ... Chicago Heights IL 60411 *TF:* 800-460-7935 ■ *Web:* www.adinoinc.com	708-481-1000		177
Adirondack Beverages Inc 701 Corporations Pk ... Scotia NY 12302 *Web:* www.adirondackbeverages.com	518-370-3621		80-2
Adirondack Community College 640 Bay Rd ... Queensbury NY 12804 *TF:* 888-786-9235 ■ *Web:* www.sunyacc.edu	518-743-2200	745-1433	162
Adirondack Correctional Facility 196 Ray Brook Rd PO Box 110 ... Ray Brook NY 12977 *Web:* www.doccs.ny.gov	518-891-1343		213
Adirondack Council 103 Hand Ave Ste 3 Ste 3 ... Elizabethtown NY 12932 *TF:* 877-873-2240 ■ *Web:* www.adirondackcouncil.org	518-873-2240	873-6675	48-13
Adirondack Mountain Club 814 Goggins Rd ... Lake George NY 12845 *TF Orders:* 800-395-8080 ■ *Web:* www.adk.org	518-668-4447		48-23
Adirondack Regional Chambers of Commerce 136 Glen St Ste 3 ... Glens Falls NY 12801 *TF:* 888-516-7247 ■ *Web:* www.adirondackchamber.org	518-798-1761	792-4147	139
Adirondack Trailways 499 Hurley Ave ... Hurley NY 12443 *TF:* 800-858-8555 ■ *Web:* www.trailwaysny.com	845-339-4230		108
Adistec 7620 NW 25 St Unit 7 ... Miami FL 33122 *Web:* www.adistec.com	786-221-2300		196
Adium Oil Company Inc 310 Blattner Dr ... Avon MN 56310	320-356-7350		579
Adizes 6404 Via Real ... Carpinteria CA 93013 *Web:* www.adizes.com	805-565-2901		194
Adjacent Technologies Inc 10415 Morado Cir Ste 120 Bldg 1 ... Austin TX 78759 *Web:* www.adjacent-tech.com	512-388-1338		180
Adjeleian Allen Rubeli Ltd 75 Albert St Ste 1005 ... Ottawa ON K1P5E7 *Web:* aar.ca	613-232-5786		261

Entry	Phone	Fax	Class
Adjustable Clamp Co 404 N Armour St ... Chicago IL 60642 *Web:* www.adjustableclamp.com	312-666-0640		758
Adjustable Forms Inc 1 E Progress Rd ... Lombard IL 60148 *Web:* www.adjustableforms.com	630-953-8700		135
Adjust-A-Brush 10445 49th St N ... Clearwater FL 33762 *Web:* www.adjust-a-brush.com	727-571-1234		361
AdKarma LLC 3806 Buttonwood Dr Ste 101 ... Columbia MO 65201	573-446-7366		5
Adkins & Kimbrough Mechanical 4415 Turin Dr ... Bessemer AL 35020 *Web:* jadkinsmechanical.com	205-432-4000		189-10
Adkins Arboretum 12610 Eveland Rd PO Box 100 ... Ridgely MD 21660 *Web:* www.adkinsarboretum.org	410-634-2847	634-2878	97
Adknowledge Inc 4600 Madison Ave 10th Fl ... Kansas City MO 64112 *TF:* 866-730-2109 ■ *Web:* www.adknowledge.com	816-931-1771		397
ADL (Anti-Defamation League) 605 Third Ave ... New York NY 10158 *TF:* 866-386-3235 ■ *Web:* www.adl.org	212-885-7700	867-0779	48-8
Adler & Adler Publishers Inc 5530 Wisconsin Ave ... Chevy Chase MD 20815	301-654-4271		637-9
Adler Display Studio Inc 7140 Windsor Blvd ... Baltimore MD 21244 *TF:* 800-356-0484 ■ *Web:* www.adlerdisplay.com	410-281-1200		7
Adler Group Inc 1400 NW 107 Ave ... Miami FL 33172 *TF:* 800-452-3537 ■ *Web:* www.adlergroup.com	305-392-4000		186
Adler Hot Oil Services Inc 5035 S 4630 E ... Vernal UT 84078 *Web:* www.adlerhotoil.com	435-828-0900		538
Adler Planetarium & Astronomy Museum 1300 S Lake Shore Dr ... Chicago IL 60605 *Web:* www.adlerplanetarium.org	312-922-7827		598
Adler School of Professional Psychology 65 E Wacker Pl Ste 2100 ... Chicago IL 60601 *Web:* www.adler.edu	312-201-5900		166
Adler Tank Rentals LLC 260 Mack Pl ... South Plainfield NJ 07080 *Web:* www.adlertankrentals.com	908-462-9800		23
Adleta Co 1645 Diplomat Dr ... Carrollton TX 75006 *TF:* 800-423-5382 ■ *Web:* www.adleta.com	972-620-5600	620-5666	361
ADM (Archer Daniels Midland Co) 4666 E Faries Pkwy ... Decatur IL 62526 *NYSE:* ADM ■ *TF:* 800-637-5843 ■ *Web:* www.adm.com	217-424-5200		185
ADM (Asphalt Drum Mixers Inc) 1 ADM Pkwy ... Huntertown IN 46748 *Web:* www.admasphaltplants.com	260-637-5729	637-3164	190
ADM (ADM Milling Co) 8000 W 110th St ... Overland Park KS 66210 *TF:* 800-422-1688 ■ *Web:* www.adm.com	913-491-9400		296-23
ADM Corn Processing Div 4666 E Faries Pkwy ... Decatur IL 62526 *TF:* 800-637-5843 ■ *Web:* www.adm.com	217-424-5200		296-23
ADM Corp 100 Lincoln Blvd ... Middlesex NJ 08846 *TF:* 800-327-0718 ■ *Web:* www.admcorporation.com	732-469-0900	469-0785	263
ADM Grain Co 4666 E Faries Pkwy ... Decatur IL 62526 *Web:* www.adm.com/en-us/pages/default.aspx	217-424-5200		275
ADM Milling Co (ADM) 8000 W 110th St ... Overland Park KS 66210 *TF:* 800-422-1688 ■ *Web:* www.adm.com	913-491-9400		296-23
ADM Natural Health & Nutrition *Archer Daniels Midland Co* 4666 Faries Pkwy ... Decatur IL 62526 **Fax:* PR ■ *TF:* 800-637-5843 ■ *Web:* www.adm.com	217-451-7231	424-5380*	799
Adm Productions Inc 40 Seaview Blvd ... Port Washington NY 11050 *Web:* www.admpro.com	516-484-6900	621-2531	514
ADM Specialty Food Ingredients Div 4666 E Faries Pkwy ... Decatur IL 62526 *TF:* 800-637-5843 ■ *Web:* www.adm.com	217-424-5200		296-17
AdMail Express Inc 31640 Hayman St ... Hayward CA 94544 *TF:* 800-273-6245 ■ *Web:* www.admail.com	800-273-6245		627
Ad-mail Inc 905 NW 17th Ave ... Portland OR 97209 *TF:* 800-456-9748 ■ *Web:* www.admailinc.com	503-223-1101		5
Admar Supply Co Inc 1950 Brighton Henriett ... Rochester NY 14623 *TF:* 800-836-2367 ■ *Web:* www.admarsupply.com	585-272-9390	272-9165	358
ADMARC 10 Desta Dr Ste 170LL ... Midland TX 79705 *Web:* admarc.com	432-687-1127		636
ADME (Association of Destination Management Executives) 11 W Monument Ave ... Dayton OH 45402 *Web:* www.adme.org	937-586-3727	586-3699	48-23
Admedia Partners 3 Park Ave ... New York NY 10016 *Web:* www.admediapartners.com	212-759-1870		401
Admerasia Inc 159 W 25th St 6th Fl ... New York NY 10001 *TF:* 800-438-7325 ■ *Web:* www.admerasia.com	212-686-3333		7
Administration for Children & Families (ACF) 370 L'Enfant Promenade SW ... Washington DC 20447 *Web:* www.acf.hhs.gov	202-401-9215	401-5450	340-10
Administration for Children & Families Regional Offices			
Atlanta 61 Forsyth St Ste 4M60 ... Atlanta GA 30303 *Web:* www.acf.hhs.gov/programs/region4	404-562-2800	562-2981	340-10
Boston JFK Federal Bldg Rm 2000 ... Boston MA 02203 *Web:* www.acf.hhs.gov	617-565-1020	565-2493	340-10
Chicago 233 N Michigan Ave Ste 400 ... Chicago IL 60601 *Web:* www.acf.hhs.gov/programs/region5	312-353-4237	353-2204	340-10
Dallas 1301 Young St Ste 914 ... Dallas TX 75202 *Web:* www.acf.hhs.gov/programs/region6	214-767-9648	767-3743	340-10
New York 26 Federal Plaza Rm 4114 ... New York NY 10278 *Web:* www.acf.hhs.gov/programs/region2	212-264-2890	264-4881	340-10
Philadelphia Public Ledger Bldg Ste 864 ... Philadelphia PA 19106 *Web:* www.acf.hhs.gov/programs/region3	215-861-4000	861-4070	340-10
San Francisco 90 Seventh St 9th Fl ... San Francisco CA 94103 *Web:* www.acf.hhs.gov/programs/region9	415-437-8400	437-8444	340-10
Administration on Aging (AoA) 1 Massachusetts Ave NW ... Washington DC 20201	202-619-0724		340-10
Administration on Aging Regional Offices (AOA)			
Region I JFK Federal Bldg Rm 2075 ... Boston MA 02203	617-565-1158		340-10
Region V 233 N Michigan Ave Ste 790 ... Chicago IL 60601 *Web:* www.acl.gov	312-938-9858	886-8533	340-10
Administrative Controls Management Inc 525 Avis Dr Ste 2 ... Ann Arbor MI 48108 *Web:* www.acmpm.com	734-995-9640		194
Administrative Resource Options Inc 200 W Adams St Ste 2000 ... Chicago IL 60606 *Web:* www.aroptions.com	312-634-0300		193
Administrative Systems Inc 5204 Fairmount Ave ... Downers Grove IL 60515	630-655-0112		47
Administrative-Maximum US Penitentiary *Florence* PO Box 8500 ... Florence CO 81226 *TF:* 877-623-8426 ■ *Web:* www.bop.gov/locations/institutions/flm	719-784-9464	784-5290	212
ADMINS Inc 1035 Cambridge St ... Cambridge MA 02141 *Web:* www.admins.com	617-494-5100		177
Admiral at the Lake 929 W Foster ... Chicago IL 60640 *Web:* admiral.kendal.org	773-433-1800		672
Admiral Beverage Corp 721 Pulliam Ave PO Box 58 ... Worland WY 82401 *Web:* www.admiralbeverage.com	307-347-4201		81-2
Admiral Craft Equipment Corp 940 S Oyster Bay Rd ... Hicksville NY 11801 **Fax Area Code:* 800 ■ *TF:* 800-223-7750 ■ *Web:* www.admiralcraft.com	516-433-3535	447-7751*	488
Admiral Exchange Company Inc 1443 Union St ... San Diego CA 92101	619-239-2165		328
Admiral Farragut Academy 501 Park St N ... Saint Petersburg FL 33710 *Web:* www.farragut.org	727-384-5500	347-5160	622
Admiral Fell Inn 888 S Broadway ... Baltimore MD 21231 *TF:* 866-583-4162 ■ *Web:* www.harbormagic.com	410-522-7377	522-0707	379
Admiral Inc 10 Taylor Ave ... Annapolis MD 21401 *TF:* 800-864-4429 ■ *Web:* www.admiralcleaners.com	410-267-8381		426
Admiral Linen Service Inc 2030 Kipling St ... Houston TX 77098 *TF:* 800-321-1948 ■ *Web:* www.admiralservices.com	713-529-2608		442
Admiral Nimitz Bookstore 328 E Main St ... Fredericksburg TX 78624 *Web:* www.thc.texas.gov	830-997-8600		565
Admiral on Baltimore 2 Baltimore Ave ... Rehoboth Beach DE 19971 *TF:* 888-882-4188 ■ *Web:* www.admiralonbaltimore.com	302-227-2103		379
Admiral Packaging Inc 10 Admiral St ... Providence RI 02908 *TF:* 800-556-6454 ■ *Web:* www.admiralpkg.com	401-274-7000	331-1910	548
Admiral Security Services Inc 5550 W Touhy Ave Ste 101 ... Skokie IL 60077 *Web:* www.admiralsecuritychicago.com	847-588-0888		693
Admiral-Merchants Motor Freight Inc 215 S 11th St ... Minneapolis MN 55403	612-332-4819		780
Admiralty Room 666 Wisconsin Ave ... Madison WI 53703 *TF:* 800-922-5512 ■ *Web:* isthmus.com	608-256-9071		671
AdMobilize LLC 1680 Michigan Ave Ste 736 ... Miami FL 33139 *TF:* 855-236-6245 ■ *Web:* www.admobilize.com	855-236-6245		387
ADMS (American Donkey & Mule Society) PO Box 1210 ... Lewisville TX 75067 *Web:* www.lovelongears.com	972-219-0781	420-9980	48-3
Adnet Adv Agency Inc 116 John St Fl 35 ... New York NY 10038 *Web:* www.adnet-nyc.com	212-587-3164		4
Adobe Associates Inc 1220 N Dutton Ave ... Santa Rosa CA 95401 *Web:* www.adobeinc.com	707-541-2300		261
Adobe Systems Inc 345 Pk Ave ... San Jose CA 95110 *NASDAQ:* ADBE ■ *TF:* 800-833-6687 ■ *Web:* www.adobe.com	408-536-6000	537-6000	178-8
Adobe Theater Inc 9813 Fourth St NW PO Box 276 ... Albuquerque NM 87114 *Web:* www.adobetheater.org	505-898-9222		572
Adobe Ventures LP 345 Park Ave ... San Jose CA 95110 *TF:* 877-722-7088 ■ *Web:* www.adobe.com	408-536-6000	537-6000	792
Adolfson & Peterson Construction Inc 6701 W 23rd St ... Minneapolis MN 55426 *TF:* 800-917-7182 ■ *Web:* www.a-p.com	952-544-1561	525-2333	186
Adolph Coors Foundation 215 Saint Paul St Ste 300 ... Denver CO 80206	303-388-1636		305
Adolphus, The 1321 Commerce St ... Dallas TX 75202 *Web:* www.adolphus.com	214-742-8200	651-3588	379
Adoption ARC Inc 4701 Pine St Ste J-7 ... Philadelphia PA 19143 *TF:* 800-884-4004 ■ *Web:* www.adoptionarc.com	215-748-1441	842-9881	48-6
Adoptive Families Magazine 108 W 39th St Ste 805 ... New York NY 10018 *TF:* 800-372-3300 ■ *Web:* www.adoptivefamilies.com	646-366-0830	366-0842	457-10
Adorama Camera Inc 42 W 18th St ... New York NY 10011 *TF:* 800-223-2500 ■ *Web:* www.adorama.com	212-741-0052	463-7223	119
Adorno-Denker Assoc Inc 4502 Broadway ... Long Island NY 11103	718-278-8660		390
ADP (Association of Directory Publishers) PO Box 209 ... Traverse City MI 49685 *TF:* 800-267-9002 ■ *Web:* www.adp.org	231-486-2182	486-2182	49-16
ADP (Automatic Data Processing Inc) 1 ADP Blvd ... Roseland NJ 07068 *NASDAQ:* ADP ■ *TF:* 800-225-5237 ■ *Web:* www.adp.com	800-225-5237		225
Adp Media Group LLC 7700 Camp Bowie W Blvd Ste B ... Fort Worth TX 76116 *TF:* 800-925-5700 ■ *Web:* www.adpmediagroup.com	817-244-2740		627
ADP Screening & Selection Services Inc 301 Remington St ... Fort Collins CO 80524 *Web:* www.adpselect.com	970-484-7722		260
ADP TotalSource Co 10200 Sunset Dr ... Miami FL 33173 *TF:* 800-447-3237 ■ *Web:* www.adp.com	305-630-1000		631
Adpay Inc 391 Inverness Pkwy Ste 300-B ... Englewood CO 80112 *Web:* www.adpay.com	303-268-1527		387
ADPEN Laboratories Inc 11757 Central Pkwy ... Jacksonville FL 32224 *Web:* www.adpen.com	904-645-9169		743

	City	State	ZIP	Phone	Fax	Class
ADPI (American Dairy Products Institute)						
116 N York St Ste 200	Elmhurst	IL	60126	630-530-8700	530-8707	49-6
Web: www.adpi.org						
Adprint International Inc						
6500 Greenbriar St	Houston	TX	77030	713-665-4578		7
TF: 800-438-7325 ■ *Web:* www.adprint.com						
Adpro International Advertising Co						
1144 Lincoln St	Brownsville	TX	78521	956-542-5800		532-2
ADRA (Adventist Development & Relief Agency)						
12501 Old Columbia Pk	Silver Spring	MD	20904	800-424-2372		48-5
TF: 800-424-2372 ■ *Web:* www.adra.org						
Adrenalin Inc 54 W 11th Ave	Denver	CO	80204	303-454-8888		344
TF: 888-757-5646 ■ *Web:* www.goadrenalin.com						
Adrenaline Family Entertainment Inc						
3325 French Park Dr Ste 6	Edmond	OK	73034	405-340-9111	340-9112	149
Adrian College 110 S Madison St	Adrian	MI	49221	517-265-5161	264-3331*	166
**Fax:* Admissions ■ *TF Admissions:* 800-877-2246 ■ *Web:* www.adrian.edu						
Adrian Dominican Sisters						
1257 E Siena Heights Dr	Adrian	MI	49221	517-266-3400		48-20
Adrian Fabricators Inc						
545 Industrial Dr	Adrian	MI	49221	517-266-5700		73
Web: adrian.cylex-usa.com						
Adrian L Merton Inc						
9011 E Hampton Dr	Capitol Heights	MD	20743	301-336-2700		189-10
Web: almertoninc.com						
Adrian Miller Direct Mktg						
43 Park Ave	Port Washington	NY	11050	516-767-9288		195
Web: adrianmiller.com						
Adriana's 771 Grand Ave	New Haven	CT	06511	203-865-6474		671
TF: 800-640-9365 ■ *Web:* adrianasnewhaven.com						
Adriance Memorial Library						
93 Market St	Poughkeepsie	NY	12601	845-485-3445		435
TF: 800-804-0092 ■ *Web:* www.poklib.org						
Adrianna Papell						
500 Seventh Ave 10th FL	New York	NY	10018	800-325-9450	714-1871*	155-21
**Fax Area Code:* 212 ■ *TF:* 800-325-9450 ■ *Web:* www.adriannapapell.com						
Adrienne Arsht Ctr for the Performing Arts of Miami-Dade County Inc						
1300 Biscayne Blvd	Miami	FL	33132	786-468-2000	468-2001	572
TF: 877-949-6722 ■ *Web:* www.arshtcenter.org						
Adrienne Electronics Corp						
7225 Bermuda Rd Unit G	Las Vegas	NV	89119	702-896-1858		647
Web: www.adrielec.com						
Adroit Investment Management Ltd						
12th Fl Canadian Western Bank Pl 10303 Jasper Ave	Edmonton	AB	T5J3N6	780-429-3500		401
Web: www.adroitinvestments.ca						
Adroit Medical Systems Inc						
1146 CaRding Machine Rd	Loudon	TN	37774	800-267-6077	267-6077	477
TF: 800-267-6077 ■ *Web:* www.adroitmedical.com						
Adroit Software Inc 23 Faulkner Rd	Shrewsbury	MA	01545	508-755-5252		180
Web: www.adroitgroup.com						
ADS Environmental Services						
4940 Research Dr	Huntsville	AL	35805	256-430-3366	430-6633	201
TF: 800-633-7246 ■ *Web:* www.adsenv.com						
ADS Machinery Corp 1201 Vine Ave NE	Warren	OH	44483	330-399-3601	399-1190	494
TF: 800-727-3321 ■ *Web:* www.adsmachinery.com						
ADS Media Group Inc						
15265 Capital Port Ste 100	San Antonio	TX	78249	210-655-6613		5
TF: 800-732-0330 ■ *Web:* www.adsmediagroup.com						
Ads Programming Services						
1 Independence Plaza Ste 820	Birmingham	AL	35209	205-803-2196		177
Web: www.adsprogramming.com						
ADS Security LP						
3001 Armory Dr Ste 100	Nashville	TN	37204	615-269-4448		692
TF: 800-448-5852 ■ *Web:* www.adssecurity.com						
ADS Tactical Inc						
Lynnwood Plaza 621 Lynnhaven Pkwy Ste 400	Virginia Beach	VA	23452	757-481-7758		449
TF: 800-948-9433 ■ *Web:* www.adsinc.com						
ADS/Transicoil 9 Iron Bridge Dr	Collegeville	PA	19426	484-902-1100	902-1150	518
TF: 800-323-7115 ■ *Web:* www.adstcoil.com						
ADSA (American Dairy Science Assn)						
1111 N Dunlap Ave	Savoy	IL	61874	217-356-5146	398-4119	48-2
TF: 888-670-2250 ■ *Web:* www.adsa.org						
ADS-B Technologies LLC						
900 Merrill Field Dr	Anchorage	AK	99501	907-258-2372		647
Web: www.ads-b.com						
Adserts Inc						
14750 W Capitol D Ste 200	Brookfield	WI	53005	262-794-9010		2
TF: 800-433-5778 ■ *Web:* adserts.com						
Adsoft Direct Inc 740 Tunbridge Rd	Danville	CA	94526	925-407-3101		463
TF: 800-438-7325 ■ *Web:* www.adsoftdirect.com						
Adsport Inc 389 E Palm Ln	Phoenix	AZ	85004	602-262-0500		7
Web: www.adsport.com						
AdStaff Media LLC						
4841 Summer Ave Ste 300	Memphis	TN	38122	901-271-6700		5
Web: adstaffmedia.com						
AdStar Inc						
4553 Glencoe Ave Ste 300	Marina del Rey	CA	90292	310-577-8255	577-8266	178-1
PINK: ADST						
Adstrategies Inc 101 Bay St Ste 201	Easton	MD	21601	410-822-2450		7
TF: 888-456-2450 ■ *Web:* www.adstrategies.com						
ADT Security Services Inc						
14200 E Exposition Ave	Aurora	CO	80012	800-246-9147		692
TF: 800-246-9147 ■ *Web:* www.adt.com						
Adtec Digital 408 Russell St	Nashville	TN	37206	615-256-6619		351
Web: www.adtecdigital.com						
Ad-tech Medical Instrument Inc						
1901 William St	Racine	WI	53404	262-634-1555		476
TF: 800-776-1555 ■ *Web:* www.adtechmedical.com						
Adtegrity Inc 408 Broadway NW	Grand Rapids	MI	49546	616-285-5429		5
Web: www.adtegrity.com						
AdTek Information Systems Inc						
500 Fifth Ave Ste 2110	New York	NY	10110	212-307-1115		180
Web: www.adtek.com						
ADTRAN Inc 901 Explorer Blvd	Huntsville	AL	35806	256-963-8000	963-8004	735
NASDAQ: ADTN ■ *TF:* 800-923-8726 ■ *Web:* www.adtran.com						
ADTRAV Travel Management						
4555 S Lake Pkwy	Birmingham	AL	35244	205-444-4800		771
TF: 800-476-2952 ■ *Web:* www.adtrav.com						
Adtron Inc 1700 Morrissey Dr	Bloomington	IL	61704	309-662-1221		5
Adult Children of Alcoholics World Service Organization Inc (ACAWSO)						
PO Box 3216	Torrance	CA	90510	562-595-7831		48-21
TF: 800-422-4453 ■ *Web:* www.adultchildren.org						
Advacare Systems 2939 N Pulaski Rd	Chicago	IL	60641	773-725-8858		475
TF: 800-427-5990 ■ *Web:* www.advacaresystems.com						
Advance America Cash Advance Centers Inc						
135 N Church St	Spartanburg	SC	29306	864-342-5600		141
NYSE: AEA ■ *TF:* 800-538-1579 ■ *Web:* www.advanceamerica.net						
Advance Auto Parts Inc						
5008 Airport Rd	Roanoke	VA	24012	877-238-2623		54
NYSE: AAP ■ *TF:* 877-238-2623 ■ *Web:* advanceautoparts.com						
Advance Automation Company Inc						
3526 N Elston Ave	Chicago	IL	60618	773-539-7633	539-7299	223
Web: www.advanceautomationco.com						
Advance Bag & Packaging Technologies						
5720 Williams Lake Rd	Waterford	MI	48329	248-674-3126	674-2630	600
TF: 800-475-2247 ■ *Web:* www.advancepac.com						
Advance Brands LLC 3540 S Blvd Ste 225	Edmond	OK	73013	405-562-1500		296-26
Web: www.advancedbrands.com						
Advance Building Maintenance						
9601 Wilshire Blvd Ste Gl25	Beverly Hills	CA	90210	310-247-0077		104
TF: 800-843-6243 ■ *Web:* www.advancemaintenance.com						
Advance Carbon Products Inc						
2036 National Ave	Hayward	CA	94545	510-293-5930	293-5939	127
TF: 800-283-1249 ■ *Web:* store.advancecarbon.com						
Advance Case Loans LLC						
205 W Wacker Dr Ste 901	Chicago	IL	60606	312-332-4100		41
Web: www.advancecaseloans.com						
Advance Central Services Inc						
1313 N Market St 10th Fl	Wilmington	DE	19001	302-830-9732		393
Advance Communications & Consulting Inc						
8803 Swigert Ct Unit A	Bakersfield	CA	93311	661-664-0177		196
TF: 800-510-2148 ■ *Web:* www.advancecomm.net						
Advance Corp Braille-Tac Div						
8200 97th St S	Cottage Grove	MN	55016	651-771-9297	771-2121	701
TF: 800-328-9451 ■ *Web:* www.advancecorp.com						
Advance Design Inc						
7100 E Vly Green Rd	Fort Washington	PA	19034	215-774-1000		5
Web: www.advancewebdesign.com						
Advance Die Casting Co						
3760 N Holton St	Milwaukee	WI	53212	414-964-0284		308
Web: www.advancediecasting.com						
Advance Digital Inc 185 Hudson St	Jersey City	NJ	07302	201-459-2888		7
Web: www.advancedigital.com						
Advance Electrical Supply Co						
263 N Oakley Blvd	Chicago	IL	60612	312-421-2300		246
Web: www.advanceelectrical.com						
Advance Energy Technologies Inc						
1 Solar Dr	Clifton Park	NY	12065	518-371-2140	371-0737	664
TF: 800-724-0198 ■ *Web:* www.advanceet.com						
Advance Engineering Co 7505 Baron Dr	Canton	MI	48187	313-537-3500		409
TF: 800-497-6388 ■ *Web:* www.adveng.net						
Advance Fiber Technologies Corp						
344 Lodi St	Hackensack	NJ	07601	201-488-2700		745-5
Advance Fire Protection Company Inc						
1451 W Lambert Rd	La Habra	CA	90631	562-691-0918		189-13
Web: firesprinkleradvisoryboard.org						
Advance Food Company Inc						
9987 Carver Rd Ste 500	Cincinnati	OH	45242	800-969-2747		299
TF: 800-969-2747 ■ *Web:* www.advancepierre.com						
Advance Graphics Equipment of York Inc						
4700 Raycom Rd	Dover	PA	17315	717-292-9183		629
Web: www.ageyork.com						
Advance Industrial Machine LLP						
W6335 Design Dr	Greenville	WI	54942	920-757-6786		757
Web: www.aim-msm.com						
Advance Insurance Company of Kansas						
1133 SW Topeka Blvd	Topeka	KS	66629	785-273-9804		391-2
TF: 800-530-5989 ■ *Web:* www.advanceinsurance.com						
Advance Lifts Inc 701 Kirk Rd	Saint Charles	IL	60174	630-584-9881	584-9405	470
TF: 800-843-3625 ■ *Web:* www.advancelifts.com						
Ad-vance Magnetics Inc						
625 Monroe St	Rochester	IN	46975	574-223-3158		295
Web: www.advancemag.com						
Advance Mechanical Contractors						
1301 E Burnett St	Signal Hill	CA	90755	562-268-5559		189-10
Web: advancemechanicalcontractors.com						
Advance Mechanical Systems Inc						
425 Algonquin Rd	Arlington Heights	IL	60005	847-593-2510		189-10
Web: www.jfahern.com						
Advance Mfg Company Inc						
8 Tpke Industrial Rd PO Box 726	Westfield	MA	01085	413-568-2411	568-6011	454
TF: 800-628-9648 ■ *Web:* www.advancemfg.com						
Advance Mold & Manufacturing Inc						
71 Utopia Rd	Manchester	CT	06042	860-432-5887		455
Web: www.advancemold.com						
Advance Notice Inc 24 Winter St	Peabody	MA	01960	978-531-6722		7
TF: 800-992-0313 ■ *Web:* www.advancenotice.com						
Advance Packaging Corp						
4459 40th St SE PO Box 888311	Grand Rapids	MI	49588	616-949-6610		100
Web: www.advancepkg.com						
Advance Paper Box Co						
6100 S Gramercy Pl	Los Angeles	CA	90047	323-750-2550	752-8133	101
TF: 800-419-6829 ■ *Web:* www.advancepaperbox.com						
Advance Petroleum Distributing Company Inc						
2451 Great SW Pkwy	Fort Worth	TX	76106	817-626-5458		579
Web: www.advancefuel.com						
Advance Printing & Graphics						
1349 Delashmut Ave	Columbus	OH	43212	614-299-9770		627
TF: 800-284-2377 ■ *Web:* www.advancecolumbus.com						
Advance Relocation & Storage Inc						
195 Sweet Hollow Rd	Old Bethpage	NY	11804	212-809-1988		393
TF: 800-448-4807 ■ *Web:* www.theadvancegrp.com						

Phone | Fax | Class

Advance Reproductions Corp
100 Flagship Dr....North Andover MA 01845 978-685-2911 685-1771 591
Web: www.advancerepro.com

Advance Research Chemicals Inc
1110 Keystone Ave....Catoosa OK 74015 918-266-6789 266-6796 143
Web: www.fluoridearc.com

Advance Reservations Inn Arizona
PO Box 950....Tempe AZ 85280 480-990-0682 990-3390 376
TF: 800-456-0682 ■ *Web:* www.azres.com

Advance Response LLC
4950 Hamilton Ave Ste 103....San Jose CA 95130 646-263-4214 393

Advance Scale of MD LLC
2400 Egg Harbor Rd....Lindenwold NJ 08021 856-627-0700 684
TF: 888-447-2253 ■ *Web:* advancescale.com

Advance Search Technical Staffing
950 Lee St Ste 205....Des Plaines IL 60016 847-706-9400 260
Web: www.advancesearch.com

Advance Tabco 200 Heartland Blvd....Edgewood NY 11717 631-242-4800 242-6900 300
TF: 800-645-3166 ■ *Web:* www.advancetabco.com

Ad-Vance Talent Solutions Inc
3911 Gulf Park Loop Ste 103....Bradenton FL 34203 941-739-8883 260
Web: ad-vance.com

Advance Tank & Construction Co
3700 E County Rd 64 PO Box 219....Wellington CO 80549 970-568-3444 568-3435 189-14
TF: 800-422-3488 ■ *Web:* www.advancetank.com

Advance Transportation Systems Inc
1125 Glendale Milford Rd....Cincinnati OH 45215 513-771-4848 311
TF: 800-878-4849 ■ *Web:* www.atslogistics.com

Advanced Alarm Systems Inc
101 Lindsey St....Fall River MA 02720 508-675-1937 693
TF: 800-442-5276 ■ *Web:* www.advancedalarmsystems.com

Advanced Analytical Consulting Group Inc
211 Congress St....Boston MA 02110 617-338-2224 194
Web: www.aacg.com

Advanced Animations PO Box 34....Stockbridge VT 05772 802-746-8974 746-8971 33
TF: 800-746-8974 ■ *Web:* www.advancedanimations.com

Advanced Auto Service & Tire Centers
1947 N Higley Rd....Mesa AZ 85205 480-985-5400 57
Web: advancedauto.com

Advanced Auto Trends 3485 Metamora Rd....Oxford MI 48371 248-628-4850 596
Web: www.advancedautotrends.com

Advanced Bionics LLC
28515 Westinghouse Pl....Valencia CA 91355 661-362-1400 362-1503 253
TF: 877-829-0026 ■ *Web:* www.advancedbionics.com

Advanced Biotechnologies Inc (ABI)
9108 Guilford Rd....Columbia MD 21046 410-792-9779 497-9773* 231
**Fax Area Code:* 301 ■ *TF:* 800-426-0764 ■ *Web:* www.abionline.com

Advanced Building & Components Inc
1541 County Rd 11....Mead NE 68041 402-624-2044 106

Advanced C4 Solutions Inc
4017 W Dr Martin Luther King Junior Blvd....Tampa FL 33614 813-282-3031 224
TF: 800-522-9226 ■ *Web:* www.ac4s.com

Advanced Cable Ties Inc
245 Suffolk Ln....Gardner MA 01440 978-630-3900 711
TF: 800-861-7228 ■ *Web:* www.advancedcableties.com

Advanced Cell Diagnostics Inc
3960 Point Eden Way....Hayward CA 94545 510-576-8800 668
TF: 877-576-3636 ■ *Web:* www.acdbio.com

Advanced Ceramics Mfg
7800 A S Nogales Hwy....Tucson AZ 85706 520-547-0850 22
Web: www.acmtucson.com

Advanced Chemistry Development Inc
110 Yonge St 14th Fl....Toronto ON M5C1T4 416-368-3435 177
TF: 800-304-3988 ■ *Web:* www.acdlabs.com

Advanced Circuits Inc
21101 E 32nd Pkwy....Aurora CO 80011 303-576-6610 224-3291* 625
**Fax Area Code:* 888 ■ *TF:* 800-979-4722 ■ *Web:* www.4pcb.com

Advanced Clinical Services LLC
10 Pkwy N Ste 350....Deerfield IL 60015 847-267-1176 174
TF: 800-264-1170 ■ *Web:* www.advancedclinical.com

Advanced Color Systems Inc
10350 SW Tualatin Rd....Tualatin OR 97062 503-612-9948 388

Advanced Components Technologies Inc
91 - 16th St S....Northwood IA 50459 641-324-2231 689

Advanced Computer Technologies LLC
101 Market Pl....Montgomery AL 36117 334-262-6882 177
Web: www.actinnovations.com

Advanced Computing Solutions Group Inc
19125 Northcreek Pkwy....Bothell WA 98011 425-609-3165 177
TF: 800-550-8007 ■ *Web:* www.acsgrp.com

Advanced Concrete Systems Inc
55 Advanced Ln....Middleburg PA 17842 570-837-3955 183
Web: www.yourbasement.com

Advanced Conversion Technology Inc
2001 Fulling Mill Rd....Middletown PA 17057 717-939-2300 767
Web: www.actpower.com

Advanced Data Systems Corp
15 Prospect St....Paramus NJ 07652 201-368-2001 180

Advanced Decorative Systems Inc
4705 Industrial Dr....Millington MI 48746 989-871-4550 247
Web: advanceddecorative.com

Advanced Defense Vehicle Systems
4590 Joslyn Rd....Lake Orion MI 48359 248-391-3200 59
Web: www.theadti.com

Advanced Design 5090 McDougall Dr SW....Atlanta GA 30336 404-699-1952 100
TF: 800-510-2523 ■ *Web:* www.stronghaven.com

Advanced Design Corp
9447B Lorton Market St....Lorton VA 22079 703-550-5510 261
Web: www.advdesign.com

Advanced Diagnostics Inc
2440 Cinnabar Loop....Anchorage AK 99507 907-344-3456 475
Web: www.adialaska.com

Advanced Digital Data Inc
6 Laurel Dr....Flanders NJ 07836 973-584-4026 584-3205 177
TF: 800-922-0972 ■ *Web:* www.addsys.com

Advanced Disposal Services Inc
90 Fort Wade Rd....Ponte Vedra Beach FL 32081 904-737-7900 360-3
Web: www.advanceddisposal.com

Advanced Distribution Systems Inc
105-107 Stonehurst Ct....Northvale NJ 07647 201-767-7350 231
Web: www.ads-outsource.com

Advanced Distributor Products LLC
2175 W Park Pl Blvd....Stone Mountain GA 30087 770-465-5560 5
Web: www.adpnow.com

Advanced Document Sciences Inc
PO Box 776049....Steamboat Springs CO 80477 970-875-0556 631
Web: www.adocs.com

Advanced Drainage Systems Inc
4640 Trueman Blvd....Hilliard OH 43026 800-821-6710 658-0204* 596
**Fax Area Code:* 614 ■ *TF:* 800-821-6710 ■ *Web:* www.ads-pipe.com

Advanced Dynamics Corp Ltd
1700 Marie Victorin....Saint-Bruno QC J3V6B9 450-653-7220 256
Web: www.advanceddynamics.com

Advanced Electronics
2601 Manhattan Beach Blvd....Redondo Beach CA 90278 310-725-0410 194
TF: 800-750-7234 ■ *Web:* www.advancedelectronics.com

Advanced Electronics Inc
721 Winston Dr....West Chicago IL 60185 630-293-3300 625
Web: www.advel.com

Advanced Energy Corp
909 Capability Dr Ste 2100....Raleigh NC 27606 919-857-9000 194
TF: 800-869-8001 ■ *Web:* www.advancedenergy.org

Advanced Energy Industries Inc
1625 Sharp Pt Dr....Fort Collins CO 80525 970-221-4670 221-5583 695
NASDAQ: AEIS ■ *TF:* 800-446-9167 ■ *Web:* www.advanced-energy.com

Advanced Engineering & Environmental Services Inc
2016 S Washington St....Grand Forks ND 58201 701-746-8087 261
Web: www.ae2s.com

Advanced Environmental Recycling Technologies Inc
914 N Jefferson St....Springdale AR 72764 479-756-7400 660
OTC: AERT ■ *Web:* aert.com

Advanced Equipment Corp
2401 W Commonwealth Ave....Fullerton CA 92833 714-635-5350 525-6083 286
TF: 800-826-3825 ■ *Web:* www.advancedequipment.com

Advanced Equities Financial Corp
311 S Wacker Dr Ste 1650....Chicago IL 60606 312-377-5300 691
Web: www.advancedequities.com

Advanced Fiberglass Technologies Inc
4400 Commerce Dr....Wisconsin Rapids WI 54494 715-421-2060 608
Web: www.ecccorrosion.com

Advanced Filtration Systems Inc
3206 Farber Dr....Champaign IL 61822 217-351-3073 454
Web: www.afsifilters.com

Advanced Focus 44 E 32nd St 4th Fl....New York NY 10016 212-217-2000 668
Web: www.advancedfocus.com

Advanced Forming Technology Inc
7040 Weld County Rd 20....Longmont CO 80504 303-833-6000 483
Web: aftmim.com

Advanced Generation Telecom Group Inc
752 Walker Rd Ste H....Great Falls VA 22066 703-757-6757 463
TF: 800-683-9847 ■ *Web:* www.adgentelecom.com

Advanced Glazings Ltd 870 King's Rd....Sydney NS B1P6R7 902-794-2899 330
TF: 800-626-3365 ■ *Web:* www.advancedglazings.com

Advanced Government Solutions Inc
2138 Priest Bridge CT Ste 4....Crofton MD 21114 240-260-4040 260-4039 261
Web: www.usgcinc.com

Advanced Green Components LLC
4005 Corporate Dr....Winchester KY 40391 859-737-6000 75
Web: www.advgreen.com

Advanced Health Media LLC (AHM)
420 Mountain Ave....New Providence NJ 07974 908-393-8700 393-8701 177
Web: www.ahmdirect.com

Advanced Heat Treat Corp
2825 MidPort Blvd....Waterloo IA 50703 319-232-5221 484
Web: ahtweb.com

Advanced Hydraulics Inc
13568 Vintage Pl....Chino CA 91710 909-590-7644 590-7049 456
TF: 888-581-8079 ■ *Web:* www.advancedhydraulicsinc.com

Advanced Image Direct
1415 S Acacia Ave....Fullerton CA 92831 714-502-3900 502-3901 459
TF: 800-540-3848 ■ *Web:* www.advancedimagedirect.com

Advanced Imaging Research Inc
4700 Lakeside Ave Ste 400....Cleveland OH 44114 216-426-1461 475
Web: www.advimg.com

Advanced Industrial Services Inc
3250 Susquehanna Trial....York PA 17406 717-764-9811 186
TF: 000-544-5000 ■ *Web:* www.ais-york.com

Advanced Information Systems Group Inc
11315 Corporate Blvd Ste 210....Orlando FL 32817 407-581-2929 581-2935 180
TF: 800-593-8359 ■ *Web:* www.aisg.com

Advanced Injection Molding LLC
4504 Macks Dr....Bossier City LA 71111 318-741-5540 596
Web: www.advancedinjectionmolding.com

Advanced Innovative Technologies LLC
530 Wilbanks Dr....Ball Ground GA 30107 770-479-1900 479-4179 744
TF: 800-222-3468 ■ *Web:* www.aitequipment.com

Advanced Insulation Concepts Inc
8055 Production Dr....Florence KY 41042 859-342-8550 14
Web: www.advancedinsulationconcepts.com

Advanced Integration LLC
4601 Hilton Corporate Dr....Columbus OH 43232 614-863-2433 350
Web: www.advint.com

Advanced Integration Technologies (AIT)
481 N Dean Ave....Chandler AZ 85226 480-940-0036 454

Advanced Laser Machining Inc
600 Cashman Dr....Chippewa Falls WI 54729 715-720-8093 492
Web: www.laser27.com

Advanced Laser Materials LLC
3115 Lucius Mccelvey....Temple TX 76504 254-773-3080 605-2
Web: www.alm-llc.com

Advanced Life Sciences Inc
1440 Davey Rd....Woodridge IL 60517 630-739-6744 739-6754 582
OTC: ADLS ■ *Web:* www.advancedlifesciences.com

Advanced Lifeline Services Pharmacy Inc
9900 Shelbyville Rd Ste 2b....Louisville KY 40223 502-423-7525 237
Web: www.alspharmacy.com

Company	Address	City	State	ZIP	Phone	Fax	Class	Details
Advanced Lighting Technologies Inc	7905 Cochran Rd Ste 300	Glenwillow	OH	44139	440-519-0500		437	*TF:* 888-440-2358 ■ *Web:* www.adlt.com
Advanced Logistics & Fulfillment LLC	8800 NE Underground Dr Pillar 252	Kansas City	MO	64161	816-452-0600		601	*Web:* advanced-logistics.net
Advanced Looseleaf Technologies Inc	1424 Somerset Ave	Dighton	MA	02715	508-669-6354	669-6143	86	*TF:* 800-339-6354 ■ *Web:* www.binder.com
Advanced Machine & Engineering Co	2500 Latham St	Rockford	IL	61103	815-962-6076	962-6483	493	*TF:* 800-225-4263 ■ *Web:* www.ame.com
Advanced Machine & Tool Corp	3706 Transportation Dr	Fort Wayne	IN	46818	260-489-3572		454	*Web:* www.amt-corp.com
Advanced Management Concepts	136 S Keowee St	Dayton	OH	45402	937-222-1024	222-5794	47	*Web:* www.advmgtconcepts.com
Advanced Manufacturing Technologies Inc	1090 Falls Rd	Grafton	WI	53024	262-375-4414		454	*Web:* www.amt-wi.com
Advanced Materials Partners Inc	45 Pine St	New Canaan	CT	06840	203-966-6415		401	*Web:* www.amplink.com
Advanced Mechanical Technology Inc	176 Waltham St	Watertown	MA	02472	617-926-6700		407	*Web:* www.amti.biz
Advanced Media Technologies Inc	3150 SW 15th St	Deerfield Beach	FL	33442	954-427-5711		647	*Web:* www.goamt.com
Advanced Medical Analysis LLC	1941 Walker Ave	Monrovia	CA	91016	626-357-8999		415	
Advanced Medical Equipment Inc	2655 S Dixie Dr	Kettering	OH	45409	937-534-1080		475	*Web:* www.advancedmedequipment.com
Advanced Medical Systems	820 Bear Tavern Rd	Ewing	NJ	08628	609-882-6889		41	*Web:* www.advmedsys.com
Advanced Medical Technology Assn	701 Pennsylvania Ave NW Ste 800	Washington	DC	20004	202-783-8700	783-8750	49-4	*Web:* www.advamed.org
Advanced Metal Components Inc	720 Empire Expy	Swainsboro	GA	30401	478-237-8994		483	*Web:* www.amcinc.net
Advanced Metals Machining LLC	1159 Midvalley Dr	Olyphant	PA	18447	570-487-2830		567	*Web:* www.advancedmetalsmachining.com
Advanced Micro Devices Inc (AMD)	1 AMD Pl PO Box 3453	Sunnyvale	CA	94088	408-749-4000		696	*NYSE: AMD* ■ *TF:* 800-538-8450 ■ *Web:* www.amd.com
Advanced Microsensors Inc	333 S St Bldg 2	Shrewsbury	MA	01545	508-770-6600		696	*Web:* www.advancedmicrosensors.com
Advanced Modern Technologies Corp	19000 Nordhoff Pl	Chatsworth	CA	91311	818-883-2082		612	*Web:* www.amtcorporation.com
Advanced Motors & Drives Inc	6268 E Molloy Rd	East Syracuse	NY	13057	315-434-9303		518	
Advanced MP Technology	1010 Calle Sombra	San Clemente	CA	92673	949-492-3113	492-9589	246	*TF:* 800-492-3113 ■ *Web:* www.advancedmp.com
Advanced Optical Systems Inc	6767 Old Madison Pike Ste 410	Huntsville	AL	35806	256-971-0036		237	*TF:* 888-800-7248 ■ *Web:* www.aos-inc.com
Advanced Orthomolecular Research Inc	3900 - 12 St NE	Calgary	AB	T2E8H9	403-250-9997		345	*TF:* 800-387-0177 ■ *Web:* www.aor.ca
Advanced Orthopro Inc	1820 N Illinois St	Indianapolis	IN	46202	317-924-4444		477	*TF:* 800-649-5998 ■ *Web:* www.advancedorthopro.com
Advanced Ozone Engineering Inc	6038 Oakwood Ave	Cincinnati	OH	45224	513-681-3871		83	
Advanced Paper Forming	541 W Rincon St	Corona	CA	92878	951-738-1800		548	*Web:* www.advancedpaper.com
Advanced Payroll Solutions LLC	201 W Passaic St Ste 202A	Rochelle Park	NJ	07662	201-587-0320		2	*Web:* www.advpayrollsolutions.com
Advanced Pension Solutions Inc	6830 Commerce Court Dr	Blacklick	OH	43004	614-501-7790	501-9860	528	
Advanced Pharmacy Concepts Inc	6899 Post Rd	North Kingstown	RI	02852	401-295-7660		237	*Web:* www.apc-rx.com
Advanced Photographic Solutions	1525 Hardeman Ln	Cleveland	TN	37312	423-479-5481		588	*TF:* 800-241-9234 ■ *Web:* www.advancedphoto.com
Advanced Plastiform Inc	535 Mack Todd Rd	Zebulon	NC	27597	919-404-2080		596	*Web:* www.advancedplastiform.com
Advanced Poly Packaging Inc	1331 Emmitt Rd	Akron	OH	44306	330-785-4000		557	*TF:* 800-754-4403 ■ *Web:* www.advancedpoly.com
Advanced Polymer Technology Corp	109 Conica Ln	Harmony	PA	16037	724-452-1330		601	*Web:* www.advpolytech.com
Advanced Polymers Inc	400 Paterson Plank Rd	Carlstadt	NJ	07072	201-933-0600		146	*Web:* www.advpolymer.com
Advanced Polymers International	3584 Walters Rd	Syracuse	NY	13209	315-451-1755		3	*Web:* www.geltac.com
Advanced Power & Controls LLC	605 E Alton Ave Ste A	Santa Ana	CA	92705	714-540-9010	540-5313	518	*TF:* 800-275-6312 ■ *Web:* www.advancedpowercontrols.com
Advanced Practice Strategies Inc	470 Atlantic Ave 14th Fl	Boston	MA	02210	617-275-7300		41	*Web:* www.aps-web.com
Advanced Precision Manufacturing Inc	2301 Estes Ave	Elk Grove Village	IL	60007	847-981-9800		454	*Web:* www.apmi.us
Advanced Pressure Systems LP	701 S Persimmon St Ste 85	Tomball	TX	77375	281-290-9950		641	*Web:* www.advancedpressuresystems.com
Advanced Probing Systems Inc	2300 Central Ave	Boulder	CO	80301	303-939-9384		594	*TF:* 800-631-0005 ■ *Web:* www.advancedprobing.com
Advanced Process Technologies Inc	150 Swendra Blvd	Cokato	MN	55321	320-286-5060		298	*Web:* www.apt-inc.com
Advanced Radiology PA	7253 Ambassador Rd	Baltimore	MD	21244	443-436-1100		415	*Web:* www.advancedradiology.com
Advanced Recovery Service	5434 King Ave Ste 200	Pennsauken	NJ	08109	856-488-8860		194	*Web:* www.advancedrecoveryservice.com
Advanced Resource Technologies Inc	1555 King St Ste 400	Alexandria	VA	22314	703-682-4740	682-4820	180	*Web:* www.team-arti.com
Advanced Resources & Construction Enterprises Inc	27 Commercial Rd	Kingfield	ME	04947	207-265-2646		480	*Web:* www.arcsystems.com
Advanced Rotorcraft Technology Inc	1330 Charleston Rd	Mountain View	CA	94043	650-968-1464		256	*Web:* www.flightlab.com
Advanced Sciences & Technologies LLC	20 E Taunton	Berlin	NJ	08009	856-719-9001		261	*Web:* adv-sci-tech.com
Advanced Scientific Concepts Inc	135 E Ortega St	Santa Barbara	CA	93101	805-966-3331		466	*TF:* 800-849-2517 ■ *Web:* www.advancedscientificconcepts.com
Advanced Sealing & Supply Co	13452 Alondra Blvd	Cerritos	CA	90703	562-802-7782		326	*Web:* www.advseal.com
Advanced Sign Co	2024 Fifth St NW	Albuquerque	NM	87102	505-246-8458		8	*Web:* www.advancedsignco.com
Advanced Solar Products Inc	270 S Main St Ste 203	Flemington	NJ	08822	908-751-5818		612	*TF:* 800-903-6130 ■ *Web:* www.advancedsolarproducts.com
Advanced Solutions International Inc	901 N Pitt St Ste 200	Alexandria	VA	22314	703-739-3100	739-3218	177	*Web:* www.advsol.com
Advanced Specialty Products	428 Clough St	Bowling Green	OH	43402	419-354-2844		358	*Web:* www.aspohio.com
Advanced Sterilization Products (ASP)	33 Technology Dr	Irvine	CA	92618	888-783-7723		477	*TF:* 888-783-7723 ■ *Web:* www.aspjj.com
Advanced Support Products Inc	20820 FM 2854 Rd	Montgomery	TX	77375	936-597-4731	597-2483	492	*TF:* 800-941-5737 ■ *Web:* www.aspbase.com
Advanced Systems Consultants Inc	4074 E Patterson Rd	Dayton	OH	45430	937-429-1428		177	*Web:* ascsoftware.com
Advanced Systems Integrators	45 Craig Dr Apt 4S	West Springfield	MA	01108	413-230-5010		201	*Web:* www.asiopen.com
Advanced Technology & Research Corp	6650 Eli Whitney Dr	Columbia	MD	21046	443-766-7888		261	*Web:* www.atrcorp.com
Advanced Technology Co	2858 E Walnut St	Pasadena	CA	91107	626-449-2696		22	*TF:* 800-447-2442 ■ *Web:* www.at-co.com
Advanced Technology for Large Structural Systems Ctr (ATLSS)	117 ATLSS Dr	Bethlehem	PA	18015	610-758-3525	758-5902	668	*Web:* www.atlss.lehigh.edu
Advanced Technology Inc	6106 W Market St	Greensboro	NC	27409	336-668-0488		492	
Advanced Technology Products Inc	12740 State Rt 4	Milford Center	OH	43045	937-349-4055		370	*Web:* atp4pneumatics.com
Advanced Technology Ventures	500 Boylston St Ste 1380	Boston	MA	02116	617-850-9700		792	*TF:* 800-792-2473 ■ *Web:* www.atvcapital.com
Advanced Technology Ventures	2884 Saind Hill Rd Ste 121	Menlo Park	CA	94025	650-321-8601	321-0934	792	*Web:* www.atvcapital.com
Advanced Telecom Services Inc	1150 First Ave Ste 105	King of Prussia	PA	19406	610-688-6000		736	*Web:* www.atsmobile.com
Advanced Testing Technologies Inc	110 Ricefield Ln	Hauppauge	NY	11788	631-231-8777		256	
Advanced Textile Composites	700 E Parker St	Scranton	PA	18509	570-207-7000	207-7070	745-7	*Web:* www.advtextile.com
Advanced Thermal Sciences Corp	3355 E La Palma Ave	Anaheim	CA	92806	714-688-4200		504	*Web:* www.atschiller.com
Advanced Trim Specialties Inc	4966 Lincoln Hwy E	Kinzers	PA	17535	717-442-8098		499	*Web:* www.atsbuild.com
Advanced Tubing Technology Inc	150 Intercraft Dr	Statesville	NC	28625	704-924-7020		595	*Web:* www.tubularproducts.com
Advanced Vacuum Company Inc	1215 Business Pkwy N	Westminster	MD	21157	410-876-8200		406	*TF:* 800-272-2525 ■ *Web:* www.advaco.com
Advanced Vessel & Alloy Inc	5420 Perimeter Rd	Valdosta	GA	31601	229-249-9370		480	*Web:* www.advancedvessel.com
Advanced Vision Research Inc	660 Main St	Woburn	MA	01801	781-932-8327		231	*Web:* www.theratears.com
Advanced Visual Systems Inc (AVS)	300 Fifth Ave	Waltham	MA	02451	781-890-4300	890-8287	178-5	*OTC: AVSC* ■ *Web:* www.avs.com
Advanced Waterjet Technologies	1035 Progress Dr	Fergus Falls	MN	56537	218-736-4611		697	*Web:* www.awjt.com

Phone | Fax | Class

Advanced Web Offset Inc
2260 Oak Ridge Way.......... Vista CA 92081 760-727-1700 174
Web: www.awoink.com
Advancedware Corp
13844 Alton Pkwy Ste 136.......... Irvine CA 92618 949-609-1240 177
Web: advancedware.com
Advancement LLC 32200 Solon Rd.......... Solon OH 44139 440-248-8550 194
TF: 866-364-3370 ■ *Web:* www.advancementllc.com
AdvancePath Academics Inc
4125 Ironbound Rd Ste 201.......... Williamsburg VA 23188 757-208-0900 242
Web: www.advancepath.com
Advansoft International Inc
415 W Golf Rd Ste 55.......... Arlington Heights IL 60005 847-952-0000 225
Web: www.adso.com
Advanta Medical Solutions LLC
10830 Guilford Rd Ste 312.......... Annapolis Junction MD 20701 240-554-1200 215
Web: www.advantamedicalsolutions.com
Advantage Business Media
100 Enterprise Dr Ste 600 PO Box 912.......... Rockaway NJ 07866 973-920-7000 920-7542* 637-9
**Fax:* Hum Res ■ *Web:* advantagemedia.com
Advantage Capital Partners
190 Carondelet Plaza Ste 1500.......... St Louis MO 63105 314-725-0800 792
Web: www.advantagecap.com
Advantage Consulting Inc
7611 Little River Tpke Ste 204 W.......... Annandale VA 22003 703-642-5153 194
Web: www.acibiz.com
Advantage Credit Inc
32065 Castle Ct Ste 300.......... Evergreen CO 80439 303-670-7993 218
TF: 800-670-7993 ■ *Web:* www.advcredit.com
Advantage Electronic Product Development
34 Garden Ctr.......... Broomfield CO 80020 303-410-0292 696
TF: 866-841-5581 ■ *Web:* www.advantage-dev.com
Advantage Engineering Inc
525 E S- 18 Rd.......... Greenwood IN 46142 317-887-0729 881-1277 14
Web: www.advantageengineering.com
Advantage Engineering LLC
910 Century Dr.......... Mechanicsburg PA 17055 717-458-0800 458-0801 256
Advantage Fund Raising Consulting Inc
208 Passaic Ave.......... Fairfield NJ 07004 973-575-9196 317
Web: sos.wa.gov
Advantage Funding Corp
1000 Parkwood Cir SE.......... Atlanta GA 30339 770-955-2274 272
TF: 800-241-2274 ■ *Web:* www.advantagefunding.com
Advantage Futures LLC
231 S Lasalle St Ste 1400.......... Chicago IL 60604 312-800-7000 169
Web: advantagefutures.com
Advantage Home Health Care Inc
4008 N Wheeling Ave.......... Muncie IN 47304 765-284-1211 363
TF: 800-884-5088 ■ *Web:* www.advantagehhc.com
Advantage Learning Solutions Inc
160-9521 Franklin Ave.......... Fort Mcmurray AB T9H3Z7 780-743-5001 449
Web: www.advantagels.ca
Advantage Limousine Services Inc
8310 Castleford St Ste 200.......... Houston TX 77040 713-983-9991 983-9959 441
Web: www.advantagelimos.com
Advantage Manufacturing Inc
616 S Santa Fe St.......... Santa Ana CA 92705 714-505-1166 518
Web: www.advantageman.com
Advantage Metals Recycling LLC
3005 Manchester Trfy.......... Kansas City MO 64129 816-861-2700 861-7670 686
TF: 866-527-4733 ■ *Web:* www.advantagerecycling.com
Advantage Mktg Inc 14 W Main St.......... Ashland OH 44805 419-281-4762 96
TF: 800-670-7479 ■ *Web:* www.advantagemkt.com
Advantage Mortgage Group Inc, The
5343 N 16th St Ste 135.......... Phoenix AZ 85016 602-953-6500 509
Web: www.tamg.biz
Advantage One Tax Consulting Inc
20610 Quarterpath Trace Cir.......... Sterling VA 20165 703-584-5533 734
Web: www.aotax.com
Advantage Payroll Services Inc
126 Merrow Rd PO Box 1330.......... Auburn ME 04211 207-784-0178 786-0490 570
TF Cust Svc: 800-876-0178 ■ *Web:* www.advantagepayroll.com
Advantage Performance Group Inc
700 Larkspur Landing Cir.......... Larkspur CA 94939 415-925-6832 925-9512 194
TF: 800-494-6646 ■ *Web:* www.advantageperformance.com
Advantage Plastics & Engineering Inc
4524 Bishop Ln.......... Louisville KY 40218 502-473-7331 256
Web: www.advantageplastics.net
Advantage Rent-A-Car
1288 Old Bayshore Hwy.......... Burlingame CA 94010 800-777-5500 126
TF Cust Svc: 800-777-5500 ■ *Web:* www.advantage.com
Advantage Resourcing 220 Norwood Pk S.......... Norwood MA 02062 781-251-8000 721
TF: 800-343-4314 ■ *Web:* www.advantageresourcing.com
Advantage RN LLC 8892 Beckett Rd.......... West Chester OH 45069 866-301-4045 260
TF: 866-301-4045 ■ *Web:* www.advantagern.com
Advantage Sci LLC
222 N Sepulveda Blvd Ste 1780.......... El Segundo CA 90245 310-536-9876 193
Web: www.advantagesci.com
Advantage Sign & Graphic Solutions
4182 Royal Ct.......... Hudsonville MI 49426 616-554-3300 896-7236 701
TF: 800-251-0929 ■ *Web:* advantagesgs.com
Advantage Title Agency Inc
201 Old Country Rd Ste 200.......... Melville NY 11747 631-424-6100 391-6
Web: www.advantagegroupny.com
Advantage Truck Accessories Inc
5400 S State Rd.......... Ann Arbor MI 48108 800-773-3110 227-8899* 61
**Fax Area Code:* 877 ■ *TF:* 800-773-3110 ■ *Web:* www.advantagetruckaccessories.com
Advantagene Inc 440 Lexington St.......... Auburndale MA 02466 617-916-5445 668
Web: www.advantagene.com
AdvantageWare Inc
425 Madison Ave Ste 1700.......... New York NY 10017-1155 212-319-1903 319-1016 809
Web: www.advantageware.com
Advantec MFS Inc 6723 Sierra Ct Ste A.......... Dublin CA 94568 925-479-0625 479-0630 18
TF: 800-334-7132 ■ *Web:* www.advantecmfs.com
Advantech Corp 380 Fairview Way.......... Milpitas CA 95035 408-519-3898 519-3899 175
TF: 888-576-9668 ■ *Web:* www.advantech.com
AdvanTech Inc 2661 Riva Rd Ste 1030.......... Annapolis MD 21401 410-266-8000 177
Web: www.advantech-inc.com

Advantech Manufacturing Inc
2450 S Commerce Dr.......... New Berlin WI 53151 262-786-1600 463
TF: 800-511-2096 ■ *Web:* www.advantechmfg.com
AdVantis Hospitality Alliance LLC
615 N Highland Ste 2A.......... Murfreesboro TN 37130 615-904-6133 707
TF: 866-218-4782 ■ *Web:* www.vistarez.com
Advantis Medical Inc
2121 Southtech Dr Ste 600.......... Greenwood IN 46143 317-859-2300 225
Web: www.advantismedical.com
Advantix Solutions Group
1202 Richardson Dr Ste 200.......... Richardson TX 75080 866-238-2684 387
TF: 866-238-2684 ■ *Web:* www.advantixsolutions.com
Advantor Systems Corp
12612 Challenger Pkwy Ste 300.......... Orlando FL 32826 407-859-3350 523-1921* 692
**Fax Area Code:* 800 ■ **Fax:* Sales ■ *TF:* 800-238-2686 ■ *Web:* www.advantor.com
Advatech Pacific Inc
10230 S 50th Pl Ste 150.......... Tempe AZ 85044 480-598-4005 598-6767 647
Web: www.advatechpacific.com
Advenir Real Estate
17501 Biscayne Blvd.......... Aventura FL 33160 305-948-3535 652
Web: advenir.net
Advent Capital Management LLC
1065 Ave of the Americas 31st Fl.......... New York NY 10018 212-482-1600 480-9655 401
TF: 888-523-8368 ■ *Web:* www.adventcap.com
Advent Design Corp
Canal St & Jefferson Ave.......... Bristol PA 19007 215-781-0500 781-0508 386
Web: adventdesign.com
Advent Electric Inc
301 E Fourth St.......... Bridgeport PA 19405 610-277-6610 358
Web: www.advent-elect.com
Advent Global Solutions Inc
12777 Jones Rd Ste 445.......... Houston TX 77070 832-678-3889 180
Web: www.adventglobal.com
Advent Industries LLC
17901 Mt Savage Rd NW.......... Frostburg MD 21532 301-689-1788 751
Web: www.firebricks.com
Advent International Corp 75 State St.......... Boston MA 02109 617-951-9400 792
Web: www.adventinternational.com
Advent Security Corp 101 Roesch Ave.......... Oreland PA 19075 215-576-7111 693
Web: www.adventsecurity.com
Advent Software Inc
600 Townsend St Ste 500 5th Fl.......... San Francisco CA 94103 415-543-7696 543-5070 178-1
NASDAQ: ADVS ■ *TF:* 800-727-0605 ■ *Web:* www.advent.com
Adventace 2166 Chardonnay Cir.......... Gibsonia PA 15044 724-443-2383 196
Web: www.adventacesms.com
Adventist Behavioral Health
14901 Broschart Rd.......... Rockville MD 20850 301-251-4500 315-3000 374-5
TF: 800-204-8600
Adventist Community Services
12501 Old Columbia Pk.......... Silver Spring MD 20904 301-680-6438 680-6125 48-5
TF: 877-227-2702 ■ *Web:* www.communityservices.org
Adventist Development & Relief Agency (ADRA)
12501 Old Columbia Pk.......... Silver Spring MD 20904 800-424-2372 48-5
TF: 800-424-2372 ■ *Web:* www.adra.org
Adventist Health 2100 Douglas Blvd.......... Roseville CA 95661 916-781-2000 353
TF: 877-336-3566 ■ *Web:* www.adventisthealth.org
Adventist Health Lodi Memorial
975 S Fairmont Ave.......... Lodi CA 95240 209-334-3411 274-0634 374-3
TF: 800-323-3360 ■ *Web:* www.lodihealth.org
Adventist HealthCare Shady Grove Medical Center
9901 Medical Ctr Dr.......... Rockville MD 20850 240-826-6000 374-3
Adventist Hinsdale Hospital
120 N Oak St.......... Hinsdale IL 60521 630-856-9000 374-3
Web: www.amitahealth.org
Adventist La Grange Memorial Hospital (ALMH)
5101 S Willow Springs Rd.......... La Grange IL 60525 708-245-9000 374-3
Web: www.keepingyouwell.com/facilities/lagrange
Adventist Media Center Inc
101 W Cochran St.......... Simi Valley CA 93065 805-955-7777 5
TF: 800-253-3002 ■ *Web:* www.adventistmediacenter.com
Adventist Medical Ctr
10123 SE Market St.......... Portland OR 97216 503-257-2500 374-3
Web: www.adventisthealth.org/nw/pages/default.aspx
Adventium Llc 320 E 35th St Apt 5b.......... New York NY 10016 212-481-9576 193
Web: www.adventium.net
Adventive Mktg Inc
417 S Arlington Heights Rd.......... Arlington Heights IL 60005 847-590-1110 194
Web: www.adventivemarketing.com
Adventure 16 Inc
4620 Alvarado Canyon Rd.......... San Diego CA 92120 619-283-2362 711
Web: www.adventure16.com
Adventure Alaska Tours Inc PO Box 64.......... Hope AK 99605 907-782-3730 782-3725 760
TF: 800-365-7057 ■ *Web:* www.adventurealaskatours.com
Adventure Aquarium One Riverside Dr.......... Camden NJ 08103 856-365-3300 365-3311 40
TF: 800-616-5297 ■ *Web:* www.adventureaquarium.com
Adventure Connection PO Box 475.......... Coloma CA 95613 530-626-7385 626-9268 760
TF: 800-556-6060 ■ *Web:* www.raftcalifornia.com
Adventure Cycling Assn
150 E Pine St PO Box 8308.......... Missoula MT 59807 406-721-1776 721-8754 48-22
TF: 800-755-2453 ■ *Web:* www.adventurecycling.org
Adventure Guild L L C, The
888 Highpoint Dr.......... Dunlap TN 37327 423-266-5709 148
Web: www.theadventureguild.com
Adventure Landing 3311 Capital Blvd.......... Raleigh NC 27604 919-872-1688 872-3408 32
Web: www.adventurelanding.com
Adventure Life South America
712 W Spruce St Ste 1.......... Missoula MT 59802 406-541-2677 541-2676 760
TF: 800-344-6118 ■ *Web:* www.adventure-life.com
Adventure Medical Kits LLC
7700 Edgewater Dr Ste 526.......... Oakland CA 94624 510-261-7414 878-2049 475
Web: www.adventuremedicalkits.com
Ad-venture Promotions LLC
2625 Regency Rd.......... Lexington KY 40503 859-263-4299 129
TF: 800-218-5488 ■ *Web:* www.ad-venturepromotions.com
Adventure Quest Laser Tag
1200 S Clearview Pkwy Ste 1106.......... New Orleans LA 70123 504-207-4444 226
Web: www.lasertagnola.com

	Phone	Fax	Class
Adventure Science Ctr 800 Ft Negley Blvd........................Nashville TN 37203 *Web:* www.adventuresci.org	615-862-5160	862-5178	520
Adventuredome 2880 Las Vegas Blvd S........Las Vegas NV 89109 *TF:* 866-456-8894 ■ *Web:* www.circuscircus.com/en/adventuredome.html	702-691-5861	794-3906	32
Adventureland Inn 305 34th Ave NW..........Altoona IA 50009 *TF:* 800-910-5382 ■ *Web:* www.adventurelandpark.com	515-265-7321	265-3506	379
Adventureland Park 305 34th Ave NW..........Altoona IA 50009 *TF:* 800-532-1286 ■ *Web:* www.adventurelandpark.com	515-266-2121	266-9831	32
Adventures Out West 1680 S 21st St....................Colorado Springs CO 80904 *TF:* 800-755-0935 ■ *Web:* www.advoutwest.com	800-755-0935		760
Adventures Unlimited Press 1 Adventure Pl............................Kempton IL 60946 *TF:* 800-718-4514 ■ *Web:* www.adventuresunlimitedpress.com	815-253-6390		690
Advertical Media LLC 14 Palm Harbor Village Way................Palm Coast FL 32137 *Web:* www.adverticalmedia.com	386-986-1600		5
Advertising Age 685 Third Ave................New York NY 10017 *Web:* www.adage.com	212-210-0100		532-3
Advertising Council Inc 815 Second Ave 9th Fl.....................New York NY 10016 *TF:* 888-200-4005 ■ *Web:* www.adcouncil.org	212-922-1500	922-1676	49-18
Advertising Premium Sales Inc 11675 Lilburn Park Rd...................Saint Louis MO 63146 *Web:* apspromos.com	314-872-7000		4
Advertising Research Foundation (ARF) 432 Park Ave S...........................New York NY 10016 *Web:* thearf.org	212-751-5656	689-1859	49-18
Advertising Specialties Institute 4800 Street Rd............................Trevose PA 19053 *TF:* 800-546-1350 ■ *Web:* www.asicentral.com	215-942-8600	953-3045	637-9
Advex Corp 121 Floyd Thompson Dr...........Hampton VA 23666 *Web:* www.advex.net	757-865-0920		295
Advice Media LLC PO Box 982064...............Park City UT 84098 *TF:* 800-260-9497 ■ *Web:* advicemedia.com	800-260-9497		631
Advics Manufacturing Ohio Inc 1650 Kingsview Dr.........................Lebanon OH 45036 *Web:* www.advics-ohio.com	513-932-7878		247
Advion BioSciences Inc 19 Brown Rd............Ithaca NY 14850 *TF:* 877-523-8466 ■ *Web:* www.advion.com	607-266-0665	266-0749	668
Adviso Consulting Inc 909 Mont-Royal E.........................Montreal QC H2J1X3 *TF:* 888-598-1881 ■ *Web:* www.adviso.ca	514-598-1881		5
Advisor & Source Newspapers 48075 Van Dyke Ave.................Shelby Township MI 48317 *TF:* 888-373-7888 ■ *Web:* www.sourcenewspapers.com	586-731-1000		532-4
Advisor Group Inc, The 3000 Mcknight E Dr......................Pittsburgh PA 15237 *Web:* www.theadvisorgroup.com	412-931-3900		652
Advisor Media Inc 4849 Viewridge Ave.......................San Diego CA 92123	858-278-5600		637-9
Advisor Today 2901 Telestar Ct............Falls Church VA 22042 *TF:* 877-866-2432 ■ *Web:* www.advisortoday.com	703-770-8267		457-5
Advisornet Financial Inc 701 Fourth Ave S Ste 1500................Minneapolis MN 55415 *Web:* advisornet.com	612-347-8600		390
Advisors Excel LLC 1300 SW Arrowhead Rd Ste 200..............Topeka KS 66604 *TF:* 866-363-9595 ■ *Web:* www.advisorsexcel.com	866-363-9595		195
Advisory Board Co, The 2445 M St NW..........................Washington DC 20037 *NASDAQ:* ABCO ■ *Web:* www.advisory.com	202-266-5600		194
Advisory Council Inc, The 1 Stiles Rd Ste 105..........................Salem NH 03079 *Web:* www.tacadvisory.com	781-791-9582		463
Advisory Council on Historic Preservation 401 F St NW Ste 308....................Washington DC 20001 *Web:* www.achp.gov	202-606-8503	606-8647	340-20
Advisory Research Holdings Inc 180 N Stetson Ave Ste 5500 180 North Stetson Avenue............Chicago IL 60601 *Web:* www.advisoryresearch.com	312-565-1414		401
Advocacy Center for Persons With Disabilities 2728 Centerview Dr Ste 102................Tallahassee FL 32301 *TF:* 800-342-0823 ■ *Web:* www.disabilityrightsflorida.org	850-488-9071		428
Advocacy Solutions LLC 4 Richmond Sq Ste 300...................Providence RI 02906 *Web:* advocacysolutionsllc.com	401-831-3700		636
Advocal 1000 Q St.......................Sacramento CA 95811 *TF:* 800-446-9121 ■ *Web:* www.advocal.com	916-446-6161		636
Advocare International LP 2801 Summit Ave.............................Plano TX 75074	972-665-5800		366
Advocate BroMenn Medical Ctr (ABMC) 1304 Franklin Ave..........................Normal IL 61761 *Web:* www.advocatehealth.com/bromenn/default.cfm?id=1	309-454-1400		374-3
Advocate Christ Medical Ctr 4440 W 95th St...........................Oak Lawn IL 60453 *TF:* 800-323-8622 ■ *Web:* www.advocatehealth.com	708-684-8000		374-3
Advocate Condell Medical Ctr (ACMC) 801 S Milwaukee Ave......................Libertyville IL 60048 *Web:* www.advocatehealth.com/condell	847-362-2900	362-1721	374-3
Advocate Good Samaritan Hospital 3815 Highland Ave..................Downers Grove IL 60515 *Web:* www.advocatehealth.com	630-275-5900		374-3
Advocate Good Shepherd Hospital (AGSH) 450 W Hwy 22............................Barrington IL 60010 *TF:* 800-775-4784 ■ *Web:* www.advocatehealth.com/gshp	847-381-9600		374-3
Advocate Hospice 1441 Branding Ave Ste 200...........Downers Grove IL 60515 *TF:* 800-564-2025 ■ *Web:* www.advocatehealth.com	630-963-6800	963-6877	371
Advocate Illinois Masonic Medical Ctr 836 W Wellington Ave......................Chicago IL 60657 *Web:* www.advocatehealth.com	773-975-1600		374-3
Advocate Lutheran General Hospital 1775 W Dempster St.....................Park Ridge IL 60068 *Web:* www.advocatehealth.com	847-723-2210		374-3
Advocate Magazine 525 W Jefferson St PO Box 895..................Boise ID 83702 *Web:* www.isb.idaho.gov	208-334-4500	334-4515	457-15
Advocate Media Inc 181 Brown's Point Rd........................Pictou NS B0K1H0 *TF:* 800-236-9526 ■ *Web:* www.advocatemediainc.com	902-485-1990		539
Advocate Sherman Hospital 1425 N Randall Rd............................Elgin IL 60123 *TF:* 800-397-9000 ■ *Web:* www.advocatehealth.com/sherman	847-742-9800		374-3
Advocate South Suburban Hospital (SSUB) 17800 S Kedzie Ave.....................Hazel Crest IL 60429 *Web:* www.advocatehealth.com/ssub	708-799-8000		374-3
Advocate Trinity Hospital 2320 E 93rd St..............................Chicago IL 60617 *Web:* www.advocatehealth.com/trin	773-967-2000		374-3
Advocate, The 7290 Blue Bonnet Blvd...................Baton Rouge LA 70810 *TF:* 800-960-6397 ■ *Web:* theadvocate.com	225-383-1111	388-0371	532-2
Advocate, The 22 N First St.....................Newark OH 43055 *TF:* 877-424-0208 ■ *Web:* www.newarkadvocate.com	740-345-4053	328-8581	532-2
Advocates for Highway & Auto Safety 750 First St NE Ste 901.................Washington DC 20002 *TF:* 877-366-0711 ■ *Web:* www.saferoads.org	202-408-1711	408-1699	48-10
Advocates for Self-Government 1010 N Tennessee St Ste 215..............Cartersville GA 30120 *TF:* 800-932-1776 ■ *Web:* theadvocates.org	770-386-8372		48-7
Advus Capital Group 16 E 34th St 15th Fl......................New York NY 10016 *Web:* www.advus.com	352-281-7509		194
Adwerks Inc 512 N Main Ave.................Sioux Falls SD 57104 *Web:* www.adwerks.com	605-357-3690		7
Adwerx Inc 307 W Main St......................Durham NC 27701 *TF:* 888-746-5678 ■ *Web:* www.adwerx.com	888-746-5678		5
Adx Computer Services Inc 315 Arden Ave Ste 2........................Glendale CA 91203 *Web:* www.adxusa.com	818-244-1121		175
Adxstudio Inc 200 - 1445 Park St..............Regina SK S4N4C5 *TF:* 800-508-7811 ■ *Web:* www.adxstudio.com	306-569-6500		225
Adynxx Inc 731 Market St Ste 420..........San Francisco CA 94103 *Web:* www.adynxx.com	415-512-7740		231
Adz Etc Inc N88w16749 Main St Ste 3............Menomonee Falls WI 53051 *Web:* www.adzetc.com	262-502-0507		7
Adzzup 2600 N Central Ave Ste 1700............Phoenix AZ 85004 *TF:* 888-723-9987 ■ *Web:* adzzup.com	888-723-9987		5
AE (Association Enterprise Inc) 1601 N Bond St Ste 303....................Naperville IL 60563 *Web:* incentivemarketing.org	630-369-7786	369-3773	47
AE Petsche Company Inc 1501 Nolan Ryan Expy.......................Arlington TX 76011 *TF:* 844-237-7600 ■ *Web:* www.aepetsche.com	844-237-7600		246
AE Stone Inc 1435 Doughty Rd...............Egg Harbor Township NJ 08234 *Web:* www.aestone.com	609-641-2781		46
A&E Television Networks LLC 235 E 45th St...........................New York NY 10017 *Web:* www.aenetworks.com	212-210-1400	210-1308	740
AE Works Ltd 6587 Hamilton Ave............Pittsburgh PA 15206 *Web:* www.ae-works.com	412-287-7333		256
AEA (American Economic Assn) 2014 Broadway Ste 305....................Nashville TN 37203 *Web:* www.aeaweb.org	615-322-2595	343-7590	49-2
AEA Advocate Magazine 345 E Palm Ln........Phoenix AZ 85004 *TF:* 800-352-5411 ■ *Web:* www.arizonaea.org	602-264-1774	240-6887	457-8
AEA Investors Inc 666 Fifth Ave 36th Fl......................New York NY 10103 *Web:* www.aeainvestors.com	212-644-5900	888-1459	405
Aearo Technologies LLC 5457 W 79th St.........................Indianapolis IN 46268 *TF:* 877-327-4332 ■ *Web:* earglobal.com	877-327-4332		576
AEB (American Egg Board) 8755 W Higgins Rd Ste 300....................Chicago IL 60631 *TF:* 888-549-2140 ■ *Web:* www.aeb.org	847-296-7043	296-7007	48-2
AEB (American Exchange Bank) 510 W Main St PO Box 818...................Henryetta OK 74437 *TF:* 888-652-3321 ■ *Web:* www.americanexchange.bank	918-652-3321	652-7057	70
AEB International Inc 654 Madison Ave Ste 1009...................New York NY 10065 *Web:* aebint.com	212-752-4647		492
AEC (Aluminum Extruders Council) 1000 N Rand Rd Ste 214....................Wauconda IL 60084 *Web:* www.aec.org	847-526-2010	526-3993	49-13
AEC (Applied Energy Company Inc) 1205 Venture Ct Ste 100.....................Carrollton TX 75006 *TF:* 800-580-1171 ■ *Web:* www.appliedenergyco.com	214-355-4200	355-4201	640
AEC Repro 44 W 39th St......................New York NY 10018 *Web:* www.aecrepro.com	928-774-8787		344
AECOM Technology Corp 555 S Flower St 37th Fl...................Los Angeles CA 90071 *Web:* www.aecom.com	213-593-8000	593-8730	261
Aecometric Corp 374 Ohio Rd...........Richmond Hill ON L4C2Z9 *Web:* aecometric.com	905-883-9555		261
Aecon Buildings Inc 19020 33rd Ave W Ste 500..................Lynnwood WA 98036 *Web:* www.aecon.com	425-774-2945		186
Aecon Group Inc 20 Carlson Ct Ste 800..........Toronto ON M9W7K6 *Web:* www.aecon.com	416-293-7004		186
AED (Alpha Epsilon Delta) 2955 S University Dr PO Box 298810 Winton-Scott 213........................Fort Worth TX 76129 *Web:* aednational.tcu.edu	817-257-4550	257-0201	48-16
AED (Academy for Educational Development) 1825 Connecticut Ave NW Ste 800...........Washington DC 20009 *Web:* www.fhi360.org	202-884-8000	884-8400	48-11
AED (Associated Equipment Distributors) 650 E Algonquin Rd Ste 305...............Schaumburg IL 60173 *TF:* 800-388-0650 ■ *Web:* www.aednet.org	630-574-0650	574-0132	49-18
AED Inc 6525 Belcrest Rd Ste 526............Hyattsville MD 20782 *Web:* www.aedworld.com	301-683-2112		463

Phone | Fax | Class

AEDC Public Affairs
100 Kindell Dr Ste B-213 ... Arnold AFB TN 37389 931-454-5655 454-6720* 743
*Fax: Hum Res ■ Web: www.arnold.af.mil

Aedes De Venustas Inc
7 Greenwich Ave ... New York NY 10014 212-206-8674 77
TF: 888-233-3715 ■ Web: aedes.com

AEE (Association of Energy Engineers)
4025 Pleasantdale Rd Ste 420 ... Atlanta GA 30340 770-447-5083 446-3969 48-12
TF: 877-407-0784 ■ Web: www.aeecenter.org

AEFK (Athletes & Entertainers for Kids)
14340 Bolsa Chica Rd Unit C ... Westminster CA 92683 562-438-5905 48-6

Aegera Therapeutics Inc
810 ch Du Golf ... Montreal QC H3E1A8 514-288-5532 288-9280 668

Aegir Systems
2151 Alessandro Dr Ste 211 ... Ventura CA 93001 805-648-2660 256
Web: www.aegir.com

Aegis Asset Management Inc
2331 W Lincoln Ave ... Anaheim CA 92801 714-635-9900 401

Aegis Assisted Living
17602 NE Union Hill Rd ... Redmond WA 98052 425-861-9993 451
TF: 888-252-3447 ■ Web: www.aegisliving.com

Aegis Communications Group Inc
8201 Ridgepoint Dr ... Irving TX 75063 972-830-1800 737
Web: www.aegisglobal.com

Aegis Film Group Inc
7510 Sunset Blvd Ste 275 ... Los Angeles CA 90046 323-848-7977 116
Web: www.aegisfilmgroup.com

Aegis Group 41451 W 11 Mile Rd ... Novi MI 48375 248-344-1450 193
TF: 800-816-6710 ■ Web: www.aegis-group.com

Aegis Power Systems Inc
805 Greenlawn Rd ... Murphy NC 28906 828-837-4029 729
Web: www.aegispower.com

Aegis Sales & Engineering Inc
5411 Industrial Rd ... Fort Wayne IN 46825 260-483-4160 757
Web: www.aegisparts.com

Aegis Sciences Corporation
515 Great Cir Rd ... Nashville TN 37228 800-533-7052 256
TF: 800-533-7052 ■ Web: www.aegislabs.com

Aegis Security Insurance Co
4507 N Front St Ste 200 ... Harrisburg PA 17110-1787 717-657-9671 657-0340 391-4
TF: 800-233-2160 ■ Web: www.aegisfirst.com

AEGIS Systems Engineering and Technology Partners Corp
1000 W Braddock Rd ... Alexandria VA 22302 571-297-1916 463
TF: 800-677-0814 ■ Web: www.asetpartners.com

Aegis Technologies Group Inc, The
410 Jan Davis Dr ... Huntsville AL 35806 256-922-0802 261
Web: aegistg.com

Aegis Technology Inc
12630 G Westminster Ave ... Santa Ana CA 92706 714-265-1238 261
Web: www.aegistech.net

AEHI Inc 14586 Central Ave ... Chino CA 91710 909-606-6998 606-6885 350
Web: www.aehiinc.com

Aehr Test Systems 400 Kato Terr ... Fremont CA 94539 510-623-9400 623-9450 695
NASDAQ: AEHR ■ TF: 800-962-4284 ■ Web: www.aehr.com

AEI (Affiliated Engineers Inc)
5802 Research Pk Blvd ... Madison WI 53719 608-238-2616 238-2614 261
Web: www.aeieng.com

AEI (American Enterprise Institute for Public Policy Research)
1150 17th St NW ... Washington DC 20036 202-862-5800 862-7177 634
TF: 800-862-5801 ■ Web: www.aei.org

AEI Speakers Bureau
214 Lincoln St Ste 113 ... Allston MA 02134 617-782-3111 708
TF: 800-447-7325 ■ Web: aeispeakers.com

AEL Financial LLC
600 N Buffalo Grove Rd ... Buffalo Grove IL 60089 847-465-2009 401
Web: aelfinancial.com

AELE (Americans for Effective Law Enforcement)
841 W Touhy Ave ... Park Ridge IL 60068 847-685-0700 685-9700 48-8
TF: 800-763-2802 ■ Web: www.aele.org

AELI (Agape English Language Institute)
1600 Park Cir Unit 116 ... Columbia SC 29201 803-445-1998 252-5500 423
Web: www.aeliusa.com

AEM (Association of Equipment Manufacturers)
6737 W Washington St Ste 2400 ... Milwaukee WI 53214 414-272-0943 272-1170 49-13
TF: 866-236-0442 ■ Web: www.aem.org

AEM Inc 6610 Cobra Way ... San Diego CA 92121 858-481-0210 253
Web: www.aem-usa.com

Aeneas Communications LLC
300 N Cumberland St Ste 200 ... Jackson TN 38301 731-554-9200 387
Web: www.aeneas.com

Aeolus Pharmaceuticals Inc
26361 Crown Valley Pkwy Ste 150 ... Mission Viejo CA 92691 949-481-9825 85
TF: 800-732-0330 ■ Web: www.aeoluspharma.com

Aeon Nexus Corp 174 Glen St ... Glens Falls NY 12801 518-338-1551 177
TF: 866-252-1251 ■ Web: www.aeonnexus.com

AEP (Association of Emergency Physicians)
911 Whitewater Dr ... Mars PA 16046 724-772-1818 49-8

AEP Industries Inc
125 Phillips Ave ... South Hackensack NJ 07606 201-641-6600 600
NASDAQ: AEPI ■ TF: 800-999-2374 ■ Web: www.aepinc.com

AEP Networks Inc
347 Elizabeth Ave Ste 100 ... Somerset NJ 08873 732-764-8858 178-12

AEP River Operations
16150 Main Cir Dr Ste 400 ... Chesterfield MO 63017 636-530-2100 530-4100 465

AEPhi (Alpha Epsilon Phi Sorority)
11 Lake Ave Ext Ste 1-A ... Danbury CT 06811 203-748-0029 748-0039 48-16
TF: 888-668-4293 ■ Web: www.aephi.org

Aeplog Inc 12800 Middle Brook Rd ... Germantown MD 20874 301-528-2800 261

Aequor Technologies Inc
377 Hoes Ln ... Piscataway NJ 08854 732-494-4999 177
Web: www.aequor.com

Aer Lingus 300 Jericho Quad Ste 130 ... Jericho NY 11753 516-622-4226 26
Web: www.aerlingus.com

Aer Mfg Inc PO Box 979 ... Carrollton TX 75011 972-417-2582 60
TF: 800-753-5237 ■ Web: www.aermanufacturing.com

AERA (American Educational Research Assn)
1430 K St NW Ste 1200 ... Washington DC 20005 202-238-3200 238-3250 49-5
TF: 800-893-7950 ■ Web: www.aera.net

Phone | Fax | Class

AERA (Automotive Engine Rebuilders Assn)
500 Coventry Ln Ste 180 ... Crystal Lake IL 60014 847-541-6550 541-5808 49-21
TF: 888-326-2372 ■ Web: www.aera.org

Aera Energy LLC 10000 Ming Ave ... Bakersfield CA 93311 661-665-5000 540
TF: 800-247-5977 ■ Web: www.aeraenergy.com

Aeration Industries International Inc
4100 Peavey Rd ... Chaska MN 55318 952-448-6789 427
Web: www.aireo2.com

Aerco International Inc
159 Paris Ave ... Northvale NJ 07647 201-768-2400 784-8073 357
TF: 800-526-0288 ■ Web: www.aerco.com

Aereon Corp 20 Nassau St Ste 223 ... Princeton NJ 08542 609-921-2131 22
Web: www.aereon.com

Aerex Industries Inc
3504 Industrial 27th St ... Ft Pierce FL 34946 772-461-0004 492
Web: www.aerexglobal.com

Aerial BioPharma LLC
9001 Aerial Ctr Pkwy Aerial Ctr Executive Pk
Ste 110 ... Morrisville NC 27560 919-460-9500 231
Web: www.aerialbio.com

Aerial Innovations Inc 3703 W Azeele St ... Tampa FL 33609 813-254-7339 196
TF: 800-223-1701 ■ Web: www.flythis.com

Aerial Photography Services Inc (APS)
2511 S Tryon St ... Charlotte NC 28203 704-333-5143 333-4911 328
Web: www.aps-1.com

Aerial Rigging & Leasing Inc
2940 Drane Field Rd ... Lakeland FL 33811 863-607-9100 358
TF: 800-821-5218 ■ Web: www.aerialrigging.com

Aerie Art Garden 71225 Aerie Rd ... Palm Desert CA 92260 760-568-6366 50-2

Aerie Inc 139 S Guild Ave Ste 101 ... Lodi CA 95240 209-339-9751 186
TF: 800-561-3357 ■ Web: www.aerieinc.com

Aerion Rental Services
1088 Hwy 65 N ... Greenbrier AR 72058 501-335-7165 23
Web: aerion.com

Aeris
2350 Mission College Blvd Ste 600 ... Santa Clara CA 95054 408-557-1993 387
Web: www.aeris.com

Aermotor Pumps Inc 293 Wright St ... Delavan WI 53115 800-230-1816 230-1816 641
TF: 800-230-1816 ■ Web: www.aermotor.com

Aero Air LLC 2050 NE 25th Ave ... Hillsboro OR 97124 503-640-3711 681-6514 13
TF: 800-448-2376 ■ Web: www.aeroair.com

Aero ALL-GAS Company Inc, The
3150 Main St ... Hartford CT 06120 860-278-2376 316
TF: 800-255-4277 ■ Web: www.allgas.com

Aero Automatic Sprinkler Co
21605 N Central Ave ... Phoenix AZ 85024 623-580-7800 610
Web: www.aerofire.com

Aero Business Group 151 S Whittier ... Wichita KS 67207 316-689-4272 454
Web: theaerogroup.com

Aero Components Inc
5124 Kaltenbrun Rd ... Fort Worth TX 76119 817-572-3003 350
Web: www.aero-components.com

Aero Controls Inc 1610 20th St NW ... Auburn WA 98001 253-269-3000 22
Web: www.aerocontrols.com

Aero Energy 230 Lincoln Way E ... New Oxford PA 17350 717-624-4311 610
Web: www.aeroenergy.com

Aero Engineering & Manufacturing Co
28217 Avenue Crocker ... Valencia CA 91355 661-295-0875 22
Web: aeroeng.com

Aero Fab 1600 W 41st St ... Baltimore MD 21211 410-467-9762 454
Web: www.netzermetalcraftinc.com

Aero Fulfillment Services Corp
3900 Aero Dr ... Mason OH 45040 513-459-3900 88
Web: www.aerofulfillment.com

Aero Gear Inc 1050 Day Hill Rd ... Windsor CT 06095 860-688-0888 285-8514 22
Web: www.aerogear.com

Aero Graphics Inc
40 W Oakland Ave ... Salt Lake City UT 84115 801-487-3273 592
TF: 800-604-2871 ■ Web: www.aero-graphics.com

Aero Grinding Inc
28300 Groesbeck Hwy ... Roseville MI 48066 586-774-6450 358
Web: aerogrinding.com

Aero Hardware & Parts Company Inc
130 Business Pk Dr ... Armonk NY 10504 914-273-8550 273-8612 770
Web: www.aerohardwareparts.com

Aero Industries Inc
4243 W Bradbury Ave ... Indianapolis IN 46241 317-244-2433 244-1311 733
TF Sales: 800-535-9545 ■ Web: www.aeroindustries.com

Aero Industries Inc
5745 Huntsman Rd
Richmond International Airport ... Richmond VA 23250 804-226-7200 236-1670 63
TF: 800-845-1308 ■ Web: www.aeroind.com

Aero Instruments & Avionics Inc
7290 Nash Rd ... North Tonawanda NY 14120 716 694 7060 22
Web: www.aeroinst.com

Aero Kool Corp 1495 SE Tenth Ave ... Hialeah FL 33010 305-887-6912 790
Web: www.aerokool.com

Aero Manufacturing Company Inc
310 Allwood Rd ... Clifton NJ 07012 973-473-5300 427
Web: www.aeromfg.com

Aero manufacturing Corp
100 Sam Fonzo Dr ... Beverly MA 01915 978-720-1000 21
Web: www.aeromanufacturing.com

Aero Mechanical Industries Inc
4901 Rockaway Blvd ... Rio Rancho NM 87124 505-896-2644 22
Web: www.aero-mechanical.net

Aero Metals Inc 1201 E Lincoln Way ... La Porte IN 46350 219-326-1976 326-1972 306
TF: 800-289-7528 ■ Web: www.aerometals.com

Aero Parts Mfg & Repair Inc
431 Rio Rancho Blvd NE ... Rio Rancho NM 87124 505-891-6600 891-6650 22
Web: www.aeroparts.aero

Aero Plastics Inc 91 Citation Dr ... Concord ON L4K2Y8 905-738-9010 738-9175 601
TF: 877-660-2376 ■ Web: www.aeroplastics.ca

Aero Products Component Services Inc
551 N 40th St ... Show Low AZ 85901 928-537-1000 770
Web: www.aeroproducts.com

Aero Rubber Company Inc
8100 W 185th St ... Tinley Park IL 60487 800-662-1009 662-4400 370
TF: 800-662-1009 ■ Web: www.aerorubber.com

Company / Address	City	State	ZIP	Phone	Fax	Class
Aero Seating Technologies LLC 5079 Walnut Grove Ave *Web:* www.aeroseating.com	San Gabriel	CA	91776	626-286-1130		22
Aero Tec Labs Inc 45 Spear Rd Industrial Pk *TF:* 800-526-5330 ■ *Web:* www.atlinc.com	Ramsey	NJ	07446	201-825-1400	825-1962	676
Aero Tech Designs Cycling Apparel 1132 Fourth Ave *TF:* 800-783-8326 ■ *Web:* www.aerotechdesigns.com	Coraopolis	PA	15108	412-262-3255		711
Aero Tech Manufacturing Inc 395 W 1100 N *Web:* www.aerotechmfg.com	North Salt Lake	UT	84054	801-292-0493		697
Aero Trades Manufacturing Corp 65 Jericho Tpke *Web:* www.aerotrades.com	Mineola	NY	11501	516-746-3360	746-3417	697
Aero Twin Inc 2403 Merrill Field Dr *Web:* www.aerotwin.com	Anchorage	AK	99501	907-274-6166	274-4285	24
Aerobics & Fitness Assn of America (AFAA) 1750 E Northrop Blvd Ste 200 *TF:* 800-446-2322 ■ *Web:* www.afaa.com	Chandler	AZ	91403	818-905-0040		48-22
Aerobiology Laboratory Associates Inc 43760 Trade Center Pl Ste 100 *Web:* www.aerobiology.net	Dulles	VA	20166	703-648-9150		416
AeroCare Holdings Inc 3325 Bartlett Blvd *Web:* www.aerocareusa.com	Orlando	FL	32811	407-206-0040		360-3
AeroCentury Corp 1440 Chapin Ave Ste 310 *NYSE: ACY* ■ *Web:* www.aerocentury.com	Burlingame	CA	94010	650-340-1888	696-3929	23
Aerocon Engineering Co 7716 Kester Ave *Web:* www.aeroconengineering.com	Van Nuys	CA	91405	818-785-2743		256
AeroControlex Group 313 Gillett St *Web:* www.aerocontrolex.com	Painesville	OH	44077	440-352-6182	354-2912	201
Aerocraft Heat Treating Co Inc 15701 Minnesota Ave *TF:* 800-949-7187 ■ *Web:* www.aerocraft-ht.com	Paramount	CA	90723	562-674-2400	633-0364	484
Aero-craft Hydraulics Inc 392 N Smith Ave *Web:* www.aero-craft.com	Corona	CA	92880	951-736-4690		790
Aerodirect Inc 860 Chaddick Dr Bldg A *Web:* www.aerodirect.com	Wheeling	IL	60090	847-325-4971		770
Aerodynamics Inc 114 Townpark Dr Ste 500 *Web:* www.flyadi.com	Kennesaw	GA	30144	404-410-7612		63
Aerodyne Alloys LLC 350 Pleasant Valley Rd *TF:* 800-243-4344 ■ *Web:* www.aerodynealloys.com	South Windsor	CT	06074	860-289-6011	289-2841	487
Aerodyne Research Inc 45 Manning Rd *Web:* www.aerodyne.com	Billerica	MA	01821	978-663-9500	663-4918	668
Aerofin Corp 4621 Murray Pl PO Box 10819 **Fax:* Sales ■ *TF:* 800-237-6346 ■ *Web:* www.aerofin.com	Lynchburg	VA	24506	434-845-7081	528-6242*	91
Aerofit Inc 1425 S Acacia Ave *Web:* www.aerofit.com	Fullerton	CA	92831	714-521-5060		22
Aeroflex Inc 35 S Service Rd PO Box 6022 *TSE: ARX* ■ *TF:* 800-843-1553 ■ *Web:* www.aeroflex.com	Plainview	NY	11803	516-694-6700	694-0658	696
Aeroflex RAD Inc 5017 N 30th St *Web:* ams.aeroflex.com	Colorado Springs	CO	80919	719-531-0800		180
Aeroflex USA Inc 282 Industrial Park Dr *Web:* www.aeroflexusa.com	Sweetwater	TN	37874	423-337-2493		370
Aeroflot Russian International Airlines 10 Rockefeller Plaza Ste 1015 *TF:* 866-879-7647 ■ *Web:* www.aeroflot.com	New York	NY	10020	212-944-2300		25
Aeroflow Inc 3165 Sweeten Creek Rd *TF:* 888-345-1780 ■ *Web:* www.aeroflowinc.com	Asheville	NC	28803	888-345-1780		475
Aeroglide Corp 100 Aeroglide Dr *TF:* 800-722-7483 ■ *Web:* www.buhlergroup.com	Cary	NC	27511	919-851-2000	851-6029	386
AeroInfo Systems Inc 200 -13575 Commerce Pkwy *Web:* www.aeroinfo.com	Richmond	BC	V6V2L1	604-232-4200		809
Aerojet PO Box 13222 *TF:* 800-637-7200 ■ *Web:* www.rocket.com	Sacramento	CA	95813	916-355-4000	351-8667	504
Aerojet Redmond Rocket Ctr 11411 139th Pl NE **Fax:* Mail Rm ■ *Web:* www.rocket.com	Redmond	WA	98052	425-885-5000	882-5804*	504
Aerojet Rocketdyne Holdings Inc 222 N Sepulveda Blvd *NYSE: GY* ■ *Web:* www.aerojetrocketdyne.com	El Segundo	CA	90245	310-252-8100		185
Aerojet Rocketdyne Inc 2001 Aerojet Rd *Web:* www.rocket.com	Rancho Cordova	CA	95742	916-355-4000		454
Aerolite Extrusion Company Inc 4605 Lake Park Rd *Web:* www.aeroext.com	Youngstown	OH	44512	330-782-1127		361
Aero-mach Laboratories Inc 7707 E Funston St *Web:* www.aeromach.com	Wichita	KS	67207	316-682-7707		22
Aeroman 139 SW 51st Terr	Cape Coral	FL	33914	239-540-0040		57
Aeromedevac Inc 681 Kenney St *Web:* www.aeromedevac.com	El Cajon	CA	92020	619-284-7910		463
Aeromedixcom LLC Po Box 14730 *TF:* 888-362-7123 ■ *Web:* www.aeromedix.com	Jackson	WY	83002	307-732-2642		459
Aeromet Industries Inc 739 S Arbogast St *TF:* 800-899-7442 ■ *Web:* www.aerometindustries.com	Griffith	IN	46319	219-924-7442		757
Aeromix Systems Inc 7135 Madison Ave W *Web:* www.aeromix.com	Golden Valley	MN	55427	763-746-8400		640
Aeromotive Inc 7805 Barton St *Web:* www.aeromotiveinc.com	Lenexa	KS	66214	913-647-7300		54
Aeronautical Accessories Inc 423 Century Ct *Web:* www.aero-access.com	Piney Flats	TN	37686	423-538-5151		20
Aeronautical Systems Inc 43671 Trade Ctr Pl Ste 100 *TF:* 800-800-2477 ■ *Web:* www.aeronautical.com	Sterling	VA	20166	703-996-8090		770
Aeronet Worldwide 42 Corporate Pk *TF:* 800-552-3869 ■ *Web:* www.aeronet.com	Irvine	CA	92606	949-474-3000		12
Aero-News Network 6001 Argyle Forest Blvd Ste 21-252 *Web:* www.aero-news.net	Jacksonville	FL	32244	863-299-8680		530
Aeronix Inc 1775 W Hibiscus Blvd Ste 200 *Web:* www.aeronix.com	Melbourne	FL	32901	321-984-1671		668
Aeropost International Services Inc 6703 NW Seventh St Ste 4567 *Web:* www.aeropost.com	Miami	FL	33126	305-592-5534		311
Aeropostale Inc 112 W 34th St Ste 22 *NYSE: ARO* ■ *Web:* www.aeropostale.com	New York	NY	10120	646-485-5410		157-5
Aeroprobe Corp 200 Technology Dr *Web:* www.aeroprobe.com	Blacksburg	VA	24073	540-443-9215	443-6525	529
AeroSat Corp 62 Rt 101A Ste 2B *Web:* www.aerosat.com	Amherst	NH	03031	603-879-0205		647
Aerosmith Aviation 321 Corporate Rd *Web:* www.aerosmithaviation.com	Longview	TX	75603	903-643-0898		63
Aerosoles Inc 201 Meadow Rd *TF:* 800-798-9478 ■ *Web:* www.aerosoles.com	Edison	NJ	08817	732-985-6900		301
AeroSolutions Group Inc 10681 Frank Marshall Ln *TF:* 800-532-0141 ■ *Web:* www.aerosolutions.com	Manassas	VA	20110	703-257-7008		770
Aerospace & Commercial Technologies Inc 970 Fm 2871 *Web:* www.aero-com-tech.com	Fort Worth	TX	76126	817-560-6600		21
Aerospace Alloys Inc 11 Britton Dr *Web:* aalloys.com	Bloomfield	CT	06002	860-882-0019		492
Aerospace America Inc 900 Harry Truman Pkwy *TF:* 800-237-6414 ■ *Web:* www.aerospaceamerica.com	Bay City	MI	48706	989-684-2121	684-4486	480
Aerospace America Magazine 1801 Alexander Bell Dr Ste 500 *TF:* 800-639-2422 ■ *Web:* www.aiaa.org	Reston	VA	20191	703-264-7500	264-7551	457-21
Aerospace Coatings International Inc 370 Knight Dr *Web:* www.aerocoatings.com	Oxford	AL	36203	256-241-2750		22
Aerospace Corp, The 2310 E El Segundo Blvd PO Box 92957 *Web:* www.aerospace.org	Los Angeles	CA	90009	310-336-5000	336-7055	668
Aerospace Dynamics International Inc 25540 Rye Canyon Rd	Valencia	CA	91355	661-257-3535		22
Aerospace Engineering & Support Inc 1307 W 2550 S *Web:* aesut.com	Ogden	UT	84401	801-394-9565		120
Aerospace Fabrications of Georgia Inc 305 Butler Industrial Dr *TF:* 800-255-0056 ■ *Web:* www.afog.com	Dallas	GA	30132	770-505-8801		697
Aerospace Industries Assn of America (AIA) 1000 Wilson Blvd Ste 1700 *TF:* 877-229-7555 ■ *Web:* www.aia-aerospace.org	Arlington	VA	22209	703-358-1000	358-1011	49-21
Aerospace Maintenance Solutions LLC 8759 Mayfield Rd *Web:* aerospacellc.com	Chesterland	OH	44026	440-729-7703		359
Aerospace Manufacturing Technologies Inc 20100 71st Ave NE *Web:* www.amtnw.com	Arlington	WA	98223	360-435-1119		454
Aerospace Medical Assn (AMA) 320 S Henry St *Web:* www.asma.org	Alexandria	VA	22314	703-739-2240	739-9652	49-8
Aerospace Museum of California 3200 Freedom Pk Dr *Web:* www.aerospaceca.org	McClellan	CA	95652	916-643-3192		520
Aerospace Products International (API) 3778 Distriplex Dr N *TF:* 888-274-2497 ■ *Web:* www.apiworldwide.com	Memphis	TN	38118	901-365-3470		22
Aero-Space Southwest Inc 21450 N Third Ave *TF:* 800-289-2779 ■ *Web:* www.aerospacesw.com	Phoenix	AZ	85027	623-582-2779		351
Aerospace Techniques Inc 1100 Country Club Rd *TF:* 800-208-8201 ■ *Web:* www.aerospacetechniques.com	Middletown	CT	06457	860-347-1200		454
Aerospace Technologies Group Inc 620 NW 35th St *Web:* www.atgshades.com	Boca Raton	FL	33431	561-244-7400		20
Aerospec Inc 505 E Alamo Dr *TF:* 888-854-2376 ■ *Web:* www.aerospecinc.com	Chandler	AZ	85225	480-892-7195		256
Aerospike Inc 2525 E Charleston Rd Ste 201 *Web:* www.aerospike.com	Mountain View	CA	94043	408-462-2376		387
Aerostar Aerospace Manufacturing Inc 2688 E Rose Garden Ln *TF:* 800-642-1572 ■ *Web:* www.aerostaraerospace.com	Phoenix	AZ	85050	602-861-1145		757
Aerotec International Inc 3007 E Chambers St *Web:* www.aerotecinternational.com	Phoenix	AZ	85040	602-253-4540		21
Aerotech Inc 101 Zeta Dr *Web:* www.aerotech.com	Pittsburgh	PA	15238	412-967-6440	967-6870	518
Aerotech Laboratories Inc 1501 W Knudsen Dr *Web:* www.emlab.com	Phoenix	AZ	85027	623-780-4800		743
Aerotech Mapping Inc 2580 Montessouri St *Web:* www.atmlv.com	Las Vegas	NV	89117	702-228-6277		727
Aerotek Inc 7301 Pkwy Dr *TF:* 888-237-6835 ■ *Web:* www.aerotek.com	Hanover	MD	21076	410-694-5100		721
Aerotron AirPower Inc 456 Aerotron Pkwy *Web:* www.aerotron.com	Lagrange	GA	30240	706-812-1700		21
Aerotronics Marketing Inc 5331 Derry Ave Ste O *Web:* www.aerotronics.net	Agoura Hills	CA	91301	818-735-6633		195
Aerovent Inc 5959 Trenton Ln *Web:* www.aerovent.com	Minneapolis	MN	55442	763-551-7500	551-7501	18

	Phone	Fax	Class
AeroVironment Inc 181 W Huntington Dr Ste 202 .... Monrovia CA 91016 *NASDAQ:* AVAV ■ *TF:* 888-833-2148 ■ *Web:* www.avinc.com	626-357-9983	359-9628	20
Aerovox Inc 167 John Vertente Blvd .... New Bedford MA 02745 *Web:* www.aerovox.com	508-994-9661	995-3000	253
Aerpio Therapeutics Inc 9987 Carver Rd Ste 420 .... Cincinnati OH 45242 *Web:* www.aerpio.com	513-985-1920		231
AerSale Inc 121 Alhambra Plaza Ste 1700 .... Coral Gables FL 33134 *Web:* www.aersale.com	305-764-3200		770
Aerus L L C 300 E Valley Dr Ste 800 .... Bristol VA 24201 *TF:* 800-243-9078 ■ *Web:* www.aerushome.com	800-243-9078		37
Aervoe Industries Inc 1100 Mark Cir .... Gardnerville NV 89410 *TF:* 800-227-0196 ■ *Web:* www.aervoe.com	775-783-3100	782-5687	550
AES (American Epilepsy Society) 342 N Main St .... West Hartford CT 06117 *TF:* 888-233-2334 ■ *Web:* www.aesnet.org	860-586-7505	586-7550	48-17
AES Corp 4300 Wilson Blvd 11th Fl .... Arlington VA 22203 *NYSE:* AES ■ *Web:* www.aes.com	703-522-1315		787
AES Electrophoresis Society 1202 Ann St .... Madison WI 53713 *TF:* 800-242-4363 ■ *Web:* www.aesociety.org	608-258-1565	258-1569	49-19
AES Safety Services 8588 Katy Fwy Ste 430 .... Houston TX 77024	979-505-0052		536
Aes, an Employment Source Inc 1335 N Main St .... Meridian ID 83642 *Web:* www.anemploymentsource.com	208-887-7740		260
AESC (Association of Energy Service Cos) 14531 Fm 529 Ste 250 .... Houston TX 77095 *TF:* 800-692-0771 ■ *Web:* www.aesc.net	713-781-0758	781-7542	48-12
Aesco Electronics Inc 2230 Picton Pkwy .... Akron OH 44312 *TF:* 877-442-6987 ■ *Web:* www.aesco.com	330-245-2630		246
AESCULAP Inc 3773 Corporate Pkwy .... Center Valley PA 18034 **Fax Area Code:* 610 ■ *TF:* 800-282-9000 ■ *Web:* www.aesculapusa.com	800-282-9000	791-6886*	476
AESP Inc 16295 NW 13th Ave .... Miami FL 33169 *TF:* 800-446-2377 ■ *Web:* www.aesp.com	305-944-7710	949-4483	253
Aesseal Inc 355 Dunavant Dr .... Rockford TN 37853 *Web:* www.aesseal.com	865-531-0192		326
Aesthetic Visual Solutions Inc 7565 Commercial Way .... Henderson NV 89011	702-248-7122		344
AESU Travel Inc 3922 Hickory Ave .... Baltimore MD 21211 *TF:* 800-638-7640 ■ *Web:* www.aesu.com	410-366-5494	366-6999	771
Aesys Technologies LLC 693 N Hills Rd .... York PA 17402 *Web:* www.aesystech.com	717-755-1081	755-0020	91
AETA (American Embryo Transfer Assn) 1800 S Oak St Ste 100 .... Champaign IL 61820 *Web:* www.aeta.org	217-398-2217	398-4119	49-8
AETC (Air Education & Training Command) 100 H St Ste 4 .... Randolph AFB TX 78150 *Web:* www.aetc.af.mil	210-652-6564	652-2027	340-4
AETEA Information Technology Inc 1445 Research Blvd Ste 210 .... Rockville MD 20850 *TF:* 888-772-3832 ■ *Web:* www.aetea.com	301-721-4200	721-1730	180
AETEK UV Systems 1229 Lakeview Ct .... Romeoville IL 60446 *TF:* 800-333-2304 ■ *Web:* www.americanultraviolet.com	630-226-4200	226-4215	437
AEterna Zentaris Inc 1405 Parc Technologique Blvd .... Quebec QC G1P4P5 *TSE:* AEZ ■ *Web:* www.aezsinc.com/en/index.php	418-652-8525		85
Aether Consulting Inc 8369 Windstone Ct .... Goodrich MI 48438 *TF:* 800-914-2259 ■ *Web:* aetherconsulting.com	586-939-8028		196
Aether Investment Partners LLC 1900 Sixteenth St Ste 825 .... Denver CO 80202 *Web:* www.aetherip.com	720-961-4190		528
Aethercomm Inc 3205 Lionshead Ave .... Carlsbad CA 92010 *Web:* www.aethercomm.com	760-208-6002		647
Aethon Inc 100 Business Center Dr .... Pittsburgh PA 15205 *TF:* 888-201-9522 ■ *Web:* www.aethon.com	412-322-2975		475
AETI (American Electric Technologies Inc) 1250 Wood Branch Park Dr Ste 600 .... Houston TX 77079 *NASDAQ:* AETI ■ *Web:* www.aeti.com	713-644-8182		254
AETN (Arkansas Educational Television Network) 350 S Donaghey Ave .... Conway AR 72034 *TF:* 800-662-2386 ■ *Web:* www.aetn.org	501-682-2386	682-4122	632
Aetna Bearing Co 1081 Sesame St .... Franklin Park IL 60131 *Web:* www.aetnabearing.com	630-694-0024		75
Aetna Felt Corp 2401 W Emaus Ave .... Allentown PA 18103 *TF:* 800-526-4451 ■ *Web:* www.aetnafelt.com	610-791-0900	791-5791	745-6
Aetna Foundation Inc 151 Farmington Ave .... Hartford CT 06156 *Web:* www.aetna.com	860-273-6382		304
Aetna Inc 151 Farmington Ave .... Hartford CT 06156 *NYSE:* AET ■ *TF:* 800-872-3862 ■ *Web:* www.aetna.com	860-273-0123		391-3
Aetna Integrated Services 646 Parsons Ave .... Columbus OH 43206 *TF:* 866-238-6201 ■ *Web:* www.aetnabuilding.com	866-238-6201		393
Aetna Plastics Corp 1702 St Clair Ave .... Cleveland OH 44114 *TF:* 800-634-3074 ■ *Web:* www.aetnaplastics.com	216-781-4421	781-4474	603
Aetna Plywood Inc 1401 St Charles Rd .... Maywood IL 60153 *TF:* 800-361-7714 ■ *Web:* www.aetnaplywood.com	708-343-1515	343-1616	613
Aetna RX Home Delivery LLC 2528 NW 19th St .... Pompano Beach FL 33069 *Web:* member.aetna.com	954-876-5000		390
AEW (AEW Capital Management LP) 2 Seaport Ln .... Boston MA 02210 *Web:* www.aew.com	617-261-9000	261-9555	401
AEW Capital Management LP (AEW) 2 Seaport Ln .... Boston MA 02210 *Web:* www.aew.com	617-261-9000	261-9555	401
Aexcel Corp 7373 Production Dr .... Mentor OH 44060 *TF:* 800-854-0782 ■ *Web:* www.aexcelcorp.com	440-974-3800	974-3808	550
AF & L Insurance Co 165 Veterans Way Ste 300 PO Box 5005 ...... Warminster PA 18974 *Web:* www.aflltc.com	215-918-0515		391-3
AFA (American Fence Association) 6404 Internationa Pkwy Ste 2250-A .... Plano TX 75093 **Fax Area Code:* 314 ■ *TF:* 800-822-4342 ■ *Web:* www.americanfenceassociation.com	800-822-4342	480-7118*	49-3
AFA (American Federation of Astrologers) 6535 S Rural Rd .... Tempe AZ 85283 *TF:* 888-301-7630 ■ *Web:* www.astrologers.com	480-838-1751	838-8293	48-18
AFA (American Finance Assn) 350 Main St ...... Malden MA 02148 *TF:* 800-835-6770 ■ *Web:* www.afajof.org	781-388-8599		49-2
AFA (Air Force Assn) 1501 Lee Hwy .... Arlington VA 22209 *TF:* 800-727-3337 ■ *Web:* www.afa.org	703-247-5800	247-5853	48-19
AFA (American Federation of Arts) 305 E 47th St 10th Fl .... New York NY 10017 *Web:* www.amfedarts.org	212-988-7700	861-2487	48-4
AFA Protective Systems Inc 155 Michael Dr .... Syosset NY 11791 *OTC:* AFAP ■ *Web:* afap.com	516-496-2322	496-2848	692
Afa Systems Inc 8 Tilbury Ct .... Brampton ON L6T3T4 *Web:* www.afasystemsinc.com	905-873-2532		757
AFAA (Aerobics & Fitness Assn of America) 1750 E Northrop Blvd Ste 200 .... Chandler AZ 91403 *TF:* 800-446-2322 ■ *Web:* www.afaa.com	818-905-0040		48-22
AFAR (American Federation for Aging Research) 55 W 39th St 16th Fl .... New York NY 10018 *TF:* 888-582-2327 ■ *Web:* www.afar.org	212-703-9977	997-0330	49-8
AFB (American Foundation for the Blind) 2 Penn Plaza .... New York NY 10001 *TF:* 800-232-5463 ■ *Web:* www.afb.org	212-502-7600	502-7777	48-17
AFC (AMPAC Fine Chemicals) MS 1007 PO Box 1718 .... Rancho Cordova CA 95741 *TF:* 800-311-9668 ■ *Web:* www.ampacfinechemicals.com	916-357-6880	353-3523	145
AFC (Automotive Finance Corp) 13085 Hamilton Crossing Blvd .... Carmel IN 46032 *TF:* 888-335-6675 ■ *Web:* www.afcdealer.com	865-384-8250		216
AFC Cable Systems Inc 960 Flaherty Dr .... New Bedford MA 02745 *TF:* 800-757-6996 ■ *Web:* www.afcweb.com	508-998-1131		813
AFC Finishing Systems Inc 250 Airport Pkwy .... Oroville CA 95965 *Web:* www.afc-ca.com	530-533-8907		295
AFC Holcroft LLC 49630 Pontiac Trail .... Wixom MI 48393 *Web:* www.afc-holcroft.com	248-624-8191	624-3710	318
AFC Industries Inc 13-16 133rd Pl .... College Point NY 11356 *TF:* 800-663-3412 ■ *Web:* www.afcindustries.com	718-747-0237		194
AFC Tool Company Inc 4900 Webster St .... Dayton OH 45414 *TF:* 800-837-8665 ■ *Web:* www.afctool.com	937-275-8700		454
AFCA (American Football Coaches Assn) 100 Legends Ln .... Waco TX 76706 *TF:* 877-557-5338 ■ *Web:* www.afca.com	254-754-9900		48-22
AFCEA (Armed Forces Communications & Electronics Assn) 4400 Fair Lakes Ct .... Fairfax VA 22033 *TF:* 800-336-4583 ■ *Web:* www.afcea.org	703-631-6100	631-4693	48-19
AFCI (Association of Film Commissioners International) 109 E 17th St .... Cheyenne WY 82001 **Fax Area Code:* 413 ■ *TF:* 888-765-5777 ■ *Web:* www.afci.org	307-637-4422	375-2903*	48-4
AFCO (Alex C Fergusson LLC) 5000 Letterkenny Rd .... Chambersburg PA 17201 **Fax Area Code:* 717 ■ *TF:* 800-345-1329 ■ *Web:* www.afcocare.us	800-345-1329	264-9182*	145
AFCO Credit Corp 14 Wall St .... New York NY 10005 *TF:* 800-288-6901 ■ *Web:* afco.com	212-401-4400	401-4436	216
Afco Industries Inc 3400 Roy St .... Alexandria LA 71302 *TF:* 800-551-6576 ■ *Web:* www.afco-ind.com	800-551-6576		482
Afco Manufacturing Corp 428 Cogshall St PO Box 230 .... Holly MI 48442 *Web:* www.afcomfg.com	248-634-4415	634-6301	480
Afco Products Inc 1030 Commerce Dr .... Lake Zurich IL 60047 *Web:* www.afco-products.com	847-299-1055	299-8455	621
Afco Steel Inc 1423 E Sixth St .... Little Rock AR 72202 *Web:* www.afcosteel.com	501-340-6200	340-6260	480
AFCOM (Association For Data Ctr Management Professionals) 742 E Chapman Ave .... Orange CA 92866	714-997-7966	997-9743	48-9
Afcon Products Inc Elec Equip 35 Sargent Dr .... Bethany CT 06524 *Web:* www.afconproducts.com	203-393-9301		14
AFCU (Andrews Federal Credit Union) 5711 Allentown Rd .... Suitland MD 20746 *TF:* 800-487-5500 ■ *Web:* www.andrewsfcu.org	301-702-5500	702-5330	219
AFD Contract Furniture Inc 810 Seventh Ave # 2 .... New York NY 10019 *Web:* www.afd-inc.com	212-721-7100	721-7175	320
AFE (Association for Facilities Engineering) 8200 Greensboro Dr Ste 400 .... McLean VA 22102 *Web:* www.afe.org	571-203-7171	766-2142	49-13
AFF (American Forest Foundation) 2000 M St NW Ste 550 .... Washington DC 20036 *TF:* 800-325-2954 ■ *Web:* www.forestfoundation.org	202-463-2462	463-2461	48-2
Affant Communication Inc Affant Communication 3146 Red Hill Ave Ste 100 .... Costa Mesa CA 92626 *Web:* www.affant.com	714-338-7100		387
Affect 60 W 38th St 4th Fl .... New York NY 10018 *Web:* www.affectstrategies.com	212-398-9680		194
AFFI (American Frozen Food Institute) 2000 Corporate Ridge Blvd Ste 1000 .... McLean VA 22102 *Web:* www.affi.org	703-821-0770	821-1350	615
Affiliated Car Rental 105 Hwy 36 .... Eatontown NJ 07724 **Fax Area Code:* 732 ■ *TF:* 800-367-5159 ■ *Web:* www.affiliatedcarrental.com	800-367-5159	380-0404*	126
Affiliated Chamber of Commerce of Greater Springfield 1441 Main St .... Springfield MA 01103 *TF:* 888-283-3757 ■ *Web:* www.myonlinechamber.com	413-787-1555	731-8530	139
Affiliated Community Medical Centers (ACMC) 101 Willmar Ave SW .... Willmar MN 56201 *TF:* 888-225-6580 ■ *Web:* www.acmc.com	320-231-5000		374-3
Affiliated Control Equipment Inc 640 Wheat Ln .... Wood Dale IL 60191 *TF:* 800-942-8753 ■ *Web:* www.affiliatedcontrol.com	630-595-4680	595-6151	55

	Phone	Fax	Class
Affiliated Engineers Inc (AEI) 5802 Research Pk Blvd ... Madison WI 53719 *Web:* www.aeieng.com	608 238 2616	238 2614	261
Affiliated Foods Inc 1401 W Farmers Ave ... Amarillo TX 79118 *TF:* 800-234-3661 ■ *Web:* www.afiama.com	806-372-3851		297-8
Affiliated Foods Midwest 1301 W Omaha Ave ... Norfolk NE 68701	402-371-0555	371-6045	297-8
Affiliated Managers Group Inc (AMG) 600 Hale St ... Prides Crossing MA 01965 *NYSE: AMG* ■ *Web:* www.amg.com	617-747-3300		360-3
Affiliated Media Inc 445 E Ohio St Ste 305 ... Chicago IL 60611 *Web:* www.affiliatedmedia.net	312-670-7200		514
Affiliated Medical Services Laboratory Inc 2916 E Central Ave ... Wichita KS 67214 *TF:* 800-876-0243 ■ *Web:* www.amsreferencelab.com	316-265-4533		415
Affina Dumont 150 E 34th St ... New York NY 10016 *TF:* 866-233-4642 ■ *Web:* www.affinia.com	212-481-7600	889-8856	379
Affinia 50 155 E 50th St ... New York NY 10022 *TF:* 866-246-2203 ■ *Web:* www.affinia.com	212-751-5710	753-1468	379
Affinia Chicago 155 E 50th St ... New York NY 10022 *TF:* 866-246-2203 ■ *Web:* www.affinia.com	212-751-5710	753-1468	379
Affinia Gardens 215 E 64th St ... New York NY 10065 *TF:* 866-233-4642 ■ *Web:* www.affinia.com	212-355-1230	758-7858	379
Affinia Manhattan 371 Seventh Ave ... New York NY 10001 *TF:* 866-246-2203 ■ *Web:* www.affinia.com	212-563-1800		379
Affinigent Inc 4 Kent Rd Ste 200 ... York PA 17402 *TF:* 800-932-3380 ■ *Web:* www.affinigent.com	717-600-0033		225
Affinimark Technologies Inc 300 George St Ste 561 ... New Haven CT 06511 *Web:* www.affinimark.com	201-676-3676		743
Affinion Group Inc 6 High Ridge Pk ... Stamford CT 06905 *TF:* 800-252-2148 ■ *Web:* www.affiniongroup.com	203-956-1000		390
Affinion Loyalty Group Inc 7814 Carousel Ln ... Richmond VA 23294 *Web:* affinion.com	804-217-6410		196
Affinitas Corp 1015 N 98th St Ste 100 ... Omaha NE 68114 *TF:* 800-369-6495 ■ *Web:* www.affinitas.net	402-505-5000		194
Affinitive LLC 135 W 26th St 8th Fl ... New York NY 10001	212-684-9100		7
Affinity 2600 N Mayfair Rd Ste 400 ... Milwaukee WI 53226 *Web:* www.affinityit.com	414-258-0200		196
Affinity Answers Corp 9266 227th Ave NE ... Redmond WA 98053 *Web:* www.colligent.com	615-298-1144		466
Affinity Circles Inc 701 B St Ste 520 ... San Diego CA 92113 *Web:* www.affinitycircles.com	650-810-1500		387
Affinity Consultants Inc 222 N Canal St ... Canal Fulton OH 44614 *Web:* www.affinityconsultants.com	330-854-9066		194
Affinity Federal Credit Union 73 Mountain View Blvd PO Box 621 ... Basking Ridge NJ 07920 *TF:* 800-325-0808 ■ *Web:* www.affinityfcu.com	800-325-0808		219
Affinity Gaming 3755 Breakthrough Way Ste 300 ... Las Vegas NV 89135 *Web:* www.affinitygaming.com	702-341-2400		132
Affinity Group Inc 2575 Vista Del Mar ... Ventura CA 93001 *Web:* www.goodsamclub.com	805-667-4100		637-9
Affinity Home Health Care Inc 121 Sandwich St ... Plymouth MA 02360 *Web:* affinityhomehealthcare.com	508-732-8988		363
Affinity Labs Inc 799 Market St Ste 500 ... San Francisco CA 94103 *Web:* www.affinitylabs.com	415-365-1400		387
Affinity Management Group LLC 10205 Westheimer Rd Ste 460 ... Houston TX 77042 *Web:* www.affinity-mgt.com	713-452-3100		194
Affinity Medical Ctr 875 Eigth St NE ... Massillon OH 44646 *TF:* 844-686-3498 ■ *Web:* www.affinitymedicalcenter.com	330-832-8761	837-6814	374-3
Affinity Wealth Management Inc 1702 Lovering Ave ... Wilmington DE 19806 *TF:* 800-825-8399 ■ *Web:* www.affinitywealth.com	302-652-6767		194
Affinium Pharmaceuticals Ltd 200 Front St W Ste 3004 ... Toronto ON M5V3K2 *Web:* pint.com	416-645-6613		668
Affirmative Insurance Holdings Inc 4450 Sojourn Dr Ste 500 ... Addison TX 75001 *OTC: AFFM* ■ *Web:* www.affirmative.com	972-728-6300		360-4
Affirmative Risk Management 4016 Stannus St PO Box 24407 ... Little Rock AR 72204 *Web:* affirmativeriskmgmt.com	501-228-0900		466
Affordable Car Rental LC 105 Hwy 36 ... Eatontown NJ 07724 *TF:* 800-367-5159 ■ *Web:* www.affiliatedcarrental.com	732-380-0888	380-0404	126
Affordable Concepts Inc 2975 W Lake Mead ... North Las Vegas NV 89032 *Web:* www.affordableconcepts.com	702-399-3330		186
Affordable Housing Update 8204 Fenton St ... Silver Spring MD 20910 *TF:* 800-666-6380 ■ *Web:* www.cdpublications.com	301-588-6380	588-6385	531-8
Affordabletours.com 11150 Cash Rd ... Stafford TX 77477 *TF:* 800-935-2620 ■ *Web:* www.affordabletours.com	281-269-2600	269-2690	772
Affton Chamber of Commerce 9815 Mackenzie Rd ... Affton MO 63123 *TF:* 800-877-1234 ■ *Web:* www.afftonchamber.com	314-631-3100		139
Affton Fabricating & Welding Company Inc 1635 Sauget Business Blvd ... Sauget IL 62206 *Web:* www.afwc.com	618-337-5450		480
Affymax Inc 19200 Stevens Creek Blvd Ste 240 ... Cupertino CA 95014 *OTC: AFFY* ■ *TF:* 800-810-0924 ■ *Web:* www.affymax.com	650-812-8700		85
Affymetrix Inc 3420 Central Expy ... Santa Clara CA 95051 *NASDAQ: AFFX* ■ *TF:* 888-362-2447 ■ *Web:* www.thermofisher.com	408-731-5000	731-5380	250
AFG (Avrett Free Ginsberg) 885 Second Ave Dag Hammarskjold Plz ... New York NY 10017 *Web:* avrettfreeginsberg.com	212-832-3800		4
Afghan Horseman 1833 Anderson St ... Vancouver BC V6H4E5 *Web:* afghanhorsemen.com	604-873-5923		671
Afghan Restaurant 2700 Jefferson Davis Hwy ... Alexandria VA 22301 *Web:* afghanrestaurantva.com	703-548-0022		671
Afghanistan 633 Third Ave 27A Fl ... New York NY 10017 *Web:* www.afghanistan-un.org	212-972-1212	972-1216	784
Afghanistan Embassy 2341 Wyoming Ave NW ... Washington DC 20008 *Web:* www.afghanembassy.us	202-483-6410	483-6488	257
AFH 3146 E Windsor Ave ... Phoenix AZ 85008 *Web:* www.azafh.com	602-956-0400		726
AFI (American Film Institute) 2021 N Western Ave ... Los Angeles CA 90027 *TF:* 866-234-3378 ■ *Web:* www.afi.com	323-856-7600	467-4578	48-4
AFI (Armed Forces Insurance Exchange) PO Box G ... Fort Leavenworth KS 66027 *TF:* 800-255-0187 ■ *Web:* www.afi.org	800-255-6792		391-4
AFI (Association of Food Industries Inc) 3301 Rt 66 Bldg C Ste 205 ... Neptune NJ 07753 *Web:* afius.org	732-922-3008	922-3590	49-6
AFI Fest 2021 N Western Ave ... Los Angeles CA 90027 *TF:* 866-234-3378 ■ *Web:* www.afi.com	323-856-7600	467-4578	282
AFIA (American Feed Industry Assn) 2101 Wilson Blvd Ste 916 ... Arlington VA 22201 *Web:* www.afia.org	703-524-0810	524-1921	48-2
AFIMAC Inc 8160 Parkhill Dr ... Milton ON L9T5V7 *TF:* 800-554-4622 ■ *Web:* afimacglobal.com	800-554-4622		194
AFIS (American Forces Information Service) 601 N Fairfax St ... Alexandria VA 22314 *Web:* www.defense.gov	703-571-3343		340-3
AFIX Technologies Inc 205 N Walnut St ... Pittsburg KS 66762 *TF:* 800-724-8380 ■ *Web:* www.afix.net	620-232-6420		179
AFJ (Alliance for Justice) 11 Dupont Cir NW 2nd Fl ... Washington DC 20036 *Web:* www.afj.org	202-822-6070		48-7
AFJ Consulting Group 5455 Wilshire Blvd Ste 2020 ... Los Angeles CA 90036 *Web:* www.afjconsulting.com	323-782-9391		734
AFL (Arena Football League) 640 N LaSalle St Ste 557 ... Chicago IL 60654 *Web:* www.arenafootball.com	312-465-2200		715-1
AFL Network Services Inc 170 Ridgeview Center Dr ... Duncan SC 29334 *Web:* www.AFLglobal.com	864-433-0333		41
AFLAC (American Family Life Assurance Company of Columbus) 1932 Wynnton Rd ... Columbus GA 31999 **Fax Area Code:* 800 ■ **Fax:* Cust Svc ■ *TF Cust Svc:* 800-992-3522 ■ *Web:* www.aflac.com	706-323-3431	448-8922*	391-2
AFLAC Inc 1932 Wynnton Rd ... Columbus GA 31999 *NYSE: AFL* ■ *TF:* 800-992-3522 ■ *Web:* www.aflac.com	706-323-3431		360-4
AFLAC PAC (American Family Life Assurance Co PAC) 1932 Wynnton Rd Ste 300 ... Columbus GA 31999 *NYSE: AFL* ■ **Fax Area Code:* 077 ■ *TF Cust Svc:* 800-992-3522 ■ *Web:* www.aflac.com	706-323-3431	442-3522*	615
AFL-CIO (American Federation of Labor & Congress of Industrial Organizations) 815 16th St NW ... Washington DC 20006 *TF:* 877-850-4959 ■ *Web:* www.aflcio.org	202-637-5000	637-5058	414
AFL-CIO Committee on Political Education 815 16th St NW ... Washington DC 20006 *TF:* 855-712-8441 ■ *Web:* www.aflcio.org	855-712-8441		615
AFM (American Federation of Musicians of the US & Canada) 1501 Broadway Ste 600 ... New York NY 10036 *TF:* 800-762-3444 ■ *Web:* www.afm.org	212-869-1330	764-6134	414
AFMA (American Fiber Manufacturers Assn Inc) 1530 Wilson Blvd Ste 690 ... Arlington VA 22209 *Web:* www.fibersource.com	703-875-0432	875-0907	49-13
AFMR (American Federation for Medical Research) 900 Cummings Ctr Ste 221-U ... Beverly MA 01915 *Web:* www.afmr.org	978-927-8330	524-8890	49-8
Afni Inc 404 Brock Dr ... Bloomington IL 61701 *TF:* 866-377-8844 ■ *Web:* www.afnicareers.com	866-377-8844		160
AFOP (Association of Farmworker Opportunity Programs) 1120 20th St NW Ste 300 ... Washington DC 20036 *Web:* afop.org	202-828-6006	828-6005	48-2
AFOSR (Air Force Office of Scientific Research) 875 N Randolph St Ste 325 ... Arlington VA 22203 *Web:* www.wpafb.af.mil	703-696-7797	696-9556	668
AFP (Agence France-Presse) 1500 K St NW Ste 600 ... Washington DC 20005 *Web:* www.afp.com	202-414-0600		530
AFP (Association of Fundraising Professionals) 4300 Wilson Blvd Ste 300 ... Arlington VA 22203 *TF:* 800-666-3863 ■ *Web:* www.afpnet.org	703-684-0410	684-0540	49-12
AFP (Association for Financial Professionals) 4520 E W Hwy Ste 750 ... Bethesda MD 20814 *Web:* www.afponline.org	301-907-2862	907-2864	49-2
AFP Advanced Food Products LLC 402 S Custer Ave ... New Holland PA 17557 *Web:* www.afpllc.com	717-355-8500		296-36
AFP International LLC 1730 Berkeley St ... Santa Monica CA 90404 *TF:* 888-895-0547 ■ *Web:* www.afproducts.com	310-559-9949		711
AFP Transformers Inc 206 Talmedge Rd ... Edison NJ 08817 *TF:* 800-843-1215 ■ *Web:* www.afp-transformers.com	732-248-0305	248-0542	767
AF&PA (American Forest & Paper Assn) 1111 19th St NW Ste 800 ... Washington DC 20036 *TF:* 800-878-8878 ■ *Web:* www.afandpa.org	202-463-2700	463-2785	48-2
Afr Labs LLC 23891 Via Fabricante Ste 607 ... Mission Viejo CA 92691 *Web:* afrlabs.com	949-462-9822		415
Afram Corp 1601 Olive St ... Saint Louis MO 63103 *Web:* www.aframcorp.com	314-645-6299		256
AFrame Digital Inc 1889 Preston White Dr Ste 101 ... Reston VA 20191 *Web:* www.aframedigital.com	571-308-0147		194
Africa Adventure Co, The 5353 N Federal Hwy Ste 300 ... Fort Lauderdale FL 33308 *TF:* 800-882-9453 ■ *Web:* www.africa-adventure.com	954-491-8877	491-9060	760
Africa Fortesa Corp 7880 San Felipe St Ste 105 ... Houston TX 77063 *TF:* 800-640-2883 ■ *Web:* www.fortesa.com	713-278-2727		536

				Phone	Fax	Class
Africa Imports 240 S Main St Unit A *TF:* 800-500-6120 ■ *Web:* www.africaimports.com	South Hackensack	NJ	07606	201-457-1995		820
Africa Oil Corp 885 W Georgia St Ste 2000 *TF:* 800-423-1625 ■ *Web:* www.africaoilcorp.com	Vancouver	BC	V6C3E8	604-689-7842		536
Africa-America Institute (AAI) 420 Lexington Ave Ste 1706 *Web:* www.aaionline.org	New York	NY	10170	212-949-5666	682-6174	48-14
Africair Inc 13551 SW 132nd Ave # 1 *Web:* www.africair.com	Miami	FL	33186	305-255-6973		770
African American Art & Culture Complex 762 Fulton St *Web:* www.aaacc.org	San Francisco	CA	94102	415-922-2049		50-2
African American Cultural Ctr of Buffalo Inc 350 Masten Ave *TF:* 800-745-3000 ■ *Web:* aaccbuffalo.org	Buffalo	NY	14209	716-884-2013		50-2
African American Historical & Cultural Museum of San Joaquin Valley 1857 Fulton St *Web:* aahcmsjv.org	Fresno	CA	93721	559-268-7102		520
African American Historical Museum & Cultural Ctr of Iowa 55 12th Ave SE *Web:* www.blackiowa.org	Cedar Rapids	IA	52406	319-862-2101		520
African American Museum 3536 Grand Ave *TF:* 800-874-3722 ■ *Web:* www.aamdallas.org	Dallas	TX	75210	214-565-9026	421-8204	520
African American Museum & Library in Oakland 659 14th St *Web:* oaklandlibrary.org	Oakland	CA	94612	510-637-0200		520
African American Museum Hall of Fame 309 Du Sable St *Web:* aahfmpeoria.org	Peoria	IL	61605	309-673-2206		520
African American Museum of the Arts 325 S Clara Ave *TF:* 800-334-4133 ■ *Web:* www.africanmuseumdeland.org	DeLand	FL	32721	386-736-4004	736-4088	520
African Burial Ground National Monument 290 Broadway 1st Fl *Web:* www.nps.gov/afbg	New York	NY	10007	212-637-2019		564
African Lion Safari & Game Farm RR 1 Ste 1 *TF:* 800-461-9453 ■ *Web:* www.lionsafari.com	Cambridge	ON	N1R5S2	519-623-2620	623-9542	823
African Safari Wildlife Park 267 S Lightner Rd *TF:* 800-521-2660 ■ *Web:* www.africansafariwildlifepark.com	Port Clinton	OH	43452	419-732-3606	734-1919	823
African Travel Inc 330 N Brand Blvd Ste 950 *TF:* 800-421-8907 ■ *Web:* www.africantravelinc.com	Glendale	CA	91203	818-507-7893	507-5802	760
African Wildlife Foundation (AWF) 1400 16th St NW Ste 120 *TF:* 888-494-5354 ■ *Web:* www.awf.org	Washington	DC	20036	202-939-3333		48-3
African-American Civil War Memorial & Museum 1200 U St NW *TF:* 800-753-9222 ■ *Web:* www.afroamcivilwar.org	Washington	DC	20001	202-667-2667	667-6771	520
African-American Museum in Philadelphia 701 Arch St *Web:* www.aampmuseum.org	Philadelphia	PA	19106	215-574-0380	574-3110	520
African-American Panoramic Experience Museum 135 Auburn Ave NE *Web:* www.apexmuseum.org	Atlanta	GA	30303	404-523-2739		520
African-American Research Library & Cultural Ctr 2650 Sistrunk Blvd	Fort Lauderdale	FL	33311	954-357-6282		50-2
Africare Inc 440 R St NW *TF:* 800-429-9493 ■ *Web:* www.africare.org	Washington	DC	20001	202-462-3614	387-1034	48-5
Afrl Hea 6030 S Kent Bldg 570	Mesa	AZ	85212	480-988-2040		610
Afro World Hair Goods Inc 7276 Natural Bridge Rd *Web:* www.afroworld.com	Normandy	MO	63121	314-474-0151		348
Afro-American Cultural Ctr 551 S Tryon St *Web:* www.ganttcenter.org	Charlotte	NC	28202	704-547-3700		50-2
Afro-American Historical Society Museum 1841 Kennedy Blvd *Web:* www.cityofjerseycity.org	Jersey City	NJ	07305	201-547-5262	547-5392	520
Afro-American Newspapers Co 2519 N Charles St **Fax Area Code: 877* ■ *TF:* 800-237-6892 ■ *Web:* www.afro.com	Baltimore	MD	21218	410-554-8200	570-9297*	637-8
AFS (American Folklore Society) 1501 Neil Ave 800 E Third St *TF:* 866-315-9403 ■ *Web:* www.afsnet.org	Bloomington	IN	47405	812-856-2379	856-2483	48-14
AFS (American Fisheries Society) 5410 Grosvenor Ln Ste 110 *Web:* www.fisheries.org	Bethesda	MD	20814	301-897-8616	897-8096	48-2
AFS (American Foundry Society) 1695 N Penny Ln *TF:* 800-537-4237 ■ *Web:* www.afsinc.org	Schaumburg	IL	60173	847-824-0181	824-2174	49-13
AFS Energy Systems 420 Oak St *Web:* www.afsenergy.com	Lemoyne	PA	17043	717-763-0286		490
AFS International Inc 71 W 23rd St 6th Fl *Web:* www.afs.org	New York	NY	10010	212-807-8686		48-11
AFSA (American Federation of School Administrators) 1101 17th St NW Ste 408	Washington	DC	20036	202-986-4209		49-5
AFSA (American Fire Sprinkler Assn) 12750 Merit Dr Ste 350 *Web:* www.firesprinkler.org	Dallas	TX	75251	214-349-5965	343-8898	49-3
AFSA (American Foreign Service Assn) 2101 E St NW *TF:* 800-704-2372 ■ *Web:* www.afsa.org	Washington	DC	20037	202-338-4045	338-6820	49-7
AFSC (Alaska Fisheries Science Ctr) 7600 Sand Point Way NE Bldg 4 *Web:* www.afsc.noaa.gov	Seattle	WA	98115	206-526-4000	526-4004	668
AFSC (American Friends Service Committee) 1501 Cherry St *TF:* 800-621-4000 ■ *Web:* www.afsc.org	Philadelphia	PA	19102	215-241-7000		48-5
AFSP (American Foundation for Suicide Prevention) 120 Wall St 22nd Fl *TF:* 888-333-2377 ■ *Web:* www.afsp.org	New York	NY	10005	212-363-3500	363-6237	48-17
AFT (American Farmland Trust) 1200 18th St *TF:* 800-431-1499 ■ *Web:* www.farmland.org	Washington	DC	20036	202-331-7300	659-8339	48-2
AFT Healthcare 555 New Jersey Ave NW *TF:* 800-238-1133 ■ *Web:* www.aft.org	Washington	DC	20001	202-879-4491		414
After Six 118 W 20th St *TF:* 800-444-8304 ■ *Web:* www.aftersix.com	New York	NY	10011	646-638-9600		155-12
Afterburner Inc 55 Ivan Allen Junior Blvd Ste 525 *Web:* www.afterburner.com	Atlanta	GA	30308	404-835-3500		193
Aftermath Claim Science Inc 4580 Weaver Pkwy Ste 200 *TF:* 800-962-6831 ■ *Web:* www.equian.com	Warrenville	IL	60555	630-922-1900		393
Afterschool.gov 370 L'Enfant Promenade SW *Web:* www.acf.hhs.gov	Washington	DC	20447	202-401-9215	205-9688	197
Afton Alps Inc 6600 Peller Ave S *Web:* www.aftonalps.com	Hastings	MN	55033	651-436-5245		378
Afton Chemical Corp 500 Spring St *TF:* 800-424-9300 ■ *Web:* www.aftonchemical.com	Richmond	VA	23219	804-788-5800	788-5184	145
Afton State Park 6959 Peller Ave S *TF:* 800-366-8917 ■ *Web:* www.dnr.state.mn.us	Hastings	MN	55033	651-436-5391	436-6912	565
AFTRA (American Federation of Television & Radio Artists) 260 Madison Ave 7th Fl *TF:* 800-638-6796 ■ *Web:* www.sagaftra.org	New York	NY	10016	212-532-0800	532-2242	414
AFX Industries LLC 522 Michigan St Ste B *Web:* www.afxindustries.com	Port Huron	MI	48060	810-966-4650	966-9522	61
AFYA Inc 8101 Sandy Spring Rd Ste 301 *Web:* www.afyainc.com	Laurel	MD	20707	301-957-3040		194
AG Body Inc 565 South 600 West *Web:* www.agbody.com	Salt Lake City	UT	84101	801-355-8053		247
AG Communications LLC 909 Church Hill Rd *Web:* www.agcomm.com	Fairfield	CT	06825	203-373-0599		463
Ag Connections Inc 1576 Killdeer Trl *Web:* www.agconnections.com	Murray	KY	42071	270-435-4369		180
AG Davis Gage & Engineering Co 6533 Sims Dr *Web:* www.agdavis-aagage.com	Sterling Heights	MI	48313	586-977-9000	977-9190	493
AG Dealer Ltd 44 Byward Market Sq *TF:* 800-665-1362 ■ *Web:* www.agdealer.com	Ottawa	ON	K1N7A2	613-596-8022		225
Ag Georgia Farm Credit PO Box 1820 *Web:* www.aggeorgia.com	Perry	GA	31069	478-987-8300		216
Ag Industries Inc 75 Chestnut St *Web:* www.agi-instore.com	North Attleboro	MA	02760	508-695-4219		697
Ag Informaton Systems 306 Primrose Ln *Web:* www.ag-is.com	Mountville	PA	17554	717-285-7105		177
Ag Leader Technology Inc 2202 S River Side Dr *Web:* agleader.com	Ames	IA	50010	515-232-5363		407
Ag Machining & Industries Inc 4607 S Windermere St *Web:* www.agmachining.com	Englewood	CO	80110	303-783-0081		697
A&G Management Inc 7779 New York Ln *Web:* aandgmanagement.com	Glen Burnie	MD	21061	410-766-8900	766-6557	655
AG Partners Inc 512 S Eigth St PO Box 467 *TF:* 800-772-2990 ■ *Web:* agpartners.net	Lake City	MN	55041	651-345-3328		447
AG Plus Inc 401 N Main PO Box 306 *Web:* www.agplusinc.com	South Whitley	IN	46787	260-723-5141		11-1
Ag Processing Inc 12700 W Dodge Rd PO Box 2047 *TF:* 800-247-1345 ■ *Web:* www.agp.com	Omaha	NE	68103	402-496-7809		296-29
Ag Russell Knives Inc 2900 S 26th St *TF:* 800-255-9037 ■ *Web:* www.agrussell.com	Rogers	AR	72758	479-631-0130		361
AG RX 751 S Rose Ave *Web:* www.agrx.com	Oxnard	CA	93030	805-487-0696	483-6146	144
AG Spanos Cos 10100 Trinity Pkwy 5th Fl *Web:* www.agspanos.com	Stockton	CA	95219	209-478-7954	473-3703	653
Ag West Supply Inc 9055 Rickreall Rd *TF:* 800-842-2224 ■ *Web:* www.agwestsupply.com	Rickreall	OR	97371	503-363-2332	363-5662	274
AGA (American Gastroenterological Assn) 4930 Del Ray Ave *TF:* 800-227-7888 ■ *Web:* www.gastro.org	Bethesda	MD	20814	301-654-2055	654-5920	49-8
AGA (American Gaming Assn) 1299 Pennsylvania Ave NW Ste 1175 *TF:* 800-994-8448 ■ *Web:* www.americangaming.org	Washington	DC	20004	202-552-2675	552-2676	48-23
AGA (American Gas Association) 400 N Capitol St NW Ste 450	Washington	DC	20001	202-824-7000	824-7097	48-12
AGA (American Galvanizers Assn) 6881 S Holly Cir Ste 108 *TF:* 800-468-7732 ■ *Web:* www.galvanizeit.org	Centennial	CO	80112	720-554-0900	554-0909	49-13
AGA (Association of Government Accountants) 2208 Mt Vernon Ave *TF:* 800-242-7211 ■ *Web:* www.agacgfm.org	Alexandria	VA	22301	703-684-6931	548-9367	49-1
Aga Khan Foundation USA (AKF) 1825 K St NW Ste 901	Washington	DC	20006	202-293-2537	785-1752	48-5
Against the Grain Brewery 401 E Main St Louisville Slugger Field *Web:* www.atgbrewery.com	Louisville	KY	40202	502-515-0174		671
AgaMatrix Inc 7C Raymond Ave *Web:* www.agamatrix.com	Salem	NH	03079	603-328-6000		743
Agape English Language Institute (AELI) 1600 Park Cir Unit 116 *Web:* www.aeliusa.com	Columbia	SC	29201	803-445-1998	252-5500	423
Agape Plastics Inc 11474 First Ave NW *Web:* www.agapeplastics.com	Grand Rapids	MI	49534	616-735-4091	735-4392	608
Agape Primary Care 3030 Towne Centre Dr Ste 200 *Web:* www.agapehomehealth.com	Mesquite	TX	75150	972-681-8420		363
Agape Tours & Charter 3306 Cumberland Ave *Web:* agapetourstx.com	Wichita Falls	TX	76309	940-767-4935		760

Name / Address	City	State	ZIP	Phone	Fax	Class
Agar Corp Inc 5150 Tacoma Dr *Web:* www.agarcorp.com	Houston	TX	77041	832-476-5100	476-5299	358
Agate Fossil Beds National Monument 301 River Rd *Web:* www.nps.gov	Harrison	NE	69346	308-668-2211	668-2318	564
Agati Inc 1219 West Lake St *TF:* 866-418-8710 ■ *Web:* www.agati.com	Chicago	IL	60607	312-829-1977		321
Agatina's 2967 Buffalo Rd *Web:* www.agatinas.com	Rochester	NY	14624	585-426-0510		671
Agatucci's 2607 N University St *Web:* agatuccis.com	Peoria	IL	61604	309-688-8200		671
Agave 242 Blvd SE *Web:* www.agaverestaurant.com	Atlanta	GA	30312	404-588-0006		671
Agawam Public Library 750 Cooper St *Web:* www.agawamlibrary.org	Agawam	MA	01001	413-789-1550	789-1552	434-3
AGB (Association of Governing Boards of Universities & Colleges) 1133 20th St NW Ste 300 *TF:* 800-356-6317 ■ *Web:* www.agb.org	Washington	DC	20036	202-296-8400	223-7053	49-5
Agb Investigative Services Inc 2033 W 95th St *TF:* 800-561-3357 ■ *Web:* agbinvestigative.com	Chicago	IL	60643	773-445-4300		177
Agbayani Construction Corp 88 Dixon Ct *Web:* www.agbayani.com	Daly City	CA	94014	415-221-2065		187
AGBU (Armenian General Benevolent Union) 55 E 59th St 7th Fl *Web:* www.agbu.org	New York	NY	10022	212-319-6383	319-6507	48-14
AGC (Armstrong Garden Centers Inc) 2200 E Rt 66 Ste 200 *Web:* www.armstronggarden.com	Glendora	CA	91740	626-914-1091		323
AGC (Associated General Contractors of America) 2300 Wilson Blvd Ste 400 *TF:* 800-242-1766 ■ *Web:* www.agc.org	Arlington	VA	22201	703-548-3118	548-3119	49-3
AGC Chemicals Americas Inc 55 E Uwchlan Ave Ste 201 *Web:* www.agcchem.com	Exton	PA	19341	610-423-4300		601
AGC Inc 106 Evansville Ave *Web:* www.agcincorporated.com	Meriden	CT	06451	203-639-7125	235-6543	677
Agcall Inc 251 Midpark Blvd SE *TF:* 877-273-4333 ■ *Web:* www.agcall.com	Calgary	AB	T2X1S3	403-256-1229		194
AGCO (AGCO Corp) 4205 River Green Pkwy *NYSE:* AGCO ■ *TF:* 877-525-4384 ■ *Web:* www.agcocorp.com	Duluth	GA	30096	770-813-9200		273
AGCO Corp (AGCO) 4205 River Green Pkwy *NYSE:* AGCO ■ *TF:* 877-525-4384 ■ *Web:* www.agcocorp.com	Duluth	GA	30096	770-813-9200		273
Agco Inc 2782 Simpson Cir	Norcross	GA	30071	770-447-6990		610
AGD (Academy of General Dentistry) 211 E Chicago Ave Ste 900 *TF:* 888-243-3368 ■ *Web:* www.agd.org	Chicago	IL	60611	312-440-4300	440-0559	49-8
Age Industries Ltd 3601 County Rd 316c *Web:* www.ageindustries.com	Cleburne	TX	76031	817-641-8178	641-2509	100
Ageatia Technology Consultancy Services Inc 850 E Higgins Rd Ste 125 *TF:* 855-243-4842 ■ *Web:* www.ageatia.com	Schaumburg	IL	60173	847-517-8415		194
AgeCare Ltd 105 20 Sunpark Plaza SE *Web:* www.agecare.ca	Calgary	AB	T2X3T2	403-873-3200		371
Agecroft Hall 4305 Sulgrave Rd *Web:* www.agecrofthall.com	Richmond	VA	23221	804-353-4241		520
Agellan Capital Partners Inc 156 Front St W Ste 303 *Web:* www.agellancapital.com	Toronto	ON	M5J2L6	416-593-6800		655
Agemark Corp 25 Avenida De Orinda *Web:* agemark.com	Orinda	CA	94563	510-548-6600		371
Agence France-Presse (AFP) 1500 K St NW Ste 600 *Web:* www.afp.com	Washington	DC	20005	202-414-0600		530
Agencia International Inc 110 W 40th St Ste 603	New York	NY	10018	212-391-1306		764
Agency for Healthcare Research & Quality 540 Gaither Rd *TF:* 800-358-9295 ■ *Web:* www.ahrq.gov	Rockville	MD	20850	301-427-1200		340-10
Agency For the Performing Arts Inc 405 S Beverly Dr *Web:* www.apa-agency.com	Beverly Hills	CA	90212	310-888-4200		708
Agency for Toxic Substances & Disease Registry 4770 Buford Hwy NE *TF:* 800-232-4636 ■ *Web:* www.atsdr.cdc.gov	Atlanta	GA	30341	800-232-4636		340-10
Agency Mabu 1003 Gateway Ave *TF:* 800-568-9346 ■ *Web:* www.agencymabu.com	Bismarck	ND	58503	701-250-0728		7
Agency Revolution 698 NW *TF:* 800-606-0477 ■ *Web:* www.agencyrevolution.com	Bend	OR	97701	800-606-0477		5
Agency Software Inc 215 W Commerce Dr *TF:* 800-342-7327 ■ *Web:* www.agencysoftware.com	Hayden Lake	ID	83835	208-762-7188	762-1265	390
agencyQ Inc 1825 K St NW Ste 500 *Web:* www.agencyq.com	Washington	DC	20006	202-776-9090		5
Agent 16 79 Fifth Ave	New York	NY	10003	212-367-3800		4
Agentis Inc 222 W Hubbard St *Web:* agentisenergy.com	Chicago	IL	60654	630-359-6210		387
Agentours Inc 126 W Portal Ave *Web:* agentours.com	San Francisco	CA	94127	415-661-5200		760
Aget Manufacturing Co 1408 E Church St *TF:* 800-832-2438 ■ *Web:* www.agetmfg.com	Adrian	MI	49221	517-263-5781	263-7154	18
AGF Burner Inc 814 Asbury Ave *Web:* www.agfburner.com	Asbury Park	NJ	07712	732-730-8090	730-8060	318
AGF Management Ltd 66 Wellington St W 31st Fl *TF:* 800-268-8583 ■ *Web:* www.agf.com	Toronto	ON	M5K1E9	905-214-8203	214-8243	401
Agfa Corp 611 River Dr *TF:* 888-274-8626 ■ *Web:* www.agfagraphics.com/gs/usa/en/internet/maings	Elmwood Park	NJ	07407	201-440-2500		591
AGFA HealthCare Corp 10 S Academy St *TF:* 877-777-2432 ■ *Web:* www.agfahealthcare.com	Greenville	SC	29601	864-421-1600		178-10
Agfinity 260 Factory Rd *TF:* 800-433-4688 ■ *Web:* www.aglandinc.com	Eaton	CO	80615	970-454-4000		276
Aggregate Industries Management Inc 7529 Standish Pl *Web:* www.aggregate-us.com	Rockville	MD	20855	301-284-3600		503-5
Aggreko 4607 W Admiral Doyle Dr *Web:* www.aggreko.com	New Iberia	LA	70560	337-367-7884		264-3
AGHE (Association for Gerontology in Higher Education) 1220 L St NW Ste 901 *Web:* www.aghe.org	Washington	DC	20005	202-289-9806		49-5
AGI (American Geological Institute) 4220 King St *Web:* www.agiweb.org	Alexandria	VA	22302	703-379-2480	379-7563	49-19
AGI (Audio General Inc) 1680 Republic Rd *TF:* 866-866-2600 ■ *Web:* www.audiogeneral.com	Huntingdon Valley	PA	19006	267-288-0300	288-0301	514
AGI (Guttmacher Institute) 125 Maiden Ln 7th Fl *TF:* 800-355-0244 ■ *Web:* www.guttmacher.org	New York	NY	10038	212-248-1111	248-1951	48-5
Agi Goldratt Institute 440 Wheelers Farms Rd Ste 304 *Web:* www.goldratt.com	Milford	CT	06461	203-624-9026		261
AGI Industries Inc 2110 S W Evangeline Thwy *Web:* www.agiindustries.com	Lafayette	LA	70508	337-233-0626		539
Agile Frameworks LLC 1826 Buerkle Rd *Web:* www.agileframeworks.com	Saint Paul	MN	55110	612-202-9011		631
Agile Manufacturing Inc 720 Industrial Park Rd	Anderson	MO	64831	417-845-6065		273
Agile Sourcing Partners Inc 2385 Railroad St *Web:* www.agilesourcingpartners.com	Corona	CA	92880	951-279-4154		612
Agile Ticketing Solutions 3810 Central Pk Ste 301 *Web:* www.agiletix.com	Hermitage	TN	37076	615-360-6700		376
AgileAssets Inc 3001 Bee Caves Rd Ste 200 *TF:* 800-877-8734 ■ *Web:* www.agileassets.com	Austin	TX	78746	512-327-4200		177
AgileCat 1818 Market St Ste 220 *Web:* www.agilecat.com	Philadelphia	PA	19103	215-508-2082		195
Agiletics Inc 585 S Ronald Reagan Blvd Ste 113 *Web:* agiletics.com	Longwood	FL	32750	407-834-5115		177
Agilis Engineering Inc 3930 Rca Blvd Ste 3000 *Web:* www.agilis.com	Palm Beach Gardens	FL	33410	561-626-8900		21
Agilith Capital Inc Victory Bldg 80 Richmond St W Ste 203 *TF:* 866-345-1231 ■ *Web:* www.agilith.com	Toronto	ON	M5H2A4	416-915-0284		528
Agility 480 Production Ave *TF:* 800-463-3339 ■ *Web:* www.agility.com/en/pages/default.aspx	Madison	AL	35758	256-772-7743		770
Agility Holdings Inc 240 Commerce	Irvine	CA	92602	714-617-6300	242-6943	12
AgilQuest Corp 9407 Hull St Rd *TF:* 888-745-7455 ■ *Web:* www.agilquest.com	Richmond	VA	23236	804-745-0467	745-6243	178-1
Agilysys NV LLC 28925 Fountain Pkwy *TF:* 800-241-8768 ■ *Web:* www.agilysys.com	Solon	OH	44139	770-810-7800		177
Agincourt Press 25 Main St	Chatham	NY	12037	518-392-2898		94
Aging Aircraft Consulting LLC 64 Green St *Web:* www.agingaircraftconsulting.com	Warner Robins	GA	31093	478-923-8786		261
Aging Life Care Association (GCM) 3275 W Ina Rd Ste 130 *TF:* 800-677-1116 ■ *Web:* www.aginglifecare.org	Tucson	AZ	85741	520-881-8008	325-7925	49-8
Aging News Alert 8204 Fenton St *TF:* 800-666-6380 ■ *Web:* cdpublications.com	Silver Spring	MD	20910	301-588-6385	588-6385	531-8
AGIS LLC 16 Poplar St *Web:* www.agismfg.com	Ambler	PA	19002	215-646-8010		326
Agissar Corp 526 Benton St *Web:* www.agissar.com	Stratford	CT	06615	203-375-8662		111
Agj Systems & Networks Inc 14257 Dedeaux Rd *Web:* www.agjsystems.com	Gulfport	MS	39503	228-392-7133		180
Ag-Land FS Inc 1505 Valle Vista Blvd *Web:* www.aglandfs.com	Pekin	IL	61554	309-346-4145		276
Ag-Land Implement Inc Hwy 63 N PO Box 31 *TF:* 800-480-2487 ■ *Web:* www.aglandimplement.com	New Hampton	IA	50659	641-394-4226	394-3936	274
AGM Container Controls Inc 3526 E Ft Lowell Rd *TF:* 800-995-5590 ■ *Web:* www.agmcontainer.com	Tucson	AZ	85716	520-881-2130	881-4983	350
AGM Industries Inc 16 Jonathan Dr *TF:* 800-225-9990 ■ *Web:* www.agmind.com	Brockton	MA	02301	508-587-3900	587-3283	811
AGMA (American Guild of Musical Artists) 1430 Broadway 14th Fl *TF:* 800-543-2462 ■ *Web:* www.musicalartists.org	New York	NY	10018	212-265-3687	262-9088	48-4
AGMA (American Gear Manufacturers Assn) 500 Montgomery St Ste 350 *Web:* www.agma.org	Alexandria	VA	22314	703-684-0211	684-0242	49-13
AGN International-North America 2851 S Parker Rd Ste 850 *TF:* 800-782-2272 ■ *Web:* www.agn.org/namain	Aurora	CO	80014	303-743-7880	743-7660	49-1
Agnes Scott College 141 E College Ave **Fax:* Admissions ■ *TF:* 800-868-8602 ■ *Web:* www.agnesscott.edu	Decatur	GA	30030	404-471-6000	471-6414*	166
Agnew Associates Inc 13033 Quaker Ave Ste A *Web:* www.agnewassociates.com	Lubbock	TX	79423	806-799-0753		261
Agnew Multilingual 741 Lakefield Rd Ste C *Web:* www.agnew.com	Westlake Village	CA	91361	805-494-3999		768
Agnico-Eagle Mines Ltd 145 King St E Ste 500 *NYSE:* AEM ■ *TF:* 888-822-6714 ■ *Web:* www.agnicoeagle.com	Toronto	ON	M5C2Y7	416-947-1212	367-4681	502
Agnik LLC 8840 Stanford Blvd Ste 1300 *Web:* www.agnik.com	Columbia	MD	21045	410-290-0864		177
AgniTEK LLC 424 Tarrow *Web:* www.agnitek.com	College Station	TX	77840	979-260-8324		180
AGO (American Guild of Organists) 475 Riverside Dr Ste 1260 *TF:* 855-631-0759 ■ *Web:* www.agohq.org	New York	NY	10115	212-870-2310	870-2163	48-4
AGO Industries Inc 500 Sovereign Rd PO Box 7132 *Web:* www.ago1.com	London	ON	N6M1A4	519-452-3780	452-3053	576

				Phone	Fax	Class

Agora Leather Products
2101 28th St N — St Petersburg FL 33713 — 727-321-0707 — 432
Web: agoraleather.com

AGP
Diana St Amelia Industrial Park Lot 18 & 19
— Guaynabo PR 00968 — 787-641-5400 — 393
Web: www.agppr.com

AGPA (American Group Psychotherapy Assn)
25 E 21st St 6th Fl — New York NY 10010 — 212-477-2677 — 979-6627 — 49-15
TF: 877-668-2472 ■ *Web:* www.agpa.org

Ag-Pro Companies 4281 US-84 — Dixie GA 31629 — 229-263-4133 — 274
Web: www.agprocompanies.com/en/boston.html

AGR Group Inc
6275 S Pearl St Ste 100-300 — Las Vegas CA 89120 — 714-245-7151 — 393
TF: 800-457-1181 ■ *Web:* www.agrgroupinc.com

AGR International Inc
615 Whitestown Rd — Butler PA 16001 — 724-482-2163 — 482-2767 — 472
Web: www.agrintl.com

AGRA Foundations Ltd 7708 Wagner Rd — Edmonton AB T6E5B2 — 780-468-3392 — 256
TF: 800-661-7227 ■ *Web:* www.agra.com

AGRA Industries Inc 1211 W Water St — Merrill WI 54452 — 715-536-9584 — 261
TF: 800-842-8033 ■ *Web:* www.agraind.com

Agracel Inc 2201 Willenborg Ave — Effingham IL 62401 — 217-342-4443 — 271
TF: 800-600-8085 ■ *Web:* agracel.com

Agralite Electric Co-op 320 Hwy 12 SE — Benson MN 56215 — 320-843-4150 — 843-3738 — 245
TF: 800-950-8375 ■ *Web:* www.agralite.coop

Agree Realty Corp
70 E Long Lake Rd — Bloomfield Hills MI 48304 — 248-737-4190 — 655
NYSE: ADC ■ *Web:* www.agreerealty.com

AgreeYa Solutions Inc 605 Coolidge Dr — Folsom CA 95630 — 916-294-0075 — 463
Web: www.agreeya.com

Agrex Inc
10975 Grandview Dr St Ste 200 — Overland Park KS 66210 — 913-851-6300 — 10-4
TF: 800-523-8181 ■ *Web:* www.agrexinc.com

Agri Beef Co 1555 Shoreline Dr Ste 320 — Boise ID 83702 — 208-338-2500 — 338-2605 — 10-1
TF: 800-657-6305 ■ *Web:* www.agribeef.com

Agri Co-op 310 Logan St — Holdrege NE 68949 — 308-995-8626 — 275
Web: www.agrico-op.com

Agri Producers Inc 205 Main St — Tampa KS 67483 — 785-965-2221 — 965-2263 — 276

agriCAREERS Inc 613 Main St PO Box 140 — Massena IA 50853 — 800-633-8387 — 779-3366* — 260
**Fax Area Code:* 712 ■ *TF:* 800-633-8387 ■ *Web:* www.agricareersinc.com

Agricenter International Inc
7777 Walnut Grove Rd Ste 9 — Memphis TN 38120 — 901-757-7777 — 232
Web: www.agricenter.org

Agricor Inc 1626 S Joaquin Dr — Marion IN 46953 — 765-662-0606 — 11-1
Web: www.agricor.org

Agricultural Commodities Inc
2224 Oxford Rd — New Oxford PA 17350 — 717-624-8249 — 280

Agricultural Marketing Service
1400 Independence Ave SW — Washington DC 20250 — 202-720-5115 — 720-8477 — 340-1
Web: www.ams.usda.gov

Agricultural Research Service
US Dept of Agriculture
1400 Independence Ave SW — Washington DC 20250 — 202-720-3656 — 720-5427 — 340-1
Web: www.ars.usda.gov

Agricultural Retailers Assn (ARA)
1156 15th St NW Ste 500 — Washington DC 20005 — 202-457-0825 — 457-0864 — 48-2
TF: 800-535-6272 ■ *Web:* www.aradc.org

Agricultural Workers Mutual Auto Insurance Co
PO Box 88 — Fort Worth TX 76101 — 817-831-9900 — 831-7565 — 391-4
TF: 800-772-7424 ■ *Web:* www.agworkers.com

Agriculture Council of America (ACA)
11020 King St Ste 205 — Overland Park KS 66210 — 913-491-1895 — 491-6502 — 48-2
TF: 800-753-9073 ■ *Web:* www.agday.org

Agri-Empire Corp 630 W Seventh St — San Jacinto CA 92583 — 951-654-7311 — 10-11
Web: www.agri-empire.com

Agri-Fab Inc 809 S Hamilton St — Sullivan IL 61951 — 800-448-9282 — 360-3
TF: 800-448-9282 ■ *Web:* www.agri-fab.com

AgriGold Hybrids
5381 Akin Rd — Saint Francisville IL 62460 — 800-262-7333 — 943-7333* — 694
**Fax Area Code:* 618 ■ *TF:* 800-262-7333 ■ *Web:* www.agrigold.com

Agri-King Inc 18246 Waller Rd — Fulton IL 61252 — 815-589-2525 — 447
TF: 800-435-9560 ■ *Web:* www.agriking.com

Agrilectric Power Inc
3063 Hwy 397 — Lake Charles LA 70615 — 337-430-0006 — 477
Web: www.agrilectric.com

Agri-Mark Inc PO Box 5800 — Lawrence MA 01842 — 978-689-4442 — 794-8304 — 296-27
TF: 800-225-0532 ■ *Web:* agrimark.coop

AgriNorthwest 6716 W Rio Grande — Kennewick WA 99336 — 509-734-1195 — 10-5
Web: www.agrinorthwest.com

Agri-Service 300 Agri-Service Way — Kimberly ID 83341 — 208-734-7772 — 734-7775 — 274
TF: 800-388-3599 ■ *Web:* www.agri-service.com

Agrium Inc 13131 Lake Fraser Dr SE — Calgary AB T2J7E8 — 403-225-7000 — 225-7609* — 200
NYSE: AGU ■ **Fax:* PR ■ *TF:* 877-247-4861 ■ *Web:* www.agrium.com

Agri-World Co-op 31545 Donald Ave — Madera CA 93636 — 559-673-1306 — 10-10

Agron Inc
2440 S Sepulveda Blvd Ste 201 — Los Angeles CA 90064 — 800-966-7697 — 34
TF: 800-966-7697 ■ *Web:* www.agron.com

AGS (American Gem Society)
8881 W Sahara Ave — Las Vegas NV 89117 — 702-255-6500 — 255-7420 — 49-4
TF: 866-805-6500 ■ *Web:* www.americangemsociety.org

AGS (Augusta Regional Airport - Bush Field)
1501 Aviation Way — Augusta GA 30906 — 706-798-3236 — 798-1551 — 27
TF: 866-289-9673 ■ *Web:* flyags.com

AGS BookWorks PO Box 460313 — San Francisco CA 94146 — 415-285-8799 — 94
Web: www.agsbookworks.com

AGS Custom Graphics Inc
8107 Bavaria Rd — Macedonia OH 44056 — 330-963-7770 — 627
TF: 800-456-9748 ■ *Web:* www.agscustomgraphics.com

Agsco Corp 160 W Hintz Rd — Wheeling IL 60090 — 847-520-4455 — 1
Web: www.agsco.com

AGSH (Advocate Good Shepherd Hospital)
450 W Hwy 22 — Barrington IL 60010 — 847-381-9600 — 374-3
TF: 800-775-4784 ■ *Web:* www.advocatehealth.com/gshp

AGSI 201 17th St NW Ste 300 — Atlanta GA 30363 — 404-816-7577 — 816-7578 — 180
TF: 800-768-2474 ■ *Web:* www.agsi.com

AgSource Cooperative Services
135 Enterprise Dr PO Box 930230 — Verona WI 53593 — 608-845-1900 — 368
Web: www.agsource.com

AGTA (American Gem Trade Assn)
3030 LBJ Fwy Ste 840 — Dallas TX 75234 — 214-742-4367 — 742-7334 — 49-4
TF: 800-972-1162 ■ *Web:* www.agta.org

AGU (American Geophysical Union)
2000 Florida Ave NW — Washington DC 20009 — 202-462-6900 — 328-0566 — 49-19
TF: 800-966-2481 ■ *Web:* www.agu.org

Agua Caliente Casino Resort Spa
32-250 Bob Hope Dr — Rancho Mirage CA 92270 — 760-321-2000 — 133
TF: 888-999-1995 ■ *Web:* www.hotwatercasino.com

Agua Caliente Cultural Museum
219 S Palm Canyon Dr — Palm Springs CA 92262 — 760-778-1079 — 520
TF: 800-347-7746 ■ *Web:* www.accmuseum.org

Agua Verde Cafe 1303 NE Boat St — Seattle WA 98105 — 206-545-8570 — 671
Web: www.aguaverde.com

Aguilar Pete (Rep D - CA)
1223 Longworth HOB — Washington DC 20515 — 202-225-3201 — 226-6962 — 342-2
Web: aguilar.house.gov

AGUIRRE Corp
10670 N Central Expwy 6th Fl — Dallas TX 75231 — 972-788-1508 — 788-1583 — 261
Web: www.aguirreroden.com

Agusta Aerospace Corp
3050 Red Lion Rd — Philadelphia PA 19114 — 215-281-1400 — 21
Web: www.agustawestland.com

AGVA (American Guild of Variety Artists)
363 Seventh Ave 17th Fl — New York NY 10001 — 212-675-1003 — 633-0097 — 48-4
TF: 800-331-0890 ■ *Web:* agvausa.com

AgVantage FS Inc 1600 Eigth St SW — Waverly IA 50677 — 319-483-4900 — 483-4992 — 276
TF: 800-346-0058 ■ *Web:* www.agvantagefs.com

Ah Computer Services Inc
7221 Aloma Ave Ste 300 — Winter Park FL 32792 — 407-671-3557 — 175
TF: 800-201-0091 ■ *Web:* ahcomputers.net

AH Harris & Son Inc 367 Alumni Rd — Newington CT 06111 — 860-665-9494 — 665-9444 — 264-3
TF: 800-382-6555 ■ *Web:* www.ahharris.com

AH Lisanti Capital Growth LLC
608 Fifth Ave Ste 301 — New York NY 10020 — 212-792-6990 — 411
Web: www.ahlisanti.com

A&h Lithoprint Inc 2540 S 27th Ave — Broadview IL 60155 — 708-345-1196 — 627
TF: 855-305-7628 ■ *Web:* www.ahlithoprint.com

AH Schreiber Co
460 W 34th St Ste 1002 — New York NY 10001 — 212-564-2700 — 155-17

AH Stephens State Historic Park
456 Alexander St NW — Crawfordville GA 30631 — 706-456-2602 — 565
Web: www.gastateparks.org

AHA (American Hydrogen Assn)
2350 W Shangri La — Phoenix AZ 85029 — 602-328-4238 — 48-12
Web: www.clean-air.org

AHA (American Heart Assn)
7272 Greenville Ave — Dallas TX 75231 — 214-373-6300 — 706-1191 — 48-17
TF: 800-242-8721 ■ *Web:* www.heart.org

AHA (American Historical Assn)
400 A St SE — Washington DC 20003 — 202-544-2422 — 544-8307 — 49-5
Web: www.historians.org

AHA (American Hospital Assn)
155 N Wacker Dr — Chicago IL 60606 — 312-422-3000 — 422-4796 — 49-8
TF: 800-424-4301 ■ *Web:* www.aha.org

AHA (American Humane Assn)
63 Inverness Dr E — Englewood CO 80112 — 303-792-9900 — 792-5333 — 48-6
TF: 800-227-4645 ■ *Web:* www.americanhumane.org

AHA (Arabian Horse Assn)
10805 E Bethany Dr — Aurora CO 80014 — 303-696-4500 — 696-4599 — 48-3
TF: 800-458-4283 ■ *Web:* www.arabianhorses.org

AHA Consulting Engineers Inc
24 Hartwell Ave 3rd Fl — Lexington MA 02421 — 781-372-3000 — 261
Web: www.aha-engineers.com

AHAM (Association of Home Appliance Manufacturers)
1111 19th St NW Ste 402 — Washington DC 20036 — 202-872-5955 — 872-9354 — 49-4
TF: 888-236-2427 ■ *Web:* www.aham.org

AHAM PAC (Association of Home Appliance Manufacturers PAC)
1111 19th St NW Ste 402 — Washington DC 20036 — 202-872-5955 — 872-9354 — 615
TF: 800-424-2970 ■ *Web:* aham.org

AHAPAC (American Hospital Assn PAC)
325 Seventh St NW — Washington DC 20004 — 202-638-1100 — 626-2345 — 615
TF: 800-424-4301 ■ *Web:* aha.org

Ahaus Tool & Engineering Inc
PO Box 280 — Richmond IN 47375 — 765-962-3571 — 962-3426 — 757
Web: www.ahaus.com

AHAVA North America 330 Seventh Ave — New York NY 10001 — 800-366-7254 — 214
TF: 800-366-7254 ■ *Web:* www.ahava.com

AHC (Association of Academic Health Centers)
1400 16th St NW Ste 720 — Washington DC 20036 — 202-265-9600 — 265-7514 — 49-8
Web: www.aahcdc.org

AHC (American Horse Council)
1616 H St NW 7th Fl — Washington DC 20006 — 202-296-4031 — 296-1970 — 48-3
TF: 800-443-0177 ■ *Web:* www.horsecouncil.org

AHC Inc 2230 N Fairfax Dr Ste 100 — Arlington VA 22201 — 703-486-0626 — 196
Web: www.ahcinc.org

AHC Media LLC
950 E Paces Ferry Rd NE Ste 2850 — Atlanta GA 30326 — 404-262-5476 — 262-5560* — 637-9
**Fax:* Cust Svc ■ *TF Cust Svc:* 800-688-2421 ■ *Web:* www.ahcmedia.com

AHCA (American Health Care Assn)
1201 L St NW — Washington DC 20005 — 202-842-4444 — 842-3860 — 49-8
TF: 800-321-0343 ■ *Web:* www.ahcancal.org

AHDI (Association for Healthcare Documentation Integrity)
4230 Kiernan Ave Ste 130 — Modesto CA 95356 — 209-527-9620 — 527-9633 — 49-8
TF: 800-982-2182 ■ *Web:* www.ahdionline.org

Ahead Hum Res Inc/Prosoft LLC
2209 Heather Ln — Louisville KY 40218 — 502-485-1000 — 177
TF: 888-749-1000 ■ *Web:* aheadhr.com

Ahead LLC 270 Samuel Barnet Blvd — New Bedford MA 02745 — 508-985-9898 — 985-2371* — 155-9
**Fax:* Cust Svc ■ *TF:* 800-282-2246 ■ *Web:* www.aheadweb.com

AheadTek Inc 6410 Via Del Oro — San Jose CA 95119 — 408-226-9991 — 226-9195 — 647
TF: 800-971-9191 ■ *Web:* www.aheadtek.com

Ahearn & Soper Inc
100 Woodbine Downs Blvd — Rexdale ON M9W5S6 — 416-675-3999 — 675-3457 — 174
TF: 800-263-4258 ■ *Web:* www.ahearn.com

Phone | Fax | Class

AHEC (American Hardwood Export Council)
42777 Trade W Dr Sterling .... Reston VA 20166 703-435-2900 435-2537 49-18
Web: www.ahec.org
Ahec 1200 N Elam Ave .... Greensboro NC 27401 336-832-8025 196
Web: gahec.org
AHEPA (American Hellenic Educational Progressive Assn)
1909 Q St NW Ste 500 .... Washington DC 20009 202-232-6300 232-2140 48-14
TF: 855-473-3512 ■ *Web:* www.ahepa.org
Ahern Adcock Devlin LLP
1650 Iowa Ave Ste 200 .... Riverside CA 92507 951-683-0672 2
Ahern Rentals Inc 4241 Arville St .... Las Vegas NV 89103 702-362-0623 264-3
TF: 800-589-6797 ■ *Web:* www.ahern.com
Ahern State Park Right Way Path .... Laconia NH 03246 603-485-2034 565
Web: www.nhstateparks.org
AHF (American Homeowners Foundation)
6776 Little Falls Rd .... Arlington VA 22213 703-536-7776 49-17
Web: www.americanhomeowners.org
AHHA (American Holistic Health Assn)
PO Box 17400 .... Anaheim CA 92817 714-779-6152 48-17
Web: www.ahha.org
AHI (Animal Health Institute)
1325 G St NW Ste 700 .... Washington DC 20005 202-637-2440 48-3
Web: www.ahi.org
AHI Facility Services Inc 625 Yuma Ct .... Dallas TX 75208 214-741-3714 104
Web: www.ahifs.com
AHI International Corp
8550 W Bryn Mawr Ave Ste 600 .... Chicago IL 60631 800-323-7373 760
TF: 800-323-7373 ■ *Web:* www.ahitravel.com
AHI Supply Inc PO Box 884 .... Friendswood TX 77549 281-331-0088 191-1
TF: 800-873-5794 ■ *Web:* www.ahi-supply.com
AHIA (Association of Healthcare Internal Auditors)
10200 W 44th Ave Ste 304 .... Wheat Ridge CO 80033 303-327-7546 422-8894 49-1
TF: 888-275-2442 ■ *Web:* www.ahia.org
AHIMA (American Health Information Management Assn)
233 N Michigan Ave Ste 2100 .... Chicago IL 60601 312-233-1100 233-1090 49-8
TF: 800-335-5535 ■ *Web:* www.ahima.org
AHIP (America's Health Insurance Plans)
601 Pennsylvania Ave NW Ste 500 .... Washington DC 20004 202-778-3200 331-7487 49-9
Web: www.ahip.org
AHJ Engineers PC 5418 N Eagle Rd Ste 140 .... Boise ID 83713 208-323-0199 261
Web: ahjengineers.com
Ahjumawi Lava Springs State Park
c/o Northern Buttes District Office
400 Glen Dr .... Oroville CA 95966 530-538-2200 565
Web: www.parks.ca.gov/?page_id=464
AHLA (Alberta Hotel & Lodging Assn)
2707 Ellwood Dr .... Edmonton AB T6X0P7 780-436-6112 436-5404 48-23
TF: 888-436-6112 ■ *Web:* www.ahla.ca
AH&LA (American Hotel & Lodging Assn)
1201 New York Ave NW Ste 600 .... Washington DC 20005 202-289-3100 48-23
Web: www.ahla.com
AHLA (American Health Lawyers Assn)
1620 Eye St NW .... Washington DC 20006 202-833-1100 833-1105 49-10
Web: www.healthlawyers.org
Ahlstrom-Munksj"
122 W Butler St Mt Holly Springs plant
.... Mount Holly Springs PA 17065 717-486-3438 557
Web: www.ahlstrom.com
AHM (Advanced Health Media LLC)
420 Mountain Ave .... New Providence NJ 07974 908-393-8700 393-8701 177
Web: www.ahmdirect.com
AHMA (American Hardware Manufacturers Assn)
801 N Plaza Dr .... Schaumburg IL 60173 847-605-1025 605-1030 49-4
Web: www.ahma.org
Ahmad's Persian 1006 Howard St .... Omaha NE 68102 402-341-9616 671
Ahmad, Zavitsanos, Anaipakos, Alavi & Mensing PC
1 Houston Ctr 1221 McKinney St Ste 3400 .... Houston TX 77010 713-655-1101 428
TF: 800-856-8153 ■ *Web:* www.azalaw.com
Ahmanson Foundation
9215 Wilshire Blvd .... Beverly Hills CA 90210 310-278-0770 305
Web: www.theahmansonfoundation.org
Ahmuty, Demers & McManus
200 IU Willets Rd .... Albertson NY 11507 516-294-5433 428
TF: 800-593-6178 ■ *Web:* www.admlaw.com
AHNA (American Holistic Nurses Assn)
2900 SW Plass Ct .... Topeka KS 66611 785-234-1712 234-1713 48-17
TF: 800-278-2462 ■ *Web:* www.ahna.org
Ahola Corp, The
6820 W Snowville Rd .... Brecksville OH 44141 440-717-7620 2
TF: 800-727-2849 ■ *Web:* www.ahola.com
Ahoskie Chamber of Commerce
310 Catherine Creek Rd .... Ahoskie NC 27910 252-332-2042 332-8617 139
Web: ahoskiechamber.net
AHP (Association for Healthcare Philanthropy)
313 Pk Ave Ste 400 .... Falls Church VA 22046 703-532-6243 532-7170 49-8
Web: www.ahp.org
AHPA (American Herbal Products Assn)
8630 Fenton St Ste 918 .... Silver Spring MD 20910 301-588-1171 588-1174 49-8
TF: 800-358-2104 ■ *Web:* www.ahpa.org
AHQA (American Health Quality Assn)
1155 21st St NW Ste 300 .... Washington DC 20006 202-331-5790 49-8
Web: www.ahqa.org
AHR Metals Inc 20 Division St .... Bessemer AL 35020 205-428-8888 697
Web: www.ahrmetals.com
AHRA (American Healthcare Radiology Administrators)
490-B Boston Post Rd Ste 200 .... Sudbury MA 01776 978-443-7591 443-8046 49-8
TF: 800-334-2472 ■ *Web:* www.ahra.org
Ahrberg Milling Co
200 S Depot St PO Box 968 .... Cushing OK 74023 918-225-0267 447
TF: 800-324-0267 ■ *Web:* www.ahrbergmilling.com
Ahresty Wilmington Corp
2627 S South St .... Wilmington OH 45177 937-382-6112 382-5871 308
Web: www.ahresty.com
AHRI - Air-Conditioning Heating & Refrigeration Institute
4100 N Fairfax Dr Ste 200 .... Arlington VA 22203 703-524-8800 528-3816 49-4
Web: www.ahrinet.org
AHS (American Headache Society)
19 Mantua Rd .... Mount Royal NJ 08061 856-423-0043 423-0082 49-8
TF: 800-582-2169 ■ *Web:* www.americanheadachesociety.org

Phone | Fax | Class

AHS (American Hiking Society)
1422 Fenwick Ln .... Silver Spring MD 20910 301-565-6704 48-23
TF: 800-972-8608 ■ *Web:* www.americanhiking.org
AHS (American Horticultural Society)
7931 E Blvd Dr .... Alexandria VA 22308 703-768-5700 768-8700 48-18
TF: 800-777-7931 ■ *Web:* www.ahs.org
AHS (American Helicopter Society International)
217 N Washington St .... Alexandria VA 22314 703-684-6777 739-9279 49-21
TF: 855-247-4685 ■ *Web:* www.vtol.org
Ah-So 1919 S Gilbert Rd .... Mesa AZ 85204 480-497-1114 671
Web: ahsomesa.com
Ahtna Engineering Services LLC
110 W 38th Ave Ste 100 .... Anchorage AK 99503 907-646-2969 261
TF: 800-397-0568 ■ *Web:* www.ahtnaes.com
Ahwatukee Foothills News
10631 S 51st St Ste 1 .... Phoenix AZ 85044 480-898-7900 532-4
Web: www.ahwatukee.com
AI Control Systems 90 Water St .... Muhlenberg PA 19605 610-921-9670 463
TF: 800-622-4326 ■ *Web:* aicontrols.com
AI Friedman Company Inc 44 W 18th St .... New York NY 10011 212-243-9000 929-7320 45
TF: 800-204-6352 ■ *Web:* www.aifriedman.com
AI Signal Research Inc
3411 Triana Blvd SW .... Huntsville AL 35805 256-551-0008 551-0099 261
Web: www.aisignal.com
AIA (AIA Corporation) 800 Winneconne Ave .... Neenah WI 54956 920-886-3700 9
Web: www.aiageared forgrowth.com
AIA (Aerospace Industries Assn of America)
1000 Wilson Blvd Ste 1700 .... Arlington VA 22209 703-358-1000 358-1011 49-21
TF: 877-229-7555 ■ *Web:* www.aia-aerospace.org
AIA (American Institute of Architects)
1735 New York Ave NW .... Washington DC 20006 202-626-7300 626-7547 48-4
TF Orders: 800-242-3837 ■ *Web:* www.aia.org
AIA (American Insurance Assn)
2101 L St .... Washington DC 20037 202-828-7100 293-1219 49-9
Web: www.aiadc.org
AIA (Archaeological Institute of America)
44 Beacon St .... Boston MA 02108 617-353-9361 353-6550 48-11
TF: 877-524-6300 ■ *Web:* www.archaeological.org
AIA Corporation (AIA) 800 Winneconne Ave .... Neenah WI 54956 920-886-3700 9
Web: www.aiagearedforgrowth.com
AIA Engineers Ltd 15310 Park Row .... Houston TX 77084 281-493-4140 261
Web: www.aiaengineering.com
AIAA (American Institute of Aeronautics & Astronautics Inc)
1801 Alexander Bell Dr Ste 500 .... Reston VA 20191 703-264-7500 264-7551 49-19
TF: 800-639-2422 ■ *Web:* www.aiaa.org
AIADA (American International Automobile Dealers Assn)
500 Montgomery St Ste 800 .... Alexandria VA 22314 703-519-7800 519-7810 49-18
TF: 800-462-4232 ■ *Web:* www.aiada.org
AIAG (Automotive Industry Action Group)
26200 Lahser Rd Ste 200 .... Southfield MI 48033 248-358-3570 358-3253 49-21
TF: 877-275-2424 ■ *Web:* www.aiag.org
AIB (Art Institute of Boston at Lesley)
29 Everett St .... Cambridge MA 02138 617-868-9600 164
TF: 800-773-0494 ■ *Web:* www.lesley.edu
AIB International Inc
1213 Bakers Way PO Box 3999 .... Manhattan KS 66505 785-537-4750 463
TF: 800-633-5137 ■ *Web:* www.aibonline.org
AIBS (American Institute of Biological Sciences)
1313 Dolley Madison Blvd Ste 402 .... McLean VA 22101 703-674-2500 674-2509 49-19
Web: www.aibs.org
AIC (American Institute of Chemists)
315 Chestnut St .... Philadelphia PA 19106 215-873-8224 925-1954 49-19
Web: www.theaic.org
AIC (American Institute of Constructors)
700 N Fairfax St Ste 510 .... Alexandria VA 22314 703-683-4999 527-3105* 49-3
**Fax Area Code:* 571 ■ *Web:* www.professionalconstructor.org
AIC (American Institute for Conservation of Historic & Artistic Works)
1156 15th St NW Ste 320 .... Washington DC 20005 202-452-9545 452-9328 48-4
Web: www.conservation-us.org
AIC International Inc
Rte 2A-Agat PO Box DR .... Hagatna GU 96932 671-565-9142 186
Web: www.aicconstruction.com
AICA (American-International Charolais Assn)
11700 NW Plaza Cir .... Kansas City MO 64153 816-464-5977 464-5759 48-2
TF: 800-270-7711 ■ *Web:* www.charolaisusa.com
AICC (American-Israel Chamber of Commerce Southeast Region)
400 Northridge Rd Ste 260 .... Atlanta GA 30350 404-843-9426 843-1416 138
Web: www.aiccse.org
AIChE (American Institute of Chemical Engineers)
120 Wall St Fl 23 .... New York NY 10005 203-702-7660 775-5177 49-19
TF Cust Svc: 800-242-4363 ■ *Web:* www.aiche.org
AICPA (American Institute of Certified Public Accountants)
1211 Ave of the Americas .... New York NY 10036 212-596-6200 596-6213 49-1
TF: 888-777-7077 ■ *Web:* www.aicpa.org
AICPCU/IIA (American Institute for CPCU & Insurance Institute of America)
720 Providence Rd Ste 100 .... Malvern PA 19355 610-644-2100 640-9576 49-9
TF: 800-644-2101 ■ *Web:* www.theinstitutes.org
AICR Newsletter 1759 R St NW .... Washington DC 20009 202-328-7744 328-7226 531-8
TF: 800-843-8114 ■ *Web:* www.aicr.org
Aid Mailing & Fulfillment
1988 Leghorn St .... Mountain View CA 94043 650-919-1999 5
TF: 800-275-8777 ■ *Web:* aidmail.com
Aid Maintenance Co
300 Roosevelt Ave .... Pawtucket RI 02860 401-722-6627 723-6860 104
TF: 800-886-6627 ■ *Web:* www.aidmaintenance.com
Aida's Bistro 2208 Fourth St SW .... Calgary AB T2S1W9 403-541-1189 671
Web: www.aidasbistro.ca
Aida-America Corp
7660 Center Point 70 Blvd .... Dayton OH 45424 937-237-2382 455
Aidells Sausage Co
1625 Alvarado St .... San Leandro CA 94577 510-614-5450 614-2287 296-26
TF: 877-243-3557 ■ *Web:* www.aidells.com
AIDS Foundation of Chicago
200 W Jackson Blvd Ste 2200 .... Chicago IL 60606 312-922-2322 305
TF: 866-895-2437 ■ *Web:* www.aidschicago.org
AIDS Healthcare Foundation
6255 W Sunset Blvd 21st Fl .... Los Angeles CA 90028 323-860-5200 305
Web: www.aidshealth.org

Name / Address	City	State	ZIP	Phone	Fax	Class
AIDS Library						
1233 Locust St 2nd Fl	Philadelphia	PA	19107	215-985-4851	985-4492	434-4
TF: 877-613-4533 ■ *Web:* www.aidslibrary.org						
AIDS United 1424 K St NW Ste 200	Washington	DC	20005	202-408-4848	408-1818	48-7
TF: 800-782-4747 ■ *Web:* www.aidsunited.org						
AIDSinfo PO Box 6303	Rockville	MD	20849	301-315-2816	519-6616	340-10
TF: 800-448-0440 ■ *Web:* www.aidsinfo.nih.gov						
Aiello Home Services Inc						
600 Old County Cir	Windsor Locks	CT	06096	860-292-2600		610
Web: www.aiellohomeservices.com						
Aiesec Canada Inc						
161 Eglinton Ave E Ste 402	Toronto	ON	M4P1J5	416-368-1001		242
Web: aiesec.ca						
AIFD (American Institute of Floral Designers)						
720 Light St	Baltimore	MD	21230	410-752-3318	752-8295	49-4
TF: 877-865-5320 ■ *Web:* www.aifd.org						
AIFP (American International Forest Products LLC)						
5560 SW 107th Ave	Beaverton	OR	97005	503-641-1611	641-2800	191-3
TF: 800-366-1611 ■ *Web:* www.lumber.com						
AIG SunAmerica Inc						
21650 Oxnard St	Woodland Hills	CA	91367	800-445-7862		360-4
TF: 800-445-7862 ■ *Web:* www-1000.aig.com						
AIG Technologies Inc						
5001 NW 13th Ave Ste B	Deerfield Beach	FL	33064	954-433-0618	426-7873*	196
**Fax Area Code:* 407 ■ *Web:* www.aigtechnologies.net						
AIGA (American Institute of Graphic Arts)						
164 Fifth Ave	New York	NY	10010	212-807-1990	807-1799	48-4
TF: 800-548-1634 ■ *Web:* www.aiga.org						
Aigner Index Inc						
23 Mac Arthur Ave	New Windsor	NY	12553	845-562-4510	562-2638	608
TF: 800-242-3919 ■ *Web:* www.aignerlabelholder.com						
AIHA (American Industrial Hygiene Assn)						
2700 Prosperity Ave Ste 250	Fairfax	VA	22031	703-849-8888	207-3561	49-13
Web: www.aiha.org						
Aiken County 828 Richland Ave W	Aiken	SC	29801	803-642-2012		338
TF: 866-876-7074 ■ *Web:* www.aikencountysc.gov						
Aiken Electric Co-op Inc						
2790 Wagener Rd	Aiken	SC	29802	803-649-6245	641-8310	245
TF Tech Supp: 877-264-5368 ■ *Web:* aikenco-op.org						
Aiken Regional Medical Centers						
302 University Pkwy	Aiken	SC	29801	803-641-5000	641-5000	374-3
TF: 800-245-3679 ■ *Web:* www.aikenregional.com						
Aiken State Natural Area						
1145 State Pk Rd	Windsor	SC	29856	803-649-2857		565
TF: 866-345-7275 ■ *Web:* www.southcarolinaparks.com						
Aiken Technical College						
2276 J Davis Hwy	Graniteville	SC	29829	803-593-9231	593-6526*	162
**Fax:* Admissions ■ *TF:* 800-246-6198 ■ *Web:* www.atc.edu						
Aiken-Bamberg-Barnwell-Edgefield Regional Library System						
314 Chesterfield St	Aiken	SC	29801	803-642-7575		434-3
Web: www.abbe-lib.org						
Aiken-Rhett House 48 Elizabeth St	Charleston	SC	29401	843-723-1159		50-3
TF: 800-789-3678 ■ *Web:* www.historiccharleston.org						
AIL (American Income Life Insurance Co)						
1200 Wooded Acres	Waco	TX	76710	254-761-6400		391-2
TF: 800-433-3405 ■ *Web:* www.ailife.com						
AILA (American Immigration Lawyers Assn)						
918 F St NW	Washington	DC	20004	202-216-2400	783-7853	49-10
TF: 800-982-2839 ■ *Web:* www.aila.org						
Aillet/Fenner/Jolly/Mcclelland Inc						
3003 Knight St Ste 120	Shreveport	LA	71105	318-425-7452		261
Web: afjmc.com						
AIM (Accuracy in Media Inc)						
4350 EW Hwy Ste 555	Bethesda	MD	20814	202-364-4401	364-4098	49-14
TF: 800-787-4567 ■ *Web:* www.aim.org						
Aim 2 Berkeley St Ste 403	Toronto	ON	M5A4J5	416-594-9393		179
TF: 866-645-2224 ■ *Web:* www.aim.ca						
Aim Computers 1819 Willow Pass Rd	Concord	CA	94520	925-687-2822		175
TF: 800-573-1874 ■ *Web:* www.aimcomp.com						
Aim Engineering & Surveying Inc						
5300 Lee Blvd	Lehigh Acres	FL	33971	239-332-4569		261
TF: 800-226-4569 ■ *Web:* aimengineering.com						
AIM Global - Assn for Automatic Identification & Mobility						
20399 Rte 19 Ste 203	Cranberry Township	PA	16066	724-934-4470	934-4495	49-19
TF: 800-878-8878 ■ *Web:* www.aimglobal.org						
Aim Meetings & Events						
212 S Henry St 2nd Fl	Alexandria	VA	22314	703-549-9500		184
Web: www.aimmeetings.com						
Aim Mro Holdings Inc						
8500 Glendale Milford Rd	Camp Dennison	OH	45111	513-831-2938	831-3859	770
Web: www.aimmro.com						
Aim Personnel Service 183 Whiting St	Hingham	MA	02043	781-740-8808		260
Web: aimpersonnel.com						
Aim Screen Printing Supply LLC						
PO Box 9645	Naperville	IL	60567	630-357-4103		687
TF: 800-233-4468 ■ *Web:* aimsupply.net						
AIM Supply Co 7337 Bryan Dairy Rd	Largo	FL	33777	727-544-6211	544-6211	385
TF: 800-999-0125 ■ *Web:* www.aimsupply.com						
Aim Systems 350 Speedvale Ave W Unit 12	Guelph	ON	N1H7M7	519-837-1072		180
TF: 800-465-2961 ■ *Web:* www.aimsystems.ca						
AIMCAL (Association of Industrial Metallizers Coaters & Laminators)						
201 Springs St	Fort Mill	SC	29715	803-802-7820	802-7821	49-13
TF: 800-443-2380 ■ *Web:* www.aimcal.org						
aimClear 9 W Superior St Ste 200	Duluth	MN	55802	218-727-4325		195
Web: www.aimclearblog.com						
Aimco 10000 SE Pine St	Portland	OR	97216	800-852-1368	582-9015	385
TF: 800-852-1368 ■ *Web:* www.aimco-global.com						
AIME (Association for Information Media & Equipment)						
PO Box 9844	Cedar Rapids	IA	52409	319-654-0608		48-4
Web: www.aime.org						
AIME (American Institute of Mining Metallurgical & Petroleum Engineers)						
12999 E Adam Aircraft Cir	Englewood	CO	80112	303-325-5185	702-0049*	48-12
**Fax Area Code:* 888 ■ *TF:* 888-702-0049 ■ *Web:* www.aimehq.org						
Aimpoint Inc 14103 Mariah Ct	Chantilly	VA	20151	703-263-9795		21
Web: www.aimpoint.com						
Aims Community College 5401 W 20th St	Greeley	CO	80634	970-330-8008	506-6958*	162
**Fax:* Admissions ■ *TF:* 800-301-5388 ■ *Web:* www.aims.edu						
Fort Lupton 260 County Rd 29 1/2	Fort Lupton	CO	80621	303-857-4022		162
Web: www.aims.edu						
AIMS Inc 235 Desiard St	Monroe	LA	71201	318-323-2467	322-3472	178-10
TF: 800-729-2467 ■ *Web:* www.aims1.com						
Aimtron Corp 555 S Vermont St	Palatine	IL	60067	630-372-7500	372-7505	625
Web: www.aimtroncorporation.com						
AIMU (American Institute of Marine Underwriters)						
14 Wall St Ste 820	New York	NY	10005	212-233-0550	227-5102	49-9
Web: www.aimu.org						
Ainley & Associates Ltd						
280 Pretty River Pkwy	Collingwood	ON	L9Y4J5	705-445-3451	445-0968	261
Web: www.ainleygroup.com						
Ainsley House 300 Grant St	Campbell	CA	95008	408-866-2119		520
Web: www.campbellmuseums.org						
Ainsworth Pet Nutrition						
984 Water St	Meadville	PA	16335	814-724-7710	337-2743	578
TF: 800-219-2558 ■ *Web:* www.ainsworthpets.com						
Aioli Bodega Espanola 1800 L St	Sacramento	CA	95811	916-447-9440		671
Web: aiolibodega.com						
AIP (American Institute of Philanthropy)						
3450 N Lake Shore Dr	Chicago	IL	60657	773-529-2300	529-0024	48-5
TF: 800-622-2520 ■ *Web:* www.charitywatch.org						
AIPAC (American Israel Public Affairs Committee)						
251 H St	Washington	DC	20001	202-639-5200		48-7
Web: aipac.org						
AIPB (American Institute of Professional Bookkeepers)						
6001 Montrose Rd Ste 500	Rockville	MD	20852	800-622-0121	541-0066	49-1
TF: 800-622-0121 ■ *Web:* www.aipb.org						
AIPC (American Italian Pasta Co)						
1251 NW Briarcliff Pkwy Ste 500	Kansas City	MO	64116	816-584-5000		296-31
Web: makesameal.com						
AIPG (American Institute of Professional Geologists)						
1400 W 122nd Ave Ste 250	Westminster	CO	80234	303-412-6205	253-9220	49-19
TF: 800-337-3140 ■ *Web:* www.aipg.org						
Aiphone Corp 1700 130th Ave NE	Bellevue	WA	98005	425-455-0510		693
Web: www.aiphone.com						
AIPLA (American Intellectual Property Law Association)						
1400 Crystal Dr Ste 600	Arlington	VA	22202	703-415-0780	415-0786	49-10
Web: www.aipla.org						
AIR (Association of Independents in Radio)						
42 Charles St 2nd Fl	Dorchester	MA	02122	617-825-4400		632
TF: 800-510-0021 ■ *Web:* www.airmedia.org						
Air & Waste Management Assn (A&WMA)						
420 Fort Duquesne Blvd						
1 Gateway Ctr 3rd Fl	Pittsburgh	PA	15222	412-904-6018	232-3450	48-12
TF: 800-270-3444 ■ *Web:* www.awma.org						
Air Apparent Inc 5432 W 104th St	Los Angeles	CA	90045	310-649-0064		772
Web: www.air-apparent.com						
Air Canada Centre 40 Bay St	Toronto	ON	M5J2X2	416-815-5500		720
TF: 800-661-8747 ■ *Web:* www.theaircanadacentre.com						
Air Center Inc 2175 Stephenson Hwy	Troy	MI	48083	248-619-7800		358
TF: 800-247-2959 ■ *Web:* teamaircenter.com						
Air Center Inc, The 270 Monroe Ave	Kenilworth	NJ	07033	908-858-5788		358
TF: 800-274-1315 ■ *Web:* www.aircenternj.com						
Air Chair Inc						
2175 N Kiowa Blvd Ste 101	Lake Havasu City	AZ	86403	928-505-2226	505-2229	710
Web: www.airchair.com						
Air Charter Team						
4151 N Mulberry Dr Ste 250	Kansas City	MO	64116	816-283-3280	283-3185	13
TF: 800-205-6610 ■ *Web:* www.aircharterteam.com						
Air Chek Inc						
1936 Butler Bridge Rd	Mills River	NC	28759	828-684-0893		196
TF: 800-247-2435 ■ *Web:* www.radon.com						
Air Cleaning Technologies Inc						
1300 W Detroit	Broken Arrow	OK	74012	918-251-8000		35
TF: 800-351-1858 ■ *Web:* www.aircleaningtech.com						
Air Combat Command						
205 Dodd Blvd Ste 101	Langley AFB	VA	23665	757-764-8346		340-4
Web: www.acc.af.mil						
Air Comfort Corp 2550 Braga Dr	Broadview	IL	60155	708-345-1900	345-2730	189-10
TF: 800-466-3779 ■ *Web:* www.aircomfort.com						
Air Compressor Solutions						
3001 Kermit Hwy	Odessa	TX	79764	432-305-0295		317
Web: www.acsir.com						
Air Compressor Supply Inc						
3916 S I-35 Service Rd	Oklahoma City	OK	73129	405-672-0382		172
Web: www.aircompressorsupplyinc.com						
Air Con Refrigeration & Heating Inc						
123 Lake St	Waukegan	IL	60085	847-336-4128		189-10
Air Conditioning Contractors of America (ACCA)						
2800 S Shirlington Rd Ste 300	Arlington	VA	22206	703-575-4477	575-8107	49-3
TF: 800-786-4452 ■ *Web:* www.acca.org						
Air Conditioning Heating & Refrigeration News						
2401 W Big Beaver Rd Ste 700	Troy	MI	48084	248-362-3700	362-0317	457-21
TF: 800-837-8337 ■ *Web:* www.achrnews.com						
Air Conditioning Products Co						
30350 Ecorse Rd	Romulus	MI	48174	734-326-0050	326-9632	697
Web: www.acpshutters.com						
Air Contact Transport Inc						
PO Box 570	Budd Lake	NJ	07828	800-765-2769	691-0127*	187
**Fax Area Code:* 973 ■ *TF:* 800-765-2769 ■ *Web:* actovernight.com						
Air Controls Bozeman Inc						
7510 Shedhorn Dr	Bozeman	MT	59718	406-587-6292		189-10
Web: aircontrolsbozeman.com						
Air Cooled Exchangers LLC						
1201 S Ninth St	Broken Arrow	OK	74012	918-251-7477		567
Web: www.ace-coolers.net						
Air Courier Dispatch						
12333 S Van Ness Ave	Hawthorne	CA	90250	607-748-9507		311
Web: www.aics.com						
Air Creebec Inc 101 Fecteau St	Val-d'or	QC	J9P0G4	819-825-8375		12
TF: 800-567-6567 ■ *Web:* www.aircreebec.ca						
Air Cruisers Co						
1747 New Jersey 34	Wall Township	NJ	07727	732-681-3527		678
Web: zodiacaerospace.com						
Air Cycle Corp 2200 Ogden Ave Ste 100	Lisle	IL	60532	800-909-9709		295
TF: 800-909-9709 ■ *Web:* www.aircycle.com						
Air Diffusion Systems 3964 Grove Ave	Gurnee	IL	60031	847-782-0044		261
Web: airdiffusion.com						

Name / Address	City	State	Zip	Phone	Fax	Class
Air Education & Training Command (AETC) 100 H St Ste 4 *Web:* www.aetc.af.mil	Randolph AFB	TX	78150	210-652-6564	652-2027	340-4
Air Force Assn (AFA) 1501 Lee Hwy *TF:* 800-727-3337 ■ *Web:* www.afa.org	Arlington	VA	22209	703-247-5800	247-5853	48-19
Air Force Chief of Staff 1670 Air Force Pentagon *TF:* 800-752-9747 ■ *Web:* www.defense.gov	Washington	DC	20330	703-571-3343		340-4
Air Force Federal Credit Union 1560 Cable Ranch Rd Ste 200 *TF:* 800-227-5328 ■ *Web:* www.airforcefcu.com	San Antonio	TX	78245	210-673-5610	673-5102	219
Air Force Magazine 1501 Lee Hwy *TF:* 800-727-3337 ■ *Web:* www.afa.org/magazine/aboutmag.asp	Arlington	VA	22209	703-247-5800	247-5853	457-12
Air Force Materiel Command 4375 Chidlaw Rd Rm N-152 *TF:* 800-225-5288 ■ *Web:* www.afmc.af.mil	Wright-Patterson AFB	OH	45433	937-257-1110		340-4
Air Force medical service 307 Boatner Rd *Web:* www.eglin.af.mil/units/eglinhospital.asp	Eglin AFB	FL	32542	850-883-9042		374-4
Air Force Office of Scientific Research (AFOSR) 875 N Randolph St Ste 325 *Web:* www.wpafb.af.mil	Arlington	VA	22203	703-696-7797	696-9556	668
Air Force Reserve Command 155 Richard Ray Blvd *Web:* www.afrc.af.mil	Robins AFB	GA	31098	478-327-1753	327-0625	340-4
Air Force Space Command 150 Vandenberg St *Web:* www.afspc.af.mil	Peterson AFB	CO	80914	719-554-3731	554-6013	340-4
Air Force Special Operations Command 229 Cody Ave Ste 103 *Web:* www.afsoc.af.mil	Hurlburt Field	FL	32544	850-884-5515		340-4
Air Georgian Ltd 2450 Derry Rd E Shell Aerocentre *Web:* www.airgeorgian.ca	Mississauga	ON	L5S1B2	905-676-1221		21
Air India 570 Lexington Ave 15th Fl *TF:* 800-223-7776 ■ *Web:* www.airindia.com	New York	NY	10022	800-223-7776		25
Air Industries Corp 12570 Knott St *TF:* 800-877-0789 ■ *Web:* www.air-industries.com	Garden Grove	CA	92841	714-892-5571	892-7904	278
Air Ivanhoe Ltd Ivanhoe Lake Air Base *TF:* 800-955-2951 ■ *Web:* www.air-ivanhoe.com	Foleyet	ON	P0M1T0	705-899-2155		239
Air Land & Sea Travel Wedding Crdn 126 N Orlando Ave *TF:* 800-799-1094 ■ *Web:* www.als-travel.com	Cocoa Beach	FL	32931	321-783-4900		775
Air Lift Co 2727 Snow Rd *TF:* 800-248-0892 ■ *Web:* www.airliftcompany.com	Lansing	MI	48917	517-322-2144		54
Air Line Pilots Assn 535 Herndon Pkwy **Fax Area Code:* 202 ■ *TF:* 877-331-1223 ■ *Web:* www.alpa.org	Herndon	VA	20170	703-689-2270	232-0438*	414
Air Liquide America LP 2700 Post Oak Blvd Ste 1800 *TF:* 877-855-9533 ■ *Web:* www.airliquide.com	Houston	TX	77056	877-855-9533		143
Air Liquide Group 2700 Post Oak Blvd *Web:* industry.airliquide.us	Houston	TX	77056	713-624-8000		256
Air Logic Power Systems LLC 1745 S 38th St Ste 100 *Web:* www.alpsleak.com	Milwaukee	WI	53215	414-671-3332		201
Air Logistics Inc 4605 Industrial Dr *TF:* 800-365-6771 ■ *Web:* www.bristowgroup.com	New Iberia	LA	70560	337-365-6771	364-8222	359
Air Mobility Command 402 Scott Dr Unit 1M8 *Web:* www.amc.af.mil	Scott AFB	IL	62225	618-229-7839		340-4
Air Monitor Corp 1050 Hopper Ave *TF:* 800-247-3569 ■ *Web:* www.airmonitor.com	Santa Rosa	CA	95403	707-544-2706	526-9970	612
Air Movement & Control Assn International Inc (AMCA) 30 W University Dr *Web:* www.amca.org	Arlington Heights	IL	60004	847-394-0150	253-0088	49-3
Air North Charter & Training Ltd 150 Condor Rd *TF:* 800-661-0407 ■ *Web:* www.flyairnorth.com	Whitehorse	YT	Y1A0M7	867-668-2228		12
Air Palm Springs 145 N Gene Autry Trail Ste 14 *TF:* 800-760-7774 ■ *Web:* www.airps.com	Palm Springs	CA	92262	800-760-7774		13
Air Products & Chemicals Inc 7201 Hamilton Blvd *NYSE:* APD ■ *TF Prod Info:* 800-345-3148 ■ *Web:* www.airproducts.com	Allentown	PA	18195	610-481-4911		143
Air Purchases Inc 24 Blanchard Rd *TF:* 800-392-6089 ■ *Web:* www.airpurchases.com	Burlington	MA	01803	781-273-2050		612
Air Quality Engineering Inc 7140 Northland Dr N *TF:* 888-883-3273 ■ *Web:* www.air-quality-eng.com	Brooklyn Park	MN	55428	763-531-9823	531-9900	18
Air Resources Laboratory 5830 University Research Ct Rm. 4204 *Web:* www.arl.noaa.gov	College Park	MD	20740	301-683-1365	713-0119	668
Air Serv International 410 Rosedale Ct Ste 190 *Web:* www.airserv.org	Warrenton	VA	20186	540-428-2323	428-2326	48-5
Air Specialists Inc 27 Hollenberg Ct *Web:* airspec.com	Bridgeton	MO	63044	636-326-5900		54
Air Sunshine Inc PO Box 22237 *TF:* 800-435-8900 ■ *Web:* www.airsunshine.com	Fort Lauderdale	FL	33335	954-434-8900		25
Air Systems International Inc 829 Juniper Crescent *TF:* 800-866-8100 ■ *Web:* www.airsystems.com	Chesapeake	VA	23320	757-424-3967		641
Air Systems of Sacramento Inc 10381 Old Placerville Rd *Web:* www.airsystems1.com	Sacramento	CA	95827	916-368-0336		35
Air T Inc 3524 Airport Rd *NASDAQ:* AIRT ■ *TF:* 800-937-5449 ■ *Web:* www.airt.net/mac	Maiden	NC	28650	828-464-8741	465-5281	546
Air Technical Industries 7501 Clover Ave *TF:* 800-321-9680 ■ *Web:* www.airtechnical.com	Mentor	OH	44060	440-951-5191	953-9237	470
Air Techniques Inc 1295 Walt Whitman Rd *TF:* 888-247-8481 ■ *Web:* www.airtechniques.com	Melville	NY	11747	516-433-7676		228
Air Tractor Inc 1524 Lelind Snow Way *Web:* www.airtractor.com	Olney	TX	76374	940-564-5616		20
Air Traffic Control Assn (ATCA) 1101 King St Ste 300 *Web:* www.atca.org	Alexandria	VA	22314	703-299-2430	299-2437	49-21
Air Transport World Magazine 8380 Colesville Rd Ste 500 **Fax Area Code:* 913 ■ *Web:* www.atwonline.com	Silver Spring	MD	20910	301-755-0200	514-3909*	457-21
Air Trek Inc 28000 A-5 Airport Rd *Web:* www.medjets.com	Punta Gorda	FL	33982	941-639-7855		30
Air Van Moving Group 2340 130th Ave NE Ste 201 *TF:* 800-989-8905 ■ *Web:* www.airvanmoving.com	Bellevue	WA	98005	425-629-4101	629-4120	519
Air Vent Inc 4117 Pinnacle Pnt Dr Ste 400 *TF:* 800-247-8368 ■ *Web:* www.airvent.com	Dallas	TX	75211	800-247-8368		697
Air Waves Inc 7750 Green Meadows Dr N *TF:* 844-543-8339 ■ *Web:* www.airwavesinc.com	Lewis Center	OH	43035	740-548-1200		627
Air Way Automation 2268 Industrial St *Web:* www.airwayautomation.com	Grayling	MI	49738	989-348-5176		494
Air Wisconsin Airlines Corp W6390 Challenger Dr Ste 203 *Web:* www.airwis.com	Appleton	WI	54914	920-739-5123		25
Air Zoo, The 6151 Portage Rd *TF:* 866-524-7966 ■ *Web:* www.airzoo.org	Portage	MI	49002	269-382-6555		520
Air2Web Inc 1230 Peachtree St NE	Atlanta	GA	30309	404-942-5300		224
Airbiquity Inc 1011 Western Ave Ste 600 *TF:* 888-334-7741 ■ *Web:* www.airbiquity.com	Seattle	WA	98104	206-219-2700	842-9259	647
Airborne Mobile Inc 3575 Saint Laurent Blvd	Montreal	QC	H2X2T7	514-289-9111		387
Airborne Systems Group 5800 Magnolia Ave *Web:* www.airborne-sys.com	Pennsauken	NJ	08109	856-663-1275	663-3028	576
AirBoss of America Corp 16441 Yonge St *TSE:* BOS ■ *Web:* www.airbossofamerica.com	Newmarket	ON	L3X2G8	905-751-1188	751-1101	677
AirBoss of America Corp Rubber Compounding 101 Glasgow St *TF:* 800-294-5723 ■ *Web:* www.airbossrubbercompounding.com	Kitchener	ON	N2G4X8	519-576-5565	576-1315	605-3
Airbrush Action Inc PO Box 438 *TF:* 800-876-2472 ■ *Web:* www.airbrushaction.com	Allenwood	NJ	08720	732-223-7878		5
Airbus Group Inc 2550 Wasser Terr Ste 9000 *Web:* northamerica.airbus-group.com	Herndon	VA	20171	703-466-5600		21
Airbus Helicopters Canada 1100 Gilmore Rd PO Box 250 *TF:* 800-267-4999 ■ *Web:* www.airbushelicopters.ca	Fort Erie	ON	L2A5M9	905-871-7772		13
Airbus Helicopters Inc 2701 Forum Dr *TF:* 800-873-0001 ■ *Web:* airbushelicoptersinc.com	Grand Prairie	TX	75052	972-641-0000		20
Airbus North America Holdings 198 Van Buren St Ste 300 *TF:* 888-340-2375 ■ *Web:* www.airbus.com	Herndon	VA	20170	703-834-3400		194
Aircastle 300 First Stamford Pl 5th Fl *NYSE:* AYR ■ *Web:* www.aircastle.com	Stamford	CT	06902	203-504-1020	504-1021	23
Aircel Corp 323 Crisp Cir *Web:* www.aircelcorp.com	Maryville	TN	37801	865-681-7066		172
AirClean Systems Inc 3248 Lake Woodard Dr *TF:* 800-849-0472 ■ *Web:* www.aircleansystems.com	Raleigh	NC	27604	919-255-3220		476
AIRCO Group 1853 S Eisenhower Ct *Web:* www.airco-ict.com	Wichita	KS	67209	316-945-0445	945-8014	770
Airco Mechanical Inc 8210 Demetre Ave *Web:* www.aircomech.com	Sacramento	CA	95828	916-381-4523		14
Aircoastal Helicopters Inc 2615 Lantana Rd Ste J	Lantana	FL	33462	561-642-6840		359
Aircom Mfg Inc 6205 E 30th St *TF:* 800-925-2426 ■ *Web:* www.aircommfg.com	Indianapolis	IN	46219	317-545-5383	542-7365	697
Aircon Corp 2873 Chelsea Ave *Web:* www.aircon-corporation.com	Memphis	TN	38108	901-452-0230		480
Aircon Engineering Inc 7 Williams St *Web:* www.airconeng.com	Cumberland	MD	21502	301-722-7269		261
Aircraft Belts Inc 1176 Telecom Dr *Web:* www.aircraftbelts.com	Creedmoor	NC	27522	919-956-4395		22
Aircraft Owners & Pilots Assn (AOPA) 421 Aviation Way *TF:* 800-872-2672 ■ *Web:* www.aopa.org	Frederick	MD	21701	301-695-2000	695-2375	49-21
Aircraft Precision Products 185 Industrial Pkwy *Web:* www.aircraftprecision.net	Ithaca	MI	48847	989-875-4186		21
Aircraft Service International Group 201 S Orange Ave Ste 1100 *Web:* www.asig.com	Orlando	FL	32801	407-648-7373		299
Aircraft Specialists Inc 6005 Propeller Ln *Web:* www.800projets.com	Sellersburg	IN	47172	812-246-4696	246-4365	63
Aircraft Technical Publishers 101 S Hill Dr **Fax:* Sales ■ *TF:* 800-227-4610 ■ *Web:* www.atp.com	Brisbane	CA	94005	415-330-9500	468-1596*	637-11
Aircraft X-Ray Labs Inc 5216 Pacific Blvd *Web:* aircraftxray.com	Huntington Park	CA	90255	323-587-4141	588-6410	743
Air-Cure Inc 8501 Evergreen Blvd *TF:* 800-547-9471 ■ *Web:* www.aircure.com	Minneapolis	MN	55433	763-717-0707		723
Airdex International Inc 8975 S Pecos Rd Ste 7A *Web:* www.airdex.com	Henderson	NV	89074	702-270-6004		601
Airdrie Stud Inc 2641 Old Frankfort Pk PO Box 487 *Web:* www.airdriestud.com	Midway	KY	40347	859-873-7270	873-6140	368
Airdrome Precision Components 3251 E Airport Way *Web:* airdrome.com	Long Beach	CA	90806	562-426-9411	492-6909	595

Name / Address	City	State	ZIP	Phone	Fax	Class
Airecon Manufacturing Corp						
5271 Brotherton Ct	Cincinnati	OH	45227	513-561-5522		697
Web: www.airecon.com						
Airefco Inc						
18755 SW Teton Ave PO Box 1349	Tualatin	OR	97062	503-692-3210	691-2392	15
TF: 800-869-1349 ■ *Web:* www.airefco.com						
Aire-Master of America Inc						
1821 N State Hwy CC	Nixa	MO	65714	417-725-2691	725-5737	310
TF: 800-525-0957 ■ *Web:* www.airemaster.com						
Aires Jewelers Co						
3 Harrison Ave	Morris Plains	NJ	07950	973-292-0950		410
Web: airesjewelers.com						
Airespring Inc						
6060 Sepulveda Blvd Ste 220	Van Nuys	CA	91411	818-786-8990		387
TF: 888-389-2899 ■ *Web:* www.airespring.com						
Airetel Staffing Inc						
415 Montgomery Rd Ste 125	Altamonte Springs	FL	32714	407-788-2015		260
Web: www.airetel.com						
Airex Corp 15 Lilac Ln	Somersworth	NH	03878	603-841-2040		767
Web: www.airex.com						
Airfasco Industries Inc						
2655 Harrison Ave SW	Canton	OH	44706	330-430-6190		454
Web: www.airfasco.com						
AirFlite Inc 3250 AirFlite Way	Long Beach	CA	90807	562-490-6200	490-6290	13
TF: 800-241-3548 ■ *Web:* www.airflight.com						
Airfloat LLC 2230 Brush College Rd	Decatur	IL	62526	217-423-6001	422-1049	207
TF: 800-888-0018 ■ *Web:* www.airfloat.com						
Airflow Sciences Corp						
12190 Hubbard St	Livonia	MI	48150	734-525-0300		261
Web: www.airflowsciences.com						
Airflow Systems Inc 11221 Pagemill Rd	Dallas	TX	75243	214-503-8008	503-9596	18
TF: 800-818-6185 ■ *Web:* www.airflowsystems.com						
Airfoil Impellers Corp						
PO Box 9966	College Station	TX	77842	979-822-6418	775-5588	18
Web: www.airfoil.com						
airG 1133 Melville St Ste 710	Vancouver	BC	V6E4E5	604-408-2228		387
TF: 866-874-8136 ■ *Web:* www.airg.com						
Airgas Inc						
259 N Radnor-Chester Rd Ste 100	Radnor	PA	19087	610-687-5253	687-1052	146
NYSE: ARG ■ *TF:* 800-255-2165 ■ *Web:* www.airgas.com						
Airgas Inc						
6055 Rockside Woods Blvd	Independence	OH	44131	216-642-6600	642-6670	385
TF: 800-562-3815 ■ *Web:* www.airgas.com						
Airgas North Central						
1250 W Washington St	West Chicago	IL	60185	630-231-9260	231-7768	385
Web: www.airgas.com						
Airgas Refrigerants Inc						
2530 Sever Rd Ste 300	Lawrenceville	GA	30043	770-717-2210		146
Web: www.airgasrefrigerants.com						
Airgas Specialty Products						
2530 Sever Rd Ste 300	Lawrenceville	GA	30043	800-295-2225	717-2222*	280
**Fax Area Code:* 770 ■ *TF:* 800-295-2225 ■ *Web:* www.airgasspecialtyproducts.com						
Airguard Industries Inc						
100 River Ridge Cir	Jeffersonville	IN	47130	866-247-4827		18
TF: 800-999-3458 ■ *Web:* clcair.com/brands-products/airguard						
AirIQ Inc						
1845 Sandstone Manor Ste 10	Pickering	ON	L1W3W9	905-831-6444		736
TF: 888-606-6444 ■ *Web:* airiq.com						
Airista LLC 913 Ridgebrook Rd	Sparks Glencoe	MD	21152	410-878-2700		21
Web: www.airistaflow.com						
Airlie Conference Ctr						
6809 Airlie Rd	Warrenton	VA	20187	540-347-1300		377
TF: 800-288-9573 ■ *Web:* www.airlie.com						
Airlie Gardens 300 Airlie Rd	Wilmington	NC	28403	910-798-7700		97
Web: airliegardens.org						
Airline Hydraulics Corp						
3557 Progress Dr	Bensalem	PA	19020	215-638-4700		22
Web: www.airlinehyd.com						
Airline Services International Inc						
5160 Explorer Dr Ste 4	Mississauga	ON	L4W4T7	905-629-4522		63
Web: www.airlineservices.com						
Airline Spares America Inc (ASA)						
1022 E Newport Ctr Dr	Deerfield Beach	FL	33442	954-429-8600	429-8388	770
Web: www.asaspares.com						
Airline Tariff Publishing Co (ATPCO)						
45005 Aviation Dr	Dulles	VA	20166	703-471-7510		16
Web: www.atpco.net						
Airlines for America (ATA)						
1301 Pennsylvania Ave NW Ste 1100	Washington	DC	20004	202-626-4000		49-21
Web: airlines.org						
Airlite Plastics Co 6110 Abbott Dr	Omaha	NE	68110	402-341-7300		596
Web: www.airliteplastics.com						
Airman Inc 51056 Century Ct	Wixom	MI	48393	248-960-1354		790
Web: www.airmaninc.com						
Airman Magazine 203 Norton St	San Antonio	TX	78226	210-925-7757	925-7219	457-12
Airmaster Fan Co 1300 Falahee Rd	Jackson	MI	49203	517-764-2300	764-3838	18
TF: 800-255-3084 ■ *Web:* www.airmasterfan.com						
Airmate Co Inc 16280 County Rd D	Bryan	OH	43506	419-636-3184	636-4210	9
TF: 800-544-3614 ■ *Web:* www.airmatecompany.com						
AirNet Communications Corp						
3950 Dow Rd Ste C	Melbourne	FL	32934	321-984-1990		735
Web: www.aircom.com						
AirNet Systems Inc						
7250 Star Check Dr	Columbus	OH	43217	614-409-4900		546
TF: 800-999-0974 ■ *Web:* www.airnet.com						
Airolite Company LLC PO Box 410	Schofield	WI	54476	715-841-8757	841-8773	491
Web: www.airolite.com						
Airosol Company Inc 1206 Illinois St	Neodesha	KS	66757	620-325-2666	325-2602	145
TF: 800-633-9576 ■ *Web:* www.airosol.com						
AirPair 875 Howard St	San Francisco	CA	94103	800-487-0668		387
TF: 800-487-0668 ■ *Web:* www.airpair.com						
Airparts Company Inc						
2310 NW 55th Ct	Fort Lauderdale	FL	33309	954-739-3575	739-9514	770
TF: 800-392-4999 ■ *Web:* www.airparts.us						
Airphrame Inc 25 Taylor St	San Francisco	CA	94102	415-857-5387		387
Web: www.airphrame.com						
AirPol Inc 1000A Lake St	Ramsey	NJ	07446	973-599-4400		261
Web: www.airpol.com						
Airport Community Schools						
11270 Grafton Rd	Carleton	MI	48117	734-869-7000	654-4014	685
Web: www.airportschools.com						
Airports Council International of North America (ACI-NA)						
1775 K St NW Ste 500	Washington	DC	20006	202-293-8500	331-1362	49-21
Web: www.aci-na.org						
Airput Inc 3819 Germantown Pk	Collegeville	PA	19426	610-454-5100		177
Web: www.airput.com						
AirRoamer Inc						
Adelaide St W Ste 354 - 157	Toronto	ON	M5H4E7	647-258-6589		224
Web: www.airroamer.com						
AirSage Inc 1330 Spring St NW Ste 400	Atlanta	GA	30309	404-809-2499		180
Web: www.airsage.com						
AirScan Inc 3505 Murrell Rd	Rockledge	FL	32955	321-631-0005		693
Web: www.airscan.com						
Air-Sea Forwarders Inc						
PO Box 90637	Los Angeles	CA	90009	310-216-1616	216-2625	12
Web: www.airseainc.com						
AIR-serv Group LLC						
1370 Mendota Heights Rd	Mendota Heights	MN	55120	651-454-0465		55
TF: 800-247-8363 ■ *Web:* www.air-serv.com						
Airship Ventures Inc						
NASA Research Pk Bldg 156	Moffett Field	CA	94035	650-969-8100	969-8101	13
Web: www.airshipventures.com						
Airspan Networks Inc						
777 Yamato Rd Ste 105	Boca Raton	FL	33431	561-893-8670	893-8671	735
OTC: AIRO ■ *Web:* www.airspan.com						
AirStar International Inc						
5273 N Commerce Ave Unit 11	Moorpark	CA	93021	805-553-9996		194
Web: www.airstarintl.com						
Airstream Inc 419 W Pike St	Jackson Center	OH	45334	937-596-6111		120
Web: www.airstream.com						
Airtech International Inc						
5700 Skylab Rd	Huntington Beach	CA	92647	714-899-8100	899-8179	386
Web: www.airtechintl.com						
Airtek Inc PO Box 466	Irwin	PA	15642	724-863-1350	864-7853	172
Web: www.airtek-inc.com						
AirTek Indoor Air Solutions Inc						
1241 Johnson Ave Ste 209	San Luis Obispo	CA	93401	877-858-6213		192
TF: 877-858-6213 ■ *Web:* www.air-tek.net						
Airtel Plaza Hotel 7277 Valjean Ave	Van Nuys	CA	91406	818-997-7676		379
TF: 877-939-9268 ■ *Web:* www.airtelplaza.com						
Airtex 259 Lower Morrisville Rd	Fallsington	PA	19054	215-295-4115		22
Web: www.airtexinteriors.com						
Airtex Consumer Products a Div of Federal Foam Technologies						
150 Industrial Pk Blvd	Cokato	MN	55321	800-851-8887	286-2428*	745-6
**Fax Area Code:* 320 ■ *TF:* 800-851-8887 ■ *Web:* www.airtex.com						
Airtex Products 407 W Main St	Fairfield	IL	62837	618-842-2111		60
TF: 800-880-3056 ■ *Web:* www.airtexproducts.com						
Air-Transport IT Services Inc						
5950 Hazeltine National Dr Ste 210	Orlando	FL	32822	407-370-4664		196
Web: www.airit.com						
AirTrav Inc						
181 Bay St Brookfield Pl PO Box 30025	Toronto	ON	M5J0A5	289-346-0071		463
Web: www.airtrav.ca						
Airtreks International LLC						
237 NE Chkalov Dr Ste 210	Vancouver	WA	98684	415-977-7100		772
Web: www.airtreks.com						
Airtrol Inc 3960 N St	Baton Rouge	LA	70806	225-383-2617	343-7986	189-10
Web: airtrolmechanical.com						
Airtronics Gage & Machine Co						
516 Slade Ave	Elgin	IL	60120	847-695-0911		455
Web: www.airtronicsgauge.com						
Airtronics Inc 1822 S Research Loop	Tucson	AZ	85710	520-881-3982		350
Web: www.airtronicsinc.com						
Airtronics Metal Products Inc						
1991 Senter Rd	San Jose	CA	95112	408-977-7800	977-7810	697
Web: www.airtronics.com						
Airvoice Wireless LLC						
2425 Franklin Rd	Bloomfield Hills	MI	48302	888-944-2355		736
TF: 888-944-2355 ■ *Web:* www.airvoicewireless.com						
Airway Heights Corrections Ctr						
11919 W Sprague Ave PO Box 1899	Airway Heights	WA	99001	509-244-6700	244-6710	213
Web: www.doc.wa.gov						
Air-Way Manufacturing Co 586 N Main St	Olivet	MI	49076	269-749-2161	749-3161	790
TF Cust Svc: 800-253-1036 ■ *Web:* www.air-way.com						
Airway Surgical Appliances Ltd						
189 Colonnade Rd	Nepean	ON	K2E7J4	613-723-4790		42
TF: 800-267-3476 ■ *Web:* www.airwaysurgical.ca						
Airways Freight Corp						
3849 W Wedington Dr	Fayetteville	AR	72704	479-442-6301	442-6522	311
TF: 800-643-3525 ■ *Web:* www.airwaysfreight.com						
AIS (American Institute of Stress, The)						
124 Pk Ave	Yonkers	NY	10703	914-963-1200		48-17
TF: 800-433-5959 ■ *Web:* www.stress.org						
AIS RealTime 4440 Bowen Blvd SE	Grand Rapids	MI	49508	877-314-1100		195
TF: 877-314-1100 ■ *Web:* www.aisservice.com						
AISC (American Institute of Steel Construction)						
1 E Wacker Dr Ste 3100	Chicago	IL	60601	312-670-2400		49-3
Web: www.aisc.org						
AISD (Amarillo Independent School District)						
7200 I- 40 W	Amarillo	TX	79106	806-326-1000	354-4378*	685
**Fax:* Hum Res ■ *Web:* www.amaisd.org						
AISES (American Indian Science & Engineering Society)						
2305 Renard SE Ste 200	Albuquerque	NM	87106	505-765-1052	765-5608	49-19
TF: 800-759-5219 ■ *Web:* www.aises.org						
AISI (American Iron & Steel Institute)						
1101 17th St NW	Washington	DC	20036	202-452-7100	463-6573	49-13
Web: www.steel.org						
Aisin Automotive Casting LLC						
4870 E Hwy 552	London	KY	40744	606-878-6523		455
Web: www.aisinauto.com						
Aisin Holdings of America Inc						
1665 E Fourth St	Seymour	IN	47274	812-524-8144	524-8146	60
Web: www.aisinworld.com						
Aisin USA Mfg Inc 1700 E Fourth St	Seymour	IN	47274	812-523-1969		60
Web: www.aisinusa.com						

Phone | Fax | Class

AIST (Association for Iron & Steel Technology)
186 Thorn Hill Rd .... Warrendale PA 15086 724-814-3000 814-3001 49-13
TF: 800-759-4867 ■ *Web:* www.aist.org

AIT (Avante International Technology Inc)
70 Washington Rd .... Princeton Junction NJ 08550 609-799-9388 799-9308 801
TF: 800-735-5040 ■ *Web:* www.aitechnology.com

AIT (Advanced Integration Technologies)
481 N Dean Ave .... Chandler AZ 85226 480-940-0036 454

AIT Worldwide Logistics
701 N Rohlwing Rd .... Itasca IL 60143 630-766-8300 311
Web: aitworldwide.com

AITC (American Institute of Timber Construction)
7012 S Revere Pkwy Ste 140 .... Centennial CO 80112 303-792-9559 792-0669 49-3
Web: www.aitc-glulam.org

AITDomains.com 421 Maiden Ln .... Fayetteville NC 28301 877-549-2881 321-1390* 396
**Fax Area Code:* 910 ■ *TF:* 877-549-2881 ■ *Web:* ait.com/domains

Aitken Products Inc
566 N Eagle St PO Box 151 .... Geneva OH 44041 440-466-5711 466-5716 14
Web: www.aitkenproducts.com

Aitkin Iron Works Inc
301 Bunker Hill Dr .... Aitkin MN 56431 218-927-2400 454
Web: www.aiw.com

AIUM (American Institute of Ultrasound in Medicine)
14750 Sweitzer Ln Ste 100 .... Laurel MD 20707 301-498-4100 498-4450 49-8
TF: 800-638-5352 ■ *Web:* www.aium.org

AIUSA (Amnesty International USA)
5 Penn Plaza 16th Fl .... New York NY 10001 212-807-8400 627-1451 48-5
TF: 866-273-4466 ■ *Web:* www.amnestyusa.org

AIV LP
7140 W Sam Houston Pkwy N Ste 100 .... Houston TX 77040 713-462-4181 385
TF: 800-447-4230 ■ *Web:* www.aivinc.com

AIW Inc
4446 Old Winter Garden Rd Ste 101 .... Orlando FL 32811 407-521-4576 445-4603 174

Aixtek 890 Cowan Rd Ste C .... Burlingame CA 94010 415-282-1188 175
Web: www.eatonassoc.com

A&J Capital Investment Inc
1609 W Valley Blvd Ste 328 .... Alhambra CA 91803 626-289-8887 401
Web: www.ajcap.com

AJ Daw Printing Ink Co
608 E Compton Blvd E .... Rancho Dmngz CA 90221 323-723-3253 388

AJ Demor & Sons Inc 2150 Eldo Rd .... Monroeville PA 15146 412-242-6125 610
Web: www.ajdemor.com

AJ Desmond & Sons Funeral Directors
2600 Crooks Rd .... Troy MI 48084 248-362-2500 362-0190 510
TF: 800-210-7135 ■ *Web:* www.desmondfuneralhome.com

AJ Funk & Co 1471 Timber Dr .... Elgin IL 60123 847-741-6760 151
Web: www.glasscleaner.com

Aj Images Inc 259 E First Ave .... Roselle NJ 07203 908-241-6900 627
TF: 800-831-7224 ■ *Web:* ajimages.com

AJ Jersey Inc
125 Saint Nicholas Ave .... South Plainfield NJ 07080 908-754-7333 358
Web: www.ajjersey.net

AJ Manufacturing Inc 1217 Oak St .... Bloomer WI 54724 715-568-2204 480
Web: www.ajdoor.com

AJ Perri Inc 1162 Pine Brook Rd .... Tinton Falls NJ 07724 732-733-2548 189-10
Web: ajperri.com

AJ Rose Manufacturing Co
38000 Chester Rd .... Avon OH 44011 440-934-7700 489
Web: www.ajrose.com

AJ Ross Creative Media 62 Wood Rd .... Sugar Loaf NY 10981 845-783-5770 4
TF: 800-723-4644 ■ *Web:* www.ajross.com

Aj Squared Security Inc
111 02 Jamaica Ave .... Jamaica NY 11418 718-849-2725 693
Web: www.aj2security.com

AJ Stationers Inc
6675 Business Pkwy Ste D .... Elkridge MD 21075 410-360-4900 535

AJ Walker Construction Co
421 S 21st St .... Mattoon IL 61938 217-235-5647 182

AJA (American Jail Assn)
1135 Professional Ct .... Hagerstown MD 21740 301-790-3930 790-2941 49-7
TF: 800-211-2754 ■ *Web:* www.americanjail.org

Ajacs Die Sales Corp
3855 Linden Ave SE .... Grand Rapids MI 49548 616-452-1469 358
TF: 800-968-6868 ■ *Web:* www.ajacs.com

Ajanta 12215 N Pennsylvania Ave .... Oklahoma City OK 73120 405-752-5283 671
Web: www.ajantacuisineofindia.com

Ajax Bldg Corp 1080 Commerce Blvd .... Midway FL 32343 850-224-9571 186
Web: www.ajaxbuildingcorp.com

A-jax Company Inc
1500 E Eighth St .... Jacksonville FL 32206 904-353-4783 350
Web: www.ajaxco.com

AJAX Electric Co
60 Tomlinson Rd .... Huntingdon Valley PA 19006 215-947-8500 947-6757 318
TF: 800-516-9916 ■ *Web:* www.ajaxelectric.com

Ajax Metal Processing Inc
4651 Bellevue St .... Detroit MI 48207 313-267-2100 267-2110 484
Web: www.ajaxmetal.com

Ajax Paving Industries Inc
1957 Crooks Rd Ste A .... Troy MI 48084 248-244-3300 574-8334* 188-4
**Fax Area Code:* 813 ■ *Web:* www.ajaxpaving.com

Ajax Santa Barbara Refrigeration & Heating
401 E Montecito St .... Santa Barbara CA 93101 805-963-1322 610
Web: ajaxrefrigerationandac.com

Ajax Tocco Magnethermic Corp
1745 Overland Ave NE .... Warren OH 44483 330-372-8511 372-8608 318
TF: 800-547-1527 ■ *Web:* www.ajaxtocco.com

Ajax United Patterns & Molds Inc
34585 Seventh St .... Union City CA 94587 510-476-8000 476-8001 608

AJC (American Jewish Committee)
165 E 56th St .... New York NY 10022 212-751-4000 750-0326 48-8
Web: www.ajc.org

AJC International
1000 Abernathy Rd NE Ste 600 .... Atlanta GA 30328 404-252-6750 252-9340 297-8
Web: www.ajcfood.com

AJCU (Association of Jesuit Colleges & Universities)
1 Dupont Cir NW Ste 405 .... Washington DC 20036 202-862-9893 48-11
Web: www.ajcunet.edu

Ajel Technologies Inc
45 Brunswick Ave Ste 222 .... Edison NJ 08817 732-476-6000 809
Web: www.ajel.com

AJH (Anna Jaques Hospital)
25 Highland Ave .... Newburyport MA 01950 978-463-1000 463-1250 374-3
TF: 800-355-7944 ■ *Web:* www.ajh.org

Ajilon Communications
970 Peachtree Industrial Blvd Ste 200 .... Suwanee GA 30024 678-482-5103 482-8849 196

Ajinomoto North America Inc
1300 N Arlington Heights Rd Ste 110 .... Itasca IL 60143 630-931-6800 296-37
Web: www.ajiusafood.com

AJL Manufacturing Corp
100 Holleder Pkwy .... Rochester NY 14615 585-254-1128 458-6400 454
Web: www.ajlmfg.com

AJLI (Association of Junior Leagues International Inc)
80 Maiden Ln Ste 305 .... New York NY 10038 212-951-8300 481-7196 48-15
TF: 800-955-3248 ■ *Web:* www.ajli.org

AJM Packaging Corp
E-4111 Andover Rd .... Bloomfield Hills MI 48302 248-901-0040 65
Web: www.ajmpack.com

Ajo Al's
Arrowhead 7458 W Bell Rd .... Glendale AZ 85308 623-334-9899 671
Web: www.ajoals.com

AJR Industries Inc
117 Gordon St .... Elk Grove Village IL 60007 847-439-0380 439-0230 454
Web: www.ajrindustries.com

AJS & Associates Inc
200 Industrial Dr .... Random Lake WI 53075 920-994-4300 200
Web: www.ajsinc.com

AJWS (American Jewish World Service)
45 W 36th St .... New York NY 10018 212-792-2900 792-2930 48-5
TF: 800-889-7146 ■ *Web:* www.ajws.org

AK Capital LLC 445 Park Ave 9th Fl .... New York NY 10022 212-333-8634 194
Web: www.akcapital.com

AK Draft Seal Ltd 7470 Buller Ave .... Burnaby BC V5J4S5 604-451-1080 234
TF: 888-520-9009 ■ *Web:* www.draftseal.com

AK Smiley Public Library
125 W Vine St .... Redlands CA 92373 909-798-7565 798-7566 434-3
TF: 800-894-7323 ■ *Web:* www.akspl.org

AK Stamping Inc 1159 US Rt 22 .... Mountainside NJ 07092 908-232-7300 232-5202 488
TF: 800-227-3258 ■ *Web:* www.akstamping.com

AK Steel Corp 9227 Centre Pt Dr .... West Chester OH 45069 513-425-5000 601-4332* 723
NYSE: AKS ■ **Fax Area Code:* 312 ■ *TF:* 800-331-5050 ■ *Web:* www.aksteel.com

AK Tube LLC 30400 E Broadway .... Walbridge OH 43465 419-661-4150 661-4380 490
TF: 800-955-8031 ■ *Web:* www.aktube.com

AKA Direct Inc 19217 SW 119th Ave .... Tualatin OR 97062 503-454-2200 5
Web: www.akadirect.com

Aka Energy Group LLC
65 Mercado St Ste 250 .... Durango CO 81301 970-764-6650 325
Web: www.akaenergy.com

AKA Enterprise Solutions
875 Sixth Ave 20th Fl .... New York NY 10001 212-502-3900 393
Web: www.akaes.com

Aka Printing & Mailing Inc
44 Joseph Mills Dr .... Fredericksburg VA 22408 540-373-1111 627
TF: 800-232-1515 ■ *Web:* akaprintingandmailing.com

Akal Global Inc 7 Infinity Loop .... Espanola NM 87532 505-692-6600 753-8689 692
TF: 888 325 2527 ■ *Web:* www.akalsecurity.com

Akamai Technologies Inc
150 Broadway .... Cambridge MA 02142 617-444-3000 444-3001 178-7
NASDAQ: AKAM ■ *TF:* 877-425-2624 ■ *Web:* www.akamai.com

Akanthos Capital Management LLC
21700 Oxnard St Ste 1520 .... Woodland Hills CA 91367 818-883-8270 401
Web: www.akanthoscapital.com

Akar Capital Management
8551 W Sunrise Blvd Ste 102A .... Plantation FL 33322 954-476-7011 690
Web: akarcapital.com

Akasaka 1450 Whalley Ave .... New Haven CT 06515 203-387-4898 671

Akashi Sushi Bar 2020 Harshman Rd .... Dayton OH 45424 937 233 8005 671
Web: akashidayton.com

Akbar 823 N Charles St .... Baltimore MD 21201 410-539-0944 671
Web: www.akbar-restaurant.com

AKC (American Kennel Club)
260 Madison Ave .... New York NY 10016 212-696-8200 696-8299 48-18
Web: www.akc.org

Ak-Chin Indian Community
42507 W Peters & Nall Rd .... Maricopa AZ 85138 520-568-1000 393
Web: www.ak-chin.nsn.us

Akdo Intertrade Inc 1435 State St .... Bridgeport CT 06605 203-336-5199 724
TF: 800-811-2536 ■ *Web:* www.akdo.com

AKEA Inc 25105 W Newberry Rd .... Newberry FL 32669 352-474-6124 186
Web: www.akeainc.com

Akebia Therapeutics Inc
245 St 1 Ste 1100 .... Cambridge MA 02142 617-871-2098 871-2099 668
Web: www.akebia.com

Akebono Brake Corp 300 Ring Rd .... Elizabethtown KY 42701 270-234-5500 247
Web: www.akebonobrakes.com

Akehurst Landscaping Service Inc
712 Philadelphia Rd .... Joppa MD 21085 410-538-4018 776
Web: www.akehurst.com

Akerman Senterfitt
Three Brickell City Centre
98 SE Seventh St Ste 1100 .... Miami FL 33131 305-374-5600 374-5095 428
Web: www.akerman.com

Akers Biosciences Inc 201 Grove Rd .... Thorofare NJ 08086 856-848-8698 231
Web: www.akersbio.com

Akers Packaging Service Inc
2820 Lefferson Rd .... Middletown OH 45044 513-422-6312 422-2829 100
TF: 800-327-7308 ■ *Web:* www.akers-pkg.com

AKF (American Kidney Fund)
6110 Executive Blvd Ste 1010 .... Rockville MD 20852 800-638-8299 881-0898* 48-17
**Fax Area Code:* 301 ■ *TF:* 800-638-8299 ■ *Web:* www.kidneyfund.org

AKF (Aga Khan Foundation USA)
1825 K St NW Ste 901 .... Washington DC 20006 202-293-2537 785-1752 48-5

AKG of America Inc 7315 Oakwood St Ext .... Mebane NC 27302 919-563-4286 358
Web: www.akg-america.com

Akhurst Machinery Ltd
1669 Foster's Way (Annacis Island) .... Delta BC V3M6S7 604-540-1430 358
TF: 888-265-4336 ■ *Web:* akhurst.com

Name / Address	City	State	Zip	Phone	Fax	Class
Akimbo Systems Inc 411 Borel Ave Ste 100	San Mateo	CA	94402	650-292-3330		387
Akin Doherty Klein & Feuge PC 8610 N New Braunfels Ste 101 *Web:* www.adkf.com	San Antonio	TX	78217	210-829-1300		2
Akin Gump Strauss Hauer & Feld LLP 1333 New Hampshire Ave NW *TF:* 800-973-1177 ■ *Web:* www.akingump.com	Washington	DC	20036	202-887-4000	887-4288	428
Akina Teppan & Sushi 195 E Alessandro Blvd	Riverside	CA	92508	951-789-0443		671
Akins Consulting Inc 2915 Red Hill Ave	Costa Mesa	CA	92626	714-424-5151		180
Akins Harvest Foods 106 F St SW *Web:* www.harvestfoodsnw.com	Quincy	WA	98848	509-787-4421		345
AKITA Drilling Ltd 1000 333 Seventh Ave SW *Web:* www.akita-drilling.com	Calgary	AB	T2P2Z1	403-292-7979		540
Akkerman Inc 58256 - 266th St *Web:* www.akkerman.com	Brownsdale	MN	55918	507-567-2261		190
AKM Semiconductor Inc 1731 Technology Dr Ste 500 *Web:* www.akm.com	San Jose	CA	95110	408-436-8580		696
Akona Consulting 137 Park Ln Ste 200 *Web:* www.akonasystems.com	Kirkland	WA	98033	425-576-0725		463
Akorn Inc 1925 W Field Ct *NASDAQ:* AKRX ■ *TF:* 800-932-5676 ■ *Web:* www.akorn.com	Lake Forest	IL	60045	847-279-6100	279-6123	231
Akoya 2325 E Carson St *Web:* www.akoyaonline.com	Pittsburgh	PA	15203	412-481-3958		344
AkPIRG (Alaska Public Interest Research Group) 737 W Fifth Ave Ste 206 *Web:* www.akpirg.org	Anchorage	AK	99501	907-278-3661		633
AKPsi (Alpha Kappa Psi) 7801 E 88th St *Web:* www.akpsi.com	Indianapolis	IN	46256	317-872-1553	872-1567	48-16
AKQA Inc 3299 K St NW *TF:* 800-561-3357 ■ *Web:* www.akqa.com	Washington	DC	20007	202-337-2572		809
AKQA Inc 360 Third St 5th Fl *Web:* www.akqa.com	San Francisco	CA	94107	415-645-9400		4
Akra Plastic Products Inc 1504 E Cedar St *TF:* 800-229-2760 ■ *Web:* akraplastics.com	Ontario	CA	91761	909-930-1999		602
AKRF Inc 440 Pk Ave S *TF:* 800-899-2573 ■ *Web:* www.akrf.com	New York	NY	10016	212-696-0670		261
Akrion Systems LLC 6330 Hedgewood Dr Ste 150 **Fax:* Sales ■ *Web:* www.akrionsystems.com	Allentown	PA	18106	610-391-9200	391-1982*	695
Akrochem Corp 255 Fountain St *TF:* 800-321-2260 ■ *Web:* www.akrochem.com	Akron	OH	44304	330-535-2100	535-8947	605-3
Akro-Mils Inc 1293 S Main St **Fax Area Code:* 330 ■ *TF:* 800-253-2467 ■ *Web:* www.akro-mils.com	Akron	OH	44301	800-253-2467	761-6348*	199
Akron Art Museum 1 S High St *Web:* www.akronartmuseum.org	Akron	OH	44308	330-376-9185	376-1180	520
Akron Auto Auction Inc 2471 Ley Dr *TF:* 800-773-0033 ■ *Web:* www.akronautoauction.com	Akron	OH	44319	330-773-8245	773-1641	51
Akron City Hall 146 S High St Rm 211 *TF:* 800-848-1300 ■ *Web:* www.akronohio.gov	Akron	OH	44308	330-375-2133	375-2468	337
Akron Civic Theatre 182 S Main St *TF:* 800-554-4549 ■ *Web:* www.akroncivic.com	Akron	OH	44308	330-535-3179	535-9828	572
Akron Community Foundation 345 W Cedar St *Web:* www.akroncf.org	Akron	OH	44307	330-376-8522		305
Akron Foundry Co 2728 Wingate Ave *Web:* www.akronfoundry.com	Akron	OH	44314	330-745-3101	745-7999	308
Akron Gasket & Packing Enterprises Inc 445 NE Ave *TF:* 800-888-2088 ■ *Web:* www.akrongasket.com	Tallmadge	OH	44278	330-633-3742		326
Akron Gear & Engineering Inc 501 Morgan Ave *Web:* www.akrongear.com	Akron	OH	44311	330-773-6608		709
Akron General Medical Ctr 400 Wabash Ave *TF:* 800-221-4601 ■ *Web:* www.akrongeneral.org	Akron	OH	44307	330-344-6000		374-3
Akron Hardware 170 Main Ave	Akron	CO	80720	970-345-6600		350
Akron Paint & Varnish Inc 1390 Firestone Pkwy *TF:* 800-772-3452 ■ *Web:* arcat.com	Akron	OH	44301	330-773-8911	773-1028	550
Akron Police - Community Relations 217 S High St Rm 402 *TF:* 800-296-3797 ■ *Web:* akronohio.gov	Akron	OH	44308	330-375-2390	375-2412	520
Akron Porcelain & Plastics Co 2739 Cory Ave PO Box 15157 *TF:* 800-737-9664 ■ *Web:* www.akronporcelain.com	Akron	OH	44314	330-745-2159	745-6688	604
Akron Public Schools 70 N Broadway Ave *Web:* www.akronschools.com	Akron	OH	44308	330-761-1661	761-3225	685
Akron Rubber Development Laboratory Inc 2887 Gilchrist Rd *TF:* 866-778-2735 ■ *Web:* www.ardl.com	Akron	OH	44305	330-794-6600		743
Akron Special Machinery Inc 2740 Cory Ave *Web:* www.polinggroup.com	Akron	OH	44314	330-753-1077		757
Akron Steel Treating Co 336 Morgan Ave *TF:* 800-364-2782 ■ *Web:* www.akronsteeltreating.com	Akron	OH	44311	330-773-8211		484
Akron Zoological Park 500 Edgewood Ave *Web:* www.akronzoo.org	Akron	OH	44307	330-375-2550	375-2575	823
Akron/Summit County Convention & Visitors Bureau 77 E Mill St *TF:* 800-245-4254 ■ *Web:* www.visitakron-summit.org	Akron	OH	44308	330-374-8900	374-7626	206
Akron-Canton Airport 5400 Lauby Rd NW *TF:* 888-434-2359 ■ *Web:* www.akroncantonairport.com	North Canton	OH	44720	330-499-4221	499-5176	27
Akron-Summit County Public Library 60 S High St *Web:* www.akronlibrary.org	Akron	OH	44326	330-643-9000		434-3
Akros Pharma Inc 302 Carnegie Ctr Ste 300 *Web:* www.akrospharma.com	Princeton	NJ	08540	609-919-9570		743
Aks Infotech Inc 8 Declan Ct *Web:* aksinfotech.net	Monmouth Junction	NJ	08852	609-301-4607		463
AKS Technologies Inc 1416 N Sam Houston Pkwy E Ste 140 *Web:* www.aks-technologies.com	Houston	TX	77032	281-987-2244		539
Aksia LLC 599 Lexington Ave 46th Fl *Web:* www.aksia.com	New York	NY	10022	212-710-5710		401
AKSM (American Kidney Stone Management Ltd) 797 Thomas Ln *TF:* 800-637-5188 ■ *Web:* www.aksm.com	Columbus	OH	43214	614-447-0281		353
AKT Enterprises 6424 Forest City Rd *TF:* 877-306-3651 ■ *Web:* www.aktenterprises.com	Orlando	FL	32810	877-306-3651		5
Aktina Medical Physics Corp 360 N Route 9W *TF:* 888-433-3380 ■ *Web:* www.aktina.com	Congers	NY	10920	845-268-0101		475
Aktion Associates Inc 1687 Woodlands Dr *Web:* www.aktion.com	Maumee	OH	43537	419-893-7001		179
AKVMA (Alaska State Veterinary Medical Assn) 1731 Bragaw St *TF:* 800-272-1813 ■ *Web:* www.akvma.org	Anchorage	AK	99508	907-563-3701		795
Akzo Nobel Chemicals Inc 10 Finderne Ave **Fax Area Code:* 908 ■ *TF:* 888-331-6212 ■ *Web:* www.akzonobel.com	Bridgewater	NJ	08807	888-331-6212	707-3664*	145
AkzoNobel Surface Chemistry LLC 525 W Van Buren St *TF Cust Svc:* 800-937-5449 ■ *Web:* www.akzonobel.com	Chicago	IL	60607	312-544-7000	544-7410	143
AkzoNobel Wood Finishes & Adhesives 2031 Nelson Miller Pkwy *Web:* www.akzonobel.com	Louisville	KY	40223	502-254-0470		550
Al Betz & Assoc Inc PO Box 665 Ste 30 *TF:* 877-402-3376 ■ *Web:* www.albetzreporting.com	Westminster	MD	21158	410-875-3376	875-2857	445
Al Biernat's 4217 Oak Lawn Ave *Web:* www.albiernats.com	Dallas	TX	75219	214-219-2201	219-2093	671
Al Boccalino 1 Yesler Way *Web:* seattleslittleitaly.com	Seattle	WA	98104	206-622-7688		671
Al C Rinaldi Inc 1718 Chestnut St *Web:* www.chopinpiano.com	Philadelphia	PA	19103	215-568-0167		526
Al Copeland Investments Inc 1001 Harimaw Ct S *TF:* 800-401-0401 ■ *Web:* www.alcopeland.com	Metairie	LA	70001	504-830-1000		670
Al Dente Pasta 491 N Palm Canyon Dr *Web:* www.aldente-palmsprings.com	Palm Springs	CA	92262	760-325-1160	325-2199	671
Al Forno Restaurant 577 S Main St *Web:* alforno.com	Providence	RI	02903	401-273-9760		671
AL Gilbert Co 304 N Yosemite Ave *TF:* 800-400-6377 ■ *Web:* farmerswarehouse.com	Oakdale	CA	95361	209-847-1721		447
Al Gordon Plumbing & Heating LC 3855 W Airline Hwy *Web:* algordonplumbing.com	Waterloo	IA	50703	319-233-3991		189-10
A&L Great Lakes Laboratories Inc 3505 Conestoga Dr *Web:* www.algreatlakes.com	Fort Wayne	IN	46808	260-483-4759		743
AL Hansen Manufacturing Co 701 Pershing Rd *Web:* www.alhansen.com	Waukegan	IL	60085	847-244-8900	244-7222	350
Al Hirschfeld Theatre 302 W 45th St *TF:* 800-432-7780 ■ *Web:* www.telecharge.com	New York	NY	10036	212-239-6262		747
Al Larson Boat Shop Inc 1046 S Seaside Ave *Web:* larsonboat.com	San Pedro	CA	90731	310-514-4100	831-4912	698
Al Neyer Inc 302 W Third St Ste 800 *TF:* 877-271-6400 ■ *Web:* www.neyer.com	Cincinnati	OH	45202	513-271-6400	271-1350	653
Al Phillips the Cleaner 3250 W Ali Baba Ln Ste C-F *Web:* www.alphillipslv.com	Las Vegas	NV	89118	702-798-7333	798-1731	426
Al Tiramisu 2014 P St NW *Web:* www.altiramisu.com	Washington	DC	20036	202-467-4466		671
Al's Garden Art Inc 311 W Citrus *Web:* www.alsgardenart.com	Colton	CA	92324	909-424-0221		364
Al's Restaurant 1200 N First St *Web:* www.alsrestaurant.net	Saint Louis	MO	63102	314-421-6399		671
ALA (Alliance for Lupus Research) 28 W 44th St Ste 501 *TF:* 800-867-1743 ■ *Web:* www.lupusresearch.org	New York	NY	10036	212-218-2840	218-2848	48-17
ALA (American Library Assn) 50 E Huron St *TF:* 800-545-2433 ■ *Web:* www.ala.org	Chicago	IL	60611	312-944-6780	944-2641	49-11
ALA (American Logistics Assn) 1133 15th St NW Ste 640 *TF:* 800-791-7146 ■ *Web:* www.ala-national.org	Washington	DC	20005	202-466-2520	296-4419	40-19
ALA (American Lung Assn) 14 Wall St *TF:* 800-586-4872 ■ *Web:* www.lung.org	New York	NY	10005	212-315-8700		48-17
ALA (Legal Management: Journal of the Assn of Legal Administrators) 75 Tri State International Ste 222 *Web:* www.alanet.org	Lincolnshire	IL	60069	847-267-1252	267-1329	457-15
ALA (Association of Legal Administrators) 75 Tri-State International Ste 222 *Web:* www.alanet.org	Lincolnshire	IL	60069	847-267-1252	267-1329	49-10
ALA (American Lighting Assn) 2050 Stemmons Fwy Ste 10046 *TF:* 800-605-4448 ■ *Web:* www.americanlightingassoc.com	Dallas	TX	75207	214-698-9898	698-9899	49-4
Ala Moana Hotel 410 Atkinson Dr *TF:* 800-367-6025 ■ *Web:* www.outrigger.com	Honolulu	HI	96814	808-955-4811	944-6839	379
Ala Moana Shopping Ctr 1450 Ala Moana Blvd *Web:* www.alamoanacenter.com	Honolulu	HI	96814	808-955-9517	955-2193	460
Alabama						
Administrative Office of Alabama Courts 300 Dexter Ave *TF:* 866-954-9411 ■ *Web:* www.alacourt.gov	Montgomery	AL	36104	334-954-5000		339-1
Agriculture & Industries Dept 1445 Federal Dr PO Box 3336 *Web:* agi.alabama.gov	Montgomery	AL	36109	334-240-7171	240-7190	339-1

Name / Address	City	State	Zip	Phone	Fax	Class
Archives & History Dept 624 Washington Ave *Web:* www.archives.state.al.us	Montgomery	AL	36130	334-242-4435		339-1
Arts Council 201 Monroe St Ste 110 *Web:* www.arts.alabama.gov	Montgomery	AL	36130	334-242-4076	240-3269	339-1
Banking Dept 401 Adams Ave Ste 680 *TF:* 866-465-2279 ■ *Web:* www.bank.state.al.us	Montgomery	AL	36104	334-242-3452	242-3500	339-1
Child Support Enforcement Div 50 N Ripley St Gordon Persons Bldg Ste 2104 *Web:* dhr.alabama.gov	Montgomery	AL	36130	334-242-1310	353-1115	339-1
Commission on Higher Education 100 N Union St PO Box 302000 *Web:* ache.alabama.gov	Montgomery	AL	36104	334-242-1998	242-0268	725
Conservation & Natural Resources Dept 64 N Union St PO Box 301450 *Web:* www.outdooralabama.com	Montgomery	AL	36130	334-242-3486		339-1
Consumer Affairs Office 11 S Union St *Web:* www.aldoi.gov	Montgomery	AL	36130	334-242-7334		339-1
Corrections Dept 301 S Ripley St PO Box 301501 *Web:* www.doc.state.al.us	Montgomery	AL	36130	334-353-3883		339-1
Crime Victims Compensation Commission 5845 Carmichael Rd *TF:* 800-541-9388 ■ *Web:* acvcc.alabama.gov	Montgomery	AL	36117	334-290-4420	290-4455	339-1
Dept of Industrial Relations 649 Monroe St *TF:* 800-548-2546 ■ *Web:* labor.alabama.gov	Montgomery	AL	36131	334-353-0515		339-1
Economic & Community Affairs Dept PO Box 5690 *Web:* adeca.alabama.gov	Montgomery	AL	36103	334-242-5100	242-5099	339-1
Education Dept 50 N Ripley St PO Box 302101 *Web:* www.alsde.edu	Montgomery	AL	36104	334-242-9700		339-1
Emergency Management Agency 5898 County Rd 41 PO Box 2160 *TF:* 800-843-0699 ■ *Web:* www.ema.alabama.gov	Clanton	AL	35046	205-280-2201	280-2410	339-1
Environmental Management Dept 1400 Coliseum Blvd *Web:* www.adem.state.al.us	Montgomery	AL	36110	334-271-7700	271-7950	339-1
Ethics Commission 100 N Union St Ste 104 *Web:* www.ethics.alabama.gov	Montgomery	AL	36104	334-242-2997	242-0248	339-1
Finance Dept 600 Dexter Ave Ste N-105 *Web:* www.finance.state.al.us	Montgomery	AL	36130	334-242-7160	353-3300	339-1
Forensic Sciences Dept 1051 Wire Rd *Web:* www.adfs.alabama.gov	Auburn	AL	36106	334-844-4648	887-7531	339-1
Higher Education Commission 100 N Union St PO Box 302000 *Web:* www.ache.state.al.us	Montgomery	AL	36130	334-242-1998	242-0268	339-1
Highway Patrol Div 301 S Ripley St PO Box 1511 *Web:* www.dps.alabama.gov	Montgomery	AL	36102	334-242-4395	277-3285	339-1
Historical Commission 468 S Perry St PO Box 300900 *Web:* www.preserveala.org	Montgomery	AL	36130	334-242-3184		339-1
Homeland Security Dept PO Box 304115	Montgomery	AL	36130	334-956-7250		339-1
Housing Finance Authority 7460 Halcyon Pointe Dr Ste 200 *TF:* 800-325-2432 ■ *Web:* www.ahfa.com	Montgomery	AL	36117	334-244-9200	244-9214	339-1
Human Resources Dept Gordon Persons Bldg 50 N Ripley St Ste 2104 *Web:* www.dhr.state.al.us	Montgomery	AL	36130	334-242-1310	353-1115	339-1
Information Services Div 64 N Union St Ste 200 *Web:* www.isd.state.al.us	Montgomery	AL	36130	334-242-2222		339-1
Insurance Dept 201 Monroe St Ste 502 PO Box 303351 *Web:* www.aldoi.gov	Montgomery	AL	36104	334-269-3550	241-4192	339-1
Labor Dept 649 Monroe St Rm 4207 *Web:* www.labor.alabama.gov	Montgomery	AL	36131	334-954-4701	242-0539	339-1
Legislature 11 S Union St *Web:* www.legislature.state.al.us	Montgomery	AL	36130	334-242-7600		339-1
Lieutenant Governor 11 S Union St Ste 725 *Web:* www.ltgov.state.al.us	Montgomery	AL	36130	334-242-7900	242-4661	339-1
Mental Health & Mental Retardation Dept 100 N Union St PO Box 301410 *TF:* 800-367-0955 ■ *Web:* mh.alabama.gov	Montgomery	AL	36130	334-242-3454	242-0725	339-1
Motor Vehicle Div 50 N Ripley St *Web:* revenue.alabama.gov/motorvehicle	Montgomery	AL	36104	334-242-9000		339-1
National Guard 1720 Congressman William L Dickinson Dr PO Box 3711 *TF:* 800-464-8273 ■ *Web:* state.nationalguard.com/alabama	Montgomery	AL	36109	334-738-3055		339-1
Pardons & Paroles Board 301 S Ripley St PO Box 302405 *Web:* www.pardons.state.al.us	Montgomery	AL	36130	334-353-7771	353-9400	339-1
Prepaid Affordable College Tuition (PACT) 100 N Union St Ste 660 *TF:* 800-252-7228 ■ *Web:* www.treasury.state.al.us	Montgomery	AL	36130	800-252-7228		725
Public Health Dept 201 Monroe St *TF:* 800-252-1818 ■ *Web:* www.adph.org	Montgomery	AL	36104	334-206-5300		339-1
Public Safety Dept PO Box 1511 *Web:* dps.alabama.gov	Montgomery	AL	36102	334-517-2800		339-1
Public Service Commission 100 N Union St RSA Union PO Box 304260 *TF:* 800-392-8050 ■ *Web:* www.psc.state.al.us	Montgomery	AL	36130	334-242-5218	242-0509	339-1
Rehabilitation Services Dept 602 S Lawrence St *TF:* 800-441-7607 ■ *Web:* www.rehab.alabama.gov	Montgomery	AL	36104	334-293-7500	293-7383	339-1
Revenue Dept 2545 Taylor Rd *Web:* www.revenue.alabama.gov	Montgomery	AL	36117	334-242-1170		339-1

Name / Address	City	State	Zip	Phone	Fax	Class
Robert Bentley Governor 600 Dexter Ave *Web:* www.governor.alabama.gov	Montgomery	AL	36130	334-242-7100		339-1
Secretary of State PO Box 5616 *Web:* www.sos.state.al.us	Montgomery	AL	36103	334-242-7200	242-4993	339-1
Securities Commission 401 Adams Ave Ste 280 *TF:* 800-222-1253 ■ *Web:* www.asc.state.al.us	Montgomery	AL	36104	334-242-2984	242-0240	339-1
Senior Services Dept 201 Monroe Ste 350 *TF:* 877-425-2243 ■ *Web:* alabamaageline.gov	Montgomery	AL	36104	334-242-5743	242-5594	339-1
State Legislature State House 11 S Union St *Web:* www.legislature.state.al.us/aliswww/default.aspx	Montgomery	AL	36130	334-242-7600		433
State Parks Div 64 N Union St Rm 538 *TF:* 800-252-7275 ■ *Web:* www.alapark.com	Montgomery	AL	36130	800-252-7275		339-1
State Port Authority 250 N Water St *Web:* www.asdd.com	Mobile	AL	36602	251-441-7234	441-7216	339-1
Tourism Department 401 Adams Ave PO Box 4927 *TF:* 800-252-2262 ■ *Web:* www.tourism.alabama.gov	Montgomery	AL	36104	334-242-4169	242-4554	339-1
Treasury Dept 600 Dexter Ave Ste S-106 *Web:* www.treasury.state.al.us	Montgomery	AL	36104	334-242-7500		339-1
Veterans Affairs Dept 770 Washington Ave, Ste 470 PO Box 1509 *Web:* www.va.state.al.us	Montgomery	AL	36104	334-242-5077	242-5102	339-1
Vital Records PO Box 5625 *Web:* www.adph.org	Montgomery	AL	36103	334-206-5418	262-9563	339-1
Weights & Measures Div 1445 Federal Dr	Montgomery	AL	36107	334-240-7133	240-7175	339-1
Workers" Compensation Div 649 Monroe St *Web:* labor.alabama.gov/wc	Montgomery	AL	36131	334-353-0515		339-1
Alabama Agricultural & Mechanical University 4900 Meridian St PO Box 1087 *TF:* 800-553-0816 ■ *Web:* www.aamu.edu	Huntsville	AL	35810	256-372-5000	372-5906	166
Alabama Agricultural & Mechanical University J F Drake Memorial Learning Resources Ctr PO Box 489 *Web:* www.aamu.edu	Normal	AL	35762	256-372-5000	372-5768	434-6
Alabama Aircraft Industries 1943 50th St N	Birmingham	AL	35212	205-592-0011		24
Alabama Art Supply Inc 1006 23rd St S *TF Cust Svc:* 800-749-4741 ■ *Web:* www.alabamaart.com	Birmingham	AL	35205	205-322-4741	254-3116	45
Alabama Assn of Realtors 522 Washington Ave PO Box 4070 *TF:* 800-446-3808 ■ *Web:* www.alabamarealtors.com	Montgomery	AL	36104	334-262-3808	263-9650	656
Alabama Ballet 2726 First Ave S *Web:* www.alabamaballet.org	Birmingham	AL	35233	205-322-4300		573-1
Alabama Card Systems Inc 500 Gene Reed Dr Ste 102 *TF:* 800-985-7507 ■ *Web:* alabamacard.com	Birmingham	AL	35215	205-833-1116	833-1160	761
Alabama Christian Academy 4700 Wares Ferry Rd *Web:* www.alabamachristian.com	Montgomery	AL	36109	334-277-1985		148
Alabama Constitution Village 109 Gates Ave *TF:* 800-678-1819 ■ *Web:* earlyworks.com	Huntsville	AL	35801	256-564-8100		520
Alabama Correctional Industries 1400 Lloyd St *TF:* 800-224-7007 ■ *Web:* www.aci.alabama.gov	Montgomery	AL	36107	334-261-3600	240-3162	630
Alabama Credit Union 220 Paul Bryant Dr E *Web:* alabamacu.com	Tuscaloosa	AL	35401	205-340-5944		219
Alabama Crown Distributing 421 Industrial Ln *TF:* 800-548-1869 ■ *Web:* georgiacrown.com	Birmingham	AL	35211	205-941-1155		81-3
Alabama Dance Theatre 1018 Madison Ave *TF:* 800-841-4273 ■ *Web:* www.alabamadancetheatre.com	Montgomery	AL	36104	334-241-2590		573-1
Alabama Democratic Party 501 Adams Ave *Web:* www.aldemocrats.org	Montgomery	AL	36104	334-262-2221		616-1
Alabama Dental Assn 836 Washington Ave *TF:* 800-489-2532 ■ *Web:* www.aldaonline.org	Montgomery	AL	36104	334-265-1684	262-6218	227
Alabama Dept of Archives & History 624 Washington Ave PO Box 300100 *Web:* www.archives.state.al.us	Montgomery	AL	36104	334-242-4435	240-3433	520
Alabama Educational Television Commission 2112 11th Ave S Ste 400 *TF:* 800-239-5233 ■ *Web:* www.aptv.org	Birmingham	AL	35205	205-328-8756	251-2192	632
Alabama Electric Company Inc 1728 Headland Ave *Web:* www.alaelectric.com	Dothan	AL	36304	334-792-5164		518
Alabama Eye Bank 500 Robert Jemison Rd *TF:* 800-423-7811 ■ *Web:* www.alabamaeyebank.org	Birmingham	AL	35209	800-423-7811		269
Alabama Farmers Co-op Inc PO Box 2227 *TF:* 888-255-2667 ■ *Web:* www.alafarm.com	Decatur	AL	35601	256-353-6843	350-1770	280
Alabama Gas Corp (Alagasco) 605 Richard Arrington Jr Blvd N *TF:* 800-292-4005 ■ *Web:* www.alagasco.com	Birmingham	AL	35203	205-326-8100		787
Alabama Goodwill Industries Inc 15810 Indianola Dr *TF:* 800-466-3945	Rockville	AL	20855	800-466-3945		256
Alabama Graphics & Engineering Supply Inc 2801 Fifth Ave S *TF:* 800-292-3806 ■ *Web:* www.algraphics.com	Birmingham	AL	35233	205-252-8505		256
Alabama Gulf Coast Zoo, The 1204 Gulf Shores Pkwy *Web:* alabamagulfcoastzoo.org	Gulf Shores	AL	36542	251-968-5732		823
Alabama Jazz Hall of Fame 1631 Fourth Ave *TF:* 800-239-2643 ■ *Web:* www.jazzhall.com	Birmingham	AL	35203	205-254-2731	254-2785	520

Name / Address	City	State	ZIP	Phone	Fax	Class
Alabama Lawyer Magazine 415 Dexter Ave *TF:* 800-354-6154 ■ *Web:* www.alabar.org	Montgomery	AL	36104	334-269-1515	261-6310	457-15
Alabama Livestock Auction Inc Hwy 80 E *Web:* www.allivestock.com	Uniontown	AL	36786	334-628-2371	628-6268	446
Alabama Media Group 200 Westside Sq Ste 100 *TF:* 800-239-5271 ■ *Web:* www.alabamamediagroup.com	Huntsville	AL	35801	256-532-4000		532-2
Alabama Medical Assn 19 S Jackson St **Fax Area Code:* 334 ■ *TF:* 800-239-6272 ■ *Web:* www.alamedical.org	Montgomery	AL	36104	800-239-6272	269-5200*	474
Alabama Metal Industries Corp (AMICO) 3245 Fayette Ave *TF:* 800-366-2642 ■ *Web:* amicoglobal.com	Birmingham	AL	35208	205-787-2611		491
Alabama Motor Express Inc 10720 E US Hwy 84 E *TF:* 800-633-7590 ■ *Web:* www.amxtrucking.com	Ashford	AL	36312	800-633-7590		780
Alabama Museum of Natural History PO Box 870340 *Web:* almnh.ua.edu	Tuscaloosa	AL	35487	205-348-7550	348-9292	520
Alabama News.net 3251 Harrison Rd *TF:* 800-467-0424 ■ *Web:* www.alabamanews.net	Montgomery	AL	36109	334-270-2834	272-6444	741-86
Alabama One Credit Union 1215 Veterans Memorial Pkwy *Web:* alabamaone.org	Tuscaloosa	AL	35404	205-759-1595		219
Alabama Outdoors Inc 3054 Independence Dr *TF:* 800-870-0011 ■ *Web:* www.alabamaoutdoors.com	Birmingham	AL	35209	205-870-1919		711
Alabama Paper Products LLC 1300 Industrial Park Dr	Tuscaloosa	AL	35401	205-339-9660		557
Alabama Pharmacy Assn 1211 Carmichael Way *TF General:* 877-877-3962 ■ *Web:* www.aparx.org	Montgomery	AL	36106	334-271-4222	271-5423	585
Alabama Public Library Service 6030 Monticello Dr *Web:* webmini.apls.state.al.us	Montgomery	AL	36130	334-213-3900	213-3993	434-5
Alabama Public Television (APT) 2112 11th Ave S Ste 400 *TF:* 800-239-5233 ■ *Web:* www.aptv.org	Birmingham	AL	35205	205-328-8756	251-2192	632
Alabama Republican Party 3505 Lorna Rd Ste 219 *TF:* 800-274-8683 ■ *Web:* www.algop.org	Birmingham	AL	35216	205-212-5900	212-5910	616-2
Alabama Rivers Alliance 2014 Sixth Ave N Ste 200 *Web:* alabamarivers.org	Birmingham	AL	35203	205-322-6395		532-5
Alabama School Journal 422 Dexter Ave *TF:* 800-392-5839 ■ *Web:* www.myaea.org	Montgomery	AL	36104	334-834-9790	262-8377	457-8
Alabama Shakespeare Festival 1 Festival Dr *TF:* 800-841-4273 ■ *Web:* www.asf.net	Montgomery	AL	36117	334-271-5300	271-5348	749
Alabama Small Business Development Consortium 1732 Fifth Ave N *Web:* www.asbdc.org	Birmingham	AL	35203	205-324-5231	324-5234	627
Alabama Southern Community College 2800 S Alabama Ave *TF:* 866-901-1117 ■ *Web:* www.ascc.edu	Monroeville	AL	36461	251-575-3156	575-5356	162
Alabama Southern Community College 30755 Hwy 43 *TF:* 800-381-3722 ■ *Web:* www.ascc.edu	Thomasville	AL	36784	334-636-9642	636-1380	162
Alabama Specialty Products Inc 152 Metal Samples Rd PO Box 8 *TF:* 888-388-1006 ■ *Web:* www.alspi.com	Munford	AL	36268	256-358-5200	358-4515	318
Alabama Sports Festival 2530 E South Blvd *TF:* 800-467-0422 ■ *Web:* www.alagames.net	Montgomery	AL	36116	334-280-0065		713
Alabama Sports Hall of Fame 2150 Richard Arrington Junior Blvd *Web:* www.ashof.org	Birmingham	AL	35203	205-323-6665	252-2212	522
Alabama State Bar 415 Dexter Ave *TF:* 800-392-5660 ■ *Web:* www.alabar.org	Montgomery	AL	36104	334-269-1515	261-6310	72
Alabama State Nurses Assn (ASNA) 360 N Hull St *TF:* 800-270-2762 ■ *Web:* www.alabamanurses.org	Montgomery	AL	36104	334-262-8321		533
Alabama State University 915 S Jackson St **Fax:* Admissions ■ *TF Admissions:* 800-253-5037 ■ *Web:* www.alasu.edu	Montgomery	AL	36104	334-229-4100	229-4984*	166
Alabama Symphony Orchestra 3621 Sixth Ave S *TF:* 800-745-3000 ■ *Web:* www.alabamasymphony.org	Birmingham	AL	35222	205-975-2787	251-6840	573-3
Alabama Theatre 1817 Third Ave N *Web:* www.alabamatheatre.com	Birmingham	AL	35203	205-252-2262		572
Alabama Theatre 4750 Hwy 17 S *TF:* 800-342-2262 ■ *Web:* www.alabama-theatre.com	North Myrtle Beach	SC	29582	843-272-1111		572
Alabama Veterinary Medical Assn 8116 Old Federal Rd Ste C *TF:* 800-272-1813 ■ *Web:* www.alvma.com	Montgomery	AL	36117	334-395-0086	270-3399	795
Alabama WMU Camp 2001 E S Blvd *Web:* alabamawmu.org	Montgomery	AL	36116	205-884-2425		239
Alabaster Caverns State Park 217036 SH 50A *Web:* www.travelok.com	Freedom	OK	73842	580-621-3381	621-3572	565
Alacare Home Health & Hospice 2400 John Hawkins Pkwy *TF:* 800-852-4724 ■ *Web:* www.alacare.com	Birmingham	AL	35244	205-981-8000	981-8743	363
Alachua County 12 SE First St 4th Fl *Web:* www.alachuacounty.us	Gainesville	FL	32601	352-374-5204		338
Alachua County Library District 401 E University Ave *TF:* 866-341-2730 ■ *Web:* www.aclib.us	Gainesville	FL	32601	352-334-3900	334-3918	434-3
Alachua County Visitors & Convention Bureau 30 E University Ave *TF:* 866-778-5002 ■ *Web:* www.visitgainesville.com	Gainesville	FL	32601	352-374-5260	338-3213	206
ALACO Ladder Co 5167 G St *TF:* 888-310-7040 ■ *Web:* www.alacoladder.com	Chino	CA	91710	909-591-7561	591-7565	421
Alacrinet Inc 530 Lytton Ave 2nd Fl *Web:* www.alacrinet.com	Palo Alto	CA	94301	650-646-2670		196
Alacritech Inc 1995 N First St Ste 200 *Web:* www.alacritech.com	San Jose	CA	95112	408-287-9997		174
Alacron Inc 71 Spit Brook Rd Ste 200 *Web:* www.alacron.com	Nashua	NH	03060	603-891-2750		253
Aladdin 651 Union Blvd *Web:* aladdinlv.com	Allentown	PA	18109	610-437-4023		671
Aladdin Bakers Inc 240 25th St *Web:* www.aladdinbakersinc.com	Brooklyn	NY	11232	718-499-1818		297-8
Aladdin Steel Inc PO Box 89 *TF:* 800-637-4455 ■ *Web:* www.aladdinsteel.com	Gillespie	IL	62033	217-839-2121	839-3823	492
Aladdin Temp-Rite LLC 250 E Main St *Web:* www.aladdintemprite.com	Hendersonville	TN	37075	615-537-3600		427
Aladdin's Eatery 2931 N High St *Web:* www.aladdinseatery.com	Columbus	OH	43202	614-262-2414		671
Aladdin's Fine Mediterranean 4240 Old Seward Hwy *Web:* www.aladdinsak.com	Anchorage	AK	99503	907-561-2373	563-5117	671
Aladdin's Natural Eatery 646 Monroe Ave *Web:* myaladdins.com/monroe.html	Rochester	NY	14607	585-442-5000		671
Alafia River State Park 14326 S County Rd 39 *Web:* www.floridastateparks.org	Lithia	FL	33547	813-672-5320		565
Alagasco (Alabama Gas Corp) 605 Richard Arrington Jr Blvd N *TF:* 800-292-4005 ■ *Web:* www.alagasco.com	Birmingham	AL	35203	205-326-8100		787
Alaglass Swimming Pools 165 Sweet Bay Rd *TF:* 877-655-7179 ■ *Web:* alaglas.com	Saint Matthews	SC	29135	877-655-7179		375
Alagnak Wild River PO Box 245 *Web:* www.nps.gov/alag	King Salmon	AK	99613	907-246-3305	246-2116	564
Alain Ducasse at the Essex House 60 W 55th St *Web:* www.alain-ducasse.com	New York	NY	10019	646-943-7373	943-7330	671
Alain Pinel Realtors Inc 12772 Saratoga-Sunnyvale Rd *Web:* www.apr.com	Saratoga	CA	95070	408-741-1111		652
Alaka'i Mechanical Corp 2655 Waiwai Loop *TF:* 800-600-1085 ■ *Web:* www.alakaimechanical.com	Honolulu	HI	96819	808-834-1085	834-1800	189-10
Alamac American Knits LLC 1885 Alamac Rd *Web:* www.alamacusa.com	Lumberton	NC	28358	910-739-2811		745-4
Alamance Community College PO Box 8000 *TF:* 877-667-7533 ■ *Web:* alamancecc.edu	Graham	NC	27253	336-578-2002	578-3964	162
Alamance County 124 W Elm St *Web:* www.alamance-nc.com	Graham	NC	27253	336-228-1312	570-6788	338
Alamance County Area Chamber of Commerce 610 S Lexington Ave *Web:* www.alamancechamber.com	Burlington	NC	27215	336-228-1338	228-1330	139
Alamance Regional Medical Ctr 1240 Huffman Mill Rd *Web:* www.armc.com	Burlington	NC	27215	336-538-7000		374-3
Alamance-Burlington School District 1712 Vaughn Rd *Web:* www.abss.k12.nc.us	Burlington	NC	27217	336-570-6060	570-6218	685
Alamar Resort Inn 311 16th St *TF:* 800-346-5681 ■ *Web:* www.alamarresortinn.net	Virginia Beach	VA	23451	757-428-7582		669
Alamar Restaurant & Marina 5999 Garden Hwy	Sacramento	CA	95837	916-922-0200		671
Alameda Animal Hospital 431 12th Ave NE *Web:* alamedaanimalhospital.com	Norman	OK	73071	405-360-0045		794
Alameda Applied Sciences Corp 3077 Teagarden St *Web:* www.aasc.net	San Leandro	CA	94577	510-483-4156		639
Alameda Bible Church Home of Victory Christian School 220 El Pueblo Rd NW *Web:* www.alamedabiblechurch.com	Albuquerque	NM	87114	505-898-2311		685
Alameda Chamber of Commerce 2210D S Shore Ctr *Web:* www.alamedachamber.com	Alameda	CA	94501	510-522-0414	522-7677	139
Alameda County 1221 Oak St Ste 555 *TF:* 800-878-1313 ■ *Web:* www.acgov.org	Oakland	CA	94612	510-272-6984	272-3784	338
Alameda County Fair Assn (ACFA) 4501 Pleasanton Ave *TF:* 800-874-9253 ■ *Web:* www.alamedacountyfair.com	Pleasanton	CA	94566	925-426-7600	426-7599	642
Alameda County Library 2450 Stevenson Blvd *TF:* 888-663-0660 ■ *Web:* aclibrary.org	Fremont	CA	94538	510-745-1500		434-3
Alameda County Medical Center-Highland Campus 1411 E 31st St *Web:* www.alamedahealthsystem.org	Oakland	CA	94602	510-437-4800		374-3
Alameda County Medical Ctr - Fairmont Hospital 15400 Foothill Blvd *Web:* www.alamedahealthsystem.org	San Leandro	CA	94578	510-895-4200		374-3
Alameda County Water District 43885 S Grimmer Blvd *TF:* 866-275-3772 ■ *Web:* www.acwd.org	Fremont	CA	94537	510-668-4200		787
Alameda Free Library 1550 Oak St *TF:* 800-222-1222 ■ *Web:* alamedaca.gov	Alameda	CA	94501	510-747-7777	337-1471	434-3
Alameda Natural Grocery 1650 Park St Unit L *TF:* 800-987-7530 ■ *Web:* www.alamedanaturalgrocery.com	Alameda	CA	94501	510-865-1500		345
Alameda Sun 3215 Encinal Ave Ste J *Web:* www.alamedasun.com	Alameda	CA	94501	510-263-1470		532-3
Alameda Times-Star 7677 Oakport St *TF:* 866-225-5277 ■ *Web:* alamedaca.gov	Oakland	CA	94621	510-208-6300		637-8
Alameda-Contra Costa Transit District 1600 Franklin St 10th Fl **Fax:* Cust Svc ■ *TF:* 877-878-8883 ■ *Web:* www.actransit.org	Oakland	CA	94612	510-891-4777	891-4705*	468
Alamo Aircraft Ltd 2538 SW 36th St PO Box 37343 *Web:* alamoaircraft.com	San Antonio	TX	78237	210-434-5577	434-1030	770

Name / Address	City	State	Zip	Phone	Fax	Class
Alamo Cafe 10060 W IH-10 *Web:* www.alamocafe.com	San Antonio	TX	78230	210-691-8827		671
Alamo Capital Financial Services 201 N Civic Dr Ste 360 *Web:* www.alamocapital.com	Walnut Creek	CA	94596	925-472-5700		690
Alamo City Chverolet 9400 San Pedro Ave *TF:* 866-635-6971 ■ *Web:* www.alamocitychevy.com	San Antonio	TX	78216	210-341-3311		57
Alamo Concrete Pavers 1008 Hoefgen *Web:* alamopavers.net	San Antonio	TX	78261	210-534-8821	534-8997	182
Alamo Group Inc 1627 E Walnut *NYSE: ALG* ■ *TF Cust Svc:* 800-788-6066 ■ *Web:* www.alamo-group.com	Seguin	TX	78155	830-379-1480	372-9683	273
Alamo Industrial Inc 1502 East Walnut St **Fax Area Code:* 830 ■ *TF:* 800-356-6286 ■ *Web:* www.alamo-industrial.com	Seguin	TX	78155	800-356-6286	379-0864*	295
Alamo Inn 2203 E Commerce St *TF:* 800-345-8082 ■ *Web:* alamoinnmotel.com	San Antonio	TX	78203	210-227-2203	222-2860	379
Alamo Iron Works Inc 943 AT&T Ctr Pkwy *TF:* 800-292-7817 ■ *Web:* www.aiwdirect.com	San Antonio	TX	78219	210-223-6161	704-8351	385
Alamo Lumber Co 10800 Sentinel Dr *TF:* 855-828-9792 ■ *Web:* alamo.doitbest.com	San Antonio	TX	78217	210-352-1300		191-3
Alamo Music Ctr 425 N Main Ave *TF:* 800-822-5010 ■ *Web:* www.alamomusic.com	San Antonio	TX	78205	210-224-1010		526
Alamo Tee's & Advertising 12814 Cogburn *TF:* 888-562-3800 ■ *Web:* alamotees.com	San Antonio	TX	78249	210-699-3800		7
Alamo Tissue Service Ltd 5844 Rocky Point Dr *TF:* 800-226-9091 ■ *Web:* www.alamotissueservice.com	San Antonio	TX	78249	210-738-2663	732-4263	545
Alamo Travel Group Inc 8930 Wurzbach Rd *TF:* 800-692-5266 ■ *Web:* www.alamotravel.com	San Antonio	TX	78240	210-593-0084	614-2448	771
Alamo, The 300 Alamo Plaza *Web:* www.thealamo.org	San Antonio	TX	78205	210-225-1391		520
Alamodome 100 Montana St *TF:* 800-884-3663 ■ *Web:* www.alamodome.com	San Antonio	TX	78203	210-207-3663	207-3646	720
Alamogordo Chamber of Commerce 1301 N White Sands Blvd *TF:* 800-826-0294 ■ *Web:* www.alamogordo.com	Alamogordo	NM	88310	575-437-6120	437-6334	139
Alamosa County 8900 Independence Way *Web:* www.alamosacounty.org	Alamosa	CO	81101	719-589-4848	589-1900	338
Alan b Harris Attorney at Law 409 N Texas Ave *TF:* 800-887-1676 ■ *Web:* alanbharris.com	Odessa	TX	79761	432-580-3118		428
Alan B Lancz & Assoc Inc 2400 N Reynolds Rd *Web:* www.ablonline.com	Toledo	OH	43615	419-536-5200	536-5401	463
Alan Davis & Associates Inc 538 Main Rd *Web:* www.alandavis.com	Hudson	QC	J0P1J0	450-458-3535		194
Alan Ferguson Assoc 1212 N Main St *Web:* alanferguson.com	High Point	NC	27262	336-889-3866		393
Alan Gordon Enterprises Inc 5625 Melrose Ave *TF:* 800-825-6684 ■ *Web:* www.alangordon.com	Hollywood	CA	90038	323-466-3561	871-2193	591
Alan Jones Auctioneers 2470 NW Dallas St *Web:* antiqueauctioncenter.com	Grand Prairie	TX	75050	972-641-7115		41
Alan Plummer & Assoc Inc 1320 S University Dr *Web:* www.apaienv.com	Fort Worth	TX	76107	817-806-1700	870-2536	261
Alan Ritchey Inc 740 S I-35 E Frontage Rd *TF:* 800-877-0273 ■ *Web:* www.alanritchey.com	Valley View	TX	76272	940-726-3276	726-5335	780
Alan Shintani Inc 94-409 Akoki St *Web:* www.alan-shintani.com	Waipahu	HI	96797	808-841-7631		186
Alan Utz & Associates Inc (AU& A) PO Box 131857 *Web:* www.auainc.com	Tyler	TX	75713	903-566-9797	566-9393	186
Alan Weber and Associates Inc 4131 Spicewood Springs Rd Ste L4 *Web:* www.alanweberassociates.com	Austin	TX	78759	512-777-2608		809
Alan White Co 506 Thomas St *TF:* 800-770-0038 ■ *Web:* www.alanwhiteco.com	Stamps	AR	71860	870-533-4471		319-2
Alan Wong's 1857 S King St *Web:* www.alanwongs.com	Honolulu	HI	96826	808-949-2526	951-9520	671
Alana's Food & Wine 2333 N High St *Web:* www.alanas.com	Columbus	OH	43202	614-294-6783		671
Alanco Technologies Inc 15575 N 83rd Way Ste 3 *OTC: ALAN* ■ *TF:* 800-368-1217 ■ *Web:* www.alanco.com	Scottsdale	AZ	85260	480-607-1010	607-1515	18
Al-Anon Family Group Inc 1600 Corporate Landing Pkwy *TF:* 888-425-2666 ■ *Web:* www.al-anon.org	Virginia Beach	VA	23454	757-563-1600	563-1655	48-21
Alaris Group Inc 4108 N 79th Ave W *Web:* www.alarisgroup.com	Duluth	MN	55810	218-730-9950		463
Alarm Security Group LLC 12301 Kiln Court Ste A *TF:* 800-888-4766 ■ *Web:* www.asgsecurity.com	Beltsville	MD	20705	301-937-8880		693
Alaska						
Arts Council 161 Klevin St Ste 102 *TF:* 888-278-7424 ■ *Web:* www.eed.state.ak.us	Anchorage	AK	99508	907-269-6610	269-6601	339-2
Attorney General PO Box 110300 *Web:* www.law.state.ak.us	Juneau	AK	99811	907-269-5100	269-5110	339-2
Banking Securities & Corporations Div 333 Willoughby Ave Fl 9 PO Box 110807 *TF:* 888-925-2521 ■ *Web:* www.commerce.alaska.gov	Juneau	AK	99801	907-465-2521	465-1230	339-2
Behavioral Health Div 3601 C St *Web:* www.hss.state.ak.us/dbh	Juneau	AK	99811	907-269-3600	269-3623	339-2
Child Support Enforcement Div 550 W Seventh Ave Ste 310 *Web:* www.csed.state.ak.us	Anchorage	AK	99501	907-269-6900	787-3220	339-2
Children's Services Office 130 Seward St Rm 406 PO Box 110630 *Web:* www.hss.state.ak.us/ocs	Juneau	AK	99811	907-465-3191	465-3397	339-2
Commerce Community & Economic Development Dept 333 W Willoughby Ave PO Box 110806 *Web:* www.commerce.alaska.gov	Juneau	AK	99811	907-465-2550	465-2974	339-2
Commission on Postsecondary Education PO Box 110510 *TF:* 800-441-2962 ■ *Web:* acpe.alaska.gov	Juneau	AK	99811	907-465-2962	465-5316	725
Corrections Dept 550 W Seventh Ave Ste 1800 *Web:* www.correct.state.ak.us	Anchorage	AK	99501	907-334-2381	465-3390	339-2
Court System 303 K St *Web:* www.courts.alaska.gov	Anchorage	AK	99501	907-264-0612		339-2
Dept of Administration,Personnel Div and Labor rel 10th Fl State Office Bldg PO Box 110201 *Web:* opd.doa.alaska.gov	Juneau	AK	99811	907-465-4430	465-2576	339-2
Education & Early Development Dept 801 W Tenth St Ste 200 PO Box 110500 *Web:* www.eed.state.ak.us	Juneau	AK	99811	907-465-2800	465-4156	339-2
Employment Security Div PO Box 115509 *TF:* 888-448-3527 ■ *Web:* www.labor.alaska.gov/estax	Juneau	AK	99811	907-465-2757	465-2374	259
Enterprise Technology Services Div State Office Bldg 5th Fl **Fax Area Code:* 907 ■ *TF:* 888-565-8680 ■ *Web:* www.alaska.gov	Juneau	AK	99811	888-565-8680	465-3450*	339-2
Environmental Conservation Dept 410 Willoughby Ave Ste 303 *Web:* www.alaska.gov	Juneau	AK	99811	907-465-5066	465-5070	339-2
Fish & Game Dept 1255 W Eigth St PO Box 25526 *Web:* www.adfg.alaska.gov	Juneau	AK	99811	907-465-4100	465-2332	339-2
Health & Social Services Dept PO Box 110601 *Web:* www.hss.state.ak.us	Juneau	AK	99811	907-465-3030	465-3068	339-2
History & Archeology Office 550 W Seventh Ave Ste 1260 *Web:* dnr.alaska.gov/parks/oha	Anchorage	AK	99501	907-269-8400	269-8901	339-2
Homeland Security & Emergency Services Div PO Box 5750 *Web:* www.ak-prepared.com	Fort Richardson	AK	99505	907-428-7000	428-7009	339-2
Housing Finance Corp 4300 Boniface Pkwy 99504 *TF:* 800-478-2432 ■ *Web:* www.ahfc.us	Anchorage	AK	99504	907-338-6100		339-2
Insurance Div PO Box 110805 *Web:* www.commerce.alaska.gov	Juneau	AK	99811	907-465-2515	465-3422	339-2
Labor & Workforce Development Dept 1016 W Sixth Ave Ste 401 *Web:* www.labor.state.ak.us	Anchorage	AK	99501	907-465-2700	465-2784	339-2
Legislative Ethics Committee 1500 W Benson Blvd Ste 230 *Web:* anchorage.akleg.gov	Anchorage	AK	99503	907-269-0111	269-0229	265
Lieutenant Governor 240 Main St Ste 301 *Web:* www.gov.state.ak.us	Juneau	AK	99811	907-465-3520		339-2
Military & Veterans Affairs Dept (DMVA) PO Box 5800 *Web:* dmva.alaska.gov	Fort Richardson	AK	99505	907-428-6896	428-7380	339-2
Motor Vehicles Div 1300 W Benson Blvd *Web:* doa.alaska.gov/dmv	Anchorage	AK	99503	907-269-5559		339-2
Natural Resources Dept 550 W Seventh Ave Ste 1260 *Web:* dnr.alaska.gov	Anchorage	AK	99501	907-269-8400	269-8917	339-2
Occupational Licensing Div 333 W Willoughby Ave 9th Fl *Web:* www.commerce.alaska.gov	Juneau	AK	99801	907-465-2550	465-2974	339-2
Parks & Outdoor Recreation Div 550 W Seventh Ave Ste 1260 *Web:* dnr.alaska.gov/parks	Anchorage	AK	99501	907-269-8400	269-8901	339-2
Parole Board 550 W Seventh Ave Ste 601 *Web:* www.correct.state.ak.us/parole-board	Anchorage	AK	99501	907-269-4642	269-4697	339-2
Permanent Fund Dividend Div 333 Willoughby Ave 11th Fl *Web:* www.pfd.alaska.gov	Juneau	AK	99811	907-465-2326	465-3470	339-2
Postsecondary Education Commission 3030 Vintage Blvd PO Box 110510 *TF:* 800-441-2962 ■ *Web:* acpe.alaska.gov	Juneau	AK	99811	907-465-2962	465-5316	339-2
Public Assistance Div 350 Main St Rm 304 PO Box 110640 *Web:* dhss.alaska.gov	Juneau	AK	99811	907-465-2680	465-5154	339-2
Real Estate Commission 550 W Seventh Ave Ste 1500 *Web:* www.commerce.alaska.gov	Anchorage	AK	99501	907-269-8160	269-8156	339-2
Regulatory Commission 550 W Eigth Ave Ste 300 *Web:* www.alaska.gov	Anchorage	AK	99501	907-276-6222	276-0160	339-2
Revenue Dept 550 W Seventh Ave Ste 1820 PO Box 110400 *Web:* www.revenue.state.ak.us	Anchorage	AK	99501	907-269-0080	276-3338	339-2
State Legislature State Capitol Ste 111 *Web:* Www.akleg.gov	Juneau	AK	99801	907-465-4648	465-2864	339-2
State Libraries Archives & Museums Div 395 Whittier St PO Box 110571 *Web:* www.eed.state.ak.us/lam	Juneau	AK	99801	907-465-2910	465-2151	339-2
State Medical Examiner 5455 Dr Martin Luther King Jr Ave *Web:* www.hss.state.ak.us/dph/sme	Anchorage	AK	99507	907-334-2200	334-2216	339-2
State Troopers Div 5700 E Tudor Rd *Web:* www.dps.state.ak.us	Anchorage	AK	99507	907-269-5511	337-2059	339-2
Supreme Court 303 K St *Web:* courts.alaska.gov/ctinfo.htm	Anchorage	AK	99501	907-264-0608	264-0878	339-2
Tourism Development Office PO Box 118004 *Web:* www.commerce.alaska.gov	Juneau	AK	99811	907-465-2510	465-2103	339-2
Transportation & Public Facilities Dept 3132 Channel Dr *Web:* www.dot.state.ak.us	Juneau	AK	99811	907-465-3900		339-2
Violent Crimes Compensation Board 240 Main St Ste 500 Court Plaza Bldg *Web:* doa.alaska.gov	Juneau	AK	99801	907-465-3040	465-2379	339-2

Name / Address	City	State	Zip	Phone	Fax	Class
Vital Statistics Bureau 5441 Commercial Blvd PO Box 110675 *Web:* dhss.alaska.gov/dph/vitalstats/pages/default.aspx	Juneau	AK	99801	907-465-3391	465-3618	339-2
Vocational Rehabilitation Div 801 W Tenth St PO Box 115516 *TF:* 800-478-2815 ■ *Web:* www.labor.state.ak.us	Juneau	AK	99801	907-465-2814	465-2856	339-2
Workers' Compensation Div 1111 W Eighth St Rm 305 *Web:* www.labor.state.ak.us/wc	Juneau	AK	99801	907-465-2790	465-2797	339-2
Alaska Aerofuel Inc 5859 Aerofuel Pl *Web:* www.alaskaaerofuel.com	Fairbanks	AK	99709	907-474-0062		316
Alaska Air Group Inc 19300 International Blvd *NYSE: ALK* ■ *TF:* 800-654-5669 ■ *Web:* www.alaskaair.com	Seattle	WA	98188	206-433-3200	392-7825	360-1
Alaska Airlines Magazine 2701 First Ave Ste 250 *Web:* www.alaskaairlinesmagazine.com	Seattle	WA	98121	206-441-5871	448-6939	457-22
Alaska Assn of Realtors 4205 Minnesota Dr *TF:* 800-478-3763 ■ *Web:* www.alaskarealtors.com	Anchorage	AK	99503	907-563-7133	561-1779	656
Alaska Aviation Heritage Museum 4721 Aircraft Dr *Web:* www.alaskaairmuseum.org	Anchorage	AK	99502	907-248-5325		520
Alaska Bar Assn 550 W Seventh Ave Ste 1900 PO Box 100279 *TF:* 800-478-4372 ■ *Web:* www.alaskabar.org	Anchorage	AK	99501	907-272-7469	272-2932	72
Alaska Bible College 248 E Elmwood Ave *TF:* 800-478-7884 ■ *Web:* www.akbible.edu	Palmer	AK	99645	907-745-3201		161
Alaska Bill Status State Capitol MS 3100 *Web:* www.legis.state.ak.us/basis	Juneau	AK	99811	907-465-4930	465-2864	433
Alaska Botanical Garden 4601 Campbell Airstrip Rd *Web:* www.alaskabg.org	Anchorage	AK	99507	907-770-3692	770-0555	97
Alaska Business Monthly 501 W Northern Lights Blvd Ste 100 *TF:* 800-770-4373 ■ *Web:* www.akbizmag.com	Anchorage	AK	99503	907-276-4373	279-2900	457-5
Alaska Clean Seas Inc 3300 C St Ste 200 *Web:* www.alaskacleanseas.org	Anchorage	AK	99503	907-659-2405		539
Alaska Club Inc, The 5201 E Tudor Rd *Web:* www.thealaskaclub.com	Anchorage	AK	99507	907-337-9550		354
Alaska Collection 509 W Fourth Ave *TF:* 888-602-3323 ■ *Web:* www.alaskaheritagetours.com	Anchorage	AK	99501	888-602-3323		760
Alaska Commercial Co 550 W 64th Ave Ste 200 *TF:* 800-563-0002 ■ *Web:* www.alaskacommercial.com	Anchorage	AK	99518	907-273-4600		345
Alaska Communications Systems Group Inc 600 Telephone Ave *NASDAQ: ALSK* ■ *TF:* 800-808-8083 ■ *Web:* www.alaskacommunications.com	Anchorage	AK	99503	907-563-8000	297-3100	736
Alaska Ctr for the Performing Arts 621 W Sixth Ave *Web:* www.myalaskacenter.com	Anchorage	AK	99501	907-263-2900	263-2927	572
Alaska Democratic Party 2602 Fairbanks St *Web:* www.alaskademocrats.org	Anchorage	AK	99503	907-258-3050		616-1
Alaska Denali Winery 11901 Industry Way Bldg A Ste 1 *Web:* denaliwinery.info	Anchorage	AK	99515	907-563-9434	563-9501	50-7
Alaska Dental Society 9170 Jewel Lake Rd Ste 203 *TF:* 800-478-4675 ■ *Web:* www.akdental.org	Anchorage	AK	99502	907-563-3003	563-3009	227
Alaska Executive Search Inc 821 N St Ste 201 *TF:* 800-938-1488 ■ *Web:* www.akexec.com	Anchorage	AK	99501	907-276-5707		260
Alaska Experience Theater & Gift Shop 333 W Fourth Ave *Web:* alaskaexperiencetheatre.com	Anchorage	AK	99501	907-272-9076		292
Alaska Fisheries Science Ctr (AFSC) 7600 Sand Point Way NE Bldg 4 *Web:* www.afsc.noaa.gov	Seattle	WA	98115	206-526-4000	526-4004	668
Alaska Humanities Forum 161 E First Ave *TF:* 800-315-6338 ■ *Web:* www.akhf.org	Anchorage	AK	99501	907-272-3979		533
Alaska Industrial Hardware Inc 2192 Viking Dr *TF:* 800-478-7201 ■ *Web:* www.aih.com/storefrontCommerce	Anchorage	AK	99501	907-276-7201	258-3054	364
Alaska Interstate Construction LLC 2525 C St ste 305 *Web:* www.aicllc.com	Anchorage	AK	99503	907-562-2792		539
Alaska Junior Theater 430 W Seventh Ave Ste 30 *Web:* www.akjt.org	Anchorage	AK	99501	907-272-7546	272-3035	573-4
Alaska Laser Printing & Mailing Services 165 E 56th Ave *Web:* www.alaskalaserprint.com	Anchorage	AK	99518	907-561-8000		5
Alaska Magazine 301 Arctic Slope Ave Ste 300 *TF:* 800-288-5892 ■ *Web:* www.alaskamagazine.com	Anchorage	AK	99518	386-246-0444		457-22
Alaska Marine Highway System 6858 Glacier Hwy PO Box 112505 *TF:* 800-642-0066 ■ *Web:* www.dot.state.ak.us/amhs	Juneau	AK	99811-2505	907-465-3941	465-8824	468
Alaska Marine Lines Inc 5615 W Marginal Way SW *TF Cust Svc:* 800-326-8346 ■ *Web:* www.lynden.com	Seattle	WA	98106	206-763-4244	764-5782	312
Alaska Medicine Magazine 4107 Laurel St *Web:* commerce.alaska.gov	Anchorage	AK	99508	907-562-0304	561-2063	457-16
Alaska Mining & Diving Supply Inc 3222 Commercial Dr *Web:* akmining.com	Anchorage	AK	99501	907-277-1741		711
Alaska Municipal League Joint Insurance Assn 807 G St Ste 356 *TF:* 800-337-3682 ■ *Web:* www.amljia.org	Anchorage	AK	99501	907-258-2625		533
Alaska Native Heritage Ctr 8800 Heritage Ctr Dr *TF:* 800-315-6608 ■ *Web:* www.alaskanative.net	Anchorage	AK	99504	907-330-8000	330-8030	520
Alaska Native Medical Ctr (ANMC) 4315 Diplomacy Dr *TF Admitting:* 800-478-6661 ■ *Web:* www.anmc.org	Anchorage	AK	99508	907-563-2662	729-1984	374-3
Alaska Native Tribal Health Consortium Inc 4000 Ambassador Dr *TF:* 800-655-4837 ■ *Web:* anthc.org	Anchorage	AK	99508	907-729-1900		363
Alaska Nurses Assn (AaNA) 3701 E Tudor Rd Ste 208 *Web:* www.aknurse.org	Anchorage	AK	99507	907-274-0827	272-0292	533
Alaska Pacific University 4101 University Dr *TF:* 800-252-7528 ■ *Web:* www.alaskapacific.edu	Anchorage	AK	99508	907-564-8248		166
Alaska Permanent Capital Management Co 900 W Fifth Ave Ste 601 *Web:* www.apcm.net	Anchorage	AK	99501	907-272-7575		194
Alaska Pharmacist's Assn 203 W 15th Ave Ste 100 *Web:* www.alaskapharmacy.org	Anchorage	AK	99501	907-563-8880	563-7880	585
Alaska Power & Telephone Co 193 Otto St PO Box 3222 *OTC: APTL* ■ *TF Cust Svc:* 800-982-0136 ■ *Web:* www.aptalaska.com	Port Townsend	WA	98368	360-385-1733	385-5177	787
Alaska Primary Care Association Inc 903 W Northern Lights Blvd Ste 200 *Web:* www.alaskapca.org	Anchorage	AK	99503	907-929-2722		138
Alaska Psychiatric Institute 3700 Piper St *Web:* dhss.alaska.gov	Anchorage	AK	99508	907-269-7100		374-5
Alaska Public Broadcasting Inc (APBI) 135 Cordova St *TF:* 888-840-0013 ■ *Web:* www.akpb.org	Anchorage	AK	99501	907-277-6300		632
Alaska Public Interest Research Group (AkPIRG) 737 W Fifth Ave Ste 206 *Web:* www.akpirg.org	Anchorage	AK	99501	907-278-3661		633
Alaska Railroad Corp 327 W Ship Creek Ave *Web:* www.alaskarailroad.com	Anchorage	AK	99501	907-265-2494		651
Alaska Regional Hospital 2801 Debarr Rd *TF:* 800-478-4450 ■ *Web:* www.alaskaregional.com	Anchorage	AK	99508	907-276-1131		374-3
Alaska Republican Party PO Box 201049 *Web:* www.alaskagop.org	Anchorage	AK	99520	907-276-4467		616-2
Alaska Salmon Bake In Alaskaland 2300 Airport Way *Web:* www.akvisit.com/salmon.html	Fairbanks	AK	99701	907-452-7274		671
Alaska Snow Removal 2134 E 88th Ave *Web:* www.akplow.com	Anchorage	AK	99507	907-349-5000	349-5008	776
Alaska State Chamber of Commerce 471 W 36th Ave *Web:* www.alaskachamber.com	Anchorage	AK	99503	907-278-2722		140
Alaska State Library PO Box 110571 *Web:* library.alaska.gov	Juneau	AK	99811	907-465-2920	465-2665	434-5
Alaska State Medical Assn 4107 Laurel St *TF:* 800-951-8712 ■ *Web:* www.asmadocs.org	Anchorage	AK	99508	907-562-0304	561-2063	474
Alaska State Museum 395 Whittier St *Web:* museums.alaska.gov	Juneau	AK	99801	907-465-2901	465-2976	520
Alaska State Veterinary Medical Assn (AKVMA) 1731 Bragaw St *TF:* 800-272-1813 ■ *Web:* www.akvma.org	Anchorage	AK	99508	907-563-3701		795
Alaska Stock Images 2505 Fairbanks St *TF:* 800-487-4285 ■ *Web:* www.alaskastock.com	Anchorage	AK	99503	907-276-1343	258-7848	593
Alaska Tanker Company LLC 15400 NW Greenbrier Pkwy Parkside Bldg Ste A400 *Web:* www.aktanker.com	Beaverton	OR	97006	503-207-0046		311
Alaska Textiles Inc 620 W Fireweed Ln *Web:* www.alaskatextiles.com	Anchorage	AK	99503	907-265-4880		791
Alaska Tour & Travel 9170 Jewel Lake Rd Ste 202 PO Box 221011 *TF:* 800-208-0200 ■ *Web:* www.alaskatravel.com	Anchorage	AK	99502	907-245-0200	245-0400	771
Alaska Travel Adventures Inc 9085 Glacier Hwy Ste 301 *TF:* 800-323-5757 ■ *Web:* www.alaskarv.com	Juneau	AK	99801	907-789-0052		771
Alaska USA Federal Credit Union 4000 Credit Union Dr PO Box 196613 *TF:* 800-525-9094 ■ *Web:* www.alaskausa.org	Anchorage	AK	99503	907-563-4567		219
Alaska Village Electric Co-op Inc 4831 Eagle St *Web:* www.avec.org	Anchorage	AK	99503	907-561-1818		245
Alaska Waterpark Company Inc 1520 O'Malley Rd *Web:* www.h2oasiswaterpark.com	Anchorage	AK	99507	907-522-4420		186
Alaska Wilderness League 122 C St NW Ste 240 *Web:* www.alaskawild.org	Washington	DC	20001	202-544-5205	544-5197	48-13
Alaska Wildlife Alliance 308 G St Ste 308 *Web:* www.akwildlife.org	Anchorage	AK	99501	907-277-0897		48-3
Alaska Wildlife Conservation Ctr Mile 79 Seward Hwy PO Box 949 *TF:* 800-478-1789 ■ *Web:* www.alaskawildlife.org	Portage	AK	99587	907-783-2025	783-2370	823
Alaska Zoo 4731 O'Malley Rd *TF:* 800-365-7057 ■ *Web:* www.alaskazoo.org	Anchorage	AK	99507	907-346-3242	346-2673	823
Alaskan Brewing Co 5429 Shaune Dr *Web:* www.alaskanbeer.com	Juneau	AK	99801	907-780-5866	780-4514	102
Alaskan Campers Inc 801 NW Kerron Ave *Web:* www.alaskancamper.net	Winlock	WA	98596	360-748-6494		120
Alaskan Copper & Brass Co 3223 Sixth Ave S *TF:* 800-552-7661 ■ *Web:* www.alascop.com	Seattle	WA	98134	206-623-5800	382-7335	492
ALBA Enterprises Inc 10260 Indiana Ct *Web:* www.albaent.com	Rancho Cucamonga	CA	91730	909-941-0600		358

Phone | Fax | Class

Alba Manufacturing Inc
8950 Seward Rd ... Fairfield OH 45011 513-874-0551 207
Web: www.albamfg.com

Alba Spectrum Technologies
1715 Wabansia ... Chicago IL 60622 773-384-9264 194
Web: www.albaspectrum.com

Alba Wheels Up International Inc
525 Washington Blvd ... Jersey City NJ 07310 201-435-7050 435-5650 311
TF: 800-633-6810 ■ *Web:* www.albawheelsup.com

Albach Company Inc 301 E Prosper St ... Chalmette LA 70043 504-271-1113 189-14
Web: www.albachco.com

Alban Tractor Co 8531 Pulaski Hwy ... Baltimore MD 21237 410-686-7777 358
TF: 800-492-6994 ■ *Web:* www.albancat.com

Albano Systems Inc
360 Bloomfield Ave Ste 308 ... Windsor CT 06095 860-688-9555 809
Web: www.albanosystems.com

Albany Area Chamber of Commerce
225 W Broad Ave ... Albany GA 31701 229-434-8700 434-8716 139
TF: 800-475-8700 ■ *Web:* www.albanyga.com

Albany Area Chamber of Commerce
435 W First Ave W ... Albany OR 97321 541-926-1517 926-7064 139
Web: www.albanychamber.com

Albany Bank & Trust Company NA
3400 W Lawrence Ave ... Chicago IL 60625 773-267-7300 267-7337 70
Web: www.albanybank.com

Albany Bedding LLC 3900 Pecan Grove Ct ... Albany GA 31701 229-420-7399 321

Albany City Hall 24 Eagle St ... Albany NY 12207 518-434-5100 434-5013 337
Web: www.albanyny.org

Albany College of Pharmacy (ACPHS)
106 New Scotland Ave ... Albany NY 12208 518-694-7221 694-7322* 166
*Fax: Admissions ■ *TF General:* 888-203-8010 ■ *Web:* www.acphs.edu

Albany County 112 State St Rm 1100 ... Albany NY 12207 518-447-7040 447-5589 338
Web: www.albanycounty.com

Albany County Convention & Visitors Bureau
25 Quackenbush Sq ... Albany NY 12207 518-434-1217 434-0887 206
TF: 800-258-3582 ■ *Web:* www.albany.org

Albany County Public Library
310 S Eigth St ... Laramie WY 82070 307-721-2580 721-2584 434-3
TF: 800-442-6757 ■ *Web:* www.albanycountylibrary.org

Albany County School 1948 E Grand Ave ... Laramie WY 82070 307-721-4400 685
Web: www.acsd1.org

Albany Democrat-Herald
600 Lyons St SW PO Box 130 ... Albany OR 97321 541-926-2211 926-4799 532-2
TF: 888-276-2017 ■ *Web:* www.democratherald.com

Albany Door Systems
975A Old Norcross Rd Ste A ... Lawrenceville GA 30046 770-338-5000 41
Web: www.assaabloyentrance.com/en/aaes/aaes

Albany Herald Publishing Company Inc
126 N Washington St ... Albany GA 31702 229-888-9300 888-9357 637-8
Web: www.albanyherald.com

Albany Industries Inc
504 N Glenfield Rd ... New Albany MS 38652 662-534-9000 534-9005 319-2
TF: 877-534-9804 ■ *Web:* www.albanyindustries.com

Albany Institute of History & Art
125 Washington Ave ... Albany NY 12210 518-463-4478 462-1522 520
Web: www.albanyinstitute.org

albany International Corp
216 Airport Dr ... Rochester NH 03867 603-330-5850 668
Web: www.albint.com

Albany International Corp
455 Patroon Creek Blvd PO Box 1907 ... Albany NY 12201 518-445-2200 445-2250 745-3
NYSE: AIN ■ *TF:* 877-327-5378 ■ *Web:* www.albint.com

Albany Law School of Union University (ALS)
80 New Scotland Ave ... Albany NY 12208 518-445-2311 167-1
TF: 800-448-3500 ■ *Web:* www.albanylaw.edu

Albany Medical Ctr 47 New Scotland Ave ... Albany NY 12208 518-262-3125 374-3
TF: 800-446-5400 ■ *Web:* www.amc.edu

Albany Memorial Hospital
600 Northern Blvd ... Albany NY 12204 518-471-3221 374-3
Web: www.nehealth.com

Albany Park Chamber of Commerce
3403 W Lauren Ave Ste 201 ... Chicago IL 60625 773-478-0202 478-0282 139
Web: northrivercommission.org/nrc2/index.php/economic-development/chamber

Albany Public Library (APL)
161 Washington Ave ... Albany NY 12210 518-427-4300 449-3386 434-3
Web: www.albanypubliclibrary.org

Albany State University
504 College Dr Rd ... Albany GA 31705 229-430-4600 166

Albany Steel Inc 566 Broadway ... Albany NY 12204 518-436-4851 436-1458 189-14
TF: 800-342-9317 ■ *Web:* www.albanysteel.net

Albany Symphony Orchestra
19 Clinton Ave PO Box 70065 ... Albany GA 12207 229-430-8933 573-3
Web: www.albanysymphony.org

Albany Visitors Assn 300 Second Ave SW ... Albany OR 97321 541-928-0911 926-1500 206
TF: 800-526-2256 ■ *Web:* www.albanyvisitors.com

Albany-Colonie Regional Chamber of Commerce
5 Computer Dr S ... Albany NY 12205 518-431-1400 431-1402 139
TF: 800-258-3582 ■ *Web:* capitalregionchamber.com

Albar Industries Inc 780 Whitney Dr ... Lapeer MI 48446 810-667-0150 608
Web: www.albar.com

Albarella Design Inc
100 Bridgepoint Dr ... South Saint Paul MN 55075 651-552-8966 344
Web: www.albarella.com

Albasha 5454 Bluebonnet Rd Ste G ... Baton Rouge LA 70809 225-292-7988 671
Web: www.albashabr.com

Albasha 1076 Main St ... Paterson NJ 07503 973-345-3700 671
Web: www.albashanj.com

Albemarle County
401 McIntire Rd ... Charlottesville VA 22902 434-296-5841 296-5800 338
TF: 800-367-7623 ■ *Web:* www.albemarle.org

Albemarle Electric Membership Corp
PO Box 69 ... Hertford NC 27944 252-426-5735 245
TF: 800-215-9915 ■ *Web:* www.aemc.coop

Albemarle Sportfishing Boats Inc
140 Midway Dr ... Edenton NC 27932 252-482-7600 90
Web: www.albemarleboats.com

Alberic Colon Auto Sales
Ave John F Kennedy Carr Ste 2 KM 3.4 ... San Juan PR 00920 877-292-4610 57
TF: 888-510-0718 ■ *Web:* albericgm.com

Phone | Fax | Class

Alberni Valley Chamber of Commerce
2533 Port Alberni Hwy ... Port Alberni BC V9Y8P2 250-724-6535 724-6560 137
Web: www.albernichamber.ca

Albert & Mackenzie A Professional Law Corp
28216 Dorothy Dr Ste 105 ... Agoura Hills CA 91301 818-575-9876 428
Web: www.albmac.com

Albert A List College of Jewish Studies
3080 Broadway ... New York NY 10027 212-678-8832 166
Web: www.jtsa.edu/list-college

Albert A Webb Assoc 3788 Mccray St ... Riverside CA 92506 951-686-1070 256
Web: www.webbassociates.com

Albert Arno Inc 5000 Claxton Ave ... St Louis MO 63120 314-383-2700 189-10
Web: albertarnostl.com

Albert at Bay Suite Hotel
435 Albert St ... Ottawa ON K1R7X4 613-238-8858 238-1433 379
TF: 800-267-6644 ■ *Web:* www.albertatbay.com

Albert C. Kobayashi Inc
94-535 Ukee St ... Waipahu HI 96797 808-671-6460 186
Web: www.ack-inc.com

Albert College 160 Dundas St W ... Belleville ON K8P1A6 613-968-5726 968-9651 622
TF: 800-952-5237 ■ *Web:* www.albertcollege.ca

Albert E. Sleeper State Park
6573 State Pk Rd ... Caseville MI 48725 989-856-4411 565
TF: 800-447-2757 ■ *Web:* www.michigan.org

Albert Einstein College of Medicine of Yeshiva University
1300 Morris Pk Ave ... Bronx NY 10461 718-430-2000 167-2
Web: www.einstein.yu.edu

Albert Einstein Healthcare Network
5501 Old York Rd ... Philadelphia PA 19141 215-456-7890 353
TF: 800-346-7834 ■ *Web:* www.einstein.edu

Albert Einstein Medical Ctr
5501 Old York Rd ... Philadelphia PA 19141 800-346-7834 374-3
TF: 800-346-7834 ■ *Web:* www.einstein.edu

Albert Fried & Company LLC
45 Broadway 24th Fl ... New York NY 10006 212-542-8266 690
Web: www.albertfried.com

Albert G's Bar-BQ 2748 S Harvard Ave ... Tulsa OK 74114 918-747-4799 671
Web: www.albertgs.com

Albert Guarnieri Co 1133 E Market St ... Warren OH 44483 330-394-5636 394-4982 297-8
TF: 800-686-2639 ■ *Web:* www.albertguarnieri.com

Albert H Notini & Sons Inc
225 Aiken St ... Lowell MA 01854 978-459-7151 458-7692 756

Albert J Marchionne Insurance Agency Inc
11 Independence Ave ... Quincy MA 02169 617-471-5010 390
Web: marchionneinsurance.com

Albert Kahn Assoc Inc
7430 Second Ave Albert Kahn Bldg ... Detroit MI 48202 313-202-7000 202-7001 261
TF: 800-833-0062 ■ *Web:* www.albertkahn.com

Albert Lea City Arena
701 Lake Chapeau Dr ... Albert Lea MN 56007 507-377-4374 720
TF: 800-345-8414 ■ *Web:* cityofalbertlea.org

Albert Lea Public Library
211 E Clark St ... Albert Lea MN 56007 507-377-4350 434-3
Web: alplonline.org

Albert Lea Seed House
1414 W Main St ... Albert Lea MN 56007 507-373-3161 373-7032 694
TF: 800-352-5247 ■ *Web:* www.alseed.com

Albert Lea Tribune, The
808 W Front St ... Albert Lea MN 56007 507-373-1411 373-0333 637-8
Web: www.albertleatribune.com

Albert Lea-Freeborn County Chamber of Commerce
2580 Bridge Ave ... Albert Lea MN 56007 507-373-3938 373-0344 139
TF: 800-345-8414 ■ *Web:* www.albertlea.org

Albert M Higley Co 2926 Chester Ave ... Cleveland OH 44114 216-861-2050 861-0030 106
Web: www.amhigley.com

Albert Moving & Storage Inc
4401 Barnett Rd ... Wichita Falls TX 76310 940-696-7000 194
Web: www.albertmovingandstorage.com

Albert R Maccani CPA
1537 S Delsea Dr ... Vineland NJ 08360 856-691-3279 2

Albert Risk Management Consultants
72 River Park St ... Needham Heights MA 02494 781-449-2866 195
Web: www.albertrisk.com

Albert Screen Print Inc 3704 Summit Rd ... Norton OH 44203 330-753-7559 745-7
Web: www.albertinc.com

Albert Tire LLC 39 Phoenix Dr ... West Deptford NJ 08086 856-663-0574 754
Web: www.alberttire.com

Albert's Organics Inc
3268 E Vernon Ave ... Vernon CA 90058 800-899-5944 297-7
TF: 800-899-5944 ■ *Web:* www.albertsorganics.com

Alberta Association of Municipal Districts & Counties
2510 Sparrow Dr ... Nisku AB T9E8N5 780-955-3639 138
Web: www.aamdc.com

Alberta Aviation Museum
11410 Kingsway Ave ... Edmonton AB T5G0X4 780-451-1175 451-1607 520
TF: 800-668-1987 ■ *Web:* www.albertaaviationmuseum.com

Alberta Bair Theater for the Performing Arts
2722 Third Ave N Ste 200 PO Box 1556 ... Billings MT 59103 406-256-8915 256-5060 572
TF: 877-321-2074 ■ *Web:* www.albertabairtheater.org

Alberta Blue Cross 10009 108th St NW ... Edmonton AB T5J3C5 780-498-8100 425-4627 391-3
TF: 800-661-6995 ■ *Web:* www.ab.bluecross.ca

Alberta Boilers Safety Assn
9410 20 Av NW ... Edmonton AB T6N0A4 780-437-9100 261
Web: www.absa.ca

Alberta Cancer Foundation
1331 29 St NW ... Calgary AB T2N4N2 403-521-3433 305
Web: albertacancer.ca

Alberta Chambers of Commerce
10025 - 102A Ave Edmonton Ctr Ste 1808 ... Edmonton AB T5J2Z2 780-425-4180 429-1061 137
TF: 800-272-8854 ■ *Web:* www.abchamber.ca

Alberta College of Art & Design
1407 14th Ave NW ... Calgary AB T2N4R3 403-284-7600 289-6682 785
TF: 800-251-8290 ■ *Web:* www.acad.ca

Alberta Enterprise Corp
10088 102 Ave ... Edmonton AB T5J2Z2 587-402-6601 402-6612 528
TF: 877-336-3474 ■ *Web:* www.alberta-enterprise.ca

Alberta Hotel & Lodging Assn (AHLA)
2707 Ellwood Dr ... Edmonton AB T6X0P7 780-436-6112 436-5404 48-23
TF: 888-436-6112 ■ *Web:* www.ahla.ca

Phone | Fax | Class

Alberta Newsprint Company Ltd
Whitecourt Plant Postal Bag 9000 10km W Hwy 43 ...... Whitecourt AB T7S1P9 780-778-7000 532-3
Web: www.albertanewsprint.com

Alberta Oil Tool 9530 60th Ave ...... Edmonton AB T6E0C1 780-434-8566 436-4329 537
TF: 877-432-3404 ■ *Web:* www.albertaoiltool.com

Alberta Oilsands Inc
815-8th Ave SW Ste 600 ...... Calgary AB T2P3P2 403-263-6700 536
Web: www.aboilsands.ca

Alberta Place Suite Hotel
10049 103rd St ...... Edmonton AB T5J2W7 780-423-1565 379

Alberta Senior Citizens Housing Association
9711 47 Ave NW ...... Edmonton AB T6E5M7 780-439-6473 138
Web: www.ascha.com

Alberta Soccer 9023 111 Ave NW ...... Edmonton AB T5B0C3 780-474-2200 138
TF: 866-250-2200 ■ *Web:* www.albertasoccer.com

Alberta Sports Hall of Fame & Museum
4200 Hwy 2 Ste 102 ...... Red Deer AB T4N1E3 403-341-8614 341-8619 522
Web: ashfm.ca

Alberta Union of Prov Employees
10451 170 St NW ...... Edmonton AB T5P4S7 780-930-3300 414
TF: 800-232-7284 ■ *Web:* www.aupe.org

Alberta Workers' Compensation Board
9912-107 St ...... Edmonton AB T5K1G5 780-498-3999 393
Web: www.wcb.ab.ca

Alberta-Pacific Forest Industries Inc
PO Box 8000 ...... Boyle AB T0A0M0 780-525-8000 638
TF: 800-661-5210 ■ *Web:* www.alpac.ca

Albertsons LLC 250 E Parkcenter ...... Boise ID 83706 208-395-6200 297-8
Web: www.albertsons.com

Albertus Magnus College
700 Prospect St ...... New Haven CT 06511 203-773-8550 773-5248* 166
*Fax: Admissions ■ *TF Admissions:* 800-578-9160 ■ *Web:* www.albertus.edu

Albertville Quality Foods Inc
130 Quality Dr ...... Albertville AL 35950 256-840-9923 840-9906 296-26
TF: 800-353-2806 ■ *Web:* www.albertvillequalityfoods.com

Albest Metal Stamping Corp
1 Kent Ave ...... Brooklyn NY 11211 718-388-6000 388-0404 488
Web: www.albest.com

Albin Marine Inc 143 River Rd ...... Cos Cob CT 06807 475-299-9504 90

Albion College 611 E Porter St ...... Albion MI 49224 517-629-1000 629-0569 166
TF: 800-858-6770 ■ *Web:* www.albion.edu

Albion Correctional Facility
3595 State School Rd ...... Albion NY 14411 585-589-5511 213
Web: nicic.gov

Albion Creative 622 SW St ...... High Point NC 27260 336-883-8028 592
Web: www.albionassociates.net

Albion Hotel 1650 James Ave ...... Miami Beach FL 33139 305-913-1000 674-0507 379
TF General: 877-782-3557 ■ *Web:* www.rubellhotels.com

Albion Industries Inc 800 N Clark St ...... Albion MI 49224 517-629-9441 350
TF: 800-835-8911 ■ *Web:* albioncasters.com

Albion International Services
2520 NW 97th Ave Ste 110 ...... Miami FL 33172 305-406-1000 195
Web: www.albionstaffing.com

Albion Laboratories Inc
101 N Main St ...... Clearfield UT 84015 801-773-4631 773-4633 447
TF: 800-453-2406 ■ *Web:* www.albionminerals.com

Albion Telephone Company Inc
225 W N St ...... Albion ID 83311 208-673-5335 387
Web: www.atcnet.net

Albona Ristorante Istriano
545 Francisco St ...... San Francisco CA 94133 415-441-1040 671
Web: albonarestaurant.com

Alborz Persian Cuisine
3300 W Anderson Ln Ste 300 ...... Austin TX 78757 512-420-2222 671
Web: www.alborzpersiancuisine.com

Albrecht- Viggiano- Zureck & Co
25 Suffolk Ct ...... Hauppauge NY 11788 631-434-9500 2
Web: www.avz.com

Albright Capital Management LLC
1101 New York Ave NW Ste 900 ...... Washington DC 20005 202-370-3500 528
Web: www.albrightcapital.com

Albright College 1621 N 13th St ...... Reading PA 19604 610-921-2381 921-7294 166
TF: 800-252-1856 ■ *Web:* www.albright.edu

Albright Memorial Library
500 Vine St ...... Scranton PA 18509 570-348-3000 348-3020 434-3
Web: www.lclshome.org

Albright Stonebridge Group
555 Thirteenth St NW Ste 300 W ...... Washington DC 20004 202-637-8600 194
Web: www.albrightstonebridge.com

Albright-Knox Art Gallery
1285 Elmwood Ave ...... Buffalo NY 14222 716-882-8700 520
Web: www.albrightknox.org

Albu & Associates Inc
2711 W Fairbanks Ave ...... Winter Park FL 32789 407-788-1450 186
Web: albu.biz

Albuquerque Academy
6400 Wyoming Blvd NE ...... Albuquerque NM 87109 505-828-3200 623
Web: www.aa.edu

Albuquerque Convention & Visitors Bureau
20 First Plaza Ste 601 ...... Albuquerque NM 87102 505-842-9918 247-9101 206
TF: 800-733-9918 ■ *Web:* visitalbuquerque.org

Albuquerque Convention Ctr
401 Second St NW ...... Albuquerque NM 87102 505-768-4575 768-3239 205
Web: www.albuquerquecc.com

Albuquerque International Sunport
2200 Sunport Blvd ...... Albuquerque NM 87106 505-244-7700 842-4278 27
Web: cabq.gov

Albuquerque Journal
7777 Jefferson St NE ...... Albuquerque NM 87109 505-823-7777 823-3994 532-2
TF: 800-990-5765 ■ *Web:* www.abqjournal.com

Albuquerque Little Theatre
224 San Pasquale SW ...... Albuquerque NM 87104 505-242-4750 572
TF: 800-242-4282 ■ *Web:* www.albuquerquelittletheatre.org

Albuquerque Public Schools (APS)
6400 Uptown Blvd NE ...... Albuquerque NM 87110 505-880-3700 889-4883* 685
*Fax: Hum Res ■ *TF:* 866-563-9297 ■ *Web:* www.aps.edu

Albuquerque Tortilla Company Inc
4300 Alexander Blvd NE ...... Albuquerque NM 87107 505-344-4011 123
Web: www.albuquerque-tortilla.com

Albuquerque Winnelson Co
3545 Princeton Dr NE ...... Albuquerque NM 87107 505-884-1553 791
TF: 800-466-7873 ■ *Web:* www.abqwinnelson.com

Alburg Dunes State Park 151 Coon Pt Rd ...... Alburg VT 05440 802-796-4170 565
TF: 800-262-5226 ■ *Web:* www.vtstateparks.com

Albury Bros Boats 1401 Broadway ...... Riviera Beach FL 33404 561-863-7006 863-7746 90
Web: www.alburybrothers.com

Alcalde & Fay
2111 Wilson Blvd 8th Fl ...... Arlington VA 22201 703-841-0626 636
Web: www.alcalde-fay.com

Alcamo Supply Corp 1152 Jericho Tpke ...... Commack NY 11725 631-543-8820 186
Web: www.alcamopools.com

Alcan Electrical & Engineering Inc
6670 Arctic Spur Rd ...... Anchorage AK 99518 907-563-3787 562-6286 186
Web: www.alcanelectric.com

Alcast Foundry Inc 2910 Fisk Ln ...... Redondo Beach CA 90278 310-542-3581 492
Web: www.alcast-foundry.com

Alcazar Networks Inc
419 State Ave Ste 3 ...... Emmaus PA 18049 484-664-2800 463
TF: 800-349-6192 ■ *Web:* www.alcazarnetworks.com

Alchem Chemical Co 5360 Tulane Dr ...... Atlanta GA 30336 404-696-9202 690
Web: www.alchemchemical.com

Alchemic Dream Inc
1751 Richardson Ste 8400 ...... Montreal QC H3K1G6 514-904-3700 904-3693 196
Web: www.alchemicdream.com

Alchemy of England
3516 Roberts Cut Off Rd ...... Fort Worth TX 76114 817-236-3141 361
TF: 800-578-1065 ■ *Web:* www.alchemyofengland.com

ALCO (Alico Inc)
10070 Daniels Interstate Ct Ste 100 ...... Fort Myers FL 33913 863-675-2966 315-2
NASDAQ: ALCO ■ *Web:* www.alicoinc.com

Alco Gas & Oil Production Equipment Ltd
5203 - 75th St ...... Edmonton AB T6E5S5 780-465-9061 539
Web: www.alcogasoil.com

ALCO Inc 6925 - 104 St ...... Edmonton AB T6H2L5 780-435-3502 403
TF: 800-563-1498 ■ *Web:* www.alcoinc.ca

Alco Industries Inc
820 Adams Ave Ste 130 ...... Norristown PA 19403 610-666-0930 757
Web: www.alcoind.com

Alco Iron & Metal Co
2140 Davis St ...... San Leandro CA 94577 510-562-1107 562-1354 686
Web: www.alcometals.com

Alco Manufacturing Corp
10584 Middle Ave ...... Elyria OH 44035 440-458-5165 458-6821 621
TF: 800-313-1821 ■ *Web:* www.alcomfgcorp.com

Alco Parking Corporation
501 Martindale St ...... Pittsburgh PA 15212 412-323-4455 562
Web: alcoparking.com

Alco Plastics Inc 160 E Pond Dr ...... Romeo MI 48065 586-752-4527 608
Web: www.alcoplastics.com

ALCO Sales & Service Co
6851 High Grove Blvd ...... Burr Ridge IL 60527 630-655-1900 194
TF: 800-323-4282 ■ *Web:* www.alcosales.com

Alcoa Inc 390 Park Ave ...... New York NY 10022 412-553-4545 485
TF: 800-523-9596 ■ *Web:* www.alcoa.com

Alcoa Inc 201 Isabella St ...... Pittsburgh PA 15212 412-553-4545 553-4498 485
NYSE: AA ■ *TF:* 800-388-4825 ■ *Web:* www.alcoa.com

Alcoa Wheel Products International
1600 Harvard Ave ...... Cleveland OH 44105 216-641-3600 483
TF: 800-242-9898 ■ *Web:* www.alcoa.com

Alcohol & Tobacco Tax & Trade Bureau
1310 G St NW Ste 300 ...... Washington DC 20220 202-453-2000 340-18
TF: 877-882-3277 ■ *Web:* www.ttb.gov

Alcoholic Beverage Control
PO Box 27491 ...... Richmond VA 23261 804-213-4565 213-4574 531-7
TF: 800-552-3200 ■ *Web:* www.abc.virginia.gov/enforce/offices.html

Alcoholics Anonymous (AA)
475 Riverside Dr 11th Fl ...... New York NY 10115 212-870-3400 870-3003 48-21
TF: 800-437-3584 ■ *Web:* www.aa.org

Alcom Printing Group Inc
140 Christopher Ln ...... Harleysville PA 19438 215-513-1600 627
Web: www.alcomprinting.com

Alcon Canada Inc
2665 Meadowpine Blvd ...... Mississauga ON L5N8C7 905-826-6700 544
TF: 800-268-4574 ■ *Web:* www.alcon.ca

Alcon Entertainment LLC
10390 Santa Monica Blvd Ste 250 ...... Los Angeles CA 90025 310-789-3040 514
Web: www.alconent.com

Alcon Laboratories Inc 6201 S Fwy ...... Fort Worth TX 76134 817-293-0450 269
TF: 800-862-5266 ■ *Web:* www.alcon.com

Alcon Tool Co 565 Crosier St ...... Akron OH 44311 330-773-9171 773-8042 493
TF: 800-852-0582 ■ *Web:* www.alcontool.com

Alcona Tool & Machine Inc PO Box 340 ...... Lincoln MI 48742 989-736-8151 736-6717 757
Web: www.alconatool.com

Alcone Marketing Group 4 Studebaker ...... Irvine CA 92618 949-770-4400 7
Web: alcone.com

Alconex Specialty Products Inc
4204 W Ferguson Rd ...... Fort Wayne IN 46809 260-744-3446 362
Web: www.alconex.com

Alcop Adhesive Label Co
826 Perkins Ln ...... Beverly NJ 08010 609-871-4400 871-3017 413
TF: 888-313-3017 ■ *Web:* alcoplabels.com

Alcopro Inc 2547 Sutherland Ave ...... Knoxville TN 37919 865-525-4900 415
TF: 800-227-9890 ■ *Web:* www.alcopro.com

Alcorn County
600 Waldron St PO Box 179 ...... Corinth MS 38834 662-286-7733 286-2548 338
Web: www.alcorncounty.org

Alcorn County Electric Power Association Inc
1909 S Tate St ...... Corinth MS 38834 662-287-4402 287-4088 245
TF: 844-741-7071 ■ *Web:* ace-power.com

Alcott Group 71 Executive Blvd ...... Farmingdale NY 11735 631-420-0100 420-1894 631
TF: 888-425-2688 ■ *Web:* www.alcottgroup.com

Alcott Whitney LLC 414 Bridge St ...... Franklin TN 37064 615-790-9155 195
Web: www.alcottwhitney.com

Phone | Fax | Class

ALCTS (Association for Library Collections & Technical Services)
50 E Huron St. . . . . Chicago IL 60611 312-280-5038 280-5033 49-11
TF: 800-545-2433 ■ *Web:* www.ala.org/alcts

Aldag Honold Mechanical Inc
3509 S Business Dr . . . . Sheboygan WI 53082 920-458-5558 458-3750 189-10
TF: 800-967-1712 ■ *Web:* www.aldaghonold.com

Aldagen Inc 2810 Meridian Pkwy Ste 148 . . . . Durham NC 27713 919-484-2571 2

AldeaVision Solutions Inc
8550 Cote de Liesse Blvd Ste 200 . . . . Saint-Laurent QC H4T1H2 514-344-5432 224
Web: aldea.tv

Aldebaran Capital LLC
10293 N Meridian St Ste 100. . . . . Indianapolis IN 46290 317-818-7827 401
TF: 888-742-7827 ■ *Web:* www.aldebarancapital.com

Aldelo LP 4641 Spyres Way Ste 4 . . . . Modesto CA 95356 209-338-5488 253
TF: 800-801-6036 ■ *Web:* www.aldelo.com

Alden & Ott Printing Inks LP
616 E Brook Dr. . . . . Arlington Heights IL 60005 847-956-6830 388
Web: www.aldenottink.com

Alden Buick Gmc Truck Inc
6 Whalers Way . . . . Fairhaven MA 02719 508-999-3300 57
Web: aldengmc.com

Alden Hauk Inc 68 Vine St . . . . Everett MA 02149 617-394-0302 627
Web: www.aldenhauk.com

Alden Hebron High School
9604 Illinois St. . . . . Hebron IL 60034 815-648-2442 685
Web: www.alden-hebron.org

Alden Research Laboratory Inc
30 Shrewsbury St. . . . . Holden MA 01520 508-829-6000 829-5939 419
Web: www.aldenlab.com

Alden Tool Company Inc 199 New Park Dr . . . . Berlin CT 06037 860-828-3556 828-8872 757
Web: www.aldentool.com

Alder Biopharmaceuticals Inc
11804 N Creek Pkwy S. . . . . Bothell WA 98011 425-205-2900 231
Web: www.alderbio.com

Alderbrook Resort & Spa 7101 E SR-106. . . . . Union WA 98592 360-898-2200 898-4610 669
TF: 800-622-9370 ■ *Web:* www.alderbrookresort.com

Alderfer Inc 382 Main St PO Box 2 . . . . Harleysville PA 19438 800-222-2319 296-26
TF Sales: 800-222-2319 ■ *Web:* www.alderfermeats.com

Alderman & Company Capital LLC
35 Warrington Round. . . . . Danbury CT 06810 203-917-4672 779-1122 401
Web: www.aldermancapital.com

Alderman Studios 325 Model Farm Rd. . . . . High Point NC 27263 336-889-6121 889-7717 590
Web: aldermancompany.com

Alderney Advisors LLC
1 Towne Sq Ste 1870 . . . . Southfield MI 48076 248-504-0690 463
Web: www.alderneyadvisors.com

Aldersgate United Methodist Church
460 W Aldersgate Dr. . . . . Nixa MO 65714 417-725-4949 48-20
Web: aldersgatechurch.com

Aldersgate Village 7220 SW Asbury Dr. . . . . Topeka KS 66614 785-478-9440 478-9104 672
TF: 000-097-6991 ■ *Web:* www.aldersgatevillage.org

Aldershot of New Mexico Inc
4884 S Main St. . . . . Mesilla Park NM 88047 575-523-8621 369

Alderson Reporting Co
1155 Connecticut Ave NW Ste 200. . . . . Washington DC 20036 202-289-2260 445
TF: 800-367-3376 ■ *Web:* www.aldersonreporting.com

Alderson-Broaddus College
101 College Hill Rd . . . . Philippi WV 26416 304-457-1700 457-6239* 166
**Fax:* Admissions ■ *TF Admissions:* 800-263-1549 ■ *Web:* www.ab.edu

Alderwood Capital LLC
505 Montgomery St 11th Fl . . . . San Francisco CA 94111 415-874-3388 70
Web: www.alderwoodcapital.com

ALDI Inc 1200 N Kirk Rd. . . . . Batavia IL 60510 630-879-8100 879-8114 345
Web: www.aldi.us

Aldila Inc 14145 Danielson St Ste B . . . . Poway CA 92064 858-513-1801 513-1870 710
OTC: ALDA ■ *TF:* 800-854-2786 ■ *Web:* www.aldila.com

Aldine Inc 150 Varick St Fl 6 . . . . New York NY 10013 212-226-2870 627
TF: 800-356-1818 ■ *Web:* aldine.com

Aldine Metal Products Corp
566 Danbury Rd Ste 1. . . . . New Milford CT 06776 860-350-2552 350-1061 482
TF: 800-215-4779 ■ *Web:* www.aldinemetal.com

Aldinger Company Inc
1440 Prudential Dr . . . . Dallas TX 75235 214-638-1808 393
Web: www.aldingerco.com

Aldo Shoes 2300 Emile Belanger . . . . Montreal QC H4R3J4 514-747-2536 301
TF: 888-818-2536 ■ *Web:* www.aldoshoes.com

Aldo Ventures Inc 7370 Viewpoint Rd . . . . Aptos CA 95003 831-662-2536 463
Web: www.aldo.com

Aldo's 306 S High St. . . . . Baltimore MD 21202 410-727-0700 671
Web: www.aldositaly.com

Aldo's Ristorante
1860 Laskin Rd. . . . . Virginia Beach VA 23454 757-491-1111 671
Web: aldosvb.com

Aldrich-Thomas Group Inc 18 N Third St . . . . Temple TX 76501 254-773-4901 652
Web: aldrich-thomas.com

Aldridge Botanical Gardens
3530 Lorna Rd . . . . Hoover AL 35216 205-682-8019 97
Web: www.aldridgegardens.com

Aldridge Electric Inc
844 E Rockland Rd . . . . Libertyville IL 60048 847-680-5200 189-4
Web: www.aldridgegroup.com

Ale Solutions Inc
1 Illinois St Ste 300 . . . . Saint Charles IL 60174 630-513-6434 652
Web: www.alesolutions.com

Ale-8-one Bottling Co 25 Carol Rd . . . . Winchester KY 40391 859-744-3484 297-8
Web: ale8one.com

Alebra Technologies Inc
3810 Pheasant Ridge Dr NE Ste 100. . . . . Minneapolis MN 55449 651-366-6140 177
TF: 888-840-2727 ■ *Web:* www.alebra.com

ALEC (American Legislative Exchange Council)
2900 Crystal Dr 6th Floor . . . . Arlington VA 22202 703-373-0933 373-0927 48-7
Web: www.alec.org

Alego Health
24651 Center Ridge Rd Ste 400 . . . . Westlake OH 44145 440-918-4570 194
TF: 855-918-4570 ■ *Web:* www.alegohealth.com

Alegria Cocina Latina Restaurant
115 Pine Ave. . . . . Long Beach CA 90802 562-436-3388 671
Web: www.alegriacocinalatina.com

Alejandra Hair Salon
14208 Palm Dr . . . . Desert Hot Springs CA 92240 954-447-9561 77
Web: www.alejandrahair.com

Alembic Global Advisors
780 Third Ave 3rd Fl. . . . . New York NY 10017 212-907-5350 401
Web: www.alembicglobal.com

Alembic Inc 3005 Wiljan Ct. . . . . Santa Rosa CA 95407 707-523-2611 523-2935 527
TF: 800-322-5893 ■ *Web:* www.alembic.com

Alemite LLC
1057-521 Corporate Ctr Dr Ste 100 . . . . Fort Mill SC 29715 803-802-0001 386
TF: 800-267-8022 ■ *Web:* www.alemite.com

Alenco Inc 16201 W 110th St . . . . Lenexa KS 66219 913-438-1902 106
Web: www.alenconline.com

Alene Candles LLC 51 Scarborough Ln . . . . Milford NH 03055 603-673-5050 364
Web: www.alene.com

Alent Technologies LLC
8201 Bondage Dr . . . . Gaithersburg MD 20882 301-520-3080 138
Web: www.alent.net

ALerCHEK Inc 15 Oak St Ste 302. . . . . Springvale ME 04083 207-490-2266 490-2210 231
TF: 877-282-9542 ■ *Web:* www.alerchek.com

Alere Inc 51 Sawyer Rd Ste 200. . . . . Waltham MA 02453 781-647-3900 231
TF: 877-441-7440 ■ *Web:* www.alere.com

Alere Medical Inc 51 Sawyer Rd Ste 200. . . . . Waltham MA 02453 781-647-3900 250
Web: www.alere.com

Alere San Diego Inc
9975 Summers Ridge Rd . . . . San Diego CA 92121 781-647-3900 231
TF: 866-284-3684 ■ *Web:* alere.com

Alere Toxicology Services Inc
1111 Newton St . . . . Gretna LA 70053 504-361-8989 743
Web: www.aleretoxicology.com

Alerion Partners 23 Old Kings Hwy S. . . . . Darien CT 06820 203-202-9900 792
Web: www.alerionpartners.com

Aleris International Inc
25825 Science Pk Dr Ste 400. . . . . Beachwood OH 44122 216-910-3400 910-3650 723
TF: 866-266-2586 ■ *Web:* www.aleris.com

Alerton 6670 185th Ave NE. . . . . Redmond WA 98052 425-869-8400 869-8445 202
Web: www.alerton.com

AlertOne Services Inc
1000 Commerce Park Dr Ste 300. . . . . Williamsport PA 17701 866-581-4540 575
TF Cust Svc: 866-581-4540 ■ *Web:* www.alert-1.com

Alerus Ctr 1200 42nd St S . . . . Grand Forks ND 58201 701-792-1200 746-6511 205
Web: www.aleruscenter.com

Alerus Financial
2300 S Columbia Rd . . . . Grand Forks ND 58201 701-795-3200 70

Alerus Retirement and Benefits
2 Pine Tree Dr Ste 400 . . . . Arden Hills MN 55112 800-795-2697 528
TF: 800-433-1685 ■ *Web:* www.alerusrb.com

Alesco Data Group LLC
5276 Summerlin Commons Way . . . . Fort Myers FL 33907 239-275-5006 4
TF: 800-701-6531 ■ *Web:* www.alescodata.com

Alessi Bakeries Inc 2909 W Cypress St . . . . Tampa FL 33609 813-879-4544 296-1
TF: 800-527-2105 ■ *Web:* www.alessibakeries.com

Aletheia House 201 Finley Ave W. . . . . Birmingham AL 35204 205-324-6502 726
TF: 800-522-7097 ■ *Web:* specialkindofcaring.org

Aleut Management Services LLC
5540 Tech Ctr Dr Ste 100 . . . . Colorado Springs CO 80919 719-531-9090 194
TF: 800-377-7765 ■ *Web:* www.aleutmgt.com

Aleutians East Borough
3380 C St Ste 205 . . . . Anchorage AK 99503 907-274-7555 276-7569 338
TF: 888-383-2699 ■ *Web:* www.aleutianseast.org

Alevistar Group Presidential Blvd . . . . Bala Cynwyd PA 19004 610-617-7800 196
Web: www.alevistar.com

Alex Alonzo Accountancy Corp
650 N First St . . . . San Jose CA 95112 408-295-3214 2

Alex C Fergusson LLC (AFCO)
5000 Letterkenny Rd. . . . . Chambersburg PA 17201 800-345-1329 264-9182* 145
**Fax Area Code:* 717 ■ *TF:* 800-345-1329 ■ *Web:* www.afcocare.us

Alex E. Paris Contracting Co
1595 Smith Township State . . . . Atlasburg PA 15004 724-947-2235 947-3820 189-3
Web: www.alexparis.com

Alex Lee Inc PO Box 800 . . . . Hickory NC 28603 828-725-4424 360-3
Web: www.alexlee.com

Alex Lyon & Son Sales Managers & Auctioneers Inc
7697 Route 31 . . . . Bridgeport NY 13030 315-633-2944 41
Web: www.lyonauction.com

Alex M Greenberg, DDS PC
18 E 48th St Rm 1702. . . . . New York NY 10017 212-319-9700 428
Web: www.dralexgreenberg.com

Alex Mccoy Plumbing
1-718 Fortune Crescent . . . . Kingston ON K7P2T3 613-546-6846 610
Web: amph.ca

Alex Nichols Agency 3800 Hampton Rd . . . . Oceanside NY 11572 516-678-9100 678-1344 12
TF: 800-545-9098 ■ *Web:* www.anaht.com

Alex Theatre 216 N Brand Blvd. . . . . Glendale CA 91203 818-243-7700 241-2089 572
TF: 800-227-2345 ■ *Web:* www.alextheatre.org

Alexa Internet Inc
Presidio Bldg 37. . . . . San Francisco CA 94129 415-561-6900 561-6795 178-7
Web: www.alexa.com

Alexa's Angels Inc 621 Innovation Cir . . . . Windsor CO 80550 970-686-7247 411
Web: www.alexas-angels.com

Alexander & Baldwin Inc
822 Bishop St. . . . . Honolulu HI 96813 808-525-6611 525-6652 185
NYSE: ALEX ■ *TF:* 866-442-6551 ■ *Web:* www.alexanderbaldwin.com

Alexander & Bonin LLC 132 Tenth Ave . . . . New York NY 10011 212-367-7474 367-7337 42
Web: www.alexanderandbonin.com

Alexander & Tom Inc 3500 Boston St . . . . Baltimore MD 21224 410-327-7400 180
Web: alextom.com

Alexander Capital Corp
900 W Castleton Rd Ste 200. . . . . Castle Rock CO 80104 303-814-0475 814-0486 216

Alexander City Chamber of Commerce
120 Tallapoosa St. . . . . Alexander City AL 35010 256-234-3461 234-0094 139
Web: www.alexandercity.org

Alexander City Outlook
548 Cherokee Rd . . . . Alexander City AL 35010 256-234-4281 96
TF: 800-613-9333 ■ *Web:* www.alexcityoutlook.com

Alexander Communications Group Inc (DIX)
712 Main St Ste 187B. . . . . Boonton NJ 07005 973-265-2300 402-6056 531-2
TF: 800-232-4317 ■ *Web:* www.downtowndevelopment.com

Name / Address	City	State	ZIP	Phone	Fax	Class
Alexander Company, The 345 W Washington Ave Ste 301 *Web:* www.alexandercompany.com	Madison	WI	53703	608-258-5580	258-5599	187
Alexander County 2000 Washington Ave *Web:* www.alexandercountyil.com	Cairo	IL	62914	618-734-0107		338
Alexander County 621 Liledoun Rd *Web:* alexandercountync.gov	Taylorsville	NC	28681	828-632-9332	632-0059	338
Alexander County Library 77 First Ave SW *Web:* www.alexanderlibrary.org	Taylorsville	NC	28681	828-632-4058		434-3
Alexander Hutton Venture Partners 1215 Fourth Ave Ste 900	Seattle	WA	98161	206-341-9800	341-9810	792
Alexander Lamar (Sen R - TN) 455 Dirksen Bldg *Web:* www.alexander.senate.gov	Washington	DC	20510	202-224-4944	228-3398	342-2
Alexander Majors Historic House & Museum 8201 State Line Rd *Web:* wornallmajors.org	Kansas City	MO	64114	816-333-5556		520
Alexander Mfg Co 12978 Tesson Ferry Rd *TF General:* 800-258-2743 ■ *Web:* www.alexandermc.com	Sappington	MO	63128	314-842-3344		9
Alexander Moulding Mill Co 250 US 281	Hamilton	TX	76531	254-386-3187		309
Alexander Oil Company Inc Intersection of 1-10 and 123 N Bypass PO Box 469 *TF:* 800-451-6734 ■ *Web:* alexander-oil.com	Seguin	TX	78155	830-379-1736		316
Alexander Open Systems Inc 12851 Foster St *TF:* 800-473-1110 ■ *Web:* www.aos5.com	Overland Park	KS	66213	913-307-2300	307-2380	174
Alexander Ramsey House (ARH) 265 S Exchange St *TF:* 800-657-3773 ■ *Web:* mnhs.org/visit	Saint Paul	MN	55102	651-296-8760		50-3
Alexander Smith Academy Inc 10255 Richmond Ave Ste 100 *Web:* www.alexandersmith.com	Houston	TX	77042	713-266-0920		685
Alexander Street Press LLC 3212 Duke St *Web:* alexanderstreet.com	Alexandria	VA	22314	703-212-8520		194
Alexander Summer LLC 205 Robin Rd Ste 120 *Web:* alexandersummer.com	Paramus	NJ	07652	201-712-1000	712-1274	655
Alexander X Kuhn & Co 123 W Front St Ste 200 *TF:* 800-784-2433 ■ *Web:* www.axk.com	Wheaton	IL	60187	630-681-8100		2
Alexander's 620 N Bruns Ln *Web:* mercedesrestaurants.com	Springfield	IL	62702	217-793-0440		671
Alexander's 105 S Jefferson St *Web:* alexandersva.com	Roanoke	VA	24011	540-982-6983		671
Alexander's Inc 210 Rt 4 E *NYSE: ALX* ■ *Web:* www.alx-inc.com	Paramus	NJ	07652	201-587-8541	708-6214	655
Alexander's Print Advantage Co 245 S 1060 W *Web:* www.alexanders.com	Lindon	UT	84042	801-224-8666		174
Alexander's Seafood Restaurant & Wine Bar 76 Queens Folly Rd *TF:* 800-234-6318 ■ *Web:* www.alexandersrestaurant.com	Hilton Head Island	SC	29928	843-785-4999		671
Alexandra Apt Hotel 77 Ryerson Ave *TF:* 800-567-1893 ■ *Web:* alexandrahotel.com	Toronto	ON	M5T2V4	416-504-2121		377
Alexandra Botanic Gardens Wellesley College 106 Central St *Web:* www.wellesley.edu	Wellesley	MA	02481	781-283-1000		97
Alexandra Park Neighbourhood Learning Centre 707 Dundas St W *Web:* www.apnlc.org	Toronto	ON	M5T2W6	416-591-7384		148
Alexandre de Paris Inc 12751 Federal Systems Park Dr *Web:* www.alexandredeparis.com	Fairfax	VA	22033	703-222-7661		77
Alexandre Mouton House/Lafayette Museum 1122 Lafayette St	Lafayette	LA	70501	337-234-2208		520
Alexandria & Arlington Bed & Breakfast Networks (AABBN) 4938 Hampden Ln Ste 164 **Fax Area Code: 202* ■ *TF:* 888-549-3415 ■ *Web:* www.aabbn.com	Bethesda	MD	20814	703-549-3415	517-9179*	376
Alexandria Archaeology Museum 105 N Union St Ste 327 *TF:* 800-367-7623 ■ *Web:* www.alexandriava.gov/historic/archaeology	Alexandria	VA	22314	703-746-4399	838-6491	520
Alexandria Black History Museum 902 Wythe St *TF:* 800-367-7623 ■ *Web:* www.alexandriava.gov/historic/blackhistory	Alexandria	VA	22314	703-838-4356	706-3999	520
Alexandria Chamber of Commerce 2834 Duke St *Web:* www.alexchamber.com	Alexandria	VA	22314	703-549-1000	549-1001	139
Alexandria City Hall 301 King St *TF:* 800-543-8911 ■ *Web:* www.alexandriava.gov	Alexandria	VA	22314	703-838-4000	838-6433	337
Alexandria Convention & Visitors Assn 221 King St *TF:* 800-388-9119 ■ *Web:* www.visitalexandriava.com	Alexandria	VA	22314	703-746-3301		206
Alexandria Daily Town Talk PO Box 7558 *TF:* 800-523-8391 ■ *Web:* www.thetowntalk.com	Alexandria	LA	71306	318-487-6397	487-6488	532-2
Alexandria Extrusion Co 401 County Rd 22 NW *TF:* 800-568-6601 ■ *Web:* alexandriaindustries.com	Alexandria	MN	56308	320-763-6537		487
Alexandria (Independent City) 301 King St Ste 2300 *Web:* alexandriava.gov	Alexandria	VA	22314	703-838-4500		338
Alexandria Industries 401 County Rd 22 NW *Web:* www.alexandriaindustries.com	Alexandria	MN	56308	320-763-6537		492
Alexandria Lakes Area Chamber of Commerce 206 Broadway *TF:* 800-235-9441 ■ *Web:* www.alexandriamn.org	Alexandria	MN	56308	320-763-3161	763-6857	139
Alexandria Moulding 20352 Powerdam Rd **Fax Area Code: 800* ■ *TF:* 866-377-2539 ■ *Web:* www.alexmo.com	Alexandria	ON	K0C1A0	613-525-2784	265-8746*	309
Alexandria National Cemetery 209 E Shamrock St *TF:* 800-827-1000 ■ *Web:* www.cem.va.gov	Pineville	LA	71360	318-449-1793	449-9327	136

Name / Address	City	State	ZIP	Phone	Fax	Class
Alexandria Real Estate Equities Inc 385 E Colorado Blvd Ste 299 *NYSE: ARE* ■ *TF:* 800-776-9437 ■ *Web:* are.com	Pasadena	CA	91101	626-578-0777		655
Alexandria State Recreation Area 57426 710th Rd *Web:* outdoornebraska.gov/alexandria	Fairbury	NE	68352	402-729-5777		565
Alexandria Symphony Orchestra 2121 Eisenhower Ave Ste 608 *Web:* www.alexsym.org	Alexandria	VA	22314	703-548-0885		573-3
Alexandria Veterans Affairs Medical Ctr 2495 Shreveport Hwy 71 N *TF:* 800-375-8387 ■ *Web:* www.alexandria.va.gov	Pineville	LA	71360	318-473-0010		374-8
Alexandria Zoological Park 3016 Masonic Dr *Web:* www.thealexandriazoo.com	Alexandria	LA	71301	318-441-6810	473-1149	823
Alexandria/Pineville Area Convention & Visitors Bureau (APACVB) 707 Main St PO Box 1070 *TF:* 800-551-9546 ■ *Web:* alexandriapinevillela.com	Alexandria	LA	71301	318-442-9546	443-1617	206
Alexandro's 2125 Missouri Blvd *Web:* alexandrosandtgs.com	Jefferson City	MO	65109	573-634-7740		671
Alexi's Grill 3550 N Central Ave Ste 120 *Web:* alexisgrill.com	Phoenix	AZ	85012	602-279-0982		671
Alexian Bros Health System 3040 Salt Creek Ln *TF:* 800-432-5005 ■ *Web:* www.alexianbrothershealth.org	Arlington Heights	IL	60005	847-818-7600		353
Alexian Bros Medical Ctr 800 Biesterfield Rd *TF:* 800-432-5005 ■ *Web:* www.alexianbrothershealth.org	Elk Grove Village	IL	60007	847-437-5500	981-5774	374-3
Alexion Pharmaceuticals Inc 352 Knotter Dr *NASDAQ: ALXN* ■ **Fax Area Code: 203* ■ *Web:* alexion.com	Cheshire	CT	06410	475-230-2596	271-8198*	85
Alexis Hotel 1007 First Ave *TF:* 866-356-8894 ■ *Web:* www.alexishotel.com	Seattle	WA	98104	206-624-4844	621-9009	379
Alexis Park Resort 375 E Harmon Ave *TF:* 800-582-2228 ■ *Web:* www.alexispark.com	Las Vegas	NV	89169	702-796-3300	796-4334	669
Alexsys Corp 14 Pebble Pl *Web:* www.alexcorp.com	Stoneham	MA	02180	781-279-0170		396
Alexza Pharmaceuticals Inc 2091 Stierlin Ct *NASDAQ: ALXA* ■ *Web:* www.alexza.com	Mountain View	CA	94043	650-944-7000	944-7999	85
ALF (American Liver Foundation) 39 Broadway *TF:* 800-465-4837 ■ *Web:* www.liverfoundation.org	New York	NY	10006	212-668-1000	483-8179	48-17
Alfa Aesar Co 26 Parkridge Rd **Fax Area Code: 800* ■ *TF:* 800-343-0660 ■ *Web:* www.alfa.com	Ward Hill	MA	01835	978-521-6300	322-4757*	145
Alfa Corp 2108 E S Blvd *TF:* 800-964-2532 ■ *Web:* www.alfainsurance.com	Montgomery	AL	36116	334-288-0375		457-1
ALFA International 2400 Pershing Rd Ste 500 *Web:* www.alfainternational.com	Kansas City	MO	64108	816-471-2121		434-3
Alfa Medical Equipment Specialists Inc 59 Madison Ave *Web:* www.sterilizers.com	Hempstead	NY	11550	516-489-3855		228
Alfa Scientific Designs Inc 13200 Gregg St *Web:* www.alfascientific.com	Poway	CA	92064	858-513-3888		476
Alfa Tec Inc 4024 22nd Ave W *Web:* www.alfatec.com	Seattle	WA	98199	206-281-9250		612
Alfa Wassermann Inc 4 Henderson Dr *TF:* 800-220-4488 ■ *Web:* www.alfawassermannus.com	West Caldwell	NJ	07006	973-882-8630		476
Alfab Inc 220 Boll Weevil Cir E *Web:* www.alfabinc.com	Enterprise	AL	36330	334-347-9516		499
AlfaLaval Inc 5400 International Trade Dr *Web:* www.alfalaval.com	Richmond	VA	23231	804-222-5300	236-3276	91
Alfalfa County 300 S Grand Ave Ste 1	Cherokee	OK	73728	580-596-3269		338
Alfalfa Electric Co-op Inc 121 E Main St *TF:* 888-736-3837 ■ *Web:* www.alfalfaelectric.com	Cherokee	OK	73728	580-596-3333	596-2464	245
Alfe Heat Treating Inc 6920 Pointe Inverness Way Ste 140 *Web:* www.al-fe.com	Fort Wayne	IN	46804	260-747-9422		484
Alfiniti Inc 1152 rue Manic *TF:* 800-334-8731 ■ *Web:* www.spectube.com	Chicoutimi	QC	G7K1A2	418-696-2545		492
Alford Motors Inc Hwy 171 *Web:* www.alfordmotors.com	Leesville	LA	71461	337-397-4144		57
Alforex Seeds 38001 County Rd 27 *TF:* 877-560-5181 ■ *Web:* www.alforexseeds.com	Woodland	CA	95695	530-666-3331	666-5317	276
Alfred A. Loeb State Park 725 Summer St NE Ste C *TF:* 800-551-6949 ■ *Web:* oregonstateparks.org	Salem	OR	97301	503-986-0707		565
Alfred Angelo Inc 1301 Virginia Dr *TF:* 888-218-0044 ■ *Web:* www.alfredangelo.com	Fort Washington	PA	19034	215-659-5300		155-21
Alfred B Maclay State Gardens 3540 Thomasville Rd *TF:* 800-257-6941 ■ *Web:* www.floridastateparks.org/maclaygardens	Tallahassee	FL	32309	850-487-4556	487-8808	97
Alfred B. Maclay Gardens State Park 14326 S County Rd 39 *Web:* www.floridastateparks.org	Lithia	FL	33547	813-672-5320		565
Alfred Hitchcock Mystery Magazine 44 Wall St Ste 904 *TF:* 800-220-7443 ■ *Web:* www.themysteryplace.com	New York	NY	10005	800-220-7443		457-11
Alfred I duPont Hospital for Children 1600 Rockland Rd *Web:* www.nemours.org	Wilmington	DE	19803	302-651-4000		374-1
Alfred M Shiver Pa 260 E Court St *Web:* shivercpa.com	Marion	NC	28752	828-652-7319		2
Alfred Mann Foundation, The 25134 Rye Canyon Loop *Web:* www.aemf.org	Valencia	CA	91355	661-702-6700		415
Alfred Manufacturing Co 4398 Elati St *Web:* alfredmfg.com	Denver	CO	80216	303-433-6385		608
Alfred Nickles Bakery Inc 26 N Main St *Web:* www.nicklesbakery.com	Navarre	OH	44662	330-879-5635	879-5896	296-1

				Phone	Fax	Class
Alfred P Sloan Foundation 630 Fifth Ave Ste 2550 *TF:* 800-401-8004 ■ *Web:* www.sloan.org	New York	NY	10111	212-649-1649	757-5117	305
Alfred Taubman Medical Library University of Michigan 1135 E Catherine St *Web:* www.lib.umich.edu	Ann Arbor	MI	48109	734-764-1210	763-1473	434-1
Alfred Williams & Co 410 S Salisbury St *Web:* alfredwilliams.com	Raleigh	NC	27601	919-832-9570		52
Alfred's Steakhouse 659 Merchant St *Web:* www.alfredssf.com	San Francisco	CA	94111	415-781-7058		671
Alfredo's Mexican Food 2849 S 14th St	Abilene	TX	79605	325-698-0104		671
Alfredo's Pizza & Pasta 251 W Baseline St *Web:* alfredospizzaandpasta.com	San Bernardino	CA	92410	909-885-0218		671
Alfresco 11710 Jefferson Ave *Web:* www.alfrescoitalianrestaurant.com	Newport News	VA	23606	757-873-0644		671
Alfresco Grills Inc 1085 Bixby Dr *TF:* 888-383-8800 ■ *Web:* www.alfrescogrills.com	City of Industry	CA	91745	323-722-7900	726-4700	106
Algeco Scotsman Inc 901 S Bond St Ste 600 *Web:* www.algecoscotsman.com	Baltimore	MD	21231	410-931-6000		106
Alger Correctional Facility N 6141 Industrial Pk Dr *Web:* www.michigan.gov/corrections	Wetmore	MI	49895	906-387-5000		213
Alger County 101 Court St *Web:* algercourthouse.com	Munising	MI	49862	906-387-2076	387-2156	338
Alger Family of Funds PO Box 8480 *TF:* 800-992-3863 ■ *Web:* www.alger.com	Boston	MA	02266	800-992-3863		528
Alger Farms Inc 950 NW Eigth St *Web:* www.algerfarms.com	Homestead	FL	33030	305-247-4334		10-5
Alger Mfg Company Inc 724 S Bon View Ave *TF:* 800-854-9833 ■ *Web:* www.alger1.com	Ontario	CA	91761	909-986-4591	983-3351	621
Algeria 326 E 48th St *Web:* www.algeria-un.org	New York	NY	10017	212-750-1960		784
Algeria Embassy 2118 Kalorama Rd NW *Web:* www.algerianembassy.org	Washington	DC	20008	202-265-2800	986-5906	257
Algo Communication Products Ltd 4500 Beedie St *TF:* 800-226-7722 ■ *Web:* www.algo.ca	Burnaby	BC	V5J5L2	604-438-3333	437-5726	246
Algo Design Inc 6455 Doris Lussier Ste 300 *TF:* 800-267-2584 ■ *Web:* www.algodesign.com	Boisbriand	QC	J7H0E8	450-681-2584		180
Algoa Correctional Ctr 8501 Fenceline Rd **Fax:* Warden ■ *TF:* 800-392-1111 ■ *Web:* mo.gov	Jefferson City	MO	65102	573-751-3911	526-1385*	213
Algoma Central Corp 63 Church St Ste 600 *Web:* www.algonet.com	St. Catharines	ON	L2R3C4	905-687-7888		312
Algoma Hardwoods Inc 1001 Perry St *TF:* 800-678-8910 ■ *Web:* www.algomahardwoods.com	Algoma	WI	54201	920-487-5221	487-3636	236
Algoma Net Co 1525 Mueller St *Web:* www.algomanet.com	Algoma	WI	54201	920-487-5577	487-2852	208
Algoma University College 1520 Queen St E *TF:* 888-254-6628 ■ *Web:* algomau.ca	Sault Sainte Marie	ON	P6A2G4	705-949-2301		354
Algonac State Park 8732 River Rd *Web:* www.michigandnr.com	Marine City	MI	48039	810-765-5605		565
Algonquin Area Public Library District 2600 Harnish *Web:* www.aapld.org	Algonquin	IL	60102	847-658-4343		434-3
Algonquin College of Applied Arts & Technology 1385 Woodroffe Ave *Web:* www.algonquincollege.com	Ottawa	ON	K2G1V8	613-727-4723		162
Algonquin Hotel 59 W 44th St *Web:* www.thealgonquin.net	New York	NY	10036	212-840-6800	944-1419	379
Algonquin Industries Inc 139 Farm St *Web:* www.algonquinindustries.com	Bellingham	MA	02019	508-966-4600		454
Algonquin Power 2845 Bristol Cir *Web:* www.algonquinpower.com	Oakville	ON	L6H7H7	905-465-4500		767
Algonquin/Lake in the Hills Chamber of Commerce 2114 W Algonquin Rd *TF:* 800-861-1055 ■ *Web:* www.alchamber.com	Lake In the Hills	IL	60156	847-658-5300	658-6546	139
Algood Food Co 7401 Trade Port Dr *TF:* 800-697-2327 ■ *Web:* www.algoodfood.com	Louisville	KY	40258	502-637-3631	637-1502	296-32
Algy Team Collection 440 NE First Ave **Fax Area Code:* 888 ■ *TF:* 800-458-2549 ■ *Web:* www.algyteam.com	Hallandale	FL	33009	954-457-8100	928-2282*	155-19
Alhambra Chamber of Commerce 104 S First St *Web:* www.alhambrachamber.org	Alhambra	CA	91801	626-282-8481	282-5596	139
Alhambra Civic Ctr Library 101 S First St *TF:* 800-477-5977 ■ *Web:* www.alhambralibrary.org	Alhambra	CA	91801	626-570-5008	457-1104	434-3
Alhambra Foundry Company Ltd 1147 Meridian Ave *Web:* www.alhambrafoundry.com	Alhambra	CA	91803	626-289-4294		751
Alhambra Hospital 100 S Raymond Ave *Web:* www.alhambrahospital.com	Alhambra	CA	91801	626-570-1606		374-3
ALI (American Laboratories Inc) 4410 S 102nd St *Web:* www.americanlaboratories.com	Omaha	NE	68127	402-339-2494		479
ALI (American Law Institute) 4025 Chestnut St *TF:* 800-253-6397 ■ *Web:* www.ali.org	Philadelphia	PA	19104	215-243-1600	243-1636	49-10
Ali Baba 404 S Craig St *Web:* www.alibabapittsburgh.com	Pittsburgh	PA	15213	412-682-2829		671
ALI's Database Consultants 1151 Williams Dr *TF:* 866-257-8970 ■ *Web:* www.aliconsultants.com	Aiken	SC	29803	803-648-5931		180
Alia Conseil Inc Place Iberville III 2960 Laurier Blvd Ste 214 *Web:* www.aliaconseil.com	Quebec	QC	G1V4S1	418-652-1737		194

				Phone	Fax	Class
Aliante Gaming LLC 7300 Aliante Pkwy *TF:* 800-627-6667 ■ *Web:* www.aliantegaming.com	North Las Vegas	NV	89084	702-692-7777		707
Alibates Flint Quarries National Monument PO Box 1460 *Web:* www.nps.gov/alfl	Fritch	TX	79036	806-857-3151	857-2319	564
Alibris Inc 1250 45th St Ste 100 *Web:* www.alibris.com	Emeryville	CA	94608	510-594-4500		95
Alice 95.5 1856 S Glenstone Ave *Web:* alice955.iheart.com	Springfield	MO	65804	417-890-5555		645-157
Alice Arts Ctr 1428 Alice St *Web:* mccatheater.com	Oakland	CA	94612	510-238-7526		520
Alice Austen House 2 Hylan Blvd *Web:* www.aliceausten.8m.com	Staten Island	NY	10305	718-816-4506	815-3959	520
Alice Chamber of Commerce (ACC) 612 E Main St PO Box 1609 *Web:* www.alicetxchamber.org	Alice	TX	78333	361-664-3454	664-2291	139
Alice Cooperstown 101 E Jackson St *Web:* www.alicecooperstown.com	Phoenix	AZ	85004	602-253-7337		671
Alice Hyde Medical Ctr 133 Pk St *Web:* www.alicehyde.com	Malone	NY	12953	518-483-3000	481-2320	374-3
Alice Lloyd College 100 Purpose Rd *TF Admissions:* 888-280-4252 ■ *Web:* www.alc.edu	Pippa Passes	KY	41844	606-368-6000		166
Alice Mfg Company Inc 208 E First Ave *Web:* www.alicemfgco.com	Easley	SC	29640	864-859-6323		745-1
Alice Public Library 401 E Third St	Alice	TX	78332	361-664-9506		434-3
Alice Travel Luxury Cruises & Tour 277 Fairfield Rd Ste 218 *TF:* 800-229-2542 ■ *Web:* www.alicetravel.com	Fairfield	NJ	07004	800-229-2542		772
Aliceville Manor 703 17th St NW *Web:* alicevillemanornursinghome.com	Aliceville	AL	35442	205-373-6307		371
Aliceville Public Library (APL) 416 Third Ave NE *Web:* pickenslibrary.com	Aliceville	AL	35442	205-373-6691	373-3731	434-3
Alico Inc (ALCO) 10070 Daniels Interstate Ct Ste 100 *NASDAQ:* ALCO ■ *Web:* www.alicoinc.com	Fort Myers	FL	33913	863-675-2966		315-2
Alidade Technology Inc 111 Knoll Dr *TF:* 877-265-1581 ■ *Web:* alidadetech.com	Collegeville	PA	19426	877-265-1581		196
Alien Technology Corp 845 Embedded Way *Web:* www.alientechnology.com	San Jose	CA	95037	408-782-3900	782-3908	647
Align Technology Inc 2560 Orchard Pkwy *NASDAQ:* ALGN ■ *TF:* 800-577-8767 ■ *Web:* www.aligntech.com	San Jose	CA	95131	408-470-1000	470-1010	228
Alignment Nashville Inc 21 White Bridge Rd Ste 201 *Web:* www.alignmentnashville.org	Nashville	TN	37205	615-585-8497		396
Alikar Gardens Resort, The 1123 Verde Dr Ste D	Colorado Springs	CO	80910	719-475-2564		210
Alimansky Capital Group Inc 12 E 44th St Ph	New York	NY	10017	212-832-7300		194
Aliments Asta Inc 511 Ave De La Gare *TF:* 800-463-1355 ■ *Web:* alimentsasta.com	St Alexandre-De-Kamouraska	QC	G0L2G0	418-495-2728	495-2879	296-26
Aliments Novali Foods Inc 3080 Rue St-Prosper	Saint-Hyacinthe	QC	J2S2A4	450-773-9944		297-8
Aliments Ouimet-Cordon Bleu Inc 8383 Rue J-Ren Ouimet *Web:* www.cordonbleu.ca	Anjou	QC	H1J2P8	514-352-3000		296-37
Alin Party Supplies Co 4139 Woodruff Ave *Web:* www.alinpartysupply.com	Lakewood	CA	90713	562-420-2489		566
Alinabal Inc 28 Woodmont Rd *TF:* 800-254-6763 ■ *Web:* www.alinabal.com	Milford	CT	06460	203-877-3241	874-5063	75
Aline Components Inc 1830 Tomlinson Rd PO Box 263 *Web:* www.alinecomponents.com	Kulpsville	PA	19443	215-368-0300	361-1400	604
ALine Inc 2206 E Gladwick St *TF:* 877-707-8575 ■ *Web:* www.alineinc.com	Rancho Dominguez	CA	90220	877-707-8575		743
ALine Systems Corp 13844 Struikman Rd *Web:* www.alinesys.com	Cerritos	CA	90703	562-229-9727		547
Alinea 1723 N Halsted St *Web:* website.alinearestaurant.com	Chicago	IL	60614	312-867-0110		671
Alinea Pharmaceuticals Inc 1 Memorial Dr Ste 1225	Cambridge	MA	02142	617-914-0123		231
Alinian Capital Group LLC 3343 W Commercial Blvd Ste 103 *Web:* www.alinian.com	Fort Lauderdale	FL	33309	954-495-2040		691
Alion Inc 870 Harbour Way S *Web:* www.alion.co	Richmond	CA	94804	510-965-0868		253
Alion Science & Technology 1750 Tysons Blvd Ste 1300 *TF:* 877-439-9227 ■ *Web:* www.alionscience.com	McLean	VA	22102	703-918-4480		261
Alioto's 3041 N Mayfair Rd *Web:* www.foodspot.com	Milwaukee	WI	53222	414-476-6900	476-6902	671
Alipes CME Inc 28 Atlantic Ave Ste 131 *Web:* www.alipes.com	Boston	MA	02110	617-303-1045		195
Aliron International Inc 5231 Massachusetts Ave *Web:* www.aliron.com	Bethesda	MD	20816	301-229-1900		194
Alisal Guest Ranch & Resort 1054 Alisal Rd *TF:* 800-425-4725 ■ *Web:* www.alisal.com	Solvang	CA	93463	805-688-6411	688-2510	669
Alisal Union Elementary School District 1205 E Market St *TF:* 800-782-7463 ■ *Web:* www.alisal.org	Salinas	CA	93905	831-753-5700	753-5709	685
ALISE (Association for Library & Information Science Education) 2150 N 107th St Ste 205 *TF:* 877-275-7547 ■ *Web:* www.alise.org	Seattle	WA	98133	206-209-5267	367-8777	49-11
Alishaev Bros Inc 20 W 47th St Ste 203 *TF:* 877-859-6020 ■ *Web:* alishaevbros.com	New York	NY	10036	877-859-6020		411
Alison Group Inc, The 2090 NE 163rd St *Web:* www.alisongroup.com	North Miami Beach	FL	33162	305-893-6255		4

Company / Address	City	State	Zip	Phone	Fax	Class
Alisto Engineering Group Inc 2737 N Main St Ste 200	Walnut Creek	CA	94597	925-279-5000		261
TF: 800-334-7275 ■ *Web:* www.alisto.com						
Alithya Group Inc 2875 Laurier Blvd Ste 1250	Quebec	QC	G1V2M2	418-650-2866		631
Web: www.alithya.com						
Alive Hospice Inc 1718 Patterson St	Nashville	TN	37203	615-327-1085	321-8902	371
TF: 800-327-1085 ■ *Web:* www.alivehospice.org						
Aljex Software Inc 463 Union Ave	Middlesex	NJ	08846	732-357-8700		179
Web: www.alcrest.com						
Aljira Ctr for Contemporary Arts 591 Broad St	Newark	NJ	07102	973-622-1600	622-6526	520
TF: 800-852-7699 ■ *Web:* www.aljira.org						
Aljon Graphics 1721 E Lambert Rd C	La Habra	CA	90631	562-694-3144		344
Web: www.aljongraphics.com						
ALK 35-151 Brunel Rd	Mississauga	ON	L4Z2H6	905-290-9952		231
TF: 800-663-0972 ■ *Web:* www.alk-abello.com						
Alken Inc 40 Hercules Dr	Colchester	VT	05446	802-655-3159		692
TF: 800-357-4777 ■ *Web:* www.polhemus.com						
Alken Industries Inc 2175 Fifth Ave	Ronkonkoma	NY	11779	631-467-2000		22
Web: www.alkenind.com						
Alken-Ziegler Inc 25575 Brest Rd	Taylor	MI	48180	734-946-4444		483
Alkermes Inc 852 Winter St	Waltham	MA	02451	781-609-6000		85
NASDAQ: ALKS ■ *TF:* 800-848-4876 ■ *Web:* www.alkermes.com						
Alkinco PO Box 278	New York	NY	10116	212-719-3070	764-7804	348
TF: 800-424-7118 ■ *Web:* www.alkincohair.com						
Alkon & Levine PC 29 Crafts St	Newton	MA	02458	617-969-6630		2
Web: alkon-levine.com						
Alkon Corp 728 Graham Dr	Fremont	OH	43420	419-333-7000		789
Web: www.alkoncorp.com						
All - Fill Inc 418 Creamery Way	Exton	PA	19341	610-524-7350		547
Web: www.all-fill.com						
All Aboard Benefits 6162 E Mockingird Ln Ste 104	Dallas	TX	75214	214-821-6677	821-6676	391-7
TF: 800-462-2322 ■ *Web:* www.allaboardbenefits.com						
All Aboard Cruises Inc 11114 SW 127th Ct	Miami	FL	33186	305-385-8657	419-4873*	771
**Fax Area Code: 786* ■ *TF:* 800-883-8657 ■ *Web:* www.allaboardcruises.com						
All Aboard Travel PO Box 90074	Chattanooga	TN	37412	423-499-9977		760
TF: 800-499-9877 ■ *Web:* www.allaboardchatt.com						
All About Kids Home Health 2102 W Teege Ave	Harlingen	TX	78550	956-412-3337		363
Web: allaboutkidshomehealth.com						
All About Packaging Inc 2200 W Everett St	Appleton	WI	54912	920-830-2700		627
TF: 800-446-1552 ■ *Web:* www.aapack.com						
All American Containers Inc 9330 NW 110th Ave	Miami	FL	33178	305-887-0797	888-4133	603
Web: allamericancontainers.com						
All American Ford Inc 520 River St	Hackensack	NJ	07601	201-487-6700		57
Web: www.allamericanfordofhackensack.com						
All American Grating Inc 3001 Grand Ave	Pittsburgh	PA	15225	412-771-6970		492
TF: 800-962-9692 ■ *Web:* www.aagrating.com						
All American Moving Group LLC PO Box 271277	Memphis	TN	38167	901-353-3900	353-4113	780
TF: 800-467-2900 ■ *Web:* www.allamericanmoving.com						
All American Poly 135 Industrial Park Cir	Lawrenceville	GA	30046	770-338-8350		600
Web: www.allampoly.com						
All American Private Security Inc 421 S Glendora Ave Ste 200	West Covina	CA	91790	626-962-9620		693
Web: www.allamericansecurity.com						
All American Recycling Corp 2 Hope St	Jersey City	NJ	07307	201-656-3363		660
Web: allamericanrecyclingcorp.com						
All American Seasonings 10600 E 54th Ave	Denver	CO	80239	303-623-2320	623-1920	296-37
TF: 800-442-4676 ■ *Web:* www.allamericanseasonings.com						
All American Ticket Service 2616 Philadelphia Pike Ste E	Claymont	DE	19703	800-669-0571	798-6552*	750
**Fax Area Code: 302* ■ *TF:* 800-669-0571 ■ *Web:* www.allamericantickets.com						
All City Metal Inc 54-01 35th St	Maspeth	NY	11378	718-472-5700		697
Web: www.allcitymetal.com						
All Classical Portland 211 SE Caruthers St Ste 200	Portland	OR	97214	503-943-5828	802-9456	645-128
TF: 888-306-5277 ■ *Web:* www.allclassical.org						
All Copy Products LLC 4141 Colorado Blvd	Denver	CO	80216	303-295-0741		45
TF: 800-332-2352 ■ *Web:* www.allcopyproducts.com						
All Creatures Animal Hospital 1894 State Rt 125	Amelia	OH	45102	513-797-7387		794
Web: www.all-creatures.com						
All Cruise Travel 1723 Hamilton Ave	San Jose	CA	95125	408-295-1200	295-2254	771
TF: 800-227-8473 ■ *Web:* www.allcruise.com						
All Custom Gasket & Materials 355 Watline Ave	Mississauga	ON	L4Z1P3	905-507-4580	507-4589	326
TF: 800-441-8193 ■ *Web:* www.allcustomgasket.com						
All Direct Mail Services Inc 15392 Cobalt St	Sylmar	CA	91342	818-833-7773		5
All Direct Travel Services Inc 19772 MacArthur Blvd Ste 150	Irvine	CA	92612	949-474-8100		772
TF: 800-862-1516 ■ *Web:* www.alldirecttravel.com						
All Flex Flexible Circuits Inc 1705 Cannon Ln	Northfield	MN	55057	507-663-7162		625
Web: www.allflexinc.com						
All Foils Inc 16100 Imperial Pkwy	Strongsville	OH	44149	440-572-3645	378-0161	492
TF: 800-521-0054 ■ *Web:* www.allfoils.com						
All Graphic Supplies 6691 Edwards Blvd	Mississauga	ON	L5T2H8	800-501-4451		791
TF: 800-501-4451 ■ *Web:* www.allgraphicsupplies.com						
All Hvac Service Company Inc 9030 Ft Hamilton Pkwy	Brooklyn	NY	11209	718-833-0148		189-10
Web: allhvac.com						
All in One Poster Co 8521 Whitaker St	Buena Park	CA	90621	714-521-7720		45
TF: 800-273-0307 ■ *Web:* www.allinoneposters.com						
All Inc 185 Plato Blvd W	Saint Paul	MN	55107	651-227-6331	292-0541	38
TF: 800-829-2127 ■ *Web:* www.allinc.com						
All Island Media Inc 1 Rodeo Dr	Edgewood	NY	11717	631-698-8400		532-3
Web: www.lipennysaver.com						
All Line Inc 16851 E Parkview Ave Unit 2	Fountain Hills	AZ	85268	480-306-6001	306-6001	208
Web: www.alllinerope.com						
All Makes Office Equipment Co 2558 Farnam St	Omaha	NE	68131	402-341-2413		321
TF: 800-341-2413 ■ *Web:* www.allmakes.com						
All Media Art Supply 417 E Main St	Kent	OH	44240	330-678-8078		45
Web: allmediaartsupply.com						
All Media Ventures 1 Quincy Ln	White Plains	NY	10605	917-806-6373	683-5090*	466
**Fax Area Code: 914* ■ *Web:* www.allmediaventures.com						
All Metals Fabricating Inc 200 Allentown Pkwy	Allen	TX	75002	972-747-1234		697
Web: www.ametals.com						
All Metals Industries Inc PO Box 807	Belmont	NH	03220	603-267-7023	267-7025	492
TF: 800-654-6043 ■ *Web:* www.allmetalsindustries.com						
All Metals Processing of Orange County Inc 8401 Standustrial St	Stanton	CA	90680	714-828-8238	828-4552	481
Web: www.allmetalsprocessing.com						
All Metals Service & Warehousing Inc 100 All Metals Dr	Cartersville	GA	30120	770-427-7379		480
Web: www.allmetals.com						
All Motorists Insurance Agency 5230 Las Virgenes Rd Ste 100	Calabasas	CA	91302	818-880-9070		390
Web: westerngeneral.com						
All Native Systems LLC 1 Mission Dr	Winnebago	NE	68071	866-323-7636		180
TF: 866-323-7636 ■ *Web:* www.allnativesystems.com						
All Needs Computer & Mailing Services Inc 8100 S 13th St	Lincoln	NE	68512	402-421-1083		5
TF: 800-921-9581 ■ *Web:* www.ancms.com						
All New Stamping Co 10801 Lower Azusa Rd	El Monte	CA	91731	800-877-7775	877-8121	488
TF: 800-877-7775 ■ *Web:* www.allnewstamping.com						
All Nippon Airways Company Ltd 2050 W 190th St Ste 100	Torrance	CA	90504	800-235-9262		25
TF: 800-235-9262 ■ *Web:* www.ana.co.jp						
All of E Solutions 2510 W Sixth St	Lawrence	KS	66049	785-832-2900		177
Web: allofe.com						
All Phase Security Inc 2959 Promenade St Ste 200	West Sacramento	CA	95691	916-375-6640		693
Web: www.allphasesecurity.com						
All Plastics & Fiberglass 8201 Zeigler Blvd	Mobile	AL	36608	251-633-2130		596
Web: www.allplastics-fiberglass.com						
All Plastics Molding Inc 15700 Midway Rd	Addison	TX	75001	972-239-2686		608
Web: www.all-plastics.com						
All Pool & Spa Inc 905 Kalanianaole Hwy	Kailua	HI	96734	808-261-8991		186
Web: www.allpoolandspa.com						
All Power Brokers Real Estate Inc 847 N Hwy 49/88 Ste 1	Jackson	CA	95642	209-223-0237		652
Web: allpower.com						
All Power Mfg Company Inc 13141 Molette St	Santa Fe Springs	CA	90670	562-802-2640		21
Web: www.allpowermfg.com						
All Products Automotive Inc 4701 W Cortland St	Chicago	IL	60639	773-889-4500		61
Web: locations.autovalue.com						
All Property Management LLC 2505 Third Ave Ste 325	Seattle	WA	98121	206-577-0029		387
Web: www.allpropertymanagement.com						
All Purpose Manufacturing Inc 614 Airport Rd	Oceanside	CA	92058	760-967-8464		320
Web: www.apmfg.net						
All Rite Industries Inc 470 Oakwood Rd	Lake Zurich	IL	60047	847-540-0300		488
Web: www.allriteindustries.com						
All Rite Ready Mix Inc 108 Williams Way	Wilder	KY	41076	859-572-9951		135
Web: www.allritereadymix.com						
All Saints Health Care 11810 Saticoy St	North Hollywood	CA	91605	818-982-4600		371
TF: 800-254-9442 ■ *Web:* www.allsaints-subacute.com						
All Seniors Care Living Centres Ltd 175 Bloor St E Ste 601	Toronto	ON	M4W3R8	416 323 3773		371
Web: www.allseniorscare.com						
All Source Security Container Mfg Corp 40 Mills Rd	Barrie	ON	L4N6H4	705-726-6460	726-5017	803-1
TF: 866-526-4579 ■ *Web:* www.allsourcemfg.com						
All Squared Web Design LLC 284 Susquehanna Trl	Allentown	PA	18104	610-351-5416		177
Web: allsquared.com						
All Star Adventures 1010 N Webb Rd	Wichita	KS	67206	316-682-3700		31
Web: www.allstarwichita.com						
All Star Consulting Inc 1111 Oak St	San Francisco	CA	94117	415-552-1400		180
Web: www.all-stars.com						
All Star Glass Co Inc 1845 Morena Blvd	San Diego	CA	92110	619-275-3343	275-6367	62-2
TF: 800-225-4184 ■ *Web:* www.allstarglass.net						
All Star Metals LLC 101 Box Car Rd	Brownsville	TX	78521	956-838-2110		492
Web: allstarmetals.wixsite.com/asm-v2						
All Star Software Systems LLC 440 Smith St	Middletown	CT	06457	860-613-1500		180
Web: www.allstarss.com/products/scanners						
All Star Team Service LLC 2 Industrial Park Dr Ste B	Waldorf	MD	20602	240-607-6209		256
All Star Wine & Spirits 579 Troy Schenectady Rd	Latham	NY	12110	518-220-9463		443
TF: 800-634-6125 ■ *Web:* www.allstarwine.com						
All State Beverage Co 130 Sixth St	Montgomery	AL	36104	334-265-0507		81-1
Web: www.allstatebeverage.com						

Company / Address	City	State	ZIP	Phone	Fax	Class
All State Fabricators Corp 1485 Elmwood Ave — *Web:* www.emiindustries.com	Cranston	RI	02910	401-785-3900		402
All State Fastener Corp 15460 E 12 Mile Rd — *TF:* 800-755-8959 ■ *Web:* www.allstatefastener.com	Roseville	MI	48066	586-773-5400		351
All States Inc 602 N 12th St — *TF Cust Svc:* 800-621-5837 ■ *Web:* cable-ties.com	Saint Charles	IL	60174	773-728-0525		608
All Steel Fabricating Company Inc 84 Creeper Hill Rd — *Web:* www.allsteelfab.com	No Grafton	MA	01536	508-839-4471		480
All Systems Installation Inc 8300 Tenth Ave N Ste A — *TF:* 800-403-4832 ■ *Web:* www.allsysinst.com	Golden Valley	MN	55427	763-593-1330		180
All Tech Engineering 1030 58th St SW — *TF:* 800-642-2024 ■ *Web:* www.alltech-eng.com	Wyoming	MI	49509	616-406-0681		454
All Terrain 2675 W Grand Ave — *Web:* www.allterrain.net	Chicago	IL	60612	312-588-3700		195
All Tile Inc 1201 Chase Ave — *TF:* 877-255-8453 ■ *Web:* www.alltile.com	Elk Grove Village	IL	60007	847-979-2500		191-1
All Tune & Lube International Inc — *ATL International Inc* 8334 Veterans Hwy — *TF Cust Svc:* 877-978-1758 ■ *Web:* www.alltuneandlube.com	Millersville	MD	21108	410-987-1011		62-5
All Waste Inc 143 Murphy Rd — *Web:* www.allwaste.com	Hartford	CT	06114	860-724-4575		192
All Weather Inc 1165 National Dr — *TF:* 800-824-5873 ■ *Web:* www.allweatherinc.com	Sacramento	CA	95834	916-928-1000	928-1165	472
All Web Cafe Inc 42 Cassatt Ave — *Web:* www.allwebcafe.com	Berwyn	PA	19312	610-644-1240		396
All Web Leads Inc 7300 FM 2222 Bldg 2 Ste 100 — **Fax Area Code:* 512 ■ *TF:* 888-522-7355 ■ *Web:* www.allwebleads.com	Austin	TX	78730	888-522-7355	349-7910*	387
All West Coach Lines 7701 Wilbur Way — *TF:* 800-843-2121 ■ *Web:* coachusa.com	Sacramento	CA	95828	916-423-4000		107
All West Communications Inc 50 W 100 N — *TF:* 866-255-9378 ■ *Web:* www.allwest.net	Kamas	UT	84036	435-783-4361		116
All West Select Sires 450 N Hill Blvd — *TF:* 800-426-2697 ■ *Web:* www.allwestselectsires.com	Burlington	WA	98233	800-426-2697		446
All World Travel Inc 314 Gilmer St — *TF:* 866-298-6067 ■ *Web:* www.allworldtravel.com	Sulphur Springs	TX	75482	903-885-0896		775
All4 Inc 2393 Kimberton Rd — *Web:* www.all4inc.com	Kimberton	PA	19442	610-933-5246		194
AllAfrica 920 M St SE — *Web:* www.allafrica.com	Washington	DC	20003	202-546-0777		530
Allagash Wilderness Waterway 106 Hogan Rd Ste 7 — *TF:* 800-332-1501 ■ *Web:* www.maine.gov	Bangor	ME	04401	207-941-4014		565
Allaire State Park PO Box 220 — *Web:* www.njparksandforests.org	Farmingdale	NJ	07727	732-938-2371		565
Allamakee County 110 Allamakee St — *TF:* 800-728-0131 ■ *Web:* www.allamakeecounty.com	Waukon	IA	52172	563-864-7454		338
Allamakee-Clayton Electric Co-op (ACEC) 229 Hwy 51 PO Box 715 — *TF:* 888-788-1551 ■ *Web:* www.acrec.com	Postville	IA	52162	563-864-7611	864-7020	245
All-American Co-op PO Box 125 — *TF:* 888-354-4058 ■ *Web:* www.allamericancoop.com	Stewartville	MN	55976	507-533-4222	280-0066	273
Allamon Tool Company Inc 18935 Freeport Dr — *TF:* 877-449-5433 ■ *Web:* www.allamontool.com	Montgomery	TX	77356	877-449-5433		539
Allamuchy Mountain State Park c/o Stephens State Pk 800 Willow Grove St — *Web:* www.njparksandforests.org	Hackettstown	NJ	07840	908-852-3790		565
Allan A Myers Inc 1805 Berks Rd PO Box 1340 — *TF:* 800-596-6118 ■ *Web:* www.allanmyers.com	Worcester	PA	19490	610-222-8800		188-4
Allan Briteway Electrical Contractors Inc 130 Algonquin Pkwy — *TF:* 800-525-4628 ■ *Web:* www.allanbriteway.com	Whippany	NJ	07981	973-781-0022	781-1744	189-4
Allan Crawford Associates Ltd 5805 Kennedy Rd — *TF:* 800-665-7301 ■ *Web:* www.aca.ca	Mississauga	ON	L4Z2G3	905-890-2010		246
Allan H. Treman State Marine Park c/o Robert H Tremin State Pk 105 Enfield Falls Rd — *Web:* parks.ny.gov/parks/35/details.aspx	Ithaca	NY	14850	607-273-3440		565
Allan Hackel Organization Inc 1330 Ctr St — *TF:* 800-970-2499 ■ *Web:* www.hackelbarter.com	Newton Center	MA	02459	617-965-4400	527-6005	6
Allan Hancock College 800 S College Dr — **Fax:* Admissions ■ *TF:* 866-342-5242 ■ *Web:* hancockcollege.edu	Santa Maria	CA	93454	805-922-6966	922-3477*	162
Lompoc Valley 1 Hancock Dr — *Web:* hancockcollege.edu	Lompoc	CA	93436	805-735-3366		162
Allan Industries Allan's Rd & Route 309 — *Web:* allanrecyclers.com	Wilkes-Barre	PA	18703	570-826-0123	829-4099	686
Allan R Nelson Consulting Engineers 17510-102 Ave 2nd Fl — *Web:* www.arneng.ab.ca	Edmonton	AB	T5S1K2	780-483-3436	489-9557	466
Allan S Feinberg An Acct Corp 16311 Ventura Blvd Ste 610	Encino	CA	91436	818-325-2800		2
Allan Stone Projects 535 W 22nd St 3rd Fl — **Fax Area Code:* 917 ■ *Web:* www.allanstoneprojects.com	New York	NY	10011	212-987-4997	421-9895*	42
Allan Tool & Machine Company Inc 1822 E Maple Rd — *TF:* 800-832-0350 ■ *Web:* allantool.com	Troy	MI	48083	248-585-2910	585-7728	621
Allana Buick & Bers Inc 990 Commercial St — *TF:* 800-378-3405 ■ *Web:* www.abbae.com	Palo Alto	CA	94303	650-543-5600		256
Allann Bros Coffee Co 1852 Fescue St SE — *Web:* www.allannbrothers.com	Albany	OR	97322	541-812-8000		297-8
Allant Group Inc, The 2056 Westings Ave Ste 500 — *TF:* 800-367-7311 ■ *Web:* www.allantgroup.com	Naperville	IL	60563	800-367-7311		194
Allbritton Communications Co 1000 Wilson Blvd Ste 2700	Arlington	VA	22209	703-647-8700		738
Allcan Distributors Inc 12612 - 124 St — *Web:* www.allcan.com	Edmonton	AB	T5L0N7	780-451-2357		480
Allcharge Inc 15 W 39th St Rm 501 — *Web:* www.allcharge.com	New York	NY	10018	212-679-9445		387
All-Clad Metalcrafters LLC 424 Morganza Rd — *TF Cust Svc:* 800-255-2523 ■ *Web:* all-clad.com	Canonsburg	PA	15317	724-745-8300	746-5035	486
Allclasses Inc 109 Kingston St 5th Fl — *Web:* allclasses.com	Boston	MA	02111	617-379-0265		387
Alle Processing Corp 56-20 59th St — *Web:* alleprocessing.com	Maspeth	NY	11378	718-894-2000		296-11
Allegacy Federal Credit Union 1691 Westbrook Plaza Dr — *TF:* 800-782-4670 ■ *Web:* www.allegacy.org	Winston-Salem	NC	27103	336-774-3400	774-3475	219
Allegan County Tourist & Recreational Council 3255 122nd Ave Ste 103 — *TF:* 888-425-5342 ■ *Web:* www.visitallegancounty.com	Allegan	MI	49010	269-686-9088		206
Allegan General Hospital 555 Linn St — *Web:* www.aghosp.org	Allegan	MI	49010	269-673-8424	686-4239	374-3
Allegan Metal Finishing Co 1274 Lincoln Rd — *Web:* www.amfco.biz	Allegan	MI	49010	269-673-6604		481
Allegan Tubular Products Inc 1276 Lincoln Rd — *Web:* www.allegantube.com	Allegan	MI	49010	269-673-6636	673-2477	595
Allegany College of Maryland 12401 Willowbrook Rd SE — **Fax:* Admissions ■ *TF:* 800-974-0203 ■ *Web:* www.allegany.edu	Cumberland	MD	21502	301-784-5000	784-5027*	162
Allegany County 7 Court St — *Web:* www.alleganyco.com	Belmont	NY	14813	585-268-7612		338
Allegany County Chamber of Commerce 24 Frederick St — *TF:* 800-425-2067 ■ *Web:* www.alleganycountychamber.com	Cumberland	MD	21502	301-722-2820	722-5995	139
Allegany County Public Library System 31 Washington St — *TF:* 800-934-2541 ■ *Web:* www.alleganycountylibrary.info	Cumberland	MD	21502	301-777-1200	777-7299	434-3
Allegany Optical LLC 17301 Vly Mall Rd — *Web:* www.alleganyoptical.com	Hagerstown	MD	21740	301-582-1771		543
Allegany State Park 2373 ASP Rt 1 Ste 3 — *Web:* parks.ny.gov/parks/73/details.aspx	Salamanca	NY	14779	716-354-9121		565
Alleghany Corp 1411 Broadway FL 34 — *NYSE:* Y ■ *Web:* www.alleghany.com	New York	NY	10018	212-752-1356		185
Alleghany Regional Hospital 1 ARH Ln — *TF:* 800-451-7210 ■ *Web:* lewisgale.com	Low Moor	VA	24457	540-862-6879		374-3
Allegheny Bradford Corp 1522 South Ave — *Web:* www.alleghenybradford.com	Lewis Run	PA	16738	814-362-2590		595
Allegheny College 520 N Main St — *TF:* 800-521-5293 ■ *Web:* www.allegheny.edu	Meadville	PA	16335	814-332-4351		166
Allegheny Design Management Inc 1154 Parks Industrial Dr — *Web:* www.alleghenydesignmgmt.com	Vandergrift	PA	15690	724-845-7336	845-9889	780
Allegheny General Hospital 320 E N Ave — *Web:* ahn.org	Pittsburgh	PA	15212	412-359-3131	359-8786	374-3
Allegheny Health Network 1301 Carlisle St — *Web:* ahn.org	Natrona Heights	PA	15065	724-224-5100	226-7385	374-3
Allegheny Institute for Public Policy 305 Mt Lebanon Blvd Ste 208 — *Web:* www.alleghenyinstitute.org	Pittsburgh	PA	15234	412-440-0079	440-0085	634
Allegheny Investments Ltd Stone Quarry Crossing 811 Camp Horne Rd Ste 100 — *Web:* www.alleghenyfinancial.com	Pittsburgh	PA	15237	412-367-3880		401
Allegheny Islands State Park c/o Point State Pk 601 Commonwealth Pl Bldg A — *Web:* www.dcnr.state.pa.us	Pittsburgh	PA	15222	412-565-2850		565
Allegheny Millwork PBT 104 Commerce Blvd — *Web:* www.alleghenymillwork.com	Lawrence	PA	15055	724-873-8700		499
Allegheny Petroleum Products Co 999 Airbrake Ave — *TF:* 800-600-2900 ■ *Web:* www.oils.com	Wilmerding	PA	15148	412-829-1990		580
Allegheny Portage Railroad National Historic Site 110 Federal Pk Rd — *Web:* www.nps.gov	Gallitzin	PA	16641	814-886-6150	884-0206	564
Allegheny Power 800 Cabin Hill Dr — *TF Cust Svc:* 800-255-3443 ■ *Web:* www.firstenergycorp.com	Greensburg	PA	15601	724-837-3000		787
Allegheny Technologies Inc 1000 Six PPG Pl — *NYSE:* ATI ■ *TF Sales:* 800-258-3586 ■ *Web:* www.atimetals.com	Pittsburgh	PA	15222	412-394-2800		723
Allegheny Valley Bank 5137 Butler St — *OTC:* AVLY ■ *TF:* 888-397-3742 ■ *Web:* www.avbpgh.com	Pittsburgh	PA	15201	412-781-0318	781-6474	360-2
Allegheny Valley School District 300 PEARL Ave — *Web:* avsdweb.org	Cheswick	PA	15024	724-274-5300		685
Allegheny Wesleyan College 2161 Woodsdale Rd — *TF:* 800-292-3153 ■ *Web:* www.awc.edu	Salem	OH	44460	330-337-6403		161
Allegheny West Conference of Seventh Day Adventists 1339 E Broad St — *Web:* www.awconf.org	Columbus	OH	43205	614-252-5271		48-20
Allegiance Capital Corp 16400 Dallas Pkwy Ste 300 — *Web:* www.allcapcorp.com	Dallas	TX	75248	214-217-7750		70
Allegiance Consultinginc 2601 Blake St Ste 110 — *Web:* www.acinow.net	Denver	CO	80205	720-947-9201		225

	Phone	Fax	Class
Allegiance Financial Group Inc 2935 Country Dr Ste 102 .... Little Canada MN 55117 *Web:* www.afg2000.com	651-294-4550		401
Allegiance Health 205 NE Ave .... Jackson MI 49201 *TF:* 800-872-6480 ■ *Web:* www.allegiancehealth.org	517-788-4800		374-3
Allegiance Security Group LLC 2900 Arendell St Ste 18 .... Morehead City NC 28557 *Web:* www.allegiancesecurityteam.com	252-247-1138	247-1139	693
Allegiant Air 8360 S Durango Dr .... Las Vegas NV 89113 *NASDAQ: ALGT* ■ *Web:* www.allegiantair.com	702-851-7300	851-7301	25
Allegiant International LLC 1710 N Main St .... Auburn IN 46706 *TF:* 866-841-3671 ■ *Web:* www.allegiantworks.com	866-841-3671		260
Allegis Capital 525 University Ave Ste 220 .... Palo Alto CA 94301 *Web:* allegiscap.com	650-687-0500	687-0234	792
Allegis Group Inc 7301 Pkwy Dr .... Hanover MD 21076 *TF:* 800-927-8090 ■ *Web:* www.allegisgroup.com	800-927-8090		721
Allegra Digital Imaging 1302 Anderson Rd .... Clawson MI 48017 *Web:* www.allegratroywest.com	248-655-0444		627
Allegra Graphic Design Group 3983 Linden Ave SE .... Grand Rapids MI 49548 *Web:* allegragr.com	616-248-4110		113
Allegra Network LLC 47585 Galleon Dr .... Plymouth MI 48170 *TF General:* 800-726-9050 ■ *Web:* allegramarketingprint.com	248-596-8600		113
Allegria Spa at the Park Hyatt Beaver Creek 100 E Thomas Pl .... Avon CO 81620 *Web:* www.allegriaspa.com	970-748-7500	748-7501	707
Allegro Coffee Co 12799 Claude Ct .... Thornton CO 80241 *TF:* 800-530-3995 ■ *Web:* www.allegro-coffee.com	303-444-4844	920-5468	296-7
Allegro Consultants Ltd 9800 JEB Stuart Pkwy Ste 106 .... Glen Allen VA 23059 *TF:* 800-597-0518 ■ *Web:* www.allegroconsultants.com	804-553-1130		196
Allegro Corp 20048 NE San Rafael St .... Portland OR 97230 **Fax:* Orders ■ *TF:* 800-288-2007 ■ *Web:* www.allegro-music.com	503-491-8480	491-8488*	523
Allegro Diagnostics Inc 6 Clock Tower Pl Ste 225 .... Maynard MA 01754 *Web:* investor.veracyte.com	978-938-4866		743
Allegro Industries 1360 Shiloh Church Rd .... Piedmont SC 29673 *TF:* 800-622-3530 ■ *Web:* www.allegrosafety.com	800-622-3530		475
Allegro Italian Kitchen 10011-109 St .... Edmonton AB T5J3S8 *Web:* www.allegroitaliankitchen.ca	780-424-6644		671
Allegro Microsystems Inc 115 NE Cutoff .... Worcester MA 01606 *Web:* www.allegromicro.com	508-853-5000		696
Allegro Ophthalmics LLC 31473 Rancho Viejo Rd Ste 204 ..... San Juan Capistrano CA 92675 *Web:* www.allegroeye.com	949-940-8130		743
Alleman Hall Mccoy Russell & Tuttle LLP 806 S W Broadway Ste 600 .... Portland OR 97205 *Web:* www.ahmrt.com	503-459-4141		428
ALLEN 525 Burbank St .... Broomfield CO 80020 *TF:* 800-876-8600 ■ *Web:* www.allencompany.net	303-469-1857	466-7437	188-4
Allen & Allen Company Inc 202 Culebra Ave .... San Antonio TX 78201 *Web:* www.lumberhardware.com	210-733-9191		362
Allen & Co Inc 1401 S Florida Ave .... Lakeland FL 33803 *TF:* 800-950-2526 ■ *Web:* alleninvestments.com	863-688-9000	616-6354	690
Allen & Company of Florida Inc 1401 S Florida Ave .... Lakeland FL 33803 *Web:* alleninvestments.com	863-688-9000		690
Allen & Gerritsen 2 Seaport Ln .... Boston MA 02210 *Web:* www.a-g.com	857-300-2000		4
Allen & Hoshall Inc 1661 International Dr Ste 100 .... Memphis TN 38120 *Web:* www.allenhoshall.com	901-820-0820	683-1001	261
Allen & Major Associates Inc 100 Commerce Way .... Woburn MA 01801 *Web:* www.allenmajor.com	781-935-6889		727
Allen & O'Hara Inc PO Box 771889 .... Memphis TN 38177 *Web:* www.allenoharadev.com	901-471-2080		653
Allen & Shariff Corp 7061 Deepage Dr .... Columbia MD 21045 *Web:* www.allenshariff.com	410-381-7100		188
Allen Agency 34-36 Elm St PO Box 578 .... Camden ME 04843	207-236-4311		390
Allen Aircraft Products Inc 6168 Woodbine Ave .... Ravenna OH 44266 *Web:* www.allenaircraft.com	330-296-9621		529
Allen and Kimbell Llp 317 E Carrillo St .... Santa Barbara CA 93101 *Web:* www.aklaw.net	805-963-8611		445
Allen Blasting & Coating Inc 1668 Old Hwy 61 .... Wever IA 52658 *TF:* 800-760-9186 ■ *Web:* allenblastingandcoating.com	319-367-5500		186
Allen Bros Inc 3737 S Halsted St .... Chicago IL 60609 *TF:* 800-548-7777 ■ *Web:* www.allenbrothers.com	773-890-5100		473
Allen C Ewing & Co 50 N Laura St Ste 3625 .... Jacksonville FL 32202 *Web:* www.allenewing.com	904-354-5573		690
Allen Chamber of Commerce 210 W McDermott Dr .... Allen TX 75013 *Web:* www.allenfairviewchamber.com	972-727-5585	727-9000	139
Allen Co 712 E Main St .... Blanchester OH 45107 *TF:* 800-329-2491 ■ *Web:* www.allenmugs.com	937-783-2491	783-4831	9
Allen Commercial Industries Inc 11301 Mosier Valley Rd .... Euless TX 76040 *Web:* www.allen-commercial.com	817-267-4919		393
Allen Communication Learning Services 55 West 900 South .... Salt Lake City UT 84101 *Web:* www.allencomm.com	801-537-7800	537-7805	178-3
Allen Correctional Ctr 3751 Lauderdale Woodyard Rd .... Kinder LA 70648 *Web:* doc.la.gov	337-639-2942		213
Allen Correctional Institution 770 W BRd St .... Columbus OH 43222 *Web:* www.drc.ohio.gov/aoci	419-224-8000	224-5828	213
Allen County 715 S Calhoun St County Courthouse Rm 201 .. Fort Wayne IN 46802 *Web:* www.allencounty.us	260-449-7245		338
Allen County 1 N Washington St .... Iola KS 66749 *TF:* 866-444-1407 ■ *Web:* www.allencounty.org	620-365-1407	365-1441	338
Allen County 301 N Main St .... Lima OH 45801 *TF:* 800-447-5375 ■ *Web:* www.allencountyohio.com	419-228-3700	222-8427	338
Allen County PO Box 115 .... Scottsville KY 42164 *TF:* 800-245-2826 ■ *Web:* www.allencountykentucky.com	270-237-4782		338
Allen County Community College 1801 N Cottonwood St .... Iola KS 66749 **Fax:* Admissions ■ *TF:* 800-444-0535 ■ *Web:* www.allencc.edu	620-365-5116	365-7406*	162
Allen County Public Library 900 Library Plaza .... Fort Wayne IN 46802 *Web:* www.acpl.lib.in.us	260-421-1200	421-1386	434-3
Allen County War Memorial Coliseum 4000 Parnell Ave .... Fort Wayne IN 46805 *TF:* 800-745-3000 ■ *Web:* www.memorialcoliseum.com	260-482-9502	484-1637	720
Allen Dell PA 202 S Rome Ave Ste 100 .... Tampa FL 33606 *TF:* 800-619-5275 ■ *Web:* www.allendell.com	813-223-5351		428
Allen Engineering Corp 819 S Fifth St .... Paragould AR 72450 *TF:* 800-643-0095 ■ *Web:* www.alleneng.com	870-236-7751		190
Allen Evans Klein International 305 Madison Ave .... New York NY 10165 *Web:* www.allenevans.com	212-983-9300		463
Allen Family Foods Inc 126 N Shipley St .... Seaford DE 19973 *Web:* allenharimllc.com/index.cfm	302-629-9163	629-0514	619
Allen Flavors Inc 23 Progress St .... Edison NJ 08820 *Web:* www.allenflavors.com	908-561-5995		297-8
Allen Furniture City Inc 7808 L St .... Omaha NE 68127 *Web:* allenshome.com	402-331-8480		321
Allen Gibbs & Houlik LC 301 N Main Ste 1700 .... Wichita KS 67202	316-267-7231		2
Allen Group 50 Washington St Ste 503 .... Norwalk CT 06854 *TF:* 800-877-4833 ■ *Web:* www.theallengroup.com	203-855-5777		462
Allen Guthrie Mchugh & Thomas Pllc 500 Lee St E Ste 800 .... Charleston WV 25301	304-345-7250		501
Allen Industries Inc 6434 Burnt Poplar Rd .... Greensboro NC 27409 *TF:* 800-967-2553 ■ *Web:* www.allenindustries.com	336-668-2791	668-7875	701
Allen Interactions Inc 1120 Centre Pointe Dr Ste 800 .... Mendota Heights MN 55120 *Web:* www.alleninteractions.com	651-203-3700		765
Allen Lumber Company Inc 502 N Main St .... Barre VT 05641 *TF:* 800-696-2666 ■ *Web:* www.allenlumbercompany.com	802-476-4156		115
Allen Lund Company Inc 4529 Angeles Crest Hwy Ste 300 .... La Canada CA 91011 *TF:* 800-777-6142 ■ *Web:* www.allenlund.com	800-777-6142		311
Allen m p General Contractors Inc 9807 Fair Oaks Blvd .... Fair Oaks CA 95628 *Web:* www.mpallen.com	916-904-5000		186
Allen Management 736 Thimble Shoals Blvd .... Newport News VA 23606 *Web:* www.apluslodging.com	757-722-2804		377
Allen Memorial Hospital 1825 Logan Ave .... Waterloo IA 50703 *TF:* 888-343-4165 ■ *Web:* unitypoint.org/waterloo/default.aspx	319-235-3941	235-3906	374-3
Allen Memorial Medical Library Case Western Reserve University 11000 Euclid Ave .... Cleveland OH 44106 *TF:* 800-423-1188 ■ *Web:* www.case.edu/chsl/allen.htm	216-368-3643		434-1
Allen Millwork Inc 6969 Fern Loop Ste 106 .... Shreveport LA 71105 *Web:* homedesigncentershreveport.com	318-629-5300	629-5301	499
Allen Morgan Health Ctr 177 N Highland Ave .... Memphis TN 38111 *Web:* trezevantmanor.org	901-325-4003		450
Allen Morris Co 121 Alhambra Plaza Ste 1600 .... Coral Gables FL 33134 *Web:* www.allenmorris.com	305-443-1000	443-1462	652
Allen Norton & Blue P A 121 Majorca Ave 3rd Fl .... Coral Gables FL 33134 *Web:* www.anblaw.com	305-445-7801		445
Allen Oil Co 1215 Old Birmingham Hwy .... Sylacauga AL 35150 *TF:* 800-723-7375 ■ *Web:* www.allenoil.com	256-245-5478		579
Allen Organ Co 150 Locust St .... Macungie PA 18062 *TF:* 800-582-4466 ■ *Web:* www.allenorgan.com	610-966-2202	965-3098	527
Allen Packaging Co 1150 Valencia Ave .... Tustin CA 92780 *Web:* www.allenpkg.com	714-259-0100		557
Allen Parish PO Box 1280 .... Oberlin LA 70655 *TF:* 888-639-4868 ■ *Web:* www.allenparish.com	337-639-4868		338
Allen Park Chamber of Commerce 6543 Allen Rd .... Allen Park MI 48101 *Web:* www.allenparkchamber.org	313-382-7303	382-4409	139
Allen Partners 500 Yale Ave N .... Seattle WA 98109 *Web:* allenpartners.com	206-812-1440		260
Allen Pattern of Michigan 202 McGrath Pl .... Battle Creek MI 49014	269-963-4131		567
Allen Premium Outlets 820 W Stacy Rd .... Allen TX 75013 *Web:* www.premiumoutlets.com	972-678-7000		460
Allen Press Inc 810 E Tenth St PO Box 1897 .... Lawrence KS 66044 *TF:* 800-627-0932 ■ *Web:* allenpress.com	785-843-1235	843-1274	47
Allen Printing Inc 415-A Spence Ln .... Nashville TN 37210 *Web:* www.allenprinting.com	615-255-2078		627
Allen Refractories Co (Inc) 131 Shackelford Rd .... Pataskala OH 43062 *Web:* www.allenrefractories.com	740-927-8000	927-9404	191-1
Allen Rick (Rep R - GA) 426 Cannon HOB .... Washington DC 20515 *Web:* allen.house.gov	202-225-2823	225-3377	342-2
Allen Systems Group Inc (ASG) 1333 Third Ave S .... Naples FL 34102 **Fax Area Code:* 800 ■ *TF:* 800-932-5536 ■ *Web:* www.asg.com	239-435-2200	325-2555*	178-12
Allen Tel Products Inc 30 TV5 Dr .... Henderson NV 89014 *Web:* www.allentel.com	702-855-5700		791

Phone | Fax | Class

Allen Turner Hyundai Inc
6000 Pensacola Blvd . . . . . Pensacola FL 32505 850-479-9667 57
Web: www.allenturnerhyundai.com

Allen University 1530 Harden St. . . . . . Columbia SC 29204 803-376-5700 376-5733* 166
**Fax:* Mail Rm ■ *TF:* 877-625-5368 ■ *Web:* www.allenuniversity.edu

Allen Ventures Inc
517 State Farm Rd . . . . . Deerfield WI 53531 608-423-9800 661
TF: 877-423-9800 ■ *Web:* www.allenventures.com

Allen Village School
706 W 42nd St . . . . . Kansas City MO 64111 816-931-0177 685
Web: www.allenvillageschool.com

Allen's Crosley Lanes
2400 E Evergreen Blvd . . . . . Vancouver WA 98661 360-693-4789 99
Web: www.crosleylanes.com

Allen's Hatchery Inc 126 N Shipley St. . . . . . Seaford DE 19973 302-629-9163 629-0514 10-8
Web: allenharimllc.com/index.cfm

Allen's of Hastings Inc
1115 W Second St . . . . . Hastings NE 68901 402-463-5633 463-5730 345
Web: www.allensuperstore.com

Allen'S Tri-State Mechanical
404 S Hayden St. . . . . . Amarillo TX 79101 806-376-8345 189-10
Web: allenstristate.com

Allen's TV Cable Service Inc
800 Victor II Blvd . . . . . Morgan City LA 70380 985-384-8335 116
Web: www.atvc.net

Allen, Summers, Simpson, Lillie & Gresham PLLC
80 Monroe Ave Ste 650 . . . . . Memphis TN 38103 901-763-4200 428
Web: www.allensummers.com

Allen-Bailey Tag & Label Inc
3177 Lehigh St. . . . . . Caledonia NY 14423 585-538-2324 548
Web: www.abtl.com

Allenberg Cotton Co
7255 Goodlett Farms Pkwy. . . . . . Cordova TN 38016 901-383-5000 383-5010 275
Web: www.ldcom.com

Allenberry Resort
1559 Boiling Springs Rd . . . . . Boiling Springs PA 17007 717-258-3211 960-5280 669
Web: www.allenberry.com

Allendale Correctional Institution
1057 Revolutionary Trl PO Box 1151 . . . . . Fairfax SC 29827 803-632-2561 213
Web: doc.sc.gov

Allendale County 526 Memorial Ave . . . . . Allendale SC 29810 803-584-3438 584-7042 338
TF: 800-733-9045 ■ *Web:* www.allendalecounty.com

Allendale Machinery Systems Inc
16 Park Way. . . . . . Upper Saddle River NJ 07458 201-327-5215 697
Web: hfoallendale.com

Allendorph Specialties Inc
201 Stanton St . . . . . Broussard LA 70518 337-232-0503 358
Web: www.allendorph.com

Allen-Edmonds Shoe Corp
201 E Seven Hills Rd . . . . . Port Washington WI 53074 262-235-6512 301
TF Cust Svc: 800-235-2348 ■ *Web:* www.allenedmonds.com

Allen Myland Inc 515 Abbott Dr. . . . . . Broomall PA 19008 610-544-0571 175
TF: 800-467-4448 ■ *Web:* www.allenmyland.com

Allensville Planing Mill Inc
108 E Main St. . . . . . Allensville PA 17002 717-483-6386 106
Web: www.apm-inc.net

Allentown Art Museum 31 N Fifth St. . . . . . Allentown PA 18101 610-432-4333 434-7409 520
Web: www.allentownartmuseum.org

Allentown Beverage Company Inc
1249 N Quebec St. . . . . . Allentown PA 18109 610-432-4581 81-1
TF: 800-573-2627 ■ *Web:* allentownbeverage.com

Allentown City Hall 435 Hamilton St . . . . . Allentown PA 18101 610-437-7539 437-7554 337
Web: www.allentownpa.gov

Allentown Equipment 1733 90th St. . . . . . Sturtevant WI 53177 800-553-3414 884-3070* 386
**Fax Area Code:* 262 ■ *TF:* 800-553-3414 ■ *Web:* www.putzmeisteramerica.com

Allentown Inc 165 County Rd . . . . . Allentown NJ 08501 609-259-7951 386
Web: www.allentowninc.com

Allentown Public Library
1210 Hamilton St . . . . . Allentown PA 18102 610-820-2400 820-0640 434-3
Web: www.allentownpl.org

Allentown School District (ASD)
31 S Penn St. . . . . . Allentown PA 18105 484-765-4000 765-4140 685
TF: 877-262-1492 ■ *Web:* www.allentownsd.org

Allentown Symphony Orchestra
23 N Sixth St . . . . . Allentown PA 18101 610-432-6715 432-6735 573-3
TF: 800-745-3000 ■ *Web:* www.millersymphonyhall.org

Allen-Vanguard Corp
2400 St Laurent Blvd . . . . . Ottawa ON K1G5B4 613-739-9646 576
TF: 800-644-9078 ■ *Web:* www.allenvanguard.com

Allerair Industries Inc
9600 Rte Transcanadienne . . . . . Saint-laurent QC H4S1V9 514-335-4277 41

Allergan Inc 2525 Dupont Dr. . . . . . Irvine CA 92612 714-246-4500 582
NYSE: AGN ■ *TF:* 800-347-4500 ■ *Web:* www.allergan.com

Allergy Partners PA 14 McDowell St . . . . . Asheville NC 28801 828-277-1300 463
Web: www.allergypartners.com

Allergy Research Group LLC
2300 N Loop Rd . . . . . Alameda CA 94502 510-263-2000 583
Web: www.allergyresearchgroup.com

Allergychoices Inc
2800 National Dr Ste 100. . . . . . Onalaska WI 54650 608-793-1580 237
TF: 866-793-1680 ■ *Web:* allergychoices.com

Allermed Laboratories Inc
7203 Convoy Ct . . . . . San Diego CA 92111 800-221-2748 231
TF: 800-221-2748 ■ *Web:* www.allermed.com

ALLETE Inc 30 W Superior St. . . . . . Duluth MN 55802 218-279-5000 360-5
NYSE: ALE ■ *TF:* 800-228-4966 ■ *Web:* www.allete.com

Allevity HR & Payroll
870 Manzanita Ct Ste A . . . . . Chico CA 95926 530-345-2486 345-8486 631
TF: 800-447-8233 ■ *Web:* www.allevityhr.com

Alley Theatre 615 Texas Ave . . . . . Houston TX 77002 713-220-5700 222-6542 572
TF: 800-745-3000 ■ *Web:* www.alleytheatre.org

Alley-Cassetty Cos Inc 2 Oldham St. . . . . . Nashville TN 37213 615-244-0440 191-1
Web: www.alley-cassetty.com

Alleyway Theatre 1 Curtain Up Alley . . . . . Buffalo NY 14202 716-852-2600 572
TF: 800-745-3000 ■ *Web:* www.alleyway.com

All-Fab Building Components Inc
1755 Dugald Rd . . . . . Winnipeg MB R2J0H3 204-661-8880 45
TF: 800-665-0335 ■ *Web:* www.all-fab.com

Allfast Fastening Systems Inc
15200 Don Julian Rd . . . . . City of Industry CA 91745 626-968-9388 968-9393 278
Web: www.allfastinc.com

Allgeier Auto Parts Inc
7650 Harrison Ave . . . . . Cincinnati OH 45247 513-353-3377 57
Web: allgeierautoparts.com

Allgood Services Inc 106 Roosevelt St . . . . . Dublin GA 31021 478-272-6271 577
TF: 800-726-0083 ■ *Web:* www.allgoodpestsolutions.com

Alli Alliance of Action Sports LLC
150 Harvester Dr Ste 140 . . . . . Burr Ridge IL 60527 304-284-0084 387
Web: www.allisports.com

Alliance Abroad Group LP
1221 S Mo Pac Expy Ste 250 . . . . . Austin TX 78746 512-457-8062 41
TF: 866-622-7623 ■ *Web:* www.allianceabroad.com

Alliance Abstract LLC
2 Mott St Ste 605 . . . . . New York NY 10013 212-962-2228 390

Alliance Advisory & Securities Inc
3390 Auto Mall Dr . . . . . Westlake Village CA 91362 805-371-8020 690
Web: www.allianceadvisory.com

Alliance Area Chamber of Commerce
210 E Main St. . . . . . Alliance OH 44601 330-823-6260 823-4434 139
Web: www.allianceohiochamber.org

Alliance Benefit Group Financial Services Corp
201 E Clark St PO Box 1206. . . . . . Albert Lea MN 56007 507-377-2919 734
Web: www.abgfs.com

Alliance Brokerage Corp 990 Wbury Rd. . . . . . Westbury NY 11590 516-333-7300 333-5698 390
Web: www.alliancebrokeragecorp.com

Alliance Carolina Tool & Mold Corp
125 Glenn Bridge Rd . . . . . Arden NC 28704 828-684-7831 757
Web: www.alliance-carolina.com

Alliance Communications Inc
15310 Amberly Dr Ste 215. . . . . . Tampa FL 33647 813-978-1992 4

Alliance Community Hospital (ACH)
200 E State St. . . . . . Alliance OH 44601 330-596-6000 374-3
Web: www.achosp.org

Alliance Construction Solutions LLC
12789 Emerson St Ste 100. . . . . . Thornton CO 80241 303-813-0035 228-7434 187
Web: www.allianceconstruction.com

Alliance Corp
2395 Meadowpine Blvd . . . . . Mississauga ON L5N7W6 905-821-4797 492
TF: 888-821-4797 ■ *Web:* www.alliancecorporation.ca

Alliance Credit Counseling Inc
10720 Sikes Pl Ste 575 . . . . . Charlotte NC 28277 704-831-4822 41
TF: 888-995-7856 ■ *Web:* www.knowdebt.org

Alliance Data Systems Corp
7500 Dallas Pkwy. . . . . . Plano TX 75024 214-494-3000 255
NYSE: ADS ■ *TF:* 800-732-0330 ■ *Web:* www.alliancedata.com

Alliance Energy Services LLC
318 Armour Rd . . . . . Kansas City MO 64116 816-421-5192 466
Web: www.alliancec3.com

Alliance Fire Protection Co
2114 E Cedar St . . . . . Tempe AZ 85281 480-966-9178 408
Web: www.afpc.com

Alliance Foods Inc 605 W Chicago Rd. . . . . . Coldwater MI 49036 517-278-2396 278-7936 345
Web: www.alliance-foods.com

Alliance for Aging Research (AAR)
750 17th St NW Ste 1100. . . . . . Washington DC 20006 202-293-2856 234-5030* 48-17
**Fax Area Code:* 770 ■ *TF:* 866-840-6283 ■ *Web:* www.agingresearch.org

Alliance for Children & Families Inc
11700 West Lake Pk Dr. . . . . . Milwaukee WI 53224 414-359-1040 359-1074 48-6
TF: 800-221-3726 ■ *Web:* www.alliance1.org

Alliance For Employee Growth & Development Inc, The
80 Cottontail Ln Ste 320. . . . . . Somerset NJ 08873 800-323-3436 193
TF: 800-323-3436 ■ *Web:* www.employeegrowth.com

Alliance for Excellent Education
1201 Connecticut Ave Ste 901 . . . . . Washington DC 20036 202-828-0828 828-0821 48-11
Web: www.all4ed.org

Alliance for International Educational & Cultural Exchange
1776 Massachusetts Ave NW Ste 620 . . . . . Washington DC 20036 202-293-6141 293-6144 48-11
TF: 888-304-9023 ■ *Web:* www.alliance-exchange.org

Alliance for Justice (AFJ)
11 Dupont Cir NW 2nd Fl. . . . . . Washington DC 20036 202-822-6070 48-7
Web: www.afj.org

Alliance for Lupus Research (ALA)
28 W 44th St Ste 501 . . . . . New York NY 10036 212-218-2840 218-2848 48-17
TF: 800-867-1743 ■ *Web:* www.lupusresearch.org

Alliance for Responsible Atmospheric Policy
2111 Wilson Blvd 8th Fl. . . . . . Arlington VA 22201 703-243-0344 243-2874 48-13
Web: www.alliancepolicy.org

Alliance for Retired Americans
815 16th St NW 4th Fl . . . . . Washington DC 20006 202-637-5399 48-6
TF: 888-373-6497 ■ *Web:* www.retiredamericans.org

Alliance for Telecommunications Industry Solutions (ATIS)
1200 G St NW Ste 500 . . . . . Washington DC 20005 202-628-6380 393-5453 49-20
TF: 800-649-1202 ■ *Web:* www.atis.org

Alliance Geotechnical Group Inc
3228 Halifax St. . . . . . Dallas TX 75247 972-444-8889 194
Web: www.aggengr.com

Alliance Grain Co 1306 W Eigth St. . . . . . Gibson City IL 60936 217-784-4284 784-8949 275
TF: 800-222-2451 ■ *Web:* www.alliance-grain.com

Alliance Health Networks
9 Exchange Pl Ste 200 . . . . . Salt Lake City UT 84111 801-355-6002 463
TF: 800-244-6224 ■ *Web:* www.alliancehealth.com

Alliance Holdings Gp LP
1717 S Boulder Ave Ste 400. . . . . . Tulsa OK 74119 918-295-1415 360-3
NASDAQ: AHGP ■ *Web:* www.ahgp.com

Alliance Holdings Inc
1021 Old York Rd 3rd Fl. . . . . . Abington PA 19001 215-706-0873 360-3
Web: www.allianceholdings.com

Alliance Home Health Care
9607 N College Ave . . . . . Indianapoli IN 46280 317-581-1100 816-3131 693
Web: alliancehomehealthcare.net

Alliance Hospitality Management LLC
1001 Wade Ave Ste 215 . . . . . Raleigh NC 27603 919-791-1801 378
Web: www.alliancehospitality.com

Alliance Imaging Inc
100 Bayview Cir Ste 400. . . . . . Newport Beach CA 92660 949-242-5300 383
TF: 800-544-3215 ■ *Web:* www.alliancehealthcareservices-us.com

Company / Address	City	State	ZIP	Phone	Fax	Class
Alliance International Forwarders Inc 7155 Old Katy Rd	Houston	TX	77024	713-428-3100		311
Alliance Investigations LLC 240 S Montezuma St Ste 103 *TF:* 800-280-2951 ■ *Web:* az-pi.com	Prescott	AZ	86303	928-717-1196		400
Alliance Laundry Systems LLC PO Box 990 *Web:* www.alliancelaundry.com	Ripon	WI	54971	920-748-3121	748-4564	427
Alliance Legal Staffing Solutions 2909 Cole Ave Ste 230 *TF:* 800-264-1170 ■ *Web:* www.alliancelegal.com	Dallas	TX	75204	214-954-1250		260
Alliance Limousine Inc 14553 Delano St Ste 210 **Fax Area Code:* 818 ■ *TF:* 800-954-5466 ■ *Web:* www.alliancelimo.net	Van Nuys	CA	91411	800-954-5466	786-8810*	441
Alliance Management Group 1901 Pennsylvania Ave NW Ste 804 *Web:* www.alliancemg.com	Washington	DC	20006	202-293-7642	293-0495	47
Alliance of Motion Picture & Television Producers (AMPTP) 15301 Ventura Blvd Bldg E *TF:* 800-541-5204 ■ *Web:* www.amptp.org	Sherman Oaks	CA	91403	818-995-3600		48-4
Alliance of Nonprofit Mailers (ANM) 1211 Connecticut Ave NW Ste 610 *Web:* www.nonprofitmailers.org	Washington	DC	20036	202-462-5132		48-7
Alliance of Professionals & Consultants Inc 8200 Brownleigh Dr *Web:* www.apc-services.com	Raleigh	NC	27617	919-510-9696		463
Alliance of Transylvanian Saxons 5393 Pearl Rd *Web:* atsaxons.com	Cleveland	OH	44129	440-842-8442		390
Alliance One International Inc 8001 Aerial Ctr Pkwy PO Box 2009 *NYSE:* AOI ■ *TF:* 800-937-5449 ■ *Web:* www.aointl.com	Morrisville	NC	27560	919-379-4300	379-4346	756
Alliance Packaging LLC 1000 SW 43rd St *Web:* www.alliancepackaging.net	Renton	WA	98057	425-291-3500		100
Alliance Paper & Food Service Inc 11058 W Addison St *Web:* www.allpfs.com	Franklin Park	IL	60131	847-349-1500		96
Alliance Pipeline Ltd Partnership 6385 Old Shady Oak Rd Ste 150 *Web:* www.alliancepipeline.com	Eden Prairie	MN	55344	952-944-3183		325
Alliance Precision Plastics 1220 Lee Rd *Web:* www.allianceppc.com	Rochester	NY	14606	585-426-5310	426-5081	757
Alliance Publishing Company Inc 40 S Linden Ave *TF:* 800-778-0098 ■ *Web:* www.the-review.com	Alliance	OH	44601	330-821-1200		532-3
Alliance Resource Partners LP 1717 S Boulder Ave Ste 400 *NASDAQ:* ARLP ■ *TF:* 800-937-5449 ■ *Web:* www.arlp.com	Tulsa	OK	74119	918-295-7600	295-7358	501
Alliance Rubber Co 210 Carpenter Dam Rd **Fax Area Code:* 501 ■ *TF:* 800-626-5940 ■ *Web:* www.rubberband.com	Hot Springs	AR	71901	800-626-5940	262-3948*	676
Alliance Scale Inc 1020 Turnpike St *Web:* www.alliancescale.com	Canton	MA	02021	781-828-8507		362
Alliance Shippers Inc 516 Sylvan Ave *Web:* alliance.com	Englewood Cliffs	NJ	07632	201-227-0400		311
Alliance Solutions Group Inc 11818 Rock Landing Dr Ste 105 *Web:* www.asg-inc.org	Newport News	VA	23606	757-223-7233		194
Alliance Source Testing LLC 214 Central Cir SW *TF:* 800-492-1613 ■ *Web:* www.stacktest.com	Decatur	AL	35603	256-351-0121		743
Alliance Support Partners Inc 5036 Commercial Cir Ste C *Web:* asp-support.com	Concord	CA	94520	925-363-5382		261
Alliance Theatre Co 1280 Peachtree St NE Woodruff Arts Ctr *Web:* www.alliancetheatre.org	Atlanta	GA	30309	404-733-4650	733-4625	749
Alliance Tickets Inc 5178 S Broadway	Englewood	CO	80113	303-781-2220		514
Alliance to Save Energy (ASE) 1850 M St NW Ste 600 *TF:* 800-862-2086 ■ *Web:* www.ase.org	Washington	DC	20036	202-857-0666	331-9588	48-12
Alliance Water Resources Inc 206 S Keene St *Web:* alliancewater.com	Columbia	MO	65251	573-874-8080		261
Alliance Winding Equipment Inc 3939 Vanguard Dr *TF:* 800-561-3357 ■ *Web:* www.alliance-winding.com	Fort Wayne	IN	46809	260-478-2200		518
Alliance Worldwide Investigative Group Inc 4 Executive Park Dr *TF:* 800-579-2911 ■ *Web:* www.allianceinvestigative.com	Clifton Park	NY	12065	518-514-2944		390
Alliance, The 810 Tate St *TF:* 877-347-0545 ■ *Web:* www.corinthalliance.com	Corinth	MS	38834	662-287-5269		139
AllianceBernstein Holding LP (AB) 1345 Ave of the Americas *NYSE:* AB ■ **Fax:* Hum Res ■ *TF Cust Svc:* 800-221-5672 ■ *Web:* www.abglobal.com/home.htm	New York	NY	10105	212-486-5800	969-2293*	401
AllianceOne Inc 4850 E St Rd Ste 300 *TF:* 866-405-7241 ■ *Web:* www.allianceoneinc.com	Trevose	PA	19053	215-354-5511		160
Alliant Consulting Inc 555 Cajon St Ste A *Web:* www.alliantconsulting.net	Redlands	CA	92373	909-792-8812		463
Alliant Co-op Data Solutions LLC 301 Fields Ln N Ctr *Web:* alliantinsight.com	Brewster	NY	10509	845-617-5500		194
Alliant Energy Corp 4902 N Biltmore Ln Ste 1000 *NYSE:* LNT ■ **Fax Area Code:* 608 ■ *TF:* 800-255-4268 ■ *Web:* www.alliantenergy.com	Madison	WI	53718	800-255-4268	458-0100*	787
Alliant Energy Ctr of Dane County 1919 Alliant Energy Ctr Way *TF:* 800-745-3000 ■ *Web:* www.alliantenergycenter.com	Madison	WI	53713	608-267-3976	267-0146	205
Alliant Insurance Services Inc 1301 Dove St *Web:* www.alliant.com	Newport Beach	CA	92660	949-756-0271		391-2
Alliant International University 10455 Pomerado Rd **Fax:* Admissions ■ *TF:* 866-825-5426 ■ *Web:* www.alliant.edu	San Diego	CA	92131	858-635-4772	635-4555*	166
Alliant Powder 2299 Snake River Ave *TF:* 800-276-9337 ■ *Web:* www.alliantpowder.com	Lewiston	ID	83501	800-379-1732		268
Allianz Global Investors of America LP 600 West Broadway Ste 250 *TF:* 800-656-6226 ■ *Web:* us.allianzgi.com	Newport Beach	CA	92101	800-656-6226		401
Allianz Life Insurance Company of North America PO Box 1344 *TF:* 800-950-5872 ■ *Web:* www.allianzlife.com	Minneapolis	MN	55416	800-950-5872		391-2
Allianz Real Estate of America 60 E 42nd St Ste 3710 *Web:* allianz-realestate.com	New York	NY	10165	203-221-8500		401
Allied 100 LLC 1800 US Hwy 51 N *Web:* www.aedsuperstore.com	Woodruff	WI	54568	715-358-2329		475
Allied Advertising Agency Inc 3700 Blanco Rd *TF:* 800-227-0627 ■ *Web:* www.alliedadvertising.com	San Antonio	TX	78212	210-732-7874		687
Allied Aerofoam Products LLC 216 Kelsey Ln *TF:* 800-338-9140 ■ *Web:* www.alliedaerofoam.com	Tampa	FL	33619	813-626-0090	569-0629	601
Allied Air Enterprises 215 Metropolitan Dr *TF:* 800-448-5872 ■ *Web:* www.alliedair.com	West Columbia	SC	29170	800-448-5872		15
Allied Automation Inc 5220 E 64th St *Web:* www.allied-automation.com	Indianapolis	IN	46220	317-253-5900		385
Allied Automotive Group 2302 ParkLake Dr Bldg 15 Ste 600	Atlanta	GA	30345	404-373-4285	370-4206	780
Allied Baltic Rubber Inc 310 Railroad Ave NE	Seville	OH	44273	330-887-7800		677
Allied Bindery LLC 32501 Dequindre Rd *TF:* 800-833-0151 ■ *Web:* www.alliedbindery.com	Madison Heights	MI	48071	248-588-5990		781
Allied Bldg Products Corp 15 E Union Ave *TF:* 800-541-2198 ■ *Web:* www.alliedbuilding.com	East Rutherford	NJ	07073	201-507-8400		191-3
Allied Blending & Ingredients 121 Royal Rd *Web:* www.alliedblending.com	Keokuk	IA	52632	319-524-1235		123
Allied Blower & Sheet Metal 1350 Polson Dr *Web:* www.alliedblower.com	Vernon	BC	V1T8H2	250-503-2533		610
Allied Body Works Inc 625 S 96th St *TF General:* 800-733-7450 ■ *Web:* www.alliedbody.com	Seattle	WA	98108	206-763-7811	763-8836	516
Allied Building Service Company of Detroit Inc 1801 Howard St *Web:* www.teamallied.com	Detroit	MI	48216	313-230-0800		104
Allied Business Consulting 295 Durham Ave Ste 212 *Web:* www.abcinc-us.com	South Plainfield	NJ	07080	908-222-7015	834-0930	194
Allied Business Intelligence Inc 249 S St *Web:* www.abiresearch.com	Oyster Bay	NY	11771	516-624-2500		668
Allied Cementing Co LLC 24 S Lincoln St	Russell	KS	67665	785-483-2627		538
Allied Chucker & Engineering Co 3529 Scheele Dr *TF:* 800-783-3637 ■ *Web:* alliedchucker.com	Jackson	MI	49202	517-787-1370	787-2878	595
Allied Concrete 1000 Harris St	Charlottesville	VA	22903	434-296-7181		182
Allied Construction Products LLC 3900 Kelley Ave *TF Cust Svc:* 800-321-1046 ■ *Web:* www.alliedcp.com	Cleveland	OH	44114	216-431-2600	431-2601	190
Allied Construction Services & Color Inc 2122 Fleur Dr PO Box 937 *TF:* 800-365-4855 ■ *Web:* www.alliedconst.com	Des Moines	IA	50304	515-288-4855	288-2069	189-9
Allied Consultants Inc 1304 W Ave *Web:* www.alliedconsultants.com	Austin	TX	78701	512-236-8535		196
Allied Container Systems Inc 201 N Civic Dr Ste 180 *TF:* 800-943-6510 ■ *Web:* www.alliedcontainer.com	Walnut Creek	CA	94596	800-943-6510		549
Allied Contractors Inc 204 E Preston St *Web:* alliedcontractor.com	Baltimore	MD	21202	410-539-6727	332-4594	189-3
Allied Controls Inc 150 E Aurora St *TF:* 800-788-0955 ■ *Web:* alliedcontrols.com	Waterbury	CT	06708	203-757-4200		203
Allied Corrosion Industries Inc 1550 Cobb Industrial Dr *TF:* 800-241-0809 ■ *Web:* www.alliedcorrosion.com	Marietta	GA	30066	770-425-1355		256
Allied Court Reporters 115 Phenix Ave *Web:* www.alliedcourtreporters.com	Cranston	RI	02920	401-946-5500	946-9228	445
Allied Electric Motor Co 924 Third Ave S *Web:* www.alliedelectric.net	Nashville	TN	37210	615-259-3892		518
Allied Electronics Inc 7151 Jack Newell Blvd S *TF:* 866-433-5722 ■ *Web:* www.alliedelec.com	Fort Worth	TX	76118	817-595-3500		246
Allied Employer Group 4400 Buffalo Gap Rd Ste 4500 *TF:* 800-495-3836 ■ *Web:* www.coemployer.com	Abilene	TX	79606	325-695-5822	692-9660	631
Allied Energy Company LLC 2700 Ishkooda Wenonah Rd *Web:* alliedenergycorp.com	Birmingham	AL	35211	205-925-6600		581
Allied Engineering & Production Corp 2421 Blanding Ave	Alameda	CA	94501	510-522-1500		454
Allied Erecting & Dismantling Company Inc 2100 Poland Ave *TF:* 800-624-2867 ■ *Web:* www.aed.cc	Youngstown	OH	44502	330-744-0808	744-3218	189-16
Allied Experiential 233 Broadway 13th Fl *Web:* www.grandcentralmarketing.com	New York	NY	10279	646-500-8741		636
Allied Fastener & Tool Inc 1130 Ng St *TF:* 877-353-3731 ■ *Web:* alliedfastener.com	Lake Worth	FL	33460	561-585-2113		350
Allied Fire & Security Inc 425 W Second Ave **Fax:* Acctg ■ *TF Acctg:* 888-333-2632 ■ *Web:* www.alliedfireandsecurity.com	Spokane	WA	99201	509-321-8778	321-8767*	692
Allied Fire Protection LP PO Box 2842 *TF:* 800-604-2600 ■ *Web:* www.alliedfireprotection.com	Pearland	TX	77588	281-485-6803	412-9668	189-10

Company / Address	City	State	ZIP	Phone	Fax	Class
ALLIED Group Inc 1100 Locust St	Des Moines	IA	50391	515-508-4211		391-4
TF: 800-532-1436 ■ *Web:* www.alliedinsurance.com						
Allied Group Inc, The 25 Amflex Dr	Cranston	RI	02921	401-946-6100		174
TF: 800-556-6310 ■ *Web:* www.thealliedgrp.com						
Allied Health Group LLC						
145 Technology Pkwy NW	Norcross	GA	30092	800-741-4674		721
TF: 800-355-6150 ■ *Web:* www.alliedhealth.com						
Allied Healthcare International Inc						
245 Pk AVe 39th Fl	New York	NY	10167	212-750-0064		363
Web: www.alliedhealthcare.com						
Allied Healthcare Products Inc						
1720 Sublette Ave	Saint Louis	MO	63110	314-771-2400	477-7701*	477
NASDAQ: AHPI ■ **Fax Area Code:* 800 ■ **Fax:* Cust Svc ■ *TF:* 800-444-3954 ■ *Web:* www.alliedhpi.com						
Allied Home Mortgage Capital Corp						
6110 Pinemont Dr	Houston	TX	77092	713-353-0400		217
Allied Hotel Properties Inc						
515 W Pender St Ste 300	Vancouver	BC	V6B6H5	604-669-5335		655
Web: www.alliedhotels.com						
Allied Insurance 1100 Locust St	Des Moines	CA	50391	800-532-1436		391-4
TF: 800-532-1436 ■ *Web:* www.alliedinsurance.com						
Allied International 13207 Bradley Ave	Sylmar	CA	91342	818-364-2333		351
TF General: 800-533-8333 ■ *Web:* www.alliedtools.com						
Allied International Corp						
7 Hill St	Bedford Hills	NY	10507	914-241-6900	241-6985	770
Web: www.alliedinter.com						
Allied International Credit Corp						
16635 Young St Unit 26	Newmarket	ON	L3X1V6	877-451-2594		160
TF: 877-451-2594 ■ *Web:* www.aiccorp.com						
Allied International NA Inc						
700 Oakmont Ln	Westmont	IL	60559	630-570-3500		519
TF: 800-444-6787 ■ *Web:* www.allied.com						
Allied Irish Banks						
1166 Ave of the Americas	New York	NY	10036	212-339-8080		70
Web: www.aib.ie						
Allied Machine & Engineering Corp						
120 Deeds Dr	Dover	OH	44622	330-343-4283		493
TF: 800-321-5537 ■ *Web:* www.alliedmachine.com						
Allied Marine & Industrial Inc						
1 Lake rd	Port Colborne	ON	L3K1A2	905-834-8275	834-5645	698
Web: www.allmind.com						
Allied Marketing Group Inc						
1555 Regal Row	Dallas	TX	75247	214-915-7000		459
Web: www.alliedmarketinggroup.com						
Allied Mechanical Services Inc						
145 N Plains Industrial Rd	Wallingford	CT	06492	269-344-0191		189-10
TF: 888-237-3017 ■ *Web:* www.alliedmechanical.com						
Allied Metals Corp 1750 Stephenson Hwy	Troy	MI	48083	248-680-2400		492
Web: www.alliedmet.com						
Allied Mineral Products Inc						
2700 Scioto Pkwy	Columbus	OH	43221	614-876-0244	876-0981	663
Web: www.alliedmineral.com						
Allied Motion Technologies Inc						
495 Commerce Dr Ste 3	Amherst	NY	14228	716-242-8634		248
NASDAQ: AMOT ■ *TF:* 888-392-5543 ■ *Web:* www.alliedmotion.com						
Allied Moulded Products Inc						
222 N Union St	Bryan	OH	43506	419-636-4217	636-2450	816
TF: 800-722-2679 ■ *Web:* www.alliedmoulded.com						
Allied Oil & Supply Inc 2209 S 24th St	Omaha	NE	68108	402-344-4343	344-4360	579
TF: 800-333-3717 ■ *Web:* www.alliedoil.com						
Allied Oil LLC						
25 Old Camplain Rd	Hillsborough	NJ	08844	908-575-7577		579
Web: www.alliedoilco.com						
Allied Oilfield Machine and Pump LLC						
202 Hulon Moreland Rd	Levelland	TX	79336	855-378-4787		538
TF: 855-378-4787 ■ *Web:* www.alliedoilfield.com						
Allied Old English Inc						
100 Markley St	Port Reading	NJ	07064	732-636-2060		123
Web: www.alliedoldenglish.com						
Allied Pacific 2951 E La Palma Ave	Anaheim	CA	92806	714-630-8145		757
Web: www.allied-pacific.com						
Allied Paper Company LLC						
5700 Plauche Ct	Harahan	LA	70123	504-733-5700		638
Web: www.alliedpapercompany.com						
Allied Personnel Services Inc						
11821 Queens Blvd Ste 310	New York	NY	11375	718-261-7979		260
TF: 800-472-8367 ■ *Web:* www.alliedpersonnel.com						
Allied Photocopy Inc						
1821 University Dr NW	Huntsville	AL	35801	256-539-2973		627
TF: 877-539-2973 ■ *Web:* alliedphotocopy.com						
Allied Pilots Association						
14600 Trinity Blvd O'Connell Bldg Ste 500	Fort Worth	TX	76155	817-302-2272		414
TF: 800-272-7456 ■ *Web:* www.alliedpilots.org						
Allied Plastic Supply LLC						
1544 Valwood Pkwy	Carrollton	TX	75006	972-241-0762		608
Web: www.alliedplastic.org						
Allied Plastics Company Inc						
2001 Walnut St	Jacksonville	FL	32206	904-359-0386	353-4746	319-1
TF Cust Svc: 800-999-0386 ■ *Web:* www.alliedplasticsco.com						
Allied Plastics Inc						
150 Holy Hill Rd	Twin Lakes	WI	53181	262-877-4700		489
Web: www.apibags.com						
Allied Power Group LLC 10131 Mills Rd	Houston	TX	77070	281-444-3535		261
TF: 888-830-3535 ■ *Web:* www.alliedpg.com						
Allied Printing Services Inc						
1 Allied Way	Manchester	CT	06045	860-643-1101		627
TF: 800-225-8777 ■ *Web:* www.alliedprinting.com						
Allied Propane Service Inc						
5000 Seaport Ave	Richmond	CA	94804	510-237-7077		579
Web: www.alliedpropaneservice.com						
Allied Property Services LLC						
2524 Ford Rd	Bristol	PA	19007	215-785-5900		290
Allied Resources Corp						
106 Pitkin St	East Hartford	CT	06108	860-290-6665		256
Web: www.alliedr.com						
Allied Sales Co 5005 E Seventh St	Austin	TX	78702	512-385-2167		541
Web: www.alliedsales.com						
Allied Screw Products Inc						
815 E Lowell Ave	Mishawaka	IN	46546	574-255-4718	255-4173	621
Web: www.aspi-nc.com						
Allied Seed LLC 9311 Hwy 45	Nampa	ID	83686	208-466-6700		276
Web: www.alliedseed.com						
Allied Services Rehabilitation Hospital						
100 Abington Executive Pk	Clarks Summit	PA	18508	570-348-1300	341-4548	374-6
TF: 888-734-2272 ■ *Web:* www.allied-services.org						
Allied Shipyard Inc 310 Ledet Ln	Larose	LA	70373	985-693-3323		698
Allied Sinterings Inc						
29 Briar Ridge Rd	Danbury	CT	06810	203-743-7502		492
Web: alliedsinterings.com						
Allied Solutions LLC						
1320 City Ctr Dr Ste 300	Carmel	IN	46032	317-706-7600	706-7606	390
Web: alliedsolutions.net						
Allied Staffing Inc						
556 n diamond bar blvd	Diamond bar	CA	91765	909-861-5200		260
Web: www.alliedstaffinginc.com						
Allied Steel Construction Co Inc						
2211 NW First Terr	Oklahoma City	OK	73107	405-232-7531	236-3705	264-3
TF: 800-522-4658 ■ *Web:* www.alliedsteelerectors.com						
Allied Steel Fabricators Inc						
4604 148th Ave NE	Redmond	WA	98052	425-861-9558		480
Web: www.alliedsteelfab.com						
Allied Supply Company Inc						
1100 E Monument Ave	Dayton	OH	45402	937-224-9833	224-5648	665
TF: 800-589-5690 ■ *Web:* www.alliedsupply.com						
Allied Systems Co 21433 SW Oregon St	Sherwood	OR	97140	503-625-2560	625-7269	273
TF: 800-285-7000 ■ *Web:* www.alliedsystems.com						
Allied Systems Holdings Inc						
2302 Parklake Dr NE	Atlanta	GA	30345	404-373-4285		360-3
TF: 800-332-4080 ■ *Web:* www.alliedholdings.com						
Allied T Pro Inc 500 Seventh Ave	New York	NY	10036	212-596-1000	313-9800	772
Web: www.alliedtpro.com						
Allied Telesyn International Corp						
19800 N Creek Pkwy Ste 100	Bothell	WA	98011	425-481-3895		176
TF: 800-424-4284 ■ *Web:* www.alliedtelesis.com						
Allied Tool & Die Company LLC						
3807 S Seventh St	Phoenix	AZ	85040	602-276-2439		697
Web: www.alliedtool.com						
Allied Tool Products						
9334 N 107th St	Milwaukee	WI	53224	414-355-8280	355-8297	455
TF: 800-558-5147 ■ *Web:* www.atptools.com						
Allied Toyotalift						
1640 Island Home Ave	Knoxville	TN	37920	865-573-0995		57
TF: 866-538-0667 ■ *Web:* www.alliedtoyotalift.com						
Allied Uniking Corporation Inc						
4750 Cromwell Ave	Memphis	TN	38118	901-365-7240		207
Allied Vaughn						
7600 Parklawn Ste 300	Minneapolis	MN	55435	952-832-3100	832-3179	658
TF: 800-323-0281 ■ *Web:* www.alliedvaughn.com						
Allied Waste Bettendorf						
6449 Valley Dr	Bettendorf	IA	52722	563-332-0050		804
Web: www.republicservices.com						
Allied Well Service Inc 2681 W Frnt St	Alice	TX	78332	361-664-6122		538
Web: www.alliedwells.com						
Allied Wheel Components						
12300 Edison Way	Garden Grove	CA	92841	714-893-4160		247
Web: www.alliedwheel.com						
AlliedCook Construction Corp						
8 US Route 1	Scarborough	ME	04074	207-772-2888		186
Web: www.alliedcook.com						
Allied-Horizontal Wireline Services LLC						
3200 Wilcrest Dr Ste 170	Houston	TX	77042	713-343-7280		536
TF: 888-494-9580 ■ *Web:* alliedhorizontal.com						
Allied-Locke Industries						
1088 Corregidor Rd	Dixon	IL	61021	815-288-1471	288-7945	620
TF: 800-435-7752 ■ *Web:* www.alliedlocke.com						
Alligato Inc						
1450-1055 W Hastings St	Vancouver	BC	V6E2E9	866-355-0187		224
TF: 866-355-0187 ■ *Web:* www.alligatomobile.com						
Alligator Adventure						
4604 Hwy 17 S Barefoot Landing	North Myrtle Beach	SC	29582	843-361-0789		823
Web: www.alligatoradventure.com						
Alligator Records & Artist Management Inc						
PO Box 60234	Chicago	IL	60660	773-973-7736	973-2088	657
TF: 800-344-5609 ■ *Web:* www.alligator.com						
Alligator Soul 114 Barnard St	Savannah	GA	31401	912-232-7899		671
Web: alligatorsoul.com						
Allina Health System						
710 E 24th St	Minneapolis	MN	55404	612-813-3600		353
TF: 800-233-8504 ■ *Web:* www.allinahealth.org						
All-Inclusive Vacations Inc						
1595 Iris St	Lakewood	CO	80215	303-980-6483		771
TF: 866-980-6483 ■ *Web:* www.all-inclusivevacations.com						
Allis Information Management Inc						
4300 W Sugnet Rd	Midland	MI	48640	989-835-5811		7
Web: www.allisinfo.com						
Allis Roller LLC 9800 S 60th St	Franklin	WI	53132	414-423-9000		190
Web: www.allis-roller.com						
Allis State Park						
284 Allis State Pk Rd	Randolph	VT	05060	802-276-3175		565
Web: www.vtstateparks.com						
Allis Tool & Machine Corp						
647 S 94th Pl	Milwaukee	WI	53214	414-453-5500		494
Web: www.allistool.com						
Allison Abrasives Inc						
141 Industry Rd	Lancaster	KY	40444	859-792-3033		1
Web: www.allisonabrasives.com						
Allison Knapp & Siekmann Ltd						
2810 Frank Scott Pkwy W	Belleville	IL	62223	618-233-2641		2
Allison Marine Contractors Inc						
9828 Hwy 182 E	Amelia	LA	70340	985-631-2000		698
Web: www.allisonmarine.net						
Allison Payment Systems LLC						
2200 Production Dr	Indianapolis	IN	46241	800-755-2440	808-2477*	110
**Fax Area Code:* 317 ■ *TF:* 800-755-2440 ■ *Web:* www.apsllc.com						
Allison Royce & Associates Inc						
PO Box 790010 Ste 760	San Antonio	TX	78279	210-564-7000	564-7001	225
Web: allisonroyce.com						

	Phone	Fax	Class
All-League Sports Photos & Lab Inc 27062 Burbank ..... Foothill Ranch CA 92610 *Web:* www.allleaguesportsphotos.com	949-598-9297		590
Allman Spry Davis Leggett & Crumpler 380 Knollwood St Ste 700 ..... Winston-salem NC 27103 *Web:* www.allmanspry.com	336-722-2300		445
Allmar Inc 287 Riverton Ave ..... Winnipeg MB R2L0N2 *TF:* 800-230-5516 ■ *Web:* www.allmar.com	204-668-1000	668-3029	236
AllMed Healthcare Management Inc 621 SW Alder St Ste 740 ..... Portland OR 97205 *TF:* 888-289-6015 ■ *Web:* allmedmd.com	503-274-9916		463
All-Med Medical Supply LLC 6321 Commerce Dr ..... Westland MI 48185 *Web:* www.amms.net	734-728-9490		475
AllMeds Inc 151 Lafayette Dr Ste 401 ..... Oak Ridge TN 37830 *TF:* 888-343-6337 ■ *Web:* www.allmeds.com	865-482-1999	481-0921	39
Allmetal Inc 1 Pierce Pl Ste 900 ..... Itasca IL 60143 *Web:* www.allmetalinc.com	630-250-8090		234
Allmetal Screw Products Corp 94 E Jefryn Blvd Ste A ..... Deer Park NY 11729 *TF:* 800-225-1396 ■ *Web:* www.allmetalcorp.com	631-243-5200	243-5307	621
Allnorth Consultants Ltd 2011 Prince George Pulpmill Rd PO Box 968 ..... Prince George BC V2L4V1 *Web:* allnorth.com	250-614-7291		261
ALLogistx International, Inc. 2130 Huntington Dr ..... South Pasadena CA 91030	323-254-9550		194
Allomatic Products Co 102 Jericho Tpke Ste 104 Floral Pk ..... Floral Park NY 11001 *TF:* 800-568-0330 ■ *Web:* www.allomatic.com	516-775-0330		61
Allor Manufacturing Inc 12534 Emerson Dr ..... Brighton MI 48116 *TF:* 888-382-6300 ■ *Web:* allorplesh.com	248-486-4500		207
Allos Therapeutics Inc 11080 Cir Pt Rd Ste 200 ..... Westminster CO 80020 *NASDAQ: ALTH*	303-426-6262		85
AlloSource 6278 S Troy Cir ..... Centennial CO 80111 *TF:* 800-557-3587 ■ *Web:* www.allosource.org	720-873-0213	873-0212	545
Allot Communications 300 Tradecenter Ste 4680 ..... Woburn MA 01801 *TF:* 877-255-6826 ■ *Web:* www.allot.com	781-939-9300	939-9393	178-10
Allout Marketing Inc 1769 Lexington Ave N PO Box 347 ..... Roseville MN 55113 *Web:* www.alloutsuccess.com	952-404-0800		195
Alloy Bellows & Precision Welding 653 Miner Rd ..... Cleveland OH 44143 *Web:* www.alloybellows.com	440-684-3000		454
Alloy Carbide Co 7827 Ave H ..... Houston TX 77012 *Web:* www.alloycarbide.com	713-923-2700	923-4652	537
Alloy Cast Products Inc 700 Swenson Dr ..... Kenilworth NJ 07033 *Web:* www.alloycastproducts.com	908-245-2255		308
Alloy Die Casting Co 6550 Caballero Blvd ..... Buena Park CA 90620 **Fax: Sales* ■ *Web:* alloydie.com	714-521-9800	521-5510*	308
Alloy Engineering & Casting Co 1700 W Washington St ..... Champaign IL 61821 **Fax Area Code: 260* ■ *TF:* 800-348-2880 ■ *Web:* www.wirco.com	217-398-3200	897-2525*	307
Alloy Engineering Co, The 844 Thacker St ..... Berea OH 44017 *Web:* www.alloyengineering.com	440-243-6800		480
Alloy Hardfacing & Engineering Company Inc 20425 Johnson Memorial Dr ..... Jordan MN 55352 *Web:* alloyhardfacing.com	952-492-5569		256
Alloy Polymers Inc (AP) 3310 Deepwater Terminal Rd ..... Richmond VA 23234 *Web:* www.alloypolymers.com	804-232-8000	230-0386	605-2
Alloy Products Corp 1045 Perkins Ave ..... Waukesha WI 53186 *Web:* www.alloyproductscorp.com	262-542-6603		298
Alloy Silverstein Financial Services 900 Kings Hwy N ..... Cherry Hill NJ 08034 *Web:* www.alloysilverstein.com	856-667-4100		401
Alloy Stainless Products Co 611 Union Blvd ..... Totowa NJ 07512 *TF:* 800-631-8372 ■ *Web:* www.alloystainless.com	973-256-1616	256-5256	595
Alloy Surfaces Company Inc 121 N Commerce Dr Chester Township .. Chester Township PA 19014 *Web:* www.alloysurfaces.com	610-497-7979		492
Alloy Ventures 400 Hamilton Ave 4th Fl ..... Palo Alto CA 94301 *Web:* www.alloyventures.com	650-687-5000	687-5010	792
Allpak Co 1010 Lake St ..... Oak Park IL 60301	708-383-7200		603
ALLParts Music Corp 13027 Brittmoore Park Dr ..... Houston TX 77041 *Web:* www.allparts.com	713-466-6414		527
All-Phase Electric Supply Co 4216 Legacy Pkwy Ste D ..... Lansing MI 48911 *Web:* all-phaselansing.com	517-394-1461		690
Allplus Computer Systems Corp 3075 NW 107th Ave ..... Doral FL 33172	305-436-3993		179
ALLPoints Inc 909 Lunt Ave ..... Schaumburg IL 60193 *Web:* allpointsinc.net	847-585-0160		189-10
ALLPoints Research Inc 200 W First St Ste 100 ..... Winston-Salem NC 27101	336-896-2200		668
All-Points Technology Corp PC 3 Saddlebrook Dr ..... Killingworth CT 06419 *Web:* www.allpointstech.com	860-663-1697		256
All-Pro Fasteners Inc 1916 Peyco Dr N ..... Arlington TX 76001 *TF:* 800-361-6627 ■ *Web:* www.apf.com	817-467-5700	467-5365	351
Allpro Parking LLC 465 Main St Lafayette Court Bldg Ste 200Annex ..... Buffalo NY 14203 *Web:* www.allproparking.com	716-849-7275		562
All-Pro Printing 11626 Prosperous Dr ..... Odessa FL 33556 *Web:* www.allproprinting.com	727-375-1502		627
Allrecipes 413 Pine St Ste 500 ..... Seattle WA 98101 *Web:* dish.allrecipes.com	206-292-3990	292-1793	637-10

	Phone	Fax	Class
Allright Tool Company Inc 6517 Georgia Rd ..... Birmingham AL 35212 *Web:* www.allrighttool.com	205-591-1468		567
Allsafe Technologies Inc 290 Creekside Dr ..... Amherst NY 14228 *Web:* www.allsafe.com	716-691-0400		596
ALLSCO Building Products Ltd 615 St George Blvd ..... Moncton NB E1E2C2 *Web:* www.allsco.com	506-853-8080		499
Allscripts Healthcare Solutions 222 Merchandise Mart Plaza Ste 2024 ..... Chicago IL 60654 *NASDAQ: MDRX* ■ *TF:* 800-654-0889 ■ *Web:* www.allscripts.com	800-654-0889		178-10
All-Search & Inspection Inc 1108 E S Union Ave ..... Midvale UT 84047 *TF:* 800-227-3152 ■ *Web:* www.all-search.com	801-984-8160	984-8170	635
Allsopp Design Inc 587 Bay Rd ..... South Hamilton MA 01982 *Web:* allsoppdesign.com	978-468-1556		344
AllSource Analysis Inc 350 Terry St Ste 300 ..... Longmont CO 80503 *Web:* www.allsourceanalysis.com	303-219-1720		466
All-South Subcontractors Inc 2678 Queenstown Rd ..... Birmingham AL 35210 *TF:* 800-873-8110 ■ *Web:* www.allsouthsub.com	205-836-8111	836-4227	189-12
AllStar Deals Inc 150 Fifth Ave 4th Fl ..... New York NY 10010 **Fax Area Code: 443*	240-876-5388	431-2508*	393
Allstar Fasteners Inc 1550 Arthur Ave ..... Elk Grove Village IL 60007 *TF:* 800-234-1444 ■ *Web:* www.allstarfasteners.com	847-640-7827		711
Allstar Fire Equipment Inc 12328 Lower Azusa Rd ..... Arcadia CA 91006 *TF:* 800-425-5787 ■ *Web:* www.allstarfire.com	626-652-0900	652-0920	679
Allstar Magnetics LLC 6205 NE 63rd St ..... Vancouver WA 98661 *TF:* 800-356-5977 ■ *Web:* www.allstarmagnetics.com	360-693-0213	693-0639	246
All-Star Recruiting LLC 6119 Lyons Rd ..... Coconut Creek FL 33073 *TF:* 800-928-0229 ■ *Web:* www.allstarrecruiting.com	800-928-0229		260
All-Star Team Realtors, The 4 Willow Bend Dr Ste 2A ..... Hattiesburg MS 39402 *Web:* deloissmith.com	601-545-3900		652
Allstar Tech 1856 Angus St ..... Regina SK S4T1Z4 *Web:* allstartech.com	306-522-7827		180
Allstate Arena 6920 Mannheim Rd ..... Rosemont IL 60018 *Web:* rosemont.com/allstate	847-635-6601	635-6606	720
Allstate Can Corp 1 Wood Hollow Rd ..... Parsippany NJ 07054 *TF:* 800-848-0272 ■ *Web:* www.allstatecan.com	973-560-9030	560-9217	124
Allstate Construction Inc 5718 Tower Rd ..... Tallahassee FL 32303 *Web:* www.allstateconstruction.com	850-514-1004	514-1206	186
Allstate Corp 2775 Sanders Rd ..... Northbrook IL 60062 *NYSE: ALL* ■ *TF:* 800-255-7828 ■ *Web:* www.allstate.com	847-402-5000		360-4
Allstate Floral & Craft Inc 14038 Park Pl ..... Cerritos CA 90703 *TF:* 800-433-4056 ■ *Web:* allstatefloral.com	562-926-2302	926-8613	293
Allstate Insurance Co 2955 Pineda Plaza Way Ste 103 ..... Melbourne FL 32940 *Web:* agents.allstate.com	321-242-1002		390
Allstate Insurance Co 2775 Sanders Rd ..... Northbrook IL 60062 *NYSE: ALL* ■ *Web:* www.allstate.com	847-402-5000		304
Allstate Leasing Inc 1 Olympic Pl ..... Towson MD 21204 *TF:* 800-223-4885 ■ *Web:* www.allstateleasing.com	800-223-4885		289
Allstate Life Insurance Co 3100 Sanders Rd Allstate W Plz ..... Northbrook IL 60062 *TF Cust Svc:* 800-366-1411 ■ *Web:* www.allstate.com	847-402-5000		391-2
Allstate Steel Company Inc 130 S Jackson Ave ..... Jacksonville FL 32220 *TF:* 800-831-9252 ■ *Web:* www.allstatesteel.com	904-781-6040		189-14
Allstate Sugar Bowl 1500 Sugar Bowl Dr ..... New Orleans LA 70112 *Web:* www.allstatesugarbowl.org	504-828-2440		181
Allsteel Inc 2210 Second Ave ..... Muscatine IA 52761 *TF Cust Svc:* 888-255-7833 ■ *Web:* www.allsteeloffice.com	563-272-4800	272-4887	319-1
Allstream Corp 200 Wellington St W ..... Toronto ON M5V3G2 *TF Cust Svc:* 888-288-2273 ■ *Web:* www.allstream.com	416-345-2000		736
Allstyle Coil Company LP 7037 Brittmore Dr ..... Houston TX 77041 *Web:* www.allstyle.com	713-466-6333		5
Allsup Inc 300 Allsup Pl ..... Belleville IL 62223 **Fax Area Code: 618* ■ *TF:* 800-854-1418 ■ *Web:* www.allsup.com	800-854-1418	236-5778*	194
All-system Aerospace Int'l Inc 75 Beacon Dr ..... Holbrook NY 11741 *Web:* allsystem.com	631-582-9200	582-9353	770
Alltech Consulting Services Inc 258 Wall St ..... Princeton NJ 08540 *Web:* www.alltechconsultinginc.com	609-945-2590		196
Alltech Inc 3031 Catnip Hill Pike ..... Nicholasville KY 40356 *TF:* 800-289-8324 ■ *Web:* www.alltech.com	859-885-9613	887-3256	584
Alltech International Inc 8298-B Old Courthouse Rd Centennial Plaza - Tysons C ..... Vienna VA 22182 *Web:* www.alltech.net	703-506-1222		177
Alltek Energy Systems 58 Hudson River Rd ..... Waterford NY 12188 *TF:* 800-238-2636 ■ *Web:* www.alltekenergy.com	518-238-2600		612
Alltek Services 4755 Drane Field Rd ..... Lakeland FL 33811 *Web:* www.allteksservices.com	863-709-0709		396
AllTek Staffing & Resource Group Inc 600 Davidson Rd ..... Pittsburgh PA 15239 *Web:* www.alltekstaffing.com	412-573-0077		194
All-Temp Refrigeration Services Inc 271 Hwy 1085 ..... Madisonville LA 70447 *TF:* 888-626-1277 ■ *Web:* www.alltempinc.com	888-626-1277		610
ALL-TEST Pro LLC 123 Spencer Plain Rd ..... Old Saybrook CT 06475 *TF:* 800-952-8776 ■ *Web:* www.alltestpro.com	860-399-4222		201

	Phone	Fax	Class
All-Tex Pipe & Supply Inc 9743 Brockbank Dallas TX 75220 *Web:* www.alltexsupply.com	214-350-5886		610
Alltranmedia Ltd 1232 Harmony St Ste 670 New Orleans LA 70115 *Web:* advercar.com	318-255-0524		5
AllTranstek LLC 1101 W 31st St Ste 200 Downers Grove IL 60515 *Web:* www.alltranstek.com	630-325-9977		463
Alltrax Inc 1111 Cheney Creek Rd Grants Pass OR 97527 *Web:* www.alltraxinc.com	541-476-3565		518
Alltronics LLC 2761 Scoll Blvd Santa Clara CA 95050 *Web:* www.alltronics.com	408-778-3868		246
All-Tronics Medical Systems Inc 3289 E 55th St Cleveland OH 44127 *Web:* www.all-tronics.net	216-429-3000		743
Allure Home Creation Co Inc 85 Fulton St Boonton NJ 07005 *Web:* www.allurehome.com	973-402-8888		361
Alluvion Staffing Inc 4190 BelFt Rd Enterprise Park Bldg Fourth Fl Ste 420 Jacksonville FL 32216 *Web:* www.alluvionstaffing.com	904-296-0626		260
Allvend Management Corp 800 W Airport Fwy 705 Irving TX 75062 *Web:* www.allvend.com	972-255-8363		463
Allview Networks LLC 8303 Arlington Dr Ste 210 Fairfax VA 22031 *TF:* 888-982-8489 ■ *Web:* www.allviewnetworks.com	888-982-8489		5
Allway Tools Inc 1255 Seabury Ave Bronx NY 10462 *TF:* 800-422-5592 ■ *Web:* www.allwaytools.com	718-792-3636	823-9640	758
All-Ways Adv Co 1442 Broad St Bloomfield NJ 07003 *TF:* 800-255-9291 ■ *Web:* www.awadv.com	973-338-0700	338-1410	4
Allways Precision Inc 14001 Van Dyke Rd Plainfield IL 60544 *TF:* 800-622-4463 ■ *Web:* allwaysprecision.com	815-577-1600		757
Allwire Inc 16395 Ave 24 1/2 PO Box 1000 Chowchilla CA 93610 *TF:* 800-255-3828 ■ *Web:* www.allwire.com	559-665-4893	665-7389	813
Ally Plm Solutions Inc 9155 Governors Way Cincinnati OH 45249 *TF:* 800-631-5961 ■ *Web:* www.allyplm.com	513-984-0480		256
Allyn & Betty Taylor Library Natural Sciences Ctr 1151 Richmond St London ON N6A3K7 *Web:* www.lib.uwo.ca/taylor	519-661-3168	661-3435	434-1
ALM (American Lawyer Media Inc) 120 Broadway 5th Fl New York NY 10271 *TF:* 877-256-2472 ■ *Web:* www.alm.com	212-457-9400		637-9
Alma 528 University Ave SE Minneapolis MN 55414 *Web:* www.restaurantalma.com	612-379-4909		671
Alma College 614 W Superior St Alma MI 48801 *TF:* 800-321-2562 ■ *Web:* www.alma.edu	989-463-7139	463-7057	166
Alma Container Corp 1000 Charles Ave Alma MI 48801 *TF:* 800-952-0178 ■ *Web:* www.almacontainer.com	989-463-2106		100
Alma de Cuba 1623 Walnut St Philadelphia PA 19103 *Web:* www.almadecubarestaurant.com	215-988-1799		671
Alma Lasers Inc 485 Half Day Rd Ste 100 Buffalo Grove IL 60089 *Web:* www.almalasers.com	224-377-2000		475
Alma Plantation Ltd 4612 Alma Rd Lakeland LA 70752	225-627-6632		296-38
Alma Products Co 2000 Michigan Ave Alma MI 48801 **Fax Area Code:* 800 ■ *TF:* 877-427-2624 ■ *Web:* www.almaproducts.com	989-463-1151	457-2719*	60
Almaco 99 M Ave Nevada IA 50201 *Web:* www.almaco.com	515-382-3506		194
Almanac, The 2600 Boyce Plaza Rd Ste 142 Pittsburgh PA 15241 **Fax:* Edit ■ *Web:* www.thealmanac.net	724-941-7725	941-8685*	532-4
Almanac, The 3525 Alameda De Las Pulgas Menlo Park CA 94025 *TF:* 800-799-4811 ■ *Web:* www.almanacnews.com	650-854-2626	854-0677	532-4
Almatis Inc 501 W Pk Rd Leetsdale PA 15056 *TF:* 800-643-8771 ■ *Web:* www.almatis.com	412-630-2800	630-2900	143
ALMC (Aurora Lakeland Medical Ctr) W3985 County Rd NN Elkhorn WI 53121 *Web:* www.aurorahealthcare.org	262-741-2000		374-3
Almeda Mall Almeda Mall 12200 Gulf Frwy Houston TX 77075 *Web:* www.almedamall.com	713-944-1010		460
Almega Cable Inc 4001 W Airport Fwy Ste 530 Bedford TX 76021	817-685-9588		116
Almet Inc 300 Hartzell Rd New Haven IN 46774 *Web:* www.almetinc.com	260-493-1556		492
Almetals Inc 51035 Grand River Ave Wixom MI 48393 *Web:* www.almetals.com	248-348-7722		492
ALMH (Adventist La Grange Memorial Hospital) 5101 S Willow Springs Rd La Grange IL 60525 *Web:* www.keepingyouwell.com/facilities/lagrange	708-245-9000		374-3
Almich & Assoc An Accountancy Corp 26463 Rancho Pkwy S Lake Forest CA 92630 *Web:* almichcpa.com	949-600-7550		2
Almighty LLC 300 Western Ave Fl 2 Boston MA 02134 *Web:* www.bealmighty.com	617-782-1511		7
Almo Corp 2709 Commerce Way Philadelphia PA 19154 *TF:* 800-345-2566 ■ *Web:* www.almo.com	215-698-4000		38
Almond Products Inc 17150 148th Ave Spring Lake MI 49456 *Web:* www.almondproducts.com	616-844-1813		481
AlmondNet Inc 134 Spring St Ste 302 New York NY 10012 **Fax Area Code:* 646 ■ *Web:* www.almondnet.com	212-219-5070	349-2778*	809
Almost Family Inc 9510 Ormsby Stn Rd Ste 300 Louisville KY 40223 *NASDAQ: AFAM* ■ *TF:* 800-828-9769 ■ *Web:* www.almostfamily.com	502-891-1000	891-8067	363
Almost Home Restaurant & Steakhouse 3310 Market St NE Salem OR 97301	503-378-0100		671
Almquist, Maltzahn, Galloway & Luth PC 1203 W Second St Grand Island NE 68802 *Web:* www.gicpas.com	308-381-1810		2
Alnara Pharmaceuticals Inc 840 Memorial Dr Cambridge MA 02139	617-349-3690		231
Alnylam Pharmaceuticals Inc 300 Third St 3rd Fl Cambridge MA 02142 *NASDAQ: ALNY* ■ *TF:* 866-330-0326 ■ *Web:* www.alnylam.com	617-551-8200	551-8101	85
ALOA (Associated Locksmiths of America) 3500 Easy St Dallas TX 75247 *TF:* 800-532-2562 ■ *Web:* www.aloa.org	214-819-9733	819-9736	49-3
Aloe Up Suncare 9700 W 76th St Ste 112 Eden Prairie MN 55344 *Web:* www.aloeup.com	952-933-7724		77
Aloft Broomfield Denver 8300 Arista Pl Broomfield CO 80021 *TF:* 866-716-8143 ■ *Web:* www.aloftbroomfielddenver.com	303-635-2000		707
Aloft Charlotte Uptown at the EpiCentre 210 E Trade St Charlotte NC 28202 *Web:* www.aloftcharlotteuptown.com	704-333-1999		297-8
Aloft Chicago O'hare 9700 Balmoral Ave Rosemont IL 60018 *TF:* 866-716-8143 ■ *Web:* www.aloftchicagoohare.com	847-671-4444		707
Aloft Group Inc 26 Parker St Newburyport MA 01950 *TF:* 800-345-8082 ■ *Web:* www.aloftgroup.com	978-462-0002		7
Alogic US LLC 1845 Ferguson Rd Allison Park PA 15101 *Web:* www.alogic-us.com	412-635-2500		196
Aloha Freight Forwarders Inc 1800 S Anderson Ave Compton CA 90220 *Web:* www.alohafreight.com	310-631-6116		311
Aloha Kitchen 2950 S Alma School Rd Ste 12 Mesa AZ 85210	480-897-2451		671
Aloha Medicinals Inc 2300 Arrowhead Dr Carson City NV 89706 *TF:* 877-835-6091 ■ *Web:* www.alohamedicinals.com	775-886-6300		231
Aloha Petroleum Ltd 1132 Bishop St Ste 1700 Honolulu HI 96813 *TF:* 800-621-4654 ■ *Web:* www.alohagas.com	808-522-9700	522-9707	113
Aloha Restaurants Inc 204 Main St Ste 960 Newport Beach CA 92661 *Web:* aloharestaurants.com	949-250-0331	673-5085	670
Aloha Shoyu Company Ltd 96-1205 Waihona St Pearl City HI 96782 *Web:* www.alohashoyu.com	808-456-5929		123
Aloha Stadium 99-500 Salt Lake Blvd Honolulu HI 96818 *Web:* www.alohastadium.hawaii.gov	808-483-2500	483-2823	720
Aloha Surf Hotel, The 444 Kanekapolei St Honolulu HI 96815 *Web:* www.alohasurfhotelwaikiki.com	808-923-0222		377
Aloha United Way Inc 200 N Vineyard Blvd Ste 700 Honolulu HI 96817 *TF:* 800-728-7825 ■ *Web:* www.auw.org	808-536-1951		226
Alon USA Energy Inc 7616 LBJ Fwy Ste 300 Dallas TX 75251 *NYSE: ALJ* ■ *Web:* www.alonusa.com	972-367-3600		580
Alonso Consulting Inc 204 Passaic Ave Fl 1 Fairfield NJ 07004 *Web:* www.alonso.com	973-575-1414		196
Alonzo King's LINES Contemporary Ballet 26 Seventh St San Francisco CA 94102 *TF:* 800-443-2623 ■ *Web:* www.linesballet.org	415-863-3040	863-1180	573-1
Alorica Inc 5 Park Plaza Ste 1100 Irvine CA 92614 *Web:* www.alorica.com	949-527-4600		178-11
Alostar Bank 3680 Grandview Pkwy Ste 200 Birmingham AL 35243 **Fax Area Code:* 866 ■ *TF:* 877-738-6391 ■ *Web:* www.alostarbank.com	877-738-6391	715-6601*	70
ALOT Inc 143 Varick St New York NY 10013 *Web:* www.alot.com	212-231-2000		387
ALP Industries Inc 1229 W Lincoln Hwy Coatesville PA 19320 *TF:* 800-220-2571 ■ *Web:* alpindustries.com	610-384-1300		678
ALP Lighting Components Inc 6333 Gross Point Rd Niles IL 60714 *Web:* alpadvantage.com	773-774-9550	774-9331	608
Alpac Inc 5752 Cedar Ridge Dr Ann Arbor MI 48103 *Web:* alpacinc.com	734-623-2866		180
Alpak Display Group 575 N Midland Ave Saddle Brook NJ 07663 *TF:* 800-275-1145 ■ *Web:* www.alpak.com	201-797-1411		8
Alpena Agency Inc 102 S Third Ave Alpena MI 49707 *Web:* alpenaagency.com	989-354-2175		390
Alpena Area Chamber of Commerce 235 W Chisholm St Alpena MI 49707 *TF:* 800-425-7362 ■ *Web:* www.alpenachamber.com	989-354-4181	356-3999	139
Alpena Area Convention & Visitors Bureau 235 W Chisholm St Alpena MI 49707 *TF:* 800-425-7362 ■ *Web:* www.visitalpena.com	989-354-4181	356-3999	206
Alpena Community College (ACC) 665 Johnson St Alpena MI 49707 *TF:* 888-468-6222 ■ *Web:* discover.alpenacc.edu	989-356-9021		162
Alpena County 720 W Chisholm St Alpena MI 49707 *TF:* 800-999-4487 ■ *Web:* www.alpenacounty.org	989-354-9500	354-9648	338
Alpena County George N Fletcher Public Library 211 N First Ave Alpena MI 49707 *TF:* 877-737-4106 ■ *Web:* alpenalibrary.org	989-356-6188	356-2765	434-3
Alpena County Regional Airport 1617 Airport Rd Alpena MI 49707 *TF:* 800-433-7300 ■ *Web:* www.alpenaairport.com	989-354-2907	358-9988	27
Alpena Oil Co Inc 235 Water St Alpena MI 49707 *TF:* 800-968-1098 ■ *Web:* www.alpenaoil.net	989-356-1098	356-9486	324
Alpena Public Schools (Inc) 2373 Gordon Rd Alpena MI 49707 *Web:* www.alpenaschools.com	989-358-5040	358-5041	685
Alpenhof Lodge 3255 W Village Dr Teton Village WY 83025 *TF:* 800-732-3244 ■ *Web:* alpenhoflodgereservations.com	307-733-3242		379
Alpern Myers Stuart LLC 14 N Sierra Madre St Ste A Colorado Springs CO 80903 *TF:* 800-973-1177 ■ *Web:* www.coloradolawyers.net	719-471-7955		428
Alpha & Omega Financial Management Consultants Inc 8580 La Mesa Blvd Ste 100 La Mesa CA 91942 *TF:* 800-755-5060 ■ *Web:* www.alpha-omega-inc.com	800-755-5060		194

Phone | Fax | Class

Alpha 1 Induction Service Ctr Inc
1525 Old Alum Creek Dr. ... Columbus OH 43209 614-253-8900 253-8981 318
TF: 800-991-2599 ■ *Web:* www.alpha1induction.com

Alpha Analytical Inc
255 Glendale Ave Ste 21 ... Sparks NV 89431 775-355-1044 794
Web: www.alpha-analytical.com

Alpha Assoc Inc 145 Lehigh Ave ... Lakewood NJ 08701 732-634-5700 634-1430 745-2
TF: 800-631-5399 ■ *Web:* www.alphainc.com

Alpha Beta Gamma International Business Honor Society
75 Grasslands Rd ... Valhalla NY 10595 914-606-6877 48-16
Web: www.abg.org

Alpha Beta Press Inc
8301 183rd St ... Tinley Park IL 60487 708-429-2000 627
Web: www.visionps.com

Alpha Bldg Corp 24850 Blanco Rd ... San Antonio TX 78260 210-491-9925 186
Web: www.alphabuilding.com

Alpha Capital Partners Ltd
122 S Michigan Ave Ste 1700 ... Chicago IL 60603 312-322-9800 792
Web: www.alphacapital.com

Alpha Card Services Inc
475 Veit Rd ... Huntingdon Valley PA 19006 866-253-2227 251
TF: 866-253-2227 ■ *Web:* www.alphacardservices.com

Alpha Chi National College Honor Scholarship Society
1210 E Race Ave ... Searcy AR 72143 501-279-4443 48-16
TF: 800-477-4225 ■ *Web:* www.harding.edu

Alpha Chi Omega
5939 Castle Creek Pkwy N Dr ... Indianapolis IN 46250 317-579-5050 579-5051 48-16
TF: 800-328-0522 ■ *Web:* www.alphachiomega.org

Alpha Chi Rho Fraternity Inc
109 Oxford Way ... Neptune NJ 07753 732-869-1895 988-5357 48-16
TF: 800-222-8733 ■ *Web:* www.alphachirho.org

Alpha Chi Sigma
2141 N Franklin Rd ... Indianapolis IN 46219 317-357-5944 351-9702 48-16
TF: 800-252-4369 ■ *Web:* www.alphachisigma.org

Alpha Cine Labs 9800 40th Ave S ... Seattle WA 98118 206-682-8230 512

Alpha Consulting Engineers Inc
115 Limekiln Rd ... New Cumberland PA 17070 717-770-2500 256
Web: alphacei.com

Alpha Corp 21351 Ridgetop Cir Ste 200 ... Dulles VA 20166 703-450-0800 450-0043 194
Web: www.alphacorporation.com

Alpha Delta Phi International Fraternity
60 S Sixth St Suite 2800 ... Minneapolis MN 55402 508-226-1832 48-16
Web: www.alphadeltaphi.org

Alpha Delta Pi
1386 Ponce de Leon Ave NE ... Atlanta GA 30306 404-378-3164 373-0084 48-16
Web: www.alphadeltapi.org

Alpha Distribution Solutions
350 Rte 61 S ... Schuylkill Haven PA 17972 570-385-0511 155-18
Web: alphadistsol.com

Alpha Distributors Inc
4700 N Ronald St ... Harwood Heights IL 60706 708-867-5200 665
TF: 800-762-4621 ■ *Web:* www.alphadist.com

Alpha Energy Solutions Inc
7200 Distribution Dr ... Louisville KY 40258 502-968-0121 610
TF: 888-212-6324 ■ *Web:* www.alphamechanicalservice.com

Alpha Engineering Associates Inc
716 Giddings Ave Ste 32 ... Annapolis MD 21401 410-295-9500 180
Web: www.alphaengr.com

Alpha Epsilon Delta (AED)
2955 S University Dr PO Box 298810
Winton-Scott 213 ... Fort Worth TX 76129 817-257-4550 257-0201 48-16
Web: aednational.tcu.edu

Alpha Epsilon Phi Sorority (AEPhi)
11 Lake Ave Ext Ste 1-A ... Danbury CT 06811 203-748-0029 748-0039 48-16
TF: 888-668-4293 ■ *Web:* www.aephi.org

Alpha Epsilon Pi Fraternity Inc
8815 Wesleyan Rd ... Indianapolis IN 46268 317-876-1913 876-1057 48-16
TF: 800-684-3608 ■ *Web:* www.aepi.org

Alpha Gallery 460C Harrison Ave ... Boston MA 02118 617-536-4465 536-5695 42
Web: www.alphagallery.com

Alpha Gamma Delta
8710 N Meridian St ... Indianapolis IN 46260 317-663-4200 48-16
Web: www.alphagammadelta.org

Alpha Gamma Rho
10101 NW Ambassador Dr ... Kansas City MO 64153 816-891-9200 891-9401 48-16
TF: 888-241-4546 ■ *Web:* www.alphagammarho.org

Alpha Grainger Manufacturing Inc
20 Discovery Way ... Franklin MA 02038 508-520-4005 520-4185 621
Web: www.agmi.com

Alpha Group, The 3767 Alpha Way ... Bellingham WA 98226 360-647-2360 671-4936* 253
*Fax: Sales ■ *TF:* 800-322-5742 ■ *Web:* www.alpha.com

Alpha I Marketing Corp
65 W Red Oak Ln ... White Plains NY 10604 914-697-5300 196
Web: www.alpha1marketing.com

Alpha Imaging Inc
4455 Glenbrook Rd ... Willoughby OH 44094 440-953-3800 953-1455 475
TF: 800-331-7327 ■ *Web:* www.alpha-imaging.com

Alpha Industries Inc
14200 Pk Meadow Dr Ste 110S ... Chantilly VA 20151 703-378-1420 378-4910 155-5
TF General: 866-631-0719 ■ *Web:* www.alphaindustries.com

Alpha Investment Consulting Group LLC
111 E Kilbourn Ave Ste 1600 ... Milwaukee WI 53202 414-319-4100 194
Web: www.alpha-investment.com

Alpha Kappa Alpha Sorority Inc
5656 S Stony Island Ave ... Chicago IL 60637 773-684-1282 48-16
TF: 800-468-3571 ■ *Web:* www.aka1908.com

Alpha Kappa Psi (AKPsi)
7801 E 88th St ... Indianapolis IN 46256 317-872-1553 872-1567 48-16
Web: www.akpsi.com

Alpha Lehigh Tool & Machine Co
41 Industrial Rd ... Alpha NJ 08865 908-454-6481 454
Web: www.alphalehigh.com

Alpha Lex Systems Integration
11100 Bradner Pl ... Porter Ranch CA 91326 818-407-9200 177
TF: 800-539-9858 ■ *Web:* alphalex.com

Alpha Marketing Inc
343 E Six Forks Rd Ste 360 ... Raleigh NC 27609 919-836-2169 195
Web: www.alphamarketing.com

Alpha Mechanical Heating & Air Conditioning Inc
4885 Greencraig Ln ... San Diego CA 92123 858-278-3500 610
Web: alphamech.com

Alpha Natural Resources Inc
1 Alpha Pl PO Box 16429 ... Bristol VA 24209 276-619-4410 501
OTC: ANR ■ *TF:* 866-322-5742 ■ *Web:* www.alphanr.com

Alpha Net Consulting LLC
3080 Olcott St Ste 235C ... Santa Clara CA 95054 408-330-0896 177
Web: anetcorp.com

Alpha Oil Inc 490 Garyray Dr ... Weston ON M9L1P8 416-745-6131 580
TF: 800-668-0220 ■ *Web:* www.alphaoil.ca

Alpha Omega International Dental Fraternity
50 W Edmonston Dr ... Rockville MD 20852 301-738-6400 738-6403 48-16
TF: 877-368-6326 ■ *Web:* www.ao.org

Alpha Omega Tours & Charters
419 N Jefferson St PO Box 97 ... Medical Lake WA 99022 509-299-5595 299-5545 760
Web: www.alphaomegatoursandcharters.com

Alpha Omicron Pi International
5390 Virginia Way ... Brentwood TN 37027 615-370-0920 371-9736 48-16
TF: 855-230-1183 ■ *Web:* www.alphaomicronpi.org

Alpha Packaging
1555 Page Industrial Blvd ... Saint Louis MO 63132 314-427-4300 427-5445 98
TF: 800-421-4772 ■ *Web:* www.alphap.com

Alpha Phi Alpha Fraternity Inc
2313 St Paul St ... Baltimore MD 21218 410-554-0040 554-0054 48-16
Web: www.apa1906.net

Alpha Phi Delta Fraternity
257E Camden-Wyoming Ave ... Staten Island NY 10308 302-538-6145 48-16
Web: www.apd.org

Alpha Phi International Fraternity
1930 Sherman Ave ... Evanston IL 60201 847-475-0663 475-6820 48-16
Web: www.alphaphi.org

Alpha Phi Omega (APO)
14901 E 42nd St ... Independence MO 64055 816-373-8667 373-5975 48-16
Web: www.apo.org

Alpha Plastics Solutions Inc
S82 W19362 Apollo Dr ... Muskego WI 53150 262-971-2774 596
Web: www.myapsi.com

Alpha Precision Machining Inc
19652 70th Ave S ... Kent WA 98032 253-395-7381 757
Web: www.alphapre.com

Alpha Pro Tech Ltd 60 Centurian Dr ... Markham ON L3R9R2 905-479-0654 228
TF: 800-749-1363 ■ *Web:* www.alphaprotech.com

Alpha Products Inc
5570 W 70th Pl ... Bedford Park IL 60638 708-594-3883 488
Web: www.alphaproductsinc.com

Alpha Q Inc 87 Upton Rd ... Colchester CT 06415 860-537-4681 537-4332 21
TF: 800-229-4243 ■ *Web:* alphaqinc.com

Alpha Rae Personnel Inc
347 W Berry St Ste 700 ... Fort Wayne IN 46802 260-426-8227 260
TF: 800-837-8940 ■ *Web:* www.alpha-rae.com

Alpha Search Advisory Partners LLC
14 Tower Pl 1st Fl ... Roslyn NY 11576 516-626-7896 260
Web: www.alphasearchadvisory.com

Alpha Sigma Alpha (ASA)
9002 Vincennes Cir ... Indianapolis IN 46268 317-871-2920 871-2924 48-16
Web: www.alphasigmaalpha.org

Alpha Sigma Phi National Fraternity
710 Adams St ... Carmel IN 46032 317-843-1911 843-2966 48-16
Web: www.alphasigmaphi.org

Alpha Sintered Metals Inc
95 Mason Run Rd ... Ridgway PA 15853 814-773-3191 776-1009 482
TF: 800-783-2420 ■ *Web:* www.alphasintered.com

Alpha Software Inc
70 BlanchaRd Rd Ste 206 ... Burlington MA 01803 781-229-4500 272-4876 178-1
Web: www.alphasoftware.com

Alpha Source Inc 6619 W Calumet Rd ... Milwaukee WI 53223 414-760-2222 475
TF: 800-654-9845 ■ *Web:* www.alphasource.com

Alpha Strategies Investment Consulting Inc
10 David St ... Ladera Ranch CA 92694 949-429-7129 195

Alpha Tau Omega Fraternity (ATO)
1 N Pennsylvania St 12th Fl ... Indianapolis IN 46204 317-684-1865 684-1862 48-16
TF: 800-798-9286 ■ *Web:* www.ato.org

Alpha Tech Inc 388 Cane Creek Rd ... Fletcher NC 28732 828-684-9709 491
Web: www.alpha.com

Alpha Tech Pet Inc
119 Russell St Ste 21 ... Littleton MA 01460 978-486-3690 237
Web: www.alphatechpet.com

Alpha Technologies Services LLC
3030 Gilchrist Rd ... Akron OH 44305 330-745-1641 848-7326 201
TF: 800-356-9886 ■ *Web:* www.alpha-technologies.com

Alpha Ten Technologies Inc
2720 Loker Ave W Ste K ... Carlsbad CA 92010 760-438-9144 187
Web: www.alphaten.com

Alpha Testing Inc
2209 Wisconsin St Ste 100 ... Dallas TX 75229 972-620-8911 620-1302 256
Web: alphatesting.com

Alpha Windward LLC
200 Lowder Brook Dr Ste 2400 ... Westwood MA 02090 781-326-8880 401
Web: www.alphawindward.com

Alpha Wire Co 711 Lidgerwood Ave ... Elizabeth NJ 07207 908-925-8000 925-5411 814
TF: 800-522-5742 ■ *Web:* www.alphawire.com

Alpha Xi Delta Women's Fraternity
8702 Founders Rd ... Indianapolis IN 46268 317-872-3500 872-2947 48-16
TF: 800-526-1870 ■ *Web:* www.alphaxidelta.org

Alphacorp Inc 21351 Ridgetop Cir ... Dulles VA 20166 801-977-8705 692
Web: www.alphacorpsecurity.com

AlphaGraphics Inc
215 S State St Ste 320 ... Salt Lake City UT 84111 801-595-7270 595-7271 627
TF: 800-955-6246 ■ *Web:* www.alphagraphics.com

AlphaKOR Group Inc 7800 Twin Oaks Dr ... Windsor ON N8N5B6 519-944-6009 180
TF: 877-944-6009 ■ *Web:* www.alphakor.com

Alphamark Advisors LLC
250 Grandview Dr Ste 175 ... Fort Mitchell KY 41017 859-957-1803 401
Web: www.alphamarkadvisors.com

Alphamicron Inc 1950 SR- 59 Ste 100 ... Kent OH 44240 330-676-0648 676-0649 194
Web: www.alphamicron.com

				Phone	Fax	Class
Alphanumeric Systems Inc 3801 Wake Forest Rd *TF:* 800-638-6556 ■ *Web:* www.alphanumeric.com	Raleigh	NC	27609	919-781-7575	872-1440	113
Alphapoint Technology Inc 6371 Business Blvd Ste 200 *Web:* www.alphapointtechnology.com	Sarasota	FL	34240	941-907-8822		177
Alphaport Inc 18013 Cleveland Pkwy Ste 170 *Web:* www.alpha-port.com	Cleveland	OH	44135	216-619-2400		194
Alphaserve Technologies LLC 104 W 27th St *Web:* www.alphaserveit.com	New York	NY	10001	212-763-5555		180
AlphaSoft Services Corp 2035 Lincoln Hwy Ste 1190	Edison	NJ	08817	925-952-6300	932-3743	180
AlphaStaff Inc 800 Corporate Dr Ste 600 *TF:* 888-335-9545 ■ *Web:* www.alphastaff.com	Fort Lauderdale	FL	33334	954-267-1760		631
Alphavax Inc 2 Triangle Dr *Web:* www.alphavax.com	Research Triangle Park	NC	27709	919-595-0400		363
Alphi Manufacturing Inc 576 Beck St *Web:* www.alphimfg.com	Jonesville	MI	49250	517-849-9945		295
Alphinat Inc Ste 680 2000 Peel *Web:* www.alphinat.com	Montreal	QC	H3A2W5	514-398-9799		177
Alphion Corp 196 Princeton Hightstown Rd Bldg 1A *Web:* www.alphion.com	Princeton Junction	NJ	08550	609-936-9001		256
Alphora Research Inc 2395 Speakman Dr Ste 2001 *Web:* www.alphoraresearch.com	Mississauga	ON	L5K1B3	905-403-0477		231
Alpin Haus Ski Shop 4850 State Hwy 30 *Web:* www.alpinhaus.com	Amsterdam	NY	12010	518-843-4400		90
Alpina Manufacturing LLC 3418 N Knox Ave *TF:* 800-915-2828 ■ *Web:* www.fastchangeframes.com	Chicago	IL	60641	773-202-8887		45
Alpina Sports Corp 93 Etna Rd *Web:* www.alpinasports.com	Lebanon	NH	03766	603-448-3101		711
Alpine Accessories Inc - Ski Snowboard Paddleboard 9219 S State Rt 31 *Web:* www.alpineaccessories.com	Lake In The Hills	IL	60156	847-854-4754		711
Alpine Adventure Trails Tours Inc 7495 Lower Thomaston Rd **Fax Area Code:* 478 ■ *TF:* 888-478-4004 ■ *Web:* www.swisshiking.com	Macon	GA	31220	888-478-4004	477-4117*	760
Alpine Air Express 1177 Alpine Air Way *Web:* www.alpine-air.com	Provo	UT	84601	801-373-1508		12
Alpine Archery 3101 N S Hwy *Web:* www.alpinearchery.com	Lewiston	ID	83501	208 746 4717		710
Alpine Bank of Colorado 2200 Grand Ave *TF:* 888-425-7463 ■ *Web:* www.alpinebank.com	Glenwood Springs	CO	81601	970-945-2424		360-2
Alpine Building Maintenance & Supply 2920 SE Loop 820 *Web:* alpinemaintenance.com	Fort Worth	TX	76140	817-795-6470	795-9833	256
Alpine Business Systems Inc 373 E Main St *Web:* alpinebiz.com	Somerville	NJ	08876	908-707-9696		180
Alpine Capital Bank 680 Fifth Ave *Web:* www.alpinecapitalbank.com	New York	NY	10019	212-328-2555		70
Alpine Communications LC 923 Humphrey St *Web:* www.alpinecom.net	Elkader	IA	52043	563-245-4000		116
Alpine Consulting Inc 1100 E Wdfield Rd *Web:* www.alpineinc.com	Schaumburg	IL	60173	847-605-0788		180
Alpine County 99 Waters St PO Box 158 *TF:* 800-894-7761 ■ *Web:* www.alpinecountyca.gov	Markleeville	CA	96120	530-694-2281	694-2491	338
Alpine Electronics of America 19145 Gramercy Pl *TF:* 800-257-4631 ■ *Web:* www.alpine-usa.com	Torrance	CA	90501	310-326-8000		52
Alpine Engineering & Design Inc 111 W Canyon Crest Rd *Web:* www.alpineeng.com	Alpine	UT	84004	801-763-8484		261
Alpine Fresh Inc 9300 NW 58th St Ste 201 *TF:* 800-292-8777 ■ *Web:* www.alpinefresh.com	Miami	FL	33178	305-594-9117	594-8506	297-7
Alpine Group Inc 1 Meadowlands Plaza *Web:* www.alpine-group.net	East Rutherford	NJ	07073	201-549-4400		360-3
Alpine Helen/White County Convention & Visitors Bureau 726 Bruckenstrasse PO Box 730 *TF:* 800-858-8027 ■ *Web:* www.helenga.org	Helen	GA	30545	706-878-2181		206
Alpine Helicopters Ltd 1295 Industrial Rd *TF:* 800-667-3852 ■ *Web:* www.alpinehelicopter.com	Kelowna	BC	V1Z1G4	250-769-4111		13
Alpine Innovations 275 N 950 E *TF:* 866-489-6788 ■ *Web:* www.alpineproducts.com	Lehi	UT	84043	801-766-4994		194
Alpine Investors 2 Embarcadero Ctr Ste 2320 *Web:* www.alpine-investors.com	San Francisco	CA	94111	415-392-9100		690
Alpine Lodge 434 Indian Creek Cir *TF:* 888-563-4388 ■ *Web:* www.alpinelodgeresort.com	Branson	MO	65616	417-338-2514		707
Alpine Lumber Co 10170 Church Ranch Way Ste 350 *TF:* 800-499-1634 ■ *Web:* www.alpinelumber.com	Westminster	CO	80021	303-451-8001	451-5232	191-3
Alpine Meats 9850 Lowr Sacramento Rd *TF:* 800-399-6328 ■ *Web:* www.alpinemeats.com	Stockton	CA	95210	209-477-2691	477-1994	473
Alpine Packaging Inc 4000 Crooked Run Rd *TF:* 844-682-2361 ■ *Web:* www.alpinepackaging.com	North Versailles	PA	15137	412-664-4000		627
Alpine Plumbing Inc 14580 W Greenfield Ave *Web:* www.alpineplumbinginc.com	Brookfield	WI	53005	262-797-4120		610
Alpine Power Systems Inc 24355 Capitol *TF:* 877-769-3762 ■ *Web:* www.alpinepowersystems.com	Redford	MI	48239	313-531-6600	531-2950	759

				Phone	Fax	Class
Alpine Resort 7715 Alpine Rd PO Box 200 *TF:* 800-707-6660 ■ *Web:* www.alpineresort.com	Egg Harbor	WI	54209	920-868-3000		669
Alpine Securities Corp 39 Exchange Pl *Web:* www.alpine-securities.com	Salt Lake City	UT	84111	801-355-5588		690
Alpine Solutions Inc 3222 Corte Malpaso Ste 204 *TF:* 855-388-1883 ■ *Web:* www.alpinesolutionsinc.com	Camarillo	CA	93012	805-388-1699		382
Alpine Testing Inc 51 W Ctr St *TF:* 844-625-7463 ■ *Web:* www.alpinetesting.com	Orem	UT	84057	844-625-7463		244
Alpine Valley Ski Area 6775 East Highland Rd *Web:* www.skialpinevalley.com	White Lake	MI	48383	248-887-2180		360-3
Alpine Valley Water Company Inc 10341 Julian Dr *Web:* www.alpinevalleyps.com	Cincinnati	OH	45215	513-672-3400		366
Alpine Woodworking Inc 9118 Davenport St NE *Web:* www.alpinewoodworking.com	Blaine	MN	55449	763-784-0333		115
Alpla Inc 289 Hwy 155 S *TF:* 800-736-1240 ■ *Web:* www.alpla.com	Mcdonough	GA	30253	770-914-1407		601
Alps Construction Inc 15745 Annico Dr *Web:* www.alpsgc.com	Homer glen	IL	60491	708-301-3366		187
Alps Sportswear Manufacturing Co 15 Union St	Lawrence	MA	01840	978-683-2438		155-3
Alqimi Technology Solutions Inc 9210 Corporate Blvd Ste 150 *Web:* www.alqimi.com	Rockville	MD	20850	301-337-0100		317
Alr Systems & Software Inc 11707 M Cir *Web:* www.alrsys.com	Omaha	NE	68137	402-891-1500		177
ALR Technologies Inc 7400 Beaufont Springs Dr Ste 300 *Web:* www.alrt.com	Richmond	VA	23225	804-554-3500		250
ALRA (American Land Rights Assn) 30218 NE 82nd Ave PO Box 400 *Web:* www.landrights.org	Battle Ground	WA	98604	360-687-3087	687-2973	48-2
Alro Steel Corp 3100 E High St *TF:* 800-877-2576 ■ *Web:* www.alro.com	Jackson	MI	49204	517-787-5500	787-6390	492
Alrod Enterprises Inc 119 N Sycamore St	Petersburg	VA	23803	804-732-3972		693
ALS (Albany Law School of Union University) 80 New Scotland Ave *TF:* 800-448-3500 ■ *Web:* www.albanylaw.edu	Albany	NY	12208	518-445-2311		167-1
ALS (American Littoral Society) 18 Hartshorne Dr Ste 1 *TF:* 800-424-8802 ■ *Web:* www.littoralsociety.org	Highlands	NJ	07732	732-291-0055	291-3551	48-13
ALSAC (American Lebanese Syrian Associated Charities) 262 Danny Thomas Pl *TF:* 800-822-6344 ■ *Web:* www.stjude.org	Memphis	TN	38105	901-578-2000	578 2805	48-5
Alsay Inc 6615 Gant St *TF:* 800-833-5969 ■ *Web:* alsaywater.com	Houston	TX	77066	281-444-6960	444-7081	189-15
ALSC (Association for Library Service to Children) 50 E Huron St *TF:* 800-545-2433 ■ *Web:* www.ala.org/alsc	Chicago	IL	60611	312-280-2163	944-7671	49-11
Alsco Inc 505 East South Temple *TF:* 800-408-0208 ■ *Web:* www.alsco.com	Salt Lake City	UT	84102	801 328 8831		787
Alsco Industries 174 Charlton Rd *Web:* www.alscoindustries.com	Sturbridge	MA	01566	508-347-1199		596
Alsea Bay Historic Interpretive Ctr 725 Summer St NE Ste C *TF:* 800-551-6949 ■ *Web:* www.oregonstateparks.org	Salem	OR	97301	800-551-6949		565
Alstate Steel Inc 203 Murry Rd SE *Web:* www.alstatesteel.com	Albuquerque	NM	87105	505-877-5454		492
Alster Communications 3062 North Cir *Web:* alster.com	Anchorage	AK	99507	907-344-9674		194
ALSTOM 1025 John St *Web:* www.alstomsignalingsolutions.com	West Henrietta	NY	14586	585-783-2000		770
ALSTOM Power Inc 200 Great Pond Dr *Web:* www.alstom.com	Windsor	CT	06095	860-688-1911	285-9611	256
Alston & Bird LLP 1201 W Peachtree St *Web:* www.alston.com	Atlanta	GA	30309	404-881-7000	881-7777	428
Alt & Witzig Engineering Inc 4105 W 99th St *Web:* www.ascet.org	Carmel	IN	46032	317-875-7000		256
ALT 92.9 Boston 55 Morrissey Blvd *Web:* www.myradio929.com	Boston	MA	02125	617-822-9600		645-23
ALT 98.7 3400 W Olive Ave Ste 550 *Web:* alt987fm.iheart.com	Burbank	CA	91505	818-559-2252		645
ALT AZ 93.3 1167 W Javelina Ave *TF:* 800-776-1070 ■ *Web:* altaz933.com	Mesa	AZ	85210	480-897-9300		645
Alt's Tool & Machine Inc 10926 Woodside Ave N *TF:* 800-599-1497 ■ *Web:* www.altstool.com	Santee	CA	92071	619-562-6653		757
ALTA (American Land Title Assn) 1828 L St NW Ste 705 *TF:* 800-787-2582 ■ *Web:* www.alta.org	Washington	DC	20036	202-296-3671	223-5843	49-10
Alta Associates Inc 8 Bartles Corner Rd *Web:* www.altaassociates.com	Flemington	NJ	08822	908-806-8442		624
Alta Bates Summit Medical Ctr (ABSMC) 2450 Ashby Ave *TF:* 800-994-6610 ■ *Web:* www.altabatessummit.org	Berkeley	CA	94705	510-204-4444		374-3
Alta Capital Management LLC 6440 South Wasatch Blvd Ste 260 *Web:* altacapital.com	Salt Lake City	UT	84121	801-274-6010		528
Alta Communications 1000 Winter St S Entrance Ste 3500	Waltham	MA	02451	617-262-7770		792
Alta Computer Data Services LLC 8823 S Redwood Rd Ste D2	West Jordan	UT	84088	801-233-0531		180
Alta Consulting Services Inc 11000 NE 33rd Pl Ste 300 *Web:* www.altaconsulting.com	Bellevue	WA	98004	425-576-1202	576-0522	631
Alta Dena Dairy 17851 E Railrd *TF Orders:* 800-535-1369 ■ *Web:* www.altadenadairy.com	City of Industry	CA	91748	800-535-1369		296-27

Name / Address	City	State	Zip	Phone	Fax	Class
Alta Devices Inc 545 Oakmead Pkwy *Web:* www.altadevices.com	Sunnyvale	CA	94085	408-988-8600		696
Alta Equipment Co 28775 Beck Rd. *TF:* 800-261-9642 ■ *Web:* www.altaequipment.com	Wixom	MI	48393	248-449-6700		358
Alta Lodge PO Box 8040 *TF Cust Svc:* 800-707-2582 ■ *Web:* www.altalodge.com	Alta	UT	84092	801-742-3500	742-3504	669
Alta Loma School District 9390 Baseline Rd *Web:* www.alsd.k12.ca.us	Alta Loma	CA	91701	909-484-5151		685
Alta Manufacturing Inc 47650 Westinghouse Dr *TF:* 800-553-3568 ■ *Web:* www.altamfg.com	Fremont	CA	94539	510-668-1870		477
Alta Mira Recovery Programs LLC 125 Bulkley Ave *Web:* www.altamirarecovery.com	Sausalito	CA	94965	415-332-1350		378
Alta Partners 1 Embarcadero Ctr 37th Fl *Web:* www.altapartners.com	San Francisco	CA	94111	415-362-4022	362-6178	792
Alta Resources 120 N Commercial St. *Fax Area Code: 920 ■ *TF:* 877-464-2582 ■ *Web:* www.altaresources.com	Neenah	WI	54956	877-464-2582	727-9954*	737
Alta Ski Lifts Co Alta Ski Area Hwy 210 Little Cottonwood Canyon *TF:* 800-453-8488 ■ *Web:* www.alta.com	Alta	UT	84092	801-359-1078		452
ALTA Systems Inc 6825 NW 18th Dr *TF:* 800-754-5641 ■ *Web:* altainc.com	Gainesville	FL	32653	352-372-2534		627
Alta Via Consulting LLC 525 Tanasi Cir. *TF:* 877-258-2842 ■ *Web:* www.altavia.com	Loudon	TN	37774	877-258-2842		177
Alta View Hospital 9660 S 1300 E *Web:* www.intermountainhealthcare.org	Sandy	UT	84094	801-501-2600		374-3
Alta Vista Gardens 1270 Vale Ter Dr *Web:* www.altavistagardens.org	Vista	CA	92084	760-945-3954		97
AltaCorp Capital Inc 410 585-8 Ave SW *Web:* www.altacorpcapital.com	Calgary	AB	T2P1G1	403-539-8600	539-8575	70
Altadena Chamber of Commerce 730 E Altadena Dr. *TF:* 800-665-2900 ■ *Web:* altadenachamber.org	Altadena	CA	91001	626-794-3988		139
Alta-Fab Structures Ltd 504-13 Ave *TF:* 800-252-7990 ■ *Web:* www.altafab.com	Nisku	AB	T9E7P6	780-955-7733		779
ALTAFF (American Library Assn) 50 E Huron St *TF:* 800-545-2433 ■ *Web:* ala.org	Chicago	IL	60611	800-545-2433		49-11
Altair Advisers LLC 303 W Madison St Ste 600 *Web:* www.altairadvisers.com	Chicago	IL	60606	312-429-3000		401
Altair Customer Intelligence 341 Cool Springs Blvd Ste 450 *TF:* 800-241-6631 ■ *Web:* www.altairci.com	Franklin	TN	37067	615-468-6800		194
Altair Engineering Inc 1820 E Big Beaver Rd *TF:* 888-222-7822 ■ *Web:* www.altair.com	Troy	MI	48083	248-614-2400	614-2411	194
Altair Nanotechnologies Inc 204 Edison Way *NASDAQ: ALTI* ■ *Web:* www.altairnano.com	Reno	NV	89502	775-856-2500		144
Altair Technology Inc 1116 W Blanco Rd *Web:* www.altairtech.com	San Antonio	TX	78232	210-764-9900		177
Altamaha Electric Membership Corp 611 W Liberty Ave PO Box 346 *TF:* 800-822-4563 ■ *Web:* www.altamahaemc.com	Lyons	GA	30436	912-526-8181		245
Altamed Health Services Corp 500 Citadel Dr Ste 490 *TF:* 877-462-2582 ■ *Web:* www.altamed.org	Los Angeles	CA	90040	323-725-8751		363
Altametrics 3191 Red Hill Ave Ste 100 *TF:* 800-676-1281 ■ *Web:* www.altametrics.com	Costa Mesa	CA	92626	800-676-1281		174
Altamira Instruments Inc 149 Delta Dr Ste 200 *Web:* www.altamirainstruments.com	Pittsburgh	PA	15238	412-963-6385		419
Altamira Technologies Corp 8201 Greensboro Dr Ste 800 *Web:* www.invertix.com	Mclean	VA	22102	703-813-2100		177
Altamont Capital Partners 400 Hamilton Ave Ste 230 *Web:* www.altamontcapital.com	Palo Alto	CA	94301	650-264-7750		196
Altamont Commuter Express (ACE) 949 E Ch St *TF:* 800-411-7245 ■ *Web:* www.acerail.com	Stockton	CA	95202	800-411-7245		468
Altamont Environmental Inc 231 Haywood St *Web:* www.altamontenvironmental.com	Asheville	NC	28801	828-281-3350		194
Altamont Pharmacy Inc 12 N Third St *Web:* altamontpharmacy.com	Altamont	IL	62411	618-483-5614		238
Altamonte Mall 451 E Altamonte Dr. *Web:* www.altamontemall.com	Altamonte Springs	FL	32701	321-280-1901		460
Altapacific Technology Group Inc 1525 E Shaw Ave Ste 201 *TF:* 800-659-3655 ■ *Web:* www.altapacific.com	Fresno	CA	93710	559-439-5700		225
AltaRock Energy Inc 2320 Marinship Way Ste 300 *Web:* www.altarockenergy.com	Sausalito	CA	94965	415-331-0130		196
Altarum Institute 3520 Green Ct Ste 300 *Web:* www.altarum.org	Ann Arbor	MI	48105	734-302-4600		544
AltaTerra Ltd 530 Lytton Ave 2nd Fl	Palo Alto	CA	94301	650-362-0440		194
AltaVista Research LLC 243 Fifth Ave Ste 235 *Web:* www.altavista-research.com	New York	NY	10016	646-435-0569		401
Altavista Wealth Management Inc 4 Vanderbilt Park Dr Ste 310 *Web:* www.altavistawealth.com	Asheville	NC	28803	828-684-2600		528
Altec Industries Inc 210 Inverness Ctr Dr. *Web:* altec.com	Birmingham	AL	35242	205-991-7733	408-8601	190
Altech Environment USA Corp 2623 Kaneville Ct *Web:* www.altechusa.com	Geneva	IL	60134	630-262-4400		201
Altech LLC 242 America Pl. *TF:* 800-264-8256 ■ *Web:* www.altecextrusions.com	Jeffersonville	IN	47130	812-282-8256	280-6070	485
Altech Services Inc 695 US Rt 46W Ste 301B *TF:* 888-725-8324 ■ *Web:* www.altechts.com	Fairfield	NJ	07004	888-725-8324	925-8725	177
Alten Construction Inc 720 12th St. *TF:* 800-360-6397 ■ *Web:* www.altenconstruction.com	Richmond	CA	94801	510-234-4200		186
AltEnergy LLC 137 Rowayton Ave *Web:* www.altenergyllc.com	Rowayton	CT	06853	203-299-1400		194
Altep Inc 7450 Remcon Cir *TF:* 800-263-0940 ■ *Web:* www.altep.com	El Paso	TX	79912	915-533-8722		177
Alter Barge Line Inc 2117 State St. *Web:* www.alterlogistics.com	Bettendorf	IA	52722	563-344-5100		313
Alter Group 5500 W Howard St *TF:* 800-531-8182 ■ *Web:* www.altergroup.com	Skokie	IL	60077	847-676-4300	676-4302	653
Alter Trading Corp 700 Office Pkwy *TF:* 888-337-2727 ■ *Web:* www.altertrading.com	Saint Louis	MO	63141	314-872-2400	872-2420	686
Altera Corp 101 Innovation Dr. *NASDAQ: ALTR* ■ *Fax: Cust Svc ■ *TF Cust Svc:* 800-767-3753 ■ *Web:* www.altera.com	San Jose	CA	95134	408-544-7000	544-6403*	696
Altera Payroll Inc 2400 Northside Crossing *TF:* 877-474-6060 ■ *Web:* www.alterapayroll.com	Macon	GA	31210	478-477-6060		2
Alte-Rego Corp 36 Tidemore Ave *Web:* www.alte-rego.com	Toronto	ON	M9W5H4	416-740-3397		600
Alterian Inc 35 E Wacker Dr Ste 200 *Web:* www.sdl.com	Chicago	IL	60601	312-704-1700		178-1
Alteris Group 26600 Telegraph Rd Ste 101 *Web:* www.alterisgroup.com	Southfield	MI	48033	248-477-5560		466
Alterman & Boop Llp 99 Hudson St 8th Fl *Web:* www.altermanandboop.com	New York	NY	10013	212-226-2800	431-3614	445
Alterna-Care 319 E Madison St # 3n *Web:* alterna-care.com	Springfield	IL	62701	217-525-3733		363
Alternative Apparel Inc 700 Lake Ave. *Web:* www.iceboxcoolstuff.com	Atlanta	GA	30307	404-522-2665	460-1260	156
Alternative Strategy Advisers LLC 601 Carlson Pkwy Ste 1125 *Web:* www.asallc.com	Minnetonka	MN	55305	952-847-2450		401
Alternative System Concepts Inc 22 Haverhill Rd PO Box 128 *TF:* 800-470-2686 ■ *Web:* www.ascinc.com	Windham	NH	03087	603-437-2234	437-2722	178-10
Alternatives for Industry Inc 2251 Whitfield Park Ave *TF:* 800-888-0866 ■ *Web:* www.afi-tools.com	Sarasota	FL	34243	941-739-6566		237
Alterra Group PO Box 201355 *Web:* www.alterra-group.com	Cleveland	OH	44120	216-539-9710		7
Alterra Real Estate Advisors LLC 540 Officenter Pl Ste 260 *Web:* www.alterrare.com	Gahanna	OH	43230	614-365-9000		652
Altest Corp 898 Faulstich Ct *Web:* www.altestcorp.com	San Jose	CA	95112	408-436-9900		757
Altfest Personal Wealth Management 445 Park Ave 6th Fl *Web:* www.altfest.com	New York	NY	10022	212-406-0850		194
Altheus Therapeutics Inc 755 Research Pkwy Ste 435	Oklahoma City	OK	73104	405-319-8180		231
Althoff Industries Inc 8001 S Rt 31 *TF:* 800-225-2443 ■ *Web:* www.althoffind.com	Crystal Lake	IL	60014	815-455-7000		189-10
Altia Inc 7222 Commerce Ctr Dr Ste 240 *TF:* 800-653-9957 ■ *Web:* www.altia.com	Colorado Springs	CO	80919	719-598-4299		177
Alticor Inc 7575 Fulton St E *Web:* www.alticor.com	Ada	MI	49355	616-787-1000		185
AltiGen Communications Inc 410 E Plumeria Dr *OTC: ATGN* ■ *TF:* 888-258-4436 ■ *Web:* www.altigen.com	San Jose	CA	95134	408-597-9000	597-9020	735
Altima Technologies Inc 2300 Cabot Dr Ste 535 *Web:* www.altimatech.com	Lisle	IL	60532	630-281-6464		764
Altimate Medical Inc 262 W First St *TF:* 800-342-8968 ■ *Web:* www.easystand.com	Morton	MN	56270	507-697-6393		476
Altira Group LLC 1675 Broadway Ste 2400 *Web:* www.altiragroup.com	Denver	CO	80202	303-592-5500	592-5519	792
Altira Inc 3225 NW 112th St *Web:* www.altira.com	Miami	FL	33167	305-687-8074		333
Altitude Digital Inc 1037 Broadway Unit B *TF:* 800-719-6242 ■ *Web:* www.altitudedigital.com	Denver	CO	80203	303-292-1414		7
Altitude Marketing 417 State Rd 2nd Fl *Web:* altitudemarketing.com	Emmaus	PA	18049	610-421-8601		195
Altium Inc 2175 Salk Ave Ste 100 *TF Sales:* 800-544-4186 ■ *Web:* www.altium.com	Carlsbad	CA	92008	760-231-0760	231-0761	178-5
Altius Broadband Inc 3314 Papermill Rd Ste 100 *TF:* 800-864-6546 ■ *Web:* www.altiuscomm.com	Phoenix	MD	21131	410-667-1638		224
Altland House 1 Ctr Sq Ste 100 *Web:* www.altlandhouse.com	Abbottstown	PA	17301	717-259-9535		671
Altman Lighting Inc 57 Alexander St *TF:* 800-425-8626 ■ *Web:* www.altmanlighting.com	Yonkers	NY	10701	914-476-7987		439
Altman Specialty Plants Inc 3742 Blue BiRd Canyon Rd *TF:* 800-773-7667 ■ *Web:* www.altmanplants.com	Vista	CA	92084	760-744-8191	744-8835	369
Altman Vilandrie & Co 225 Franklin St 24th Fl *Web:* www.altvil.com	Boston	MA	02110	617-753-7200		463
Altman Weil Inc PO Box 625 *TF:* 866-886-3600 ■ *Web:* www.altmanweil.com	Newtown Square	PA	19073	610-359-9900	359-0467	194
Altmas Products 1201 Francisco St *TF:* 800-537-7239 ■ *Web:* www.altmansproducts.com	Torrance	CA	90502	310-559-4093		612
Altmeyer Home Stores Inc 6515 Rt 22 *TF:* 800-394-6628 ■ *Web:* www.bedbathhome.com	Delmont	PA	15626	724-468-3434	468-3233	362
Alt-N Technologies Ltd 4550 State Hwy 360 Ste 100 *Web:* www.altn.com	Grapevine	TX	76051	817-601-3222		180
Alto Cinco 526 Westcott St. *Web:* www.altocinco.net	Syracuse	NY	13210	315-422-6399		671

Name / Address	City	State	Zip	Phone	Fax	Class
Alto Consulting & Training 7210 Metro Blvd *Web:* www.altoconsulting.com	Minneapolis	MN	55439	952-831-6604		196
Alto Development Corp 5206 Asbury Rd PO Box 758 *TF:* 800-323-4035 ■ *Web:* aemedical.com	Farmingdale	NJ	07727	732-938-2266		476
Alto Products Corp 1 Alto Way *Web:* www.altousa.com	Atmore	AL	36502	251-368-7777		61
Altocloud Inc 800 W El Camino Real *Web:* www.altocloud.com	Mountain View	CA	94040	650-492-5218		387
Alton Baker Park 1820 Roosevelt Blvd *Web:* www.eugene-or.gov/altonbakerpark	Eugene	OR	97402	541-682-4800		564
Alton Memorial Hospital 1 Memorial Dr *TF:* 800-994-6610 ■ *Web:* www.altonmemorialhospital.org	Alton	IL	62002	618-463-7311		374-3
Alton Mental Health Ctr 4500 College Ave	Alton	IL	62002	618-474-3200	474-3807	374-5
Alton National Cemetery 600 Pearl St *TF:* 800-535-1117 ■ *Web:* www.cem.va.gov	Alton	IL	62003	314-845-8320		136
Alton Regional Convention & Visitors Bureau (ARCVB) 200 Piasa St *TF:* 800-258-6645 ■ *Web:* www.visitalton.com	Alton	IL	62002	618-465-6676	465-6151	206
Alton Steel Inc 5 Cut St *Web:* www.altonsteel.com	Alton	IL	62002	618-463-4490		492
Altona Correctional Facility 555 Devil Den Rd *Web:* www.doccs.ny.gov/faclist.html	Altona	NY	12910	518-236-7841		213
Altoona Area Public Library 1600 Fifth Ave *Web:* www.altoonalibrary.org	Altoona	PA	16602	814-946-0417	946-3230	434-3
Altoona Ctr 1020 Green Ave *Web:* www.myaltoonacenterfornursingcare.com	Altoona	PA	16601	814-946-2700	946-1420	230
Altoona Mirror 301 Cayuga Ave *TF:* 800-222-1962 ■ *Web:* www.altoonamirror.com	Altoona	PA	16602	814-946-7411	946-7540	532-2
Altoona Regional Health System Altoona Hospital 620 Howard Ave *TF:* 877-855-8152 ■ *Web:* www.altoonaregional.org	Altoona	PA	16601	814-889-2011		374-3
Altoona VA Medical Ctr 2907 Pleasant Vly Blvd **Fax Area Code:* 814 ■ *TF:* 877-626-2500 ■ *Web:* www.altoona.va.gov	Altoona	PA	16602	877-626-2500	940-7898*	374-8
Altoona-Blair County Chamber of Commerce 3900 Industrial Pk Dr Ste 12 *Web:* www.blairchamber.com	Altoona	PA	16602	814-943-8151	943-5239	139
Altoros Systems 830 Stewart Dr Ste 119 *TF:* 855-258-6767 ■ *Web:* www.altoros.com	Sunnyvale	CA	94085	650-395-7002		194
Altos Ventures 2882 Sand Hill Rd Ste 100 *Web:* altos.vc	Menlo Park	CA	94025	650-234-9771		792
Alto-Shaam Inc W 164 N 9221 Water St PO Box 450 *TF:* 800-329-8744 ■ *Web:* www.alto-shaam.com	Menomonee Falls	WI	53052	262-251-3800	251-7067	298
Altotech Ventures LLC 205 De Anza Blvd Ste 14 *Web:* www.altotechventures.com	San Mateo	CA	94402	650-574-1870		792
Altour International Inc 80 Pine St # 17 *Web:* www.altour.com	New York	NY	10005	212-509-2375		772
ALTRAN 2525 Rt 130 S *Web:* www.altran-na.com	Cranbury	NJ	08512	609-409-9790		743
ALTRES Inc 967 Kapiolani Blvd *Web:* www.altres.com	Honolulu	HI	96814	808-591-4940	591-4914	721
Altria Group Inc 6601 W Broad St *NYSE:* MO ■ *TF:* 800-732-0330 ■ *Web:* www.altria.com	Richmond	VA	23230	804-274-2200		185
Altrius Capital Management Inc 1323 Commerce Dr *Web:* www.altrius-capital.com	New Bern	NC	28562	252-638-7598		796
Altron Inc 6700 Bunker Lake Blvd NW *Web:* www.altroninc.com	Anoka	MN	55303	763-427-7735		625
Altronic Inc 712 Trumbull Ave *Web:* www.altronicinc.com	Girard	OH	44420	330-545-9768	545-9005	247
Altru Apparel 718 Gladys Ave Ste 2 *Web:* altruapparel.com	Los Angeles	CA	90021	213-622-0588		157-6
Altru Hospital 1200 S Columbia Rd *TF:* 800-732-4277 ■ *Web:* www.altru.org	Grand Forks	ND	58201	701-780-5000		374-3
Altruent Systems 1017 Passport Wayy *Web:* www.altruent.com	Cary	NC	27513	919-828-4419		174
Altschul & Altschul Inc 18 E 12th St Frnt 1 *Web:* www.altschul.biz	New York	NY	10003	212-924-1505		428
Altura Communication Solutions LLC 1335 S Acacia Ave *Web:* www.alturacs.com	Fullerton	CA	92831	714-948-8400		246
Altura Homecare & Rehabilitation 4308 Carlisle Blvd NE Ste 202 *Web:* www.alturahomecare.com	Albuquerque	NM	87107	505-884-0383		363
Alturas Analytics Inc 1324 Alturas Dr *TF:* 877-344-1279 ■ *Web:* www.alturasanalytics.com	Moscow	ID	83843	208-883-3400		743
Alturdyne Inc 660 Steele St *Web:* www.alturdyne.com	El Cajon	CA	92020	619-440-5531	442-0481	262
AlturnaMATS Inc 701 E Spring St Mailbox #9 *TF:* 800-438-9336 ■ *Web:* www.alturnamats.com	Titusville	PA	16354	814-827-8884		296
Altus Air Force Base 305 E Ave *Web:* www.altus.af.mil	Altus Afb	OK	73523	580-482-8100	481-5966	497-1
Altus Alliance LLC 719 Second Ave The Millennium Tower 14th Fl *Web:* www.altusalliance.com	Seattle	WA	98104	206-438-1890		194
Altus Consulting Corp 38699 Old Wheatland Rd *TF:* 800-300-4505 ■ *Web:* www.altuscc.com	Waterford	VA	20197	703-929-4000		463
Alu-Bra Foundry Inc 630 E Green St *Web:* alubra.com	Bensenville	IL	60106	630-766-3112		492
Aluchem Inc 1 Landy Ln *TF:* 800-336-8519 ■ *Web:* www.aluchem.com	Cincinnati	OH	45215	513-733-8519		487
Alum Creek State Park 3615 S Old State Rd *Web:* alum-creek-state-park.org	Delaware	OH	43015	740-548-4631		565
Aluma Tower Company Inc 1639 Old Dixie Hwy *Web:* www.alumatower.com	Vero Beach	FL	32960	772-567-3423		647
Alumacraft Boat Co 315 St Julien St *Web:* www.alumacraft.com	Saint Peter	MN	56082	507-931-1050		90
Aluma-Form Inc 3625 Old Getwell Rd *Web:* www.alumaform.com	Memphis	TN	38118	901-362-0100	794-9515	816
Alum-A-Lift Inc 7909 US Hwy 78 *Web:* www.alum-a-lift.com	Winston	GA	30187	770-489-0328		256
Alum-alloy Company Inc 603 S Hope Ave *Web:* www.webstercorp.com	Ontario	CA	91761	909-986-0410		492
Alumawall Inc 1701 S Seventh St Ste 9 *TF:* 800-826-3825 ■ *Web:* www.alumawall.com	San Jose	CA	95112	408-292-6353		492
Alumaweld Boats Inc 1601 Ave F *TF:* 800-401-2628 ■ *Web:* www.alumaweldboats.com	White City	OR	97503	541-826-7171	830-6907	90
Alumicor Ltd 290 Humberline Dr *TF:* 877-258-6426 ■ *Web:* www.alumicor.com	Toronto	ON	M9W5S2	416-745-4222		481
Alumi-Guard Inc 2401 Corporate Blvd *Web:* www.alumi-guard.com	Brooksville	FL	34604	352-754-8555		567
AluminArt Products Ltd 1 Summerlea Rd *Web:* www.aluminart.com	Brampton	ON	L6T4V2	905-791-7521		350
Aluminum & Stainless Inc PO Box 3484 *TF:* 800-252-9074 ■ *Web:* www.aluminumandstainless.com	Lafayette	LA	70502	337-837-4381		492
Aluminum Assn Inc 1525 Wilson Blvd Ste 600 *Web:* www.aluminum.org	Arlington	VA	22209	703-358-2960	358-2961	49-13
Aluminum Coil Anodizing Corp 501 E Lake St *Web:* www.acacorp.com	Streamwood	IL	60107	630-837-4000	837-0814	481
Aluminum Distributing 2930 SW Second Ave *TF:* 866-825-9271 ■ *Web:* www.adimetal.com	Fort Lauderdale	FL	33315	954-523-6474		492
Aluminum Extruded Shapes Inc 10549 Reading Rd *Web:* www.alum-ext.com	Cincinnati	OH	45241	513-563-2205		492
Aluminum Extruders Council (AEC) 1000 N Rand Rd Ste 214 *Web:* www.aec.org	Wauconda	IL	60084	847-526-2010	526-3993	49-13
Aluminum Extrusions Inc 140 Matthews Dr	Senatobia	MS	38668	662-562-6663		492
Aluminum Ladder Co 1430 W Darlington St *TF:* 800-752-2526 ■ *Web:* www.aluminumladder.com	Florence	SC	29501	843-662-2595	661-0972	487
Aluminum Line Products Co 24460 Sperry Cir *TF:* 800-321-3154 ■ *Web:* www.aluminumline.com	Westlake	OH	44145	440-835-8880	835-8879	697
Aluminum Precision Products Inc 3333 W Warner St *TF:* 800-411-8983 ■ *Web:* www.aluminumprecision.com	Santa Ana	CA	92704	714-546-8125	540-8662	483
Aluminum Resources Inc 789 Swan Dr *Web:* www.aluminumresources.com	Smyrna	TN	37167	615-355-6500		492
Alumni Center, The 1241 University Dr N *TF:* 800-279-0971 ■ *Web:* www.ndsualumni.com	Fargo	ND	58102	701-231-6800		671
ALung Technologies Inc 2500 Jane St Ste 1 *Web:* www.alung.com	Pittsburgh	PA	15203	412-697-3370		250
Alutiiq LLC 3909 Arctic Blvd Ste 400 *TF:* 800-829-8547 ■ *Web:* www.alutiiq.com	Anchorage	AK	99503	907-222-9500	222-9501	360-3
Alva-Amco Pharmacal Cos Inc 7711 Merrimac Ave *TF:* 800-792-2582 ■ *Web:* www.alva-amco.com	Niles	IL	60714	847-663-0700		582
Alvah Bushnell Co 519 E Chelten Ave *TF:* 800-255-7434 ■ *Web:* www.bushnellco.com	Philadelphia	PA	19144	215-842-9520	843-7725	560
Alvarado Hospital Medical Ctr 6655 Alvarado Rd *TF:* 800-258-2723 ■ *Web:* www.alvaradohospital.com	San Diego	CA	92120	619-287-3270		374-3
Alvarado Mfg Company Inc 12660 Colony St *TF:* 800-423-4143 ■ *Web:* www.alvaradomfg.com	Chino	CA	91710	909-591-8431	628-1403	491
Alvarado Street Bakery 2225 S Mcdowell Blvd Ext *Web:* www.alvaradostreetbakery.com	Petaluma	CA	94954	707-283-0300		68
Alvarado's Mexican Restaurant 11641 S Western Ave *Web:* www.alvaradosmexican.com	Oklahoma City	OK	73170	405-692-2007		671
Alvarez & Associates Llc 8601 Georgia Ave Ste 510	Silver Spring	MD	20910	301-565-3443		174
Alvarez & Marsal Holdings LLC 600 Lexington Ave 8th Fl *Web:* www.alvarezandmarsal.com	New York	NY	10022	212-759-4433	759-5532	194
Alvarez Technology Group Inc 209 Pajaro St Ste A *Web:* www.alvareztg.com	Salinas	CA	93901	831-753-7677		177
Alvarez, Sambol, Winthrop & Madson PA 390 N Orange Ave *Web:* www.awtspa.com	Orlando	FL	32801	407-210-2796		428
Alvernia College 540 Upland Ave *TF:* 888-258-3764 ■ *Web:* www.alvernia.edu	Reading	PA	19611	610-796-8200	790-2873	166
Alverno College PO Box 343922 *TF:* 800-933-3401 ■ *Web:* www.alverno.edu	Milwaukee	WI	53234	414-382-6100		166
Alverson, Taylor, Mortensen & Sanders 7401 W Charleston Blvd *Web:* www.alversontaylor.com	Las Vegas	NV	89117	702-384-7000		428
Alvesta 500 Oakmead Pkwy *Web:* www.alvesta.com	Sunnyvale	CA	94085	408-331-4800		253
Alvin & Company Inc 1335 Blue Hills Ave **Fax Area Code:* 800 ■ *TF:* 800-444-2584 ■ *Web:* www.alvinco.com	Bloomfield	CT	06002	860-243-8991	777-2896*	43
Alvin Ailey American Dance Theater 405 W 55th St *TF:* 800-718-2787 ■ *Web:* www.alvinailey.org	New York	NY	10019	212-405-9000	405-9001	573-1
Alvin C York Campus 3400 Lebanon Pike *TF:* 800-273-8255 ■ *Web:* www.va.gov/directory/guide/facility.asp?ID=94	Murfreesboro	TN	37129	615-867-6000	225-4901	374-8

Name / Address	City	State	Zip	Phone	Fax	Class
Alvin Goldfarb Jeweler of Seattle Inc 305 Bellevue Way NE *Web:* agjeweler.com	Bellevue	WA	98004	425-454-9393		410
Alvin H Butz Inc 840 W Hamilton St Ste 600 *Web:* www.butz.com	Allentown	PA	18101	610-395-6871	395-3363	186
Alvin Hollis & Co 1 Hollis St *TF:* 800-649-5090 ■ *Web:* www.alvinhollis.com	South Weymouth	MA	02190	781-335-2100	335-6134	316
Alvin's Island - Tropical Department Stores 216 Lincon Rd Miami Beach *Web:* www.alvinsisland.com	Miami	FL	33139	305-531-9766		157-5
Alvine Engineering Inc 1102 Douglas On The Mall *Web:* www.alvine.com	Omaha	NE	68102	402-346-7007		256
Alvin-Manvel Area Chamber of Commerce 105 W Willis St *Web:* alvinmanvelchamber.com	Alvin	TX	77511	281-331-3944	585-8662	139
Alvopetro Energy Ltd 332 - 6 Ave SW Ste 1175 *Web:* www.alvopetro.com	Calgary	AB	T2P0B2	587-794-4224		536
Al-Wali Corp 401 Thornton Rd *Web:* www.newleaf-dist.com	Lithia Springs	GA	30122	770-948-7845		530
Alwan Printing 7825 S Roberts Rd *Web:* alwanprinting.com	Bridgeview	IL	60455	708-598-9600		627
Always a Good Sign 407 Bloomfield Dr Ste 3 *Web:* alwaysagoodsign.com	West Berlin	NJ	08091	856-753-7800		701
Alweather Windows & Doors Ltd 27 Troop Ave *Web:* www.awwd.ca	Dartmouth	NS	B3B2A7	902-468-2605		234
Aly Centrifuge Inc 6126 Private Rd 902 *Web:* www.alycentrifuge.com	Celina	TX	75009	972-382-4400		536
Alyeska Pipeline Service Co *Alaska Corp, The* 3700 Centerpoint Dr PO Box 196660	Anchorage	AK	99503	907-787-8700		597
Alyeska Prince Hotel & Resort 1000 Arlberg Ave PO Box 249 *TF:* 800-880-3880 ■ *Web:* www.alyeskaresort.com	Girdwood	AK	99587	907-754-1111		669
ALZA Corp 700 Eubanks Dr *Web:* jnj.com	Vacaville	CA	95688	707-453-6400		743
Alzheimer's Assn 225 N Michigan Ave Fl 17 **Fax Area Code:* 866 ■ *TF:* 800-272-3900 ■ *Web:* www.alz.org	Chicago	IL	60601	312-335-8700	699-1246*	48-17
AM (Ackerman McQueen Inc) 1601 NW Expy Ste 1100 *TF:* 800-438-7325 ■ *Web:* www.am.com	Oklahoma City	OK	73118	405-843-7777	848-8034	4
AM 1300 THE ZONE 3601 S Congress Ave Bldg F *Web:* am1300thezone.iheart.com	Austin	TX	78704	512-684-7300	684-7441	645-14
AM 1400 Solid gold soul 500 Corporate Pkwy Ste 200 *Web:* www.am1400solidgoldsoul.com	Amherst	NY	14226	716-843-0600		645
AM 570 LA Sports 3400 W Olive Ave Ste 550 *TF:* 866-987-2570 ■ *Web:* am570lasports.iheart.com	Burbank	CA	91505	818-559-2252		645
AM 740 KTRH Newsradio 2000 W Loop S Ste 300 *Web:* www.ktrh.com	Houston	TX	77027	713-212-8000		645-75
AM 900 CHML 875 Main St W *Web:* 900chml.com	Hamilton	ON	L8S4R1	905-521-9900	540-2452	645
AM Best Co Ambest Rd *TF:* 800-424-2378 ■ *Web:* www.ambest.com	Oldwick	NJ	08858	908-439-2200	439-3296	637-10
AM Facility Services 8481 Bash St Ste 1700 *Web:* www.amincorporated.com	Indianapolis	IN	46250	317-578-2290		104
AM General LLC 105 N Niles Ave PO Box 7025 *Web:* www.amgeneral.com	South Bend	IN	46617	574-237-6222		59
AM Kinney 150 E Fourth St *TF:* 800-265-3682 ■ *Web:* www.amkinney.com	Cincinnati	OH	45202	513-421-2265		261
AM New York 330 W 34th St 17th Fl *Web:* www.amny.com	New York	NY	10001	212-239-5555	239-2828	532-2
AM Pappas & Assoc 2520 Meridian Pkwy *Web:* www.pappasventures.com	Durham	NC	27713	919-998-3300	998-3301	792
AM Private Investments Inc 45 Pine St E Wing *Web:* www.aminet.com	New Canaan	CT	06840	203-972-5095		401
AM Resorts LLC 7 Campus Blvd *TF:* 800-247-5645 ■ *Web:* www.amresorts.com	Newtown Square	PA	19073	610-359-6500		707
AM Skier Agency Inc 209 Main Ave *Web:* amskier.com	Hawley	PA	18428	570-226-4571		390
A&M Supply Corp 6701 90th Ave N	Pinellas Park	FL	33782	727-541-6631	546-3617	820
A-M Systems Inc 131 Business Park Loop *TF:* 800-426-1306 ■ *Web:* a-msystems.com	Sequim	WA	98382	360-683-8300		477
AM Technical Solutions Inc 2213 RR 620 N Ste 105 *TF:* 888-729-1548 ■ *Web:* www.amts.com	Austin	TX	78734	888-729-1548		393
AM Todd Co 1717 Douglas Ave *TF:* 800-968-2603 ■ *Web:* www.wildflavors.com	Kalamazoo	MI	49007	269-343-2603	343-3399	479
Am860 The Answer 5211 W Laurel St Ste 101 *TF:* 800-520-1234 ■ *Web:* am860theanswer.com	Tampa	FL	33607	813-639-1903	639-1272	645-162
AMA (Aerospace Medical Assn) 320 S Henry St *Web:* www.asma.org	Alexandria	VA	22314	703-739-2240	739-9652	49-8
AMA (American Marketing Assn) 311 S Wacker Dr Ste 5800 *TF:* 800-262-1150 ■ *Web:* www.ama.org	Chicago	IL	60606	312-542-9000	542-9001	49-18
AMA (American Medical Assn) 515 N State St *TF:* 800-621-8335 ■ *Web:* www.ama-assn.org	Chicago	IL	60610	312-464-5000	464-4184	49-8
AMA (American Motorcyclist Assn) 13515 Yarmouth Dr *TF:* 800-262-5646 ■ *Web:* www.americanmotorcyclist.com	Pickerington	OH	43147	614-856-1900	856-1920	48-22
AMA (Academy of Model Aeronautics) 5161 E Memorial Dr *TF:* 800-435-9262 ■ *Web:* www.modelaircraft.org	Muncie	IN	47302	765-287-1256	289-4248	48-18
AMA Plastics Inc 1100 Citrus St *Web:* amaplastics.com	Riverside	CA	92507	951-734-5600		604
Amac Enterprises 5909 W 130th St *Web:* www.amacent.com	Cleveland	OH	44130	216-362-1880		484
AMACO (American Art Clay Co) 6060 Guion Rd *TF:* 800-374-1600 ■ *Web:* www.amaco.com	Indianapolis	IN	46254	317-244-6871	248-9300	43
Amada America Inc 7025 Firestone Blvd *TF:* 800-626-6612 ■ *Web:* www.amada.com	Buena Park	CA	90621	714-739-2111	739-4099	456
Amada Capital Corp 7025 Firestone Blvd *Web:* www.amadacapital.com	Buena Park	CA	90621	714-739-2111		216
Amadas Industries Inc 1100 Holland Rd *Web:* www.amadas.com	Suffolk	VA	23434	757-539-0231	934-3264	273
Amadeus 122 E Washington St *TF:* 800-344-7829 ■ *Web:* www.amadeusrestaurant.com	Ann Arbor	MI	48104	734-665-8767		671
Amadeus North America Inc 3470 NW 82nd Ave Ste 1000 *TF:* 888-262-3387 ■ *Web:* www.amadeus.com	Miami	FL	33122	305-499-6000	499-6889	335
Amadeus Spa at the Marriott Napa Valley 3425 Solano Ave *Web:* marriott.com	Napa	CA	94558	707-254-3330		707
Amador County 810 Ct St *TF:* 800-775-9772 ■ *Web:* www.co.amador.ca.us	Jackson	CA	95642	209-223-6470	257-0619	338
Amador County Chamber of Commerce 115 Main St PO Box 596 *TF General:* 800-822-9466 ■ *Web:* amadorchamber.com	Jackson	CA	95642	209-223-0350		139
Amador County Library 530 Sutter St *Web:* www.co.amador.ca.us	Jackson	CA	95642	209-223-6400		434-3
Amador County Unified School District 217 Rex Ave *Web:* www.amadorcoe.org	Jackson	CA	95642	209-223-1750		685
AMAG Pharmaceuticals Inc 61 Mooney St *AMEX: AVM*	Cambridge	MA	02138	617-497-2070		231
AMAG Technology Inc 20701 Manhattan Pl *TF:* 800-889-9138 ■ *Web:* www.amag.com	Torrance	CA	90501	310-518-2380	834-0685	692
Amak Brake LLC 1765 Cleveland Ave	Glasgow	KY	42141	270-678-6766		247
Amal Law Group LLC 7804 W College Dr Ste 3n *Web:* amallaw.com	Palos Heights	IL	60463	708-361-3600		428
Amalfi 143 N Brea Ave *Web:* www.amalfila.com	Los Angeles	CA	90036	323-938-2504		671
Amalfi 1351 W 86th St *Web:* www.amalfiristoranteitaliano.com	Indianapolis	IN	46260	317-253-4034		671
Amalfi Semiconductor Inc 475 Alberto Way Ste 200	Los Gatos	CA	95032	408-399-5360		696
Amalfi's 4703 NE Fremont St *Web:* www.amalfisrestaurant.com	Portland	OR	97213	503-284-6747		671
Amalgamated Bank of Chicago 30 N LaSalle *Web:* www.aboc.com	Chicago	IL	60602	312-822-3000	267-8767	70
Amalgamated Bank of New York 275 Seventh Ave *TF:* 800-662-0860 ■ *Web:* www.amalgamatedbank.com	New York	NY	10001	800-662-0860		70
Amalgamated Dairies Ltd 79 Water St *Web:* www.adl.ca	Summerside	PE	C1N1A6	902-888-5088		578
Amalgamated Life Insurance Co 730 Broadway *Web:* www.amalgamatedlife.com	New York	NY	10003	212-539-5826		391-2
Amalgamated Sugar Co LLC 1951 S Saturn Way Ste 100 *Web:* www.amalgamatedsugar.com	Boise	ID	83709	208-383-6500	383-6688	296-38
Amalgamated Transit Union (ATU) 10000 New Hampshire Ave *TF:* 888-240-1196 ■ *Web:* www.atu.org	Silver Spring	MD	20903	202-537-1645	244-7824	414
Aman Environmental Construction Inc 614 E Edna Pl *Web:* www.amanenvironmental.com	Covina	CA	91723	626-967-4287		189-5
Amana Appliances Inc 2800 220th Trl *TF Cust Svc:* 800-843-0304 ■ *Web:* www.amana.com	Amana	IA	52204	319-622-5511	622-2180	15
Amana Colonies 622 46th Ave *TF:* 800-579-2294 ■ *Web:* www.amanacolonies.com	Amana	IA	52203	319-622-7622		10-4
Amanda's Fonda 3625 W Colorado Ave	Colorado Springs	CO	80904	719-227-1975		671
Amangani Resort 1535 NE Butte Rd *TF:* 877-734-7333 ■ *Web:* www.aman.com/resorts/amangani	Jackson	WY	83001	307-734-7333	734-7332	669
Amani Fahmy-Jensen CPA PC 763 N St	White Plains	NY	10605	914-948-1880		2
Amann Business Systems Inc 1901 Jefferson Hwy *Web:* amannsystems.com	New Orleans	LA	70121	504-836-6800		396
Amano Cincinnati Inc 140 Harrison Ave *TF:* 800-526-2559 ■ *Web:* www.amano.com	Roseland	NJ	07068	973-403-1900	364-1086	111
Amano Enzyme USA Company Ltd 1415 Madeline Ln *Web:* www.amano-enzyme.co.jp	Elgin	IL	60124	847-649-0101		390
Amara Resort LLC 100 Amara Ln *Web:* www.amararesort.com	Sedona	AZ	86336	928-282-4828		378
Amaram Technology Corp 8230 Boone Blvd Ste 445 *Web:* www.amaram.com	Vienna	VA	22182	703-288-4113	879-7555	177
Amaranth Medical Inc 1145 Terra Bella Ave Ste A *Web:* amaranthmedical.com	Mountain View	CA	94043	650-965-3830		476
Amarillo Biosciences Inc 4134 Business Pk Dr *Web:* www.amarbio.com	Amarillo	TX	79110	806-376-1741	376-9301	85
Amarillo Botanical Gardens 1400 Streit Dr *Web:* www.amarillobotanicalgardens.org	Amarillo	TX	79106	806-352-6513		97
Amarillo Chamber of Commerce 1000 S Polk St *Web:* www.amarillo-chamber.org	Amarillo	TX	79101	806-373-7800	373-3909	139
Amarillo Civic Ctr 401 S Buchanan St *TF:* 800-692-1338 ■ *Web:* amarillociviccenter.com	Amarillo	TX	79101	806-378-4297	378-4234	205

Phone | Fax | Class

Amarillo Club 600 S Tyler St Amarillo TX 79101 806-373-4361 671
Web: amarilloclub.net
Amarillo College
2201 S Washington St Amarillo TX 79109 806-371-5000 371-5066 162
TF: 800-227-8784 ■ *Web:* www.actx.edu
Amarillo Convention & Visitor Council
1000 S Polk St Amarillo TX 79101 806-374-1497 206
TF: 800-692-1338 ■ *Web:* www.visitamarillo.com
Amarillo Economic Development Corp
801 S Fillmore Ste 205 Amarillo TX 79101 806-379-6411 463
TF: 800-333-7892 ■ *Web:* www.amarilloedc.com
Amarillo Gear Co 2401 W Sundown Ln Amarillo TX 79118 806-622-1273 622-3258 709
Web: www.amarillogear.com
Amarillo Globe News PO Box 2091 Amarillo TX 79166 806-376-4488 373-0810 532-2
TF: 800-692-4052 ■ *Web:* amarillo.com
Amarillo Independent School District (AISD)
7200 I- 40 W Amarillo TX 79106 806-326-1000 354-4378* 685
**Fax:* Hum Res ■ *Web:* www.amaisd.org
Amarillo Museum of Art
2200 S Van Buren St Amarillo TX 79109 806-371-5050 520
TF: 800-383-4712 ■ *Web:* www.amarilloart.org
Amarillo National Bank
410 S Taylor Plaza 1 Amarillo TX 79101 806-378-8000 378-8066* 70
**Fax:* Cust Svc ■ *TF:* 800-253-1031 ■ *Web:* www.anb.com
Amarillo Opera 2223 S Van Buren St Amarillo TX 79109 806-372-7464 573-2
Web: www.amarilloopera.org
Amarillo Public Library
413 SE Fourth Ave Amarillo TX 79101 806-378-3054 378-9327 434-3
TF: 800-687-9737 ■ *Web:* www.amarillolibrary.org
Amarillo Wind Machine Co 20513 Ave 256 Exeter CA 93221 559-592-4256 592-4194 273
TF: 800-311-4498 ■ *Web:* www.amarillowind.com
Amarillo Zoo 700 Comanchero Trail Amarillo TX 79107 806-381-7911 381-7901 823
Web: zoo.amarillo.gov
A-Mark Precious Metals Inc
429 Santa Monica Blvd Ste 230 Santa Monica CA 90401 310-587-1485 319-0317 360-3
Web: www.amark.com
Amash Justin (Rep R - MI)
114 Cannon Bldg Washington DC 20515 202-225-3831 225-5144 342-2
Web: amash.house.gov
Amason & Assoc Inc
1810 Rice Mine Rd NE Ste 100 Tuscaloosa AL 35406 205-345-9626 610
Web: www.amason-associates.com
Amatech Inc 1460 Grimm Dr Erie PA 16501 814-452-0010 601
Web: www.amatechinc.com
Amateur Athletic Union of the US (AAU)
1910 Hotel Plaza Blvd Lake Buena Vista FL 32830 407-934-7200 934-7242 48-22
TF: 800-228-4872 ■ *Web:* www.aausports.org
Amateur Trapshooting Assn (ATA)
601 W National Rd Vandalia OH 45377 937-898-4638 898-5472 48-22
TF: 800-671-8042 ■ *Web:* www.shootata.com
Amatex Corp 1032 Stambridge St Norristown PA 19404 610-277-6100 277-6106 745-3
TF: 800-441-9680 ■ *Web:* www.amatex.com
Amato Legal Search Inc
2321 Old Maple Ct Ellicott City MD 21042 410-750-7550 428
Web: www.amatolegalsearch.com
AmaWaterways 26010 Mureau Rd Calabasas CA 91302 800-626-0126 760
TF: 800-626-0126 ■ *Web:* www.amawaterways.com
Amax Engineering Corp
1565 Reliance Way Fremont CA 94539 510-651-8886 651-4119 173-2
TF Cust Svc: 800-889-2629 ■ *Web:* www.amax.com
Amax Nutrasource Inc
14291 E Don Julian Rd City Of Industry CA 91746 626-961-6600 345
TF: 800-893-5306 ■ *Web:* www.amaxnutrasource.com
Amazing Mail-print Ctr
2130 S Seventh Ave Ste 170 Phoenix AZ 85007 888-681-1214 5
TF: 888-681-1214 ■ *Web:* amazingmail.com
Amazing Media Inc
133 Eglin Pkwy SE Ft Walton Beach FL 32563 850-833-2648 5
Amazing Recycled Products Inc
PO Box 312 Denver CO 80201 303-295-1004 699-2102 661
TF: 800-241-2174 ■ *Web:* amazingrecycled.blogspot.in
Amazon.com Inc
1200 12th Ave S Ste 1200 Seattle WA 98144 206-266-1000 95
NASDAQ: AMZN ■ *TF Cust Svc:* 800-201-7575 ■ *Web:* www.amazon.com
AMB Financial Corp 8230 Hohman Ave Munster IN 46321 219-836-5870 836-5883 360-2
OTC: AMFC ■ *TF:* 800-436-5113 ■ *Web:* www.ambfinancial.com
AMBA (American Malting Barley Assn)
740 N Plankinton Ave Ste 830 Milwaukee WI 53203 414-272-4640 49-6
Web: www.ambainc.org
AMBAC Assurance Corp
1 State St Plaza New York NY 10004 212-658-7470 208-3414 391-5
TF: 800-221-1854 ■ *Web:* www.ambac.com
AMBAC Financial Group Inc
1 State St Plaza New York NY 10004 212-668-0340 509-9190 360-4
OTC: ABKFQ ■ *TF:* 800-221-1854 ■ *Web:* www.ambac.com
AMBAC International Inc
910 Spears Creek Ct Elgin SC 29045 803-735-1400 735-2163 60
TF: 800-628-6894 ■ *Web:* ambacdiesel.com
Ambar 350 Ludlow Ave Cincinnati OH 45220 513-281-7000 281-7001 671
Web: www.ambarindia.com
Ambarella Inc 2975 San Ysidro Way Santa Clara CA 95054 408-734-8888 696
Web: www.ambarella.com
Ambasoft 23505 Crenshaw Blvd Torrance CA 90505 310-326-4160 177
Ambassador Capital Management LLC
500 Griswold St Ste 2800 Detroit MI 48226 313-961-3111 401
Ambassador Dining Room
3811 Canterbury Rd Baltimore MD 21218 410-366-1484 671
Web: www1.nyc.gov
Ambassador Duty Free Store
707 Patricia St Windsor ON N9B0B5 519-977-9100 977-7811 241
Web: www.ambassadordutyfree.com
Ambassador Financial Group Inc
1605 N Cedar Crest Blvd Ste 508 Allentown PA 18104 610-351-1633 401
Web: www.ambfg.com
Ambassador Hotel
2308 W Wisconsin Ave Milwaukee WI 53233 414-345-5000 379
TF: 888-322-3326 ■ *Web:* www.ambassadormilwaukee.com
Ambassador Hotel Inc 2040 Kuhio Ave Honolulu HI 96815 808-941-7777 378
Web: www.ambassadorwaikiki.com

Ambassador Speakers Bureau
PO Box 50358 Nashville TN 37205 615-370-4700 661-4344 708
Web: www.ambassadorspeakers.com
Ambassador Theaters 219 W 49th St New York NY 10019 212-239-6200 747
TF: 800-745-3000 ■ *Web:* ambassadortheater.com
Ambella Home Collection Corporate Office
4910 Lakawana St Dallas TX 75247 214-631-8901 321
Amber Assn Partners LLC
801 N Fairfax St Ste 211 Alexandria VA 22314 703-299-0000 299-9233 47
Web: amberllc.com
Amber Diagnostics Inc
2180 Premier Row Orlando FL 32809 407-438-7847 475
TF: 866-919-2959 ■ *Web:* www.amberusa.com
Amber India 377 Santana Row Ste 1140 San Jose CA 95128 408-248-5400 671
Web: www.amber-india.com
Amber Lotus Publishing PO Box 11329 Portland OR 97211 503-284-6400 284-6417 130
TF: 800-326-2375 ■ *Web:* www.amberlotus.com
Amber Precision Instruments Inc
746 San Aleso Ave Sunnyvale CA 94085 408-752-0199 407
Web: www.amberpi.com
Amber Resources LLC 1543 W 16th St Long Beach CA 90813 562-432-3946 579
Web: amberresources.com
Amber Road Inc
1 Meadowlands Plaza East Rutherford NJ 07073 201-935-8588 39
Web: www.amberroad.com
Amber Rose 1400 Valley St Dayton OH 45404 937-228-2511 671
Web: www.theamberrose.com
Amber Waves Inc 11 S Ave W Richardton ND 58652 701-974-4230 77
Web: www.amberwavesinc.com
Amberton University 1700 Eastgate Dr Garland TX 75041 972-279-6511 279-9773 166
Web: www.amberton.edu
AmberWave Inc 13 Garabedian Dr Salem NH 03079 603-870-8700 180
Web: www.amberwave.com
AMBEST Inc 5115 Maryland Way Brentwood TN 37027 615-371-5187 324
TF: 800-910-7220 ■ *Web:* www.am-best.com
Ambiance Day Spa & Salon
1777 Monte Vista Ave Claremont CA 91711 909-625-5535 77
Web: www.claremontclub.com
Ambiance Models & Talent Inc
6918 Shallowford Rd Ste 300 Chattanooga TN 37421 423-265-2121 507
Web: www.ambiancemodels.com
AmbiCom Holdings Inc 500 Alder Dr Milpitas CA 95035 408-321-0822 407
Web: www.ambicom.com
Ambient Consulting LLC
10900 Wayzata Blvd Ste 850 Minneapolis MN 55305 763-582-9000 582-7901 225
Web: www.ambientconsulting.com
Ambient Healthcare Inc
15851 SW 41st St Ste 500 Davie FL 33331 954-389-1126 389-1129 238
TF: 800-670-6922 ■ *Web:* www.ambienthealth.com
Ambiente Wine Importing Company Inc
2314 Rutland Dr Ste 205 Austin TX 78758 512-835-2299 80-3
Web: www.ambientewine.com
AmbioPharm Inc 1024 Dittman Ct North Augusta SC 29842 415-921-3593 41
Web: www.ambiopharm.com
Ambit Consulting
225 W Eighth Ave Ste 300 Vancouver BC V6J1Y6 604-662-3130 194
Web: ambit-consulting.com
Ambit Energy LP 1801 N Lamar St Ste 200 Dallas TX 75202 877-282-6248 787
TF: 877-282-6248 ■ *Web:* ww2.ambitenergy.com
Ambit Pacific Recycling Inc
16228 S Figueroa St Gardena CA 90248 310-538-3798 660
Web: www.ambitpacific.com
Ambius Inc
485 E Half Day Rd Ste 450 Buffalo Grove IL 60089 847-634-4258 104
Web: www.ambius.com
Ambix Manufacturing Inc
71 Hobbs St Ste 104 Conway NH 03818 603-452-5247 393
Web: www.ambixllc.com
Ambler Growth Strategy Conslnt
3432 Reading Ave Hammonton NJ 08037 609-567-9669 463
TF: 800-832-7090 ■ *Web:* ambler.com
Amboy Bancorp 3590 US Hwy 9 S Old Bridge NJ 08857 732-591-8700 591-0705 360-2
TF: 800-942-6269 ■ *Web:* www.amboybank.com
Amboy National Bank
3590 US Hwy 9 S Old Bridge NJ 08857 732-591-8700 591-0705 70
TF: 800-942-6269 ■ *Web:* www.amboybank.com
Ambrado Inc
1301 W President George Bush Hwy Ste 150 Richardson TX 75080 972-696-6800 647
Web: www.ambrado.com
Ambrico & Company PA
425 W Colonial Dr Ste 305 Orlando FL 32804 407-316-8900 2
Ambriola Company Inc
7 Patton Dr West Caldwell NJ 07006 800-962-8224 297-4
TF: 800-962-8224 ■ *Web:* www.ambriola.com
Ambrose Engineering Inc
W66n215 Commerce Ct Cedarburg WI 53012 262-377-7602 261
Web: AMBROSEENGINEERING.COM
Ambrose Printing Co
210 Cumberland Bend Nashville TN 37228 615-256-1151 627
TF: 800-334-6524 ■ *Web:* www.ambroseprint.com
Ambrosia 467 Elmwood Ave Buffalo NY 14222 716-881-2196 671
Ambrosia 1401 Simonton St Key West FL 33040 305-293-0304 671
Web: keywestambrosia.com
Ambrosia House Tropical Lodging
622 Fleming St Key West FL 33040 305-296-9838 296-2425 379
TF: 800-535-9838 ■ *Web:* www.ambrosiakeywest.com
Ambrosia Restaurant 174 E Broadway Eugene OR 97401 541-342-4141 671
Web: www.ambrosiarestaurant.com
Ambrx Inc 10975 N Torrey Pines Rd La Jolla CA 92037 858-875-2400 238
Web: www.ambrx.com
Ambry 3016 E Commercial Blvd Fort Lauderdale FL 33308 954-771-7342 671
Web: ambryrestaurant.net
AMBS 3003 Benham Ave Elkhart IN 46517 574-295-3726 167-3
TF: 800-964-2627 ■ *Web:* www.ambs.edu
Ambush Boarding Co
2555 Cobb Place Ln NW Kennesaw GA 30144 770-420-9111 711
Web: www.ambushboardco.com

Phone | Fax | Class

AMC (Augusta Medical Ctr)
78 Medical Ctr Dr PO Box 1000 Fishersville VA 22939 540-932-4000 374-3
TF: 800-932-0262 ■ *Web:* www.augustahealth.com

AMC (Appalachian Mountain Club) 5 Joy St Boston MA 02108 617-523-0655 523-0722 48-13
TF Orders: 800-262-4455 ■ *Web:* www.outdoors.org

AMC Industries LLC 1120 N 28th St Tampa FL 33605 813-989-9663 321
Web: www.amcind.com

AMC Institute
700 N Fairfax St Ste 510 Alexandria VA 22314 215-564-3484 963-9785 49-12
TF: 800-927-5007 ■ *Web:* amcinstitute.org

Amc Management Group Inc
34 Abby Rd Farmingdale NJ 07727 732-938-5457 463
Web: www.amcinc.biz

Amc Network LLC
708 Gravenstein Hwy N Ste 184 Sebastopol CA 95472 707-829-9484 184
Web: www.amcnetwork.com

AMC Networks Inc 11 Penn Plaza 2nd Fl New York NY 10001 212-324-8500 740
NASDAQ: AMCX ■ *Web:* www.amcnetworks.com

AMC Star Theatres
25333 W 12-Mile Rd Southfield MI 48034 248-368-1802 748
TF: 888-262-4386 ■ *Web:* www.amctheatres.com

AMC Theatres PO Box 725489 Atlanta GA 31139-9923 888-440-4262 748
TF: 888-440-4262 ■ *Web:* www.amctheatres.com

AMCA (Air Movement & Control Assn International Inc)
30 W University Dr Arlington Heights IL 60004 847-394-0150 253-0088 49-3
Web: www.amca.org

Amcep Metals 4484 E Tennessee St Tucson AZ 85714 520-748-1900 748-2752 686
TF: 800-757-5211 ■ *Web:* amcepmetals.com

Amcest Nationwide Monitoring
1017 Walnut St Roselle NJ 07203 800-631-7370 196
TF: 800-631-7370 ■ *Web:* www.amcest.com

AmCheck Inc 5030 E Sunrise Dr Phoenix AZ 85044 480-763-5900 734
Web: www.amcheck.com

AmChel Communications Inc
1703 Martinez Ln Wylie TX 75098 972-442-1030 429-7985 480
TF: 866-388-6959 ■ *Web:* www.amchel.com

AMCHP (Association of Maternal & Child Health Programs)
2030 M St NW Ste 350 Washington DC 20036 202-775-0436 49-7
Web: www.amchp.org

AMCI 4755 Alla Rd Ste 1000 Marina Del Rey CA 90292 855-486-5527 7
TF: 855-486-5527 ■ *Web:* www.amciglobal.com

Amcom Data Processing Inc
2 Annabel Ln Ste 130 San Ramon CA 94583 925-328-0322 180
Web: www.amcom.biz

Amcom Software Inc
10400 Yellow Cir Dr Eden Prairie MN 55343 952-230-5200 230-5510 178-7
TF: 800-852-8935 ■ *Web:* spok.com

Amcon Block & Precast Inc
2211 Hwy 10 S Saint Cloud MN 56304 320-251-6030 362
TF: 888-251-6030 ■ *Web:* www.amconblock.com

AMCON Distributing Co 7405 Irvington Rd Omaha NE 68122 402-331-3727 331-4834 756
NYSE: DIT ■ *TF:* 888-201-5997 ■ *Web:* www.amcon.com

Amcor Ltd 935 Technology Dr Ste 100 Ann Arbor MI 48108 734-428-9741 601
TF: 800-333-7680 ■ *Web:* www.amcor.com

Amcor Packaging
935 Technology Dr Ste 100 Ann Arbor MI 48108 734-428-9741 562-6059* 98
**Fax Area Code: 714* ■ *Web:* www.amcor.com/petpackaging

AMCP (Academy of Managed Care Pharmacy)
100 N Pitt St Ste 400 Alexandria VA 22314 703-683-8416 683-8417 49-8
TF: 800-827-2627 ■ *Web:* www.amcp.org

AMCS Corp 135 US Hwy 202-206 Ste 12 Bedminster NJ 07921 908-719-6560 261
TF: 800-982-0136 ■ *Web:* www.amcscorp.com

AMD (Advanced Micro Devices Inc)
1 AMD Pl PO Box 3453 Sunnyvale CA 94088 408-749-4000 696
NYSE: AMD ■ *TF:* 800-538-8450 ■ *Web:* www.amd.com

AMD (World Millwork Alliance)
10047 Robert Trent Jones Pkwy New Port Richey FL 34655 727-372-3665 372-2879 49-3
Web: worldmillworkalliance.com

AMD Industries Inc 4620 W 19th St Cicero IL 60804 708-863-8900 233
TF: 800-367-9999 ■ *Web:* www.amdpop.com

AMDA (American Medical Directors Assn)
11000 Broken Land Pkwy Ste 400 Columbia MD 21044 410-740-9743 740-4572 49-8
TF: 800-876-2632 ■ *Web:* www.paltc.org

Amdocs Ltd
1390 Timberlake Manor Pkwy Chesterfield MO 63017 314-212-7000 212-7500 178-10
NYSE: DOX ■ *Web:* www.amdocs.com

AMDTechnologies Inc
1 Commerce Valley Dr E Markham ON L3T7X6 905-882-2600 882-2620 625
Web: www.amd.com

AME (Applied Molecular Evolution Inc)
10300 Campus Pt Dr Ste 200 San Diego CA 92121 858-597-4990 85

AME (Association for Mfg Excellence)
3701 W Algonquin Rd Ste 225 Rolling Meadows IL 60008 224-232-5980 232-5981 49-12
Web: www.ame.org

AME Inc 2467 Coltharp Rd PO Box 909 Fort Mill SC 29716 803-548-7766 548-7448 188-6
TF: 800-849-7766 ■ *Web:* www.ameonline.com

AME Label Corp 25155 W Ave Stanford Valencia CA 91355 661-257-2200 257-7981 413
TF: 866-278-9268 ■ *Web:* www.amelabel.com

AME Services Inc 23 Barreca St Norco LA 70079 504-712-3220 104

Amec Foster Wheeler
1002 Walnut St Ste 200 Boulder CO 80302 303-443-7839 225
Web: www.amecfw.com

AMECO (American Equipment Co)
4775 Technology Way Ste 208 Boca Raton FL 33431 561-997-2080 997-2110 770
Web: www.ameco.net

Amedica Corp
1885 West 2100 South Salt Lake City UT 84119 855-839-3500 250
TF: 855-839-3500 ■ *Web:* www.amedica.com

Amedisys 209 Tenth Ave S Ste 512 Nashville TN 37203 423-587-9484 587-9408 371
TF: 800-464-0020 ■ *Web:* www.amedisys.com

Amedisys Inc
5959 S Sherwood Forest Blvd Ste 300 Baton Rouge LA 70816 225-292-2031 352
NASDAQ: AMED ■ *TF:* 800-464-0020 ■ *Web:* www.amedisys.com

Amegy Bancorp Inc 4400 Post Oak Pkwy Houston TX 77027 713-235-8800 360-2
Web: amegybank.com

Amegy Bank of Texas
4400 Post Oak Pkwy Houston TX 77027 713-235-8800 70
TF: 800-287-0301 ■ *Web:* www.amegybank.com

Amel's Restaurant 435 McNeilly Rd Pittsburgh PA 15226 412-563-3466 671
Web: www.amelsrestaurantpgh.com

Amelia County
16360 Dunn St Ste 101 Amelia Courthouse VA 23002 804-561-3039 561-6039 338
Web: www.ameliacova.com

Amelia Island Book Festival
PO Box 15286 Fernandina Beach FL 32035 904-624-1665 281
Web: www.ameliaislandbookfestival.org

Amelia Island Museum of History
233 S Third St Fernandina Beach FL 32034 904-261-7378 261-9701 520
TF: 800-862-9297 ■ *Web:* ameliamuseum.org

Amelia Island Plantation
39 Beach Lagoon Rd Amelia Island FL 32034 904-261-6161 669
TF: 800-834-4900 ■ *Web:* www.villasofameliaisland.com

Amelia Island State Park
12157 Heckscher Dr Jacksonville FL 32226 904-251-2320 565
Web: www.floridastateparks.org/park/Amelia-Island

Amelia Island-Fernandina Beach-Yulee Chamber of Commerce
961687 Gateway Blvd Ste 101-G Fernandina Beach FL 32034 904-261-3248 261-6997 139
TF: 800-226-3542 ■ *Web:* www.islandchamber.com

Amelia's 235 S Main St Ste 107 Gainesville FL 32601 352-373-1919 671
Web: www.ameliasgainesville.com

Amelia's Bistro 187 Warren St Jersey City NJ 07302 201-332-2200 671
Web: ameliasbistro.com

Amendia Inc 1755 W Oak Pkwy Marietta GA 30062 678-445-3784 475
TF: 877-755-3329 ■ *Web:* www.amendia.com

Amer Technology Inc
5717 Northwest Pkwy San Antonio TX 78249 210-256-7070 177
Web: www.amersolutions.com

AmerCable Inc 350 Bailey Rd El Dorado AR 71730 870-862-4919 862-9613 813
TF: 800-643-1516 ■ *Web:* www.amercable.com

AMERCO 1325 Airmotive Way Ste 100 Reno NV 89502 775-688-6300 688-6338 185
NASDAQ: UHAL ■ *Web:* www.amerco.com

Amerco Real Estate Co
2727 N Central Ave Ste 500 Phoenix AZ 85004 602-263-6555 653
Web: www.amercorealestate.com

Ameren Corp 1901 Chouteau Ave Saint Louis MO 63103 314-621-3222 360-5
NYSE: AEE ■ *TF:* 800-552-7583 ■ *Web:* ameren.com

Amerequip Corp 1015 Calumet Ave Kiel WI 53042 920-894-2000 894-3799 273
TF: 800-831-7158 ■ *Web:* www.amerequip.com

Ameresco Canada Inc
90 Sheppard Ave E North York ON M2N3A1 416-512-7700 466
TF: 888-483-7267 ■ *Web:* www.ameresco.ca

Ameresco Inc 111 Speen St Ste 410 Framingham MA 01701 508-661-2200 661-2201 192
TF: 866-263-7372 ■ *Web:* www.ameresco.com

Amerex Corp
7595 Gadsden Hwy PO Box 81 Trussville AL 35173 205-655-3271 678
Web: www.amerex-fire.com

Amerex Energy Services LLC
1 Sugar Creek Ctr Blvd Ste 700 Sugar Land TX 77478 281-340-5200 194
Web: www.amerexenergy.com

Amerge Corp 1406 W Sixth St Ste 200 Cleveland OH 44113 216-928-6007 928-6008 41

Americ Machinery Corp 820 Walnut Ave Vallejo CA 94592 253-236-8555 111
Web: www.americmachinery.com

America Chung Nam Inc
1163 Fairway Dr City of Industry CA 91789 909-839-8383 553
Web: www.acni.net

America First Credit Union
1344 W 4675 S Ogden UT 84405 801-627-0900 778-8079* 219
**Fax: Hum Res* ■ *TF:* 800-999-3961 ■ *Web:* www.americafirst.com

America II Electronics Inc
2600 118th Ave N Saint Petersburg FL 33716 727-573-0900 572-9696 246
TF: 800-767-2637 ■ *Web:* www.americaii.com

America Online Inc (AOL) 22000 AOL Way Dulles VA 20166 703-265-1000 398
Web: www.aol.com

America Outdoors 5816 Kingston Pk Knoxville TN 37919 865-558-3595 558-3598 48-23
TF: 800-524-4814 ■ *Web:* www.americaoutdoors.org

America The Beautiful Dreamer Inc
9700 NE 126th Ave Vancouver WA 98682 360-816-0167 321
Web: www.atbd.com

America's Best Franchising Inc
50 Glenlake Pkwy Ste 350 Atlanta GA 30328 770-393-2662 393-2480 379

America's Blood Centers (ABC)
725 15th St NW Ste 700 Washington DC 20005 202-393-5725 393-1282 49-8
TF: 888-872-5663 ■ *Web:* www.americasblood.org

America's Call Center Inc
7901 Baymeadows Way Ste 14 Jacksonville FL 32256 904-224-2000 737
TF: 800-598-2580 ■ *Web:* www.webcallusa.com

America's Car-Mart Inc
802 SE Plaza Ave Ste 200 Bentonville AR 72712 479-464-9944 273-7556 57
NASDAQ: CRMT ■ *Web:* www.car-mart.com

America's Choice Home Loans LP
8584 Katy Fwy Ste 200 Houston TX 77024 713-463-6779 652
Web: www.achlonline.com

America's Community Bankers (ACB)
1120 Connecticut Ave NW Washington DC 20036 800-226-5377 49-2
TF: 800-226-5377 ■ *Web:* www.aba.com

America's Ctr Convention Ctr
701 Convention Plaza Ste 300 Saint Louis MO 63101 314-342-5036 342-5040 205
TF: 800-325-7962 ■
Web: www.explorestlouis.com/americascenter/public.asp

America's Essential Hospitals (NAPH)
1301 Pennsylvania Ave NW Ste 950 Washington DC 20004 202-585-0100 585-0101 49-8
Web: essentialhospitals.org

America's Health Insurance Plans (AHIP)
601 Pennsylvania Ave NW Ste 500 Washington DC 20004 202-778-3200 331-7487 49-9
Web: www.ahip.org

America's Natural Gas Alliance
701 Eighth St NW Ste 800 Washington DC 20001 202-789-2642 944-1920 536
Web: www.naturalgassolution.org

America's Packard Museum
420 S Ludlow St Dayton OH 45402 937-226-1710 520
Web: www.americaspackardmuseum.org

America's Promise - the Alliance for Youth
909 N Washington St Ste 400 Alexandria VA 22314 703-684-4500 48-6
Web: www.americaspromise.org

America's Second Harvest
35 E Wacker Dr Ste 2000 Chicago IL 60601 312-263-2303 263-5626 48-5
TF: 800-771-2303 ■ *Web:* www.feedingamerica.org

				Phone	Fax	Class
America-Israel Chamber of Commerce - Chicago 247 S State St Ste 1325 *TF:* 800-645-3433 ■ *Web:* www.israeltrade.org	Chicago	IL	60604	312-641-2937	641-2941	138
Americal Corp 389 Americal Rd	Henderson	NC	27537	252-762-2000		155-10
Ameri-Cal Floral Inc 94 San Miguel Canyon Rd *Web:* www.americal.com	Watsonville	CA	95076	831-728-4205		369
Americall 1502 Tacoma Ave S *TF:* 800-964-3556 ■ *Web:* www.americall.com	Tacoma	WA	98402	253-272-4111		41
American Academy for Cerebral Palsy & Developmental Medicine (AACPDM) 555 E Wells St Ste 1100 *TF:* 800-274-2237 ■ *Web:* www.aacpdm.org	Milwaukee	WI	53202	414-918-3014	276-2146	48-17
American Academy for Liberal Education (AALE) 1200 G St NW Ste 883 *Web:* www.aale.org	Washington	DC	20005	202-434-8971	452-8620	48-1
American Academy McAllister Institute of Funeral Service 619 W 54th St 2nd Fl *TF:* 866-932-2264 ■ *Web:* www.funeraleducation.org	New York	NY	10019	212-757-1190	765-5923	800
American Academy of Actuaries 1100 17th St NW 7th Fl *Web:* www.actuary.org	Washington	DC	20036	202-223-8196	872-1948	49-9
American Academy of Addiction Psychiatry (AAAP) 400 Massasoit Ave 2nd Fl Ste 307 *TF:* 800-263-6317 ■ *Web:* www.aaap.org	East Providence	RI	02914	401-524-3076	272-0922	49-15
American Academy of Allergy Asthma & Immunology (AAAAI) 555 E Wells St Ste 1100 *TF:* 800-654-2452 ■ *Web:* www.aaaai.org	Milwaukee	WI	53202	414-272-6071	272-6070	49-8
American Academy of Art 332 S Michigan Ave 3rd Fl *TF:* 888-461-0600 ■ *Web:* www.aaart.edu	Chicago	IL	60604	312-461-0600	294-9570	164
American Academy of Arts & Letters 633 W 155th St *Web:* www.artsandletters.org	New York	NY	10032	212-368-5900		48-4
American Academy of Arts & Sciences 136 Irving St *TF:* 800-666-2211 ■ *Web:* www.amacad.org	Cambridge	MA	02138	617-576-5000	576-5050	48-4
American Academy of Audiology (AAA) 11730 Plaza America Dr Ste 300 *TF:* 800-222-2336 ■ *Web:* www.audiology.org	Reston	VA	20190	703-790-8466	790-8631	49-8
American Academy of Child & Adolescent Psychiatry (AACAP) 3615 Wisconsin Ave NW *TF:* 800-333-7636 ■ *Web:* www.aacap.org	Washington	DC	20016	202-966-7300	966-2891	49-15
American Academy of Cosmetic Dentistry (AACD) 402 W Wilson St *TF:* 800-543-9220 ■ *Web:* www.aacd.com	Madison	WI	53703	608-222-8583	222-9540	49-8
American Academy of Cosmetic Surgery (AACS) 225 W Wacker Dr Ste 650 *Web:* www.cosmeticsurgery.org	Chicago	IL	60606	312-981-6760	981-6787	49-8
American Academy of Dental Group Practice (AADGP) 2525 E Arizona Biltmore Cir Ste 127 *TF:* 800-475-2098 ■ *Web:* www.aadgp.org	Phoenix	AZ	85016	602-381-1185	381-1093	49-8
American Academy of Dermatology (AAD) 930 E Woodfield Rd *TF:* 800-868-2472 ■ *Web:* www.aad.org	Schaumburg	IL	60173	847-330-0230	330-0050	49-8
American Academy of Disability Evaluating Physicians (AADEP) 223 W Jackson Blvd Ste 1104 *TF:* 800-456-6095 ■ *Web:* www.iaime.org	Chicago	IL	60606	312-663-1171	663-1175	49-8
American Academy of Dramatic Arts 120 Madison Ave *TF:* 800-463-8990 ■ *Web:* aada.edu	New York	NY	10016	212-686-9244		164
American Academy of English 530 Golden Gate Ave *Web:* www.aae.edu	San Francisco	CA	94102	415-567-0189	567-1475	423
American Academy of Environmental Engineers 130 Holiday Ct Ste 100	Annapolis	MD	21401	410-266-3311		48-12
American Academy of Facial Plastic & Reconstructive Surgery (AAFPRS) 310 S Henry St *Web:* aafprs.org	Alexandria	VA	22314	703-299-9291	299-8898	49-8
American Academy of Family Physicians (AAFP) 11400 Tomahawk Creek Pkwy *TF:* 800-274-2237 ■ *Web:* www.aafp.org	Leawood	KS	66211	913-906-6000	906-6075	49-8
American Academy of Home Care Physicians (AAHCP) PO Box 1037 *Web:* aahcm.org	Edgewood	MD	21040	410-676-7966	676-7980	49-8
American Academy of Hospice & Palliative Medicine (AAHPM) 4700 West Lake Ave *Web:* www.aahpm.org	Glenview	IL	60025	847-375-4712		49-8
American Academy of Medical Acupuncture (AAMA) 1970 E Grand Ave Ste 330 *Web:* www.medicalacupuncture.org	El Segundo	CA	90245	310-364-0193		48-17
American Academy of Neurology (AAN) 1080 Montreal Ave *TF:* 800-879-1960 ■ *Web:* www.aan.com	Saint Paul	MN	55116	651-695-1940	695-2791	49-8
American Academy of Nurse Practitioners (AANP) PO Box 12846 *TF:* 800-981-2491 ■ *Web:* www.aanp.org	Austin	TX	78711	512-442-4262	442-6469	49-8
American Academy of Ophthalmology Governmental Affairs Div 20 F St NW Ste 400 *TF:* 866-561-8558 ■ *Web:* www.aao.org	Washington	DC	20001	202-737-6662	737-7061	615
American Academy of Ophthalmology 655 Beach St *TF:* 866-561-8558 ■ *Web:* www.aao.org	San Francisco	CA	94109	415-561-8500	561-8575	49-8
American Academy of Optometry (AAO) 6110 Executive Blvd Ste 506 *Web:* www.aaopt.org	Rockville	MD	20852	301-984-1441	984-4737	49-8
American Academy of Orthopaedic Surgeons (AAOS) 6300 N River Rd *TF:* 800-346-2267 ■ *Web:* www.aaos.org	Rosemont	IL	60018	847-823-7186	823-8125	49-8
American Academy of Orthotists & Prosthetists (AAOP) 1331 H St NW Ste 501 *Web:* www.oandp.org	Washington	DC	20005	202-380-3663	380-3447	49-8
American Academy of Otolaryngology-Head & Neck Surgery (AAO-HNS) 1650 Diagonal Rd *TF:* 877-722-6467 ■ *Web:* www.entnet.org	Alexandria	VA	22314	703-836-4444	683-5100	49-8
American Academy of Pain Management (AAPM) 13947 Mono Way Ste A *TF:* 888-519-9901 ■ *Web:* www.aapainmanage.org	Sonora	CA	95370	209-533-9744	533-9750	49-8

				Phone	Fax	Class
American Academy of Pediatric Dentistry (AAPD) 211 E Chicago Ave Ste 1600 *TF:* 800-974-3084 ■ *Web:* www.aapd.org	Chicago	IL	60611	312-337-2169	337-6329	49-8
American Academy of Pediatrics (AAP) 141 NW Pt Blvd *TF:* 800-433-9016 ■ *Web:* www.aap.org	Elk Grove Village	IL	60007	847-434-4000	434-8000	49-8
American Academy of Periodontology (AAP) 737 N Michigan Ave Ste 800 *TF:* 800-282-4867 ■ *Web:* www.perio.org	Chicago	IL	60611	312-787-5518	787-3670	49-8
American Academy of Physical Medicine & Rehabilitation (AAPM&R) 9700 W Bryn Mawr Ave Ste 200 *Web:* www.aapmr.org	Rosemont	IL	60018	847-737-6000		49-8
American Academy of Physician Assistants (AAPA) 2318 Mill Rd Ste 1300 *Web:* www.aapa.org	Alexandria	VA	22314	703-836-2272	684-1924	615
American Academy of Physician Assistants (AAPA) 950 N Washington St *TF:* 800-692-2326 ■ *Web:* www.aapa.org	Alexandria	VA	22314	703-836-2272	684-1924	49-8
American Academy of Psychiatry & the Law (AAPL) 1 Regency Dr PO Box 30 *TF:* 800-331-1389 ■ *Web:* www.aapl.org	Bloomfield	CT	06002	860-242-5450	286-0787	49-15
American Academy of Religion (AAR) 825 Houston Mill Rd NE Ste 300 *Web:* www.aarweb.org	Atlanta	GA	30329	404-727-3049	727-7959	48-20
American Academy of Sleep Medicine (AASM) 2510 N Frontage Rd Ste 920 *Web:* www.aasmnet.org	Darien	IL	60561	708-492-0930	492-0943	48-17
American Accessories International Inc 550 W Main St Ste 825 *Web:* americanaccessoriesintl.com	Knoxville	TN	37902	865-525-9100		361
American Accounts & Advisers PO Box 250 *TF:* 866-714-0489 ■ *Web:* www.amaccts.com	Cottage Grove	MN	55016	651-287-6100	287-6190	160
American Acctg Assn 5717 Bessie Dr *Web:* www.aaahq.org	Sarasota	FL	34233	941-921-7747	923-4093	49-1
American Achievement Corp 7211 Cir S Rd *TF:* 800-531-5055 ■ *Web:* www.artcarved.com	Austin	TX	78745	512-444-0571		409
American Acrylic Corp 400 Sheffield Ave *Web:* www.americanacrylic.com	West Babylon	NY	11704	631-422-2200		596
American Actuator Corp (AAC) 89 Selleck St *Web:* www.americanactuator.com	Stamford	CT	06902	203-324-6334		456
American Adoption Congress (AAC) PO Box 42730 *TF:* 800-735-2929 ■ *Web:* www.americanadoptioncongress.org	Washington	DC	20015	202-483-3399		48-6
American Adv Federation (AAF) 1101 Vermont Ave NW Ste 500 *TF:* 800-999-2231 ■ *Web:* www.aaf.org	Washington	DC	20005	202-898-0089	898-0159	49-18
American Advisors Group 3800 W Chapman Ave 3rd Fl *TF:* 866-948-0003 ■ *Web:* www.americanadvisorsgroup.com	Orange	CA	92868	866-948-0003		215
American Aerogel Corp 460 Buffalo Rd Ste 200A *Web:* www.aerosafeglobal.com	Rochester	NY	14611	585-328-2140		480
American Aerospace Controls Inc 570 Smith St *TF:* 888-873-8559 ■ *Web:* www.a-a-c.com	Farmingdale	NY	11735	631-694-5100		256
American Aerospace Technologies INC 14 Union Hill Rd *Web:* americanaerospace.com	Conshohocken	PA	19428	610-225-2604		256
American AgCredit (ACA) PO Box 1120 *TF:* 800-800-4865 ■ *Web:* www.agloan.com	Santa Rosa	CA	95402	707-545-1200		216
American Agencies Company Inc 21 E Ogden Ave Ste 201	Westmont	IL	60559	630-493-1776	493-1781	160
American Agricultural Economics Assn (AAEA) 555 E Wells St Ste 1100 *Web:* www.aaea.org	Milwaukee	WI	53202	414-918-3190		48-2
American Agricultural Insurance Co 1501 E Woodfield Rd Ste 300 W *Web:* www.aaic.com	Schaumburg	IL	60173	847-969-2900	969-2752	391-4
American Agriculturist 5227-B Baltimore Pike *TF:* 800-441-1410 ■ *Web:* www.americanagriculturist.com	Littlestown	PA	17340	717-359-0150	359-0250	457-1
American Air Charter Inc 577 Bell Ave *TF:* 888-532-2710 ■ *Web:* www.americanaircharter.com	Chesterfield	MO	63005	636-532-2707	532-1486	13
American Air Distributing Inc 830 S Bolmar St *Web:* aa.com	West Chester	PA	19382	610-918-7090		610
American Aircraft Products Inc 15411 S Broadway *Web:* www.americanaircraft.com	Gardena	CA	90248	310-532-7434		697
American Airlines Arena 601 Biscayne Blvd *Web:* www.aaarena.com	Miami	FL	33132	786-777-1000		720
American Airlines CR Smith Museum 4601 Hwy 360 at FAA Rd *TF:* 877-277-6484 ■ *Web:* www.crsmithmuseum.org	Fort Worth	TX	76155	817-967-1560	967-5737	520
American Airlines Ctr 2500 Victory Ave *TF:* 800-745-3000 ■ *Web:* www.americanairlinescenter.com	Dallas	TX	75219	214-222-3687		720
American Airlines Employees Federal Credit Union 4151 Amon Carter Blvd PO Box 155489 *TF:* 800-533-0035 ■ *Web:* www.aacreditunion.org	Fort Worth	TX	76155	817-952-4500		219
American Airlines Inc 4333 Amon Carter Blvd **Fax:* Cust Svc ■ *TF:* 800-433-7300 ■ *Web:* www.aa.com	Fort Worth	TX	76155	817-963-1234	967-4162*	25
American Airlines Theatre 227 W 42nd St *Web:* www.roundabouttheatre.org	New York	NY	10036	212-719-1300	869-8817	747
American Alliance for Health Physical Education Recreation & Dance (AAH-PERD) 1900 Assn Dr *TF:* 800-213-7193 ■ *Web:* shapeamerica.org	Reston	VA	20191	703-476-3400	476-9527	48-22
American Alloy Fabrication Inc 2842 Jordan Ln NW *Web:* www.americanalloy.com	Huntsville	AL	35816	256-837-6369		295

	Phone	Fax	Class
American Alpine Club 710 Tenth St Ste 15 .... Golden CO 80401 *Web:* americanalpineclub.org	303-384-0112		434-3
American Aluminum Co 230 Sheffield St .... Mountainside NJ 07092 *TF:* 800-257-8174 ■ *Web:* www.amalco.com	908-233-3500	233-3241	482
American Aluminum Extrusion Company LLC 5253 McCurry Rd .... Roscoe IL 61073 *TF:* 877-896-2236 ■ *Web:* www.americanaluminum.com	815-525-3100	525-3101	492
American Amateur Baseball Congress (AABC) 100 W Broadway .... Farmington NM 87401 *Web:* www.aabc.us	505-327-3120		48-22
American Ambulance Assn (AAA) 8400 Westpark Dr Fl 2 .... McLean VA 22102 *TF:* 800-523-4447 ■ *Web:* www.the-aaa.org	703-610-9018		49-21
American Ambulance Service Inc 1 American Way .... Norwich CT 06360 *TF:* 800-394-2533 ■ *Web:* www.americanamb.com	860-886-1463		30
American Amicable Life Insurance Co PO Box 2549 .... Waco TX 76702 *TF:* 800-736-7311 ■ *Web:* americanamicable.com	254-297-2777		391-2
American Amusement Machine Assn (AAMA) 450 E Higgins Rd Ste 201 .... Elk Grove Village IL 60007 *Web:* www.coin-op.org	847-290-9088	290-9121	48-23
American Angus Assn (AAA) 3201 Frederick Ave .... Saint Joseph MO 64506 *TF:* 800-821-5478 ■ *Web:* www.angus.org	816-383-5100	233-9703	48-2
American Animal Care Center 37177 Fremont Blvd .... Fremont CA 94536	510-791-0464		794
American Animal Hospital Assn (AAHA) 12575 W Bayaud Ave .... Lakewood CO 80228 *TF:* 800-252-2242 ■ *Web:* www.aaha.org/default.aspx	303-986-2800	986-1700	48-3
American Anthropological Assn (AAA) 2200 Wilson Blvd Ste 600 .... Arlington VA 22201 *Web:* www.americananthro.org	703-528-1902	528-3546	49-5
American Antiquarian Society (AAS) 185 Salisbury St .... Worcester MA 01609 *Web:* www.americanantiquarian.org	508-755-5221	753-3311	48-4
American Antique Mall 3130 E Grant Rd .... Tucson AZ 85716 *Web:* www.americanantiquemall.com	520-326-3070		460
American Anti-Slavery Group, The 198 Tremont St .... Boston MA 02116 **Fax Area Code:* 270 ■ *TF:* 800-884-0719 ■ *Web:* www.iabolish.org	617-426-8161	964-2716*	48-5
American Apparel & Footwear Assn (AAFA) 740 sixth St NW 3rd and 4th Fl .... Washington DC 22209 **Fax Area Code:* 703 ■ *TF:* 800-520-2262 ■ *Web:* www.aafaglobal.org	202-853-9080	522-6741*	49-4
American Apparel LLC 747 Warehouse St .... Los Angeles CA 90021 *TF:* 888-747-0070 ■ *Web:* www.americanapparel.net	213-488-0226		155-12
American Arbitration Assn Inc (AAA) 1633 Broadway 10th Fl .... New York NY 10019 *TF:* 800-778-7879 ■ *Web:* www.adr.org	212-716-5800		41
American Architectural Manufacturers Assn (AAMA) 1827 Walden Office Sq Ste 550 .... Schaumburg IL 60173 *Web:* www.aamanet.org	847-303-5664	303-5774	49-3
American Arium 14811 Myford Rd .... Tustin CA 92780	714-731-1661		696
American Art Clay Co (AMACO) 6060 Guion Rd .... Indianapolis IN 46254 *TF:* 800-374-1600 ■ *Web:* www.amaco.com	317-244-6871	248-9300	43
American Artists Group Inc PO Box 49313 .... Athens GA 30604 **Fax Area Code:* 270 ■ *Web:* www.americanartistsgroup.com	706-227-0708	637-3105*	130
American Arts Alliance *Performing Arts Alliance* 1211 Connecticut Ave NW Ste 200 .... Washington DC 20036 *Web:* www.theperformingartsalliance.org	202-207-3850	833-1543	48-4
American Artstone Co 2025 N Broadway St .... New Ulm MN 56073 *TF:* 800-967-2076 ■ *Web:* www.american-artstone.com	507-233-3700		183
American Asphalt Paving Co 500 Chase Rd .... Shavertown PA 18708 *Web:* www.amerasphalt.com	570-696-1181	696-3486	46
American Assembly 475 Riverside Dr Ste 456 .... New York NY 10115 *Web:* www.americanassembly.org	212-870-3500	870-3555	634
American Assets Inc 11455 El Camino Real .... San Diego CA 92130 *Web:* www.americanassetstrust.com	858-350-2600		655
American Assn for Accreditation of Ambulatory Surgery Facilities Inc (AAAASF) 5101 Washington St Ste 2F PO Box 9500 .... Gurnee IL 60031 *TF:* 888-545-5222 ■ *Web:* www.aaaasf.org	847-775-1985		48-1
American Assn for Adult & Continuing Education (AAACE) 1827 Powers Ferry Rd Bldg 14 Ste 100 .... Atlanta GA 30339 *Web:* www.aaace.org	678-271-4319		49-5
American Assn for Cancer Research (AACR) 615 Chestnut St 17th Fl .... Philadelphia PA 19106 *TF:* 866-423-3965 ■ *Web:* www.aacr.org	215-440-9300		49-8
American Assn for Clinical Chemistry Inc (AACC) 1850 K St NW Ste 625 .... Washington DC 20006 *TF Cust Svc:* 800-892-1400 ■ *Web:* www.aacc.org	202-857-0717	887-5093	49-19
American Assn for Geriatric Psychiatry (AAGP) 7910 Woodmont Ave Ste 1050 .... Bethesda MD 20814 *Web:* www.aagponline.org	301-654-7850	654-4137	49-15
American Assn for Justice (AAJ) 777 Sixth St NW Ste 200 .... Washington DC 20001 *TF:* 800-424-2725 ■ *Web:* www.justice.org	202-965-3500		49-10
American Assn for Justice PAC 777 Sixth St NW Ste 200 .... Washington DC 20001 *TF:* 800-622-1791 ■ *Web:* www.justice.org	202-965-3500		615
American Assn for Marriage & Family Therapy (AAMFT) 112 S Alfred St .... Alexandria VA 22314 *Web:* www.aamft.org	703-838-9808	838-9805	48-6
American Assn for Respiratory Care (AARC) 9425 N MacArthur Blvd Ste 100 .... Irving TX 75063 *TF:* 800-272-3900 ■ *Web:* www.aarc.org	972-243-2272	484-2720	49-8
American Assn for State & Local History (AASLH) 1717 Church St .... Nashville TN 37203 *Web:* www.aaslh.org	615-320-3203	327-9013	48-4
American Assn for the Advancement of Science (AAAS) 1200 New York Ave NW .... Washington DC 20005 *Web:* www.aaas.org	202-326-6400	682-0816	49-19
American Assn for Thoracic Surgery (AATS) 900 Cummings Ctr Ste 221-U .... Beverly MA 01915 *TF:* 800-424-5249 ■ *Web:* www.aats.org	978-927-8330	522-8469	49-8
American Assn of Acupunture & Oriental Medicine (AAAOM) PO Box 162340 .... Sacramento CA 95816 *TF:* 866-455-7999 ■ *Web:* www.aaaomonline.org	916-443-4770		48-17
American Assn of Adv Agencies (AAAA) 1065 Ave of the Americas 16th Fl .... New York NY 10018 *TF:* 800-537-4180 ■ *Web:* www.aaaa.org	212-682-2500	682-8391	49-18
American Assn of Airport Executives (AAAE) 601 Madison St Ste 400 .... Alexandria VA 22314 *TF:* 800-609-7374 ■ *Web:* www.aaae.org	703-824-0500	820-1395	49-21
American Assn of Cereal Chemists Inc (AACC) 3340 Pilot Knob Rd .... Saint Paul MN 55121 *TF:* 800-328-7560 ■ *Web:* www.aaccnet.org/default.aspx	651-454-7250	454-0766	49-6
American Assn of Colleges for Teacher Education (AACTE) 1307 New York Ave NW Ste 300 .... Washington DC 20005 *Web:* www.aacte.org	202-293-2450	457-8095	49-5
American Assn of Colleges of Nursing (AACN) 1 Dupont Cir NW Ste 530 .... Washington DC 20036 *Web:* www.aacn.nche.edu	202-463-6930	785-8320	49-5
American Assn of Colleges of Osteopathic Medicine (AACOM) 5550 Friendship Blvd Ste 310 .... Chevy Chase MD 20815 *TF:* 800-356-7836 ■ *Web:* www.aacom.org	301-968-4100	968-4101	49-8
American Assn of Colleges of Podiatric Medicine (AACPM) 15850 Crabbs Branch Way Ste 320 .... Rockville MD 20855 *Web:* www.aacpm.org	301-948-9760	948-1928	49-8
American Assn of Collegiate Registrars & Admissions Officers (AACRAO) 1 Dupont Cir NW Ste 520 .... Washington DC 20036 *TF:* 800-222-4922 ■ *Web:* www.aacrao.org	202-293-9161	872-8857	49-5
American Assn of Critical-Care Nurses (AACN) 101 Columbia .... Aliso Viejo CA 92656 *TF:* 800-809-2273 ■ *Web:* www.aacn.org	949-362-2000	362-2020	49-8
American Assn of Crop Insurers (AACI) 1 Massachusetts Ave NW Ste 800 .... Washington DC 20001 *Web:* www.cropinsurers.com	202-789-4100	408-7763	49-9
American Assn of Daily Money Managers (AADMM) 174 Crestview Dr .... Bellefonte PA 16823 **Fax Area Code:* 814 ■ *TF:* 877-326-5991 ■ *Web:* www.aadmm.com	877-326-5991	355-2452*	49-2
American Assn of Endodontists (AAE) 211 E Chicago Ave Ste 1100 .... Chicago IL 60611 *TF:* 800-872-3636 ■ *Web:* www.aae.org	312-266-7255	266-9867	49-8
American Assn of Engineering Societies (AAES) 1620 'I' St NW Ste 210 .... Washington DC 20006 *TF Orders:* 888-400-2237 ■ *Web:* www.aaes.org	202-296-2237	296-1151	49-19
American Assn of Equine Practitioners (AAEP) 4075 Iron Works Pkwy .... Lexington KY 40511 *TF:* 800-443-0177 ■ *Web:* www.aaep.org	859-233-0147	233-1968	48-3
American Assn of Family & Consumer Sciences (AAFCS) 400 N Columbus St Ste 202 .... Alexandria VA 22314 *TF:* 800-424-8080 ■ *Web:* www.aafcs.org	703-706-4600	706-4663	49-5
American Assn of Franchisees & Dealers (AAFD) PO Box 10158 .... Palm Desert CA 92255 **Fax Area Code:* 866 ■ *TF:* 800-733-9858 ■ *Web:* www.aafd.org	619-209-3775	855-1988*	49-18
American Assn of Gynecological Laparoscopists (AAGL) 6757 Katella Ave .... Cypress CA 90630 *TF:* 800-554-2245 ■ *Web:* www.aagl.org	714-503-6200	503-6201	49-8
American Assn of Immunologists (AAI) 9650 Rockville Pike .... Bethesda MD 20814 *Web:* www.aai.org	301-634-7178	634-7887	49-8
American Assn of Individual Investors (AAII) 625 N Michigan Ave Ste 1900 .... Chicago IL 60611 *TF:* 800-428-2244 ■ *Web:* www.aaii.com	312-280-0170	280-9883	49-2
American Assn of Insurance Services (AAIS) 1745 S Naperville Rd .... Wheaton IL 60189 *TF:* 800-564-2247 ■ *Web:* www.aaisonline.com	630-681-8347	681-8356	49-9
American Assn of Integrated Healthcare Delivery Systems Inc (AAIHDS) 4435 Waterfront Dr Ste 101 .... Glen Allen VA 23060 *TF:* 888-491-8833 ■ *Web:* www.aaihds.org	804-747-5823	747-5316	49-8
American Assn of Law Libraries (AALL) 53 W Jackson Blvd Ste 940 .... Chicago IL 60604 *TF:* 800-285-2221 ■ *Web:* www.aallnet.org	312-939-4764	431-1097	49-11
American Assn of Managing General Agents (AAMGA) 610 Freedom Business Ctr Ste 110 .... King of Prussia PA 19406 *Web:* www.aamga.org	610-992-0022	992-0021	49-9
American Assn of Medical Assistants (AAMA) 20 N Wacker Dr Ste 1575 .... Chicago IL 60606 *TF:* 800-228-2262 ■ *Web:* www.aama-ntl.org	312-899-1500	899-1259	49-8
American Assn of Medical Review Officers (AAMRO) PO Box 12873 .... Research Triangle Park NC 27709 *TF:* 800-489-1839 ■ *Web:* www.aamro.com	919-489-5407	490-1010	49-8
American Assn of Medical Society Executives (AAMSE) 1000 Westgate Dr Ste 252 .... St. Paul MN 55114 *Web:* www.aamse.org	651-288-3432	290-2266	49-8
American Assn of Motor Vehicle Administrators (AAMVA) 4301 Wilson Blvd Ste 400 .... Arlington VA 22203 *TF:* 800-221-9253 ■ *Web:* www.aamva.org	703-522-4200	522-1553	49-7
American Assn of Museums (AAM) 1575 Eye St NW Ste 400 .... Washington DC 20005 *TF:* 866-226-2150 ■ *Web:* www.aam-us.org	202-289-1818	289-6578	48-4
American Assn of Naturopathic Physicians (AANP) 818 18th St Ste 250 .... Washington DC 20006 *TF:* 866-538-2267 ■ *Web:* www.naturopathic.org	202-237-8150	237-8152	48-17
American Assn of Neurological Surgeons (AANS) 5550 Meadowbrook Dr .... Rolling Meadows IL 60008 *TF:* 888-566-2267 ■ *Web:* www.aans.org	847-378-0500	378-0600	49-8
American Assn of Neuromuscular & Electrodiagnostic Medicine (AANEM) 2621 Superior Dr NW .... Rochester MN 55901 *TF:* 844-347-3277 ■ *Web:* www.aanem.org	507-288-0100	288-1225	49-8
American Assn of Neuroscience Nurses (AANN) 4700 West Lake Ave .... Glenview IL 60025 *TF:* 888-557-2266 ■ *Web:* www.aann.org	847-375-4733	375-6430	49-8
American Assn of Nurse Anesthetists (AANA) 222 S Prospect Ave .... Park Ridge IL 60068 *TF:* 855-526-2262 ■ *Web:* www.aana.com	847-692-7050	692-6968	49-8

	Phone	Fax	Class
American Assn of Oral & Maxillofacial Surgeons (AAOMS) 9700 W Bryn Mawr Ave .... Rosemont IL 60018 *TF:* 800-822-6637 ■ *Web:* www.aaoms.org	847-678-6200	678-6286	49-8
American Assn of Orthodontists (AAO) 401 N Lindbergh Blvd. .... Saint Louis MO 63141 *TF:* 800-424-2841 ■ *Web:* www.mylifemysmile.org	314-993-1700		49-8
American Assn of Orthodontists PAC 401 N Lindbergh Blvd. .... Saint Louis MO 63141 *TF:* 800-424-2841 ■ *Web:* www.aaoinfo.org	314-993-1700	997-1745	615
American Assn of Pharmaceutical Scientists (AAPS) 2107 Wilson Blvd Ste 700 .... Arlington VA 22201 *TF:* 877-998-2277 ■ *Web:* www.aaps.org	703-243-2800	243-9650	49-19
American Assn of Physics Teachers (AAPT) 1 Physics Ellipse .... College Park MD 20740 *TF:* 800-446-8923 ■ *Web:* www.aapt.org	301-209-3311	209-0845	49-5
American Assn of Poison Control Centers (AAPCC) 3201 New Mexico Ave Ste 310 .... Washington DC 20016 *TF:* 800-222-1222 ■ *Web:* www.aapcc.org	800-222-1222		49-8
American Assn of Port Authorities (AAPA) 1010 Duke St .... Alexandria VA 22314 *Web:* www.aapa-ports.org	703-684-5700	684-6321	49-21
American Assn of Professional Landmen (AAPL) 4100 Fossil Creek Blvd. .... Fort Worth TX 76137 *TF:* 888-566-2275 ■ *Web:* www.landman.org	817-847-7700	847-7704	48-12
American Assn of School Administrators (AASA) 801 N Quincy St Ste 700 .... Arlington VA 22203 *TF:* 800-771-1162 ■ *Web:* www.aasa.org	703-528-0700	841-1543	49-5
American Assn of School Librarians (AASL) 50 E Huron St .... Chicago IL 60611 *TF:* 800-545-2433 ■ *Web:* www.ala.org/aasl	312-280-4386	664-7459	49-11
American Assn of State Colleges & Universities (AASCU) 1307 New York Ave NW 5th Fl .... Washington DC 20005 *TF:* 800-558-3417 ■ *Web:* www.aascu.org	202-293-7070	296-5819	49-5
American Assn of State Highway & Transportation Officials (AASHTO) 444 N Capitol St NW Ste 249 .... Washington DC 20001 *Web:* www.transportation.org	202-624-5800	624-5806	49-7
American Assn of Suicidology (AAS) 5221 Wisconsin Ave NW 2nd Fl .... Washington DC 20015 *Web:* www.suicidology.org	202-237-2280	237-2282	48-17
American Assn of Teachers of French (AATF) 302 N Granite St .... Marion IL 62959 *Web:* www.frenchteachers.org	618-453-5731		49-5
American Assn of Teachers of German (AATG) 112 Haddontowne Ct Ste 104 .... Cherry Hill NJ 08034 *TF:* 800-835-6770 ■ *Web:* www.aatg.org	856-795-5553	795-9398	49-5
American Assn of Teachers of Spanish & Portuguese (AATSP) 900 Ladd Rd .... Walled Lake MI 48390 *Web:* www.aatsp.org	248-960-2180	960-9570	49-5
American Assn of Textile Chemists & Colorists (AATCC) 1 Davis Dr PO Box 12215 .... Research Triangle Park NC 27709 *Web:* www.aatcc.org	919-549-8141	549-8933	49-13
American Assn of University Professors (AAUP) 1133 Nineteenth St Ste 200 .... Washington DC 20036 *TF:* 800-424-2973 ■ *Web:* www.aaup.org	202-737-5900	737-5526	49-5
American Assn of University Women (AAUW) 1111 16th St NW .... Washington DC 20036 *TF:* 800-326-2289 ■ *Web:* www.aauw.org	202-785-7700	872-1425	49-5
American Assn of Variable Star Observers (AAVSO) 49 Bay State Rd .... Cambridge MA 02138 *TF:* 888-802-7827 ■ *Web:* www.aavso.org	617-354-0484	354-0665	49-19
American Assn on Intellectual & Developmental Disabilities (AAIDD) 444 N Capitol St NW Ste 846 .... Washington DC 20001 *TF:* 800-424-3688 ■ *Web:* www.aaidd.org	202-387-1968	387-2193	48-17
American Association for Homecare 2011 Crystal Dr Ste 725 .... Arlington VA 22202 *TF:* 800-988-4484 ■ *Web:* www.aahomecare.org	703-836-6263	836-6730	49-8
American Association for Justice 777 Sixth St NW Ste 200 .... Washington DC 20001 *TF:* 800-424-2727 ■ *Web:* www.justice.org	202-965-3500	625-7084	531-7
American Association for Laboratory Accreditation (A2LA) 5301 Buckeystown Pike Ste 350 .... Frederick MD 21704 *TF:* 800-321-2211 ■ *Web:* www.a2la.org	301-644-3248	662-2974	49-19
American Association for Laboratory Animal Science (AALAS) 9190 Crestwyn Hills Dr .... Memphis TN 38125 *Web:* www.aalas.org	901-754-8620	753-0046	49-19
American Association for Physical Activity & Recreation (AAPAR) 1900 Assn Dr .... Reston VA 20191 *TF:* 800-213-7193 ■ *Web:* shapeamerica.org/aapar	703-476-3400	476-9527	48-23
American Association for the Study of Liver Diseases (AASLD) 1001 N Fairfax St Ste 400 .... Alexandria VA 22314 *Web:* www.aasld.org	703-299-9766	299-9622	49-8
American Association of Bioanalysts (AAB) 906 Olive St Ste 1200 .... Saint Louis MO 63101 *TF:* 800-457-3332 ■ *Web:* www.aab.org	314-241-1445	241-1449	49-8
American Association of Bovine Practitioners (AABP) 1130 E Main St Ste 302 .... Ashland OH 44805 *Web:* www.aabp.org	419-496-0685	496-0697	48-2
American Association of Clinical Endocrinologists (AACE) 245 Riverside Ave Ste 2000 .... Jacksonville FL 32202 *TF:* 800-435-7352 ■ *Web:* www.aace.com	904-353-7878	353-8185	49-8
American Association of Colleges of Nursing 1 Dupont Cir NW Ste 530 .... Washington DC 20036 *TF:* 800-441-1414 ■ *Web:* www.aacn.nche.edu	202-887-6791	887-8476	48-1
American Association of Community Colleges (AACC) 1 Dupont Cir NW Ste 410 .... Washington DC 20036 *Web:* www.aacc.nche.edu	202-728-0200	833-2467	49-5
American Association of Drugless Practitioners (AADP) 2200 Market St Ste 803 .... Galveston TX 77550 *TF:* 888-764-2237 ■ *Web:* www.aadp.net	409-621-2600		48-17
American Association of Exporters & Importers (AAEI) 1050 17th St NW Ste 810 .... Washington DC 20036 *Web:* www.aaei.org	202-857-8009	857-7843	49-18
American Association of Nurse Anesthetists PAC (AANAPAC) 222 S Prospect Ave. .... Park Ridge IL 60068 *TF:* 855-526-2262 ■ *Web:* aana.com	847-692-7050	692-6968	615
American Association of Petroleum Geologists (AAPG) 1444 S Boulder Ave PO Box 979 .... Tulsa OK 74119 *TF:* 800-364-2274 ■ *Web:* www.aapg.org	918-584-2555	560-2665	48-12

	Phone	Fax	Class
American Association of Physician Specialists Inc (AAPS) 5550 W Executive Dr Ste 400 .... Tampa FL 33609 *TF:* 800-232-3188 ■ *Web:* www.aapsus.org	813-433-2277	830-6599	49-8
American Association of Political Consultants (AAPC) 8400 W pk Dr 2nd Fl .... McLean VA 22102 *Web:* www.theaapc.org	703-245-8020		48-7
American Association of Preferred Provider Organizations (AAPPO) 974 Breckenridge Ln Ste 162 .... Louisville KY 40202 *Web:* nasho.org	502-403-1122	403-1129	49-8
American Association of Tissue Banks (AATB) 8200 Greensboro Dr Ste 320 .... McLean VA 22101 *TF:* 800-767-7643 ■ *Web:* www.aatb.org	703-827-9582	356-2198	49-8
American Astronomical Society (AAS) 2000 Florida Ave NW Ste 400 .... Washington DC 20009 *Web:* www.aas.org	202-328-2010	234-2560	49-19
American Athletic Inc (AAI) 200 American Ave .... Jefferson IA 50129 *TF:* 800-247-3978 ■ *Web:* www.americanathletic.com	800-247-3978		346
American Augers Inc 135 US Rt 42 .... West Salem OH 44287 *TF:* 800-324-4930 ■ *Web:* www.americanaugers.com	419-869-7107	869-7727	57
American Auto Accessories Inc 35-06 Leavitt St .... Flushing NY 11354 **Fax Area Code:* 347	718-886-6600	625-8600*	60
American Autoimmune Related Disease Assn (AARDA) 22100 Gratiot Ave .... Eastpointe MI 48021 *TF:* 800-598-4668 ■ *Web:* www.aarda.org	586-776-3900	776-3903	48-17
American Automatrix Inc 1 Technology Ln .... Export PA 15632 *Web:* www.aamatrix.com	724-733-2000		407
American Automobile Assn Inc (AAA) 1000 AAA Dr .... Heathrow FL 32746 *Web:* www.aaa.com	407-444-4240	444-4247	48-23
American Automobile Association, Inc. 321 Whittington Pkwy .... Louisville KY 40222 *TF:* 800-727-2552 ■ *Web:* www.aaa.com	502-582-3311	584-1455	53
American Aviation 2495 Broad St .... Brooksville FL 34604 *Web:* www.americanaviation.com	352-796-5173	799-4681	63
American Baby Magazine 375 Lexington Ave .... New York NY 10017 *Web:* www.parents.com	212-499-2000		457-11
American Backflow Specialties 3940 Home Ave .... San Diego CA 92105 *TF:* 800-662-5356 ■ *Web:* www.americanbackflow.com	619-527-2525		612
American Bakers Assn PAC 601 Pennsylvania Ave NW Ste 230 .... Washington DC 20004 *Web:* americanbakers.org	202-789-0300	898-1164	615
American Baler Co 800 E Centre St .... Bellevue OH 44811 *TF:* 800-843-7512 ■ *Web:* www.americanbaler.com	419-483-5790	483-3815	386
American Ballet Theatre (ABT) 890 Broadway 3rd Fl .... New York NY 10003 *Web:* www.abt.org	212-477-3030	254-5938	573-1
American Bank 4029 W Tilghman St .... Allentown PA 18104 *Web:* ambk.com	610-366-1800		70
American Bank Ctr 1901 N Shoreline Blvd .... Corpus Christi TX 78401 *TF:* 800-745-3000 ■ *Web:* www.americanbankcenter.com	361-826-4700	826-4905	205
American Bank of Commerce 610 W Fifth St .... Austin TX 78701 *Web:* www.theabcbank.com	512-391-5500		70
American Banker Magazine 1 State St Plaza 27th Fl .... New York NY 10004 *TF:* 800-221-1809 ■ *Web:* www.americanbanker.com	212-803-8200		457-5
American Bankers Assn (ABA) 1120 Connecticut Ave NW .... Washington DC 20036 *TF Cust Svc:* 800-226-5377 ■ *Web:* www.aba.com	202-663-5000		49-2
American Bankers Assn PAC (ABAPAC) 1120 Connecticut Ave NW .... Washington DC 20036 **Fax Area Code:* 202 ■ *TF:* 800-226-5377 ■ *Web:* www.aba.com/default.htm	800-226-5377	663-7544*	615
American Banknote Corp 2200 Fletcher Ave .... Fort Lee NJ 07024 *Web:* www.abnote.com	203-941-4090	496-4568	627
American Bankruptcy Institute (ABI) 66 Canal Ctr Plaza Ste 600 .... Alexandria VA 22314 *Web:* www.abi.org	703-739-0800	739-1060	49-10
American Baptist Assn (ABA) 4605 N State Line Ave .... Texarkana TX 75503 *TF:* 800-264-2482 ■ *Web:* www.abaptist.org	903-792-2783	792-8128	48-20
American Baptist Churches USA PO Box 851 .... Valley Forge PA 19482 *TF:* 800-222-3872 ■ *Web:* www.abc-usa.org	610-768-2000	768-2275	48-20
American Baptist College 1800 Baptist World Ctr Dr .... Nashville TN 37207 *Web:* www.abcnash.edu	615-256-1463		161
American Baptist News Service PO Box 851 .... Valley Forge PA 19482 *TF:* 800-222-3872 ■ *Web:* www.abc-usa.org	610-768-2000		530
American Baptist Seminary of the West 2606 Dwight Way .... Berkeley CA 94704 *Web:* www.absw.edu	510-841-1905	841-2446	167-3
American Bar Assn (ABA) 321 N Clark St .... Chicago IL 60654 *TF:* 800-285-2221 ■ *Web:* www.americanbar.org	312-988-5000		49-10
American Baseball Coaches Assn (ABCA) 108 S University Ave Ste 3 .... Mount Pleasant MI 48858 *Web:* www.abca.org	989-775-3300		48-22
American Battle Monuments Commission Courthouse Plaza II Ste 500 2300 Clarendon Blvd .... Arlington VA 22201 *Web:* www.abmc.gov	703-696-6900	696-6666	340-20
American Behavioral Benefits Managers 2204 Lakeshore Dr Ste 135 .... Birmingham AL 35209 *TF:* 800-925-5327 ■ *Web:* www.americanbehavioral.com	205-871-7814	868-9600	462
American Benefits Council 1501 M St NW Ste 600 .... Washington DC 20005 *TF:* 877-829-5500 ■ *Web:* www.americanbenefitscouncil.org	202-289-6700	289-4582	49-2
American Beverage Assn 1101 16th St NW .... Washington DC 20036 *Web:* www.ameribev.org	202-463-6732		49-6

Name / Address	City	State	Zip	Phone	Fax	Class
American Beverage Assn PAC 1101 16th St NW *Web:* www.ameribev.org	Washington	DC	20036	202-463-6732		615
American Beverage Corp 1 Daily Way *Web:* www.ambev.com	Verona	PA	15147	412-828-9020	828-3462	80-2
American Beverage Licensees (ABL) 5101 River Rd Ste 108 *Web:* www.ablusa.org	Bethesda	MD	20816	301-656-1494	656-7539	49-6
American Bible Society 1865 Broadway *TF:* 800-322-4253 ■ *Web:* www.americanbible.org	New York	NY	10023	212-408-1200	408-1512	637-3
American Bicycle Assn (ABA) 1645 W Sunrise Blvd *TF:* 866-650-4867 ■ *Web:* www.usabmx.com	Gilbert	AZ	85233	480-961-1903	961-1842	48-22
American Biltrite Inc 57 River St *OTC: ABLT* ■ *TF:* 800-284-3325 ■ *Web:* www.ambilt.com	Wellesley Hills	MA	02481	781-237-6655	237-6880	291
American Biltrite Inc Tape Products Div (ABI) 105 Whittendale Dr **Fax Area Code:* 888 ■ *TF:* 888-224-6325 ■ *Web:* www.abitape.com	Moorestown	NJ	08057	856-778-0700	224-6325*	732
American Bin & Conveyor Inc 221 Front St *Web:* www.americanconveyor.com	Burlington	WI	53105	262-763-0123		492
American Bio Medica Corp (ABMC) 122 Smith Rd *OTC: ABMC* ■ *TF General:* 800-227-1243 ■ *Web:* www.abmc.com	Kinderhook	NY	12106	518-758-8158	758-8172	85
American Biodiesel Inc 171 Saxony Rd Ste 202 *Web:* www.communityfuels.com	Encinitas	CA	92023	760-942-9306		579
American Biologics 1180 Walnut Ave *TF:* 800-227-4473 ■ *Web:* www.americanbiologics.com	Chula Vista	CA	91911	619-429-8200	429-8004	419
American Blimp Corp 1900 NE 25th Ste 8 *Web:* www.americanblimp.com	Hillsboro	OR	97124	503-693-1611		20
American BOA Inc 1420 Redi Rd *TF:* 800-856-4580 ■ *Web:* www.americanboa.com	Cumming	GA	30040	770-889-9400		480
American Board Assembly Inc 5456 Endeavour Ct *Web:* www.americanboard.com	Moorpark	CA	93021	805-523-0274	523-1185	625
American Board of Internal Medicine (ABIM) 510 Walnut St Ste 1700 *TF:* 800-441-2246 ■ *Web:* www.abim.org	Philadelphia	PA	19106	215-446-3500	446-3590	48-1
American Board of Medical Specialties (ABMS) 353 N Clark St Ste 1400 *Web:* www.abms.org	Chicago	IL	60654	312-436-2600		48-1
American Boat & Yacht Council Inc (ABYC) 613 Third St Ste 10 *TF:* 800-678-4333 ■ *Web:* www.abycinc.org	Annapolis	MD	21403	410-990-4460	990-4466	49-21
American Boiler Manufacturers Assn (ABMA) 8221 Old Courthouse Rd Ste 207 *TF:* 800-227-1966 ■ *Web:* www.abma.com	Vienna	VA	22182	703-356-7172		49-13
American Bolt & Screw Manufacturing Corp 14650 Miller Ave Ste 200 *TF:* 800-325-0844 ■ *Web:* www.absfasteners.com	Fontana	CA	92336	909-390-0522		350
American Bonanza Society (ABS) 1922 Midfield Rd *Web:* www.bonanza.org	Wichita	KS	67206	316-945-1700	945-1710	48-18
American Book Co 11130 Kingston Pk Ste 1-183 *Web:* www.americanbookco.com	Knoxville	TN	37934	865-966-7454	675-0557	96
American Booksellers Assn (ABA) 200 White Plains Rd Ste 600 *TF:* 800-637-0037 ■ *Web:* www.bookweb.org	Tarrytown	NY	10591	914-591-2665	591-2720	49-18
American Borate Corp 5700 Cleveland St Ste 350 *TF:* 800-486-1072 ■ *Web:* www.americanborate.com	Virginia Beach	VA	23462	757-490-2242	490-1548	503-1
American Botanical Council 6200 Manor Rd *TF:* 800-373-7105 ■ *Web:* www.abc.herbalgram.org	Austin	TX	78723	512-926-4900	926-2345	48-17
American Boychoir School 19 Lambert Dr *TF:* 800-627-7468 ■ *Web:* www.americanboychoir.org	Princeton	NJ	08540	609-924-5858	924-5812	622
American Brain Tumor Assn (ABTA) 2720 River Rd *TF:* 800-886-2282 ■ *Web:* www.abta.org	Des Plaines	IL	60018	847-827-9910	827-9918	48-17
American Brass Manufacturing Co 5000 Superior Ave *TF:* 800-431-6440 ■ *Web:* www.americanbrass.com	Cleveland	OH	44103	216-431-6565	431-9420	609
American Bridge Co 1000 American Bridge Way **Fax: Acctg* ■ *Web:* www.americanbridge.net	Coraopolis	PA	15108	412-631-1000	631-2000*	180-4
American Bright Optoelectronics Corp 13815-C Magnolia Ave *Web:* www.americanbrightled.com	Chino	CA	91710	909-628-5050		253
American Broach & Machine Co 575 S Mansfield *Web:* www.americanbroach.com	Ypsilanti	MI	48197	734-961-0300	961-9999	493
American Broadband Communications LLC 153 W Dave Dugas Rd *Web:* www.americanbroadband.com	Sulphur	LA	70665	337-583-2111		387
American Brush Company Inc 300 Industrial Blvd *Web:* www.americanbrush.com	Claremont	NH	03743	603-542-9951		103
American Buckskin Registry Assn Inc (ABRA) 1141 Hartnell Ave *TF:* 800-458-4283 ■ *Web:* www.americanbuckskin.org	Redding	CA	96002	530-223-1420		48-3
American Building Supply Inc 8360 Elder Creek Rd *Web:* abs-hardware.com	Sacramento	CA	95828	916-503-4100		499
American Buildings Co 1150 State Docks Rd *TF:* 888-307-4338 ■ *Web:* www.americanbuildings.com	Eufaula	AL	36027	334-687-2032	688-2261	105
American Bullion Inc 12301 Wilshire Blvd Ste 650 *TF:* 800-326-9598 ■ *Web:* www.americanbullion.com	Los Angeles	CA	90025	310-689-7720		792
American Bureau of Shipping (ABS) 16855 Northchase Dr *Web:* www.eagle.org	Houston	TX	77060	281-877-5800	877-5803	49-21
American Burn Assn (ABA) 625 N Michigan Ave Ste 2550 *Web:* www.ameriburn.org	Chicago	IL	60611	312-642-9260	642-9130	49-8
American Business Conference (ABC) 1828 L St NW Ste 908 *Web:* www.americanbusinessconference.org	Washington	DC	20036	202-822-9300	467-4070	49-12
American Business Systems Inc 315 Littleton Rd **Fax Area Code:* 978 ■ *TF:* 800-356-4034 ■ *Web:* www.abs-software.com	Chelmsford	MA	01824	800-356-4034	250-8027*	178-1
American Business Women's Assn (ABWA) 11050 Roe Ave Ste 200 **Fax Area Code:* 913 ■ *TF:* 800-228-0007 ■ *Web:* www.abwa.org	Overland Park	KS	66211	800-228-0007	660-0101*	49-12
American Cabaret Theatre 121 Monument Cir Ste 516 *Web:* www.thecabaret.org	Indianapolis	IN	46204	317-275-1169		572
American Cable Company Inc 231 E Luzerne St *Web:* www.americancableco.com	Philadelphia	PA	19124	215-456-0700		116
American Camp Assn (ACA) 5000 State Rd 67 N *TF:* 800-428-2267 ■ *Web:* www.acacamps.org	Martinsville	IN	46151	765-342-8456	342-2065	48-23
American Campus Communities Inc 12700 Hill Country Blvd Ste T-200 *NYSE: ACC* ■ *Web:* www.americancampus.com	Austin	TX	78738	512-732-1000	732-2450	654
American Cancer Society (ACS) 250 William St NW *TF:* 800-227-2345 ■ *Web:* www.cancer.org	Atlanta	GA	30303	404-320-3333		48-17
American Cancer Society Hope Lodge of Baltimore 636 W Lexington St *TF:* 888-227-6333 ■ *Web:* www.cancer.org	Baltimore	MD	21201	410-547-2522		372
American Cancer Society Hope Lodge of Buffalo 197 Summer St *Web:* www.cancer.org	Buffalo	NY	14222	716-882-9244		372
American Cancer Society Hope Lodge of Charleston 269 Calhoun St *TF:* 800-227-2345 ■ *Web:* www.cancer.org	Charleston	SC	29401	843-958-0930	958-9054	372
American Cancer Society Hope Lodge of Marshfield 611 W Doege St *Web:* www.cancer.org	Marshfield	WI	54449	715-486-9100		372
American Cancer Society Hope Lodge of Rochester 411 Second St NW *Web:* www.cancer.org	Rochester	MN	55901	507-529-4673		372
American Cancer Society Hope Lodge Worcester 7 Oak St *TF:* 800-227-2345 ■ *Web:* www.cancer.org	Worcester	MA	01609	508-792-2985		372
American Cancer Society Joe Lee Griffin Hope Lodge 1104 Ireland Way *TF:* 800-227-2345 ■ *Web:* www.cancer.org	Birmingham	AL	35205	205-558-7860		372
American Cancer Society Joseph S. & Jeannette M. Silber Hope Lodge 11432 Mayfield Rd *Web:* www.cancer.org	Cleveland	OH	44106	216-844-4673		372
American Cancer Society Winn-Dixie Hope Lodge 250 Williams St NW *TF:* 800-227-2345 ■ *Web:* www.cancer.org	Atlanta	GA	30303	404-327-9200		372
American Canoe Assn (ACA) 503 Sophia St Ste 100 **Fax Area Code:* 888 ■ *TF:* 888-229-3792 ■ *Web:* www.americancanoe.org	Fredericksburg	VA	22401	540-907-4460	229-3792*	48-22
American Capital Group Inc 23382 Mill Creek Dr Ste 115 *TF:* 877-814-6871 ■ *Web:* www.acgcapital.com	Laguna Hills	CA	92653	949-271-5800		792
American Capital Partners LLC 205 Oser Ave *TF:* 800-393-0493 ■ *Web:* www.americancapitalpartners.com	Hauppauge	NY	11788	631-851-0918		401
American Capital Strategies Ltd 2 Bethesda Metro Ctr 14th Fl *NASDAQ: ACAS* ■ *Web:* www.americancapital.com	Bethesda	MD	20814	301-951-6122	654-6714	216
American Career College Inc 151 Innovation Dr *TF:* 877-832-0790 ■ *Web:* americancareercollege.edu	Irvine	CA	92617	949-783-4800		166
American Cargo Express Inc PO Box 483 *Web:* www.americancargoexpress.com	Elizabeth	NJ	07207	908-351-3400		449
American Carrier Equipment Trailer Sales LLC 2285 E Date Ave *TF:* 800-344-2174 ■ *Web:* www.americancarrierequipment.com	Fresno	CA	93706	559-442-1500		779
American Cast Iron Pipe Co (ACIPCO) 1501 31st Ave N *TF:* 800-442-2347 ■ *Web:* www.american-usa.com	Birmingham	AL	35207	205-325-7701		307
American Casting & Manufacturing Corp 51 Commercial St *TF:* 800-342-0333 ■ *Web:* seals.com	Plainview	NY	11803	516-349-7010	349-8389	326
American Cause, The 501 Church St Ste 315 *Web:* www.theamericancause.org	Vienna	VA	22180	703-255-2632	255-2219	48-7
American Cave Conservation Assn 119 E Main St *Web:* www.hiddenrivercave.com	Horse Cave	KY	42749	270-786-1466		48-13
American Century Investments Inc PO Box 419200 **Fax: Cust Svc* ■ *TF:* 800-345-2021 ■ *Web:* www.americancentury.com	Kansas City	MO	64141	816-531-5575	340-7962*	401
American Century Proprietary Holdings Inc PO Box 419200 *TF:* 800-345-2021 ■ *Web:* www.americancentury.com	Kansas City	MO	64141	816-531-5575		528
American Ceramic Society (ACerS) 600 N Cleveland Ave # 210 *TF:* 866-721-3322 ■ *Web:* www.ceramics.org	Westerville	OH	43082	614-890-4700	899-6109	48-4
American Certified Equipment Inc 1650 Swan Lake Rd *Web:* www.valveworksusa.com	Bossier City	LA	71111	318-425-0266		789
American Cetacean Society (ACS) 745 W Paseo Del Mar *Web:* www.acsonline.org	San Pedro	CA	90731	310-548-6279		48-3
American Chamber of Commerce Executives (ACCE) 4875 Eisenhower Ave Ste 250 *TF:* 800-394-2223 ■ *Web:* www.acce.org	Alexandria	VA	22304	703-998-0072	212-9512	49-12
American Chemet Corp 740 Waukegan Rd *TF:* 800-421-8661 ■ *Web:* www.chemet.com	Deerfield	IL	60015	847-948-0800	948-0811	143

Organization	Address	City	State	ZIP	Phone	Fax	Class	TF / Web
American Chemical Society (ACS)	1155 16th St NW	Washington	DC	20036	202-872-4600	872-4615	49-19	*TF:* 800-227-5558 ■ *Web:* www.acs.org
American Chiropractic Assn (ACA)	1701 Clarendon Blvd 2nd Fl	Arlington	VA	22209	703-276-8800	243-2593	49-8	*TF:* 800-986-4636 ■ *Web:* www.acatoday.org
American Chiropractic Assn PAC (ACA-PAC)	1701 Clarendon Blvd	Arlington	VA	22209	703-276-8800	243-2593	615	*TF:* 800-986-4636 ■ *Web:* www.acatoday.org
American Chiropractor, The	8619 NW 68Th St	Miami	FL	33166	888-369-1396		530	*TF:* 888-369-1396 ■ *Web:* www.theamericanchiropractor.com
American Choral Directors Assn (ACDA)	545 Couch Dr	Oklahoma City	OK	73102	405-232-8161	232-8162	48-4	*Web:* www.acda.org
American Chrome Co	518 W Crossroads Pkwy	Bolingbrook	IL	60440	630-685-2200		492	*TF:* 800-562-4488 ■ *Web:* www.americanchrome.com
American Chronic Pain Assn (ACPA)	PO Box 850	Rocklin	CA	95677	800-533-3231	652-8190*	48-17	**Fax Area Code:* 916 ■ *TF:* 800-533-3231 ■ *Web:* theacpa.org
American Cinematographer Magazine	1782 N Orange Dr	Los Angeles	CA	90028	323-969-4333	876-4973	457-9	*TF:* 800-448-0145 ■ *Web:* www.theasc.com
American City Business Journals Inc	120 W Morehead St Ste 400	Charlotte	NC	28202	704-973-1000		637-9	*Web:* www.bizjournals.com
American Civil Constructors Inc	4901 S Windemere St	Littleton	CO	80120	303-795-2582	347-1844	188-4	*Web:* www.accbuilt.com
American Civil Liberties Union (ACLU)	125 Broad St 18th Fl	New York	NY	10004	212-549-2500	549-2580	48-8	*TF:* 877-867-1025 ■ *Web:* www.aclu.org
American Classic Agency	201 Atp Tour Blvd	Ponte Vedra	FL	32082	904-285-4030		390	*Web:* www.aclassic.com
American Classic Sales	1142 South 2475 West	Salt Lake City	UT	84104	801-977-3935		710	
American Clay Enterprises LLC	2418 Second St SW	Albuquerque	NM	87102	505-243-5300		503-6	*TF:* 866-404-1634 ■ *Web:* www.americanclay.com
American Cleaning Solutions	39-30 Review Ave	Long Island	NY	11101	718-392-8080	482-9366	151	*TF:* 888-929-7587 ■ *Web:* www.cleaning-solutions.com
American Cleft Palate-Craniofacial Assn	1504 E Franklin St Ste 102	Chapel Hill	NC	27514	919-933-9044	933-9604	49-8	*Web:* www.acpa-cpf.org
American Clock & Watch Museum	100 Maple St	Bristol	CT	06010	860-583-6070		520	*TF:* 800-733-2767 ■ *Web:* www.clockmuseum.org
American Club, The	419 Highland Dr	Kohler	WI	53044	920-457-8000	457-0299	669	*TF:* 800-344-2838 ■ *Web:* www.americanclubresort.com
American Coach Limousine	1100 Jorie Blvd Ste 314	Oak Brook	IL	60523	630 620 0001		441	*TF:* 888-709-5466 ■ *Web:* www.americancoachlimousine.com
American Coal Ash Assn (ACAA)	15200 E Girard Ave Ste 3050	Aurora	CO	80014	720-870-7897	870-7889	48-12	*Web:* www.acaa-usa.org
American Coalition for Clean Coal Electricity (ACCCE)	1152 15th St NW Ste 400	Washington	DC	20005	202-459-4800		48-12	*Web:* americaspower.org
American Coalition for Fathers & Children (ACFC)	1718 M St NW Ste 1187	Washington	DC	20036	800-978-3237		48-6	*TF:* 800-978-3237 ■ *Web:* www.acfc.org
American Coil Spring Co	1041 E Keating Ave	Muskegon	MI	49442	231-726-4021		719	*TF:* 800-633-8078 ■ *Web:* americancoil.com
American Coin Merchandising Inc	325 Interlocken Pkwy	Broomfield	CO	80021	303-444-2559		55	
American Coke & Coal Chemicals Institute (ACCCI)	25 Massachusetts AveNW Ste 800	Washington	DC	20001	202-452-7198	463-6573	48-12	*Web:* www.accci.org
American College	270 S Bryn Mawr Ave	Bryn Mawr	PA	19010	610-526-1000	526-1300*	800	**Fax:* Admissions ■ *TF:* 888-263-7265 ■ *Web:* www.theamericancollege.edu
American College Health Assn (ACHA)	1362 Mellon Rd Ste 180	Hanover	MD	21076	410-859-1500	859-1510	49-8	*Web:* www.acha.org
American College of Allergy Asthma & Immunology (ACAAI)	85 W Algonquin Rd Ste 550	Arlington Heights	IL	60005	847-427-1200	427-1294	49-8	*Web:* www.acaai.org
American College of Cardiology (ACC)	2400 N St NW	Washington	DC	20037	202-375-6000	375-7000	49-8	*TF Cust Svc:* 800-253-4636 ■ *Web:* www.acc.org
American College of Chest Physicians (ACCP)	3300 Dundee Rd	Northbrook	IL	60062	847-498-1400	498-5460	49-8	*TF:* 800-343-2227 ■ *Web:* www.chestnet.org
American College of Clinical Pharmacy (ACCP)	13000 W 87th St Pkwy	Lenexa	KS	66215	913-492-3311	492-0088	49-8	*Web:* www.accp.com
American College of Dentists (ACD)	839J Quince Orchard Blvd Ste J	Gaithersburg	MD	20878	301-977-3223	977-3330	49-8	*Web:* www.acd.org
American College of Emergency Physicians (ACEP)	1125 Executive Cir PO Box 619911	Dallas	TX	75261	972-550-0911	580-2816	49-8	*TF:* 800-798-1822 ■ *Web:* www.acep.org
American College of Eye Surgeons/American Board of Eye Surgery (ACES)	334 E Lake Rd Ste 135	Palm Harbor	FL	34685	727-366-1487	836-9783	49-8	*TF:* 800-223-2233 ■ *Web:* www.aces-abes.org
American College of Foot & Ankle Surgeons (ACFAS)	8725 W Higgins Rd Ste 555	Chicago	IL	60631	773-693-9300	693-9304	49-8	*TF:* 800-421-2237 ■ *Web:* www.acfas.org
American College of Forensic Examiners International (ACFEI)	2750 E Sunshine St	Springfield	MO	65804	417-881-3818	881-4702	49-8	*TF:* 800-423-9737 ■ *Web:* www.acfei.com
American College of Gastroenterology (ACG)	6400 Goldsboro Rd Ste 450	Bethesda	MD	20817	301-263-9000	263-9025	49-8	*Web:* gi.org
American College of Healthcare Executives (ACHE)	1 N Franklin St Ste 1700	Chicago	IL	60606	312-424-2800	424-0023	49-8	*Web:* www.ache.org
American College of Managed Care Medicine (ACMCM)	4435 Waterfront Dr Ste 101	Glen Allen	VA	23060	804-527-1905	747-5316	49-8	*TF:* 888-491-8833 ■ *Web:* www.acmcm.org
American College of Musicians	808 Rio Grande St	Austin	TX	78701	512-478-5775		48-4	*Web:* www.pianoguild.com
American College of Nurse-Midwives (ACNM)	8403 Colesville Rd Ste 1550	Silver Spring	MD	20910	240-485-1800	485-1818	49-8	*TF:* 800-468-3571 ■ *Web:* www.midwife.org
American College of Nutrition	300 S Duncan Ave Ste 225	Clearwater	FL	33755	727-446-6086	446-6202	49-8	*Web:* americancollegeofnutrition.org
American College of Obstetricians & Gynecologists (ACOG)	409 12th St SW PO Box 96920	Washington	DC	20090	202-863-1648		49-8	*Web:* acog.org
American College of Occupational & Environmental Medicine (ACOEM)	25 NW Pt Blvd Ste 700	Elk Grove Village	IL	60007	847-818-1800	818-9266	49-8	*Web:* www.acoem.org
American College of Orgonomy	4419 Rt 27	Princeton	NJ	08545	732-821-1144	821-0174	766	*Web:* www.orgonomy.org
American College of Osteopathic Family Physicians (ACOFP)	330 E Algonquin Rd Ste 1	Arlington Heights	IL	60005	847-952-5100	228-9755	49-8	*TF:* 800-323-0794 ■ *Web:* www.acofp.org
American College of Physician Executives (ACPE)	400 N Ashley Dr Ste 400	Tampa	FL	33602	813-287-2000	287-8993	49-8	*TF:* 800-562-8088 ■ *Web:* www.physicianleaders.org
American College of Physicians (ACP)	190 N Independence Mall W	Philadelphia	PA	19106	215-351-2400	351-2594	49-8	*TF:* 800-523-1546 ■ *Web:* www.acponline.org
American College of Preventive Medicine (ACPM)	455 Massachusetts Ave NW	Washington	DC	20001	202-466-2044	466-2662	49-8	*Web:* www.acpm.org
American College of Psychiatrists	122 S Michigan Ave # 1360	Chicago	IL	60603	312-662-1020	662-1025	49-15	*TF:* 800-382-8270 ■ *Web:* www.acpsych.org
American College of Radiology (ACR)	1892 Preston White Dr	Reston	VA	20191	703-648-8900		49-8	*TF:* 800-227-5463 ■ *Web:* www.acr.org
American College of Rheumatology (ACR)	2200 Lake Blvd NE	Atlanta	GA	30319	404-633-3777	633-1870	49-8	*Web:* www.rheumatology.org
American College of Sports Medicine (ACSM)	401 W Michigan St PO Box 1440	Indianapolis	IN	46202	317-637-9200	634-7817	49-8	*Web:* www.acsm.org
American College of Surgeons (ACS)	633 N St Clair St	Chicago	IL	60611	312-202-5000	202-5001	49-8	*TF:* 800-621-4111 ■ *Web:* www.facs.org
American College of Trust & Estate Counsel (ACTEC)	901 15th St NW Ste 525	Washington	DC	20005	202-684-8460	684-8459	49-10	*Web:* www.actec.org
American College Personnel Assn (ACPA)	1 Dupont Cir NW Ste 300	Washington	DC	20036	202-835-2272	296-3286	49-5	*TF:* 800-228-5424 ■ *Web:* www.myacpa.org
American Combustion Industries Inc	7100 Holladay Tyler Rd Ste 233	Glenn Dale	MD	20769	301-779-3400		256	*Web:* www.aci.com
American Commerce Insurance Co	3590 Twin Creeks Dr	Columbus	OH	43204	614-308-3366	308-3365	391-4	*TF:* 800-848-2945 ■ *Web:* www.mapfreinsurance.com
American Commercial Barge Lines Inc	1701 E Market St	Jeffersonville	IN	47130	800-457-6377		314	*TF:* 800-457-6377 ■ *Web:* www.bargeacbl.com
American Composers Alliance Inc (ACA)	802 W 190th St Ste 1B	New York	NY	10040	212-925-0458		48-4	*Web:* www.composers.com
American Composers Orchestra	240 W 35th St Ste 405	New York	NY	10001	212-977-8495	977-8995	573-3	*Web:* www.americancomposers.org
American Composites Inc	9730 NW 114th Way	Medley	FL	33178	305-888-7281		22	*Web:* www.qualityfrp.com
American Composites Manufacturers Assn (ACMA)	3033 Wilson Blvd Ste 420	Arlington	VA	22201	703-525-0743	525-0743	49-13	*Web:* www.acmanet.org
American Computer & Digital Components	440 Cloverleaf Dr	Baldwin Park	CA	91706	626-336-1899		696	*Web:* www.acdi.com
American Concrete Institute International (ACI)	38800 Country Club Dr PO Box 9094	Farmington Hills	MI	48331	248-848-3700	848-3701	49-3	*Web:* www.concrete.org
American Concrete Pavement Assn (ACPA)	5420 Old OrchaRd Rd Ste A-100	Skokie	IL	60077	847-966-2272	966-9970	49-3	*TF:* 800-281-7899 ■ *Web:* www.acpa.org
American Concrete Pipe Assn	8445 Freeport Pkwy Ste 350	Irving	TX	75063	972-506-7216	506-7682	49-3	*Web:* www.concretepipe.org
American Conference of Governmental Industrial Hygienists (ACGIH)	1330 Kemper Meadows Dr	Cincinnati	OH	45240	513-742-2020	742-3355	49-7	*Web:* www.acgih.org
American Conservative Union, The (ACU)	1331 H St NW Ste 500	Washington	DC	20005	202-347-9388		48-7	*Web:* www.conservative.org
American Conservatory of Music	252 Wildwood Rd	Hammond	IN	46324	219-931-6000		166	*Web:* www.americanconservatory.edu
American Conservatory Theater (ACT)	30 Grant Ave 6th Fl	San Francisco	CA	94108	415-834-3200	749-2291	573-4	*Web:* www.act-sf.org
American Consulting Inc	7260 Shadeland Stn	Indianapolis	IN	46256	317-547-5580	543-0270	261	*Web:* www.structurepoint.com
American Consumer Industries Inc (ACI)	1105 N Market St Ste 1150	Wilmington	DE	19801	303-495-2665		787	*Web:* www.aciinc.net

Company	City	State	Zip	Phone	Fax	Class
American Consumers Inc 55 Hannah Way *Web:* shoprite-ga.com	Rossville	GA	30741	706-861-3347		345
American Contract Bridge League (ACBL) 6575 Windchase Blvd *TF Sales:* 800-264-2743 ■ *Web:* www.acbl.org	Horn Lake	MS	38637	662-253-3100	253-3187	48-18
American Converters Inc 5360 Main St NE *Web:* www.amconvas.com	Fridley	MN	55421	763-574-1044		601
American Coolair Corp 3604 Mayflower St *TF:* 877-250-2822 ■ *Web:* www.coolair.com	Jacksonville	FL	32205	904-389-3646	387-3449	14
American Cooling Technology Inc 715 Willow Springs Ln *Web:* www.actusa.us.com	York	PA	17406	717-767-2775		14
American Copak Corp 9175 Eton Ave *Web:* www.americancopak.com	Chatsworth	CA	91311	818-576-1000	882-1637	549
American Cord & Webbing Co 88 Century Dr *Web:* www.acw1.com	Woonsocket	RI	02895	401-762-5500	762-5514	745-5
American Correctional Assn (ACA) 206 N Washington St Ste 200 *TF:* 800-222-5646 ■ *Web:* www.aca.org	Alexandria	VA	22314	703-224-0000		49-7
American Corrugated Products Inc 4700 Alkire Rd *TF:* 800-248-6840	Columbus	OH	43228	614-870-2000		100
American Cotton Growers Textile Div (ACG) PO Box 2827 *TF:* 800-333-8011 ■ *Web:* pcca.com/services/denim	Lubbock	TX	79408	806-763-8011	762-7400	745-1
American Council for an Energy-Efficient Economy (ACEEE) 529 14th St NW Ste 600 *Web:* www.aceee.org	Washington	DC	20045	202-507-4000	429-2248	48-7
American Council for Capital Formation (ACCF) 1001 Connecticut Ave NW Ste 620 *Web:* www.accf.org	Washington	DC	20036	202-293-5811	785-8165	49-2
American Council for Construction Education (ACCE) 1717 N Loop 1604 E Ste 320 *Web:* www.acce-hq.org	San Antonio	TX	78232	210-495-6161	495-6168	48-1
American Council for Voluntary International Action 1400 16th St NW Ste 210 *Web:* www.interaction.org	Washington	DC	20036	202-667-8227	667-8236	48-5
American Council of Engineering Cos (ACEC) 1015 15th St NW 8th Fl *TF:* 800-338-1391 ■ *Web:* www.acec.org	Washington	DC	20005	202-347-7474	898-0068	49-19
American Council of Hypnotist Examiners 3435 Camino del Rio S Ste 316 **Fax Area Code:* 818 ■ *Web:* www.hypnotistexaminers.org	San Diego	CA	92108	619-280-7200	247-9379*	49-15
American Council of Independent Laboratories (ACIL) 1875 I St NW Ste 500 *TF:* 800-368-1131 ■ *Web:* www.acil.org	Washington	DC	20006	202-887-5872	887-0021	49-19
American Council of Life Insurers (ACLI) 101 Constitution Ave NW Ste 700 W *Web:* www.acli.com	Washington	DC	20001	202-624-2000		49-9
American Council of the Blind (ACB) 1155 15th St NW Ste 1004 *TF:* 800-424-8666 ■ *Web:* www.acb.org	Washington	DC	20005	202-467-5081	467-5085	48-17
American Council of the Blind (ACB) 2200 Wilson Blvd Ste 650 **Fax Area Code:* 703 ■ *TF:* 800-424-8666 ■ *Web:* www.acb.org	Arlington	VA	22201	202-467-5081	465-5085*	48-11
American Council on Education (ACE) 1 Dupont Cir NW Ste 800 *Web:* www.acenet.edu	Washington	DC	20036	202-939-9300	833-4760	49-5
American Council on Exercise (ACE) 4851 Paramount Dr *TF:* 800-825-3636 ■ *Web:* www.acefitness.org	San Diego	CA	92123	858-576-6500	576-6564	48-17
American Council on Science & Health (ACSH) 110 E 42nd St Ste 1300 *TF:* 866-905-2694 ■ *Web:* www.acsh.org	New York	NY	10017	212-362-7044	362-4919	49-19
American Council on the Teaching of Foreign Languages (ACTFL) 1001 N Fairfax St Ste 200 *TF:* 844-685-4373 ■ *Web:* www.actfl.org	Alexandria	VA	22314	703-894-2900	894-2905	49-5
American Councils for International Education 1776 Massachusetts Ave NW Ste 700 *Web:* www.americancouncils.org	Washington	DC	20036	202-833-7522	833-7523	49-5
American Counseling Assn (ACA) 5999 Stevenson Ave *TF:* 800-347-6647 ■ *Web:* www.counseling.org	Alexandria	VA	22304	703-823-9800	823-0252	49-15
American Craft Council 72 Spring St 6th Fl *TF:* 800-836-3470 ■ *Web:* www.craftcouncil.org	New York	NY	10012	212-274-0630		48-4
American Crane & Equipment Corp 531 Old Swede Rd **Fax:* Sales ■ *TF:* 877-877-6778 ■ *Web:* www.americancrane.com	Douglassville	PA	19518	610-385-6061	385-3191*	470
American Crane & Tractor Parts Inc 2200 State Line Rd *Web:* www.actparts.com	Kansas City	KS	66103	913-371-8585		54
American Cruise Lines 741 Boston Post Rd Ste 200 *TF:* 800-814-6880 ■ *Web:* www.americancruiselines.com	Guilford	CT	06437	203-453-6800	453-0417	221
American Crystal Sugar Co 101 Third St N *TF:* 800-774-2678 ■ *Web:* www.crystalsugar.com	Moorhead	MN	56560	218-236-4400		296-38
American Culinary Federation Inc (ACF) 180 Ctr Pl Way *TF:* 800-624-9458 ■ *Web:* www.acfchefs.org	Saint Augustine	FL	32095	904-824-4468	825-4758	49-6
American Custom Drying Co 109 Elbow Ln *Web:* www.americancustomdrying.com	Burlington	NJ	08016	609-387-3933		172
American Cybersystems Inc (ACS) 2400 Meadowbrook Pkwy **Fax Area Code:* 877 ■ *Web:* www.acsicorp.com	Duluth	GA	30096	770-493-5588	270-6248*	194
American Cylinder Company Inc 481 S Governors Hwy *Web:* www.americancylinder.com	Peotone	IL	60468	708-258-3935	258-3980	223
American Dairy Goat Assn (ADGA) 209 W Main St PO Box 865 *TF:* 800-306-8937 ■ *Web:* www.adga.org	Spindale	NC	28160	828-286-3801	287-0476	48-2
American Dairy Products Institute (ADPI) 116 N York St Ste 200 *Web:* www.adpi.org	Elmhurst	IL	60126	630-530-8700	530-8707	49-6
American Dairy Science Assn (ADSA) 1111 N Dunlap Ave *TF:* 888-670-2250 ■ *Web:* www.adsa.org	Savoy	IL	61874	217-356-5146	398-4119	48-2
American Dehydrated Foods Inc 3801 E Sunshine *TF:* 800-456-3447 ■ *Web:* www.adf.com	Springfield	MO	65809	417-881-7755		619
American Dental Assistants Assn (ADAA) 140 N Bloomingdale Rd *TF:* 877-874-3785 ■ *Web:* www.adaausa.org	Bloomingdale	IL	60108	312-541-1550		49-8
American Dental Assn (ADA) 211 E Chicago Ave *TF:* 800-621-8099 ■ *Web:* www.ada.org	Chicago	IL	60611	312-440-2500		49-8
American Dental Assn 1111 14th St NW Ste 1100 *TF:* 800-353-2237 ■ *Web:* www.ada.org	Washington	DC	20005	202-898-2424	898-2437	615
American Dental Education Assn (ADEA) 1400 K St NW Ste 1100 *TF:* 800-353-2237 ■ *Web:* www.adea.org	Washington	DC	20005	202-289-7201	289-7204	49-5
American Dental Hygienists' Assn (ADHA) 444 N Michigan Ave Ste 3400 *TF:* 800-243-2342 ■ *Web:* www.adha.org	Chicago	IL	60611	312-440-8900	467-1806	49-8
American Dental Partners Inc 401 Edgewater Pl Ste 430 *NASDAQ: ADPI* ■ *TF:* 800-838-6563 ■ *Web:* www.amdpi.com	Wakefield	MA	01880	781-213-6500	224-4216	463
American Derringer Corp 127 N Lacy Dr *TF:* 800-575-0535 ■ *Web:* www.amderringer.com	Waco	TX	76705	254-799-9111	799-7935	284
American Design Drafting Assn (ADDA) 105 E Main St *Web:* www.adda.org	Newbern	TN	38059	731-627-0802	627-9321	48-4
American Diabetes Assn (ADA) 1701 N Beauregard St *TF:* 800-232-3472 ■ *Web:* www.diabetes.org	Alexandria	VA	22311	703-549-1500		48-17
American Die Technology Inc 3870 Lakefield Dr *Web:* www.amdie.com	Suwanee	GA	30024	770-623-6111		567
American Direct Mail Corp 350 Hudson St *Web:* www.americandirectmarketing.com	New York	NY	10014	212-924-5400		629
American Direct Procurement Inc 11000 Lakeview Ave *Web:* www.americandirectco.com	Lenexa	KS	66219	913-677-5588		191-3
American Distilling & Mfg Company Inc 31 E High St *Web:* www.americandistilling.com	East Hampton	CT	06424	860-267-4444		583
American Donkey & Mule Society (ADMS) PO Box 1210 *Web:* www.lovelongears.com	Lewisville	TX	75067	972-219-0781	420-9980	48-3
American Douglas Metals Inc 783 Thorpe Rd *TF:* 800-428-0023 ■ *Web:* www.americandouglasmetals.com	Orlando	FL	32824	407-855-6590	857-3290	492
American Drill Bushings Co (ADB) 5740 Hunt Rd *TF:* 800-423-4425 ■ *Web:* www.americandrillbushing.com	Valdosta	GA	31606	229-253-8928	253-8929	493
American Dryer Corp 88 Currant Rd *Web:* adclaundry.com	Fall River	MA	02720	508-678-9000	678-9447	427
American Dynamics Flight Systems Inc 8264 Preston Ct Ste A *Web:* www.adflightsystems.com	Jessup	MD	20794	301-358-0747		21
American Eagle Energy Corp 2549 W Main St Ste 202	Littleton	CO	80120	303-798-5235		536
American Eagle Federal Credit Union 417 Main St *TF:* 800-842-0145 ■ *Web:* www.americaneagle.org	East Hartford	CT	06118	860-568-2020	568-2020	219
American Eagle Outfitters Inc 77 Hot Metal St *NYSE: AEO* ■ *TF Cust Svc:* 888-232-4535 ■ *Web:* www.ae.com	Pittsburgh	PA	15203	412-432-3300		157-4
American Eagle Steel Corp 716 Giddings Ave *Web:* www.americaneaglesteel.com	Annapolis	MD	21401	410-573-0335		791
American Economic Assn (AEA) 2014 Broadway Ste 305 *Web:* www.aeaweb.org	Nashville	TN	37203	615-322-2595	343-7590	49-2
American Ecotech LLC 100 Elm St Factory D *TF:* 877-247-0403 ■ *Web:* www.americanecotech.com	Warren	RI	02885	877-247-0403		196
American Educational Products Inc 401 Hickory St PO Box 2121 *TF:* 800-289-9299 ■ *Web:* www.amep.com	Fort Collins	CO	80522	970-484-7445	484-1198	243
American Educational Research Assn (AERA) 1430 K St NW Ste 1200 *TF:* 800-893-7950 ■ *Web:* www.aera.net	Washington	DC	20005	202-238-3200	238-3250	49-5
American Educator Magazine 555 New Jersey Ave NW *TF:* 800-238-1133 ■ *Web:* www.aft.org	Washington	DC	20001	202-879-4400		457-8
American Egg Board (AEB) 8755 W Higgins Rd Ste 300 *TF:* 888-549-2140 ■ *Web:* www.aeb.org	Chicago	IL	60631	847-296-7043	296-7007	48-2
American Egyptian Cooperation Foundation 1535 W Loop S	Houston	TX	77027	713-624-7113		138
American Electric Power Company Inc 1 Riverside Plaza *NYSE: AEP* ■ *TF Cust Svc:* 800-277-2177 ■ *Web:* www.aep.com	Columbus	OH	43215	614-716-1000		360-5
American Electric Supply Inc 361 Maple St *Web:* www.amelect.com	Corona	CA	92880	951-734-7910	737-9906	246
American Electric Technologies Inc (AETI) 1250 Wood Branch Park Dr Ste 600 *NASDAQ: AETI* ■ *Web:* www.aeti.com	Houston	TX	77079	713-644-8182		254
American Electronic Components 1101 Lafayette St *TF:* 888-847-6552 ■ *Web:* www.aecsensors.com	Elkhart	IN	46516	574-295-6330	293-8013	247
American Embryo Transfer Assn (AETA) 1800 S Oak St Ste 100 *Web:* www.aeta.org	Champaign	IL	61820	217-398-2217	398-4119	49-8

Name / Address	City	State	Zip	Phone	Fax	Class
American Emergency Vehicles						
165 American Way	Jefferson	NC	28640	336-982-9824		59
Web: www.aev.com						
American Emo Trans Inc						
2600 Hutchison McDonald Rd	Charlotte	NC	28269	704-359-0045		787
Web: americanemotrans.com						
American Endodontic Society						
265 N Main St	Glen Ellyn	IL	60137	773-519-4879	858-0525*	49-8
**Fax Area Code:* 630 ■ *TF:* 800-325-8649 ■ *Web:* www.aesoc.com						
American Engineering Testing Inc						
550 Cleveland Ave N.	Saint Paul	MN	55114	651-659-9001		261
TF: 800-972-6364 ■ *Web:* www.amengtest.com						
American Enterprise Institute for Public Policy Research (AEI)						
1150 17th St NW	Washington	DC	20036	202-862-5800	862-7177	634
TF: 800-862-5801 ■ *Web:* www.aei.org						
American Environmental Container Corp						
2302 Lasso Ln	Lakeland	FL	33801	863-666-3020		100
TF: 800-535-7946 ■ *Web:* www.sanjuanpools.com						
American Epilepsy Society (AES)						
342 N Main St	West Hartford	CT	06117	860-586-7505	586-7550	48-17
TF: 888-233-2334 ■ *Web:* www.aesnet.org						
American Equipment Co						
2106 Anderson Rd	Greenville	SC	29611	864-295-7800		264-3
Web: www.ameco.com						
American Equipment Co (AMECO)						
4775 Technology Way Ste 208	Boca Raton	FL	33431	561-997-2080	997-2110	770
Web: www.ameco.net						
American Equity Investment Life Insurance Co						
6000 Westown Pkwy	West Des Moines	IA	50266	515-221-0002		391-2
TF: 888-221-1234 ■ *Web:* www.american-equity.com						
American Esoteric Laboratories Inc						
1701 Century Ctr Cove	Memphis	TN	38134	901-405-8200		415
Web: www.ael.com						
American Excelsior Co 850 Ave H E	Arlington	TX	76011	800-777-7645	649-7816*	601
**Fax Area Code:* 817 ■ *TF:* 800-777-7645 ■ *Web:* www.americanexcelsior.com						
American Exchange Bank (AEB)						
510 W Main St PO Box 818	Henryetta	OK	74437	918-652-3321	652-7057	70
TF: 888-652-3321 ■ *Web:* www.americanexchange.bank						
American Exchanger Services Inc						
1950 Innovation Way	Hartford	WI	53027	262-670-6645		268
Web: www.amexservices.com						
American Executive Management Inc						
30 Federal St	Salem	MA	01970	978-744-5923		194
Web: www.americanexecutive.us						
American Express Centurion Bank						
4315 South 2700 West	Salt Lake City	UT	84184	801-945-3000		70
TF: 800-343-3548 ■ *Web:* www.americanexpress.com						
American Express Company Inc						
World Financial Ctr 200 Vesey St	New York	NY	10285	212-640-2000	640-0404	215
NYSE: AXP ■ *TF:* 800-528-4800 ■ *Web:* www.americanexpress.com						
American Express Travel Service Co						
PO Box 981535	El Paso	TX	10285	212-640-5574	640-0404	771
Web: travel.americanexpress.com						
American Exteriors LLC						
7100 E Belleview Ave	Littleton	CO	80120	303-794-6369		235
TF: 800-794-6369 ■ *Web:* www.amext.com						
American Fabricators Inc						
570 Metroplex Dr	Nashville	TN	37211	615-831-8700		697
Web: www.americanfabricators.com						
American Factory Direct Furniture Outlets Inc						
210 New Camellia Blvd.	Covington	LA	70433	985-845-2465		321
Web: www.afd-furniture.com						
American Family Association						
PO Box 2440	Tupelo	MS	38803	662-844-5036		644
TF: 800-326-4543 ■ *Web:* www.afa.net						
American Family Care						
3700 Cahaba Beach Rd.	Birmingham	AL	35242	205-403-8902		352
TF: 800-258-7535 ■ *Web:* www.afcurgentcare.com						
American Family Life Assurance Co PAC (AFLAC PAC)						
1932 Wynnton Rd Ste 300	Columbus	GA	31999	706-323-3431	442-3522*	615
NYSE: AFL ■ **Fax Area Code:* 877 ■ *TF Cust Svc:* 800-992-3522 ■ *Web:* www.aflac.com						
American Family Life Assurance Company of Columbus (AFLAC)						
1932 Wynnton Rd	Columbus	GA	31999	706-323-3431	448-8922*	391-2
**Fax Area Code:* 800 ■ **Fax:* Cust Svc ■ *TF Cust Svc:* 800-992-3522 ■ *Web:* www.aflac.com						
American Family Life Insurance Co						
6000 American Pkwy	Madison	WI	53783	608-249-2111		391-2
TF: 800-692-6326 ■ *Web:* www.amfam.com						
American Family Mutual Insurance Co						
6000 American Pkwy	Madison	WI	53783	608-249-2111		391-2
TF Cust Svc: 800-374-0008 ■ *Web:* www.amfam.com						
American Fan Company Inc						
2933 Symmes Rd	Fairfield	OH	45014	513-874-2400	870-6249	18
TF: 866-771-6266 ■ *Web:* www.americanfan.com						
American Farm Bureau Federation						
600 Maryland Ave SW Ste 1000-W	Washington	DC	20024	202-406-3600		48-2
TF: 800-327-6287 ■ *Web:* www.fb.org						
American Farmland Trust (AFT)						
1200 18th St.	Washington	DC	20036	202-331-7300	659-8339	48-2
TF: 800-431-1499 ■ *Web:* www.farmland.org						
American Faucet & Coating Corp						
3280 Corporate Vw.	Vista	CA	92081	760-598-5895		612
TF: 800-621-8383 ■ *Web:* www.sigmafaucet.com						
American Federation for Aging Research (AFAR)						
55 W 39th St 16th Fl.	New York	NY	10018	212-703-9977	997-0330	49-8
TF: 888-582-2327 ■ *Web:* www.afar.org						
American Federation for Medical Research (AFMR)						
900 Cummings Ctr Ste 221-U	Beverly	MA	01915	978-927-8330	524-8890	49-8
Web: www.afmr.org						
American Federation of Arts (AFA)						
305 E 47th St 10th Fl	New York	NY	10017	212-988-7700	861-2487	48-4
Web: www.amfedarts.org						
American Federation of Astrologers (AFA)						
6535 S Rural Rd	Tempe	AZ	85283	480-838-1751	838-8293	48-18
TF: 888-301-7630 ■ *Web:* www.astrologers.com						
American Federation of Government Employees						
80 F St NW	Washington	DC	20001	202-737-8700	639-6441	414
TF: 888-844-2343 ■ *Web:* www.afge.org						
American Federation of Labor & Congress of Industrial Organizations (AFL-CIO)						
815 16th St NW	Washington	DC	20006	202-637-5000	637-5058	414
TF: 877-850-4959 ■ *Web:* www.aflcio.org						
American Federation of Musicians of the US & Canada (AFM)						
1501 Broadway Ste 600	New York	NY	10036	212-869-1330	764-6134	414
TF: 800-762-3444 ■ *Web:* www.afm.org						
American Federation of Police & Concerned Citizens						
6350 Horizon Dr	Titusville	FL	32780	321-264-0911	264-0033	49-7
TF: 800-435-7352 ■ *Web:* www.afp-cc.org						
American Federation of School Administrators (AFSA)						
1101 17th St NW Ste 408	Washington	DC	20036	202-986-4209		49-5
American Federation of State County & Municipal Employees						
1625 L St NW	Washington	DC	20036	202-429-1000	429-1293	414
TF: 800-772-1105 ■ *Web:* www.afscme.org						
American Federation of Teachers						
555 New Jersey Ave NW	Washington	DC	20001	202-879-4400		457-8
TF: 800-238-1133 ■ *Web:* www.aft.org						
American Federation of Television & Radio Artists (AFTRA)						
260 Madison Ave 7th Fl	New York	NY	10016	212-532-0800	532-2242	414
TF: 800-638-6796 ■ *Web:* www.sagaftra.org						
American Feed Industry Assn (AFIA)						
2101 Wilson Blvd Ste 916	Arlington	VA	22201	703-524-0810	524-1921	48-2
Web: www.afia.org						
American Felt & Filter Co						
361 Walsh Ave	New Windsor	NY	12553	845-561-3560	563-4422	745-6
TF: 800-769-7778 ■ *Web:* www.affco.com						
American Fence Association (AFA)						
6404 Internationa Pkwy Ste 2250-A	Plano	TX	75093	800-822-4342	480-7118*	49-3
**Fax Area Code:* 314 ■ *TF:* 800-822-4342 ■ *Web:* www.americanfenceassociation.com						
American Fence Inc 2502 N 27th Ave	Phoenix	AZ	85009	602-272-2333		191-2
TF: 888-691-4565 ■ *Web:* www.americanfence.com						
American Fiber & Finishing Inc						
PO Box 2488	Albemarle	NC	28001	704-983-6102	983-1850	745-1
Web: www.affinc.com						
American Fiber Manufacturers Assn Inc (AFMA)						
1530 Wilson Blvd Ste 690	Arlington	VA	22209	703-875-0432	875-0907	49-13
Web: www.fibersource.com						
American Fidelity Assurance Co						
2000 N Classen Blvd	Oklahoma City	OK	73106	405-523-2000		360-4
TF: 800-654-8489 ■ *Web:* americanfidelity.com						
American Fidelity Life Insurance Co						
500 S Palafox Ste 200	Pensacola	FL	32502	850-456-7401	453-5440	391-2
Web: www.amfisite.com						
American Film Institute (AFI)						
2021 N Western Ave	Los Angeles	CA	90027	323-856-7600	467-4578	48-4
TF: 866-234-3378 ■ *Web:* www.afi.com						
American Finance Assn (AFA) 350 Main St	Malden	MA	02148	781-388-8599		49-2
TF: 800-835-6770 ■ *Web:* www.afajof.org						
American Financial Group Inc						
301 E Fourth St	Cincinnati	OH	45202	513-579-2121	579-2580	360-4
NYSE: AFG ■ *Web:* www.afginc.com						
American Financial Printing Inc						
404 Industrial Blvd	Minneapolis	MN	55413	612-378-0711		781
Web: www.afpi.com						
American Fire Protection						
4019 E Summit Ln	Nampa	ID	83687	208-463-0209		610
Web: www.firesafetyboise.com						
American Fire Sprinkler Assn (AFSA)						
12750 Merit Dr Ste 350	Dallas	TX	75251	214-349-5965	343-8898	49-3
Web: www.firesprinkler.org						
American First National Bank						
9999 Bellaire Blvd	Houston	TX	77036	713-596-2888		70
Web: www.afnb.com						
American Fisheries Society (AFS)						
5410 Grosvenor Ln Ste 110	Bethesda	MD	20814	301-897-8616	897-8096	48-2
Web: www.fisheries.org						
American Fitness Magazine						
1750 E Northrop Blvd Ste 200	Chandler	AZ	85286	800-446-2322		457-13
TF: 800-446-2322 ■ *Web:* www.afaa.com						
American Fleet & Retail Graphics Inc						
780 S Milliken Ave Ste G	Ontario	CA	91761	909-937-7570		344
Web: www.amgraph.biz						
American Floor Products Company Inc						
7977 Cessna Ave	Gaithersburg	MD	20879	800-342-0424	987-0422*	291
**Fax Area Code:* 301 ■ *TF:* 800-342-0424 ■ *Web:* www.afco-usa.com						
American Fluorescent Corp						
2345 Ernie Krueger Cir	Waukegan	IL	60087	847-249-5970	249-2618	439
TF: 800-873-2326 ■ *Web:* www.afxinc.com						
American Folk Art Museum						
2 Lincoln Sq	New York	NY	10023	212-265-1040		520
Web: www.folkartmuseum.org						
American Folklore Society (AFS)						
1501 Neil Ave 800 E Third St	Bloomington	IN	47405	812-856-2379	856-2483	48-14
TF: 866-315-9403 ■ *Web:* www.afsnet.org						
American Food & Vending Corp						
124 Metropolitan Pk Dr	Syracuse	NY	13088	315-457-9950		299
TF: 800-466-9261 ■ *Web:* www.afvusa.com						
American Foods Group Inc						
544 Acme St	Green Bay	WI	54302	920-437-6330		473
TF: 800-345-0293 ■ *Web:* www.americanfoodsgroup.com						
American Football Coaches Assn (AFCA)						
100 Legends Ln	Waco	TX	76706	254-754-9900		48-22
TF: 877-557-5338 ■ *Web:* www.afca.com						
American Forces Information Service (AFIS)						
601 N Fairfax St	Alexandria	VA	22314	703-571-3343		340-3
Web: www.defense.gov						
American Foreign Service Assn (AFSA)						
2101 E St NW	Washington	DC	20037	202-338-4045	338-6820	49-7
TF: 800-704-2372 ■ *Web:* www.afsa.org						
American Foreign Service Protective Assn						
1620 L St	Washington	DC	20036	202-833-4910		49-7
Web: www.afspa.org						
American Forest & Paper Assn (AF&PA)						
1111 19th St NW Ste 800	Washington	DC	20036	202-463-2700	463-2785	48-2
TF: 800-878-8878 ■ *Web:* www.afandpa.org						
American Forest Foundation (AFF)						
2000 M St NW Ste 550	Washington	DC	20036	202-463-2462	463-2461	48-2
TF: 800-325-2954 ■ *Web:* www.forestfoundation.org						

	Phone	Fax	Class
American Forest Management Inc 407 N Pike Rd E PO Box 1919 .... Sumter SC 29151 *Web:* www.americanforestmanagement.com	803-773-5461	773-4248	302
American Forests 1220 L St NW Ste 750 .... Washington DC 20005 *TF:* 800-368-5748 ■ *Web:* www.americanforests.org	202-737-1944		48-13
American Fork Hospital 170 N 1100 E .... American Fork UT 84003 *TF:* 800-530-5090 ■ *Web:* www.intermountainhealthcare.org	801-763-3300	855-3548	374-3
American Foundation for AIDS Research (AmFAR) 120 Wall St 13th Fl .... New York NY 10005 *Web:* www.amfar.org	212-806-1600	806-1601	48-17
American Foundation for Suicide Prevention (AFSP) 120 Wall St 22nd Fl .... New York NY 10005 *TF:* 888-333-2377 ■ *Web:* www.afsp.org	212-363-3500	363-6237	48-17
American Foundation for the Blind (AFB) 2 Penn Plaza .... New York NY 10001 *TF:* 800-232-5463 ■ *Web:* www.afb.org	212-502-7600	502-7777	48-17
American Foundry Group Inc 14602 S Grant .... Bixby OK 74008 *Web:* www.americanfoundry.com	918-366-4401		492
American Foundry Society (AFS) 1695 N Penny Ln .... Schaumburg IL 60173 *TF:* 800-537-4237 ■ *Web:* www.afsinc.org	847-824-0181	824-2174	49-13
American Freight Ohio Inc 2770 Lexington Ave .... Mansfield OH 44904 *TF:* 800-420-2337 ■ *Web:* www.americanfreight.us	419-884-2224		321
American Friends Service Committee (AFSC) 1501 Cherry St .... Philadelphia PA 19102 *TF:* 800-621-4000 ■ *Web:* www.afsc.org	215-241-7000		48-5
American Frozen Food Institute (AFFI) 2000 Corporate Ridge Blvd Ste 1000 .... McLean VA 22102 *Web:* www.affi.org	703-821-0770	821-1350	615
American Fuel Cell & Coated Fabrics Co 601 Firestone Dr .... Magnolia AR 71753 *Web:* www.amfuel.com	870-234-3381		22
American Fuji Seal Inc 1051 Bloomfield Rd .... Bardstown KY 40004 *Web:* www.fujiseal.co.jp/americas/index.html	502-348-9211		596
American Furniture Warehouse Co 8501 Grant St .... Thornton CO 80229 *TF:* 888-615-9415 ■ *Web:* www.afw.com/en	303-289-3300		321
American Furukawa Inc 47677 Galleon Dr .... Plymouth MI 48170 *Web:* www.americanfurukawa.com	734-446-2200		54
American Galvanizers Assn (AGA) 6881 S Holly Cir Ste 108 .... Centennial CO 80112 *TF:* 800-468-7732 ■ *Web:* www.galvanizeit.org	720-554-0900	554-0909	49-13
American Gaming & Electronics 556 W Taylor Rd .... Romeoville IL 60446 **Fax Area Code: 708* ■ *TF:* 800-336-6630 ■ *Web:* www.agegaming.com	815-919-8184	290-2200*	322
American Gaming Assn (AGA) 1299 Pennsylvania Ave NW Ste 1175 .... Washington DC 20004 *TF:* 800-994-8448 ■ *Web:* www.americangaming.org	202-552-2675	552-2676	48-23
American Gas Assn 400 N Capitol St NW .... Washington DC 20001 *TF:* 800-846-6242 ■ *Web:* www.aga.org	202-824-7000		615
American Gas Association (AGA) 400 N Capitol St NW Ste 450 .... Washington DC 20001	202-824-7000	824-7097	48-12
American Gasket & Rubber Co 119 E Commerce Dr .... Schaumburg IL 60173 *Web:* agr.tekni-plex.com	847-882-8333		326
American Gastroenterological Assn (AGA) 4930 Del Ray Ave .... Bethesda MD 20814 *TF:* 800-227-7888 ■ *Web:* www.gastro.org	301-654-2055	654-5920	49-8
American Gear Manufacturers Assn (AGMA) 500 Montgomery St Ste 350 .... Alexandria VA 22314 *Web:* www.agma.org	703-684-0211	684-0242	49-13
American Gelbvieh Assn 10900 Dover St .... Westminster CO 80021 *TF:* 800-529-0900 ■ *Web:* www.gelbvieh.org	303-465-2333	465-2339	48-2
American Gem Society (AGS) 8881 W Sahara Ave .... Las Vegas NV 89117 *TF:* 866-805-6500 ■ *Web:* www.americangemsociety.org	702-255-6500	255-7420	49-4
American Gem Trade Assn (AGTA) 3030 LBJ Fwy Ste 840 .... Dallas TX 75234 *TF:* 800-972-1162 ■ *Web:* www.agta.org	214-742-4367	742-7334	49-4
American General Media Corp 1400 Easton Dr Ste 144 .... Bakersfield CA 93309 *Web:* www.americangeneralmedia.com	661-328-1410		645-10
American General Supplies Inc 7840 Airpark Rd .... Gaithersburg MD 20879	301-590-9200	590-3069	770
American Geological Institute (AGI) 4220 King St .... Alexandria VA 22302 *Web:* www.agiweb.org	703-379-2480	379-7563	49-19
American Geophysical Union (AGU) 2000 Florida Ave NW .... Washington DC 20009 *TF:* 800-966-2481 ■ *Web:* www.agu.org	202-462-6900	328-0566	49-19
American Geothermal Systems Inc 8650 Spicewood Springs Rd .... Austin TX 78759 *Web:* www.amgeosystems.com	512-219-1465		194
American GFM Corp 1200 Cavalier Blvd .... Chesapeake VA 23323 *Web:* www.agfm.com	757-487-2442		455
American Gilsonite Co 29950 S Bonanza Hwy .... Bonanza UT 84008 *Web:* www.americangilsonite.com	435-789-1921		601
American Girl Inc 8400 Fairway Pl .... Middleton WI 53562 *TF Orders:* 800-845-0005 ■ *Web:* www.americangirl.com	608-836-4848		762
American Glass Distributors 3901 Airline Dr .... Houston TX 77022 *TF:* 800-570-3303 ■ *Web:* www.allamericanglass.com	713-692-8522		54
American GNC Corp 888 E Easy St .... Simi Valley CA 93065 *TF:* 800-773-8321 ■ *Web:* www.americangnc.com	805-582-0582		237
American Golf Corp 2951 28th St .... Santa Monica CA 90405 *TF:* 800-238-7267 ■ *Web:* www.americangolf.com	310-664-4000		655
American Gramaphone LLC 9130 Mormon Bridge Rd .... Omaha NE 68152	402-457-4341	457-4332	657
American Granby Inc 7652 Morgan Rd .... Liverpool NY 13090 **Fax: Acctg* ■ *TF:* 800-776-2266 ■ *Web:* www.americangranby.com	315-451-1100	451-1876*	612
American Greetings Corp 1 American Rd .... Cleveland OH 44144 *NYSE: AM* ■ *TF Sales:* 800-777-4891 ■ *Web:* www.corporate.americangreetings.com	216-252-7300	252-6778	130
American Grinding & Machine Co 2000 N Mango Ave .... Chicago IL 60639 *TF:* 877-988-4343 ■ *Web:* www.americangrinding.com	773-889-4343	889-3781	454
American Group Psychotherapy Assn (AGPA) 25 E 21st St 6th Fl .... New York NY 10010 *TF:* 877-668-2472 ■ *Web:* www.agpa.org	212-477-2677	979-6627	49-15
American Growers Cooling Co 1225 Abbott St .... Salinas CA 93901	831-753-6555		803-2
American Guard Services Inc 1299 E Artesia Blvd .... Carson CA 90746 *TF:* 800-662-7372 ■ *Web:* www.americanguardservices.com	310-645-6200		400
American Guild of Musical Artists (AGMA) 1430 Broadway 14th Fl .... New York NY 10018 *TF:* 800-543-2462 ■ *Web:* www.musicalartists.org	212-265-3687	262-9088	48-4
American Guild of Organists (AGO) 475 Riverside Dr Ste 1260 .... New York NY 10115 *TF:* 855-631-0759 ■ *Web:* www.agohq.org	212-870-2310	870-2163	48-4
American Guild of Variety Artists (AGVA) 363 Seventh Ave 17th Fl .... New York NY 10001 *TF:* 800-331-0890 ■ *Web:* agvausa.com	212-675-1003	633-0097	48-4
American Gypsum Co 3811 Turtle Creek Blvd Ste 1200 .... Dallas TX 75219 *TF:* 866-439-5800 ■ *Web:* www.americangypsum.com	214-530-5500		347
American Hardware Manufacturers Assn (AHMA) 801 N Plaza Dr .... Schaumburg IL 60173 *Web:* www.ahma.org	847-605-1025	605-1030	49-4
American Hardwood Export Council (AHEC) 42777 Trade W Dr Sterling .... Reston VA 20166 *Web:* www.ahec.org	703-435-2900	435-2537	49-18
American Harvest Baking Company Inc 823 Est Gate Dr Ste 3 .... Mt Laurel NJ 08054 *Web:* www.ahbfoods.com	856-642-9955		68
American Headache Society (AHS) 19 Mantua Rd .... Mount Royal NJ 08061 *TF:* 800-582-2169 ■ *Web:* www.americanheadachesociety.org	856-423-0043	423-0082	49-8
American Health Assoc 671 Ohio Pk Ste K .... Cincinnati OH 45245 *TF:* 800-522-7556 ■ *Web:* www.themedlab.com	800-522-7556		415
American Health Care Assn (AHCA) 1201 L St NW .... Washington DC 20005 *TF:* 800-321-0343 ■ *Web:* www.ahcancal.org	202-842-4444	842-3860	49-8
American Health Care Assn PAC 1201 L St NW .... Washington DC 20005 *Web:* ahcancal.org	202-842-4444	842-3860	615
American Health Information Management Assn (AHIMA) 233 N Michigan Ave Ste 2100 .... Chicago IL 60601 *TF:* 800-335-5535 ■ *Web:* www.ahima.org	312-233-1100	233-1090	49-8
American Health Lawyers Assn (AHLA) 1620 Eye St NW .... Washington DC 20006 *Web:* www.healthlawyers.org	202-833-1100	833-1105	49-10
American Health Quality Assn (AHQA) 1155 21st St NW Ste 300 .... Washington DC 20006 *Web:* www.ahqa.org	202-331-5790		49-8
American Healthcare Radiology Administrators (AHRA) 490-B Boston Post Rd Ste 200 .... Sudbury MA 01776 *TF:* 800-334-2472 ■ *Web:* www.ahra.org	978-443-7591	443-8046	49-8
American Hearing Research Foundation 275 N York St Ste 401 .... Elmhurst IL 60126 *Web:* www.american-hearing.org	630-617-5079		48-17
American Heart Assn (AHA) 7272 Greenville Ave .... Dallas TX 75231 *TF:* 800-242-8721 ■ *Web:* www.heart.org	214-373-6300	706-1191	48-17
American Heat Treating Inc 16 Commerce Dr .... Monroe CT 06468 *Web:* www.americanheattreating.com	203-268-1750		484
American Helicopter Museum & Education Ctr 1220 American Blvd W .... West Chester PA 19380 *Web:* www.americanhelicopter.museum	610-436-9600		520
American Helicopter Society International (AHS) 217 N Washington St .... Alexandria VA 22314 *TF:* 855-247-4685 ■ *Web:* www.vtol.org	703-684-6777	739-9279	49-21
American Hellenic Educational Progressive Assn (AHEPA) 1909 Q St NW Ste 500 .... Washington DC 20009 *TF:* 855-473-3512 ■ *Web:* www.ahepa.org	202-232-6300	232-2140	48-14
American Herbal Products Assn (AHPA) 8630 Fenton St Ste 918 .... Silver Spring MD 20910 *TF:* 800-358-2104 ■ *Web:* www.ahpa.org	301-588-1171	588-1174	49-8
American Hereford Assn 1501 Wyandotte St .... Kansas City MO 64108 *Web:* www.hereford.org	816-842-3757	842-6931	48-2
American Heritage Bank 2 S Main PO Box 1408 .... Sapulpa OK 74067 *Web:* www.ahb-ok.com	918-224-3210		70
American Highway Users Alliance 1920 L St NW Ste 525 .... Washington DC 20036 *TF:* 800-388-0650 ■ *Web:* www.highways.org	202-857-1200	857-1220	49-21
American Hiking Society (AHS) 1422 Fenwick Ln .... Silver Spring MD 20910 *TF:* 800-972-8608 ■ *Web:* www.americanhiking.org	301-565-6704		48-23
American Historical Assn (AHA) 400 A St SE .... Washington DC 20003 *Web:* www.historians.org	202-544-2422	544-8307	49-5
American Historical Society of Germans from Russia 631 D St .... Lincoln NE 68502 *TF:* 800-234-8861 ■ *Web:* www.ahsgr.org	402-474-3363	474-7229	48-14
American Hobby Craft Distributors Inc 2040 W N Ln .... Phoenix AZ 85021	602-861-1239		44
American Holistic Health Assn (AHHA) PO Box 17400 .... Anaheim CA 92817 *Web:* www.ahha.org	714-779-6152		48-17
American Holistic Nurses Assn (AHNA) 2900 SW Plass Ct .... Topeka KS 66611 *TF:* 800-278-2462 ■ *Web:* www.ahna.org	785-234-1712	234-1713	48-17

Phone | Fax | Class

American Home Base 428 Childers St. Pensacola FL 32534 850-857-0860 484-8661 737
TF General: 800-549-0595 ■ *Web:* www.amhomebase.com

American Home Furnishings
3535 Menaul Blvd NE. Albuquerque NM 87107 505-883-2211 816-6521 321
TF: 800-854-6755 ■ *Web:* www.americanhome.com

American Home Shield
889 Ridge Lake Blvd PO Box 851. Memphis TN 38120 901-537-8000 367
TF: 800-776-4663 ■ *Web:* www.ahs.com

American Homeowners Foundation (AHF)
6776 Little Falls Rd. Arlington VA 22213 703-536-7776 49-17
Web: www.americanhomeowners.org

American HomePatient Inc
5200 Maryland Way Ste 400. Brentwood TN 37027 615-221-8884 363
TF: 800-890-7271 ■ *Web:* www.ahom.com

American Homestar Corp
2450 S Shore Blvd Ste 300. League City TX 77573 281-334-9700 334-9737* 505
**Fax:* Acctg ■ *Web:* www.americanhomestar.com

American Honda Motor Company Inc
1919 Torrance Blvd. Torrance CA 90501 310-783-3170 59
TF: 800-999-1009 ■ *Web:* www.honda.com

American Horse Council (AHC)
1616 H St NW 7th Fl. Washington DC 20006 202-296-4031 296-1970 48-3
TF: 800-443-0177 ■ *Web:* www.horsecouncil.org

American Horticultural Society (AHS)
7931 E Blvd Dr. Alexandria VA 22308 703-768-5700 768-8700 48-18
TF: 800-777-7931 ■ *Web:* www.ahs.org

American Hose & Rubber Co
3645 E 44th St. Tucson AZ 85713 520-514-1666 370
TF: 800-272-7537 ■ *Web:* amhose.com

American Hospital Assn (AHA)
155 N Wacker Dr. Chicago IL 60606 312-422-3000 422-4796 49-8
TF: 800-424-4301 ■ *Web:* www.aha.org

American Hospital Assn PAC (AHAPAC)
325 Seventh St NW. Washington DC 20004 202-638-1100 626-2345 615
TF: 800-424-4301 ■ *Web:* aha.org

American Hotel & Lodging Assn (AH&LA)
1201 New York Ave NW Ste 600. Washington DC 20005 202-289-3100 48-23
Web: www.ahla.com

American Hotel Register Co
100 S Milwaukee Ave. Vernon Hills IL 60061 847-743-3000 688-9108* 559
**Fax Area Code:* 800 ■ **Fax:* Sales ■ *TF:* 800-323-5686 ■ *Web:* www.americanhotel.com

American Humane Assn (AHA)
63 Inverness Dr E. Englewood CO 80112 303-792-9900 792-5333 48-6
TF: 800-227-4645 ■ *Web:* www.americanhumane.org

American Hydrogen Assn (AHA)
2350 W Shangri La. Phoenix AZ 85029 602-328-4238 48-12
Web: www.clean-air.org

American Hytech Corp
Headquarters 125 UPark Rd. Pittsburgh PA 15238 412-826-3333 177

American Immigration Lawyers Assn (AILA)
918 F St NW. Washington DC 20004 202-216-2400 783-7853 49-10
TF: 800-982-2830 ■ *Web:* www.aila.org

American Importing Company Inc
550 Kasota Ave SE. Minneapolis MN 55414 612-331-7000 805
Web: www.amportfoods.com

American Income Life Insurance Co (AIL)
1200 Wooded Acres. Waco TX 76710 254-761-6400 391-2
TF: 800-433-3405 ■ *Web:* www.ailife.com

American Indian College Fund
8333 Greenwood Blvd. Denver CO 80221 303-426-8900 426-1200 48-11
TF: 800-776-3863 ■ *Web:* www.collegefund.org

American Indian College of the Assemblies of God
10020 N 15th Ave. Phoenix AZ 85021 602-944-3335 943-8299 166
TF: 800-621-7440 ■ *Web:* www.aicag.edu

American Indian Science & Engineering Society (AISES)
2305 Renard SE Ste 200. Albuquerque NM 87106 505-765-1052 765-5608 49-19
TF: 800-759-5219 ■ *Web:* www.aises.org

American Industrial Hygiene Assn (AIHA)
2700 Prosperity Ave Ste 250. Fairfax VA 22031 703-849-8888 207-3561 49-13
Web: www.aiha.org

American Instants Inc
117 Bartley Flanders Rd. Flanders NJ 07836 973-584-8811 805
Web: www.americaninstants.com

American Institute for Cancer Research
1759 R St NW. Washington DC 20009 202-328-7744 328-7226 668
TF: 800-843-8114 ■ *Web:* www.aicr.org

American Institute for Conservation of Historic & Artistic Works (AIC)
1156 15th St NW Ste 320. Washington DC 20005 202-452-9545 452-9328 48-4
Web: www.conservation-us.org

American Institute for CPCU & Insurance Institute of America (AICPCU/IIA)
720 Providence Rd Ste 100. Malvern PA 19355 610-644-2100 640-9576 49-9
TF: 800-644-2101 ■ *Web:* www.theinstitutes.org

American Institute of Aeronautics & Astronautics Inc (AIAA)
1801 Alexander Bell Dr Ste 500. Reston VA 20191 703-264-7500 264-7551 49-19
TF: 800-639-2422 ■ *Web:* www.aiaa.org

American Institute of Architects (AIA)
1735 New York Ave NW. Washington DC 20006 202-626-7300 626-7547 48-4
TF Orders: 800-242-3837 ■ *Web:* www.aia.org

American Institute of Biological Sciences (AIBS)
1313 Dolley Madison Blvd Ste 402. McLean VA 22101 703-674-2500 674-2509 49-19
Web: www.aibs.org

American Institute of Certified Public Accountants (AICPA)
1211 Ave of the Americas. New York NY 10036 212-596-6200 596-6213 49-1
TF: 888-777-7077 ■ *Web:* www.aicpa.org

American Institute of Chemical Engineers (AIChE)
120 Wall St Fl 23. New York NY 10005 203-702-7660 775-5177 49-19
TF Cust Svc: 800-242-4363 ■ *Web:* www.aiche.org

American Institute of Chemists (AIC)
315 Chestnut St. Philadelphia PA 19106 215-873-8224 925-1954 49-19
Web: www.theaic.org

American Institute of Constructors (AIC)
700 N Fairfax St Ste 510. Alexandria VA 22314 703-683-4999 527-3105* 49-3
**Fax Area Code:* 571 ■ *Web:* www.professionalconstructor.org

American Institute of Floral Designers (AIFD)
720 Light St. Baltimore MD 21230 410-752-3318 752-8295 49-4
TF: 877-865-5320 ■ *Web:* www.aifd.org

American Institute of Food Distribution
10 Mountainview Rd Ste S125. Upper Saddle River NJ 07458 201-791-5570 791-5222 49-6
Web: www.foodinstitute.com

Phone | Fax | Class

American Institute of Graphic Arts (AIGA)
164 Fifth Ave. New York NY 10010 212-807-1990 807-1799 48-4
TF: 800-548-1634 ■ *Web:* www.aiga.org

American Institute of Marine Underwriters (AIMU)
14 Wall St Ste 820. New York NY 10005 212-233-0550 227-5102 49-9
Web: www.aimu.org

American Institute of Mining Metallurgical & Petroleum Engineers (AIME)
12999 E Adam Aircraft Cir. Englewood CO 80112 303-325-5185 702-0049* 48-12
**Fax Area Code:* 888 ■ *TF:* 888-702-0049 ■ *Web:* www.aimehq.org

American Institute of Philanthropy (AIP)
3450 N Lake Shore Dr. Chicago IL 60657 773-529-2300 529-0024 48-5
TF: 800-622-2520 ■ *Web:* www.charitywatch.org

American Institute of Physics
1 Physics Ellipse. College Park MD 20740 301-209-3100 209-0843 49-19
TF: 800-892-8259 ■ *Web:* www.aip.org

American Institute of Professional Bookkeepers (AIPB)
6001 Montrose Rd Ste 500. Rockville MD 20852 800-622-0121 541-0066 49-1
TF: 800-622-0121 ■ *Web:* www.aipb.org

American Institute of Professional Geologists (AIPG)
1400 W 122nd Ave Ste 250. Westminster CO 80234 303-412-6205 253-9220 49-19
TF: 800-337-3140 ■ *Web:* www.aipg.org

American Institute of Steel Construction (AISC)
1 E Wacker Dr Ste 3100. Chicago IL 60601 312-670-2400 49-3
Web: www.aisc.org

American Institute of Stress, The (AIS)
124 Pk Ave. Yonkers NY 10703 914-963-1200 48-17
TF: 800-433-5959 ■ *Web:* www.stress.org

American Institute of Timber Construction (AITC)
7012 S Revere Pkwy Ste 140. Centennial CO 80112 303-792-9559 792-0669 49-3
Web: www.aitc-glulam.org

American Institute of Ultrasound in Medicine (AIUM)
14750 Sweitzer Ln Ste 100. Laurel MD 20707 301-498-4100 498-4450 49-8
TF: 800-638-5352 ■ *Web:* www.aium.org

American Institutes for Research
1000 Thomas Jefferson St NW. Washington DC 20007 202-403-5000 403-5454 668
TF: 877-334-3499 ■ *Web:* www.air.org

American Insurance Assn (AIA)
2101 L St. Washington DC 20037 202-828-7100 293-1219 49-9
Web: www.aiadc.org

American Insurance Assn PAC
2101 L St NW Ste 400. Washington DC 20037 202-828-7100 293-1219 615
Web: www.aiadc.org

American Intellectual Property Law Association (AIPLA)
1400 Crystal Dr Ste 600. Arlington VA 22202 703-415-0780 415-0786 49-10
Web: www.aipla.org

American InterContinental University
Atlanta
6600 Peachtree Dunwoody Rd
500 Embassy Row NE. Atlanta GA 30328 404-965-6500 166
TF: 800-491-0182 ■ *Web:* www.aiuniv.edu
Dunwoody
6600 Peachtree-Dunwoody Rd 500 Embassy Row Atlanta GA 30328 404-965-6500 695-4538* 166
**Fax Area Code:* 866 ■ **Fax:* Admissions ■ *TF:* 855-377-1888 ■ *Web:* www.aiuniv.edu

American InterContinental University Los Angeles
231 N Martingale Rd 6th Fl. Schaumburg IL 60173 877-701-3800 166
TF: 877-701-3800 ■ *Web:* www.aiuniv.edu

American Intercontinental University South Florida
2250 N Commerce Pkwy. Weston FL 33326 954-446-6100 166
TF: 855-377-1888 ■ *Web:* www.aiuniv.edu

American Interiors 302 S Byrne Rd. Toledo OH 43615 419-535-1808 320
Web: www.aminteriors.com

American International Automobile Dealers Assn (AIADA)
500 Montgomery St Ste 800. Alexandria VA 22314 703-519-7800 519-7810 49-18
TF: 800-462-4232 ■ *Web:* www.aiada.org

American International College
1000 State St. Springfield MA 01109 413-205-3201 205-3051* 166
**Fax:* Admissions ■ *TF Admissions:* 800-242-3142 ■ *Web:* www.aic.edu

American International Forest Products LLC (AIFP)
5560 SW 107th Ave. Beaverton OR 97005 503-641-1611 641-2800 191-3
TF: 800-366-1611 ■ *Web:* www.lumber.com

American International Inc
1040 Avendia Acaso. Camarillo CA 93012 805-388-6800 388-7950 253
TF: 800-336-6500 ■ *Web:* www.aius.net

American International Radio Inc
3601 E Algonquin Rd Ste 800. Rolling Meadows IL 60008 847-818-9999 681
Web: www.airadio.com

American International Rattlesnake Museum
202 San Felipe NW Ste A. Albuquerque NM 87104 505-242-6569 242-6569 520
Web: www.rattlesnakes.com

American Iron & Steel Institute (AISI)
1101 17th St NW. Washington DC 20036 202-452-7100 463-6573 49-13
Web: www.steel.org

American Iron & Steel Institute PAC
1140 Connecticut Ave NW Ste 705. Washington DC 20036 202-452-7100 463-6573 615
Web: www.steel.org

American Iron Magazine
1010 Summer St. Stamford CT 06905 203-425-8777 457-3
TF Cust Svc: 877-693-3572 ■ *Web:* www.aimag.com

American Islamic College
640 W Irving Pk Rd. Chicago IL 60613 773-281-4700 281-8552* 166
**Fax:* Admissions ■ *Web:* www.aicusa.edu

American Israel Public Affairs Committee (AIPAC)
251 H St. Washington DC 20001 202-639-5200 48-7
Web: aipac.org

American Italian Pasta Co (AIPC)
1251 NW Briarcliff Pkwy Ste 500. Kansas City MO 64116 816-584-5000 296-31
Web: makesameal.com

American Jail Assn (AJA)
1135 Professional Ct. Hagerstown MD 21740 301-790-3930 790-2941 49-7
TF: 800-211-2754 ■ *Web:* www.americanjail.org

American Jazz Museum
1616 E 18th St. Kansas City MO 64108 816-474-8463 520
Web: americanjazzmuseum.org

American Jersey Cattle Assn
6486 E Main St. Reynoldsburg OH 43068 614-861-3636 861-8040 48-2
TF: 800-952-5200 ■ *Web:* www.usjersey.com

American Jewish Committee (AJC)
165 E 56th St. New York NY 10022 212-751-4000 750-0326 48-8
Web: www.ajc.org

Name / Address	City	State	Zip	Phone	Fax	Class
American Jewish Congress 745 Fifth Ave 30th Fl *Web:* www.ajcongress.org	New York	NY	10151	212-879-4500	758-1633	48-7
American Jewish Historical Society 101 Newbury St *TF:* 800-392-6100 ■ *Web:* www.ajhs.org	Boston	MA	02116	617-226-1245		520
American Jewish Joint Distribution Committee (JDC) 711 Third Ave 10th Fl *Web:* www.jdc.org	New York	NY	10017	212-687-6200	370-5467	48-5
American Jewish World Service (AJWS) 45 W 36th St *TF:* 800-889-7146 ■ *Web:* www.ajws.org	New York	NY	10018	212-792-2900	792-2930	48-5
American Journal of Pathology 9650 Rockville Pk *Web:* www.asip.org	Bethesda	MD	20814	301-634-7130		194
American Journal of Psychiatry 1000 Wilson Blvd Ste 1825 *TF:* 800-368-5777 ■ *Web:* psychiatryonline.org	Arlington	VA	22209	703-907-7300	907-1085	457-16
American Journalism Review *University of Maryland* 1117 Journalism Bldg *Web:* www.ajr.org	College Park	MD	20742	301-405-8805		457-5
American Kennel Club (AKC) 260 Madison Ave *Web:* www.akc.org	New York	NY	10016	212-696-8200	696-8299	48-18
American Kennel Club Library 260 Madison Ave 4th Fl *Web:* www.akc.org	New York	NY	10016	212-696-8200		434-4
American Kennel Club Museum of the Dog 1721 S Mason Rd *Web:* www.akc.org	Saint Louis	MO	63131	314-821-3647		520
American Key Products Inc 1 Reuten Dr *Web:* www.akfponline.com	Closter	NJ	07624	201-767-8022		791
American Kidney Fund (AKF) 6110 Executive Blvd Ste 1010 **Fax Area Code:* 301 ■ *TF:* 800-638-8299 ■ *Web:* www.kidneyfund.org	Rockville	MD	20852	800-638-8299	881-0898*	48-17
American Kidney Stone Management Ltd (AKSM) 797 Thomas Ln *TF:* 800-637-5188 ■ *Web:* www.aksm.com	Columbus	OH	43214	614-447-0281		353
American Labor Museum/Botto House National Landmark 83 Norwood St *Web:* www.labormuseum.net	Haledon	NJ	07508	973-595-7953	595-7291	520
American Laboratories Inc (ALI) 4410 S 102nd St *Web:* www.americanlaboratories.com	Omaha	NE	68127	402-339-2494		479
American Laboratory 395 Oyster Pt Blvd Ste 321 *Web:* www.americanlaboratory.com	South San Francisco	CA	94080	650-243-5600		457-19
American Laminates 3142 Talbot Ave, Bldg D *Web:* www.americanlaminates.com	Riverbank	CA	95367	209-869-2536		200
American Laminators 600 Applegate St PO Box 297 *Web:* www.americanlaminators.com	Drain	OR	97435	541-836-2000	836-7144	817
American Land Rights Assn (ALRA) 30218 NE 82nd Ave PO Box 400 *Web:* www.landrights.org	Battle Ground	WA	98604	360-687-3087	687-2973	48-2
American Land Title Assn (ALTA) 1828 L St NW Ste 705 *TF:* 800-787-2582 ■ *Web:* www.alta.org	Washington	DC	20036	202-296-3671	223-5843	49-10
American Landmark Properties 8114 Lawndale Ave *Web:* www.americanlandmark.com	Skokie	IL	60076	847-568-0808		652
American Lands Alliance 726 Seventh St SE *Web:* www.americanlands.org	Washington	DC	20003	202-547-9400		48-13
American Language Communication Ctr 229 W 36th St *Web:* www.learnenglish.com	New York	NY	10018	212-736-2373	947-6403	423
American Laser Skincare 24555 Hallwood Ct *Web:* www.americanlaser.com	Farmington Hills	MI	48335	248-426-8250	426-0129	810
American Latvian Assn Inc 400 Hurley Ave *Web:* www.alausa.org	Rockville	MD	20850	301-340-1914	340-8732	48-14
American Law Institute (ALI) 4025 Chestnut St *TF:* 800-253-6397 ■ *Web:* www.ali.org	Philadelphia	PA	19104	215-243-1600	243-1636	49-10
American Law Label Inc 1674 S Research Loop Ste 436 *Web:* www.americanlawlabel.com	Tucson	AZ	85710	520-546-6200	546-6203	413
American Lawn Mower Co 2100 N Grandville Ave *Web:* www.americanlawnmower.com	Muncie	IN	47303	765-288-6624		429
American Lawyer Media Inc (ALM) 120 Broadway 5th Fl *TF:* 877-256-2472 ■ *Web:* www.alm.com	New York	NY	10271	212-457-9400		637-9
American Lebanese Syrian Associated Charities (ALSAC) 262 Danny Thomas Pl *TF:* 800-822-6344 ■ *Web:* www.stjude.org	Memphis	TN	38105	901-578-2000	578-2805	48-5
American Lecithin Company Inc 115 Hurley Rd Unit 2B *TF:* 800-364-4416 ■ *Web:* www.americanlecithin.com	Oxford	CT	06478	203-262-7100	262-7101	296-29
American LegalNet Inc 16501 Ventura Blvd Ste 615 *TF:* 800-293-2771 ■ *Web:* alncorp.com	Encino	CA	91436	818-817-9225		428
American Legion Auxiliary 8945 N Meridian St 2nd Fl *TF:* 800-504-4098 ■ *Web:* www.alaforveterans.org	Indianapolis	IN	46260	317-569-4500	569-4502	48-19
American Legion, The 700 N Pennsylvania St *TF Cust Svc:* 800-433-3318 ■ *Web:* www.legion.org	Indianapolis	IN	46204	317-630-1200	630-1223	48-19
American Legislative Exchange Council (ALEC) 2900 Crystal Dr 6th Floor *Web:* www.alec.org	Arlington	VA	22202	703-373-0933	373-0927	48-7
American Liberty Hospitality Inc 10700 Richmond Ave Ste 120 *Web:* www.amliberty.com	Houston	TX	77042	713-977-5556		379
American Library Assn (ALTAFF) 50 E Huron St *TF:* 800-545-2433 ■ *Web:* ala.org	Chicago	IL	60611	800-545-2433		49-11
American Library Assn (ALA) 50 E Huron St *TF:* 800-545-2433 ■ *Web:* www.ala.org	Chicago	IL	60611	312-944-6780	944-2641	49-11
American Lifts 532 E Baili Ct	Greensburg	IN	47240	812-663-4085		470
American Lighting Assn (ALA) 2050 Stemmons Fwy Ste 10046 *TF:* 800-605-4448 ■ *Web:* www.americanlightingassoc.com	Dallas	TX	75207	214-698-9898	698-9899	49-4
American Limousines Inc 4401 E Fairmount Ave *TF:* 800-787-1690 ■ *Web:* www.amerlimo.com	Baltimore	MD	21224	410-522-0400		441
American List Counsel Inc 750 College Rd E Ste 201 *TF:* 800-252-5478 ■ *Web:* www.alc.com	Princeton	NJ	08540	609-580-2871	580-2888	5
American Littoral Society (ALS) 18 Hartshorne Dr Ste 1 *TF:* 800-424-8802 ■ *Web:* www.littoralsociety.org	Highlands	NJ	07732	732-291-0055	291-3551	48-13
American Liver Foundation (ALF) 39 Broadway *TF:* 800-465-4837 ■ *Web:* www.liverfoundation.org	New York	NY	10006	212-668-1000	483-8179	48-17
American Locker Group Inc 815 S Main St *OTC:* ALGI ■ *TF:* 800-828-9118 ■ *Web:* www.americanlocker.com	Grapevine	TX	76051	817-329-1600	421-8618	692
American Locker Security Systems Inc 608 Allen St *TF Sales:* 800-828-9118 ■ *Web:* www.americanlocker.com	Jamestown	NY	14701	800-828-9118		692
American Logistics Assn (ALA) 1133 15th St NW Ste 640 *TF:* 800-791-7146 ■ *Web:* www.ala-national.org	Washington	DC	20005	202-466-2520	296-4419	48-19
American Louver Co 7700 N Austin Ave **Fax Area Code:* 847 ■ *TF:* 800-772-0355 ■ *Web:* www.americanlouver.com	Skokie	IL	60077	800-772-0355	966-8074*	439
American Lubrication Equipment Corp 11212A McCormick Rd PO Box 1350 **Fax Area Code:* 800 ■ *TF:* 888-252-9300 ■ *Web:* americanlube.com	Hunt Valley	MD	21030	888-252-9300	759-2637*	541
American Lumber Distributors & Brokers Inc 2405 Republic Blvd *Web:* www.americanlumber1.com	Birmingham	AL	35201	205-791-0155		752
American Lung Assn (ALA) 14 Wall St *TF:* 800-586-4872 ■ *Web:* www.lung.org	New York	NY	10005	212-315-8700		48-17
American Machine & Tool Company Inc 400 Spring St *TF:* 888-268-7867 ■ *Web:* www.amtpump.com	Royersford	PA	19468	610-948-3800		641
American Machine Tool Distributors' Assn (AMTDA) 1445 Research Blvd Ste 450 *Web:* www.amtonline.org	Rockville	MD	20850	301-738-1200		49-18
American Made Cutlery 905 Industrial Rd *TF:* 800-311-9690 ■ *Web:* americanmadecutlery.com	Waverly	IA	50677	319-352-2080		362
American Malting Barley Assn (AMBA) 740 N Plankinton Ave Ste 830 *Web:* www.ambainc.org	Milwaukee	WI	53203	414-272-4640		49-6
American Marazzi Tile Inc 359 Clay Rd *TF:* 800-289-8453 ■ *Web:* marazziusa.com	Sunnyvale	TX	75182	972-232-3801	226-5629	751
American Marketing Assn (AMA) 311 S Wacker Dr Ste 5800 *TF:* 800-262-1150 ■ *Web:* www.ama.org	Chicago	IL	60606	312-542-9000	542-9001	49-18
American Marking Systems Inc 1015 Paulison Ave PO Box 1677 *TF:* 800-782-6766 ■ *Web:* www.ams-stamps.com	Clifton	NJ	07011	973-478-5600	478-0039	467
American Massage Therapy Assn (AMTA) 500 Davis St Ste 900 *TF:* 877-905-2700 ■ *Web:* www.amtamassage.org	Evanston	IL	60201	847-864-0123	864-1178	48-17
American Mathematical Society (AMS) 201 Charles St *TF Cust Svc:* 800-321-4267 ■ *Web:* www.ams.org	Providence	RI	02904	401-455-4000	331-3842	49-19
American Mechanical Services 13300 Mid Atlantic Blvd *Web:* www.amsofusa.com	Laurel	MD	20708	301-206-5070		189-10
American Media Inc 4 New York Plaza *Web:* www.americanmediainc.com	New York	NY	10004	212-545-4800		637-9
American Media International LLC 2609 Tucker St *Web:* ami-media.com	Burlington	NC	27215	336-229-5554		512
American Medical Alarms Inc 4414 SE 16th Pl Ste 4 *Web:* www.americanmedicalalarms.com	Cape Coral	FL	33904	239-540-4655		475
American Medical Assn (AMA) 515 N State St *TF:* 800-621-8335 ■ *Web:* www.ama-assn.org	Chicago	IL	60610	312-464-5000	464-4184	49-8
American Medical Assn PAC 25 Massachusetts Ave NW # 600 *TF:* 800-621-8335 ■ *Web:* ama-assn.org	Washington	DC	20001	312-464-4430		615
American Medical Directors Assn (AMDA) 11000 Broken Land Pkwy Ste 400 *TF:* 800-876-2632 ■ *Web:* www.paltc.org	Columbia	MD	21044	410-740-9743	740-4572	49-8
American Medical Group Assn (AMGA) 1422 Duke St *Web:* www.amga.org	Alexandria	VA	22314	703-838-0033	548-1890	49-8
American Medical ID 949 Wakefield Ste 100 *TF:* 800-363-5985 ■ *Web:* www.americanmedical-id.com	Houston	TX	77018	800-363-5985		475
American Medical Informatics Assn (AMIA) 4720 Montgomery Ln Ste 500 *Web:* www.amia.org	Bethesda	MD	20814	301-657-1291	657-1296	49-8
American Medical News 515 N State St *Web:* www.amednews.com	Chicago	IL	60654	312-464-4429		457-16
American Medical Rehabilitation Providers Assn (AMRPA) 1710 N St NW *TF:* 888-346-4624 ■ *Web:* www.amrpa.org	Washington	DC	20036	202-223-1920	223-1925	49-8
American Medical Response (AMR) 6200 S Syracuse Way Ste 200 *TF:* 877-244-4890 ■ *Web:* www.amr.net	Greenwood Village	CO	80111	303-495-1200		30
American Medical Student Assn (AMSA) 1902 Assn Dr *TF:* 800-767-2266 ■ *Web:* www.amsa.org	Reston	VA	20191	703-620-6600	620-5873	49-5

				Phone	Fax	Class
American Medical Supplies Inc						
751 Park of Commerce Dr Ste 126	Boca Raton	FL	33487	561-362-7105		475
American Medical Technologies Inc						
5655 Bear Ln	Corpus Christi	TX	78405	800-359-1959		228
OTC: ADLI ■ *TF:* 800-359-1959						
American Medical Technologists (AMT)						
10700 W Higgins Rd Ste 150	Rosemont	IL	60018	847-823-5169	823-0458	49-8
TF: 800-275-1268 ■ *Web:* www.americanmedtech.org						
American Medical Writers Assn (AMWA)						
30 W Gude Dr Ste 525	Rockville	MD	20850	301-294-5303	294-9006	49-14
Web: www.amwa.org						
American Megatrends Inc (AMI)						
5555 Oakbrook Pkwy Bldg 200	Norcross	GA	30093	770-246-8600	246-8790	176
TF: 800-828-9264 ■ *Web:* www.ami.com						
American Memorial Park						
PO Box 5198-CHRB	Saipan	MP	96950	670-234-7207	234-6698	564
Web: www.nps.gov/amme						
American Mensa Ltd						
1229 Corporate Dr W	Arlington	TX	76006	817-607-0060	649-5232	48-15
TF: 800-666-3672 ■ *Web:* www.us.mensa.org						
American Mental Health Counselors Assn (AMHCA)						
801 N Fairfax St Ste 304	Alexandria	VA	22314	703-548-6002	548-4775	49-15
TF: 800-326-2642 ■ *Web:* www.amhca.org						
American Metal & Plastics Inc						
450 32nd St SW	Grand Rapids	MI	49548	616-452-6061	452-3835	489
Web: www.ampi-gr.com						
American Metal Bearing Co						
7191 Acacia Ave	Garden Grove	CA	92841	714-892-5527	898-3217	620
TF: 800-888-3048 ■ *Web:* www.ambco.net						
American Metal Crafters LLC						
695 High St	Middletown	CT	06457	860-343-1960		198
TF: 800-840-9243 ■ *Web:* www.americanmetalcraftersllc.com						
American Metal Fab Inc						
55515 Franklin Dr	Three Rivers	MI	49093	269-279-5108		689
Web: www.americanmetalfab.com						
American Metal Market LLC						
225 Park Ave S 6th Fl	New York	NY	10003	212-213-6202		345
Web: www.amm.com						
American Metal Technologies LLC						
8213 Durand Ave	Sturtevant	WI	53177	262-633-1756		454
TF: 800-313-1821 ■ *Web:* www.amermetals.com						
American Metalcraft Inc						
3708 N River Rd Ste 800	Franklin Park	IL	60131	800-333-9133	333-6046	488
TF: 800-333-9133 ■ *Web:* www.amnow.com						
American Metals Corp						
1499 Parkway Blvd	West Sacramento	CA	95691	916-371-7700		492
Web: www.american-steel.com						
American Meteorological Society (AMS)						
45 Beacon St	Boston	MA	02108	617-227-2425	742-8718	49-19
TF: 800-824-0405 ■ *Web:* www.ametsoc.org						
American Metro Bank 4878 N Broadway	Chicago	IL	60640	773-769-6868		70
Web: www.americanmetrobank.com						
American Micro Products Inc						
4288 Armstrong Blvd	Batavia	OH	45103	513-732-2674		567
Web: www.american-micro.com						
American Migraine Foundation (ACHE)						
19 Mantua Rd	Mount Royal	NJ	08061	856-423-0043	423-0082	48-17
Web: americanmigrainefoundation.org						
American Millwork Corp 4840 Beck Dr	Elkhart	IN	46516	574-295-4158	293-5378	499
Web: www.americanmillwork.com						
American Miniature Horse Assn (AMHA)						
5601 S IH- 35 W	Alvarado	TX	76009	817-783-5600	783-6403	48-3
Web: www.amha.org						
American Mktg Services & Consultant						
939 Tower Rd	Mundelein	IL	60060	847-566-4545		194
Web: amscinc.com						
American Modern Home Insurance Co						
PO Box 5323	Cincinnati	OH	45201	513-943-7200		391-4
TF: 800-543-2644 ■ *Web:* www.amig.com						
American Modular Systems Inc						
787 Spreckels Ave	Manteca	CA	95336	209-825-1921		186
Web: www.americanmodular.com						
American Modular Technologies (AMT)						
6306 Old 421 Rd PO Box 1069	Liberty	NC	27298	336-622-6200	622-6473	105
Web: www.americanmodulartechnologies.com						
American Moistening Company Inc						
10402 Rodney St	Pineville	NC	28134	704-889-7281		610
TF: 800-948-5540 ■ *Web:* www.amco.com						
American Montessori Society (AMS)						
281 Pk Ave S 6th Fl	New York	NY	10010	212-358-1250	358-1256	48-11
TF: 800-632-4121 ■ *Web:* www.amshq.org						
American Morgan Horse Assn (AMHA)						
4066 Shelburne Rd Ste 5	Shelburne	VT	05482	802-985-4944	985-8897	48-3
TF: 888-436-3700 ■ *Web:* www.morganhorse.com						
American Motel Management						
2200 Northlake Pkwy Ste 277	Tucker	GA	30084	770-939-1801	939-1419	655
TF: 800-580-8258 ■ *Web:* www.americanmotelonline.com						
American Motive Power Inc						
9431 Foster Wheeler Rd	Dansville	NY	14437	585-335-3131		650
Web: www.americanmotivepower.com						
American Motorcyclist Assn (AMA)						
13515 Yarmouth Dr	Pickerington	OH	43147	614-856-1900	856-1920	48-22
TF: 800-262-5646 ■ *Web:* www.americanmotorcyclist.com						
American Moving & Storage Assn (AMSA)						
1611 Duke St	Alexandria	VA	22314	703-683-7410	683-7527	49-21
TF: 888-849-2672 ■ *Web:* www.promover.org						
American Municipal Power Inc						
1111 Schrock Rd Ste 100	Columbus	OH	43229	614-540-1111	540-1113	787
Web: www.amppartners.org						
American Muscle 7 Lee Blvd	Malvern	PA	19355	610-251-2397		791
TF: 888-332-7930 ■ *Web:* www.americanmuscle.com						
American Museum of Fly Fishing						
4104 Main Rd	Manchester	VT	05254	802-362-3300	362-3308	522
TF: 800-333-1550 ■ *Web:* www.amff.com						
American Museum of Natural History						
Library Central Pk W at 79th St	New York	NY	10024	212-769-5400	769-5009	434-4
Web: www.amnh.org						
American Museum of Science & Energy						
300 S Tulane Ave	Oak Ridge	TN	37830	865-576-3200	576-0024	520
TF: 800-257-8235 ■ *Web:* amse.org						
American Music Therapy Assn Inc (AMTA)						
8455 Colesville Rd Ste 1000	Silver Spring	MD	20910	301-589-3300	589-5175	48-17
Web: www.musictherapy.org						
American Musical Supply PO Box 152	Spicer	MN	56288	320-796-2088		526
TF: 800-458-4076 ■ *Web:* www.americanmusical.com						
American Musicological Society (AMS)						
6010 College Stn	Brunswick	ME	04011	207-798-4243	798-4254	48-4
TF: 888-421-1442 ■ *Web:* www.ams-net.org						
American Mutual Share Insurance Corp						
5656 Frantz Rd	Dublin	OH	43017	614-764-1900		390
Web: www.excessshare.com						
American National Bank 628 Main St	Danville	VA	24541	434-792-5111		360-2
NASDAQ: AMNB ■ *TF:* 800-240-8190 ■ *Web:* www.amnb.com						
American National Bank PO Box 2139	Omaha	NE	68103	402-457-1077		70
TF Cust Svc: 800-279-0007 ■ *Web:* american.bank						
American National CattleWomen Inc (ANCW)						
200 NW 66th St	Oklahoma City	OK	73116	303-850-3441		48-2
Web: www.ancw.org						
American National Insurance Co						
1 Moody Plaza	Galveston	TX	77550	409-763-4661		391-2
NASDAQ: ANAT ■ *Web:* www.americannational.com						
American National Logistics Inc						
202 N San Jacinto St	Rockwall	TX	75087	972-772-3132		194
Web: www.anlinc.com						
American National Property & Casualty Co						
1949 E Sunshine St	Springfield	MO	65899	417-887-0220	887-1801*	391-4
**Fax:* Hum Res ■ *TF:* 800-333-2860 ■ *Web:* www.anpac.com						
American National Rubber Co						
Main & High St	Ceredo	WV	25507	304-453-1311	453-2347*	677
**Fax:* Sales ■ *TF Cust Svc:* 800-624-3410 ■ *Web:* www.anr-co.com						
American National Standards Institute (ANSI)						
25 W 43rd St 4th fl	New York	NY	10036	212-642-4900	398-0023	48-1
TF: 800-374-3818 ■ *Web:* www.ansi.org						
American Natural Soda Ash Corp						
15 Riverside Ave	Westport	CT	06880	203-226-9056	227-1484	144
Web: www.ansac.com						
American Naturopathic Medical Assn (ANMA)						
PO Box 96273	Las Vegas	NV	89193	702-450-3477		48-17
Web: www.anma.org						
American Needle Inc						
1275 Busch Pkwy	Buffalo Grove	IL	60089	847-215-0011		155-9
Web: www.shop.americanneedle.com						
American Nephrology Nurses Assn (ANNA)						
200 E Holly Ave	Sewell	NJ	08080	856-256-2320	589-7463	49-8
TF: 888-600-2662 ■ *Web:* www.annanurse.org						
American Neurological Assn (ANA)						
1120 Rte 73 Ste 200	Mount Laurel	NJ	08054	856-380-6892		49-8
Web: myana.org						
American Nickeloid Co 2900 Main St	Peru	IL	61354	815-223-0373	223-5344	481
TF: 800-645-5643 ■ *Web:* www.nickeloid.com						
American Nuclear Insurers (ANI)						
95 Glastonbury Blvd Ste 300	Glastonbury	CT	06033	860-682-1301		49-9
Web: www.amnucins.com						
American Nuclear Society (ANS)						
555 N Kensington Ave	La Grange Park	IL	60526	708-352-6611	352-0499	49-19
TF: 800-323-3044 ■ *Web:* www.ans.org						
American Numismatic Society						
75 Varick St 11th Fl	New York	NY	10013	212-571-4470	571-4479	520
Web: www.numismatics.org						
American Nursery & Landscape Assn (ANLA)						
1000 Vermont Ave NW Ste 300	Washington	DC	20005	202-789-2900	789-1893	48-2
Web: americanhort.org						
American Nurses Assn (ANA)						
8515 Georgia Ave Ste 400	Silver Spring	MD	20910	301-628-5000	628-5001	49-8
TF: 800-274-4262 ■ *Web:* nursingworld.org						
American Nurses Assn California (ANA\C)						
1121 L St Ste 409	Sacramento	CA	95814	916-447-0225		533
Web: www.anacalifornia.org						
American Nurses Assn PAC (ANA PAC)						
8515 Georgia Ave Ste 400	Silver Spring	MD	20910	301-628-5000	628-5001	615
TF: 800-274-4262 ■ *Web:* www.nursingworld.org						
American Nutrition Inc 2813 Wall Ave	Ogden	UT	84401	801-394-3477		578
TF: 800-257-4530 ■ *Web:* www.anibrands.com						
American Occupational Therapy Assn Inc (AOTA)						
4720 Montgomery Ln PO Box 31220	Bethesda	MD	20824	301-652-2682	652-7711	49-8
TF: 800-877-1383 ■ *Web:* www.aota.org						
American Office Equipment Company Inc						
309 N Calvert St	Baltimore	MD	21202	410-539-7529		321
Web: www.americanoffice.com						
American Oil Chemists Society (AOCS)						
2710 S Boulder PO Box 17190	Urbana	IL	61802	217-359-2344	351-8091	48-12
TF: 866-535-2730 ■ *Web:* www.aocs.org						
American Organization for Bodywork Therapies of Asia (AOBTA)						
PO Box 343 Ste 408	West Berlin	NJ	08091	856-809-2953		48-17
Web: www.aobta.org						
American Organization of Nurse Executives (AONE)						
155 N Wacker Dr Ste 400	Chicago	IL	60606	312-422-2800	422-4503	49-8
Web: www.aone.org						
American Orthodontics Corp						
1714 Cambridge Ave	Sheboygan	WI	53081	920-457-5051	457-1485	228
TF: 800-558-7687 ■ *Web:* www.americanortho.com						
American Orthopaedic Society for Sports Medicine (AOSSM)						
6300 N River Rd Ste 500	Rosemont	IL	60018	847-292-4900	292-4905	49-8
TF: 877-321-3500 ■ *Web:* www.sportsmed.org						
American Ortho-Tech Inc						
1320 Mason Ave	Daytona Beach	FL	32117	386-258-0401		477
American Orthotic & Prosthetic Assn (AOPA)						
330 John Carlyle St Ste 200	Alexandria	VA	22314	571-431-0876	431-0899	48-17
Web: www.aopanet.org						
American Osteopathic Assn (AOA)						
142 E Ontario St	Chicago	IL	60611	312-202-8000	202-8200	49-8
TF: 800-621-1773 ■ *Web:* www.osteopathic.org						
American Outdoor Products Inc						
6350 Gunpark Dr	Boulder	CO	80301	800-641-0500		296-37
TF: 800-641-0500 ■ *Web:* www.backpackerspantry.com						

Name / Address	Phone	Fax	Class
American Outfitters Ltd 3700 Sunset Ave. Waukegan IL 60087 *TF:* 800-397-6081 ■ *Web:* www.americanoutfitters.com	847-623-3959		711
American Overseas Book Company Inc 550 Walnut St. Norwood NJ 07648 *TF:* 800-571-9554 ■ *Web:* www.aobc.com	201-767-7600		96
American Overseas Marine Corp 100 Newport Ave Ext. Quincy MA 02171 *Web:* gdamsea.com	617-786-8300	472-4925	313
American Pacific Corp (AMPAC) 3883 Howard Hughes Pkwy Ste 700 Las Vegas NV 89169 *NASDAQ: APFC* ■ *Web:* www.apfc.com	702-735-2200		145
American Packaging Corp 777 Driving Pk Ave. Rochester NY 14613 *TF:* 800-551-8801 ■ *Web:* www.ampkcorp.com	585-254-9500	254-5801	548
American Packaging Corp Extrusion Div 777 Driving Pk Ave. Rochester NY 14613 *TF:* 800-551-8801 ■ *Web:* www.ampkcorp.com	585-254-9500	254-5801	548
American Packing & Gasket Co (APG) 6039 Armour Dr PO Box 213 Houston TX 77020 *TF:* 800-888-5223 ■ *Web:* callapg.com	713-675-5271	675-2730	326
American Pain Society (APS) 4700 West Lake Ave Glenview IL 60025 *Web:* www.americanpainsociety.org	847-375-4715	375-6479	48-17
American Paint Horse Assn (APHA) 2800 Meacham Blvd. Fort Worth TX 76137 *Web:* www.apha.com	817-834-2742	834-3152	48-3
American Pallet Inc 1001 Knox Rd Oakdale CA 95361 *Web:* www.americanpallet.com	209-847-6122	847-6154	551
American Panel Corp 5800 SE 78th St Ocala FL 34472 *TF:* 800-327-3015 ■ *Web:* www.americanpanel.com	352-245-7055	245-0726	664
American Paper & Twine Co 7400 Cockrill Bend Blvd. Nashville TN 37209 **Fax Area Code: 877* ■ *TF:* 800-251-2437 ■ *Web:* shopapt.com	615-350-9000	413-5055*	559
American Paper Recycling Corp 87 Central St. Mansfield MA 02048 *TF Cust Svc:* 800-762-6790 ■ *Web:* aprcorp.com	800-762-6790		660
American Park & Recreation Society (APRS) 22377 Belmont Ridge Rd Ashburn VA 20148 *TF:* 800-765-3110 ■ *Web:* www.arcat.com	703-858-0784	858-0794	48-23
American Parkinson Disease Assn (APDA) 135 Parkinson Ave Staten Island NY 10305 *TF:* 800-223-2732 ■ *Web:* www.apdaparkinson.org	718-981-8001	981-4399	48-17
American Pavilion 1706 Warrington Ave Danville IL 61832 *TF:* 800-424-9699 ■ *Web:* www.americanpavilion.com	217-443-0800	443-9619	733
American Paving Company Inc 315 N Thorne PO Box 4348 Fresno CA 93706 *Web:* www.americanpavingco.com	559-268-9886		188-4
American Payroll Assn (APA) 660 N Main Ave Ste 100 San Antonio TX 78205 *Web:* americanpayroll.org	210-226-4600	226-4027	49-12
American Peanut Shellers Assn 2336 Lake Pk Dr Albany GA 31707 *Web:* www.peanut-shellers.org	229-888-2508	888-5150	49-6
American Permanent Ware Inc 729 Third Ave Dallas TX 75226 *TF:* 800-527-2100 ■ *Web:* www.apwwyott.com	214-421-7366	565-0976	298
American Pet Products Manufacturers Assn (APPMA) 255 Glenville Rd Greenwich CT 06831 *TF:* 800-452-1225 ■ *Web:* www.americanpetproducts.org	203-532-0000	532-0551	49-4
American Petroleum Institute (API) 1220 L St NW Washington DC 20005 *TF:* 800-526-4233 ■ *Web:* www.api.org	202-682-8000		48-12
American Pharmacists Assn PAC 2215 Constitution Ave NW Washington DC 20037 *TF:* 800-237-2742 ■ *Web:* www.pharmacist.com	202-628-4410	783-2351	615
American Pharmacists Association 2215 Constitution Ave NW Washington DC 20037 *TF:* 800-237-2742 ■ *Web:* www.pharmacist.com	202-628-4410	783-2351	49-8
American Philatelic Society (APS) 100 Match Factory Pl Bellefonte PA 16823 *Web:* www.stamps.org	814-933-3803	933-6128	48-18
American Philosophical Society (APS) 104 S Fifth St Philadelphia PA 19106 *Web:* www.amphilsoc.org	215-440-3400		48-11
American Photo Magazine 1633 Broadway 43rd Fl. New York NY 10019 *TF:* 800-274-4514 ■ *Web:* www.popphoto.com	212-767-6000	767-5602	457-14
American Physical Security Group LLC 1030 Goodworth Dr Apex NC 27539 *Web:* www.americanpsg.com	919-363-1894		234
American Physical Society (APS) 1 Physics Ellipse College Park MD 20740 *TF:* 866-918-1164 ■ *Web:* www.aps.org	301-209-3200	209-0865	49-19
American Physical Therapy Assn (APTA) 1111 N Fairfax St Alexandria VA 22314 *TF:* 800-999-2782 ■ *Web:* www.apta.org	703-684-2782	706-8536	49-8
American Physiological Society (APS) 9650 Rockville Pk. Bethesda MD 20814 *Web:* www.the-aps.org	301-634-7164	634-7241	49-8
American Phytopathological Society, The (APS) 3340 Pilot Knob Rd Saint Paul MN 55121 *TF:* 800-328-7560 ■ *Web:* www.apsnet.org/pages/default.aspx	651-454-7250	454-0766	49-19
American Pilots' Assn 499 S Capitol St SW Ste 409 Washington DC 20003 *Web:* www.americanpilots.org	202-484-0700	484-9320	49-21
American Pipe & Supply Company Inc 4100 Eastlake Blvd Birmingham AL 35217 *Web:* www.americanpipe-mt.com	205-252-9460		612
American Planning Assn (APA) 1030 15th St NW Washington DC 20005 *Web:* www.planning.org	202-872-0611	872-0643	49-17
American Plastic Molding Corp 965 S Elm St. Scottsburg IN 47170 *Web:* www.apmc.com	812-752-7000	752-5155	604
American Plastic Toys Inc 799 Ladd Rd Walled Lake MI 48390 *TF:* 800-521-7080 ■ *Web:* www.americanplastictoys.com	248-624-4881		762
American Plastics Group Inc 715 W Pk Rd Union MO 63084 *TF:* 800-528-2121 ■ *Web:* www.americanplasticsgroup.com	636-583-2583		604
American Players Theater 5950 Golf Course Rd PO Box 819 Spring Green WI 53588 *Web:* www.americanplayers.org	608-588-2361	588-7085	572
American Playground Corp 2328 Jefferson St Anderson IN 46016 *TF:* 800-541-1602 ■ *Web:* american-playground.net	765-642-0288	649-7162	346
American Pneumatic Tool Inc 9949 Tabor Pl Santa Fe Springs CA 90670 *TF:* 800-532-7402 ■ *Web:* www.apt-tools.com	562-204-1555	204-1773	759
American Podiatric Medical Assn (APMA) 9312 Old Georgetown Rd Bethesda MD 20814 *TF:* 800-275-2762 ■ *Web:* www.apma.org	301-581-9200	530-2752	49-8
American Polarity Therapy Assn (APTA) 122 N Elm St Ste 512 Greensboro NC 27401 *TF:* 800-437-0620 ■ *Web:* www.polaritytherapy.org	336-574-1121	574-1151	48-17
American Polarizers Inc 141 S Seventh St Reading PA 19602 *TF:* 800-736-9031 ■ *Web:* www.apioptics.com	610-373-5177	373-2229	544
American Police Hall of Fame & Museum 6350 Horizon Dr Titusville FL 32780 *Web:* www.aphf.org	321-264-0911	264-0033	520
American Political Science Assn (APSA) 1527 New Hampshire Ave NW Washington DC 20036 *Web:* www.apsanet.org	202-483-2512	483-2657	49-5
American Polywater Corp 11222 60th St N Stillwater MN 55082 *TF:* 800-328-9384 ■ *Web:* www.polywater.com	651-430-2270	430-3634	145
American Pool Enterprises Inc 11515 Cronridge Dr # Q Owings Mills MD 21117 *Web:* www.americanpool.com	443-471-1190		271
American Poolplayers Assn Inc (APA) 1000 Lake St Louis Blvd Ste 325 Lake Saint Louis MO 63367 *Web:* www.poolplayers.com	636-625-8611	625-2975	48-22
American Porcelain Enamel Co 203 W Church St Crandall TX 75114	972-427-6654		701
American Portfolios Holdings Inc 4250 Veterans Memorial Hwy Ste 420E Holbrook NY 11741 *Web:* www.americanportfolios.com	631-439-4600		401
American Portwell Technology Inc 44200 Christy St. Fremont CA 94538 *TF:* 877-278-8899 ■ *Web:* www.portwell.com	510-403-3399		174
American Postal Workers Union 1300 L St NW Washington DC 20005 *Web:* www.apwu.org	202-842-4200		414
American Postal Workers Union PAC (COPA) 1300 L St NW Washington DC 20005 *Web:* apwu.org	202-842-4200		615
American Power Conversion Corp (APC) 132 Fairgrounds Rd West Kingston RI 02892 *TF Cust Svc:* 800-788-2208 ■ *Web:* www.apc.com	401-789-5735	789-3710	253
American Power Pull Corp 550 W Linfoot St PO Box 109 Wauseon OH 43567 *TF:* 800-808-5922 ■ *Web:* www.americanpowerpull.com	419-335-7050	335-7070	470
American Precision Prototyping Inc 19503 E Sixth St Tulsa OK 74108	918-266-1004		454
American Press 4900 Hwy 90 E Lake Charles LA 70615 *TF News Rm:* 800-442-2511 ■ *Web:* www.americanpress.com	337-494-4080		532-2
American Printing House for the Blind 1839 Frankfort Ave PO Box 6085 Louisville KY 40206 *TF:* 800-223-1839 ■ *Web:* www.aph.org	502-895-2405	899-2274	637-10
American Process Lettering Inc 30 Bunting Ln. Primos PA 19018 *Web:* amprosports.com	610-623-9000		594
American Product Distributors Inc (APD) 8350 Arrowridge Blvd. Charlotte NC 28273 *TF:* 800-849-5842 ■ *Web:* www.americanproduct.com	704-522-9411		534
American Products Company Inc 610 Rahway Ave Union NJ 07083 *TF:* 800-232-3198 ■ *Web:* www.amerprod.com	908-687-4100	687-0037	621
American Products Inc (API) 13909 Lynmar Blvd. Tampa FL 33626 *Web:* www.americanprod.com	813-925-0144		295
American Products LLC 597 Evergreen Rd Strafford MO 65757 *TF:* 855-736-2135 ■ *Web:* www.amprod.us	417-736-2135	736-2662	488
American Professional Services Inc 111 Harrison Ave Oklahoma City OK 73104 *Web:* www.americanpi.net	405-636-4222	632-7667	400
American Profol Inc 4333 C St SW Cedar Rapids IA 52404 *Web:* www.americanprofol.com	319-365-0599		600
American Prospect 1710 Rhode Island Ave NW 12th Fl Washington DC 20036 *Web:* www.prospect.org	202-776-0730		457-17
American Proteins Inc 4705 Leland Dr Cumming GA 30041 *Web:* www.americanproteins.com	770-886-2250	886-2296	447
American Psychiatric Assn (APA) 1000 Wilson Blvd Ste 1825 Arlington VA 22209 *TF:* 888-357-7924 ■ *Web:* www.psychiatry.org	703-907-7300	907-1085	49-15
American Psychiatric Nurses Assn (APNA) 1555 Wilson Blvd Ste 530 Arlington VA 22209 *TF:* 866-243-2443 ■ *Web:* www.apna.org	703-243-2443	243-3390	49-8
American Psychiatric Publishing Inc 1000 Wilson Blvd Ste 1825 Arlington VA 22209 *TF:* 800-368-5777 ■ *Web:* www.appi.org	703-907-7322	907-1091	637-9
American Psychoanalytic Assn (APsaA) 309 E 49th St New York NY 10017 *Web:* www.apsa.org	212-752-0450	593-0571	49-15
American Psychological Assn (APA) 750 First St NE Washington DC 20002 *TF:* 800-374-2721 ■ *Web:* www.apa.org	202-336-5500	336-5962	49-15
American Public Communications Council Inc (APCC) 625 Slaters Ln Ste 104 Alexandria VA 22314	703-739-1322	739-1324	49-20
American Public Gas Assn (APGA) 201 Massachusetts Ave NE Ste C-4 Washington DC 20002 *TF:* 800-927-4204 ■ *Web:* www.apga.org	202-464-2742	464-0246	48-12

Name / Address	City	State	Zip	Phone	Fax	Class
American Public Health Assn (APHA) 800 'I' St NW *Web:* www.apha.org	Washington	DC	20001	202-777-2742	777-2533	49-8
American Public Human Services Assn (APHSA) 1133 19th St NW Ste 400 *Web:* www.aphsa.org	Washington	DC	20036	202-682-0100	289-6555	49-7
American Public Life Insurance Co 2305 Lakeland Dr PO Box 925 *TF:* 800-256-8606 ■ *Web:* ampublic.com	Jackson	MS	39205	601-936-6600		391-5
American Public Power Assn (APPA) 1875 Connecticut Ave Ste 1200 *Web:* www.publicpower.org	Washington	DC	20009	202-467-2900	467-2910	48-12
American Public Television (APT) 55 Summer St 4th Fl *Web:* aptonline.org/aptweb.nsf/home?readform	Boston	MA	02110	617-338-4455	338-5369	632
American Public Transportation Assn (APTA) 1666 K St NW Ste 1100 *Web:* www.apta.com	Washington	DC	20006	202-496-4800	496-4321	49-21
American Public University System (AMU) 111 W Congress St *TF:* 877-777-9081 ■ *Web:* www.amu.apus.edu	Charles Town	WV	25414	304-724-3700		167
American Public Works Assn (APWA) 2345 Grand Blvd Ste 700 *TF:* 800-848-2792 ■ *Web:* www.apwa.net	Kansas City	MO	64108	816-472-6100	472-1610	49-7
American Qualex Scientific Products (AQSP) 920-A Calle Negocio *Web:* www.aqsp.com	San Clemente	CA	92673	949-492-8298		231
American Quality Schools Corp 910 W Van Buren St *Web:* www.aqs.org	Chicago	IL	60607	312-226-3355		685
American Quarter Horse Assn (AQHA) 1600 Quarter Horse Dr *TF:* 800-291-7323 ■ *Web:* www.aqha.com	Amarillo	TX	79104	806-376-4811	349-6411	48-3
American Rabbit Breeders Assn (ARBA) PO Box 5667 *TF:* 800-753-9448 ■ *Web:* www.arba.net	Bloomington	IL	61702	309-664-7500	664-0941	48-3
American Radio Relay League (ARRL) 225 Main St *TF:* 888-277-5289 ■ *Web:* www.arrl.org	Newington	CT	06111	860-594-0200	594-0259	49-14
American Radiolabeled Chemicals Inc (ARC) 101 ARC Dr *TF:* 800-331-6661 ■ *Web:* www.arc-inc.com	Saint Louis	MO	63146	314-991-4545	991-4692	145
American Railcar Industries Inc 100 Clark St *NASDAQ: ARII* ■ *TF:* 800-489-9888 ■ *Web:* www.americanrailcar.com	Saint Charles	MO	63301	636-940-6000	940-6030	650
American Railway Engineering & Maintenance-of-Way Assn (AREMA) 4501 Forbes Blvd Ste 130	Lanham	MD	20706	301-459-3200		49-21
American Raisin Packers Inc 2335 Chandler St PO Box 30 *TF:* 800-967-5743 ■ *Web:* americanraisinpacking.com	Selma	CA	93662	559-896-4760	896-8942	11-1
American Ramp Sales Co 601 S Mckinley Ave *TF:* 800-949-2024 ■ *Web:* www.americanrampcompany.com	Joplin	MO	64801	417-206-6816		295
American Realty Investors Inc 1603 Lyndon B Johnson Fwy Ste 800 One Hickory Ctr *NYSE: ARL* ■ *TF:* 800-400-6407 ■ *Web:* www.americanrealtyinvest.com	Dallas	TX	75234	469-522-4200	522-4299	655
American Recreation Coalition (ARC) 1225 New York Ave NW Ste 450 *Web:* www.funoutdoors.com	Washington	DC	20005	202-682-9530	682-9529	48-23
American Recycled Plastic Inc 773 N Union Grove Rd *TF:* 866-417-5821 ■ *Web:* www.itsrecycled.com	Friendsville	TN	37737	865-738-3439	738-3731	661
American Recycling of Georgia LLC 4785 Fulton Industrial Blvd	Atlanta	GA	30336	404-691-1117		548
American Red Ball Transit Company Inc PO Box 1127 *TF:* 800-733-8139 ■ *Web:* www.redball.com	Indianapolis	IN	46206	800-733-8139		519
American Red Cross 2025 E St NW *TF:* 800-257-7575 ■ *Web:* www.redcross.org	Washington	DC	20006	202-303-4498	303-0044	48-5
American Red Cross In Greater New York (Inc) 520 W 49th St *TF:* 877-733-2767 ■ *Web:* www.redcross.org	New York	NY	10019	877-733-2767		352
American Red Cross Pacific NorthWest Blood Service 3131 N Vancouver Ave *TF:* 800-733-2767 ■ *Web:* www.redcrossblood.org	Portland	OR	97227	503-284-1234		417
American Reeling Devices Inc 15 Airpark Vista Blvd *TF Sales:* 800-354-7335 ■ *Web:* americanreeling.net	Dayton	NV	89403	800-354-7335		117
American Refining Group Inc 77 N Kendall Ave *Web:* www.amref.com	Bradford	PA	16701	814-368-1200		580
American Refrigeration Supplies 2632 E Chambers St *Web:* store.arsnet.com/arsweb/en-us	Phoenix	AZ	85040	602-243-2792	243-2893	665
American Refugee Committee (ARC) 430 Oak Grove St Ste 204 *TF:* 800-875-7060 ■ *Web:* www.arcrelief.org	Minneapolis	MN	55403	612-872-7060	607-6499	48-5
American Registry for Internet Numbers (ARIN) 3635 Concorde Pkwy Ste 200 *Web:* www.arin.net	Chantilly	VA	20151	703-227-9840		48-9
American Registry of Diagnostic Medical Sonographers (ARDMS) 1401 Rockville Pike Ste 600 *TF:* 800-541-9754 ■ *Web:* www.ardms.org	Rockville	MD	20852	301-738-8401	738-0312	49-8
American Relays Inc 15537 S Blackburn Ave *Web:* www.americanrelays.com	Norwalk	CA	90650	562-944-0447	944-0590	203
American Reliance Inc (AMREL) 3445 Fletcher Ave *Web:* www.amrel.com	El Monte	CA	91731	626-443-6818		529
American Religious Town Hall Meeting Inc PO Box 180118 *TF:* 800-783-9828 ■ *Web:* www.americanreligious.org	Dallas	TX	75218	214-328-9828	328-3042	451
American Renal Assoc Inc 500 Cummings Ctr Ste 6550 *TF:* 877-997-3625 ■ *Web:* www.americanrenal.com	Beverly	MA	01915	978-922-3080		353
American Renolit Corp 1207 E Lincolnway *Web:* laminatefinder.com	LaPorte	IN	46350	219-324-6886	324-5332	599

Name / Address	City	State	Zip	Phone	Fax	Class
American Rental Assn (ARA) 1900 19th St *TF:* 800-334-2177 ■ *Web:* www.ararental.org	Moline	IL	61265	309-764-2475	764-1533	49-4
American Repertory Ballet 7 Livingston Ave *Web:* www.americanrepertoryballet.org	New Brunswick	NJ	08901	732-249-1254	249-8475	573-1
American Repertory Theatre (ART) 64 Brattle St *Web:* www.americanrepertorytheater.org	Cambridge	MA	02138	617-495-2668	495-1705	749
American Republic Insurance Co 601 Sixth Ave **Fax Area Code:* 515 ■ *TF Cust Svc:* 800-247-2190	Des Moines	IA	50309	800-247-2190	247-2435*	391-2
American Research & Management Co 145 Front St *TF:* 800-426-0501 ■ *Web:* www.arm-co.com	Marion	MA	02738	508-748-1665		401
American Residential Services LLC 9010 Maier Rd Ste 105 *TF:* 866-399-2885 ■ *Web:* www.ars.com	Laurel	MD	20723	901-271-9700		189-10
American Resort Development Assn (ARDA) 1201 15th St NW Ste 400 *Web:* www.arda.org	Washington	DC	20005	202-371-6700	289-8544	49-17
American Rifleman Magazine 11250 Waples Mill Rd *TF:* 800-672-3888 ■ *Web:* americanrifleman.org	Fairfax	VA	22030	800-672-3888		457-20
American Ring Company Inc 19 Grosvenor Ave	East Providence	RI	02914	401-438-9060	438-3806	408
American River Bankshares 3100 Zinfandel Dr Ste 450 *NASDAQ: AMRB* ■ *TF:* 800-544-0545 ■ *Web:* www.americanriverbank.com	Rancho Cordova	CA	95670	800-544-0545		360-2
American River College 4700 College Oak Dr **Fax:* Admissions ■ *TF:* 800-700-4144 ■ *Web:* www.arc.losrios.edu	Sacramento	CA	95841	916-484-8011	484-8864*	162
American River Ventures 2270 Douglas Blvd Ste 212 *Web:* www.arventures.com	Roseville	CA	95661	916-780-2828		792
American Rivers 1101 14th St NW Ste 1400 *TF:* 877-347-7550 ■ *Web:* www.americanrivers.org	Washington	DC	20005	202-347-7550	347-9240	48-13
American Road & Transportation Builders Assn (ARTBA) 1219 28th St NW *TF:* 800-636-2377 ■ *Web:* www.artba.org	Washington	DC	20007	202-289-4434	289-4435	49-3
American Road Insurance Co, The 1 American Rd	Dearborn	MI	48126	313-322-3000		391-4
American Road Machinery Inc 401 Bridge St *Web:* www.americanroadmachinery.com	Minerva	OH	44657	330-868-7724		190
American Robotics Corp 880 Peru Ave Unit 2 *Web:* www.swapbox.com	San Francisco	CA	94112	562-546-2659		387
American Rock Mechanics Assn (ARMA) 600 Woodland Terr *Web:* www.armarocks.org	Alexandria	VA	22302	703-683-1808	683-1815	49-19
American Roentgen Ray Society (ARRS) 44211 Slatestone Ct *TF:* 800-438-2777 ■ *Web:* www.arrs.org	Leesburg	VA	20176	703-729-3353	729-4839	49-8
American Roller Bearing Co 400 Second Ave NW *Web:* www.amroll.com	Hickory	NC	28601	828-624-1460		75
American Roller Co 1440 13th Ave *TF:* 800-285-6750 ■ *Web:* www.americanroller.com	Union Grove	WI	53182	262-878-8665	878-1932	677
American Rose Society (ARS) 8877 Jefferson Paige Rd *TF:* 800-637-6534 ■ *Web:* rose.org	Shreveport	LA	71119	318-938-5402	938-5405	48-18
American Royal Assn 1701 American Royal Ct *TF:* 866 844 2295 ■ *Web:* www.americanroyal.com	Kansas City	MO	64102	816-221-9800	221-8189	48-2
American Running Assn 4405 E W Hwy Ste 405 *TF:* 800-776-2732 ■ *Web:* www.americanrunning.org	Bethesda	MD	20814	301-913-9517	913-9520	48-22
American Saddlebred Horse Assn (ASHA) 4083 Iron Works Pkwy *TF:* 800-829-4438 ■ *Web:* www.asha.net	Lexington	KY	40511	859-259-2742	259-1628	48-3
American Saddlebred Museum 4083 Iron Works Pkwy *TF:* 800-829-4438 ■ *Web:* www.asbmuseum.org	Lexington	KY	40511	859-259-2746	255-4909	520
American Safety Clothing Inc 30 E Park Ave *Web:* americansafetyclothingmfg.com	Sellersville	PA	18960	215-257-7667		477
American Safety Technologies Inc 565 Eagle Rock Ave *TF:* 800-631-7841 ■ *Web:* www.astantislip.com	Roseland	NJ	07068	973-403-2600	403-1108	550
American Sales Company Inc 4201 Walden Ave *Web:* www.americansalescompany.net	Lancaster	NY	14086	716-686-7000	685-6144	335
American Sanitary Partition Corp 300 Enterprise St PO Box 99 *Web:* www.am-sanitary-partition.com	Ocoee	FL	34761	407-656-0611	656-8189	286
American Savings Bank FSB 1001 Bishop St *TF:* 800-272-2566 ■ *Web:* www.asbhawaii.com	Honolulu	HI	96813	808-627-6900		70
American Scale Service & Supply Co 8590 W 14th Ave *TF:* 800-709-5656 ■ *Web:* www.ameriscale.com	Lakewood	CO	80215	303-232-5656		362
American Scholar Magazine 1606 New Hampshire Ave NW *TF:* 800-745-8379 ■ *Web:* www.pbk.org	Washington	DC	20009	202-265-3808	986-1601	457-10
American School Counselor Assn (ASCA) 1101 King St Ste 625 *TF:* 800-306-4722 ■ *Web:* www.schoolcounselor.org	Alexandria	VA	22314	703-683-2722	683-1619	49-5
American School Health Assn (ASHA) 7918 Jones Branch Dr Ste 300 *Web:* www.ashaweb.org	McLean	VA	44240	703-506-7675	506-3266	49-5
American Science & Engineering Inc 829 Middlesex Tpke *NASDAQ: ASEI* ■ *Web:* www.as-e.com	Billerica	MA	01821	978-262-8700		692
American Scientist Magazine 3106 E NC Hwy 54 PO Box 13975 *TF:* 800-243-6534 ■ *Web:* www.americanscientist.org	Research Triangle Park	NC	27709	919-549-4691	549-0090	457-19

Organization	Phone	Fax	Class
American Seafoods Holdings LLC 2025 First Ave Ste 900 Seattle WA 98121 *TF:* 800-275-2019 ■ *Web:* www.americanseafoods.com	206-374-1515	374-1516	285
American Seal & Engineering Company Inc 295 Indian River Rd Orange CT 06477 *Web:* www.ameriseal.com	203-789-8819		529
American Seating Co 401 American Seating Ctr NW Grand Rapids MI 49504 *TF Cust Svc:* 800-748-0268 ■ *Web:* www.americanseating.com	616-732-6600	732-6401	319-3
American Security Products Inc 11925 Pacific Ave Fontana CA 92337 *TF:* 800-421-6142 ■ *Web:* www.amsecusa.com	951-685-9680	685-9685	692
American Seed Trade Assn (ASTA) 1701 Duke St Ste 275 Alexandria VA 22304 *TF:* 888-890-7333 ■ *Web:* www.betterseed.org	703-837-8140	837-9365	48-2
American Seminar Leaders Assn (ASLA) 2405 E Washington Blvd Pasadena CA 91104 *TF:* 800-801-1886 ■ *Web:* www.asla.com	626-791-1211	791-0701	49-12
American Seniors Housing Assn (ASHA) 5225 Wisconsin Ave NW Ste 502 Washington DC 20015 *Web:* www.seniorshousing.org	202-237-0900	237-1616	48-6
American SensoRx Inc 31 N Monroe St Ridgewood NJ 07410 *Web:* www.americansensorx.com	201-447-8999		256
American Services Inc 1300 Rutherford Rd Greenville SC 29609 *TF:* 877-292-7450 ■ *Web:* www.american-services-inc.com	864-292-7450		693
American Shared Hospital Services 4 Embarcadero Ctr Ste 3700 San Francisco CA 94111 *NYSE: AMS* ■ *TF:* 800-735-0641 ■ *Web:* www.ashs.com	415-788-5300	788-5660	264-4
American Sheep Industry Assn (ASI) 9785 Maroon Cir Ste 360 Englewood CO 80112 *TF:* 800-228-5262 ■ *Web:* www.sheepusa.org	303-771-3500	771-8200	48-2
American Shetland Pony Club (ASPC) 81B E Queenwood Rd Ste 2 Morton IL 61550 *Web:* shetlandminiature.com	309-263-4044	263-5113	48-3
American Shore & Beach Preservation Assn (ASBPA) 5460 Beaujolais Ln Fort Myers FL 33919 *TF:* 800-331-1600 ■ *Web:* www.asbpa.org	239-489-2616	489-9917	48-13
American Short Line & Regional Railroad Assn (ASLRRA) 50 F St NW Ste 7020 Washington DC 20001 *Web:* www.aslrra.org	202-628-4500	628-6430	49-21
American Shorthorn Assn 7607 NW Prairie View Rd Kansas City MO 64151 *Web:* www.shorthorn.org	816-599-7777	599-7782	48-3
American Showa Inc 707 W Cherry St Sunbury OH 43074 *Web:* www.amshowa.com	740-965-1133		247
American SIDS Institute 528 Raven Way Naples FL 34110 *Web:* www.sids.org	239-431-5425	431-5536	48-6
American Silk Mills Corp 75 Stark St Plains PA 18705 *Web:* www.americansilk.com	570-822-7147	829-7044	745-1
American Simmental Assn (ASA) One Genetics Way Bozeman MT 59718 *Web:* www.simmental.org	406-587-4531	587-9301	48-2
American Slate Co 1900 Olympic Blvd Walnut Creek CA 94596 *Web:* www.americanslate.com	925-977-4880		724
American Sleep Apnea Assn (ASAA) 6856 Eastern Ave NW Ste 203 Washington DC 20012 *TF:* 888-293-3650 ■ *Web:* www.sleepapnea.org	202-293-3650	293-3656	48-17
American Society for Adolescent Psychiatry (ASAP) 1737 Omar Dr Mesquite TX 75150 *Web:* adolescent-psychiatry.org	972-613-0985		49-15
American Society for Aesthetic Plastic Surgery, The (ASAPS) 11262 Monarch St Garden Grove CA 92841 *TF:* 800-364-2147 ■ *Web:* www.surgery.org	562-799-2356	799-1098	49-8
American Society for Biochemistry & Molecular Biology Inc (ASBMB) 9650 Rockville Pk Bethesda MD 20814 *Web:* www.asbmb.org	301-634-7145	634-7126	49-19
American Society for Bone & Mineral Research (ASBMR) 2025 M St NW Ste 800 Washington DC 20036 *Web:* www.asbmr.org	202-367-1161	367-2161	49-8
American Society for Cell Biology (ASCB) 8120 Woodmont Ave Ste 750 Bethesda MD 20814 *Web:* www.ascb.org	301-347-9300	347-9310	49-19
American Society for Clinical Pathology (ASCP) 33 W Monroe St Ste 1600 Chicago IL 60603 *TF Cust Svc:* 800-621-4142 ■ *Web:* www.ascp.org	312-541-4999	541-4998	49-8
American Society for Colposcopy & Cervical Pathology (ASCCP) 152 W Washington St Hagerstown MD 21740 *TF:* 800-787-7227 ■ *Web:* www.asccp.org	301-733-3640		49-8
American Society for Dermatologic Surgery (ASDS) 5550 Meadowbrook Dr Ste 120 Rolling Meadows IL 60008 *TF:* 800-714-1374 ■ *Web:* www.asds.net	847-956-0900	956-0999	49-8
American Society for Engineering Education (ASEE) 1818 N St NW Ste 600 Washington DC 20036 *Web:* www.asee.org	202-331-3500	265-8504	49-19
American Society for Gastrointestinal Endoscopy (ASGE) 1520 Kensington Rd Ste 202 Oak Brook IL 60523 *TF:* 866-353-2743 ■ *Web:* www.asge.org	630-573-0600	573-0691	49-8
American Society for Histocompatibility & Immunogenetics (ASHI) 15000 Commerce Pkwy Ste C Mount Laurel NJ 08054 *Web:* www.ashi-hla.org	856-638-0428	439-0525	49-8
American Society for Horticultural Science (ASHS) 1018 Duke St Alexandria VA 22314 *TF:* 800-331-1600 ■ *Web:* www.ashs.org	703-836-4606	836-2024	48-2
American Society for Laser Medicine & Surgery Inc (ASLMS) 2100 Stewart Ave Ste 240 Wausau WI 54401 *TF:* 877-258-6028 ■ *Web:* www.aslms.org	715-845-9283	848-2493	49-8
American Society for Microbiology (ASM) 1752 N St NW Washington DC 20036 *TF:* 800-546-2416 ■ *Web:* www.asm.org	202-737-3600		49-8
American Society for Nondestructive Testing Inc (ASNT) 1711 Arlingate Ln PO Box 28518 Columbus OH 43228 *TF Orders:* 800-222-2768 ■ *Web:* www.asnt.org	614-274-6003	274-6899	49-19
American Society for Nutrition (ASNS) 9211 Corporate Blvd Ste 300 Rockville MD 20850 *TF:* 800-627-8723 ■ *Web:* www.nutrition.org	301-634-7050	634-7894	49-6
American Society for Parenteral & Enteral Nutrition (ASPEN) 8630 Fenton St Ste 412 Silver Spring MD 20910 *TF:* 800-727-4567 ■ *Web:* www.nutritioncare.org	301-587-6315	587-2365	49-8
American Society for Pharmacology & Experimental Therapeutics (ASPET) 9650 Rockville Pk Bethesda MD 20814 *TF:* 800-422-4633 ■ *Web:* www.aspet.org	301-634-7060	634-7061	49-8
American Society for Photobiology (ASP) PO Box 1897 Lawrence KS 66044 *TF:* 800-627-0326 ■ *Web:* www.photobiology.org	785-843-1234	843-1274	49-19
American Society for Photogrammetry & Remote Sensing, The (ASPRS) 5410 Grosvenor Ln Ste 210 Bethesda MD 20814 *Web:* www.asprs.org	301-493-0290	493-0208	49-19
American Society for Public Administration (ASPA) 1301 Pennsylvania Ave NW Ste 840 Washington DC 20004 *TF:* 800-765-7755 ■ *Web:* www.aspanet.org	202-393-7878	638-4952	49-7
American Society for Quality (ASQ) 600 N Plankinton Ave Milwaukee WI 53203 *TF:* 800-248-1946 ■ *Web:* www.asq.org	414-272-8575	272-1734	49-13
American Society for Reproductive Medicine (ASRM) 1209 Montgomery Hwy Birmingham AL 35216 *TF:* 800-654-2452 ■ *Web:* www.asrm.org	205-978-5000	978-5005	49-8
American Society for Surgery of the Hand (ASSH) 822 W Washington Blvd Chicago IL 60607 **Fax Area Code:* 847 ■ *Web:* www.assh.org	312-880-1900	384-1435*	49-8
American Society for the Prevention of Cruelty to Animals (ASPCA) 424 E 92nd St New York NY 10128 *TF:* 800-582-5979 ■ *Web:* www.aspca.org	212-876-7700		48-3
American Society for Therapeutic Radiology & Oncology (ASTRO) 8280 Willow Oaks Corporate Dr Ste 500 Fairfax VA 22031 *TF:* 800-962-7876 ■ *Web:* www.astro.org	703-502-1550	502-7852	49-8
American Society of Abdominal Surgeons (ASAS) 824 Main St Second Fl Ste 1 Melrose MA 02176 *Web:* www.abdominalsurg.org	781-665-6102	665-4127	49-8
American Society of Access Professionals (ASAP) 1444 'I' St NW Ste 700 Washington DC 20005 *Web:* www.accesspro.org	202-712-9054	216-9646	48-8
American Society of Addiction Medicine (ASAM) 11400 Rockville Pike Ste 200 Rockville MD 20852 *Web:* www.asam.org	301-656-3920	656-3815	49-8
American Society of Agricultural Consultants (ASAC) 605 Columbus Ave South New Prague WI 56071 *Web:* www.agconsultants.org	952-758-5811		48-2
American Society of Agronomy (ASA) 5585 Guilford Rd Madison WI 53711 *TF:* 866-359-9161 ■ *Web:* www.agronomy.org	608-273-8080	273-2021	48-2
American Society of Andrology (ASA) 1100 E Woodfield St Ste 350 Schaumburg IL 60173 *Web:* www.andrologysociety.org	847-517-1050	517-7229	49-8
American Society of Anesthesiologists (ASA) 520 N NW Hwy Park Ridge IL 60068 *Web:* www.asahq.org	847-825-5586	825-1692	49-8
American Society of Animal Science (ASAS) 1111 N Dunlap Ave Savoy IL 61874 *Web:* www.asas.org	217-356-9050	398-4119	48-2
American Society of Appraisers (ASA) 555 Herndon Pkwy Ste 125 Herndon VA 20170 *TF:* 800-272-8258 ■ *Web:* www.appraisers.org	703-478-2228	742-8471	49-17
American Society of Artists PO Box 1326 Palatine IL 60078 *TF:* 800-284-9484 ■ *Web:* www.americansocietyofartists.info	312-751-2500		48-4
American Society of Assn Executives (ASAE) 1575 'I' St NW Washington DC 20005 *TF:* 888-950-2723 ■ *Web:* www.asaecenter.org	202-626-2723		49-12
American Society of Business Publication Editors (ASBPE) 214 N Hale St Wheaton IL 60187 *TF:* 800-255-8141 ■ *Web:* www.asbpe.org	630-510-4588	510-4501	49-16
American Society of Cataract & Refractive Surgery (ASCRS) 4000 Legato Rd Ste 700 Fairfax VA 22033 *TF:* 877-996-4464 ■ *Web:* www.ascrs.org	703-591-2220	591-0614	49-8
American Society of Cinematographers (ASC) 1782 N Orange Dr Hollywood CA 90028 *TF:* 800-448-0145 ■ *Web:* www.theasc.com	323-969-4333	882-6391	48-4
American Society of Civil Engineers (ASCE) 1801 Alexander Bell Dr Reston VA 20191 *TF:* 800-548-2723 ■ *Web:* www.asce.org	703-295-6300	295-6211	457-21
American Society of Clinical Hypnosis (ASCH) 140 N Bloomingdale Rd Bloomingdale IL 60108 *TF:* 800-227-6963 ■ *Web:* www.asch.net	630-980-4740	351-8490	49-8
American Society of Clinical Oncology (ASCO) 2318 Mill Rd Ste 800 Alexandria VA 22314 **Fax Area Code:* 703 ■ *TF:* 888-282-2552 ■ *Web:* www.asco.org	571-483-1300	299-0255*	49-8
American Society of Consultant Pharmacists (ASCP) 1321 Duke St Alexandria VA 22314 *TF:* 800-355-2727 ■ *Web:* www.ascp.com	703-739-1300	739-1321	49-8
American Society of Dermatopathology, The 111 Deer Lake Rd Ste 100 Deerfield IL 60015 *Web:* www.asdp.org	847-686-2231	480-9282	49-8
American Society of Echocardiography (ASE) 2100 Gateway Centre Blvd Ste 310 Morrisville NC 27560 *Web:* www.asecho.org	919-861-5574	882-9900	49-8
American Society of Farm Managers & Rural Appraisers (ASFMRA) 950 S Cherry St Ste 508 Denver CO 80246 *TF:* 800-888-8827 ■ *Web:* www.asfmra.org	303-758-3513	758-0190	48-2
American Society of Golf Course Architects (ASGCA) 125 N Executive Dr Ste 106 Brookfield WI 53005 *Web:* www.asgca.org	262-786-5960	786-5919	48-22
American Society of Health-System Pharmacists (ASHP) 7272 Wisconsin Ave Bethesda MD 20814 *TF:* 866-279-0681 ■ *Web:* www.ashp.org	301-664-8700	664-8877	49-8
American Society of Heating Refrigerating & Air-Conditioning Engineers Inc (ASHRAE) 1791 Tullie Cir NE Atlanta GA 30329 *TF Cust Svc:* 800-527-4723 ■ *Web:* www.ashrae.org	404-636-8400	321-5478	49-3
American Society of Hematology (ASH) 1900 M St NW Ste 200 Washington DC 20036 *Web:* www.hematology.org	202-776-0544	776-0545	49-8
American Society of Home Inspectors (ASHI) 932 Lee St Ste 101 Des Plaines IL 60016 *TF:* 800-743-2744 ■ *Web:* www.homeinspector.org	847-759-2820	759-1620	49-3

Phone | Fax | Class

American Society of Human Genetics (ASHG)
9650 Rockville Pike ... Bethesda MD 20814 301-634-7300 634-7079 49-19
Web: www.ashg.org

American Society of Hypertension (ASH)
148 Madison Ave 5th Fl ... New York NY 10016 212-696-9099 696-0711 49-8
TF: 800-654-2452 ■ *Web:* www.ash-us.org

American Society of Ichthyologists & Herpetologists
PO Box 1897 ... Lawrence KS 66044 785-843-1235 843-1274 49-19
Web: www.asih.org

American Society of Indexers (ASI)
1628 E Southern Ave Ste 9-223 ... Tempe AZ 85282 480-245-6750 49-16
Web: www.asindexing.org

American Society of Interior Designers (ASID)
608 Massachusetts Ave ... Washington DC 20002 202-546-3480 546-3240 48-4
Web: www.asid.org

American Society of International Law, The (ASIL)
2223 Massachusetts Ave NW ... Washington DC 20008 202-939-6000 797-7133 49-10
TF: 800-828-7571 ■ *Web:* www.asil.org

American Society of Landscape Architects (ASLA)
636 'I' St NW ... Washington DC 20001 202-898-2444 898-1185 48-2
TF: 888-999-2752 ■ *Web:* www.asla.org

American Society of Limnology & Oceanography (ASLO)
5400 Bosque Blvd Ste 680 ... Waco TX 76710 254-399-9635 776-3767 49-19
TF: 800-929-2756 ■ *Web:* www.aslo.org

American Society of Media Photographers (ASMP)
150 N Second St ... Philadelphia PA 19106 215-451-2767 451-0880 49-14
Web: www.asmp.org

American Society of Military Comptrollers (ASMC)
415 N Alfred St ... Alexandria VA 22314 703-549-0360 549-3181 48-19
TF: 800-462-5637 ■ *Web:* www.asmconline.org

American Society of Naval Engineers (ASNE)
1452 Duke St ... Alexandria VA 22314 703-836-6727 836-7491 49-21
Web: www.navalengineers.org

American Society of Neuroradiology (ASNR)
2210 Midwest Rd Ste 207 ... Oak Brook IL 60523 630-574-0220 574-0661 49-8
Web: www.asnr.org

American Society of News Editors (ASNE)
11690-B Sunrise Vly Dr ... Reston VA 20191 703-453-1122 453-1133 49-14
Web: www.asne.org

American Society of Notaries (ASN)
PO Box 5707 ... Tallahassee FL 32314 850-671-5164 671-5165 49-12
Web: www.notaries.org

American Society of Nuclear Cardiology (ASNC)
4550 Montgomery Ave Ste 780-N ... Bethesda MD 20814 301-215-7575 215-7113 49-8
Web: www.asnc.org

American Society of Pension Professionals & Actuaries (ASPPA)
4245 N Fairfax Dr Ste 750 ... Arlington VA 22203 703-516-9300 516-9308 49-12
Web: www.asppa.org

American Society of PeriAnesthesia Nurses (ASPAN)
90 Frontage Rd ... Cherry Hill NJ 08034 856-616-9600 616-9601 49-8
TF: 877-737-9696 ■ *Web:* www.aspan.org

American Society of Plant Biologists (ASPB)
15501 Monona Dr ... Rockville MD 20855 301-251-0560 49-19
Web: my.aspb.org

American Society of Plastic Surgeons (ASPS)
444 E Algonquin Rd ... Arlington Heights IL 60005 847-228-9900 228-9131 49-8
TF: 888-475-2784 ■ *Web:* www.plasticsurgery.org

American Society of Professional Estimators (ASPE)
2525 Perimeter Pl Dr Ste 103 ... Nashville TN 37214 615-316-9200 316-9800 49-3
TF: 888-378-6283 ■ *Web:* www.aspenational.org

American Society of Radiologic Technologists (ASRT)
15000 Central Ave SE ... Albuquerque NM 87123 505-298-4500 298-5063 49-8
TF: 800-444-2778 ■ *Web:* www.asrt.org

American Society of Regional Anesthesia & Pain Medicine (ASRA)
239 Fourth Ave Ste 1714 ... Pittsburgh PA 15222 412-471-2718 471-7503 49-8
TF: 855-795-2772 ■ *Web:* www.asra.com

American Society of Safety Engineers (ASSE)
1800 E Oakton St ... Des Plaines IL 60018 847-699-2929 768-3434 49-19
Web: www.asse.org

American Society of Travel Agents (ASTA)
1101 King St Ste 200 ... Alexandria VA 22314 703-739-2782 684-8319 48-23
TF: 800-275-2782 ■ *Web:* www.asta.org

American Society of Travel Agents PAC
1101 King St Ste 490 ... Alexandria VA 22314 703-739-2782 838-8467 615
TF: 800-275-2782 ■ *Web:* www.asta.org

American Society of Tropical Medicine & Hygiene
111 Deer Lake Rd Ste 100 ... Deerfield IL 60015 847-480-9592 480-9282 49-8
Web: www.astmh.org

American Society on Aging (ASA)
575 Market St Ste 2100 ... San Francisco CA 94105 415-974-9600 974-0300 48-6
TF: 800-537-9728 ■ *Web:* www.asaging.org

American Sociological Assn (ASA)
1307 New York Ave ... Washington DC 20005 202-383-9005 638-0882 49-5
TF: 800-524-9400 ■ *Web:* www.asanet.org

American Software Inc
470 E Paces Ferry Rd ... Atlanta GA 30305 404-261-4381 264-5206 178-1
NASDAQ: AMSWA ■ *TF:* 800-726-2946 ■ *Web:* www.amsoftware.com

American Solar Energy Society (ASES)
2525 Arapahoe Ave Ste E4 253 ... Boulder CO 80302 303-443-3130 48-12
Web: www.ases.org

American Solutions for Business
31 E Minnesota Ave E ... Glenwood MN 56334 800-862-3690 634-5265* 534
**Fax Area Code:* 320 ■ *TF:* 800-862-3690 ■ *Web:* home.americanbus.com

American Southern Insurance Co
3715 Northside Pkwy NW Bldg 400 Ste 800 ... Atlanta GA 30327 404-266-9599 266-8327 391-4
TF: 800-241-1172 ■ *Web:* www.amsou.com

American Soybean Assn (ASA)
12125 Woodcrest Executive Dr Ste 100 ... Saint Louis MO 63141 314-576-1770 576-2786 48-2
TF: 800-688-7692 ■ *Web:* www.soygrowers.com

American Specialties Inc (ASI)
441 Saw Mill River Rd ... Yonkers NY 10701 914-476-9000 476-0688 609
Web: www.americanspecialties.com

American Specialty Health Plans
10221 Wateridge Cir ... San Diego CA 92121 800-848-3555 391-3
TF: 800-848-3555 ■ *Web:* www.ashcompanies.com

American Spectator Magazine
933 N Kenmore St Ste 405 ... Arlington VA 22201 703-807-2011 457-17
TF: 800-524-3469 ■ *Web:* www.spectator.org

American Spectrum Realty Inc
2401 Fountain View 7th Fl ... Houston TX 77057 713-706-6200 706-6251 655
NYSE: AQQ

American Speech-Language-Hearing Assn (ASHA)
2200 Research Blvd ... Rockville MD 20850 301-296-5700 296-8580 49-8
TF: 800-498-2071 ■ *Web:* www.asha.org

American Spice Trade Assn (ASTA)
1101 17th St NW Ste 700 ... Washington DC 20036 202-331-2460 463-8998 49-6
Web: www.astaspice.org

American Spirit 1776 D St NW ... Washington DC 20006 202-628-1776 628-0820 457-10
TF: 800-424-8200 ■
Web: dar.org/national-society/american-spirit-magazine

American Spirit Graphics Corp
801 SE Ninth St ... Minneapolis MN 55414 612-623-3333 623-9314 627
Web: www.asgc.com

American Spoon Foods Inc
1668 Clarion Ave ... Petoskey MI 49770 231-347-9030 296-20
TF: 800-222-5886 ■ *Web:* www.spoon.com

American Sport Art Museum & Archives
1 Academy Dr ... Daphne AL 36526 251-626-3303 626-3874 520
Web: www.asama.org

American Sportfishing Assn (ASA)
1001 N Fairfax St Ste 501 ... Alexandria VA 22314 703-519-9691 519-1872 49-4
Web: www.asafishing.org

American Sportfishing Assnn PAC (ASA PAC)
225 Reinekers Ln Ste 420 ... Alexandria VA 22314 703-519-9691 519-1872 615
Web: www.asafishing.org

American Sports 74 Albe Dr Ste 1 ... Newark DE 19702 302-369-9480 250-4024 710
TF: 866-207-3179 ■ *Web:* www.americansports.com

American Sports Institute (ASI)
116 E Blithedale Ave ... Mill Valley CA 94941 415-383-5750 48-22

American Spring Wire Corp
26300 Miles Rd ... Cleveland OH 44128 216-292-4620 718
Web: www.americanspringwire.com

American Staffing Assn (ASA)
277 S Washington St Ste 200 ... Alexandria VA 22314 703-253-2020 253-2053 49-12
Web: www.americanstaffing.net

American Stage
163 Third St N ... Saint Petersburg FL 33701 727-823-1600 821-2444 572
TF: 800-435-7352 ■ *Web:* www.americanstage.org

American Stainless & Supply LLC
815 State Rd ... Cheraw SC 29520 843-537-5231 605-2
Web: americanstainlessandsupply.com

American Stair Corp Inc
642 Forestwood Dr ... Romeoville IL 60446 800-872-7824 372-3684* 491
**Fax Area Code:* 815 ■ *TF:* 800-872-7824 ■ *Web:* www.americanstair.com

American Standard Cos Inc
1 Centennial Ave ... Piscataway NJ 08855 800-442-1902 360-3
TF: 800-442-1902 ■ *Web:* www.americanstandard-us.com

American Standard Cos Inc Bath & Kitchen Products Div
1 Centennial Ave PO Box 6820 ... Piscataway NJ 08855 800-442-1902 611
TF: 800-442-1902 ■ *Web:* www.americanstandard-us.com

American Standard Insurance Company of Wisconsin
6000 American Pkwy ... Madison WI 53783 608-249-2111 391-2
TF: 800-692-6326 ■ *Web:* www.amfam.com

American Standards Testing Bureau Inc
40 Water St ... New York NY 10274 212-943-3160 825-2250 743

American State Bank 1401 Ave Q ... Lubbock TX 79401 806-767-7000 360-2
TF: 800-531-1401 ■ *Web:* www.prosperitybankusa.com

American States Water Co
630 E Foothill Blvd ... San Dimas CA 91773 909-394-3600 360-5
NYSE: AWR ■ *TF:* 800-999-4033 ■ *Web:* www.aswater.com

American Statistical Assn (ASA)
732 N Washington St ... Alexandria VA 22314 703-684-1221 684-2037 49-19
TF: 888-231-3473 ■ *Web:* www.amstat.org

American Steamship Co
500 Essjay Rd
Centerpointe Corporate Pk ... Williamsville NY 14221 716-635-0222 635-0220 314
Web: www.americansteamship.com

American Steel & Aluminum Company Inc
3545 E Main St ... Grand Prairie TX 75050 972-264-1533 492
Web: www.asafab.com

American Steel Corp
4884 S Desert View Dr ... Apache Junction AZ 85220 480-474-0100 492
Web: www.americansteelcorporation.com

American Steel Fabricators Inc
2686 Industrial Ave ... North Charleston SC 29405 843-747-2860 480

American Steel Products Inc
5620 NE 65th Ave ... Portland OR 97218 503-288-8420 492
Web: www.americansteelonline.com

American Stone Virginia LLC
8179 Arba Ave ... Ruther Glen VA 22546 804-448-9460 183
Web: www.asiprecast.com

American String Teachers Association (ASTA)
4155 Chain Bridge Rd ... Fairfax VA 22030 703-279-2113 279-2114 49-5
TF: 800-821-7303 ■ *Web:* www.astaweb.com

American Strip Steel Inc
901 Coopertown Rd ... Delanco NJ 08075 800-526-1216 412-1442* 492
**Fax Area Code:* 908 ■ *TF:* 800-526-1216 ■ *Web:* www.americanstrip.com

American Structural Metals Inc
777 Lehmann Way PO Box 40 ... Somerset WI 54025 715-247-5950 480
Web: www.asm-mmf.com

American Studies Assn (ASA)
1120 19th St NW Ste 301 ... Washington DC 20036 202-467-4783 467-4786 49-5
TF: 800-468-3571 ■ *Web:* www.theasa.net

American Subcontractors Assn Inc (ASA)
1004 Duke St ... Alexandria VA 22314 703-684-3450 836-3482 49-3
TF: 866-378-8866 ■ *Web:* www.asaonline.com

American Superconductor Corp
64 Jackson Rd ... Devens MA 01434 978-842-3000 815
Web: www.amsc.com

American Supply Assn PAC (ASA PAC)
1200 N Arlington Heights Rd Ste 150 ... Itasca IL 60143 630-467-0000 615
Web: www.asa.net

American Surplus Inc
1 Noyes Ave Bldg B ... Rumford RI 02916 401-434-4355 321
TF: 800-876-3736 ■ *Web:* www.americansurplus.com

Phone | Fax | Class

American Suzuki Motor Corp
3251 Imperial Hwy ... Brea CA 92821 714-996-7040 517
Web: www.suzuki.com

American Swedish Historical Museum
1900 Pattison Ave ... Philadelphia PA 19145 215-389-1776 389-7701 520
TF: 800-222-4750 ■ *Web:* www.americanswedish.org

American Swedish Institute, The (ASI)
2600 Pk Ave ... Minneapolis MN 55407 612-871-4907 871-8682 520
TF: 800-798-6032 ■ *Web:* www.asimn.org

American Symphony Orchestra
263 W 38 St 10th Fl ... New York NY 10018 212-868-9276 868-9277 573-3
Web: www.americansymphony.org

American Synthetic Fiber LLC
312 S Holland Dr ... Pendergrass GA 30567 706-693-2422 683
Web: www.asfiber.com

American Systems Corp
14151 Pk Meadow Dr Ste 500 ... Chantilly VA 20151 703-968-6300 968-5151 180
TF: 800-733-2721 ■ *Web:* www.americansystems.com

American Tank & Fabricating Co (AT&F)
12314 Elmwood Ave ... Cleveland OH 44111 216-252-1500 251-4963 723
TF: 800-544-5316 ■ *Web:* www.atfco.com

American Target Advertising Inc
9625 Surveyor Ct Ste 400 ... Manassas VA 20110 703-392-7676 5
Web: americantarget.com

American Tcb 7560 Lindbergh Dr ... Gaithersburg MD 20879 301-216-1500 193
Web: wll.com

American Technical Ceramics Corp
1 Norden Ln ... Huntington Station NY 11746 631-622-4700 622-4748 249
Web: www.atceramics.com

American Technology Network Corp
1341 San Mateo Ave ... South San Francisco CA 94080 650-875-0130 544
TF: 800-910-2862 ■ *Web:* www.atncorp.com

American Technology Services Inc
2751 Prosperity Ave 6th Fl ... Fairfax VA 22031 703-876-0300 177
Web: www.networkats.com

American Telecare
15159 Technology Dr ... Eden Prairie MN 55344 952-897-0000 153
Web: www.americantelecare.com

American Telecast Corp
835 Springdale Dr Ste 206 ... Exton PA 19341 610-430-7800 4
Web: www.americantelecast.com

American Textile Co 10 N Linden St ... Duquesne PA 15110 412-948-1020 948-1002 746
TF Cust Svc: 800-289-2826 ■ *Web:* www.americantextile.com

American Textile History Museum
491 Dutton St ... Lowell MA 01854 978-441-0400 441-1412 520
Web: www.athm.org

American Textile Machinery Assn (ATMA)
201 Pk Washington Ct ... Falls Church VA 22046 703-538-1789 49-13
TF: 800-225-4324 ■ *Web:* www.atmanet.org

American Theological Library Assn (ATLA)
300 S Wacker Dr Ste 2100 ... Chicago IL 60606 312-454-5100 454-5505 48-20
TF: 888-665-2852 ■ *Web:* www.atla.com

American Therapeutic Recreation Assn (ATRA)
629 N Main St ... Hattiesburg MS 39401 601-450-2872 582-3354 48-17
TF: 800-433-5255 ■ *Web:* www.atra-online.com

American Thermoplastic Co (ATC)
106 Gamma Dr ... Pittsburgh PA 15238 800-245-6600 86
TF: 800-245-6600 ■ *Web:* www.binders.com

American Thermoplastic Extrusion Co
4851 NW 128th St Rd ... Opa Locka FL 33054 305-769-9566 769-1998 599

American Thoracic Society (ATS)
61 Broadway 4th Fl ... New York NY 10006 212-315-8600 315-6498 49-8
TF: 866-316-2673 ■ *Web:* www.thoracic.org

American Time & Signal Co 140 Third St ... Dassel MN 55325 320-275-2101 411
Web: www.american-time.com

American Tinnitus Assn (ATA)
522 SW Fifth Ave Ste 825 ... Portland OR 97204 503-248-9985 248-0024 48-17
TF: 800-634-8978 ■ *Web:* www.ata.org

American Tire Depot
14407 Alondra Blvd ... La Mirada CA 92833 562-677-3950 677-3956 755
TF: 855-899-3764 ■ *Web:* www.americantiredepot.com

American Tool & Mold Inc
1700 Sunshine Dr ... Clearwater FL 33765 727-447-7377 447-0125 757
Web: www.a-t-m.com

American Torch Tip Co
6212 29th St E ... Bradenton FL 34203 941-753-7557 811
Web: americantorchtip.com

American Tort Reform Assn (ATRA)
1101 Connecticut Ave NW Ste 400 ... Washington DC 20036 202-682-1163 682-1022 49-10
Web: www.atra.org

American Tower Corp
116 Huntington Ave 11th Fl ... Boston MA 02116 617-375-7500 375-7575 170
NYSE: AMT ■ *TF:* 877-282-7483 ■ *Web:* www.americantower.com

American Town Network LLC
43 Ruane St ... Fairfield CT 06824 203-256-3390 532-3
TF: 800-331-8923 ■ *Web:* www.americantowns.com

American Trademark Construction Services Inc
200 Lau Pkwy ... Englewood OH 45315 937-832-8885 186
TF: 800-257-5540 ■ *Web:* www.atcs-online.com

American Traffic Safety Services Assn (ATSSA)
15 Riverside Pkwy Ste 100 ... Fredericksburg VA 22406 540-368-1701 368-1717 49-21
TF: 800-272-8772 ■ *Web:* www.atssa.com

American Traffic Solutions Inc
42 Oriental St ... Providence RI 02908 401-274-5658 178-10
OTC: NEST

American Trails PO Box 491797 ... Redding CA 96049 530-547-2060 547-2035 48-23
TF: 866-363-7226 ■ *Web:* www.americantrails.org

American Trails West (ATW)
92 Middle Neck Rd ... Great Neck NY 11021 516-487-2800 487-2855 760
TF: 800-645-6260 ■ *Web:* www.atwteentours.com

American Train Dispatchers Assn
4239 W 150th St ... Cleveland OH 44135 216-251-7984 414

American Translators Assn (ATA)
225 Reinekers Ln Ste 590 ... Alexandria VA 22314 703-683-6100 683-6122 49-5
Web: www.atanet.org

American Trim 1005 W Grand Ave ... Lima OH 45801 419-228-1145 996-4850 488
Web: www.amtrim.com

American Trucking Assn (ATA)
950 N Glebe Rd Ste 210 ... Arlington VA 22203 703-838-1700 49-21
TF: 800-282-5463 ■ *Web:* www.trucking.org

American Trust Administrators Inc
255 NW Blue Pkwy Ste 100 ... Lees Summit MO 64063 816-251-7700 391-2
Web: www.ataamerica.com

American Tubing Inc 2191 Ford Ave ... Springdale AR 72764 479-756-1291 567
Web: www.americantubing.com

American Turned Products Inc
7626 Klier Dr ... Fairview PA 16415 814-474-4200 474-4718 621
Web: www.atpteam.com

American TV & Appliance of Madison Inc
2404 W Beltline Hwy ... Madison WI 53713 608-271-1000 35
Web: www.americantv.com

American Twisting Co
1675 Stieve Dr ... South Haven MI 49090 269-637-8581 548
Web: americantwisting.com

American Type Culture Collection (ATCC)
10801 University Blvd PO Box 1549 ... Manassas VA 20108 703-365-2700 365-2701 668
TF Cust Svc: 800-638-6597 ■ *Web:* www.atcc.org

American Ultraviolet Co
40 Morristown Rd ... Bernardsville NJ 07924 908-696-1130 696-1131 811
TF: 800-288-9288 ■ *Web:* www.americanultraviolet.com

American Uniform Co
4363 Ocoee St N Ste 3 ... Cleveland TN 37312 423-476-6561 155-19

American United Life Insurance Co
1 American Sq 510A PO Box 368 ... Indianapolis IN 46206 317-285-1877 391-2
TF: 800-537-6442 ■ *Web:* www.oneamerica.com

American University
4400 Massachusetts Ave NW ... Washington DC 20016 202-885-1000 885-2558 166
TF: 800-829-1040 ■ *Web:* www.american.edu

American University Washington College of Law
4801 Massachusetts Ave NW ... Washington DC 20016 202-274-4101 274-4107 167-1
TF: 800-995-6423 ■ *Web:* www.wcl.american.edu

American Urban Radio Networks
960 Penn Ave 4th Fl ... Pittsburgh PA 15222 412-456-4000 456-4040 646
TF: 800-456-4211 ■ *Web:* www.aurn.com

American Urethane Inc 1905 Betson Ct ... Odenton MD 21113 410-672-2100 672-2191 604
Web: www.americanurethane.com

American Urological Assn (AUA)
1000 Corporate Blvd ... Linthicum MD 21090 410-689-3700 689-3800 49-8
TF: 866-746-4282 ■ *Web:* www.auanet.org

American Utility Management Inc
2211 S York Rd Ste 320 ... Oak Brook IL 60523 866-520-1245 218-1401* 463
**Fax Area Code:* 603 ■ *TF:* 866-520-1245 ■ *Web:* www.aum-inc.com

American Valve & Hydrant Manufacturing Company LP
3525 Hollywood St ... Beaumont TX 77701 409-832-7721 789
Web: www.avhmc.com

American Vanguard Corp
4695 MacArthur Ct ... Newport Beach CA 92660 949-260-1200 145
NYSE: AVD ■ *Web:* www.american-vanguard.com

American Veterinary Medical Assn (AVMA)
1931 N Meacham Rd Ste 100 ... Schaumburg IL 60173 847-925-8070 925-1329 49-8
TF: 800-248-2862 ■ *Web:* www.avma.org

American Veterinary Medical Assn PAC (AVMA)
1910 Sunderland Pl NW ... Washington DC 20036 202-789-0007 842-4360 615
TF: 800-321-1473 ■ *Web:* www.avma.org

American Visionary Art Museum
800 Key Hwy ... Baltimore MD 21230 410-244-1900 244-5858 520
Web: www.avam.org

American Volkssport Assn (AVA)
1001 Pat Booker Rd Ste 101 ... Universal City TX 78148 210-659-2112 659-1212 48-22
TF: 855-999-5200 ■ *Web:* www.ava.org

American Warehouses Inc
1918 Collingsworth St ... Houston TX 77009 713-228-6381 228-5913 803-1
TF: 800-987-0482 ■ *Web:* www.americanwarehouses.com

American Warmblood Registry (AWR)
PO Box 1332 ... DeLeon Springs FL 32130 406-734-5499 667-0516* 48-3
**Fax Area Code:* 775 ■ *TF:* 800-575-1669 ■ *Web:* www.americanwarmblood.com

American Warming & Ventilating Inc
7301 International Dr ... Holland OH 43528 419-865-5000 865-1375 697
Web: www.awv.com

American Waste Digest Corp
226 King St ... Pottstown PA 19464 610-326-9480 532-3
Web: www.americanwastedigest.com

American Watchmakers-Clockmakers Institute (AWI)
701 Enterprise Dr ... Harrison OH 45030 513-367-9800 367-1414 49-4
TF: 866-367-2924 ■ *Web:* awci.com

American Water Ski Hall of Fame & Museum
1251 Holy Cow Rd ... Polk City FL 33868 863-324-2472 324-3996 522
TF: 800-533-2972 ■ *Web:* usawaterskifoundation.org

American Water Works Assn (AWWA)
6666 W Quincy Ave ... Denver CO 80235 303-794-7711 347-0804 48-12
TF: 800-926-7337 ■ *Web:* www.awwa.org

American Water Works Co Inc
1025 Laurel Oak Rd ... Voorhees NJ 08043 856-346-8200 346-8360 360-5
NYSE: AWK ■ *TF:* 888-282-6816 ■ *Web:* www.amwater.com

American Waterways Operators (AWO)
801 N Quincy St Ste 200 ... Arlington VA 22203 703-841-9300 841-0389 49-21
Web: www.americanwaterways.com

American Welding Society (AWS)
550 NW 42nd Ave ... Miami FL 33126 305-443-9353 443-7559 49-3
TF: 800-443-9353 ■ *Web:* www.aws.org

American West Homes
250 Pilot Rd Ste 140 ... Las Vegas NV 89119 702-736-6434 653
Web: www.americanwesthomes.com

American Whitewater (AW) PO Box 1540 ... Cullowhee NC 28723 828-586-1930 586-2840 48-23
TF: 866-262-8429 ■ *Web:* americanwhitewater.org

American Wilbert Vault Corp
7525 W 99th Pl ... Bridgeview IL 60455 708-366-3210 366-3281 134
TF: 800-328-5040 ■ *Web:* www.americanwilbert.com

American Wind Energy Assn (AWEA)
1501 M St NW Ste 1000 ... Washington DC 20005 202-383-2500 383-2505 48-12
Web: www.awea.org

American Wind Power Ctr
1701 Canyon Lake Dr ... Lubbock TX 79403 806-747-8734 520
Web: www.windmill.com

Phone | Fax | Class

American Window & Glass Inc
2716 Lynch Rd, Evansville IN 47711 — 812-464-9400 | 464-3131 | 608
TF: 877-671-6943 ■ *Web:* www.americanwindowandglass.com

American Wire Producers Assn (AWPA)
801 N Fairfax St Ste 211, Alexandria VA 22314 — 703-299-4434 | 299-9233 | 49-13
Web: www.awpa.org

American Wire Rope & Sling
3122 Engle Rd, Fort Wayne IN 46809 — 866-578-4700 | | 492
TF: 866-578-4700 ■ *Web:* www.awrsling.com

American Woman's Society of Certified Public Accountants (AWSCPA)
1430 Yale St, Houston OH 77008 — 713-893-5685 | | 49-1
Web: www.awscpa.org

American Wood Dryers Inc
15495 SE Formor Ct, Clackamas OR 97015 — 503-655-1955 | | 454
Web: www.drykilns.us

American Wood Fibers Inc
9841 Broken Land Pkwy Ste 302, Columbia MD 21046 — 410-290-8700 | | 820
Web: www.awf.com

American Woodmark Corp
3102 Shawnee Dr, Winchester VA 22601 — 540-665-9100 | 665-9176 | 115
NASDAQ: AMWD ■ *TF:* 800-255-4204 ■ *Web:* www.americanwoodmark.com

American Youth Soccer Organization (AYSO)
19750 S Vermont Ave Ste 200, Torrance CA 90502 — 800-872-2976 | 525-1155* | 48-22
**Fax Area Code:* 310 ■ *TF:* 800-872-2976 ■ *Web:* ayso.org

American Zettler Inc 75 Columbia, Aliso Viejo CA 92656 — 949-831-5000 | 831-8642 | 203
Web: www.azettler.com

American Zoetrope 916 Kearny St, San Francisco CA 94133 — 415-788-1700 | | 514
Web: www.zoetrope.com

Americana Tickets NY 1535 Broadway, New York NY 10036 — 212-581-6660 | | 750
TF: 800-833-3121 ■ *Web:* www.americanaticketsny.com

American-Arab Anti Discrimination Committee (ADC)
1990 M St NW Ste 610, Washington DC 20036 — 202-244-2990 | 244-3196 | 48-8
TF: 800-253-3931 ■ *Web:* www.adc.org

AmericanChurch Inc 525 McClurg Rd, Huntington IN 46750 — 800-446-3035 | 275-5771* | 263
**Fax Area Code:* 877 ■ *TF:* 800-446-3035 ■ *Web:* www.americanchurch.com

American-Indonesian Chamber of Commerce
317 Madison Ave Ste 1619, New York NY 10017 — 212-687-4505 | 687-5844 | 138
Web: www.aiccusa.org

American-International Charolais Assn (AICA)
11700 NW Plaza Cir, Kansas City MO 64153 — 816-464-5977 | 464-5759 | 48-2
TF: 800-270-7711 ■ *Web:* www.charolaisusa.com

American-Israel Chamber of Commerce & Industry of Minnesota
13100 Wayzata Blvd, Minnetonka MN 55305 — 952-593-8666 | | 138
Web: www.aiccmn.org

American-Israel Chamber of Commerce Southeast Region (AICC)
400 Northridge Rd Ste 260, Atlanta GA 30350 — 404-843-9426 | 843-1416 | 138
Web: www.aiccse.org

Americanna Co 29 Aldrin Rd, Plymouth MA 02360 — 508-747-5550 | | 9
TF Cust Svc: 888-747-5550 ■ *Web:* www.americanna.com

Americano Beach Resort
1260 N Atlantic Ave, Daytona Beach FL 32118 — 386-255-7431 | 253-9513 | 669
TF: 800-874-1824 ■ *Web:* www.thesuitesatamericanobeach.com

American-Russian Chamber of Commerce & Industry
1101 Pennsylvania Ave NW 6th Fl, Washington DC 20004 — 202-756-4943 | 362-4634 | 138
Web: www.arcci.org

Americans for Democratic Action (ADA)
1625 K St NW Ste 210, Washington DC 20006 — 202-785-5980 | 785-5969 | 48-7
TF: 855-712-8441 ■ *Web:* www.adaction.org

Americans for Effective Law Enforcement (AELE)
841 W Touhy Ave, Park Ridge IL 60068 — 847-685-0700 | 685-9700 | 48-8
TF: 800-763-2802 ■ *Web:* www.aele.org

Americans for Fair Taxation
PO Box 4929, Clearwater FL 33758 — 800-324-7829 | | 48-7
TF: 800-324-7829 ■ *Web:* www.fairtax.org

Americans for Nonsmokers' Rights (ANR)
2530 San Pablo Ave Ste J, Berkeley CA 94702 — 510-841-3032 | 841-3071 | 48-17
TF: 800-735-2966 ■ *Web:* www.no-smoke.org

Americans for Peace Now (APN)
1101 14th St NW 6th Fl, Washington DC 20005 — 202-728-1893 | 728-1895 | 48-7
TF: 877-429-0678 ■ *Web:* www.peacenow.org

Americans for Tax Reform (ATR)
722 12th St NW Ste 4, Washington DC 20005 — 202-785-0266 | 785-0261 | 48-8
Web: www.atr.org

Americans for the Arts
1000 Vermont Ave NW 6th Fl, Washington DC 20005 — 202-371-2830 | 371-0424 | 48-4
Web: americansforthearts.org

Americans United for Separation of Church & State
518 C St NE, Washington DC 20002 — 202-466-3234 | 466-2587 | 48-7
TF: 800-875-3707 ■ *Web:* www.au.org

AmericanTours International LLC (ATI)
6053 W Century Blvd, Los Angeles CA 90045 — 310-641-9953 | 216-5807 | 760
Web: www.americantours.com

AmericanWest Bank 2237 NW 57th St, Seattle WA 98107 — 206-784-2200 | | 70
Web: www.bannerbank.com

Americarb Inc 1025 Faultless Dr, Ashland OH 44805 — 419-281-5800 | | 127
Web: www.americarb.com

Americare Certified Special Services Inc
5923 Strickland Ave, Brooklyn NY 11234 — 718-535-3100 | | 363
Web: www.americareny.com

AmeriCare Medical Inc 1938 Woodslee Dr, Troy MI 48083 — 248-280-2020 | | 363
TF: 800-732-5569 ■ *Web:* www.americaremedical.com

Americare Systems Inc 214 N Scott St, Sikeston MO 63801 — 573-471-1113 | | 451
Web: www.americareusa.net

AmeriCares Foundation
88 Hamilton Ave, Stamford CT 06902 — 203-658-9500 | | 48-5
TF: 800-486-4357 ■ *Web:* www.americares.org

Americas electric cooperatives (NRECA)
4301 Wilson Blvd, Arlington VA 22203 — 703-907-5939 | | 48-12
Web: www.nreca.coop

Americas Floor Source
3442 Millennium Ct, Columbus OH 43219 — 614-237-3181 | | 131
Web: www.americasfloorsource.com

Americas Society 680 Pk Ave 68th St, New York NY 10065 — 212-628-3200 | 628-3200 | 48-11
Web: www.as-coa.org

Americas Styrenics LLC
24 Waterway Ave Ste 1200, Woodlands TX 77380 — 832-616-7800 | | 146
TF: 844-512-1212 ■ *Web:* www.amsty.com

Phone | Fax | Class

AmericasMart
240 Peachtree St NW Ste 2200, Atlanta GA 30303 — 404-220-3000 | | 205
TF: 800-285-6278 ■ *Web:* www.americasmart.com

Americh Corp 13212 Saticoy St, North Hollywood CA 91605 — 818-982-1711 | | 610
Web: www.americh.com

Americhem Inc
2000 Americhem Way, Cuyahoga Falls OH 44221 — 330-929-4213 | 929-4144 | 143
TF: 800-228-3476 ■ *Web:* www.americhem.com

Americhip Inc 19032 S Vermont Ave, Los Angeles CA 90248 — 310-323-3697 | | 195
Web: www.americhip.com

AmeriChoice Corp
8045 Leesburg Pk 6th Fl, Vienna VA 22182 — 703-506-3555 | 506-3556 | 391-3
Web: www.americhoice.com

AmericInn International LLC
250 Lake Dr E, Chanhassen MN 55317 — 952-294-5000 | 294-5001 | 379
TF Resv: 800-634-3444 ■ *Web:* www.americinn.com

Americo Federal Credit Union
4101 Main St, Erie PA 16511 — 814-899-6608 | | 219
Web: americofcu.com

Americo Financial Life & Annuity Insurance Co
PO Box 410288, Kansas City MO 64141 — 800-231-0801 | | 391-2
TF: 800-231-0801 ■ *Web:* www.americo.com

Americo Life Inc 300 W 11th St, Kansas City MO 64105 — 816-391-2000 | | 360-4
TF General: 800-231-0801 ■ *Web:* www.americo.com

Americo Manufacturing Company Inc
6224 N Main St, Acworth GA 30101 — 770-974-7000 | | 1
Web: www.americomfg.com

AmeriCom Inc PO Box 2146, Sandy UT 84091 — 801-571-2446 | 257-6643* | 736
**Fax Area Code:* 775 ■ *TF:* 800-820-6296 ■ *Web:* www.americom.com

Americomm 804 Greenbrier Cir, Chesapeake VA 23320 — 757-622-2724 | | 5
TF: 800-527-6757 ■ *Web:* americommllc.com

Americor Press 880 Louis Dr, Warminster PA 18974 — 215-259-1600 | | 627
TF: 800-788-8511 ■ *Web:* www.americorpress.com

Americorp Financial LLC
877 S Adams Rd, Birmingham MI 48009 — 248-723-4500 | | 194
Web: www.eamericorp.com

Americtraining Inc 4315 Brook Rd NW, Lancaster OH 43130 — 740-756-7461 | | 196
Web: www.ameritraining.com

Americu Credit Union
1916 Black River Blvd, Rome NY 13440 — 315-356-3000 | | 219
Web: americu.org

Ameridial Inc
4535 Strausser St NW, North Canton OH 44720 — 800-445-7128 | 497-5500* | 737
**Fax Area Code:* 330 ■ *TF:* 800-445-7128 ■ *Web:* www.ameridial.com

Ameridrives 1802 Pittsburgh Ave, Erie PA 16502 — 814-480-5000 | 453-5891 | 620
TF: 800-352-0141 ■ *Web:* www.ameridrives.com

AmeriDrives International
1802 Pittsburgh Ave, Erie PA 16502 — 814-480-5000 | 453-5891 | 620
TF: 800-352-0141 ■ *Web:* www.ameridrives.com

AmeriFab Inc 3501 E Ninth St, Indianapolis IN 46201 — 317-231-0100 | | 492
Web: www.amerifabinc.com

AmeriFactors
215 Celebration Pl Ste 340, Celebration FL 34747 — 407-566-1150 | 566-1250 | 272
TF: 800-884-3863 ■ *Web:* www.amerifactors.com

Ameri-Fax Corp 6520 W 20th Ave Unit 2, Hialeah FL 33016 — 305-828-1701 | 824-1606 | 554
TF: 800-262-8214 ■ *Web:* www.posconcepts.com

Ameriflex Inc 2390 Railroad St, Corona CA 92880 — 951-737-5557 | | 492
Web: www.ameriflex.com

Ameriflight Inc
1515 W 20th St PO Box 612763, DFW Airport TX 75261 — 818-847-0000 | 846-3950* | 12
**Fax:* Cust Svc ■ *TF:* 800-800-4538 ■ *Web:* w3.ameriflight.com

Ameri-Force Inc
9485 Regency Sq Blvd Ste 300, Jacksonville FL 32225 — 904-353-1773 | | 360-2
Web: www.ameriforce.com

Ameri-Forge Group Inc
13770 Industrial Rd, Houston TX 77015 — 713-393-4200 | | 483
Web: www.ameriforge.com

AmeriGas Inc 460 N Gulph Rd, King of Prussia PA 19406 — 610-337-7000 | | 316
Web: www.amerigas.com

AmeriGas Partners LP
460 N Gulph Rd, King of Prussia PA 19406 — 610-337-7000 | 992-3259 | 316
NYSE: APU ■ *TF:* 800-427-4968 ■ *Web:* www.amerigas.com

AmeriGas Propane Inc PO Box 965, Valley Forge PA 19482 — 610-337-7000 | | 579
TF: 800-934-6802 ■ *Web:* www.amerigas.com

Amerigo Nashville 1920 W End Ave, Nashville TN 37203 — 615-320-1740 | | 671
TF: 800-321-2211 ■ *Web:* www.amerigo.net

AMERIgreen Energy Inc
1862 Charter Ln Ste 101, Lancaster PA 17601 — 717 945 1392 | | 536
TF: 888-423-8357 ■ *Web:* www.amerigreen.com

AMERIGROUP Corp
4425 Corporation Ln, Virginia Beach VA 23462 — 757-490-6900 | | 391-3
NYSE: AGP ■ *TF:* 800-600-4441 ■ *Web:* www.amerigroup.com

Ameriguard Security Services Inc
5470 W Spruce Ave Ste 102, Fresno CA 93722 — 559-271-5984 | | 693
Web: ameriguard.publishpath.com

AmeriHealth Casualty
1700 Market St Ste 700, Philadelphia PA 19103 — 215-587-1901 | 587-1826 | 353
Web: www.amerihealthcasualty.com

AmeriHealth Mercy Health Plan
8040 Carlson Rd Ste 500, Harrisburg PA 17112 — 717-651-3540 | | 352
TF: 888-991-7200 ■ *Web:* amerihealthcaritaspa.com

Ameril-Co Carriers Inc
1702 E Overland, Scottsbluff NE 69361 — 308-635-3157 | | 780
TF: 800-445-5400 ■ *Web:* www.americo-carriers.com

Amerijet International Inc
2800 S Andrews Ave, Fort Lauderdale FL 33316 — 954-320-5300 | | 12
TF: 800-927-6059 ■ *Web:* www.amerijet.com

Ameri-Kart Corp 17196 State Rd 120, Bristol IN 46507 — 574-848-7462 | | 596
Web: www.ameri-kart.com

Amerikohl Mining Inc 202 Sunset Dr, Butler PA 16001 — 724-282-2339 | 282-3226 | 501
Web: www.amerikohl.com

Amerilab Technologies Inc
2765 Niagara Ln N, Minneapolis MN 55447 — 763-525-1262 | | 583
Web: www.amerilabtech.com

Amerilist Inc 978 Route 45 Ste L2, Pomona NY 10970 — 845-362-6737 | | 317
TF: 800-457-2899 ■ *Web:* www.amerilist.com

AmerillumBrands 3728 Maritime Way, Oceanside CA 92056 — 760-727-7675 | | 439
TF: 800-439-0549 ■ *Web:* www.amerillum.com

Company	Phone	Fax	Class
Amerilodge 1040 W Hamlin Rd .... Rochester Hills MI 48309 *Web:* amerilodgegroup.com	248-601-2500		377
Amerimade Technology Inc 449 Mtn Vista Pkwy .... Livermore CA 94551 *TF:* 800-938-3824 ■ *Web:* www.amerimade.com	925-243-9090	243-9266	608
Amerimax Bldg Products Inc 5208 Tennyson Pkwy .... Plano TX 75024 **Fax Area Code:* 800 ■ *Web:* www.amerimaxbp.com	469-366-3200	448-8391*	480
Amerimax Home Products Inc 450 Richardson Dr .... Lancaster PA 17603 *TF:* 800-347-2586 ■ *Web:* www.amerimax.com	717-299-3711		480
Ameripack Inc 107 N Gold Dr.............. Robbinsville NJ 08691 *TF:* 800-456-7963 ■ *Web:* www.ameripack.com	609-259-7004		5
AmeriPark LLC 3200 Cobb Galleria Pkwy Ste 299 .... Atlanta GA 30339 *Web:* www.ameripark.com	678-303-5962		192
AmeriPoint Title Inc 10101 Reunion Pl Ste 250 .... San Antonio TX 78216	210-340-2921		391-6
AmeriPride Services Inc 10801 Wayzata Blvd .... Minnetonka MN 55305 *TF Cust Svc:* 800-750-4628 ■ *Web:* www.ameripride.com	952-738-4200	738-4252	442
Ameriprise Brokerage 70400 Ameriprise Financial Ctr .... Minneapolis MN 55474 *TF:* 800-535-2001 ■ *Web:* www.ameriprise.com	800-535-2001		690
Ameriprise Financial Inc 834 Ameriprise Financial Ctr .... Minneapolis MN 55474 *NYSE: AMP* ■ *TF:* 866-673-3673 ■ *Web:* www.ameriprise.com	612-671-3131		401
Ameriprise Financial Services Inc 70100 Ameriprise Financial Ctr .... Minneapolis MN 55474 *TF:* 866-483-8434 ■ *Web:* www.ameriprise.com	866-483-8434		401
Ameriqual Group LLC 18200 Hwy 41 N .... Evansville IN 47725 *Web:* ameriqualgroup.com	812-867-1444		296-36
Ameris Bank 24 Second Ave SE PO Box 3668................ Moultrie GA 31768 *TF:* 866-616-6020 ■ *Web:* www.amerisbank.com	866-616-6020		186
AMERIS Health Systems LLC 1114 17th Ave S Ste 205 .... Nashville TN 37212 *Web:* www.amerishealth.com	615-327-4440		363
AMERISAFE Inc 2301 Hwy 190 W............. DeRidder LA 70634 *NASDAQ: AMSF* ■ *TF:* 800-256-9052 ■ *Web:* www.amerisafe.com	337-463-9052		391-4
Ameriserv Financial 216 Franklin St PO Box 520.................. Johnstown PA 15907 *NASDAQ: ASRV* ■ *TF:* 800-837-2265 ■ *Web:* www.ameriserv.com	814-533-5300		70
Amerisource Bergen 1300 Morris Dr Ste 100 .... Chesterbrook PA 19087 *NYSE: ABC* ■ *TF:* 800-829-3132 ■ *Web:* www.amerisourcebergen.net	610-727-7000	727-3600	238
Amerispa 90 Rue de Stanstead St Ste 101 .... Bromont QC J2L1K6 *TF:* 866-263-7477 ■ *Web:* www.amerispa.ca	450-534-2717		706
AmeriSpan Unlimited 1334 Walnut St 6 Fl .... Philadelphia PA 19107 *TF:* 800-879-6640 ■ *Web:* www.amerispan.com	215-751-1100	751-1986	423
AmeriSpec Inc 3839 Forest Hill Irene Rd .... Memphis TN 38125 *TF:* 877-769-5217 ■ *Web:* www.amerispec.com	877-769-5217		365
Ameristar Casino & Hotel 3200 N Ameristar Dr....................... Kansas City MO 64161 *TF:* 888-777-8700 ■ *Web:* www.ameristar.com	816-414-7000		379
Ameristar Casino Hotel Council Bluffs 2200 River Rd.............................. Council Bluffs IA 51501 *TF:* 866-667-3386 ■ *Web:* www.ameristar.com	712-328-8888		133
Ameristar Casino Hotel Vicksburg 4116 Washington St........................ Vicksburg MS 39180 *TF:* 800-700-7770 ■ *Web:* www.ameristar.com	601-638-1000		133
Ameristar Casinos Inc 3773 Howard Hughes Pkwy Ste 490-S......... Las Vegas NV 89169 *NASDAQ: ASCA* ■ *TF:* 888-708-5699 ■ *Web:* www.ameristar.com	702-567-7000		132
Ameristar Fence Products Inc 1555 N Mingo Rd............................ Tulsa OK 74116 *TF:* 888-333-3422 ■ *Web:* www.ameristarfence.com	918-835-0898		491
Amerisure Insurance Co 26777 Halsted Rd Ste 200 .... Farmington Hills MI 48331 *TF:* 800-257-1900 ■ *Web:* www.amerisure.com	248-615-9000	615-8548	391-4
Amerit Fleet Solutions Inc 4000 Executive Pkwy Ste 240............... San Ramon CA 94583 *Web:* www.kelleyamerit.com	925-913-4160		393
Amerita Inc 20 Fairbanks Ste 173 .... Irvine CA 92618 *TF:* 800-218-5604 ■ *Web:* www.ameritaiv.com	949-273-6528		363
Ameritas Direct 5900 'O' St .... Lincoln NE 68510 *TF:* 800 555-4655 ■ *Web:* www.ameritasdirect.com	800-555-4655		391-2
Ameritas Life Insurance Corp 5900 'O' St .... Lincoln NE 68510 **Fax:* Hum Res ■ *TF:* 800-745-1112 ■ *Web:* www.ameritas.com	402-467-1122	467-7935*	391-2
Ameritek USA Inc 125 130th St SE Ste 200...................... Everett WA 98208 *Web:* www.ameritek.org	425-379-2580		476
Ameritel Inn Boise Towne Square 7965 W Emerald St.......................... Boise ID 83704 *TF:* 800-600-6001 ■ *Web:* www.ameritelinns.com	208-378-7000		379
Ameritel Inn Pocatello 1440 Bench Rd.............................. Pocatello ID 83201 *TF:* 800-600-6001 ■ *Web:* www.ameritelinns.com	208-234-7500		379
Ameritox Ltd 7090 Samuel Morse Dr Ste 300.............. Columbia MD 21046 *Web:* www.ameritox.com	443-220-0115		225
Ameritube Master Distribution LLC 1000 N Hwy 77.............................. Hillsboro TX 76645 *Web:* www.ameritube.com	254-580-9888		492
Amerivon Holdings LLC 2815 Townsgate Rd Ste 225 .... Westlake Village CA 91361 *Web:* www.amerivon.com	805-719-4800		195
AmeriWater Inc 1303 Stanley Ave............... Dayton OH 45404 *TF:* 800-535-5585 ■ *Web:* ameriwater.com	937-461-8833		45
Ameriwood Industries Inc 410 E S First St........................... Wright City MO 63390 *TF General:* 800-489-3351 ■ *Web:* www.ameriwood.com	636-745-3351		319-2
Amernet 315 Montgomery St .... San Francisco CA 94104 *Web:* www.amer.net	415-616-5100		387
Amerril Energy LLC 3721 Briarpark Dr Ste 155 .... Houston TX 77042	713-660-1620		536
AmerTac 1 Rt 17 S .... Saddle River NJ 07458 *Web:* www.amertac.com	201-934-3224		350
Amery Regional Medical Ctr 265 Griffin St E............................. Amery WI 54001 *TF:* 800-424-5273 ■ *Web:* www.amerymedicalcenter.org	715-268-8000	268-0311	353
Ames 1327 Northbrook Pkwy Ste 400........... Suwanee GA 30024 *TF:* 800-408-2801 ■ *Web:* www.amestools.com	800-303-1827		758
Ames Chamber of Commerce 1601 Golden Aspen Dr Ste 110 .... Ames IA 50010 *TF:* 800-288-7470 ■ *Web:* www.ameschamber.com	515-232-2310	232-6716	139
Ames Community School District 415 Stanton Ave .... Ames IA 50014 *Web:* www.ames.k12.ia.us	515-268-6600	268-6633	685
Ames Corp 19 Ames Blvd.................... Hamburg NJ 07419 *Web:* www.theamescorp.com	973-827-9101	827-8893	677
Ames Fire & Waterworks 1427 N Market Blvd Ste 9.................. Sacramento CA 95834 *Web:* www.amesfirewater.com	916-928-0123	928-9333	609
Ames Laboratory 111 TASF .... Ames IA 50011 *Web:* www.ameslab.gov	515-294-9557	294-3226	668
Ames National Corp 405 Fifth St PO Box 846...................... Ames IA 50010 *NASDAQ: ATLO* ■ *Web:* www.amesnational.com	515-232-6251	663-3033	360-2
Ames Nowell State Park Linwood St........... Abington MA 02351 *Web:* www.mass.gov	781-857-1336		565
Ames Public Library 515 Douglas Ave............ Ames IA 50010 *Web:* www.amespubliclibrary.org	515-239-5630	232-4571	434-3
Ames Supply Co 1936C University Ln............... Lisle IL 60532	630-964-2440	964-0497	385
Ames True Temper Inc 465 Railroad Ave.......................... Camp Hill PA 17011 *TF:* 800-393-1846 ■ *Web:* www.ames.com	800-393-1846		758
Amesbury Group Inc 57 S Hunt Rd........... Amesbury MA 01913 *Web:* www.amesbury.com	978-834-3262		326
Ametco Manufacturing Corp 4326 Hamann Industrial Pky................ Willoughby OH 44094 *TF:* 800-321-7042 ■ *Web:* www.ametco.com	800-321-7042		488
Ametek Advanced Industries Inc 4550 Southeast Blvd......................... Wichita KS 67210 *Web:* www.advancedindustries.com	316-522-0424		22
AMETEK Aerospace & Defense 50 Fordham Rd........................... Wilmington MA 01887 *Web:* www.ametekaerospaceanddefense.com	978-988-4771		472
AMETEK Automation & Process Technologies 1080 N Crooks .... Clawson MI 48017 *TF:* 800-635-0289 ■ *Web:* www.ametekapt.com	248-435-0700	435-8120	201
Ametek HDR Power Systems Inc 3563 Interchange Rd....................... Columbus OH 43204 *TF:* 888-797-2685 ■ *Web:* www.hdrpower.com	614-308-5500	308-5506	253
Ametek HSA Inc 7841 NW 56th St .... Miami FL 33166 *Web:* www.highstandardaviation.com	305-599-8855		22
AMETEK Inc 1100 Cassatt Rd PO Box 1764......... Berwyn PA 19312 *NYSE: AME* ■ **Fax Area Code:* 215 ■ *TF:* 800-473-1286 ■ *Web:* www.ametek.com	610-647-2121	323-9337*	360-3
Ametek Inc 7800 Equitable Dr.............. Minneapolis MN 55344 *Web:* ametekemc.com	612-426-3555		253
AMETEK Inc 485 Oberlin Ave, S............... Lakewood NJ 08701 *TF:* 800-936-8100 ■ *Web:* www.ametek-ecp.com	732-370-9100		815
AMETEK Inc Chemical Products Div 455 Corporate Blvd........................... Newark DE 19702 *TF Orders:* 800-441-7777 ■ *Web:* www.ametekfpp.com	302-456-4431	456-4444	745-3
AMETEK Inc Dixson Div 287 27 Rd............................ Grand Junction CO 81503 *TF:* 888-302-0639 ■ *Web:* www.ametekvis.com	970-242-8863	245-6267	495
AMETEK Inc Test & Calibration Instruments Div 8600 Somerset Dr.............................. Largo FL 33773 *TF:* 800-733-5427 ■ *Web:* www.ametek.com	727-538-6132	538-6121	472
AMETEK Inc Westchester Plastics Div 42 Mountain Ave...................... Nesquehoning PA 18240 *TF:* 800-936-8100 ■ *Web:* www.ametek-westchesterplas.com	570-645-6900	645-6959	599
AMETEK National Controls Corp 1725 Western Dr...................... West Chicago IL 60185 *TF:* 800-323-2593 ■ *Web:* ametekncc.com	630-231-5900	231-1377	203
AMETEK Power Instruments 50 Fordham Rd........................... Wilmington MA 01887 **Fax:* Cust Svc ■ *Web:* www.ametekpower.com	978-988-4903	988-4944*	201
AMETEK Process & Analytical Instruments 150 Freeport Rd .... Pittsburgh PA 15238 *Web:* www.ametekpi.com	412-828-9040	826-0399	201
AMETEK Rotron Mil-Aero Products Div 55 Hasbrouck Ln .... Woodstock NY 12498 *Web:* www.ametekaerodefense.com	845-679-1371	679-1371	18
AMETEK Sensor Technology Drexelbrook Div 205 Keith Valley Rd......................... Horsham PA 19044 *TF Cust Svc:* 800-553-9092 ■ *Web:* www.drexelbrook.com	215-674-1234	674-2731	495
AMETEK Solidstate Controls 875 Dearborn Dr........................... Columbus OH 43085 *TF:* 800-635-7300 ■ *Web:* www.solidstatecontrolsinc.com	614-846-7500	885-3990	253
AMETEK Specialty Metal Products 21 Toelles Rd .... Wallingford CT 06492 *Web:* www.ametekmetals.com	203-265-6731		485
AMETEK Technical & Industrial Products 100 E Erie St................................. Kent OH 44240 *Web:* www.ametekdfs.com	330-673-3452		18
AMETEK US Gauge 820 Pennsylvania Blvd..................... Feasterville PA 19053 *Web:* www.ametekusg.com	215-355-6900	354-1802	472
Ameublements Tanguay Inc 7200 Rue Armand-Viau .... Quebec QC G2C2A7 *Web:* www.tanguay.ca	418-847-4411	847-4848	321
Amex Inc 2724 Summer St NE............... Minneapolis MN 55413 *Web:* www.amexinc.com	612-331-3063	331-3180	174
Amex International Inc 1615 L St NW Ste 340 .... Washington DC 20036 *Web:* www.amexdc.com	202-429-0222		770
Amex World Trade Corp 18765 SW 78th Ct .... Cutler Bay FL 33157 *Web:* www.amexworldtrade.com	305-238-3010		54

	Phone	Fax	Class

AMF Bakery Systems
2115 W Laburnum Ave ... Richmond VA 23227 804-355-7961 355-1074 207
TF: 800-225-3771 ■ *Web:* www.amfbakery.com

AMF Bowling Worldwide Inc
7313 Bell Creek Rd ... Mechanicsville VA 23111 800-342-5263 99
TF: 800-342-5263 ■ *Web:* www.amf.com

AmFAR (American Foundation for AIDS Research)
120 Wall St 13th Fl ... New York NY 10005 212-806-1600 806-1601 48-17
Web: www.amfar.org

Amfed Cos LLC
576 Highland Colony Pkwy ... Ridgeland MS 39157 601-853-4949 853-2727 390
TF: 800-264-8085 ■ *Web:* www.amfed.com

Amfine Chemical Corp
10 Montnview Rd Ste 215N ... Upper Saddle River NJ 07458 201-818-0159 818-0259 146
Web: www.amfine.com

Amfirst Bank NA Mccook 602 W B St ... Mccook NE 69001 308-345-1555 70
Web: amfirstbank.com

AMFM Inc 240 Capitol St Ste 500 ... Charleston WV 25301 304-344-1623 463
TF: 800-348-1623 ■ *Web:* www.amfmwv.com

AMG (Affiliated Managers Group Inc)
600 Hale St ... Prides Crossing MA 01965 617-747-3300 360-3
NYSE: AMG ■ *Web:* www.amg.com

AMG (Association Management Group Inc)
8400 Westpark Dr 2nd Fl ... McLean VA 22102 703-610-9000 610-9005 47
Web: www.amg-inc.com

AMG Inc
301 Jefferson Ridge Pkwy Lynchpin Industrial Ctr
... Lynchburg VA 24501 434-385-7525 454
Web: www.amg-inc.net

AMG Industries Inc
200 Commerce Dr ... Mount Vernon OH 43050 740-397-4044 397-3092* 489
**Fax:* Mail Rm ■ *TF:* 800-222-4357 ■ *Web:* www.amgindustries.com

AMG Medical Inc 8505 Dalton ... Montreal QC H4T1V5 514-737-5251 477
TF: 800-363-2381 ■ *Web:* www.amgmedical.com

AMG Resources Corp
2 Robinson Plaza # 350 ... Pittsburgh PA 15205 412-777-7300 331-0972 686
TF: 877-395-8338 ■ *Web:* www.amgresources.com

AMGA (American Medical Group Assn)
1422 Duke St ... Alexandria VA 22314 703-838-0033 548-1890 49-8
Web: www.amga.org

Am-Gard Security Inc 600 Main St ... Pittsburgh PA 15215 412-781-5800 693
TF: 800-554-0412 ■ *Web:* www.am-gard.com

Amgen Canada Inc
6775 Financial Dr Ste 100 ... Mississauga ON L5N0A4 905-285-3000 285-3100 85
TF: 800-665-4273 ■ *Web:* www.amgen.ca

Amgen Inc 1 Amgen Ctr Dr ... Thousand Oaks CA 91320 805-447-1000 85
TF: 800-563-9798 ■ *Web:* www.amgen.com

Amglo Kemlight Laboratories Inc
215 Gateway Rd ... Bensenville IL 60106 630-350-9470 350-9474 437
Web: www.amglo.com

Amgraf Inc 1501 Oak St ... Kansas City MO 64108 816-474-4797 180
TF: 800-304-4797 ■ *Web:* amgraf.com

AMHA (American Miniature Horse Assn)
5601 S IH- 35 W ... Alvarado TX 76009 817-783-5600 783-6403 48-3
Web: www.amha.org

AMHA (American Morgan Horse Assn)
4066 Shelburne Rd Ste 5 ... Shelburne VT 05482 802-985-4944 985-8897 48-3
TF: 888-436-3700 ■ *Web:* www.morganhorse.com

AMHCA (American Mental Health Counselors Assn)
801 N Fairfax St Ste 304 ... Alexandria VA 22314 703-548-6002 548-4775 49-15
TF: 800-326-2642 ■ *Web:* www.amhca.org

Amherst Alarm Inc
435 Lawrence Bell Dr ... Amherst NY 14221 716-632-4600 693
Web: www.amherstalarm.com

Amherst Area Chamber of Commerce
28 Amity St ... Amherst MA 01002 413-253-0700 256-0771 139
TF: 800-593-4052 ■ *Web:* www.amherstarea.com

Amherst Capital Partners LLC
Brown St Centre 255 E Brown St Ste 120 ... Birmingham MI 48009 248-642-5660 642-9247 194

Amherst Chamber of Commerce
400 Essjay Rd Ste 150 ... Williamsville NY 14221 716-632-6905 632-0548 139
Web: www.amherst.org

Amherst College 220 S Pleasant St ... Amherst MA 01002 413-542-2000 542-2040* 166
**Fax:* Admissions ■ *TF:* 866-542-4438 ■ *Web:* www.amherst.edu

Amherst College Frost Library
PO Box 5000 ... Amherst MA 01002 413-542-2373 542-2662 434-6
Web: www.amherst.edu/library

Amherst County 153 Washington St ... Amherst VA 24521 434-946-9400 946-9370 338
Web: www.countyofamherst.com

Amherst County Chamber of Commerce
154 S Main St ... Amherst VA 24521 434-946-0990 946-0879 139
Web: www.amherstvachamber.com

Amherst County Virgina
382 S Main St PO Box 370 ... Amherst VA 24521 434-946-9400 946-9348 434-3
Web: www.countyofamherst.com

Amherst Museum
3755 Tonawanda Creek Rd ... Amherst NY 14228 716-689-1440 689-1409 520
Web: www.bnhv.org

Amherst Public Library
350 John James Audubon Pkwy ... Amherst NY 14228 716-689-4922 689-6116 434-3
Web: buffalolib.org

Amherst Town Library 14 Main St ... Amherst NH 03031 603-673-2288 672-6063 434-3
TF: 800-545-2433 ■ *Web:* www.amherstlibrary.org

Amherst Veterinary Hospital
311 Willow St ... Amherst NS B4H3Y3 434-929-1010 794
Web: wi-net.com

AMI (American Megatrends Inc)
5555 Oakbrook Pkwy Bldg 200 ... Norcross GA 30093 770-246-8600 246-8790 176
TF: 800-828-9264 ■ *Web:* www.ami.com

Ami 4407 Wheeler Ave ... Alexandria VA 22304 703-370-4606 5
Web: amidirect.com

Ami Adini & Assoc Inc
4609 Russell Ave ... Los Angeles CA 90027 323-913-4073 194
TF: 888-400-4260 ■ *Web:* www.amiadini.com

AMI Asset Management Corp
10866 Wilshire Blvd Ste 770 ... Los Angeles CA 90024 424-320-4000 401
Web: www.amiassetmanagement.com

AMI Bearings Inc
570 N Wheeling Rd ... Mount Prospect IL 60056 847 759 0620 385
Web: www.amibearings.com

AMI Environmental
8802 S 135Th St Ste 100 ... Omaha NE 68138 402-397-5001 463
Web: www.amienvironmental.com

Ami Imaging Systems Inc
7815 Telegraph Rd ... Bloomington MN 55438 952-828-0080 415
Web: www.ami-imaging.com

AMI Mechanical Inc
12141 Pennsylvania St ... Thornton CO 80241 303-280-1401 610
Web: www.amimechanical.com

AMI Metals Inc
1738 General George Patton Dr ... Brentwood TN 37027 615-377-0400 492
TF: 800-727-1903 ■ *Web:* www.amimetals.com

AMIA (American Medical Informatics Assn)
4720 Montgomery Ln Ste 500 ... Bethesda MD 20814 301-657-1291 657-1296 49-8
Web: www.amia.org

Amica at City Centre
380 Princess Royal Dr ... Mississauga ON L5B4M9 905-803-8100 371
TF: 800-541-0966 ■ *Web:* www.amica.ca

Amica Mutual Insurance Co
100 Amica Way ... Lincoln RI 02865 800-652-6422 391-4
TF: 800-652-6422 ■ *Web:* www.amica.com

Amicalola Electric Membership Corp
544 Hwy 515 S ... Jasper GA 30143 706-253-5200 245
TF: 800-282-7411 ■ *Web:* www.amicalolaemc.com

Amicalola Falls State Park & Lodge
418 Amicalola Falls State Pk Rd ... Dawsonville GA 30534 706-265-4703 565
Web: www.gastateparks.org

Amicci's of Little Italy
231 S High St ... Baltimore MD 21202 410-528-1096 671
Web: www.amiccis.com

Amici 3343 W Cary St ... Richmond VA 23221 804-353-4700 671
Web: www.amicirva.com

Amici Milano Restaurant
600 Chesnut Ave ... Trenton NJ 08611 609-396-6300 396-3926 671
Web: www.amicimilano.com

Amick Farms Inc 2079 Batesburg Hwy ... Batesburg SC 29006 803-532-1400 10-8
TF: 800-926-4257 ■ *Web:* www.amickfarms.com

AMICO (Alabama Metal Industries Corp)
3245 Fayette Ave ... Birmingham AL 35208 205-787-2611 491
TF: 800-366-2642 ■ *Web:* amicoglobal.com

Amico Corp 85 Fulton Way ... Richmond Hill ON L4B2N4 905-764-0800 641
TF: 877-462-6426 ■ *Web:* www.amico.com

Amico Group 2199 Blackacre Dr RR #1 ... Oldcastle ON N0R1L0 519-737-1577 261
TF: 800-733-5683 ■ *Web:* www.amicoaffiliates.com

Amicus Technology
2118 Wilshire Blvd Ste 430 ... Santa Monica CA 90403 310-670-4962 179
TF: 800-440-1904 ■ *Web:* www.amicustech.com

Amidon Graphics 1966 Benson Ave ... Saint Paul MN 55116 651-690-2401 690-4009 627
TF: 800-328-6502 ■ *Web:* www.amidongraphics.com

amidus LLC
Research and Technology Park 1450 S Rolling Rd
... Baltimore MD 21227 410-926-0520 455-5901 463
Web: amidus.com

Amigo Farms Inc 4245 E Hwy 80 ... Yuma AZ 85365 928-726-3738 726-3744 10-11
TF: 800-293-0071 ■ *Web:* www.amigofarms.com

Amigo Mexican Restaurant
3805 Ringgold Rd ... Chattanooga TN 37412 423-624-4345 671
Web: amigorestaurantonline.com

Amigos Canning Company Inc
4669 Hwy 90 W ... San Antonio TX 78237 210-798-5360 798-5365 296-36
Web: www.amigosfoods.com

Amigos de las Americas
1000 W Loop S Ste 1325 ... Houston TX 77027 713 782 5290 48-5
TF: 800-231-7796 ■ *Web:* www.amigoslink.org

Amigos Library Services
14400 Midway Rd ... Dallas TX 75244 972-851-8000 991-6061 387
TF: 800-843-8482 ■ *Web:* www.amigos.org

Amigos Meat Distributors-East LP
611 Crosstimber ... Houston TX 77022 713-928-3111 297-9
Web: www.amigosfoods.biz

Amika Mobile Corp 700 March Rd Ste 203 ... Ottawa ON K2K2V9 613-599-4445 179
Web: www.amikamobile.com

Aminex Therapeutics Inc
11335 NE 122nd Ste 105 ... Kirkland WA 98034 425-286-4222 582
Web: www.aminextx.com

Amini Innovation Corp 8725 Rex Rd ... Pico Rivera CA 90660 562-222-2500 222-2525 320
Web: www.amini.com

Aminian Business Services Inc 50 Tesla ... Irvine CA 92618 949-724-1155 113
TF: 888-800-5207 ■ *Web:* www.aminian.com

Amino Transport Inc
223 NE Loop 820 Ste 101 ... Hurst TX 76053 800-304-3360 194
TF: 800-304-3360 ■ *Web:* www.aminotransport.com

AMIPAC (North American Meat Institute)
1150 Connecticut Ave NW ... Washington DC 20036 202-587-4200 587-4300 615
TF: 800-611-6100 ■ *Web:* www.meatinstitute.org

Amira International 15005 E Layton Pl ... Aurora CO 80015 303-400-3982 501
Web: amira.com.au

Amirit Technologies Inc
271 US Hwy 46 Ste C103 ... Fairfield NJ 07004 973-575-7557 828-0205 194

Amirsys Inc
2180 South 1300 East Ste 405 ... Salt Lake City UT 84106 801-485-6500 41
Web: www.amirsys.com

Amistad National Recreation Area
4121 Hwy 90 W ... Del Rio TX 78840 830-775-7491 778-9248 564
TF: 800-444-7275 ■ *Web:* www.nps.gov

Amistar Automation Inc
1269 Linda Vista ... San Marcos CA 92078 760-471-1700 471-9065 695
Web: www.amistarautomation.com

AMITA Corp 2650 Queensview Dr Ste 250 ... Ottawa ON K2B8H6 613-742-6482 196
Web: www.amita.com

Amite County PO Box 680 ... Liberty MS 39645 601-657-8022 657-8288 338
TF: 800-748-9837 ■ *Web:* www.amitecounty.ms

Amitron Inc
2001 Landmeier Rd ... Elk Grove Village IL 60007 847-290-9800 625
Web: www.amitroncorp.com

Name / Address	City	State	Zip	Phone	Fax	Class
Amity Foundation of California						
2260 Watson Way	Vista	CA	92083	888-508-9269		305
TF: 888-508-9269						
Amity Machine of Alburtis						
3750 Chestnut Rd	Alburtis	PA	18011	610-966-3115		454
Web: www.amityindustries.com						
Amivest Capital Management						
703 Market St 18th Fl	San Francisco	CA	94103	800-541-7774	541-9760*	401
**Fax Area Code:* 415 ■ *TF:* 800-541-7774 ■ *Web:* www.wrapmanager.com						
Amiya						
160 Green St						
Harborside Financial Ctr Plz 5	Jersey City	NJ	07311	201-433-8000	433-8866	671
Web: www.amiyarestaurant.com						
AMJ Campbell International						
1445 Courtneypark Dr E	Mississauga	ON	L5T2E3	905-670-6683		314
TF: 800-363-6683 ■ *Web:* www.amj-international.com						
Amj Industries Inc						
4000 Auburn St Unit 104	Rockford	IL	61101	815-654-9000		358
Web: amjindustries.com						
AMK Drives & Controls Inc						
5631 S Laburnum Ave	Richmond	VA	23231	804-222-0323	222-0339	518
Web: amk-group.com/en						
Amkor Technology Inc 1900 S Price Rd	Chandler	AZ	85248	480-821-5000		696
NASDAQ: AMKR ■ *Web:* www.amkor.com						
AML Partners LLC 4 Grand Cove Way	Edgewater	NJ	07020	201-484-8835		466
TF: 866-790-5095 ■ *Web:* www.amlpartners.com						
AMLI Residential						
200 W Monroe St Ste 2200	Chicago	IL	60606	312-283-4700		654
Web: www.amli.com						
AMLI Residential Properties Trust						
200 W Monroe St Ste 2200	Chicago	IL	60606	312-283-4700	283-4720	653
Web: www.amli.com						
Ammann & Whitney Inc 96 Morton St	New York	NY	10014	212-462-8500	929-5356	261
Web: www.ammann-whitney.com						
Ammar's Inc 710 S College Ave	Bluefield	VA	24605	276-322-4686	326-1060	229
Web: www.magicmartstores.com						
Ammeraal Beltech USA						
7501 N St Louis Ave	Skokie	IL	60076	847-673-6720	673-6373	370
TF Cust Svc: 800-323-4170 ■ *Web:* www.ammeraalbeltech.com						
Ammo Alley LLC 11562 County Rd 395	Hartsburg	MO	65039	573-634-6196		711
Web: www.wholesalehunter.com						
Ammunition						
1500 Sansome St RoundHouse 1	San Francisco	CA	94111	415-632-1170		194
Web: www.ammunitiongroup.com						
AMN Healthcare Services Inc						
12400 High Bluff Dr Ste 100	San Diego	CA	92130	866-871-8519		721
NYSE: AHS ■ *TF:* 866-871-8519 ■ *Web:* www.amnhealthcare.com						
Amneal Pharmaceuticals LLC						
85 Adams Ave	Hauppauge	NY	11788	631-952-0214	656-1009	582
NYSE: IPAH						
Amnesty International USA (AIUSA)						
5 Penn Plaza 16th Fl	New York	NY	10001	212-807-8400	627-1451	48-5
TF: 866-273-4466 ■ *Web:* www.amnestyusa.org						
Amnet Inc						
219 W Colorado Ave Ste 200	Colorado Springs	CO	80903	719-442-6683		174
Web: www.amnet.net						
Amnet Technology Solutions						
26 Fahey St	Stamford	CT	06907	203-355-2400		180
Web: www.amnetsystems.com						
Amnicon Falls State Park						
4279 County Hwy U	South Range	WI	54874	715-398-3000		565
Web: dnr.wi.gov/topic/parks/name/amnicon						
AMOA (Amusement & Music Operators Assn)						
380 Terra Cotta Rd Ste F	Crystal Lake	IL	60012	847-428-7699	428-7719	48-23
TF: 800-937-2662 ■ *Web:* amoa.memberclicks.net						
AMOA-National Dart Assn (NDA)						
10070 W 190th Pl Ste 200	Mokena	IL	60448	800-808-9884	226-1310*	48-22
**Fax Area Code:* 708 ■ *TF:* 800-808-9884 ■ *Web:* www.ndadarts.com						
Amoco Federal Credit Union						
PO Box 889	Texas City	TX	77592	409-948-8541		219
TF: 800-231-6053 ■ *Web:* www.amocofcu.org						
Amodei Mark (Rep R - NV)						
332 Cannon HOB	Washington	DC	20515	202-225-6155	225-5679	342-2
Web: amodei.house.gov						
Amon Carter Museum						
3501 Camp Bowie Blvd	Fort Worth	TX	76107	817-738-1933		520
TF: 800-573-1933 ■ *Web:* www.cartermuseum.org						
Amon G Carter Foundation						
201 Main St Ste 1945	Fort Worth	TX	76102	817-332-2783	332-2787	305
TF: 800-591-9663 ■ *Web:* www.agcf.org						
Amoray Dive Resort Inc						
104250 Overseas Hwy	Key Largo	FL	33037	305-451-3595		707
TF: 800-426-6729 ■ *Web:* www.amoray.com						
Amore 6931 Snider Plaza	Dallas	TX	75205	214-739-0502		671
Web: amoreitalian.net						
Amorim Cork Composites 26112 110th St	Trevor	WI	53179	262-862-2311		209
Web: www.amorimcorkcomposites.com/index.php						
Amorim Industrial Solutions Inc						
26112 110th St	Trevor	WI	53179	262-862-2311		820
Web: www.amorimcorkcomposites.com						
Amoroso's Baking Co						
845 S 55th St	Philadelphia	PA	19143	215-471-4710		296-1
Web: www.amorosobaking.com						
Amory Engineers PC						
PO Box 1768 25 Depot St	Duxbury	MA	02332	781-934-0178		261
Web: amoryengineers.com						
Amos Press Inc 911 S Vandemark Rd	Sidney	OH	45365	937-498-2111	498-0812	637-9
TF: 866-468-1622 ■ *Web:* www.amosmedia.com						
Amos-Hill Assoc Inc 112 Shelby Ave	Edinburgh	IN	46124	812-526-2671	526-5865	613
TF: 800-745-1778 ■ *Web:* www.amoshill.com						
Amot Controls Corp 8824 Fallbrook Dr	Houston	TX	77064	281-940-1800	559-9419*	201
**Fax Area Code:* 713 ■ *Web:* www.amotusa.com						
Amotec Inc 1701 E 12th St Ste 103	Cleveland	OH	44114	440-250-4600		194
Web: www.amotecinc.com						
AMP (Applied Measurement Professionals Inc)						
18000 W 105th St	Olathe	KS	66061	913-895-4600	895-4650	47
TF: 800-345-6559 ■ *Web:* www.goamp.com						
AMP (Automatic Machine Products Co)						
400 Constitution Dr	Taunton	MA	02780	508-822-4226	822-4476	621
Web: www.ampcomp.com						
AMP 1037 4131 N Central Expy Ste 1000	Dallas	TX	75204	214-525-7000		645-44
TF: 877-787-1037 ■ *Web:* amp1037.cbslocal.com						
AMP Agency 77 N Washington St	Boston	MA	02114	617-723-8929		4
Web: www.ampagency.com						
Amp Machinery Systems Inc						
1098 Chetwood Dr	Carol Stream	IL	60188	630-213-8970		358
Web: www.ampmachinery.com						
AMPAC (American Pacific Corp)						
3883 Howard Hughes Pkwy Ste 700	Las Vegas	NV	89169	702-735-2200		145
NASDAQ: APFC ■ *Web:* www.apfc.com						
AMPAC Fine Chemicals (AFC)						
MS 1007 PO Box 1718	Rancho Cordova	CA	95741	916-357-6880	353-3523	145
TF: 800-311-9668 ■ *Web:* www.ampacfinechemicals.com						
Ampac Packaging LLC						
12025 Tricon Rd	Cincinnati	OH	45246	513-671-1777	671-2920*	66
**Fax:* Cust Svc ■ *TF:* 800-543-7030 ■ *Web:* www.ampaconline.com						
Ampac Seed Co 32727 Hwy 99 E	Tangent	OR	97389	541-928-1651	928-2430	694
TF: 800-547-3230 ■ *Web:* www.ampacseed.com						
Ampacet Corp 660 White Plains Rd	Tarrytown	NY	10591	914-631-6600	631-7197	143
TF Cust Svc: 800-888-4267 ■ *Web:* www.ampacet.com						
Ampco Manufacturers Inc						
9 Burbidge St Ste 101	Coquitlam	BC	V3K7B2	604-472-3800		627
TF: 800-663-5482 ■ *Web:* www.ampcomfg.com						
Ampco Metal Inc						
1117 E Algonquin Rd	Arlington Heights	IL	60005	847-437-6000	437-6008	485
TF: 800-844-6008 ■ *Web:* www.ampcometal.com						
Ampco Products Inc 11400 NW 36th Ave	Miami	FL	33167	305-821-5700	642-5300*	286
**Fax Area Code:* 866 ■ *Web:* www.ampco.com						
Ampco Pumps Company Inc						
2045 W Mill Rd	Glendale	WI	53209	414-643-1852		641
TF: 800-737-8671 ■ *Web:* www.ampcopumps.com						
Ampco-Pittsburgh Corp						
600 Grant St Ste 4600	Pittsburgh	PA	15219	412-456-4400		674
NYSE: AP ■ *Web:* www.ampcopittsburgh.com						
Ampcus Inc						
14900 Conference Center Dr Ste 203	Chantilly	VA	20151	703-637-7299		180
Web: www.ampcus.com						
AMPERAGE Marketing						
6711 Chancellor Dr	Cedar Falls	IA	50613	319-268-9151		195
Web: www.amperagemarketing.com/?ref=meandv						
Ampersand Art Supply						
1235 S Loop 4 Ste 400	Buda	TX	78610	512-322-0278	322-9928	43
TF: 800-822-1939 ■ *Web:* www.ampersandart.com						
Ampersand Capital Partners						
55 William St Ste 240	Wellesley	MA	02481	781-239-0700	239-0824	792
TF: 800-477-6834 ■ *Web:* www.ampersandcapital.com						
Ampex Casting Corp 23 W 47th St Ste 4	New York	NY	10036	212-719-1318		407
Ampex Corp 26460 Corporate Ave	Hayward	CA	94545	650-367-2011	367-4669*	658
**Fax:* Hum Res ■ *Web:* www.ampex.com						
Ampex Data Systems Corp						
500 Broadway	Redwood City	CA	94063	650-367-2011	367-3106	173-8
TF: 800-752-7590 ■ *Web:* www.ampex.com						
Amphastar Pharmaceuticals Inc						
11570 Sixth St	Rancho Cucamonga	CA	91730	909-980-9484		582
TF: 800-423-4136 ■ *Web:* www.amphastar.com						
Amphenol Aerospace 40-60 Delaware Ave	Sidney	NY	13838	607-563-5011	563-5157	253
TF: 800-678-0141 ■ *Web:* www.amphenol-aerospace.com						
Amphenol Corp 358 Hall Ave	Wallingford	CT	06492	203-265-8900		815
NYSE: APH ■ *TF:* 877-267-4366 ■ *Web:* www.amphenol.com						
Amphenol Optimize Manufacturing Co						
482 N Moriposa Rd Bldg Bldg. A	Nogales	AZ	85621	520-397-7015	397-7014	466
TF: 800-288-4746 ■ *Web:* www.amphenol-optimize.com						
Amphenol PCD 72 Cherry Hill Dr	Beverly	MA	01915	978-624-3400	927-1513*	253
**Fax:* Sales ■ *TF:* 800-472-4225 ■ *Web:* www.amphenolpcd.com						
Amphenol RF 4 Old Newtown Rd	Danbury	CT	06810	203-743-9272	796-2032	253
TF: 800-627-7100 ■ *Web:* www.amphenolrf.com						
Amphenol Sine Systems						
44724 Morley Dr	Clinton Township	MI	48036	586-465-3131		253
Web: www.amphenol-sine.com						
Amphenol Spectra-Strip 720 Sherman Ave	Hamden	CT	06514	203-281-3200	281-5872	253
TF: 800-846-6400 ■ *Web:* www.spectra-strip.com						
Amphenol-Tuchel Electronics						
6900 Haggerty Rd Ste 200	Canton	MI	48187	734-451-6400		253
TF: 800-380-8052 ■ *Web:* www.amphenol.info						
AMPI 315 N Broadway	New Ulm	MN	56073	507-354-8295		297-4
TF: 800-533-3580 ■ *Web:* www.ampi.com						
Amplicon Express Inc						
2345 NE Hopkins Ct	Pullman	WA	99163	509-332-8080		743
TF: 877-332-8080 ■ *Web:* ampliconexpress.com						
Amplified Geochemical Imaging LLC						
210 Executive Dr Ste 1	Newark	DE	19702	302-266-2428		539
Web: www.agisurveys.net						
Amplifier Technologies Inc						
1749 Chapin Rd	Montebello	CA	90640	323-278-0001	278-0083	52
TF: 800-947-4434 ■ *Web:* www.bgw.com						
AmpliPhi Biosciences Corp						
3579 Valley Centre Dr Ste 100	San Diego	CA	92130	858-829-0829		85
OTC: APHB ■ *TF:* 877-795-3647 ■ *Web:* www.ampliphibio.com						
AmpliVox Sound Systems LLC						
3995 Commercial Ave	Northbrook	IL	60062	847-498-9000	498-6691	52
TF: 800-267-5486 ■ *Web:* www.ampli.com						
Ampls 1164 N Kraemer Pl	Anaheim	CA	92806	714-630-1313		463
TF: 800-794-6245 ■ *Web:* ampls.com						
AMPORTS 2901 Childs St	Baltimore	MD	21226	410-350-0400		465
Web: www.amports.com						
Ampronix Inc 15 Whatney	Irvine	CA	92618	949-273-8000		475
TF: 800-400-7972 ■ *Web:* www.ampronix.com						
Amptech Inc 201 Glocheski Dr	Manistee	MI	49660	231-464-5492		179
Web: www.amptechinc.com						
AMPTP (Alliance of Motion Picture & Television Producers)						
15301 Ventura Blvd Bldg E	Sherman Oaks	CA	91403	818-995-3600		48-4
TF: 800-541-5204 ■ *Web:* www.amptp.org						
AmQuip Crane Rental LLC						
1150 Northbrook Dr Ste 100	Trevose	PA	19053	215-639-9200		23
Web: www.amquip.com						

	Phone	Fax	Class
AMR (American Medical Response) 6200 S Syracuse Way Ste 200 Greenwood Village CO 80111 *TF:* 877-244-4890 ■ *Web:* www.amr.net	303-495-1200		30
AMR Corp 4333 Amon Carter Blvd PO Box 619616 Fort Worth TX 76155 *OTC:* AAMRQ ■ *TF:* 800-535-5225 ■ *Web:* www.aa.com	817-963-1234	967-4162	360-1
AMR Management Services 201 E Main St Ste 1405 Lexington KY 40507 *Web:* www.amrms.com	859-514-9150	514-9207	47
AmRad Engineering Inc 32 Hargrove Grade Palm Coast FL 32137 *TF:* 800-445-6033 ■ *Web:* www.americanradionic.com	386-445-6000	445-6871	253
AMRCON 92 Broad St Keyport NJ 07735 *Web:* www.amrcon.com	732-705-5057		396
AMREL (American Reliance Inc) 3445 Fletcher Ave El Monte CA 91731 *Web:* www.amrel.com	626-443-6818		529
AmRent PO Box 163250 Columbus OH 43215 *TF:* 800-324-4595 ■ *Web:* www.amrent.com	855-202-0113		635
AMREP Corp 300 Alexander Pk Ste 204 Princeton NJ 08540 *NYSE:* AXR ■ *Web:* www.amrepcorp.com	609-716-8200		653
AMREP Southwest Inc 333 New Mexico 528 Ste 400 Rio Rancho NM 87124 *Web:* www.amrepsw.com	505-896-9009		653
AMRESCO Commercial Finance LLC 412 E Parkcenter Blvd Boise ID 83706 *Web:* www.amresco.com	208-333-2000	333-2050	216
Amresco Inc 6681 Cochran Rd Solon OH 44139 *TF:* 800-448-4442 ■ *Web:* www.amresco-inc.com	440-349-1313	349-3255	231
Amridge University 1200 Taylor Rd Montgomery AL 36117 *TF:* 888-790-8080 ■ *Web:* www.amridgeuniversity.edu	334-387-3877	387-3878	166
AMRO Fabrication Corp 1430 Adelia Ave South El Monte CA 91733 *Web:* www.amrofab.com	626-579-2200		529
Amro Music Stores 2910 Poplar Ave Memphis TN 38111 *TF General:* 800-626-2676 ■ *Web:* www.amromusic.com	901-323-8888		526
AmRod Corp 60 Pennsylvania Ave Kearny NJ 07032 *Web:* www.amrod.com	973-344-3806		492
Amron LLC 920 Amron Ave Antigo WI 54409 *Web:* www.nationaldefensecorp.com	715-623-4176		807
AMRPA (American Medical Rehabilitation Providers Assn) 1710 N St NW Washington DC 20036 *TF:* 888-346-4624 ■ *Web:* www.amrpa.org	202-223-1920	223-1925	49-8
AMS (American Montessori Society) 281 Pk Ave S 6th Fl New York NY 10010 *TF:* 800-632-4121 ■ *Web:* www.amshq.org	212-358-1250	358-1256	48-11
AMS (American Musicological Society) 6010 College Stn Brunswick ME 04011 *TF:* 888-421-1442 ■ *Web:* www.ams-net.org	207-798-4243	798-4254	48-4
AMS (American Mathematical Society) 201 Charles St Providence RI 02904 *TF Cust Svc:* 800-321-4267 ■ *Web:* www.ams.org	401-455-4000	331-3842	49-19
AMS (American Meteorological Society) 45 Beacon St Boston MA 02108 *TF:* 800-824-0405 ■ *Web:* www.ametsoc.org	617-227-2425	742-8718	49-19
Ams Controls Inc 12180 Prichard Farm Rd Maryland Heights MO 63043 *Web:* www.amscontrols.com	314-344-3144		358
AMS Entertainment 152 Aero Camino Ste E Goleta CA 93117 *Web:* www.ams-events.com	805-899-4000		181
AMS Filling Systems 2500 Chestnut Tree Rd Honey Brook PA 19344 *TF:* 800-647-5390 ■ *Web:* www.amsfilling.com	610-942-4200		547
AMS Genetics Inc 1515 Livingstone Rd PO Box 12 Hudson WI 54016 *Web:* www.amsgenetics.com	240-329-0169	469-4231	11-2
AMS Health Sciences Inc 4000 N Lindsay Oklahoma City OK 73105 *TF:* 800-426-4267 ■ *Web:* www.amsonline.com	405-842-0131	843-4935	296-11
Ams Mechanical Systems Inc 140 E Tower Dr Burr Ridge IL 60527 *TF:* 800-794-5033 ■ *Web:* www.amsmechanicalsystems.com	630-887-7700	887-0770	261
AMS Plastics Inc 1530 Hilton Head Rd Ste 205 El Cajon CA 92019 *Web:* www.amsplastics.com	619-713-2000	713-2975	604
Ams Production Machining Inc 800 Andico Rd Plainfield IN 46168 *Web:* www.amsmachining.com	317-838-9273		757
AMS.NET Inc 502 Commerce Way Livermore CA 94551 **Fax Area Code:* 925 ■ *TF:* 800-893-3660 ■ *Web:* www.ams.net	800-893-3660	245-6150*	177
AMSA (American Medical Student Assn) 1902 Assn Dr Reston VA 20191 *TF:* 800-767-2266 ■ *Web:* www.amsa.org	703-620-6600	620-5873	49-5
AMSA (American Moving & Storage Assn) 1611 Duke St Alexandria VA 22314 *TF:* 888-849-2672 ■ *Web:* www.promover.org	703-683-7410	683-7527	49-21
AmSafe Inc 1043 N 47th Ave Phoenix AZ 85043 *Web:* www.amsafe.com	602-850-2850	850-2812	678
Amscan Inc 80 Grasslands Rd Elmsford NY 10523 *TF:* 800-444-8887 ■ *Web:* www.amscan.com	914-345-2020	345-3884	566
Amsco Windows Inc 1880 S 1045 W Salt Lake City UT 84104 *TF:* 800-748-4661 ■ *Web:* www.amscowindows.com	801-978-5000	974-0498	234
Amsco-Wire Products Co 610 Grand Ave Ridgefield NJ 07657	201-945-5618		621
Amset Technical Consulting 1864 S Elmhurst Rd Mount Prospect IL 60056 *TF:* 888-982-6783 ■ *Web:* www.amsetusa.com	847-229-1155		261
Amsher 4524 Southlake Pkwy Ste 15 Birmingham AL 35244 *TF:* 844-227-4627 ■ *Web:* www.amsher.com	205-322-4110		160
AMSL (Association Management Solutions LLC) 48377 Freemont Blvd Ste 117 Fremont CA 94538 *Web:* www.amsl.com	510-492-4000		47
Amsoil Inc 925 Tower Ave Superior WI 54880 *TF Sales:* 800-777-7094 ■ *Web:* www.amsoil.com	715-392-7101	392-5225	541
AMSplus Inc 400 Washington St Braintree MA 02184 *TF:* 888-239-9575 ■ *Web:* www.amsplus.com	888-239-9575		225
Amstan Logistics 101 Knightsbridge Dr Hamilton OH 45011 *TF:* 800-322-5546 ■ *Web:* www.amstan.com	513-863-4627		780
AMSTED Industries Inc 180 N Stetson St Ste 1800 Chicago IL 60601 *Web:* www.amsted.com	312-645-1700		307
Amsted Rail Company Inc 311 S Wacker Dr Ste 5300 Chicago IL 60606 *Web:* www.amstedrail.com	312-922-4501		770
Amstek Metal LLC 2408 W Mcdonough Joliet IL 60436 *TF:* 800-551-9473 ■ *Web:* www.amstekmetal.com	815-725-2520		492
Amstel House 30 Market St New Castle DE 19720 *Web:* www.newcastlehistory.org	302-322-2794	322-8923	50-3
Amsterdam Hospitality 888 Seventh Ave 20th Fl New York NY 10019	212-292-3600		379
Amsterdam Nursing Home Corp 1060 Amsterdam Ave New York NY 10025 *Web:* www.amsterdamcares.com	212-316-7700		371
Amsterdam Printing & Litho Corp 166 Wallins Corners Rd Amsterdam NY 12010 *TF Cust Svc:* 800-833-6231 ■ *Web:* www.amsterdamprinting.com	800-203-9917		9
Amster-Kirtz Co 2830 Cleveland Ave NW Canton OH 44709 *TF:* 800-257-9338 ■ *Web:* www.amsterkirtz.com	330-535-6021		297-8
AmSurg Corp 1A Burton Hills Blvd Nashville TN 37215 *NASDAQ:* AMSG ■ *TF:* 800-945-2301 ■ *Web:* www.amsurg.com	615-665-1283	665-0755	352
AMSUS (Association of Military Surgeons of the United States) 9320 Old Georgetown Rd Bethesda MD 20814 *TF:* 800-761-9320 ■ *Web:* www.amsus.org	301-897-8800	530-5446	49-8
AMT (American Medical Technologists) 10700 W Higgins Rd Ste 150 Rosemont IL 60018 *TF:* 800-275-1268 ■ *Web:* www.americanmedtech.org	847-823-5169	823-0458	49-8
AMT (Association for Mfg Technology) 7901 Westpark Dr McLean VA 22102 *TF:* 800-524-0475 ■ *Web:* www.amtonline.org	703-893-2900	893-1151	49-12
AMT (American Modular Technologies) 6306 Old 421 Rd PO Box 1069 Liberty NC 27298 *Web:* www.americanmodulartechnologies.com	336-622-6200	622-6473	105
AMT Datasouth Corp 803 Camarillo Springs Rd Ste D Camarillo CA 93012 *TF:* 800-215-9192 ■ *Web:* www.amtdatasouth.com	805-388-5799	484-5282	173-6
AMT Machine Systems Ltd 868 Fwy Dr N Columbus OH 43229 *TF:* 866-204-0660 ■ *Web:* www.amtmachinesystems.com	614-635-8050		256
AMTA (American Music Therapy Assn Inc) 8455 Colesville Rd Ste 1000 Silver Spring MD 20910 *Web:* www.musictherapy.org	301-589-3300	589-5175	48-17
AMTA (American Massage Therapy Assn) 500 Davis St Ste 900 Evanston IL 60201 *TF:* 877-905-2700 ■ *Web:* www.amtamassage.org	847-864-0123	864-1178	48-17
AMTDA (American Machine Tool Distributors' Assn) 1445 Research Blvd Ste 450 Rockville MD 20850 *Web:* www.amtonline.org	301-738-1200		49-18
Amtec Precision Products Inc 1355 Holmes Rd Elgin IL 60123 *Web:* www.amtecprecision.com	847-695-8030		621
Amtech Systems Inc 131 S Clark Dr Tempe AZ 85281 *NASDAQ:* ASYS ■ *Web:* www.amtechsystems.com	480-967-5146	968-3763	695
AMTEK Information Service Inc 4001 Sherwood Houston TX 77092 *Web:* www.amtekusa.com	713-956-0100		463
AMTEL 900 Lafayette St Ste 506 Santa Clara CA 95050 *Web:* www.amtelnet.com	408-615-0522		196
Amtelco 4800 Curtin Dr McFarland WI 53558 *TF:* 800-356-9148 ■ *Web:* www.amtelco.com	608-838-4194	838-8367	735
Amtex Corp 832 East Walnut St Garland TX 75040 *Web:* www.amtexcorp.com	972-276-7626		360-3
Amtex Enterprises Inc 4699 Old Ironsides Dr Ste 270 Santa Clara CA 95054 *Web:* amtexenterprises.com	408-734-4050		177
AmTex Machine Products Inc 4517 Brittmoore Rd Houston TX 77041 *Web:* amtexmachine.com	713-896-4488	896-6363	358
Amtex Precision Fabrication 3920 Bahler Ave Manvel TX 77578 *Web:* www.amtexprecision.com	281-489-7042		697
Amtex Security Inc 1001 Third St Ste 8 Corpus Christi TX 78404 *Web:* www.amtexsecurity.com	361-882-1222	371-5206	400
Amtex Systems Inc 50 Broad St Ste 801 New York NY 10004 *Web:* www.amtexsystems.com	212-269-6448	269-6458	180
Amthor Steel 1717 Gaskell Ave Erie PA 16503 *TF:* 800-831-9252 ■ *Web:* www.amthorsteel.com	814-452-4700		492
AMTIS Inc 12124 High Tech Ave Ste 150 Orlando FL 32817 *Web:* www.amtisinc.com	407-513-9490		463
Amtote International Inc 11200 Pepper Rd Hunt Valley MD 21031 *TF:* 800-345-1566 ■ *Web:* www.amtote.com	410-771-8700		322
Am-Touch Dental 28703 Industry Dr Valencia CA 91355 *TF:* 800-350-4568 ■ *Web:* www.amtouch.com	661-294-1213		228
Amtrol Inc 1400 Div Rd West Warwick RI 02893 *Web:* www.amtrol.com	401-884-6300	885-2567	91
AmTrust Bank 1801 E Ninth St Cleveland OH 44114 *TF:* 888-696-4444 ■ *Web:* www.mynycb.com	216-736-3480	987-8732	70
Amtrust Realty Corp 250 Broadway Rm 3001 New York NY 10007 *Web:* www.amtrustre.com	212-732-4776		652
AMU (American Public University System) 111 W Congress St Charles Town WV 25414 *TF:* 877-777-9081 ■ *Web:* www.amu.apus.edu	304-724-3700		167
Amundi Smith Breeden 280 S Mangum St Ste 301 Durham NC 27701 *Web:* www.amundismithbreeden.com	919-967-7221		401
Amuneal Manufacturing Corp 4737 Darrah St Philadelphia PA 19124 *TF:* 800-755-9843 ■ *Web:* www.amuneal.com	215-535-3000		697
Amunix Operating Inc 500 Ellis St Mountain View CA 94043 *Web:* www.amunix.com	650-428-1800		668

				Phone	Fax	Class
Amusement & Music Operators Assn (AMOA) 380 Terra Cotta Rd Ste F *TF:* 800-937-2662 ■ *Web:* amoa.memberclicks.net	Crystal Lake	IL	60012	847-428-7699	428-7719	48-23
Amvac Chemical Corp 4100 E Washington Blvd *TF:* 800-424-9300 ■ *Web:* www.amvac-chemical.com	Los Angeles	CA	90023	323-264-3910	268-1028	280
AMVC Management Services LLC 508 Market St *Web:* www.amvcms.com	Audubon	IA	50025	712-563-2080		194
AMVETS 4647 Forbes Blvd *TF:* 877-726-8387 ■ *Web:* www.amvets.org	Lanham	MD	20706	301-459-9600	459-7924	48-19
Amvic Inc 501 McNicoll Ave *TF:* 877-470-9991 ■ *Web:* www.amvicsystem.com	Toronto	ON	M2H2E2	416-410-5674		183
AMWA (American Medical Writers Assn) 30 W Gude Dr Ste 525 *Web:* www.amwa.org	Rockville	MD	20850	301-294-5303	294-9006	49-14
Amway Corp 7575 Fulton St E *TF:* 800-253-6500 ■ *Web:* www.amway.com	Ada	MI	49355	616-787-4000	787-7550	366
Amway Grand Plaza Hotel 187 Monroe Ave NW *TF:* 800-253-3590 ■ *Web:* www.amwaygrand.com	Grand Rapids	MI	49503	616-774-2000	776-6489	379
AMX Corp 3000 Research Dr *TF:* 855-269-8585 ■ *Web:* www.amx.com	Richardson	TX	75082	469-624-8585		203
Amx LLC 3000 Reseach Dr *Web:* amx.com	Richardson	TX	75082	469-624-8000		52
Amy's Ice Creams 3500 Guadalupe St *Web:* www.amysicecreams.com	Austin	TX	78705	512-458-6895		381
Amy's Kitchen Inc PO Box 449 *TF:* 800-323-7738 ■ *Web:* www.amys.com	Petaluma	CA	94953	707-781-6600		296-36
Amylin Pharmaceuticals Inc 9360 Towne Ctr Dr *NASDAQ: AMLN* ■ *Web:* www.bms.com	San Diego	CA	92121	858-552-2200		582
AMZ Financial Insurance Services LLC 4944 Windplay Dr Ste 115 *Web:* amzfinancial.com	El Dorado Hills	CA	95762	916-939-3765		463
Amzak Corp 1 N Federal Hwy Ste 400 *Web:* www.amzak.com	Boca Raton	FL	33432	561-953-4164	338-7677	188-10
Amzi! inc 83 Vance Crescent Ext *TF:* 800-963-9963 ■ *Web:* www.amzi.com	Asheville	NC	28806	828-350-0350		178-2
AN Deringer Inc 64 N Main St *TF:* 800-448-8108 ■ *Web:* www.anderinger.com	Saint Albans	VT	05478	802-524-8110		449
ANA (American Neurological Assn) 1120 Rte 73 Ste 200 *Web:* myana.org	Mount Laurel	NJ	08054	856-380-6892		49-8
ANA (Acoustic Neuroma Assn) 600 Peachtree Pkwy Ste 108 *TF:* 877-200-8211 ■ *Web:* www.anausa.org	Cumming	GA	30041	770-205-8211	205-0239	48-17
ANA (American Nurses Assn) 8515 Georgia Ave Ste 400 *TF:* 800-274-4262 ■ *Web:* nursingworld.org	Silver Spring	MD	20910	301-628-5000	628-5001	49-8
ANA (Association of National Advertisers) 708 Third Ave 33rd Fl *TF:* 800-914-4194 ■ *Web:* www.ana.net	New York	NY	10017	212-697-5950	687-7310	49-18
Ana Consultants LLC 5000 Thompson Terr	Colleyville	TX	76034	817-335-9900		261
ANA PAC (American Nurses Assn PAC) 8515 Georgia Ave Ste 400 *TF:* 800-274-4262 ■ *Web:* www.nursingworld.org	Silver Spring	MD	20910	301-628-5000	628-5001	615
Ana Properties 3630 N Josey Ln Ste 217	Carrollton	TX	75007	972-939-0610		256
ANAC (American Nurses Assn California) 1121 L St Ste 409 *Web:* www.anacalifornia.org	Sacramento	CA	95814	916-447-0225		533
AnaBios Corporation Inc San Diego Science Ctr 3030 Bunker Hill St Ste 312 *Web:* www.anabios.com	San Diego	CA	92109	858-366-8608		743
Anabliss Inc 4055 Tejon St Ste 203 *Web:* anabliss.com	Denver	CO	80211	303-825-4441		344
Anabolic Laboratories Inc 17802 Gillette Ave *Web:* www.anaboliclabs.com	Irvine	CA	92614	949-863-0340		743
ANAC (Association of Nurses in AIDS Care) 3538 Ridgewood Rd *TF:* 800-260-6780 ■ *Web:* www.nursesinaidscare.org	Akron	OH	44333	330-670-0101	670-0109	49-8
Anachemia Canada Inc 255 Rue Norman *Web:* www.anachemia.com	Lachine	QC	H8R1A3	514-489-5711		690
Anacom General Corp 1240 S Claudina St **Fax: Sales* ■ *TF:* 800-955-9540 ■ *Web:* www.anacom-medtek.com	Anaheim	CA	92805	714-774-8484	774-7388*	392
Anacom Inc 3000 Tasman Dr *Web:* www.anacominc.com	Santa Clara	CA	95054	408-519-2062		196
Anacomp Inc 15378 Ave of Science *OTC: ANMP* ■ *Web:* www.anacomp.com	San Diego	CA	92128	858-716-3400		496
Anaconda-Deer Lodge County 800 S Main *Web:* adlc.us	Anaconda	MT	59711	406-563-4000	563-4001	338
Anacortes Public Library 1220 Tenth St	Anacortes	WA	98221	360-293-1910		434-3
Anadarko Bank & Trust Co 110 W Oklahoma Ave *Web:* www.bocokonline.com	Anadarko	OK	73005	405-247-3311		70
Anadarko Petroleum Corp 1201 Lake Robbins Dr *NYSE: APC* ■ *TF:* 800-800-1101 ■ *Web:* www.anadarko.com	Spring	TX	77380	832-636-1000		536
Anadigm Inc 2036 N Gilbert Rd Ste 2-417 *Web:* www.anadigm.com	Mesa	AZ	85203	480-422-0191	659-3511	246
Anagram International Inc 7700 Anagram Dr *Web:* www.anagramballoon.com	Eden Prairie	MN	55344	952-949-5600		600
Anaheim Automation 910 E Orangefair Ln *TF Sales:* 800-345-9401 ■ *Web:* www.anaheimautomation.com	Anaheim	CA	92801	714-992-6990	992-0471	203
Anaheim Chamber of Commerce 2400 E Katella Ave Ste 725 *Web:* www.anaheimchamber.org	Anaheim	CA	92806	714-758-0222	758-0468	139
Anaheim City Hall 200 S Anaheim Blvd *Web:* www.anaheim.net	Anaheim	CA	92805	714-765-5162	765-5164	337
Anaheim Convention Ctr 800 W Katella Ave *Web:* www.anaheim.net	Anaheim	CA	92802	714-765-8950	765-8965	205
Anaheim Custom Extruders 4640 E La Palma Ave *TF Cust Svc:* 800-229-2760 ■ *Web:* acextrusions.com	Anaheim	CA	92807	714-693-8508	693-9531	600
Anaheim Ducks 2695 E Katella Ave **Fax Area Code:* 714 ■ *TF:* 877-945-3946 ■ *Web:* ducks.nhl.com	Anaheim	CA	92806	877-945-3946	940-2953*	716
Anaheim Elementary School District 1001 SE St *Web:* anaheimelementary.org	Anaheim	CA	92805	714-517-7500		685
Anaheim Extrusion Company Inc 1330 N Kraemer Blvd PO Box 6380 *TF:* 800-660-3318 ■ *Web:* www.anaheimextrude.com	Anaheim	CA	92806	714-630-3111	630-0443	485
Anaheim Hotel, The 1700 S Harbor Blvd *TF:* 800-631-4144 ■ *Web:* www.anaheimplazahotel.com	Anaheim	CA	92802	714-772-5900	772-8386	379
Anaheim Indoor Marketplace 1440 S Anaheim Blvd *Web:* www.anaheimindoormarketplace.com	Anaheim	CA	92805	714-999-0888	999-0885	460
Anaheim Manufacturing Co 25300 Al Moen Dr *TF Cust Svc:* 800-767-6293 ■ *Web:* www.anaheimmfg.com	North Olmsted	OH	44070	800-767-6293	454-4406	36
Anaheim Marriott 700 W Convention Way *TF:* 800-845-5279 ■ *Web:* www.marriott.com	Anaheim	CA	92802	714-750-8000	750-9100	671
Anaheim Memorial Medical Ctr 1111 W La Palma Ave *Web:* www.memorialcare.org	Anaheim	CA	92801	714-774-1450		374-3
Anaheim Public Library 500 W Broadway *Web:* www.anaheim.net/902/library	Anaheim	CA	92805	714-765-1880	765-1730	434-3
Anaheim Union High School District (AUHSB) 501 N Crescent Way **Fax: Admin* ■ *Web:* www.auhsd.us	Anaheim	CA	92801	714-999-3511	520-9752*	685
Anaheim University 1240 S State College Blvd Rm 110 *TF:* 800-955-6040 ■ *Web:* www.anaheim.edu	Anaheim	CA	92806	714-772-3330		165
Anaheim White House 887 S Anaheim Blvd *Web:* www.anaheimwhitehouse.com	Anaheim	CA	92805	714-772-1381	772-7062	671
Anaheim/Orange County Visitor & Convention Bureau 800 W Katella Ave *TF:* 855-405-5020 ■ *Web:* visitanaheim.org	Anaheim	CA	92802	714-765-8888	991-8963	206
AnaJet LLC 3050 Redhill Ave *Web:* www.anajet.com	Costa Mesa	CA	92626	714-662-3200		194
Anakena Solutions Inc 18345 Ventura Blvd *Web:* www.anakenasolutions.com	Tarzana	CA	91356	310-929-7869		180
Ana-Lab Corp PO Box 9000 *Web:* www.ana-lab.com	Kilgore	TX	75663	903-984-0551	984-5914	743
Analog Devices Inc 3 Technology Way *NASDAQ: ADI* ■ *TF:* 800-262-5643 ■ *Web:* www.analog.com	Norwood	MA	02062	781-329-4700	461-3113	696
Analogix Semiconductor Inc 3211 Scott Blvd Ste 103 *Web:* www.analogix.com	Santa Clara	CA	95054	408-988-8848		696
Analynk Wireless LLC 790 Cross Pointe Rd *Web:* www.analynk.com	Columbus	OH	43230	614-755-5091		179
Analysis Group Inc 111 Huntington Ave 10th Fl *Web:* www.analysisgroup.com	Boston	MA	02199	617-425-8000	425-8001	194
Analystik 1430 Rue Belanger *Web:* www.analystik.ca	Montreal	QC	H2G1A4	514-278-2727		180
Analyte Health Inc 328 S Jefferson St Ste 770 *Web:* www.analytehealth.com	Chicago	IL	60661	312-477-3000		418
Analytic Investors LLC 555 W Fifth St 50th Fl *TF:* 800-618-1872 ■ *Web:* www.aninvestor.com	Los Angeles	CA	90013	213-688-3015	688-8856	401
Analytica Group-environmental Laboratories 4307 Arctic Blvd *Web:* www.analyticagroup.com	Anchorage	AK	99503	907-258-2155		743
Analytical Design Service Corp 540 Avis Dr Ste E *Web:* www.adsc-usa.com	Ann Arbor	MI	48108	734-761-2626		256
Analytical Graphics Inc 220 Vly Creek Blvd *TF:* 800-220-4785 ■ *Web:* www.agi.com	Exton	PA	19341	610-981-8000	981-8001	177
Analytical Group Inc, The 16638 N 90th St *Web:* www.analyticalgroup.com	Scottsdale	AZ	85260	480-483-7505		195
Analytical Industries Inc 2855 Metropolitan Pl *Web:* www.aii1.com	Pomona	CA	91767	909-392-6900		295
Analytical Mechanics Associates Inc 303 Butler Farm Rd Ste 104A *Web:* www.ama-inc.com	Hampton	VA	23666	757-865-0000	865-1881	177
Analytical Perspectives LLC 2714 Exchange Dr *Web:* www.ultratrace.com	Wilmington	NC	28405	910-794-2822		794
Analytical Sensors & Instruments Ltd 12800 Pk One Dr *Web:* www.asi-sensors.com	Sugar Land	TX	77478	281-565-8818	565-8811	419
Analytical Spectral Devices Inc 2555 55th St Ste 100 *Web:* www.asdi.com	Boulder	CO	80301	303-444-6522		419
Analytics Corp 10329 Stony Run Ln *TF:* 800-888-8061 ■ *Web:* analyticscorp.com	Ashland	VA	23005	804-365-3000		743
Anamet Inc 26102 Eden Landing Rd *Web:* anametinc.com	Hayward	CA	94545	510-887-8811		261
Ananke Inc 14 Imperial Pl Ste 202 *Web:* www.ananke.com	Providence	RI	02906	401-331-2780		196
Anaqua Grill 555 S Alamo St **Fax Area Code:* 817 ■ *TF:* 800-845-5279	San Antonio	TX	78205	210-229-1000	778-2049*	671
Anara Spa at the Hyatt Regency Kauai 1571 Poipu Rd *Web:* www.anaraspa.com	Koloa	HI	96756	808-742-1234		707
Anaren Microwave Inc 6635 Kirkville Rd *NASDAQ: ANEN* ■ *TF:* 800-544-2414 ■ *Web:* www.anaren.com	East Syracuse	NY	13057	315-432-8909	432-9121	253

Name / Address	City	State	ZIP	Phone	Fax	Class
Anasazi Heritage Ctr 27501 Hwy 184 *Web:* www.blm.gov	Dolores	CO	81323	970-882-5600	882-7035	50-2
Anasazi State Park Museum 460 North Hwy 12 *Web:* www.stateparks.utah.gov	Boulder	UT	84716	435-335-7308		565
AnaSpec Inc 34801 Campus Dr *TF:* 800-452-5530 ■ *Web:* www.anaspec.com	Fremont	CA	94555	510-791-9560	791-9572	231
Anastasi Trucking & Paving Inc 4430 Walden St *Web:* www.anastasitrucking.com	Lancaster	NY	14086	716-683-5003	683-5045	189-5
Anasteel & Supply Company LLC 2272 Mabros Industrial Pkwy *Web:* www.anasteel.com	Ellenwood	GA	30294	404-675-9501		480
Anasys Instruments Corp 325 Chapala St *Web:* www.anasysinstruments.com	Santa Barbara	CA	93101	805-730-3310	730-3300	668
Anatech Electronics Inc 70 Outwater Ln *Web:* www.anatechelectronics.com	Garfield	NJ	07026	973-772-4242		262
Anatech Ltd 771 Crosspoint Dr *Web:* www.anatechltd.com	Denver	NC	28037	704-489-1488		54
Anatek Labs Inc 1282 Alturas Dr *TF:* 800-334-5493 ■ *Web:* www.anateklabs.com	Moscow	ID	83843	208-883-2839		743
Anatolia 48 White Bridge Rd *Web:* www.anatolia-restaurant.com	Nashville	TN	37205	615-356-1556	356-1551	671
Anatolia's 992 Willamette St *Web:* poppisanatolia.com	Eugene	OR	97401	541-343-9661		671
Anatom-e Information Systems Ltd 7505 Fannin St Ste 422 *Web:* www.anatom-e.com	Houston	TX	77054	469-231-4568		743
Anatometal 411 Ingalls St *Web:* www.anatometal.com	Santa Cruz	CA	95060	831-454-9880		411
Ancero LLC 1001 Briggs Rd Ste 220 *Web:* www.ancero.com	Mount Laurel	NJ	08054	856-210-5800		387
Ancestry.com 360 W 4800 N *TF Cust Svc:* 800-262-3787 ■ *Web:* www.ancestry.com	Provo	UT	84604	801-705-7000	705-7001	397
Anchan Thai Kitchen 936 King St W *Web:* www.youngthailand.com	Toronto	ON	M5V1P5	416-366-8424		671
Anchin Block & Anchin LLP 1375 Broadway *Web:* www.anchin.com	New York	NY	10018	212-840-3456	840-7066	2
Anchor Animal Hospital Inc 750 State Rd *Web:* anchoranimalhospital.com	North Dartmouth	MA	02747	508-996-3731		794
Anchor Bank 1055 Wayzata Blvd E *TF:* 800-425-5150 ■ *Web:* www.anchorlink.com	Wayzata	MN	55391	952-473-4606		70
Anchor Bar 651 Delaware Ave *TF:* 866-248-9623 ■ *Web:* www.anchorbar.com	Buffalo	NY	14202	716-883-1134		671
Anchor Bay Entertainment Inc 9242 Beverly Blvd Ste 201 *TF:* 877-230-2756 ■ *Web:* www.anchorbayentertainment.com	Beverly Hills	CA	90210	424-204-4166		511
Anchor Bay Packaging Corp 30905 23 Mile Rd *TF:* 800-280-0780 ■ *Web:* www.anchorbaypackaging.com	New Baltimore	MI	48047	586-949-4040	949-9998	100
Anchor Bay School District 5201 County Line Rd Ste 100 *Web:* www.anchorbay.misd.net	Casco Township	MI	48064	586-725-2861	725-0290	685
Anchor Bay Veterinary Center PC 36755 Green St *Web:* www.anchorbayvetcenter.com	New Baltimore	MI	48047	586-725-7700		794
Anchor Benefit Consulting Inc 2400 Maitland Ctr Pkwy Ste 111 *TF:* 800-845-7629 ■ *Web:* anchorbenefit.com	Maitland	FL	32751	407-667-8766		194
Anchor Brake Shoe Co 1920 Downs Dr *Web:* www.nyab.com	West Chicago	IL	60185	630-293-1110		650
Anchor Brewing Co 1705 Mariposa St *Web:* www.anchorbrewing.com	San Francisco	CA	94107	415-863-8350	552-7094	102
Anchor Capital Advisors LLC 1 Post Office Sq Ste 3850 *Web:* www.anchorcapital.com	Boston	MA	02109	617-338-3800		401
Anchor Commercial Bank 13951 US Hwy One *Web:* www.anchorcommercialbank.com	Juno Beach	FL	33408	561-383-3150		70
Anchor Computer Inc 1900 New Hwy *TF:* 800-728-6262 ■ *Web:* www.anchorcomputer.com	Farmingdale	NY	11735	631-293-6100	293-0891	178-10
Anchor Construction Corp 2254 25th Place NE *Web:* www.anchorconst.com	Washington	DC	20018	202-269-6694		186
Anchor Coupling Inc 5520 13th St *Web:* www.anchorcoupling.com	Menominee	MI	49858	906-863-2671	863-3242	621
Anchor Fabrication Ltd 1200 Lawson Rd *TF:* 800-635-0386 ■ *Web:* anchorfabrication.com	Fort Worth	TX	76131	800-635-0386		480
Anchor Financial Group 415 Fallowfield Rd Ste 300 *Web:* www.anchorfinancialgroup.com	Camp Hill	PA	17011	717-975-0509		390
Anchor Glass Container Corp 401 E Jackson St Ste 1100 *Web:* www.anchorglass.com	Tampa	FL	33602	813-884-0000		330
Anchor Hocking Co 519 Pierce Ave *TF:* 800-562-7511 ■ *Web:* www.oneida.com/anchor-hocking	Lancaster	OH	43130	740-681-6900		334
Anchor Hospital 5454 Yorktowne Dr *TF:* 866-667-8797 ■ *Web:* www.anchorhospital.com	Atlanta	GA	30349	770-991-6044		726
Anchor Industries Inc 1100 Burch Dr *TF:* 800-544-4445 ■ *Web:* www.anchorinc.com	Evansville	IN	47725	812-867-2421	867-1429	733
Anchor Marketing Inc 2726 17th Ave S *Web:* www.anchorwebsite.com	Grand Forks	ND	58208	701-787-8230		177
Anchor Packaging Inc 13515 Barrett Pkwy Dr *Web:* www.anchorpackaging.com	Saint Louis	MO	63021	314-822-7800		601
Anchor Paper Company Inc 480 Broadway St *TF:* 800-652-9755 ■ *Web:* www.anchorpaper.com	Saint Paul	MN	55101	651-298-1311	298-0060	553
Anchor Products Company Inc 52 Official Rd *Web:* www.anchorsurgical.com	Addison	IL	60101	630-543-9124		476
Anchor QEA LLC 720 Olive Way Ste 1900 *Web:* www.anchorqea.com	Seattle	WA	98101	206-287-9130	287-9131	194
Anchor Realty Associates Inc 1113 W Baker Rd Ste D *Web:* har.com	Baytown	TX	77521	281-427-4747		652
Anchor Subaru LLC 949 Eddie Dowling Hwy *Web:* anchorsubaru.com	North Smithfield	RI	02896	401-769-1199		57
Anchor Tampa Inc 3907 W Osborne Ave *TF:* 800-879-8685 ■ *Web:* www.anchortampa.com	Tampa	FL	33614	813-879-8685		186
Anchor Tool & Die Co 12200 Brookpark Rd *TF:* 888-341-8910 ■ *Web:* www.anchor-mfg.com	Cleveland	OH	44130	216-362-1850	265-7833	757
Anchorage Alaska Bed & Breakfast Assn (AABBA) PO Box 242623 *TF:* 888-584-5147 ■ *Web:* www.anchorage-bnb.com	Anchorage	AK	99524	907-272-5909		376
Anchorage Chamber of Commerce 1016 W Sixth Ave Ste 303 *TF:* 800-327-5774 ■ *Web:* www.anchoragechamber.org	Anchorage	AK	99501	907-272-2401	272-4117	139
Anchorage City Hall 632 W Sixth Ave *Web:* www.muni.org	Anchorage	AK	99501	907-343-4431		337
Anchorage Convention & Visitors Bureau 524 W Fourth Ave *TF:* 800-478-6657 ■ *Web:* www.anchorage.net	Anchorage	AK	99501	907-276-4118		206
Anchorage Correctional Complex 1400 E Fourth Ave *Web:* www.correct.state.ak.us	Anchorage	AK	99501	907-269-4100	269-4208	213
Anchorage Daily News 1001 Northway Dr *TF:* 800-478-4200 ■ *Web:* www.adn.com	Anchorage	AK	99508	907-257-4200		532-2
Anchorage Municipality 632 W Sixth Ave # 250 *Web:* www.muni.org	Anchorage	AK	99501	907-343-4311	343-4313	338
Anchorage Museum of History & Art 625 C St *Web:* www.anchoragemuseum.org	Anchorage	AK	99501	907-929-9200	929-9290	520
Anchorage Opera 1507 Spar Ave *Web:* www.anchorageopera.org	Anchorage	AK	99501	907-279-2557	279-7798	573-2
Anchorage Press 540 E Fifth Ave *TF:* 800-800-7754 ■ *Web:* www.anchoragepress.com	Anchorage	AK	99501	907-561-7737	561-7777	532-4
Anchorage School District 3580 E Tudor Rd *Web:* www.asdk12.org	Anchorage	AK	99507	907-742-4000	742-4176	685
Anchorage Symphony Orchestra 400 D St Ste 230 *Web:* www.anchoragesymphony.org	Anchorage	AK	99501	907-274-8668	272-7916	573-3
Anchorage Uptown Suites 235 E Second Court *Web:* www.anchorageuptownsuites.com	Anchorage	AK	99501	907-279-4232		379
Anchor-Harvey Components LLC 600 W Lamm Rd *TF:* 888-367-4464 ■ *Web:* www.anchorharvey.com	Freeport	IL	61032	815-233-3833		483
Anchor-In 1 S St *Web:* anchorin.com	Hyannis	MA	02601	508-775-0357	775-1313	379
Ancient Cedars Spa at the Wickaninnish Inn 500 Osprey Ln PO Box 250 *TF:* 800-333-4604 ■ *Web:* www.wickinn.com	Tofino	BC	V0R2Z0	250-725-3113	725-3110	707
Ancilla Systems Inc 1419 S Lake Pk Ave *TF:* 800-952-2355 ■ *Web:* www.ancilla.org	Hobart	IN	46342	219-947-8500	947-4037	353
Ancillary Care Services 222 W Las Colinas Blvd Ste 500N *NASDAQ:* ANCI ■ **Fax Area Code:* 806 ■ *TF:* 844-516-3335	Irving	TX	75039	844-516-3335	473-3228*	363
Ancira Winton Chevrolet 6111 Bandera Rd *TF General:* 800-299-5286 ■ *Web:* chevroletancira.com	San Antonio	TX	78238	210-762-4545		57
ANCO Insurance 1111 Briarcrest Dr PO Box 3889 **Fax Area Code:* 936 ■ *TF:* 800-749-1733 ■ *Web:* www.anco.com	Bryan	TX	77802	979-776-2626	327-3219*	390
Anco Products Inc (API) 2500 S 17th St *TF:* 800-837-2626 ■ *Web:* www.ancoproductsinc.com	Elkhart	IN	46517	574-293-5574	295-6235	389
Ancora Psychiatric Hospital 301 Spring Garden Rd *Web:* nj.gov	Hammonton	NJ	08037	609-561-1700	561-2509	374-5
Ancra International LLC 4880 W Rosecrans Ave *TF:* 800-973-5092 ■ *Web:* www.ancra-llc.com	Hawthorne	CA	90250	310-973-5000	973-1138	678
ANCW (American National CattleWomen Inc) 200 NW 66th St *Web:* www.ancw.org	Oklahoma City	OK	73116	303-850-3441		48-2
Andaloro, Smith & Krueger LLP N19W24400 Riverwood Dr Ste 200 *Web:* www.askcpas.com	Waukesha	WI	53188	262-544-2000		2
Andaluca 407 Olive Way *Web:* www.andaluca.com	Seattle	WA	98101	206-382-6999	382-6997	671
Andalusia Health (ARH) 849 S Three Notch St PO Box 760 *Web:* www.andalusiaregional.com	Andalusia	AL	36420	334-222-8466	222-6983	374-3
Andaluz 125 Second St NW *Web:* www.hotelandaluz.com	Albuquerque	NM	87102	505-242-9090		379
ANDalyze Inc 2109 S Oak St Ste 102 *Web:* www.andalyze.com	Champaign	IL	61820	217-328-0045		407
Andantex USA Inc 1705 Valley Rd *Web:* www.andantex.com	Wanamassa	NJ	07712	732-493-2812		770
Andaz 5th Avenue 485 Fifth Ave 41st St *Web:* newyork5thavenue.andaz.hyatt.com/en/hotel/home.html	New York	NY	10017	212-601-1234		378
Andaz San Diego 600 F St *Web:* sandiego.andaz.hyatt.com	San Diego	CA	92101	619-849-1234	531-7955	379
Andcor Companies Inc 825 Wayzata Blvd E *TF:* 800-642-9940 ■ *Web:* www.andcor.com	Wayzata	MN	55391	952-404-8060		260
Andela 147 Lexington Ave, PH *Web:* andela.com	New York	NY	10016	212-848-9800		260
Andersen Bakery Inc 30703 San Clemente St *Web:* www.andersenbakery.com	Hayward	CA	94544	510-429-7100		345

Name / Address	City	State	Zip	Phone	Fax	Class
Andersen Construction Company Inc 6712 N Cutter Cir *Web:* www.andersen-const.com	Portland	OR	97217	503-283-6712		186
Andersen Corp 100 Fourth Ave N *TF:* 888-888-7020 ■ *Web:* www.andersenwindows.com	Bayport	MN	55003	651-264-5150		236
Andersen Manufacturing Inc 3125 N Yellowstone Hwy *TF:* 800-635-6106 ■ *Web:* andersenhitches.com	Idaho Falls	ID	83401	208-523-6460		647
Andersen Products Inc 3202 Caroline Dr *Web:* www.anpro.com	Haw River	NC	27258	336-376-3000		475
Andersen Sterilizers Inc 3154 Caroline Dr *Web:* www.andcal.com	Haw River	NC	27258	336-376-8622		476
Anderson & Vreeland Inc 8 Evans St *TF:* 800-994-5993 ■ *Web:* andersonvreeland.com	Fairfield	NJ	07004	973-227-2270		628
Anderson America Corp 10710 Southern Loop Blvd *TF:* 800-828-1004 ■ *Web:* www.andersonamerica.com	Pineville	NC	28134	704-522-1823		358
Anderson Area Chamber of Commerce 907 N Main St Ste 200 *TF:* 800-422-1955 ■ *Web:* www.andersonscchamber.com	Anderson	SC	29621	864-226-3454	226-3300	139
Anderson Area Chamber of Commerce 7850 Five Mile Rd *TF:* 800-353-2226 ■ *Web:* www.andersonareachamber.org	Cincinnati	OH	45230	513-474-4802	474-4857	139
Anderson Automatics Inc 6401 Welcome Ave N *TF:* 800-752-1768 ■ *Web:* www.andersonautomatics.com	Minneapolis	MN	55429	763-533-2206	533-0320	621
Anderson Brass Co 1629 W Bobo Newsome Hwy *TF:* 800-476-9876 ■ *Web:* www.andersonbrass.com	Hartsville	SC	29550	843-332-4111	332-3752	789
Anderson Bros Construction Company Inc 11325 State Hwy 210 *Web:* www.andersonbrothers.com	Brainerd	MN	56401	218-829-1768	829-7607	188-4
Anderson Brule Architects Inc 325 S First St Fl 4 *TF:* 800-853-9318 ■ *Web:* www.aba-arch.com	San Jose	CA	95113	408-298-1885		41
Anderson Center For Autism Inc 4885 Route 9 PO Box 367 *Web:* www.andersoncenterforautism.org	Staatsburg	NY	12580	845-889-4034		371
Anderson Chemical Co 325 S Davis *TF:* 800-366-2477 ■ *Web:* www.accomn.com	Litchfield	MN	55355	320-693-2477	693-8238	145
Anderson Cleaning 144 Garing Rd	Chicora	PA	16025	724-445-2849		256
Anderson Coach & Travel 1 Anderson Plaza *TF:* 800-345-3435 ■ *Web:* www.goanderson.com	Greenville	PA	16125	724-588-8310	588-0257	760
Anderson Columbia Co Inc 871 NW Guerdon St *Web:* www.andersoncolumbia.com	Lake City	FL	32055	386-752-7585	755-5430	188-4
Anderson Communications 1691 Phoenix Blvd Ste 390 *Web:* www.andercom.com	Atlanta	GA	30349	404-766-8000		4
Anderson Concrete Corp 400 Frank Rd *Web:* www.andersonconcrete.com	Columbus	OH	43207	614-443-0123	443-4001	182
Anderson Cook Inc 17650 15-Mile Rd *Web:* www.andersoncook.com	Fraser	MI	48026	586-293-0800		456
Anderson Copper & Brass Co 7231 W Laraway Rd *TF:* 800-323-5284 ■ *Web:* andersonfittings.com	Frankfort	IL	60423	708-535-9030		609
Anderson County PO Box 8002 PO Box 8002 *TF:* 800-447-5375 ■ *Web:* www.andersoncountysc.org	Anderson	SC	29624	864-260-4000		338
Anderson County 100 N Main St Rm 111 *TF:* 800-523-2701 ■ *Web:* www.andersoncountychamber.org	Clinton	TN	37716	865-457-5400		338
Anderson County 100 E Fourth Ave *Web:* andersoncountyks.org	Garnett	KS	66032	785-448-6841		338
Anderson County 151 S Main St *Web:* andersoncountyclerk.ky.gov	Lawrenceburg	KY	40342	502-839-3041	839-3043	338
Anderson County 500 N Church St *Web:* www.co.anderson.tx.us	Palestine	TX	75801	903-723-7403	723-4625	338
Anderson County Chamber of Commerce 245 N Main St Ste 200 *TF:* 800-870-3481 ■ *Web:* www.andersoncountychamber.org	Clinton	TN	37716	865-457-2559	463-7480	139
Anderson County Library 300 S McDuffie St *Web:* www.andersonlibrary.org	Anderson	SC	29621	864-260-4500		434-3
Anderson County Public Library 114 N Main St *Web:* www.andersonpubliclibrary.org	Lawrenceburg	KY	40342	502-839-6420		434-3
Anderson Dairy Inc 801 Searles Ave *Web:* www.andersondairy.com	Las Vegas	NV	89101	702-642-7507	642-3480	296-27
Anderson Daymon Worldwide LLC 1301 Fourth Ave NW Ste 100 *Web:* www.adww.com	Issaquah	WA	98027	425-313-1505		708
Anderson DDB Health & Lifestyle 33 Bloor St E *Web:* www.andersonddb.com	Toronto	ON	M4W3H1	416-960-3830		5
Anderson Development Co 1415 E Michigan St *Web:* www.andersondevelopment.com	Adrian	MI	49221	517-263-2121	263-1000	145
Anderson Economic Group LLC 1555 Watertower Pl Ste 100 *Web:* www.andersoneconomicgroup.com	East Lansing	MI	48823	517-333-6984	333-7058	256
Anderson Electric Inc PO Box 758 *Web:* www.anderson-electric.com	Springfield	IL	62705	217-529-5471	529-0412	189-4
Anderson Engineering of New Prague Inc 20526 330th St *Web:* aenpi.com	New Prague	MN	56071	507-364-7373		261
Anderson Equipment Co 1000 Washington Pk *TF:* 800-414-4554 ■ *Web:* www.andersonequip.com	Bridgeville	PA	15017	412-343-2300		358
Anderson Erickson Dairy Co 2420 E University Ave *TF:* 800-234-6455 ■ *Web:* www.aedairy.com	Des Moines	IA	50317	515-265-2521	263-6301	296-27
Anderson Farms Inc 4600 Second St	Davis	CA	95618	530-753-5695		10-11
Anderson Forest Products Inc 1267 Old Edmonton Rd *TF:* 800-489-6778 ■ *Web:* www.afp-usa.com	Tompkinsville	KY	42167	270-487-6778	487-8953	551
Anderson Gallery 907 W Franklin St *Web:* arts.vcu.edu/andersongallery	Richmond	VA	23284	804-828-1522		520
Anderson Global Inc 500 W Sherman Blvd *Web:* www.andersonglobal.com	Muskegon Heights	MI	49444	231-733-2164	733-1288	567
Anderson H Thomas 6160 Saint Andrews Rd *Web:* hthomasanderson.com	Columbia	SC	29212	803-798-9586		428
Anderson Hardwood Floors PO Box 1155 *Web:* www.andersonfloors.com	Clinton	SC	29325	864-833-6250		613
Anderson Hospital 6800 SR 162 *Web:* www.andersonhospital.org	Maryville	IL	62062	618-288-5711		374-3
Anderson Independent-Mail 1000 Williamston Rd *TF:* 800-859-6397 ■ *Web:* www.independentmail.com	Anderson	SC	29621	864-224-4321	260-1276	532-2
Anderson International Corp 4545 Boyce Pkwy *Fax Area Code: 330 ■ *TF:* 800-336-4730 ■ *Web:* www.andersonintl.net	Stow	OH	44224	216-641-1112	688-0117*	298
Anderson Japanese Gardens 318 Spring Creek Rd *Web:* andersongardens.org	Rockford	IL	61107	815-229-9390		97
Anderson Lake Conservation Area 647 N State Hwy 100 *Web:* dnr.illinois.gov/Lands/Landmgt/PARKS/R1/ANDERSON.HTM	Astoria	IL	61501	309-759-4484		565
Anderson LeNeave & Co 6000 Fairview Rd Ste 625 *Web:* www.andersonleneave.com	Charlotte	NC	28210	704-552-9212		194
Anderson Machinery Company Inc 6535 Leopard St *Web:* www.andersonmachinerytexas.com	Corpus Christi	TX	78409	361-289-6043	289-6047	358
Anderson Machining Service Inc 211 Collins Rd *Web:* www.basinprecision.com	Jefferson	WI	53549	920-674-6003		454
Anderson Marketing Group 7420 Blanco Rd Ste 200 *Web:* www.andadv.com	San Antonio	TX	78216	210-223-6233		7
Anderson Merchandisers LP 421 SE 34th Ave *Web:* www.amerch.com	Amarillo	TX	79103	806-376-6251		530
Anderson Pacific Engineering Construction Inc 1390 Norman Ave *Web:* www.andpac.com	Santa Clara	CA	95054	408-970-9900	970-9975	256
Anderson Partners Advertising 444 Regency Parkway Dr Ste 311 *TF:* 800-551-9737 ■ *Web:* www.andersonpartners.com	Omaha	NE	68114	402-341-4807	341-2846	4
Anderson Perry & Assoc Inc 1901 N Fir St *Web:* www.andersonperry.com	La Grande	OR	97850	541-963-8309		256
Anderson Power Products 13 Pratts Junction Rd *Web:* www.andersonpower.com	Sterling	MA	01564	978-422-3600		596
Anderson Precision Inc 20 Livingston Ave *Web:* www.andersonprecision.com	Jamestown	NY	14701	716-484-1148		621
Anderson Printing & Mailing 139 S Mechanic St *Web:* www.printanderson.com	Jackson	MI	49201	517-787-4562		627
Anderson Public Library 111 E 12th St *Web:* www.and.lib.in.us	Anderson	IN	46016	765-641-2456	641-2197	434-3
Anderson Ranch Arts Center 5263 Owl Creek Rd PO Box 5598 *TF:* 800-525-6363 ■ *Web:* www.andersonranch.org	Snowmass Village	CO	81615	970-923-3181	923-3871	50-2
Anderson Rowe & Buckley Inc 2833 Third St	San Francisco	CA	94107	415-282-1625		189-10
Anderson Satuloff Machado 20700 Ventura Blvd Ste 205 *Web:* asmmcpa.com	Woodland Hills	CA	91364	818-710-0622		2
Anderson Security Agency Ltd 2555 W Morningside Dr *Web:* www.andersonsecurity.com	Phoenix	AZ	85023	602-331-7000		693
Anderson Shumaker Co 824 S Central Ave *Web:* www.andersonshumaker.com	Chicago	IL	60644	773-287-0874		390
Anderson Symphony Orchestra (ASO) 1124 Meridian Plaza *Web:* www.andersonsymphony.org	Anderson	IN	46016	765-644-2111		573-3
Anderson Technologies Inc 14000 172nd St *Web:* www.andtec.com	Grand Haven	MI	49417	616-844-2505		596
Anderson Tool & Engineering Co Inc 1735 W 53 St *Web:* www.iupui.edu	Anderson	IN	46013	765-643-6691		454
Anderson Trucking Service Inc 725 Opportunity St PO Box 1377 *TF:* 800-328-2316 ■ *Web:* www.atsinc.com	Saint Cloud	MN	56301	320-255-7400	255-7494	780
Anderson Truss Company Inc 780 Louisville Rd *Web:* www.andersontrusscompany.com	Alcoa	TN	37701	865-983-9485		817
Anderson Tube Company Inc 1400 Fairgrounds Rd *TF:* 800-523-2258 ■ *Web:* www.atube.com	Hatfield	PA	19440	215-855-0118		612
Anderson University 1100 E Fifth St *Fax: Admissions ■ *TF Admissions:* 800-428-6414 ■ *Web:* www.anderson.edu	Anderson	IN	46012	765-649-9071	641-4091*	166
Anderson Wood Products Co 1381 Beech St *TF:* 800-678-6056 ■ *Web:* www.andersonwood.com	Louisville	KY	40211	502-778-5591	778-5599	499
Anderson's BBQ House 5410 Harry Hines Blvd *Web:* www.mikeandersonsbbq.com	Dallas	TX	75235	214-630-0735		671
Anderson, Eckstein & Westrick Inc 51301 Schoenherr Rd *TF:* 800-427-5100 ■ *Web:* www.aewinc.com	Shelby Township	MI	48315	586-726-1234		261
Anderson, Julian & Hull LLP C W Moore Plaza 250 S Fifth St Ste 700 *Web:* www.ajhlaw.com	Boise	ID	83707	208-344-5800		428
Anderson, O'Brien, Bertz, Skrenes & Golla 1257 Main St *Web:* www.andlaw.com	Stevens Point	WI	54481	715-344-0890		428

Phone | Fax | Class

Anderson, Zeigler, Disharoon, Gallagher & Gray PC
50 Old Courthouse Sq 5th Fl . . . Santa Rosa CA 95404 707-545-4910 428
Web: andersonzeigler.com

Anderson/Madison County Visitors & Convention Bureau
6335 S Scatterfield Rd . . . Anderson IN 46013 765-643-5633 206
TF: 800-533-6569 ■ *Web:* www.visitandersonmadisoncounty.com

Anderson-DuBose Co 5300 Tod Ave SW . . . Lordstown OH 44481 440-248-8800 824-2256* 300
**Fax Area Code:* 330 ■ *Web:* anderson-dubose.com

Andersons Inc
1947 Briarfield Blvd PO Box 119 . . . Maumee OH 43537 419-893-5050 185
NASDAQ: ANDE ■ *TF:* 800-537-3370 ■ *Web:* www.andersonsinc.com

Anderson-Tully 1725 N Washington St . . . Vicksburg MS 39183 601-629-3283 629-3284 188-5
TF: 800-454-6270 ■ *Web:* www.andersontully.com

Anderson-Tully Co
775 Ridgelake Blvd Ste 1050 . . . Memphis TN 38120 901-576-1400 683
Web: www.andersontully.com

Andersonville National Historic Site
496 Cemetery Rd . . . Andersonville GA 31711 229-924-0343 924-1086 564
Web: www.nps.gov/ande

Andes Candies Inc 1400 E Wisconsin St . . . Delavan WI 53115 262-728-9121 296-8

Andex Industries Inc
1911 Fourth Ave N . . . Escanaba MI 49829 800-338-9882 786-3133* 88
**Fax Area Code:* 906 ■ *TF:* 800-338-9882 ■ *Web:* www.andex.net

Andiamo 322 Garfield St . . . Santa Fe NM 87501 505-995-9595 671
Web: andiamosantafe.com

Andiamo 5950 Santo Rd . . . San Diego CA 92124 858-277-3501 671
Web: andiamo-ristorante.com

Andiamo 400 Renaissance Ctr Ste A403 . . . Detroit MI 48243 313-567-6700 567-6701 671
Web: www.andiamoitalia.com

Andiamo Partners 17 State St 8th Fl . . . New York NY 10004 212-488-1595 260
Web: www.andiamogo.com

Andina 1314 NW Glisan St . . . Portland OR 97209 503-228-9535 671
Web: www.andinarestaurant.com

Andis Co 1800 Renaissance Blvd . . . Sturtevant WI 53177 262-884-2600 884-1100 37
TF: 800-558-9441 ■ *Web:* www.andis.com

Andor Technology Plc (USA)
425 Sullivan Ave Ste No3 . . . South Windsor CT 06074 860-290-9211 419
Web: www.andor.com

Andorra Embassy
2 United Nations Plaza 25th Fl . . . New York NY 10017 212-750-8064 750-6630 257
Web: www.embassy.org/embassies/ad.html

Andover Co, The 95 Old River Rd . . . Andover MA 01810 978-475-3300 390
Web: andovercos.com

Andover Coils LLC 310 N Earl Ave . . . Lafayette IN 47904 765-447-1157 518
Web: www.andovercoils.com

Andover College
265 Western Ave . . . South Portland ME 04106 207-774-6126 774-1715 800
TF: 800-639-3110 ■ *Web:* kaplanuniversity.edu

Andover Corp 4 Commercial Dr . . . Salem NH 03079 603-893-6888 544
Web: www.andcorp.com

Andover Healthcare Inc 9 Fanaras Dr . . . Salisbury MA 01952 978-465-0044 462-0003 476
TF: 800-432-6686 ■ *Web:* www.andovercoated.com

Andover Newton Theological School
210 Herrick Rd . . . Newton Center MA 02459 617-964-1100 167-3
TF: 800 964 2687 ■ *Web:* www.ants.edu

Andover Village Retirement Community Inc
486 S Main St . . . Andover OH 44003 440-293-5416 793
Web: www.andovervillage.com

Andpak Inc 400 Jarvis Dr . . . Morgan Hill CA 95037 408-782-2500 88
Web: www.andpak.com

AndPlus LLC
257 Turnpike Rd Ste 201 . . . Southborough MA 01772 508-425-7533 196
Web: www.andplus.com

Andra Partners LLC
2550 Meridian Blvd Ste 200 . . . Franklin TN 37067 615-567-8090 463
TF: 800-213-0154 ■ *Web:* www.andrapartners.com

Andre's 401 S Sixth St . . . Las Vegas NV 89101 702-385-5016 385-1742 671
Web: andrelv.com

Andre's 1235 Morena Blvd . . . San Diego CA 92110 619-275-4114 276-4245 671
Web: www.andresrestaurantsd.com

Andrea Obston Marketing Communications LLC
3 Regency Dr . . . Bloomfield CT 06002 860-243-1447 636
TF: 800-237-9151 ■ *Web:* www.aomc.com

Andreas 268 Thayer St . . . Providence RI 02906 401-331-7879 331-7300 671
Web: andreasri.com

Andreas Furniture Company Inc
114 Dover Rd NE . . . Sugarcreek OH 44681 330-852-2494 321
TF: 800-846-7448 ■ *Web:* www.andreasfurniture.com

Andreini & Co 220 W 20th Ave . . . San Mateo CA 94403 650-573-1111 378-4361 390
TF: 800-969-2522 ■ *Web:* www.andreini.com

Andreou & Casson Ltd
661 West Lake St Ste 2n . . . Chicago IL 60661 312-935-2001 428
Web: www.andreou-casson.com

Andretti Green Racing
7615 Zionsville Rd . . . Indianapolis IN 46268 317-872-2700 787
Web: www.andrettiautosport.com

Andrew Associates Inc 6 Pearson Way . . . Enfield CT 06082 860-253-0000 5
Web: andrewdm.com

Andrew College 501 College St . . . Cuthbert GA 39840 800-664-9250 162
TF: 800-664-9250 ■ *Web:* www.andrewcollege.edu

Andrew County PO Box 206 . . . Savannah MO 64485 816-324-3624 324-6154 338
Web: www.andrewcounty.org

Andrew Edson & Associates Inc
89 Bounty Ln . . . Jericho NY 11753 516-931-0873 636
Web: www.edsonpr.com

Andrew G Gordon Inc 306 Washington St . . . Norwell MA 02061 781-659-2262 390
TF: 866-243-2259 ■ *Web:* agordon.com

Andrew Garrett Inc
52 Vanderbilt Ave Ste 510 . . . New York NY 10017 212-682-8833 690
Web: www.andrewgarrett.com

Andrew Jackson State Park
196 Andrew Jackson Pk Rd . . . Lancaster SC 29720 803-285-3344 565
Web: www.southcarolinaparks.com

Andrew Low House, The
329 Abercorn St . . . Savannah GA 31401 912-233-6854 50-3
TF: 800-721-1240 ■ *Web:* www.andrewlowhouse.com

Andrew Moore & Associates
1132 Old York Rd . . . Abington PA 19001 215-885-3500 420
Web: www.moore4law.com

Andrew R Mancini Assoc Inc
129 Odell Ave . . . Endicott NY 13760 607-754-7070 786-0410 360-2
Web: andrewmancini.com

Andrew Seybold Inc
315 Meigs Rd Ste A-267 . . . Santa Barbara CA 93109 805-898-2460 466
Web: www.andrewseybold.com

Andrew T Johnson Company Inc
15 Tremont Pl . . . Boston MA 02108 617-742-1610 523-0719 240
Web: www.andrewtjohnson.com

Andrew Technologies LLC
1421 Edinger Ave Ste D . . . Tustin CA 92780 888-959-7674 475
TF: 888-959-7674 ■ *Web:* hydrasolve.com

Andrew Tool & Machining Inc
15300 28th Ave N . . . Plymouth MN 55447 763-559-0402 454
Web: www.andrewtool.com

Andrew W Mellon Foundation
140 E 62nd St . . . New York NY 10065 212-838-8400 888-4172 305
Web: www.mellon.org

Andrew's 228 228 S Adams St . . . Tallahassee FL 32301 850-222-3444 222-2433 671
TF: 800-628-2866 ■ *Web:* www.andrewsdowntown.com

Andrews & Hamilton Company Inc
3829 S Miami Blvd . . . Durham NC 27703 919-787-4100 358
TF: 800-443-6866 ■ *Web:* www.storageequip.com

Andrews County
215 NW First St PO Box 727 . . . Andrews TX 79714 432-524-1426 338
Web: www.co.andrews.tx.us

Andrews Distribution Co
13650 Copus Rd . . . Bakersfield CA 93313 661-858-2266 858-2965 11-1
Web: www.andrewsaginc.com

Andrews Excavating Inc
5 W Willow Rd . . . Willow Street PA 17584 717-464-3329 464-4963 189-5
TF: 800-730-6822 ■ *Web:* andrewsexcavating.com

Andrews Federal Credit Union (AFCU)
5711 Allentown Rd . . . Suitland MD 20746 301-702-5500 702-5330 219
TF: 800-487-5500 ■ *Web:* www.andrewsfcu.org

Andrews Hammock Powell Inc
250 Charter Ln . . . Macon GA 31210 478-405-8301 256
TF: 800-948-1952 ■ *Web:* www.ahpengr.com

Andrews Hooper Pavlik Plc
5300 Gratiot Rd . . . Saginaw MI 48638 989-497-5300 2
TF: 888-754-8478 ■ *Web:* ahpplc.com

Andrews Hotel 624 Post St . . . San Francisco CA 94109 415-563-6877 928-6919 379
TF: 800-926-3739 ■ *Web:* www.andrewshotel.com

Andrews Industrial Controls
108 Rosslyn Rd . . . Carnegie PA 15106 412-279-5335 407
TF: 800-269-1750 ■ *Web:* www.andrewsic.com

Andrews Kurth LLP
600 Travis St Chase Towers Ste 4200 . . . Houston TX 77002 713-220-4200 220-4285 428
TF: 800-973-1177 ■ *Web:* www.andrewskurth.com

Andrews Logistics Inc
2445 E Southlake Blvd . . . Southlake TX 76092 817-527-2770 194
TF: 866-536-1234 ■ *Web:* www.andrewslogistics.com

Andrews McMeel Universal
1130 Walnut . . . Kansas City MO 64106 816-581-7500 932-6684 530
TF: 800-273-8255 ■ *Web:* www.amuniversal.com

Andrews Osborne Academy
38588 Mentor Ave . . . Willoughby OH 44094 440-942-3600 622
Web: www.andrewsosborne.org

Andrews Products Inc
431 Kingston Ct . . . Mount Prospect IL 60056 847-759-0190 759-0848 517
Web: www.andrewsproducts.com

Andrews University
3976 Rose Dr . . . Berrien Springs MI 49103 269-471-7771 471-2670 166
TF: 800-253-2874 ■ *Web:* www.andrews.edu

Andrews University James White Library
4190 Admin Dr . . . Berrien Springs MI 49104 269-471-3264 471-6166 434-6
TF: 800-253-2874 ■ *Web:* www.andrews.edu/library

Andrews University Seventh-day Adventist Theological Seminary
4145 E Campus Cir Dr
Andrews University . . . Berrien Springs MI 49104 269-471-3537 471-6202 167-3
TF: 800-253-2874 ■ *Web:* www.andrews.edu/sem

Andrews Van Lines Inc
310 S Seventh St . . . Norfolk NE 68701 402-371-5440 519
TF Cust Svc: 800-228-8146 ■ *Web:* www.andrewsvanlines.com

Andrie Inc 561 E Western Ave . . . Muskegon MI 49442 231-728-2226 726-6747 314
TF: 800-722-2421 ■ *Web:* www.andrietg.com

Andritz Inc 35 Sherman St . . . Muncy PA 17756 770-640-2500 454
Web: www.andritz.com

Andritz Kusters Inc
201 Zima Pk Dr . . . Spartanburg SC 29301 864-587-4848 744
TF: 800-598-5189 ■ *Web:* www.andritz.com

Andro Diagnostics Inc 101 14th St . . . Galveston TX 77550 409-762-0422 743

Android Industries
2155 Executive Hills Dr . . . Auburn Hills MI 48326 248-732-0000 247
Web: www.android-ind.com

Andromed Inc 5003 Levy St . . . Saint Laurent QC H4R2N9 514-336-0043 475
Web: www.andromed.com

Androscoggin Home Health Services Inc
PO Box 819 . . . Lewiston ME 04243 207-777-7740 363
TF: 800-482-7412 ■ *Web:* www.ahch.org

Androscoggin Wayside Park
1607 Berlin Rd . . . Errol NH 03579 603-538-6707 565
Web: www.nhstateparks.org

Andrus on Hudson
185 Old Broadway . . . Hastings On Hudson NY 10706 914-478-3700 478-3541 672
TF: 800-616-8044 ■ *Web:* andrusonhudson.org

Andrus Planetarium
511 Warburton Ave Hudson River Museum . . . Yonkers NY 10701 914-963-4550 963-8558 598
Web: www.hrm.org/planetarium.html

Andrus Transportation Services LLC
3185 East Deseret Dr North . . . Saint George UT 84790 435-673-1566 360-2
TF: 800-888-5838 ■ *Web:* www.andrustrans.com

Andy & Bax 324 SE Grand Ave . . . Portland OR 97214 503-234-7538 239-8817 711
Web: www.andyandbax.com

Name / Address	City	State	ZIP	Phone	Fax	Class
Andy Frain Services Inc 761 Shoreline Dr	Aurora	IL	60504	630-820-3820		693
TF: 877-707-4771 ■ *Web:* www.andyfrain.com						
Andy J Egan Company Inc 2001 Waldorf NW	Grand Rapids	MI	49544	616-791-9952		595
Web: www.andyegan.com						
Andy Rice Photography 7226 Rue De Roark	La Jolla	CA	92037	858-459-8458		590
Web: www.andyricephoto.com						
Andy Warhol Foundation For The Visual Arts Inc 65 Bleecker St 7th Fl.	New York	NY	10012	212-387-7555		305
Web: www.warholfoundation.org						
Andy Warhol Museum 117 Sandusky St	Pittsburgh	PA	15212	412-237-8300	237-8340	520
TF: 800-232-2789 ■ *Web:* www.warhol.org						
Andy Williams Moon River Theatre 2500 Hwy 76	Branson	MO	65616	417-334-1800	337-9627	572
TF: 800-666-6094 ■ *Web:* www.andywilliamspac.com						
Andy's Mediterranean Grille 906 Nassau St	Cincinnati	OH	45206	513-281-9791		671
Web: www.andyskabob.com						
Anel Corp 3244 Hwy 51	Winona	MS	38967	662-283-1540		492
TF: 800-325-5089 ■ *Web:* www.anelcorp.com						
Anemostat 1220 Watsoncenter Rd PO Box 4938	Carson	CA	90745	310-835-7500	835-0448	234
TF: 877-423-7426 ■ *Web:* www.anemostat.com						
ANERA (ANERA) 1111 14th St NW Ste 400	Washington	DC	20005	202-266-9700	266-9701	48-5
Web: www.anera.org						
Anesthesia Service Inc 1821 N Classen Blvd	Oklahoma City	OK	73106	405-525-3588		475
TF: 800-336-3356 ■ *Web:* www.anesthesiaservice.com						
ANEXIO Technology Services Inc 5 W Hargett St 11th FL	Raleigh	NC	27601	844-208-6512		196
TF: 844-208-6512 ■ *Web:* www.anexio.com						
Anfield Inc 5625 Dillard Dr Ste 217	Cary	NC	27518	919-851-8681		344
ANG Federal Credit Union PO Box 170204	Birmingham	AL	35217	205-841-4525	841-4545	219
TF: 800-237-6211 ■ *Web:* www.angfcu.org						
Angarai International Inc 9111 Edmonston Rd Ste 305	Greenbelt	MD	20770	410-472-5000		196
TF: 800-512-9180 ■ *Web:* www.angarai-intl.com						
Angel Baby Brokerage 26 Red Ball Trl.	Coffeen	IL	62017	217-534-2557		796
TF: 800-519-3386 ■ *Web:* www.angelbabybrokerage.com						
Angel Fire Resort PO Box 130	Angel Fire	NM	87710	575-377-6401		669
TF: 800-633-7463 ■ *Web:* www.angelfireresort.com						
Angel Healthcare 5828 Balcones Dr Ste 105	Austin	TX	78731	512-453-6449		363
Angel Medical Systems Inc 788 Shrewsbury Ave Suite 2144	Tinton Falls	NJ	07724	732-542-5551	463-2606*	363
**Fax Area Code:* 801 ■ *Web:* www.angel-med.com						
Angel of The Winds Casino 3438 Stoluckquamish Ln	Arlington	WA	98223	360-474-9740		132
TF: 800-465-4329 ■ *Web:* www.angelofthewinds.com						
Angel Plants Inc 560 W Deer Park Ave	Dix Hills	NY	11746	631-242-7788		292
Web: www.angelplants.com						
Angel Printing & Reproduction Inc 1400 W 57th St.	Cleveland	OH	44102	216-631-5225		627
Web: www.angelprinting.com						
Angel Reyes & Associates PC 5950 Berkshire Ln Ste 410	Dallas	TX	75225	214-278-6026	526-7910	41
Web: www.reyeslaw.com						
Angel Sales Inc 4147 N Ravenswood Ave	Chicago	IL	60613	773-883-8858	883-8889	328
Web: www.angelsales.com						
Angel Stadium 2000 Gene Autry Way	Anaheim	CA	92806	714-940-2000	940-2244	720
TF: 866-800-1275 ■ *Web:* losangeles.angels.mlb.com						
Angela Hospice Home Care 14100 Newburgh Rd.	Livonia	MI	48154	734-464-7810	464-6930	371
TF General: 866-464-7810 ■ *Web:* www.angelahospice.org						
Angeles Contractor Inc 783 Phillips Dr	City of Industry	CA	91748	626-923-3800	923-3801	186
Web: www.angelescontractor.com						
Angeles Investment Advisors LLC 429 Santa Monica Blvd Ste 650	Santa Monica	CA	90401	310-393-6300		401
Web: www.angelesadvisors.com						
Angeli Caffe 7274 Melrose Ave.	Los Angeles	CA	90046	323-936-9086		671
Angelina County Junior College District Texas 3500 S First St	Lufkin	TX	75904	936-639-1301		166
Web: www.angelina.edu						
Angelina's 1563 E Fremont St	Stockton	CA	95205	209-948-6609		671
TF: 800-422-3548 ■ *Web:* www.angelinas.com						
Angelina's Ristorante 399 Ellis St.	Staten Island	NY	10307	718-227-2900	227-3329	671
Web: angelinasristorante.com						
Angelina's Ristorante Italiano 11 Depot St.	Concord	NH	03301	603-228-3313		671
Web: www.angelinasrestaurant.com						
Angelini Osteria 7313 Beverly Blvd.	Los Angeles	CA	90036	323-297-0070		671
Web: www.angeliniosteria.com						
Angell & Company Pllc 5700 Crooks Rd Ste 102	Troy	MI	48098	248-649-8720	649-8727	2
Web: angellcompany.com						
Angell & Giroux Inc 2727 Alcazar St.	Los Angeles	CA	90033	323-269-8596		482
Web: www.angellandgiroux.com						
Angell & Phelps Chocolate Factory 154 S Beach St	Daytona Beach	FL	32114	386-252-6531		671
TF: 800-969-2634 ■ *Web:* angellandphelps.com						
Angell's Bar & Grill 999 W Main St	Boise	ID	83702	208-342-4900		671
TF: 800-243-4622 ■ *Web:* www.angellsbarandgrill.com						
Angelo & O'Brien Pa 340 N Ave E	Cranford	NJ	07016	908-276-8300		2
Angelo Gordon & Co 245 Park Ave.	New York	NY	10167	212-692-2000		41
Web: www.angelogordon.com						
Angelo Iafrate Construction Co 26300 Sherwood Ave	Warren	MI	48091	586-756-1070	756-0467	188-4
TF: 800-561-3357 ■ *Web:* www.iafrate.com						
Angelo State University 2601 W Ave N ASU Stn 11014	San Angelo	TX	76909	325-942-2041	942-2078*	166
**Fax:* Admissions ■ *TF:* 800-946-8627 ■ *Web:* www.angelo.edu						
Angelo State University Henderson Library 2025 S Johnson St.	San Angelo	TX	76909	325-942-2051	942-2198	434-6
TF: 800-946-8627 ■ *Web:* www.angelo.edu						
Angelo's 4107 S Providence Rd	Columbia	MO	65203	573-443-6100		671
Web: angelospizzaandsteak.com						
Angelo's 305 Main St	Evansville	IN	47708	812-428-6666	428-6699	671
Web: angelosevansville.com						
Angelo's Fairmount Tavern 2300 Fairmount Ave	Atlantic City	NJ	08401	609-344-2439	348-1043	671
Web: www.angelosfairmounttavern.com						
Angels of the Valley Hospice Care 2600 Foothill Blvd Ste 202	La Crescenta	CA	91214	818-542-3070	542-3071	793
TF: 888-344-0880 ■ *Web:* www.angelsofthevalley.com						
Angels Unaware Inc, The 4918 W Linebaugh Ave.	Tampa	FL	33624	813-963-2529		371
Web: www.angelsunaware.com						
Angelus Block Co Inc 11374 Tuxford St	Sun Valley	CA	91352	818-767-8576	768-3124	183
Web: www.angelusblock.com						
Angie Brewer & Associates LC 9104 58th Dr E	Bradenton	FL	34202	941-757-4300		195
TF: 800-893-1222 ■ *Web:* www.angiebrewer.com						
Angie's Cantina 11 E Buchanan St	Duluth	MN	55802	218-727-6117		671
TF: 800-706-7672 ■ *Web:* www.grandmasrestaurants.com/littleangies						
Angler Restaurant 312 Talbot St	Ocean City	MD	21842	410-289-7424		671
TF: 800-322-3065 ■ *Web:* angleroc.net						
Angles Gallery 2754 S La Cienega Blvd	Los Angeles	CA	90034	310-396-5019	202-6330	42
Web: www.anglesgallery.com						
Anglin Flewelling Rasmussen Campbell & Trytten LLP 301 N Lake Ave Ste 600	Pasadena	CA	91101	626-535-1900		428
Web: www.afrct.com						
Angola 820 Second Ave 12th Fl	New York	NY	10017	212-861-5656	861-9295	784
Web: www.un.int						
Angola Embassy 2108 16th St NW	Washington	DC	20009	202-785-1156	822-9049	257
Web: www.angola.org						
Angola Wire Products Inc 803 Wohlert St	Angola	IN	46703	260-665-9447	665-6182	286
TF: 800-800-7225 ■ *Web:* www.angolawire.com						
ANGOSS Software Corp Ste 200 111 George St	Toronto	ON	M5A2N4	416-593-1122		177
Web: www.angoss.com						
Angotti's 725 Burnet Ave	Syracuse	NY	13203	315-472-8403		671
Angstrom Graphics Inc 4437 E 49th St	Cleveland	OH	44125	216-271-5300	271-7650	627
TF: 800-634-1262 ■ *Web:* www.angstromgraphics.com						
Angstrom Lighting 12224 Montague St	Pacoima	CA	91331	323-960-0113		722
Web: www.angstromlighting.com						
Angstrom Precision Metals Inc 8229 Tyler Blvd.	Mentor	OH	44060	440-255-6700		60
Angstrom Sciences Inc 40 S Linden St.	Duquesne	PA	15110	412-469-8466		492
Web: www.angstromsciences.com						
Angstrom Technologies Inc 7880 Foundation Dr	Florence	KY	41042	859-282-0020	282-8577	145
TF Cust Svc: 800-543-7358 ■ *Web:* www.angtech.com						
Anguil Environmental Systems Inc 8855 N 55th St	Milwaukee	WI	53223	414-365-6400	365-6410	18
TF: 800-488-0230 ■ *Web:* www.anguil.com						
Anguilla Tourist Marketing Office 246 Central Ave	White Plains	NY	10606	914-287-2400		775
TF: 800-553-4939 ■ *Web:* ivisitanguilla.com						
Angus Barn 9401 Glenwood Ave	Raleigh	NC	27617	919-781-2444	783-5568	671
TF: 800-277-2270 ■ *Web:* www.angusbarn.com						
Angus Systems Group Ltd 1125 Leslie St.	Toronto	ON	M3C2J6	416-385-8550	385-8551	393
TF: 877-442-6487 ■ *Web:* www.angus-systems.com						
Angus, The 1101 Scenic Hwy.	Pensacola	FL	32503	850-432-0539		671
Web: www.anguspensacola.com						
Anheuser-Busch Cos Inc 1 Busch Pl.	Saint Louis	MO	63118	314-577-2000	525-0810	80-1
TF: 800-342-5283 ■ *Web:* www.anheuser-busch.com						
Anheuser-Busch InBev 250 Pk Ave	New York	NY	10177	212-573-8800		102
Web: www.ab-inbev.com						
Anheuser-Busch Inc 900 John St.	West Henrietta	NY	14586	585-427-0090		81-1
Web: www.lakebeverage.com						
Anholt Technologies Inc 440 Church Rd	Avondale	PA	19311	610-268-2758		273
Web: anholt.com						
ANI (American Nuclear Insurers) 95 Glastonbury Blvd Ste 300	Glastonbury	CT	06033	860-682-1301		49-9
Web: www.amnucins.com						
ANI Pharmaceuticals Inc 210 Main St W	Baudette	MN	56623	302-482-8644		418
Web: www.anipharmaceuticals.com						
Aniakchak National Monument & Preserve PO Box 245	King Salmon	AK	99613	907-246-3305	246-2116	564
Web: www.nps.gov/ania						
Anika Therapeutics Inc 32 Wiggins Ave.	Bedford	MA	01730	781-457-9000	305-9720	479
NASDAQ: ANIK ■ *TF:* 800-299-7089 ■ *Web:* www.anikatherapeutics.com						
Animal & Plant Health Inspection Service (APHIS) *National Veterinary Services Laboratories* 4700 River Rd	Riverdale	MD	20737	844-820-2234		743
TF: 844-820-2234 ■ *Web:* www.aphis.usda.gov						
Animal Alliance of Canada 221 Broadview Ave	Toronto	ON	M4M2G3	416-462-9541	462-9647	48-3
Web: www.animalalliance.ca						
Animal Ark Wildlife Sanctuary & Nature Ctr 1265 Deerlodge Rd	Reno	NV	89508	775-970-3111	366-5771*	823
**Fax Area Code:* 866 ■ *TF:* 866-366-5771 ■ *Web:* www.animalark.org						
Animal Eye Specialty Clinic 3421 Forest Hill Blvd W	Palm Beach	FL	33406	561-967-5966		794
Web: www.animaleyespecialtyclinic.com						
Animal Health Institute (AHI) 1325 G St NW Ste 700	Washington	DC	20005	202-637-2440		48-3
Web: www.ahi.org						
Animal Hospital Inc 5001 N 12th Ave	Pensacola	FL	32504	850-479-2900		794
Web: www.petcarehospital.com						
Animal Hospital of Pittsford PC 2816 Monroe Ave Ste 2	Rochester	NY	14618	585-271-7700		794
Web: www.pittsfordvet.com						

Name / Address	City	State	Zip	Phone	Fax	Class
Animal Medical Center of Somerset County Inc						
1911 N Center Ave	Somerset	PA	15501	814-443-6070		794
TF: 800-767-0677 ■ Web: www.amcdocs.com						
Animal Medical Center, The						
510 E 62nd St Fl 2	New York	NY	10065	212-838-8100		794
Web: www.amcny.org						
Animal Protection of New Mexico Inc Foundation						
Po Box 11395	Albuquerque	NM	87192	505-265-2322		305
TF: 800-473-5220 ■ Web: apnm.org						
Animal Supply Company LLC						
32001 32nd Ave S Ste 420	Federal Way	WA	98001	253-237-0400		297-8
TF: 800-323-2963 ■ Web: www.animalsupplycompany.com						
Animal Welfare Association						
509 Centennial Blvd	Voorhees	NJ	08043	856-424-2288		794
TF: 800-646-4773 ■ Web: www.awanj.org						
Animas Corp 200 Lawrence Dr	West Chester	PA	19380	610-644-8990		477
TF: 877-937-7867 ■ Web: www.animas.com						
Animated Designs LLC						
31336 Via Colinas Ste 103	Westlake Village	CA	91362	818-889-2348		4
Web: www.anides.com						
Animated Story Boards Ltd						
1001 Ave of the Americas 24 Fl	New York	NY	10018	212-595-0400		514
Web: www.animatedstoryboards.com						
Animation Mentor						
1400 65th St Ste 250	Emeryville	CA	94608	877-326-4628		764
TF: 877-326-4628 ■ Web: www.animationmentor.com						
Animax Interactive LLC						
6627 Valjean Ave	Van Nuys	CA	91406	818-570-0820		637-10
Web: www.animaxent.com						
Anis Cafe & Bistro 2974 Grandview Ave	Atlanta	GA	30305	404-233-9889		671
Web: www.anisbistro.com						
Anita Borg Institute for Women and Technology (IWT)						
1501 Page Mill Rd MS 1105	Palo Alto	CA	94304	650-352-7500	852-8172	48-9
Web: anitaborg.org						
Anita Purves Nature Ctr						
1505 N Broadway	Urbana	IL	61801	217-384-4062	384-1052	50-5
TF: 800-745-3000 ■ Web: www.urbanaparks.org						
Anitox Corp 1055 Progress Cir	Lawrenceville	GA	30043	678-376-1055		146
Web: www.anitox.com						
Anixter Inc 2301 Patriot Blvd	Glenview	IL	60026	224-521-8000	521-8100	189-4
TF: 800-492-1212 ■ Web: www.anixter.com						
Anka Behavioral Health Inc						
1850 Gateway Blvd Ste 900	Concord	CA	94520	925-825-4700		104
Web: www.ankabhi.org						
Anklesaria Group Inc 1172 Cuchara Dr	Del Mar	CA	92014	858-755-7119		244
Web: www.anklesaria.com						
Ankmar LLC 4200 Monaco St	Denver	CO	80216	303-321-6051		364
TF: 800-640-8061 ■ Web: www.dhpace.com						
Ankom Technology 2052 Oneil Rd	Macedon	NY	14502	315-986-8090		419
Web: www.ankom.com						
Ankor Energy LLC						
1615 Poydras St Ste 1100	New Orleans	LA	70112	504-596-3700		538
Web: www.ankorenergy.com						
ANL (Argonne National Laboratory)						
9700 S Cass Ave	Argonne	IL	60439	630-252-2000		668
TF: 800-632-8990 ■ Web: www.anl.gov						
ANLA (American Nursery & Landscape Assn)						
1000 Vermont Ave NW Ste 300	Washington	DC	20005	202-789-2900	789-1893	48-2
Web: americanhort.org						
Anlin Industries 1665 Tollhouse Rd	Clovis	CA	93611	559-322-1531		499
TF: 800-287-7996 ■ Web: www.anlin.com						
ANM (Alliance of Nonprofit Mailers)						
1211 Connecticut Ave NW Ste 610	Washington	DC	20036	202-462-5132		48-7
Web: www.nonprofitmailers.org						
ANMA (American Naturopathic Medical Assn)						
PO Box 96273	Las Vegas	NV	89193	702-450-3477		48-17
Web: www.anma.org						
ANMC (Alaska Native Medical Ctr)						
4315 Diplomacy Dr	Anchorage	AK	99508	907-563-2662	729-1984	374-3
TF Admitting: 800-478-6661 ■ Web: www.anmc.org						
AnMed Health 800 N Fant St	Anderson	SC	29621	864-512-1000		374-3
Web: www.anmedhealth.org						
Ann & Hope Inc 1 Ann & Hope Way	Cumberland	RI	02864	877-228-7824		229
TF: 877-228-7824 ■ Web: www.curtainandbathoutlet.com						
Ann Arbor Area Convention & Visitors Bureau						
120 W Huron St	Ann Arbor	MI	48104	734-995-7281	995-7283	206
TF: 800-888-9487 ■ Web: www.visitannarbor.org						
Ann Arbor Art Ctr 117 W Liberty St	Ann Arbor	MI	48104	734-994-8004	994-3610	50-2
Web: www.annarborartcenter.org						
Ann Arbor City Hall 301 E Huron St	Ann Arbor	MI	48104	734-794-6000	994-1765	337
Web: www.a2gov.org						
Ann Arbor Civic Ballet						
3900 E Jackson	Ann Arbor	MI	48103	734-668-8066		573-1
Ann Arbor Civic Theatre						
322 W Ann St	Ann Arbor	MI	48104	734-971-0605	971-2769	572
Web: www.a2ct.org						
Ann Arbor Distribution						
1942 Mcgregor Rd	Ypsilanti	MI	48198	734-484-0100		463
Web: annarbordist.com						
Ann Arbor District Library (AADL)						
343 S Fifth Ave	Ann Arbor	MI	48104	734-327-4200	327-8309	434-3
TF: 800-230-4085 ■ Web: www.aadl.org						
Ann Arbor Film Festival						
217 N First St	Ann Arbor	MI	48104	734-995-5356		282
Web: www.aafilmfest.org						
Ann Arbor Symphony Orchestra						
220 E Huron St Ste 470	Ann Arbor	MI	48104	734-994-4801	994-3949	573-3
TF: 800-745-3000 ■ Web: www.a2so.com						
Ann Arbor Transportation Authority						
2700 S Industrial Hwy	Ann Arbor	MI	48104	734-973-6500	973-6338	468
TF: 800-835-4603 ■ Web: www.theride.org						
Ann Clark Ltd 453 Quality Ln	Rutland	VT	05701	802-773-7886		362
Web: www.annclarkcookiecutters.com						
Ann Coppel Productions LLC						
PO Box 17144	Seattle	WA	98127	206-282-7720		514
Web: www.anncoppelproductions.com						
Ann Inc 7 Times Sq	New York	NY	10036	212-541-3300	541-3299	157-6
NYSE: ANN ■ TF: 800-677-6788 ■ Web: www.anninc.com						
Ann Mcgee-cooper & Assoc Inc						
4236 Hockaday Dr	Dallas	TX	75229	214-357-8550		104
Web: www.amca.com						
Ann Norton Sculpture Gardens						
253 Barcelona Rd	West Palm Beach	FL	33401	561-832-5328	835-9305	50-3
Web: www.ansg.org						
Ann Sacks Tile & Stone Inc						
8120 NE 33rd Dr	Portland	OR	97211	503-281-7751	287-8807	751
TF: 800-278-8453 ■ Web: www.annsacks.com						
ANNA (American Nephrology Nurses Assn)						
200 E Holly Ave	Sewell	NJ	08080	856-256-2320	589-7463	49-8
TF: 888-600-2662 ■ Web: www.annanurse.org						
Anna Griffin Inc 99 Armour Dr	Atlanta	GA	30324	404-817-8170		552-2
TF: 888-817-8170 ■ Web: www.annagriffin.com						
Anna Jaques Hospital (AJH)						
25 Highland Ave	Newburyport	MA	01950	978-463-1000	463-1250	374-3
TF: 800-355-7944 ■ Web: www.ajh.org						
Anna Kustera Gallery 520 W 21st St	New York	NY	10011	212-989-0082		42
Web: www.annakustera.com						
Anna Maria College 50 Sunset Ln	Paxton	MA	01612	800-344-4586		166
TF: 800-344-4586 ■ Web: www.annamaria.edu						
Anna Maria of Aurora Inc						
889 N Aurora Rd	Aurora	OH	44202	330-562-6171		371
Web: www.annamariaofaurora.com						
Anna's Greek Cuisine 7370 Sawmill Rd	Columbus	OH	43235	614-799-2207		671
Web: annasgreekfood.com						
Anna's Trattoria						
304 Seabreeze Blvd	Daytona Beach	FL	32118	386-239-9624		671
Annabelle Candy Company Inc						
27211 Industrial Blvd	Hayward	CA	94545	510-783-2900	785-7675	297-3
TF: 800-228-2800 ■ Web: annabellecandy.com						
Annals of Internal Medicine Magazine						
190 N Independence Mall W	Philadelphia	PA	19106	215-351-2400		457-16
TF: 800-523-1546 ■ Web: www.annals.org						
Annan & Bird Lithographers Ltd						
1060 Tristar Dr	Mississauga	ON	L5T1H9	905-670-0604		627
TF: 800-565-5618 ■ Web: www.annan-bird.com						
Annandale Chamber of Commerce						
7263 Maple Pl Ste 207	Annandale	VA	22003	703-256-7232	256-7233	139
TF: 800-357-2110 ■ Web: www.annandalechamber.com						
Annandale Millwork Allied Systems						
220 Arbor Ct	Winchester	VA	22602	540-665-9600		499
TF: 800-798-7859 ■ Web: amcasc.com						
Annapolis & Anne Arundel County Chamber of Commerce						
134 Holiday Ct Ste 316	Annapolis	MD	21401	410-266-3960	266-8270	139
TF: 800-624-8887 ■ Web: www.annearundelchamber.org						
Annapolis & Anne Arundel County Conference & Visitors Bureau (AAACCVB)						
26 W St	Annapolis	MD	21401	410-280-0445	263-9591	206
TF: 888-302-2852 ■ Web: www.visitannapolis.org						
Annapolis Accommodations						
41 Maryland Ave	Annapolis	MD	21401	410-263-3262	263-1703	376
TF: 800-981-8234 ■ Web: www.stayannapolis.com						
Annapolis Bancorp Inc						
1000 Bestgate Rd	Annapolis	MD	21401	410-224-4455	278-6265*	360-2
NASDAQ: ANNB ■ *Fax Area Code: 000 ■ TF: 000-555-5455 ■ Web: www.fnb-online.com						
Annapolis Capital Ltd 9 Avenue SW	Calgary	AB	T2P0T1	403-231-4430		528
Web: www.annapoliscapital.ca						
Annapolis City Hall						
160 Duke of Gloucester St	Annapolis	MD	21401	410-263-7007	216-0284	337
Web: www.annapolis.gov						
Annapolis Harbour Shopping Ctr						
2512A Solomon'S Island Rd	Annapolis	MD	21401	410-266-5857		460
Web: www.annapolisharbourcenter.com						
Annapolis Maritime Museum						
723 Second St PO Box 3088	Annapolis	MD	21403	410-295-0104		520
Web: www.amaritime.org						
Annapolis Micro Systems Inc						
190 Admiral Cochrane Dr	Annapolis	MD	21401	410-841-2514	841-2518	668
Web: www.annapmicro.com						
Annapolis Opera Inc						
801 Chase St						
Maryland Hall for the Creative Arts	Annapolis	MD	21401	410-267-8135	267-6440	573-2
Web: www.annapolisopera.org						
Annapolis Summer Garden Theatre						
143 Compromise St	Annapolis	MD	21401	410-268-9212		572
Web: www.summergarden.com						
Annapolis Symphony Orchestra						
801 Chase St Maryland Hall	Annapolis	MD	21401	410-269-1132	263-0616	573-3
TF: 800-955-5566 ■ Web: www.annapolissymphony.org						
Annapurna Chai House						
1620 St Michaels	Santa Fe	NM	87505	505-988-9688		671
Web: www.chaishoppe.com						
Annco Services Inc						
8892 152nd Pl S	Delray Beach	FL	33446	561-638-2540	638-3993	422
TF: 800-736-4255 ■ Web: www.anncoservices.com						
Anne Arundel County 44 Calvert St	Annapolis	MD	21401	410-222-7000		338
Web: www.aacounty.org						
Anne Arundel County Public Library						
5 Harry S Truman Pkwy	Annapolis	MD	21401	410-222-7371	222-7188	434-3
Web: aacpl.net						
Anne Arundel Medical Ctr						
2001 Medical Pkwy	Annapolis	MD	21401	443-481-1000		374-3
TF: 800-735-2258 ■ Web: www.aahs.org						
Anne Klein & Assoc Inc						
1000 Atrium Way Ste 102	Mount Laurel	NJ	08054	856-866-0411		636
Web: www.akleinpr.com						
Anne Kolb Nature Ctr						
751 Sheridan St	Hollywood	FL	33019	954-357-5161		50-5
Web: www.floridanaturepictures.com						
Anne Koplik Designs Inc 173 Main St	Brewster	NY	10509	845-279-8244		411
Web: annekoplik.com						
Anne Murray Centre 36 Main St	Springhill	NS	B0M1X0	902-597-8614	597-2001	520
TF: 800-337-5764 ■ Web: www.annemurraycentre.com						
Annenberg Ctr for the Performing Arts						
3680 Walnut St	Philadelphia	PA	19104	215-898-3900		572
Web: www.annenbergcenter.org						
Annenberg Foundation						
101 W Elm St Ste 640	Conshohocken	PA	19428	610-341-9066	964-8688	305
Web: www.annenberg.org						

Phone | Fax | Class

Annenberg Media
1301 Pennsylvania Ave NW ste302 ... Washington DC 20004 800-532-7637 783-0333* 632
*Fax Area Code: 202 ■ TF: 800-532-7637 ■ Web: www.learner.org

Annenberg Theater
101 Museum Dr Palm Springs Art Museum ... Palm Springs CA 92262 760-325-4490 572
Web: www.psmuseum.org

Annese & Associates Inc
747 Pierce Rd Ste 2 ... Clifton Park NY 12065 518-371-9000 225
Web: www.annese.com

Annett Wayside Park Cathedral Rd ... Rindge NH 03461 603-485-2034 565
TF: 800-846-3677 ■ Web: www.nhstateparks.org

Annette Willis Insurance Agency Inc
18401 NW 27th Ave ... Miami FL 33056 305-625-2403 390
Web: annettewillisinsurance.com

Annex Brands Inc
7580 Metropolitan Dr Ste 200 ... San Diego CA 92108 619-563-4800 113
TF: 877-722-5236 ■ Web: www.gopackagingstore.com

Annex Pro Inc 49 Dunlevy Ave Ste 220 ... Vancouver BC V6A3A3 604-682-6639 526
TF: 800-682-6639 ■ Web: www.annexpro.com

Annex Wealth Management LLC
12700 W Bluemound Rd Ste 200 ... Elm Grove WI 53122 262-786-6363 463
Web: annexwealth.com

Annie E Casey Foundation
701 St Paul St ... Baltimore MD 21202 410-547-6600 547-6624 305
TF: 800-222-1099 ■ Web: www.aecf.org

Annie Penn Hospital 618 S Main St ... Reidsville NC 27320 336-951-4000 951-4561 374-3
TF: 866-391-2734 ■ Web: www.conehealth.com

Annie Wright School 827 N Tacoma Ave ... Tacoma WA 98403 253-272-2216 572-3616 622
Web: aw.org

Annie's Thai Castle
3195 Roswell Rd NE ... Atlanta GA 30305 404-264-9546 671
Web: www.anniesthaifood.com

Annin & Co 105 Eisenhower Pkwy ... Roseland NJ 07068 973-228-9400 228-4905 287
TF: 888-252-4569 ■ Web: www.annin.com

Anning Johnson Company Inc
1959 Anson Dr ... Melrose Park IL 60160 708-681-1300 681-1310 189-9
TF: 800-628-4145 ■ Web: www.anningjohnson.com

Anniston Sportswear Corp PO Box 189 ... Anniston AL 36201 256-236-1551 831-9414 155-12
TF: 866-814-9253 ■ Web: www.annistonstar.com

Anniston Star
4305 McClellan Blvd PO Box 2285 ... Anniston AL 36206 256-236-1551 241-1991 532-2
TF: 866-814-9253 ■ Web: www.annistonstar.com

Annmarie Garden
13480 Dowell Rd PO Box 99 ... Dowell MD 20629 410-326-4640 326-4887 97
Web: www.annmariegarden.org

Annodyne Inc 920 Harvest Dr Ste 240 ... Blue Bell PA 19422 215-540-9110 7
Web: www.annodyne.com

AnnTaylor Inc 7 Times Sq ... New York NY 10036 212-541-3300 157-6
TF: 800-342-5266 ■ Web: www.anntaylor.com

Annual Reviews 4139 El Camino Way ... Palo Alto CA 94306 650-493-4400 855-9815 637-9
TF: 800-523-8635 ■ Web: www.annualreviews.org

Annuvia Inc 1725 Clay St Ste 100 ... San Francisco CA 94109 866-364-7940 41
TF: 866-364-7940 ■ Web: www.annuvia.com

Ano-Coil Corp 60 E Main St ... Rockville CT 06066 860-871-1200 872-0534 781
Web: www.anocoil.com

Anoka Area Chamber of Commerce
12 Bridge Sq ... Anoka MN 55303 763-421-7130 421-0577 139
Web: www.anokaareachamber.com

Anoka County 325 E Main St ... Anoka MN 55303 763-422-7350 422-6919 338
Web: anokacounty.us

Anoka County Library 711 County Rd 10 ... Blaine MN 55434 763-717-3267 717-3259 434-3
Web: www.anokacounty.us/1758/Library

Anoka Technical College 1355 W Hwy 10 ... Anoka MN 55303 763-433-1100 576-7701* 800
*Fax: Admissions ■ TF: 800-627-3529 ■ Web: www.anokatech.edu

Anoka-Hennepin Independent School District 11
2727 N Ferry St ... Anoka MN 55303 763-506-1000 506-1003 685
TF: 800-729-6164 ■ Web: www.anoka.k12.mn.us

Anoka-Ramsey Community College
11200 Mississippi Blvd NW ... Coon Rapids MN 55433 763-433-1100 433-1521 162
TF: 800-627-3529 ■ Web: www.anokaramsey.edu
Cambridge 300 Polk St S ... Cambridge MN 55008 763-433-1100 433-1841* 162
*Fax: Admissions ■ TF: 800-627-3529 ■ Web: www.anokaramsey.edu

Anomatic Corp 1650 Tamarack Rd ... Newark OH 43055 740-522-2203 481
Web: www.anomatic.com

Anonymizer Inc
6755 Mira Mesa Blvd Ste 123-164 ... San Diego CA 92121 888-270-0141 525
TF: 888-270-0141 ■ Web: www.anonymizer.com

Anonymous Content LLC
3532 Hayden Ave ... Culver City CA 90232 310-558-6000 558-2724 514
Web: www.anonymouscontent.com

Anoplate Inc 459 Pulaski St 475 ... Syracuse NY 13204 315-471-6143 471-7132 621
Web: anoplate.com

Another Printer Inc 10 Bush River Ct ... Columbia SC 29210 803-798-1380 627
TF: 888-689-6399 ■ Web: anotherprinterinc.com

Anova Home Health Care Services Inc
1229 Silver Ln Ste 201 ... Pittsburgh PA 15136 412-859-8801 363
Web: www.anovahomehealth.com

ANR (Americans for Nonsmokers' Rights)
2530 San Pablo Ave Ste J ... Berkeley CA 94702 510-841-3032 841-3071 48-17
TF: 800-735-2966 ■ Web: www.no-smoke.org

ANR Pipeline Co 717 Texas St ... Houston TX 77002 888-427-2875 325
TF: 800-827-5267 ■ Web: www.anrpl.com

Anrad Corp 4950 Levy St ... St Laurent QC H4R2P1 514-856-6920 743

Anresco Inc 1375 Van Dyke Ave ... San Francisco CA 94124 415-822-1100 41
TF: 800-359-0920 ■ Web: anresco.com

Anritsu Co 490 Jarvis Dr ... Morgan Hill CA 95037 408-778-2000 776-1744 248
TF: 800-267-4878 ■ Web: www.anritsu.com/en-GB

ANRO Inc 931 S Matlack St ... West Chester PA 19382 610-687-1200 627
TF: 800-355-2676 ■ Web: www.anro.com

Anron Air Systems Inc
440 Wyandanch Ave ... West Babylon NY 11704 631-643-3433 491-6983 189-10
TF: 800-421-0389 ■ Web: anronac.com

ANS (American Nuclear Society)
555 N Kensington Ave ... La Grange Park IL 60526 708-352-6611 352-0499 49-19
TF: 800-323-3044 ■ Web: www.ans.org

ANSA McAL (US) Inc 11403 NW 39th St ... Doral FL 33178 305-599-8766 360-3
Web: www.ansamcal.com

Ansar Group Inc, The
240 S Eigth St ... Philadelphia PA 19107 215-922-6088 922-6463 475
TF: 888-883-7804 ■ Web: www.ans-hrv.com

Ansatel Communications Inc
940 Kingsway ... Vancouver BC V5V3C4 604-872-6500 224
TF: 866-872-6500 ■ Web: ansatel.com

Anschutz Family foundation, The
555 Seventeenth St Ste 2400 ... Denver CO 80202 303-293-2338 305
Web: www.anschutzfamilyfoundation.org

Ansco & Assoc LLC
5250 Triangle Pkwy NW ... Norcross GA 30092 404-508-5700 186
Web: www.anscoinc.com

Ansel Adams Gallery, The
9031 Village Dr ... Yosemite National Park CA 95389 209-372-4413 522
TF: 800-436-7275 ■ Web: www.anseladams.com

Ansell Healthcare Inc
111 S Wood Ave Ste 210 ... Iselin NJ 08830 732-345-5400 219-5114 576
TF: 800-365-2282 ■ Web: www.ansell.com

Ansell Sandel Medical Solutions LLC
19736 Dearborn St ... Chatsworth CA 91311 818-534-2500 475
Web: www.sandelmedical.com

Ansen Corp 100 Chimney Pt Dr ... Ogdensburg NY 13669 315-393-3573 393-7638 625
Web: www.ansencorp.com

Ansett Aircraft Spares & Services Inc
12675 Encinitas Ave ... Sylmar CA 91342 818-362-1100 246
TF: 800-950-1411 ■ Web: www.ansettspares.com

ANSI (American National Standards Institute)
25 W 43rd St 4th fl ... New York NY 10036 212-642-4900 398-0023 48-1
TF: 800-374-3818 ■ Web: www.ansi.org

Ansira Inc 2300 Locust St ... Saint Louis MO 63103 314-783-2300 5
Web: ansira.com

Ansol Inc
4250 Pacific Hwy PO Box 82044 Ste 118 ... San Diego CA 92110 619-523-2040 393
Web: www.ansolinc.com

Anson Community Hospital
500 Morven Rd ... Wadesboro NC 28170 704-994-4500 374-3
Web: carolinashealthcare.org

Anson County 101 S Greene St ... Wadesboro NC 28170 704-994-3201 338
Web: www.co.anson.nc.us

Anson County School District
320 Camden Rd ... Wadesboro NC 28170 704-694-4417 694-7479 780
Web: www.ansonschools.org

Anson Industries Inc
1959 Anson Dr ... Melrose Park IL 60160 708-681-1300 681-1310 189-12
Web: www.ansonindustries.com

Anson Shirt Co Cloud Ave ... Wadesboro NC 28170 704-694-5148 155-19

Ansonia Nature & Recreation Ctr
10 Deerfield Ln ... Ansonia CT 06401 203-736-1053 50-5
TF: 800-200-2882 ■ Web: www.ansonianaturecenter.org

Anson-Stoner Inc
111 E Fairbanks Ave ... Winter Park FL 32789 407-629-9484 7
Web: www.anson-stoner.com

Anstiss & Company PC 1115 Westford St ... Lowell MA 01851 978-452-2500 2
Web: anstisscpa.com

Answer Co, The
233 Nelson's Crescent Ste 502 ... New Westminister BC V3L0E4 604-473-9166 179
Web: www.theanswerco.com

Answer Heating & Cooling Inc
8490 Midland Rd ... Freeland MI 48623 989-695-9461 610
Web: www.answersos.com

Answer One Inc 2216 Young Dr Ste 3 ... Lexington KY 40505 859-269-3482 179
TF: 800-517-7395 ■ Web: answerone.biz

AnswerDash Inc
4000 Mason Rd New Ventures Facility Fluke Hall
... Seattle WA 98195 800-311-5786 387
TF: 800-311-5786 ■ Web: www.answerdash.com

AnswerLive LLC 1101 Cherryville ... Shelby NC 28150 704-333-8880 481-1280 393
TF: 800-472-4495 ■ Web: www.answerlive.com

AnswerOn Inc 1707 Main St Ste 500 ... Longmont CO 80501 720-684-4900 177
Web: www.answeron.com

Answerport Inc
10200 N Port Washington Rd Ste 101 ... Milwaukee WI 53092 414-289-9100 194
Web: www.answerport.com

Answers Corp 237 W 35th St Ste 1101 ... New York NY 10001 646-502-4777 502-4778 178-7
TF: 888-885-5008 ■ Web: www.answers.com

Answers in Genesis Ky Inc
2800 Bullittsburg Church Rd ... Petersburg KY 41080 859-727-2222 48-20
Web: www.answersingenesis.org

Answers Research Inc
380 Stevens Ave Ste 214 ... Solana Beach CA 92075 858-792-4660 792-1075 466
Web: www.answersresearch.com

AnswersMedia Inc
30 N Racine Ave Ste 300 ... Chicago IL 60607 312-421-0113 5
Web: www.answersmediainc.com

ANSYS Inc 275 Technology Dr ... Canonsburg PA 15317 724-746-3304 514-9494 178-5
NASDAQ: ANSS ■ TF: 800-937-3321 ■ Web: www.ansys.com

Antaean Solutions LLC
11700 Preston Rd Ste 600-213 ... Dallas TX 75230 214-987-3439 194
Web: www.antaeans.com

Antaeus Capital Inc
1100 Glendon Ave PH Ste 9 ... Los Angeles CA 90024 310-443-9000 690
Web: www.antaeuscap.com

Antarctica Asset Management Ltd
1560 Broadway Ste 1111 ... New York NY 10003 212-925-1419 219-8266 194
Web: www.antarcticaam.com

Antares Development Corp
6243 W Ih 10 870 ... San Antonio TX 78201 210-736-2220 177
Web: www.antares-corp.com

Antares Pharma Inc
3905 Annapolis Ln N Ste 105 ... Minneapolis MN 55447 763-475-7700 476
AMEX: AIS ■ Web: www.antarespharma.com

Antares Technology Solutions Inc
8772 Quarters Lake Rd Bldg 13 ... Baton Rouge LA 70898 225-922-7748 180
Web: www.antaresnet.com

Antea Group
5910 Rice Creek Pkwy Ste 100 ... Saint Paul MN 55126 651-639-9449 639-9473 667
TF: 800-477-7411 ■ Web: www.anteagroup.com

Antec Inc 47900 Fremont Blvd ... Fremont CA 94538 510-770-1200 770-1288 253
TF: 800-222-6832 ■ Web: www.antec.com

Name / Address	City	State	Zip	Phone	Fax	Class
Antedo Inc 1475 Saratoga Ave Ste 190 *Web:* www.antedo.com	San Jose	CA	95129	408-253-1870		647
Antelope County 501 Main St. *Web:* antelopecounty.nebraska.gov	Neligh	NE	68756	402-887-4410	887-4719	338
Antelope Island State Park 4528 W 1700 S. *Web:* www.stateparks.utah.gov	Syracuse	UT	84075	801-773-2941		565
Antelope Valley Board of Trade 41319-12th St W Ste 104 *Web:* www.avbot.org	Palmdale	CA	93551	661-947-9033		139
Antelope Valley Chambers of Commerce 554 W Lancaster Blvd *TF:* 800-944-2200 ■ *Web:* lancasterchamber.org	Lancaster	CA	93534	661-948-4518	949-1212	139
Antelope Valley College 3041 W Ave K **Fax:* Admissions ■ *Web:* www.avc.edu	Lancaster	CA	93536	661-722-6300	722-6531*	162
Antelope Valley Hospital 1600 W Ave J *Web:* www.avhospital.org	Lancaster	CA	93534	661-949-5000		374-3
Antelope Valley Indian Museum State Historic Park Antelope Vly Fwy Ave M *Web:* www.avim.parks.ca.gov	Perris	CA	92571	661-946-3055		565
Antelope Valley Press 37404 Sierra Hwy *TF:* 888-874-2527 ■ *Web:* www.avpress.com	Palmdale	CA	93550	661-273-2700	947-4870	532-2
Antenna Factory Inc 931 Albion Ave	Schaumburg	IL	60193	312-242-1727		350
Antenna House Inc 3844 Kennett Pk Ste 200 *TF:* 800-517-3001 ■ *Web:* rainbowpdf.com	Greenville	DE	19807	302-427-2456		809
Antenna Products 101 SE 25th Ave *NASDAQ: ANTP* ■ *Web:* www.antennaproducts.com	Mineral Wells	TX	76067	940-325-3301	325-0716	360-3
Antenna Products Corp 101 SE 25th Ave *Web:* www.antennaproducts.com	Mineral Wells	TX	76067	940-325-3301	325-0716	647
Antenna Technology Communications Inc 450 N McKemy Ave *Web:* www.atci.com	Chandler	AZ	85226	480-844-8501		647
Antennas for Communications 2499 SW 60 Ave *Web:* www.afcsat.com	Ocala	FL	34474	352-687-4121	687-1203	647
Antex Electronics Corp 19160 Van Ness Ave *Web:* www.antex.com	Torrance	CA	90501	310-532-3092		625
Anthelio Healthcare Solutions Inc 5400 LBJ Fwy Ste 200 *TF:* 855-268-4354 ■ *Web:* www.antheliohealth.com	Dallas	TX	75240	214-257-7000		363
Anthem 537 E Pete Rose Way Ste 100 *Web:* www.anthemww.com	Cincinnati	OH	45202-3378	513-784-0066		344
Anthem Blue Cross & Blue Shield 2015 Staples Mill Rd *TF:* 800-451-1527 ■ *Web:* www.anthem.com	Richmond	VA	23230	804-354-7000		391-3
Anthem Blue Cross & Blue Shield Maine 2 Gannett Dr *TF Cust Svc:* 800-482-0966 ■ *Web:* www.anthem.com	South Portland	ME	04106	207-822-7000	822-7375	391-3
Anthem Blue Cross & Blue Shield of Connecticut 370 Bassett Rd *TF:* 800-922-1742 ■ *Web:* www.anthem.com	North Haven	CT	06473	800-922-4670		391-3
Anthem Blue Cross & Blue Shield of Nevada 9133 W Russell Rd **Fax Area Code:* 800 ■ *TF:* 800-332-3842 ■ *Web:* www.anthem.com	Las Vegas	NV	89148	702-228-2583	763-3142*	391-3
Anthem Blue Cross Blue Shield Colorado 700 Broadway *TF:* 800-654-9338 ■ *Web:* www.anthem.com	Denver	CO	80273	303-831-2131	764-7047	391-3
Anthem Heatlh Services Inc 57 Karner Rd	Albany	NY	12205	518-862-1247		363
Anthem Inc 120 Monument Cir *TF:* 800-999-7222 ■ *Web:* www.antheminc.com	Indianapolis	IN	46204	317-488-6000		462
Anthem Insurance Cos Inc 120 Monument Cir Ste 200 *TF:* 800-331-1476 ■ *Web:* www.anthem.com	Indianapolis	IN	46204	317-488-6000		360-4
Anthem Life Insurance Co 6740 N High St Ste 200 *TF:* 800-551-7265 ■ *Web:* www.anthem.com	Worthington	OH	43085	614-436-0688		391-2
Anthem Mktg Corp 549 W Randolph Ste 700 *Web:* www.anthemedge.com	Chicago	IL	60661	312-441-0382		194
Anthony & Sylvan Pools Corp 3739 Easton Rd Rt 611 *TF:* 800-366-7958 ■ *Web:* www.anthonysylvan.com	Doylestown	PA	18901	215-489-5600		728
Anthony Forest Products Co 309 N Washington Ave *TF:* 800-221-2326 ■ *Web:* www.anthonyforest.com	El Dorado	AR	71730	870-862-3414		683
Anthony International 12391 Montera Ave *TF:* 800-772-0900 ■ *Web:* www.anthonyintl.com	Sylmar	CA	91342	818-365-9451	361-9611	329
Anthony Liftgates Inc 1037 W Howard St *Web:* www.anthonyliftgates.com	Pontiac	IL	61764	815-842-3383		54
Anthony Louis Ctr 115 Forestview Ln *Web:* www.anthonylouiscenter.com	Plymouth	MN	55441	763-542-9212	542-9248	726
Anthony Marano Company Inc 3000 S Ashland Ave *Web:* www.anthonymarano.com	Chicago	IL	60608	773-321-7500		297-7
Anthony Ostlund Baer & Louwagie PA 3600 Wells Fargo Bldg 90 S Seventh St *TF:* 800-973-1177 ■ *Web:* anthonyostlund.com	Minneapolis	MN	55402	612-349-6969		428
Anthony Timberlands Inc 111 S Plum St PO Box 137 *Web:* www.anthonytimberlands.com	Bearden	AR	71720	870-687-3611	687-2283	683
Anthony Underwood Inc 4006 Bessemer Hwy *Web:* anthonyunderwood.com	Bessemer	AL	35020	205-424-4033		57
Anthony Wayne Board of Education PO Box 2487 *Web:* www.anthonywayneschools.org	Whitehouse	OH	43571	419-877-5377		685
Anthony Wayne Business Exchange 3508 Stellhorn Rd Ste *Web:* www.anthonywayne.com	Fort Wayne	IN	46815	260-485-1990		196
Anthony's 7220 F St *Web:* www.anthonyssteakhouse.com	Omaha	NE	68127	402-331-7575		671
Anthony's at Point Defiance 5910 N Waterfront Dr *Web:* www.anthonys.com	Tacoma	WA	98407	253-752-9700		671
Anthony's Fish Grotto 1360 N Harbor Dr *Web:* www.anthonysfishgrotto.com	San Diego	CA	92101	619-232-5103		671
Anthony's Pier 66 2201 Alaskan Way *Web:* www.anthonys.com	Seattle	WA	98121	206-448-6688		671
Anthony-Thomas Candy Co 1777 Arlingate Ln *TF:* 877-226-3921 ■ *Web:* www.anthony-thomas.com	Columbus	OH	43228	614-274-8405		296-8
Anthro Corp 10450 SW Manhasset Dr **Fax Area Code:* 800 ■ *TF:* 800-325-3841 ■ *Web:* www.anthro.com	Tualatin	OR	97062	503-691-2556	325-0045*	319-1
Antibodies Inc PO Box 1560 **Fax Area Code:* 530 ■ *TF:* 800-824-8540 ■ *Web:* www.antibodiesinc.com	Davis	CA	95617	800-824-8540	758-6307*	85
Antica Posta 519 E Paces Ferry Rd *Web:* www.anticaposta.com	Atlanta	GA	30305	404-262-7112	262-7335	671
AntiCancer Inc 7917 Ostrow St *TF:* 800-511-2555 ■ *Web:* www.anticancer.com	San Diego	CA	92111	858-654-2555	268-4175	231
Antico Forno 93 Salem St *Web:* www.anticofornoboston.com	Boston	MA	02113	617-723-6733		671
Anti-Defamation League (ADL) 605 Third Ave *TF:* 866-386-3235 ■ *Web:* www.adl.org	New York	NY	10158	212-885-7700	867-0779	48-8
Antietam Cable Television Inc 1000 Willow Cir *Web:* www.antietamcable.com	Hagerstown	MD	21740	301-797-5000		116
Antietam National Battlefield 5831 Dunker Church Rd PO Box 158 *Web:* www.nps.gov/anti	Sharpsburg	MD	21782	301-432-5124	432-4590	564
Antigone Books 411 N Fourth Ave *Web:* www.antigonebooks.com	Tucson	AZ	85705	520-792-3715	882-8802	95
Antigua & Barbuda 305 E 47th St 6th Fl *Web:* antigua-barbuda.org	New York	NY	10017	212-541-4117		784
Embassy 3216 New Mexico Ave NW *TF:* 866-978-7299 ■ *Web:* www.antigua-barbuda.org	Washington	DC	20016	202-362-5122	362-5225	257
Antigua & Barbuda Dept of Tourism & Trade 305 E 47th St 6th Fl *TF:* 888-268-4227 ■ *Web:* www.antigua-barbuda.org	New York	NY	10017	212-541-4117	541-4789	775
Antigua Group Inc, The 16651 N 84 Ave *TF:* 800-528-3133 ■ *Web:* www.antigua.com	Peoria	AZ	85382	623-523-6000		155-12
Antillean Marine Shipping Corp 3038 NW N River Dr *TF:* 888-633-6361 ■ *Web:* www.antillean.com	Miami	FL	33142	305-633-6361		313
Antimite Associates Inc 5867 Pine Ave *TF:* 800-974-2847 ■ *Web:* www.antimitepestcontrol.com	Chino Hills	CA	91709	909-606-2300		577
Antioch Baptist Church 1057 Texas Ave	Shreveport	LA	71101	318-222-7090		50-1
Antioch Chamber of Commerce 101 H St #4 *Web:* www.antiochchamber.com	Antioch	CA	94509	925-757-1800	757-5286	139
Antioch International Inc 410 Winding View *Web:* www.antioch-intl.com	New Braunfels	TX	78132	402-289-2217		256
Antioch Speedway 1201 W Tenth St *Web:* www.antiochspeedway.com	Antioch	CA	94509	925-779-9220	779-9213	515
Antioch University 900 Dayton St *Web:* www.antiochsea.edu	Yellow Springs	OH	45387	937-769-1340		166
Antiochian Orthodox Christian Archdiocese of North America 358 Mountain Rd *TF:* 888-421-1442 ■ *Web:* www.antiochian.org	Englewood	NJ	07631	201-871-1355	871-7954	48-20
Antiok Holdings Inc 34 Shining Willow Way # 132 *Web:* www.antiok.com	La Plata	MD	20646	301-743-2100		624
Antique Automobile Club of America (AACA) 501 W Governor Rd PO Box 417 *TF:* 800-211-4371 ■ *Web:* www.aaca.org	Hershey	PA	17033	717-534-1910	534-9101	48-18
Antique Car Museum/Grovewood Gallery 111 Grovewood Rd *Web:* www.grovewood.com	Asheville	NC	28804	828-253-7651		520
Antique Collectors Club 116 Pleasant St *TF:* 800-254-4100 ■ *Web:* businessfinder.masslive.com	EastHampton	MA	01027	413-529-0861		637-2
Antique Mall 1251 S Virginia St *TF:* 888-316-6255 ■ *Web:* www.antiquemalls.com	Reno	NV	89502	775-324-4141		460
Antique Powerland Museum 3995 Brooklake Rd NE *TF:* 800-778-7956 ■ *Web:* www.antiquepowerland.com	Brooks	OR	97303	503-393-2424	393-2424	520
Antique Street Lamps Inc 2011-B W Rundberg Ln *Web:* antiquestreetlamps.acuitybrands.com	Austin	TX	78758	512-977-8444	977-9622	439
Antique Trader 700 E State St *TF:* 800-258-0929 ■ *Web:* www.antiquetrader.com	Iola	WI	54990	715-445-2214	445-4087	457-14
Antique Village 10203 Chamberlayne Rd *Web:* www.antiquevillageva.com	Mechanicsville	VA	23116	804-746-8914		460
Antique World 11111 Main St *Web:* www.antiqueworldmarket.com	Clarence	NY	14031	716-759-8483		460
Antiques Mall of Madison 4748 Cottage Grove Rd *Web:* www.antiquesmadison.com	Madison	WI	53716	608-222-2049		460
Antiquity 112 Romero St NW *Web:* antiquityrestaurant.com	Albuquerque	NM	87104	505-247-3545		671
Antitrust & Trade Regulation Daily 1801 S Bell St *TF:* 800-372-1033 ■ *Web:* www.bna.com/atrc	Arlington	VA	22202	800-372-1033		531-2
Antler Inn 43 W Pearl St PO Box 575 *TF:* 800-483-8667 ■ *Web:* www.townsquareinns.com	Jackson	WY	83001	307-733-2535		379
Antoine du Chez 2700 E Second Ave *Web:* www.antoineduchez.com	Denver	CO	80206	303-320-6012	996-1061	707

Name / Address	City	State	Zip	Phone	Fax	Class
Antoine's 713 St Louis St	New Orleans	LA	70130	504-581-4422		671
Web: www.antoines.com						
Anton & Michel PO Box 4917	Carmel	CA	93921	831-624-2406		671
Web: www.carmelsbest.com/antonmichel						
Anton Cabinetry 2002 W Pioneer Pkwy	Pantego	TX	76013	817-460-8681		115
TF: 800-321-6854 ■ *Web:* www.antoncabinetry.com						
Anton'S Cleaners Inc 500 Clark Rd	Tewksbury	MA	01876	978-851-3721		426
Web: antons.com						
Anton/Bauer Inc 14 Progress Dr	Shelton	CT	06484	203-929-1100		591
TF: 800-422-3473 ■ *Web:* www.antonbauer.com						
Antone's Italian Cafe						
4837 Mahoning Ave	Austintown	OH	44515	330-793-0707		671
Web: chadanthonys.com						
Antonelli Institute						
300 Montgomery Ave	Erdenheim	PA	19038	215-836-2222	836-2794	164
TF: 800-722-7871 ■ *Web:* www.antonelli.edu						
Antonello Ristorante						
3800 S Plaza Dr	Santa Ana	CA	92704	714-751-7153		671
Web: www.antonello.com						
Antoni's Italian Cafe						
1118 Coolidge Blvd Ste A	Lafayette	LA	70503	337-232-8384		671
Antonio's Garlic Clove						
2206 Fourth St SW	Calgary	AB	T2S1W9	403-228-0866		671
Antonio's Mexican Village						
840 Paredes Rd	Brownsville	TX	78521	956-542-6504		671
Antonios' of Nashville						
7097 Old HaRding Pike	Nashville	TN	37221	615-646-9166		671
Web: antoniosofnashville.com						
Antonucci & Assoc Arch & Engrs						
50 Fifth Ave	Pelham	NY	10803	914-636-4000		261
Web: www.aa-ae.com						
Antrim County 203 E Cayuga St	Bellaire	MI	49615	231-533-6353	533-6935	338
Web: www.antrimcounty.org						
Antrim Energy Inc 610-301 8 Ave SW	Calgary	AB	T2P1C5	403-264-5111		536
TF: 800-311-0721 ■ *Web:* www.antrimenergy.com						
Antron Engineering & Machine Co Inc						
170 Mechanic St	Bellingham	MA	02019	508-966-2803		261
Web: www.antroneng.com						
Antronix Inc 440 Forsgate Dr	Cranbury	NJ	08512	609-860-0160		647
Web: www.antronix.net						
Antwerp Diamond Distributors						
6 E 45th St Ste 302	New York	NY	10017	212-319-3300		411
TF: 800-223-0444						
Anvasion Inc 53 Taylor Rd	Bethel	CT	06801	203-770-3415		463
Web: anvasion.com						
Anvil Cases						
15730 Salt Lake Ave	City of Industry	CA	91745	626-968-4100	968-1703	453
TF: 800-359-2684 ■ *Web:* www.anvilcase.com						
Anvil Corp 1675 W Bakerview Rd	Bellingham	WA	98226	360-671-1450		261
Web: www.anvilcorp.com						
Anvil Media Inc 310 NE Failing St	Portland	OR	97212	503-595-6050		6
Web: www.anvilmediainc.com						
Anvil Mountain Correctional Ctr						
1810 Ctr Creek Rd PO Box 730	Nome	AK	99762	907-443-2241	443-5195	213
Web: www.correct.state.ak.us						
Anworth Mortgage Asset Corp						
1299 Ocean Ave 2nd Fl	Santa Monica	CA	90401	310-255-4493	434-0070	654
NYSE: ANH ■ *Web:* www.anworth.com						
Anxiety Disorders Assn of America (ADAA)						
8730 Georgia Ave Ste 600	Silver Spring	MD	20910	240-485-1001	485-1035	48-17
TF: 800-922-8947 ■ *Web:* www.adaa.org						
Any Budget Printing & Mailing						
8170 Ronson Rd Ste L	San Diego	CA	92111	858-278-3151		627
TF: 800-767-8951 ■ *Web:* www.anybudget.com						
Any Lab Test Now						
235 Bloomfield Dr 110 Bldg	B Lititz	PA	17543	717-823-6787		415
Web: www.anylabtestnow.com						
AnyDoc Software Inc						
5404 Cypress Ctr Dr Ste 140	Tampa	FL	33609	888-495-2638	222-0018*	178-7
**Fax Area Code:* 813 ■ *TF:* 888-495-2638 ■ *Web:* www.onbase.com/en/product/onbaseanydoc						
Anytime Fitness Inc						
12181 Margo Ave S	Hastings	MN	55033	651-438-5000		354
Web: www.anytimefitness.com						
Any-Time Home Care Inc						
127 S Broadway PO Box 995	Nyack	NY	10960	845-353-8280		363
Web: anytimehomecare.com						
ANZ 1177 Ave of the Americas 6th Fl	New York	NY	10036	212-801-9800	801-9163	70
Web: www.anz.com						
Anza ElectricCo-op Inc						
58470 Hwy 371 PO Box 391909	Anza	CA	92539	951-763-4333	763-5297	245
TF: 844-311-7201 ■ *Web:* www.anzaelectric.org						
Anza Inc 312 Ninth Ave SE Ste B	Watertown	SD	57201	605-886-3889		701
Web: www.anza.com						
Anza-Borrego Desert State Park						
200 Palm Canyon Dr	Borrego Springs	CA	92004	760-767-5311	767 3427	565
Web: www.parks.ca.gov/?page_id=638						
Anzu 222 Mason St Hotel Nikko	San Francisco	CA	94102	415-394-1100	394-1102	671
Web: www.hotelnikkosf.com						
AO Precision Mfg LLC						
1870 Mason Ave	Daytona Beach	FL	32117	386-274-5882		350
Web: www.aopmfg.com						
AO Reed & Co 4777 Ruffner St	San Diego	CA	92111	858-565-4131	292-6958	189-10
Web: www.aoreed.com						
AO Smith Corp						
11270 W Pk Pl Ste 170 PO Box 245008	Milwaukee	WI	53224	414-359-4000	359-4180	518
NYSE: AOS ■ *TF:* 800-359-4065 ■ *Web:* www.aosmith.com						
AO Smith Electrical Products Co						
531 N Fourth St	Tipp City	OH	45371	937-667-2431	667-5030	518
TF: 800-543-9450 ■ *Web:* www.centuryelectricmotor.com						
AO Smith Water Products Co						
500 Tennessee Waltz Pkwy	Ashland City	TN	37015	800-527-1953	792-2163*	36
**Fax Area Code:* 615 ■ *TF:* 800-527-1953 ■ *Web:* www.hotwater.com						
AOA (American Osteopathic Assn)						
142 E Ontario St	Chicago	IL	60611	312-202-8000	202-8200	49-8
TF: 800-621-1773 ■ *Web:* www.osteopathic.org						
AoA (Administration on Aging)						
1 Massachusetts Ave NW	Washington	DC	20201	202-619-0724		340-10
AOA (Administration on Aging Regional Offices)						
Region I JFK Federal Bldg Rm 2075	Boston	MA	02203	617-565-1158		340-10

Name / Address	City	State	Zip	Phone	Fax	Class
Aoa Products LLC 3711 King Rd	Toledo	OH	43617	419-350-1244		358
Web: www.aoaproductsllc.com						
AOAC International						
481 N Frederick Ave Ste 500	Gaithersburg	MD	20877	301-924-7077	924-7089	49-19
TF: 800-379-2622 ■ *Web:* www.aoac.org						
AOAExcel Inc						
243 N Lindbergh Blvd Fl 1	St. Louis	MO	63141	800-365-2219		387
TF: 800-365-2219 ■ *Web:* www.aoa.org/aoaexcel?sso=y						
AOBTA (American Organization for Bodywork Therapies of Asia)						
PO Box 343 Ste 408	West Berlin	NJ	08091	856-809-2953		48-17
Web: www.aobta.org						
AOC (Association of Old Crows)						
1000 N Payne St Ste 300	Alexandria	VA	22314	703-549-1600	549-2589	48-19
TF: 800-247-5626 ■ *Web:* www.crows.org						
AOC Holding Company Inc						
4506 State 359 and Loop 20	Laredo	TX	78042	956-722-5251		316
TF: 800-722-5251 ■ *Web:* www.argpetro.com						
AOC LLC 955 Tennessee 57	Collierville	TN	38017	901-854-2800	854-1183	605-2
Web: www.aoc-resins.com						
AOC Wine Bar & Restaurant						
8700 W Third St	Los Angeles	CA	90048	310-859-9859		671
Web: www.aocwinebar.com						
AOCA (Automotive Oil Change Assn)						
330 N Wabash Ave Ste 2000	Chicago	IL	60611	312-321-5132	673-6832	49-21
TF: 800-230-0702 ■ *Web:* www.aoca.org						
AOCS (American Oil Chemists Society)						
2710 S Boulder PO Box 17190	Urbana	IL	61802	217-359-2344	351-8091	48-12
TF: 866-535-2730 ■ *Web:* www.aocs.org						
AODME (Association of Osteopathic Directors & Medical Educators)						
142 E Ontario St	Chicago	IL	60611	312-202-8211	202-8224	49-8
TF: 800-621-1773 ■ *Web:* www.aodme.org						
Aok Networking LLC 820 Clark St	Oviedo	FL	32765	407-249-1989		196
TF: 800-747-8433 ■ *Web:* www.aoknetworking.com						
A-Ok Rentals Inc						
950 Bloomfield Ave	West Caldwell	NJ	07006	973-575-7900	575-7847	310
Web: www.affiliatedcarrental.com						
AOL (America Online Inc) 22000 AOL Way	Dulles	VA	20166	703-265-1000		398
Web: www.aol.com						
AOL Canada Inc 99 Spadina Ave Ste 200	Toronto	ON	M5V3P8	416-263-8100	263-8102	224
TF: 888-265-6306 ■ *Web:* www.aol.ca						
AOM (Academy of Management)						
235 Elm Rd PO Box 3020	Briarcliff Manor	NY	10510	914-923-2607	923-2615	49-12
TF: 800-633-4931 ■ *Web:* aom.org						
AOML (Atlantic Oceanographic & Meteorological Laboratory)						
4301 Rickenbacker Cswy	Miami	FL	33149	305-361-4300	361-4449	668
Web: www.aoml.noaa.gov						
Aon Corp 200 E Randolph St	Chicago	IL	60601	312-381-1000		360-4
TF: 877-384-4276 ■ *Web:* www.aon.com						
Aon Risk Services Inc						
200 E Randolph St	Chicago	IL	60601	312-381-1000		390
TF: 877-384-4276 ■ *Web:* www.aon.com						
AONE (American Organization of Nurse Executives)						
155 N Wacker Dr Ste 400	Chicago	IL	60606	312-422-2800	422-4503	49-8
Web: www.aone.org						
AOPA (Aircraft Owners & Pilots Assn)						
421 Aviation Way	Frederick	MD	21701	301-695-2000	695-2375	49-21
TF: 800-872-2672 ■ *Web:* www.aopa.org						
AOPA (American Orthotic & Prosthetic Assn)						
330 John Carlyle St Ste 200	Alexandria	VA	22314	571-431-0876	431-0899	48-17
Web: www.aopanet.org						
AOPA Pilot Magazine						
421 Aviation Way	Frederick	MD	21701	301-695-2000	695-2375	457-14
TF: 800-872-2672 ■ *Web:* www.aopa.org						
AORN Inc 2170 S Parker Rd Ste 300	Denver	CO	80231	303-755-6300	750-3212*	49-8
**Fax:* Cust Svc ■ *TF:* 800-755-2676 ■ *Web:* www.aorn.org						
Aos Thermal Compounds LLC						
22 Meridian Rd Ste 6	Eatontown	NJ	07724	732-389-5514		579
TF: 888-662-7337 ■ *Web:* www.aosco.com						
AOSS Medical Supply Inc						
4971 Central Ave	Monroe	LA	71203	318-325-8290		475
Web: www.aossmedical.com						
AOSSM (American Orthopaedic Society for Sports Medicine)						
6300 N River Rd Ste 500	Rosemont	IL	60018	847-292-4900	292-4905	49-8
TF: 877-321-3500 ■ *Web:* www.sportsmed.org						
AOTA (American Occupational Therapy Assn Inc)						
4720 Montgomery Ln PO Box 31220	Bethesda	MD	20824	301-652-2682	652-7711	49-8
TF: 800-877-1383 ■ *Web:* www.aota.org						
AP (Ace Personnel) 5909 Woodson Rd	Mission	KS	66202	913-384-1100		721
Web: www.acepersonnel.com						
AP (Alloy Polymers Inc)						
3310 Deepwater Terminal Rd	Richmond	VA	23234	804-232-8000	230-0386	605-2
Web: www.alloypolymers.com						
AP (Associated Press) 450 W 33rd St	New York	NY	10001	212-621-1500		530
Web: www.ap.org						
AP Exhaust Technologies Inc						
300 Dixie Trial	Goldsboro	NC	27530	919-580-2000		60
TF: 800-277-2787 ■ *Web:* www.apemissions.com						
AP International Enterprise Inc						
3301 SR- 66	Neptune	NJ	07753	732-918-7001		527
Web: www.apintl.com						
AP Nonweiler Co						
3321 County Rd A PO Box 1007	Oshkosh	WI	54903	920-231-0850		550
TF: 800-445-6810 ■ *Web:* apnonweiler.com						
ap Services LLC, The						
562 Watertown Ave Ste 3	Waterbury	CT	06708	203-596-7553		41
Web: www.therapservices.net						
APA (American Poolplayers Assn Inc)						
1000 Lake St Louis Blvd Ste 325	Lake Saint Louis	MO	63367	636-625-8611	625-2975	48-22
Web: www.poolplayers.com						
APA (At-sea Processors Assn)						
4039 21st Ave W Ste 400	Seattle	WA	98199	206-285-5139	285-1841	49-6
Web: www.atsea.org						
APA (Architectural Precast Assn)						
6710 Winkler Rd Ste 8	Fort Myers	FL	33919	239-454-6989	454-6787	49-3
Web: www.archprecast.org						
APA (American Planning Assn)						
1030 15th St NW	Washington	DC	20005	202-872-0611	872-0643	49-17
Web: www.planning.org						

Name	Address	City	State	ZIP	Phone	Fax	Class
APA (American Psychiatric Assn)	1000 Wilson Blvd Ste 1825 *TF:* 888-357-7924 ■ *Web:* www.psychiatry.org	Arlington	VA	22209	703-907-7300	907-1085	49-15
APA (American Psychological Assn)	750 First St NE *TF:* 800-374-2721 ■ *Web:* www.apa.org	Washington	DC	20002	202-336-5500	336-5962	49-15
APA (American Payroll Assn)	660 N Main Ave Ste 100 *Web:* americanpayroll.org	San Antonio	TX	78205	210-226-4600	226-4027	49-12
APA - Engineered Wood Assn	7011 S 19th St *Web:* www.apawood.org	Tacoma	WA	98466	253-565-6600	565-7265	49-3
APA Search Inc	1 Byram Brook Pl Ste 103 *Web:* www.apasearch.com	Armonk	NY	10504	914-273-6000		260
APA Services	4150 International Plaza Tower I Ste 510 *TF:* 877-425-5023 ■ *Web:* www.apaservices.net	Fort Worth	TX	76109	877-425-5023		734
A-Pac Manufacturing Company Inc	2719 Courier NW *TF:* 800-272-2634 ■ *Web:* www.polybags.com	Grand Rapids	MI	49534	800-272-2634		345
Apache Capital Management LLC	230 Park Ave Ste 1518 *Web:* www.apachecapital.com	New York	NY	10169	212-972-0991		401
Apache Corp	2000 Post Oak Blvd Ste 100 *NYSE: APA* ■ *TF:* 800-272-2434 ■ *Web:* www.apachecorp.com	Houston	TX	77056	713-296-6000		536
Apache County	75 W Cleveland St *TF:* 800-304-4452 ■ *Web:* www.co.apache.az.us	Saint Johns	AZ	85936	928-337-4364	337-2771	338
Apache Farmers Co-op	230 W Floyd PO Box 332 *Web:* www.apachecoop.com	Apache	OK	73006	580-588-3110	588-9277	275
Apache Greyhound Park	3801 E Washington *TF:* 800-772-0852 ■ *Web:* phoenixgreyhoundpark.com	Phoenix	AZ	85034	480-982-2371		133
Apache Hose & Belting Co Inc	4805 Bowling St SW *TF Sales:* 800-553-5455 ■ *Web:* www.apache-inc.com	Cedar Rapids	IA	52404	319-365-0471	365-2522	370
Apache Junction Chamber of Commerce, The	567 W Apache Trl PO Box 1747 *Web:* www.ajchamber.com	Apache Junction	AZ	85120	480-982-3141	982-3234	139
Apache Junction Public Library	1177 N Idaho Rd *Web:* www.ajpl.org	Apache Junction	AZ	85119	480-983-6012		434-3
Apache Junction/Gold Canyon News, The	1075 S Idaho Rd Ste 102 *Web:* ajnews.com	Apache Junction	AZ	85119	480-982-7799		532-4
Apache Software Foundation (ASF)	1901 Munsey Dr *Web:* www.apache.org	Forest Hill	MD	21050	410-420-0140	803-2258	48-9
Apache Stainless Equipment Corp	200 W Industrial Dr PO Box 538 *TF:* 800-444-0398 ■ *Web:* www.apachestainless.com	Beaver Dam	WI	53916	920-356-9900	887-0206	386
Apacheta Corp	53 W Baltimore Pk Ste 200 *Web:* www.apacheta.com	Media	PA	19063	610-558-5852		809
Apac-ks Wilkerson Crane Rental	12790 E 36th St N *Web:* www.wilkersoncranerental.com	Tulsa	OK	74116	918-437-9500		188
APACVB (Alexandria/Pineville Area Convention & Visitors Bureau)	707 Main St PO Box 1070 *TF:* 800-551-9546 ■ *Web:* alexandriapinevillela.com	Alexandria	LA	71301	318-442-9546	443-1617	206
Apalachee Correctional Institution	35 Apalachee Dr *Web:* dc.state.fl.us	Sneads	FL	32460	850-718-0688	593-6445	213
Apalachicola Bay Chamber of Commerce	122 Commerce St *Web:* www.apalachicolabay.org	Apalachicola	FL	32320	850-653-9419	653-8219	139
Apantec LLC	4500 N Cannon Ave *Web:* www.apantec.com	Lansdale	PA	19446	267-436-3091		639
Aparaa Corp	14900 Landmark Blvd Ste 630 *TF:* 888-441-2535 ■ *Web:* www.aparaa.com	Dallas	TX	75254	888-441-2535		177
Apartment Association	333 W Broadway Ste 101 *Web:* www.apt-assoc.com	Long Beach	CA	90802	562-426-8341		414
Apartment Investment & Management Co	4582 S Ulster St Pkwy Ste 1100 *NYSE: AIV* ■ *TF General:* 888-789-8600 ■ *Web:* www.aimco.com	Denver	CO	80237	303-691-4350	759-3226	655
APBI (Alaska Public Broadcasting Inc)	135 Cordova St *TF:* 888-840-0013 ■ *Web:* www.akpb.org	Anchorage	AK	99501	907-277-6300		632
APC (Association of Professional Chaplains)	1701 E Woodfield Rd Ste 400 *Web:* www.professionalchaplains.org	Schaumburg	IL	60173	847-240-1014	240-1015	48-20
APC (American Power Conversion Corp)	132 Fairgrounds Rd *TF Cust Svc:* 800-788-2208 ■ *Web:* www.apc.com	West Kingston	RI	02892	401-789-5735	789-3710	253
APC Hegeman	8-12 Dietz St Ste 201 *Web:* www.eap-counseling.com	Oneonta	NY	13820	607-432-9039		462
APC Integrated Services Inc	770 SPIRIT OF SAINT LOUIS Blvd *TF:* 888-294-7886 ■ *Web:* www.apcisg.com	Chesterfield	MO	63005	888-294-7886		317
Apc Paper Company Inc	130 Sullivan St *Web:* www.apcpapergroup.com	Claremont	NH	03743	603-542-0411		557
APCC (American Public Communications Council Inc)	625 Slaters Ln Ste 104	Alexandria	VA	22314	703-739-1322	739-1324	49-20
APCO Bulletin	351 N Williamson Blvd *TF:* 888-272-6911 ■ *Web:* www.apcointl.org	Daytona Beach	FL	32114	386-322-2500	322-2501	531-8
APCO Employees Credit Union	750 17th St N *TF:* 800-249-2726 ■ *Web:* www.apcocu.org	Birmingham	AL	35203	205-257-3601		219
Apco Extruders Inc	180 National Rd *TF Orders:* 800-942-8725	Edison	NJ	08817	732-287-3000	287-1421	548
APCO Graphics Inc	388 Grant St SE *TF:* 877-988-2726 ■ *Web:* www.apcosigns.com	Atlanta	GA	30312	404-688-9000		701
Apco Products Inc	PO Box 236 *TF:* 800-869-0194 ■ *Web:* www.apco-products.com	Essex	CT	06426	860-767-2108	767-7259	233
APCO Worldwide	700 12th St *Web:* www.apcoworldwide.com	Washington	DC	20005	202-778-1000		636

Name	Address	City	State	ZIP	Phone	Fax	Class
APCOM Inc	125 SE Pkwy *TF:* 800-251-3535 ■ *Web:* www.apcom-inc.com	Franklin	TN	37064	615-794-5574	791-0660	202
APCON Inc	9255 SW Pioneer Ct *TF:* 800-624-6808 ■ *Web:* www.apcon.com	Wilsonville	OR	97070	503-682-4050		174
APD (American Product Distributors Inc)	8350 Arrowridge Blvd *TF:* 800-849-5842 ■ *Web:* www.americanproduct.com	Charlotte	NC	28273	704-522-9411		534
APDA (American Parkinson Disease Assn)	135 Parkinson Ave *TF:* 800-223-2732 ■ *Web:* www.apdaparkinson.org	Staten Island	NY	10305	718-981-8001	981-4399	48-17
APEL International Inc	11201 Ampere Ct *Web:* www.apelfilters.com	Louisville	KY	40299	502-240-0443		791
Apel Steel Corp	2345 Second Ave NW *Web:* www.apelsteel.net	Cullman	AL	35058	256-739-6280		492
Apelles LLC	3700 Corporate Dr Ste 240 *TF:* 800-825-4425 ■ *Web:* www.apellesnow.com	Columbus	OH	43231	614-899-7322		317
Apelon Inc	750 Main St Ste 1500 *Web:* www.apelon.com	Hartford	CT	06103	203-431-2530	431-2523	475
Aperia Technologies Inc	1616 Rollins Rd *Web:* www.aperiatech.com	Burlingame	CA	94010	415-494-9624		755
Aperio Group LLC	3 Harbor Dr Ste 315 *Web:* www.aperiogroup.com	Sausalito	CA	94965	415-339-4300		401
Aperio Insights LLC	6057 Preston Haven Dr *Web:* aperioinsights.com	Dallas	TX	75230	469-363-0109		195
Aperion Information Technologies Inc	90 S Washington St *Web:* www.aperion.com	Oxford	MI	48371	248-969-9791		196
Aperto Networks Inc	598 Gibraltar Dr *Web:* www.apertonet.com	Milpitas	CA	95035	408-719-9977	719-9970	736
Aperture Venture Partners	645 Madison Ave 20th Fl *Web:* www.aperturevp.com	New York	NY	10022	212-758-7325	319-8779	792
Apetito Canada Ltd	12 Indell Ln *TF:* 800-268-8199 ■ *Web:* apetito.ca	Brampton	ON	L6T3Y3	905-799-1022		297-8
Apex Advertising Inc	2959 Old Tree Dr *TF:* 800-666-5556 ■ *Web:* www.apexadv.com	Lancaster	PA	17603	717-396-7100		7
Apex Airtronics Inc	2465 Atlantic Ave	Brooklyn	NY	11207	718-485-8560		647
Apex Anodizing Nev Inc	280 Coney Island Dr Ste B *Web:* apexanodizing.com	Sparks	NV	89431	775-355-8121		481
Apex Asset Management LLC	2501 Oregon Pike Ste 201 *TF:* 888-592-2149 ■ *Web:* www.apexasset.com	Lancaster	PA	17601	717-519-1770		195
Apex Behavioral Health Western Wayne PLLC	1547 S Wayne Rd *Web:* www.apexwesternwayne.com	Westland	MI	48186	734-729-3133		726
Apex Bioscienceinc	2810 Meridian Pkwy	Durham	NC	27713	919-405-4000		583
Apex Broach & Machine Co	22862 Hoover Rd *Web:* www.apbsi.com	Warren	MI	48089	586-758-2626	758-2627	403
Apex Broadcasting Inc	2294 Clements Ferry Rd *Web:* www.apexbroadcasting.com	Charleston	SC	29492	843-972-1100		645-10
Apex Business Machines & Supplies	352 Riverside Dr *TF:* 800-361-2697 ■ *Web:* apexbiz.com	Sudbury	ON	P3E1H7	705-674-4472		177
Apex Capital LLC	25 Orinda Way Ste 300	Orinda	CA	94563	925-253-1800		401
Apex Co	100 Main St *Web:* www.theapexcompanies.com	Pawtucket	RI	02860	401-729-7200		229
Apex Color	200 N Lee St *TF:* 800-367-6790 ■ *Web:* www.apexcolor.net	Jacksonville	FL	32204	800-367-6790		110
Apex Companies LLC	15850 Crabbs Branch Way Ste 200 *Web:* www.apexcos.com	Rockville	MD	20855	301-417-0200	975-0169	261
Apex Composites LLC	5322 John Lucas Dr *Web:* www.apexcomposites.com	Burlington	ON	L7L6A6	905-331-8042		22
Apex Computer Systems Inc	13875 Cerritos Corp Dr Ste A *Web:* www.acsi2000.com	Cerritos	CA	90703	562-926-6820		196
Apex CoVantage LLC	198 Van Buren St 200 Presidents Plz *Web:* apexcovantage.com	Herndon	VA	20170	703-709-3000		178-12
Apex Digital Imaging Inc	16057 Tampa Palms Blvd W *TF:* 866-973-3034 ■ *Web:* www.apexdigitalimaging.com	Tampa	FL	33647	813-973-3034		701
Apex Distribution Inc	407 - 2 St SW Ste 550 *Web:* www.apexdistribution.com	Calgary	AB	T2P2Y3	403-268-7333		540
APEX Financial Services Inc	11800 Singletree Ln Ste 314 *Web:* www.apexfsi.com	Eden Prairie	MN	55344	952-238-1315		41
Apex Group	1201 1201 K St Ste 750 St Ste 750 *Web:* theapexgroup.net	Sacramento	CA	95814	916-444-3116		636
Apex Homes Inc	7172 Rt 522 *TF:* 800-326-9524 ■ *Web:* www.apexhomesofpa.com	Middleburg	PA	17842	570-837-2333	837-2346	186
Apex Industries Inc	100 Millennium Blvd *TF:* 800-268-3331 ■ *Web:* www.apexindustries.com	Moncton	NB	E1E2G8	506-857-1620		480
Apex Information Management Consultants Inc	4515 Culver Rd Ste 310 *Web:* www.apeximc.com	Rochester	NY	14622	585-225-8430		177
Apex Innovations Inc	19951 W 162nd St *Web:* www.apex-innovations.com	Olathe	KS	66062	913-254-0250		177
Apex Machine Co	3000 NE 12th Terr *Web:* www.apexmachine.com	Fort Lauderdale	FL	33334	954-566-1572	563-2844	629
Apex Machine Tool Co	1790 New Britain Ave *Web:* www.apexmachinetool.com	Farmington	CT	06032	860-677-2884		529
Apex Maritime Ord	1900 E Golf Rd *Web:* apexshipping.com	Schaumburg	IL	60173	630-227-9818		311

Company / Address	City	ST	ZIP	Phone	Fax	Class
Apex Mechanical Systems Inc 7440 Trade St — *Web:* www.apexmech.com	San Diego	CA	92121	858-536-8700		610
Apex Medical Technologies Inc 10064 Mesa Ridge Court Ste 202 — *Web:* www.apexmedtech.com	San Diego	CA	92121	858-535-0012		476
Apex Mills Corp 168 Doughty Blvd — *TF:* 800-989-2739 ■ *Web:* www.apexmills.com	Inwood	NY	11096	516-239-4400	239-4951	745-4
Apex Oil Company Inc 8235 Forsyth Blvd Ste 400 — *Web:* www.apexoil.com	Quebec	MO	63105	314-889-9600	854-8539	579
Apex Packing & Rubbr Co 1855 New Hwy Ste D — *TF:* 800-645-9110 ■ *Web:* apexgaskets.com	Farmingdale	NY	11735	631-420-8150		358
Apex Paper Box Co 5601 Walworth Ave — *TF Cust Svc:* 800-438-2269 ■ *Web:* boxit.com	Cleveland	OH	44102	216-631-6900	416-2145	101
Apex Piping Systems Inc 302 Falco Dr — *TF:* 888-995-2739 ■ *Web:* www.apexpiping.com	Wilmington	DE	19804	302-995-6136		610
Apex Precision Technologies Inc 8824 Union Mills Dr — *Web:* www.apexprecision.com	Camby	IN	46113	317-821-1000		639
Apex Resources Inc 549 Stonegate Dr — *Web:* apexr.com	Katy	TX	77494	832-786-7492		539
Apex Software Inc 37 Antrim Rd	Pittston	PA	18640	570-830-5893		177
Apex Software Solutions LLC 5039 Beckwith Blvd Ste 109 — *Web:* www.apexwin.com	San Antonio	TX	78249	210-699-6666		525
Apex Spring & Stamping Corp 11420 First Ave NW — *Web:* www.apexspring.com	Grand Rapids	MI	49534	616-453-5463		492
APEX Systems Inc 4400 Cox Rd Ste 100 — *Web:* www.apexsystems.com/Pages/default.aspx	Glen Allen	VA	23060	804-254-2600	254-7290	721
Apex Tool Works Inc 3200 Tollview Dr — *Web:* www.apextool.com	Rolling Meadows	IL	60008	847-394-5810	394-2739	757
Apex Venture Partners 225 W Washington St Ste 1500 — *TF:* 800-719-4664 ■ *Web:* www.apexvc.com	Chicago	IL	60606	312-857-2800	857-1800	792
Apex3 Security 500 W Madison Ste 2750 — *Web:* www.apex3security.com	Chicago	IL	60661	773-867-9204		693
Apex-Petroleum Corp 9500 Arena Dr Ste 360 — *Web:* www.apexpetroleum.com	Upper Marlboro	MD	20744	301-773-9009		579
APG (Automation Products Group Inc) 1025 W 1700 N — *TF:* 888-525-7300 ■ *Web:* www.apgsensors.com	Logan	UT	84321	435-753-7300	753-7490	201
APG (American Packing & Gasket Co) 6039 Armour Dr PO Box 213 — *TF:* 800-888-5223 ■ *Web:* callapg.com	Houston	TX	77020	713-675-5271	675-2730	326
APG Cash Drawer LLC 5250 Industrial Blvd NE — *Web:* cashdrawer.com	Minneapolis	MN	55421	763-571-5000	571-5771	488
APG Office Furnishings Inc 12075 Northwest Blvd Ste 100 — *Web:* www.apgof.com	Cincinnati	OH	45246	513-621-9111		321
APG Security Inc 116 N Broadway — *Web:* www.apgsecurity.com	South Amboy	NJ	08879	732-553-1537		693
APGA (American Public Gas Assn) 201 Massachusetts Ave NE Ste C-4 — *TF:* 800-927-4204 ■ *Web:* www.apga.org	Washington	DC	20002	202-464-2742	464-0246	48-12
Apgar Brothers Trucking Co 200 Apgar Dr	Somerset	NJ	08873	732-356-3900		780
APHA (American Paint Horse Assn) 2800 Meacham Blvd — *Web:* www.apha.com	Fort Worth	TX	76137	817-834-2742	834-3152	48-3
APHA (American Public Health Assn) 800 'I' St NW — *Web:* www.apha.org	Washington	DC	20001	202-777-2742	777-2533	49-8
ApHC (Appaloosa Horse Club) 2720 W Pullman Rd — *TF:* 888-304-7768 ■ *Web:* www.appaloosa.com	Moscow	ID	83843	208-882-5578	882-8150	48-3
APHIS (Animal & Plant Health Inspection Service) *National Veterinary Services Laboratories* 4700 River Rd — *TF:* 844-820-2234 ■ *Web:* www.aphis.usda.gov	Riverdale	MD	20737	844-820-2234		743
APHL (Association of Public Health Laboratories) 8515 Georgia Ave Ste 700 — *TF:* 800-899-2278 ■ *Web:* www.aphl.org	Silver Spring	MD	20910	240-485-2745	485-2700	49-7
APHSA (American Public Human Services Assn) 1133 19th St NW Ste 400 — *Web:* www.aphsa.org	Washington	DC	20036	202-682-0100	289-6555	49-7
API (Anco Products Inc) 2500 S 17th St — *TF:* 800-837-2626 ■ *Web:* www.ancoproductsinc.com	Elkhart	IN	46517	574-293-5574	295-6235	389
API (American Petroleum Institute) 1220 L St NW — *TF:* 800-526-4233 ■ *Web:* www.api.org	Washington	DC	20005	202-682-8000		48-12
API (Aerospace Products International) 3778 Distriplex Dr N — *TF:* 888-274-2497 ■ *Web:* www.apiworldwide.com	Memphis	TN	38118	901-365-3470		22
API Construction Co 1100 Old Hwy 8 NW — *TF:* 800-223-4922 ■ *Web:* www.apiconst.com	New Brighton	MN	55112	651-636-4320	636-0312	189-9
API Delevan 270 Quaker Rd — *Web:* www.delevan.com	East Aurora	NY	14052	716-652-3600	652-4814	253
API Foils Inc 329 New Brunswick Ave — *Web:* www.apigroup.com	Rahway	NJ	07065	732-382-6800		295
APi Group Inc 1100 Old Hwy 8 NW — *TF:* 800-223-4922 ■ *Web:* www.apigroupinc.com	New Brighton	MN	55112	800-223-4922		185
API Heat Transfer Inc 2777 Walden Ave — *TF:* 877-274-4328 ■ *Web:* www.apiheattransfer.com	Buffalo	NY	14225	716-684-6700	684-2129	91
Api Security Services & Investigations Inc 867 High St Ste D — *Web:* apisecurity.us	Worthington	OH	43085	614-310-1980		693
APi Supply Inc 624 Arthur St NE — *Web:* www.apisupplyinc.com	Minneapolis	MN	55413	612-379-8000	379-8038	264-3
APi Systems Group Inc 10575 Vista Park Rd — *TF General:* 877-828-1200 ■ *Web:* www.afpgusa.com/api-systems-group.php	Dallas	TX	75238	214-291-1200	291-1340	692
APIC (Association for Professionals in Infection Control & Epidemiology Inc) 1275 K St NW Ste 1000 — *TF:* 800-650-9883 ■ *Web:* www.apic.org	Washington	DC	20005	202-789-1890	789-1899	49-8
Apio Inc PO Box 727 — *TF Sales:* 800-454-1355 ■ *Web:* www.apioinc.com	Guadalupe	CA	93434	800-454-1355		296-21
Apkudo LLC 3500 Boston St Ste 333 — *Web:* www.apkudo.com	Baltimore	MD	21224	410-777-8612		387
APL (Aliceville Public Library) 416 Third Ave NE — *Web:* pickenslibrary.com	Aliceville	AL	35442	205-373-6691	373-3731	434-3
APL (Albany Public Library) 161 Washington Ave — *Web:* www.albanypubliclibrary.org	Albany	NY	12210	518-427-4300	449-3386	434-3
APL Access & Security Inc 115 S William Dillard Dr — *TF:* 866-873-2288 ■ *Web:* www.aplsecurity.com	Gilbert	AZ	85233	480-497-9471		693
APL Logistics Inc 16220 N Scottsdale Rd Ste 300 — **Fax Area Code:* 602 ■ *TF:* 866-896-2005 ■ *Web:* www.apllogistics.com	Scottsdale	AZ	85254	866-896-2005	586-4861*	449
Aplicare Inc 550 Research Pkwy	Meriden	CT	06450	203-630-0500		583
Aplix Inc 12300 Steele Creek Rd — *Web:* www.aplix.com	Charlotte	NC	28273	704-588-1920	588-1941	594
APLU (Association of Public & Land-grant Universities) 1307 New York Ave NW Ste 400 — *Web:* www.aplu.org	Washington	DC	20005	202-478-6040	478-6046	49-5
Aplus 3680 Victoria St N — *TF:* 877-275-8763 ■ *Web:* www.aplus.net	Shoreview	MN	55126	858-410-6929		398
A-Plus Printing & Graphic Center Inc 6561 NW 18th Ct — *Web:* www.a-plusprinting.com	Plantation	FL	33313	954-327-7315		627
APlus Technologies Inc 10015 Old Columbia Rd Ste B — *Web:* www.aplustechnologies.com	Columbia	MD	21046	410-290-6233		177
APM Hexseal Corp 44 Honeck St — *TF:* 800-498-9034 ■ *Web:* www.apmhexseal.com	Englewood	NJ	07631	201-569-5700	569-4106	326
APM Systems 1313 S Pennsylvania Ave — *Web:* apmsystems.com	Morrisville	PA	19067	215-295-1097		311
APMA (American Podiatric Medical Assn) 9312 Old Georgetown Rd — *TF:* 800-275-2762 ■ *Web:* www.apma.org	Bethesda	MD	20814	301-581-9200	530-2752	49-8
Apmetrix Inc 2815 Forbs Ave STE 107-40 — *TF:* 800-490-3184 ■ *Web:* www.apmetrix.com	Hoffman Estates	IL	60192	312-416-0950		387
APMP (Association of Proposal Management Professionals) PO Box 668 — *Web:* www.apmp.org	Dana Point	CA	92629	949-493-9398		49-12
APN (Americans for Peace Now) 1101 14th St NW 6th Fl — *TF:* 877-429-0678 ■ *Web:* www.peacenow.org	Washington	DC	20005	202-728-1893	728-1895	48-7
APN Consulting Inc 475 Wall St — *Web:* www.apnconsultinginc.com	Princeton	NJ	08540	609-924-3400		194
Apn Healthcare Inc 320 W Hefner Rd — *Web:* www.apnhealthcare.com	Oklahoma City	OK	73114	405-418-8500		361
APN Media LLC PO Box 20113 — *TF:* 800-470-7599 ■ *Web:* www.ohranger.com	New York	NY	10023	212-581-3380	245-4226	637-9
APNA (American Psychiatric Nurses Assn) 1555 Wilson Blvd Ste 530 — *TF:* 866-243-2443 ■ *Web:* www.apna.org	Arlington	VA	22209	703-243-2443	243-3390	49-8
APO (Alpha Phi Omega) 14901 E 42nd St — *Web:* www.apo.org	Independence	MO	64055	816-373-8667	373-5975	48-16
Apogee Consulting Group PA 1151 Kildaire Farm Rd Ste 120 — *Web:* www.acg-pa.com	Cary	NC	27511	919-858-7420		256
Apogee Designs Ltd 101 S Kane St — *Web:* www.apogeedesigns.com	Baltimore	MD	21224	410-633-6336		596
Apogee Enterprises Inc 4400 W 78th St Ste 520 — *NASDAQ: APOG* ■ *TF:* 877-752-3432 ■ *Web:* www.apog.com	Minneapolis	MN	55435	952-835-1874		329
Apogee Software Inc 1999 S Bascom Ave Ste 250 — *Web:* www.apogee.com	Campbell	CA	95008	408-369-9001	369-9018	178-6
Apogee Technology Inc 129 Morgan Dr — *OTC: ATCS* ■ *Web:* www.apogeebio.com	Norwood	MA	02062	781-551-9450	769-9107	696
Apollo Athletics Inc 1428 S Central Park Ave — *Web:* www.apolloathletics.com	Anaheim	CA	92802	714-533-8118		360-3
Apollo Cafe 1310 E Brady St — *TF:* 800-558-7171 ■ *Web:* apollocafe.com	Milwaukee	WI	53202	414-272-2233	272-2344	671
Apollo Chemical Company LLC 1105 Southerland St — *TF:* 800-374-3827 ■ *Web:* www.apollochemical.com	Graham	NC	27253	336-226-1161	226-7494	145
Apollo Design Technology Inc 4130 Fourier Dr — *Web:* www.apollodesign.net	Fort Wayne	IN	46818	260-497-9191	497-9192	722
Apollo Distributing Co 128 Passaic Ave — *Web:* www.apollodist.com	Fairfield	NJ	07004	973-228-5000		361
Apollo Graphics 6501 SW Macadam Ave — *TF:* 800-463-3339 ■ *Web:* www.apollographicsprinting.com	Portland	OR	97239	503-288-9191		627
Apollo Group Inc 4025 E Elwood St — *NASDAQ: APOL* ■ *TF:* 800-990-2765 ■ *Web:* www.apollo.edu	Phoenix	AZ	85040	800-990-2765		242
Apollo Health Street Inc 2 Brighton Rd Ste 300	Clifton	NJ	07012	973-405-5002		317
Apollo Industries Inc 83 N End Dr	Wallingford	VT	05773	802-446-3466		536
Apollo Oil LLC 1175 Early Dr — *TF:* 800-473-5823 ■ *Web:* www.apollooil.com	Winchester	KY	40391	859-744-5444		316
Apollo PACS Inc 7700 Leesburg Pike Ste 419 — *Web:* www.apolloei.com	Falls Church	VA	22043	703-288-1474		177
Apollo Plastics Corp 5333 N Elston Ave — *Web:* spcmfg.com	Chicago	IL	60630	773-282-9222	282-2763	604

	Phone	Fax	Class
Apollo Professional Svc 29 Stiles Rd Ste 302 .... Salem NH 03079 *TF:* 866-277-3343 ■ *Web:* www.apollopros.com	866-277-3343		201
Apollo Retail Specialists LLC 1234 Tech Blvd .... Tampa FL 33619 *Web:* www.apolloretail.com	813-712-2525		393
Apollo Theater 2540 N Lincoln Ave .... Chicago IL 60614 *Web:* www.apollochicago.com	773-935-6100		572
Apollo Theatre 253 W 125th St .... New York NY 10027 *TF:* 800-745-3000 ■ *Web:* www.apollotheater.org	212-531-5300	749-2743	572
Apollo Wood Products 7225 Edison Ave .... Ontario CA 92335 *Web:* www.apollowoodproducts.com	909-371-9510		660
ApolloMD Inc 5665 New Northside Dr Ste 320 .... Atlanta GA 30328 *Web:* www.apollomd.com	770-874-5400	874-5433	353
Apollo-Ridge School District PO Box 219 .... Spring Church PA 15686 *Web:* www.apolloridge.com	724-478-6000		685
Apologetics Press Inc 230 Landmark Dr .... Montgomery AL 36117 *Web:* www.apologeticspress.org	334-272-8558		532-3
APOS Systems Inc 100 Conestoga College Blvd Ste 1118 .... Kitchener ON N2P2N6 *Web:* www.apos.com	519-894-2767		177
Apostle Pictures 568 Broadway Ste 601 .... New York NY 10012 *Web:* www.apostlenyc.com	212-541-4323		514
Apostolic Assembly of The Faith In Christ Jesus 10807 Laurel St .... Rancho Cucamonga CA 91730 *Web:* www.apostolicassembly.org	909-987-3013		48-20
Apostolic Bible Institute Inc 6944 Hudson Blvd N .... Saint Paul MN 55128 *Web:* www.apostolic.org	651-739-7686		166
Apostolic Christian Restmor Inc 1500 Parkside Ave .... Morton IL 61550 *Web:* www.acrestmor.org	309-284-1400	266-7877	450
Apotex Corp 2400 N Commerce Pkwy Ste 400 .... Weston FL 33326 **Fax Area Code:* 800 ■ *TF:* 877-427-6839 ■ *Web:* www.apotex.com	877-427-6839	706-5576*	583
Apotex Fermentation Inc 50 Scurfield Blvd .... Winnipeg MB R3Y1G4 *TF:* 800-363-8805 ■ *Web:* www.apoferm.com	204-989-6830		743
Apotex Inc 150 Signet Dr .... Toronto ON M9L1T9 *TF:* 800-268-4623 ■ *Web:* www.apotex.com	416-749-9300	401-3849	582
Apotex Pharmachem Inc 34 Spalding Dr .... Brantford ON N3T6B8 *Web:* www.apotexpharmachem.com	519-756-8942	753-3051	479
Apothecary Products 11750 12th Ave S Burnsville .... Burnsville MN 55337 *TF:* 800-328-2742 ■ *Web:* www.apothecaryproducts.com	800-328-2742	328-1584	214
Apothecary Shoppe, The 82 S 1100 E #104 .... Salt Lake City UT 84102 *Web:* www.mygnp.com	801-521-6353		237
APPA (American Public Power Assn) 1875 Connecticut Ave Ste 1200 .... Washington DC 20009 *Web:* www.publicpower.org	202-467-2900	467-2910	48-12
APPA (Association of Higher Education Facilities Officers) 1643 Prince St .... Alexandria VA 22314 *TF:* 800-336-3097 ■ *Web:* www.appa.org	703-684-1446	549-2772	49-5
Appalachian Behavioral Healthcare 100 Hospital Dr .... Athens OH 45701 *TF:* 800-372-8862 ■ *Web:* mha.ohio.gov	740-594-5000		374-5
Appalachian Brewing Co 50 N Cameron St .... Harrisburg PA 17101 *TF:* 800-377-1277 ■ *Web:* www.abcbrew.com	717-221-1080	221-1083	671
Appalachian Electric Co-op 1109 Hill Dr .... New Market TN 37820 *TF:* 800-325-8925 ■ *Web:* aecoop.org	865-475-2032	475-0888	245
Appalachian Electronic Instruments Inc 100 Aei Dr .... Fairlea WV 24902 *Web:* www.aei-wv.com	304-647-5855		201
Appalachian Mountain Club (AMC) 5 Joy St .... Boston MA 02108 *TF Orders:* 800-262-4455 ■ *Web:* www.outdoors.org	617-523-0655	523-0722	48-13
Appalachian National Scenic Trail PO Box 807 .... Harpers Ferry WV 25425 *Web:* www.nps.gov/appa	304-535-6331	535-2667	564
Appalachian Regional Healthcare Service (ARH) 80 Hospital Dr PO Box 8086 .... Barbourville KY 40906 *TF:* 888-654-0015 ■ *Web:* www.arh.org	859-226-2440		353
Appalachian School of Law 1169 Edgewater Dr .... Grundy VA 24614 *TF:* 800-895-7411 ■ *Web:* www.asl.edu	276-935-4349		167-1
Appalachian State University *Belk Library* 218 College St PO Box 32026 .... Boone NC 28608 **Fax:* Administration ■ *TF:* 877-423-0086 ■ *Web:* www.library.appstate.edu	828-262-2300	262-3001*	434-6
Appalachian Stove & Fabricators Inc 329 Emma Rd .... Asheville NC 28806 *Web:* www.appalachianstove.com	828-253-0164		357
Appalachian Timber Services Inc 393 EDGAR Givens Pkwy .... Sutton WV 26601 *TF:* 800-272-8437 ■ *Web:* www.atstimber.com	304-765-7393		818
Appalachian Trail Conservancy (ATC) 799 Washington St PO Box 807 .... Harpers Ferry WV 25425 *TF Sales:* 888-287-8673 ■ *Web:* appalachiantrail.org	304-535-6331	535-2667	48-23
Appalachian Wood Products Inc 171 Loop Rd .... Clearfield PA 16830 *TF:* 800-844-1280 ■ *Web:* www.appwood.com	814-765-2003	765-4751	499
Appaloosa Horse Club (ApHC) 2720 W Pullman Rd .... Moscow ID 83843 *TF:* 888-304-7768 ■ *Web:* www.appaloosa.com	208-882-5578	882-8150	48-3
Appaloosa Management LP 51 John F Kennedy Pkwy .... Short Hills NJ 07078 *Web:* www.amlp.com	973-701-7000		403
Apparatus Inc 1401 N Meridian St .... Indianapolis IN 46202 *Web:* apparatus.net	317-254-8488		271
Apparel Finishing America 250 Belmont Ave .... Haledon NJ 07508 *Web:* www.apparelgroup.org	973-942-6800		426
Apparelmaster 123 Harrison Ave .... Harrison OH 45030 *TF:* 877-543-1678 ■ *Web:* companycasuals.com	513-202-1600		442
Apparent Technologies Inc 11202 Georgian Dr Unit A .... Austin TX 70753 *Web:* www.apparenttech.com	512-873-0023		454
AppDetex 501 W Grove St .... Boise ID 83702 *TF:* 855-693-3839 ■ *Web:* www.appdetex.com	855-693-3839		196
Appeal-Democrat 1530 Ellis Lake Dr PO Box 431 .... Marysville CA 95901 **Fax:* News Rm ■ *TF:* 800-831-2345 ■ *Web:* www.appeal-democrat.com	530-741-2345	749-8390*	532-2
Appetez 825 W Roseburg Ave .... Modesto CA 95350	209-577-5099		671
APPI Energy 224 Phillip Morris Dr Ste 402 .... Salisbury MD 21804 *TF:* 800-520-6685 ■ *Web:* www.appienergy.com	800-520-6685		194
Appian Analytics Inc 2000 Crow Canyon Pl Ste 300 .... San Ramon CA 94583 *TF:* 877-757-7646 ■ *Web:* www.appianalytics.com	877-757-7646		624
Appian Corp 11955 Democracy Dr Ste 1700 .... Reston VA 20190 *Web:* www.appian.com	703-442-8844		178-1
Appian Digital 3102, Church St .... Burlington NC 27215 *Web:* www.appiandigital.com	336-538-4747		180
Applanix Corp 85 Leek Cresent .... Richmond Hill ON L4B3B3 *TF:* 800-225-9977 ■ *Web:* www.applanix.com	905-709-4600		387
Apple & Assoc Inc 395 Saint Thomas Ch Rd PO Box 996 .... Chapin SC 29036 *Web:* www.appleassoc.com	803-932-2000		260
Apple & Eve Inc Two Seaview Blvd .... Port Washington NY 11050 *TF:* 800-969-8018 ■ *Web:* www.appleandeve.com	516-621-1122	621-2164	296-20
Apple Bank for Savings 122 E 42nd St .... New York NY 10168 *TF:* 800-824-0710 ■ *Web:* www.applebank.com	914-902-2775		70
Apple Blossom Hill Inc 10150 Clyde Rd .... Fenton MI 48430	810-632-5590		793
Apple Creek Banc Corp 3 W Main St PO Box 237 .... Apple Creek OH 44606 *TF:* 888-327-7533 ■ *Web:* www.applecreekbank.com	330-698-2631		70
Apple Discount Drugs 404 N Fruitland Blvd .... Salisbury MD 21801 *TF:* 800-424-8401 ■ *Web:* www.appledrugs.com	410-749-8401		23
Apple Farm Bakery 2015 Monterey St .... San Luis Obispo CA 93401 *TF:* 800-255-2040 ■ *Web:* www.applefarm.com	805-544-2040		378
Apple Farm Service Inc 10120 W Versailles Rd .... Covington OH 45318 *TF:* 800-860-4851 ■ *Web:* www.applefarmservice.com	937-526-4851		274
Apple Federal Credit Union 4029 Ridge Top Rd .... Fairfax VA 22030 *Web:* applefcu.org	703-788-4800		219
Apple Inc 1 Infinite Loop .... Cupertino CA 95014 *NASDAQ: AAPL* ■ **Fax:* Mail Rm ■ *TF Cust Svc:* 800-275-2273 ■ *Web:* www.apple.com	408-996-1010	996-0275*	173-2
Apple Jade 300 N Clippert St .... Lansing MI 48912 *Web:* www.applejadelansing.com	517-332-1111		671
Apple Printing & Advertising Specialties Inc 5055 NW Tenth Ter .... Fort Lauderdale FL 33309 *Web:* appleprinting.com	954-776-5091		7
Apple Rehab 21 Waterville Rd .... Avon CT 06001 *TF General:* 800-873-1013 ■ *Web:* www.apple-rehab.com	860-927-5368		450
Apple River Canyon State Park 8763 E Canyon Rd .... Apple River IL 61001 *Web:* www.dnr.illinois.gov/Parks/Pages/ArgyleLake.aspx	815-745-3302		565
Apple Rock Adv & Promotion 7602 Business Park Dr .... Greensboro NC 27409 *Web:* www.applerock.com	336-232-4800		4
Apple Rubber Products Inc 310 Erie St .... Lancaster NY 14086 *TF Cust Svc:* 800-828-7745 ■ *Web:* www.applerubber.com	716-684-6560	684-8302	326
Apple Saddlery 1875 Innes Rd .... Ottawa ON K1B4C6 *TF:* 800-867-8225 ■ *Web:* www.applesaddlery.com	613-744-4040		711
Apple Spice Junction West Valley 2235 South 1300 West Ste A .... Salt Lake City UT 84119 *Web:* www.applespice.com	801-359-8821		194
Apple Tree Enterprises Inc 195 Underwood Rd .... Fletcher NC 28732 *Web:* www.appletreeautos.com	828-684-4400		57
Apple Tree Inn 9508 N Div St .... Spokane WA 99218 *TF:* 800-323-5796 ■ *Web:* www.appletreeinnmotel.com	509-466-3020		379
Apple Vacations Inc 101 NW Pt Blvd .... Elk Grove Village IL 60007 **Fax Area Code:* 847 ■ *TF:* 800-517-2000 ■ *Web:* www.applevacations.com	800-517-2000	640-1950*	771
Apple Valley Chamber of Commerce 16010 Apple Valley Rd .... Apple Valley CA 92307 *TF:* 800-872-0222 ■ *Web:* avchamber.org	760-242-2753	242-0303	139
Apple Valley Chamber of Commerce 14800 Galaxie Ave Ste 101 .... Apple Valley MN 55124 *TF:* 800-301-9435 ■ *Web:* www.applevalleychamber.com	952-432-8422		139
Apple Valley Medical Clinic Ltd 14655 Galaxie Ave .... Apple Valley MN 55124 *TF:* 800-233-8504 ■ *Web:* www.applevalleymedicalcenter.com	952-432-6161		237
Apple Valley Unified School District (AVUSD) 12555 Navajo Rd .... Apple Valley CA 92308 *Web:* www.avusd.org	760-247-8001		685
Appleby College 540 Lakeshore Rd W .... Oakville ON L6K3P1 *Web:* www.appleby.on.ca	905-845-4681	845-9505	622
Applegate Insulation Manufacturing Inc 1000 Highview Dr .... Webberville MI 48892 *TF:* 800-627-7536 ■ *Web:* www.applegateinsulation.com	517-521-3545	521-3597	389
Applegate Livestock Equipment Inc 902 S State Rd 32 .... Union City IN 47390 *TF:* 800-354-9502 ■ *Web:* www.applegatelivestock.com	765-964-4631		273
Appleone 990 Knox St .... Torrance CA 90502 *Web:* www.appleone.com	310-516-1572		2
AppleOne Employment Services Inc 327 West Broadway PO Box 29048 .... Glendale CA 91209 **Fax Area Code:* 818 ■ *TF:* 800-872-2677 ■ *Web:* www.appleone.com	800-872-2677	265-5514*	721
AppleOne Services Ltd 50 Paxman Rd Ste 8 .... Etobicoke ON M9C1B7 *Web:* www.appleone.ca	416-622-0100	622-6327	2
Apples of Gold Center for Learning 604 Liberty St .... Pella IA 50219 *Web:* www.applesofgold.biz	641-620-1160		194

Company / Address	City	State	Zip	Phone	Fax	Class
Appleton Coated LLC 540 Prospect St *Web:* www.appletoncoated.com	Combined Locks	WI	54113	920-788-3550		557
Appleton Group Wealth Management LLC 100 W Lawrence St Ste 306 *TF:* 866-993-7727 ■ *Web:* www.appletongrouponline.com	Wisconsin	WI	54911	920-993-7727		401
Appleton Medical Ctr 1818 N Meade St *TF:* 800-236-4101 ■ *Web:* www.thedacare.org	Appleton	WI	54911	920-731-4101	738-6319	374-3
Appleton Papers Inc 825 E Wisconsin Ave PO Box 359 *Web:* www.appvion.com	Appleton	WI	54912	920-734-9841		552-1
Appleton Partners Inc 1 Post Office Sq 6th Fl *TF:* 800-338-0745 ■ *Web:* www.appletonpartners.com	Boston	MA	02109	617-338-0700		401
Applewood Books Inc 1 River Rd *TF General:* 800-277-5312 ■ *Web:* www.applewoodbooks.com	Carlisle	MA	01741	800-277-5312		637-2
Applewood Centers Inc 2525 E 22nd St *TF:* 800-424-0182 ■ *Web:* www.applewoodcenters.org	Cleveland	OH	44115	216-696-5800		726
Applewood Manor Inn 62 Cumberland Cir *TF:* 800-442-2197 ■ *Web:* www.applewoodmanor.com	Asheville	NC	28801	828-254-2244	254-0899	379
Applewood Seed Co 5380 Vivian St *Web:* www.applewoodseed.com	Arvada	CO	80002	303-431-7333	467-7886	694
Applewood the CS Mott Estate 1400 E Kearsley St *Web:* www.ruthmottfoundation.org	Flint	MI	48503	810-233-0170	233-7022	50-3
Appliance Recycling Centers of America Inc 7400 Excelsior Blvd *NASDAQ: ARCI* ■ *TF:* 800-452-8680 ■ *Web:* www.arcainc.com	Minneapolis	MN	55426	952-930-9000	930-1800	660
Applicant Insight Ltd 5396 School Rd PO Box 458 *TF:* 800-771-7703 ■ *Web:* applicantinsight.com	New Port Richey	FL	34652	800-771-7703	890-6454	635
Applicantpro 3688 campus dr Ste 150 *Web:* www.applicantpro.com	Eagle Mountain	UT	84005	801-766-0174		225
Application Consulting Group 1639 NJ-10 Ste 107 *Web:* www.acgi.com	Parsippany	NJ	07054	973-898-0012	898-6647	39
Applied Aerodynamics Inc 2265 Valley Branch Cir *Web:* www.appliedaero.com	Farmers Branch	TX	75234	972-620-4319		22
Applied Aerospace Structures Corp (AASC) 3437 S Airport Way PO Box 6189 *Web:* www.aascworld.com	Stockton	CA	95206	209-982-0160	983-3375	504
Applied Analysis Inc 515 Groton Rd Ste 101 *Web:* www.discover-aai.com	Westford	MA	01821	978-392-4500		261
Applied Broadband Inc 1881 Ninth St Canyon Ctr Ste 125 *Web:* www.appliedbroadband.com	Boulder	CO	80302	303-449-2033		196
Applied Business Software 2847 Gundry Ave *TF:* 800-833-3343 ■ *Web:* www.themortgageoffice.com	Signal Hill	CA	90755	562-426-2188		177
Applied Cad Knowledge Inc 18 Westech Dr *TF:* 800-796-3628 ■ *Web:* www.appliedcad.com	Tyngsboro	MA	01879	978-649-9800		177
Applied Capital Inc 3700 Rio Grande Blvd NW Ste 4 *Web:* www.appliedcapital.net	Albuquerque	NM	87107	505-342-1840	342-2246	272
Applied Card Systems 50 Applied Card Way **Fax Area Code: 484* ■ *TF:* 866-227-5627 ■ *Web:* www.appliedcard.com	Glen Mills	PA	19342	866-227-5627	840-2758*	215
Applied Ceramics Inc 48630 Milmont Dr *Web:* www.appliedceramics.net	Fremont	CA	94538	510-249-9700		174
Applied Clinical Intelligence LLC 251 St Asaphs Rd 3 Bala Plaza W Ste 402 *TF:* 800-468-9283 ■ *Web:* www.aciclinical.com	Bala Cynwyd	PA	19004	484-429-7200		193
Applied Coatings Inc 661 Route 23 S *Web:* www.appliedcustomcoatings.com	Wayne	NJ	07470	973-628-8600		596
Applied Computer Research Inc (ACR) PO Box 41730 *Web:* www.itmarketintelligence.com	Phoenix	AZ	85080	602-885-5311		637-11
Applied Control Engineering Inc 700 Creek View Rd *Web:* ace-net.com	Newark	DE	19711	302-738-8800		261
Applied Cos 28020 Avenue Stanford *Web:* www.appliedcompanies.net	Valencia	CA	91355	661-257-0090		14
Applied Data Resources Inc 1303 N Glenville Dr	Richardson	TX	75081	972-238-8111		658
Applied Data Trends Inc 107-A Clinton Ave *Web:* www.adt-it.com	Huntsville	AL	35801	256-319-0700		180
Applied Diagnostics Inc 1140 Business Center Dr Ste 370 *TF:* 855-239-8378 ■ *Web:* www.applieddiagnostics.com	Houston	TX	77043	713-271-4133	271-6885	415
Applied Dynamics International Inc 3800 Stone School Rd *TF:* 888-465-4329 ■ *Web:* www.adi.com	Ann Arbor	MI	48108	734-973-1300	668-0012	178-2
Applied Educational Systems Inc 208 Bucky Dr *TF:* 800-220-2175 ■ *Web:* www.aeseducation.com	Lititz	PA	17543	800-220-2175		194
Applied Energy Company Inc (AEC) 1205 Venture Ct Ste 100 *TF:* 800-580-1171 ■ *Web:* www.appliedenergyco.com	Carrollton	TX	75006	214-355-4200	355-4201	640
Applied Energy Group Inc 1377 Motor Pkwy Ste 401 *Web:* www.appliedenergygroup.com	Islandia	NY	11749	631-434-1414		194
Applied Energy Solutions LLC 1 Technology Pl **Fax:* Sales ■ *TF:* 800-836-2132 ■ *Web:* www.appliedenergysol.com	Caledonia	NY	14423	585-538-4421	538-6345*	74
Applied Engineering Inc 2008 E Hwy 50 *TF:* 800-630-9644 ■ *Web:* www.appliedeng.com	Yankton	SD	57078	605-665-4425	665-1479	482
Applied Fiber Inc PO Box 1339 *TF:* 800-226-5394 ■ *Web:* www.appliedfiber.com	Leesburg	GA	31763	229-759-8301		544
Applied Flow Technology Corp 2955 Professional Pl Ste 301 *TF:* 800-589-4943 ■ *Web:* www.aft.com	Colorado Springs	CO	80904	719-686-1000		261
Applied Fusion Inc 1915 Republic Ave *TF:* 800-704-1078 ■ *Web:* appliedfusioninc.com	San Leandro	CA	94577	510-351-4511	351-0692	811
Applied Imaging Inc 5282 E Paris SE *TF:* 800-521-0983 ■ *Web:* www.appliedimaging.com	Grand Rapids	MI	49512	616-554-5200		225
Applied Industrial Technologies Inc 1 Applied Plaza Eulid Ave *NYSE: AIT* ■ *Web:* www.applied.com	Cleveland	OH	44115	216-426-4000		385
Applied Innovations Corp 1001 Yamato Rd Ste 300W *Web:* www.appliedi.net	Boca Raton	FL	33431	561-981-8196		225
Applied Instrument Technologies Inc 2121 Aviation Dr *Web:* www.aitanalyzers.com	Upland	CA	91786	909-204-3700		419
Applied Integrated Technologies Inc 7120 Samuel Morse Dr Ste 150 *Web:* www.ait-i.com	Columbia	MD	21046	410-872-0022	872-0044	177
Applied Knowledge Group Inc 2100 Reston Pkwy Ste 400 *Web:* www.akgroup.com	Reston	VA	20191	703-860-1145		321
Applied Laboratories Inc 3240 N Indianapolis Rd PO Box 2127 *Web:* www.appliedlabs.com	Columbus	IN	47202	812-372-2607	372-2631	418
Applied Laser Technologies 8404 Venture Cir *TF:* 888-359-3002 ■ *Web:* www.aplaser.com	Schofield	WI	54476	715-359-3002		492
Applied LNG 31111 Agoura Rd Ste 208 *TF:* 800-609-1702 ■ *Web:* www.appliedlng.com	Westlake Village	CA	91361	818-450-3650		536
Applied Logic Inc 11475 Olde Cabin Rd Ste 100 *TF:* 844-478-7225 ■ *Web:* www.appliedlogicinc.com	St. Louis	MO	63141	844-478-7225		809
Applied Marketing Research Inc 420 W 98th St *TF:* 800-381-5599 ■ *Web:* www.appliedmr.com	Kansas City	MO	64114	816-442-1010		195
Applied Materials Inc 3050 Bowers Ave PO Box 58039 *NASDAQ: AMAT* ■ *TF:* 800-447-1762 ■ *Web:* www.appliedmaterials.com	Santa Clara	CA	95054	408-727-5555		695
Applied Materials/Semitool 655 W Reserve Dr *Web:* www.appliedmaterials.com	Kalispell	MT	59901	406-752-2107		695
Applied Math Modeling Inc 75 S Main St Ste 7 PO Box 144 *Web:* www.coolsimsoftware.com	Concord	NH	03301	603-369-3793		261
Applied Measurement Professionals Inc (AMP) 18000 W 105th St *TF:* 800-345-6559 ■ *Web:* www.goamp.com	Olathe	KS	66061	913-895-4600	895-4650	47
Applied Mechanical Systems Inc 5598 Wolf Creek Pk *TF:* 888-854-3073 ■ *Web:* www.appliedmechanicalsys.com	Dayton	OH	45426	937-854-3073		610
Applied Medical Technology Inc 8000 Katherine Blvd *TF:* 800-869-7382 ■ *Web:* www.appliedmedical.net	Brecksville	OH	44141	440-717-4000		475
Applied Membranes Inc 2450 Business Park Dr *TF:* 800-321-9321 ■ *Web:* www.appliedmembranes.com	Vista	CA	92081	760-727-3711	727-4427	612
Applied Merchandising Concepts LLC 15 Beechwood Ave *Web:* www.appliedmerchandising.com	New Rochelle	NY	10801	914-738-5200		393
Applied Mfg Technologies Inc 219 Kay Industrial Dr *Web:* www.robotprogrammers.com	Orion	MI	48359	248-409-2000		256
Applied Micro Circuits Corp 215 Moffett Pk Dr *NASDAQ: AMCC* ■ *Web:* www.apm.com	Sunnyvale	CA	94089	408-542-8600	542-8601	696
Applied Minds LLC 2937 N Ontario St *TF:* 800-447-9778 ■ *Web:* appliedminds.com	Burbank	CA	91504	818-545-1400		180
Applied Molecular Evolution Inc (AME) 10300 Campus Pt Dr Ste 200	San Diego	CA	92121	858-597-4990		85
Applied OLAP Inc 3322 SW Memorial Pkwy Ste 647 *Web:* www.appliedolap.com	Huntsville	AL	35801	256-885-4371		177
Applied Physics Laboratory University of Washington 1013 NE 40th St PO Box 355640 *Web:* www.apl.washington.edu	Seattle	WA	98105	206-543-1300	543-6785	668
Applied Physics Systems Inc 281 E Java Dr *Web:* www.appliedphysics.com	Sunnyvale	CA	94089	650-965-0500		256
Applied Plastics Company Inc 7320 S Sixth St *TF:* 800-959-0445 ■ *Web:* www.appliedplasticsinc.com	Oak Creek	WI	53154	414-764-2900	764-8606	599
Applied Power Technologies Inc 470 Vandell Way Ste A *Web:* www.apt4power.com	Campbell	CA	95008	408-342-0790		196
Applied Process Cooling Corp 555 Price Ave **Fax Area Code: 707* ■ *TF:* 877-231-6406 ■ *Web:* www.apcco.net	Redwood City	CA	94063	650-595-0665	433-1310*	664
Applied Process Inc 12202 Newburgh Rd *Web:* www.appliedprocess.com	Livonia	MI	48150	734-464-8000		484
Applied Research & Technology 215 Tremont St *TF:* 800-775-2427 ■ *Web:* artproaudio.com	Rochester	NY	14608	585-436-2720	436-3942	52
Applied Research Co 53 W Jackson Blvd Ste 337 *Web:* www.appliedresearch.com	Chicago	IL	60604	312-922-7882		169
Applied Research Laboratory 1800 Alexander Bell Dr Ste 256 **Fax Area Code: 814* ■ *Web:* www.arl.psu.edu	Reston	VA	20191	703-939-8670	865-3105*	668
Applied Sciences Group Inc 4455 Genesee St Bldg 6 Ste 103 *TF:* 877-274-9811 ■ *Web:* www.asgrp.com	Buffalo	NY	14225	716-626-5100	626-0629	180
Applied Services & Information Systems Inc 209 Business Park Dr *TF:* 800-848-8218 ■ *Web:* www.asisinfo.net	Virginia Beach	VA	23462	757-498-0100		225
Applied Skills & Knowledge 100 W Hanover Ave	Cedar Knolls	NJ	07927	973-631-1607		195

Phone | Fax | Class

Applied Software Inc
3919 National Dr Ste 200 .... Burtonsville MD 20866 888-624-8439 177
TF: 888-624-8439 ■ *Web:* www.magview.com

Applied Statistics & Management Inc
31515 Rancho Pueblo Rd Ste 205 .... Temecula CA 92592 951-699-4600 809
Web: www.mdstaff.com

Applied Systems Engineering Inc
1480 Hickory St Ste 106 .... Niceville FL 32578 850-729-7550 256
Web: aseifl.com

Applied Systems Inc
200 Applied Pkwy .... University Park IL 60484 708-534-5575 534-8016* 178-11
**Fax:* Hum Res ■ *TF Sales:* 800-786-1362 ■ *Web:* www.appliedsystems.com

Applied Technical Services Inc
6300 Merrill Creek Pkwy #A100 .... Everett WA 98203 425-249-5555 625
Web: www.atslab.com

Applied Technology & Management Inc
5550 NW 111th Blvd .... Gainesville FL 32653 800-275-6488 261
TF: 800-275-6488 ■ *Web:* www.appliedtm.com

Applied Thermal Systems
8401 73rd Ave N Ste 74 .... Brooklyn Park MN 55428 763-535-5545 612
TF: 800-479-4783 ■ *Web:* www.apptherm.com

Applied Thin-Film Products Inc
3439 Edison Way .... Fremont CA 94538 510-661-4287 481
Web: www.thinfilm.com

Applied Voice & Speech Technologies Inc
27042 Towne Centre Dr Ste 200 .... Foothill Ranch CA 92610 949-699-2300 179
TF: 800-499-6544 ■ *Web:* www.avst.com

Appling County 69 Tippins St .... Baxley GA 31513 912-367-8100 367-8161 338
TF: 800-673-6338 ■ *Web:* www.baxley.org

Appling County School District
249 Blackshear Hwy .... Baxley GA 31513 912-367-8600 685
Web: www.appling.k12.ga.us

APPMA (American Pet Products Manufacturers Assn)
255 Glenville Rd .... Greenwich CT 06831 203-532-0000 532-0551 49-4
TF: 800-452-1225 ■ *Web:* www.americanpetproducts.org

appMobi Inc
35-37 E Orange St Ste 202 .... Lancaster PA 17602 717-666-3151 387

APPNET.COM 7883 NC Hwy 105 S .... Boone NC 28607 828-963-7286 783-3293* 180
**Fax Area Code:* 800 ■ *TF:* 888-926-4584 ■ *Web:* www.appnet.com

AppNeta Inc 285 Summer St 4th Fl .... Boston MA 02210 800-508-5233 809
TF: 800-664-4401 ■ *Web:* www.appneta.com

Appomattox Court House National Historical Park
Hwy 24 PO Box 218 .... Appomattox VA 24522 434-352-8987 352-8330 564
Web: www.nps.gov/apco

Appomattox Regional Library
209 E Cawson St .... Hopewell VA 23860 804-458-6329 434-3
Web: www.arls.org

Appperfect Corp
20065 Stevens Creek Blvd Ste 2A .... Cupertino CA 95014 408-252-4100 225
Web: www.appperfect.com

Appraisal Institute
550 W Van Buren St Ste 1000 .... Chicago IL 60607 312-335-4100 335-4400 49-17
TF: 888-756-4624 ■ *Web:* www.appraisalinstitute.org

Appraisal Journal
200 W Madison Ste 1500 .... Chicago IL 60606 888-756-4624 335-4400* 457-5
**Fax Area Code:* 312 ■ *TF:* 888-756-4624 ■ *Web:* www.appraisalinstitute.org

Appraisers Assn of America (AAA)
386 Pk Ave S Ste 2000 .... New York NY 10016 212-889-5404 889-5503 49-12
Web: appraisersassociation.org

Apprimus Inc 291 Rt 22 E Ste 20 .... Lebanon NJ 08833 908-236-8885 809
Web: www.apprimus.biz

Apprio Inc 425 Third St SW .... Washington DC 20024 202-684-8266 180
Web: www.apprioinc.com

Apprise Software Inc
3101 Emrick Blvd Ste 301 .... Bethlehem PA 18020 610-991-3900 177
Web: www.apprise.com

Appro International Inc
901 Fifth Ave Ste 1000 .... Seattle WA 98164 206-701-2000 299-9174 173-8
TF: 800-950-2729 ■ *Web:* www.cray.com

Approach Information Technology Inc
2027 Blue Heron Dr .... Melbourne FL 32940 321-242-6780 196
TF: 800-958-6556 ■ *Web:* www.approachit.com

Approva Corp
13454 Sunrise Vly Dr Ste 500 .... Herndon VA 20171 703-956-8300 178-9
Web: www.infor.com

Appsec Consulting Inc
6110 Hellyer Ave Ste 100 .... San Jose CA 95138 408-224-1110 177
TF: 800-487-3363 ■ *Web:* www.appsecconsulting.com

AppsHosting Inc
13772 Goldenwest St Ste 321 .... Westminster CA 92683 877-625-6610 387
TF: 877-625-6610

AppTech Corp
2011 Palomar Airport Rd Ste 102 .... Carlsbad CA 92011 877-720-0022 177
TF: 877-720-0022 ■ *Web:* apptechcorp.com

App-Techs Corp 505-B Willow Ln .... Lancaster PA 17601 717-735-0848 174
Web: www.app-techs.com

Apptopia Inc 71 Summer St .... Boston MA 02110 617-758-8165 387
Web: apptopia.com

Apptricity Corp
5605 N Macarthur Blvd Ste 900 .... Irving TX 75038 214-596-0601 177
Web: www.apptricity.com

AppWorx Corp 2475 140th Avene NE .... Bellevue WA 98005 425-644-2121 809
Web: www.automic.com

APPX Software Inc
11363 San Jose Blvd Ste 301 .... Jacksonville FL 32223 904-880-5560 880-6635 178-1
TF: 800-879-2779 ■ *Web:* www.appx.com

APQC 123 N Post Oak Ln Ste 300 .... Houston TX 77024 713-681-4020 681-8578 49-12
TF: 800-776-9676 ■ *Web:* www.apqc.org

APRA (Automotive Parts Remanufacturers Assn)
4215 Lafayette Ctr Dr Ste 3 .... Chantilly VA 20151 703-968-2772 968-2878 49-21
TF: 877-734-4827 ■ *Web:* www.apra.org

Apria Healthcare Group Inc
26220 Enterprise Ct .... Lake Forest CA 92630 949-639-2000 363
TF: 800-277-4288 ■ *Web:* www.apria.com

Apricorn Inc 12191 Kirkham Rd .... Poway CA 92064 858-513-2000 513-2020 173-8
TF: 800-458-5448 ■ *Web:* www.apricorn.com

Apricus Biosciences
11975 El Camino Real Ste 300 .... San Diego CA 92130 858-222-8041 866-0482 85
NASDAQ: APRI ■ *Web:* www.apricusbio.com

Phone | Fax | Class

Apriva Inc
8501 N Scottsdale Rd Ste 110 .... Scottsdale AZ 85253 480-421-1210 177
TF: 877-277-0728 ■ *Web:* www.apriva.com

APRO (Association of Progressive Rental Organizations)
1504 Robin Hood Trl .... Austin TX 78703 512-794-0095 794-0097 49-18
TF: 800-204-2776 ■ *Web:* www.rtohq.org

APRS (American Park & Recreation Society)
22377 Belmont Ridge Rd .... Ashburn VA 20148 703-858-0784 858-0794 48-23
TF: 800-765-3110 ■ *Web:* www.arcat.com

APS (Aerial Photography Services Inc)
2511 S Tryon St .... Charlotte NC 28203 704-333-5143 333-4911 328
Web: www.aps-1.com

APS (American Pain Society)
4700 West Lake Ave .... Glenview IL 60025 847-375-4715 375-6479 48-17
Web: www.americanpainsociety.org

APS (Albuquerque Public Schools)
6400 Uptown Blvd NE .... Albuquerque NM 87110 505-880-3700 889-4883* 685
**Fax:* Hum Res ■ *TF:* 866-563-9297 ■ *Web:* www.aps.edu

APS (American Philatelic Society)
100 Match Factory Pl .... Bellefonte PA 16823 814-933-3803 933-6128 48-18
Web: www.stamps.org

APS (American Philosophical Society)
104 S Fifth St .... Philadelphia PA 19106 215-440-3400 48-11
Web: www.amphilsoc.org

APS (American Physical Society)
1 Physics Ellipse .... College Park MD 20740 301-209-3200 209-0865 49-19
TF: 866-918-1164 ■ *Web:* www.aps.org

APS (American Physiological Society)
9650 Rockville Pk .... Bethesda MD 20814 301-634-7164 634-7241 49-8
Web: www.the-aps.org

APS (American Phytopathological Society, The)
3340 Pilot Knob Rd .... Saint Paul MN 55121 651-454-7250 454-0766 49-19
TF: 800-328-7560 ■ *Web:* www.apsnet.org/pages/default.aspx

APS (Arizona Public Service Co)
400 N Fifth St PO Box 53999 .... Phoenix AZ 85004 602-371-7171 787
TF: 800-253-9405 ■ *Web:* www.aps.com

APS Healthcare Inc
8403 Colesville Rd .... Silver Spring MD 20910 301-563-5633 462

APS Healthcare Inc
44 S Broadway Ste 12 .... White Plains NY 10601 914-288-4700 462
TF: 800-305-3720

APS Materials Inc 4011 Riverside Dr .... Dayton OH 45405 937-278-6547 481
Web: www.apsmaterials.com

APS Technology Inc 7 Laser Ln .... Wallingford CT 06492 860-613-4450 284-7428* 261
**Fax Area Code:* 203 ■ *Web:* www.aps-tech.com

APSA (American Political Science Assn)
1527 New Hampshire Ave NW .... Washington DC 20036 202-483-2512 483-2657 49-5
Web: www.apsanet.org

APsaA (American Psychoanalytic Assn)
309 E 49th St .... New York NY 10017 212-752-0450 593-0571 49-15
Web: www.apsa.org

Apsara 71 Rue D'Auteuil .... Quebec QC G1R4C3 418-694-0232 671
Web: restaurantapsara.com

Apscreen Inc
PO Box 80639 .... Rancho Santa Margarita CA 92688 949-646-4003 277-2733* 635
**Fax Area Code:* 888 ■ *TF:* 800-277-2733 ■ *Web:* www.apscreen.com

APSP (Association of Pool & Spa Professionals)
2111 Eisenhower Ave Ste 500 .... Alexandria VA 22314 703-838-0083 549-0493 49-4
TF: 800-323-3996 ■ *Web:* www.apsp.org

APT (Association for Play Therapy)
3198 Willow Ave Ste 110 .... Clovis CA 93612 559-294-2128 294-2129 49-15
TF: 800-347-6647 ■ *Web:* www.a4pt.org

APT (Alabama Public Television)
2112 11th Ave S Ste 400 .... Birmingham AL 35205 205-328-8756 251-2192 632
TF: 800-239-5233 ■ *Web:* www.aptv.org

APT (American Public Television)
55 Summer St 4th Fl .... Boston MA 02110 617-338-4455 338-5369 632
Web: aptonline.org/aptweb.nsf/home?readform

APT Foundation
1 Long Wharf Dr Ste 321 .... New Haven CT 06511 203-781-4600 726
TF: 855-378-4373 ■ *Web:* aptfoundation.org

A-P-T Research Inc
4950 Research Dr NW .... Huntsville AL 35805 256-327-3373 256
Web: www.apt-research.com

APTA (American Polarity Therapy Assn)
122 N Elm St Ste 512 .... Greensboro NC 27401 336-574-1121 574-1151 48-17
TF: 800-437-0620 ■ *Web:* www.polaritytherapy.org

APTA (American Physical Therapy Assn)
1111 N Fairfax St .... Alexandria VA 22314 703-684-2782 706-8536 49-8
TF: 800-999-2782 ■ *Web:* www.apta.org

APTA (American Public Transportation Assn)
1666 K St NW Ste 1100 .... Washington DC 20006 202-496-4800 496-4321 49-21
Web: www.apta.com

Aptara Inc 3110 Fairview Pk Dr .... Falls Church VA 22042 703-352-0001 781
Web: www.aptaracorp.com

AptarGroup Inc
475 W Terra Cotta Ave Ste E .... Crystal Lake IL 60014 815-477-0424 477-0481 154
NYSE: ATR ■ *TF:* 800-401-1957 ■ *Web:* www.aptar.com

Aptech Computer Systems Inc
135 Delta Dr .... Pittsburgh PA 15238 412-963-7440 178-11
TF: 800-245-0720 ■ *Web:* www.aptech-inc.com

Aptech Systems Inc
30741 Third Ave Ste 160 .... Black Diamond WA 98010 360-886-7100 809
Web: www.aptech.com

APTI (Association for Psychological Type International)
230 Washington Ave Extn Ste 101 .... Albany NY 12203 518-320-7416 49-15
Web: www.aptinternational.org

Aptima Inc 12 Gill St Ste 1400 .... Woburn MA 01801 781-935-3966 668
Web: www.aptima.com

Aptium Oncology 8201 Beverly Blvd .... Los Angeles CA 90048 323-866-3340 352
Web: www.aptiumoncology.com

Apto Solutions Inc
1910 MacArthur Blvd .... Atlanta GA 30318 404-605-0992 463
TF: 800-806-7578 ■ *Web:* www.aptosolutions.com

Aptos Chamber of Commerce
7605-A Old Dominion Ct .... Aptos CA 95003 831-688-1467 688-6961 139
TF: 800-862-2543 ■ *Web:* www.aptoschamber.com

	Phone	Fax	Class
APTS (Association of Public Television Stations) 2100 Crystal Dr Ste 700 Arlington VA 22202 *TF:* 800-346-6484 ■ *Web:* www.apts.org	202-654-4200	654-4236	49-14
AptSoft Corp 20 Burlington Mall Rd Burlington MA 01803	781-270-4900		525
APVA Preservation Virginia 204 W Franklin St Richmond VA 23220 *Web:* preservationvirginia.org	804-648-1889	775-0802	48-13
APWA (American Public Works Assn) 2345 Grand Blvd Ste 700 Kansas City MO 64108 *TF:* 800-848-2792 ■ *Web:* www.apwa.net	816-472-6100	472-1610	49-7
APX Enclosures Inc 200 Oregon St Mercersburg PA 17236 *Web:* www.apx-enclosures.com	717-328-9399		697
Apx Power Markets Inc 224 Airport Pkwy Ste 600 San Jose CA 95110 *Web:* www.apx.com	408-517-2100		225
AQ Pharmaceuticals Inc 11555 Monarch St Garden Grove CA 92841 *Web:* www.aqpharmaceuticals.com	714-903-1000		479
Aq Technologies 60 E Van Buren Chicago IL 60605 *TF:* 800-914-2259 ■ *Web:* www.aqtechnologies.com	312-867-5400		317
AQHA (American Quarter Horse Assn) 1600 Quarter Horse Dr Amarillo TX 79104 *TF:* 800-291-7323 ■ *Web:* www.aqha.com	806-376-4811	349-6411	48-3
AQL Decorating Company Inc 215 Bergen Blvd Fairview NJ 07022 *Web:* www.aqldecorating.com	201-941-1610		88
Aqs Management Systems Inc 2167 Northdale Blvd NW Coon Rapids MN 55433 *Web:* www.aqsperformance.com	651-633-7902		463
AQSP (American Qualex Scientific Products) 920-A Calle Negocio San Clemente CA 92673 *Web:* www.aqsp.com	949-492-8298		231
AQT Solutions Inc 860 Napa Valley Corporate Way Ste R Napa CA 94558 *Web:* www.aqtsolutions.com	707-265-7800		809
Aqtis 533 Rue Ontario E Montreal QC H2L1N8 *Web:* www.aqtis.qc.ca	514-844-2113		138
Aqua America Inc 762 W Lancaster Ave Bryn Mawr PA 19010 *NYSE: WTR* ■ *TF:* 877-987-2782 ■ *Web:* www.aquaamerica.com	877-987-2782		787
Aqua Bamboo 2425 Kuhio Ave Honolulu HI 96815 *TF:* 855-747-0754 ■ *Web:* www.aquaresorts.com	808-922-7777	943-8555	379
Aqua Bath Company Inc 921 Cherokee Ave Nashville TN 37207 *TF:* 800-232-2284 ■ *Web:* www.aquabath.com	615-227-0017		610
Aqua Blue 1564 Holcomb Bridge Rd Roswell GA 30076 *Web:* www.aquablueatl.com	770-643-8886		671
Aqua Cal Inc 2737 24th St N Saint Petersburg FL 33713 *TF:* 800-786-7751 ■ *Web:* www.aquacal.com	727-823-5642		14
Aqua Data Inc 95 Fifth Ave Pincourt QC J7W5K8 *TF:* 800-567-9003 ■ *Web:* www.aquadata.com	514-425-1010	425-3506	242
Aqua Finance Inc 1 Corporate Dr Ste 300 Wausau WI 54401 *Web:* www.aquafinance.com	715-848-5425		194
Aqua Hospitality Corp 445 Seaside Ave Honolulu HI 96815 *TF:* 855-747-0755 ■ *Web:* www.aquaresorts.com	808-923-2345	943-8555	379
Aqua Hotel & Lounge 1530 Collins Ave Miami Beach FL 33139 *Web:* www.aquamiami.com	305-538-4361		379
Aqua Hotels & Resorts Inc 1850 Ala Moana Blvd Honolulu HI 96815 *Web:* www.aquaresorts.com	808-943-9291		378
Aqua Pharmaceuticals LLC 158 W Gay St Ste 310 West Chester PA 19380 *Web:* www.aquapharm.com	610-644-7000		238
Aqua Rehab Inc 2145 rue Michelin Laval QC H7L5B8 *TF:* 800-661-3472 ■ *Web:* www.aquarehab.com	450-687-3472		242
Aqua Science Engineers Inc 55 Oak Ct Ste 220 Danville CA 94526	925-820-9391		261
AQUA TERRA Consultants Inc 2685 Marine Way Ste 1314 Mountain View CA 94043 *Web:* www.aquaterra.com	650-962-1864		256
Aqua Test Inc 28620 Maple Valley Black Diamond Rd SE Maple Valley WA 98038 *Web:* aquatestinc.com	425-432-9360		743
Aqua Waikiki Pearl Hotel 415 Nahua St Waikiki Beach HI 96815 *Web:* www.aquawaikikipearl.com	808-922-1616		378
Aqua Waikiki Wave 2299 Kuhio Ave Honolulu HI 96815 *TF:* 855-747-0754 ■ *Web:* www.aquaresorts.com	808-922-1262	943-8555	379
Aqua-Aerobic Systems Inc 6306 N Alpine Rd Loves Park IL 61111 *TF:* 800-940-5008 ■ *Web:* www.aqua-aerobic.com	815-654-2501	654-2508	806
AquaCap Inc 4 Hillman Dr Ste 190 Chadds Ford PA 19317	610-361-2800	361-6168	238
Aqua-Chem Inc 3001 E Governor John Sevier Hwy Knoxville TN 37914 *Web:* www.aqua-chem.com	865-544-2065		610
Aqua-Dyne Inc 3620 W 11th St Houston TX 77008 *TF:* 800-826-9274 ■ *Web:* www.aqua-dyne.com	713-864-6929	864-0313	641
Aquae Sulis Spa at the JW Marriott Resort Las Vegas 221 N Rampart Blvd Las Vegas NV 89144 *TF:* 877-869-8777 ■ *Web:* www.marriott.com	702-869-7807		707
Aquafine Corp 29010 Avenue Paine Valencia CA 91355 *Web:* www.aquafineuv.com	661-257-4770		427
Aquafor Beech Ltd 2600 Skymark Ave Bldg 6 Ste 202 Mississauga ON L4W5B2 *Web:* www.aquaforbeech.com	905-629-0099		261
Aquagrill Inc 210 Spring St New York NY 10012 *Web:* www.aquagrill.com	212-274-0505	274-0587	671
Aqua-Leisure Industries Inc PO Box 239 Avon MA 02322 *TF:* 866-807-3998 ■ *Web:* www.aqualeisure.com	866-807-3998		710
Aqualified LLC 525 Webb Industrial Dr Ste 211 Marietta GA 30062 *TF:* 800-585-4021 ■ *Web:* www.aqualified.com	800-585-4021		261
Aqualung America Inc 2340 Cousteau Ct Vista CA 92083 *TF:* 800-446-2671 ■ *Web:* www.aqualung.com	760-597-5000	597-4900	710
Aquantia Corp 105 E Tasman Dr San Jose CA 95134 *Web:* www.aquantia.com	408-228-8300		194

	Phone	Fax	Class
Aquarian Capital LLC 5345 Annabel Ln Plano TX 75093 *Web:* www.aquariancapital.com	469-361-2177		668
Aquarion Co 835 Main St Bridgeport CT 06604 *TF:* 800-732-9678 ■ *Web:* www.aquarion.com	203-336-7662		787
Aquarium Fish Magazine 3 Burroughs Irvine CA 92618	949-855-8822	855-3045	457-14
Aquarium of the Bay The Embarcadero at Beach St Pier 39 San Francisco CA 94133 *Web:* www.aquariumofthebay.org	415-623-5300	623-5324	40
Aquarium of the Pacific 100 Aquarium Way Long Beach CA 90802 *TF:* 800-481-3470 ■ *Web:* www.aquariumofpacific.org	562-590-3100		40
Aquarius Casino Resort 1900 S Casino Dr Laughlin NV 89029 *TF:* 888-662-5825 ■ *Web:* www.aquariuscasinoresort.com	702-298-5111		133
Aquarius Imaging LLC 3810 Inverrary Blvd Lauderhill FL 33319 *Web:* www.aquariusimaging.com	954-777-2729		177
Aquascape Environmental 605 Mauldin Dr Woodstock GA 30188 *TF:* 800-241-4113 ■ *Web:* www.aquascape.net	678-445-0077		196
Aquatec Inc 1235 Shappert Dr Machesney Park IL 61115 *Web:* www.aquatecinc.com	815-654-1500		358
Aquatech Consultancy Inc 1 Commercial Blvd Ste 201 Novato CA 94949 *Web:* www.noleak.com	415-884-2121		261
Aquaterra Spa at the Surf & Sand Resort 1555 S Coast Hwy Laguna Beach CA 92651 *TF:* 877-741-5908 ■ *Web:* www.surfandsandresort.com	949-376-2772		707
Aquaterra Technologies Inc PO Box 774 West Chester PA 19381 *TF:* 800-581-7204 ■ *Web:* aquaterra-tech.com	610-431-5733		196
Aquatherm Industries Inc 1940 Rutgers University Blvd Lakewood NJ 08701 **Fax Area Code: 732* ■ *TF:* 800-535-6307 ■ *Web:* www.warmwater.com	800-535-6307	905-9899*	357
Aquatic Development Group Inc 13 Green Mountain Dr Cohoes NY 12047 *Web:* www.aquaticgroup.com	518-783-0038		697
Aquatic Informatics Inc 570 Granville St Ste 1100 Vancouver BC V6C3P1 *TF:* 877-870-2782 ■ *Web:* aquaticinformatics.com	604-873-2782		146
Aquatrol Inc 237 N Euclid Way Ste H Anaheim CA 92801 *Web:* aquatrol.com	714-533-3381		237
Aquaveo LLC 3210 N Canyon Rd Ste 300 Provo UT 84604 *Web:* www.aquaveo.com	801-691-5528		256
Aquavit 65 E 55th St New York NY 10022 *Web:* www.aquavit.org	212-307-7311		671
Aqueduct Medical Inc 665 Third St Ste 20 San Francisco CA 94107 *TF:* 877-365-4325 ■ *Web:* www.aqueductmedical.com	877-365-4325		475
Aquent LLC 711 Boylston St Boston MA 02116 **Fax Area Code: 208* ■ *TF:* 855-767-6333 ■ *Web:* www.aquent.com	617-535-5000	429-6244*	721
Aqueos Corp 101 Millstone Rd Broussard LA 70518 *TF:* 800-999-5099 ■ *Web:* www.aqueossubsea.com	337-714-0033		539
Aqui Cal-Mex Grill 1145 Lincoln Ave San Jose CA 95125 *Web:* aquicalmex.com	408-995-0381		671
Aquila Commercial LLC 1717 W Sixth St Austin TX 78703 *Web:* www.aquilacommercial.com	512-684-3800		652
Aquila Drilling Co LP 2525 Kell Blvd Ste 405 Wichita Falls TX 76308 *TF:* 800-637-1278 ■ *Web:* aquiladrilling.com	940-761-3153		540
Aquila Group of Funds 380 Madison Ave Ste 2300 New York NY 10017 *TF:* 800-437-1020 ■ *Web:* www.aquilafunds.com	212-697-6666		528
Aquilent Inc 1100 W St Laurel MD 20707 *Web:* www.aquilent.com	301-939-1000		196
Aquinas & More Catholic Goods Inc 4727 N Academy Blvd Ste A Colorado Springs CO 80918 *Web:* www.aquinasandmore.com	719-495-7493		45
Aquinas College 4210 HaRding Rd Nashville TN 37205 *TF Admissions:* 800-649-9956 ■ *Web:* aquinascollege.edu	615-297-7545		166
Aquinas Institute of Theology 23 S Spring Ave Saint Louis MO 63108 *TF:* 800-977-3869 ■ *Web:* www.ai.edu	314-256-8800	256-8888	167-3
Aquinex Services Llc 991 US Hwy 22 Ste 200 Bridgewater NJ 08807 *Web:* aquinex.com	201-633-3208		206
Aquion Water Treatment Products LLC 101 S Gary Ave Roselle IL 60007 *Web:* aquion.com	847-437-9400	437-1594	806
Aquionics Inc 21 Kenton Lands Rd Erlanger KY 41018 *Web:* www.aquionics.com	859-341-0710		427
Aquitaine 569 Tremont St Boston MA 02118 *Web:* www.aquitaineboston.com	617-424-8577		671
AquiTec International 547 W Jackson Blvd 9th Fl Chicago IL 60661	312-264-1900	264-1991	178-1
Aqumin LLC 7676 Woodway Dr Ste 325 Houston TX 77063 *Web:* www.aqumin.com	713-781-2121		809
Aqwest 8276 Eagle Rd Larkspur CO 80118 *Web:* www.aqwest.com	303-681-0456		261
AR 160 Schoolhouse Rd Souderton PA 18964 **Fax Area Code: 866* ■ *TF:* 800-933-8181 ■ *Web:* www.arworld.us	215-723-8181	859-0582*	647
A-r Editions Inc 1600 Aspen Cmns Ste 100 Middleton WI 53562 *TF:* 800-736-0070 ■ *Web:* www.areditions.com	608-836-9000	831-8200	523
AR Medicom Inc 1200 55th Ave Lachine QC H8T3J8 *Web:* www.medicom.com	514-636-6262		475
A&R Partners Inc 201 Baldwin Ave San Mateo CA 94401 *Web:* www.arpartners.com	650-762-2800		636
AR Systems 297 E Harrison St Corona CA 92879 *Web:* www.autoretail.com	951-465-7700		180
AR Thomson Group 3420 189 St Surrey BC V3Z1A7 *Web:* www.arthomson.com	604-507-6050	507-6098	326
AR Wilfley & Sons Inc 7350 E Progress Pl Ste 200 Englewood CO 80111 *TF:* 800-525-9930 ■ *Web:* www.wilfley.com	303-779-1777	779-1277	641
ARA (American Rental Assn) 1900 19th St Moline IL 61265 *TF:* 800-334-2177 ■ *Web:* www.ararental.org	309-764-2475	764-1533	49-4

	Phone	Fax	Class
ARA (Agricultural Retailers Assn) 1156 15th St NW Ste 500 .... Washington DC 20005 *TF:* 800-535-6272 ■ *Web:* www.aradc.org	202-457-0825	457-0864	48-2
ARA (Awards and Personalization Assn) 8735 W Higgins Rd Ste 300 .... Chicago IL 60631 *TF:* 800-344-2148 ■ *Web:* awardspersonalization.org/default.aspx	847-375-4800	375-6480	49-4
ARA (Automotive Recyclers Assn) 9113 Church St Ste 20N .... Manassas VA 20110 *TF:* 888-385-1005 ■ *Web:* www.a-r-a.org	571-208-0428	208-0430	49-21
Arab American Institute (AAI) 1600 K St NW Ste 601 .... Washington DC 20006 *Web:* www.aaiusa.org	202-429-9210	429-9214	48-8
Arabel Inc 16301 NW 49th Ave .... Hialeah FL 33014 *TF Sales:* 800-759-5959 ■ *Web:* www.arabel.com	305-623-8302	624-0714	191-2
Arabia Steamboat Museum 400 Grand Blvd .... Kansas City MO 64106 *Web:* www.1856.com	816-471-1856		520
Arabian Horse Assn (AHA) 10805 E Bethany Dr .... Aurora CO 80014 *TF:* 800-458-4283 ■ *Web:* www.arabianhorses.org	303-696-4500	696-4599	48-3
Arabian Horse World Magazine 1316 Tamson Dr Ste 101 .... Cambria CA 93428 *TF:* 800-955-9423 ■ *Web:* arabianhorseworld.com	805-771-2300	927-6522	457-14
ArabMedicare.com PO Box 12547 .... Research Triangle Park NC 27709 *Web:* www.arabmedicare.com	919-781-5838		393
Arachne Web Technologies 3324 Alpine Dr .... Ann Arbor MI 48108 *Web:* www.arachneweb.com	734-975-8490		396
Arachnid Inc 6212 Material Ave .... Loves Park IL 61111 *TF:* 800-435-8319 ■ *Web:* www.bullshooter.com	815-654-0212	654-0447	322
Aradigm Corp 3929 Pt Eden Way .... Hayward CA 94545 *OTC: ARDM* ■ *Web:* www.aradigm.com	510-265-9000	265-0277	476
Aragon Elastomers LLC 740 S Pierce Ave .... Louisville CO 80027 *Web:* www.aragonelastomers.com	303-666-9519		601
Aragon Ventures Inc 1455 Adams Dr .... Menlo Park CA 94025	650-566-8000		401
Aram A. Kaz Co, The 365 Silas Deane Hwy .... Wethersfield CT 06109 *TF:* 800-969-2251 ■ *Web:* www.aramkaz.com	860-529-6900		393
ARAMARK Corp 1101 Market St .... Philadelphia PA 19107 *TF:* 800-388-3300 ■ *Web:* www.aramark.com	215-238-3000		185
ARAMARK Uniform & Career Apparel LLC 2860 Rudder Rd .... Memphis TN 38118 *TF:* 800-272-6275 ■ *Web:* www.aramarkuniform.com	800-272-6275		271
Aramco Services Co 9009 W Loop S .... Houston TX 77096 *Web:* www.aramcoservices.com	713-432-4000	432-4146	536
Aramsco Inc 1480 Grandview Ave .... Paulsboro NJ 08086 *TF:* 800-767-6933 ■ *Web:* www.aramsco.com	856-686-7700		146
Aranda Tooling Inc 15301 Springdale St .... Huntington Beach CA 92649 *Web:* www.arandatooling.com	714-379-6565	379-6570	488
Arandell Inc N 82 W 13118 Leon Rd .... Menomonee Falls WI 53051 *TF:* 800-558-8724 ■ *Web:* www.arandell.com	262-255-4400		627
Aransas County 301 N Live Oak St .... Rockport TX 78382 *Web:* www.aransascounty.org	361-790-0122	790-0119	338
Arapahoe Community College 5900 S Santa Fe Dr .... Littleton CO 80160 **Fax:* Admissions ■ *TF:* 888-800-9198 ■ *Web:* www.arapahoe.edu	303-797-0100	797-5970*	162
Arapahoe Philharmonic 5601 S Broadway Ste 345 .... Littleton CO 80121 *Web:* www.arapahoe-phil.org	303-781-1892		573-3
Ararat Rock Products Co 525 Quarry Rd .... Mount Airy NC 27030	336-786-4693		503-5
Arata Expositions Inc 15928 Tournament Dr .... Gaithersburg MD 20877 *Web:* www.arataexpo.com	301-921-0800		184
Arazoza Brothers Corp 15901 SW 242nd St .... Homestead FL 33031 *TF:* 800-238-1510 ■ *Web:* www.arazozabrothers.com	305-246-3223		293
ARB Inc 26000 Commercentre Dr .... Lake Forest CA 92630 *Web:* www.arbinc.com	949-598-9242		188-9
ARBA (American Rabbit Breeders Assn) PO Box 5667 .... Bloomington IL 61702 *TF:* 800-753-9448 ■ *Web:* www.arba.net	309-664-7500	664-0941	48-3
Arbco Industries Inc 2040 Borland Rd .... Export PA 15632 *Web:* www.arbcowheels.com	724-327-6300		596
Arbec Forest Products Inc 8770, Langelier Blvd Ste 216 .... Saint-leonard QC H1P3C6 *Web:* www.arbec.ca	514-327-3350		683
Arbella Insuranc 1100 Crown Colony Dr PO Box 699103 .... Quincy MA 02269 *TF:* 800-972-5348 ■ *Web:* www.arbella.com	617-328-2800	328-2970	391-4
Arben Group LLC 175 Marble Ave .... Pleasantville NY 10570 *Web:* arbengroup.com	914-741-5459	741-2923	189-14
Arbill PO Box 820542 .... Philadelphia PA 19154 *TF:* 800-523-5367 ■ *Web:* www.arbill.com	800-523-5367	426-5808	679
Arbitech LLC 15330 Barranca Pkwy .... Irvine CA 92618 *Web:* www.arbitech.com	949-376-6650		174
Arbitration Forums Inc 3350 Buschwood Pk Dr Ste 295 .... Tampa FL 33618 *TF Cust Svc:* 800-967-8889 ■ *Web:* www.arbfile.org	813-931-4004	931-4618	41
Arbitron Inc 9705 Patuxent Woods Dr .... Columbia MD 21046 *NYSE: ARB* ■ *TF:* 800-543-7300 ■ *Web:* www.arbitron.com	410-312-8000		466
Arbon Steel & Service Co Inc 2355 Bond St .... University Park IL 60484 *Web:* www.arbonsteel.com	708-534-6800	534-6826	492
Arbonne International 9400 Jeronimo Rd .... Irvine CA 92618 *Web:* arbonne.com	949-770-2610		76
Arbor Acres 1240 Arbor Rd .... Winston-Salem NC 27104 *TF:* 866-658-2724 ■ *Web:* www.arboracres.org	336-724-7921		672
Arbor Associates Inc 15 Court Sq Ste 1050 .... Boston MA 02108 *Web:* www.arbor-associates.com	617-227-8829		260
Arbor Brewing Co 114 E Washington St .... Ann Arbor MI 48104 *TF:* 800-685-0909 ■ *Web:* www.arborbrewing.com	734-213-1393		671

	Phone	Fax	Class
Arbor Capital Management Inc 1400 W Benson Blvd Ste 575 .... Anchorage AK 99503 *Web:* www.acminc.com	907-222-7581		401
Arbor Centers for Eyecare 2640 W 183rd St .... Homewood IL 60430 *TF:* 866-798-6633 ■ *Web:* www.arboreyecare.com	708-798-6633		237
Arbor Crest Wine Cellars 4705 N Fruithill Rd .... Spokane WA 99217 *Web:* www.arborcrest.com	509-927-9463	927-0574	50-7
Arbor Hospice & Home Care 2366 Oak Vly Dr .... Ann Arbor MI 48103 *TF:* 888-992-2273 ■ *Web:* www.arborhospice.org	734-662-5999	662-2330	371
Arbor House 300 Main St .... Lewiston ME 04240 *Web:* www.cmmc.org	207-795-0111		372
Arbor Lodge State Historical Park 2600 Arbor Ave .... Nebraska City NE 68410 *Web:* www.arbordayfarm.org/attractions/arbor-lodge.cfm	402-873-7222		565
Arbor Masters Tree & Landscape Inc 8250 Cole Pkwy .... Shawnee KS 66227 *Web:* www.arbormasters.com	913-441-8888		776
Arbor Partners LLC 130 S First St .... Ann Arbor MI 48104 *Web:* www.arborpartners.com	734-668-9000	669-4195	792
Arbor Press LLC 4303 Normandy Ct .... Royal Oak MI 48073 *Web:* www.arboroakland.com	248-549-0150		627
Arbor Realty Trust Inc 333 Earle Ovington Blvd Ste 900 .... Uniondale NY 11553 *NYSE: ABR* ■ *TF:* 877-952-7267 ■ *Web:* www.arbor.com	516-506-4200		654
Arbor Research & Trading LLC 1000 Hart Rd Ste 260 .... Barrington IL 60010 *Web:* www.arborresearch.com	847-304-1550		668
Arbor Rose Senior Care 6063 E Arbor Ave .... Mesa AZ 85206 *Web:* www.milestoneretirement.com	480-630-3647		793
Arbor Solutions Inc 1345 Monroe Ave NW Ste 309 .... Grand Rapids MI 49505 *Web:* www.arbsol.com	616-451-2500		196
Arbor Tree Surgery Inc 802 Paso Robles St .... Paso Robles CA 93446 *TF:* 800-247-8733 ■ *Web:* www.arbortree.com	805-239-1239		776
Arborcrest Gardens Inc 205 Evergreen Ln .... Boone NC 28607 *TF:* 800-488-0444 ■ *Web:* www.arborcrestgardens.org	828-265-4873		40
Arboretum & Botanic Garden 1156 High St .... Santa Cruz CA 95064 *Web:* arboretum.ucsc.edu	831-427-2998	427-1524	97
Arboretum at California State University Fresno 2351 E Barstow Ave .... Fresno CA 93740 *Web:* www.fresnostate.edu	559-278-7422	278-7698	97
Arboretum at Flagstaff 4001 S Woody Mtn Rd .... Flagstaff AZ 86001 *Web:* www.thearb.org	928-774-1442	774-1441	97
Arboretum at Penn State 336 Forest Resources Bldg .... University Park PA 16802 *Web:* www.arboretum.psu.edu	814-865-9118	865-3725	97
Arboretum at Penn State Behrend 4701 College Dr .... Erie PA 16563 *Web:* www.psbehrend.psu.edu	814-898-6160	898-6461	97
Arboretum of the Barnes Foundation 300 N Latch's Ln .... Merion PA 19066 *Web:* www.barnesfoundation.org	610-667-0290		97
Arboretum Ventures 303 Detroit St .... Ann Arbor MI 48104	734-998-3688	998-3689	792
Arboretum, The Arboretum Rd University of Guelph .... Guelph ON N1G2W1 *TF:* 877-674-1610 ■ *Web:* www.uoguelph.ca/arboretum	519-824-4120	763-9598	97
Arbors East Subacute 5500 E Broad St .... Columbus OH 43213 *Web:* arborseastskillednursing.com	614-575-9003		450
Arbors of Hop Brook 403 W Ctr St .... Manchester CT 06040 *Web:* www.arborsct.com	860-647-9343		672
Arborwell Inc 2337 American Ave .... Hayward CA 94545 *TF:* 800-800-3329 ■ *Web:* www.arborwell.com	510-881-4260		776
Arbutus Park Retirement Community 207 Ottawa St .... Johnstown PA 15904 *Web:* arbutusparkmanor.com	814-266-8621		672
Arbutus Software Inc 6450 Roberts St .... Burnaby BC V5G4E1 *TF:* 877-333-6336 ■ *Web:* www.arbutussoftware.com	604-437-7873		179
Arby's Restaurant Group Inc 1155 Perimeter Ctr W .... Atlanta GA 30338 *Web:* arbys.com	678-514-4100		670
ARC (Association Resource Ctr) 555 Capitol Mall Ste 755 PO Box 276567 .... Sacramento CA 95814 *Web:* www.4arc.com	916-932-2200	932-2209	47
ARC (American Recreation Coalition) 1225 New York Ave NW Ste 450 .... Washington DC 20005 *Web:* www.funoutdoors.com	202-682-9530	682-9529	48-23
ARC (American Radiolabeled Chemicals Inc) 101 ARC Dr .... Saint Louis MO 63146 *TF:* 800-331-6661 ■ *Web:* www.arc-inc.com	314-991-4545	991-4692	145
ARC (ARC Document Solutions) ARC 1981 N Broadway Ste 385 .... Walnut Creek CA 94596 *NYSE: ARC* ■ *Web:* www.e-arc.com	925-949-5100	949-5101	781
ARC (American Refugee Committee) 430 Oak Grove St Ste 204 .... Minneapolis MN 55403 *TF:* 800-875-7060 ■ *Web:* www.arcrelief.org	612-872-7060	607-6499	48-5
ARC 1981 N Broadway Ste 385 .... Walnut Creek CA 94596 *NYSE: ARC* ■ *Web:* www.e-arc.com	925-949-5100	949-5101	240
Arc Aspicio LLC 1725 I St NW Ste 300 .... Washington DC 20006 *Web:* www.arcaspicio.com	703-465-2060		196
ARC Automotive Inc 1729 Midpark Rd Ste D .... Knoxville TN 37921 *Web:* www.arcautomotive.com	865-583-7600		60
Arc Baltimore, The 7215 York Rd .... Baltimore MD 21212 *Web:* www.thearcbaltimore.org	410-296-2272		49-15
ARC Disposal & Recycling Company Inc 2101 S Busse Rd .... Mount Prospect IL 60056 *Web:* www.republicservices.com	847-981-0091		804
ARC Document Solutions (ARC) ARC 1981 N Broadway Ste 385 .... Walnut Creek CA 94596 *NYSE: ARC* ■ *Web:* www.e-arc.com	925-949-5100	949-5101	781

				Phone	Fax	Class
ARC Document Solutions 6300 Gulfton St *Web:* www.e-arc.com	Houston	TX	77081	713-782-8580		781
ARC Global Document Management 1431 NW 17th Ave *Web:* www.e-arc.com	Portland	OR	97209	503-227-3424	223-4254	240
Arc Human Services Inc 201 S Johnson Rd *TF:* 800-328-6481 ■ *Web:* www.aadvantageinc.org	Houston	PA	15342	724-745-3010		793
ARC Industries Inc 2879 Johnstown Rd **Fax Area Code: 614* ■ *TF:* 800-734-7007 ■ *Web:* www.arcind.com	Columbus	OH	43219	800-734-7007	342-5680*	721
Arc Machines Inc 10500 Orbital Way *Web:* www.arcmachines.com	Pacoima	CA	91331	818-896-9556	890-3724	811
ARC Medical Devices Inc 8-3071 No 5 Rd *Web:* arcmedicaldevices.com	Richmond	BC	V6X2T4	604-222-9577		794
Arc of Stanly County, The 350 Pee Dee Ave Ste A *TF:* 800-230-7525 ■ *Web:* www.monarchnc.org	Albemarle	NC	28001	704-986-1500		49-15
Arc of the US 1010 Wayne Ave Ste 650 *TF:* 800-433-5255 ■ *Web:* www.thearc.org	Silver Spring	MD	20910	301-565-3842	565-3843	48-17
ARC Pressure Data Inc 3718 Warschun Rd *Web:* www.arcpressure.com	Aubrey	TX	76277	940-565-8090		539
ARC Properties Inc 1401 Broad St *Web:* www.arcproperties.com	Clifton	NJ	07013	973-249-1000	249-1001	655
ARC Resources Ltd 308 Fourth Ave SW Ste 1200 *TSE: ARX* ■ *TF:* 888-272-4900 ■ *Web:* www.arcresources.com	Calgary	AB	T2P0H7	403-503-8600		675
Arc San Joaquin Inc 41 W Yokuts Ave *TF:* 800-847-3030 ■ *Web:* www.arc-sj.org	Stockton	CA	95207	209-955-1625		260
Arc Tech Inc 14100 Park Meadow Dr *Web:* www.arctech.com	Chantilly	VA	20151	703-222-0820		268
Arc Technologies 185 Vallecitos De Oro *Web:* www.arc-tech.com	San Marcos	CA	92069	760-744-7400		454
ARC Technology Solutions LLC 165 Ledge St Ste 4 *Web:* www.arcserv.com	Nashua	NH	03060	603-883-3027		295
ARC the Hotel Ottawa 140 Slater St *TF:* 800-699-2516 ■ *Web:* www.arcthehotel.com	Ottawa	ON	K1P5H6	613-238-2888	235-8421	379
Arc Worldwide 35 W Wacker Dr *Web:* www.arcww.com	Chicago	IL	60601	312-220-5959	220-6212	7
Arca Biopharma Inc 11080 CirPoint Rd Ste 140 *NASDAQ: ABIO* ■ *Web:* arcabio.com	Westminister	CO	80020	720-940-2100	208-9261	668
Arcade Partners LLC 62 La Salle Rd Ste 304 *Web:* www.arcadepartners.com	West Hartford	CT	06107	860-236-6320		401
Arcadia 100 W San Carlos St *Web:* michaelmina.net	San Jose	CA	95113	408-278-4555		671
Arcadia Assn of Realtors Inc 601 S First Ave *Web:* theaar.com	Arcadia	CA	91006	626-446-2115		652
Arcadia Biosciences Inc 202 Cousteau Pl Ste 200 *Web:* www.arcadiabio.com	Davis	CA	95618	530-756-7077		743
Arcadia Chamber of Commerce 388 W Huntington Dr *TF:* 800-838-3006 ■ *Web:* arcadiacachamber.org	Arcadia	CA	91007	626-447-2159	445-0273	139
Arcadia Content 6454 Quinpool Rd Ste 301 *Web:* arcadiacontent.com	Halifax	NS	B3L1A9	902-446-3414		514
Arcadia Convalescent Hospital Inc 1601 S Baldwin Ave *Web:* www.arcadiahealthcarecenter.com	Arcadia	CA	91007	626-445-2170		371
Arcadia Data Inc 999 Baker way Ste 220 *Web:* www.arcadiadata.com	San Manteo	CA	94404	408-340-5919		396
Arcadia Farms Cafe 7014 E First Ave *Web:* arcadiafarmscafe.com	Scottsdale	AZ	85251	480-941-5665		671
Arcadia Mfg Group Inc 80 Cohoes Ave *Web:* www.arcadiamfg.com	Green Island	NY	12183	518-434-6213		480
Arcadia Resources Inc 9320 Priority Way W Dr *Web:* www.arcadiaresourcesinc.com	Indianapolis	IN	46240	317-569-8234		260
Arcadia Retirement Residence 1434 Punahou St *Web:* arcadia.org/companies/arcadia	Honolulu	HI	96822	808-941-0941	949-4965	672
Arcadia Solutions LLC 20 Blanchard Rd Unit 10 *Web:* www.arcadiasolutions.com	Burlington	MA	01803	781-202-3600		196
Arcadia University 450 S Easton Rd **Fax: Admissions* ■ *TF:* 877-272-2342 ■ *Web:* www.arcadia.edu	Glenside	PA	19038	215-572-2900	881-8767*	166
Arcadis 630 Plaza Dr Ste 200 *Web:* www.arcadis.com//en/united-states/cookie-wall	Highlands Ranch	CO	80129	720-344-3500		192
Arcady Bay Partners LLC 40417 Aldie Springs Dr *Web:* www.arcadybay.com	Aldie	VA	20105	703-359-4773		691
Arcamed LLC 5101 Decatur Blvd Ste A *Web:* www.arcamed.com	Indianapolis	IN	46241	317-910-1822	375-7717	475
Arcane Technologies Inc 918 Monticello Ave *Web:* www.arcanetech.com	Charlottesville	VA	22902	434-979-7979		180
Arcata Associates Inc 2588 Fire Mesa St *Web:* www.arcataassoc.com	Las Vegas	NV	89128	702-642-9500	968-2237	261
ArcBest (ABC) 3801 Old Greenwood Rd *NASDAQ: ARCB* ■ **Fax Area Code: 479* ■ *TF:* 800-610-5544 ■ *Web:* arcb.com	Fort Smith	AR	72903	800-610-5544	785-6124*	780
Arcca Inc 2288 Second St Pk *Web:* www.arcca.com	Penns Park	PA	18943	215-598-9750		256
ArcelorMittal Burns Harbor LLC 250 W US Hwy 12 *TF:* 800-621-4366 ■ *Web:* www.arcelormittal.com	Burns Harbor	IN	46304	219-787-2120		492
Arcestra Inc 197 Spadina Ave Ste 200 *Web:* www.arcestra.com	Toronto	ON	M5T2C8	416-596-9561		387
Arcet Equipment Company Inc 1700 Chamberlayne Ave *TF:* 800-388-0302 ■ *Web:* arc3gases.com	Richmond	VA	23222	800-388-0302		201
Arch Chemicals Inc 1200 Old Lower River Rd PO Box 800 *NYSE: ARJ* ■ *TF:* 800-638-8174 ■ *Web:* lonza.com	Charleston	TN	37310	423-780-2724	780-2330	145
Arch Communications Inc 1327 Hampton Ave *Web:* archcom.net	St. Louis	MO	63139	314-645-8000		393
Arch Crown Tags Inc 460 Hillside Ave *TF:* 800-526-8353 ■ *Web:* www.archcrown.com	Hillside	NJ	07205	973-731-6300	731-2228	413
Arch Framing & Design Inc 7844 Manchester Rd Ste *Web:* www.archframing.com	Saint Louis	MO	63143	314-447-3300		45
Arch Insurance Group Inc 1 Liberty Plaza 53rd Fl *TF:* 866-993-9978 ■ *Web:* www.archcapgroup.com	New York	NY	10006	212-651-6500		391-2
Arch Language Network Inc 1885 University Ave W Ste 75 *TF:* 800-835-6870 ■ *Web:* www.archlanguage.com	Saint Paul	MN	55104	651-789-7897		768
Arch Street Meeting House 320 Arch St *Web:* www.archstreetfriends.org	Philadelphia	PA	19106	215-413-1804		50-1
ARCH Venture Partners 8755 W Higgins Rd Ste 1025 *Web:* www.archventure.com	Chicago	IL	60631	773-380-6600	380-6606	792
Archadeck 2924 Emerywood Pkwy Ste 101 *TF:* 800-722-4668 ■ *Web:* www.archadeck.com	Richmond	VA	23294	804-353-6999		189-2
Archaeological Institute of America (AIA) 44 Beacon St *TF:* 877-524-6300 ■ *Web:* www.archaeological.org	Boston	MA	02108	617-353-9361	353-6550	48-11
Archaeology Magazine 36-36 33rd St *TF:* 877-275-9782 ■ *Web:* www.archaeology.org	Long Island	NY	11106	718-472-3050	472-3051	457-19
Archangel Systems Inc 1635 Pumphrey Ave *Web:* www.archangel.com	Auburn	AL	36832	334-826-8008		529
Arch-Con Corp 1335 W Gray Ste 300 *Web:* www.arch-con.com	Houston	TX	77019	713-533-1900		186
Archdale-Trinity Chamber of Commerce 213 Balfour Dr *TF:* 800-626-2672 ■ *Web:* www.archdaletrinitychamber.com	Archdale	NC	27263	336-434-2073	431-5845	139
Archdiocese of Louisville 212 E College St *Web:* www.archlou.org	Louisville	KY	40203	502-585-3291		48-20
Archdiocese of Newark 171 Clifton Ave *Web:* www.rcan.org	Newark	NJ	07104	973-497-4126		48-20
Archdiocese of Philadelphia 222 N 17th St *Web:* archphila.org	Philadelphia	PA	19103	215-965-4636		48-20
Archdiocese of Portland in Oregon 2838 E Burnside St *Web:* www.archdpdx.org	Portland	OR	97214	503-234-5334		48-20
Archdiocese of Saint Paul & Minneapolis 226 Summit Ave *TF:* 877-290-1605 ■ *Web:* www.archspm.org	Saint Paul	MN	55102	651-291-4411		48-20
Archdiocese of San Francisco 1 Peter Yorke Way *Web:* www.sfarchdiocese.org	San Francisco	CA	94109	415-614-5500		48-20
Archer Advanced Rubber Components Inc 2860 Lowery St *Web:* www.archerseal.com	Winston-Salem	NC	27101	336-996-7776		326
Archer Communications Inc 252 Alexander St *TF:* 800-398-3029 ■ *Web:* www.archercom.com	Rochester	NY	14607	585-461-1570		7
Archer Daniels Midland Co (ADM) 4666 E Faries Pkwy *NYSE: ADM* ■ *TF:* 800-637-5843 ■ *Web:* www.adm.com	Decatur	IL	62526	217-424-5200		185
Archer Daniels Midland Co 5550 Maplewood Dr *Web:* adm.com	Windsor	ON	N9C0B9	519-972-8100	972-2337	297-8
Archer Daniels Midland Company 77 W Wacker Dr *TF:* 800-637-5843 ■ *Web:* www.adm.com	Chicago	IL	60601	217-424-5200		296-8
Archer Group, The 600 N King St Ste 600 *Web:* www.archer-group.com	Wilmington	DE	19801	302-429-9120		7
Archer Screw Products Inc 11341 Melrose Ave *TF:* 800-952-7897 ■ *Web:* www.archerscrew.com	Franklin Park	IL	60131	847-451-1150		454
Archer Wire International Corp 7300 S Narragansett Ave *Web:* www.archerwire.com	Bedford Park	IL	60638	708-563-1700	563-1740	73
Archer/Malmo Adv Inc 65 Union Ave Ste 500 *Web:* www.archermalmo.com	Memphis	TN	38103	901-523-2000		4
Archi's Thai Kitchen 6360 W Flamingo Rd *Web:* archithai.com	Las Vegas	NV	89103	702-880-5550		671
Archibald Bush Foundation 332 Minnesota St Ste E-900 *Web:* www.bushfoundation.org	Saint Paul	MN	55101	651-227-0891	297-6485	305
Archibald Gray & McKay Ltd 3514 White Oak Rd *TF:* 800-336-9708 ■ *Web:* www.agm.on.ca	London	ON	N6E2Z9	519-685-5300		256
Archibus Inc 18 Tremont St *Web:* www.archibus.com	Boston	MA	02108	617-227-2508	227-2509	177
Archie Comic Publications Inc 325 Fayette Ave *Web:* www.archiecomics.com	Mamaroneck	NY	10543	914-381-5155	381-4015	637-5
Archie McPhee & Co 10915 47th Ave W *Web:* mcphee.com	Mukilteo	WA	98275	425-349-3009		195
Archie Moore's Bar & Restaurant 188 1/2 Willow St *Web:* www.archiemoores.com	New Haven	CT	06511	203-773-9870		671
Archimede Gruden USA Inc 51 Newark St Ste 302	Hoboken	NJ	07030	201-798-0222		194
ArchiPAC 1735 New York Ave NW *Web:* www.aia.org	Washington	DC	20006	202-626-7300	626-7547	615

Name / Address	City	State	ZIP	Phone	Fax	Class
Archipelago Holdings LLC						
100 S Wacker Dr Ste 1800	Chicago	IL	60606	312-960-1696		252
Archi-Tech Systems Inc						
275 Phillips Blvd Ste 140	Ewing	NJ	08618	609-882-2447		224
TF: 800-235-4471 ■ *Web:* www.archi-tech.com						
Architectual Engineering Consultants Inc						
40801 Hwy 6 24 Ste 214	Avon	CO	81620	970-748-8520		256
Web: www.aec-vail.com						
Architectural & Transportation Barriers Compliance Board						
1331 F St NW Ste 1000	Washington	DC	20004	202-272-0080	272-0081	340-20
TF: 800-872-2253 ■ *Web:* www.access-board.gov						
Architectural Brass Co						
1130 Donald Lee Hollowell Pkwy NW	Atlanta	GA	30318	404-351-0594		295
Web: www.architecturalbrass.com						
Architectural Bronze Aluminum Corp						
655 Deerfield Rd Ste 100	Deerfield	IL	60015	800-339-6581	266-7301*	777
**Fax Area Code: 847* ■ *TF:* 800-339-6581 ■ *Web:* www.architecturalbronze.com						
Architectural Builders Hardware Manufacturing						
1222 Ardmore Ave Apt W	Itasca	IL	60143	630-875-9900		350
TF: 800-932-9224 ■ *Web:* www.abhmfg.com						
Architectural Building Supply Co						
2965 S Main St	Salt Lake City	UT	84115	801-486-3481		350
Web: www.absdoors.com						
Architectural Ceramics Inc						
800 E Gude Dr Ste F	Rockville	MD	20850	301-762-4140		191-1
Web: www.architecturalceramics.net						
Architectural Digest						
1 World Trade Ctr	New York	NY	10007	800-365-8032		457-2
TF: 800-365-8032 ■ *Web:* www.architecturaldigest.com						
Architectural Floor Systems Inc						
595 Supreme Dr	Bensenville	IL	60106	877-437-3567		131
TF: 877-437-3567 ■ *Web:* www.gerflorusa.com						
Architectural Polymers						
1220 Little Gap Rd	Palmerton	PA	18071	610-824-3322		590
Web: www.architecturalpolymers.com						
Architectural Precast Assn (APA)						
6710 Winkler Rd Ste 8	Fort Myers	FL	33919	239-454-6989	454-6787	49-3
Web: www.archprecast.org						
Architectural Record Magazine						
350 Fifth Ave Ste 6000	New York	NY	10118	646-849-7100	849-7148	457-2
Web: www.architecturalrecord.com						
Architectural Surfaces Inc						
5801 Midway Park NE	Albuquerque	NM	87109	505-889-0124		290
Web: www.architectstudio.com						
Architectural Woodwork Institute (AWI)						
46179 Westlake Dr Ste 120	Potomac Falls	VA	20165	571-323-3636	323-3630	49-3
Web: www.awinet.org						
Architecture Technology Corp (ATC)						
9971 Vly View Rd	Eden Prairie	MN	55344	952-829-5864		178-1
Web: www.atcorp.com						
Architecture Technology Corp						
9971 Valley View Rd Ste 500	Eden Prairie	MN	55344	607-257-1975		180
Web: www.atc-nycorp.com						
Architelos Inc						
43622 Merchant Mill Terr	Leesburg	VA	20176	310-418-7162		387
Architex International						
3333 Commercial Ave	Northbrook	IL	60062	847-205-1333		361
TF: 800-621-0827 ■ *Web:* www.architex-ljh.com						
Architrave Interiors Inc						
1337 Ocean Ave Ste D	Santa Monica	CA	90401	310-395-5657		393
Web: architraveinteriors.com						
Archive-cd LLC 910 Beverly Way	Jacksonville	OR	97530	541-899-5704		177
TF: 800-323-1868 ■ *Web:* www.archive-cd.com						
Archives of American Art						
750 Ninth St NW Ste 2200	Washington	DC	20001	202-633-7940		48-4
Web: www.aaa.si.edu						
Archmill House Inc 1276 Osprey Dr	Ancaster	ON	L9G4V5	905-648-7330		7
Web: www.archmillhouse.com						
Archon Group LP 6011 Connection Dr	Irving	TX	75039	972-368-2200		345
Archonix Systems LLC						
30 Lake Ctr Executive Park 401 Rt 73 N Ste 105	Marlton	NJ	08053	856-787-0020		177
TF: 800-862-2627 ■ *Web:* www.archonixsystems.com						
Archrival Inc 720 O St	Lincoln	NE	68508	402-435-2525		7
TF: 800-410-5205 ■ *Web:* www.archrival.com						
Archstone-Smith Trust						
9200 E Panorama Cir Ste 400	Englewood	CO	80112	303-708-5959	708-5999	655
Archway Marketing Services Inc						
19850 S Diamond Lake Rd	Rogers	MN	55374	763-428-3300		463
TF: 866-779-9855 ■ *Web:* www.archway.com						
Archway Programs Inc PO Box 668	Atco	NJ	08004	856-767-5757		685
Web: www.archwayprograms.org						
Archway Systems Inc						
2134 Main St Ste 160	Huntington Beach	CA	92648	714-374-0440		177
Web: www.archwaysystems.com						
ARCI (Association of Racing Commissioners International)						
1510 Newtown Pike # 210	Lexington	KY	40511	859-224-7070		49-7
TF: 800-532-0383 ■ *Web:* www.arci.com						
Arclyte Technologies Inc						
953 S Meridian	Alhambra	CA	91803	626-281-2220		196
Web: arclyte.com						
ARCO Coffee Co 2206 Winter St	Superior	WI	54880	715-392-4771	392-4776	296-7
TF: 800-283-2726 ■ *Web:* www.arcocoffee.com						
Arco Electric Products Corp						
2325 E Michigan Rd	Shelbyville	IN	46176	317-398-9713	398-2655	518
TF: 800-428-4370 ■ *Web:* www.arco-electric.com						
Arco Ideas & Design Inc						
212 N Tennessee St	Cartersville	GA	30120	770-386-2799		711
Web: www.arcoideas.com						
Arco Products Co						
4661 W Saluson Ave	Los Angeles	CA	90043	213-670-5136		580
Web: arco.com						
Arcobasso Foods Inc						
8850 Pershall Rd	Hazelwood	MO	63042	314-381-8083		297-8
Web: www.arcobasso.com						
Arcodoro 5000 Westheimer Rd Ste 120	Houston	TX	77056	713-621-6888		671
Web: www.arcodoro.com						

Name / Address	City	State	ZIP	Phone	Fax	Class
Arcodoro & Pomodoro						
5000 Westheimer Ste 120	Houston	TX	77056	713-621-6888		671
Web: www.arcodoro.com						
Arcomm Communications Corp						
462 W Main St 3	Hillsboro	NH	03244	603-464-4600		175
Web: arcomm1.com						
ARCON Corp 260 Bear Hill Rd Ste 200	Waltham	MA	02451	781-890-3330		225
Web: www.arcon.com						
Arcos Industries 1 Arcos Dr	Mount Carmel	PA	17851	570-339-5200	339-5206	811
TF: 800-233-8460 ■ *Web:* www.arcos.us						
ARC-PA (Accreditation Review Commission on Education for the Physician Assistant Inc)						
12000 Findley Rd Ste 240	Duluth	GA	30097	770-476-1224	476-1738	48-1
Web: www.arc-pa.org						
Arcsine Engineering 950 Executive Way	Redding	CA	96002	530-222-7204		261
Web: www.arc-sine.com						
Arcsoft Inc 46601 Fremont Blvd	Fremont	CA	94538	510-440-9901		180
Web: arcsoft.com						
Arctern Inc 10332 Main St Ste 150	Fairfax	VA	22030	703-738-6669		260
Web: www.arctern.com						
Arctic Cat Inc						
601 Brooks Ave S	Thief River Falls	MN	56701	218-681-8558		705
NASDAQ: ACAT ■ *Web:* www.arcticcat.com						
Arctic Cir Restaurants Inc PO Box 339	Midvale	UT	84047	801-561-3620		670
Web: www.acburger.com						
Arctic Combustion Ltd						
2283 Argentia Rd Unit 25	Mississauga	ON	L5N5Z2	905-858-4604		612
TF: 800-462-9058 ■ *Web:* www.arctic-combustion.com						
Arctic Ease 200 Shell Ln Ste 204	Phoenixville	PA	19460	484-924-9186		238
Web: www.arcticease.com						
Arctic Engineering Company Inc						
8410 Minnesota St	Merrillville	IN	46410	219-947-4999		261
Web: arcticengineering.com						
Arctic Glacier Holdings Inc						
625 Henry Ave	Winnipeg	MB	R3A0V1	204-772-2473		578
TF: 888-573-9237 ■ *Web:* www.arcticglacier.com						
Arctic Glacier USA Inc						
1654 Marthaler Ln	West Saint Paul	MN	55118	651-455-0410		380
Arctic Hunter Energy Inc						
1610 675 W Hastings St	Vancouver	BC	V6B1N2	604-681-3131		536
Web: www.arctichunter.com						
Arctic Industries Inc 9731 NW 114th Way	Miami	FL	33178	305-883-5581	883-4651	14
TF: 800-325-0123 ■ *Web:* arcticwalkins.com						
Arctic Information Technology Inc						
3500 Eide St Ste 300	Anchorage	AK	99503	907-261-9500		317
Web: www.arcticit.com						
Arctic Research Consortium of the US (ARCUS)						
3535 College Rd Ste 101	Fairbanks	AK	99709	907-474-1600	474-1604	668
Web: www.arcus.org						
Arctic Slope Regional Corp						
1230 Agvik St PO Box 129	Barrow	AK	99723	907-852-8633	852-5733	538
TF: 800-770-2772 ■ *Web:* www.asrc.com						
Arctic Star Refrigeration Mfg Company Inc						
3540 W Pioneer Pkwy	Arlington	TX	76013	817-274-1396	277-4828	664
TF: 800-229-6562 ■ *Web:* www.arcticstar.com						
Arctic Storm Management Group LLC						
2727 Alaskan Way Pier 69	Seattle	WA	98121	206-547-6557	547-3165	285
TF: 800-929-0908 ■ *Web:* www.arcticstorm.com						
Arctic Wolf Networks Inc						
440 Wolfe Rd Mail Stop 147	Sunnyvale	CA	94085	888-272-8429		196
TF: 888-272-8429 ■ *Web:* arcticwolf.com						
ArcticDx Inc						
MaRS Centre S Tower 101 College St Ste 200	Toronto	ON	M5G1L7	866-964-5182		416
TF: 866-964-5182 ■ *Web:* www.arcticdx.com						
Arc-tronics Inc						
1150 Pagni Dr	Elk Grove Village	IL	60007	847-437-0211	437-0181	625
Web: www.arc-tronics.com						
Arcturus Advisors						
1643 Plantation Oaks Ln	Fernandina Beach	FL	32034	866-593-2207		41
TF: 866-593-2207 ■ *Web:* www.arcturusadvisors.com						
ARCUS (Arctic Research Consortium of the US)						
3535 College Rd Ste 101	Fairbanks	AK	99709	907-474-1600	474-1604	668
Web: www.arcus.org						
Arcus Capital Partners LLC						
3060 Peachtree Rd NW Ste 1880	Atlanta	GA	30305	404-949-2111		251
TF: 800-388-2855 ■ *Web:* www.arcuscp.com						
Arcus Foundation 402 E Michigan Ave	Kalamazoo	MI	49007	269-373-4373		303
Web: www.arcusfoundation.org						
Arcus LLC 8170 Adams Dr	Hummelstown	PA	17036	717-703-3200		193
ARCVB (Alton Regional Convention & Visitors Bureau)						
200 Piasa St	Alton	IL	62002	618-465-6676	465-6151	206
TF: 800-258-6645 ■ *Web:* www.visitalton.com						
Arcways Inc 1076 Ehlers Rd	Neenah	WI	54956	920-725-2667		499
Web: www.arcways.com						
Arcweb Technologies LLC						
234 Market St 5th Fl	Philadelphia	PA	19106	800-846-7980		463
TF: 800-846-7980 ■ *Web:* arcweb.co						
Ard Group Inc 116 John St Apt 602	New York	NY	10038	212-571-1111		193
Web: www.ardcareers.com						
ARD Inc 159 Bank St Ste 300	Burlington	VT	05401	802-658-5050		463
ARDA (American Resort Development Assn)						
1201 15th St NW Ste 400	Washington	DC	20005	202-371-6700	289-8544	49-17
Web: www.arda.org						
Ardea Biosciences Inc						
4939 Directors Pl	San Diego	CA	92121	858-652-6500	625-0760	85
TF: 800-735-9277 ■ *Web:* ardeabio.com						
ARDEC (US Army Armament Research Development & Engineering Ctr)						
Technical & Industrial Liaison Officer	Picatinny	NJ	07806	973-724-9623	328-2996	668
Web: www.pica.army.mil						
Ardelyx Inc 34175 Ardenwood Blvd	Fremont	CA	94555	510-745-1700		231
Web: www.ardelyx.com						
Arden Asset Management LLC						
375 Park Ave 32nd Fl	New York	NY	10152	212-751-5252		401
Web: www.ardenglobalfunds.com						
Arden Cos						
30400 Telegraph Rd Ste 200	Bingham Farms	MI	48025	248-415-8500	415-8520	746
TF: 800-876-7336 ■ *Web:* www.ardencompanies.com						
Arden Engineering Constructors LLC						
505 Narragansett Pk Dr	Pawtucket	RI	02861	401-727-3500	727-3540	189-10
TF: 800-991-2998 ■ *Web:* www.ardeneng.com						

	Phone	Fax	Class
Arden Engineering Inc 1878 N Main St. Orange CA 92865 Web: www.cadenceaerospace.com	714-998-6410		22
Arden Group Inc 2020 S Central Ave. Compton CA 90220 NASDAQ: ARDNA	310-638-2842		360-3
Arden Jewelry Manufacturing Co 10 Industrial Ln Johnston RI 02919 Web: www.ardenjewelry.com	401-274-9800		408
Arden Realty Inc 11601 Wilshire Blvd 4th Fl. Los Angeles CA 90025	310-966-2600	966-2699	655
Arden Theatre Co 40 N Second St Philadelphia PA 19106 Web: www.ardentheatre.org	215-922-8900	922-7011	749
Ardent Health Services 1 Burton Hills Blvd Ste 250 Nashville TN 37215 Web: www.ardenthealth.com	615-296-3000		353
Ardent Media Inc 522 E 82nd St New York NY 10028	212-861-1501		94
Ardent Sound Inc 33 S Sycamore St. Mesa AZ 85202 Web: www.ardentsound.com	480-649-1806		194
Ardenwood Historic Farm 34600 Ardenwood Blvd Fremont CA 94555 TF: 888-327-2757 ■ Web: www.ebparks.org	510-544-2797	796-0231	520
Ardeo 3311 Connecticut Ave NW Washington DC 20008 Web: www.ardeobardeo.com	202-244-6750		671
ARDEX Inc 400 Ardex Park Dr. Aliquippa PA 15001 Web: www.ardex.com	724-203-5000		183
Ardham Technologies Inc 5411 Jefferson St NE Ste 200 Albuquerque NM 87109 TF: 800-877-7868 ■ Web: www.ardham.com	505-872-9040		180
Ardica Technologies Inc 2325 Third St Ste 424 San Francisco CA 94107 Web: www.ardica.com	415-568-9270		253
ARDL Inc 400 Aviation Dr Mount Vernon IL 62864 Web: www.ardlinc.com	618-244-3235		256
Ardmore Associates LLC 33 N Dearborn St Ste 1720 Chicago IL 60602 Web: www.ardmoreassociates.com	312-795-1400		261
Ardmore Banking Advisors 44 E Lancaster Ave Second Fl PO Box 533 Ardmore PA 19003 Web: www.ardmoreadvisors.com	610-649-4643	649-2217	194
Ardmore Farms Inc 1915 N Woodland Blvd DeLand FL 32724 TF: 800-557-0220 ■ Web: www.juice4u.com	330-753-2293	848-4287	296-20
Ardmore Telephone Company Inc 30190 Ardmore Ave Ardmore AL 35739 Web: www.ardmore.net	256-423-2131		387
ARDMS (American Registry of Diagnostic Medical Sonographers) 1401 Rockville Pike Ste 600 Rockville MD 20852 TF: 800-541-9754 ■ Web: www.ardms.org	301-738-8401	738-0312	49-8
Ardour Capital Investments LLC 26 BRdway Ste 1107 New York City NY 10004 Web: www.ardourcapital.com	212-375-2950		690
Ards Trucking Company Inc 4190 Alligator Rd Timmonsville SC 29161 TF: 877-273-7297 ■ Web: www.ardtrucking.com	843-393-5101		780
Ardsley Musical Instrument Service Ltd 219 Sprain Rd. Scarsdale NY 10583 Web: www.ardsleymusic.com	914-693-6639		526
Ardus Medical Inc 11297 Grooms Rd Cincinnati OH 45242 Web: www.ardusmedical.com	513-469-7867	469-2329	475
ARE (Association for Research & Enlightenment) 215 67th St. Virginia Beach VA 23451 TF: 800-333-4499 ■ Web: www.edgarcayce.org	757-428-3588	422-6921	48-17
ARE (Association for Retail Environment) 4651 Sheridan St Ste 470 Hollywood FL 33021 Web: www.retailenvironments.org	954-893-7300	893-7500	49-3
Area 51 Esg Inc 51 Post Irvine CA 92618 TF: 877-476-8751 ■ Web: www.area51esg.com	949-387-0051		246
Area Agency On Aging 9549 Koger Blvd Gadsden Bldg Ste 100 St Petersburg FL 33702 TF: 800-963-5337 ■ Web: www.agingcarefl.org	727-570-9696	234-4401	450
Area Agency On Aging 10b Inc 1550 Corporate Woods Pkwy Uniontown OH 44685 TF: 800-421-7277 ■ Web: www.directionhomeakroncanton.org	330-896-9172	896-6644	450
Area Circulation Inc 5656 Shell Rd. Virginia Beach VA 23455	757-499-8330		463
Area Development Magazine 400 Post Ave Ste 304 Westbury NY 11590 TF: 800-735-2732 ■ Web: www.areadevelopment.com	516-338-0900	338-0100	457-5
Area Development Partnership 1 Convention Ctr Plaza Hattiesburg MS 39401 TF: 800-238-4288 ■ Web: www.theadp.com	601-296-7500	296-7505	139
Area Erectors Inc 2323 Harrison Ave. Rockford IL 61104 TF: 800-270-2732 ■ Web: www.areaerectors.com	815-398-6700	398-6787	189-14
Area Mental Health Ctr 531 Campusview Garden City KS 67846 TF: 800-279-3645 ■ Web: compassbh.org	620-276-7689		726
Area Metropolitan Ambulance Authority 551 E Berry St. Fort Worth TX 76110 Web: www.medstar911.org	817-923-3700		30
Area Temps Inc 1228 Euclid Ave. Cleveland OH 44115 TF: 866-995-5627 ■ Web: www.areatemps.com	440-646-1333		721
Area Trade Bindery Co 157 W Providencia Ave. Burbank CA 91502	818-846-6041		92
Area Wide Communication 3850 Broadway St. Portsmouth VA 23703 TF: 800-299-7293 ■ Web: areawidecomm.com	757-638-3327		196
Area Wide Technologies Inc 2110 Clearlake Blvd Ste 100. Champaign IL 61822 Web: areawidetech.com	217-359-8041		180
Areacall Inc 7803 Stratford Rd Bethesda MD 20814 TF: 800-205-6268 ■ Web: www.areacall.com	301-657-2718		116
Areias Systems Inc 5900 Butler Ln Ste 280 Scotts Valley CA 95066 Web: www.areiasys.com	831-440-9800		256
Arellano Construction Co 7051 SW 12th St Miami FL 33144 TF: 800-746-9554 ■ Web: www.ohlarellano.com/en	305-994-9901		360-3
AREMA (American Railway Engineering & Maintenance-of-Way Assn) 4501 Forbes Blvd Ste 130 Lanham MD 20706	301-459-3200		49-21
Arena Energy 4200 RES Forest Dr Ste 500 The Woodlands TX 77381 Web: www.arenaenergy.com	281-681-9500	681-9503	538
Arena Football League (AFL) 640 N LaSalle St Ste 557 Chicago IL 60654 Web: www.arenafootball.com	312-465-2200		715-1
Arena Hotel 817 The Alameda San Jose CA 95126 Web: www.pacifichotels.com	408-294-6500	294-6585	379
Arena Pharmaceuticals Inc 6166 Nancy Ridge Dr San Diego CA 92121 NASDAQ: ARNA ■ Web: www.arenapharm.com	858-453-7200		85
Arena Stage 1101 Sixth St SW Washington DC 20024 Web: www.arenastage.org	202-554-9066	488-4056	572
Arenac County PO Box 747 Standish MI 48658 TF: 800-232-5216 ■ Web: www.arenaccountygov.com	989-846-4626		338
Arend Laukhuf & Stoller Inc 117 N Main St Paulding OH 45879 Web: www.brsw-cpa.com	419-399-3686		2
Arends & Sons Inc 715 S Sangamon Ave Gibson City IL 60936 TF: 800-637-6052 ■ Web: www.arends-sons.com	217-784-4241	784-8749	274
Arenson Office Furnishings Inc 1115 Broadway 6th Fl. New York NY 10010 Web: www.aof.com	646-395-3563		321
Arenson Office Furniture 8185 Camino Santa Fe San Diego CA 92121 TF: 800-851-0189 ■ Web: www.arensonof.com	858-453-2411		321
Ares Corp 1440 Chapin Ave Ste 390 Burlingame CA 94010 Web: www.arescorporation.com	650-401-7100	401-7101	113
Ares Management LLC 2000 Ave of the Stars 12th Fl Los Angeles CA 90067 Web: www.aresmgmt.com	310-201-4100	201-4170	463
Ares Printing & Packaging Corp 63 Flushing Ave Unit 224 Brooklyn NY 11205 Web: www.aresny.com	718-858-8760		627
Ares Sportswear Ltd 3704 Lacon Rd Hilliard OH 43026 TF: 800-439-8614 ■ Web: www.areswear.com	614-767-1950		687
Arete Corp PO Box 1299 Center Harbor NH 03226 Web: www.arete-microgen.com	603-253-9797	253-9799	792
Arete Development Inc 20 Industrial Rd Fairfield NJ 07004	973-244-0037		610
Arete Inc 65 S Main St Bldg E Pennington NJ 08534 TF: 800-834-1377 ■ Web: www.areteinc.com	609-737-1212		174
Arete Industries Inc 7260 Osceola St Westminster CO 80030 Web: www.areteindustries.com	303-427-8688		536
Aretech LLC 21730 Red Rum Dr Ste 112 Ashburn VA 20147 Web: www.aretechllc.com	571-292-8889		350
AREVA Inc 4800 Hampden Ln Ste 1100 Bethesda MD 20814 Web: www.areva.com	301-841-1600		787
AREVA Transnuclear Inc 7135 Minstrel Way Ste 300 Columbia MD 21045 Web: www.transnuclear.com	410-910-6900		261
ARF (Advertising Research Foundation) 432 Park Ave S New York NY 10016 Web: thearf.org	212-751-5656	689-1859	49-18
Arfa Enterprises Inc 4300 Haddonfield Rd Pennsauken NJ 08002	856-486-0550		324
ARG Recovery LLC 3308 Preston Rd Ste 350-215 Plano TX 75093 Web: www.argrecovery.com	972-335-2090		194
ARG Trucking Corp 369 Bostwick Rd Phelps NY 14532 *Fax: Hum Res ■ TF: 800-334-1314 ■ Web: www.wadhams.com	315-789-8871	789-8879*	780
Arganteal Corp 9226 Knoll Crest Loop Austin TX 78759	512-801-6729		196
Argen Corp, The 5855 Oberlin Dr San Diego CA 92121 TF: 800-375-9077 ■ Web: www.argen.com	858-455-7900		228
Argenia LLC 11524 Fairview Rd Little Rock AR 72212 TF: 800-482-5968 ■ Web: argenia.com	501-227-9670		390
Argent Associates Inc 140 Fieldcrest Ave Edison NJ 08837 TF: 800-287-4666 ■ Web: www.argentassociates.com	732-512-9009		224
Argent Wealth Management 404 Wyman St Ste 375 Waltham MA 02451 Web: www.argentwm.com	781-290-4900		194
Argentina			
Consulate General 2200 W Loop S Ste 1025 Houston TX 77027 Web: www.chous.mrecic.gov.ar	713-871-8935		257
Consulate General 5055 Wilshire Blvd Ste 210 Los Angeles CA 90036 Web: clang.mrecic.gob.ar	323-954-9155	934-9076	257
Consulate General 12 W 56th St New York NY 10019	212-603-0400	541-7746	257
Consulate General 245 Peachtree Ctr Ave NE Ste 2450 Atlanta GA 30303 Web: www.catla.cancilleria.gov.ar	404-880-0805	880-0806	257
Embassy 1600 New Hampshire Ave NW Washington DC 20009 Web: www.embassyofargentina.us	202-238-6400	332-3171	257
Argentine Santa Fe Industries Credit Union 4150 Kansas Ave Kansas City KS 66106	913-342-9039		219
Argentum Group, The 60 Madison Ave Ste 701 New York NY 10010 Web: www.argentumgroup.com	212-949-6262	949-8294	402
Arges Imaging Inc 129 N Hill Ave Pasadena CA 91106	626-529-3766		228
ARGI Investment Services LLC 1914 Stanley Gault Pkwy Louisville KY 40223 TF: 866-568-9719 ■ Web: www.argifinancialgroup.com	502-753-0609		401
Argie Cooper Public Library 100 S Main St. Shelbyville TN 37160 Web: www.acolibrary.com	931-684-7323	685-4848	434-3
Argo & Lehne Jewelers Inc 3100 Tremont Rd Columbus OH 43221 TF: 800-438-6677 ■ Web: argolehne.com	614-457-6261		410
Argo Data Resource Corp 1500 N Greenville Ave Richardson TX 75081 Web: www.argodata.com	972-866-3300	866-3301	177

	Phone	Fax	Class
Argo Inc 455 N Cityfront Plaza Dr Ste 2000 .... Chicago IL 60611 *Web:* www.argoconsulting.com	312-988-9220		463
Argo International Corp 160 Chubb Ave.............................. Lyndhurst NJ 07071 *TF:* 877-274-6468 ■ *Web:* www.argointl.com	201-561-7010		246
Argo Marketing Group 64 Lisbon St .... Lewiston ME 04240 *Web:* www.argocontact.com	207-514-0744		195
Argo Products Co 3500 Goodfellow Blvd .... Saint Louis MO 63120 *Web:* www.argoproducts.com	314-385-1803	385-1808	488
Argo Sales Ltd 717-7th Ave SW Ste 1300......... Calgary AB T2P0Z3 *Web:* www.argosales.com	403-265-6633		358
Argo Systems Inc 2964 Peachtree Rd............. Atlanta GA 30305 *Web:* sintecmedia.com	404-869-4575		180
ARGO Systems LLC 1362 Mellon Rd Ste 100...................... Hanover MD 21076 *Web:* www.argo-sys.com	410-768-2444		261
Argo Translation Inc 2420 Ravine Way Ste 200..................... Glenview IL 60025 *TF:* 888-961-9291 ■ *Web:* www.argotrans.com	847-901-4075		768
Argon ST Inc 12701 Fair Lakes Cir Ste 800................... Fairfax VA 22033 *Web:* www.argonst.com	703-322-0881		735
Argon Technologies Inc 4612 Wesley St.............................. Greenville TX 75401 *TF:* 888-651-1010 ■ *Web:* www.argontech.com	903-455-5036		261
Argonaut Constructors Inc 360 Sutton Pl ....Santa Rosa CA 95407 *Web:* www.argonautconstructors.com	707-542-4862	542-3210	188-10
Argonaut Hotel 495 Jefferson St........... San Francisco CA 94109 *TF:* 866-415-0704 ■ *Web:* www.argonauthotel.com	415-563-0800		379
Argonaut Inc 576 Folsom St.............. San Francisco CA 94105 *Web:* www.argonautinc.com	415-633-8200		5
Argonaut, The PO Box 11209............Marina del Rey CA 90295 *Web:* argonautnews.com	310-822-1629		532-4
Argonne National Laboratory (ANL) 9700 S Cass Ave............................ Argonne IL 60439 *TF:* 800-632-8990 ■ *Web:* www.anl.gov	630-252-2000		668
Argos Computer Systems Inc 110 W 32nd St Fl 7......................... New York NY 10001 *Web:* argosnyc.com	212-594-5400		180
Argos Systems Inc 19 Crosby Dr .... Bedford MA 01730 *Web:* www.argos.com	781-271-9111		225
Argosy Publishing Inc 109 Oak St............... Newton MA 02464 *TF:* 800-343-2887 ■ *Web:* www.argosypublishing.com	617-527-9999		627
Argosy University 1515 Central Pkwy..............Eagan MN 55121 *Fax: Admissions ■ *TF:* 888-844-2004 ■ *Web:* argosy.edu	651-846-2882	994-7956*	166
Argosy University Hawaii 400 ASB Tower 1001 Bishop St .... Honolulu HI 96813 *TF:* 888-323-2777 ■ *Web:* www.argosy.edu	808-536-5555	536-5505	800
Argosy's Alton Belle Casino 1 Piasa St .... Alton IL 62002 *TF:* 800-711-4263 ■ *Web:* www.argosyalton.com	800-711-4263		133
Arguedas Cassman & Headley 803 Hearst Ave .... Berkeley CA 94710 *Web:* www.achlaw.com	510-845-3000		428
Argus 75 Central St............................. Boston MA 02109	617-261-7676		4
Argus Connection Inc 1111 W N Carrier Pkwy Ste 300............ Grand Prairie TX 75050 *TF:* 800-421-3746 ■ *Web:* www.argusx.com	469-471-0035		225
Argus Interactive Agency Inc 217 N Main St Ste 200...................... Santa Ana CA 92701 *TF:* 866-595-9597 ■ *Web:* www.argusinteractive.com	866-595-9597		530
Argus Leader 200 S Minnesota Ave............Sioux Falls SD 57104 *Fax: Edit ■ *Web:* www.argusleader.com	605-331-2200	331-2294*	532-2
Argus Machine Company Ltd 5820 97th St NW .... Edmonton AB T6E3J1 *TF:* 888-434-9451 ■ *Web:* www.argusmachine.com	780-434-9451		539
Argus Research Co 61 Broadway Ste 1910 .... New York NY 10006 *Web:* www.argusresearch.com	212-425-7500		218
Argus Supply Co 46400 Continental Dr .... Chesterfield MI 48047 *TF:* 800-873-0456 ■ *Web:* argus-hazco.com	586-840-3200		23
Argyle Lake State Park 640 Argyle Pk Rd .... Colchester IL 62326 *Web:* www.dnr.illinois.gov/Parks/Pages/ArgyleLake.aspx	309-776-3422		565
Argyle Security Inc 12903 Delivery Dr........................ San Antonio TX 78247 *Web:* isisecurity.com	210-495-5245		692
ARH (Alexander Ramsey House) 265 S Exchange St .... Saint Paul MN 55102 *TF:* 800-657-3773 ■ *Web:* mnhs.org/visit	651-296-8760		50-3
ARH (Appalachian Regional Healthcare Service) 80 Hospital Dr PO Box 8086................Barbourville KY 40906 *TF:* 888-654-0015 ■ *Web:* www.arh.org	859-226-2440		353
ARH (Andalusia Health) 849 S Three Notch St PO Box 760 ....Andalusia AL 36420 *Web:* www.andalusiaregional.com	334-222-8466	222-6983	374-3
ARH (Whitesburg Appalachian Regional Hospital) 240 Hospital Rd .... Whitesburg KY 41858 *Web:* arh.org/locations/whitesburg.aspx	606-633-3500		374-3
ARH Regional Medical Ctr 100 Medical Ctr Dr.......................... Hazard KY 41701 *TF:* 800-456-3452 ■ *Web:* www.arh.org	606-439-1331	439-6682	374-3
ARHMF 2525 Ponce De Leon Blvd PO Box 1225...... Coral Gables FL 33134 *Web:* arhmf.com	305-779-3560		445
ARHP (Association of Reproductive Health Professionals) 1901 L St NW Ste 300 .... Washington DC 20036 *TF:* 877-311-8972 ■ *Web:* www.arhp.org	202-466-3825	466-3826	49-8
ARI (Autism Research Institute) 4182 Adams Ave............................ San Diego CA 92116 *TF:* 866-366-3361 ■ *Web:* www.autism.com	619-281-7165	563-6840	48-17
ARi Industries Inc 381 Ari Ct .... Addison IL 60101 *TF:* 800-237-6725 ■ *Web:* www.ariindustries.biz	630-953-9100		201
ARI Network Services Inc 10850 W Pk Pl Ste 1200..................... Milwaukee WI 53224 *TF:* 877-805-0803 ■ *Web:* www.arinet.com	414-973-4300	283-4357	178-10
Ari Products Inc 102 Gaither Dr Ste 3 .... Mount Laurel NJ 08054 *Web:* www.ariproducts.com	856-234-0757		291
Aria Athletic Club & Spa 1300 Westhaven Dr............................ Vail CO 81657 *TF:* 888-824-5772 ■ *Web:* vailcascade.com/colorado-mountain-spa.php	970-479-5942	476-7405	707
Aria Communications Corp 717 W Saint Germain St..................... St. Cloud MN 56301 *TF:* 800-955-9924 ■ *Web:* www.ariacallsandcards.com	800-955-9924		737
Aria Group Inc 17395 Daimler St.................. Irvine CA 92614 *TF:* 800-905-7329 ■ *Web:* www.aria-group.com	949-475-2915		261
Aria Health Bucks County Campus 380 N Oxford Valley Rd.................... Langhorne PA 19047 *Web:* www.ariahealth.org	215-949-5000		374-3
Aria Health System *Frankford Campus* 4900 Frankford Ave .... Philadelphia PA 19124 *Web:* www.ariahealth.org	215-831-2000		374-3
Aria Medical 1330 W Blanco Rd .... San Antonio TX 78232 *Web:* www.ariamedical.com	210-281-9602		475
Aria Restaurant 490 E Paces Ferry Rd NE .... Atlanta GA 30305 *Web:* www.aria-atl.com	404-233-7673		671
Aria Solutions Inc 110 - 12th Ave SW Ste 600 .... Calgary AB T2R0G7 *TF:* 866-235-1181 ■ *Web:* www.ariasolutions.com	403-235-0227		624
Aria Tuscan Grill 100 N Tryon St .... Charlotte NC 28202 *Web:* www.sonomarestaurants.net	704-376-8880		671
ARIAD Pharmaceuticals Inc 26 Landsdowne St .... Cambridge MA 02139 *NASDAQ: ARIA* ■ *Web:* www.ariad.com	617-494-0400	494-8144	85
Arial Software LLC 1501 Stampede Ave Ste 9005.................... Cody WY 82414 *Web:* www.arialsoftware.com	949-218-3852		525
Arias & Associates Inc 142 Chula Vista Dr....................... San Antonio TX 78232 *Web:* www.ariasinc.com	210-308-5884		261
Ariat International Inc 3242 Whipple Rd .... Union City CA 94587 *Web:* ariat.com	510-477-7000		301
Ariba Inc 807 11th Ave...................... Sunnyvale CA 94089 *NASDAQ: ARBA* ■ *TF:* 866-772-7422 ■ *Web:* www.ariba.com	650-390-1000		39
Aribex Inc 744 S 400 E............................ Orem UT 84097 *TF:* 866-340-5522 ■ *Web:* aribex.com	801-226-5522		228
Aridis Pharmaceuticals LLC 5941 Optical Ct........................... San Jose CA 95138 *Web:* www.aridispharma.com	408-385-1742		85
Ariel Corp 35 Blackjack Rd Ext .... Mount Vernon OH 43050 *Web:* www.arielcorp.com	740-397-0311		172
Ariel Group Inc, The 1050 Waltham St Ste 600.................... Lexington MA 02421 *Web:* www.arielgroup.com	781-761-9000		194
Ariel Partners LLC 1501 BRdway 12th fl........................ New York NY 10036 *Web:* www.arielpartners.com	646-467-7394		177
Ariel Restaurant 2072 Drummond St........... Montreal QC H3G1W9 *Web:* www.arielrestaurant.com	514-282-9790		671
Ariel Technologies 1980 E Lohman Ave .... Las Cruces NM 88001 *TF:* 877-524-6860 ■ *Web:* arielusa.com	877-524-6860		175
Ariens Co 655 W Ryan St .... Brillion WI 54110 *TF:* 800-678-5443 ■ *Web:* www.ariens.com	920-756-2141	756-2407	429
Aries Computer Solutions Inc 2211 Sheridan Dr Ste 203 .... Buffalo NY 14223 *TF:* 800-364-4905 ■ *Web:* www.customswebclearance.com	716-876-4004		809
Aries Electronics Inc 2609 Bartram Rd .... Bristol PA 19007 *Fax Area Code: 908 ■ *Web:* www.arieselec.com	215-781-9956	996-3891*	253
Aries Industries Inc 550 Elizabeth St .... Waukesha WI 53186 *Web:* www.ariesindustries.com	262-896-7205		647
Arima Boats 7510 Bree Dr.................. Bremerton WA 98312 *Web:* www.arimaboats.com	360-813-3600		90
Arimed Orthotics & Prosthetics Inc 302 Livingston St .... Brooklyn NY 11217 *TF:* 800-333-0109 ■ *Web:* www.arimed.com	718-875-8754		477
ARIN (American Registry for Internet Numbers) 3635 Concorde Pkwy Ste 200................. Chantilly VA 20151 *Web:* www.arin.net	703-227-9840		48-9
ARINC Inc 2551 Riva Rd .... Annapolis MD 21401 *TF:* 866-321-6060 ■ *Web:* www.arinc.com	410-266-4000	573-3300	681
Aring Equipment Company Inc 13001 W Silver Spring Dr....................... Butler WI 53007 *Web:* www.aringequipment.com	262-781-3770		358
Arion Systems Inc 15040 Conference Ctr Dr Ste 200.............. Chantilly VA 20151 *Web:* www.arionsys.com	703-815-1130		261
Ariosa Diagnostics Inc 5945 Optical Ct............................ San Jose CA 95138 *TF:* 855-927-4672 ■ *Web:* www.ariosadx.com	855-927-4672		418
Aris Horticulture Inc 115 Third St SE .... Barberton OH 44203 *Fax Area Code: 330 ■ *TF:* 800-232-9557 ■ *Web:* www.arishort.com	800-232-9557	745-3098*	369
ARISE Technologies Corp 65 Northland Rd........................... Waterloo ON N2V1Y8 *Web:* www.arisetech.com	519-725-2244		192
Arista Industries Inc 557 Danbury Rd............ Wilton CT 06897 *Web:* www.aristaindustries.com	203-761-1009		296-25
Arista Information Systems Inc 1105 Fairchild Rd...................... Winston-Salem NC 27105 *TF:* 800-742-5877 ■ *Web:* www.aristainfo.com	336-776-1105		5
Aristatek Inc 710 E Garfield St Ste 220 .... Laramie WY 82070 *TF:* 877-912-2200 ■ *Web:* www.aristatek.com	307-721-2126		177
Ariste Medical Inc 20 S Dudley Ste 900 .... Memphis TN 38103 *Web:* www.aristemedical.com	901-866-1400	866-1702	363
Aristech Acrylics LLC 7350 Empire Dr ....Florence KY 41042 *Web:* www.aristechacrylics.com	859-283-1501		600
Aristo Cast Inc 7400 Research Dr................ Almont MI 48003 *Web:* www.aristo-cast.com	810-798-2900		492

Name / Address	City	State	ZIP	Phone	Fax	Class
Aristo's 224 South 1300 East Web: aristosslc.com	Salt Lake City	UT	84102	801-581-0888		671
Aristocrat Technologies 7230 Amigo St TF: 800-748-4156 ■ Web: www.aristocrat.com	Las Vegas	NV	89119	702-270-1000	270-1001	322
Aristotle Capital Management LLC 11100 Santa Monica Blvd Ste 1700 TF: 877-478-4722 ■ Web: www.aristotlecap.com	Los Angeles	CA	90025	310-478-4005	478-8496	401
Aristotle Inc 205 Pennsylvania Ave SE *Fax: Sales ■ TF Sales: 800-296-2747 ■ Web: www.aristotle.com	Washington	DC	20003	202-543-8345	543-6407*	178-11
Arizon Structures 11880 Dorsett Rd Web: www.arizoncompanies.com	St. Louis	MO	63043	314-739-0037		256
Arizona						
Administrative Office of the Cts 1501 W Washington St Web: www.azcourts.gov	Phoenix	AZ	85007	602-452-3300		339-3
Agriculture Dept 1688 W Adams St TF: 800-294-0308 ■ Web: agriculture.az.gov	Phoenix	AZ	85007	602-542-4373	542-5420	339-3
Arts Commission 417 W Roosevelt St Web: azarts.gov	Phoenix	AZ	85003	602-255-5882	256-0282	339-3
Attorney General 1275 W Washington St Web: www.azag.gov	Phoenix	AZ	85007	602-542-5025	542-4085	339-3
Boxing Commission 1110 W Washington St Ste 450 Web: boxingandmma.az.gov	Phoenix	AZ	85007	602-364-1700	364-1703	339-3
Children Youth & Families Div 1789 W Jefferson St TF: 866-229-5553 ■ Web: www.azdes.gov	Phoenix	AZ	85007	602-542-0419		339-3
Consumer Protection & Antitrust Unit 1275 W Washington St Web: www.azag.gov	Phoenix	AZ	85007	602-542-5025	542-4579	339-3
Corrections Dept 1601 W Jefferson St Web: corrections.az.gov	Phoenix	AZ	85007	602-542-5497	542-2859	339-3
Criminal Justice Commission 1110 W Washington St Ste 230 Web: www.azcjc.gov	Phoenix	AZ	85007	602-364-1146	364-1175	339-3
Education Dept 1535 W Jefferson St TF: 800-352-4558 ■ Web: www.azed.gov	Phoenix	AZ	85007	602-542-5393	542-5010	339-3
Emergency & Military Affairs Dept 5636 E McDowell Rd Web: www.azdema.gov	Phoenix	AZ	85008	602-267-2700	267-2954	339-3
Employment Administration PO Box 6123 Web: www.azdes.gov	Phoenix	AZ	85005	602-542-3957	542-2491	259
Executive Clemency Board 1645 W Jefferson Ste 101 Web: boec.az.gov	Phoenix	AZ	85007	602-542-5656	542-5680	339-3
Financial Institutions 2910 N 44th St Ste 310 TF: 800-544-0708 ■ Web: www.azdfi.gov	Phoenix	AZ	85018	602-771-2800	381-1225	339-3
Game & Fish Dept 5000 W Carefree Hwy Web: www.azgfd.com	Phoenix	AZ	85086	602-942-3000		339-3
Government Information Technology Agency 100 N 15th Ave Ste 440 Web: www.azdfi.gov	Phoenix	AZ	85007	602-364-4482	364-4799	339-3
Health Services Dept 150 N 18th Ave Web: www.azdhs.gov	Phoenix	AZ	85007	602-542-1025	542-0883	339-3
Highway Patrol Div 2222 W Encanto Blvd Web: www.azdps.gov	Phoenix	AZ	85005	602-223-2000		339-3
Historic Preservation Office 1100 W Washington St Web: www.azstateparks.com	Phoenix	AZ	85007	602-542-4009		339-3
Housing Dept 1110 W Washington St Ste 310 Web: azhousing.gov	Phoenix	AZ	85007	602-771-1000	771-1002	339-3
Industrial Commission 800 W Washington St Web: www.ica.state.az.us	Phoenix	AZ	85007	602-542-4661		339-3
Insurance Dept 2910 N 44th St 2nd Fl Ste 210 Web: azinsurance.gov	Phoenix	AZ	85018	602-364-2499	364-2505	339-3
Land Dept 1616 W Adams St Web: land.az.gov	Phoenix	AZ	85007	602-542-4631		339-3
Legislature Arizona State Capitol Complex 1700 W Washington St 1700 W Washington St TF: 800-352-8404 ■ Web: www.azleg.state.az.us	Phoenix	AZ	85007	602-926-3559		339-3
Lottery 4740 E University Dr TF: 800-639-8783 ■ Web: arizonalottery.com	Phoenix	AZ	85034	480-921-4400		452
Medical Board 9545 Doubletree Ranch Rd TF: 877-255-2212 ■ Web: www.azmd.gov	Scottsdale	AZ	85258	480-551-2700	551-2828	339-3
Motor Vehicle Div PO Box 2100 MD 555M Web: www.azdot.gov/mvd	Phoenix	AZ	85001	602-255-0072		339-3
Nursing Board 4747 N Seventh St Ste 200 Web: www.azbn.gov	Phoenix	AZ	85014	602-771-7800	771-7888	339-3
Office of the Governor 1700 W Washington St Web: azgovernor.gov	Phoenix	AZ	85007	602-542-4331		339-3
Postsecondary Education Commission 2020 N Central Ave Ste 650 Web: highered.az.gov	Phoenix	AZ	85004	602-258-2435	258-2483	339-3
Racing Dept 1110 W Washington St Ste 450 Web: racing.az.gov	Phoenix	AZ	85007	602-364-1700	364-1703	712
Real Estate Dept 2910 N 44th St Ste 100 Web: www.re.state.az.us	Phoenix	AZ	85018	602-771-7799	468-0562	339-3
Rehabilitation Services Admin 1789 W Jefferson St 2nd Fl NW TF: 800-563-1221 ■ Web: des.az.gov	Phoenix	AZ	85007	602-542-3332		339-3
Revenue Dept 1600 W Monroe St Web: www.azdor.gov	Phoenix	AZ	85007	602-255-3381		339-3
Secretary of State 1700 W Washington St W Wing 7th Fl TF: 800-458-5842 ■ Web: www.azsos.gov	Phoenix	AZ	85007	602-542-4285	542-1575	339-3
Securities Div 1300 W Washington St 3rd Fl TF: 866-837-4399 ■ Web: www.azinvestor.gov	Phoenix	AZ	85007	602-542-4242		339-3
State Boards Office 1400 W Washington St Web: ppse.az.gov	Phoenix	AZ	85007	602-542-5709	542-1253	339-3
State Parks 1300 W Washington St Web: www.azstateparks.com	Phoenix	AZ	85007	602-542-4174		339-3
Supreme Court 1501 W Washington St Web: azcourts.gov	Phoenix	AZ	85007	602-542-9300	542-9480	339-3
Tourism Office 1110 W Washington St Ste 155 TF: 888-520-3434 ■ Web: visitarizona.com	Phoenix	AZ	85007	602-364-3700	364-3701	339-3
Treasurer 1700 W Washington St 1st Fl TF: 877-365-8310 ■ Web: www.aztreasury.gov	Phoenix	AZ	85007	602-542-7800	542-7176	339-3
Veterans" Service Dept 3839 N Third St Ste 200 Web: www.azdvs.gov	Phoenix	AZ	85012	602-255-3373		339-3
Vital Records Office 1818 W Adams St TF: 888-816-5907 ■ Web: www.azdhs.gov	Phoenix	AZ	85007	602-364-1300		339-3
Weights & Measures Dept 4425 W Olive Ave Ste 134 Web: www.azdwm.gov	Glendale	AZ	85302	602-771-4938		339-3
Arizona Art Supply 4025 N 16th St TF: 877-264-9514 ■ Web: www.arizonaartsupply.com	Phoenix	AZ	85016	602-264-9514		45
Arizona Assn of Realtors 255 E Osborne Rd Ste 200 TF: 800-426-7274 ■ Web: www.aaronline.com	Phoenix	AZ	85012	602-248-7787	351-2474	656
Arizona Attorney Magazine 4201 N 24th St Ste 200 TF: 866-482-9227 ■ Web: www.myazbar.org/AZAttorney	Phoenix	AZ	85016	602-252-4804	271-4930	457-15
Arizona Automobile Dealers Association 4701 N 24th St Ste B3 TF: 800-678-3875 ■ Web: www.aada.com	Phoenix	AZ	85016	602-468-0888		138
Arizona Bankers Assn 111 W Monroe St Ste 440 TF: 800-873-4722 ■ Web: www.azbankers.org	Phoenix	AZ	85003	602-258-1200		138
Arizona Biltmore Resort & Spa 2400 E Missouri TF: 800-950-0086 ■ Web: www.arizonabiltmore.com	Phoenix	AZ	85016	602-955-6600	381-7600	669
Arizona Bridge To Independent Living 5025 E Washington St Ste 200 Web: ability360.org	Phoenix	AZ	85034	602-256-2245		363
Arizona Cardinals 8701 S Hardy Dr TF: 800-999-1402 ■ Web: www.azcardinals.com	Tempe	AZ	85284	602-379-0101		715-3
Arizona Chamber of Commerce & Industry 3200 N Central Ave Ste 1125 TF: 866-275-5816 ■ Web: www.azchamber.com	Phoenix	AZ	85012	602-248-9172	265-1262	140
Arizona Charlie's Boulder Casino & Hotel 4575 Boulder Hwy TF: 888-236-9066 ■ Web: www.arizonacharliesboulder.com	Las Vegas	NV	89121	702-951-5800		379
Arizona Charlie's Decatur Casino & Hotel 740 S Decatur Blvd Web: www.arizonacharliesdecatur.com	Las Vegas	NV	89107	702-258-5200	258-5192	133
Arizona Community Foundation 2201 E Camelback Rd Ste 405B TF: 800-222-8221 ■ Web: www.azfoundation.org	Phoenix	AZ	85016	602-381-1400	381-1575	303
Arizona Components Company Inc 2901 W McDowell Rd Web: www.azcompco.com	Phoenix	AZ	85009	602-269-5655		246
Arizona Correctional Industries 3701 W Cambridge Ave TF: 800-992-1738 ■ Web: aci.az.gov	Phoenix	AZ	85009	602-272-7600	255-3108	630
Arizona Coyotes Hockey Club 9400 W Maryland Ave TF: 877-448-4483 ■ Web: coyotes.nhl.com	Glendale	AZ	85305	623-772-3200	772-3201	716
Arizona Culinary Institute 10585 N 114th St Ste 401 TF: 866-294-2433 ■ Web: www.azculinary.edu	Scottsdale	AZ	85259	480-603-1066		163
Arizona Daily Star 4850 S Pk Ave TF: 800-695-4492 ■ Web: tucson.com	Tucson	AZ	85714	520-573-4343	573-4107	532-2
Arizona Daily Sun 1751 S Thompson St TF: 800-367-3524 ■ Web: www.azdailysun.com	Flagstaff	AZ	86001	928-774-4545	774-4790	532-2
Arizona Dental Assn 3193 N Drinkwater Blvd TF: 800-866-2732 ■ Web: www.azda.org	Scottsdale	AZ	85251	480-344-5777	344-1442	227
Arizona Diamondbacks 401 E Jefferson St Web: arizona.diamondbacks.mlb.com	Phoenix	AZ	85004	602-462-6500		713
Arizona Doll & Toy Museum 5847 W Myrtle Ave	Glendale	AZ	85301	623-939-6186		520
Arizona Energy Masters 219 W Lone Cactus TF: 800-435-7764 ■ Web: www.arizonaenergymasters.com	Phoenix	AZ	85027	602-427-0007		192
Arizona Farm Bureau Federation 325 S Higley Rd Web: www.azfb.org	Higley	AZ	85296	480-635-3600		391-4
Arizona Federal Credit Union PO Box 60070 TF: 800-523-4603 ■ Web: www.arizonafederal.org	Phoenix	AZ	85082	602-683-1000		219
Arizona Golf Resort & Conference Ctr 425 S Power Rd TF: 800-528-8282 ■ Web: www.arizonagolfresort.com	Mesa	AZ	85206	480-832-3202	981-0151	669
Arizona Grand Resort 8000 S Arizona Grand Pkwy TF: 866-267-1321 ■ Web: www.arizonagrandresort.com	Phoenix	AZ	85044	602-438-9000	431-6535	669
Arizona Highways Magazine 2039 W Lewis Ave *Fax Area Code: 602 ■ TF: 800-543-5432 ■ Web: www.arizonahighways.com	Phoenix	AZ	85009	800-543-5432	254-4505*	457-22
Arizona Historical Society Museum 1300 N College Ave Web: www.arizonahistoricalsociety.org	Tempe	AZ	85281	480-929-0292	967-5450	520
Arizona Historical Society Pioneer Museum 2340 N Ft Valley Rd TF: 800-842-7293 ■ Web: www.arizonahistoricalsociety.org	Flagstaff	AZ	86001	928-774-6272	774-1596	520
Arizona Home Care LLC 1626 S Edward Dr Web: www.azhomecare.com	Tempe	AZ	85281	602-252-5000		237

	City	St	Zip	Phone	Fax	Class
Arizona Inn 2200 E Elm St	Tucson	AZ	85719	520-325-1541	881-5830	379
TF: 800-933-1093 ■ *Web:* arizonainn.com						
Arizona Jewish Post						
3822 E River Rd Ste 300	Tucson	AZ	85718	520-319-1112		532-3
TF: 800-910-0664 ■ *Web:* www.jewishtucson.org						
Arizona Leather Company Inc						
4235 Schaefer Ave	Chino	CA	91710	909-993-5101		321
TF: 888-669-5328 ■ *Web:* www.arizonaleather.com						
Arizona Library Assn (AzLA)						
950 E Baseline Rd Ste 104-1025	Tempe	AZ	85283	480-609-3999		435
Web: www.azla.org						
Arizona Limousines Inc						
8900 N Central Ave Ste 101	Phoenix	AZ	85020	602-267-7097	870-3388	441
TF: 800-678-0033 ■ *Web:* www.arizonalimos.com						
Arizona Materials LLC 3636 S 43rd Ave	Phoenix	AZ	85009	602-278-4444		182
Web: www.arizonamaterials.com						
Arizona Medical Assn, The (ArMA)						
810 W Bethany Home Rd	Phoenix	AZ	85013	602-246-8901	242-6283	474
TF: 800-482-3480 ■ *Web:* www.azmed.org						
Arizona Mills 5000 Arizona Mills Cir	Tempe	AZ	85282	480-491-7300	491-7400	460
TF: 877-746-6642 ■ *Web:* simon.com/mall/arizona-mills						
Arizona Natural Resources						
2525 E BeaRdsley Rd	Phoenix	AZ	85050	602-569-6900	569-9697	214
TF: 800-201-9208 ■ *Web:* www.arizonanaturalresources.com						
Arizona Nurses Assn (AzNA)						
1850 E Southern Ave Ste 1	Tempe	AZ	85282	480-831-0404	839-4780	533
Web: www.aznurse.org						
Arizona Osteopathic Medical Assn						
5150 N 16th St Ste A122	Phoenix	AZ	85016	602-266-6699		533
TF: 888-266-6699 ■ *Web:* az-osteo.org						
Arizona Partsmaster Inc						
7125 W Sherman St	Phoenix	AZ	85043	602-233-3580	233-3607	612
TF: 888-924-7278 ■ *Web:* www.azpartsmaster.com						
Arizona Pharmacy Assn						
1845 E Southern Ave	Tempe	AZ	85282	480-838-3385	838-3557	585
Web: www.azpharmacy.org						
Arizona Precision Sheet Metal						
2140 W Pinnacle Peak Rd	Phoenix	AZ	85027	623-516-3700	516-3701	697
TF: 800-443-7039 ■ *Web:* www.apsm-jit.com						
Arizona Public Service Co (APS)						
400 N Fifth St PO Box 53999	Phoenix	AZ	85004	602-371-7171		787
TF: 800-253-9405 ■ *Web:* www.aps.com						
Arizona Publishing Cos PO Box 1950	Phoenix	AZ	85004	602-444-8000		637-8
TF: 800-331-9303 ■ *Web:* www.azcentral.com						
Arizona Rattlers 201 E Jefferson St	Phoenix	AZ	85004	602-514-8383		715-1
Web: www.azrattlers.com						
Arizona Republic 200 E Van Buren St	Phoenix	AZ	85004	602-444-8000	444-8044*	532-2
*Fax: News Rm ■ *TF:* 800-331-9303 ■ *Web:* www.azcentral.com						
Arizona Republican Party						
3501 N 24th St	Phoenix	AZ	85016	602-957-7770	224-0932	616-2
Web: az.gop						
Arizona Scholarship Fund						
4850 E Baseline Rd Ste 112	Mesa	AZ	85206	480-497-4564		305
TF: 800-477-8237 ■ *Web:* www.azscholarships.org						
Arizona Science Ctr						
600 E Washington St	Phoenix	AZ	85004	602-716-2000	716-2099	520
Web: www.azscience.org						
Arizona Sports & Tourism Authority						
1 Cardinals Dr	Glendale	AZ	85305	623-433-7500		772
Web: www.az-sta.com						
Arizona State Capitol Museum						
1700 W Washington St	Phoenix	AZ	85007	602-542-4675	256-7985	520
TF: 800-228-4710 ■ *Web:* azlibrary.gov/azcm						
Arizona State Hospital						
2500 E Van Buren St	Phoenix	AZ	85008	602-244-1331	220-6355	374-5
TF: 877-588-5163 ■ *Web:* www.azdhs.gov/azsh						
Arizona State Library						
1700 W Washington St Ste 300	Phoenix	AZ	85007	602-542-4035		434-5
Web: www.azlibrary.gov						
Arizona State Museum						
1013 E University Blvd University of Arizona	Tucson	AZ	85721	520-621-6302		520
Web: www.statemuseum.arizona.edu						
Arizona State Prison Complex-Douglas						
6911 N BDI Blvd PO Box 3867	Douglas	AZ	85607	520-364-7521	364-7445	213
Web: corrections.az.gov						
Arizona State Prison Complex-Eyman						
4374 E Butte Ave	Florence	AZ	85132	520-868-0201	868-0276	213
TF: 866-333-2039 ■ *Web:* corrections.az.gov						
Arizona State Prison Complex-Florence						
1305 E Butte Ave PO Box 629	Florence	AZ	85132	520-868-4011	868-5333	213
Web: corrections.az.gov						
Arizona State Prison Complex-Lewis						
26700 S Highway 85 PO Box 70	Buckeye	AZ	85326	623-386-6160	386-7332	213
Web: corrections.az.gov/location/98/lewis						
Arizona State Prison Complex-Perryville						
2105 N Citrus Rd	Goodyear	AZ	85395	623-853-0304		213
Arizona State Prison Complex-Phoenix						
2500 E Van Buren St PO Box 52109	Phoenix	AZ	85008	602-685-3100	542-3965	213
Web: corrections.az.gov/location/105/phoenix						
Arizona State Prison Complex-Safford						
896 S Crook Rd	Safford	AZ	85546	928-428-4698	428-3235	213
Web: corrections.az.gov						
Arizona State Prison Complex-Winslow						
2100 S Hwy 87	Winslow	AZ	86047	928-289-9551	289-2951	213
Web: az.gov						
Arizona State Prison Complex-Yuma						
7125 E Juan Sanchez Blvd	San Luis	AZ	85349	928-627-8871	627-6703	213
Web: corrections.az.gov						
Arizona State Retirement System						
3300 N Central Ave	Phoenix	AZ	85012	602-240-2000		528
TF: 800-621-3778 ■ *Web:* www.azasrs.gov						
Arizona State University						
550 E Tyler Mall PO Box 871404	Tempe	AZ	85287	480-965-6891	965-8102	598
Web: asu.edu						
East 7001 E Williams Field Rd	Mesa	AZ	85212	480-727-1118		166
Web: campus.asu.edu/polytechnic						
Hayden Library 300 E Orange Mall	Tempe	AZ	85281	480-965-3417	965-9169	434-6
TF: 800-728-0209 ■ *Web:* www.asu.edu						
Sandra Day O'Connor College of Law						
PO Box 877906	Tempe	AZ	85287	480-727-8856	727-7930	167-1
TF: 855-278-5080 ■ *Web:* www.law.asu.edu						
West PO Box 37100	Phoenix	AZ	85069	602-543-5500	543-8312*	166
*Fax: Admissions ■ *TF:* 855-278-5080 ■ *Web:* www.asu.edu						
Arizona State University Art Museum						
10th St & Mill Ave						
Nelson Fine Arts Ctr Arizona State University	Tempe	AZ	85287	480-965-2787	965-5254	520
TF: 855-278-5080 ■ *Web:* www.asuartmuseum.asu.edu						
Arizona State Veterans Home						
4141 N Third St	Phoenix	AZ	85012	602-248-1550		793
Web: dvs.az.gov						
Arizona Technology Council						
2800 N Central Ave Ste 1920	Phoenix	AZ	85004	602-343-8324		78
Web: www.aztechcouncil.org						
Arizona Veterinary Medical Assn						
100 W Coolidge St	Phoenix	AZ	85013	602-242-7936	249-3828	795
TF: 800-272-1813 ■ *Web:* www.azvma.org						
Arizona Western College 2020 S Ave 8 E	Yuma	AZ	85366	928-317-6000	344-7543	162
TF: 888-293-0392 ■ *Web:* www.azwestern.edu						
Arizona Wholesale Supply Co						
2020 E University Dr	Phoenix	AZ	85034	602-258-7901	258-8335	612
TF: 866-977-6849 ■ *Web:* www.arizonawholesalesupply.com						
Arizona Wing Commemorative Air Force Museum						
2017 N Greenfield Rd Falcon Field	Mesa	AZ	85215	480-924-1940		520
Web: azcaf.org						
Arizona-Sonora Desert Museum Inc						
2021 N Kinney Rd	Tucson	AZ	85743	520-883-1380		522
TF: 800-288-3861 ■ *Web:* www.desertmuseum.org						
ARJ Infusion Services Inc						
10049 Lakeview Ave	Lenexa	KS	66219	866-451-8804		237
TF: 866-451-8804 ■ *Web:* www.arjinfusion.com						
Arjobex America Mill						
10901 Westlake Dr	Charlotte	NC	28273	800-765-9278		557
TF: 800-765-9278 ■ *Web:* www.polyart.com						
ARK Diagnostics Inc						
48089 Fremont Blvd	Fremont	CA	94538	510-270-6270	270-6298	363
TF: 877-869-2320 ■ *Web:* www.ark-tdm.com						
Ark Restaurants Corp						
85 Fifth Ave 14th Fl	New York	NY	10003	212-206-8800	206-8814	670
NASDAQ: ARKR ■ *Web:* www.arkrestaurants.com						
ARK Solutions Inc						
1939 Roland Clarks Pl Ste 300	Reston	VA	20191	703-657-0670		463
Web: www.arksolutionsinc.com						
Ark Technologies Inc						
3655 Ohio Ave	Saint Charles	IL	60174	630-377-8855		492
Web: www.arktechno.com						
Ark TeleServices 2 E Merrick Rd	Valley Stream	NY	11580	800-898-5367		393
TF: 800-898-5367 ■ *Web:* www.arktele.com						
Ark Valley Electric Co-op Assn						
10 E Tenth St	South Hutchinson	KS	67504	620-662-6661		245
TF: 888-297-9212 ■ *Web:* www.arkvalley.com						
Arkadin Inc 5 Concourse Pkwy Ste 1600	Atlanta	GA	30328	866-551-1432		387
TF: 866-551-1432 ■ *Web:* www.arkadin.com						
Arkanova Energy Corp						
305 Camp Craft Rd Ste 525	West Lake Hills	TX	78746	512-222-0975		536
Web: www.arkanovaenergy.com						
Arkansas						
Administrative Office of the Cts						
625 Marshall St	Little Rock	AR	72201	501-682-9400	682-9410	339-4
TF: 800-950-8221 ■ *Web:* courts.arkansas.gov						
Aging & Adult Services Div						
PO Box 1437 Slot S-530	Little Rock	AR	72203	501-682-2441		339-4
TF: 800-482-8049 ■ *Web:* www.daas.ar.gov						
Arts Council 1100 N St Ste 1500	Little Rock	AR	72201	501-324-9150	324-9207	339-4
Web: www.arkansasarts.org						
Attorney General						
323 Ctr St Ste 200	Little Rock	AR	72201	501-682-2007	682-8084	339-4
TF Consumer Info: 800-482-8982 ■ *Web:* arkansasag.gov						
Bank Dept 400 HaRdin Rd Ste 100	Little Rock	AR	72211	501-324-9019	324-9028	339-4
Web: banking.arkansas.gov						
Bureau of Standards						
4608 W 61st St	Little Rock	AR	72209	501-225-1598		339-4
Web: plantboard.arkansas.gov/Standards						
Child Support Enforcement Office						
1509 W Seventh St	Little Rock	AR	72201	501-682-8398		339-4
Web: dfa.arkansas.gov						
Children & Family Services Div						
Slot S560 PO Box 1437	Little Rock	AR	72203	501-682-8008	682-6968	339-4
Web: humanservices.arkansas.gov						
Consumer Protection Div						
323 Ctr St Ste 200	Little Rock	AR	72201	501-682-2007		339-4
TF: 800-482-8982 ■ *Web:* arkansasag.gov						
Contractors Licensing Board						
4100 RichaRds Rd	North Little Rock	AR	72117	501-372-4661	372-2247	339-4
Web: aclb.arkansas.gov						
Cosmetology Board						
4815 W Markham St Slot 8 Ste 108	Little Rock	AR	72201	501-682-2168	682-5640	339-4
Web: www.accessarkansas.org						
Crime Victims Reparations Board						
323 Ctr St Ste 200	Little Rock	AR	72201	501-682-2007		339-4
TF: 800-482-8982 ■ *Web:* arkansasag.gov						
Development Finance Authority						
900 W Capitol Ste 310	Little Rock	AR	72201	501-682-5900	682-5859	339-4
Web: www.arkansas.gov						
Education Dept 4 Capitol Mall	Little Rock	AR	72201	501-682-4475		339-4
Web: arkansased.org						
Environmental Quality Dept						
5301 Northshore Dr	Little Rock	AR	72118	501-682-0744	682-0880	339-4
TF: 888-233-0326 ■ *Web:* www.adeq.state.ar.us						
Ethics Commission						
501 Woodlane St Ste 301n	Little Rock	AR	72203	501-324-9600		265
TF: 800-422-7773 ■ *Web:* www.arkansasethics.com						
Financial Aid Office						
114 Silas Hunt Hall	Fayetteville	AR	72701	479-575-3806	575-7790	725
Web: finaid.uark.edu						
Game & Fish Commission						
2 Natural Resource Dr	Little Rock	AR	72205	501-223-6300		339-4
TF: 800-364-4263 ■ *Web:* www.agfc.com						

Entry	City	State	ZIP	Phone	Fax	Class
General Assembly State Capitol Bldg *Web:* www.arkleg.state.ar.us	Little Rock	AR	72201	501-682-6107	682-2917	339-4
Governor State Capitol Rm 250 *Web:* www.arkansas.com/exit.axd?url=www.governor.arkansas.gov	Little Rock	AR	72201	501-682-2345	682-1382	339-4
Heritage Dept 1100 N St Ste 1500 *Web:* www.arkansasheritage.com	Little Rock	AR	72201	501-324-9150	324-9154	339-4
Higher Education Dept 423 Main St Ste 400 *Web:* www.adhe.edu	Little Rock	AR	72201	501-371-2000		339-4
Highway & Transportation Dept 10324 I-30 *TF:* 800-245-1672 ■ *Web:* www.arkansashighways.com	Little Rock	AR	72209	501-569-2000	569-2400	339-4
Human Services Dept PO Box 1437 *Web:* humanservices.arkansas.gov	Little Rock	AR	72203	501-682-1001		339-4
Information Systems Dept (DIS) 1 Capitol Mall PO Box 3155 *Web:* www.dis.arkansas.gov	Little Rock	AR	72201	501-682-9990	682-4310	339-4
Insurance Dept 1200 W Third St *TF:* 800-282-9134 ■ *Web:* insurance.arkansas.gov	Little Rock	AR	72201	501-371-2600	371-2618	339-4
Labor Dept 10421 W Markham St *Web:* www.labor.ar.gov	Little Rock	AR	72205	501-682-4500	682-4506	339-4
Lieutenant Governor 500 Woodlane St Ste 270 State Capitol *Web:* www.ltgovernor.arkansas.gov	Little Rock	AR	72201	501-682-2144		339-4
Natural Resources Commission 101 E Capitol Ste 350 *Web:* www.anrc.arkansas.gov	Little Rock	AR	72201	501-682-1611	682-3991	339-4
Parks & Tourism Dept 1 Capitol Mall ỳSte 4A-900 *TF:* 800-628-8725 ■ *Web:* www.arkansas.com	Little Rock	AR	72201	501-682-7777	324-1525	339-4
Public Accountancy Board 101 E Capitol Ave Ste 450 *Web:* www.arkansas.gov	Little Rock	AR	72201	501-682-1520	682-5538	339-4
Real Estate Commission 612 S Summit St *Web:* arec.arkansas.gov	Little Rock	AR	72201	501-683-8010	683-8020	339-4
Rehabilitation Services 525 W Capitol Ave *TF:* 800-330-0632 ■ *Web:* ace.arkansas.gov	Little Rock	AR	72201	501-296-1600	296-1655	339-4
Revenue Div 1816 W Seventh St Rm 2380 Ledbetter Bldg PO Box 1272 *Web:* www.dfa.arkansas.gov	Little Rock	AR	72203	501-682-7030	682-7599	339-4
Secretary of State 500 Woodlane Ave Ste 256 *Web:* www.sos.arkansas.gov	Little Rock	AR	72201	501-682-1010	682-3510	339-4
Securities Dept 201 E Markham St Ste 300 *TF:* 800-981-4429 ■ *Web:* securities.arkansas.gov	Little Rock	AR	72201	501-324-9260	324-9268	339-4
State Medical Board 1401 West Capitol Ave Ste 340 *TF:* 888-228-1233 ■ *Web:* www.armedicalboard.org	Little Rock	AR	72201	501-296-1802	296-1805	339-4
State Police 1 State Police Plaza Dr *Web:* www.asp.state.ar.us	Little Rock	AR	72209	501-618-8000		339-4
Supreme Court 625 Marshall St 1320 Justice Bldg *Web:* courts.arkansas.gov/cotc	Little Rock	AR	72201	501-682-6849	682-6877	339-4
Treasurer 500 Woodlane State Capitol Ste 220 *Web:* www.artreasury.gov	Little Rock	AR	72201	501-682-5888	682-9692	339-4
Veterans Affairs Dept 2200 Fort Roots Dr Bldg 65 Rm 119 *Web:* www.veterans.arkansas.gov	North Little Rock	AR	72114	501-370-3820		339-4
Vital Records Div 4815 W Markham St Slot 44 *Web:* www.healthy.arkansas.gov	Little Rock	AR	72205	501-661-2174	663-2832	339-4
Arkansas Alligator Farm & Petting Zoo 847 Whittington Ave *TF:* 800-750-0000 ■ *Web:* www.alligatorfarmzoo.com	Hot Springs	AR	71901	501-623-6172		823
Arkansas Anatomic Pathology Services pa 411 E Matthews Ave *TF:* 800-764-0447 ■ *Web:* www.dapsonline.com	Jonesboro	AR	72401	870-930-3518		418
Arkansas Arts Ctr 501 E Ninth St *Web:* www.arkarts.com	Little Rock	AR	72202	501-372-4000	375-8053	520
Arkansas Automatic Sprinklers Inc 185 Arena Rd *Web:* www.arautosprinklers.com	Cabot	AR	72023	501-843-9392		693
Arkansas Baptist Foundation 10 Remington Dr *TF:* 800-838-2272 ■ *Web:* abf.org	Little Rock	AR	72204	501-376-0732		48-20
Arkansas Bar Assn 2224 Cottondale Ln *TF:* 800-609-5668 ■ *Web:* arkbar.com	Little Rock	AR	72202	501-375-4606	375-4901	72
Arkansas Blue Cross Blue Shield PO Box 2181 **Fax Area Code:* 501 ■ *TF:* 800-238-8379	Little Rock	AR	72203	800-238-8379	378-2969*	391-3
Arkansas Business LP 122 E Second St *TF:* 888-322-6397 ■ *Web:* www.arkansasbusiness.com	Little Rock	AR	72201	501-372-1443	375-7933	457-5
Arkansas Capital Corp Group 200 S Commerce St Ste 400 *TF:* 800-216-7237 ■ *Web:* www.arcapital.com	Little Rock	AR	72201	501-374-9247	374-9425	216
Arkansas Children's Hospital 1 Children's Way *Web:* www.archildrens.org	Little Rock	AR	72202	501-364-1100		374-1
Arkansas City Area Chamber of Commerce PO Box 795 *TF:* 800-794-4780 ■ *Web:* www.arkcity.org	Arkansas City	KS	67005	620-442-0230		139
Arkansas City Convention & Visitors Bureau 106 S Summit St PO Box 795 *TF:* 800-794-4780 ■ *Web:* www.arkcity.org	Arkansas City	KS	67005	620-442-0230		206
Arkansas Correctional Industries (ACI) 6841 W 13th St *TF:* 877-635-7213 ■ *Web:* www.acicatalog.com	Pine Bluff	AR	71602	870-730-0385	850-8440	630
Arkansas County 101 Court Sq	De Witt	AR	72042	870-673-2418		338
Arkansas Data Services 27 Macarthur Dr *Web:* www.ark-data-services.com	Conway	AR	72032	501-327-8000		177
Arkansas Democrat-Gazette 121 E Capital St *TF Cust Svc:* 800-482-1121 ■ *Web:* www.arkansasonline.com	Little Rock	AR	72203	501-378-3400	372-4765	532-2
Arkansas Democratic Party 1300 W Capitol Ave *TF:* 800-995-3386 ■ *Web:* www.arkdems.org	Little Rock	AR	72201	501-374-2361		616-1
Arkansas Department of Correction 302 Wackenhut Way *Web:* www.adc.arkansas.gov	Newport	AR	72112	870-523-2639	523-6202	213
Arkansas Dept of Corrections Delta Regional Unit 425 W Capitol Ave Ste 1620 *TF:* 800-482-1127 ■ *Web:* www.arkansas.gov	Little Rock	AR	72201	501-324-8900		213
Arkansas Dept of Corrections East Arkansas Regional Unit 326 Lee 601 PO Box 180 *Web:* adc.arkansas.gov/pages/default.aspx	Brickeys	AR	72320	870-295-4700	295-6564	213
Arkansas Dept of Corrections Maximum Security Unit 2501 State Farm Rd *TF:* 866-801-3435 ■ *Web:* www.arkansas.gov	Tucker	AR	72168	501-842-3800	842-1977	213
Arkansas Dept of Corrections North Central Unit 10 Prison Cir *Web:* adc.arkansas.gov	Calico Rock	AR	72519	870-297-4311	297-4322	213
Arkansas Dept of Corrections Varner Unit PO Box 600 PO Box 600 *Web:* adc.arkansas.gov	Grady	AR	71644	870-575-1800	479-3803	213
Arkansas Dept of Corrections Wrightsville Unit PO Box 1000 *Web:* adc.arkansas.gov	Wrightsville	AR	72183	501-897-5806	897-5716	213
Arkansas Distributing Company LLC 800 E Barton Ave	West Memphis	AR	72301	870-735-3506	735-0052	81-1
Arkansas Educational Television Network (AETN) 350 S Donaghey Ave *TF:* 800-662-2386 ■ *Web:* www.aetn.org	Conway	AR	72034	501-682-2386	682-4122	632
Arkansas Educator Magazine 1500 W Fourth St *TF:* 800-632-0624 ■ *Web:* aeaonline.org	Little Rock	AR	72201	501-375-4611	375-4620	457-8
Arkansas Federal Credit Union 2424 Marshall Rd *Web:* afcu.org	Jacksonville	AR	72076	501-982-1000		219
Arkansas Graphics Inc 800 S Gaines St *TF:* 877-918-4847 ■ *Web:* www.arkansasgraphics.com	Little Rock	AR	72201	501-376-8436		627
Arkansas Headwaters Recreation Area 307 W Sackett Ave *Web:* cpw.state.co.us	Salida	CO	81201	719-539-7289		565
Arkansas Hospice 14 Parkstone Cir *TF:* 877-257-3400 ■ *Web:* www.arkansashospice.org	North Little Rock	AR	72116	501-748-3333		371
Arkansas Juvenile Access & Treatment Ctr 425 W Capitol Ste 1620 *TF:* 877-727-3468 ■ *Web:* www.arkansas.gov	Little Rock	AR	72201	501-324-8900	324-8904	412
Arkansas Lawyer Magazine 2224 Cottondale Ln *TF:* 800-609-5668 ■ *Web:* arkbar.com	Little Rock	AR	72202	501-375-4606	375-4901	457-15
Arkansas Lions Eye Bank & Laboratory 4301 W Markham St Ste 523 *Web:* eye.uams.edu	Little Rock	AR	72205	501-686-5822	686-7037	269
Arkansas Methodist Medical Ctr 900 W KingsFwy *Web:* www.myammc.org	Paragould	AR	72451	870-239-7000	239-7202	374-3
Arkansas Municipal League 301 W Second St *TF:* 800-876-4552 ■ *Web:* www.arml.org	North Little Rock	AR	72114	501-374-3484		474
Arkansas Museum of Natural Resources 3853 Smackover Hwy *TF:* 888-287-2757 ■ *Web:* www.arkansasstateparks.com	Smackover	AR	71762	870-725-2877		565
Arkansas Museum of Science & History *Museum of Discovery* 500 President Clinton Ave Ste 150 *Web:* museumofdiscovery.org	Little Rock	AR	72201	501-396-7050	396-7054	520
Arkansas Northeastern College 2501 S Div St PO Box 1109 **Fax:* Admissions ■ *TF:* 800-955-2289 ■ *Web:* www.anc.edu	Blytheville	AR	72316	870-762-1020	763-1654*	162
Arkansas Nurses Assn (ARNA) 1123 S University Ste 800 *Web:* www.arna.org	Little Rock	AR	72204	501-244-2363	244-9903	533
Arkansas Pharmacists Assn 417 S Victory St *Web:* www.arpharmacists.org	Little Rock	AR	72201	501-372-5250		585
Arkansas Poly Inc 1248 S 28th St *TF:* 800-364-5036 ■ *Web:* www.arkpoly.com	Van Buren	AR	72956	479-474-5036		345
Arkansas Post Museum 5530 Hwy 165 S *Web:* www.arkansasstateparks.com	Gillett	AR	72055	870-548-2634		565
Arkansas Post National Memorial 1741 Old Post Rd *Web:* www.nps.gov	Gillett	AR	72055	870-548-2207	548-2431	564
Arkansas Power Electronics International Inc 535 W Research Ctr Blvd Ste 209 *Web:* apei.net	Fayetteville	AR	72701	479-443-5759		256
Arkansas Power Steering & Hydraulics Inc 900 Fiber Optic Dr *TF:* 800-734-9411 ■ *Web:* apshyd.com	North Little Rock	AR	72117	501-372-4828		112
Arkansas Precast Corp 2601 Cory Dr	Jacksonville	AR	72076	501-982-1547		183
Arkansas Realtors Assn 11224 Executive Ctr Dr *TF:* 888-333-2206 ■ *Web:* www.arkansasrealtors.com	Little Rock	AR	72211	501-225-2020	225-7131	656
Arkansas Repertory Theatre 601 Main St PO Box 110 *TF:* 866-684-3737 ■ *Web:* www.therep.org	Little Rock	AR	72201	501-378-0445	378-0012	573-4
Arkansas River Valley Regional Library 501 N Front St *Web:* www.arvrls.com	Dardanelle	AR	72834	479-229-4418	229-2595	434-3
Arkansas State Dental Assn 7480 Hwy 107 *TF:* 800-501-2732 ■ *Web:* www.arkansasdentistry.org	Sherwood	AR	72120	501-834-7650	834-7657	227
Arkansas State Hospital 4313 W Markham St *Web:* humanservices.arkansas.gov	Little Rock	AR	72205	501-686-9000	682-1197	374-5

Phone | Fax | Class

Arkansas State Library
900 W Capitol Ste 100 .... Little Rock AR 72201 501-682-2053 682-1529 434-5
Web: www.library.arkansas.gov

Arkansas State University
PO Box 1630 .... State University AR 72467 870-972-3024 972-3406 166
TF: 800-382-3030 ■ *Web:* www.astate.edu

Arkansas State University Mountain Home
1600 S College St.......... Mountain Home AR 72653 870-508-6100 508-6287 162
TF: 800-482-5964 ■ *Web:* www.asumh.edu

Arkansas State University Museum
PO Box 490 .... State University AR 72467 870-972-2074 972-2793 520
TF: 800-342-2923 ■ *Web:* www.astate.edu/museum

Arkansas State University Newport
7648 Victory Blvd.......... Newport AR 72112 870-512-7800 512-7825* 162
**Fax:* Admissions ■ *TF:* 800-976-1676 ■ *Web:* www.asun.edu

Arkansas Steel Associates LLC
2803 Van Dyke Rd .... Newport AR 72112 870-523-3693 492
TF: 800-962-2902 ■ *Web:* www.arkansassteel.com

Arkansas Symphony Orchestra
2417 N Tyler St PO Box 7328.......... Little Rock AR 72217 501-666-1761 666-3193 573-3
Web: www.arkansassymphony.org

Arkansas Times
201 E Markham Ste 200.......... Little Rock AR 72201 501-375-2985 375-3623 532-5
Web: www.arktimes.com

Arkansas Trailer Manufacturing Co
3200 S Elm St.......... Little Rock AR 72204 501-666-5417 666-1787 779
Web: arkansastrailer.com

Arkansas Valley Communications
1201 E Eigth St.......... Russellville AR 72801 479-968-1502 647
TF: 800-442-1924 ■ *Web:* www.avc-wireless.com

Arkansas Valley Correctional Facility (AVCF)
12750 Colorado 96 PO Box 1000.......... Crowley CO 81033 719-267-3520 267-5024 213
Web: www.doc.state.co.us

Arkansas Valley Electric Co-op Corp
1811 W Commercial St PO Box 47.......... Ozark AR 72949 479-667-2176 667-5238 245
TF: 800-468-2176 ■ *Web:* www.avecc.com

Arkansas Valley Petroleum Inc
8336 E 73rd St Ste 100.......... Tulsa OK 74133 918-252-0508 250-4921 579
TF: 800-888-1389 ■ *Web:* arkvalprop.com

Arkansas Valley Regional Medical Ctr (AVRMC)
1100 Carson Ave .... La Junta CO 81050 719-384-5412 383-6005 374-3
TF: 877-696-6775 ■ *Web:* www.avrmc.org

Arkansas Veterinary Medical Assn
PO Box 17687 .... Little Rock AR 72222 501-868-3036 868-3034 795
TF: 800-272-1813 ■ *Web:* www.arkvetmed.org

Arkay Packaging Corp 350 E Pk Dr.......... Roanoke VA 24019 540-977-3031 977-2503 101
TF: 800-780-4707 ■ *Web:* www.arkay.com

Arkel International Inc
1048 Florida Blvd.......... Baton Rouge LA 70802 225-343-0525 261
Web: www.arkel.com

Arkos Field Services LP
919 Milam Ste 825.......... Houston TX 77002 832-783-5400 538
Web: www.arkos.com

Arkwin Industries Inc 686 Main St .... Westbury NY 11590 516-333-2640 334-6786* 790
**Fax:* Sales ■ *TF:* 800-284-2551 ■ *Web:* www.arkwin.com

ARL (US Army Research Laboratory)
Attn: AMSRD-ARL-O-PA 2800 Powder Mill Rd .... Adelphi MD 20783 301-394-2500 394-1174 668
Web: www.arl.army.mil

ARL (Association of Research Libraries)
21 Dupont Cir NW Ste 800.......... Washington DC 20036 202-296-2296 872-0884 49-5
Web: www.arl.org

Arland Tool & Manufacturing Inc
PO Box 207 .... Sturbridge MA 01566 508-347-3368 487
Web: www.arland.com

Arlans Market Inc 6500 Fm 2100 .... Crosby TX 77532 281-328-4868 345
Web: www.arlansmarket.com

Arledge & Assoc Inc 309 N Bryant Ave .... Edmond OK 73034 405-348-0615 348-0931 2
Web: www.jmacpas.com

Arley Wholesale Inc 700 N S Rd .... Scranton PA 18504 570-344-9874 191-1
Web: www.arleywholesale.com

Arlington Arts Ctr (AAC)
3550 Wilson Blvd.......... Arlington VA 22201 703-248-6800 248-6849 50-2
Web: www.arlingtonartscenter.org

Arlington Baptist College
3001 W Div St .... Arlington TX 76012 817-461-8741 274-1138* 166
**Fax:* Admissions ■ *TF:* 800-899-0012 ■ *Web:* arlingtonbaptistcollege.edu

Arlington Capital Management Inc
21 S Evergreen Ave Ste 210 .... Arlington Heights IL 60005 847-670-4030 194
TF: 855-471-5796 ■ *Web:* www.arlington-capital.com

Arlington Capital Partners
5425 Wisconsin Ave Ste 200 .... Chevy Chase MD 20015 202-337-7500 337-7525 403
Web: www.arlingtoncap.com

Arlington Central School District
144 Todd Hill Rd.......... LaGrangeville NY 12540 845-486-4460 486-4457 685
TF: 800-993-8982 ■ *Web:* www.arlingtonschools.org

Arlington Chamber of Commerce
2009 14th St N Ste 111 .... Arlington VA 22201 703-525-2400 139
Web: www.arlingtonchamber.org

Arlington Chamber of Commerce
505 E Border St .... Arlington TX 76010 817-275-2613 701-0893 139
TF: 800-275-8777 ■ *Web:* www.arlingtontx.com

Arlington Chamber of Commerce
611 Massachusetts Ave .... Arlington MA 02474 781-643-4600 646-5581 139
Web: www.arlcc.org

Arlington Coal & Lumber Company Inc
41 Pk Ave.......... Arlington MA 02476 781-643-8100 643-7414 364
TF: 800-649-8101 ■ *Web:* www.arlcoal.com

Arlington Computer Products Inc
851 Commerce Ct.......... Buffalo Grove IL 60089 847-541-6333 180
TF Orders: 800-548-5105 ■ *Web:* www.arlingtoncp.com

Arlington Connection 1606 King St.......... Alexandria VA 22314 703-778-9431 532-4
Web: www.connectionnewspapers.com

Arlington Convention & Visitors Bureau
1905 E Randol Mill Rd.......... Arlington TX 76011 817-265-7721 206
TF: 800-433-5374 ■ *Web:* www.arlington.org

Arlington Convention Ctr
1200 Ballpark Way .... Arlington TX 76011 817-459-5000 459-5091 205
Web: webapps.arlingtontx.gov/tmp/acc

Arlington County
2100 Clarendon Blvd Ste 300.......... Arlington VA 22201 703-228-3130 228-7430 338
Web: www.arlingtonva.us

Arlington County Central Library
1015 N Quincy St.......... Arlington VA 22201 703-228-5990 434-3
Web: www.arlingtonva.us

Arlington Hat Co Inc 4725 34th St.......... Long Island NY 11101 718-361-3000 361-8713 155-9

Arlington Heights Chamber of Commerce
311 S Arlington Heights Rd Ste 20.......... Arlington Heights IL 60005 847-253-1703 139

Arlington Heights Memorial Library
500 N Dunton Ave.......... Arlington Heights IL 60004 847-392-0100 506-2650 434-3
Web: www.ahml.info

Arlington Historical Museum
1805 S Arlington Ridge Rd.......... Arlington VA 22202 703-892-4204 520
Web: www.arlingtonhistoricalsociety.org

Arlington House-Robert E Lee Memorial
George Washington Memorial Pkwy Turkey Run Pk . McLean VA 22101 703-235-1530 235-1546 564
Web: www.nps.gov/arho

Arlington Industries Inc
1616 Lakeside Dr.......... Waukegan IL 60085 847-689-2754 689-1616 534
TF: 800-323-4147 ■ *Web:* www.arli.com

Arlington Industries Inc
1 Stauffer Industrial Pk.......... Scranton PA 18517 570-562-0270 562-0646 815
TF: 800-233-4717 ■ *Web:* www.aifittings.com

Arlington Iron Works 9127 Euclid Ave.......... Manassas VA 20110 703-368-3193 480
Web: www.arlingtonironworks.com

Arlington Machine & Tool Co
90 New Dutch Ln .... Fairfield NJ 07004 973-276-1377 757
Web: www.arlingtonmachine.com

Arlington Memorial Hospital
800 W Randol Mill Rd .... Arlington TX 76012 817-960-6100 374-3
Web: www.texashealth.org

Arlington Metals Corp
11355 Franklin Ave.......... Franklin Park IL 60131 847-451-9100 451-9676 482
Web: www.arlingtonmetals.com

Arlington Museum of Art
201 W Main St .... Arlington TX 76010 817-275-4600 520
TF: 800-303-3047 ■ *Web:* www.arlingtonmuseum.org

Arlington Park
2200 W Euclid Ave PO Box 7 .... Arlington Heights IL 60006 847-385-7500 385-7251 642
TF: 800-935-9935 ■ *Web:* www.arlingtonpark.com

Arlington Plating Co
600 S Vermont St PO Box 974 .... Palatine IL 60067 847-359-1490 481
Web: www.arlingtonplating.com

Arlington Public Library
101 W Abram St PO Box 90231 .... Arlington TX 76004 817-459-6961 434-3
Web: www.arlingtonlibrary.org

Arlington Residence Court Hotel
1200 N Courthouse Rd.......... Arlington VA 22201 703-524-4000 707
TF: 800-275-2866 ■ *Web:* www.arlingtoncourthotel.com

Arlington Resort Hotel & Spa
239 Central Ave .... Hot Springs AR 71901 501-623-7771 669
TF: 800-643-1502 ■ *Web:* www.arlingtonhotel.com

Arlington School District
315 N French Ave.......... Arlington WA 98223 360-618-6200 618-6221 685
TF: 877-766-4753 ■ *Web:* www.asd.wednet.edu

Arlington Steak House 1724 W Div St.......... Arlington TX 76012 817-275-7881 275-7881 671

Arlington Toyota Inc
10939 Atlantic Blvd .... Jacksonville FL 32225 904-721-3000 57
Web: www.arlingtontoyota.com

Arlington (TX) City Hall
101 W Abram St.......... Arlington TX 76010 817-275-3271 459-6116 337
TF: 800-275-8777 ■ *Web:* www.arlington-tx.gov/government/city-hall

Arlo G. Lott Trucking Inc 257 S 100 E .... Jerome ID 83338 208-324-5053 324-0668 780
TF: 800-443-5688 ■ *Web:* arloglotttrucking.com

Arlon Graphics 2811 S Harbor Blvd .... Santa Ana CA 92704 714-540-2811 329-2756* 3
**Fax Area Code:* 800 ■ *TF:* 800-232-7161 ■ *Web:* www.arlon.com

ARM (Associated Risk Managers)
2 Pierce Pl .... Itasca IL 60143 630-285-4324 285-3590 49-9
TF: 800-735-5441 ■ *Web:* www.armiweb.com

ARM (Association of Rotational Molders International)
800 Roosevelt Rd Ste C-312.......... Glen Ellyn IL 60137 630-942-6589 790-3095 49-13
Web: www.rotomolding.org

ARM Inc 141 Caspian Ct.......... Sunnyvale CA 94089 408-734-5600 734-5050 696
Web: www.arm.com

ArMA (Arizona Medical Assn, The)
810 W Bethany Home Rd .... Phoenix AZ 85013 602-246-8901 242-6283 474
TF: 800-482-3480 ■ *Web:* www.azmed.org

ARMA (American Rock Mechanics Assn)
600 Woodland Terr.......... Alexandria VA 22302 703-683-1808 683-1815 49-19
Web: www.armarocks.org

ARMA (Asphalt Roofing Manufacturers Assn)
529 14th St NW Ste 750.......... Washington DC 20045 202-207-0917 223-9741 49-3
TF: 800-247-6637 ■ *Web:* www.asphaltroofing.org

ARMA International
11880 College Blvd Ste 450.......... Overland Park KS 66210 913-341-3808 341-3742 49-12
TF: 800-422-2762 ■ *Web:* www.arma.org

Armacell LLC 7600 Oakwood St Ext.......... Mebane NC 27302 919-304-3846 601
Web: www.armacell.us

Armada Group Inc, The
325 Soquel Ave Ste A.......... Santa Cruz CA 95062 800-408-2120 344
TF: 800-408-2120 ■ *Web:* www.thearmadagroup.com

Armada Hoffler
222 Central Pk Ave Ste 2100 .... Virginia Beach VA 23462 757-366-4000 186
Web: www.armadahoffler.com

Armada Oil & Gas Company Inc
3335 Greenfield Rd.......... Melvindale MI 48122 313-582-1777 579
Web: www.armadaoil.com

Armada Rubber Mfg Co
24586 Armada Ridge Rd PO Box 579.......... Armada MI 48005 586-784-9135 784-5023 677
Web: www.armadarubber.com

Armadillo Enterprises Inc
4924 W Waters Ave.......... Tampa FL 33634 813-600-3920 526
Web: www.armadilloent.com

ArmaLite Inc 745 S Hanford St .... Geneseo IL 61254 309-944-6939 807
Web: www.armalite.com

Armand Manufacturing Inc
2399 Silver Wolf Dr .... Henderson NV 89011 702-565-7500 565-3838 66
TF: 800-669-9811 ■ *Web:* www.armandmfg.com

	Phone	Fax	Class
Armando's Mexican Restaurant 4242 W Vernor Hwy .... Detroit MI 48209 *Web:* www.mexicantown.com	313-554-0666		671
Armandos 2630 Westheimer Rd .... Houston TX 77098 *Web:* www.armandosrestaurant.com	713-520-1738		671
Armani's Restaurant 2900 Bayport Dr .... Tampa FL 33607 *Web:* www.hyatt.com	813-207-6800		671
Armanino Foods of Distinction Inc 30588 San Antonio St .... Hayward CA 94544 *OTC:* AMNF ■ *TF:* 800-255-5855 ■ *Web:* www.armaninofoods.com	510-441-9300	441-0101	296-36
Armanino LLP 12667 Alcosta Blvd Ste 500 .... San Ramon CA 94583 *Web:* www.armaninollp.com	925-790-2600	790-2601	2
Armanta Inc 350 Mt Kemble Ave .... Morris Township NJ 07960 *TF:* 800-432-1255 ■ *Web:* www.armanta.com	973-326-9600		809
Armatron International Inc 15 Highland Ave .... Malden MA 02148 *TF:* 800-343-3280 ■ *Web:* www.flowtron.com	781-321-2300		429
Armature Dns 2000 Inc 11001 Jean Meunier .... Montreal QC H1G4S7 *TF:* 800-363-7996 ■ *Web:* www.dns-2000.com	514-324-1141		791
Armbrae Academy 1400 Oxford St .... Halifax NS B3H3Y8 *Web:* www.armbrae.ns.ca	902-423-7920		685
Armbrecht Jackson LLP 63 S Royal St Riverview Plaza 13th Fl .... Mobile AL 36602 *TF:* 800-973-1177 ■ *Web:* www.ajlaw.com	251-405-1300		428
Armbrust International Ltd 735 Allens Ave .... Providence RI 02905 *Web:* www.armbrustintl.com	401-781-3300		409
Armbrust Paper Tubes Inc 6255 S Harlem Ave .... Chicago IL 60638 *Web:* www.tubesrus.com	773-586-3232		125
Armec Corp 8113 Beaver Ridge Rd .... Knoxville TN 37931 *Web:* armec.us	865-483-9969		454
Armed Forces Communications & Electronics Assn (AFCEA) 4400 Fair Lakes Ct .... Fairfax VA 22033 *TF:* 800-336-4583 ■ *Web:* www.afcea.org	703-631-6100	631-4693	48-19
Armed Forces Financial Network LLC 11601 Roosevelt Blvd TA-94 .... Saint Petersburg FL 33716 *Web:* www.affn.org	727-227-2880		225
Armed Forces Insurance Exchange (AFI) PO Box G .... Fort Leavenworth KS 66027 *TF:* 800-255-0187 ■ *Web:* www.afi.org	800-255-6792		391-4
Armed Forces Retirement Home - Gulfport 1800 Beach Dr .... Gulfport MS 39507 **Fax Area Code:* 202 ■ *TF:* 800-422-9988 ■ *Web:* www.afrh.gov	800-422-9988	541-7519*	672
Armed Forces Retirement Home - Washington 3700 N Capitol St NW .... Washington DC 20011 **Fax Area Code:* 202 ■ *TF Admissions:* 800-422-9988 ■ *Web:* www.afrh.gov/afrh	800-422-9988	541-7519*	450
Armed Response Team, The 6201 Pan American Fwy NE Ste 237 .... Albuquerque NM 87109 *Web:* www.armedresponseteam.com	505-237-2278		693
Armed Services Mutual Benefit Assn (ASMBA) PO Box 160384 .... Nashville TN 37216 *TF:* 800-251-8434 ■ *Web:* www.asmba.com	615-851-0800	851-9484	48-19
Armelle Supermarket 140 W Boynton Beach Blvd .... Boynton Beach FL 33435	561-739-6543		297-8
Armellini Express Lines Inc 3446 SW Armellini Ave .... Palm City FL 34990 **Fax:* Cust Svc ■ *TF:* 800-327-7887 ■ *Web:* www.armellini.com	772-287-0575	221-3284*	780
Armen Computing Ltd 286 Bethany Ct .... Inman SC 29349 **Fax Area Code:* 212 ■ *TF:* 800-372-6078	800-372-6078	537-0444*	809
Armenia 119 E 36th St .... New York NY 10016 *Web:* www.un.int	212-686-9079	686-3934	784
Armenia Embassy 2225 R St NW .... Washington DC 20008 *Web:* www.armeniaemb.org	202-319-1976		257
Armenian Assembly of America 734 15th St NW Ste 500 .... Washington DC 20005 *Web:* www.aaainc.org	202-393-3434	638-4904	48-14
Armenian Church of America 630 Second Ave .... New York NY 10016 *Web:* www.armenianchurch.org	212-686-0710	779-3558	48-20
Armenian General Benevolent Union (AGBU) 55 E 59th St 7th Fl .... New York NY 10022 *Web:* www.agbu.org	212-319-6383	319-6507	48-14
Arment Dietrich Public Relations PO Box 13013 Ste 4n .... Chicago IL 60613 *Web:* www.armentdietrich.com	312-878-6406		636
Armentor Glenn Law Corp 300 Stewart St .... Lafayette LA 70501 *TF:* 800-960-5551 ■ *Web:* www.glennarmentor.com	337-233-1471		428
Armijo High School 824 Washington St .... Fairfield CA 94533 *Web:* www.fsusd.org	707-422-7500		685
Armin Industries 1500 N La Fox St .... South Elgin IL 60177 *TF:* 800-427-3607 ■ *Web:* www.armin-ind.com	847-742-1864	742-0253	757
Armistead Mechanical Inc 168 Hopper Ave .... Waldwick NJ 07463 *TF:* 800-587-5267 ■ *Web:* www.armisteadmechanical.com	201-447-6740	447-6744	189-10
Armm Inc 17744 Sampson Ln .... Huntington Beach CA 92647 *Web:* www.armminc.com	714-848-8190		476
Armor Group Inc, The 4600 N Mason-Montgomery Rd .... Mason OH 45040 *TF:* 800-255-0393 ■ *Web:* www.thearmorgroup.com	800-255-0393		318
Armor Protective Packaging 951 Jones St .... Howell MI 48843 *TF:* 800-365-1117 ■ *Web:* www.armorvci.com	517-546-1117		557
Armor Security Inc 2601 Stevens Ave S .... Minneapolis MN 55408 *Web:* www.armorsecurity.com	612-870-4142		45
Armortex Inc 5926 Corridor Pkwy .... Schertz TX 78154 *Web:* www.armortex.com	210-661-8306	661-8308	194
Armory Art Ctr 1700 Parker Ave .... West Palm Beach FL 33401 *Web:* www.armoryart.org	561-832-1776	832-0191	50-2
Armour Group Inc 350 E Las Olas Blvd Ste 800 .... Fort Lauderdale FL 33301 *Web:* www.thearmourgroup.com	954-767-2030		330
Armour Risk Management Inc 1880 JFK Blvad Ste 801 .... Philadelphia PA 19103 *Web:* www.armourholdings.com	215-665-5000		391-4
Armour Transportation Systems Inc 689 Edinburgh Dr .... Moncton NB E1E2L4 *TF:* 800-561-7987 ■ *Web:* www.armour.ca	506-857-0205		23
Arms Acres 75 Seminary Hill Rd .... Carmel NY 10512 *TF:* 800-989-2676 ■ *Web:* www.armsacres.com	845-225-3400		726
Arms Control Assn 1313 L St NW Ste 130 .... Washington DC 20005 *Web:* www.armscontrol.org	202-463-8270	463-8273	48-5
Arms Family Museum of Local History 648 Wick Ave .... Youngstown OH 44502 *Web:* www.mahoninghistory.org	330-743-2589	743-7210	520
Armstrong Ambulance Service Inc 87 Mystic St .... Arlington MA 02474 *Web:* armstrongambulance.com	781-648-0612		30
Armstrong Atlantic State University 11935 Abercorn St .... Savannah GA 31419 *TF:* 800-633-2349 ■ *Web:* www.armstrong.edu	800-633-2349		166
Armstrong Bros Holding Company Inc 8530 M 60 .... Union City MI 49094	517-741-4471		491
Armstrong Consultants Inc 861 Rood Ave .... Grand Junction CO 81501 *Web:* www.armstrongconsultants.com	970-242-0101		256
Armstrong County 100 Trice St PO Box 189 .... Claude TX 79019 *Web:* www.co.armstrong.tx.us	806-226-3221		338
Armstrong County 450 E Market St .... Kittanning PA 16201 *TF:* 800-368-1066 ■ *Web:* www.co.armstrong.pa.us	724-543-2500		338
Armstrong County Chamber of Commerce 124 Market St .... Kittanning PA 16201 *TF:* 800-379-7448 ■ *Web:* allekiskistrong.com	724-543-1305		139
Armstrong County Memorial Hospital (ACMH) 1 Nolte Dr .... Kittanning PA 16201 *Web:* www.acmh.org	724-543-8500	543-8704	374-3
Armstrong County Tourist Bureau 125 Market St Ste 2 .... Kittanning PA 16201 *TF:* 888-265-9954 ■ *Web:* www.armstrongcounty.com	724-543-4003	545-3119	206
Armstrong Donohue & Ceppos 204 Monroe St Ste 101 .... Rockville MD 20850 *Web:* www.adclawfirm.com	301-251-0440		428
Armstrong Engineering Assoc Inc PO Box 566 .... West Chester PA 19381 *TF:* 800-343-3082 ■ *Web:* www.rmarmstrong.com	610-436-6080	436-0374	91
Armstrong Garden Centers Inc (AGC) 2200 E Rt 66 Ste 200 .... Glendora CA 91740 *Web:* www.armstronggarden.com	626-914-1091		323
Armstrong Group of Cos 1 Armstrong Pl .... Butler PA 16001 *Web:* www.armstrongonewire.com	724-283-0925		116
Armstrong International Inc 2081 SE Ocean Blvd 4th Fl .... Stuart FL 34996 *TF:* 866-738-5125 ■ *Web:* www.armstronginternational.com	772-286-7175	286-1001	789
Armstrong Lumber Co Inc 2709 Auburn Way N .... Auburn WA 98002 *TF:* 800-868-9066 ■ *Web:* www.armstrong-homes.com	253-833-6666		817
Armstrong Medical Industries Inc 575 Knightsbridge Pkwy .... Lincolnshire IL 60069 *TF Cust Svc:* 800-323-4220 ■ *Web:* www.armstrongmedical.com	847-913-0101	913-0138	477
Armstrong Mfg Co 2700 SE Tacoma St .... Portland OR 97202 *TF:* 800-426-6226 ■ *Web:* www.armstrongblue.com	503-228-8381	228-8384	494
Armstrong Mold Corp 6910 Manlius Ctr Rd .... East Syracuse NY 13057 *Web:* www.armstrongmold.com	315-437-1517	437-9198	757
Armstrong Oil and Gas Inc 1421 BLk St .... Denver CO 80202 *Web:* www.armstrongoilandgas.com	303-623-1821		538
Armstrong Partnership LP 23 Prince Andrew Pl .... Toronto ON M3C2H2 *TF:* 800-463-7828 ■ *Web:* www.armstrongpartnership.com	416-444-3050		195
Armstrong Pumps Inc 93 E Ave .... North Tonawanda NY 14120 *Web:* armstrongfluidtechnology.com	716-693-8813		641
Armstrong Redwoods State Reserve 17000 Armstrong Woods Rd .... Guerneville CA 95446 *Web:* www.parks.ca.gov/default.asp?page_id=450	707-869-2015	869-5629	565
Armstrong School District 181 Heritage Park Dr Ste 2 .... Kittanning PA 16201 *Web:* www.asd.k12.pa.us	724-548-7200		685
Armstrong Shaw Associates Inc 237 Elm St .... New Canaan CT 06840 *Web:* www.armstrongshaw.com	203-972-9600		401
Armstrong Systems & Consulting 5101 Tremont Ave Ste A .... Davenport IA 52807	563-386-9090		608
Armstrong World Industries Inc 2500 Columbia Ave .... Lancaster PA 17603 *NYSE:* AWI ■ *TF Cust Svc:* 800-233-3823 ■ *Web:* www.armstrong.com	717-397-0611		291
Armtec Defense Products Co 85-901 Ave 53 .... Coachella CA 92236 *TF:* 800-341-2333 ■ *Web:* esterline.com	760-398-0143	398-3896	807
Army & Navy Academy 2605 Carlsbad Blvd .... Carlsbad CA 92008 *TF:* 888-762-2338 ■ *Web:* www.armyandnavyacademy.org	760-729-2385	434-5948	622
Army & Navy Club, The 901 17th St NW .... Washington DC 20006 *Web:* www.armynavyclub.org	202-628-8400		42
Army Aviation Assn of America (AAAA) 593 Main St .... Monroe CT 06468 *Web:* www.quad-a.org	203-268-2450	268-5870	48-19
Army Distaff Foundation 6200 Oregon Ave NW .... Washington DC 20015 *TF:* 800-541-4255 ■ *Web:* www.armydistaff.org	202-541-0149		48-19
ARMY Magazine 2425 Wilson Blvd .... Arlington VA 22201 *TF:* 800-336-4570 ■ *Web:* www.ausa.org	703-841-4300	525-9039	457-12
Army Residence Community 7400 Crestway .... San Antonio TX 78239 *TF:* 800-725-0083 ■ *Web:* www.armyresidence.com	210-646-5316		672
ARN (Association of Rehabilitation Nurses) 4700 West Lake Ave .... Glenview IL 60025 *TF:* 800-229-7530 ■ *Web:* www.rehabnurse.org	847-375-4710	375-6481	49-8

Name / Address	City	State	ZIP	Phone	Fax	Class
ARNA (Arkansas Nurses Assn) 1123 S University Ste 800 *Web:* www.arna.org	Little Rock	AR	72204	501-244-2363	244-9903	533
Arnaud's 813 Bienville St *TF:* 866-230-8895 ■ *Web:* www.arnaudsrestaurant.com	New Orleans	LA	70112	504-523-5433		671
Arneg Canada Inc 18 Rue Richelieu *TF:* 800-363-3439 ■ *Web:* arneg.ca	Lacolle	QC	J0J1J0	450-246-3837	246-2368	610
Arneg LLC 750 Old Hargrave Rd *Web:* www.arnegusa.com	Lexington	NC	27295	336-956-5300		610
Arnellwest Inc Main St & 600 S *Web:* www.arnell-west.com	Salt Lake City	UT	84111	801-975-9966		186
Arnerich Massena & Associates Inc 2045 NE Martin Luther King Jr Blvd *Web:* arnerichmassena.com	Portland	OR	97212	503-239-0475		401
Arneson River Theatre 418 Villita St *Web:* getcreativesanantonio.com	San Antonio	TX	78205	210-207-8614		572
Arnie's Inc 722 Leonard St NW *TF:* 800-442-1162 ■ *Web:* www.arniesrestaurants.com	Grand Rapids	MI	49503	616-454-3098		296-1
Arnima Design 518 N Tampa St Ste 320 *Web:* arnima.com	Tampa	FL	33602	813-341-3500		177
Arnoff Moving & Storage Inc 1282 Dutchess Tpke *TF:* 800-633-6683 ■ *Web:* www.arnoff.com	Poughkeepsie	NY	12603	845-471-1504	452-3606	519
Arnold & Assoc 14275 Midway Rd Ste 170 *TF:* 800-535-6329 ■ *Web:* www.elarnoldandassociates.com	Addison	TX	75001	972-991-1144		256
Arnold & Itkin LLP 6009 Memorial Dr *TF:* 888-493-1629 ■ *Web:* www.arnolditkin.com	Houston	TX	77007	713-222-3800		428
Arnold & Mabel Beckman Foundation 100 Academy Dr *Web:* www.beckman-foundation.org	Irvine	CA	92617	949-721-2222		305
Arnold & Porter Kaye Scholer LLP 250 W 55th St *Web:* www.kayescholer.com	New York	NY	10019	212-836-8000	836-8689	428
Arnold & Porter Kaye Scholer LLP 601 Massachusetts Ave NW *Web:* www.arnoldporter.com	Washington	DC	20001	202-942-5000	942-5999	428
Arnold Air Force Base 100 Kindel Dr Ste B-213 *Web:* www.arnold.af.mil	Arnold	TN	37389	931-454-3000		497-1
Arnold Arboretum of Harvard University 125 Arborway *Web:* arboretum.harvard.edu	Jamaica Plain	MA	02130	617-524-1718	524-1418	97
Arnold Construction Corp 700 Gervais St *Web:* www.arnoldconstruction.net	Columbia	SC	29201	803-731-4321		186
Arnold Engineering Inc 345 Cessna Cir Ste 102 *Web:* www.arnoldeng.com	Corona	CA	92880	951-898-0999		256
Arnold Lumber Co 251 Fairgrounds Rd *TF:* 800-339-0116 ■ *Web:* www.arnold.myeshowroom.com	West Kingston	RI	02092	401-783-2266	792-3610	191-3
Arnold Machinery Co 2975 West 2100 South *TF Cust Svc:* 800-821-0548 ■ *Web:* www.arnoldmachinery.com	Salt Lake City	UT	84119	801-972-4000	972-4371	358
Arnold Motor Supply & The Merrill Co 601 First Ave S W *Web:* www.arnoldmotorsupply.com	Spencer	IA	51301	712-262-1141		61
Arnold Palmer Hospital for Children & Women 92 W Miller St *TF:* 800-648-3818 ■ *Web:* www.orlandohealth.com	Orlando	FL	32806	407-649-9111		374-1
Arnold Refrigeration Inc 1122 N Cherry *TF:* 800-441-1170 ■ *Web:* arnoldrefrigeration.com	San Antonio	TX	78202	210-225-5493	225-2605	109-10
Arnold Sanders Consulting Engineers Inc 12651 Mcgregor Blvd Ste 103 *Web:* arnoldsanders.com	Fort Myers	FL	33919	239-267-3666		261
Arnold State Recreation Area PO Box 117 *Web:* www.outdoornebraska.ne.gov/parks	Anselmo	NE	68813	308-749-2235		565
Arnold Steel Company Inc 79 Randolph Rd *Web:* www.arnoldsteel.com	Howell	NJ	07731	732-363-1079		492
Arnold Supply Inc 2409 Pasadena Blvd *Web:* www.arnoldsupply.com	Pasadena	TX	77502	713-477-3333		358
Arnold Transportation Services Inc 9523 Florida Mining Blvd *TF:* 800-846-4321 ■ *Web:* www.arnoldtrans.com	Jacksonville	FL	32257	972-986-3154		780
Arnold Walker & Arnold & Company PC 915 N Jefferson Ave *TF:* 800-256-5518 ■ *Web:* www.awacpa.com	Mount Pleasant	TX	75455	903-572-6606		2
Arnot Ogden Medical Ctr 600 Roe Ave *TF:* 800-952-2662 ■ *Web:* www.arnothealth.org	Elmira	NY	14905	607-737-4100	737-4447	374-3
Arnprior Aerospace Inc 107 Baskin Dr E *Web:* www.arnprioraerospace.com	Arnprior	ON	K7S3M1	613-623-4267		21
Arns Law Firm, The 515 Folsom St Fl 3 *TF:* 800-495-7800 ■ *Web:* www.arnslaw.com	San Francisco	CA	94105	415-495-7800		428
Arnstein & Lehr LLP 120 S Riverside Plaza Ste 1200 *Web:* www.arnstein.com	Chicago	IL	60606	312-876-7100		445
Aro Welding 48500 Structural Dr *Web:* www.arotechnologies.com	Chesterfield	MI	48051	586-949-9353	949-4493	811
Arobella Medical LLC 5929 Baker Rd Ste 470 *Web:* www.advcircuit.com	Minnetonka	MN	55345	952-345-6840		250
Arobotech Systems Inc 1524 E Avis Dr *Web:* www.arobotech.com	Madison Heights	MI	48071	248-588-9080		757
AROG Pharmaceuticals LLC 12400 Coit Rd *Web:* www.arogpharma.com	Dallas	TX	75251	214-593-0500		582
Aromaland Inc 1326 Rufina Cir *TF:* 800-933-5267 ■ *Web:* www.aromaland.com	Santa Fe	NM	87507	505-438-0402		77
Aronoff Ctr for the Arts 650 Walnut St *Web:* www.cincinnatiarts.org	Cincinnati	OH	45202	513-721-3344	977-4150	572
Aronov Realty 3500 Eastern Blvd *Web:* www.aronov.com	Montgomery	AL	36116	334-277-1000	272-0747	655
Aronson & Co 805 King Farm Blvd Ste 300 *Web:* www.aronsonllc.com	Rockville	MD	20850	301-231-6200	231-7630	2
Aronson + Johnson + Ortiz LP 230 S Broad St 20th Fl *Web:* www.ajopartners.com	Philadelphia	PA	19102	215-546-7500		690
Aroostook Home Health Services 658 Main St Ste 2 *TF:* 877-688-9977 ■ *Web:* aroostookhomehealthservices.com	Caribou	ME	04736	207-492-8290	492-8245	363
Aroostook Medical Ctr, The (TAMC) 140 Academy St *Web:* www.tamc.org	Presque Isle	ME	04769	207-768-4000		374-3
Aroostook State Park 87 State Pk Rd *Web:* www.maine.gov	Presque Isle	ME	04769	207-768-8341		565
Arora & Assoc PC 1200 Lenox Dr Ste 200 *Web:* www.arorapc.com	Lawrence Township	NJ	08648	609-844-1111		256
Around The Clock Care 5353 Truxtun Ave *Web:* www.bakersfieldcare.com	Bakersfield	CA	93309	661-324-4277		363
AroundWire.Com LLC 9455 De Soto Ave *TF:* 888-382-3793 ■ *Web:* www.aroundwire.com	Chatsworth	CA	91311	888-382-3793		387
Arowana Consulting Inc 1550 Park Ave Ste 202 *Web:* www.arowanaconsulting.com	South Plainfield	NJ	07080	732-412-3567		177
Arpa International Film Festival 2919 Maxwell St *Web:* www.affma.org	Los Angeles	CA	90027	323-663-1882	663-1882	282
ARPAC Group 9511 W River St *TF:* 800-496-7210 ■ *Web:* www.arpac.com	Schiller Park	IL	60176	847-678-9034	671-7006	547
Arpin International Group Inc 4372 Post Rd *TF:* 800-323-1963 ■ *Web:* www.arpinintl.com	East Greenwich	RI	02818	401-885-4600		360-3
Arque Capital Ltd 7501 E McCormick Pkwy *Web:* www.arquecapital.com	Scottsdale	AZ	85258	602-971-9000		690
Arquitectonica International Corp 2900 Oak Ave *Web:* arquitectonica.com	Miami	FL	33133	305-372-1812	372-1175	261
ArQule Inc 19 Presidential Way *NASDAQ: ARQL* ■ *TF:* 800-373-7827 ■ *Web:* www.arqule.com	Woburn	MA	01801	781-994-0300	376-6019	85
Arradiance Inc 142 N Rd Ste F-150 *Web:* www.arradiance.com	Sudbury	MA	01776	978-369-8291		253
Array BioPharma Inc 3200 Walnut St *NASDAQ: ARRY* ■ *TF:* 877-633-2436 ■ *Web:* www.arraybiopharma.com	Boulder	CO	80301	303-381-6600	449-5376	85
Array Healthcare Facilities Solutions 2520 Renaissance Blvd Ste 110 *Web:* www.array-architects.com	King of Prussia	PA	19406	610-270-0599		261
Array Marketing 45 Progress Ave *TF:* 800-295-4120 ■ *Web:* www.arraymarketing.com	Toronto	ON	M1P2Y6	416-299-4865	292-9759	233
Arrayent Inc 2317 Broadway St *Web:* www.arrayent.com	Redwood City	CA	94063	650-260-4520		256
Arrayworks Inc 135 Wood Rd	Braintree	MA	02184	781-849-9797		177
Arrendale Associates Inc 20484 Chartwell Ctr Dr Ste G *Web:* www.aaita.com	Cornelius	NC	28031	704-895-8025		177
Arribas Bros Inc 1500 Live Oak Ln *Web:* www.arribas.com	Orlando	FL	32830	407-828-4840		327
Arrington Jodey (Rep R - TX) 1029 Longworth HOB *Web:* arrington.house.gov	Washington	DC	20515	202-225-4005	225-9615	342-2
Arrington Manufacturing LLC 67 Motorsport Dr *Web:* www.shophemi.com	Martinsville	VA	24112	276-666-6767		247
Arris 60 Decibel Rd *TF:* 800-233-2267 ■ *Web:* www.arris.com	State College	PA	16801	814-238-2461		647
Arris Group Inc 3871 Lakefield Dr *NASDAQ: ARRS* ■ *TF:* 866-362-7747 ■ *Web:* www.arris.com	Suwanee	GA	30024	678-473-2000	473-8470	647
ARRL (American Radio Relay League) 225 Main St *TF:* 888-277-5289 ■ *Web:* www.arrl.org	Newington	CT	06111	860-594-0200	594-0259	49-14
Arr-maz Custom Chemicals Inc 9189 stevedoring rd *Web:* m.arrmaz.com	Convent	LA	70723	863-578-1206		579
Arro Consulting Inc 108 W Airport Rd *TF:* 800-536-1401 ■ *Web:* www.thearrogroup.com	Lititz	PA	17543	717-569-7021		261
ArroHealth 49 Wireless Blvd Ste 140 *TF:* 866-449-8844 ■ *Web:* www.arrohealth.com	Hauppauge	NY	11788	631-780-5000		393
Arrone Appel CPA Professional 2425 Balsam Dr *Web:* appel-cpa.com	Boulder	CO	80304	303-545-5755		2
Arrow Electric Company Inc 317 Wabasso Ave *TF:* 888-999-5591 ■ *Web:* www.arrowelectric.com	Louisville	KY	40209	502-367-0141	361-8613	189-4
Arrow Electronics Corp 7459 S Lima St *NYSE: ARW* ■ *Web:* www.arrow.com	Englewood	CO	80112	303-824-4000		174
Arrow Electronics, Inc 9201 East Dry Creek Rd *Web:* www.arrowecs.com	Centennial	CO	80112	303-824-4000		174
Arrow Energy Services Inc 4030 Columbus Dr *Web:* www.arrowenergyservices.com	Kalkaska	MI	49646	231-258-4596		540
Arrow Engine Co 2301 E Independence St *TF:* 800-331-3662 ■ *Web:* www.arrowengines.com	Tulsa	OK	74110	918-583-5711		262
Arrow Environmental Services Inc 6225 Tower Ln *TF:* 888-424-2324 ■ *Web:* www.arrowservices.com	Sarasota	FL	34240	888-424-2324		577
Arrow Fastener Co Inc 271 Mayhill St *TF:* 800-776-2228 ■ *Web:* www.arrowfastener.com	Saddle Brook	NJ	07663	201-843-6900	843-3911	758
Arrow Financial Corp 250 Glen St *NASDAQ: AROW* ■ *TF:* 888-444-0058 ■ *Web:* www.arrowfinancial.com	Glens Falls	NY	12801	518-415-4307		360-2
Arrow Florist & Park Avenue Greenhouses Inc 757 Pk Ave *TF:* 800-556-7097 ■ *Web:* www.arrowflorist.net	Cranston	RI	02910	401-785-1900	785-4120	292

	Phone	Fax	Class
Arrow Freight Management Inc 1001 Berryville st, El Paso TX 79928 *TF:* 888-598-9891 ■ *Web:* www.arrowelp.com	888-598-9891		311
Arrow Gear Company Inc 2301 Curtiss St., Downers Grove IL 60515 *Web:* www.arrowgear.com	630-969-7640	969-0253	22
Arrow International Inc 2400 Bernville Rd, Reading PA 19605 *Web:* www.arrowintl.com	610-378-0136		476
Arrow Lock Co 100 Arrow Dr., New Haven CT 06511 *TF:* 800-839-3157 ■ *Web:* www.arrowlock.com	800-839-3157	421-6615	350
Arrow Pneumatics Inc 2111 W 21st St, Broadview IL 60155 *Web:* www.arrowpneumatics.com	708-343-9595		18
Arrow Road Construction Co 3401 S Busse Rd, Mount Prospect IL 60056 *TF:* 800-523-4417 ■ *Web:* www.arrowroad.com	847-437-0700	437-0779	188-4
Arrow Rock State Historic Site PO Box 1, Arrow Rock MO 65320 *Web:* www.mostateparks.com	660-837-3330		565
Arrow Security Patrols 60 Knickerbocker Ave, Bohemia NY 11716 *Web:* www.arrowsecurity.net	631-675-2430		693
Arrow Staffing Services 499 W State St, Redlands CA 92373 *Web:* www.arrowstaffing.com	909-792-1252		260
Arrow Stage Lines 720 E Norfolk Ave, Norfolk NE 68701 *TF:* 800-672-8302 ■ *Web:* www.arrowstagelines.com	402-371-3850		107
Arrow Strategies LLC 27777 Franklin Rd Ste 1200, Southfield MI 48034 *Web:* www.arrowstrategies.com	248-502-2500		180
Arrow Surfboards 1115 Thompson Ave Ste 7, Santa Cruz CA 95062 *Web:* www.arrowsurfshop.com	831-462-2791		710
Arrow Tank & Engineering Co 650 N Emerson St., Cambridge MN 55008 *TF:* 888-892-7769 ■ *Web:* www.arrowtank.com	763-689-3360	689-1263	91
Arrow Tool & Stamping Company Inc 4548 W Mitchell St., Milwaukee WI 53214 *Web:* www.arrowtool.com	414-383-5710		697
Arrow Trading Inc 5290 NW 20th Terr Hngr 57-101, Fort Lauderdale FL 33309 *Web:* www.arrowtrading.com	954-771-9366		770
Arrow Truck Sales Inc 3200 Manchester Trfy, Kansas City MO 64129 *TF:* 800-311-7144 ■ *Web:* www.arrowtruck.com	816-923-5000		57
Arrow Tru-Line Inc 2211 S Defiance St., Archbold OH 43502 *TF:* 877-285-7253 ■ *Web:* www.arrowtruline.com	419-446-2785	445-2068	488
Arrow Uniform Rental Inc 6400 Monroe Blvd, Taylor MI 48180 *TF:* 888-332-7769 ■ *Web:* www.arrowuniform.com	313-299-5000		442
Arrow United Industries 450 Riverside Dr., Wyalusing PA 18853 *Web:* www.arrowunited.com	570-746-1888	746-9286	697
Arrow Value Recovery 9101 Burnet Rd Ste 203, Austin TX 78758 *TF:* 800-393-7627 ■ *Web:* www.arrowvaluerecovery.com	800-393-7627		660
Arrowac Fisheries Inc 4039 21st Ave W Ste 200 Fisherman's Commerce Bldg, Seattle WA 98199 *Web:* www.arrowac-merco.com	206-282-5655		297-5
Arrowhead Agency 16155 N 83rd Ave Ste 205, Peoria AZ 85382 *Web:* arrowhead.agency	623-979-3000		4
Arrowhead Containers Inc 4330 Clary Blvd, Kansas City MO 64130 *TF:* 888-861-9225 ■ *Web:* www.smcpackaging.com	816-861-8050		100
Arrowhead Conveyor Corp 3255 Medalist Dr PO Box 2408, Oshkosh WI 54903 *Web:* www.arrowheadsystems.com	920-235-5562		207
Arrowhead Electric Co-op Inc 5401 W Hwy 61 PO Box 39, Lutsen MN 55612 *TF:* 800-864-3744 ■ *Web:* www.aecimn.com	218-663-7239	663-7850	245
Arrowhead Library System 430 E High St Ste 200, Milton WI 53548 *TF:* 855-352-9003 ■ *Web:* www.als.lib.wi.us	608-868-2872	868-2875	434-3
Arrowhead Plastic Engineering Inc 2909 S Hoyt Ave, Muncie IN 47302 *Web:* www.arrowheadinc.com	765-286-0533	286-1681	604
Arrowhead Products Corp 4411 Katella Ave, Los Alamitos CA 90720 *Web:* www.arrowheadproducts.net	714-828-7770		22
Arrowhead Promotion & Fulfillment Company Inc 1105 SE Eighth St., Grand Rapids MN 55744 *Web:* www.apfco.com	218-327-1165		195
Arrowhead Regional Medical Ctr 400 N Pepper Ave, Colton CA 92324 *TF:* 855-422-8029 ■ *Web:* www.arrowheadmedcenter.org	909-580-1000		374-3
Arrowhead Stadium 1 Arrowhead Dr, Kansas City MO 64129 **Fax:* PR ■ *Web:* www.chiefs.com/arrowhead	816-920-9300	923-4719*	720
Arrowhead State Park 3995 Main Pk Rd, Canadian OK 74425 *Web:* www.travelok.com	918-339-2204	339-7236	565
Arrowhead Towne Ctr 7700 W Arrowhead Towne Ctr., Glendale AZ 85308 *TF:* 800-251-5866 ■ *Web:* www.arrowheadtownecenter.com	623-979-7777		460
Arrow-Magnolia International 2646 Rodney Ln, Dallas TX 75229 *TF:* 800-527-2101 ■ *Web:* www.arrowmagnolia.com	972-247-7111	484-2896	151
Arrowpoint Capital Whitehall Corporate Ctr Ste 3 3600 Arco Corporate Dr, Charlotte NC 28273 *TF:* 866-236-7750 ■ *Web:* www.arrowpointcap.com	704-522-2000		391-4
Arrowsight Inc 45 Kensico Dr 2nd Fl, Mount Kisco NY 10549 *Web:* arrowsight.com	212-869-8282		366
Arrowwood Resort & Conference Ctr 2100 Arrowwood Ln NW, Alexandria MN 56308 *TF Resv:* 866-386-5263 ■ *Web:* www.arrowwoodresort.com	320-762-1124	762-0133	669

	Phone	Fax	Class
Arroyo Chop House 536 S Arroyo Pkwy, Pasadena CA 91105 *Web:* www.arroyochophouse.com	626-577-7463		671
ARRS (American Roentgen Ray Society) 44211 Slatestone Ct, Leesburg VA 20176 *TF:* 800-438-2777 ■ *Web:* www.arrs.org	703-729-3353	729-4839	49-8
ARS (American Rose Society) 8877 Jefferson Paige Rd, Shreveport LA 71119 *TF:* 800-637-6534 ■ *Web:* rose.org	318-938-5402	938-5405	48-18
ARS Adv Inc 1001 Reads Lake Rd, Chattanooga TN 37415 *Web:* aislerocket.com	423-875-3743		6
ARS National Services Inc 201 W Grand Ave, Escondido CA 92025 *TF:* 800-456-5053 ■ *Web:* www.arsnational.com	800-456-5053		393
ARS Technologies Inc 98 N Ward St, New Brunswick NJ 08901 *Web:* www.arstechnologies.com	732-296-6620		463
ARSC (Association for Recorded Sound Collections) PO Box 543, Annapolis MD 21404 *Web:* www.arsc-audio.org	410-757-0488		48-4
Arsee Engineers Inc 9715 Kincaid Dr, Fishers IN 46037 *Web:* arsee-engineers.com	317-594-5152		261
Arsenal Capital Partners 100 Park Ave 31st Fl., New York NY 10017 *Web:* www.arsenalcapital.com	212-771-1717		696
ART (American Repertory Theatre) 64 Brattle St, Cambridge MA 02138 *Web:* www.americanrepertorytheater.org	617-495-2668	495-1705	749
Art & Logic Inc 2 N Lake Ave Ste 1050, Pasadena CA 91101 *Web:* www.artandlogic.com	626-427-7184		180
Art Academy of Cincinnati 1212 Jackson St., Cincinnati OH 45202 *TF:* 800-323-5692 ■ *Web:* www.artacademy.edu	513-562-6262	562-8778	164
Art And Creative Materials Institute Inc, The (ACMI) 99 Derby St Ste 200, Hingham MA 02043 *Web:* www.acminet.org	781-293-4100	294-0808	48-18
Art Anderson Assoc Inc 202 Pacific Ave, Bremerton WA 98337 *Web:* www.artanderson.com	360-479-5600		256
Art Brands LLC 225 Business Ctr Dr, Blacklick OH 43004 *TF:* 877-755-4278 ■ *Web:* www.artbrands.com	614-755-4278		687
Art Calendar 1500 Pk Ctr Dr, Orlando FL 32835 *Web:* www.professionalartistmag.com	407-563-7000	563-7099	457-2
Art Center Kalamazoo Institute 314 S Park St, Kalamazoo MI 49007 *Web:* www.kiarts.org	269-349-7775		520
Art Cir Public Library 3 E St, Crossville TN 38555 *TF:* 800-250-8618 ■ *Web:* www.artcirclelibrary.info	931-484-6790	484-2350	434-3
Art Connection Inc 2860 Ctr Port Cir, Pompano Beach FL 33064 *Web:* www.artconnectionusa.com	954-977-8177		820
Art Corner, The 264 Washington St., Salem MA 01970 *Web:* artcornersalem.com	978-745-9524		45
Art Craft Display Inc 500 Business Centre Dr, Lansing MI 48917 *TF:* 800-878-0710 ■ *Web:* artcraftdisplay.com	517-485-2221		226
Art Ctr College of Design 1700 Lida St., Pasadena CA 91103 *TF:* 800-242-8721 ■ *Web:* www.artcenter.edu	626-396-2200	795-0578	164
Art Ctr of Corpus Christi 100 N Shoreline Blvd, Corpus Christi TX 78401 *Web:* www.artcentercc.org	361-884-6406		50-2
Art Dealers Assn of America (ADAA) 205 Lexington Ave Ste 901, New York NY 10016 **Fax Area Code:* 646 ■ *TF:* 800-272-8258 ■ *Web:* www.artdealers.org	212-488-5550	688-6809*	48-4
Art Directors Club Inc 106 W 29th St, New York NY 10001 *Web:* adcglobal.org	212-643-1440		533
Art Directors Guild (ADG) 11969 Ventura Blvd Ste 200, Studio City CA 91604 *Web:* www.adg.org	818-762-9995	762-9997	48-4
Art Display Co Inc 401 Hampton Park Blvd, Capitol Heights MD 20743 *TF:* 800-421-1256 ■ *Web:* www.artdisplayco.com	240-765-1400		344
Art Emporium 2928 Granville St, Vancouver BC V6H3J7 *Web:* www.theartemporium.ca	604-738-3510		42
Art Essentials 32 E Victoria St., Santa Barbara CA 93101 *Web:* www.sbartessentials.com	805-965-5456		45
Art for Everyday Inc 420 Canarctic Dr, Toronto ON M3J2V3 *Web:* artforeveryday.com	416-645-5120	645-5121	820
ART Furniture Inc 1165 Auto Ctr Dr, Ontario CA 91761 *Web:* www.arthomefurnishings.com	909-390-1039		321
Art Gallery of Ontario 317 Dundas St W, Toronto ON M5T1G4 *TF:* 877-225-4246 ■ *Web:* www.ago.net	416-979-6660		305
Art Guild Inc 300 Wolf Dr, West Deptford NJ 08086 *Web:* www.artguildinc.com	856-853-7500		701
Art Hardware 119 E Costilla, Colorado Springs CO 80903 *TF:* 800-544-5960 ■ *Web:* arthardware.wordpress.com	719-635-2348		45
Art in America Magazine 110 Greene St 2nd floor, New York NY 10012 **Fax Area Code:* 773 ■ *TF Cust Svc:* 800-925-8059 ■ *Web:* www.artinamericamagazine.com	212-398-1690	442-4531*	457-2
Art Institute of Atlanta 6600 Peachtree Dunwoody Rd NE 100 Embassy Row, Atlanta GA 30328 *TF:* 800-275-4242 ■ *Web:* www.artinstitutes.edu/atlanta	770-394-8300	394-0008	164
Art Institute of Boston at Lesley (AIB) 29 Everett St, Cambridge MA 02138 *TF:* 800-773-0494 ■ *Web:* www.lesley.edu	617-868-9600		164
Art Institute of California			
Inland Empire 674 E Brier Dr, San Bernardino CA 92408 *TF:* 800-353-0812 ■ *Web:* www.artinstitutes.edu/inland-empire	909-915-2100		164
Los Angeles 2900 31st St, Santa Monica CA 90405 *TF:* 888-646-4610 ■ *Web:* www.artinstitutes.edu/los-angeles	310-752-4700		164
Orange County 3601 W Sunflower Ave, Santa Ana CA 92704 *Web:* www.artinstitutes.edu	714-830-0200	556-1923	164
San Diego 7650 Mission Valley Rd, San Diego CA 92108 **Fax Area Code:* 619 ■ *TF:* 888-624-0300 ■ *Web:* www.artinstitutes.edu/san-diego	858-598-1200	291-3206*	164
San Francisco 1170 Market St., San Francisco CA 94102 *TF:* 888-493-3261 ■ *Web:* www.artinstitutes.edu/san-francisco	415-865-0198	863-6344	164

Name / Address	City	State	ZIP	Phone	Fax	Class
Art Institute of Charlotte 3 Lake Pointe Plaza 2110 Water Ridge Pkwy; *TF:* 800-872-4417 ■ *Web:* www.artinstitutes.edu	Charlotte	NC	28217	704-357-8020	357-1514	164
Art Institute of Chicago 111 S Michigan Ave; *Web:* www.artic.edu	Chicago	IL	60603	312-443-3600		520
Art Institute of Colorado 1200 Lincoln St; *TF:* 800-275-2420 ■ *Web:* www.artinstitutes.edu/denver	Denver	CO	80203	303-837-0825		164
Art Institute of Dallas 8080 Pk Ln Ste 100; **Fax Area Code:* 800 ■ *TF:* 800-275-4243 ■ *Web:* www.artinstitutes.edu	Dallas	TX	75231	214-692-8080	275-4243*	164
Art Institute of Fort Lauderdale 1799 SE 17th St; *TF:* 800-275-7603 ■ *Web:* www.artinstitutes.edu/fort-lauderdale	Fort Lauderdale	FL	33316	954-463-3000		164
Art Institute of Houston 1900 Yorktown St; *TF:* 800-275-4244 ■ *Web:* www.artinstitutes.edu	Houston	TX	77056	713-623-2040	966-2700	164
Art Institute of Indianapolis 3500 Depauw Blvd; *TF:* 866-441-9031 ■ *Web:* www.artinstitutes.edu	Indianapolis	IN	46268	317-613-4800		164
Art Institute of Las Vegas 2350 Corporate Cir; *TF:* 800-833-2678 ■ *Web:* www.artinstitutes.edu	Henderson	NV	89074	702-369-9944		164
Art Institute of New York City 218-232 W 40th St; *Web:* www.artinstitutes.edu/new-york	New York	NY	10018	212-226-5500		164
Art Institute of Ohio *Cincinnati* 8845 Governor's Hill Dr Ste 100; *TF:* 866-613-5184 ■ *Web:* www.artinstitutes.edu	Cincinnati	OH	45249	513-833-2400		164
Art Institute of Philadelphia 1622 Chestnut St; *TF:* 800-275-2474 ■ *Web:* www.artinstitutes.edu	Philadelphia	PA	19103	215-567-7080		164
Art Institute of Pittsburgh 420 Blvd of the Allies; *TF:* 800-275-2470 ■ *Web:* www.artinstitutes.edu	Pittsburgh	PA	15219	412-263-6600	263-6667	164
Art Institute of Portland 1122 NW Davis St; **Fax:* Admissions ■ *TF:* 888-228-6528 ■ *Web:* www.artinstitutes.edu	Portland	OR	97209	503-228-6528	227-1945*	164
Art Institute of Seattle 2323 Elliott Ave; *TF:* 800-275-2471 ■ *Web:* www.artinstitutes.edu	Seattle	WA	98121	206-448-0900		164
Art Institute of Tampa 4401 N Himes Ave Ste 150; *TF:* 866-703-3277 ■ *Web:* www.artinstitutes.edu	Tampa	FL	33614	855-784-1269		164
Art Institute of Washington 1820 N Ft Myer Dr; *TF:* 877-303-3771 ■ *Web:* www.artinstitutes.edu/arlington	Arlington	VA	22209	703-358-9550	358-9759	164
Art Institutes International Minnesota, The 15 S Ninth St; *TF:* 800-777-3643 ■ *Web:* www.artinstitutes.edu	Minneapolis	MN	55402	612-332-3361	332-3934	164
Art Iron Inc 860 Curtis St; *TF:* 800-472-1113 ■ *Web:* www.artiron.com	Toledo	OH	43609	419-241-1261		492
Art Lithocraft Co 219 W 18th St; *Web:* www.artlithocraft.com	Kansas City	MO	64108	816-421-8335		628
Art Material Services Inc 625 Joyce Kilmer Ave; *TF:* 888-522-5526 ■ *Web:* www.artmaterialservice.com	New Brunswick	NJ	08901	732-545-8888		362
Art Moehn 2200 Seymour Rd; *Web:* artmoehn.com	Jackson	MI	49201	517-455-7721		516
Art Morrison Enterprises Inc 5301 Eighth St E; *TF:* 888-640-0516 ■ *Web:* www.artmorrison.com	Fife	WA	98424	253-922-7188		57
Art Museum of the University of Memphis 142 Communication & Fine Arts Bldg The University of Memphis; *Web:* www.memphis.edu	Memphis	TN	38152	901-678-2224	678-5118	520
Art of The Knot Inc 5893 Sunset Dr	South Miami	FL	33143	305-667-2000		131
Art Optical Contact Lens Inc PO Box 1848; *Web:* www.artoptical.com	Grand Rapids	MI	49501	616-453-1888	453-8702	542
Art Placement Inc 228 Third Ave S Ste 228; *TF:* 800-363-0546 ■ *Web:* www.artplacement.com	Saskatoon	SK	S7K1L9	306-664-3385	933-2521	42
Art Resource Inc 65 Bleecker St 12th Fl; *TF:* 888-505-8666 ■ *Web:* www.artres.com	New York	NY	10012	212-505-8700		624
Art Supply Warehouse 6672 Westminster Blvd; *TF:* 800-854-6467 ■ *Web:* www.artsupplywarehouse.com	Westminster	CA	92683	714-891-3626		45
Art4Orm Inc 2636 NW 26th Ave Ste 201	Portland	OR	97210	503-228-1399		344
ARTA Travel 5700 W Plano Pkwy Ste 1400; *Web:* www.artatravel.com	Plano	TX	75093	972-422-4000	422-2331	772
Artafact LLC 43165 Sabercat; *TF:* 800-618-3228 ■ *Web:* www.artafact.com	Fremont	CA	94539	510-651-9178		466
ARTBA (American Road & Transportation Builders Assn) 1219 28th St NW; *TF:* 800-636-2377 ■ *Web:* www.artba.org	Washington	DC	20007	202-289-4434	289-4435	49-3
Artbeats Software Inc 1405 N Myrtle Rd; *TF:* 800-444-9392 ■ *Web:* www.artbeats.com	Myrtle Creek	OR	97457	541-863-4429		225
ArtCentre of Plano, The 901 18th St; *Web:* www.artcentreofplano.org	Plano	TX	75074	972-423-7809		50-2
Artco 1 Staery Pl; *Web:* www.artcoprinting.com	Rexburg	ID	83441	208-359-1000		687
Artco-Bell Corp 1302 Industrial Blvd; *TF:* 877-778-1811 ■ *Web:* www.artcobell.com	Temple	TX	76504	254-778-1811		319-3
Artcraft Company Inc, The 200 John L Dietsch Blvd; *TF:* 800-659-4042 ■ *Web:* www.artcraft.com	North Attleboro	MA	02763	508-695-4042		429
Art-Craft Optical Company Inc 57 Goodway Dr S; *TF:* 800-828-8288 ■ *Web:* www.artcraftoptical.com	Rochester	NY	14623	585-546-6640	546-5133	542
Artcraft Signs Co 1717 S Acoma St; *Web:* www.artcraftsign.com	Denver	CO	80223	303-777-7771	778-7175	701
ARTEC Consultants Inc 114 W 26th St Ste 11; *Web:* www.artecconsultants.com	New York	NY	10001	212-242-0120		722
Artech Information Systems LLC 360 Mt Kemble Ave Ste 2000; *TF:* 800-950-9496 ■ *Web:* www.artechinfo.com	Morristown	NJ	07960	973-998-2500	998-2599	721
Artech Photography Studio 3404 Bath Rd	Perry	MI	48872	517-625-5177		590
Artel 25 Bradley Dr; *TF:* 888-406-3463 ■ *Web:* www.artel-usa.com	Westbrook	ME	04092	207-854-0860		250
Artel Video Systems Corp 5B Lyberty Way; *TF:* 800-225-0228 ■ *Web:* www.artel.com	Westford	MA	01886	978-263-5775	263-9755	647
Artemis International Solutions Corp 401 Congress Ave Ste 2650; *Web:* www.aisc.com	Austin	TX	78701	512-201-8222		178-1
Artemis Solutions Group Inc 2501 Coolidge Rd Ste 503; *Web:* artemis-solutions.com	East Lansing	MI	48823	517-336-9925		177
Artemus Group 317 Office Square Ln Ste 202B; **Fax Area Code:* 757 ■ *TF:* 866-744-7101 ■ *Web:* www.artemus.us	Virginia Beach	VA	23462	866-744-7101	257-0668*	313
Artemus W Ham Concert Hall 4505 Maryland Pkwy; *Web:* www.unlv.edu/pac	Las Vegas	NV	89154	702-895-2787	895-4714	572
Arteriocyte Medical Systems Inc 7100 Euclid Ave Research & Development Ctr; *Web:* www.arteriocyte.com	Cleveland	OH	44103	216-456-9640		475
Artesian Resources Corp 664 Churchmans Rd; *NASDAQ: ARTNA* ■ *TF:* 800-332-5114 ■ *Web:* www.artesianwater.com	Newark	DE	19702	302-453-6900	453-6957	360-5
Artex Risk Solutions Inc 2 Pierce Pl; *Web:* www.artexrisk.com	Itasca	IL	60143	630-694-5050		317
Artforum International Magazine 350 Seventh Ave; *TF:* 800-966-2783 ■ *Web:* www.artforum.com	New York	NY	10001	212-475-4000	529-1257	457-2
Arthaus Foundation 3840 S Ridgewood Ave; *Web:* arthaus.org	Port Orange	FL	32129	386-767-0076		522
Arthrex Inc 1370 Creekside Blvd; *TF:* 800-934-4404 ■ *Web:* www.arthrex.com	Naples	FL	34108	239-643-5553	598-5534	477
Arthritis Foundation 1330 W Peachtree St Ste 100; *TF:* 800-283-7800 ■ *Web:* www.arthritis.org	Atlanta	GA	30309	404-872-7100	872-0457	48-17
Arthroscopy Assn of North America (AANA) 9400 W Higgins Rd Ste 200; *TF:* 877-924-0305 ■ *Web:* www.aana.org	Rosemont	IL	60018	847-292-2262	292-2268	49-8
Arthur Agency Inc 104 E Jackson St	Carbondale	IL	62901	618-351-1599		463
Arthur Blank & Co Inc 225 Rivermoor St; *TF:* 800-776-7333 ■ *Web:* www.abnote.com	Boston	MA	02132	617-325-9600	327-1235	9
Arthur Bryant Barbecue 1702 Village W Pkwy; *Web:* arthurbryantsbbq.com	Kansas City	KS	66111	913-788-7500		671
Arthur Bryant's Barbeque 1727 Brooklyn Ave; *Web:* arthurbryantsbbq.com	Kansas City	MO	64127	816-231-1123		671
Arthur Consulting Group Inc 31355 Oak Crest Dr Ste 200; *TF:* 800-677-9792 ■ *Web:* www.arthurconsulting.com	Westlake Village	CA	91361	818-735-4800		734
Arthur County 205 Fir St; *Web:* arthurcounty.nebraska.gov	Arthur	NE	69121	308-764-2201		338
Arthur D Little Inc 1 Federal St Ste 2810; *Web:* www.adlittle.com	Boston	MA	02110	617-532-9550	261-6630	194
Arthur Dyson & Assoc 1295 N Wishon Ave; *TF:* 800-375-5283 ■ *Web:* www.arthurdyson.com	Fresno	CA	93728	559-486-3582	486-3582	261
Arthur F Schultz Co 939 W 26th St; *Web:* www.arthurfschultz.com	Erie	PA	16508	814-454-8171	454-3052	35
Arthur Financial Services LLC 1516 E Palm Valley Blvd Bldg B Ste 1; *Web:* www.arthurfinancial.com	Round Rock	TX	78664	512-218-6948		251
Arthur G James Cancer Hospital & Richard J Solove Research Institute *Bone Marrow Transplant Program* 300 W Tenth Ave Ste 519; **Fax Area Code:* 614 ■ *TF:* 800-293-5066 ■ *Web:* cancer.osu.edu	Columbus	OH	43210	800-293-5066	293-4044*	769
Arthur Groom & Company Inc 262 E Ridgewood Ave; *Web:* www.arthurgroom.com	Ridgewood	NJ	07450	201-670-0300		410
Arthur J Gallagher & Co 2 Pierce Pl; *NYSE: AJG* ■ *TF:* 888-285-5106 ■ *Web:* www.ajg.com	Itasca	IL	60143	630-773-3800	285-4000	390
Arthur J Rogers & Co 1559 Elmhurst Rd; *Web:* www.arthurjrogers.com	Elk Grove Village	IL	60007	847-297-2200		652
Arthur J. Glatfelter Agency Inc PO Box 2726; *TF:* 800-233-1957 ■ *Web:* www.glatfelters.com	York	PA	17405	717-741-0911	741-4160	390
Arthur Kill Correctional Facility 2911 Arthur Kill Rd; *Web:* metro.org	Staten Island	NY	10309	718-356-7333		213
Arthur Langhus Layne LLC 1718 S Cheyenne; *Web:* www.all-llc.com	Tulsa	OK	74119	918-382-7581		194
Arthur p Jones & Associates Inc 98 Cottage St; *TF:* 800-531-6500 ■ *Web:* www.apjones.com	Easthampton	MA	01027	413-527-2388		160
Arthur Rutenberg Homes Inc 13922 58th St N; *Web:* www.arthurrutenberghomes.com	Clearwater	FL	33760	727-536-5900		187
Arthur State Bank 100 E Main St PO Box 769; *TF:* 877-226-5246 ■ *Web:* www.arthurstatebank.com	Union	SC	29379	864-427-1213	429-8537	70
Arthur Vining Davis Foundations 225 Water St; *Web:* www.avdf.org	Jacksonville	FL	32202	904-359-0670	359-0675	305
Arthur W Wood Company Inc 50 Congress St Ste 300; *Web:* www.arthurwood.com	Boston	MA	02109	617-542-0500		194

	Phone	Fax	Class
Arthur, Chapman, Kettering, Smetak & Pikala PA 500 Young Quinlan Bldg 81 S Ninth St . . . . Minneapolis MN 55402 *TF:* 800-916-9262 ■ *Web:* www.arthurchapman.com	612-339-3500		428
Artichoke Cafe 424 Central SE . . . . Albuquerque NM 87102 *TF:* 800-838-3006 ■ *Web:* www.artichokecafe.com	505-243-0200	243-3365	671
Articulon 2841 Plaza Pl . . . . Raleigh NC 27612 *Web:* www.articulon.com	919-232-5008		636
Artillery Company of Newport Military Museum 23 Clark St . . . . Newport RI 02840 *Web:* www.newportartillery.org	401-846-8488		520
Artimex Iron Company Inc 315 Cypress Ln . . . . El Cajon CA 92020 *Web:* www.artimexiron.com	619-444-3155		480
Artisan Books & Bindery 509 Pendleton Point Rd . . . . Islesboro ME 04848 *Web:* www.artisanbooksandbindery.com	207-734-6852		95
Artisan Cinema & Sound LLC 15876 N 76th St Ste 100 . . . . Scottsdale AZ 85260 *Web:* www.artisanaz.com	480-538-1071	538-1072	748
Artisan Colour Inc 8970 E Bahia Dr . . . . Scottsdale AZ 85260 *TF:* 800-274-2422 ■ *Web:* blog.artisanhd.com	480-948-0009		781
Artisan Communications Inc 12400 Hwy W Hwy 71 Ste 350-407 . . . . Austin TX 78738 *Web:* www.artisan.tv	512-600-4200		387
Artisan Controls Corp 111 Canfield Ave Bldg B15-18 . . . . Randolph NJ 07869 *TF:* 800-457-4950 ■ *Web:* www.artisancontrols.com	973-598-9400		203
Artisan Funds PO Box 8412 . . . . Boston MA 02266 *TF Cust Svc:* 800-344-1770 ■ *Web:* www.artisanpartners.com/individual-investors.html	800-344-1770		528
Artisan Hotel & Spa 1501 W Sahara Ave . . . . Las Vegas NV 89102 *Web:* www.theartisanhotel.com	702-214-4000		378
Artisan Industries Inc 73 Pond St . . . . Waltham MA 02451 *Web:* www.artisanind.com	781-893-6800		256
Artisan Laboratories Inc 2532 SE Hawthorne Blvd . . . . Portland OR 97214 *TF:* 800-222-6721 ■ *Web:* www.artisandental.com	503-238-6006		476
Artisan Partners Limited Partnership 875 E Wisconsin Ave Ste 800 . . . . Milwaukee WI 53202 *Web:* www.artisanpartners.com	414-390-6100		528
Artisan's Bank 2961 Centerville Rd . . . . Wilmington DE 19808 *TF:* 800-282-8255 ■ *Web:* www.artisansbank.com	302-658-6881	654-0559	70
Artisans Inc PO Box 1059 . . . . Calhoun GA 54526 *TF:* 800-311-8756 ■ *Web:* www.artisanscarpet.com	715-322-5285		131
Artist Brand Canvas 2448 Loma Ave . . . . South El Monte CA 91733 *TF Orders:* 888-579-2704 ■ *Web:* www.artistbrandcanvas.com	626-579-2740		43
Artist Point 901 Timberline Dr . . . . Lake Buena Vista FL 32830 *Web:* disneyworld.disney.go.com	407-824-3200		671
Artist's Magazine, The 4700 E Galbraith Rd . . . . Cincinnati OH 45236 *TF:* 800-422-2550 ■ *Web:* www.artistsnetwork.com	513-531-2222	891-7153	457-2
Artistic Carton Co 1975 Big Timber Rd . . . . Elgin IL 60123 *TF:* 800-735-7225 ■ *Web:* www.artisticcarton.com	847-741-0247	741-8529	100
Artistic Checks PO Box 40003 . . . . Colorado Springs CO 80935 *TF:* 800-824-3255 ■ *Web:* www.artisticchecks.com	800-824-3255		142
Artistic Frame Corp 979 Third Ave 17th Fl . . . . New York NY 10022 *Web:* www.artisticframe.com	212-289-2100	289-2101	319-1
Artistic Maintenance Inc 23676 Birtcher Dr . . . . Lake Forest CA 92630 *Web:* www.artisticmaintenance.com	949-581-9817		422
Artistic Media Partners Inc 5520 E 75th St . . . . Indianapolis IN 46250 *Web:* www.artisticradio.com	317-594-0600	594-9567	643
Artistic Stone Kitchen & Bath Inc 2973 Teagarden St . . . . San Leandro CA 94577 *Web:* www.artisticstoneinc.com	510-483-1298		361
Artistica Metal Designs Inc 3200 Golf Course Dr . . . . Ventura CA 93003 *Web:* artisticahome.com	805-850-1100		492
Artistry in Motion Inc 15101 Keswick St . . . . Van Nuys CA 91405 *TF:* 800-992-7755 ■ *Web:* www.artistryinmotion.com	818-994-7388	994-7688	554
Artists Club, The 13118 NE Fourth St . . . . Vancouver WA 98684 *TF:* 800-574-1323 ■ *Web:* www.knitpicks.com	800-574-1323		761
Artists for Humanity Inc 100 W Second St . . . . Boston MA 02127 *TF:* 800-942-2677 ■ *Web:* www.afhboston.org	617-268-7620		260
Artists Repertory Theatre 1516 SW Alder St . . . . Portland OR 97205 *Web:* www.artistsrep.org	503-241-9807	241-8268	573-4
Artizen Inc 200 Main St Ste #21A . . . . Redwood City CA 94063 *Web:* www.artizen.com	650-261-9400		260
Artkraft Strauss LLC 1776 Broadway Ste 1810 . . . . New York NY 10019 *Web:* www.artkraft.com	212-265-5155	265-5159	233
Artlite Office Supply Co 1860 Chshire Bridge Rd NE . . . . Atlanta GA 30324 *Web:* www.artlite.net	404-875-7271	875-2623	535
Artman Lutheran Home 250 N Bethlehem Pk . . . . Ambler PA 19002 *Web:* www.libertylutheran.org	215-643-6335		48-20
Artmart 2355 S Hanley Rd . . . . Saint Louis MO 63144 *Web:* www.artmartstl.com	314-781-9999		45
ARTnews Magazine 48 W 38th St 9th Fl . . . . New York NY 10018 *TF:* 800-284-4625 ■ *Web:* artnews.com	212-398-1690	819-0394	457-2
Artonomy 544 W Liberty St Ste A . . . . Cincinnati OH 45214 *TF:* 800-333-2607 ■ *Web:* www.artonomyinc.com	513-651-2787		522
Artos Engineering Co 21605 Gateway Ct . . . . Brookfield WI 53045 *TF:* 800-283-5564 ■ *Web:* www.artosengineering.com	262-252-4545	252-4544	494
Artpark 450 S Fourth St . . . . Lewiston NY 14092 *TF:* 877-325-5787 ■ *Web:* www.artpark.net	716-754-9000	754-2741	572
Art-Phyl Creations 16250 NW 48th Ave . . . . Hialeah FL 33014 *TF:* 800-327-8318 ■ *Web:* hookstoresales.com	305-624-2333		233
Arts & Business Council of Americans for the Arts 1 E 53rd St 2nd Fl . . . . New York NY 10022 *Web:* americansforthearts.org	212-223-2787	980-4857	48-4
ARTS Anonymous PO Box 230175 . . . . New York NY 10023 *Web:* www.artsanonymous.org	718-251-3828		48-21
Arts Center of Cannon County Inc, The 1424 John Bragg Hwy . . . . Woodbury TN 37190 *Web:* www.artscenterofcc.com	615-563-2787		522
Arts Club of Chicago, The 201 E Ontario St . . . . Chicago IL 60611 *Web:* artsclubchicago.org	312-787-3997		522
Arts Ctr of Coastal Carolina 14 Shelter Cove Ln . . . . Hilton Head Island SC 29928 *TF:* 888-860-2787 ■ *Web:* www.artshhi.com	843-686-3945	842-7877	572
Arts Foundation of Cape Cod, The 396 Main St Ste 10 . . . . Hyannis MA 02601 *Web:* www.artsfoundation.org	508-362-0066		305
Arts Midwest 2908 Hennepin Ave Ste 200 . . . . Minneapolis MN 55408 *TF:* 800-814-0506 ■ *Web:* www.artsmidwest.org	612-341-0755		720
Artsicle Inc 25 W 13th St . . . . New York NY 10011 *Web:* www.artsicle.com	646-470-4219		387
ArtSouth 5825 SW 68th St Ste 2 Office 202 . . . . South Miami FL 33143 *Web:* www.artsouthhomestead.org	305-247-9406	247-7308	50-2
ARTspace 165 King St W . . . . Chatham ON N7M1E4 *Web:* www.artspacechathamkent.com	519-352-1064		520
Artspace Inc 201 E Davie St . . . . Raleigh NC 27601 *Web:* www.artspacenc.org	919-821-2787		520
Artspace.com Markets Inc 915 Broadway Ste 602 . . . . New York NY 10010 *Web:* www.artspace.com	212-675-5804		690
Arts-Way Mfg Co Inc 5556 Hwy 9 PO Box 288 . . . . Armstrong IA 50514 *NASDAQ: ARTW* ■ *TF:* 800-535-4517 ■ *Web:* www.artsway-mfg.com	712-864-3131	864-3154	273
Artus Corp PO Box 511 . . . . Englewood NJ 07631 *Web:* www.artuscorp.com	201-568-1000	568-8865	326
ArtVoice 810 Main St . . . . Buffalo NY 14202 *Web:* www.artvoice.com	716-881-6604	881-6682	532-5
Artwork Conversion Software Inc 417 Ingalls St . . . . Santa Cruz CA 95060 *Web:* www.artwork.com	831-426-6163		177
Artworks Around Town Gallery & Art Ctr 2200 Market St . . . . Wheeling WV 26003 *Web:* www.artworksaroundtown.org	304-233-7540		50-2
Aruba Networks Inc 1344 Crossman Ave . . . . Sunnyvale CA 94089 *NASDAQ: ARUN* ■ *TF:* 800-943-4526 ■ *Web:* www.arubanetworks.com	408-227-4500	752-0626	177
Aruba Petroleum Inc 555 Republic Dr Ste 505 . . . . Plano TX 75074 *Web:* www.arubapetroleum.com	972-312-9366		536
Aruba Tourism Authority 1750 Powder Springs St Ste 190 . . . . Marietta GA 30064 *TF:* 800-862-7822 ■ *Web:* www.aruba.com	404-892-7822		775
Arugula 953 Farmington Ave . . . . West Hartford CT 06107 *Web:* arugula-bistro.com	860-561-4888		671
Arun's 4156 N Kedzie Ave . . . . Chicago IL 60618 *Web:* www.arunsthai.com	773-539-1909		671
Arundel FSB 333 E Patapsco Ave . . . . Baltimore MD 21225 *Web:* arundelfederal.com	410-355-9300	355-0335	70
Arup Laboratories 500 Chipeta Way . . . . Salt Lake City UT 84108 *Web:* www.aruplab.com	801-583-2787		418
Arup North America Ltd 560 Mission St Ste 700 . . . . San Francisco CA 94105 *Web:* www.arup.com	415-957-9445		256
Aruze Gaming America Inc 745 Grier Dr . . . . Las Vegas NV 89119 *Web:* www.aruzegaming.com	702-361-3166		761
Arvada Chamber of Commerce 7305 Grandview Ave . . . . Arvada CO 80002 *Web:* www.arvadachamber.org	303-424-0313	424-5370	139
Arvada Ctr for the Arts & Humanities 6901 Wadsworth Blvd . . . . Arvada CO 80003 *TF:* 800-659-2656 ■ *Web:* www.arvadacenter.org	720-898-7200	898-7204	572
Arvan Inc 14083 S Normandie Ave . . . . Gardena CA 90249 *Web:* www.arvaninc.com	310-327-1818	324-6634	22
Arvato Digital Services LLC 29011 Commerce Ctr Dr . . . . Valencia CA 91355 *TF:* 800-223-1478 ■ *Web:* www.arvato.com	800-223-1478		393
Arvco Container Corp 845 Gibson St . . . . Kalamazoo MI 49001 *TF:* 800-968-9127 ■ *Web:* www.arvco.com	269-381-0900	381-2919	100
Arvin Sango Inc 2905 Wilson Ave . . . . Madison IN 47250 *Web:* www.arvinsango.com	812-265-2888	273-8339	488
ArvinMeritor Inc 2135 W Maple Rd . . . . Troy MI 48084 *NYSE: MTOR* ■ *TF:* 800-535-5560 ■ *Web:* www.meritor.com	248-435-1000	435-1393	60
Arvinyl Metal Laminates Corp 233 N Sherman Ave . . . . Corona CA 92882 **Fax Area Code: 951* ■ *TF:* 800-278-4695 ■ *Web:* www.arvinyl.com	800-278-4695	371-7118*	485
Arvizu Advertising & Promotions Inc 3111 N Central Ave Ste 1240 . . . . Phoenix AZ 85012 *Web:* www.arvizu.com	602-279-4669		4
ARVO (Association for Research in Vision & Ophthalmology) 12300 Twinbrook Pkwy Ste 250 . . . . Rockville MD 20852 *TF:* 888-503-1050 ■ *Web:* www.arvo.org	240-221-2900	221-0370	49-8
Arvon Inc 5544 Greenwich Rd Ste 102 . . . . Virginia Beach VA 23462 *TF:* 800-388-8255 ■ *Web:* www.arvon.com	757-499-9900		260
Arw Engineers Inc 1594 W Park Cir Ste 100 . . . . Ogden UT 84404 *Web:* www.arwengineers.com	801-782-6008		261
ARW Optical Corp 2021 Capital Dr . . . . Wilmington NC 28405 *TF:* 800-983-7174 ■ *Web:* arwoptical.com	910-452-7373		237
Arwood Machine Corp 95 Parker St . . . . Newburyport MA 01950 *Web:* www.arwoodmachine.com	978-463-3777		454
ARX Networks Corp 37100 Central Cy . . . . Newark CA 94560 *TF:* 800-972-2175 ■ *Web:* www.arxnetworks.com	650-403-4279		180

Name / Address	City	State	ZIP	Phone	Fax	Class
Arxis Technology Inc						
2468 Tapo Canyon Rd	Simi Valley	CA	93063	805-306-7800		196
Web: www.arxistechnology.com						
Arzel Zoning Technology Inc						
4801 Commerce Pkwy	Cleveland	OH	44128	216-831-6068		201
TF: 800-611-8312 ■ *Web:* www.arzelzoning.com						
A&S Engineers Inc						
10377 Stella Link Rd	Houston	TX	77025	713-942-2700		261
Web: as-engineers.com						
A&S Mold & Die Corp 9705 Eton Ave	Chatsworth	CA	91311	818-341-5393		596
Web: www.aandsmold.com						
As Soon As Possible Inc						
1750 W 96th St	Bloomington	MN	55431	952-564-2727		781
Web: www.asap.net						
AS220 115 Empire St	Providence	RI	02903	401-831-9327	454-7445	572
Web: www.as220.org						
ASA (Autism Society of America)						
4340 EW Hwy Ste 350	Bethesda	MD	20814	301-657-0881	657-0869	48-17
TF: 800-328-8476 ■ *Web:* www.autism-society.org						
ASA (Acoustical Society of America)						
1305 Walt Whitman Rd Ste 300	Melville	NY	11747	516-576-2360	576-2377	49-19
TF: 800-828-8840 ■ *Web:* www.acousticalsociety.org						
ASA (American Studies Assn)						
1120 19th St NW Ste 301	Washington	DC	20036	202-467-4783	467-4786	49-5
TF: 800-468-3571 ■ *Web:* www.theasa.net						
ASA (American Society of Andrology)						
1100 E Woodfield St Ste 350	Schaumburg	IL	60173	847-517-1050	517-7229	49-8
Web: www.andrologysociety.org						
ASA (Airline Spares America Inc)						
1022 E Newport Ctr Dr	Deerfield Beach	FL	33442	954-429-8600	429-8388	770
Web: www.asaspares.com						
ASA (Alpha Sigma Alpha)						
9002 Vincennes Cir	Indianapolis	IN	46268	317-871-2920	871-2924	48-16
Web: www.alphasigmaalpha.org						
ASA (American Sportfishing Assn)						
1001 N Fairfax St Ste 501	Alexandria	VA	22314	703-519-9691	519-1872	49-4
Web: www.asafishing.org						
ASA (American Simmental Assn)						
One Genetics Way	Bozeman	MT	59718	406-587-4531	587-9301	48-2
Web: www.simmental.org						
ASA (American Society of Agronomy)						
5585 Guilford Rd	Madison	WI	53711	608-273-8080	273-2021	48-2
TF: 866-359-9161 ■ *Web:* www.agronomy.org						
ASA (American Society of Anesthesiologists)						
520 N NW Hwy	Park Ridge	IL	60068	847-825-5586	825-1692	49-8
Web: www.asahq.org						
ASA (American Society of Appraisers)						
555 Herndon Pkwy Ste 125	Herndon	VA	20170	703-478-2228	742-8471	49-17
TF: 800-272-8258 ■ *Web:* www.appraisers.org						
ASA (American Society on Aging)						
575 Market St Ste 2100	San Francisco	CA	94105	415-974-9600	974-0300	48-6
TF: 800-537-9728 ■ *Web:* www.asaging.org						
ASA (American Sociological Assn)						
1307 New York Ave	Washington	DC	20005	202-383-9005	638-0882	49-5
TF: 800-524-9400 ■ *Web:* www.asanet.org						
ASA (American Soybean Assn)						
12125 Woodcrest Executive Dr Ste 100	Saint Louis	MO	63141	314-576-1770	576-2786	48-2
TF: 800-688-7692 ■ *Web:* www.soygrowers.com						
ASA (American Statistical Assn)						
732 N Washington St	Alexandria	VA	22314	703-684-1221	684-2037	49-19
TF: 888-231-3473 ■ *Web:* www.amstat.org						
ASA (American Subcontractors Assn Inc)						
1004 Duke St	Alexandria	VA	22314	703-684-3450	836-3482	49-3
TF: 866-378-8866 ■ *Web:* www.asaonline.com						
ASA (Automotive Service Assn)						
1901 Airport Fwy	Bedford	TX	76021	800-272-7467	685-0225*	49-21
**Fax Area Code:* 817 ■ *TF Cust Svc:* 800-272-7467 ■ *Web:* www.asashop.org						
ASA (American Staffing Assn)						
277 S Washington St Ste 200	Alexandria	VA	22314	703-253-2020	253-2053	49-12
Web: www.americanstaffing.net						
ASA Alloys Inc 81 Steinway Blvd	Etobicoke	ON	M9W6H6	416-213-0000		492
TF: 800-387-9166 ■ *Web:* www.asaalloys.com						
ASA Computers Inc						
645 National Ave	Mountain View	CA	94043	650-230-8000	230-8090	176
TF: 800-732-5727 ■ *Web:* www.asacomputers.com						
ASA Controls Inc						
10051 Simonson Rd Ste 8	Harrison	OH	45030	513-353-3101		189-10
Web: asacontrols.com						
ASA Entertainment LLC						
201 N Riverside Dr Ste C	Indialantic	FL	32903	321-722-9300		226
Web: www.asaentertainment.com						
ASA International Ltd 10 Speen St	Framingham	MA	01701	508-626-2727	626-0645	178-11
ASA PAC (American Sportfishing Assnn PAC)						
225 Reinekers Ln Ste 420	Alexandria	VA	22314	703-519-9691	519-1872	615
Web: www.asafishing.org						
ASA PAC (American Supply Assn PAC)						
1200 N Arlington Heights Rd Ste 150	Itasca	IL	60143	630-467-0000		615
Web: www.asa.net						
Asa Solutions Inc						
2155 W Pinnacle Peak Rd Ste 201	Phoenix	AZ	85027	480-922-9532		177
Web: www.asasolutions.com						
ASA Tire Master Software						
651 S Stratford Dr	Meridian	ID	83642	208-855-0781		174
TF: 800-241-8472 ■ *Web:* www.asatire.com						
ASAA (American Sleep Apnea Assn)						
6856 Eastern Ave NW Ste 203	Washington	DC	20012	202-293-3650	293-3656	48-17
TF: 888-293-3650 ■ *Web:* www.sleepapnea.org						
ASAC (American Society of Agricultural Consultants)						
605 Columbus Ave	South New Prague	WI	56071	952-758-5811		48-2
Web: www.agconsultants.org						
ASAE (American Society of Assn Executives)						
1575 'I' St NW	Washington	DC	20005	202-626-2723		49-12
TF: 888-950-2723 ■ *Web:* www.asaecenter.org						
Asah 2125 Hwy 33	Trenton	NJ	08690	609-890-1400		474
TF: 800-955-2321 ■ *Web:* www.asah.org						
Asahi 4520 W Market St	Greensboro	NC	27407	336-855-8883		671
Asahi Beer USA Inc						
3625 Del Amo Blvd Ste 250	Torrance	CA	90503	310-214-9051	542-5108	102
Web: www.asahibeerusa.com						
Asahi Kasei America Inc						
800 Third Ave 30th Fl	New York	NY	10022	212-371-9900	371-9050	605-2
Web: www.ak-america.com						
Asahi Kasei Plastics North America Inc						
900 E Van Riper Rd	Fowlerville	MI	48836	517-223-2000	223-2002	605-2
TF Cust Svc: 800-993-5382 ■ *Web:* akplastics.com						
ASAHP (Association of Schools of Allied Health Professions)						
122 C St NW Ste 650	Washington	DC	20001	202-237-6481	237-6485	49-8
Web: www.asahp.org						
ASAM (American Society of Addiction Medicine)						
11400 Rockville Pike Ste 200	Rockville	MD	20852	301-656-3920	656-3815	49-8
Web: www.asam.org						
ASANA STUDIO 5701 Yukon St	Arvada	CO	80002	303-431-6311		148
Web: asanastudio.com						
Asano of Hawaii Corp						
3159 Koapaka St Ste D	Honolulu	HI	96819	808-836-3939		379
ASAP (American Society of Access Professionals)						
1444 'I' St NW Ste 700	Washington	DC	20005	202-712-9054	216-9646	48-8
Web: www.accesspro.org						
ASAP (American Society for Adolescent Psychiatry)						
1737 Omar Dr	Mesquite	TX	75150	972-613-0985		49-15
Web: adolescent-psychiatry.org						
ASAP Industries LLC 908 Blimp Rd	Houma	LA	70363	985-851-7272		358
TF: 800-938-1488 ■ *Web:* asapind.net						
Asap Personnel Services Inc						
10301 N Rodney Parham Rd	Little Rock	AR	72227	501-537-2727		260
Web: asapworksforme.com						
Asap Printing Corp						
643 Billinis Rd	Salt Lake City	UT	84119	801-263-2727		627
Web: www.asapprintingcorp.com						
ASAP Solutions Group LLC						
3885 Holcomb Bridge Rd	Norcross	GA	30092	770-246-1718		179
TF: 800-867-4378 ■ *Web:* www.myasap.com						
ASAP Ventures LLC						
132 King St Ste 200	Alexandria	VA	22314	703-837-5150		463
Web: www.asapventures.com						
ASAPS (American Society for Aesthetic Plastic Surgery, The)						
11262 Monarch St	Garden Grove	CA	92841	562-799-2356	799-1098	49-8
TF: 800-364-2147 ■ *Web:* www.surgery.org						
ASAS (American Society of Abdominal Surgeons)						
824 Main St Second Fl Ste 1	Melrose	MA	02176	781-665-6102	665-4127	49-8
Web: www.abdominalsurg.org						
ASAS (American Society of Animal Science)						
1111 N Dunlap Ave	Savoy	IL	61874	217-356-9050	398-4119	48-2
Web: www.asas.org						
Asbarez Armenian Daily						
419 W Colorado St	Glendale	CA	91204	818-500-9363		532-2
Web: www.asbarez.com						
ASBMB (American Society for Biochemistry & Molecular Biology Inc)						
9650 Rockville Pk	Bethesda	MD	20814	301-634-7145	634-7126	49-19
Web: www.asbmb.org						
ASBMR (American Society for Bone & Mineral Research)						
2025 M St NW Ste 800	Washington	DC	20036	202-367-1161	367-2161	49-8
Web: www.asbmr.org						
ASBO (Association of School Business Officials International)						
11401 N Shore Dr	Reston	VA	20190	866-682-2729	478-0205*	49-5
**Fax Area Code:* 703 ■ *TF:* 866-682-2729 ■ *Web:* asbointl.org						
ASBPA (American Shore & Beach Preservation Assn)						
5460 Beaujolais Ln	Fort Myers	FL	33919	239-489-2616	489-9917	48-13
TF: 800-331-1600 ■ *Web:* www.asbpa.org						
ASBPE (American Society of Business Publication Editors)						
214 N Hale St	Wheaton	IL	60187	630-510-4588	510-4501	49-16
TF: 800-255-8141 ■ *Web:* www.asbpe.org						
Asbury Automotive Group Inc						
2905 Premiere Pkwy Ste 300	Duluth	GA	30097	770-418-8200		57
NYSE: ADG ■ *Web:* www.asburyauto.com						
Asbury College 1 Macklem Dr	Wilmore	KY	40390	859-858-3511	858-3921*	166
**Fax:* Admissions ■ *TF Admissions:* 800-888-1818 ■ *Web:* www.asbury.edu						
Asbury Graphite Mills Inc						
405 Old Main St	Asbury	NJ	08802	908-537-2155	537-2908	500
Web: asbury.com						
Asbury Methodist Village						
201 Russell Ave	Gaithersburg	MD	20877	301-216-4100		672
TF: 800-327-2879 ■ *Web:* www.asburymethodistvillage.org						
Asbury Park Chamber of Commerce						
1201 Springwood Ave	Asbury Park	NJ	07712	732-775-7676	775-7675	139
Web: www.asburyparkchamber.com						
Asbury Park Press 3601 Hwy 66	Neptune	NJ	07754	732-922-6000	922-4818*	532-2
**Fax:* News Rm ■ *TF:* 800-883-7737 ■ *Web:* www.app.com						
Asbury Theological Seminary						
204 N Lexington Ave	Wilmore	KY	40390	859-858-3581		167-3
TF: 800-227-2879 ■ *Web:* www.asburyseminary.edu						
ASC (American Society of Cinematographers)						
1782 N Orange Dr	Hollywood	CA	90028	323-969-4333	882-6391	48-4
TF: 800-448-0145 ■ *Web:* www.theasc.com						
ASC (Adhesive & Sealant Council Inc)						
7101 Wisconsin Ave Ste 990	Bethesda	MD	20814	301-986-9700	986-9795	49-13
Web: www.ascouncil.org						
ASC Capacitors 301 W O St	Ogallala	NE	69153	308-284-3611	284-8324	253
TF: 800-347-4572 ■ *Web:* www.ascapacitor.com						
ASC Global Technologies						
4430 Laven Way	Colorado Springs	CO	80920	719-321-4975		45
ASC Industries Inc						
1227 Corporate Dr W	Arlington	TX	76006	817-640-1300	649-2685	770
TF: 800-989-9830 ■ *Web:* www.ascintl.com						
ASC Profiles Inc						
2110 Enterprise Blvd	West Sacramento	CA	95691	916-372-0933		697
TF Cust Svc: 800-360-2477 ■ *Web:* www.ascprofiles.com						
ASC Signal Corp 1120 Jupiter Rd Ste 102	Plano	TX	75074	214-291-7654		701
Web: www.cpii.com/division.cfm/13						
ASCA (American School Counselor Assn)						
1101 King St Ste 625	Alexandria	VA	22314	703-683-2722	683-1619	49-5
TF: 800-306-4722 ■ *Web:* www.schoolcounselor.org						
ASCB (American Society for Cell Biology)						
8120 Woodmont Ave Ste 750	Bethesda	MD	20814	301-347-9300	347-9310	49-19
Web: www.ascb.org						
ASCC Inc 15 Ogle View Rd	Cranberry Township	PA	16066	724-772-2722		196
Web: asccinc.com						

	City	State	Zip	Phone	Fax	Class
ASCCP (American Society for Colposcopy & Cervical Pathology) 152 W Washington St *TF:* 800-787-7227 ■ *Web:* www.asccp.org	Hagerstown	MD	21740	301-733-3640		49-8
ASCD (Association for Supervision & Curriculum Development) 1703 N Beauregard St *TF:* 800-933-2723 ■ *Web:* www.ascd.org	Alexandria	VA	22311	703-578-9600	575-5400	49-5
ASCDI (Association of Service & Computer Dealers International) 131 NW First Ave *TF:* 800-393-2505 ■ *Web:* www.ascdi.com	Delray Beach	FL	33444	561-266-9016	431-6302	48-9
ASCE (American Society of Civil Engineers) 1801 Alexander Bell Dr *TF:* 800-548-2723 ■ *Web:* www.asce.org	Reston	VA	20191	703-295-6300	295-6211	457-21
Ascedia Inc 161 S First St *TF:* 800-928-4406 ■ *Web:* www.ascedia.com	Milwaukee	WI	53204	414-292-3200		224
Ascend Advisory Group LLC 6760 Perimeter Dr *Web:* www.ascendadvisory.com	Dublin	OH	43016	614-784-6000		194
Ascend Analytics LLC 1877 Broadway Ste 706 *TF:* 800-628-1628 ■ *Web:* www.ascendanalytics.com	Boulder	CO	80302	303-415-1400		463
Ascend Federal Credit Union 520 Airpark Dr PO Box 1210 *TF:* 800-342-3086 ■ *Web:* www.ascendfcu.org	Tullahoma	TN	37388	931-455-5441		219
Ascend Hr Solutions 450 East 1000 North *Web:* www.ascendhr.com	North Salt Lake	UT	84054	801-299-6400		2
Ascend Laboratories 339 Jefferson Ave Ste 101 *Web:* www.ascendlaboratories.com	Parsippany	NJ	07054	201-476-1977		231
Ascend Marketing LLC 3904 W Vickery Blvd *Web:* ascend-marketing.com	Fort Worth	TX	76107	817-886-0014		636
Ascend Therapeutics Inc 607 Herndon Pkwy Ste 110 *TF:* 888-412-5751 ■ *Web:* www.ascendtherapeutics.com	Herndon	VA	20170	703-471-4744		231
Ascendant Advisors LLC 4 Oaks Pl 1330 Post Oak Blvd Ste 1550 *TF:* 800-552-6010 ■ *Web:* www.ascendantadvisors.com	Houston	TX	77056	800-552-6010		528
Ascendant Engineering Solutions 12303 Technology Blvd Ste 925 *Web:* aesaustin.com	Austin	TX	78727	512-371-5704		256
Ascendant Pictures 406 Wilshire Blvd *Web:* www.ascendantpictures.com	Santa Monica	CA	90401	310-288-4600		514
Ascendbridge Solutions 50 Acadia Ave *TF:* 800-668-2374 ■ *Web:* www.ascendbridge.com	Markham	ON	L3R0B3	905-944-0047		179
Ascendiant Capital Group LLC 18881 Von Karman Ave 16th Fl *Web:* www.ascendiant.com	Irvine	CA	92612	949-259-4900		463
Ascendum Solutions LLC 10290 Alliance Rd *Web:* www.ascendum.com	Cincinnati	OH	45242	513-792-5100		196
Ascension Chamber of Commerce 1006 W Hwy 30 *Web:* www.ascensionchamber.com	Gonzales	LA	70737	225-647-7487	647-5124	139
Ascension Health 4600 Edmundson Rd *Web:* ascension.org	Saint Louis	MO	63134	314-733-8000	733-8000	353
Ascension Health Ventures LLC 101 S Hanley Rd Ste 200 *Web:* ascensionventures.org	Clayton	MO	63105	314-733-8100		792
Ascension Industries 1254 Erie Ave *Web:* www.asmfab.com	North Tonawanda	NY	14120	716-693-9381	693-9882	482
Ascension Parish 208 E Railroad St *Web:* www.ascensionparish.net	Gonzales	LA	70737	225-621-5709	621-5704	338
Ascent Aviation Group Inc 1 Mill St *Web:* www.ascent1.com	Parish	NY	13131	315-625-7299		579
Ascent Biomedical Ventures 142 W 57th St Ste 4A *Web:* www.ankarcapital.com	New York	NY	10019	212-303-1680		77
Ascent Capital Group Inc 5251 DTC Pkwy Ste 1000 *Web:* www.ascentcapitalgroupinc.com	Greenwood Village	CO	80111	303-628-5600		692
Ascent Capital Management LLC 2796 NW Clearwater Dr Ste 200 *Web:* www.ascentcap.com	Bend	OR	97703	541-382-4847		194
Ascent Hospitality 3616 S Bogan Rd Ste 201 *Web:* www.ascent-hospitality.com	Buford	GA	30519	706-529-6900		378
Ascent LLC 2350 Ball Dr *Web:* www.ascent-corp.com	St. Louis	MO	63146	314-989-1011		463
Ascent Media Group Inc 520 Broadway 5th Fl *Web:* ascentcapitalgroupinc.com	Santa Monica	CA	90401	310-434-7000	434-7007	512
Ascent Real Estate 2900 N Park Way *Web:* ascentrealestate.net	San Diego	CA	92104	619-814-3420		652
Ascent Services Group, The 1001 Galaxy Way Ste 405 *Web:* www.ascentsg.com	Concord	CA	94520	925-627-4900		180
Ascent Solar Technologies Inc 12300 Grant St *Web:* www.ascentsolar.com	Thornton	CO	80241	720-872-5000		696
Ascent Venture Partners 255 State St Fl 5 *Web:* www.ascentvp.com	Boston	MA	02109	617-720-9400	720-9401	792
Ascenta Health Ltd 4-15 Garland Ave *TF:* 866-224-1775 ■ *Web:* www.nutrasea.ca	Dartmouth	NS	B3B0A6	902-435-7329	435-3513	345
Ascenta Therapeutics Inc 101 Lindenwood Dr Ste 405	Malvern	PA	19355	610-408-0301	725-1515	231
Ascentek Inc 12 Betnr Industrial Dr *Web:* www.ascentek.com	Pittsfield	MA	01201	413-496-9900		396
Ascentium Capital LLC 23970 Hwy 59 N *TF:* 866-722-8500 ■ *Web:* www.ascentiumcapital.com	Kingwood	TX	77339	866-722-8500		509
Ascentive LLC 50 S 16th St Ste 3575 *TF:* 800-842-4084 ■ *Web:* www.ascentive.com	Philadelphia	PA	19102	215-320-6000		177
Ascentra Credit Union 1710 Grant St *TF:* 800-426-5241 ■ *Web:* ascentra.org	Bettendorf	IA	52722	563-355-0152		219
ASCG Inc 300 W 31st Ave *Web:* www.whpacific.com	Anchorage	AK	99503	907-339-6500	339-5327	261
ASCH (American Society of Clinical Hypnosis) 140 N Bloomingdale Rd *TF:* 800-227-6963 ■ *Web:* www.asch.net	Bloomingdale	IL	60108	630-980-4740	351-8490	49-8
Ascher Bros Company Inc 3033 W Fletcher St *TF:* 800-734-8055 ■ *Web:* www.ascherbrothers.com	Chicago	IL	60618	773-588-0001	588-5350	189-8
Aschinger Electric Co 877 Horan Dr *Web:* www.aschinger.com	Fenton	MO	63026	636-343-1211		189-4
ASCIS (Academie Ste Cecile International School) 925 Cousineau Rd *Web:* academiestececile.ca	Windsor	ON	N9G1V8	519-969-1291	969-7953	622
ASCLA (Association of Specialized & Co-op Library Agencies) 50 E Huron St *TF:* 800-545-2433 ■ *Web:* www.ala.org/ascla	Chicago	IL	60611	312-280-4395	944-8085	49-11
ASCO (Association of Schools & Colleges of Optometry) 6110 Executive Blvd Ste 420 *Web:* optometriceducation.org	Rockville	MD	20852	301-231-5944	770-1828	49-8
ASCO (American Society of Clinical Oncology) 2318 Mill Rd Ste 800 **Fax Area Code:* 703 ■ *TF:* 888-282-2552 ■ *Web:* www.asco.org	Alexandria	VA	22314	571-483-1300	299-0255*	49-8
ASCO Sintering Co 2750 Garfield Ave *Web:* www.ascosintering.com	Commerce	CA	90040	323-725-3550		350
ASCO Valve Inc 50-60 Hanover Rd *Web:* www.asco.com/en-us	Florham Park	NJ	07932	973-966-2000		201
Ascom (US) Inc 598 Airport Blvd Ste 300 *Web:* www.ascom.us	Morrisville	NC	27560	919-234-2500		647
Ascot Enterprises Inc 503 S Main St *Web:* www.ascotent.com	Nappanee	IN	46550	574-773-7751	773-2894	746
Ascot Staffing 1939 Harrison St Ste 150 *TF:* 800-579-7967 ■ *Web:* www.ascotstaffing.com	Oakland	CA	94612	510-839-9520		260
ASCP (American Society of Consultant Pharmacists) 1321 Duke St *TF:* 800-355-2727 ■ *Web:* www.ascp.com	Alexandria	VA	22314	703-739-1300	739-1321	49-8
ASCP (American Society for Clinical Pathology) 33 W Monroe St Ste 1600 *TF Cust Svc:* 800-621-4142 ■ *Web:* www.ascp.org	Chicago	IL	60603	312-541-4999	541-4998	49-8
ASCRS (American Society of Cataract & Refractive Surgery) 4000 Legato Rd Ste 700 *TF:* 877-996-4464 ■ *Web:* www.ascrs.org	Fairfax	VA	22033	703-591-2220	591-0614	49-8
Ascutney State Park 1826 Black Mtn Rd *Web:* www.vtstateparks.com	Windsor	VT	05089	802-674-2060		565
ASD (Allentown School District) 31 S Penn St *TF:* 877-262-1492 ■ *Web:* www.allentownsd.org	Allentown	PA	18105	484-765-4000	765-4140	685
ASD 600 Corporate Pointe Ste 1000, 10th Fl *TF:* 800-421-4511 ■ *Web:* www.asdonline.com	Culver	CA	90230	323-817-2200	957-1131	184
ASD Data Services LLC PO Box 1184 *TF:* 877-742-7297 ■ *Web:* www.asd.com	Manchester	TN	37349	877-742-7297		637-6
ASDS (American Society for Dermatologic Surgery) 5550 Meadowbrook Dr Ste 120 *TF:* 800-714-1374 ■ *Web:* www.asds.net	Rolling Meadows	IL	60008	847-956-0900	956-0999	49-8
ASE (American Society of Echocardiography) 2100 Gateway Centre Blvd Ste 310 *Web:* www.asecho.org	Morrisville	NC	27560	919-861-5574	882-9900	49-8
ASE (Alliance to Save Energy) 1850 M St NW Ste 600 *TF:* 800-862-2086 ■ *Web:* www.ase.org	Washington	DC	20036	202-857-0666	331-9588	48-12
ASEC International Inc 267 Riverchase Way *TF:* 800-883-8235 ■ *Web:* asecinternational.com	Lexington	SC	29072	803-939-4809		396
ASEE (American Society for Engineering Education) 1818 N St NW Ste 600 *Web:* www.asee.org	Washington	DC	20036	202-331-3500	265-8504	49-19
Asel Art Supply 2701 Cedar Springs *TF:* 888-273-5278 ■ *Web:* www.aselart.com	Dallas	TX	75201	214-871-2425	871-0007	45
Asen Marketing & Advertising Inc 18 Emory Pl Ste 100 *Web:* www.asenmarketing.com	Knoxville	TN	37917	865-769-0006		195
Asentinel Lackawanna Ave Ste 2B *TF:* 877-571-4737 ■ *Web:* www.tangoe.com/asentinel	Parsippany	NJ	07054	973-257-0300	257-0302	174
Aseptico Inc 8333 216th St SE *Web:* www.aseptico.com	Woodinville	WA	98072	425-487-3157		475
AseraCare Hospice 5220 Tennyson Pkwy Ste 400 *TF:* 800-261-3467 ■ *Web:* www.aseracare.com	Plano	TX	75024	972-372-6300		371
AseraCare Hospice of Milwaukee 5220 Tennyson Pkwy Ste 400 *TF:* 800-598-5132 ■ *Web:* www.aseracare.com	Plano	TX	75024	262-785-1356		371
Asereth Medical Services Inc 257 Fair Oaks Ave Ste 100 *Web:* www.asereth.com	Pasadena	CA	91105	626-449-0099		260
ASES (American Solar Energy Society) 2525 Arapahoe Ave Ste E4 253 *Web:* www.ases.org	Boulder	CO	80302	303-443-3130		48-12
ASF (Apache Software Foundation) 1901 Munsey Dr *Web:* www.apache.org	Forest Hill	MD	21050	410-420-0140	803-2258	48-9
ASF (Atlantic Salmon Federation) PO Box 5200 *TF:* 800-565-5666 ■ *Web:* www.asf.ca	Saint Andrews	NB	E5B3S8	506-529-1033		48-3
ASFMRA (American Society of Farm Managers & Rural Appraisers) 950 S Cherry St Ste 508 *TF:* 800-888-8827 ■ *Web:* www.asfmra.org	Denver	CO	80246	303-758-3513	758-0190	48-2
ASG (Allen Systems Group Inc) 1333 Third Ave S **Fax Area Code:* 800 ■ *TF:* 800-932-5536 ■ *Web:* www.asg.com	Naples	FL	34102	239-435-2200	325-2555*	178-12
ASG Renaissance 22226 Garrison St *TF:* 800-238-0890 ■ *Web:* www.asgren.com	Dearborn	MI	48124	313-565-4700	565-4701	261
ASGCA (American Society of Golf Course Architects) 125 N Executive Dr Ste 106 *Web:* www.asgca.org	Brookfield	WI	53005	262-786-5960	786-5919	48-22

Name / Address	City	State	Zip	Phone	Fax	Class
ASGE (American Society for Gastrointestinal Endoscopy)						
1520 Kensington Rd Ste 202	Oak Brook	IL	60523	630-573-0600	573-0691	49-8
TF: 866-353-2743 ■ *Web:* www.asge.org						
ASH (American Society of Hypertension)						
148 Madison Ave 5th Fl	New York	NY	10016	212-696-9099	696-0711	49-8
TF: 800-654-2452 ■ *Web:* www.ash-us.org						
ASH (American Society of Hematology)						
1900 M St NW Ste 200	Washington	DC	20036	202-776-0544	776-0545	49-8
Web: www.hematology.org						
Ash Brokerage Corp						
7609 W Jefferson Blvd	Fort Wayne	IN	46804	260-478-0600		390
Web: www.ashbrokerage.com						
Ash Creek Associates Inc						
3015 SW First Ave	Portland	OR	97201	503-924-4704	943-6357	192
Ash Creek Enterprises LLC						
1110 Broadbridge Ave	Stratford	CT	06615	203-331-1685		387
Web: www.ashcreek.com						
Ash Grove Cement Co						
8900 Indian Creek Pkwy	Overland Park	KS	66210	913-451-8900		135
OTC: ASHG ■ *TF:* 800-545-1882 ■ *Web:* www.ashgrove.com						
Ash Hollow State Historical Park						
PO Box 70	Lewellen	NE	69147	308-778-5651		565
Web: outdoornebraska.gov/ashhollow						
Ash Stevens Inc 5861 John C Lodge Fwy	Detroit	MI	48202	313-872-6400		231
Web: www.ashstevens.com						
ASHA (American School Health Assn)						
7918 Jones Branch Dr Ste 300	McLean	VA	44240	703-506-7675	506-3266	49-5
Web: www.ashaweb.org						
ASHA (American Seniors Housing Assn)						
5225 Wisconsin Ave NW Ste 502	Washington	DC	20015	202-237-0900	237-1616	48-6
Web: www.seniorshousing.org						
ASHA (American Speech-Language-Hearing Assn)						
2200 Research Blvd	Rockville	MD	20850	301-296-5700	296-8580	49-8
TF: 800-498-2071 ■ *Web:* www.asha.org						
ASHA (American Saddlebred Horse Assn)						
4083 Iron Works Pkwy	Lexington	KY	40511	859-259-2742	259-1628	48-3
TF: 800-829-4438 ■ *Web:* www.asha.net						
Ashaway Line & Twine Manufacturing Co						
24 Laurel St	Ashaway	RI	02804	401-377-2221	377-9091	208
TF: 800-556-7260 ■ *Web:* www.ashawayusa.com						
Ashbaugh Beal LLP						
4400 Columbia Ctr 701 Fifth Ave	Seattle	WA	98104	206-386-5900		428
TF: 800-745-5901 ■ *Web:* ashbaughbeal.com						
Ashbrook Ctr						
401 College Ave Ashland University	Ashland	OH	44805	419-289-5411		634
TF: 877-289-5411 ■ *Web:* www.ashbrook.org						
Ashbrook Simon-Hartley LP						
11600 E Hardy	Houston	TX	77093	281-449-0322		192
Web: www.alfalaval.com/as-h						
Ashburn Consulting LLC						
43848 Goshen Farm Ct	Leesburg	VA	20176	703-652-9120		180
Web: www.ashburnconsulting.com						
Ashbury College 362 Mariposa Ave	Rockcliffe	ON	K1M0T3	613-749-5954		685
Web: www.ashbury.ca						
Ashbury Images						
1661 Tennessee St Ste 3G	San Francisco	CA	94107	415-885-2742		184
TF: 800-533-4183 ■ *Web:* www.ashburyimages.org						
Ashcroft Inc 250 E Main St	Stratford	CT	06614	203-378-8281		407
TF: 800-328-8258 ■ *Web:* www.ashcroftinc.com						
Ashe County Chamber of Commerce						
1 N Jefferson Ave Ste C PO Box 31	West Jefferson	NC	28694	336-846-9550		338
TF: 888-343-2743 ■ *Web:* ashechamber.com						
Asheboro Elastics Corp 150 N Pk St	Asheboro	NC	27203	336-629-2626	629-3782	745-4
TF: 800-328-6569 ■ *Web:* www.aecnarrowfabrics.com						
Asher Agency Inc 535 W Wayne St	Fort Wayne	IN	46802	260-424-3373		636
Web: www.asheragency.com						
Asher's Chocolates 80 Wambold Rd	Souderton	PA	18964	215-721-3000	721-3265	296-8
TF: 800-223-4420 ■ *Web:* www.ashers.com						
Asheville Area Chamber of Commerce						
36 Montford Ave	Asheville	NC	28802	828-258-6101	251-0926	139
TF: 888-314-1041 ■ *Web:* www.ashevillechamber.org						
Asheville Art Museum						
175 Biltmore Ave	Asheville	NC	28801	828-253-3227		520
Web: ashevilleart.org						
Asheville Catholic School						
12 Culvern St	Asheville	NC	28804	828-252-7896		685
Web: www.ashevillecatholic.org						
Asheville Chevrolet Inc						
205 Smokey Pk Hwy	Asheville	NC	28806	828-665-4444		57
TF: 866-921-1073 ■ *Web:* www.ashevillechevrolet.com						
Asheville Citizen Times						
14 O'Henry Ave	Asheville	NC	28801	828-252-5611	251-0585	532-2
TF: 800-672-2472 ■ *Web:* www.citizen-times.com						
Asheville City Hall						
70 Ct Plaza PO Box 7148	Asheville	NC	28802	828-259-5600	259-5499	337
TF: 800-662-7952 ■ *Web:* www.ashevillenc.gov						
Asheville Community Theatre						
35 E Walnut St	Asheville	NC	28801	828-254-1320	252-4723	572
TF: 800-595-4849 ■ *Web:* www.ashevilletheatre.org						
Asheville Racquet Club Inc						
200 Racquet Club Rd	Asheville	NC	28803	828-274-3361		354
Web: ashevilleracquetclub.com						
Asheville Regional Airport						
61 Terminal Dr Ste 1	Fletcher	NC	28732	828-684-2226	684-3404	27
TF: 866-719-3910 ■ *Web:* www.flyavl.com						
Asheville Savings Bank S S B						
PO Box 652	Asheville	NC	28802	828-254-7411	252-1512	70
TF: 800-222-3230 ■ *Web:* www.ashevillesavings.com						
Asheville School						
360 Asheville School Rd	Asheville	NC	28806	828-254-6345		622
Web: www.ashevilleschool.org						
Asheville Symphony Orchestra						
87 Haywood St PO Box 2852	Asheville	NC	28802	828-254-7046	254-1761	573-3
Web: www.ashevillesymphony.org						
Asheville-Buncombe Library System						
67 Haywood St	Asheville	NC	28801	828-250-4746		434-3
Web: www.buncombecounty.org/governing/depts/library						
Asheville-Buncombe Technical Community College						
340 Victoria Rd	Asheville	NC	28801	828-254-1921	251-6718*	162
**Fax:* Admissions ■ *Web:* www.abtech.edu						
Madison 4646 US Hwy 25-70	Marshall	NC	28753	828-649-2947	281-9859	162
Web: www.abtech.edu						
Ashfall Fossil Beds State Historical Park						
86930 517th Ave	Royal	NE	68773	402-893-2000		565
Web: ashfall.unl.edu						
Ashfield Capital Partners LLC						
801 Montgomery St Ste 200	San Francisco	CA	94133	415-391-4747	391-1234	401
TF: 877-391-4747 ■ *Web:* www.ashfield.com						
Ashford Hospitality Trust Inc						
14185 Dallas Pkwy Ste 1100	Dallas	TX	75254	972-490-9600	980-2705	654
NYSE: AHT ■ *Web:* www.ahtreit.com						
Ashford Stud 5095 Frankfort Rd	Versailles	KY	40383	859-873-7088	879-5756	368
TF: 800-976-1034 ■ *Web:* www.coolmore.com						
Ashford University 400 N Bluff Blvd	Clinton	IA	52732	563-242-4023		166
TF: 800-242-4153 ■ *Web:* www.ashford.edu						
ASHG (American Society of Human Genetics)						
9650 Rockville Pike	Bethesda	MD	20814	301-634-7300	634-7079	49-19
Web: www.ashg.org						
ASHI (American Society for Histocompatibility & Immunogenetics)						
15000 Commerce Pkwy Ste C	Mount Laurel	NJ	08054	856-638-0428	439-0525	49-8
Web: www.ashi-hla.org						
ASHI (American Society of Home Inspectors)						
932 Lee St Ste 101	Des Plaines	IL	60016	847-759-2820	759-1620	49-3
TF: 800-743-2744 ■ *Web:* www.homeinspector.org						
Ashiana Indian Restaurant						
12610 Briar Forest Rd	Houston	TX	77077	281-679-5555		671
Web: ashianarestaurant.net						
Ashir Capital Inc 40 Wall St 59th Fl	New York	NY	10005	212-269-2300		70
Ashkenazy Acquisition Corp						
150 E 58th St 39th Fl	New York	NY	10155	212-213-4444		528
TF: 800-421-3483 ■ *Web:* www.aacrealty.com						
Ashland 1745 Cottage St	Ashland	OH	44805	859-815-3333		145
Web: www.ashland.com						
Ashland Addison Florist Co						
1640 W Fulton St	Chicago	IL	60612	312-432-1800		292
TF: 800-348-1157 ■ *Web:* www.ashaddflorist.com						
Ashland Alliance Chamber of Commerce						
1733 Winchester Ave	Ashland	KY	41101	606-324-5111	325-4607	139
TF: 800-233-3826 ■ *Web:* www.ashlandalliance.com						
Ashland Community & Technical College						
1400 College Dr	Ashland	KY	41101	606-326-2000	326-2192*	162
**Fax:* Admissions ■ *TF:* 800-928-4256 ■ *Web:* www.ashland.kctcs.edu						
Ashland Construction Co						
4601 Atlantic Ave	Raleigh	NC	27604	919-872-7500		186
Web: www.ashlandconstruction.com						
Ashland County 142 W Second St	Ashland	OH	44805	419-282-4242		338
Web: www.ashlandcounty.org						
Ashland County 201 W Main St Rm 202	Ashland	WI	54806	715-682-7015	682-7078	338
Web: www.co.ashland.wi.us						
Ashland County West Holmes Career Ctr						
1783 St Rt 60	Ashland	OH	44805	419-289-3313		165
Web: www.acwhcc.org						
Ashland Distribution Co						
5200 Blazer Pkwy PO Box 2219	Columbus	OH	43216	614-790-3333		146
Web: www.ashland.com						
Ashland Hardware Systems						
545 E John Carpenter Fwy Ste 610	Irving	TX	75062	469-621-9830		608
Web: www.ashlandhardware.com						
Ashland Inc						
50 E River Ctr Blvd PO Box 391	Covington	KY	41012	859-815-3333		185
NYSE: ASH ■ *TF:* 877-546-2782 ■ *Web:* www.ashland.com						
Ashland Independent School District						
1820 Hickman St	Ashland	KY	41105	606-327-2706	327-2705	685
TF: 800-752-6200 ■ *Web:* www.ashland.kyschools.us						
Ashland Industries Inc						
1115 Rail Dr PO Box 717	Ashland	WI	54806	715-682-4622		190
Web: www.ashlandind.com						
Ashland Lumber Company Inc						
134 Front St	Ashland	MA	01721	508-881-2660		364
Ashland Partners						
4400 Livingston Rd	Central Point	OR	97502	541-857-8800		393
Web: www.ashlandpartners.com						
Ashland Springs Hotel 212 E Main St	Ashland	OR	97520	541-488-1700	488-0240	379
TF: 888-795-4545 ■ *Web:* www.ashlandspringshotel.com						
Ashland Theological Seminary						
910 Ctr St	Ashland	OH	44805	419-289-5161	289-5969	167-3
Web: www.ashland.edu						
Ashland University 401 College Ave	Ashland	OH	44805	419-289-4142	289-5999	166
TF: 800-882-1548 ■ *Web:* www.ashland.edu						
Ashland University Library						
509 College Ave	Ashland	OH	44805	419-289-5400	289-5422	434-6
TF: 866-434-5222 ■ *Web:* www.ashland.edu						
Ashland-The Henry Clay Estate						
120 Sycamore Rd	Lexington	KY	40502	859-266-8581		50-3
Web: www.henryclay.org						
Ashlar Inc						
9600 Great Hills Trl Ste 150W-1625	Austin	TX	78759	512-250-2186	250-5811	178-5
TF: 800-877-2745 ■ *Web:* www.ashlar.com						
Ashley County 215 E Jefferson St	Hamburg	AR	71646	870-853-2000		338
Web: local.arkansas.gov						
Ashley Furniture Industries Inc						
1 Ashley Way	Arcadia	WI	54612	608-323-6225	323-6008	319-2
TF: 800-477-2222 ■ *Web:* www.ashleyfurniture.com						
Ashley Hall School						
172 Rutledge Ave	Charleston	SC	29403	843-722-4088		685
TF: 800-847-1582 ■ *Web:* ashleyhall.org						
Ashley Lighting Inc 405 Industrial Dr	Trumann	AR	72472	870-483-6181	483-7140	439
Web: ashleylighting.com						
Ashley Madison Agency, The						
2300 Yonge St	Toronto	ON	M4P1E4	866-742-2218		226
TF: 866-742-2218 ■ *Web:* www.ashleymadison.com						
Ashley Ward Inc 7490 Easy St	Mason	OH	45040	513-398-1414	398-1125	621
TF: 800-951-9276 ■ *Web:* www.ashleyward.com						
Ashley-Chicot Electric Co-op Inc						
307 E Jefferson St	Hamburg	AR	71646	870-853-5212		245
TF: 800-281-5212 ■ *Web:* www.ashley-chicot.com						

Name	Address	City	State	Zip	Phone	Fax	Class	Other
Ashmore Inn & Suites	4019 S Loop 289	Lubbock	TX	79423	806-785-0060		379	*Web:* www.ashmoreinn.com
Ashoka the Great	9474 Black Mountain Rd	San Diego	CA	92126	858-695-9749		671	*Web:* ashokasd.com
ASHP (American Society of Health-System Pharmacists)	7272 Wisconsin Ave	Bethesda	MD	20814	301-664-8700	664-8877	49-8	*TF:* 866-279-0681 ■ *Web:* www.ashp.org
ASHRAE (American Society of Heating Refrigerating & Air-Conditioning Engineers Inc)	1791 Tullie Cir NE	Atlanta	GA	30329	404-636-8400	321-5478	49-3	*TF Cust Svc:* 800-527-4723 ■ *Web:* www.ashrae.org
Ashram, The	PO Box 8009	Calabasas	CA	91372	818-222-6900		673	*Web:* www.theashram.com
ASHS (American Society for Horticultural Science)	1018 Duke St	Alexandria	VA	22314	703-836-4606	836-2024	48-2	*TF:* 800-331-1600 ■ *Web:* www.ashs.org
Ashta Chemicals Inc	3509 Middle Rd	Ashtabula	OH	44004	440-997-5221	992-0151	143	*TF Cust Svc:* 800-492-5082 ■ *Web:* www.ashtachemicals.com
Ashtabula Area Chamber of Commerce	4536 Main Ave	Ashtabula	OH	44004	440-998-6998	992-8216	139	*TF:* 800-337-6746 ■ *Web:* www.ashtabulachamber.net
Ashtabula Area City School District	2630 W 13th St	Ashtabula	OH	44004	440-992-1200	992-1209	685	*Web:* www.aacs.net
Ashtabula County District Library	335 W 44th St	Ashtabula	OH	44004	440-997-9341	992-7714	434-3	*Web:* www.acdl.info
Ashtabula County Medical Ctr (ACMC)	2420 Lake Ave	Ashtabula	OH	44004	440-997-2262	997-6644	374-3	*TF:* 800-722-3330 ■ *Web:* www.acmchealth.org
Ashtabula Rubber Co	2751 W Ave	Ashtabula	OH	44004	440-992-2195	992-7829	677	*Web:* www.ashtabularubber.com
Ashtead Technology Inc	19407 Pk Row Ste 170	Houston	TX	77084	281-398-9533		193	*TF:* 800-242-3910 ■ *Web:* www.ashtead-technology.com
Ashton College	1190 Melville St	Vancouver	BC	V6E3W1	604-899-0803		162	*Web:* www.ashtoncollege.ca
Ashton Company Inc, The	2727 S Country Club Rd PO Box 26927	Tucson	AZ	85713	520-624-5500	791-9059	186	*Web:* www.ashtoncoinc.com
Ashton Gardens Houston	21919 Inverness Forest Blvd	Houston	TX	77073	281-362-0011		184	*TF:* 800-475-2637 ■ *Web:* www.ashtongardens.com
Ashton Hotel	610 Main St	Fort Worth	TX	76102	817-332-0100		379	*Web:* www.theashtonhotel.com
Ashton Metzler & Assoc	PO Box 1640	Sanibel	FL	33957	239-395-3152		41	*Web:* www.ashtonmetzler.com
Ashton Staffing Inc	3590 Cherokee St Ste 303	Kennesaw	GA	30144	770-419-1776		260	*TF:* 800-264-1170 ■ *Web:* www.ashtonstaffing.com
Ashton-Potter (USA) Ltd	2855 Broadway St	Buffalo	NY	14227	716-633-2000		627	*Web:* www.ashtonpotter.com
Ashwaubenon School District	1055 Griffiths Ln	Green Bay	WI	54304	920-492-2900	492-2911	685	*Web:* www.ashwaubenon.k12.wi.us
Ashwood Management Partners LLC	1325 Howard Ave	Burlingame	CA	94010	650-867-0076		463	*Web:* www.ashwoodmp.com
ASI (American Swedish Institute, The)	2600 Pk Ave	Minneapolis	MN	55407	612-871-4907	871-8682	520	*TF:* 800-798-6032 ■ *Web:* www.asimn.org
ASI (American Sports Institute)	116 E Blithedale Ave	Mill Valley	CA	94941	415-383-5750		48-22	
ASI (American Society of Indexers)	1628 E Southern Ave Ste 9-223	Tempe	AZ	85282	480-245-6750		49-16	*Web:* www.asindexing.org
ASI (American Sheep Industry Assn)	9785 Maroon Cir Ste 360	Englewood	CO	80112	303-771-3500	771-8200	48-2	*TF:* 800-228-5262 ■ *Web:* www.sheepusa.org
ASI (American Specialties Inc)	441 Saw Mill River Rd	Yonkers	NY	10701	914-476-9000	476-0688	609	*Web:* www.americanspecialties.com
ASI Automation LLC	475 Applejack Ct	Sparta	MI	49345	616-887-8201		261	
ASI Computer Systems Inc	5250 Nordic Dr	Cedar Falls	IA	50613	319-266-7688		180	*Web:* www.asicomp.com
Asi Constructors Inc	1850 E Platteville Blvd	Pueblo West	CO	81007	719-647-2821	647-2890	186	*Web:* www.asiconstructors.com
ASI Corp	48289 Fremont Blvd	Fremont	CA	94538	510-226-8000	445-4157*	174	*Fax: Sales ■ *TF:* 800-200-0274 ■ *Web:* www.asipartner.com
ASI DataMyte Inc	2800 Campus Dr Ste 60	Plymouth	MN	55441	763-553-1040	760-7232*	178-10	*Fax Area Code: 844 ■ *TF:* 800-455-4359 ■ *Web:* www.asidatamyte.com
Asi Networks Inc	19331 E Walnut Dr N	City Of Industry	CA	91748	800-251-1336		180	*TF:* 800-251-1336 ■ *Web:* www.asi-networks.com
Asi System Integration Inc	48 W 37th St	New York	NY	10018	866-308-3920	629-3944*	113	*Fax Area Code: 212 ■ *TF:* 866-308-3920 ■ *Web:* www.asisystem.com
Asi Technologies	209 Progress Dr	Montgomeryville	PA	18936	215-661-1002		350	*Web:* www.asidrives.com
Asi Technologies Inc	5848 N 95th Ct	Milwaukee	WI	53225	414-464-6200	464-9863	234	*TF:* 800-558-7068 ■ *Web:* www.asidoors.com
Asia America MultiTechnology Assn (AAMA)	1270 Oakmead Pkwy	Sunnyvale	CA	94085	408-736-2554		49-13	*Web:* www.aamasv.com
Asia Pacific Capital	345 S Figueroa St Ste 100	Los Angeles	CA	90071	213-680-8811		528	*Web:* www.apccusa.com
Asia Pacific Center for Security	2058 Maluhia Rd	Honolulu	HI	96815	808-971-8900		693	*Web:* www.apcss.org
Asian American Business Development Center Inc	80 Wall St Ste 418	New York	NY	10005	212-966-0100		194	*Web:* www.aabdc.com

Name	Address	City	State	Zip	Phone	Fax	Class	Other
Asian American Civic Association Inc	87 Tyler St Fl 5	Boston	MA	02111	617-426-9492		554	*TF:* 800-977-9873 ■ *Web:* www.aaca-boston.org
Asian American Legal Defense & Education Fund (AALDEF)	99 Hudson St 12th Fl	New York	NY	10013	212-966-5932	966-4303	48-8	*TF:* 800-966-5946 ■ *Web:* www.aaldef.org
Asian Art Museum	200 Larkin St Civic Ctr Plz	San Francisco	CA	94102	415-581-3500	581-4700	520	*TF:* 800-965-2030 ■ *Web:* www.asianart.org
Asian Cultures Museum	1809 N Chaparral St	Corpus Christi	TX	78401	361-881-8827		520	*Web:* www.asianculturesmuseum.org
Asian Inc Social Svc Crdntr	1167 Mission St Fl 4	San Francisco	CA	94103	415-928-5910		194	*Web:* www.asianinc.org
Asian Mint	11617 N Central Expy Ste 135	Dallas	TX	75243	214-363-6655		671	*Web:* www.asianmint.com
Asian Pacific American Legal Center of Southern California	1145 Wilshire Blvd Fl 2	Los Angeles	CA	90017	213-977-7500		428	*TF:* 800-520-2356 ■ *Web:* advancingjustice-la.org
Asian Television Network (ATN)	330 Cochrane Dr	Markham	ON	L3R8E4	905-948-8199	948-8108	740	*Web:* www.asiantelevision.com
Asian University for Women	1100 Massachusetts Ave Ste 3	Cambridge	MA	02138	617-914-0500		166	*Web:* asian-university.org
Asiana Cafe	130 E Putnam Ave	Greenwich	CT	06830	203-622-6833	861-2680	671	*Web:* www.asianacafe.com
Asiana Cuisine Enterprises Inc	1447 W 178th St	Gardena	CA	90248	310-327-2233		297-8	*Web:* acesushi.com
asiaSF	201 Ninth St	San Francisco	CA	94103	415-255-2742		671	*Web:* www.asiasf.com
Asiatico & Associates Pllc	5850 Granite Pkwy Ste 900	Plano	TX	75024	214-570-0700		428	*TF:* 800-555-1234 ■ *Web:* baalegal.com
Asico LLC	26 Plaza Dr	Westmont	IL	60559	630-986-8032	986-0065	5	*Web:* www.asico.com
Asics America Corp	29 Parker Ste 100	Irvine	CA	92618	949-453-8888	453-0292	301	*TF:* 800-333-8404 ■ *Web:* www.asics.com/us/en-us
ASID (American Society of Interior Designers)	608 Massachusetts Ave	Washington	DC	20002	202-546-3480	546-3240	48-4	*Web:* www.asid.org
ASIL (American Society of International Law, The)	2223 Massachusetts Ave NW	Washington	DC	20008	202-939-6000	797-7133	49-10	*TF:* 800-828-7571 ■ *Web:* www.asil.org
Asilomar State Beach & Conference Grounds	804 Crocker Ave	Pacific Grove	CA	93950	831-646-6440		565	*Web:* www.parks.ca.gov/default.asp?page_id=566
ASIS International	1625 Prince St	Alexandria	VA	22314	703-519-6200	519-6299	49-12	*Web:* www.asisonline.org
Asist Translation Services	4891 Sawmill Rd Ste 200	Columbus	OH	43235	614-451-6744		768	*Web:* www.asisttranslations.com
ASIWPCA (Association of State & Interstate Water Pollution Control Administrators)	1221 Connecticut Ave NW 2nd Fl	Washington	DC	20036	202-756-0600		49-7	*Web:* www.acwa-us.org
Ask Associates Inc	1201 Wakarusa Ste C-1	Lawrence	KS	66049	785-841-8194		738	*TF:* 800-315-4333 ■ *Web:* www.askusa.com
ASK Plastics Inc	9750 Ashton Rd	Philadelphia	PA	19114	215-969-0800		604	*Web:* www.askplastics.com
ASK Services Inc	42180 Ford Rd Ste 101	Canton	MI	48187	734-983-9040	983-9041	400	*TF:* 888-416-1313 ■ *Web:* www.ask-services.com
Ask Telemarketing Inc	5815 Carmichael Rd	Montgomery	AL	36117	334-387-2758		737	*TF:* 800-897-9880 ■ *Web:* www.asktelemarketing.com
Ask.com	555 12th St Ste 500	Oakland	CA	94607	510-985-7400		397	*TF:* 800-611-4827 ■ *Web:* www.ask.com
Aski Capital Inc	419 Notre Dame Ave	Winnipeg	MB	R3B1R3	204-987-7180		138	*TF:* 866-987-7180 ■ *Web:* www.askifinancial.ca
Askins Family LTP	208 S Blanding St	Lake City	SC	29560	843-394-8555		189-8	
AskMencom Solutions Canada Inc	4200 St Laurent Ste 801	Montreal	QC	H2W2R2	514-908-2552	843-3650	4	*Web:* in.askmen.com
ASKO Appliances Inc	PO Box 44848	Madison	WI	53744	800-898-1879		36	*TF:* 800-898-1879 ■ *Web:* askona.com
ASKO Inc	501 W Seventh Ave	Homestead	PA	15120	412-461-4110	461-5400	493	*TF:* 800-321-1310 ■ *Web:* www.askoinc.com
ASL Distribution Services Ltd	2160 Buckingham Rd	Oakville	ON	L6H6M7	905-829-5141		478	*TF:* 800-387-7995 ■ *Web:* www.asldistribution.com
ASL Marketing	2 Dubon Ct	Farmingdale	NY	11735	516-248-6100		195	*Web:* www.aslmarketing.com
ASL Services	3700 Commerce Blvd Ste 216	Kissimmee	FL	34741	407-518-7900		701	*TF:* 888-744-6275 ■ *Web:* www.aslservices.com
ASLA (American Seminar Leaders Assn)	2405 E Washington Blvd	Pasadena	CA	91104	626-791-1211	791-0701	49-12	*TF:* 800-801-1886 ■ *Web:* www.asla.com
ASLA (American Society of Landscape Architects)	636 'I' St NW	Washington	DC	20001	202-898-2444	898-1185	48-2	*TF:* 888-999-2752 ■ *Web:* www.asla.org
ASLMS (American Society for Laser Medicine & Surgery Inc)	2100 Stewart Ave Ste 240	Wausau	WI	54401	715-845-9283	848-2493	49-8	*TF:* 877-258-6028 ■ *Web:* www.aslms.org
ASLO (American Society of Limnology & Oceanography)	5400 Bosque Blvd Ste 680	Waco	TX	76710	254-399-9635	776-3767	49-19	*TF:* 800-929-2756 ■ *Web:* www.aslo.org
ASLRRA (American Short Line & Regional Railroad Assn)	50 F St NW Ste 7020	Washington	DC	20001	202-628-4500	628-6430	49-21	*Web:* www.aslrra.org
ASLU LLC	12087 Landon Dr	Mira Loma	CA	91752	951-934-4200		711	*Web:* www.activerideshop.com
ASM (American Society for Microbiology)	1752 N St NW	Washington	DC	20036	202-737-3600		49-8	*TF:* 800-546-2416 ■ *Web:* www.asm.org
ASM America Inc	3440 E University Dr	Phoenix	AZ	85034	602-470-5700		695	*Web:* www.asm.com

Name / Address	City	State	ZIP	Phone	Fax	Class
Asm Consulting Services						
22 Sunnyhill Rd	Emerald Hills	CA	94062	650-780-9321		190
ASM Industries Inc Pacer Pumps Div						
41 Industrial Cir	Lancaster	PA	17601	717-656-2161	656-0477	641
TF Cust Svc: 800-233-3861 ■ *Web:* www.pacerpumps.com						
ASM International						
9639 Kinsman Rd	Materials Park	OH	44073	440-338-5151	338-4634	49-13
TF: 800-336-5152 ■ *Web:* www.asminternational.org						
ASMBA (Armed Services Mutual Benefit Assn)						
PO Box 160384	Nashville	TN	37216	615-851-0800	851-9484	48-19
TF: 800-251-8434 ■ *Web:* www.asmba.com						
ASMC (American Society of Military Comptrollers)						
415 N Alfred St	Alexandria	VA	22314	703-549-0360	549-3181	48-19
TF: 800-462-5637 ■ *Web:* www.asmconline.org						
ASME International Gas Turbine Institute (IGTI)						
6525 the Corners Pkwy	Norcross	GA	30092	404-847-0072	847-0151	49-19
Web: www.asme.org						
ASML US Inc 8555 S River Pkwy	Tempe	AZ	85284	480-383-4422		695
Web: www.asml.com						
ASMO North America LLC						
470 Crawford Rd	Statesville	NC	28625	704-878-6663		518
Web: www.densocorp-na.com/locations/anam						
ASMP (American Society of Media Photographers)						
150 N Second St	Philadelphia	PA	19106	215-451-2767	451-0880	49-14
Web: www.asmp.org						
ASN (American Society of Notaries)						
PO Box 5707	Tallahassee	FL	32314	850-671-5164	671-5165	49-12
Web: www.notaries.org						
ASNA (Alabama State Nurses Assn)						
360 N Hull St	Montgomery	AL	36104	334-262-8321		533
TF: 800-270-2762 ■ *Web:* www.alabamanurses.org						
ASNC (American Society of Nuclear Cardiology)						
4550 Montgomery Ave Ste 780-N	Bethesda	MD	20814	301-215-7575	215-7113	49-8
Web: www.asnc.org						
ASNE (American Society of News Editors)						
11690-B Sunrise Vly Dr	Reston	VA	20191	703-453-1122	453-1133	49-14
Web: www.asne.org						
ASNE (American Society of Naval Engineers)						
1452 Duke St	Alexandria	VA	22314	703-836-6727	836-7491	49-21
Web: www.navalengineers.org						
ASNR (American Society of Neuroradiology)						
2210 Midwest Rd Ste 207	Oak Brook	IL	60523	630-574-0220	574-0661	49-8
Web: www.asnr.org						
ASNS (American Society for Nutrition)						
9211 Corporate Blvd Ste 300	Rockville	MD	20850	301-634-7050	634-7894	49-6
TF: 800-627-8723 ■ *Web:* www.nutrition.org						
ASNT (American Society for Nondestructive Testing Inc)						
1711 Arlingate Ln PO Box 28518	Columbus	OH	43228	614-274-6003	274-6899	49-19
TF Orders: 800-222-2768 ■ *Web:* www.asnt.org						
Asnuntuck Community College						
170 Elm St	Enfield	CT	06082	860-253-3000	253-3014*	162
**Fax:* Admissions ■ *TF:* 800-501-3967 ■ *Web:* www.asnuntuck.edu						
ASO (Anderson Symphony Orchestra)						
1124 Meridian Plaza	Anderson	IN	46016	765-644-2111		573-3
Web: www.andersonsymphony.org						
ASO LLC 300 Sarasota Ctr Blvd	Sarasota	FL	34240	941-379-0300	378-9040	477
Web: www.asocorp.com						
Asolo Repertory Theatre						
5555 N Tamiami Tr	Sarasota	FL	34243	941-351-9010	351-5796	749
TF: 800-361-8388 ■ *Web:* www.asolorep.org						
Asotin County 135 Second St	Asotin	WA	99402	509-243-2016	243-4978	338
TF: 800-933-2128 ■ *Web:* www.co.asotin.wa.us						
ASP (American Society for Photobiology)						
PO Box 1897	Lawrence	KS	66044	785-843-1234	843-1274	49-19
TF: 800-627-0326 ■ *Web:* www.photobiology.org						
ASP (Advanced Sterilization Products)						
33 Technology Dr	Irvine	CA	92618	888-783-7723		477
TF: 888-783-7723 ■ *Web:* www.aspjj.com						
ASP (Association of Shareware Professionals)						
PO Box 1522	Martinsville	IN	46151	765-349-4740	301-3756*	48-9
**Fax Area Code:* 815 ■ *Web:* www.asp-software.org						
ASP Global						
3450 Atlanta Industrial Pkwy Ste 250	Atlanta	GA	30331	404-620-6924	699-6080	475
Web: www.anatomysupply.com						
ASP Inc 460 Brant St Ste 212	Burlington	ON	L7R4B6	905-333-4242	481-1966*	693
**Fax Area Code:* 416 ■ *TF:* 877-552-5535 ■ *Web:* www.security-asp.com						
ASPA (Association of Specialized & Professional Accreditors)						
3304 N Broadway St Ste 214	Chicago	IL	60657	773-857-7900		48-1
TF: 800-228-5424 ■ *Web:* www.aspa-usa.org						
ASPA (American Society for Public Administration)						
1301 Pennsylvania Ave NW Ste 840	Washington	DC	20004	202-393-7878	638-4952	49-7
TF: 800-765-7755 ■ *Web:* www.aspanet.org						
ASPAN (American Society of PeriAnesthesia Nurses)						
90 Frontage Rd	Cherry Hill	NJ	08034	856-616-9600	616-9601	49-8
TF: 877-737-9696 ■ *Web:* www.aspan.org						
Aspasie Inc						
221 Saint-Georges	Saint-barnabe-nord	QC	G0X2K0	819-379-2157		195
Web: www.aspasie.com						
ASPB (American Society of Plant Biologists)						
15501 Monona Dr	Rockville	MD	20855	301-251-0560		49-19
Web: my.aspb.org						
ASPC (American Shetland Pony Club)						
81B E Queenwood Rd Ste 2	Morton	IL	61550	309-263-4044	263-5113	48-3
Web: shetlandminiature.com						
ASPCA (American Society for the Prevention of Cruelty to Animals)						
424 E 92nd St	New York	NY	10128	212-876-7700		48-3
TF: 800-582-5979 ■ *Web:* www.aspca.org						
ASPCA Animal Poison Control Ctr						
424 E 92nd St	New York	NY	10128	212-876-7700		48-3
TF: 888-426-4435 ■ *Web:* www.aspca.org						
ASPE (American Society of Professional Estimators)						
2525 Perimeter Pl Dr Ste 103	Nashville	TN	37214	615-316-9200	316-9800	49-3
TF: 888-378-6283 ■ *Web:* www.aspenational.org						
ASPE Inc 114 Edinburgh S Dr Ste 200	Cary	NC	27511	877-800-5221		764
TF: 877-800-5221 ■ *Web:* aspetraining.com						
Aspect Automation LLC						
1185 Willow Lake Blvd	Saint Paul	MN	55110	651-643-3700		407
Web: www.aspectautomation.com						

Name / Address	City	State	ZIP	Phone	Fax	Class
Aspect Business Solutions						
7550 IH 10 W 14th Fl	San Antonio	TX	78229	210-298-5000	298-5001	84
Web: www.4aspect.com						
Aspect Consulting Inc						
20140 Vly Forge Cir	King Of Prussia	PA	19406	610-783-0600		177
Web: www.aspect-consulting.com						
Aspects Inc 9441 Opal Ave	Mentone	CA	92359	909-794-7722		286
ASPEN (American Society for Parenteral & Enteral Nutrition)						
8630 Fenton St Ste 412	Silver Spring	MD	20910	301-587-6315	587-2365	49-8
TF: 800-727-4567 ■ *Web:* www.nutritioncare.org						
Aspen Art Museum 590 N Mill St	Aspen	CO	81611	970-925-8050	925-8054	520
Web: aspenartmuseum.org						
Aspen Canyon Ranch 13206 County Rd 3	Parshall	CO	80468	970-725-3600		239
TF: 800-321-1357 ■ *Web:* www.aspencanyon.com						
Aspen Chamber Resort Assn						
425 Rio Grande Pl	Aspen	CO	81611	970-925-1940	920-1173	139
TF: 800-670-0792 ■ *Web:* www.aspenchamber.org						
Aspen Chamber Symphony						
225 Music School Rd	Aspen	CO	81611	970-925-3254		573-3
Web: www.aspenmusicfestival.com						
Aspen Environmental Group						
5020 Chesebro Rd Ste 200	Agoura Hills	CA	91301	818-597-3407		194
Web: www.aspeneg.com						
Aspen Equipment Co						
9150 Pillsbury Ave S	Bloomington	MN	55420	952-888-2525		59
Web: www.aspenequipment.com						
Aspen Graphics Inc 4795 Oakland St	Denver	CO	80239	303-371-2345		627
Aspen Group Inc, The						
1100 Wayne Ave Ste 1200	Silver Spring	MD	20910	301-650-6200		225
Web: www.theaspengroupinc.com						
Aspen Grove						
7301 S Santa Fe Dr Ste 550	Littleton	CO	80120	303-794-0640	798-0238	460
Aspen Hill Club						
14501 Homecrest Rd	Silver Spring	MD	20906	301-598-5200		42
Web: www.aspenhillclub.com						
Aspen Institute						
1 DuPont Cir NW Ste 700	Washington	DC	20036	202-736-5823	467-0790	634
Web: www.aspeninstitute.org						
Aspen Marketing Services						
1240 N Ave	West Chicago	IL	60185	630-293-9600	293-9600	4
TF: 800-848-0212 ■ *Web:* www.aspenms.com						
Aspen Meadows Resort 845 Meadows Rd	Aspen	CO	81611	970-925-4240		669
TF: 800-452-4240 ■ *Web:* www.aspenmeadows.com						
Aspen Medical Products 6481 Oak Cyn	Irvine	CA	92618	949-681-0200	681-0222	476
TF: 800-295-2776 ■ *Web:* www.aspenmp.com						
Aspen Networks Inc						
3777 Stevens Creek Blvd	Santa Clara	CA	95051	408-246-4059		180
TF: 800-746-9370 ■ *Web:* www.aspen-networks.com						
Aspen Opera Theater 225 Music School Rd	Aspen	CO	81611	970-925-3254		573-2
Web: www.aspenmusicfestival.com						
Aspen Optical Inc 1050 W Main St Ste 102	Mesa	AZ	85201	480-894-8770		543
Web: www.aspenoptical.com						
Aspen Products Inc						
4231 Clary Blvd	Kansas City	MO	64130	816-921-0234		558
Web: www.aspenpro.com						
Aspen Santa Fe Ballet 0245 Sage Way	Aspen	CO	81611	970-925-7175	925-1127	573-1
TF: 866-449-0464 ■ *Web:* www.aspensantafeballet.com						
Aspen Ski & Board Co						
1170 L Powell Rd	Lewis Center	OH	43035	614-848-6600		711
TF: 877-861-0777 ■ *Web:* aspenskiandboard.com						
Aspen Skiing Co 117 ABC	Aspen	CO	81611	970-925-1220		669
TF: 855-754-2863 ■ *Web:* www.aspensnowmass.com						
Aspen Square Management Inc						
380 Union St	West Springfield	MA	01089	413-781-0712		177
Web: www.aspensquare.com						
Aspen Surgical 6945 Southbelt Dr SE	Caledonia	MI	49316	616-698-7100		477
TF: 888-364-7004 ■ *Web:* www.aspensurgical.com						
Aspen Technology Inc						
200 Wheeler Rd	Burlington	MA	01803	781-221-6400		178-5
NASDAQ: AZPN ■ *TF:* 888-996-7100 ■ *Web:* www.aspentech.com						
Aspen Times 310 E Main St	Aspen	CO	81611	970-925-3414		532-2
TF: 800-525-6200 ■ *Web:* www.aspentimes.com						
Aspen Waste Systems Inc						
2951 Weeks Ave SE	Minneapolis	MN	55414	612-884-8000	884-8010	804
Web: www.aspenwaste.com						
ASPET (American Society for Pharmacology & Experimental Therapeutics)						
9650 Rockville Pk	Bethesda	MD	20814	301-634-7060	634-7061	49-8
TF: 800-422-4633 ■ *Web:* www.aspet.org						
Aspex Inc 1984 Isaac Newton Sq W	Reston	VA	20190	703-956-9343		177
Web: aspex.com						
ASPH (Association of Schools of Public Health)						
1900 M St NW Ste 710	Washington	DC	20036	202-296-1099	296-1252	49-5
Web: www.asph.org						
Asphalt Drum Mixers Inc (ADM)						
1 ADM Pkwy	Huntertown	IN	46748	260-637-5729	637-3164	190
Web: www.admasphaltplants.com						
Asphalt Green 555 E 90th St	New York	NY	10128	212-369-8890		354
Web: www.agtri.com						
Asphalt Institute						
2696 Research Pk Dr	Lexington	KY	40511	859-288-4960	288-4999	49-3
Web: www.asphaltinstitute.org						
Asphalt Materials Inc PO Box 5	West Jordan	UT	84084	801-561-4231	561-7795	46
Web: asphaltmaterials.net						
Asphalt Roofing Manufacturers Assn (ARMA)						
529 14th St NW Ste 750	Washington	DC	20045	202-207-0917	223-9741	49-3
TF: 800-247-6637 ■ *Web:* www.asphaltroofing.org						
Asphalt Specialists Inc						
1780 Highwood E	Pontiac	MI	48340	248-334-4570	334-4135	189-3
Web: www.asipaving.com						
ASPIRA Assn Inc						
1444 'I' St NW Ste 800	Washington	DC	20005	202-835-3600	835-3613	48-14
Web: www.aspira.org						
Aspirus Wausau Hospital						
333 Pine Ridge Blvd	Wausau	WI	54401	715-847-2121		374-3
TF: 800-283-2881 ■ *Web:* www.aspirus.org						
Asplundh Tree Expert Co						
708 Blair Mill Rd	Willow Grove	PA	19090	215-784-4200		776
TF: 800-248-8733 ■ *Web:* www.asplundh.com						

Phone | Fax | Class

Asponte Technology Inc
11523 Palmbrush Trl Ste 137 .... Lakewood Ranch FL 34202 888-926-9434 180
TF: 888-926-9434 ■ *Web:* www.asponte.com

ASPPA (American Society of Pension Professionals & Actuaries)
4245 N Fairfax Dr Ste 750 .... Arlington VA 22203 703-516-9300 516-9308 49-12
Web: www.asppa.org

ASPR (Association of Staff Physician Recruiters)
1000 Westgate Dr Ste 252 .... Saint Paul MN 55114 800-830-2777 49-8
TF: 800-830-2777 ■ *Web:* www.aspr.org

ASPRS (American Society for Photogrammetry & Remote Sensing, The)
5410 Grosvenor Ln Ste 210 .... Bethesda MD 20814 301-493-0290 493-0208 49-19
Web: www.asprs.org

ASPS (American Society of Plastic Surgeons)
444 E Algonquin Rd .... Arlington Heights IL 60005 847-228-9900 228-9131 49-8
TF: 888-475-2784 ■ *Web:* www.plasticsurgery.org

Aspyr Media Inc
1250 S Capital of Texas Hwy Ste 650 .... Austin TX 78746 512-708-8100 708-9595 179
Web: www.aspyr.com

Aspyra Inc
4360 Pk Terr Dr Ste 100 .... Westlake Village CA 91361 800-437-9000 880-4398* 178-10
OTC: APYI ■ **Fax Area Code:* 818 ■ *TF:* 800-437-9000 ■ *Web:* www.aspyra.com

ASQ (American Society for Quality)
600 N Plankinton Ave .... Milwaukee WI 53203 414-272-8575 272-1734 49-13
TF: 800-248-1946 ■ *Web:* www.asq.org

ASR Analytics LLC 1389 Canterbury Way .... Potomac MD 20854 301-738-9502 194
Web: www.asranalytics.com

ASR Constructors Inc 5230 Wilson St .... Riverside CA 92509 951-779-6580 194
Web: asrconstructors.com

ASR International Corp
580 Old Willets Path .... Hauppauge NY 11788 631-231-1086 463
Web: www.asrintl.com

ASRA (American Society of Regional Anesthesia & Pain Medicine)
239 Fourth Ave Ste 1714 .... Pittsburgh PA 15222 412-471-2718 471-7503 49-8
TF: 855-795-2772 ■ *Web:* www.asra.com

ASRC Energy Services Inc 3900 C St .... Anchorage AK 99503 907-339-6200 539
Web: www.asrcenergy.com

ASRM (American Society for Reproductive Medicine)
1209 Montgomery Hwy .... Birmingham AL 35216 205-978-5000 978-5005 49-8
TF: 800-654-2452 ■ *Web:* www.asrm.org

ASRT (American Society of Radiologic Technologists)
15000 Central Ave SE .... Albuquerque NM 87123 505-298-4500 298-5063 49-8
TF: 800-444-2778 ■ *Web:* www.asrt.org

ASSA ABLOY 110 Sargent Dr .... New Haven CT 06511 800-377-3948 777-9042* 234
**Fax Area Code:* 203 ■ **Fax:* Sales ■ *TF:* 800-377-3948 ■ *Web:* www.assaabloydss.com

Assa Abloy of Canada Ltd
160 Four Vly Dr .... Vaughan ON L4K4T9 905-738-2466 350
TF: 800-461-3007 ■ *Web:* www.assaabloy.ca

ASSA Inc 110 Sargent Dr .... New Haven CT 06511 203-624-5225 892-3256* 350
**Fax Area Code:* 800 ■ *TF:* 800-235-7482 ■ *Web:* www.assalock.com

Assabet Valley Chamber of Commerce
18 Church St PO Box 578 .... Hudson MA 01749 978-568-0360 562-4118 139
Web: www.assabetvalleychamber.org

Assaggio 95-1249 Meheula Pkwy .... Mililani HI 96789 808-623-5115 671
Web: assaggiohi.com

Assaggio 29 Prince St .... Boston MA 02113 617-227-7380 742-3512 671
Web: www.assaggioboston.com

Assaggio Ristorante 2010 Fourth Ave .... Seattle WA 98121 206-441-1399 671
Web: www.assaggioseattle.com

Assante Financial Management Ltd
4145 N Service Rd Ste 100 .... Burlington ON L7L6A3 905-335-2291 401
Web: assante.com

Assateague Island National Seashore
7206 National Seashore Ln PO Box 38 .... Berlin MD 21811 410-641-1441 564
Web: www.nps.gov/asis

Assateague State Park
7307 Stephen Decatur Hwy .... Berlin MD 21811 410-641-2120 260-8595 565
TF: 888-432-2267 ■ *Web:* dnr2.maryland.gov

Assay Technology Inc
1382 Stealth St .... Livermore CA 94551 925-461-8880 639
TF: 800-833-1258 ■ *Web:* www.assaytech.com

ASSE (American Society of Safety Engineers)
1800 E Oakton St .... Des Plaines IL 60018 847-699-2929 768-3434 49-19
Web: www.asse.org

Assembled Products
300 Hastings Dr .... Buffalo Grove IL 60089 847-215-1948 697
Web: www.aproducts.com

Assemblies of God (A/G)
1445 N Boonville Ave .... Springfield MO 65802 417-862-2781 48-20
TF: 800-641-4310 ■ *Web:* www.ag.org

Assemblies of God Theological Seminary
1435 N Glenstone Ave .... Springfield MO 65802 417-268-1000 268-1001 167-3
TF: 800-467-2487 ■ *Web:* www.agts.edu

Assemblies Unlimited Inc
143 Covington Dr .... Bloomingdale IL 60108 630-980-0200 41
Web: www.assemblies.com

Assembly of Turkish American Assn (ATAA)
1526 18th St NW .... Washington DC 20036 202-483-9090 483-9092 48-14
TF: 800-627-7692 ■ *Web:* www.ataa.org

Assess IT 12137 Travertine Ct .... Poway CA 92064 949-491-1269 193
Web: assessit.com

Assess-IT Inc 273 Pine Wood Ct .... Marietta GA 30068 510-717-9655 463
Web: www.assess-it.com

Assessment Technology Inc
6700 E Speedway Blvd .... Tucson AZ 85710 520-323-9033 225
TF: 800-367-4762 ■ *Web:* www.ati-online.com

Asset 15050 Ave of Science .... San Diego CA 92128 888-303-8755 367
TF: 888-303-8755 ■ *Web:* amsfmo.com

Asset Acceptance Capital Corp (AACC)
28405 Van Dyke Ave .... Warren MI 48093 586-939-9600 160
NASDAQ: AACC ■ *TF:* 800-545-9931 ■ *Web:* www.assetacceptance.com

Asset Allocation & Management Co
30 W Monroe St 3rd Fl .... Chicago IL 60603 312-263-2900 401
TF: 800-541-7774 ■ *Web:* www.aamcompany.com

Asset Appraisal Services Inc
344 N 115th St .... Omaha NE 68154 402-390-0505 41
Web: www.assetappraisalservices.com

Asset Based Lending Consultant
1641 NW 71st Terr .... Hollywood FL 33024 954-962-0099 194
Web: www.ablc.net

Asset Communications Inc
1764 Prospector Ave. .... Park City UT 84060 435-645-9108 463
Web: assetcommunications.com

Asset Consulting Group LLC
231 S Bemiston Ave 14th Fl .... St Louis MO 63105 314-862-4848 401
Web: www.acgnet.com

Asset Management Ventures
2100 Geng Rd Ste 200 .... Palo Alto CA 94303 650-621-8808 792
Web: www.assetman.com

Asset Plus Co 675 Bering Dr Ste 200 .... Houston TX 77057 713-782-5800 268-5111 653
Web: www.assetpluscorp.com

Asset Preservation Advisors Inc
3344 Peachtree Rd Ste 2050 .... Atlanta GA 30326 404-261-1333 528
TF: 800-833-8985 ■ *Web:* assetpreservationadvisors.com

Asset Protection Associates Inc
2305 Old Milton Pkwy .... Alpharetta GA 30009 678-566-0222 693
Web: www.assetprotectionassociates.net

Asset Sales Inc
301 Post Office Dr Ste C .... Indian Trail NC 28079 704-821-4315 41
Web: www.asset-sales.com

Asset Staffing Inc
14 NE First Ave Ste 1209 .... Miami FL 33132 305-371-5969 260
Web: www.assetstaffing.com

Asset Strategy Consultants LLC
6 N Park Dr Ste 208 .... Hunt Valley MD 21030 410-528-8282 401
TF: 866-344-8282 ■ *Web:* www.assetstrategyconsultants.com

Assetbuilder Inc 1255 W 15th St Ste 1000 .... Plano TX 75075 972-535-4040 401
Web: assetbuilder.com

AssetMark Inc 1655 Grant St 10th Fl .... Concord CA 94520 800-664-5345 401
TF: 800-664-5345 ■ *Web:* www.assetmark.com

AssetPoint LLC 770 Pelham Rd .... Greenville SC 29615 864-679-3500 809
Web: assetpoint.com

ASSETT Inc 11220 Assett Loop Ste 204 .... Manassas VA 20109 703-365-8950 180
Web: www.assett.net

Assette LLC 1 Faneuil Hall 4th Fl .... Boston MA 02109 617-723-6161 177
Web: www.assette.com

ASSH (American Society for Surgery of the Hand)
822 W Washington Blvd .... Chicago IL 60607 312-880-1900 384-1435* 49-8
**Fax Area Code:* 847 ■ *Web:* www.assh.org

ASSI Security Inc
1370 Reynolds Ave Ste 201 .... Irvine CA 92614 949-955-0244 693
Web: www.assisecurity.com

Assicurazioni Generali US Branch
250 Greenwich St 33rd Fl .... New York NY 10007 212-602-7600 587-9537 360-4
TF: 800-777-9656 ■ *Web:* www.generaliusa.com

Assiniboine Gordon Inn on the Park
1975 Portage Ave .... Winnipeg MB R3J0J9 204-888-4806 897-9870 379
TF: 800-665-6373 ■ *Web:* gordonhotels.com

Assiniboine Park Zoo
55 Pavilion Crescent .... Winnipeg MB R3P2N6 204-927-8080 823
TF: 877-927-6006 ■ *Web:* www.assiniboinepark.ca/zoo

ASSIST Aviation Solutions LLC
117 Perimeter Rd .... Nashua NH 03063 603-505-4668 693
TF: 800-561-2726 ■ *Web:* www.assist-us.com

Assist Cornerstone Technologies Inc
150 W Civic Ctr Dr Ste 601 .... Sandy UT 84070 800-732-0136 177
TF: 800-732-0136 ■ *Web:* www.assistcornerstone.com

Assist-2-Sell Inc 1610 Meadow Wood Ln .... Reno NV 89502 775-688-6060 823-8823 652
TF: 800-528-7816 ■ *Web:* www.assist2sell.com

Associated Administrators LLC
911 Ridgebrook Rd .... Sparks MD 21152 410-683-6500 390
Web: www.associated-admin.com

Associated Agencies Inc
1701 Golf Rd Tower 3 7th Fl .... Rolling Meadows IL 60008 847-427-8400 427-3559 390
Web: www.assocagencies.com

Associated Aircraft Mfg & Sales Inc
2735 NW 63rd Ct .... Fort Lauderdale FL 33309 954-772-6606 57
Web: www.aamsi.com

Associated Bag Co 400 W Boden St .... Milwaukee WI 53207 800-926-6100 926-4610 66
TF: 800-926-6100 ■ *Web:* www.associatedbag.com

Associated Banc-Corp
1305 Main St .... Stevens Point WI 54481 920-491-7000 360-2
NYSE: ASB ■ *TF PR:* 800-236-8866 ■ *Web:* www.associatedbank.com

Associated Bank
1305 Main St MS 7721 .... Stevens Point WI 54481 262-879-0133 70
TF: 866-536-3222 ■ *Web:* www.associatedbank.com

Associated Bank 2870 Holmgren Way .... Green Bay WI 54304 262-879-0133 70
TF: 800-728-3501 ■ *Web:* www.associatedbank.com

Associated Bank Green Bay NA
200 N Adams St .... Green Bay WI 54301 920-433-3200 70
TF: 800-728-3501 ■ *Web:* www.associatedbank.com

Associated Bank Illinois NA
612 N Main St .... Rockford IL 61103 815 987-3500 70
TF: 800-236-8866 ■ *Web:* www.associatedbank.com

Associated Bank Milwaukee
401 E Kilbourn Ave .... Milwaukee WI 53202 414-271-1786 70
TF: 800-236-8866 ■ *Web:* www.associatedbank.com

Associated Behavioral Health
4700 42nd Ave SW Ste 470 .... Seattle WA 98116 206-935-1282 671-6496* 462
**Fax Area Code:* 425 ■ *TF:* 800-858-6702 ■ *Web:* www.abhc.com

Associated Bodywork & Massage Professionals (ABMP)
25188 Genesee Trl Rd Ste 200 .... Golden CO 80401 303-674-8478 667-8260* 48-17
**Fax Area Code:* 800 ■ *TF:* 800-458-2267 ■ *Web:* www.abmp.com

Associated Builders & Contractors Inc (ABC)
4250 Fairfax Dr .... Arlington VA 22203 703-812-2000 812-8235 49-3
TF: 877-889-5627 ■ *Web:* www.abc.org

Associated Building Maintenance Company Inc
2140 Priest Bridge Ct .... Crofton MD 21114 410-721-1818 104
Web: www.abmcoinc.com

Associated Ceramics & Technology Inc
400 N Pike Rd .... Sarver PA 16055 724-353-1585 353-1050 249
Web: www.associatedceramics.com

Associated Church Press The (ACP)
924 Woodcrest Way .... Oviedo FL 32765 407-341-6615 386-3236 49-16
Web: www.theacp.org

Associated Clinical Laboratories
1526 Peach St .... Erie PA 16501 814-461-2420 415
Web: www.associatedclinicallabs.com

				Phone	Fax	Class
Associated Collegiate Press (ACP)						
2221 University Ave SE Ste 121	Minneapolis	MN	55414	612-625-8335	626-0720	48-11
Web: www.studentpress.org						
Associated Communications & Research Services Inc (ACRS)						
817 NE 63rd St	Oklahoma City	OK	73105	405-843-9966		196
Associated ElectricCo-op Inc						
2814 S Golden PO Box 754	Springfield	MO	65801	417-881-1204		245
Web: www.aeci.org						
Associated Electrics Inc						
26021 Commercentre Dr	Lake Forest	CA	92630	949-544-7500		711
TF: 800-705-2215 ■ Web: www.teamassociated.com						
Associated Energy Systems						
8621 S 180th St	Kent	WA	98032	425-251-9190		362
Web: www.aes4home.com						
Associated Engineering Group Ltd						
9888 Jasper Ave Ste 500	Edmonton	AB	T5J5C6	780-451-7666	454-7698	256
Web: www.ae.ca						
Associated Equipment Corp						
5043 Farlan Ave	Saint Louis	MO	63115	314-385-5178	385-3254	248
TF: 800-949-1472 ■ Web: associatedequip.com						
Associated Equipment Distributors (AED)						
650 E Algonquin Rd Ste 305	Schaumburg	IL	60173	630-574-0650	574-0132	49-18
TF: 800-388-0650 ■ Web: www.aednet.org						
Associated Fabrics Corp						
15-01 Pollitt Dr Unit 7	Fair Lawn	NJ	07410	800-232-4077	710-3850*	594
*Fax Area Code: 866 ■ TF: 800-232-4077 ■ Web: www.afc-fabrics.com						
Associated Floors 32 Morris Ave	Springfield	NJ	07081	800-800-4320		189-2
TF: 800-800-4320 ■ Web: www.associnť.com						
Associated Food Stores Inc						
1850 West 2100 South	Salt Lake City	UT	84119	801-973-4400		297-8
TF Cust Svc: 888-574-7100 ■ Web: www.afstores.com						
Associated General Contractors of America (AGC)						
2300 Wilson Blvd Ste 400	Arlington	VA	22201	703-548-3118	548-3119	49-3
TF: 800-242-1766 ■ Web: www.agc.org						
Associated General Contractors PAC						
2300 Wilson Blvd Ste 400	Arlington	VA	22201	703-548-3118	548-3119	615
TF: 800-242-1767 ■ Web: www.agc.org						
Associated Global Systems Inc						
3333 New Hyde Pk Rd	New Hyde Park	NY	11042	516-627-8910		449
TF Cust Svc: 800-645-8300 ■ Web: www.agsystems.com						
Associated Grocers Inc						
8600 Anselmo Ln	Baton Rouge	LA	70810	225-444-1000	763-6194	297-8
TF: 800-637-2021 ■ Web: www.agbr.com						
Associated Grocers of Florida Inc						
1141 SW 12th Ave	Pompano Beach	FL	33069	954-876-3000		297-8
Web: www.agfla.com						
Associated Grocers of New England Inc						
11 Co-op Way	Pembroke	NH	03275	603-223-6710		297-8
TF: 800-242-2248 ■ Web: www.agne.com						
Associated Grocers of the South						
3600 Vanderbilt Rd	Birmingham	AL	35217	205-841-6781		297-8
TF: 800-695-6051 ■ Web: www.agsouth.com						
Associated Hotels LLC						
1 N LaSalle St Ste 1015	Chicago	IL	60602	312-782-6008	782-2356	379
TF: 800-546-7866 ■ Web: www.associatedhotelsllc.com						
Associated Hygienic Products LLC						
3400 River Green Ct Ste 600	Duluth	GA	30096	770-497-9800		558
TF General: 800-757-0927 ■ Web: www.ahp-dsg.com						
Associated Industries						
11347 Vanowen St	North Hollywood	CA	91605	818-760-1000	760-2142	647
TF: 800-775-0000 ■ Web: www.associated-ind.com						
Associated Industries Management Services Inc						
1206 N Lincoln Ste 200	Spokane	WA	99201	509-326-6885		194
TF: 800-720-4291 ■ Web: www.aiin.com						
Associated Industries Of Massachusetts Mutual Insurance Com						
PO Box 4070	Burlington	MA	01803	781-221-1600	270-5599	391-4
TF: 866-270-3354 ■ Web: www.aimmutual.com						
Associated Locksmiths of America (ALOA)						
3500 Easy St	Dallas	TX	75247	214-819-9733	819-9736	49-3
TF: 800-532-2562 ■ Web: www.aloa.org						
Associated Materials Inc						
3773 State Rd	Cuyahoga Falls	OH	44223	330-929-1811		697
TF: 800-257-4335 ■ Web: www.associatedmaterials.com						
Associated Materials Inc Alside Div						
PO Box 2010	Akron	OH	44309	800-922-6009		235
TF Cust Svc: 800-922-6009 ■ Web: www.alside.com						
Associated Packaging Inc						
435 Calvert Dr	Gallatin	TN	37066	615-452-2131	452-7890	385
Web: www.associatedpackaging.com						
Associated Pallets Inc						
71 Premium Dr	South Carrollton	KY	42374	270-754-4087		200
Web: www.associatedpallet.com						
Associated Petroleum Carriers Inc						
PO Box 2808	Spartanburg	SC	29304	864-573-9301		780
TF Cust Svc: 800-573-9301 ■ Web: www.apccorporate.com						
Associated Petroleum Products						
2320 Milwaukee Way	Tacoma	WA	98421	253-627-6179		579
Web: www.associatedpetroleum.com						
Associated Press						
1100 13th St NW Ste 700	Washington	DC	20005	202-641-9000		646
TF: 800-824-5498 ■ Web: www.ap.org						
Associated Press (AP) 450 W 33rd St	New York	NY	10001	212-621-1500		530
Web: www.ap.org						
Associated Press Inc, The						
121 SW Salmon St #1450	Portland	OR	97204	503-228-2169		530
Web: www.ap.org						
Associated Risk Managers (ARM)						
2 Pierce Pl	Itasca	IL	60143	630-285-4324	285-3590	49-9
TF: 800-735-5441 ■ Web: www.armiweb.com						
Associated Southwest Investors Inc						
6501 Americas Pkwy NE	Albuquerque	NM	87110	505-247-4050		403
Associated Steel Corp						
18200 Miles Rd	Cleveland	OH	44128	800-321-9300	475-6067*	351
*Fax Area Code: 216 ■ TF: 800-321-9300 ■ Web: www.associatedsteel.com						
Associated Steel Workers Ltd						
1714 Silva St	Honolulu	HI	96819	808-841-8323	845-3690	482
Web: www.aswcranes.com						

				Phone	Fax	Class
Associated Students UCLA						
308 Westwood Plaza	Los Angeles	CA	90095	310-825-7711		95
Web: www.asucla.ucla.edu						
Associated Television International						
4401 Wilshire Blvd	Los Angeles	CA	90010	323-556-5600		514
Web: www.associatedtelevision.com						
Associated Venture Investors Management						
130 Lytton Ave Ste 210	Palo Alto	CA	94301	650-687-0235		792
Web: pinnacleven.com						
Associated Wholesale Grocers Inc						
5000 Kansas Ave	Kansas City	KS	66106	913-288-1000		297-8
Web: www.awginc.com						
Associated Wholesalers Inc						
PO Box 67	Robesonia	PA	19551	610-693-3161	693-3171*	297-8
*Fax: Orders ■ TF: 800-927-7771 ■ Web: www.awiweb.com						
Association & Society Management International Inc						
201 Pk Washington Ct	Falls Church	VA	22046	703-533-0251	241-5603	47
Web: www.asmii.com						
Association Associates Inc						
Mercerville Rd Bldg B Ste 514	Trenton	NJ	08619	609-890-9207	581-8244	47
Web: www.hq4u.com						
Association Enterprise Inc (AE)						
1601 N Bond St Ste 303	Naperville	IL	60563	630-369-7786	369-3773	47
Web: incentivemarketing.org						
Association for Advanced Life Underwriting (AALU)						
11921 Freedom Dr Ste 1100	Reston	VA	20190	703-641-9400	641-9885	49-9
TF: 888-275-0092 ■ Web: www.aalu.org						
Association for Advanced Training in the Behavioral Sciences (AATBS)						
5126 Ralston St	Ventura	CA	93003	805-676-3030	676-3033	49-5
TF: 800-472-1931 ■ Web: aatbs.com						
Association for Applied & Therapeutic Humor (AATH)						
65 Enterprise	Aliso Viejo	CA	92656	815-708-6587	715-6931*	48-17
*Fax Area Code: 949 ■ TF: 888-747-2284 ■ Web: www.aath.org						
Association for Applied Psychophysiology & Biofeedback (AAPB)						
10200 W 44th Ave Ste 304	Wheat Ridge	CO	80033	303-422-8436	422-8894	49-8
TF: 800-477-8892 ■ Web: www.aapb.org						
Association for Asian Studies (AAS)						
825 Victors Way Ste 310	Ann Arbor	MI	48108	734-665-2490	665-3801	48-11
TF: 800-316-2739 ■ Web: www.asian-studies.org						
Association for Assessment & Accreditation of Laboratory Animal Care International						
5283 Corporate Dr Ste 203	Frederick	MD	21703	301-696-9626	696-9627	48-1
TF: 800-926-0066 ■ Web: www.aaalac.org						
Association for Behavioral & Cognitive Therapies (ABCT)						
305 Seventh Ave 16th Fl	New York	NY	10001	212-647-1890	647-1865	49-15
TF: 800-685-2228 ■ Web: www.abct.org/home						
Association for Biblical Higher Education (AABC)						
5850 T G Lee Blvd Ste 130	Orlando	FL	32822	407-207-0808		48-1
TF: 800-525-1611 ■ Web: www.abhe.org						
Association for Business Communication						
181 Turner St NW	Blacksburg	VA	24061	540-231-1939		49-12
TF: 000-010-7243 ■ Web: www.businesscommunication.org						
Association for Career & Technical Education (ACTE)						
1410 King St	Alexandria	VA	22314	703-683-3111	683-7424	49-5
TF: 800-826-9972 ■ Web: www.acteonline.org						
Association for Childhood Education International (ACEI)						
1101 16th St NW Ste 300	Washington	DC	20036	202-372-9986	570-2212*	49-5
*Fax Area Code: 301 ■ TF: 800-423-3563 ■ Web: www.acei.org						
Association for Children with Down Syndrome Inc (ACDS)						
4 Fern Pl	Plainview	NY	11803	516-933-4700	933-9524	48-17
TF: 800-342-9871 ■ Web: www.acds.org						
Association for Clinical Pastoral Education (ACPE)						
1549 Clairmont Rd Ste 103	Decatur	GA	30033	404-320-1472		48-1
Web: www.acpe.edu						
Association for Communications Technology Professionals in Higher Education (ACUTA)						
152 W Zandale Dr Ste 200	Lexington	KY	40503	859-278-3338	278-3268	49-5
Web: www.acuta.org						
Association for Computing Machinery (ACM)						
2 Penn Plaza Ste 701	New York	NY	10121	212-626-0500	944-1318	48-9
TF: 800-342-6626 ■ Web: www.acm.org						
Association for Continuing Higher Education (ACHE)						
1700 Asp Ave	Norman	OK	73072	800-807-2243		49-5
TF: 800-807-2243 ■ Web: www.acheinc.org						
Association for Co-op Operations Research & Development (ACORD)						
1 Blue Hill Plaza PO Box 1529	Pearl River	NY	10965	845-620-1700	620-3600	49-9
TF: 800-444-3341 ■ Web: www.acord.org						
Association for Corporate Growth (ACG)						
125 S Wacker Dr Ste 3100	Chicago	IL	60606	312-957-4260		49-12
TF: 877-358-2220 ■ Web: www.acg.org						
Association for Couples in Marriage Enrichment (ACME)						
PO Box 21374	Winston-Salem	NC	27120	800-634-8325		48-6
TF: 800-634-8325 ■ Web: www.bettermarriages.org						
Association For Data Ctr Management Professionals (AFCOM)						
742 E Chapman Ave	Orange	CA	92866	714-997-7966	997-9743	48-9
Association for Death Education & Counseling (ADEC)						
111 Deer Lake Rd Ste 100	Deerfield	IL	60015	847-509-0403	480-9282	49-8
Web: www.adec.org						
Association for Facilities Engineering (AFE)						
8200 Greensboro Dr Ste 400	McLean	VA	22102	571-203-7171	766-2142	49-13
Web: www.afe.org						
Association for Financial Professionals (AFP)						
4520 E W Hwy Ste 750	Bethesda	MD	20814	301-907-2862	907-2864	49-2
Web: www.afponline.org						
Association for Gerontology in Higher Education (AGHE)						
1220 L St NW Ste 901	Washington	DC	20005	202-289-9806		49-5
Web: www.aghe.org						
Association for Healthcare Documentation Integrity (AHDI)						
4230 Kiernan Ave Ste 130	Modesto	CA	95356	209-527-9620	527-9633	49-8
TF: 800-982-2182 ■ Web: www.ahdionline.org						
Association for Healthcare Philanthropy (AHP)						
313 Pk Ave Ste 400	Falls Church	VA	22046	703-532-6243	532-7170	49-8
Web: www.ahp.org						
Association for Information Media & Equipment (AIME)						
PO Box 9844	Cedar Rapids	IA	52409	319-654-0608		48-4
Web: www.aime.org						
Association for Iron & Steel Technology (AIST)						
186 Thorn Hill Rd	Warrendale	PA	15086	724-814-3000	814-3001	49-13
TF: 800-759-4867 ■ Web: www.aist.org						

	Phone	Fax	Class
Association for Library & Information Science Education (ALISE) 2150 N 107th St Ste 205 .... Seattle WA 98133 *TF:* 877-275-7547 ■ *Web:* www.alise.org	206-209-5267	367-8777	49-11
Association for Library Collections & Technical Services (ALCTS) 50 E Huron St.................................Chicago IL 60611 *TF:* 800-545-2433 ■ *Web:* www.ala.org/alcts	312-280-5038	280-5033	49-11
Association for Library Service to Children (ALSC) 50 E Huron St.................................Chicago IL 60611 *TF:* 800-545-2433 ■ *Web:* www.ala.org/alsc	312-280-2163	944-7671	49-11
Association for Linen Management 2161 Lexington Rd Ste 2 .... Richmond KY 40475 *TF:* 800-669-0863 ■ *Web:* www.almnet.org	859-624-0177	624-3580	49-4
Association for Macular Diseases Inc 210 E 64th St 8th Fl ....New York NY 10065 *TF:* 800-829-0500 ■ *Web:* www.macula.org	212-605-3719		48-17
Association for Maximum Service Television (MSTV) 1776 Massachusetts Ave NW...............Washington DC 20036	202-861-0344		49-14
Association for Mfg Excellence (AME) 3701 W Algonquin Rd Ste 225..........Rolling Meadows IL 60008 *Web:* www.ame.org	224-232-5980	232-5981	49-12
Association for Mfg Technology (AMT) 7901 Westpark Dr................................McLean VA 22102 *TF:* 800-524-0475 ■ *Web:* www.amtonline.org	703-893-2900	893-1151	49-12
Association for Play Therapy (APT) 3198 Willow Ave Ste 110 .... Clovis CA 93612 *TF:* 800-347-6647 ■ *Web:* www.a4pt.org	559-294-2128	294-2129	49-15
Association for Postal Commerce 1901 Ft Myer Dr .... Arlington VA 22209 *Web:* www.postcom.org	703-524-0096	524-1871	49-18
Association for Practical & Professional Ethics 618 E Third St.......................... Bloomington IN 47405 *Web:* www.indiana.edu	812-855-4848		49-5
Association for Professionals in Infection Control & Epidemiology Inc (APIC) 1275 K St NW Ste 1000 .... Washington DC 20005 *TF:* 800-650-9883 ■ *Web:* www.apic.org	202-789-1890	789-1899	49-8
Association for Psychological Type International (APTI) 230 Washington Ave Extn Ste 101 .... Albany NY 12203 *Web:* www.aptinternational.org	518-320-7416		49-15
Association for Recorded Sound Collections (ARSC) PO Box 543 .... Annapolis MD 21404 *Web:* www.arsc-audio.org	410-757-0488		48-4
Association for Research & Enlightenment (ARE) 215 67th St...........................Virginia Beach VA 23451 *TF:* 800-333-4499 ■ *Web:* www.edgarcayce.org	757-428-3588	422-6921	48-17
Association for Research in Vision & Ophthalmology (ARVO) 12300 Twinbrook Pkwy Ste 250............... Rockville MD 20852 *TF:* 888-503-1050 ■ *Web:* www.arvo.org	240-221-2900	221-0370	49-8
Association for Retail Environment (ARE) 4651 Sheridan St Ste 470.................. Hollywood FL 33021 *Web:* www.retailenvironments.org	954-893-7300	893-7500	49-3
Association for Supervision & Curriculum Development (ASCD) 1703 N Beauregard St...................... Alexandria VA 22311 *TF:* 800-933-2723 ■ *Web:* www.ascd.org	703-578-9600	575-5400	49-5
Association for the Advancement of Artificial Intelligence (AAAI) 445 Burgess Dr Ste 100.................... Menlo Park CA 94025 *TF:* 800-548-4664 ■ *Web:* www.aaai.org	650-328-3123	321-4457	48-9
Association for the Advancement of Computing in Education (AACE) PO Box 1545 .... Chesapeake VA 23327 **Fax Area Code:* 703 ■ *TF:* 800-352-5397 ■ *Web:* www.aace.org	757-366-5606	997-8760*	49-5
Association for the Advancement of Medical Instrumentation (AAMI) 4301 N Fairfax Dr Ste 301 .... Arlington VA 22203 *TF:* 800-332-2264 ■ *Web:* www.aami.org	703-525-4890	276-0793	49-8
Association for the Advancement of the Blind & Retarded (AABR) 1508 College Pt Blvd ....College Point NY 11356 *Web:* www.aabr.org	718-321-3800		48-17
Association for Vascular Access (AVA) 5526 W 13400 S Ste 229..................... Herriman UT 84096 *TF:* 877-924-2821 ■ *Web:* www.avainfo.org	801-792-9079	601-8012	49-8
Association for Women in Communications (AWC) 1717 E Republic Rd Ste A...................Springfield MO 65804 *Web:* www.womcom.org	417-886-8606		49-14
Association for Women in Science Inc (AWIS) 1321 Duke St Ste 210...................... Alexandria VA 22314 *TF:* 866-736-7343 ■ *Web:* www.awis.org	703-894-4490	894-4489	49-19
Association for Women's Rights in Development (AWID) 215 Spadina Ave Ste 150 .... Toronto ON M5T2C7 *Web:* www.awid.org	416-594-3773	594-0330	48-8
Association Headquarters Inc 1120 Rt 73 Ste 200.......................Mount Laurel NJ 08054 *Web:* ahredchair.com	856-439-0500	439-0525	47
Association Management & Communications 349 Granada Rd ....West Palm Beach FL 33401	561-802-4310		47
Association Management Ctr 8735 W Higgins Rd Ste 300 ....Chicago IL 60631 *Web:* www.connect2amc.com	847-375-4700		47
Association Management Group Inc (AMG) 8400 Westpark Dr 2nd Fl .... McLean VA 22102 *Web:* www.amg-inc.com	703-610-9000	610-9005	47
Association Management Magazine 1575 'I' St NW.......................... Washington DC 20005 *TF:* 888-950-2723 ■ *Web:* www.asaecenter.org	202-371-0940		457-5
Association Management Resources 2123 University Park Dr Ste 100............... Okemos MI 48864 *Web:* www.managedbyamr.com	734-677-2270		47
Association Management Solutions LLC (AMSL) 48377 Freemont Blvd Ste 117 .... Fremont CA 94538 *Web:* www.amsl.com	510-492-4000		47
Association Management Specialists 275 E Hillcrest Dr Ste 215 .... Thousand Oaks CA 91360 *Web:* www.assoc-mgmt.net	805-557-1111		47
Association Management Systems Inc 214 N Hale St................................ Wheaton IL 60187 *Web:* www.association-mgmt.com	630-510-4500	510-4501	47
Association of Academic Health Centers (AHC) 1400 16th St NW Ste 720................. Washington DC 20036 *Web:* www.aahcdc.org	202-265-9600	265-7514	49-8
Association of Advanced Rabbinical & Talmudic Schools (AARTS) 11 Broadway............................... New York NY 10004	212-363-1991		49-5
Association of Alternative Newsweeklies (AAN) 115615th St NW........................... Washington DC 20005 *TF:* 866-415-0704 ■ *Web:* www.altweeklies.com	202-289-8484	289-2004	49-14
Association of American Chambers of Commerce in Latin America 1615 H St NW........................... Washington DC 20062 *TF:* 800-638-6582 ■ *Web:* www.aaccla.org	202-463-5485	463-3126	138
Association of American Colleges & Universities (AAC&U) 1818 R St NW........................... Washington DC 20009 *Web:* www.aacu.org	202-387-3760	265-9532	49-5
Association of American Geographers (AAG) 1710 16th St NW .... Washington DC 20009 *TF:* 800-696-7353 ■ *Web:* www.aag.org	202-234-1450	234-2744	49-19
Association of American Indian Physicians (AAIP) 1225 Sovereign Row Ste 103 ....Oklahoma City OK 73108 *Web:* www.aaip.org	405-946-7072	946-7651	49-8
Association of American Law Schools (AALS) 1201 Connecticut Ave NW Ste 800........... Washington DC 20036 *Web:* www.aals.org	202-296-8851	296-8869	49-5
Association of American Medical Colleges (AAMC) 2450 N St NW........................... Washington DC 20037 *TF:* 800-273-8255 ■ *Web:* www.aamc.org	202-828-0400	828-1125	49-5
Association of American Publishers Inc (AAP) 71 Fifth Ave...............................New York NY 10003 *TF:* 866-271-4968 ■ *Web:* www.publishers.org	212-255-0200	255-7007	49-16
Association of American Railroads (AAR) 425 Third St SW......................... Washington DC 20024 *TF:* 800-533-6644 ■ *Web:* www.aar.org	202-639-2100	639-2286	49-21
Association of American Universities (AAU) 1200 New York Ave NW Ste 550............. Washington DC 20005 *Web:* www.aau.edu	202-408-7500	408-8184	49-5
Association of American University Presses 28 W 36th St Ste 602 ....New York NY 10018 *TF:* 800-678-2120 ■ *Web:* www.aaupnet.org	212-989-1010	989-0975	49-16
Association of Certified Fraud Examiners (ACFE) 716 W Ave .... Austin TX 78701 *TF:* 800-245-3321 ■ *Web:* www.acfe.com	512-478-9000	478-9297	49-1
Association of Children's Museums (ACM) 2711 Jefferson Davis Hwy Ste 600............. Arlington VA 22202 *Web:* www.childrensmuseums.org	703-224-3100		48-4
Association of Christian Schools International (ACSI) 731 Chapel Hills Dr .... Colorado Springs CO 80920 *TF Cust Svc:* 800-367-0798 ■ *Web:* www.acsi.org	719-528-6906		49-5
Association of Civilian Technicians (ACT) 12620 Lake Ridge Dr ....Woodbridge VA 22192 *TF:* 800-729-3277 ■ *Web:* www.actnat.com	703-494-4845	494-0961	48-19
Association of Clinical Research Professionals (ACRP) 999 Canal Center Plaza Ste 800.............. Alexandria VA 22314 *TF:* 888-508-5731 ■ *Web:* www.acrpnet.org	703-254-8100	254-8101	49-8
Association of College & Research Libraries (ACRL) 50 E Huron St...............................Chicago IL 60611 *TF:* 800-545-2433 ■ *Web:* www.ala.org/acrl/aboutacrl	312-280-2519	280-2520	49-11
Association of College & University Housing Officers International (ACUHO-I) 941 Chatham Ln Ste 318 .... Columbus OH 43221 *Web:* www.acuho-i.org	614-292-0099	292-3205	49-5
Association of College Unions International (ACUI) 120 W Seventh St 1 City Ctr Ste 200 .... Bloomington IN 47404 *TF:* 800-228-5424 ■ *Web:* www.acui.org	812-245-2284	245-6710	49-5
Association of Collegiate Business Schools & Programs (ACBSP) 11520 W 119th St...................... Overland Park KS 66213 *Web:* www.acbsp.org	913-339-9356	339-6226	48-1
Association of Collegiate Schools of Architecture (ACSA) 1735 New York Ave NW 3rd Fl ....Washington DC 20006 *TF:* 877-426-6323 ■ *Web:* www.acsa-arch.org	202-785-2324	628-0448	49-5
Association of Community Cancer Centers (ACCC) 11600 Nebel St Ste 201 .... Rockville MD 20852 *Web:* www.accc-cancer.org	301-984-9496	770-1949	49-8
Association of Community College Trustees (ACCT) 1101 17th St NW Ste 300..................Washington DC 20036 *TF:* 866-895-2228 ■ *Web:* www.acct.org	202-775-4667	223-1297	49-5
Association of Consulting Chemists & Chemical Engineers (ACC&CE) 514 Corrigan Way.............................Cary NJ 27519 *Web:* www.chemconsult.org	908-500-9333		49-19
Association of Consulting Foresters of America (ACF) 312 Montgomery St Ste 208................. Alexandria VA 22314 *TF:* 888-540-8733 ■ *Web:* www.acf-foresters.org	703-548-0990	548-6395	48-2
Association of Corporate Counsel (ACC) 1025 Connecticut Ave NW Ste 200...........Washington DC 20036 *TF:* 877-647-3411 ■ *Web:* www.acc.com	202-293-4103	293-4701	49-10
Association of Corporate Travel Executives (ACTE) 515 King St Ste 440 .... Alexandria VA 22314 *Web:* www.acte.org	703-683-5322	683-2720	48-23
Association of Destination Management Executives (ADME) 11 W Monument Ave ....Dayton OH 45402 *Web:* www.adme.org	937-586-3727	586-3699	48-23
Association of Directory Publishers (ADP) PO Box 209 .... Traverse City MI 49685 *TF:* 800-267-9002 ■ *Web:* www.adp.org	231-486-2182	486-2182	49-16
Association of Emergency Physicians (AEP) 911 Whitewater Dr .... Mars PA 16046	724-772-1818		49-8
Association of Energy Engineers (AEE) 4025 Pleasantdale Rd Ste 420 .... Atlanta GA 30340 *TF:* 877-407-0784 ■ *Web:* www.aeecenter.org	770-447-5083	446-3969	48-12
Association of Energy Service Cos (AESC) 14531 Fm 529 Ste 250.......................Houston TX 77095 *TF:* 800-692-0771 ■ *Web:* www.aesc.net	713-781-0758	781-7542	48-12
Association of Equipment Manufacturers (AEM) 6737 W Washington St Ste 2400 ....Milwaukee WI 53214 *TF:* 866-236-0442 ■ *Web:* www.aem.org	414-272-0943	272-1170	49-13
Association of Farmworker Opportunity Programs (AFOP) 1120 20th St NW Ste 300.................Washington DC 20036 *Web:* afop.org	202-828-6006	828-6005	48-2
Association of Film Commissioners International (AFCI) 109 E 17th St ....Cheyenne WY 82001 **Fax Area Code:* 413 ■ *TF:* 888-765-5777 ■ *Web:* www.afci.org	307-637-4422	375-2903*	48-4
Association of Flight Attendants 501 Third St NW.......................... Washington DC 20001 *TF:* 800-424-2401 ■ *Web:* afacwa.org	202-434-1300	434-1319	414

	Phone	Fax	Class
Association of Food Industries Inc (AFI) 3301 Rt 66 Bldg C Ste 205 .... Neptune NJ 07753 *Web:* afius.org	732-922-3000	922-3590	49-6
Association of Fundraising Professionals (AFP) 4300 Wilson Blvd Ste 300 .... Arlington VA 22203 *TF:* 800-666-3863 ■ *Web:* www.afpnet.org	703-684-0410	684-0540	49-12
Association of Governing Boards of Universities & Colleges (AGB) 1133 20th St NW Ste 300 .... Washington DC 20036 *TF:* 800-356-6317 ■ *Web:* www.agb.org	202-296-8400	223-7053	49-5
Association of Government Accountants (AGA) 2208 Mt Vernon Ave .... Alexandria VA 22301 *TF:* 800-242-7211 ■ *Web:* www.agacgfm.org	703-684-6931	548-9367	49-1
Association of Healthcare Internal Auditors (AHIA) 10200 W 44th Ave Ste 304 .... Wheat Ridge CO 80033 *TF:* 888-275-2442 ■ *Web:* www.ahia.org	303-327-7546	422-8894	49-1
Association of Higher Education Facilities Officers (APPA) 1643 Prince St .... Alexandria VA 22314 *TF:* 800-336-3097 ■ *Web:* www.appa.org	703-684-1446	549-2772	49-5
Association of Home Appliance Manufacturers (AHAM) 1111 19th St NW Ste 402 .... Washington DC 20036 *TF:* 888-236-2427 ■ *Web:* www.aham.org	202-872-5955	872-9354	49-4
Association of Home Appliance Manufacturers PAC (AHAM PAC) 1111 19th St NW Ste 402 .... Washington DC 20036 *TF:* 800-424-2970 ■ *Web:* aham.org	202-872-5955	872-9354	615
Association of Independents in Radio (AIR) 42 Charles St 2nd Fl .... Dorchester MA 02122 *TF:* 800-510-0021 ■ *Web:* www.airmedia.org	617-825-4400		632
Association of Industrial Metallizers Coaters & Laminators (AIMCAL) 201 Springs St .... Fort Mill SC 29715 *TF:* 800-443-2380 ■ *Web:* www.aimcal.org	803-802-7820	802-7821	49-13
Association of Jesuit Colleges & Universities (AJCU) 1 Dupont Cir NW Ste 405 .... Washington DC 20036 *Web:* www.ajcunet.edu	202-862-9893		48-11
Association of Jewish Libraries PO Box 1118 .... Teaneck NJ 07666 *Web:* www.jewishlibraries.org	201-371-3255		49-11
Association of Junior Leagues International Inc (AJLI) 80 Maiden Ln Ste 305 .... New York NY 10038 *TF:* 800-955-3248 ■ *Web:* www.ajli.org	212-951-8300	481-7196	48-15
Association of Legal Administrators (ALA) 75 Tri-State International Ste 222 .... Lincolnshire IL 60069 *Web:* www.alanet.org	847-267-1252	267-1329	49-10
Association of Maternal & Child Health Programs (AMCHP) 2030 M St NW Ste 350 .... Washington DC 20036 *Web:* www.amchp.org	202-775-0436		49-7
Association of Military Surgeons of the United States (AMSUS) 9320 Old Georgetown Rd .... Bethesda MD 20814 *TF:* 800-761-9320 ■ *Web:* www.amsus.org	301-897-8800	530-5446	49-8
Association of National Advertisers (ANA) 708 Third Ave 33rd Fl .... New York NY 10017 *TF:* 800-914-4194 ■ *Web:* www.ana.net	212-697-5950	687-7310	49-18
Association of Nurses in AIDS Care (ANAC) 3538 Ridgewood Rd .... Akron OH 44333 *TF:* 800-260-6780 ■ *Web:* www.nursesinaidscare.org	330-670-0101	670-0109	49-8
Association of Old Crows (AOC) 1000 N Payne St Ste 300 .... Alexandria VA 22314 *TF:* 800-247-5626 ■ *Web:* www.crows.org	703-549-1600	549-2589	48-19
Association of Osteopathic Directors & Medical Educators (AODME) 142 E Ontario St .... Chicago IL 60611 *TF:* 800-621-1773 ■ *Web:* www.aodme.org	312-202-8211	202-8224	49-8
Association of Performing Arts Presenters 1211 Connecticut Ave NW Ste 200 .... Washington DC 20036 *TF:* 888-820-2787 ■ *Web:* www.apap365.org	202-833-2787	833-1543	48-4
Association of Pool & Spa Professionals (APSP) 2111 Eisenhower Ave Ste 500 .... Alexandria VA 22314 *TF:* 800-323-3996 ■ *Web:* www.apsp.org	703-838-0083	549-0493	49-4
Association of Professional Ball Players of America 101 S Kraemer Ave Ste 112 .... Placentia CA 92870 *Web:* www.apbpa.org	714-528-2012	528-2037	48-22
Association of Professional Chaplains (APC) 1701 E Woodfield Rd Ste 400 .... Schaumburg IL 60173 *Web:* www.professionalchaplains.org	847-240-1014	240-1015	48-20
Association of Professional Flight Attendants 1004 W Euless Blvd .... Euless TX 76040 *Web:* www.apfa.org	817-540-0108	540-2077	414
Association of Progressive Rental Organizations (APRO) 1504 Robin Hood Trl .... Austin TX 78703 *TF:* 800-204-2776 ■ *Web:* www.rtohq.org	512-794-0095	794-0097	49-18
Association of Proposal Management Professionals (APMP) PO Box 668 .... Dana Point CA 92629 *Web:* www.apmp.org	949-493-9398		49-12
Association of Public & Land-grant Universities (APLU) 1307 New York Ave NW Ste 400 .... Washington DC 20005 *Web:* www.aplu.org	202-478-6040	478-6046	49-5
Association of Public Health Laboratories (APHL) 8515 Georgia Ave Ste 700 .... Silver Spring MD 20910 *TF:* 800-899-2278 ■ *Web:* www.aphl.org	240-485-2745	485-2700	49-7
Association of Public Television Stations (APTS) 2100 Crystal Dr Ste 700 .... Arlington VA 22202 *TF:* 800-346-6484 ■ *Web:* www.apts.org	202-654-4200	654-4236	49-14
Association of Public-Safety Communications Officials International Inc 351 N Williamson Blvd .... Daytona Beach FL 32114 *TF:* 888-272-6911 ■ *Web:* www.apcointl.org	386-322-2500	322-2501	49-7
Association of Racing Commissioners International (ARCI) 1510 Newtown Pike # 210 .... Lexington KY 40511 *TF:* 800-532-0383 ■ *Web:* www.arci.com	859-224-7070		49-7
Association of Rehabilitation Nurses (ARN) 4700 West Lake Ave .... Glenview IL 60025 *TF:* 800-229-7530 ■ *Web:* www.rehabnurse.org	847-375-4710	375-6481	49-8
Association of Reproductive Health Professionals (ARHP) 1901 L St NW Ste 300 .... Washington DC 20036 *TF:* 877-311-8972 ■ *Web:* www.arhp.org	202-466-3825	466-3826	49-8
Association of Research Libraries (ARL) 21 Dupont Cir NW Ste 800 .... Washington DC 20036 *Web:* www.arl.org	202-296-2296	872-0884	49-5
Association of Rotational Molders International (ARM) 800 Roosevelt Rd Ste C-312 .... Glen Ellyn IL 60137 *Web:* www.rotomolding.org	630-942-6589	790-3095	49-13
Association of School Business Officials International (ASBO) 11401 N Shore Dr .... Reston VA 20190 *Fax Area Code: 703 ■ *TF:* 866-682-2729 ■ *Web:* asbointl.org	866-682-2729	478-0205*	49-5
Association of Schools & Colleges of Optometry (ASCO) 6110 Executive Blvd Ste 420 .... Rockville MD 20852 *Web:* optometriceducation.org	301-231-5944	770-1828	49-8
Association of Schools of Allied Health Professions (ASAHP) 122 C St NW Ste 650 .... Washington DC 20001 *Web:* www.asahp.org	202-237-6481	237-6485	49-8
Association of Schools of Public Health (ASPH) 1900 M St NW Ste 710 .... Washington DC 20036 *Web:* www.asph.org	202-296-1099	296-1252	49-5
Association of Science-Technology Centers Inc (ASTC) 1025 Vermont Ave NW Ste 500 .... Washington DC 20005 *Web:* www.astc.org	202-783-7200	783-7207	49-19
Association of Service & Computer Dealers International (ASCDI) 131 NW First Ave .... Delray Beach FL 33444 *TF:* 800-393-2505 ■ *Web:* www.ascdi.com	561-266-9016	431-6302	48-9
Association of Shareware Professionals (ASP) PO Box 1522 .... Martinsville IN 46151 *Fax Area Code: 815 ■ *Web:* www.asp-software.org	765-349-4740	301-3756*	48-9
Association of Social Work Boards (ASWB) 400 S Ridge Pkwy Ste B .... Culpeper VA 22701 *TF:* 800-225-6880 ■ *Web:* www.aswb.org	540-829-6880		49-7
Association of Specialized & Co-op Library Agencies (ASCLA) 50 E Huron St .... Chicago IL 60611 *TF:* 800-545-2433 ■ *Web:* www.ala.org/ascla	312-280-4395	944-8085	49-11
Association of Specialized & Professional Accreditors (ASPA) 3304 N Broadway St Ste 214 .... Chicago IL 60657 *TF:* 800-228-5424 ■ *Web:* www.aspa-usa.org	773-857-7900		48-1
Association of Staff Physician Recruiters (ASPR) 1000 Westgate Dr Ste 252 .... Saint Paul MN 55114 *TF:* 800-830-2777 ■ *Web:* www.aspr.org	800-830-2777		49-8
Association of State & Interstate Water Pollution Control Administrators (ASIWPCA) 1221 Connecticut Ave NW 2nd Fl .... Washington DC 20036 *Web:* www.acwa-us.org	202-756-0600		49-7
Association of State & Territorial Health Officials (ASTHO) 2231 Crystal Dr Ste 450 .... Arlington VA 22202 *Fax Area Code: 571 ■ *Web:* www.astho.org	202-371-9090	527-3189*	49-7
Association of State & Territorial Solid Waste Management Officials (ASTSWMO) 444 N Capitol St NW Ste 315 .... Washington DC 20001 *Web:* www.astswmo.org	202-624-5828	624-7875	49-7
Association of State Wetland Managers 32 Tandberg Trail Ste 2A .... Windham ME 04062 *TF:* 800-451-6027 ■ *Web:* www.aswm.org	207-892-3399	892-3089	49-7
Association of Support Professionals, The 38954 Proctor Blvd Ste 396 .... Sandy OR 97005 *Web:* www.asponline.com	503-668-9004		48-9
Association of Surgical Technologists (AST) 6 W Dry Creek Cir Ste 200 .... Littleton CO 80120 *TF:* 800-637-7433 ■ *Web:* www.ast.org	303-694-9130	694-9169	49-8
Association of Talent Agents 9255 Sunset Blvd Ste 930 .... Los Angeles CA 90069 *Web:* www.agentassociation.com	310-274-0628	274-5063	48-4
Association of Test Publishers 601 Pennsylvania Ave NW Ste 900 .... Washington DC 20004 *TF:* 866-240-7909 ■ *Web:* www.testpublishers.org	866-240-7909		49-5
Association of the US Army (AUSA) 2425 Wilson Blvd .... Arlington VA 22201 *TF:* 800-336-4570 ■ *Web:* www.ausa.org	703-841-4300	525-9039	48-19
Association of the Wall & Ceiling Industries International (AWCI) 513 W Broad St Ste 210 .... Falls Church VA 22046 *TF:* 800-233-8990 ■ *Web:* www.awci.org	703-538-1600	534-8307	49-3
Association of Theological Schools in the US & Canada (ATS) 10 Summit Pk Dr .... Pittsburgh PA 15275 *TF:* 800-621-7440 ■ *Web:* www.ats.edu	412-788-6505	788-6510	49-5
Association of Universities for Research in Astronomy (AURA) 1200 New York Ave NW Ste 350 .... Washington DC 20005 *TF:* 888-624-8373 ■ *Web:* www.aura-astronomy.org	202-483-2101	483-2106	49-5
Association of University Centers on Disabilities (AUCD) 1100 Wayne Ave Ste 1000 .... Silver Spring MD 20910 *TF:* 888-572-2249 ■ *Web:* www.aucd.org	301-588-8252	588-2842	49-5
Association of University Programs in Health Administration (AUPHA) 2000 N 14th St Ste 780 .... Arlington VA 22201 *TF:* 877-275-6462 ■ *Web:* www.aupha.org	703-894-0941	894-0941	49-8
Association of University Technology Managers (AUTM) 111 Deer Lake Rd Ste 100 .... Deerfield IL 60015 *Web:* www.autm.net	847-559-0846	480-9282	49-19
Association of Vacuum Equipment Manufacturers (AVEM) 201 Pk Washington Ct .... Falls Church VA 22046 *Web:* www.avem.org	703-538-3543	241-5603	49-13
Association of Vineyard Churches 5115 Grove W Blvd .... Stafford TX 77477 *Web:* www.vineyardusa.org	281-313-8463		48-20
Association of Washington Business PO Box 658 .... Olympia WA 98507 *TF:* 800-521-9325 ■ *Web:* www.awb.org	360-943-1600	943-5811	140
Association of Water Technologies (AWT) 9707 Key W Ave Ste 100 .... Rockville MD 20850 *Web:* www.awt.org	301-740-1421	990-9771	48-2
Association of Western Pulp & Paper Workers 1430 SW Clay St .... Portland OR 97208 *Web:* www.awppw.org	503-228-7486		414
Association of Women's Health Obstetric & Neonatal Nurses (AWHONN) 2000 L St NW Ste 740 .... Washington DC 20036 *TF:* 800-673-8499 ■ *Web:* www.awhonn.org	202-261-2400	728-0575	49-8
Association of Zoos & Aquariums (AZA) 8403 Colesville Rd Ste 710 .... Silver Spring MD 20910 *TF:* 800-323-6593 ■ *Web:* www.aza.org	301-562-0777	562-0888	48-3
Association on American Indian Affairs (AAIA) 966 Hungerford Dr Ste 12-B .... Rockville MD 20850 *Web:* www.indian-affairs.org	240-314-7155	314-7159	457-17
Association Resource Ctr (ARC) 555 Capitol Mall Ste 755 PO Box 276567 .... Sacramento CA 95814 *Web:* www.4arc.com	916-932-2200	932-2209	47
Association Resource Group 7926 Jones Branch Dr Ste 1150 .... Mc Lean VA 22102 *Web:* www.myarg.com	703-734-3500		387

Company	Phone	Fax	Class
Association Resources Inc 342 N Main St .... West Hartford CT 06117 *Web:* www.associationresources.com	860-586-7500	586-7550	47
Association Solutions Ltd 1111 Burlington Ave Ste 108 .... Lisle IL 60532	630-241-3100	241-0142	47
Assumption College 500 Salisbury St .... Worcester MA 01609 *TF:* 888-882-7786 ■ *Web:* www.assumption.edu	508-767-7000	799-4412	166
Assumption College for Sisters 350 BernaRdsville Rd .... Mendham NJ 07945 *Web:* www.acs350.org	973-543-6528	543-1738	162
Assumption Parish 4813 Hwy 1 PO Box 520 .... Napoleonville LA 70390 *TF:* 800-315-9513 ■ *Web:* www.assumptionla.com	985-369-7435	369-2972	338
Assurance Investment Management LLC 1920 Georgetown Rd .... Hudson OH 44236 *Web:* www.assureim.com	330-650-1750		463
Assurance Manufacturing Co 9010 Evergreen Blvd .... Minneapolis MN 55433 *Web:* www.assurancemfg.com	763-780-4252		488
Assurance Operations Corp 2005 Liberty Ave .... Lawrenceburg TN 38464 *Web:* www.assuranceoperations.com	931-766-7750		567
AssuranceAmerica Corp 5500 I- N Pkwy Ste 600 .... Atlanta GA 30328 *TF:* 800-450-7857 ■ *Web:* www.assuranceamerica.com	770-952-0200		391-4
Assurant Employee Benefits 2323 Grand Blvd .... Kansas City MO 64108 *TF:* 800-733-7879 ■ *Web:* www.assurantemployeebenefits.com	816-474-2345	881-8996	391-2
Assurant Group 11222 Quail Roost Dr .... Miami FL 33157 *TF:* 800-852-2244 ■ *Web:* www.assurant.com	305-253-2244		360-4
Assurant Inc 1 Chase Manhattan Plaza .... New York NY 10005 *NYSE: AIZ* ■ *Web:* www.assurant.com	212-859-7000		360-4
Assurant Solutions 440 Mt Rushmore Rd .... Rapid City SD 57701 *Web:* www.assurantsolutions.com	770-763-1000	859-4403	391-5
Assured Document Destruction Inc 8050 Arville St Ste 105 .... Las Vegas NV 89139 *Web:* shreddinglv.com	702-614-0001		317
Assured Guaranty Corp 31 W 52nd St .... New York NY 10019 *TF:* 800-778-7879 ■ *Web:* www.assuredguaranty.com	212-974-0100	581-3268	391-5
Assured Packaging Inc 6080 Vipond Dr .... Mississauga ON L5T2V4 *TF:* 800-665-4273 ■ *Web:* www.assuredpackaging.com	905-565-1410		393
Assured Pharmacy Inc 11100 Ash St Ste 200 .... Leawood KS 66211 *OTC: APHYQ* ■ *Web:* www.assuredrxservices.com	913-602-8344		237
Assurex International 8200 E 32nd St N .... Wichita KS 67226 *Web:* www.truenorth.net	316-266-6222		401
Assurity Life Insurance Co PO Box 82533 .... Lincoln NE 68501 *TF:* 800-869-0355 ■ *Web:* assurity.com	402-476-6500		390
AST (Association of Surgical Technologists) 6 W Dry Creek Cir Ste 200 .... Littleton CO 80120 *TF:* 800-637-7433 ■ *Web:* www.ast.org	303-694-9130	694-9169	49-8
AST Bearings 115 Main Rd .... Montville NJ 07045 *TF:* 800-526-1250 ■ *Web:* www.astbearings.com	973-335-2230	335-6987	75
AST Products Inc 9 Linnell Cir .... Billerica MA 01821 *TF:* 877-667-4500 ■ *Web:* www.astp.com	978-667-4500		481
AST Sports Science Inc 120 Capitol Dr .... Golden CO 80401 *TF:* 800-627-2788 ■ *Web:* www.ast-ss.com	303-278-1420	278-1417	799
ASTA (American Seed Trade Assn) 1701 Duke St Ste 275 .... Alexandria VA 22304 *TF:* 888-890-7333 ■ *Web:* www.betterseed.org	703-837-8140	837-9365	48-2
ASTA (American String Teachers Association) 4155 Chain Bridge Rd .... Fairfax VA 22030 *TF:* 800-821-7303 ■ *Web:* www.astaweb.com	703-279-2113	279-2114	49-5
ASTA (American Society of Travel Agents) 1101 King St Ste 200 .... Alexandria VA 22314 *TF:* 800-275-2782 ■ *Web:* www.asta.org	703-739-2782	684-8319	48-23
ASTA (American Spice Trade Assn) 1101 17th St NW Ste 700 .... Washington DC 20036 *Web:* www.astaspice.org	202-331-2460	463-8998	49-6
Asta Funding Inc 210 Sylvan Ave .... Englewood Cliffs NJ 07632 *NASDAQ: ASFI* ■ *TF:* 866-389-7627 ■ *Web:* www.astafunding.com	201-567-5648		272
A-Star Staffing Inc 2835 Camino Del Rio S Ste 220 .... San Diego CA 92108 *TF:* 800-720-2870 ■ *Web:* www.astarstaffing.com	619-574-7600		260
Astatech Inc 2525 Pearl Buck Rd .... Bristol PA 19007 *TF:* 800-387-2269 ■ *Web:* www.astatechinc.com	215-785-3197		196
ASTC (Association of Science-Technology Centers Inc) 1025 Vermont Ave NW Ste 500 .... Washington DC 20005 *Web:* www.astc.org	202-783-7200	783-7207	49-19
Astea International Inc 240 Gibraltar Rd .... Horsham PA 19044 *NASDAQ: ATEA* ■ *TF:* 800-878-4657 ■ *Web:* www.astea.com	215-682-2500	682-2515	178-1
Astec Inc 4101 Jerome Ave .... Chattanooga TN 37407 *Web:* www.astecinc.com	423-867-4210		190
Astec Industries Inc 1725 Shepherd Rd .... Chattanooga TN 37421 *NASDAQ: ASTE* ■ *TF:* 800-272-7100 ■ *Web:* www.astecindustries.com	423-899-5898	899-4456	190
ASTECH Engineered Products Inc 3030 Red Hill Ave .... Santa Ana CA 92705	949-250-1000		480
As-Tech Industries 24296 Gibson .... Warren MI 48089 *Web:* as-techindustries.com	586-754-6100		697
Astek Corp 5055 Corporate Plaza Dr .... Colorado Springs CO 80919 *Web:* www.simtek.com	719-260-1625		194
Astellas Pharma US Inc 1 Astellas Way .... Northbrook IL 60062 **Fax Area Code:* 877 ■ *TF:* 800-695-4321 ■ *Web:* www.astellas.us	800-695-4321	829-7942*	85
AstenJohnson 4399 Corporate Rd .... Charleston SC 29405 *TF:* 800-529-7990 ■ *Web:* www.astenjohnson.com	843-747-7800	202-6278	745-3
Aster Group Inc 434-B Copperfield Blvd .... Concord NC 28025	704-262-9200		809
Astex Pharmaceuticals 4140 Dublin Blvd Ste 200 .... Dublin CA 94568 *Web:* astx.com	925-560-0100	560-0101	85
Asthma & Allergy Foundation of America (AAFA) 8201 Corporate Dr Ste 1000 .... Landover MD 20785 *TF:* 800-727-8462 ■ *Web:* www.aafa.org	202-466-7643	466-8940	48-17
ASTHO (Association of State & Territorial Health Officials) 2231 Crystal Dr Ste 450 .... Arlington VA 22202 **Fax Area Code:* 571 ■ *Web:* www.astho.org	202-371-9090	527-3189*	49-7
Asti Trattoria 408C E 43rd St .... Austin TX 78751 *Web:* www.astiaustin.com	512-451-1218		671
Astia Inc 1 Market Plaza Spear Twr 24th Fl .... San Francisco CA 94105 *Web:* www.astia.org	415-421-5500		10-3
Asticou Inn 15 Peabody Dr .... Northeast Harbor ME 04662 *TF:* 800-258-3373 ■ *Web:* www.asticou.com	207-276-3344		379
Astley Gilbert Ltd 42 Carnforth Rd .... Toronto ON M4A2K7 *Web:* www.astleygilbert.com	416-288-8666		627
ASTM International 100 Barr Harbor Dr PO Box C700 ..... West Conshohocken PA 19428 *TF:* 800-814-1017 ■ *Web:* www.astm.org	610-832-9500	832-9555	49-19
Aston Hotel & Resorts Sunvalley 333 S Main St .... Ketchum ID 83340 *TF:* 877-997-6667 ■ *Web:* www.astonhotels.com	208-622-6400		669
Aston Hotels & Resorts 2155 Kalakaua Ave Ste 500 .... Honolulu HI 96815 *TF:* 800-775-4228 ■ *Web:* www.astonhotels.com	808-931-1400	931-1414	379
Aston MonteLago Village Resort 30 Strada di Villaggio .... Henderson NV 89011	702-564-4700		655
Aston Veterinarian Hospital 5200 Pennell Rd .... Media PA 19063 *Web:* www.astonvet.com	610-494-5800		794
ASTONE Inc 2300 Tulare St Ste 210 .... Fresno CA 93721	559-375-7100		195
Astor & Sanders Corp 9900 Belward Campus Dr Ste 275 .... Rockville MD 20850 *Web:* www.astor-sanders.com	301-838-3420		387
Astor Crowne Plaza 739 Canal St .... New Orleans LA 70130 *TF:* 877-408-9661 ■ *Web:* www.astorneworleans.com	504-962-0500	962-0503	379
Astor Home For Children, The 6339 Mill St PO Box 5005 .... Rhinebeck NY 12572 *Web:* www.astorservices.org	845-871-1000		48-15
Astor Hotel, The 924 E Juneau Ave .... Milwaukee WI 53202 *TF:* 800-558-0200 ■ *Web:* astormilwaukee.com	414-271-4220	271-6370	379
Astoria Financial Corp 1 Astoria Federal Plaza .... Lake Success NY 11042 *NYSE: AF* ■ *TF:* 800-967-7140 ■ *Web:* astoriafederal.com	516-327-3000		360-2
Astoria Ford 710 W Marine Dr .... Astoria OR 97103 *TF:* 888-760-9303 ■ *Web:* www.astoriaford.net	503-325-6411		57
Astoria-Pacific Inc 15130 SE 82nd Dr .... Clackamas OR 97015 *TF:* 800-536-3111 ■ *Web:* www.astoria-pacific.com	503-657-3010		292
Astoundry Inc 2441 Bartlett St .... Houston TX 77098 *Web:* astoundry.com	713-520-6200		809
Astra Associates Inc 6500 Dobry Dr .... Sterling Heights MI 48314 *Web:* www.midwestinstrument.com	248-254-6500		201
Astra Foods Inc 6430 Market St .... Upper Darby PA 19082 *Web:* www.astrafoods.com	610-352-4400		297-8
Astra Group Corporation 5913 Woodson Rd .... Mission KS 66202	913-378-1900		2
Astral Media Inc 1800 McGill College Ste 600 .... Montreal QC H3A3J6 *Web:* www.bellmedia.ca	514-939-5000	939-1515	116
Astralloy Steel Products Inc 1550 Red Hollow Rd .... Birmingham AL 35215 *Web:* www.astralloy.com	205-853-0300		492
AstraZeneca Canada Inc 1004 Middlegate Rd .... Mississauga ON L4Y1M4 *TF:* 800-565-5877 ■ *Web:* www.astrazeneca.ca	905-277-7111	270-3248	582
AstraZeneca Pharmaceuticals LP 1800 Concord Pk PO Box 15437 .... Wilmington DE 19850 *TF:* 800-236-9933 ■ *Web:* www.astrazeneca-us.com	800-236-9933		582
Astrix Technology Group 125 Half Mile Rd Ste 200 .... Red Bank NJ 07701 *Web:* www.astrixsoftware.com	732-661-0400		396
ASTRO (American Society for Therapeutic Radiology & Oncology) 8280 Willow Oaks Corporate Dr Ste 500 .... Fairfax VA 22031 *TF:* 800-962-7876 ■ *Web:* www.astro.org	703-502-1550	502-7852	49-8
Astro Chemicals Inc 126 Memorial Dr .... Springfield MA 01104 *Web:* www.astrochemicals.com	413-781-7240	781-7246	146
Astro Craft Inc 7509 Spring Grove Rd .... Spring Grove IL 60081 *TF:* 800-644-5660 ■ *Web:* www.astrocraft.com	815-675-1500		358
Astro Industries Inc 4403 Dayton-Xenia Rd .... Dayton OH 45432 **Fax:* Sales ■ *TF:* 800-543-5810 ■ *Web:* www.astro-ind.com	937-429-5900	429-4054*	813
Astro Machine Works Inc 470 Wenger Dr .... Ephrata PA 17522 *Web:* www.astromachineworks.com	717-738-4281		454
Astro Manufacturing & Design Corp 34459 Curtis Blvd .... Eastlake OH 44095 *Web:* www.astromfg.com	440-946-8171		295
Astro Mechanical Contractors Inc 603 S Marshall Ave .... El Cajon CA 92020 *Web:* astro-mech.com	619-442-9686		610
Astro Met Inc 9974 Springfield Pk .... Cincinnati OH 45215 *TF:* 800-706-8849 ■ *Web:* www.astromet.com	513-772-1242	772-9080	500
Astro Pak Corp 270 E Baker St Ste 100 .... Costa Mesa CA 92626 **Fax Area Code:* 714 ■ *TF:* 888-278-7672 ■ *Web:* www.astropak.com	888-278-7672	434-1376*	743
Astro Seal Inc 827 Palmyrita Ave # B .... Riverside CA 92507 *TF:* 800-394-5808 ■ *Web:* www.astroseal.com	951-787-6670	787-6677	621
Astro Shapes Inc 65 Main St .... Struthers OH 44471 *Web:* www.astroshapes.com	330-755-1414		492
Astro Studios Inc 348 Sixth St .... San Francisco CA 94103 *TF:* 800-274-1376 ■ *Web:* www.astrostudios.com	415-487-6787		463
Astro Tool & Machine Company Inc 810 Martin St .... Rahway NJ 07065 *Web:* www.astrotoolco.com	732-382-2450	382-6394	757
Astrodyne Corp 375 Forbes Blvd .... Mansfield MA 02048 *TF:* 800-823-8082 ■ *Web:* www.astrodynetdi.com	508-964-6300		256

Phone | Fax | Class

Astrofoam Molding Company Inc
4117 Calle Tesoro .... Camarillo CA 93012 805-482-7276 482-6599 601
Web: www.astrofoam.com

Astron Wireless Technologies Inc
22560 Glenn Dr Ste 114 .... Sterling VA 20164 703-450-5517 57
Web: www.astronwireless.com

Astronautics Corp of America
4115 N Teutonia Ave PO Box 523 .... Milwaukee WI 53201 414-449-4000 447-8231 529
TF: 800-490-9010 ■ Web: www.astronautics.com

Astronics Corp 130 Commerce Way .... East Aurora NY 14052 716-805-1599 655-0309 438
NASDAQ: ATRO ■ TF: 800-937-5449 ■ Web: www.astronics.com

Astronomical Society of the Pacific
390 Ashton Ave .... San Francisco CA 94112 415-337-1100 337-5205 48-11
TF: 800-335-2624 ■ Web: www.astrosociety.org

Astrophysics Inc
21481 Ferrero Pkwy .... City Of Industry CA 91789 909-598-5488 692
Web: www.astrophysicsinc.com

Astrotech Corp
401 Congress Ave Ste 1650 .... Austin TX 78701 512-485-9530 485-9531 504
NASDAQ: ASTC ■ Web: www.astrotechcorp.com

Astrup Drug Inc 1305 First Ave SW .... Austin MN 55912 507-433-4586 433-7003 238
TF: 800-803-1503 ■ Web: www.astrupdrug.com

ASTSWMO (Association of State & Territorial Solid Waste Management Officials)
444 N Capitol St NW Ste 315 .... Washington DC 20001 202-624-5828 624-7875 49-7
Web: www.astswmo.org

Astyra Corp 411 E Franklin St Ste 105 .... Richmond VA 23219 804-433-1100 260
Web: www.astyra.com

ASU Group, The 2120 University Park Dr .... Okemos MI 48805 517-349-2212 194
TF: 800-968-0278 ■ Web: www.asugroup.com

ASU Keer cultural Ctr
6110 N Scottsdale Rd .... Scottsdale AZ 85253 480-596-2660 572
Web: www.asukerr.com

Asuka Japanese Cuisine
7381 Market St .... Boardman OH 44512 330-629-8088 671
Web: asukajapanese.com

Asuragen Inc 2150 Woodward St Ste 100 .... Austin TX 78744 512-681-5200 681-5201 476
Web: www.asuragen.com

Asure Software 110 Wild Basin Rd .... Austin TX 78746 512-437-2700 437-2365 178-7
NASDAQ: ASUR ■ TF: 888-323-8835 ■ Web: www.asuresoftware.com

Asurion Canada Inc 1222 Main St 2nd Fl .... Moncton NB E1C1H6 506-386-9204 386-9154 393

ASUSTeK Computer International
800 Corporate Way .... Fremont CA 94539 510-739-3777 608-4555 625
Web: www.asus.com

ASW Global LLC 3375 Gilchrist Rd .... Mogadore OH 44260 330-733-6291 803-1
TF: 888-826-5087 ■ Web: www.aswglobal.com

ASWB (Association of Social Work Boards)
400 S Ridge Pkwy Ste B .... Culpeper VA 22701 540-829-6880 49-7
TF: 800-225-6880 ■ Web: www.aswb.org

Asylum Research Corp
6310 Hollister Ave .... Santa Barbara CA 93117 805-696-6466 419
Web: www.asylumresearch.com

Asylum, The 72 Palm Ave .... Burbank CA 91502 323-850-1214 514
Web: www.theasylum.cc

Asynchrony Solutions Inc
900 Spruce St Ste 700 .... St. Louis MO 63102 314-678-2200 41
TF: 800-220-0733 ■ Web: www.asynchrony.com

AT & T Inc
175 E Houston St PO Box 2933 .... San Antonio TX 78299 210-821-4105 736
NYSE: AT&T ■ TF: 800-351-7221 ■ Web: www.att.com

AT & T Park
24 Willie Mays Plaza .... San Francisco CA 94107 415-972-2000 720

AT Clayton & Co Inc 300 Atlantic St .... Stamford CT 06901 203-658-1200 658-1201 553
Web: www.atclayton.com

At First Site Inc
4449 Easton Way 2nd Fl .... Columbus OH 43219 614-479-0000 809
Web: www.af3web.net

At Health Inc
14175 W Indian School Rd Suite B4-103 .... Goodyear AZ 85395 623-266-4997 322-0498 356
TF: 888-284-3258 ■ Web: www.athealth.com

AT Kearney Inc 227 W Adams St Ste 2500 .... Chicago IL 60606 312-648-0111 223-6200 194
Web: www.atkearney.com

At Last Naturals Inc
401 Columbus Ave .... Valhalla NY 10595 800-527-8123 747-3791* 214
*Fax Area Code: 914 ■ TF: 800-527-8123 ■ Web: www.atlastnaturals.com

At Rosewood 284 Troy Rd .... Rensselaer NY 12144 518-286-1621 286-1691 450
TF: 800-772-5969 ■ Web: www.rosewoodrehabilitation.com

ATA (American Tinnitus Assn)
522 SW Fifth Ave Ste 825 .... Portland OR 97204 503-248-9985 248-0024 48-17
TF: 800-634-8978 ■ Web: www.ata.org

ATA (Airlines for America)
1301 Pennsylvania Ave NW Ste 1100 .... Washington DC 20004 202-626-4000 49-21
Web: airlines.org

ATA (Amateur Trapshooting Assn)
601 W National Rd .... Vandalia OH 45377 937-898-4638 898-5472 48-22
TF: 800-671-8042 ■ Web: www.shootata.com

ATA (American Trucking Assn)
950 N Glebe Rd Ste 210 .... Arlington VA 22203 703-838-1700 49-21
TF: 800-282-5463 ■ Web: www.trucking.org

ATA (American Translators Assn)
225 Reinekers Ln Ste 590 .... Alexandria VA 22314 703-683-6100 683-6122 49-5
Web: www.atanet.org

Ata Career Education
10180 Linn Sta Rd Ste A200 .... Louisville KY 40223 502-371-8330 162
Web: www.ata.edu

Ata Engineering Inc
11995 El Camino Real Ste 200 .... San Diego CA 92130 858-480-2000 261
Web: ata-e.com

ATA Ventures
4300 El Camino Real Ste 205 .... Los Altos CA 94022 650-594-0189 594-0257 792
Web: www.ataventures.com

ATAA (Assembly of Turkish American Assn)
1526 18th St NW .... Washington DC 20036 202-483-9090 483-9092 48-14
TF: 800-627-7692 ■ Web: www.ataa.org

ATAC Corp 2770 De La Cruz Blvd .... Santa Clara CA 95050-2624 408-736-2822 727-8447 809
Web: www.atac.com

Ataco Steel Products Corp
PO Box 270 .... Cedarburg WI 53012 262-377-3000 377-3452 488
TF: 800-536-4822 ■ Web: www.atacosteel.com

Atalanta Corp 1 Atalanta Plaza .... Elizabeth NJ 07206 908-351-8000 297-8
Web: www.atalantacorp.com

Atalanta Investment Co Inc
601 Fairview Blvd .... Incline Village NV 89451 775-833-1836 833-1890 402

Atalanta/Sosnoff Capital LLC
101 Pk Ave 6th Fl .... New York NY 10178 212-867-5000 922-1820 401
TF: 800-730-6001 ■ Web: www.atalantasosnoff.com

Atalasoft Inc
116 Pleasant St Ste 321 .... Easthampton MA 01027 413-572-4443 177
Web: www.atalasoft.com

Atamian Manufacturing Corp
910 Plainfield St .... Providence RI 02909 401-944-9614 488
Web: www.atamianmfg.com

ATAP Inc 130 Industry way .... Eastaboga AL 36260 256-362-2221 362-2221 470
TF: 800-362-2827 ■ Web: www.atap.com

Atari Inc 475 Park Ave S .... New York NY 10016 212-726-6500 178-3
Web: www.atari.com

ATAS International Inc
6612 Snowdrift Rd .... Allentown PA 18106 610-395-8445 395-9342 491
TF: 800-468-1441 ■ Web: www.atas.com

Atascadero Chamber of Commerce
6904 El Camino Real .... Atascadero CA 93422 805-466-2044 466-9218 139
TF: 877-204-9830 ■ Web: www.atascaderochamber.org

Atascadero State Hospital
10333 S Camino Real .... Atascadero CA 93422 805-468-2000 468-3386 374-5
TF: 844-210-6207 ■ Web: dsh.ca.gov

Atascosa County
1 Courthouse Cir Dr Ste 102 .... Jourdanton TX 78026 830-767-2511 769-1021 338

ATC (Athens Technical College)
800 US Hwy 29 N .... Athens GA 30601 706-355-5000 369-5756 800
Web: athenstech.edu

ATC (American Thermoplastic Co)
106 Gamma Dr .... Pittsburgh PA 15238 800-245-6600 86
TF: 800-245-6600 ■ Web: www.binders.com

ATC (Appalachian Trail Conservancy)
799 Washington St PO Box 807 .... Harpers Ferry WV 25425 304-535-6331 535-2667 48-23
TF Sales: 888-287-8673 ■ Web: appalachiantrail.org

ATC (Architecture Technology Corp)
9971 Vly View Rd .... Eden Prairie MN 55344 952-829-5864 178-1
Web: www.atcorp.com

ATC Inc 4037 Guion Ln .... Indianapolis IN 46268 317-328-8492 639
Web: www.atcinc.net

ATC Lighting & Plastics Inc
101 Parker Dr .... Andover OH 44003 440-293-4064 293-4591 438
TF: 800-533-8333 ■ Web: www.atc-lighting-plastics.com

ATCA (Air Traffic Control Assn)
1101 King St Ste 300 .... Alexandria VA 22314 703-299-2430 299-2437 49-21
Web: www.atca.org

ATCC (American Type Culture Collection)
10801 University Blvd PO Box 1549 .... Manassas VA 20108 703-365-2700 365-2701 668
TF Cust Svc: 800-638-6597 ■ Web: www.atcc.org

Atcc 757 Barbershop Rd .... Edinburg VA 22824 540-984-8443 693

Atchafalaya Measurement Inc
124 Credit Dr .... Scott LA 70583 337-237-7675 539
Web: atchafalayameasurement.com

Atchison County 423 N Fifth St .... Atchison KS 66002 913-367-1653 367-0227 338
Web: www.atchisoncountyks.org

Atchison County
405 S Main St PO Box 243 .... Rock Port MO 64482 660-744-6562 744-6564 338
TF: 800-989-4115 ■ Web: www.atchisoncounty.org

Atchison-Holt Electric Co-op
18585 Industrial Rd PO Box 160 .... Rock Port MO 64482 660-744-5344 245
TF: 888-744-5366 ■ Web: www.ahec.coop

ATCO Gas & Pipelines Ltd
10035 - 105 St .... Edmonton AB T5J2V6 780-424-5222 787
Web: www.atcogas.com

ATCO Industries Inc
7300 Fifteen Mile Rd .... Sterling Heights MI 48312 586-795-9595 803-1
Web: www.atcoindustries.com

ATCO Ltd 700 909 11th Ave SW .... Calgary AB T2R1N6 403-292-7500 292-7532 787
TSE: ACO/X ■ TF: 800-242-3447 ■ Web: www.atco.com

ATCO Power Ltd 919-11 Ave SW Ste 400 .... Calgary AB T2R1P3 403-209-6900 767
Web: www.atcopower.com

ATCO Products Inc
189-V Frelinghuysen Ave .... Newark NJ 07114 973-242-5757 242-0131 350
Web: www.atcoproducts.com

ATCO Properties & Management Inc
555 Fifth Ave 16th Fl .... New York NY 10017 212-687-5154 463
Web: www.atco555.com

Atco Raceway 1000 Jackson Rd .... Atco NJ 08004 856-768-2167 515
Web: atcodragway.rocks

Atco Rubber Products Inc
7101 Atco Dr .... Fort Worth TX 76118 817-595-2894 370
TF: 800-877-3828 ■ Web: www.atcoflex.com

Atcoflex Inc 14261 172nd Ave .... Grand Haven MI 49417 616-842-4661 842-4623 370
Web: www.atcoflexinc.com

ATD (Atlantic Tool & Die Co)
19963 Progress Dr .... Strongsville OH 44149 440-238-6931 488
Web: www.atlantictool.com

ATD Austin PO Box 13324 .... Austin TX 78711 512-395-8101 4
Web: theredphonebook.com

ATD Engineering & Machine LLC
533 N Ct St .... Au Gres MI 48703 989-876-7161 876-7162 494
Web: www.atdemllc.com

ATD-American Co 135 Greenwood Ave .... Wyncote PA 19095 215-576-1380 523-2300* 320
*Fax Area Code: 800 ■ TF: 866-283-9327 ■ Web: www.atdamerican.com

A-Team Advertising Advisors LLC
Four Park Ave Ste 15R .... New York NY 10016 646-530-8670 856-8929* 7
*Fax Area Code: 866

ATEC Group 1762 Central Ave Ste 300 .... Albany NY 12205 518-452-3700 174

ATEC Inc 12600 Executive Dr .... Stafford TX 77477 281-276-2700 240-2682 621
TF: 800-873-0001 ■ Web: www.atec.com

A-tech Security Inc
4616 Hawkins St NE .... Albuquerque NM 87109 505-821-5777 77
Web: www.atechsecurity.com

ATEK Access Technologies LLC
10025 Valley View Rd Ste 190 .... Eden Prairie MN 55344 763-553-7700 693
Web: atekcompanies.com

				Phone	Fax	Class
ATEL Capital Group 600 California St 6th Fl	San Francisco	CA	94108	415-989-8800	989-3796	216
TF: 800-543-2835 ■ *Web:* www.atel.com						
Ateliers Lesage Inc (les) 1330 Rue Soucy	Saint-hubert	QC	J4T1A3	450-445-5088		757
Web: aterliersiesage.com						
Atelka Inc 1000 St Antoine St W Ste 500	Montreal	QC	H3C3R7	514-448-4905		393
Web: www.atelka.com						
ATEN 23 Hubble	Irvine	CA	92618	949-428-1111	428-1100	173-1
Web: www.aten-usa.com						
Ater Wynne LLP 1331 NW Lovejoy St Lovejoy Bldg Ste 900	Portland	OR	97209	503-226-1191		428
Web: aterwynne.com						
ATF (Bureau of Alcohol Tobacco Firearms & Explosives) 650 Massachusetts Ave NW	Washington	DC	20226	202-927-8210		340-14
Web: www.atf.gov						
AT&F (American Tank & Fabricating Co) 12314 Elmwood Ave	Cleveland	OH	44111	216-252-1500	251-4963	723
TF: 800-544-5316 ■ *Web:* www.atfco.com						
Atfocus 394 Old Orchard Grove	Toronto	ON	M5M2E9	416-485-4220		193
TF: 866-349-2661 ■ *Web:* atfocus.ca						
ATG Technologies Inc 2639 N Monroe St Cedars Bldg B Ste 200	Tallahassee	FL	32303	800-775-7790		393
TF: 800-775-7790 ■ *Web:* www.patlive.com						
Ath Power Consulting Corp 9 Bartlet St	Andover	MA	01810	978-474-6464		463
TF: 800-523-1288 ■ *Web:* www.athpower.com						
Athabasca University 1 University Dr	Athabasca	AB	T9S3A3	780-675-6111	675-6174	785
TF: 800-788-9041 ■ *Web:* www.athabascau.ca						
Athana International Inc 602 Faye	Redondo Beach	CA	90277	310-539-7280	539-6596	658
TF: 800-421-1591 ■ *Web:* www.athana.com						
Athanor Group Inc 921 E California Ave	Ontario	CA	91761	909-467-1205	467-1208	621
Athavale Lystad & Assoc Inc 6720-B Rockledge Dr Ste 160	Bethesda	MD	20817	301-816-3237		256
Web: www.alaengr.com						
Athea Laboratories Inc 1900 W Cornell St	Milwaukee	WI	53209	800-743-6417	354-9219*	145
**Fax Area Code:* 414 ■ *TF:* 800-743-6417 ■ *Web:* www.athea.com						
Athena Automation Ltd 372 New Enterprise Way	Vaughan	ON	L4H0S8	905-265-0277		261
Web: www.athenaautomation.com						
Athena Controls Inc 5145 Campus Dr	Plymouth Meeting	PA	19462	610-828-2490	828-7084	201
TF: 800-782-6776 ■ *Web:* www.athenacontrols.com						
Athena Diagnostics Inc 377 Plantation St 2nd Fl	Worcester	MA	01605	508-756-2886		231
TF: 800-394-4493 ■ *Web:* www.athenadiagnostics.com						
Athena Engineering Inc 456 E Foothill Blvd	San Dimas	CA	91773	909-599-0947	599-5018	189-4
TF: 877-777-4778 ■ *Web:* www.athenaengineering.net						
Athena Pallas 556 22nd St S	Arlington	VA	22202	703-521-3870		671
Web: www.athenapallas.com						
Athenaeum of Ohio 6616 Beechmont Ave	Cincinnati	OH	45230	513-231-2223	231-3254	167-3
TF: 800-888-1818 ■ *Web:* www.mtsm.org						
Athenaeum of Philadelphia 219 S Sixth St	Philadelphia	PA	19106	215-925-2688	925-3755	434-4
Web: www.philaathenaeum.org						
Athenaeum, The 201 Prince St	Alexandria	VA	22314	703-548-0035		50-3
Web: www.nvfaa.org						
athenahealth Inc 311 Arsenal St	Watertown	MA	02472	617-402-1000	402-1099	178-1
NASDAQ: ATHN ■ *TF:* 800-981-5084 ■ *Web:* www.athenahealth.com						
Athene's 3618 W Broadway	Vancouver	BC	V6R2B7	604-731-4135		671
Web: www.athenes.ca						
Atheneum Suite Hotel & Conference Ctr 1000 Brush Ave	Detroit	MI	48226	313-962-2323	962-2424	379
TF: 800-772-2323 ■ *Web:* www.atheneumsuites.com						
Athenian 252 E 2500 S	Ogden	UT	84401	801-621-4911		671
Athenian Garden 6940 22nd Ave N	Saint Petersburg	FL	33710	727-345-7040		671
Web: www.atheniangardens.com						
Athenian School 2100 Mt Diablo Scenic Blvd	Danville	CA	94506	925-837-5375		622
Web: www.athenian.org						
Athens 13600 Snow Rd	Brookpark	OH	44142	216-676-8500		296-2
TF: 800-837-5683 ■ *Web:* www.athens.com						
Athens Area Chamber of Commerce 449 E State St Ste 1	Athens	OH	45701	740-594-2251	594-2252	139
TF: 877-360-3608 ■ *Web:* www.athenschamber.com						
Athens Area Chamber of Commerce 246 W Hancock Ave	Athens	GA	30601	706-549-6800	549-5636	139
Web: www.athensga.com						
Athens Banner-Herald 1 Press Pl	Athens	GA	30601	706-549-0123	208-2246	532-2
TF: 800-533-4252 ■ *Web:* onlineathens.com						
Athens City School District 25 S Plains Rd	The Plains	OH	45780	740-797-4544		685
Web: www.athenscity.k12.oh.us						
Athens Convention & Visitors Bureau 300 N Thomas St	Athens	GA	30601	706-357-4430	546-8040	206
TF: 800-653-0603 ■ *Web:* www.visitathensga.com						
Athens County Board of Developmental Disabilities 801 W Union St	Athens	OH	45701	740-594-3539		338
Web: athenscbdd.org						
Athens County Convention & Visitors Bureau 667 E State St	Athens	OH	45701	740-592-1819	593-7365	206
TF: 800-878-9767 ■ *Web:* www.athensohio.com						
Athens Messenger, The 9300 Johnson Rd	Athens	OH	45701	740-592-6612	592-4647	637-8
Web: www.athensmessenger.com						
Athens Newspaper Inc 14 N Court St	Athens	GA	45701	706-549-6800		637-8
Web: athensga.com						
Athens on Fourth Avenue 500 N Fourth Ave	Tucson	AZ	85705	520-624-6886		671
Web: athenson4thave.com						
Athens Regional Medical Ctr 1114 W Madison Ave	Athens	TN	37303	423-745-1411		374-3
TF: 800-855-2880 ■ *Web:* starrregional.com						
Athens Services 14048 Valley Blvd	La Puente	CA	91746	626-336-3636		804
TF: 888-336-6100 ■ *Web:* www.athensservices.com						
Athens State Bank 6530 N State Rt 29	Springfield	IL	62707	217-487-7766	487-7733	70
TF: 800-367-7576 ■ *Web:* athensstatebank.com						
Athens Steel Inc 200 Dairy Pak Rd	Athens	GA	30607	706-552-3850		492
Web: www.athenssteel.com						
Athens Technical College (ATC) 800 US Hwy 29 N	Athens	GA	30601	706-355-5000	369-5756	800
Web: athenstech.edu						
Athens/Clarke County Library 2025 Baxter St	Athens	GA	30606	706-613-3650	613-3660	434-3
Web: athenslibrary.org						
Athens-Clarke County 325 E Washington St Rm 200 PO Box 1868	Athens	GA	30601	706-613-3031	613-3033	338
Web: www.athensclarkecounty.com						
Athens-Limestone Hospital 700 W Market St	Athens	AL	35611	256-233-9292	233-9278	374-3
TF: 800-522-0272 ■ *Web:* www.athenslimestonehospital.com						
Atherton Baptist Homes 214 S Atlantic Blvd	Alhambra	CA	91801	626-863-1224		672
TF: 800-340-4178 ■ *Web:* www.abh.org						
Atherton Hotel 125 S Atherton St State College	Pennsylvania	PA	16801	814-231-2100		671
Web: www.athertonhotel.net						
Athey & Company PA 1015 N Pearl St	Bridgeton	NJ	08302	856-451-8277		2
Web: www.atheycocpa.com						
Athletes & Entertainers for Kids (AEFK) 14340 Bolsa Chica Rd Unit C	Westminster	CA	92683	562-438-5905		48-6
Athletes in Action 651 Taylor Dr	Xenia	OH	45385	937-352-1000		48-15
Web: athletesinaction.org						
Athletic Supply Co 16101 NE 87th St	Redmond	WA	98052	425-882-1456	497-4727	711
TF: 800-732-9259 ■ *Web:* www.kimmelathletic.com						
Athletic Training Equipment Company Inc 655 Spice Island Dr	Sparks	NV	89431	775-352-2800		711
Web: www.atecsports.com						
AtHomeNet Inc PO Box 1405	Suwanee	GA	30024	770-904-7930		225
Web: www.athomenet.com						
Athreya Inc 100 Jersey Ave Ste A 103	New Brunswick	NJ	08901	732-246-2700		180
Web: athreyainc.com						
ATI (AmericanTours International LLC) 6053 W Century Blvd	Los Angeles	CA	90045	310-641-9953	216-5807	760
Web: www.americantours.com						
ATI Allegheny Ludlum Corp 100 River Rd	Brackenridge	PA	15014	724-224-1000		723
TF Sales: 800-258-3586 ■ *Web:* www.atimetals.com						
ATI Ambulance 8400 W 183rd Pl	Tinley Park	IL	60487	708-802-8101		30
Web: www.traceambulance.com						
ATI Industrial Automation Export Co 1031 Goodworth Dr	Apex	NC	27539	919-772-0115	772-8259	201
Web: www.ati-ia.com						
ATI Ladish Company Inc 5481 S Packard Ave	Cudahy	WI	53110	414-747-2611		483
TF: 800-444-5427 ■ *Web:* www.atimetals.com						
ATI Precision Finishing 499 Delaware Ave	Rochester	PA	15074	724-775-1664		481
Web: www.atimetals.com						
Atigeo LLC 800 Bellevue Way NE Ste 600	Bellevue	WA	98004	425-635-3900		177
Web: www.atigeo.com						
ATIS (Alliance for Telecommunications Industry Solutions) 1200 G St NW Ste 500	Washington	DC	20005	202-628-6380	393-5453	49-20
TF: 800-649-1202 ■ *Web:* www.atis.org						
ATIS Elevator Inspections LLC 1976 Innerbelt Business Ctr	St. Louis	MO	63114	855-755-2847		393
TF: 855-755-2847 ■ *Web:* www.atis.com						
Atiwa Computer Leasing Exchange 6950 Portwest Dr Ste 100	Houston	TX	77024	713-467-9390		179
TF: 800-428-2532 ■ *Web:* www.atiwa.com						
Atkins & Pearce Inc 1 Braid Way	Covington	KY	41017	859-356-2001	356-2395	208
TF: 800-837-7477 ■ *Web:* www.atkinsandpearce.com						
Atkins Nutritionals Inc 1050 17th St Ste 1000	Denver	CO	80265	303-633-2840		799
TF: 800-628-5467 ■ *Web:* www.atkins.com						
Atkinson & Assoc Insurance Inc 1537 Brantley Rd Bldg C	Fort Myers	FL	33907	239-437-5555		390
Web: atkinsoninsurance.com						
Atkinson Andelson Loya Ruud & Romo A Professional Law Corp 12800 Towne Ctr Dr	Cerritos	CA	90703	562-653-3200		428
Web: www.aalrr.com						
Atkinson Candy Co 1608 W Frank Ave	Lufkin	TX	75904	936-639-2333	639-2337	296-8
Web: www.atkinsoncandy.com						
Atkinson Conway & Gagnon Inc 420 L St Ste 500	Anchorage	AK	99501	907-276-1700		428
TF: 800-478-1900 ■ *Web:* www.acglaw.com						
Atkinson County PO Box 518	Pearson	GA	31642	912-422-3391	422-3429	338
TF: 800-858-2224 ■ *Web:* www.atkinsoncounty.org						
Atkinson County School System 98 Roberts Ave E	Pearson	GA	31642	912-422-7373	422-7369	685
TF: 800-639-0850 ■ *Web:* www.atkinson.k12.ga.us						
Atkinson Freight Lines Co 2950 State Rd	Bensalem	PA	19020	215-639-2678		780
Atkinson Industries Inc 1801 E 27th St Terr	Pittsburg	KS	66762	620-231-6900	231-7154	729
Web: www.azz.com						
Atkinson Lake State Recreation Area PO Box 508	Bassett	NE	68714-0508	402-684-2921		565
Web: www.travelnenebraska.com						
Atkinson Trading Co 3911 W Saragosa St	Chandler	AZ	85226	480-899-9597		327
Atkinson's Mirror and Glass 909 N Orchard St	Boise	ID	83706	208-375-3762	375-3774	234
TF: 800-221-3748 ■ *Web:* www.atkinsonsmirrorandglass.com						
Atkinson-Baker Inc (ABI) 500 N Brand Blvd 3rd Fl	Glendale	CA	91203	818-551-7300		445
TF: 800-288-3376 ■ *Web:* www.depo.com						

Name / Address	City	State	Zip	Phone	Fax	Class
ATL Inc W140 N9504 Fountain Blvd; *Web:* www.atlco.com	Menomonee Falls	WI	53051	262-255-6150		393
ATLA (American Theological Library Assn) 300 S Wacker Dr Ste 2100; *TF:* 888-665-2852 ■ *Web:* www.atla.com	Chicago	IL	60606	312-454-5100	454-5505	48-20
Atlanta Airlines Terminal Corp Hartsfield-Jackson Atlanta International Airport PO Box 45170; *Web:* www.aatc.org	Atlanta	GA	30320	404-530-2100		25
Atlanta Area Chamber of Commerce 101 N East St; *Web:* www.atlantatexas.org	Atlanta	TX	75551	903-796-3296		139
Atlanta Athletic Club 1930 Bobby Jones Dr; *TF:* 800-858-9940 ■ *Web:* www.atlantaathleticclub.org	Johns Creek	GA	30097	770-448-2166		354
Atlanta Attachment Company Inc 362 Industrial Pk Dr; *TF:* 877-206-5116 ■ *Web:* www.atlatt.com	Lawrenceville	GA	30045	770-963-7369	963-7641	36
Atlanta Ballet 1695 Marietta Blvd NW; *TF:* 800-278-4447 ■ *Web:* www.atlantaballet.com	Atlanta	GA	30318	404-873-5811	874-7905	573-1
Atlanta Botanical Garden 1345 Piedmont Ave NE; *Web:* atlantabg.org	Atlanta	GA	30309	404-876-5859	876-7472	97
Atlanta Bread Co 1200 Wilson Way Ste 100; *Web:* www.atlantabread.com	Smyrna	GA	30082	770-432-0933		68
Atlanta Business Chronicle 3423 Piedmont Rd Ste 400; *TF:* 800-282-7411 ■ *Web:* www.bizjournals.com	Atlanta	GA	30305	404-249-1000	249-1048	457-5
Atlanta Capital Management Company LLC 1075 Peachtree St NW Ste 2100; *Web:* www.atlcap.com	Atlanta	GA	30309	404-876-9411	872-1672	401
Atlanta Carrier Hotel 56 Marietta St; *Web:* www.56marietta.com	Atlanta	GA	30303	404-869-8992		377
Atlanta Casework Systems Inc 3815 Evans Rd; *Web:* www.atlcasework.com	Cumming	GA	30040	770-887-4766		200
Atlanta City Hall 55 Trinity Ave SW Ste 2500; *TF:* 800-897-1910 ■ *Web:* www.atlantaga.gov	Atlanta	GA	30303	404-330-6004	658-6893	337
Atlanta Civic Ctr 395 Piedmont Ave NE; *TF:* 877-430-7596	Atlanta	GA	30308	404-523-6275		572
Atlanta Commercial Tire Inc 146 Forest Pkwy; *Web:* www.actire.com	Forest Park	GA	30297	404-675-9998		54
Atlanta Contemporary Art Ctr 535 Means St NW; *Web:* atlantacontemporary.org	Atlanta	GA	30318	404-688-1970		50-2
Atlanta Convention & Visitors Bureau 233 Peachtree St NE Ste 1400; *Web:* www.atlanta.net	Atlanta	GA	30303	404-521-6600		206
Atlanta Cutlery Corp 2147 Gees Mill Rd; *TF:* 800-883-0300 ■ *Web:* www.atlantacutlery.com	Conyers	GA	30013	770-922-3700	760-8993	222
Atlanta Daily World Inc 875 Old Roswell Rd Ste C 100; *Web:* www.atlantadailyworld.com	Roswell	GA	30076	404-761-1114		532-3
Atlanta Dragway 500 E Ridgeway Rd; *Web:* www.atlantadragway.com	Commerce	GA	30529	706-335-2301		515
Atlanta Falcons 4400 Falcon Pkwy; *Web:* www.atlantafalcons.com	Flowery Branch	GA	30542	770-965-3115	965-3185	715-3
Atlanta Fish Market 265 Pharr Rd NE; *Web:* www.buckheadrestaurants.com	Atlanta	GA	30305	404-240-1833		671
Atlanta Fixture & Sales Co 3185 NE Expy; *TF:* 800-282-1977 ■ *Web:* www.atlantafixture.com	Atlanta	GA	30341	770-455-8844	986-9202	300
Atlanta Fuel Co 2324 Donald Lee Hollowell Pkwy; *Web:* atlantafuel.com	Atlanta	GA	30318	404-792-9888		316
Atlanta Grill 181 Peachtree St NE; *Web:* www.ritzcarlton.com	Atlanta	GA	30303	404-659-0400		671
Atlanta Hardwood Corp 5596 Riverview Rd SE; *TF:* 800-476-5393 ■ *Web:* www.hardwoodweb.com	Mableton	GA	30126	404-792-2290		364
Atlanta Hawks Centennial Tower 101 Marietta St NW Ste 1900; *Web:* www.nba.com/hawks	Atlanta	GA	30303	404-827-3800	827-3880	714-1
Atlanta History Ctr 130 W Paces Ferry Rd; *Web:* www.atlantahistorycenter.com	Atlanta	GA	30305	404-814-4000		520
Atlanta Hospital Hospitality House 1815 S Ponce De Leon Ave NE; *TF:* 855-286-9658 ■ *Web:* www.atlhhh.org	Atlanta	GA	30307	404-377-6333		372
Atlanta International Consulting Group (aicg) 1401 Peachtree St NE Ste 500; *Web:* www.aicginc.com	Atlanta	GA	30309	404-872-4884		194
Atlanta Intown Real Estate Services 181 Tenth St NE; *Web:* www.atlantaintown.com	Atlanta	GA	30309	404-881-1810		652
Atlanta Journal-Constitution 223 Perimeter Ctr Pkwy NE; *TF:* 800-933-9771 ■ *Web:* www.ajc.com	Atlanta	GA	30346	404-526-5151	526-5746	532-2
Atlanta Magazine 260 Peachtree St Ste 300; *TF:* 800-930-3019 ■ *Web:* www.atlantamagazine.com	Atlanta	GA	30303	404-527-5500	527-5575	457-22
Atlanta Medical Ctr 303 Pkwy Dr NE	Atlanta	GA	30312	404-265-4000		374-3
Atlanta Metropolitan College 1630 Metropolitan Pkwy SW; **Fax:* Admissions ■ *Web:* www.atlm.edu	Atlanta	GA	30310	404-756-4000	756-4407*	162
Atlanta Motor Speedway PO Box 500; *TF:* 877-926-7849 ■ *Web:* www.atlantamotorspeedway.com	Hampton	GA	30228	770-946-4211	946-3928	515
Atlanta Petroleum Equipment Co 4732 N Royal Atlanta Dr; *TF:* 800-562-4060 ■ *Web:* www.atlantapetroleum.com	Tucker	GA	30084	770-491-6644		539
Atlanta Pops Orchestra PO Box 49493; *Web:* atlantapops.com	Atlanta	GA	30359	404-636-0020		573-3
Atlanta Postal Credit Union 501 Pulliam St SW Ste 350; *TF:* 800-849-8431 ■ *Web:* www.apcu.com	Atlanta	GA	30312	404-768-4126	768-0815	219
Atlanta Public Schools 130 Trinity Ave SW; *Web:* www.atlanta.k12.ga.us	Atlanta	GA	30303	404-802-3500	802-1803	685
Atlanta State Park 927 Pk Rd 42; *Web:* tpwd.texas.gov/state-parks/atlanta	Atlanta	TX	75551	903-796-6476		565
Atlanta Symphony Orchestra 1280 Peachtree St NE Ste 4074; *TF:* 800-745-3000 ■ *Web:* www.atlantasymphony.org	Atlanta	GA	30309	404-733-4900	733-4901	573-3
Atlanta Toyota Inc 2345 Pleasant Hill Rd; *Web:* www.atlantatoyota.com	Duluth	GA	30096	770-476-8282		57
Atlanta-Fulton Public Library 1 Margaret Mitchell Sq; *Web:* www.afpls.org/locations/locations2	Atlanta	GA	30303	404-730-1700		434-3
Atlantech Online Inc 1010 Wayne Ave Ste 630; *TF:* 800-256-1612 ■ *Web:* www.atlantech.net	Silver Spring	MD	20910	301-589-3060		225
Atlantic & Pacific Management 11075 Carmel Mtn Rd Ste 200; *Web:* www.apcompanies.com	San Diego	CA	92129	858-672-3100		652
Atlantic Air Enterprises Inc 856 Elston St; *Web:* www.atlanticairent.com	Rahway	NJ	07065	732-381-4000		697
Atlantic American Corp 4370 Peachtree Rd NE; *NASDAQ:* AAME ■ *TF:* 800-241-1439 ■ *Web:* www.atlam.com	Atlanta	GA	30319	404-266-5500		360-4
Atlantic Automotive Corp 23 Walker Ave; *Web:* www.mileonecorporate.com	Baltimore	MD	21208	410-602-6177		57
Atlantic Aviation 17725 John F Kennedy Blvd; *TF:* 800-774-1433 ■ *Web:* www.atlanticaviation.com	Houston	TX	77032	281-443-3434		63
Atlantic Aviation Services 19711 Campus Dr Ste 100 John Wayne Airport; *TF:* 800-872-2672 ■ *Web:* www.atlanticaviation.com	Santa Ana	CA	92707	949-851-5061		63
Atlantic Battery Company Inc 309 Main St; *TF:* 800-698-5483 ■ *Web:* www.atlanticbatterycompany.com	Watertown	MA	02472	617-924-2868		74
Atlantic Bay Mortgage Group 596 Lynnhaven Pkwy Ste 102; *TF:* 866-877-3143 ■ *Web:* www.atlanticbay.com	Virginia Beach	VA	23452	757-213-1660		217
Atlantic Beverage Co 3775 Park Ave; *Web:* atlanticbeverageco.com	Edison	NJ	08820	732-548-5800		805
Atlantic Blueberry Co 7201 Weymouth Rd; *Web:* www.atlanticblueberry.com	Hammonton	NJ	08037	609-561-8600	561-5033	315-1
Atlantic British Ltd Halfmoon Light Industrial Pk 6 Enterprise Ave; *TF:* 800-533-2210 ■ *Web:* www.roverparts.com	Clifton Park	NY	12065	518-664-6169		57
Atlantic Bulk Carrier Corp PO Box 112; *TF:* 800-966-0030 ■ *Web:* www.atlanticbulk.com	Providence Forge	VA	23140	804-966-5459	966-5081	449
Atlantic Center For The Arts Inc 1414 Art Ctr Ave; *TF:* 800-393-0975 ■ *Web:* atlanticcenterforthearts.org	New Smyrna Beach	FL	32168	386-427-6975		327
Atlantic City Aquarium 800 N New Hampshire Ave; *Web:* acaquarium.com	Atlantic City	NJ	08401	609-348-2880		40
Atlantic City Bar & Grill 1219 Pacific Ave; *Web:* www.acbarandgrill.com	Atlantic City	NJ	08401	609-348-8080		671
Atlantic City City Hall 1301 Bacharach Blvd; *Web:* www.cityofatlanticcity.org	Atlantic City	NJ	08401	609-347-5300	347-6408	337
Atlantic City Convention & Visitors Authority 2314 Pacific Ave; *TF:* 888-228-4748 ■ *Web:* www.atlanticcitynj.com	Atlantic City	NJ	08401	609-348-7100		206
Atlantic City Free Public Library 1 N Tennessee Ave; *TF:* 800-621-3362 ■ *Web:* acfpl.org	Atlantic City	NJ	08401	609-345-2269	345-5570	434-3
Atlantic City International Airport (ACY) 101 Atlantic City International Airport Ste 106; *Web:* www.sjta.com	Egg Harbor Township	NJ	08234	609-645-7895		27
Atlantic City Racing Course (ACRC) 4501 Black Horse Pk; *Web:* acracecourse.com	Mays Landing	NJ	08330	609-641-2190		642
Atlantic Club, The 1904 Atlantic Ave; *Web:* www.theatlanticclub.com	Manasquan	NJ	08736	732-223-2100		354
Atlantic Coast Bank (ACFC) 505 Haines Ave; *NASDAQ:* ACFC ■ *TF:* 800-342-2824 ■ *Web:* www.atlanticcoastbank.net	Waycross	GA	31501	912-283-4711		360-2
Atlantic Concrete Products Inc 8900 Old Rt 13 PO Box 129; *Web:* www.atlanticconcrete.com	Tullytown	PA	19007	215-945-5600	946-3102	183
Atlantic Construction Fabrics Inc 2831 CaRdwell Rd; *TF:* 800-448-3636 ■ *Web:* www.acfenvironmental.com	Richmond	VA	23234	804-271-2363	743-7779	190
Atlantic Constructors Inc 1401 Battery Brooke Pkwy; *Web:* acibuilds.com	Richmond	VA	23237	804-222-3400	222-6638	189-10
Atlantic Container Line (ACL) 50 Cardinal Dr; *TF:* 800-225-1235 ■ *Web:* www.aclcargo.com	Westfield	NJ	07090	908-518-5300	518-7321	313
Atlantic Cordage Corp 35 Mileed Way; *TF:* 800-999-8489 ■ *Web:* www.atlantic-group.com	Avenel	NJ	07001	732-574-0700		492
Atlantic Corporate Interiors Inc (ACI) 7001 Muirkirk Meadows Dr Ste A; *Web:* www.aciinc.com	Beltsville	MD	20705	301-931-3600	931-3601	321
Atlantic Council of the United States 1101 15th St NW 11th Fl; *TF:* 800-311-9410 ■ *Web:* www.atlanticcouncil.org	Washington	DC	20005	202-463-7226	463-7241	634
Atlantic County 5901 E Main St; *Web:* www.aclink.org	Mays Landing	NJ	08330	609-641-7867	625-4738	338

	Phone	Fax	Class
Atlantic County Historical Society Museum 907 Shore Rd .... Somers Point NJ 08244 *Web:* www.atlantic-county.org	609-927-5218	927-5218	520
Atlantic County Library-Mays Landing 40 Farragut Ave........ Mays Landing NJ 08330 *TF:* 800-852-7899 ■ *Web:* www.atlanticlibrary.org	609-625-2776	625-8143	434-3
Atlantic Credit & Finance Inc 3353 Orange Ave .... Roanoke VA 24012 *TF:* 800-888-9419 ■ *Web:* www.atlanticcreditfinance.com	540-772-7800	772-7895	160
Atlantic Eyrie Lodge 6 Norman Rd .... Bar Harbor ME 04609 **Fax Area Code:* 207 ■ *TF:* 800-422-2883 ■ *Web:* www.atlanticeyrielodge.com	800-422-2883	288-8500*	379
Atlantic Firearms LLC 10337 Bunting Rd........ Bishopville MD 21813 *Web:* www.atlanticfirearms.com	410-352-5183	352-3374	711
Atlantic Forest Products LLC 1600 Sparrows Point .... Baltimore MD 21230 *Web:* www.atlanticforest.com	410-752-8092		690
Atlantic Gasket Corp 3908 Frankford Ave........ Philadelphia PA 19124 *TF:* 800-229-8881 ■ *Web:* www.atlanticgasket.com	215-533-6400	533-4130	326
Atlantic Health System 475 South St........ Morristown NJ 07960 *TF:* 800-247-9580 ■ *Web:* www.atlantichealth.org	973-971-5000	290-7561	374-3
Atlantic India Rubber Co 1437 Kentucky Rt 1428........ Hagerhill KY 41222 *TF:* 800-476-6638 ■ *Web:* www.atlanticindia.com	606-789-9115	789-9098	677
Atlantic Inertial Systems Inc 250 Knotter Dr .... Cheshire CT 06410 *Web:* www.atlanticinertial.com	203-250-3676		256
Atlantic Information Services Inc 1100 17th St NW Ste 300........ Washington DC 20036 *TF:* 800-521-4323 ■ *Web:* www.aishealth.com	202-775-9008	331-9542	637-9
Atlantic International University 900 Ft St Mall........ Honolulu HI 96813 *TF:* 800-993-0066 ■ *Web:* www.aiu.edu	808-924-9567		166
Atlantic Lift Truck Inc 2945 Whittington Ave........ Baltimore MD 21230 *TF:* 800-638-4566 ■ *Web:* www.atlanticlift.com	410-644-7777		385
Atlantic Mills Inc 1295 Towbin Ave .... Lakewood NJ 08701 *Web:* www.atlanticmills.com	732-363-9281		557
Atlantic Monthly Magazine 600 New Hampshire Ave NW .... Washington DC 20037 *TF Cust Svc:* 800-234-2411 ■ *Web:* www.theatlantic.com	202-266-6000		457-11
Atlantic Oakes 119 Eden St .... Bar Harbor ME 04609 *TF:* 800-356-3585 ■ *Web:* www.barharbor.com	207-288-5801		669
Atlantic Oceanographic & Meteorological Laboratory (AOML) 4301 Rickenbacker Cswy .... Miami FL 33149 *Web:* www.aoml.noaa.gov	305-361-4300	361-4449	668
Atlantic Optical Company Inc 20801 Nordhoff St .... Chatsworth CA 91311 *TF:* 800-423-5175 ■ *Web:* www.ce-tru.com	818-407-1890		543
Atlantic Packaging Co 806 N 23rd St........ Wilmington NC 28405 *TF:* 800-722-5841 ■ *Web:* www.atlanticpkg.com	910-343-0624		553
Atlantic Palace Suites Hotel 1507 Boardwalk .... Atlantic City NJ 08401 *TF:* 800-527-8483 ■ *Web:* www.atlanticpalacesuites.com	609-344-1200	345-0733	379
Atlantic Paper & Twine Co Inc 85 York Ave........ Pawtucket RI 02860 *TF:* 800-613-0950 ■ *Web:* www.atlanticpaper.com	401-725-0950		559
Atlantic Personnel Search Inc 9624 Pennsylvania Ave........ Upper Marlboro MD 20772 *TF:* 877-229-5254 ■ *Web:* www.atlanticpersonnel.com	301-599-2108		193
Atlantic Pharmaceuticals Inc 1 Glenlake Pkwy Ste 700 .... Atlanta GA 30328 *Web:* www.atlanticpharma.com	678-638-6170		743
Atlantic Premium Shutters 29797 Beck Rd .... Wixom MI 48393 *TF:* 866-288-2726 ■ *Web:* thetapcogroup.com/brands/atlantic	248-668-6408		699
Atlantic Prsnnel Tnant Scrning 8895 N Military Trl Ste 6........ Palm Beach Gardens FL 33410 *Web:* www.atlanticscreening.com	561-776-1804		196
Atlantic Publishing Co 315 E Washington St .... Starke FL 32091 **Fax Area Code:* 352 ■ *TF:* 800-814-1132 ■ *Web:* www.atlantic-pub.com	800-814-1132	622-1875*	637-2
Atlantic Realty Partners Inc 3438 Peachtree Rd........ Atlanta GA 30326 *Web:* www.goarp.com	404-591-2900		652
Atlantic Relocation Systems Inc 1314 Chattahoochee Ave NW .... Atlanta GA 30318 *TF Cust Svc:* 800-241-1140 ■ *Web:* www.atlanticrelocation.com	404-351-5311	350-6530	519
Atlantic Salmon Federation (ASF) PO Box 5200 .... Saint Andrews NB E5B3S8 *TF:* 800-565-5666 ■ *Web:* www.asf.ca	506-529-1033		48-3
Atlantic Sands Hotel 101 N Boardwalk .... Rehoboth Beach DE 19971 *TF:* 800-422-0600 ■ *Web:* www.atlanticsandshotel.com	302-227-2511		379
Atlantic Scale Co Inc 136 Washington Ave........ Nutley NJ 07110 *Web:* atlanticscale.com	973-661-7090	661-3651	361
Atlantic School of Theology 660 Francklyn St........ Halifax NS B3H3B5 *Web:* www.astheology.ns.ca	902-423-6939	492-4048	167-3
Atlantic Services Group Inc 2131 K St NW Ste 200 .... Washington DC 20037	202-466-5050	466-7194	441
Atlantic Sign Media Inc 111 Trail One ste 101........ Burlington NC 27215 *Web:* atlanticsignmedia.com	336-584-1375		701
Atlantic Skyline 4605 Brookfield Corporate Dr........ Chantilly VA 20151 *TF:* 800-326-8287 ■ *Web:* www.atlanticexhibits.com	703-802-6800		393
Atlantic Software Technologies Inc 340 Madison Ave 19th Fl .... New York NY 10173 *Web:* www.astworld.com	212-682-4160		177
Atlantic Spas & Billiards 8721 Glenwood Ave .... Raleigh NC 27617 *TF:* 800-849-8827 ■ *Web:* www.atlanticspasandbilliards.com	919-783-7447	783-0146	375
Atlantic Speakers Bureau 980 Rt 730........ Scotch Ridge NB E3L5L2 *Web:* www.atlanticspeakersbureau.com	506-465-0990		708
Atlantic Sportswear Inc 36 Waldron Way........ Portland ME 04103 *TF:* 800-941-3759 ■ *Web:* atlanticsportswearinc.com	207-797-5028		687
Atlantic Spring PO Box 650 .... Flemington NJ 08822 *TF:* 877-231-6474 ■ *Web:* www.mw-ind.com	908-788-5800	788-0511	719
Atlantic Tape Company Inc 611 Hwy 74 S Ste 300 .... Peachtree City GA 30269 *Web:* www.atlantictape.com	770-461-3557		557
Atlantic Testing Laboratories Ltd 6431 US Hwy 11........ Canton NY 13617 *Web:* www.atlantictesting.com	315-386-4578	386-1012	261
Atlantic Tire & Supply Company Inc 1430 Saint Georges Ave .... Avenel NJ 07001 *Web:* www.emcar.com	732-381-0100		57
Atlantic Tool & Die Co (ATD) 19963 Progress Dr........ Strongsville OH 44149 *Web:* www.atlantictool.com	440-238-6931		488
Atlantic Tower Group of Cos Inc 6260 Pine Slash Rd .... Mechanicsville VA 23116 *Web:* www.atlantic-tower.com	804-550-7490	559-6041	170
Atlantic Track & Turnout Co 270 N Broad St........ Bloomfield NJ 07003 *TF:* 800-631-1274 ■ *Web:* www.atlantictrack.com	973-748-5885	748-4520	770
Atlantic Trust 100 International Dr 23rd Fl .... Baltimore MD 21202 *TF:* 866-644-4144 ■ *Web:* www.cibcatlantictrust.com	202-783-4144	737-5487	401
Atlantic Union College 338 Main St .... South Lancaster MA 01561 *TF:* 800-282-2030 ■ *Web:* www.auc.edu	978-368-2000	368-2517	166
Atlantic Veal & Lamb Inc 275 Morgan Ave .... Brooklyn NY 11211 *Web:* atlanticveal.com	718-599-6400		473
Atlantic Ventilating & Equipment Co 25 Sebethe Dr........ Cromwell CT 06416	860-635-1300		697
Atlantic Webworks & Consulting Inc 331 S Swing Rd .... Greensboro NC 27409 *Web:* www.atlanticwebworks.com	336-855-8572		180
Atlantic Wildfowl Heritage Museum 1113 Atlantic Ave .... Virginia Beach VA 23451 *Web:* www.awhm.org	757-437-8432		520
Atlantic Zeiser Inc 15 Patton Dr........ West Caldwell NJ 07006 *Web:* www.atlanticzeiser.com	973-228-0800	228-9064	111
Atlantic, The 601 N Ft Lauderdale Beach Blvd........ Fort Lauderdale FL 33304 *Web:* www.atlantichotelfl.com	954-567-8020	567-8040	379
Atlantica Oak Island Resort & Conference Ctr 36 Treasure Dr PO Box 6 .... Western Shore NS B0J3M0 *TF:* 800-565-5075 ■ *Web:* www.atlanticaoakisland.com	902-627-2600	627-2020	669
Atlanticare Regional Medical Ctr 1925 Pacific Ave........ Atlantic City NJ 08401 *Web:* atlanticare.org	609-344-4081		374-3
Atlantic-Pacific Capital Inc 102 Greenwich Ave 2nd Fl .... Greenwich CT 06830 *Web:* www.apcap.com	203-862-9182		401
Atlantis Casino Resort 3800 S Virginia St .... Reno NV 89502 *TF:* 800-723-6500 ■ *Web:* www.atlantiscasino.com	775-825-4700		669
Atlantis Energy Systems Inc 4517 Industry St........ Poughkeepsie NY 12603 *Web:* www.atlantisenergy.com	916-438-2930		357
Atlantis Restaurant 3648 King St .... Alexandria VA 22302 *Web:* alexandriaitalianfood.com	703-671-0250		671
Atlantis Seafood Steakhouse 3800 S Virginia St Atlantis Casino Resort........ Reno NV 89502 **Fax Area Code:* 775 ■ *TF:* 800-723-6500 ■ *Web:* www.atlantiscasino.com	800-723-6500	827-1518*	671
Atlantix Global Systems 1 Sun Ct........ Norcross GA 30092 *TF:* 877-552-8526 ■ *Web:* www.atlantixglobal.com	770-248-7700	448-7726	174
Atlas Advertising LLC 1128 Grant St .... Denver CO 80203 *TF:* 800-543-4402 ■ *Web:* www.atlas-advertising.com	303-292-3300		7
Atlas Advisors LLC 140 E 45th St 18th Fl .... New York NY 10017 *Web:* www.atlasadvisors.com	212-471-4100		690
Atlas Air Worldwide Holdings Inc 2000 Westchester Ave........ Purchase NY 10577 *NASDAQ: AAWW* ■ *TF:* 866-434-1617 ■ *Web:* www.atlasair.com	914-701-8000	701-8001	12
Atlas Aircraft Center 115 Flight Line Ave........ Portsmouth NH 03801 *Web:* www.planesense.com	603-501-7700		23
Atlas Bistro 2515 N Scottsdale Rd Ste 18 .... Scottsdale AZ 85257 *Web:* www.azeats.com	480-990-2433		671
Atlas Bolt & Screw Co 1628 Troy Rd........ Ashland OH 44805 *TF:* 800-321-6977 ■ *Web:* www.atlasfasteners.com	419-289-6171	289-2564	278
Atlas Bronze 445 Bunting Ave........ Trenton NJ 08611 *TF:* 800-478-0887 ■ *Web:* www.atlasbronze.com	609-599-1402		492
Atlas Brown Investment Advisors Inc 333 E Main St - 400........ Louisville KY 40202 *TF:* 866-871-0334 ■ *Web:* www.atlasbrown.com	502-271-2900		194
Atlas Butler Heating & Cooling 4849 Evanswood Dr........ Columbus OH 43229 **Fax Area Code:* 800 ■ *Web:* www.atlasbutler.com	614-294-8600	387-6223*	610
Atlas Carpet Mills Inc 2200 Saybrook Ave........ Los Angeles CA 90040 *TF:* 800-272-8527 ■ *Web:* www.atlascarpetmills.com	323-724-9000	724-4526	131
Atlas Companies, The 5101 Commerce Crossing Dr........ Louisville KY 40229 *TF:* 800-225-5752 ■ *Web:* www.atlas-co.com	502-779-2100		111
Atlas Concrete Products 65 Burritt St .... New Britain CT 06053 *TF:* 800-774-1112 ■ *Web:* www.atlasconcrete.com	860-224-2244	224-2255	360-3
Atlas Construction Group 8218 E 121st St S........ Bixby OK 74008 *Web:* www.atlasgc.com	918-369-3910		186
Atlas Construction Supply Inc 4640 Brinnell St .... San Diego CA 92111 *TF:* 877-588-2100 ■ *Web:* www.atlasform.com	858-277-2100	277-0585	191-1
Atlas Container Corp 8140 Telegraph Rd........ Severn MD 21144 *TF:* 800-394-4894 ■ *Web:* www.atlascontainer.com	410-551-6300	551-2703	100

Company	City	State	ZIP	Phone	Fax	Class
Atlas Copco Comptec LLC 46 School Rd *Web:* www.atlascopco.us	Voorheesville	NY	12186	518-765-3344		172
Atlas Copco North America LLC 7 Campus Dr Ste 200 *TF:* 800-732-6762 ■ *Web:* www.atlascopco.us	Parsippany	NJ	07054	973-397-3400		360-3
Atlas Copco Tools & Assembly Systems 3301 Cross Creek Pkwy *TF:* 800-859-3746 ■ *Web:* atlascopco.com/us/tools/us	Auburn Hills	MI	48326	248-373-3000	373-3001	759
Atlas Cylinder Corp 500 S Wolf Rd *TF:* 800-892-1008 ■ *Web:* parker.com	Des Plaines	IL	60016	847-298-2400	294-2655	223
Atlas Distributing Corp 44 Southbridge St *TF:* 800-649-6221 ■ *Web:* www.atlasdistributing.com	Auburn	MA	01501	508-791-6221		81-1
Atlas Environmental Services Inc 9032 Olive Dr *TF:* 800-909-8733 ■ *Web:* www.atlastree.com	Spring Valley	CA	91977	619-463-1707		776
Atlas Foundry Company Inc 601 N Henderson Ave *Web:* www.atlasfdry.com	Marion	IN	46952	765-662-2525	662-2902	307
Atlas Global Bistro 3111 Woodward Ave	Detroit	MI	48201	313-831-2241		671
Atlas Heating & Ventilating Company 407 Cabot St *Web:* www.atlasheat.com	South San Francisco	CA	94080	650-873-7000		612
Atlas Industrial Holdings LLC 5275 Sinclair Rd *Web:* www.atlascos.com	Columbus	OH	43229	614-841-4500		207
Atlas Legal Research Lp 14241 Dallas Pkwy Ste 650 *Web:* www.atlaslegal.com	Dallas	TX	75254	214-526-8811		428
Atlas Machine & Supply Inc 7000 Global Dr *Web:* www.atlasmachine.com	Louisville	KY	40258	502-584-7262		454
Atlas Machining & Welding Inc 777 Smith Ln *Web:* www.atlasmw.com	Northampton	PA	18067	610-262-1374		757
Atlas Match LLC 1801 S Airport Cir *TF:* 800-628-2426 ■ *Web:* www.atlasmatch.com	Euless	TX	76040	817-354-7474		9
Atlas Metal Industries 1135 NW 159th Dr *TF Cust Svc:* 800-762-7565 ■ *Web:* www.atlasfoodserv.com	Miami	FL	33169	305-625-2451	623-0475	298
Atlas Mfg 2950 Weeks Ave SE *TF:* 800-245-6440 ■ *Web:* www.atlasmfg.com	Minneapolis	MN	55414	612-331-2566	331-1295	697
Atlas Minerals & Chemicals Inc 1227 Valley Rd *TF Cust Svc:* 800-523-8269 ■ *Web:* www.atlasmin.com	Mertztown	PA	19539	610-682-7171	682-9200	3
Atlas Model Railroad Company Inc 378 Florence Ave *TF Orders:* 800-872-2521 ■ *Web:* www.atlasrr.com	Hillside	NJ	07205	908-687-0880	687-8857	762
Atlas Oil Co 24501 Ecorse Rd *TF:* 800-878-2000 ■ *Web:* www.atlasoil.com	Taylor	MI	48180	313-292-5500	731-0264	579
Atlas Pacific Engineering Co 1 Atlas Ave *TF:* 800-588-5438 ■ *Web:* www.atlaspacific.com	Pueblo	CO	81001	719-948-3040		298
Atlas Paper Mills LLC 3301 NW 107th St *TF:* 800-562-2860 ■ *Web:* www.atlaspapermills.com	Miami	FL	33167	305-636-5740		558
Atlas Performing Arts Center 1333 H St NE *Web:* atlasarts.org	Washington	DC	20002	202-399-7993		708
Atlas Railroad Construction LLC 1370 Washington Pike Ste 202 **Fax Area Code:* 585 ■ *TF:* 800-324-6625 ■ *Web:* gwrr.com	Bridgeville	PA	15017	412-677-2020	785-6206*	188-8
Atlas Refinery Inc 142 Lockwood St *Web:* www.atlasrefinery.com	Newark	NJ	07105	973-589-2002	589-7377	145
Atlas Roofing Corp 2322 Valley Rd *TF Cust Svc:* 800-478-0258 ■ *Web:* www.atlasroofing.com	Meridian	MS	39307	601-483-7111	483-7344	40
Atlas Roofing Falcon Foam Div 8240 Byron Ctr Rd SW **Fax Area Code:* 616 ■ *TF:* 800-917-9138 ■ *Web:* atlaseps.com	Byron Center	MI	49315	800-917-9138	878-9942*	600
Atlas Scientific Technologies Inc 2430 University Blvd W *Web:* www.atlasscitech.com	Jacksonville	FL	32217	904-731-0241		194
Atlas Sheet Metal Inc 19 Musick *Web:* atlassheetmetal.com	Irvine	CA	92618	949-600-8787		610
Atlas Sound 1601 Jack McKay Blvd **Fax Area Code:* 800 ■ *TF:* 800-876-3333 ■ *Web:* www.atlasied.com	Ennis	TX	75119	972-875-8413	765-3435*	52
Atlas Steel Products Co 7990 Bavaria Rd *TF:* 800-444-1682 ■ *Web:* www.atlassteel.com	Twinsburg	OH	44087	330-425-1600	425-1611	492
Atlas Systems Inc 5712 Cleveland St Ste 200 *TF:* 800-567-7401 ■ *Web:* www.atlas-sys.com	Virginia Beach	VA	23462	757-467-7872		177
Atlas Technologies Inc 3100 Cotter Ave *Web:* www.atlastechnologies.com	Fenton	MI	48430	810-629-6663	629-8145	456
Atlas Testing Laboratories Inc 9820 Sixth St *TF:* 800-832-8677 ■ *Web:* www.atlastesting.com	Rancho Cucamonga	CA	91730	909-373-4130		743
Atlas Tool Inc 29880 Groesbeck Hwy *TF:* 800-375-8181 ■ *Web:* www.atlastool.com	Roseville	MI	48066	586-778-3570	778-3931	757
Atlas Travel International Inc 1 Maple St Ste 3 *TF:* 800-362-8626 ■ *Web:* www.atlastravel.com	Milford	MA	01757	508-478-8626		775
Atlas Tube 1855 E 122nd St *TF:* 800-733-5683 ■ *Web:* www.atlastube.com	Chicago	IL	60633	773-646-4500	646-6128	490
Atlas Tubular LP 1710 S Hwy 77 *Web:* www.atlastubular.com	Robstown	TX	78380	361-387-7505	387-4613	490
Atlas Van Lines Inc 1212 St George Rd **Fax:* Cust Svc ■ *TF:* 800-638-9797 ■ *Web:* www.atlasvanlines.com	Evansville	IN	47711	812-424-2222	421-7129*	519
Atlas Water Systems Inc 301 Second Ave *TF:* 888-877-0561 ■ *Web:* atlaswater.com	Waltham	MA	02451	781-373-4700		806
Atlas Welding & Boiler Repair Inc 2373 Tiebout Ave	Bronx	NY	10458	718-365-6600		189-10
Atlas World Group Inc 1212 St George Rd *TF:* 800-252-8885 ■ *Web:* www.atlasvanlines.com	Evansville	IN	47711	812-424-2222	421-7129	360-3
AtlasBanc Holdings Corp 301 S Missouri Ave *Web:* www.atlasbanc.com	Clearwater	FL	33756	727-446-6660		691
AtlasPower Inc 10 Futurity Pl *Web:* www.atlaspower.com	Tijeras	NM	87059	505-286-9625		261
Atlatl Inc 3000 Croasdaile Dr *Web:* sehhey.com	Durham	NC	27705	919-384-0514		177
ATLSS (Advanced Technology for Large Structural Systems Ctr) 117 ATLSS Dr *Web:* www.atlss.lehigh.edu	Bethlehem	PA	18015	610-758-3525	758-5902	668
Atlus USA Inc 199 Technology Dr *Web:* www.atlus.com	Irvine	CA	92618	949-788-0455		553
Atm Merchant Systems 1667 Helm Dr *TF:* 888-878-8166 ■ *Web:* www.atmms.com	Las Vegas	NV	89119	702-837-8787		69
ATMA (American Textile Machinery Assn) 201 Pk Washington Ct *TF:* 800-225-4324 ■ *Web:* www.atmanet.org	Falls Church	VA	22046	703-538-1789		49-13
Atmac Mechanical Services LP 1201 Summit Ave *Web:* www.atmac.com	Plano	TX	75074	214-428-1544		189-10
Atmel Corp 2325 Orchard Pkwy *NASDAQ: ATML* ■ *TF:* 800-579-1639 ■ *Web:* www.atmel.com	San Jose	CA	95131	408-441-0311	436-4200	696
Atmos Energy Corp 5430 LBJ Fwy Ste 1800 *NYSE: ATO* ■ *TF:* 888-286-6700 ■ *Web:* www.atmosenergy.com	Dallas	TX	75240	972-934-9227		360-5
Atmos Tech Industries LLC 1108 Pollack Ave *TF:* 800-452-8510 ■ *Web:* www.atmostech.com	Ocean	NJ	07712	732-493-8400		186
Atmosphere 1620 Piedmont Ave *Web:* www.atmospherebistro.com	Atlanta	GA	30324	678-702-1620		671
ATN (Asian Television Network) 330 Cochrane Dr *Web:* www.asiantelevision.com	Markham	ON	L3R8E4	905-948-8199	948-8108	740
AT-NET Services Inc 9625-D Southern Pine Blvd *Web:* www.expertip.net	Charlotte	NC	29273	704-831-2500		396
AtNetPlus Inc 1000 Campus Dr Ste 700 *Web:* www.atnetplus.com	Stow	OH	44224	330-945-5685		225
ATO (Alpha Tau Omega Fraternity) 1 N Pennsylvania St 12th Fl *TF:* 800-798-9286 ■ *Web:* www.ato.org	Indianapolis	IN	46204	317-684-1865	684-1862	48-16
Atoka County PO Box 900 *Web:* atokaok.org	Atoka	OK	74525	580-889-3341	889-7584	338
Atom Group LLC, The 33 Jewell Ct Ste 6 *Web:* www.theatomgroup.com	Portsmouth	NH	03801	603-501-0003		226
Atomic Aquatics Inc 16742 Burke Ln *Web:* atomicaquatics.com	Huntington Beach	CA	92647	714-375-1433		711
Atomic Cartoons Inc 112 W Sixth Sve *Web:* www.atomiccartoons.com	Vancouver	BC	V5Y1K6	604-734-2866		33
Atomic Design 277 Alexander St Ste 208 *Web:* www.atomicdesign.net	Rochester	NY	14607	585-271-8661		195
Atomic Direct LLC 1219 SE Lafayette St *TF:* 800-722-3590 ■ *Web:* atomicdirect.com	Portland	OR	97202	503-296-6131		7
Atomic Object LLC 941 Wealthy St SE *Web:* www.atomicobject.com	Grand Rapids	MI	49506	616-776-6020		177
Atomic Testing Museum 755 E Flamingo Rd *Web:* www.nationalatomictestingmuseum.org	Las Vegas	NV	89119	702-794-5151	794-5155	520
Atomic USA 2030 Lincoln Ave **Fax Area Code:* 801 ■ *TF:* 800-258-5020 ■ *Web:* www.atomic.com	Ogden	UT	84401	800-258-5020	334-4503*	710
AtomicLeads.com 4926 Windy Hill Dr *Web:* www.atomicleads.com	Raleigh	NC	27609	919-439-4900		195
Atom-Jet Industries Ltd 2110 Park Ave *TF:* 800-573-5048 ■ *Web:* atomjet.com	Brandon	MB	R7B0R9	204-728-8590		273
Atossa Genetics Inc 2345 Eastlake Ave E Ste 201 *Web:* www.atossagenetics.com	Seattle	WA	98102	206-588-0256		582
Atotech USA Inc 1750 Overview Dr *Web:* www.atotech.com/en	Rock Hill	SC	29730	803-817-3500	817-3666	253
AtoZdatabases com PO Box 27757 *TF:* 877-428-0101 ■ *Web:* www.atozdatabases.com	Omaha	NE	68127	877-428-0101		393
Atp Electronics Inc 750 N Mary Ave *Web:* www.atpinc.com	Sunnyvale	CA	94085	408-732-5000	732-5055	173-8
ATP Oil & Gas Corp 4600 Post Oak Pl Ste 200 *OTC: ATPAQ*	Houston	TX	77027	713-622-3311		536
ATP Tour Inc 201 ATP Tour Blvd *Web:* www.atpworldtour.com	Ponte Vedra Beach	FL	32082	904-285-8000	285-5966	48-22
ATPCO (Airline Tariff Publishing Co) 45005 Aviation Dr *Web:* www.atpco.net	Dulles	VA	20166	703-471-7510		16
ATP-USA Mfg LLC 600 Putnam Pike Ste 8	Greenville	RI	02858	401-767-3100		301
ATR (Americans for Tax Reform) 722 12th St NW Ste 4 *Web:* www.atr.org	Washington	DC	20005	202-785-0266	785-0261	48-8
Atr Inc 6405 Cypresswood Dr Ste 250 *Web:* www.atrco.com	Spring	TX	77379	281-370-9540		809
ATRA (Automatic Transmission Rebuilders Assn) 2400 Latigo Ave *TF:* 866-464-2872 ■ *Web:* www.atra.com	Oxnard	CA	93030	805-604-2000	604-2003	49-21
ATRA (American Therapeutic Recreation Assn) 629 N Main St *TF:* 800-433-5255 ■ *Web:* www.atra-online.com	Hattiesburg	MS	39401	601-450-2872	582-3354	48-17
ATRA (American Tort Reform Assn) 1101 Connecticut Ave NW Ste 400 *Web:* www.atra.org	Washington	DC	20036	202-682-1163	682-1022	49-10
ATRAHAN Transformation Inc 860 Chemin Des Acadiens *TF:* 800-995-2274 ■ *Web:* www.atrahan.com	Yamachiche	QC	G0X3L0	819-296-3791		473
Atrenne Integrated Solutionsÿ 9210 Science Ctr Dr *Web:* www.abelconn.com	New Hope	MN	55428	763-533-3533	536-0349	625
Atrex Inc 175 Industrial Loop S *TF:* 800-874-4505 ■ *Web:* www.atrexinc.com	Orange Park	FL	32073	904-264-9086		647
Atria 137 Main St PO Box 561 *Web:* www.atriamv.com	Edgartown	MA	02539	508-627-5850		671

Company	City	State	Zip	Phone	Fax	Class
Atria Campana del Rio 1550 E River Rd *Web:* www.atriaseniorliving.com	Tucson	AZ	85718	520-445-4447		672
Atria Chandler Villas 101 S Yucca St *Web:* www.atriaseniorliving.com	Chandler	AZ	85224	480-899-7650		672
Atria Meridian Assisted Living Community 3061 Donnelly Dr *Web:* www.atriaseniorliving.com	Lantana	FL	33462	561-902-1085		672
Atria Rancho Park 801 Cypress Way *Web:* atriaranchopark.com	San Dimas	CA	91773	626-275-4376		672
Atria Senior Living Group 300 E Market St Ste 100 *Web:* www.atriaseniorliving.com	Louisville	KY	40202	502-779-4700		451
AtriCure Inc 6217 Centre Pk Dr *NASDAQ: ATRC* ■ *TF:* 888-347-6403 ■ *Web:* www.atricure.com	West Chester	OH	45069	513-755-4100	755-4567	85
Atrilogy Solutions Group Inc 1 Jenner Ste 240 *Web:* www.atrilogy.com	Irvine	CA	92618	949-777-4700	777-4777	463
Atrion Corp 1 Allentown Pkwy *NASDAQ: ATRI* ■ *TF:* 800-627-0226 ■ *Web:* www.atrioncorp.com	Allen	TX	75002	972-390-9800	396-7581	476
Atrion Medical Products Inc 1426 Curt Francis Rd *Web:* www.atrionmedical.com	Arab	AL	35016	256-586-1580		596
Atris Inc 1151 S Trooper Rd Ste E *TF:* 800-724-3384 ■ *Web:* www.atris.biz	Norristown	PA	19403	800-724-3384		735
Atrium Cos Inc 3890 W NW Hwy Ste 500 *TF:* 800-938-1000 ■ *Web:* atrium.com	Dallas	TX	75220	214-630-5757		234
Atrium Holding Co 6900 E Camelback Rd Ste 607	Scottsdale	AZ	85251	480-222-6035		379
Atrium Hotel 18700 MacArthur Blvd *TF:* 800-854-3012 ■ *Web:* www.atriumhotel.com	Irvine	CA	92612	949-833-2770		379
Atrium Medical Corp 5 Wentworth Dr *TF:* 800-528-7486 ■ *Web:* www.atriummed.com	Hudson	NH	03051	603-880-1433	880-6718	476
Atrium Medical Ctr 1 Medical Ctr Dr *TF:* 800-338-4057 ■ *Web:* www.atriummedcenter.org	Middletown	OH	45005	513-424-2111		374-3
Atrium Staffing Services Ltd 71 Fifth Ave 3rd Fl *Web:* www.atriumstaff.com	New York	NY	10003	212-292-0550		260
ATS (American Thoracic Society) 61 Broadway 4th Fl *TF:* 866-316-2673 ■ *Web:* www.thoracic.org	New York	NY	10006	212-315-8600	315-6498	49-8
ATS (Association of Theological Schools in the US & Canada) 10 Summit Pk Dr *TF:* 800-621-7440 ■ *Web:* www.ats.edu	Pittsburgh	PA	15275	412-788-6505	788-6510	49-5
Ats All Tire Supply Co 6600 Long Point Rd Ste 101 *TF:* 888-339-6665 ■ *Web:* www.alltiresupply.com	Houston	TX	77055	888-339-6665		54
ATS Group LLC 1200 Atwater Dr Ste 170 *TF:* 800-237-8274 ■ *Web:* www.theatsgroup.com	Malvern	PA	19355	484-320-4302		196
ATS Systems Inc 30222 Esperanza *TF:* 800-321-1833 ■ *Web:* www.ats-s.com	Rancho Santa Margarita	CA	92688	949-888-1744		697
Ats Systems Oregon Inc 2121 NE Jack London St *TF:* 800-564-6253 ■ *Web:* www.atsautomation.com	Corvallis	OR	97330	541-758-3329		386
Ats Tech Solutions Inc 2550 Limestone Pky Ste F *TF:* 800-433-5778 ■ *Web:* www.atstech.net	Gainesville	GA	30501	770-538-2900		175
ATS Tours 300 Continental Blvd Ste 350 *TF:* 888-410-5770 ■ *Web:* travel2-us.com	El Segundo	CA	90245	888-410-5770		760
Atsco ReMfg Inc 4525 N 43rd Ave *Web:* www.atscoreman.com	Phoenix	AZ	85031	623-842-4047		61
Atscott Manufacturing Company Inc 1150 Holstein Dr NE *TF:* 800-362-3550 ■ *Web:* www.atscott.com	Pine City	MN	55063	320-629-2501		757
At-sea Processors Assn (APA) 4039 21st Ave W Ste 400 *Web:* www.atsea.org	Seattle	WA	98199	206-285-5139	285-1841	49-6
ATSI Inc 415 Commerce Dr *Web:* atsi.com	Amherst	NY	14228	716-691-9200		261
Atsim Inc 1825 George Ave Ste 1F	Annapolis	MD	21401	410-990-1711		261
ATSSA (American Traffic Safety Services Assn) 15 Riverside Pkwy Ste 100 *TF:* 800-272-8772 ■ *Web:* www.atssa.com	Fredericksburg	VA	22406	540-368-1701	368-1717	49-21
AT&T Ctr 1 AT&T Ctr Pkwy *TF Resv:* 800-745-3000 ■ *Web:* www.attcenter.com	San Antonio	TX	78219	210-444-5000		720
ATT Metrology Services Inc 30210 SE 79th St Ste 100 *TF:* 888-320-7011 ■ *Web:* www.attinc.com	Issaquah	WA	98027	425 867 5356		23
Attac Consulting Group 301 E Liberty St Ste 605 *Web:* attacconsulting.com	Ann Arbor	MI	48104	734-214-2990		196
Attachments International Inc 9 Industrial Park Dr *Web:* www.attachments.com	Pelican Rapids	MN	56572	218-863-6444		190
Attala County 230 W Washington St *Web:* attalacounty.net	Kosciusko	MS	39090	662-289-2921	289-7662	338
Attc Manufacturing Inc 10455 State Rd 37 *Web:* www.attcmanufacturing.com	Tell City	IN	47586	812-547-5060		247
Attema Sales Inc 117 E 13th St *Web:* www.attemamarketing.com	Pella	IA	50219	641-628-1787		195
Attendee Management Inc 15572 Ranch Rd 12 Ste 1 *TF:* 877-947-5174 ■ *Web:* attendeenet.com	Wimberley	TX	78676	512-847-5174		624
Attention Software Inc 2175 N Academy Cir Ste 100 *Web:* www.attentionsoftware.com	Colorado Springs	CO	80909	719-591-9110		180
Attentus Medical Sales Inc 5750 N Sam Houston Pkwy E Ste 406 *Web:* www.attentusmedical.com	Houston	TX	77032	281-776-5188		475
Attic Technologies Inc 1199 Amboy Ave Tano Professional Bldg *Web:* www.attictechnologies.com	Edison	NJ	08837	732-767-0660		94
Attic, The 3441 E Broadway *Web:* theatticonbroadway.com	Long Beach	CA	90803	562-433-0153		671
Attica Correctional Facility 639 Exchange St PO Box 149 *Web:* www.doccs.ny.gov/faclist.html	Attica	NY	14011	585-591-2000		213
Attica Hydraulic Exchange Inc 48175 Gratiot Ave *TF:* 800-422-4279 ■ *Web:* www.ahx1.com	Chesterfield	MI	48051	586-949-4240		358
AtticSalt Greetings Inc PO Box 5773 **Fax Area Code: 866* ■ *TF:* 888-345-6005 ■ *Web:* www.atticsaltgreetings.com	Topeka	KS	66605	888-345-6005	333-0225*	130
Attitude Measurement Corp 721 Arbor Way Ste 190 *TF:* 800-222-1577 ■ *Web:* www.amcglobal.com	Blue Bell	PA	19422	610-238-9200		466
Attleboro Public Library 74 N Main St *Web:* www.sailsinc.org	Attleboro	MA	02703	508-222-0157	226-3326	434-3
Attodyne Inc 1 Westside Dr Unit 6 *TF:* 800-656-6381 ■ *Web:* www.attodynelasers.com	Toronto	ON	M9C1B2	416-840-9096		757
Attorney Aid Divorce & Bankruptcy Center Inc 3605 Long Beach Blvd Ste 300 *TF:* 877-905-5297 ■ *Web:* www.attorneyaid.com	Long Beach	CA	90807	562-988-0885		428
Attorney General 102 W Water St *Web:* attorneygeneral.delaware.gov	Dover	DE	19904	302-739-4211		428
Attorney Resource 3300 Oak Lawn Ave Ste 510 *Web:* www.attorneyresource.com	Dallas	TX	75219	214-922-8050	871-3041	721
Attorney's Title Insurance Fund Inc 6545 Corporate Ctr Blvd *TF:* 800-336-3863 ■ *Web:* thefund.com	Orlando	FL	32822	407-240-3863	240-0750	391-6
Attorneys at Law Vandeventer Black LLP 8 Juniper Trl *Web:* www.vanblk.com	Kitty Hawk	NC	27949	252-261-5055		445
Attraction Inc 672 Rue du Parc *TF:* 800-567-6095 ■ *Web:* www.attraction.com	Lac-Drolet	QC	G0Y1C0	819-549-2477	549-2734	155-3
Attraction Media Inc 5455 de Gaspe Ave Ste 805 *Web:* www.attraction.ca	Montreal	QC	H2T3B3	514-846-1222		514
Attronica Computers Inc 15867 Gaither Dr *Web:* www.attronica.com	Gaithersburg	MD	20877	301-417-0070		180
Attune Foods Inc 900 Kearny St Ste 600 *Web:* www.attunefoods.com	San Francisco	CA	94133	415-486-2101		296-25
Attunity Inc 70 BlanchaRd Rd **Fax Area Code: 877* ■ *TF:* 866-288-8648 ■ *Web:* www.attunity.com	Burlington	MA	01803	781-730-4070	896-2760*	178-1
Attwood Corp 1016 N Monroe St *TF:* 844-808-5704 ■ *Web:* www.attwoodmarine.com	Lowell	MI	49331	616-897-9241	897-8358	350
ATU (Amalgamated Transit Union) 10000 New Hampshire Ave *TF:* 888-240-1196 ■ *Web:* www.atu.org	Silver Spring	MD	20903	202-537-1645	244-7824	414
ATW (American Trails West) 92 Middle Neck Rd *TF:* 800-645-6260 ■ *Web:* www.atwteentours.com	Great Neck	NY	11021	516-487-2800	487-2855	760
ATW Companies Inc 55 Service Ave *TF:* 800-226-3553 ■ *Web:* www.atwcompanies.com	Warwick	RI	02886	401-244-1002		492
Atwater Brewing Co 237 Joseph Campau Ave *Web:* atwaterbeer.com	Detroit	MI	48207	313-877-9205		671
Atwater Chamber of Commerce 1181 Third St *TF:* 844-269-9688 ■ *Web:* atwaterchamberofcommerce.com	Atwater	CA	95301	209-358-4251		139
Atwater Kent Museum 15 S Seventh St *Web:* www.philadelphiahistory.org	Philadelphia	PA	19106	215-685-4830	685-4837	520
Atwood & Cherny PC 101 Huntington Ave 25th Fl *TF:* 800-973-1177 ■ *Web:* www.atwoodcherny.com	Boston	MA	02199	617-262-6400		41
Atwood Cafe 1 W Washington St *Web:* atwoodrestaurant.com	Chicago	IL	60602	312-368-1900		671
Atwood Mobile Products 1120 N Main St *TF:* 800-546-8759 ■ *Web:* www.atwoodmobile.com	Elkhart	IN	46514	574-264-2131		60
Atwood Oceanics Inc 15011 Katy Fwy Ste 800 *NYSE: ATW* ■ *Web:* www.atwd.com	Houston	TX	77094	281-749-7800		540
Atwoods Distributing Inc 5400 Owen K Garriott *Web:* www.atwoods.com	Enid	OK	73703	580-233-3702		293
ATX Networks Corp 1-501 Clements Rd W *TF:* 800-565-7488 ■ *Web:* www.atxnetworks.com	Ajax	ON	L1S7H4	905-428-6068		647
At-your-service Software Inc 450 Bronxville Rd *Web:* www.ayssoftware.com	Bronxville	NY	10708	914-337-9030		177
aTyr Pharma Inc 3545 General Atomics Ct Ste 250 *Web:* www.atyrpharma.com	San Diego	CA	92121	858-731-8389		668
Atzl Scatassa & Zigler Land Surveyors & Engineers PC 234 N Main St	New City	NY	10956	845-634-4694		727
AU& A (Alan Utz & Associates Inc) PO Box 131857 *Web:* www.auainc.com	Tyler	TX	75713	903-566-9797	566-9393	186
Au Authum Ki Inc 4645 S Ash Ave Ste I1	Tempe	AZ	85282	480-497-1997	377-1143	685
Au Bon Pain 19 Fid Kennedy Ave *TF:* 800-825-5227 ■ *Web:* www.aubonpain.com	Boston	MA	02210	617-423-2100	423-7879	68
Au Naturel Wellness & Medical Spa at the Brookstreet Hotel 525 Legget Dr *TF:* 888-826-2220 ■ *Web:* www.brookstreethotel.com	Ottawa	ON	K2K2W2	613-271-1800		707
Au Petit Coin Breton 1029 Rue Saint-Jean *Web:* aupetitcoinbreton.com	Quebec	QC	G1R1R6	418-694-0758		671
Au Ptit Marche De Notre Dame 552 Rue Notre Dame	Bon-Conseil	QC	J0C1A0	819-336-2686		297-8
Au Sable Woodworking Company 6677 Frederic St PO Box 108	Frederic	MI	49733	989-348-7086		777
AUA (American Urological Assn) 1000 Corporate Blvd *TF:* 866-746-4282 ■ *Web:* www.auanet.org	Linthicum	MD	21090	410-689-3700	689-3800	49-8
Auberge Bonaparte 447 St-francois-xavier *Web:* www.bonaparte.com	Montreal	QC	H2Y2T1	514-844-1448		377

Phone | Fax | Class

Auberge De La Fontaine b & b Inn
1301 Rue Rachel E .... Montreal QC H2J2K1 514-597-0166 707
TF: 800-597-0597 ■ *Web:* www.aubergedelafontaine.com

Auberge du Soleil
180 Rutherford Hill Rd .... Rutherford CA 94573 707-963-1211 963-8764 379
TF: 800-348-5406 ■ *Web:* aubergedusoleil.aubergeresorts.com

Auberge du Tresor 20 Rue Sainte-Anne .... Quebec QC G1R3X2 418-694-1876 694-0563 671
TF: 800-566-1876 ■ *Web:* www.aubergedutresor.com

Auberge du Vieux-Port
97 Rue de la Commune E .... Montreal QC H2Y1J1 514-876-0081 876-8923 379
TF: 888-660-7678 ■ *Web:* www.aubergeduvieuxport.com

Auberge et spa Le Nordik Inc
16 ch Nordik .... Old Chelsea QC J9B2P7 819-827-1111 354
TF: 866-575-3700 ■ *Web:* www.lenordik.com

Auberge Resorts LLC
591 Redwood Hwy Ste 3150 .... Mill Valley CA 94941 415-380-3460 378
Web: www.aubergeresorts.com

Auberge Saint-Antoine
8 rue Saint-Antoine .... Quebec QC G1K4C9 418-692-2211 692-1177 379
TF: 888-692-2211 ■ *Web:* www.saint-antoine.com

Aubrey Silvey Enterprises Inc
371 Hamp Jones Rd .... Carrollton GA 30117 770-834-0738 834-1055 188-10
Web: www.silvey.com

Auburn Area Chamber of Commerce
1103 High St .... Auburn CA 95603 530-885-5616 885-5854 139
Web: www.auburnchamber.net

Auburn Area Chamber of Commerce
25 Second St NW .... Auburn WA 98001 253-833-0700 735-4091 139
TF: 800-395-0144 ■ *Web:* www.auburnareawa.org

Auburn Career Ctr 8140 Auburn Rd .... Painesville OH 44077 440-357-7542 507
TF: 800-954-8742 ■ *Web:* www.auburncc.org

Auburn Chamber of Commerce
714 E Glenn Ave .... Auburn AL 36830 334-887-7011 821-5500 139
Web: www.auburnchamber.com

Auburn City School District
PO Box 3270 .... Auburn AL 36831 334-887-2100 887-2107 685
TF: 866-632-9992 ■ *Web:* www.auburnschools.org

Auburn Cord Duesenberg Museum
1600 S Wayne St .... Auburn IN 46706 260-925-1444 925-6266 520
TF: 800-745-3000 ■ *Web:* www.automobilemuseum.org

Auburn Corp 10490 164th Pl .... Orland Park IL 60467 708-349-7676 191-3
TF: 800-393-1826 ■ *Web:* www.auburncorp.com

Auburn Correctional Facility
135 State St PO Box 618 .... Auburn NY 13021 315-253-8401 213
Web: www.doccs.ny.gov/faclist.html

Auburn Gear Inc 400 E Auburn Dr .... Auburn IN 46706 260-925-3200 925-4725 709
Web: www.auburngear.com

Auburn Journal Inc 1030 High St .... Auburn CA 95603 530-885-5656 532-3
TF: 800-284-3233 ■ *Web:* www.auburnjournal.com

Auburn Leather Co 125 N Caldwell St .... Auburn KY 42206 270-542-4116 542-7107 431
TF: 800-635-0617 ■ *Web:* www.auburnleather.com

Auburn Manor 501 Oak St N .... Chaska MN 55318 952-448-9303 371
Web: www.auburnhomes.org

Auburn Manufacturing Co
29 Stack St .... Middletown CT 06457 860-346-6677 346-1334 326
TF: 800-427-5387 ■ *Web:* www.auburn-mfg.com

Auburn Memorial Hospital 17 Lansing St .... Auburn NY 13021 315-255-7011 255-7382 374-3
Web: www.auburnhospital.org

Auburn Public Library 49 Spring St .... Auburn ME 04210 207-333-6640 333-6644 434-3
Web: www.auburnpubliclibrary.org

Auburn Public Library 749 E Thach Ave .... Auburn AL 36830 334-501-3190 434-3
TF: 800-888-2726 ■ *Web:* www.auburnalabama.org

Auburn Publishers Inc 25 Dill St .... Auburn NY 13021 315-253-5311 253-6031 637-8
TF: 800-878-5311 ■ *Web:* www.auburnpub.com

Auburn Regional Medical Ctr
202 N Div St .... Auburn WA 98001 253-833-7711 697-7293 374-3
TF: 866-268-7223 ■ *Web:* www.multicare.org

Auburn State Recreation Area
501 El Dorado St .... Auburn CA 95603 530-885-4527 565
Web: www.parks.ca.gov/default.asp?page_id=502

Auburn Supply Co 3850 W 167th St .... Markham IL 60428 708-596-9800 596-0981 612
Web: www.auburnsupply.com

Auburn Systems LLC 8 Electronics Ave .... Danvers MA 01923 978-777-2460 201
TF: 800-255-5008 ■ *Web:* www.auburnsys.com

Auburn Union School District
255 Epperle Ln .... Auburn CA 95603 530-885-7242 885-5170 685
Web: www.auburn.k12.ca.us

Auburn University
202 Mary Martin Hall .... Auburn University AL 36849 334-844-6425 844-6436* 166
**Fax:* Admissions ■ *TF Admissions:* 866-389-6770 ■ *Web:* www.auburn.edu
Montgomery 7440 E Dr .... Montgomery AL 36117 334-244-3000 244-3795 166
TF: 800-227-2649 ■ *Web:* www.aum.edu
Ralph Brown Draughon Library
231 Mell St .... Auburn University AL 36849 334-844-4500 434-6
Web: www.lib.auburn.edu

Auburn Vacuum Forming Company Inc
40 York St .... Auburn NY 13021 315-253-2440 596
Web: www.avfco.com

Auburn-Opelika Tourism Bureau
714 E Glenn Ave .... Auburn AL 36830 334-887-8747 821-5500 206
TF: 866-880-8747 ■ *Web:* www.aotourism.com

AUCD (Association of University Centers on Disabilities)
1100 Wayne Ave Ste 1000 .... Silver Spring MD 20910 301-588-8252 588-2842 49-5
TF: 888-572-2249 ■ *Web:* www.aucd.org

Aucoin & Associates Inc
433 N C C Duson St .... Eunice LA 70535 337-457-7366 256

Aucoin-Hart 1525 Metairie Rd .... Metairie LA 70005 504-834-9999 410
TF: 800-992-8743 ■ *Web:* aucoinhart.com

Audability Inc
5915 Airport Rd Ste 700 .... Mississauga ON L4V1T1 416-915-1301 387
Web: www.audability.com

Audax Labs 101 Huntington Ave .... Boston MA 02199 617-859-1500 194
Web: www.audaxgroup.com

Audcomp Computer Systems
611 Tradewind Dr Ste 100 .... Ancaster ON L9G4V5 905-304-1775 179
Web: www.audcomp.com

Audi of America 3800 Hamlin Rd .... Auburn Hills MI 48326 888-237-2834 59
TF: 888-237-2834 ■ *Web:* www.audiusa.com

Phone | Fax | Class

Audible Inc 1 Washington Pk .... Newark NJ 07102 973-820-0400 395
TF: 888-283-5051 ■ *Web:* www.audible.com

Audience Communication Inc
174 Spadina Rd Ste 101 .... Toronto ON M5T2C2 416-703-3737 224
TF: 800-249-4656 ■ *Web:* www.audienceinc.ca

Audience Partners LLC
414 Commerce Dr Ste 100 .... Fort Washington PA 19034 484-928-1010 366
Web: www.audiencepartners.com

AudienceScience Inc
1120 112th Ave NE Ste 400 .... Bellevue WA 98004 425-201-3900 171
Web: www.audiencescience.com

Audient Inc 20532 Crescent Bay Dr .... Lake Forest CA 92630 949-830-9412 256

Audio Acoustics Inc
800 N Cedarbrook Ave .... Springfield MO 65802 417-869-0770 246
Web: www.aaius.com

Audio Advisor 3427 Kraft Ave SE .... Grand Rapids MI 49512 616-254-8870 254-8875 194
TF: 800-942-0220 ■ *Web:* www.audioadvisor.com

Audio America Inc
15132 Park Of Commerce Blvd Ste 100 .... Jupiter FL 33478 561-863-7704 52
Web: www.audioamerica.com

Audio Authority Corp 2048 Mercer Rd .... Lexington KY 40511 859-233-4599 387
TF: 800-322-8346 ■ *Web:* www.audioauthority.com

Audio Command Systems 694 Main St .... Westbury NY 11590 516-997-5800 997-2195 52
TF: 800-382-2939 ■ *Web:* www.audiocommand.com

Audio Direct
2004 E Irvington Rd Ste 264 .... Tucson AZ 85714 888-628-3467 35
TF Cust Svc: 888-628-3467 ■ *Web:* www.audio-direct.com

Audio Engineering Society
60 E 42nd St Rm 2520 .... New York NY 10165 212-661-8528 682-0477 49-19
TF: 800-541-7299 ■ *Web:* www.aes.org

Audio General Inc (AGI)
1680 Republic Rd .... Huntingdon Valley PA 19006 267-288-0300 288-0301 514
TF: 866-866-2600 ■ *Web:* www.audiogeneral.com

Audio Research Corp
3900 Annapolis Ln N .... Plymouth MN 55447 763-577-9700 577-0323 52
Web: www.audioresearch.com

Audio Video Systems Inc
14566 Lee Rd .... Chantilly VA 20151 703-263-1002 263-0722 514
Web: www.avsinc.net

Audio Visual Dynamics
424 Sand Shore Rd .... Hackettstown NJ 07840 973-993-8500 194
Web: avdusa.com

AudioCodes Inc 27 World'S Fair Dr .... Somerset NJ 08873 732-469-0880 729
Web: audiocodes.com

Audio-Digest Foundation
1577 E Chevy Chase Dr .... Glendale CA 91206 818-240-7500 240-7379 766
TF: 800-423-2308 ■ *Web:* www.audio-digest.org

Audiokinetic Inc
409 St-Nicolas St Ste 300 .... Montreal QC H2Y2P4 514-499-9100 225
Web: www.audiokinetic.com

AudioQuest Inc 2621 White Rd .... Irvine CA 92614 949-585-0111 253
TF: 800-747-2770 ■ *Web:* www.audioquest.com

Audiosears Corp 2 S St .... Stamford NY 12167 607-652-7305 652-3653 52
TF: 800-533-7863 ■ *Web:* www.audiosears.com

Audio-technica Us Inc 1221 Commerce Dr .... Stow OH 44224 330-686-2600 688-3752 246
TF: 800-667-3745 ■ *Web:* www.audio-technica.com

Audio-Video Corp 213 Broadway .... Albany NY 12204 518-449-7213 449-1205 52
Web: www.audiovideocorp.com

Audiovox Corp 180 Marcus Blvd .... Hauppauge NY 11788 631-231-7750 52
NASDAQ: VOXX ■ *TF:* 800-645-4994 ■ *Web:* www.voxxintl.com

Audit & Adjustment Company Inc
20700 44th Ave W Ste 100 .... Lynnwood WA 98036 425-776-9797 535
TF: 800-526-1074 ■ *Web:* www.audit-adjustment.com

Audit Bureau of Circulations (ABC)
48 W Seegers Rd .... Arlington Heights IL 60005 224-366-6939 605-0483* 49-18
**Fax Area Code:* 847 ■ *TF:* 800-759-6397 ■ *Web:* www.auditedmedia.com

Audit Group Inc, The
16141 Swingley Ridge Rd Ste 310 .... Chesterfield MO 63017 636-536-6333 463
Web: theauditgroup.com

Audit Integrity Inc
11111 Santa Monica Blvd Ste 220 .... Los Angeles CA 90025 310-444-8820 194

Audit Logistics LLC
1172 W Century Dr Ste 245 .... Louisville CO 80027 303-951-9000 2
Web: www.auditlogistics.com

Audit Technology Group
1850 W Winchester Rd .... Libertyville IL 60048 847-281-8703 734
Web: www.atgaudits.com

Auditorium Theatre 50 E Congress Pkwy .... Chicago IL 60605 312-341-2310 572
TF: 800-982-2787 ■ *Web:* www.auditoriumtheatre.org

Audits & Systems Inc C/O
464 Central Rd .... Northfield IL 60093 847-446-5244 734

Audrain County
101 N Jefferson St Rm 101 .... Mexico MO 65265 573-473-5820 581-2380 338
TF: 800-392-0815 ■ *Web:* www.audraincounty.org

Audubon County 318 Leroy St Ste 6 .... Audubon IA 50025 712-563-4275 338
Web: www.iowacourts.gov

Audubon House & Tropical Garden
250 Whitehead St .... Key West FL 33040 305-294-2116 520
TF: 800-428-3826 ■ *Web:* www.audubonhouse.com

Audubon Magazine 225 Varick St 7th Fl .... New York NY 10014 212-979-3000 477-9069 457-19
TF Cust Svc: 800-274-4201 ■ *Web:* www.audubon.org

Audubon Metals LLC 3055 Ohio Dr .... Henderson KY 42420 270-830-6622 485
Web: www.audubonmetals.com

Audubon Naturalist Society
8940 Jones Mill Rd .... Chevy Chase MD 20815 301-652-9188 951-7179 48-13
TF: 888-744-4723 ■ *Web:* www.audubonnaturalist.org

Audubon Nature Institute
6500 Magazine St .... New Orleans LA 70118 504-581-4629 823
TF: 800-774-7394 ■ *Web:* audubonnatureinstitute.org

Auer Precision Inc 1050 W Birchwood Ave .... Mesa AZ 85210 480-834-4637 621
Web: www.auerprecision.com

Auer Steel & Heating Supply Co
2935 W Silver Spring Dr .... Milwaukee WI 53209 414-463-1234 463-0303 14
TF: 800-242-0406 ■ *Web:* www.auersteel.com

Auerbach Grayson & Company LLC
25 W 45th St .... New York NY 10036 212-557-4444 690
Web: agco.com

Auerr Zajac & Assoc LLP 29 Dean Ave .... Franklin MA 02038 508-528-1305 2
Web: auerr-zajaccpa.com

Name / Address	Phone	Fax	Class
Augenblick & Company Pc 368 W Bridge St .... New Hope PA 18938 *Web:* augenblickpc.com	215-862-9153		528
Augeo Affinity Marketing Inc 2561 Territorial Rd .... St. Paul MN 55114 *Web:* www.augeomarketing.com	651-917-9143		195
Augie Leopold Adv Specialties Inc 3214 Roman St .... Metairie LA 70001 *Web:* augieleopold.com	504-836-0525		4
Augie's Front Burner 109 S Fifth St .... Springfield IL 62701 *TF:* 800-545-7300 ■ *Web:* www.augiesfrontburner.com	217-544-6979		671
Auglaize & Mercer Counties Convention & Visitors Bureau 900 Edgewater Dr .... Saint Marys OH 45885 *TF:* 800-860-4726 ■ *Web:* www.seemore.org	419-394-1294		206
Auglaize County 209 S Blackhoof St Ste 201 .... Wapakoneta OH 45895 *TF:* 877-836-3206 ■ *Web:* www.auglaizecounty.org	419-739-6710		338
Augmentum Inc 1065 E Hillsdale Blvd Ste 413 .... Foster City CA 94404 *Web:* augmentum.com	650-578-9221		225
Augsburg College 2211 Riverside Ave .... Minneapolis MN 55454 *TF:* 800-788-5678 ■ *Web:* www.augsburg.edu	612-330-1000	330-1590	166
Augsburg Fortress 510 Marquette Ave Ste 800 .... Minneapolis MN 55402 **Fax Area Code:* 800 ■ *TF:* 800-328-4648 ■ *Web:* www.augsburgfortress.org	612-330-3300	722-7766*	637-3
August 301 Tchoupitoulas St .... New Orleans LA 70130 *Web:* www.restaurantaugust.com	504-299-9777		671
August Arace & Sons Inc 642 Third Ave .... Elizabeth NJ 07202	908-354-1626		189-10
August Capital 2480 Sand Hill Rd Ste 101 .... Menlo Park CA 94025 *Web:* www.augustcap.com	650-234-9900	234-9910	792
August Inc 354 Congress Park Dr .... Centerville OH 45459 *TF:* 800-318-5242 ■ *Web:* www.augustinc.com	937-434-2520		321
August Lang & Husak Inc 4630 Montgomery Ave Ste 400 .... Bethesda MD 20814 *Web:* www.alhadv.com	301-657-2772		7
August Law Group PC 19200 Von Karman Ste 900 .... Irvine CA 92612 *Web:* www.augustlawgroup.com	949-752-7772		41
August Mack Environmental Inc 1302 N Meridian St Ste 300 .... Indianapolis IN 46202 *Web:* www.augustmack.com	317-916-8000		194
August Moon 2269 Lexington Rd .... Louisville KY 40206 *Web:* www.augustmoonbistro.com	502-456-6569		671
August Moon Chinese Restaurant 1300 S Milton Rd .... Flagstaff AZ 86001 *TF:* 800-847-6020 ■ *Web:* augustmoonflagstaff.com	928-774-5280		671
August Schell Brewing Co 1860 Schell Rd .... New Ulm MN 56073 *Web:* www.schellsbrewery.com	507-354-5528		298
August Wilson 245 W 52nd St .... New York NY 10019 *Web:* www.telecharge.com	212-239-6200		747
August Winter & Sons Inc 2323 N Roemer Rd .... Appleton WI 54911 *TF:* 800-236-8882 ■ *Web:* www.augustwinter.com	920-739-8881	739-2230	189-13
Augusta Ballet Inc 1301 Greene St .... Augusta GA 30901 *Web:* www.augustaballet.org	706-261-0555		573-1
Augusta Chronicle 725 Broad St .... Augusta GA 30901 **Fax:* News Rm ■ *TF:* 866-249-8223 ■ *Web:* chronicle.augusta.com	706-724-0851	722-7403*	532-2
Augusta Chronicle, The 725 Broad St .... Augusta GA 30901 *Web:* www.augustachronicle.com	706-722-5620		532-3
Augusta Civic Ctr 16 Cony St .... Augusta ME 04330 *Web:* www.augustamaine.gov	207-626-2405		205
Augusta Correctional Ctr 1821 Estaline Valley Rd .... Craigsville VA 24430 *Web:* vadoc.virginia.gov	540-997-7000		213
Augusta County 18 Government Center Ln .... Verona VA 24482 *Web:* www.co.augusta.va.us	540-245-5600	245-5621	338
Augusta County Library 1759 Jefferson Hwy .... Fishersville VA 22939 *Web:* www.augustacountylibrary.org	540-885-3961		434-3
Augusta Fiberglass Coatings Inc 86 Lake Cynthia Rd .... Blackville SC 29817 *Web:* www.augustafiberglass.com	803-284-2246		596
Augusta Flooring Inc 202 Bobby Jones Expy .... Martinez GA 30907 *Web:* augustafloor.com	706-650-0400		290
Augusta (GA) Municipal Hall 535 Telfair St .... Augusta GA 30901 *Web:* www.augustaga.gov	706-821-2300	826-4790	337
Augusta Grill 1818 Augusta Rd .... Greenville SC 29605 *Web:* www.augustagrill.com	864-242-0316		671
Augusta Mall 3450 Wrightsboro Rd .... Augusta GA 30909 *Web:* www.augustamall.com	706-731-8850		460
Augusta Medical Ctr (AMC) 78 Medical Ctr Dr PO Box 1000 .... Fishersville VA 22939 *TF:* 800-932-0262 ■ *Web:* www.augustahealth.com	540-932-4000		374-3
Augusta Metro Chamber of Commerce 1 Tenth St Ste 120 .... Augusta GA 30901 *TF:* 888-639-8188 ■ *Web:* augustametrochamber.com	706-821-1300	821-1330	139
Augusta Metropolitan Convention & Visitors Bureau 1450 Greene St Ste 560 .... Augusta GA 30901 *TF:* 800-726-0243 ■ *Web:* visitaugusta.com	706-823-6600	823-6609	206
Augusta Museum of History 560 Reynolds St .... Augusta GA 30901 *Web:* www.augustamuseum.org	706-722-8454	724-5192	520
Augusta National Inc 2604 Washington Rd .... Augusta GA 30904 *Web:* masters.com	706-667-6000		360-3
Augusta Opera 1215 Troupe St .... Augusta GA 30904	706-364-9114		573-2
Augusta Players, The 1301 Greene St Ste 304 PO Box 2352 .... Augusta GA 30901 *TF:* 800-968-4332 ■ *Web:* augustaplayers.org	706-826-4707		573-4
Augusta Regional Airport - Bush Field (AGS) 1501 Aviation Way .... Augusta GA 30906 *TF:* 866-289-9673 ■ *Web:* flyags.com	706-798-3236	798-1551	27

Name / Address	Phone	Fax	Class
Augusta State Airport 16 Cony St .... Augusta ME 04330 *Web:* www.augustamaine.gov	207-626-2306		27
Augusta State University 2500 Walton Way .... Augusta GA 30904 *TF:* 800-341-4373 ■ *Web:* www.augusta.edu	706-737-1632	667-4355	166
Augusta Technical College 3200 Augusta Tech Dr .... Augusta GA 30906 **Fax:* Admissions ■ *Web:* www.augustatech.edu	706-771-4000	771-4034*	800
Augustana College 639 38th St .... Rock Island IL 61201 **Fax:* Admissions ■ *TF:* 800-798-8100 ■ *Web:* www.augustana.edu	309-794-7000	794-7174*	166
Augustana College 2001 S Summit Ave .... Sioux Falls SD 57197 **Fax:* Admissions ■ *TF:* 800-727-2844 ■ *Web:* www.augie.edu	605-274-0770	274-5518*	166
Augusta-Richmond County 535 Telfair St .... Augusta GA 30901 *Web:* www.augustaga.gov	706-821-2300	826-4790	338
Augusta-Richmond County Library 823 Telfair St .... Augusta GA 30901 *Web:* arcpls.org	706-821-2600	724-6762	434-3
Augustine 532 Gibson Dr Ste 250 .... Roseville CA 95678 *Web:* www.augustineideas.com	916-774-9600		7
Augustine Casino 84-001 Ave 54 .... Coachella CA 92236 *TF:* 888-752-9294 ■ *Web:* www.augustinecasino.com	760-391-9500		133
Augustus C Long Health Sciences Library Columbia University Medical Ctr 701 W 168th St .... New York NY 10032 *Web:* library.cumc.columbia.edu	212-305-3605		434-1
AUHSB (Anaheim Union High School District) 501 N Crescent Way .... Anaheim CA 92801 **Fax:* Admin ■ *Web:* www.auhsd.us	714-999-3511	520-9752*	685
Aui Contractors LLC 4775 N Fwy .... Fort Worth TX 76106 *Web:* www.auipartners.com	817-926-4377	926-4387	187
Auld & White Constructors LLC 4168 Southpoint Pkwy Ste 101 .... Jacksonville FL 32216 *TF:* 800-795-1747 ■ *Web:* www.auld-white.com	904-296-2555		186
Aulick Leasing Corp 305 Ninth Ave PO Box 1369 .... Scottsbluff NE 69361 *Web:* www.aulickleasing.com	308-220-4000		126
Aultman Hospital 2600 Sixth St SW .... Canton OH 44710 *Web:* www.aultman.org	330-452-9911		374-3
Aumtech Inc 710 Old Bridge Tpke .... East Brunswick NJ 08816 *TF:* 800-439-4815 ■ *Web:* aumtech.com	732-254-1875		180
Aunt Chilada's Easy Street Cafe 69 Pope Ave .... Hilton Head Island SC 29928 *Web:* auntchiladashhi.com	843-785-7700		671
Aunt Emma's 700 E St .... Chula Vista CA 91910 *Web:* www.auntemmaspancakes.com	619-427-2722		671
Auntie Pasto's Restuarant 1099 S Beretania St .... Honolulu HI 96814 *Web:* www.auntiepastos.com	808-523-8855		671
AUPHA (Association of University Programs in Health Administration) 2000 N 14th St Ste 780 .... Arlington VA 22201 *TF:* 877-275-6462 ■ *Web:* www.aupha.org	703-894-0941	894-0941	49-8
AURA (Association of Universities for Research in Astronomy) 1200 New York Ave NW Ste 350 .... Washington DC 20005 *TF:* 888-624-8373 ■ *Web:* www.aura-astronomy.org	202-483-2101	483-2106	49-5
Aura Advance Technologies Inc 1742 Tenth Ave SW .... Calgary AB T3C0J8 *Web:* auraadvanced.com	403-269-6123		175
Aura Systems Inc 1310 E Grand Ave .... El Segundo CA 90245 *OTC:* AUSI ■ *TF:* 800-909-2872 ■ *Web:* www.aurasystems.com	310-643-5300	643-7457	518
Auraria Higher Education Ctr 1068 Ninth St Pk .... Denver CO 80204 *Web:* www.ahec.edu	303-556-2400		166
Aurelia Osborn Fox Memorial Hospital 1 Norton Ave .... Oneonta NY 13820 *Web:* www.bassett.org	607-432-2000		374-3
Aurelio's Pizza 18162 Harwood Ave .... Homewood IL 60430 *Web:* www.aureliospizza.com	708-798-8050		670
Aurelius Capital Management LP 535 Madison Ave 22nd Fl .... New York NY 10022 *Web:* www.aurelius-capital.com	646-445-6500		528
Aureole 3950 Las Vegas Blvd S .... Las Vegas NV 89119 *Web:* www.charliepalmer.com	702-632-7401		671
Aureole 135 W 42nd St .... New York NY 10036 *TF:* 800-889-7188 ■ *Web:* www.charliepalmer.com	212-319-1660		671
Auric Systems International 85 Grove St .... Peterborough NH 03458 *Web:* www.auricsystems.com	603-924-6079		253
Aurico Reports Inc 116 W Eastman St .... Arlington Heights IL 60004 *TF:* 866-255-1852 ■ *Web:* www.aurico.com	866-255-1852		400
Auritt Communications 555 Eigth Ave Rm 709 .... New York NY 10018 *Web:* auritt.com	212-302-6230		514
Aurora Area Convention & Visitors Bureau 43 W Galena Blvd .... Aurora IL 60506 *TF:* 800-477-4369 ■ *Web:* www.enjoyaurora.com	630-897-5581		206
Aurora Aviation 22785 Airport Rd NE .... Aurora OR 97002 *TF:* 800-760-0924 ■ *Web:* www.auroraaviation.com	503-678-1217	678-1219	63
Aurora Bearing Co 901 Aucutt Rd .... Montgomery IL 60538 *Web:* www.aurorabearing.com	630-859-2030		75
Aurora Blacktop Inc 1065 Sard Ave .... Montgomery IL 60538	630-892-9389		189-3
Aurora Chamber of Commerce 14305 E Alameda Ave Ste 300 .... Aurora CO 80012 *Web:* www.aurorachamber.org	303-344-1500	344-1564	139
Aurora Chamber of Commerce 43 W Galena Blvd .... Aurora IL 60506 *TF:* 866-947-8081 ■ *Web:* www.aurorachamber.com	630-256-3180	256-3189	139
Aurora Chamber of Commerce 14483 Yonge St .... Aurora ON L4G0P3 *Web:* www.aurorachamber.on.ca	905-727-7262	841-6217	137
Aurora City Hall 15151 E Alameda Pkwy .... Aurora CO 80012 *TF:* 800-895-4999 ■ *Web:* www.auroragov.org	303-739-7015	739-7594	337
Aurora Computer Technology Inc 6 Schubert St .... Staten Island NY 10305 *TF:* 800-541-6519 ■ *Web:* auroracomputer.com	718-981-2363		180

Listing	Phone	Fax	Class
Aurora Contractors Inc 100 Raynor Ave. Ronkonkoma NY 11779 *TF:* 866-423-2197 ■ *Web:* www.auroracontractors.com	631-981-3785		610
Aurora Co-op Elevator Co 605 12th St PO Box 209 Aurora NE 68818 *TF:* 800-642-6795 ■ *Web:* www.auroracoop.com	402-694-2106	694-6943	275
Aurora Cord & Cable Co 325 S Union St. Aurora IL 60505 *Web:* www.auroracord.com	630-851-1616	851-1626	438
Aurora Corp of America 3500 Challenger St. Torrance CA 90503 *TF:* 800-327-8508 ■ *Web:* www.auroracorp.com	310-793-5650		534
Aurora County 401 N Main St PO Box 366 Plankinton SD 57368 *Web:* ujs.sd.gov	605-942-7165	942-7170	338
Aurora Diagnostics LLC 11025 RCA Ctr Dr Ste 300 Palm Beach Gardens FL 33410 *Web:* www.auroradx.com	561-626-5512		415
Aurora Flight Sciences Corp 9950 Wakeman Dr Manassas VA 20110 *Web:* www.aurora.aero	703-369-3633		22
Aurora Fox Arts Ctr 9900 E Colfax Ave. Aurora CO 80010 *TF:* 800-250-2525 ■ *Web:* www.aurorafoxartscenter.org	303-739-1970	739-1975	572
Aurora Funds 3100 Tower Blvd Durham NC 27707 *Web:* www.aurorafunds.com	919-484-0400		792
Aurora Health Care Inc 750 W Virginia St PO Box 341880 Milwaukee WI 53234 *Web:* www.aurorahealthcare.org	414-647-3000	649-7982	353
Aurora History Museum 15051 E Alameda Pkwy Aurora CO 80012 *Web:* www.auroragov.org	303-739-6660	739-6657	520
Aurora Instruments Ltd 1001 E Pender St Vancouver BC V6A1W2 *Web:* www.aurorabiomed.com	604-215-8700		111
Aurora Investment Management LLC 300 N LaSalle St 52nd Fl Chicago IL 60654 *Web:* www.aurorallc.com	312-762-6700		401
Aurora Lakeland Medical Ctr (ALMC) W3985 County Rd NN Elkhorn WI 53121 *Web:* www.aurorahealthcare.org	262-741-2000		374-3
Aurora Las Encinas Hospital 2900 E Del Mar Blvd. Pasadena CA 91107 *TF:* 800-792-2345 ■ *Web:* www.lasencinashospital.com	626-795-9901	792-2919	374-5
Aurora Metals Divison LLC 1995 Greenfield Ave Montgomery IL 60538 *Web:* www.aurorametals.com	630-844-4900	844-6839	308
Aurora National Life Assurance Co PO Box 4490 Hartford CT 06147 **Fax Area Code:* 803 ■ *TF:* 800-265-2652 ■ *Web:* www.auroralife.com	800-265-2652	333-2311*	391-2
Aurora Networks Inc 5400 Betsy Ross Dr Santa Clara CA 95054 *TF:* 866-362-7747 ■ *Web:* www.aurora.com	408-235-7000		735
Aurora Organic Dairy Corp 1919 14th St Ste 300 Boulder CO 80302 *Web:* www.auroraorganic.com	720-564-6296		296-25
Aurora Packing Company Inc 125 S Grant St North Aurora IL 60542 *Web:* aurorabeef.com	630-897-0551		297-9
Aurora Pictures Inc 5249 Chicago Ave. Minneapolis MN 55417 *TF:* 800-346-9487 ■ *Web:* www.aurorapictures.com	612-821-6490		514
Aurora Public Library 101 S River St. Aurora IL 60506 *Web:* www.aurora.lib.il.us	630-264-4100	896-3209	434-3
Aurora Public Library 14949 E Alameda Pkwy Aurora CO 80014 *Web:* www.odyssey.aurora.lib.co.us	303-739-6600	739-6586	434-3
Aurora Reservoir 5800 S Powhaton Rd Aurora CO 80016 *TF:* 800-583-2137 ■ *Web:* www.auroragov.org	303-690-1286		50-5
Aurora Sentinel 14305 E Alameda Ave Ste 200 Aurora CO 80012 *TF:* 855-269-4484 ■ *Web:* www.aurorasentinel.com	303-750-7555	750-7699	532-4
Aurora Sinai Medical Ctr 945 N 12th St Milwaukee WI 53201 *TF:* 888-863-5502 ■ *Web:* www.aurorahealthcare.org	414-219-2000		374-3
Aurora Symphony Orchestra PO Box 441481 Aurora CO 80044 *Web:* www.aurorasymphony.org	303-873-6622		573-3
Aurora Systems Consulting Inc 2510 W 237th St Ste 202 Torrance CA 90505 *TF:* 888-282-0696 ■ *Web:* www.aurorait.com	888-282-0696		463
Aurora Textile Finishing Co 911 N Lake St PO Box 70 Aurora IL 60507 *TF:* 800-864-0303 ■ *Web:* www.auroratextile.com	630-892-7651		745-7
Aurora University 347 S Gladstone Ave Aurora IL 60506 *TF:* 800-742-5281 ■ *Web:* www.aurora.edu	630-844-5533		166
Aurora VNA Zilber Family Hospice 1155 N Honey Creek Pkwy Wauwatosa WI 53213 *TF:* 888-206-6955 ■ *Web:* www.aurorahealthcare.org	414-615-5900		371
Aurora Worldwide Development Corp 2810 Crossroads Dr Ste 3100 Madison WI 53718 *Web:* www.aurorawdc.com	608-268-3470		463
Auroros Inc 8420 Honeycutt Rd Ste 200 Raleigh NC 27615 *Web:* www.aurorosinc.com	919-841-0553	841-0299	194
Aurotech Inc 6909 Timber Creek Ct Clarksville MD 21029 *Web:* www.aurotechcorp.com	301-854-1326		194
Aurum Ceramic Dental Laboratories Ltd 115 17 Ave SW Calgary AB T2S0A1 *TF:* 800-665-8815 ■ *Web:* www.aurumgroup.com	403-228-5120		418
Auryn Inc 6033 W Century Blvd Ste 808 Los Angeles CA 90045	310-649-4278		514
AUS Inc 155 Gaither Dr Mount Laurel NJ 08054 *Web:* ausinc.com	856-234-9200		360-3
AUSA (Association of the US Army) 2425 Wilson Blvd Arlington VA 22201 *TF:* 800-336-4570 ■ *Web:* www.ausa.org	703-841-4300	525-9039	48-19
Ausco Products Inc 2245 Pipestone Rd Benton Harbor MI 49022 *Web:* www.auscoproducts.com	269-926-0700		247
Ausdal Financial Partners 220 N Main St Ste 400 Davenport IA 52801 *Web:* www.ausdal.com	563-326-2064		690
Ausland Builders Inc 3935 Highland Ave Grants Pass OR 97526 *Web:* auslandgroup.com	541-476-3788		186
Ausley McMullen 123 S Calhoun St. Tallahassee FL 32302 *Web:* ausley.com	850-224-9115		428
Austad's Golf 2801 E Tenth St Sioux Falls SD 57103 *TF Cust Svc:* 800-444-1234 ■ *Web:* www.austads.com	605-331-4653		711
Austal USA LLC 100 Addsco Rd. Mobile AL 36602 *Web:* www.austal.com	251-434-8000		698
AustarPharma LLC 300 Columbus Cir Unit F Ste F Edison NJ 08837 *Web:* www.austarpharma.com	732-225-8850		582
Aus-Tex Printing & Mailing 2431 Forbes Dr. Austin TX 78754 *TF:* 800-472-7581 ■ *Web:* www.austex.com	512-476-7581		627
Austin & Williams 125 Kennedy Dr Ste 100 Hauppauge NY 11788 *Web:* www.austin-williams.com	631-231-6600		7
Austin Aerotech Repair Services Inc 2005 Windy Terr Cedar Park TX 78613 *Web:* www.austinaerotech.com	512-335-6000		246
Austin American-Statesman 305 S Congress Ave Austin TX 78704 *TF:* 800-445-9898 ■ *Web:* www.statesman.com	512-445-4040	445-3679	532-2
Austin Associates LLC 7205 W Central Ave Toledo OH 43617 *Web:* www.austinassociates.com	419-841-8521		401
Austin Bridge & Road Inc 6330 Commerce Dr Ste 150 Irving TX 75063 *Web:* www.austin-ind.com	214-596-7300		188-4
Austin Business Journal 111 Congress Ave Ste 750 Austin TX 78701 **Fax:* Edit ■ *TF:* 800-687-1747 ■ *Web:* www.bizjournals.com	512-494-2500	494-2525*	457-5
Austin Business Printing 404 W Powell Ln Austin TX 78753 *TF:* 800-305-6368 ■ *Web:* www.abpcreative.com	512-836-6902		627
Austin Chamber Music Ctr 3814 Medical Pkwy Austin TX 78756 *Web:* www.austinchambermusic.org	512-454-7562	454-0029	573-3
Austin Chamber of Commerce 535 E Fifth St Austin TX 78701 *Web:* www.austinchamber.com	512-478-9383	478-9615	139
Austin Chemical Company Inc 1565 Barclay Blvd. Buffalo Grove IL 60089 *Web:* www.austinchemical.com	847-520-9600		146
Austin Children's Museum 201 Colorado St Austin TX 78701 *Web:* thinkeryaustin.org	512-472-2499		521
Austin Chronicle PO Box 4189 Austin TX 78765 *Web:* www.austinchronicle.com	512-454-5766	458-6910	532-5
Austin City Hall PO Box 1088 Austin TX 78767 *TF:* 800-591-6474 ■ *Web:* www.austintexas.gov	512-974-2000		337
Austin Civic Orchestra PO Box 27132 Austin TX 78755 *TF:* 800-460-0610 ■ *Web:* www.austincivicorchestra.org	512-200-2261		573-3
Austin Co 6095 Parkland Blvd Cleveland OH 44124 *Web:* www.theaustin.com	440-544-2600		186
Austin College 900 N Grand Ave. Sherman TX 75090 **Fax:* Admissions ■ *TF:* 800-526-4276 ■ *Web:* www.austincollege.edu	903-813-3000	813-3197*	166
Austin Commercial Inc 3535 Travis Ste 300 Dallas TX 75204 *Web:* www.austin-ind.com	214-443-5700		186
Austin Community College (ACC) 5930 Middle Fiskville Rd Austin TX 78752 **Fax:* Admissions ■ *TF:* 877-442-3522 ■ *Web:* www.austincc.edu	512-223-7000	223-7665*	162
Cypress Creek 5930 Middle Fiskville Rd. Austin TX 78752 *TF:* 800-561-3357 ■ *Web:* www.austincc.edu	512-223-4222	223-2048	162
Eastview 3401 Webberville Rd. Austin TX 78702 **Fax:* Admissions ■ *TF:* 888-626-1697 ■ *Web:* austincc.edu/locations/campuses/eastview-campus	512-223-5100	223-5900*	162
Northridge 11928 Stonehollow Dr. Austin TX 78758 *TF:* 888-626-1697 ■ *Web:* austincc.edu/locations/campuses/northridge-campus	512-223-4000		162
Pinnacle 7748 Hwy 290 W. Austin TX 78736 *TF:* 888-626-1697 ■ *Web:* austincc.edu/locations/campuses/pinnacle-campus	512-223-8001	223-8122	162
Rio Grande 1212 Rio Grande Austin TX 78701 *TF:* 888-626-1697 ■ *Web:* austincc.edu/locations/campuses/rio-grande-campus	512-223-3000		162
Riverside 1020 Grove Blvd Austin TX 78741 **Fax:* Admissions ■ *TF:* 888-626-1697 ■ *Web:* austincc.edu/locations/campuses/riverside-campus	512-223-6000	223-6767*	162
Austin Convention & Visitors Bureau 301 Congress Ave Ste 200 Austin TX 78701 *TF:* 800-926-2282 ■ *Web:* www.austintexas.org	512-474-5171	583-7282	206
Austin Convention Ctr 500 E Cesar Chavez St Austin TX 78701 *TF:* 800-282-3388 ■ *Web:* www.austinconventioncenter.com	512-404-4000	404-4416	205
Austin County 1 E Main St. Bellville TX 77418 *Web:* www.austincounty.com	979-865-5911	865-8786	338
Austin Creek State Recreation Area 17000 Armstrong Woods Rd. Guerneville CA 95446 *Web:* www.parks.ca.gov/default.asp?page_id=452	707-869-2015		565
Austin Daily Herald Inc 310 NE Second St. Austin MN 55912 *Web:* www.austindailyherald.com	507-433-8851	437-8644	637-8
Austin Davis & Mitchell Attorneys at Law 109 Cherry St Dunlap TN 37327 *Web:* austindavismitchell.com	423-949-4159		428
Austin Elementary School 1900 Duncan St Pampa TX 79065 *Web:* www.pampaisd.net	806-669-4760		685
Austin Enviro Group 6802 Manzanita St. Austin TX 78759 *TF:* 800-564-0362 ■ *Web:* www.aegaustin.com	512-913-0077		226
Austin Exploration Inc 10333 Westoffice Dr Houston TX 77042 *Web:* austinex.com	713-780-7141	780-3118	727

Phone | Fax | Class

Austin Film Festival
1801 Salina St Ste 210 . . . Austin TX 78702 — 512-478-4795 — 478-6205 — 282
TF: 800-310-3378 ■ *Web:* www.austinfilmfestival.com

Austin Graduate School of Theology
7640 Guadalupe St . . . Austin TX 78752 — 512-476-2772 — 476-3919 — 166
TF: 866-287-4723 ■ *Web:* www.austingrad.edu

Austin Graphics Inc
1198 Second Ave E . . . Owen Sound ON N4K2J1 — 519-376-2116 — 344
TF: 800-265-6964 ■ *Web:* www.austingraphics.ca

Austin Industrial Inc
2801 E 13th S PO Box 87888 . . . La Porte TX 77571 — 713-641-3400 — 641-2424 — 188-9
TF: 866-308-2592 ■ *Web:* www.austin-ind.com

Austin Industries Inc
3535 Travis St Ste 300 . . . Dallas TX 75204 — 214-443-5500 — 360-3
Web: www.austin-ind.com

Austin Jewish Academy 7300 Hart Ln . . . Austin TX 78731 — 512-735-8350 — 685
Web: www.austinjewishacademy.org

Austin Land & Cattle Co
1205 N Lamar Blvd . . . Austin TX 78703 — 512-472-1813 — 671
Web: alcsteaks.com

Austin Museum of Art Downtown
700 Congress Ave . . . Austin TX 78701 — 512-453-5312 — 520
TF: 800-432-7136 ■ *Web:* thecontemporaryaustin.org

Austin Museum of Art Laguna Gloria
3809 W 35th St . . . Austin TX 78703 — 512-458-8191 — 520
Web: thecontemporaryaustin.org

Austin Opera
3009 Industrial Terr Ste 100 . . . Austin TX 78758 — 512-472-5927 — 573-2
Web: austinopera.org

Austin Organs Inc 156 Woodland St . . . Hartford CT 06105 — 860-522-8293 — 524-9828 — 527
TF: 800-582-4466 ■ *Web:* www.austinorgans.com

Austin Peay State University
601 College St . . . Clarksville TN 37044 — 931-221-7661 — 221-6168* — 166
*Fax: Admissions ■ *TF Admissions:* 800-844-2778 ■ *Web:* www.apsu.edu

Austin Powder Co
25800 Science Pk Dr Ste 300 . . . Cleveland OH 44122 — 216-464-2400 — 464-4418 — 268
TF: 800-321-0752 ■ *Web:* www.austinpowder.com

Austin Presbyterian Theological Seminary
100 E 27th St . . . Austin TX 78705 — 512-472-6736 — 167-3
Web: www.austinseminary.edu

Austin Public Library 800 Guadalupe St . . . Austin TX 78701 — 512-974-7400 — 434-3
Web: library.austintexas.gov

Austin Pump & Supply Co PO Box 17037 . . . Austin TX 78760 — 512-442-2348 — 442-2932 — 385
TF: 800-252-9692 ■ *Web:* www.austinpump.com

Austin State Hospital
4110 Guadalupe St . . . Austin TX 78751 — 512-452-0381 — 419-2163 — 374-5
TF: 866-407-3773 ■ *Web:* www.dshs.texas.gov

Austin Straubel International Airport
2077 Airport Dr Ste 18 . . . Green Bay WI 54313 — 920-498-4800 — 498-8799 — 27
Web: www.co.brown.wi.us

Austin Symphony Orchestra
1101 Red River St . . . Austin TX 78701 — 512-476-6064 — 476-6242 — 573-3
TF: 888-462-3787 ■ *Web:* www.austinsymphony.org

Austin Tape & Label Inc
3350 Cavalier Trl . . . Stow OH 44224 — 330-928-7999 — 787
Web: www.austintape.com

Austin Test Inc Dba Bridge 360
10801 N MoPac Expy Bldg 1 Ste 320 . . . Austin TX 78759 — 512-837-8798 — 177
Web: www.bridge360.com

Austin Trust Co
336 S Congress Ave Ste 100 . . . Austin TX 78704 — 512-478-2121 — 478-2616 — 69
Web: www.austintrust.com

Austin Ventures 300 W Sixth St Ste 2300 . . . Austin TX 78701 — 512-485-1900 — 792
TF: 800-694-4460 ■ *Web:* www.austinventures.com

Austin White Lime Company Ltd
14001 McNeil Round Rock Rd . . . Austin TX 78728-6310 — 800-553-5463 — 440
TF: 800-553-5463 ■ *Web:* www.austinwhitelime.com

Austin Zoo 10807 Rawhide Trail . . . Austin TX 78736 — 512-288-1490 — 288-3972 — 823
TF: 800-410-4444 ■ *Web:* www.austinzoo.org

Austin-Bergstrom International Airport (ABIA)
3600 Presidential Blvd . . . Austin TX 78719 — 512-530-2242 — 27
Web: www.ci.austin.tx.us

AustinMohawk & Company Inc
2175 Beechgrove Pl . . . Utica NY 13501 — 315-793-3000 — 793-9370 — 91
TF: 800-765-3110 ■ *Web:* www.austinmohawk.com

Austins Entertainment Center LP
16231 N Ih-35 . . . Pflugerville TX 78660 — 512-670-9600 — 31
Web: www.austinspark.com

Austin-Westran LLC 602 E Blackhawk Dr . . . Byron IL 61010 — 815-234-2811 — 234-3009 — 779

Australia 150 E 42nd St 33rd Fl . . . New York NY 10017 — 212-351-6600 — 351-6610 — 784
Web: unny.mission.gov.au
Consulate General
2029 Century Pk E Ste 3150 . . . Los Angeles CA 90067 — 310-229-2300 — 257
Web: www.losangeles.consulate.gov.au
Consulate General
150 E 42nd St 34th Fl . . . New York NY 10017 — 212-351-6500 — 351-6501 — 257
Web: www.newyork.usa.embassy.gov.au
Consulate General 1000 Bishop St PH . . . Honolulu HI 96813 — 808-529-8100 — 529-8142 — 257
TF: 866-343-3086 ■ *Web:* www.usa.embassy.gov.au/whwh/hawaiicg.html
Embassy 2005 Massachusetts Ave NW . . . Washington DC 20036 — 202-558-2216 — 318-0771 — 257
TF: 800-345-6541 ■ *Web:* www.visahq.com

Australian American Chamber of Commerce of Houston
1300 McGowen St Ste 120 . . . Houston TX 77004 — 713-527-9688 — 415-0545* — 138
*Fax Area Code: 832 ■ *Web:* www.aacc-houston.org

Australian Consulate General
Consulate General
123 N Wacker Dr Ste 1330 . . . Chicago IL 60606 — 312-419-1480 — 419-1499 — 257
Web: australia.visahq.com

Australian-American Chamber of Commerce - San Francisco
PO Box 471285 . . . San Francisco CA 94147 — 415-485-6718 — 138
TF: 800-662-4455 ■ *Web:* sfaussies.com

Austria 600 Third Ave 31st Fl . . . New York NY 10016 — 917-542-8400 — 949-1840* — 784
*Fax Area Code: 212 ■ *Web:* www.bmeia.gv.at
Consulate General
3524 International Ct NW . . . Washington DC 20008 — 202-895-6700 — 257
Web: www.austria.org
Consulate General
11859 Wilshire Blvd Ste 501 . . . Los Angeles CA 90025 — 310-444-9310 — 477-9897 — 257
TF: 800-255-2414 ■ *Web:* www.austria.org
Consulate General 31 E 69th St . . . New York NY 10021 — 212-933-5140 — 585-1992 — 257
Web: www.bmeia.gv.at/botschaft/gk-new-york.html
Embassy 3524 International Ct NW . . . Washington DC 20008 — 202-895-6700 — 895-6750 — 257
TF: 800-255-2414 ■ *Web:* www.austria.org

Austrian & Assoc Inc
2530 Superior Ave Ste 202 . . . Cleveland OH 44114 — 216-621-6631 — 261

Austrian Tourist Office PO Box 1142 . . . New York NY 10108 — 212-944-6880 — 730-4568 — 775
TF: 800-221-9831 ■ *Web:* www.austria.info/us

Austro Mold Inc 3 Rutter St . . . Rochester NY 14606 — 585-458-1410 — 458-0963 — 757

Autec Inc 2500 W Front St . . . Statesville NC 28677 — 704-871-9141 — 427
Web: www.autec-carwash.com

Authenex Inc 1413 Grant Rd . . . Mountain View CA 94040 — 650-641-1198 — 224
Web: www.authenex.com

AuthenTec Inc 100 Rialto Pl # 100 . . . Melbourne FL 32901 — 321-308-1300 — 696

Authentech Software Developers Inc
11285 Palmer Ln . . . Twinsburg OH 44087 — 330-425-4538 — 177
Web: authentech.com

Authentic Pine Floors Inc
4042 Hwy 42 . . . Locust Grove GA 30248 — 800-283-6038 — 752
TF: 800-283-6038 ■ *Web:* www.authenticpinefloors.com

Authenticity Consulting Inc
4008 Lake Dr Ave N . . . Minneapolis MN 55422 — 763-971-8890 — 463
TF: 800-971-2250 ■ *Web:* www.authenticityconsulting.com

Authentidate Holding Corp
300 Connell Dr Fl 5 . . . Berkeley Heights NJ 07922 — 908-787-1700 — 787
TF: 800-864-6210 ■ *Web:* www.authentidate.com

Authentify Inc
8745 W Higgins Rd Ste 240 . . . Chicago IL 60631 — 773-243-0300 — 177
Web: www.authentify.com

Authentix Inc 4355 Excel Pkwy Ste 100 . . . Addison TX 75001 — 469-737-4400 — 737-4409 — 692
Web: www.authentix.com

Author House
1663 Liberty Dr Ste 200 . . . Bloomington IN 47403 — 812-339-6000 — 339-6554 — 637-2
TF: 888-728-8467 ■ *Web:* www.authorhouse.com

Author Services Inc
7051 Hollywood Blvd . . . Hollywood CA 90028 — 323-466-3310 — 463
TF: 800-624-6504 ■ *Web:* authorservicesinc.com

Authorize.Net Corp PO Box 8999 . . . San Francisco CA 94128 — 801-492-6450 — 492-6489 — 178-7
TF: 877-447-3938 ■ *Web:* www.authorize.net

Authors Guild Bulletin
31 E 32nd St 7th Fl . . . New York NY 10016 — 212-563-5904 — 564-5363 — 531-2
TF: 800-444-6544 ■ *Web:* www.authorsguild.org

Autism Research Institute (ARI)
4182 Adams Ave . . . San Diego CA 92116 — 619-281-7165 — 563-6840 — 48-17
TF: 866-366-3361 ■ *Web:* www.autism.com

Autism Society of America (ASA)
4340 EW Hwy Ste 350 . . . Bethesda MD 20814 — 301-657-0881 — 657-0869 — 48-17
TF: 800-328-8476 ■ *Web:* www.autism-society.org

Autistic Treatment Center Inc
10503 Metric Dr . . . Dallas TX 75243 — 972-644-2076 — 148
TF: 877-666-2747 ■ *Web:* www.atcoftexas.org

AUTM (Association of University Technology Managers)
111 Deer Lake Rd Ste 100 . . . Deerfield IL 60015 — 847-559-0846 — 480-9282 — 49-19
Web: www.autm.net

Auto Barn 13 Harbor Pk Dr . . . Port Washington NY 11050 — 516-484-9500 — 54
Web: www.autobarn.net

Auto Builders
5715 Corporate Way . . . West Palm Beach FL 33407 — 561-622-3515 — 186
TF: 800-378-5946 ■ *Web:* www.autobuilders.com

Auto Cast Inc
4565 Spartan Industrial Dr SW . . . Grandville MI 49418 — 616-534-4941 — 308
Web: www.autocastinc.com

Auto Ch 332 W Broadway Ste 1604 . . . Louisville KY 40202 — 502-992-0200 — 992-0201 — 740
Web: www.theautochannel.com

Auto Chlor System
450 Ferguson Dr . . . Mountain View CA 94043 — 650-967-3085 — 386
Web: www.autochlor.com

Auto Clerk Inc 936 Dewing Ave Ste G . . . Lafayette CA 94549 — 925-284-1005 — 177
TF: 800-656-7509 ■ *Web:* www.autoclerk.com

Auto Club of America Corp (ACA)
9411 N Georgia St . . . Oklahoma City OK 73120 — 405-751-4430 — 751-4462 — 53
TF: 800-411-2007 ■ *Web:* www.autoclubofamerica.com

Auto Club of New York Inc
1415 Kellum Pl . . . Garden City NY 11530 — 516-746-7730 — 53
Web: www.aaa.com

Auto Club Speedway 9300 Cherry Ave . . . Fontana CA 92335 — 909-429-5000 — 429-5500 — 515
TF: 800-944-7223 ■ *Web:* autoclubspeedway.com

Auto Comm Engineering Corp
109 Evergreen Dr . . . Houma LA 70364 — 985-876-1855 — 256
Web: auto-comm.com

Auto Crane Co PO Box 580697 . . . Tulsa OK 74158 — 918-836-0463 — 516
TF: 888-848-5445 ■ *Web:* www.autocrane.com

Auto Credit Express Inc
3271 Five Points Dr Ste 200 . . . Auburn Hills MI 48326 — 248-370-6600 — 57
Web: www.autocreditexpress.net

Auto Data Direct Inc
1379 Cross Creek Cir . . . Tallahassee FL 32301 — 850-877-8804 — 224
TF: 866-923-3123 ■ *Web:* www.add123.com

Auto Europe 39 Commercial St . . . Portland ME 04101 — 207-842-2000 — 842-2222 — 126
TF: 800-223-5555 ■ *Web:* www.autoeurope.com

Auto Export Shipping Inc
187 Mill Ln Ste 103 . . . Mountainside NJ 07092 — 908-436-2150 — 96
TF: 800-829-4933 ■ *Web:* aesshipping.com

Auto FX Software
130 Inverness Plaz Ste 510 . . . Birmingham AL 35242 — 205-980-0056 — 980-1121 — 178-8
TF: 800-839-2008 ■ *Web:* www.autofx.com

Auto Internet Marketing Inc
2495 Enterprise Rd Ste 201 . . . Clearwater FL 33763 — 727-791-0825 — 195
Web: www.autointernetmarketing.com

Auto Lenders Liquidation Center
104 Rt 73 . . . Voorhees NJ 08043 — 888-305-5968 — 57
TF: 888-305-5968 ■ *Web:* www.autolenders.com

Auto Mall, The 800 Putney Rd . . . Brattleboro VT 05301 — 802-275-4510 — 57
Web: www.brattautomall.com

Auto Meter Products Inc 413 W Elm St . . . Sycamore IL 60178 — 815-895-8141 — 895-6786 — 495
TF: 866-248-6356 ■ *Web:* www.autometer.com

				Phone	Fax	Class
Auto Parts Warehouse Inc						
1073 E Artesia Blvd	Carson	CA	90746	310-884-5000	604-5088	61
Web: www.apwks.com						
Auto Profit Masters						
250 E Dry Creek Rd	Littleton	CO	80122	303-795-5838		463
TF: 866-826-7911 ■ *Web:* autoprofitmasters.com						
Auto Quotes						
8800 Baymeadows Way W Ste 500	Jacksonville	FL	32256	904-384-2279		57
Web: aqnet.com						
Auto Supply Company Inc						
1032 Winston St	Greensboro	NC	27405	336-275-6193		57
Web: www.ascodc.com						
Auto Toy Store, The						
727 N Federal Hwy	Fort Lauderdale	FL	33304	954-379-2886		57
Web: www.thenewautotoystore.com						
Auto Truck Inc						
1420 Brewster Creek Blvd	Bartlett	IL	60103	630-860-5600	860-5631	516
TF: 877-284-4440 ■ *Web:* www.autotruck.com						
Autobahn Freight Lines Ltd						
27 Automatic Rd	Brampton	ON	L6S5N8	416-741-5454	741-0155	311
TF: 877-989-9994 ■ *Web:* www.autobahnfreight.com						
Autobell Car Wash Inc						
1521 E Third St	Charlotte	NC	28204	704-527-9274	333-0526	62-1
TF: 800-582-8096 ■ *Web:* www.autobell.com						
Autobus Girardin Inc						
4000 Girardin St	Drummondville	QC	J2E0A1	819-477-3222		108
Web: www.girardinbluebird.com						
Autobytel Inc 18872 MacArthur Blvd	Irvine	CA	92612	949-225-4500	225-4541	58
NASDAQ: ABTL ■ *TF:* 888-422-8999 ■ *Web:* www.autobytel.com						
Autocam Corp 4070 E Paris Ave	Kentwood	MI	49512	616-698-0707	698-6876	60
TF: 800-747-6978 ■ *Web:* www.autocam.com						
Autocar LLC 551 S Washington St	Hagerstown	IN	47346	765-489-5499		247
Web: www.autocartruck.com						
AutoCom Associates						
74 W Long Lake Rd Ste 103	Bloomfield Hills	MI	48304	248-647-8621		636
TF: 800-667-6167 ■ *Web:* www.usautocom.com						
Autodesk Inc 111 McInnis Pkwy	San Rafael	CA	94903	415-507-5000	507-5100	178-5
NASDAQ: ADSK ■ *TF Tech Supp:* 800-964-6432 ■ *Web:* www.autodesk.com						
Autodessys Inc 2011 Riverside Dr	Columbus	OH	43221	614-488-8838	488-0848	178-8
Web: www.formz.com						
Autodie LLC 44 Coldbrook St NW	Grand Rapids	MI	49503	616-454-9361		757
Web: www.autodie.com						
Autodraft Inc 2815 Baird Rd	Fairport	NY	14450	585-389-1900		180
TF: 800-989-5028 ■ *Web:* www.adraft.com						
AutoFair Automotive Group						
200 Keller St	Manchester	NH	03103	603-634-1000		57
Web: www.autofair.com						
Autofusion Corp						
6215 Ferris Sq Ste 200	San Diego	CA	92121	858-270-9444		58
TF: 800-410-7354 ■ *Web:* www.autofusion.com						
autograph Inc 999 N NorthLk Way	Seattle	WA	98103	571-354-7273		195
Web: www.autograph.me						
Auto-Graphics Inc 430 N Vineyard Ave	Ontario	CA	91764	909-595-7004	595-3506	781
TF: 800-776-6939 ■ *Web:* www4.auto-graphics.com						
Autoimmune Inc 1199 Madia St	Pasadena	CA	91103	626-792-1235		502
OTC: AIMM ■ *Web:* www.autoimmuneinc.com						
Autoimmune Technologies LLC						
1010 Common St Ste 1705	New Orleans	LA	70112	504-529-9944	529-8982	85
Web: www.autoimmuno.com						
Autoland 170 Rt 22 E	Springfield	NJ	07081	973-467-2900		57
TF Sales: 877-813-7239 ■ *Web:* www.1800autoland.com						
Autoliv Inc 3350 Airport Rd	Ogden	UT	84405	801-625-8200		678
NYSE: ALV ■ *Web:* www.autoliv.com						
Autologue Computer Systems Inc						
8452 Commonwealth Ave	Buena Park	CA	90621	714-522-3551		177
Web: www.autologue.com						
AutoManager Inc						
7301 Topanga Canyon Blvd Ste 200	Canoga Park	CA	91303	310-207-2202		809
TF: 800-300-2808 ■ *Web:* www.automanager.com						
Automann Inc 850 Randolph Rd	Somerset	NJ	08873	201-529-4996		57
Web: www.automann.com						
Automark Marking Systems						
13475 Lakefront Dr	Earth City	MO	63045	314-739-0430		467
Web: www.automark.com						
Automatan Inc 2911 Apache Dr	Plover	WI	54467	715-341-6501		261
TF: 800-521-0007 ■ *Web:* www.automatan.com						
Automated Assembly Corp						
20777 Kensington Blvd	Lakeville	MN	55044	952-469-6556		48-20
Web: www.autoassembly.com						
Automated Benefit Services Inc						
8220 Irving Rd	Sterling Heights	MI	48312	586-693-4300		390
Web: www.abs-tpa.com						
Automated Bldg Components Inc						
2359 Grant Rd	North Baltimore	OH	45872	419-257-2152	257-2779	817
TF: 800-837-2152 ■ *Web:* www.abctruss.com						
Automated Conveyor Systems Inc						
3850 Southland Dr	West Memphis	AR	72301	870-732-5050	732-5191	207
TF: 800-881-6750 ■ *Web:* www.automatedconveyors.com						
Automated Equipment						
5140 Moundview Dr	Red Wing	MN	55066	651-385-2271		298
Web: autoequipllc.com						
Automated Financial Systems Inc						
123 Summit Dr	Exton	PA	19341	484-875-1250	524-7977*	178-11
**Fax Area Code:* 610 ■ *TF:* 800-201-0461 ■ *Web:* www.afsvision.com						
Automated Logic Corp						
1150 Roberts Rd N	Kennesaw	GA	30144	770-429-3000		202
Web: www.automatedlogic.com						
Automated Media Services Corp						
110 Commerce Dr	Allendale	NJ	07401	201-934-6666		514
Web: www.3gtv.com						
Automated Medical Systems Inc						
2310 N Patterson St Bldg H	Valdosta	GA	31602	800-256-3240		179
TF: 800-256-3240 ■ *Web:* automedical.com						
Automated Packaging Systems Inc						
10175 Phillip Pkwy	Streetsboro	OH	44241	330-528-2000	342-2400	547
TF Sales: 800-527-0733 ■ *Web:* www.autobag.com						
Automated Precision Inc						
15000 Johns Hopkins Dr	Rockville	MD	20850	240-268-0400		295
Web: www.apisensor.com						
Automated Presort Inc						
1400 Centre Cir Dr	Downers Grove	IL	60515	630-620-7678		4
Automated Products Inc						
1812 Karau Dr	Marshfield	WI	54449	715-387-3426	387-6588	817
TF: 800-426-0870 ■ *Web:* apiebs.com						
Automated Quality Technologies Inc						
563 Shoreview Park Rd	St Paul	MN	55126	651-484-6544		697
TF: 800-250-9297 ■ *Web:* www.lionprecision.com						
Automated Records Management Systems Inc						
1850 Enterprise Dr	De Pere	WI	54115	920-339-0135		803-1
Web: www.arms4rim.com						
Automated Trading Desk LLC						
11 eWall St	Mount Pleasant	SC	29464	843-789-2000		177
Web: www.atdesk.com						
Automated Voice Systems Inc (AVSI)						
17059 El Cajon Ave	Yorba Linda	CA	92886	714-524-4488		52
Automatic Data Processing Inc (ADP)						
1 ADP Blvd	Roseland	NJ	07068	800-225-5237		225
NASDAQ: ADP ■ *TF:* 800-225-5237 ■ *Web:* www.adp.com						
Automatic Fire Protection Inc						
4582 Old Christoval Rd	San Angelo	TX	76904	325-651-9000		610
Web: www.automaticfireprotection.com						
Automatic Fire Sprinkler Inc						
7272 Mars Dr	Huntington Beach	CA	92647	714-841-2066		610
TF: 800-436-2066						
Automatic Funds Transfer Services						
151 S Landers St Ste C	Seattle	WA	98134	206-254-0975	254-0968	69
TF: 800-275-2033 ■ *Web:* www.afts.com						
Automatic Ice & Beverage Inc						
1400 Tuscaloosa Ave SW	Birmingham	AL	35211	205-787-9640		665
Web: aibnow.com						
Automatic Machine Products Co (AMP)						
400 Constitution Dr	Taunton	MA	02780	508-822-4226	822-4476	621
Web: www.ampcomp.com						
Automatic Power Inc						
10810 W Little York Rd Ste 130	Houston	TX	77041	713-228-5208	228-3717	439
Web: www.automaticpower.com						
Automatic Products Corp						
2735 Forest Ln	Garland	TX	75042	972-272-6422	494-0533	621
Web: www.ap-corp.com						
Automatic Products International Ltd						
165 Bridgepoint Dr	Saint Paul	MN	55075	800-523-8363		55
TF: 800-523-8363 ■ *Web:* www.automaticproducts.com						
Automatic Slim's 83 S Second St	Memphis	TN	38103	901-525-7948		671
Web: www.automaticslimsmemphis.com						
Automatic Spring Products Corp						
803 Taylor Ave	Grand Haven	MI	49417	616-842-7800	842-4380	718
Web: www.automaticspring.com						
Automatic Sprinkler of Texas Inc						
1147 S Cedar Ridge Dr	Duncanville	TX	75137	972-298-2772		610
Web: www.autosprinkleroftx.com						
Automatic Supply 4877 SR- 261	Newburgh	IN	47630	812-858-1809		429
Web: www.automaticirrigation.com						
Automatic Systems Inc						
9230 E 47th St	Kansas City	MO	64133	816-356-0660	356-5730	207
TF: 800-366-3488 ■ *Web:* www.asi.com						
Automatic Transmission Rebuilders Assn (ATRA)						
2400 Latigo Ave	Oxnard	CA	93030	805-604-2000	604-2003	49-21
TF: 800-404-2872 ■ *Web:* www.atra.com						
Automatic Valve Corp 41144 Vincenti Ct	Novi	MI	48375	248-474-6700	474-6732	789
TF: 800-558-5950 ■ *Web:* www.automaticvalve.com						
Automatika Inc 137 Delta Dr	Pittsburgh	PA	15238	412-968-1022		393
Web: www.automatika.com						
Automation & Control Technology Inc						
6141 Avery Rd	Dublin	OH	43016	614-495-1120		194
Web: www.autocontroltech.com						
Automation & Modular Components Inc						
10301 Enterprise Dr	Davisburg	MI	48350	248-922-4740		207
Web: www.amcautomation.com						
Automation Engineering LLC						
1100 W Grand Ave	Salina	KS	67401	785-309-0505		190
Web: www.bcd.com						
Automation Image Inc						
2650 Vly View Ln Ste 100	Dallas	TX	75234	972-247-8816	243-2814	180
Web: www.automationimage.com						
Automation International Inc						
1020 Bahls St	Danville	IL	61832	217-446-9500	446-6855	811
Web: www.automation-intl.com						
Automation Nth 491 Waldron Rd	La Vergne	TN	37086	615-793-7704		201
TF: 866-800-4271 ■ *Web:* www.automationnth.com						
Automation Plastics Corp 150 Lena Dr	Aurora	OH	44202	330-562-5148		608
Web: www.automationplastics.com						
Automation Products Group Inc (APG)						
1025 W 1700 N	Logan	UT	84321	435-753-7300	753-7490	201
TF: 888-525-7300 ■ *Web:* www.apgsensors.com						
Automation Service						
13871 Parks Steed Dr	Earth City	MO	63045	314-785-6600	785-6610	201
TF: 800-325-4808 ■ *Web:* www.automationservice.com						
Automation Services & Controls Inc						
16765 Park Cir Dr	Chagrin Falls	OH	44023	440-543-8146		261
TF: 800-645-8146 ■ *Web:* www.ascdrives.com						
Automation Systems Interconnect Inc						
4700 Wport Dr Ste 500	Mechanicsburg	PA	17055	717-249-5581		201
Web: www.asi-ez.com						
Automation Technologies Inc						
8219 Leesburg Pk	Vienna	VA	22182	703-883-1410	883-1435	180
Web: www.ati4it.com						
Automation Technology Inc						
2001 Gateway Pl	San Jose	CA	95110	408-350-7020		178-7
Web: www.intertek.com						
Automation Tool Co 101 Mill Dr	Cookeville	TN	38501	931-528-5417		207
Web: www.automationtool.com						
AutoMedx Inc						
12321 Middlebrook Rd Ste 150	Germantown	MD	20874	301-916-9508		250
Web: www.automedx.biz						
Autometrix Precision Cutting Systems Inc						
12098 Charles Dr	Grass Valley	CA	95945	530-477-5065		111
TF: 800-635-3080 ■ *Web:* www.autometrix.com						

Name / Address	City	State	ZIP	Phone	Fax	Class
Automobile Club of Southern California 2601 S Figueroa St *TF:* 800-400-4222 ■ *Web:* www.aaa.com	Los Angeles	CA	90007	213-741-3686		53
Automobile Consumer Services Inc 6249 Stewart Rd *TF:* 800-223-4882 ■ *Web:* www.acscorp.com	Cincinnati	OH	45227	513-527-7700	527-7705	58
Automobile Magazine 120 E Liberty St *Web:* www.automobilemag.com	Ann Arbor	MI	48104	310-531-9900		457-3
Automobile Racing Club of America 8117 Lewis Ave *TF:* 800-385-2503 ■ *Web:* www.arcaracing.com	Temperance	MI	48182	734-847-6726		57
Automotion Inc 11000 Lavergne Ave *Web:* www.automotionconveyors.com	Oak Lawn	IL	60453	708-229-3700		207
Automotive Aftermarket Industry Assn (AAIA) 7101 Wisconsin Ave *TF:* 800-936-8906 ■ *Web:* autocare.org	Bethesda	MD	20814	301-654-6664	654-3299	49-21
Automotive Distribution Network 3085 Fountainside Dr Ste 210 *TF:* 800-727-8112 ■ *Web:* www.networkhq.org	Germantown	TN	38138	901-682-9090		49-18
Automotive Distributors Company Inc 2981 Morse Rd **Fax Area Code:* 614 ■ *TF:* 800-421-5556 ■ *Web:* www.adw1.com	Columbus	OH	43231	800-421-5556	476-9469*	61
Automotive Engine Rebuilders Assn (AERA) 500 Coventry Ln Ste 180 *TF:* 888-326-2372 ■ *Web:* www.aera.org	Crystal Lake	IL	60014	847-541-6550	541-5808	49-21
Automotive Engineered Products Inc 7149 Mission Gorge Rd **Fax Area Code:* 909 ■ *Web:* www.jbaheaders.com	San Diego	CA	92120	619-229-7797	599-6424*	489
Automotive Executive Magazine 8400 Westpark Dr *Web:* insidenova.com	McLean	VA	22102	703-821-7150		457-21
Automotive Finance Corp (AFC) 13085 Hamilton Crossing Blvd *TF:* 888-335-6675 ■ *Web:* www.afcdealer.com	Carmel	IN	46032	865-384-8250		216
Automotive Hall of Fame 21400 Oakwood Blvd *Web:* www.automotivehalloffame.org	Dearborn	MI	48124	313-240-4000	240-8641	520
Automotive Industry Action Group (AIAG) 26200 Lahser Rd Ste 200 *TF:* 877-275-2424 ■ *Web:* www.aiag.org	Southfield	MI	48033	248-358-3570	358-3253	49-21
Automotive Information Ctr 18872 MacArthur Blvd *TF:* 888-422-8999 ■ *Web:* www.autobytel.com	Irvine	CA	92612	888-422-8999		58
Automotive Mfg & Supply Co 90 Plant Ave Ste 1 *Web:* www.amscovf.com	Hauppauge	NY	11788	631-435-1400		61
Automotive News Magazine 1155 Gratiot Ave *TF:* 877-812-1584 ■ *Web:* www.autonews.com	Detroit	MI	48207	313-446-0450	446-0383	457-21
Automotive Oil Change Assn (AOCA) 330 N Wabash Ave Ste 2000 *TF:* 800-230-0702 ■ *Web:* www.aoca.org	Chicago	IL	60611	312-321-5132	673-6832	49-21
Automotive Parts Headquarters 2959 Clearwater Rd *TF:* 800-247-0339 ■ *Web:* www.autopartshq.com	Saint Cloud	MN	56301	320-252-5411	252-4256	61
Automotive Parts Remanufacturers Assn (APRA) 4215 Lafayette Ctr Dr Ste 3 *TF:* 877-734-4827 ■ *Web:* www.apra.org	Chantilly	VA	20151	703-968-2772	968-2878	49-21
Automotive Quality & Logistics Inc 14744 Jib St *Web:* www.aql-inc.com	Plymouth	MI	48170	734-459-1670		194
Automotive Racing Products Inc 1863 Eastman Ave *TF:* 800-826-3045 ■ *Web:* www.arp-bolts.com	Ventura	CA	93003	805-339-2200	650-0742	350
Automotive Recyclers Assn (ARA) 9113 Church St Ste 20N *TF:* 888-385-1005 ■ *Web:* www.a-r-a.org	Manassas	VA	20110	571-208-0428	208-0430	49-21
Automotive Resources Inc 12775 Randolph Ridge Ln *TF:* 800-562-3250 ■ *Web:* www.ari-hetra.com	Manassas	VA	20109	703-359-6265		295
Automotive Resources International 4001 Leadenhall Rd *Web:* www.arifleet.com	Mount Laurel	NJ	08054	856-778-1500		289
Automotive Service Assn (ASA) 1901 Airport Fwy **Fax Area Code:* 817 ■ *TF Cust Svc:* 800-272-7467 ■ *Web:* www.asashop.org	Bedford	TX	76021	800-272-7467	685-0225*	49-21
Automotive Service Inc 910 Mtn Home Rd PO Box 2157 *Web:* www.reladyne.com/locations/automotiveserviceinc	Sinking Spring	PA	19608	610-678-3421	678-3515	316
Automotive Training Center-Exton Campus 114 Pickering Way *TF:* 888-321-8992 ■ *Web:* www.autotraining.edu	Exton	PA	19341	610-363-6716		166
AutoNation Inc 200 SW First Ave Ste 1600 *NYSE: AN* ■ *Web:* www.autonation.com/pages/homepage.aspx	Fort Lauderdale	FL	33301	954-769-7000		57
Autonet Mobile Inc 3636 N Laughlin Rd Ste 150 *TF:* 800-977-2107 ■ *Web:* www.autonetmobile.com	Santa Rosa	CA	95403	415-223-0316		645-10
Auto-Owners Insurance Co 6101 Anacapri Blvd *TF:* 800-346-0346 ■ *Web:* www.auto-owners.com	Lansing	MI	48917	517-323-1200	323-8796	391-4
Autopacific Inc 2991 Dow Ave *Web:* www.autopacific.com	Tustin	CA	92780	714-838-4234		195
Autoquip Corp 1058 W Industrial Rd *TF:* 888-811-9876 ■ *Web:* www.autoquip.com	Guthrie	OK	73044	405-282-5200	282-8105	470
Autorama Inc 5389 Poplar Ave *TF:* 888-356-7636 ■ *Web:* www.mbofmemphis.com	Memphis	TN	38119	901-345-6211		57
AutoRevo LTD 7920 Belt Line Rd Ste 450 *TF:* 888-311-7386 ■ *Web:* www.autorevo.com	Dallas	TX	75254	972-715-8600		57
Autoscan Inc 4040 23rd Ave W *TF:* 800-270-0724 ■ *Web:* www.autoscaninc.com	Seattle	WA	98199	206-282-1616		196
AutoSeis Inc 2101 Midway Rd Ste 310	Carrollton	TX	75006	972-332-3388		407
AutoStar 1338 Foothill Dr	Salt Lake City	CT	84108	801-232-2311	746-8367	654
Autostar Solutions Inc 1300 Summit Ave Ste 800 *TF:* 800-682-2215 ■ *Web:* www.autostarsolutions.com	Fort Worth	TX	76102	800-682-2215		174
Autostrade International of Virginia O&M Inc 45305 Catalina Ct Ste 102	Sterling	VA	20166	703-904-8001		188-4
Autoswage Products Inc 726 River Rd *TF:* 800-480-9198 ■ *Web:* www.autoswage.com	Shelton	CT	06484	203-929-1401	929-6187	482
Autotether Inc 3 Inspiration Ln Unit B3 *TF:* 800-969-6352 ■ *Web:* www.autotether.com	Chester	CT	06412	860-526-1700		45
Autotool 7875 Corporate Blvd *Web:* www.autotoolinc.com	Plain City	OH	43064	614-733-0222		454
Autotrol Corp 365 E Prairie St *TF:* 800-228-6207 ■ *Web:* www.autotrol.com	Crystal Lake	IL	60014	815-459-3080	459-3227	518
Autotronics U S A LLC 700 N Benton Ave *TF:* 800-454-7498 ■ *Web:* www.autotronics.net	Springfield	MO	65802	417-864-4400		324
Autotruck Federal Credit Union 3611 Newburg Rd *TF:* 800-459-2328 ■ *Web:* www.autotruckfcu.org	Louisville	KY	40218	502-459-8981	458-0371	219
AutoTruckToys.com 2814 W Wood St *TF:* 800-544-6194 ■ *Web:* www.autotrucktoys.com	Paris	TN	38242	731-642-3535		791
AutoVIN Inc 13085 Hamilton Crossing Blvd Ste 500 **Fax Area Code:* 678 ■ *TF:* 866-585-8080 ■ *Web:* www.autovin.com	Carmel	IN	46032	866-585-8080	585-8201*	58
AutoVision Wireless Inc 360 Deerhide Crescent *TF:* 866-514-8030 ■ *Web:* www.autovisionwireless.com	Toronto	ON	M9M2Y6	416-747-4444	747-4443	225
AutoWeek Magazine 1155 Gratiot Ave *TF Circ:* 888-288-6954 ■ *Web:* www.autoweek.com	Detroit	MI	48207	313-446-6000	446-0347	457-3
AutoZone Inc 123 S Front St *NYSE: AZO* ■ *TF:* 800-288-6966 ■ *Web:* www.autozone.com	Memphis	TN	38103	901-495-6500		54
Autrans Corp 611 Enon Springs Rd *Web:* www.autranscanada.com	Smyrna	TN	37167	615-459-0770		54
Autry Greer & Sons Inc 2850 W Main St *TF:* 800-999-7750 ■ *Web:* www.greers.com	Mobile	AL	36612	251-457-8655	456-3744	345
Autry National Ctr Museum of the American West 4700 Western Heritage Way *Web:* theautry.org	Los Angeles	CA	90027	323-667-2000	660-5721	520
Autumn Harp Inc 26 Thompson Dr *TF:* 800-448-8106 ■ *Web:* www.autumnharp.com	Essex Junction	VT	05452	802-857-4600	857-4601	214
Autumn Press Inc 945 Camelia St *Web:* www.autumnpress.com	Berkeley	CA	94710	510-654-4545		627
Auven Therapeutics Management LLP 6501 Redhook Plaza Ste 201 *Web:* www.auventx.com	Saint Thomas	VI	00802	340-779-6908		528
Auvil Fruit Co Inc 21902 SR 97 *Web:* www.auvilfruit.com	Orondo	WA	98843	509-784-1033		315-3
Aux Anciens Canadiens 34 rue Saint-Louis Casier postal 175 succursale Haute-Ville *Web:* www.auxancienscanadiens.qc.ca	Quebec	QC	G1R4P3	418-692-1627	692-5419	671
Auyuittuq National Park PO Box 353 *Web:* www.pc.gc.ca	Pangnirtung	NU	X0A0R0	867-473-2500	473-8612	563
AV & R 269 Prince St *Web:* avr-aerospace.com	Montreal	QC	H3C2N4	514-788-1420		21
AV Homes Inc 8601 N Scottsdale Rd Ste 225 *NASDAQ: AVHI* ■ *TF:* 800-284-6637 ■ *Web:* www.avhomesinc.com	Scottsdale	AR	85253	480-214-7400		653
AV Nackawic Inc 103 Pinder Rd *Web:* www.av-group.ca	Nackawic	NB	E6G1W4	506-575-3314		638
AVA (Academy of Vocal Arts) 1920 Spruce St *TF:* 800-356-7372 ■ *Web:* www.avaopera.org	Philadelphia	PA	19103	215-735-1685	732-2189	573-2
AVA (Association for Vascular Access) 5526 W 13400 S Ste 229 *TF:* 877-924-2821 ■ *Web:* www.avainfo.org	Herriman	UT	84096	801-792-9079	601-8012	49-8
AVA (American Volksspott Assn) 1001 Pat Booker Rd Ste 101 *TF:* 855-999-5200 ■ *Web:* www.ava.org	Universal City	TX	78148	210-659-2112	659-1212	48-22
AVA Electronics Corp 4000 Bridge St	Drexel Hill	PA	19026	610-284-2500		815
Ava Pork Products Inc 383 W John St Hicksville *Web:* www.avapork.com	Hicksville	NY	11802	516-750-1500	750-1501	297-9
AVAD Canada Ltd 205 Courtneypark Dr W *TF:* 866-523-2823 ■ *Web:* ca.avad.com	Mississauga	ON	L5W0A5	866-523-2823		174
Availl Technologies Inc 1960 Old Gatesburg Rd *Web:* www.availtec.com	State College	PA	16803	814-234-3394		261
Availink Inc 20201 Century Blvd Ste 160 *Web:* www.availink.com	Germantown	MD	20874	301-515-6716		256
Avala Marketing Group Inc 1078 Headquarters Pk *Web:* www.avalamarketing.com	Fenton	MO	63026	636-343-9988		195
Avalanche Creative Svcs Inc 135 W 29th St *Web:* www.avalanchecreative.tv	New York	NY	10001	212-206-9335		514
Avaleris Inc 1400-45 O'Connor St *TF:* 800-867-1389 ■ *Web:* www.avaleris.com	Ottawa	ON	K1P1A4	613-237-9695		196
Avalex Technologies Corp 2665 Gulf Breeze Pkwy *Web:* www.avalex.com	Gulf Breeze	FL	32563	850-470-8464		21
Avalign Technologies Inc 272 E Deerpath Rd Ste 208 *TF:* 855-282-5446 ■ *Web:* www.avaligntech.com	Lake Forest	IL	60045	855-282-5446		475
Avalon Capital Management 495 Seaport Ct Ste 106 *Web:* www.avaloncapital.com	Redwood City	CA	94063	650-306-1500		401
Avalon Consulting LLC 5600 Tennyson Pkwy Ste 230 *TF:* 800-499-6544 ■ *Web:* www.avalonconsult.com	Plano	TX	75024	469-424-3449		196
Avalon Copy Centers of America Inc 901 N State St *TF:* 800-431-2584 ■ *Web:* www.teamavalon.com	Syracuse	NY	13208	315-471-3333		113
Avalon Corporate Furnished Apartments 1553 Empire Blvd *TF:* 800-934-9763 ■ *Web:* www.rochesterfurnished.com	Webster	NY	14580	585-671-4421	671-9771	379
Avalon Development Corp 130 Goldstream Rd *Web:* www.avalonalaska.com	Fairbanks	AK	99708	907-457-5159		393

Company / Address	City	State	ZIP	Phone	Fax	Class
Avalon Fortress Security Corp 9697 NW East River Rd *TF:* 844-788-9111 ■ *Web:* www.avalonsecurity.com	Minneapolis	MN	55433	763-767-9111	231-8466	693
Avalon Holdings Corp 1 American Way *NYSE: AWX* ■ *Web:* www.avalonholdings.com	Warren	OH	44484	330-856-8800	856-8480	804
Avalon Hotel, The 16 E 32nd St *TF:* 800-315-4642 ■ *Web:* www.avalonhotelnyc.com	New York	NY	10016	212-299-7000		378
Avalon Motel Corp 1529 Broadway *Web:* avalon-motel.com	Saugus	MA	01906	781-233-4200		379
Avalon Pontoon Boats 903 Michigan Ave *Web:* boatersbook.com	Alma	MI	48801	989-463-2112		90
Avalon Shutters Inc 725 S Lugo Ave *Web:* www.avalonshutters.com	San Bernardino	CA	92408	909-888-8227		499
Avalon Travel Publishing 1700 Fourth St *Web:* www.avalontravelbooks.com	Berkeley	CA	94710	510-595-3664		637-2
Avalon Trust Co 125 Lincoln Ave Ste 301 *Web:* www.avalontrust.com	Santa Fe	NM	87501	505-983-1111		401
Avalon Ventures 1134 Kline St *Web:* www.avalon-ventures.com	La Jolla	CA	92037	858-348-2180		690
Avalon Vision Solutions LLC 422 Thornton Rd Ste 104 *Web:* www.avalonvision.com	Lithia Springs	GA	30122	770-944-8445		407
Avalonerie 16 W Tenth St *TF:* 888-295-4949 ■ *Web:* www.avalonerie.com	Erie	PA	16501	814-459-2220	459-2322	379
Avalotis Co 400 Jones St *TF:* 800-317-2519 ■ *Web:* www.avalotis.com	Verona	PA	15147	412-828-9666		189-8
Avanade Inc 818 Stewart St *TF:* 844-282-6233 ■ *Web:* www.avanade.com	Seattle	WA	98101	206-239-5600		39
Avancen MOD Corp 1156 Bowman Rd Ste 200 *TF:* 800-607-1230 ■ *Web:* www.avancen.com	Mount Pleasant	SC	29464	800-607-1230		250
Avancent Consulting Corp 1896 Kentucky Ave *Web:* www.avancent.com	Winter Park	FL	32789	407-897-8664		196
Avangate Inc 555 Twin Dolphin Dr Ste 155 *Web:* www.avangate.com	Redwood Shores	CA	94065	650-249-5280		387
Avani Media Inc 80 Liberty Ship Way Ste 25 *Web:* www.avanimedia.com	Sausalito	CA	94965	415-331-2150		196
AVANIR Pharmaceuticals 30 Enterprise Ste 400 *NASDAQ: AVNR* ■ *Web:* www.avanir.com	Aliso Viejo	CA	92656	949-389-6700	643-6800	85
Avanquest Software USA 1333 W 120th Ave *TF:* 800-011-2312 ■ *Web:* www.avanquest.com	Westminster	CO	80234	800-011-2312		178-7
Avansis Ventures LLC 12710 Popes Head Rd *Web:* www.avansis.com	Clifton	VA	20124	703-796-0222		792
Avant Business Services 60 E 42nd St Lowr Level *Web:* www.nymessenger.com	New York	NY	10165	212-687-5145		41
Avant Inc 4667 Mission St *Web:* avantexperience.com	San Francisco	CA	94112	415-349-4840		196
Avant Ministries 10000 N Oak Trafficway *TF:* 800-468-1892 ■ *Web:* www.avantministries.org	Kansas City	MO	64155	816-734-8500		48-20
Avant Solution, The 22511 Telegraph Rd Ste 115 *Web:* avantsolution.com	Southfield	MI	48033	248-423-0052		177
Avant Strategies LLC 81 Pondfield Rd Ste 156 *Web:* avantstrategies.net	Bronxville	NY	10708	914-861-3131		195
Avant Systems Group 815-1661 Portage Ave *Web:* avant.ca	Winnipeg	MB	R3J3T7	204-789-9596		180
Avante Group Inc 4601 Sheridan St Ste 540N *Web:* www.avantecenters.com	Hollywood	FL	33021	954-987-7180		371
Avante International Technology Inc (AIT) 70 Washington Rd *TF:* 800-735-5040 ■ *Web:* www.aitechnology.com	Princeton Junction	NJ	08550	609-799-9388	799-9308	801
Avante Security Inc 1959 Leslie St *Web:* www.avantesecurity.com	Toronto	ON	M3B2M3	416-923-6984		693
Avante Solutions Inc 728 W Jackson Ste 105 *Web:* www.avantesolutions.com	Chicago	IL	60661	312-715-1080		445
Avantec Vascular Corp 605 W California Ave *Web:* www.avantecvascular.com	Sunnyvale	CA	94086	408-329-5400		476
Avantech Inc 95-A Sunbelt Blvd *Web:* www.avantechinc.com	Columbia	SC	29203	803-407-7171		358
Avanti 4620 Grandview Ave *Web:* avanticheyenne.com	Cheyenne	WY	82009	307-634-3432		671
Avanti Corp 6621 Richmond Hgwy Ste 200 *Web:* www.avanticorporation.com	Alexandria	VA	22306	703-765-0060	765-0694	194
Avanti Destinations Inc 1629 SW Salmon St **Fax Area Code:* 800 ■ *TF:* 800-422-5053 ■ *Web:* www.avantidestinations.com	Portland	OR	97205	503-295-1100	422-9505*	771
Avanti Engineering Inc 200 West Lake Dr *TF:* 800-521-3320 ■ *Web:* www.avantiengineering.com	Glendale Heights	IL	60139	630-260-1333	260-1762	621
Avanti Environmental Inc 10842 Noel St Ste 108 *Web:* www.avantienvironmental.com	Los Alamitos	CA	90720	714-730-3320		194
Avanti Foods 109 Depot St *TF:* 800-243-3739 ■ *Web:* www.avantifoods.com	Walnut	IL	61376	815-379-2155	379-9357	296-36
Avanti Polar Lipids Inc 700 Industrial Pk Dr *TF:* 800-227-0651 ■ *Web:* www.avantilipids.com	Alabaster	AL	35007	205-663-2494	663-0756	479
Avanti Press Inc 155 W Congress St Ste 200 **Fax Area Code:* 800 ■ *TF:* 800-228-2684 ■ *Web:* www.avantipress.com	Detroit	MI	48226	313-961-0022	875-9690*	130
Avanti's 2728 E Thomas Rd *Web:* www.avanti-az.com	Phoenix	AZ	85016	602-956-0900		671
Avantia Inc 9655 Sweet Vly Dr *Web:* www.avantia-inc.com	Valley View	OH	44125	216-901-9366		196
Avantica Technologies 2680 Bayshore Pkwy Ste 416 *TF:* 877-372-1955 ■ *Web:* www.avantica.net	Mountain View	CA	94043	650-248-9678		196
Avantpage Translations 1138 Villaverde Ln *TF:* 877-269-5264 ■ *Web:* www.avantpage.com	Davis	CA	95618	530-750-2040		317
Avantus 15 W Strong St Ste 20A **Fax Area Code:* 800 ■ *TF:* 800-600-2510 ■ *Web:* www.advantagecredit.com	Pensacola	FL	32501	850-470-9336	600-2508*	178-10
Avanzado LLC 25330 Interchange Ct *TF:* 800-913-1058 ■ *Web:* www.avanzadollc.com	Farmington Hills	MI	48335	800-913-1058		459
Avascent Group, The 1615 L St NW Ste 1200 *Web:* www.avascent.com	Washington	DC	20036	202-452-6990		463
Avatar Engineering Inc 14360 W 96th Terr *Web:* avatar-eng.com	Lenexa	KS	66215	913-897-6757		256
Avatar Management Services Inc 8157 Bavaria Dr E *TF:* 800-728-2827 ■ *Web:* www.avatarms.com	Macedonia	OH	44056	330-963-3900		463
Avatar Studios Inc 2675 Scott Ave Ste G *Web:* www.avatar-studios.com	Saint Louis	MO	63103	314-533-2242	533-3349	514
Avatier Corp 2603 Camino Ramon Ste 110 *TF:* 800-609-8610 ■ *Web:* www.avatier.com	San Ramon	CA	94583	925-217-5170	275-0853	178-12
AVAX Technologies Inc 2000 Hamilton St Ste 204 *Web:* avax-tech.com	Philadelphia	PA	19130	215-241-9760	241-9684	85
Avaxia Biologics Inc 128 Spring St Ste 620 *Web:* www.avaxiabiologics.com	Lexington	MA	02421	781-861-0062		668
Avaya Government Solutions Inc 12730 Fair Lakes Cir *TF:* 800-492-6769 ■ *Web:* www.avaya.com/avayagov	Fairfax	VA	22033	703-653-8000	653-8001	178-10
Avaya Inc 211 Mt Airy Rd *TF:* 866-462-8292 ■ *Web:* www.avaya.com	Basking Ridge	NJ	07920	908-953-6000		176
Avazpour Networking Services Inc 10895 Grandview Dr	Overland Park	KS	66210	913-498-8777	491-7407	39
Avborne Accessory Group 7500 NW 26th St *Web:* www.avborne.com	Miami	FL	33122	305-593-6038		22
AVCF (Arkansas Valley Correctional Facility) 12750 Colorado 96 PO Box 1000 *Web:* www.doc.state.co.us	Crowley	CO	81033	719-267-3520	267-5024	213
Avchem Inc 5757 Phantom Dr Ste 300 *Web:* www.avchem.com	Hazelwood	MO	63042	314-880-2700		146
Avcom SMT Inc 213 E Broadway *Web:* www.avcomsmt.com	Westerville	OH	43081	614-882-8176		668
Avcorp Industries Inc 10025 River Way *TF:* 866-781-3111 ■ *Web:* www.avcorp.com	Delta	BC	V4G1M7	604-582-1137	582-2620	22
AvCraft Technical Services Inc 3301 Mustang St *Web:* www.avcrafttechnical.com	Myrtle Beach	SC	29577	843-232-1338		20
Ave Intervision LLC 1840 W State St *TF:* 800-448-9126 ■ *Web:* www.amvonet.com	Alliance	OH	44601	800-448-9126		685
Ave Maria University 5050 Ave Maria Blvd **Fax:* Admissions ■ *TF:* 877-283-8648 ■ *Web:* avemaria.edu	Naples	FL	34119	239-280-2500	280-2556*	166
Ave Maria University School of Law 1025 Commons Cir *Web:* www.avemarialaw.edu	Naples	FL	34119	239-687-5300		167-1
Avec Restaurant 615 W Randolph St *Web:* www.avecrestaurant.com	Chicago	IL	60661	312-377-2002		671
Aveda Corp 4000 Pheasant Ridge Dr *TF:* 800-644-4831 ■ *Web:* www.aveda.com	Blaine	MN	55449	800-644-4831		214
Avedis Zildjian Co 22 Longwater Dr *TF:* 800-229-8672 ■ *Web:* www.zildjian.com	Norwell	MA	02061	781-871-2200		527
AVEM (Association of Vacuum Equipment Manufacturers) 201 Pk Washington Ct *Web:* www.avem.org	Falls Church	VA	22046	703-538-3543	241-5603	49-13
Avemco Insurance Co 411 Aviation Way *TF:* 800-874-9125 ■ *Web:* avemco.com	Frederick	MD	21701	301-694-5700		391-4
Avenal State Prison 1 Kings Hwy PO Box 8 *Web:* cdcr.ca.gov	Avenal	CA	93204	559-386-0587		213
Avendra LLC 702 King Farm Blvd Ste 600 *Web:* www.avendra.com	Rockville	MD	20850	301-825-0500	825-0497	379
Avenger Aircraft & Services LLC 103 N Main St Ste 106 *Web:* www.avengeraircraft.com	Greenville	SC	29601	864-232-8073		194
Aventura Hospital 20900 Biscayne Blvd *TF:* 800-523-5772 ■ *Web:* www.aventurahospital.com	Aventura	FL	33180	305-682-7000		374-3
Aventura Mall 19501 Biscayne Blvd *Web:* aventuramall.com	Aventura	FL	33180	305-935-1110		460
Aventure International Aviation Services LLC 108 International Dr *Web:* aventureaviation.com	Peachtree City	GA	30269	770-632-7930		21
Avenue Bistro Restaurant 6710 W Central Ave *Web:* centralavenuebistro.com	Toledo	OH	43617	419-841-5944	842-1435	671
Avenue Inn & Spa 33 Wilmington Ave *TF:* 800-433-5870 ■ *Web:* www.avenueinn.com	Rehoboth Beach	DE	19971	800-433-5870		379
Avenue Magazine 79 Madison Ave 16th Fl *Web:* www.avenuemagazine.com	New York	NY	10016	212-268-8600		457-11
Avenue Marketing & Communication 363 W Erie St #4E Chicago, *Web:* www.avenue-inc.com	Chicago	IL	60654	312-787-8300		5
Avenue Plaza Resort 2111 St Charles Ave *TF:* 800-614-8685 ■ *Web:* www.avenueplazaresort.com	New Orleans	LA	70130	504-566-1212		379

Name	Address	City	State	ZIP	Phone	Fax	Class	Details
Avenue Staffing	7000 57th Ave N Ste 120	Crystal	MN	55428	763-537-6104		260	*Web:* www.avenuestaffing.com
Avenue Stores Inc	365 W Passaic St	Rochelle Park	NJ	07662	201-845-0880		157-6	*TF:* 888-843-2836 ■ *Web:* www.avenue.com
Avenue100 Media Solutions Inc	1601 Trapelo Rd Ste 202	Waltham	MA	02451	781-683-3300		242	*Web:* avenue100.com
Avenues Mall	10300 Southside Blvd	Jacksonville	FL	32256	904-363-3054	363-3058	460	*Web:* www.simon.com
Aveo Pharmaceuticals Inc	75 Sidney St	Cambridge	MA	02139	617-299-5000	995-4995	668	*NASDAQ: AVEO* ■ *Web:* www.aveooncology.com
Aveox Inc	2265A Ward Ave.	Simi Valley	CA	93065	805-915-0200		518	*Web:* www.aveox.com
Avera	1325 S Cliff Ave PO Box 5045	Sioux Falls	SD	57105	605-322-8000		374-3	*Web:* www.avera.org/mckennan
Avera Health	3900 W Avera Dr	Sioux Falls	SD	57108	605-322-4700	322-4799	353	*Web:* www.avera.org
Avera Queen of Peace Hospital	525 N Foster St	Mitchell	SD	57301	605-995-2000	995-2441	374-3	*TF:* 888-531-1685 ■ *Web:* www.avera.org/queen-of-peace
Avera Sacred Heart Hospital	501 Summit	Yankton	SD	57078	605-668-8000		374-3	*Web:* www.avera.org/sacred-heart
Avera Saint Luke's Hospital	305 S State St	Aberdeen	SD	57401	605-622-5000	622-5127	374-3	*TF:* 800-658-3535 ■ *Web:* www.avera.org/st-lukes-hospital
Avere Systems Inc	5000 Mcknight Rd Ste 404	Pittsburgh	PA	15237	412-894-2570		173-8	*TF:* 888-882-8373 ■ *Web:* www.averesystems.com
Averitt Air Inc	625 Hngr Ln Hngr 4 Nashville International Airport	Nashville	TN	37217	615-399-8077		21	*Web:* www.averittair.com
Averitt Express Inc	1415 Neal St	Cookeville	TN	38501	800-283-7488		780	*TF:* 800-283-7488 ■ *Web:* www.averittexpress.com
Avery Abrasives Inc	2225 Reservoir Ave.	Trumbull	CT	06611	203-372-3513		1	*Web:* www.averyabrasives.com
Avery County	4501 Tynecastle Hwy Unit 2Intersection of NC 105 & NC 184	Banner Elk	NC	28604	828-898-5605		338	*Web:* www.averycounty.com
Avery Dennison	207 Goode Ave	Glendale	CA	91203-1222	800-444-4947		745-5	*TF:* 800-444-4947 ■ *Web:* www.rbis.averydennison.com
Avery Dennison Corp	17700 Foltz Industrial Pkwy	Strongsville	OH	44149	440-878-7000		413	
Avery Dennison Corp	207 Goode Ave	Glendale	CA	91203	626-304-2000		732	*NYSE: AVY* ■ *TF Cust Svc:* 888-567-4387 ■ *Web:* www.averydennison.com
Avery Dennison Fastener Div	224 Industrial Rd	Fitchburg	MA	01420	800-225-5913	848-2169	608	*TF:* 800-225-5913 ■ *Web:* www.fastener.averydennison.com
Avery Dennison Microreplication Div	207 Goode Ave	Glendale	CA	91203	626-304-2000		240	*Web:* www.averydennison.com
Avery Dennison Specialty Tapes	250 Chester St	Painesville	OH	44077	866-462-8379	358-4469*	732	**Fax Area Code:* 888 ■ *TF:* 866-462-8379 ■ *Web:* tapes.averydennison.com
Avery Dennison Worldwide Graphics Div	207 Goode Ave Bldg 8	Glendale	CA	91205	440-358-3700		552-1	*TF:* 800-443-9380 ■ *Web:* www.averydennison.com/en/home.html
Avery Dennison Worldwide Office Products Div	207 Goode Ave	Glendale	CA	91203	626-304-2000	848-2169*	534	**Fax Area Code:* 800 ■ *TF:* 800-462-8379 ■ *Web:* www.averydennison.com
Avery Outdoors Inc	335 Cumberland St	Memphis	TN	38112	901-454-2567		711	*Web:* www.averyoutdoors.com
Avery Point Mktg Solutions	244 Upton Rd	Colchester	CT	06415	860-537-2440		194	
Avery Research Ctr for African-American History & Culture	125 Bull St	Charleston	SC	29424	843-953-7609	953-7607	520	*Web:* www.cofc.edu
Avery Weigh-Tronix Inc	1000 Armstrong Dr	Fairmont	MN	56031	507-238-4461	238-8258*	684	**Fax:* Mktg ■ *TF:* 800-458-7062 ■ *Web:* www.averyweigh-tronix.com
Avery/Mitchell Correctional Ctr	600 Amity Pk Rd	Spruce Pine	NC	28777	828-765-0229	765-0946	213	
Aves Audio Visual Systems Inc	PO Box 500	Sugar Land	TX	77487	281-295-1300	295-1310	38	*TF:* 800-365-2837 ■ *Web:* www.avesav.com
Avesta Computer Services Ltd	1 Executive Dr Ste 120	Somerset	NJ	08873	201-369-9400		196	*TF:* 888-283-7821 ■ *Web:* www.avestacs.com
AVF Consulting Inc	1220-A E Joppa Rd Ste 240	Baltimore	MD	21286	410-296-5100		180	*TF:* 800-296-2747 ■ *Web:* www.avfconsulting.com
Avfinity LLC	11782 Jollyville Rd.	Austin	TX	78759	512-535-3416		387	*Web:* www.avfinity.com
AVG Automation	4140 Utica St	Bettendorf	IA	52722	877-774-3279		253	*TF:* 877-774-3279 ■ *Web:* avg.net/index.htm
AVI Casino Enterprise Inc	10000 Aha Macav Pkwy	Laughlin	NV	89029	702-535-5555		452	*TF:* 800-562-4142 ■ *Web:* www.avicasino.com
Avi Systems Inc	9675 W 76th St Ste 200	Eden Prairie	MN	55344	952-949-3700	949-6000	647	*TF:* 800-488-4954 ■ *Web:* www.avisystems.com
Aviagen Group	5015 Bradford Dr.	Huntsville	AL	35805	256-890-3800	890-3919	10-8	*Web:* aviagen.com
Aviall Inc	2750 Regent Blvd Dallas Fort Worth Airport	Dallas	TX	75261	972-586-1985	586-1361	770	*Web:* www.aviall.com
Aviat Aircraft Inc	672 S Washington	Afton	WY	83110	307-885-3151		529	*Web:* www.aviataircraft.com
Aviation Brake Services Inc	7274 NW 34th St	Miami	FL	33122	305-594-4677		22	*Web:* www.aviationbrake.com
Aviation Capital Group Corp	840 Newport Ctr Dr Ste 300	Newport Beach	CA	92660	949-219-4600	759-5675	23	*Web:* www.aviationcapitalgroup.com
Aviation Devices & Electronic Components LLC	1810 Mony St	Fort Worth	TX	76102	817-738-9161		57	*Web:* www.avdec.com
Aviation Ground Equipment Corp	53 Hanse Ave	Freeport	NY	11520	516-546-0003		57	*TF:* 800-758-0044 ■ *Web:* www.aviationgroundequip.com
Aviation Institute of Maintenance	3001 Grant Ave	Philadelphia	PA	19114	215-676-7700		800	*Web:* www.aviationmaintenance.edu
Aviation Institute of Maintenance Houston	7651 Airport Blvd	Houston	TX	77061	713-644-7777		800	*TF:* 888-349-5387 ■ *Web:* www.aviationmaintenance.edu
Aviation Leasing Group	8080 Ward Pkwy Ste 407	Kansas City	MO	64114	816-931-7300		23	
Aviation Management Systems Inc	155 Fleet St	Portsmouth	NH	03801	603-431-3362	433-7650	463	*Web:* amsinc.aero
Aviation Materials Management Inc	2581 Rulon White Blvd	Ogden	UT	84404	801-782-8450		529	*Web:* www.avmat.com
Aviation Museum of Kentucky	4020 Airport Rd	Lexington	KY	40510	859-231-1219		520	*TF:* 800-960-7200 ■ *Web:* www.aviationky.org
Aviation Partners Inc	7213 Perimeter Rd S	Seattle	WA	98108	206-762-1171		529	*Web:* www.aviationpartners.com
Aviation Spares & Services I	8920 152nd Ave NE	Redmond	WA	98052	425-869-7799		770	*Web:* www.assic.com
Aviation Supplies & Academics Inc	7005 132nd Pl SE	Newcastle	WA	98059	425-235-1500		637-2	*TF:* 800-272-2359 ■ *Web:* asa2fly.com
Aviation Systems of Northwest Florida Inc	175 E Olive Rd	Pensacola	FL	32514	800-759-0953		21	*TF:* 800-759-0953 ■ *Web:* lsijax.com
Aviation Week & Space Technology Magazine	1200 G St NW	Washington	DC	20005	800-525-5003		457-19	*TF:* 800-525-5003 ■ *Web:* www.aviationweek.com
AviationWeek	1200 G St NW Ste 900	Washington	DC	20005	800-525-5003	383-2438*	531-13	**Fax Area Code:* 202 ■ *TF:* 800-525-5003 ■ *Web:* www.aviationweek.com/businessaviation.aspx
Avibank Manufacturing Inc	11500 Sherman Way	North Hollywood	CA	91605	818-392-2100	255-2094	278	*TF:* 800-627-3999 ■ *Web:* www.avibank.com
Avicenna Technology Inc	1602 Benson Rd	Montevideo	MN	56265	320-269-5588		454	*Web:* www.avicennatech.com
Avid Identification Systems Inc	3185 Hamner Ave	Norco	CA	92860	951-371-7505		10-3	*Web:* www.avidid.com
Avid Inc	50 Founders Plaza	East Hartford	CT	06108	860-528-1988		344	*Web:* www.avidinc.com
Avid Neo Geo	108 Lake Ave	Orlando	FL	32801	407-246-0092		4	*Web:* www.avidneogeo.com
Avid Payment Solutions	950 S Old Woodward Ste 220	Birmingham	MI	48009	888-855-8644	671-9773*	255	**Fax Area Code:* 866 ■ *TF:* 888-855-8644 ■ *Web:* www.avidpays.com
Avid Radiopharmaceuticals Inc	3711 Market St 7th Fl	Philadelphia	PA	19104	215-298-0700		231	*Web:* www.avidrp.com
Avid Technology Inc	65-75 Network Dri	Burlington	MA	01803	978-640-6789	640-3366	178-8	*NASDAQ: AVID* ■ *TF:* 800-949-2843 ■ *Web:* www.avid.com
Avideon Corp	PO Box 4830	Baltimore	MD	21211	888-368-1237		195	*TF:* 888-368-1237 ■ *Web:* www.avideon.com
Avidex Industries LLC	13555 Bel-Red Rd Ste 226	Bellevue	WA	98005	425-643-0330		52	*Web:* www.avidex.com
Avidian Technologies Inc	2053 152nd Ave NE	Redmond	WA	98052	206-686-3001		177	*TF:* 800-860-5534 ■ *Web:* avidian.com
Avidyne Corp	55 Old Bedford Rd Ste 101	Lincoln	MA	01773	781-402-7400		22	*Web:* www.avidyne.com
Avila Retail Development & Management LLC	5001 Ellison St NE	Albuquerque	NM	87109	505-341-3753		292	*Web:* www.avilaretail.com
Avila University	11901 Wornall Rd	Kansas City	MO	64145	816-501-2400	501-2453	166	*TF:* 866-943-5787 ■ *Web:* www.avila.edu
Avila's	4714 Maple Ave.	Dallas	TX	75219	214-520-2700		671	
Avilar Technologies Inc	6760 Alexander Bell Dr Ste 105	Columbia	MD	21046	410-290-0008		177	*Web:* www.avilar.com
Aviles Engineering Corp	5790 Windfern Rd.	Houston	TX	77041	713-895-7645	895-7943	256	*Web:* www.avilesengineering.com
Avineon Inc	4825 Mark Ctr Dr Ste 700	Alexandria	VA	22311	703-671-1900	671-1901	177	*Web:* www.avineon.com
Aviojet Corp	76 Brookside Dr	Upper Saddle River	NJ	07458	201-825-3111	825-6950	770	*Web:* www.aviojet.com
Avion Solutions Inc	4905 Research Dr NW	Huntsville	AL	35805	256-721-7006		261	*Web:* avionsolutions.com
Avion Technologies Inc	1203 Lorimar Dr	Mississauga	ON	L5S1M9	905-670-1570	670-1568	709	*Web:* www.avion-tech.com
Avionic Instruments Inc	1414 Randolph Ave.	Avenel	NJ	07001	732-388-3500	382-4996	253	*TF:* 800-468-3571 ■ *Web:* www.avionicinstruments.com
Avionics & Systems Integration Group LLC	10 Collins Industrial Pl Ste 3b	North Little Rock	AR	72113	501-771-9388		529	*Web:* asigllc.com
Avionics Test & Analysis Corp	4540 E Hwy 20 Ste 6	Niceville	FL	32578	850-897-4553	897-4331	261	*Web:* www.avtest.com

Name / Address	Phone	Fax	Class
Avior Computing Corp Nashua Airport 11 Perimeter Rd . . . . . Nashua NH 03063 *Web:* www.aviorcomputing.com	603-886-8145		177
Avior Integrated Products Inc 1001 Autoroute 440 Ouest . . . . . Laval QC H7L3W3 *TF:* 800-463-4920 ■ *Web:* www.avior.ca	450-629-6200		21
Aviotrade Inc 10850 NW 21st St Ste 230 & 240. . . . . Miami FL 33172 *Web:* www.aviotrade.com	305-717-5000		492
Avis Furniture Co 1410 Union Ave . . . . . Kansas City MO 64101 *Web:* www.avisfurniture.com	816-421-5939		321
Avis Industrial Corp 1909 S Main St . . . . . Upland IN 46989 *Web:* www.avisindustrial.com	765-998-8100	998-8111	60
Avis Rent A Car System Inc 6 Sylvan Way . . . . . Parsippany NJ 07054 *Fax: Sales ■ *TF:* 800-331-1212 ■ *Web:* www.avis.com	973-496-3500	496-3444*	126
Avisen Securities Inc 3620 American River Dr Ste 145. . . . . Sacramento CA 95864 *TF:* 800-230-7704 ■ *Web:* www.avisensecurities.com	916-480-2747		690
Avista Adventist Hospital 100 Health Pk Dr . . . . . Louisville CO 80027 *Web:* avistahospital.org	303-673-1000		374-3
Avista Corp 1411 E Mission St . . . . . Spokane WA 99202 *NYSE: AVA* ■ *TF:* 800-936-6629 ■ *Web:* www.avistacorp.com	509-489-0500		787
Avista Corporation 1411 E Mission St. . . . . Spokane WA 99252 *Fax Area Code: 509 ■ *TF:* 800-227-9187 ■ *Web:* www.avistautilities.com	800-227-9187	495-8725*	787
Avista Resort 300 N Ocean Blvd. . . . . North Myrtle Beach SC 29582 *TF:* 866-573-2062 ■ *Web:* www.avistaresort.com	843-249-2521		377
AvistaHotels.com 5353 Conroy Rd Ste 200 . . . . . Orlando FL 32811 *Web:* www.avistahotels.com	407-581-5457	581-7777	377
Avistar Communications Corp 1855 S Grant St 4th Fl . . . . . San Mateo CA 94402 *OTC: AVSR* ■ *Web:* www.avistar.com	650-525-3300	525-1360	178-7
Avitus Group PO Box 81590 . . . . . Billings MT 59108 *TF:* 800-454-2446 ■ *Web:* www.avitusgroup.com	800-454-2446		734
Avjobs Inc PO Box 260830. . . . . Littleton CO 80163 *Fax Area Code: 888 ■ *TF:* 888-624-8691 ■ *Web:* www.avjobs.com	303-683-2322	624-8691*	260
Avl Powertrain Engineering Inc 47519 Halyard Dr . . . . . Plymouth MI 48170 *Web:* www.avl.com	734-414-9600		153
Avl Systems Design LLC 14901 Bristol Park Blvd . . . . . Edmond OK 73013 *TF:* 800-935-3920 ■ *Web:* www.avl1.com	405-749-1866		180
AVM LP 777 Yamato Rd. . . . . Boca Raton FL 33431 *Web:* www.avmlp.com	561-544-4600		690
AVMA (American Veterinary Medical Assn PAC) 1910 Sunderland Pl NW . . . . . Washington DC 20036 *TF:* 800-321-1473 ■ *Web:* www.avma.org	202-789-0007	842-4360	615
AVMA (American Veterinary Medical Assn) 1931 N Meacham Rd Ste 100. . . . . Schaumburg IL 60173 *TF:* 800-248-2862 ■ *Web:* www.avma.org	847-925-8070	925-1329	49-8
AvMed 4300 NW 89th Blvd . . . . . Gainesville FL 32606 *TF:* 800-346-0231 ■ *Web:* www.avmed.org	352-372-8400		391-3
AVMetrics LLC 90 W Cochran St Ste C. . . . . Simi Valley CA 93065 *Web:* www.avmetrics.net	805-421-5056		466
AVN Media Network Inc 9400 Penfield Ave. . . . . Chatsworth CA 91311 *Web:* www.avnmedianetwork.com	818-718-5788		637-9
Avnet Electronics Marketing Inc 2211 S 47th St . . . . . Phoenix AZ 85034 *TF:* 888-924-6832 ■ *Web:* avnetexpress.avnet.com	480-643-2000		253
Avnet Inc 2211 S 47th St . . . . . Phoenix AZ 85034 *NYSE: AVT* ■ *TF:* 888-822-8638 ■ *Web:* www.avnet.com	480-643-2000		246
Avnet Technology Solutions 8700 S Price Rd . . . . . Tempe AZ 85284 *TF:* 800-409-1483 ■ *Web:* www.ats.avnet.com	480-794-6500		174
Avoca Group 179 Nassau St Ste 3a . . . . . Princeton NJ 08542 *TF:* 800-595-0735 ■ *Web:* www.theavocagroup.com	609-252-9020	252-9022	194
Avocet Hospitality Group 38 Ctr St. . . . . Folly Beach SC 29439 *TF:* 800-905-6290 ■ *Web:* avocethospitality.com	843-588-6699		377
Avogadro Group LLC, The 2825 Verne Roberts Cir. . . . . Antioch CA 94509 *Web:* www.avogadrogroup.com	925-680-4300		192
Avon Bearings Inc 1500 Nagle Rd . . . . . Avon OH 44011 *Web:* www.kaydonbearings.com	440-871-2500		75
Avon Free Public Library 281 Country Club Rd . . . . . Avon CT 06001 *TF:* 800-200-2882 ■ *Web:* www.avonctlibrary.info	860-673-9712	675-6364	434-3
Avon Health Ctr Inc 652 W Avon Rd . . . . . Avon CT 06001 *TF:* 800-889-6008 ■ *Web:* avonhealthcenter.com	860-673-2521		450
Avon Old Farms School 500 Old Farms Rd . . . . . Avon CT 06001 *TF:* 800-464-2866 ■ *Web:* www.avonoldfarms.com	860-404-4100	675-6051	622
Avon Park Correctional Institution 8100 County Rd 64 E . . . . . Avon Park FL 33825 *Web:* dc.state.fl.us	863-453-3174	453-1511	213
Avon Products Inc 360 W 31st St. . . . . New York NY 10011 *NYSE: AVP* ■ *TF Cust Svc:* 800-367-2866 ■ *Web:* www.avon.com	212-282-7000		214
Avondale House 3611 Cummins St. . . . . Houston TX 77027 *TF:* 800-245-1255 ■ *Web:* www.avondalehouse.org	713-993-9544		685
Avonworth School District 258 Josephs Ln . . . . . Pittsburgh PA 15237 *Web:* www.avonworth.k12.pa.us	412-369-8738	369-8746	685
Avotus Corp 409 Matheson Blvd E. . . . . Mississauga ON L4Z2H2 *Web:* www.avotus.com	905-890-9199		224
Avow Hospice Inc 1095 Whippoorwill Ln. . . . . Naples FL 34105 *TF:* 800-378-0596 ■ *Web:* www.avowcares.org	239-261-4404		371
Avox Systems Inc 225 Erie St. . . . . Lancaster NY 14086 *Web:* www.avoxsys.com	716-683-5100		22
Avoyelles Correctional Ctr 1630 Prison Rd. . . . . Cottonport LA 71327 *Web:* doc.la.gov	318-876-2891	876-4220	213
Avoyelles Journal 105 N Main St. . . . . Marksville LA 71351 *TF:* 800-565-4321 ■ *Web:* avoyellestoday.com	318-253-5413	253-7223	532-4
Avoyelles Parish 675 Government St. . . . . Marksville LA 71351 *Web:* avoyellesso.org	318-253-8085		338
Avoyelles Parish Library 104 N Washington St . . . . . Marksville LA 71351 *Web:* www.avoyelles.lib.la.us	318-253-7559		434-3
AVR Inc 14698 Galaxy Ave . . . . . Apple Valley MN 55124 *TF:* 800-369-6787 ■ *Web:* www.avrconcrete.com	952-432-7132		182
Avrett Free Ginsberg (AFG) 885 Second Ave Dag Hammarskjold Plz. . . . . New York NY 10017 *Web:* avrettfreeginsberg.com	212-832-3800		4
Avrick Direct Inc PO Box 1449. . . . . Goleta CA 93116 *Web:* www.avrickdirect.com	805-683-6551		463
Avrio Capital Inc Crowfoot West Business Centre 400 Crowfoot Crescent NW Ste 500 . . . . . Calgary AB T3G5H6 *Web:* www.avriocapital.com	403-215-5492		528
AVRMC (Arkansas Valley Regional Medical Ctr) 1100 Carson Ave . . . . . La Junta CO 81050 *TF:* 877-696-6775 ■ *Web:* www.avrmc.org	719-384-5412	383-6005	374-3
AVS (Advanced Visual Systems Inc) 300 Fifth Ave. . . . . Waltham MA 02451 *OTC: AVSC* ■ *Web:* www.avs.com	781-890-4300	890-8287	178-5
AVS Companies 750 Morse Ave . . . . . Elk Grove Village IL 60007 *TF:* 800-441-0009 ■ *Web:* www.americanvending.com	847-439-9400	439-9405	55
Avs Group 3120 S Ave . . . . . La Crosse WI 54601 *Web:* www.avsgroup.com	608-787-8101		194
AVS Inc 60 Fitchburg Rd. . . . . Ayer MA 01432 *TF:* 800-772-0710 ■ *Web:* www.avsinc.com	978-772-0710	772-6462	318
AVS Installations LLC 400 Raritan Ctr Pkwy Ste D. . . . . Edison NJ 08837 *TF:* 800-218-9177 ■ *Web:* www.avsillc.com	732-634-7903		180
AVS Science & Technology Society 120 Wall St 32nd Fl . . . . . New York NY 10005 *Web:* www.avs.org	212-248-0200	248-0245	49-19
AVSI (Automated Voice Systems Inc) 17059 El Cajon Ave . . . . . Yorba Linda CA 92886	714-524-4488		52
Avsi Group 4464 w 12th st . . . . . Houston TX 77055 *TF:* 800-835-7365 ■ *Web:* www.avsigroup.com	713-200-8300		23
Avstar Aviation Ltd 12 N Haven Ln . . . . . East Northport NY 11731 *TF:* 800-575-2359 ■ *Web:* www.avstaraviation.com	631-499-0048		13
Avt Simulation Inc 2603 Challenger Tech Ct Ste 180. . . . . Orlando FL 32826 *Web:* www.avtsim.com	407-381-5311		256
Avtec Inc 6 Industrial Pk . . . . . Cahokia IL 62206 *TF:* 800 552 8832 ■ *Web:* www.avteclighting.com	618-337-7800	337-7976	438
Avtech Corp 3400 Wallingford Ave N. . . . . Seattle WA 98103 *TF:* 800-687-4568 ■ *Web:* www.avtcorp.com	206-695-8000	695-8011	647
Avtech Software Inc 16 Cutler St Cutler Mill. . . . . Warren RI 02885 *TF:* 888-220-6700 ■ *Web:* www.avtech.com	401-847-6700		177
Avtron Aerospace Inc 7900 E Pleasant Valley Rd . . . . . Cleveland OH 44131 *TF:* 800-783-7871 ■ *Web:* www.avtronaero.com	216-750-5152		21
Avue Technologies Corp 3560 Bridgeport Way W Ste 3B . . . . . University Place WA 98466 *Web:* www.avuetech.com	253-573-1877		178-1
AVUSD (Apple Valley Unified School District) 12555 Navajo Rd . . . . . Apple Valley CA 92308 *Web:* www.avusd.org	760-247-8001		685
Avval Inc 1235 Windham Pkwy . . . . . Romeoville IL 60446 *Web:* www.avval.com	630 343 6060		177
Avvo Inc 705 Fifth Ave S Ste 600 . . . . . Seattle WA 98104 *Web:* www.avvo.com	206-734-4111		387
AVX Corp 801 17th Ave S . . . . . Myrtle Beach SC 29577 *NYSE: AVX* ■ *Web:* www.avx.com	843-448-9411		253
AW (American Whitewater) PO Box 1540 . . . . . Cullowhee NC 28723 *TF:* 866-262-8429 ■ *Web:* americanwhitewater.org	828-586-1930	586-2840	48-23
AW Chesterton Co 500 Unicorn Pk Dr . . . . . Woburn MA 01801 *TF:* 888-400-4872 ■ *Web:* www.chesterton.com	781-438-7000	438-8971	326
AW Mercer Inc 104 Industrial Dr PO Box 508. . . . . Boyertown PA 19512 *TF:* 800-344-8858 ■ *Web:* www.awmercer.com	610-367-8460	367-7491	697
AW Shucks 3601 Greenville Ave. . . . . Dallas TX 75206 *Web:* www.awshucksdallas.com	214-821-9449		671
Aw Transmission Engineering USA Inc 14920 Keel St. . . . . Plymouth MI 48170 *Web:* www.awtec.com	734-454-1710	454-1091	60
AW Zengeler Cleaners 550 Dundee Rd . . . . . Northbrook IL 60062 *Web:* www.zengelercleaners.com	847-272-6550		426
Award Hardwood Floors LLP 401 N 72nd Ave . . . . . Wausau WI 54401	715-849-8080		290
Award Products Inc 4830 N Front St . . . . . Philadelphia PA 19120 *Web:* directory.hawaiitribune-herald.com	215-457-9414		777
Award Solutions Inc 2100 Lakeside Blvd . . . . . Richardson TX 75082 *Web:* awardsolutions.com	972-664-0727		194
Award Winner Group 202 W Third St . . . . . Mount Vernon NY 10550 *Web:* www.awardwinnergroup.com	914-664-7134	668-2858	453
Awards and Personalization Assn (ARA) 8735 W Higgins Rd Ste 300 . . . . . Chicago IL 60631 *TF:* 800-344-2148 ■ *Web:* awardspersonalization.org/default.aspx	847-375-4800	375-6480	49-4
Aware Inc 40 Middlesex Tpke . . . . . Bedford MA 01730 *NASDAQ: AWRE* ■ *Web:* www.aware.com	781-276-4000	276-4001	696
Awareness Technology Inc PO Box 1679 . . . . . Palm City FL 34991 *Web:* www.awaretech.com	772-283-6540	283-8020	544
AwaySys Inc 207 Los Angeles Ave # 105 . . . . . Moorpark CA 93021 *Web:* www.awaysys.com	805-242-2007		463
Awbury Arboretum & Historic Estate 1 Awbury Rd Francis Cope House . . . . . Philadelphia PA 19138 *Web:* www.awbury.org	215-849-2855		97
AWC (Association for Women in Communications) 1717 E Republic Rd Ste A. . . . . Springfield MO 65804 *Web:* www.womcom.org	417-886-8606		49-14
AWC Commercial Window Coverings Inc 825 Williamson Ave . . . . . Fullerton CA 92832 *TF:* 800-252-2280 ■ *Web:* www.awc-cwc.com	714-879-3880	879-8419	189-1

Company	City	State	Zip	Phone	Fax	Class
AWC Inc 6655 Exchequer Dr *Web:* www.awc-inc.com	Baton Rouge	LA	70809	225-752-1100		463
AWCI (Association of the Wall & Ceiling Industries International) 513 W Broad St Ste 210 *TF:* 800-233-8990 ■ *Web:* www.awci.org	Falls Church	VA	22046	703-538-1600	534-8307	49-3
AWEA (American Wind Energy Assn) 1501 M St NW Ste 1000 *Web:* www.awea.org	Washington	DC	20005	202-383-2500	383-2505	48-12
Awecomm Technologies L L C 165 Kirts Blvd Ste 400 *TF:* 800-574-0902 ■ *Web:* www.awecomm.com	Troy	MI	48084	248-404-9910		224
AWF (African Wildlife Foundation) 1400 16th St NW Ste 120 *TF:* 888-494-5354 ■ *Web:* www.awf.org	Washington	DC	20036	202-939-3333		48-3
Awful Arthur's Seafood Co 6078 Mechanicsville Tpke *Web:* www.awfularthurs.com	Mechanicsville	VA	23111	804-559-4370		671
aWhere Inc 4891 Independence St Ste 275 *Web:* www.awhere.com	Wheat Ridge	CO	80033	303-279-9293		463
AWHONN (Association of Women's Health Obstetric & Neonatal Nurses) 2000 L St NW Ste 740 *TF:* 800-673-8499 ■ *Web:* www.awhonn.org	Washington	DC	20036	202-261-2400	728-0575	49-8
AWI (American Watchmakers-Clockmakers Institute) 701 Enterprise Dr *TF:* 866-367-2924 ■ *Web:* awci.com	Harrison	OH	45030	513-367-9800	367-1414	49-4
AWI (Architectural Woodwork Institute) 46179 Westlake Dr Ste 120 *Web:* www.awinet.org	Potomac Falls	VA	20165	571-323-3636	323-3630	49-3
AWID (Association for Women's Rights in Development) 215 Spadina Ave Ste 150 *Web:* www.awid.org	Toronto	ON	M5T2C7	416-594-3773	594-0330	48-8
AWIS (Association for Women in Science Inc) 1321 Duke St Ste 210 *TF:* 866-736-7343 ■ *Web:* www.awis.org	Alexandria	VA	22314	703-894-4490	894-4489	49-19
A&WMA (Air & Waste Management Assn) 420 Fort Duquesne Blvd 1 Gateway Ctr 3rd Fl *TF:* 800-270-3444 ■ *Web:* www.awma.org	Pittsburgh	PA	15222	412-904-6018	232-3450	48-12
AWNEX Inc 260 Valley St Ste 100 *Web:* www.awnexinc.com	Ball Ground	GA	30107	770-704-7140		350
Awningtec USA Inc 3265 Highway 62 NW *Web:* www.awningtecusa.com	Corydon	IN	47112	812-734-0423		697
AWO (American Waterways Operators) 801 N Quincy St Ste 200 *Web:* www.americanwaterways.com	Arlington	VA	22203	703-841-9300	841-0389	49-21
AWP (AWP) George Mason Univ MS 1E3 *Web:* awpwriter.org	Fairfax	VA	22030	703-993-4301	993-4302	48-11
AWP Inc 826 Overholt Rd *TF:* 800-343-2650 ■ *Web:* www.awptrafficsafety.com	Kent	OH	44240	800-343-2650		693
Awp Industries Inc 616 Industrial Rd *Web:* www.awpind.com	Frankfort	KY	40601	502-695-0070		488
AWP Windows and Doors 8130 NW 74th Ave *Web:* www.awpwindowsanddoors.com	Medley	FL	33166	305-887-2646	883-1309	234
AWPA (American Wire Producers Assn) 801 N Fairfax St Ste 211 *Web:* www.awpa.org	Alexandria	VA	22314	703-299-4434	299-9233	49-13
AWR (American Warmblood Registry) PO Box 1332 **Fax Area Code: 775* ■ *TF:* 800-575-1669 ■ *Web:* www.americanwarmblood.com	DeLeon Springs	FL	32130	406-734-5499	667-0516*	48-3
Awrey Bakeries Inc 12301 Farmington Rd *TF:* 800-950-2253 ■ *Web:* www.awrey.com	Livonia	MI	48150	734-522-1100		68
AWS (American Welding Society) 550 NW 42nd Ave *TF:* 800-443-9353 ■ *Web:* www.aws.org	Miami	FL	33126	305-443-9353	443-7559	49-3
AWSCPA (American Woman's Society of Certified Public Accountants) 1430 Yale St *Web:* www.awscpa.org	Houston	OH	77008	713-893-5685		49-1
AWT (Association of Water Technologies) 9707 Key W Ave Ste 100 *Web:* www.awt.org	Rockville	MD	20850	301-740-1421	990-9771	48-2
AWT World Trade Inc 4321 N Knox Ave *Web:* www.awt-gpi.com	Chicago	IL	60641	773-777-7100	777-0909	629
AWWA (American Water Works Assn) 6666 W Quincy Ave *TF:* 800-926-7337 ■ *Web:* www.awwa.org	Denver	CO	80235	303-794-7711	347-0804	48-12
Axa Distributors LLC 1290 Ave of the Americas	New York	NY	10104	212-314-3731	314-3583	391-2
AXA Equitable Life Insurance Co 1290 Ave of the Americas *TF:* 800-800-9882 ■ *Web:* us.axa.com	New York	NY	10104	212-554-1234		391-2
AXA Rosenberg Investment Management LLC 4 Orinda Way Bldg E *Web:* www.axa-im.com/en/equities/rosenberg-equities	Orinda	CA	94563	925-254-6464		401
Axcelis Technologies Inc 108 Cherry Hill Dr *NASDAQ: ACLS* ■ *Web:* www.axcelis.com	Beverly	MA	01915	978-787-4000	787-4200	695
Axcept Media LLC 411 N Washington Ave Ste 208 *TF:* 800-767-9660 ■ *Web:* axceptmedia.com	Minneapolis	MN	55401	612-279-1310		195
Axcera Corp 103 Freedom Dr *TF:* 800-215-2614 ■ *Web:* www.axcera.com	Lawrence	PA	15055	724-873-8100	873-8105	647
Axcesor Inc 2260 Dakota Dr *Web:* www.axcesor.com	Grafton	WI	53024	262-375-7530		246
Axcet HR Solutions *Axet* 8325 Lenexa Dr Ste 410 *TF:* 800-801-7557 ■ *Web:* www.axcethr.com	Lenexa	KS	66214	913-383-2999	383-2949	631
Axcient Inc 1161 San Antonio Rd *TF:* 800-715-2339 ■ *Web:* www.axcient.com	Mountain View	CA	94043	800-715-2339		177
Axel Plastics Research Laboratories Inc 5820 Broadway *TF:* 800-332-2935 ■ *Web:* www.axelplastics.com	Woodside	NY	11377	718-672-8300		541
Axens North America Inc 650 College Rd E Ste 1200 *Web:* www.axens.net	Princeton	NJ	08540	609-243-8700		256
Axeon Specialty Products LLC 750 Washington Blvd Ste 600 *TF:* 855-378-4958 ■ *Web:* www.axeonsp.com	Stamford	CT	06901	855-378-4958		579
Axesstel Inc 6815 Flanders Dr Ste 210 *OTC: AXST* ■ *Web:* www.axesstel.com	San Diego	CA	92121	858-625-2100	625-2110	735
AXH air-coolers LLC 2230 E 49th St *Web:* www.axh.com	Tulsa	OK	74105	918-712-8268		539
AXIA Consulting LLC 1391 W Fifth Ave Ste 320 *TF:* 866-937-5550 ■ *Web:* www.axiaconsulting.net	Columbus	OH	43212	614-675-4050		196
Axia Public Relations 222 E Forsyth St *Web:* www.axiapr.com	Jacksonville	FL	32202	904-416-1500		636
Axia Strategies Inc 8688 Eagle Creek Cir *Web:* www.axiastrategies.com	Savage	MN	55378	952-945-3535		463
Axial Inc 902 Broadway 19th Fl *TF:* 800-860-4519 ■ *Web:* www.axial.net	New York	NY	10003	800-860-4519		691
AXIAL360 3500 Marmenco Ct *TF:* 800-965-0577 ■ *Web:* www.axial360.com	Baltimore	MD	21230	410-789-5300		5
Axiam Inc 58 Blackburn Ctr *Web:* www.axiam.com	Gloucester	MA	01930	978-281-3550		20
Axian Inc 9600 SW Nimbus Ave *Web:* www.axian.com	Beaverton	OR	97008	503-644-6106		196
Axian Technology 21622 N 14th Ave *Web:* www.axiantech.com	Phoenix	AZ	85027	623-580-0800		454
Axikin Pharmaceuticals Inc 6185 Cornerstone Ct Ste 106 *Web:* www.axikin.com	San Diego	CA	92121	858-458-1890		668
Axim Systems Inc 15 Diamond Rd *Web:* www.axim.com	Lexington	MA	02420	781-430-0429		196
Axiobionics 6111 Jackson Rd Ste 200 *TF:* 800-552-3539 ■ *Web:* www.axiobionics.com	Ann Arbor	MI	48103	734-327-2946		250
Axiom Education LLC 4 Research Dr *TF:* 800-246-9567 ■ *Web:* www.axiomeducation.com	Shelton	CT	06484	203-242-3070		387
Axiom Label 1360 W Walnut Pkwy *TF:* 800-882-5104 ■ *Web:* www.axiomlabel.com	Compton	CA	90220	310-603-8910		88
Axiom Marketing Inc 624 E Park Ave *TF:* 800-861-9940 ■ *Web:* www.axmarketing.com	Libertyville	IL	60048	847-362-5656		195
Axiom Memory Solutions LLC 15 Chrysler *TF:* 888-658-3326 ■ *Web:* www.axiomupgrades.com	Irvine	CA	92618	949-581-1450		174
Axiom Resource Management Inc 5203 Leesburg Pk Ste 300 *TF:* 800-566-9305 ■ *Web:* www.axiom-rm.com	Falls Church	VA	22041	703-208-3000		194
Axiom Software Ltd 400 Columbus Ave *TF:* 800-588-8805 ■ *Web:* www.axiomsw.com	Valhalla	NY	10595	914-769-8800		177
AXIOM Systems Inc 241 E Fourth St Ste 200 *Web:* www.axiom-systems.com	Frederick	MD	21701	301-815-5220		177
Axiom Technology Group Inc 2077 Miner St, Ste 204 *Web:* axiomtechgroup.com	Des Plaines	IL	60016	630-861-1000		196
Axiom Xcell Inc 13230 Evening Creek Dr Ste 217 *Web:* www.axiomxcell.com	San Diego	CA	92128	858-683-6100		656
AxioMx Inc 688 E Main St *Web:* www.axiomxinc.com	Branford	CT	06405	203-208-1918		231
Axion BioSystems Inc 1819 Peachtree Rd NE Ste 350 *Web:* www.axionbiosystems.com	Atlanta	GA	30309	404-477-2557		261
Axion International Holdings Inc 4005 All American Way *Web:* www.axionintl.com	Zanesville	OH	43701	740-452-2500	452-5488	608
Axios HR 528 Fourth St NW *Web:* www.axiosincorporated.com	Grand Rapids	MI	49504	616-949-2525		194
Axios Products Inc 353 Veterans Hwy Ste 204 *Web:* www.axios.com	Commack	NY	11725	631-864-3666	864-3693	180
Axis Communications Inc (ACI) 100 Apollo Dr *TF:* 800-444-2947 ■ *Web:* www.axis.com	Chelmsford	MA	01824	978-614-2000	614-2100	176
Axis Construction Corp 125 Laser Ct *Web:* www.theaxisgroup.com	Hauppauge	NY	11788	631-243-5970	243-5973	685
Axis Dance Co 1428 Alice St Ste 200 *TF:* 800-838-3006 ■ *Web:* www.axisdance.org	Oakland	CA	94612	510-625-0110	625-0321	573-1
AXIS Financial Services Inc 2774 Gateway Rd *Web:* www.axisservicing.com	Carlsbad	CA	92009	760-929-6680		401
Axis Jet 6133 Freeport Blvd *TF:* 800-553-8638 ■ *Web:* www.axisjet.com	Sacramento	CA	95822	916-391-5000		23
AXIS Personal Trainers Inc 550 Ravenswood Ave *Web:* www.axispt.com	Menlo Park	CA	94025	650-463-1920		354
Axis Technical Group Inc 300 S Ahrbor Blvd *Web:* axistechnical.com	Anaheim	CA	92805	714-491-2636		225
Axis Teknologies 8800 Roswell Rd Bldg A Ste 265	Sandy Springs	GA	30350	678-441-0260		194
Axiscades 3008 W Willow Knolls Dr *Web:* axis-inc.com	Peoria	IL	61614	309-691-3988		261
Axletree Solutions Inc 2 King Arthur Court Lakeside W Ste A-1 *TF:* 800-781-3591 ■ *Web:* www.axletrees.com	North Brunswick	NJ	08902	732-296-0001		177
Axley 2 E Mifflin St Ste 200 *TF:* 800-368-5661 ■ *Web:* www.axley.com	Madison	WI	53703	608-257-5661	257-5444	445
Axley & Rode LLP 1307 S First St *Web:* www.axleyrode.com	Lufkin	TX	75901	936-634-6621	634-8183	2
Axmen 7655 US Hwy 10 W *Web:* www.axmen.com	Missoula	MT	59808	406-728-7020		316
AXON Connected LLC 2322 Blue Stone Hills Dr Ste 20 *Web:* www.axonconnected.com	Harrisonburg	VA	22801	540-558-8596		743
Axon Pressure Products Inc 8909 Jackrabbit Rd *TF:* 800-626-4999 ■ *Web:* www.axonep.com	Houston	TX	77095	281-855-3200		539

				Phone	Fax	Class
Axon Sports LLC 2100 Stewart Ave Ste 201 *Web:* www.axonsports.com	Wausau	WI	54401	715-848-1024		387
Axonify Inc 460 Phillip St Ste 300 *TF:* 866-317-1992 ■ *Web:* www.axonify.com	Waterloo	ON	N2L5J2	519-585-1200		242
Axsess Energy Group Llc 18 Sawmill Dr *Web:* www.axsessgroup.com	Northborough	MA	01532	508-351-9050		196
Axson North America Inc 31200 Stephenson Hwy *Web:* www.axson-technologies.com/us/index.html	Madison Heights	MI	48071	248-588-2270	588-5909	3
Axsun Inc 4900 Armand Frappier *TF:* 888-992-9786 ■ *Web:* www.axsungroup.com	Saint-Hubert	QC	J3Z1G5	450-445-3003		311
Axsun Technologies Inc 1 Fortune Dr *TF:* 866-462-9786 ■ *Web:* www.axsun.com	Billerica	MA	01821	978-262-0049	262-0035	696
AXT Inc 4281 Technology Dr *NASDAQ: AXTI* ■ *Web:* www.axt.com	Fremont	CA	94538	510-438-4700	353-0668	696
Axton Inc 441 Derwent Pl Annacis Business Pk *Web:* www.axton.ca	Delta	BC	V3M5Y9	604-522-2731		295
Axxess International 1804 Alstep Dr Ste *Web:* axxessintl.com	Mississauga	ON	L5S1W1	905-672-0270		449
Axxiem Corp 578 Warburton Ave *Web:* www.axxiem.com	Hastings On Hudson	NY	10706	914-478-7600		177
Axxis Inc 1295 Bandana Blvd Ste 120 *Web:* www.axxispetro.com	St. Paul	MN	55108	651-644-8280		177
AXYS Technologies Inc 2045 Mills Rd *TF:* 877-792-7878 ■ *Web:* www.axystechnologies.com	Sidney	BC	V8L5X2	250-655-5850		608
Axyz Automation Inc 2844 E Kemper Rd *TF:* 800-527-9670 ■ *Web:* www.axyz.com	Cincinnati	OH	45241	513-771-7444		180
AY McDonald Manufacturing Co 4800 Chavenelle Rd *TF Cust Svc:* 800-292-2737 ■ *Web:* www.aymcdonald.com	Dubuque	IA	52002	563-583-7311	588-0720	505
Aya Kitchens & Baths Ltd 1551 Caterpillar Rd *TF:* 866-292-4968 ■ *Web:* www.ayakitchens.com	Mississauga	ON	L4X2Z6	905-848-1999	848-5127	819
Ayalogic Inc 530 S Main St Ste 1731	Akron	OH	44311	330-253-2700	253-3055	225
Ayanna Plastics & Engineering 4701 110th Ave N *Web:* www.ayannaplastics.com	Clearwater	FL	33762	727-561-4329		607
aycan Medical Systems LLC 693 East Ave *Web:* www.aycanus.com	Rochester	NY	14607	585-473-1350		475
Ayco Company LP 1 Wall St *Web:* www.ayco.com	Albany	NY	12205	518-464-2000		401
Ayers Meetings & Events Inc 19727 Whitewind Dr *Web:* www.ayersme.com	Houston	TX	77094	281-492-7272		184
Aylus Networks Inc 6 Technology Park Dr *Web:* www.aylus.com	Westford	MA	01886	978-392-4730		177
Aylward Enterprises Inc 401 Industrial Dr *Web:* www.aylward.com	New Bern	NC	28562	252-633-5757		231
Ayn Rand Institute, Endowment 2121 Alton Pkwy Ste 250 *Web:* www.aynrand.org	Irvine	CA	92606	949-222-6550		305
Ayoka LLC 1161 W Corporate Dr Ste 303 *Web:* www.ayokasystems.com	Arlington	TX	76006	817-210-4042		180
Ayothaya Thai Cuisine 7555 W Sand Lake *Web:* www.ayothayathai.com	Orlando	FL	32819	407-345-0040		671
Ayres Assoc Inc 3433 Oakwood Hills Pkwy *Web:* www.ayresassociates.com	Eau Claire	WI	54701	715-834-3161		261
Ayres Hotel Anaheim 2550 E Katella Ave *TF:* 800-595-5692 ■ *Web:* www.ayreshotels.com	Anaheim	CA	92806	714-634-2106		379
AYSO (American Youth Soccer Organization) 19750 S Vermont Ave Ste 200 *Fax Area Code: 310 ■ *TF:* 800-872-2976 ■ *Web:* ayso.org	Torrance	CA	90502	800-872-2976	525-1155*	48-22
Ayzenberg Group Inc 49 E Walnut St *Web:* www.ayzenberg.com	Pasadena	CA	91103	626-584-4070		7
AZ Countertops Inc 1445 S Hudson Ave *TF:* 800-266-3524 ■ *Web:* azcountertopsinc.com	Ontario	CA	91762	909-983-5386		724
A-Z Sponge & Foam Products Ltd 811 Cundy Ave Annacis Island *TF:* 800-665-3990 ■ *Web:* www.a-zfoam.com	Delta	BC	V3M5P6	604-525-1665	525-1081	601
AZA (Association of Zoos & Aquariums) 8403 Colesville Rd Ste 710 *TF:* 800-323-6593 ■ *Web:* www.aza.org	Silver Spring	MD	20910	301-562-0777	562-0888	48-3
Azalea Software Inc 1512 California Ave SW *Web:* www.azalea.com	Seattle	WA	98116	206-341-9500		396
Azalea State Reserve 15336 Hwy 101 PO Box 2006 *Web:* www.parks.ca.gov/default.asp?page_id=420	Trinidad	CA	95570	707-677-3132		565
Azar Computer Software Services Inc 1200 Regal Row *Web:* www.azarinc.com	Austin	TX	78748	512-476-5085		179
Azar Nut Co 1800 NW Dr *TF:* 800-351-8178	El Paso	TX	79912	915-877-4079		296-28
Azar's 2501 N Monroe St *Web:* azarsrestaurant.com	Spokane	WA	99205	509-326-7171		671
Azavar Technologies 55 E Jackson Ste 2100 *Web:* www.azavar.com	Chicago	IL	60604	312-583-0100		194
Azaya Therapeutics Inc 12500 Network Blvd Ste 207 *Web:* www.azayatherapeutics.com	San Antonio	TX	78249	210-341-6600	341-6619	668
Azco Inc PO Box 567 *TF:* 800-236-2500 ■ *Web:* www.azco-inc.com	Appleton	WI	54912	920-734-5791	734-7432	189-10
Azcon Corp 820 W Jackson Blvd Ste 425 *Web:* azcon.net	Chicago	IL	60607	312-559-3100	559-1543	686
Azerbaijan 866 UN Plaza Ste 560 *Web:* www.un.int	New York	NY	10017	212-371-2559	371-2784	784
Azerbaijan Embassy 2741 34th St NW *Web:* www.azembassy.us	Washington	DC	20008	202-337-3500		257
Azevan Pharmaceuticals Inc 116 Research Dr *Web:* www.azevan.com	Bethlehem	PA	18015	610-419-1057		231
Azimuth Inc 3741 Morgantown Industrial Pk *TF:* 800-522-9226 ■ *Web:* www.azimuthinc.com	Morgantown	WV	26501	304-292-3700		261
Azimuth Systems Inc 35 Nagog Pk *Web:* www.azimuthsystems.com	Acton	MA	01720	978-263-6610	263-5352	224
Azimuth Three Communications 127 Delta Park Blvd *Web:* www.az3.com	Brampton	ON	L6T5M8	905-793-7793		480
Aziza 5800 Geary Blvd *Web:* www.aziza-sf.com	San Francisco	CA	94121	415-752-2222		671
AzLA (Arizona Library Assn) 950 E Baseline Rd Ste 104-1025 *Web:* www.azla.org	Tempe	AZ	85283	480-609-3999		435
Azmark Aero Systems LLC 944 Guadalupe Rd *Web:* www.azmark.aero	Gilbert	AZ	85233	480-926-8969		21
AzNA (Arizona Nurses Assn) 1850 E Southern Ave Ste 1 *Web:* www.aznurse.org	Tempe	AZ	85282	480-831-0404	839-4780	533
Aznar Financial Advisors 21 Lakeview Dr *Web:* www.aznaradvisors.com	Morris Plains	NJ	07950	973-540-8850		401
Azon USA Inc 643 W Crosstown Pkwy *TF:* 800-788-5942 ■ *Web:* www.azonintl.com	Kalamazoo	MI	49008	269-385-5942	373-9295	386
Azonix Corp 900 Middlesex Tpke Bldg 6 *TF:* 800-967-5558 ■ *Web:* www.azonix.com	Billerica	MA	01821	978-670-6300	670-8855	201
Aztalan Engineering Inc 100 S Industrial Dr *Web:* www.aztalan.com	Lake Mills	WI	53551	920-648-3411		757
Aztalan State Park 1213 S Main St *Web:* dnr.wi.gov	Lake Mills	WI	53551	920-648-8774	648-5166	565
Aztec Building Systems Inc 3361 Deskin Dr *Web:* www.aztecbuildingsystems.com	Norman	OK	73069	405-329-0255		186
Aztec Communications Ltd 6830 Barney Rd *Web:* www.azteccom.com	Houston	TX	77092	713-462-6707		256
Aztec Energy Partners Inc 1951 Honey Creek Commons *Web:* aztec-energy.com	Conyers	GA	30013	770-760-1100		194
Aztec Engineering Group Inc 4561 E Mcdowell Rd *Web:* aztec.us	Phoenix	AZ	85008	602-454-0402		261
Aztec Facility Services Inc 11000 S Wilcrest Dr Ste 125 *Web:* www.aztec1.com	Houston	TX	77099	281-668-9000		256
Aztec International Inc 3010 Henson Rd *Fax Area Code: 615 ■ *TF:* 800-369-5357 ■ *Web:* www.candlemaking.com	Knoxville	TN	37921	865-588-5357	538-2062*	151
Aztec Landscaping Inc 7980 Lemon Grove Way *Web:* www.azteclandscaping.com	Lemon Grove	CA	91945	619-464-3303		104
Aztec Ruins National Monument 725 Ruins Rd *Web:* www.nps.gov	Aztec	NM	87410	505-334-6174	334-6372	564
Aztec Supply 954 N Batavia St *TF:* 800-836-3210 ■ *Web:* www.mezzaninesandmore.com	Orange	CA	92867	714-771-6580	771-3013	603
Aztec Well Servicing Company Inc 300 Legion Rd PO Box 100 *Web:* www.aztecwell.com	Aztec	NM	87410	505-334-6194		540
Azteca 12911 Main St *Web:* www.theazteca.com	Garden Grove	CA	92840	714-638-3790		671
Azteca 4801 Tacoma Mall Blvd *Web:* aztecamex.com	Tacoma	WA	98409	253-472-0246		671
Azteca America Inc 1139 Grand Central Ave *Web:* www.aztecaamerica.com	Glendale	CA	91201	818-241-5400	247-0190	116
Azteca Foods Inc 5005 S Nagle Ave *Web:* www.aztecafoods.com	Chicago	IL	60638	708-563-6600		296-35
Azteca Mexican Restaurants 15735 Ambaum Blvd SW *Web:* www.aztecamex.com	Seattle	WA	98166	206-243-7021		670
Aztech Innovations Inc 805 Bayridge Dr	Kingston	ON	K7P1T5	613-384-9400		261
Aztech Labs Inc 4005 Clipper Ct *Web:* www.aztech.com	Fremont	CA	94538	510-683-9800	683-9803	173-3
Aztech Technologies Inc 5 McCrea Hill Rd *Web:* www.aztechtech.com	Ballston Spa	NY	12020	518-885-5385		196
AzTx Cattle Co PO Box 390 *TF:* 800-999-5065 ■ *Web:* www.aztx.com	Hereford	TX	79045	806-364-8871	364-3842	10-1
Azul 500 Brickell Key Dr *Web:* www.mandarinoriental.com	Miami	FL	33131	305-913-8358		671
Azul 7 Inc 800 Hennepin Ave Ste 700 *Web:* azul7.com	Minneapolis	MN	55403	612-767-4335		4
Azul Partners Inc 625 N Michigan Ave Ste 1220 *Web:* www.azulpartners.com	Chicago	IL	60657	773-525-7406		195
Azul Systems Inc 1600 Plymouth St *Web:* www.azul.com	Mountain View	CA	94043	650-230-6500	230-6600	173-2
Azulstar Inc 1051 Jackson St Ste D *TF:* 800-778-7879 ■ *Web:* www.azulstar.com	Grand Haven	MI	49417	616-842-2763		387

				Phone	Fax	Class
Azure Green Consultants LLC 409 E Pioneer *Web:* www.azuregreenconsultants.com	Puyallup	WA	98372	253-770-3144		256
Azure Horizons Inc 7115 N Ave Ste 185 *TF:* 877-494-6070 ■ *Web:* www.azure-horizons.com	Oak Park	IL	60302	877-494-6070		180
Azure Solutions Inc 1010 W Hamlin Rd *Web:* azuresol.com	Rochester Hills	MI	48309	248-651-8210		180
Azurea Inc 365 Gus Hipp Blvd *Web:* www.dragonpoint.com	Rockledge	FL	32955	321-631-0610		196
Azusa Chamber of Commerce 240 W Foothill Blvd *TF:* 800-443-2153 ■ *Web:* www.azusachamber.org	Azusa	CA	91702	626-334-1507	334-5217	139
Azusa City Library 729 N Dalton Ave *TF:* 800-984-4636 ■ *Web:* www.ci.azusa.ca.us	Azusa	CA	91702	626-812-5232	334-4868	434-3
Azusa Pacific University 901 E Alosta Ave PO Box 7000 *TF:* 800-825-5278 ■ *Web:* www.apu.edu	Azusa	CA	91702	626-969-3434	812-3096	166
AZZ Inc 3100 W Seventh St Ste 500 *TF:* 800-732-0330 ■ *Web:* www.azz.com	Fort Worth	TX	76107	817-810-0095	336-5354	729
Azzur Group LLC 726 Fitzwatertown Rd Ste 6 *Web:* www.azzur.com/consulting	Willow Grove	PA	19090	610-363-0422		393

B

				Phone	Fax	Class
B - A Bolton Hill Bistro 1501 Bolton St *Web:* www.b-bistro.com	Baltimore	MD	21217	410-383-8600		671
B & B Agency of Boston 47 Commercial Wharf Ste 3 *TF:* 800-248-9262 ■ *Web:* www.boston-bnbagency.com	Boston	MA	02110	800-248-9262		376
B & b Automotive Inc 301 W Market St *Web:* www.bbauto.org	Aberdeen	WA	98520	360-533-4113		57
B & B Boats Inc 3568 Old Winter Garden Rd	Orlando	FL	32805	407-299-2190		90
B & B Discount Sales Co 712 S Broadway	Oklahoma City	OK	73109	405-232-3578		791
B & B Electronics Manufacturing Co PO Box 1040 *TF:* 800-346-3119 ■ *Web:* www.bb-elec.com	Ottawa	IL	61350	815-433-5100	433-5109	696
B & B Express Printing Inc 7519 W Kennewick Ave A *Web:* www.bbprinting.com	Kennewick	WA	99336	509-783-7383		627
B & b Medical Services Inc 5401 S Sheridan Rd Ste 204 *TF:* 800-372-9548 ■ *Web:* www.bandbmedical.com	Tulsa	OK	74145	800-372-9548		146
B & B Molders LLC 58471 Fir Rd S *Web:* www.bandbmolders.com	Mishawaka	IN	46544	574-259-7838		596
B & B Paper Converters Inc 12500 Elmwood Ave *Web:* bbpaper.com	Cleveland	OH	44111	216-941-8100		554
B & B Petroleum LLC 19153 HAEIDD Dr *Web:* www.bbpetroleum.com	Hammond	LA	70401	985-230-9959		538
B & B Precision Manufacturing Inc 310 W Main St *Web:* www.bbprecision.com	Avon	NY	14414	585-226-6226		454
B & b Printing Company Inc 521 Research Rd *TF:* 800-882-1844 ■ *Web:* www.bbprintnet.com	Richmond	VA	23236	804-794-8273		627
B & b Selectcom Inc 1109 S Fremont Ave *Web:* bbselectcom.com	Tucson	AZ	85719	520-882-0911		54
B & B Trade Distribution Centre 1950 Oxford St E *TF:* 800-265-0382 ■ *Web:* bbtrade.ca	London	ON	N5V2Z8	519-679-1770		610
B & B Wrecking & Excavating Inc 4510 E 71st St Ste 6 *Web:* www.bbwrecking.net	Cleveland	OH	44105	216-429-1700	429-1717	189-5
B & C Transportation Inc 427 Continental Dr *TF:* 877-812-2287 ■ *Web:* bctransportation.net	Maryville	TN	37804	865-983-4653		107
B & D Litho of Arizona 3820 N 38th Ave *TF:* 800-735-0375 ■ *Web:* www.bndlithoaz.com	Phoenix	AZ	85019	602-269-2526		627
B & F System Inc 3920 S Walton Walker *Web:* www.maxam.com	Dallas	TX	75236	214-333-2111	333-1511	361
B & G Foods Inc 4 Gatehall Dr Ste 110 *NYSE: BGS* ■ *Web:* www.bgfoods.com	Parsippany	NJ	07054	973-401-6500		296-20
B & G House of Printing Inc 1825 W 169th St Ste A *TF:* 800-882-1844 ■ *Web:* bgprinting.com	Gardena	CA	90247	310-532-1533		627
B & G Mfg Company Inc 3067 Unionville Pk **Fax:* Sales ■ *TF:* 800-366-3067 ■ *Web:* www.bgmfg.com	Hatfield	PA	19440	215-822-1921	822-1006*	278
B & G Oysters 550 Tremont St *Web:* www.bandgoysters.com	Boston	MA	02116	617-423-0550		671
B & G Security International 6631 Hwy 42 *Web:* www.bgsecurity.com	Rex	GA	30273	770-507-6409		692
B & H Manufacturing Co 3461 Roeding Rd *TF:* 888-643-0444 ■ *Web:* www.bhlabeling.com	Ceres	CA	95307	209-556-6160	537-6854	547
B & H Manufacturing Inc 141 County Rd 34 E *TF:* 800-240-3288 ■ *Web:* www.bhmfg.com	Jackson	MN	56143	507-847-2802		273
B & H Photo-Video-Pro Audio Corp 420 Ninth Ave *TF:* 800-947-9954 ■ *Web:* www.bhphotovideo.com	New York	NY	10001	212-444-6615	239-7770	119
B & I Contractors Inc 2701 Prince St *TF:* 800-677-1997 ■ *Web:* bandiflorida.com	Fort Myers	FL	33916	239-332-4646	332-5928	189-10
B & J Parking Lot Maintenance 12207 Inkster Rd *Web:* www.bandjmaint.com	Taylor	MI	48180	734-941-7570		562

				Phone	Fax	Class
B & K Electric Wholesale 1225 S Johnson Dr *Web:* www.bk-electric.com	City Of Industry	CA	91745	626-965-5040		253
B & L Wholesale Supply Inc 70 Hartford St *Web:* www.blwholesale.com	Rochester	NY	14605	585-546-6616		191-4
B & M Roofing of Colorado Inc 3768 Eureka Way *Web:* www.bmroofing.com	Frederick	CO	80516	303-443-5843	938-9642	189-12
B & O Railroad Museum 901 W Pratt St *TF:* 866-468-7630 ■ *Web:* www.borail.org	Baltimore	MD	21223	410-752-2490	752-2499	520
B & R Eckel's Transport Ltd 5514B - 50 Ave *TF:* 800-661-3290 ■ *Web:* www.breckels.com	Bonnyville	AB	T9N2K8	780-826-3889		539
B & S Logging Inc 4411 NW Elliott Ln	Prineville	OR	97754	541-447-3175		448
B & W Engineering Corp 3303 Harbor Blvd *Web:* b-w-engineering.com	Costa Mesa	CA	92626	714-540-9975		261
B & W Fluid Dynamics Inc 901 Seaco Ave	Deer Park	TX	77536	281-534-9300		256
B & W Press Inc 401 E Main St *TF:* 877-246-3467 ■ *Web:* www.bwpress.com	Georgetown	MA	01833	978-352-6100	352-5955	263
B & W Tile Mfg Company Inc 14600 S Western Ave *Web:* www.bwtile.com	Gardena	CA	90249	310-538-9579		751
B 104 1541 Alta Dr 4th Fl *Web:* www.b104.com	Whitehall	PA	18052	610-434-1742	434-6288	645
B 98.7 434 Bearcat Dr *Web:* www.b987.com	Salt Lake City	UT	84115	801-485-6700		645-142
B b C Security & Communication Inc 401 Mclean Ave *Web:* bbcsecurity.com	Yonkers	NY	10705	914-969-4000		693
B Berger Co 1380 Highland Rd *TF Cust Svc:* 800-288-8400 ■ *Web:* duralee.com	Macedonia	OH	44056	330-425-3838		594
B Braun Medical Inc 824 12th Ave *TF:* 800-523-9676 ■ *Web:* www.bbraunusa.com	Bethlehem	PA	18018	610-691-5400	997-5510	476
B C & G Weithman Construction Company Inc 2171 E Mansfield St	Bucyrus	OH	44820	419-562-8027		186
B C L of Texas 2212 S Congress Ave *Web:* www.bcloftexas.org	Austin	TX	78704	512-912-9884		196
B C Szerlip Insurance Agency Inc 34 Sycamore Ave *Web:* bcszerlip.com	Little Silver	NJ	07739	732-842-2020		390
B C Teachers Federation 100 - 550 W Sixth Ave *Web:* www.bctf.ca	Vancouver	BC	V5Z4P2	604-871-2283		414
B Carroll Reece Museum PO Box 70660 *TF:* 855-590-3878 ■ *Web:* www.etsu.edu/reece	Johnson City	TN	37614	423-439-4392	439-4283	520
B D N Industrial Hygiene Consultants Inc 8105 Valleywood Ln *TF:* 800-968-0123 ■ *Web:* bdnihc.com	Portage	MI	49024	269-329-1237		196
B Designs Letterpress 23 Noel St *Web:* www.bdesignsletterpress.com	Amesbury	MA	01913	978-388-1052		130
B E Meyers & Co Inc 9461 Willows Rd NE *TF:* 800-327-5648 ■ *Web:* www.bemeyers.com	Redmond	WA	98052	425-881-6648		544
B e p Consulting Inc 1006 West Lake St *Web:* bepinc.com	Chicago	IL	60607	312-850-3140		196
B E Peterson Inc 40 Murphy Dr Avon Industrial Pk *Web:* www.bepeterson.com	Avon	MA	02322	508-436-7900		492
B Frank Joy LLC 5355 Kilmer Pl *Web:* www.bfjoy.com	Hyattsville	MD	20781	301-779-9400		188-10
B G Consultants Inc 4806 Vue Du Lac Pl *Web:* www.bgcons.com	Manhattan	KS	66503	785-537-7448	537-8793	261
B G m Engineering Inc 14100 Simone Dr *Web:* bgmengineering.net	Shelby Township	MI	48315	586-532-8670		256
B Green Innovations Inc 750 Hwy 34 *Web:* bgreeninnovations.com	Matawan	NJ	07747	732-441-7700		180
B H G Inc PO Box 309 *TF:* 800-658-3485 ■ *Web:* www.bhgnews.com	Garrison	ND	58540	701-463-2201		627
B H Suhr & Company Inc 840 Custer *Web:* bhsuhr.com	Evanston	IL	60202	847-864-6315		727
B i d Designs 1525 Perimeter Pkwy NW Ste 125 *Web:* bid-designs.com	Huntsville	AL	35806	256-489-2815		196
B J Bindery 833 S Grand Ave *TF:* 800-400-3105 ■ *Web:* www.bjbindery.com	Santa Ana	CA	92705	714-835-7342		535
B Jcc Inspections 1000 Banks Draw *TF:* 877-248-6006 ■ *Web:* www.bjccinspections.com	Rexford	MT	59930	406-882-4825		261
B Line Express Inc 7065 Long View Rd *Web:* www.blinex.com	Columbia	MD	21044	301-596-9290		809
B M C Bil Mac Corp 2995 44th St SW *Web:* www.bmcbil-mac.com	Grandville	MI	49418	616-538-1930		454
B M Ross & Assoc Ltd 62 N St *TF:* 888-524-2641 ■ *Web:* www.bmross.net	Goderich	ON	N7A2T4	519-524-2641		256
B Ma Media Group 4091 Erie St *Web:* www.bmamedia.com	Willoughby	OH	44094	440-975-4262		194
B Oma Suburban Chicago 1515 E Woodfield Rd Ste 110 *Web:* www.bomasuburbanchicago.com	Schaumburg	IL	60173	847-995-0970		533
B P Lesky Distributing Company Inc 120 Western Maryland Pkwy	Hagerstown	MD	21740	301-733-0787		443
B Riley & Company LLC 11100 Santa Monica Blvd Ste 800 *Web:* www.brileyco.com	Los Angeles	CA	90025	310-966-1444		690
B Sharp Technologies Inc 1 Valleybrook Dr Ste 206 *TF:* 866-994-2499 ■ *Web:* www.bsharp.com	Toronto	ON	M3B2S7	416-445-7162		177
B Squared Inc 104 W 29th St 7th Fl *Web:* www.bsqu.com	New York	NY	10001	212-777-2044		626

Name / Address	City	State	Zip	Phone	Fax	Class
B Street Theatre 2711 B St	Sacramento	CA	95816	916-443-5300		572
Web: www.bstreettheatre.org						
B Swing Inc 700 Washington Ave N	Minneapolis	MN	55401	612-752-1160		177
Web: www.bswing.com						
B W Smith Structural Engineers						
12435 Ventura Ct	Studio City	CA	91604	818-505-9409		261
B Z Plumbing Company Inc						
1901 Aviation Blvd	Lincoln	CA	95648	916-645-1600		610
B'nai B'rith International						
2020 K St NW 7th Fl	Washington	DC	20006	202-857-6600	857-6609	48-20
TF: 888-388-4224 ■ *Web:* www.bnaibrith.org						
B'nai B'rith Klutznick National Jewish Museum						
1120 20th St NW	Washington	DC	20036	202-857-6600		520
TF: 888-388-4224 ■ *Web:* www.bnaibrith.org						
B'Nai B'Rith Magazine						
2020 K St NW 7th Fl	Washington	DC	20006	202-857-6600		457-18
TF: 888-388-4224 ■ *Web:* www.bnaibrith.org						
B'nai B'rith Youth Organization (BBYO)						
2020 K St NW	Washington	DC	20006	202-857-6633	857-6568	48-20
Web: www.bbyo.org						
B. E. Smith Inc 8801 Renner Ave	Lenexa	KS	66219	855-296-6318		193
TF: 855-296-6318 ■ *Web:* www.besmith.com						
B. Green & Co 1300 S Monroe St	Baltimore	MD	21230	410-539-6134		345
Web: www.bgreenco.com						
B. H. Craig Construction Company Inc						
835 Wall St	Florence	AL	35630	256-766-3350	767-0367	186
Web: www.bhcraigconst.com						
B. Schoenberg & Company Inc						
345 Kear St	Yorktown	NY	10598	914-962-1200		603
TF: 800-770-2801 ■ *Web:* www.bschoenberg.info						
B.C. Advantage (VCC) Funds Ltd						
Ste 410 221 W Esplanade Ste 410	North Vancouver	BC	V7M3J3	604-688-6877		528
Web: www.bcadvantagefunds.com						
B.C. Government & Service Employees' Union						
4911 Canada Way	Burnaby	BC	V5G3W3	604-291-9611		414
TF: 800-663-1674 ■ *Web:* www.bcgeu.ca						
B.R. Fries & Associates Inc						
34 W 32nd St	New York	NY	10001	212-563-3300		261
Web: www.brfries.com						
B104.7 Syracuse's Country Station						
500 Plum St Ste 400	Syracuse	NY	13204	315-472-9797		645-160
TF: 844-289-7234 ■ *Web:* b1047.iheart.com						
B2 Digital Media LLC						
3183 Airway Ave Ste F101	Costa Mesa	CA	92627	949-945-3005		631
Web: www.b2digitalmedia.com						
B2 Environmental Inc						
10838 Old Mill Rd Ste A	Omaha	NE	68154	402-330-0763		196
Web: www.b2environmental.com						
B2 Gold Corp						
595 Burrard St Ste 3100 PO Box 49143	Vancouver	BC	V7X1J1	604-681-8371	681-6209	502
TF: 800-310-8855 ■ *Web:* www.b2gold.com						
B-21 Liquors Inc						
43380 US Hwy 19 N	Tarpon Springs	FL	34689	727-937-5049		443
Web: b-21.com						
B27 Resources 1417 Gables Ct	Plano	TX	75075	214-473-8580		194
Web: www.b27resources.com						
B2B Staffing Services Inc						
4141 Ball Rd #150	Cypress	CA	90630	714-243-4104		260
Web: www.b2bstaffingservices.com						
B2B Workforce Inc						
200 N Pt Ctr E Ste 150	Alpharetta	GA	30022	770-667-7200		113
B2B2C 2700 Michelin St Ste 255	Laval	QC	H7L5Y1	514-908-5420		224
Web: www.b2b2c.ca						
b2b2dot0 Inc 7474 Creedmoor Rd Ste 108	Raleigh	NC	27613	919-676-7429		393
Web: www.b2b2dot0.com						
B2i Technologies Inc						
2000 N Central Expy Ste 209	Plano	TX	75074	972-234-9200		809
Web: www.b2itech.com						
B3 Solutions LLC						
1225 W Beaver St Ste 108	Jacksonville	FL	32204	904-695-4241		463
TF: 800-780-4707 ■ *Web:* b3solutions.com						
B93.9 new county						
3100 Smoketree Ct Ste 700	Raleigh	NC	27604	919-878-1500		645-131
Web: b939country.iheart.com						
BA Consulting Group Ltd						
45 St Clair Ave W Ste 300	Toronto	ON	M4V1K9	416-961-7110		261
Web: www.bagroup.com						
BA Robinson Company Ltd 619 Berry St	Winnipeg	MB	R3H0S2	204-784-0150		612
TF: 866-903-6275 ■ *Web:* www.barobinson.com						
Baa Indianapolis LLC						
2500 S High School Rd Ste 100	Indianapolis	IN	46241	317-487-5025		194
Web: www.indianapolisairport.com						
Baader-Johnson						
2955 Fairfax Trafficway	Kansas City	KS	66115	913-621-3366		298
TF: 800-288-3434 ■ *Web:* www.baader.com						
Baan Sawan 2135 Devine St	Columbia	SC	29205	803-252-8992		671
Web: baansawan.blogspot.com						
Baan Thai 3235 N Anthony Blvd	Fort Wayne	IN	46805	260-471-2929		671
Web: baanthaiin.com						
Baan Thai Restaurant 1924 SW BRdway	Portland	OR	97201	902-446-4301		671
Web: www.baanthai.ca						
BAASS Business Solutions BC Inc						
305-9600 Cameron St	Burnaby	BC	V3J7N3	604-420-1099		179
Web: www.baass.com						
BAB Inc 500 Lake Cook Rd Ste 475	Deerfield	IL	60015	800-251-6101	405-8140*	670
OTC: BABB ■ **Fax Area Code:* 847 ■ *TF:* 800-251-6101 ■ *Web:* www.babcorp.com						
Babb Lumber Company Inc						
6652 Highway 41	Ringgold	GA	30736	706-935-2411		818
Web: www.babb.com						
Babbo 110 Waverly Pl	New York	NY	10011	212-777-0303		671
Web: www.babbonyc.com						
Babbo Italian Eatery						
20211 N 67th Ave	Glendale	AZ	85308	623-566-9898	566-5561	671
Web: babboitalian.com						
BABC (British-American Business Council)						
52 Vanderbilt Ave 20th Fl	New York	NY	10017	212-661-4060	661-4074	138
Web: www.babc.org						
Babcock & Jenkins Inc						
1233 NW 12th Ave Ste 100	Portland	OR	97209	503-382-8013		7
Web: www.bnj.com						
Babcock & Wilcox Co						
20 S Van Buren Ave	Barberton	OH	44203	330-753-4511	860-1886	91
TF: 800-222-2625 ■ *Web:* www.babcock.com						
Babcock Galleries						
233 Broadway 26th Fl	New York	NY	10279	212-767-1852	767-1857	42
Web: www.artnet.com						
Babcock Law Firm						
10101 Siegen Ln Ste 3C	Baton Rouge	LA	70810	225-819-3737		428
Web: www.stephenbabcock.com						
Babcock Lumber Co 2220 Palmer St	Pittsburgh	PA	15218	412-351-3515		499
Web: www.babcocklumber.com						
Babcock Power Inc						
6 Kimball Ln Ste 210	Lynnfield	MA	01940	978-646-3300	646-3301	91
TF: 800-523-0480 ■ *Web:* www.babcockpower.com						
Babcock Power Services Inc						
6 Kimball Ln Ste 210	Lynnfield	MA	01940	508-852-7100		256
Web: babcockpower.com						
Babcock State Park 486 Babcock Rd	Clifftop	WV	25831	304-438-3004		565
TF: 800-225-5982 ■ *Web:* www.babcocksp.com						
Babcock-Davis 9300 73rd Ave N	Brooklyn Park	MN	55428	763-488-9247	488-9248	234
TF: 888-412-3726 ■ *Web:* www.babcockdavis.com						
Babe Ruth Birthplace Museum						
216 Emory St	Baltimore	MD	21230	410-727-1539	727-1652	522
Web: baberuthmuseum.org						
Babe Ruth League Inc						
1770 Brunswick Pk PO Box 5000	Trenton	NJ	08638	609-695-1434	695-2505	48-22
TF: 800-880-3142 ■ *Web:* www.baberuthleague.org						
Babe Winkelman Productions						
PO Box 407	Brainerd	MN	56401	800-333-0471		742
TF: 800-333-0471 ■ *Web:* www.winkelman.com						
Babe's Grill & Bar 5614 Schroeder Rd	Madison	WI	53711	608-274-7300		671
Web: www.babesmadison.com						
Babette's Cafe 573 N Highland Ave	Atlanta	GA	30307	404-523-9121		671
Web: www.babettescafe.com						
Babich & Assoc 6030 E Mockingbird Ln	Dallas	TX	75206	214-823-9999		260
TF: 800-615-7320 ■ *Web:* www.babich.com						
Babin Brian (Rep R - TX)						
316 Cannon HOB	Washington	DC	20515	202-225-1555	226-0396	342-2
Web: babin.house.gov						
Babin Machine Works Inc						
2510 N Ninth St	Beaumont	TX	77703	409-892-1231		455
Babin's Seafood House						
17485 Tomball Pkwy	Houston	TX	77064	281-477-9300		671
Web: www.babinsseafood.com						
Babson College 231 Forest St	Babson Park	MA	02457	781-235-1200	239-4006*	166
**Fax:* Admissions ■ *TF Admissions:* 800-488-3696 ■ *Web:* www.babson.edu						
Babush Neiman Komman Johnson LLP						
5909 Peachtree Dunwoody 800	Atlanta	GA	30328	770-261-1900		2
Web: www.bnkj.com						
Baby Jogger Co						
8575 Magellan Pkwy Ste 1000	Richmond	VA	23227	800-241-1848	262-6277*	64
**Fax Area Code:* 804 ■ *TF:* 800-241-1848 ■ *Web:* www.babyjogger.com						
Baby Kay's Cajun Kitchen						
2051 S Dobson Rd	Mesa	AZ	85202	480-800-4811		671
Web: www.babykayscajunkitchen.com						
Baby Trend Inc 1567 S Campus Ave	Ontario	CA	91761	800-328-7363	773-0108*	64
**Fax Area Code:* 909 ■ *TF Cust Svc:* 800-328-7363 ■ *Web:* www.babytrend.com						
Baby's Dream Furniture Inc						
411 Industrial Blvd	Buena Vista	GA	31803	229-649-4404	649-2007	319-2
TF: 800-835-2742 ■ *Web:* www.babysdream.com						
BabyCenter LLC 163 Freelon St	San Francisco	CA	94107	415-537-0900	537-0909	356
TF: 866-732-8243 ■ *Web:* www.babycenter.com						
BAC (International Union of Bricklayers & Allied Craftworkers)						
1776 eye St NW	Washington	DC	20006	202-783-3788	393-0219	414
TF: 888-880-8222 ■ *Web:* www.bacweb.org						
Bac Sales Inc 1871 Route 9H	Hudson	NY	12534	518-828-6363		612
Web: www.bacsales.com						
Baca County 741 Main St	Springfield	CO	81073	719-523-4372		338
Web: www.springfieldcolorado.com						
Bacall's Cafe 6118 Hamilton Ave	Cincinnati	OH	45224	513-541-8804		671
Web: www.bacallscafe.com						
Bacara Resort & Spa						
8301 Hollister Ave	Santa Barbara	CA	93117	805-968-0100	968-1800	669
TF: 855-968-0100 ■ *Web:* meritagecollection.com/bacararesort						
Bacardi Bottling Corp						
12200 N Main St	Jacksonville	FL	32218	904-757-1290		81-3
Bacardi 2701 S Le Jeune Rd	Coral Gables	FL	33134	305-573-8511	573-7507*	80-1
**Fax:* Hum Res ■ *Web:* www3.bacardi.com/us/en						
Bacarella Transportation Service						
225 Masarik Ave	Stratford	CT	06615	203-375-1180		366
TF: 800-463-3339 ■ *Web:* www.btxair.com						
Bacaro 921 Pearl St	Boulder	CO	80302	303-444-4888		671
Bacaro 113 N Walnut St	Champaign	IL	61820	217-398-6982		671
Web: www.bacarowinelounge.com						
BACC (British-American Chamber of Commerce Great Lakes Region)						
4700 Millenia Blvd Ste 175	Orlando	FL	32839	216-621-0222		138
Web: www.baccohio.org						
BACC (Belgian-American Chamber of Commerce in the US)						
1177 Ave of the Americas 7th Fl	New York	NY	10036	212-541-0771		138
Web: www.belcham.org						
Baccala Concrete Corp 100 Armento St	Johnston	RI	02919	401-231-8300	232-3965	182
TF: 866-705-2382 ■ *Web:* baccalaconcrete.com						
Baccarat Casino 10128 104th Ave	Edmonton	AB	T5J4Y8	780-413-3178		133
Web: www.gatewaycasinos.com						
Baccarat New York LLC 20 W 53rd St	New York	NY	10019	212-790-8800		707
TF: 866-957-5139 ■ *Web:* www.baccarathotels.com						
Bacchanalia 1198 Howell Mill Rd	Atlanta	GA	30318	404-365-0410	365-8020	671
Web: starprovisions.com						
Bacchanalia 2413 S Oakley Ave	Chicago	IL	60608	773-254-6555		671
Web: www.bacchanaliainchicago.com						
BACCHUS Network, The						
111 K St NE 10th fl	Washington	DC	20002	303-871-0901		48-17
Web: www.naspa.org						
Bacchus Restaurant 925 E Wells St	Milwaukee	WI	53202	414-765-1166		671
Web: www.bacchusmke.com						

Name / Address	City	State	ZIP	Phone	Fax	Class
Bacco's 263 Pk Ave *Web:* baccosristorante.com	Rochester	NY	14607	585-442-5090		671
Bach Pharma Inc 800 Turnpike St Ste 300 *Web:* www.bachpharma.com	North Andover	MA	01845	978-794-5510		238
Bacharach Inc 621 Hunt Vly Cir *TF:* 800-736-4666 ■ *Web:* www.bacharach-inc.com	New Kensington	PA	15068	724-334-5000	334-5001	201
Bacharach Institute for Rehabilitation 61 W Jimmie Leads Rd *TF:* 800-899-1142 ■ *Web:* www.bacharach.org	Pomona	NJ	08240	609-652-7000	652-7487	374-6
Bachelor Controls Inc 123 N Washington Ave *Web:* bachelorcontrols.com	Sabetha	KS	66534	785-284-3482		261
Bachem Bioscience Inc 3132 Kashiwa St *TF:* 888-422-2436 ■ *Web:* www.bachem.com	Torrance	CA	90505	310-539-4171		479
Bachem-Peninsula Laboratories Inc 312 Kashiwa St *TF:* 800-922-1516 ■ *Web:* www.bachem.com	Torrence	CA	90505	650-801-6090	595-4071	231
Bachi Co 1201 Ardmore Ave *TF:* 800-797-4992 ■ *Web:* www.bachiwinder.com	Itasca	IL	60143	630-773-5600	773-5621	494
Bachman Machine Company Inc 4321 N Broadway *Web:* www.bachmanmachine.com	St Louis	MO	63147	314-231-4221		483
Bachman's Inc 6010 Lyndale Ave S *TF:* 888-222-4626 ■ *Web:* www.bachmans.com	Minneapolis	MN	55419	612-861-7311	861-7748	292
Bachmann Construction Company Inc 1201 S Stoughton Rd *Web:* bachmannconstruction.net	Madison	WI	53716	608-222-8869		186
Bachmann Industries Inc 1400 E Erie Ave *TF Cust Svc:* 800-356-3910 ■ *Web:* www.bachmanntrains.com	Philadelphia	PA	19124	215-533-1600	744-4699	762
Bachmann Software & Service 270 Sparta Ave Ste 104 *Web:* www.bachmannsoftware.com	Sparta	NJ	07871	973-729-9427		177
Bachus & Schanker LLC 123 N College Ave Ste 211 *Web:* coloradolaw.net	Fort Collins	CO	80524	970-223-9802		445
Baci 18748 Beach Blvd *TF:* 800-499-9982 ■ *Web:* www.bacirestaurant.com	Huntington Beach	CA	92648	714-965-1194		671
Back Bay Grill 65 Portland St *TF:* 800-876-9293 ■ *Web:* www.backbaygrill.com	Portland	ME	04101	207-772-8833		671
Back Country Horsemen of America (BCHA) PO Box 1367 *TF:* 888-893-5161 ■ *Web:* www.bcha.org	Graham	WA	98338	360-832-2461		48-23
Back Home Again Inc 291 N State Rd 2	Valparaiso	IN	46383	219-477-4333		363
Back Porch Grill, The 4810 Central Ave *Web:* www.backporchgrill.com	Hot Springs	AR	71913	501-525-0885		671
Back Stage Magazine 770 Broadway *Web:* www.backstage.com	New York	NY	10003	212-493-4420		457-9
Back to Basics Learning Dynamics Inc 6 Stone Hill Rd *Web:* backtobasicslearning.com	Wilmington	DE	19803	302-594-0754		768
Back To Bed Inc 700 Hill Top Dr *Web:* www.backtobed.com	Itasca	IL	60143	630-931-4602		321
Back Yard Burgers Inc 500 Church St Ste 200 *TF:* 800-292-6939 ■ *Web:* www.backyardburgers.com	Nashville	TN	37219	615-620-2300	620-2301	670
BackBay Communications Inc 20 Park Plaza Ste 801 *Web:* www.backbaycommunications.com	Boston	MA	02116	617-556-9982		636
Backblaze Inc 500 Ben Franklin Ct *TF:* 800-874-2458 ■ *Web:* www.backblaze.com	San Mateo	CA	94401	650-352-3738		45
Backbone Media LLC 69 Milk St Ste 306 *Web:* backbonemedia.com	Westborough	MA	01581	508-366-2100		636
Backbone State Park 1282 120th St *Web:* www.iowadnr.gov	Strawberry Point	IA	52076	563-924-2000		565
Backchannelmedia Inc 105 S St *Web:* backchannelmedia.com	Boston	MA	02111	617-210-8100		6
Backcountry Gear LLC 1855 W Second Ave *TF:* 800-953-5499 ■ *Web:* www.backcountrygear.com	Eugene	OR	97402	541-485-4007		711
Backcountry.com 2607 S 3200 W Ste A *TF Orders:* 800-409-4502 ■ *Web:* www.backcountry.com	West Valley City	UT	84119	800-409-4502		459
Backer Springfield Inc 4700 John Bragg Hwy *Web:* backer-springfield.com	Murfreesboro	TN	37127	615 907 6900		815
Background Bureau Inc 2019 Alexandria Pike *TF:* 800-854-3990 ■ *Web:* www.backgroundbureau.com	Highland Heights	KY	41076	859-781-3400	781-9540	635
Background Information Services Inc 1800 30th St Ste 204 *TF:* 800-433-6010 ■ *Web:* www.bisi.com	Boulder	CO	80301	303-442-3960	442-1004	635
Backing Up Classics Auto Museum 4545 Concord Pkwy S *Web:* www.backingupclassics.com	Concord	NC	28027	704-788-9500		520
BackOffice Associates LLC 75 Perseverance Way *Web:* www.boaweb.com	Hyannis	MA	02601	508-430-7100		177
Backpacker Magazine 2520 55th St Ste 210 *Web:* www.backpacker.com	Boulder	CO	80301	610-967-8296		457-14
Backroads 801 Cedar St *TF:* 800-462-2848 ■ *Web:* www.backroads.com	Berkeley	CA	94710	510-527-1555	527-1444	760
Backroads Magazine 160 Co Rd 521 *Web:* www.backroadsusa.com	Newton	NJ	07860	973-948-4176	948-0823	457-3
Backstreet Cafe 1103 S Shepherd Dr *Web:* www.backstreetcafe.net	Houston	TX	77019	713-521-2239		671
Backstrom McCarley Berry & Company LLC 115 Sansome St Mezzanine A *Web:* www.bmcbco.com	San Francisco	CA	94104	415-392-5505		401
Backtrack Inc 8850 Tyler Blvd *TF:* 800-991-9694 ■ *Web:* backtracker.com	Mentor	OH	44060	440-205-8280		260
Backupify Inc 17 Sellers St *TF:* 800-571-4984 ■ *Web:* www.backupify.com	Cambridge	MA	02139	800-571-4984		809
Backus Meyer & Branch LLP 116 Lowell St *TF:* 800-472-3675 ■ *Web:* www.backusmeyer.com	Manchester	NH	03104	603-668-7272		428
Backus Turner International 3116 N Federal Hwy *Web:* www.backusturner.com	Lighthouse Point	FL	33064	305-573-9996		195
Backwoods 3300 N IH35 Ste 149 *Web:* www.backwoods.com	Austin	TX	78705	512-583-1700		711
Backwoods Guns & Wildlife Taxidermy Inc 3322 Us Rt 60	Huntington	WV	25705	304-521-6888		711
Backyard Adventures Inc 14201 I-27 *Web:* www.crownofminnesota.com	Amarillo	TX	79119	612-781-6505		711
Backyard Broadcasting 4237 Salisbury Rd Ste 225 *Web:* www.bybradio.com	Jacksonville	FL	32216	904-674-0260		643
Bacompt Systems Inc 12742 Hamilton Crossing Blvd *TF:* 800-466-6245 ■ *Web:* www.bacompt.com	Carmel	IN	46032	317-574-7474		781
Bacon County 504 N Pierce St PO Box 450 *Web:* www.almaone.com	Alma	GA	31510	912-632-5859	632-7710	338
Bacon Don (Rep R - NE) 1516 Longworth HOB *TF:* 888-221-7452 ■ *Web:* bacon.house.gov	Washington	DC	20515	202-225-4155		342-2
Bacon Free Library 58 Eliot St *Web:* baconfreelibrary.org	South Natick	MA	01760	508-653-6730		434-3
Bacon Veneer Co 6951 High Grove Blvd *TF:* 800-443-7995 ■ *Web:* www.baconveneer.com	Burr Ridge	IL	60527	630-323-1414	323-1499	613
Bacone College 2299 Old Bacone Rd **Fax:* Admissions ■ *TF Admissions:* 888-682-5514 ■ *Web:* www.bacone.edu	Muskogee	OK	74403	918-683-4581	781-7416*	166
Bacon-Universal Company Inc 918 Ahua St *TF:* 800-352-3508 ■ *Web:* www.baconuniversal.com	Honolulu	HI	96819	808-839-7202	834-8110	358
Bacova Guild Ltd 1000 Commerce Ctr Dr *Web:* www.bacova.com	Covington	VA	24426	540-863-2600		131
Bactolac Pharmacutical Inc 7 Oser Ave *Web:* www.bactolac.com	Hauppague	NY	11788	631-951-4908		583
BACVA (Baltimore Area Convention & Visitors Assn) 100 Light St 12th Fl *TF:* 877-225-8466 ■ *Web:* www.baltimore.org	Baltimore	MD	21202	410-659-7300	727-2308	206
Bad Ass Coffee Co of Hawaii Inc 155 W Malvern Ave *Web:* badasscoffeestore.com	Salt Lake City	UT	84115	801-463-1966	463-2606	310
Bad Boy Furniture Warehouse Ltd 500 Fenmar Dr *Web:* www.badboy.ca	Weston	ON	M9L2V5	416-667-7546		321
Bad Boy Inc 102 Industrial Dr *Web:* www.badboymowers.com	Batesville	AR	72501	870-698-0090		194
Bad Dog Tools 24 Broadcommon Rd *TF:* 800-252-1330 ■ *Web:* baddogtools.com	Bristol	RI	02809	401-253-1330		350
Badawest Restaurant 4018 Corruna Rd	Flint	MI	48532	810-232-2479		671
Badcock's Economy Furniture Store Inc 3931 RCA Blvd *Web:* badcocksfl.com	Palm Beach Gardens	FL	33410	561-694-8588		321
Baden Gage & Schroeder LLC 6920 Pointe Inverness Way Ste 300 *Web:* www.badencpa.com	Fort Wayne	IN	46804	260-422-2551	422-7862	2
Baden Steelbar & Bolt Corp 852 Big Sewickly Crk Rd R *Web:* www.badensteel.com	Sewickley	PA	15143	724-266-3003		350
Bader Group Inc, The 5090 Shoreham Pl #108 *Web:* www.badergroup.com	San Deigo	CA	92122	619-501-9586		193
Bader Rutter 1433 N Water St Ste 100 *Web:* www.baderrutter.com	Milwaukee	WI	53202	262-784-7200	938-5595	4
Badge A Minit Ltd 345 N Lewis Ave *TF:* 800-223-4103 ■ *Web:* www.badgeaminit.com	Oglesby	IL	61348	815-883-8822	883-9696	456
Badger Air Brush Co 9128 Belmont Ave *TF:* 800-247-2787 ■ *Web:* www.badgerairbrush.com	Franklin Park	IL	60131	847-678-3104	671-4352	43
Badger Bus 5501 Femrite Dr *TF:* 800-442-8259 ■ *Web:* www.badgerbus.com	Madison	WI	53718	608-255-1511		107
Badger Coaches Inc 5501 Femrite Dr *TF:* 800-442-8259 ■ *Web:* www.badgerbus.com	Madison	WI	53718	608-255-1511		760
Badger Daylighting Corp 1300 E US Hwy 136 Ste E *TF:* 877-322-3437 ■ *Web:* badgerinc.com	Pittsboro	IN	46167	877-322-3437		539
Badger Express LLC 181 Quality Ct *TF:* 800-972-0084 ■ *Web:* www.badgerexpress.com	Fall River	WI	53932	920-484-5808		192
Badger Foundry Co 1058 E Mark St *TF:* 800-654-5773 ■ *Web:* www.badgerfoundry.com	Winona	MN	55987	507-452-5760	452-6469	307
Badger Land Car Wash Equipment & Supplies LLC 300A E Oak St *Web:* www.badgerlandcarwashequipment.com	Oak Creek	WI	53154	414-764-4250		406
Badger Liquor Company Inc 850 S Morris St *TF:* 800-242-9708 ■ *Web:* www.badgerliquor.com	Fond du Lac	WI	54936	920-923-8160	923-8169	81-3
Badger Meter Inc 4545 W Brown Deer Rd *NYSE: BMI* ■ *TF:* 800-876-3837 ■ *Web:* www.badgermeter.com	Milwaukee	WI	53224	414-355-0400		495
Badger Mining Corp 409 S Church St CA Chier Resource Ctr *TF:* 800-932-7263 ■ *Web:* www.badgerminingcorp.com	Berlin	WI	54923	920-361-2388	361-2826	502
Badger Mutual Insurance Co 1635 W National Ave *TF:* 800-837-7833 ■ *Web:* www.badgermutual.com	Milwaukee	WI	53204	414-383-1234		390
Badger Plug Company Inc N1045 Technical Dr PO Box 199 *Web:* www.badgerplug.com	Greenville	WI	54942	920-757-7300		612
Badger Press Inc 100 E Blackhawk Dr *Web:* badgergroup.com	Fort Atkinson	WI	53538	920-563-5144		627
Badger Sportswear Inc 111 Badger Ln *TF:* 888-871-0990 ■ *Web:* www.badgersport.com	Statesville	NC	28625	704-871-0990		155-3

Phone | Fax | Class

Badger State Ethanol LLC
820 W 17th St PO Box 317 . . . Monroe WI 53566 608-329-3900 144
Web: www.badgerstateethanol.com

Badger State Industries (BSI)
3099 E Washington Ave PO Box 8990 . . . Madison WI 53708 608-240-5200 240-3320 630
TF: 800-862-1086 ■ *Web:* www.buybsi.com

Badger Truck Ctr Inc
2326 W St Paul Ave . . . Milwaukee WI 53233 414-344-9500 57
Web: www.badgertruck.com

Badger West Wine & Spirits LLC
5400 Old Town Hall Rd . . . Eau Claire WI 54701 715-836-8600 836-8609 81-3
TF: 800-472-6674 ■ *Web:* www.badgerliquor.com

Badgley Phelps & Bell Inc
1420 Fifth Ave Ste 3200 . . . Seattle WA 98101 206-623-6172 401
TF: 800-869-7173 ■ *Web:* badgley.com

Badia Spices Inc 1400 NW 93rd Ave . . . Doral FL 33172 305-629-8000 123
Web: www.badia-spices.com

Badiyan Inc 720 W 94th St . . . Minneapolis MN 55420 952-888-5507 514
Web: www.badiyan.com

Badlands National Park
25216 Ben Reifel Rd PO Box 6 . . . Interior SD 57750 605-433-5361 433-5404 564
Web: www.nps.gov/badl

Badorf Shoe Co Inc 1958 Auction Rd . . . Manheim PA 17545 717-653-0155 301
TF: 800-325-1545 ■ *Web:* www.badorfshoe.com

BAE Systems Aerospace & Defense Group Inc
7822 S 46th St . . . Phoenix AZ 85044 602-643-7233 21
Web: www.baesystems.com

BAE Systems Analytical Solutions Inc
308 Voyager Way . . . Huntsville AL 35806 256-890-8000 890-0000 194

BAE Systems Electronics & Integrated Solutions
65 Spit Brook Rd . . . Nashua NH 03060 603-885-4321 21
Web: www.baesystems.com

BAE Systems OASYS LLC
645 Harvey Rd Ste 9 . . . Manchester NH 03103 603-232-8221 544

BAE Systems Simula Inc 7822 S 46th St . . . Phoenix AZ 85044 602-643-7233 21

Baer Supply Co
909 Forest Edge Dr . . . Vernon Hills IL 60061 847-913-2237 913-2230 351
TF: 800-944-2237 ■ *Web:* www.baersupply.com

Baer's Furniture Co Inc
1589 Northwest 12th Ave . . . Pompano Beach FL 33069 954-582-4200 321
Web: baers.com

Baerlocher production USA LLC
5890 Highland Ridge Dr . . . Cincinnati OH 45232 513-482-6300 143
Web: www.baerlocher.com

Baesman Group Inc 274 Marconi Blvd . . . Columbus OH 43215 614-771-2300 195
Web: www.baesman.com

BAF Industries Inc 1451 Edinger Ave . . . Tustin CA 92780 714-258-8055 151
TF: 800-437-9893 ■ *Web:* www.prowax.com

Bag Makers Inc 6606 S Union Rd . . . Union IL 60180 800-458-9031 458-9023 66
TF: 800-458-9031 ■ *Web:* www.bagmakersinc.com

Bag to Earth Inc 201 Richmond Blvd . . . Napanee ON K7R3Z9 613-354-1330 557
Web: bagtoearth.com

Bagatelle 115 Duval St . . . Key West FL 33040 305-296-6609 671
Web: www.bagatellekeywest.com

Bagby Elevator Company Inc
4240 First Ave S . . . Birmingham AL 35222 205-591-4245 256
Web: www.bagbyelevator.com

BagcraftPapercon 3900 W 43rd St . . . Chicago IL 60632 773-254-8000 254-8204 554
TF: 800-621-8468 ■ *Web:* www.bagcraft.com

Bagdad Roller Mills Inc
5740 Elmburg Rd . . . Bagdad KY 40003 502-747-8968 447
TF: 800-928-3333 ■ *Web:* www.bagdadrollermillsfeed.com

Baggett Transportation Co
2 S 32nd St . . . Birmingham AL 35233 888-224-4388 780
TF: 800-633-8982 ■ *Web:* www.baggetttransport.com

Baghouse & Industrial Sheet Metal Services Inc
1731 Pomona Rd . . . Corona CA 92880 951-272-6610 272-1241 18
Web: www.1888baghouse.com

Bag-Packinc 9486 Sutton Pl . . . Hamilton OH 45011 513-346-3900 596
Web: www.bagpackinc.com

Bagwell Marketting 13211 Deer Run Trl . . . Dallas TX 75243 972-480-8192 7
Web: www.oklahoma-advertising.com

Bahama Breeze 8849 International Dr . . . Orlando FL 32819 407-248-2499 671
TF: 877-500-9715 ■ *Web:* www.bahamabreeze.com

Bahama Buck's Franchise Corp
5741 50th St . . . Lubbock TX 79424 806-771-2189 771-2190 381
Web: www.bahamabucks.com

BAHAMA Consulting Corp
4651 Nicols Rd Ste 200 . . . Eagan MN 55122 651-994-7900 177
Web: bahama-consulting.com

Bahama House
2001 S Atlantic Ave . . . Daytona Beach Shores FL 32118 888-687-1894 248-0991* 379
**Fax Area Code:* 386 ■ *TF:* 888-687-1894 ■ *Web:* www.daytonabahamahouse.com

Bahamas
Consulate General 25 SE Second Ave . . . Miami FL 33131 800-224-2627 257
TF: 800-224-2627 ■ *Web:* bahamas.com
Consulate General 231 E 46th St . . . New York NY 10017 212-421-6420 257
Web: www.bahamasny.net
Embassy 2220 Massachusetts Ave NW . . . Washington DC 20008 202-319-2660 319-2668 257
Web: www.bahamasembdc.org

Bahamas Tourism Office
1200 S Pine Island Rd Ste 750 . . . Plantation FL 33324 954-236-9292 236-9282 775
TF: 800-327-7678 ■ *Web:* www.bahamas.com

Bahia Honda State Park
36850 Overseas Hwy . . . Big Pine Key FL 33043 305-872-2353 565
Web: www.floridastateparks.org

Bahia Mar Beach Resort & Yachting Ctr
801 Seabreeze Blvd . . . Fort Lauderdale FL 33316 954-764-2233 523-5424 669
TF: 888-802-2442 ■ *Web:* doubletree3.hilton.com

Bahia Mar Resort & Conference Ctr
6300 Padre Blvd . . . South Padre Island TX 78597 800-926-6926 669
TF: 800-926-6926 ■ *Web:* pirentals.com

Bahia Resort Hotel
998 W Mission Bay Dr . . . San Diego CA 92109 858-488-0551 488-7055 669
TF: 800-576-4229 ■ *Web:* www.bahiahotel.com

Bahl & Gaynor Investment Counsel
255 East Fifth St Ste 2700 . . . Cincinnati OH 45202 513-287-6100 287-6110 401
TF: 800-341-1810 ■ *Web:* www.bahl-gaynor.com

Phone | Fax | Class

Bahn Thai Restaurant
1319 S Monroe St . . . Tallahassee FL 32301 850-224-4765 671

Bahn Thai Restaurant
944 Williamson St Ste 4 . . . Madison WI 53703 608-256-0202 671

Bahwan CyberTek Inc
209 W Central St 312 . . . Natick MA 01760 508-652-0001 177
Web: www.bahwancybertek.com

BAI 115 S LaSalle St Ste 3300 . . . Chicago IL 60603 800-224-9889 457-5
TF: 800-224-9889 ■ *Web:* www.bai.org/bankingstrategies/about.asp

BAI (Bank Administration Institute)
115 S LaSalle St Ste 3300 . . . Chicago IL 60603 312-683-2464 683-2373* 49-2
**Fax:* Cust Svc ■ *TF Cust Svc:* 800-224-9889 ■ *Web:* www.bai.org

Baier Marine Company Inc
2920 Airway Ave . . . Costa Mesa CA 92626 800-455-3917 350
TF: 800-455-3917 ■ *Web:* www.baiermarine.com

Bailard Biehl & Kaiser Group
950 Tower Ln Ste 1900 . . . Foster City CA 94404 650-571-5800 573-7128 401
TF: 800-224-5273 ■ *Web:* www.bailard.com

Bailey & Galyen 1901 W Airport Fwy . . . Bedford TX 76021 817-288-1101 428
TF: 800-215-8795 ■ *Web:* www.galyen.com

Bailey & Glasser LLP
209 Capitol St . . . Charleston WV 25301 304-345-6555 428
Web: www.baileyglasser.com

Bailey Bridges Inc 119 40th St, NE . . . Fort Payne AL 35967 256-845-7516 480
Web: www.baileybridge.com

Bailey Cavalieri LLC
10 W Broad St Ste 2100 . . . Columbus OH 43215 614-221-3155 428
Web: baileycav.com

Bailey Company Inc, The
501 Cowan St . . . Nashville TN 37207 800-342-1665 358
TF: 800-342-1665 ■ *Web:* www.baileycompany.com

Bailey County 300 S First St . . . Muleshoe TX 79347 806-272-3044 272-3538 338
Web: www.co.bailey.tx.us

Bailey Farms LLC 549 Karem Dr . . . Marshall WI 53559 800-655-1705 578
TF: 800-655-1705 ■ *Web:* www.baileyfarmspets.com

Bailey House Inc 180 Christopher St . . . New York NY 10014 212-337-3000 195
Web: www.baileyhouse.org

Bailey Lauerman & Assoc Inc
1299 Farnam St Ste 1400 . . . Lincoln NE 68102 402-514-9400 4
Web: www.baileylauerman.com

Bailey Matthews Shell Museum
3075 Sanibel-Captiva Rd PO Box 1580 . . . Sanibel FL 33957 239-395-2233 395-6706 520
TF: 888-679-6450 ■ *Web:* www.shellmuseum.org

Bailey Metal Products Ltd
1 Caldari Rd . . . Concord ON L4K3Z9 905-738-9267 307
Web: www.bmp-group.com

Bailey Properties 106 Aptos Beach Dr . . . Aptos CA 95003 831-688-7009 652
TF: 800-347-6830 ■ *Web:* www.baileyproperties.com

Bailey's 185 Lombard Ave . . . Winnipeg MB R3B0W4 204-944-1180 671
TF: 800-431-6067 ■ *Web:* www.baileysprimedining.com

Bailey's Express Inc
61 Industrial Pk Rd . . . Middletown CT 06457 860-632-0388 632-9089 780
TF: 800-523-3758 ■ *Web:* www.baileysxpress.com

Bailey's Seafood & Grill
5520-A Johnston St . . . Lafayette LA 70503 337-988-6464 671
Web: www.baileyscss.com

Bailey, Javins & Carter Lc
213 Hale St . . . Charleston WV 25301 304-345-0346 428
Web: www.baileyjavinscarter.com

Bailey-Parks Urethane Inc
184 Gilbert Ave . . . Memphis TN 38106 901-774-7930 610
Web: www.baileyparks.com

Baileys Furniture Outlet Inc
350 W Intl Airport Rd Ste 100 . . . Anchorage AK 99518 907-563-4083 321
Web: www.baileysfurniture.com

Bailiwick Data Systems Inc
4260 Norex Dr . . . Chaska MN 55318 952-556-5502 196
Web: www.bailiwick.com

Baille Lumber Co
4002 Legion Dr PO Box 6 . . . Hamburg NY 14075 716-649-2850 649-2811 191-3
TF: 800-950-2850 ■ *Web:* www.baillie.com

Baillio's Inc 5301 Menaul Blvd NE . . . Albuquerque NM 87110 505-883-7511 39
TF: 800-540-7511 ■ *Web:* baillios.com

Baily International Inc
1122 SR-3 . . . Natl Stock Yards IL 62071 618-271-1122 123
Web: www.bailyinc.com

Bain & Co 131 Dartmouth St . . . Boston MA 02116 617-572-2000 572-2427 194
Web: www.bain.com

Bain & Holden Tire Company Inc
100 N Amhurst Pl . . . Englewood TN 37329 423-887-7932 57

Bain Capital Inc 200 Clarendon St . . . Boston MA 02116 617-516-2000 516-2010 792
Web: baincapital.com

Bain Freibaum & Company LLC
3515 N Arnoult Rd . . . Metairie LA 70002 504-568-0086 2
Web: www.bainfreibaumcpa.com/index.html

Bain Pest Control Service Inc
1320 Middlesex St . . . Lowell MA 01851 978-452-9621 577
TF: 800-272-3661 ■ *Web:* bainpestcontrol.com

Bainbridge-Decatur County Chamber of Commerce
PO Box 755 . . . Bainbridge GA 39818 229-246-4774 243-7633 139
TF: 800-243-4774 ■ *Web:* www.bainbridgega.com

Baird & Warner Inc
120 S LaSalle St Ste 2000 . . . Chicago IL 60603 312-368-1855 368-1490 652
TF: 888-661-1176 ■ *Web:* www.bairdwarner.com

Baird & Wilson Sheet Metal Inc
2703 Bond St . . . Knoxville TN 37917 865-523-9982 697
Web: www.bairdandwilson.com

Baird Hampton & Brown Inc
6300 Ridglea Pl Ste 700 . . . Fort Worth TX 76116 817-338-1277 338-9245 256
Web: www.bhbinc.com

Baird Patrick & Company Inc
305 Plaza 10 . . . Jersey City NJ 07311 201-680-7300 680-7301 690
TF: 800-221-7747 ■ *Web:* www.bairdpatrick.com

Baird-Neece Packing Corp 60 SE St . . . Porterville CA 93257 559-784-3393 11-1

BairesDev 1999 S Bascom Ave, Ste 700 . . . Campbell CA 95008 408-600-1331 196
Web: www.bairesdev.com

Baisch & Skinner Inc
2721 Lasalle St . . . Saint Louis MO 63104 314-664-1212 292
TF: 800-523-0013 ■ *Web:* www.baischandskinner.com

	Phone	Fax	Class

Baisch Engineering Inc
809 Hyland Ave. .... Kaukauna WI 54130 920-766-3521 256
Web: www.baisch.com
Baja 104 14th St .... Hoboken NJ 07030 201-653-0610 671
Baja Cafe Dos
1310 S Federal Hwy .... Deerfield Beach FL 33441 954-596-1305 671
Web: www.bajacafefl.com
Baja Duty Free (BDF)
4590 Border Village Rd. .... San Ysidro CA 92173 619-428-6671 241
Web: www.bajadutyfree.com
Baja Expeditions Inc 3096 Palm St .... San Diego CA 92104 858-581-3311 220
TF: 800-843-6967 ■ Web: www.bajaex.com
Baja Foods LLC 636 W Root St .... Chicago IL 60609 773-376-9030 297-6
Baja Fresh 320 Commerce Ste 100 .... Irvine CA 92602 949-270-8900 671
TF: 877-225-2373 ■ Web: www.bajafresh.com
Baja Marine Corp
1653 Whichards Beach Rd .... Washington NC 27889 252-975-2000 90
Web: www.bajamarine.com
BAJobs com 652 Bair Is Rd Ste 301 .... Redwood City CA 94063 650-298-8100 298-8101 260
Web: www.bajobs.com
Baka Communications Inc
630 The East Mall .... Etobicoke ON M9B4B1 416-641-2800 196
TF: 866-884-3329 ■ Web: www.baka.ca
Bake'n Joy Foods Inc
351 Willow St .... North Andover MA 01845 978-683-1414 683-1713 296-16
TF: 800-666-4937 ■ Web: www.bakenjoy.com
Baker & McKenzie LLP
300 E Randolph St Ste 5000 .... Chicago IL 60601 312-861-8800 861-2899 428
Web: www.bakermckenzie.com
Baker & Sons Equipment Co
45381 SR- 145 .... Lewisville OH 43754 740-567-3317 57
Web: www.bakerandsons.com
Baker & Taylor Inc
2550 W Tyvola Rd Ste 300 .... Charlotte NC 28217 800-775-1800 998-3316* 96
*Fax Area Code: 704 ■ TF: 800-775-1800 ■ Web: www.btol.com
Baker Book House Company Inc
6030 E Fulton St .... Ada MI 49301 616-676-9185 676-9573 637-3
TF Orders: 800-877-2665 ■ Web: www.bakerpublishinggroup.com
Baker Book House Company Inc Revell Div
6030 E Fulton St .... Ada MI 49301 616-676-9185 676-9573 637-3
TF Orders: 800-877-2665 ■ Web: bakerpublishinggroup.com
Baker Botts LLP
910 Louisiana St 1 Shell Plz .... Houston TX 77002 713-229-1234 229-1522 428
Web: www.bakerbotts.com
Baker Boy Bake Shop Inc 170 Gta Dr .... Dickinson ND 58601 701-225-4444 578
Web: www.bakerboy.com
Baker Charlie (R)
State House Office of the Governorÿ Rm 360 .... Boston MA 02133 617-725-4005 727-9725 343
Web: www.mass.gov/governor
Baker College
Auburn Hills 1500 University Dr .... Auburn Hills MI 48326 248-340-0600 340-0608* 166
*Fax: Admissions ■ TF: 888-429-0410 ■ Web: www.baker.edu
Cadillac 9600 E 13th St .... Cadillac MI 49601 231-876-3100 876-3440 166
TF: 888-313-3463 ■ Web: www.baker.edu
Clinton Township
34950 Little Mack Ave .... Clinton Township MI 48035 586-791-6610 166
TF: 888-272-2842 ■ Web: www.baker.edu
Flint 1050 W Bristol Rd .... Flint MI 48507 800-964-4299 766-4255* 166
*Fax Area Code: 810 ■ *Fax: Admissions ■ TF: 800-964-4299 ■ Web: www.baker.edu
Jackson 2800 Springport Rd .... Jackson MI 49202 517-788-7800 788-6187 166
TF: 888-343-3683 ■ Web: www.baker.edu
Owosso 1020 S Washington St .... Owosso MI 48867 989-729-3350 729-3359* 166
*Fax: Admissions ■ TF: 800-879-3797 ■ Web: www.baker.edu
Port Huron 3403 Lapeer Rd .... Port Huron MI 48060 810-985-7000 985-7066 166
TF: 888-262-2442 ■ Web: www.baker.edu
Baker Commodities Inc
4020 Bandini Blvd .... Vernon CA 90058 323-268-2801 296-12
Web: www.bakercommodities.com
Baker Communications Inc
10101 SW Fwy #630 .... Houston TX 77074 713-627-7700 587-2051 765
TF: 877-253-8506 ■ Web: www.bakercommunications.com
Baker Company Inc 175 Gatehouse Rd .... Sanford ME 04073 207-324-8773 324-3869 420
TF: 800-992-2537 ■ Web: www.bakerco.com
Baker Concrete Construction Inc
900 N Garver Rd .... Monroe OH 45050 513-539-4000 539-4380 189-3
TF: 800-539-2224 ■ Web: www.bakerconcrete.com
Baker Correctional Institution
20706 US Hwy 90 .... Sanderson FL 32087 386-719-4500 758-5759 213
Web: myflorida.com
Baker County 1995 Third St Ste 150 .... Baker City OR 97814 541-523-8207 523-8240 338
Web: www.bakercounty.org
Baker County 339 E Macclenny Ave .... Macclenny FL 32063 904-259-8113 338
Web: www.bakercountyfl.org
Baker County Visitors & Convention Bureau
490 Campbell St .... Baker City OR 97814 541-523-3356 523-9187 206
TF: 800-523-1235 ■ Web: www.visitbaker.com
Baker Creek State Park
863 Baker Creek Rd .... McCormick SC 29835 864-443-2457 565
Web: southcarolinaparks.com/bakercreek/default.aspx
Baker Distributing Co
14610 Breakers Dr Ste 100 .... Jacksonville FL 32258 800-217-4698 612
TF: 844-289-0033 ■ Web: www.bakerdist.com
Baker Donelson Bearman Caldwell & Berkowitz PC
165 Madison Ave 1st Tennessee Bldg Ste 2000 .... Memphis TN 38103 901-526-2000 577-2303 428
TF: 800-973-1177 ■ Web: www.bakerdonelson.com
Baker Electric Inc 111 Jackson Ave .... Des Moines IA 50315 515-288-6774 288-2226 189-4
Web: www.bakerelectric.com
Baker Foodservice Design Inc
2220 E Paris Ave SE .... Grand Rapids MI 49546 616-942-4011 463
TF: 800-968-4011 ■ Web: www.bakergroup.com
Baker Group 4224 Hubbell Ave .... Des Moines IA 50317 515-262-4000 266-1025 189-10
TF: 855-262-4000 ■ Web: www.thebakergroup.com
Baker Hostetler LLP
1900 E Ninth St National City Ctr Ste 3200 .... Cleveland OH 44114 216-621-0200 696-0740 428
Web: www.bakerlaw.com
Baker Hughes Inc (BHI)
2929 Allen Pkwy Ste 1200 .... Houston TX 77019 713-439-8600 539
NYSE: BHI ■ TF: 800-229-7447 ■ Web: www.bakerhughes.com
Baker Hughes Inc
12645 W Airport Blvd .... Sugar Land TX 77478 281-276-5400 145
TF: 877-369-8296 ■ Web: www.bakerhughes.com
Baker Hughes INTEQ
17015 Aldine Westfield Rd .... Houston TX 77073 713-625-4200 538
TF: 800-411-9705 ■ Web: www.bakerhughes.com
Baker Implement Co 421 E Main St .... Portageville MO 63873 573-379-5455 379-5313 274
Web: www.bakerimplement.com
Baker Institute for Animal Health
Cornell University College of Veterinary Medicine
235 Hungerford Hill Rd .... Ithaca NY 14853 607-256-5600 256-5608 668
Web: www.vet.cornell.edu/baker
Baker Iron & Metal Company Inc
740 Rock Castle Ave .... Lexington KY 40505 859-255-5676 252-3590 686
Web: www.bakeriron.com
Baker Krizner Financial Planning
2230 N Limestone St .... Springfield OH 45503 937-390-8750 463
TF: 888-390-8753 ■ Web: www.bakerkrizner.com
Baker Manock & Jensen
5260 N Palm Ste 421 .... Fresno CA 93704 559-432-5400 428
TF: 800-336-3375 ■ Web: www.bakermanock.com
Baker McMillen Co 3688 Wyoga Lake Rd .... Stow OH 44224 330-923-8300 820
Web: www.baker-mcmillen.com
Baker Metal Products Inc
11140 Zodiac Ln .... Dallas TX 75229 972-241-3553 480
Web: bakermetal.com
Baker Motor Company Inc
1511 Savannah Hwy .... Charleston SC 29407 843-852-4000 57
Web: www.bakermotorcompany.com
Baker Perkins Inc
3223 Kraft Ave SE .... Grand Rapids MI 49512 616-784-3111 784-0973 298
Web: bakerperkins.com
Baker Products
55480 Hwy 21 N PO Box 128 .... Ellington MO 63638 573-663-7711 821
TF: 800-548-6914 ■ Web: www.baker-online.com
Baker Ready Mix & Building Materials
2800 Frenchmen St .... New Orleans LA 70122 504-947-8081 182
TF: 800-393-6343 ■ Web: www.bakerreadymix.com
Baker Rock Resources
21880 SW Farmington Rd .... Beaverton OR 97007 503-642-2531 46
TF: 800-340-7625 ■ Web: www.baker-rock.com
Baker Roofing Co 517 Mercury St .... Raleigh NC 27603 919-828-2975 828-9352 189-12
TF: 800-849-4096 ■ Web: www.bakerroofing.com
Baker Septic Installations
7740 S George Blvd .... Sebring FL 33875 863-385-0917 610
Web: bakersseptictanks.com
Baker Sheet Metal Corp
3541 Argonne Ave .... Norfolk VA 23509 757-853-4325 697
Web: www.bakersheetmetal.com
Baker Sterchi Cowden Rice LLC
1010 Market St Ste 950 .... Saint Louis MO 63101 314-231-2925 445
Web: bscr-law.com
Baker Storey McDonald Properties Inc
3011 Armory Dr Ste 120 .... Nashville TN 37204 615-373-9511 505
Web: www.bsmproperties.com
Baker Tankhead Inc 10405 N fwy .... Fort Worth TX 76177 817-232-8030 480
TF: 866-232-8030 ■ Web: www.bakertankhead.com
Baker Tilly 8219 Leesburg Pk Ste 800 .... Vienna VA 22182 703-923-8300 2
Web: www.bakertilly.com
Baker Travel Inc
23832 Rockfield Blvd .... Lake Forest CA 92630 949-458-1818 775
Baker Triangle 341 Highway 80 E .... Mesquite TX 75150 972-289-5534 289-4580 189-9
TF: 800-458-3480 ■ Web: www.bakertriangle.com
Baker University 618 E Eighth St .... Baldwin City KS 66006 785-594-6451 165
TF: 800-873-4282 ■ Web: www.bakeru.edu
Baker's Burgers Inc
1875 Business Ctr Dr .... San Bernardino CA 92408 909-884-5233 670
Web: www.bakersdrivethru.com
Baker's Ribs 2223 S Voss Rd .... Houston TX 77057 713-977-8725 671
Web: www.bakersribs.com
Baker, Keener & Nahra LLP
633 W Fifth St Ste 5500 .... Los Angeles CA 90071 213-241-0900 428
Web: www.bknlawyers.com
Bakercorp
3020 Old Ranch Pkwy Ste 220 .... Seal Beach CA 90740 562-430-6262 430-4865 264-2
Web: www.bakercorp.com
Baker-Meekins Company Inc, The
1404 Front Ave .... Lutherville Timonium MD 21093 410-823-2600 401
Web: www.bakcrmcckins.com
Bakers Pride Oven Company Inc
30 Pine St .... New Rochelle NY 10801 914-576-0200 427
Web: www.bakerspride.com
Bakersfield Californian Inc
1707 Eye St .... Bakersfield CA 93301 661-395-7500 4
Web: www.bakersfield.com
Bakersfield City Hall
1600 Truxtun Ave .... Bakersfield CA 93301 661-326-3751 324-1850 337
Web: bakersfieldcity.us
Bakersfield City School District
1300 Baker St .... Bakersfield CA 93305 661-631-4600 326-1485 685
Web: www.bcsd.com
Bakersfield College
1801 Panorama Dr .... Bakersfield CA 93305 661-395-4011 395-4500* 162
*Fax: Admissions ■ Web: www.bakersfieldcollege.edu
Bakersfield Magazine Inc
1601 New Stine Rd Ste 200 .... Bakersfield CA 93309 661-834-4126 95
Web: www.bakersfieldmagazine.net
Bakersfield Memorial Hospital
420 34th St .... Bakersfield CA 93301 661-327-4647 374-3
Web: www.bakersfieldmemorial.org
Bakersfield Museum of Art
1930 R St .... Bakersfield CA 93301 661-323-7219 520
Web: www.bmoa.org
Bakersfield News Observer
1219 20th St .... Bakersfield CA 93301 661-324-9466 532-4
Bakersfield Pipe & Supply Inc
3301 Zachary Ave .... Shafter CA 93263 661-589-9141 589-3739 596
Web: www.bakersfieldpipe.com

Phone | Fax | Class

Bakersfield Symphony Orchestra
1328 34th St Ste A — Bakersfield CA 93301 — 661-323-7928 — 323-7331 — 573-3
Web: www.bsonow.org

Bakerwell Inc
6295 Maxtown Rd Ste 300 — Westerville OH 43082 — 614-898-7590 — 536
Web: www.bakerwell.com

Bakery Barn Inc 111 Terence Dr — Pittsburgh PA 15236 — 412-655-1113 — 297-8
Web: bakery-barn.net

Bakery Confectionery Tobacco Workers & Grain Millers International Union
10401 Connecticut Ave — Kensington MD 20895 — 301-933-8600 — 946-8452 — 414
Web: www.bctgm.org

Bakewise Brands Inc
1688 N Wayneport Rd — Macedon NY 14502 — 315-986-9999 — 296-1

Bakke Norman 1200 Heritage Dr — New Richmond WI 54017 — 715-246-3800 — 445
Web: www.bakkenorman.com

Bakken, The 3537 Zenith Ave S — Minneapolis MN 55416 — 612-926-3878 — 927-7265 — 520
Web: www.thebakken.org

Baklund R&D LLC 13835 200th St — Hutchinson MN 55350 — 320-587-0743 — 587-0928 — 350

Bal Seal Engineering Company Inc
19650 Pauling — Foothill Ranch CA 92610 — 949-460-2100 — 460-2300 — 326
TF: 800-366-1006 ■ *Web:* www.balseal.com

Bala Consulting Engineers Inc
443 S Gulph Rd — King Of Prussia PA 19406 — 610-649-8000 — 256
Web: www.bala.com

Balance 2200 California St NW — Washington DC 20008 — 202-797-0021 — 354
Web: www.balancegym.com

Balance Day Spa LLC
3111 Battleground Ave — Greensboro NC 27408 — 336-574-2556 — 77
Web: www.balancedayspa.com

Balance Financial Inc
1800 - 112th Ave NE Ste 260-E — Bellevue WA 98004 — 425-458-4400 — 458-4011 — 387

Balance Innovations LLC
11011 Eicher Dr — Lenexa KS 66219 — 913-599-1177 — 628
TF: 800-366-5241 ■ *Web:* balanceinnovations.com

Balance Rock Inn 21 Albert Meadow — Bar Harbor ME 04609 — 207-288-2610 — 288-5534 — 379
TF: 800-753-0494 ■ *Web:* www.balancerockinn.com

Balance Technology Inc
7035 Jomar Dr — Whitmore Lake MI 48189 — 734-769-2100 — 769-2542 — 494
Web: www.balancetechnology.com

BalancePoint Inc
9201 Ward Pkwy Ste 200 — Kansas City MO 64114 — 816-268-1400 — 196
TF: 800-403-3302 ■ *Web:* www.balancepointcorp.com

Balancing Pool
2350, 330 - Fifth Ave SW — Calgary AB T2P0L4 — 403-539-5350 — 706
Web: www.balancingpool.ca

Balasa Dinverno Foltz LLC
500 Park Blvd Ste 1400 — Itasca IL 60143 — 630-875-4900 — 41
TF: 800-840-4740 ■ *Web:* www.bdfllc.com

Balax Inc PO Box 96 — North Lake WI 53064 — 262-966-2355 — 966-1028 — 493
Web: www.balax.com

Balazs Analytical Laboratory
46409 Landing Pkwy — Fremont CA 94538 — 510-624-4000 — 743
Web: www.balazs.com

Balboa City Schools 525 Hawthorn St — San Diego CA 92101 — 619-298-2990 — 685
Web: www.balboaschool.com

Balboa Instruments Inc 1382 Bell Ave — Tustin CA 92780 — 714-384-0382 — 203
Web: www.balboainstruments.com

Balboa Park 1549 El Prado Ste 1 — San Diego CA 92101 — 619-239-0512 — 50-5
Web: www.balboapark.org

Balboa Park Inn 3402 Pk Blvd — San Diego CA 92103 — 619-298-0823 — 379
TF: 800-938-8181 ■ *Web:* www.balboaparkinn.com

Balboa Records Inc
10900 Washington Blvd — Culver City CA 90232 — 310-204-3792 — 204-0886 — 657
Web: www.balboarecords.com

Balboa Travel Management Inc
5414 Oberlin Dr Ste 300 — San Diego CA 92121 — 858-678-3300 — 678-3399 — 771
TF: 800-359-8773 ■ *Web:* www.balboa.com

Balcan Plastics Ltd
9340 Meaux St — Saint Leonard QC H1R3H2 — 514-326-0200 — 326-4565 — 601
TF: 877-422-5226 ■ *Web:* www.balcan.com

Balch & Bingham LLP
1901 Sixth Ave N Ste 1500 — Birmingham AL 35203 — 205-251-8100 — 428
Web: www.balch.com

Balch Petroleum Contractors & Builders Inc
930 Ames Ave — Milpitas CA 95035 — 408-942-8686 — 580
TF: 800-454-6131 ■ *Web:* www.balchpetroleum.com

Balchem Corp
52 Sunrise Pk Rd PO Box 600 — New Hampton NY 10958 — 845-326-5613 — 326-5742 — 479
NASDAQ: BCPC ■ *TF:* 877-407-8289 ■ *Web:* www.balchem.com

Balcom Agency, The
1500 Ballinger St — Fort Worth TX 76102 — 817-877-9933 — 4
Web: www.balcomagency.com

Balcones Dermatology Associates PA
7800 N Mopac Expy Ste 315 — Austin TX 78759 — 512-459-4869 — 237
Web: www.balconesdermatology.com

Balcones Resources Inc
9301 Johnny Morris Rd — Austin TX 78724 — 512-472-3355 — 660
TF: 800-727-4246 ■ *Web:* www.balconesresources.com

Bald Eagle State Park 149 Main Pk Rd — Howard PA 16841 — 814-625-2775 — 565
Web: www.dcnr.state.pa.us

Bald Head Island Rentals LLC
21 Keelson Row — Bald Head Island NC 28461 — 910-457-1702 — 652
Web: www.baldheadislandrentals.com

Bald Mountain Recreation Area
1330 E Greenshield Rd — Lake Orion MI 48360 — 248-693-6767 — 565
Web: www.michigandnr.com

Bald Point State Park
146 PO Box Cut — Alligator Point FL 32346 — 850-349-9146 — 565
Web: www.floridastateparks.org

Baldknobbers Restaurant 645 MO-165 — Branson MO 65616 — 417-231-4999 — 671
Web: www.baldknobbers.com

Baldomero Lopez State Veterans' Nursing Home
6919 Pkwy Blvd — Land O Lakes FL 34639 — 813-558-5000 — 793
Web: floridavets.org

Baldor Electric Co
5711 RS Boreham Jr St PO Box 2400 — Fort Smith AR 72901 — 479-646-4711 — 648-5792 — 518
Web: www.baldor.com

Baldwin & Clarke Corporate Finance Inc
Coldstream Park 116B S River Rd — Bedford NH 03110 — 603-668-4353 — 70
Web: baldwinclarke.com

Baldwin & Lyons Inc
111 Congressional Blvd Ste 500 — Carmel IN 46032 — 317-636-9800 — 632-9444 — 391-4
NASDAQ: BWINB ■ *TF:* 800-644-5501 ■ *Web:* www.baldwinandlyons.com

Baldwin & Shell Construction Co Inc
1000 W Capitol PO Box 1750 — Little Rock AR 72201 — 501-374-8677 — 375-7649 — 186
Web: www.baldwinshell.com

Baldwin Aviation Safety & Compliance
11 Palmetto Pkwy — Hilton Head Island SC 29926 — 843-342-5434 — 302
Web: www.baldwinaviation.com

Baldwin C. Mark Atty.
112 Old Bridge St — Jacksonville NC 28540 — 910-455-4065 — 428

Baldwin County 322 Courthouse Sq — Bay Minette AL 36507 — 251-937-9561 — 580-2500 — 338
TF: 800-403-4872 ■ *Web:* www.baldwincountyal.gov

Baldwin County
121 N Wilkinson St Ste 314 — Milledgeville GA 31061 — 478-445-4791 — 445-6320 — 338
Web: www.baldwincountyga.com

Baldwin County Electric Membership Corp
19600 Hwy 59 — Summerdale AL 36580 — 251-989-6247 — 989-0148 — 245
TF: 800-837-3374 ■ *Web:* www.baldwinemc.org

Baldwin Filters 4400 Hwy 30 — Kearney NE 68847 — 800-822-5394 — 828-4453 — 60
TF: 800-822-5394 ■ *Web:* www.baldwinfilter.com

Baldwin Hackett & Meeks Inc
11602 W Ctr Rd — Omaha NE 68144 — 402-333-3300 — 177
Web: www.bhmi.com

Baldwin Hardware Corp
841 E Wyomissing Blvd — Reading PA 19611 — 610-777-7811 — 350
TF: 800-566-1986 ■ *Web:* www.baldwinhardware.com

Baldwin Haspel Burke & Mayer LLC
Energy Ctr 1100 Poydras St Ste 3600 — New Orleans LA 70163 — 504-569-2900 — 428
TF: 800-424-8802 ■ *Web:* www.bhbmlaw.com

Baldwin Intl
30403 Bruce Industrial Pkwy — Solon OH 44139 — 440-248-9500 — 492
Web: www.russelmetals.com/en

Baldwin Metals Company Inc
1901 W Commerce St — Dallas TX 75208 — 214-747-6722 — 697
TF: 800-642-2541 ■ *Web:* baldwinmetals.com

Baldwin Park Medical Ctr
1011 Baldwin Pk Blvd — Baldwin Park CA 91706 — 626-851-1011 — 374-3
Web: healthy.kaiserpermanente.org

Baldwin Public Library
300 W Merrill St — Birmingham MI 48009 — 248-647-1700 — 434-3
TF: 800-246-8464 ■ *Web:* www.baldwinlib.org

Baldwin Richardson Foods Company Inc
1 Tower Ln Ste 2390 — Oakbrook Terrace IL 60181 — 630-607-1780 — 296-25
TF Cust Svc: 866-644-2732 ■ *Web:* www.brfoods.com

Baldwin State Prison
140 Laying Farm Rd — Hardwick GA 31034 — 478-445-5218 — 445-6507 — 213
Web: dcor.state.ga.us

Baldwin Technology Co Inc
2 Trap Falls Rd Ste 402 — Shelton CT 06484 — 314-863-6640 — 726-2132 — 629
NYSE: BLD ■ *Web:* www.baldwintech.com

Baldwinsville Public Library
33 E Genesee St — Baldwinsville NY 13027 — 315-635-5631 — 635-6760 — 434-3
TF: 800 388 2000 ■ *Web:* www.bville.lib.ny.us

Baldwin-Wallace College 275 Eastland Rd — Berea OH 44017 — 440-826-2222 — 826 3830* — 166
**Fax:* Admissions ■ *TF:* 877-292-7759 ■ *Web:* www.bw.edu

Bale Chevrolet Co
13101 Chenal Pkwy — Little Rock AR 72211 — 501-221-9191 — 57
Web: balechevrolet.com

Balfour 7211 Cir S Rd — Austin TX 78745 — 800-225-3687 — 409
TF: 800-225-3087 ■ *Web:* www.balfour.com

Balfour Beatty Construction (BBC)
3100 McKinnon St 10th Fl — Dallas TX 75201 — 214-451-1000 — 186
Web: balfourbeattyus.com

Balfour Beatty Construction
7901 SW Sixth Ct Ste 200 — Fort Lauderdale FL 33324 — 954-585-4000 — 186
TF: 800-816-8847 ■ *Web:* www.balfourbeattyus.com

Balfour Beatty Inc
999 Peachtree St NE Ste 200 — Atlanta GA 30309 — 404-875-0356 — 188-4
Web: www.balfourbeatty.com

Balfour Lumber Company Inc
800 W Clay St — Thomasville GA 31792 — 229-226-6086 — 683
Web: balfourlumber.com

Bali Cafe 109 NE Second Ave — Miami FL 33132 — 305-358-5751 — 671

Bali Steak & Seafood 2005 Kalia Rd — Honolulu HI 96815 — 808-949-4321 — 671
TF: 800-445-8667 ■ *Web:* www.hiltonhawaiianvillage.com

Balihoo Inc 404 S Eighth St Ste 300 — Boise ID 83702 — 866-446-9914 — 179
TF: 866-446-9914 ■ *Web:* balihoo.com

Balkamp Inc 2601 S Holt Rd — Indianapolis IN 46241 — 317-244-7241 — 61
Web: www.balkamp.com

Ball Aerospace & Technologies Corp
1600 Commerce St — Boulder CO 80301 — 303-939-4000 — 460-2315* — 529
**Fax:* Mail Rm ■ *Web:* www.ball.com/aerospace

Ball Automotive Group
1935 National City Blvd — National City CA 91950 — 619-474-6431 — 57
Web: www.ballauto.com

Ball Beauty Supplies
416 N Fairfax Ave — Los Angeles CA 90036 — 323-655-2330 — 77
TF: 800-588-0244 ■ *Web:* www.ballbeauty.com

Ball Bounce & Sport Inc/Hedstrom Plastics
1 Hedstrom Dr — Ashland OH 44805 — 419-289-9310 — 281-3371 — 762
TF: 800-765-9665 ■ *Web:* www.hedstrom.com

Ball Chain Mfg Company Inc
741 S Fulton Ave — Mount Vernon NY 10550 — 914-664-7500 — 664-7460 — 483
TF: 800-377-3948 ■ *Web:* www.ballchain.com

Ball Corp 10 Longs Peak Dr — Broomfield CO 80021 — 303-469-3131 — 185
NYSE: BLL ■ *Web:* www.ball.com

Ball Heating & Air 8332 W Oaklawn Rd — Biloxi MS 39532 — 228-392-5432 — 610
Web: www.callballthatsall.com

Ball Homes LLC 3609 Walden Dr — Lexington KY 40517 — 859-268-1191 — 187
TF: 888-268-1101 ■ *Web:* www.ballhomes.com

Ball Horticultural Co
622 Town Rd — West Chicago IL 60185 — 630-231-3600 — 231-3605 — 293
TF: 800-879-2255 ■ *Web:* www.ballhort.com

Ball Janik 101 SW Main St Ste 1100 — Portland OR 97204 — 503-228-2525 — 428
Web: www.bjllp.com

	Phone	Fax	Class
Ball Kirk & Holm Pc 3324 Kimball Ave .... Waterloo IA 50704 *TF:* 800-272-3900 ■ *Web:* www.ballkirkholm.com	319-234-2638		428
Ball Metal Food Container LLC 300 W Greger St............................ Oakdale CA 95361	209-847-8073		124
Ball State University 2000 W University Ave....................... Muncie IN 47306 **Fax:* Admissions ■ *TF:* 800-382-8540 ■ *Web:* cms.bsu.edu	765-289-1241	285-1632*	166
Ball Tire & Gas Inc 620 S Ripley Blvd .... Alpena MI 49707 *TF:* 800-952-3553 ■ *Web:* balltire.net	989-354-4186	356-2080	755
Ball Watch USA 1131 Fourth St N .... Saint Petersburg FL 33701 *Web:* www.ballwatchusa.com	727-896-4278		411
Ballantine and Company Inc PO Box 805 .... Carlisle MA 01741	978-369-1772	369-9179	195
Ballantine Corp, The 55 Lane Rd Ste 350 .... Fairfield NJ 07004 *TF:* 800-669-6801 ■ *Web:* ballantine.com	973-305-1500		5
Ballantine House 49 Washington St.............. Newark NJ 07102 *Web:* www.newarkmuseum.org	973-596-6550	642-0459	50-3
Ballantine Laboratories Inc 312 Old Allerton Rd .... Annandale NJ 08801 *Web:* www.ballantinelabs.com	908-713-7742	713-7743	743
Ballantyne Resort Hotel 10000 Ballantyne Commons Pkwy .... Charlotte NC 28277 *TF:* 866-248-4824 ■ *Web:* www.theballantynehotel.com	704-248-4000	248-4005	669
Ballantyne Strong Inc 13710 FNB Pkwy .... Omaha NE 68154 *NYSE:* BTN ■ *TF General:* 800-424-1215 ■ *Web:* ballantynestrong.com	800-424-1215		591
Ballard Alliance 2208 NW Market St Ste 100..................... Seattle WA 98107 *Web:* www.ballardchamber.com	206-784-9705	783-8154	139
Ballard Care & RehabilitationCtr 820 NW 95th St .... Seattle WA 98117 *Web:* genesishcc.com	206-782-0100		450
Ballard Direct 7000 W Palmetto Park Rd Ste 210 .... Boca Raton FL 33433 *Web:* www.ballarddirect.com	914-262-6951		195
Ballard Group Inc, The 2525 S Wadsworth Blvd Ste 200 .... Lakewood CO 80227 *TF:* 800-393-6343 ■ *Web:* www.theballardgroup.com	303-988-4514		261
Ballard Petroleum LLC 845 12th St W........... Billings MT 59102 *TF:* 800-561-3357 ■ *Web:* www.ballardpetroleum.com	406-259-8790		536
Ballard Power Systems Inc 9000 Glenlyon Pkwy.......................... Burnaby BC V5J5J8 *NASDAQ:* BLDP ■ *Web:* www.ballard.com	604-454-0900	412-4700	253
Ballard Spahr Andrews & Ingersoll LLP 1735 Market St 51st Fl................... Philadelphia PA 19103 *Web:* www.ballardspahr.com	215-665-8500	864-8999	428
Ballard Technology Inc 11400 Airport Rd Ste 201..................... Everett WA 98204 *Web:* www.ballardtech.com	425-339-0281		529
Ballard's Farm Sausage Inc 7275 Right Fork Wilson Creek .... Wayne WV 25570 *TF General:* 800-346-7675 ■ *Web:* www.ballardsfarm.com/main.htm	304-272-5147	272-5336	296-26
Ballco Manufacturing Inc 2375 E Liberty Rd........................... Aurora IL 60502 *Web:* www.ballcomfg.com	630-898-1600		790
Ballet Arizona 2835 E Washington St .... Phoenix AZ 85034 *Web:* www.balletaz.org	602-381-0184	381-0189	573-1
Ballet Arkansas 1521 Merrill Dr.............. Little Rock AR 72211 *Web:* www.balletarkansas.org	501-223-5150		573-1
Ballet Austin 501 W Third St..................... Austin TX 78701 *Web:* www.balletaustin.org	512-476-9051		573-1
Ballet British Columbia 677 Davie St 6th Fl....................... Vancouver BC V6B2G6 *TF:* 800-236-5588 ■ *Web:* www.ballettbc.com	604-732-5003	732-4417	573-1
Ballet Chicago 17 N State St Ste 1900 .... Chicago IL 60602 *Web:* www.balletchicago.org	312-251-8838	251-8840	573-1
Ballet Hispanico of New York 167 W 89th St............................ New York NY 10024 *Web:* www.ballethispanico.org	212-362-6710	362-7809	573-1
Ballet Idaho 501 S Eigth St....................... Boise ID 83702 *Web:* www.balletidaho.org	208-343-0556	424-3129	573-1
Ballet Lubbock 5702 Genoa Ave Ste A9 .... Lubbock TX 79424 *TF:* 800-692-4035 ■ *Web:* www.balletlubbock.org	806-785-3090	785-3309	573-1
Ballet Magnificat 5406 I-55 N................. Jackson MS 39211 *TF:* 866-617-3257 ■ *Web:* www.balletmagnificat.com	601-977-1001	977-8948	573-1
Ballet Mississippi 201 E Pascagoula St Ste 106 PO Box 1787 .... Jackson MS 39215 *TF:* 800-968-4332 ■ *Web:* www.balletms.com	601-960-1560	960-2135	573-1
Ballet Quad Cities 613 17th St............. Rock Island IL 61201 *Web:* www.balletquadcities.com	309-786-3779	786-2677	573-1
Ballet Tech 890 Broadway .... New York NY 10003 **Fax Area Code:* 646 ■ *Web:* ballettech.org	212-777-7710	537-2629*	573-1
Ballet Tennessee 3202 Kelly's Ferry Rd.................... Chattanooga TN 37419 *Web:* www.ballettennessee.org	423-821-2055		573-1
Ballet Theatre Foundation American Ballet Theatre 890 Broadway Third Fl .... New York NY 10003 *Web:* www.abt.org	212-477-3030	254-5938	48-4
Ballet Theatre of Maryland 801 Chase St Maryland Hall for the Creative Arts............ Annapolis MD 21401 *Web:* www.balletmaryland.org	410-263-8289	626-1835	573-1
Ballet Theatre of New Mexico 6913 Natalie NE .... Albuquerque NM 87110 *Web:* www.btnm.org	505-888-1054		573-1
Ballet West 50 West 200 South............. Salt Lake City UT 84101 *Web:* www.balletwest.org	801-323-6900	359-3504	573-1
Ballet Western Reserve 218 W Boardman St PO Box 1684 .... Youngstown OH 44501 *Web:* www.balletwesternreserve.org	330-744-1934		573-1
BalletMet Columbus 322 Mt Vernon Ave....... Columbus OH 43215 *TF:* 800-417-1057 ■ *Web:* www.balletmet.org	614-229-4860		573-1
Ballew's Aluminum Products Inc 2 Shelter Dr .... Greer SC 29650 *TF:* 800-231-6666 ■ *Web:* www.ballews.com	864-272-4453		697

	Phone	Fax	Class
Ballinger 833 Chestnut St Ste 1400.................. Philadelphia PA 19107 *Web:* www.ballinger.com	215-446-0900		261
Ballistic Recovery Systems Inc 380 Airport Rd .... South St. Paul MN 55075 *Web:* www.brsparachutes.com	651-457-7491		20
Ballon Stoll Bader & Nadler PC 729 Seventh Ave 17th Fl.................... New York NY 10019 *Web:* www.ballonstoll.com	212-575-7900		428
Balloons Everywhere Inc 16474 Greeno Rd .... Fairhope AL 36532 **Fax Area Code:* 251 ■ *TF:* 800-239-2000 ■ *Web:* www.balloons.com	800-239-2000	210-2105*	566
Balls Bluff National Cemetery Rt 7 .... Leesburg VA 22075 *Web:* www.cem.va.gov	540-825-0027	825-6684	136
Balls Food Stores Inc 5300 Speaker Rd .... Kansas City KS 66106 *Web:* www.henhouse.com	913-321-4223		345
Bally Fitness 8700 W Bryn Mawr Ave .... Chicago IL 60631 *Web:* www.ballyfitness.com	773-380-3000		354
Bally Refrigerated Boxes Inc 135 Little Nine Rd...................... Morehead City NC 28557 *Web:* www.ballyrefboxes.com	252-240-2829	240-0384	14
Bally Ribbon Mills 23 N Seventh St............... Bally PA 19503 *Web:* www.ballyribbon.com	610-845-2211	845-8013	745-5
Bally's Atlantic City 1900 Pacific Ave.......................... Atlantic City NJ 08401 *TF:* 800-772-7777 ■ *Web:* www.caesars.com/ballys-ac	609-340-2000		669
Bally's Casino Tunica 1450 Bally's Blvd .... Robinsonville MS 38664 *TF:* 866-422-5597 ■ *Web:* www.ballystunica.com	866-422-5597		133
Bally's Las Vegas 3645 Las Vegas Blvd S.................... Las Vegas NV 89109 *TF Resv:* 800-522-4700 ■ *Web:* www.caesars.com/ballys-las-vegas	702-967-4111		133
Ballymore Co 501 Gunnard Carlson Dr.................... Coatesville PA 19365 *TF:* 800-762-8327 ■ *Web:* www.ballymore.com	610-593-5062	593-8615	421
Balmoral Hall School 630 Westminster Ave .... Winnipeg MB R3C3S1 *Web:* www.balmoralhall.com	204-784-1600	774-5534	622
Balmoral Inn 120 Balmoral Ave.................... Biloxi MS 39531 *TF:* 800-393-9131 ■ *Web:* www.balmoralinn.com	228-388-6776		379
Balmoral Park 26435 S Dixie Hwy .... Crete IL 60417 *Web:* www.balmoralpark.com	708-672-1414		642
Balmorhea State Park PO Box 15............. Toyahvale TX 79786 *Web:* tpwd.texas.gov/state-parks/balmorhea	432-375-2370		565
Balnea Spa 319 chemin du Lac Gale .... Bromont QC J2L2S5 *TF:* 866-734-2110 ■ *Web:* www.balnea.ca	450-534-0604		226
Balon Corp 3245 S Hattie Ave .... Oklahoma City OK 73129 *Web:* www.balon.com	405-677-3321		789
Balsams Resort, The 1000 Cold Spring Rd .... Dixville Notch NH 03576 *Web:* www.thebalsams.com	603-255-2500		377
BalTec Corp 121 Hillpointe Dr Ste 900.................. Canonsburg PA 15317 *TF:* 800-447-4838 ■ *Web:* www.baltecorporation.com	724-873-5757		358
Balthazar 80 Spring St........................ New York NY 10012 *Web:* www.balthazarny.com	212-965-1414		671
Baltimore Alarm & Security 5314 Reistertown Rd........................ Baltimore MD 21215	443-602-8141		692
Baltimore Area Convention & Visitors Assn (BACVA) 100 Light St 12th Fl .... Baltimore MD 21202 *TF:* 877-225-8466 ■ *Web:* www.baltimore.org	410-659-7300	727-2308	206
Baltimore Behavioral Health (BBH) 1101 W Pratt St .... Baltimore MD 21223 *TF:* 800-789-2647 ■ *Web:* baltimorecity.md.networkofcare.org	410-962-7180	962-7194	726
Baltimore Book Festival 10 E Baltimore St 10th Fl .... Baltimore MD 21202 *Web:* baltimorebookfestival.com	410-752-8632	385-0361	281
Baltimore Business Journal 36 S Charles St Ste 2500..................... Baltimore MD 21201 *Web:* www.bizjournals.com	410-576-1161	752-3112	457-5
Baltimore City Community College 2901 Liberty Heights Ave .... Baltimore MD 21215 **Fax:* Admissions ■ *TF:* 888-203-1261 ■ *Web:* www.bccc.edu	410-462-8300	462-8345*	162
Baltimore City Paper 812 Pk Ave .... Baltimore MD 21201 *TF:* 800-456-8900 ■ *Web:* citypaper.com	410-523-2300	523-2222	532-5
Baltimore City Public Schools 200 E N Ave .... Baltimore MD 21202 **Fax Area Code:* 410 ■ *TF:* 800-422-0009 ■ *Web:* www.baltimorecityschools.org	443-984-2000	545-0897*	685
Baltimore Convention Ctr 1 W Pratt St .... Baltimore MD 21201 *TF:* 800-327-4414 ■ *Web:* www.bccenter.org	410-649-7000	649-7008	205
Baltimore County 401 Bosley Ave .... Towson MD 21204 *TF:* 800-332-6347 ■ *Web:* baltimorecountymd.gov	410-887-2139		338
Baltimore County Chamber of Commerce 102 W Pennsylvania Ave Ste 101 .... Towson MD 21204 *Web:* www.baltcountychamber.com	410-825-6200	821-9901	139
Baltimore County Public Library 320 York Rd .... Towson MD 21204 *TF:* 800-705-3493 ■ *Web:* www.bcpl.info	410-887-6100	887-6103	434-3
Baltimore County Revenue Authority 115 Towsontown Blvd E .... Baltimore MD 21286 *TF:* 888-246-5384 ■ *Web:* www.baltimoregolfing.com	410-887-3127	296-7459	562
Baltimore County Visitor Ctr 400 Washington Ave.......................... Towson MD 21204 *Web:* www.enjoybaltimorecounty.com	410-887-2849		206
Baltimore Credit & Collection Services Inc 6400 Baltimore National Pk Ste 469........... Baltimore MD 21228 *Web:* www.bccs2.com	410-549-6444		218
Baltimore Development Corp 36 S Charles St Ste 2100..................... Baltimore MD 21201 *Web:* www.baltimoredevelopment.com	410-837-9305		393
Baltimore Gas & Electric Co 110 W Fayette St............................ Baltimore MD 21201 *TF:* 800-685-0123 ■ *Web:* www.bge.com	410-470-7433		787
Baltimore International College 17 Commerce St.............................. Baltimore MD 21202 *TF:* 800-624-9926 ■ *Web:* www.stratford.edu	410-752-4710		163

Entry	City	State	ZIP	Phone	Fax	Class
Baltimore Life Cos 10075 Red Run Blvd *TF:* 800-628-5433 ■ *Web:* www.baltlife.com	Owings Mills	MD	21117	410-581-6600		391-2
Baltimore Magazine 1000 Lancaster St Ste 400 **Fax Area Code: 410 ■ TF Cust Svc:* 800-935-0838 ■ *Web:* www.baltimoremagazine.net	Baltimore	MD	21202	443-873-3900	625-0280*	457-22
Baltimore Museum of Art 10 Art Museum Dr *TF:* 800-735-2964 ■ *Web:* www.artbma.org	Baltimore	MD	21218	443-573-1700	573-1582	520
Baltimore Museum of Industry 1415 Key Hwy *Web:* www.thebmi.org	Baltimore	MD	21230	410-727-4808	727-4869	520
Baltimore National Cemetery 5501 Frederick Ave *TF:* 800-535-1117 ■ *Web:* www.cem.va.gov/cems/nchp/baltimore.asp	Baltimore	MD	21228	410-644-9696	644-1563	136
Baltimore Polytechnic Institute 1400 W Cold Spring Ln *Web:* www.bpi.edu	Baltimore	MD	21209	410-396-7026		685
Baltimore Ravens 1101 Russell St *Web:* www.baltimoreravens.com	Baltimore	MD	21230	410-261-7283		715-3
Baltimore Rigging Company Inc, The 6601 Tributary St *TF:* 800-626-2150 ■ *Web:* www.baltimorerigging.com	Baltimore	MD	21224	443-696-4001	696-4006	189-1
Baltimore Streetcar Museum 1901 Falls Rd *Web:* www.baltimoremd.com	Baltimore	MD	21211	410-547-0264	547-0264	520
Baltimore Sun 501 N Calvert St *TF:* 800-829-8000 ■ *Web:* www.baltimoresun.com	Baltimore	MD	21278	410-332-6000	332-6455	532-2
Baltimore Symphony Orchestra 1212 Cathedral St *TF:* 877-276-1444 ■ *Web:* www.bsomusic.org	Baltimore	MD	21201	410-783-8100		573-3
Baltimore Teachers Union 5800 Metro Dr Ste 200 *TF:* 800-332-6347 ■ *Web:* www.baltimoreteachers.org	Baltimore	MD	21215	410-358-6600		260
Baltimore Times 2513 N Charles St *TF:* 800-944-7403 ■ *Web:* baltimoretimes-online.com	Baltimore	MD	21218	410-366-3900	243-1627	532-4
Baltimore Washington Medical Ctr 301 Hospital Dr *TF:* 800-994-6610 ■ *Web:* www.mybwmc.org	Glen Burnie	MD	21061	410-787-4000	595-1958	374-3
Baltimore/Washington Corridor Chamber of Commerce 312 Marshall Ave Ste 104 *Web:* www.baltwashchamber.org	Laurel	MD	20707	301-725-4000	725-0776	139
Baltimore/Washington International Thurgood Marshall Airport (BWI) PO Box 8766 *TF:* 800-435-9294 ■ *Web:* www.bwiairport.com	Baltimore	MD	21240	410-859-7111	768-9452	27
Baltz & Co 49 W 23rd St Fl 9 *Web:* www.baltzco.com	New York	NY	10010	212-982-8300		636
Balzekas Museum of Lithuanian Culture 6500 S Pulaski Rd *Web:* www.balzekasmuseum.org	Chicago	IL	60629	773-582-6500	582-5133	520
Balzer Pacific Equipment Co 2136 SE Eigth Ave *TF:* 800-442-0966 ■ *Web:* www.balzerpacific.com	Portland	OR	97214	503-232-5141	232-9556	358
BAM (Brooklyn Academy of Music) 30 Lafayette Ave *Web:* www.bam.org	Brooklyn	NY	11217	718-636-4100		572
Bama Pie Ltd 5377 E 66th St N *Web:* www.bama.com	Tulsa	OK	74117	918-592-0778		296-1
Bama Sea Products 756 28th St S *TF:* 800-833-3474 ■ *Web:* www.bamasea.com	Saint Petersburg	FL	33712	727-327-3474	322-0580	296-14
Bama Theatre 600 Greensboro Ave *Web:* www.tuscarts.org	Tuscaloosa	AL	35401	205-758-5195	345-2787	572
Bambara Restaurant 202 S Main St *Web:* www.bambara-slc.com	Salt Lake City	UT	84101	801-363-5454		671
Bamberg County 2340 Main Hwy *Web:* www.bambergsc.com	Bamberg	SC	29003	803-245-5128	245-5156	338
Bamberger Polymers Inc 2 Jericho Plaza Ste 109 *TF:* 800-888-8959 ■ *Web:* www.bambergerpolymers.com	Jericho	NY	11753	516-622-3600	622-3610	603
Bamboo Court 4935 Centennial Blvd *Web:* bamboocourtcoloradosprings.com	Colorado Springs	CO	80919	719-599-7383		671
Bamboo Garden 1200 Yellowstone Ave *Web:* orderbamboogarden.com	Pocatello	ID	83201	208-238-2331		671
Bamboo Restaurant 10835 Venice Blvd *Web:* bamboorestaurant.net	Los Angeles	CA	90034	310-287-0668		671
Bamboo Solutions 11417 Sunset Hills Rd Ste 105 *Web:* www.bamboosolutions.com	Reston	VA	20190	703-964-2002		177
Bamboo Stix 2243 N Tyler Rd Ste 101 *Web:* www.bamboostix.com	Wichita	KS	67205	316-722-8886		671
Bamboo Worldwide Inc 30 N Racine Ste 300 *TF:* 800-652-6555 ■ *Web:* www.bambooworldwide.com	Chicago	IL	60607	773-227-4848		463
BAMC (Brooke Army Medical Ctr) 3551 Roger Brooke Dr *TF:* 800-443-2262 ■ *Web:* www.bamc.amedd.army.mil	Fort Sam Houston	TX	78234	210-916-4141		374-4
BAMC (Bay Area Medical Ctr) 3100 Shore Dr *TF:* 888-788-2070 ■ *Web:* bamc.org	Marinette	WI	54143	715-735-4200		374-3
Bamco Inc 30 Baekeland Ave *Web:* www.gobamco.com	Middlesex	NJ	08846	732-302-0889		480
Ban Thai 340 N Charles St *Web:* www.banthai.us	Baltimore	MD	21201	410-727-7971		671
Ban Thai 792 Eastgate S Dr	Cincinnati	OH	45245	513-752-3200		671
Ban Thai 15726 100th Ave *Web:* www.banthai.com	Edmonton	AB	T5P0L1	780-444-9345		671
Banacol Marketing Corp 355 Alhambra Cir Ste 1510 *TF:* 877-324-7619	Coral Gables	FL	33134	305-441-9036	446-4291	297-7
Banana Banner Signs 3148 Duke St *Web:* bananabanner.com	Alexandria	VA	22314	703-522-6262		701
Banana Blossom Thai 4228 Pk Blvd *Web:* www.bananablossomthai.com	Oakland	CA	94602	510-336-0990		671
Banana Leaf 820 W Broadway *Web:* www.bananaleaf-vancouver.com	Vancouver	BC	V5Z1J9	604-731-6333		671
Bananas at Large 1504 Fourth St *Web:* www.bananas.com	San Rafael	CA	94901	415-457-7600		526
Banc Statements Inc 4700 Birmingham St *Web:* www.bsisite.com	Birmingham	AL	35217	205-956-5004		70
Banca IMI Securities Corp 1 William St *Web:* www.bancaimi.com	New York	NY	10004	212-326-1100		690
Bancker Construction Corp 218 Blydenburgh Rd *TF:* 800-767-7565 ■ *Web:* www.bancker.com	Islandia	NY	11749	631-582-8880	582-3698	188-10
Bancography Inc 2301 First Ave N Ste 103 *Web:* www.bancography.com	Birmingham	AL	35203	205-251-3227		256
Bancorp Bank 409 Silverside Rd Ste 105 *NASDAQ: TBBK* ■ *TF Cust Svc:* 866-255-9831 ■ *Web:* thebancorp.com	Wilmington	DE	19809	302-385-5000		70
Bancorp Rhode Island 1 Turks Head Pl *NASDAQ: BARI* ■ *Web:* www.bankri.com	Providence	RI	02903	401-456-5000		360-2
BancorpSouth Inc 2910 W Jackson St *NYSE: BXS* ■ *TF:* 888-797-7711 ■ *Web:* www.bancorpsouth.com	Tupelo	MS	38801	662-680-2000	678-7263	360-2
Bancroft & Sons Transportation Inc 3390 High Prairie Rd *Web:* www.bancroftandsons.com	Grand Prairie	TX	75050	972-790-3777		5
Bancroft Bag Inc 425 Bancroft Blvd *TF:* 800-551-4950 ■ *Web:* www.bancroftbag.com	West Monroe	LA	71292	318-387-2550		65
Bancroft Construction Co 1300 N Grant Ave Ste 110 *Web:* www.bancroftconstruction.com	Wilmington	DE	19806	302-655-3434	655-4599	188-7
Bancroft Fund Ltd 65 Madison Ave Ste 550 *NYSE: BCV*	Morristown	NJ	07960	973-631-1177		405
Band Digital Inc 150 N Michigan Ave Ste 300 *Web:* banddigital.com	Chicago	IL	60601	312-981-6000		195
Banda Group International LLC 1799 E Queen Creek Rd Ste 1 *Web:* www.bandagroupintl.com	Chandler	AZ	85286	480-636-8734		194
Bandana's Bar-B-Q 11750 Gravois Rd *Web:* www.bandanasbbq.com	Saint Louis	MO	63127	314-849-1162		671
Bandar 845 Fourth Ave *Web:* www.bandarrestaurant.com	San Diego	CA	92101	619-238-0101		671
Bandera County Convention & Visitors Bureau 126 State Hwy 16 S PO Box 171 *TF:* 800-364-3833 ■ *Web:* www.banderacowboycapital.com	Bandera	TX	78003	830-796-3045		206
Bandera Electric Co-op Inc 3172 State Hwy 16 N **Fax Area Code: 830* ■ *TF:* 866-226-3372 ■ *Web:* banderaelectric.com	Bandera	TX	78003	866-226-3372	460-3030*	245
Bandido's Inc 6060 E State Blvd *Web:* www.bandidos.com	Fort Wayne	IN	46815	260-493-0607		671
Bandimere Speedway 3051 S Rooney Rd *TF:* 888-737-5253 ■ *Web:* www.bandimere.com	Morrison	CO	80465	303-697-6001	697-0815	515
Bandit Industries Inc 6750 W Millbrook Rd *TF:* 800-952-0178 ■ *Web:* www.banditchippers.com	Remus	MI	49340	989-561-2270	561-2273	190
Bandit Lites Inc 2233 Sycamore Dr *Web:* www.banditlites.com	Knoxville	TN	37921	865-971-3071		41
Band-It-IDEX Inc 4799 Dahlia St *TF:* 800-525-0758 ■ *Web:* www.band-it-idex.com	Denver	CO	80216	303-320-4555	333-6549	350
BandMerch LLC 3120 W Empire Ave *Web:* www.bandmerch.com	Burbank	CA	91504	818-736-4800		5
Bandung Indonesian Restaurant 600 Williamson St *Web:* www.bandungrestaurant.com	Madison	WI	53703	608-255-6910		671
Bandy Carroll Hellige Advertising Inc 307 W Muhammad Ali Blvd *Web:* www.bch.com	Louisville	KY	40202	502-589-7711		7
Bandy Inc 201 S International Rd *Web:* www.bandyco.com	Garland	TX	75042	972-272-5455		697
Bane Machinery Inc PO Box 541355 *TF:* 800-594-2263 ■ *Web:* www.banemachinery.com	Dallas	TX	75354	214-352-2468	352-2460	358
Banetti Inc 55 NE 94th St *TF:* 855-855-7800 ■ *Web:* www.banetti.com	Miami	FL	33138	855-855-7800		180
Banff Adventures Unlimited 211 Bear St Bison Courtyard *TF:* 800-644-8888 ■ *Web:* www.banffadventures.com	Banff	AB	T1L1A8	403-762-4554		760
Banff Centre for Arts and Creativity 107 Tunnel Mtn Dr PO Box 1020 *TF:* 800-884-7574 ■ *Web:* www.banffcentre.ca	Banff	AB	T1L1H5	403-762-6100		377
Banff Mountain Book Festival 107 Tunnel Mountain Dr PO Box 1020 Stn 38 *Web:* www.banffcentre.ca	Banff	AB	T1L1H5	403-762-6100	762-6277	281
Banff National Park PO Box 900 *TF:* 877-737-3783 ■ *Web:* www.pc.gc.ca	Banff	AB	T1L1K2	403-762-1550	762-1551	563
Banfield the Pet Hospital 18101 SE Sixth Way *TF:* 866-894-7927 ■ *Web:* www.banfield.com	Vancouver	WA	98683	866-894-7927		794
Bang Printing Inc 3323 Oak St *TF:* 800-328-0450 ■ *Web:* www.bangprinting.com	Brainerd	MN	56401	218-829-2877	829-7145	626
Bangkok 54 2919 Columbia Pk *Web:* www.bangkok54restaurant.com	Arlington	VA	22204	703-521-4070		671
Bangkok Bistro 715 N Glebe Rd *Web:* www.bangkokbistrodc.com	Arlington	VA	22203	703-243-9669		671
Bangkok Cafe 1203 S Holden Rd	Greensboro	NC	27407	336-855-9370		671
Bangkok City 1129 E Walnut St *Web:* wordpress.com	Springfield	MO	65806	417-799-1221		671
Bangkok Cuisine 32166 Woodward Ave	Royal Oak	MI	48073	248-439-0529		671
Bangkok Garden 18 Elm St *TF:* 800-461-3333 ■ *Web:* www.bangkokgarden.ca	Toronto	ON	M5G1G7	416-977-6748		671
Bangkok Gardens 811 Cherry St *Web:* www.bangkokgardens.com	Columbia	MO	65201	573-874-3284		671
Bangkok House 318 N Kings Hwy	Myrtle Beach	SC	29577	843-626-5384		671
Bangkok Restaurant 3255 W Hammer Ln Ste 18	Stockton	CA	95209	209-476-8616		671

Name / Address	City	State	Zip	Phone	Fax	Class
Bangkok Restaurant 1492-A Piedmont Ave NE *Web:* www.bangkokatl.com	Atlanta	GA	30309	404-874-2514		671
Bangkok Thai Cuisine 3426 E Fourth St *Web:* bangkokthaicuisinelbc.com	Long Beach	CA	90814	562-433-0093		671
Bangkok View 1233 28th St SW	Wyoming	MI	49509	616-531-8070		671
Bangladesh Consulate General 4201 Wilshire Blvd Ste 605 *Web:* www.bangladeshconsulatela.com	Los Angeles	CA	90010	323-932-0100	932-9703	257
Bangladesh Mission to the United Nations 820 Second Ave Diplomat Ctr 4th Fl *Web:* www.un.int	New York	NY	10017	212-867-3434	972-4038	784
Bangor City Hall 73 Harlow St *TF:* 800-829-4477 ■ *Web:* www.bangormaine.gov	Bangor	ME	04401	207-992-4200	945-4449	337
Bangor Daily News 491 Main St PO Box 1329 *TF:* 800-432-7964 ■ *Web:* www.bangordailynews.com	Bangor	ME	04402	207-990-8000		532-2
Bangor Electronics Co 614 Joy St	Bangor	MI	49013	269-427-7944		458
Bangor Hydro Electric Co PO Box 932 *TF:* 800-499-6600 ■ *Web:* emeramaine.com	Bangor	ME	04402	207-945-5621		787
Bangor International Airport 287 Godfrey Blvd *TF:* 866-359-2264 ■ *Web:* www.flybangor.com	Bangor	ME	04401	207-992-4600	945-3607	27
Bangor Museum & History Ctr 159 Union St *Web:* www.bangorhistoricalsociety.org	Bangor	ME	04401	207-942-1900		520
Bangor Public Library 145 Harlow St *Web:* www.bpl.lib.me.us	Bangor	ME	04401	207-947-8336	947-8336	434-3
Bangor Region Chamber of Commerce 208 Maine Ave *Web:* www.bangorregion.com	Bangor	ME	04401	207-947-0307	990-1427	139
Bangor Savings Bank 99 Franklin St *TF:* 877-226-4671 ■ *Web:* www.bangor.com	Bangor	ME	04401	207-942-5211		70
Bangor Symphony Orchestra PO Box 1441 *TF General:* 800-639-3221 ■ *Web:* www.bangorsymphony.org	Bangor	ME	04402	207-942-5555	990-1272	573-3
Bangor Theological Seminary 159 State St *TF:* 800-287-6781 ■ *Web:* www.bts.edu	Portland	ME	04101	207-942-6781	990-1267	167-3
Bangs Ambulance Service Inc 205 W Green St *Web:* www.bangsambulance.com	Ithaca	NY	14850	607-273-1161		30
Banik Communications Inc 121 Fourth St N Ste 1B *Web:* banik.com	Great Falls	MT	59401	406-454-3422		7
Banjo Corp 150 Banjo Dr *Web:* www.banjocorp.com	Crawfordsville	IN	47933	765-362-7367		641
Bank Administration Institute (BAI) 115 S LaSalle St Ste 3300 **Fax:* Cust Svc ■ *TF Cust Svc:* 800-224-9889 ■ *Web:* www.bai.org	Chicago	IL	60603	312-683-2464	683-2373*	49-2
Bank Advisory Group LLC, The 15100 Gebron Dr *Web:* www.bankadvisory.com	Austin	TX	78734	512-263-8800		196
Bank Capital Corp 5055 N 32nd St *Web:* biltmorebankaz.com	Phoenix	AZ	85018	602-992-5055		360-2
Bank Financial 6415 W 95th St *TF:* 800-894-6900 ■ *Web:* www.bankfinancial.com	Chicago Ridge	IL	60415	800-894-6900		70
Bank First National PO Box 10 *Web:* www.bankfirstnational.com	Manitowoc	WI	54221	920-684-6611		70
Bank Independent 710 S Montgomery Ave *TF:* 877-865-5050 ■ *Web:* www.bibank.com	Sheffield	AL	35660	256-386-5000		360-2
Bank Leumi USA 579 Fifth Ave *TF:* 800-892-5430 ■ *Web:* www.leumiusa.com	New York	NY	10017	917-542-2343		70
Bank Midwest NA 1111 Main St *Web:* www.bankmw.com	Kansas City	MO	64105	816-471-9800		70
Bank Mutual Corp 4949 W Brown Deer Rd *NASDAQ: BKMU* ■ **Fax Area Code:* 608 ■ *TF:* 844-256-8684 ■ *Web:* www.bankmutual.com	Milwaukee	WI	53223	414-354-1500	251-0580*	360-2
Bank of Albuquerque 201 Third St NW *TF:* 800-583-0709 ■ *Web:* www.bankofalbuquerque.com	Albuquerque	NM	87102	505-855-0855	222-8481	70
Bank of America Business Capital 1 Bryant Pk *Web:* www.bofaml.com	New York	NY	10036	860-659-3200		216
Bank of America Card Services PO Box 2493 *TF:* 800-732-9194 ■ *Web:* www.bankofamerica.com	Norfolk	VA	23501	800-732-9194		215
Bank of America Pavilion 290 Northern Ave *Web:* www.bostonpavilion.net	Boston	MA	02210	617-728-1600		572
Bank of America Stadium 800 S Mint St *Web:* www.panthers.com	Charlotte	NC	28202	704-358-7000		720
Bank of Bartlett Inc 6281 Stage Rd *Web:* bankofbartlett.com	Bartlett	TN	38134	901-302-6600		70
Bank of Bennington (Bennington NE) 12212 N 156th St *Web:* www.bankbenn.com	Bennington	NE	68007	402-238-2245		70
Bank of Bennington, The 155 North St *Web:* www.thebankofbennington.com	Bennington	VT	05201	802-442-8121		70
Bank of Blue Valley PO Box 26128 *Web:* www.bankbv.com	Overland Park	KS	66225	913-338-1000		70
Bank of Cashton 723 Main St *Web:* bankofcashton.com	Cashton	WI	54619	608-654-5121		70
Bank of Commerce Holdings 1901 Churn Creek Rd *NASDAQ: BOCH* ■ *TF:* 800-421-2575 ■ *Web:* www.reddingbankofcommerce.com	Redding	CA	96002	530-224-3333		360-2
Bank of Delmar Inc 2245 Northwood Dr *Web:* www.bankofdelmarvahb.com	Salisbury	MD	21801	410-548-1100		70
Bank of Denver 810 E 17th Ave *Web:* thebankofdenver.com	Denver	CO	80218	303-572-3600		70
Bank of Erath 105 W Edwards *Web:* bankoferath.com	Erath	LA	70533	337-937-5816		70
Bank of Florence Museum 8502 N 30th St *TF:* 800-799-4889 ■ *Web:* www.historicflorence.org/attractions.php	Omaha	NE	68112	402-496-9923		520
Bank of Gleason 203 Main St PO Box 231 *Web:* www.gleasononline.com	Gleason	TN	38229	731-648-5506	648-5090	70
Bank of Glen Burnie, The 101 Crain Hwy SE *Web:* www.thebankofglenburnie.com	Glen Burnie	MD	21061	410-766-3300		70
Bank of Gravett 211 SE Main St *Web:* bankofgravett.net	Gravette	AR	72736	479-787-5251		70
Bank of Hawaii Corp 130 Merchant St 20th Fl *NYSE: BOH* ■ *TF:* 888-643-3888 ■ *Web:* www.boh.com	Honolulu	HI	96813	888-643-3888		360-2
Bank of Hazlehurst PO Box 628 *Web:* www.bankofhazlehurst.com	Hazlehurst	GA	31539	912-375-4228		70
Bank of Herrin, The 101 S Park Ave	Herrin	IL	62948	618-942-6666		70
Bank of Holly Springs PO Box 250 *Web:* www.bankofhollysprings.com	Holly Springs	MS	38635	662-252-2511	252-1816	70
Bank of Kirksville 214 S Franklin *Web:* bankofkirksville.com	Kirksville	MO	63501	660-665-7766		70
Bank of Landisburg, The 100 N Carlisle St PO Box 179 *Web:* www.bankoflandisburg.com	Landisburg	PA	17040	717-789-3213		70
Bank of Louisiana 300 St Charles Ave *TF:* 866-392-9952 ■ *Web:* www.bankoflouisiana.com	New Orleans	LA	70130	504-592-0600	592-0606	70
Bank of Marin 504 Tamalpais Dr *NASDAQ: BMRC* ■ *TF:* 800-654-5111 ■ *Web:* www.bankofmarin.com	Corte Madera	CA	94925	415-927-2265		70
Bank of Mauston, The 503 Gateway Ave *Web:* www.bankofmauston.com	Mauston	WI	53948	608-847-6200		70
Bank of McKenney 20718 First St *OTC: BOMK* ■ *TF:* 800-528-2273 ■ *Web:* www.bankofmckenney.com	McKenney	VA	23872	804-478-4434	478-4704	70
Bank of Montreal (BMO) 100 King St W 1 First Canadian Pl 19th Fl *NYSE: BMO* ■ *TF:* 800-340-5021 ■ *Web:* www.bmo.com	Toronto	ON	M5X1A1	416-867-6785	867-6793	70
Bank of Montreal 3 Times Sq *TF:* 877-225-5266 ■ *Web:* www.bmocm.com	New York	NY	10036	877-225-5266		70
Bank of Morton 366 S Fourth St PO Box 229 *Web:* www.bankofmorton.com	Morton	MS	39117	601-732-8944	732-8599	70
Bank of Napa 2007 Redwood Rd Ste 101 *Web:* www.thebankofnapa.com	Napa	CA	94558	707-257-7777		70
Bank of Nevada 2700 W Sahara Ave *TF:* 877-299-2265	Las Vegas	NV	89102	702-248-4200	248-8661	70
Bank of New Glarus 501 First St *Web:* www.thebankofnewglarus.bank	New Glarus	WI	53574	608-527-5205		70
Bank of North Dakota 1200 Memorial Hwy *TF:* 800-472-2166 ■ *Web:* bnd.nd.gov	Bismarck	ND	58504	701-328-5600	328-5632	70
Bank of Nova Scotia 1 Liberty Plaza 26th Fl *TSE: BNS* ■ *TF:* 800-472-6842 ■ *Web:* www.scotiabank.com	New York	NY	10006	212-225-5000		70
Bank of Oak Ridge 2211 Oak Ridge Rd *OTC: BKOR* ■ *Web:* www.bankofoakridge.com	Oak Ridge	NC	27310	336-644-9944		70
Bank of Oklahoma NA PO Box 2300 *TF:* 800-234-6181 ■ *Web:* www.bankofoklahoma.com	Tulsa	OK	74192	918-588-6010		70
Bank of South Carolina Corp 256 Meeting St *NASDAQ: BKSC* ■ *TF:* 800-523-4175 ■ *Web:* www.banksc.com	Charleston	SC	29401	843-724-1500		360-2
Bank of Springfield 2600 Adlai Stevenson Dr *TF:* 877-698-3278 ■ *Web:* www.bankwithbos.com	Springfield	IL	62703	217-529-5555		70
Bank of Stockton PO Box 1110 *TF:* 800-941-1494 ■ *Web:* www.bankofstockton.com	Stockton	CA	95201	209-929-1600		70
Bank of Sunset & Trust Co 863 Napoleon Ave *TF:* 800-264-5578 ■ *Web:* www.bankofsunset.com	Sunset	LA	70584	337-662-5222	662-5705	70
Bank of Tampa, The 601 Bayshore Blvd *Web:* bankoftampa.com	Tampa	FL	33606	813-872-1216		70
Bank of Tescott, The 600 S Santa Fe	Salina	KS	67401	785-825-1621		70
Bank of the Cascades 121 N Ninth St *Web:* botc.com	Boise	ID	83702	208-343-7848		70
Bank of the Orient 233 Sansome St *TF:* 877-275-3342 ■ *Web:* www.bankorient.com/home	San Francisco	CA	94104	415-338-0843	338-0619	186
Bank of the Ozarks Inc 12615 Chenal Pkwy PO Box 8811 *NASDAQ: OZRK* ■ *TF:* 800-274-4482 ■ *Web:* www.bankozarks.com	Little Rock	AR	72211	501-978-2265		360-2
Bank of the Sierra PO Box 1930 *TF Cust Svc:* 888-454-2265 ■ *Web:* www.bankofthesierra.com	Porterville	CA	93258	559-782-4900		70
Bank of Tokyo-Mitsubishi Ltd 1251 Ave of the Americas *Web:* www.bk.mufg.jp	New York	NY	10020	212-782-4000		70
Bank of Tuscaloosa 2200 Jack Warner Pkwy *Web:* www.synovus.com/local/tuscaloosa-al	Tuscaloosa	AL	35401	205-345-6200		70
Bank Of Utica 222 Genesee St *OTC: BKUT* ■ *TF:* 800-442-1028 ■ *Web:* www.bankofutica.com	Utica	NY	13502	315-797-2700	797-2707	70
Bank of Walterboro 1100 N Jeffries Blvd *Web:* bankofwalterboro.com	Walterboro	SC	29488	843-549-2265		70
Bank Street College Library 610 W 112th St *Web:* www.bankstreet.edu	New York	NY	10025	212-875-4400		162
Bank Street Group LLC, The 4 Landmark Sq 3rd Fl *Web:* www.bankstreet.com	Stamford	CT	06901	203-252-2800		70
BANK W Holdings LLC 5 Bedford Farms Dr Ste 304 *Web:* www.bankwholdings.com	Bedford	NH	03110	603-792-2345		260
Bank2 909 S Meridian *Web:* bank2.bank	Oklahoma City	OK	73108	405-946-2265		70
Bank-A-Count Corp 1666 Main St PO Box 167 *Web:* www.bank-a-count.com	Rudolph	WI	54475	715-435-3131		781
BankAtlantic Bancorp Inc 401 E Las Olas Blvd Ste 800 *Web:* www.bbxcapital.com	Fort Lauderdale	FL	33301	954-940-4000		360-2

Phone | Fax | Class

Bankcard Central Inc
1321 Burlington St .... Kansas City MO 64116 816-221-1133 225
Web: www.bankcardcentral.com

BankCard Services
21281 S Western Ave .... Torrance CA 90501 213-365-1122 395
TF: 888-339-0100 ■ *Web:* www.Navyzebra.com

Bankers Business Management Services Inc
8121 Georgia Ave Ste 950 .... Silver Spring MD 20910 301-565-0601 194
Web: www.bankersbms.com

Bankers Data Services Inc 521 W 11th St......... Alma GA 31510 912-632-2060 396
TF: 888-458-8652 ■ *Web:* www.bdsalma.com

Bankers Fidelity Life Insurance Co
4370 Peachtree Rd NE .... Atlanta GA 30319 800-241-1439 391-2
NASDAQ: AAME ■ *TF:* 866-458-7504 ■ *Web:* bankersfidelity.com

Bankers Financial Products Corp
201 N Main St Ste 4 .... Fort Atkinson WI 53538 800-348-1831 622-8741 401
TF: 800-348-1831 ■ *Web:* www.rate-watch.com

Bankers Insurance LLC 4490 Cox Rd .... Glen Allen VA 23060 804-497-3634 391-2
Web: www.bankersinsurance.net

Bankers Life & Casualty Co
111 E Wacker Dr Ste 2100 .... Chicago IL 60601 312-396-6000 391-2
TF: 800-231-9150 ■ *Web:* www.bankerslife.com

Bankers Life Fieldhouse
125 S Pennsylvania St .... Indianapolis IN 46204 317-917-2500 720
TF: 800-745-3000 ■ *Web:* www.bankerslifefieldhouse.com

Bankers Petroleum Ltd
Suite, 800,-777 8 Ave SW .... Calgary AB T2P3R5 403-513-2699 538
Web: www.bankerspetroleum.com

Bankers' Bank 7700 Mineral Point Rd .... Madison WI 53717 608-833-5550 70
TF: 800-388-5550 ■ *Web:* www.bankersbankusa.com

Bank-Fund Staff Federal Credit Union
PO Box 27755 .... Washington DC 20038 202-458-4300 522-1528 219
TF: 800-923-7328 ■ *Web:* www.bfsfcu.org

Banking Daily 1801 S Bell St.................. Arlington VA 22202 703-341-5777 531-1
TF: 800-372-1033

Banko Beverage Co
5001 Crackersport Rd........................ Allentown PA 18104 610-434-0147 391-1276 81-1

Bankoh Investment Services Inc
130 Merchant St Ste 850 .... Honolulu HI 96813 808-537-8500 402
Web: www.boh.com

Bankruptcy Management Solutions Inc
5 Peters Canyon Rd Ste 200 .... Irvine CA 92606 800-634-7734 463
TF: 800-634-7734 ■ *Web:* www.bmsadvantage.com

Banks com Inc
575 Market St Ste 900 .... San Francisco CA 94105 415-744-6700 744-6718 196
Web: www.bankofsf.com

Banks County Schools
1989 Historic Homer Hwy.................... Commerce GA 30529 706-677-2224 685
Web: www.banks.k12.ga.us

Banks Hardwoods Inc 69937 M-103........ White Pigeon MI 49099 269-483-2323 820
Web: www.bankshardwoods.com

Banks Jim (Rep R - IN)
509 Cannon HOB .... Washington DC 20515 202-225-4436 342-2
Web: banks.house.gov

Banks Pest Control Inc
215 Golden State Ave .... Bakersfield CA 93301 661-323-7858 577
TF: 800-662-6300 ■ *Web:* bankspest.com

Bankshot Sports Organization
330-U N Stonestreet Ave Ste 504.............. Rockville MD 20852 301-309-0260 309-0263 710
TF: 800-933-0140 ■ *Web:* www.bankshot.com

Banksys Management Inc
2750 Peachtree Industrial .... Duluth GA 30097 678-957-1234 180
Web: www.banksys.net

BankTEL Systems LLC
319 Park Creek Dr .... Columbus MS 39705 662-245-1007 809
Web: banktel.com

Bankwest 420 S Pierre St........................ Pierre SD 57501 605-224-7391 224-7393 70
TF: 800-253-0362 ■ *Web:* www.bankwest-sd.com

Bankwest Corp
2050 N California Blvd .... Walnut Creek CA 94596 925-933-7810 70
TF: 888-389-8668 ■ *Web:* www.bankofthewest.com

Bannack State Park 4200 Bannack Rd .... Dillon MT 59725 406-834-3413 834-3548 565

Banneker-Douglas Museum
84 Franklin St........................ Annapolis MD 21401 410-216-6180 974-2553 520
Web: bdmuseum.maryland.gov

Banner & Witcoff Ltd
10 S Wacker Dr Ste 3000 .... Chicago IL 60606 312-463-5000 428
Web: bannerwitcoff.com

Banner Bank
10 S First Ave PO Box 907 .... Walla Walla WA 99362 509-527-3636 70
TF: 800-272-9933 ■ *Web:* www.bannerbank.com

Banner Baywood Medical Ctr
6644 E Baywood Ave .... Mesa AZ 85206 480-981-2000 374-3
Web: www.bannerhealth.com

Banner Behavioral Health Hospital
7575 E Earll Dr .... Scottsdale AZ 85251 480-941-7500 374-5
TF: 800-254-4357 ■ *Web:* www.bannerhealth.com

Banner Boswell Medical Ctr
10401 W Thunderbird Blvd.................... Sun City AZ 85351 623-977-7211 374-3
Web: www.bannerhealth.com

Banner County PO Box 67.................... Harrisburg NE 69345 308-436-5265 338

Banner Day Camp
1225 Riverwoods Rd........................ Lake Forest IL 60045 847-295-4900 121
Web: www.bannerdaycamp.com

Banner Del E Webb Memorial Hospital
14502 W Meeker Blvd .... Sun City West AZ 85375 623-214-4000 214-4105 374-3
TF: 800-254-4357 ■ *Web:* www.bannerhealth.com

Banner Desert Medical Ctr
1400 S Dobson Rd .... Mesa AZ 85202 480-512-3000 374-3
Web: www.bannerhealth.com

Banner Engineering Corp
9714 Tenth Ave N .... Minneapolis MN 55441 763-544-3164 544-3213 253
TF: 888-373-6767 ■ *Web:* www.bannerengineering.com

Banner Equipment Company Inc
1370 Bungalow Rd .... Morris IL 60450 815-941-9600 57
Web: www.bannerbeer.com

Banner Good Samaritan Medical Ctr
1111 E McDowell Rd .... Phoenix AZ 85006 602-839-2000 374-3
Web: www.bannerhealth.com

Banner Life Insurance Co
1701 Research Blvd .... Rockville MD 20850 301-279-4800 391-2
TF: 800-638-8428 ■ *Web:* www.lgamerica.com

Banner Marsh State Fish & Wildlife Area
19721 N US 24........................ Canton IL 61520 309-647-9184 565
Web: www.dnr.illinois.gov/Parks/Pages/BannerMarsh.aspx

Banner Personnel Service Inc
53 W Jackson Blvd Ste 1219 .... Chicago IL 60604 312-922-5400 347-1206 260
Web: www.bannerpersonnel.com

Banner Pharmacaps Inc
4815 Emperor Blvd........................ Durham NC 27265 336-812-3442 582
Web: www.patheon.com

Banner Retail Marketing Group LLC
16201 E Indiana Ave ste 3240 .... Spokane Valley WA 99216 800-843-9271 214-1963* 7
**Fax Area Code:* 801 ■ *TF:* 800-843-9271 ■ *Web:* www.bannerretail.com

Banner Supply Co 7195 NW 30th St.............. Miami FL 33122 305-593-2946 477-2775 191-3
TF: 888-511-4004 ■ *Web:* www.bannersupply.com

Banner Thunderbird Medical Ctr (BTMC)
5555 W ThunderbiRd Rd .... Glendale AZ 85306 602-839-2000 865-5930 374-3
Web: www.bannerhealth.com

Banner Welder Inc
N 117 W 18200 Fulton Dr................. Germantown WI 53022 262-253-2900 811
TF: 800-721-7068 ■ *Web:* www.bannerweld.com

Banner Wholesale Grocers Inc
3000 S Ashland Ave Ste 300 .... Chicago IL 60608 312-421-2650 345
TF: 844-421-2650 ■ *Web:* www.bannerwholesale.com

Banner, The
26381 S Tamiami Trail .... Bonita Springs FL 34134 239-213-6000 532-4

Banner-Gazette
490 E State Rd 60 PO Box 38.................... Pekin IN 47165 812-967-3176 967-3194 532-4
TF: 800-889-3390 ■ *Web:* www.gbpnews.com

Banner-Press PO Box 585.................... Brenham TX 77834 979-836-7956 830-8577 532-2
Web: www.brenhambanner.com

Banning Museum, The 401 E 'M' St .... Wilmington CA 90744 310-548-7777 520
TF: 800-905-2030 ■ *Web:* banningmuseum.org

Banning State Park
61101 Banning Pk Rd PO Box 643............ Sandstone MN 55072 320-245-2668 245-0251 565
Web: www.dnr.state.mn.us

Bannister & Assoc Inc 34 N High St......... New Albany OH 43054 614-895-1355 895-3466 47
Web: www.bannister.com

Bannister Family House
406 Dickinson St .... San Diego CA 92103 619-543-7977 543-7937 372
TF: 800-926-8273 ■ *Web:* health.ucsd.edu

Bannister's Wharf 1 Bannister's Wharf........... Newport RI 02840 401-846-4500 849-8750 50-6
TF: 800-395-1343 ■ *Web:* www.bannistersnewport.com

Bannock County PO Box 4016 .... Pocatello ID 83205 208-236-7211 236-7363 338
Web: www.bannockcounty.us

Bannockburn Baptist Church
7100 Brodie Ln........................ Austin TX 78745 512-892-2703 48-20
Web: bbcfamily.com

Banorte Securities International Ltd
140 E 45th St 32nd Fl........................ New York NY 10017 212-484-5200 401
Web: www.banortesecurities.com

Banque, The 1849 E Little Creek Rd .... Norfolk VA 23518 757-480-3600 671
Web: thebanque.com

Bansley & Kiener LLP
8745 W Higgins Rd Ste 200 .... Chicago IL 60631 312-263-2700 2
Web: www.bk-cpa.com

Bantam Group Inc 50 Bay Colony Dr .... Westwood MA 02090 781-329-2020 449
Web: www.bantamgroup.com

Banterra Corp 1404 US Rt 45 S................ Eldorado IL 62930 618-273-9346 70
TF: 877-541-2265 ■ *Web:* www.banterrabank.com

Bantrel Inc 700 Sixth Ave SW Ste 1400............ Calgary AB T2P0T8 403-290-5000 261
Web: www.bantrel.com

Bantu Inc 8133 Lessburg Pk Ste 250.............. Vienna VA 22182 703-766-4577 828-1726* 261
**Fax Area Code:* 888 ■ *Web:* www.bantu.com

Banyan Air Service
5360 NW 20th Terr.................... Fort Lauderdale FL 33309 954-491-3170 771-0281 63
TF: 800-200-2031 ■ *Web:* www.banyanair.com

Banyan Communications Inc
3569 New Town Lake Dr.................. Saint Charles MO 63301 636-946-3456 514
Web: www.banyancom.com

Banyan International Corp
11629 49th Pl W........................ Mukilteo WA 98275 325-677-1372 475
TF: 888-782-8548 ■ *Web:* www.statkit.com

Banyan Medical Systems Inc
4106 S 87th St........................ Omaha NE 68127 402-403-4400 180
TF: 866-225-7790 ■ *Web:* www.banyanmedicalsystems.com

Banyan Resort 323 Whitehead St .... Key West FL 33040 305-296-7786 294-1107 669
TF: 866-371-9222 ■ *Web:* www.thebanyanresort.com

Banyan Water Inc 11002-B Metric Blvd........... Austin TX 78758 800-276-1507 463
TF: 800-276-1507 ■ *Web:* www.banyanwater.com

Baoding 4722 Sharon Rd Ste F................ Charlotte NC 28210 704-552-8899 552-8828 671
Web: baodingsouthpark.com

Bap Geon LLC
3310 Austin Bluffs Pkwy............. Colorado Springs CO 80918 713-227-1544 54
TF: 800-827-7455 ■ *Web:* www.bap-geon.com

Bapitst Campus Ministry Unc Charlotte
1328 John Kirk Dr .... Charlotte NC 28262 704-547-7472 48-20
Web: bcmcharlotte.org

Bapko Metal Fabricators Inc
838 N Cypress St........................ Orange CA 92867 714-639-9380 492
Web: www.bapko.com

Baptist Bible College
628 E Kearney St .... Springfield MO 65803 800-228-5754 268-6694* 161
**Fax Area Code:* 417 ■ **Fax:* Admissions ■ *TF:* 800-228-5754 ■ *Web:* gobbc.edu

Baptist Bible Fellowship International (BBFI)
720 E Kearney St .... Springfield MO 65803 417-862-5001 865-0794 48-20
Web: www.bbfi.org

Baptist College of Florida
5400 College Dr........................ Graceville FL 32440 850-263-3261 263-7506* 166
**Fax:* Admissions ■ *TF:* 800-328-2660 ■ *Web:* www.baptistcollege.edu

Baptist Easley Hospital
200 Fleetwood Dr........................ Easley SC 29640 864-442-7200 374-3
Web: www.palmettohealth.org

Baptist General Convention of Texas
7557 Rambler Rd Ste 1200.................... Dallas TX 75231 888-244-9400 48-20
TF: 888-244-9400 ■ *Web:* texasbaptists.org

				Phone	Fax	Class
Baptist Health 1 Trillium Way *TF:* 800-395-4435 ■ *Web:* www.baptisthealth.com	Corbin	KY	40701	606-528-1212	528-3223	374-3
Baptist Health Louisville 4000 Kresge Way **Fax Area Code:* 859 ■ *Web:* www.baptisthealth.com	Louisville	KY	40207	502-897-8100	276-3765*	374-3
Baptist Health Medical Ctr 3333 Spring Hill Dr *Web:* www.baptist-health.com	North Little Rock	AR	72117	501-202-3000		374-3
Baptist Health Paducah (WBH) 2501 Kentucky Ave **Fax Area Code:* 859 ■ *Web:* www.baptisthealth.com/paducah/pages/default.aspx	Paducah	KY	42003	270-575-2100	276-3765*	374-3
Baptist Health South Florida Inc 5000 University Dr *TF:* 800-622-2838 ■ *Web:* www.baptisthealth.net	Coral Gables	FL	33146	786-662-7000		353
Baptist Healthcare System 4007 Kresge Way *TF:* 800-873-4575 ■ *Web:* www.baptisthealth.com/pages/home.aspx	Louisville	KY	40207	502-897-8100		353
Baptist Hospital 1000 W Moreno St *Web:* www.ebaptisthealthcare.org	Pensacola	FL	32501	850-434-4011		374-3
Baptist Hospital of Miami 8900 N Kendall Dr SW **Fax Area Code:* 305 ■ *TF:* 800-994-6610 ■ *Web:* www.baptisthealth.net	Miami	FL	33176	786-596-1960	598-5910*	374-3
Baptist Housing 6165 Hwy 17 Ste 125 *TF:* 800-950-9675 ■ *Web:* www.baptisthousing.org	Delta	BC	V4K5B8	604-940-1960		371
Baptist Medical Ctr 1225 N State St *TF:* 800-948-6262 ■ *Web:* www.mbhs.org	Jackson	MS	39202	601-968-1000		374-3
Baptist Medical Ctr 800 Prudential Dr *TF:* 800-222-1222 ■ *Web:* www.baptistjax.com	Jacksonville	FL	32207	904-202-2000		374-3
Baptist Medical Ctr 111 Dallas St *TF:* 866-309-2873 ■ *Web:* www.baptisthealthsystem.com	San Antonio	TX	78205	210-297-7000		374-3
Baptist Medical Ctr South 2105 E S Blvd *TF:* 800-356-9596 ■ *Web:* www.baptistfirst.org	Montgomery	AL	36116	334-288-2100		374-3
Baptist Memorial Health Care Corp 350 N Humphreys Blvd *TF:* 800-422-7847 ■ *Web:* www.baptistonline.org	Memphis	TN	38120	901-227-5920		353
Baptist Memorial Hospital DeSoto 7601 Southcrest Pkwy *Web:* www.baptistonline.org	Southaven	MS	38671	662-772-4000		374-3
Baptist Memorial Hospital Golden Triangle 2520 Fifth St N *TF:* 800-422-7847 ■ *Web:* www.baptistonline.org	Columbus	MS	39705	662-244-1000	244-1651	374-3
Baptist Memorial Hospital Memphis 6019 Walnut Grove Rd *Web:* www.baptistonline.org	Memphis	TN	38120	901-226-5000	226-5618	374-3
Baptist Memorial Hospital North Mississippi 2301 S Lamar Blvd *Web:* www.baptistonline.org	Oxford	MS	38655	662-232-8100	232-8391	374-3
Baptist Memorial Hospital Union City 1201 Bishop St *TF:* 800-344-2470 ■ *Web:* www.baptistonline.org/facilities/unioncity	Union City	TN	38261	731-885-2410	884-8603	374-3
Baptist Memorial Hospital Union County 200 Hwy 30 W *Web:* www.baptistonline.org	New Albany	MS	38652	662-538-7631	538-2591	374-3
Baptist Mid-Missions 7749 Webster Rd *Web:* www.bmm.org	Cleveland	OH	44130	440-826-3930	826-4457	48-20
Baptist Missionary Assn of America (BMA) 611 Locust Ave *TF:* 800-333-1442 ■ *Web:* bmamissions.org	Conway	AR	72034	501-455-4977		48-20
Baptist Missionary Assn Theological Seminary 1530 E Pine St *TF:* 800-259-5673 ■ *Web:* www.bmats.edu	Jacksonville	TX	75766	903-586-2501	586-0378	167-3
Baptist Press 901 Commerce St *TF:* 800-222-3872 ■ *Web:* www.sbc.net	Nashville	TN	37203	615-244-2355		530
Baptist Rehabilitation Germantown 2100 Exeter Rd *Web:* www.baptistonline.org	Germantown	TN	38138	901-757-1350		374-6
Baptist Theological Seminary at Richmond 8040 Villa Park Dr Ste 250 *Web:* www.btsr.edu	Richmond	VA	23228	804-355-8135		167-3
Baptist Trinity Home Care & Hospice 6019 Walnut Grove Rd *TF:* 800-422-7847 ■ *Web:* www.baptistonline.org	Memphis	TN	38120	901-226-5000		371
Baptist University of the Americas 8019 S Pan Am Expy *TF:* 800-721-1396 ■ *Web:* www.bua.edu	San Antonio	TX	78224	210-924-4338	924-2701	161
Baptist Village of Hugo 1200 W Finley St *Web:* baptistvillage.org	Hugo	OK	74743	580-326-8383		48-20
Baptist World Alliance 405 N Washington St *Web:* www.bwanet.org	Falls Church	VA	22046	703-790-8980	893-5160	48-20
Bar Americain 152 W 52nd St *Web:* www.baramericain.com	New York	NY	10019	212-265-9700		671
Bar Engineering Company Ltd 5237 70th Ave *TF:* 800-275-4934 ■ *Web:* www.bareng.ca	Lloydminster	AB	T9V3N6	780-875-1683		261
Bar G Feed Yard 275 FM 1057 Rd *TF:* 800-569-3736 ■ *Web:* bar-g.com	Summerfield	TX	79085	806-357-2241		10-1
Bar Green Inc 619 E Westinghouse Blvd *Web:* www.bargreeninc.com	Charlotte	NC	28273	704-552-6483	552-1403	194
Bar Harbor Bankshares 82 Main St PO Box 400 *NYSE:* BHB ■ *TF:* 888-853-7100 ■ *Web:* www.bhbt.com	Bar Harbor	ME	04609	207-288-3314	288-2626	360-2
Bar Harbor Chamber of Commerce 2 Cottage St *TF:* 888-540-9990 ■ *Web:* www.barharborinfo.com	Bar Harbor	ME	04609	207-288-5103	667-9080	139
Bar Harbor Hotel-Bluenose Inn 90 Eden St *TF:* 800-445-4077 ■ *Web:* barharborhotel.com	Bar Harbor	ME	04609	207-288-3348	288-2183	379
Bar Harbor Inn Oceanfront Resort Newport Dr *TF:* 800-248-3351 ■ *Web:* www.barharborinn.com	Bar Harbor	ME	04609	207-288-3351		669
Bar Harbor Lobster Bakes 10 State Hwy 3 PO Box 152 *Web:* www.barharborlobsterbakes.com	Hulls Cove	ME	04644	207-288-4055	288-5767	671
Bar Harbor Town Hall 93 Cottage St *TF:* 800-232-4733 ■ *Web:* www.barharbormaine.gov	Bar Harbor	ME	04609	207-288-4098	288-4461	337
Bar Italian Ristorante-Caffe 13 Maryland Plaza *Web:* www.baritaliastl.com	Saint Louis	MO	63108	314-361-7010		671
Bar Lazy J Guest Ranch 447 County Rd 3 PO Box N *TF:* 800-396-6279 ■ *Web:* www.barlazyj.com	Parshall	CO	80468	970-725-3437	725-0121	239
Bar Method, The 3333 Fillmore St *Web:* barmethod.com	San Francisco	CA	94123	415-441-6333		354
Bar None Auction Inc 4751 Power Inn Rd **Fax Area Code:* 916 ■ *TF:* 866-372-1700 ■ *Web:* www.barnoneauction.com	Sacramento	CA	95826	866-372-1700	383-6865*	187
Bar Productscom Inc 1990 Lake Ave SE *TF:* 800-256-6396 ■ *Web:* www.barproducts.com	Largo	FL	33771	727-584-2093		321
Bar XH Air Inc 575 Palmer Rd NE (Esso Avitat) *Web:* www.barxh.com	Calgary	AB	T2E7G4	403-291-3227		23
Baraboo BanCorp Inc, The 101 Third Ave	Baraboo	WI	53913	608-356-7703		70
Baracci Solutions Inc 24 Boul De La Concorde E *TF:* 800-463-3339 ■ *Web:* www.baracci.com	Laval	QC	H7G4X2	450-662-8700		225
Barada Associates Inc 130 E Second St *Web:* baradainc.com	Rushville	IN	46173	765-932-5917		463
Baraga Correctional Facility 13924 Wadaga Rd *TF:* 800-326-4537 ■ *Web:* www.michigan.gov/corrections	Baraga	MI	49908	906-353-7070		213
Baraga County 16 N Third St *Web:* www.baragacounty.org/contactlocation	L'Anse	MI	49946	906-524-6183		338
Baraga State Park 1300 US Hwy 41 S *Web:* www.michigandnr.com	Baraga	MI	49908	906-353-6558		565
Baranov Museum, The 101 Marine Way *Web:* www.baranovmuseum.org	Kodiak	AK	99615	907-486-5920		520
Barantec Inc 777 Passaic Ave Fl 4 *Web:* www.barantec.com	Clifton	NJ	07012	973-779-8774		203
Baraonda 710 Peachtree St *Web:* www.baraondaatlanta.com	Atlanta	GA	30308	404-879-9962		671
Barattas 2320 S Union St *Web:* barattas.com	Des Moines	IA	50315	515-243-4516		671
Barbacoa Grill 276 W Bobwhite Ct *Web:* www.barbacoa-boise.com	Boise	ID	83706	208-338-5000		671
Barbados *Consulate General* 2121 Poncedaleon Blvd Ste 1300 *Web:* www.foreign.gov.bb	Coral Gables	FL	33134	305-442-1994	455-7975	257
Barbara Ann Karmanos Cancer Institute 4100 John R St *TF:* 800-527-6266 ■ *Web:* www.karmanos.org	Detroit	MI	48201	800-527-6266		668
Barbara B Mann Performing Arts Hall 13350 FSW Pkwy *TF:* 800-440-7469 ■ *Web:* www.bbmannpah.com	Fort Myers	FL	33919	239-489-3033	481-4620	572
Barbara Gladstone Gallery 515 W 24th St *Web:* www.gladstonegallery.com	New York	NY	10011	212-206-9300	206-9301	42
Barbara Katz Sportswear Co 2240 SW 19th St Ste 601 *Web:* barbarakatz.com	Boca Raton	FL	33431	561-391-1066	391-5284	157-6
Barbara Mathes Gallery 22 E 80th St *Web:* barbaramathesgallery.com	New York	NY	10075	212-570-4190	570-4191	42
Barbara Timken Ccna 304 Timberwood Cir	Lafayette	LA	70508	337-989-2653		297-8
Barbaricum LLC 819 Seventh St NW *Web:* barbaricum.com	Washington	DC	20001	202-393-0873		196
Barbaron Inc 107 NE Fourth St *TF:* 800-413-5500 ■ *Web:* www.barbaron.com	Crystal River	FL	34429	352-795-9010		188-3
Barbato's Restaurant 7472 New Perry Hwy *Web:* www.barbatos.com	Erie	PA	16510	814-864-9999		670
Barber & Assoc 1308 Sumac Dr *Web:* www.barberandassociates.com	Knoxville	TN	37919	865-388-5296		708
Barber Bros Contracting Company LLC 2636 Dougherty Dr *TF:* 800-624-8287 ■ *Web:* www.barber-brothers.com	Baton Rouge	LA	70805	225-355-5611	355-5615	188-4
Barber Dairies Inc 36 Barber Ct *Web:* www.barbersdairy.com	Homewood	AL	35209	205-942-2351		296-27
Barber Martin & Associates 7400 beuafont springs Dr *TF:* 800-928-7315 ■ *Web:* www.barbermartin.com	Richmond	VA	23225	804-320-3232		7
Barber Mfg 1824 Brown St *Web:* www.barbermfg.com	Anderson	IN	46016	765-643-6905		718
Barber Vintage Motorsports Museum 6030 Barber Motorsports Pkwy *Web:* www.barbermuseum.org	Leeds	AL	35094	205-699-7275		520
Barber's Poultry Inc 810 E 50th Ave *Web:* www.barberspoultry.com	Denver	CO	80216	303-466-7338	466-6960	619
Barberian's Steak House 7 Elm St *Web:* www.barberians.com	Toronto	ON	M5G1H1	416-597-0335	597-1407	671
Barber-Nichols Inc 6325 W 55th Ave *Web:* www.barber-nichols.com	Arvada	CO	80002	303-421-8111	420-4679	621
Barbers Hill ISD (BHISD) 9600 Eagle Dr PO Box 1108 *Web:* www.bhisd.net	Mont Belvieu	TX	77580	281-576-2221		685
Barbers Point Coast Guard Air Station 1 Coral Sea Rd *Web:* www.uscg.mil	Kapolei	HI	96707	808-682-2771		158
Barbershop Harmony Society 110 Seventh Ave N *TF:* 800-876-7464 ■ *Web:* www.barbershop.org	Nashville	TN	37203	615-823-3993	313-7619	48-18
Barberton South Summitt Chamber of Commerce 211 Second St NW *Web:* www.southsummitchamber.org	Barberton	OH	44203	330-745-3141		139
Barbette 1600 West Lake St *Web:* www.barbette.com	Minneapolis	MN	55408	612-827-5710		671
Barbizon International LLC 4950 W Kennedy Blvd Ste 210 *TF:* 888-999-9404 ■ *Web:* www.barbizonmodeling.com	Tampa	FL	33609	888-999-9404		507

Company	City	State	Zip	Phone	Fax	Class
Barbour County 8 N Main St	Philippi	WV	26416	304-457-3454	457-5983	338
TF: 800-433-0567 ■ *Web:* barbourcounty.wv.gov						
Barbour Publishing Inc 1810 Barbour Dr PO Box 719	Uhrichsville	OH	44683	740-922-6045		95
Web: www.barbourbooks.com						
Barbour Welting Company Div Barbour Corp 1001 N Montello St	Brockton	MA	02301	508-583-8200	583-4113	301
TF: 800-955-9649 ■ *Web:* www.barbourcorp.com						
Barboursville Veterans Home 512 Water St	Barboursville	WV	25504	304-736-1027	736-1093	793
TF: 800-669-8477 ■ *Web:* veterans.wv.gov						
Bar-B-Q Shop, The 1782 Madison Ave	Memphis	TN	38104	901-272-1277		671
TF: 877-372-8237 ■ *Web:* dancingpigs.com						
Barbuto 775 Washington St	New York	NY	10014	212-924-9700	924-9300	671
Web: www.barbutonyc.com						
BARC Electric Co-op 84 High St PO Box 264	Millboro	VA	24460	800-846-2272		245
TF: 800-846-2272 ■ *Web:* www.barcelectric.com						
Barcalounger Corp 2829 W Andrew Johnson Hwy Ste 210	Morristown	TN	37814	423-353-1288	353-1291	361
Web: www.barcalounger.com						
Barcelona 263 E Whittier St	Columbus	OH	43206	614-443-3699	444-0539	671
Web: www.barcelonacolumbus.com						
Barcelona Restaurant & Wine Bar 4180 Black Rock Tpke	Fairfield	CT	06824	203-255-0800		671
Web: www.barcelonawinebar.com						
Barchart.com Inc 330 S Wells Ste 618	Chicago	IL	60606	312-554-8122		317
TF: 800-238-5814 ■ *Web:* www.barchart.com						
Barclay College 607 N Kingman St	Haviland	KS	67059	620-862-5252	862-5403	161
TF: 800-862-0226 ■ *Web:* www.barclaycollege.edu						
Barclay Damon, LLP 200 Delaware Ave Ste 1200	Buffalo	NY	14202	716-856-5500	856-5510	445
Web: www.damonmorey.com						
Barclay Hotel 1348 Robson St	Vancouver	BC	V6E1C5	604-688-8850		379
Web: www.barclayhotel.com						
Barclay Prime 237 S 18th St	Philadelphia	PA	19103	215-732-7560	732-7560	671
Web: www.barclayprime.com						
Barclay Products Ltd 4000 Porett Dr Ste B	Gurnee	IL	60031	847-244-1234		609
TF: 800-446-9700 ■ *Web:* www.barclayproducts.com						
Barclay Water Management Inc 55 Chapel St	Newton	MA	02458	617-926-3400		145
Web: www.barclaywm.com						
Barclays 745 Seventh Ave	New York	NY	10019	212-526-7000	412-7300*	690
**Fax:* Hum Res ■ *TF:* 888-227-2275 ■ *Web:* www.investmentbank.barclays.com						
Barco Electronic Systems Pvt Ltd 11101 Trade Ctr Dr	Rancho Cordova	CA	95670	916-859-2500	859-2515	173-4
TF: 888-414-7226 ■ *Web:* barco.com						
BARCO Industries Inc 1020 MacArthur Rd	Reading	PA	19605	800-234-8665	374-6320*	758
**Fax Area Code:* 610 ■ *TF Cust Svc:* 800-234-8665 ■ *Web:* www.barcotools.com						
Barco Rent a Truck 717 South 5600 West	Salt Lake City	UT	84104	801-532-7777		770
TF: 800-453-4761 ■ *Web:* www.barcorentatruck.com						
Barco Uniforms 350 W Rosecrans Ave	Gardena	CA	90248	310-323-7315		155-19
TF: 800-262-1559 ■ *Web:* www.barcouniforms.com						
Barcoding Inc 2220 Boston St	Baltimore	MD	21231	410-385-8532		179
TF: 888-412-7226 ■ *Web:* www.barcoding.com						
Barcom Inc 400B Chickamauga Rd	Chattanooga	TN	37421	423-855-1822		180
Web: www.barcominc.com						
Barcontrol Systems & Services Inc 113 Edinburgh Ct	Greenville	SC	29607	864-421-0050		177
TF: 800-947-4362 ■ *Web:* www.barcontrol.com						
BarcoView LLC 3059 Premiere Pkwy	Duluth	GA	30097	678-475-8000		173-4
TF: 800-553-0961 ■ *Web:* www.barco.com						
Bard Access Systems Inc 605 North 5600 West	Salt Lake City	UT	84116	801-522-5000		476
TF: 800-443-5505 ■ *Web:* www.bardaccess.com						
BARD Advertising Inc 4900 Lincoln Dr	Edina	MN	55436	952-345-8000		7
Web: www.bardadvertising.com						
Bard College PO Box 5000	Annandale-on-Hudson	NY	12504	845-758-7472	758-5208	166
TF: 800-872-7423 ■ *Web:* www.bard.edu						
Bard Consulting LLC 555 Montgomery St Ste 1288	San Francisco	CA	94111	415-421-2822		196
Web: www.bardconsulting.com						
Bard Electrophysiology Inc 55 Technology Dr	Lowell	MA	01851	978-441-6202		475
Bard Inc Peripheral Vascular 1625 W Third St	Tempe	AZ	85281	480-894-9515	966-7062	476
TF: 800-321-4254 ■ *Web:* www.bardpv.com						
BARD Materials 2021 325th Ave PO Box 246	Dyersville	IA	52040	563-875-7145	875-7860	182
Web: bardmaterials.com						
Bard Mfg Co Inc 1914 Randolph Dr	Bryan	OH	43506	419-636-1194	636-2640	15
TF: 800-563-5660 ■ *Web:* www.bardhvac.com						
Bard Rao + Athanas Consulting Engineers Inc 10 Guest St 4th Fl	Boston	MA	02135	617-254-0016	924-9339	261
Web: www.brplusa.com						
Bardane Manufacturing Co 317 Delaware St PO Box 70	Jermyn	PA	18433	570-876-4844	876-1938	308
Web: www.bardane.com						
Bardel Entertainment Inc 548 Beatty St	Vancouver	BC	V6B2L3	604-669-5589		514
Web: bardel.ca						
Barden & Robeson Corp 103 Kelly Ave	Middleport	NY	14105	716-735-3732	735-3752	106
TF: 800-724-0141 ■ *Web:* www.bardenhomes.com						
Barden Corp 200 Pk Ave	Danbury	CT	06810	203-744-2211	744-3756	620
TF: 800-243-1060 ■ *Web:* www.bardenbearings.com						
Bardes Plastics Inc 5225 W Clinton Ave	Milwaukee	WI	53223	800-558-5161	354-6331*	602
**Fax Area Code:* 414 ■ *TF Cust Svc:* 800-558-5161 ■ *Web:* www.bardesplastics.com						
Bardex Corp 6338 Lindmar Dr	Goleta	CA	93117	805-964-7747		537
Web: www.bardex.com						
Bardon Supplies Ltd 405 College St E PO Box 1023	Belleville	ON	K8N4Z6	613-966-5643		612
TF: 800-750-2723 ■ *Web:* www.bardonsupplies.com						
Bardons & Oliver Inc 5800 Harper Rd	Solon	OH	44139	440-498-5800	498-2001	455
Web: www.bardonsoliver.com						
Bardwil Home 1071 Sixth Ave 4th Fl	New York	NY	10018	212-944-1870	869-3599	746
Web: bardwilhome.com						
Bare Bones Software Inc 73 Princeton St Ste 206	North Chelmsford	MA	01863	978-251-0500		177
Web: www.barebones.com						
Bare Hill Correctional Facility 181 Brand Rd	Malone	NY	12953	518-483-8411		213
Barefoot Landing 4898 Hwy 17 S	North Myrtle Beach	SC	29582	843-272-8349	272-1052	50-6
Web: www.bflanding.com						
Barefoot Resort & Golf 4980 Barefoot Resort Bridge Rd	North Myrtle Beach	SC	29582	843-390-3200	390-3213	669
TF: 866-638-4818 ■ *Web:* www.barefootgolf.com						
Barenbrug USA Inc 33477 Hwy 99 E PO Box 239	Tangent	OR	97389	541-926-5801	926-9435*	694
**Fax:* Sales ■ *Web:* www.barenbrug.com						
Barfield Inc 4101 NW 29th St	Miami	FL	33142	305-894-5300	894-5301	24
TF: 800-321-1039 ■ *Web:* www.barfieldinc.com						
Barfield Murphy Shank & Smith PC 1121 Riverchase Office Rd	Birmingham	AL	35244	205-982-5500		2
Web: bmss.com						
Barg Coffin Lewis & Trapp LLP 350 California St 22nd Fl	San Francisco	CA	94104	415-228-5400		428
Web: www.bargcoffin.com						
Bargain Supply Co 844 E Jefferson St	Louisville	KY	40206	502-562-5000	562-5051	351
TF: 800-322-5226 ■ *Web:* www.bargainsupply.com						
Barge Cauthen & Assoc Inc 6606 Charlotte Pk Ste 210	Nashville	TN	37209	615-356-9911		256
Web: bargecauthen.com						
Barge Waggoner Sumner & Cannon 211 Commerce St Ste 600	Nashville	TN	37201	615-254-1500	255-6572	261
Web: www.bargewaggoner.com						
Barger Packaging Inc 2901 Oakland Ave	Elkhart	IN	46517	888-525-2845		601
TF: 888-525-2845 ■ *Web:* www.bargerpackaging.com						
Bargreen Coffee Co 2821 Rucker Ave	Everett	WA	98201	425-252-3161		296-7
TF: 800-884-3161 ■ *Web:* bargreenscoffee.com						
Bargreen Ellingson Inc 2925 70th Ave E	Fife	WA	98424	253-722-2600	896-3620	300
TF: 866-722-2665 ■ *Web:* www.bargreen.com						
Bariatrix Nutrition Corp 40 Allen Rd	South Burlington	VT	05403	802-862-9242		123
Web: www.bariatrix.com						
Bari-Jay Fashions Inc 1277 Bridge St Unit 1B	New Dundee	ON	N0B2E0	800-735-5808	467-9970*	155-21
**Fax Area Code:* 888 ■ *TF:* 800-735-5808 ■ *Web:* www.barijay.com						
Baring Asset Management Co Inc 470 Atlantic Ave Independence Wharf	Boston	MA	02210	617-946-5200		401
Web: www.barings.com						
Baritz & Colman LLP 1075 Broken Sound Pkwy NW Ste 102	Boca Raton	FL	33487	561-864-5100		428
TF: 800-962-2873 ■ *Web:* www.baritzcolman.com						
Barix Clinics 135 S Prospect St	Ypsilanti	MI	48198	734-547-4700		810
TF: 800-282-0066 ■ *Web:* www.barixclinics.com						
Barkan & Barkan Company LPA 81 S Fourth St Ste 300	Columbus	OH	43215	614-441-8565		428
Web: www.barkanlaw.net						
Barkcamp State Park 65330 Barkcamp Rd	Belmont	OH	43718	740-404-4064		565
Web: www.ohiodnr.com						
Barker & Williamson 603 Cidco Rd	Cocoa	FL	32926	321-639-1510	445-6031	647
Web: www.bwantennas.com						
Barker Air & Hydraulics Inc 1308 Miller Rd	Greenville	SC	29607	864-288-3537		641
TF: 800-922-3324 ■ *Web:* www.barkerair.com						
Barker Blue Digital Imaging Inc 363 N Amphlett Blvd	San Mateo	CA	94401	650-696-2100		627
Web: www.barkerblue.com						
Barker Brothers Inc 1666 Summerfield St	Ridgewood	NY	11385	718-456-6400		1
Web: www.barkerbuff.com						
Barker Business Systems Inc 650 S Rock Blvd Ste 17	Reno	NV	89502	775-856-1771		535
Web: www.e-totalprint.com						
Barker Contracting 3619 E Speedway Blvd Ste 101	Tucson	AZ	85719	520-323-3831	323-3834	186
Web: www.barkermorrissey.com						
Barker Martin PS 719 Second Ave Ste 1200	Seattle	WA	98104	360-756-9806		428
TF: 888-381-9806 ■ *Web:* www.barkermartin.com						
Barker Specialty Products LLC 27 Realty Dr	Cheshire	CT	06410	203-272-2222		296-5
Web: www.barkerspecialty.com						
BarkerGilmore LLC 1387 Fairport Rd Ste 845	Fairport	NY	14450	585-598-6555		721
TF: 800-713-7278 ■ *Web:* www.barkergilmore.com						
Barkley 1740 Main St	Kansas City	MO	64108	816-842-1500		4
TF: 800-444-8768 ■ *Web:* barkleyus.com						
Barkley Co PO Box 5540	Yuma	AZ	85365	928-782-2571	782-4656	10-11
Web: www.barkleycompany.com						
Barkman Honey 120 Santa Fe St	Hillsboro	KS	67063	800-364-6623		296-24
TF: 800-364-6623 ■ *Web:* barkmanhoney.com						
Barksdale Air Force Base 555 Davis Ave W	Barksdale	LA	71110	318-456-1015		497-1
Web: www.barksdale.af.mil						
Barksdale Inc 3211 Fruitland Ave	Los Angeles	CA	90058	323-589-6181	589-3463	201
TF: 800-835-1060 ■ *Web:* www.barksdale.com						
Barletta & Assoc Inc 1313 Campbell Rd Ste F	Houston	TX	77055	713-464-7700	464-3696	652
Web: www.barlettainc.com						
Barletta Lou (Rep R - PA) 2049 Rayburn HOB	Washington	DC	20515	202-225-6511	226-6250	342-2
Web: barletta.house.gov						
Barley House 132 N Main St	Concord	NH	03301	603-228-6363		671
Web: thebarleyhouse.com						
Barley's Smokehouse & Brewpub 1130 Dublin Rd	Columbus	OH	43215	614-485-0227		671
Web: www.smokehousebrewing.com						
Barley, Snyder, Senft & Cohen LLC 126 E King St	Lancaster	PA	17602	717-299-5201		428
Web: www.barley.com						

Company / Address	City	State	Zip	Phone	Fax	Class
Barlovento LLC 431 Technology Dr *Web:* barloventollc.com	Dothan	AL	36303	334-983-9979	983-9983	186
Barlow 1305 Grand Dd SE *TF:* 800-688-1202 ■ *Web:* www.barlowtruckline.com	Faucett	MO	64448	816-238-3373		780
Barlow Garsek & Simon LLP 920 Foch St *Web:* www.bgsfirm.com	Fort Worth	TX	76107	817-731-4500		428
Barlow, Josephs & Holmes Ltd 101 Dyer St Fl 5 *Web:* barjos.com	Providence	RI	02903	401-273-4446		428
Barmon Door & Plywood Inc 2508 Hartford Dr	Lake Stevens	WA	98258	425-334-1222		613
Barn Furniture Mart Inc 6206 N Sepulveda Blvd *TF:* 888-302-2276 ■ *Web:* www.barnfurnituremart.com	Van Nuys	CA	91411	818-780-4070		321
Barna Log Homes LLC 22459 Alberta St *Web:* www.barnahomes.com	Oneida	TN	37841	423-215-1390		106
Barna, Guzy & Steffen Ltd 400 Northtown Financial Plaza 200 Coon Rapids Blvd *TF:* 800-678-4574 ■ *Web:* www.bgs.com	Coon Rapids	MN	55433	763-780-8500		428
Barnacle Bill's 14 Castillo Dr *Web:* www.barnaclebillsonline.com	Saint Augustine	FL	32084	904-824-3663		671
Barnacle Historic State Park, The 3485 Main Hwy *Web:* www.floridastateparks.org	Coconut Grove	FL	33133	305-442-6866	442-6872	565
Barnard & Sons Construction LLC 3054 Simpson Hwy 13 PO Box 517 *Web:* www.barnardandsons.com	Mendenhall	MS	39114	601-847-2420	847-0110	685
Barnard College Columbia University 3009 Broadway **Fax:* Admissions ■ *Web:* www.barnard.edu	New York	NY	10027	212-854-2014	854-6220*	166
Barnard Construction Company Inc PO Box 99 *TF:* 800-992-5030 ■ *Web:* www.barnard-inc.com	Bozeman	MT	59771	406-586-1995	586-3530	188-10
Barnegat Lighthouse State Park PO Box 167 *Web:* www.njparksandforests.org	Barnegat Light	NJ	08006	609-494-2016		565
Barnes & Conti Assoc Inc 940 Dwight Way Ste 15 *Web:* www.barnesconti.com	Berkeley	CA	94710	510-644-0911		194
Barnes & Jones Corp 91 Pacella Pk Dr *Web:* www.barnesandjones.com	Randolph	MA	02368	781-963-8000	963-3322	357
Barnes & Noble College Bookstores Inc 120 Mtn View Blvd *TF:* 800-478-9515 ■ *Web:* www.bncollege.com	Basking Ridge	NJ	07920	908-991-2665		95
Barnes & Noble Inc 122 Fifth Ave *NYSE:* BKS ■ *Web:* www.barnesandnoble.com	New York	NY	10011	212-633-3300		95
Barnes & Thornburg 11 S Meridian St *TF:* 800-236-1352 ■ *Web:* www.btlaw.com	Indianapolis	IN	46204	317-236-1313	231-7433	428
Barnes Advertising Corp 1580 Fairview Rd *TF:* 800-458-1410 ■ *Web:* barnesadvertisingcorp.com	Zanesville	OH	43701	740-453-6836		7
Barnes Aerospace 169 Kennedy Rd *Web:* www.barnesaerospace.com	Windsor	CT	06095	860-298-7740	298-7738	21
Barnes Alarm Systems Inc 3201 Flagler Ave Ste 503 *Web:* www.barnesalarmsystems.net	Key West	FL	33040	305-294-6753		693
Barnes Bullets Inc 38 N Frontage Rd *Web:* www.barnesbullets.com	Mona	UT	84645	435-856-1000		711
Barnes Communications Inc 1 Yonge St Ste 1504 *Web:* www.barnesir.com	Toronto	ON	M5E1E5	416-367-5000	367-5390	194
Barnes County 230 Fourth St NW Rm 202 *TF:* 800-352-0867 ■ *Web:* www.co.barnes.nd.us	Valley City	ND	58072	701-845-8500		338
Barnes Distribution 1301 E Ninth St Ste 700 *TF:* 800-726-9626 ■ *Web:* classc.mscdirect.com	Cleveland	OH	44114	216-416-7200		385
Barnes Farming Corp 7840 Old Bailey Hwy **Fax Area Code:* 252 ■ *TF:* 800-367-2799 ■ *Web:* www.farmpak.com	Spring Hope	NC	27882	800-367-2799	459-9020*	10-11
Barnes Foundation 300 N Latch's Ln *Web:* www.barnesfoundation.org	Merion	PA	19066	610-667-0290	664-4026	520
Barnes Group Inc 123 Main St *NYSE:* B ■ *TF:* 800-480-9198 ■ *Web:* barnesgroupinc.com	Bristol	CT	06011	860-583-7070		718
Barnes International Inc 814 Chestnut St PO Box 1203 *TF:* 800-435-4877 ■ *Web:* www.barnesintl.com	Rockford	IL	61105	815-964-8661	964-5074	455
Barnes Investment Advisory Inc 7250 N 16th St Ste 412 *Web:* www.barnesinvest.com	Phoenix	AZ	85020	602-248-9099		528
Barnes Lodge 4520 Clayton Ave *TF:* 800-551-3492 ■ *Web:* www.barnesjewish.org	Saint Louis	MO	63110	314-652-4319		372
Barnes Transportation Services Inc 2309 Whitley Rd **Fax Area Code:* 252 ■ *TF:* 800-898-5897 ■ *Web:* www.barnestransport.com	Wilson	NC	27895	800-898-5897	291-2787*	360-2
barnesandnoble.com Inc 122 Fifth Ave *TF:* 800-843-2665 ■ *Web:* www.barnesandnoble.com	New York	NY	10011	212-414-6000		95
Barnes-Jewish Hospital 1 Barnes-Jewish Hospital Plaza *Web:* www.barnesjewish.org	Saint Louis	MO	63110	314-362-5000		374-3
Barnes-Jewish Saint Peters Hospital 4901 Forest Park Ave *TF:* 800-536-2653 ■ *Web:* www.bjc.org	St. Louis	MI	63108	314-747-9322		374-3
Barnet Associates LLC 2 Round Lake Rd *TF:* 888-827-7070 ■ *Web:* www.barnetassociates.com	Ridgefield	CT	06877	888-827-7070		317
Barnet-Dulaney Eye Ctr 4800 N 22nd St *TF:* 866-742-6581 ■ *Web:* www.goodeyes.com	Phoenix	AZ	85016	602-955-1000		798
Barnett & Murphy Inc 1323 Brookhaven Dr *Web:* www.bmdm.com	Orlando	FL	32803	407-650-0264		7
Barnett & Ramel Optical Co 7154 N 16th St *TF:* 800-228-9732 ■ *Web:* www.broptical.com	Omaha	NE	68112	800-228-9732		543
Barnett Contracting Inc 7703 Bagby Ave *Web:* www.barnettcontracting.com	Waco	TX	76712	254-666-7117	666-7119	256
Barnett Cox & Assoc 711 Tank Farm Rd Ste 210 *Web:* www.barnettcox.com	San Luis Obispo	CA	93401	805-545-8887		7
Barnett Engineering Ltd 7710 5 St SE Ste 215 *TF:* 800-268-2646 ■ *Web:* barnett-engg.com	Calgary	AB	T2H2L9	403-255-9544		261
Barnett Inc 801 W Bay St *TF:* 888-803-4467 ■ *Web:* www.ebarnett.com	Jacksonville	FL	32204	904-899-0156		612
Barnett Millworks Inc 4915 Hamilton Blvd *Web:* www.barnettmillworks.com	Theodore	AL	36582	251-443-7710		499
Barnett Tool & Engineering 2238 Palma Dr *Web:* www.barnettclutches.com	Ventura	CA	93003	805-642-9435		256
Barney J Belleci 26555 Carmel Rancho Blvd	Carmel	CA	93923	831-624-6466		390
Barney Trucking Inc 235 State Rt 24 *TF:* 800-524-7930 ■ *Web:* www.barneytrucking.com	Salina	UT	84654	800-524-7930		685
Barney's Pumps Inc 2965 Barney's Pumps Pl *TF:* 800-273-1182 ■ *Web:* www.barneyspumps.com	Lakeland	FL	33812	863-665-8500	666-3858	641
Barneys New York Inc 575 Fifth Ave *Web:* www.barneys.com	New York	NY	10017	212-450-8700		157-4
Barnhardt Mfg Co 1100 Hawthorne Ln **Fax Area Code:* 704 ■ *TF:* 800-277-0377 ■ *Web:* www.barnhardt.net	Charlotte	NC	28205	800-277-0377	342-1892*	228
Barnhart 1641 California St *Web:* www.barnhartusa.com	Denver	CO	80202	303-626-7200		4
Barnhart Crane & Rigging Co 1701 Dunn Ave *TF:* 800-727-0149 ■ *Web:* www.barnhartcrane.com	Memphis	TN	38106	901-775-3000		190
Barnhart Display Inc 1170 Charming St *Web:* www.barnhartdisplay.com	Maitland	FL	32751	407-637-2060	637-2053	464
Barnhill Bolt Company Inc 2500 Princeton Dr NE *TF:* 800-472-3900 ■ *Web:* www.barnhillbolt.com	Albuquerque	NM	87107	505-884-1808		350
Barnhill Contracting Co 4325 Pleasant Valley Rd *Web:* www.barnhillcontracting.com	Raleigh	NC	27612	252-823-1021		188-4
Barnsco Inc 2609 Willowbrook *Web:* www.barnsco.com	Dallas	TX	75220	214-352-9091		480
Barnsider 5202 N Main St *Web:* barnsider-restaurant.com	Dayton	OH	45415	937-277-1332		671
Barnsider Management Corp 15 A Newbury St Rte 1 *Web:* www.barnsiderrestaurants.com	Danvers	MA	01923	978-777-3885		463
Barnsley Gardens 597 Barnsley Gardens Rd *TF:* 877-773-2447 ■ *Web:* www.barnsleyresort.com	Adairsville	GA	30103	770-773-7480	773-1779	669
Barnstable County PO Box 427 *TF:* 800-642-2423 ■ *Web:* www.barnstablecounty.org	Barnstable	MA	02630	508-362-2511		338
Barnstead Inn 349 Bonnet St *TF:* 800-331-1619 ■ *Web:* www.barnsteadinn.com	Manchester Center	VT	05255	802-362-1619		379
Barnum Financial Group 6 Corporate Dr *Web:* www.barnumfinancialgroup.com	Shelton	CT	06484	203-513-6000		401
Barnum Museum 820 Main St *Web:* www.barnum-museum.org	Bridgeport	CT	06604	203-331-1104	331-0079	520
Barnum Sales and Marketing 2720 Beechwood Dr SE *Web:* barnumsales.com	Grand Rapids	MI	49506	616-949-9408		636
Barnwell County 57 Wall St *Web:* www.barnwellcountysc.us	Barnwell	SC	29812	803-541-1020		338
Barnwell Garden & Art Ctr 601 Clyde Fant Pkwy	Shreveport	LA	71101	318-673-7703		50-2
Barnwell Industries Inc 1100 Alakea St Ste 2900 *NYSE:* BRN ■ *Web:* www.brninc.com	Honolulu	HI	96813	808-531-8400	531-7181	536
Barnwell State Park 223 State Pk Rd *Web:* www.southcarolinaparks.com	Blackville	SC	29817	803-284-2212		565
Barnwell Whaley Patterson & Helms LLC 288 Meeting St *TF:* 800-237-2000 ■ *Web:* www.barnwell-whaley.com	Charleston	SC	29401	843-577-7700		428
Baroan Technologies 385 Falmouth Ave *Web:* www.baroan.com	Elmwood Park	NJ	07407	201-796-0404		180
Barokas Public Relations 71 Columbia St Ste 325 *TF:* 800-719-8080 ■ *Web:* www.barokas.com	Seattle	WA	98104	206-264-8220		636
Barolo Grill 3030 E Sixth Ave *Web:* www.barologrilldenver.com	Denver	CO	80206	303-393-1040		671
Barometer Capital Management Inc 1 University Ave Ste 1910 Ste 1800 PO Box 25 *Web:* www.barometercapital.ca	Toronto	ON	M5J2P1	416-601-6888		401
Baron Brothers Nursery Inc 7568 Santa Rosa Rd *TF:* 800-561-3357 ■ *Web:* www.baronbrothers.com	Camarillo	CA	93012	805-484-0085		323
Baron Funds 767 Fifth Ave 49th Fl *TF:* 800-992-2766 ■ *Web:* www.baronfunds.com	New York	NY	10153	212-583-2000	583-2150	528
Baron Metal Industries Inc 101 Ashbridge Cir *TF:* 800-263-7515 ■ *Web:* www.baronmetal.com	Woodbridge	ON	L4L3R5	416-749-2111		480
Baron Mfg Company LLC 1200 Capitol Dr *TF:* 800-368-8585 ■ *Web:* www.baronsnaps.com	Addison	IL	60101	630-628-9110		350
Baron Oilfield Supply Ltd 9515-108 St *TF:* 888-532-5661 ■ *Web:* www.baronoilfield.ca	Grande Prairie	AB	T8V5R7	780-532-5661		358
Baron Services Inc 4930 Research Dr *Web:* www.baronweather.com	Huntsville	AL	35805	256-881-8811		529
Baron Sign Manufacturing 900 W 13th St *Web:* www.baronsign.com	Riviera Beach	FL	33404	561-863-7446		186
Baron Spices Inc 1440 Kentucky Ave *Web:* www.baronspices.com	Saint Louis	MO	63110	314-535-9020		297-8

Name / Address	City	State	ZIP	Phone	Fax	Class
Barona Resort & Casino						
1932 Wildcat Canyon Rd	Lakeside	CA	92040	619-443-2300		133
TF: 888-722-7662 ■ *Web:* www.barona.com						
Barone Galasso & Assoc Inc						
710 W Ivy	San Diego	CA	92101	619-232-2100		653
Baronne Plaza Hotel						
201 Baronne St	New Orleans	LA	70112	504-522-0083		379
Web: www.baronneplaza.com						
Barr & Barr Inc 460 W 34th St	New York	NY	10001	212-563-2330	967-2297	186
Web: www.barrandbarr.com						
Barr Andy (Rep R - KY)						
1427 Longworth HOB	Washington	DC	20515	202-225-4706		342-2
Web: barr.house.gov						
Barr Engineering Co						
4700 W 77th St	Minneapolis	MN	55435	952-832-2600	832-2601	261
TF: 800-632-2277 ■ *Web:* www.barr.com						
Barr Lake State Park						
13401 Picadilly Rd	Brighton	CO	80603	303-659-6005		565
Web: cpw.state.co.us						
Barr Systems LLC 4500 NW 27th Ave	Gainesville	FL	32606	352-491-3100		174
Web: www.barrsystems.com						
Barracks, The 43 Pinkney St	Annapolis	MD	21401	410-267-7619		50-3
Web: www.annapolis.org						
Barragan Nanette (Rep D-CA)						
1320 Longworth HOB	Washington	DC	20515	202-225-8220		342-2
Web: barragan.house.gov						
Barragan's 814 S Central Ave	Glendale	CA	91204	818-243-1103		671
Web: barragansrestaurants.com						
Barran Liebman LLP						
601 SW Second Ave Ste 2300	Portland	OR	97204	503-228-0500		428
Web: www.barran.com						
Barrancas National Cemetery						
Naval Air Stn 1 Cemetery Rd	Pensacola	FL	32508	850-453-4108	453-4635	136
Web: www.cem.va.gov						
Barrantagh Investment Management Inc						
100 Yonge St Ste 1700	Toronto	ON	M5C2W1	416-868-6295		528
Web: www.barrantagh.com						
Barrasso John (Sen R - WY)						
307 Dirksen Bldg	Washington	DC	20510	202-224-6441	224-1724	342-2
Web: www.barrasso.senate.gov						
Barratt's Chapel & Museum						
6362 Bay Rd	Frederica	DE	19946	302-335-5544		520
Web: www.barrattschapel.org						
Barre Opera House 6 N Main St PO Box 583	Barre	VT	05641	802-476-8188	476-5648	572
Web: www.barreoperahouse.org						
Barre y Lane LLC						
9318 Drawbridge Rd	Mechanicsville	VA	23116	804-723-4035		116
Web: www.barreylane.com						
Barren County 117 N Public Sq Ste 1A	Glasgow	KY	42141	270-651-3783	651-1083	338
Web: www.barrencounty.ky.gov						
Barrent Group, The 3056 104th Sreet	Urbandale	IA	50322	515-276-2527		317
TF: 800-734-4667 ■ *Web:* www.barrentgroup.com						
Barresi's 4111 Webster Ave	Cincinnati	OH	45236	513-793-2540		671
Web: www.barresis.com						
Barrett & Co 42 Weybosset St Ste 2	Providence	RI	02903	401-351-1000		401
TF: 800-556-7078 ■ *Web:* www.barrett.net						
Barrett & Company Pllc						
4910 NW Camas Meadows Dr	Camas	WA	98607	360-210-5100		2
Barrett & McNagny LLP						
215 E Berry St	Fort Wayne	IN	46802	260-423-9551		428
Web: www.barrettlaw.com						
Barrett Business Services Inc						
8100 NE Pkwy Dr Ste 200	Vancouver	WA	98662	360-828-0700	828-0701	631
NASDAQ: BBSI ■ *TF:* 800-494-5669 ■ *Web:* www.barrettbusiness.com						
Barrett Carpet Mills Inc						
2216 Abutment Rd	Dalton	GA	30721	800-241-4064		131
TF: 800-241-4064 ■ *Web:* kraustlooring.com/barrett						
Barrett Distribution Centers Inc						
15 Freedom Way	Franklin	MA	02038	508-553-8800		803-1
Web: www.barrettdistribution.com						
Barrett Engineered Pumps Inc						
1695 National Ave	San Diego	CA	92113	619-232-7867		641
TF: 800-603-0399 ■ *Web:* www.barrettpump.com						
Barrett Group LLC, The						
100 Jefferson Blvd Ste 310	Warwick	RI	02888	401-921-5443		260
Web: www.careerchange.com						
Barrett Industries Corp						
3 Becker Farm Rd Ste 307	Roseland	NJ	07068	973-533-1001	533-1020	188-4
Web: www.barrettpaving.com						
Barrett Oil Inc 2126 W Bay St	Savannah	GA	31415	912-234-7231		316
Web: www.barrettoilsavannah.com						
Barrett Outdoor Communications Inc						
381 Highland St	West Haven	CT	06516	203-932-4601		8
Web: www.barrettoc.com						
Barrett Trailers Inc						
1831 Hardcastle Blvd	Purcell	OK	73080	405-527-5050	527-3206	779
Web: www.barrett-trailers.com						
Barrette Outdoor Living Inc						
740 N Main St	Bulls Gap	TN	37711	440-891-0790		596
Web: www.barretteoutdoorliving.com						
Barrette-Chapais Ltee						
CP 248 Km 346 Rt 113	Chapais	QC	G0W1H0	418-745-2545		683
Web: www.barrette-chapais.qc.ca						
Barrick Gold Corp						
TD Canada Trust Tower 161 Bay St PO Box 212	Toronto	ON	M5J2S1	416-861-9911	861-2492	502
NYSE: ABX ■ *TF:* 800-720-7415 ■ *Web:* www.barrick.com						
Barrick Goldstrike Mines Inc PO Box 29	Elko	NV	89803	416-861-9911		502
Web: www.barrick.com						
Barrie House Coffee Company Inc						
4 Warehouse ln	Elmsford	NY	10523	800-876-2233		297-2
TF: 800-876-2233 ■ *Web:* www.barriehouse.com						
Barrie Public Library 60 Worsley St	Barrie	ON	L4M1L6	705-728-1010		435
TF: 800-222-8477 ■ *Web:* library.barrie.ca						
Barriere Construction Co LLC						
1 Galleria Blvd Ste 1650	Metairie	LA	70001	504-581-7283	581-2270	188-4
TF: 866-645-3060 ■ *Web:* www.barriere.com						
Barrington Area Chamber of Commerce						
325 N Hough St	Barrington	IL	60010	847-381-2525	381-2540	139
Web: www.barringtonchamber.com						

Name / Address	City	State	ZIP	Phone	Fax	Class
Barrington Bank & Trust Company Na						
201 S Hough St	Barrington	IL	60010	847-842-4500	304-6697	70
Web: www.barringtonbank.com						
Barrington Hotel & Suites						
263 Shepherd of the Hills Expy	Branson	MO	65616	417-334-8866		379
TF: 800-760-8866 ■ *Web:* www.barringtonhotel.com						
Barrington Management Company Inc						
10401 N Meridian St Ste 210	Indianapolis	IN	46290	317-581-0300		652
Web: www.barringtonmanagement.com						
Barrington Research Associates Inc						
161 N Clark St Ste 2950	Chicago	IL	60601	312-634-6000		401
Web: brai.com						
Barrington's 7822 Fairview Rd	Charlotte	NC	28226	704-364-5755		671
Web: www.barringtonsrestaurant.com						
Barrio Cafe 2814 N 16th St	Phoenix	AZ	85006	602-636-0240		671
Web: www.barriocafe.com						
Barrio Logan College Institute						
1625 Newton Ave Ste 200	San Diego	CA	92113	619-232-4686		196
TF: 800-774-7744 ■ *Web:* blci.org						
Barrios Technology Inc						
16441 Space Ctr Blvd Ste B-100	Houston	TX	77058	281-280-1900	280-1901	668
Web: www.barrios.com						
Barris, Sott, Denn & Driker PLLC						
333 W Fort St Ste 1200	Detroit	MI	48226	313-965-9725		428
TF: 877-529-8750 ■ *Web:* www.bsdd.com						
Barrister Digital Solutions LLC						
1700 K St NW Ste B100	Washington	DC	20006	202-289-7279		113
BarristerBooks Inc 615 Florida St	Lawrence	KS	66044	866-808-5635		95
TF: 866-808-5635 ■ *Web:* www.barristerbooks.com						
Barron & Newburger PC						
1212 Guadalupe St Ste 104	Austin	TX	78701	512-476-9103		428
Web: www.bnpclaw.com						
Barron County 330 E LaSalle Ave	Barron	WI	54812	715-537-6210	537-6817	338
Barron Electric Co-op						
1434 State Hwy 25 N	Barron	WI	54812	715-537-3171		245
TF: 800-322-1008 ■ *Web:* www.barronelectric.com						
Barron Motor Inc						
1850 McCloud Pl NE	Cedar Rapids	IA	52402	319-393-6220		61
Barron's Educational Series Inc						
250 Wireless Blvd	Hauppauge	NY	11788	631-434-3311	434-3723	637-2
TF: 800-645-3476 ■ *Web:* www.barronseduc.com						
Barron's Wholesale Tire Inc						
1302 Eastport Rd	Jacksonville	FL	32218	904-696-1200		755
Web: www.barrontire.com						
Barrow County 233 E Broad St	Winder	GA	30680	770-307-3005	307-3141	338
TF: 800-436-7442 ■ *Web:* www.barrowga.org						
Barrow County Chamber of Commerce						
PO Box 456	Winder	GA	30680	770-867-9444	867-6366	139
Web: www.barrowchamber.com						
Barrow County News						
189 W Athens St Ste 22	Winder	GA	30680	770-867-7557		532-4
Web: www.barrowcountynews.com						
Barrow Hanley Mewhinney & Strauss LLC						
2200 Ross Ave 31st Fl	Dallas	TX	75201	214-665-1900		401
TF: 800-543-0407 ■ *Web:* www.barrowhanley.com						
Barrow Utilities & Electric Co-op Inc (BUECI)						
1295 Agvik St PO Box 449	Barrow	AK	99723	907-852-6166		245
Web: www.bueci.org						
Barry Assoc Inc 17 Halls Mill Rd	Preston	CT	06365	860-889-8943		189-10
Barry Better Menswear						
125 John W Morrow Pkwy Ste 242B	Gainesville	GA	30501	770-534-7685		155-12
Web: barrysmenswear.com						
Barry Bunker Chevrolet Inc						
1307 N Wabash Ave	Marion	IN	46952	866-726-5519		57
TF Sales: 866-603-8625 ■ *Web:* barrybunker.com						
Barry Callebaut USA LLC						
400 Industrial Pk Rd	Saint Albans	VT	05478	802-524-9711	524-5148	296-8
TF: 866 443 0460 ■ *Web:* www.barry-callebaut.com						
Barry County 220 W State St	Hastings	MI	49058	269-945-1290	945-0209	338
TF: 800-662-9278 ■ *Web:* barrycounty.org						
Barry County Clerk 700 Main St Ste 2	Cassville	MO	65625	417-847-2561		338
TF: 800-726-7390 ■ *Web:* barrycountycollector.com						
Barry Electric Co-op						
4015 Main St PO Box 307	Cassville	MO	65625	866-847-2333		245
TF: 866-847-2333 ■ *Web:* barryelectric.com						
Barry Financial Group Inc						
40 SE Fifth St Ste 600	Boca Raton	FL	33432	561-368-9120		401
Web: www.talkmoney.com						
barry r. epstein associates Inc						
11922 Waterwood Dr	Boca Raton	FL	33428	561-852-0000	451-0000	636
Web: www.publicrelations.nu						
Barry S. Nussbaum Company Inc						
13151 Emily Rd	Dallas	TX	75240	972-437-9900		405
Barry Strock Consulting Associates Inc						
154 Rosemont St	Albany	NY	12206	518-459-4252		180
Barry University						
11300 NE Second Ave	Miami Shores	FL	33161	305-899-3000	899-2971*	166
**Fax:* Admissions ■ *TF:* 800-756-6000 ■ *Web:* www.barry.edu						
Barry Memorial Library						
11300 NE Second Ave	Miami Shores	FL	33161	305-899-3000		434-6
TF: 800-756-6000 ■ *Web:* www.barry.edu/libraryservices						
Orlando 1650 Sandlake Rd Ste 390	Orlando	FL	32809	407-438-4150	438-9774*	166
**Fax:* Admissions ■ *TF:* 800-756-6000 ■ *Web:* barry.edu						
Tallahassee						
325 John Knox Rd Bldg A	Tallahassee	FL	32303	850-385-2279	385-7576*	166
**Fax:* Admissions ■ *TF:* 800-756-6000 ■ *Web:* barry.edu						
Barry University Dwayne O Andreas School of Law						
6441 E Colonial Dr	Orlando	FL	32807	321-206-5600		167-1
TF: 800-756-6000 ■ *Web:* www.barry.edu						
Barry W James & Associates LLP						
721 E Texas Ave	Baytown	TX	77520	281-420-1040		734
Web: www.bwjames.com						
Barry's Bootcamp						
1106 N La Cienega Blvd	West Hollywood	CA	90069	310-360-6262		354
Web: www.barrysbootcamp.com						
Barrymore Theatre 2090 Atwood Ave	Madison	WI	53704	608-241-8633		572
TF: 800-745-3000 ■ *Web:* www.barrymorelive.com						

Name / Address	City	State	Zip	Phone	Fax	Class
Barry-owen Co Inc 5625 Smithway St.	Los Angeles	CA	90040	323-724-4800	724-4996	292
TF: 800-682-6682 ■ *Web:* www.barryowen.com						
Barry-Wehmiller Cos Inc 8020 Forsyth Blvd	Saint Louis	MO	63105	314-862-8000	862-2744*	547
**Fax:* Sales ■ *TF:* 800-781-7820 ■ *Web:* www.barrywehmiller.com						
Barry-Wehmiller Cos Inc Accraply Div 3580 Holly Ln N	Plymouth	MN	55447	763-557-1313	519-9656	547
TF: 800-328-3997 ■ *Web:* www.accraply.com						
Bar-S Foods Co PO Box 29049	Phoenix	AZ	85038	800-699-4115		296-26
TF: 800-699-4115 ■ *Web:* www.bar-s.com						
Barse & Company Inc 7800 John Carpenter Fwy	Dallas	TX	75247	214-631-0925		411
Web: barse.com						
Barshop & Oles Company Inc 801 Congress Ave Ste 300	Austin	TX	78701	512-477-1212		652
Web: www.barshopoles.com						
BARSKA Optics 1721 Wright Ave.	La Verne	CA	91750	909-445-8168		543
TF: 800-894-9703 ■ *Web:* www.barska.com/index.html						
Barson Group Pa 60 E Main St PO Box 8018	Somerville	NJ	08876	908-203-9800		2
Web: barsongroup.com						
Barstow College 2700 Barstow Rd	Barstow	CA	92311	760-252-2411	252-1875	162
TF: 877-823-2378 ■ *Web:* barstow.edu						
Barstow School, The 11511 State Line Rd	Kansas City	MO	64114	816-942-3255		685
Web: www.barstowschool.org						
Bart Morrill CPA PC 24 S 200 E PO Box 355	Roosevelt	UT	84066	435-725-1900		2
Web: morrillcpa.com						
Bar-T-5 Covered Wagon Cook Out & Wild West Show 812 Cache Creek Dr	Jackson	WY	83001	307-733-5386	739-9183	671
TF: 800-772-5386 ■ *Web:* www.bart5.com						
Barta - Schoenewald Inc 3805 Calle Tecate	Camarillo	CA	93012	805-389-1935	389-1165	518
Web: www.a-m-c.com						
Bartech Group 17199 N Laurel Park Dr Ste 224	Livonia	MI	48152	734-953-5050		721
TF: 800-828-4410 ■ *Web:* www.bartechgroup.com						
Bartell & Bartell Ltd 432 Rolling Rdg Dr	State College	PA	16801	814-861-6606		463
TF: 800-472-3272 ■ *Web:* bartellbartell.com						
Bartell Hotels 4875 N Harbor Dr	San Diego	CA	92106	619-224-1556		707
TF: 800-345-9995 ■ *Web:* www.bartellhotels.com						
Bartell Machinery Systems LLC 6321 Elmer Hill Rd	Rome	NY	13440	315-336-7600	336-0947	494
TF: 800-537-8473 ■ *Web:* www.bartellmachinery.com						
Bartender Magazine PO Box 158	Liberty Corner	NJ	07938	908-766-6006	766-6607*	457-21
**Fax:* Edit ■ *Web:* www.bartender.com						
Barter Depot 1107 W Veterans Hwy	Jackson	NJ	08527	732-833-2273		750
Web: barterdepot.com						
Barter Theatre 127 W Main St	Abingdon	VA	24210	276-628-3991	619-3335	749
Web: www.bartertheatre.com						
Barth Electric Company Inc 1934 N Illinois St	Indianapolis	IN	46202	317-924-6226	923-6938	189-4
TF: 800-666-6226 ■ *Web:* www.barthelectric.com						
Barth Industries Company LP 12650 Brookpark Rd	Cleveland	OH	44130	216-267-1950		454
Web: barthindustries.com						
Bartha Visual 600 N Cassady Ave	Columbus	OH	43219	614-252-7455		23
TF: 800-513-1209 ■ *Web:* bartha.com						
Bartholomew County 234 Washington St PO Box 924	Columbus	IN	47201	812-379-1600	379-1675	338
Web: www.bartholomewco.com						
Bartholomew County Public Library 536 Fifth St.	Columbus	IN	47201	812-379-1255		434-3
TF: 800-685-0524 ■ *Web:* mybcpl.org						
Bartholomew County Rural Electric Membership Corp 1697 W Deaver Rd	Columbus	IN	47201	812-372-2546		245
TF: 800-927-5672 ■ *Web:* www.bcremc.com						
Bartizan Corp 217 Riverdale Ave	Yonkers	NY	10705	914-965-7977	965-7746	534
TF: 800-899-2278 ■ *Web:* www.bartizan.com						
Bartko Zankel Tarrant & Miller 1 Embarcadero Ctr Ste 800	San Francisco	CA	94111	415-956-1900	956-1152	445
Web: www.bzbm.com						
Bartle & Gibson Company Ltd 13475 Ft Rd NW	Edmonton	AB	T5A1C6	780-472-2850		612
TF: 800-661-5615 ■ *Web:* www.bartlegibson.com						
Bartlesville Area Chamber of Commerce 201 S Keeler Ave.	Bartlesville	OK	74003	918-336-8708	337-0216	139
TF: 800-593-5573 ■ *Web:* www.bartlesville.com						
Bartlesville Public Library 600 S Johnstone Ave	Bartlesville	OK	74003	918-338-4161		434-3
Web: www.bartlesville.lib.ok.us						
Bartlett & Co 600 Vine St Ste 2100	Cincinnati	OH	45202	513-621-4612	621-6462	401
TF: 800-800-4612 ■ *Web:* www.bartlett1898.com						
Bartlett & Co 4900 Main St Ste 12	Kansas City	MO	64112	816-753-6300		296-23
TF: 800-888-6300 ■ *Web:* www.bartlettandco.com						
Bartlett & West Engineers Inc 1200 SW Executive Dr	Topeka	KS	66615	785-272-2252		261
TF: 888-200-6464 ■ *Web:* www.bartwest.com						
Bartlett Arboretum & Gardens 151 Brookdale Rd	Stamford	CT	06903	203-322-6971	595-9168	97
Web: www.bartlettarboretum.org						
Bartlett Area Chamber of Commerce 2969 Elmore Pk Rd	Bartlett	TN	38134	901-372-9457	372-9488	139
Web: www.bartlettchamber.org						
Bartlett Chamber of Commerce 138 S Oak Ave	Bartlett	IL	60103	630-830-0324	830-9724	139
Web: www.bartlettchamber.com						
Bartlett Dairy Inc 105-03 150th St.	Jamaica	NY	11435	718-658-2299	725-2527	296-27
Web: www.bartlettny.com						
Bartlett Electric Co-op Inc 27492 Texas 95	Bartlett	TX	76511	254-527-3551	527-3221	245
Web: www.bartlettec.coop						
Bartlett High School 701 W Schick Rd	Bartlett	IL	60103	630-372-4700		685
Web: www.u-46.org						
Bartlett Holdings Inc 60 Industrial Park Rd	Plymouth	MA	02360	508-746-6464		256
Web: www.excelscaffold.com						
Bartlett State Jail 1018 Arnold Dr	Bartlett	TX	76511	254-527-3300		213
Bartolotta Ristorante diMare 3131 Las Vegas Blvd S	Las Vegas	NV	89109	702-770-9966		671
Web: www.wynnlasvegas.com						
Barton & Loguidice PC 290 Elwood Davis Rd	Liverpool	NY	13088	315-457-5200		261
Web: bartonandloguidice.com						
Barton Air Fabrications Inc 394 Sherman Ave N	Hamilton	ON	L8L6N7	905-524-2234	526-6580	454
Web: www.bartonairfab.com						
Barton Assoc Inc 701 Richmond Ave	Houston	TX	77006	713-961-9111		266
Web: www.bartona.com						
Barton Brescome Inc 69 Defco Park Rd	North Haven	CT	06473	203-239-4901		80-3
TF: 800-922-4840 ■ *Web:* www.brescomebarton.com						
Barton College PO Box 5000	Wilson	NC	27893	252-399-6300	399-6572	166
TF: 800-345-4973 ■ *Web:* www.barton.edu						
Barton Cotton Inc 3030 Waterview Ave	Baltimore	MD	21230	800-348-1102	536-0491*	317
**Fax Area Code:* 410 ■ *TF:* 800-638-4652 ■ *Web:* www.bartoncotton.com						
Barton County 1400 Main St Ste 202	Great Bend	KS	67530	620-793-1835	793-1990	338
Web: www.bartoncounty.org						
Barton County 1004 Gulf St.	Lamar	MO	64759	417-682-3529	682-4100	338
Web: www.bartoncounty.com						
Barton County Community College 245 NE 30th Rd	Great Bend	KS	67530	620-792-2701	786-1160*	162
**Fax:* Admissions ■ *TF:* 800-722-6842 ■ *Web:* www.bartonccc.edu						
Barton County Electric Co-op 91 US-160	Lamar	MO	64759	417-682-5636		245
TF: 800-286-5636 ■ *Web:* www.bartonelectric.com						
Barton County Feeders Inc 1164 SE 40th Rd.	Ellinwood	KS	67526	620-564-2200		10-1
Web: bartoncountyfeeders.com						
Barton Creek Square Mall 2901 S Capital of Texas Hwy.	Austin	TX	78746	512-327-7040	328-0923	460
TF: 800-408-8424 ■ *Web:* www.simon.com						
Barton Heights Veterinary Hospital 117 Terrace Dr	Stroudsburg	PA	18360	570-424-6773		794
Web: www.bartonheights.com						
Barton Joe (Rep R - TX) 2107 Rayburn HOB	Washington	DC	20515	202-225-2002	225-3052	342-2
Web: joebarton.house.gov						
Barton Library 200 E Fifth St	El Dorado	AR	71730	870-863-5447		434-3
Barton Malow Enterprises Inc 26500 American Dr.	Southfield	MI	48034	248-436-5000	436-5001	186
TF: 800-261-6270 ■ *Web:* www.bartonmalow.com						
Barton Solvents Inc 1920 NE Broadway Ave.	Des Moines	IA	50313	515-265-7998	265-0259	146
TF: 800-728-6488 ■ *Web:* www.barsol.com						
Barton Staffing Solutions Inc 723 Aurora Ave.	Aurora	IL	60505	630-897-3591		260
TF: 800-264-1170 ■ *Web:* bartonstaffing.com						
Barton Supply Inc 1260 Marlkress Rd PO Box 2240	Cherry Hill	NJ	08034	856-429-6500		612
TF: 800-328-5519 ■ *Web:* bartonsupply.com						
Barton W Stone Christian Home 873 Grove St.	Jacksonville	IL	62650	217-479-3400	243-8553	450
TF: 800-397-1313 ■ *Web:* heritageofcare.com						
Barton Warnock Visitor Ctr PO Box 375 HC 70	Terlingua	TX	79852	432-424-3327		565
Web: tpwd.texas.gov						
Barton, Klugman & Oetting LLP 350 S Grand Ave Ste 2200	Los Angeles	CA	90071	213-621-4000		428
Web: bkolaw.com						
Bartons Club 93 93 Jackpot	Jackpot	NV	89825	775-755-2341		452
TF: 800-258-2937 ■ *Web:* www.bartonsclub93.com						
Bartow County 135 W Cherokee Ave Ste 251	Cartersville	GA	30120	770-387-5030	387-5023	338
TF: 800-436-7442 ■ *Web:* www.bartowga.org						
Bartow County Public Library 429 W Main St	Cartersville	GA	30120	770-382-4203		434-3
TF: 800-729-5700 ■ *Web:* www.bartowlibraryonline.org						
Bartow Ford Co 2800 US Hwy 98 N	Bartow	FL	33830	863-533-0425		57
Web: bartowford.com						
Bartow-Pell Mansion Museum 895 Shore Rd Pelham Bay Pk	Bronx	NY	10464	718-885-1461	885-9164	520
Web: www.bartowpellmansionmuseum.org						
Bartram's Garden 54th St & Lindbergh Blvd	Philadelphia	PA	19143	215-729-5281	729-1047	97
Web: www.bartramsgarden.org						
Barts Water Sports 7581 E 800 N	North Webster	IN	46555	574-834-7666		711
TF: 800-348-5016 ■ *Web:* www.bartswatersports.com						
Bartush-Schnitzius Foods Co 1137 N Kealy St	Lewisville	TX	75057	972-219-1270		297-8
Web: www.bartushfoods.com						
Baruch College 55 Lexington Ave at 24th St	New York	NY	10010	646-312-1000	312-1362	166
TF: 800-273-8255 ■ *Web:* www.baruch.cuny.edu						
Baruch College The William & Anita Newman Library 151 E 25th St	New York	NY	10010	646-312-1600		434-6
Web: www.baruch.cuny.edu						
Basalite Concrete Products LLC 605 Industrial Way	Dixon	CA	95620	707-678-1901	678-6268	183
TF: 800-776-6690 ■ *Web:* www.basalite.com						
Basalt Regional Library 14 Midland Ave.	Basalt	CO	81621	970-927-4311		434-3
Web: basaltrld.org						
Basch Subscriptions Inc 10 Ferry St Ste 429	Concord	NH	03301	603-229-0662		366
Web: www.basch.com						
Basco Shower Enclosures 7201 Snider Rd.	Mason	OH	45040	513-573-1900		329
TF: 800-543-1938 ■ *Web:* www.bascoshowerdoor.com						
Bascom Palmer Eye Institute 900 NW 17th St	Miami	FL	33136	305-326-6000		374-7
TF: 800-329-7000 ■ *Web:* www.bascompalmer.org/site						
Bascom-Turner Instrument 111 Downey St	Norwood	MA	02062	781-769-9660		612
TF: 800-225-3298 ■ *Web:* www.bascomturner.com						

Phone | Fax | Class

BASD (Boyertown Area School District)
911 Montgomery Ave ..... Boyertown PA 19512 610-367-6031 369-7620 186
Web: www.boyertownasd.org

Base Camp Franchising
170 S 1000 E ..... Salt Lake City UT 84102 801-359-0071 157-1
Web: basecampfranchising.com

Base One International Corp
44 E 12th St Apt 3B ..... New York NY 10003 212-673-2511 809
Web: www.boic.com

Base One Technologies Inc
30 Church St Ste 28 ..... New Rochelle NY 10801 914-633-0200 180
Web: www.base-one.com

Baseball America Magazine
4319 S Alston Ave Ste 103 ..... Durham NC 27713 919-682-9635 457-20
Web: baseballamerica.com

Baseball Express Inc
5750 NW Pkwy Ste 100 ..... San Antonio TX 78249 210-348-7000 525-9339 711
TF: 800-937-4824 ■ *Web:* www.baseballexpress.com

Baseball Hall of Fame
910 S Third St ..... Minneapolis MN 55415 612-375-9707 522
TF: 888-375-9707 ■ *Web:* www.domeplus.com

Baseball Reliquary PO Box 1850 ..... Monrovia CA 91017 626-791-7647 522
Web: www.baseballreliquary.org

BASF 100 Milverton Dr 5th Fl ..... Mississauga ON L5R4H1 289-360-1300 360-6000 143
TF Cust Svc: 866-485-2273 ■ *Web:* www2.basf.us/basf-canada

BASF Corp 100 Campus Dr ..... Florham Park NJ 07932 973-245-6000 895-8002 143
TF: 800-526-1072 ■ *Web:* www.basf.com

BASF Corp/Bldg Systems
889 Valley Pk Dr ..... Shakopee MN 55379 952-496-6000 3
TF Cust Svc: 800-433-9517 ■ *Web:* www.master-builders-solutions.basf.us/en-us

Basham Industries 10325 SR 56 ..... Coalmont TN 37313 931-692-3218 155-21
Web: www.bashamindustries.com/contact.htm

Bashas Inc 22402 S Bashas Rd ..... Chandler AZ 85248 480-895-9350 345
TF: 800-755-7292 ■ *Web:* www.bashas.com

Bashlin Industries Inc PO Box 867 ..... Grove City PA 16127 724-458-8340 458-8342 351
Web: www.bashlin.com

Basi Italia 811 Highland St ..... Columbus OH 43215 614-294-7383 671
Web: basi-italia.com

Basic Adhesives Inc 60 Webro Rd ..... Clifton NJ 07012 973-614-9000 3
Web: www.elektromek.com

Basic Aluminum Castings Co
1325 E 168th St ..... Cleveland OH 44110 216-481-5606 481-7031 308
TF: 800-888-2044 ■ *Web:* www.basicaluminum.com

Basic American Foods
2185 N California Blvd Ste 215 ..... Walnut Creek CA 94596 925-472-4000 296-18
Web: www.baf.com

Basic Carbide Corp 900 Main St ..... Lowber PA 15660 724-446-1630 446-1656 1
TF: 800-426-4291 ■ *Web:* www.basiccarbide.com

Basic Commerce & Industries
304 Harper Dr Ste 203 ..... Moorestown NJ 08057 856-778-1660 261
TF: 800-828-1120 ■ *Web:* www.bcisse.com

Basic Commodities Inc
863 S Orlando Ave ..... Winter Park FL 32789 407-629-2000 169
TF: 800-338-7006 ■ *Web:* basiccommodities.com

Basic Components Inc
1201 S Second Ave ..... Mansfield TX 76063 817-473-7224 473-3388 191-2
TF: 800-452-1780 ■ *Web:* www.basiccomp.com

Basic Energy Services Inc
500 W Illinois Ste 800 Ste 800 ..... Midland TX 79701 432-620-5500 539
NYSE: BAS ■ *Web:* www.basicenergyservices.com

Basic Food Flavors Inc
3950 E Craig Rd ..... North Las Vegas NV 89030 702-643-0043 275
Web: www.basicfoodflavors.com

Basic Metals Inc
W180 N11819 River Ln ..... Germantown WI 53022 262-255-0034 492
TF: 800-989-1996 ■ *Web:* www.basicmetals.com

Basic Pay LLC 231 W 29th St Ste 503 ..... New York NY 10001 212-684-8827 684-6036 570
Web: www.basicpayllc.com

Basic Plumbing Inc
1409 Mechanical Blvd ..... Garner NC 27529 919-662-1082 610
Web: www.basicplumbinginc.com

Basic Resources Inc
928 12th St Ste 700 ..... Modesto CA 95354 209-521-9771 188-4

Basic Rubber & Plastics Co
8700 Boulder Ct ..... Walled Lake MI 48390 248-360-7400 360-7101 326
Web: www.basicrubber.com

Basic Software Systems
905 N Kings Hwy ..... Texarkana TX 75501 903-792-4421 179
TF: 800-252-4476 ■ *Web:* www.basic-software.com

Basic Systems Inc 9255 Cadiz Rd ..... Cambridge OH 43725 740-432-3001 192
TF: 800-307-8422 ■ *Web:* www.basic-systems.com

Basicgrey LLC 377 Marshall Way ..... Layton UT 84041 801-544-1116 344
Web: www.basicgrey.com

Basil
Basil Thai Restaurant 460 King St ..... Charleston SC 29403 843-724-3490 671
Web: www.eatatbasil.com

Basil's 2324 Grand Canal Blvd ..... Stockton CA 95207 209-478-6290 671

Basil's Restaurant & Tapas Bar
2985 Grandview Ave NE ..... Atlanta GA 30305 404-233-9755 671
Web: www.basils.net

Basilica of Saint Mary of the Immaculate Conception, The
232 Chapel St ..... Norfolk VA 23504 757-622-4487 50-1
Web: www.basilicaofsaintmary.org

Basilica of the Assumption
409 Cathedral St ..... Baltimore MD 21201 410-727-3565 50-1
Web: americasfirstcathedral.org

Basilius Inc 4338 S Ave ..... Toledo OH 43615 419-536-5810 711
Web: www.basilius.com

Basin Disposal Inc
2021 N Commercial Ave ..... Pasco WA 99301 509-547-2476 547-8617 804
TF: 800-642-6447 ■ *Web:* www.basindisposal.com

Basin Electric Power Co-op
1717 E IH- Ave ..... Bismarck ND 58501 701-223-0441 224-5336 245
Web: www.basinelectric.com

Basin Harbor Club
4800 Basin Harbor Rd ..... Vergennes VT 05491 802-475-2311 475-6545 669
TF: 800-622-4000 ■ *Web:* www.basinharbor.com

Basin Holdings US LLC
The Chrysler Bldg 405 Lexington Ave 71st Fl ..... New York NY 10174 212-695-7376 256
Web: www.basinholdings.com

Basin Printing 1437 E Second Ave ..... Durango CO 81301 970-247-5212 627
Web: www.basinprinting.com

Basin Tire & Auto Inc
2700 E Main St ..... Farmington NM 87402 505-326-2231 385-2460* 62-5
**Fax Area Code:* 970 ■ *TF:* 800-832-9832 ■ *Web:* directoryplus.com

Basis International Ltd
5901 Jefferson St NE ..... Albuquerque NM 87109 505-345-5232 345-5082 178-12
TF Orders: 800-423-1394 ■ *Web:* www.basis.com

Basis Technology Corp 1 Alewife Ctr ..... Cambridge MA 02140 617-386-2000 177
TF: 800-697-2062 ■ *Web:* www.basistech.com

Baskerville-Donovan Inc
449 W Main St ..... Pensacola FL 32502 850-438-9661 261
Web: www.baskervilledonovan.com

Baskin Auto Truck & Tractor Inc
1844 Hwy 51 S ..... Covington TN 38019 901-476-2626 476-2658 57
TF: 877-476-2626 ■ *Web:* www.baskintrandtr.com

Baskin-Robbins Inc 130 Royall St ..... Canton MA 02021 781-737-3000 381
TF: 800-859-5339 ■ *Web:* www.baskinrobbins.com

Baskow & Assoc 2948 E Russell Rd ..... Las Vegas NV 89120 702-733-7818 772
Web: www.baskow.com

Basler Electric Co 12570 Rt 143 ..... Highland IL 62249 618-654-2341 654-2351 203
Web: www.basler.com

Basler Flight Service
Wittman Regional Airport PO Box 2464 ..... Oshkosh WI 54903 920-236-7827 236-7833 63
TF: 800-564-6322 ■ *Web:* www.baslerflightservice.com

Basler Turbo Conversions LLC
255 W 35th St ..... Oshkosh WI 54902 920-236-7820 235-0381 24
Web: www.baslerturbo.com

Basmat Inc 1531 240th St ..... Harbor City CA 90710 310-325-2063 325-9682 697
Web: www.mcstarlite.com

Basque Museum & Cultural Ctr
611 W Grove St ..... Boise ID 83702 208-343-2671 520
Web: www.basquemuseum.com

Bass & Associates PC
3936 E Ft Lowell Rd Ste 200 ..... Tucson AZ 85712 520-577-1544 41
Web: www.bass-associates.com

Bass Doherty & Finks PC
40 Soldiers Field Pl ..... Boston MA 02135 617-787-5551 41
Web: www.bassdoherty.com

Bass Karen (Rep D - CA)
2241 Rayburn HOB ..... Washington DC 20515 202-225-7084 225-2422 342-2
Web: bass.house.gov

Bass Performance Hall
4th & Calhoun Sts ..... Fort Worth TX 76102 817-212-4300 810-9294 572
TF: 877-212-4280 ■ *Web:* www.basshall.com

Bass Player Magazine
28 E 28th St 12th Fl ..... New York NY 10016 212-378-0400 378-0470 457-9
TF Cust Svc: 866-246-3595 ■ *Web:* www.bassplayer.com

Bass Pro Shops Outdoor World
1935 S Campbell Ave ..... Springfield MO 65807 417-887-7334 885-0072 711
Web: www.basspro.com

Bass River State Forest
762 Stage Rd ..... Tuckerton NJ 08087 609-296-1114 565
Web: www.njparksandforests.org

Bass, Nixon & Kennedy Inc
6310 Chapel Hill Rd 250 ..... Raleigh NC 27607 919-851-4422 261
TF: 800-524-5905 ■ *Web:* www.bnkinc.com

Bassett Furniture Industries Inc
3525 Fairystone Pk Hwy PO Box 626 ..... Bassett VA 24055 877-525-7070 319-2
NASDAQ: BSET ■ *TF:* 877-525-7070 ■ *Web:* www.bassettfurniture.com

Bassett Healthcare Network
1 Atwell Rd ..... Cooperstown NY 13326 607-547-3456 547-3921 374-3
TF: 800-227-7388 ■ *Web:* www.bassett.org

Bassett Mirror Company Inc PO Box 627 ..... Bassett VA 24055 276-629-3341 332
Web: www.bassettmirror.com

Bassett Printing Corp
3321 Fairystone Park Hwy ..... Bassett VA 24055 800-336-5102 627
TF: 800-336-5102

Bassham Wholesale Egg Company Inc
5409 Hemphill St ..... Fort Worth TX 76115 817-921-1600 297-8
Web: www.basshamfoods.com

Bassler Energy Services Inc
8050 Hwy 21 W ..... Caldwell TX 77836 979-535-4593 311
Web: www.basslerenergyservices.com

Bassmaster
3500 Blue Lake Dr Ste 330 ..... Birmingham FL 35243 877-227-7872 457-20
TF: 877-227-7872 ■
Web: www.bassmaster.com/topics/bassmaster%20magazine

Basta 2195 Broad St ..... Cranston RI 02905 401-461-2300 671
Web: bastaonbroad.com

Basta's Trattoria 410 NW 21st Ave ..... Portland OR 97209 503-274-1572 671
Web: www.bastastrattoria.com

Bastian Co 15 Eagle St ..... Phelps NY 14532 315-548-2300 9
TF: 800-463-4255 ■ *Web:* www.bastiancompany.com

Bastian Solutions (BMH)
10585 N Meridian St 3rd Fl ..... Indianapolis IN 46290 317-575-9992 575-8596 55
TF: 800-772-0464 ■ *Web:* www.bastiansolutions.com

Bastian Trucking Inc 440 S Main ..... Aurora UT 84620 435-529-7453 780
TF: 800-452-5126 ■ *Web:* www.bastiantrucking.com

Bastion Capital Corp
1901 Ave of the Stars ..... Los Angeles CA 90067 310-788-5700 403

Bastion Infrastructure Group
801 - 1 Richmond St W ..... Toronto ON M5H3W4 416-583-2600 528
Web: www.bastionfunds.com

Bastion Technologies Inc
17625 El Camino Real Ste 330 ..... Houston TX 77058 281-283-9330 283-9333 256
Web: www.bastiontechnologies.com

Bastrop Chamber of Commerce
927 Main St ..... Bastrop TX 78602 512-303-0558 303-0305 139
Web: www.bastropchamber.com

Bastrop County 804 Pecan St ..... Bastrop TX 78602 512-581-4000 338
Web: www.co.bastrop.tx.us

Bastrop Isd 906 Farm St ..... Bastrop TX 78602 512-772-7100 685
Web: www.bisdtx.org

Bastrop State Park 3005 Hwy 21 E ..... Bastrop TX 78602 512-321-2101 565
Web: tpwd.texas.gov

	Phone	Fax	Class
Bastrop-Morehouse Parish Chamber of Commerce 110 N Franklin St .... Bastrop LA 71220 *TF:* 800-228-5150 ■ *Web:* bastroplacoc.org	318-281-3794		139
BasWare Inc 60 Long Ridge Rd .... Stamford CT 06902 *Web:* www.basware.com	203-487-7900		177
Bat Assoc Inc 5151 Brook Hollow Pkwy Ste 250 .... Norcross GA 30071 *Web:* www.batassociates.com	770-242-3908		256
Bat Conservation International (BCI) 500 N Capital of Texas Hwy .... Austin TX 78746 *TF:* 800-538-2287 ■ *Web:* batcon.org	512-327-9721	327-9724	48-3
Bataan Memorial Museum 1050 Old Pecos Trl .... Santa Fe NM 87505 *TF:* 800-396-4104 ■ *Web:* bataanmuseum.com	505-474-1670	474-1670	520
Batavia Container Inc 1400 Paramount Pkwy .... Batavia IL 60510 *Web:* www.bataviacontainer.com	630-879-2100		100
Batavia Downs 8315 Pk Rd .... Batavia NY 14020 *Web:* www.westernotb.com	585-343-3750		642
Batavia Public Library District 10 S Batavia Ave .... Batavia IL 60510 *Web:* www.batavia.lib.il.us	630-879-1393		434-3
Batavia VA Medical Ctr 222 Richmond Ave .... Batavia NY 14020 *TF:* 800-273-8255 ■ *Web:* www.buffalo.va.gov	585-297-1000	297-1069	374-8
Batching Systems Inc 50 Jibsail Dr .... Prince Frederick MD 20678 *Web:* www.batchingsystems.com	410-414-8111		547
BatchMaster Software Inc 24461 Ridge Rt Dr Ste 210 .... Laguna Hills CA 92653 *Web:* www.batchmaster.com	949-583-1646	271-4620	178-10
Bateman Gordon & Sands Inc 3050 N Federal Hwy .... Lighthouse Point FL 33064	954-941-0900		390
Bates College 2 Andrews Rd .... Lewiston ME 04240 **Fax:* Admissions ■ *TF:* 888-522-8371 ■ *Web:* www.bates.edu	207-786-6255	786-6025*	166
Bates College Ladd Library 48 Campus Ave .... Lewiston ME 04240 *Web:* www.bates.edu	207-786-6226	786-6055	434-6
Bates Communications Inc 40 Grove St Ste 310 .... Wellesley MA 02482 *Web:* www.bates-communications.com	781-235-8239		195
Bates Coughtry Reiss LLP 2601 Saturn St Ste 210 .... Brea CA 92821 *Web:* bcrcpas.com	714-871-2422		2
Bates County 1 N Delaware St .... Butler MO 64730 *TF:* 800-726-7390 ■ *Web:* www.batescounty.net	660-679-3371	679-9922	338
Bates Creative Group Llc 1119 E W Hwy .... Silver Spring MD 20910 *Web:* www.batescreativegroup.com	301-495-8844		463
Bates Ford 1673 W Main St .... Lebanon TN 37087 *TF:* 888-834-4671 ■ *Web:* tonybatesfordsales.com	888-834-4671		57
Bates Technical College 1101 S Yakima Ave .... Tacoma WA 98405 *Web:* www.bates.ctc.edu	253-680-7000		162
Bates Technologies Inc 9059 Technology Ln .... Fishers IN 46038 *Web:* www.batestech.com	317-841-2400		246
Bates Troy Health Care Linen Supply 151 Laurel Ave .... Binghamton NY 13905 *TF:* 800-473-5340 ■ *Web:* www.batestroy.com	607-723-5333		442
Bates White LLC 1300 Eye St N W Ste 600 .... Washington DC 20005 *Web:* www.bateswhite.com	202-408-6110		463
Bates-Scofield Homestead 45 Old King's Hwy N .... Darien CT 06820 *Web:* darienhistorical.org	203-655-9233		50-3
Batesville Casket Co 1 Batesville Blvd .... Batesville IN 47006 *TF Cust Svc:* 800-622-8373 ■ *Web:* www.batesville.com	812-934-7500		134
Batesville Memorial Public Library (BMPL) 131 N Walnut St .... Batesville IN 47006 *Web:* www.ebatesville.com/library	812-934-4706	934-6288	434-3
Batesville Tool & Die Inc 177 Six Pine Ranch Rd .... Batesville IN 47006 *Web:* btdinc.com	812-934-5616		483
Bath & Beyond, The 77 Connecticut St .... San Francisco CA 94107 *TF:* 800-696-6662 ■ *Web:* www.bathandbeyond.com	415-552-5001		362
Bath & Body Works 7 Limited Pkwy E .... Reynoldsburg OH 43068 *TF:* 800-395-1001 ■ *Web:* www.bathandbodyworks.com	800-395-1001		214
Bath County PO Box 39 .... Owingsville KY 40360 *Web:* bathcounty.ky.gov/pages/default.aspx	606-674-2613	674-9526	338
Bath County PO Box 309 .... Warm Springs VA 24484 *TF:* 888-823-1710 ■ *Web:* www.bathcountyva.org	540-839-7221	839-7222	338
Bath House Cultural Ctr (BHCC) 521 E Lawther Dr .... Dallas TX 75218 *Web:* www.dallasculture.org/bathhouseculturecenter	214-670-8749	670-8751	50-2
Bath Iron Works Corp 700 Washington St .... Bath ME 04530 *Web:* gdbiw.com	207-443-3311		698
Bath National Cemetery VA Medical Ctr .... Bath NY 14810 *Web:* www.cem.va.gov	607-664-4853	664-4761	136
Bath Veterans Affairs Medical Ctr 76 Veterans Ave .... Bath NY 14810 *TF:* 877-845-3247 ■ *Web:* www.bath.va.gov	607-664-4000		374-8
Bath-and-Body.com 1073 Exchange St .... Boise ID 83716	208-345-5136		214
Bathcraft Inc 1610 James P Rodgers Dr .... Valdosta GA 31601 *Web:* www.bathcraft.com	229-333-0805		609
Bathcrest Inc 265E 3900 S .... Salt Lake City UT 84107 *TF:* 855-662-7220 ■ *Web:* www.bathcrest.com	855-662-7220		189-11
Bath-Tec Inc PO Box 1118 .... Ennis TX 75120 *TF:* 800-526-3301 ■ *Web:* www.bathtec.com	972-646-5279		375
Bathtub Billy's 630 Ridge Rd W .... Rochester NY 14615 *Web:* www.bathtubbillys.com	585-865-6510		671
Baton Rouge Ballet Theatre 10745 Linkwood Ct PO Box 82288 .... Baton Rouge LA 70884 *Web:* www.batonrougeballet.org	225-766-8379		573-1

	Phone	Fax	Class
Baton Rouge Business Report 9029 Jefferson Hwy .... Baton Rouge LA 70809 *Web:* www.businessreport.com	225-928-1700	926-1329	457-5
Baton Rouge City Hall 222 St Louis St Ste 301 .... Baton Rouge LA 70802 *TF:* 800-368-3749 ■ *Web:* www.brgov.com	225-389-3100	389-5203	337
Baton Rouge Community College (BRCC) 201 Community College Dr .... Baton Rouge LA 70806 *TF:* 866-217-9823 ■ *Web:* www.mybrcc.edu	225-216-8000	216-8010	162
Baton Rouge Convention & Visitors Bureau 359 Third St .... Baton Rouge LA 70801 *TF:* 800-527-6843 ■ *Web:* www.visitbatonrouge.com	225-383-1825		206
Baton Rouge General Medical Ctr (BRGMC) 3600 Florida Blvd .... Baton Rouge LA 70806 *Web:* www.brgeneral.org	225-387-7000		374-3
Baton Rouge Little Theater 7155 Florida Blvd .... Baton Rouge LA 70806 *Web:* theatrebr.org	225-924-6496		573-4
Baton Rouge Machine Works 12612 Ronaldson Rd .... Baton Rouge LA 70807 *Web:* www.brmw.net	225-775-2542		567
Baton Rouge Metropolitan Airport 9430 Jackie Cochran Dr Ste 300 .... Baton Rouge LA 70807 *Web:* www.flybtr.com	225-355-0333	355-2334	27
Baton Rouge Regional Eye Bank 7777 Hennessy Blvd Ste 1005 .... Baton Rouge LA 70808 *Web:* www.eyebankbr.org	225-766-8996	765-4366	269
Baton Rouge Rehab Hospital 8595 United Plaza Blvd .... Baton Rouge LA 70809	225-927-0567		374-6
BATS 8050 Marshall Dr Ste 120 .... Lenexa KS 66214 *Web:* www.batstrading.com	913-815-7000		691
Batson Acctg & Tax pa 20 Washington Pk .... Greenville SC 29601 *Web:* www.batsontax.net	864-235-6824		2
Batson-Cook Co 817 Fourth Ave PO Box 151 .... West Point GA 31833 *Web:* www.batson-cook.com	706-643-2500	643-2199	186
Batsto Historic Village 31 Batsto Rd .... Hammonton NJ 08037 *TF:* 800-852-7899 ■ *Web:* www.batstovillage.org	609-561-0024	567-8116	50-3
Batta Environmental Associates Inc Delaware Industrial Park 6 Garfield Way .... Newark DE 19713 *TF:* 800-494-2273 ■ *Web:* www.battaenv.com	302-737-3376		261
Battalia Winston International 555 Madison Ave 19th Fl .... New York NY 10022 *TF:* 800-570-3118 ■ *Web:* www.battaliawinston.com	212-308-8080	308-1309	266
Battambang 850 Broadway .... Oakland CA 94607 *Web:* themenupage.com	510-839-8815		671
Battelle Memorial Institute Inc 505 King Ave .... Columbus OH 43201 *TF:* 800-201-2011 ■ *Web:* www.battelle.org	614-424-6424		668
Battelle Rippe Kingston LLP 2000 W Dorothy Ln .... Cincinnati OH 45202 *Web:* rsmus.com	937-298-0201		2
Battelle Ventures 100 Princeton S Corp Ctr Ste 150 .... Ewing NJ 08628	609-921-1456	921-8703	792
Battenfeld Grease & Oil Corp of New York 1174 Erie Ave PO Box 728 .... North Tonawanda NY 14120 *TF:* 800-652-0550 ■ *Web:* www.battenfeld-grease.com	716-695-2100	695-0367	541
Battenfeld-American Inc 1575 Clinton St .... Buffalo NY 14206	716-822-8410		541
Battered Women's Justice Project 1801 Nicollet Ave S Ste 102 .... Minneapolis MN 55403 *TF:* 800-903-0111 ■ *Web:* www.bwjp.org	612-824-8768	824-8965	49-10
Battery Handling Systems Inc 1488 Page Industrial Ct .... Saint Louis MO 63132 *Web:* www.bhs1.com	314-423-7091		74
Battery Systems Inc 12322 Monarch St .... Garden Grove CA 92841 *Web:* www.batterysystems.net	310-667-9320		61
Battery Ventures 1 Marina Pk Dr Ste 1100 .... Boston MA 02210 *TF:* 800-449-0645 ■ *Web:* www.battery.com	617-948-3600	948-3601	792
Battery Wharf Hotel & Spa, The 3 Battery Wharf .... Boston MA 02109 *TF:* 877-794-6218 ■ *Web:* www.batterywharfhotelboston.com	617-994-9000		707
Battle Creek Area Chamber of Commerce 1 Riverwalk Ctr ste 3A 34 W Jackson St .... Battle Creek MI 49017 *TF:* 800-397-2240 ■ *Web:* www.battlecreek.org	269-962-4076	962-6309	139
Battle Creek Enquirer 77 E Michigan Ave Ste 101 .... Battle Creek MI 49017 *TF:* 800-333-4139 ■ *Web:* www.battlecreekenquirer.com	269-964-7161		532-2
Battle Creek/Calhoun County Convention & Visitors Bureau 77 E Michigan Ave Ste 100 .... Battle Creek MI 49017 *TF:* 800-397-2240 ■ *Web:* www.battlecreekvisitors.org	269-962-2240		206
Battle Ground Lake State Park 18002 NE 249th St .... Battle Ground WA 98604 *TF:* 888-226-7688 ■ *Web:* www.parks.wa.gov	360-687-4621		565
Battle Island State Park 2150 State Rt 48 .... Fulton NY 13069 *Web:* parks.ny.gov/parks/44/details.aspx	315-593-3408		565
Battle Medialab Inc 117 E Boca Raton Rd .... Boca Raton FL 33432 *Web:* battlemedialab.com	561-395-1555		180
Battle of Lexington State Historic Site 1101 Deleware .... Lexington MO 64067 *Web:* www.mostateparks.com	660-259-4654		565
Battle of the Windmill National Historic Site 370 Vankoughnet St .... Prescott ON K0E1T0 *Web:* www.pc.gc.ca/eng/lhn-nhs/on/windmill/index.aspx	613-925-2896	925-1536	563
Battle River Regional Div 5402 48a Ave .... Camrose AB T4V0L3 *TF:* 800-262-4869 ■ *Web:* www.brsd.ab.ca	780-672-6131		685
Battle Road Research Ltd 465 Waverley Oaks Rd Ste 209 .... Waltham MA 02452 *Web:* www.battleroad.com	781-894-0705		401
Battlefield Farms Inc 23190 Clarks Mtn Rd .... Rapidan VA 22733 **Fax Area Code:* 540 ■ *TF:* 800-722-0744 ■ *Web:* www.battlefieldfarms.com	800-722-0744	854-6486*	369

Name / Address	Phone	Fax	Class
Battlefield Mall 2825 S Glenstone Ave. Springfield MO 65004 *TF:* 800-228-5754 ■ *Web:* www.simon.com	417-883-7777	883-2641	460
Battlefords Chamber of Commerce PO Box 1000 Jcts of Hws 16 & 40 E. North Battleford SK S9A3E6 *Web:* www.battlefordschamber.com	306-445-6226	445-6633	137
Battlefords Union Hospital 1092 107th St. North Battleford SK S9A1Z1 *Web:* buhfoundation.com	306-446-6600		374-2
Battle-Friedman House & Gardens 1010 Greensboro Ave. Tuscaloosa AL 35401 *Web:* www.historictuscaloosa.org	205-758-6138		50-3
Battleground National Cemetery 6625 Georgia Ave NW. Washington DC 20012 *Web:* www.nps.gov	202-829-4650		136
Battleground Restaurant Group Inc 1337 Winstead Pl. Greensboro NC 27408 *Web:* www.brginc.com	336-272-9355	272-5568	670
Battleship Texas SHS 3523 Independence Pkwy S 3523 Independence Pkwy. La Porte TX 77571 *Web:* tpwd.texas.gov	281-479-2431	479-5618	520
Battlespace Simulations Inc 26525 Harmony Hills. San Antonio TX 78260 *Web:* www.battlespacesims.com	210-179-2656		809
Batuta Inc 1s450 Summit Ave Ste 210. Oakbrook Terrace IL 60181 *Web:* www.batuta.org	630-827-2500		180
Baudville Inc 5380 52nd St SE. Grand Rapids MI 49512 *TF Orders:* 800-728-0888 ■ *Web:* www.baudville.com	616-698-0889	698-0554	178-1
Baue Funeral Homes 620 Jefferson St. Saint Charles MO 63301 *TF:* 888-724-0073 ■ *Web:* baue.com	636-940-1000	946-3084	510
BAUER 100 Domain Dr. Exeter NH 03833 *TF:* 800-362-3146 ■ *Web:* www.bauer.com	603-430-2111	430-3010	710
Bauer Built Inc PO Box 248. Durand WI 54736 *TF:* 800-268-5114 ■ *Web:* www.bauerbuilt.com	715-672-4295		755
Bauer Compressors Inc 1328 Azalea Garden Rd. Norfolk VA 23502 *Web:* www.bauercomp.com	757-855-6006	855-6224	172
Bauer Howden Inc 175 Century Dr. Bristol CT 06010 *Web:* www.bauerct.com	860-583-9100		22
Bauer Manufacturing Inc 100 N Fm 3083 Rd. Conroe TX 77303 *Web:* www.bauer-conroe.com	936-539-5030		697
Bauer Premium Fly Reels 585 Clover Ln Ste 1. Ashland OR 97520 *TF:* 888-484-4165 ■ *Web:* www.bauerflyreel.com	541-488-8246	488-8244	710
Bauer Publishing Co LP 270 Sylvan Ave. Englewood Cliffs NJ 07632 **Fax Area Code:* 201 ■ *TF:* 800-530-2689 ■ *Web:* www.bauerpublishing.com	212-764-3344	569-5303*	637-9
Bauer Sheet Metal & Fabricating Inc 1550 Evanston. Muskegon MI 49442 *Web:* www.bauersheetmetal.com	231-773-3244		697
Bauer-Pileco Inc 100 N FM 3083 E. Conroe TX 77303 *TF:* 800-474-5326 ■ *Web:* www.bauerpileco.com	713-691-3000	691-0089	386
Bauerschmidt & Sons Inc 11920 Merrick Blvd. Jamaica NY 11434 *Web:* www.bauerschmidtandsons.com	718-528-3500		499
Bauerware LLC 3886 17th St. San Francisco CA 94114 *TF:* 877-864-5662 ■ *Web:* bauerware.com	415-864-3886		362
Baugo Community School Indiana 29125 County Rd 22 W. Elkhart IN 46517	574-293-8583		685
Bauhaus USA Inc 1 Bauhaus Dr. Saltillo MS 38866 *Web:* www.bauhaususa.com	662-869-2664	869-5910	319-2
Baum Machine Inc N253 Stoney Brook Rd. Appleton WI 54915 *Web:* www.baummachine.com	920-738-6613		757
Baum Textile Mills Inc 812 Jersey Ave. Jersey City NJ 07310 *TF:* 866-842-7631 ■ *Web:* www.baumtextile.com	201-659-0444	659-9719	594
Bauman Associates Ltd PO Box 1225. Eau Claire WI 54702 *TF:* 888-952-2866 ■ *Web:* baumancpa.com	715-834-2001		2
Bauman Rare Books 535 Madison Ave Frnt 1. New York NY 10022 *Web:* www.baumanrarebooks.com	212-751-0011		95
Baumann & De Groot Inc 116 E Lakewood Blvd. Holland MI 49424 *Web:* baumannanddegroot.com	616-355-6550		189-10
Baumer Foods Inc 2424 Edenborn Ave Ste 510. Metairie LA 70001 *Web:* www.baumerfoods.com	504-482-5761		296-20
Baumfolder Corp 1660 Campbell Rd. Sidney OH 45365 *TF:* 800-543-6107 ■ *Web:* www.baumfolder.com	937-492-1281	492-7280	556
Baumgarten's 144 Ottley Dr. Atlanta GA 30324 **Fax Area Code:* 480 ■ *TF:* 800-247-5547 ■ *Web:* www.b3.net	404-874-7675	964-1279*	534
Baumhower's of Tuscaloosa 500 Harper Lee Dr. Tuscaloosa AL 35404 *Web:* www.baumhowers.com	205-556-5658	556-5639	671
Bausch & Lomb Inc 1400 N Goodman St. Rochester NY 14609 **Fax Area Code:* 585 ■ *TF:* 800-553-5340 ■ *Web:* www.bausch.com	800-553-5340	338-6896*	542
Bausch & Lomb Pharmaceuticals Inc 8500 Hidden River Pkwy. Tampa FL 33637 *TF Cust Svc:* 800-323-0000 ■ *Web:* www.bausch.com	800-553-5340		582
Bau-Xi Gallery 3045 Granville St. Vancouver BC V6H3J9 *TF:* 800-933-6339 ■ *Web:* www.bau-xi.com	604-733-7011		42
Bavarian Autosport Inc 275 Constitution Ave. Portsmouth NH 03801 *TF:* 800-535-2002 ■ *Web:* www.bavauto.com	603-427-2002		54
Bavarian Grill 221 W Parker Rd. Plano TX 75023 *Web:* www.bavariangrill.com	972-881-0705		671
Bavarian Inn 713 S Main St. Frankenmuth MI 48734 *Web:* www.bavarianinn.com	989-652-9941		671
Bavarian Inn 855 N Fifth St. Custer SD 57730 *Web:* www.bavarianinnsd.com	605-673-2802		379
Bavarian Point Restaurant 4815 E Main St. Mesa AZ 85205 *Web:* www.bavarianpoint.net	480-830-0999		671
Bavarian World 595 Valley Rd. Reno NV 89512 *Web:* bavarianworldreno.com	775-323-7646		671
Bawmann Group Inc, The 1755 High St. Denver CO 80218 *Web:* gotoamtbg.com	303-320-7790	320-7661	636
Bax Engineering Co 221 Point W Blvd. Saint Charles MO 63301 *TF:* 800-444-0522 ■ *Web:* www.baxengineering.com	636-928-5552		261
Baxter & Woodman Inc 8678 Ridgefield Rd. Crystal Lake IL 60012 *Web:* baxterwoodman.com	815-459-1260	455-0450	261
Baxter Chrysler Jeep Inc 17950 Burt St. Omaha NE 68118 *Web:* baxterchryslerjeepdodge.net	402-493-7800		57
Baxter Corp 7125 Mississauga Rd. Mississauga ON L5N0C2 *TF:* 866-234-2345 ■ *Web:* www.baxter.ca	905-369-6000		231
Baxter County 1 E Seventh St Fl 1 Baxter County Courthouse. Mountain Home AR 72653 *Web:* www.baxtercounty.org	870-425-3475		338
Baxter Enterprises 466 Baxter Ln. Winchester TN 37398 *Web:* www.baxterent.com	931-962-8687		596
Baxter Healthcare Corp 1 Baxter Pkwy. Deerfield IL 60015 **Fax Area Code:* 224 ■ *Web:* www.baxter.com	847-948-2000	948-1813*	476
Baxter International Inc 1 Baxter Pkwy. Deerfield IL 60015 *NYSE:* BAX ■ *TF:* 800-422-9837 ■ *Web:* www.baxter.com	847-948-2000	948-3948	477
Baxter Planning Systems Inc 7801 N Capital of Texas Hwy Ste 250. Austin TX 78731 *Web:* bybaxter.com	512-323-5959		178-10
Baxter Regional Medical Ctr 624 Hospital Dr. Mountain Home AR 72653 *TF:* 800-695-3627 ■ *Web:* www.baxterregional.org	870-424-1000		374-3
Baxter State Park 64 Balsam Dr. Millinocket ME 04462 *Web:* baxterstatepark.org	207-723-5140		565
Baxter, Baker, Sidle, Conn & Jones PA 120 E Baltimore St Ste 2100. Baltimore MD 21202 *Web:* www.bbcolaw.com	410-385-8122		428
BaxterBoo 7025 S Fulton St Ste 150. Centennial CO 80112 *TF:* 888-887-0063 ■ *Web:* www.baxterboo.com	888-887-0063		690
Bay Area Chamber of Commerce 901 Saginaw St. Bay City MI 48708 *Web:* www.baycityarea.com	989-893-4567	895-5594	139
Bay Area Chamber of Commerce 145 Central Ave. Coos Bay OR 97420 *Web:* coosbaynorthbendcharlestonchamber.com	541-266-0868	267-6704	139
Bay Area Discovery Museum 557 McReynolds Rd. Sausalito CA 94965 *Web:* bayareadiscoverymuseum.org	415-339-3900		521
Bay Area Economics 1285 66th St. Emeryville CA 94608 *TF:* 800-440-8265 ■ *Web:* www.bae1.com	510-547-9380		194
Bay Area Exhibits Inc 1735 Technology Dr Ste 250. San Jose CA 95110 *Web:* www.baexhibits.com	408-566-8888		393
Bay Area Hospital 1775 Thompson Rd. Coos Bay OR 97420 *TF:* 800-798-0799 ■ *Web:* www.bayareahospital.org	541-269-8111		374-3
Bay Area Legal Aid 1735 Telegraph Ave. Oakland CA 94612 *Web:* baylegal.org	510-663-4755		428
Bay Area Medical Ctr (BAMC) 3100 Shore Dr. Marinette WI 54143 *TF:* 888-788-2070 ■ *Web:* bamc.org	715-735-4200		374-3
Bay Area Rapid Transit District 300 Lakeside Dr. Oakland CA 94612 *Web:* www.bart.gov	510-464-6000		468
Bay Area Renaissance Festival at Mosi 11315 N 46th St. Tampa FL 33617 *Web:* bayarearenfest.com	813-983-0111		720
Bay Area Reporter 395 Ninth St. San Francisco CA 94103 *TF:* 800-640-4829 ■ *Web:* www.ebar.com	415-861-5019		532-3
Bay Associates Group Inc 1432 Front Ave. Lutherville MD 21093 *Web:* www.bayassociates.com	410-825-6616		612
Bay Bank 2328 W Joppa Rd. Lutherville MD 21093 *NASDAQ:* BYBK ■ *TF:* 800-222-6566 ■ *Web:* www.baybankmd.com	410-494-2580		360-2
Bay Banks of Virginia Inc 100 S Main St PO Box 1869. Kilmarnock VA 22482 *OTC:* BAYK ■ *Web:* www.bankoflancaster.com	804-435-1171		70
Bay Business Credit 1460 Maria Ln Ste 300. Walnut Creek CA 94596 *Web:* baybizcr.com	925-256-9003		70
Bay Cast Inc 2611 Ctr Ave. Bay City MI 48708 *Web:* www.baycast.com	989-892-0511		307
Bay City Flower Company Inc 2265 Cabrillo Hwy S. Half Moon Bay CA 94019 *TF Sales:* 800-399-5858 ■ *Web:* www.baycityflower.com	650-726-5535		369
Bay City Public Schools 910 N Walnut St. Bay City MI 48706 *Web:* www.bcschools.net	989-686-9700		685
Bay City Recreation Area 3582 State Pk Dr. Bay City MI 48706 *Web:* www.michigandnr.com	989-684-3020		565
Bay City Tribune 2901 16th St. Bay City TX 77414 *TF:* 800-794-0427 ■ *Web:* www.baycitytribune.com	979-245-5555	245-1537	532-2
Bay Club Company, The 150 Greenwich St. San Francisco CA 94111 *TF:* 800-224-0240 ■ *Web:* bayclubs.com/sanfrancisco	415-433-2200		354
Bay Club Hotel & Marina 2131 Shelter Island Dr. San Diego CA 92106 *TF:* 800-672-0800 ■ *Web:* www.bayclubhotel.com	619-224-8888	225-1604	379
Bay Club Ownership Resort Inc, The 69-450 Waikoloa Beach Dr. Waikoloa Village HI 96738 *Web:* thebayclub.hgvc.com	808-886-7979		378
Bay Computer Associates Inc 136 Frances Ave. Cranston RI 02910 *Web:* www.baycomp.com	401-461-1484		177
Bay Correctional Facility 5400 Bayline Dr. Panama City FL 32404 *Web:* dc.state.fl.us	850-769-1455	769-1942	213
Bay Corrugated Container Inc 1655 W Seventh St. Monroe MI 48161 *Web:* www.baycorr.com	734-243-5400		100

	Phone	Fax	Class
Bay County 515 Ctr Ave Ste 101 ....Bay City MI 48708 *TF:* 877-229-9960 ■ *Web:* www.baycounty-mi.gov	989-895-4280	895-4284	338
Bay County 840 W 11th St................. Panama City FL 32401 *Web:* www.co.bay.fl.us	850-248-8140		338
Bay County Chamber of Commerce 235 W Fifth St.......................... Panama City FL 32401 *Web:* www.panamacity.org	850-785-5206	763-6229	139
Bay County Library System 500 Ctr Ave................................Bay City MI 48708 *Web:* www.baycountylibrary.org	989-894-2837	894-2021	434-3
Bay County Medical Care Facility 564 W Hampton Rd ....Essexville MI 48732 *TF:* 800-327-4693 ■ *Web:* www.baycountymcf.com	989-892-3591	892-6991	450
Bay County Public Library 898 W 11th St.......................... Panama City FL 32401 *TF:* 800-955-8771 ■ *Web:* www.nwrls.lib.fl.us	850-522-2100		434-3
Bay Craft Inc 1785 Langley Ave .... DeLand FL 32724 *Web:* www.baycraftinc.com	386-943-8877		90
Bay de Noc Community College 2001 N Lincoln Rd ....Escanaba MI 49829 **Fax:* Admissions ■ *TF:* 800-221-2001 ■ *Web:* mybay.baycollege.edu	906-786-5802	786-8515*	162
Bay Diesel Corp 3736 Cook Blvd .... Chesapeake VA 23323 *Web:* www.baydiesel.com	757-485-0075		698
Bay Dynamics Inc 595 Market St Ste 920 .... San Francisco CA 94105 *Web:* www.baydynamics.com	415-912-3130		194
Bay Electric Company Inc 627 36th St........................... Newport News VA 23607 *Web:* www.bayelectricco.com	757-595-2300	595-6112	186
Bay Glen Animal Hospital P C 1616 Clear Lake City Blvd ....Houston TX 77062 *Web:* www.bayglenvet.com	281-410-2611		794
Bay Harbor Inn & Suites *Daddy O Miami* 9660 E Bay Harbor Dr .... Bay Harbor Islands FL 33154 *Web:* www.daddyohotel.com/miami	305-868-4141		379
Bay Hill Golf Club & Lodge 9000 Bay Hill Blvd ....Orlando FL 32819 *TF:* 888-422-9445 ■ *Web:* www.bayhill.com	407-876-2429	876-1035	669
Bay Houston Towing Co 2243 Milford St.........Houston TX 77253 *TF:* 800-324-3755 ■ *Web:* www.bayhouston.com	713-529-3755	529-2591	465
Bay Industries Inc 2929 Walker Dr........... Green Bay WI 54311 *Web:* www.baycompanies.com	920-406-4000		499
Bay Island Sportswear Inc 225 By Pass 72 NW .... Greenwood SC 29649 *Web:* www.bayislandsportswear.com	864-229-1298		594
Bay Landing Hotel 1550 Bayshore Hwy Fl 2...................... Burlingame CA 94010 *TF:* 888-220-0301 ■ *Web:* www.baylandinghotel.com	650-259-9000	259-9099	378
Bay Leaf 935 W Hamilton St..................Allentown PA 18101 *TF:* 800-903-6385 ■ *Web:* www.allentownbayleaf.com	610-433-4211		671
Bay Logistics Inc 1202 Pontaluna Rd.......................Spring Lake MI 49456 *Web:* www.baylogistics.com	231-799-1015		803-1
Bay MarketForce LLC 215 N Main St Ste 140.....................West Bend WI 53095 *Web:* www.baymarketforce.com	262-335-1718		195
Bay Meadows Racing Assn 2600 S Delaware St ....San Mateo CA 94403 *Web:* baymeadows.com	650-573-4500		642
Bay Mechanical Inc 2696 Reliance Dr Ste 200...............Virginia Beach VA 23452 *TF:* 888-229-6324 ■ *Web:* www.baymechanical.com	757-468-6700	468-0377	189-10
Bay Medical Ctr 615 N Bonita Ave .... Panama City FL 32401 *Web:* www.baymedical.org	850-769-1511		374-3
Bay Microsystems Inc 2055 Gateway Pl Ste 650 .... San Jose CA 95110 *Web:* baymicrosystems.com	408-437-0400		180
Bay Mills Community College 12214 West Lakeshore Dr.................. Brimley MI 49715 *TF:* 800-844-2622 ■ *Web:* www.bmcc.edu	906-248-3354	248-3351	165
Bay Mills Resort & Casinos 11386 West Lakeshore Dr.................. Brimley MI 49715 *TF:* 888-422-9645 ■ *Web:* www.baymillscasinos.com	888-422-9645		452
Bay Minette Public Library 205 W Second St .... Bay Minette AL 36507 *Web:* cityofbayminette.org	251-580-1648	937-0339	434-3
Bay News 1624 N Meadowcrest Blvd .... Crystal River FL 34429 *Web:* www.baynews9.com	352-563-2052		530
Bay Park Hotel 1425 Munras Ave............ Monterey CA 93940 *TF Resv:* 800-338-3564 ■ *Web:* www.bayparkhotel.com	831-649-1020	373-4258	379
Bay Partners 10600 N De Anza Blvd Ste 100...............Cupertino CA 95014 *Web:* www.baypartners.com	408-725-2444	446-4502	792
Bay Path College 588 Longmeadow St....... Longmeadow MA 01106 *TF:* 800-782-7284 ■ *Web:* www.baypath.edu	800-782-7284		166
Bay Pines National Cemetery 10000 Bay Pines Blvd................. Saint Petersburg FL 33708 *TF:* 800-827-1000 ■ *Web:* www.cem.va.gov	800-827-1000		136
Bay Pointe Nursing Pavilion 4201 31st St S .... Saint Petersburg FL 33712 *TF:* 800-955-8771 ■ *Web:* baypointenursingpavilion.com	727-867-1104	867-9837	450
Bay Polymer Corp 44530 S Grimmer Blvd ....Fremont CA 94538 *Web:* www.baypolymer.com	510-490-1791	490-5914	608
Bay Regional Juvenile Detention Ctr 450 E 11th St .... Panama City FL 32401 *TF:* 800-355-2280 ■ *Web:* www.djj.state.fl.us	850-872-4706	873-7099	412
Bay Regional Medical Ctr (BRMC) 1900 Columbus Ave..........................Bay City MI 48708 *TF:* 800-656-3950 ■ *Web:* www.mclaren.org	989-894-3000		374-3
Bay Ship & Yacht Co 2900 Main St Ste 2100........................Alameda CA 94501 *Web:* www.bay-ship.com	510-337-9122	337-0154	698
Bay Shipbuilding Co 605 N Third Ave ....Sturgeon Bay WI 54235 *Web:* bayshipbuildingcompany.com	920-743-5524		698

	Phone	Fax	Class
Bay Shore Chamber of Commerce 77 E Main St PO Box 5110................... Bay Shore NY 11706 *TF:* 800-332-6367 ■ *Web:* www.bayshorecommerce.com	631-665-7003		139
Bay Shore Systems Inc 14206 N Ohio St............................Rathdrum ID 83858 *Web:* eventbrite.com/e	208-687-3311		190
Bay Standard Manufacturing Inc 24485 Marsh Creek Rd.....................Brentwood CA 94513 *Web:* www.baystandard.com	925-634-1181		350
Bay State College 122 Commonwealth Ave........Boston MA 02116 *TF:* 800-815-3276 ■ *Web:* www.baystate.edu	617-217-9000	249-0400	800
Bay State Computers Inc 16901 Melford Blvd Ste 329...................Bowie MD 20716 *TF:* 800-266-3783 ■ *Web:* www.bayst.com	301-352-7878	352-6925	180
Bay State Correctional Ctr 28 Clark St ....Norfolk MA 02056 *Web:* mass.gov	508-668-1687	668-1687	213
Bay State Envelope Inc 440 Chauncy St ....Mansfield MA 02048 *TF:* 800-462-6220 ■ *Web:* www.baystateenvelope.com	508-337-8900		627
Bay State Integrated Technology Inc 22 Settlers Dr .... Lakeville MA 02347 *TF:* 800-244-7592 ■ *Web:* www.baystatetechnology.com	508-947-1478		180
Bay State Milling Co 100 Congress St............Quincy MA 02169 **Fax Area Code:* 617 ■ *TF:* 800-553-5687 ■ *Web:* www.baystatemilling.com	800-553-5687	479-8910*	296-23
Bay Swiss Mfg Company Inc 5 Airpark Vista Blvd ....Dayton NV 89403 *TF:* 800-247-3207 ■ *Web:* www.bayswiss.com	775-246-7100	246-7104	621
Bay Technical Assoc Inc 5239 Ave A................. Long Beach Industrial Park MS 39560 *TF:* 800-523-2702 ■ *Web:* www.baytech.net	228-563-7334		174
Bay Tek Games Inc 1077 E Glenbrook Dr..........Pulaski WI 54162 *Web:* www.bay-tek.com	920-822-3951		31
Bay Valley Hotel & Resort 2470 Old Bridge Rd ....Bay City MI 48706 *TF:* 888-241-4653 ■ *Web:* www.bayvalley.com	989-686-3500		669
Bay View Food Products Inc 2606 N Huron Rd .... Pinconning MI 48650 *Web:* www.bayviewfoods.com	989-879-3555		296-19
Bay View Plaza Furniture Inc 2181 E Pass Rd ....Gulfport MS 39507 *TF:* 800-748-9852 ■ *Web:* bayviewfurniture.com	228-896-4400		321
Bay View State Park 10901 Bay View-Edison Rd .... Mount Vernon WA 98273 *Web:* www.parks.wa.gov	360-757-0227		565
Bay Village 8400 Vamo Rd ....Sarasota FL 34231 *Web:* www.bayvillage.org	941-966-5611		672
Bay Watch Resort & Conference Ctr 2701 S Ocean Blvd.................... North Myrtle Beach SC 29582 *TF:* 844-887-9448 ■ *Web:* oceanaresorts.com	843-272-4600		669
Bay Wolf Restaurant 3853 Piedmont Ave ....Oakland CA 94611 *Web:* www.baywolf.com	510-655-6004		671
Bayada Nurses Home Care Specialists 290 Chester Ave..........................Moorestown NJ 08057 *TF:* 877-591-1527 ■ *Web:* www.bayada.com	856-231-1000	231-1955	363
Bayard Firm, The 222 Delaware Ave Ste 900 .... Wilmington DE 19801 *Web:* www.bayardfirm.com	302-655-5000		428
Bayaud Industries Inc 333 W Bayaud Ave.........Denver CO 80223 *TF:* 800-337-3242 ■ *Web:* www.bayaudenterprises.org	303-830-6885		317
Baybank Corp 104 S Tenth St .... Gladstone MI 49837 *Web:* baybank.us	906-428-4040		70
Baybutt Construction Corp 25 Avon St ....Keene NH 03431 *Web:* www.baybutt.com	603-352-6846	352-6633	186
Bayco Products Inc 640 Sanden Blvd ....Wylie TX 75098 *TF:* 800-233-2155 ■ *Web:* www.baycoproducts.com	469-326-9400		437
Baycrest Centre For Geriatric Care 3560 Bathurst St........................... Toronto ON M6A2E1 *TF:* 800-668-2785 ■ *Web:* www.baycrest.org	416-785-2500		371
Bayer Built Woodworks Inc 24614 Hwy 71 .... Belgrade MN 56312 *Web:* www.bayerbuilt.com	320-254-3651	254-3601	191-3
Bayer Corp 100 Bayer Blvd.................... Whippany NJ 07981 *Web:* www.bayer.us	862-404-3000		582
Bayer CropScience 2 TW Alexander Dr .... Research Triangle Park NC 27709 *TF:* 800-331-2867 ■ *Web:* www.cropscience.bayer.us	919-549-2000		85
Bayer Inc 77 Belfield Rd..................... Toronto ON M9W1G6 *TF:* 800-622-2937 ■ *Web:* www.bayer.ca	416-248-0771		582
Bayer MaterialScience LLC 100 Bayer Rd .... Pittsburgh PA 15205	412-777-2000	777-3899	605-2
Bayerkohler & Graff Ltd 11132 Zealand Ave N ....Champlin MN 55316 *TF:* 866-315-2771 ■ *Web:* bayergraff.com	763-427-2542		734
Bayer-Risse Engineering Inc 78 Rt 173 W .... Hampton NJ 08827 *Web:* bayer-risse.com	908-735-2255		261
Bayfield County PO Box 878................. Washburn WI 54891 *TF:* 800-447-4094 ■ *Web:* www.bayfieldcounty.org	715-373-6100	373-6153	338
Bayfield Electric Co-op Inc 68460 District St..........................Iron River WI 54847 *TF:* 800-278-0166 ■ *Web:* www.bayfieldelectric.com	715-372-4287	372-4318	245
BAY-FM 94.5 (AC) 190 Pk Ctr Plaza Ste 200 .... San Jose CA 95113 *TF:* 800-948-5229 ■ *Web:* www.kbay.com	408-287-5775		645-146
Bayforce Technology Solutions Inc 5100 W Kennedy Blvd Ste 425.................. Tampa FL 33609 *Web:* www.bayforce.com	813-386-0663		260
Bayfront Inn 138 Avenida Menendez................Saint Augustine FL 32084 *TF:* 800-727-4656 ■ *Web:* www.bayfrontinn.com	904-824-1681		379
Bayhead Products Corp 173 Crosby Rd ....Dover NH 03820 *TF:* 800-229-4323 ■ *Web:* www.bayheadproducts.com	603-742-3000	743-4701	470
Bayhealth Medical Ctr 21 W Clarke Ave..........Milford DE 19963 *TF:* 877-453-7107 ■ *Web:* www.bayhealth.org	302-430-5738		374-3
Bayland Buildings Inc PO Box 13571 .... Green Bay WI 54307 *TF:* 800-488-6903 ■ *Web:* baylandbuildings.com	920-498-9300		186

Phone | Fax | Class

Bayless Engineering Inc
26100 Ave Hall .... Valencia CA 91355 661-257-3373 454
Web: www.baylessengineering.com
Bayley Construction Co
8005 SE 28th St Ste 100 .... Mercer Island WA 98040 206-621-8884 343-7728 186
Web: www.bayley.net
Baylis Medical Company Inc
5959 Trans-Canada Hwy .... Montreal QC H4T1A1 514-488-9801 477
TF: 800-850-9801 ■ *Web:* www.baylismedical.com
Bayliss Machine & Welding Co
2901 Eighth Ave N .... Birmingham AL 35203 205-323-6121 454
Web: www.baylissmachine.com
Bayloff Stamped Products
5910 Belleville Rd. .... Belleville MI 48111 734-397-9116 489
Web: www.bayloff.com
Baylor All Saints Medical Ctr
1400 Eigth Ave .... Fort Worth TX 76104 817-926-2544 374-3
Web: baylorhealth.com
Baylor College of Medicine
1 Baylor Plaza MS BCM365 .... Houston TX 77030 713-798-7766 798-1518 167-2
Web: www.bcm.edu
Baylor County
301 N Washington PO Box 31 .... Seymour TX 76380 940-889-3148 889-8882 338
TF: 800-633-0852 ■ *Web:* www.cityofseymour.org
Baylor Health Care System
3500 Gaston Ave. .... Dallas TX 75246 214-820-0111 353
Web: www.baylorhealth.com
Baylor Institute for Rehabilitation
909 N Washington Ave .... Dallas TX 75246 214-820-9300 374-6
Web: www.baylorhealth.com
Baylor Medical Center (TMC)
4343 N Josey Ln. .... Carrollton TX 75010 972-492-1010 374-3
Baylor Medical Ctr at Garland
2300 Marie Curie Blvd .... Garland TX 75042 972-487-5000 374-3
Web: baylorhealth.com
Baylor Medical Ctr at Irving
1901 N MacArthur Blvd .... Irving TX 75061 972-579-8100 374-3
Web: www.baylorhealth.com/physicianslocations/irving
Baylor Plaza Hotel 3600 Gaston Ave .... Dallas TX 75246 214-820-4561 372
TF: 800-422-9567 ■ *Web:* www.baylorhealth.com
Baylor Regional Medical Ctr at Grapevine
1650 W College St .... Grapevine TX 76051 817-481-1588 374-3
TF: 800-422-9567 ■ *Web:* www.baylorhealth.com
Baylor Trucking Inc 9269 E State Rd 48 .... Milan IN 47031 812-623-2020 780
TF: 800-322-9567 ■ *Web:* www.baylortrucking.com
Baylor University
1301 S University Parks Dr. .... Waco TX 76798 254-710-3718 710-1066 166
TF: 800-229-5678 ■ *Web:* www.baylor.edu
Baylor University
Title IX Office
Clifton Robinson Tower Ste 285 .... Waco TX 76798 254-710-8454 710-2316 167-1
TF: 800-229-5678 ■ *Web:* baylor.edu
Baylor University Medical Ctr at Dallas
3500 Gaston Ave. .... Dallas TX 75246 214-820-0111 374-3
Web: www.baylorhealth.com
Baylor University Moody Memorial Library & Jones Library
One Bear Pl PO Box 97148 .... Waco TX 76798 254-710-2112 434-6
Web: www.baylor.edu/lib
Baylor Women's Correctional Institution
660 Baylor Blvd .... New Castle DE 19720 302-577-3004 213
Baymont Inn & Suites
3101 Scott Futrell Dr .... Charlotte NC 28208 704-533-9441 378
Web: www.baymontinns.com
Bayne Machine Works Inc
910 Fork Shoals Rd .... Greenville SC 29605 864-288-3877 454
Web: www.baynethinline.com
Bayona 430 Rue Dauphine .... New Orleans LA 70112 504-525-4455 522-0589 671
Web: www.bayona.com
Bayonne Chamber of Commerce 621 Ave C ..... Bayonne NJ 07002 201-436-4333 139
Web: www.bayonnenj.org
Bayonne Free Public Library 697 Ave C .... Bayonne NJ 07002 201-858-6970 434-3
Web: www.bayonnenj.org
Bayonne Medical Ctr 29th St & Ave E .... Bayonne NJ 07002 201-858-5000 858-5000 374-3
Web: bayonnemedicalcenter.org
Bayou Bay Seafood House
7117 Chapman Hwy .... Knoxville TN 37920 865-573-7936 671
Web: bayoubayseafoodhouseknoxville.com
Bayou Bend Collection & Gardens
6003 Memorial Dr .... Houston TX 77007 713-639-7750 520
Web: www.mfah.org/bayoubend
Bayou City Pump Inc 109 N Richey .... Pasadena TX 77506 713-472-7722 472-7713 641
Web: www.bayoucitypumpco.com
Bayou Coating LLC
12710 Leisure Rd .... Baton Rouge LA 70807 225-775-3018 567
Web: www.bayoullc.com
Bayou Companies LLC, The
5200 Curtis Ln .... New Iberia LA 70560 337-369-3761 539
TF: 800-619-4807 ■ *Web:* www.bayoucompanies.com
Bayou Manor 4141 S Braeswood Blvd. .... Houston TX 77025 713-666-2651 672
TF: 800-252-9240 ■ *Web:* houstonretirement.org
Bayou Microsystems LLC 209 Abby Rd .... Thibodaux LA 70301 985-414-3949 177
Web: www.bayoumicro.com
Bayou Perma-Pipe Canada Ltd
5233 39th St. .... Camrose AB T4V4R5 780-672-2345 481
Web: www.permapipe.com
Bayou Segnette State Park
7777 Westbank Expy. .... Westwego LA 70094 504-736-7140 565
TF: 888-677-2296 ■ *Web:* www.crt.state.la.us
Bayou State Oil Corp 1115 Hawn Ave .... Shreveport LA 71107 318-222-0737 536
Bay-Pointe Technology Ltd
2662 Brecksville Rd .... Richfield OH 44286 330-659-6400 525
Web: baypointetechnology.com
BayPort Credit Union Inc
3711 Huntington Ave .... Newport News VA 23607 757-928-8850 219
TF: 800-928-8801 ■ *Web:* www.bayportcu.org/home.html
Bays Corp PO Box 1455 .... Chicago IL 60690 312-346-5757 296-1
TF: 800-367-2297 ■ *Web:* www.bays.com

Phone | Fax | Class

Bays Mountain Planetarium & Observatory
853 Bays Mtn Pk Rd .... Kingsport TN 37660 423-229-9447 224-2589 598
Web: baysmountain.com
Bayshore Community Hospital
727 N Beers St .... Holmdel NJ 07733 732-739-5900 374-3
Web: www.bayshorehospital.org
Bayshore Concrete Products Corp
1134 Bayshore Rd .... Cape Charles VA 23310 757-331-2300 183
Web: www.usa.skanska.com
Bayshore Medical Ctr
4000 Spencer Hwy .... Pasadena TX 77504 713-359-2000 359-1004 374-3
TF: 800-639-7353 ■ *Web:* www.bayshoremedical.com
Bayshore Recycling Corp
75 Crows Mill Rd .... Keasbey NJ 08832 732-738-6000 660
TF: 800-797-2878 ■ *Web:* bayshorerecycling.com
Bayshore Town Ctr
5800 N Bayshore Dr Ste A256 .... Glendale WI 53217 414-963-8780 460
Web: www.bayshoretowncenter.com
Bayshore Transportation System Inc
901 Dawson Dr. .... Newark DE 19713 302-366-0220 780
TF: 800-523-3319 ■ *Web:* www.bayshoreallied.com
Bayside Fuel Oil Depot Corp
1776 Shore Pkwy .... Brooklyn NY 11214 718-372-9800 581
Web: www.baysidedepot.com
Bayside Interiors Inc
3220 Darby Common .... Fremont CA 94539 510-438-9171 438-9375 189-9
Web: www.baysideinteriors.com
Bayside Marketplace 401 Biscayne Blvd .... Miami FL 33132 305-577-3344 50-6
Web: www.baysidemarketplace.com
Bayside Resort Hotel
225 Massachusetts 28 .... West Yarmouth MA 02673 508-775-5669 775-8862 669
TF: 800-243-1114 ■ *Web:* www.baysideresort.com
Bayside Solutions Inc
6160 Stoneridge Mall Rd Ste 320 .... Pleasanton CA 94588 800-220-0074 260
TF: 800-220-0074 ■ *Web:* www.baysidesolutions.com
Bayside State Prison 4293 Rt 47 .... Leesburg NJ 08327 856-785-0040 785-2559 213
Web: state.nj.us
BaySpec Inc 1101 McKay Dr .... San Jose CA 95131 408-512-5928 246
Web: www.bayspec.com
Baystar Hotel Group
500N Westshore Blvd Ste 740 .... Largo FL 33609 727-585-3333 132
Web: baystarhotels.com
Baystate Franklin Medical Ctr
164 High St .... Greenfield MA 01301 413-773-0211 374-3
Web: www.baystatehealth.org
Baystate Medical Ctr
759 Chestnut St .... Springfield MA 01199 413-794-0000 374-3
Web: www.baystatehealth.org
Baystate Visiting Nurse Association & Hospice
50 Maple St .... Springfield MA 01199 413-794-6411 371
TF: 800-249-8298 ■ *Web:* www.baystatehealth.org
Bayswater Point State Park
1479 Point Breeze Pl .... Far Rockaway NY 11601 718-967-1976 565
Web: parks.ny.gov/parks/86/details.aspx
Baytec Service LLC 4761 Hwy 146 200 .... Bacliff TX 77518 800-560-2334 316
TF: 800-560-2334 ■ *Web:* www.bayteccontainers.com
Baytex Energy Corp
2800 520 - Third Ave SW .... Calgary AB T2P0R3 587-952-3000 536
TF: 800-524-5521 ■ *Web:* www.baytexenergy.com
Baytown Chamber of Commerce
1300 Rolling Brook Ste 400 .... Baytown TX 77521 281-422-8359 428-1758 139
Web: www.baytownchamber.com
Bayview 11 W Aloha St. .... Seattle WA 98119 206-284-7330 672
Web: www.bayviewcommunity.org
Bayview Capital Group LLC
214 Minnetonka Ave S .... Wayzata MN 55391 952-345-2000 690
Web: www.bayviewcap.com
Bayview Environmental Services Inc
6925 San Leandro St .... Oakland CA 94621 510-562-6181 63
Web: www.bayviewenvironmental.com
Bayview Glen Public School
42 Limcombe Dr. .... Markham ON L3T2V5 905-889-2448 685
Web: www.yrdsb.ca
Bayview Limousine Service
15701 Nelson Pl S .... Seattle WA 98188 206-824-6200 277-5895* 441
**Fax Area Code: 425* ■ *TF:* 800-606-7880 ■ *Web:* www.bayviewlimo.com
Bayview Opera House
4705 Third St .... San Francisco CA 94124 415-824-0386 572
Web: www.bvoh.org
Bayview Press 30 Knox St PO Box 153 .... Thomaston ME 04861 207-354-9919 354-9919 130
TF: 800-903-2346 ■ *Web:* www.bayviewpress.com
Bayway Lincoln-mercury Inc
12333 Gulf Fwy .... Houston TX 77034 888-262-9275 57
TF: 888-262-9275 ■ *Web:* clickmotive.com
Bayway Lumber & Home Center (inc)
400 Ashton Ave. .... Linden NJ 07036 908-486-4480 683
Web: www.baywaylumber.com
Baywood Homes 1140 Sheppard Ave W .... North York ON M3K2A2 416-999-9999 186
Baywood Hotels Inc
7871 Belle Point Dr .... Greenbelt MD 20770 301-345-8700 378
Web: www.baywoodhotels.com
Bazaar del Mundo 4133 Taylor St. .... San Diego CA 92110 619-296-3161 50-6
Web: www.bazaardelmundo.com
Bazelon Less & Feldman PC
1 S Broad St Ste 1500 .... Philadelphia PA 19107 215-568-1155 428
Web: www.bazless.com
BAZI Inc 1730 Blake St Ste 305 .... Denver CO 80202 303-316-8577 296-11
Web: www.drinkbazi.com
Bazo's Fresh Mexican Grill
4014 Dutchmans Ln .... Louisville KY 40207 502-899-9600 671
Web: bazosgrill.com
Bazon Cox & Associates Inc
1244 Executive Blvd .... Chesapeake VA 23320 757-410-2128 180
TF: 800-769-1763 ■ *Web:* bazoncox.com
Bazz Houston Co
12700 Western Ave. .... Garden Grove CA 92841 714-898-2666 898-1389 488
TF: 800-385-9608 ■ *Web:* www.bazz-houston.com
Bazzirk Inc 1027 E Riverside Dr. .... Austin TX 78704 512-418-8500 7
TF: 800-252-5400 ■ *Web:* www.bazzirk.com

Name / Address	City	State	ZIP	Phone	Fax	Class
BB & T Corp 200 W Second St NYSE: BBT ■ TF: 800-226-5228 ■ Web: bbt.investorroom.com/corporate-information	Winston-Salem	NC	27101	336-733-1470		360-2
B&B Contractors & Developers Inc 2781 Salt Springs Rd Web: www.bbcdonline.com	Youngstown	OH	44509	330-270-5020	270-5035	186
B&B Image Group 1712 Marshall St NE TF: 888-788-9461 ■ Web: www.bbimagegroup.com	Minneapolis	MN	55413	612-788-9461		344
BB King's Blues Club 143 Beale St Web: www.bbkings.com	Memphis	TN	38103	901-524-5464	524-5454	671
B&B Manufacturing Company Inc 27940 Beale Ct Web: www.bbmfg.com	Valencia	CA	91355	661-257-2161		454
Bb Riverboats Inc 101 Riverboat Row TF: 800-261-8586 ■ Web: www.bbriverboats.com	Newport	KY	41071	859-261-8500		749
BB's Restaurant & Bar 1019 Hendricks Ave Web: www.bbsrestaurant.com	Jacksonville	FL	32207	904-306-0100	306-0118	671
BBB Tank Services Inc 9225 Leopard St Web: www.bbbtankservices.com	Corpus Christi	TX	78409	361-241-1001		770
BBC (Balfour Beatty Construction) 3100 McKinnon St 10th Fl Web: balfourbeattyus.com	Dallas	TX	75201	214-451-1000		186
BBC America 1120 Ave of the Americas Web: www.bbcamerica.com	New York	NY	10036	212-705-9300		740
BBC Engineering Inc 8650 Business Park Dr Web: forteandtablada.com/company_history_bbce.asp	Shreveport	LA	71105	318-798-3344		256
BBCC (Brantford Brant Chamber of Commerce) 77 Charlotte St Web: www.brantfordbrantchamber.com	Brantford	ON	N3T2W8	519-753-2617	753-0921	137
Bbdo Atlanta Inc 3500 Lenox Rd NE Ste 1900 Web: bbdoatl.com	Atlanta	GA	30326	404-231-1700		4
BBDO Worldwide Inc 1285 Ave of the Americas Web: www.bbdo.com	New York	NY	10019	212-459-5000		4
BBF (Brother's Brother Foundation) 1200 Galveston Ave TF: 800-435-7352 ■ Web: www.brothersbrother.org	Pittsburgh	PA	15233	412-321-3160	321-3325	48-5
BBFI (Baptist Bible Fellowship International) 720 E Kearney St Web: www.bbfi.org	Springfield	MO	65803	417-862-5001	865-0794	48-20
BBGM 1825 K St NW Ste 300 Web: www.bbg-bbgm.com	Washington	DC	20006	202-452-1644	452-1647	261
BBH (Baltimore Behavioral Health) 1101 W Pratt St TF: 800-789-2647 ■ Web: baltimorecity.md.networkofcare.org	Baltimore	MD	21223	410-962-7180	962-7194	726
BBH Consulting Inc 80 E Antelope Dr Web: www.bbhconsulting.com	Layton	UT	84041	801-779-4405		317
BBH Solutions Inc 121 E 24th St Web: www.bbhsolutions.com	New York	NY	10010	212-475-7100		180
BBL (BBL Construction Services Inc) 302 Washington Ave Ext Web: www.bblinc.com	Albany	NY	12203	518-452-8200		186
Bbl Co 2194 Detwiler Rd Web: www.bblco.com	Kulpsville	PA	19443	215-256-6812		595
BBL Construction Services Inc (BBL) 302 Washington Ave Ext Web: www.bblinc.com	Albany	NY	12203	518-452-8200		186
BBL Hospitality LLC 302 Washington Ave Ext Web: www.bblhospitality.com	Albany	NY	12203	518-640-6464		378
BBQ Revue 4725 Madison Rd	Cincinnati	OH	45227	513-871-3500		671
BBR Benefits Solutions LLC 8150 Perry Hwy Ste 100 Web: bbrbenefits.com	Pittsburgh	PA	15237	412-847-3100		390
Bbr Creative Inc 300 Rue Beauregard TF: 800-561-3357 ■ Web: www.bbrcreative.com	Lafayette	LA	70508	337-233-1515		344
BBS Securities Inc 4100 Yonge St Ste 507 Web: www.bbssecurities.com	Toronto	ON	M2P2B5	416-235-0200		690
BBU (Beefmaster Breeders United) 6800 Pk Ten Blvd Ste 290-W Web: www.beefmasters.org	San Antonio	TX	78213	210-732-3132	732-7711	48-2
BBVCC (Greater Bentonville Area Chamber of Commerce) 200 E Central St PO Box 330 Web: www.bbvchamber.com	Bentonville	AR	72712	479-273-2841	273-2180	139
BBYO (B'nai B'rith Youth Organization) 2020 K St NW Web: www.bbyo.org	Washington	DC	20006	202-857-6633	857-6568	48-20
BC (Buehler Planetarium & Observatory) 3501 SW Davie Rd Web: www.broward.edu/locations/central/buehler.jsp	Davie	FL	33314	954-201-6681		598
BC Clark Northpark 12042 N May Ave TF: 800-742-5877 ■ Web: www.bcclark.com	Oklahoma City	OK	73120	405-755-4040		410
BC Investment Management Corp 2940 Jutland Rd Sawmill Point Web: www.bcimc.com	Victoria	BC	V8T5K6	250-356-0263		528
BC Johnson Associates LLC 3702 Old Chocolate Bayou Rd Web: www.bcjohnson.com	Manvel	TX	77578	281-489-4894		463
BC Lions 10605 135th St Web: www.bclions.com	Surrey	BC	V3T4C8	604-930-5466	583-7882	715-2
Bc Maritime Employers Assn 349 Railway St Web: www.bcmea.com	Vancouver	BC	V6A1A4	604-688-1155		138
BC One Call Ltd 4259 Canada Way Ste 130 TF: 800-474-6886 ■ Web: www.bconecall.bc.ca	Burnaby	BC	V5G1H3	604-257-1900		194
BC Plumbing Co 1215 S Seventh St Web: bcplumbing.net	Louisville	KY	40203	502-634-9725		189-10
BC Public School Employers' Assn 400-1333 W Broadway Web: www.bcpsea.bc.ca	Vancouver	BC	V6H4C1	604-730-4507	730-0787	624
BC Systems Inc 200 Belle Mead Rd Web: www.bcpowersys.com	Setauket	NY	11733	631-751-9370		668
BC Transit 520 Gorge Rd E TF: 800-373-6393 ■ Web: www.bctransit.com	Victoria	BC	V8W2P3	250-385-2551	995-5639	468
BC Wire Rope & Rigging 2720 E Regal Park Dr TF: 800-669-5919 ■ Web: www.bcwirerope.com	Anaheim	CA	92806	800-669-5919		492
BCA (Buddhist Churches of America) 1710 Octavia St Web: buddhistchurchesofamerica.org	San Francisco	CA	94109	415-776-5600	771-6293	48-20
BCAA (British Columbia Automobile Assn) 4567 Canada Way TF: 800-222-4357 ■ Web: www.bcaa.com	Burnaby	BC	V5G4T1	604-268-5000		53
BCB Bancorp Inc 104-110 Ave C NASDAQ: BCBP ■ Web: www.bcbcommunitybank.com	Bayonne	NJ	07002	201-823-0700	339-0403	360-2
BCBG Max Azria 2761 Fruitland Ave Web: www.bcbg.com	Vernon	CA	90058	323-589-2224		277
BCC (Benning Construction Co Inc) 4695 S Atlanta Rd Web: www.benningnet.com	Atlanta	GA	30339	404-792-1911		186
BCC (Brevard Community College) *Cocoa* 1519 Clearlake Rd *Fax: Admissions ■ TF: 888-747-2802 ■ Web: www.easternflorida.edu	Cocoa	FL	32922	321-632-1111	433-7357*	162
Bcc Engineering Inc 6401 SW 87th Ave Ste 200 TF: 800-746-9554 ■ Web: www.bcceng.com	Miami	FL	33173	305-670-2350		261
BCC Planetarium & Obersvatory 1519 Clearlake Rd Web: www.easternflorida.edu	Cocoa	FL	32922	321-433-7373		598
BCC Research LLC 49 Walnut Pk Bldg 2 TF: 866-285-7215 ■ Web: www.bccresearch.com	Wellesley	MA	02481	781-489-7301	489-7308	637-9
BCCR (Brown College of Court Reporting & Medical Transcription) 1900 Emery St NW Ste 200 TF: 800-849-0703 ■ Web: www.bccr.edu	Atlanta	GA	30318	404-876-1227	876-4415	800
BCCVB (Bucks County Conference & Visitors Bureau) 3207 St Rd TF: 800-836-2825 ■ Web: www.visitbuckscounty.com	Bensalem	PA	19020	215-639-0300	642-3277	206
BCD Travel USA LLC 6 Concourse Pkwy Web: www.bcdtravel.us	Atlanta	GA	30328	678-441-5200		772
BCE Inc 1 CARREFOUR ALEXANDER-GRAHAM-BELL Bldg A, 4th Fl TF: 888-932-6666 ■ Web: www.bce.ca	Verdun	QC	H3E3B3	888-932-6666		787
BCER Engineering Inc 5420 Ward Rd Ste 200 Web: www.bcer.com	Arvada	CO	80002	303-422-7400		256
BCF LLP 25th Fl 1100 Rene-Levesque Blvd W TF: 866-511-8501 ■ Web: www.bcf.ca	Montreal	QC	H3B5C9	514-397-8500		428
BCF Solutions Inc 2300 Ninth St S Ste 200 Web: bcfsolutions.com	Arlington	VA	22204	703-717-9912		317
Bcg Attorney Search 175 S Lake Ave Unit 200 TF: 800-298-6440 ■ Web: www.bcgsearch.com	Pasadena	CA	91101	800-298-6440		260
Bcg Engineering & Consulting Inc 3012 26th St Web: www.bcgengineers.com	Metairie	LA	70002	504-454-3866		261
BCH (Boulder Community Hospital) 1100 Balsam Ave Web: www.bch.org	Boulder	CO	80301	303-440-2273		374-3
BCH Mechanical Inc 6354 118th Ave N Web: www.bchmechanical.com	Largo	FL	33773	727-546-3561	545-1801	189-10
BCHA (Back Country Horsemen of America) PO Box 1367 TF: 888-893-5161 ■ Web: www.bcha.org	Graham	WA	98338	360-832-2461		48-23
BCI (Bat Conservation International) 500 N Capital of Texas Hwy TF: 800-538-2287 ■ Web: batcon.org	Austin	TX	78746	512-327-9721	327-9724	48-3
BCI Burke Company Inc 660 Van Dyne Rd TF: 800-356-2070 ■ Web: www.bciburke.com	Fond du Lac	WI	54937	920-921-9220		346
BCI Inc 848 Marshall Phelps Rd Web: www.thebutlerco.com	Windsor	CT	06095	860-688-8024		776
Bci Staffing Inc 11800 Northfall Ln Ste 1405 TF: 800-579-7967 ■ Web: www.bci-it.com	Alpharetta	GA	30009	678-393-8536		193
BCinteriors 3550 Frontier Ave Ste C2 Web: www.bcinteriors.com	Boulder	CO	80301	303-443-3666		320
BCIU (Business Council for International Understanding) 1212 Ave of the Americas 10th Fl Web: www.bciu.org	New York	NY	10036	212-490-0460	697-8526	49-12
BCLC (British Columbia Lottery Corp) 74 W Seymour St TF: 866-815-0222 ■ Web: www.bclc.com	Kamloops	BC	V2C1E2	250-828-5500	828-5631	452
Bcls 100 Technology Way Ste 110 Web: www.bcls.lib.nj.us	Mount Laurel	NJ	08054	856-439-2520	439-2523	139
BCM Energy Partners Inc 5005 Riverway Ste 350	Houston	TX	77056	713-623-2003		540
BCM Resources Corp 1040 W Georgia St TF: 888-646-0144 ■ Web: www.bcmresources.com	Vancouver	BC	V6E4H1	604-646-0144		502
BCM Technologies 1709 Dryden Rd Ste 1790 Web: www.bcmtechnologies.com	Houston	TX	77030	713-795-0105	795-4602	792
B&CMA (Biscuit & Cracker Manufacturers Assn) 6325 Woodside Ct Ste 125 *Fax Area Code: 410 ■ Web: www.thebcma.org	Columbia	MD	21046	443-545-1645	290-8585*	49-6
BCN (Bliss Clearing Niagara) 1004 E State St TF: 800-642-5477 ■ Web: www.bcntechserv.com	Hastings	MI	49058	269-948-3300	948-3313	456
Bcn Transportation Services 3650 W Liberty Rd TF: 800-891-9911 ■ Web: www.bcnservices.com	Ann Arbor	MI	48103	734-994-4100		463
BCNS Technologies 116 Highwood Ave Web: computernetworking-repair.com	Henderson	NV	89002	702-566-5321		177
Bco Inc 799 Middlesex Tpke TF: 800-937-4688 ■ Web: www.bco-inc.com	Billerica	MA	01821	978-663-2525		631
BCP International Ltd 1800 N Beauregard St Ste 350	Alexandria	VA	22311	703-575-7300		588

Name / Address	City	State	ZIP	Phone	Fax	Class
BCP Veterinary Pharmacy 1614 Webster St *TF:* 800-481-1729 ■ *Web:* www.bcpvetpharm.com	Houston	TX	77003	713-771-1144		237
BCRS Assoc LLC 77 Water St *Web:* bcrsllc.com	New York	NY	10005	212-440-0800		734
BCS (Birmingham Board of Education) 2015 Pk Pl N *TF:* 800-628-6673 ■ *Web:* www.bhamcityschools.org	Birmingham	AL	35203	205-231-4600		685
Bcs Engineering 25 Grosvenor St *Web:* www.bcsengineering.com	Athens	OH	45701	740-331-4481		177
BCS Inc 8920 Stephens Rd Ste 200 *Web:* www.bcs-hq.com	Laurel	MD	20723	410-997-7778		194
BCS Prosoft Inc 2700 Lockhill Selma *TF:* 800-882-6705 ■ *Web:* www.bcsprosoft.com	San Antonio	TX	78230	210-308-5505		179
BCSCVB (Experience Bryan College Station) 715 University Dr E *TF:* 800-777-8292 ■ *Web:* www.visitaggieland.com	College Station	TX	77840	979-260-9898	260-9800	206
BCSD (Binghamton City School District) 164 Hawley St PO Box 2126 *Web:* binghamtonschools.org	Binghamton	NY	13902	607-762-8100		685
BCSIA (Belfer Ctr for Science & International Affairs) Harvard Univ John F Kennedy School of Government 79 JFK St *Web:* www.belfercenter.org	Cambridge	MA	02138	617-495-1400	495-8963	634
BCT Partners LLC 105 Lock St *Web:* www.bctpartners.com	Newark	NJ	07103	973-622-0900		463
BCVB (Bloomington Convention & Visitors Bureau) 7900 International Dr Ste 990 *TF:* 800-346-4289 ■ *Web:* www.bloomingtonmn.org	Bloomington	MN	55425	952-858-8500	858-8854	206
BCW Diversified 514 E 31st St *TF:* 800-433-4229 ■ *Web:* www.bcwsupplies.com	Anderson	IN	46016	765-644-2033	649-2884	627
BCWSA (Bucks County Water & Sewer Authority) 1275 Almshouse Rd **Fax Area Code:* 267 ■ *TF:* 800-222-2068 ■ *Web:* www.bcwsa.net	Warrington	PA	18976	215-343-2538	200-0339*	806
BD Biosciences 2350 Qume Dr *TF:* 800-223-8226 ■ *Web:* www.bdbiosciences.com	San Jose	CA	95131	408-432-9475	954-2347	419
BD Biosciences PharMingen 10975 Torreyana Rd **Fax Area Code:* 619 ■ *TF:* 800-848-6227 ■ *Web:* www.bdbiosciences.com	San Diego	CA	92121	858-812-8800	812-8888*	85
BD Diagnostics 7 Loveton Cir *Web:* www.bd.com	Sparks	MD	21152	410-316-4000	316-4066	231
B&D Industries Inc 9720 Bell Ave SE *TF:* 866-315-8349 ■ *Web:* www.banddindustries.com	Albuquerque	NM	87123	505-299-4464		246
BD Medical 9450 S State St *TF:* 888-237-2762 ■ *Web:* www.bd.com	Sandy	UT	84070	801-565-2300		476
BDA (Bensinger DuPont & Assoc) 134 N LaSalle St Ste 2200 *TF:* 800-227-8620 ■ *Web:* www.bensingerdupont.com	Chicago	IL	60602	312-726-8620	726-1061	462
BDA (Bensussen Deutsch & Assoc Inc) 15525 Woodinville-Redmond Rd NE *TF:* 800-451-4764 ■ *Web:* www.bdainc.com	Woodinville	WA	98072	425-492-6111		466
BDA Sports Management 700 Ygnacio Valley Rd Ste 330 *Web:* www.bdasports.com	Walnut Creek	CA	94596	925-279-1040		393
Bdc Computer Services LLC 399 Lakeview Ave *TF:* 877-233-4877 ■ *Web:* www.bdecomputer.com	Clifton	NJ	07011	973-772-8507		175
BDEC (Burke-Divide Electric Co-op Inc) 9549 Hwy 5 W *TF:* 800-472-2983 ■ *Web:* www.bdec.coop	Columbus	ND	58727	701-939-6671	939-6666	245
BDF (Baja Duty Free) 4590 Border Village Rd *Web:* www.bajadutyfree.com	San Ysidro	CA	92173	619-428-6671		241
Bdf 91 Washington St *Web:* www.bdf.com	Morristown	NJ	07960	973-898-9800		231
BDNA Corp 339 N Bernardo Ave Ste 206 *Web:* www.bdna.com	Mountain View	CA	94043	650-625-9530		387
BDO Capital Advisors LLC 1888 Century Park E *Web:* www.bdocap.com	Los Angeles	CA	90067	310-557-0300	557-8253	70
BDP International Inc 510 Walnut St *TF:* 800-627-5502 ■ *Web:* www.bdpinternational.com	Philadelphia	PA	19106	215-629-8900	629-8940	449
B-D-R Transport Inc 7994 US Rt 5 *TF:* 800-421-0126 ■ *Web:* www.bdrtransport.com	Westminster	VT	05158	802-463-0606		780
BDS Engineering Inc 6859 Federal Blvd *Web:* www.bdsengineering.com	Lemon Grove	CA	91945	619-582-4992		256
BDS Marketing Inc 10 Holland *TF:* 800-633-3070 ■ *Web:* www.bdsmktg.com	Irvine	CA	92618	949-472-6700		195
BDSI (BioDelivery Sciences International Inc) 4131 Parklake Ave Ste 225 *NASDAQ:* BDSI ■ *Web:* www.bdsi.com	Raleigh	NC	27612	919-582-9050	582-9051	85
BE Implement Co 1645 FM 403 PO Box 752 *TF:* 800-725-5435 ■ *Web:* www.beimplement.com	Brownfield	TX	79316	806-637-3594	637-8992	274
Be Media 655 Hawaii St *Web:* www.bemedia.com	El Segundo	CA	90245	310-725-8500		317
Be Original 1520 Lake Louella Rd *Web:* beoriginal.com	Suwanee	GA	30024	770-813-9933		344
BEA (Bureau of Economic Analysis) 1441 L St NW *TF:* 800-727-9540 ■ *Web:* www.bea.gov	Washington	DC	20005	202-606-9900	606-5311	340-2
BEA (Broadcast Education Assn) 1771 N St NW *Web:* www.beaweb.org	Washington	DC	20036	202-429-5355	609-9940	49-5
Beach Camera 203 Rt 22 E *TF:* 800-572-3224 ■ *Web:* www.beachcamera.com	Green Brook	NJ	08812	732-968-6400	968-7709	119
Beach Colony Resort 5308 N Ocean Blvd *TF General:* 800-222-2141 ■ *Web:* www.beachcolony.com	Myrtle Beach	SC	29577	843-449-4010	449-2810	669
Beach Ford Inc 2717 Virginia Beach Blvd *Web:* beachfordvirginiabeach.com	Virginia Beach	VA	23452	757-486-2717		57
Beach Haven Inn 4740 Mission Blvd *Web:* www.beachhaveninn.com	San Diego	CA	92109	858-272-3812	272-3532	379
Beach Manufacturing Co PO Box 129 *TF:* 800-543-5942 ■ *Web:* www.beachmfgco.com	Donnelsville	OH	45319	937-882-6372	882-6153	60
Beach Mold & Tool Inc 999 Progress Blvd *Web:* www.beachmold.com	New Albany	IN	47150	812-945-2688		596
Beach Oil Co 631 US Hwy 76 *Web:* www.beachoil.com	Clarksville	TN	37041	931-358-9303	358-9331	579
Beach Properties of Hilton Head 64 Arrow Rd *TF:* 800-671-5155 ■ *Web:* www.beach-property.com	Hilton Head Island	SC	29928	843-671-5155		656
Beach Realty & Construction 4826 N Croatan Hwy *TF:* 800-635-1559 ■ *Web:* www.beachrealtync.com	Kitty Hawk	NC	27949	252-261-3815		652
Beach Terrace Motor Inn 3400 Atlantic Ave *TF:* 800-841-8416 ■ *Web:* www.beachterrace.com	Wildwood	NJ	08260	609-522-8100		378
Beach.com Inc 5 Penn Plaza 23rd Fl *Web:* www.beach.com	New York	NY	10001	212-835-1529		387
Beachbody LLC 3301 Exposition Blvd *Web:* www.beachbody.com	Santa Monica	CA	90404	310-883-9000		6
Beachcomber Resort Hotel & Villas 1200 S Ocean Blvd *TF:* 800-231-2423 ■ *Web:* www.beachcomberresort.com	Pompano Beach	FL	33062	954-941-7830	942-7680	669
Beachcomber Restaurant 2 A St	Saint Augustine	FL	32080	904-471-3744		671
Beacher's Lodge 6970 A1A S *TF:* 800-527-8849 ■ *Web:* www.beacherslodge.com	Saint Augustine	FL	32080	904-471-8849	471-3002	379
Beaches Restaurant & Bar 1919 SE Columbia River Dr *Web:* www.beachesrestaurantandbar.com	Vancouver	WA	98661	360-699-1592		671
Beachhead Solutions Inc 1955 The Alameda *Web:* www.beachheadsolutions.com	San Jose	CA	95126	408-496-6936		177
Beachwood Systems Consulting Inc 13315 Broadway Ave *Web:* www.beachsys.com	Cleveland	OH	44125	216-823-1800		194
Beacon Acctg Group LLC 10 Pidgeon Hill Dr Ste 110 *Web:* beaconaccountinggroup.com	Sterling	VA	20165	703-430-7666		2
Beacon Advanced Eye Care Center 1320 Shelfer St *Web:* www.beaconvisioncenter.com	Leesburg	FL	34748	352-728-8318		543
Beacon Application Services Corp 959 Concord St Ste 250 *TF:* 800-561-3357 ■ *Web:* www.beaconservices.com	Framingham	MA	01701	508-663-4433		41
Beacon Assoc Inc 900-A S Main St Ste 102 *Web:* www.beaconassociates.net	Bel Air	MD	21014	410-638-7279	638-7662	194
Beacon Consulting Group Inc 125 High St 25th Fl *Web:* www.beaconcgi.com	Boston	MA	02110	617-523-4030		354
Beacon Container Corp 700 W First St *TF:* 800-422-8383 ■ *Web:* www.beaconcontainer.com	Birdsboro	PA	19508	610-582-2222	582-3992	100
Beacon Credit Union PO Box 627 *TF:* 800-762-3136 ■ *Web:* www.beaconcu.org	Wabash	IN	46992	260-563-7443		219
Beacon Electric Supply 9630 Chesapeake Dr *Web:* www.beaconelectric.com	San Diego	CA	92123	858-279-9770	279-9908	246
Beacon Energy Services Inc 2685 Temple Ave *Web:* www.beaconenergyservices.com	Signal Hill	CA	90755	562-997-3087		261
Beacon Fasteners & Components 198 W Carpenter Ave *Web:* www.beaconfasteners.com	Wheeling	IL	60090	847-353-2000	541-1789	350
Beacon Financial Partners 25800 Science Park Dr Ste 100 *TF:* 866-568-3951 ■ *Web:* www.beaconplanners.com	Beachwood	OH	44122	216-910-1850		194
Beacon Health System 615 N Michigan St *TF:* 800-850-7913 ■ *Web:* www.qualityoflife.org	South Bend	IN	46601	574-647-1000	647-3670	374-3
Beacon Hill Financial Corp 120 Water St *Web:* www.beaconhillfinancial.com	Boston	MA	02109	617-973-6900		401
Beacon Hill Staffing Group LLC 152 Bowdoin St *Web:* www.beaconhillstaffing.com	Boston	MA	02108	617-326-4000	227-1220	631
Beacon Hotel 720 Ocean Dr *TF:* 877-674-8200 ■ *Web:* www.beaconsouthbeach.com	Miami Beach	FL	33139	305-674-8200		379
Beacon Hotel & Corporate Quarters 1615 Rhode Island Ave NW *TF:* 800-821-4367 ■ *Web:* www.beaconhotelwdc.com	Washington	DC	20036	202-296-2100		379
Beacon House 19 Myrtle St *Web:* rogerson.org	Boston	MA	02114	617-523-8295		372
Beacon House 1301 N Third St *TF:* 800-562-9753 ■ *Web:* www.upbeaconhouse.org	Marquette	MI	49855	906-225-7100	225-4903	372
Beacon Industries Inc 12300 Old Tesson Rd *TF:* 800-454-7159 ■ *Web:* www.beacontechnology.com	Saint Louis	MO	63128	314-487-7600	487-0100	21
Beacon Medaes 1800 Overview Dr *TF:* 888-463-3427 ■ *Web:* www.beaconmedaes.com	Rock Hill	SC	29730	803-817-5600		250
Beacon Occupational Health & Safety Services Inc 800 Cordova St *Web:* www.beaconohss.com	Anchorage	AK	99501	907-222-7612		194
Beacon Partnerships Inc PO Box 3801 *Web:* www.beaconpartnerships.com	Oakton	VA	22124	703-596-5220		463
Beacon Pointe Advisors LLC 500 Newport Ctr Dr Ste 125 *Web:* www.bpadvisors.com	Newport Beach	CA	92660	949-718-1600		401
Beacon Power Corp 65 Middlesex Rd	Tyngsboro	MA	01879	978-694-9121		253
Beacon Press Inc 24 Farnsworth St *TF:* 800-253-9646 ■ *Web:* www.beacon.org	Boston	MA	02210	617-742-2110	723-3097	637-2
Beacon Products LLC 2041 58th Ave Cir E *TF:* 800-345-4928 ■ *Web:* www.beaconproducts.com	Bradenton	FL	34203	800-345-4928		362
Beacon Rock State Park 34841 State Rd 14 *TF:* 888-226-7688 ■ *Web:* parks.state.wa.us/474/Beacon-Rock	Skamania	WA	98648	509-427-8265	427-8265	565

Name / Address	City	State	Zip	Phone	Fax	Class
Beacon Roofing Supply Inc 1 Lakeland Pk Dr	Peabody	MA	01960	978-535-7668		191-4
NASDAQ: BECN ■ *TF:* 877-645-7663 ■ *Web:* www.beaconroofingsupply.com						
Beacon Technologies Inc 1441 Donelson Pk	Nashville	TN	37217	615-301-5020		179
Web: beacontech.net						
Beacon Trust Co 163 Madison Ave Ste 600	Morristown	NJ	07960	973-377-8090		401
TF: 866-377-8090 ■ *Web:* www.beacontrust.com						
Beacon Wireless Solutions Inc 206 Laird Dr Ste 207	Toronto	ON	M4G3W5	416-696-7555		647
TF: 866-867-7770 ■ *Web:* www.beaconwireless.net						
Beacon, The 205 SE Catawba Rd Ste G	Port Clinton	OH	43452	419-732-2154	734-5382	532-4
TF: 800-521-2660 ■ *Web:* www.thebeacon.net						
Bead Bazaar USA Inc 687 Lofstrand Ln Ste H	Rockville	MD	20850	301-610-6022		411
Web: beadkit.com						
Bead Industries Inc 11 Cascade Blvd	Milford	CT	06460	203-301-0270	301-0280	487
TF: 800-297-4851 ■ *Web:* www.beadindustries.com						
Beadle County 450 Third St SW	Huron	SD	57350	605-353-8405		338
Web: beadle.sdcounties.org						
Beadles Lumber Company Inc 900 Sixth St NE PO Box 3457	Moultrie	GA	31776	229-985-6996		683
TF: 800-763-2400 ■ *Web:* www.beadleslumber.com						
Beaird Group 236 S Washington St	Naperville	IL	60540	630-637-0430		463
Web: www.beairdgroup.com						
Beal Bank SSB 6000 Legacy Dr	Plano	TX	75024	469-467-5000		70
Web: www.bealbank.com						
Beal College 99 Farm Rd	Bangor	ME	04401	207-947-4591	947-0208	800
TF: 800-660-7351 ■ *Web:* www.bealcollege.edu						
Beale Memorial Library 701 Truxtun Ave	Bakersfield	CA	93301	661-868-0701	868-0799	434-3
TF: 800-984-4636 ■ *Web:* www.kerncountylibrary.org						
Beale Street Historic District 203 Beale St Ste 300	Memphis	TN	38103	901-526-0115		50-6
Web: www.bealestreet.com						
Beall Corp 9200 N Ramsey Blvd	Portland	OR	97203	855-219-5686	289-3528*	779
**Fax Area Code:* 503 ■ *TF:* 855-219-5686 ■ *Web:* www.bealltrailers.com						
Beall Woods State Park 9285 Beall Woods Ave	Mount Carmel	IL	62863	618-298-2442		565
Web: www.dnr.illinois.gov/Parks/Pages/BeallWoods.aspx						
Beall's Inc 1806 38th Ave E	Bradenton	FL	34208	941-747-2355		229
Web: www.beallsinc.com						
Beals-Martin & Associates Inc 2596 Bay Rd Ste A	Redwood City	CA	94063	650-364-8141		187
TF: 800-879-7730 ■ *Web:* www.bealsmartin.com						
Beam 24 School St	Boston	MA	02108	617-523-0500		194
Web: www.beamland.com						
Beam Construction Company Inc 601 E Main St	Cherryville	NC	28021	704-435-3206	435-8412	685
Web: www.beamconstruction.com						
Beam Engineering For Advanced 809 S Orlando Ave	Winter Park	FL	32789	407-629-1282		261
Web: www.beamco.com						
Beam Inc 510 Lake Cook Rd	Deerfield	IL	60015	847-948-8888		80-1
Web: www.jimbeam.com						
Beam Industries 1700 W Second St	Webster City	IA	50595	515-832-4620		788
TF: 800-369-2326 ■ *Web:* www.beamvac.com						
Beam Mack Sales & Service Inc 2674 W Henrietta Rd	Rochester	NY	14623	585-424-4860		780
TF: 877-650-8789 ■ *Web:* www.beammack.com						
Beam, Longest & Neff LLC 8126 Castleton Rd	Indianapolis	IN	46250	317-849-5832		261
Web: www.b-l-n.com						
Beamers Hells Canyon Tours 1451 Bridge St	Clarkston	WA	99403	509-758-4800	758-3643	760
TF: 800-522-6966 ■ *Web:* www.hellscanyontours.com						
Beamie's 865 Reynolds St	Augusta	GA	30901	706-724-6593		671
BeamPines Inc 232 Madison Ave 10th Fl	New York	NY	10016	212-476-4100		194
Web: www.beampines.com						
Beamz Interactive Inc 15354 N 83rd Way Ste 101	Scottsdale	AZ	85260	480-424-2053		527
Web: thebeamz.com						
Bean, Kinney & Korman A Professional Corp 2300 Wilson Blvd The Navy League Bldg 7th Fl	Arlington	VA	22201	703-525-4000		428
TF: 800-926-7926 ■ *Web:* www.beankinney.com						
Beans & Barley 1901 E N Ave	Milwaukee	WI	53202	414-270-7070		671
Web: www.beansandbarley.com						
Beanstream Internet Commerce Inc 1803 Douglas St Ste 200	Victoria	BC	V8T5C3	888-472-2072	472-2330*	225
**Fax Area Code:* 250 ■ *TF:* 888-472-0811 ■ *Web:* www.beanstream.com						
Beantree Learning 43629 Greenway Corporate Dr	Ashburn	VA	20147	571-223-3110		685
Web: beantreelearning.com						
Bear Branch Elementary School 8909 Fm 1488 Rd	Magnolia	TX	77354	281-356-4771		685
Web: www.magnoliaisd.org						
Bear Brook State Park 157 Deerfield Rd	Allenstown	NH	03275	603-271-3556	271-3553	565
Web: www.nhstateparks.org						
Bear Butte State Park 20250 Hwy 79 PO Box 688	Sturgis	SD	57785	605-347-5240		565
Web: gfp.sd.gov/state-parks/directory/bear-butte						
Bear Cartage & Intermodal Inc 8600 Joliet Rd	Mccook	IL	60525	708-924-9093		314
TF: 800-561-3357 ■ *Web:* www.bearcartage.com						
Bear Cat Mfg Inc 3650 Sabin Brown Rd	Wickenburg	AZ	85390	928-684-7851		190
Web: www.bearcatmfg.com						
Bear Creek Lake State Park 22 Bear Creek Lake Rd	Cumberland	VA	23040	804-492-4410		565
TF: 800-933-7275 ■ *Web:* dcr.virginia.gov						
Bear Creek Mountain Resort 101 Doe Mtn Ln	Macungie	PA	18062	610-641-7101		378
TF: 866-754-2822 ■ *Web:* www.bcmountainresort.com						
Bear Creek Nature Ctr 245 Bear Creek Rd	Colorado Springs	CO	80906	719-520-6387	636-8968	50-5
Web: adm.elpasoco.com/parks						
Bear Forest Products Inc 4685 Brookhollow Cir	Riverside	CA	92509	951-727-1767		690
Web: www.bearforestproducts.com/home						
Bear Head Lake State Park 9301 Bear Head State Pk Rd	Ely	MN	55731	218-365-7229		565
Web: www.dnr.state.mn.us						
Bear Island Paper Company LLC 10026 Old Ridge Rd	Ashland	VA	23005	804-227-3394		557
Web: www.paperage.com						
Bear Lake County 7 E Ctr St PO Box 190	Paris	ID	83261	208-945-2212		338
Web: www.bearlakecounty.info						
Bear Lake State Park 1030 N Bear Lake Blvd	Garden City	UT	84028	435-946-3343		565
Web: www.stateparks.utah.gov						
Bear Mountain Golf Course 43101 Gold Mine Dr PO Box 77	Big Bear Lake	CA	92315	844-462-2327		669
TF: 844-462-2327 ■ *Web:* www.bigbearmountainresort.com						
Bear Mountain State Park Palisades Pkwy Rt 9W N	Bear Mountain	NY	10911	845-786-2701		565
Web: parks.ny.gov/parks/13/details.aspx						
Bear Mountain Trailside Museums & Zoo Bear Mtn State Pk Rt 9 W	Bear Mountain	NY	10911	845-786-2701		520
TF: 800-762-8687 ■ *Web:* www.trailsidezoo.org						
Bear Pond Books 77 Main St	Montpelier	VT	05602	802-229-0774		95
Web: www.bearpondbooks.com						
Bear River State Park 601 Bear River Dr	Evanston	WY	82930	307-789-6547		565
Bear Staffing Services Inc 47 S Broad St	Woodbury	NJ	08096	866-580-2327		260
TF: 866-580-2327 ■ *Web:* www.bearstaff.com						
Bear State Bank 600 Hwy 71 S	Mena	AR	71953	479-394-3838		70
Web: www.bearstatebank.com/home/home						
Bear Used Office Furniture 256 E Jericho Tpke	Mineola	NY	11501	516-741-7666		645-10
Web: www.computer-furniture.com						
BearCom Bldg Services 7022 S 400 W	Midvale	UT	84047	801-569-9500	569-8400	152
Web: bearcomservices.com						
Bearcom Inc 4009 Distribution Dr Ste 200	Garland	TX	75041	800-527-1670		246
TF Sales: 800-527-1670 ■ *Web:* www.bearcom.com						
Beard Implement Co 216 Frederick St	Arenzville	IL	62611	217-997-5514		274
TF: 800-626-6409 ■ *Web:* www.beardimplement.com						
Beard St Clair Gaffney PA 2105 Coronado St	Idaho Falls	ID	83404	208-523-5171		445
Web: www.beardstclair.com						
Bearden Antique Mall 310 Mohican St	Knoxville	TN	37919	865-584-1521		460
Beardsley Architects + Engineers 64 S St	Auburn	NY	13021	315-253-7301		256
Web: www.beardsley.com						
Beardsley Zoo 1875 Noble Ave	Bridgeport	CT	06610	203-394-6565		823
Web: www.beardsleyzoo.org						
Bearing Belt & Chain Inc 729 E Buckeye	Phoenix	AZ	85034	602-252-6541		770
Web: bbcarizona.com						
Bearing Distributors Inc 8000 Hub Pkwy	Cleveland	OH	44125	216-642-9100	642-9573	385
TF: 888-423-4872 ■ *Web:* www.bdi-usa.com						
Bearing Headquarters Co 2550 S 25th Ave	Broadview	IL	60155	708-681-4400	681-4462	385
Web: www.bearingheadquarters.com						
Bearing Inspection Inc 4500 Mt Pleasant NW	North Canton	OH	44720	234-262-3000		75
TF Cust Svc: 800-416-8881 ■ *Web:* www.timken.com						
Bearing Service & Supply Inc 1327 N Market	Shreveport	LA	71107	318-424-1447		791
Web: www.bearserco.com						
Bearing Service Co of Pennsylvania 630 Alpha Dr RIDC Park	Pittsburgh	PA	15238	412-963-7710	963-8005	75
TF: 800-783-2327 ■ *Web:* www.bearing-service.com						
Bearing Technologies Ltd 1141 Jaycox Rd	Avon	OH	44011	440-937-4770		247
Web: www.brgtec.com						
Bearings & Drives Inc 607 Lower Poplar St PO Box 4325	Macon	GA	31208	478-746-7623		385
Web: www.bdindustrial.com						
Bearings Ltd 2100 Pacific St	Hauppauge	NY	11788	631-273-8200		385
Web: www.bearingslimited.com						
Bearsch Compeau Knudson Architects & Engineers PC 41 Chenango St	Binghamton	NY	13901	607-772-0007		256
Web: www.bckpc.com						
Bearse Manufacturing Co 3815 W Cortland St	Chicago	IL	60647	773-235-8710	235-8716	67
Web: www.bearseusa.com						
Bearskin Airlines 1475 W Walsh St	Thunder Bay	ON	P7E4X6	807-577-1141		25
TF: 800-465-2327 ■ *Web:* www.bearskinairlines.com						
Beartooth Electric Co-op Inc 1306 N Broadway St PO Box 1110	Red Lodge	MT	59068	406-446-2310	446-3934	245
TF: 800-472-9821 ■ *Web:* beartoothec.coopwebbuilder2.com						
Beartown State Forest 69 Blue Hill Rd	Monterey	MA	01245	413-528-0904		565
Web: www.mass.gov						
Beartown State Park HC 64 PO Box 189	Hillsboro	WV	24946	304-653-4254	653-4254	565
TF General: 800-225-5982 ■ *Web:* www.beartownstatepark.com						
Beary Landscaping Inc 15001 W 159th St	Lockport	IL	60491	815-838-4100	838-3200	192
Web: bearylandscaping.com						
Beasley Allen Crow Methvin 218 Commerce St	Montgomery	AL	36104	334-269-2343		428
TF: 800-898-2034 ■ *Web:* www.beasleyallen.com						
Beasley Broadcast Group Inc 3033 Riviera Dr Ste 200	Naples	FL	34103	239-263-5000	263-8191	643
NASDAQ: BBGI ■ *Web:* www.bbgi.com						
Beasley Direct Marketing Inc 15227 Perry Ln	Morgan Hill	CA	95037	408-782-0046		225
Web: www.beasleydirect.com						

Entry	City	State	ZIP	Phone	Fax	Class
Beasley Forest Products Inc 712 Uvalda Hwy *Web:* www.beasleyforestproducts.com	Hazlehurst	GA	31539	912-375-5174		683
Beasley Heating & Air 57 Wc Beasley Ln	Coats	NC	27521	919-894-4248		189-10
Beasley Mitchell Co 509 S Main St Ste A *Web:* www.bmc-cpa.com	Las Cruces	NM	88004	575-528-6700		2
Beatitudes Campus of Care 1610 W Glendale Ave *TF:* 800-432-4040 ■ *Web:* beatitudescampus.org	Phoenix	AZ	85021	602-995-2611		672
Beatport LLC 2399 Blake St Ste 170 *Web:* www.beatport.com	Denver	CO	80205	720-974-9500		526
Beattie Farmers Union Cooperative Assn PO Box 79 *Web:* www.beattiecoop.com	Beattie	KS	66406	785-353-2237		48-2
Beatty Group International 9800 Beaverton Hillsdale Ste 105 *TF:* 800-285-6215 ■ *Web:* www.beattygroup.com	Beaverton	OR	97005	503-644-3340		384
Beatty Joyce (Rep D - OH) 133 Cannon HOB *Web:* beatty.house.gov	Washington	DC	20515	202-225-4324	225-1984	342-2
Beatty Machine & Mfg Company Inc 940 150th St *Web:* www.beattymachine.com	Hammond	IN	46327	219-931-3000	937-1662	456
Beatty Management Company Inc 6824 Elm St Ste 200 *Web:* www.beattycos.com	Mclean	VA	22101	703-821-0500		652
Beau Rivage Resort & Casino 875 Beach Blvd *TF:* 888-750-7111 ■ *Web:* www.beaurivage.com	Biloxi	MS	39530	228-386-7111	386-7414	669
Beauchamp Construction Co 2100 Ponce De Leon Blvd Ste 825 *Web:* www.beauchampco.com	Coral Gables	FL	33134	305-445-0819	447-0941	186
Beauchamp Distributing Co 1911 S Santa Fe Ave *Web:* www.beauchampdist.com	Compton	CA	90221	310-639-5320		81-1
Beaudin Le Prohon Inc 6171 Boul Bourque *Web:* www.leprohon.com	Sherbrooke	QC	J1N1H2	819-563-2454		610
Beaufort County 102 Ribaut Rd *Web:* www.co.beaufort.sc.us	Beaufort	SC	29902	843-255-5050		338
Beaufort County Board of Education 321 Smaw Rd *Web:* www.beaufort.k12.nc.us	Washington	NC	27889	252-946-6593		685
Beaufort County Community College 5337 Hwy 264 E **Fax:* Admissions ■ *Web:* beaufortccc.edu	Washington	NC	27889	252-946-6194	940-6393*	162
Beaufort County North Carolina 121 W Third St *Web:* www.co.beaufort.nc.us	Washington	NC	27889	252-946-0079	946-7722	338
Beaufort Memorial Hospital 955 Ribaut Rd *TF:* 877-532-6472 ■ *Web:* www.bmhsc.org	Beaufort	SC	29902	843-522-5200		374-3
Beaufort National Cemetery 1601 Boundary St *TF:* 800 273 8255 ■ *Web:* www.cem.va.gov	Beaufort	SC	29902	843-524-3925	524-8538	136
Beaufort-Jasper Water & Sewer Authority 6 Snake Rd *Web:* www.bjwsa.org	Okatie	SC	29909	843-987-9200		806
Beaufurn LLC 5269 US Hwy 158 *TF:* 888-766-7706 ■ *Web:* www.beaufurn.com	Advance	NC	27006	888-766-7706		321
Beaujolais Bistro 753 Riverside Dr *Web:* www.beaujolaisbistro.com	Reno	NV	89503	775-323-2227		671
Beaulieu of America Inc 1502 Coronet Dr PO Box 1248 *TF:* 800-227-7211 ■ *Web:* usa.beaulieuflooring.com	Dalton	GA	30722	800-227-7211		131
Beaulieu Vineyard 1960 St Helena Hwy *TF:* 800-373-5896 ■ *Web:* www.bvwines.com	Rutherford	CA	94573	707-967-5233		80-3
Beaumont at Bryn Mawr 601 N Ithan Ave *Web:* www.beaumontretirement.com	Bryn Mawr	PA	19010	610-526-7000	525-0293	672
Beaumont Chamber of Commerce 1110 Pk St *Web:* www.bmtcoc.org	Beaumont	TX	77701	409-838-6581	833-6718	139
Beaumont Chamber of Commerce 726 Beaumont Ave *Web:* www.beaumontcachamber.com	Beaumont	CA	92223	951-845-9541	769-9080	139
Beaumont Civic Ctr Complex 701 Main St *TF:* 800-782-3081 ■ *Web:* www.discoverbeaumont.com	Beaumont	TX	77701	409-838-3435		205
Beaumont Convention & Visitors Bureau 505 Willow St *TF:* 800-392-4401 ■ *Web:* www.beaumontcvb.com	Beaumont	TX	77701	409-880-3749		206
Beaumont Enterprise 380 Main St *Web:* www.beaumontenterprise.com	Beaumont	TX	77701	409-838-2888	880-0757	532-2
Beaumont Juvenile Correctional Ctr 3500 Beaumont Rd	Beaumont	VA	23014	804-556-3316		412
Beaumont Library District 125 E Eigth St	Beaumont	CA	92223	951-845-1357		434-3
Beaumont Public Library System 801 Pearl St *TF:* 800-633-9363 ■ *Web:* beaumonttexas.gov/departments/library	Beaumont	TX	77701	409-838-6606	838-6838	434-3
Beaumont Rice Mills Inc 1800 Pecos St *Web:* bmtricemills.com	Beaumont	TX	77701	409-832-2521	832-6927	296-23
Beaumont School 3301 N Park Blvd *Web:* www.beaumontschool.org	Cleveland Heights	OH	44118	216-321-2954		685
Beauregard Electric Co-op Inc 1010 E First St *TF:* 800-367-0275 ■ *Web:* www.beci.org	DeRidder	LA	70634	337-463-6221	463-2809	245
Beauregard Parish PO Box 100 *Web:* beauregardclerk.org	DeRidder	LA	70634	337-463-8595	462-3916	338
Beauregard Parish Library 205 S Washington Ave *TF:* 800-524-6239 ■ *Web:* www.library.beau.org	DeRidder	LA	70634	337-463-6217	462-5434	434-3
Beauregard-Keyes House 1113 Chartres St *Web:* bkhouse.org	New Orleans	LA	70116	504-523-7257	523-7257	50-3
Beaute Craft Supply Co 600 W Maple Rd	Troy	MI	48084	248-362-0400		76
BeautiControl Inc 2121 Midway Rd PO Box 815189 **Fax Area Code:* 972 ■ **Fax:* Sales ■ *TF:* 800-232-8841 ■ *Web:* shop.beauticontrol.com	Carrollton	TX	75006	800-232-8841	960-7923*	214
Beautiful Restaurant, The 2260 Cascade Rd SW *Web:* www.beautifulrestaurant-atlanta.com	Atlanta	GA	30311	404-752-5931	758-4767	671
Beauti-Vue Products Inc 8555 194th Ave **Fax Area Code:* 800 ■ *TF:* 800-558-9431 ■ *Web:* www.beautivue.com	Bristol	WI	53104	262-857-2306	329-9431*	87
Beauty Bar LLC 2919 W Central Ave *Web:* www.beauty-bar.com	Toledo	OH	43606	419-537-5400		77
Beauty Brands Inc 4600 Madison St Ste 400 *TF:* 877-640-2248 ■ *Web:* www.beautybrands.com	Kansas City	MO	64112	816-531-2266		77
Beauty Collection Inc 7862 Burnet Ave *Web:* beautycollection.com	Van Nuys	CA	91405	818-785-7447		77
Beauty Craft Supply & Equipment Co 11110 Bren Rd W *TF:* 800-328-5010 ■ *Web:* www.beautycraft.com	Minnetonka	MN	55343	952-935-4420		77
Beauty Management Inc 270 Beavercreek Rd *Web:* www.perfectlooksalons.com	Oregon City	OR	97045	503-723-3200		77
Beauty Schools of America 1176 SW 67 Ave *Web:* www.bsa.edu	Miami	FL	33144	305-824-2070		77
Beauvais Manor On The Park 3625 Magnolia Ave *Web:* www.beauvaismanor.com	Saint Louis	MO	63110	314-771-2990		672
Beaver Aerospace & Defense Inc 11850 Mayfield St *Web:* www.beaver-online.com	Livonia	MI	48150	734-853-5003	853-5043	223
Beaver County PO Box 338 *Web:* www.okcounties.org	Beaver	OK	73932	580-625-3151		338
Beaver County 810 Third St Courthouse *Web:* www.beavercountypa.gov	Beaver	PA	15009	724-728-5700		338
Beaver County 105 E Ctr St PO Box 1013 *Web:* beaver.utah.gov	Beaver	UT	84713	435-438-6490	438-6462	338
Beaver County Chamber of Commerce 798 Turnpike St *TF:* 800-756-9161 ■ *Web:* beavercountychamber.com	Beaver	PA	15009	724-775-3944	728-9737	139
Beaver County Times 400 Fair Ave **Fax:* Edit ■ *Web:* www.timesonline.com	Beaver	PA	15009	724-775-3200	775-4180*	532-2
Beaver Creek Cooperative Telephone Co 15223 Henrici Rd *Web:* www.bctelco.com	Oregon City	OR	97045	503-632-3113		387
Beaver Creek Lodge 26 Avon Dale Ln *TF:* 800-525-7280 ■ *Web:* www.beavercreeklodge.net	Beaver Creek	CO	81620	970-845-9800	845-8242	379
Beaver Creek Nature Area 48351 264th St *TF:* 800-710-2267 ■ *Web:* gfp.sd.gov	Valley Springs	SD	57068	605-223-7660	773-6245	565
Beaver Creek State Park 12021 Echo Dell Rd *Web:* www.ohiodnr.com	East Liverpool	OH	43920	330-385-3091		565
Beaver Creek Valley State Park 15954 County Rd 1 *Web:* www.dnr.state.mn.us	Caledonia	MN	55921	507-724-2107	724-2107	565
Beaver Dam Community Hospital 707 S University Ave *Web:* www.bdch.com	Beaver Dam	WI	53916	920-887-7181	887-7973	374-3
Beaver Dam State Park 14548 Beaver Dam Ln *Web:* www.dnr.illinois.gov/parks/pages/beaverdam.aspx	Plainview	IL	62685	217-854-8020		565
Beaver Dam State Park PO Box 985 *Web:* www.parks.nv.gov	Caliente	NV	89008	775-728-4460		565
Beaver Dunes State Park Hwy 270 N *TF:* 800-654-8240 ■ *Web:* www.travelok.com	Beaver	OK	73932	580-625-3373		565
Beaver Express Service LLC 4310 Oklahoma Ave PO Box 1147 *TF:* 800-593-2328 ■ *Web:* www.beaverexpress.com	Woodward	OK	73802	580-256-6460	256-6239	780
Beaver Island State Park 2136 W Oakfield Rd *Web:* parks.ny.gov/parks/56/details.aspx	Grand Island	NY	14072	716-773-3271		565
Beaver Lake Nature Ctr 8477 E Mud Lake Rd *Web:* www.onondagacountyparks.com	Baldwinsville	NY	13027	315-638-2519	638-7488	50-5
Beaver Lake State Park 3850 70th St SE *Web:* www.parkrec.nd.gov/parks/blsp/blsp.html	Wishek	ND	58495	701-452-2752		565
Beaver Mfg Company Inc 12 Ed Needham Dr *Web:* www.beaverloc.com	Mansfield	GA	30055	770-786-1622		548
Beaver Run Resort & Conference Ctr 620 Village Rd *TF:* 800-525-2253 ■ *Web:* www.beaverrun.com	Breckenridge	CO	80424	970-453-6000		669
Beaver Steel Services Inc 1200 Arch St *Web:* www.beaversteel.com	Carnegie	PA	15106	412-429-8860		492
Beaver Street Brewery 11 S Beaver St *TF:* 800-450-9535 ■ *Web:* www.beaverstreetbrewery.com	Flagstaff	AZ	86001	928-779-0079		671
Beaver Street Fisheries Inc 1741 W Beaver St *TF:* 800-874-6426 ■ *Web:* beaverstreetfisheries.com	Jacksonville	FL	32209	904-354-8533		296-13
Beavercreek Board of Education 3040 Kemp Rd *Web:* www.beavercreek.k12.oh.us	Dayton	OH	45431	937-426-1522	429-7517	685
Beavercreek Chamber of Commerce 3210 Beaver-Vu Dr *TF:* 800-698-3120 ■ *Web:* www.beavercreekchamber.org	Beavercreek	OH	45431	937-426-2202	426-2204	139
Beaverhead County 2 S Pacific St Ste 16 *TF:* 800-346-5437 ■ *Web:* www.beaverheadcounty.org	Dillon	MT	59725	406-683-3700	683-3728	338
Beaverhead Rock State Park c/o Bannack State Pk 4200 Bannack Rd *Web:* stateparks.mt.gov	Dillon	MT	59725	406-834-3413		565

	Phone	Fax	Class
Beavers Bend Resort Park PO Box 10 Broken Bow OK 74728 *TF:* 800-435-5514 ■ *Web:* www.beaversbend.com	580-494-6300		565
Beavertail Hill State Park 3201 Spurgin Rd FWP Reg 2 Ofc Missoula MT 59804 *Web:* stateparks.mt.gov	406-542-5500		565
Beaverton Area Chamber of Commerce 12655 SW Ctr St Ste 140 Beaverton OR 97005 *Web:* www.beaverton.org	503-644-0123	526-0349	139
Beaverton City Library 12375 SW Fifth St Beaverton OR 97005 *Web:* www.beavertonlibrary.org	503-644-2197		434-3
Beaverton Foods Inc 7100 NW Century Blvd Hillsboro OR 97124 *TF:* 800-223-8076 ■ *Web:* www.beavertonfoods.com	503-646-8138		296-19
Beavertooth Oak Inc 401 S Fir St Medford OR 97501 *TF:* 800-306-1942 ■ *Web:* www.beavertooth.net	541-779-1942		191-3
Beavertown Block Company Inc 3612 Paxtonville Rd Middleburg PA 17842 *TF:* 800-597-2565 ■ *Web:* www.beavertownblock.net	570-837-1744	837-1591	183
Beazer Homes USA Inc 1000 Abernathy Rd Ste 1200 Atlanta GA 30328 *NYSE: BZH* ■ *Web:* www.beazer.com	770-829-3700		653
Beazley 30 Batterson Park Rd Farmington CT 06032 *Web:* www.beazley.com	860-677-3700		390
Beb Software Systems 1806 Swift Ave Ste 200 Kansas City MO 64116 *TF:* 800-660-5241 ■ *Web:* www.bebsoft.com	816-452-4222		179
Bebco Industries Inc 4725 Lawndale La Marque TX 77568 *Web:* www.okbebco.com	409-935-5743		106
bebe stores Inc 400 Valley Dr Brisbane CA 94005 *NASDAQ: BEBE* ■ *TF:* 877-232-3777 ■ *Web:* www.bebe.com	415-715-3900		155-21
Beber Silverstein Group 89 NE 27th St Unit 119 Miami FL 33137 *Web:* www.thinkbsg.com	305-856-9800		7
Bec Legal Systems 175 Tri County Pkwy Ste 120 Cincinnati OH 45246 *Web:* www.beclegal.com	513-948-1500		180
Becerra Xavier (Rep D - CA) 1226 Longworth Bldg Washington DC 20515 *Web:* becerra.house.gov	202-225-6235		342-2
Becharas Bros Coffee Co Inc 14501 Hamilton Ave Highland Park MI 48203 *TF:* 800-944-9675 ■ *Web:* www.becharas.com	313-869-4700	869-7940	297-2
Bechdon Company Inc, The 300 Commerce Dr Upper Marlboro MD 20774 *Web:* www.bechdon.com	301-249-0900		454
Becherer Kannett & Schweitzer The Water Tower 1255 Powell St Emeryville CA 94608 *Web:* bkscal.com	510-658-3600		428
Becher-Hoppe Associates Inc 330 Fourth St Wausau WI 54403 *Web:* www.becherhoppe.com	715-845-8000		261
Bechik Products Inc 860 Blue Gentian Rd Ste 140 Eagan MN 55121 *TF:* 800-328-6569 ■ *Web:* www.bechik.com	651-698-0364	698-1009	471
Becht Engineering Company Inc 22 Church St PO Box 300 Liberty Corner NJ 07938 *Web:* www.becht.com	908-580-1119		256
Bechta Group Ltd 1001 17th St Ste 1210 Denver CO 80202 *Web:* bglfc.com	303-860-0990		271
Bechtel Corp 50 Beale St San Francisco CA 94105 *Web:* www.bechtel.com	415-768-1234	768-9038	261
Bechtel North America 3000 Post Oak Blvd Houston TX 77056 *Web:* www.bechtel.com	713-235-2000	960-9031	261
Bechtel Petroleum & Chemical 3000 Post Oak Blvd Houston TX 77056 *Web:* www.bechtel.com	713-235-2000		188-9
Beck & Hofer Construction Inc 618 E Maple St Sioux Falls SD 57104 *Web:* beckandhofer.com	605-336-0118		186
Beck Aluminum Corp 300 Allen Bradley Dr Mayfield Heights OH 44124 *Web:* www.beckaluminum.com	216-861-4455		492
Beck and Tysver Pllc 2900 Thomas Ave S Ste 100 Minneapolis MN 55416 *Web:* bitlaw.com	612-915-9633		445
Beck Cultural Exchange Ctr Inc 1927 Dandridge Ave Knoxville TN 37915 *TF:* 800-845-5665 ■ *Web:* beckcenter.net	865-524-8461	524-8462	50-2
Beck Group, The 1807 Ross Ave Ste 500 Dallas TX 75201 *TF:* 800-864-7717 ■ *Web:* www.beckgroup.com	214-303-6200	303-6300	186
Beck Mack & Oliver LLC 360 Madison Ave 18th Fl New York NY 10017 *Web:* www.beckmack.com	212-661-2640		401
Beck Mfg 330 E Ninth St Waynesboro PA 17268 *Web:* www.beckmfg.com	717-762-9141	762-9153	595
Beck Oil Co 3345 Main St Keokuk IA 52632 *Web:* www.beckoilco.com	319-524-9237		324
Beck Paul Associates pa 12 Kulick Rd Fairfield NJ 07004 *TF:* 800-989-5525 ■ *Web:* www.pbanj.com	973-276-1700		261
Beck Suppliers Inc 1000 N Frnt St Fremont OH 43420 *TF:* 800-648-0357 ■ *Web:* www.beckoil.com	419-332-5527		581
Beck/Arnley Worldparts Inc 2375 Midway Ln Smyrna TN 37167 *Web:* www.beckarnley.com	615-220-3200		54
Beckart Environmental Inc 6900 46th St Kenosha WI 53144 *Web:* beckart.com	262-656-7680		261
Becker & Mayer! Ltd 11120 NE 33rd Pl # 101 Bellevue WA 98004 *Web:* www.beckermayer.com	425-827-7120	828-9659	94
Becker Arena Products Inc 6611 W Hwy 13 Savage MN 55378 *TF:* 800-234-5522 ■ *Web:* www.beckerarena.com	952-890-2690		186
Becker Avionics Inc 10376 Usa Today Way Miramar FL 33025 *Web:* www.becker-avionics.com	954-450-3137		57
Becker Bros Inc 401 Main St Ste 110 Peoria IL 61602 *Web:* bccinc.net	309-674-1200	674-5454	186
Becker Capital Management Inc 1211 S W Fifth Ave Ste 2185 Portland OR 97204 *TF:* 800-551-3998 ■ *Web:* www.beckercap.com	503-223-1720		401
Becker College 61 Sever St Worcester MA 01609 **Fax: Admissions* ■ *TF:* 877-523-2537 ■ *Web:* www.becker.edu	508-791-9241	890-1500*	166
Becker Communications 119 Merchant St Ste 300 Honolulu HI 96813 *Web:* www.beckercommunications.com	808-533-4165	537-4990	637-9
Becker County 915 Lake Ave Detroit Lakes MN 56501 **Fax: Acctg* ■ *TF:* 800-438-0576 ■ *Web:* www.co.becker.mn.us	218-846-7311	846-7257*	338
Becker Electric Supply Inc 1341 E Fourth St Dayton OH 45402 *TF:* 800-762-9515 ■ *Web:* www.beckerelectric.com	937-226-1341	226-1790	246
Becker Media 144 Linden St Ste 110 Oakland CA 94607 *Web:* www.beckermedia.net	510-465-6200		195
Becker Transportation Inc 1501 S Bulington Ave Hastings NE 68901	402-461-4454		314
Becker"s ASC Review 35 E Wacker Dr Ste 1782 Chicago IL 60601 *TF:* 800-417-2035 ■ *Web:* www.beckersasc.com	800-417-2035		194
Beckerman & Co 430 Lake Ave Colonia NJ 07067 *Web:* www.beckermanco.com	732-499-9200		390
Beckers Tax Service & Financial Management Company Inc 5625 Cypress Creek Pkwy Ste 321 Houston TX 77069 *TF:* 800-209-2974 ■ *Web:* tenfortyplus.com	281-397-7777		226
Becket & Lee LLP 16 General Warren Blvd Malvern PA 19355 *Web:* www.becket-lee.com	610-644-7800		428
Becket Fund for Religious Liberty 1350 Connecticut Ave NW Ste 605 Washington DC 20036 *Web:* www.becketlaw.org	202-955-0095	955-0090	48-8
Beckett Air Inc 37850 Beckett Pkwy North Ridgeville OH 44039 *TF:* 800-831-7839 ■ *Web:* www.beckettair.com	440-327-9999	327-3569	18
Beckett Corp 3250 Skyway Cir N Irving TX 75038 *TF:* 888-232-5388 ■ *Web:* www.beckettpumps.com	972-871-8000	871-8888	641
Beckett Fine Art Ltd 33 Hazelton Ave Ste 212 Toronto ON M5R2E3 *Web:* www.beckettfineart.com	416-922-5582		42
Beckett Football Card Monthly 4635 McEwen Rd Dallas TX 75244 *Web:* www.beckett.com	972-991-6657	991-8930	457-20
Beck-Ford Construction LP 6750 MayaRd Rd Houston TX 77041 *Web:* www.beck-ford.com	713-896-7774	937-1942	360-2
Beckham County PO Box 67 Sayre OK 73662 *Web:* beckham.okcounties.org	580-928-2457	928-2467	338
Beckley Appalachian Regional Hospital 306 Stanaford Rd Beckley WV 25801 *Web:* www.arh.org	304-255-3000		374-3
Beckley-Raleigh County Chamber of Commerce 245 N Kanawha St Beckley WV 25801 *TF:* 877-987-3847 ■ *Web:* www.brccc.com	304-252-7328	252-7373	139
Beckman & Gast Company Inc 282 W Kremer-Hoying Rd PO Box 307 Saint Henry OH 45883 *Web:* www.beckmangast.com	419-678-4195		296-20
Beckman Coulter Genomics 36 Cherry Hill Dr Danvers MA 01923 *Web:* www.beckmangenomics.com	978-867-2600		231
Beckman Production Services Inc 3786 Beebe Rd Kalkaska MI 49646 *Web:* www.beckmanproduction.com	231-258-9524		539
Beckmann Converting Inc 14 Pk Dr Amsterdam NY 12010 *TF:* 800-777-1667 ■ *Web:* www.beckmannconverting.com	518-842-0073	842-0282	745-2
Beckmann's Old World Bakery Ltd 104 Bronson St Ste 6 Santa Cruz CA 95062 *Web:* www.beckmannsbakery.com	831-423-9242		345
Beckmanxmo 376 Morrison Rd Columbus OH 43213 *TF:* 800-864-2232 ■ *Web:* beckmanxmo.com	614-864-2232	864-3305	627
Beckmill Research LLC 108 Deer Dr Lexington VA 24450 *Web:* beckmill.com	540-463-6200		196
Becknell Wholesale Co 504 E 44th St Lubbock TX 79404 *Web:* www.becknell.com	806-747-3201		350
Becks Bookstores Inc 4520 N Broadway Chicago IL 60640 *Web:* www.becksbooks.com	773-784-7963	784-0066	95
Becks Furniture Inc 11840 Folsom Blvd Rancho Cordova CA 95742 *Web:* www.becksfurniture.com	916 353 5000		321
Beckta Dining & Wine 150 Elgin St Ottawa ON K2P1L4 *Web:* www.beckta.com	613-238-7063		671
Beco Concrete Products Inc 4855 New Baumgartner Rd St. Louis MO 63129	314-892-7400		183
Beco Equipment Co 5555 Dahlia St Commerce CO 80022 *Web:* www.becoequipment.com	303-288-2613	288-5776	264-3
Beco Management Inc 5410 Edson Ln Ste 200 Rockville MD 20852 *Web:* beconet.com	301-816-1500	816-1501	652
Be-Cool Inc 310 Woodside Ave Essexville MI 48732 *TF:* 800-691-2667 ■ *Web:* www.becool.com	989-895-9699		612
BECS Technology Inc 9487 Dielman Rock Island Industrial Dr Saint Louis MO 63132 *Web:* www.becs.com	314-567-0088		201
Becterm Inc 4780 Boul Henri-bourassa Quebec QC G1H3A7 *Web:* becterm.com	418-622-6777		196
Becton Dickinson & Co 1 Becton Dr Franklin Lakes NJ 07417 *NYSE: BDX* ■ *TF Cust Svc:* 888-237-2762 ■ *Web:* www.bd.com	201-847-6800		477
Becton Healthcare Resources Inc 5674 Stoneridge Dr Ste 116 Pleasanton CA 94588 *Web:* www.bhrcorp.org	925-520-0005		194
Bed & Breakfast Assn of Downtown Toronto PO Box 190 Stn B Toronto ON M5T2W1 *Web:* www.bnbinfo.com	416-410-3938	483-8822	376
Bed & Breakfast Atlanta 790 N Ave Ste 202 Atlanta GA 30306 *TF:* 800-967-3224 ■ *Web:* www.bedandbreakfastatlanta.com	404-875-0525	876-6544	376

	Phone	Fax	Class
Bed & Breakfast Cape Cod PO Box 2250....... Mashpee MA 02649 *TF:* 800-556-3815 ■ *Web:* www.bookcapecod.com	508-255-3824		376
Bed Bath & Beyond Inc 650 Liberty Ave...........Union NJ 07083 *NASDAQ: BBBY* ■ *TF:* 800-462-3966 ■ *Web:* www.bedbathandbeyond.com	908-688-0888		362
Bed Wood & Parts LLC 8345 Madisonville Rd....................Hopkinsville KY 42240 *TF:* 877-206-9663 ■ *Web:* bedwoodandparts.com	270-424-3000		57
BedandBreakfast.com 700 Brazos St Ste B-700....................... Austin TX 78701 *TF Sales:* 800-462-2632 ■ *Web:* www.bedandbreakfast.com	512-322-2700	320-0883	773
Bedco Inc 4600 Bree Rd.................... East China MI 48054 *Web:* www.bedcoinc.com	810-329-2292	329-4017	456
Bedell Frazier Investment Counselling LLC 2 Walnut Creek Ctr 200 Pringle Ave Ste 555.................................Walnut Creek CA 94596 *Web:* www.bedellinvest.com	925-932-0344		401
Beden-Baugh Products Inc 105 Lisbon Rd .... Laurens SC 29360 *TF:* 866-598-5794 ■ *Web:* www.naclsolutions.com	864-682-3136		199
Bederson LLP 347 Mt Pleasant Ave.......... West Orange NJ 07052 *Web:* www.bederson.com	973-736-3333		734
Bedford Area Chamber of Commerce 305 E Main St.............................. Bedford VA 24523 *TF:* 800-828-1120 ■ *Web:* www.bedfordareachamber.com	540-586-9401		139
Bedford Consulting Group Inc 145 Adelaide St W Ste 400.................... Toronto ON M5H4E5 *Web:* www.bedfordgroup.com	416-963-9000		193
Bedford County 200 S Juliana St .... Bedford PA 15522 *Web:* www.bedfordcountypa.org	814-623-4807	623-4831	338
Bedford County 100 N Cannon Blvd...........Shelbyville TN 37160 *Web:* www.shelbyvilletn.com	931-684-3482	684-3483	338
Bedford County Chamber of Commerce 125 South Juliana St .... Bedford PA 15522 *Web:* bedfordcountychamber.com	814-623-2233	623-6089	139
Bedford County Visitors Bureau 131 S Juliana St............................ Bedford PA 15522 *TF:* 800-765-3331 ■ *Web:* www.visitbedfordcounty.com	814-623-1771	623-1671	206
Bedford Court 3701 International Dr ....Silver Spring MD 20906 *Web:* www.sunriseseniorliving.com	301-598-2900		672
Bedford Gazette 424 W Penn St................ Bedford PA 15522 *TF:* 800-242-4250 ■ *Web:* www.bedfordgazette.com	814-623-1151		532-3
Bedford Hills Correctional Facility 247 Harris Rd ....Bedford Hills NY 10507 *Web:* www.doccs.ny.gov/faclist.html	914-241-3100		213
Bedford (Independent City) 215 E Main St.............................. Bedford VA 24523 *Web:* www.bedfordva.gov/reversion.shtml	540-587-6001		338
Bedford Industries Inc 1659 Rowe Ave..........................Worthington MN 56187 *TF Cust Svc:* 877-233-3673 ■ *Web:* bedford.com	507-376-4136	376-6742	548
Bedford Laboratories Inc 300 Northfield Rd .... Bedford OH 44146 *TF:* 800-562-4797	440-232-3320	232-6264	479
Bedford Machine & Tool Inc 2103 John Williams Blvd .... Bedford IN 47421 *TF:* 800-264-1948 ■ *Web:* www.bedfordmachine.com	812-275-1948		491
Bedford Management Co 196 Bedford Ave........................... Brooklyn NY 11249 *Web:* bedfordmanagement.com	718-388-0025		463
Bedford Materials Co Inc 7676 Allegheny Rd.....................Manns Choice PA 15550 *Fax Area Code: 814 ■ *TF:* 800-773-4276 ■ *Web:* www.bedfordmaterials.com	800-773-4276	623-9199*	816
Bedford Precision Inc 12704 NE 124th St #49 ....Kirkland WA 98034 *Web:* www.bedfordprecision.com	425-823-9700		454
Bedford Public Library 1323 K St.............. Bedford IN 47421 *TF:* 800-382-9841 ■ *Web:* www.bedlib.org	812-275-4471		434-3
Bedford Public Schools 1623 W Sterns Rd........................ Temperance MI 48182 *Web:* www.bedford.k12.mi.us	734-850-6000	850-6099	685
Bedford Recycling Cener 904 Summit Ln .... Bedford IN 47421 *Web:* www.bedfordrecycling.com	812-275-6883		492
Bedford Reinforced Plastics Inc 264 Reynoldsdale Rd .... Bedford PA 15522 *Web:* www.bedfordplastics.com	814-623-8125		596
Bedford Road Pharmacy Inc 11306 Bedford Rd NE.....................Cumberland MD 21502 *TF:* 800-788-6693 ■ *Web:* www.pharmacareofcumberland.com	301-777-1771	777-0119	238
Bedford Rural Electric Co-op Inc 8846 Lincoln Hwy........................... Bedford PA 15522 *TF:* 800-808-2732 ■ *Web:* www.bedfordrec.com	814-623-5101	623-7983	245
Bedford Technology LLC 2424 Armour Rd PO Box 609..............Worthington MN 56187 *TF:* 800-721-9037 ■ *Web:* plasticboards.com	507-372-5558	372-5726	661
Bedford Underwriters Ltd 315 E Mill St.............................Plymouth WI 53073 *Web:* bedfordunderwriters.com	920-892-8795		390
Bedford Village Inn 2 Olde Bedford Way .... Bedford NH 03110 *TF:* 800-852-1166 ■ *Web:* www.bedfordvillageinn.com	603-472-2001		671
Bedford-Stuyvesant Community Legal Services Corp 1368 Fulton St .... Brooklyn NY 11216 *Web:* www.restorationplaza.org	718-636-6900		41
Bedoukian Research Inc 21 Finance Dr.........Danbury CT 06810 *Web:* www.bedoukian.com	203-830-4000	830-4010	145
Bedroc Inc 3351 Aspen Grove Dr Ste 350 ....Franklin TN 37067 *TF:* 800-217-5420 ■ *Web:* www.bedroc.com	615-815-1785		631
Bedrock International LLC 9929 Lackman Rd............................Lenexa KS 66219 *Web:* www.kcstone.com	913-438-7625		191-1
Bedrock Prime 1309 N Wilson Rd Ste A.......... Radcliff KY 40160 *TF:* 866-334-5914 ■ *Web:* www.bedrockprime.com	270-351-8043		177
Bedroom Store Inc 2440 Adie Rd .... Maryland Heights MO 63043 *Web:* www.thebedroomstore.com	314-822-2617		321
BeDynamic Inc 1725 Westlake Ave N Ste 150................... Seattle WA 98109 *Web:* bedynamic.com	206-458-6950		132
Bee County Chamber of Commerce 1705 N St Mary .... Beeville TX 78102 *Web:* www.beecountychamber.org	361-358-3267		139
Bee Steel Inc 2090 Celebration Dr Ste 209 ....Grand Rapids MI 49525 *Web:* www.beesteelinc.com	616-363-6694		492
Bee Trucking Inc 9540 Ball St ....San Antonio TX 78217	210-646-7211		780
Bee-alive Inc 151 N Rte 9 W...................Congers NY 10920 *TF:* 800-543-2337 ■ *Web:* www.beealive.com	800-543-2337		231
Beebe Medical Ctr 424 Savannah Rd............ Lewes DE 19958 *Web:* beebehealthcare.org	302-645-3300		374-3
Beech Fork State Park 5601 Long Branch Rd....................Barboursville WV 25504 *Web:* www.beechforksp.com	304-528-5794		565
Beecher Hill LLC 9991 Beecher Hill Rd ....Peshastin WA 98847 *TF:* 866-414-0559 ■ *Web:* beecherhill.com	509-548-0559		379
Beecher Investors Inc 1266 E Main St Ste 700R .... Stamford CT 06902 *Web:* www.beecherinvestors.com	203-539-6281		401
Beech-Nut Nutrition Corp 1 Nutritious Pl .... Amsterdam NY 12010 *TF:* 800-233-2468 ■ *Web:* www.beechnut.com	800-233-2468		296-36
Beechwood Hotel 363 Plantation St...........Worcester MA 01605 *TF:* 800-344-2589 ■ *Web:* www.beechwoodhotel.com	508-754-5789		379
Beecken Petty O'Keefe & Co 131 S Dearborn St Ste 2800...................Chicago IL 60603 *Web:* www.bpoc.com	312-435-0300		792
Beed's Lake State Park 1422 165th St Pk .... Hampton IA 50441 *Web:* www.iowadnr.gov	641-456-2047		565
Beef Belt Feeders Inc 1350 E Rd 70...........Scott City KS 67871	620-872-3059		10-1
Beef Magazine 7900 International Dr Ste 300...............Minneapolis MN 55425 *TF Cust Svc:* 800-722-5334 ■ *Web:* beefmagazine.com	952-851-9329	851-4601	457-1
Beef Northwest Feeders Inc 3455 Victorio Rd.............................Nyssa OR 97913 *Web:* www.beefnw.com	541-372-2101	372-5661	10-1
Beef O'Bradys Inc 5660 W Cypress St Ste A...................... Tampa FL 33607 *TF:* 800-728-8878 ■ *Web:* www.beefobradys.com	813-226-2333		670
Beef Products Inc 891 Two Rivers Dr...................... Dakota Dunes SD 57049 *Web:* www.beefproducts.com	605-217-8000	217-8001	296-26
Beefeaters Inc 1110 Brickell Ave Ste 302.......... Miami FL 33131 *Web:* beefeaters.com	305-967-8826		366
Beefmaster Breeders United (BBU) 6800 Pk Ten Blvd Ste 290-W ....San Antonio TX 78213 *Web:* www.beefmasters.org	210-732-3132	732-7711	48-2
Beehive Botanicals Inc 16297 W Nursery Rd ....Hayward WI 54843 *TF:* 800-233-4483 ■ *Web:* www.beehivebotanicals.com	715-634-4274		799
Beehive Specialty Co 8701 Wall St Ste 900 .... Austin TX 78754 *TF:* 866-898-8774 ■ *Web:* www.beehivespecialty.com	512-912-7940	997-7944	4
Beekley Corp 1 Prestige Ln..................... Bristol CT 06010 *TF:* 800-233-5539 ■ *Web:* www.beekley.com	860-583-4700		476
Beekman Arms-delamater Inn Inc 6387 Mill St............................. Rhinebeck NY 12572 *TF:* 800-222-2909 ■ *Web:* www.beekmandelamaterinn.com	845-876-7077		707
Beelman Truck Co 1 Racehorse Dr......................East Saint Louis IL 62205 *TF Sales:* 800-541-5918 ■ *Web:* www.beelman.com	618-646-5300		780
Beemac Trucking 2747 Litionville Rd...........Ambridge PA 15003 *TF:* 800-282-8781 ■ *Web:* beemactrucking.com	724-266-8781	266-5638	685
Beemer Precision Inc 230 New York Dr PO Box 3080.......... Fort Washington PA 19034 *TF:* 800-836-2340 ■ *Web:* www.oilite.com	215-646-8440	283-3397	620
Beemsterboer Slag Corp 3411 Sheffield Ave .... Hammond IN 46327 *Web:* www.beemslag.com	219-931-7462		779
Beena Vision Systems Inc 600 Pinnacle Ct .... Norcross GA 30071 *Web:* www.beenavision.com	678-597-3156		544
BeenVerified Inc 307 Fifth Ave 16th Fl ....New York NY 10016 *TF:* 888-579-5910 ■ *Web:* www.beenverified.com	888-579-5910		317
Beer Institute 440 First St NW Ste 350...................Washington DC 20001 *TF:* 800-379-2739 ■ *Web:* www.beerinstitute.org	202-737-2337	737-7004	49-6
Beer Nuts Inc 103 N Robinson St .... Bloomington IL 61701 *Web:* www.beernuts.com	309-827-8580		296-28
Beere Precision Products Inc 4915 21st St.................................Racine WI 53406 *TF:* 800-348-0101 ■ *Web:* www.beere.com	262-632-0472		791
Beer-wells Real Estate Services Inc 430 N Center St ....Longview TX 75601	903-753-2191		652
Beeson & Assoc Inc 7711 Cambridge Ct ....Crestwood KY 40014	502-241-8460		194
Beet Sugar Development Foundation 800 Grant St Ste 300 ....Denver CO 80203 *Web:* www.bsdf-assbt.org	303-832-4460	832-4468	48-2
Beetling Design Corp 2131 Hartley Ave........................... Coquitlam BC V3K6Z3 *Web:* www.beetling.com	604-525-6777		361
Beeville Independent School District 201 N St Marys St .... Beeville TX 78102 *Web:* www.beevilleisd.net	361-358-7111	358-7837	780
Beezley Management LLC 23632 Calabasas Rd Ste 105 .... Calabasas CA 91302 *TF:* 800-451-2502 ■ *Web:* www.beezleymanagement.com	818-591-8555		195
Beggar's Banquet 218 Abbott Rd .... East Lansing MI 48823 *TF:* 800-345-8082 ■ *Web:* www.beggarsbanquet.com	517-351-4540		671
Beggs & Lane RLLP 501 Commendencia St....................... Pensacola FL 32502 *Web:* www.beggslane.com	850-432-2451		445

	City	State	ZIP	Phone	Fax	Class
Beghou Consulting 1880 Oak Ave *Web:* www.beghouconsulting.com	Evanston	IL	60201	847-864-5480		463
Beginnings For Parents 156 Wind Chime Ct Ste A *TF:* 800-541-4327 ■ *Web:* www.ncbegin.org	Raleigh	NC	27615	919-715-4092	715-4093	48-17
Begley, Carlin & Mandio LLP 680 Middletown Blvd *Web:* www.begleycarlin.com	Langhorne	PA	19047	215-750-0110		428
Begneaud Manufacturing Inc 306 E Amedee Dr *TF:* 800-358-8970 ■ *Web:* www.begno.com	Lafayette	LA	70583	337-237-5069		295
Behan Communications Inc 86 Glen St *TF:* 800-872-7245 ■ *Web:* www.behancommunications.com	New York	NY	12801	518-792-3856		636
Behavior LLC 40 W 27th St Rm 1200 Ste 401 *Web:* www.behaviordesign.com	New York	NY	10001	212-532-4002		177
Behavioral Science Technology Inc 417 Bryant Cir *TF:* 800-548-5781 ■ *Web:* www.bstsolutions.com	Ojai	CA	93023	805-646-0166		194
Behlen Building Systems 4025 E 23rd St *TF:* 800-228-0340 ■ *Web:* www.behlenbuildingsystems.com	Columbus	NE	68601	800-228-0340		186
Behlen Manufacturing Co 4025 E 23rd St *Web:* www.behlenmfg.com	Columbus	NE	68601	402-564-3111	563-7405	105
Behler-Young Co 4900 Clyde Pk SW *TF:* 800-627-4499 ■ *Web:* www.behler-young.com	Grand Rapids	MI	49509	616-531-3400	531-1453	612
Behnke Center for Contemporary Performance 100 W Roy St PO Box 19515 *Web:* www.ontheboards.org	Seattle	WA	98119	206-217-9886	217-9887	572
Behnke Lubricants Inc W134N5373 Campbell Dr *Web:* www.jax.com	Menomonee Falls	WI	53051	262-781-8850		579
Behnke Nurseries Co 11300 Baltimore Ave *Web:* www.behnkes.com	Beltsville	MD	20705	301-937-1100	937-8034	323
Behr Process Corp 3400 W Segerstrom Ave *TF:* 800-854-0133 ■ *Web:* www.behr.com	Santa Ana	CA	92704	714-545-7101	241-1002	550
Behrens Manufacturing Co 1250 E Sanborn St *Web:* www.behrensmfg.com	Winona	MN	55987	507-454-4664	452-2106	488
Behringer Corp 17 Ridge Rd *Web:* www.behringersystems.com	Branchville	NJ	07826	973-948-0226		492
Behringer Saws Inc 721 Hemlock Rd *Web:* www.behringersaws.com	Morgantown	PA	19543	610-286-9777		351
Behrman House Inc 11 Edison Pl *Web:* behrmanhouse.com	Springfield	NJ	07081	973-379-7200		637-2
BEI Engineering Group Inc Dba Banks Engineering 10511 Six Mile Cypress Pkwy	Fort Myers	FL	33966	239-939-5490		261
BEI Precision Systems & Space Company Inc 1100 Murphy Dr *Web:* www.beiprecision.com	Maumelle	AR	72113	501-851-4000	851-5452	248
BEI Technologies 2470 Coral St *Web:* www.beikimco.com	Vista	CA	92081	760-597-6300		223
BEI Technologies Inc Industrial Encoder Div 7230 Hollister Ave *TF Sales:* 800-350-2727 ■ *Web:* www.beiied.com	Goleta	CA	93117	805-968-0782	968-3154	253
Beier Radio Inc 1150 N Causeway Blvd *Web:* www.beieris.com	Mandeville	LA	70471	504-341-0123		770
Beijing 92 Rue de la Gauchetiere O *Web:* www.restaurantbeijing.net	Montreal	QC	H2Z1C1	514-861-2003		671
Beirut 4082 Monroe St *Web:* beirutrestaurant.com	Toledo	OH	43606	419-473-0885		671
Beirut Restaurant 1385 Robert St S *Web:* www.beirutrestaurantanddeli.com	Saint Paul	MN	55118	651-457-4886		671
Beisser's Inc 3705 SE Beisser Dr *TF:* 800-383-1058 ■ *Web:* www.beisserlumber.com	Grimes	IA	50111	515-986-4422		364
Beistle Co 1 Beistle Plaza *TF:* 800-445-2131 ■ *Web:* www.beistle.com	Shippensburg	PA	17257	717-532-2131	532-7789	566
Beiswenger Hoch & Associates Inc 510 Shotgun Rd *Web:* www.bhaeng.us	Sunrise	FL	33326	954-334-9000		186
Beiter's Inc 560 Montgomery Pk *Web:* www.beiters.com	South Williamsport	PA	17702	570-326-2073		321
Beitler-Mckee Optical Co 160 S 22nd St *TF:* 800-989-4700 ■ *Web:* beitlermckee.com	Pittsburgh	PA	15203	412-481-4700		542
Beitzel Corp 12072 Bittinger Rd *Web:* www.beitzelcorp.com	Grantsville	MD	21536	301-245-4107		186
BE&K Building Group 1031 S Caldwell St Ste 100 *Web:* www.bekbg.com	Charlotte	NC	28203	704-412-9300	659-4161	186
Bek Business Solutions 723 Memorial Hwy *Web:* www.bekbusiness.com	Bismarck	ND	58504	701-255-2032		180
Bekaert Corp 3200 W Market St Ste 303 *Web:* www.bekaert.com	Akron	OH	44333	330-867-3325	873-3424	813
Bekins Van Lines LLC 8010 Castleton Rd *TF:* 800-456-8092 ■ *Web:* www.bekins.com	Indianapolis	IN	46250	800-456-8092		519
Bekker Compliance Consulting Partners LLC 19360 Rinaldi St Ste 453 *Web:* www.bccp-llc.com	Porter Ranch	CA	91326	818-836-1291		194
Bekum America Corp 1140 W Grand River Ave PO Box 567 *Web:* www.bekumamerica.com	Williamston	MI	48895	517-655-4331		604
Bel Air Finishing Supply Corp 101 Circuit Dr *Web:* www.belairfinishing.com	North Kingstown	RI	02852	401-667-7902		481
Bel Air Investment Advisors LLC 1999 Ave of the Stars Ste 2800 *Web:* www.belair-llc.com	Los Angeles	CA	90067	310-229-1500		401
Bel Air Mall 3299 Bel Air Mall *TF:* 800-275-8777 ■ *Web:* www.shopatbelairmall.com	Mobile	AL	36606	251-478-1893		460
Bel Fuse Inc 206 Van Vorst St *NASDAQ: BELFA* ■ *TF:* 800-235-3873 ■ *Web:* www.belfuse.com	Jersey City	NJ	07302	201-432-0463	432-9542	729
Bel Stewart Connector 11118 Susquehanna Trl S *TF:* 800-323-9612 ■ *Web:* www.belfuse.com	Glen Rock	PA	17327	717-235-7512	235-7954	253
Bel/Kaukauna USA 1500 E N Ave *Web:* www.kaukaunacheese.com	Little Chute	WI	54140	920-788-3524		296-5
Belac LLC 420 Commerce Blvd *Web:* www.belac.com	Oldsmar	FL	34677	813-749-3200		21
Belair Produce Company Inc 7226 Pkwy Dr *TF:* 888-782-8008 ■ *Web:* www.belairproduce.com	Hanover	MD	21076	410-782-8000		297-7
Bel-Aire Mechanical Inc 4201 N 47th Ave *Web:* belairemechanical.com	Phoenix	AZ	85031	623-846-8600		610
Belaire Products Inc 763 S Broadway St	Akron	OH	44311	330-253-3116	376-7790	9
Belamar Hotel, The 3501 Sepulveda Blvd *Web:* www.thebelamar.com	Manhattan Beach	CA	90266	310-750-0300		707
Belanger Inc 1001 Doheny Ct *Web:* www.belangerinc.com	Northville	MI	48167	248-349-7010		427
Bel-Art Products Inc 661 Rte 23 S *TF:* 800-423-5278 ■ *Web:* www.belart.com	Wayne	NJ	07440	973-694-0500	694-7199	420
Belarus 136 E 67th St 4th Fl *Web:* www.un.int	New York	NY	10021	212-535-3420	734-4810	784
Belarus Embassy 1619 New Hampshire Ave NW *Web:* belarusfacts.by/belembassy	Washington	DC	20009	202-986-1606	986-1805	257
Belarus Tractor International Inc 7842 N Faulkner Rd *TF:* 800-356-2336 ■ *Web:* www.belarus.com	Milwaukee	WI	53224	800-356-2336		274
Belcam Inc Delagar Div 27 Montgomery St *TF:* 800-328-3006 ■ *Web:* www.belcamshop.com	Rouses Point	NY	12979	518-297-3366	297-3366	214
Belcan Corp 10200 Anderson Way *TF:* 800-423-5226 ■ *Web:* belcan.com	Cincinnati	OH	45242	513-891-0972		261
Belco Industries Inc 9138 W Belding Rd *Web:* www.belcoind.com	Belding	MI	48809	616-794-0410		318
Belco Mfg Company Inc 2303 Taylors Valley Rd *TF:* 800-251-8265 ■ *Web:* www.belco-mfg.com	Belton	TX	76513	254-933-9000	939-2644	199
Belco Packaging Systems Inc 910 S Mountain Ave *TF:* 800-833-1833 ■ *Web:* www.belcopackaging.com	Monrovia	CA	91016	626-357-9566	359-3440	547
Belcourt Castle 657 Bellevue Ave *Web:* www.belcourtcastle.com	Newport	RI	02840	401-846-0669	846-5345	50-3
Belden Brick & Supply Company Inc 620 Leonard St NW *Web:* www.beldenbrickandsupply.com	Grand Rapids	MI	49504	616-459-8367		362
Belden Brick Company Inc 700 Tuscarawas St W *TF:* 800-762-5728 ■ *Web:* www.beldenbrick.com	Canton	OH	44702	330-456-0031	456-2694	150
Belden Inc 2200 US Hwy 27 S *TF:* 800-235-3362 ■ *Web:* www.belden.com	Richmond	IN	47374	765-983-5200	983-5294	814
Belding Tank Technologies Inc 200 N Gooding St PO Box 160 *TF:* 800-253-4252 ■ *Web:* www.beldingtank.com	Belding	MI	48809	616-794-1130	794-3666	610
Beldon 100 S Canyonwood Dr **Fax Area Code: 210* ■ *TF:* 855-971-6936 ■ *Web:* www.beldon.com	Dripping Springs	TX	78620	512-337-1820	341-2959*	189-12
Belfair State Park 3151 NE SR 300 Rt 300 *Web:* www.parks.wa.gov	Belfair	WA	98528	360-275-0668		565
Belfast Area Chamber of Commerce 14 Main St *TF:* 877-338-9015 ■ *Web:* www.belfastmaine.org	Belfast	ME	04915	207-338-5900	338-3808	139
Belfer Ctr for Science & International Affairs (BCSIA) Harvard Univ John F Kennedy School of Government 79 JFK St *Web:* www.belfercenter.org	Cambridge	MA	02138	617-495-1400	495-8963	634
Belfint Lyons & Shuman PA 1011 Centre Rd Ste 310 *Web:* belfint.com	Wilmington	DE	19805	302-225-0600		2
BelFlex Staffing Network 11591 Goldcoast Dr *Web:* www.belflex.com	Cincinnati	OH	45249	513-241-8367		260
BELFOR (Canada) Inc 3300 Bridgeway St *TF:* 888-432-1123 ■ *Web:* www.belfor.com	Vancouver	BC	V5K1H9	604-432-1123		667
Belford's Savannah 315 W St Julian St *TF:* 800-517-9007 ■ *Web:* www.belfordssavannah.com	Savannah	GA	31401	912-233-2626		671
Belfort Furniture Inc 22250 and 22267 Shaw Rd *Web:* www.belfortfurniture.com	Dulles	VA	20166	703-406-7600		321
Belfort Instrument Co 727 S Wolfe St *Web:* www.belfortinstrument.com	Baltimore	MD	21231	410-342-2626		639
Belgian Draft Horse Corp of America 125 Southwood Dr *TF:* 800-831-9910 ■ *Web:* www.belgiancorp.com	Wabash	IN	46992	260-563-3205		48-3
Belgian Tourist Office 300 E 42nd St *Web:* www.belgium-tourism.be	New York	NY	10017	212-758-8130	355-7675	775
Belgian-American Chamber of Commerce in the US (BACC) 1177 Ave of the Americas 7th Fl *Web:* www.belcham.org	New York	NY	10036	212-541-0771		138
Belgium 1 Dag Hammarskj"ld Plaza 885 Second Ave 41st Fl *Web:* www.diplomatie.be/newyorkun	New York	NY	10017	212-378-6300	681-7618	784
Consulate General 6100 Wilshire Blvd Ste 1200 *Web:* www.diplomatie.be/losangeles	Los Angeles	CA	90048	323-857-1244		257
Consulate General 230 Peachtree St NW Ste 2710 *Web:* www.diplomatie.belgium.be/united_states	Atlanta	GA	30303	404-659-2150		257
Embassy 3330 Garfield St NW	Washington	DC	20008	202-333-6900	338-4960	257
Belham Management Industries 9307 Monroe Rd **Fax Area Code: 787* ■ *Web:* www.bmienergy.com	Charlotte	NC	28270	704-815-4246	763-5397*	463

Name / Address	City	State	Zip	Phone	Fax	Class
Belhaven College 1500 Peachtree St PO Box 153 *Fax: Admissions ■ *TF:* 800-960-5940 ■ *Web:* www.belhaven.edu	Jackson	MS	39202	601-968-5940	968-0946*	166
Beliefnet 999 Waterside Dr Ste 1900 *TF:* 800-311-2458 ■ *Web:* www.beliefnet.com	Norfolk	VA	23510	800-311-2458		171
Believe In Tomorrow National Children's Foundation 6601 Frederick Rd *TF:* 800-933-5470 ■ *Web:* www.believeintomorrow.org	Baltimore	MD	21228	410-744-1032	744-1984	48-6
Believe Wireless LLC 9722 Groffs Mill Dr Ste 112 *Web:* www.believewireless.com	Owings Mills	MD	21117	410-902-0070		225
Belitec Inc 3320 boul Gene-H-Kruger *Web:* www.belitec.ca	Trois-Rivieres	QC	G9A4M3	819-373-3880		535
Beliveau, Fradette, Doyle & Gallant PA 91 Bay St *TF:* 800-900-4250 ■ *Web:* www.beliveau-fradette.com	Manchester	NH	03104	603-623-1234		428
Belize 675 Third Ave Ste 1911 *Web:* www.belizemission.com	New York	NY	10017	212-986-1240	593-0932	784
Belize Embassy 2535 Massachusetts Ave NW *Web:* www.embassyofbelize.gov.bz	Washington	DC	20008	202-332-9636	332-6888	257
Belk Farms 57800 Desert Cactus Dr	Thermal	CA	92274	760-399-5951		10-4
Belk Inc 2801 W Tyvola Rd *OTC:* BLKIB ■ *Web:* www.belk.com	Charlotte	NC	28217	704-357-1000		229
Belknap County 34 County Dr *TF:* 800-678-1333 ■ *Web:* www.belknapcounty.org	Laconia	NH	03246	603-527-5400	527-5409	338
Belknap White Group Inc, The 111 Plymouth St *Web:* www.belknapwhite.com	Mansfield	MA	02048	508-337-2700		364
Bell & Evans 154 W Main St PO Box 39 *TF:* 800-837-2778 ■ *Web:* www.bellandevans.com	Fredericksburg	PA	17026	717-865-6626	865-7046	619
Bell Aerospace Services Inc 1305 Airport Fwy Ste 123	Bedford	TX	76021	817-278-0750		529
Bell Aliant Regional Communications 1505 Barrington St Maritime Ctr *TSE:* BA ■ *TF:* 800-555-1212 ■ *Web:* aliant.bell.ca	Halifax	NS	B3J3K5	800-267-1110		736
Bell Aviation Inc 2404 Edmund Hwy *Web:* www.bellaviation.com	West Columbia	SC	29170	803-822-4114	822-8970	57
Bell Canada 1050 Beaver Hall Hill *TF:* 800-667-0123 ■ *Web:* www.bell.ca	Montreal	QC	H2Z1S4	800-667-0123		736
Bell Chamber of Commerce 4401 Gage Ave	Bell	CA	90201	323-560-8755		139
Bell Construction 255 Wilson Pike Cir	Brentwood	TN	37027	615-373-4343	373-9224	188-4
Bell Container Corp 615 Ferry St *TF:* 800-892-4040 ■ *Web:* www.bellcontainer.com	Newark	NJ	07105	973-344-4400	344-0817	100
Bell County 101 E Central Ave PO Box 768 *TF:* 800-460-2355 ■ *Web:* www.bellcountytx.com	Belton	TX	76513	254-939-3521	933-5179	338
Bell County PO Box 157 *Web:* www.bellcountyclerk.ky.gov	Pineville	KY	40977	606-337-6143	337-5415	338
Bell County Chamber of Commerce PO Box 788 *Web:* www.bellcountychamber.net	Middlesboro	KY	40965	606-248-1075	248-8851	139
Bell County Expo Ctr 301 W Loop 121 *TF:* 800-479-0338 ■ *Web:* www.bellcountyexpo.com	Belton	TX	76513	254-933-5353	933-5354	205
Bell Electrical Contractors Inc 128 Millwell Dr *Web:* www.bellelectrical.com	Maryland Heights	MO	63043	314-739-7744		189-4
Bell Equipment Inc 511 Fourth St *Web:* belleq.com	Nezperce	ID	83543	208-937-2402	937-2118	274
Bell Ford Inc 2401 W Bell Rd *TF:* 800-688-1776 ■ *Web:* www.bellford.com	Phoenix	AZ	85023	602-457-2144		57
Bell Fork Lift Inc 34660 Centaur Dr *Web:* www.bellforklift.com	Clinton Township	MI	48035	586-415-5200		770
Bell Foundry Co 5310 Southern Ave *Web:* www.bfco.com	Southgate	CA	90280	323-564-5701		492
Bell Gardens Chamber of Commerce 7535 Perry Rd *Web:* www.bellgardenschamber.org	Bell Gardens	CA	90201	562-806-2355		139
Bell Gas Inc 1811 SE Main St	Roswell	NM	88203	575-622-1733		579
Bell Geospace Inc 400 N Sam Houston Pkwy E Ste 325 *TF:* 800-672-4774 ■ *Web:* bellgeo.com	Houston	TX	77060	281-591-6900		539
Bell Harbor International Conference Ctr 2211 Alaskan Way Pier 66 *TF:* 888-772-4422 ■ *Web:* www.bellharbor.com	Seattle	WA	98121	206-441-6666	441-6665	205
Bell Helicopter Textron Inc 600 E Hurst Blvd (State Hwy 10) *TF:* 888-874-5884 ■ *Web:* www.bellhelicopter.com	Hurst	TX	76053	817-280-2011	280-2321	20
Bell Investment Advisors 1111 Broadway Ste 1630 *TF:* 800-700-0089 ■ *Web:* www.bellinvest.com	Oakland	CA	94607	510-433-1066		401
Bell Lifestyle Products Inc 3164 Pepper Mill Ct *TF:* 800-333-7995 ■ *Web:* www.belllifestyleproducts.com	Mississauga	ON	L5L4X4	800-333-7995		711
Bell Litho Inc 370 Crossen Ave *TF:* 800-952-3306 ■ *Web:* www.bell-litho.com	Elk Grove Village	IL	60007	847-952-3300		781
Bell Lumber & Pole Co 778 First St NW PO Box 120786 *TF:* 877-633-4334 ■ *Web:* www.blpole.com	New Brighton	MN	55112	651-633-4334	633-8852	818
Bell Media Inc *Bell Media Inc* 299 Queen St W *Web:* www.bellmedia.ca	Toronto	ON	M5V2Z5	416-924-6664		740
Bell MTS 333 Main St *Web:* www.mts.ca	Winnipeg	MB	R3C3V6	204-225-5687		224
Bell Museum of Natural History 10 Church St SE *Web:* www.bellmuseum.umn.edu	Minneapolis	MN	55455	612-626-9660		520
Bell Nursery Inc 3838 Bell Rd *TF:* 800-736-5608 ■ *Web:* www.bellnursery.com	Burtonsville	MD	20866	301-421-1500		369
Bell Photographers 341 Garfield St *Web:* www.bellphoto.com	Idaho Falls	ID	83401	208-524-4601		590
Bell Pipe & Supply 215 E Ball Rd *Web:* www.bellpipe.com	Anaheim	CA	92805	714-772-3200		610
Bell Products Inc 722 Soscol Ave *Web:* www.bellproducts.com	Napa	CA	94559	707-255-1811		610
Bell Shoals Baptist Church of Brandon Inc 2102 Bell Shoals Rd *Web:* bellshoals.com	Brandon	FL	33511	813-689-4229		48-20
Bell Supply Inc 7221 Rt 130 *TF:* 888-834-2371 ■ *Web:* www.bellsupplyinc.com	Pennsauken	NJ	08110	856-663-3900	665-2196	690
Bell Techlogix 5777 Decatur Blvd *Fax Area Code: 888 ■ *TF:* 866-782-2355 ■ *Web:* www.belltechlogix.com	Indianapolis	IN	46241	317-333-7777	890-9494*	180
Bell Tower Hotel 300 S Thayer St *TF:* 800-562-3559 ■ *Web:* www.belltowerhotel.com	Ann Arbor	MI	48104	734-769-3010	769-4339	379
Bell Tower Inn 1235 Second St SW *TF:* 800-448-7583 ■ *Web:* www.rochesterlodging.com	Rochester	MN	55902	507-289-2233	289-2233	379
Bell Trans 1900 Industrial Rd *Web:* www.airportshuttlelasvegas.com	Las Vegas	NV	89102	702-739-7990		184
Bell, Nunnally & Martin 3232 McKinney Ave Ste 1400 *TF:* 800-973-1177 ■ *Web:* www.bellnunnally.com	Dallas	TX	75204	214-740-1400		428
Bella Fresca Restaurant 6307 Line Ave *Web:* www.bellafresca.com	Shreveport	LA	71106	318-865-6307		671
Bella Italia 6407 Iron Bridge Rd *Web:* work-telephone-manners.com	Richmond	VA	23234	804-743-1116		671
Bella Mia Restaurant & Bar 58 S First St	San Jose	CA	95113	408-280-1993		671
Bella Monica 3121 EdwaRds Mill Rd Ste 103 *Web:* www.bellamonica.com	Raleigh	NC	27612	919-881-9778		671
Bella Napoli 6331 N Mesa St	El Paso	TX	79912	915-584-3321		671
Bella Via 47-46 Vernon Blvd	Long Island	NY	11101	718-361-7510		671
Bella Vista 53 Maryland St	Winnipeg	MB	R3G1C3	204-775-4485		671
Bella Vista Mexican Restaurant 127 E 20th Ave	Denver	CO	80205	303-297-9020		671
Bella Web Design Inc 3605 Sandy Plains Rd Ste 240-121 *Web:* www.bellawebdesign.com	Marietta	GA	30066	770-509-8797		180
Bellagio Hotel & Casino 3600 Las Vegas Blvd S *TF:* 888-987-7111 ■ *Web:* www.bellagio.com	Las Vegas	NV	89109	702-693-7111	693-8585	669
Bellamy Automotive Group Inc 145 Industrial Blvd *Web:* bellamystrickland.com	Mcdonough	GA	30253	770-954-3000		57
Bellamy Management Services LLC 901 D St SW Ste 1009 *Web:* www.bms-llc.com	Washington	DC	20024	202-863-2270		261
Bellamy Software Ltd 13220 St Albert Trail Ste 310 *Web:* www.bellamysoftware.com	Edmonton	AB	T5L4W1	780-489-5756		525
Bellarmine University 2001 Newburg Rd *TF:* 800-274-4723 ■ *Web:* www.bellarmine.edu	Louisville	KY	40205	502-272-8000		166
Bellasera Hotel 221 Ninth St S *TF:* 844-898-4184 ■ *Web:* www.sunstream.com/naples/bellasera	Naples	FL	34102	239-649-7333		379
Bellatrix Exploration Ltd 1920 800 Fifth Ave SW *Web:* www.bellatrixexploration.com	Calgary	AB	T2P3T6	403-266-8670		539
Bellco First Federal Credit Union 7600 E OrchaRd Rd Ste 400N *TF:* 800-235-5261 ■ *Web:* www.bellco.org	Greenwood Village	CO	80111	303-689-7800		219
Bellco Glass Inc 340 Edrudo Rd *TF:* 800-257-7043 ■ *Web:* www.bellcoglass.com	Vineland	NJ	08360	856-691-1075	691-3247	333
Belle Bonfils Memorial Blood Ctr 717 Yosemite St *TF:* 800-365-0006 ■ *Web:* www.bonfils.org	Denver	CO	80230	303-341-4000		89
Belle Chasse Academy Inc 100 Fifth St *Web:* www.bellechasseacademy.com	Belle Chasse	LA	70037	504-433-5850		685
Belle Fourche Area Community Center 1111 National St *TF:* 800-396-5007 ■ *Web:* www.bellefourche.org	Belle Fourche	SD	57717	605-892-2467		354
Belle Fourche Pipeline 455 N Poplar St *Web:* truecos.com	Casper	WY	82601	307-237-9301	266-0252	597
Belle Grove Historic District 623 Garrison Ave Rm 331 *Web:* www.fortsmithar.gov	Fort Smith	AR	72902	479-784-2266	784-2462	50-3
Belle Haven Country Club Inc 6023 Ft Hunt Rd *Web:* www.bellehavencc.com	Alexandria	VA	22307	703-329-1448		31
Belle Isle State Park 1632 Belle Isle Rd *Web:* www.dcr.virginia.gov/state-parks/belle-isle#general_information	Lancaster	VA	22503	804-462-5030		565
Belle Meade Plantation 5025 Harding Pk *TF:* 800-270-3991 ■ *Web:* www.bellemeadeplantation.com	Nashville	TN	37205	615-356-0501	356-0501	520
Belle of Baton Rouge Casino 103 France St *TF:* 800-676-4847 ■ *Web:* www.belleofbatonrouge.com	Baton Rouge	LA	70802	800-676-4847		133
Belle Tire Inc 1000 Enterprise Dr *TF:* 888-462-3553 ■ *Web:* www.belletire.com	Allen Park	MI	48101	313-271-9400		62-5
Belle W Baruch Institute for Marine & Coastal Sciences University of S Carolina 712 Main St Rm 607 *Web:* artsandsciences.sc.edu	Columbia	SC	29208	803-777-5288	777-3935	668
Belleclaire Hotel Corp 250 W 77th St *TF:* 800-643-5553 ■ *Web:* www.hotelbelleclaire.com	New York	NY	10024	212-362-7700		378
Bellefonte Area School District 318 N Allegheny St *TF:* 866-632-9992 ■ *Web:* www.basd.net	Bellefonte	PA	16823	814-355-4814		685
Bellefonte Intervalley Chamber of Commerce 320 W High St *Web:* www.bellefonte.com	Bellefonte	PA	16823	814-355-2917		139
Belle-Pak Packaging Inc 7465 Birchmount Rd *TF:* 800-565-2137 ■ *Web:* www.belle-pak.com	Markham	ON	L3R5X9	905-475-5151	475-9295	601
Belleplain State Forest County Route 550 PO Box 450 *Web:* www.njparksandforests.org/parks/belle.html	Woodbine	NJ	08270	609-861-2404		565

Name	Address	City	State	Zip	Phone	Fax	Class	TF / Web
Belleview-South Marion Chamber of Commerce	5331 SE Abshier Blvd	Belleview	FL	34420	352-245-2178		139	Web: belleviewsouthmarionchamber.org
Belleville Area Chamber of Commerce	248 Main St	Belleville	MI	48111	734-697-7151	697-1415	139	TF: 800-692-2274 ■ Web: www.bellevilleareachamber.org
Belleville Chamber of Commerce	5 Moira St E	Belleville	ON	K8P2S3	613-962-4597	962-3911	137	TF: 888-852-9992 ■ Web: www.bellevillechamber.ca
Belleville General Hospital	265 Dundas St E	Belleville	ON	K8N5A9	613-969-7400	968-8234	374-2	TF: 800-483-2811 ■ Web: www.qhc.on.ca
Belleville News-Democrat	120 S Illinois St	Belleville	IL	62220	618-234-1000	236-9773	532-2	TF: 800-642-3878 ■ Web: www.bnd.com
Belleville Public Library	1327 19th St	Belleville	KS	66935	785-527-5305	527-5305	434-3	Web: www.bellevillepl.blogspot.in
Belleville Public Library	221 Washington Ave	Belleville	NJ	07109	973-450-3434	759-6731	434-3	Web: www.bellepl.org
Belleville Shoe Manufacturing Co	100 Premier Dr	Belleville	IL	62220	618-233-5600	257-1112	301	Web: www.bellevilleboot.com
Belleville Wire Cloth Inc	18 Rutgers Ave	Cedar Grove	NJ	07009	973-239-0074	239-3985	688	TF: 800-631-0490 ■ Web: www.bwire.com
Bellevue Arts Museum	510 Bellevue Way NE	Bellevue	WA	98004	425-519-0770	637-1799	520	TF: 800-367-2648 ■ Web: www.bellevuearts.org
Bellevue Botanical Garden	12001 Main St	Bellevue	WA	98005	425-452-2750		97	Web: www.bellevuebotanical.org
Bellevue Chamber of Commerce	1102 Galvin Rd S	Bellevue	NE	68005	402-898-3000	291-8729	139	Web: www.bellevuenebraska.com
Bellevue Chamber of Commerce	330 112th Ave NE Ste 100	Bellevue	WA	98004	425-454-2464	462-4660	139	TF: 800-624-3555 ■ Web: www.bellevuechamber.org
Bellevue Club Hotel	11200 SE Sixth St	Bellevue	WA	98004	425-454-4424	688-3101	379	TF: 800-579-1110 ■ Web: www.bellevueclub.com
Bellevue Community College	3000 Landerholm Cir SE	Bellevue	WA	98007	425-564-1000	564-4065*	162	*Fax: Admissions ■ Web: www.bellevuecollege.edu
Bellevue Drug Co	254 Bellevue Ave	Hammonton	NJ	08037	609-561-0825		237	Web: bellevuedrug.com
Bellevue Hospital Ctr	462 First Ave	New York	NY	10016	212-562-4141		374-5	Web: nyc.gov
Bellevue House National Historic Site	35 Centre St	Kingston	ON	K7L4E5	613-545-8666	545-8721	563	Web: www.pc.gc.ca/eng/lhn-nhs/on/bellevue/index.aspx
Bellevue Leader	604 Fort Crook Rd N	Bellevue	NE	68005	402-733-7300	733-9116	532-4	TF: 800-284-6397 ■ Web: www.omaha.com
Bellevue Mechanical Inc	1331 120th Ave NE	Bellevue	WA	98005	425-453-2140		261	Web: www.bmimech.com
Bellevue Public Library	1003 Lincoln Rd	Bellevue	NE	68005	402-293-3157	293-3163	434-3	Web: www.bellevuelibrary.org
Bellevue State Park	800 Carr Rd	Wilmington	DE	19809	302-761-6963	761-6951	565	Web: www.destateparks.com
Bellevue University	1000 Galvin Rd S	Bellevue	NE	68005	402-293-2000	557-5438*	166	*Fax: Admissions ■ TF: 800-756-7920 ■ Web: www.bellevue.edu
Bellflower Chamber of Commerce	16730 Bellflower Blvd	Bellflower	CA	90706	562-867-1744	866-7545	139	TF: 800-341-3060 ■ Web: www.bellflowerchamber.com
Bellflower Medical Center	9542 E Artesia Blvd	Bellflower	CA	90706	562-273-1800		374-3	
Bellia Office Furniture Inc	1047 N Broad St	Woodbury	NJ	08096	856-845-2234		320	TF: 800-830-0801 ■ Web: www.bellia.net
Bellin College of Nursing	3201 Eaton Rd	Green Bay	WI	54311	920-433-6699	433-1922	166	TF: 800-236-8707 ■ Web: www.bellincollege.edu
Bellin Hospital	744 S Webster Ave	Green Bay	WI	54301	920-433-3500		374-3	Web: www.bellin.org
Bellingham Herald	1155 N State St	Bellingham	WA	98225	360-676-2600	756-2826*	532-2	*Fax: News Rm ■ Web: www.bellinghamherald.com
Bellingham Marine Industries Inc	1001 C St	Bellingham	WA	98225	360-676-2800	734-2417	188-5	TF: 800-733-5679 ■ Web: www.bellingham-marine.com
Bellingham Public Library	100 Blackstone St	Bellingham	MA	02019	508-966-1660	966-3189	434-3	TF: 800-392-6090 ■ Web: www.bellinghamlibrary.org
Bellingham Public Library	210 Central Ave	Bellingham	WA	98225	360-778-7323		434-3	Web: www.bellinghampubliclibrary.org
Bellingham/Whatcom Chamber of Commerce & Industry	119 N Commercial St Ste 110	Bellingham	WA	98225	360-734-1330	734-1332	139	Web: bellingham.com
Bellingrath Gardens & Home	12401 Bellingrath Garden Rd	Theodore	AL	36582	251-973-2217	973-0540	97	TF: 800-247-8420 ■ Web: bellingrath.org
Bellini	495 Central Ave	Scarsdale	NY	10583	914-472-7336		319-2	Web: www.bellini.com
Bellino Fine Linens	18 W Forest Ave	Englewood	NJ	07631	201-568-5255		361	Web: bellinofinelinens.com
Bellisio Foods Inc	1201 Harman Pl Ste 302	Minneapolis	MN	55403	612-371-8222		296-36	Web: www.bellisiofoods.com
Bellisio's Italian Restaurant & Wine Bar	405 Lake Ave S	Duluth	MN	55802	218-727-4921		671	Web: www.grandmasrestaurants.com
Bell-Mark Corp	331 Changebridge Rd	Pine Brook	NJ	07058	973-882-0202	808-4616	547	TF: 800-345-9999 ■ Web: www.bell-mark.com
Bellmont Cabinet Co	13610 52nd St E Ste 300	Sumner	WA	98390	253-321-3011		653	Web: bellmontcabinets.com
Bellmoor, The	6 Christian St	Rehoboth Beach	DE	19971	302-227-5800		379	TF: 800-425-2355 ■ Web: www.thebellmoor.com
Bello Vita	2927 N Roan St	Johnson City	TN	37601	423-282-8600		671	
Bellomy Research Inc	175 Sunnynoll Ct	Winston-Salem	NC	27106	800-443-7344		195	TF: 800-443-7344 ■ Web: www.bellomyresearch.com
Bellsoft Inc	3545 Cruise Rd Ste 102	Lawrenceville	GA	30044	770-935-4152		177	Web: www.bellsoftinc.com
Bellus Health Inc	275 Armand Frappier Blvd	Laval	QC	H7V4A7	450-680-4500	680-4501	85	TSE: BLU ■ Web: www.bellushealth.com
Bellwyck Packaging Inc	21 Finchdene Sq	Toronto	ON	M1X1A7	416-752-1210		393	Web: www.bellwyck.ca
Belmar	464 S Teller St	Lakewood	CO	80226	303-742-1520	987-7693	50-6	Web: www.belmarcolorado.com
Bel-Mar Wire Products Inc	2343 N Damen Ave	Chicago	IL	60647	773-342-3800	342-0038	286	TF: 800-249-9450 ■ Web: www.belmarwire.net
Belmark Inc	600 Heritage Rd PO Box 5310	De Pere	WI	54115	920-336-2848	336-4577	113	Web: www.belmark.com
Belmont Abbey College	100 Belmont-Mt Holly Rd	Belmont	NC	28012	704-461-6748		166	TF: 888-222-0110 ■ Web: www.belmontabbeycollege.edu
Belmont Brewing Co	25 39th Pl	Long Beach	CA	90803	562-433-3891	434-0604	671	Web: www.belmontbrewing.com
Belmont Chamber of Commerce	1059 Alameda De Las Pulgas	Belmont	CA	94002	650-595-8696	204-6232	139	Web: www.belmontchamber.org
Belmont County	101 W Main St	Saint Clairsville	OH	43950	740-695-2121		338	Web: www.belmontcountyohio.org/county-departments
Belmont Courthouse State Historic Site	c/o Fallon Region Headquarters 16799 Lahontan Dam	Fallon	NV	89406	775-867-3001		565	Web: parks.nv.gov
Belmont Ctr for Comprehensive Treatment	4200 Monument Rd	Philadelphia	PA	19131	215-877-2000		374-5	TF: 800-841-7363 ■ Web: www.einstein.edu
Belmont Hall & Restaurant	718 Grove St	Manchester	NH	03103	603-625-8540		671	Web: www.belmontrestaurant.com
Belmont Icehouse LLC	3116 Commerce St Ste D	Dallas	TX	75226	972-755-3200		7	Web: www.belmonticehouse.com
Belmont Lake State Park	PO Box 247	Babylon	NY	11702	631-667-5055		565	Web: parks.ny.gov/parks/88/details.aspx
Belmont Mansion	1900 Belmont Blvd	Nashville	TN	37212	615-460-5459		50-3	Web: www.belmontmansion.com
Belmont Metals Inc	330 Belmont Ave	Brooklyn	NY	11207	718-342-4900		492	Web: www.belmontmetals.com
Belmont Park	2150 Hempstead Tpke	Elmont	NY	11003	516-488-6000		642	TF: 800-888-3536 ■ Web: www.nyra.com
Belmont Shore	200 Nieto Ave Ste 200-B	Long Beach	CA	90803	562-434-3066		460	Web: www.belmontshore.org
Belmont Textile Machinery Co	1212 W Catawba St	Mount Holly	NC	28120	704-827-5836	827-8551	744	
Belmont Trading Company Inc	900 Corporate Grove Dr	Buffalo Grove	IL	60089	847-412-9690	412-9692	246	Web: www.belmont-trading.com
Belmont University	1900 Belmont Blvd	Nashville	TN	37212	615-460-6000	460-5434*	166	*Fax: Admissions ■ TF: 800-563-6765 ■ Web: www.belmont.edu
Belmont Village LP	8554 Katy Fwy Ste 200	Houston	TX	77024	713-463-1700		345	Web: www.belmontvillage.com
Beloit College	700 College St	Beloit	WI	53511	608-363-2500	363-2075*	166	*Fax: Admissions ■ TF Admissions: 800-331-4943 ■ Web: www.beloit.edu
Beloit Convention & Visitors Bureau	500 Public Ave	Beloit	WI	53511	608-365-4838	365-6850	206	Web: www.visitbeloit.com
Beloit Daily News	149 State St	Beloit	WI	53511	608-365-8811	365-1420	532-2	TF: 800-356-3411 ■ Web: www.beloitdailynews.com
Beloit Health System	1969 W Hart Rd	Beloit	WI	53511	608-363-5724	363-5702	374-3	TF: 800-637-2641 ■ Web: www.beloithealthsystem.org
Beloit Public Library	605 Eclipse Blvd	Beloit	WI	53511	608-364-2905		434-3	Web: www.als.lib.wi.us
Beloit Regional Hospice	655 Third St Ste 200	Beloit	WI	53511	608-363-7421	363-7426	371	TF: 877-363-7421 ■ Web: www.beloitregionalhospice.com
Belpointe Capital	125 Greenwich Ave	Greenwich	CT	06830	203-629-3300		77	TF: 800-244-7469 ■ Web: www.belpointe.com
Bel-Ray Company LLC	PO Box 526	Farmingdale	NJ	07727	732-938-2421	938-4232	541	Web: www.belray.com
Bel-Rea Institute of Animal Technology	1681 S Dayton St	Denver	CO	80247	303-751-8700	751-9969	800	TF: 800-950-8001 ■ Web: belrea.edu
Belrock Construction Ltd	185 Adesso Dr	Concord	ON	L4K3C4	905-669-9481		186	Web: www.belrock.com
Belshaw Adamatic Bakery	814 44th St NW Ste 103	Auburn	WA	07724	206-322-5474		298	TF: 800-578-2547 ■ Web: www.belshaw-adamatic.com
Belshaw Bros Inc	1750 22nd Ave S	Seattle	WA	98144	206-322-5474	322-5425	298	TF: 800-578-2547 ■ Web: www.belshaw-adamatic.com
Belshire Environmental Services Inc	25971 Towne Centre Dr	Foothill Ranch	CA	92610	949-460-5200		63	TF: 800-995-8220 ■ Web: www.belshire.com
Belson Outdoors Inc	111 N River Rd	North Aurora	IL	60542	630-897-8489	897-0573	319-4	TF: 800-323-5664 ■ Web: www.belson.com
Belstar Inc	8408 Arlington Blvd Ste 200	Fairfax	VA	22031	703-645-0280		261	Web: www.belstar.com

	Phone	Fax	Class
Belstra Milling Company Inc 424 15th St .... Demotte IN 46310 *Fax Area Code: 219 ■ TF: 800-276-2789 ■ Web: www.belstramilling.com	800-276-2789	907-5227*	447
Belt Collins 2153 N King St Ste 200 .... Honolulu HI 96819 Web: www.beltcollins.com	808-521-5361	538-7819	261
Belt Railway Co of Chicago 6900 S Central Ave .... Bedford Park IL 60638 TF: 877-772-5772 ■ Web: www.beltrailway.com	708-496-4000		651
Belt Tech Industrial Inc 2574 E 700 S .... Washington IN 47501 TF: 877-554-2358 ■ Web: belttech1.com	812-644-7623		358
Belterra Casino Resort 777 Belterra Dr .... Florence IN 47020 TF: 888-235-8377 ■ Web: www.belterracasino.com	812-427-7777		669
Belterra Corp 1638 Fosters Way .... Delta BC V3M6S6 TF: 888-860-5600 ■ Web: www.belterra.ca	604-540-1950		370
Belting Industries Company Inc 20 Boright Ave .... Kenilworth NJ 07033 TF: 800-843-2358 ■ Web: www.beltingindustries.com	908-272-8591	272-3825	370
Beltline Bar 16 28th St SE .... Grand Rapids MI 49548 Web: beltlinebar.com	616-245-0494		671
Belton Industries Inc 1205 Hanby Rd PO Box 127 .... Belton SC 29627 TF: 800-845-8753 ■ Web: www.beltonindustries.com	864-338-5711	338-5594	745-3
Belton School District 110 W Walnut St .... Belton MO 64012 Web: www.beltonschools.org	816-489-7000		685
Beltone Electronics Corp 2601 Patriot Blvd .... Glenview IL 60026 TF: 800-235-8663 ■ Web: www.beltone.com	847-832-3300		477
Beltrami County 619 Beltrami Ave NW Courthouse .... Bemidji MN 56601 Web: www.co.beltrami.mn.us	218-333-4120		338
Beltrami Electric Co-op Inc 4111 Technology Dr NW .... Bemidji MN 56601 TF: 800-955-6083 ■ Web: www.beltramielectric.com	218-444-2540	444-3676	245
Beltservice Corp 4143 Rider Trl N .... Earth City MO 63045 TF: 800-727-2358 ■ Web: www.beltservice.com	314-344-8500	344-8511	207
Beltsville Human Nutrition Research Ctr USDA/ARS BARC-E Bldg 307-C Rm 117 10300 Baltimore Blvd .... Beltsville MD 20705 Web: www.ars.usda.gov	301-504-8157	504-9381	668
Beltzville State Park 2950 Pohopoco Dr .... Lehighton PA 18235 Web: www.dcnr.state.pa.us	610-377-0045		565
Beluga Composites Corp 6830 du Parc Ave Ste 572 .... Montreal QC H3N1W7	514-278-7856		582
Belvac Production Machinery Inc 237 Graves Mill Rd .... Lynchburg VA 24502 TF: 800-423-5822 ■ Web: www.belvac.com	434-239-0358		494
Belvedere Hotel 319 W 48th St .... New York NY 10036 TF: 800-492-8122 ■ Web: www.newyorkhotel.com	212-245-7000	245-4455	379
Belvedere Terminals Inc 138 107th Ave Ste 313 .... Treasure Island FL 33706 TF: 800-716-8515 ■ Web: www.belvedereterminals.com	800-716-8515		538
Belvedere USA Corp 1 Belvedere Blvd .... Belvidere IL 61008 TF: 800-435-5491 ■ Web: www.belvedere.com	800-435-5491	626-9750	76
Belvedere, The 9882 S Santa Monica Blvd .... Beverly Hills CA 90212 Web: peninsula.com	310-975-2736	788-2319	671
Belvedere, The 107 Eigth Ave SW .... Calgary AB T2P1B4 Web: www.thebelvedere.ca	403-265-9595		671
Belvedere-Tiburon Public Library 1501 Tiburon Blvd .... Tiburon CA 94920 TF: 800-838-3006 ■ Web: www.beltiblibrary.org	415-789-2665	789-2650	434-3
Belvest USA Inc 5 E 57th St .... New York NY 10022 Web: www.belvest.com	212-317-0460		157-2
Belvidere Area Chamber of Commerce 130 S State St Ste 300 .... Belvidere IL 61008 TF: 800-477-4369 ■ Web: www.belviderechamber.com	815-544-4357	547-7654	139
Belwave Communications 4132 Edgehill Rd .... Fort Worth TX 76116	817-737-3124		225
Belwith International Ltd 3100 Broadway Ave .... Grandville MI 49418 TF: 800-235-9484 ■ Web: www.belwith.com	800-235-9484		350
Belz Enterprises 100 Peabody Pl Ste 1400 .... Memphis TN 38103 TF: 800-561-3357 ■ Web: www.belz.com	901-767-4780		653
Bema Inc 744 N Oaklawn Ave .... Elmhurst IL 60126 Web: bemaprint.com	630-279-7800	279-0284	66
Bemco Inc 2255 Union Pl .... Simi Valley CA 93065 Web: www.bemcoinc.com	805-583-4970	583-5033	703
Bcme International LLC 7333 Ronson Rd .... San Diego CA 92111 Web: www.beme.net	858-751-0580		361
Bement & Company PC 39 E Eagle Ridge Dr Ste 200 .... North Salt Lake UT 84054 Web: bementcompany.com	801-936-1900		2
Bement School 94 Main St PO Box 8 .... Deerfield MA 01342 TF: 877-405-3949 ■ Web: www.bement.org	413-774-7061	774-7863	622
Bemidji Area Chamber of Commerce 300 Bemidji Ave .... Bemidji MN 56601 TF: 800-458-2223 ■ Web: www.bemidji.org	218-444-3541	444-4276	139
Bemidji Ind School District 31 502 Minnesota Ave NW .... Bemidji MN 56601 Web: www.bemidji.k12.mn.us	218-333-3100	333-3129	685
Bemidji State University 1500 Birchmont Dr NE .... Bemidji MN 56601 TF Admissions: 800-475-2001 ■ Web: www.bemidjistate.edu	218-755-2001	755-4048	166
Bemis Assoc Inc 1 Bemis Way .... Shirley MA 01464 Web: www.bemisworldwide.com	978-425-6761		3
Bemis Balkind LLC 6135 Wilshire Blvd .... Los Angeles CA 90048 Web: www.bemisbalkind.com	323-965-4800		4
Bemis Company Inc 1 Neenah Ctr Fourth Fl PO Box 669 .... Neenah WI 54957 NYSE: BMS ■ TF: 800-558-7651 ■ Web: www.bemis.com	920-727-4100		548
Bemis Company Inc Paper Packaging Div 2445 Deer Pk Blvd .... Omaha NE 68105 TF: 800-541-4303 ■ Web: www.bemispaper.com	800-541-4303		65
Bemis Ctr for Contemporary Arts 724 S 12th St .... Omaha NE 68102 Web: www.bemiscenter.org	402-341-7130	341-9791	50-2
Bemis Manufacturing Co 300 Mill St .... Sheboygan Falls WI 53085 TF: 800-558-7651 ■ Web: www.bemismfg.com	920-467-4621	467-8573	319-4
Bemis Public Library 6014 S Datura St .... Littleton CO 80120 TF: 800-895-1999 ■ Web: www.littletongov.org	303-795-3961	795-3996	434-3
BEMSCO Inc 1193 South 400 West .... Salt Lake City UT 84101 Web: www.bemsco.com	801-487-7455		487
Ben & Jerry's Homemade Inc 30 Community Dr .... South Burlington VT 05403 Web: www.benjerry.com	802-846-1500		296-25
Ben Amun Company Inc 246 W 38th St Fl 12a .... New York NY 10018 Web: www.ben-amun.com	212-944-6480		410
Ben Arnold Beverage Company LP 101 Beverage Blvd .... Ridgeway SC 29130 *Fax: Cust Svc ■ TF Acctg: 888-262-9787 ■ Web: www.charmer-sunbelt.com	803-337-3500	337-5310*	81-3
Ben Bridge Jeweler Inc PO Box 1908 .... Seattle WA 98111 TF Cust Svc: 888-917-9171 ■ Web: www.benbridge.com	888-448-1912		410
Ben Davis Chevrolet 931 W Seventh St .... Auburn IN 46706 Web: bendavischevrolet.net	260-570-4327		57
Ben Dyer Associates Inc 11721 Woodmore Rd Ste 200 .... Mitchellville MD 20721 TF: 800-345-3132 ■ Web: www.bendyer.com	301-430-2000		261
Ben Hawes State Park 400 Boothfield Rd .... Owensboro KY 42301 Web: www.kentuckytourism.com	270-687-7137	687-7138	565
Ben Hill County 402A E Pine St .... Fitzgerald GA 31750 TF: 800-248-8863 ■ Web: www.benhillcounty.com	229-426-5100	426-5630	338
Ben Hill Griffin Inc 72 N Ave .... Frostproof FL 33843	863-635-1327		315-2
Ben Hur Construction Co 3783 Rider Trail S .... Saint Louis MO 63045 Web: www.benhurconstruction.com	314-298-8007		189-14
Ben Lippen School 7401 Monticello Rd .... Columbia SC 29203 Web: www.benlippen.com	803-807-4000	744-1387	622
Ben Lomond Suites LLC 2510 Washington Blvd .... Ogden UT 84401 TF: 877-627-1900 ■ Web: benlomondsuites.com	801-627-1900		379
Ben M Muller Realty Company Inc 1971 E Beltline Ave NE Ste 240 .... Grand Rapids MI 49525 Web: mullerrealty.com	616-456-7114		652
Ben Moss Jewellers 300-201 Portage Ave .... Winnipeg MB R3B3K6 TF: 888-236-6677 ■ Web: www.benmoss.com	204-947-6682	988-0148	410
Ben O'neal Company Inc 3003 Tenth Ave .... Chattanooga TN 37407 TF: 800-962-5803 ■ Web: www.benonealcompany.com/home.html	423-624-3359		295
Ben Taub General Hospital 1504 Taub Loop .... Houston TX 77030 Web: www.harrishealth.org	713-873-2000		374-3
Ben Tire Distributors Ltd 203 E Madison St PO Box 158 .... Toledo IL 62468 *Fax Area Code: 217 ■ TF: 800-252-8961 ■ Web: www.bentire.com	800-252-8961	849-3019*	755
Benaka Inc 7 Lawrence St .... New Brunswick NJ 08901 Web: www.benakainc.com	732-246-7060		186
Benaroya Research Institute 1201 Ninth Ave .... Seattle WA 98101 Web: www.benaroyaresearch.org	206-342-6500		743
Benbow Lake State Recreation Area 1600 Hwy 101 .... Garberville CA 95542 Web: www.parks.ca.gov/default.asp?page_id=426	707-923-3238		565
Bench & Bar of Minnesota Magazine 600 Nicollet Mall Ste 380 .... Minneapolis MN 55402 TF: 800-366-4812 ■ Web: mnbenchbar.com	612-333-1183	333-4927	457-15
Benchmarc360 Inc 6340 Sugarloaf Pkwy Ste 200 .... Atlanta GA 30097-4329 Web: www.benchmarc360.com	678-291-0011		232
Benchmark Automation LLC 380 Commerce Blvd .... Bogart GA 30622 Web: www.benchmarkautomation.net	706-208-0814		358
Benchmark Brands Inc 5250 Triangle Pkwy Ste 200 .... Norcross GA 30092	770-242-1254		301
Benchmark Construction Company Inc 4121 Oregon Pike PO Box 806 .... Brownstown PA 17508 Web: www.benchmarkgc.com	717-626-9559		186
Benchmark Electronics Inc 3000 Technology Dr .... Angleton TX 77515 NYSE: BHE ■ TF: 800-322-2885 ■ Web: www.bench.com	979-849-6550		625
Benchmark Group 4053 Maple Rd .... Amherst NY 14226 TF: 800-876-0160 ■ Web: www.benchmarkgrp.com	716-833-4986	833-2954	654
Benchmark Hospitality International 4 Waterway Sq Ste 300 .... The Woodlands TX 77380 Web: www.benchmarkresortsandhotels.com	281-367-5757		379
Benchmark International 2710 W Fifth Ave .... Eugene OR 97402 TF: 800-248-4393 ■ Web: www.benchmark-intl.com	541-484-9212	344-2735	743
Benchmark Network Solutions Inc 1931 Evans Rd .... Cary NC 27513 TF: 800-934-1174 ■ Web: www.benchmark-net.com	919-678-8595		180
Benchmark Plus Management LLC 820 A St Ste 700 .... Tacoma WA 98402 Web: www.bpfunds.com	253-573-0657		401
Benchmark Technologies International Inc 411 Hackensack Ave Fl 8 .... Hackensack NJ 07601 TF: 800-265-8254 ■ Web: www.btiworld.com	201-996-0077		194
Benchworks Inc 860 High St .... Chestertown MD 21620 Web: www.benchworks.com	410-810-8862		7
Benco Dental Co 295 CenterPoint Blvd .... Pittston PA 18640 TF: 800-462-3626 ■ Web: www.benco.com	800-462-3626		475
Benco Electric Co-op 20946 549 Ave PO Box 8 .... Mankato MN 56002 TF: 888-792-3626 ■ Web: www.benco.org	507-387-7963		245
Benco Steel Inc 2710 Highway 70 E .... Hickory NC 28602 Web: www.bencosteel.com	828-328-1714		492

Entry	City	State	ZIP	Phone	Fax	Class
Bend Chamber of Commerce 777 NW Wall St Ste 200 — *TF:* 800-905-2363 ■ *Web:* www.bendchamber.org	Bend	OR	97703	541-382-3221	385-9929	139
Bend Garbage & Recycling Inc 20835 NE Montana St PO Box 504 — *TF:* 800-743-5002 ■ *Web:* www.bendgarbage.com	Bend	OR	97709	541-382-2263	383-3640	804
Bend Metro Parks & Recreation District 200 NW Pacific Park Ln — *Web:* bendparksandrec.org	Bend	OR	97701	541-389-7275		31
Bend Research Inc 64550 Research Rd — *Web:* www.bendresearch.com	Bend	OR	97701	541-382-4100	382-2713	668
BendaGrace Stulz & Company PC 38800 Van Dyke Ave	Sterling Heights	MI	48312	586-883-6240		2
Bendco Inc 801 Houston Ave — *TF:* 800-288-2363 ■ *Web:* www.bendco.com	Pasadena	TX	77502	713-473-1557	473-1882	595
Bendel Executive Suites 213 Bendel Rd — *Web:* www.bendelexec.com	Lafayette	LA	70503	337-261-0604	233-4296	379
Bender Consulting Services Inc 3 Penn Ctr W Ste 223 — *Web:* www.benderconsult.com	Pittsburgh	PA	15276	412-787-8567		180
Bender Engineering Inc 10037 E River St — *TF:* 800-255-5675 ■ *Web:* www.maintstar.com	Irvine	CA	92618	949-458-7560		261
Bender Group 345 Parr Cir — *TF:* 800-621-9402 ■ *Web:* www.bendergroup.com	Reno	NV	89512	775-788-8800	788-8811	449
Bender Lumber Company Inc 3120 Brock Ln — *Web:* www.benderlumber.com	Bedford	IN	47421	812-279-9737		191-3
Bender Plumbing Supplies Inc 550 Grand Ave — *TF:* 800-441-9287 ■ *Web:* www.benderplumbing.com	New Haven	CT	06511	203-787-4288		612
Bender Rbt Inc 17 Cardinale Ln — *Web:* www.benderrbt.com	Queensbury	NY	12804	518-743-8755		177
Bender/Helper Impact (BHI) 11500 W Olympic Blvd Ste 655 — *Web:* www.bhimpact.com	Los Angeles	CA	90064	310-473-4147		636
Bendigo State Park 533 State Pk Rd — *Web:* www.dcnr.state.pa.us	Johnsonburg	PA	15845	814-965-2646		565
Bendix Commercial Vehicle Systems LLC 901 Cleveland St — *TF:* 800-247-2725 ■ *Web:* www.bendix.com	Elyria	OH	44035	440-329-9000	329-9557	61
Bendpak Inc 1645 Lemonwood Dr — *Web:* www.bendpak.com	Santa Paula	CA	93060	805-933-9970		256
Bendsen Signs & Graphics Inc 1506 E McBride Ave — *TF:* 866-275-6407 ■ *Web:* www.bsg1946.com	Decatur	IL	62526	217-877-2345	877-2347	344
BendTec Inc 366 Garfield Ave — *TF:* 800-236-3832 ■ *Web:* www.bendtec.com	Duluth	MN	55802	218-722-0205		595
Benecaid Health Benefit Solutions Inc 185 The W Mall Ste 800 — *TF:* 877-797-7448 ■ *Web:* www.benecaid.com	Toronto	ON	M9C5L5	416-626-8786		391-3
BeneCard Services Inc 3131 Princeton Pike Bldg 2B Ste 103 — *Web:* www.benecard.com	Lawrenceville	NJ	08648	609-219-0400		390
Benedetto Guitars Inc 10 Mall Terr Ste A — *Web:* benedettoguitars.com	Savannah	GA	31406	912-692-1400		194
Benedict College 1600 Harden St — *TF:* 800-868-6598 ■ *Web:* www.benedict.edu	Columbia	SC	29204	803-253-5000		166
Benedict Group Inc 900 Small Dr — *Web:* www.benedictgroup.com	Elizabeth City	NC	27909	303-747-6690		177
Benedict Inn Retreat & Conference Ctr 1402 Southern Ave — *Web:* benedictine.com	Beech Grove	IN	46107	317-788-7581		673
Benedictine College 1020 N Second St — **Fax:* Admissions ■ *TF:* 800-467-5340 ■ *Web:* www.benedictine.edu	Atchison	KS	66002	913-367-5340	367-5462*	166
Benedictine Health System 503 E Third St Ste 400 — *TF:* 800-833-7208 ■ *Web:* www.bhshealth.org	Duluth	MN	55805	218-786-2370	786-2373	353
Benedictine University 5700 College Rd — *TF:* 888-829-6363 ■ *Web:* www.ben.edu	Lisle	IL	60532	630-829-6300	829-6301	166
Benefact Consulting Group 6285 Northam Dr Ste 200 — *TF:* 855-829-2225 ■ *Web:* www.benefact.ca	Mississauga	ON	L4V1X5	855-829-2225		463
Beneficial Financial Group 55 N 300 W — **Fax:* Cust Svc ■ *TF:* 800-233-7979 ■ *Web:* www.beneficialfinancialgroup.com	Salt Lake City	UT	84145	801-933-1100	531-3317*	391-2
Beneficial Mutual Savings Bank 530 Walnut St — *TF:* 800-784-8490 ■ *Web:* www.thebeneficial.com	Philadelphia	PA	19106	215-864-6000		70
Benefis Health Care *West Campus* 1101 26th St S — *Web:* www.benefis.org	Great Falls	MT	59405	406-455-5000		374-3
Benefis HealthSystems *East Campus* 1101 26th St S — *Web:* www.benefis.org	Great Falls	MT	59405	406-455-5000	455-4587	374-3
Benefis Peace Hospice of Montana 2600 15th Ave S — *Web:* www.benefis.org	Great Falls	MT	59405	406-455-3040		371
Benefit & Risk Management Services Inc 10860 Gold Ctr Dr Ste 300 — *TF:* 888-326-2555 ■ *Web:* www.brmsonline.com	Rancho Cordova	CA	95670	916-858-2950		390
Benefit Administrative Services International Corp 9246 Portage Industrial Dr — *Web:* www.basiconline.com	Portage	MI	49024	269-327-1922		734
Benefit Advantage Inc 3431 Commodity Ln — *TF:* 800-686-6829 ■ *Web:* www.benefitadvantage.com	Green Bay	WI	54304	920-339-0351		463
Benefit Communications Inc 2126 21st Ave S — **Fax Area Code:* 615 ■ *TF:* 800-489-3786 ■ *Web:* benefitcommunications.com	Nashville	TN	37204	800-489-3786	383-7917*	390
Benefit Concepts Inc 1173 Brittmoore Rd — *Web:* www.mybciteam.com	Houston	TX	77043	713-728-7200	728-7201	390
Benefit Coordinators Corporation of California 2 Robinson Plaza Ste 200 — *Web:* www.benxcel.com	Pittsburgh	PA	15205	412-276-1111		251
BeneFit Cosmetics 225 Bush St — *TF Cust Svc:* 800-781-2336 ■ *Web:* www.benefitcosmetics.com	San Francisco	CA	94104	415-781-8153		214
Benefit Express Services LLC 1700 E Golf Rd Ste 1000 — *TF:* 800-282-3232 ■ *Web:* www.benefitexpress.info	Schaumburg	IL	60173	847-637-1550		177
Benefit Recovery Group 6745 Lenox Center Ct Ste 100 — *TF:* 866-384-4051 ■ *Web:* brgsubro.com	Memphis	TN	38115	866-384-4051		445
Benefit Resource Group LLC 5985 Home Gardens Dr Ste A — *Web:* benresgroup.com	Reno	NV	89502	775-688-4400		390
Benefit Services Group Inc, The N25 W23050 Paul Rd — *Web:* www.bsg.com	Pewaukee	WI	53072	262-521-5700		401
BenefitHelp Solutions Inc 10505 SE 17th Ave — *TF:* 888-398-8057 ■ *Web:* www.benefithelpsolutions.com	Milwaukie	OR	97222	503-219-3679		535
BenefitMall 3450 Lakeside Dr Ste 400 — *TF:* 877-729-6299 ■ *Web:* www.benefitmall.com	Miramar	FL	33027	954-874-4800		2
BenefitMall Inc 4851 LBJ Fwy Ste 1100 — *TF:* 888-338-6293 ■ *Web:* www.benefitmall.com	Dallas	TX	75244	469-791-3300	791-3313	178-10
Benefits Data Trust 1500 Market St Ste 550 — *Web:* bdtrust.org	Philadelphia	PA	19103	215-207-9100		403
Benefits Div Inc 125 S Swoope Ave Ste 210 — *Web:* benefits-division.com	Maitland	FL	32751	407-629-9085		390
Benefits Plus Consulting Group Inc 1807 Pine St Fl 1 — *Web:* benefitsplusconsulting.com	Philadelphia	PA	19103	215-564-0288		401
Benefitvision Inc 4522 RFD — *TF:* 800-810-2200 ■ *Web:* www.benefitvision.com	Long Grove	IL	60047	800-810-2200		196
Benelogic LLC 2118 Greenspring Dr — *Web:* www.benelogic.com	Timonium	MD	21093	443-322-2494		177
Benemax Inc 7 W Mill St — *TF:* 800-528-1530 ■ *Web:* www.benemax.com	Medfield	MA	02052	800-528-1530		194
Benenson Strategy Group LLC 777 Third Ave 33rd Fl — *Web:* www.bsgco.com	New York	NY	10017	212-702-8777		615
Beneplace Inc 9020 N Capitol of Texas Hwy Bldg 2 Ste 200 — *Web:* bp.beneplace.com	Austin	TX	78759	512-346-3300		390
Benesch 205 N Michigan Ave Ste 2400 — *Web:* web.benesch.com	Chicago	IL	60601	312-565-0450		261
Benesyst Inc 800 Washington Ave N 8th Fl — *TF:* 866-786-3366 ■ *Web:* www.benesyst.net	Minneapolis	MN	55401	800-422-4661		256
Beneteau America Inc 24 N Market St Ste 201 — *Web:* www.beneteau.com/us	Charleston	SC	29401	843-805-5000		90
Benetech Inc 2245 Sequoia Dr — *Web:* benetechglobal.com	Aurora	IL	60506	630-844-1300		360-3
Benetrends Inc 1180 Welsh Rd — *TF:* 866-423-6387 ■ *Web:* www.benetrends.com	North Wales	PA	19454	267-498-0059		463
Benevity Social Ventures Inc 402 11th Ave Ste 100 — *Web:* www.benevity.com	Calgary	AB	T2G0Y4	403-237-7875		195
Benevolent & Protective Order of Elks of the USA 2750 N Lakeview Ave — *Web:* www.elks.org	Chicago	IL	60614	773-755-4700	755-4790	48-15
Benevolent Life Insurance Company Inc 1624 Milam St	Shreveport	LA	71103	318-425-1522		391-2
Benewah County 701 College Ave — *TF:* 800-983-0937 ■ *Web:* www.idaho.gov	Saint Maries	ID	83861	208-245-3212	245-9152	338
Benfield Electric Supply Company Inc 25 Lafayette Ave — *Web:* www.benfieldelectric.com	North White Plains	NY	10603	914-948-6660	993-0558	246
Bengal Energy Ltd 715 Fifth Ave SW Ste 2000 — *Web:* bengalenergy.ca	Calgary	AB	T2P2X6	403-205-2526		540
Benham & Green Capital Management LLC 1299 Prospect St Ste 301	La Jolla	CA	92037	858-551-3130		401
Benicia Capitol State Historic Park 115 W G St — *Web:* www.parks.ca.gov/default.asp?page_id=475	Benicia	CA	94510	707-745-3385		565
Benicia Chamber of Commerce 601 First St Ste 100 — *Web:* www.beniciachamber.com	Benicia	CA	94510	707-745-2120	745-2275	139
Benicia Fabrication & Machine Inc 101 E Ch Rd — *Web:* www.beniciafab.com	Benicia	CA	94510	707-745-8111	745-8102	91
Benicia Public Library 150 E 'L' St — *TF:* 800-656-4673 ■ *Web:* www.ci.benicia.ca.us	Benicia	CA	94510	707-746-4343	747-8122	434-3
Benicia State Recreation Area 1 State Park Rd — *Web:* www.parks.ca.gov/default.asp?page_id=476	Benicia	CA	94510	707-648-1911		565
Benihana 1100 W Eighth Ave — *Web:* www.benihana.com	Anchorage	AK	99501	907-222-5212		671
Benihana 912 Ridgelake Blvd — *Web:* www.benihana.com	Memphis	TN	38120	901-767-8980		671
Benihana 229 Peachtree St NE — *Web:* www.benihana.com	Atlanta	GA	30303	404-522-9629		671
Benihana 5400 Whitehall St — *Web:* www.benihana.com	Irving	TX	75038	972-550-0060		671
Benihana of Tokyo 165 SW Temple — *TF:* 800-366-3684 ■ *Web:* www.benihana.com	Salt Lake City	UT	84101	801-322-2421		671
Benin 125 E 38th St — *Web:* www.un.int	New York	NY	10016	212-684-1339	684-2058	784
Benin Embassy 2124 Kalorama Rd NW — *Web:* www.beninembassy.us	Washington	DC	20008	202-232-6656	265-1996	257
Benise-Dowling & Assoc Inc 5068 Snapfinger Woods Dr — *Web:* www.benise-dowling.com	Decatur	GA	30035	770-981-4237	593-0342	189-8

Listing	City	State	ZIP	Phone	Fax	Class
Benjamin Development Company Inc 377 Oak St Ste 110 *Web:* www.benjamindevco.com	Garden City	NY	11530	516-745-0150		186
Benjamin Franklin Institute of Technology 41 Berkeley St *TF:* 877-400-2348 ■ *Web:* www.bfit.edu	Boston	MA	02116	617-423-4630	482-3706	800
Benjamin Franklin Plumbing 410 22nd St E Ste 920 *TF:* 800-471-0809 ■ *Web:* www.benjaminfranklinplumbing.com	Bradenton	FL	34208	941-366-9692		310
Benjamin H Moore & Company Inc 720 N Maitland Ave Ste 105 *Web:* bhmcpapa.com	Maitland	FL	32751	407-644-3119		2
Benjamin Manufacturing 3215 S Sweetwater Rd *TF:* 800-343-1756 ■ *Web:* www.benjaminmfg.com	Lithia Springs	GA	30122	770-941-1433		610
Benjamin Moore & Co 101 Paragon Dr *TF:* 800-344-0400 ■ *Web:* www.benjaminmoore.com	Montvale	NJ	07645	201-573-9600	573-9046	550
Benjamin N Cardozo School of Law Yeshiva University 55 Fifth Ave Brookdale Ctr *TF:* 800-232-5463 ■ *Web:* www.cardozo.yu.edu	New York	NY	10003	212-790-0200	790-0256	167-1
Benjamin Office Supply & Services Inc 760 E Gude Dr *Web:* www.benjaminofficesupply.com	Rockville	MD	20850	301-340-1384		535
Benjamin Plumbing Inc 2870 Commerce Park Dr *Web:* benjaminplumbing.com	Madison	WI	53719	608-271-7071		189-10
Benjamin Rush State Park 15001 Roosevelt Blvd *Web:* www.dcnr.state.pa.us	Philadelphia	PA	19154	215-639-4538		565
Benjamin Schlesinger & Associates LLC 3 Bethesda Metro Ctr Ste 700 *Web:* www.bsaenergy.com	Bethesda	MD	20814	301-951-7266		194
Benjamin West 428 CTC Blvd *Web:* www.benjaminwest.com	Louisville	CO	80027	303-530-3885		320
Benjamin, The 125 E 50th St *TF:* 866-222-2366 ■ *Web:* www.thebenjamin.com	New York	NY	10022	212-715-2500		379
Benji's 4001 Rosedale Hwy	Bakersfield	CA	93308	661-328-0400		671
Benjy's 2424 Dunstan Rd *Web:* www.benjys.com	Houston	TX	77005	713-522-7602	522-7655	671
Benko & Piane CPA'S 8301 Florence Ave Ste 316	Downey	CA	90240	562-923-9231		2
Benlan Inc 2760 Brighton Rd Winston Business Pk *Web:* www.benlan.com	Oakville	ON	L6H5T4	905-829-5004		476
Benlee Dunright 30383 Ecorse Rd *Web:* www.benlee.com	Romulus	MI	48174	734-722-8100		120
Benner Metals Corp 1220 S State College Blvd *Web:* www.bennermetals.com	Fullerton	CA	92831	714-879-6477		492
Benner-Nawman Inc 3450 Sabin Brown Rd *TF:* 800-992-3833 ■ *Web:* www.bnproducts.com	Wickenburg	AZ	85390	928-684-2813	684-7041	286
Bennet Michael F (Sen D - CO) 261 Hart Senate Office Bldg *Web:* www.baldwin.senate.gov	Washington	DC	20510	202-224-5852	224-9787	342-2
Bennett & Middendorf Ltd 901 York *Web:* bennettandmiddendorf.com	Quincy	IL	62301	217-222-1142		2
Bennett & Pless Inc 47 Perimeter Ctr E Ste 110 *Web:* www.bennett-pless.com	Atlanta	GA	30346	678-990-8700		261
Bennett Auto Supply Inc 3141 SW Tenth St **Fax Area Code:* 899 ■ **Fax:* Hum Res ■ *Web:* www.bennettauto.com	Pompano Beach	FL	33069	954-335-8700	924-0003*	54
Bennett Brothers Inc 30 E Adams St *TF:* 800-621-2626 ■ *Web:* www.bennettbrothers.com	Chicago	IL	60603	312-263-4800		411
Bennett College 900 E Washington St **Fax:* Admissions ■ *TF Admissions:* 800-413-5323 ■ *Web:* www.bennett.edu	Greensboro	NC	27401	336-370-8624	517-2166*	166
Bennett County 201 State St *Web:* www.bennettcosheriff.org/deputies.html	Martin	SD	57551	605-685-6516	685-2255	338
Bennett Enterprises Inc PO Box 670 *Web:* www.bennett-enterprises.com	Perrysburg	OH	43552	419-874-1933		379
Bennett Jones LLP 855 Second St S W 4500 Bankers Hall E *TF:* 800-222-6479 ■ *Web:* www.bennettjones.ca	Calgary	AB	T2P4K7	403-298-3100		428
Bennett Lumber Products Inc 3759 Hwy 6 PO Box 130 *TF:* 800-789-0029 ■ *Web:* blpi.com	Princeton	ID	83857	208-875-1121	875-0191	683
Bennett Metal Products Inc 700 Rackaway St PO Box 34 *Web:* bennettmetal.com	Mount Vernon	IL	62864	618-244-1911		481
Bennett Mfg Company Inc 13315 Railroad St *Web:* www.bennettmfg.com	Alden	NY	14004	716-937-9161	937-3137	286
Bennett Mineral Co PO Box 28 *Web:* www.bennettmineral.com	Walkerton	VA	23177	804-769-0546		761
Bennett Oil Co 810 E Sheldon St *TF:* 800-428-4512 ■ *Web:* www.bennettoil.com	Prescott	AZ	86301	928-445-1181		581
Bennett Packaging 220 NW Space Center Cir *Web:* www.bennettpackaging.com	Lees Summit	MO	64064	816-379-5001		100
Bennett Pointe Grill & Bar 4625 Hillsborough Rd *Web:* www.bpgrill.com	Durham	NC	27705	919-382-9431		671
Bennett Pump Co 1218 Pontaluna Rd *TF:* 800-235-7618 ■ *Web:* bennettpump.com	Spring Lake	MI	49456	231-798-1310	799-6202	639
Bennett Spring State Park 26250 Hwy 64A *Web:* www.mostateparks.com	Lebanon	MO	65536	417-532-4338		565
Bennett Tool & Die Company Inc 910 Cherokee Ave	Nashville	TN	37207	615-227-5291		697
Bennett's Bar-B-Que Inc 3538 Peoria St Ste 508 *Web:* www.bennettsbbq.com	Aurora	CO	80010	303-792-3088		670
Bennet-Tec Information Systems Inc 50 Jericho Tpke *Web:* www.bennet-tec.com	Jericho	NY	11753	516-997-5596		177
Bennett-Thrasher PC 3625 Cumberland Blvd *Web:* btcpa.net	Atlanta	GA	30339	770-396-2200		2
Bennigan's 5151 Beltline Rd Ste 300 *TF:* 800-442-1162 ■ *Web:* bennigans.com	Dallas	TX	75254	469-248-4419		670
Benning Construction Co Inc (BCC) 4695 S Atlanta Rd *Web:* www.benningnet.com	Atlanta	GA	30339	404-792-1911		186
Bennington Area Chamber of Commerce 100 Veterans Memorial Dr *Web:* www.bennington.com	Bennington	VT	05201	802-447-3311	447-1163	139
Bennington College 1 College Dr *TF:* 800-833-6845 ■ *Web:* www.bennington.edu	Bennington	VT	05201	802-442-5401	447-4269	166
Bennington County 100 Veterans Memorial Dr *Web:* www.bennington.com	Bennington	VT	05201	802-447-3311	447-1163	338
Bennington Johnson Biermann & Craigmile LLC 3500 Republic Plaza 370 17th St Ste 3500	Denver	CO	80202	303-629-5200		428
Bennington Museum 75 Main St *TF:* 800-205-8033 ■ *Web:* www.bennington.com	Bennington	VT	05201	802-447-1571	442-8305	520
Benny Hinn Ministries PO Box 162000 *TF:* 800-433-1900 ■ *Web:* www.bennyhinn.org	Irving	TX	75016	877-777-7710		48-20
Benny Whitehead Inc 3265 S Eufaula Ave *TF:* 800-633-7617 ■ *Web:* www.bwitruck.com	Eufaula	AL	36027	334-687-8055	687-1345	360-2
Benny's Inc 340 Waterman Ave *Web:* www.hellobennys.com	Smithfield	RI	02917	401-231-1000		54
BenQ America Corp 15375 Barranca Ste A205 *TF:* 866-600-2367 ■ *Web:* www.benq.us	Irvine	CA	92618	949-255-9500	255-9600	173-7
BENS (Business Executives for National Security) 1030 15th St NW Ste 200 *Web:* www.bens.org	Washington	DC	20005	202-296-2125	296-2490	49-12
Bensenville Community Public Library 200 S Church Rd *Web:* benlib.org	Bensenville	IL	60106	630-766-4642	766-0788	434-3
Bensimon Byrne Inc 225 Wellington St W *Web:* bensimonbyrne.com	Toronto	ON	M5V3G7	416-922-2211		7
Bensinger Consulting 625 W Deer Valley Rd Ste 103-185 *Web:* www.bensingerconsulting.com	Phoenix	AZ	85027	602-237-8500	237-8600	196
Bensinger DuPont & Assoc (BDA) 134 N LaSalle St Ste 2200 *TF:* 800-227-8620 ■ *Web:* www.bensingerdupont.com	Chicago	IL	60602	312-726-8620	726-1061	462
Benson County PO Box 213 *Web:* www.bensoncountynd.com/contact.htm	Minnewaukan	ND	58351	701-473-5345	473-5571	338
Benson Industries LLC 1650 NW Naito Pkwy Ste 250 *Web:* www.bensonglobal.com	Portland	OR	97209	503-226-7611		189-6
Benson Mktg Group 2700 Napa Vly Corporate Dr Ste H *Web:* www.bensonmarketing.com	Napa	CA	94558	707-254-9292		194
Benson Piombo & Co 300 Tamal Plaza Ste 180 *Web:* www.bensonpiombo.com	Corte Madera	CA	94925	415-924-2292		2
Benson Steel Ltd 72 Commercial Rd *TF:* 800-462-9058 ■ *Web:* www.bensonsteel.com	Bolton	ON	L7E1K4	905-857-0684		400
Benson Stone Co 1100 11th St *TF:* 800-561-3357 ■ *Web:* www.bensonstone.com	Rockford	IL	61104	815-227-2000	227-2001	724
Benson's Bakery Inc 134 Elder St *Web:* www.bensonsbakery.com	Bogart	GA	30622	770-725-5711		68
Benson's Gourmet Seasonings PO Box 638 *TF:* 800-325-5619 ■ *Web:* www.bensonsgourmetseasonings.com	Azusa	CA	91702	626-969-4443	969-2912	296-37
Benson, The 309 SW Broadway *TF:* 800-663-1144 ■ *Web:* www.coasthotels.com	Portland	OR	97205	503-228-2000	471-3920	379
Bensussen Deutsch & Assoc Inc (BDA) 15525 Woodinville-Redmond Rd NE *TF:* 800-451-4764 ■ *Web:* www.bdainc.com	Woodinville	WA	98072	425-492-6111		466
Bent County 725 Bent Ave *TF:* 800-424-1554 ■ *Web:* www.bentcounty.org	Las Animas	CO	81054	719-456-1600	456-0375	338
Bent Gate Mountaineering 1313 Washington Ave *TF:* 877-236-8428 ■ *Web:* www.bentgate.com	Golden	CO	80401	303-271-9382		711
Bent Image Lab LLC 2729 SE Division St *Web:* bentimagelab.com	Portland	OR	97202	503-228-6206		514
Bent River Machine Inc 951 Rio Torcido *Web:* www.bent-river.com	Clarkdale	AZ	86324	928-634-7568		757
Bent's Old Fort National Historic Site 35110 Hwy 194 E *Web:* www.nps.gov/beol	La Junta	CO	81050	719-383-5010	383-2129	564
Bentara 76 Orange St	New Haven	CT	06510	203-562-2511		671
Bentley College 175 Forest St **Fax:* Admissions ■ *Web:* www.bentley.edu	Waltham	MA	02452	781-891-2244	891-3414*	166
Bentley Historical Library 1150 Beal Ave *TF:* 866-233-6661 ■ *Web:* www.bentley.umich.edu	Ann Arbor	MI	48109	734-764-3482	936-1333	434-4
Bentley Hotel New York 500 E 62nd St *Web:* www.hotelbentleynewyork.com	New York	NY	10065	212-644-6000		379
Bentley Mfg Company Inc 520 Pk Industrial Dr *TF:* 800-424-2425 ■ *Web:* www.gasketsonline.com	La Habra	CA	90631	562-501-2955	697-5319	326
Bentley Motors Inc 2200 Ferdinand Porsche Dr *Web:* www.bentleymotors.com	Herndon	VA	20171	703-364-7990		59
Bentley Prince Street 14641 E Don Julian Rd **Fax Area Code:* 626 ■ *TF:* 800-423-4709 ■ *Web:* www.bentleymills.com	City of Industry	CA	91746	800-423-4709	956-0937*	131
Bentley Systems Inc 685 Stockton Dr *TF:* 800-236-8539 ■ *Web:* www.bentley.com	Exton	PA	19341	610-458-5000	458-1060	178-5
Bentley World Packaging Ltd 4080 N Port Washington Rd *Web:* www.bentleywp.com	Milwaukee	WI	53212	414-967-8000	967-8001	549
Bently Holdings Corp 240 Stockton St *Web:* www.kamalaspa.com	San Francisco	CA	94108	415-288-0202		652
Bently Nevada Inc 1631 Bently Pkwy S	Minden	NV	89423	775-782-3611		536

Company	City	State	Zip	Phone	Fax	Class
Bento 1306 University Blvd	Tuscaloosa	AL	35401	205-758-7426		671
Benton & Assoc Inc 1970 W Lafayette Ave *Web:* www.bentonassociates.com	Jacksonville	IL	62650	217-245-4146		256
Benton Convention Ctr 301 W Fifth St *Web:* twincityquarter.com	Winston-Salem	NC	27101	336-727-2976		205
Benton County 215 E Central St Ste 217 *Web:* www.bentoncountyar.gov	Bentonville	AR	72712	479-271-1013	271-1019	338
Benton County 205 NW Fifth St Ste 111 *Web:* www.co.benton.or.us	Corvallis	OR	97330	541-766-6800	766-6893	338
Benton County 615 Hwy 23 PO Box 189 *Web:* www.co.benton.mn.us	Foley	MN	56329	320-968-5205	968-5353	338
Benton County 7122 W Okanogan Pl Bldg A *Web:* www.co.benton.wa.us	Kennewick	WA	99336	509-735-3591	736-3066	338
Benton County 111 E Fourth St *Web:* www.bentoncountyiowa.org	Vinton	IA	52349	319-472-2439	472-2913	338
Benton County 1231 Hirsch Pkwy PO Box 852 *Web:* www.bentoncomo.com	Warsaw	MO	65355	660-438-8412	438-8413	338
Benton Foundation 1625 K St NW 11th Fl *TF:* 800-424-9836 ■ *Web:* www.benton.org	Washington	DC	20006	202-638-5770	638-5771	305
Benton Foundry Inc 5297 SR 487 *TF:* 800-652-7539 ■ *Web:* www.bentonfoundry.com	Benton	PA	17814	570-925-6711	925-6929	307
Benton Rural Electric Assn (BREA) 402 Seventh St PO Box 1150 *TF:* 800-221-6987 ■ *Web:* www.bentonrea.org	Prosser	WA	99350	509-786-2913	786-0291	245
Bentonville Plastics Inc 607 SW A St *Web:* www.bentonvilleplastics.com	Bentonville	AR	72712	479-273-7272		608
Bentsen-Rio Grande Valley State Park 2800 S Bensen Palm Dr *TF:* 800-792-1112 ■ *Web:* www.theworldbirdingcenter.com	Mission	TX	78572	956-585-1107		565
Bentz Whaley Flessner 7251 Ohms Ln *TF:* 800-921-0111 ■ *Web:* www.bwf.com	Minneapolis	MN	55439	952-921-0111	921-0109	317
Benucci's 3349 Monroe Ave *Web:* www.benuccis.com	Rochester	NY	14618	585-264-1300		671
Benz Communications LLC 209 Mississippi St *TF:* 888-550-5251 ■ *Web:* www.benzcommunications.com	San Francisco	CA	94107	888-550-5251		193
Benz Oil Inc 2724 W Hampton Ave *Web:* www.benz.com	Milwaukee	WI	53209	414-442-2900	442-8388	541
Benz Research & Development Corp 6447 Parkland Dr *Web:* www.benzrd.com	Sarasota	FL	34243	941-758-8256		544
Benzel's Pretzel Bakery Inc 5200 Sixth Ave *TF:* 800-344-4438 ■ *Web:* www.benzels.com	Altoona	PA	16602	814-942-5062	942-4133	296-9
Benzie County 448 Ct Pl *TF:* 800-315-3593 ■ *Web:* www.benzieco.net	Beulah	MI	49617	231-882-9671	882-5941	338
Benziger Family Winery 1883 London Ranch Rd *TF:* 800-883-2800 ■ *Web:* www.benziger.com	Glen Ellen	CA	95442	707-935-3000	935-3016	80-3
Bepex International LLC 333 Taft St NE *Web:* www.bepex.com	Minneapolis	MN	55413	612-331-4370		298
Beppe & Gianni's Tratoria 1646 E 19th Ave *Web:* beppeandgiannis.net	Eugene	OR	97403	541-683-6661		671
BeQuick Software Inc 601 Heritage Dr Ste 442 *Web:* www.bequick.com	Jupiter	FL	33458	561-721-9600		177
Bera Ami (Rep D - CA) 1431 Longworth HOB *Web:* bera.house.gov	Washington	DC	20515	202-225-5716	226-1298	342-2
Berber Food Mfg 425 Hester St *Web:* www.miranchoretail.com	San Leandro	CA	94577	510-553-0444		123
Berbiglia Inc 1114 W 103 St *Web:* www.berbiglia.com	Kansas City	MO	64114	816-942-0070		443
Berchtold Equipment Co Inc 330 E 19th St *TF:* 800-691-7817 ■ *Web:* www.berchtold.com	Bakersfield	CA	93305	661-323-7817	325-4059	274
Berco Inc 1120 Montrose Ave *Web:* bercodesigns.com	Saint Louis	MO	63104	314-772-4700		320
Berco of America Inc W229 N1420 Wwood Dr *Web:* www.bercoamerica.com	Waukesha	WI	53186	262-524-2222		358
Berding & Weil LLP 2175 N California Blvd Ste 500 *TF:* 800-838-2090 ■ *Web:* www.berding-weil.com	Walnut Creek	CA	94596	925-838-2090		428
Berdon LLP 360 Madison Ave 8th Fl *TF:* 800-309-2110 ■ *Web:* www.berdonllp.com	New York	NY	10017	212-832-0400	371-1159	2
Berea City School District 390 Fair St *Web:* www.berea.k12.oh.us	Berea	OH	44017	216-898-8300	898-8551	685
Berea College 101 Chestnut St **Fax:* Admissions ■ *TF:* 800-326-5948 ■ *Web:* www.berea.edu	Berea	KY	40403	859-985-3500	985-3512*	166
Berean Baptist Church Unaffiliated Inc 517 Glensford Dr *Web:* bereanbaptistchurch.org	Fayetteville	NC	28314	910-868-5156		48-20
Bereaved Parents of the USA PO Box 95 *Web:* www.bereavedparentsusa.org	Park Forest	IL	60466	708-748-7866		48-21
Beredco LLC 2020 N Bramblewood *Web:* www.beredco.com	Wichita	KS	67206	316-265-2856	681-4732	536
Berendsen Fluid Power 401 S Boston Ave Ste 1200 *TF:* 800-360-2327 ■ *Web:* www.bfpna.com	Tulsa	OK	74103	918-592-3781	581-5080	385
Berenergy Corp 1888 Sherman St	Denver	CO	80203	303-295-2323		540
Berenfield Containers 3300 N Hutchinson St *Web:* www.berenfield.com	White Hall	AR	71602	870-247-2800		198
Berenson Corp 2495 Main St *TF:* 800-333-0578 ■ *Web:* www.berensonhardware.com	Buffalo	NY	14214	716-833-3100	833-2402	350
Beretta USA Corp 17601 Beretta Dr *TF:* 800-237-3882 ■ *Web:* www.berettausa.com	Accokeek	MD	20607	301-283-2191	283-0189	284
BERG Chilling Systems Inc 51 Nantucket Blvd *Web:* www.berg-group.com	Toronto	ON	M1P2N5	416-755-2221		610
Berg Co 2160 Industrial Dr *Web:* www.bergliquorcontrols.com	Monona	WI	53713	608-221-4281	221-1416	664
Berg Equipment Co 2700 W Veterans Pkwy *TF:* 800-494-1738 ■ *Web:* www.bergequipment.com	Marshfield	WI	54449	715-384-2151	387-6777	273
Berg Furniture 120 E Gloucester Pike *Web:* www.bergfurniture.com	Barrington	NJ	08007	856-310-0511		319-2
Berg Hill Greenleaf & Ruscitti LLP 1712 Pearl St *TF:* 800-473-9050 ■ *Web:* www.bhgrlaw.com	Boulder	CO	80302	303-402-1600		428
Berg Steel Corp 4306 Normandy Ct *Web:* www.bergsteel.com	Royal Oak	MI	48073	248-549-6066	549-1374	492
Berg Steel Pipe Corp 5315 W 19th St *TF:* 800-619-4807 ■ *Web:* www.bergpipe.com	Panama City	FL	32401	850-769-2273	763-9683	490
Berg's Ski & Snowboard Shop 367 W 13th Ave *TF:* 800-800-1953 ■ *Web:* www.bergsskishop.com	Eugene	OR	97401	541-683-1300		711
Bergad Inc 747 Eljer Way *TF:* 888-476-8664 ■ *Web:* www.bergad.com	Ford City	PA	16226	724-763-2883		471
Bergaila & Associates Inc 1155 Dairy Ashford Rd Ste 600 *Web:* www.bergaila.com	Houston	TX	77079	281-496-0803	496-4705	721
Bergamot Inc 820 E Wisconsin St **Fax:* Sales ■ *TF Cust Svc:* 800-922-6733 ■ *Web:* www.bergamot.net	Delavan	WI	53115	262-728-5572	728-3750*	9
Bergdorf Goodman Inc 754 Fifth Ave *TF Cust Svc:* 888-774-2424 ■ *Web:* www.bergdorfgoodman.com	New York	NY	10019	212-753-7300		157-4
Berge Ford 460 E Auto Ctr Dr *Web:* www.bergefordfleet.com	Mesa	AZ	85204	480-497-1111		57
Bergelectric Corp 5650 W Centinela Ave *Web:* www.bergelectric.com	Los Angeles	CA	90045	310-337-1377		189-4
Bergen Briller Group LLC, The 1787 Wrightstown Rd *Web:* www.bbgsearch.com	Newtown	PA	18940	215-369-4190		260
Bergen Community College 400 Paramus Rd **Fax:* Admissions ■ *TF:* 877-612-5381 ■ *Web:* www.bergen.edu	Paramus	NJ	07652	201-447-7200	670-7973*	162
Bergen County 1 Bergen County Plaza Rm 580 *Web:* www.co.bergen.nj.us	Hackensack	NJ	07601	201-336-6000		338
Bergen County Community Action Program I 241 Moore St *Web:* www.greaterbergen.org	Hackensack	NJ	07601	201-968-0200		379
Bergen County Zoological Park 216 Forest Ave *Web:* co.bergen.nj.us	Paramus	NJ	07652	201-336-7257	336-7247	823
Bergen Regional Medical Ctr 230 E Ridgewood Ave *Web:* www.bergenregional.com	Paramus	NJ	07652	201-967-4000		374-3
Bergenfield Public School District 225 W Clinton Ave *Web:* www.bergenfield.org	Bergenfield	NJ	07621	201-385-8801		186
Berger & Company PA 95 Thames Blvd	Bergenfield	NJ	07621	201-384-6667		2
Berger & Montague PC 1622 Locust St *TF:* 800-424-6690 ■ *Web:* www.bergermontague.com	Philadelphia	PA	19103	215-875-3000		428
Berger Assoc PC 1700 Bedford St Ste 101 *Web:* bergerassociatespc.com	Stamford	CT	06905	203-325-9727		2
Berger Bldg Products Inc 805 Pennsylvania Blvd *TF Cust Svc:* 800-523-8852 ■ *Web:* www.bergerbp.com	Feasterville	PA	19053	215-355-1200	355-7738	697
Berger Engineering Co 10900 Shady Trl *Web:* www.berger-engr.com	Dallas	TX	75220	214-358-4451	351-2954	189-4
Berger Singerman PA 350 E Las Olas Blvd Ste 1000 *TF:* 800-900-4250 ■ *Web:* www.bergersingerman.com	Fort Lauderdale	FL	33301	954-525-9900		445
Berger Transfer & Storage Inc 2950 Long Lake Rd **Fax Area Code:* 651 ■ *TF:* 877-268-2101 ■ *Web:* www.bergerallied.com	Saint Paul	MN	55113	877-268-2101	639-2277*	519
Berger/ABAM Engineers Inc 33301 Ninth Ave S Ste 300 *Web:* www.abam.com	Federal Way	WA	98003	206-431-2300	431-2250	261
Bergeson LLP 303 Almaden Blvd Ste 500 *Web:* be-law.com	San Jose	CA	95110	408-291-6200		445
Bergey & Co 8938 Worcester Hwy *Web:* bergeycpa.com	Berlin	MD	21811	410-641-1101	641-2012	2
Bergey Windpower Co 2200 Industrial Blvd *Web:* www.bergey.com	Norman	OK	73069	405-364-4212		567
Bergey's Inc 462 Harleysville Pike *TF:* 800-237-4397 ■ *Web:* www.bergeys.com	Souderton	PA	18964	215-723-6071	723-4963	62-5
Berggruen Holdings Inc 1114 Ave of the Americas 41st Fl *Web:* www.berggruenholdings.com	New York	NY	10036	212-380-2230		360-3
Berghammer Construction Corp 4750 N 132nd St *TF:* 800-558-9441 ■ *Web:* berghammer.com	Butler	WI	53007	262-790-4750		186
Bergin Fruit & Nut Company Inc 2000 Energy Park Dr *Web:* berginfruit.com	St Paul	MN	55108	651-642-1234		10-11
Bergin Glass Impressions Inc 2511 Napa Vly Corporate Dr Ste 111 *Web:* www.berginglass.com	Napa	CA	94558	707-224-0111		362
Bergkamp Inc 3040 Emulsion Dr *Web:* www.bergkampinc.com	Salina	KS	67401	785-825-1375		492
Berglund Construction 8410 S Chicago Ave *Web:* www.berglundco.com	Chicago	IL	60617	773-374-1000	374-0701	189-3

Phone | Fax | Class

Bergman Jack (Rep R - MI)
414 Cannon HOB ... Washington DC 20515 202-225-4735 342-2
Web: bergman.house.gov
Bergman Luggage Co
401 NE Northgate Way Ste 914 ... Seattle WA 98125 206-365-5775 453
TF: 800-299-8864 ■ *Web:* www.bergmanluggage.com
Bergman Real Estate LLC 2013 15th St ... Troy NY 12180 518-636-4725 652
Web: adkreal.com
Bergmann Assoc Inc
28 E Main St 200 1st Federal Plaza ... Rochester NY 14614 585-232-5135 261
TF: 800-724-1168 ■ *Web:* www.bergmannpc.com
Berg-Oliver Associates Inc
14701 St Mary's Ln Ste 400 ... Houston TX 77079 281-589-0898 261
Web: www.bergoliver.com
Bergquist Co 18930 W 78th St ... Chanhassen MN 55317 952-835-2322 835-4156 253
TF: 800-347-4572 ■ *Web:* www.bergquistcompany.com
Bergseth Bros Co 1211 47th St N ... Fargo ND 58102 701-232-8818 81-1
Web: bergsethbeer.com
Bergstrom Automotive 1 Neenah Ctr ... Neenah WI 54956 920-725-4444 57
Web: www.bergstromauto.com
Bergstrom Jewelers Inc
1695 W End Blvd ... St Louis Park MN 55416 952-767-0606 410
Web: bergstromjewelers.com
Bergstrom Manufacturing Co
2390 Blackhawk Rd ... Rockford IL 61125 815-874-7821 874-2144 15
Web: www.bergstrominc.com
Bergstrom of Kaukauna 2929 Lawe St ... Kaukauna WI 54130 866-939-0130 57
TF: 866-939-0130 ■ *Web:* www.bergstromchryslerjeep.com/contact-form.htm
Berico Fuels Inc
2200 E Bessemer Ave ... Greensboro NC 27405 336-273-8663 316
TF: 800-868-3835 ■ *Web:* berico.com
Berico Technologies LLC
1501 Lee Hwy, Ste 303 ... Arlington VA 22209 703-224-8300 809
Web: www.bericotechnologies.com
Bering Air 1470 Sepalla Dr PO Box 1650 ... Nome AK 99762 907-443-5464 443-5919 25
TF: 800-478-5422 ■ *Web:* www.beringair.com
Bering Straits Information Technology LLC
4600 Debarr Rd ... Anchorage AK 99508 907-563-3788 177
Web: www.beringstraits.com
Beringea LLC
32330 W 12 Mile Rd ... Farmington Hills MI 48334 248-489-9000 792
Web: www.beringea.com
Berje Inc 700 Blair Rd ... Bloomfield NJ 07003 973-748-8980 680-9618 145
Web: www.berjeinc.com
Berkadia Commercial Mortgage LLC
118 Welsh Rd ... Horsham PA 19044 215-328-3200 225
Web: www.berkadia.com
Berkel & Co Contractors Inc
PO Box 335 ... Bonner Springs KS 66012 913-422-5125 441-0402 188-2
Web: www.berkelandcompany.com
Berkeley Art Museum & Pacific Film Archive
2120 Oxford St Ste 2250 ... Berkeley CA 94720 510-642-0808 642-4889 520
Web: www.bampfa.berkeley.edu
Berkeley Chamber of Commerce
1834 University Ave ... Berkeley CA 94703 510-549-7000 549-1789 139
TF: 800-847-4823 ■ *Web:* www.berkeleychamber.com
Berkeley City College 2050 Ctr St ... Berkeley CA 94704 510-981-2800 841-7333 162
Web: berkeleycitycollege.edu
Berkeley College
Garrett Mountain
44 Rifle Camp Rd ... Woodland Park NJ 07424 973-278-5400 278-9141 800
TF: 800-446-5400 ■ *Web:* www.berkeleycollege.edu
Paramus 64 E Midland Ave ... Paramus NJ 07652 201-967-9667 265-6446 800
TF: 800-446-5400 ■ *Web:* www.berkeleycollege.edu
Woodbridge 430 Rahway Ave ... Woodbridge NJ 07095 732-750-1800 750-0652 800
TF: 800-446-5400 ■ *Web:* www.berkeleycollege.edu
Berkeley College New York City
3 E 43rd St ... New York NY 10017 212-986-4343 818-1079 800
TF: 800-446-5400 ■ *Web:* www.berkeleycollege.edu
Berkeley College White Plains
99 Church St ... White Plains NY 10601 914-694-1122 328-9469 800
TF: 800-446-5400 ■ *Web:* www.berkeleycollege.edu
Berkeley Communications Corp
1321 67th St ... Emeryville CA 94608 510-644-1599 194
TF: 877-237-5266 ■ *Web:* www.berkcom.com
Berkeley County
1003 Hwy 52 PO Box 6122 ... Moncks Corner SC 29461 843-719-4234 338
Web: www.berkeleycountysc.gov
Berkeley County Chamber of Commerce
PO Box 968 ... Moncks Corner SC 29461 843-761-8238 899-6491 139
TF: 800-882-0337 ■ *Web:* www.berkeleysc.org
Berkeley County Council
400 W Stephen St Ste 201 ... Martinsburg WV 25401 304-264-1923 267-1794 338
Web: www.berkeleycountycomm.org
Berkeley County Library
1003 Hwy 52 ... Moncks Corner SC 29461 843-719-4223 434-3
Berkeley Electric Co-op Inc
551 Rembert C Dennis Blvd ... Moncks Corner SC 29461 843-761-8200 245
Web: www.berkeleyelectric.coop
Berkeley Farms Inc 25500 Clawiter Rd ... Hayward CA 94545 510-265-8600 296-27
Web: www.berkeleyfarms.com
Berkeley Forge & Tool Inc
1331 E Shore Hwy ... Berkeley CA 94710 510-526-5034 525-9014 483
Web: www.berkforge.com
Berkeley Hills Real Estate Inc
1714 Solano Ave ... Berkeley CA 94707 510-524-9888 652
Web: www.berkhills.com
Berkeley Hotel, The 1200 E Cary St ... Richmond VA 23219 804-780-1300 648-4728 379
TF: 888-780-4422 ■ *Web:* www.berkeleyhotel.com
Berkeley International Capital Corp
650 California St 26th Fl ... San Francisco CA 94108 415-249-0450 792
Web: www.berkeleyvc.com
Berkeley Public Library
2090 Kittredge St ... Berkeley CA 94704 510-981-6100 981-6111 434-3
TF: 800-870-3663 ■ *Web:* www.berkeleypubliclibrary.org
Berkeley Pumps 293 Wright St ... Delavan WI 53115 262-728-5551 426-9446* 641
**Fax Area Code:* 800 ■ **Fax:* Cust Svc ■ *TF:* 888-782-7483 ■ *Web:* www.berkeleypumps.com

Berkeley Repertory Theatre
2025 Addison St ... Berkeley CA 94704 510-647-2949 647-2975 749
Web: www.berkeleyrep.org
Berkeley Sensor & Actuator Ctr (BSAC)
University of California
403 Cory Hall MC Ste 1774 ... Berkeley CA 94720 510-643-6690 643-6637 668
Web: www-bsac.eecs.berkeley.edu
Berkeley Symphony Orchestra
1942 University Ave Ste 207 ... Berkeley CA 94704 510-841-2800 841-5422 573-3
Web: www.berkeleysymphony.org
Berkeley Varitronics Systems Inc
255 Liberty St Liberty Corporate Pk ... Metuchen NJ 08840 732-548-3737 177
TF: 888-737-4287 ■ *Web:* www.bvsystems.com
Berkeleys Northside Travel Inc
1824 Euclid Ave ... Berkeley CA 94709 510-843-1000 772
TF: 800-575-3411 ■ *Web:* www.berkeley4travel.com
Berkhemer Clayton Inc
241 S Figueroa St Ste 300 ... Los Angeles CA 90012 213-621-2300 193
TF: 800-713-7278 ■ *Web:* www.berkhemerclayton.com
Berklee College of Music
1140 Boylston St ... Boston MA 02215 617-747-2221 747-2047* 166
**Fax:* Admissions ■ *TF:* 800-421-0084 ■ *Web:* www.berklee.edu
Berklee Performance Ctr
136 Massachusetts Ave ... Boston MA 02115 617-747-2261 572
TF: 800-237-5533 ■ *Web:* www.berklee.edu
Berkley Industries 9938 Pigeon Rd ... Bay Port MI 48720 989-656-2171 595
TF: 800-852-4925 ■ *Web:* www.avci.net
Berkley Medical Resources Inc
700 Mtn View Dr ... Smithfield PA 15478 724-564-5002 476
TF: 800-835-2442 ■ *Web:* www.business.com
Berkley Risk Administrators Company LLC
222 S Ninth St Ste 1300 ... Minneapolis MN 55402 612-766-3000 390
TF: 800-449-7707 ■ *Web:* www.berkleyrisk.com
Berkley Screw Machine Products Inc
2100 Royce Haley Dr ... Rochester Hills MI 48309 248-853-0044 853-1532 621
Berkot Super Foods 20005 Wolf Rd ... Mokena IL 60448 708-479-7411 345
Web: www.berkotfoods.com
Berkowitz Dick Pollack & Brant LLP
200 S Biscayne Blvd 6th Fl ... Miami FL 33131-5351 305-379-7000 379-8200 2
TF: 800-999-1272 ■ *Web:* www.bpbcpa.com
Berkowitz Oliver Williams Shaw & Eisenbrandt LLP
Crown Ctr 2600 Grand Blvd Ste 1200 ... Kansas City MO 64108 816-561-7007 428
Web: www.berkowitzoliver.com
Berkowsky & Associates Inc
2551 US Hwy 130 ... Cranbury NJ 08512 609-655-2400 186
Web: www.berkowsky.com
Berks & Beyond Employment Services Inc
926 Penn Ave ... Wyomissing PA 19610 610-376-9675 193
Web: www.berksandbeyond.com
Berks County
Law Library 633 Ct St 10th Fl ... Reading PA 19601 610-478-3370 478-6375 338
Web: www.co.berks.pa.us
Berks Packing Company Inc
307-323 Bingaman St PO Box 5919 ... Reading PA 19610 800-882-3757 378-1210* 296-26
**Fax Area Code:* 610 ■ *TF:* 800-882-3757 ■ *Web:* www.berksfoods.com
Berks VNA 1170 Berkshire Blvd ... Wyomissing PA 19610 855-843-8627 378-9762* 371
**Fax Area Code:* 610 ■ *TF:* 855-843-8627 ■ *Web:* www.hhcminc.org
Berkshire & Burmeister Attorneys at Law
1301 S 75th St Ste 100 ... Omaha NE 68124 402-827-7000 827-7001 445
Web: www.berkshire-law.com
Berkshire Advisors Inc
2240 Ridgewood Rd ... Wyomissing PA 19610 610-376-6970 401
TF: 800-560-4325 ■ *Web:* www.berkshireadvisors.net
Berkshire Athenaeum 1 Wendell Ave ... Pittsfield MA 01201 413-499-9480 499-9489 434-3
TF: 800-925-7737 ■ *Web:* www.berkshire.net
Berkshire Bancorp Inc 160 Broadway ... New York NY 10038 212-791-5362 360-2
NASDAQ: BERK ■ *Web:* www.berkbank.com
Berkshire Bank PO Box 1308 ... Pittsfield MA 01202 413-443-5601 443-3587 70
TF: 800-773-5601 ■ *Web:* www.berkshirebank.com
Berkshire Blanket Inc 44 E Main St ... Ware MA 01082 413-967-5964 442
Web: www.berkshireblanket.com
Berkshire Botanical Garden
5 W Stockbridge Rd PO Box 826 ... Stockbridge MA 01262 413-298-3926 97
Web: www.berkshirebotanical.org
Berkshire Chamber of Commerce
66 Allen St ... Pittsfield MA 01201 413-499-4000 139
Web: 1berkshire.com
Berkshire Community College
1350 W St ... Pittsfield MA 01201 413-499-4660 447-7840 162
Web: www.berkshirecc.edu
Berkshire County 66 Allen St ... Pittsfield MA 01201 413-499-4000 338
Web: 1berkshire.com
Berkshire Eagle
75 S Church St PO Box 1171 ... Pittsfield MA 01202 413-447-7311 499-3419 532-2
TF: 800-234-7404 ■ *Web:* www.berkshireeagle.com
Berkshire Gas Company Inc
115 Cheshire Rd ... Pittsfield MA 01201 413-442-1511 787
TF: 800-292-5012 ■ *Web:* www.berkshiregas.com
Berkshire General Store, The
25 Edison Dr ... Wayne NJ 07470 973-696-6204 155-10
Web: www.berkshiregeneralstore.com
Berkshire Hathaway Group (BHG)
3555 Farnam St ... Omaha NE 68131 888-395-6349 298-1915* 391-4
**Fax Area Code:* 212 ■ *TF:* 800-223-2064 ■ *Web:* berkshirehathaway.com
Berkshire Hathaway Homestates Cos (BHHC)
PO Box 2048 ... Omaha NE 68103 888-495-8949 391-4
TF: 888-495-8949 ■ *Web:* www.bhhc.com
Berkshire Hathaway Inc
3555 Farnam St Ste 1440 ... Omaha NE 68131 402-346-1400 346-3375 185
NYSE: BRK/A ■ *TF:* 800-223-2064 ■ *Web:* www.berkshirehathaway.com
Berkshire Health & Rehabilitation Ctr
705 Clearview Dr ... Vinton VA 24179 540-982-6691 450
TF: 800-321-1245 ■ *Web:* www.berkshirehealthrehab.com
Berkshire Hills Bancorp Inc
24 N St ... Pittsfield MA 01201 413-443-5601 360-2
NYSE: BHLB ■ *TF:* 800-773-5601 ■ *Web:* www.berkshirebank.com

Name / Address	City	State	ZIP	Phone	Fax	Class
Berkshire Industries Inc 109 Apremont Way Web: www.berkshireindustries.com	Westfield	MA	01085	413-568-8676		621
Berkshire Medical Ctr 725 N St Web: www.berkshirehealthsystems.org	Pittsfield	MA	01201	413-447-2000		374-3
Berkshire Property Advisors LLC 1150 Sanctuary Pkwy Ste 150 TF: 800-330-4020 ■ Web: www.berkshirecommunities.com	Alpharetta	MA	30009	617-646-2300	646-2375	655
Berkshire Refrigerated Warehousing 4550 S Packers Ave	Chicago	IL	60609	773-254-2424		803-2
Berkshire School 245 N Undermountain Rd Web: www.berkshireschool.org	Sheffield	MA	01257	413-229-8511	229-1028	622
Berkshire Theatre Festival 83 E Main St Web: www.berkshiretheatregroup.org	Stockbridge	MA	01262	413-298-5576		749
Berlin Industries Inc 175 Mercedes Dr Web: www.berlinindustries.com	Carol Stream	IL	60188	630-682-0600		627
Berlin Metals LLC 3200 Sheffield Ave TF: 800-754-8867 ■ Web: www.berlinmetals.com	Hammond	IN	46327	219-933-0111	933-0692	492
Berlin Pacific 400 W 47th Ste 3AB Web: www.berlinpacific.com	New York	NY	10036	212-247-2502		463
Berlin Steel Construction Co 76 Depot Rd PO Box 428 TF: 800-816-6108 ■ Web: www.berlinsteel.com	Kensington	CT	06037	860-828-3531	828-5253	480
Berline 423 N Main St Ste 300 Web: www.berline.com	Royal Oak	MI	48067	248-593-4744		5
Berliner Photography LLC 314 N La Brea Ave	Los Angeles	CA	90036	323-857-1282		590
Berlin-Ichthyosaur State Park HC 61 Web: www.parks.nv.gov	Austin	NV	89310	775-964-2440		565
Berlin-Wheeler Inc 2942A SW Wanamaker Dr Web: www.berlinwheeler.com	Topeka	KS	66614	785-271-1000		160
Berliss Bearing Co 644 Rt 10 Po Box 45 Web: www.berliss.com	Livingston	NJ	07039	973-992-4242	992-6669	75
Berlitz Languages Inc 400 Alexander Pk Web: www.berlitz.com	Princeton	NJ	08540	609-514-9650	514-9689	423
Berman & Larson Associates 38 E Ridgewood Ave Ste 209 Web: jobsbl.com	Ridgewood	NJ	07450	201-909-0906		260
Berman Moving & Storage Inc 23800 Corbin Dr TF: 800-333-0582 ■ Web: www.bermanmovers.com	Cleveland	OH	44128	216-663-8816		312
Berman Myles L Law Offices 4665 Macarthur Ct Ste 240 Web: www.topgundui.com	Newport Beach	CA	92660	949-640-1860		428
Bermello Ajamil & Partners 2601 S Bayshore Dr Web: www.bermelloajamil.com	Miami	FL	33133	305-859-2050	859-9638	261
Bermo Inc 4501 Ball Rd NE Web: www.bermo.com	Circle Pines	MN	55014	763-786-7676	785-2159	488
Bermuda Dept of Tourism 675 Third Ave 20th Fl TF: 800-223-6106 ■ Web: www.gotobermuda.com	New York	NY	10017	212-818-9800	983-5289	775
Bermuda Village 142 Bermuda Village Dr TF Mktg: 800-843-5433 ■ Web: www.bermudavillage.net	Advance	NC	27006	800-843-5433		672
Bern's Steak House 1208 S Howard Ave Web: www.bernssteakhouse.com	Tampa	FL	33606	813-251-2421		671
Bernalillo County 1 Civic Plaza NW 10th Fl TF: 800-545-6566 ■ Web: www.bernco.gov	Albuquerque	NM	87102	505-468-7000	768-4329	338
Bernard Chaus Inc 530 Seventh Ave 18th Fl Web: chausny.com	New York	NY	10018	646-562-4700		155-21
Bernard Food Industries Inc 1125 Hartrey Ave TF: 800-323-3663 ■ Web: www.bernardfoods.com	Evanston	IL	60204	847-869-5222	869-5315	296-18
Bernard L Madoff Investment Securities Co 45 Rockefeller Ctr 11th Fl TF: 800-334-1343 ■ Web: www.madofftrustee.com	New York	NY	10111	212-230-2424		690
Bernard N Ackerman CPA PA 596 Herrons Ferry Rd 5th fl Web: www.bnacpa.com	Rock Hill	SC	29730	803-366-8371		2
Bernard Welding Equipment 449 W Corning Rd Web: www.bernardwelds.com	Beecher	IL	60401	708-946-2281		811
Bernard Zell Anshe Emet Day School 3751 N Broadway St Web: www.bernardzell.org	Chicago	IL	60613	773-281-1858	281-4709	297-7
Bernard'O Restaurant 12457 Rancho BernaRdo Rd Web: bernardorestaurant.wordpress.com	San Diego	CA	92128	858-487-7171		671
Bernard's Grove 187 Long Pond Rd Web: www.bernardsgrove.com	Rochester	NY	14612	585-227-6405		671
Bernardo Fashions LLC 463 Seventh Ave 7th Fl Web: www.bernardofashions.com	New York	NY	10018	212-594-3900		432
Bernards Bros Inc 555 First St Web: www.bernards.com	San Fernando	CA	91340	818-898-1521		186
Bernards Inn 27 Mine Brook Rd TF: 888-766-0002 ■ Web: www.bernardsinn.com	Bernardsville	NJ	07924	908-766-0002	766-4604	379
Bernards Township Board of Education 101 Peachtree Rd Web: www.bernardsboe.com	Basking Ridge	NJ	07920	908-204-2600		685
Bernardus Lodge 415 Carmel Valley Rd TF: 800-223-2533 ■ Web: www.bernardus.com	Carmel Valley	CA	93924	831-658-3400		379
Bernatello's PO Box 729 TF: 800-666-9455 ■ Web: www.bernatellos.com	Maple Lake	MN	55358	952-831-6622	831-6606	296-21
Berndt & Associates PC 30500 Van Dyke Ave Ste 702 TF: 800-850-1079 ■ Web: www.berndtlegal.com	Warren	MI	48093	586-558-9000		428
Berndt Group Ltd, The 3618 Falls Rd Web: www.berndtgroup.net	Baltimore	MD	21211	410-889-5854		177

Name / Address	City	State	ZIP	Phone	Fax	Class
Berne Apparel Co 2501 E 850 N TF: 800-843-7657 ■ Web: www.berneapparel.com	Ossian	IN	46774	888-772-3763		155-19
Berne Cooperative Association Inc 158 W Main St Web: www.bernecoopassoc.com	Ute	IA	51060	712-885-2249		324
Berner Foods Inc 2034 E Factory Rd TF: 800-819-8199 ■ Web: www.bernerfoods.com	Dakota	IL	61018	815-563-4222	563-4017	296-5
Berney Office Solutions LLC 10690 John Knight Close TF: 800-383-9362 ■ Web: www.berney.com	Montgomery	AL	36117	334-271-4750		627
Berney-Karp Inc 3350 E 26th St TF: 800-237-6395 ■ Web: www.ceramic-source.com	Los Angeles	CA	90058	323-260-7122	260-7245	334
Bernhard LLC 13641 Airline Hwy Web: www.bernhardmechanical.com	Baton Rouge	LA	70817	225-752-0785		189-10
Bernhardt Furniture Company Inc 1839 Morganton Blvd TF: 888-901-2655 ■ Web: www.bernhardt.com	Lenoir	NC	28645	828-758-9811		319-1
Bernheim Arboretum & Research Forest 2499 Clermont Rd PO Box 130 Web: bernheim.org	Clermont	KY	40110	502-955-8512		97
Bernheimer-Lincoln Insurance Group 779 Farmington Ave Web: bernheimerinsurance.com	West Hartford	CT	06119	860-232-3810		390
Bernice State Park 901 State Pk Rd Web: www.travelok.com	Grove	OK	74344	918-786-9447	787-5634	565
Bernicke & Associates Ltd 1565 Bluestem Blvd Web: www.bernicke.com	Altoona	WI	54701	715-832-1173		401
Bernie & Phyl's Furniture 308 E Main St TF: 800-318-9806 ■ Web: www.bernieandphyls.com	Norton	MA	02766	508-286-4000		321
Bernina of America Inc 3702 Prairie Lake Ct Web: www.bernina.com	Aurora	IL	60504	630-978-2500		37
Berns Co 1250 W 17th St TF: 800-421-3773 ■ Web: www.thebernsco.com	Long Beach	CA	90813	562-437-0471	436-1074	470
Bernsohn & Fetner LLC 625 W 51st St Web: bfbuilding.com	New York	NY	10019	212-315-4330		610
Bernstein Crisis Management Inc 700 S Myrtle Ave Ste 404 Web: www.bernsteincrisismanagement.com	Monrovia	CA	91016	626-825-3838		463
Bernstein-Rein 4600 Madison Ave Ste 1500 Web: www.b-r.com	Kansas City	MO	64112	816-756-0640	399-6000	4
Berntsen Brass & Aluminum Foundry Inc 2334 Pennsylvania Ave Web: www.berntsen-foundry.com	Madison	WI	53704	608-249-9233		492
Bernzott Capital Advisors 888 W Ventura Blvd Ste B TF: 800-856-2646 ■ Web: www.bernzott.com	Camarillo	CA	93010	805-389-9445		194
Beroe Inc 338 Raleigh St TF: 800-245-5507 ■ Web: www.beroeinc.com	Holly Springs	NC	27540	919-605-3435		466
Beronio Lumber Co 2525 Marin St Web: www.beronio.com	San Francisco	CA	94124	415-824-4300		364
Beroth Oil Co 20 W 32nd St Web: www.berothoil.com	Winston-Salem	NC	27105	336-757-7600		580
Berr Pet Supply Inc 929 N Market Blvd TF: 888-237-7738 ■ Web: berrpet.com	Sacramento	CA	95834	916-921-0145		237
Berrien County 201 N Davis St Ste 105 Web: www.berriencountygeorgia.com	Nashville	GA	31639	229-686-7461	686-7819	338
Berrien County 701 Main St Web: www.berriencounty.org	Saint Joseph	MI	49085	269-983-7111	982-8642	338
Berrien Resa 711 Saint Joseph Ave Web: www.berrienresa.org	Berrien Springs	MI	49103	269-471-7725		685
Berry PO Box 959 Web: www.berryplastics.com	Evansville	IN	47706	812-424-2904		199
Berry & Berry Law Offices 2930 Lakeshore Ave Web: berryandberry.com	Oakland	CA	94610	510-250-0200		428
Berry Aviation Inc 1807 Airport Dr TF: 800-229-2379 ■ Web: www.berryaviation.com	San Marcos	TX	78666	512-353-2379	353-2593	13
Berry Bros General Contractors Inc 1414 River Rd	Berwick	LA	70342	985-384-8770		10-3
Berry Coffee Co 14825 Martin Dr Web: www.berrycoffee.com	Eden Prairie	MN	55344	952-937-8697		297-8
Berry College 2277 Martha Berry Hwy NW *Fax: Admissions ■ TF: 800-237-7942 ■ Web. www.berry.edu	Mount Berry	GA	30149	706-232-5374	290-2178*	166
Berry Dunn Mcneil & Parker 100 Middle St 4th Fl TF: 800-908-4490 ■ Web: www.berrydunn.com	Portland	ME	04101	207-775-2387	774-2375	2
Berry Global Inc 101 Oakley St TF: 877-662-3779 ■ Web: www.berryplastics.com	Evansville	IN	47710	812-424-2904	424-0128	199
Berry Hill Mansion 700 Louisville Rd	Frankfort	KY	40601	502-564-3000		50-3
Berry Metal Co 2408 Evans City Rd Web: www.berrymetal.com	Harmony	PA	16037	724-452-8040		492
Berry Oil 3193 Leigh Ave Web: www.berryoil.net	Tetonia	ID	83452	208-456-2271		579
Berry Petroleum Co 1999 Broadway Ste 3700 NYSE: BRY	Denver	CO	80202	303-825-3344	999-4401	536
Berry Plastics 44 Oneil St	EastHampton	MA	01027	413-527-1250		604
Berry-Hill Galleries Inc 11 E 70th St Web: www.berry-hill.com	New York	NY	10021	212-744-2300	744-2838	42
Berryman Products Inc 3800 E Randol Mill Rd TF: 800-433-1704 ■ Web: www.berrymanproducts.com	Arlington	TX	76011	817-640-2376	640-4850	146
Berry-Shino Securities Inc 15100 N 78th Way Ste 100 Web: www.berry-shino.com	Scottsdale	AZ	85260	480-315-3660		690
Berryville Chamber of Commerce 506 S Main PO Box 402 Web: www.berryvillear.com	Berryville	AR	72616	870-423-3704		139

	Phone	Fax	Class
Berryville Graphics 25 Jack Enders Blvd, Berryville VA 22611 *Web:* www.bcprintcroamcrica.com	540-955-2750	955-2633	626
Bert & Ernie's Saloon 361 N Last Chance Gulch, Helena MT 59601 *Web:* www.bertanderniesofhelena.com	406-443-5680		671
Bert R Huncilman & Son 115 Security Pkwy, New Albany IN 47150	812-945-3544		697
Bert R Hybels Inc 3322 Grand Prairie Rd, Kalamazoo MI 49006 *Web:* www.hybels.com	269-382-4921		292
Berta's 3928 Twiggs St, San Diego CA 92110 *Web:* www.bertasinoldtown.com	619-295-2343		671
Bertch Cabinet Manufacturing Inc 4747 Crestwood Dr, Waterloo IA 50702 *TF:* 800-728-4327 ■ *Web:* www.bertch.com	319-296-2987	296-2315	115
Bertech-Kelex 640 Maple Ave, Torrance CA 90503 *Web:* www.bertech.com	310-787-0337		246
Bertek Systems Inc 133 Bryce Blvd, Fairfax VT 05454 *TF:* 800-367-0210 ■ *Web:* www.berteksystems.com	802-752-3170		627
Bertelkamp Automation Inc 6321 Baum Dr, Knoxville TN 37919 *Web:* www.bertelkamp.com	865-588-7691		358
Bertelsmann Inc 1540 Broadway 24th Fl, New York NY 10036 *Web:* www.bertelsmann.com	212-782-1000		360-3
Bertelsmann SE & Co 1745 Broadway, New York NY 10019 **Fax Area Code:* 912 ■ *Web:* www.bertelsmann.com	490-524-1800	466-7013*	637-9
Berthel Fisher Companies 4201 42nd St NE Ste 100, Cedar Rapids IA 52402 *TF:* 800-356-5234 ■ *Web:* www.berthel.com	319-447-5700	447-4250	690
Bertie County 106 Dundee St PO Box 530, Windsor NC 27983 *Web:* www.co.bertie.nc.us	252-794-5300	794-5327	338
Bertling Logistics Inc 19054 Kenswick Dr, Humble TX 77338 *Web:* www.bertling.com	281-774-2300		194
Bertrand at Mister A's 2550 Fifth Ave 12th Fl, San Diego CA 92103 *Web:* www.asrestaurant.com	619-239-1377	239-1379	671
Berts Bikes & Sports 4050 Southwestern Blvd, Orchard Park NY 14127 *TF:* 800-255-9982 ■ *Web:* www.bertsbikes.com	716-646-0028		711
Bertsche Engineering Corp 711 Dartmouth Ln, Buffalo Grove IL 60089 *Web:* www.bertsche.com	847-537-8757		261
Bertucci's Restaurant Corp 155 Otis St, Northborough MA 01532 *Web:* www.bertuccis.com	508-351-2500		670
Bertuccio Farms 2410 Airline Hwy, Hollister CA 95023 *Web:* www.thefarmbertuccios.com	831-636-0821		315-3
Berwick Electric Co 3450 N Nevada Ave Ste 100, Colorado Springs CO 80907 *Web:* www.berwickelectric.com	719-632-7683	471-9660	189-4
Berwick Hospital Ctr, The 701 E 16th St, Berwick PA 18603 *TF:* 800-654-5988 ■ *Web:* commonwealthhealth.net	570-759-5000	759-3473	374-3
Berwind Group 1500 Market St 3000 Ctr Sq W, Philadelphia PA 19102 *Web:* www.berwind.com	215-563-2800	575-2314	185
Berwind Natural Resources Corp 509 15th St, Windber PA 15963	814-467-4519		501
Berwyn Development Corp 3322 S Oak Pk Ave 2nd Fl, Berwyn IL 60402 *Web:* www.berwyn.net	708-788-8100	788-0966	139
Berwyn Public Library (BPL) 2701 S Harlem Ave, Berwyn IL 60402 *Web:* www.berwynlibrary.org	708-795-8000	795-8101	434-3
Bescast Inc 4600 E 355th St, Willoughby OH 44094 *Web:* www.bescast.com	440-946-5300		306
Besco Electric Supply Co 711 S 14th St, Leesburg FL 34748 *Web:* www.bescolights.com	352-787-4542	365-0554	362
Besen Group LLC, The 10127 Ebenshire Ct, Oakton VA 22124 *Web:* www.thebesengroup.com	703-981-8168		463
Beshenich Muir & Associates LLC 121A Cherokee St, Leavenworth KS 66048 *Web:* www.bma-1.com	913-904-1880		463
Besicorp Ltd 1151 Flatbush Rd, Kingston NY 12401 *Web:* www.besicorp.com	845-336-7700		357
Besl Transfer Co 5700 Este Ave, Cincinnati OH 45232 *TF:* 800-456-2375 ■ *Web:* www.besl.com	513-242-3456	242-4013	780
Besly Cutting Tools Inc 16200 Woodmint Ln, South Beloit IL 61080 *TF:* 800-435-2965 ■ *Web:* www.besly.com	815-389-2231	389-1339	493
Bessamaire 10145 Philipp Pkwy Unit B, Streetsboro OH 44241 **Fax Area Code:* 440 ■ *TF:* 800-321-5992 ■ *Web:* www.bessamaire.com	800-321-5992	439-1625*	664
Besse Forest Products Group Inc 933 N Eigth St, Gladstone MI 49837 *Web:* www.bessegroup.com	906-428-3113		448
Bessemer Area Chamber of Commerce 321 N 18th St, Bessemer AL 35020 *TF:* 888-423-7736 ■ *Web:* www.bessemerchamber.com	205-425-3253	425-4979	139
Bessemer Hall of History 1905 Alabama Ave, Bessemer AL 35020 *TF:* 800-777-0369 ■ *Web:* www.bhamrails.info	205-426-1633		520
Bessemer Public Library 400 19th St, Bessemer AL 35020 *TF:* 800-488-7033 ■ *Web:* www.bessemerlibrary.org	205-428-7882		434-3
Bessemer Trust Co 630 Fifth Ave, New York NY 10111 *TF:* 866-271-7403 ■ *Web:* www.bessemertrust.com	212-708-9100	265-5826	401
Besser Co 801 Johnson St, Alpena MI 49707 *TF:* 800-530-9980 ■ *Web:* www.besser.com	989-354-4111	354-3120	386
Bessie Smith Cultural Ctr 200 E Martin Luther King Blvd, Chattanooga TN 37403 *TF:* 800-322-3344 ■ *Web:* www.bessiesmithcc.org	423-266-8658	267-1076	520
Bessire & Associates Inc 7621 Little Ave Ste 106, Charlotte NC 28226 *TF:* 800-797-7355 ■ *Web:* bessire.com	704-341-1423		193
Best & Flanagan LLP 60 S Sixth St Ste 2700, Minneapolis MN 55402 *Web:* www.bestlaw.com	612-339-7121	339-5897	428
Best Access Systems 6161 E 75th St, Indianapolis IN 46250 *TF:* 855-365-2407 ■ *Web:* www.bestaccess.com	317-849-2250		350
Best Aire LLC 3648 Rockland Cir, Millbury OH 43447 *TF:* 800-314-4755 ■ *Web:* www.best-aire.com	419-726-0055		316
Best Banner Sign Graphics Inc 630 Canion St, Austin TX 78752 *Web:* www.bannersigngraphics.com	512-458-5348		45
Best Bath Systems 723 Garber St, Caldwell ID 83605 *TF:* 866-333-8657 ■ *Web:* bestbath.com	208-342-6823	333-8657	375
Best Buy Company Inc 7601 Penn Ave S, Minneapolis MN 55423 *NYSE:* BBY ■ **Fax:* Cust Svc ■ *TF:* 888-237-8289 ■ *Web:* www.bestbuy.com	612-291-1000	292-2323*	35
Best Buys Direct Inc 1044 State Rt 23 Ste 310, Wayne NJ 07470 *Web:* www.bestbuysdirect.com	973-628-8100		514
Best Chevrolet Inc 128 Derby St, Hingham MA 02043 *TF:* 866-208-7873 ■ *Web:* www.thebestchevy.com	866-208-7873		57
Best Choice Software Inc 2112 First St W, Bradenton FL 34208 *Web:* www.bestchoicesoftware.com	941-747-5858		179
Best Cleaners Inc 469 Albany Shaker Rd, Albany NY 12211 *Web:* www.bestcleanersny.com	518-459-7440		426
Best Cutting Die Co 8080 Mccormick Blvd, Skokie IL 60076 *Web:* www.bestcuttingdie.com	847-675-5522		697
Best Data Products Inc 20740 Plummer St, Chatsworth CA 91311 *Web:* diamondmm.com	818-773-9600	773-9619	173-3
Best Distributing Company Inc PO Box 128, Goldsboro NC 27533 *Web:* www.bestdistributing.com	919-735-1651		191-4
BEST Flow Line Equipment 9298 Baythorne Dr, Houston TX 77041 *Web:* www.bestswivel.com	713-690-4511		358
Best Friends Pet Care Inc 520 Main Ave, Norwalk CT 06851 *Web:* www.bestfriendspetcare.com	203-849-1010		794
Best Friends Veterinary Ctr 2082 Cheyenne Ct, Grafton WI 53024 *Web:* www.bestfriendsvet.com	262-375-0130		794
Best Image Marketing Inc 2222 Park Pl Blvd, Clearlake CA 95422 *TF:* 800-996-0411 ■ *Web:* connect.homes.com	707-995-5050		195
Best Impressions Catalog Co 345 N Lewis Ave, Oglesby IL 61348 *TF:* 800-635-2378 ■ *Web:* www.bestimpressions.com	815-883-3532		791
Best Label Co 2900 Faber St, Union City CA 94587 *TF:* 800-637-5333 ■ *Web:* www.bestlabel.com	510-489-5400	489-2914	413
Best Life & Health Insurance Co 2505 McCabe Way, Irvine CA 92614 *TF:* 800-433-0088 ■ *Web:* www.bestlife.com	949-253-4080		391-2
Best Line Oil Co Inc 219 N 20th St, Tampa FL 33605 *TF:* 800-382-1811 ■ *Web:* www.bestlineoil.com	813-248-1044		579
Best Maid Products Inc PO Box 1809, Fort Worth TX 76101 *TF:* 800-447-3581 ■ *Web:* www.bestmaidproducts.com	817-335-5494		296-19
Best Maids 842 Lemay Ferry Rd, Saint Louis MO 63125	314-544-6180		256
Best Material Handling Inc 7150 Oak Valley Dr, Colorado Springs CO 80919 *TF:* 800-933-5270 ■ *Web:* www.best-materials.com	719-599-9191		321
Best Metal Products Co 3570 Raleigh Dr SE, Grand Rapids MI 49512 *Web:* www.bestmetalproducts.com	616-942-7141		223
Best Plumbing Specialties 3039 Ventrie Ct, Myersville MD 21773 *TF:* 800-448-6710 ■ *Web:* www.bestplumbingonline.com	800-448-6710		612
Best Plumbing Tile & Stone 49 Rt 138, Somers NY 10589 *Web:* www.bestplg.com	914-232-2020		610
Best Press Inc 4201 Airborn Dr, Addison TX 75001 *TF:* 800-638-3508 ■ *Web:* www.bestpress.com	972-930-1000		627
Best Priced Products Inc 3 Westchester Plaza, Elmsford NY 10523 *TF:* 800-824-2939 ■ *Web:* www.bpp2.com	914-345-3800		407
Best Provision Company Inc 144 Avon Ave, Newark NJ 07108 *TF:* 000-631-4466 ■ *Web:* www.bestprovision.com	973-242-5000	648-0041	296-26
Best Registration Services Inc 1418 S Third St, Louisville KY 40208 *TF:* 800-977-3475 ■ *Web:* www.bestregistrar.com	502-637-4528		396
Best Reports Inc PO Box 546, Richmond IL 60071 *Web:* www.bestreports.net	815-678-2703	839-7440	635
Best Sweet Inc 288 Mazeppa Rd, Mooresville NC 28115 *TF:* 888-211-5530 ■ *Web:* www.bestco.com	704-664-4300		296-8
Best Telecom Inc 262 E End Ave, Beaver PA 15009 *TF:* 888-365-2273 ■ *Web:* www.besttelecom.com	888-365-2273		387
Best Theratronics Ltd 413 March Rd, Ottawa ON K2K0E4 *TF:* 866-792-8598 ■ *Web:* www.theratronics.ca	613-591-2100		476
Best Travel Inc 8600 W Bryn Mawr Ave, Chicago IL 60631 *Web:* www.besttravel.com	773-380-0150	380-7028	771
Best Vascular 4350 International Blvd Ste A, Norcross GA 30093 *TF:* 800-668-6783 ■ *Web:* www.bestvascular.com	770-717-0904	717-1283	476
Best Way Disposal 2577 Kentucky Ave, Indianapolis IN 46221 *Web:* www.bestway-disposal.com	317-484-3365		660
Best Way Logistics 14004 Century Ln, Grandview MO 64030 *TF:* 877-923-7892 ■ *Web:* bestwaylogistics.com	816-767-8008		314
Best Western Chincoteague Island 7105 Maddox Blvd, Chincoteague Island VA 23336 *TF:* 800-553-6117 ■ *Web:* www.bestwestern.com	757-336-6557	336-6558	379
Best Western Edgewater 2400 London Rd, Duluth MN 55812 *Web:* www.zmchotels.com	218-728-3601		378
Best Western Grandma's Feather Bed 9300 Glacier Hwy, Juneau AK 99801 *TF:* 888-781-5005 ■ *Web:* www.grandmasfeatherbed.com	907-789-5005		671

	City	State	Zip	Phone	Fax	Class
Best Western Inn of the Ozarks 207 W Van Buren	Eureka Springs	AR	72632	479-253-9768	253-9768	669
TF: 800-552-3785 ■ *Web:* www.bestwestern.com						
Best Western InnTowner, The 2424 University Ave	Madison	WI	53726	608-233-8778		378
TF: 800-258-8321 ■ *Web:* inntowner.com						
Best Western International Inc 6201 N 24th Pkwy	Phoenix	AZ	85016	602-957-4200		379
TF: 800-528-1234 ■ *Web:* www.bestwestern.com						
Best Western Plus Heritage Inn 151 E McLeod Rd	Bellingham	WA	98226	360-647-1912		378
Web: www.bestwesternheritageinn.com						
Best Western Victorian Inn 487 Foam St	Monterey	CA	93940	831-373-8000	655-8174	379
TF: 800-232-4141 ■ *Web:* www.victorianinn.com						
Best Yet Market Inc 1 Lexington Ave	Bethpage	NY	11714	516-570-5300		345
Web: bestmarket.com						
Best's Review Ambest Rd	Oldwick	NJ	08858	908-439-2200	439-3363	457-5
TF: 800-424-2378 ■ *Web:* www.ambest.com/review						
Best's Underwriting Newsletter Ambest Rd	Oldwick	NJ	08858	908-439-2200		531-1
Web: www3.ambest.com/buglcem						
Best, Vanderlaan & Harrington 25 E Washington St Ste 800	Chicago	IL	60602	312-819-1100		428
TF: 800-351-4316 ■ *Web:* www.bestfirm.com						
Bestar Inc 4220 Villeneuve St	Lac-Megantic	QC	G6B2C3	819-583-1017		319-1
TF: 888-823-7827 ■ *Web:* www.bestar.ca						
Bestforms Inc 1135 Avenida Acaso	Camarillo	CA	93012	805-383-6993	987-5280	110
TF: 800-350-0618 ■ *Web:* www.bestforms.com						
BestIT 5716 Corsa Ave	Westlake Village	CA	91362	818-699-1668		196
Web: www.bestit.com						
Bestmark Inc 5500 Feltl Rd Ste 200	Minnetonka	MN	55343	952-922-3890		196
Web: www.bestmark.com						
Bestolife Corp 2777 Stemmons Fwy Ste 1800	Dallas	TX	75207	214-583-0271	631-3047	3
TF: 855-243-9164 ■ *Web:* www.bestolife.com						
Best-One Tire & Service LLC 101 N Polk St	Monroe	IN	46772	260-692-6171		755
Web: www.bestonetire.com						
BestPass Inc 828 Washington Ave	Albany	NY	12203	518-458-1579		393
TF: 888-410-9696 ■ *Web:* www.bestpass.com						
Best-Rite Mfg 2885 Lorraine Ave	Temple	TX	76501	800-749-2258	697-6258	286
TF: 800-749-2258 ■ *Web:* www.moorecoinc.com						
Bestronics Inc 197 Woodland Pkwy Ste 104-477	San Marcos	CA	92078	760-585-4040		45
Web: www.bestronics.com						
BestTel 360 E First St Ste 904	Tustin	CA	92780	714-612-7333		387
Web: www.besttel.net						
BestTransport.com Inc 400 W Wilson Bridge Rd Ste 100	Columbus	OH	43085	614-888-2378		224
TF: 800-548-3745 ■ *Web:* www.besttransport.com						
Best-Wade Petroleum Inc 201 Dodge Dr	Ripley	TN	38063	731-635-9661		581
Web: www.bestwade.com						
Bestway Enterprises Inc 3877 Luker Rd	Cortland	NY	13045	607-753-8261	753-9948	780
Web: www.bestwaylumber.com						
Bestway Inc 12400 Coit Rd Ste 950	Dallas	TX	75251	214-630-6655	630-8404	264-2
TF: 800-316-4567 ■ *Web:* www.bestwayrto.com						
Bestway Systems Inc 5755 Granger Rd Ste 400	Independence	OH	44131	216-398-6090		449
Web: www.bestwaysystems.com						
Bestway Tours & Safaris 8678 Greenall Ave	Burnaby	BC	V5J3M6	604-264-7378	264-7774	760
TF: 800-663-0844 ■ *Web:* www.bestway.com						
BestWeek Life/Health Newsletter Ambest Rd	Oldwick	NJ	08858	908-439-2200	439-3363	531-1
Web: www.ambest.com						
Bestwill Corp 439 Wald	Irvine	CA	92618	949-502-5700		612
TF: 800-325-4170 ■ *Web:* www.bestwill.com						
Besty Ross House 239 Arch St	Philadelphia	PA	19106	215-686-1252		50-3
Web: historicphiladelphia.org						
BET Networks & BET Interactive LLC 1235 W St NE	Washington	DC	20018	202-608-2000		740
Web: www.bet.com						
Beta Alpha Psi 220 Leigh Farm Rd	Durham	NC	27707	919-402-4044	402-4040	48-16
TF: 800-362-5066 ■ *Web:* www.bap.org						
Beta Analytic Inc 4985 SW 74th Ct	Miami	FL	33155	305-667-5167		743
Web: www.betalabservices.com						
Beta Beta Beta National Biological Honor Society Univ of N Alabama PO Box 5079	Florence	AL	35632	256-765-6220	765-6221	48-16
Web: www.tri-beta.org						
Beta Fluid Systems Inc 1209 Freeway Dr	Reidsville	NC	27320	336-342-0306		22
Beta Gamma Sigma Inc (BGS) 125 Weldon Pkwy	Maryland Heights	MO	63043	314-432-5650	432-7083	48-16
TF: 800-337-4677 ■ *Web:* www.betagammasigma.org						
Beta LaserMike Inc 8001 Technology Blvd	Dayton	OH	45424	937-233-9935	233-7284	472
TF: 800-886-9935 ■ *Web:* www.betalasermike.com						
Beta Phi Mu *Florida State Univ College of Information* 3141 Chestnut St	Philadelphia	PA	19104	215-895-2492	895-2494	48-16
Web: beta-phi-mu.org						
Beta Research Corp 6400 Jericho Tpke	Syosset	NY	11791	516-935-3800		668
Web: www.betaresearch.com						
Beta Screen Corp 707 Commercial Ave	Carlstadt	NJ	07072	201-939-2400	939-7656	591
TF: 800-272-7336 ■ *Web:* www.betascreen.com						
Beta Shim Co 11 Progress Dr	Shelton	CT	06484	203-926-1150	929-5509	488
Web: www.betashim.com						
Beta Soft Systems Inc 42808 Christy St Ste 101	Fremont	CA	94538	510-744-1700		180
TF: 800-368-1322 ■ *Web:* www.betasoftsystems.com						
Beta Systems Software of North America Inc 8300 Greensboro Dr Ste L1-633	McLean	VA	22102	703-889-1240	889-1241	178-12
Web: www.betasystems.com						
Beta Theta Pi 5134 Bonham Rd	Oxford	OH	45056	800-800-2382	523-2381*	48-16
**Fax Area Code:* 513 ■ *TF:* 800-800-2382						
Betach Solutions Inc 12 Manning Close NE	Calgary	AB	T2E7N6	403-984-2473		196
TF: 800-867-1389 ■ *Web:* www.betach.com						
Betachem Inc 58 Ware Rd	Upper Saddle River	NJ	07458	201-327-4100		479
Betacom Inc 9331 E Fowler Ave Ste F	Thonotosassa	FL	33592	813-986-4922		194
Web: www.betacominc.com						
Betar Inc 100 Randolph Rd	Somerset	NJ	08873	908-359-4200	359-1010	621
Web: www.betar.net						
Beta-tech Consulting Inc 1553 Markham Way	Sacramento	CA	95818	916-443-0300		194
Web: beta-techconsulting.com						
Bete Fog Nozzle Inc 50 Greenfield St	Greenfield	MA	01301	413-772-0846	772-6729	350
TF: 800-235-0049 ■ *Web:* www.bete.com						
Beth Ahabah Museum & Archives 1109 W Franklin St	Richmond	VA	23220	804-353-2668		520
Web: www.bethahabah.org						
Beth Israel Deaconess Hospital-Milton 199 Reedsdale Rd	Milton	MA	02186	617-696-4600	696-7380	374-3
TF: 800-462-5540 ■ *Web:* www.bidmilton.org						
Beth Israel Deaconess Medical Ctr (BIDMC) 330 Brookline Ave	Boston	MA	02215	617-667-7000		374-3
TF: 800-667-5356 ■ *Web:* www.bidmc.org						
Beth Medrash Govoha of America Inc 901 Madison Ave	Lakewood	NJ	08701	732-364-4212		48-20
Beth Ramacher Development Ctr 710 N Hughes Ave	Fresno	CA	93728	559-497-3955		685
TF: 800-293-0703 ■ *Web:* www.fcoe.org						
Bethany Bible College 26 Western St	Sussex	NB	E4E1E6	506-432-4400	432-4425	785
TF: 888-432-4444 ■ *Web:* www.kingswood.edu						
Bethany College 31 E Campus Dr	Bethany	WV	26032	304-829-7000	829-7142*	166
**Fax:* Admissions ■ *TF:* 800-922-7611 ■ *Web:* www.bethanywv.edu						
Bethany College 335 E Swensson St	Lindsborg	KS	67456	785-227-3311	227-8993*	166
**Fax:* Admissions ■ *TF Admissions:* 800-826-2281 ■ *Web:* www.bethanylb.edu						
Bethany House Publishers 11400 Hampshire Ave S	Bloomington	MN	55438	616-676-9185	676-9573	637-3
TF: 800-328-6109 ■ *Web:* bakerpublishinggroup.com						
Bethany Lutheran College 700 Luther Dr	Mankato	MN	56001	507-344-7000	344-7376*	166
**Fax:* Admissions ■ *TF:* 800-944-3066 ■ *Web:* www.blc.edu						
Bethany Republican-Clipper 202 N 16 St	Bethany	MO	64424	660-425-6325	425-3441	532-4
Web: www.bethanyclipper.com						
Bethany Retreat House 2202 Lituanica Ave	East Chicago	IN	46312	219-398-5047	398-9329	673
TF: 800-444-8910 ■ *Web:* www.bethanyretreathouse.org						
Bethany Theological Seminary 615 National Rd W	Richmond	IN	47374	765-983-1800	983-1840	167-3
TF: 800-287-8822 ■ *Web:* www.bethanyseminary.edu						
Bethany Village 325 Wesley Dr	Mechanicsburg	PA	17055	717-766-0279		672
Web: www.bethanyvillage.org						
Bethea Baptist Retirement Community 157 Home Ave	Darlington	SC	29532	843-393-2867	393-2458	672
TF: 877-393-2867 ■ *Web:* bethearetirement.com						
Bethel Baptist Church 1196 N Academy St	Galesburg	IL	61401	309-342-3166		48-20
Web: www.mybethel.com						
Bethel College 1001 W McKinley Ave	Mishawaka	IN	46545	574-807-7000	807-7000*	166
**Fax:* Admissions ■ *TF Admissions:* 800-422-4101 ■ *Web:* www.bethelcollege.edu						
Bethel College 300 E 27th St	North Newton	KS	67117	316-283-2500	284-5286*	166
**Fax:* Admissions ■ *TF:* 800-522-1887 ■ *Web:* www.bethelks.edu						
Beth-El College of Nursing & Health Sciences 1420 Austin Bluffs Pkwy	Colorado Springs	CO	80918	719-255-8227	262-4416	166
TF: 800-990-8227 ■ *Web:* uccs.edu/~bethel						
Bethel Inn & Country Club 21 Broad St PO Box 49	Bethel	ME	04217	207-824-2175	824-2233	669
TF: 800-654-0125 ■ *Web:* www.bethelinn.com						
Bethel Seminary 3949 Bethel Dr	Saint Paul	MN	55112	651-638-6400	638-6002	167-3
TF: 800-255-8706 ■ *Web:* www.bethel.edu/seminary						
Bethel University 325 Cherry Ave	McKenzie	TN	38201	731-352-4000	352-4241*	166
**Fax:* Admissions ■ *Web:* www.bethelu.edu						
Bethel University 3900 Bethel Dr	Saint Paul	MN	55112	651-638-6400	635-1490*	166
**Fax:* Admissions ■ *TF:* 800-255-8706 ■ *Web:* www.bethel.edu						
Bethel World Outreach Ministries International Inc 8252 Georgia Ave	Silver Spring	MD	20910	301-588-8099		48-20
Web: cityofhope.bwomi.org						
Bethesda Christian University 730 N Euclid	Anaheim	CA	92801	714-517-1945		161
Web: buc.edu						
Bethesda Home 408 E Main St	Goessel	KS	67053	620-367-2291		371
TF: 800-555-1212 ■ *Web:* www.bethesdahome.org						
Bethesda Hospital 2951 Maple Ave	Zanesville	OH	43701	740-454-4000		374-3
TF: 800-322-4762 ■ *Web:* genesishcs.org						
Bethesda Ministries 2200 Peacock Rd	Richmond	IN	47374	765-939-2975		48-20
Web: mybwc.org						
Bethesda North Hospital 10500 Montgomery Rd	Cincinnati	OH	45242	513-569-5400		374-3
Web: www.trihealth.com						
Bethesda Softworks LLC 1370 Piccard Dr Ste 120	Rockville	MD	20850	301-926-8300	926-8010	178-6
Web: www.bethsoft.com						
Bethlehem Area Public Library 11 W Church St	Bethlehem	PA	18018	610-867-3761	867-2767	434-3
TF: 800-732-0999 ■ *Web:* www.bapl.org						
Bethlehem Chamber of Commerce 318 Delaware Ave Ste 11	Delmar	NY	12054	518-439-0512	475-0910	139
Web: www.bethlehemchamber.com						
Bethlehem Construction Inc 5505 Tichenal Rd	Cashmere	WA	98815	509-782-1001		186
TF: 800-627-1613 ■ *Web:* www.bethlehemconstruction.com						
Bethpage Federal Credit Union 899 S Oyster Bay Rd	Bethpage	NY	11714	800-628-7070	349-6828*	219
**Fax Area Code:* 516 ■ *TF:* 800-628-7070 ■ *Web:* www.bethpagefcu.com						
Bethpage State Park Bethpage Pkwy	Farmingdale	NY	11735	516-249-0701	753-0413	565
TF: 800-456-2267 ■ *Web:* parks.ny.gov/parks/108/details.aspx						
Bethune Memorial House National Historic Site 235 John St N	Gravenhurst	ON	P1P1G4	705-687-4261	687-4935	563
Web: www.pc.gc.ca/eng/lhn-nhs/on/bethune/index.aspx						

Phone | Fax | Class

Bethune-Cookman College
640 Dr Mary McLeod Bethune Blvd .... Daytona Beach FL 32114 386-481-2900 481-2601* 166
*Fax: Admissions ■ *TF Admissions:* 800-448-0228 ■ *Web:* www.cookman.edu

Betis Group Inc 1420 Beverly Rd Ste 330 .... McLean VA 22101 703-532-2008 177
Web: www.betis.com

Betson Enterprises Inc
303 Patterson Plank Rd .... Carlstadt NJ 07072 201-438-1300 438-4837 55
TF: 800-524-2343 ■ *Web:* www.betson.com

Betsy Hotel 1440 Ocean Dr .... Miami Beach FL 33139 305-531-6100 379
TF: 866-792-3879 ■ *Web:* www.thebetsyhotel.com

Betsy Johnson Regional Hospital
803 Tilghman Dr, Ste 100 PO Box 1706 .... Dunn NC 28334 910-892-7161 374-3
Web: myharnetthealth.org

Bettcher Industries Inc PO Box 336 .... Vermilion OH 44089 440-965-4422 298
TF: 800-321-8763 ■ *Web:* www.bettcher.com

Bette & Cring LLC
22 Century Hill Dr Ste 201 .... Latham NY 12110 518-213-1010 186
TF: 800-872-7878 ■ *Web:* www.bettecring.com

Bettendorf Community School District
3311 18th St .... Bettendorf IA 52722 563-359-3681 359-3685 685
Web: www.bettendorf.k12.ia.us

Bettendorf Office Products Inc
3280 Middle Rd .... Bettendorf IA 52722 563-359-3487 359-8901 45
TF: 800-468-7280 ■ *Web:* www.bettoffice.com

Bettendorf Public Library
2950 Learning Campus Dr .... Bettendorf IA 52722 563-344-4175 344-4185 434-3
Web: www.bettendorflibrary.com

Bettendorf-Stanford 1370 W Main St .... Salem IL 62881 618-548-3555 361
TF: 800-548-2253 ■ *Web:* www.bettendorfstanford.com

Better Baked Foods Inc
56 Smedley St .... North East PA 16428 814-725-8778 296-1
Web: www.betterbaked.com

Better Banks 10225 N Knoxville Ave .... Peoria IL 61615 309-243-1000 70
Web: betterbanks.com

Better Business Bureau In Alaska Oregon & Western Washington
341 W Tudor Rd Ste 209 .... Anchorage AK 99503 907-562-0704 79
Web: bbb.org/alaskaoregonwesternwashington

Better Business Bureau Inc
1000 Broadway Ste 625 .... Oakland CA 94607 510-844-2000 844-2100 79
TF: 866-411-2221 ■ *Web:* bbb.org/greater-san-francisco

Better Business Bureau of Acadiana
4007 W Congress St Ste B .... Lafayette LA 70506 337-981-3497 981-7559 79
TF: 800-557-7392 ■ *Web:* bbb.org/acadiana

Better Business Bureau of Arkansas
12521 Kanis Rd .... Little Rock AR 72211 501-664-7274 664-0024 79
Web: bbb.org

Better Business Bureau of Ark-La-Tex
401 Edwards St Ste 135 .... Shreveport LA 71101 318-797-1330 79
TF: 800-372-4222 ■ *Web:* bbb.org/shreveport

Better Business Bureau of Asheville/Western North Carolina
112 Executive Pk .... Asheville NC 28801 828-253-2392 252-5039 79
TF: 800-452-2882 ■ *Web:* bbb.org/asheville

Better Business Bureau of Brazos Valley & Deep East Texas
418 Tarrow .... College Station TX 77840 979-260-2222 79
Web: bbb.org/bryan

Better Business Bureau of Canton Region/West Virginia
1434 Cleveland Ave NW .... Canton OH 44703 330-454-9401 456-8957 79
TF: 800-362-0494 ■ *Web:* bbb.org/canton

Better Business Bureau of Central & Eastern Kentucky
1460 Newtown Pk .... Lexington KY 40511 859-259-1008 259-1639 79
TF: 800-866-6668 ■ *Web:* bbb.org/lexington

Better Business Bureau of Central Alabama & the Wiregrass Area
2101 Highland Ave Ste 410 .... Birmingham AL 35205 205-558-2222 558-2239 79
TF: 800-824-5274 ■ *Web:* bbb.org/csal

Better Business Bureau of Central Alabama & the Wiregrass Area Dothan Branch
1971 S Brannon Stand Rd .... Dothan AL 36305 334-794-0492 794-0659 79
Web: bbb.org/csal

Better Business Bureau of Central East Texas
3600 Old BullaRd Rd Bldg 1 .... Tyler TX 75701 903-581-5704 534-8644 79
TF: 800-443-0131 ■ *Web:* bbb.org/east-texas

Better Business Bureau of Central East Texas
102 Commander Ste 7 .... Longview TX 75605 903-758-3222 534-8644 79
TF: 800-443-0131 ■ *Web:* bbb.org/east-texas

Better Business Bureau of Central Florida
1600 S Grant St .... Longwood FL 32750 407-621-3300 786-2625 79
Web: bbb.org/central-florida

Better Business Bureau of Central Georgia
277 ML King Jr Blvd Ste 102 .... Macon GA 31201 478-742-7999 742-8191 79
TF: 800-422-2811 ■ *Web:* bbb.org/central-georgia

Better Business Bureau of Central Illinois
8100 N University Peoria .... Peoria IL 61615 309-688-3741 681-7290 79
TF: 800-763-4222 ■ *Web:* bbb.org/central-illinois

Better Business Bureau of Central Indiana
151 N Delaware St .... Indianapolis IN 46204 317-488-2222 488-2224 79
TF: 866-463-9222 ■ *Web:* bbb.org/indy

Better Business Bureau of Central Louisiana & Ark-La-Tex
5220-C Rue Verdun .... Alexandria LA 71303 318-473-4494 473-8906 79
TF General: 800-372-4222 ■ *Web:* bbb.org/shreveport

Better Business Bureau of Central New England & Northeast Connecticut
340 Main St Ste 802 .... Worcester MA 01608 508-755-3340 754-4158 79

Better Business Bureau of Central North Carolina
3608 W Friendly Ave .... Greensboro NC 27410 336-852-4240 852-7540 79
Web: bbb.org/greensboro

Better Business Bureau of Central Northeast Northwest & Southwest Arizona
4428 N 12th St .... Phoenix AZ 85014 602-264-1721 263-0997 79
TF: 877-291-6222 ■ *Web:* bbb.org/phoenix

Better Business Bureau of Central Ohio
1169 Dublin Rd .... Columbus OH 43215 614-486-6336 486-6631 79
TF: 800-759-2400 ■ *Web:* bbb.org/centralohio

Better Business Bureau of Central Oklahoma
17 S Dewey Ave .... Oklahoma City OK 73102 405-239-6081 235-5891 79
TF: 800-654-7757 ■ *Web:* bbb.org/oklahoma-city

Better Business Bureau of Central Texas
1805 Rutherford Ln Ste 100 .... Austin TX 78754 512-445-2911 445-2096 79
TF: 800-621-0508 ■ *Web:* bbb.org/central-texas

Better Business Bureau of Central Virginia
720 Moorefield Pk Dr Ste 300 .... Richmond VA 23236 804-648-0016 320-0248 79
TF: 800-533-5501 ■ *Web:* bbb.org/richmond

Better Business Bureau of Chicago & Northern Illinois
330 N Wabash Ave Ste 2006 .... Chicago IL 60611 312-832-0500 832-9985 79
Web: bbb.org/chicago

Better Business Bureau of Cincinnati
7 W Seventh St Ste 1600 .... Cincinnati OH 45202 513-421-3015 621-0907 79
TF: 800-388-2222 ■ *Web:* bbb.org/cincinnati

Better Business Bureau of Coastal North & South Carolina
1121 Third Ave Ste 203 .... Conway SC 29526 843-488-2227 488-0998 79
Web: bbb.org/myrtle-beach

Better Business Bureau of Connecticut
29 Berlin Rd .... Wallingford CT 06416 860-740-4500 740-4515 79
Web: bbb.org/connecticut

Better Business Bureau of Dayton/Miami Valley
15 W Fourth St Ste 300 .... Dayton OH 45402 937-222-5825 222-3338 79
TF: 800-776-5301 ■ *Web:* bbb.org/dayton

Better Business Bureau of Delaware
60 Reads Way .... New Castle DE 19720 302-221-5255 221-5265 79
Web: bbb.org/delaware

Better Business Bureau of Detroit & Eastern Michigan
26777 Central Pk Blvd Ste 100 .... Southfield MI 48076 248-223-9400 356-5135 79
Web: bbb.org/detroit

Better Business Bureau of Eastern Massachusetts Maine Rhode Island & Vermont
290 Donald Lynch Blvd Ste 102 .... Marlborough MA 01752 508-652-4800 652-4820 79
TF: 800-422-2811 ■ *Web:* bbb.org/boston

Better Business Bureau of Eastern Missouri & Southern Illinois
211 N Broadway Ste 2060 .... Saint Louis MO 63102 314-645-3300 645-2666 79
Web: bbb.org/stlouis

Better Business Bureau of Eastern North Carolina
5540 Munford Rd Ste 130 .... Raleigh NC 27612 919-277-4222 277-4221 79
TF: 800-452-2777 ■ *Web:* bbb.org/raleigh-durham

Better Business Bureau of Eastern Oklahoma
1722 S Carson Ave Ste 3200 .... Tulsa OK 74119 918-492-1266 492-1276 79
TF: 800-955-5100 ■ *Web:* bbb.org/tulsa

Better Business Bureau of Eastern Ontario & the Outaouais Inc
700 Industrial Ave Unit 505 .... Ottawa ON K1G0Y9 613-237-4856 78

Better Business Bureau of Eastern Pennsylvania
1880 JFK Blvd Ste 1330 .... Philadelphia PA 19103 215-985-9313 563-4907 79
Web: bbb.org/washington-dc-eastern-pa

Better Business Bureau of El Paso
720 Arizona Ave .... El Paso TX 79902 915-577-0191 577-0209 79
TF: 800-621-0508 ■ *Web:* bbb.org/elpaso

Better Business Bureau of Greater East Tennessee
255 N Peters Rd Ste A PO Box 31377 .... Knoxville TN 37923 865-692-1600 692-1590 79
Web: bbb.org/knoxville

Better Business Bureau of Greater Iowa Quad Cities & Sioux Land Region
505 Fifth Ave Ste 950 .... Des Moines IA 50309 515-243-8137 243-2227 79
TF: 800-239-1642 ■ *Web:* www.bbb.org/iowa

Better Business Bureau of Greater Kansas City
8080 Ward Pkwy Ste 401 .... Kansas City MO 64114 816-421-7800 472-5442 79
TF: 877-606-0695 ■ *Web:* bbb.org/kansas-city

Better Business Bureau of Greater Maryland
502 S Sharp St Ste 1200 .... Baltimore MD 21201 410-347-3990 347-3936 79
TF: 800-579-6239 ■ *Web:* bbb.org/greater-maryland

Better Business Bureau of Greater New Orleans
710 Baronne St Ste C .... New Orleans LA 70113 504-581-6222 524-9110 79
Web: bbb.org/new-orleans

Better Business Bureau of Hampton Roads
586 Virginian Dr .... Norfolk VA 23505 757-531-1300 531-1388 79
Web: bbb.org/norfolk

Better Business Bureau of Hawaii
1132 Bishop St Ste 615 .... Honolulu HI 96813 808-536-6956 628-3970 79
TF: 877-222-6551 ■ *Web:* bbb.org/hawaii

Better Business Bureau of Heartland
11811 P St .... Omaha NE 68137 402-391-7612 391-7535 79
TF: 800-649-6814 ■ *Web:* bbb.org/nebraska

Better Business Bureau of Kansas Inc
345 N Riverview St Ste 720 .... Wichita KS 67203 316-263-3146 263-3063 79
TF: 800-856-2417 ■ *Web:* bbb.org/nebraska

Better Business Bureau of Louisville Southern Indiana
844 S Fourth St .... Louisville KY 40203 502-583-6546 589-9940 79
TF: 800-388-2222 ■ *Web:* bbb.org/louisville

Better Business Bureau of Maine
290 Donald Lynch Blvd Ste 102 .... Marlborough MA 01752 508-652-4800 652-4820 79
TF: 800-422-2811 ■ *Web:* www.bbb.org/boston

Better Business Bureau of Metro Washington DC & Eastern Pennsylvania
1411 K St NW Ste 1000 .... Washington DC 20005 202-393-8000 393-1198 79
TF: 800-864-1224 ■ *Web:* bbb.org/washington-dc-eastern-pa

Better Business Bureau of Metropolitan Atlanta
503 Oak Pl Ste 590 .... Atlanta GA 30349 404-766-0875 768-1085 79
Web: bbb.org/atlanta

Better Business Bureau of Metropolitan Dallas & Northeast Texas
1601 Elm St Ste 3838 .... Dallas TX 75201 214-220-2000 740-0321 79
TF: 800-444-0686 ■ *Web:* bbb.org/dallas

Better Business Bureau of Metropolitan Houston
1333 W Loop S Ste 1200 .... Houston TX 77027 713-868-9500 867-4947 79
TF: 800-876-7060 ■ *Web:* bbb.org/houston

Better Business Bureau of Metropolitan New York
257 Pk Ave S .... New York NY 10010 212-533-6200 477-4912 79
TF: 800-684-3322 ■ *Web:* bbb.org/new-york-city

Better Business Bureau of Middle Tennessee Inc
201 Fourth Ave N Ste 100 .... Nashville TN 37219 615-242-4222 250-4245 79
TF: 800-615-9720 ■ *Web:* bbb.org/nashville

Better Business Bureau of Minnesota & North Dakota
220 River Ridge Cir S .... Burnsville MN 55337 651-699-1111 695-2488 79
TF: 800-646-6222 ■ *Web:* bbb.org/minnesota

Better Business Bureau of New Jersey
1700 Whitehorse-Hamilton Sq Rd Ste D-5 .... Trenton NJ 08690 609-588-0808 588-0546 79
TF: 888-494-4009 ■ *Web:* bbb.org/new-jersey

Better Business Bureau of North Central Texas
4245 Kemp Blvd Ste 900 .... Wichita Falls TX 76308 940-691-1172 691-1175 79
Web: bbb.org/wichita-falls

Better Business Bureau of Northeast California
3075 Beacon Blvd .... West Sacramento CA 95691 916-443-6843 443-0376 79
TF: 866-334-6272 ■ *Web:* bbb.org/northeast-california

Better Business Bureau of Northeast Florida & The Southeast Atlantic
4417 Beach Blvd Ste 202 .... Jacksonville FL 32207 904-721-2288 79
TF: 800-713-6661 ■ *Web:* bbb.org/north-east-florida

	Phone	Fax	Class
Better Business Bureau of Northeast Louisiana 1900 N 18th St Ste 411 . . . . . Monroe LA 71201 *TF:* 800-372-4222 ■ *Web:* bbb.org/north-east-louisiana	318-387-4600		79
Better Business Bureau of Northeast Ohio 2800 Euclid Ave 4th Fl . . . . . Cleveland OH 44115 *TF:* 800-233-0361 ■ *Web:* bbb.org/cleveland	216-241-7678	861-6365	79
Better Business Bureau of Northeastern & Central Pennsylvania 1054 Oak St . . . . . Scranton PA 18508 *Web:* bbb.org/washington-dc-eastern-pa	570-342-5100	342-1282	79
Better Business Bureau of Northern Alabama 107 Lincoln St . . . . . Huntsville AL 35804 *Web:* bbb.org/northern-alabama	256-533-1640	533-1177	79
Better Business Bureau of Northern Colorado & East Central Wyoming 8020 S County Rd 5 Ste 100 . . . . . Fort Collins CO 80528 *TF:* 800-564-0371 ■ *Web:* bbb.org/wyoming-and-northern-colorado	970-484-1348	221-1239	79
Better Business Bureau of Northern Indiana 4011 Parnell Ave. . . . . . Fort Wayne IN 46805 *TF:* 800-552-4631 ■ *Web:* bbb.org/northernindiana	260-423-4433	423-3301	79
Better Business Bureau of Northern Nevada 4834 Sparks Blvd Ste 102 . . . . . Sparks NV 89436 *Web:* bbb.org/reno	775-322-0657	322-8163	79
Better Business Bureau of Northwest 1000 Stn Dr Ste 222 . . . . . Dupont WA 98327 *Web:* bbb.org/alaskaoregonwesternwashington	206-431-2222	431-2200	79
Better Business Bureau of Northwest Florida 912 E Gadsden St . . . . . Pensacola FL 32501 *TF:* 800-729-9226 ■ *Web:* bbb.org/northwest-florida	850-429-0002	429-0006	79
Better Business Bureau of Northwest Indiana 7863 Broadway Ste 124 . . . . . Merrillville IN 46410 *Web:* bbb.org/northernindiana	260-423-4433	423-3301	79
Better Business Bureau of Northwest North Carolina 500 W Fifth St Ste 202 . . . . . Winston-Salem NC 27101 *TF:* 800-777-8348 ■ *Web:* bbb.org/northwestern-north-carolina	336-725-8348	777-3727	79
Better Business Bureau of Northwest Ohio & Southeast Michigan 7668 King's Pt Rd . . . . . Toledo OH 43617 *TF:* 800-743-4222 ■ *Web:* bbb.org/toledo	419-531-3116	578-6001	79
Better Business Bureau of Quebec 1565 Boul de l'Avenir Ste 206 . . . . . Laval QC H7S2N5 **Fax Area Code: 450* ■ *Web:* www.occq-qcco.com	514-905-3893	663-6316*	78
Better Business Bureau of Rockford 330 N Wabash Ave Ste 3120 . . . . . Chicago IL 60611 *TF:* 800-955-5100 ■ *Web:* www.bbb.org/chicago	312-832-0500	832-9985	79
Better Business Bureau of San Diego & Imperial Counties 5050 Murphy Canyon Rd Ste 110 . . . . . San Diego CA 92123 *Web:* bbb.org/sdoc	858-637-6199	496-2141	79
Better Business Bureau of Saskatchewan 980 Albert St Ste 201 . . . . . Regina SK S4R2P7 *TF:* 888-352-7601 ■ *Web:* bbb.org/saskatchewan	306-352-7601	565-6236	78
Better Business Bureau of South Central Louisiana 748 Main St . . . . . Baton Rouge LA 70802 *Web:* bbb.org/baton-rouge	225-346-5222	346-1029	79
Better Business Bureau of South Texas 1333 W Loop S Ste 1200 . . . . . Houston TX 77027 *TF:* 800-705-3994 ■ *Web:* bbb.org/houston	713-868-9500	867-4947	79
Better Business Bureau of Southeast Florida & the Caribbean 4411 Beacon Cir Ste 4 . . . . . West Palm Beach FL 33407 *TF:* 866-966-7226 ■ *Web:* bbb.org/south-east-florida	561-842-1918	845-7234	79
Better Business Bureau of Southeast Tennessee & Northwest Georgia 508 N Market St . . . . . Chattanooga TN 37405 *TF:* 800-548-4456 ■ *Web:* bbb.org/chattanooga	423-266-6144	267-1924	79
Better Business Bureau of Southeast Texas 550 Fannin St Ste 100 . . . . . Beaumont TX 77701 *TF:* 800-685-7650 ■ *Web:* bbb.org/southeast-texas	409-835-5348	838-6858	79
Better Business Bureau of Southern Alberta 1709 8 Ave NE Ste 5 . . . . . Calgary AB T2E0S9 *Web:* www.bbb.org/calgary	403-531-8784	640-2514	78
Better Business Bureau of Southern Arizona 434 S Williams Blvd Ste 102 . . . . . Tucson AZ 85711 *TF:* 800-697-4733 ■ *Web:* bbb.org/tucson	520-888-5353	888-6262	79
Better Business Bureau of Southern Colorado 25 N Wahsatch Ave. . . . . . Colorado Springs CO 80903 *TF:* 800-571-0371 ■ *Web:* bbb.org/southern-colorado	719-636-1155	636-5078	79
Better Business Bureau of Southern Nebraska 3 Wilson Blvd Ste 1 . . . . . Omaha NE 68137 *Web:* bbb.org/nebraska	402-436-2345	476-8221	79
Better Business Bureau of Southern Nevada 6040 S Jones Blvd . . . . . Las Vegas NV 89118 *TF:* 800-449-8693 ■ *Web:* bbb.org/southern-nevada	702-320-4500	320-4560	79
Better Business Bureau of Southern Piedmont Carolinas 13860 Ballantyne Corporate Pl Ste 225 . . . . . Charlotte NC 28277 *TF:* 800-432-1000 ■ *Web:* bbb.org/charlotte	704-927-8611	927-8615	79
Better Business Bureau of Southwest Idaho & Eastern Oregon 1200 N Curtis Rd . . . . . Boise ID 83706 *TF:* 800-218-1001 ■ *Web:* bbb.org/snakeriver	208-342-4649	342-5116	79
Better Business Bureau of Southwest Louisiana Inc 2309 E Prien Lake Rd . . . . . Lake Charles LA 70601 *TF:* 800-542-7085 ■ *Web:* bbb.org/lakecharles	337-478-6253	474-8981	79
Better Business Bureau of Southwest Missouri 430 S Glenstone Ave. . . . . . Springfield MO 65802 *TF:* 800-286-3932 ■ *Web:* bbb.org/southwestern-missouri	417-862-4222	869-5544	79
Better Business Bureau of the Abilene Area 3300 S 14th St Ste 307 . . . . . Abilene TX 79605 *TF:* 800-705-3994 ■ *Web:* bbb.org/abilene	325-691-1533	691-0309	79
Better Business Bureau of the Akron Inc 222 W Market St . . . . . Akron OH 44303 *TF:* 800-825-8887 ■ *Web:* bbb.org/akron	330-253-4590	253-6249	79
Better Business Bureau of the Bakersfield Area 1601 H St Ste 101 . . . . . Bakersfield CA 93301 *TF:* 800-675-8118 ■ *Web:* bbb.org/central-california-inland-empire	661-322-2074	322-8318	79
Better Business Bureau of the Denver-Boulder Metro Area 1020 Cherokee St . . . . . Denver CO 80204 *TF:* 800-356-6333 ■ *Web:* bbb.org/denver	303-758-2100	758-8321	79
Better Business Bureau of the Maritime Provinces 1888 Brunswick St Ste 805 . . . . . Halifax NS B3J3J8 *Web:* bbb.org/atlantic-provinces	902-422-6581	429-6457	78
Better Business Bureau of the Mid-Hudson 150 White Plains Rd Ste 107 . . . . . Tarrytown NY 10591 *Web:* bbb.org/new-york-city	914-333-0550	333-7519	79
Better Business Bureau of the Mid-South 3693 Tyndale Dr . . . . . Memphis TN 38125 *TF:* 800-222-8754 ■ *Web:* bbb.org/memphis	901-759-1300	757-2997	79
Better Business Bureau of the San Angelo Area 3134 Executive Dr. . . . . . San Angelo TX 76904 *TF:* 800-252-5555 ■ *Web:* bbb.org/san-angelo	325-949-2989	949-3514	79
Better Business Bureau of the Santa Clara Valley 1112 S Bascom Ave . . . . . San Jose CA 95128 *Web:* bbb.org/losangelessiliconvalley	408-278-7400	278-7444	79
Better Business Bureau of the South Central Area 1800 NE Loop 410 Ste 400 . . . . . San Antonio TX 78217 *Web:* bbb.org/central-texas	210-828-9441	828-3101	79
Better Business Bureau of the South Plains of Texas 3333 66th St . . . . . Lubbock TX 79413 *TF:* 800-687-7890 ■ *Web:* bbb.org/south-plains-texas	806-763-0459	744-9748	79
Better Business Bureau of the Southeast Atlantic 6555 Abercorn St Ste 120 . . . . . Savannah GA 31405 *Web:* bbb.org/north-east-florida	912-354-7521		79
Better Business Bureau of the Southwest 2625 Pennsylvania St NE Ste 2050 . . . . . Albuquerque NM 87110 *Web:* bbb.org/new-mexico-southwest-colorado	505-326-6501	346-0696	79
Better Business Bureau of the Texas Panhandle 600 S Tyler Ste 1300 . . . . . Amarillo TX 79101 *TF:* 800-621-0508 ■ *Web:* bbb.org/amarillo	806-379-6222	379-8206	79
Better Business Bureau of the Tri-Counties PO Box 129 . . . . . Santa Barbara CA 93102 *TF:* 800-955-5100 ■ *Web:* bbb.org/santa-barbara	805-963-8657	962-8557	79
Better Business Bureau of the Tri-Parish Area 801 Barrow St Ste 400 . . . . . Houma LA 70360 *TF:* 800-533-5501 ■ *Web:* bbb.org/new-orleans	985-868-3456		79
Better Business Bureau of Upstate New York 100 Bryant Woods S . . . . . Amherst NY 14228 *TF:* 800-828-5000 ■ *Web:* bbb.org/upstate-new-york	716-881-5222	883-5349	79
Better Business Bureau of Utah 5673 S Redwood Rd . . . . . Salt Lake City UT 84123 *TF:* 800-456-3907 ■ *Web:* bbb.org/utah	801-892-6009	892-6002	79
Better Business Bureau of Vancouver Island 220-1175 Cook St Ste 220 . . . . . Victoria BC V8V4A1 *TF:* 877-826-4222 ■ *Web:* bbb.org/vancouver-island	250-386-6348	386-2367	78
Better Business Bureau of West Central Ohio 219 N McDonel St . . . . . Lima OH 45801 *TF:* 800-462-0468 ■ *Web:* www.bbb.org	419-223-7010		79
Better Business Bureau of West Florida 2655 McCormick Dr . . . . . Clearwater FL 33759 *TF:* 800-525-1447 ■ *Web:* bbb.org/west-florida	727-535-5522	539-6301	79
Better Business Bureau of West Georgia-East Alabama PO Box 2587 . . . . . Columbus GA 31902 *Web:* bbb.org/columbus-georgia	706-324-0712		79
Better Business Bureau of Western Massachusetts 35 Ctr St Ste 203 . . . . . Chicopee MA 01013 *TF:* 866-566-9222 ■ *Web:* bbb.org/central-western-massachusetts	866-566-9222		79
Better Business Bureau of Western Pennsylvania 400 Holiday Dr Ste 220 . . . . . Pittsburgh PA 15220 *TF:* 800-345-3890 ■ *Web:* bbb.org/pittsburgh	412-456-2700	922-8656	79
Better Business Bureau of Wisconsin 10101 W Greenfield Ave Ste 125 . . . . . Milwaukee WI 53214 *Web:* bbb.org/wisconsin	414-847-6000	302-0355	79
Better Business Bureau Online *Council of Better Business Bureaus, The* 4200 Wilson Blvd Ste 800 . . . . . Arlington VA 22203 *TF:* 800-459-8875 ■ *Web:* www.bbb.org	703-276-0100	525-8277	79
Better Business Bureau Serving Central & Northern Alberta 16102 100 Ave NW . . . . . Edmonton AB T5P0L3 *Web:* www.bbb.org/edmonton	780-482-2341	482-1150	78
Better Business Bureau Serving Central California 4201 W Shaw Ave Ste 107 . . . . . Fresno CA 93722 *TF:* 800-675-8118 ■ *Web:* bbb.org/central-california-inland-empire	559-222-8111	228-6518	79
Better Business Bureau Serving Eastern Washington North Idaho & Montana Inc 152 S Jefferson St Ste 200 . . . . . Spokane WA 99201 *Web:* www.bbb.org	509-455-4200		79
Better Business Bureau Serving Mainland British Columbia 788 Beatty St Ste 404 . . . . . Vancouver BC V6B2M1 *TF:* 888-803-1222 ■ *Web:* www.bbb.org/mbc	604-682-2711	681-1544	78
Better Business Bureau Serving Western Michigan 40 Pearl St NW Ste 354 . . . . . Grand Rapids MI 49503 *Web:* bbb.org/western-michigan	616-774-8236	774-2014	79
Better Business Bureau Serving Western Ontario 190 Wortley Rd Ste 206 . . . . . London ON N6C4Y7 *TF:* 877-283-9222 ■ *Web:* bbb.org/western-ontario	519-673-3222	673-5966	78
Better Business Bureau Serving Winnipeg & Manitoba 1030B Empress St . . . . . Winnipeg MB R3G3H4 *TF:* 800-385-3074 ■ *Web:* www.bbb.org/manitoba	204-989-9010	989-9016	78
Better Business Bureau Upstate South Carolina 408 N Church St Ste C . . . . . Greenville SC 29601 *TF:* 800-363-3115 ■ *Web:* bbb.org/upstatesc	864-242-5052		79
Better Hearing Institute (BHI) 1444 I St NW Ste 700 . . . . . Washington DC 20005 *TF:* 800-639-3884 ■ *Web:* www.betterhearing.org	202-449-1100		48-17
Better Home Products Ltd 534 Eccles Ave . . . . . South San Francisco CA 94080 *Web:* www.betterhomeproducts.com	650-827-9270		351
Better Homes & Gardens Wood Magazine 1716 Locust St . . . . . Des Moines IA 50309 *TF:* 800-374-9663 ■ *Web:* www.woodmagazine.com	800-374-9663		457-14
Better Investing PO Box 220 . . . . . Royal Oak MI 48068 *TF:* 877-275-6242 ■ *Web:* www.betterinvesting.org	248-583-6242	583-4880	49-2
Better Label & Products Inc 3333 Empire Blvd SW. . . . . . Atlanta GA 30354 *TF:* 800-448-1813 ■ *Web:* www.betterlabel.com	404-763-8440		627
Better Made Snack Foods Inc 10148 Gratiot Ave. . . . . . Detroit MI 48213 *TF:* 800-332-2394 ■ *Web:* www.bmchips.com	313-925-4774	925-6028	296-35
Better Management Corp (BMC) 4321 State Rt7 . . . . . New Waterford OH 44445 *TF:* 877-293-4300 ■ *Web:* www.bmcbulk.com	330-921-4301		660
Better Packages Inc 255 Canal St PO Box 711 . . . . . Shelton CT 06484 *TF:* 800-237-9151 ■ *Web:* www.betterpackages.com	203-926-3722	926-3706	111

	City	State	Zip	Phone	Fax	Class
Better Sleep Council 501 Wythe St *Web:* www.bettersleep.org	Alexandria	VA	22314	703-683-8371	683-4503	48-17
Better World Books Inc 55740 Currant Rd *Web:* www.betterworldbooks.com	Mishawaka	IN	46545	574-252-5303		95
Betteridge Jewelers Inc 117 Greenwich Ave *Web:* www.betteridge.com	Greenwich	CT	06830	203-869-0124		410
Bettinger Company Inc, The 1515 Market St Ste 935 *Web:* www.bettingerco.com	Philadelphia	PA	19102	215-564-0700		631
Bettinger Farms Inc 11602 Frankfort Rd **Fax Area Code:* 567 ■ *TF:* 855-629-7661 ■ *Web:* bettingersgreenhouse.com	Swanton	OH	43558	419-829-2771	202-2125*	369
Betts Industries Inc 1800 Pennsylvania Ave W *TF:* 800-482-2678 ■ *Web:* www.bettsind.com	Warren	PA	16365	814-723-1250	723-7030	595
Betts Patterson & Mines PS 1 Convention Pl 701 Pk St Ste 1400 *Web:* bpmlaw.com	Seattle	WA	98101	206-292-9988		445
Betty Brinn Children's Museum 929 E Wisconsin Ave *Web:* www.bbcmkids.org	Milwaukee	WI	53202	414-390-5437	291-0906	521
Betty Dain Creations Inc 9701 NW 112 Ave Ste 10 *TF General:* 800-327-5256 ■ *Web:* www.bettydain.com	Miami	FL	33178	305-769-3451		76
Betty Ford Alpine Gardens 183 Gore Creek Dr *Web:* bettyfordalpinegardens.org	Vail	CO	81657	970-476-0103		97
Betty Machine Co 324 Freehill Rd *TF:* 800-264-3480 ■ *Web:* www.bettymachine.com	Hendersonville	TN	37075	615-826-6004	826-6262	621
Betz Industries Inc 2121 Bristol Ave NW *Web:* www.betzindustries.com	Grand Rapids	MI	49504	616-453-4429		492
Beulah Heights University 892 Berne St SE PO Box 18145 **Fax:* Admissions ■ *TF:* 888-777-2422 ■ *Web:* www.beulah.edu	Atlanta	GA	30316	404-627-2681	564-5290*	161
Beusa Energy 4 Waterway Sq Pl Ste 900 *Web:* www.beusaenergy.com	The Woodlands	TX	77380	281-296-1500		536
Beutler Air Conditioning Service 855 National Dr Ste 109 *Web:* www.beutler.com	Sacramento	CA	95834	916-696-8721	646-2200	189-10
Beval Saddlery Ltd 50 Pine St *Web:* www.beval.com	New Canaan	CT	06840	203-966-7828		711
Bevco Precision Manufacturing Co 21320 Doral Rd *TF:* 800-864-2991 ■ *Web:* www.bevco.com	Waukesha	WI	53186	262-798-9200		319-1
Bevco Sales International Inc 9354 194 St *TF:* 800-663-0090 ■ *Web:* bevco.net	Surrey	BC	V4N4E9	604-888-1455		358
Bevel Design Company Inc 8600 La Salle Rd Ste 330 *TF:* 800-648-8479 ■ *Web:* beveldesign.com	Towson	MD	21286	443-279-9900		358
Beverage Capital Corp 2209 Sulphur Spring Rd *Web:* www.beveragecapital.com	Baltimore	MD	21227	410-242-7404		805
Beverage Distributors Co 14200 E Moncrieff Pl **Fax Area Code:* 334 ■ *TF General:* 888-262-9787 ■ *Web:* www.charmer-sunbelt.com	Aurora	CO	80011	303-371-3421	270-5983*	81-3
Beverage Marketing Corp 850 Third Ave Ste 13C *TF:* 800-275-4630 ■ *Web:* www.beveragemarketing.com	New York	NY	10022	212-688-7640	826-1255	195
Beverage-Air Corp 3779 Champion Blvd *TF:* 800-845-9800 ■ *Web:* www.beverage-air.com	Winston-Salem	NC	27105	336-245-6400	245-6453	664
Beveridge & Diamond PC 1350 I St NW Ste 700 *Web:* www.bdlaw.com	Washington	DC	20005	202-789-6000		428
Beveridge Seay Inc 2000 P St NW Ste 700 *Web:* www.bevseay.com	Washington	DC	20036	202-822-3800		393
Beverly Beach State Park 198 NE 123rd St *TF:* 800-452-5687 ■ *Web:* www.oregonstateparks.org	Newport	OR	97365	800-452-5687		565
Beverly Chamber of Commerce 100 Cummings Ctr Ste 107K *TF:* 800-924-8167 ■ *Web:* www.greaterbeverlychamber.com	Beverly	MA	01915	978-232-9559	232-9372	139
Beverly Hills Cafe 7321 Miami Lakes Dr *Web:* www.thebeverlyhillscafe.com	Miami Lakes	FL	33014	305-558-8201		671
Beverly Hills Chamber of Commerce Santa Monica Blvd 2nd Fl *TF:* 800-342-5397 ■ *Web:* www.beverlyhillschamber.com	Beverly Hills	CA	90210	310-248-1000	248-1020	139
Beverly Hills Courier 8840 W Olympic Blvd *Web:* www.bhcourier.com	Beverly Hills	CA	90211	310-278-1322	271-5118	532-4
Beverly Hills Film Festival 9663 Santa Monica Blvd Ste 777 *Web:* www.beverlyhillsfilmfestival.com	Beverly Hills	CA	90210	310-779-1206		282
Beverly Hills Hotel 9641 Sunset Blvd *TF:* 800-650-1842 ■ *Web:* www.dorchestercollection.com	Beverly Hills	CA	90210	310-276-2251	887-2887	379
Beverly Hills Plaza Hotel 10300 Wilshire Blvd *TF:* 800-800-1234 ■ *Web:* www.beverlyhillsplazahotel.com	Los Angeles	CA	90024	310-275-5575		378
Beverly Hills Public Library 444 N Rexford Dr *TF:* 800-238-0172 ■ *Web:* www.beverlyhills.org	Beverly Hills	CA	90210	310-288-2220	278-3387	434-3
Beverly Hills Transfer & Storage Co 15500 S Main St *TF:* 800-999-7114 ■ *Web:* www.beverlyhillstransfer.com	Gardena	CA	90248	800-999-7114		519
Beverly Hills Unified School District 255 S Lasky Dr *TF:* 800-444-9995 ■ *Web:* www.bhusd.org	Beverly Hills	CA	90212	310-551-5100	277-6137	685
Beverly Hills Wealth Management LLC 9454 Wilshire Blvd	Beverly Hills	CA	90212	310-859-1600		401
Beverly Hilton 9876 Wilshire Blvd *TF:* 800-605-8896 ■ *Web:* www.beverlyhilton.com	Beverly Hills	CA	90210	310-274-7777	285-1313	379
Beverly Hospital 309 W Beverly Blvd *TF:* 800-618-6664 ■ *Web:* www.beverly.org	Montebello	CA	90640	323-726-1222	725-4338	374-3
Beverly Hospital 85 Herrick St *Web:* www.beverlyhospital.org	Beverly	MA	01915	978-922-3000		374-3
Beverly National Cemetery 916 Bridgeboro Rd **Fax Area Code:* 609 ■ *Web:* www.cem.va.gov/cems/nchp/beverly.asp	Beverly	NJ	08010	215-504-5610	871-4691*	136
Beverly Public Library 32 Essex St *TF:* 800-829-3676 ■ *Web:* www.noblenet.org	Beverly	MA	01915	978-921-6062		434-3
Beverly Wilshire - A Four Seasons Hotel 9500 Wilshire Blvd *TF:* 800-545-4000 ■ *Web:* www.fourseasons.com/beverlywilshire	Beverly Hills	CA	90212	310-275-5200	274-2851	379
Bevilacqua Research Corp 4901 Corporate Dr NW *Web:* www.brc2.com	Huntsville	AL	35805	256-882-6229		809
Bevill State Community College 2631 Temple Ave N **Fax:* Admissions ■ *TF:* 800-648-3271 ■ *Web:* www.bscc.edu	Fayette	AL	35555	205-932-3221	932-3294*	162
Jasper 1411 Indiana Ave **Fax:* Admissions ■ *TF:* 800-648-3271 ■ *Web:* www.bscc.edu	Jasper	AL	35501	205-387-0511	387-5191*	162
Bevin Bros 10 Bevin Rd *Web:* www.bevinbells.com	East Hampton	CT	06424	860-267-4431		527
Bevin Matt (R) 700 Capitol Ave Ste 100ÿ *Web:* governor.ky.gov	Frankfort	KY	40601	502-564-2611	564-2517	343
Bevmax Wines & Liquors 835 E Main St *Web:* www.bevmax.com	Stamford	CT	06902	203-357-9151		443
BevMo! 1401 Willow Pass Rd Ste 900 *Web:* www.bevmo.com	Concord	CA	94520	925-609-6000		443
Bewabic State Park 720 Idlewild Rd *Web:* www.michigandnr.com	Crystal Falls	MI	49920	906-875-3324		565
Bexar Appraisal District 411 N Frio St *Web:* www.bcad.org	San Antonio	TX	78207	210-224-8511		41
Bexar County 100 Dolorosa St *TF:* 800-877-8339 ■ *Web:* www.bexar.org	San Antonio	TX	78205	210-335-2011	335-2252	338
Bexel Corp 2701 N Ontario St *Web:* www.bexel.com	Burbank	CA	91504	818-565-4399		525
Bexil Corp 11 Hanover Sq *OTC:* BXLC ■ *TF:* 800-937-5449 ■ *Web:* www.bexil.com	New York	NY	10005	212-785-0400	363-1101	360-4
Bexion Pharmaceuticals LLC 632 Russell St *Web:* www.bexionpharma.com	Covington	KY	41011	859-757-1652		231
Bexley City School District 348 S Cassingham Rd *TF:* 800-282-1780 ■ *Web:* www.bexleyschools.org	Columbus	OH	43209	614-231-7611		685
Bexley Hall Seminary 1407 E 60th St *TF:* 800-275-8235 ■ *Web:* www.bexleyseabury.edu	Chicago	IL	60637	773-380-6780	380-6788	167-3
Bexley Public Library 2411 E Main St *Web:* www.bexlib.org	Bexley	OH	43209	614-231-9709		434-3
Beyer Barber Co 1136 Hamilton St Ste 103 *Web:* www.beyerbarber.com	Allentown	PA	18101	610-435-9577		77
Beyer Blinder Belle Architects & Planners LLC 41 E 11th St 20th Fl *Web:* www.beyerblinderbelle.com	New York	NY	10271	212-777-7800	475-7424	261
Beyer Construction Ltd 3080 S Calhoun Rd *Web:* www.beyer.com	New Berlin	WI	53151	262-789-6040		186
Beyer Don (Rep D - VA) 1119 Longworth HOB *Web:* beyer.house.gov	Washington	DC	20515	202-225-4376	225-0017	342-2
Beyond Components 5 Carl Thompson Rd *TF:* 800-971-4242 ■ *Web:* www.beyondcomponents.com	Westford	MA	01886	800-971-4242	929-2302	246
Beyond Digital Imaging 36 Apple Creek Blvd *TF:* 888-689-1888 ■ *Web:* www.bdimaging.com	Markham	ON	L3R4Y4	905-415-1888	415-1583	701
Beyond Ink LLC 82 Middle St *Web:* www.beyondink.com	Portland	ME	04112	207-699-5775		631
Beyond Marketing 2001 Main St Ste 301 *Web:* www.beyondmk.com	Wheeling	WV	26003	304-232-4544		636
Beyond Pesticides 701 E St SE Ste 200 *TF:* 866-260-6653 ■ *Web:* www.beyondpesticides.org	Washington	DC	20003	202-543-5450	543-4791	48-13
Beyond Pix Studios 950 Battery St *Web:* beyondpix.com	San Francisco	CA	94111	415-434-1027	434-1032	512
Beyond Quota LLC 537 King Muir Rd *Web:* www.beyond-quota.com	Lake Forest	IL	60045	847-234-9475		463
Beyond Roi Inc 512 Brookfield Rd *Web:* getbeyondroi.com	Raleigh	NC	27615	919-615-4200		196
Beyond Spots & Dots 1034 Fifth Ave *Web:* www.beyondspotsanddots.com	Pittsburgh	PA	15219	412-281-6215		4
Beyond the Arc Inc 2600 Tenth St Ste 616 *TF:* 877-676-3743 ■ *Web:* www.beyondthearc.com	Berkeley	CA	94710	877-676-3743		463
Beyond Yoga 10559C Jefferson Blvd *Web:* www.beyondyoga.com	Culver City	CA	90232	310-882-6476		148
Beyond.com Inc 1060 First Ave Ste 100 *Web:* www.beyond.com	King of Prussia	PA	19406	610-878-2800		260
Bezek-Durst-Seiser Inc 3330 C St Ste 200 *Web:* bdsak.com	Anchorage	AK	99503	907-562-6076		261
BF Inkjet Media Inc 116 Bethea Rd #322 *Web:* www.bfinkjet.com	Fayetteville	GA	30214	770-719-2051		481
BF Nashville 1101 Kermit Dr Ste 310	Nashville	TN	37217	615-399-9700		670
Bf Shaw Printing Co 1586 Barber Greene Rd *Web:* www.shawmedia.com	De Kalb	IL	60115	815-756-4841		532-3
Bfa Systems Inc 3325 Triana Blvd PO Box 1527 *Web:* www.bfasystems.com	Huntsville	AL	35805	256-922-8791		261

Name / Address	City	State	ZIP	Phone	Fax	Class
BFC Forms Service Inc 1051 N Kirk Rd *TF:* 800-774-6840 ■ *Web:* www.bfcprint.com	Batavia	IL	60510	630-879-9240		627
BFG 665 Broadway Ste 300 *Web:* www.bfgcom.com	New York	NY	10012	843-837-9115		7
BFG Supply Co LLC PO Box 479 *TF:* 800-883-0234 ■ *Web:* www.bfgsupply.com	Burton	OH	44021	440-834-1883		276
BFGoodrich Tires Inc PO Box 19001 *TF:* 877-788-8899 ■ *Web:* www.bfgoodrichtires.com	Greenville	SC	29602	877-788-8899		755
Bfi Print Communications Holding Co 602 Bedford St *Web:* www.bfiprint.com	Whitman	MA	02382	781-447-1199		627
BFMA (Business Forms Management Assn) 3800 Old Cheney Rd Ste 101-285 **Fax Area Code:* 877 ■ *TF:* 888-367-3078 ■ *Web:* www.bfma.org	Lincoln	NE	68516	402-216-0479	204-5979*	49-12
Bframe Data Systems Inc 3057 Peachtree Industrial Blvd Ste 200 *TF:* 800-833-1059 ■ *Web:* www.bframe.com	Duluth	GA	30097	678-387-0100		177
BFS Business Printing Inc 76 South St *TF:* 800-561-3357 ■ *Web:* www.bfsprinters.com	Boston	MA	02111	617-482-7770		627
BFS Industries LLC 200 Industrial Dr *TF:* 800-331-1956 ■ *Web:* www.bfs-ind.com	Butner	NC	27509	919-575-6711	575-4275	357
B&G Equipment Company Inc 135 Region S Dr *TF:* 800-544-8811 ■ *Web:* www.bgequip.com	Jackson	GA	30233	678-688-5601		295
BG Financial Services Group 160 Main St *Web:* www.nsfgma.com	Gloucester	MA	01930	978-675-9941		401
B-G Mechanical Service Inc 12 Second Ave *TF:* 800-992-7386 ■ *Web:* www.bgmechanical.com	Chicopee	MA	01020	413-888-1500	594-2983	189-10
BG National Plumbing & Heating 200 Montrose Rd *Web:* www.bgnational.com	Westbury	NY	11590	516-334-8282		610
BG Products Inc 740 S Wichita St *TF:* 800-961-6228 ■ *Web:* www.bgprod.com	Wichita	KS	67213	316-265-2686	265-1082	541
BGA (Lincoln Botanical Garden & Arboretum) University of Nebraska 1309 N 17th St *TF:* 800-742-8800 ■ *Web:* www.unl.edu/bga	Lincoln	NE	68588	402-472-2679	472-9615	97
BGBC Partners LLP 300 N Meridian St Ste 1100 *Web:* bgbc.us	Indianapolis	IN	46204	317-633-4700		734
BGC 199 Water St One Seaport Plaza *Web:* www.bgcmarketdata.com	New York	NY	10038	212-829-4840		251
BGC Partners Inc 499 Pk Ave *NASDAQ:* BGCP ■ *Web:* www.bgcpartners.com	New York	NY	10022	646-346-7000	346-6919	644
BGCC (Bowling Green Chamber of Commerce) 130 S Main St PO Box 31 *Web:* www.bgchamber.net	Bowling Green	OH	43402	419-353-7945	353-3693	139
BGCS (Bowling Green City Schools) 137 Clough St *Web:* www.bgcs.k12.oh.us	Bowling Green	OH	43402	419-352-3576	352-1701	685
BGD Cos Inc 5323 Lakeland Ave N *TF:* 800-699-3537 ■ *Web:* www.bgdcompanies.com	Minneapolis	MN	55429	612-338-6804	338-4942	319-1
BGE 10777 Westheimer Rd Ste 400 *Web:* www.browngay.com	Houston	TX	77042	281-558-8700	558-9701	261
BGF Industries Inc 3802 Robert Porcher Way **Fax Area Code:* 336 ■ *TF:* 800-476-4845 ■ *Web:* www.bgf.com	Greensboro	NC	27410	800-476-4845	545-0233*	745-3
BGH (Buchanan General Hospital) 1535 Slate Creek Rd *TF:* 800-552-7096 ■ *Web:* www.bgh.org	Grundy	VA	24614	276-935-1000	935-1354	374-3
BGIS North America 7400 Birchmount Rd *Web:* www.brookfieldgis.com	Markham	ON	L3R4E6	905-943-4100		271
BGK Finishing Systems 4131 Pheasant Ridge Dr NE *Web:* www.carlisleft.com/en/brands/bgk	Minneapolis	MN	55449	763-784-0466	784-1362	470
BGL Asset Services LLC 1611 S Isabella Rd *Web:* www.bglas.com	Mt Pleasant	MI	48858	989-772-8888		261
BGO Architects Inc 4202 Beltway Dr *Web:* www.bgoarchitects.com	Addison	TX	75001	214-520-8878		393
BGR Holding LLC 601 Thirteenth St NW The Homer Bldg Eleventh Fl S *Web:* www.bgrdc.com	Washington	DC	20005	202-333-4936	833-9392	194
BGR Inc 6392 Gano Rd *TF:* 800-628-9195 ■ *Web:* www.packbgr.com	West Chester	OH	45069	513-755-7100	755-7855	559
BGS (Beta Gamma Sigma Inc) 125 Weldon Pkwy *TF:* 800-337-4677 ■ *Web:* www.betagammasigma.org	Maryland Heights	MO	63043	314-432-5650	432-7083	48-16
BGSU (BGSU) 1001 E Wooster St *TF:* 866-246-6732 ■ *Web:* bgsu.edu/library.html	Bowling Green	OH	43403	419-372-2051	372-0475	434-6
BGT (Hunt-Morgan House) 201 N Mill St *Web:* www.bluegrasstrust.org/huntmorgantours.html	Lexington	KY	40507	859-253-0362	259-9210	50-3
BH (Bristol Hospital) 41 Brewster Rd *Web:* www.bristolhospital.org	Bristol	CT	06010	860-585-3000	585-3053	374-3
BH Aircraft Company Inc 2230 Smithtown Ave *Web:* www.bhaircraft.com	Ronkonkoma	NY	11779	631-981-4200	981-0221	21
BH Electronics Inc 12219 Wood Lake Dr *Web:* www.bhelectronics.com	Burnsville	MN	55337	952-894-9590	894-9380	253
BH Media Group Inc 1314 Douglas St Ste 1500 *Web:* bhmginc.com	Omaha	NE	68102	402-444-1517		532-3
BH Solutions Group Inc 1000 S Cleveland Massillon Rd Ste 2 *Web:* www.bhsolutionsgroup.com	Akron	OH	44333	330-666-6970		260
B-H Transfer Co 750 Sparta Rd PO Box 151 *TF:* 800-342-6462 ■ *Web:* www.b-htransfer.com	Sandersville	GA	31082	478-552-5119		449
Bhan Thai 1324 Peabody Ave *Web:* www.bhanthairestaurant.com	Memphis	TN	38104	901-272-1538		671
Bharat Forge America 2807 S ML King Jr Blvd	Lansing	MI	48910	517-393-5300		483
Bhargava Wealth Management 609 White Pine Rd *TF:* 800-289-9999 ■ *Web:* www.bhargavacapital.com	Franklin Lakes	NJ	07417	201-897-0085		226
BHCC (Bath House Cultural Ctr) 521 E Lawther Dr *Web:* www.dallasculture.org/bathhouseculturecenter	Dallas	TX	75218	214-670-8749	670-8751	50-2
BHE Consulting 276 Libbey Industrial Pkwy *Web:* www.bheconsulting.com	Weymouth	MA	02189	781-340-5871		261
BHE Environmental Inc 11733 Chesterdale Rd *Web:* www.powereng.com	Cincinnati	OH	45246	513-326-1500	326-1550	256
BHG (Berkshire Hathaway Group) 3555 Farnam St **Fax Area Code:* 212 ■ *TF:* 800-223-2064 ■ *Web:* berkshirehathaway.com	Omaha	NE	68131	888-395-6349	298-1915*	391-4
BHHC (Berkshire Hathaway Homestates Cos) PO Box 2048 *TF:* 888-495-8949 ■ *Web:* www.bhhc.com	Omaha	NE	68103	888-495-8949		391-4
BHI (Bender/Helper Impact) 11500 W Olympic Blvd Ste 655 *Web:* www.bhimpact.com	Los Angeles	CA	90064	310-473-4147		636
BHI (Baker Hughes Inc) 2929 Allen Pkwy Ste 1200 *NYSE:* BHI ■ *TF:* 800-229-7447 ■ *Web:* www.bakerhughes.com	Houston	TX	77019	713-439-8600		539
BHI (Better Hearing Institute) 1444 I St NW Ste 700 *TF:* 800-639-3884 ■ *Web:* www.betterhearing.org	Washington	DC	20005	202-449-1100		48-17
BHISD (Barbers Hill ISD) 9600 Eagle Dr PO Box 1108 *Web:* www.bhisd.net	Mont Belvieu	TX	77580	281-576-2221		685
BHK Securities LLC 2200 Lakeshore Dr Ste 250 *TF:* 888-529-2610 ■ *Web:* www.bhkllc.com	Birmingham	AL	35209	205-322-2025		690
BHN Corp 435 Madison Ave *Web:* www.bhncorp.com	Memphis	TN	38103	901-521-9500	521-9507	189-9
BHP Billiton Petroleum (Americas) Inc 1360 Post Oak Blvd Ste 150 *TF:* 800-359-1692 ■ *Web:* www.bhpbilliton.com	Houston	TX	77056	713-961-8500	961-8400	536
BHW Sheet Metal Co 113 Johnson St *Web:* bhwsm.com	Jonesboro	GA	30236	770-471-9303		697
BI Inc 6400 Lookout Rd *TF:* 800-241-2911 ■ *Web:* www.bi.com	Boulder	CO	80301	303-218-1000	218-1250	692
BI Nutraceuticals 2550 El Presidio St *TF:* 800-546-6113 ■ *Web:* www.botanicals.com	Long Beach	CA	90810	310-669-2100	637-3644	479
BIA (Bureau of Indian Affairs) 1849 C St NW MS 4004 MIB *Web:* www.bia.gov	Washington	DC	20240	202-208-7163	208-5320	340-13
BIA (Brick Industry Assn) 1850 Centennial Pk Dr Ste 301 *TF:* 866-644-1293 ■ *Web:* www.gobrick.com	Reston	VA	20191	703-620-0010	620-3928	49-18
BIA (Bureau of Indian Affairs Regional Offices) *Alaska Region* 3601 C St Ste 1100 *TF:* 800-645-8397 ■ *Web:* www.bia.gov	Anchorage	AK	99503	907-271-1536	271-1349	340-13
Bia Digital Partners Lp 15120 Enterprise Ct *Web:* www.biadigitalpartners.com	Chantilly	VA	20151	703-227-9600		690
Biaggi's 5990 University Ave *Web:* www.biaggis.com	West Des Moines	IA	50266	515-221-9900		671
Biaggi's 6401 E Lloyd Expy Ste 3 *Web:* www.biaggis.com	Evansville	IN	47715	812-421-0800		671
Biaggi's 4010 W Jefferson Blvd *Web:* www.biaggis.com	Fort Wayne	IN	46804	260-459-6700		671
Biaggi's 1611 Aspen Commons *Web:* www.biaggis.com	Madison	WI	53562	608-664-9288		671
Biaggi's Ristorante 320 Collins Rd NE *Web:* biaggis.com	Cedar Rapids	IA	52402	319-393-6593		671
Biaggi's Ristorante Italiano 1705 Clearwater Ave *Web:* www.biaggis.com	Bloomington	IL	61704	309-664-2148	664-2149	670
Biaggi's Ristorante Italiano 13655 California St *Web:* biaggis.com	Omaha	NE	68154	402-965-9800		671
Biagio 155 King St E *Web:* www.biagioristorante.com	Toronto	ON	M5C1G9	416-366-4040		671
Bialik Hebrew Day School 2760 Bathurst St *Web:* bialik.ca	Toronto	ON	M6B3A1	416-783-3346		685
Biamp Systems Inc 9300 SW Gemini Dr **Fax Area Code:* 503 ■ *TF:* 800-826-1457 ■ *Web:* www.biamp.com	Beaverton	OR	97008	800-826-1457	626-0281*	52
Bianchi Kasavan & Pope LLP 243 Sixth St Ste 220 *Web:* www.bkpcpa.com	Hollister	CA	95023	831-638-2111		2
Bianchi PR Inc 888 W Big Beaver Rd Ste 777 *Web:* www.bianchipr.com	Troy	MI	48084	248-269-1122		636
Bianchis Pizzeria 128 E Front St *Web:* www.bianchispizzeria.com	Hattiesburg	MS	39401	601 450 1263		671
Biar Inc 2506 S Philippe Ave *Web:* www.biar.us/index.html	Gonzales	LA	70737	225-647-4300		358
Bi-ax Intl Inc 596 Cedar Ave *TF:* 800-265-5586 ■ *Web:* www.biaxinc.com	Wingham	ON	N0G2W0	519-357-1818		600
Biax-Fiberfilm Corp N1001 Tower View Dr *TF:* 800-365-7391 ■ *Web:* www.biax-fiberfilm.com	Greenville	WI	54942	920-757-9000		454
Biba 2801 Capitol Ave *TF:* 800-755-6266 ■ *Web:* www.biba-restaurant.com	Sacramento	CA	95816	916-455-2422	455-0542	671
Bibb Country Correctional Facility 565 Bibb Ln *Web:* doc.alabama.gov	Brent	AL	35034	205-926-5252		213
Bibb County 157 SW Davidson Dr *Web:* www.bibbal.com	Centreville	AL	35042	205-926-3114		338
Bibb County 700 Poplar St *Web:* maconbibb.us	Macon	GA	31201	478-751-7400		338
Bibbero Systems Inc 1300 N McDowell Blvd *TF:* 800-242-2376 ■ *Web:* www.bibbero.com	Petaluma	CA	94954	707-778-3131	778-0824	627
Bibby Financial Services 600 TownPark Ln Ste 450 *TF:* 877-882-4229 ■ *Web:* www.bibbyusa.com	Kennesaw	GA	30144	877-882-4229		272

Phone | Fax | Class

Bible Broadcasting Network Inc
11530 Carmel Commons Blvd PO Box 7300 .... Charlotte NC 28226 704-523-5555 643
TF: 800-888-7077 ■ *Web:* www.bbnradio.org

Bible League 3801 Eagle Nest Dr .... Crete IL 60417 817-595-1664 48-20
TF: 866-825-4636 ■ *Web:* www.bibleleague.org

Bible Way Fellowship Baptist Church
10120 Hartsook St .... Houston TX 77034 713-943-2215 48-20
Web: www.bibleway1.org

Biblical Archaeology Review
4710 41st St NW .... Washington DC 20016 202-364-3300 364-2636 457-18
TF: 800-221-4644 ■ *Web:* www.biblicalarchaeology.org

Biblical Theological Seminary
200 N Main St .... Hatfield PA 19440 215-368-5000 368-2301 167-3
TF: 800-235-4021 ■ *Web:* www.biblical.edu

Bibliotheques Publiques de L'Estrie Inc
4155 Rue Brodeur.......... Sherbrooke QC J1L1K4 819-565-9744 565-9157 436
Web: www.reseaubiblioduquebec.qc.ca

BIC Corp 1 BIC Way Ste 1.......... Shelton CT 06484 203-783-2000 571
Web: www.bicworld.com

Bice Ristorante 5601 Universal Blvd .... Orlando FL 32819 212-688-1999 752-1329 670
Web: www.bice-orlando.com

Bicentennial Capitol Mall State Park
600 James Robertson Pkwy .... Nashville TN 37243 615-741-5280 565
Web: www.state.tn.us

Bicitis Group Inc 426 Herrick Dr.......... Dover NJ 07801 973-250-2394 180
Web: www.bicitisgroup.com

Bickel's Snack Foods
1120 Zinns Quarry Rd.......... York PA 17404 717-843-0738 296-35
TF: 800-233-1933 ■ *Web:* www.bickelssnacks.com

Bickelhaupt Arboretum 340 S 14th St .... Clinton IA 52732 563-242-4771 97
Web: bick-arb.org

Bickford's Family Restauarants Inc
37 Oak St Ext .... Brockton MA 02301 800-969-5653 583-2120* 670
**Fax Area Code:* 508 ■ *TF:* 800-969-5653 ■ *Web:* www.bickfords.com

BICO Drilling Tools Inc
1604 Greens Rd .... Houston TX 77032 281-590-6966 540
Web: www.bicodrilling.com

Bi-Coastal Media LLC 140 N Main St .... Lakeport CA 95453 707-263-6113 263-0939 643
Web: www.bicoastalmedia.com

Bicom Inc 755 Main St.......... Monroe CT 06468 203-268-4484 625
Web: www.bicominc.com

Bicon LLC 501 Arborway .... Boston MA 02130 617-524-4443 228
TF: 800-882-4266 ■ *Web:* www.bicon.com

Bi-Con Services Inc
10901 Clay Pike Rd .... Derwent OH 43733 740-685-2542 189-3
Web: www.biconservices.com

Bi-County Scale & Equipment Co
75 Kean St .... West Babylon NY 11704 631-643-2300 296-26
Web: www.bicountyscale.com

Bicycle Garage of Indy Inc
4340 E 82nd St.......... Indianapolis IN 46250 317-842-4140 711
TF: 800-238-7389 ■ *Web:* bgifitness.com

Bicycle Warehouse 4670 Santa Fe St .... San Diego CA 92109 858-273-7300 711
TF: 800-257-1759 ■ *Web:* www.bicyclewarehouse.com

Bicycling Magazine 400 S Tenth St.......... Emmaus PA 18098 800-666-2806 457-14
TF: 800-666-2806 ■ *Web:* www.bicycling.com

Biddeford Blankets 300 Terr Dr.......... Mundelein IL 60060 800-789-6441 566-6431* 746
**Fax Area Code:* 847 ■ *TF:* 800-789-6441 ■ *Web:* biddefordblankets.com

Biddeford-Saco Chamber of Commerce & Industry
28 Water St Ste 101 .... Biddeford ME 04005 207-282-1567 139
TF: 800-565-0121 ■ *Web:* www.biddefordsacochamber.org

Biddeford-Saco-OOB Courier
457 Alfred St.......... Biddeford ME 04005 207-282-4337 532-4
Web: www.biddefordsacooobcourier.com

Biddle Precision Components Inc
701 S Main St.......... Sheridan IN 46069 317-758-4451 758-5260 621
TF: 800-428-4387 ■ *Web:* www.emcprecision.com

Bidlake Agency Inc
2905 Millennium Ste 3.......... Billings MT 59102 406-245-6224 390
Web: billingsinsurance.com

BIDMC (Beth Israel Deaconess Medical Ctr)
330 Brookline Ave.......... Boston MA 02215 617-667-7000 374-3
TF: 800-667-5356 ■ *Web:* www.bidmc.org

BidMed LLC 321 N Clark St Ste 2550.......... Chicago IL 60654 773-840-8140 475
Web: bidmed.com

Bid-Well Corp PO Box 97 .... Canton SD 57013 800-843-9824 987-2605* 190
**Fax Area Code:* 605 ■ *TF:* 800-843-9824 ■ *Web:* www.terex.com

Bidwell Industrial Group Inc
2055 S Main St.......... Middletown CT 06457 860-346-9283 347-8775 111
Web: www.bidwellinc.com

Bidwell-Sacramento River State Park
12105 River Rd.......... Chico CA 95973 530-342-5185 565
Web: www.parks.ca.gov/default.asp?page_id=463

Biederlack of America
11501 Bedford Rd NE.......... Cumberland MD 21502 301-759-3633 746

Bielecky Bros Inc 979 Third Ave .... New York NY 10022 212-753-2355 751-9369 319-2
TF: 800-318-9806 ■ *Web:* www.bieleckybrothers.com

bieMEDIA LLC 511 Broadway.......... Denver CO 80203 303-825-2275 742
Web: biemedia.com

Bienville House Hotel
320 Decatur St .... New Orleans LA 70130 504-529-2345 525-6079 379
TF: 800-535-7836 ■ *Web:* www.bienvillehouse.com

Bienville Parish
100 Courthouse Dr Rm 100 .... Arcadia LA 71001 318-263-2123 338
TF: 800-433-9064 ■ *Web:* www.bienvilleparish.org

Bierlein Cos Inc 2000 Bay City Rd .... Midland MI 48642 989-496-0066 496-0144 189-16
TF: 800-336-6626 ■ *Web:* www.bierlein.com

Bierschbach Equipment & Supply Co
PO Box 1444 .... Sioux Falls SD 57101 605-332-4466 191-1
TF: 800-843-3707 ■ *Web:* bierschbach.com

Biery Cheese Co 6544 Paris Ave.......... Louisville OH 44641 330-875-3381 296-5
Web: www.bierycheese.com

Biesanz Stone Co Inc 4600 Goodview Rd .... Winona MN 55987 507-454-4336 454-8140 724
Web: www.biesanzstone.com

Biewer Lumber LLC 812 S Riverside.......... Saint Clair MI 48079 810-329-4789 818
Web: www.biewerlumber.com

BIF New York Inc 465 Barell Ave.......... Carlstadt NJ 07072 201-933-7777 320
Web: www.bifnewyork.com

Biff Duncan Associates Inc
450 Shrewsbury Plaza .... Shrewsbury NJ 07702 732-876-0263 261
Web: www.biffduncan.com

Biflex Intimates Group
180 Madison Ave 6th Fl .... New York NY 10016 212-532-8340 155-18

BIFMA (Business & Institutional Furniture Manufacturers Assn)
678 Front Ave NW Ste 150.......... Grand Rapids MI 49504 616-285-3963 49-13

BIG 100 1801 Rockville Pk .... Rockville MD 20852 240-747-2700 645
TF: 800-493-1003 ■ *Web:* wbig.iheart.com

Big 3 Packaging LLC
4201 Torresdale Ave.......... Philadelphia PA 19124 215-743-4201 601
Web: big3packaging.com

Big 3 Precision Products Inc
2923 S Wabash Ave .... Centralia IL 62801 618-533-3251 567
Web: big3precision.com

Big 5 Sporting Goods Corp
2525 E El Segundo Blvd.......... El Segundo CA 90245 310-536-0611 711
NASDAQ: BGFV ■ *TF:* 800-898-2994 ■ *Web:* big5sportinggoods.com

Big 6 Drilling Co 7500 San Felipe St.......... Houston TX 77063 713-783-2300 540
Web: www.big6drilling.com

Big 920, The 12100 W Howard Ave.......... Milwaukee WI 53228 414-545-8900 645
Web: thebig920.iheart.com

BIG 98, The 55 Music Sq W.......... Nashville TN 37203 615-664-2400 645-108
Web: thebig98.iheart.com

Big 98.5 119 W Naylor Mill Rd.......... Salisbury MD 21801 410-202-8102 645
Web: www.bigclassicrock.com

Big 98.7 2720 Seventh Ave S .... Fargo ND 58103 701-237-4500 235-9082 645-58
Web: www.big987.com

Big Apple Bagels
500 Lake Cook Rd Ste 475.......... Deerfield IL 60015 847-948-7520 405-8140 68
TF: 800-251-6101 ■ *Web:* www.babcorp.com

Big Apple Car Inc 169 Bay 17th St.......... Brooklyn NY 11214 718-331-9500 314
TF: 800-251-5001 ■ *Web:* www.bigapplecar.com

Big Apple Circus
1 Metrotech Ctr 3rd Fl .... Brooklyn NY 11201 646-793-9313 149
TF: 888-541-3750 ■ *Web:* www.bigapplecircus.org

Big Arm State Park
490 N Meridian Rd.......... Kalispell MT 59901 406-752-5501 565
Web: www.fwp.mt.gov

Big Art's BBQ 2796 Struble Rd.......... Cincinnati OH 45251 513-825-4811 671

Big B Lumberteria
6600 Brentwood Blvd.......... Brentwood CA 94513 925-634-2442 634-9839 364
Web: www.bigblumber.com

Big Bang ERP Inc 105 De Louvain W .... Montreal QC H2N1A3 514-360-4408 196
TF: 844-361-4408 ■ *Web:* www.bigbangerp.com

Big Basin Redwoods State Park
21600 Big Basin Way.......... Boulder Creek CA 95006 831-338-8860 565
Web: www.parks.ca.gov

Big Beam Emergency Systems Inc
290 E Prairie St PO Box 518.......... Crystal Lake IL 60039 815-459-6100 459-6126 439
TF: 800-209-6357 ■ *Web:* www.bigbeam.com

Big Bear Oil Company Inc
11685 Pebble Hills Blvd.......... El Paso TX 79936 915-921-1905 579
Web: www.ysletadelsurpueblo.org

Big Ben British Pub & Restaurant
2000 S Blvd .... Charlotte NC 28203 704-817-9697 671
Web: www.bigbenpub.com

Big Bend Community College
7662 Chanute St.......... Moses Lake WA 98837 509-793-2222 762-6243* 162
**Fax:* Admissions ■ *TF:* 877-745-1212 ■ *Web:* www.bigbend.edu

Big Bend Electric Co-op
1373 N Hwy 261 PO Box 348.......... Ritzville WA 99169 509-659-1700 659-1404 245
TF: 866-844-2363 ■ *Web:* www.bbec.org

Big Bend National Park
PO Box 129 .... Big Bend National Park TX 79834 432-477-2251 477-1175 564
Web: www.nps.gov/bibe

Big Bend Natural History Assn
PO Box 196 .... Big Bend National Park TX 79834 432-477-2236 48-13
Web: www.bigbendbookstore.org

Big Bend of the Colorado State Recreation Area
4220 S Needles Hwy Ste 3 .... Laughlin NV 89209 702-298-1859 565
Web: parks.nv.gov/parks/big-bend-of-the-colorado

Big Bend Ranch State Park
PO Box 2319 .... Presidio TX 79845 432-229-3416 565
Web: tpwd.texas.gov/state-parks/big-bend-ranch

Big Bend State Fish & Wildlife Area
PO Box 181 .... Prophetstown IL 61277 815-537-2270 565
Web: www.dnr.state.il.us

Big Bend Telephone Company Inc
808 N Fifth St .... Alpine TX 79830 800-520-0092 116
TF: 800-520-0092 ■ *Web:* www.bigbend.net

Big Bog State Recreation Area
55716 Hwy 72 NE.......... Waskish MN 56685 218-647-8592 647-8730 565
Web: www.dnr.state.mn.us

Big Bone Lick State Park 3380 Beaver Rd .... Union KY 41091 859-384-3522 565
Web: www.parks.ky.gov

Big Boy Restaurants International LLC
4199 Marcy St .... Warren MI 48091 586-759-6000 670
Web: www.bigboy.com

Big Brothers Big Sisters of SJC
308 N Locke Ave.......... Farmington NM 87401 505-326-1508 79

Big Buck Brewery & Steakhouse Inc
550 S Wisconsin Ave .... Gaylord MI 49735 989-732-5781 670
Web: www.bigbuck.com

Big C Lumber Inc
50860 Princess Way PO Box 176.......... Granger IN 46530 574-277-4550 191-3
TF: 888-297-0010 ■ *Web:* www.bigclumber.com

Big Cat Energy Corp
121 Merino Stree, PO Box 500.......... Upton WY 82730 307-468-9369 536
Web: www.bigcatenergy.com

Big Cedar Lodge 612 Devil's Pool Rd .... Ridgedale MO 65739 417-335-2777 335-2340 669
Web: www.bigcedar.com

Big Ceramic Store LLC 543 Vista Blvd.......... Sparks NV 89434 775-351-2888 690
Web: www.bigceramicstore.com

Big Country Autoland
4004 Spur Business 84 .... Snyder TX 79549 325-573-5456 57
Web: bigcountryautoland.com

Name / Address	City	State	ZIP	Phone	Fax	Class
Big Country Electric Co-op 1010 W S First St PO Box 518	Roby	TX	79543	325-776-2244		245
TF: 888-662-2232 ■ *Web:* bigcountry.net						
Big Creek Lumber 3564 Hwy 1	Davenport	CA	95017	831-457-5015	423-2800	191-3
Web: www.big-creek.com						
Big Creek Software LLC 201 N Third St Ste E	Polk City	IA	50226	515-984-6243		177
Web: www.bigcreek.com						
Big Creek State Park 8794 NW 125th Ave	Polk City	IA	50226	515-984-6473	984-9320	565
Web: www.iowadnr.gov						
Big Cypress National Preserve 33100 Tamiami Trl E	Ochopee	FL	34141	239-695-2000	695-3901	564
Web: www.nps.gov						
Big Cypress Tree State Park 295 Big Cypress Rd	Greenfield	TN	38230	731-235-2700		565
Web: www.state.tn.us						
Big d Floor Covering Supplies 7261 Lampson Ave	Garden Grove	CA	92841	714-894-2443	934-6078	290
TF: 866-894-2443 ■ *Web:* bigdsupply.com						
Big D Ranch 7590 S 10 Mile Rd	Meridian	ID	83642	208-888-1710	888-0075	10-3
Web: www.bigdranch.com						
Big Daddy Drayage Inc 575 Ave P	Newark	NJ	07105	973-522-1717		311
Web: www.bigdaddydrayage.com						
Big Daddy O's Beach BBQ 2333 Roosevelt Blvd	Oxnard	CA	93035	805-984-0014		671
Big Deahl Productions Inc 1450 N Dayton St	Chicago	IL	60642	312-587-1071		514
Web: www.bigdeahl.com						
Big Deer State Park 1467 Boulder Beach Rd	Groton	VT	05046	802-584-3822		565
TF: 888-409-7579 ■ *Web:* www.vtstateparks.com/htm/bigdeer.cfm						
Big Delta State Historical Park c/o Northern Area Office 3700 Airport Way	Fairbanks	AK	99709	907-451-2695		565
Web: www.dnr.alaska.gov						
Big Dog Logistics LLP 1235 N Loop W Ste 500	Houston	TX	77008	713-996-8171		314
Big Dogs 519 Lincoln County Pkwy	Lincolnton	NC	28092	800-244-3647		155-3
TF: 800-244-3647 ■ *Web:* www.bigdogs.com						
Big Dutchman Inc 3900 John F Donnelly Dr	Holland	MI	49424	616-392-5981		273
Web: www.bigdutchmanusa.com						
Big Easy New Orleans Style Sandwiches 1915 N Central Expy Ste 200	Plano	TX	75075	972-424-5261		671
Web: www.bigeasyplano.com						
Big Enterprises Inc 105 Paul Mellon Ct	Waldorf	MD	20602	301-843-7030		256
Big Fish Grill 20298 Coastal Hwy	Rehoboth Beach	DE	19971	302-227-3474		671
TF: 800-441-1329 ■ *Web:* www.bigfishgrill.com						
Big Fitness 5 Progress St	Seekonk	MA	02771	401-885-5200		354
TF: 800-383-2008 ■ *Web:* www.bigfitness.com						
Big Five Tours & Expeditions 1551 SE Palm Ct	Stuart	FL	34994	772-287-7995	287-5990	760
TF: 800-244-3483 ■ *Web:* www.bigfive.com						
Big Flat Electric Co-op Inc 333 S Seventh St	Malta	MT	59538	406-654-2040		245
TF: 800-242-2040 ■ *Web:* www.bigflatelectric.com						
Big Fly Inc 13940 Cedar Rd Ste 227	Cleveland	OH	44118	323-875-2273		21
Web: www.bigflyaviation.com						
Big Foot Beach State Park 1452 Wells St	Lake Geneva	WI	53147	262-248-2528		565
TF: 888-936-7463 ■ *Web:* www.dnr.wi.gov						
Big Foot Productions Inc 3709 36th Ave	Long Island	NY	11101	718-729-1900	729-8638	514
Web: www.bigfootnyc.com						
Big Four Restaurant 1075 California St	San Francisco	CA	94108	415-771-1140		671
TF: 800-424-8292 ■ *Web:* big4restaurant.com						
Big Freight Systems Inc 360 Hwy 12 N	Steinbach	MB	R5G1A6	204-326-3434		311
Web: www.bigfreight.com						
Big Frey Promotional Products 420 Lake Cook Rd Ste 117	Deerfield	IL	60015	800-888-1636		7
TF: 800-888-1636 ■ *Web:* www.bigfrey.com						
Big G Cereals PO Box 9452 PO Box 9452	Minneapolis	MN	55440	800-248-7310	764-8330*	296-4
**Fax Area Code:* 763 ■ **Fax:* PR ■ *TF:* 800-248-7310 ■ *Web:* www.generalmills.com						
Big G Express Inc 190 Hawkins Dr	Shelbyville	TN	37160	800-684-9140		780
TF: 800-955-9140 ■ *Web:* www.biggexpress.com						
Big Girls Bras Etcetera Inc 3540 NW 56th St Ste 207	Lauderdale	FL	33309	954-484-2701		157-6
TF: 866-352-4494 ■ *Web:* www.biggerbras.com						
Big Hill Pond State Park 1435 John Howell Rd	Pocahontas	TN	38061	731-645-7967		565
Web: www.state.tn.us						
Big Hole National Battlefield 16425 Hwy 43 W	Wisdom	MT	59761	406-689-3155	689-3151	564
Web: www.nps.gov						
Big Horn County 420 W C St	Basin	WY	82410	307-568-2357	568-9375	338
TF: 800-500-2324 ■ *Web:* www.bighorncountywy.gov						
Big Horn County 121 W Third St	Hardin	MT	59034	406-665-9735	665-9706	338
TF: 800-833-8503 ■ *Web:* www.bighorncountymt.gov/departments/treasurer						
Big Horn Energy 376 33rd St	Cody	WY	82414	307-587-5613		271
Big Horn Energy Services II LLC 4321 Greenville Cir	Midland	TX	79707	432-312-4071		536
Web: www.bighornenergyservices.com						
Big Horn Inc 1222 E 38th St	Chattanooga	TN	37407	423-867-4800		350
Big Horn Rural Electric Co-op 208 S Fifth St PO Box 270	Basin	WY	82410	307-568-2419		245
TF: 800-564-2419 ■ *Web:* www.bighornrea.com						
Big Huge Games Inc 1954 Greenspring Dr Ste 520	Timonium	MD	21093	410-842-0028	842-0047	174
Web: www.bighugegames.com						
Big Kaiser Precision Tooling Inc 641 Fargo Ave	Elk Grove Village	IL	60007	847-228-7660	228-0881	493
TF: 888-866-5776 ■ *Web:* www.bigkaiser.com						
Big L Corp 620 S Main St PO Box 134	Sheridan	MI	48884	989-291-3232	291-3421	364
Web: www.big-l-lumber.com						
Big Lagoon State Park 12301 Gulf Beach Hwy	Pensacola	FL	32507	850-492-1595		565
Web: www.floridastateparks.org/biglagoon						
Big Lake Public Library 3140 S Big Lake Rd	Big Lake	AK	99652	907-892-6475		434-3
Big Lake State Park 204 Lake Shore Dr	Craig	MO	64437	660-442-3770		565
Web: www.mostateparks.com						
Big League Dreams USA LLC 16333 Fairfield Ranch Rd	Chino Hills	CA	91709	909-287-6900		717
Web: www.bigleaguedreams.com						
Big Lots Inc (BLI) 300 Phillipi Rd	Columbus	OH	43228	614-278-6800	278-8322	791
NYSE: BIG ■ *TF:* 877-998-1697 ■ *Web:* www.biglots.com						
Big M Inc 12 Vreeland Ave	Totowa	NJ	07512	973-890-0021		157-6
TF: 800-695-1788 ■ *Web:* mandee.com						
Big m p G Inc 811 E Vienna Ave	Milwaukee	WI	53212	414-332-3900		5
TF: 800-558-5580 ■ *Web:* www.bigmpg.com						
Big Meadows 1000 Longmoor Ave	Savanna	IL	61074	815-273-2238		371
Web: www.bigmeadows.biz						
Big Mountain Imaging 4725 Copper Sage St	Las Vegas	NV	89115	702-739-7318		317
Web: bigmountain.com						
Big Muddy River Correctional Ctr 251 N Hwy 37 PO Box 1000	Ina	IL	62846	618-437-5300	437-5627	213
Web: illinois.gov						
Big Night Entertainment Group 33 Union St 2nd Fl	Boston	MA	02108	617-338-4343		720
Web: www.bneg.com						
Big O Tires LLC 21609 N Highway 99 C	Lynnwood	WA	98036	425-778-6899		755
Web: www.bigotires.com						
Big Oak Tree State Park 13640 S Hwy 102	East Prairie	MO	63845	573-649-3149		565
Web: www.mostateparks.com						
Big Pocono State Park c/o Tobyhanna State Park Complex 114 Campground Rd	Tobyhanna	PA	18466	570-894-8336		565
Web: www.dcnr.state.pa.us						
Big Rapids Products 1313 Maple St	Big Rapids	MI	49307	231-796-3593		247
Web: www.brproducts.com						
Big Red Liquors Inc 1110 N College Ave	Bloomington	IN	47404	812-332-0653		443
Web: www.bigredliquors.com						
Big Ridge State Park 1015 Big Ridge Rd	Maynardville	TN	37807	865-992-5523		565
TF: 800-471-5305 ■ *Web:* tnstateparks.com/parks/campground/big-ridge						
Big River Oil Company Inc 1920 Orchard Ave	Hannibal	MO	63401	573-221-0226		579
Web: www.bigriveroil.com						
Big River Resources West Burlington LLC 15210 103rd St	West Burlington	IA	52655	319-753-1100	753-1103	10-5
Web: www.bigriverresources.com						
Big River State Forest RR 1 PO Box 118	Keithsburg	IL	61442	309-374-2496		565
Web: dnr.illinois.gov/Lands/Landmgt/PARKS/R1/BIGRIVER.HTM						
Big River Zinc Corp 2401 Mississippi Ave	Sauget	IL	62201	618-274-5000		485
TF: 800-274-4002 ■ *Web:* www.bigriverzinc.com						
Big Rock Sports LLC 173 Hankison Dr	Newport	NC	28570	252-808-3500	726-8352	710
TF: 800-334-2661 ■ *Web:* www.bigrocksports.com						
Big Run State Park 10368 Savage River Rd 10368 Savage River Rd	Swanton	MD	21561	301-895-5453		565
Web: dnr.maryland.gov/publiclands/Pages/western/bigrun.aspx						
Big Sandy Community & Technical College 1 Bert T Combs Dr	Prestonsburg	KY	41653	606-886-3863		162
TF: 888-641-4132 ■ *Web:* www.bigsandy.kctcs.edu						
Mayo 513 Third St	Paintsville	KY	41240	606-789-5321		162
Web: www.kctcs.net						
Big Sandy Rural Electric Cooperative Corp 504 11th St	Paintsville	KY	41240	606-789-4095	789-5454	245
TF: 888-789-7322 ■ *Web:* www.bigsandyrecc.com						
Big Sandy Superstore Arena 1 Civic Ctr Plaza	Huntington	WV	25701	304-696-5990		720
Web: www.bigsandyarena.com						
Big Saver Foods Inc 4260 Charter St	Vernon	CA	90058	323-582-7222		345
Web: www.bigsaverfoods.com						
Big Shoals State Park 11330 SE County Rd 135	White Springs	FL	32096	386-397-4331		565
TF: 877-635-3655 ■ *Web:* www.floridastateparks.org						
Big Sioux Recreation Area 410 Pk Ave	Brandon	SD	57005	605-582-7243		565
Web: gfp.sd.gov/state-parks/directory/big-sioux						
Big Six Farms 5575 Zenith Mill Rd	Fort Valley	GA	31030	478-825-7504	825-1194	315-3
Big Sky Construction Company Inc 507 Exposition Ave	Dallas	TX	75226	972-226-4704		187
TF: 800-544-4576 ■ *Web:* www.bigskyconstruction.com						
Big Sky Engineering Inc 429 Venture Ct	Verona	WI	53593	608-848-9898		256
Web: www.bigskyeng.com						
Big Sky Resort 50 Big Sky Resort Rd	Big Sky	MT	59716	406-995-5000	995-5001	669
TF: 800-548-4486 ■ *Web:* www.bigskyresort.com						
Big Sky Technologies 9325 Sky Pk Ct Ste 120	San Diego	CA	92123	858-715-5000		178-7
TF: 800-736-2751 ■ *Web:* www.bigskytech.com						
Big South Fork National River & Recreation Area 4564 Leatherwood Rd	Oneida	TN	37841	423-569-9778	569-5505	564
Web: www.nps.gov						
Big Spring 215 W Third St PO Box 3359	Big Spring	TX	79720	432-264-6032	264-6047	206
TF: 866-222-7100 ■ *Web:* www.bigspringtx.com						
Big Spring Cafe 3507 Governors Dr	Huntsville	AL	35806	256-539-9994		671
Web: www.bigspringcafe.com						
Big Spring Independent School District 708 E 11th Pl	Big Spring	TX	79720	432-264-3600	264-3646	685
TF: 866-632-9992 ■ *Web:* www.bsisd.esc18.net						
Big Spring School District 45 Mt Rock Rd	Newville	PA	17241	717-776-2000		360-2
Web: www.bigspringsd.org						
Big Spring State Hospital 1901 N Hwy 87	Big Spring	TX	79720	432-267-8216	268-7263	374-5
Web: www.dshs.texas.gov/mhhospitals/BigSpringSH/default.shtm						

	Phone	Fax	Class
Big Spring State Park c/o Colonel Denning State Pk 1599 Doubling Gap Rd ... Newville PA 17241 *Web:* www.dcnr.state.pa.us	717-776-5272		565
Big Spring State Park 1 Scenic Dr ... Big Spring TX 79720 *Web:* tpwd.texas.gov/state-parks/big-spring	432-263-4931		565
Big Stone County 20 SE Second St ... Ortonville MN 56278 *Web:* www.bigstonecounty.org	320-839-6376		338
Big Stone Island Nature Area c/o Hartford Beach State Pk 13672 Hartford Beach Rd ... Corona SD 57227 *Web:* gfp.sd.gov/state-parks/directory/big-stone	605-432-6374		565
Big Stone Lake State Park 35889 Meadowbrook State Pk Rd ... Ortonville MN 56278 *TF:* 888-646-6367 ■ *Web:* www.dnr.state.mn.us	320-839-3663	839-3676	565
Big Talbot Island State Park 12157 Heckscher Dr ... Jacksonville FL 32226 *Web:* www.floridastateparks.org/bigtalbotisland	904-251-2320		565
Big Ten Conference 5440 Park Pl ... Rosemont IL 60018 *TF:* 800-745-3000 ■ *Web:* bigten.org	847-696-1010		206
Big Texan Steak Ranch 7701 I-40 E ... Amarillo TX 79118 *TF Cust Svc:* 800-657-7177 ■ *Web:* www.bigtexan.com	806-372-6000		671
Big Thicket National Preserve 6044 FM 420 ... Kountze TX 77625 *Web:* www.nps.gov/bith	409-951-6700	951-6714	564
Big Think Studios 1426 18th St ... San Francisco CA 94107 *Web:* www.bigthinkstudios.com	415-934-1111		7
Big Timberworks Inc 1 Rabel Ln ... Gallatin Gateway MT 59730 *TF:* 800-763-4639 ■ *Web:* bigtimberworks.com	406-763-4639		286
Big W Sales 1040 W Charter Way ... Stockton CA 95206 *Web:* www.bigwsales.com	209-464-9493		274
Big West Oil LLC 333 W Center St ... North Salt Lake UT 84054 *Web:* www.bigwestoil.com	801-296-7700		580
Big Y Foods Inc 2145 Roosevelt Ave ... Springfield MA 01102 *TF Cust Svc:* 800-828-2688 ■ *Web:* www.bigy.com	413-784-0600		345
Biga on the Banks 203 S St Mary's St ... San Antonio TX 78205 *TF:* 800-962-4263 ■ *Web:* www.biga.com	210-225-0722		671
Bigbend Hospice 1723 Mahan Ctr Blvd ... Tallahassee FL 32308 *TF:* 800-772-5862 ■ *Web:* www.bigbendhospice.org	850-878-5310		371
BigByte Corp 47400 Seabridge Dr ... Fremont CA 94538 *TF:* 800-536-6425 ■ *Web:* www.bigbytecorp.com	510-249-1100		175
BigCountry 107.3 3811 Rogers Ave Ste C ... Fort Smith AR 72903 *Web:* bigcountry1073.com	479-452-0681	452-0873	645-61
Big-D Construction Corp 404 West 400 South ... Salt Lake City UT 84101 *TF:* 800-748-4481 ■ *Web:* www.big-d.com	801-415-6000	415-6900	188-7
Bigelow & Co 500 N Commercial St ... Manchester NH 03101 *Web:* www.bigelowcpa.com	603-627-7659		2
Bigelow Hollow State Park & Nipmuck State Forest c/o Shenipsit State Forest 166 Chestnut Hill Rd ... Stafford Springs CT 06076 *Web:* www.ct.gov	860-684-3430		565
Bigelow Management Inc 4640 S Eastern Ave ... Las Vegas NV 89119 *Web:* budgetsuites.com	702-450-1000		379
Bigelow Tea 201 Black Rock Tpke ... Fairfield CT 06825 *TF:* 888-244-3569 ■ *Web:* www.bigelowtea.com	888-244-3569		296-40
Bigeye Direct Inc 13860 Redskin Dr ... Herndon VA 20171 *Fax Area Code: 866 ■ *Web:* www.bigeyedirect.com	703-955-3017	654-2797*	195
BIG-FM 95.7 12100 W Howard Ave ... Greenfield WI 53228 *Web:* 957bigfm.ihcart.com	414-545-8900		645
Bigge Crane & Rigging Co 10700 Bigge Ave ... San Leandro CA 94577 *TF:* 888-337-2444 ■ *Web:* bigge.com	510-277-4747	639-4053	189-1
Biggers Chevrolet 1385 E Chicago St ... Elgin IL 60120 *TF:* 866-431-1555 ■ *Web:* www.biggerschevy.com	847-742-9000	742-0061	57
Biggins Lacy Shapiro & Company LLC 47 Hulfish St Ste 400 ... Princeton NJ 08542 *Web:* www.blsstrategies.com	609-924-9775		194
Biggs Cardosa Assoc Inc 865 The Alameda ... San Jose CA 95126 *Web:* biggscardosa.com	408-296-5515		261
Biggs Plumbing Co 1615 Dungan Ln ... Austin TX 78754 *Web:* biggsplumbing.com	512-837-5955		189-10
Biggs/Gilmore Communications 261 E Kalamazoo Ave ... Kalamazoo MI 49007	269-349-7711		7
BiggsKofford & Co 630 Southpointe Ct Ste 200 ... Colorado Springs CO 80906 *Web:* www.biggskofford.com	719-579-9090		2
Bigham Brothers Inc 705 E Slaton Rd ... Lubbock TX 79452 *Web:* www.bighambrothers.com	806-745-0384		273
Bighorn Airways Inc 912 W Brundage Ln ... Sheridan WY 82801 *TF:* 800-451-5333 ■ *Web:* www.bighornairways.com	307-672-3421		13
Bighorn Canyon National Recreation Area 5 Ave B PO Box 7458 ... Fort Smith MT 59035 *Web:* www.nps.gov/bica	406-666-2412	666-2415	564
Bighorn Resort 1801 Majestic Ln ... Billings MT 59102 *Web:* www.thebighornresort.com	406-839-9300		378
Biglari Holdings Inc 175 E Houston St Ste 1300 ... San Antonio TX 78205 *NYSE:* BH ■ *Web:* www.biglariholdings.com	210-344-3400		360-3
BigLever Software Inc 10500 Laurel Hill Cove ... Austin TX 78730 *Web:* www.biglever.com	512-426-2227		177
Bigmouth 244 Kearny St Fl 6 ... San Francisco CA 94108 *Web:* www.bigmouth.com	415-394-6680		7
Bigotes 1821 E Abram St ... Arlington TX 76010	817-274-1350		671
Bigrentz Inc 1063 Mcgaw Ave Ste 200 ... Irvine CA 92614 *TF:* 855-999-5438 ■ *Web:* www.bigrentz.com	855-999-5438		23
BigTent Design Inc 350 Brannan St 3rd Fl ... San Francisco CA 94107 *Web:* www.bigtent.com	415-992-6550		387

	Phone	Fax	Class
Bihler of America Inc 85 Industrial Rd ... Phillipsburg NJ 08865 *Web:* www.bihler.com	908-213-9001		190
Bihrle Applied Research Inc 81 Research Dr ... Hampton VA 23666 *Web:* www.bihrle.com	757-766-2416		256
BII (Burgess Industries Inc) 7500 Boone Ave N Ste 111 ... Brooklyn Park MN 55428 *TF:* 800-233-2589 ■ *Web:* www.burgessind.com	763-553-7800	553-9289	629
Bijan Boutique 420 N Rodeo Dr ... Beverly Hills CA 90210 *Web:* www.bijan.com	310-273-6544	273-6535	574
Bijou Grille, The 643 Main St ... Buffalo NY 14203 *TF:* 800-745-3000 ■ *Web:* www.bijougrille.com	716-847-1512	852-3041	671
BIK&Co 7600 County Line Rd Ste 6 ... Burr Ridge IL 60527 *Web:* www.bikcpa.com	847-362-4310		2
Bike Friday Travel Systems 3364 W 11th Ave ... Eugene OR 97402 *TF:* 800-777-0258 ■ *Web:* bikefriday.com	541-687-0487		775
Bike Gallery Portland Inc 5329 NE Sandy Blvd ... Portland OR 97213 *Web:* bikegallery.com	503-281-9800		711
Bike USA Inc 2811 Brodhead Rd ... Bethlehem PA 18020 *Web:* www.bikeusainc.com	610-868-7652		711
Biko 3920 Ravens Crest Dr ... Plainsboro NJ 08536 *Web:* www.bikotech.biz	617-910-0160		193
Bilbrey Insurance Services Inc 5701 Greendale Rd ... Johnston IA 50131 *TF:* 800-383-0116 ■ *Web:* icapiowa.com	800-383-0116		390
Bilco Tool Corp 30076 Dequindre Rd ... Warren MI 48092 *Web:* www.bilcotool.com	586-574-9300	574-9340	757
Bilenky Cycle Works Inc 5319 N Second St ... Philadelphia PA 19120 *TF:* 844-889-8823 ■ *Web:* www.bilenky.com	215-329-4744		711
Bilicki Law Firm Pc, The 1285 N Main St ... Jamestown NY 14701 *TF:* 800-851-2812 ■ *Web:* www.bilickilaw.com	716-664-5600		428
Bilingual Education Institute 6060 Richmond Ave Ste 180 ... Houston TX 77057 *Web:* www.bei.edu	713-789-4555		764
Bilirakis Gus M (Rep R - FL) 2112 Rayburn HOB ... Washington DC 20515 *Web:* bilirakis.house.gov	202-225-5755	225-4085	342-2
Bil-Jax Inc 125 Taylor Pkwy ... Archbold OH 43502 *TF:* 800-537-0540 ■ *Web:* www.biljax.com	419-445-8915	445-0367	491
Bilkays Express Co 2400 Bedle Pl ... Linden NJ 07036 *TF:* 800-526-4006 ■ *Web:* Www.bilkays.com	908-289-2400	289-6364	780
Bill & Hillary Clinton National Airport 1 Airport Dr ... Little Rock AR 72202 *TF:* 800-897-1910 ■ *Web:* www.fly-lit.com	501-372-3439	372-0612	27
Bill & Melinda Gates Foundation PO Box 23350 ... Seattle WA 98102 *TF:* 800-728-3843 ■ *Web:* www.gatesfoundation.org	206-709-3100	709-3180	305
Bill & Ralphs Inc 118 B & R Dr ... Sarepta LA 71071	318-539-2071		297-8
Bill Abbott Inc 500 W Ctr ... Monticello IL 61856 *Web:* billabbottinc.com	217-762-2576		57
Bill Baggs Cape Florida State Park 1200 S Crandon Blvd ... Key Biscayne FL 33149 *Web:* www.floridastateparks.org	305-361-5811		565
Bill Barrett Corp 1099 18th St Ste 2300 ... Denver CO 80202 *NYSE:* BBG ■ *TF:* 800-826-6762 ■ *Web:* www.billbarrettcorp.com	303-293-9100	291-0420	538
Bill Black Chevrolet Cadillac Inc 601 E Bessemer Ave ... Greensboro NC 27405 *Web:* billblackauto.com	336-275-9641		57
Bill Collins 4220 Bardstown Rd ... Louisville KY 40218 *TF:* 888-327-9095 ■ *Web:* billcollinsford.net	502-459-9550		57
Bill Currie Ford Inc 5815 N Dale Mabry Hwy ... Tampa FL 33614 *Web:* billcurrieford.com	813-872-5555		57
Bill Dunbar & Associates LLC 2601 Fortune Cir E Ste 301A ... Indianapolis IN 46241 *TF:* 800-411-4281 ■ *Web:* www.billdunbar.com	317-247-8014		463
Bill Farris Insurance Agency Inc 390 Cypress Gardens Blvd ... Winter Haven FL 33880 *Web:* www.statefarm.com	863-299-2153		390
Bill Good Marketing Inc 6891 S 700 W Ste 100 ... Midvale UT 84047 *Web:* www.billgoodmarketing.com	801-572-1480		195
Bill Graham Civic Auditorium 99 Grove St ... San Francisco CA 94102 *Web:* billgrahamcivicauditorium.com	415-624-8900		572
Bill Hwang's Restaurant 879 Canton Rd ... Akron OH 44312	330-784-7167		671
Bill Johnson's Big Apple 3757 E Van Buren St ... Phoenix AZ 85008 *Web:* www.billjohnsons.com	602-275-2107		671
Bill Lee's Bamboo Chopsticks 1203 18th St ... Bakersfield CA 93301 *Web:* www.billlees.com	661-324-9441	324-7811	671
Bill Miller Bar-B-Q Inc 2750 Bill Miller Ln PO Box 839925 ... San Antonio TX 78223 *Fax: Sales ■ *TF:* 800-339-3111 ■ *Web:* www.billmillerbbq.com	210-225-4461	302-1533*	670
Bill Penney Toyota 4808 University Dr NW ... Huntsville AL 35816 *Web:* www.billpenneytoyota.com	256-837-1111		57
Bill Pollard Jr CPA 79 E Eleventh St ... Tracy CA 95376 *Web:* billpollardcpa.com	209-832-5110		2
Bill Smith Auto Parts 400 Ash St ... Danville IL 61832 *Web:* www.billsmithauto.com	217-442-0156		54
Bill Snethkamp Lansing Dodge Inc 6131 S Pennsylvania Ave ... Lansing MI 48911 *TF:* 888-685-2185 ■ *Web:* www.billsnethkamp.com	888-685-2185		57
Bill Spoon's Barbecue 5524 S Blvd ... Charlotte NC 28217 *Web:* spoonsbarbecue.com	704-525-8865		671
Bill Stasek Chevrolet Inc 700 W Dundee Rd ... Wheeling IL 60090 *Web:* www.stasekchevrolet.com	847-537-7000		57
Bill T Jones/Arnie Zane Dance Co 219 W 19th St ... New York NY 10011 *Web:* www.newyorklivearts.org	212-691-6500	633-1974	573-1

Name / Address	City	State	ZIP	Phone	Fax	Class
Bill's Distributing Ltd 5900 Packer Dr NE	Menomonie	WI	54751	715-235-5820		297-8
Bill.com Inc 1810 Embarcadero Rd *Web:* www.bill.com	Palo Alto	CA	94303	650-621-7700		177
Billco Manufacturing Inc 100 Halstead Blvd. *Web:* www.billco-mfg.com	Zelienople	PA	16063	724-452-7390	452-0217	386
Billerica Public Library 15 Concord Rd *Web:* www.billericalibrary.org	Billerica	MA	01821	978-671-0948		434-3
Billiard Congress of America 12303 Airport Way Ste 140 *TF:* 800-343-1329 ■ *Web:* bca-pool.com	Broomfield	CO	80021	303-243-5070	243-5075	48-22
Billings Area Chamber of Commerce 815 S 27th St *TF:* 855-328-9116 ■ *Web:* www.billingschamber.com	Billings	MT	59101	406-245-4111	245-7333	139
Billings C'mon Inn Hotel 2020 Overland Ave *TF:* 800-655-1170 ■ *Web:* www.cmoninn.com	Billings	MT	59102	406-655-1100		379
Billings Capital Management LLC 1001 Nineteenth St N 19th Fl *TF:* 800-785-7914 ■ *Web:* www.billingscap.com	Arlington	VA	22209	703-962-1871		528
Billings City Hall 210 N 27th St *Web:* www.ci.billings.mt.us	Billings	MT	59101	406-657-8210	657-8390	337
Billings Clinic 2800 Tenth Ave N *TF:* 800-332-7156 ■ *Web:* www.billingsclinic.com	Billings	MT	59101	406-238-2501		374-3
Billings Convention & Visitors Bureau 815 S 27th St PO Box 31177 *TF:* 800-735-2635 ■ *Web:* www.visitbillings.com	Billings	MT	59107	406-245-4111	245-7333	206
Billings County 495 Fourth St PO Box 168 *Web:* www.billingscountynd.gov	Medora	ND	58645	701-623-4377	623-4761	338
Billings Gazette 401 N 28th St *TF:* 800-543-2505 ■ *Web:* www.billingsgazette.com	Billings	MT	59101	406-657-1200	657-1208	532-2
Billings Livestock Commission Co 2443 N Frontage Rd *Web:* www.billingslivestock.com	Billings	MT	59101	406-245-4151		446
Billings Logan International Airport 1901 Terminal Cir *TF:* 800-331-3131 ■ *Web:* www.ci.billings.mt.us	Billings	MT	59105	406-657-8495	657-8438	27
Billings Nissan 2100 King Ave W *Web:* billingsnissan.com	Billings	MT	59102	406-655-1111		57
Billings Studio Theatre (BST) 1500 Rimrock Rd *TF:* 800-227-7368 ■ *Web:* www.billingsstudiotheatre.com	Billings	MT	59102	406-248-1141		572
Billings Symphony 2721 Second Ave N *TF:* 800-871-9929 ■ *Web:* www.billingssymphony.org	Billings	MT	59101	406-252-3610	252-3353	573-3
Billings Times 2919 Montana Ave *TF:* 800-325-8276 ■ *Web:* billingstimes.net	Billings	MT	59101	406-245-4994	245-5115	532-4
Billingsley House Museum 6900 Green Landing Rd *Web:* pgparks.com	Upper Marlboro	MD	20772	301-627-0730		522
Billions Corp, The 3522 W Armitage Ave *TF:* 800-254-2543 ■ *Web:* billions.com	Chicago	IL	60647	312-997-9999		463
Billows Electric Supply 9100 State Rd *TF:* 866-398-1162 ■ *Web:* www.billows.com	Philadelphia	PA	19136	215-332-9700	338-8320	246
Billpro Management Systems Inc 30575 Euclid Ave *TF:* 800-736-0587 ■ *Web:* www.billpro.net	Wickliffe	OH	44092	440-516-3776		177
Bills Engineering Inc 1124 Ft St Mall Ste 200 *Web:* billsengineering.com	Honolulu	HI	96813	808-792-2022		261
Billups Inc 340 Oswego Pointe Dr Ste 101 *Web:* billups.com	Lake Oswego	OR	97034	503-454-0714	454-0716	6
Billy Bob's Texas 2520 Rodeo Plaza *Web:* billybobstexas.com	Fort Worth	TX	76164	817-624-7117		720
Billy Graham Evangelistic Assn 1 Billy Graham Pkwy *TF:* 877-247-2426 ■ *Web:* www.billygraham.org	Charlotte	NC	28201	704-401-2432		48-20
Billy Heroman's Flowerland 10812 N Harrell'S Ferry Rd *Web:* www.billyheromans.com	Baton Rouge	LA	70816	225-272-7673		292
Billy's 1301 H St *Web:* www.billysrestaurant.com	Lincoln	NE	68508	402-474-0084		671
Billy's Hickory Pit Bar B-Q 101 Cochran Rd	Lexington	KY	40502	859-269-9593		671
BI-LO LLC 5050 Edgewood Ct *TF:* 800-967-9105 ■ *Web:* www.bi-lo.com	Jacksonville	SC	32203	800-768-4438		345
Bilotta Home Center Inc 564 Mamaroneck Ave *Web:* bilotta.com	Mamaroneck	NY	10543	914-381-7734		362
Biloxi City Hall PO Box 429 *Web:* www.biloxi.ms.us	Biloxi	MS	39533	228-435-6254	435-6129	337
Biloxi Little Theatre 220 Lee St *Web:* www.4blt.org	Biloxi	MS	39530	228-432-8543	392-7639	573-4
Biloxi National Cemetery 400 Veterans Ave *Web:* www.cem.va.gov	Biloxi	MS	39531	228-388-6668	523-5784	136
Biltmore Construction Company Inc 1055 Ponce De Leon Blvd *Web:* www.biltmoreconstruction.com	Belleair	FL	33756	727-585-2084		685
Biltmore Greensboro Hotel 111 W Washington St *TF General:* 800-332-0303 ■ *Web:* www.thebiltmoregreensboro.com	Greensboro	NC	27401	336-272-3474		379
Biltmore Hotel & Conference Ctr of the Americas 1200 Anastasia Ave *TF Cust Svc:* 800-727-1926 ■ *Web:* www.biltmorehotel.com	Coral Gables	FL	33134	305-445-1926		669
Biltmore Hotel & Suites 2151 Laurelwood Rd *TF:* 800-255-9925 ■ *Web:* www.hotelbiltmore.com	Santa Clara	CA	95054	408-988-8411		379
Biltmore Hotel Oklahoma 401 S Meridian Ave *TF:* 800-522-6620 ■ *Web:* www.biltmoreokc.com	Oklahoma City	OK	73108	405-947-7681		379
Biltmore Suites 205 W Madison St *TF:* 800-868-5064 ■ *Web:* www.biltmoresuites.com	Baltimore	MD	21201	410-728-6550	728-5829	379
Biltrite Corp 51 Sawyer Rd *TF:* 800-877-8775 ■ *Web:* www.biltrite.com	Waltham	MA	02454	781-647-1700	647-4205	676
Bimac Corp 3034 Dryden Rd *TF:* 800-966-3853 ■ *Web:* www.bimac.com	Dayton	OH	45439	937-299-7333	299-7367	306
Bi-Mart Corp 220 S Seneca Rd *Web:* www.bimart.com	Eugene	OR	97402	541-344-0681		237
Bimbo Bakeries USA PO Box 976 **Fax Area Code:* 610 ■ *TF:* 800-984-0989 ■ *Web:* www.bimbobakeriesusa.com	Horsham	PA	19044	800-984-0989	320-9286*	296-1
Bimbo Bakery USA 2069 Aldergrove Ave *Web:* bimbobakeriesusa.com	Escondido	CA	92029	760-489-8433		68
Bimeda-MTC Animal Health Inc 420 Beaverdale Rd *TF:* 888-524-6332 ■ *Web:* www.bimedamtc.com	Cambridge	ON	N3C2W4	519-654-8000	654-8001	584
Bimini Twist 8480 Okeechobee Blvd *Web:* mybiminitwist.com	West Palm Beach	FL	33411	561-784-2660	784-2660	671
Bi-Mor Stations Inc 1890 S Pacific Hwy	Medford	OR	97501	541-772-2053		324
Bimsym Ebusiness Solutions 3466 Progress Dr Ste 218 *Web:* bimsym.com	Bensalem	PA	19020	215-639-7040		180
Bin 26 Enoteca 26 Charles St *Web:* www.bin26.com	Boston	MA	02114	617-723-5939		671
BIN 36 161 N Jefferson St *Web:* www.bin36.com	Chicago	IL	60661	312-995-6560		671
Bin 941 Tapas Parlour 941 Davie St *Web:* www.bin941.ca	Vancouver	BC	V6Z1B9	604-683-1246		671
Binary Group Inc 1911 Ft Myer Dr Ste 300 *Web:* www.binarygroup.com	Arlington	VA	22209	571-480-4444	480-4445	387
Binary Pulse Inc 3545 Harbor Gateway S Ste 102 *Web:* www.binarypulse.com	Costa Mesa	CA	92626	714-429-0110		4
Bindagraphics Inc 2701 Wilmarco Ave *TF:* 800-326-0300 ■ *Web:* www.bindagraphics.com	Baltimore	MD	21223	410-362-7200	362-7233	92
Binder Metal Products Inc 14909 S Broadway *TF:* 800-233-0896 ■ *Web:* www.bindermetal.com	Gardena	CA	90248	323-321-4835		295
Binder Park Zoo 7400 Div Dr *TF:* 800-537-2929 ■ *Web:* www.binderparkzoo.org	Battle Creek	MI	49014	269-979-1351	979-8834	823
Binders 284 S Sharon Amity Rd *TF:* 888-472-6866 ■ *Web:* www.bindersart.com	Charlotte	NC	28211	888-472-6866		543
Bindery Associates Inc 2025 Horseshoe Rd *Web:* www.binderyassociates.com	Lancaster	PA	17602	717-295-7443		5
Bindtech Inc 1232 Antioch Pk *Web:* www.bindtechinc.com	Nashville	TN	37211	615-834-0404		92
Binetti & Feerick CPAs PA 381 Broadway Ste 45	Westwood	NJ	07675	201-664-9151		2
Bing Design 126 E Ctr College St *TF:* 800-223-2203 ■ *Web:* www.bingdesign.com	Yellow Springs	OH	45387	937-767-2521		225
Bing's 1952 Kensington Ave *Web:* www.bingsrestaurant.net	Buffalo	NY	14215	716-839-5788		671
Bingham County 501 N Maple St Ste 205 *Web:* www.co.bingham.id.us	Blackfoot	ID	83221	208-782-3013		338
Bingham Osborn & Scarborough LLC 345 California St Ste 1100 *Web:* www.bosinvest.com	San Francisco	CA	94104	415-781-8535		194
Binghampton Zoo at Ross Park 60 Morgan Rd *Web:* www.rossparkzoo.com	Binghamton	NY	13903	607-724-5461		823
Binghamton City School District (BCSD) 164 Hawley St PO Box 2126 *Web:* binghamtonschools.org	Binghamton	NY	13902	607-762-8100		685
Binghamton Knitting Co Inc 11 Alice St **Fax Area Code:* 607 ■ *TF:* 877-746-3368 ■ *Web:* www.binghamtonknitting.com	Binghamton	NY	13904	877-746-3368	722-4621*	155-16
Binghamton Press Co Vestal Pkwy E *Web:* www.pressconnects.com	Binghamton	NY	13902	607-798-1234		532-3
Binghamton University 4400 Vestal Pkwy E **Fax:* Admissions ■ *TF:* 800-782-0289 ■ *Web:* www.binghamton.edu	Binghamton	NY	13902	607-777-2000	777-4445*	166
Binh-Le 5903 E 31st St	Tulsa	OK	74135	918-835-7722		671
Binion's Gambling Hall & Hotel 128 E Fremont St *TF:* 800-937-6537 ■ *Web:* www.binions.com	Las Vegas	NV	89101	702-382-1600		133
Binkley & Barfield Inc 1710 Seamist Dr *Web:* www.binkleybarfield.com	Houston	TX	77008	713-869-3433		256
Binkley & Hurst LP 133 Rothsville Stn Rd *TF:* 800-414-4705 ■ *Web:* www.binkleyhurst.com	Lititz	PA	17543	717-626-4705		429
Binovia Corp 8631 F St *Web:* www.binovia.com	Omaha	NE	68127	402-331-0202		180
Binsons Hospital Supplies Inc 26834 Lawrence *Web:* www.binsons.com	Center Line	MI	48015	586-755-2300		475
Binswanger Glass 965 Ridge Lake Blvd Ste 305 *TF:* 800-365-9922 ■ *Web:* www.binswangerglass.com	Memphis	TN	38120	800-365-9922		329
Bio Agri Mix LP 11 Ellens St *Web:* www.bioagrimix.com	Mitchell	ON	N0K1N0	519-348-9865		794
BIO Analytics 65 Broad St *Web:* www.bio4analytics.com	Stamford	CT	06901	203-327-0800		194
Bio Compression Systems Inc 120 W Commercial Ave *TF:* 800-888-0908 ■ *Web:* www.biocompression.com	Moonachie	NJ	07074	201-939-0716		476
Bio Medic Data Systems Inc 1 Silas Rd *TF:* 800-526-2637 ■ *Web:* www.bmds.com	Seaford	DE	19973	302-628-4100	628-4110	84
Bio Medical Innovations 814 Airport Way *TF:* 800-201-3958 ■ *Web:* www.leadlok.com	Sandpoint	ID	83864	800-201-3958		250
Bio Medware 3526 W Liberty Rd Ste 100 *TF:* 800-663-1334 ■ *Web:* www.biomedware.com	Ann Arbor	MI	48103	734-913-1098		196

Company / Address	City	State	Zip	Phone	Fax	Class
Bio Rem Usa Inc						
2496 W Royalton Rd	Broadview Heights	OH	44147	440-230-9542		196
Web: biorem.com						
Bio/Data Corp PO Box 347	Horsham	PA	19044	215-441-4000	443-8820	419
TF: 800-257-3282 ■ *Web:* www.biodatacorp.com						
BioAdvance 3711 Market St Fl 8	Philadelphia	PA	19104	215-966-6214		792
Web: www.bioadvance.com						
Bioanalytical Systems Inc						
2701 Kent Ave	West Lafayette	IN	47906	765-463-4527	497-1102	419
NASDAQ: BASI ■ *TF:* 800-845-4246 ■ *Web:* www.basinc.com						
Bio-Botanica Inc 75 Commerce Dr	Hauppauge	NY	11788	631-231-5522	231-7332	479
TF: 800-645-5720 ■ *Web:* www.bio-botanica.com						
Biobridges LLC						
167 Worcester St Ste 211	Wellesley	MA	02481	781-416-0909		225
Web: www.biobridges.com						
BioCardia Inc 125 Shoreway Rd Ste B	San Carlos	CA	94070	650-226-0120		476
TF: 800-624-1179 ■ *Web:* www.biocardia.com						
Biocare Inc 122 Clair Dr	Piedmont	SC	29673	864-295-9000		83
Biocare Medical LLC 4040 Pike Ln	Concord	CA	94520	925-603-8000		582
TF: 800-799-9499 ■ *Web:* biocare.net						
Biocell Laboratories Inc						
2001 University Dr	Rancho Dominguez	CA	90220	310-537-3300		231
TF: 800-222-8382 ■ *Web:* www.biocell.com						
BioCell Technology LLC						
4695 Macarthur Ct 11th Fl	Newport Beach	CA	92660	714-632-1231		345
Web: www.biocelltechnology.com						
Biocentric Inc 700 Collings Ave	Collingswood	NJ	08107	856-854-3500		463
TF: 866-624-6236 ■ *Web:* www.biocentricinc.com						
Biocept Inc						
5810 Nancy Ridge Dr Ste 150	San Diego	CA	92121	858-320-8200		583
Web: www.biocept.com						
Bio-Chem Fluidics Inc 85 Fulton St	Boonton	NJ	07005	973-263-3001		201
TF: 800-323-4340 ■ *Web:* www.biochemfluidics.com						
Biocoat Inc 211 Witmer Rd	Horsham	PA	19044	215-734-0888		476
Web: www.biocoat.com						
BioCryst Pharmaceuticals Inc						
2190 Pkwy Lake Dr	Birmingham	AL	35244	205-444-4600	444-4640	85
NASDAQ: BCRX ■ *TF:* 800-361-0912 ■ *Web:* www.biocryst.com						
BioCure Inc 2975 Gateway Dr Ste 100	Norcross	GA	30071	678-966-3400		476
Web: www.biocure.com						
BioDelivery Sciences International Inc (BDSI)						
4131 Parklake Ave Ste 225	Raleigh	NC	27612	919-582-9050	582-9051	85
NASDAQ: BDSI ■ *Web:* www.bdsi.com						
Bio-Detek Inc						
525 Narragansett Park Dr	Pawtucket	RI	02861	401-729-1400		250
Web: www.bio-detek.com						
Biodex Medical Systems Inc						
20 Ramsay Rd	Shirley	NY	11967	631-924-9000	924-8355	476
TF: 800-224-6339 ■ *Web:* www.biodex.com						
Biodiversity Research Institute						
276 Canco Rd	Portland	ME	04103	207-839-7600		196
Web: www.briloon.org						
Bioethics Legal Review						
1617 JFK Blvd Ste 1750	Philadelphia	PA	19103	215-557-2300		531-7
TF: 877-256-2472 ■ *Web:* www.lawjournalnewsletters.com						
Biofilm Inc 3225 Executive Ridge	Vista	CA	92081	760-727-9030		231
Web: astroglide.com						
Biofit Engineered Products						
15500 Biofit Way	Bowling Green	OH	43402	419-823-1089	823-1342	319-1
TF: 800-597-0246 ■ *Web:* www.biofit.com						
BioFlex Laser Therapy						
411 Horner Ave	Etobicoke	ON	M8W4W3	416-251-1055		476
TF: 888-557-4004 ■ *Web:* www.bioflexlaser.com						
BioFlorida						
525 Okeechobee Blvd Ste 1500	West Palm Beach	FL	33401	561-653-3839		743
TF: 800-822-6344 ■ *Web:* www.bioflorida.com						
BioForce Nanosciences						
1615 Golden Aspen Dr Ste 101	Ames	IA	50010	515-233-8333		250
Web: www.bioforcenano.com						
Bioforest Technologies Inc						
59 Industrial Park Crescent	Sault Sainte Marie	ON	P6B5P3	705-942-5824		302
Web: bioforest.ca						
BioGenex Laboratories Inc						
4600 Norris Canyon Rd	San Ramon	CA	94583	925-275-0550		231
TF: 800-421-4149 ■ *Web:* www.biogenex.com						
BIOgroupUSA Inc 1059 Broadwy Ste F	Dunedin	FL	34698	727-789-1646		610
Web: www.biobagusa.com						
Biohelix Corp 500 Cummings Ste 5550	Beverly	MA	01915	858-552-1100	592-9020*	231
**Fax Area Code:* 740 ■ *TF:* 800-874-1517 ■ *Web:* www.biohelix.com						
BioHorizons Inc						
2300 Riverchase Ctr	Birmingham	AL	35244	205-967-7880	870-0304	477
TF: 888-246-8338 ■ *Web:* www.biohorizons.com						
Bioionix Inc 4603 Triangle St	Mcfarland	WI	53558	608-838-0300		612
Web: www.bioionix.com						
BIO-key International Inc						
300 Nickerson Rd	Marlborough	MA	01752	508-460-4000		84
Web: www.bio-key.com						
Biokinetics & Assoc Ltd						
2470 Don Reid Dr	Ottawa	ON	K1H1E1	613-736-0384		256
Web: www.biokinetics.com						
Biola University 13800 Biola Ave	La Mirada	CA	90639	562-903-6000	903-4709*	166
**Fax:* Admissions ■ *TF Admissions:* 800-652-4652 ■ *Web:* www.biola.edu						
Bio-Lab Inc						
1725 N Brown Rd PO Box 30000	Lawrenceville	GA	30043	678-502-4000		143
TF: 800-859-7946 ■ *Web:* www.biolabinc.com						
BioLase Inc 4 Cromwell	Irvine	CA	92618	888-424-6527		424
TF: 888-424-6527 ■ *Web:* www.biolase.com						
BioLegend Inc 11080 Roselle St	San Diego	CA	92121	858-455-9588		668
TF: 877-246-5343 ■ *Web:* www.biolegend.com						
BioLife Solutions Inc						
3303 Monte Villa Pkwy Ste 310	Bothell	WA	98021	425-402-1400		85
Web: biolifesolutions.com						
Bioline USA Inc 305 Constitution Dr	Taunton	MA	02780	508-880-8990		194
Web: www.bioline.com						
bioLytical Laboratories Inc						
1108 - 13351 Commerce Pkwy	Richmond	BC	V6V2X7	604-204-6784		668
TF: 866-674-6784 ■ *Web:* www.biolytical.com						
BioMarin Pharmaceutical Inc						
105 Digital Dr	Novato	CA	94949	415-506-6700	382-7889	85
NASDAQ: BMRN ■ *Web:* www.biomarin.com						
Biomarine Inc 456 Creamery Way	Exton	PA	19341	610-524-8800	524-8807	576
TF: 800-378-2287 ■ *Web:* www.neutronicsinc.com						
BioMarker Pharmaceuticals Inc						
5941 Optical Ct	San Jose	CA	95138	408-257-2000		668
Web: www.biomarkerinc.com						
BioMarker Strategies LLC						
855 N Wolfe St Ste 603	Baltimore	MD	21205	410-522-1008		418
Web: www.biomarkerstrategies.com						
BioMed Realty Trust Inc						
17190 Bernardo Ctr Dr	San Diego	CA	92128	858-485-9840	485-9843	654
NYSE: BMR ■ *Web:* www.biomedrealty.com						
Biomere 57 Union St	Worcester	MA	01608	508-459-7544		10-3
Web: brmcro.com						
Biomerica Inc 1533 Monrovia Ave	Newport Beach	CA	92663	949-645-2111		231
OTC: BMRA ■ *TF Cust Svc:* 800-854-3002 ■ *Web:* www.biomerica.com						
BioMerieux Inc 595 Anglum Rd	Hazelwood	MO	63042	314-731-8500		476
TF: 800-634-7656 ■ *Web:* www.biomerieux.com						
Biomerix Corp 47757 Fremont Blvd	Fremont	CA	94538	510-933-3450	933-3451	668
Web: www.biomerix.com						
Biomet Inc 56 E Bell Dr PO Box 587	Warsaw	IN	46582	574-267-6639	267-8137	477
TF: 800-348-9500 ■ *Web:* www.biomet.com						
Biomet Microfixation Inc						
1520 Tradeport Dr	Jacksonville	FL	32218	904-741-4400	741-4500	476
TF: 800-874-7711 ■ *Web:* www.biomet.com						
Biometrix Inc 2419 Ocean Ave	San Francisco	CA	94127	415-333-0522	333-0532	418
Web: biometrixinc.com						
Bio-Microbics Inc 8450 Cole Pkwy	Shawnee	KS	66227	913-422-0707		427
Web: www.biomicrobics.com						
BioMimetic Systems Inc						
810 Memorial Dr Ste 106	Cambridge	MA	02139	617-758-2505		256
Web: www.biomimetic-systems.com						
Biomod Concepts Inc						
1821B Lavoisier	Sainte-julie	QC	J3E1Y6	514-905-5848		466
Web: www.biomod.com						
BioMotiv 20600 Chagrin Blvd Ste 210	Cleveland	OH	44122	216-455-3200		238
Web: www.biomotiv.com						
Biomune Co 8906 Rosehill Rd	Lenexa	KS	66215	913-894-0230	894-0236	584
TF: 800-999-0297 ■ *Web:* ceva.us						
Bion Enterprises Ltd						
455 State St Ste 100	Des Plaines	IL	60016	847-544-5044		743
Biondo Investment Advisors LLC						
540 Routes 6 & 209	Milford	PA	18337	570-296-5525		194
Web: www.thebiondogroup.com						
Bionetics Corp, The						
101 Production Dr Ste 100	Yorktown	VA	23693	757-873-0900		261
TF: 800-868-0330 ■ *Web:* www.bionetics.com						
BioNJ						
1255 Whitehorse-Mercerville Rd						
Building B-Ste 514	Trenton	NJ	08619	609-890-3185	581-8244	463
Web: bionj.org						
Bionomic Industries Inc						
777 Corporate Dr	Mahwah	NJ	07430	201-529-1094		261
Web: bionomicind.com						
Bionostics Inc 7 Jackson Rd	Devens	MA	01434	978 772 7070	772 7072	231
TF General: 800-776-3856 ■ *Web:* www.bionostics.com						
BioNumerik Pharmaceuticals Inc						
8023 Vantage Dr Ste Lobby 1	San Antonio	TX	78230	210-614-1701	614-2892	85
Web: www.bionumerik.com						
Bioo Scientific Corp						
3913 Todd Ln Ste 312	Austin	TX	78744	512-707-8993		85
Web: www.biooscientific.com						
BIOPAC Systems Inc 42 Aero Camino	Goleta	CA	93117	805-685-0066		743
TF: 877-524-6722 ■ *Web:* www.biopac.com						
Biopass Medical Systems Inc						
7401 Wiles Rd Ste 222	Coral Springs	FL	33067	954-575-1588		261
TF: 800-544-4455 ■ *Web:* www.biopass.com						
Bio-Pharm Inc 2091 Hartel St	Levittown	PA	19057	215-949-3711		231
Web: www.bio-pharminc.com						
Biophysical Society (BPS)						
9650 Rockville Pk	Bethesda	MD	20814	301-634-7114	634-7133	49-19
Web: www.biophysics.org						
BioPro Inc 2929 Lapeer Rd	Port Huron	MI	48060	810-982-7777		477
TF: 800-252-7707 ■ *Web:* www.bioproimplants.com						
BioProcess Algae LLC 1811 Aksarben Dr	Omaha	NE	68106	402-916-9559	884-8776	580
Web: www.bioprocessalgae.com						
BiOptix Inc 1775 38th St	Boulder	CO	80301	303-545-5550		419
Web: www.bioptix.com						
Bioqual Corp 4 Research Ct	Rockville	MD	20850	301-251-2801	251-1260	85
TF: 800-225-5600 ■ *Web:* www.bioqual.com						
Bioquant Image Analysis Corp						
5611 Ohio Ave	Nashville	TN	37209	615-350-7866		514
TF: 800-221-0549 ■ *Web:* www.bioquant.com						
BIOQUELL Inc 702 Electronic Dr Ste 200	Horsham	PA	19044	215-682-0225		743
Web: www.bioquell.com						
Bio-Rad Laboratories						
1000 Alfred Nobel Dr	Hercules	CA	94547	510-724-7000	741-5824*	231
NYSE: BIO ■ **Fax:* Cust Svc ■ *TF:* 800-424-6723 ■ *Web:* www.bio-rad.com						
Bio-Recovery Corp						
1863 Pond Rd Ste 4	Ronkonkoma	NY	11779	888-471-4204		83
TF: 800-556-0621 ■ *Web:* www.biorecovery.com						
Bio-Reference Laboratories Inc						
481 Edward H Ross Dr	Elmwood Park	NJ	07407	800-229-5227	791-1941*	416
NASDAQ: BRLI ■ **Fax Area Code:* 201 ■ *TF:* 800-229-5227 ■ *Web:* www.bioreference.com						
BioReliance Corp 14920 Broschart Rd	Rockville	MD	20850	301-738-1000	610-2590	85
TF: 800-553-5372 ■ *Web:* www.bioreliance.com						
Bio-Research Products Inc						
323 W Cherry St	North Liberty	IA	52317	319-626-6707		743
TF: 800-326-3511 ■ *Web:* www.bio-researchprod.com						
BioResource International Inc						
4222 Emperor Blvd Ste 460	Durham	NC	27703	919-993-3389		668
Web: www.briworldwide.com						
Bios Cos 309 E Dewey	Sapulpa	OK	74066	918-227-8390		363
Web: bioscorp.com						
Biosafe Engineering						
5750 W 80th St	Indianapolis	IN	46278	317-858-8099	858-8202	111
TF: 888-858-8099 ■ *Web:* biosafeeng.com						

	Phone	Fax	Class
Biosan Laboratories Inc 1950 Tobsal Ct..........Warren MI 48091 *TF:* 800-253-6800 ■ *Web:* www.biosan.com	586-755-8970		743
BioSante Pharmaceuticals Inc 111 Barclay Blvd.........................Lincolnshire IL 60069 *NASDAQ: BPAX* ■ *Web:* www.biospace.com	847-478-0500		582
Bio-Scene Recovery 13191 Meadow St NE........................Alliance OH 44601 *TF:* 877-380-5500 ■ *Web:* www.bioscene.com	330-823-5500		83
BioScience 1444 'I' St NW Ste 200...........Washington DC 20005 *TF:* 800-992-2427 ■ *Web:* www.aibs.org/bioscience	202-628-1500	628-1509	457-19
Bioscreen Testing Services Inc 3904 Del AMO Blvd Ste 801...................Torrance CA 90503 *Web:* www.bioscreen.com	310-214-0043	370-3642	333
BioScrip 1600 Broadway Ste 950..............Denver CO 80202 *NASDAQ: BIOS* ■ *TF:* 877-409-2301 ■ *Web:* www.bioscrip.com	720-697-5200		586
Bioseal 167 W Orangethorpe Ave...............Placentia CA 92870 *TF:* 800-441-7325 ■ *Web:* www.biosealnet.com	714-528-4695		476
Biosense Webster Inc 3333 S Diamond Canyon Rd..............Diamond Bar CA 91765 *TF:* 800-729-9010 ■ *Web:* www.biosensewebster.com	909-839-8500	468-2905	476
Bio-Serv 3 Foster Ln Ste 201...............Flemington NJ 08822 *TF:* 800-996-9908 ■ *Web:* www.bio-serv.com	908-284-2155	284-4753	584
Biosign Technologies Inc 14-3715 Laird Rd.......................Mississauga ON L5L0A3	416-218-9800		476
Biosonics Inc 4027 Leary Way NW...............Seattle WA 98107 *Web:* www.biosonicsinc.com	206-782-2211		201
BioSpace Inc 90 New Montgomery St Ste 414...........San Francisco CA 94105 *TF:* 888-246-7722 ■ *Web:* www.biospace.com	877-277-7585		397
BiosPacific Inc 5980 Horton St Ste 225....................Emeryville CA 94608 *TF:* 800-344-6686 ■ *Web:* www.biospacific.com	510-652-6155	652-4531	231
BioSpecifics Technologies Corp 35 Wilbur St..............................Lynbrook NY 11563 *NASDAQ: BSTC* ■ *Web:* www.biospecifics.com	516-593-7000	593-7039	582
Biostat International Inc 14506 University Point Pl Ste A.................Tampa FL 33613 *Web:* biostatinternational.com	813-979-1619		194
BioStratum Inc 4825 Creekstone Dr Ste 200..................Durham NC 27703 *Web:* www.biostratum.com	919-572-6515		743
Biosynexus Inc 9298 Gaither Rd............Gaithersburg MD 20877	301-330-5800		231
Biosystems LLC 651 S Main St..............Middletown CT 06457	860-344-1079	344-1068	477
Biotab Nutraceuticals Inc 401 E Huntington Dr......................Monrovia CA 91016	626-775-6334		345
Biotech Clinical Laboratories Inc 25775 Meadowbrook..........................Novi MI 48375 *Web:* biotechclinical.com	248-912-1700		743
BioTechLogic Inc 717 Indian Rd..............Glenview IL 60025 *Web:* www.biotechlogic.com	847-730-3475		85
BioTechniques 52 Vanderbilt Ave 7th Fl....................New York NY 10017 *TF:* 800-606-6246 ■ *Web:* biotechniques.com	212-520-2777		457-19
Biotechnology Industry Organization 1201 Maryland Ave SW Ste 900............Washington DC 20024 *TF:* 866-356-5155 ■ *Web:* www.bio.org	202-962-9200	488-6301	49-19
Biotechnology Software 140 Huguenot St 3rd Fl...................New Rochelle NY 10801 *TF:* 800-654-3237 ■ *Web:* www.liebertpub.com	914-740-2100		531-3
BioTek Instruments Inc 100 Tigan St PO Box 998....................Winooski VT 05404 *TF:* 888-451-5171 ■ *Web:* www.biotek.com	802-655-4740	655-7941	419
BioTeknica Inc 250 Bird Rd Ste 216....................Coral Gables FL 33146 *TF:* 800-542-0650 ■ *Web:* www.bioteknica.com	305-445-2080		466
Biothera Pharmaceuticals 3388 Mike Collins Dr Ste A.....................Eagan MN 55121 *TF:* 877-699-5100 ■ *Web:* www.biothera.com	651-675-0300		743
bioTheranostics Inc 9640 Towne Centre Dr Ste 200.............San Diego CA 92121 *TF:* 877-886-6739 ■ *Web:* www.biotheranostics.com	858-587-5870		743
BioTime Inc 101 Atlantic Ave Ste 102...........Alameda CA 94501 *Web:* www.biotimeinc.com	510-521-3390		85
Bio-Tissue 7000 SW 97th Ave Ste 211.............Miami FL 33173 *TF:* 888-296-8858 ■ *Web:* www.biotissue.com	305-412-4430	412-4429	545
Biotools Inc 17546 Bee Line Hwy...............Jupiter FL 33458 *TF:* 866-286-6571 ■ *Web:* www.btools.com	561-625-0133		583
BioUrja Trading LLC 1080 Eldridge Pkwy Ste 1175..................Houston TX 77077 *TF:* 800-469-9051 ■ *Web:* www.biourja.com	832-775-9000		580
BioVascular Inc 12230 El Camino Real Ste 100...............San Diego CA 92130 *Web:* www.biovascularinc.com	858-455-5000		668
Bioventures Investors 70 Walnut St Ste 302.........................Wellesley MA 02481 *Web:* www.bioventuresinvestors.com	617-252-3443	621-7993	792
Bioventus LLC 4721 Emperor Blvd Ste 100........Durham NC 27703 *Web:* www.bioventusglobal.com	919-474-6700		477
Biovet Inc 4375 Ave Beaudry.............Saint-Hyacinthe QC J2S8W2 *TF:* 888-824-6838 ■ *Web:* biovet.ca	450-771-7291	771-4158	584
Biovet USA Inc 1502 E 122nd St...............Burnsville MN 55337 *TF:* 877-824-6838 ■ *Web:* www.biovet.ca	952-884-3113		584
BioVid Corp 10 Canal St Ste 136...................Bristol PA 19007 *Web:* biovid.com	609-750-1400		195
Biovision Technologies 64 E Uwchlan Ave # 273............................Exton PA 19341 *Web:* www.biovis.com	610-524-9740		419
BioWa Inc 9420 Athena Cir ....La Jolla CA 92037 *Web:* kyowa-kirin.com/biowa	858-952-7200		743
Bio-west Inc 1063 W 1400 N..........................Logan UT 84321 *Web:* bio-west.com	435-752-4202		196
BioXcel Corp 780 E Main St.......................Branford CT 06405 *Web:* www.bioxcel.com	203-433-4086		194
BioZone Laboratories Inc 580 Garcia Ave............................Pittsburg CA 94565 *Web:* www.biozonelabs.com	925-473-1000		418
BioZyme Inc 6010 Stockyards Expy...........Saint Joseph MO 64504 *TF:* 800-821-3070 ■ *Web:* www.biozymeinc.com	816-238-3326	238-7549	447
BIPAC (Business-Industry Political Action Committee) 1707 L St NW Ste 350....................Washington DC 20036 *Web:* www.bipac.org	202-833-1880	833-2338	615
Bi-Petro Inc 3150 Executive Park Dr.....................Springfield IL 62794 *Web:* www.bipetro.com	217-535-0181		581
Bi-Phase Technologies 2945 Lone Oak Dr..............................St Paul MN 55121 *Web:* www.bi-phase.com	952-886-6450		247
Birach Broadcasting Corp Tower 14 Ste 1190........................Southfield MI 48075 *Web:* www.birach.com	248-557-3500	557-2950	643
Birch Aquarium at Scripps 2300 Expedition Way ....La Jolla CA 92037 *TF:* 800-877-1911 ■ *Web:* www.aquarium.ucsd.edu	858-534-3474	534-7114	40
Birch Bay State Park 5105 Helwig Rd............Blaine WA 98230 *Web:* www.parks.wa.gov	360-371-2800		565
Birch Communications Inc 2300 Main St 6th Fl.......................Kansas City MO 64108 *TF:* 866-424-5100 ■ *Web:* www.birch.com	816-300-3000		736
Birch Hill Investment Advisors LLC 24 Federal St 10th Fl..........................Boston MA 02110 *TF:* 800-441-3453 ■ *Web:* www.birchhilladvisors.com	617-502-8300		401
Birch Lake State Recreation Area c/o Northern Area Office 3700 Airport Way.......Fairbanks AK 99709 *Web:* www.dnr.alaska.gov/parks/units/birch.htm	907-451-2695		565
Birch Point Beach State Park c/o Bureau of Parks & Lands 22 State House Sta 18 Elkins Ln................Augusta ME 04333 *Web:* maine.gov/dacf/mgs/index.shtml	207-941-4014		565
Birch Tree Promotions 5 tyng st...........Newburyport MA 01950 *Web:* www.birchtreepromotions.com	978-270-3852		636
Birchard Public Library of Sandusky County 423 Croghan St...............................Fremont OH 43420 *Web:* www.birchard.lib.oh.us	419-334-7101	334-4788	434-3
Birchcraft Studios Inc 10 Railroad St..............................Abington MA 02351 **Fax Area Code: 800* ■ *TF:* 800-333-0405 ■ *Web:* www.birchcraft.com	781-878-5152	678-5151*	130
Birches 641 S Montford Ave..................Baltimore MD 21224 *Web:* www.birchesrestaurant.com	410-732-3000		671
Birchwood automative group 35D-3965 Portage Ave.........................Winnipeg MB R3K2H7 *Web:* birchwood.ca	204-832-1676		57
Birchwood Foods 6009 Goshen Springs Rd....................Norcross GA 30071 *Web:* www.bwfoods.com	770-448-9101		473
Birchwood Laboratories Inc 7900 Fuller Rd...........................Eden Prairie MN 55344 *TF:* 800-328-6156 ■ *Web:* www.birchwoodcasey.com	952-937-7900	937-7979	145
Birchwood Manor 111 N Jefferson Rd.........Whippany NJ 07981 *Web:* birchwoodmanor.com	973-887-1414		671
Birchwood Plaza 1426 W Birchwood..............Chicago IL 60626 *TF:* 800-321-1245 ■ *Web:* www.birchwoodplaza.com	773-274-4405		672
Bird Electronic Corp 30303 Aurora Rd ....Solon OH 44139 *TF:* 866-695-4569 ■ *Web:* birdrf.com	440-248-1200	248-5426	248
Bird Marella Boxer Wolpert Nessim Drooks & Lincenberg PC 1875 Century Park E 23rd Fl...............Los Angeles CA 90067 *Web:* www.birdmarella.com	310-201-2100		41
Bird Precision 1 Spruce St PO Box 540569...................Waltham MA 02454 *TF Cust Svc:* 800-454-7369 ■ *Web:* www.birdprecision.com	781-894-0160	894-6308	620
Bird Solutions International 1338 N Melrose Dr Ste H........................Vista CA 92083 *TF:* 800-210-9514 ■ *Web:* www.birdsolutions.com	760-758-9747		577
Bird Studies Canada 115 Front St PO Box 160.................Port Rowan ON N0E1M0 *TF:* 888-448-2473 ■ *Web:* www.bsc-eoc.org	519-586-3531	586-3532	48-3
Bird Technologies Group Inc 30303 Aurora Rd ....Solon OH 44139 *TF:* 866-695-4569 ■ *Web:* birdrf.com	440-248-1200	248-5426	248
Birdair Inc 65 Lawrence Bell Dr Ste 100...................Amherst NY 14221 *TF:* 800-622-2246 ■ *Web:* www.birdair.com	716-633-9500	633-9850	189-12
Birdie Golf Balls Golf Equipment 208 Margate Ct..............................Margate FL 33063 *TF:* 800-333-7271 ■ *Web:* www.birdiegolfballstore.com	954-973-2741		711
Birds & Blooms 5400 S 60th St..............Greendale WI 53129 *TF:* 888-860-8040 ■ *Web:* www.birdsandblooms.com	888-860-8040		457-14
Birdsall Tool & Gage Co 24735 Crestview Ct ....Farmington Hills MI 48335 *Web:* www.birdsalltool.com	248-474-5150		757
Birdsong Corp 612 Madison Ave...................Suffolk VA 23434 *TF:* 800-227-5980 ■ *Web:* www.birdsong-peanuts.com	757-539-3456		275
Birdsong Gregory LLC 715 N Church St Ste 101 ....Charlotte NC 28202 *Web:* www.birdsonggregory.com	704-332-2299		4
BirdWatching Magazine 25 Braintree Hill Office Pk Ste 404.............Braintree MA 02184 *TF:* 877-252-8141 ■ *Web:* www.birdwatchingdaily.com	877-252-8141		457-14
Birdwing Spa 21398 575th Ave ....Litchfield MN 55355 *Web:* www.birdwingspa.com	320-693-6064	693-7026	706
Birk Manufacturing 14 Capitol Dr Colton Rd Industrial Park Exit 71 of East Lyme CT 06333 *Web:* www.birkmfg.com	860-739-4170		14
Birken Manufacturing Co 3 Old Windsor Rd............................Bloomfield CT 06002 *TF:* 800-777-2213 ■ *Web:* www.birken.net	860-242-2211	242-2749	621
Birket Engineering Inc 162 W Plant St........................Winter Garden FL 34787 *TF:* 800-622-4326 ■ *Web:* www.birket.com	407-290-2000		261
Birko Corp 9152 Yosemite St.................Henderson CO 80640 *Web:* www.birkocorp.com	303-289-1090		146
Birks 1240 du Sq-Phillips St.....................Montreal QC H3B3H4 *TF:* 800-758-2511 ■ *Web:* www.birksandmayors.com	800-758-2511		410
Birmingham Beverage Company Inc 211 Citation Ct.........................Birmingham AL 35209 *Web:* alabev.com	205-942-9403		81-1

Listing	City	State	ZIP	Phone	Fax	Class
Birmingham Board of Education (BCS) 2015 Pk Pl N TF: 800-628-6673 ■ Web: www.bhamcityschools.org	Birmingham	AL	35203	205-231-4600		685
Birmingham Botanical Gardens 2612 Ln Pk Rd TF: 800-215-1700 ■ Web: www.bbgardens.org	Birmingham	AL	35223	205-414-3900		97
Birmingham Business Alliance 505 N 20th St Ste 200 Web: birminghambusinessalliance.com	Birmingham	AL	35203	205-324-2100	324-2560	139
Birmingham Business Journal 2140 11th Ave S Ste 205 Web: www.bizjournals.com	Birmingham	AL	35205	205-322-0000	322-0040	457-5
Birmingham City Hall 710 N 20th St Web: www.birminghamal.gov	Birmingham	AL	35203	205-254-2000	254-2926	337
Birmingham Civil Rights Institute 520 16th St N TF: 866-328-9696 ■ Web: www.bcri.org	Birmingham	AL	35203	205-328-9696	323-5219	520
Birmingham Festival Theater 1901 1/2 11th Ave S PO Box 55321 Web: www.bftonline.org	Birmingham	AL	35205	205-933-2383		573-4
Birmingham International Airport 5900 Messer Airport Hwy Web: flybirmingham.com	Birmingham	AL	35212	205-595-0533	599-0538	27
Birmingham International Forest Products LLC 300 Riverhills Business Pk TF: 800-767-2437 ■ Web: www.bifp.com	Birmingham	AL	35242	205-972-1500	972-1461	191-3
Birmingham Museum of Art 2000 Eigth Ave N TF: 800-732-6845 ■ Web: www.artsbma.org	Birmingham	AL	35203	205-254-2565		520
Birmingham News 1731 First Ave N TF: 800-568-4123 ■ Web: www.alabamamediagroup.com	Birmingham	AL	35203	205-325-4444		532-2
Birmingham Public Library 2100 Pk Pl Web: www.bham.lib.al.us	Birmingham	AL	35203	205-226-3600		434-3
Birmingham Race Course 1000 John Rogers Dr TF: 800-998-8238 ■ Web: www.birminghamracecourse.com	Birmingham	AL	35210	205-838-7500	838-7407	133
Birmingham Rail & Locomotive Company Inc PO Box 530157 TF: 800-241-2260 ■ Web: www.bhamrail.com	Birmingham	AL	35253	205-424-7245	424-7436	770
Birmingham Times 115 Third Ave W Web: birminghamtimes.com	Birmingham	AL	35204	205-251-5158	323-2294	532-4
Birmingham VA Medical Ctr 700 S 19th St *Fax: Admitting ■ Web: www.birmingham.va.gov	Birmingham	AL	35233	205-933-8101	933-4498*	374-8
Birmingham Vending Co 540 Second Ave N TF: 800-288-7635 ■ Web: www.bhmvending.com	Birmingham	AL	35204	205-324-7526	322-6639	55
Birmingham Zoo 2630 Cahaba Rd TF: 800-458-8085 ■ Web: www.birminghamzoo.com	Birmingham	AL	35223	205-879-0409	879-9426	823
Birmingham-Bloomfield Chamber of Commerce 725 S Adams Rd Ste 130 Web: www.bbcc.com	Birmingham	MI	48009	248-644-1700	644-0286	139
Birmingham-Jefferson Convention Complex 2100 Richard Arrington Jr Blvd N Web: www.bjcc.org	Birmingham	AL	35203	205-458-8400		205
Birmingham-Southern College 900 Arkadelphia Rd *Fax: Admissions ■ TF: 800-523-5793 ■ Web: www.bsc.edu	Birmingham	AL	35254	205-226-4600	226-3074*	166
Birmingham-Toledo Inc 3620 Vann Rd TF: 800-824-2187 ■ Web: birminghamtoledo.com	Birmingham	AL	35235	205-655-1881		358
Birnbach Communications Inc 20 Devereux St Ste 3A Web: www.birnbachcom.com	Marblehead	MA	01945	781-639-6701		636
Birnbaum Interpreting Services 8730 Georgia Ave Ste 210 TF: 800-471-6441 ■ Web: www.bisworld.com	Silver Spring	MD	20910	301-587-8885		768
Birner Dental Management Services Inc 1777 S Harrison St Ste 1400 TF: 877-898-1083 ■ Web: www.perfectteeth.com	Denver	CO	80210	303-691-0680	691-0889	463
Birnie Bus Service Inc 248 Otis St TF: 800-734-3950 ■ Web: birniebus.com	Rome	NY	13441	315-336-3950		109
BIRO Mfg Co 1114 W Main St Web: www.birosaw.com	Marblehead	OH	43440	419-798-4451	798-9106	298
Biron Groupe Sante Inc 4105-F Blvd Matte Web: www.biron.ca	Brossard	QC	J4Y2P4	514-866-6146		418
Birtcher Anderson Realty Management 31910 Del Obispo Ste 260 Web: birtcheranderson.com	San Juan Capistrano	CA	92675	949-545-0500		652
Birthday Direct 120 Commerce St TF: 888-491-9185 ■ Web: www.birthdaydirect.com	Muscle Shoals	AL	35661	256-381-0310		292
Birthday In A Box Inc 7951 Cessna Ave TF: 800-237-6545 ■ Web: www.birthdayinabox.com	Gaithersburg	MD	20879	800-237-6545		195
BIS Computer Solutions Inc 2428 Foothill Blvd TF: 800-929-5589 ■ Web: www.biscomputer.com	La Crescenta	CA	91214	818-248-5023		177
Biscayne National Park 9700 SW 328th St Web: www.nps.gov/bisc	Homestead	FL	33033	305-230-1144	230-1190	564
Biscayne Nature Ctr 6767 Crandon Blvd Web: www.biscaynenaturecenter.org	Key Biscayne	FL	33149	305-361-6767	365-8434	50-5
Biscayne Rod Manufacturing Inc 425 E Ninth St TF: 866-969-0808 ■ Web: www.biscaynerod.com	Hialeah	FL	33010	305-884-0808		710
Bischoff Insurance Agency Inc 1300 Oakridge Dr Ste 100 TF: 888-229-5558 ■ Web: bradbischoff.com	Fort Collins	CO	80525	970-223-9400		390
Bisco Dental Products (Canada) Inc 2571 Smith St TF: 800-667-8811 ■ Web: www.biscocanada.com	Richmond	BC	V6X2J1	604-276-8662		475
Bisco Environmental Inc 135 Robert Treat Paine Dr Web: www.biscoenv.com	Taunton	MA	02780	508-738-5100		567
Bisco Industries Inc 1500 N Lakeview Ave TF: 800-323-1232 ■ Web: www.biscoind.com	Anaheim	CA	92807	800-323-1232		246
Biscom Inc 321 Billerica Rd TF: 800-477-2472 ■ Web: www.biscom.com	Chelmsford	MA	01824	978-250-1800	250-4449	173-3
Biscotti's Restaurant 3556 St Johns Ave Web: www.biscottis.net	Jacksonville	FL	32205	904-387-2060	387-0051	671
Biscuit & Cracker Manufacturers Assn (B&CMA) 6325 Woodside Ct Ste 125 *Fax Area Code: 410 ■ Web: www.thebcma.org	Columbia	MD	21046	443-545-1645	290-8585*	49-6
Biscuitville Inc 1414 Yanceyville St Web: www.biscuitville.com	Greensboro	NC	27405	336-553-3700		670
Bisetti's Italian Restaurant 120 S College Ave Web: www.bisettis.com	Fort Collins	CO	80524	970-493-0086		671
BISG (Book Industry Study Group Inc) 1412 Broadway 21st Fl Ofc 19 Web: www.bisg.org	New York	NY	10018	646-336-7141	336-6214	49-16
Bishop & Associates Inc 1209 Fox Glen Dr Web: www.bishopinc.com	St. Charles	IL	60174	630-443-2702		466
Bishop Distributing Co 5200 36th St SE TF Cust Svc: 800-748-0363 ■ Web: www.bishopdistributing.com	Grand Rapids	MI	49512	800-748-0363		361
Bishop George Ahr High School 1 Tingley Ln Web: www.bgahs.org	Edison	NJ	08820	732-549-1108		685
Bishop Hearth & Home Inc 1948 Vanderhorn Dr Web: www.bishophome.com	Memphis	TN	38134	901-384-0070		362
Bishop International Airport G-3425 W Bristol Rd TF: 800-433-7300 ■ Web: www.bishopairport.org	Flint	MI	48507	810-235-6560	233-3065	27
Bishop Kelly Foundation Inc 7009 W Franklin Rd Web: www.bk.org	Boise	ID	83709	208-375-6010		685
Bishop Loughlin Memorial High School 357 Clermont Ave Web: blmhs.org	Brooklyn	NY	11238	718-857-2700		685
Bishop Machine Works Inc 1780 Iris Dr SW Web: www.bishopmachineworks.com	Conyers	GA	30094	770-483-7673		697
Bishop Miege High School 5041 Reinhardt Dr Web: www.bishopmiege.com	Roeland Park	KS	66205	913-262-2700		685
Bishop Mike (Rep R - MI) 428 Cannon HOB Web: mikebishop.house.gov	Washington	DC	20515	202-225-4872	225-5820	342-2
Bishop Museum 1525 Bernice St Web: www.bishopmuseum.org	Honolulu	HI	96817	808-847-3511		520
Bishop O'Dowd High School 9500 Stearns Ave Web: www.bishopodowd.org	Oakland	CA	94605	510-577-9100		685
Bishop Paiute Gaming Corp 2742 N Sierra Hwy Web: www.bishoppaiutetribe.com	Bishop	CA	93514	760-873-4150		452
Bishop Partners Ltd 28 W 44th St #1120 TF: 800-446-3037 ■ Web: www.bishoppartners.com	New York	NY	10036	212-986-3419	575-1050	266
Bishop Rob (Rep R - UT) 123 Cannon Bldg Web: robbishop.house.gov	Washington	DC	20515	202-225-0453	225-5857	342-2
Bishop Sanford D Jr (Rep D - GA) 2407 Rayburn HOB Web: bishop.house.gov	Washington	DC	20515	202-225-3631	225-2203	342-2
Bishop Spencer Place Redevelopment Corp 4301 Madison Ave Web: www.bishopspencerplace.org	Kansas City	MO	64111	816-931-4277		672
Bishop State Community College 351 N Broad St TF: 800-523-7000 ■ Web: bishop.edu	Mobile	AL	36603	251-405-7000		162
Baker-Gaines Central 1365 Dr ML King Jr Ave Web: bishop.edu	Mobile	AL	36603	251-662-5400	405-4427	162
Southwest 925 Dauphin Island Pkwy Web: bishop.edu	Mobile	AL	36605	251-665-4100		162
Bishop Strachan School 298 Lonsdale Rd Web: www.bss.on.ca	Toronto	ON	M4V1X2	416-483-4325	481-5632	622
Bishop Whelan Elementary School 244 rue de la Presentation	Dorval	QC	H9S3L6	514-634-0550		685
Bishop's 2183 W Fourth Ave Web: www.bishopsonline.com	Vancouver	BC	V6K1N7	604-738-2025		671
Bishop's College School 80 chemin Moulton Hill TF: 877-570-7542 ■ Web: www.bishopscollegeschool.com	Sherbrooke	QC	J1M1Z8	819-566-0227		622
Bishop's Ranch 5297 Westside Rd Web: www.bishopsranch.org	Healdsburg	CA	95448	707-433-2440	433-3431	673
Bishop's University 2600 College St Web: www.ubishops.ca	Sherbrooke	QC	J1M1Z7	819-822-9600	822-9661	785
Bishop-Wisecarver Corp 2104 Martin Way TF: 888-580-8272 ■ Web: www.bwc.com	Pittsburg	CA	94565	925-439-8272	439-5931	620
Bismarck Civic Ctr 315 S Fifth St	Bismarck	ND	58504	701-355-1370		205
Bismarck Expressway Suites 180 E Bismarck Expy TF: 888-774-5566 ■ Web: expresswayhotels.com	Bismarck	ND	58504	701-222-3311	222-3311	379
Bismarck Mandan Chamber of Commerce 1640 Burnt Boat Dr Web: www.bismarckmandan.com	Bismarck	ND	58502	701-223-5660	255-6125	139
Bismarck Municipal Airport 2301 University Dr Bldg 17 PO Box 991 Web: www.bismarckairport.com	Bismarck	ND	58502	701-355-1800	221-6886	27
Bismarck State College 1500 Edwards Ave *Fax: Admissions ■ TF: 800-445-5073 ■ Web: www.bismarckstate.edu	Bismarck	ND	58501	701-224-5400	224-5643*	162
Bismarck Tribune 707 E Front Ave *Fax: Edit ■ TF: 866-476-5348 ■ Web: www.bismarcktribune.com	Bismarck	ND	58504	701-223-2500	223-2063*	532-2

	Phone	Fax	Class
Bismarck Veterans Memorial Public Library 515 N Fifth St ... Bismarck ND 58501	701-355-1480		434-3
Bismarck-Burleigh Public Health 500 E Front St ... Bismarck ND 58504 *Web:* www.bismarcknd.gov	701-355-1540	221-6883	337
Bismarck-Mandan Convention & Visitors Bureau 1600 Burnt Boat Dr ... Bismarck ND 58503 *TF:* 800-767-3555 ■ *Web:* www.discoverbismarckmandan.com	701-222-4308	222-0647	206
Bismarck-Mandan Symphony Orchestra 215 N Sixth St ... Bismarck ND 58501 *Web:* www.bismarckmandansymphony.org	701-258-8345	258-8345	573-3
Bison Bookbinding and Letterpress 112 Grand Ave ... Bellingham WA 98225 *Web:* bisonbookbinding.com	360-734-0481		92
Bison Capital Asset Management LLC 233 Wilshire Blvd Ste 425 ... Santa Monica CA 90401 *Web:* www.bisoncapital.com	310-260-6573		401
Bison Gear & Engineering Corp 3850 Ohio Ave ... Saint Charles IL 60174 *TF:* 800-282-4766 ■ *Web:* www.bisongear.com	630-377-4327	377-6777	709
Bison Inc 603 L St ... Lincoln NE 68508 **Fax Area Code:* 800 ■ *TF:* 800-247-7668 ■ *Web:* www.bisoninc.com	402-474-3353	638-0698*	710
Bison Turf 1211 N University Dr ... Fargo ND 58102 *Web:* thebisonturfnd.com	701-235-9118		671
Bisque Imports 1 Belmont Ave ... Belmont NC 28012 *TF:* 888-568-5991 ■ *Web:* www.bisqueimports.com	704-829-9290		361
Bissell Inc 2345 Walker NW ... Grand Rapids MI 49544 **Fax:* Hum Res ■ *TF:* 800-237-7691 ■ *Web:* www.bissell.com	616-453-4451	791-0662*	788
Bissell Professional Group Inc 3512 N Croatan Hwy ... Kitty Hawk NC 27949 *TF:* 800-366-8201 ■ *Web:* www.bissellprofessionalgroup.com	252-261-3266		261
Bissett Resource Consultants Ltd 250 839 - 5 Ave SW ... Calgary AB T2P3C8	403-294-1888		261
Bisso Marine Company Inc 11311 Neeshaw Dr ... Houston TX 77065 *Web:* www.bissomarine.com	281-897-1500		313
Bisso Towboat Company Inc 13969 River Rd ... Luling LA 70070 *Web:* www.bissotowing.com	504-861-1411		465
Bi-State Development Agency 707 N First St ... Saint Louis MO 63102 *TF:* 800-342-9299 ■ *Web:* www.metrostlouis.org	314-982-1400		468
Bistro 17 1617 SE 17th St ... Fort Lauderdale FL 33316 *Web:* marriott.com	954-626-1748	626-1717	671
Bistro 5 5 Playstead Rd ... West Medford MA 02155 *Web:* www.bistro5.com	781-395-7464		671
Bistro 821 821 Fifth Ave S ... Naples FL 34102 *Web:* www.bistro821.com	239-261-5821	261-1972	671
Bistro Aix 1440 San Marco Blvd ... Jacksonville FL 32207 *Web:* www.bistrox.com	904-398-1949		671
Bistro Aix 3340 Steiner St ... San Francisco CA 94123 *Web:* www.bistroaix.com	415-202-0100		671
Bistro An American Cafe 1103 E Front Ave ... Bismarck ND 58504 *Web:* www.bistro1100.com	701-224-8800	224-0398	671
Bistro Bella Vita 44 Grandville Ave SW ... Grand Rapids MI 49503 *Web:* www.bistrobellavita.com	616-222-4600	222-4601	671
Bistro Bis 15 E St NW ... Washington DC 20001 *Web:* www.bistrobis.com	202-661-2700		671
Bistro by the Tracks 215 Brookview Centre Way Ste 109 ... Knoxville TN 37919 *Web:* www.bistrobythetracks.com	865-558-9500		671
Bistro Enzo 1502 Rehberg Ln ... Billings MT 59102 *Web:* bistroenzobillings.com	406-651-0999		671
Bistro Jeanty 6510 Washington St ... Yountville CA 94599 *Web:* www.bistrojeanty.com	707-944-0103	944-0370	671
Bistro Mezzaluna 1821 SE Tenth Ave ... Fort Lauderdale FL 33316 *Web:* www.bistromezzaluna.com	954-522-9191		671
Bistro Pastis 2153 Fourth Ave W ... Vancouver BC V6K1N7 *Web:* www.bistropastis.com	604-731-5020		671
Bistro Romano 120 Lombard St ... Philadelphia PA 19147 *TF:* 800-292-4301 ■ *Web:* www.bistroromano.com	215-925-8880		671
Bistro Vendome 1420 Larimer St ... Denver CO 80202 *Web:* www.bistrovendome.com	303-825-3232	825-3240	671
Bit by Bit Computing 5233 Mccandlish Rd ... Grand Blanc MI 48439 *Web:* bitbybitcomputing.com	810-694-7477		177
BIT MedTech operation 15870 Bernardo Ctr Dr ... San Diego CA 92127 *Web:* www.calmedtech.com	858-613-1200		475
Bit of Britain Inc 141 Union School Rd ... Oxford PA 19363 *TF:* 800-550-1110 ■ *Web:* www.bitofbritain.com	610-998-0400		711
Bit of Germany 1901 Flower St ... Bakersfield CA 93305	661-325-8874		671
BITCO Insurance Cos 320 18th St ... Rock Island IL 61201 **Fax Area Code:* 309 ■ *TF:* 800-475-4477 ■ *Web:* www.bitco.com	800-475-4477	786-3847*	391-4
Bite 100 Montgomery Ste 1103 ... San Francisco CA 94104 *Web:* www.biteglobal.com	415-365-0222		636
bitHeads Inc 1309 Carling Ave ... Ottawa ON K1Z7L3 *TF:* 855-622-3232 ■ *Web:* www.bitheads.com	613-722-3232		180
Bithgroup Technologies Inc 113 W Monument St ... Baltimore MD 21201 *TF:* 800-677-1997 ■ *Web:* www.bithgroup.com	410-962-1188		463
Bitlab LLC 1144 Parkwood Ave ... Park Ridge IL 60068 *Web:* bitlab.com	847-823-5070		179
BitNami 650 Mission St 3rd Fl ... San Francisco CA 94105 *Web:* bitnami.com	415-318-3470		387
BitRage NOVIS Corp 6816 Southpoint Pkwy Bldg 301 ... Jacksonville FL 32216	904-674-0062		693
BITS 3190 Fairview Park Dr Ste 350 ... Falls Church VA 22042 *Web:* www.thebitsgroup.com	703-822-0970		196
Bits & Bytes Computer Services 1987 Hendersonville Rd Ste B ... Asheville NC 28803 *TF:* 800-341-8067 ■ *Web:* bitsbyte.com	828-684-8953		175
Bits n Bytes Computer Systems 3201 Double C Dr ... Norman OK 73069 *Web:* www.bnbtech.com	405-292-5408		180
Bittenbender Consrtuction Lp 5 N Columbus Blvd Pier 5 ... Philadelphia PA 19106 *Web:* www.bittenbenderconstruction.com	215-925-8900		186
Bitter Creek Ale House 246 N Eigth St ... Boise ID 83702 *Web:* bcrfl.com	208-429-6340		671
Bitterman Scales LLC 413 Radcliff Rd ... Willow Street PA 17584 *TF:* 877-464-3009 ■ *Web:* www.bittermanscales.com	717-464-3009		362
Bitterroot Valley Chamber of Commerce 105 E Main St ... Hamilton MT 59840 *Web:* bitterrootchamber.com	406-363-2400	363-2402	139
Bittersweet Ski Resort Snowline 600 River Rd ... Otsego MI 49078 *Web:* www.skibittersweet.com	269-694-2032		707
BitWise Inc 1515 Woodfield Rd Ste 740 ... Schaumburg IL 60173 *Web:* www.bitwiseglobal.com	847-969-1500		177
Bitwise Solutions Inc 569 Aviator Dr ... Fort Worth TX 76179 *Web:* www.bitwise.com	817-577-4866		809
Bitworks LLC 126 Tower Rd ... Waterbury CT 06710 *Web:* www.bitworksusa.net	203-756-9513		180
Bitz-Ee Mama's 7023 N 58th Ave ... Glendale AZ 85301 *Web:* www.bitz-eemamas.com	623-931-0562		671
Bitzer Products Co 2714 S Ninth Ave ... Broadview IL 60155 *Web:* www.bitzerproducts.com	708-345-0795		454
Bitzer US Inc 4031 Chamblee Rd ... Oakwood GA 30566 *Web:* www.bitzer.de/us/us/?country=us	770-718-2900		172
Bix Beiderbecke Memorial Society PO Box 3688 ... Davenport IA 52808 *TF:* 888-249-5487 ■ *Web:* www.bixsociety.org	563-324-7170	326-1732	48-4
Bix Pix Entertainment Inc 11630 Tuxford St ... Sun Valley CA 91352 *Web:* www.bixpix.com	818-252-7474	252-7410	33
Bix Produce Co 1415 L'Orient St ... Saint Paul MN 55117 *TF:* 800-642-9514 ■ *Web:* www.bixproduce.com	651-487-8000		297-7
Bix Restaurant 56 Gold St ... San Francisco CA 94133 *Web:* www.bixrestaurant.com	415-433-6300	433-4574	671
Bixby International Corp 1 Preble Rd ... Newburyport MA 01950 *Web:* www.bixbyintl.com	978-462-4100		600
Bixby Knolls Towers 3737 Atlantic Ave ... Long Beach CA 90807 *TF:* 800-545-1833 ■ *Web:* www.bixbyknollstowers.org	562-426-6123	426-2571	672
Bixel & Co 8721 Sunset Blvd Ste 101 ... Los Angeles CA 90069 *TF:* 855-854-9830 ■ *Web:* www.bixelco.com	310-854-3828		184
Bixler Inc 1600 Tysons Blvd Ste 800 ... McLean VA 22102 *Web:* www.bixler.com	703-894-3000	894-3001	809
Biz Print 600 W Front St ... Boise ID 83702 *Web:* bizprint.com	208-338-9746		627
Bizcaya Grill 3300 SW 27th Ave ... Miami FL 33133 *Web:* ritzcarlton.com	305-644-4675		671
Bizco Technologies Inc 7950 "O" St ... Lincoln NE 68510 *Web:* www.bizco.com	402-323-4800		179
BIZDOC Capital Group 5024 Night Hawk Dr NE ... Rio Rancho NM 87144 *TF:* 844-249-3621 ■ *Web:* www.bizdoccapital.com	844-249-3621		463
Bizerba USA Inc 31 Gordon Rd ... Piscataway NJ 08854 *Web:* www.bizerba.com	732-565-6000		407
Bizfin 50 Mclaughlin Dr ... Greensburg PA 15601 *Web:* www.bizfin.com	724-836-6827		194
BizLand Inc 70 BlanchaRd Rd ... Burlington MA 01803 *TF:* 800-249-5263 ■ *Web:* www.bizland.com	800-249-5263		39
Bizlink Technology Inc 3400 Gateway Blvd ... Fremont CA 94538 *TF:* 800-326-4193 ■ *Web:* www.bizlinktech.com	510-252-0786	252-1178	815
BizNet Technology Inc 8125 SW 120th St ... Miami FL 33156 *Web:* www.biznettechnology.com	305-256-2024		180
Bizphyx Inc 1910 Poplar Dr ... Wylie TX 75098 *Web:* www.bizphyx.com	972-429-5560		194
Bizport Ltd 9 N Third St ... Richmond VA 23219 *Web:* www.bizportdoes.com	804-780-1060		463
BizQuest LLC 2100 E Rt 66 Ste 200 ... Glendora CA 91740 *TF:* 888-280-3815 ■ *Web:* www.bizquest.com	888-280-3815		393
BizSpeed Inc 3050 Royal Blvd S Ste 130 ... Alpharetta GA 30022 *Web:* www.bizspeed.com	678-287-3310		180
BizWest 3180 Sterling Cir Ste 201 ... Boulder CO 80301 *TF:* 800-440-3506 ■ *Web:* bizwest.com	303-440-4950	440-8954	457-5
BizWest 141 S College Ave ... Fort Collins CO 80524 *TF:* 800-433-4688 ■ *Web:* bizwest.com	970-221-5400	221-5432	457-5
BizXchange Inc 3600 136th Pl SE Ste 270 ... Bellevue WA 98006 *Web:* www.bizx.com	425-998-5055		691
Bizzuka Inc 105 Chapel Dr Ste 300 ... Lafayette LA 70506 *Web:* www.bizzuka.com	337-216-4423		177
BJ's On the Water 115 75th St ... Ocean City MD 21842 *TF:* 800-227-0525 ■ *Web:* www.bjsonthewater.com	410-524-7575	524-7624	671
BJ's Restaurant & Brewhouse 461 Esplanade Dr ... Oxnard CA 93030 *Web:* www.bjsrestaurants.com	805-485-1124		671
BJ's Restaurants Inc 7755 Ctr Ave Ste 300 ... Huntington Beach CA 92647 *NASDAQ: BJRI* ■ *TF:* 800-962-4284 ■ *Web:* bjsrestaurants.com	714-500-2400	848-8287	670
BJC HealthCare 4901 Forest Pk Ave ... Saint Louis MO 63108 *Web:* www.bjc.org	314-286-2000		353
Bjork Construction Company Inc 4420 Enterprise Pl ... Fremont CA 94538 *TF:* 800-499-4917 ■ *Web:* www.bjorkconstruction.com	510-656-4688		378
BJW Berghorst & Sons 11430 James St ... Holland MI 49424 *TF:* 800-542-0378 ■ *Web:* www.berghorst.com	616-772-2114		612
BKF Engineers 255 Shoreline Dr Ste 200 ... Redwood City CA 94065 *Web:* www.bkf.com	650-482-6300	482-6399	261

Name / Address	City	State	ZIP	Phone	Fax	Class
BKI (Burk-Kleinpeter Inc)						
4176 Canal St	New Orleans	LA	70119	504-486-5901		261
Web: www.bkiusa.com						
bkm Officeworks						
9201 Spectrum Ctr Blvd Ste 100	San Diego	CA	92123	858-569-4700		321
Web: www.bkmofficeworks.com						
BKR International						
19 Fulton St Ste 401	New York	NY	10038	212-964-2115	964-2133	49-1
TF: 800-257-4685 ■ *Web:* www.bkr.com						
B&L Associates Inc 13 Tech Cir	Natick	MA	01760	508-651-1404		177
TF: 800-406-4333 ■ *Web:* www.bandl.com						
BL Bistro 2203 S Austin St	Amarillo	TX	79109	806-355-7838		671
Web: www.blbistro.com						
BL Cos 355 Research Pkwy	Meriden	CT	06450	203-630-1406	630-2615	261
TF: 800-301-3077 ■ *Web:* www.blcompanies.com						
BL Downey Company LLC						
2125 Gardner Rd	Broadview	IL	60155	708-345-8000		481
TF: 800-323-1206 ■ *Web:* www.bldowney.com						
BL Harbert International Inc						
820 Shades Creek Pkwy Ste 3000	Birmingham	AL	35209	205-802-2800	802-2801	186
Web: blharbert.com						
BL Harbert International LLC						
820 Shades Creek Pkwy Ste 3000	Birmingham	AL	35209	404-841-4000		256
Web: www.bharbert.com						
B&L Pipeco Services						
11707 Hwy 152 W PO Box 778 PO Box 778	Pampa	TX	79066	806-665-0061	665-2231	492
Web: www.bl-supply.com						
Blach Construction Co						
469 El Cmino Real Ste 100	Santa Clara	CA	95050	408-244-7100	244-2220	186
Web: www.blach.com						
Blach Distributing Co 131 W Main St	Elko	NV	89801	775-738-7111		81-1
TF: 800-310-5099 ■ *Web:* www.abwholesaler.com						
Blachford Corp 401 Ctr Rd	Frankfort	IL	60423	905-823-3200	231-8321*	541
**Fax Area Code:* 630 ■ *TF:* 800-241-8334 ■ *Web:* www.blachford.com						
Blachly-Lane Inc PO Box 70	Junction City	OR	97448	541-688-8711	688-8958	245
TF: 800-446-8418 ■ *Web:* www.blachlylane.coop						
Black & Soli PC CPA						
81 W Esperanza Blvd Ste E	Green Valley	AZ	85614	520-625-5988		2
Web: blackandsoli.com						
Black & Veatch 11401 Lamar Ave	Overland Park	KS	66211	913-458-2000		188-7
Web: www.bv.com						
Black Angus						
10907 N Rodney Parham Rd	Little Rock	AR	72212	501-228-7800		671
Web: blackanguscafe.com						
Black Archives Research Ctr & Museum						
445 Gamble St Rm 207	Tallahassee	FL	32307	850-599-3020		520
TF: 800-448-4762 ■ *Web:* cis.famu.edu						
Black Bart International LLC						
155 Blue Heron Blvd E Ste R2	West Palm Beach	FL	33404	561-842-4550		711
TF: 866-289-7050 ■ *Web:* blackbartlures.com						
Black Barts Steakhouse Saloon						
2760 E Butler Ave	Flagstaff	AZ	86004	928-779-3142		671
Web: www.blackbartssteakhouse.com						
Black Bashor & Porsch LLP						
270 E Connelly Blvd	Sharon	PA	16146	724-981-7510		2
Web: bbpcpa.com						
Black Bear Casino Resort						
1785 Hwy 210 PO Box 777	Carlton	MN	55718	218-878-2327	878-2414	133
TF: 888-771-0777 ■ *Web:* www.blackbearcasinohotel.com						
Black Bear Diner 1880 Shasta St	Redding	CA	96001	602-843-1921		671
Web: www.blackbeardiner.com						
Black Bear Diner 2323 S Virginia St	Reno	NV	89502	775-827-5570		671
Web: www.blackbeardiner.com						
Black Box Corp 1000 Pk Dr	Lawrence	PA	15055	724-746-5500	321-0746*	176
NASDAQ: BBOX ■ **Fax Area Code:* 800 ■ *TF:* 877-877-2269 ■ *Web:* www.blackbox.com						
Black Box Inc 2777 Loker Ave W Unit A	Carlsbad	CA	92010	760-804-3300		711
Web: www.blackboxdist.com						
Black Box Principals Inc						
83 Cairns Pl	Belle Mead	NJ	08502	201-914-0374		463
Black Butte Ranch						
12930 Hawks BeaRd Rd PO Box 8000	Black Butte Ranch	OR	97759	541-595-1252	595-2077	669
TF: 866-901-2961 ■ *Web:* www.blackbutteranch.com						
Black Canyon Capital LLC						
2000 Ave of the Stars 11th Fl	Los Angeles	CA	90067	310-272-1800		690
Web: www.blackcanyoncapital.com						
Black Canyon of the Gunnison National Park						
102 Elk Creek	Gunnison	CO	81230	970-641-2337	641-3127	564
Web: www.nps.gov/blca						
Black Classic Press PO Box 13414	Baltimore	MD	21203	410-242-6954		637-2
Web: www.blackclassicbooks.com						
Black Clawson Converting Machinery Inc						
46 N First St	Fulton	NY	13069	315-598-7121	593-0396	556
Web: www.davis-standard.com						
Black Cultural Centre for Nova Scotia						
10 Cherry Brook Rd	Cherry Brook	NS	B2Z1A8	902-434-6223	434-2306	520
TF: 800-465-0767 ■ *Web:* web1.bccnsweb.com						
Black Diamond Paving Inc						
41550 Boscell Rd	Fremont	CA	94538	510-770-1150		183
Web: www.blackdiamondpaving.com						
Black Diane (Rep R - TN)						
1131 Longworth HOB	Washington	DC	20515	202-225-4231	225-6887	342-2
Web: black.house.gov						
Black Elk Energy LLC						
11451 Katy Fwy Ste 500	Houston	TX	77079	281-598-8600		539
Black Enterprise Magazine						
130 Fifth Ave	New York	NY	10011	212-242-8000	886-9610	457-5
TF Cust Svc: 800-727-7777 ■ *Web:* www.blackenterprise.com						
Black Equipment Co Inc						
1187 Burch Dr	Evansville	IN	47716	812-477-6481		112
Web: www.blackequipment.com						
Black Forest Decor LLC PO Box 297	Jenks	OK	74037	800-605-0915		791
TF: 800-605-0915 ■ *Web:* www.blackforestdecor.com						
Black Forest Inn 1 E 26th St	Minneapolis	MN	55404	612-872-0812	872-0423	671
Web: www.blackforestinnmpls.com						
Black Gold						
4320 18th Ave S Grand Forks	Grand Forks	ND	58201	701-792-3414	772-0749	10-11
Web: blackgoldfarms.com						
Black Hat Inc 1932 First Ave Ste 204	Seattle	WA	98101	206-443-5489		692
TF: 866-203-8081 ■ *Web:* www.blackhat.com						
Black Hawk College						
East 1501 State Hwy 78	Kewanee	IL	61443	309-852-5671	856-6005*	162
**Fax:* Admissions ■ *TF:* 800-233-5671 ■ *Web:* www.bhc.edu						
Quad Cities 6600 34th Ave	Moline	IL	61265	309-796-5000	796-5209*	162
**Fax:* Admissions ■ *TF:* 800-334-1311 ■ *Web:* www.bhc.edu						
Black Hawk County 316 E Fifth St	Waterloo	IA	50703	319-833-3012		338
TF: 800-696-5123 ■ *Web:* www.co.black-hawk.ia.us						
Black Hawk State Park 228 S Blossom	Lake View	IA	51450	712-657-8712	657-2289	565
Web: www.iowadnr.gov						
Black Hawk Station Casino						
141 Gregory St PO Box 417	Black Hawk	CO	80422	303-582-5582	582-5590	133
Web: blackhawkcolorado.com						
Black Hills Bentonite LLC PO Box 9	Mills	WY	82644	307-265-3740		503-2
TF Orders: 800-700-8666 ■ *Web:* www.bhbentonite.com						
Black Hills Caverns 2600 Cavern Rd	Rapid City	SD	57702	605-343-0542		50-5
TF: 800-837-9358 ■ *Web:* www.blackhillscaverns.com						
Black Hills Corp 625 Ninth St	Rapid City	SD	57701	605-721-1700		360-5
NYSE: BKH ■ *TF:* 866-264-8003 ■ *Web:* www.blackhillscorp.com						
Black Hills Electric Co-op						
25191 Co-op Way PO Box 792	Custer	SD	57730	605-673-4461	673-3147	245
TF: 800-742-0085 ■ *Web:* www.bhec.com						
Black Hills Health & Education Ctr						
PO Box 19	Hermosa	SD	57744	605-255-4101	255-4687	706
TF Cust Svc: 866-757-0160 ■ *Web:* bhhec.org						
Black Hills National Cemetery						
20901 Pleasant Vly Dr	Sturgis	SD	57785	605-347-3830	720-7298	136
Web: www.cem.va.gov						
Black Hills Pioneer 315 Seaton Cir	Spearfish	SD	57783	605-642-2761		532-2
Web: bhpioneer.com						
Black Hills Shooters Supply Inc						
2875 Creek Dr	Rapid City	SD	57703	605-348-4477		711
Web: www.bhshooters.com						
Black Hills State University						
1200 University St Unit 9502	Spearfish	SD	57799	605-642-6343	642-6254	166
TF: 800-255-2478 ■ *Web:* www.bhsu.edu						
Black History Museum & Cultural Ctr of Virginia						
00 Clay St	Richmond	VA	23220	804-780-9093		520
Web: www.blackhistorymuseum.org						
Black Horse Pike Regional School District						
580 Erial Rd	Blackwood	NJ	08012	856-227-4105	227-6835	685
Web: www.bhprsd.org						
Black Letter Discovery Inc						
33 New Montgomery St Ste 950	San Francisco	CA	94105	415-946-2470		194
Web: www.blackletterdiscovery.com						
Black Madonna Shrine						
100 St Joseph Hill Rd PO Box 181	Pacific	MO	63069	636-938-5361		50-1
Web: www.franciscancaring.org/blackmadonnashri.html						
Black Mann & Graham LLP						
2905 Corporate Cir	Flower Mound	TX	75028	972-353-4174		428
Black McCuskey Souers & Arbaugh						
1000 United Bank Plaza	Canton	OH	44702	330-456-8341		445
Web: bmsa.com						
Black Mesa State Park & Nature Preserve						
County Rd 325	Kenton	OK	73946	580-426-2222	426-2405	565
Web: www.travelok.com						
Black Millwork Company Inc						
220 W Crescent Ave	Allendale	NJ	07401	201-934-0100		499
Web: www.blackmillwork.com						
Black Moshannon State Park						
4216 Beaver Rd	Philipsburg	PA	16866	814-342-5960		565
Web: www.dcnr.state.pa.us						
Black Mountain Ranch						
4000 Conger Mesa Rd	McCoy	CO	80463	970-653-4226		239
TF: 800-967-2401 ■ *Web:* www.blackmtnranch.com						
Black Mountain-Swannanoa Chamber of Commerce						
201 E State St	Black Mountain	NC	28711	828-669-2300	669-1407	139
TF: 800-669-2301 ■ *Web:* www.exploreblackmountain.com						
Black Olive 814 S Bond St	Baltimore	MD	21231	410-276-7141	276-7143	671
Web: www.theblackolive.com						
Black Pearl, The Bannister's Wharf	Newport	RI	02840	401-846-5264		671
Web: www.blackpearlnewport.com						
Black Pest Prevention Inc						
605 Springbrook Rd	Charlotte	NC	28217	704-522-9222		577
Web: www.blackpest.com						
Black Point Inn Resort						
510 Black Pt Rd	Scarborough	ME	04074	207-883-2500	883-9976	669
TF: 800-258-3373 ■ *Web:* www.blackpointinn.com						
Black Prince Distillery Inc						
691 Clifton Ave	Clifton	NJ	07011	973-365-2050	365-0746	80-1
TF: 800-666-9463 ■ *Web:* www.blackprincedistillery.com						
Black Radio Network 166 Madison Ave	New York	NY	10016	212-686-6850	686-7308	644
TF: 866-342-6892 ■ *Web:* www.blackradionetwork.com						
Black Ridge Oil & Gas						
110 N fifth St Ste 410	Minnetonka	MN	55403	952-426-1241		536
Web: www.blackridgeoil.com						
Black River Asset Management LLC						
9320 Excelsior Blvd	Hopkins	MN	55343	952-984-3863		792
Web: www.black-river.com						
Black River Electric Co-op						
2600 Hwy 67 PO Box 31	Fredericktown	MO	63645	573-783-3381		245
TF: 800-392-4711 ■ *Web:* www.brec.coop						
Black River Electric Co-op						
1121 N Pike Rd W PO Box 130	Sumter	SC	29151	803-469-8060		245
Web: www.blackriver.coop						
Black River Manufacturing Inc						
2625 20th St	Port Huron	MI	48060	810-982-9812	982-2074	60
Web: www.blackrivermfg.biz						
Black River State Forest						
W10325 Hwy 12	Black River	WI	53707	608-266-2621	275-3338	565
TF: 888-936-7463 ■ *Web:* dnr.wi.gov						
Black River Technical College						
1410 Hwy 304 E	Pocahontas	AR	72455	870-248-4000	248-4100	162
TF: 866-890-6933 ■ *Web:* www.blackrivertech.org						
Black Rock Cable 1512 Fairview St	Bellingham	WA	98229	360-738-3116		116
Black Rock Mountain State Park						
3085 Black Rock Mtn Pkwy	Mountain City	GA	30562	706-746-2141		565
Web: www.gastateparks.org						

Phone | Fax | Class

Black Rock State Park
c/o Topsmead State Forest PO Box 1081 ... Litchfield CT 06759 860-283-8088 565
Web: www.ct.gov

Black Sand Technologies Inc
3316 Bee Cave Rd Ste C ... Austin TX 78746 512-329-9400 390
Web: www.blacksand.com

Black Sandy State Park
6563 Hauser Dam Rd c/o Helena Area Resource Office (HARO)
PO Box 200701 ... Helena MT 59620 406-444-2535 565
Web: stateparks.mt.gov

Black Srebnick Kornspan & Stumpf PA
201 S Biscayne Blvd Ste 1300 ... Miami FL 33131 305-371-6421 428
Web: www.royblack.com

Black Swan Energy Ltd
Ste 1200 Bow Vly Sq III 255 - Fifth Ave SW
Ste 1200 ... Calgary AB T2P3G6 403-930-4400 536
Web: www.blackswanenergy.com

Black Swan Inn 746 E Ctr St ... Pocatello ID 83201 208-233-3051 379
TF: 800-424-3337 ■ *Web:* www.blackswaninn.com

Black Tomato 11 George St ... Ottawa ON K1N8W5 613-789-8123 671
Web: www.theblacktomato.com

Black's Tire Service Inc
30 Bitmore Rd ... Whiteville NC 28472 910-642-4123 54
Web: www.blackstire.com

BlackBag Technologies Inc
300 Piercy Rd ... San Jose CA 95138 408-844-8890 180
Web: www.blackbagtech.com

Blackbaud Inc
2000 Daniel Island Dr ... Charleston SC 29492 843-216-6200 216-6100 178-1
NASDAQ: BLKB ■ *TF:* 800-468-8996 ■ *Web:* www.blackbaud.com

BlackBerry Ltd 2200 University Ave E ... Waterloo ON N2K0A7 519-888-7465 888-7884 173-2
NASDAQ: BBRY ■ *Web:* ca.blackberry.com

Blackbird 619 W Randolph St ... Chicago IL 60661 312-715-0708 671
Web: www.blackbirdrestaurant.com

Blackboard Inc 1899 L St NW 5th Fl ... Washington DC 20036 202-463-4860 463-4863 178-3
TF: 800-424-9299 ■ *Web:* www.blackboard.com

BlackBook Media Corp 29 E 19th St ... New York NY 10003 212-334-1800 532-3
Web: bbook.com

Blackbourn 200 Fourth Ave N ... Edgerton MN 56128 800-842-7550 442-4313* 86
**Fax Area Code: 507* ■ *TF:* 800-842-7550 ■ *Web:* www.blackbourn.com

Blackbridge Partners LLC
800 W Cummings Pk Ste 2000 ... Woburn MA 01801 617-273-2404 70
Web: www.blackbridgepartners.com

BlackBrush Oil & Gas LP
18615 Tuscany Stone Ste 300 ... San Antonio TX 78258 210-495-5577 536
Web: www.blackbrushenergy.com

Blackburn College 700 College Ave ... Carlinville IL 62626 217-854-3231 854-3713* 166
**Fax: Admissions* ■ *TF:* 800-233-3550 ■ *Web:* www.blackburn.edu

Blackburn Correctional Complex
3111 Spurr Rd ... Lexington KY 40511 859-246-2366 246-2376 213
TF: 800-808-1213 ■ *Web:* corrections.ky.gov

Blackburn Elementary School
4377 W N Carolina 10 ... Newton NC 28658 704-462-1344 685
Web: www.catawbaschools.net

Blackburn Marsha (Rep R - TN)
2266 Rayburn Bldg ... Washington DC 20515 202-225-2811 225-3004 342-2
Web: blackburn.house.gov

Blackburn Radio Inc
700 Richmond St Ste 102 ... London ON N6A5C7 519-679-8680 360-2
Web: blackburnradio.com

Blackburn's Fabrication Inc
2467 Jackson Pk ... Columbus OH 43223 614-875-0784 492
Web: blackburnsfab.com

Blackburn's Physicians Pharmacy Inc
301 Corbet St ... Tarentum PA 15084 724-224-9100 224-9124 476
TF: 800-472-2440 ■ *Web:* www.blackburnsmed.com

Blackcomb Aviation LP
Vancouver International Airport 4360 Agar Dr
... Richmond BC V7B1A3 604-273-5311 21
Web: www.blackcombhelicopters.com

Blackfin Technology Inc
1702 W Fairview Ave ... Boise ID 83702 208-338-1581 177

Blackfoot Inn 5940 Blackfoot Trl SE ... Calgary AB T2H2B5 403-252-2253 252-3574 379
TF: 800-661-1151 ■ *Web:* www.hotelblackfoot.com

Blackfoot Livestock Auction
93 Rich Ln ... Blackfoot ID 83221 208-785-0500 446
Web: www.blackfootlivestockauction.com

Blackfoot School District 55
270 E Bridge St ... Blackfoot ID 83221 208-785-8800 785-8809 685
Web: www.d55.k12.id.us

Blackford County
110 W Washington St ... Hartford City IN 47348 765-348-1620 348-7222 338
Web: gov.blackfordcounty.org

Blackhawk Bank PO Box 719 ... Beloit WI 53511 608-364-4534 69
TF: 888-769-2600 ■ *Web:* www.blackhawkbank.com

Blackhawk Equipment Co 5295 Vivian St ... Arvada CO 80002 303-421-3000 172
Web: www.blackhawkequipment.com

Blackhawk Machine Products Inc
6 Industrial Dr ... Smithfield RI 02917 401-232-7563 232-0770 621
Web: www.blackhawk-machine.com

Blackhawk Management Corp
1335 Regents Pk Dr ... Houston TX 77058 281-286-5751 463
Web: www.blackhawkmgmt.com

Blackhawk Technical College
6004 S County Rd G ... Janesville WI 53546 608-758-6900 743-4407 800
TF: 800-498-1282 ■ *Web:* www.blackhawk.edu

BlackInk IT
1101 E 16th St Ste 300 ... Indianapolis IN 46202 317-472-8000 472-8010 225
Web: blackinkit.com

Blackledge Furniture
233 SW Second St ... Corvallis OR 97333 541-753-4851 321
TF: 800-782-4851 ■ *Web:* www.blackledgefurniture.com

Blacklion International Inc
10605 Park Rd ... Charlotte NC 28210 704-541-1148 321
Web: www.blacklion.com

Blackman Kallick 10 S Riverside Plaza ... Chicago IL 60606 312-207-1040 2
TF: 866-939-3921 ■ *Web:* www.plantemoran.com

Blackman Plumbing Supply Company Inc
3480 Sunrise Hwy ... Wantagh NY 11793 516-785-6000 612
Web: www.blackman.com

Blackmer 1809 Century Ave ... Grand Rapids MI 49503 616-241-1611 241-3752 641
TF: 888-363-7886 ■ *Web:* www.psgdover.com

Blackmore Company Inc
10800 Blackmore Ave ... Belleville MI 48111 734-483-8661 608
TF: 800-874-8660 ■ *Web:* www.blackmoreco.com

BlackPlanet.com 205 Hudson St 6th Fl ... New York NY 10013 212-431-4477 505-3478 171
Web: www.blackplanet.com

BlackRock Inc 601 Union St ... Seattle WA 98101 206-613-6700 792
NYSE: BLK ■ *TF:* 800-441-7450 ■ *Web:* www.blackrock.com/corporate

BlackRock Inc 40 E 52nd St ... New York NY 10022 212-810-5300 401
NYSE: BLK ■ *Web:* www.blackrock.com

Blacksands Petroleum Inc
Ste 410 25025 I-45 N ... The Woodlands TX 77380 713-554-4491 536

Blacksburg High
750 Imperial St ... Christiansburg VA 24073 540-382-5100 381-6127 685
Web: www.mcps.org

Blackstone Group 345 Pk Ave ... New York NY 10154 212-583-5000 583-5749 690
Web: www.blackstone.com

Blackstone Group Inc, The
332 S Michigan Ave Ste 1610 ... Chicago IL 60604 312-419-0400 466
Web: www.bgglobal.com

Blackstone Industries Inc
16 Stoney Hill Rd ... Bethel CT 06801 203-792-8622 796-7861 759
TF: 800-272-2885 ■ *Web:* www.blackstoneind.com

Blackstone Restaurant & Brewery
1918 W End Ave ... Nashville TN 37203 615-327-9969 671
Web: blackstone-pub.com

Blackstone River & Canal Heritage State Park
287 Oak St ... Uxbridge MA 01569 508-278-7604 565
Web: www.mass.gov

Blackstone Valley Chamber of Commerce
110 Church St ... Whitinsville MA 01588 508-234-9090 234-5152 139
TF: 800-841-0919 ■ *Web:* www.blackstonevalley.org

Blacktail Mountain Ski Area LLC
13990 Blacktail Rd ... Lakeside MT 59922 406-844-0999 379
Web: www.blacktailmountain.com

Blackthorn Restaurant & Pub
2134 Seneca St ... Buffalo NY 14210 716-825-9327 671
Web: blackthornrestaurant.com

Blackton Inc 1714 Alden Rd ... Orlando FL 32803 407-898-2661 131
Web: www.blacktoninc.com

Blackwater Falls State Park PO Box 490 ... Davis WV 26260 304-259-5216 565
Web: www.blackwaterfalls.com

Blackwater River State Park
7720 Deaton Bridge Rd ... Holt FL 32564 850-983-5363 565
Web: www.floridastateparks.org

Blackwell Burke PA
431 S Seventh St 2500 ... Minneapolis MN 55415 612-343-3200 428
Web: www.blackwellburke.com

Blackwell Engineering
566 E Market St ... Harrisonburg VA 22801 540-432-9555 261
Web: www.blackwellengineering.com

Blackwell Plastics Inc 5606 Cavanaugh ... Houston TX 77021 713-643-6577 596
Web: www.blackwellplastics.com

Blackwell, The 2110 Tuttle Pk Pl ... Columbus OH 43210 614-247-4000 247-4040 379
TF: 866-247-4003 ■ *Web:* www.theblackwell.com

Blade 541 N Superior St ... Toledo OH 43660 419-724-6000 724-6439 532-2
TF: 800-245-3317 ■ *Web:* www.toledoblade.com

Blade Creative Branding Inc
150 Laird Dr ... Toronto ON M4G3V7 416-467-4770 7
TF: 800-392-5233 ■ *Web:* www.bladecreativebranding.com

Blade Energy Partners Ltd
2600 Network Blvd Ste 550 ... Frisco TX 75034 972-712-8407 712-8408 192
TF: 800-849-1545 ■ *Web:* www.blade-energy.com

Blade HQ 400 S 1000 E Ste E ... Lehi UT 84043 801-768-0232 362
Web: www.bladehq.com

Blade Technologies Inc
10820 Sunset Office Dr Ste 101 ... St. Louis MO 63127 314-752-7999 225
TF: 800-634-5184 ■ *Web:* www.bladetechinc.com

Bladen Community College PO Box 266 ... Dublin NC 28332 910-879-5556 879-5513 162
Web: www.bladencc.edu

Bladen County
166 E Broad St Rm 109 ... Elizabethtown NC 28337 910-862-6700 862-6767 338
Web: www.bladennc.govoffice3.com

Blade-Tech Industries Inc
5530 184th St E ... Puyallup WA 98375 253-655-8059 711
TF: 877-331-5793 ■ *Web:* www.blade-tech.com

Bladon Springs State Park
3921 Bladon Rd ... Bladon Springs AL 36919 251-754-9207 754-9207 565
TF: 800-252-7275 ■ *Web:* www.alapark.com/parks

Bladwin Tammy (Sen D - WI)
709 Hart Senate Office Bldg ... Washington DC 20510 202-224-5653 342-2
Web: www.baldwin.senate.gov

Blain Supply Inc 3507 E Racine St ... Janesville WI 53547 608-754-2821 274
TF: 800-210-2370 ■ *Web:* www.farmandfleet.com

Blaine Construction Corp
6510 Deane Hill Dr ... Knoxville TN 37919 865-693-8900 691-7606 186
Web: www.blaineconstruction.com

Blaine County 145 Lincoln Ave ... Brewster NE 68821 308-547-2222 547-2228 338
TF: 800-657-2113 ■ *Web:* www.blainecounty.ne.gov

Blaine County 420 Ohio St ... Chinook MT 59523 406-442-9830 357-2199 338
TF: 800-666-6124 ■ *Web:* blainecounty-mt.gov

Blaine County
206 First Ave S Blaine County Courthouse ... Hailey ID 83333 208-788-5505 788-5501 338
Web: www.co.blaine.id.us

Blaine County 212 N Weigle ... Watonga OK 73772 580-623-5890 338
Web: www.watonga.com

Blaine Tech Services Inc
1680 Rogers Ave ... San Jose CA 95112 408-573-0555 194
TF: 800-545-7558 ■ *Web:* www.blainetech.com

Blaine Warren Advertising LLC
7120 Smoke Ranch Rd ... Las Vegas NV 89128 702-435-6947 7
Web: www.blainewarren.com

Blaine's Art Supply 1025 Photo Ave ... Anchorage AK 99503 907-561-5344 562-5988 45
TF: 866-561-4278 ■ *Web:* www.blainesart.com

Listing	City	State	Zip	Phone	Fax	Class
Blair Academy 2 Pk St PO Box 600	Blairstown	NJ	07825	908-362-6121		622
Web: www.blair.edu						
Blair Cedar & Novelty Works Inc						
680 W US Hwy 54	Camdenton	MO	65020	573-346-2235	346-5534	328
TF: 800-325-3943 ■ *Web:* www.blaircedar.com						
Blair Concrete Services						
1410-B Diggs Dr	Raleigh	NC	27603	919-833-9088		189-3
Web: www.donleyinc.com						
Blair County 423 Allegheny St	Hollidaysburg	PA	16648	814-693-3000	693-3033	338
TF: 800-400-4271 ■ *Web:* www.blairco.org						
Blair Museum of Lithopanes						
5403 Elmer Dr 5403 Elmer Dr	Toledo	OH	43615	419-245-1356		520
Web: www.lithophanemuseum.org						
Blair Rubber Co 5020 Panther Pkwy	Seville	OH	44273	800-321-5583		131
TF: 800-321-5583 ■ *Web:* www.blairrubber.com						
Blair, Church & Flynn Consulting Engineers						
451 Clovis Ave Ste 200	Clovis	CA	93612	559-326-1400		261
Web: www.bcf-engr.com						
Blair-HSM Group of Cos						
3671 Horseblock Rd	Medford	NY	11763	631-924-6600		22
Web: www.blair-hsm.com						
Blaise Alexander Chevrolet Inc						
933 Broad St	Montoursville	PA	17754	570-368-8677		57
Web: blaisealexander.com						
Blake International USA Rigs LLC						
410 S Van Ave	Houma	LA	70363	985-274-2200		539
Web: www.blakeinternationalrigs.com						
Blake Medical Ctr 2020 59th St W	Bradenton	FL	34209	941-792-6611		374-3
TF: 800-523-5827 ■ *Web:* www.blakemedicalcenter.com						
Blake Real Estate Co						
1150 Connecticut Ave, NW	Washington	DC	20036	202-778-0400		186
Web: www.blakereal.com						
Blake School 110 Blake Rd S	Hopkins	MN	55343	952-988-3405	988-3455	623
Web: www.blakeschool.org						
Blakely Construction Company Inc						
2830 W I-20	Odessa	TX	79703	432-381-3540		539
TF: 800-604-9339 ■ *Web:* www.blakelycc.com						
Blakely New York 136 W 55th St	New York	NY	10019	212-245-1800	582-8332	379
TF: 800-735-0710 ■ *Web:* www.blakelynewyork.com						
Blakeslee Arpaia Chapman Inc						
200 N Branford Rd	Branford	CT	06405	203-488-2500		183
TF: 800-922-6203 ■ *Web:* bac-inc.com						
Blakeslee Prestress Inc						
Rt 139 McDermott Rd PO Box 510	Branford	CT	06405	203-481-5306	481-3562	183
Web: www.blakesleeprestress.com						
Blakeslee-Lane Inc 916 N Charles St	Baltimore	MD	21201	410-727-8800		809
Web: www.blakesleeadv.com						
Blakinger Byler & Thomas PC						
28 Penn Sq	Lancaster	PA	17603	717-299-1100		428
TF: 800-828-9093 ■ *Web:* www.blakingerthomas.com						
Blalock Walters PA 802 11th St W	Bradenton	FL	34205	941-748-0100		428
Web: blalockwalters.com						
Blanchard Compact Equipment						
1410 Ashville Hwy	Spartanburg	SC	29303	864-582-1245		274
TF: 888-799-3606 ■ *Web:* www.blanchardmachinery.com						
Blanchard Valley Hospital						
1900 S Main St	Findlay	OH	45840	419-423-4500		374-3
Web: www.bvhealthsystem.org						
Blanco America Inc						
110 Mt Holly By-Pass	Lumberton	NJ	08048	800-451-5782		362
TF: 800-451-5782 ■ *Web:* www.blanco-germany.com/en_us/en_us/home.html						
Blanco County						
101 E Pecan Dr PO Box 65	Johnson City	TX	78636	830-868-0973	868-2084	338
Web: www.co.blanco.tx.us						
Blanco State Park PO Box 493	Blanco	TX	78606	830-833-4333		565
Web: tpwd.texas.gov/state-parks/blanco						
Bland Correctional Ctr						
256 Bland Farm Rd	Bland	VA	24315	276-688-3341		213
Web: vadoc.virginia.gov						
Bland County 612 Main St Ste 104	Bland	VA	24315	276-688-4622	688-9758	338
TF: 800-519-3468 ■ *Web:* www.blandcountyva.gov						
Bland Farms Inc						
1126 Raymond Bland Rd	Glennville	GA	30427	912-654-1330		297-7
Web: www.blandfarms.com						
Blandford Nature Ctr						
1715 Hillburn Ave NW	Grand Rapids	MI	49504	616-735-6240		50-5
Web: blandfordnaturecenter.org						
Blane Canada Ltd PO Box 4408	Wheaton	IL	60189	630-462-9222		195
Web: www.blanecanada.com						
Blaney McMurtry LLP						
Maritime Life Tower 2 Queen St E Ste 1500	Toronto	ON	M5C3G5	416-593-1221		428
Web: www.blaney.com						
Blank Park Zoo 7401 SW Ninth St	Des Moines	IA	50315	515-285-4722		823
TF: 800-226-3369 ■ *Web:* www.blankparkzoo.com						
Blank Quilting Corp						
Blank Quilting 49 W 37th St 14th fl	New York	NY	10018	800-294-9495	679-4578*	594
*Fax Area Code: 212 ■ *TF:* 800-294-9495 ■ *Web:* blankquilting.net						
Blank Rome LLP						
1 Logan Sq 130 N 18th St	Philadelphia	PA	19103	215-569-5500	569-5555	428
TF: 800-973-1177 ■ *Web:* www.blankrome.com						
Blank Wesselink Cook & Associates Inc						
2623 E Pershing Rd	Decatur	IL	62526	217-428-0973		261
Blanke Industries Inc						
1099 Brown St Ste 103	Wauconda	IL	60084	847-487-2780		419
TF: 800-239-6584 ■ *Web:* www.blankeindustries.com						
Blanks Printing & Imaging Inc						
2343 N Beckley	Dallas	TX	75208	214-741-3905	741-6105	781
TF: 800-325-7651 ■ *Web:* www.blanks.com						
Blanks/USA Inc 7700 68th Ave N #7	Minneapolis	MN	55428	800-328-7311		560
TF: 800-328-7311 ■ *Web:* www.laserblanks.com						
BLANKSPACES Mid Wilshire						
5405 Wilshire Blvd	Los Angeles	CA	90036	323-330-9505		23
Web: www.blankspaces.com						
Blanski Peter Kronage & Zoch						
7500 Olson Memorial Hwy Ste 200	Minneapolis	MN	55427	763-546-6211		2
Blanton & Assoc Inc						
5 Lakeway Centre Ct Ste 200	Austin	TX	78734	512-264-1095		194
TF: 888-863-5881 ■ *Web:* www.blantonassociates.com						
Blanton Museum of Art						
200 E Martin Luther King Jr Blvd						
University of Texas at Austin	Austin	TX	78701	512 471 7324	471 7023	520
Web: blantonmuseum.org						
Blantyre 16 Blantyre Rd PO Box 995	Lenox	MA	01240	413-637-3556		379
TF: 844-881-0104 ■ *Web:* blantyre.com						
Blarney Castle Oil Co						
12218 W St PO Box 246	Bear Lake	MI	49614	231-864-3111		539
Web: www.blarneycastleoil.com						
Blaser Die Casting Co						
5700 Third Ave S	Seattle	WA	98108	206-767-7800		308
Blaser Swisslube Inc 31 Hatfield Ln	Goshen	NY	10924	845-294-3200		536
TF: 800-726-3845 ■ *Web:* www.blaser.com						
Blasingame, Burch, Garrard & Ashley PC						
440 College Ave	Athens	GA	30603	706-354-4000		428
TF: 866-354-3544 ■ *Web:* www.bbgbalaw.com						
Blast Advanced Media						
950 Reserve Dr Ste 150	Roseville	CA	95678	916-724-6701		180
TF: 888-252-7866 ■ *Web:* www.blastam.com						
Blast Communications Inc						
1444 N Farnsworth Ave Ste 304	Aurora	IL	60505	630-375-9600		224
Web: www.blastcomm.com						
Blast Inc						
220 Chatham Business Dr PO Box 818	Pittsboro	NC	27312	919-533-0143	542-5955	178-7
TF: 800-242-5278 ■ *Web:* www.blast.com						
Blast Intermediate Unit 17						
2400 Reach Rd	Williamsport	PA	17701	570-323-8561		685
Web: www.iu17.org						
Blast Radius 515 Richards St	Vancouver	BC	V6B2Z5	604-647-6500		7
TF: 866-473-6800 ■ *Web:* www.blastradius.com						
Blattel Communications						
250 Montgomery St Ste 1200	San Francisco	CA	94104	415-397-4811		636
Web: www.blattel.com						
Blattner Steel Company Inc						
2100 Rust Ave	Cape Girardeau	MO	63703	573-339-1129		492
TF: 800-442-0777 ■ *Web:* www.blattnersteel.com						
Blauch Bros Inc 911 Chicago Ave	Harrisonburg	VA	22802	540-434-2589		610
TF: 888-881-3939 ■ *Web:* blauchbrothers.com						
Blauer Mfg Co Inc 20 Aberdeen St	Boston	MA	02215	617-536-6606	536-6948	155-19
TF: 800-225-6715 ■ *Web:* www.blauer.com						
Blauvelt State Park						
Palisades Interstate Park Commission						
Adminstration Bldg Rt 9 W	Bear Mountain	NY	10911	845-359-0544		565
Web: parks.ny.gov/parks/49/details.aspx						
Blax Inc 6600 St-Urbain	Montreal	QC	H2S3G8	514-523-4600		180
Web: www.blax.ca						
Blaylock Oil Company Inc						
724 S Flagler Ave	Homestead	FL	33030	305-247-7249		581
Web: www.blaylockoil.com						
Blaze Energy Ltd						
900 - Sixth Ave SW Ste 1010	Calgary	AB	T2P3K2	403-264-0877		536
Web: www.blazeenergy.com						
Blaze Fireplaces of Northern California Inc						
101 Cargo Way	San Francisco	CA	94124	415-495-2002		361
Web: www.blazefireplaces.com						
Blaze Marketing Solutions Ltd						
1000 Windmill Rd Ste 32	Dartmouth	NS	B3B1L7	902-468-0537		195
Web: blazemarketing.com						
Blazer Industries Inc PO Box 489	Aumsville	OR	97325	503-749-1900	749-3969	106
TF: 877-211-3437 ■ *Web:* www.blazerind.com						
BlazeTech Corp 29B Montvale Ave	Woburn	MA	01801	781-759-0700		192
TF: 800-341-2334 ■ *Web:* www.blazetech.com						
Blazing Editions 42 Ladd St	East Greenwich	RI	02818	401-885-4329		522
Web: www.blazing.com						
Blazing Technologies Inc						
4631A Morgantown Rd	Mohnton	PA	19540	484-722-4800		697
Web: www.blazingtech.net						
Blecher & Collins						
515 S Figueroa St Ste 1750	Los Angeles	CA	90071	213-622-4222		428
TF: 800-817-2949 ■ *Web:* www.blechercollins.com						
Bleckley County 112 N Second St	Cochran	GA	31014	478-934-3200		338
Web: www.bleckley.org						
Bledsoe Cattle Co 41726 US 385	Wray	CO	80758	970-332-4955		10-1
Bledsoe County PO Box 205	Pikeville	TN	37367	423-447-2791		338
Web: www.pikeville-bledsoe.com						
Bledsoe Creek State Park						
400 Zieglers Ft Rd	Gallatin	TN	37066	615-452-3706		565
Web: www.state.tn.us						
Bledsoe Telephone Co-op Corp (BTC)						
338 Cumberland Ave PO Box 609	Pikeville	TN	37367	423-447-2121	447-2498	736
TF: 888-382-1222 ■ *Web:* www.bledsoe.net						
Blekko Inc						
130 Marine Pkwy Ste 200	Redwood City	CA	94065	650-631-3845		225
Web: blekko.com						
Blencowe Group Inc, The						
915 Lady St Ste 444	Columbia	SC	29201	803-779-5866		35
TF: 800-345-7743 ■ *Web:* blencowe.com						
Blendco Systems LLC 1 Pearl Buck Ct	Bristol	PA	19007	215-781-3600		146
Web: www.blendco.com						
Blendex Company Inc						
11208 Electron Dr	Louisville	KY	40299	502-267-1003	267-1024	296-23
TF: 800-626-6325 ■ *Web:* www.blendex.com						
Blenheim Pharmacal Inc						
119 Creamery Rd	North Blenheim	NY	12131	805-477-9866		463
Web: bpipack.com						
Blenko Glass Co PO Box 67	Milton	WV	25541	304-743-9081		334
TF: 877-425-3656 ■ *Web:* www.blenko.com						
Blennerhassett Island Historical State Park						
137 Juliana St	Parkersburg	WV	26101	304-420-4800		565
Web: www.blennerhassettislandstatepark.com						
Blentech Corp 2899 Dowd Dr	Santa Rosa	CA	95407	707-523-5949		298
Web: www.blentech.com						
Bless Your Heart 3701 19th St	Lubbock	TX	79410	806-791-2211		671
Blessey Marine Services Inc						
1515 River Oaks Rd E	Harahan	LA	70123	504-734-1156		763
Web: www.blessey.com						
Blessing Health System PO Box 7005	Quincy	IL	62305	217-223-1200		371
TF: 800-222-9913 ■ *Web:* www.blessinghospital.org						

	Phone	Fax	Class
Blessing Hospital Broadway at 11th St ... Quincy IL 62301 *TF:* 866-460-3933 ■ *Web:* www.blessinghospital.org	217-223-8400	223-6891	374-3
BlessingWhite Inc 23 Orchard Rd ... Skillman NJ 08558 *Web:* blessingwhite.com	908-904-1000		463
BLET (Brotherhood of Locomotive Engineers & Trainmen) 1370 Ontario St Mezzanine Level ... Cleveland OH 44113 *TF:* 877-772-5772 ■ *Web:* www.ble-t.org	216-241-2630	241-6516	414
Bleublancrouge Inc 606 rue Cathcart bureau 1007 ... Montreal QC H3B1K9 *Web:* www.bleublancrouge.ca	514-875-7007		636
Bley LLC 700 Chase Ave ... Elk Grove Village IL 60007 *Web:* acmeind.com	847-290-0117		454
Bleyhl Farm Service Inc 940 E Wine Country Rd ... Grandview WA 98930 *TF Cust Svc:* 800-862-6806 ■ *Web:* www.bleyhl.com	509-882-2248	882-4208	276
Bleyl & Assoc 1715 S Capital Of Texas Hwy Ste 109 ... Austin TX 78746 *Web:* bleylengineering.com	512-328-7878	328-7884	256
Blf Marketing LLC 220 Athens Way Ste 110 ... Nashville TN 37228 *Web:* blfmarketing.com	615-726-2360		7
BLI (Bulk Lift International Inc) 1013 Tamarac Dr ... Carpentersville IL 60110 *TF:* 800-879-2247 ■ *Web:* www.bulklift.com	847-428-6059	428-7180	67
BLI (Big Lots Inc) 300 Phillipi Rd ... Columbus OH 43228 *NYSE: BIG* ■ *TF:* 877-998-1697 ■ *Web:* www.biglots.com	614-278-6800	278-8322	791
Blickman Inc 500 US Hwy 46 E ... Clifton NJ 07011 *Web:* www.blickman.com	973-330-0557		475
Blind Center, The 1001 N Bruce St ... Las Vegas NV 89101 *TF:* 800-922-9334 ■ *Web:* www.blindcenter.org	702-642-6000		34
Blind Tiger Brewery & Restaurant 417 SW 37th St ... Topeka KS 66611 *Web:* www.blindtiger.com	785-267-2739	267-7527	671
Blinn College 902 College Ave ... Brenham TX 77833 **Fax:* Admissions ■ *Web:* www.blinn.edu	979-830-4000	830-4110*	162
Blinn Farrell & Co 60 Bailey Blvd ... Haverhill MA 01830 *Web:* blinnfarrell.com	978-372-8518		2
Blish-Mize Co 223 S Fifth St ... Atchison KS 66002 *TF:* 800-995-0525 ■ *Web:* www.blishmize.com	913-367-1250	367-0667	351
Bliss & Nyitray Inc 800 Douglas Rd Ste 300 ... Coral Gables FL 33134 *Web:* www.bniengineers.com	305-442-7086		261
Bliss Clearing Niagara (BCN) 1004 E State St ... Hastings MI 49058 *TF:* 800-642-5477 ■ *Web:* www.bcntechserv.com	269-948-3300	948-3313	456
Bliss Communications Inc PO Box 5001 ... Janesville WI 53547 *Web:* www.blissnet.net	608-754-3311		643
Bliss Direct Media 641 15Th Ave NE ... Saint Joseph MN 56374 *TF:* 800-578-7947 ■ *Web:* www.blissdirect.com	320-271-1600		387
Bliss Mcknight Inc 2801 E Empire ... Bloomington IL 61704 *Web:* blissmcknight.com	309-663-1393		390
Bliss Triune Enterprises Llc 4595 Mt Vernon Dr ... Los Angeles CA 90043 *Web:* blisstriune.com	323-291-6607		226
Blissfield Manufacturing Co 626 Depot St ... Blissfield MI 49228 *TF Cust Svc:* 800-626-1772 ■ *Web:* www.blissfield.com	517-486-2121		14
Blistex Inc 1800 Swift Dr ... Oak Brook IL 60523 *TF Cust Svc:* 800-837-1800 ■ *Web:* www.blistex.com	800-837-1800		582
Blithewold Mansion Gardens & Arboretum 101 Ferry Rd Rt 114 ... Bristol RI 02809 *Web:* www.blithewold.org	401-253-2707	253-0412	97
Blitman & King Llp 16 Main St W Ste 500 ... Rochester NY 14614 *Web:* www.bklawyers.com	585-232-5600		445
Blitt & Gaines Pc 661 Glenn Ave ... Wheeling IL 60090 *TF:* 888-920-0620 ■ *Web:* www.blittandgaines.com	847-403-4900		428
Blizzard Internet Marketing Inc 1001 Grand Ave Ste 005 ... Glenwood Springs CO 81601 *TF:* 888-840-5893 ■ *Web:* www.blizzardinternet.com	970-928-7875	928-7874	225
BLM (Bureau of Land Management) 1849 C St NW Rm 5665 ... Washington DC 20240 *TF:* 800-246-8101 ■ *Web:* www.blm.gov	202-208-3801	208-5242	340-13
Bloch Industries 140 Commerce Dr ... Rochester NY 14623 *TF:* 800-499-7871 ■ *Web:* www.blochindustries.com	585-334-9600		115
Block & Company Inc 1111 S Wheeling Rd ... Wheeling IL 60090 *Web:* www.blockandcompany.com	847-537-7200		567
Block Communications Inc 405 Madison Ave Ste 2100 ... Toledo OH 43604 *Web:* www.blockcommunications.com	419-724-6212		360-3
Block Engineering Inc 377 Simarano Dr ... Marlborough MA 01752 *Web:* www.blockeng.com	508-251-3100		419
Block Hawley Commercial Real Estate Services LLC 16253 Swingley Ridge Rd Ste 150 ... Chesterfield MO 63017 *Web:* www.blockllc.com/blockhawley	636-534-2900		652
Block Insurance Agency Inc 2333 Highland St ... Allentown PA 18104 *Web:* blockins.com	610-433-4131	433-1531	390
Block Iron & Supply Co Po Box 557 ... Oshkosh WI 54903 *Web:* www.blockiron.com	920-231-8645		351
Block Landsman 33 N LaSalle St Ste 1400 ... Chicago IL 60602 *Web:* www.block-landsman.com	312-251-1144		445
Block Scientific Inc 1620 Ocean Ave Unit 3 ... Bohemia NY 11716 *Web:* www.blockscientific.com	631-589-1118		475
Block Steel Corp 6101 Oakton St ... Skokie IL 60077 *Web:* www.blocksteel.com	847-966-3000	966-5906	723
Block Vision Holdings Corp 120 W Fayette St Ste 700 ... Baltimore MD 21201 *Web:* www.blockvision.com	410-752-0121		393
Blocker & Wallace Service LLC 1472 Rogers Ave ... Memphis TN 38114 *TF:* 800-843-0551 ■ *Web:* www.blockerandwallace.com	901-274-0708		791
Blodgett Supply Co Inc 100 Ave D PO Box 759 ... Williston VT 05495 *TF:* 888-888-3424 ■ *Web:* www.blodgettsupply.com	802-864-9831	229-5105	38
Bloedel Reserve, The 7571 NE Dolphin Dr ... Bainbridge Island WA 98110 *Web:* bloedelreserve.org	206-842-7631		97
Bloedorn Lumber Company Inc PO Box 1077 ... Torrington WY 82240 *Web:* www.bloedornlumber.com	307-532-2151		364
BlogHer Inc 805 Veterans Blvd Ste 305 ... Redwood City CA 94063 *Web:* www.blogher.com	650-363-2564		387
Blogster.com LLC 20545 Ctr Ridge Rd Ste 135 ... Rocky River OH 44116 *Web:* www.blogster.com	440-333-7805	333-7806	387
Blohm Creative Partners 1331 E Grand River Ave Ste 210 ... East Lansing MI 48823 *TF:* 800-261-1537 ■ *Web:* www.blohmcreative.com	517-333-4900		7
Blommer Chocolate Co 600 W Kinzie St ... Chicago IL 60610 *TF:* 800-621-1606 ■ *Web:* www.blommer.com	312-226-7700		296-8
Blonder Home Accents 3950 Prospect Ave ... Cleveland OH 44115	216-431-3561		802
Blonder Tongue Laboratories Inc 1 Jake Brown Rd ... Old Bridge NJ 08857 *NYSE: BDR* ■ *TF:* 877-407-8033 ■ *Web:* www.blondertongue.com	732-679-4000	679-4353	647
Blood & Marrow Transplant Group of Georgia (BMTGA) 5670 Peachtree Dunwoody Rd Ste 1000 ... Atlanta GA 30342 *Web:* www.bmtga.com	404-255-1930	255-1939	769
Blood Assurance Inc 705 E Fourth St ... Chattanooga TN 37403 *TF:* 800-962-0628 ■ *Web:* www.bloodassurance.org	423-756-0966		89
Blood Bank Computer Systems Inc 1002 15th St SW Ste 120 ... Auburn WA 98001 *TF:* 800-763-8352 ■ *Web:* www.bbcsinc.com	253-333-0046		476
Blood Bank of Alaska 4000 Laurel St ... Anchorage AK 99508 *Web:* www.bloodbankofalaska.org	907-222-5600	563-1371	89
Blood Bank of Delmarva 100 Hygeia Dr ... Newark DE 19713 *TF:* 800-548-4009 ■ *Web:* www.delmarvablood.org	302-737-8405	737-8233	89
Blood Bank of Hawaii 2043 Dillingham Blvd ... Honolulu HI 96819 *TF:* 800-372-9966 ■ *Web:* www.bbh.org	808-845-9966		89
Blood Bank of the Redwoods 2324 Bethards Dr ... Santa Rosa CA 95405 *TF:* 888-393-4483 ■ *Web:* www.bloodcenters.org	707-545-1222		89
Blood Centers of the Pacific 250 Bush St Ste 136 ... San Francisco CA 94104 *TF:* 888-393-4483 ■ *Web:* www.bloodcenters.org	415-567-6400		89
Blood Ctr of Northcentral Wisconsin 211 Forest St ... Wausau WI 54403	715-842-0761		89
Blood Ctr, The 2609 Canal St ... New Orleans LA 70112 *TF:* 800-862-5663 ■ *Web:* www.thebloodcenter.org	504-524-1322	592-1580	89
Blood Donor Ctr at Presbyterian/St Luke's Medical Ctr 1719 E 19th Ave ... Denver CO 80218 *TF:* 800-231-2222 ■ *Web:* www.pslmc.com	303-839-6000		769
Blood Group Alliance Inc 1300 Division Rd Ste 102 ... West Warwick RI 02893	401-381-0600	381-0016	194
Blood Systems Laboratories 2424 W Erie Dr ... Tempe AZ 85282 *TF:* 800-288-2199 ■ *Web:* www.bloodsystemslaboratories.org	602-343-7000		417
BloodCenter of Wisconsin 638 N 18th St ... Milwaukee WI 53233 *TF:* 877-232-4376 ■ *Web:* www.bcw.edu	414-933-5000		89
Blood-Horse Magazine PO Box 911088 ... Lexington KY 40591 *TF:* 800-866-2361 ■ *Web:* www.bloodhorse.com	859-278-2361	276-4450	457-14
Bloodroot 85 Ferris St ... Bridgeport CT 06605 *Web:* www.bloodroot.com	203-576-9168		671
BloodSource 1608 Q St ... Sacramento CA 95811 *TF:* 800-995-4420 ■ *Web:* www.bloodsource.org	916-456-1500		89
Bloom Engineering Co Inc 5460 Curry Rd ... Pittsburgh PA 15236 *Web:* www.bloomeng.com	412-653-3500	653-2253	318
Bloomberg LP 731 Lexington Ave ... New York NY 10022 *Web:* www.bloomberg.com	212-318-2000	893-5000	530
Bloomfield Bakers 16100 Foothill Blvd ... Azusa CA 91702	626-610-2253		345
Bloomfield College 467 Franklin St ... Bloomfield NJ 07003 *TF:* 800-848-4555 ■ *Web:* www.bloomfield.edu	973-748-9000	748-0916	166
Bloomfield Public Library 90 Broad St ... Bloomfield NJ 07003 *Web:* bplnj.org	973-566-6200		434-3
Bloomfield Township Public Library 1099 Lone Pine Rd ... Bloomfield Hills MI 48302 *TF:* 800-318-2596 ■ *Web:* www.btpl.org	248-642-5800		434-3
Blooming Color Inc 230 Eisenhower Ln N ... Lombard IL 60148 *TF:* 800-709-8773 ■ *Web:* www.bloomingcolor.com	630-705-9200		92
Bloomingdale's 1000 Third Ave ... New York NY 10022 *TF:* 800-777-0000 ■ *Web:* www.bloomingdales.com	212-705-2000	705-2805	229
Bloomington City Hall 401 N Morton St ... Bloomington IN 47404 *TF:* 800-772-1213 ■ *Web:* www.bloomington.in.gov	812-339-2261	349-3570	337
Bloomington Convention & Visitors Bureau (BCVB) 7900 International Dr Ste 990 ... Bloomington MN 55425 *TF:* 800-346-4289 ■ *Web:* www.bloomingtonmn.org	952-858-8500	858-8854	206
Bloomington Monroe County Convention Ctr 302 S College Ave ... Bloomington IN 47403 *Web:* www.bloomingtonconvention.com	812-336-3681	349-2981	205
Bloomington Public Library 205 E Olive St ... Bloomington IL 61701 *Web:* blpl.ent.sirsi.net	309-828-6091		434-3
Bloomington Speedway 5185 S Fairfax Rd ... Bloomington IN 47401 *Web:* www.bloomingtonspeedway.com	812-824-7400	824-7400	515
Bloomington/Monroe County Convention & Visitors Bureau 2855 N Walnut St ... Bloomington IN 47404 *TF:* 800-800-0037 ■ *Web:* www.visitbloomington.com	812-334-8900	334-2344	206
Bloomington-Normal Area Convention & Visitors Bureau 3201 CIRA Dr Ste 201 ... Bloomington IL 61704 *TF:* 800-433-8226 ■ *Web:* www.visitbn.org	309-665-0033	661-0743	206

	City	State	Zip	Phone	Fax	Class
Bloomington-Normal Seating Co 2031 Warehouse Rd *Web:* www.bnseating.com	Normal	IL	61761	309-663-5350		59
BloomNation LLC 8889 W Olympic Blvd *TF:* 877-702-5666 ■ *Web:* www.bloomnation.com	Beverly Hills	CA	90211	877-702-5666		292
BloomNet Inc 1 Old Country Rd Ste 500 *TF:* 866-256-6663 ■ *Web:* www.mybloomnet.net	Carle Place	NY	11514	866-256-6663		387
Bloomsburg Area Chamber of Commerce 238 Market St *TF:* 800-275-6401 ■ *Web:* www.bloomsburg.org	Bloomsburg	PA	17815	570-784-2522	784-2661	139
Bloomsburg Carpet Industries Inc 4999 Columbia Blvd *TF:* 800-233-8773 ■ *Web:* www.bloomsburgcarpet.com	Bloomsburg	PA	17815	570-784-9188		131
Bloomsburg University 400 E Second St **Fax:* Admissions ■ *TF:* 888-651-6117 ■ *Web:* www.bloomu.edu	Bloomsburg	PA	17815	570-389-3900	389-4795*	166
Bloomsbury Bistro 509 W Whitaker Mill Rd Ste 101 *Web:* www.bloomsburybistro.com	Raleigh	NC	27608	919-834-9011	834-9096	671
Blossman Gas Inc 4601 Hanshaw Rd **Fax Area Code:* 518 ■ *TF:* 800-256-7762 ■ *Web:* www.blossmangas.com	Ocean Springs	MS	39564	228-872-8747	483-0141*	316
Blossman Oil Company Inc 711 E Boston St *Web:* www.blossmanoil.com	Covington	LA	70433	985-898-2663		324
Blossom Bucket, The 13305 Wooster St NW	North Lawrence	OH	44666	330-834-2551		292
Blossom Chevrolet Inc 1850 N Shadeland Ave *Web:* www.blossomchevrolet.com	Indianapolis	IN	46219	317-357-1121		57
Blossom Music Ctr Tickets 1145 W Steels Corners Rd *TF:* 800-745-3000 ■ *Web:* www.livenation.com	Cuyahoga Falls	OH	44223	330-920-8040		572
Blossom Restaurant 171 E Bay St *Web:* magnolias-blossom-cypress.com	Charleston	SC	29401	843-722-9200		671
Blough Tech Inc 119 S Broad St *TF:* 800-957-0554 ■ *Web:* www.bloughtech.com	Cairo	GA	39828	229-377-8825		180
Blount County 341 Ct St *TF:* 800-458-9529 ■ *Web:* www.blounttn.org	Maryville	TN	37804	865-273-5700	273-5705	338
Blount County 220 Second Ave E Rm 106 *Web:* www.co.blount.al.us	Oneonta	AL	35121	205-625-4160		338
Blount County Chamber of Commerce 201 S Washington St *TF:* 855-257-3964 ■ *Web:* www.blountchamber.com	Maryville	TN	37804	865-983-2241	984-1386	139
Blount County Public Library 508 N Cusick St *Web:* www.blountlibrary.org	Maryville	TN	37804	865-982-0981		434-3
Blount County Schools 204 Second Ave E *Web:* www.blountboe.net	Oneonta	AL	35121	205-625-4102		685
Blount County-Oneonta Chamber of Commerce 225 Second Ave E *Web:* bocc.publishpath.com	Oneonta	AL	35121	205-274-2153	274-2099	139
Blount Hospitality House 610 Madison St *Web:* www.blounthospitalityhouse.org	Huntsville	AL	35801	256-534-7014		372
Blount International Inc 4909 SE International Way *Web:* www.blount.com	Portland	OR	97222	503-653-8881		360-3
Blount Mansion 200 W Hill Ave *Web:* www.blountmansion.org	Knoxville	TN	37901	865-525-2375	546-5315	50-3
Blount Memorial Hospital 907 E Lamar Alexander Pkwy *TF:* 800-448-0219 ■ *Web:* www.blountmemorial.org	Maryville	TN	37804	865-983-7211		374-3
Blount Outdoor Products Group 4909 SE International Way *Web:* blount.com	Portland	OR	97222	503-653-8881		429
Blount Seafood Corp 630 Currant Rd *TF Hotline:* 800-274-2526 ■ *Web:* www.blountseafood.com	Fall River	MA	02720	774-888-1300	888-1399	296-14
Blount Small Ship Adventures 461 Water St *TF:* 800-556-7450 ■ *Web:* blountsmallshipadventures.com	Warren	RI	02885	401-247-0955		220
Blow Fly Inn 1201 Washington Ave *Web:* blow-fly-inn.com	Gulfport	MS	39507	228-265-8225		671
Blow Molded Products Inc 4720 Felspar St *Web:* www.blowmoldedproducts.com	Riverside	CA	92509	951-360-6055		608
Blow Molded Specialties Inc 222 Bronder Dr *Web:* www.blowmolded.com	Foley	MN	56329	320-968-7251		596
Blower Application Company Inc N 114 W 19125 Clinton Dr *TF:* 800-959-0880 ■ *Web:* www.bloapco.com	Germantown	WI	53022	262-255-5580	255-3446	386
Blowfish 355 Santana Row Ste 1010 *Web:* www.blowfishsushi.com	San Jose	CA	95128	408-345-3848		671
Blowfish Direct LLC 11130 Holder St *TF:* 877-725-6934 ■ *Web:* www.blowfishshoes.com	Cypress	CA	90630	877-725-6934		690
Blowing Rock Chamber of Commerce PO Box 406 *TF:* 877-750-4636 ■ *Web:* www.blowingrock.com	Blowing Rock	NC	28605	828-295-7851		139
BLR (Business & Legal Reports Inc) 141 Mill Rock Rd E *TF:* 800-727-5257 ■ *Web:* www.blr.com	Old Saybrook	CT	06475	860-510-0100	510-7225	637-9
BLT Enterprises Inc 501 Spectrum Cir *Web:* www.blt-enterprises.com	Oxnard	CA	93030	805-278-8220		358
BLT Prime 111 E 22nd St *TF:* 800-855-2880 ■ *Web:* bltrestaurants.com	New York	NY	10010	212-995-8500		671
Blu 4 Avery St 4th Fl *Web:* www.blurestaurant.com	Boston	MA	02111	617-375-8550		671
Bluberi Gaming & Technologies inc 2120 Rue Letendre *Web:* www.bluberi.com	Drummondville	QC	J2C7E9	819-475-5155		133
Blue & Co 12800 N Meridian St Ste 400 *TF:* 800-717-2583 ■ *Web:* www.blueandco.com	Carmel	IN	46032	317-848-8920	573-2458	2
Blue & Gray Bar & Grill 2 Baltimore St	Gettysburg	PA	17325	717-334-1999		671
Blue 9 Capital 145 Hudson St Ste 401 *Web:* www.blue9capital.com	New York	NY	10013	212-798-0400		690
Blue Adobe Grille 10885 N Frank Lloyd Wright Blvd *Web:* www.blueadobegrille.com	Scottsdale	AZ	85259	480-314-0550		671
Blue Banner Company Inc 2601 Third St *Web:* pe.com	Riverside	CA	92507	951-686-2422		315-2
Blue Barn Theatre 1106 S Tenth St *Web:* www.bluebarn.org	Omaha	NE	68102	402-345-1576		572
Blue Beacon International Inc 500 Graves Blvd *Web:* www.bluebeacon.com	Salina	KS	67401	785-825-2221	825-0801	62-1
Blue Bell Creameries Inc PO Box 1807 *Web:* www.bluebell.com	Brenham	TX	77834	979-836-7977		296-25
Blue Bird Bistro 1700 Summit St *Web:* bluebirdbistro.com	Kansas City	MO	64108	816-221-7559		671
Blue Bird Corp 402 Blue Bird Blvd *Web:* www.blue-bird.com	Fort Valley	GA	31030	478-825-2021		516
Blue Bird Inc 10135 Mill Rd *TF:* 800-828-4106 ■ *Web:* bluebirdpears.net	Peshastin	WA	98847	509-548-1700	548-0288	315-3
Blue Box Group Inc 119 Pine St Ste 200 *TF:* 800-613-4305 ■ *Web:* www.blueboxcloud.com	Seattle	WA	98101	800-613-4305		387
Blue C Communications 3183-C Airway Ave *Web:* www.bluecusa.com	Costa Mesa	CA	92626	714-540-5700		7
Blue Cactus Bar & Grill 2 ByWard Market *TF:* 800-665-2274 ■ *Web:* www.bluecactusbarandgrill.com	Ottawa	ON	K1N7A1	613-241-7061		671
Blue Canoe Inc 390 Lake Benbow Dr *Web:* www.bluecanoe.com	Garberville	CA	95542	707-923-1373		157-2
Blue Canoe Properties LLC 2120 16th Ave S	Birmingham	AL	35205	205-918-0921		652
Blue Care Network of Michigan 20500 Civic Ctr Dr **Fax:* Cust Svc ■ *TF:* 800-662-6667 ■ *Web:* bcbsm.com	Southfield	MI	48076	248-799-6400	799-6969*	391-3
Blue Cat Design Mastwoods Rd *TF:* 888-258-3228 ■ *Web:* www.bluecatdesign.com	Port Hope	ON	L1A3V5	905-753-1017	753-2777	7
Blue Chip Casino Inc 777 Blue Chip Dr *TF:* 888-879-7711 ■ *Web:* www.bluechipcasino.com	Michigan City	IN	46360	219-879-7711		133
Blue Chip Computer Systems 6733 S Sepulveda Blvd Ste 150 *Web:* www.bccs.com	Los Angeles	CA	90045	310-410-0126		177
Blue Chip Venture Co 312 Walnut St Ste 1120 *TF:* 800-719-4664 ■ *Web:* www.bcvc.com	Cincinnati	OH	45202	513-723-2300		792
Blue Corn Cafe 716 Ninth St *Web:* bluecorncafedurham.com	Durham	NC	27705	919-286-9600		671
Blue Cross & Blue Shield Assn 225 N Michigan Ave *TF:* 888-630-2583 ■ *Web:* www.bcbs.com	Chicago	IL	60601	312-297-6000		49-9
Blue Cross & Blue Shield of Alabama 450 Riverchase Pkwy E *TF:* 800-292-8868 ■ *Web:* www.bcbsal.org	Birmingham	AL	35244	205-988-2200		391-3
Blue Cross & Blue Shield of Kansas City 2301 Main St **Fax:* Hum Res ■ *TF:* 800-892-6048 ■ *Web:* www.bluekc.com	Kansas City	MO	64108	816-395-2222	395-2726*	391-3
Blue Cross & Blue Shield of Michigan 600 Lafayette Blvd E *TF:* 855-237-3501 ■ *Web:* www.bcbsm.com	Detroit	MI	48226	313-225-9000		391-3
Blue Cross & Blue Shield of Mississippi PO Box 1043 *TF:* 800-222-8046 ■ *Web:* www.bcbsms.com	Jackson	MS	39215	601-932-3704	939-7035	391-3
Blue Cross & Blue Shield of Montana 560 N Pk Ave PO Box 4309 *TF:* 800-447-7828 ■ *Web:* www.bcbsmt.com	Helena	MT	59604	406-437-5000		391-3
Blue Cross & Blue Shield of Nebraska 1919 Aksarben Dr PO Box 3248 *TF:* 800-422-2763 ■ *Web:* www.nebraskablue.com	Omaha	NE	68180	402-982-7000		391-3
Blue Cross & Blue Shield of New Mexico PO Box 27630 *TF:* 800-835-8699 ■ *Web:* www.bcbsnm.com	Albuquerque	NM	87125	505-291-3500		391-3
Blue Cross & Blue Shield of North Carolina 1965 Ivory Creek Blvd *TF Cust Svc:* 800-446-8053 ■ *Web:* www.bcbsnc.com	Durham	NC	27702	919-489-7431		391-3
Blue Cross & Blue Shield of Oklahoma 1215 S Boulder Ave *TF Cust Svc:* 800-942-5837 ■ *Web:* www.bcbsok.com	Tulsa	OK	74119	918-560-3500		391-3
Blue Cross & Blue Shield of Rhode Island 500 Exchange St *TF:* 800-637-3718 ■ *Web:* www.bcbsri.com	Providence	RI	02903	401-459-1000		391-3
Blue Cross & Blue Shield of Texas Inc 1001 E Lookout Dr *TF:* 800-521-2227 ■ *Web:* www.bcbstx.com	Richardson	TX	75082	972-766-6900		391-3
Blue Cross & Blue Shield of Vermont 445 Industrial Ln *TF Cust Svc:* 800-247-2583 ■ *Web:* www.bcbsvt.com	Montpelier	VT	05602	802-223-6131		391-3
Blue Cross Blue Shield of Arizona 2444 W Las Palmaritas Dr **Fax:* Cust Svc ■ *TF:* 800-232-2345 ■ *Web:* www.azblue.com	Phoenix	AZ	85021	602-864-4400	864-4041*	391-3
Blue Cross Blue Shield of Delaware PO Box 1991 *TF:* 800-572-4400 ■ *Web:* www.highmarkbcbsde.com	Wilmington	DE	19899	800-876-7639		391-3
Blue Cross Blue Shield of Georgia 3350 Peachtree Rd NE *TF Cust Svc:* 800-441-2273 ■ *Web:* www.bcbsga.com	Atlanta	GA	30326	404-842-8000		391-3
Blue Cross Blue Shield of Illinois 300 E Randolph St *TF:* 800-972-8382 ■ *Web:* www.bcbsil.com	Chicago	IL	60601	312-653-6000		391-3
Blue Cross Blue Shield of Kansas 1133 SW Topeka Blvd *TF:* 800-432-0216 ■ *Web:* www.bcbsks.com	Topeka	KS	66629	785-291-7000	290-0711	391-3
Blue Cross Blue Shield of Louisiana 5525 Reitz Ave *TF:* 800-599-2583 ■ *Web:* bcbsla.com	Baton Rouge	LA	70898	225-295-3307	295-2054	391-3
Blue Cross Blue Shield of Massachusetts 401 Pk Dr **Fax Area Code:* 800 ■ **Fax:* PR ■ *TF:* 800-262-2583 ■ *Web:* www.bluecrossma.com	Boston	MA	02215	617-246-5000	636-9494*	391-3

	Phone	Fax	Class

Blue Cross Blue Shield of North Dakota
4510 13th Ave S .... Fargo ND 58121 701-282-1100 391-3
TF: 800-342-4718 ■ *Web:* www.bcbsnd.com
Blue Cross Blue Shield of Wyoming
4000 House Ave .... Cheyenne WY 82001 307-634-1393 778-8582 391-3
TF: 800-851-9145 ■ *Web:* www.bcbswy.com
Blue Cross of California
2 Gannett Dr .... South Portland ME 04106 800-482-0966 438-6811* 391-3
**Fax Area Code:* 888 ■ *TF:* 800-999-3643 ■ *Web:* www.anthem.com
Blue Cross of Idaho 3000 E Pine Ave .... Meridian ID 83642 208-345-4550 331-7311 391-3
TF: 800-274-4018 ■ *Web:* www.bcidaho.com
Blue Cross of Northeastern Pennsylvania
19 N Main St .... Wilkes-Barre PA 18711 800-577-3742 200-6710* 391-3
**Fax Area Code:* 570 ■ *TF Cust Svc:* 800-577-3742 ■ *Web:* www.bcnepa.com
Blue Danube Restaurant
Elm & Adeline Sts .... Trenton NJ 08611 609-393-6133 393-1596 671
Web: www.bluedanuberestaurant.net
Blue Diamond Growers 1802 C St .... Sacramento CA 95811 916-442-0771 10-10
Web: www.bluediamond.com
Blue Dog Printing & Design
1039 Andrew Dr .... West Chester PA 19380 610-430-7992 627
Web: getbluedog.com
Blue Dolphin Energy Co
801 Travis St Ste 2100 .... Houston TX 77002 713-568-4725 536
OTC: BDCO
Blue Door Consulting
21 W New York Ave .... Oshkosh WI 54901 920-230-2583 194
Web: www.bluedoorconsulting.com
Blue Dot Energy Services LLC
Route 76 E .... Bridgeport WV 26330 304-842-3829 23
Web: www.bluedotinc.com
Blue Earth County 204 S Fifth St .... Mankato MN 56001 507-304-4000 338
TF: 800-222-1222 ■ *Web:* www.co.blue-earth.mn.us
Blue Fin 1567 Broadway .... New York NY 10036 212-918-1400 671
Web: bluefinnyc.com
Blue Fire Capital LLC
311 S Wacker Dr Ste 2000 .... Chicago IL 60606 312-242-0500 690
Web: www.bluefirecap.com
Blue Fountain Media Inc
102 Madison Ave 2nd Fl .... New York NY 10016 212-260-1978 225
TF: 800-278-0816 ■ *Web:* www.bluefountainmedia.com
Blue Frog Solutions Inc
555 S Andrews Ave Ste 202 .... Pompano Beach FL 33069 954-788-0700 177
Blue Garnet Assoc LLC
8055 W Manchester Ave Ste 430 .... Playa Del Rey CA 90293 310-439-1930 194
Web: www.bluegarnet.net
Blue Generation Div of M Rubin & Sons Inc
34-01 38th Ave .... Long Island NY 11101 718-361-2800 361-2680 155-19
TF: 888-336-4687 ■ *Web:* www.bluegeneration.com
Blue Giant Equipment Corp
85 Heart Lake Rd S .... Brampton ON L6W3K2 905-457-3900 358
TF: 800-668-7078 ■ *Web:* www.bluegiant.com
Blue Ginger 583 Washington St .... Wellesley MA 02482 781-283-5790 671
TF: 800-522-6379 ■ *Web:* www.ming.com
Blue Goose Cantina 4757 W Pk Blvd .... Plano TX 75093 972-596-8882 671
Web: www.bluegoosecantina.com
Blue Granite Inc
2750 Old Centre Rd Ste 150 .... Portage MI 49024 877-817-0736 180
TF: 877-817-0736 ■ *Web:* www.blue-granite.com
Blue Grass Airport 4000 Terminal Dr .... Lexington KY 40510 859-425-3100 233-1822 27
TF: 800-800-4000 ■ *Web:* www.bluegrassairport.com
Blue Grass Chemical Specialties LP
895 Industrial Blvd .... New Albany IN 47150 812-948-1115 145
Blue Grass Energy Co-op Corp
1201 Lexington Rd .... Nicholasville KY 40356 859-885-4191 885-2854 245
TF: 888-546-4243 ■ *Web:* www.bgenergy.com
Blue Grass Quality Meats
2645 Commerce Dr .... Crescent Springs KY 41017 859-331-7100 331-7100 296-26
Web: www.bluegrassqualitymeats.com
Blue Grass Regional Library
104 E Sixth St .... Columbia TN 38401 931-388-9282 981-4587* 434-3
**Fax Area Code:* 865 ■ *TF:* 888-345-5575
Blue Grass Regional Mental Health-Mental Retardation Board Inc
1351 Newtown Pike Bldg 1 .... Lexington KY 40511 859-253-1686 255-4866 48-6
TF: 800-928-8000 ■ *Web:* www.bluegrass.org
Blue Grass Stockyard
375 Lisle Industrial Ave PO Box 1023 .... Lexington KY 40588 859-255-7701 255-5495 446
TF: 800-621-3972 ■ *Web:* www.bgstockyards.com
Blue Grass Tours Inc
817 Enterprise Dr .... Lexington KY 40510 859-233-2152 760
TF: 800-448-5728 ■ *Web:* www.bluegrasstours.com
Blue Grotto 210 Atwells Ave .... Providence RI 02903 401-272-9030 671
TF: 800-294-7709 ■ *Web:* www.bluegrottorestaurant.com
Blue Harbor Resort & Conference Center
725 Blue Harbor Dr .... Sheboygan WI 53081 920 452 2900 370
Web: www.blueharborresort.com
Blue Haven Resort 1851 Lake Shore Dr .... Branson MO 65616 417-334-3917 707
Web: www.branson.com
Blue Heaven 729 Thomas St .... Key West FL 33040 305-296-8666 671
Web: www.blueheavenkw.com
Blue Hill 75 Washington Pl .... New York NY 10011 212-539-1776 671
Web: bluehillfarm.com
Blue Hills Hospital 500 Vine St .... Hartford CT 06112 860-293-6400 726
Web: www.ct.gov
Blue Hills Reservation 695 Hillside St .... Milton MA 02186 617-698-1802 565
Web: www.mass.gov
Blue Hive Inc 7 Coppage Dr .... Worcester MA 01603 508-581-9560 8
Web: www.blue-hive.com
Blue Horizon Hotel 1225 Robson St .... Vancouver BC V6E1C3 604-688-1411 688-4461 379
TF: 800-663-1333 ■ *Web:* www.bluehorizonhotel.com
Blue Iceberg LLC
146 W 29th St Studio 11W .... New York NY 10001 212-337-9920 7
Web: www.blue-iceberg.com
Blue Iguana 165 SW Temple .... Salt Lake City UT 84101 801-533-8900 671
Web: www.blueiguanarestaurant.net
Blue Interactive Agency
608 SW Fourth Ave .... Fort Lauderdale FL 33315 954-779-2801 5
TF: 800-311-8252 ■ *Web:* www.blueinteractiveagency.com

	Phone	Fax	Class

Blue Ion LLC 73 1/2 Wentworth St .... Charleston SC 29401 843-727-0310 180
Web: www.blueion.com
Blue Jeans Network Inc
516 Clyde Ave .... Mountain View CA 94043 408-550-2828 387
Web: www.bluejeans.com
Blue Knob State Park 124 Pk Rd .... Imler PA 16655 814-276-3576 565
Web: www.dcnr.state.pa.us
Blue Lakes Charters & Tours
12154 N Saginaw Rd .... Clio MI 48420 810-686-4287 686-9772 107
TF: 800-282-4287 ■ *Web:* www.bluelakes.com
Blue Lan Group Inc 79 Sandwich Rd .... Plymouth MA 02360 508-747-0433 317
TF: 800-573-1874 ■ *Web:* www.bluelangroup.com
Blue Lance Inc 410 Pierce St .... Houston TX 77002 713-255-4800 178-12
TF: 800-856-2583 ■ *Web:* www.bluelance.com
Blue Licks Battlefield State Resort Park
10299 Maysville Rd .... Carlisle KY 40311 859-289-5507 565
TF: 800-443-7008 ■ *Web:* www.parks.ky.gov
Blue Line Engineering Co
525 E Colorado Ave .... Colorado Springs CO 80903 719-447-1373 256
Web: www.bluelineengineering.com
Blue Lion Restaurant
160 N Millward St .... Jackson WY 83001 307-733-3912 671
Web: www.bluelionrestaurant.com
Blue Lotus Creative
7971 Columbia St .... Vancouver BC V5Z2X5 604-306-8701 195
Web: www.bluelotuscreative.com
Blue Lotus Sidc Llc
509 Village Rd W .... Princeton Junction NJ 08550 609-716-4615 180
TF: 800-319-8862 ■ *Web:* www.bluelotussidc.com
Blue Magnet Partners LLC
11030 Jones Bridge Rd Ste 206 .... Alpharetta GA 30022 770-265-9858 194
Blue Marlin 101 N Hamilton St .... Madison WI 53703 608-255-2255 671
Blue Marlin 1200 Lincoln St .... Columbia SC 29201 803-799-3838 671
Web: www.bluemarlincolumbia.com
Blue Mermaid Cafe
119 Billy Mitchell Blvd .... Brownsville TX 78521 956-544-2157 671
Blue Mermaid Chowder House & Bar
471 Jefferson St .... San Francisco CA 94109 415-771-2222 671
Web: www.argonauthotel.com
Blue Mesa Grill
1600 S University Dr .... Fort Worth TX 76107 817-332-6372 671
Web: www.bluemesagrill.com
Blue Mine Group
12626 High Bluff Dr Ste 450 .... San Diego CA 92130 858-792-2633 225
Blue Moon Bar & Grill
2535 University Ave .... Madison WI 53705 608-233-0441 671
Web: www.bluemoonbar.com
Blue Moon Fish Co
4405 W Tradewinds Ave .... Lauderdale-by-the-Sea FL 33308 954-267-9888 267-9006 671
Web: www.bluemoonfishco.com
Blue Moon Hotel 944 Collins Ave .... Miami Beach FL 33139 305-673-2262 534-1546 379
TF: 800-553-7739 ■ *Web:* www.bluemoonhotel.com
Blue Moon Restaurant
35 Baltimore Ave .... Rehoboth Beach DE 19971 302-227-6515 671
TF: 800-317-3222 ■ *Web:* www.bluemoonrehoboth.com
Blue Mound State Park
4350 Mounds Pk Rd .... Blue Mounds WI 53517 608-437-5711 565
Web: dnr.wi.gov
Blue Mounds State Park 1410 161st St .... Luverne MN 56156 507-283-1307 283-1306 565
TF: 888-646-6367 ■ *Web:* www.dnr.state.mn.us
Blue Mountain Air Inc
707 Aldridge Rd .... Vacaville CA 95688 800-889-2085 610
TF: 800-889-2085 ■ *Web:* www.bluemountainair.net
Blue Mountain Arts Inc PO Box 4549 .... Boulder CO 80306 303-449-0536 130
TF Sales: 800-545-8573 ■ *Web:* www.sps.com
Blue Mountain College
PO Box 160 .... Blue Mountain MS 38610 662-685-4771 685-4776* 166
**Fax:* Admissions ■ *TF:* 800-235-0136 ■ *Web:* www.bmc.edu
Blue Mountain Community College
2411 NW Carden Ave PO Box 100 .... Pendleton OR 97801 541-276-1260 278-5871* 162
**Fax:* Admissions ■ *TF:* 888-441-7232 ■ *Web:* www.bluecc.edu
Blue Mountain Growers Inc
231 E Broadway Ave .... Milton-Freewater OR 97862 541-938-3391 315-3
Blue Mountain Quality Resources Inc
475 Rolling Ridge Dr Ste 200 .... State College PA 16801 814-234-2417 234-7077 177
TF: 800-982-2388 ■ *Web:* coolblue.com
Blue Mountain School District Inc
PO Box 188 .... Orwigsburg PA 17961 570-366-0515 685
Web: www.bmsd.org
Blue Mountain Wallcoverings Inc
15 Akron Rd .... Etobicoke ON M8W1T3 416-251-1678 002
Web: www.blmtn.com
Blue Nile 545 W Nine-Mile Rd .... Ferndale MI 48220 248-547-6699 671
TF: 800-275-8777 ■ *Web:* www.bluenilemi.com
Blue Nile Ethiopian Restaurant - Ann Arbor, The
221 E Washington St .... Ann Arbor MI 48104 734-998-4746 671
TF: 800-477-2757 ■ *Web:* www.bluenilemi.com
Blue Nile Inc 705 Fifth Ave S Ste 900 .... Seattle WA 98104 206-336-6700 410
NASDAQ: NILE ■ *TF:* 800-242-2728 ■ *Web:* www.bluenile.com
Blue North Fisheries Inc
2930 Westlake Ave N .... Seattle WA 98109 206-352-9252 352-9380 285
Web: bluenorth.com
Blue Ocean Press Inc
6299 NW 27th Way .... Fort Lauderdale FL 33309 954-973-1819 627
TF: 800-910-4283 ■ *Web:* www.blueoceanpress.com
Blue Owl Restaurant, The
6116 Second St .... Kimmswick MO 63053 636-464-3128 671
TF: 800-624-5426 ■ *Web:* www.theblueowl.com
Blue Parrot Bistro
35 Chambersburg St .... Gettysburg PA 17325 717-337-3739 671
Web: blueparrotbistro.com
Blue Parrot Inn 409 Angela St .... Key West FL 33040 305-296-0033 379
TF: 800-549-4430 ■ *Web:* www.blueparrotinn.com
Blue Parrott Bar & Grille
1934 W Sixth St .... Wilmington DE 19805 302-655-8990 655-9488 671
Web: www.blueparrotgrille.com
Blue Pillar Inc
9025 N River Rd Ste 150 .... Indianapolis IN 46240 888-234-3212 192
TF: 888-234-3212 ■ *Web:* bluepillar.com

				Phone	Fax	Class
Blue Plate Communications Inc PO Box 4214 *Web:* www.blueplate.com	Dedham	MA	02027	781-453-0330		636
Blue Plate, The 3218 Mission St *Web:* www.blueplatesf.com	San Francisco	CA	94110	415-282-6777		671
Blue Point Capital Partners 127 Public Sq Ste 5100 *Web:* www.bluepointcapital.com	Cleveland	OH	44114	216-535-4700		401
Blue Point Coastal Cuisine 565 Fifth Ave. *Web:* cohnrestaurants.com	San Diego	CA	92101	619-233-6623		671
Blue Point Grill 258 Nassau St *Web:* bluepointgrill.com	Princeton	NJ	08542	609-921-1211		671
Blue Point Grille 700 W St Clair Ave *TF:* 800-468-3571 ■ *Web:* hrcleveland.com	Cleveland	OH	44113	216-875-7827		671
Blue Print Automation Inc 16037 Innovation Dr. *Web:* www.blueprintautomation.com	South Chesterfield	VA	23834	804-520-5400		547
Blue Quill Angler Inc 1532 Bergen Pkwy *TF:* 800-435-5353 ■ *Web:* www.bluequillangler.com	Evergreen	CO	80439	303-674-4700		711
Blue Restaurant & Bar 206 N College St *Web:* www.bluecharlotte.com	Charlotte	NC	28202	704-927-2583		671
Blue Rhino Studio Inc 3277 Sun Dr. *Web:* www.rhinocentral.com	Eagan	MN	55121	651-287-0900		393
Blue Ribbon 97 Sullivan St *Web:* www.blueribbonrestaurants.com	New York	NY	10012	212-274-0404		671
Blue Ribbon Home Warranty Inc 95 S Wadsworth Blvd *TF:* 800-571-0475 ■ *Web:* blueribbonhomewarranty.com	Lakewood	CO	80226	303-986-3900	986-3152	367
Blue Ribbon Meats Inc 3316 W 67th Pl. *Web:* blueribbonmeats.com	Cleveland	OH	44102	216-631-8850		296-26
Blue Ribbon Products Fishng Tackl Dlr 1701 W Academy St *TF:* 800-334-9114 ■ *Web:* www.bettstackle.net	Fuquay Varina	NC	27526	919-552-2226		711
Blue Ribbon Tag & Label Corp 4035 N 29th Ave. *TF:* 800-433-4974 ■ *Web:* www.blueribbonlabel.com	Hollywood	FL	33020	954-922-9292	922-9977	413
Blue Ribbon Travel-american 3601 W 76th St Ste 190 *TF:* 800-626-5309 ■ *Web:* www.blueribbontravel.com	Minneapolis	MN	55435	952-835-2724		775
Blue Ridge Bank & Trust Co 4240 Blue Ridge Blvd Ste 100 *TF:* 800-569-4287 ■ *Web:* www.blueridgebank.com	Kansas City	MO	64133	816-358-5000		70
Blue Ridge Beverage Company Inc 44-46 Barley Dr *Web:* www.blueridgebeverage.com	Salem	VA	24153	540-380-2000		81-1
Blue Ridge Brewing Co 217 N Main St *Web:* www.blueridgebrewing.com	Greenville	SC	29601	864-232-4677	232-4680	671
Blue Ridge Builders Supply Inc 5221 Rockfish Gap Tpke *Web:* www.brbs.net	Charlottesville	VA	22903	434-823-1387		290
Blue Ridge Community College 180 W Campus Dr *TF:* 800-223-3271 ■ *Web:* www.blueridge.edu	Flat Rock	NC	28731	828-694-1700	694-1690	162
Transylvania 45 Oak Pk Dr *Web:* www.blueridge.edu	Brevard	NC	28712	828-883-2520		162
Blue Ridge Community College Harrisonburg 160 N Mason St *Web:* www.brcc.edu	Harrisonburg	VA	22802	540-432-3690		162
Blue Ridge Electric Membership Corp 1216 Blowing Rock Blvd. *TF:* 800-451-5474 ■ *Web:* blueridgeemc.com	Lenoir	NC	28645	828-758-2383	758-2699	245
Blue Ridge Farms Inc 3301 Atlantic Ave	Brooklyn	NY	11208	718-827-9000		123
Blue Ridge Grain & Mktg Inc 2545 Flintridge Rd Ste 120	Gainesville	GA	30501	770-535-2864		194
Blue Ridge Grill 1261 W Paces Ferry Rd *TF:* 800-961-3119 ■ *Web:* www.blueridgegrill.com	Atlanta	GA	30327	404-233-5030		671
Blue Ridge Internet Works 321 E Main St. *Web:* www.brnets.com	Charlottesville	VA	22902	434-817-0707		387
Blue Ridge Landscape & Design Inc 172-12 Imboden Dr *Web:* www.blueridgelandscape.com	Winchester	VA	22603	540-869-0000		776
Blue Ridge Mountain Cabinets 1101 Franklin St. *Web:* www.blueridgemountaincabinets.com	Rocky Mount	VA	24151	540-489-1000		115
Blue Ridge Optics LLC 1617 Longwood Ave. *Web:* www.blueridgeoptics.com	Bedford	VA	24523	540-586-8526		529
Blue Ridge Partners Management Consulting LLC 1350 Beverly Rd Ste 115 *Web:* www.blueridgepartners.com	Mclean	VA	22101	703-448-1881		194
Blue Ridge Public Television 1215 McNeil Dr *TF:* 888-332-7788 ■ *Web:* www.blueridgepbs.org	Roanoke	VA	24015	540-344-0991	344-2148	632
Blue Ridge Real Estate Co PO Box 940 *OTC:* BLRGZ	Blakeslee	PA	18610	570-443-8433		655
Blue Ridge School 273 Mayo Dr *Web:* blueridgeschool.com	Saint George	VA	22935	434-985-2811		622
Blue Ridge Tool & Machine Company Inc 115 Hollow Oaks Ln *TF:* 800-922-6274 ■ *Web:* www.blueridgetool.com	Easley	SC	29642	864-859-4758		454
Blue Ridge X-Ray Company Inc 120 Vista Blvd *TF:* 800-727-7290 ■ *Web:* www.blueridgex-ray.com	Arden	NC	28704	800-727-7290		475
Blue River State Recreation Area 3019 Apple St. *Web:* outdoornebraska.gov/blueriver	Lincoln	NE	68503	402-471-0641		565
Blue Rock Advisors Inc 445 E Lake St Ste 120. *Web:* blue-rock.com	Wayzata	MN	55391	952-229-8700		401
Blue Rock State Park 7924 Cutler Lake Rd *Web:* www.ohiodnr.com	Blue Rock	OH	43720	740-674-4794		565
Blue Rock Technologies 800 Kirts Blvd *TF:* 866-390-8200 ■ *Web:* www.bluerocktech.com	Troy	MI	48084	248-786-6100		225
Blue Seal Feeds Inc 2905 US Hwy 61 N. *TF Cust Svc:* 866-647-1212 ■ *Web:* www.blueseal.com	Muscatine	IA	52761	866-647-1212		447
Blue Shield of California 50 Beale St **Fax:* Hum Res ■ *Web:* www.blueshieldca.com	San Francisco	CA	94105	415-229-5000	229-6230*	391-3
Blue Skies Consulting LLC 100 Blue Skies Dr Belen Alexander Airport (E80) *Web:* www.blueskies.aero	Belen	NM	87002	505-864-3700		196
Blue Sky Agency 950 Joseph E Lowery Blvd Ste 30. *Web:* blueskyagency.com	Atlanta	GA	30318	404-876-0202		4
Blue Sky Cleaners 1111 Elliott Ave W *Web:* www.blueskycleaners.com	Seattle	WA	98119	206-838-8433		426
Blue Sky Cycling Inc 2530 Randolph St. *TF:* 800-585-4137 ■ *Web:* www.blueskycycling.com	Huntington Park	CA	90255	323-585-3934		711
Blue Sky Energy Inc 2598 Fortune Way Ste K *TF:* 800-493-7877 ■ *Web:* www.blueskyenergyinc.com	Vista	CA	92081	760-597-1642		610
Blue Sky Industries Inc 595 Monterey Pass Rd *Web:* www.blueskyindustries.com	Monterey Park	CA	91754	213-620-9950		360-3
Blue Sky Pest Control 3050 S Country Club Dr Ste 7 *Web:* blueskypest.com	Mesa	AZ	85210	480-635-8492		577
Blue Sky Sports Center of Euless LLC 7801 Main St *Web:* www.blueskysportscenter.com	The Colony	TX	75056	469-384-3400		711
Blue Sky Studios Inc 1 American Ln *Web:* www.blueskystudios.com	Greenwich	CT	06831	203-992-6000	992-6001	33
Blue Sky Swimwear 729 E International Speedway Blvd. *TF Orders:* 800-799-6445 ■ *Web:* www.blueskyswimwear.com	Daytona Beach	FL	32118	386-255-2590	253-5938	155-17
Blue Spoon 89 Congress St *Web:* bluespoonme.com	Portland	ME	04101	207-773-1116		671
Blue Spring State Park 2100 W French Ave. *Web:* www.floridastateparks.org	Orange City	FL	32763	386-775-3663		565
Blue Springs Chamber of Commerce 1000 W Main St *Web:* bluespringschamber.com	Blue Springs	MO	64015	816-229-8558	229-1244	139
Blue Springs State Park 2595 Alabama 10 *Web:* www.alapark.com	Clio	AL	36017	334-397-4875	397-4875	565
Blue Star Automobile Stores Inc 2001 S State St.	Chicago	IL	60616	312-225-7174		54
Blue Star Contemporary Arts Ctr 116 Blue Star Rd. *Web:* www.bluestarart.org	San Antonio	TX	78204	210-227-6960		50-2
Blue Star Growers Inc 200 Blue Star Rd.	Cashmere	WA	98815	509-782-2922		315-3
Blue Star Plastics Inc 801 Nandino Blvd. *Web:* www.bluestarplastics.com	Lexington	KY	40511	859-255-0714		608
Blue Star, The 1645 S Tejon St *Web:* www.thebluestar.net	Colorado Springs	CO	80905	719-632-1086		671
Blue State Digital LLC 406 Seventh St NW 3rd Fl *Web:* bluestatedigital.com	Washington	DC	20004	202-449-5600		7
Blue Stone Strategy Group LLC 2214 N Central Ave ITCA/El Encanto Bldg Ste 130 *Web:* www.bluestonestrategy.com	Phoenix	AZ	85004	949-476-8828	861-7419	463
Blue Sun Biodiesel LLC 1687 Cole Blvd Ste 100 *Web:* www.gobluesun.com	Lakewood	CO	80401	303-865-7700		579
Blue Talon Bistro 420 Prince George St *Web:* www.bluetalonbistro.com	Williamsburg	VA	23185	757-476-2583		671
Blue Tangerine Solutions Inc 1380 Sarno Rd Ste B *TF:* 800-870-4293 ■ *Web:* www.bluetangerinesolutions.com	Melbourne	FL	32935	321-309-6900		180
Blue Tape Inc 16101 College Oak *Web:* www.blue-tape.com	San Antonio	TX	78249	210-222-0580		627
Blue Technologies 5885 Grant Ave *Web:* www.bluetechnologiesinc.com	Cleveland	OH	44105	216-271-4800		112
Blue Tee Corp 250 Park Ave S.	New York	NY	10003	212-598-0880		360-3
Blue Telescope 236 W 30 St 7th Fl. *Web:* www.blue-telescope.com	New York	NY	10001	212-675-7702		195
Blue Tent Mktg 218 E Valley Rd Ste 205 *Web:* bluetent.com	Carbondale	CO	81623	970-704-3240		194
Blue Turtle Studio 4884 Broiles Rd *Web:* www.blueturtlestudio.com	Christiana	TN	37037	615-585-5757		130
Blue Tusk 165 Walton St *Web:* www.bluetusk.com	Syracuse	NY	13202	315-472-1934		671
Blue Valley Public Safety Inc 509 James Rollo Dr *Web:* bluevalleypublicsafety.com	Grain Valley	MO	64029	816-847-7502		237
Blue Valley Tele-Communications Inc 1559 Pony Express Hwy *Web:* www.bluevalley.net	Home	KS	66438	785-799-3311		737
Blue Water Area Chamber of Commerce 512 McMorran Blvd *TF:* 800-361-0526 ■ *Web:* www.bluewaterchamber.com	Port Huron	MI	48060	810-985-7101	985-7311	139
Blue Water Cafe 1095 Hamilton St. *Web:* www.bluewatercafe.net	Vancouver	BC	V6B5T4	604-688-8078		671
Blue Water Grill 31 Union Sq W *Web:* bluewatergrillnyc.com	New York	NY	10003	212-675-9500		671
Blue Water Resort 291 S Shore Dr. *TF:* 800-367-9393 ■ *Web:* www.redjacketresorts.com/blue-water-resort.php	South Yarmouth	MA	02664	508-398-2288		669

	Phone	Fax	Class
Blue Water Sailing Magazine 747 Aquidneck Ave Ste 201 Ste 201.......... Middletown RI 02842 *TF:* 888-800-7245 ■ *Web:* www.bwsailing.com	401-847-7612	845-8580	457-4
Blue Wave Marketing and Promotion 107 South St Ste 2F.........................Boston MA 02111 *Web:* www.bluewavemarketing.com	617-576-3100		195
Blue Williams LLP 3421 N Causeway Blvd Ste 900.................Metairie LA 70002 *TF:* 800-326-4991 ■ *Web:* bluewilliams.com	504-831-4091		428
Blue Zebra Appointment Setting 25 Pequot Ave Ste A.................. Port Washington NY 11050 **Fax Area Code:* 516 ■ *TF:* 800-755-0094 ■ *Web:* www.bluezebraappointmentsetting.com	800-755-0094	345-0298*	7
BlueAlly 8609 Westwood Center Dr Ste 100.............. Vienna VA 22182 *TF:* 888-768-2060 ■ *Web:* www.blueally.com	888-768-2060		260
BlueArc Corp 50 Rio Robles Dr................ San Jose CA 95134 *Web:* www.hds.com	408-576-6600		173-8
Blueberry Lake State Recreation Site 23 Richardson Hwy.......................... Valdez AK 99686 *Web:* dnr.alaska.gov	907-269-8400		565
Bluebonnet Trail Elementary 11316 Farmhaven Rd......................... Austin TX 78754 *TF:* 800-842-7708 ■ *Web:* www.manorisd.net	512-278-4125		305
Bluebonnet Waste Control PO Box 223845....... Dallas TX 75222	214-748-5221	748-6886	804
Bluechip Athletic Solutions LLC 5885 Glenridge Dr Ste 115.....................Atlanta GA 30328 *Web:* bas-llc.net	404-941-2510		225
BlueCross BlueShield of Tennessee Inc 1 Cameron Hill Cir.................... Chattanooga TN 37402 *TF:* 800-848-0298 ■ *Web:* www.bcbst.com	800-565-9140		219
BlueCross BlueShield of Western New York 257 W Genesee St ....Buffalo NY 14202 *TF:* 800-888-0757 ■ *Web:* bcbswny.com	716-887-6900	887-7912	391-3
Bluecube Information Technology 10521 S Parker Rd, Ste F...................... Parker CO 80134 *Web:* www.bluecubeit.com	720-463-3800		196
Bluedial.com 3622 N Rancho Dr.............. Las Vegas NV 89130 *Web:* www.bluedial.com	702-645-5260		410
Bluedog Design LLC 403 N Carpenter St ....Chicago IL 60642 *Web:* www.bluedogdesign.com	312-243-1101		195
Bluefield College 3000 College Dr............. Bluefield VA 24605 **Fax:* Admissions ■ *TF:* 800-872-0175 ■ *Web:* www.bluefield.edu	276-326-3682	326-4395*	166
Bluefield Regional Medical Ctr (BRMC) 500 Cherry St............................ Bluefield WV 24701 *TF:* 800-994-6610 ■ *Web:* www.bluefieldregional.net	304-327-1100		374-3
Bluefield State College 219 Rock St........... Bluefield WV 24701 **Fax:* Admissions ■ *TF:* 800-654-7798 ■ *Web:* bluefieldstate.edu	304-327-4000	325-7747*	166
Bluefly Inc 42 W 39th St 9th Fl ....New York NY 10018 *NASDAQ: BFLY* ■ *TF Cust Svc:* 877-258-3359 ■ *Web:* www.bluefly.com	212-944-8000	354-3400	157-6
BlueGenesisCom Corp 5915 Airport Rd Ste 1100................. Mississauga ON L4V1T1 *Web:* www.bluegenesis.com	905-673-3232		387
Blue-Grace Logistics LLC 2846 S Falkenburg Rd ....Riverview FL 33578 *TF:* 800-697-4477 ■ *Web:* www.mybluegrace.com	800-697-4477		311
Bluegrass Cellular Inc 2902 Ring Rd ....Elizabethtown KY 42701 *TF:* 800-928-2355 ■ *Web:* www.bluegrasscellular.com	270-769-0339		736
Bluegrass Community & Technical College *Cooper Campus* 470 Cooper Dr ....Lexington KY 40506 *TF:* 866-774-4872 ■ *Web:* www.bluegrass.kctcs.edu	859-246-6200	246-4666	162
Bluegrass Scenic Railroad & Museum 175 Beasley Rd Woodford County Pk...........Versailles KY 40383 *Web:* www.bgrm.org	859-873-2476	873-0408	520
Bluegrassnet Development Corp 321 E Breckinridge St......................Louisville KY 40203 *Web:* www.bluegrass.net	502-589-4638		225
Bluegreen Corp 4960 Conference Way N Ste 100 .... Boca Raton FL 33431 *NYSE: BXG* ■ *TF:* 800-456-2582 ■ *Web:* bluegreenvacations.com	561-912-8000	912-8100	753
Blueharbor Bank 106 Corporate Park Dr .... Mooresville NC 28117 *TF:* 877-322-8228 ■ *Web:* www.blueharborbank.com	704-662-7700		70
BlueHornet Networks Inc 2355 Northside Dr Ste B250................. San Diego CA 92108 *TF:* 866-586-3755 ■ *Web:* www.bluehornet.com	619-295-1856		195
Bluehour 250 NW 13th Ave ....Portland OR 97209 *Web:* www.bluehouronline.com	503-226-3394		671
BlueLight Analytics Inc 24-2625 Joseph Howe Dr.......................Halifax NS B3L4G4 *Web:* curingresin.com	902-407-4242		228
BlueLine IT Group Inc 189 N Water St...........................Rochester NY 14604	585-730-5977	790-5978	631
BlueLine Services LLC 448 East 6400 South Ste 425.............Salt Lake City UT 84107 *Web:* www.blueline-services.com	801-575-8378		415
Blueline Simulations LLC 218 e bearss ave............................ Tampa FL 33613 *Web:* www.bluelinesims.com	813-269-7467		463
BlueLink Marketing LLC 306 W 37th St 11th Fl......................New York NY 10018 **Fax Area Code:* 917	212-730-5785	210-3778*	393
Bluelinx Holdings Inc 4300 Wildwood Pkwy ....Atlanta GA 30339 *Web:* www.bluelinxco.com	770-953-7000		690
Bluelock LLC 6325 Morenci Trl ....Indianapolis IN 46268 *TF:* 888-402-2583 ■ *Web:* www.bluelock.com	888-402-2583		180
Bluemetal Architects Inc 44 Pleasant St........................... Watertown MA 02472 *TF:* 866-252-0111 ■ *Web:* www.bluemetal.com	866-252-0111		196
Bluenose Inn & Suites 636 Bedford Hwy........... Halifax NS B3M2L8 *TF:* 800-553-5339	800-565-2301		379
Blueox Corp 38 N Canal St...................... Oxford NY 13830 *TF:* 877-233-8176 ■ *Web:* www.blueoxenergy.com	877-233-8176		579
BluePearl Veterinary Partners LLC 3000 Busch Lake Blvd .... Tampa FL 33614 *Web:* bluepearlvet.com	813-933-8944		794

	Phone	Fax	Class
Bluepoint Leadership Development Ltd 25 Whitney Dr................................Milford OH 45150 *TF:* 888-221-8685 ■ *Web:* www.bluepointleadership.com	513-683-4702		194
BluePoint Venture Marketing 17 Draper Rd ....Wayland MA 01778 *Web:* www.bluepointmktg.com	978-509-8444		636
BluePointe 3344 Peachtree Rd.................... Atlanta GA 30326 *Web:* www.buckheadrestaurants.com	404-261-6456		671
BluePointe Capital Management LLC 400 S El Camino Real Ste 760 ....San Mateo CA 94402 *Web:* www.bluepointecapital.com	650-293-4545		690
Blueport Commerce Inc 500 Harrison Ave Ste 3R......................Boston MA 02118 *Web:* www.furniture.com	617-275-7200		459
Blueprint Ventures 601 Gateway Blvd Ste 1140 .... South San Francisco CA 94080	415-901-4000		792
BlueRange Technology Inc 9241 Globe Ctr Dr Ste 100..................Morrisville NC 27560 *TF:* 877-928-4800 ■ *Web:* www.bluerangetech.com	877-928-4800		631
BlueRun Ventures 545 Middlefield Rd Ste 250 .... Menlo Park CA 94025 *Web:* brv.com	650-462-7250		792
BlueRush Media Group Corp 75 Sherbourne St .... Toronto ON M5A2P9 *Web:* www.bluerush.com/en	416-203-0618		195
BlueScope Construction Inc 1540 Genessee St.........................Kansas City MO 64102 *TF:* 800-488-6903 ■ *Web:* www.bluescopeconstruction.com	816-245-6000	245-6099	186
Bluescope Steel Americas LLC 111 W Ocean Blvd ....Long Beach CA 90802 *Web:* www.bhpsteel.com	562-491-1441		492
BlueScreen LLC 137 N Larchmont Ste 508..................Los Angeles CA 90004 *Web:* www.bluescreen.com	323-467-7572		722
Blueslice Networks Inc 1751 Richardson St Ste 7500................. Montreal QC H3K1G6 *Web:* www.blueslice.com	514-935-9700	932-9701	174
Bluesocket Inc 1 Burlington Woods Dr Ste 210 ....Burlington MA 01803 *Web:* www.adtran.com	781-328-0888		252
BlueSpire Strategic Marketing 7650 Edinborough Way Ste 500............Minneapolis MN 55435 *TF:* 800-727-6397 ■ *Web:* bluespiremarketing.com	800-727-6397		5
Bluestar Resort & Golf LLC 8800 N Gainey Ctr Dr Ste 350 ....Scottsdale AZ 85258 *TF:* 800-345-8082 ■ *Web:* www.bluestargolf.com	480-348-6519		707
Bluestem 900 Westport Rd...................Kansas City MO 64111 *Web:* kansascitymenus.com/goodbye.html	816-561-1101		671
Bluestem Brands Inc 6509 Flying Cloud Dr....................Eden Prairie MN 55344 *Web:* bluestembrands.silkroad.com	952-656-3700		737
Bluestem Electric Co-op Inc 614 E Hwy 24 PO Box 5 .... Wamego KS 66547 *TF:* 800-558-1580 ■ *Web:* www.bluestemelectric.com	785-456-2212		245
Bluestone & Hockley Real Estate Services 9320 SW Barbur Blvd Ste 300 ....Portland OR 97219 *Web:* www.bluestonehockley.com	503-222-3800		652
Bluestone Engineering Inc 1990 N California Blvd Ste 830 ....Walnut Creek CA 94596 *Web:* www.bergersongroup.com	925-932-7053		256
Bluestone Industries Inc 10030 Green Level Church Rd Ste 802..............Cary NC 27519 **Fax Area Code:* 631 ■ *Web:* bluestoneind.com	919-267-9276	218-4600*	360-3
Bluestone National Scenic River PO Box 246 PO Box 246.....................Glen Jean WV 25846 *Web:* www.nps.gov/blue	304-465-0508	465-0591	564
BlueStone Natural Resources LLC 2100 S Utica Ste 200 .... Tulsa OK 74114 *TF:* 800-270-7007 ■ *Web:* www.bluestone-nr.com	918-392-9200		539
Bluestone State Park HC 78.................... Hinton WV 25951 *Web:* www.bluestonesp.com	304-466-2805		565
Bluestorm Technologies Inc 455 Court St.........................Binghamton NY 13904 *Web:* www.bluestormtech.com	607-762-5401		180
BlueSun Inc 5500 N Service Rd Ste 1107..................Burlington ON L7L6W6 *TF:* 800-387-0073 ■ *Web:* www.bluesun.ca	905-333-3353		179
BlueTie Inc 2480 Browncroft Blvd Ste 2b ....Rochester NY 14625 *TF:* 800-258-3843 ■ *Web:* www.bluetie.com	585-586-2000	586-2268	225
BlueView Inc 1306 S Denver........................ Tulsa OK 74119 *Web:* www.blueviewagency.com	918-592-1400		180
Bluewater Adventures Ltd 252 E First St Ste 3.................. North Vancouver BC V7L1B3 *TF:* 888-877-1770 ■ *Web:* www.bluewateradventures.ca	604-980-3800	980-1800	220
Bluewater Bay Resort 2000 Bluewater Blvd..........................Niceville FL 32578 *Web:* www.bwbresort.com	850-897-3241		669
Bluewater Energy Inc 3459 Acworth Due W Rd Ste 206 ....Acworth GA 30101 *Web:* bluewaterenergysolutions.com	678-594-2058		463
Bluewater Industries Inc 5300 Memorial Ste 550 ....Houston TX 77007	713-802-2060		41
Bluewater Mfg Inc 4064 Peavey Rd.............Chaska MN 55318 *Web:* www.bluewater-mfg.com	952-448-2935		172
BlueWater Partners LLC 146 Monroe Ctr St NW Ste 701 ....Grand Rapids MI 49503 *Web:* www.bluewaterpartners.com	616-988-9444		251
Bluewater Resort 2001 S Ocean Blvd.....................Myrtle Beach SC 29577	843-626-8345		669
Bluewater Resort & Casino 11300 Resort Dr.............................. Parker AZ 85344 *Web:* www.bluewaterfun.com	928-669-7000		378
Bluewater Ropes Inc 209 Lovvorn Rd......... Carrollton GA 30117 *Web:* www.bluewaterropes.com	770-834-7515		208
Bluewater Thermal Solutions 126 Millport Cir Ste 102.................. Greenville SC 29607 *TF:* 877-990-0050 ■ *Web:* www.bluewaterthermal.com	864-990-0050	990-0056	484

Phone | Fax | Class

Blue-White Industries Ltd
5300 Business Dr — Huntington Beach CA 92649 — 714-893-8529 — 894-9492 — 201
TF: 800-022-2110 ■ Web: www.bluwhite.com

Blueye Corp 1321 N Wood St — Chicago IL 60622 — 773-342-1200 — 177
Web: www.blueye.com

Bluezoo
1500 Epcot Resorts Blvd
PO Box 22653 — Lake Buena Vista FL 32830 — 407-934-1111 — 671
Web: www.swandolphin.com/bluezoo

Bluff Point State Park
c/o Ft Trumbull State Pk 90 Walbach St — New London CT 06320 — 860-444-7591 — 565
Web: www.ct.gov

Bluffton Flying Service Co
1080 Navajo Dr — Bluffton OH 45817 — 419-358-7045 — 13
TF: 800-742-5877 ■ Web: www.blufftonflyingservice.com

Bluffton Motor Works LLC
410 E Spring St — Bluffton IN 46714 — 260-827-2200 — 518
TF: 800-579-8527 ■ Web: www.blmworks.com

Bluffton Today
52 Persimmon St PO Box 4869 — Bluffton SC 29910 — 843-815-0800 — 815-0898 — 532-4
Web: blufftontoday.com

Bluffton University 1 University Dr — Bluffton OH 45817 — 419-358-3000 — 358-3081* — 166
*Fax: Admissions ■ TF: 800-488-3257 ■ Web: www.bluffton.edu

Blum & Fink Inc 333 Seventh Ave — New York NY 10001 — 212-695-2606 — 155-7

Blum Inc 7733 Old Plank Rd — Stanley NC 28164 — 704-827-1345 — 350
TF: 800-438-6788 ■ Web: www.blum.com

Blum Rod (Rep R - IA)
1108 Longworth HOB — Washington DC 20515 — 202-225-2911 — 342-2
Web: blum.house.gov

Blum Shapiro
29 S Main St PO Box 272000 — West Hartford CT 06107 — 860-561-4000 — 521-9241 — 2

Blumberg Capital
501 Folsom St Ste 400 — San Francisco CA 94105 — 415-905-5000 — 194
Web: www.blumbergcapital.com

BlumbergExcelsior Inc
16 Court St 14th Fl — Brooklyn NY 11241 — 212-431-5000 — 104
Web: www.blumberg.com

Blume Mechanical LLC
11300 43rd St N — Clearwater FL 33762 — 727-544-5993 — 35
Web: www.blumemechanical.com

Blumen Gardens Inc 403 Edward St — Sycamore IL 60178 — 815-895-3737 — 293
Web: blumengardens.com

Blumenauer Earl (Rep D - OR)
1111 Longworth Bldg — Washington DC 20515 — 202-225-4811 — 225-8941 — 342-2
Web: blumenauer.house.gov

Blumenthal Lansing Co
30 Two Bridges Rd Ste 110 — Fairfield NJ 07004 — 201-935-6220 — 594
TF: 800-553-4158 ■ Web: www.buttons.com

Blumenthal Richard (Sen D - CT)
706 Hart Senate Office Bldg — Washington DC 20510 — 202-224-2823 — 224-9673 — 342-2
Web: www.blumenthal.senate.gov

Blumerich Communications Service
6403 W Pierson Rd — Flushing MI 48433 — 810-659-5000 — 736
TF: 800-478-9191 ■ Web: www.blumerich.com

Blunt Rochester Lisa (Rep D - DE)
1123 Longworth HOB — Washington DC 20515 — 202-225-4165 — 342-2
Web: bluntrochester.house.gov

Blunt Roy (Sen R - MO)
260 Russell Bldg — Washington DC 20510 — 202-224-5721 — 224-8149 — 342-2
Web: www.blunt.senate.gov

Blur Studio 3960 Ince Blvd — Culver City CA 90232 — 424-298-4800 — 298-4801 — 33
Web: www.blur.com

Bluteau DeVenney & Company Inc
5670 Spring Garden Rd Ste 901A — Halifax NS B3J1H6 — 902-425-0467 — 41
TF: 877-210-9800 ■ Web: www.bluteaudevenney.com

Blutek Power Inc 300-1 SR- 17 S Ste B2 — Lodi NJ 07644 — 973-594-1800 — 518
Web: www.blutekpower.com

Bluware Inc 16285 Park 10 Pl Ste 300 — Houston TX 77084 — 713-335-1500 — 177
TF: 800-776-7263 ■ Web: www.bluware.com

BluWater Bistro 102 Lakeside Ave — Seattle WA 98122 — 206-328-2233 — 671
Web: www.bluwaterbistro.com

Blyth Academy 300 John St Ste 276 — Thornhill ON L3T5W4 — 905-889-8081 — 623
Web: blytheducation.com

Blythe Area Chamber of Commerce
207 E Hobsonway — Blythe CA 92225 — 760-922-8166 — 922-4010 — 139
TF: 800-433-3243 ■ Web: www.blythechamberofcommerce.com

Blythe Construction Inc
2911 N Graham St — Charlotte NC 28206 — 704-375-8474 — 375-7814 — 188-4
TF: 800-521-2651 ■ Web: www.blytheconstruction.com

Blythe Park Elementary School
735 Leesley Rd — Riverside IL 60546 — 708-447-2168 — 685
Web: www.district96.org

Blytheco LLC 23161 Mill Creek Dr — Laguna Hills CA 92653 — 949-583-9500 — 583-0649 — 180
TF: 800-425-9843 ■ Web: www.blytheco.com

Blythewood Oil Company Inc
4118 US Hwy 21 S — Ridgeway SC 29130 — 803-754-3319 — 579

BMA (Business Marketing Assn)
708 Third Ave 33rd Fl — New York NY 10017 — 212-697-5950 — 687-7310 — 49-18
Web: www.marketing.org

BMA (Baptist Missionary Assn of America)
611 Locust Ave — Conway AR 72034 — 501-455-4977 — 48-20
TF: 800-333-1442 ■ Web: bmamissions.org

BMA Communications LLC
115 Trolley Ct — Pittsburgh PA 15237 — 412-391-4332 — 195
Web: www.bmacommunications.com

BMC (Better Management Corp)
4321 State Rt7 — New Waterford OH 44445 — 330-921-4301 — 660
TF: 877-293-4300 ■ Web: www.bmcbulk.com

BMC Group Inc 600 First Ave Ste 300 — Seattle WA 98104 — 206-516-3300 — 261
Web: www.bmcgroup.com

BMC Software Inc 2101 City W Blvd — Houston TX 77042 — 713-918-8800 — 918-8000 — 178-1
NASDAQ: BMC ■ TF: 800-841-2031 ■ Web: www.bmc.com

BMDA (Building Material Dealers Assn)
1006 SE Grand Ave Ste 301 — Portland OR 97214 — 503-208-3763 — 49-3
TF: 888-960-6329 ■ Web: www.bmda.com

Bme Assocs 10 Liftbridge Ln E — Fairport NY 14450 — 585-377-7360 — 261
Web: www.bmepc.com

Bmea Enterprises Inc 13370 Kirkham Way — Poway CA 92064 — 858-513-6584 — 321

BMF (Buchanan Metal Forming Inc)
103 W Smith St — Buchanan MI 49107 — 269-695-3836 — 695-3830 — 483
Web: www.bmfcorp.com

BMG (Buford Media Group LLC)
6125 Paluxy Dr — Tyler TX 75703 — 903-561-4411 — 116

BMG Aviation Inc 984 S Kirby Rd — Bloomington IN 47403 — 812-825-7979 — 825-7978 — 63
TF: 888-457-3787 ■ Web: www.bmgaviation.com

BMG Metals Inc 950 Masonic Ln — Richmond VA 23231 — 804-226-1024 — 222-3693 — 492
TF: 800-552-1510 ■ Web: www.bmgmetals.com

Bmg of Kansas Inc 606 Commerce Dr — Hesston KS 67062 — 620-327-4038 — 697

BMH (Bastian Solutions)
10585 N Meridian St 3rd Fl — Indianapolis IN 46290 — 317-575-9992 — 575-8596 — 55
TF: 800-772-0464 ■ Web: www.bastiansolutions.com

BMH Books
1104 Kings Hwy PO Box 544 — Winona Lake IN 46590 — 800-348-2756 — 637-8
TF: 800-348-2756 ■ Web: www.bmhbooks.com

BMI (Book Manufacturers Institute Inc)
PO Box 731388 Ste 1-B — Ormond Beach FL 32173 — 386-986-4552 — 986-4553 — 49-16
Web: bomi.memberclicks.net

BMI (Broadcast Music Inc)
250 Greenwich St 7 World Trade Ctr — New York NY 10007 — 212-220-3000 — 220-4474 — 48-4
Web: www.bmi.com

BMI (Brotherhood Mutual Insurance Co)
6400 Brotherhood Way PO Box 2589 — Fort Wayne IN 46825 — 800-333-3735 — 391-4
TF Cust Svc: 800-333-3735 ■ Web: www.brotherhoodmutual.com

BMI Educational Services PO Box 800 — Dayton NJ 08810 — 732-329-6991 — 986-9393* — 96
*Fax Area Code: 800 ■ TF: 800-222-8100 ■ Web: www.bmionline.com

Bmi Gaming Inc
3500 NW Boca Raton Blvd Ste 721 — Boca Raton FL 33431 — 561-391-7200 — 892-2268 — 322
Web: www.bmigaming.com

BMI Imaging Systems
1115 E Arques Ave — Sunnyvale CA 94085 — 408-736-7444 — 736-4397 — 496
TF: 800-359-3456 ■ Web: www.bmiimaging.com

BMM International LLC
815 Pilot Rd Ste G — Las Vegas NV 89119 — 702-407-2420 — 463
TF: 800-603-1374 ■ Web: www.bmm.com

BMO (Bank of Montreal)
100 King St W 1 First Canadian Pl 19th Fl — Toronto ON M5X1A1 — 416-867-6785 — 867-6793 — 70
NYSE: BMO ■ TF: 800-340-5021 ■ Web: www.bmo.com

Bmo Bankcorp Inc 111 W Monroe St — Chicago IL 60603 — 888-340-2265 — 360-2
TF: 888-340-2265 ■ Web: www.bmoharris.com

BMO Financial Corp
1 First Canadian Pl 21st Fl — Toronto ON M5X1A1 — 416-359-4440 — 216
TF: 800-553-0332 ■ Web: www.bmo.com

BMO Harris Bank 111 W Monroe St — Chicago IL 60603 — 847-238-2265 — 70
TF: 888-340-2265 ■ Web: www.bmoharris.com

BMO Harris Bank 770 N Water St — Milwaukee WI 53202 — 414-765-7569 — 360-2
NYSE: BMO ■ TF: 855-732-3414 ■ Web: www.bmoharris.com

BMO Harris Bradley Ctr
1001 N Fourth St — Milwaukee WI 53203 — 414-227-0400 — 720
Web: www.bmoharrisbradleycenter.com

BMP America Inc 11625 Maple Ridge Rd — Medina NY 14103 — 585-798-0950 — 798-4272 — 629
Web: www.bmpworldwide.com

BMPL (Batesville Memorial Public Library)
131 N Walnut St — Batesville IN 47006 — 812-934-4706 — 934-6288 — 434-3
Web: www.ebatesville.com/library

BMS (Broadcast Microwave Services Inc)
12305 Crosthwaite Cir — Poway CA 92064 — 858-391-3050 — 391-3049 — 224
TF: 800-669-9667 ■ Web: bms-inc.com

Bms Communications Inc
4133 Guardian St — Simi Valley CA 93063 — 805-526-1141 — 256

BMS Consulting Inc
209 Starling Ave — Martinsville VA 24112 — 276-666-9425 — 463
Web: www.bmsbenefits.com

Bms Management Inc
1200 W Commerce Way — Lincoln NE 68521 — 402-474-4014 — 88
TF: 800-780-4707 ■ Web: www.bmslogisticsinc.com

BMT Aerospace USA Inc 18559 Malyn Blvd — Fraser MI 48026 — 586-285-7700 — 709
Web: www.bmtaerospace.com

Bmt Fleet Technology Ltd 311 Legget Dr — Kanata ON K2K1Z8 — 613-592-2830 — 261
Web: www.fleetech.com

BMTGA (Blood & Marrow Transplant Group of Georgia)
5670 Peachtree Dunwoody Rd Ste 1000 — Atlanta GA 30342 — 404-255-1930 — 255-1939 — 769
Web: www.bmtga.com

BMW Constructors Inc
1740 W Michigan St — Indianapolis IN 46222 — 317-267-0400 — 189-10
Web: www.bmwcnstrs.com

BMW Manufacturing Co 1400 Hwy 101 S — Greer SC 29651 — 864-802-6000 — 59
Web: www.bmwusfactory.com

BMW Motorcycle Owners of America
PO Box 3982 — Ballwin MO 63022 — 636-394-7277 — 391-1811 — 48-18
Web: www.bmwmoa.org

BMW of Darien 140 Ledge Rd — Darien CT 06820 — 203-656-1804 — 57
TF: 855-349-6240 ■ Web: www.bmwdarien.com

BMW of Manhattan Inc 555 W 57th St — New York NY 10019 — 212-586-2269 — 54
TF: 877-855-4607 ■ Web: www.bmwnyc.com

BMW of North America LLC
300 Chestnut Ridge Rd — Woodcliff Lake NJ 07677 — 201-307-4000 — 307-4095 — 59
TF: 800-831-1117 ■ Web: www.bmwusa.com

BMW Toronto 11 Sunlight Park Rd — Toronto ON M4M1B5 — 416-623-4269 — 57
Web: bmwtoronto.ca

BMWED (Brotherhood of Maintenance of Way Employees)
41475 Gardenbrook Rd — Novi MI 48375 — 248-662-2660 — 662-2659 — 414
Web: www.bmwe.org/default.aspx

BNA Bank 133 E Bankhead — New Albany MS 38652 — 662-534-8171 — 70
Web: bnabank.com

BNA Consulting Inc
635 S State St — Salt Lake City UT 84111 — 801-532-2196 — 261
TF: 800-999-9574 ■ Web: www.bnaconsulting.com

BNBS Inc 11600 Otter Creek S Rd — Mabelvale AR 72103 — 501-224-1992 — 535
Web: bnbsolutionsinc.com

BNBuilders Inc 2601 Fourth Ave Ste 350 — Seattle WA 98121 — 206-382-3443 — 186
TF: 800-726-3811 ■ Web: www.bnbuilders.com

BNC Bancorp 1226 Eastchester Dr — High Point NC 27265 — 336-476-9200 — 360-2
NASDAQ: BNCN ■ Web: www.bankofnc.com

BNC National Bank 322 E Main Ave — Bismarck ND 58501 — 701-250-3000 — 250-3028 — 70
TF: 800-262-2265 ■ Web: www.bncbank.com

Phone | Fax | Class

BNCCORP Inc 322 E Main Ave Bismarck ND 58501 701-250-3040 222-3653 360-2
OTC: BNCC ■ *TF:* 800-297-4575 ■ *Web:* www.bnccorp.com

BNEINC (Boddie-Noell Enterprises Inc)
1021 Noell Ln PO Box 1908 Rocky Mount NC 27804 252-937-2000 670
Web: www.bneinc.com

BNI Coal Ltd
1637 Burnt Boat Dr PO Box 897 Bismarck ND 58503 701-222-8828 222-1547 501
TF: 800-533-7492 ■ *Web:* www.bnicoal.com

bNimble Technologies
45987 Paseo Padre Pkwy Ste 7 Fremont CA 94539 510-870-2312 178-12
Web: www.bnimbletech.com

BNL (Brookhaven National Laboratory)
PO Box 5000 Upton NY 11973 631-344-8000 344-3000 668
Web: www.bnl.gov

BNL Inc
11760 Armistead Filler Ln Lovettsville VA 20180 540-822-5569 180
Web: www.bnlinc.com

Bnl Industries Inc
30 Industrial Park Rd Vernon CT 06066 860-870-6222 789
Web: www.bnl.com

BNN (Business News Network)
299 Queen St W Toronto ON M5V2Z5 416-384-6600 740
TF: 855-326-6266 ■ *Web:* www.bnn.ca

BNP Associates Inc
14 Fairfield Dr Ste 103 Brookfield CT 06804 203-792-3000 261
Web: www.bnpassociates.com

BNP Paribas 787 Seventh Ave New York NY 10019 212-841-3000 841-2146 690
Web: group.bnpparibas

BNR (Brave New Restaurant)
2300 Cottondale Ln Ste 105 Little Rock AR 72202 501-663-2677 671
Web: www.bravenewrestaurant.com

BNSF (Burlington Northern & Santa Fe Railway)
2650 Lou Menk Dr Fort Worth TX 76131 800-795-2673 648
TF: 800-795-2673 ■ *Web:* www.bnsf.com

BNSF (Burlington Northern Santa Fe Corp)
500 New Jersey Ave NW Ste 550 Washington DC 20001 202-347-8662 347-8675 615
TF: 800-964-9386 ■ *Web:* www.bnsf.com

BNSF Logistics LLC
4700 S Thompson Ste A202 Springdale AR 72764 888-285-4514 225
TF: 888-285-4514 ■ *Web:* www.bnsflogistics.com

BNX Shipping Inc 910 E 236th St Carson CA 90745 310-764-0999 311
Web: bnxlogistics.bkihost.net

BNY MELLON 1 Wall St New York NY 10286 212-495-1784 360-2
NYSE: BK ■ *Web:* www.bnymellon.com

BNZ Materials Inc
6901 S Pierce St Ste 260 Littleton CO 80128 303-978-1199 978-0308 662
TF: 800-999-0890 ■ *Web:* www.bnzmaterials.com

Bo Ling's 4701 Jefferson St Kansas City MO 64112 816-753-1718 671
Web: www.bolings.com

Bo Loong Restaurant
3922 St Clair Ave Cleveland OH 44114 216-391-3113 671

BO's Fish Wagon 801 Caroline St Key West FL 33040 305-294-9272 671
Web: bosfishwagon.com

BOA Editions Ltd
250 N Goodman St Ste 306 Rochester NY 14607 585-546-3410 546-3913 637-2
Web: www.boaeditions.org

Boa Technology Inc 1760 Platte St Denver CO 80202 303-455-5126 194
TF: 844-203-1297 ■ *Web:* www.boatechnology.com

Boa-Franc Inc 1255-98th St Saint-georges QC G5Y8J5 418-227-1181 290
TF: 800-463-1303 ■ *Web:* www.boa-franc.com

Boar's Head Inn 200 Ednam Dr Charlottesville VA 22903 434-296-2181 972-6024 669
TF: 800-476-1988 ■ *Web:* www.boarsheadinn.com

Boar's Head Provisions Company Inc
1819 Main St Ste 800 Sarasota FL 34236 941-955-0994 296-26
Web: www.boarshead.com

Board of Overseers of The Bar
97 Winthrop St Augusta ME 04330 207-623-1121 445
TF: 800-506-6631 ■ *Web:* mebaroverseers.org

Board of Supervisors 201 State St Boone IA 50036 515-433-0500 338

BoardBookit Inc 1 Altoona Pl Pittsburgh PA 15228 412-436-5180 387
Web: www.boardbookit.com

Boarder to Boarder Trucking Inc
PO Box 328 Edinburg TX 78541 956-316-4444 685
TF: 800-678-8789 ■ *Web:* www.btbtrucking.com

Boardman Inc
1135 S McKinley Ave Oklahoma City OK 73108 405-634-5434 492
Web: www.boardmaninc.com

Boardman Park 375 BoaRdman-Poland Rd Boardman OH 44512 330-726-8107 726-4562 50-1
Web: www.boardmanpark.com

Boardman Town Crier 240 Franklin St SE Warren OH 44483 330-629-6200 629-6210 532-4
TF: 800-837-6397 ■ *Web:* www.towncrieronline.com

Boardroom Communications Inc
Bank Of America Plaza 1776 N Pine Island Rd
Ste 320 Fort Lauderdale FL 33322 954-370-8999 636
TF: 877-773-4761 ■ *Web:* www.boardroompr.com

Boardroom Events LLC
5409 Overseas Hwy #295 Marathon FL 33050 786-361-0454 393
Web: www.boardroomevents.com

Boardroom Inc 281 Tresser Blvd 8th Fl Stamford CT 06901 203-973-5900 967-3086 637-9
TF: 800-274-5611 ■ *Web:* bottomlineinc.com

Boardroom Insiders Inc PO Box 847 Fort Mill SC 94114 415-643-5327 466
Web: www.boardroominsiders.com

Boardwalk Pipeline Partners LP
3800 Frederica St Owensboro KY 42301 270-686-3620 325
NYSE: BWP ■ *TF:* 866-913-2122 ■ *Web:* bwpmlp.com

Boardwalk Plaza Hotel
2 Olive Ave Rehoboth Beach DE 19971 302-227-7169 227-0561 379
TF: 800-332-3224 ■ *Web:* www.boardwalkplaza.com

Boart Longyear Co
2640 W 1700 S Salt Lake City UT 84104 801-972-6430 977-3374 190
TF: 800-453-8740 ■ *Web:* www.boartlongyear.com

Boat Owners Assn of the US
880 S Pickett St Alexandria VA 22304 703-823-9550 48-22
TF: 800-395-2628 ■ *Web:* www.boatus.com

boathouse group Inc 260 Charles St Waltham MA 02453 781-663-6600 7
Web: www.boathouseinc.com

Boathouse, The 101 Palm Blvd Isle of Palms SC 29451 843-886-8000 671
Web: www.boathouserestaurants.com

Boating Life Magazine
460 N Orlando Ave Ste 200 Winter Park FL 32789 515-237-3697 457-4
Web: www.boatingmag.com

Boating Magazine 1633 Broadway New York NY 10019 212-767-4818 457-4
Web: www.boatingmag.com

BOB 105.9 9471 Three Rivers Rd Ste A Gulfport MS 39503 228-388-2001 645-69
Web: www.bob1059.com

BOB 94.9 WRBT 600 Corporate Cir Harrisburg PA 17110 717-540-8800 645-71
Web: bob949.iheart.com

Bob Allen Ford 9239 Metcalf Ave Overland Park KS 66212 913-381-3000 57
TF: 888-573-6364 ■ *Web:* www.boballenford.com

Bob Barker Company Inc
PO Box 429 Fuquay Varina NC 27526 800-334-9880 594
TF: 800-334-9880 ■ *Web:* www.bobbarker.com

Bob Brown Chevrolet Inc
3600 111th St Urbandale IA 50322 515-278-7800 57
Web: bobbrownchevy.com

Bob Bullock Texas State History Museum
1800 N Congress Ave Austin TX 78701 512-936-8746 520
Web: www.thestoryoftexas.com

Bob Davidson Ford Lincoln
1845 E Joppa Rd Baltimore MD 21234 410-661-6400 668-4306 57
TF: 877-885-7890 ■ *Web:* www.bobdavidsonford.com

Bob Evans Farms Inc 3776 S High St Columbus OH 43207 800-939-2338 670
NASDAQ: BOBE ■ *TF:* 800-939-2338 ■ *Web:* www.bobevans.com

Bob Feller Museum
310 Mill St PO Box 160 Van Meter IA 50261 515-996-2644 522
Web: www.bobfellermuseum.org

Bob Fisher Chevrolet Inc
4111 Pottsville Pike Reading PA 19605 610-370-6683 57
Web: www.bobfisherchev.com

Bob Harris Oil Co 905 S Main St Cleburne TX 76033 817-558-0615 655

Bob Hart Consulting LLC
5126 W Evans Creek Rd Rogue River OR 97537 541-582-8890 194

Bob Inc 8740 49th Ave N North Minneapolis MN 55428 763-533-2261 533-1735 454
Web: www.bobmfg.com

Bob J Johnson & Associates Inc
16420 W Hardy Rd Ste 100 Houston TX 77060 281-873-5555 612
Web: www.bjja.com

Bob Jones University
1700 Wade Hampton Blvd Greenville SC 29614 864-242-5100 232-9258* 166
**Fax Area Code:* 800 ■ **Fax:* Admissions ■ *TF Admissions:* 800-252-6363 ■ *Web:* www.bju.edu

Bob Jones University Museum & Gallery
Bob Jones University
1700 Wade Hampton Blvd Greenville SC 29614 864-770-1331 520
Web: www.bjumg.org

Bob Mills Furniture Company LLC
3600 W Reno Ave Oklahoma City OK 73107 405-947-6500 321
Web: bobmillsfurniture.com

Bob Reeves Brass Mouthpieces
25574 Rye Canyon Rd Ste D Valencia CA 91355 661-775-8820 711
TF: 800-837-0980 ■ *Web:* www.bobreeves.com

Bob Ross auto group 85 Loop Rd Centerville OH 45459 937-433-0990 516
Web: www.bobrossauto.com

Bob Schmitt Homes Inc
9095 Gatestone Rd North Ridgeville OH 44039 440-327-9495 187
Web: www.bobschmitthomes.com

Bob Sight Ford Inc
610 NW Blue Pkwy Lees Summit MO 64063 816-524-6550 57
Web: www.bobsightford.com

Bob Stall Chevrolet 7601 Alvarado Rd La Mesa CA 91942 619-460-1311 57
TF: 800-295-2695 ■ *Web:* www.bobstall.com

Bob Straub State Park US 101 Pacific City OR 97135 800-551-6949 565
TF: 800-551-6949 ■ *Web:* www.oregonstateparks.org

Bob Sumerel Tire Company Inc
1257 Cox Ave Erlanger KY 41018 859-283-2700 755
Web: www.bobsumereltire.com

BOB the (Big Old Bldg)
20 Monroe Ave NW Grand Rapids MI 49503 616-356-2000 493-2011 50-6
TF: 800-242-9790 ■ *Web:* www.thebob.com

Bob Ward & Sons Inc 3015 Paxson St Missoula MT 59801 406-728-3220 711
TF: 800-800-5083 ■ *Web:* www.bobwards.com

Bob Wolfe Partners Tpg
202 San Vicente Blvd Apt 16 Santa Monica CA 90402 310-260-1340 7
Web: www.bwp-tpg.com

Bob's Barricades Inc 921 Shotgun Rd Sunrise FL 33326 954-423-2627 295
TF: 800-432-5031 ■ *Web:* www.bobsbarricades.com

Bob's Discount Furniture Inc
428 Tolland Tpke Manchester CT 06042 860-645-3208 321
Web: www.mybobs.com

Bob's Red Mill Natural Foods Inc
13521 SE Pheasant Ct Milwaukie OR 97222 503-654-3215 653-1339 296-4
TF: 800-553-2258 ■ *Web:* www.bobsredmill.com

Bob's Sporting Goods 1111 Hudson St Longview WA 98632 360-425-3870 636-4334 229
TF: 800-292-5551 ■ *Web:* www.bobsmerch.com

Bob's Steak & Chop House
4300 Lemmon Ave Dallas TX 75219 214-528-9446 671
Web: www.bobs-steakandchop.com

Bob's Steak & Chop House
5760 Legacy Dr Ste B1 Plano TX 75024 972-608-2627 671
Web: www.bobs-steakandchop.com

Bob's Stores Inc 160 Corporate Ct Meriden CT 06450 203-235-5775 157-2
TF: 866-333-2627 ■ *Web:* www.bobstores.com

Bob's Transport & Storage Company Inc
7980 Tar Bay Dr Jessup MD 20794 410-799-0832 799-0951 780
Web: www.bobstransport.com

Boba House 332 S Tate St Greensboro NC 27403 336-379-7444 671
Web: www.bobahouse.com

Bobak's Chicago Sausagelogists
4551 W Adams St Chicago IL 60624 773-735-5334 296-26
Web: www.bobak.com

Bobber Interactive Corp
2505 Third Ave Ste 300A Seattle WA 98121 206-443-3863 387
Web: www.bobberinteractive.com

Bobby Brown State Park
2509 Bobby Brown State Pk Rd Elberton GA 30635 706-213-2046 565
Web: www.gastateparks.org/info/bobbybrown

Bobby Flay Steak 1 Borgata Way Atlantic City NJ 08401 609-317-1000 671
Web: www.bobbyflaysteak.com

Company	City	State	ZIP	Phone	Fax	Class
Bobby Jones 2625 N Berkeley Lake Rd NW Bldg 200 Ste 100 *TF Cust Svc:* 800-776-0076 ■ *Web:* www.bobbyjones.com	Duluth	GA	30096	888-776-0076		155-3
Bobby Rahal Automotive Group 10701 Perry Hwy *Web:* www.bobbyrahal.com	Wexford	PA	15090	724-935-9300		483
Bobby Riggs Tennis Museum 875 Santa Fe Dr *Web:* bobbyriggs.net	Encinitas	CA	92024	760-473-2672		522
Bobby Rubino's Place for Ribs 2501 N Federal Hwy *Web:* www.bobbyrubinos.com	Pompano Beach	FL	33064	954-781-7550		670
Bobby Valentine's Sports Gallery Cafe 225 Main St	Stamford	CT	06901	203-348-0010		671
Bobby Wilkerson Inc 222 S Main St *TF:* 800-631-1999 ■ *Web:* www.wilkersons.com	Stuttgart	AR	72160	800-631-1999		410
BobCAD-CAM Inc 28200 US Hwy 19 N Ste E *Web:* www.bobcad.com	Clearwater	FL	33761	727-442-3554		177
Bobcat Central Inc 3516 Newton Rd *Web:* www.bobcatcentral.com	Stockton	CA	95205	209-466-9631		45
Bobcat Co 250 E Beaton Dr *Web:* www.bobcat.com	West Fargo	ND	58078	701-241-8700		516
Bobcat of Atlanta 6972 Best Friend Rd *Web:* www.bobcatofatlanta.com	Atlanta	GA	30340	770-242-6500		791
Bobcat of Boston Inc 20 Concord St *TF:* 800-287-8590 ■ *Web:* www.bobcatboston.com	North Reading	MA	01864	978-664-3727		791
Bobcat of St. Louis 401 W Outer Rd *Web:* www.bobcatofstl.com	Valley Park	MO	63088	636-225-2900		690
Bobcats Basketball LLC 333 E Trade St *Web:* www.timewarnercablearena.com	Charlotte	NC	28202	704-688-9000		717
Bobco Metals Co 2000 S Alameda St *TF:* 877-952-6226 ■ *Web:* bobcometal.com	Los Angeles	CA	90058	877-952-6226		492
Bobeck Real Estate Company Inc 3333 W Hamilton Rd	Fort Wayne	IN	46814	260-432-1000		652
Bobit Business Media 3520 Challenger St **Fax:* Hum Res ■ *Web:* www.bobitbusinessmedia.com	Torrance	CA	90503	310-533-2400	533-2500*	637-9
Bob-Leon Plastics Inc 5151 Franklin Blvd *TF:* 800-301-0211 ■ *Web:* www.bob-leon.com	Sacramento	CA	95820	916-452-4063	452-3759	286
Bobo Construction Inc 9728 Kent St *TF:* 800-768-5594 ■ *Web:* www.boboconstructioninc.com	Elk Grove	CA	95624	916-685-2285		187
Bobrick Washroom Equipment Inc 11611 Hart St *Web:* www.bobrick.com	North Hollywood	CA	91605	818-764-1000	765-2700	487
BOC International Inc 23 Drydock Ave *TF:* 800-675-8074 ■ *Web:* www.bocintl.com	Boston	MA	02210	617-345-0050		449
BOC Partners Inc 1030 South Ave W *TF:* 800-901-4970 ■ *Web:* bocpartners.com	Westfield	NJ	07090	908-232-2177		7
Boc Plastics Inc 90 Piedmont Industrial Dr Ste 100 *Web:* www.bocplastics.com	Winston-Salem	NC	27107	336-767-0277		596
Boc Water Hydraulics Inc 12024 Salem-Warren Rd *Web:* www.bocwaterhydraulics.com	Salem	OH	44460	330-332-4444		790
Boca Biolistics LLC 5001 NW 13th Ave Ste H *Web:* bocabio.com	Pompano Beach	FL	33064	954-449-6126	429-2998	743
Boca Communications LLC 2159 Powell St	San Francisco	CA	94133	415-738-7718		636
Boca Del Lupo 1422 William St *TF:* 800-838-3006 ■ *Web:* bocadellupo.com	Vancouver	BC	V5L2P7	604-684-2622		747
Boca Pharmacal Inc 3550 NW 126th Ave *TF:* 800-354-8460	Coral Springs	FL	33065	800-354-8460		583
Boca Raton Historical Society & Museum 71 N Federal Hwy *TF:* 800-778-0080 ■ *Web:* www.bocahistory.org	Boca Raton	FL	33432	561-395-6766		522
Boca Raton Museum of Art 501 Plaza Real Mizner Pk *TF:* 866-481-1689 ■ *Web:* www.bocamuseum.org	Boca Raton	FL	33432	561-392-2500	391-6410	520
Boca Raton Public Library 400 NW Second Ave *Web:* www.myboca.us/957/Library	Boca Raton	FL	33432	561-393-7852		434-3
Boca Raton Regional Hospital 800 Meadows Rd *Web:* www.brrh.com	Boca Raton	FL	33486	561-395-7100		374-3
Boca Raton Rehabilitation Ctr 755 Meadows Rd *Web:* bocaratonhealthandrehab.com	Boca Raton	FL	33486	561-391-5200	391-0685	450
Boca Raton Resort & Club 501 E Camino Real *TF:* 888-543-1224 ■ *Web:* www.bocaresort.com	Boca Raton	FL	33432	561-447-3000	447-5073	669
Bocada Inc 5555 Lakeview Dr *TF:* 866-262-2321 ■ *Web:* www.bocada.com	Kirkland	WA	98033	425-818-4400	898-2402	387
Bocados Restaurant 1312 W Alabama St *Web:* www.bocadoshouston.com	Houston	TX	77006	713-523-5230		671
Bocarsly Emden Cowan Esmail & Arndt LLP 633 W Fifth St 70th Fl *Web:* bocarslyemden.com	Los Angeles	CA	90071	213-239-8000		445
Boccardo Law Firm Inc, The 111 W Saint John St Ste 400 *TF:* 800-662-9807 ■ *Web:* www.boccardo.com	San Jose	CA	95113	800-662-9807		445
Boces Lower Hudson Regional Information Ctr 44 Executive *TF:* 800-722-5797 ■ *Web:* www.lhric.org	Elmsford	NY	10523	914-592-4203		685
Bock & Clark Corp 3550 W Market St Ste 200 *TF:* 800-787-8397 ■ *Web:* www.bockandclark.com	Akron	OH	44333	330-665-4821		727
Bock Water Heaters Inc 110 S Dickinson St *TF:* 800-794-2491 ■ *Web:* www.bockwaterheaters.com	Madison	WI	53703	608-257-2225		36

Company	City	State	ZIP	Phone	Fax	Class
Bockorny Group Inc 1101 16th St NW Ste 500 *Web:* www.bockornygroup.com	Washington	DC	20036	202-659-9111	659-6387	194
Bockstael Construction (1979) Ltd 1505 Dugald Rd *Web:* www.bockstael.com	Winnipeg	MB	R2J0H3	204-233-7135		186
Bocook Engineering Inc 312 Tenth St *Web:* bocook.com	Paintsville	KY	41240	606-789-5961		256
Bocotek Inc 2420 Comanche Rd NE Ste G1b *Web:* bocotek.com	Albuquerque	NM	87107	505-237-0528		175
Boda Plumbing Inc 1909 Tower Industrial Dr *TF:* 800-882-7779 ■ *Web:* www.bodaplumbing.com	Monroe	NC	28110	704-291-9097		610
Boddie-Noell Enterprises Inc (BNEINC) 1021 Noell Ln PO Box 1908 *Web:* www.bneinc.com	Rocky Mount	NC	27804	252-937-2000		670
Bode Concrete 385 Mendell St *TF:* 800-244-4653 ■ *Web:* www.bodegravel.com	San Francisco	CA	94124	415-920-7100		182
Bode North America Inc 660 John Dodd Rd *Web:* www.bodenorthamerica.com	Spartanburg	SC	29303	864-578-9683		60
Bodean Seafood Restaurant 3376 E 51st St *TF:* 800-234-8828 ■ *Web:* www.bodean.net	Tulsa	OK	74135	918-749-1407		671
Bodega 442 Granby St *Web:* www.bodegaongranby.com	Norfolk	VA	23510	757-622-8527		671
Bodega Bay Lodge 103 Coast Hwy 1 *TF Resv:* 888-875-2250 ■ *Web:* www.bodegabaylodge.com	Bodega Bay	CA	94923	707-875-3525		379
Bodega Latina Corp 14601B Lakewood Blvd *Web:* elsupermarkets.com	Paramount	CA	90723	562-616-8800		345
Bodega Restaurant 30 Baldwin St *Web:* www.bodegarestaurant.com	Toronto	ON	M5T1L3	416-977-1287	408-1941	671
Boden Inc PO Box 3292 *TF:* 866-291-3363 ■ *Web:* www.bodeninc.com	Princeton	NJ	08820	866-291-3363		809
Bodhtree Solutions Inc 210 Hammond Ave *Web:* www.bodhtree.com	Fremont	CA	94539	408-954-8700		177
Bodie State Historic Park PO Box 515 *Web:* www.parks.ca.gov	Bridgeport	CA	93517	760-647-6445		565
Bodine Aluminum Inc 2100 Walton Rd *Web:* www.bodinealuminum.com	St. Louis	MO	63114	314-423-8200		492
Bodine Co PO Box 460 *TF:* 800-223-5728 ■ *Web:* www.bodine.com	Collierville	TN	38027	901-853-7211	853-5009	767
Bodine Electric Co 201 Northfield Rd *TF:* 800-726-3463 ■ *Web:* www.bodine-electric.com	Northfield	IL	60093	773-478-3515	478-3232	518
Bodines Casino 5650 S Carson St *Web:* bodinescarson.com	Carson City	NV	89701	775-885-7777		452
Bodman PLC 1901 Saint Antoine St Sixth Fl at Ford Field *Web:* www.bodmanlaw.com	Detroit	MI	48226	313-259-7777		428
Bodwell High School 955 Harbourside Dr *Web:* www.bodwell.edu	North Vancouver	BC	V7P3S4	604-924-5056		685
Body & Soul 42 Pleasant St **Fax Area Code:* 603 ■ *Web:* www.marthastewart.com	Watertown	MA	02472	617-449-5506	647-0116*	457-18
Body Bar Inc 1942 Broadway St *Web:* www.bodybars.com	Boulder	CO	80302	303-938-6865		711
Body By Jake Global LLC 11611 San Vicente Blvd Ste 515	Los Angeles	CA	90049	310-571-7101		345
Body Logic Fitness Studio 2102 E Main Ste 110 *Web:* www.bodylogicfit.com	Puyallup	WA	98372	253-224-7001		354
Body Shop, The 5036 One World Way *TF:* 800-263-9746 ■ *Web:* www.thebodyshop.in	Wake Forest	NC	27587	919-554-4900		214
Body Tech 19815 La Grange Rd *TF:* 800-289-8879 ■ *Web:* bodytechtotalfitness.com	Mokena	IL	60448	708-478-5054		354
Body, The 250 W 57th St *Web:* www.thebody.com	New York	NY	10107	212-541-8500	541-4911	356
Body/Mind Restoration Retreats 56 Lieb Rd *Web:* www.bodymindretreats.com	Spencer	NY	14883	607-277-7779		706
Body-Borneman Insurance PO Box 584 *Web:* www.body-borneman.com	Boyertown	PA	19512	610-367-1100	367-1140	390
Body-Solid Inc 1900 Des Plaines Ave *TF:* 800-833-1227 ■ *Web:* www.bodysolid.com	Forest Park	IL	60130	708-427-3500	427-3556	267
Boeck & Assoc Inc 930 Town Centre Dr *Web:* boeckinsurance.com	Medford	OR	97504	541-770-9400		390
BoeFly LLC 50 W 72nd St Ste C6 *TF:* 800-277-3158 ■ *Web:* www.boefly.com	New York	NY	10023	800-277-3158		387
Boehl Stopher & Graves LLP 400 W Market St Ste 2300 *Web:* www.bsg-law.com	Louisville	KY	40202	502-589-5980		428
Boehm Pressed Steel Co 5440 Wegman Dr *TF:* 800-936-3227 ■ *Web:* www.boehmstampings.com	Valley City	OH	44280	800-936-3227		488
Boehringer Ingelheim Ltd 5180 S Service Rd *TF:* 800-268-9243 ■ *Web:* www.boehringer-ingelheim.com	Burlington	ON	L7L5H4	905-639-0333		582
Boehringer Ingelheim Pharmaceuticals Inc 900 Ridgebury Rd **Fax:* Cust Svc ■ *TF:* 800-243-0127 ■ *Web:* www.boehringer-ingelheim.com	Ridgefield	CT	06877	203-798-9988	791-6234*	582
Boehringer Ingelheim Vetmedica Inc 2621 N Belt Hwy *TF:* 800-821-7467 ■ *Web:* www.bi-vetmedica.com	Saint Joseph	MO	64506	816-233-2571		584
Boeing Co, The 100 N Riverside Plaza *NYSE:* BA ■ *Web:* www.boeing.com	Chicago	IL	60606	312-544-2000		20
Boeing Company Commercial Airplane Group PO Box 3707 *Web:* www.boeing.com/commercial	Seattle	WA	98124	206-655-2121		20
Boeing Phantom Works PO Box 2515 *Web:* www.boeing.com	Seal Beach	CA	90740	562-797-2020		529

Name / Address	City	State	ZIP	Phone	Fax	Class
Boekel Scientific 855 Pennsylvania Blvd *TF:* 800-336-6929 ■ *Web:* www.boekelsci.com	Feasterville	PA	19053	215-396-8200	396-8264	420
Boelte-Hall Litho Inc 4710 Roe Pkwy *Web:* boelte.com	Roeland Park	KS	66205	913-766-7700		627
Boelter Cos Inc N22W23685 Ridgeview Pkwy W *TF:* 800-263-5837 ■ *Web:* www.boelter.com	West Waukesha	WI	53188	262-523-6200	523-6003	300
Boelter Industries Inc 202 Galewski Dr. *Web:* www.wspackaging.com	Winona	MN	55987	507-452-2315		101
Boenning & Scattergood Inc 200 Barr Harbor Dr Four Tower Bridge Ste 300 *TF:* 800-883-1212 ■ *Web:* www.boenninginc.com	West Conshohocken	PA	19428	610-832-1212		401
Boerner Botanical Gardens 9400 Boerner Dr *TF:* 800-733-2622 ■ *Web:* www.boernerbotanicalgardens.org	Hales Corners	WI	53130	414-525-5601		97
Boesen the Florist 3422 Beaver Ave *TF:* 800-274-4761 ■ *Web:* www.boesen.com	Des Moines	IA	50310	515-274-4761		292
Boething Treeland Farms Inc 23475 Long Valley Rd. *Web:* boethingtreeland.com	Woodland Hills	CA	91367	818-883-1222	712-6979	752
Bogachiel State Park 185983 Hwy 101 *Web:* www.parks.wa.gov	Forks	WA	98331	360-374-6356		565
Bogart & Brownell 7648 Standish Pl Ste 320 *Web:* www.bogartandbrownell.com	Rockville	MD	20855	301-444-4500		390
Bogen Communications International Inc 50 Spring St *OTC:* BOGN ■ *TF:* 800-999-2809 ■ *Web:* www.bogen.com	Ramsey	NJ	07446	201-934-8500	934-6532	52
Boggy Depot State Park 475 S Pk Ln *Web:* www.travelok.com	Atoka	OK	74525	580-889-5625	889-7868	565
Bogle Vineyards & Winery 37783 County Rd 144 *Web:* www.boglewinery.com	Clarksburg	CA	95612	916-744-1139	744-1187	50-7
Bognet Construction Associates Inc 1911 N Ft Myer Dr Ste 705 *Web:* www.bognet.com	Arlington	VA	22209	703-807-0007		186
Bogota School District 1 Henry C Luthin Pl	Bogota	NJ	07603	201-441-4800		685
Boh Bros Construction Co LLC 730 S Tonti St *TF:* 800-284-3377 ■ *Web:* www.bohbros.com	New Orleans	LA	70119	504-821-2400	821-0714	188-4
Bohanan's Prime Steaks & Seafood 219 E Houston St 2nd Fl. *Web:* www.bohanans.com	San Antonio	TX	78205	210-472-2600	472-2276	671
Bohannan Huston Inc 7500 Jefferson St NE *TF:* 800-877-5332 ■ *Web:* www.bhinc.com	Albuquerque	NM	87109	505-823-1000	798-7988	178-5
Boheme, The 325 S Orange Ave *TF:* 866-663-0024 ■ *Web:* www.grandbohemianhotel.com/theboheme	Orlando	FL	32801	407-313-9000		671
Bohemian Cafe 1406 S 13th St *Web:* www.bohemiancafe.net	Omaha	NE	68108	402-342-9838		671
Bohemian Hotel Celebration 700 Bloom St *TF:* 888-249-4007 ■ *Web:* www.celebrationhotel.com	Celebration	FL	34747	407-566-6000	566-1844	379
Bohle Co, The 1625 Stanford St	Santa Monica	CA	90404	310-785-0515	277-2066	636
Bohler Engineering PC 35 Technology Dr *Web:* www.atlantictraffic.com	Warren	NJ	07059	908-668-8300		256
Bohler-Uddeholm North America 2505 Millenium Dr *TF:* 800-638-2520 ■ *Web:* www.bucorp.com	Elgin	IL	60124	630-883-3100	883-3101	492
Bohn & Dawson Inc 3500 Tree Ct Industrial Blvd *Web:* www.bohnanddawson.com	Saint Louis	MO	63122	636-225-5011	825-6111	480
Bohnert Equipment Company Inc 1010 S Ninth St *Web:* www.bohnert.com	Louisville	KY	40203	502-584-3391		57
Bohr Dahm Greif & Assoc PC 1845 51st St NE *Web:* bdgcpas.com	Cedar Rapids	IA	52402	319-366-8400		2
Bohrens Moving & Storage Inc 3 Applegate Dr *TF:* 800-326-4736 ■ *Web:* www.bohrensmoving.com	Robbinsville	NJ	08691	609-208-1470	208-1471	519
Boies Schiller & Flexner LLP 5301 Wisconsin Ave NW *Web:* bsfllp.com	Washington	DC	20015	202-237-2727	237-6131	428
Boiling Springs Savings Bank (BSSB) 25 Orient Way *TF:* 888-388-7459 ■ *Web:* www.bssbank.com	Rutherford	NJ	07070	201-939-5000	939-3957	70
Boiling Springs State Park 207745 Boiling Springs Rd *Web:* www.travelok.com	Woodward	OK	73801	580-256-7664	256-4338	565
Boingo Wireless Inc 10960 Wilshire Blvd Ste 800 *TF:* 800-880-4117 ■ *Web:* www.boingo.com	Los Angeles	CA	90024	310-586-5180		177
Boiron-Borneman Inc 6 Campus Blvd *Web:* www.boironusa.com	Newtown Square	PA	19073	610-325-7464		231
Bois Blanc Island Lighthouse National Historic Site 30 Victoria St *Web:* www.pc.gc.ca/eng/lhn-nhs/on/boisblanc/index.aspx	Lachine	QC	N9V2Z2	519-736-5416	736-6603	563
Bois BSL Energie Inc 1081 Rue Industrielle CP4 *Web:* www.smartlog.ca	Mont-joli	QC	G5H3T9	418-775-5360		290
Boisaco Inc 648, Chemin du Moulin *Web:* www.boisaco.com	Sacre-Coeur	QC	G0T1Y0	418-236-4633		683
Boise Airport 3201 Airport Way *Web:* www.cityofboise.org	Boise	ID	83705	208-383-3110		27
Boise Art Museum 670 Julia Davis Dr *Web:* www.boiseartmuseum.org	Boise	ID	83702	208-345-8330	345-2247	520
Boise Bible College 8695 W Marigold St *TF:* 800-893-7755 ■ *Web:* www.boisebible.edu	Boise	ID	83714	208-376-7731	376-7743	161
Boise Cascade LLC 1111 W Jefferson St Ste 300 *Web:* www.bc.com	Boise	ID	83702	208-384-6161		557
Boise Centre on the Grove 850 W Front St *Web:* www.boisecentre.com	Boise	ID	83702	208-336-8900	336-8803	205
Boise City Hall 150 N Capitol Blvd *TF:* 800-377-3529 ■ *Web:* www.cityofboise.org	Boise	ID	83702	208-384-4422	384-4420	337
Boise City Independent School District 8169 W Victory Rd *Web:* www.boiseschools.org	Boise	ID	83709	208-854-4000	854-4003	685
Boise Convention & Visitors Bureau 250 S Fifth St Ste 300 *TF:* 800-635-5240 ■ *Web:* www.boise.org	Boise	ID	83702	208-344-7777		206
Boise County 420 Main St PO Box 1300 *Web:* www.boisecounty.us	Idaho City	ID	83631	208-392-4431	392-4473	338
Boise Metro Chamber of Commerce PO Box 2368 *Web:* www.boisechamber.org	Boise	ID	83701	208-472-5205	472-5201	139
Boise Philharmonic Assn Inc 516 S Ninth St *Web:* boisephil.org	Boise	ID	83702	208-344-7849	336-9078	573-3
Boise Public Library 715 S Capitol Blvd *Web:* www.boisepubliclibrary.org	Boise	ID	83702	208-972-8200	384-4025	434-3
Boise State University 1910 University Dr *Web:* my.boisestate.edu	Boise	ID	83725	208-426-1000		166
Boise VA Medical Center 500 W Fort St *TF:* 866-437-5093 ■ *Web:* www.boise.va.gov	Boise	ID	83702	208-422-1000		374-8
Boise Valley Feeders LLC 1555 Shoreline Dr Ste 320 **Fax Area Code:* 800 ■ *TF:* 800-657-6305 ■ *Web:* www.agribeef.com	Boise	ID	83702	208-338-2605	657-6305*	10-1
Boise Weekly 523 Broad St *Web:* www.boiseweekly.com	Boise	ID	83702	208-344-2055	342-4733	532-5
Boiseries Raymond Inc 11880, 56e Ave *TF:* 800-361-6577 ■ *Web:* www.boiseriesraymond.com	Montreal	QC	H1E2L6	514-494-1141	494-9666	499
Boise-Winnemucca Stages Inc 1230 W Bannock St *TF:* 800-448-5692 ■ *Web:* www.boise-winnemuccastages.com	Boise	ID	83702	208-336-3300	336-3303	107
Boite a Fleur De Laval Inc La 3266 Boul Sainte-Rose *TF:* 800-784-3495 ■ *Web:* alaboiteafleurs.com	Laval	QC	H7P4K8	450-622-0341		292
Bo-Jac Seed Co 245 County Rd 1500 E	Mount Pulaski	IL	62548	217-792-5001		10-11
Bojangles' Restaurants Inc 9432 Southern Pine Blvd *TF:* 800-366-9921 ■ *Web:* www.bojangles.com	Charlotte	NC	28273	704-335-1804		670
Bojo Engineering 473 Sapena Ct Ste 19 *Web:* www.bojoinc.com	Santa Clara	CA	95054	408-844-8211		261
Bokam Engineering Inc 2720 S Shannon St *TF:* 800-201-2011 ■ *Web:* www.bokam.com	Santa Ana	CA	92704	714-513-2200		261
Boker's Inc 3104 Snelling Ave *TF:* 800-927-4377 ■ *Web:* www.bokers.com	Minneapolis	MN	55406	612-729-9365		621
Boksa Marine Design 16132 Churchview Dr Ste 205 *Web:* boksamarinedesign.com	Lithia	FL	33547	813-654-9800		261
Boland 30 W Watkins Mill Rd *TF:* 800-552-6526 ■ *Web:* www.boland.com	Gaithersburg	MD	20878	240-306-3000		610
Boland Balloon Post Mills Airport PO Box 51 *Web:* www.myairship.com	Post Mills	VT	05058	802-333-9254	333-9254	28
Boland Marine & Mfg Company Inc 1000 Tchoupitoulas St *Web:* www.bolandmarine.com	New Orleans	LA	70130	504-581-5800	581-5814	698
Bolanos & Company Inc 8708 Killam Indus Blvd *Web:* www.bolanos.com	Laredo	TX	78045	956-722-0976		311
Bold Ideas 645 N Michigan Ave Ste 800	Chicago	IL	60611	312-280-0440		317
Bold Planning Solutions Llc 1116 Sklar Dr E *TF:* 800-257-8881 ■ *Web:* www.boldplanning.com	Venice	FL	34293	941-497-3110		809
Boldcap Ventures LLC 750 Lexington Ave 6th Fl **Fax Area Code:* 917 ■ *Web:* www.boldcap.com	New York	NY	10022	212-730-5498	591-0880*	792
Bolden Lipkin PC 3993 Huntingdon Pk. *TF:* 888-947-3750 ■ *Web:* blicpa.com	Huntingdon Valley	PA	19006	215-947-3750		2
Bolder Graphics 5375 50 St SE *Web:* www.boldergraphics.com	Calgary	AB	T2C3W1	403-299-9400		627
Bolder Technology Inc 4740 Hancock Dr *Web:* bolder.com	Boulder	CO	80303	303-447-8677		196
Boldfocus Inc 1900 S Norfolk St Ste 350 *Web:* www.boldfocus.com	San Mateo	CA	94403	650-212-2653		180
Boldt Carlisle & Smith LLC 1255 Lee St SE Ste 210 *Web:* www.bcsllc.com	Salem	OR	97302	503-585-7751		2
Bolduc Leroux Inc 3365 des Entreprises Blvd *Web:* www.bolducleroux.ca	Terrebonne	QC	J6X4J9	450-477-3413		492
Boler Co 500 Pk Blvd Ste 450 *TF:* 800-728-7828 ■ *Web:* hendrickson-intl.com	Itasca	IL	60143	630-773-9111	773-9121	360-3
Boler Equipment Service Inc 4611 Sinclair Ave *Web:* www.boler.net	Midland	TX	79707	432-694-0660	694-2120	579
Bolero Assoc 1820 W Orangewood Ave *TF:* 800-775-5325 ■ *Web:* www.boleroassociates.com	Orange	CA	92868	714-634-4441		463
Boley Tool & Machine Works Inc 1044 Spring Bay Rd *Web:* boleytool.com	East Peoria	IL	61611	309-694-2722		493
Bolger LLC 3301 Como Ave SE *TF:* 866-264-3287 ■ *Web:* www.bolgerinc.com	Minneapolis	MN	55414	651-645-6311	645-1750	627
Bolin Marketing & Advertising 2523 Wayzata Blvd Ste 300 *TF:* 800-876-6264 ■ *Web:* www.bolinmarketing.com	Minneapolis	MN	55405	612-374-1200		7
Boling Furniture Co 311 NE Church Rd *TF:* 800-540-6008 ■ *Web:* bolingfurniture.com	Mount Olive	NC	28365	919-635-2400	635-4845	319-1

	Phone	Fax	Class
Bolingbrook Area Chamber of Commerce & Industry			
201 Canterbury Ln Unit B .... Bolingbrook IL 60440	630-226-8420	226-8426	139
TF: 800 216 1110 ■ *Web:* www.bolingbrookchamber.org			
Bolivar County 200 S Ct St .... Cleveland MS 38732	662-846-5877	846-5880	338
Web: www.co.bolivar.ms.us			
Bolivar County Library			
104 S Leflore Ave .... Cleveland MS 38732	662-843-2774	843-4701	434-3
Web: www.bolivar.lib.ms.us			
Bolivar Medical Ctr 901 Hwy 8 E .... Cleveland MS 38732	662-846-0061	846-2380	374-3
Web: www.bolivarmedical.com			
Bolivarian Republic of Venezuela			
Consulate General			
545 Boylston St 3rd Fl .... Boston MA 02116	617-266-9368		257
Web: www.embavenez-us.org/_boston			
Bolivia 801 Second Ave 4th Fl Ste 402 .... New York NY 10017	212-682-8132		784
Web: www.unohrlls.org			
Consulate General			
800 Second Ave Ste 300 .... New York NY 10017	212-687-0530	687-0532	257
Web: www.bolivianyc.org			
Embassy 3014 Massachusetts Ave NW .... Washington DC 20008	202-483-4410	328-3712	257
Bollard Group LLC, The 1 Joy St .... Boston MA 02108	617-720-5800		194
Web: www.bollard.com			
Bolle Inc 9200 Cody St .... Overland Park KS 66214	913-752-3400	752-3550	542
TF: 800-423-3537 ■ *Web:* www.bolle.com			
Boller Construction Company Inc			
3045 Washington St .... Waukegan IL 60085	847-662-5566		187
Web: www.bollerconstruction.com			
Bolles School 7400 San Jose Blvd .... Jacksonville FL 32217	904-733-9292	739-9929	622
Web: www.bolles.org			
Bollinger Algiers Inc			
434 Powder St .... New Orleans LA 70114	504-362-7960	361-1679	698
Web: www.bollingershipyards.com			
Bollinger County 207 Mayfield Dr .... Marble Hill MO 63764	573-238-1174		338
TF: 800-777-0068 ■ *Web:* bcmnh.org			
Bollinger Gretna 4640 Peters Rd .... Harvey LA 70058	504-367-8080		698
TF: 800-829-2002 ■ *Web:* bollingershipyards.com			
Bollinger Insurance 101 JFK Pkwy .... Short Hills NJ 07078	973-467-0444		390
Web: www.bollingerinsurance.com			
Bollinger Mill State Historic Site			
113 Bollinger Mill Rd .... Burfordville MO 63739	573-243-4591		565
Web: www.mostateparks.com			
Bollinger Shipyards Inc			
8365 Louisiana 308 .... Lockport LA 70374	985-532-2554	532-7225	698
Web: www.bollingershipyards.com			
Bollinger, Lach & Associates Inc			
333 Pierce Rd Ste 200 .... Itasca IL 60143	630-438-6400		261
Web: www.bollingerlach.com			
Bollman Hat Co 110 E Main St .... Adamstown PA 19501	717-484-4361		155-9
Web: www.bollmanhats.com			
Bollus Lynch LLP 89 Shrewsbury St .... Worcester MA 01604	508-755-7107		2
Web: www.bolluslynch.com			
Bolnick & Snow LLP			
39 Old Doansburg Rd .... Brewster NY 10509	845-279-6300		2
Web: bolnickandsnow.com			
Bolon Hart & Buehler Inc			
100 E Broad St Ste 2450 .... Columbus OH 43215	614-228-2691		2
Web: bhbcpa.com			
Bolsa Chica Ecological Reserve			
3842 Warner Ave .... Huntington Beach CA 92649	714-846-1114	846-4065	823
Web: www.bolsachica.org			
Bolsan Company Inc			
163 Linnwood Rd .... Eighty Four PA 15330	724-225-0446		567
Web: www.bolsan.com			
Bolt Products Inc			
16725 E Johnson Dr .... City Of Industry CA 91745	626-961-4401		351
TF: 800-423-6503 ■ *Web:* www.boltproducts.com			
Bolt Public Relations			
2911 State St Ste K .... Carlsbad CA 92008	760-730-7400		636
Web: www.boltpr.com			
BOLT Solutions Inc			
90 Park Ave Ste 1700 .... New York NY 10016	212-608-4646		626
Web: boltinc.com			
Bolt Staffing Service Inc			
3427 Broadway St Ste F4 .... American Canyon CA 94503	707-552-7800		260
Web: www.boltstaffing.com			
Bolt Technology Corp 4 Duke Pl .... Norwalk CT 06854	203-853-0700	854-9601	537
NASDAQ: BOLT			
Boltaron Performance Products LLC			
1 General St .... Newcomerstown OH 43832	740-498-5900		601
Web: www.boltaron.com			
Bolte Real Estate Inc & Bolte Insurance Inc			
134 E Second St .... Port Clinton OH 43452	419-732-3111		390
Web: bolterealty.com			
Bolthouse Farms			
7200 E Brundage Ln .... Bakersfield CA 93307	800-467-4683	366-2834*	10-11
**Fax Area Code:* 661 ■ **Fax:* Sales ■ *TF:* 800-467-4683 ■ *Web:* www.bolthouse.com			
Bolton & Co			
3475 E Foothill Blvd Ste 100 .... Pasadena CA 91107	626-799-7000	441-3233	390
TF: 800-439-9337 ■ *Web:* www.boltonco.com			
Bolton & Hay Inc 2701 Delaware Ave .... Des Moines IA 50317	515-265-2554		300
TF: 800-362-1861 ■ *Web:* www.boltonhay.com			
Bolton & Menk Inc 1960 Premier Dr .... Mankato MN 56001	507-625-4171	625-4177	261
Web: www.bolton-menk.com			
Bolton Construction & Service of WNC Inc			
169 Elk Mtn Rd .... Asheville NC 28804	828-253-3621		186
TF: 800-466-3337 ■ *Web:* boltonservicewnc.com			
Bolton Metal Products Co			
2042 Axemann Rd .... Bellefonte PA 16823	814-355-6217	355-6219	485
Web: www.boltonmetalproducts.com			
Bolton Oil Company Ltd 1316 54th St .... Lubbock TX 79412	806-747-1629		541
Web: www.boltonoil.com			
Bolton, Sullivan, Taylor & Weber LLP			
1023 N Mallard .... Palestine TX 75801	903-729-2229		2
Web: bstwcpa.com			
Bolttech Mannings			
501 Mosside Blvd .... North Versailles PA 15137	724-872-4873	829-1834*	385
**Fax Area Code:* 412 ■ *TF:* 888-846-8827 ■ *Web:* www.bolttechmannings.com			

	Phone	Fax	Class
BOMA (Building Owners & Managers Assn International)			
1101 15th St NW Ste 800 .... Washington DC 20005	202-408-2662	326-6377	49-17
TF: 800-426-6292 ■ *Web:* www.boma.org			
Bo-mac Contractors Ltd			
1020 Lindbergh Dr .... Beaumont TX 77707	409-842-2125		188
TF: 800-526-6221 ■ *Web:* www.bomaccontractors.com			
Bomag Americas Inc			
125 Blue Granite Pkwy .... Ridgeway SC 61443	803-337-0700	337-0800	190
TF: 800-782-6624 ■ *Web:* www.bomag.com			
Bomaine Corp 20731 S Fordyce Ave .... Carson CA 90810	310-537-1979		360-2
Boman Kemp Basement Window Systems			
2393 S 1900 W .... Ogden UT 84401	801-731-0615		480
Web: www.boman-kemp.com			
Bomanite Corp			
8777 Auburn Folsom Rd Ste 108 .... Granite Bay CA 95746	303-369-1115		183
Web: www.bomanite.com			
Bomar Inc 73 SW St .... Charlestown NH 03603	603-826-5791	826-4125	350
Bomarko Inc 1955 N Oak Rd .... Plymouth IN 46563	574-936-9901		548
Web: www.bomarko.com			
Bomb Magazine 80 Hanson Pl Ste 703 .... Brooklyn NY 11217	718-636-9100	636-9200	457-2
Web: bombmagazine.org			
Bombard Electric LLC 3570 W Post Rd .... Las Vegas NV 89118	702-263-3570		261
Web: www.bombardelectric.com			
Bombardier Aerospace			
400 Cote-Vertu Ouest .... Dorval QC H4S1Y9	514-855-5000	855-7401	20
TF General: 866-855-5001 ■ *Web:* www.bombardier.com			
Bombardier Aerospace Learjet			
1 Learjet Way .... Wichita KS 67209	316-946-2000	946-2220	20
TF: 800-289-5327 ■ *Web:* businessaircraft.bombardier.com			
Bombardier Capital Inc			
1 Learjet Way Mailstop 1 .... Wichita KS 05446	802-764-5232	855-8385*	216
**Fax Area Code:* 514 ■ **Fax:* Sales ■ *TF:* 800-949-5568 ■ *Web:* www.bombardier.com			
Bombardier Inc			
800 RenT-LTvesque Blvd W .... Montreal QC H3B1Y8	514-861-9481	861-7769	20
TSE: BBD/B ■ *Web:* www.bombardier.com			
Bombardier Recreational Products (BRP)			
565 de la Montagne .... Valcourt QC J0E2L0	450-532-2211	532-5133	710
TF: 800-946-0332 ■ *Web:* www.brp.com			
Bombardier Transportation North America			
1101 Parent St .... Saint-Bruno QC J3V6E6	450-441-2020	441-1515	650
Web: www.bombardier.com			
Bombay Club 815 Connecticut Ave NW .... Washington DC 20006	202-659-3727		671
Bombay Cricket Club Restaurant			
1925 SE Hawthorne Blvd .... Portland OR 97214	503-231-0740		671
Web: www.bombaycricketclubrestaurant.com			
Bombay Cuisine 1420 Lake Dr .... Grand Rapids MI 49506	616-456-7055		671
Bombay Curry Company			
2607 Mt Vernon Ave .... Alexandria VA 22301	703-836-6363		671
Web: www.bombaycurrycompany.com			
Bombay Deluxe			
555 W Northern Lights Blvd .... Anchorage AK 99503	907-277-1200		671
Web: www.bombaydeluxe.com			
Bombay House 463 N University Ave .... Provo UT 84601	801-373-6677		671
TF: 800-786-1000 ■ *Web:* bombayhouse.com			
Bombay House 2731 Parleys Way .... Salt Lake City UT 84109	801-581-0222		671
Web: www.bombayhouse.com			
Bombay Mahal			
1001 Rue Jean-Talon Ouest .... Montreal QC H3N1T2	514-273-3331		671
Web: www.restaurantbombaymahal.ca			
Bombet Cashio & Assoc			
11220 N Harrells Ferry Rd .... Baton Rouge LA 70816	225-275-0796	272-3631	400
TF: 800-256-5333 ■ *Web:* www.bombet.com			
Bomco Inc 125 Gloucester Ave .... Gloucester MA 01930	978-283-9000		483
Web: www.bomco.com			
Bomel Construction Company Inc			
8195 E Kaiser Blvd .... Anaheim Hills CA 92808	714-921-1660	921-1943	189-3
Web: www.bomelconstruction.com			
Bomgaars 1805 Zenith .... Sioux City IA 51103	712-226-5000	277-1247	791
Web: www.bomgaars.com			
Bommarito Automotive Group			
15736 Manchester Rd .... Ellisville MO 63011	636-391-7200	394-3241	57
TF: 800-367-2209 ■ *Web:* www.bommarito.com			
Bommer Industries Inc PO Box 187 .... Landrum SC 29356	864-457-3301	457-2487	350
TF: 800-334-1654 ■ *Web:* www.bommer.com			
Bomoseen State Park			
22 Cedar Mtn Rd .... Fair Haven VT 05743	802-265-4242		565
Web: www.vtstateparks.com			
Bon Air Juvenile Correctional Ctr			
1900 Chatsworth Ave .... Bon Air VA 23235	804-323-2550	323-2440	412
Web: www.djj.virginia.gov			
Bon Appetit Management Co			
100 Hamilton Ave Ste 400 .... Palo Alto CA 94301	650-798-8000	798-8090	299
TF: 800-765-9419 ■ *Web:* www.bamco.com			
Bon Chef Inc 205 SR- 94 .... Lafayette NJ 07848	973-383-8848		481
Web: www.bonchef.com			
Bon Homme County			
300 W 18th Ave PO Box 6 .... Tyndall SD 57066	605-589-4215	589-4245	338
Web: ujs.sd.gov			
Bon Homme Yankton Electric Assn			
134 S Lidice St .... Tabor SD 57063	605-463-2507	463-2419	245
TF: 800-925-2929 ■ *Web:* www.byelectric.com			
Bon Secour Fisheries Inc			
17449 County Rd 49 S .... Bon Secour AL 36511	251-949-7411	949-6478	297-5
Web: www.bonsecourfisheries.com			
Bon Secours Community Hospital			
160 E Main St .... Port Jervis NY 12771	845-858-7000	858-7415	374-3
TF: 866-522-4984 ■ *Web:* www.bonsecourscommunityhosp.org			
Bon Secours Health System Inc			
1505 Marriottsville Rd .... Marriottsville MD 21104	410-442-5511	442-1082	353
Web: bonsecours.com/healthsystem			
Bon Secours International			
150 Kingsley Ln .... Norfolk VA 23505	757-889-2273		374-3
Web: bshr.com			
Bon Secours Maryview Medical Ctr			
3636 High St .... Portsmouth VA 23707	757-398-4444		374-3
Web: bonsecours.com/hampton-roads			
Bon Secours Memorial Regional Medical Ctr			
8260 Atlee Rd .... Mechanicsville VA 23116	804-764-6000	764-6420	374-3
Web: richmond.bonsecours.com			

				Phone	Fax	Class
Bon Secours Saint Francis Hospital 2095 Henry Tecklenburg Dr *TF:* 800-863-2273 ■ *Web:* rsfh.com	Charleston	SC	29414	843-402-1000		374-3
Bon Secours Saint Mary's Hospital 5801 Bremo Rd *TF:* 877-342-1500 ■ *Web:* richmond.bonsecours.com	Richmond	VA	23226	804-285-2011	559-0356	374-3
Bon Secours Virginia HealthSource Inc 7229 Forest Ave Ste 208 *Web:* richmond.bonsecours.com	Richmond	VA	23226	804-673-2727		194
Bon Secours Wellness Arena 650 N Academy St *Web:* bonsecoursarena.com	Greenville	SC	29601	864-241-3800		720
Bon Ton Cafe 401 Magazine St *Web:* www.thebontoncafe.com	New Orleans	LA	70130	504-524-3386		671
Bon Venture Services Inc 34 Ironia Rd *Web:* www.bonventure.net	Flanders	NJ	07836	973-584-5699		95
Bon Voyage Travel 1640 E River Rd Ste 115 *TF:* 800-439-7963 ■ *Web:* bvtravel.com	Tucson	AZ	85718	520-797-1110	797-2408	771
Bonadio Group, The 171 Sully's Trail Ste 201 *TF:* 877-917-3077 ■ *Web:* www.bonadio.com	Pittsford	NY	14534	585-381-1000	381-3131	2
Bonafide Security Solutions 3605 N 126th St *Web:* www.bonafidesafe.com	Brookfield	WI	53005	262-790-9400		693
Bonair Daydreams PO Box 1522 *TF:* 888-226-6247 ■ *Web:* www.bonairdaydreams.com	Wrightsville Beach	NC	28480	910-617-3887	509-4108	130
Bonaire Government Tourist Office 80 Broad St Ste 3202 32nd Fl *TF:* 877-267-2572 ■ *Web:* www.infobonaire.com	New York	NY	10004	212-956-5912	956-5913	775
Bonal Technologies Inc 1300 N Campbell Rd *Web:* www.bonal.com	Royal Oak	MI	48067	248-582-0900		811
Bonamici Suzanne (Rep D - OR) 439 Cannon Bldg *Web:* bonamici.house.gov	Washington	DC	20515	202-225-0855	225-9497	342-2
Bonanno, Savino & Davies PC 105 Chestnut St Ste 32 *Web:* www.bsdcpa.com	Needham	MA	02492	781-449-3919		2
Bonanza Beverage Co 6333 Ensworth St *Web:* www.bonanzabev.com	Las Vegas	NV	89119	702-361-4166		81-1
Bonanza Creek Country Guest Ranch 523 Bonanza Creek Rd *TF:* 800-476-6045 ■ *Web:* www.bonanzacreekcountry.com	Martinsdale	MT	59053	406-572-3366	572-3366	239
Bonanza Inc 400 E Pine St Ste 215 *Web:* www.bonanza.com	Seattle	WA	98122	425-654-1521	654-1521	393
Bonanza Press Inc 19860 141st Pl NE *TF:* 800-233-0008 ■ *Web:* www.bonanzapress.com	Woodinville	WA	98072	425-486-3399		627
Bonanza Trade & Supply 6853 Lankershim Blvd *TF:* 888-965-6577 ■ *Web:* www.stonetooling.com	North Hollywood	CA	91605	818-765-6577		194
Bonanzaville USA 1351 Main Ave W *Web:* www.bonanzaville.org	West Fargo	ND	58078	701-282-2822	282-7606	520
BonAppeThai 245 W Pearl St *Web:* bonappethai.com	Jackson	WY	83001	307-734-0245		671
Bonari & Company CPAs 3724 Lakeside Dr Ste 201 *Web:* bonaricpas.com	Reno	NV	89509	775-322-5850		2
Bonaventure Tours 8 Boudreau Ln *TF:* 800-561-1213 ■ *Web:* www.aboutbonaventuretours.com	Haute-Aboujagane	NB	E4P5N1	506-532-3674	532-6487	760
Bond Andiola & Co 39 State Rt 12 3rd Fl *Web:* www.bac-cpa.com	Flemington	NJ	08822	908-782-0023		2
Bond Bros Inc 145 Spring St *Web:* www.bondbrothers.com	Everett	MA	02149	617-387-3400	389-1412	186
Bond Consulting Services 3450 Spring St Ste 108 *TF:* 800-997-9921 ■ *Web:* www.bondconsultingservices.com	Long Beach	CA	90806	562-988-3451		177
Bond County 200 W College Ave *Web:* www.bondcountyil.com	Greenville	IL	62246	618-664-3208	664-2257	338
Bond Digital 2419 N Ashland Ave *Web:* www.bondgrp.com	Chicago	IL	60614	773-549-2710		7
Bond Optics LLC 76 Etna Rd PO Box 422 *Web:* www.bondoptics.com	Lebanon	NH	03766	603-448-2300	448-5489	544
Bond Place Hotel 65 Dundas St E *TF:* 800-268-9390 ■ *Web.* bondplace.ca	Toronto	ON	M5B2G8	416-362-6061		379
Bond Printing Company Inc 104 Plain St *TF:* 800-649-5090 ■ *Web:* www.bondprinting.com	Hanover	MA	02339	781-871-3990		627
Bond Pro LLC 1501 E Second Ave *TF:* 888-789-4985 ■ *Web:* www.cumberlandtech.com	Tampa	FL	33605	888 789 4985		391-5
Bond Tool & Engineering 6190 N Riverview Dr *Web:* www.bondtool.com	Kalamazoo	MI	49004	269-344-5164		256
Bondcote Corp PO Box 729 *TF:* 800-368-2160 ■ *Web:* www.bondcote.com	Pulaski	VA	24301	540-980-2640	980-5636	745-2
Bonded Concrete Inc 303 Rt 155 *TF:* 800-252-8589 ■ *Web:* www.bondedconcrete.com	Watervliet	NY	12189	518-273-5800		182
Bondfield Construction Company Ltd 407 Basaltic Rd *Web:* www.bondfield.com	Concord	ON	L4K4W8	416-667-8422		186
Bondhus Corp 1400 E Broadway St PO Box 660 *TF Cust Svc:* 800-328-8310 ■ *Web:* www.bondhus.com	Monticello	MN	55362	763-295-2162	295-4440	758
Bondioli & Pavesi Inc 10252 Sycamore Dr *Web:* bondioli-pavesi.com	Ashland	VA	23005	804-550-2224		429
Bone & Joint Hospital 1111 N Dewey Ave *Web:* www.boneandjoint.com	Oklahoma City	OK	73103	405-272-9671		374-7
Bone Bank Allografts 4808 Research Dr *TF Sales:* 800-397-0088 ■ *Web:* www.bonebank.com	San Antonio	TX	78240	210-696-7616	696-7609	545
Bone McAllester Norton PLLC 511 Union St Nashville City Ctr Ste 1600 *Web:* www.bonelaw.com	Nashville	TN	37219	615-238-6300		428
Bone's Restaurant 3130 Piedmont Rd NE *TF:* 800-982-1980 ■ *Web:* www.bonesrestaurant.com	Atlanta	GA	30305	404-237-2663	233-5704	671
Bonefish Capital LLC Rosewood Court 2101 Cedar Springs Rd Ste 1050 *Web:* www.bonefishcapital.com	Dallas	TX	75201	214-347-0780		463
Bonefish Grill 3665 Henderson Blvd *Web:* www.bonefishgrill.com	Tampa	FL	33609	813-876-3535		670
Bonefish Grill 3491 Thomasville Rd *Web:* www.bonefishgrill.com	Tallahassee	FL	32309	850-297-0460		671
Bonefish Grill 4501 E 82nd St *Web:* www.bonefishgrill.com	Indianapolis	IN	46250	317-863-3474		671
Bonefish Grill 620 W Edison Ave Ste 100 *Web:* www.bonefishgrill.com	Mishawaka	IN	46545	574-259-2663		671
Bonefish Grill 2100 Koury Blvd *Web:* www.bonefishgrill.com	Greensboro	NC	27407	336-851-8900		671
Bonell Manufacturing Co 13521 S Halsted St *TF:* 800-323-3110 ■ *Web:* www.bonellmfg.com	Riverdale	IL	60827	708-849-1770	849-3434	674
Bonfiglioli USA 3541 Hargrave Ct *Web:* www.bonfiglioliusa.com	Hebron	KY	41048	859-334-3333		709
Bonfire 999 Market St *Web:* www.bonfirerestaurant.com	Paterson	NJ	07513	973-278-2400		671
Bonfire, The 7009 Coastal Hwy *Web:* www.thebonfirerestaurant.com	Ocean City	MD	21842	410-524-7171		671
Bonfit America Inc 5741 Buckingham Pkwy Unit A *TF:* 800-526-6348 ■ *Web:* www.bonfit.com	Culver City	CA	90230	310-204-7880		568
Bongards' Creameries 13200 County Rd 51 *Web:* www.bongards.com	Norwood	MN	55368	952-466-5521		296-5
Bongo Room 1470 N Milwaukee Ave *Web:* www.thebongoroom.com	Chicago	IL	60622	773-489-0690		671
Bongos Cuban Cafe 420 Jefferson Ave *Web:* www.bongoscubancafe.com	Miami Beach	FL	33139	305-695-7000		670
Bongos Cuban Cafe 1498 E Buena Vista Dr *Web:* www.bongoscubancafe.com	Lake Buena Vista	FL	32830	407-828-0999		671
Bonham Area Chamber of Commerce 327 N Main *Web:* www.fannincountytexas.com	Bonham	TX	75418	903-583-4811	583-7972	139
Bonham State Park 1363 State Pk 24 *Web:* tpwd.texas.gov/state-parks/bonham	Bonham	TX	75418	903-583-5022		565
Bonhams & Butterfields 220 San Bruno Ave *TF:* 800-223-2854 ■ *Web:* www.bonhams.com	San Francisco	CA	94103	415-861-7500	861-8951	51
Bonhouse 4713 Kirkwood Hwy	Wilmington	DE	19808	302-633-1218		671
Bonipak 1850 W Stowell Rd *TF:* 800-561-3357 ■ *Web:* www.bonipak.com	Santa Maria	CA	93458	805-925-2585	922-7982	10-11
Bonita Pioneer Packaging Products Inc 7333 SW Bonita Rd *TF:* 800-677-7725 ■ *Web:* www.bonitapioneer.com	Portland	OR	97224	800-677-7725	323-6027	65
Bonita Springs Area Chamber of Commerce 25071 Chamber of Commerce Dr *TF:* 800-226-2943 ■ *Web:* www.bonitaspringschamber.com	Bonita Springs	FL	34135	239-992-2943	992-5011	139
Bonitz Contracting Company Inc 645 Rosewood Dr *Web:* www.bonitz.us	Columbia	SC	29201	803-799-0181	748-9223	189-2
Bonland Industries Inc 50 Newark-Pompton Tpke *TF:* 800-232-6600 ■ *Web:* www.bonlandhvac.com	Wayne	NJ	07470	973-694-3211	628-1120	189-12
Bonnell Aluminum 25 Bonnell St *TF:* 800-846-8885 ■ *Web:* www.bonlalum.com	Newnan	GA	30263	770-253-2020		485
Bonnell's 4259 Bryant Irvin Rd *Web:* bonnellstexas.com	Fort Worth	TX	76109	817-738-5489		671
Bonner Chevrolet Company Inc 694 Wyoming Ave *Web:* www.bonnerchevrolet.com	Kingston	PA	18704	570-763-4799		57
Bonner County 215 S First Ave *TF:* 800-433-0567 ■ *Web:* bonnercounty.us	Sandpoint	ID	83864	208-265-1432		338
Bonnet House Museum & Garden 900 N Birch Rd *Web:* www.bonnethouse.org	Fort Lauderdale	FL	33304	954-563-5393	561-4174	520
Bonnett Wholesale Florists 119 Eigth St E *Web:* www.bonnettwholesale.com	Milan	IL	61264	309-787-4401		292
Bonnette Page & Stone Corp 91 Bisson Ave *Web:* www.bpsnh.com	Laconia	NH	03246	603-524-3411	524-4641	186
Bonneville Collections 6026 S Fashion Point Dr *TF:* 800-660-6138 ■ *Web:* www.bonncoll.com	Ogden	UT	84403	801-621-7880		160
Bonneville County 605 N Capital Ave *TF:* 800-294-4214 ■ *Web:* www.co.bonneville.id.us	Idaho Falls	ID	83402	208-529-1350		338
Bonneville International Corp 55 N 300 W *Web:* www.bonneville.com	Salt Lake City	UT	84101	801-575-7500		643
Bonneville Transloaders Inc (BTI) 642 S Federal Blvd *Web:* www.bonntran.com	Riverton	WY	82501	307-856-7480	856-4623	648
Bonnie Castle Resort 31 Holland St *TF:* 800-955-4511 ■ *Web:* www.bonniecastle.com	Alexandria Bay	NY	13607	315-482-4511		669
Bonnie Heneson Communications Inc 9199 Reisterstown Rd Ste 212C *Web:* www.bonnieheneson.com	Owings Mills	MD	21117	410-654-0000		4
Bonnie Lure State Recreation Area 11321 SW Terwilliger Blvd *TF:* 800-551-6949 ■ *Web:* www.oregonstateparks.org	Portland	OR	97219	800-551-6949		565
Bonnie's Beef & Seafood Co 6867 Gulf Fwy *Web:* www.bonniesbeefandseafood.com	Houston	TX	77087	713-641-2397		671

Name / Address	City	State	Zip	Phone	Fax	Class
Bono's Pit Bar-B-Q 10645 Phillips Hwy Ste 200 *Web:* www.bonosbarbq.com	Jacksonville	FL	32256	904-880-8310	880-8373	670
Bonocore Technology Partners LLC 29 Meadow Ridge Dr *Web:* www.bonocore.com	Corte Madera	CA	94925	415-806-7008		463
Bonsai Artransport Inc 509 Mccormick Dr Ste O *TF:* 800-207-3714 ■ *Web:* www.bonsai-finearts.com	Glen Burnie	MD	21061	410-768-2787		200
Bonsai Japanese Steak House 1925 Lakeland Dr *Web:* facebook.com	Jackson	MS	39216	601-981-0606		671
Bonset America Corp 6107 Corporate Park Dr *Web:* www.bonset.com	Brown Summit	NC	27214	336-375-0234		600
Bonstone Materials Corp 707 Swan Dr *TF:* 800-425-2214 ■ *Web:* bonstone.com	Mukwonago	WI	53149	262-363-9877		3
Bonterra Dining & Wine Room 1829 Cleveland Ave *Web:* www.bonterradining.com	Charlotte	NC	28203	704-333-9463		671
Bonterra Energy Corp 1015 - Fourth St SW Ste 901 *TF:* 800-511-3447 ■ *Web:* www.bonterraenergy.com	Calgary	AB	T2R1J4	403-262-5307		536
Bonterra Trattoria 1016 Eigth St SW *Web:* www.bonterra.ca	Calgary	AB	T2R1K2	403-262-8480		671
Bontex Inc 12918 Whitehorse Ln *OTC: BOTX* ■ *TF:* 800-438-5868 ■ *Web:* www.bontex.com	St. Louis	MO	63131	314-965-8059		601
Bon-Ton Stores Inc 2801 E Market St *NASDAQ: BONT* ■ *TF:* 800-945-4438 ■ *Web:* www.bonton.com	York	PA	17402	717-757-7660		229
Book Depot Inc 67 Front St N *TF:* 888-402-7323 ■ *Web:* www.bookdepot.com	Thorold	ON	L2V1X3	905-680-7230		96
Book Exchange Inc 152 Willey St *TF:* 800-339-7691 ■ *Web:* www.bookexchangewv.com	Morgantown	WV	26505	304-292-7354		95
Book Industry Study Group Inc (BISG) 1412 Broadway 21st Fl Ofc 19 *Web:* www.bisg.org	New York	NY	10018	646-336-7141	336-6214	49-16
Book Loft 631 S Third St *Web:* www.bookloft.com	Columbus	OH	43206	614-464-1774		95
Book Manufacturers Institute Inc (BMI) PO Box 731388 Ste 1-B *Web:* bomi.memberclicks.net	Ormond Beach	FL	32173	386-986-4552	986-4553	49-16
Book Marketing Update PO Box 2887 *Web:* www.bookmarket.com	Taos	NM	87571	575-751-3398	751-3398	531-10
Book Passage 51 Tamal Vista Blvd *TF:* 800-999-7909 ■ *Web:* www.bookpassage.com	Corte Madera	CA	94925	415-927-0960		95
Book Publishing Report 60 Long Ridge Rd Ste 300 *Web:* www.bookpublishingreport.com	Stamford	CT	06902	203-325-8193	325-8915	531-11
Book Revue 313 New York Ave *Web:* www.bookrevue.com	Huntington	NY	11743	631-271-1442	271-5890	95
Book Soup 8818 Sunset Blvd *Web:* www.booksoup.com	West Hollywood	CA	90069	310-659-3110	659-3410	95
Book Systems Inc 4901 University Sq Ste 3 *Web:* www.booksys.com	Huntsville	AL	35816	256-533-9746		180
Book Television 299 Queen St W *Web:* www.booktelevision.com	Toronto	AB	M5V2Z5	416-384-8000	591-5117	740
Bookazine Company Inc 75 Hook Rd *TF:* 800-221-8112 ■ *Web:* www.bookazine.com	Bayonne	NJ	07002	201-339-7777	339-7778	96
BookBuyers 317 Castro St *TF:* 800-909-6161 ■ *Web:* www.bookbuyers.com	Mountain View	CA	94041	650-968-7323		95
Booker Arceneaux & Laskowski LLP 1100 NW Loop 410 Ste 207	San Antonio	TX	78213	210-341-2538		2
Booker Cory A (Sen D - NJ) 359 Dirksen Senate Office Bldg *Web:* www.booker.senate.gov/?p=contact	Washington	DC	20510	202-224-3224	224-8378	342-2
Booker T Washington Insurance Co 1728 Third Ave N	Birmingham	AL	35203	205-328-5454		391-2
Booker T. Washington National Monument 12130 Booker T Washington Hwy *Web:* www.nps.gov/bowa	Hardy	VA	24101	540-721-2094	721-8311	564
Booker T. Washington State Park 5801 Champion Rd *Web:* www.state.tn.us	Chattanooga	TN	37416	423-894-4955		565
Bookkeeping Express Enterprises LLC 671 N Glebe Rd Ste 1610 *Web:* www.bookkeepingexpress.com	Arlington	VA	22203	703-766-5757		2
BookLender.com 8453 Tyco Rd # P *Web:* www.booksfree.com	Vienna	VA	22182	703-748-2390		93
Booklist Magazine 50 E Huron St *TF:* 800-545-2433 ■ *Web:* www.ala.org	Chicago	IL	60611	800-545-2433		457-11
Bookman Road Elementary School 1245 Bookman Rd *TF:* 800-421-3481 ■ *Web:* www.richland2.org	Elgin	SC	29045	803-699-1724		685
Bookmans Entertainment Exchange 8034 N 19th Ave *Web:* www.bookmans.com	Phoenix	AZ	85021	602-433-0255		95
BookPal LLC 18101 Von Karman Ave Ste 1240 *TF:* 866-522-6657 ■ *Web:* book-pal.com	Irvine	CA	92612	866-522-6657		95
BookPeople 603 N Lamar *TF:* 800-853-9757 ■ *Web:* www.bookpeople.com	Austin	TX	78703	512-472-5050	482-8495	95
Books & Books 265 Aragon Ave *Web:* www.booksandbooks.com	Coral Gables	FL	33134	305-442-4408		95
Books Inc 2251 Chestnut St *Web:* www.booksinc.net	San Francisco	CA	94123	415-931-3633		95
Books of Discovery 2539 Spruce St *TF:* 800-775-9227 ■ *Web:* www.booksofdiscovery.com	Boulder	CO	80302	800-775-9227		95
Books on the Square 471 Angell St *TF:* 888-669-9660 ■ *Web:* www.booksq.com	Providence	RI	02906	401-331-9097		95
Books-A-Million Inc 402 Industrial Ln *NASDAQ: BAMM* ■ *TF:* 800-201-3550 ■ *Web:* www.booksamillion.com	Birmingham	AL	35211	205-942-3737		95
Booksource Inc 1230 Macklind Ave **Fax Area Code: 800* ■ *TF:* 800-444-0435 ■ *Web:* www.booksource.com	Saint Louis	MO	63110	314-647-0600	647-1923*	96
Booman Floral 2302 Bautista Ave *TF:* 800-549-0158 ■ *Web:* www.boomanfloral.com	Vista	CA	92084	760-630-4170		292
Boomer Consulting 610 Humboldt St *TF:* 800-739-9998 ■ *Web:* www.boomer.com	Manhattan	KS	66502	785-537-2358		194
Boomer Project 2601 Floyd Ave *Web:* www.boomerproject.com	Richmond	VA	23220	804-358-8981		194
Boomerang Grille 9200 S Western *Web:* www.boomeranggrille.com	Oklahoma City	OK	73139	405-378-7049		670
Boomerang Management Enterprises LLC 1935 Samco Rd Ste 104 *Web:* boomerangme.com	Rapid City	SD	57702	605-718-2666		256
Boomers & Beyond Inc 1998 Ruffin Mill Rd *TF:* 800-958-8324 ■ *Web:* www.firststreetonline.com	Colonial Heights	VA	23834	804-524-9888		195
Boomtown Casino & Hotel Reno 2100 Garson Rd *TF Resv:* 800-648-3790 ■ *Web:* boomtownreno.com	Verdi	NV	89439	775-345-6000		133
Boomtown Casino Biloxi 676 Bayview Ave *TF:* 800-627-0777 ■ *Web:* www.boomtownbiloxi.com	Biloxi	MS	39530	228-435-7000		133
Boomtown Casino New Orleans 4132 Peters Rd *TF:* 800-366-7711 ■ *Web:* www.boomtownneworleans.com	Harvey	LA	70058	504-366-7711		133
Boomtown Hotel Casino 300 Riverside Dr *Web:* www.boomtownbossier.com	Bossier City	LA	71111	318-746-0711		133
Boomtown Inc 2100 Garson Rd *TF:* 800-648-3790 ■ *Web:* www.boomtownreno.com	Verdi	NV	89439	775-345-6000		132
Boomtown Internet Group Inc 111 Rosemary Ln *TF:* 888-454-3330 ■ *Web:* www.boomtownig.com	Glenmoore	PA	19343	888-454-3330		194
Boon Edam Inc 402 McKinney Pkwy *Web:* www.boonedam.us	Lillington	NC	27546	910-814-3800		407
Boondocks Restaurant 3948 S Peninsula Dr *TF:* 800-442-1162 ■ *Web:* boondocks-restaurant.com	Wilbur by the Sea	FL	32127	386-760-9001		671
Boone County 222 S Fourth St *TF:* 800-330-0755 ■ *Web:* www.co.boone.ne.us	Albion	NE	68620	402-395-2055		338
Boone County 601 N Main St *TF:* 877-225-7077 ■ *Web:* www.boonecountyil.org	Belvidere	IL	61008	815-547-4770	547-3579	338
Boone County 2950 E Washington St *TF:* 800-372-7172 ■ *Web:* www.boonecountyky.org	Burlington	KY	41005	859-334-2242	334-2193	338
Boone County 801 E Walnut St *TF:* 800-552-7583 ■ *Web:* www.showmeboone.com	Columbia	MO	65201	573-886-4270	886-4254	338
Boone County 100 N Main St Ste 201 *Web:* boonecountyar.com	Harrison	AR	72601	870-741-8428	741-9724	338
Boone County 116 W Washington St *TF:* 800-582-8440 ■ *Web:* boonecounty.in.gov	Lebanon	IN	46052	765-483-4458	483-5243	338
Boone County 200 State St *Web:* www.boonecountywv.org	Madison	WV	25130	304-369-7350		338
Boone County Chamber of Commerce 221 N Lebanon St *TF:* 800-382-1039 ■ *Web:* www.boonechamber.org	Lebanon	IN	46052	765-482-1320	482-3114	139
Boone County Convention & Visitors Bureau PO Box 644 *TF:* 800-634-2650 ■ *Web:* www.boonecvb.com	Lebanon	IN	46052	765-484-8572		206
Boone County Historical Society Museum 3801 Ponderosa St *Web:* boonehistory.org	Columbia	MO	65201	573-443-8936		520
Boone County Rural Electric Membership Corp 1207 Indianapolis Ave *TF:* 800-897-7362 ■ *Web:* www.bremc.com	Lebanon	IN	46052	765-482-2390	482-7869	245
Boone Electric Co-op 1413 Rangeline St *TF:* 800-225-8143 ■ *Web:* www.booneelectric.coop	Columbia	MO	65201	573-449-4181		245
Boone Hall Plantation & Gardens 1235 Long Pt Rd *Web:* boonehallplantation.com	Mount Pleasant	SC	29464	843-884-4371	884-0475	50-3
Boone Hospital Ctr 1600 E Broadway *TF:* 800-735-2966 ■ *Web:* www.boone.org	Columbia	MO	65201	573-815-8000		374-3
Boone Newspapers Inc 15222 Freeman's Bend Rd *Web:* www.boonenewspapers.com	Tuscaloosa	AL	35475	205-330-4100	330-4140	637-0
Boone Oakley LLC 1445 S Mint St *Web:* booneoakley.com	Charlotte	NC	28203	704-333-9797		7
Boone Printing & Graphics Inc 70 S Kellogg Ave *TF:* 800-423-1618 ■ *Web:* boonegraphics.net	Goleta	CA	93117	805-683-2349		627
Boone Station State Historic Site 240 Gentry Rd *Web:* www.parks.ky.gov	Lexington	KY	40502	859-527-3131		565
Boone Tavern Hotel of Berea College 100 S Main St *TF:* 800-366-9358 ■ *Web:* www.boonetavernhotel.com	Berea	KY	40404	859-985-3700		379
Boonshoft Museum of Discovery 2600 DeWeese Pkwy *TF:* 800-832-3474 ■ *Web:* www.boonshoftmuseum.org	Dayton	OH	45414	937-275-7431	275-5811	520
Boonville Correctional Ctr 1216 E Morgan St **Fax: Warden* ■ *TF:* 800-392-8486 ■ *Web:* doc.mo.gov	Boonville	MO	65233	660-882-6521	882-7825*	213
Boos Dental Laboratory 1000 Boone Ave N Ste 660 *TF:* 800-333-2667 ■ *Web:* www.dentalservices.net	Golden Valley	MN	55427	763-544-1446	546-1392	415
Boost Motor Group Inc 3080 Yonge St *TF:* 877-266-7841 ■ *Web:* www.boostmotorgroup.com	Toronto	ON	M4N3N1	416-487-7000		177
Boost Rewards 811 E Fourth St Ste B *TF:* 800-324-9756 ■ *Web:* www.boostrewards.com	Dayton	OH	45402	800-324-9756		195
Boostability Inc 2600 W Executive Pkwy Ste 200 *TF:* 800-261-1537 ■ *Web:* www.boostability.com	Lehi	UT	84043	800-261-1537		5
Boot Hill Casino & Resort 4000 W Comanche St *Web:* boothillcasino.com	Dodge City	KS	67801	620-682-7777		452
Boot Hill Museum 500 W Wyatt Earp Blvd *Web:* www.boothill.org	Dodge City	KS	67801	620-227-8188		520
BootBarn Inc 620 Pan American Dr *Web:* www.bootbarn.com	Livingston	TX	77351	936-327-2405		229
Booth 4900 Nautilus Ct N Ste 220 *TF:* 800-332-6684 ■ *Web:* www.boothco.com	Boulder	CO	80301	303-581-1408		5

Phone | Fax | Class

Booth Bay Marketing
1220 Valley Forge Rd Ste 45 Phoenixville PA 19460 610-933-5112 195
Web: www.boothbay.com

Booth Creek Ski Holdings Inc
950 Red Sand Stone Rd Ste 43 Vail CO 81657 530-550-5100 787
Web: www.boothcreek.com

Booth Manufacturing Co
3101 Industrial Ave 2 Fort Pierce FL 34946 772-465-4441 547

Booth Production Services Inc
5768 Remington Dr Winston-Salem NC 27104 336-766-1961 514
Web: www.boothproductionservices.com

Booth Theatre 222 W 45th St New York NY 10036 212-239-6200 747
TF: 800-432-7780 ■ *Web:* www.telecharge.com

Booth's Bowery 3657 S Nova Rd Port Orange FL 32129 386-761-9464 671
Web: www.boothsbowery.com

Bootheel Petroleum Company Inc
623 N SR- 25 PO Box 187 Dexter MO 63841 573-624-4160 580
Web: www.bootheelpetroleum.com

Bootz Industries PO Box 18010 Evansville IN 47719 812-423-5401 429-2254 609
Web: www.bootz.com

Booz Allen Hamilton Inc
8283 Greensboro Dr McLean VA 22102 703-902-5000 902-3333 194
TF: 866-390-3908 ■ *Web:* www.boozallen.com

Boozman John (Sen R - AR)
141 Hart Senate Office Bldg Washington DC 20510 202-224-4843 342-2
Web: www.boozman.senate.gov

BOP (Brookfield Properties Corp)
181 Bay St Ste 330 Toronto ON M5J2T3 416-369-2300 369-2301 655
NYSE: BPO ■ *TF:* 800-387-0825 ■ *Web:* www.brookfieldproperties.com

BOPI 1705 S Veterans Pkwy Bloomington IL 61701 309-662-3395 627
Web: www.bopi.com

Bopp-Busch Mfg Co 545 E Huron Rd Au Gres MI 48703 989-876-7121 876-6555 488
Web: www.boppbusch.com

Borak Inc Dba Northfield Pharm
601 Water St S Northfield MN 55057 507-663-0344 237

Boral Industries Inc
200 Mansell Ct E Ste 310 Roswell GA 30076 770-645-4500 360-3
Web: boral.com.au

Boral Material Technologies Inc
45 NE Loop 410 Ste 700 San Antonio TX 78216 210-349-4069 146
TF: 800-964-0951 ■ *Web:* www.boralmti.com

Borbet Alabama Inc 979 W Veterans Blvd Auburn AL 36832 334-502-9400 247

Borbon Inc 7312 Walnut Ave Buena Park CA 90620 714-994-0170 994-0641 189-8
TF: 800-675-1118 ■ *Web:* www.borbon.net

Bordallo Madeleine (Rep D - GU)
2441 Rayburn Bldg Washington DC 20515 202-225-1188 226-0341 342-2
Web: bordallo.house.gov

Borden Dairy Co
8750 N Central Expy Ste 400 Dallas TX 75231 214-459-1100 296-25
Web: www.lalafoods.com

Borden Ladner Gervais LLP
40 King St W Toronto ON M5H3Y4 416-367-6000 41
TF: 800-268-8326 ■ *Web:* www.blg.com

Borden Office Equipment Co
141 N Fifth St Steubenville OH 43952 740-283-3321 320
Web: www.bordenofficeequipment.com

Border Field State Park
1500 Monument Rd San Diego CA 92154 619-575-3613 565
Web: www.parks.ca.gov/default.asp?page_id=664

Border Gold Corp 15234 N Bluff Rd White Rock BC V4B3E6 604-535-3287 691
TF: 888-312-2288 ■ *Web:* www.bordergold.com

Border Grill Las Vegas
3950 Las Vegas Blvd S
Mandalay Bay Resort & Casino Las Vegas NV 89119 702-632-7403 632-6945 671
Web: www.bordergrill.com

Border States Electric Supply
105 25th St N Fargo ND 58102 701-293-5834 246
TF: 800-800-0199 ■ *Web:* www.borderstates.com

Border States Paving Inc 4101 N 32nd St Fargo ND 58102 701-237-4860 237-0233 188-4
Web: borderstatespaving.com

Border Valley Trading Ltd
604 E Mead Rd Brawley CA 92227 760-344-6700 344-4305 10
Web: www.bordervalley.com

Bordercomm Partners LP
6842 Industrial Ave El Paso TX 79915 915-779-3000 194
Web: bordercomm.com

BorderJump LLC
631 Second Ave S Ste 200 Nashville TN 37210 615-346-9373 742-2529 393

Borderland Construction Company Inc
400 E 38 St Tucson AZ 85713 520-623-0900 623-0232 188-4
Web: borderland-inc.com

Borderland State Park
Massapoag Ave North Easton MA 02356 508-238-6566 565
Web: www.mass.gov

Borderland Tours 2875 W Hilltop Rd Portal AZ 85632 520-558-2351 760
Web: www.borderland-tours.com

Bordner PJ Company Inc
2100 Wales Rd NE Massillon OH 44646 330-832-7522 345

Boreal Genomics Inc
5150 El Camino Real Los Altos CA 94022 604-822-8268 231
TF: 800-681-5644 ■ *Web:* www.borealgenomics.com

Borealis Compounds LLC
176 Thomas Rd Port Murray NJ 07865 908-850-6200 77
Web: www.borealisgroup.com

Borealis Ventures 10 Allen St Hanover NH 03755 603-643-1500 792
Web: www.borealisventures.com

Borek Business Solutions
1144 Willagillespie Rd Ste 28 Eugene OR 97401 541-345-3883 686-5800 196

Borek Construction Ltd
9690 Rd 223 PO Box 870 Dawson Creek BC V1G4H8 250-782-5561 188
Web: www.borekltd.com

Borel Private Bank & Trust Co
160 Bovet Rd San Mateo CA 94402 650-378-3700 70
Web: www.bostonprivate.com

Boren, Oliver & Coffey LLP
59 N Jefferson St Martinsville IN 46151 765-342-0147 428
TF: 800-403-9971 ■ *Web:* boclawyers.com

Borenson and Assoc 330 Schantz Rd Allentown PA 18104 610-398-6908 196
Web: borenson.com

Borer Financial Communication LLC
615 Fifth St Ste 210 Carlstadt NJ 07072 201-939-9297 225
Web: borerfinancial.com

Borg Compressed Steel Corp
1032 N Lewis Ave Tulsa OK 74110 918-587-2511 686
Web: yaffeco.net

Borg Indak Inc 701 Enterprise Dr Delavan WI 53115 262-728-5531 153
TF: 800-433-5778 ■ *Web:* www.borgindak.com

Borgata Hotel Casino & Spa
1 Borgata Way Atlantic City NJ 08401 609-317-1000 317-1039 379
TF: 877-786-9900 ■ *Web:* www.theborgata.com

Borger High School 600 W First St Borger TX 79007 806-273-1029 685
Web: www.borgerisd.net

Borgeson Universal Company Inc
91 Technology Park Dr Torrington CT 06790 860-482-8283 723
Web: borgeson.com

Borgess Medical Ctr 1521 Gull Rd Kalamazoo MI 49048 269-226-7000 226-5966 374-3
Web: www.borgess.com

Borghese 3 E 54th St New York NY 10022 212-659-5300 214
Web: www.borghese.com

Borghesi Building & Engineering Company Inc
2155 E Main St Torrington CT 06790 860-482-7613 256
Web: www.borghesibuilding.com

BorgWarner Automatic Transmission Systems
3800 Automation Ave Auburn Hills MI 48326 248-754-9600 60
Web: www.borgwarner.com

BorgWarner Inc 3850 Hamlin Rd Auburn Hills MI 48326 248-754-9200 60
NYSE: BWA ■ *Web:* www.borgwarner.com

BorgWarner Morse TEC 800 Warren Rd Ithaca NY 14850 607-257-6700 60
Web: www.borgwarner.com

BorgWarner TorqTransfer Systems
3800 Automation Ave Auburn Hills MI 48326 248-754-9600 60
Web: www.borgwarner.com

Borgwarner Turbo Systems
1849 Brevard Rd Arden NC 28704 828-684-4000 247
Web: www.turbodriven.com

Boricua College 3755 Broadway New York NY 10032 212-694-1000 694-1015* 166
**Fax:* Admissions ■ *TF:* 800-920-4593 ■ *Web:* www.boricuacollege.edu

Borin Manufacturing Inc
5741 Buckingham Pkwy Unit B Culver City CA 90230 310-822-1000 111
Web: borin.com

Borinquen Coast Guard Air Station
260 GuaRd Rd Aguadilla PR 00603 787-890-8400 158
Web: www.uscg.mil/d7/airstaborinquen

Borla Performance Industries Inc
500 Borla Dr Johnson City TN 37604 423-979-4000 979-4099 60
TF: 877-462-6752 ■ *Web:* www.borla.com

Born Free USA United with Animal Protection Institute
1122 S St Sacramento CA 95814 916-447-3085 48-3
TF: 800-348-7387 ■ *Web:* bornfreeusa.org

Born Into It Inc 112 Burlington St Woburn MA 01801 781-491-0707 157-6
Web: www.chowdaheadz.com

Boro Construction
400 Feheley Dr King Of Prussia PA 19406 610-272-7400 186
Web: www.boroconstruction.com

Borrie's 1800 Smelter Ave Black Eagle MT 59414 406-761-0300 671

Borroughs Corp 3002 N Burdick St Kalamazoo MI 49004 269-342-0161 342-4161 286
TF: 800-748-0227 ■ *Web:* www.borroughs.com

Borsheim's Inc 120 Regency Pkwy Omaha NE 68114 402-391-0400 391-6694 410
TF: 800-642-4438 ■ *Web:* www.borsheims.com

Borton & Sons Inc 2550 Borton Rd Yakima WA 98903 509-966-3905 315-3
Web: www.bortonfruit.com

Borton LC 200 E First Ave Hutchinson KS 67501 620-669-8211 685
Web: borton.biz

Bortz Media & Sports Group Inc
5105 DTC Pkwy Ste 200 Greenwood Village CO 80111 303-893-9902 893-9913 194
Web: www.bortz.com

Borzynski Bros Distributing Inc
10508 Kraut Rd Franksville WI 53126 262-886-1623 10-11

BOS Innovations Ltd
888 E Belvidere Rd Ste 218 Grayslake IL 60030 847-665-1080 690
Web: www.blacklight.com

BOS Solutions Ltd
635-8th Ave SW Ste 1200 Calgary AB T2P3M3 403-234-8103 261
Web: www.bos-solutions.com

Bosch & Associates LLC 111 Beach Rd Fairfield CT 06824 203-255-8700 193
Web: www.boschllc.com

Bosch Automotive Proving Grounds
2104 Indiana 2 New Carlisle IN 46552 574-654-4000 743
Web: www.bosch.us

Bosch Rexroth 14001 S Lakes Dr Charlotte NC 44691 330-263-3300 263-3333 790
TF: 800-739-7684 ■ *Web:* www.boschrexroth.com/en/us

Bosch Rexroth Corp
5150 Prairie Stone Pkwy Hoffman Estates IL 60192 847-645-3600 645-6201 518
TF: 800-860-1055 ■ *Web:* www.boschrexroth.com/en/us

Bosch Rexroth Corp Piston Pump Div
8 Southchase Ct Fountain Inn SC 29644 864-967-2777 967-8900 640
Web: boschrexroth.com

Bosch Security Systems
130 Perinton Pkwy Fairport NY 14450 585-223-4060 223-9180 692
TF: 800-289-0096 ■ *Web:* us.boschsecurity.com

Bosch Thermotechnology
340 Mad River Pk Waitsfield VT 05673 800-283-3787 357
TF: 800-283-3787 ■ *Web:* www.bosch-climate.us

Boscobel Marketing Communications Inc
8606 Second ave Silver Spring MD 20910 301-588-2900 7
TF: 800-261-1537 ■ *Web:* www.boscobel.com

Boscogen Inc 11 Morgan Ste B Irvine CA 92618 949-380-4317 791
TF: 800-719-9878 ■ *Web:* www.boscogen.com

Boscos Squared 827 S Main Memphis TN 38106 901-278-0087 671
Web: www.boscosbeer.com

Boscov's Dept Stores
4500 Perkiomen Ave Reading PA 19606 610-779-2000 229
Web: www.boscovs.com

Bose Corp The Mountain Framingham MA 01701 508-766-1099 820-3465 52
TF Sales: 800-379-2073 ■ *Web:* global.bose.com

Bose McKinney & Evans LLP
111 Monument Cir Ste 2700 Indianapolis IN 46204 317-684-5000 428
Web: www.boselaw.com

Name / Address	City	State	ZIP	Phone	Fax	Class
Bo-Sherrel Company Inc 3340 Tree Swallow Pl	Fremont	CA	94555	510-792-0354		735
Boskovich Farms Inc 711 Diaz Ave *TF:* 800-555-5211 ■ *Web:* www.boskovichfarms.com	Oxnard	CA	93030	805-487-2299	487-5189	10-11
Bosmere Inc 323 Corban Ave SW *Web:* bosmereusa.com	Concord	NC	28025	704-784-1608		429
Bosnia & Herzegovina *Embassy* 2109 E St NW *Web:* www.bhembassy.org	Washington	DC	20037	202-337-1500	337-1502	257
Bosque County PO Box 617 *TF:* 800-848-2886 ■ *Web:* www.bosquecounty.us	Meridian	TX	76665	254-435-2382	435-2152	338
Boss Chair Inc 5353 Jillson St *TF:* 800-593-1888 ■ *Web:* www.bosschair.com	Commerce	CA	90040	323-262-1919		321
Boss Hawg's 2833 SW 29th St *Web:* www.bosshawgsbbq.com	Topeka	KS	66614	785-273-7300		671
Boss Industries Inc 1761 Genesis Dr *Web:* www.bossair.com	Laporte	IN	46350	219-324-7776		172
Boss Law Firm APLC, The 409 Camino del Rio S Ste 201 *Web:* bosslawfirm.com	San Diego	CA	92108	619-234-1776		428
Bossa Nova Technologies LLC 606 Venice Blvd Ste B *Web:* www.bossanovatech.com	Venice	CA	90291	310-577-8113		196
Bossard Memorial Library 7 Spruce St *Web:* www.bossard.lib.oh.us	Gallipolis	OH	45631	740-446-7323	446-1701	434-3
Bosse Mattingly Constructors Inc 2116 Plantside Dr *Web:* www.bmconstructors.com	Louisville	KY	40299	502-671-0995		186
Bosse Sports 141 Boston Post Rd *TF:* 800-841-4358 ■ *Web:* bossesports.com	Sudbury	MA	01776	978-443-4613		354
Bosselman Inc 3123 W Stolley Park Rd Ste A *Web:* www.bosselman.com	Grand Island	NE	68801	308-381-2800		345
Bosserman Aviation Equipment Inc 2327 SR- 568 *Web:* www.bossermanaviationequip.com	Carey	OH	43316	419-396-0250		57
Bosshardt Realty Services LLC 5542 NW 43rd St *TF:* 800-284-6110 ■ *Web:* www.bosshardtrealty.com	Gainesville	FL	32653	352-371-6100		652
Bossier Chamber of Commerce 710 Benton Rd *TF:* 800-659-2955 ■ *Web:* www.bossierchamber.com	Bossier City	LA	71111	318-746-0252	746-0357	139
Bossier Civic Ctr 620 Benton Rd *Web:* www.bossiercity.org	Bossier City	LA	71111	318-741-8900	741-8910	205
Bossier Parish Community College 6220 E Texas St *Web:* www.bpcc.edu	Bossier City	LA	71111	318-678-6000	678-6390	162
Bossier Parish Library (BPL) 2206 Beckett St *TF:* 800-745-3000 ■ *Web:* www.bossierlibrary.org	Bossier City	LA	71111	318-746-1693	746-7768	434-3
Bossier Press Tribune 4250 Viking Dr *TF:* 800-552-8502 ■ *Web:* www.bossierpress.com	Bossier City	LA	71111	318-747-7900	747-5298	532-4
Bossong Hosiery Mills Inc 840 W Salisbury St	Asheboro	NC	27203	336-625-2175		155-10
Bost Mike (Rep R - IL) 1440 Longworth HOB *Web:* bost.house.gov	Washington	DC	20515	202-225-5661	225-0285	342-2
Boston Academy of English 38 Chauncy St 8th Fl **Fax Area Code:* 617 ■ *TF:* 800-704-9313 ■ *Web:* www.bostonacademyofenglish.com	Boston	MA	02111	800-704-9313	695-9349*	423
Boston Academy of English inc 38 Chauncy St 8th Fl **Fax Area Code:* 617 ■ *TF:* 800-704-9313 ■ *Web:* bostonacademyofenglish.com	Boston	MA	02111	800-704-9313	695-9349*	423
Boston Advisors Inc 1 Liberty Sq 10th Fl *TF:* 800-523-5903 ■ *Web:* www.bostonadvisors.com	Boston	MA	02109	617-348-3100	348-0081	401
Boston African-American National Historic Site 14 Beacon St Ste 401 *Web:* www.nps.gov	Boston	MA	02108	617-742-5415	720-0848	564
Boston Architectural College 320 Newbury St **Fax:* Admissions ■ *TF:* 877-585-0100 ■ *Web:* www.the-bac.edu	Boston	MA	02115	617-585-0100	585-0100*	800
Boston Athenaeum 10 1/2 Beacon St *Web:* www.bostonathenaeum.org	Boston	MA	02108	617-227-0270		434-4
Boston Ballet 19 Clarendon St *Web:* www.bostonballet.org	Boston	MA	02116	617-695-6950	695-6995	573-1
Boston Baptist College 950 Metropolitan Ave *TF:* 888-235-2014 ■ *Web:* boston.edu	Boston	MA	02136	617-364-3510		166
Boston Barricade Company Inc 1151 19th St *Web:* www.bostonbarricade.com	Vero Beach	FL	32960	772-569-7202		295
Boston Beanery Restaurants Inc 63 Don Knotts Blvd *Web:* www.bostonbeanery.com	Morgantown	WV	26508	304-594-0095		670
Boston Bed Company Inc, The 1113 Commonwealth Ave	Boston	MA	02215	617-782-3830		321
Boston Beer Co 1 Design Ctr Pl Ste 850 *NYSE:* SAM ■ *TF:* 888-661-2337 ■ *Web:* www.bostonbeer.com	Boston	MA	02210	617-368-5000	368-5500	102
Boston Benefit Partners LLC 177 Milk St Ste 305 *Web:* www.bosben.com	Boston	MA	02109	617-570-9100		463
Boston Bruins 100 Legends Way *TF:* 800-745-3000 ■ *Web:* bruins.nhl.com	Boston	MA	02114	617-624-1900	523-7184	716
Boston Business Journal 160 Federal St 12th Fl *Web:* www.bizjournals.com	Boston	MA	02110	617-330-1000		457-5
Boston Capital Ventures 84 State St Ste 320	Boston	MA	02109	617-227-6550		792
Boston Celtics 226 Cswy St 4th Fl *Web:* www.nba.com	Boston	MA	02114	617-854-8000	367-4286	714-1
Boston Centerless Inc 11 Presidential Way *TF:* 800-343-4111 ■ *Web:* www.bostoncenterless.com	Woburn	MA	01801	781-994-5000		454
Boston Children's Museum 308 Congress St *Web:* www.bostonchildrensmuseum.org	Boston	MA	02210	617-426-6500	426-1944	521
Boston City Hall 1 City Hall Plaza *Web:* www.cityofboston.gov	Boston	MA	02201	617-635-4601	248-1937	337
Boston College 140 Commonwealth Ave *TF:* 800-360-2522 ■ *Web:* www.bc.edu	Chestnut Hill	MA	02467	617-552-3100	552-0798	166
Boston College Law School 885 Centre St *TF:* 800-321-2211 ■ *Web:* www.bc.edu	Newton	MA	02459	617-552-8550	552-2615	167-1
Boston College Libraries 140 Commonwealth Ave *Web:* www.bc.edu/libraries	Chestnut Hill	MA	02467	617-552-4472		434-6
Boston Color Graphics LLC 755 Middlesex Tpke *TF:* 800-767-0067 ■ *Web:* www.bcgconnect.com	Billerica	MA	01821	800-767-0067		781
Boston Common Hotel & Conference Ctr 40 Trinity Pl *TF:* 800-238-0767 ■ *Web:* www.bostoncommonhotel.com	Boston	MA	02116	617-933-7700		378
Boston Conservatory at Berklee 8 Fenway **Fax:* Admissions ■ *Web:* www.bostonconservatory.edu	Boston	MA	02215	617-536-6340	247-3159*	166
Boston Consulting Group, The Exchange Pl 31st Fl *Web:* www.bcg.com	Boston	MA	02109	617-973-1200		194
Boston Consumers Checkbook 185 Franklin St *TF:* 888-382-1222 ■ *Web:* www.checkbook.org	Boston	MA	02110	888-382-1222		95
Boston Convention & Exhibition Ctr 415 Summer St *Web:* massconvention.com	Boston	MA	02210	617-954-2000	954-2299	205
Boston Ctr for the Arts 539 Tremont St *Web:* www.bcaonline.org	Boston	MA	02116	617-426-5000	426-5336	572
Boston Duck Tours Ltd 4 Copley Pl Ste 310 *TF:* 800-226-7442 ■ *Web:* www.bostonducktours.com	Boston	MA	02116	617-450-0065		760
Boston Electronics Corp 91 Boylston St *Web:* www.boselec.com	Brookline	MA	02445	617-566-3821		179
Boston Endoscopy Center LLC 175 Worcester St (Rte 9) *Web:* www.gmed.com/bec	Wellesley Hills	MA	02481	617-936-7693		415
Boston Engineering Corp 300 Bear Hill Rd *Web:* www.boston-engineering.com	Waltham	MA	02451	781-466-8010		261
Boston Event Guide.com 475 Hillside Ave *Web:* www.bostoneventguide.com	Needham Heights	MA	02494	781-444-7771		194
Boston Family Office LLC, The 88 Broad St 2nd Fl *TF:* 800-900-4401 ■ *Web:* www.bosfam.com	Boston	MA	02110	617-624-0800		401
Boston Film Festival 126 S St *Web:* www.bostonfilmfestival.org	Rockport	MA	01966	617-523-8388		282
Boston Financial Data Services 2000 Crown Colony Dr *TF:* 888-772-2337 ■ *Web:* www.bostonfinancial.com	Quincy	MA	02169	617-483-5000		401
Boston Foundation 75 Arlington St 10th Fl *Web:* www.tbf.org	Boston	MA	02116	617-338-1700	338-1604	303
Boston Globe 135 Morrissey Blvd *TF:* 800-423-8058 ■ *Web:* www.boston.com	Boston	MA	02125	617-929-2000		532-2
Boston Globe, The PO Box 55819 PO Box 2378 *TF:* 888-694-5623 ■ *Web:* www.bostonglobe.com	Boston	MA	02205	888-694-5623		281
Boston Group 400 Riverside Ave *TF:* 800-225-1633 ■ *Web:* www.bostonretail.com	Medford	MA	02155	800-225-1633		286
Boston Harbor Association, The 374 Congress St Ste 307 *TF:* 800-439-2370 ■ *Web:* www.tbha.org	Boston	MA	02210	617-482-1722		804
Boston Harbor Hotel 70 Rowes Wharf *TF:* 800-752-7077 ■ *Web:* www.bhh.com	Boston	MA	02110	617-439-7000	330-9450	379
Boston Harbor Islands National Recreation Area 408 Atlantic Ave Ste 228 *TF:* 877-874-2478 ■ *Web:* www.nps.gov	Boston	MA	02110	617-223-8666	223-8671	564
Boston Illiquid Securities Offering Network Inc 205 Portland St Ste 200 *Web:* www.bison.co	Boston	MA	02114	617-752-1921		387
Boston Inc 2917 Business Park Dr *Web:* www.furnitureappliancemart.com	Stevens Point	WI	54482	715-342-2895		321
Boston Industrial Consulting 89 Newbury St *Web:* bicinc.com	Danvers	MA	01923	978-739-0399		261
Boston Jetsearch Inc 200 Hanscom Dr Ste 207 *Web:* www.bostonjetsearch.com	Bedford	MA	01730	781-274-0074		261
Boston Language Institute Inc 648 Beacon St Kenmore Sq *TF:* 877-998-3500 ■ *Web:* www.bostonlanguage.com	Boston	MA	02215	617-262-3500	262-3595	768
Boston Logic Technology Partners Inc 81 Wareham St *Web:* www.bostonlogic.com	Boston	MA	02118	617-266-9166		177
Boston Market Corp 14103 Denver W Pkwy *TF General:* 866-977-9090 ■ *Web:* www.bostonmarket.com	Golden	CO	80401	303-278-9500		670
Boston Market Strategies Inc 500 Cummings Ctr Ste 3150 *Web:* www.bmsi3.com	Beverly	MA	01915	781-245-7773		194
Boston Marriott Copley Place 110 Huntington Ave *Web:* marriott.com	Boston	MA	02116	617-236-5800		379
Boston Medical Ctr 1 Boston Medical Ctr Pl *TF:* 800-249-2007 ■ *Web:* www.bmc.org	Boston	MA	02118	617-638-8000		374-3
Boston Millennia Partners 30 Rowes Wharf Ste 400 *Web:* www.bostonmillenniapartners.com	Boston	MA	02110	617-428-5150	428-5160	792
Boston Modern Orchestra Project 376 Washington St *Web:* www.bmop.org	Malden	MA	02148	781-324-0397		573-3

	Phone	Fax	Class
Boston National Historical Park Charlestown Navy Yard........Boston MA 02129 *Web:* www.nps.gov/bost	617-242-5601	242-6006	564
Boston Organics 50 Terminal St........Charlestown MA 02129 *Web:* bostonorganics.com	617-242-1700		297-8
Boston Park Plaza Hotel & Towers 50 Pk Plaza........Boston MA 02116 *TF:* 800-225-2008 ■ *Web:* www.bostonparkplaza.com	617-426-2000		379
Boston Partners 909 Third Ave 32nd Fl........New York NY 10022 *TF:* 800-225-5291 ■ *Web:* www.robecoinvest.com	212-908-9500		690
Boston Partners Financial Group LLC 138 River Rd Ste 310........Andover MA 01810 *TF:* 800-387-2747 ■ *Web:* www.bostonpartnersfinancialgroup.com	978-689-9303		390
Boston Philharmonic Orchestra 236 Huntington Ave Ste 210........Boston MA 02115 *Web:* www.bostonphil.org	617-236-0999	236-8613	573-3
Boston Phoenix, The 126 Brookline Ave........Boston MA 02215 *Web:* thephoenix.com	617-536-5390		532-5
Boston Pizza Restaurants LP 1501 LBJ Fwy Ste 450........Dallas TX 75234 *TF:* 866-277-8721 ■ *Web:* www.bostons.com	972-484-9022	484-7630	670
Boston Pops 301 Massachusetts Ave Symphony Hall........Boston MA 02115 *TF:* 888-266-1200 ■ *Web:* www.bso.org	617-266-1492		573-3
Boston Portfolio Advisors Inc 800 Corporate Dr Ste 408........Fort Lauderdale FL 33334 *Web:* www.bostonportfolio.com	954-938-3000		401
Boston Private Financial Holdings Inc 10 Post Office Sq........Boston MA 02109 *NASDAQ: BPFH* ■ *TF:* 855-738-8916 ■ *Web:* www.bostonprivate.com	617-912-1900		360-2
Boston Properties Inc 800 Boylston St........Boston MA 02199 *NYSE: BXP* ■ *Web:* www.bostonproperties.com	617-236-3300		655
Boston Public Library 700 Boylston St Copley Sq........Boston MA 02116 *Web:* www.bpl.org	617-536-5400		434-3
Boston Sand & Gravel Company Inc 100 N Washington St........Boston MA 02114 *OTC: BSND* ■ *TF:* 800-624-2724 ■ *Web:* www.bostonsand.com	617-227-9000		182
Boston Scientific Corp 300 Boston Scientific Way........Marlborough MA 01752 *NYSE: BSX* ■ *TF:* 800-876-9960 ■ *Web:* www.bostonscientific.com	508-683-4000		476
Boston Ship Repair Inc 32A Drydock Ave........Boston MA 02210 *Web:* www.northeastship.com/main_boston.html	617-330-5045		698
Boston Store Inc 2400 N Mayfair Rd........Milwaukee WI 53226 *Web:* news.bonton.com/ecommupgrade/siteupgrade_bos.html	414-453-7500		229
Boston Strategies International Inc 445 Washington St........Wellesley MA 02482 *Web:* www.bostonstrategies.com	781-250-8150		463
Boston Symphony Hall 301 Massachusetts Ave........Boston MA 02115 *TF:* 888-266-1200 ■ *Web:* www.bso.org	617-266-1492		572
Boston Symphony Orchestra 301 Massachusetts Ave Symphony Hall........Boston MA 02115 *TF:* 888-266-1200 ■ *Web:* www.bso.org	617-266-1492	638-9367	573-3
Boston Systems & Solutions Llc 241 Winter St Ste 2........Haverhill MA 01830 *Web:* www.bsscorp.com	978-469-0002		180
Boston University Mugar Memorial Library 771 Commonwealth Ave........Boston MA 02215 *TF:* 800-922-9999 ■ *Web:* www.bu.edu/library	617-353-3710	353-2084	434-6
Boston University School of Law 765 Commonwealth Ave........Boston MA 02215 *TF:* 800-321-2211 ■ *Web:* www.bu.edu/law	617-353-3100	353-0578	167-1
Boston University School of Medicine 715 Albany St........Boston MA 02118 **Fax:* Admissions ■ *Web:* www.bumc.bu.edu	617-638-8000	638-5258*	167-2
Boston University School of Medicine Alumni Medical Library 72 East Concord St Fl 2........Boston MA 02118 *Web:* www.bumc.bu.edu/busm/about/library	617-638-1950		434-1
Boston Warehouse Trading Corp 59 Davis Ave........Norwood MA 02062 *TF:* 888-923-2982 ■ *Web:* www.bwtc.com	781-769-8550	769-9468	361
Boston Whaler Inc 100 Whaler Way........Edgewater FL 32141 *TF:* 877-294-5645 ■ *Web:* www.bostonwhaler.com	877-294-5645		90
Boston's Best Chimney Sweep 76 Bacon St........Waltham MA 02451 *TF Cust Svc:* 800-660-6708 ■ *Web:* www.bestchimney.com	781-893-6611		152
Bostons Weekly Dig 242 E Berkeley St 5th Fl........Boston MA 02118 *Web:* digboston.com	617-426-8942	426-8942	532-5
Bostwick Laboratories 4355 Innslake Dr........Glen Allen VA 23060 *Web:* www.bostwicklaboratories.com	804-967-9225		418
Bostwick-Braun Co 7349 Crossleigh Ct........Toledo OH 43617 **Fax Area Code:* 419 ■ *TF:* 800-777 9640 ■ *Web:* bostwick braun.com	800-777-9640	259-3622*	351
Boswell Bay State Marine Park PO Box 1247........Soldotna AK 99669 *Web:* dnr.alaska.gov/parks/units/pwssmp/smpcord.htm	907-262-5581		565
Boswell Engineering 330 Phillips Ave........South Hackensack NJ 07606 *Web:* www.boswellengineering.com	201-641-0770	641-1831	261
Boswell's Party Supplies Danville 1901 Cam Ramon........Danville CA 94526 *Web:* www.boswells-party.com	925-866-1644		226
Bosworth Steel Erectors Inc 4001 Jaffee St........Dallas TX 75216 *Web:* www.bosworthsteel.com	214-371-3700	371-1020	189-14
Bot Home Automation Inc 1523 26th St........Santa Monica CA 90404 *Web:* www.ring.com	310-929-7085		693
Botanas 816 S Fifth St........Milwaukee WI 53204 *Web:* www.botanasrestaurant.com	414-672-3755		671
Botanic Garden of Smith College Smith College........NorthHampton MA 01063 *Web:* www.smith.edu/garden	413-585-2740	585-2744	97
Botanic gardenÿat Georgia Southern University 1505 Bland Ave PO Box 8039........Statesboro GA 30460 *Web:* academics.georgiasouthern.edu	912-871-1149	871-1777	97
Botanica the Wichita Gardens 701 N Amidon Ave........Wichita KS 67203 *Web:* www.botanica.org	316-264-0448		97
Botanical Garden of the Ozarks 4703 N Crossover Rd PO Box 10407........Fayetteville AR 72764 *Web:* www.bgozarks.org	479-750-2620		97
Botanical Gardens at Asheville 151 WT Weaver Blvd........Asheville NC 28804 *Web:* www.ashevillebotanicalgardens.org	828-252-5190		97
Botanical Laboratories Inc 1441 W Smith Rd........Ferndale WA 98248 *TF:* 800-232-4005 ■ *Web:* www.wellesse.com	360-384-5656	384-1140	582
Botanical Research Institute of Texas 1700 University Dr........Fort Worth TX 76102 *Web:* www.brit.org	817-332-4441	332-4112	97
Botetourt County 1 W Main St........Fincastle VA 24090 *Web:* www.co.botetourt.va.us	540-473-8220		338
Botetourt County Chamber of Commerce 13 W Main St........Fincastle VA 24090 *Web:* botetourtchamber.com	540-473-8280	473-8365	139
Bothell/Kenmore Reporter 11630 Slater Ave NE Stes 8-9........Kirkland WA 98034 *Web:* www.bothell-reporter.com	425-483-3732		532-4
Bothe-Napa Valley State Park 3801 St Helena Hwy........Calistoga CA 94515 *Web:* www.parks.ca.gov/default.asp?page_id=477	707-942-4575		565
Bothwell Lodge State Historic Site 19349 Bothwell State Pk Rd........Sedalia MO 65301 *Web:* www.mostateparks.com	660-827-0510		565
Bothwell Regional Health Ctr 601 E 14th St........Sedalia MO 65301 *TF:* 800-635-9194 ■ *Web:* www.brhc.org	660-826-8833		374-3
Botnay Bay Computer 177 Bartlett St........Portsmouth NH 03801 *Web:* botnaybay.com	603-436-6035		196
Botsford Hospital 28050 Grand River Ave........Farmington Hills MI 48336 *Web:* www.botsford.org	248-471-8000		374-3
Botswana 154 E 46th St........New York NY 10017 *Web:* botswanaun.org	212-889-2277	725-5061	784
Botswana Embassy 1531 New Hampshire Ave NW........Washington DC 20036 *Web:* www.botswanaembassy.org	202-244-4990	244-4164	257
Bott Radio Network 10550 Barkley St Ste 100........Overland Park KS 66212 *TF:* 800-875-1903 ■ *Web:* www.bottradionetwork.com	913-642-7770	642-1319	643
Bottega 2240 Highland Ave S........Birmingham AL 35205 *Web:* bottegarestaurant.com	205-939-1000		671
Bottega Veneta Inc 699 Fifth Ave........New York NY 10022 *Web:* www.bottegaveneta.com	212-371-5511		430
Botticelli Italian Restaurant 523 Main St........Rapid City SD 57701 *Web:* botticelliristorante.net	605-348-0089		671
Bottineau Convention & Visitor Bureau 519 Main St Ste 1........Bottineau ND 58318 *TF:* 800-735-6932 ■ *Web:* www.bottineau.com	701-228-3849	228-5130	206
Bottineau County 314 W Fifth St........Bottineau ND 58318 *Web:* www.bottineau.com	701-228-3618		338
Bottini Fuel Oil Co 2785 W Main St........Wappingers Falls NY 12590 *Web:* www.bottinifuel.com	845-297-5580		316
Bottlemate Inc 2095 Leo Ave........Commerce CA 90040 *Web:* www.bottlemate.com	323-887-9009		333
Bottom Line/Personal 3 Landmark Sq 8th Fl........Stamford CT 06901 **Fax Area Code:* 203 ■ **Fax:* Edit ■ *TF Cust Svc:* 800-678-5835 ■ *Web:* bottomlineinc.com	800-274-5611	967-3621*	531-6
Bottomline Technologies 325 Corporate Dr........Portsmouth NH 03801 *NASDAQ: EPAY* ■ *TF:* 800-243-2528 ■ *Web:* www.bottomline.com	603-436-0700	436-0300	178-1
Botz Deal & Company PC 2 Wbury Dr........Saint Charles MO 63301 *Web:* www.botzdeal.com	636-946-2800		2
Bouchaine Vineyards Inc 1075 Buchli Station Rd........Napa CA 94559 *Web:* www.bouchaine.com	707-252-9065		443
Bouchard Transportation Company Inc 58 S Service Rd Ste 150........Melville NY 11747 *Web:* www.bouchardtransport.com	631-390-4900	390-4905	314
Bouchee Mission St and Seventh Ave........Carmel-By-The-Sea CA 93923 *Web:* www.andresbouchee.com	831-626-7880		671
Boucher & James Inc 1456 Ferry Rd Bldg 500 Ste 500........Doylestown PA 18901 *Web:* bjengineers.com	215-345-9400		261
Boucher Brothers Management Inc 1451 Ocean Dr Ste 205........Miami Beach FL 33139 *Web:* www.boucherbrothers.com	305-535-8177		23
Boucher Group Inc 4141 S 108th St........Greenfield WI 53228 *TF:* 800-210-7559 ■ *Web:* www.boucher.com	414-427-4141	427-4140	57
Bouchey Financial Group Ltd 1819 Fifth Ave........Troy NY 12180 *TF:* 800-783-0339 ■ *Web:* www.boucheyfinancial.com	518-720-3333		401
Boudin Bakery 50 Francisco St Ste 200........San Francisco CA 94133 *Web:* www.boudinbakery.com	415-882-1849		68
Boudreau-Espley-Pitre Corp 1040 Lorne St Unit 3........Sudbury ON P3C4R9 *TF:* 877-675-7720 ■ *Web:* www.bestech.com	705-675-7720		261
Boudro's On the Riverwalk 421 E Commerce St........San Antonio TX 78205 *Web:* www.boudros.com	210-224-8484	225-2839	671
Boulanger, Roland & Cie Ltd 235 rue St-Louis........Warwick QC J0A1M0 *Web:* www.boulanger.qc.ca	819-358-4100		279
Boulder Adventure Lodge (A-Lodge) 91 Four Mile Canyon Rd........Boulder CO 80302 *TF:* 800-556-3446 ■ *Web:* boulder-utah.com	435-335-7460		379

Phone Fax Class

Boulder Arts & Crafts
1421 Pearl St Mall Boulder CO 80302 303-443-3683 460
TF: 866-656-2667 ■ Web: www.boulderartsandcrafts.com

Boulder Ballet 2590 Walnut St Ste 10 Boulder CO 80302 303-443-0028 573-1
Web: www.boulderballet.org

Boulder Beach State Park
44 Stillwater Rd Groton VT 05046 802-584-3823 565
Web: www.vtstateparks.com

Boulder Beer Co 2880 Wilderness Pl Boulder CO 80301 303-444-8448 102
Web: www.boulderbeer.com

Boulder Book Store 1107 Pearl St Boulder CO 80302 303-447-2074 447-3946 95
TF: 800-244-4651 ■ Web: www.boulderbookstore.com

Boulder Chamber of Commerce
2440 Pearl St Boulder CO 80302 303-442-1044 938-8837 139
TF: 800-258-7597 ■ Web: www.boulderchamber.com

Boulder ChopHouse & Tavern
921 Walnut St Boulder CO 80302 303-443-1188 671
Web: www.boulderchophouse.com

Boulder City Hall PO Box 791 Boulder CO 80306 303-441-3388 441-4478 337
Web: bouldercolorado.gov

Boulder City/Hoover Dam Museum
1305 Arizona St Boulder City NV 89005 702-294-1988 520
TF: 800-680-5851 ■ Web: www.bcmha.org

Boulder Community Hospital (BCH)
1100 Balsam Ave Boulder CO 80301 303-440-2273 374-3
Web: www.bch.org

Boulder Convention & Visitors Bureau
2440 Pearl St Boulder CO 80302 303-442-2911 938-2098 206
TF: 800-444-0447 ■ Web: www.bouldercoloradousa.com

Boulder Cork 3295 30th St Boulder CO 80301 303-443-9505 443-0193 671
Web: www.bouldercork.com

Boulder Country Day School
4820 Nautilus Ct N Boulder CO 80301 303-527-4931 685
Web: bouldercountryday.org

Boulder County 1750 33rd St Ste 201 Boulder CO 80301 303-413-7770 413-7775 338
Web: www.bouldercounty.org

Boulder Daily Camera 1048 Pearl St Boulder CO 80302 303-442-1202 449-9358 532-2
Web: www.dailycamera.com

Boulder Innovation Group Inc
4824 Sterling Dr Boulder CO 80301 303-447-0248 407
Web: www.imageguided.com

Boulder Museum of Contemporary Art
1750 13th St Boulder CO 80302 303-443-2122 520
Web: www.bmoca.org

Boulder Philharmonic Orchestra
2590 Walnut St Boulder CO 80302 303-449-1343 443-9203 573-3
Web: www.boulderphil.org

Boulder Public Library
1001 Arapahoe Ave Boulder CO 80302 303-441-3100 434-3
Web: www.boulderlibrary.org

Boulder Reservoir 5565 N 51st St Boulder CO 80301 303-441-3461 441-1807 50-5
Web: www.bouldercolorado.gov

Boulder Station Hotel & Casino
4111 Boulder Hwy Las Vegas NV 89121 702-432-7777 133
TF: 800-683-7777 ■ Web: boulderstation.sclv.com

Boulder Weekly 690 S Lashley Ln Boulder CO 80305 303-494-5511 494-2585 532-5
Web: boulderweekly.com

Boulders Resort & Golden Door Spa
34631 N Tom Darlington Dr Scottsdale AZ 85262 480-488-9009 669
TF: 000-579-2001 ■ Web: www.theboulders.com

Boulevard 1 Mission St San Francisco CA 94105 415-543-6084 495-2936 671
Web: www.boulevardrestaurant.com

Boulevard Brewing Co 2501 SW Blvd Kansas City MO 64108 816-474-7095 102
Web: www.boulevard.com

Boulevard Club The
1491 Lake Shore Blvd W Toronto ON M6K3C2 416-532-3341 354
Web: www.boulevardclub.com

Boulevard Mall 3528 S Maryland Pkwy Las Vegas NV 89169 702-735-7430 460
TF: 800-321-8400 ■ Web: www.boulevardmall.com

Boulevard Mall 730 Alberta Dr Amherst NY 14226 716-834-8600 460
Web: www.boulevard-mall.com

Boulevard Pizzeria & Italian Eatery
2935 Virginia Beach Blvd Virginia Beach VA 23452 757-463-1311 671
Web: blvdpizzavb.com

Bouley 163 Duane St New York NY 10013 212-964-2525 671
Web: www.davidbouley.com

Bou-Matic PO Box 8050 Madison WI 53708 608-222-3484 273
Web: www.boumatic.com

Bounce Ideas Inc 102 Conference Blvd Toronto ON M1C2E7 416-286-6656 317
Web: www.bounceideas.ca

BounceU 1166 S Gilbert Rd Gilbert AZ 85296 480-632-9663 31
Web: www.bounceu.com

Bound to Stay Bound Books Inc (BTSB)
1880 W Morton Ave Jacksonville IL 62650 217-245-5191 747-2872* 92
*Fax Area Code: 800 ■ TF: 800-637-6586 ■ Web: www.btsb.com

Bound'ry 911 20th Ave S Nashville TN 37212 615-321-3043 671
Web: boundrynashville.com

Boundary County PO Box 419 Bonners Ferry ID 83805 208-267-5504 267-7814 338
Web: www.boundarycountyid.org

Boundary County School District
6577 Main St Ste 101 Bonners Ferry ID 83805 208-267-3146 302
Web: bcsd101.com

Boundless Network Inc
200 E Sixth St Ste 300 Austin TX 78701 512-472-9200 472-9204 194
Web: www.boundlessnetwork.com

Bounty Print Ltd 6359 Bayne St Halifax NS B3K2V6 902-453-0300 627
TF: 800-337-5764 ■ Web: www.bountyprint.com

Bountyland Petroleum Inc
1510 Blue Ridge Blvd Ste 202 Seneca SC 29672 864-647-7282 581
Web: mybountyland.com

Bourbon & Boots Inc
314 Main St 2th FL North Little Rock AR 72114 855-623-3562 690
TF: 877-791-8079 ■ Web: www.bourbonandboots.com

Bourbon County 210 S National Ave Fort Scott KS 66701 620-223-3800 223-5832 338
Web: bourboncountyks.org

Bourbon House Seafood & Oyster Bar
144 Bourbon St New Orleans LA 70130 504-522-0111 671
Web: www.bourbonhouse.com

Bourbon Orleans - A Wyndham Historic Hotel
717 Orleans St New Orleans LA 70116 504-523-2222 571-4666 379
TF: 866-513-9744 ■ Web: www.bourbonorleans.com

Bourdon Forge Company Inc
99 Tuttle Rd Middletown CT 06457 860-632-2740 632-7247 350
TF: 800-419-6829 ■ Web: www.bourdonforge.com

Bourgault Industries Ltd
1 mile NE side Hwy 368 St. Brieux SK S0K3V0 306-275-2300 273
TF: 800-288-1117 ■ Web: www.bourgault.com

Bourn & Koch Inc 2500 Kishwaukee St Rockford IL 61104 815-965-4013 965-0019 455
TF: 800-535-0135 ■ Web: www.bourn-koch.com

Bourne Brothers Printing Company Inc
5276 Hwy 42 Hattiesburg MS 39401 601-582-1808 627
TF: 800-928-2086 ■ Web: www.bournebrothers.com

Bourne Industries Inc
491 S Comstock St Corunna MI 48817 989-743-3461 599
TF: 800-474-3524 ■ Web: www.bourneindustries.com

Bourns Inc 1200 Columbia Ave Riverside CA 92507 951-781-5690 781-5006 625
TF: 877-426-8767 ■ Web: www.bourns.com

Bouten Construction Co 627 N Napa St Spokane WA 99202 509-535-3531 535-6047 297-7
Web: www.boutenconstruction.com

Bouthillette Parizeau
9825 Verville St Montreal QC H3L3E1 514-383-3747 256
Web: www.bpa.ca

Boutique Spa at the Ritz-Carlton Georgetown
3100 S St NW Washington DC 20007 202-912-4175 707
TF: 800-241-3333 ■ Web: www.ritzcarlton.com

Boutwell Owens & Co Inc
251 Authority Dr Fitchburg MA 01420 978-343-3067 101
Web: www.boutwellowens.com

Bouvier Kelly Inc
212 S Elm St Ste 200 Greensboro NC 27401 336-275-7000 636
TF: 800-707-1457 ■ Web: www.bouvierkelly.com

Bovie Medical Corp
734 Walt Whitman Rd Ste 207 Melville NY 11747 631-421-5452 250
NYSE: BVX ■ TF: 800-537-2790 ■ Web: www.boviemedical.com

Bovine's 3979 Hwy 17 Business Murrells Inlet SC 29576 843-651-2888 671
Web: www.bovinesrestaurant.com

Bow Engineering & Development Inc
1953 S Beretania St Ph A Honolulu HI 96826 808-941-8853 261
Web: www.bowengineering.com

Bow Plastics Ltd 5700 Cote de Liesse Montreal QC H4T1B1 514-735-5671 607
TF: 800-852-8527 ■ Web: www.bow-group.com

Bowden Manufacturing Corp
4590 Beidler Rd Willoughby OH 44094 440-946-1770 757
TF: 800-876-8970 ■ Web: bowdenmfg.com

Bowden Oil Company Inc PO Box 145 Sylacauga AL 35150 256-245-5611 249-2975 316
TF: 800-280-0393 ■ Web: www.bowdenoil.com

Bowditch Ford Inc
11291 Jefferson Ave Newport News VA 23601 757-595-2211 54
TF: 866-399-2616 ■ Web: bowditchford.com

Bowdoin College 5000 College Stn Brunswick ME 04011 207-725-3000 725-3101* 166
*Fax: Admissions ■ TF: 000-029-1040 ■ Web: www.bowdoin.edu

Bowdoin College Hawthorne-Longfellow Library
3000 College Stn Brunswick ME 04011 207-725-3280 725-3083 434-6
TF: 800-537-6066 ■ Web: library.bowdoin.edu

Bowdoin College Museum of Art
9400 College Stn Brunswick ME 04011 207-725-3275 520
Web: www.bowdoin.edu

Bowdoin Group Inc, The
40 William St Wellesley MA 02481 781-239-9933 721
Web: www.bowdoingroup.com

BOWE Bell + Howell 760 S Wolf Rd Wheeling IL 60090 847-675-7600 340-8852* 173-7
*Fax Area Code: 585 ■ TF: 800-220-3030 ■ Web: www.bellhowell.net

Bowen & Bowen
16 W 445 S Frontage Rd Burr Ridge IL 60527 630-325-9800 2
Web: bowencpa.com

Bowen & Watson Inc PO Box 877 Toccoa GA 30577 706-886-3197 886-3010 186
Web: www.bowen-watson.com

Bowen Advisors Inc
25 Recreation Park Dr Ste 210 Hingham MA 02043 617-245-1660 70
Web: www.bowenadvisors.com

Bowen Engineering Corp
8802 N Meridian St Indianapolis IN 46260 317-842-2616 841-4257 188-7
Web: www.bowenengineering.com

Bowen Group 10 Ctr St Ste 103 Stafford VA 22556 540-658-0490 463
Web: www.thebowengroup.com

Bowen Workforce Solutions Inc
602 12 Ave SW Ste 700 Calgary AB T2R1J3 403-262-1156 260
TF: 866-837-2465 ■ Web: www.bowenworks.ca

Bowen, Hanes & Company Inc
The Forum 3290 Northside Pkwy Ste 880 Atlanta GA 30327 404-995-0507 528
Web: www.bowenhanes.com

Bowers & Burrows Oil Co
213 Young St Henderson NC 27536 252-492-0181 316
Web: bbfuels.net

Bowers Envelope Co
5331 N Tacoma Ave Indianapolis IN 46220 317-253-4321 263
TF: 800-333-4321 ■ Web: www.bowersenvelope.com

Bowers Kidseum, The 1802 N Main St Santa Ana CA 92706 714-480-1520 521
Web: bowers.org/index.php/visit/kidseum/about-kidseum

Bowers Manufacturing Co
6565 S Sprinkle Rd Portage MI 49002 269-323-2565 492
Web: www.bowers-mfg.com

Bowers Museum of Cultural Art
2002 N Main St Santa Ana CA 92706 714-567-3600 567-3603 520
Web: www.bowers.org

Bowerston Shale Co, The PO Box 199 Bowerston OH 44695 740-269-2921 269-5456 150
TF: 800-225-2749 ■ Web: www.bowerstonshale.com

Bowhead 4900 Seminary Rd Ste 1200 Alexandria VA 22311 703-413-4226 22
Web: www.bowheadsupport.com

Bowie County 710 James Bowie Dr New Boston TX 75570 903-628-6700 628-6729 338
Web: www.co.bowie.tx.us

Bowie Industries Inc 1004 E Wise St Bowie TX 76230 940-872-1106 872-4792 273
TF: 800-433-0934 ■ Web: www.bowieindustries.com

Bowie State University
14000 Jericho Pk Rd Bowie MD 20715 301-860-4000 860-3518 166
TF: 877-772-6943 ■ Web: www.bowiestate.edu

Name	Address	City	State	ZIP	Phone	Fax	Class
Bowie-Cass Electric Co-op Inc	117 N St *TF:* 800-794-2919 ■ *Web:* www.bcec.com	Douglassville	TX	75560	903-846-2311		245
Bowl America Inc	6446 Edsall Rd *NYSE:* BWL.A ■ *Web:* www.bowl-america.com	Alexandria	VA	22312	703-941-6300		99
Bowl-A-Roll Lanes	1560 Jefferson Rd *Web:* www.bowl-a-roll.com	Rochester	NY	14623	585-427-7250		99
Bowles Mattress Co Inc	1220 Watt St *TF:* 800-223-7509 ■ *Web:* www.bowlesmattress.com	Jeffersonville	IN	47130	812-288-8614		471
Bowlin Travel Centers Inc	150 Louisiana NE *OTC:* BWTL ■ *TF:* 800-448-1240 ■ *Web:* www.bowlintc.com	Albuquerque	NM	87108	505-266-5985		8
Bowling Green Area Chamber of Commerce	710 College St *TF:* 866-330-2422 ■ *Web:* www.bgchamber.com	Bowling Green	KY	42101	270-781-3200	843-0458	139
Bowling Green Chamber of Commerce (BGCC)	130 S Main St PO Box 31 *Web:* www.bgchamber.net	Bowling Green	OH	43402	419-353-7945	353-3693	139
Bowling Green City Schools (BGCS)	137 Clough St *Web:* www.bgcs.k12.oh.us	Bowling Green	OH	43402	419-352-3576	352-1701	685
Bowling Green Independent School District	1211 Ctr St *Web:* b-g.k12.ky.us	Bowling Green	KY	42101	270-746-2200		685
Bowling Green Public Library	201 W Locust St *Web:* www.bgmopl.org	Bowling Green	MO	63334	573-324-5030		434-3
Bowling Green State University	1001 E Wooster St *TF:* 866-246-6732 ■ *Web:* www.bgsu.edu	Bowling Green	OH	43403	419-372-2531	372-6955	166
Bowling Green State University Firelands	1 University Dr **Fax:* Admissions ■ *Web:* www.firelands.bgsu.edu	Huron	OH	44839	419-433-5560	433-9696*	162
Bowling Portfolio Management LLC	4030 Smith Rd Ste 140 *TF:* 800-835-9556 ■ *Web:* www.bowlingpm.com	Cincinnati	OH	45209	513-871-7776		401
Bowling Proprietors' Assn of America (BPAA)	621 Six Flags Dr PO Box 5802 **Fax Area Code:* 817 ■ *TF:* 800-343-1329 ■ *Web:* www.bpaa.com	Arlington	TX	76011	800-343-1329	633-2940*	48-23
Bowlmor	222 W 44th St *Web:* www.bowlmor.com	New York	NY	10036	212-777-2214		31
Bowman & Company LLP	601 White Horse Rd *Web:* www.bowmanllp.com	Voorhees	NJ	08043	856-435-6200		2
Bowman Barrett & Associates Inc	130 E Randolph St Ste 2650 *Web:* bbandainc.com	Chicago	IL	60601	312-228-0100		261
Bowman Consulting Group	14020 Thunderbolt Pl # 300 *Web:* www.bowmanconsulting.com	Chantilly	VA	20151	703-464-1000		727
Bowman County	104 First St NW Ste 3 *Web:* www.bowmannd.com	Bowman	ND	58623	701-523-3450	523-5443	338
Bowman Foster & Associates P C	4 Interstate Corporate Ctr *Web:* www.bfa-eng.com	Norfolk	VA	23502	757-466-7400		261
Bowman Hollis Manufacturing Inc	2925 Old Steele Creek Rd *TF:* 888-269-2358 ■ *Web:* www.bowmanhollis.com	Charlotte	NC	28208	704-374-1500	333-5520	744
Bowman Lake State Park	745 Bliven Sherman Rd *Web:* parks.ny.gov/parks/76	Oxford	NY	13830	607-334-2718		565
Bowman Mfg Company Inc	17301 51st Ave NE *TF:* 800-962-4660 ■ *Web:* www.bowmandispensers.com	Arlington	WA	98223	360-435-5005		608
Bowman Plating Company Inc	2631 126th St *Web:* www.bowmanplating.com	Compton	CA	90222	310-639-4343		481
Bowman's Hill Wildflower Preserve	1635 River Rd PO Box 685 *Web:* www.bhwp.org	New Hope	PA	18938	215-862-2924	862-1846	97
Bowmanville Zoological Park Ltd	340 King St E	Bowmanville	ON	L1C3K5	905-623-5655	623-0957	823
Bowne AE & T Group	235 E Jericho Tpke *Web:* www.bownegroup.com	Mineola	NY	11501	516-746-2350		256
Bowring Ranch State Historical Park	Hwy 61	Merriman	NE	69218	308-684-3428		565
Bowser Morner Inc	1419 Miami St *Web:* www.bowser-morner.com	Toledo	OH	43605	419-691-4800		261
Bowser's Lucky Dog Casino	3140 Dredge Dr *Web:* orofinogroup.com	Helena	MT	59602	406-442-1555		443
Box Butte County	7006 Otoe Rd	Alliance	NE	69301	308-762-4607	762-2867	338
Box Elder County	01 S Main St *TF:* 877-390-2326 ■ *Web:* www.boxeldercounty.org	Brigham City	UT	84302	435-734-3300	723-7562	338
Boxer Hotel, The	107 Merrimac St *Web:* www.theboxerboston.com	Boston	MA	02114	617-624-0202		707
Boxerwood Nature Ctr & Woodland Garden	963 Ross Rd *Web:* www.boxerwood.org	Lexington	VA	24450	540-463-2697		97
Boxes of St Louis Inc	1833 Knox Ave *Web:* www.boxesinc.com	Saint Louis	MO	63139	314-781-2600		100
Boxwood Hall State Historic Site	1073 E Jersey St *Web:* www.state.nj.us/dep/parksandforests/historic	Elizabeth	NJ	07201	908-282-7617		565
Boxworks Technologies Inc	2065 Pkwy Blve *TF:* 877-495-2250 ■ *Web:* boxworks.com	Salt Lake City	UT	84119	801-214-6100		180
BOXX Modular Inc	555 Jubilee Ln Bldg A *Web:* www.boxxmodularus.com	Lewisville	TX	75056	972-492-4040		106
Boy Scouts of America (BSA)	1325 W Walnut Hill Ln PO Box 152079 *TF:* 800-323-0732 ■ *Web:* www.scouting.org	Irving	TX	75015	972-580-2000		48-15
Boyajian Inc	144 Will Dr *TF General:* 800-965-0665 ■ *Web:* www.boyajianinc.com	Canton	MA	02021	781-828-9966		296-41

Name	Address	City	State	ZIP	Phone	Fax	Class
Boyar's Intrinsic Value Research LLC	6 E 32nd St 7th Fl *Web:* boyarresearch.com	New York	NY	10016	212-995-8300		401
Boyarsky Silbert & Silverman PA	6151 Executive Blvd	Rockville	MD	20852	301-231-0535		2
Boyce & Bynum Pathology Laboratories PC	200 Portland St *Web:* www.bbpllab.com	Columbia	MO	65201	573-886-4600		415
Boyce Thompson Arboretum	37615 US Hwy 60 *TF:* 877-763-5315 ■ *Web:* cals.arizona.edu	Superior	AZ	85273	520-689-2723	689-5858	97
Boyce Thompson Institute for Plant Research Inc	Cornell University 533 Twr Rd *Web:* btiscience.org	Ithaca	NY	14853	607-254-1234	254-1242	668
Boyd & Assoc Inc	6319 Colfax Ave *Web:* www.boydsecurity.com	North Hollywood	CA	91606	818-752-1888		693
Boyd Bros Transportation Inc	3275 Alabama 30 *TF:* 800-700-2693 ■ *Web:* www.boydbros.com	Clayton	AL	36016	334-775-1400		780
Boyd Brothers Inc	425 E 15th St *TF:* 800-677-2693 ■ *Web:* www.boyd-printing.com	Panama City	FL	32405	850-763-1741		77
Boyd Coffee Co	19730 NE Sandy Blvd *TF Cust Svc:* 800-545-4077 ■ *Web:* www.boyds.com	Portland	OR	97230	503-666-4545		296-7
Boyd Corp	6325 San Pedro Ave *Web:* www.boydlightingsa.com	San Antonio	TX	78216	210-344-9222		439
Boyd County	PO Box 26 *TF:* 800-424-9300 ■ *Web:* boydcounty.ne.gov	Butte	NE	68722	402-775-2391	775-2146	338
Boyd County Public Library	1740 Central Ave *Web:* www.thebookplace.org	Ashland	KY	41101	606-329-0518	329-0578	434-3
Boyd Gaming Corp	3883 Howard Hughes Pkwy 9th Fl *NYSE:* BYD ■ *TF:* 800-522-4700 ■ *Web:* boydgaming.com	Las Vegas	NV	89169	702-792-7200		132
Boyd Group Inc, The	3570 Portage Ave *TF:* 800-385-5451 ■ *Web:* www.boydgroup.com	Winnipeg	MB	R3K0Z8	204-895-1244		62
Boyd Jones Construction Co	4360 Nicholas St *Web:* www.boydjones.biz	Omaha	NE	68131	402-553-1804		186
Boyd Lake State Park	3720 N County Rd Ste 11-C *Web:* cpw.state.co.us	Loveland	CO	80538	970-669-1739		565
Boyd Lighting Co	944 Folsom St *TF:* 800-736-7672 ■ *Web:* www.boydlighting.com	San Francisco	CA	94107	415-778-4300	778-4319	439
Boydell Development Co	743 Beaubien St	Detroit	MI	48226	313-964-0333		652
Boyden & Youngblutt Adv & Mktg Inc	120 W Superior St *Web:* b-y.net	Fort Wayne	IN	46802	260-422-4499		4
Boyden Caverns	5350 Moaning Cave Rd *TF:* 866-762-2837 ■ *Web:* www.caverntours.com	Vallecito	CA	95251	209-736-2708	736-0330	50-5
Boyden World Corp	50 Broadway *TF:* 877-226-9336 ■ *Web:* www.boyden.com	Hawthorne	NY	10532	914-747-0093	747-0108	266
Boyds Philadelphia	1818 Chestnut St *Web:* www.boydsphila.com	Philadelphia	PA	19103	215-564-9000		157-3
Boyer & Associates Inc	3525 Plymouth Blvd Ste 207 *Web:* www.boyerassoc.com	Plymouth	MN	55447	763-412-4300		177
Boyer Candy Inc	821 17th St *Web:* www.boyercandies.com	Altoona	PA	16602	814-944-9401		296-8
Boyer Consulting Inc	708 Cheyenne Dr	Naperville	IL	60565	630-445-5560		463
Boyer Petroleum Co	1817 Hull Ave *TF:* 800-532-1480 ■ *Web:* www.boyerpetroleum.com	Des Moines	IA	50313	515-243-4450		580
Boyer's Food Markets Inc	301 S Warren St *Web:* www.boyersfood.com	Orwigsburg	PA	17961	570-366-1477		345
Boyertown Area School District (BASD)	911 Montgomery Ave *Web:* www.boyertownasd.org	Boyertown	PA	19512	610-367-6031	369-7620	186
Boyett Petroleum	601 McHenry Ave *TF:* 800-545-9212 ■ *Web:* www.boyett.net	Modesto	CA	95350	209-577-6000	577-6040	579
Boyhood Home of President Woodrow Wilson	419 Seventh St *TF:* 800-325-5446 ■ *Web:* www.wilsonboyhoodhome.org	Augusta	GA	30901	706-722-9828		50-3
Boykin Contracting Inc	167 Lott Ct	West Columbia	SC	29169	803-926-4930		610
Boykin Management Co	8015 W Kenton Cir Ste 220 *Web:* www.boykin.com	Huntersville	NC	28078	704-896-2880		194
Boylan Indoor Tennis	4000 Saint Francis Dr *Web:* www.boylan.org	Rockford	IL	61103	815-877-4273		354
Boyle & Stoll CPAs PC	3755 Brickway Blvd *Web:* boyle-stoll.com	Santa Rosa	CA	95403	707-571-1951		2
Boyle Brendan (Rep D - PA)	1133 Longworth HOB *Web:* boyle.house.gov	Washington	DC	20515	202-225-6111	226-0611	342-2
Boyle County	321 W Main St *Web:* www.boyleky.com	Danville	KY	40422	859-238-1110	238-1108	338
Boyle County Public Library	307 W Broadway *Web:* boylepublib.org	Danville	KY	40422	859-236-8466	236-7692	434-3
Boyle Energy Services & Technology Inc	28 Locke Rd *TF:* 800-428-8872 ■ *Web:* www.boyleenergy.com	Concord	NH	03301	603-227-5200		256
Boyle Fredrickson SC	840 N Plankinton Ave *Web:* www.boylefred.com	Milwaukee	WI	53203	414-225-9755		428
Boyle Investment Co	5900 Poplar Ave Ste 100 *Web:* www.boyle.com	Memphis	TN	38119	901-767-0100	766-4299	655
Boyle Ogata Bregman	17461 Derian Ave Ste 202 *Web:* www.bobsearch.com	Irvine	CA	92614	949-474-0115		260
Boyle Software Inc	42 W 24th St *Web:* www.boylesoftware.com	New York	NY	10010	212-691-0609		180

Phone | Fax | Class

Boyne Country Sports
1200 Bay View Rd. Petoskey MI 49770 | 231-439-4906 | | 711
TF: 800-462-6963 ■ *Web:* www.boyne.com

Boyne Highlands Resort
600 Highlands Dr. Harbor Springs MI 49740 | 231-526-3000 | 526-3100 | 669
TF: 800-462-6963 ■ *Web:* www.boyne.com

Boyne Mountain Resort
3951 Charlevoix Ave. Petoskey MI 49770 | 231-439-4750 | 439-4786 | 669
TF: 800-462-6963 ■ *Web:* www.boyneresorts.com

Boynton Beach City Library
208 S Seacrest Blvd. Boynton Beach FL 33435 | 561-742-6390 | | 434-3
Web: www.boyntonlibrary.org

Boynton Beach Mall
801 N Congress Ave. Boynton Beach FL 33426 | 561-736-7902 | | 460
TF: 877-746-6642 ■ *Web:* www.simon.com

Boynton Restaurant and Spirits
117 Highland St. Worcester MA 01609 | 508-756-5432 | | 671
Web: boyntonrestaurant.com

Boys & Girls Club of Zionsville
1575 Mulberry st. Zionsville IN 46077 | 317-873-6670 | | 652
Web: www.bagcoz.org

Boys & Girls Clubs of America
1275 Peachtree St NE. Atlanta GA 30309 | 404-487-5700 | | 48-15
Web: www.bgca.org

Boys Arnold & Company Inc
1272 Hendersonville Rd. Asheville NC 28803 | 828-274-1542 | | 401
Web: manageyourinvestments.com

Boys Town 14100 Crawford St. Boys Town NE 68010 | 402-498-1300 | | 48-6
TF: 800-448-3000 ■ *Web:* www.boystown.org

Boysen State Park 15 Ash St. Shoshoni WY 82649 | 307-876-2796 | | 565

Bozard Ford Co
540 Outlet Mall Blvd. St Augustine FL 32084 | 904-824-1641 | | 57
Web: bozardford.com

Bozeman Area Chamber of Commerce
2000 Commerce Way. Bozeman MT 59715 | 406-586-5421 | 586-8286 | 139
Web: www.bozemanchamber.com

Bozeman Deaconess Hospital
915 Highland Blvd. Bozeman MT 59715 | 406-585-5000 | 585-1070 | 374-3
Web: www.bozemanhealth.org

Bozeman Public Library 626 E Main St. Bozeman MT 59715 | 406-582-2400 | 582-2424 | 434-3
Web: www.bozemanlibrary.org

Bozeman School District 7 PO Box 520. Bozeman MT 59771 | 406-522-6000 | | 685
Web: www.bsd7.org

Bozzuto Group 7850 Walker Dr Ste 400. Greenbelt MD 20770 | 301-220-0100 | | 187
TF General: 866-698-7513 ■ *Web:* www.bozzuto.com

Bozzuto's Inc 275 School House Rd. Cheshire CT 06410 | 203-272-3511 | 250-2880* | 297-8
OTC: BOZZ ■ **Fax:* Sales ■ *TF:* 800-458-5114 ■ *Web:* www.bozzutos.com

BP Canada Energy Co 240 Fourth Ave SW. Calgary AB T2P2H8 | 403-233-1359 | 233-1476* | 536
**Fax:* Mail Rm ■ *TF:* 877-833-1359 ■ *Web:* www.bp.com

BP Canada Energy Resources Co
240- Fourth Ave SW. Calgary AB T2P2H8 | 403-233-1313 | | 536

BP Environmental Inc
8615 Commerce Dr Unit 1. Easton MD 21601 | 410-819-0010 | | 192
Web: www.bpenvironmental.net

BP Exploration (Alaska) Inc (BPXA)
PO Box 196612. Anchorage AK 99519 | 907-561-5111 | | 597
Web: www.bp.com

B&P Littleford 1000 Hess Ave. Saginaw MI 48601 | 989-757-1300 | | 146
Web: www.bpprocess.com

BP Logix Inc 410 S Melrose Dr Ste 100. Vista CA 92081 | 760-643-4121 | | 225
Web: www.bplogix.com

BP Lubricants USA Inc 1500 Valley Rd. Wayne NJ 07470 | 973-633-2200 | | 541
TF: 800-333-3991 ■ *Web:* www.bp.com

BP MotorClub PO Box 4441. Carol Stream IL 60197 | 800-334-3300 | | 53
TF: 800-334-3300 ■ *Web:* www.bpmotorclub.com

BP Pipelines (North America) Inc
150 W Warrenville Rd. Naperville IL 60563 | 630-536-2532 | | 580
TF: 800-872-2672 ■ *Web:* www.bp.com

BP PLC 28100 Torch Pkwy. Warrenville IL 60555 | 800-333-3991 | | 580
NYSE: BP ■ *TF:* 800-333-3991 ■ *Web:* www.bp.com

BP Prudhoe Bay Royalty Trust
101 Barclay St. New York NY 10007 | 212-815-6908 | | 538
NYSE: BPT

BP Solar International Inc
630 Solarex Ct. Frederick MD 21703 | 301-698-4200 | | 696

BPA
Bonneville Power Administration
905 NE 11th Ave. Portland OR 97232 | 503-230-3000 | | 340-9
TF: 800-282-3713 ■ *Web:* www.bpa.gov

BPA Worldwide
100 BeaRd Sawmill Rd 6th Fl. Shelton CT 06484 | 203-447-2800 | 447-2900 | 49-18
Web: www.bpaww.com

BPAA (Bowling Proprietors' Assn of America)
621 Six Flags Dr PO Box 5802. Arlington TX 76011 | 800-343-1329 | 633-2940* | 48-23
**Fax Area Code:* 817 ■ *TF:* 800-343-1329 ■ *Web:* www.bpaa.com

BPDI Corp 1000 S Lynndale Dr Apt O. Appleton WI 54914 | 920-830-7897 | | 95
Web: www.bookworldstores.com

BPI Communications LLC
121 W Long Lake Rd Ste 100. Bloomfield Hills MI 48304 | 248-645-0001 | | 5
Web: www.bpicommunications.com

BPI Inc 612 S Trenton Ave. Pittsburg PA 15221 | 412-334-8554 | 371-9984 | 192
Web: www.bpiminerals.com

BPI Information Systems
6055 W Snowville Rd. Brecksville OH 44141 | 440-717-4112 | | 138
TF: 800-870-4340 ■ *Web:* www.bpiohio.com

BPL (Brentwood Public Library)
34 Second Ave. Brentwood NY 11717 | 631-273-7883 | | 434-3
Web: brentwoodnylibrary.org

BPL (Brooklyn Public Library)
496 Franklin Ave. Brooklyn NY 11238 | 718-623-0012 | | 434-3
Web: bklynlibrary.org

BPL (Berwyn Public Library)
2701 S Harlem Ave. Berwyn IL 60402 | 708-795-8000 | 795-8101 | 434-3
Web: www.berwynlibrary.org

BPL (Bossier Parish Library)
2206 Beckett St. Bossier City LA 71111 | 318-746-1693 | 746-7768 | 434-3
TF: 800-745-3000 ■ *Web:* www.bossierlibrary.org

BPM Inc 200 W Front St. Peshtigo WI 54157 | 715-582-4551 | 582-4853 | 557
TF: 800-826-0494 ■ *Web:* www.bpmpaper.com

BPMLLP (Burr Pilger & Mayer LLP)
600 California St Ste 1300. San Francisco CA 94108 | 415-421-5757 | 288-6288 | 2
Web: www.bpmcpa.com

BPR Inc 4655 Wilfrid-Hamel Blvd. Quebec QC G1P2J7 | 418-871-8151 | | 668
Web: bpr.ca

BPRR (Buffalo & Pittsburgh Railroad Inc)
1200-C Scottsville Rd Ste 200. Rochester NY 14624 | 585-463-3307 | 477-4947* | 648
**Fax Area Code:* 800 ■ *TF:* 800-603-3385 ■ *Web:* www.gwrr.com

BPS (Biophysical Society)
9650 Rockville Pk. Bethesda MD 20814 | 301-634-7114 | 634-7133 | 49-19
Web: www.biophysics.org

BPXA (BP Exploration (Alaska) Inc)
PO Box 196612. Anchorage AK 99519 | 907-561-5111 | | 597
Web: www.bp.com

BPZ Resources Inc
580 Westlake Park Blvd Two Westlake Bldg
Ste 525. Houston TX 77079 | 281-556-6200 | 556-6377 | 536

BQ6 Media Group 110 Gibraltar Rd. Horsham PA 19044 | 267-965-2000 | | 195

BR (Business Roundtable)
300 New Jersey Ave NW Ste 800. Washington DC 20001 | 202-872-1260 | 466-3509 | 49-12
Web: businessroundtable.org

BR Amon & Sons Inc W 2950 State Rd 11. Elkhorn WI 53121 | 262-723-2547 | | 188-4

BR Funsten & Co 5200 Watt Ct Ste B. Fairfield CA 94534 | 209-825-5375 | 825-4916 | 361
TF: 888-261-2871 ■ *Web:* www.brfunsten.com

BR Kreider & Son Inc 63 Kreider Ln. Manheim PA 17545 | 717-898-7651 | | 189-5
Web: www.brkreider.com

Br Printers Inc 10154 toebben dr. Independence KY 41051 | 859-292-1700 | | 627
Web: www.brprinters.com

B&R Stores Inc 4554 W St. Lincoln NE 68503 | 402-464-6297 | | 345
Web: www.russmarket.com

Brabazon Pumps & Compressor
2484 Century Rd. Green Bay WI 54303 | 920-498-6020 | | 172
TF: 800-825-3222 ■ *Web:* www.brabazon.com

Brabham Oil Company Inc 525 Midway St. Bamberg SC 29003 | 803-245-2471 | | 581
TF: 800-832-5660 ■ *Web:* www.brabhamoil.com

Brabo & Carlsen LLP
1111 E Tahquitz Canyon Way. Palm Springs CA 92262 | 760-320-0848 | | 2
Web: brabo-carlsen.com

Bracalente Mfg Group
20 W Creamery Rd. Trumbauersville PA 18970 | 215-536-3077 | 536-4844 | 621
Web: www.bracalente.com

Bracco Diagnostics Inc
259 Prospect Plns Rd. Cranbury NJ 08512 | 609-514-2200 | | 582
Web: corporate.bracco.com

Brace Management Group Inc
9500 Arena Dr Ste 250. Upper Marlboro MD 20774 | 301-772-7600 | | 193
Web: www.bracemgmt.com

Bracewell & Giuliani LLP
711 Louisiana St Ste 2300. Houston TX 77002 | 713-223-2300 | 404-3970* | 428
**Fax Area Code:* 800 ■ *Web:* www.bracewell.com

Bracewell Engineering Inc
PO Box 21. San Juan Bautista CA 95045 | 831-623-2526 | | 261
Web: bracewellengineering.com

Bracing Systems Inc
4N350 Old Gary Ave. Hanover Park IL 60133 | 630-665-2732 | | 480
Web: www.bracingsystems.com

Brack Capital Real Estate
853 Broadway 2nd Fl. New York NY 10003 | 212-308-7200 | | 652
Web: www.brack capital.com

Bracken County
116 W Miami St PO Box 264. Brooksville KY 41004 | 606-735-2300 | 735-2615 | 338
Web: brackencounty.ky.gov/Pages/index.aspx

Brackenridge Hospital 601 E 15th St. Austin TX 78701 | 512-324-7000 | | 374-3
Web: www.seton.net

Bracker's Dept Store 60 N Morley Ave. Nogales AZ 85621 | 520-287-3631 | | 229

Brackett Builders Inc 185 Marybill Dr S. Troy OH 45373 | 937-339-7505 | | 186
Web: www.brackettbuilders.com

Brackett Inc
7115 SE Forbes Ave Bldg 451 J St. Topeka KS 66619 | 785-862-2205 | 862-1127 | 629
TF: 800-255-3506 ■ *Web:* www.brackett-inc.com

Braco Window Cleaning Service Inc
1 Braco International Blvd. Wilder KY 41076 | 859-442-6000 | 442-6001 | 152
TF: 800-969-4300 ■ *Web:* www.bracowindowcleaning.com

Brad Montgomery Productions Inc
6574 S Zeno Ct. Aurora CO 80016 | 303-691-0726 | | 196
Web: www.bradmontgomery.com

Brad Peters Agency Inc
2028 N State St. Belvidere IL 61008 | 815-544-2950 | | 390

Bradbury & Stamm Construction Company Inc
7110 Second St NW. Albuquerque NM 87107 | 505-765-1200 | 842-5419 | 186
Web: www.bradburystamm.com

Bradbury Company Inc 1200 E Cole. Moundridge KS 67107 | 620-345-6394 | | 456
TF: 800-397-6394 ■ *Web:* bradburygroup.com

Bradbury Mountain State Park
528 Hallowell Rd. Pownal ME 04069 | 207-688-4712 | | 565
Web: www.maine.gov

Bradbury Science Museum
1350 Central PO Box 1663. Los Alamos NM 87545 | 505-667-4444 | 665-6932 | 520
Web: www.lanl.gov

Bradco Inc 107-11th Ave PO Box 997. Holbrook AZ 86025 | 928-524-3976 | | 579
TF: 800-442-4770 ■ *Web:* www.bradcoinc.com

Braddock Hospital
12500 Willowbrook Rd. Cumberland MD 21502 | 240-964-7000 | | 374-3
TF: 888-369-1122 ■ *Web:* www.wmhs.com

Braden Farms Inc 6940 Hughson Ave. Hughson CA 95326 | 209-883-4061 | | 10-10

Braden Mfg LLC 5199 N Mingo Rd. Tulsa OK 74117 | 800-272-3360 | 272-7414* | 480
**Fax Area Code:* 918 ■ *TF:* 800-272-3360 ■ *Web:* www.braden.com

Braden Sutphin Ink Co
3650 E 93rd St. Cleveland OH 44105 | 216-271-2300 | | 388
TF: 800-289-6872 ■ *Web:* www.bsink.com

Braden-Burry Expediting Ltd
18 Yellowknife Airport 100 McMillan St. Yellowknife NT X1A3T2 | 867-766-8666 | | 314
TF: 866-746-4223 ■ *Web:* www.bbex.com

BradenCarco Gearmatic Paccar Winch Div
800 E Dallas St. Broken Arrow OK 74012 | 918-251-8511 | 259-1575 | 190
Web: www.paccarwinch.com

Bradford & Barthel LLP
2518 River Plaza Dr. Sacramento CA 95833 | 916-569-0790 | | 428
Web: www.bradfordbarthel.com

Name / Address	City	State	Zip	Phone	Fax	Class
Bradford & Bigelow Inc 3 Perkins Way *TF:* 800-727-2326 ■ *Web:* www.bradford-bigelow.com	Newburyport	MA	01950	978-904-3100		626
Bradford & Galt Inc 11457 Olde Cabin Rd Ste 200 *TF:* 800-997-4644 ■ *Web:* bradfordandgalt.com	Saint Louis	MO	63141	314-997-4644		196
Bradford Allen 200 S Michigan Ave 18th Fl *Web:* www.bradfordallen.com	Chicago	IL	60604	312-994-5700		652
Bradford Area School District Inc PO Box 375 *Web:* www.bradfordareaschools.org	Bradford	PA	16701	814-362-3841		685
Bradford Cos 9400 N Central Expy Ste 500 *TF:* 800-258-5525 ■ *Web:* www.bradford.com	Dallas	TX	75231	972-776-7000	776-7083	655
Bradford County 945 N Temple Ave *Web:* www.bradford-co-fla.org	Starke	FL	32091	904-966-6280	964-4454	338
Bradford County 301 Main St Courthouse *TF:* 800-468-2433 ■ *Web:* www.bradfordcountypa.org	Towanda	PA	18848	570-265-1727	265-1729	338
Bradford Health Services 2101 Magnolia Ave S Ste 518 *TF:* 800-217-2849 ■ *Web:* www.bradfordhealth.com	Birmingham	AL	35205	205-251-7753		726
Bradford Industries Inc 1857 Middlesex St *Web:* www.bradfordind.com	Lowell	MA	01851	978-459-4100	459-2597	745-2
Bradford Licensing Associates 7 Oak Pl Ste 1 *Web:* www.bradfordlicensing.com	Montclair	NJ	07042	973-509-0200		618
Bradford Printing & Finishing LLC 460 Bradford Rd	Bradford	RI	02808	401-377-2231		745-7
Bradford Regional Medical Ctr 116 Interstate Pk *Web:* www.brmc.com	Bradford	PA	16701	814-368-4143		374-3
Bradford School 2469 Stelzer Rd *TF:* 800-678-7981 ■ *Web:* www.bradfordschoolcolumbus.edu	Columbus	OH	43219	614-416-6200		800
Bradford Scott Data Corp 1001 Chestnut Hills Pkwy Ste 1 *TF:* 800-430-5120 ■ *Web:* www.bradfordscott.com	Fort Wayne	IN	46814	260-625-5107		396
Bradford Soap Works Inc 200 Providence St *Web:* www.bradfordsoap.com	West Warwick	RI	02893	401-821-2141		214
Bradford Technologies Inc 302 Piercy Rd *TF:* 866-445-8367 ■ *Web:* www.bradfordsoftware.com	San Jose	CA	95138	408-360-8520		177
Bradford White Corp 725 Talamore Dr *TF:* 800-523-2931 ■ *Web:* www.bradfordwhite.com	Ambler	PA	19002	215-641-9400	641-1612	36
Bradford-O'Keefe Funeral Homes Inc 675 E Howard Ave *Web:* www.bradfordokeefe.com	Biloxi	MS	39530	228-374-5650		510
Bradham Bros Inc 6128 Rozzelles Ferry Rd *Web:* bradhambrothers.com	Charlotte	NC	28214	704-392-8056		189-10
Bradhart Products Inc 7747 Lochlin Dr *Web:* www.bradhart.com	Brighton	MI	48116	248-437-8700		454
Bradington-Young 1340 14th Ave Ct SW *TF:* 800-468-8730 ■ *Web:* www.bradington-young.com	Hickory	NC	28602	704-435-5881	435-4276	319-2
Bradley & Assoc 201 S Capitol Ave Ste 910 *TF:* 800-228-0844 ■ *Web:* www.bradleycpa.com	Indianapolis	IN	46225	317-237-5500		734
Bradley & Riley PC PO Box 2804 *Web:* bradleyriley.com	Cedar Rapids	IA	52406	319-363-0101		428
Bradley Arant Boult Cummings LLP 1819 Fifth Ave N *Web:* www.bradley.com	Birmingham	AL	35203	205-521-8000		428
Bradley Boulder Inn 2040 16th St *Web:* www.thebradleyboulder.com	Boulder	CO	80302	303-545-5200		379
Bradley Caldwell Inc 200 Kiwanis Blvd **Fax:* Cust Svc ■ *TF Cust Svc:* 800-257-9100 ■ *Web:* www.bradleycaldwell.com	Hazleton	PA	18202	570-455-7511	455-0385*	276
Bradley Corp W 142 N 9101 Fountain Blvd *TF:* 800-272-3539 ■ *Web:* www.bradleycorp.com	Menomonee Falls	WI	53051	262-251-6000	251-5817	609
Bradley County 155 N Ocoee St *Web:* www.bradleyco.net	Cleveland	TN	37311	423-728-7226	478-8845	338
Bradley County 101 E Cedar St *Web:* www.countycriminal.com/court-records	Warren	AR	71671	870-226-6743		338
Bradley Graphic Solutions Inc 941 Mill Rd *TF:* 800-638-8223 ■ *Web:* bradleygraphics.net	Bensalem	PA	19020	215-638-8771		627
Bradley Hospital 1011 Veterans Memorial Pkwy *TF:* 800-561-3357 ■ *Web:* www.bradleyhospital.org	East Providence	RI	02915	401-432-1000	432-1500	374-1
Bradley House 11321 Old Seward Hwy *Web:* alaskabradleyhouse.com	Anchorage	AK	99515	907-336-7177	336-7178	671
Bradley Inn 3063 Bristol Rd *TF:* 800-942-5560 ■ *Web:* www.bradleyinn.com	New Harbor	ME	04554	207-677-2105	677-3367	379
Bradley J Mcdonough CPA 2645 Frederica St Ste 200	Owensboro	KY	42301	270-852-2733		2
Bradley Mj and Associates Inc 47 Jct Sq Dr *Web:* www.mjbradley.com	Concord	MA	01742	978-369-5533		196
Bradley Petroleum Inc 7268 S Tucson Way *Web:* www.bradleygas.com	Centennial	CO	80112	303-792-3444		580
Bradley Plumbing & Heating Inc 431 Hackel Dr	Montgomery	AL	36117	334-271-0700		189-10
Bradley Pulverizer Company Inc 123 S Third St *Web:* www.bradleypulverizer.com	Allentown	PA	18105	610-434-5191		491
Bradley University 1501 W Bradley Ave *TF Admissions:* 800-447-6460 ■ *Web:* www.bradley.edu	Peoria	IL	61625	309-676-7611	677-2797	166
Bradley-Sciocchetti Inc 4420 N Crescent Blvd *TF:* 800-950-4822 ■ *Web:* www.bsihvac.com	Pennsauken	NJ	08109	856-663-3022		196
Bradmark Technologies Inc 4265 San Felipe St Ste 700 *TF:* 800-621-2808 ■ *Web:* www.bradmark.com	Houston	TX	77027	713-621-2808	621-1639	178-1

Name / Address	City	State	Zip	Phone	Fax	Class
Brad-Pak Enterprises Inc 124 S Ave *Web:* brad-pak.com	Garwood	NJ	07027	908-233-1234		76
Bradshaw Advertising 811 NW 19th Ave *Web:* bradshawads.com	Portland	OR	97209	503-221-5000		7
Bradshaw Consulting Services Inc 2170 Woodside Exec Ct *Web:* www.bcs-gis.com	Aiken	SC	29803	803-641-0960		180
Bradshaw International Inc 9409 Buffalo Ave *Web:* www.bradshawintl.com	Rancho Cucamonga	CA	91730	909-476-3884		730
Bradshaw- Smith & Co 5851 W Charleston *Web:* www.bradshawsmith.com	Las Vegas	NV	89146	702-878-9788		2
Bradshaw State Jail 3900 W Loop 571 N *Web:* www.cca.com	Henderson	TX	75652	903-655-0880	655-0500	213
Bradshaw-Chambers County Public Library 3419 20th Ave *TF:* 800-959-0717 ■ *Web:* www.chamberscountylibrary.org	Valley	AL	36854	334-768-2161		434-3
Brady Campaign to Prevent Gun Violence 1225 'I' St NW Ste 1100 *TF:* 800-732-0999 ■ *Web:* www.bradycampaign.org	Washington	DC	20005	202-898-0792	371-9615	48-7
Brady Chapman Holland & Assoc Inc 10055 W Gulf Bank *Web:* bch-insurance.com	Houston	TX	77040	713-688-1500		390
Brady Coated Products 6555 W Good Hope Rd PO Box 571 **Fax Area Code:* 800 ■ *TF:* 800-662-1191 ■ *Web:* www.bradyid.com	Milwaukee	WI	53201	414-358-6600	292-2289*	732
Brady Connolly & Masuda Pc 211 Landmark Dr Ste C2 *Web:* bcm-law.com	Normal	IL	61761	309-862-4914		428
Brady Corp 6555 W Good Hope Rd *NYSE:* BRC ■ **Fax Area Code:* 800 ■ **Fax:* Cust Svc ■ *TF Cust Svc:* 800-541-1686 ■ *Web:* www.bradycorp.com	Milwaukee	WI	53223	414-358-6600	292-2289*	413
Brady Enterprises Inc 167 Moore Rd	East Weymouth	MA	02189	781-337-5000		296-15
Brady Identification Solutions 6555 W Good Hope Rd **Fax Area Code:* 800 ■ **Fax:* Cust Svc ■ *TF Cust Svc:* 800-537-8791 ■ *Web:* www.bradyid.com	Milwaukee	WI	53223	414-358-6600	292-2289*	178-1
Brady Industries Inc 7055 Lindell Rd *TF:* 800-293-4698 ■ *Web:* www.bradyindustries.com	Las Vegas	NV	89118	702-876-3990	876-1580	406
Brady Kevin (Rep R - TX) 1011 Longworth HOB *Web:* kevinbrady.house.gov	Washington	DC	20515	202-225-4901	225-5524	342-2
Brady Marketing Co 1331N California Blvd Ste 320 *TF:* 800-543-7549 ■ *Web:* www.bradymarketing.com	Walnut Creek	CA	94596	925-676-1300	676-3082	38
Brady Martz & Assoc PC 401 Demers Ave Ste 300 *Web:* www.bradymartz.com	Grand Forks	ND	58201	701-775-4685	795-7498	2
Brady Oilfield Services LP 23 Marion Ave PO Box 83 *Web:* www.brady.sk.ca	Oxbow	SK	S0C2B0	306-458-2344		539
Brady Palmer Label Corp 1791 Rt 6 Carmel PO Box 490 PO Box 490 **Fax Area Code:* 845 ■ *TF:* 800-783-3097	New York	NY	10512	800-783-3097	225-1823*	627
Brady Robert (Rep D - PA) 2004 Rayburn HOB *Web:* www.brady.house.gov	Washington	DC	20515	202-225-4731	225-0088	342-2
Brady Sullivan Properties LLC 670 N Commercial St *Web:* www.bradysullivan.com	Manchester	NH	03101	603-622-6223		652
Braen Stone Co 400 Central Ave PO Box 8310 *Web:* braenstone.com	Haledon	NJ	07508	973-595-6250	595-7087	503-5
Braff Group, The 1665 Washington Rd Ste 3 *TF:* 888-922-5169 ■ *Web:* www.thebraffgroup.com	Pittsburgh	PA	15228	412-833-5733		476
Braff Harris & Sukoneck 305 Broadway Fl 7 *Web:* bhs-law.com	New York	NY	10007	212-822-1478		445
Bragg Financial Advisors Inc 1031 S Caldwell St Ste 200 *Web:* www.braggfinancial.com	Charlotte	NC	28203	704-377-0261		401
Bragg Live Food Products Inc PO Box 7 *Web:* bragg.com	Santa Barbara	CA	93102	805-968-1020		297-8
Bragg's Electric Construction Company Inc 3000 Cantrell Rd *Web:* cdicon.com	Little Rock	AR	72202	501-666-6166		256
Bragg-Mitchell Mansion 1906 Springhill Ave *Web:* www.braggmitchellmansion.com	Mobile	AL	36607	251-471-6364		520
Brahma Compression Ltd 43rd Ave SE Ste 1310 *Web:* www.brahmacompression.com	Calgary	AB	T2G2A2	403-287-6990		112
Braille Battery Inc 6935 15th St E Ste 115 *Web:* www.braillebattery.com	Sarasota	FL	34243	941-312-5047		74
Braille Institute of America Inc 741 N Vermont Ave *TF:* 800-272-4553 ■ *Web:* www.brailleinstitute.org	Los Angeles	CA	90029	323-663-1111	663-0867	48-11
Brain Injury Assn of America 1608 Spring Hill Rd Ste 110 *TF:* 800-444-6443 ■ *Web:* www.biausa.org	Vienna	VA	22182	703-761-0750	761-0755	48-17
Brain Research Institute 695 Charles Young Dr S *Web:* www.bri.ucla.edu	Los Angeles	CA	90095	310-825-5061	206-5855	668
BrainCells Inc 3636 Nobel Dr Ste 215 *Web:* www.braincellsinc.com	San Diego	CA	92122	858-812-7700		668
Brainerd Baptist Church 300 Brookfield Ave *Web:* brainerdbaptist.org	Chattanooga	TN	37411	423-624-2606		48-20
Brainerd Compressor Rebuilders Inc 3034 Sandbrook St *TF:* 800-228-4138 ■ *Web:* www.brainerdcompressor.com	Memphis	TN	38116	800-228-4138		14
Brainerd Industries Inc 680 Precision Ct *TF:* 800-790-0430 ■ *Web:* www.brainerdindustries.com	Miamisburg	OH	45342	937-228-0488		483

Phone | Fax | Class

Brainerd International Raceway
5523 Birchdale Rd ... Brainerd MN 56401 218-824-7223 824-7240 515
TF: 866-444-4455 ■ Web: www.brainerdraceway.com

Brainerd Lakes Area Chamber of Commerce
7393 State Hwy 371 PO Box 356 ... Brainerd MN 56401 218-829-2838 829-8199 139
TF: 800-450-2838 ■ Web: www.explorebrainerdlakes.com

Brainerd Mfg Company Inc
140 Business Pk Dr ... Winston-Salem NC 27107 336-769-4077 350
TF: 800-652-7277 ■ Web: www.libertyhardware.com

Brainin Advance Industries Inc
48 Frank Mossberg Dr ... Attleboro MA 02703 508-226-1200 226-8703 815
Web: www.pepbrainin.com

BrainLAB Inc
5 Westbrook Corporate Ctr ... Westchester IL 60154 708-409-1343 409-1619 382
TF: 800-784-7700 ■ Web: www.brainlab.com

Brains II Canada Inc
165 Konrad Crescent ... Markham ON L3R9T9 905-946-8700 175
Web: www.brainsiisolutions.com

Brains On Fire Inc 148 River St ... Greenville SC 29601 864-676-9663 195
TF: 800-438-7325 ■ Web: www.brainsonfire.com

Brainsport The Running Store
704 Broadway Ave ... Saskatoon SK S7N1B4 306-244-0955 711
Web: www.brainsport.ca

Brainstorm Internet Inc
640 Main Ave Ste 201 ... Durango CO 81301 970-247-1442 225
Web: www.gobrainstorm.net

Braintree Laboratories Inc
60 Columbian St W ... Braintree MA 02185 781-843-2202 476
Web: www.braintreelabs.com

Brainworks Software Inc
100 S Main St ... Sayville NY 11782 631-563-5000 178-1
TF: 800-755-1111 ■ Web: www.brainworks.com

BrainX Inc 45 Rincon Dr Ste 103-3B ... Camarillo CA 93012 805-384-1001 177
Web: www.brainx.com

Brake Resources Inc 835 Texas Ct ... O'Fallon MO 63366 636-240-3211 247
Web: www.bti-bri.com

Brake Supply Company Inc
5501 Foundation Blvd ... Evansville IN 47725 812-467-1000 385
TF: 800-457-5788 ■ Web: www.brake.com

Brake Systems Inc 2221 NE Hoyt St ... Portland OR 97232 503-236-2116 454
Web: www.brakesystemsinc.com

Brakebush Bros Inc N4993 Sixth Dr ... Westfield WI 53964 608-296-2121 296-3192 619
TF: 800-933-2121 ■ Web: www.brakebush.com

Brakeley Briscoe Inc
322 W Bellevue Ave Ste 204 ... San Mateo CA 94402 650-344-8883 317
TF: 800-416-3086 ■ Web: www.brakeleybriscoe.com

Brakewell Steel Fabricator Inc
55 Leone Ln ... Chester NY 10918 845-469-9131 469-7618 482
TF: 888-914-9131 ■ Web: www.brakewell.com

Brakke Consulting Inc
2735 Villa Creek Ste 140 ... Dallas TX 75234 972-243-4033 194
TF: 877-399-6354 ■ Web: www.brakkeconsulting.com

Brakur Custom Cabinetry
18656 Route 59 ... Shorewood IL 60404 815-436-4970 115
Web: www.brakur.com

Bramble Inn 2019 Main St ... Brewster MA 02631 508-896-7644 671
Web: www.brambleinn.com

Bramble Park Zoo
800 Tenth St NW PO Box 910 ... Watertown SD 57201 605-882-6269 882-5232 823
Web: www.brambleparkzoo.com

Bramco Inc 1801 Watterson Trail ... Louisville KY 40232 502-493-4300 219
Web: www.bramco.com

Brame Specialty Company Inc PO Box 27 ... Durham NC 27702 919-683-1331 682-6034 559
TF: 800-533-2041 ■ Web: www.brameco.com

Brammer Engineering Inc
400 Texas St Bank One Bldg Ste 600 ... Shreveport LA 71101 318-429-2345 539
Web: www.brammer.com

Brampton Board of Trade
36 Queen St E Ste 101 ... Brampton ON L6V1A2 905-451-1122 450-0295 137
Web: www.bramptonbot.com

Brampton Brick Ltd 225 Wanless Dr ... Brampton ON L7A1E9 905-840-1011 840-1535 150
TSE: BBLA ■ TF: 800-230-5511 ■ Web: www.bramptonbrick.com

Brampton (City of) 2 Wellington St W ... Brampton ON L6Y4R2 905-874-2000 707
Web: www.brampton.ca

Bramson ORT College
69-30 Austin St ... Forest Hills NY 11375 718-261-5800 800

Branagh Inc 750 Kevin Ct ... Oakland CA 94621 510-638-6455 562-8371 186
Web: www.branaghinc.com

Branbury State Park
3570 Lake Dunmore Rd Rt 53 ... Brandon VT 05733 802-247-5925 565
Web: www.vtstateparks.com

Branch Banking & Trust Company of South Carolina
301 College St ... Greenville SC 29601 800-226-5228 70
TF: 800-226-5228 ■ Web: www.bbt.com

Branch County 31 Div St ... Coldwater MI 49036 517-279-4301 278-4130 338
TF: 800-968-9333 ■ Web: www.countyofbranch.com

Branch Group Inc
442 Rutherford Ave NE ... Roanoke VA 24016 540-982-1678 186
Web: www.branchgroup.com

Branch Highways Inc
442 Rutherford Ave ... Roanoke VA 24016 540-982-1678 982-4216 188-4
TF: 800-353-3747 ■ Web: www.branchhighways.com

Branch Manufacturing Co
6420 Pine St ... North Branch MN 55056 651-674-4441 674-4442 697
TF: 800-242-2679 ■ Web: www.branchmfg.com

Branched Oak State Recreation Area
12000 W Branched Oak Rd ... Raymond NE 68428 402-783-3400 565
Web: outdoornebraska.gov

Brand Advisor 512 Union St ... San Francisco CA 94133 415-393-0800 194
Web: www.brandadvisors.com

Brand Electric Inc 6274 E 375 S ... Lafayette IN 47905 765-296-3437 194
Web: www.brandelectric.com

Brand Energy & Infrastructure Services Inc
1325 Cobb International Dr Ste A-1 ... Kennesaw GA 30152 678-285-1400 514-0285* 491
*Fax Area Code: 770 ■ TF: 855-746-4477 ■ Web: www.beis.com

Brand Hydraulics Company Inc
2332 S 25th St ... Omaha NE 68106 402-344-4434 790
TF: 800-232-6298 ■ Web: www.brand-hyd.com

Brand Innovation Group
8902 Airport Dr Pyramid Plazaa Ste A ... Fort Wayne IN 46809 260-469-4060 7
Web: www.gotobig.com

Brand Institute Inc
200 SE First St 12th Fl ... Miami FL 33131 305-374-2500 466
Web: www.brandinst.com

Brand Integrity 60 Park Ave ... Rochester NY 14607 585-442-5404 194
Web: www.brandintegrity.com

Brand Iron 821 22nd St ... Denver CO 80205 303-534-1901 195
TF: 800-343-6405 ■ Web: brandiron.net

Brand Launcher Inc 4703 Falls Rd ... Baltimore MD 21209 410-235-7070 7
Web: www.brandlauncher.com

Brand Library & Art Ctr
1601 W Mountain St ... Glendale CA 91201 818-548-2051 520
TF: 800-576-0744 ■ Web: www.glendaleca.gov

Brand Pharm 79 Madison Ave ... New York NY 10016 212-684-0909 4

Brand Protection Agency LLC
8750 N Central Expwy Ste 720 ... Dallas TX 75231 866-339-5657 534-1756* 195
*Fax Area Code: 972 ■ TF: 866-339-5657 ■ Web: brandprotectionagency.com

Brand Sense Partners LLC
10441 Jefferson Blvd Ste 100 ... Culver City CA 90232 310-867-7222 195
Web: bsp.com

Brand Thunder LLC 6588 Dalmore Ln ... Dublin OH 43016 614-408-8202 387
Web: brandthunder.com

Brandamplitude Llc
3467 Notre Dame Path ... Stevensville MI 49127 269-429-6526 195
Web: brandamplitude.com

Branded Emblem Co Inc
7920 Foster St ... Overland Park KS 66204 913-648-0573 648-7444 258
Web: www.campdavid.com

Brandeis Machinery & Supply Co
1801 Watterson Trl ... Louisville KY 40299 502-493-4380 499-3180 358
Web: www.brandeismachinery.com

Brandeis University 415 S St ... Waltham MA 02454 781-736-3500 736-3536 166
TF: 800-622-0622 ■ Web: www.brandeis.edu

BrandEquity International
7 Great Meadow Rd ... Newton MA 02462 800-969-3150 344
TF: 800-969-3150 ■ Web: www.brandequity.com

Brander Engineering Inc
975 Hansen Rd ... Green Bay WI 54304 920-499-0260 261
Web: branderti.com

Brandermill Woods
14311 Brandermill Woods Trl ... Midlothian VA 23112 804-744-1173 744-4894 672
Web: www.brandermillwoods.com

Brandes Investment Partners LP
11988 El Camino Real Ste 500 ... San Diego CA 92130 858-755-0239 755-0916 401
TF: 800-237-7119 ■ Web: www.brandes.com

Branding Brand 2313 E Carson St ... Pittsburgh PA 15203 888-979-5018 387
TF: 888-979-5018 ■ Web: www.brandingbrand.com

Branding Farm, The 1378 Main St ... Venice CA 90291 310-822-6888 5
Web: branding.farm

BrandingBusiness Inc One Wrigley ... Irvine CA 92618 949-273-6330 7
Web: www.brandingbusiness.com

BrandJuice Consulting Inc
1700 E 17th Ave Ste 200 ... Denver CO 80218 303-629-0560 466
Web: brandjuice.com

Brandmovers Inc
2120 Powers Ferry Rd SE # 300 ... Atlanta GA 30339 888-463-4933 631
TF: 888-463-4933 ■ Web: www.brandmovers.com

Brandon Advertising
3023 Church St ... Myrtle Beach SC 29577 843-916-2000 7
TF: 800-228-9290 ■ Web: www.thebrandonagency.com

Brandon Assoc
20 Commonwealth Ave Ste 901 ... Boston MA 02116 857-362-7360 636
Web: www.brandonassociatesllc.com

Brandon Assocs Ltd 26 Sarah Dr ... Farmingdale NY 11735 631-293-1414 256
Web: www.brandonassociates.com

Brandon Business Machines Inc
505 W Robertson St ... Brandon FL 33511 813-689-1950 175
TF: 800-585-1768 ■ Web: www.bbmusa.com

Brandon Chamber of Commerce
1043 Rosser Ave ... Brandon MB R7A0L5 204-571-5340 571-5347 137
Web: www.brandonchamber.ca

Brandon College
944 Market St 2nd Fl ... San Francisco CA 94102 415-391-5711 391-3918 423
Web: www.brandoncollege.com

Brandon Hall School
1701 Brandon Hall Dr ... Atlanta GA 30350 770-394-8177 622
Web: www.brandonhall.org

Brandon Regional Health Ctr
150 McTavish Ave E ... Brandon MB R7A2B3 204-578-4000 374-2
Web: www.brandonrha.mb.ca

Brandon Regional Hospital
119 Oakfield Dr ... Brandon FL 33511 813-681-5551 374-3
TF: 800-733-0429 ■ Web: www.brandonhospital.com

Brandon School Division 1031 Sixth St ... Brandon MB R7A4K5 204-729-3955 685
Web: www.bsd.ca

Brandon Technology Consulting Inc
3012 Business Park Cir Ste 700 ... Goodlettsville TN 37072 615-757-1200 463
Web: www.brandontci.com

Brandon University 270 18th St ... Brandon MB R7A6A9 204-728-9520 728-7346 785
TF: 800-862-6307 ■ Web: www.brandonu.ca

Brandpoint 850 5Th St S ... Hopkins MN 55343 877-374-5270 5
TF: 877-374-5270 ■ Web: www.brandpoint.com

BrandsMart USA Corp 3200 SW 42nd St ... Hollywood FL 33312 800-432-8579 35
TF: 800-432-8579 ■ Web: www.brandsmartusa.com

Brandstand Group Inc
686 Yorktown Rd ... Lewisberry PA 17339 717-932-4178 671

Brandstream 8353 160th Ave NE ... Redmond WA 98052 425-497-1404 457-3899* 463
*Fax Area Code: 720 ■ Web: www.brandstream.com

Brandt Box & Paper Company Inc
6 W Crisman Rd ... Columbia NJ 07832 908-496-4500 100
Web: www.brandtboxnj.com

Brandt Consolidated Inc
211 IL-125 ... Pleasant Plains IL 62677 217-476-3438 280
Web: www.brandt.co

Brandt Holdings Co 4650 26th Ave S Ste E ... Fargo ND 58104 701-237-6000 360-3
Web: www.brandtholdings.com

	Phone	Fax	Class
Brandt Ronat & Co 60 Mcleod St .... Merritt Island FL 32953 *Web:* brc60.com	321-453-3101		7
Brandt Technologies Inc 231 W Grand Ave .... Bensenville IL 60106 *Web:* www.brandttech.com	630-787-1800		146
Brandt Tractor Ltd Hwy 1 E PO Box 3856 .... Regina SK S4P3R8 *TF:* 888-227-2638 ■ *Web:* www.brandt.ca	306-791-7777		111
Brandtailers 17838 Fitch .... Irvine CA 92614 *Web:* www.brandtailers.com	949-442-0500		7
Brandtjen & Kluge Inc 539 Blanding Woods Rd .... Saint Croix Falls WI 54024 *TF:* 800-826-7320 ■ *Web:* www.kluge.biz	715-483-3265	483-1640	629
Brandweek Magazine 770 Broadway 7th Fl .... New York NY 10003 *Web:* www.adweek.com	212-493-4171		457-5
Brandx Internet LLC 927 Sixth St Apt 4 .... Santa Monica CA 90403 *TF:* 800-899-4125 ■ *Web:* www.brandx.net	310-395-5500		225
Brandy's 1500 E Cedar Ave Ste 40 .... Flagstaff AZ 86004 *Web:* www.brandysrestaurant.com	928-779-2187		671
Brandywine Capital Assoc 113 East Evans St .... West Chester PA 19380 *TF:* 888-344-2920 ■ *Web:* www.brandywinecap.com	610-344-2910		401
Brandywine Conservancy Inc US Rt 1 .... Chadds Ford PA 19317 *Web:* www.brandywine.org/conservancy	610-388-2700		520
Brandywine Creek State Park PO Box 3782 .... Greenville DE 19807 *Web:* www.destateparks.com	302-577-3534		565
Brandywine Global Investment Management LLC 2929 Arch St 8th Fl .... Philadelphia PA 19104 *TF:* 800-348-2499 ■ *Web:* www.brandywineglobal.com	215-609-3500	609-3501	401
Brandywine Hospital 201 Reeceville Rd .... Coatesville PA 19320 *TF:* 800-430-3762 ■ *Web:* www.brandywinehospital.com	610-383-8000		374-3
Brandywine Investment Group Homalite Div 11 Brookside Dr .... Wilmington DE 19804 *TF:* 800-346-7802 ■ *Web:* www.homalite.com	302-652-3686	652-4578	600
Brandywine Machine Company Inc 300 Creek Rd .... Downingtown PA 19335 *TF:* 800-523-7128 ■ *Web:* www.bramcostainless.com	800-523-7128		454
Brandywine Nursing & Rehabilitation Ctr Inc 505 Greenbank Rd .... Wilmington DE 19808 *Web:* www.brandywinenursing.org	302-998-0101		363
Brandywine Realty Trust 555 E Lancaster Ave Ste 100 .... Radnor PA 19087 *NYSE: BDN* ■ *TF:* 866-426-5400 ■ *Web:* www.brandywinerealty.com	610-325-5600	325-5622	655
Brandywine River Museum 1 Hoffman's Mill Rd .... Chadds Ford PA 19317 *Web:* www.brandywine.org/museum	610-388-2700	388-1197	520
Brandywine Valley Baptist Church 7 Mt Lebanon Rd .... Wilmington DE 19803 *Web:* brandywineonline.org	302-478-4255		48-20
Brandywine Valley Fabricators Inc Brandywine Vly Fab .... Coatesville PA 19320 *Web:* www.brandywinevalleyfab.com	610-384-7440		480
Brandywine Zoo 1001 N Pk Dr .... Wilmington DE 19802 *Web:* www.brandywinezoo.org	302-571-7747	571-7787	823
Branford Hills Health Care Ctr 189 Alps Rd .... Branford CT 06405 *Web:* www.bhhcc.com	203-481-6221	483-1893	450
Branham Corp 207 Eiler Ave .... Louisville KY 40214 *Web:* www.branhamcorp.com	502-366-0326		207
Branigan Cultural Ctr 501 N Main St PO Box 20000 .... Las Cruces NM 88004 *Web:* www.las-cruces.org	575-541-2154	541-2152	50-2
Branksome Hall 10 Elm Ave .... Toronto ON M4W1N4 *Web:* www.branksome.on.ca	416-920-9741	920-5390	622
Brann & Isaacson 184 Main St .... Lewiston ME 04243 *TF:* 800-225-6964 ■ *Web:* www.brannlaw.com	207-786-3566		428
Brann's Steakhouse & Grille 401 Leonard St NW .... Grand Rapids MI 49504 *Web:* www.branns.com	616-454-9368		671
Brannan Island State Recreation Area 17645 State Hwy 160 .... Rio Vista CA 94571 *Web:* www.parks.ca.gov/default.asp?page_id=487	916-777-7701		565
Brannan Paving Coltd 111 Elk Dr PO Box 3403 .... Victoria TX 77903 *TF:* 800-626-7064 ■ *Web:* www.brannanpaving.com	361-573-3130	573-6211	186
Brannan Sand & Gravel Co 2500 Brannan Way .... Denver CO 80229 *Web:* www.brannan1.com	303-534-1231	534-1231	46
Brannen Banks of Florida Inc PO Box 1929 .... Inverness Fl 34451 *TF:* 866-546-8273 ■ *Web:* www.brannenbanks.com	352-726-1221	726-1156	360-2
Brannen Brothers-flutemakers Inc 58 Dragon Ct .... Woburn MA 01801 *Web:* brannenflutes.com	781-935-9522		527
Branom Instrument Co 5500 Fourth Ave S .... Seattle WA 98108 *TF:* 800-767-6051 ■ *Web:* www.branom.com	206-762-6050		358
Branson 41 Eagle Rd .... Danbury CT 06813 *TF:* 800-732-9262 ■ *Web:* www.emersonindustrial.com	800-732-9262		782
Branson Cafe 120 W Main St .... Branson MO 65616 *TF:* 800-287-2462 ■ *Web:* downtownbransoncafe.com	417-334-3021		671
Branson City Hall 110 W Maddux St Ste 205 .... Branson MO 65616 *TF:* 800-520-5544 ■ *Web:* www.cityofbranson.org	417-334-3345	335-4354	337
Branson Daily News 200 Industrial Pk Dr .... Hollister MO 65672 *Web:* bransontrilakesnews.com	417-334-3161		532-2
Branson Fowlkes & Company Inc 3300 Chimney Rock Rd Ste 100-B .... Houston TX 77056 *Web:* www.bransonfowlkes.com	713-780-0606		401
Branson's Best Reservations 2875 Green Mtn Dr .... Branson MO 65616 *TF:* 800-335-2555 ■ *Web:* www.bransonbest.com	417-339-2204		376

	Phone	Fax	Class
Branson/Lakes Area Chamber of Commerce PO Box 1897 .... Branson MO 65615 *TF:* 800-214-3661 ■ *Web:* www.bransonchamber.com	417-334-4084	334-4139	139
Branson/Lakes Area Lodging Assn PO Box 430 .... Branson MO 65615 *Web:* blala.clubexpress.com	417-559-3869	335-3643	376
Brant Securities Ltd Ste 300-220 Bay St Ste 300 .... Toronto ON M5J2W4 *TF:* 888-544-9318 ■ *Web:* www.brantsec.com	416-596-4545		690
Branter Thibodeau & Associate 674 Mt Hope Ave Ste 1 .... Bangor ME 04401 *Web:* btacpa.com	207-947-3325		2
Brantford Brant Chamber of Commerce (BBCC) 77 Charlotte St .... Brantford ON N3T2W8 *Web:* www.brantfordbrantchamber.com	519-753-2617	753-0921	137
Brantley Janson Yost & Ellison CPA 1617 S 325th St .... Federal Way WA 98003 *Web:* www.brantleyjanson.com	253-838-3484		2
Brantley Partners 3550 Lander Rd Ste 300 .... Cleveland OH 44124	216-464-8400	464-8405	792
Bran-Zan Holdings Inc 1548 Barclay Blvd .... Buffalo Grove IL 60089 *TF:* 866-266-9670 ■ *Web:* www.branzan.com	866-266-9670		299
Brasfield & Gorrie LLC 3021 Seventh Ave S .... Birmingham AL 35233 *TF:* 800-239-8017 ■ *Web:* www.brasfieldgorrie.com	205-328-4000	251-1304	186
Brasher Motor Company of Weimar Inc 1700 I- 10 .... Weimar TX 78962 *TF:* 800-783-1746 ■ *Web:* www.brashermotors.com	979-725-8515	725-8118	57
Brasitas 954 E Main St .... Stamford CT 06902 *Web:* www.brasitas.com	203-323-3176		671
Brass Ring Capital Inc 301 Carlson Pkwy Ste 265 .... Minnetonka MN 55305 *Web:* www.brassringcapital.com	952-473-2710		401
Brass-Craft Manufacturing Co 39600 Orchard Hill Pl .... Novi MI 48375 *Web:* www.brasscraft.com	248-305-6000		609
Brasseler USA 1 Brasseler Blvd .... Savannah GA 31419 *TF:* 800-841-4522 ■ *Web:* www.brasselerusa.com	800-841-4522		228
Brasserie Margaux 401 Lenora St .... Seattle WA 98121 *Web:* www.margauxseattle.com	206-219-2224		671
Brasstech Inc 2001 Carnegie Ave .... Santa Ana CA 92705 *Web:* www.brasstech.com	949-417-5207	417-5208	609
Brasstown Valley Resort 6321 US Hwy 76 .... Young Harris GA 30582 *TF:* 800-201-3205 ■ *Web:* www.brasstownvalley.com	706-379-9900	379-9999	669
Braswell Drugs Inc 1107 S Tyler St .... Covington LA 70433	985-892-0818		237
Braswell Food Co 226 N Zetterower Ave .... Statesboro GA 30458 *TF:* 800-673-9388 ■ *Web:* www.braswells.com	912-764-6191		296-20
Bratcher Heating & Air Conditioning Inc 1210 Ft Jesse Rd .... Normal IL 61761 *Web:* www.bratchercomfort.com	309-454-1611		189-10
Bratt Decor Inc 5 N Haven St .... Baltimore MD 21224 *Web:* www.brattdecor.com	703-448-6833		321
Brattle Group Inc, The 44 Brattle St .... Cambridge MA 02138 *TF:* 800-754-9452 ■ *Web:* www.brattle.com	617-864-7900		194
Brattleboro Area Chamber of Commerce 180 Main St .... Brattleboro VT 05301 *TF:* 877-254-4565 ■ *Web:* www.brattleborochamber.org	802-254-4565	254-5675	139
Brattleboro Memorial Hospital Inc 17 Belmont Ave .... Brattleboro VT 05301 *TF:* 866-972-5266 ■ *Web:* www.bmhvt.org	802-257-0341		374-3
Bratton Corp 2801 E 85th St .... Kansas City MO 64132 *Web:* www.brattonsteel.com	816-363-1014		189-14
Brauer Material Handling Systems Inc 226 Molly Walton Dr .... Hendersonville TN 37075 **Fax Area Code:* 615 ■ *TF:* 800-645-6083 ■ *Web:* www.braueronline.com	800-645-6083	859-2937*	385
Braun Industries Inc 1170 Production Dr .... Van Wert OH 45891 *TF:* 877-344-9990 ■ *Web:* www.braunambulances.com	877-344-9990		59
Braun Intertec Corp 11001 Hampshire Ave S .... Bloomington MN 55438 *TF:* 800-279-6100 ■ *Web:* www.braunintertec.com	952-995-2000		261
Bravado International Group Merchandising Services Inc 1755 Broadway 2nd Fl .... New York NY 10019 *Web:* www.bravadousa.com	212-445-3400		7
Brave New Restaurant (BNR) 2300 Cottondale Ln Ste 105 .... Little Rock AR 72202 *Web:* www.bravenewrestaurant.com	501-663-2677		671
Brave River Solutions Inc 875 Centerville Rd Bldg 3 .... Warwick RI 02886 *Web:* www.braveriver.com	401-828-6611		180
BraveMatters 3334 W Main St Ste 404 .... Norman OK 73072 *TF:* 888-315-5982 ■ *Web:* www.bravematters.com	888-315-5982		466
Braverman & Co 331 Madison Ave .... New York NY 10017 *Web:* www.braverlaw.net	212-682-2900		41
Braverman Financial Assoc 2173 Embassy Dr .... Lancaster PA 17603 *Web:* www.bravermanfinancial.com	717-399-4030		194
Bravo Highland Village Shopping Center South Plaza, Upper Level I-55 N Exit 100 Northside Dr .... Jackson MS 39211 *Web:* www.bravobuzz.com	601-982-8111	362-2990	671
Bravo 98-115 Kaonohi St .... Aiea HI 96701 *Web:* www.bravorestaurant.com	808-487-5544		671
BRAVO | BRIO Restaurant Group 777 Goodale Blvd Ste 100 .... Columbus OH 43212 *TF:* 888-852-3753 ■ *Web:* www.bbrg.com/index.html	614-326-7944	326-7943	670
Bravo Sports Corp 12801 Carmenita Rd .... Santa Fe Springs CA 90670 *TF Cust Svc:* 800-234-9737 ■ *Web:* www.bravosportscorp.com	562-484-5100		710
Bravo Wellness LLC 20445 Emerald Pkwy Dr SW Ste 400 .... Cleveland OH 44135 *Web:* www.bravowell.com	216-658-9500		363
Brawner Paper Company Inc 5702 Armour Dr .... Houston TX 77020 *TF:* 800-962-9384 ■ *Web:* www.brawnerpaper.com	713-675-6584		553

	Phone	Fax	Class
Braxton Automotive Group Inc 1604 Howell Mill Rd NW .... Atlanta GA 30318 *Web:* www.braxtonautogroup.com	404-367-4767		57
Braxton County 300 Main St PO Box 486 .... Sutton WV 26601 *Web:* www.braxtoncounty.wv.gov	304-765-2833	765-2947	338
Braxton Design Group 1622 Beckoning Ridge Rd .... Charlottesville VA 22901 *Web:* braxtondesigngroup.com	434-977-7999		187
Braxton Mfg Company Inc 858 Echo Lake Rd .... Watertown CT 06795 *Web:* www.braxtonmfg.com	860-274-6781		483
Braxton Technologies LLC 6 N Tejon St Ste 220 .... Colorado Springs CO 80903 *Web:* www.braxtontech.com	719-380-8488		196
Bray International Inc 13333 Westland E Blvd .... Houston TX 77041 *Web:* www.bray.com	281-894-5454		789
Bray Real Estate 637 N Ave .... Grand Junction CO 81501 *TF:* 888-760-4251 ■ *Web:* www.brayandco.com	970-242-8450		652
Brayton Energy Llc 75 Lafayette Rd # B .... Hampton NH 03842 *Web:* www.braytonenergy.com	603-601-0450		261
Brazi's Italian Restaurant 201 Food Terminal Plaza .... New Haven CT 06511 *Web:* brazis.com	203-498-2488		671
Brazil 747 Third Ave 9th Fl .... New York NY 10017 *Web:* www.un.int	212-372-2600	371-5716	784
Consulate General 300 Montgomery St Ste 300 .... San Francisco CA 94104	415-981-8170		257
Consulate General 175 Purchase St .... Boston MA 02110 *Web:* www.consulatebrazil.org	617-542-4004		257
Consulate General 1233 W Loop S Ste 1150 .... Houston TX 77027 *TF:* 800-326-2289 ■ *Web:* houston.itamaraty.gov.br	713-961-3063	961-3070	257
Consulate General 8484 Wilshire Blvd Ste 300 .... Beverly Hills CA 90211 *TF:* 877-782-5477 ■ *Web:* losangeles.itamaraty.gov.br	323-651-2664	651-1274	257
Consulate General of Brazil in Miami 3150 SW 38th Ave 1st Fl .... Miami FL 33146 *Web:* miami.itamaraty.gov.br	305-285-6200	285-6240	257
Embassy 3006 Massachusetts Ave NW .... Washington DC 20008 *Web:* washington.itamaraty.gov.br	202-238-2700		257
Brazilian Court, The 301 Australian Ave .... Palm Beach FL 33480 *TF:* 800-552-0335 ■ *Web:* www.thebraziliancourt.com	561-655-7740	655-0801	379
Brazilian Grill 680 Main St .... Hyannis MA 02601 *Web:* www.braziliangrill-capecod.com	508-771-0109		671
Brazilian Travel Service (BTS) 16 W 46th St 2nd Fl .... New York NY 10036 *TF:* 800-342-5746 ■ *Web:* www.btstravelonline.com	212-764-6161	719-4142	16
Brazilian-American Chamber of Commerce Inc 509 Madison Ave Ste 304 .... New York NY 10022 *Web:* www.brazilcham.com	212-751-4691	751-7692	138
Brazilian-American Chamber of Commerce of Florida PO Box 310030 .... Miami FL 33231 *TF:* 800-741-1420 ■ *Web:* www.brazilchamber.org	305-579-9030	579-9756	138
Brazoria County 111 E Locust St .... Angleton TX 77515 *Web:* brazoriacountytx.gov	979-849-5711		338
Brazoria County Library System 451 N Velasco Ste 250 .... Angleton TX 77515 *Web:* bcls.lib.tx.us	979-864-1505		434-3
Brazoria Telephone Co 314 W Texas St .... Brazoria TX 77422 *Web:* www.btel.com	979-798-2121		736
Brazos Bend State Park 21901 FM 762 .... Needville TX 77461 *Web:* tpwd.texas.gov/state-parks/brazos-bend	409-553-5101		565
Brazos Bookstore 2421 Bissonnet .... Houston TX 77005 *Web:* www.brazosbookstore.com	713-523-0701		95
Brazos County 300 E 26th St Ste 120 .... Bryan TX 77803 *Web:* www.brazoscountytx.gov	979-361-4224		338
Brazos Telecommunications Inc 109 N Ave D .... Olney TX 76374 *TF:* 800-687-3222 ■ *Web:* www.brazosnet.com	940-564-5659		196
Brazos Urethane Inc 1031 Sixth St N .... Texas City TX 77590 *TF:* 866-527-2967 ■ *Web:* www.brazosurethane.com	409-965-0011	948-1511	189-12
Brazos Valley Radio 1240 E Villa Maria Rd .... Bryan TX 77802 *Web:* www.brazosradio.com	979-776-1240		643
Brazosport Area Chamber of Commerce 300 Abner Jackson Pkwy .... Lake Jackson TX 77566 *Web:* www.brazosport.org	979-285-2501	285-2505	139
Brazosport College 500 College Dr .... Lake Jackson TX 77566 *Fax: Admissions ■ *TF:* 877-717-7873 ■ *Web:* www.brazosport.edu	979-230-3000	230-3443*	162
Brazosport Facts 720 S Main St .... Clute TX 77531 *TF:* 800-864-8340 ■ *Web:* www.thefacts.com	979-265-7411	265-9052	532-2
Brazosport Regional Health System (BRHS) 100 Medical Dr .... Lake Jackson TX 77566 *Web:* brazosportregional.org	979-297-4411		374-3
BRB Contractors Inc 3805 NW 25th St .... Topeka KS 66618 *TF:* 800-722-3145 ■ *Web:* www.brbcontractors.com	785-232-1245	235-8045	188-10
BRB Publications Inc PO Box 27869 .... Tempe AZ 85285 *TF:* 800-929-3811 ■ *Web:* www.brbpub.com	480-829-7475		637-2
BRC Imagination Arts 2711 Winona Ave .... Burbank CA 91504 *Web:* www.brcweb.com	818-841-8084		514
BRC Investment Management LLC 8400 E Prentice Ave Ste 1401 .... Greenwood Village CO 80111 *Web:* www.brcinvest.com	303-414-1100		796
BRC Rubber Group Inc PO Box 227 .... Churubusco IN 46723 *Web:* www.brcrp.com	260-693-2171	693-6511	677
BRCC (Baton Rouge Community College) 201 Community College Dr .... Baton Rouge LA 70806 *TF:* 866-217-9823 ■ *Web:* www.mybrcc.edu	225-216-8000	216-8010	162
Brd Solutions 101 Trenton Cir .... Canonsburg PA 15317 *Web:* www.brdsolutions.net	724-941-6375		195
BREA (Benton Rural Electric Assn) 402 Seventh St PO Box 1150 .... Prosser WA 99350 *TF:* 800-221-6987 ■ *Web:* www.bentonrea.org	509-786-2913	786-0291	245
Brea Chamber of Commerce 1 Civic Ctr Cir .... Brea CA 92821 *Web:* www.breachamber.com	714-529-4938		139
Brea Mall 1065 Brea Mall .... Brea CA 92821 *TF:* 800-409-3175 ■ *Web:* www.simon.com	714-990-2732		460
Bread for the World 425 Third St SW Ste 1200 .... Washington DC 20024 *TF Cust Svc:* 800-822-7323 ■ *Web:* www.bread.org	202-639-9400	639-9401	48-5
Bread Loaf Corp 1293 Rt 7 S .... Middlebury VT 05753 *Web:* breadloaf.com	802-388-9871	388-3815	194
Breadbox Food Stores Inc 9100 Bolton Ln .... Knoxville TN 37922	865-531-6053		345
Breadfruit Tree 8095 Rio Blanco Rd .... Stockton CA 95219 *Web:* www.breadfruittree.com	209-952-7361		671
Breakaway Press Inc 9620 Topanga Canyon Pl .... Chatsworth CA 91311 *Web:* www.breakawaypress.com	818-727-7388		627
Breakaway Tours 337 Queen St W .... Toronto ON M5V2A4 *TF:* 800-465-4257 ■ *Web:* www.breakawaytours.com	416-915-9880		760
Breaker Group Inc, The 32 Mill St .... Mount Holly NJ 08060 *TF:* 800-456-4822 ■ *Web:* www.breakergroup.com	609-267-1330		180
Breakers at Waikiki, The 250 Beach Walk .... Honolulu HI 96815 *TF:* 800-426-0494 ■ *Web:* www.breakers-hawaii.com	808-923-3181	923-7174	379
Breakers Hotel & Restaurant 1507 Ocean Ave .... Spring Lake NJ 07762 *Web:* www.breakershotel.com	732-449-7700		378
Breakers Hotel & Suites 105 Second St .... Rehoboth Beach DE 19971 *TF:* 800-441-8009 ■ *Web:* www.thebreakershotel.com	302-227-6688	227-2013	379
Breakers Palm Beach, The 1 S County Rd .... Palm Beach FL 33480 *TF:* 888-273-2537 ■ *Web:* www.thebreakers.com	877-724-3188		707
Breakers Resort 3002 N Ocean Blvd .... Myrtle Beach SC 29577 *TF:* 800-952-4507 ■ *Web:* www.breakers.com	843-448-8082	626-5001	669
Breakers Resort Inn 16th & Oceanfront .... Virginia Beach VA 23451 *TF:* 800-237-7532 ■ *Web:* www.breakersresort.com	757-428-1821	422-9602	669
Breakers, The 1 S County Rd .... Palm Beach FL 33480 *TF:* 888-273-2537 ■ *Web:* www.thebreakers.com	561-655-6611	659-8403	669
Breakeven Inc 355 Apple Creek Blvd Ste 200 .... Markham ON L3R9X7 *Web:* www.causeview.com	905-752-1500		305
Breaks Interstate Park 627 Commission Cir PO Box 100 .... Breaks VA 24607 *Web:* www.breakspark.com	276-865-4413		565
Breakthrough Collaborative 545 Sansome St Ste 700 .... San Francisco CA 94111 *Web:* www.breakthroughcollaborative.org	415-442-0600		48-11
Breakthrough Management Group Inc 1200 17th St Ste 180 .... Denver CO 80202 *TF:* 800-467-4462	303-827-0010	827-0011	194
Breakthrough Urban Ministries 3330 W Carroll Ave .... Chicago IL 60624 *Web:* breakthrough.org	773-722-1144		48-20
Breakwater Inn 1711 Glacier Ave .... Juneau AK 99801	907-586-6303		379
Brearley School 610 E 83rd St .... New York NY 10028 *Web:* www.brearley.org	212-744-8582		623
Breathe Technologies Inc 175 Technology Dr Ste 100 .... Irvine CA 92618 *Web:* www.breathetechnologies.com	949-988-7700		475
Breathitt County PO Box 227 .... Jackson KY 41339 *TF:* 800-930-8727 ■ *Web:* www.breathittcounty.com	606-666-5060	666-7018	338
Breault Research Organization Inc 6400 E Grant Rd Ste 350 .... Tucson AZ 85715 *Web:* www.breault.com	520-721-0500		261
BREC (Butler Rural Electric Co-op Inc) 3888 Still-Beckett Rd .... Oxford OH 45056 *TF:* 800-255-2732 ■ *Web:* www.butlerrural.coop	513-867-4400		245
BREC's Baton Rouge Zoo 3601 Thomas Rd .... Baton Rouge LA 70807 *Web:* www.brzoo.org	225-775-3877	775-3931	823
Brechan Enterprises Inc 2705 Mill Bay Rd .... Kodiak AK 99615 *Web:* www.brechanconstructionllc.com	907-486-3215	486-4889	188-4
Breck's PO Box 65 .... Guilford IN 47022 *TF:* 800-644-5505 ■ *Web:* www.brecks.com	513-354-1511	354-1505	323
Breckenridge Grand Vacations LLC PO Box 6879 .... Breckenridge CO 80424 *Web:* www.breckenridgegrandvacations.com	970-547-3630		378
Breckenridge Village 36851 Ridge Rd .... Willoughby OH 44094 *Web:* www.ohioliving.org/communities/ohio-living-breckenridge-village	440-942-4342		672
Breckinridge Capital Advisors Inc 125 High St Oliver St Tower Fl 4 .... Boston MA 02110 *Web:* www.breckinridge.com	617-443-0779		401
Breckinridge County PO Box 227 .... Hardinsburg KY 40143 *Web:* www.breckinridgecountyky.com	270-756-2269	756-2364	338
Breckinridge County School District 86 Airport Rd .... Hardinsburg KY 40143 *TF:* 800-325-1713 ■ *Web:* breckinridgecountyky.com	270-756-2186		685
Breckinridge Inn 2800 Breckinridge Ln .... Louisville KY 40220 *Web:* www.breckinridgeinn.com	502-456-5050	451-1577	379
Brecksville Broadview Hts Csd 6638 Mill Rd .... Brecksville OH 44141 *Web:* www.bbhcsd.org	440-740-4000		685
Bredero Shaw A ShawCor Co 3838 N Sam Houston Pkwy E Ste 300 .... Houston TX 77032 *Web:* www.brederoshaw.com	281-886-2350	886-2353	481
Bredet Services Inc 1660 N Service Rd E Ste 105 .... Oakville ON L6H7G3 *TF:* 800-372-6174 ■ *Web:* www.bredetservices.com	905-337-7233		180
Bredy Consulting Services 50 Union St .... Andover MA 01810 *TF:* 800-785-5165 ■ *Web:* www.bnmc.net	978-482-2020		179
Breeden Homes Inc 366 E 40th Ave .... Eugene OR 97405	541-686-9431	686-0918	187
B-Reel 401 Broadway 24th Fl .... New York NY 10013 *Web:* www.b-reel.com	212-966-6186		514

Phone | Fax | Class

Breen Energy Solutions LLC
104 Broadway St. Carnegie PA 15106 412-431-4499 256
Web: www.breenes.com

Breen Engineering Inc
1983 W 190th St. Torrance CA 90504 310-464-8404 261
Web: www.breeneng.com

Breese Publishing Co
8060 Old US Hwy 50 Breese IL 62230 618-526-7211 526-2590 637-8
Web: www.breesepub.com

Breeze Newspaper
2510 Del Prado Blvd. Cape Coral FL 33904 239-574-1110 637-8
TF: 800-772-1213 ■ *Web:* www.breezenewspapers.com

Breeze-Eastern Corp 35 Melanie Ln Whippany NJ 07981 973-602-1001 470
TF: 800-929-1919 ■ *Web:* www.breeze-eastern.com

BreezeGo Inc 3332 Southside Blvd Jacksonville FL 32216 904-998-4066 174
Web: www.breezego.com

Breezy Hill Nursery Inc 7530 288th Ave Salem WI 53168 262-537-2111 776
TF: 800-236-4242 ■ *Web:* www.breezyhillnursery.com

Breezy Point Resort
9252 Breezy Pt Dr. Breezy Point MN 56472 218-562-7811 562-4510 669
TF: 800-432-3777 ■ *Web:* www.breezypointresort.com

Breg Inc 2885 Loker Ave E Carlsbad CA 92010 760-599-3000 329-2734* 48-2
**Fax Area Code:* 800 ■ *TF:* 800-897-2734 ■ *Web:* www.breg.com

Brehm Communications Inc
16644 W Bernardo Dr # 300. San Diego CA 92127 858-451-6200 451-3814 637-8
Web: www.brehmcommunications.com

Brehm Preparatory School
950 S Brehm Ln Carbondale IL 62901 618-457-0371 529-1248 622
Web: www.brehm.org

Breiholz Construction Co
1527 Maine St Des Moines IA 50309 515-288-6077 186
Web: www.breiholz.com

Breitburn Energy Partners LP
515 S Flower St Ste 4800 Los Angeles CA 90071 213-225-5900 225-5916 538
NASDAQ: BBEP ■ *TF:* 800-732-0330 ■ *Web:* www.breitburn.com

Breitling Energy Corp
Ste 12000 1910 PACIFIC Ave Ste 12000 Dallas TX 75201 214-716-2600 536
TF: 866-884-0224 ■ *Web:* www.breitlingenergy.com

Brek Manufacturing Co 1513 W 132nd St Gardena CA 90249 310-329-7638 529
Web: www.brek.aero

Bremen Castings Inc 500 N Baltimore St. Bremen IN 46506 800-837-2411 546-5016* 307
**Fax Area Code:* 574 ■ *TF:* 800-837-2411 ■ *Web:* www.bremencastings.com

Bremer County 415 E Bremer Ave Waverly IA 50677 319-352-0130 338
Web: www.co.bremer.ia.us

Bremer Financial Corp
380 St Peter St Saint Paul MN 55102 800-908-2265 312-3675* 69
**Fax Area Code:* 651 ■ *TF:* 800-908-2265 ■ *Web:* www.bremer.com

Bremer Whyte Brown & O'Meara LLP
20320 SW Birch St 2nd Fl Newport Beach CA 92660 949-221-1000 428
Web: www.bremerwhyte.com

Bremerton Area Chamber of Commerce
286 Fourth St Bremerton WA 98337 360-479-3579 479-1033 139
TF: 800-323-0130 ■ *Web:* www.bremertonchamber.org

Bremerton Washington
50 Magnuson Way Bremerton WA 98310 360-473-5376 706
Web: www.ci.bremerton.wa.us

Bremner Biscuit Co 4600 Joliet St. Denver CO 80239 303-371-8180 296-9
TF: 866-972-6879 ■ *Web:* www.bremnerbiscuitco.com

Bren Events Ctr 100 Bren Events Ctr. Irvine CA 92697 949-824-5050 572
Web: www.ucirvinesports.com/bren/index

Brenau University
500 Washington St Gainesville GA 30501 770-534-6299 538-4701* 166
**Fax:* Admissions ■ *TF:* 800-252-5119 ■ *Web:* www.brenau.edu

Brendan T. Byrne State Forest
PO Box 215 New Lisbon NJ 08064 609-726-1191 565
Web: www.njparksandforests.org/parks/byrne.html

Brendan Vacations 21625 Prairie St Chatsworth CA 91311 800-687-1002 760
TF: 800-687-1002 ■ *Web:* www.brendanvacations.com

Brendan's Camarillo LLC
1755 E Daily Dr Camarillo CA 93010 805-383-4100 378
Web: brendans.com

Brenden Theatres 531 Davis St Vacaville CA 95688 707-469-0180 748
Web: www.brendentheatres.com

Brendle Sprinkler Co Inc
3635 Montgomery St Montgomery AL 36109 334-270-8571 277-7967 189-13
Web: www.brendlesprinkler.com

Brenham Oil & Gas Corp
601 Cien Rd Ste 235. Kemah TX 77565 281-334-9479 536
Web: www.brenhamoil.com

Brenham Wholesale Grocery Co
602 W First St. Brenham TX 77833 979-836-7925 830-0346 297-8
TF: 800-392-4869 ■ *Web:* www.brenhamwholesale.com

Brenham/Washington County Convention & Visitor Bureau
314 S Austin St. Brenham TX 77833 979-836-3695 836-2540 206
TF: 888-273-6426 ■ *Web:* www.brenhamtexas.com

Brennan & Clark LLC
721 E Madison Ste 200 Villa Park IL 60181 630-279-7600 160
TF: 800-858-7600 ■ *Web:* brennanclark.com

Brennan House Historic Home
631 S Fifth St Louisville KY 40202 502-540-5145 540-5165 50-3

Brennan J m Inc
2101 W Saint Paul Ave Milwaukee WI 53201 414-342-3829 610
Web: www.jmbrennan.com

Brennan Manna & Diamond LLC
75 E Market St Akron OH 44308 330-253-5060 428
Web: www.bmdllc.com

Brennan's of Houston 3300 Smith St. Houston TX 77006 713-522-9711 671
Web: www.brennanshouston.com

Brenneman Printing Inc
1909 Olde Homestead Ln Lancaster PA 17601 717-299-2847 627
TF: 800-222-2423 ■ *Web:* www.brennemaninc.com

Brenner Group Inc, The
19200 Stevens Creek Blvd Ste 200. Cupertino CA 95014 408-873-3400 401
Web: thebrennergroup.com

Brenner Oil Co 12948 Quincy St Holland MI 49424 616-399-9742 538
Web: www.brenneroil.com

Brenner Printing Inc
1234 Triplett St. San Antonio TX 78216 210-349-4024 627
TF: 877-349-4024 ■ *Web:* www.brennerprinting.com

Brenner Tank LLC
450 Arlington Ave. Fond du Lac WI 54935 920-922-5020 779
Web: www.brennertank.com

Brenner's Steakhouse 10911 Katy Fwy Houston TX 77079 713-465-2901 671
Web: www.brennerssteakhouse.com

Brenner-Fiedler & Associates Inc
4059 Flat Rock Dr. Riverside CA 92505 800-843-5558 358
TF: 800-843-5558 ■ *Web:* www.brenner-fiedler.com

Brenntag Canada Inc 43 Jutland Rd Toronto ON M8Z2G6 416-243-9615 243-9731 146
TF: 866-516-9707 ■ *Web:* www.brenntag.ca/en

Brenntag Mid-South Inc
1405 Hwy 136 W Henderson KY 42420 270-830-1200 827-3990* 146
**Fax:* Hum Res ■ *Web:* www.brenntagmid-south.com

Brenntag North America Inc
5083 Pottsville Pk PO Box 13786. Reading PA 19605 610-926-6100 146
TF: 800-220-6262 ■ *Web:* www.brenntag.com

Brenntag Northeast Inc 81 W Huller Ln Reading PA 19605 610-926-4151 926-4160 146
Web: www.brenntag.com

Brenntag Southeast Inc
5083 Pottsville Pk. Reading PA 19605 610-926-6100 146
Web: www.brenntagmid-south.com

Brenntag Southwest Inc
1000 Coolidge St South Plainfield NJ 75604 903-759-7151 759-3145 146
TF: 800-732-0562 ■ *Web:* www.brenntag.com

Brent Adams & Assoc 119 Lucknow Sq. Dunn NC 28334 910-892-8177 445
TF: 800-434-8399 ■ *Web:* brentadams.com

Brent House Hotel
1512 Jefferson Hwy New Orleans LA 70121 504-842-4140 842-4160 379
TF: 800-535-3986 ■ *Web:* www.brenthouse.com

Brent's Place 11980 E 16th Ave Aurora CO 80010 720-343-2800 831-4567* 372
**Fax Area Code:* 303 ■ *Web:* www.brentsplace.org

Brentech Inc
9340 Carmel Mtn Rd Ste C. San Diego CA 92129 858-484-7314 175
TF: 800-709-0440 ■ *Web:* www.brentech-inc.com

Brenton Arboretum
25141 260th St. Dallas Center IA 50063 515-992-4211 992-3303 97
Web: www.thebrentonarboretum.org

Brenton LLC 4750 County Rd 13 NE Alexandria MN 56308 320-852-7705 852-7621 547
TF: 800-535-2730 ■ *Web:* www.brentonengineering.com

Brenton Productions Inc
179 Gasoline Alley Ste 102A Mooresville NC 02777 800-572-7798 463
TF: 800-572-7798 ■ *Web:* www.brentontv.com

Bren-Tronics Inc 10 Brayton Ct. Commack NY 11725 631-499-5155 499-5504 74
Web: www.bren-tronics.com

Brentwood Acquisition Corp
453 Industrial Way Molalla OR 97038 503-829-7366 115
Web: www.brentwoodjackson.com

Brentwood Assoc
11150 Santa Monica Blvd Ste 1200 Los Angeles CA 90025 310-477-6611 477-1011 403
Web: www.brentwood.com

Brentwood Capital Advisors LLC
5000 Meridian Blvd Ste 350. Franklin TN 37067 615-224-3830 401
Web: www.brentwoodcap.com

Brentwood Christian School Association of Parents, Teachers & Friends
11908 N Lamar Blvd. Austin TX 78753 512-835-5983 685

Brentwood College School
2735 Mt Baker Rd. Mill Bay BC V0R2P1 250-743-5521 743-2911 622
Web: www.brentwood.bc.ca

Brentwood Group Ltd, The
1980 Willamette Falls Dr Ste 260 West Linn OR 97068 503-697-8136 721
Web: www.brentwoodgroup.com

Brentwood High School Pto
5304 Murray Ln Brentwood TN 37027 615-472-4220 685
Web: brentwoodpto.membershiptoolkit.com

Brentwood Hospital
1006 Highland Ave Shreveport LA 71101 318-678-7500 227-9296 374-5
TF: 877-678-7500 ■ *Web:* www.brentwoodbehavioral.com

Brentwood Industries Inc
500 Spring Ridge Dr. Reading PA 19610 610-374-5109 199
Web: www.brentwoodindustries.com

Brentwood Industries Inc Polychem Systems Div
500 Spring Ridge Dr. Reading PA 19610 610-374-5109 806
Web: brentwoodindustries.com

Brentwood North Nursing & Rehabilitation Ctr
3705 Deerfield Rd. Riverwoods IL 60015 847-947-9000 450
Web: brentwoodnorthrehab.com

Brentwood Originals Inc
20639 S Fordyce Ave Carson CA 90810 310-637-6804 639-9710 746
TF: 800-663-5965 ■ *Web:* www.brentwoodoriginals.com

Brentwood Plastics Inc
8734 Suburban Tracks St. Louis MO 63144 314-968-1135 596
Web: www.brentwoodplastics.com

Brentwood Public Library (BPL)
34 Second Ave Brentwood NY 11717 631-273-7883 434-3
Web: brentwoodnylibrary.org

Brentwood School
100 S Barrington Pl Los Angeles CA 90049 310-476-9633 476-4087 685
Web: www.bwscampus.com

Brentwood Subacute Rehabilitation Ctr
5400 W 87th St. Burbank IL 60459 708-423-1200 450
Web: savaseniorcare.com

Brescia University 717 Frederica St. Owensboro KY 42301 270-685-3131 686-4314* 166
**Fax:* Admissions ■ *TF Admissions:* 877-273-7242 ■ *Web:* brescia.edu

Brescia University College
1285 Western Rd London ON N6G1H2 519-432-8353 858-5137 785
Web: www.brescia.uwo.ca

Bresser's Cross Index Directory Co
684 W Baltimore St. Detroit MI 48202 313-874-0570 874-3510 637-6
TF: 800-995-0570 ■ *Web:* www.bressers.com

Bresslergroup 1216 Arch St 7th Fl Philadelphia PA 19107 215-561-5100 261
Web: www.bresslergroup.com

Bretford Manufacturing Inc
11000 Seymour Ave Franklin Park IL 60131 847-678-2545 343-1779* 319-3
**Fax Area Code:* 800 ■ *TF:* 800-521-9614 ■ *Web:* www.bretford.com

Brethren Press 1451 Dundee Ave Elgin IL 60120 800-441-3712 667-8188 637-3
TF: 800-441-3712 ■ *Web:* www.brethrenpress.com

Bretthauer Oil Co
453 SW Washington St. Hillsboro OR 97123 503-648-2531 579
TF: 800-359-3113 ■ *Web:* www.bretthauer.com

Phone Fax Class

Brevard College 1 Brevard College Dr .... Brevard NC 28712 828-883-8292 884-3790* 166
**Fax:* Admissions ■ *TF Admissions:* 800-527-9090 ■ *Web:* www.brevard.edu

Brevard Community College (BCC)
Cocoa 1519 Clearlake Rd .... Cocoa FL 32922 321-632-1111 433-7357* 162
**Fax:* Admissions ■ *TF:* 888-747-2802 ■ *Web:* www.easternflorida.edu
Melbourne 3865 N Wickham Rd ....Melbourne FL 32935 321-632-1111 433-5770* 162
**Fax:* Admissions ■ *TF:* 888-747-2802 ■ *Web:* www.easternflorida.edu
Palm Bay 250 Community College Pkwy........ Palm Bay FL 32909 321-632-1111 433-5325* 162
**Fax:* Admissions ■ *TF:* 888-747-2802 ■ *Web:* www.easternflorida.edu
Titusville 1311 N US 1...................... Titusville FL 32796 321-632-1111 433-5115 162
TF: 888-747-2802 ■ *Web:* www.easternflorida.edu

Brevard Correctional Institution
855 Camp Rd .... Cocoa FL 32927 321-634-6000 213
Web: dc.state.fl.us

Brevard County
2725 Judge Fran Jamieson Way.................. Viera FL 32940 321-264-6750 264-6751 338
Web: www.brevardfl.gov

Brevard County Tourism Development
2725 Judge Fran Jamieson Way Ste 150 ....Melbourne FL 32940 321-637-5492 617-7391 206
TF: 800-955-8771 ■ *Web:* www.brevardfl.gov

Brevard Eye Center Inc
665 S Apollo Blvd..........................Melbourne FL 32901 321-984-3200 237
Web: www.brevardeye.com

Brevard Regional Juvenile Detention Ctr
5225 DeWitt Ave................................ Cocoa FL 32927 321-690-3400 412

Brevard Zoo 8225 N Wickham Rd ....Melbourne FL 32940 321-254-9453 259-5966 823
Web: brevardzoo.org

Brevard-Transylvania Chamber of Commerce
175 E Main St.................................. Brevard NC 28712 828-883-3700 883-8550 139
TF: 800-648-4523 ■ *Web:* www.brevardncchamber.org

Brevium Inc
11602 S Redwood Rd Ste B205 ....Riverton UT 84095 801-302-2299 261
Web: brevium.com

Brew Media Relations
588 Broadway Ste 1004 ....New York NY 10012 212-677-4835 636
Web: www.brewpr.com

Brewer & Pritchard PC
3 Riverway 18th Fl ....Houston TX 77056 713-209-2950 428
TF: 800-445-8710 ■ *Web:* www.bplaw.com

Brewer Co 1354 US Hwy 50.....................Milford OH 45150 513-576-6300 46
TF: 800-394-0017 ■ *Web:* www.brewercote.com

Brewer Oil Co 2701 Candelaria NE .... Albuquerque NM 87107 505-884-2040 579
Web: www.breweroil.com

Brewer Science Inc 2401 Brewer Dr .... Rolla MO 65401 573-364-0300 550
Web: www.brewerscience.com

Brewer-Cantelmo Company Inc
55 W 39th St Ste 205 ....New York NY 10018 212-244-4600 244-1640 453
Web: www.brewer-cantelmo.com

Brewer-Garrett Company (Inc)
6800 Eastland Rd ....Cleveland OH 44130 440-243-3535 243-9993 189-10
Web: www.brewer-garrett.com

Brewer-Hendley Oil Co
207 N Forest Hills School Rd .... Marshville NC 28103 704-233-2600 579
Web: brewerhendley.com

Brewers Art 1106 N Charles St ....Baltimore MD 21201 410-547-6925 671
Web: www.thebrewersart.com

Brewery Arts Ctr 449 W King St...............Carson City NV 89703 775-883-1976 572
TF: 800-747-4697 ■ *Web:* www.breweryarts.org

Brewhouse Brew Pub & Grill
939 Getchell St.............................. Helena MT 59601 406-457-9390 457-0206 671
Web: atthebrewhouse.com

Brewmatic Co
20333 S Normandie Ave PO Box 2959 ....Torrance CA 90509 310-787-5444 787-5412 298
TF: 800-421-6860 ■ *Web:* www.brewmatic.com

Brewster Academy 80 Academy Dr .... Wolfeboro NH 03894 603-569-7200 569-7272 622
TF: 800-842-9961 ■ *Web:* www.brewsteracademy.org

Brewster County 201 W Ave E .... Alpine TX 79830 432-837-3366 837-6217 338
Web: brewstercountytx.com

Brewster Place 1205 SW 29th St................Topeka KS 66611 785-274-3350 672
Web: brewsterliving.org

Brewster Rocky Mountain Adventures
PO Box 370 .... Banff AB T1L1A5 403-762-5454 673-2100 760
Web: www.brewsteradventures.com

Brewster Technology
1591 Route 22 Bldg 1........................Brewster NY 10509 845-279-9400 225
Web: www.brewstertech.net

Brewster Travel Canada
100 Gopher St PO Box 1140....................... Banff AB T1L1J3 403-762-6700 762-6750 760
TF: 866-606-6700 ■ *Web:* www.brewster.ca

Brewster Village 3300 W Brewster St........... Appleton WI 54914 920-832-5400 832-4922 450
Web: www.outagamie.org

Brewster WaLLPaper Corp
67 Pacella Park Dr ....Randolph MA 02368 781-963-4800 550
Web: www.brewsterwallcovering.com

Brewton-Parker College
201 David-Eliza Fountain Cir Hwy 280
PO Box 197 .... Mount Vernon GA 30445 912-583-2241 583-3598* 166
**Fax:* Admissions ■ *TF:* 800-342-1087 ■ *Web:* www.bpc.edu

Breyer Stephen G
US Supreme Ct Bldg 1 1st St NE ....Washington DC 20543 202-479-3000 341-4
Web: www.supremecourt.gov

BRG (Business Resource Group)
10440 N Central Expy Ste 1150 .... Dallas TX 75231 214-777-5100 194
TF: 888-391-9166 ■ *Web:* www.brg.com

BRGMC (Baton Rouge General Medical Ctr)
3600 Florida Blvd.......................... Baton Rouge LA 70806 225-387-7000 374-3
Web: www.brgeneral.org

BRHS (Brazosport Regional Health System)
100 Medical Dr..........................Lake Jackson TX 77566 979-297-4411 374-3
Web: brazosportregional.org

Briad Group, The 78 Okner Pkwy .... Livingston NJ 07039 973-597-6433 597-6422 670
Web: www.briad.com

Brian Gavin Diamonds
7322 SW Frwy Ste 1810 - Arena One..............Houston TX 77074 713-574-6666 410
Web: www.briangavindiamonds.com

Brian Loncar & Associates PC
1104 Travis St.......................... Wichita Falls TX 76301 877-239-4878 445
TF: 877-239-4878 ■ *Web:* www.brianloncar.com

Brian Patrick Conry PC
534 SW Third Ave Ste 711 ....Portland OR 97204 503-274-4430 428
Web: www.brianpatrickconry.com

Brian's Toys W730 State Rd 35 ....Fountain City WI 54629 608-687-7572 292
Web: www.brianstoys.com

Briar Cliff University
3303 Rebecca St........................... Sioux City IA 51104 712-279-5321 279-1632* 166
**Fax:* Admissions ■ *TF:* 800-662-3303 ■ *Web:* www.briarcliff.edu

Briar Hill Stone Co, The
12470 State Rt 520 PO Box 457 ....Glenmont OH 44628 330-377-5100 724
TF: 800-225-2749 ■ *Web:* www.briarhillstone.com

Briar Ridge Country Club Inc
123 Country Club Dr ....Schererville IN 46375 219-322-1605 706
Web: www.briarridgecc.com

Briarcliffe College 1055 Stewart Ave........... Bethpage NY 11714 516-918-3600 165
TF: 855-512-5333 ■ *Web:* www.briarcliffe.edu

Briarhurst Manor
404 Manitou Ave...................... Manitou Springs CO 80829 719-685-1864 685-9638 671
TF: 877-685-1448 ■ *Web:* www.briarhurst.com

Briarlane Rental Property Management Inc
85 Spy Ct Ste 100.......................... Markham ON L3R4Z4 905-944-9406 652
Web: www.briarlane.ca

BriarTek Inc 3129 Mt Vernon Ave .... Alexandria VA 22305 703-548-7892 180
Web: www.briartek.com

Briarwood College
2279 Mt Vernon Rd........................Southington CT 06489 860-628-4751 628-6444* 166
**Fax:* Admissions ■ *TF:* 800-952-2444 ■ *Web:* www.lincolncollegene.edu

BRIC Engineered Systems Ltd
1101 Wentworth St W Ste D1 .... Oshawa ON L1J8P7 888-625-8880 256
TF: 888-625-8880 ■ *Web:* www.briceng.com

Bricco 241 Hanover St ....Boston MA 02113 617-248-6800 671
Web: www.bricco.com

Bricco 1 W Exchange St ....Akron OH 44308 330-475-1600 671
Web: www.briccoakron.com

Brice Bldg Company Inc
201 Sunbelt Pkwy........................Birmingham AL 35211 205-930-9911 186

Brice's Crossroads National Battlefield Site
2680 Natchez Trace Pkwy .... Tupelo MS 38804 662-680-4025 680-4033 564
TF: 800-305-7417 ■ *Web:* www.nps.gov/brcr

Brick Alley Pub & Restaurant
140 Thames St ....Newport RI 02840 401-849-6334 848-5640 671
Web: www.brickalley.com

Brick Bodies Fitness Services Inc
2430 Broad Ave .... Timonium MD 21093 410-252-8058 560-3299 354
TF: 866-952-7425 ■ *Web:* www.brickbodies.com

Brick Gentry Law Firm
6701 Westown Pkwy Ste 100 ....West Des Moines IA 50266 515-274-1450 428
TF: 800-558-7605 ■ *Web:* www.brickgentrylaw.com

Brick Industry Assn (BIA)
1850 Centennial Pk Dr Ste 301.................. Reston VA 20191 703-620-0010 620-3928 49-18
TF: 866-644-1293 ■ *Web:* www.gobrick.com

Brick Oven 111 East 800 North ....Provo UT 84606 801-374-8800 671
Web: www.brickovenrestaurants.com

Brick Pit 5456 Old Shell Rd ....Mobile AL 36608 251-343-0001 671

Brick Store Museum 117 Main St ....Kennebunk ME 04043 207-985-4802 520
Web: www.brickstoremuseum.org

Brick Township Chamber of Commerce
270 Chambers Bridge Rd .... Brick NJ 08723 732-477-4949 477-5788 139
TF: 877-539-2020 ■ *Web:* brickchamber.com

Brickell Financial Services Motor Club Inc
7300 Corporate Ctr Dr Ste 601...................Miami FL 33126 305-392-4300 392-4301 53
TF: 800-262-7262 ■ *Web:* www.road-america.com

Bricker & Eckler LLP 100 S Third St .... Columbus OH 43215 614-227-2300 428
TF: 800-447-5375 ■ *Web:* www.bricker.com

Brickforce Staffing Inc
2 Ethel Rd Ste 204-B .... Edison NJ 08817 732-819-7770 260
TF: 800-264-1170 ■ *Web:* www.brickforce.com

BrickKicker Inc 849 N Ellsworth St.......... Naperville IL 60563 800-821-1820 365
TF: 800-821-1820 ■ *Web:* www.brickkicker.com

Brickner Motors Inc
16450 County Rd A ....Marathon WI 54448 715-842-5611 57
Web: bricknermotors.net

Bricks 1695 S Virginia St .... Reno NV 89502 775-786-2277 671
TF: 800-717-4143 ■ *Web:* bricksrestaurant.com

Bricktown 2 S Mickey Mantle Dr...........Oklahoma City OK 73104 405-236-8666 50-6
Web: welcometobricktown.com

Bricktown Brewery
1 N Oklahoma Ave ....Oklahoma City OK 73104 405-232-2739 671
Web: www.bricktownbrewery.com

Brickyard Crossing Golf Resort & Inn
4400 W 16th St.......................Indianapolis IN 46222 317-492-6417 669
Web: brickyardcrossing.com

Brickyard VFX 2054 Broadway ....Santa Monica CA 90404 310-453-5722 530
Web: www.brickyardvfx.com

Bricmont Inc
500 Technology Dr
Southpointe Industrial Pk..................Canonsburg PA 15317 724-746-2300 261
Web: www.andritz.com

Bridal Guide Magazine
228 E 45th St 11th Fl ....New York NY 10017 212-838-7733 308-7165 457-11
TF: 800-472-7744 ■ *Web:* www.bridalguide.com

Bridal Veil Falls State Scenic Viewpoint
I-84.. Bridal Veil OR 97010 800-551-6949 565
TF: 800-551-6949 ■ *Web:* www.oregonstateparks.org

Bridenstine Jim (Rep R - OK)
216 Cannon HOB ....Washington DC 20515 202-225-2211 342-2
Web: bridenstine.house.gov

Bridg.com
11390 W Olympic Blvd Ste 450 ....Los Angeles CA 90064 855-455-5522 5
TF: 855-455-5522 ■ *Web:* bridg.com

Bridge Bank 55 Almaden Blvd Ste 200 .... San Jose CA 95113 408-423-8500 423-8520 360-2
NASDAQ: BBNK ■ *TF General:* 866-273-4265 ■ *Web:* www.bridgebank.com

Bridge Capital LLC Micro Beach Rd.............. Saipan MP 96950 670-322-2222 186
Web: www.bccnmi.com

Bridge City Food Mktg Inc
110 SE Second Ave..........................Portland OR 97214 503-239-8024 297-8

Bridge Community Bank
200 S Cherry ....Mechanicsville IA 52306 563-432-7291 360-2
Web: www.bridge.bank

Name / Address	City	State	Zip	Phone	Fax	Class
Bridge Consulting Group LLC						
11 Pebble Beach Way	Washington	NJ	07882	908-689-7513		466
Bridge Diagnostics Inc						
5398 Manhattan Cir	Boulder	CO	80303	303-494-3230		261
Web: www.bridgetest.com						
Bridge Home Health & Hospice						
15100 Birchaven Ln	Findlay	OH	45840	419-423-5351	423-8967	371
TF: 800-982-3306 ■ *Web:* www.bvhealthsystem.org						
Bridge Kitchenware Inc						
B 198 Mt Pleasant Ave	East Hanover	NJ	07936	973-884-9000		362
Web: www.bridgekitchenware.com						
Bridge Metrics LLC 830 S Greenville Ave	Allen	TX	75002	877-801-7158		466
TF: 877-801-7158 ■ *Web:* www.bridgemetrics.com						
Bridge Personnel Services						
2800 W Higgins Rd Ste 680	Hoffman Estates	IL	60195	847-885-9696		260
Web: www.bridgepersonnel.com						
Bridge Restaurant 31 Locust St	Dubuque	IA	52001	563-557-7280		671
TF: 800-365-9155 ■ *Web:* www.bridgerest.com						
Bridge-Between Retreat Ctr, The						
4471 Flaherty Ln	Denmark	WI	54208	920-864-7230	864-7044	673
Web: www.bridge-between.com						
Bridgeborn LLC						
596 Lynnhaven Pkwy Ste 100	Virginia Beach	VA	23452	757-437-5000		434-3
Web: www.bridgeborn.com						
Bridgeforce Inc						
101 Ponds Edge Dr Ste 100	Chadds Ford	PA	19317	610-616-3106		196
Web: www.bridgeforce.com						
Bridgeline Digital 80 BlanchaRd Rd	Burlington	MA	01803	781-376-5555	376-5033	180
TF: 800-603-9936 ■ *Web:* www.bridgelinedigital.com						
Bridgepoint Education Inc						
13500 Evening Creek Dr N Ste 600	San Diego	CA	92128	858-486-1710	408-2903	242
NYSE: BPI ■ *TF:* 866-475-0317 ■ *Web:* www.bridgepointeducation.com						
Bridgepoint Merchant Banking						
816 P St Ste 200	Lincoln	NE	68508	402-817-7900		690
Web: bridgepointmb.com						
BridgePort Brewing Co						
1318 NW Northrup St	Portland	OR	97209	503-241-7179		102
TF: 888-834-7546 ■ *Web:* www.bridgeportbrew.com						
Bridgeport City Hall 999 Broad St	Bridgeport	CT	06604	203-576-7201	576-3913	337
TF: 800-978-2828 ■ *Web:* bridgeportct.gov						
Bridgeport Fittings Inc						
705 Lordship Blvd	Stratford	CT	06615	203-377-5944	381-3488	816
Web: www.bptfittings.com						
Bridgeport Hospital 267 Grant St	Bridgeport	CT	06610	203-384-3000	384-3046	374-3
TF: 800-688-4954 ■ *Web:* www.bridgeporthospital.org						
Bridgeport Inc 1432 Old W Main St	Red Wing	MN	55066	651-388-1264		321
Web: www.bridgeport.com						
Bridgeport News 3506 S Halsted st	Chicago	IL	60609	773-927-0025		532-4
TF: 877-828-3838 ■ *Web:* www.bridgeportnews.net						
Bridgeport News 1000 Bridgeport Ave	Shelton	CT	06484	203-926-2080		532-4
TF Advestisement: 855-247-8573 ■ *Web:* thebridgeportnews.com						
Bridgeport Public Library						
925 Broad St	Bridgeport	CT	06604	203-576-7403	576-8255	434-3
Web: www.bportlibrary.org						
Bridgeport Regional Business Council						
10 Middle St Ste 1401	Bridgeport	CT	06604	203-335-3800		139
Web: www.brbc.org						
Bridger LLC						
2009 Chenault Dr Ste 100	Carrollton	TX	75006	214-722-6960		449
Web: www.bridgergroup.com						
Bridger Steel Inc 1558 Amsterdam Rd	Belgrade	MT	59714	406-388-9555		697
Web: bridgersteel.com						
Bridger Valley Extreme Access						
40014 Business Loop 1-80 PO Box 399	Mountain View	WY	82939	307-786-2800	786-4362	245
TF: 800-276-3481 ■ *Web:* bvea.coop						
Bridgers & Paxton Consulting Engineers Inc						
4600-C Montgomery Blvd NE	Albuquerque	NM	87109	505-883-4111		256
Web: www.bpce.com						
Bridges Consulting Inc						
2701 Technology Dr Ste 210	Annapolis Junction	MD	20701	240-646-1100		463
Web: www.bridges-inc.com						
Bridges Investment Counsel Inc						
256 Durham Plaza 8401 W Dodge Rd Ste 256	Omaha	NE	68114	402-397-4700		528
Web: www.bridgesfund.com						
Bridges Public Charter School						
100 Gallatin St NE	Washington	DC	20011	202-545-0515		685
Web: bridgespcs.org						
Bridges Restaurant						
1696 Duranleau St	Vancouver	BC	V6H3S4	604-687-4400		671
TF: 800-663-0666 ■ *Web:* www.bridgesrestaurant.com						
BRIDGES USA Inc 477 N Fifth St	Memphis	TN	38105	901-452-5600		260
Web: www.bridgesusa.org						
Bridgestone Aircraft Tire USA Inc						
802 S Ayersville Rd	Mayodan	NC	27027	336-548-8100	548-7441	24
Web: www.bridgestone.com						
Bridgestone Americas Holding Inc						
535 Marriott Dr	Nashville	TN	37214	615-937-1000	937-3621	754
TF Cust Svc: 877-201-2373 ■ *Web:* www.bridgestoneamericas.com/en/index						
Bridgestone Arena 501 Broadway	Nashville	TN	37203	615-770-2000		720
TF: 800-356-4840 ■ *Web:* www.bridgestonearena.com						
Bridgestone Canada Inc						
5770 Hurontario St Ste 400	Mississauga	ON	L5R3G5	905-890-1990		755
Web: www.bridgestone.com						
Bridgestone Golf Inc						
15320 Industrial Pk Blvd NE	Covington	GA	30014	770-787-7400		710
TF: 800-358-6319 ■ *Web:* www.bridgestonegolf.com						
Bridgestone Multimedia Group Inc						
300 N McKemy Ave	Chandler	AZ	85226	480-940-5777		511
Web: gobmg.com						
Bridgestone Retail Operations LLC						
535 Marriott Dr Ste 300	Nashville	TN	60108	877-201-2373		54
TF: 877-201-2373 ■ *Web:* www.bsro.com						
BridgeSTOR LLC 18060 Old Coach Dr	Poway	CA	92064	858-375-7076	613-9141	173-8
TF: 800-280-8204 ■ *Web:* www.bridgestor.com						
Bridgeton Area Chamber of Commerce						
76 Magnolia Ave PO Box 1063	Bridgeton	NJ	08302	856-455-1312	453-9795	139
Web: www.baccnj.com						

Name / Address	City	State	Zip	Phone	Fax	Class
Bridgetown Printing Co						
5300 N Channel Ave	Portland	OR	97217	503-863-5300		627
Web: www.bridgetown.com						
Bridgewater & Area Chamber of Commerce						
373 King St	Bridgewater	NS	B4V1B1	902-543-4263	543-1156	137
Web: www.bridgewaterchamber.com						
Bridgewater Assoc Inc						
1 Glendinning Pl	Westport	CT	06880	203-226-3030	291-7300	401
Web: www.bridgewater.com						
Bridgewater College						
402 E College St	Bridgewater	VA	22812	540-828-5375	828-5481	166
TF: 800-759-8328 ■ *Web:* www.bridgewater.edu						
Bridgewater Hotel 723 First Ave	Fairbanks	AK	99701	800-528-4916	452-6126*	379
**Fax Area Code:* 907 ■ *TF:* 800-528-4916 ■ *Web:* www.fountainheadhotels.com						
Bridgewater Interiors LLC						
4617 W Fort St	Detroit	MI	48209	313-842-3300		689
Web: bridgewater-interiors.com						
Bridgewater State College						
131 Summer St	Bridgewater	MA	02325	508-531-1000	531-1746*	166
**Fax:* Admissions ■ *Web:* www.bridgew.edu						
Bridgewater State College Maxwell Library						
10 Shaw Rd	Bridgewater	MA	02325	508-531-1392		434-6
Web: www.bridgew.edu/library						
Bridgewater State Hospital						
20 Admin Rd	Bridgewater	MA	02324	508-279-4500		374-5
TF: 800-450-2208 ■ *Web:* mass.gov						
BridgeWave Communications Inc						
3350 Thomas Rd	Santa Clara	CA	95054	408-567-6900		647
Web: www.bridgewave.com						
Bridge-world Language Center Inc, The						
110 Second St S Ste 213	Waite Park	MN	56387	320-259-9239		768
TF: 800-835-6870 ■ *Web:* www.bridgelanguage.com						
Bridgford Foods Corp 1308 N Patt St	Anaheim	CA	92801	714-526-5533	526-4360	296-26
NASDAQ: BRID ■ *TF:* 800-854-3255 ■ *Web:* www.bridgford.com						
Bridgton Academy PO Box 292	North Bridgton	ME	04057	207-647-3322		622
Web: www.bridgtonacademy.org						
Bridle Trails State Park						
5300 116th Ave NE	Kirkland	WA	98033	425-649-4275		565
Web: www.parks.wa.gov						
Bridon Cordage LLC 909 E 16th St	Albert Lea	MN	56007	507-377-1601		208
TF: 800-533-6002 ■ *Web:* www.bridoncordage.com						
Briefing.com Inc						
401 N Michigan Ste 2910	Chicago	IL	60611	312-670-4463		404
TF General: 800-752-3013 ■ *Web:* www.briefing.com						
Briercrest College & Seminary						
510 College Dr	Caronport	SK	S0H0S0	306-756-3200	756-5500	167-3
Web: www.briercrest.ca						
Brierley & Partners						
5465 Legacy Dr Ste 300	Plano	TX	75024	214-760-8700	743-5511	5
TF: 800-899-8700 ■ *Web:* www.brierley.com						
Brierley Associates LLC						
990 S Broadway Ste 222	Denver	CO	80209	303-703-1405		261
TF: 800-364-2059 ■ *Web:* brierleyassociates.com						
Briess Malting Co 625 S Irish Rd	Chilton	WI	53014	920-849-7711	849-4277	461
TF: 800-657-0806 ■ *Web:* www.briess.com						
Brigantine Restaurants Inc						
7889 Ostrow St	San Diego	CA	92111	858-268-1030	268-5727	670
TF: 800-442-1162 ■ *Web:* www.brigantine.com						
Briggs & Stratton Corp						
12301 W Wirth St	Milwaukee	WI	53222	414-259-5333		262
NYSE: BGG ■ *TF:* 800-444-7774 ■ *Web:* www.briggsandstratton.com						
Briggs & Veselka Co						
9 Greenway Plaza Ste 1700	Houston	TX	77046	713-667-9147		2
Web: bvccpa.com						
Briggs Auto Group Inc						
2312 Stagg Hill Rd	Manhattan	KS	66502	785-537-8330		54
TF: 800-257-4004 ■ *Web:* www.briggsauto.com						
Briggs Boat Works Inc 370 Harbor Rd	Wanchese	NC	27981	252-473-2393	473-2392	90
Web: www.briggsboatworks.com						
Briggs Capital LLC						
858 Washington St Ste 100	Dedham	MA	02026	781-493-6581		401
Web: www.briggscapital.com						
Briggs Equipment 10540 N Stemmons Fwy	Dallas	TX	75220	214-630-0808	631-3560	385
TF: 800-606-1833 ■ *Web:* www.briggsequipment.us						
Briggs Inc 1501 Broadway	New York	NY	10036	212-354-9440		184
Web: www.briggsnyc.com						
Briggs Industrial Equipment						
10550 N Stemmons Fwy	Dallas	TX	75220	214-630-0808		385
TF: 800-516-9206 ■ *Web:* www.briggsindustrial.com						
Briggs Lawrence County Public Library						
321 S Fourth St	Ironton	OH	45638	740-532-1124		434-3
TF: 800-582-7277 ■ *Web:* www.briggslibrary.com						
Briggs Plumbing						
597 Old Mt Holly Rd	Goose Creek	SC	29445	800-888-4458	627-4449	611
TF: 800-888-4458 ■ *Web:* www.briggsplumbing.com						
Brigham & Women's Hospital						
75 Francis St	Boston	MA	02115	617-732-5500		374-7
TF: 800-722-5520 ■ *Web:* www.brighamandwomens.org						
Brigham Young University						
730 E University Pkwy	Provo	UT	84604	801-422-7700		166
Lee Library 2060 HBLL	Provo	UT	84602	801-422-2905	422-0466*	434-6
**Fax:* Admin ■ *Web:* www.lib.byu.edu						
Brigham Young University Hawaii						
55-220 Kulanui St	Laie	HI	96762	808-293-3211	293-3741*	166
**Fax:* Admissions ■ *Web:* www.byuh.edu						
Brigham Young University Idaho						
525 S Ctr	Rexburg	ID	83460	866-672-2984	496-1220*	166
**Fax Area Code:* 208 ■ **Fax:* Admissions ■ *TF:* 866-672-2984 ■ *Web:* www.byui.edu						
Bright Chair Co 51 Railroad Ave	Middletown	NY	10940	845-343-2196		319-1
TF: 888-524-5997 ■ *Web:* www.brightchair.com						
Bright Co-op Inc 803 W Seale St	Nacogdoches	TX	75964	936-564-8378	564-3281	763
TF: 800-562-0730 ■ *Web:* www.brightcoop.com						
Bright Horizon Resources LLC						
6120 S Yale Ave Ste 900	Tulsa	OK	74136	918-879-3200		536
TF: 800-935-9935 ■ *Web:* www.bhrep.com						
Bright Horizons Family Solutions LLC						
200 Talcott Ave S	Watertown	MA	02472	617-673-8000	673-8001	148
TF: 800-324-4386 ■ *Web:* www.brighthorizons.com						

Name / Address	City	State	Zip	Phone	Fax	Class
Bright Ideas in Broad Ripple Inc 7425 Westfield Blvd	Indianapolis	IN	46240	317-257-4111		328
Web: www.bright-ideas.org						
Bright Image Corp 2830 S18th Ave	Broadview	IL	60155	888-449-5656	449-1155*	203
*Fax Area Code: 708 ■ TF: 888-449-5656 ■ Web: www.touchandglow.com						
Bright Lights USA Inc 145 Shreve Ave	Barrington	NJ	08007	856-546-5656		529
Web: www.brightlightsusa.com						
Bright of America Inc 300 Greenbrier Rd	Summersville	WV	26651	304-872-3000		558
Bright Pest Control Co 4340 Sanita Ct	Louisville	KY	40213	502-452-9600		577
Web: brightpest.com						
Bright Trading LLC 4850 Harrison Dr	Las Vegas	NV	89121	702-739-1393	739-1398	113
Web: www.stocktrading.com						
Bright View Technologies 5151 Mccrimmon Pkwy Ste 200	Morrisville	NC	27560	919-228-4370		253
Web: www.brightviewtechnologies.com						
Bright Wood Corp 335 NW Hess St PO Box 828	Madras	OR	97741	541-475-2243	475-7086	499
Web: www.brightwood.com						
Brightergy LLC 1712 Main St FL 7	Kansas City	MO	64108	816-866-0555		192
Web: brightergy.com						
BrightHouse LLC 675 Ponce de Leon Ave Ste 9700	Atlanta	GA	30308	404-240-2500		195
Web: www.thinkbrighthouse.com						
Brightleaf Square Gregson & Main Sts Ste 24	Durham	NC	27701	919-682-9229	688-1953	50-6
Web: www.historicbrightleaf.com						
Brightlight Pictures Inc 2400 Boundary Rd The Bridge Studios	Burnaby	BC	V5M3Z3	604-628-3000		514
Web: www.brightlightpictures.com						
BrightMove Inc 320 High Tide Dr # 201	Saint Augustine	FL	32080	877-482-8840		196
TF: 877-482-8840 ■ Web: www.brightmove.com						
Brighton Chrysler Plymouth Dodge Inc 9827 E Grand River	Brighton	MI	48116	810-355-4161		57
Brighton Cromwell LLC 111 Canfield Ave Bldg C 1-10	Randolph	NJ	07869	973-252-4100		314
Web: www.brightoncromwell.com						
Brighton Feed & Saddlery 370 N Main St	Brighton	CO	80601	303-659-0721		711
Web: www.brightonsaddlery.com						
Brighton Ford Inc 8240 W Grand River	Brighton	MI	48114	810-227-1171		57
TF: 888-644-9991 ■ Web: brightonford.com						
Brighton Jones LLC 506 Second Ave Ste 1800	Seattle	WA	98104	206-329-5546		401
Web: www.brightonjones.com						
Brighton Memorial Library 2300 Elmwood Ave	Rochester	NY	14618	585-784-5300	784-5333	434-3
Web: www.brightonlibrary.org						
Brighton Recreation Area 6360 Chilson Rd	Howell	MI	48843	810-229-6566		565
Web: www.michigandnr.com						
Brighton Securities Corp 1703 Monroe Ave	Rochester	NY	14618	585-473-3590		690
TF: 800-388-1703 ■ Web: www.brightonsecurities.com						
Brighton State Park 102 State Park Rd	Island Pond	VT	05846	802-723-4360		565
Web: www.vtstateparks.com						
Brightons Orangerie 550 Light St	Baltimore	MD	21202	866-766-3782	659-5925*	671
*Fax Area Code: 410 ■ TF: 866-766-3782 ■ Web: sonesta.com						
BrightSign LLC 16795 Lark Ave Ste 200	Los Gatos	CA	95032	408-852-9263		407
Web: www.brightsign.biz						
Brightsource Energy Inc 1999 Harrison St Ste 2150	Oakland	CA	94612	510-550-8161	550-8165	245
Web: www.brightsourceenergy.com						
Brightstar Corp 9725 NW 117th Ave Ste 300	Miami	FL	33178	305-421-6000		246
Web: brightstar.com						
Brigtsen's 723 Dante St	New Orleans	LA	70118	504-861-7610		671
TF: 800-672-6124 ■ Web: www.brigtsens.com						
Brilex Industries Inc PO Box 749	Youngstown	OH	44501	330-744-1114	744-1125	480
Web: www.brilex.com						
Briljent LLC 7615 W Jefferson Blvd	Fort Wayne	IN	46804	260-434-0990		765
Web: www.briljent.com						
Brill J Michael & Assoc 5053 Ritter Rd Ste 200	Mechanicsburg	PA	17055	717-691-0200		727
Web: www.jmichaelbrill.com						
Brill Securities Inc 152 W 57th St 16th Fl	New York	NY	10019	212-957-5700		690
TF: 800-933-0800 ■ Web: www.brillsec.com						
Brillacademic Publishers Inc 2 liberty Sq 11th Fl	Boston	MA	02109	617-263-2323	263-2324	637-2
TF: 800-337-9255 ■ Web: www.brill.com						
Brillcast Inc 3400 Wentworth Dr SW	Grand Rapids	MI	49519	616-534-4977	534-0880	308
TF: 800-327-8474 ■ Web: www.brillcast.com						
Brilliance Audio 1704 Eaton Dr	Grand Haven	MI	49417	616-846-5256		658
Web: www.brillianceaudio.com						
Brilliance Educator Supplies & Resources Inc 8679 Sudley Rd	Manassas	VA	20110	571-292-2331		535
Brilliant Digital Entertainment Inc 14011 Ventura Blvd Ste 501	Sherman Oaks	CA	91423	818-386-2179		178-8
Web: www.globalfileregistry.com						
Brilliant Jewelers/Mjj Inc 902 Broadway 18th Fl	New York	NY	10010	212-353-2326		411
Web: www.mjjbrilliant.com						
Brilliant Store Inc 933 Corporate Way	Fremont	CA	94539	510-668-0398		225
Web: www.brilliant-electronics.com						
Brillio 100 Town Sq Pl Ste 308	Jersey City	NJ	07310	800-317-0575		463
TF: 800-317-0575 ■ Web: www.brillio.com						
Brillion Iron Works Inc 1900 North St	Marysville	KS	66508	920-756-2121	756-3062	273
TF: 855-320-0373 ■ Web: landoll.com						
Brim's Snack Foods 3045 Bartlett Corporate Dr Ste 101	Bartlett	TN	38133	901-377-9016		297-8
Web: www.brimsnacks.com						
Brimar Industries Inc 64 Outwater Ln	Garfield	NJ	07026	800-274-6271		627
TF: 800-274-6271 ■ Web: www.brimar.com						
Bri-Mar Mfg LLC 1002 Wayne Ave	Chambersburg	PA	17201	717-261-0922		770
Web: www.bri-mar.com						
Brimfield State Forest 86 Dearth Hill Rd	Brimfield	MA	01010	413-267-9687		565
Web: www.mass.gov						
Brimley State Park 9200 W 6-Mile Rd	Brimley	MI	49715	906-248-3422		565
Web: www.michigandnr.com						
Brimmer Burek & Keelan LLP 5601 Mariner St Ste 200	Tampa	FL	33609	813-282-3400		2
Web: www.bbkm.com						
Brimtek Inc 21660 Red Rum Dr Ste 105	Ashburn	VA	20147	571-918-4921		196
TF: 800-738-8258 ■ Web: www.brimtek.com						
Brinderson 3330 Harbor Blvd Ste 100	Costa Mesa	CA	92626	714-466-7100		188-7
Web: www.brinderson.com						
Brine Group Staffing Solutions Inc 800 District Ave Ste 120	Burlington	MA	01803	781-272-3400		260
Web: brinegroup.com						
Brinjac Engineering Inc 114 N Second St	Harrisburg	PA	17101	717-233-4502	233-0833	261
TF: 877-274-6526 ■ Web: www.brinjac.com						
Brink Constructors Inc 2950 N Plaza Dr	Rapid City	SD	57702	605-342-6966	342-5905	189-4
Web: www.brinkred.com						
Brink's Inc PO Box 619031	Dallas	TX	75261	469-549-6000		693
TF: 800-274-6575 ■ Web: www.brinks.com/en						
Brink's Inc 1801 Bayberry Ct PO Box 18100	Richmond	VA	23226	804-289-9600	289-9770*	185
NYSE: BCO ■ *Fax: Mail Rm ■ TF Sales: 800-274-6575 ■ Web: www.brinks.com/en						
Brinker Brown Fastener & Supply Inc 12290 Crystal Commerce Loop	Fort Myers	FL	33966	239-939-3535		385
TF: 800-527-5530 ■ Web: www.brinkerbrown.com						
Brinker International Inc 6820 LBJ Fwy	Dallas	TX	75240	972-980-9917	770-9593	670
NYSE: EAT ■ TF: 800-983-4637 ■ Web: www.brinker.com						
Brinkman International Group Inc 167 Ames St	Rochester	NY	14611	585-235-4545	235-6568	295
Web: www.brinkmanig.com						
Brinkman Tool & Die Inc 325 Kiser St	Dayton	OH	45404	937-222-1161	222-2079	757
Web: www.brinkmantool.com						
Brinkmann Corp 4215 McEwen Rd	Dallas	TX	75244	972-387-4939	770-8545	439
TF: 800-527-0717						
Brinkmann Instruments Inc 1819 Underwood Blvd	Delran	NJ	08075	856-764-7300		419
Web: www.lauda-brinkmann.com						
Brinly-Hardy Co 3230 Industrial Pkwy	Jeffersonville	IN	47130	812-218-7200	218-6085	429
TF: 800-626-5329 ■ Web: www.brinly.com						
Brintons USA 1000 Cobb Pl Blvd Bldg 200 Ste 200	Kennesaw	GA	30144	678-594-9300		131
Web: brintons.net						
Brio Tuscan Grille 3993 Easton Stn St	Columbus	OH	43219	614-416-4745		671
Web: www.brioitalian.com						
Briohn Building Corp 3885 N Brookfield Rd Ste 200	Brookfield	WI	53045	262-790-0500		186
Web: www.briohn.com						
Brioni Roman Style USA Corp 610 Fifth Ave Ste 404	New York	NY	10020	212-332-6900		157-6
Web: brioni.com						
Brioschi Inc 19-01 Pollitt Dr	Fair Lawn	NJ	07410	201-796-4226		582
Brisar Industries Inc 150 E Seventh St	Paterson	NJ	07524	973-278-2500		88
TF: 800-928-1963 ■ Web: www.brisar.com						
Briscoe County PO Box 555	Silverton	TX	79257	806-823-2134	823-2359	338
Web: www.co.briscoe.tx.us						
BriskHeat Corp 1055 Gibbard Ave	Columbus	OH	43201	614-294-3376	294-3807	318
TF: 800-848-7673 ■ Web: www.briskheat.com						
Bristol Aluminum 5514 Bristol Emilie Rd	Levittown	PA	19057	215-946-3160		362
TF: 800-338-5532 ■ Web: www.bristolaluminum.com						
Bristol Bar & Grille Inc 1321 BaRdstown Rd	Louisville	KY	40204	502-456-1702		670
Web: bristolbarandgrille.com						
Bristol Bay Borough PO Box 189	Naknek	AK	99633	907-246-4224	246-6633	338
TF: 800-478-2316 ■ Web: www.bristolbayboroughak.us						
Bristol Broadcasting Company Inc 901 E Valley Dr	Bristol	VA	24201	276-669-8112	669-0541	643
Web: www.bristolbroadcasting.com						
Bristol Chamber of Commerce 20 Volunteer Pkwy	Bristol	TN	37620	423-989-4850	989-4867	139
Web: www.bristolchamber.com						
Bristol Community College 777 Elsbree St	Fall River	MA	02720	508-678-2811	730-3255*	162
*Fax: Admissions ■ Web: www.bristol.mass.edu						
Attleboro 11 Field St	Attleboro	MA	02703	508-226-2484	222-7638	162
Web: bristolcc.edu						
New Bedford 777 Elsbree St	Fall River	MA	02720	508-678-2811		162
Web: www.bristolcc.edu						
Bristol Compressors Inc 15185 Industrial Park Rd	Bristol	VA	24202	276-466-4121		14
TF: 855-601-0894 ■ Web: www.bristolcompressors.com						
Bristol Construction Services LLC 111 W 16th Ave Fl 3	Anchorage	AK	99501	907-563-0013		186
TF: 877-563-0013 ■ Web: www.bristol-companies.com						
Bristol County 9 Ct St	Taunton	MA	02780	508-824-9681	821-3101	338
Web: countyofbristol.net						
Bristol County 10 Ct St	Bristol	RI	02809	401-253-7000	253-3080	338
Web: www.bristolri.us						
Bristol Environmental Inc 1123 Beaver St	Bristol	PA	19007	215-788-6040		667
TF: 800-807-0614 ■ Web: www.beigroup.com						
Bristol Farms 915 E 230th St	Carson	CA	90745	310-233-4700		345
Web: www.bristolfarms.com						
Bristol Harbor Group Inc 99 Poppasquash Rd Unit H	Bristol	RI	02809	401-253-4318		261
TF: 800-356-6955 ■ Web: www.bristolharborgroup.com						

				Phone	Fax	Class
Bristol Herald-Courier 320 Bob Morrison Blvd *TF:* 888-228-2098 ■ *Web:* www.heraldcourier.com	Bristol	VA	24201	276-669-2181	669-3696	532-2
Bristol Hospital (BH) 41 Brewster Rd *Web:* www.bristolhospital.org	Bristol	CT	06010	860-585-3000	585-3853	374-3
Bristol Hotel 1055 First Ave. *TF:* 800-662-4477 ■ *Web:* www.thebristolsandiego.com	San Diego	CA	92101	619-232-6141	232-0118	379
Bristol (Independent City) 497 Cumberland St Rm 210 *Web:* www.bristolva.org	Bristol	VA	24201	276-645-7321	821-6097	338
Bristol Industries 630 E Lambert Rd. **Fax:* Sales ■ *TF:* 800-543-2614 ■ *Web:* www.bristol-ind.com	Brea	CA	92821	714-990-4121	529-6726*	278
Bristol Instruments Inc 50 Victor Heights Pkwy. *Web:* www.bristol-inst.com	Victor	NY	14564	585-924-2620		544
Bristol Memorial Works Inc 797 King St.	Bristol	CT	06010	860-583-1654		724
Bristol Metals LP 390 Bristol Metals Rd *TF:* 800-222-3312 ■ *Web:* www.brismet.com	Bristol	TN	37620	423-989-4700		490
Bristol Motor Speedway 151 Speedway Blvd *TF:* 866-415-4158 ■ *Web:* www.bristolmotorspeedway.com	Bristol	TN	37620	423-989-6933	764-1646	515
Bristol Products Corp 700 Shelby St. *TF Orders:* 800-336-8775 ■ *Web:* www.bristolproducts.com	Bristol	TN	37620	423-968-4140	968-2084	155-1
Bristol Public Library 701 Goode St *Web:* www.bristol-library.org	Bristol	VA	24201	276-645-8780	669-5593	434-3
Bristol Public Library 5 High St. *TF:* 877-603-7323 ■ *Web:* bristollib.com	Bristol	CT	06010	860-584-7787	584-7696	434-3
Bristol Regional Medical Ctr 1 Medical Pk Blvd. *Web:* www.wellmont.org	Bristol	TN	37620	423-844-1121		374-3
Bristol West Insurance Group 900 S Pine Island Rd Ste 600 *TF:* 888-888-0080 ■ *Web:* www.bristolwest.com	Davie	FL	33324	888-888-0080	888-0070	391-2
Bristol, The 200 Boylston St *TF:* 800-819-5053 ■ *Web:* www.fourseasons.com	Boston	MA	02116	617-338-4400	423-0154	671
Bristol-Donald Company Inc 50 Roanoke Ave *TF:* 800-455-1445 ■ *Web:* www.bristoldonald.com	Newark	NJ	07105	973-589-2640	589-2610	516
Bristol-Myers Squibb Canada Inc 2344 Alfred-Nobel Blvd Ste 300 *TF Cust Svc:* 800-267-0005 ■ *Web:* www.bmscanada.ca	Montreal	QC	H4S0A4	514-333-3200		582
Bristol-Myers Squibb Co 345 Pk Ave *NYSE:* BMY ■ *TF:* 800-332-2056 ■ *Web:* www.bms.com	New York	NY	10154	212-546-4000		582
Bristol-Warren Regional School District 151 State St *Web:* www.bw.k12.ri.us	Bristol	RI	02809	401-253-4000		685
Briston Construction LLC 309 E Tenth Dr *Web:* www.bristonconstruction.com	Mesa	AZ	85210	480-776-5810		186
Bristow Academy Inc 365 Golden Knights Blvd *Web:* www.bristowgroup.com	Titusville	FL	32780	321-385-2919		148
Bristow Alaska Inc 1915 Donald Ave. *TF:* 800-686-4080 ■ *Web:* www.bristowgroup.com	Fairbanks	AK	99701	907-452-1197	452-4539	359
BRIT Systems Inc 1909 Hi Line Dr *Web:* www.brit.com	Dallas	TX	75207	214-630-0636		475
Brit's Pub & Eating Establishment 1110 Nicollet Mall *Web:* www.britspub.com	Minneapolis	MN	55403	612-332-3908	332-8032	671
Brita Products Co 1221 Broadway *TF:* 800-242-7482 ■ *Web:* www.brita.com	Oakland	CA	94612	510-271-7000	832-1463	806
Britax Child Safety Inc 4140 Pleasant Rd *TF:* 888-427-4829 ■ *Web:* us.britax.com	Fort Mill	NC	29708	704-409-1700		64
Brite Pharmacy Inc 8317 37th Ave.	Jackson Heights	NY	11372	718-424-1101		237
Briteline Extrusions Inc 575 Beech Hill Rd *Web:* www.briteline.net	Summerville	SC	29485	843-873-4410		492
Brite-Line LLC 10660 E 51st Ave *TF:* 888-201-6448 ■ *Web:* www.brite-line.com	Denver	CO	80239	888-201-6448	208-0758	732
Britestar Business Solutions Inc 1305 Governors Ct Ste B *Web:* britestarbusiness.com	Abingdon	MD	21009	410-679-0441		317
BriteVision Media LLC 50 First St Ste 600 **Fax Area Code:* 888 ■ *TF:* 877-479-7777 ■ *Web:* www.britevision.com	San Francisco	CA	94105	877-479-7777	755-5282*	8
Britex Fabrics LLC 146 Geary St. *Web:* www.britexfabrics.com	San Francisco	CA	94108	415-392-2910	392-3906	270
British Airways Executive Club PO Box 300743 **Fax Area Code:* 212 ■ *TF:* 800-452-1201 ■ *Web:* www.britishairways.com	Jamaica	NY	11430	800-452-1201	251-6767*	26
British Columbia Automobile Assn (BCAA) 4567 Canada Way *TF:* 800-222-4357 ■ *Web:* www.bcaa.com	Burnaby	BC	V5G4T1	604-268-5000		53
British Columbia Chamber of Commerce 750 W Pender St Ste 1201 *Web:* www.bcchamber.org	Vancouver	BC	V6C2T8	604-683-0700	683-0416	137
British Columbia Lottery Corp (BCLC) 74 W Seymour St *TF:* 866-815-0222 ■ *Web:* www.bclc.com	Kamloops	BC	V2C1E2	250-828-5500	828-5631	452
British Columbia Place Stadium 777 Pacific Blvd *Web:* www.bcplace.com	Vancouver	BC	V6B4Y8	604-669-2300		720
British Columbia Sports Hall of Fame & Museum 777 Pacific Blvd S *Web:* www.bcsportshalloffame.com	Vancouver	BC	V6B4Y8	604-687-5520	687-5510	522
British Columbia Wildlife Park 9077 Dallas Dr *Web:* www.bcwildlife.org	Kamloops	BC	V2C6V1	250-573-3242	573-2406	823
British Columbia's Women's Hospital & Health Centre 4500 Oak St *TF:* 888-300-3088 ■ *Web:* www.bcwomens.ca	Vancouver	BC	V6H3N1	604-875-2424		374-2
British Standards Institution, The 12110 Sunset Hills Rd Ste 200 *TF:* 800-862-4977 ■ *Web:* www.bsigroup.com	Reston	VA	20190	703-437-9000		457-5
British-American Business Council (BABC) 52 Vanderbilt Ave 20th Fl *Web:* www.babc.org	New York	NY	10017	212-661-4060	661-4074	138
British-American Business Council of Los Angeles 15303 Ventura Blvd Ste 1040 **Fax Area Code:* 818 ■ *Web:* www.babcla.org	Sherman Oaks	CA	91403	310-312-1962	995-4124*	138
British-American Chamber of Commerce Great Lakes Region (BACC) 4700 Millenia Blvd Ste 175 *Web:* www.baccohio.org	Orlando	FL	32839	216-621-0222		138
British-American Chamber of Commerce of Miami 501 Brickell Key Dr Ste 410	Miami	FL	33131	305-377-0992		138
Britt Trucking & Construction Co 1900 Seminole Rd	Lamesa	TX	79331	806-872-3353		780
Brittain Engineering 56 Third St NW *Web:* www.brittainengineering.com	Hickory	NC	28601	828-328-1813		256
Brittany Pointe Estates 1001 S Valley Forge Rd *TF:* 800-504-2287 ■ *Web:* www.actsretirement.org	Lansdale	PA	19446	215-855-4109		672
Britten Woodworks 1954 N Betsie River Rd *Web:* www.brittenwoodworks.com	Interlochen	MI	49643	231-275-5457		115
Britto Agency The 234 W 56th St Fl 5 *Web:* thebrittoagency.com	New York	NY	10019	212-977-6772		195
Britto Central Inc 818 Lincoln Rd *Web:* www.britto.com	Miami	FL	33139	305-531-8821		522
Britton Lumber Company Inc 7 Ely Rd PO Box 389 *TF:* 800-343-5300 ■ *Web:* www.brittonlumber.com	Fairlee	VT	05045	802-333-4388	333-4295	191-3
Brivo Systems LLC 7700 Old Georgetown Rd Ste 300 *TF Tech Supp:* 866-692-7486 ■ *Web:* www.brivo.com	Bethesda	MD	20814	301-664-5242		692
Brixmor Property Group 420 Lexington Ave 7th Fl *TF:* 800-468-7526 ■ *Web:* brixmor.com	New York	NY	10170	212-869-3000		655
BRK Brands Inc 3901 Liberty St Rd. *TF:* 800-323-9005 ■ *Web:* www.firstalert.com	Aurora	IL	60504	630-851-7330		283
BRMC (Bay Regional Medical Ctr) 1900 Columbus Ave *TF:* 800-656-3950 ■ *Web:* www.mclaren.org	Bay City	MI	48708	989-894-3000		374-3
BRMC (Bluefield Regional Medical Ctr) 500 Cherry St *TF:* 800-994-6610 ■ *Web:* www.bluefieldregional.net	Bluefield	WV	24701	304-327-1100		374-3
Broaching Industries Inc 25755 Dhondt Ct *Web:* www.broachingindustries.com	Chesterfield	MI	48051	586-949-3775		454
Broad Oak Energy II LLC 1707 Market Pl Ste 320 *TF:* 800-554-2143 ■ *Web:* www.broadoakenergy.com	Irving	TX	75063	972-444-8808		192
Broad River Correctional Institution 4460 Broad River Rd. *TF:* 800-983-7174 ■ *Web:* www.doc.sc.gov	Columbia	SC	29210	803-896-2234		213
Broad River Electric Co-op Inc 811 Hamrick St. *TF:* 866-687-2667 ■ *Web:* www.broadriverelectric.com	Gaffney	SC	29342	864-489-5737	487-7808	245
Broad Street Grille at the Chattanoogan 1201 Broad St. *Web:* www.chattanooganhotel.com	Chattanooga	TN	37402	423-424-3700		671
Broadband Capital Management LLC 712 Fifth Ave 22nd Fl *Web:* www.broadbandcapital.com	New York	NY	10019	212-759-2020		690
Broadband Dynamics LLC 8757 E Via De Commercio *TF:* 888-801-1034 ■ *Web:* www.broadbanddynamics.net	Scottsdale	AZ	85258	888-801-1034	801-1038	387
Broadband Express LLC 374 Westdale Ave *TF:* 800-875-2225 ■ *Web:* www.broadbandexpress.com	Westerville	OH	43082	614-823-6464		260
Broadband Forum 48377 Fremont Blvd Ste 117 *Web:* www.broadband-forum.org	Fremont	CA	94538	510-492-4020		48-9
Broadband Solutions Inc 1886 Commerce Dr *Web:* www.broadband-solutions.com	De Pere	WI	54115	920-339-8056		116
Broadband Specialists Inc 1700 Peachtree Rd *TF:* 800-331-0578 ■ *Web:* bsicable.com	Balch Springs	TX	75180	972-329-1280		196
Broadcast Communications Media Inc 3101 Ocean Park Blvd Ste 309 *Web:* www.bcmedia.tv	Santa Monica	CA	90405	310-452-6585		393
Broadcast Education Assn (BEA) 1771 N St NW *Web:* www.beaweb.org	Washington	DC	20036	202-429-5355	609-9940	49-5
Broadcast Electronics Inc 4100 N 24th St *Web:* www.bdcast.com	Quincy	IL	62305	217-224-9600	224-9607	647
Broadcast Engineering Magazine 9800 Metcalf Ave *Web:* tvtechnology.com	Overland Park	KS	66212	212-378-0400		457-9
Broadcast Equipment Corp 1035 44th Dr *Web:* www.becny.com	Long Island	NY	11101	718-784-5540		116
Broadcast International Group 10458 NW 31st Terr *Web:* www.bigmiami.com	Doral	FL	33172	305-599-2112		647
Broadcast Microwave Services Inc (BMS) 12305 Crosthwaite Cir *TF:* 800-669-9667 ■ *Web:* bms-inc.com	Poway	CA	92064	858-391-3050	391-3049	224
Broadcast Music Inc (BMI) 250 Greenwich St 7 World Trade Ctr. *Web:* www.bmi.com	New York	NY	10007	212-220-3000	220-4474	48-4
Broadcast Promotions Inc 1775 Bald Hill Rd	Warwick	RI	02886	401-826-3600		393
Broadcast Sports Inc 7455 Race Rd *Web:* broadcastsportsinc.com	Hanover	MD	21076	410-564-2600		514
Broadcast Technical Services Inc 7219 Gessner Dr. *Web:* www.btshouston.com	Houston	TX	77040	832-467-0002		224
Broadcaster Press Inc, The 201 W Cherry St *Web:* www.broadcasteronline.com	Vermillion	SD	57069	605-624-4429		532-3

Phone | Fax | Class

Broadcasters Letter
1400 Independence Ave SW . . . . Washington DC 20250 202-720-4623 720-5773 531-11
Web: www.usda.gov

Broadcasting Board of Governors
330 Independence Ave SW . . . . Washington DC 20237 202-203-4545 203-4585 340-20
Web: www.bbg.gov
International Broadcasting Bureau
330 Independence Ave SW . . . . Washington DC 20237 202-203-4000 340-20
Web: www.bbg.gov
Voice of America
330 Independence Ave SW . . . . Washington DC 20237 202-203-4545 340-20
Web: www.voanews.com

Broadcom Corp 1320 Ridder Park Dr . . . . Irvine CA 92617 408-433-8000 926-5203* 696
NASDAQ: BRCM ■ **Fax Area Code:* 949 ■ *TF:* 877-673-9442 ■ *Web:* www.broadcom.com

Broaddus & Associates
1301 S Capital of Texas Hwy Ste A 302 . . . . . . Austin TX 78746 512-329-8822 329-8242 261
Web: broaddusassociates.com

Broadfield Distributing Inc
67A Glen Cove Ave. . . . . Glen Cove NY 11542 516-676-2378 671-3092 246
TF: 800-634-5178 ■ *Web:* www.broadfield.com

Broadgate Inc 830 Kirts Blvd Ste 400. . . . . Troy MI 48084 248-918-0110 463
Web: www.broadgateinc.com

Broadhurst Theatre 235 W 44th St . . . . New York NY 10036 212-239-6200 747
TF: 800-447-7400 ■ *Web:* telecharge.com/go.aspx?md=102&pid=7793

Broadjam Inc 6401 Odana Rd . . . . Madison WI 53719 608-271-3633 225
Web: www.broadjam.com

Broadlawns Medical Ctr
1801 Hickman Rd. . . . . Des Moines IA 50314 515-282-2200 282-3589 374-3
Web: www.broadlawns.org

Broadleaf Services Inc 6 Fortune Dr. . . . . Billerica MA 01821 866-337-7733 425-5280* 180
**Fax Area Code:* 781 ■ *TF:* 866-337-7733 ■ *Web:* www.broadleafservices.com

Broadley-James Corp 19 Thomas . . . . Irvine CA 92618 949-829-5555 475
Web: www.broadleyjames.com

Broadman & Holman Publishers
127 Ninth Ave N MSN 114. . . . . Nashville TN 37234 800-448-8032 251-3914* 637-3
**Fax Area Code:* 615 ■ *TF:* 800-448-8032 ■ *Web:* www.bhpublishinggroup.com

Broadmead 13801 York Rd . . . . Cockeysville MD 21030 410-527-1900 672
Web: www.broadmead.org

Broadmoor LLC 2740 N Arnoult Rd . . . . Metairie LA 70002 504-885-5400 187
Web: www.broadmoorllc.com

Broadmoor, The 1 Lake Ave . . . . Colorado Springs CO 80906 719-577-5775 577-5738 669
TF: 866-837-9520 ■ *Web:* www.broadmoor.com

Broadnet Teleservices LLC
1805 Shea Ctr Dr Ste 160. . . . . Highlands Ranch CO 80129 877-579-4929 116
TF: 877-579-4929 ■ *Web:* www.broadnet.com

BroadSoft Inc
9737 Washingtonian Blvd Ste 350 . . . . . . Gaithersburg MD 20877 301-977-9440 178-1
NASDAQ: BSFT ■ *Web:* www.broadsoft.com

BroadSpan Capital
1450 Brickell Ave Ste 2620. . . . . Miami FL 33131 305-424-3400 70
Web: www.brocap.com

Broadstone Real Estate LLC
530 Clinton Sq . . . . Rochester NY 14604 585-287-6500 655
Web: www.broadstone.com

Broadus Oil Corp of Illinois
201 Dannys Dr Ste 5. . . . . Streator IL 61364 815-673-5515 579
Web: www.broadusoil.com

Broadview Media Inc 201 S Union St. . . . . . . Montgomery AL 36104 334-223-5708 513

Broadview Networks Holdings Inc
800 Westchester Ave Ste N-501 . . . . Rye Brook NY 10573 914-922-7000 736
TF: 800-260-8766 ■ *Web:* www.broadviewnet.com

BroadVision Inc
1600 Seaport Blvd Ste 550. . . . . Redwood City CA 94063 650-295-0716 39
NASDAQ: BVSN ■ *Web:* www.broadvision.com

BroadVoice Inc
9221 Corbin Ave Ste 255 . . . . Northridge CA 91324 888-325-5875 387
TF: 888-325-5875 ■ *Web:* www.broadvoice.com

Broadwater Athletic Clubs & Hot Springs
4920 W US Hwy 12 . . . . Helena MT 59601 406-443-5777 354
Web: www.thebroadwater.com

Broadway at the Beach
1325 Celebrity Cir . . . . Myrtle Beach SC 29577 843-444-3200 50-6
TF: 800-386-4662 ■ *Web:* www.broadwayatthebeach.com

Broadway Bank 1177 NE Loop 410. . . . . San Antonio TX 78209 210-283-6500 70
Web: broadway.bank

Broadway Ctr for the Performing Arts
901 Broadway. . . . . Tacoma WA 98402 253-591-5890 591-2013 572
TF: 800-291-7593 ■ *Web:* www.broadwaycenter.org

Broadway Electric Service Company Inc
1800 N Central St. . . . . Knoxville TN 37917 865-524-1851 189-4
Web: besco.com

Broadway Electrical Company Inc
295 Freeport St. . . . . Boston MA 02122 617-288-7900 288-4169 189-4
Web: www.broadelec.com

Broadway Financial Corp
4800 Wilshire Blvd. . . . . Los Angeles CA 90010 323-634-1700 634-1728 360-2
NASDAQ: BYFC ■ *TF:* 888-988-2265 ■ *Web:* www.broadwayfederalbank.com

Broadway In Chicago 24 W Randolph St. . . . . Chicago IL 60601 312-977-1700 977-0519 572
TF: 800-359-2525 ■ *Web:* www.broadwayinchicago.com

Broadway Laundry Cleaners
548 N Broadway St. . . . . Greenville MS 38701 662-332-5988 426
Web: www.linenservice.com

Broadway League, The
729 Seventh Ave 5th Fl. . . . . New York NY 10019 212-764-1122 944-2136 48-4
TF: 866-442-9878 ■ *Web:* www.broadwayleague.com

Broadway Marketing Ltd 80 Fuller Rd . . . . Albany NY 12205 518-489-3226 195
Web: www.broadwaymarketing.com

Broadway Mechanical 873 81st Ave. . . . . Oakland CA 94621 510-746-4000 610
TF: 800-862-4930 ■ *Web:* www.broadwaymechanical.com

Broadway Oyster Bar
736 S Broadway . . . . Saint Louis MO 63102 314-621-8811 621-1995 671
Web: www.broadwayoysterbar.com

Broadway Plaza Hotel 1155 Broadway . . . . New York NY 10001 212-679-7665 378
TF: 877-504-6835 ■ *Web:* www.broadwayplazahotel.com

Broadway Services Inc
3709 E Monument St . . . . Baltimore MD 21205 410-563-6900 563-6960 104
Web: www.broadwayservices.com

Broadway Video Inc 1619 Broadway . . . . New York NY 10019 212-265-7600 512
Web: www.broadwayvideo.com

Broadway.com 729 Seventh Ave . . . . New York NY 10019 212-541-8457 541-4892 750
TF: 800-276-2392 ■ *Web:* broadway.com

Broan-NuTone LLC 926 W State St . . . . Hartford WI 53027 262-673-4340 673-8709 37
TF Cust Svc: 800-558-1711 ■ *Web:* www.broan.com

Broaster Company LLC, The
2855 Cranston Rd. . . . . Beloit WI 53511 608-365-0193 296
Web: www.broaster.com

Brocade Communications Systems Inc
130 Holger Way . . . . San Jose CA 95134 408-333-8000 333-8101 176
NASDAQ: BRCD ■ *TF:* 800-752-8061 ■ *Web:* www.brocade.com

Brochsteins Inc 11530 Main St . . . . Houston TX 77025 713-666-2881 499
Web: www.brochsteins.com

Brock & Company Inc
257 Great Vly Pkwy. . . . . Malvern PA 19355 610-647-5656 647-0867 670
TF: 866-468-2783 ■ *Web:* www.brockco.com

Brock & Scott PLLC
1315 Westbrook Plaza Dr . . . . Winston-salem NC 27103 336-760-5526 428
Web: www.brockandscott.com

Brock Cabinets Inc
2218 Wingate Rd . . . . Fayetteville NC 28304 910-424-1776 115
Web: www.brockcabinets.com

Brock Capital Group LLC
521 Fifth Ave 39th Fl . . . . New York NY 10175 212-209-3000 41
Web: www.brockcapital.com

Brock Grain Systems
611 N Higbee St PO Box 2000 . . . . Milford IN 46542 574-658-4191 658-4133 273
Web: www.brockgrain.com

Brock Group
10343 Sam Houston Park Dr Ste 200. . . . . Houston TX 77705 281-807-8200 807-8201 189-8
TF: 800-600-9675 ■ *Web:* www.brockgroup.com

Brock Solutions Inc 86 Ardelt Ave . . . . Kitchener ON N2C2C9 519-571-1522 571-1721 261
TF: 877-702-7625 ■ *Web:* www.brocksolutions.com

Brock University
1812 Sir Isaac Brock Way. . . . . Saint Catharines ON L2S3A1 905-688-5550 988-5488 785
TF: 800-465-3959 ■ *Web:* www.brocku.ca

Brock-McVey Co 1100 Brock-McVey Dr. . . . . Lexington KY 40509 859-255-1412 612
Web: www.brockmcvey.com

Brockton Area Workforce Investment Board Inc
34 School St. . . . . Brockton MA 02301 508-584-3234 260
Web: bawib.org

Brockton Hospital 680 Centre St . . . . Brockton MA 02302 508-941-7000 374-3
Web: www.signature-healthcare.org

Brockton Public Library 304 Main St . . . . Brockton MA 02301 508-580-7890 580-7898 434-3
TF: 800-645-8333 ■ *Web:* www.brocktonpubliclibrary.org

Brockton Symphony Orchestra
PO Box 1407 . . . . Brockton MA 02303 508-588-3841 573-3
Web: www.brocktonsymphony.org

Brockville General Hospital
75 Charles St . . . . Brockville ON K6V1S8 613-345-5645 374-2
TF: 800-567-7415 ■ *Web:* www.bgh-on.ca

Brockway-Smith Co (BWAY) 146 Dascomb Rd . . . . Andover MA 01810 978-475-7100 826-0606* 499
**Fax Area Code:* 732 ■ *TF:* 800-225-7912 ■ *Web:* www.brosco.com

Broco Inc 10868 Bell Ct. . . . . Rancho Cucamonga CA 91730 909-483-3222 483-3233 485
TF: 800-845-7259 ■ *Web:* www.broco-rankin.com

Broco Products Inc
18624 Syracuse Ave. . . . . Cleveland OH 44110 216-531-0880 411
TF: 800-321-0837 ■ *Web:* brocoproducts.com

Broda Construction Ltd
4271 - Fifth Ave E. . . . . Prince Albert SK S6V7V6 306-764-5337 188
Web: www.brodagroup.com

Brodart Co 500 Arch St . . . . Williamsport PA 17701 570-326-2461 178-10
TF: 800-233-8467 ■ *Web:* www.brodart.com

Broders Southside Pasta Bar
5000 Penn Ave S . . . . Minneapolis MN 55419 612-925-9202 671
Web: www.broders.com

Brodhead Steel Products Co
143 S Linden Ave . . . . South San Francisco CA 94080 650-871-8251 492
Web: www.brodheadsteel.com

Brodock Press Inc 502 Court St. . . . . Utica NY 13502 315-735-9577 627
Web: www.brodock.com

Brody School of Medicine at East Carolina University
600 Moye Blvd . . . . Greenville NC 27834 252-744-1020 744-1926* 167-2
**Fax:* Admissions ■ *TF:* 800-722-3281 ■ *Web:* www.ecu.edu/med

Brody Transportation Co Inc
621 S Bentalou St. . . . . Baltimore MD 21223 410-947-7000 778

Broedell Plumbing Supply Inc
1601 Commerce Ln . . . . Jupiter FL 33458 561-743-6663 743-4644 612
TF: 800-683-6363 ■ *Web:* www.broedell.com

Broetje Orchards 1111 Fishhook Pk Rd . . . . Prescott WA 99348 509-749-2217 315-3
Web: www.firstfruits.com

Brogan & Partners Advertising Consultancy Inc
800 N Old Woodward Ave Ste 100 . . . . Birmingham MI 48009 248-341-8200 195
Web: www.brogan.com

Brogan Cadillac Co 112 Route 46 E. . . . . Totowa NJ 07512 973-785-4300 57
Web: brogancadillac.com

Brogan Tennyson Group Inc
2245 US Hwy 130 Ste 102 . . . . Dayton NJ 08810 732-355-0700 7
TF: 800-561-3357 ■ *Web:* www.brogantennyson.com

Broich Enterprises Inc
6440 City W Pkwy . . . . Eden Prairie MN 55344 952-941-2270 941-3066 665
TF: 800-853-3508 ■ *Web:* www.arcticairco.com

Broken Acres Electronics
1005 E Strub Rd . . . . Sandusky OH 44870 419-621-8277 175
Web: www.brokenacres.com

Broken Arrow Chamber of Commerce
210 N Main Ste C. . . . . Broken Arrow OK 74012 918-251-1518 251-1777 139
Web: www.brokenarrow.org

Broken Arrow Communications Inc
8316 Corona Loop NE . . . . Albuquerque NM 87113 505-877-2100 877-2101 681
Web: www.bacom-inc.com

Broken Arrow Electric Supply Inc
2350 W Vancouver . . . . Broken Arrow OK 74012 918-258-3581 251-3799 246
TF: 800-616-1326 ■ *Web:* www.baes.com

Broker Restaurant, The 821 17th St. . . . . Denver CO 80202 303-292-5065 292-2652 671
Web: www.thebrokerrestaurant.com

Brokers Group LLC, The
512 Executive Dr. . . . . Princeton NJ 08540 609-924-8900 260
Web: www.talonpro.com

Phone | Fax | Class

Brokers International Financial Services LLC
102 SE 13th St .... Panora IA 50216 641-755-4635 693
TF: 877-886-1939 ■ *Web:* www.brokersifs.com

Brokers Logistics Ltd
1000 Hawkins Blvd .... El Paso TX 79915 915-778-7751 194
Web: www.brokerslogistics.com

Brokers Worldwide 701C Ashland Ave .... Folcroft PA 19032 610-461-3661 459
TF: 800-624-5287 ■ *Web:* asendiausa.com

Brolite Products Inc 1900 S Pk Ave .... Streamwood IL 60107 630-830-0340 296-42
TF: 888-276-5483 ■ *Web:* www.bakewithbrolite.com

Bromley Communications LLC
401 E Houston St 5th Fl .... San Antonio TX 78205 210-244-2000 4

Bromley Group LLC, The
15 W 26th St 3rd Fl .... New York NY 10010 212-696-1100 195
TF: 800-585-8367 ■ *Web:* tbg-world.com

Bromley Mountain Ski Resort
3984 Vt Rt 11 .... Peru VT 05152 802-824-5522 378
Web: www.bromley.com

Bromma Inc
4400 Ben Franklin Blvd Ste 200 .... Durham NC 27704 919-471-4000 295
Web: www.bromma.com

Bronco Billy's Casino
233 E Bennett Ave .... Cripple Creek CO 80813 719-689-2142 133
TF: 877-989-2142 ■ *Web:* www.broncobillyscasino.com

Bronco Mfg LLC 4953 S 48th W Ave .... Tulsa OK 74107 918-446-7196 539
Web: www.broncomfg.com

Bronco Wine Co 6342 Bystrum Rd .... Ceres CA 95307 209-538-3131 538-2178 80-3
TF: 855-874-2394 ■ *Web:* classicwinesofcalifornia.com

Broncus Medical Inc
1400 N Shoreline Blvd Ste 8 .... Mountain View CA 94043 650-428-1600 371
Web: www.broncus.com

Brondell Inc 1159 Howard St .... San Francisco CA 94103 415-315-9000 320
TF: 888-542-3355 ■ *Web:* brondell.com

Broniec Assoc Inc
4855 Peachtree Industrial Blvd Ste 215 .... Norcross GA 30092 770-729-9664 2
TF: 800-432-8348 ■ *Web:* www.broniec.com

Bronner Bros Inc
2141 Powers Ferry Rd .... Marietta GA 30067 770-988-0015 953-0848 214
TF: 800-241-6151 ■ *Web:* www.bronnerbros.com

Bronson Methodist Hospital
601 John St .... Kalamazoo MI 49007 269-341-7654 374-3
TF: 800-276-6766 ■ *Web:* www.bronsonhealth.com

Bronx Chamber of Commerce
1200 Waters Pl Ste 106 .... Bronx NY 10461 718-828-3900 139
Web: www.bronxmall.com

Bronx Charter School for Excellence
1960 Benedict Ave .... Bronx NY 10462 718-828-7301 685
Web: bronxexcellence.org

Bronx Community College
2155 University Ave .... Bronx NY 10453 718-289-5100 289-6003* 162
**Fax:* Admissions ■ *TF:* 866-888-8777 ■ *Web:* www.bcc.cuny.edu

Bronx Council on the Arts 1738 Hone Ave .... Bronx NY 10461 718-931-9500 409-6445 460
TF: 866-564-5226 ■ *Web:* bronxarts.org

Bronx County 851 Grand Concourse Ste 301 .... Bronx NY 10451 718-590-3500 338
Web: www.nyc.gov

Bronx County Historical Society
3309 Bainbridge Ave .... Bronx NY 10467 718-881-8900 881-4827 520
Web: www.bronxhistoricalsociety.org

Bronx Defenders, The 860 Courtlandt Ave .... Bronx NY 10451 718-838-7878 708
TF: 800-597-7980 ■ *Web:* www.bronxdefenders.org

Bronx Library Ctr 310 E Kings Bridge Rd .... Bronx NY 10458 718-579-4244 930-0983* 434-3
**Fax Area Code:* 212 ■ *TF:* 800-342-3688 ■ *Web:* www.nypl.org

Bronx Museum of the Arts
1040 Grand Concourse .... Bronx NY 10456 718-681-6000 681-6181 520
Web: www.bronxmuseum.org

Bronx Psychiatric Ctr 1500 Waters Pl .... Bronx NY 10461 718-931-0600 862-4858 374-5
TF: 800-597-8481 ■ *Web:* omh.ny.gov

Bronx Zoo 2300 Southern Blvd .... Bronx NY 10460 718-220-5100 823
TF: 800-433-4149 ■ *Web:* www.bronxzoo.com

BronxCare Family Wellness Center
1276 Fulton Ave .... Bronx NY 10456 718-590-1800 374-3
TF: 877-451-9361 ■ *Web:* www.bronxcare.org

Bronze Craft Corp 37 Will St .... Nashua NH 03060 603-883-7747 883-0222 350
TF: 800-488-7747 ■ *Web:* www.bronzecraft.com

Brook Consulting Services Inc
2 Quimby Ln .... Flemington NJ 08822 908-284-9836 196
TF: 800-578-9765 ■ *Web:* brookconsultingservice.com

Brook Environmental & Engineering Corp
11419 Cronridge Dr Ste 10 .... Owings Mills MD 21117 410-356-5073 743
Web: www.carrollcountytimes.com

Brook Farm Veterinary Center
2371 Route 22 .... Patterson NY 12563 845-878-4833 794
TF: 800-388-8255 ■ *Web:* www.brookfarmveterinarycenter.com

Brook Furniture Rental Inc
100 N Field Dr Ste 220 .... Lake Forest IL 60045 847-810-4000 264-2
TF: 877-285-7368 ■ *Web:* www.bfr.com

Brook House 920 Elmridge Ctr Dr .... Rochester NY 14626 585-723-9988 671

Brook Mays Music Co
8605 John Carpenter Fwy .... Dallas TX 75247 214-631-0928 905-4964 526
TF Cust Svc: 800-637-8966 ■ *Web:* www.brookmays.com

Brookdale 111 Westwood Pl Ste 400 .... Brentwood TN 37027 615-221-2250 221-2289 672
TF: 866-785-9025 ■ *Web:* brookdale.com

Brookdale Community College
765 Newman Springs Rd .... Lincroft NJ 07738 732-842-1900 224-2271* 162
**Fax:* Admissions ■ *TF:* 866-767-9512 ■ *Web:* www.brookdalecc.edu

Brookdale Group, The
3455 Peachtree Rd NE Ste 700 .... Atlanta GA 30326 404-364-8080 528
Web: www.brookdalegroup.com

Brookdale Plastics 9909 S Shore Dr .... Plymouth MN 55441 763-797-1000 596
Web: www.brookdaleplastics.com

Brookdale University Hospital & Medical Ctr
1 Brookdale Plaza .... Brooklyn NY 11212 718-240-5000 374-3
Web: www.brookdalehospital.org

Brookdale Westlake Village
28550 Westlake Village Dr .... Westlake OH 44145 440-835-4367 672
TF: 855-308-2432 ■
Web: www.brookdale.com/en/communities/brookdale-westlake-village.html

Brooke Alexander Editions
59 Wooster St .... New York NY 10012 212-925-4338 941-9565 42
Web: www.baeditions.com

Brooke Army Medical Ctr (BAMC)
3551 Roger Brooke Dr .... Fort Sam Houston TX 78234 210-916-4141 374-4
TF: 800-443-2262 ■ *Web:* www.bamc.amedd.army.mil

Brooke Chase Associates Inc
1543 Second St Ste 201 .... Sarasota FL 34236 877-374-0039 721
TF: 877-374-0039 ■ *Web:* www.brookechase.com

Brooke County 632 Main St .... Wellsburg WV 26070 304-737-3661 338
Web: www.brookewv.org

Brooke County Schools
1201 Pleasant Ave .... Wellsburg WV 26070 304-737-3481 780
Web: www.edline.net/pages/brookecountyschools

Brooke Distributors Inc
16250 NW 52nd Ave .... Hialeah FL 33014 305-624-9752 38
TF: 800-275-8792 ■ *Web:* brookedist.com

Brooke Ocean Technology Ltd
461 Windmill Rd .... Dartmouth NS B3A1J9 902-468-2928 261
Web: www.brooke-ocean.com

Brooke Private Equity Associates
20 Custom House St Ste 610 .... Boston MA 02110 617-227-3160 227-4128 401
Web: www.brookepea.com

Brookfield Engineering Lab Inc
11 Commerce Blvd .... Middleboro MA 02346 508-946-6200 946-6262 201
TF: 800-628-8139 ■ *Web:* www.brookfieldengineering.com

Brookfield Fabricating Corp
111 Stanbury Industrial Dr .... Brookfield MO 64628 660-258-2214 480
Web: www.brookfieldfabricating.com

Brookfield Properties Corp (BOP)
181 Bay St Ste 330 .... Toronto ON M5J2T3 416-369-2300 369-2301 655
NYSE: BPO ■ *TF:* 800-387-0825 ■ *Web:* www.brookfieldproperties.com

Brookfield Properties Inc
181 Bay St Ste 330 PO Box 770 .... Toronto ON M5J2T3 416-359-8555 359-8596 655
NYSE: BPO ■ *Web:* www.brookfieldofficepropertiescanada.com

Brookfield Public Library
1900 N Calhoun Rd .... Brookfield WI 53005 262-782-4140 796-6670 434-3
Web: www.ci.brookfield.wi.us/index.aspx?NID=38

Brookfield Zoo 3300 Golf Rd .... Brookfield IL 60513 708-688-8000 823

Brookgreen Gardens
1931 Brookgreen Dr .... Murrells Inlet SC 29576 843-235-6000 235-6039 97
TF: 800-849-1931 ■ *Web:* www.brookgreen.org

Brookhaven at Lexington
1010 Waltham St .... Lexington MA 02421 781-863-9660 672
Web: brookhavenatlexington.org

Brookhaven College
3939 Vly View Ln .... Farmers Branch TX 75244 972-860-4700 860-4886* 162
**Fax:* Admitting ■ *TF:* 800-827-1000 ■ *Web:* www.brookhavencollege.edu

Brookhaven Memorial Hospital Medical Ctr
101 Hospital Rd .... Patchogue NY 11772 631-654-7100 374-3
Web: www.brookhavenhospital.org

Brookhaven National Laboratory (BNL)
PO Box 5000 .... Upton NY 11973 631-344-8000 344-3000 668
Web: www.bnl.gov

Brookhaven School District
326 E Court St .... Brookhaven MS 39601 601-833-6661 833-4154 685
Web: www.brookhaven.k12.ms.us

Brookhaven-Lincoln County Chamber of Commerce
230 S Whitworth Ave .... Brookhaven MS 39601 601-833-1411 833-1412 139
TF: 800-613-4667 ■ *Web:* brookhavenchamber.org

Brookings County 314 Sixth Ave .... Brookings SD 57006 605-696-8205 696-8211 338
Web: www.brookingscountysd.gov

Brookings Institution
1775 Massachusetts Ave NW .... Washington DC 20036 202-797-6000 797-6004 634
TF: 800-275-1447 ■ *Web:* www.brookings.edu

Brookings Public Library
515 Third St .... Brookings SD 57006 605-692-9407 434-3
Web: www.brookingslibrary.org

Brookline Bank PO Box 470469 .... Brookline MA 02445 617-730-3520 360-2
NASDAQ: BRKL ■ *TF Cust Svc:* 877-668-2265 ■ *Web:* www.brooklinebank.com

Brookline Booksmith 279 Harvard St .... Brookline MA 02446 617-566-6660 95
Web: www.brooklinebooksmith.com

Brookline Chamber of Commerce
251 Harvard St Ste 1 .... Brookline MA 02446 617-739-1330 739-1200 139
TF: 800-832-3747 ■ *Web:* www.brooklinechamber.com

Brookline College
2445 W Dunlap Ave Ste 100 .... Phoenix AZ 85021 602-242-6265 685
TF: 800-793-2428 ■ *Web:* brooklinecollege.edu

Brookline Public Library
361 Washington St .... Brookline MA 02445 617-730-2370 434-3
TF: 800-447-8844 ■ *Web:* www.brooklinelibrary.com

Brooklyn Academy of Music (BAM)
30 Lafayette Ave .... Brooklyn NY 11217 718-636-4100 572
Web: www.bam.org

Brooklyn Ascend Charter School
205 Rockaway Pkwy .... Brooklyn NY 11212 718-240-9162 685
Web: www.ascendlearning.org

Brooklyn Botanic Garden
1000 Washington Ave .... Brooklyn NY 11225 718-623-7200 97
Web: www.bbg.org

Brooklyn Bottling Co 643 S Rd .... Milton NY 12547 845-795-2171 296-20

Brooklyn Brewery, The 79 N 11th St .... Brooklyn NY 11211 718-486-7422 486-7440 102
TF: 800-544-1809 ■ *Web:* www.brooklynbrewery.com

Brooklyn Chamber of Commerce
335 Adams St Ste 2700 .... Brooklyn NY 11201 718-875-1000 237-4274 139
Web: www.ibrooklyn.com

Brooklyn College 2900 Bedford Ave .... Brooklyn NY 11210 718-951-5000 951-4506* 166
**Fax:* Admissions ■ *Web:* www.brooklyn.cuny.edu

Brooklyn College Library
2900 Bedford Ave .... Brooklyn NY 11210 718-951-5335 951-4540 434-6
Web: library.brooklyn.cuny.edu

Brooklyn Correctional Institution
59 Hartford Rd .... Brooklyn CT 06234 860-779-2600 213
Web: ct.gov

Brooklyn Ctr for the Performing Arts
PO Box 100843 .... Brooklyn NY 11210 718-951-4600 572
Web: www.brooklyncenter.com

	City	State	ZIP	Phone	Fax	Class
Brooklyn Cyclones						
1904 Surf Ave MCU Pk	Brooklyn	NY	11224	718-449-8497		717
Web: www.brooklyncyclones.com						
Brooklyn Gallery of Coins & Stamps Inc						
8725 Fourth Ave	Brooklyn	NY	11209	718-745-5701	745-2775	711
Web: brooklyngallery.com						
Brooklyn Historical Society						
128 Pierrepont St	Brooklyn	NY	11201	718-222-4111		520
TF: 800-371-3238 ■ *Web:* www.brooklynhistory.org						
Brooklyn Hospital Ctr 121 DeKalb Ave	Brooklyn	NY	11201	718-250-8000		374-3
Web: www.tbh.org						
Brooklyn International Film Festival						
180 S Fourth St Ste 2S	Brooklyn	NY	11211	718-486-8181		282
Web: www.brooklynfilmfestival.org						
Brooklyn Law School 250 Joralemon St	Brooklyn	NY	11201	718-780-7906	780-0395*	167-1
**Fax:* Admissions ■ *Web:* www.brooklaw.edu						
Brooklyn Legal Services Corp						
105 Court St Fl 3	Brooklyn	NY	11201	718-237-5500		428
Web: www.legalservicesnyc.org/our-program/brooklyn						
Brooklyn Museum of Art						
200 Eastern Pkwy	Brooklyn	NY	11238	718-638-5000	501-6136	520
Web: www.brooklynmuseum.org						
Brooklyn Navy Yard Development Corp						
63 Flushing Ave Bldg 292 3rd Fl	Brooklyn	NY	11205	718-907-5900	643-9296	655
TF: 800-339-9113 ■ *Web:* brooklynnavyyard.org						
Brooklyn Products Inc						
171 Wamplers Lake Rd	Brooklyn	MI	49230	517-592-2185		247
Web: www.brooklynproducts.com						
Brooklyn Public Library (BPL)						
496 Franklin Ave	Brooklyn	NY	11238	718-623-0012		434-3
Web: bklynlibrary.org						
Brooklyn Seafood Steak & Oyster House						
1212 Second Ave	Seattle	WA	98101	206-224-7000		671
Web: thebrooklyn.com						
Brooklyn Tabernacle 17 Smith St	Brooklyn	NY	11201	718-290-2000		48-20
Web: www.brooklyntabernacle.org						
Brooklyn-Irish Hills Chamber of Commerce						
131 N Main St PO Box 805	Brooklyn	MI	49230	517-592-8907		139
Web: irishhills.com						
Brookman LLC						
61 Rhode Island Ave NW	Washington	DC	20001	301-515-0450		196
Web: www.brookman.com						
Brookmont Capital Management LLC						
2000 McKinney Ave Ste 1230	Dallas	TX	75201	214-953-0190		401
Web: www.brookmontcapital.com						
Brooks & District Chamber of Commerce						
403-2 Ave W Ste 4	Brooks	AB	T1R1B4	403-362-7641	362-6893	137
Web: www.brookschamber.ab.ca						
Brooks & Sparks Inc 21020 Park Row Dr	Katy	TX	77449	281-578-9595		261
Web: www.brooksandsparks.com						
Brooks and Freund LLC						
5661 Independence Cir Ste 1	Fort Myers	FL	33912	239-939-5251		187
TF: 800-741-3114 ■ *Web:* www.brooksandfreund.com						
Brooks Automation Inc						
15 Elizabeth Dr	Chelmsford	MA	01824	978-262-2400	262-2500	695
NASDAQ: BRKS ■ *TF:* 800-698-6149 ■ *Web:* www.brooks.com						
Brooks Automation Inc Polycold Systems						
3800 Lakeville Hwy	Petaluma	CA	94954	707-769-7000	769-1380	14
TF: 800-698-6149 ■ *Web:* www.brooks.com						
Brooks Borg Skiles Architecture Engineering						
317 Sixth Ave Ste 400	Des Moines	IA	50309	515-244-7167		256
Web: www.bbsae.com						
Brooks Construction Company Inc						
6525 Ardmore Ave	Fort Wayne	IN	46809	260-478-1990		191-2
Web: www.brooks1st.com						
Brooks County 100 E Miller St	Falfurrias	TX	78355	361-325-5604		338
Web: co.brooks.tx.us						
Brooks Elementary School						
3225 Sangamon Dr	Dekalb	IL	60115	815-754-9936		685
Web: www.dist428.org						
Brooks Equipment Company Inc						
10926 David Taylor Dr Ste 300	Charlotte	NC	28269	800-826-3473	433-9265	679
TF: 800-826-3473 ■ *Web:* www.brooksequipment.com						
Brooks Group, The						
10 W 37th St 16th Fl	New York	NY	10018	212-768-0860		195
Web: www.brookspr.com						
Brooks Harbour & Assoc Inc						
9342 Lindale Ave	Baton Rouge	LA	70815	225-927-7430		256
Web: www.arthursrestaurant.com						
Brooks Instrument LLC 407 W Vine St	Hatfield	PA	19440	215-362-3500		407
TF: 800-950-2468 ■ *Web:* www.brooksinstrument.com						
Brooks International Speakers Bureau						
763 Santa Fe Dr	Denver	CO	80204	303-825-8700		708
TF: 800-713-7278 ■ *Web:* www.brooksinternational.com						
Brooks Lake Lodge & Guest Ranch						
458 Brooks Lake Rd	Dubois	WY	82513	866-213-4022		239
TF: 866-213-4022 ■ *Web:* www.brookslake.com						
Brooks Memorial Hospital						
529 Central Ave	Dunkirk	NY	14048	716-366-1111		374-3
TF: 800-366-0717 ■ *Web:* www.brookshospital.org						
Brooks Memorial State Park						
2465 Hwy 97	Goldendale	WA	98620	509-773-4611		565
Web: www.parks.wa.gov						
Brooks Mfg Co 2120 Pacific St	Bellingham	WA	98229	360-733-1700	734-6668	818
TF: 800-843-7657 ■ *Web:* www.brooksmfg.com						
Brooks Mo (Rep R - AL)						
2400 Rayburn HOB	Washington	DC	20515	202-225-4801		342-2
Web: brooks.house.gov						
Brooks Rand Labs LLC						
18804 N Crk Pkwy Ste 100	Bothell	WA	98011	206-632-6206		743
Web: brooksapplied.com						
Brooks Resources Corp						
409 NW Franklin Ave	Bend	OR	97701	541-382-1662	385-3285	653
TF: 877-475-9779 ■ *Web:* brooksresources.com						
Brooks School						
1160 Great Pond Rd	North Andover	MA	01845	978-725-6300		622
Web: www.brooksschool.org						

	City	State	ZIP	Phone	Fax	Class
Brooks Sports Inc						
19910 N Creek Pkwy Ste 200	Bothell	WA	98011	800-227-6657		301
TF: 800-227-6657 ■ *Web:* www.brooksrunning.com						
Brooks Stevens & Pope P A						
5121 Kingdom Way Ste 300	Raleigh	NC	27607	919-481-9103		445
Web: www.bsp-pa.com						
Brooks Susan W (Rep R - IN)						
1505 Longworth Bldg	Washington	DC	20515	202-225-2276	225-0016	342-2
Web: susanwbrooks.house.gov						
Brooks Tropicals Inc						
18400 SW 256th St PO Box 900160	Homestead	FL	33090	305-247-3544	246-5827*	315-4
**Fax:* Sales ■ *TF:* 800-327-4833 ■ *Web:* www.brookstropicals.com						
Brooks Utility Products Group						
23847 Industrial Park Dr	Farmington Hills	MI	48335	248-477-0250		639
TF: 888-687-3008 ■ *Web:* www.brooksutility.com						
Brooks, McGinnis & Company LLC						
2 Premier Plaza 5607 Glenridge Dr Ste 650	Atlanta	GA	30342	404-531-4940		2
Web: brooksmcginnis.com						
Brooks, Pierce, McLendon, Humphrey & Leonard LLP						
230 N Elm St Ste 2000	Greensboro	NC	27401	336-373-8850		428
Web: www.brookspierce.com						
Brooksfilms Ltd						
9336 W Washington Blvd	Culver City	CA	90232	310-202-3292		514
Brookshire Bros Ltd						
1201 Ellen Trout Dr	Lufkin	TX	75904	936-634-8155	279-3374*	345
**Fax Area Code:* 979 ■ *TF:* 855-467-7837 ■ *Web:* www.brookshirebrothers.com						
Brookshire Grocery Co						
1600 W SW Loop 323	Tyler	TX	75701	903-534-3000		345
Web: brookshires.com						
Brookshire Suites 120 E Lombard St	Baltimore	MD	21202	410-625-1300		379
TF: 855-345-5033 ■ *Web:* www.brookshiresuites.com						
Brookside by Day 3313 S Peoria Ave	Tulsa	OK	74105	918-745-9989		671
Web: brooksidebyday.com						
Brookside Equipment 7707 Mosley Rd	Houston	TX	77017	713-943-7100		755
Web: www.brooksideusa.com						
Brookside Gardens 1800 Glenallan Ave	Wheaton	MD	20902	301-962-1400	962-7878	97
TF: 800-366-2012 ■ *Web:* www.montgomeryparks.org						
Brookside Inn 1297 S Perry St	Castle Rock	CO	80104	303-688-2500		379
Web: www.bsmc.com						
Brookside Lumber & Supply Co						
500 Logan Rd PO Box 327	Bethel Park	PA	15102	412-835-7610	835-8672	191-3
Web: www.brooksidelumber.com						
Brookside Resort 463 E Pkwy	Gatlinburg	TN	37738	865-436-5611		669
TF: 800-251-9597 ■ *Web:* brooksideresort.com						
Brooks-Jeffrey Computer Store						
19 Medical Plaza	Mountain Home	AR	72653	870-425-8064		175
TF: 800-506-8064 ■ *Web:* www.bjmweb.com						
Brooks-ransom Assoc						
7415 N Palm Ave Ste 100	Fresno	CA	93711	559-449-8444		256
Web: www.brooksransom.com						
Brookstone Capital Management						
1745 S Naperville Rd Ste 200	Wheaton	IL	60189	630-653-1400		194
Web: www.brookstonecm.com						
Brookstone Inc 1 Innovation Way	Merrimack	NH	03054	866-576-7337		327
TF Cust Svc: 800-846-3000 ■ *Web:* www.brookstone.com						
Brookstone LP 3715 Dacoma St	Houston	TX	77092	713-683-8800	680-0088	186
Web: www.brookstone-tx.com						
Brookstown Inn						
200 Brookstown Ave	Winston-Salem	NC	27101	336-725-1120	773-0147	379
TF: 800-845-4262 ■ *Web:* www.brookstowninn.com						
Brookstreet Hotel 525 Legget Dr	Ottawa	ON	K2K2W2	613-271-1800		379
TF: 888-826-2220 ■ *Web:* www.brookstreethotel.com						
Brooksville Regional Hospital						
17240 Cortez Blvd	Brooksville	FL	34601	352-796-5111		374-3
Web: bayfrontbrooksville.com						
Brookville Lake PO Box 100	Brookville	IN	47012	765-647-2657		565
Web: www.in.gov						
Brookwood Companies Inc						
485 Madison Ave Ste 500	New York	NY	10022	212-551-0100	472-0294*	594
**Fax Area Code:* 646 ■ *Web:* www.brookwoodcos.net						
Brookwood Laminating 275 Putnam Rd	Wauregan	CT	06387	860-774-5001	774-5002	745-2
TF: 800-247-6658 ■ *Web:* www.brookwoodcos.com						
Brookwood Middle School						
1020 Hunters Ridge Dr	Genoa City	WI	53128	262-279-1053		685
TF: 800-774-7778 ■ *Web:* www.genoacityschools.org						
Brookwood Program Management LLC						
1819 Peachtree Rd NE Ste 501	Atlanta	GA	30309	404-350-9988	605-8906	463
Web: www.brookwoodpm.com						
Broom Street Theatre						
1119 Williamson St	Madison	WI	53703	608-244-8338		572
TF: 800-745-3000 ■ *Web:* bstonline.org						
Broome Community College						
901 Front St	Binghamton	NY	13905	607-778-5000	778-5442*	162
**Fax:* Admissions ■ *TF:* 800-836-0689 ■ *Web:* www.sunybroome.edu						
Broome County 44 Hawley St	Binghamton	NY	13901	607-778-2451	778-2243	338
Web: www.gobroomecounty.com						
Broome County Veterans Memorial Arena						
1 Stuart St	Binghamton	NY	13901	607-778-1528		720
Web: broomearenaforum.com						
Broome Employment Center						
171 Frnt St	Binghamton	NY	13905	607-778-2136		260
TF: 800-522-4369 ■ *Web:* www.broometiogaworks.com						
Broomfield Colorado						
1 DesCombes Dr	Broomfield	CO	80020	303-469-3301	438-6296	338
Web: www.ci.broomfield.co.us						
Broomfield Chamber of Commerce						
105 Edgeview Dr Ste 410	Denver	CO	80021	303-466-1775	466-4481	139
Web: www.broomfieldchamber.com						
Bros & Co 4860 S Lewis Ave	Tulsa	OK	74105	918-743-8822		4
Web: www.broco.com						
Brose North America Inc						
3933 Automation Ave	Auburn Hills	MI	48326	248-339-4000	339-4099	360-3
Web: www.brose.com						
Bro-Tex Inc 800 Hampden Ave	Saint Paul	MN	55114	651-645-5721	646-1876	508
TF: 800-328-2282 ■ *Web:* www.brotex.com						
Brother International Corp						
100 Somerset Corporate Blvd	Bridgewater	NJ	08807	908-704-1700	704-8235	111
TF Cust Svc: 877-552-6255 ■ *Web:* www.brother-usa.com						

Phone | Fax | Class

Brother Sebastian's Steak House
1350 S 119th St — Omaha NE 68144 — 402-330-0300 — 330-4814 — 671
Web: www.brothersebastians.com

Brother's Brother Foundation (BBF)
1200 Galveston Ave — Pittsburgh PA 15233 — 412-321-3160 — 321-3325 — 48-5
TF: 800-435-7352 ■ *Web:* www.brothersbrother.org

Brotherhood Bank & Trust
756 Minnesota Ave — Kansas City MO 66101 — 913-321-4242 — 70
TF: 855-522-6722 ■ *Web:* www.brotherhoodbank.com

Brotherhood Mutual Insurance Co (BMI)
6400 Brotherhood Way PO Box 2589 — Fort Wayne IN 46825 — 800-333-3735 — 391-4
TF Cust Svc: 800-333-3735 ■ *Web:* www.brotherhoodmutual.com

Brotherhood of Locomotive Engineers & Trainmen (BLET)
1370 Ontario St Mezzanine Level — Cleveland OH 44113 — 216-241-2630 — 241-6516 — 414
TF: 877-772-5772 ■ *Web:* www.ble-t.org

Brotherhood of Maintenance of Way Employees (BMWED)
41475 Gardenbrook Rd — Novi MI 48375 — 248-662-2660 — 662-2659 — 414
Web: www.bmwe.org/default.aspx

Brotherhood of Railroad Signalmen
917 Shenandoah Shores Rd — Front Royal VA 22630 — 540-622-6522 — 622-6532 — 49-21
Web: www.brs.org

Brotherhood Winery
100 Brotherhood Plaza Dr PO Box 190 — Washingtonville NY 10992 — 845-496-3661 — 80-3
TF: 800-724-3960 ■ *Web:* www.brotherhood-winery.com

Brothers Inc 1000 Sussex Blvd — Broomall PA 19008 — 610-328-0670 — 328-6218 — 189-4
TF: 866-276-7462 ■ *Web:* brotherselectric.com

Brothers Produce Inc 3173 Produce Row — Houston TX 77023 — 713-924-4196 — 921-3060 — 297-7
Web: www.brothersproduce.com

Brothers Property Corp
2 Alhambra Plaza Ste 1280 — Coral Gables FL 33134 — 305-285-1035 — 653
Web: www.brothersproperty.com

Brotman Financial Group Inc
16 Greenmeadow Dr Ste 201 — Timonium MD 21093 — 410-252-4555 — 528
Web: www.brotmanfinancial.com

Brotman Medical Center
3828 Delmas Terr — Culver City CA 90232 — 310-836-7000 — 374-3

Broudy Precision Equipment Co
9 Union Hill Rd — West Conshohocken PA 19428 — 610-825-7200 — 111
Web: www.broudyprecision.com

Broughton Foods 1701 Green St — Marietta OH 45750 — 740-373-4121 — 296-27
TF: 800-303-3400 ■ *Web:* www.broughtonfoods.com

Broughton Hospital
1000 S Sterling St — Morganton NC 28655 — 828-433-2111 — 374-5
Web: ncdhhs.gov

Broussard Bros Inc
25817 Louisiana Hwy 333 — Abbeville LA 70510 — 337-893-5303 — 264-3
TF: 800-299-5303 ■ *Web:* www.broussardbrothers.com

Broussard's Restaurant
819 Rue Conti — New Orleans LA 70112 — 504-581-3866 — 581-3873 — 671
Web: www.broussards.com

Broward Community College
Central 3501 SW Davie Rd — Davie FL 33314 — 954-201-7350 — 162
Web: www.broward.edu
Downtown Ctr
111 E Las Olas Blvd — Fort Lauderdale FL 33301 — 954-201-7350 — 201-7466* — 162
**Fax:* Admissions ■ *TF:* 888-654-6482 ■ *Web:* www.broward.edu
North 1000 Coconut Creek Blvd — Coconut Creek FL 33066 — 954-201-2240 — 201-2242* — 162
**Fax:* Admissions ■ *TF:* 888-654-6482 ■ *Web:* www.broward.edu
Pines 16957 Sheridan St — Pembroke Pines FL 33331 — 954-201-3601 — 201-3614 — 162
Web: www.broward.edu/locations/pines
South
7200 Hollywood/Pines Blvd — Pembroke Pines FL 33024 — 954-201-8835 — 201-8060* — 162
**Fax:* Admissions ■ *Web:* www.broward.edu

Broward County
115 S Andrews Ave Rm 409 — Fort Lauderdale FL 33301 — 954-357-7000 — 338
Web: www.broward.org

Broward County Chamber of Commerce
2425 E Commercial Blvd #103 — Fort Lauderdale FL 33308 — 954-565-5750 — 139
Web: www.browardbiz.com

Broward County Historical Commission
151 SW Second St — Fort Lauderdale FL 33301 — 954-765-4670 — 765-4437 — 520
TF: 866-682-2258 ■ *Web:* www.broward.org

Broward County Library
100 S Andrews Ave — Fort Lauderdale FL 33301 — 954-357-7444 — 434-3
TF: 800-266-2278 ■ *Web:* www.broward.org/library/pages/default.aspx

Broward County Public Schools
600 SE Third Ave — Fort Lauderdale FL 33301 — 754-321-0000 — 321-2701 — 685
Web: www.browardschools.com

Broward Ctr for the Performing Arts
201 SW Fifth Ave — Fort Lauderdale FL 33312 — 954-462-0222 — 572
Web: www.browardcenter.org

Broward Fire Equipment & Service Inc
101 SW Sixth St — Fort Lauderdale FL 33301 — 954-467-6625 — 467-6640 — 679
TF: 800-866-3473 ■ *Web:* www.browardfire.com

Brower Mechanical Inc 4060 Alvis Ct — Rocklin CA 95677 — 916-624-0808 — 610
TF: 877-816-6649 ■ *Web:* www.browermechanical.com

Brown & Bigelow Inc
345 Plato Blvd E — Saint Paul MN 55107 — 651-293-7000 — 9
TF Cust Svc: 800-628-1755 ■ *Web:* www.brownandbigelow.com

Brown & Brown Agency of Insurance Professionals Inc
208 N Mill — Pryor OK 74361 — 918-825-3295 — 390
Web: www.bbinsurance.com

Brown & Brown Inc
220 S Ridgewood Ave — Daytona Beach FL 32114 — 386-252-9601 — 390
NYSE: BRO ■ *Web:* www.bbinsurance.com

Brown & Brown Insurance PO Box 1718 — Tacoma WA 98401 — 253-396-5500 — 396-4500 — 391-4
TF: 800-562-8171 ■ *Web:* www.bbtacoma.com

Brown & Caldwell Consulting Engineers
201 N Civic Dr Ste 115 — Walnut Creek CA 94596 — 925-937-9010 — 937-9026 — 261
TF: 800-727-2224 ■ *Web:* www.brownandcaldwell.com

Brown & Charbonneau LLP
420 Exchange Ste 270 — Irvine CA 92602 — 714-505-3000 — 428
Web: bc-llp.com

Brown & Connery LLP 360 Haddon Ave — Westmont NJ 08108 — 856-854-8900 — 428
TF: 800-447-5375 ■ *Web:* brownconnery.com

Brown & Haley PO Box 1596 — Tacoma WA 98401 — 800-426-8400 — 296-8
TF: 800-426-8400 ■ *Web:* www.brown-haley.com

Brown & Michaels
400 M T Bank Bldg Ste 400 — Ithaca NY 14850 — 607-256-2000 — 428
Web: www.bpmlegal.com

Brown & Miller Racing Solutions LLC
4005 Dearborn Pl NW — Concord NC 28027 — 704-793-4319 — 57
Web: www.bmrs.net

Brown & Saenger
711 W Russell St PO Box 84040 — Sioux Falls SD 57118 — 605-336-1960 — 332-0963 — 320
TF: 800-952-3509 ■ *Web:* www.brown-saenger.com

Brown & Streza LLP 40 Pacifica 15th Fl — Irvine CA 92618 — 949-453-2900 — 41
Web: www.brownandstreza.com

Brown Anthony (Rep D - MD)
1505 Longworth HOB — Washington DC 20515 — 202-225-8699 — 342-2
Web: anthonybrown.house.gov

Brown Armstrong Accountancy Corp
4200 Truxtun Ave Ste 300 — Bakersfield CA 93309 — 661-324-4971 — 2
Web: www.bacpas.com

Brown Automotive Group LP
4300 S Georgia — Amarillo TX 79110 — 806-353-7211 — 57
TF: 888-388-6728 ■ *Web:* smallerprofit.com

Brown Bros Harriman & Co
140 Broadway — New York NY 10005 — 212-483-1818 — 70
Web: www.bbh.com

Brown Brown & Associates PA
551 Ave K SE — Winter Haven FL 33880 — 863-299-1500 — 299-7599 — 2
Web: ronaldbrowncpa.com

Brown Bus Co 2111 E Sherman Ave — Nampa ID 83686 — 208-466-4181 — 466-2861 — 109
TF: 800-574-1580 ■ *Web:* www.brownbuscompany.com

Brown Coach Inc 50 Venner Rd — Amsterdam NY 12010 — 518-843-4700 — 843-3600 — 107
TF: 800-424-4700 ■ *Web:* www.browntours.com

Brown College of Court Reporting & Medical Transcription (BCCR)
1900 Emery St NW Ste 200 — Atlanta GA 30318 — 404-876-1227 — 876-4415 — 800
TF: 800-849-0703 ■ *Web:* www.bccr.edu

Brown County 25 Market St Ste 1 — Aberdeen SD 57401 — 605-626-7105 — 626-4010 — 338
Web: www.brown.sd.us

Brown County
800 Mt Orab Pike Ste 101 — Georgetown OH 45121 — 937-378-3956 — 378-6324 — 338
Web: www.browncountyohio.gov

Brown County 305 E Walnut Ste 120 — Green Bay WI 54301 — 920-448-4016 — 448-4498 — 338
TF: 800-362-9082 ■ *Web:* www.co.brown.wi.us

Brown County 601 Oregon St — Hiawatha KS 66434 — 785-742-2581 — 742-7705 — 338
Web: ks-brown.manatron.com

Brown County 200 Ct St Rm 4 — Mount Sterling IL 62353 — 217-773-2713 — 773-3648 — 338
Web: www.illinoiscourts.gov

Brown County PO Box 85 — Nashville IN 47448 — 812-988-0234 — 338
Web: thebrowncountychamber.org

Brown County 14 S State St PO Box 248 — New Ulm MN 56073 — 507-233-6600 — 359-1430 — 338
Web: www.co.brown.mn.us

Brown County Chamber of Commerce
PO Box 21606 — Georgetown OH 45121 — 937-378-4784 — 378-1634 — 139
Web: www.browncountyohiochamber.com

Brown County Convention & Visitors Bureau
10 N Van Buren St PO Box 840 — Nashville IN 47448 — 812-988-7303 — 206
TF: 800-753-3255 ■ *Web:* www.browncounty.com

Brown County Court 148 W Fourth St — Ainsworth NE 69210 — 402-387-2864 — 382-3374 — 338
Web: supremecourt.nebraska.gov

Brown County Inn 51 State Rd 46 — Nashville IN 47448 — 812-988-2291 — 379
TF: 800-772-5249 ■ *Web:* www.browncountyinn.com

Brown County Library 515 Pine St — Green Bay WI 54301 — 920-448-4400 — 434-3
Web: www.co.brown.wi.us

Brown County Rural Electric Assn
24386 State Hwy 4 PO Box 529 — Sleepy Eye MN 56085 — 507-794-3331 — 794-4282 — 245
TF: 800-658-2368 ■ *Web:* www.browncountyrea.coop

Brown County State Park
1405 State Rd 46 W PO Box 608 — Nashville IN 47448 — 812-988-6406 — 565
Web: www.in.gov

Brown Dairy Equipment
6500 W Gerwoude Dr — Mc Bain MI 49657 — 231-825-4144 — 429
Web: browndairyequip.com

Brown Dog Cafe 5893 Pfeiffer Rd — Cincinnati OH 45242 — 513-794-1610 — 671
Web: www.browndogcafe.com

Brown Edmund G. Jr. (D)
State Capitol Bldg Ste 1173 — Sacramento CA 95814 — 916-445-2841 — 558-3160 — 343
Web: gov.ca.gov

Brown Foundation Inc 2217 Welch St — Houston TX 77019 — 713-523-6867 — 523-2917 — 305
Web: www.brownfoundation.org

Brown Gibbons Lang & Co LLC
1375 E Ninth St Ste 2500 — Cleveland OH 44114 — 216-241-2800 — 241-7417 — 403
Web: www.bglco.com

Brown Graham & Company PC
7431 Continental Pkwy — Amarillo TX 79114 — 806-355-8241 — 2
Web: www.bgc-cpa.com

Brown Greer PLC 115 S 15th St — Richmond VA 23219 — 804-521-7200 — 445
Web: browngreer.com

Brown Hay & Stephens PO Box 2459 — Springfield IL 62705 — 217-544-8491 — 445
Web: www.bhslaw.com

Brown Hotel, The 335 W Broadway St — Louisville KY 40202 — 502-583-1234 — 379
TF: 888-888-5252 ■ *Web:* www.brownhotel.com

Brown Industries Inc
205 W Industrial Blvd — Dalton GA 30720 — 706-277-1977 — 627
TF: 800-241-4698 ■ *Web:* www.brownind.com

Brown International Corporation LLC
333 Ave M NW — Winter Haven FL 33881 — 863-299-2111 — 296
Web: www.brown-intl.com

Brown Investment Advisory & Trust Co
901 S Bond St Ste 400 — Baltimore MD 21231 — 410-537-5400 — 401
TF: 800-645-3923 ■ *Web:* www.brownadvisory.com

Brown Jordan Co 9860 Gidley St — El Monte CA 91731 — 800-743-4252 — 319-4
TF: 800-743-4252 ■ *Web:* www.brownjordan.com

Brown Kate (D)
900 Court St N State Capitol Bldg Rm 160 — Salem OR 97301 — 503-378-4582 — 378-8970 — 343
Web: www.oregon.gov/gov/pages/index.aspx

Brown Ken J Realtors
1618 S Western St — Amarillo TX 79106 — 806-352-5617 — 652

Brown Machine LLC 330 N Ross St — Beaverton MI 48612 — 989-435-7741 — 146
TF: 877-702-4142 ■ *Web:* www.brown-machine.com

Brown Mackie College
Fort Wayne 3000 E Coliseum Blvd — Fort Wayne IN 46805 — 260-484-4400 — 484-2678 — 800
TF General: 866-433-2289 ■ *Web:* www.brownmackie.edu

				Phone	Fax	Class
Merrillville						
1000 E 80th Pl Ste 205M	Merrillville	IN	46410	219-769-3321	738-1076	800
TF: 800-258-3321 ■ *Web:* www.brownmackie.edu						
South Bend 3454 Douglas Rd	South Bend	IN	46635	574-237-0774	237-3585	800
TF: 800-743-2447 ■ *Web:* www.brownmackie.edu						
Brown Mackie College Akron						
755 White Pond Dr	Akron	OH	44320	330-869-3600	869-3650	800
TF: 800-799-7387 ■ *Web:* www.brownmackie.edu						
Brown Mackie College Atlanta						
4370 Peachtree Rd NE	Atlanta	GA	30319	404-799-4500		800
TF: 877-479-8419 ■ *Web:* www.brownmackie.edu						
Brown Mackie College Bettendorf						
2119 E Kimberly Rd	Bettendorf	IA	52722	563-344-1500		800
TF: 888-420-1652 ■ *Web:* www.brownmackie.edu						
Brown Mackie College Canton						
4300 Munson Ave NW	North Canton	OH	44718	330-494-1214	494-8112	800
Web: www.brownmackie.edu						
Brown Mackie College Cincinnati						
1011 Glendale-Milford Rd	Cincinnati	OH	45215	513-771-2424	771-3413	800
Web: www.brownmackie.edu						
Brown Mackie College Findlay						
1700 Fostoria Ave Ste 100	Findlay	OH	45840	419-423-2211	423-0725	800
TF: 800-842-3687 ■ *Web:* www.brownmackie.edu						
Brown Mackie College Hopkinsville						
4001 Ft Campbell Blvd	Hopkinsville	KY	42240	270-886-1302	886-3544	800
TF: 800-359-4753 ■ *Web:* www.brownmackie.edu						
Brown Mackie College Lenexa						
9705 Lenexa Dr	Lenexa	KS	66215	913-768-1900	495-9555	800
TF: 800-635-9101 ■ *Web:* www.brownmackie.edu						
Brown Mackie College Louisville						
3605 Fern Valley Rd	Louisville	KY	40219	502-968-7191	357-9956	800
TF: 800-999-7387 ■ *Web:* www.brownmackie.edu						
Brown Mackie College Miami						
3700 Lakeside Dr	Miramar	FL	33027	305-341-6600		800
TF: 866-505-0335 ■ *Web:* www.brownmackie.edu						
Brown Mackie College Northern Kentucky						
309 Buttermilk Pk	Fort Mitchell	KY	41017	859-341-5627		800
TF: 800-888-1445 ■ *Web:* www.brownmackie.edu						
Brown Mackie College Salina						
2106 S Ninth St	Salina	KS	67401	785-825-5422		800
TF: 800-365-0433 ■ *Web:* www.brownmackie.edu/salina.aspx						
Brown Mackie College Tucson						
4585 E Speedway Blvd Ste 204	Tucson	AZ	85712	520-319-3300		800
TF: 800-727-4161 ■ *Web:* www.brownmackie.edu						
Brown Medical School						
222 Richmond St 1st Fl	Providence	RI	02912	401-863-2149	863-5096	167-2
Web: brown.edu						
Brown Mfg Corp 6001 E Hwy 27	Ozark	AL	36360	800-633-8909	795-3029*	273
**Fax Area Code:* 334 ■ *TF:* 800-633-8909 ■ *Web:* www.brownmfgcorp.com						
Brown Packing Company Inc						
116 Willis St	Gaffney	SC	29341	864-489-5723		296-26
Brown Packing Company Inc						
1 Dutch Vly Dr	South Holland	IL	60473	708-849-7990		10-3
Brown Palace Hotel 321 17th St	Denver	CO	80202	303-297-3111		379
TF: 800-321-2599 ■ *Web:* www.brownpalace.com						
Brown Parker & Demarinis Adv Inc						
1825 NW Corporate Blvd Ste 250	Boca Raton	FL	33431	888-527-3226		4
TF: 888-527-3226 ■ *Web:* bpdadvertising.com						
Brown Precision Inc 90 Shields Rd	Huntsville	AL	35811	256-746-0533		21
Web: www.brownprecisioninc.com						
Brown Produce Co IL 37	Farina	IL	62838	618-245-3301		619
Brown Room at Congress Hall						
251 Beach Ave	Cape May	NJ	08204	609-884-8421		377
Web: www.caperesorts.com						
Brown Schultz Sheridan & Fritz						
210 Grandview Ave	Camp Hill	PA	17011	717-761-7171		2
Web: bssf.com						
Brown Sherrod (Sen D - OH)						
713 Hart Bldg	Washington	DC	20510	202-224-2315	228-6321	342-2
Web: www.brown.senate.gov						
Brown Smith Wallace LLC						
6 Cityplace Dr Ste 900	St Louis	MO	63141	314-983-1200		390
Web: bswllc.com						
Brown Sprinkler Corp						
4705 Pinewood Rd	Louisville	KY	40218	502-968-6274		189-10
Web: www.brownsprinkler.com						
Brown Stove Works Inc						
1422 Carolina Ave	Cleveland	TN	37320	423-476-6544	476-6599	36
TF All: 800-251-7485 ■ *Web:* www.brownstoveworksinc.com						
Brown Sugar Cafe 1033 Commonwealth Ave	Boston	MA	02215	617-787-4242		671
Web: www.brownsugarcafe.com						
Brown Swiss Cattle Breeders Assn of the USA						
800 Pleasant St	Beloit	WI	53511	608-365-4474	365-5577	48-2
Web: www.brownswissusa.com						
Brown &Tedstrom Inc						
1700 Broadway Ste 500	Denver	CO	80290	303-863-7231		401
TF: 800-883-9361 ■ *Web:* www.brown-tedstrom.com						
Brown University 45 Prospect St	Providence	RI	02912	401-863-2378	863-9300*	166
**Fax:* Admissions ■ *Web:* www.brown.edu						
Brown University						
Sheridan Center for Teaching & Learning, The						
201 Thayer St Seventh Fl PO Box 1912	Providence	RI	02912	401-863-1219	863-6976	434-1
Web: www.brown.edu						
Brown University Rockefeller Library						
10 Prospect St	Providence	RI	02912	401-863-2165	863-1272	434-6
Web: www.brown.edu						
Brown Vs Board of Education National Historic Site						
1515 SE Monroe St	Topeka	KS	66612	785-354-4273	354-7213	564
Web: www.nps.gov						
Brown Wood Preserving Company Inc						
6201 Camp Ground Rd	Louisville	KY	40216	502-448-2337	448-9944	818
TF: 800-537-1765 ■ *Web:* www.bwpole.com						
Brown Wood Products Co						
7040 N Lawndale Ave	Lincolnwood	IL	60712	800-328-5858	884-0423	820
TF: 800-328-5858 ■ *Web:* www.brownwoodinc.com						
Brown's Bakery 1226 Versailles Rd	Lexington	KY	40508	859-225-8400		296-1
Web: www.brownbakery.com						
Brown's Cleaners						
1223 Montana Ave	Santa Monica	CA	90403	310-451-8531		426
Brown's Wharf Inn						
121 Atlantic Ave	Boothbay Harbor	ME	04538	207-633-5440	633-5440	379
TF: 800-334-8110 ■ *Web:* www.brownswharfinn.com						
Brown, Garganese, Weiss & D'Agresta PA						
111 N Orange Ave Ste 2000	Orlando	FL	32802	407-425-9566		428
Web: www.orlandolaw.net						
Brown-Atchison Electric Co-op Assn Inc						
1712 Central Ave PO Box 230	Horton	KS	66439	785-486-2117		245
Web: www.baelectric.com						
Brownback Sam (R)						
300 SW Tenth Ave ÿ Ste 212S	Topeka	KS	66612	785-296-3232	296-7973	343
Web: www.governor.ks.gov						
Browne & Co 100 Esna Pk Dr	Markham	ON	L3R1E3	905-475-6104		300
TF: 866-306-3672 ■ *Web:* www.browneco.com						
Browne & Miller Literary Assoc LLC						
52 Village Pl	Hinsdale	IL	60521	312-922-3063		444
Web: www.browneandmiller.com						
Browne Academy 5917 Telegraph Rd	Alexandria	VA	22310	703-960-3000		685
Web: www.browneacademy.org						
Browne-Halco Inc						
788 Morris Tpke Ste 202	Short Hills	NJ	07078	973-232-1065		300
TF: 888-289-1005 ■ *Web:* www.halco.com						
Brownell & Company Inc						
423 E Haddam-Moodus Rd	Moodus	CT	06469	860-873-8625	873-1944	208
Web: www.brownellco.com						
Brownell World Travel						
216 Summit Blvd Ste 220	Birmingham	AL	35243	205-802-6222		771
TF: 800-999-3960 ■ *Web:* www.brownelltravel.com						
Brownfields Capital LLC						
1125 17th St Ste 2350	Denver	CO	80202	303-534-2100		528
Brown-Forman 850 Dixie Hwy	Louisville	KY	40210	502-585-1100	774-7188	185
NYSE: BFB ■ *TF:* 800-831-9146 ■ *Web:* www.brown-forman.com						
Brownie Baker, The						
4870 W Jacquelyn Ave	Fresno	CA	93722	559-277-7070		297-8
Web: www.browniebaker.com						
Browning Arms Co 1 Browning Pl	Morgan	UT	84050	801-876-2711		229
Web: www.browning.com						
Browning Equipment Inc						
800 E Main St	Purcellville	VA	20132	540-338-7123	338-5835	274
Web: www.browningequipment.com						
Browning Kaleczyc Berry and Hoven P C						
800 N Last Chance Gulch Ste 101	Helena	MT	59601	406-443-6820		445
Web: www.bkbh.com						
Browning Phyllis Co						
14855 Blanco Rd	San Antonio	TX	78209	210-408-2500		463
Web: www.phyllisbrowning.com						
Browning School Inc 52 E 62nd St	New York	NY	10065	212-838-6280	355-5602	685
Web: www.browning.edu						
Brownlee Distributing Company Inc						
34401 Groesbeck Hwy	Clinton Twp	MI	48035	586-792-9100		54
Web: bdcfederated.com						
Brownlee Fryett 396 11th Ave SW Fl 7	Calgary	AB	T2R0C5	403-232-8408		428
Web: www.brownleelaw.com						
Brownley Julia (Rep D - CA)						
1019 Longworth Bldg	Washington	DC	20515	202-225-5811	225-1100	342-2
Web: juliabrownley.house.gov						
Brownlie & Braden LLC						
2820 Ross Tower 500 N Akard	Dallas	TX	75201	214-219-4650		194
TF: 888-339-4650 ■ *Web:* www.brownliebraden.com						
Browns Corner Short Stop						
5550 Auburn Way S	Auburn	WA	98092	253-833-7185		297-8
Web: 76.com						
Browns Medical Imaging 9880 Pflumm Rd	Lenexa	KS	66215	913-888-0710		475
Web: www.brownsmedicalimaging.com						
Brownstein Group Inc						
215 S Broad St	Philadelphia	PA	19107	215-735-3470		7
Web: m.brownsteingroup.com						
Brownstone Furniture						
3435 Regatta Blvd	Richmond	CA	94804	510-236-0703		321
Web: brownstonefurniture.com						
Brownstone House 351 W Broadway	Paterson	NJ	07522	973-595-8582		671
Web: www.thebrownstone.com						
Brownstone Real Estate Co						
1840 Fishburn Rd	Hershey	PA	17033	717-533-6222		652
TF: 877-533-6222 ■ *Web:* www.brwnstone.com						
Brownstown Electric Supply Company Inc						
690 E State Rd 250 PO Box L	Brownstown	IN	47220	812-358-4555	358-2484	787
TF: 800-742-8492 ■ *Web:* www.brownstown.com						
Brown-Strauss Steel 2495 Uravan St	Aurora	CO	80011	303-371-2200		492
TF Sales: 800-677-2778 ■ *Web:* www.brown-strauss.com						
Brownsville Area School Dist						
5 Falcon Dr	Brownsville	PA	15417	724-785-2021	785-4333	685
Web: www.basd.org						
Brownsville Chamber of Commerce						
1600 University Blvd	Brownsville	TX	78520	956-542-4341	504-3348	139
Web: www.brownsvillechamber.com						
Brownsville City Hall						
1001 E Elizabeth St	Brownsville	TX	78520	956-548-6000	546-4021	337
Web: www.cob.us						
Brownsville Convention & Visitors Bureau						
650 Ruben M Torres Sr Blvd	Brownsville	TX	78521	956-546-3721		206
TF: 800-626-2639 ■ *Web:* brownsville.org						
Brownsville Herald, The						
1135 E Van Buren St	Brownsville	TX	78520	956-542-4301	542-0840	532-2
TF: 800-488-4301 ■ *Web:* www.brownsvilleherald.com						
Brownsville Independent School District						
1900 E Price Rd	Brownsville	TX	78521	956-548-8000	548-8019	685
Web: www.bisd.us						
Brownsville Public Library						
4320 Southmost Rd	Brownsville	TX	78521	956-548-1055	548-0684	434-3
Web: www.bpl.us						
Browntown-Cadiz Springs State Recreation Area						
PO Box 36	Browntown	WI	53522	608-966-3777		565
Web: www.cadizsprings.com						
Browntrout Publishers Inc						
201 Continental Blvd	El Segundo	CA	90245	310-607-9010	607-9011	637-2
TF: 800-777-7812 ■ *Web:* www.browntrout.com						

Name / Address	City	State	Zip	Phone	Fax	Class
Brown-Wilbert Inc 2280 Hamline Ave N *Web:* www.brownwilbert.com/register.asp	Saint Paul	MN	55113	651-631-1234		134
Brownwood Area Chamber of Commerce 600 E Depot St *Web:* www.brownwoodchamber.org	Brownwood	TX	76801	325-646-9535	643-6686	139
Brownwood Public Library 600 Carnegie Blvd *Web:* www.brownwoodpubliclibrary.com	Brownwood	TX	76801	325-646-0155	646-6503	434-3
Brownwood Regional Medical Ctr 1501 Burnet Dr *Web:* www.brmc-cares.com	Brownwood	TX	76801	325-646-8541		374-3
Browsersoft Inc 450 Navajo Ln *TF:* 800-914-2259 ■ *Web:* browsersoft.com	Shawnee Mission	KS	66217	913-851-2453		225
Brox Industries Inc 1471 Methuen St *TF:* 800-370-7828 ■ *Web:* www.broxindustries.com	Dracut	MA	01826	978-454-9105	805-9720	188-4
Broyhill Asset Management LLC 800 Golfview Pk *Web:* www.broyhillasset.com	Lenoir	NC	28645	828-758-6100		401
Broyhill Co 1 N Market Sq *TF:* 800-228-1003 ■ *Web:* www.broyhill.com	Dakota City	NE	68731	402-987-3412	987-3601	273
Broyhill Furniture Industries Inc 3483 Hickory Blvd *TF Cust Svc:* 800-225-0265 ■ *Web:* www.broyhillfurniture.com	Hudson	NC	28638	800-225-0265		319-2
Broyles Kight & Ricafort PC 8250 Haverstick Rd Ste 100 *TF:* 888-834-2692 ■ *Web:* www.bkrlaw.com	Indianapolis	IN	46240	317-571-3600		428
BRP (Bombardier Recreational Products) 565 de la Montagne *TF:* 800-946-0332 ■ *Web:* www.brp.com	Valcourt	QC	J0E2L0	450-532-2211	532-5133	710
BRP Manufacturing Co 637 N Jackson St *TF:* 800-858-0482 ■ *Web:* www.brpmfg.com	Lima	OH	45801	419-228-4441	222-5010	676
Brph Cos Inc 5700 N Harbor City Blvd Ste 400 *Web:* www.brph.com	Melbourne	FL	32940	321-254-7666		780
BRProud 10000 Perkins Rd *Web:* www.brproud.com	Baton Rouge	LA	70810	225-766-3233	768-9293	741-13
BRT Extrusions Inc 1818 N Main St *Web:* www.brtextrusions.com	Niles	OH	44446	330-544-0244		492
BRT Realty Trust 60 Cutter Mill Rd Ste 303 *NYSE:* BRT ■ *TF:* 800-450-5816 ■ *Web:* www.brtrealty.com	Great Neck	NY	11021	516-466-3100		509
Brubaker & Associates Inc 7626 Hammerly Blvd *TF:* 800-649-5475 ■ *Web:* www.brubakerandassociates.com	Houston	TX	77055	713-464-4666		196
Brubaker-Mann Inc 36011 Soap Mine Rd *Web:* brubakermann.com	Barstow	CA	92311	760-256-2520	256-0127	500
Bruce & Merrilees Electric Co 930 Cass St *TF:* 800-652-5560 ■ *Web:* www.bruceandmerrilees.com	New Castle	PA	16101	724-652-5566	652-8290	189-4
Bruce E Brooks & Associates Inc 2209 Chestnut St *TF:* 800-345-6202 ■ *Web:* www.brucebrooks.com	Philadelphia	PA	19103	215-569-0400		261
Bruce Foods Corp PO Box 1030 *TF:* 800-299-9082 ■ *Web:* www.brucefoods.com	New Iberia	LA	70561	337-365-8101	369-9026	296-20
Bruce Fox Inc 1909 McDonald Ln *Web:* www.brucefox.com	New Albany	IN	47150	812-945-3511		777
Bruce Hersh CPA Accountancy Corp 17547 Ventura Blvd	Encino	CA	91316	818-905-0533		2
Bruce Industries Inc 101 Evans Ave *Web:* www.bruceind.com	Dayton	NV	89403	775-246-0101		438
Bruce Mau Design Inc 745 Fifth Ave 19th FL *Web:* www.brucemaudesign.com	NewYork	NY	10022	416-306-6401		344
Bruce Museum of Arts & Science 1 Museum Dr *Web:* www.brucemuseum.org	Greenwich	CT	06830	203-869-0376	869-0963	520
Bruce R Smith Ltd 973 St Johns Rd W *Web:* www.brsmith.com	Simcoe	ON	N3Y4K1	519-426-0904		478
Bruce Supply Corp 8805 18th Ave *Web:* www.brucesupplyplumbing.com	Brooklyn	NY	11214	718-259-4900	256-5082	612
Bruce Telecom 3145 Hwy 21 PO Box 80 *TF:* 866-517-2000 ■ *Web:* www.brucetelecom.com	Tiverton	ON	N0G2T0	519-368-2000		736
Brucemore 2160 Linden Dr SE *Web:* www.brucemore.org	Cedar Rapids	IA	52403	319-362-7375		50-3
Bruceton Farm Service Inc 1768 Mileground Rd *Web:* www.bfscompanies.com	Morgantown	WV	26505	304-291-6980		297-8
Bruckmann Rosser Sherrill & Company LLC 126 E 56th St 29th Fl *Web:* www.brs.com	New York	NY	10022	212-521-3700		360-3
Bruderer Inc 1200 Hendricks Cswy *Web:* www.bruderer.com	Ridgefield	NJ	07657	201-941-2121	886-2010	456
Brudi Bolzoni Auramo Inc 17635 Hoffman Way *TF:* 800-358-5438 ■ *Web:* www.bolzoni-auramo.com	Homewood	IL	60430	708-957-8809		295
Bruegger's Enterprises 93 Church St *Web:* www.brueggers.com	Burlington	VT	05401	802-860-1995		68
Bruel & Kjaer 2815 Colonnades Ct Ste A *Web:* www.bksv.com/en	Norcross	GA	30071	770-209-4423		248
Bruen Deldin Didio Assoc 3 Starr Ridge Rd *Web:* bddinsurance.com	Brewster	NY	10509	845-279-5151		390
Bruen Productions International Inc 5235 Gulf Stream Court 2nd Fl *Web:* www.bruen.com	Loveland	CO	80538	970-593-6300		5
Brueton Industries Inc 146 Hanse Ave *TF Cust Svc:* 800-221-6783 ■ *Web:* www.brueton.com	Freeport	NY	11520	516-379-3400	543-4520	319-2
Bruin Plastics Company Inc 61 Joslin Rd *Web:* www.bruinplastics.com	Glendale	RI	02826	401-568-3081		600
Bruker Daltonics Inc 40 Manning Rd *TF:* 800-672-7676 ■ *Web:* www.bruker.com	Billerica	MA	01821	978-663-3660	667-5993	419
Brule County 300 S Courtland St Ste 111 *Web:* brulecounty.org	Chamberlain	SD	57325	605-734-4580		338
Brule River State Forest 6250 S Ranger Rd *Web:* www.dnr.wi.gov	Brule	WI	54820	715-372-5678	372-4836	565
Brulin Holding Co 2920 Dr AJ Brown Ave *TF:* 800-776-7149 ■ *Web:* www.brulin.com	Indianapolis	IN	46205	317-923-3211	925-4596	145
Brumback Library 215 W Main St *Web:* www.brumbacklib.com	Van Wert	OH	45891	419-238-2168	238-3180	434-3
Brumbaugh Body Co 1 Jennifer Rd	Duncansville	PA	16635	814-696-9552		516
Bruml Capital Corp 1801 E Ninth St Ste 1620 *Web:* www.brumlcapital.com	Cleveland	OH	44114	216-771-6660		690
Brumlow Mills Inc 734 S River St *Web:* www.brumlowcarpet.com	Calhoun	GA	30701	706-625-4428		131
Brundage Management Company Inc 254 Spencer Ln *Web:* www.brundagemgt.com	San Antonio	TX	78201	210-735-9393	735-2061	803-1
Bruneau Dunes State Park 27608 Sand Dunes Rd *Web:* www.parksandrecreation.idaho.gov	Mountain Home	ID	83647	208-366-7919		565
Bruneau Group 390 Rideau St *Web:* www.bruneaugroup.com	Ottawa	ON	K1N9P4	613-562-3646		445
Brunei Darussalam *Embassy* 3520 International Ct NW *Web:* www.bruneiembassy.org	Washington	DC	20008	202-237-1838	885-0560	257
Bruner Corp 3637 Lacon Rd *Web:* www.brunercorp.com	Hilliard	OH	43026	614-334-9000	334-9001	14
Brunet Island State Park 23125 255th St *Web:* dnr.wi.gov/newurl.html	Cornell	WI	54732	715-239-6888		565
Brunet-Garcia Advertising Inc 1510 Hendricks Ave *TF:* 866-346-1977 ■ *Web:* www.brunetgarcia.com	Jacksonville	FL	32207	904-346-1977		7
Bruning & Federle Mfg Co 2503 Northside Dr *Web:* www.bruning-federle.com	Statesville	NC	28625	704-873-7237		18
Brunini 190 E Capitol St The Pinnacle Bldg Ste 100 *Web:* www.brunini.com	Jackson	MS	39201	601-948-3101		445
Brunk House 5705 Salem-Dallas Hwy NW	Salem	OR	97304	503-371-8586		50-3
Brunk Industries Inc 1225 Sage St *Web:* www.brunkindustries.com	Lake Geneva	WI	53147	262-248-8873		483
Brunner Inc 11 Stanwix St 5th Fl *Web:* www.brunnerworks.com	Pittsburgh	PA	15222	412-995-9500		7
Bruno Enterprises Inc 379 Amherst St Ste 163 *Web:* www.bei.tc	Nashua	NH	03063	603-235-2624		180
Bruno Scheidt Inc 71 W 23rd St Fl 4	New York	NY	10010	212-741-8290		805
Bruno Skorheim 9665 Chesapeake Dr Ste 470 *Web:* www.brunoskorheim.com	San Diego	CA	92123	858-300-3141		2
Bruno White Entertainment Inc 9460 Delegates Dr Ste 101 *Web:* www.brunowhite.com	Orlando	FL	32837	407-352-5555		514
Bruno's 9462 N MacArthur Blvd *Web:* brunosristorante.com	Irving	TX	75063	972-556-2465		671
Brunsell Bros Ltd 4611 W Beltline Hwy *Web:* www.brunsell.com	Madison	WI	53711	608-275-7171		364
Bruns-Gutzwiller Inc 305 John St *Web:* www.bruns-gutzwiller.com	Batesville	IN	47006	812-934-2105	934-2107	189-7
BRUNS-PAK Corp 999 New Durham Rd *TF:* 800-374-2766 ■ *Web:* bruns-pak.com	Edison	NJ	08817	732-248-4455		261
Brunswick & The Golden Isles of Georgia Visitors Bureau 4 Glynn Ave *TF:* 800-933-2627 ■ *Web:* www.goldenisles.com	Brunswick	GA	31520	912-265-0620	265-0629	206
Brunswick Area Chamber of Commerce 1324 Pearl Rd M2 *Web:* www.brunswickareachamber.org	Brunswick	OH	44212	330-225-8411		139
Brunswick Bank & trust 439 Livingston Ave *Web:* www.brunswickbank.com	New Brunswick	NJ	08901	732-247-5800		360-2
Brunswick Boat Group 800 S Gay St 17th Fl *Web:* brunswick.com	Knoxville	TN	37929	865-582-2200		90
Brunswick Box Company Inc 852 Planters Rd	Lawrenceville	VA	23868	434-848-2222		551
Brunswick City School District 3643 Ctr Rd *Web:* www.bcsoh.org	Brunswick	OH	44212	330-225-7731	273-0507	685
Brunswick Community College 50 College Rd *TF:* 800-754-1050 ■ *Web:* www.brunswickcc.edu	Bolivia	NC	28422	910-755-7300		162
Brunswick Corp 1 N Field Ct *NYSE:* BC ■ *Web:* www.brunswick.com	Lake Forest	IL	60045	847-735-4700	735-4765	710
Brunswick Corp Mercury Marine Div W 6250 Pioneer Rd *TF:* 866-408-6372 ■ *Web:* www.mercurymarine.com	Fond du Lac	WI	54935	920-929-5040		262
Brunswick Corp Sea Ray Group 26125 N Riverwoods Blvd Ste 500 *Web:* www.brunswick.com	Mettawa	IL	60045	847-735-4700	735-4765	90
Brunswick County 250 Grey Water Rd *TF:* 800-442-7033 ■ *Web:* www.brunswickcountync.gov	Bolivia	NC	28422	910-253-2657	253-2022	338
Brunswick County 216 N Main St *Web:* www.brunswickco.com	Lawrenceville	VA	23868	434-848-2215	848-4307	338
Brunswick County Board of Education 35 Referendum Dr *TF:* 800-662-7030 ■ *Web:* www.bcswan.net	Bolivia	NC	28422	910-253-2900		685
Brunswick County Chamber of Commerce 114 Wall St *TF:* 800-426-6644 ■ *Web:* www.brunswickcountychamber.org	Shallotte	NC	28459	910-754-6644	754-6539	139
Brunswick County Library 109 W Moore St *Web:* www.brunswickcountync.gov/library	Southport	NC	28461	910-457-6237		434-3
Brunswick Cove Inc 1478 River Rd SE *Web:* www.brunswickcove.com	Winnabow	NC	28479	910-371-9894		186
Brunswick Electric Membership Corp 795 Ocean Hwy PO Box 826 *TF:* 800-842-5871 ■ *Web:* www.bemc.org	Shallotte	NC	28459	910-754-4391	755-4299	245

Phone Fax Class

Brunswick Floors 3550 Darien Hwy .... Brunswick GA 31525 912-265-0222 191-4
Web: www.brunswickfloors.com

Brunswick Historical Society
605 Brunswick Rd. .... Troy NY 12180 518-279-4024 522
Web: townofbrunswick.org

Brunswick Laboratories LLC
200 Turnpike Rd .... Southborough MA 01772 508-281-6660 743
Web: www.brunswicklabs.com

Brunswick News PO Box 1557 .... Brunswick GA 31521 912-265-8320 280-0926 532-2
Web: goldenisles.news

Brunswick School Inc 100 Maher Ave .... Greenwich CT 06830 203-625-5800 41
TF: 800-546-9425 ■ *Web:* www.brunswickschool.org

Brunswick-Glynn County Library
208 Gloucester St .... Brunswick GA 31520 912-279-3740 261-3849 434-3

Brunswick-Golden Isles Chamber of Commerce
1505 Richmond St 2nd Fl .... Brunswick GA 31520 912-265-0620 265-0629 139
TF: 888-453-5955 ■ *Web:* www.brunswickgoldenisleschamber.com

Brunton Enterprises Inc
8815 Sorensen Ave .... Santa Fe Springs CA 90670 562-945-0013 696-7620 189-14
Web: www.plas-tal.com

Brush Art Corp 343 W US Hwy 24 .... Downs KS 67437 785-454-3383 7
Web: www.brushart.com

Brush Creek Ranch
66 Brush Creek Ranch Rd .... Saratoga WY 82331 307-327-5284 327-5970 239
Web: www.brushcreekranch.com

Brush Research Mfg Company Inc
4642 Floral Dr .... Los Angeles CA 90022 323-261-2193 268-6587 103
TF: 800-572-6501 ■ *Web:* www.brushresearch.com

Brushes Corp 5400 Smith Rd .... Cleveland OH 44142 216-267-8084 267-9077 103
Web: www.brushescorp.com

Brushfoil LLC 1 Shoreline Dr Unit 6 .... Guilford CT 06437 203-453-7403 601
TF: 800-493-2321 ■ *Web:* www.brushfoil.com

Brushtech Inc 4 Matt Ave .... Plattsburgh NY 12901 518-563-8420 563-0581 103
Web: brushtechbrushes.com

Brushy Creek State Recreation Area
2802 Brushy Creek Rd .... Lehigh IA 50557 515-543-8298 843-8395 565
Web: www.iowadnr.gov

Bruss Co 3548 N Kostner Ave .... Chicago IL 60641 773-282-2900 297-9
TF: 800-621-3882 ■ *Web:* bruss.com

Bruss North American Inc
600 Progress Dr .... Russell Springs KY 42642 270-858-2600 247
Web: www.bruss.de

Brutger Equities Inc
100 Fourth Ave S .... Saint Cloud MN 56301 320-252-6262 377
Web: www.brutgerequities.com

Bry-Air Inc 10793 SR 37 W .... Sunbury OH 43074 740-965-2974 965-5470 14
TF: 877-427-9247 ■ *Web:* www.bry-air.com

Bryan City School District
1350 Fountain Grove Dr .... Bryan OH 43506 419-636-6973 633-6280 48-11
Web: www.bryan.k12.oh.us

Bryan College 140 Landes Way .... Dayton TN 37321 423-775-2041 775-7199 166
TF: 800-277-9522 ■ *Web:* www.bryan.edu

Bryan County PO Box 1789 .... Durant OK 74702 580-924-2202 338
Web: www.ok.gov

Bryan County 51 N Courthouse St .... Pembroke GA 31321 912-653-3819 653-4691 338
TF: 800-501-0155 ■ *Web:* www.bryancountyga.org

Bryan Health 1600 S 48th St .... Lincoln NE 68506 402-481-7333 374-3
TF: 800-742-7844 ■ *Web:* www.bryanhealth.com

Bryan Hospital (CHWC) 433 W High St .... Bryan OH 43506 419-636-1131 630-2155 374-3
Web: www.chwchospital.org

Bryan LGH Medical Ctr West
2300 S 16th St .... Lincoln NE 68502 402-481-1111 374-3
Web: www.bryanhealth.com

Bryan Mills Iradesso Inc
1129 Leslie St .... Toronto ON M3C2K5 416-447-4740 4
Web: www.bmir.com

Bryan Public Library 201 E 26th St .... Bryan TX 77803 979-209-5600 434-3
Web: www.bcslibrary.org

Bryan Steam LLC 783 Chili Ave .... Peru IN 46970 765-473-6651 473-3074 91
Web: www.bryanboilers.com

Bryan Systems 14020 US 20A Hwy .... Montpelier OH 43543 800-745-2796 780
TF: 800-745-2796 ■ *Web:* www.bryansystems.com

Bryan W Whitfield Memorial Hospital
105 Hwy 80 E PO Box 890 .... Demopolis AL 36732 334-289-4000 374-3
TF: 800-453-2395 ■ *Web:* www.bwwmh.com

Bryan-College Station Chamber of Commerce
4001 E 29th St Ste 175 .... Bryan TX 77802 979-260-5200 139
Web: www.bcschamber.org

Bryan-College Station Eagle
1729 Briarcrest Dr .... Bryan TX 77802 979-776-4444 776-8923 532-2
TF: 800-299-7355 ■ *Web:* theeagle.com

Bryant & Stratton College
Cleveland 3121 Euclid Ave .... Cleveland OH 44115 216-771-1700 771-7787 800
TF: 866-948-0571 ■ *Web:* www.bryantstratton.edu
Eastlake 35350 Curtis Blvd .... Eastlake OH 44095 440-510-1112 306-2015 800
Web: www.bryantstratton.edu
Parma 12955 Snow Rd .... Parma OH 44130 216-265-3151 265-0325 800
Web: www.bryantstratton.edu

Bryant & Stratton College Albany
1259 Central Ave .... Albany NY 12205 518-437-1802 437-1048 800
TF: 800-836-5627 ■ *Web:* www.bryantstratton.edu

Bryant & Stratton College Amherst
3650 Millersport Hwy .... Getzville NY 14068 716-625-6300 800
TF: 800-669-3328 ■ *Web:* www.bryantstratton.edu

Bryant & Stratton College Buffalo
465 Main St Ste 400 .... Buffalo NY 14203 716-884-9120 884-0091 800
Web: www.bryantstratton.edu

Bryant & Stratton College Greece
150 Bellwood Dr .... Rochester NY 14606 585-720-0660 800
Web: www.bryantstratton.edu

Bryant & Stratton College Henrietta
1225 Jefferson Rd .... Rochester NY 14623 585-292-5627 292-6015 800
TF: 800-677-1323 ■ *Web:* www.bryantstratton.edu

Bryant & Stratton College Milwaukee
310 W Wisconsin Ave Ste 500-E .... Milwaukee WI 53203 414-276-5200 276-3930 800
TF: 866-948-0571 ■ *Web:* www.bryantstratton.edu

Bryant & Stratton College Richmond
8141 Hull St Rd .... Richmond VA 23235 804-745-2444 745-6884 800
TF: 866-948-0571 ■ *Web:* www.bryantstratton.edu

Bryant & Stratton College Southtowns
200 Rod Tail .... Orchard Park NY 14127 716-677-9500 677-9599 800
Web: www.bryantstratton.edu

Bryant & Stratton College Syracuse
953 James St .... Syracuse NY 13203 315-472-6603 474-4383 800
Web: www.bryantstratton.edu

Bryant & Stratton College Syracuse North
8687 Carling Rd .... Liverpool NY 13090 315-652-6500 800
TF: 800-836-5627 ■ *Web:* www.bryantstratton.edu

Bryant & Stratton College Virginia Beach
301 Ctr Pt Dr .... Virginia Beach VA 23462 757-499-7900 499-9977 800
TF: 800-333-4268 ■ *Web:* www.bryantstratton.edu

Bryant Bureau
18600 Florence St Ste C6a .... Roseville MI 48066 586-772-6452 260
Web: bryantbureau.net

Bryant Christie Inc
500 Union St Ste 701 .... Seattle WA 98101 206-292-6340 196
Web: www.bryantchristie.com

Bryant Convenience Inc 510 Bryant St .... Denver CO 80204 303-534-1379 297-8

Bryant Grinder 65 Pearl St .... Springfield VT 05156 802-885-5161 885-9444 455
TF: 800-352-0050 ■ *Web:* www.bryantgrinder.com

Bryant Katt & Assoc PC 6211 O St .... Lincoln NE 68510 402-486-1040 2
Web: bka-cpa.com

Bryant Park Hotel 40 W 40th St .... New York NY 10018 212-869-0100 869-4446 379
TF: 877-640-9300 ■ *Web:* www.bryantparkhotel.com

Bryant Phil (R) PO Box 139 .... Jackson MS 39205 601-359-3150 359-3741 343
Web: www.governorbryant.ms.gov/Pages/default.aspx

Bryant Rubber Corp
1112 Lomita Blvd .... Harbor City CA 90710 310-530-2530 530-9143 605-3
Web: www.bryantrubber.com

Bryant Staffing 377 Hoes Ln Ste 200 .... Piscataway NJ 08854 732-981-0440 260
Web: www.bryantstaffing.com

Bryant University 1150 Douglas Pk .... Smithfield RI 02917 401-232-6000 232-6741* 166
**Fax:* Admissions ■ *TF Admissions:* 800-622-7001 ■ *Web:* www.bryant.edu

Bryce Canyon National Park
PO Box 640201 .... Bryce Canyon UT 84764 435-834-5322 834-4102 564
Web: www.nps.gov

Bryce Corp 4505 Old Lamar Ave .... Memphis TN 38118 901-369-4400 548
TF: 800-238-7277 ■ *Web:* www.brycecorp.com

BryCoat Inc 207 Vollmer Ave .... Oldsmar FL 34677 727-490-1000 550
TF: 800-989-8788 ■ *Web:* www.brycoat.com

Brycon Corp 134 Rio Rancho Blvd NE .... Rio Rancho NM 87124 505-892-6163 186
Web: www.brycon.com

Brydan Solutions Inc
8550 W Desert Inn Rd Ste 102-176 .... Las Vegas NV 89117-4401 702-966-2774 966-2758 175
Web: www.brydansolutions.com

Bryley Systems Inc 12 Main St .... Hudson MA 01749 978-562-6077 175
Web: www.bryley.com

BryLin Hospitals 1263 Delaware Ave .... Buffalo NY 14209 716-886-8200 374-5
TF: 800-727-9546 ■ *Web:* www.brylin.com

Bryn Mawr Bank Corp
801 Lancaster Ave .... Bryn Mawr PA 19010 610-525-1700 520-7278* 360-2
NASDAQ: BMTC ■ **Fax:* Cust Svc ■ *TF:* 855-381-2631 ■ *Web:* www.bmtc.com

Bryn Mawr Capital Management Inc
1 Town Pl Ste 200 .... Bryn Mawr PA 19010 484-380-8100 194
Web: www.brynmawrcap.com

Bryn Mawr College 101 N Merion Ave .... Bryn Mawr PA 19010 610-526-5000 526-7471* 166
**Fax:* Admissions ■ *Web:* www.brynmawr.edu

Bryn Mawr Hospital
130 S Bryn Mawr Ave .... Bryn Mawr PA 19010 610-526-3000 374-3
Web: www.mainlinehealth.org/bmh

Bryn Mawr Rehab Hospital
414 Paoli Pike .... Malvern PA 19355 484-596-5400 374-6
TF: 866-225-5654 ■ *Web:* www.mainlinehealth.org

Brynwood Partners LP
8 Sound Shore Dr Ste 265 .... Greenwich CT 06830 203-622-1790 402
Web: www.brynwoodpartners.com

Brytex Building Systems Inc
5610 97 St .... Edmonton AB T6E3J1 780-437-7970 186
TF: 800-399-3831 ■ *Web:* www.brytex.com

B&S Aircraft Alloys Inc 10 Aerial Way .... Syosset NY 11791 516-681-2400 492
Web: www.bsaa.com

BSA (Boy Scouts of America)
1325 W Walnut Hill Ln PO Box 152079 .... Irving TX 75015 972-580-2000 48-15
TF: 800-323-0732 ■ *Web:* www.scouting.org

BSA Life Structures
9365 Counselors Row .... Indianapolis IN 46240 317-819-7878 261
Web: www.bsalifestructures.com

BSAC (Berkeley Sensor & Actuator Ctr)
University of California
403 Cory Hall MC Ste 1774 .... Berkeley CA 94720 510-643-6690 643-6637 668
Web: www-bsac.eecs.berkeley.edu

BS&B Safety Systems LLC 7455 E 46th St .... Tulsa OK 74145 918-622-5950 789
Web: www.bsbsystems.com

BSC America Inc 803 Bel Air Rd .... Bel Air MD 21014 800-764-7400 463
TF: 800-764-7400 ■ *Web:* www.bscamerica.com

BSCAI (Building Service Contractors Assn International)
401 N Michigan Ave Ste 2200 .... Chicago IL 60611 312-321-5167 673-6735 49-13
TF: 800-368-3414 ■ *Web:* www.bscai.org

BSD Medical Corp (BSDM)
2188 West 2200 South .... Salt Lake City UT 84119 801-972-5555 250
NASDAQ: BSDM

BSDM (BSD Medical Corp)
2188 West 2200 South .... Salt Lake City UT 84119 801-972-5555 250
NASDAQ: BSDM

BSG Team Ventures Inc
224 Clarendon St Ste 41 .... Boston MA 02116 617-266-4333 260
TF: 800-767-3263 ■ *Web:* www.bostonsearchgroup.com

BSI (Badger State Industries)
3099 E Washington Ave PO Box 8990 .... Madison WI 53708 608-240-5200 240-3320 630
TF: 800-862-1086 ■ *Web:* www.buybsi.com

BSI (Burner Systems International Inc)
3600 Cummings Rd .... Chattanooga TN 37419 423-822-3600 357
Web: www.burnersystems.com

BSI (Building Service Inc)
W222 N630 Cheaney Rd .... Waukesha WI 53186 262-955-6400 393
TF: 866-353-3600 ■ *Web:* www.buildingservice.com

	Phone	Fax	Class
BSI Constructors Inc 6767 SW Ave.......... Saint Louis MO 63143 *Web:* www.bsistl.com	314-781-7820	781-1354	186
BSK & Assoc 550 W Locust Ave ....Fresno CA 93650 *Web:* www.bskinc.com	559-497-2880		261
Bsm Engineers PO Box 502....................Astoria OR 97103 *Web:* bsmengineering.com	503-325-8065		261
BSM Media Inc 1002 NE First St Ste 300 ....Pompano Beach FL 33060 *Web:* www.bsmmedia.com	954-943-2322		195
BSM Wireless Inc 75 International Blvd Ste 100 .... Toronto ON M9W6L9 *TF:* 866-768-4771 ■ *Web:* www.bsmwireless.com	416-675-1201		692
BSN Medical Inc 5825 Carnegie Blvd........... Charlotte NC 28209 *TF:* 800-552-1157 ■ *Web:* www.bsnmedical.com	704-554-9933		477
BSQUARE Corp 110 110th Ave NE...............Bellevue WA 98004 *NASDAQ: BSQR* ■ *TF:* 888-820-4500 ■ *Web:* www.bsquare.com	425-519-5900		178-2
BSSB (Boiling Springs Savings Bank) 25 Orient Way.............................Rutherford NJ 07070 *TF:* 888-388-7459 ■ *Web:* www.bssbank.com	201-939-5000	939-3957	70
BST (Billings Studio Theatre) 1500 Rimrock Rd .... Billings MT 59102 *TF:* 800-227-7368 ■ *Web:* www.billingsstudiotheatre.com	406-248-1141		572
BT Americas Inc 2160 E Grand Ave .... El Segundo CA 90245 *Web:* www.globalservices.bt.com	408-330-2700	330-2701	394
BT Bones 2280 Shepherd Hill Expy ....Branson MO 65616	417-335-2002		671
BT Conferencing Inc 150 Newport Ave Ext, Ste 301............North Quincy MA 02171 *TF:* 866-770-8777 ■ *Web:* www.btconferencing.com	866-770-8777		360-3
BT Mancini Co Inc Brookman Div 876 S Milpitas Blvd ....Milpitas CA 95035 *TF:* 800-955-4324 ■ *Web:* www.btmancini.com	408-942-7900		186
B&t Service Station Contractors 630 S Frontage Rd .... Nipomo CA 93444 *TF:* 888-862-2552 ■ *Web:* btssc.com	805-929-8944		324
BTA (Business Technology Assn) 12411 Wornall Rd Ste 200................Kansas City MO 64145 *TF:* 800-325-7219 ■ *Web:* www.bta.org	816-941-3100	941-2829	49-18
BTA Oil Producers LLC 104 S Pecos ....Midland TX 79701 *TF:* 800-688-3753 ■ *Web:* www.btaoil.com	432-682-3753		536
BTAS Inc 3572 Dayton-Xenia Rd Ste 210.............Beavercreek OH 45432 *Web:* www.btas.com	937-431-9431		194
BTC (Bledsoe Telephone Co-op Corp) 338 Cumberland Ave PO Box 609 ....Pikeville TN 37367 *TF:* 888-382-1222 ■ *Web:* www.bledsoe.net	423-447-2121	447-2498	736
Btd Mfg Inc 1111 13th Ave SE............Detroit Lakes MN 56501 *TF:* 866-562-3986 ■ *Web:* www.btdmfg.com	866-562-3986		488
BTE Technologies Inc 7455-L New Ridge Rd........................Hanover MD 21076 *Web:* www.btetech.com	410-850-0333		250
B-tec Solutions Inc 913 Cedar Ave ....Croydon PA 19021 *TF:* 800-523-1430 ■ *Web:* www.btecsolutions.com	215-785-2400		454
BTECH Inc 10 Astro Pl ....Rockaway NJ 07866 *Web:* www.btechinc.com	973-983-1120		57
BTF Enterprises Inc 3540 Soquel Ave Ste A.....................Santa Cruz CA 95062 *Web:* www.btfenterprises.com	831-464-4880	464-4881	47
BTG International Inc 5 Tower Bridge 300 Barr Harbor Dr Ste 810......................... West Conshohocken PA 19428 *Web:* www.btgplc.com	610-278-1660	278-1605	792
BTI (Bonneville Transloaders Inc) 642 S Federal Blvd ....Riverton WY 82501 *Web:* www.bonntran.com	307-856-7480	856-4623	648
BTI Group 4 N Second St Ste 560.............San Jose CA 95113 *TF:* 800-622-0192 ■ *Web:* www.btigroupma.com	408-246-1102		196
BTIG LLC 600 Montgomery St 6th Fl .... San Francisco CA 94111 *Web:* wwwca01.btig.com	415-248-2200		690
BTL Machine Inc 1168 Sherborn St ....Corona CA 92879 *Web:* www.btlmachine.com	951-808-9929		454
BTM Capital Corp 111 Huntington Ave............Boston MA 02199	617-573-9000		216
Btm Global Consulting 330 S Second Ave Ste 450................Minneapolis MN 55401 *Web:* www.btmglobal.com	612-238-8800		225
BTM Solutions Inc 572 Yorkville Rd E .... Columbus MS 39702 *TF:* 800-909-9381 ■ *Web:* www.btmsolutions.com	662-328-2400		177
BTMC (Banner Thunderbird Medical Ctr) 5555 W ThunderbiRd Rd .... Glendale AZ 85306 *Web:* www.bannerhealth.com	602-839-2000	865-5930	374-3
BTR Capital Management Inc 550 Kearny St Ste 510 .... San Francisco CA 94108 *Web:* www.btrcap.com	415-989-0100		528
BTS (IEEE Broadcast Technology Socicty) 445 Hoes Ln.............................Piscataway NJ 08854 *TF:* 800-678-4333 ■ *Web:* bts.ieee.org	732-562-5407	981-1769	49-19
BTS (Brazilian Travel Service) 16 W 46th St 2nd Fl.......................New York NY 10036 *TF:* 800-342-5746 ■ *Web:* www.btstravelonline.com	212-764-6161	719-4142	16
BTS Asset Management Inc 420 Bedford St Ste 340.....................Lexington MA 02420 *TF:* 800-343-3040 ■ *Web:* www.btsmanagement.com	800-343-3040		401
Bts Consulting Group Ltd 355 Glen Arms Dr...........................Danville CA 94526 *Web:* btsconsultinggroup.com	925-837-1730		196
BTS USA Inc 300 Stamford Pl Ste 425........... Stamford CT 06902 *TF:* 800-445-7089 ■ *Web:* www.bts.com	203-316-2740		194
BTSB (Bound to Stay Bound Books Inc) 1880 W Morton Ave ....Jacksonville IL 62650 **Fax Area Code:* 800 ■ *TF:* 800-637-6586 ■ *Web:* www.btsb.com	217-245-5191	747-2872*	92
BTU International Inc 23 Esquire Rd ....North Billerica MA 01862 *NASDAQ: BTUI* ■ *TF:* 800-998-0666 ■ *Web:* www.btu.com	978-667-4111	667-9068	695
Btu Management Inc 534 La Crosse St......... Mauston WI 53948 *Web:* btumanagement.com	608-847-4600		189-10
Bubba Gump Shrimp Co 99 S Market St ....Charleston SC 29401 *Web:* www.bubbagump.com	843-723-5665		671

	Phone	Fax	Class
Bubba Gump Shrimp Co 401 Biscayne Blvd........ Miami FL 33132 *Web:* www.bubbagump.com	305-379-8866		671
Bubba Gump Shrimp Co LLC 2501 Seawall Blvd ....Galveston TX 77550 *TF:* 800-552-6379 ■ *Web:* www.bubbagump.com	409-766-4952		670
Bubba's 100 Flat Creek Dr ....Jackson Hole WY 83001 *Web:* www.bubbasjh.com	307-733-2288		671
Bubble Technology Industries Inc 31278 Hwy 17 .... Chalk River ON K0J1J0 *Web:* www.bubbletech.ca	613-589-2456		639
BubbleLife Media LLC 7850 Collin McKinney Pkwy Ste 300 .... McKinney TX 75070 *Web:* www.bubblelife.com	214-233-0740		5
Buca di Beppo 1204 Harmon Pl ....Minneapolis MN 55403 *Web:* www.bucadibeppo.com	612-288-0138	341-0496	670
Buca Inc 1204 Harmon Pl...................Minneapolis MN 55403 *Web:* www.bucadibeppo.com	612-288-0138	341-0496	670
Buca's Tuscan Roadhouse 4 Depot Rd.......... Harwich MA 02645 *Web:* www.bucasroadhouse.com	508-432-6900		671
Buccaneer State Park 1150 S Beach Blvd.........................Waveland MS 39576 *Web:* www.mdwfp.com	228-467-3822		565
Buchalter Nemer Pc 1000 Wilshire Blvd.......................Los Angeles CA 90017 *Web:* www.buchalter.com	213-891-0700	896-0400	428
Buchanan Automotive Group 707 S Washington Blvd Ste 900...............Sarasota FL 34236 *Web:* www.buchananautogroup.com	941-364-9500		57
Buchanan County 1012 Walnut St PO Box 950...................Grundy VA 24614 *Web:* www.buchanancountyonline.com	276-935-6503	935-4479	338
Buchanan County 210 Fifth Ave NE .... Independence IA 50644 *Web:* www.buchanancountyiowa.org	319-334-5989		338
Buchanan County 411 Jules St............. Saint Joseph MO 64501 *Web:* www.co.buchanan.mo.us	816-271-1437	271-1535	338
Buchanan County Public Library 1185 Poe Town St...........................Grundy VA 24614 *Web:* www.bcplnet.org	276-935-5721		434-3
Buchanan General Hospital (BGH) 1535 Slate Creek Rd.........................Grundy VA 24614 *TF:* 800-552-7096 ■ *Web:* www.bgh.org	276-935-1000	935-1354	374-3
Buchanan Hardwoods Inc 600 Baptist Line Rd .... Aliceville AL 35442 *Web:* www.buchananhardwoods.com	205-373-8710		291
Buchanan Hauling & Rigging 4625 Industrial Rd .... Fort Wayne IN 46825 *TF:* 888-544-4285 ■ *Web:* www.buchananhauling.com	260-471-1877		780
Buchanan Ingersoll & Rooney PC 301 Grant St 1 Oxford Ctr 20th Fl............. Pittsburgh PA 15219-1410 *Web:* www.bipc.com	412-562-8800	562-1041	428
Buchanan Metal Forming Inc (BMF) 103 W Smith St ....Buchanan MI 49107 *Web:* www.bmfcorp.com	269-695-3836	695-3830	483
Buchanan Technologies Inc 1026 Texan Trl .... Grapevine TX 76051 *TF:* 888-730-2774 ■ *Web:* www.buchanan.com	972-869-3966		180
Buchanan Vern (Rep R - FL) 2104 Rayburn Bldg.......................Washington DC 20515 *Web:* buchanan.house.gov	202-225-5015	226-0828	342-2
Buchanan's Birthplace State Park c/o Cowans Gap State Pk 6235 Aughwick Rd...Fort Loudon PA 17224 *Web:* www.dcnr.state.pa.us	717-485-3948		565
Buchbinder Tunick & Company LLP 1 Penn Plaza Ste 5335 ....New York NY 10119 *Web:* www.buchbinder.com	212-695-5003		711
Bucher & Christian Consulting Inc 9777 N College Ste 1300...................Indianapolis IN 46280 *TF:* 866-363-1132 ■ *Web:* www.bcforward.com	866-363-1132		194
Bucher Elementary School 450 Candlewyck Rd ....Lancaster PA 17601 *Web:* www.mtwp.net	717-569-4291		685
Buchheit Inc 33 Perry County Rd 540.....................Perryville MO 63775 *Web:* www.buchheitonline.com	573-547-1010		191-2
Buck & Knobby Equipment Co 6220 Sterns Rd.........................Ottawa Lake MI 49267 *TF:* 855-213-2825 ■ *Web:* www.buckandknobby.com	734-856-2811	856-2709	264-3
Buck Chuck Co 2155 Traversefield Dr .... Traverse City MI 49686 **Fax Area Code:* 231 ■ *TF:* 800-228-2825 ■ *Web:* buckchuck.com	800-228-2825	947-4953*	493
Buck Company Inc 897 Lancaster Pk..........Quarryville PA 17566 *Web:* www.buckcompany.com	717-284-4114	284-3737	307
Buck Creek State Park 1901 Buck Creek Ln ....Springfield OH 45502 *Web:* www.ohiodnr.com	937-322-5284		565
Buck Distributing Company Inc 15827 Commerce Ct.................Upper Marlboro MD 20774 *TF Cust Svc:* 800-750-2825 ■ *Web:* www.buckdistributing.com	301-952-0400		81-1
Buck Island Reef National Monument 2100 Church St Ste 100 ....Christiansted VI 00820 *Web:* www.nps.gov/buis	340-773-1460	773-5995	564
Buck Ken (Rep R - CO) 1130 Longworth HOB.....................Washington DC 20515 *Web:* buck.house.gov	202-225-4676	225-5870	342-2
Buck Knives Inc 660 S Lochsa St.............Post Falls ID 83854 *TF:* 800-326-2825 ■ *Web:* www.buckknives.com	208-262-0500		222
Buck Owens' Crystal Palace Steakhouse 2800 Buck Owens Blvd....................Bakersfield CA 93308 *Web:* www.buckowens.com	661-328-7560		671
Buck's Pizza Franchising Corp Inc PO Box 405 .... Du Bois PA 15801 *TF:* 800-310-8848 ■ *Web:* www.buckspizza.com	800-310-8848		670
Buck's Pocket State Park 393 County Rd 174.........................Grove Oak AL 35975 *TF:* 800-760-4089 ■ *Web:* www.alapark.com	256-659-2000	659-2000	565
Buck's Restaurant 425 W Ormsby Ave.........Louisville KY 40203 *Web:* www.bucksrestaurantandbar.com	502-637-5284		671

	Phone	Fax	Class
Buckeye Book Fair 205 W Liberty St ... Wooster OH 44691 *Web:* www.buckeyebookfair.com	330-262-3244		281
Buckeye Boxes Inc 601 N Hague Ave ... Columbus OH 43204 *Web:* www.buckeyeboxes.com	614-274-8484		66
Buckeye Broadband 5566 Southwick Blvd ... Toledo OH 43614 *Web:* www.buckeyecablesystem.com	419-724-9802	724-7074	116
Buckeye Business Products Inc 3830 Kelley Ave ... Cleveland OH 44114 **Fax Area Code:* 216 ■ *TF:* 800-837-4323 ■ *Web:* www.buckeyebusiness.com	800-837-4323	881-6105*	628
Buckeye Career Ctr 545 University Dr NE ... New Philadelphia OH 44663 *TF:* 800-227-1665 ■ *Web:* www.buckeyecareercenter.org	330-339-2288		162
Buckeye Container Inc 3350 Long Rd ... Wooster OH 44691 *TF:* 800-968-6894	330-264-6336	264-0127	100
Buckeye Corrugated Inc 275 Springside Dr ... Akron OH 44333 *Web:* www.bcipkg.com	330-576-0590	576-0600	100
Buckeye Diamond Logistics Inc 15 Sprague Rd ... South Charleston OH 45368 *Web:* www.buckeyediamond.com	937-462-8361		200
Buckeye Fabric Finishing Co 1260 E Main St ... Coshocton OH 43812 *Web:* www.buckeyefabric.com	740-622-3251		745-7
Buckeye Fire Equipment Co 110 Kings Rd ... Kings Mountain NC 28086 *Web:* www.buckeyef.com	704-739-7415	739-7418	678
Buckeye International Inc 2700 Wagner Pl ... Maryland Heights MO 63043 *TF:* 800-321-2583 ■ *Web:* www.buckeyeinternational.com	314-291-1900	298-2850	151
Buckeye Lake State Park 2905 Liebs Island Rd ... Millersport OH 43046 *Web:* www.ohiodnr.com	740-467-2690		565
Buckeye Machine Fabricators Inc 610 E Lima St ... Forest OH 45843 *Web:* www.buckeyemachine.com	419-273-2521		757
Buckeye Mt Holly LLC 100 Buckeye Dr ... Mt Holly NC 28120	704-822-6400		557
Buckeye Nissan Inc 3820 Pkwy Ln ... Hilliard OH 43026 *TF:* 800-686-4391 ■ *Web:* buckeyenissan.com	614-771-2345		57
Buckeye Nutrition 330 E Schultz Ave ... Dalton OH 44618 *TF:* 800-417-6460 ■ *Web:* www.buckeyenutrition.com	800-417-6460		447
Buckeye Pacific LLC 4386 SW Macadam Ave Ste 200 ... Portland OR 97207 *TF:* 800-767-9191 ■ *Web:* www.buckeyepacific.com	503-274-2284	274-2284	191-3
Buckeye Partners LP 5 Tek Pk 9999 Hamilton Blvd ... Breinigsville PA 18031 *NYSE:* BPL ■ *Web:* www.buckeye.com	610-904-4000		597
Buckeye Partners LP 1 Greenway Plaza Ste 600 ... Houston TX 77046 *Web:* www.buckeye.com	832-615-8600		597
Buckeye Payroll Services 5749 Park Ctr Ct ... Toledo OH 43615 *Web:* www.buckeyepayroll.com	419-472-7377		2
Buckeye Power Sales Company Inc 6850 Commerce Ct Dr ... Blacklick OH 43004 *TF:* 800-523-3587 ■ *Web:* www.buckeyepowersales.com	614-861-6000		620
Buckeye Pumps Inc 1311 Freese Works Pl ... Galion OH 44833 *Web:* www.buckeyepumps.com	419-468-7866		358
Buckeye Rural Electric Co-op 4848 State Rt 325 PO Box 200 ... Patriot OH 45658 *TF:* 800-231-2732 ■ *Web:* www.buckeyerec.coop	740-379-2025		245
Buckeye ShapeForm 555 Marion Rd ... Columbus OH 43207 *TF:* 800-728-0776 ■ *Web:* www.buckeyeshapeform.com	614-445-8433	445-8224	254
Buckeye Snack Food Co 11677 Chesterdale Rd ... Cincinnati OH 45246	513-458-6200		296-9
Buckeye Tools & Supply Company Inc 400 Gargrave Rd ... Dayton OH 45449 *Web:* www.buckeyetools.com	937-847-8888		351
Buckham Memorial Library 11 Div St E ... Faribault MN 55021 *TF:* 800-658-2354 ■ *Web:* www.ci.faribault.mn.us	507-334-2089		434-3
Buckhannon-Upshur Chamber of Commerce 14 E Main St ... Buckhannon WV 26201 *TF:* 800-225-5982 ■ *Web:* www.buchamber.com	304-472-1722		139
Buckhead Beef of Florida 355 Progress Rd ... Auburndale FL 33823 *Web:* buckheadbeef.com	863-508-1050		297-9
Buckhead Capital Management LLC 3330 Cumberland Blvd Ste 650 ... Atlanta GA 30339 *Web:* www.buckheadcapital.com	404-720-8800	720-8802	401
Buckhead Diner 3073 Piedmont Rd NE ... Atlanta GA 30305 *Web:* www.buckheadrestaurants.com	404-262-3336		671
Buckhorn Inc 55 W Techne Ctr Dr ... Milford OH 45150 *TF:* 800-543-4454 ■ *Web:* www.buckhorninc.com	513-831-4402	831-5474	199
Buckhorn Lake State Resort Park 4441 Ky Hwy 1833 ... Buckhorn KY 41721 *TF:* 800-325-0058 ■ *Web:* www.parks.ky.gov	606-398-7510		565
Buckhorn Rubber Products Inc 5151 Industrial Dr ... Hannibal MO 63401 *Web:* www.buckhornrubber.com	573-221-8933		677
Buckhorn Saloon & Museum 318 E Houston St ... San Antonio TX 78205 *TF:* 800-354-4629 ■ *Web:* www.buckhornmuseum.com	210-247-4000	247-4020	520
Buckhorn State Park W8450 Buckhorn Pk Ave ... Necedah WI 54646 *Web:* dnr.wi.gov/newurl.html	608-565-2789		565
Buckingham Branch Railroad Co PO Box 336 ... Dillwyn VA 23936 *Web:* www.buckinghambranch.com	434-983-3300		649
Buckingham Browne & Nichols School 46 Belmont St ... Watertown MA 02472 *Web:* www.bbns.org	617-547-6100		685
Buckingham Correctional Ctr 1349 Correctional Ctr Rd ... Dillwyn VA 23936 *Web:* vadoc.virginia.gov	434-983-4400		213
Buckingham County 13360 W James Anderson Hwy ... Buckingham VA 23921 *TF:* 800-440-6116 ■ *Web:* buckinghamcountyva.org	434-969-4242	969-1638	338
Buckingham Family of Financial Services, The 8182 Maryland Ave Ste 900 ... St Louis MO 63105 *Web:* www.bamadvisorservices.com	314-725-0455	725-7022	401
Buckingham Hotel 101 W 57th St ... New York NY 10019 *Web:* tripadvisor.com.au	212-246-1500		379
Buckingham's BBQ 2002 S Campbell Ave ... Springfield MO 65807 *Web:* buckinghambbq.com	417-886-9979		671
Buckingham's Restaurant & Oasis 2820 W Hwy 76 ... Branson MO 65616 *TF:* 800-725-2236 ■ *Web:* clarionhotelbranson.com	417-337-7777		671
Buckle Inc 2407 W 24th St ... Kearney NE 68845 *NYSE:* BKE ■ *TF:* 800-626-1255 ■ *Web:* www.buckle.com	308-236-8491	236-4493	157-4
Buckles-Smith 801 Savaker Ave ... San Jose CA 95126 *TF:* 800-833-7362 ■ *Web:* www.buckles-smith.com	408-280-7777		246
Buckley Associates Inc 385 King St ... Hanover MA 02339 *Web:* www.buckleyonline.com	781-878-5000		14
Buckley Broadcasting Corp 166 W Putnam Ave ... Greenwich CT 06830	203-661-4307		643
Buckley Energy Group Ltd 154 Admiral St ... Bridgeport CT 06605 *TF:* 800-937-2682 ■ *Web:* www.santaenergy.com	800-937-2682		316
Buckley Gent Macdonald & Cary PC 100 Great Oaks Blvd Ste 121 ... Albany NY 12203	518-437-0430	437-1157	2
Buckley Industries Inc 1850 E 53rd St N ... Wichita KS 67219 *TF:* 800-835-2779 ■ *Web:* www.buckleyind.com	316-744-7587	744-8463	603
Buckley Oil Company Inc 1809 Rock Island St ... Dallas TX 75207 *TF:* 800-721-4147 ■ *Web:* www.buckleyoil.com	214-421-4147		581
Buckley Powder Co 42 Inverness Dr E ... Englewood CO 80112 *TF:* 800-333-2266 ■ *Web:* www.buckleypowder.com	303-790-7007		268
Buckley School, The 3900 Stansbury Ave ... Sherman Oaks CA 91423 *Web:* www.buckley.org	818-783-1610		685
Buckley's 5355 Poplar Ave ... Memphis TN 38119 *Web:* www.buckleysgrill.com	901-683-4538		671
Bucklin Tractor & Implement Co 115 W Railroad PO Box 127 ... Bucklin KS 67834 *TF:* 800-334-4823 ■ *Web:* www.btiequip.com	620-826-3271	826-3760	273
Buckman Buckman & Reid Inc 174 Patterson Ave ... Shrewsbury NJ 07702 *TF:* 800-531-0303 ■ *Web:* www.buckmanbuckman.com	732-530-0303		401
Buckman Enochs Coss & Assoc 590 Enterprise Dr ... Lewis Center OH 43035 *Web:* becsearch.com	614-825-6215		260
Buckman Laboratories Inc 1256 N McLean Blvd ... Memphis TN 38108 *TF:* 877-282-5626 ■ *Web:* www.buckman.com	901-278-0330		145
Bucknell University 701 Moore Ave ... Lewisburg PA 17837 *TF:* 800-222-1222 ■ *Web:* www.bucknell.edu	570-577-2000		166
Bucknell University Bertrand Library 69 Coleman Hall Rd ... Lewisburg PA 17837 *Web:* www.bucknell.edu/isr	570-577-1557	577-3313	434-6
Buckner International 700 N Pearl St Ste 1200 ... Dallas TX 75201 *TF:* 800-442-4800 ■ *Web:* www.buckner.org	214-758-8000		48-6
Buckrail Lodge 110 E Karns Ave PO Box 23 ... Jackson WY 83001 *Web:* www.buckraillodge.com	307-733-2079		379
Bucks County 55 E Ct St ... Doylestown PA 18901 *TF:* 888-942-8257 ■ *Web:* www.buckscounty.org	215-348-6000		338
Bucks County Community College 275 Swamp Rd ... Newtown PA 18940 **Fax:* Admissions ■ *Web:* www.bucks.edu	215-968-8000	968-8110*	162
Bristol 1280 New Rodgers Rd ... Bristol PA 19007 *Web:* www.bucks.edu	215-781-3939		162
Upper County 1 Hillendale Dr ... Perkasie PA 18944 *Web:* www.bucks.edu	215-258-7700		162
Bucks County Conference & Visitors Bureau (BCCVB) 3207 St Rd ... Bensalem PA 19020 *TF:* 800-836-2825 ■ *Web:* www.visitbuckscounty.com	215-639-0300	642-3277	206
Bucks County Free Library 150 S Pine St ... Doylestown PA 18901 *TF:* 800-233-3401 ■ *Web:* www.buckslib.org	215-348-9081	348-4760	434-3
Bucks County Water & Sewer Authority (BCWSA) 1275 Almshouse Rd ... Warrington PA 18976 **Fax Area Code:* 267 ■ *TF:* 800-222-2068 ■ *Web:* www.bcwsa.net	215-343-2538	200-0339*	806
Buckskin Mountain State Park 5476 Hwy 95 ... Parker AZ 85344	928-667-3231		565
Bucktail State Park c/o Region 1 Office ... Emporium PA 15834 *Web:* www.dcnr.state.pa.us	814-486-3365		565
Bucshon Larry (Rep R - IN) 1005 Longworth Bldg ... Washington DC 20515 *Web:* bucshon.house.gov	202-225-4636	225-3284	342-2
Bud Industries Inc 4605 E 355th St ... Willoughby OH 44094 *Web:* www.budind.com	440-946-3200	951-4015	254
Bud K Worldwide 475 US Hwy 319 S ... Moultrie GA 31768 *TF:* 877-428-3599 ■ *Web:* www.budk.com	866-246-7164		350
Bud Weiser Motors Inc 2676 Milwaukee Rd ... Beloit WI 53511 *Web:* budweisermotors.com	608-466-4172		57
Bud Werner Memorial Library 1289 Lincoln Ave ... Steamboat Springs CO 80487 *Web:* www.steamboatlibrary.org	970-879-0240		434-3
Bud's Best Cookies Inc 2070 Pkwy Office Cir ... Hoover AL 35244 *Web:* www.budsbestcookies.com	205-987-4840		297-8
Bud's Seafood Grill 314 Lincoln Ctr ... Stockton CA 95207 *Web:* www.budsseafood.com	209-956-0270		671
Budco Inc 2004 N Yellowood Ave ... Broken Arrow OK 74012 *TF:* 800-747-7307 ■ *Web:* www.budcobank.com	800-747-7307		459
Budd Bay Cafe 525 Columbia St NW ... Olympia WA 98501 *TF:* 800-442-1162 ■ *Web:* www.buddbaycafe.com	360-357-6963		671
Budd Larner P C 150 John F Kennedy Pkwy ... Short Hills NJ 07078 *Web:* www.buddlarner.com	973-379-4800	379-7734	428

Name / Address	City	State	Zip	Phone	Fax	Class
Budd Ted (Rep R - NC)						
118 Cannon HOB	Washington	DC	20515	202-225-4531		342-2
Web: budd.house.gov						
Buddakan 325 Chestnut St	Philadelphia	PA	19106	215-574-9440	574-8994	671
Web: www.buddakan.com						
Buddha's Veggie Restaurant						
5802 MacLeod Trail SW	Calgary	AB	T2H0J8	403-252-8830		671
Web: www.buddhasveggie.com						
Buddhist Churches of America (BCA)						
1710 Octavia St	San Francisco	CA	94109	415-776-5600	771-6293	48-20
Web: buddhistchurchesofamerica.org						
Buddy Group Inc, The						
722 Lombard St Ste 202	San Francisco	CA	94133	415-240-4160		5
Web: www.thebuddygroup.com						
Buddy H Coffey CPA PC						
201 N Thornton Ave	Dalton	GA	30720	706-226-7924		2
Buddy Holly Ctr 1801 Crickets Ave	Lubbock	TX	79401	806-775-3560	767-0732	520
Web: www.mylubbock.us						
Buddy Lee Attractions Inc						
38 Music Sq E Ste 300	Nashville	TN	37203	615-244-4336		731
Web: www.buddyleeattractions.com						
Buddy Moore Trucking Inc						
PO Box 10047	Birmingham	AL	35202	205-949-2260		780
TF: 877-366-6566 ■ *Web:* www.buddymooretrucking.com						
Buddy Rogers Music Inc						
6891 Simpson Ave	Cincinnati	OH	45239	513-729-1950	728-6010	526
TF: 800-536-2263 ■ *Web:* www.buddyrogers.com						
Buddy's Bar-B-Q 5806 Kingston Pk	Knoxville	TN	37919	865-584-1924	588-7211	670
Web: www.buddysbarbq.com						
Buddy's Home Furnishings						
6608 E Adamo Dr	Tampa	FL	33619	866-779-5085		264-2
TF: 866-779-5085 ■ *Web:* www.buddyrents.com						
Buddy's Italian Restaurant						
626 E Lewis St	Pocatello	ID	83201	208-233-1172		671
Buddy's Kitchen Inc						
12105 Nicollet Ave	Burnsville	MN	55337	952-894-2540		296-36
Web: www.buddyskitchen.com						
House Budget Committee						
207 Cannon House Office Bldg	Washington	DC	20515	202-226-7270		342-1
Web: www.budget.house.gov						
Budget 1 Hour Signs Inc						
2535 E Indian School Rd	Phoenix	AZ	85016	602-955-4686		701
Web: budgetsignsaz.com						
Budget Blinds Inc 1927 N Glassell St	Orange	CA	92865	714-637-2100		87
TF: 800-800-9250 ■ *Web:* www.budgetblinds.com						
Budget Finance Co						
1849 Sawtelle Blvd	Los Angeles	CA	90025	310-696-4050		217
TF: 800-225-6267 ■ *Web:* www.bfcloans.com						
Budget Host Inn 116 Kenyon Rd W	Fort Dodge	IA	50501	515-955-8501		379
Web: budgethost.com						
Budget Host International						
2307 Roosevelt Dr	Arlington	TX	76016	817-861-6088	861-6089	379
TF: 800-283-4678 ■ *Web:* www.budgethost.com						
Budget Rent A Car System Inc						
6 Sylvan Way	Parsippany	NJ	07054	800-283-4382		126
TF: 800-527-0700 ■ *Web:* www.budget.com						
Budget Suites of America						
2770 N Hwy 360	Grand Prairie	TX	75050	972-647-2500		379
TF: 866-877-2000 ■ *Web:* www.budgetsuites.com						
Budget, The						
134 N Factory St PO Box 249	Sugarcreek	OH	44681	330-852-4634	852-4421	532-4
TF: 800-915-0042 ■ *Web:* www.thebudgetnewspaper.com						
Budney Industries Inc PO Box 8316	Berlin	CT	06037	860-828-1950	828-7528	21
Web: www.budney.com						
Budreck Truck Lines Inc						
2642 Joseph Ct	University Park	IL	60484	708-496-0522	496-0568	186
TF: 800-621-0013 ■ *Web:* www.budreck.com						
Buds Salads 2428 Harrison Ave	Dallas	TX	75215	214-428-1200		345
Web: www.buds-salads.com						
Budway Enterprises Inc 13600 Napa St	Fontana	CA	92335	909-463-0500		314
Web: www.budway.net						
Budzar Industries Inc						
38241 Willoughby Pkwy	Willoughby	OH	44094	440-918-0505		201
Web: www.budzar.com						
BUECI (Barrow Utilities & Electric Co-op Inc)						
1295 Agvik St PO Box 449	Barrow	AK	99723	907-852-6166		245
Web: www.bueci.org						
Buehler Food Markets Inc						
1401 Old Mansfield Rd	Wooster	OH	44691	330-264-4355		345
TF: 800-998-4438 ■ *Web:* www.buehlers.com						
Buehler Ltd 41 Waukegan Rd	Lake Bluff	IL	60044	847-295-6500	295-7979	419
TF Sales: 800-283-4537 ■ *Web:* buehler.com						
Buehler Motor Inc						
860 Aviation Pkwy Ste 300	Morrisville	NC	27560	919-380-3333	380-3256	518
TF: 800-327-7727 ■ *Web:* www.buehlermotor.com						
Buehler Moving & Storage						
3899 Jackson St	Denver	CO	80205	303-388-4000	388-0296	519
TF: 800-234-6683 ■ *Web:* www.buehlercompanies.com						
Buehler Planetarium & Observatory (BC)						
3501 SW Davie Rd	Davie	FL	33314	954-201-6681		598
Web: www.broward.edu/locations/central/buehler.jsp						
Buena Park Convention & Visitors Office						
6601 Beach Blvd	Buena Park	CA	90621	800-541-3953		206
TF: 800-541-3953 ■ *Web:* www.visitbuenapark.com						
Buena Park Downtown						
8308 On The Mall	Buena Park	CA	90620	714-503-5000	761-0748	460
Web: www.buenaparkdowntown.com						
Buena Vista Hospitality Group Inc						
6750 Forum Dr Ste 316	Orlando	FL	32821	407-352-7161	352-2413	669
Web: www.bvhg.com						
Buena Vista Motor Inn						
1599 Lombard St	San Francisco	CA	94123	415-923-9600		378
TF: 800-835-4980 ■ *Web:* www.buenavistamotorinn.com						
Buena Vista Museum of Natural History						
2018 Chester Ave	Bakersfield	CA	93301	661-324-6350	324-7522	520
Web: www.sharktoothhill.org						
Buena Vista Regional Medical Ctr						
PO Box 309	Storm Lake	IA	50588	712-732-4030		374-3
TF: 877-401-8030 ■ *Web:* www.bvrmc.org						
Buena Vista University						
610 W Fourth St	Storm Lake	IA	50588	712-749-2253	749-2035	166
TF: 800-383-9600 ■ *Web:* www.bvu.edu						
Buescher State Park PO Box 75	Smithville	TX	78957	512-237-2241		565
Web: tpwd.texas.gov/state-parks/buescher						
Buettner Bros Lumber Co						
700 Seventh Ave SW	Cullman	AL	35055	256-734-4221		817
Web: bblumber.net						
Buff & Shine Manufacturing Inc						
2139 E Del Amo Blvd	Rancho Dominguez	CA	90220	310-886-5111		295
TF: 800-659-2833 ■ *Web:* www.buffandshine.com						
Buff Restaurant 2600 Canyon Blvd	Boulder	CO	80302	303-442-9150		671
Web: www.buffrestaurant.com						
Buffa Louie's 114 S Indiana Ave	Bloomington	IN	47408	812-333-3030	334-3945	671
Web: www.buffalouies.com						
Buffalo & Erie County Botanical Gardens						
2655 S Pk Ave	Buffalo	NY	14218	716-827-1584		97
Web: www.buffalogardens.com						
Buffalo & Erie County Naval & Military Park						
1 Naval Park Cove	Buffalo	NY	14202	716-847-1773		50-4
TF: 800-244-8684 ■ *Web:* www.buffalonavalpark.org						
Buffalo & Erie County Public Library						
1 Lafayette Sq	Buffalo	NY	14203	716-858-8900	858-6211	434-3
Web: www.buffalolib.org						
Buffalo & Pittsburgh Railroad Inc (BPRR)						
1200-C Scottsville Rd Ste 200	Rochester	NY	14624	585-463-3307	477-4947*	648
**Fax Area Code:* 800 ■ *TF:* 800-603-3385 ■ *Web:* www.gwrr.com						
Buffalo Abrasives Inc						
960 Erie Ave	North Tonawanda	NY	14120	716-693-3856		295
TF: 800-635-8856 ■ *Web:* www.buffaloabrasives.com						
Buffalo Air Handling Co						
467 Zane Snead Dr	Amherst	VA	24521	434-946-7455		18
Web: www.buffaloair.com						
Buffalo Bill Historical Ctr						
720 Sheridan Ave	Cody	WY	82414	307-587-4771		520
TF: 800-487-2692 ■ *Web:* centerofthewest.org						
Buffalo Bill Memorial Museum						
987 1/2 Lookout Mtn Rd	Golden	CO	80401	303-526-0744	526-0197	520
Web: www.buffalobill.org						
Buffalo Bill Ranch State Historical Park						
2921 Scouts Rest Ranch Rd	North Platte	NE	69101	308-535-8035		565
Web: outdoornebraska.gov						
Buffalo Bill State Park 47 Lakeside Rd	Cody	WY	82414	307-587-9227		565
Buffalo Bill's Resort & Casino						
31900 Las Vegas Blvd S	Primm	NV	89019	702-386-7867		133
TF: 888-774-6668 ■ *Web:* primmvalleyresorts.com						
Buffalo Bills						
Ralph Wilson Stadium 1 Bills Dr	Orchard Park	NY	14127	716-648-1800		715-3
TF: 877-228-4257 ■ *Web:* www.buffalobills.com						
Buffalo City Hall 65 Niagara Sq	Buffalo	NY	14202	716-851-4200	851-4360	337
TF: 800-541-2437 ■ *Web:* www.ci.buffalo.ny.us						
Buffalo Computer Graphics Inc						
4185 Bayview Rd	Blasdell	NY	14219	716-822-8668		180
Web: www.buffalocomputergraphics.com						
Buffalo County 407 S Second St	Alma	WI	54610	608-685-6209	685-6213	338
Web: www.buffalocounty.com						
Buffalo County Nebraska						
1512 Central Ave PO Box 1270	Kearney	NE	68848	308-236-1224	233-3649	338
Web: buffalocounty.ne.gov						
Buffalo Dental Manufacturing Company Inc						
159 Lafayette Dr	Syosset	NY	11791	516-496-7200		228
TF: 800-828-0203 ■ *Web:* www.buffalodental.com						
Buffalo Design Collaborative Group, The						
443 Delaware Ave	Buffalo	NY	14202	716-923-7000		226
Web: www.schneiderdesign.com						
Buffalo Economic Renaissance Corp						
920 City Hall	Buffalo	NY	14202	716-842-6923		138
Buffalo Engineering PC						
4245 Union Rd	Cheektowaga	NY	14225	716-633-5300		261
Web: buffaloengineering.com						
Buffalo Feeders LLC						
US Hwy 64 PO Box 409	Buffalo	OK	73834	580-735-2511		10-1
Web: www.buffalofeeders.com						
Buffalo Fire Historical Museum						
1850 William St	Buffalo	NY	14206	716-892-8400		520
Web: bfhsmuseum.com						
Buffalo Games Inc						
220 James E Casey Dr	Buffalo	NY	14206	855-895-4290		762
TF: 855-895-4290 ■ *Web:* www.buffalogames.com						
Buffalo General Hospital 100 High St	Buffalo	NY	14203	716-859-5600		374-3
TF: 800-506-6480 ■ *Web:* www.kaleidahealth.org						
Buffalo Grill 1611 Rebsamen Pk Rd	Little Rock	AR	72211	501-296-9535		671
Web: www.buffalogrilllr.com						
Buffalo Grove Area Chamber of Commerce						
50 1/2 Raupp Blvd PO Box 7124	Buffalo Grove	IL	60089	847-541-7799	541-7819	139
Web: www.bglcc.org						
Buffalo Grove Park District						
530 Bernard Dr	Buffalo Grove	IL	60089	847-850-2100		31
TF: 800-526-0844 ■ *Web:* bgparks.org						
Buffalo Hospital Supply Company Inc						
4039 Genesee St	Buffalo	NY	14225	716-626-9400	626-4307	475
Web: www.buffalohospital.com						
Buffalo Industries Inc						
99 S Spokane St	Seattle	WA	98134	206-682-9900	682-9907	745-8
TF: 800-683-0052 ■ *Web:* www.buffaloindustries.com						
Buffalo Lodging Associates LLC						
570 Delaware Ave	Buffalo	NY	14202	716-858-3163		378
Web: www.buffalolodging.com						
Buffalo Museum of Science						
1020 Humboldt Pkwy	Buffalo	NY	14211	716-896-5200	897-6723	520
TF: 866-291-6660 ■ *Web:* www.sciencebuff.org						
Buffalo National River						
402 N Walnut St Ste 136	Harrison	AR	72601	870-741-5443	741-7286	564
TF: 800-447-7538 ■ *Web:* www.nps.gov						
Buffalo News 1 News Plaza PO Box 100	Buffalo	NY	14240	716-849-4444	856-5150	532-2
TF: 800-777-8640 ■ *Web:* buffalonews.com						
Buffalo Niagara Convention & Visitors Bureau						
403 Main St Ste 630	Buffalo	NY	14203	716-852-2356	852-0131	206
TF: 800-283-3256 ■ *Web:* www.visitbuffaloniagara.com						

				Phone	Fax	Class
Buffalo Niagara Convention Ctr 153 Franklin St Convention Ctr Plz	Buffalo	NY	14202	716-855-5555	855-3158	205
TF: 800-995-7570 ■ *Web:* www.buffaloconvention.com						
Buffalo Niagara International Airport 4200 Genesee St	Cheektowaga	NY	14225	716-630-6000	630-6070	27
TF: 877-359-2642 ■ *Web:* www.buffaloairport.com						
Buffalo Niagara Partnership 665 Main St Ste 200	Buffalo	NY	14203	716-852-7100	852-2761	139
TF: 844-308-9165 ■ *Web:* www.thepartnership.org						
Buffalo Pharmacies Inc 1479 Kensington Ave	Buffalo	NY	14215	716-832-0599		237
Web: www.buffalopharmacies.com						
Buffalo Phil's 1149 University Blvd	Tuscaloosa	AL	35401	205-758-3318		671
Web: buffalophils.com						
Buffalo Philharmonic Orchestra 499 Franklin St	Buffalo	NY	14202	716-885-0331	885-9372	573-3
Web: www.bpo.org						
Buffalo Printing Co 2620/30 Elmwood Ave	Kenmore	NY	14217	716-877-9444		627
Web: www.buffaloprinting.com						
Buffalo Psychiatric Ctr 400 Forest Ave	Buffalo	NY	14213	716-885-2261	885-4852	374-5
TF: 800-597-8481 ■ *Web:* www.omh.ny.gov						
Buffalo Public Schools 712 City Hall	Buffalo	NY	14202	716-816-3500		685
Web: buffaloschools.org						
Buffalo Pumps Inc 874 Oliver St	North Tonawanda	NY	14120	716-693-1850	693-6303	641
TF: 800-942-6326 ■ *Web:* www.buffalopumps.com						
Buffalo Raceway 5600 McKinley Pkwy	Hamburg	NY	14075	716-649-1280	649-0033	642
TF: 800-237-1205 ■ *Web:* www.buffaloraceway.com						
Buffalo River State Park 155 S St Hwy 10	Glyndon	MN	56547	218-498-2124	498-2583	565
Web: www.dnr.state.mn.us						
Buffalo Rock Co 111 Oxmoor Rd	Birmingham	AL	35209	205-942-3435		81-2
TF: 800-822-9799 ■ *Web:* www.buffalorock.com						
Buffalo Rock State Park & Effigy Tumuli 1300 N 27th Rd PO Box 2034	Ottawa	IL	61350	815-433-2220		565
Web: www.dnr.illinois.gov/parks/pages/buffalorock.aspx						
Buffalo Run Casino 1000 Buffalo Run Blvd	Miami	OK	74354	918-542-7140		132
Web: www.buffalorun.com						
Buffalo Sabres HSBC Arena 1 Seymour H Knox III Plaza	Buffalo	NY	14203	716-855-4100		716
TF: 888-467-2273 ■ *Web:* sabres.nhl.com						
Buffalo Seminary 205 Bidwell Pkwy	Buffalo	NY	14222	716-885-6780		165
TF: 800-682-9857 ■ *Web:* buffaloseminary.org						
Buffalo Services Inc 2100 Veterans Blvd	Mccomb	MS	39648	601-249-3013	249-3013	345
Web: www.buffaloservices.com						
Buffalo Specialties Inc 10706 Craighead Dr	Houston	TX	77025	713-271-6107		687
TF: 800-256-0838 ■ *Web:* buffspec.com						
Buffalo Spree Magazine 100 Corporate Pkwy Ste 220	Buffalo	NY	14226	716-783-9119	783-9983	457-22
TF: 855-697-7733 ■ *Web:* www.buffalospree.com						
Buffalo State College 1300 Elmwood Ave	Buffalo	NY	14222	716-878-4000	878-6100*	166
**Fax:* Admissions ■ *Web:* www.buffalostate.edu						
Buffalo State College EH Butler Library 1300 Elmwood Ave	Buffalo	NY	14222	716-878-6314	878-3134	434-6
Web: www.buffalostate.edu/library						
Buffalo Supply Inc 1050A Coal Creek Dr	Lafayette	CO	80026	800-366-1812		238
TF: 800-366-1812 ■ *Web:* www.buffalosupply.com						
Buffalo Veneer & Plywood Company Inc 501 Sixth Ave NE	Buffalo	MN	55313	763-682-1822	682-9769	613
TF: 800-964-3667 ■ *Web:* www.buffaloveneerandplywood.com						
Buffalo Wild Wings Inc 5500 Wayzata Blvd Ste 1600	Minneapolis	MN	55416	952-593-9943	593-9787	670
NASDAQ: BWLD ■ *Web:* www.buffalowildwings.com						
Buffalo Wire Works Co 1165 Clinton St	Buffalo	NY	14206	716-826-4666	826-8271	688
TF: 800-828-7028 ■ *Web:* www.buffalowire.com						
Buffalo Zoological Gardens 300 Parkside Ave	Buffalo	NY	14214	716-837-3900		823
Web: www.buffalozoo.org						
Buffalo's Franchise Concepts Inc 9606 Santa Monica Blvd Penthouse	Beverly Hills	CA	90210	310-319-1850	319-1863	670
Web: www.buffalos.com						
Buffelen Woodworking Co 1901 Taylor Way	Tacoma	WA	98421	253-627-1191		499
TF: 800-423-8810 ■ *Web:* www.buffelendoor.com						
Buford Goff & Associates Inc 1331 Elmwood Ave	Columbia	SC	29201	803-254-6302		261
Web: bgainc.com						
Buford Media Group LLC (BMG) 6125 Paluxy Dr	Tyler	TX	75703	903-561-4411		116
Buford-Thompson Co 1450 N Jim Wright Fwy Ft Worth	White Settlement	TX	76108	817-467-4981	467-5619	186
Web: www.buford-thompson.com						
Bug Off Exterminators Inc 1064 NW 54th St	Fort Lauderdale	FL	33309	954-772-8338		577
Web: bugoffexterminatorsflorida.com						
Bug Tracker 2030 Blvd Pie-IX Ste 307	Montreal	QC	H1V2C8	514-496-0093		631
Web: www.bug-tracker.com						
Bugaboo Creek Steak House 24 Bangor Mall Blvd	Bangor	ME	04401	207-945-5515		671
Web: bugaboocreek.com						
Bugcrowd Inc 921 Front St 1st Fl	San Francisco	CA	94111	650-260-8443		196
TF: 888-361-9734 ■ *Web:* bugcrowd.com						
Buglisi Dance Theatre 229 W 42nd St Ste 502	New York	NY	10036	212-719-3301	719-3302	573-1
TF: 800-754-0797 ■ *Web:* www.buglisi-foreman.org						
BUG-O Systems Inc 161 Hillpointe Dr	Canonsburg	PA	15317	412-331-1776	331-0383	811
TF: 800-245-3186 ■ *Web:* www.bugo.com						
Bug-Out Service Inc 5951 Arlington Expwy	Jacksonville	FL	32211	904-743-8272		577
Web: bugoutservice.com						
Buhler Inc 13105 12th Ave N	Plymouth	MN	55441	763-847-9900	847-9911	201
TF: 800-722-7483 ■ *Web:* www.buhlergroup.com						
Buhler Versatile Inc 1260 Clarence Ave	Winnipeg	MB	R3T1T2	204-661-8711	654-2503	273
Web: www.buhlerindustries.com						
Build-A-Bear Workshop Inc 1954 Innerbelt Business Ctr Dr	Saint Louis	MO	63114	314-423-8000		761
NYSE: BBW ■ *TF:* 888-560-2327 ■ *Web:* www.buildabear.com						
BuildASign.com 11525B Stonehollow Dr Ste 220	Austin	TX	78758	512-374-9850		177
TF: 800-330-9622 ■ *Web:* www.buildasign.com						
BuildBlock Building Systems LLC 9701 N Broadway Ext	Oklahoma City	OK	73114	405-840-3386		183
Web: www.buildblock.com						
BuildCentral Inc 200 W Madison St Ste 1110	Chicago	IL	60606	312-223-1600		5
Web: www.buildcentral.com						
Builder Fusion Inc 424 W 800 N Ste 202	Orem	UT	84057	801-765-0191		317
Web: www.builderfusion.com						
Builder Homesite Inc 11900 Ranch Rd 620 N	Austin	TX	78750	512-371-3800		195
Web: www.builderhomesite.com						
Builder Magazine 1 Thomas Cir NW Ste 600	Washington	DC	20005	202-452-0800	785-1974	457-21
TF: 800-325-6180 ■ *Web:* www.builderonline.com						
BuilderGuru Contracting Inc 2124 Priest Bridge Dr Ste 14	Crofton	MD	21114	410-923-1379		186
Web: www.builderguru.com						
Builders Design & Leasing Inc 7601 Lindbergh Dr	Gaithersburg	MD	20879	301-590-1100		393
Web: www.buildersdesign.com						
Builders FirstSource Inc 2001 Bryan St Ste 1600	Dallas	TX	75201	214-880-3500	880-3599	191-3
NASDAQ: BLDR ■ *Web:* www.bldr.com						
Builders General Supply Co 15 Sycamore Ave	Little Silver	NJ	07739	800-570-7227		191-3
TF: 800-570-7227 ■ *Web:* www.buildersgeneral.com						
Builders Hardware & Specialty Company Inc 2002 W 16th St	Erie	PA	16505	814-453-4736		191-2
Web: www.builders-hardware.net						
Builders Hardware & Supply Company Inc 1516 15th Ave W	Seattle	WA	98119	206-281-3700		351
TF: 800-828-1437 ■ *Web:* www.builders-hardware.com						
Builders Redi-Mix Inc 30701 W 10 Mile Rd Ste 500 PO Box 2900	Farmington Hills	MI	48333	888-988-4400		182
TF: 888-988-4400 ■ *Web:* www.superiormaterialsllc.com						
Building & Construction Trades Dept AFL-CIO 815 16th St NW Ste 600	Washington	DC	20006	202-347-1461	628-0724	49-3
Web: www.bctd.org						
Building 19 Inc 319 Lincoln St	Hingham	MA	02043	781-749-6900		791
Web: www.building19.com						
Building Block Computer 3209 Terminal Dr Ste 100	Saint Paul	MN	55121	651-687-9435		734
Web: www.bbcusa.com						
Building Bridges at Wilcat Way 1525 NE Wildcat Way	Bentonville	AR	72712	479-254-5277		186
Building Design & Construction Magazine 3030 W Salt Creek Ln Ste 201	Arlington Heights	IL	60005	847-391-1000	390-0408	457-21
TF: 888-811-3288 ■ *Web:* www.bdcnetwork.com						
Building Earth Sciences Inc 5545 Derby Dr	Irondale	AL	35210	205-836-6300		256
Web: www.buildingandearth.com						
Building Industry Credit Association 10601 Civic Center Dr	Rancho Cucamonga	CA	91730	213-251-1100	986-3903	218
TF: 800-722-2422 ■ *Web:* www.bicanet.com						
Building Leaders Inc PO Box 408263 Ste 200b	Chicago	IL	60640	773-769-4409		261
Web: www.buildingleaders.com						
Building Maintenance Services LLC 1541 S Beretania St Ste 204	Honolulu	HI	96826	808-983-1250		104
Web: www.bmsnationwide.com						
Building Material Dealers Assn (BMDA) 1006 SE Grand Ave Ste 301	Portland	OR	97214	503-208-3763		49-3
TF: 888-960-6329 ■ *Web:* www.bmda.com						
Building Owners & Managers Assn International (BOMA) 1101 15th St NW Ste 800	Washington	DC	20005	202-408-2662	326-6377	49-17
TF: 800-426-6292 ■ *Web:* www.boma.org						
Building Performance Institute Inc 107 Hermes Rd Ste 210	Malta	NY	12020	518-899-2727		194
TF: 877-274-1274 ■ *Web:* www.bpihomeowner.org						
Building Products Corp 950 Freeburg Ave	Belleville	IL	62220	618-233-4427	233-2031	182
TF: 800-233-1996 ■ *Web:* www.buildingproductscorp.com						
Building Products Plus 12317 Almeda Rd	Houston	TX	77045	800-460-8627	433-7068*	818
**Fax Area Code:* 713 ■ *TF:* 800-460-8627 ■ *Web:* www.buildingproductsplus.com						
Building Restoration Inc 2423 Ravine Rd	Kalamazoo	MI	49004	269-345-0567		104
Web: www.gobri.com						
Building Service Contractors Assn International (BSCAI) 401 N Michigan Ave Ste 2200	Chicago	IL	60611	312-321-5167	673-6735	49-13
TF: 800-368-3414 ■ *Web:* www.bscai.org						
Building Service Inc (BSI) W222 N630 Cheaney Rd	Waukesha	WI	53186	262-955-6400		393
TF: 866-353-3600 ■ *Web:* www.buildingservice.com						
BuildingSearch.com Inc 90 Railway Ave	Campbell	CA	95008	408-426-8424		387
Web: www.buildingsearch.com						
BuildingStars Inc 33 Worthington Access Dr	Maryland Heights	MO	63043	314-991-3356		310
Web: www.buildingstars.com						
Bukit Energy Inc 2310, 700 - Second St SW Scotia Tower	Calgary	AB	T2P2W2	403-930-2250		536
Web: www.bukitenergy.com						

	Phone	Fax	Class
Bula Forge & Machine Inc 3001 W 121st St, Cleveland OH 44111 *Web:* www.bulaforge.com	216-252-7600		483
Bulbman 3101 Orange Grove Ave, North Highlands CA 95660 *TF:* 800-245-2852 ■ *Web:* www.bulbman.com	916-920-3234		752
Bulfinch Cos Inc 250 First Ave Ste 200, Needham Heights MA 02494 *Web:* www.bulfinch.com	781-707-4000		652
Bulgaria 11 E 84th St, New York NY 10028	212-737-4790		784
Consulate General 121 E 62nd St, New York NY 10065 *Web:* bulgaria-embassy.org	212-935-4646	319-5955	257
Embassy 1621 22nd St NW, Washington DC 20008 *Web:* www.bulgaria-embassy.org	202-387-0174	234-7973	257
Bul-Go-Gi House 8813 92 St NW, Edmonton AB T6C3P9 *Web:* www.edmontonkoreanfood.com	780-466-2330		671
Bulk Chemicals Inc 1074 Stinson Dr, Reading PA 19605 *Web:* www.bulkchemicals.com	610-926-4128		146
Bulk Connection Inc 15 Allen St, Mystic CT 06355 *TF:* 800-543-2855 ■ *Web:* www.bulkconnection.com	860-572-9111		311
Bulk Foods.com 3040 Hill Ave, Toledo OH 43607 *Web:* www.bulkfoods.com	419-531-6887		345
Bulk Lift International Inc (BLI) 1013 Tamarac Dr, Carpentersville IL 60110 *TF:* 800-879-2247 ■ *Web:* www.bulklift.com	847-428-6059	428-7180	67
Bulk Solutions Inc 4040 Waring Rd, Lakeland FL 33811 *TF:* 800-345-1159 ■ *Web:* bulksol.com	863-248-1136		463
Bulk Transit Corp 7177 Industrial Pkwy, Plain City OH 43064 *TF:* 800-345-2855 ■ *Web:* www.bulktransit.com	614-873-4632	873-3393	780
Bulkmatic Transport Co 2001 N Cline Ave, Griffith IN 46319 **Fax Area Code:* 219 ■ *TF:* 800-535-8505 ■ *Web:* www.bulkmatic.com	800-535-8505	972-7655*	780
Bulkmatic Transport Co 205 Butler Cir SW, Vernon AL 35592	205-695-7132		780
Bulk-pack Inc 1025 N Ninth St, Monroe LA 71201 *TF:* 800-498-4215 ■ *Web:* www.bulk-pack.com	318-387-3260	387-6362	100
Bull & Bear Capital Advisors Inc 8659 Nathans Cove Ct, Jacksonville FL 32256 *Web:* www.bullbearcapital.com	904-363-3600		194
Bull HN Information Systems Inc 285 Billerica Rd, Billerica MA 01824 *Web:* www.bull.com	978-294-6000	244-0085	180
Bull Island Realty Inc 29 Holloway Rd, Poquoson VA 23662 *Web:* bullislandrealty.com	757-868-4663		652
Bull Mktg Group LLC 79 S Milwaukee Ave, Wheeling IL 60090	847-520-1182		194
Bull Moose Tube Co 1819 Clarkson Rd Ste 100, Chesterfield MO 63017 *TF:* 800-325-4467 ■ *Web:* www.bullmoosetube.com	636-537-2600		490
Bull Ring of Santa Fe, The 150 Washington Ave, Santa Fe NM 87501 *Web:* santafebullring.com	505-983-3328		671
Bull Shoals-White River State Park 140 Boat Dock Cove Rd, Bull Shoals AR 72169 *Web:* www.arkansasstateparks.com	870-431-5521		565
Bull Wealth Management Group Inc 4100 Yonge St Ste 612, Toronto ON M2P2B5 *TF:* 866-623-2053 ■ *Web:* www.bullwealth.com	416-223-2053		690
Bull's Eye Saloon & Restaurant 3734 Kirkwood Hwy, Wilmington DE 19808 *Web:* www.bullseyesaloon.com	302-633-6557		671
Bull's Island Recreation Area 2185 Daniel Bray Hwy, Stockton NJ 08559 *Web:* www.njparksandforests.org	609-397-2949		565
Bullard Abrasives Inc 6 Carol Dr, Lincoln RI 02865 *TF:* 800-227-4469 ■ *Web:* www.bullardabrasives.com	401-333-3000		1
Bullard Co 1898 Safety Way, Cynthiana KY 41031 *TF:* 800-227-0423 ■ *Web:* www.bullard.com	859-234-6611	234-4352	576
Bullard Construction Inc PO Box 575, Addison TX 75001 *Web:* www.bullardconstruction.com	972-661-8474	661-8985	186
Bullards Beach State Park PO Box 569, Bandon OR 97411 *TF:* 800-551-6949 ■ *Web:* oregonstateparks.org	541-347-2209		565
Bulldawg Mktg Inc 115 Eastbend Ct, Mooresville NC 28117 *Web:* www.bulldawgmarketing.com	704-660-6441		194
Bulldog Automation 653 Riverside St, Portland ME 04103 *Web:* bulldogautomation.com	207-772-9561		261
Bulldog Bag Ltd 13631 Vulcan Way, Richmond BC V6V1K4 *TF:* 800-665-1944 ■ *Web:* www.bulldogbag.com	604-273-8021		601
Bulldog Hiway Express 3390 Buffalo Ave, Charleston SC 29418 *TF:* 800-331-9515 ■ *Web:* www.bulldoghiway.com	843-744-1651	529-3345	449
Bulldog Marine 1133 Lake Oconee Pkwy, Eatonton GA 31024 *Web:* www.bulldogmarine.biz	706-923-0404		261
Bulldog Solutions LLC 7600 N Capital of Texas Hwy Bldg C Ste 250, Austin TX 78731 *TF:* 877-402-9199 ■ *Web:* www.bulldogsolutions.com	877-402-9199		5
Bullen Cos 1640 Delmar Dr PO Box 37, Folcroft PA 19032 *TF:* 800-444-8900 ■ *Web:* bullenonline.com	610-534-8900	534-8912	151
Bullet Guard Corp 3963 Commerce Dr, West Sacramento CA 95691 *Web:* www.bulletguard.com	916-373-0402		320
Bullet Weights Inc 182 S Apollo Dr, Alda NE 68810 *Web:* www.bulletweights.com	308-382-7436	382-2906	710
Bulletin Daily 211 N Main St, Colfax WA 99111 *Web:* www.colfax.com	509-397-3332		532-3
Bulletin, The 1777 SW Chandler Ave, Bend OR 97702 *TF:* 800-503-3933 ■ *Web:* www.bendbulletin.com	541-382-1811	385-5804	532-2
Bulley & Andrews LLC 1755 W Armitage Ave, Chicago IL 60622 *TF:* 800-561-3357 ■ *Web:* www.bulley.com	773-235-2433	235-2471	186
Bullfrog Films Inc 372 Dautrich Rd, Reading PA 19606 *TF:* 800-543-3764 ■ *Web:* www.bullfrogfilms.com	610-779-8226		514
Bullhead Area Chamber of Commerce 1251 Hwy 95, Bullhead City AZ 86429 *TF:* 800-987-7457 ■ *Web:* bullheadareachamber.com	928-754-4121	754-5514	139
Bullhead City Bee 1905 Lakeside Dr, Bullhead City AZ 86442 *Web:* www.bullheadcitybee.com	928-763-9339		77
Bullhorn Inc 33-41 Farnsworth St 5th Fl, Boston MA 02210 *TF:* 800-206-7934 ■ *Web:* www.bullhorn.com	617-478-9100		177
Bullis Charter School 102 W Portola Ave, Los Altos CA 94022 *Web:* www.bullischarterschool.com	650-947-4939		685
Bullitt County 300 S Buckman St, Shepherdsville KY 40165 *TF:* 800-526-2068 ■ *Web:* www.bullittcounty.org	502-543-2262		338
Bullitt County Chamber of Commerce 295 N Buckman St PO Box 1656, Shepherdsville KY 40165 *Web:* www.bullittchamber.org	502-543-6727	543-1765	139
Bullivant Houser Bailey PC 888 SW Fifth Ave Ste 300, Portland OR 97204 *Web:* www.bullivant.com	503-228-6351		428
Bulloch & Bulloch Inc 309 Cash Memorial Blvd, Forest Park GA 30297 *TF:* 800-339-8177 ■ *Web:* www.jphallexpress.com	404-762-5063		25
Bulloch County 20 Siebald St, Statesboro GA 30458 *Web:* www.bullochcounty.net	912-764-6245	764-8634	338
Bulloch County Board of Education 150 Williams Rd Ste A, Statesboro GA 30458 *Web:* www.bulloch.k12.ga.us	912-212-8500	764-8436	685
Bullock County 106 Conecuh Ave PO Box 87, Union Springs AL 36089 *Web:* www.bullockcountyal.com	334-738-5411		338
Bullock County Correctional Facility 104 Bullock Dr PO Box 5107, Union Springs AL 36089 *TF:* 800-292-6678 ■ *Web:* alabama.gov	334-738-5625	738-5020	213
Bullock Creek Public Schools 1420 S Badour Rd, Midland MI 48640 *TF:* 800-999-3199 ■ *Web:* www.bcreek.k12.mi.us	989-631-9022	631-2882	685
Bullock Steve (D) *State Capitol* PO Box 200801, Helena MT 59620 *Web:* governor.mt.gov	406-444-3111	444-5529	343
Bullock's Bar-B-Que 3330 Quebec Dr, Durham NC 27705 *Web:* www.bullocksbbq.com	919-383-3211		671
Bullseye Database Mktg LLC 5546 S 104th E Ave, Tulsa OK 74146 *Web:* www.bullseyedm.com	918-587-1731		194
Bullseye Glass Co 3722 SE 21st Ave, Portland OR 97202 *TF:* 888-220-3002 ■ *Web:* www.bullseyeglass.com	503-232-8887		329
Bullseye Marketing Group 125 E Main St Ste 205, Mount Kisco NY 10549 *Web:* www.bullseyegroup.biz	914-242-8288		195
Bullseye Strategy 110 E Broward Blvd Ste 1550, Fort Lauderdale FL 33301 *Web:* www.bullseyestrategy.com	954-591-8999		194
Bulltick Capital Markets 701 Brickell Ave Ste 2550, Miami FL 33131 *Web:* bulltick.com	305-533-1541	533-1008	691
Bullwacker's 653 Cannery Row, Monterey CA 93940	831-373-1353		671
Bully Hill Vineyards 8843 Greyton H Taylor Memorial Dr, Hammondsport NY 14840 *TF:* 800-441-4241 ■ *Web:* www.bullyhillvineyards.com	607-868-3610	868-3205	80-3
Bulova Corp Empire State Bldg 350 Fifth Ave, Woodside NY 10118 **Fax Area Code:* 718 ■ *TF:* 800-228-5682 ■ *Web:* www.bulova.com	212-497-1875	204-3546*	153
Bulow Creek State Park 3351 Old Dixie Hwy, Ormond Beach FL 32174 *Web:* www.floridastateparks.org/bulowcreek	386-676-4050		565
Bulow Plantation Ruins Historic State Park 3501 Old Kings Rd, Flagler Beach FL 32136 *Web:* www.floridastateparks.org	386-517-2084		565
Bumble Bee Seafoods Inc PO Box 85362, San Diego CA 92186 *TF:* 800-800-8572 ■ *Web:* www.bumblebee.com	858-715-4000		296-13
Bunch/Shoemaker Inc 7026 Old Katy Rd No 152, Houston TX 77024 *Web:* bunchshoemaker.com	713-426-2850		321
Bunches 14 1/2 N Santa Cruz Ave, Los Gatos CA 95030 *Web:* buncheslosgatos.com	408-395-5451		292
Buncombe Correctional Ctr 2988 Riverside Dr, Asheville NC 28804 *Web:* www.doc.state.nc.us	828-645-7630		213
Buncombe County 205 College St Ste 300, Asheville NC 28801 *TF:* 800-334-9880 ■ *Web:* www.buncombecounty.org	828-250-4100	250-6077	338
Bundy Group 24 Walnut Ave, Roanoke VA 24016 *Web:* bundygroup.com	540-342-2151		194
Bunge Ltd 50 Main St, White Plains NY 10606 *NYSE:* BG ■ *Web:* www.bunge.com	914-684-2800		296-29
Bunim/Murray Productions 6007 Sepulveda Blvd, Van Nuys CA 91411 *Web:* www.bunim-murray.com	818-756-5100		514
Bunker Clark Winnell Nuorala PC 2301 Mitchell Park Dr, Petoskey MI 49770 *Web:* bcwncpa.com	231-347-3963		2
Bunker Hill Community College			
Charlestown 250 New Rutherford Ave, Boston MA 02129 **Fax:* Admissions ■ *TF:* 877-218-8829 ■ *Web:* www.bhcc.mass.edu	617-228-2000	228-2082*	162
Chelsea 70 Everett Ave, Chelsea MA 02150 *Web:* www.bhcc.mass.edu	617-228-2101	228-2106	162
Bunker Hill Monument Monument Sq, Charlestown MA 02129 *Web:* www.nps.gov	617-242-5641	242-6006	50-4
Bunkers International Corp 1071 S Sun Dr Ste 3, Lake Mary FL 32746	407-328-7757	328-0045	465
Bunnell Inc 436 Lawndale Dr, Salt Lake City UT 84115 *TF:* 800-800-4358 ■ *Web:* www.bunl.com	801-467-0800		476
Bunnery Bakery & Restaurant, The 130 N Cache Dr, Jackson WY 83001 *Web:* bunnery.com/restaurant2.php	307-733-5474		671
Bunn-O-Matic Corp 1400 Stevenson Dr, Springfield IL 62703 *TF:* 800-637-8606 ■ *Web:* www.bunn.com	217-529-6601		37
Buns Over Texas 6045 SW 34th, Amarillo TX 79109 *TF:* 800-383-4712 ■ *Web:* bunsovertexas.com	806-358-6808		671

	Phone	Fax	Class
Buntin Group, The 716 Division St............Nashville TN 37203 Web: www.buntingroup.com	615-244-5720	244-6511	4
Bunting Bearings Corp 1001 Holland Pk Blvd........................Holland OH 43528 TF: 888-286-8464 ■ Web: www.buntingbearings.com	419-866-7000	866-0653	308
Bunting Door & Hardware Company Inc 6650 Business Pkwy Ste C....................Elkridge MD 21237 Web: www.buntingdoor.com	410-574-8123	574-8171	351
Bunting Magnetics Co 500 S Spencer Ave.......Newton KS 67114 TF: 800-835-2526 ■ Web: buntingmagnetics.com	316-284-2020	283-4975	485
Buon Appetito 1609 India St.................San Diego CA 92101 Web: www.sandiegouniontribune.com	619-238-9880		671
Buon Giorno Ristorante Italiano 823 17th Ave SW...........................Calgary AB T2T0A1 Web: buongiornoristoranteitaliano.ca	403-244-5522		671
Buona Terra 2535 N California Ave..............Chicago IL 60647 Web: www.buona-terra.com	773-289-3800		671
Buona Vita Inc 1 S Industrial Blvd............Bridgeton NJ 08302 Web: www.buonavitainc.com	856-453-7972		297-8
Burbank Central Library 110 N Glenoaks Blvd........................Burbank CA 91502 Web: www.burbank.lib.ca.us	818-238-5600		434-3
Burbank Chamber of Commerce 200 W Magnolia Blvd........................Burbank CA 91502 TF: 800-495-5005 ■ Web: www.burbankchamber.org	818-846-3111	846-0109	139
Burbank Roofing Supply Inc 700 N Victory Blvd..........................Burbank CA 91502 Web: www.roofingdealer.com	818-840-8851		191-4
Burbank Town Ctr 201 E Magnolia Blvd..........Burbank CA 91502 Web: www.burbanktowncenter.com	818-566-8556	566-7936	460
Burbank Water & Power 164 W Magnolia Blvd........................Burbank CA 91502 TF: 800-342-5397 ■ Web: www.burbankwaterandpower.com	818-238-3700		539
Burberry Ltd (New York) 9 E 57th St...........New York NY 10022 TF: 800-282-2200 ■ Web: www.burberry.com	212-407-7100		157-4
Burch & Company Inc 4151 N Mulberry Dr Ste 235................Kansas City MO 64116 Web: www.burchco.com	816-842-4660		690
Burch & Cracchiolo PA 702 E Osborn Rd Ste 200.....................Phoenix AZ 85014 Web: www.bcattorneys.com	602-274-7611		428
Burch Fabrics Group 4200 Brockton Dr SE....................Grand Rapids MI 49512 TF: 800-841-8111 ■ Web: www.burchfabrics.com	616-698-2800		594
Burch Industries Inc 21381 Charles Craft Ln PO Box 1049..........Laurinburg NC 28352 TF: 800-477-3346 ■ Web: www.burchindustries.com	910-844-3688	844-3689	664
Burch Porter & Johnson Pllc 130 North Ct Ave..........................Memphis TN 38103 Web: www.bpjlaw.com	901-524-5000	524-5024	428
Burchell Nursery Inc, The 12000 Hwy 120.............................Oakdale CA 95361 TF: 800-828-8733 ■ Web: www.burchellnursery.com	209-845-8733	847-0284	292
Burchfield Group Inc, The 1295 Northland Dr Ste 350.....................St Paul MN 55120 TF: 800-778-1359 ■ Web: www.burchfieldgroup.com	651-389-5640		194
Burchfield-Penney Art Ctr *Buffalo State College* 1300 Elmwood Ave............................Buffalo NY 14222 TF: 800-349-9099 ■ Web: www.burchfieldpenney.org	716-878-6011	878-6003	50-2
Burckhardt Compression (US) Inc 7240 Brittmoore Rd Ste 100...................Houston TX 77041 Web: www.burckhardtcompression.com	281-582-1050		358
Burco Molding Inc 15015 Herriman Blvd.......................Noblesville IN 46060	317-773-5699		608
Burd & Fletcher 3000 W Geospace Dr.....................Independence MO 64056 TF: 800-821-2776 ■ Web: www.burdfletcher.com	816-257-0291		101
Burdeshaw Associates Ltd 4701 Sangamore Rd Ste N100.................Bethesda MD 20816 Web: www.burdeshaw.com	301-229-5800		194
Burdette Beckmann Inc 5851 Johnson St..........................Hollywood FL 33021 TF: 888-575-7413 ■ Web: www.bbiteam.com	954-983-4360		123
Burdette Ketchum 1023 Kings Ave..........Jacksonville FL 32207 Web: www.burdetteketchum.com	904-645-6200		7
Burdine-Anderson Corp 1528 Resource Dr.........................Burlington KY 41005 Web: www.burdine-anderson.com	859-371-4985		454
Burdiss Lettershop Services Co 9765 Widmer Rd..............................Lenexa KS 66215 Web: www.burdiss.com	913-492-0545		5
Bureau County 700 S Main St.................Princeton IL 61356 TF: 800-916-3330 ■ Web: www.bureaucounty-il.com	815-866-3606		338
Bureau of Alcohol Tobacco Firearms & Explosives (ATF) 650 Massachusetts Ave NW................Washington DC 20226 Web: www.atf.gov	202-927-8210		340-14
Bureau of Alcohol Tobacco Firearms & Explosives Regional Offices			
Atlanta Field Div 2600 Century Pkwy NE.......................Atlanta GA 30345 Web: www.atf.gov	404-417-2600	417-2601	340-14
Baltimore Field Div 31 Hopkins Plaza 5th Fl...................Baltimore MD 21201 Web: www.atf.gov/baltimore-field-division	410-779-1700		340-14
Boston Field Div 10 Causeway St Ste 791.........Boston MA 02222	617-557-1200	557-1201	340-14
Charlotte Field Div 6701 Carmel Rd Ste 200....................Charlotte NC 28226 Web: www.atf.gov	704-716-1800	716-1801	340-14
Chicago Field Div 525 W Van Buren St Ste 600.................Chicago IL 60607 Web: www.atf.gov	312-846-7200	846-7201	340-14
Columbus Field Div 37 W Broad St Ste 200.....................Columbus OH 43215 Web: www.atf.gov	614-827-8400	827-8401	340-14
Dallas Field Div 1114 Commerce St Rm 303......................Dallas TX 75242 Web: www.atf.gov	469-227-4300	227-4330	340-14
Denver Field Div 950 17th St Ste 1800...........Denver CO 80202 Web: www.atf.gov	303-575-7600	575-7601	340-14
Detroit Field Div 1155 Brewery Pk Blvd Ste 300.................Detroit MI 48207 Web: www.atf.gov	313-202-3400	202-3445	340-14
Houston Field Div 333 W Loop N # 111.........Houston TX 77024 Web: www.atf.gov	713-220-2157		340-14
Kansas City Group V 2600 Grand Ave Ste 280................Kansas City MO 64108 Web: www.atf.gov	816-559-0850	559-0831	340-14
Louisville Field Div 600 Martin Luther King Pl #322............Louisville KY 40202 Web: www.atf.gov	502-753-3400	753-3401	340-14
Miami Field Div 11410 NW 20 St Ste 201.........Miami FL 33172 Web: www.atf.gov	305-597-4800	597-4801	340-14
Nashville Field Div 5300 Maryland Way Ste 200..............Brentwood TN 37027 Web: www.atf.gov/nashville-field-division	615-565-1400	565-1401	340-14
New Orleans Field Div 1 Galleria Blvd Ste 1700....................Metairie LA 70001	504-841-7000	841-7159	340-14
Philadelphia Field Div 601 Walnut St........................Philadelphia PA 19106 Web: www.atf.gov	215-446-7800	446-7811	340-14
Phoenix Field Div 201 E Washington St Ste 940...............Phoenix AZ 85004 Web: www.atf.gov	602-776-5400	776-5429	340-14
Saint Paul Field Div 30 E Seventh St Ste 1900................Saint Paul MN 55101 Web: www.atf.gov	651-726-0200	726-0201	340-14
Tampa Field Div 400 N Tampa St Ste 2100........Tampa FL 33602 Web: www.atf.gov	813-202-7300	202-7301	340-14
Washington (DC) Field Div 1401 H St NW Ste 900..................Washington DC 20226 Web: www.atf.gov/field/washington	202-648-8010	648-8001	340-14
Bureau of Consular Affairs 2201 C St NW SA 17 9th Fl................Washington DC 20522 TF: 888-407-4747 ■ Web: travel.state.gov	202-501-4444		340-16
Office of Children's Issues SA-17 Ninth Fl........................Washington DC 20522 TF: 888-407-4747 ■ Web: www.travel.state.gov	202-501-4444	485-6221	340-16
Passport Services 600 19th St NW 1st Fl, Sidewalk Level.....Washington DC 20006 TF: 888-874-7793 ■ Web: travel.state.gov	877-487-2778		340-16
Bureau of Diplomatic Security DS Public Affairs Bureau of Diplomatic Security..............Washington DC 20522 Web: www.state.gov	571-345-2502		340-16
Bureau of East Asian & Pacific Affairs 2201 C St NW Rm 2236......................Washington DC 20520 Web: www.state.gov/p/eap	202-895-3500		340-16
Bureau of Economic Analysis (BEA) 1441 L St NW...........................Washington DC 20005 TF: 800-727-9540 ■ Web: www.bea.gov	202-606-9900	606-5311	340-2
Bureau of Engraving & Printing 14th & C Sts SW........................Washington DC 20228 *Fax Area Code: 202 ■ TF: 877-874-4114 ■ Web: www.moneyfactory.gov	877-874-4114	874-3177*	340-18
Bureau of Indian Affairs (BIA) 1849 C St NW MS 4004 MIB................Washington DC 20240 Web: www.bia.gov	202-208-7163	208-5320	340-13
Bureau of Indian Affairs Regional Offices (BIA)			
Alaska Region 3601 C St Ste 1100...........Anchorage AK 99503 TF: 800-645-8397 ■ Web: www.bia.gov	907-271-1536	271-1349	340-13
Eastern Oklahoma Region 3100 W Peak Blvd PO Box 8002...........Muskogee OK 74402 TF: 800-645-8397 ■ Web: www.bia.gov	918-781-4600	781-4604	340-13
Eastern Region 545 Marriott Dr Ste 700.....................Nashville TN 37214 TF: 800-495-4655 ■ Web: www.bia.gov	615-564-6700	564-6701	340-13
Great Plains Region 115 Fourth Ave SE.......................Aberdeen SD 57401 TF: 800-221-0827 ■ Web: www.bia.gov	605-226-7343	226-7446	340-13
Midwest Region 5600 American Blvd W Ste 500..........Bloomington MN 55347 Web: www.bia.gov	612-713-4400	713-4401	340-13
Navajo Region 301 W Hill St.....................Gallup NM 87301 Web: www.bia.gov	505-863-8314	863-8324	340-13
Northwest Region 911 NE 11th Ave............Portland OR 97232 TF: 800-645-8397 ■ Web: www.bia.gov	503-231-6702	231-2201	340-13
Pacific Region 2800 Cottage Way...........Sacramento CA 95825 TF: 800-645-8397 ■ Web: www.bia.gov	916-978-6000	978-6099	340-13
Rocky Mountain Region 316 N 26th St..........Billings MT 59101 TF: 800-645-8397 ■ Web: www.bia.gov	406-247-7943	247-7976	340-13
Southern Plains Region PO Box 368..........Anadarko OK 73005 TF: 800-645-8465 ■ Web: www.indianaffairs.gov	405-247-6673	247-5611	340-13
Southwest Region 1001 Indian School Rd NW.............Albuquerque NM 87104 Web: www.bia.gov	505-563-3103	563-3101	340-13
Western Region 2600 N Central Ave FL 8 Ste 310.............Phoenix AZ 85008 TF: 800-495-4655 ■ Web: www.bia.gov	602-379-6600	379-4413	340-13
Bureau of Industry & Security 1401 Constitution Ave NW Rm 4065.........Washington DC 20230 Web: www.bis.doc.gov	202-622-2480		340-2
Bureau of International Labor Affairs 200 Constitution Ave NW..................Washington DC 20210 Web: www.dol.gov/ilab	202-693-4770	693-4780	340-15
Bureau of Labor Statistics 2 Massachusetts Ave NE..................Washington DC 20212 TF: 800-877-8339 ■ Web: www.bls.gov	202-691-5200	691-7890	340-15
Consumer Price Index 2 Massachusetts Ave NE..................Washington DC 20212 TF: 800-877-8339 ■ Web: www.bls.gov/cpi	202-691-5200	691-6325	340-15
Bureau of Labor Statistics Regional Offices			
Mid-Atlantic Information Office 170 S Independence Mall W Ste 610 E.....Philadelphia PA 19106 Web: www.bls.gov/ro3	215-597-3282	861-5720	340-15
Midwest Information Office 230 S Dearborn St Ste 960.................Chicago IL 60604 TF: 800-877-8339 ■ Web: www.bls.gov	312-353-1880	353-1886	340-15

Phone | Fax | Class

Mountain-Plains Information Office
2300 Main St Ste 1190 .... Kansas City MO 64108 816-285-7000 285-7009 340-15
TF: 800-487-9004 ■ Web: www.bls.gov/ro7
New England Information Office
JFK Federal Bldg Ste E-310 .... Boston MA 02203 617-565-2327 565-4182 340-15
Web: www.bls.gov/ro1
New York-New Jersey Information Office
201 Varick St Rm 808 .... New York NY 10014 646-264-3600 337-2532* 340-15
*Fax Area Code: 212 ■ TF: 800-877-8339 ■ Web: www.bls.gov/ro2
Southeast Information Office
61 Forsyth St .... Atlanta GA 30303 404-893-4222 893-4221 340-15
TF: 800-347-3764 ■ Web: www.bls.gov
Southwest Information Office
Federal Bldg 525 Griffin St Rm 221 .... Dallas TX 75202 972-850-4800 767-8881* 340-15
*Fax Area Code: 214 ■ Web: www.bls.gov/ro6
Western Information Office
PO Box 193766 .... San Francisco CA 94119 415-625-2270 625-2351 340-15
TF: 800-877-8339 ■ Web: www.bls.gov

Bureau of Land Management (BLM)
1849 C St NW Rm 5665 .... Washington DC 20240 202-208-3801 208-5242 340-13
TF: 800-246-8101 ■ Web: www.blm.gov
Wild Horse & Burro Program
1849 C St NW Rm. 5665 .... Washington DC 20240 202-208-3801 340-13
TF: 866-468-7826 ■ Web: www.blm.gov

Bureau of Land Management Regional Offices
Alaska State Office
222 W Seventh Ave Ste 13 .... Anchorage AK 99513 907-271-5960 271-3684 340-13
TF: 800-877-8339 ■ Web: www.blm.gov
Arizona State Office
1 N Central Ave Ste 800 .... Phoenix AZ 85004 602-417-9200 417-9556 340-13
Web: www.blm.gov
California State Office
2800 Cottage Way Ste W-1834 .... Sacramento CA 95825 916-978-4400 978-4416 340-13
Web: www.blm.gov
Colorado State Office
2850 Youngfield St .... Lakewood CO 80215 303-239-3600 239-3933 340-13
Web: www.blm.gov
Eastern States Office
7450 Boston Blvd .... Springfield VA 22153 703-440-1600 340-13
TF: 800-370-3936 ■ Web: www.blm.gov
Idaho State Office 1387 S Vinnell Way .... Boise ID 83709 208-373-4000 373-3899 340-13
Web: www.blm.gov
Montana State Office
5001 Southgate Dr .... Billings MT 59101 406-896-5000 340-13
Web: www.blm.gov
Nevada State Office 1340 Financial Blvd .... Reno NV 89502 775-861-6400 861-6606 340-13
Web: www.blm.gov
Oregon/Washington State Office
333 SW First Ave .... Portland OR 97204 503-808-6001 808-6422 340-13
Web: www.blm.gov
Wyoming State Office
5353 Yellowstone Rd PO Box 1828 .... Cheyenne WY 82003 307-775-6256 775-6129 340-13
Web: www.blm.gov

Bureau of National Affairs Inc
1801 S Bell St .... Arlington VA 22202 703-341-3000 637-2
TF: 800-372-1033 ■ Web: www.bna.com

Bureau of Reclamation 1849 C St NW .... Washington DC 20240 202-513-0501 340-13
Web: www.usbr.gov

Bureau of Reclamation Regional Offices
Great Plains Region 2021 Fourth Ave .... Billings MT 59107 406-247-7600 247-7793 340-13
Web: www.usbr.gov
Lower Colorado Region
PO Box 61470 .... Boulder City NV 89006 702-293-8411 293-8333 340-13
Web: www.usbr.gov
Mid-Pacific Region
2800 Cottage Way Federal Bldg .... Sacramento CA 95825 916-978-5000 978-5005 340-13
TF: 800-967-4222 ■ Web: www.usbr.gov
Pacific Northwest Region
1150 N Curtis Rd Ste 100 .... Boise ID 83706 208-378-5012 378-5019 340-13
Web: www.usbr.gov
Upper Colorado Region
125 S State St Rm 6107 .... Salt Lake City UT 84138 801-524-3600 524-5499 340-13
TF: 800-645-8465 ■ Web: www.usbr.gov/uc

Bureau of the Public Debt
PO Box 7015 .... Parkersburg WV 26106 800-722-2678 340-18
TF: 800-722-2678
TreasuryDirect PO Box 7015 .... Parkersburg WV 26106 844-284-2676 340-18
TF: 844-284-2676 ■ Web: www.savingsbonds.gov

Burford Ranch 1443 W Sample Ave .... Fresno CA 93711 559-431-0902 10-4

Burg Simpson Eldredge Hersh Jardine PC
40 Inverness Dr E .... Englewood CO 80112 303-792-5595 428
Web: www.burgsimpson.com

Burgeonvest Bick Securities Ltd
21 King St W Ste 1100 .... Hamilton ON L8P4W7 905-528-6505 401
TF: 888-866 3608 ■ Web: www.burgeonvest.com

Burger & Brown Engineering Inc
4500 E 142nd St .... Grandview MO 64030 816-878-6675 454
TF: 800-764-3518 ■ Web: www.smartflow-usa.com

Burger King Corp 5505 Blue Lagoon Dr .... Miami FL 33126 305-378-3000 670
TF: 866-394-2493 ■ Web: www.bk.com

Burger's Ozark Country Cured Hams Inc
32819 hwy 87 .... California MO 65018 573-796-3134 796-3137 296-26
TF: 800-203-4424 ■ Web: www.smokehouse.com

Burgerville USA 109 W 17th St .... Vancouver WA 98660 888-827-8369 670
TF: 888-827-8369 ■ Web: www.burgerville.com

Burgess & Niple Inc 5085 Reed Rd .... Columbus OH 43220 614-459-2050 261
Web: www.burgessniple.com

Burgess Adv & Associates Inc
1290 Congress St .... Portland ME 04102 207-775-5227 4
Web: www.burgessadv.com

Burgess Falls State Natural Area
4000 Burgess Falls Dr .... Sparta TN 38583 931-432-5312 565
Web: www.state.tn.us

Burgess Group LLC, The
1727 King St .... Alexandria VA 22314 703-894-1800 809
Web: www.burgessgroup.com

Burgess Industries Inc (BII)
7500 Boone Ave N Ste 111 .... Brooklyn Park MN 55428 763-553-7800 553-9289 629
TF: 800-233-2589 ■ Web: www.burgessind.com

Phone | Fax | Class

Burgess Michael (Rep R - TX)
2336 Rayburn HOB .... Washington DC 20515 202-225-7772 225-2919 342-2
Web: burgess.house.gov

Burgess Pigment Company Inc
525 Beck Blvd PO Box 349 .... Sandersville GA 31082 478-552-2544 552-4274 500
TF: 800-841-8999 ■ Web: www.burgesspigment.com

Burgess Sales & Supply Inc
2121 W Morehead St .... Charlotte NC 28208 704-333-8933 351
Web: www.burgesssales.com

Burgess Speciality Fabrication Inc
8222 Fawndale Ln .... Houston TX 77040 713-462-0293 697
Web: www.burgessfab.com

Burgess Steel LLC 200 W Forest Ave .... Englewood NJ 07631 201-871-3500 690
Web: www.burgesssteel.com

Burgess-Norton Manufacturing Co
737 Peyton St .... Geneva IL 60134 630-232-4100 621
Web: www.burgessnorton.com

Burghardt Sporting Goods
14660 W Capitol Dr .... Brookfield WI 53005 262-790-1170 711
TF: 866-790-6606 ■ Web: www.burghardtsportinggoods.com

Burgiss Group LLC, The
111 River St Fl 10th .... Hoboken NJ 07030 201-427-9600 180
Web: burgiss.com

Burgum Doug (R)
Dept 101, 600 E Boulevard Ave .... Bismarck ND 58505 701-328-2200 328-2205 343
Web: www.governor.nd.gov

Burgundy Asset Management Ltd
Bay Wellington Tower Brookfield Pl 181 Bay St
Ste 4510 .... Toronto ON M5J2T3 416-869-3222 690
TF: 888-480-1790 ■ Web: www.burgundyasset.com

Burgundy Group Inc, The
2420 S Power Rd Ste 103 .... Mesa AZ 85209 480-325-7700 180
TF: 800-573-1874 ■ Web: www.tbginc.com

Burien Toyota Collision Center
15025 First Ave S .... Burien WA 98148 206-243-0700 54
TF: 800-561-3357 ■ Web: www.burientoyota.com

Burkart-Phelan Inc 2 Shaker Rd .... Shirley MA 01464 978-425-4500 425-9800 527
TF: 800-347-7461 ■ Web: www.burkart.com

Burke & Assoc Professional Property Management
4974 N Fresno St Ste 106 .... Fresno CA 93726 559-225-6075 652

Burke & Herbert Bank & Trust Co
100 S Fairfax St .... Alexandria VA 22314 703-751-7701 70
TF: 877-440-0800 ■ Web: www.burkeandherbertbank.com

Burke & Schindler PLL
901 Adams Crossing .... Cincinnati OH 45202 513-455-8200 2
Web: www.burkecpa.com

Burke Beverages Inc 4900 S Vernon Ave .... McCook IL 60525 708-688-2000 81-1
Web: www.burkebev.com

Burke County PO Box 310 .... Bowbells ND 58721 701-377-2718 338
Web: www.burkecountynd.com

Burke County PO Box 89 .... Waynesboro GA 30830 706-554-2324 554-0350 338
TF: 800-436-7442 ■ Web: www.burkecounty-ga.gov

Burke County Chamber of Commerce
110 E Meeting St .... Morganton NC 28655 828-437-3021 437-1613 139
Web: burkecountychamber.org

Burke County Public Library
204 S King St .... Morganton NC 28655 828-437-5638 433-1914 434-3
Web: www.bcpls.org

Burke County Public Schools
789 Burke Veterans Pkwy .... Waynesboro GA 30830 706-554-5101 554-8051 685
Web: www.burke.k12.ga.us

Burke E Porter Machinery Co
730 Plymouth Ave NE .... Grand Rapids MI 49505 616-234-1200 459-1032 386
TF: 800-562-9133 ■ Web: www.bepco.com

Burke Handling Systems 431 Hwy 49 S .... Jackson MS 39218 601-939-6600 770
TF: 800-222-5400 ■ Web: www.burkehandling.com

Burke Inc 500 W Seventh St .... Cincinnati OH 45203 513-241-5663 684-7500 466
Web: www.burke.com

Burke Inc 1800 Merriam Ln .... Kansas City KS 66106 800-255-4147 722-2614* 477
*Fax Area Code: 913 ■ TF Sales: 800-255-4147 ■ Web: burkebariatric.com

Burke International Tours Inc
PO Box 890 .... Newton NC 28658 828-465-3900 760
TF: 800-476-3900 ■ Web: www.burkechristiantours.com

Burke Lake Recreation Area
29145 Burke Lake Rd .... Burke SD 57523 605-223-7660 565
Web: www.gfp.sd.gov

Burke Mountain Operating Co
223 Sherburne Lodge Rd .... East Burke VT 05832 802-626-7300 378
Web: qburke.com

Burke Museum of Natural History & Culture
University of Washington
17th Ave NE & NE 45th St .... Seattle WA 98195 206-543-5590 685-3039 520
TF: 800-411-9671 ■ Web: www.burkemuseum.org

Burke Rehabilitation Hospital
785 Mamaroneck Ave .... White Plains NY 10605 914-597-2500 374-6
TF: 888-992-8753 ■ Web: www.burke.org

Burke-Divide Electric Co-op Inc (BDEC)
9549 Hwy 5 W .... Columbus ND 58727 701-939-6671 939-6666 245
TF: 800-472-2983 ■ Web: www.bdec.coop

Burkett & Wong Engineers
9449 Balboa Ave Ste 270 .... San Diego CA 92123 619-299-5550 261
Web: www.bwesd.com

Burkett Engineering Inc
105 E Robinson St Ste 501 .... Orlando FL 32801 407-246-1260 261
Web: burkettengineering.com

Burkett Oil Company Inc
6788 Best Friend Rd .... Norcross GA 30071 770-447-8030 579
TF: 800-228-1786 ■ Web: www.burkettoil.com

Burkett's Office Supplies Inc
8520 Younger Creek Dr .... Sacramento CA 95828 916-387-8900 535
Web: www.burkettsoffice.com

Burkhalter Travel Agency
6501 Mineral Pt Rd .... Madison WI 53705 608-833-5200 771
TF: 800-556-9286 ■ Web: www.burkhaltertravel.com

Burkhart Advertising Inc
1335 Mishawaka Ave .... South Bend IN 46615 574-233-2101 7
TF: 800-777-8122 ■ Web: www.burkhartadv.com

Name / Address	City	State	Zip	Phone	Fax	Class
Burkhart Dental Supply Co 2502 S 78th St TF Cust Svc: 800-562-8176 ■ Web: www.burkhartdental.com	Tacoma	WA	98409	253-474-7761	472-4773	476
Burkhart Group Ltd, The 412 S Broadleigh Rd Web: burkhartgrp.com	Columbus	OH	43209	614-397-8788		180
Burkina Faso 866 UN Plaza Ste 326 Web: www.burkina-onu.org	New York	NY	10017	212-308-4720	308-4690	784
Burkina Faso Embassy 2005 Massachusetts Ave NW TF: 800-345-6541 ■ Web: www.visahq.com	Washington	DC	20008	202-332-5577	667-1882	257
Burk-Kleinpeter Inc (BKI) 4176 Canal St Web: www.bkiusa.com	New Orleans	LA	70119	504-486-5901		261
Burkland Inc 6520 S State Rd Web: burklandinc.com	Goodrich	MI	48438	810-636-2233		489
Burkle North America Inc 11105 Knott Ave Web: burkleamerica.com	Cypress	CA	90630	714-379-5090		770
Burklund Distributors Inc 2500 N Main St Ste 3 TF: 800-322-2876 ■ Web: www.burklund.com	East Peoria	IL	61611	309-694-1900		297-3
Burks Tractor Co Inc 3140 Kimberly Rd TF: 800-247-7419 ■ Web: www.burkstractor.com	Twin Falls	ID	83301	208-733-5543	734-9852	274
Burl Capital LLC 1 International Pl 7th Fl Web: www.burlcapital.com	Boston	MA	02110	617-936-3358		194
Burleigh County 514 E Thayer Ave PO Box 1055 TF: 877-222-6682 ■ Web: www.ndcourts.gov	Bismarck	ND	58502	701-222-6690	222-6758	338
Burleson Area Chamber of Commerce 1044 SW Wilshire Blvd TF: 800-227-2345 ■ Web: burlesonchamber.com	Burleson	TX	76028	817-295-6121	295-6192	139
Burleson County 100 W Buck St Ste 203 Web: www.co.burleson.tx.us	Caldwell	TX	77036	979-567-2329	567-2376	338
Burley Tobacco Growers Cooperative Assn 620 S Broadway TF: 800-561-7710 ■ Web: www.burleytobacco.com	Lexington	KY	40508	859-252-3561		48-2
Burlingame Chamber of Commerce 417 California Dr Web: www.burlingamechamber.org	Burlingame	CA	94010	650-344-1735	344-1763	139
Burlington Chamber of Commerce 414 Locust St Ste 201 Web: www.burlingtonchamber.com	Burlington	ON	L7S1T7	905-639-0174	333-3956	137
Burlington City Hall 149 Church St Web: www.burlingtonvt.gov	Burlington	VT	05401	802-865-7000	865-7014	337
Burlington Coat Factory 1830 Rt 130 N TF: 855-355-2875 ■ Web: burlingtoncoatfactory.com	Burlington	NJ	08016	609-387-7800		362
Burlington College 351 N Ave TF: 800-862-9616	Burlington	VT	05401	800-862-9616		166
Burlington County 49 Rancocas Rd Web: www.co.burlington.nj.us	Mount Holly	NJ	08060	609-265-5122	265-0696	338
Burlington County Library 5 Pioneer Blvd TF: 800-365-0580 ■ Web: www.bcls.lib.nj.us	Mount Holly	NJ	08060	609-267-9660	267-4091	434-3
Burlington County Times 4284 US-130 Web: www.phillyburbs.com	Willingboro	NJ	08046	609-871-8000		532-2
Burlington Drug Company Inc 91 Catamount Dr TF: 800-330-0703 ■ Web: www.burlingtondrug.com	Milton	VT	05468	802-893-5105		231
Burlington Engineering Inc 220 W Grove Ave Web: www.burlingtoneng.com	Orange	CA	92865	714-921-4045		256
Burlington Free Press 100 Bank St TF: 800-427-3124 ■ Web: www.burlingtonfreepress.com	Burlington	VT	05401	802-863-3441	660-1802	532-2
Burlington Hawk Eye Co 800 S Main St PO Box 10 TF: 800-397-1708 ■ Web: www.thehawkeye.com	Burlington	IA	52601	319-754-8461	754-6824	637-8
Burlington International Airport 1200 Airport Dr	South Burlington	VT	05403	802-863-2874	863-7947	27
Burlington Mall 75 Middlesex Tpke TF: 877-746-6642 ■ Web: www.simon.com/mall/?id=146	Burlington	MA	01803	781-272-8667		460
Burlington Medical Supplies Inc 3 Elmhurst St Web: www.burmed.com	Newport News	VA	23603	757-888-8994		475
Burlington Northern & Santa Fe Railway (BNSF) 2650 Lou Menk Dr TF: 800-795-2673 ■ Web: www.bnsf.com	Fort Worth	TX	76131	800-795-2673		648
Burlington Northern Santa Fe Corp (BNSF) 500 New Jersey Ave NW Ste 550 TF: 800-964-9386 ■ Web: www.bnsf.com	Washington	DC	20001	202-347-8662	347-8675	615
Burlington Public Library 22 Sears St TF: 800-422-2462 ■ Web: www.burlington.org	Burlington	MA	01803	781-270-1690	229-0406	434-3
Burlington Public Library 210 Ct St Web: www.burlington.lib.ia.us	Burlington	IA	52601	319-753-1647		434-3
Burlington/Alamance County Convention & Visitors Bureau 200 S Main St PO Box 519 TF: 800-637-3804 ■ Web: www.visitalamance.com	Burlington	NC	27216	336-570-1444	228-1330	206
Burlington/West Burlington Area Chamber of Commerce 610 N Fourth St Ste 200 Web: www.greaterburlington.com	Burlington	IA	52601	319-752-6365	752-6454	139
Burma Bibas Inc 597 Fifth Ave 10th Fl Web: www.burmabibas.com	New York	NY	10017	212-750-2500		155-13
Burmax Co 28 Barretts Ave *Fax Area Code: 631 ■ TF: 800-645-5118 ■ Web: www.burmax.com	Holtsville	NY	11742	800-645-5118	289-7590*	76
Burnaby Board of Trade 4555 Kings Way Ste 201 Web: www.bbot.ca	Burnaby	BC	V5H4T8	604-412-0100	412-0102	137
Burnaby Hospital 3935 Kincaid St Web: www.fraserhealth.ca	Burnaby	BC	V5G2X6	604-453-1910		374-2
Burnaby Lake Greenhouses Ltd 17250 80 Ave Web: www.burlake.com	Surrey	BC	V4N6J6	604-576-2088		192
Burnac Corp 44 St Clair Ave W Web: www.burnac.com	Toronto	ON	M4V3C9	416-964-3600		652
Burndy LLC 47 E Industrial Park Dr TF: 800-346-4175 ■ Web: www.burndy.com	Manchester	NH	03109	800-346-4175		815
Burner Systems International Inc (BSI) 3600 Cummings Rd Web: www.burnersystems.com	Chattanooga	TN	37419	423-822-3600		357
Burnet Consolidated Independent School District 208 E Brier Ln Web: www.burnet.txed.net	Burnet	TX	78611	512-756-2124	756-7498	780
Burnet County 220 S Pierce St TF: 800-970-6638 ■ Web: www.burnetcountytexas.org	Burnet	TX	78611	512-756-5420	756-5410	338
Burnet Middle School 8401 Hathaway Dr Web: www.austinisd.org	Austin	TX	78757	512-414-3225		685
Burnett & Son Meat Co Inc 1420 S Myrtle Ave Web: www.burnettandson.com	Monrovia	CA	91016	626-357-2165		473
Burnett County 7410 County Rd K TF: 800-788-3164 ■ Web: www.burnettcounty.com/gov	Siren	WI	54872	715-349-2181	349-2830	338
Burnett Dairy Co-op 11631 SR- 70 TF: 800-854-2716 ■ Web: www.burnettdairy.com	Grantsburg	WI	54840	715-689-2468	689-2135	296-5
Burnett Specialists 9800 Richmond Ave Ste 800 Web: www.burnettspecialists.com	Houston	TX	77042	713-977-4777	977-7533	631
Burnette Foods Inc 701 US Hwy 31 Web: www.burnettefoods.com	Elk Rapids	MI	49629	231-264-8116		296-20
Burnetts Staffing Inc 2710 Ave E E Web: www.burnetts.com	Arlington	TX	76011	817-385-8880		260
Burney Co 121 Rowell Ct Web: www.burney.com	Falls Church	VA	22046	703-241-5611		403
Burney Forest Products 35586 Highway 299E	Burney	CA	96013	530-335-5107		683
Burnham & Flower Group Inc 315 S Kalamazoo Mall TF: 888-748-7966 ■ Web: hfgroup.com	Kalamazoo	MI	49007	269-381-1173		390
Burnham Composite Structures Inc 6262 W 34th St S Web: www.burnhamcs.com	Wichita	KS	67215	316-946-5900		22
Burnham Financial Services LLC 2038 Saranac Ave Web: burnhambenefitadvisors.com	Lake Placid	NY	12946	518-523-8100		390
Burnham Holdings Inc 1241 Harrisburg Ave PO Box 3245 Web: www.burnhamholdings.com	Lancaster	PA	17604	717-390-7800		357
Burnham Industrial Contractors Inc 3229 Babcock Blvd Web: www.burnhamindustrial.net	Pittsburgh	PA	15237	412-366-6622		189-9
Burnham Marketing LLC 1 Amber Ridge Rd Web: www.burnhammarketing.com	Chestnut Ridge	NY	10977	917-204-6999		195
Burnham Nationwide Inc The Burnham Ctr 111 W Washington St Ste 450 Web: burnhamnationwide.com	Chicago	IL	60602	312-407-7990		194
Burnham Park Animal Hospital 1025 S State St Web: www.chicagovet.net	Chicago	IL	60605	312-663-9200		794
Burnham Point State Park 34075 NYS Rt 12E Web: parks.ny.gov/parks/57/details.aspx	Cape Vincent	NY	13618	315-654-2522		565
Burning Glass International Inc 1 Lewis Wharf Web: www.burning-glass.com	Boston	MA	02110	617-227-4800		260
Burning Man 1900 Third St Web: burningman.org	San Francisco	CA	94158	415-865-3800		520
Burns & McBride Inc 240 S DuPont Hwy TF: 800-756-5110 ■ Web: www.burnsandmcbride.com	New Castle	DE	19720	302-656-5110		316
Burns & McDonnell 9400 Ward Pkwy TF: 800-718-2492 ■ Web: www.burnsmcd.com	Kansas City	MO	64114	816-333-9400		261
Burns Bog Conservation Society 7953 120 St TF: 888-850-6264 ■ Web: www.burnsbog.org	Delta	BC	V4C6P6	604-572-0373		138
Burns Burns Walsh & Walsh PA 704 Topeka Ave TF: 888-528-3186 ■ Web: bbwwlaw.com	Lyndon	KS	66451	785-828-4418		428
Burns Controls Co 13735 Beta Rd TF: 800-442-2010 ■ Web: www.burnscontrols.com	Dallas	TX	75244	972-233-6712		358
Burns Cooley Dennis Inc 551 Sunnybrook Rd Web: www.bcdgeo.com	Ridgeland	MS	39157	601-856-9911		256
Burns Engineering Inc 10201 Bren Rd E TF: 800-328-3871 ■ Web: www.burnsengineering.com	Minnetonka	MN	55343	952-935-4400		256
Burns Janitor Service 1631 W Hill St TF: 800-323-4358 ■ Web: www.burnsjanitor.com	Louisville	KY	40210	502-585-4548		104
Burns Motor Freight Inc 500 Seneca Trl N TF: 800-598-5674 ■ Web: www.burnsmotorfreight.com	Marlinton	WV	24954	304-799-6106	799-4257	780
Burns Pest Elimination Inc 2620 W Grovers Ave TF: 877-971-4782 ■ Web: burnspestelimination.com	Phoenix	AZ	85053	602-971-4782		577
Burns Power Tools 350 Mariano Bishop Blvd Web: www.burnstools.com	Fall River	MA	02721	508-675-0381		190
Burns Printing Inc 6131 Industrial Heights Dr TF: 866-288-5618 ■ Web: www.burnsmp.com	Knoxville	TN	37909	865-584-2265		627
Burns, Delatte & Mccoy Inc 320 Westcott St Ste 100 Web: www.bdmi-ce.com	Houston	TX	77007	713-861-3016		261
Burnsteads, The 11980 NE 24th St Ste 200 Web: www.burnstead.com	Bellevue	WA	98005	425-454-1900		187
Burnsville Chamber of Commerce 350 W Burnsville Pkwy Ste 425 TF: 800-521-6055 ■ Web: www.burnsvillechamber.com	Burnsville	MN	55337	952-435-6000	435-6972	139
Burnsville Ctr 1178 Burnsville Ctr Web: www.burnsvillecenter.com	Burnsville	MN	55306	952-435-8182		460

Phone | Fax | Class

Burpee Museum of Natural History
737 N Main St ... Rockford IL 61103 815-965-3433 520
Web: www.burpee.org

Burr & Forman LLP
420 N 20th St Ste 3400 ... Birmingham AL 35203 205-251-3000 41
Web: www.burr.com

Burr Oak State Park
10220 Burr Oak Lodge Rd ... Glouster OH 45732 740-767-3570 565
Web: www.ohiodnr.com

Burr Oak Tool Inc 405 W S St ... Sturgis MI 49091 269-651-9393 651-4324 455
TF: 800-861-8864 ■ *Web:* www.burroak.com

Burr Pilger & Mayer LLP (BPMLLP)
600 California St Ste 1300 ... San Francisco CA 94108 415-421-5757 288-6288 2
Web: www.bpmcpa.com

Burr Pond State Park
384 Burr Mtn Rd ... Torrington CT 06790 860-482-1817 565
Web: www.ct.gov

Burr Richard (Sen R - NC)
217 Russell Senate Office Bldg ... Washington DC 20510 202-224-3154 228-2981 342-2
Web: www.burr.senate.gov

Burr Truck & Trailer Sales Inc
2901 Vestal Rd ... Vestal NY 13850 607-729-2211 729-4375 57
Web: www.burrtruck.com

Burrell 233 N Michigan Ave Ste 2900 ... Chicago IL 60601 312-297-9600 4
Web: www.burrell.com

Burrell Consultng Group Inc
1001 Enterprise Way Ste 100 ... Roseville CA 95678 916-783-8898 256
Web: www.burrellcg.com

Burrell Imaging
1311 Merrillville Rd ... Crown Point IN 46307 219-663-3210 662-0915 588
TF: 800-348-8732 ■ *Web:* www.burrellprolabs.com

BurrellesLuce
30 B Vreeland Rd PO Box 674 ... Florham Park NJ 07932 973-992-6600 992-7675 387
TF: 800-631-1160 ■ *Web:* www.burrellesluce.com

Burris Company Inc 331 E Eigth St ... Greeley CO 80631 970-356-1670 356-8702 544
TF: 888-228-7747 ■ *Web:* www.burrisoptics.com

Burris Logistics
501 SE Fifth St PO Box 219 ... Milford DE 19963 302-839-5157 839-5175 803-2
TF: 800-805-8135 ■ *Web:* www.burrislogistics.com

Burritt on the Mountain
3101 Burritt Dr ... Huntsville AL 35801 256-536-2882 532-1784 520
TF: 800-428-2343 ■ *Web:* www.burrittonthemountain.com

Burroughs Wellcome Fund
21 TW Alexander Dr
PO Box 13901 ... Research Triangle Park NC 27709 919-991-5100 991-5160 304
Web: www.bwfund.org

Burroughs-Ross-Colville Co
301 Depot St ... McMinnville TN 37110 931-473-2111 473-5350 820

Burrow Global LLC
6200 Savoy Dr Ste 800 ... Houston TX 77036 713-963-0930 186
Web: www.burrowglobal.com

Burrows Paper Corp 501 W Main St ... Little Falls NY 13365 315-823-2300 823-3892 557
TF: 800-272-7122 ■ *Web:* www.burrowspaper.com

Burrows Paper Corp Packaging Group
2000 Commerce Ctr Dr ... Franklin OH 45005 937-746-1933 746-0344 548
TF: 800-732-1933 ■ *Web:* www.burrowspaper.com

Burrtec Waste Industries Inc
9890 Cherry Ave ... Fontana CA 92335 909-429-4200 429-4291 804
TF: 888-287-7832 ■ *Web:* www.burrtec.com

Burrus Research Associates Inc
557 Cottonwood Ave ... Hartland WI 53029 262-367-0949 367-7163 463
Web: www.burrus.com

Bursich Associates Inc
2129 E High St ... Pottstown PA 19464 610-323-4040 261
Web: www.bursich.com

Bursma Electronic Distributing Inc
2851 Buchanan Ave SW ... Grand Rapids MI 49548 616-831-0080 38
TF: 800-777-2604 ■ *Web:* www.bursma.com

Burst Communication Inc
8200 S Akron St Ste 108 ... Centennial CO 80112 303-649-9600 649-9890 246
Web: www.burstvideo.com

Burst Marketing LLC
122 Industrial Park Rd 2nd Fl ... Albany NY 12206 518-279-7950 5
Web: www.burstmarketing.net

Burstek 12801 Westlinks Dr Ste 101 ... Fort Myers FL 33913 239-495-5900 174
TF: 800-709-2551 ■ *Web:* www.burstek.com

Burt County Attorney
111 N 13th St Ste 12 ... Tekamah NE 68061 402-374-2955 374-2956 338
Web: www.burtcounty.ne.gov

Burt County Public Power District
613 N 13th St ... Tekamah NE 68061 402-374-2631 245
TF: 888-835-1620 ■ *Web:* www.burtcoppd.com

Burt Lake State Park
6635 State Pk Dr ... Indian River MI 49749 231-238-9392 565
Web: www.michigandnr.com

Burt Lumber Co 911 Greensboro Hwy ... Washington GA 30673 706-678-1531 683
Web: www.burtlumbercompany.com

Burt Martin Arnold Securities Inc
608 Silver Spur Rd Ste 100 ... Rolling Hills Estates CA 90274 310-544-3545 690
Web: www.bmasecurities.com

Burtco Inc 185 Rt 123 ... Westminster Station VT 05159 802-722-3358 183
TF: 800-451-4401 ■ *Web:* burtcoselfstorage.com

Burtech Plumbing 102 Second St ... Encinitas CA 92024 760-634-5134 634-5154 261
Web: burtechpipelineanddrains.com

Burton & Mayer Inc
W140 N9000 Lilly Rd ... Menomonee Falls WI 53051 262-781-0770 627
TF: 800-236-1770 ■ *Web:* www.burtonmayer.com

Burton Computer Resources Inc
400 N 16th Ave ... Laurel MS 39440 601-428-0205 180
Web: www.burtoncomputer.com

Burton Cummings Theatre 364 Smith St ... Winnipeg MB R3B2H2 204-956-5656 572
Web: burtoncummingstheatre.ca

Burton Industries Inc
9821 Cedar Falls Rd ... Hazelhurst WI 54531 715-356-5767 729
Web: www.burtonindustries.com

Burton Lumber Corp 835 Wilson Rd ... Chesapeake VA 23324 757-545-4613 545-8852 236
TF: 800-347-5444 ■ *Web:* burton-lumber.com

Burton Neil & Assoc
1060 Andrew Dr Ste 160 ... West Chester PA 19380 610-696-2120 445
TF: 866-696-2120 ■ *Web:* www.attorneys-network.com

Burton-Taylor International Consulting LLC
1319 Thornapple Dr Mezzanine Level ... Osprey FL 34229 646-201-4152 194
Web: www.burton-taylor.com

Burundi 336 E 45th St 12th Fl ... New York NY 10017 212-499-0001 499-0006 784
Web: burundi-un.org

Burundi Embassy
2233 Wisconsin Ave NW Ste 212 ... Washington DC 20007 202-342-2574 342-2578 257
TF: 800-862-7822 ■ *Web:* www.burundiembassy-usa.org

Buryanek Recreation Area
27450 Buryanek Rd ... Burke SD 57523 605-337-2587 565
Web: www.gfp.sd.gov/state-parks/directory/buryanek

Bus 100.3, The 2141 Grand Ave ... Des Moines IA 50312 515-245-8900 645-48
Web: thebusfm.iheart.com

Bus Andrews Truck Equipment Inc
2828 N E Ave ... Springfield MO 65803 417-869-1541 869-1656 57
TF: 800-273-0733 ■ *Web:* busandrews.com

Buscemi Co, International LLC
PO Box 88065 ... Los Angeles CA 90009 310-568-1011 311
Web: buscemico.com

Busch Agricultural Resources Inc
2101 26th St S ... Moorhead MN 56560 218-233-8531 10-5
Web: www.anheuser-busch.com

Busch Distributors Inc
7603 State Rt 270 ... Pullman WA 99163 509-339-6600 339-6616 581
TF: 800-752-2295 ■ *Web:* www.buschdist.com

Busch Electronics
739 Kasota Ave SE ... Minneapolis MN 55414 651-288-2580 791
Web: www.buschelectronics.com

Busch Gardens Williamsburg
1 Busch Gardens Blvd ... Williamsburg VA 23185 757-229-4386 253-3399* 32
*Fax: Mktg ■ *TF:* 800-343-7946 ■ *Web:* www.buschgardens.com

Busch Industries Inc
900 E Paris Ave SE ... Grand Rapids MI 49546 616-957-3737 480

Busch LLC 516 Viking Dr ... Virginia Beach VA 23452 757-463-7800 358
Web: www.buschvacuum.com/us/en

Busch Precision Inc
8200 N Faulkner Rd ... Milwaukee WI 53224 414-362-7300 757
Web: www.buschprecision.com

Busch Semiconductor Vacuum Group LLC
18430 Sutter Blvd ... Morgan Hill CA 95037 408-782-0800 696
Web: www.buschvacuum.com/nl/en/company/busch-svg

Busch Stadium 700 Clark St ... Saint Louis MO 63102 314-345-9600 720
Web: stlouis.cardinals.mlb.com

Busch Vacuum Technics Inc
1740 Lionel Bertrand ... Boisbriand QC J7H1N7 450-435-6899 641
TF: 800-363-6360 ■ *Web:* www.busch.ca

Busch's Inc 2240 S Main St ... Ann Arbor MI 48103 734-214-8088 345
Web: www.buschs.com

Busche Performance Group
1563 E State Rd 8 ... Albion IN 46701 260-636-7030 295
Web: www.busche-cnc.com

Buschman Corp 4100 Payne Ave Ste 1 ... Cleveland OH 44103 216-431-6633 557
Web: buschmancorp.com

Buscomm Inc 11696 Lilburn Park Rd ... Saint Louis MO 63146 314-567-7755 177
TF: 800-283-7755 ■ *Web:* www.buscomminc.com

Buse Timber & Sales Inc
3812 28th Pl NE ... Everett WA 98201 425-258-2577 259-6956 683
TF: 800-305-2577 ■ *Web:* www.busetimber.com

Busek Company Inc 11 Tech Cir ... Natick MA 01760 508-655-5565 194
Web: www.busek.com

Bush Barn Art Ctr 600 Mission St SE ... Salem OR 97302 503-581-2228 371-3342 50-2
TF: 800-901-7173 ■ *Web:* www.salemart.org

Bush Bros & Co 1016 E Weisgarber Rd ... Knoxville TN 37909 865-588-7685 296-20
Web: www.bushbeans.com

Bush Construction Corp
4029 Ironbound Rd Ste 200 ... Williamsburg VA 23188 757-220-2874 187

Bush Consulting Group 34 S Main St ... Cleveland OH 44022 330-337-6104 194
Web: bushconsultinggroup.com

Bush House Museum 600 Mission St SE ... Salem OR 97302 503-363-4714 520
Web: www.oregonlink.com/bush_house

Bush Inc 2581 Hickory Blvd SE ... Lenoir NC 28645 828-728-4224 57
Web: www.roosterbush.com

Bush Industries Inc 1 Mason Dr ... Jamestown NY 14701 716-665-2000 319-2
TF: 800-950-4782 ■ *Web:* www.bushfurniture.com

Bush Intercontinental Airport
2800 N Terminal Rd ... Houston TX 77032 281-233-3000 27
Web: www.fly2houston.com/iah

Bush Ross PA 1801 N Highland Ave ... Tampa FL 33602 813-224-9255 428
TF: 800-856-7413 ■ *Web:* www.bushross.com

Bush School, The 3400 E Harrison St ... Seattle WA 98112 206-322-7978 685
Web: bush.edu

Bush-Holley House 39 Strickland Rd ... Cos Cob CT 06807 203-869-6899 861-9720 50-3
TF: 800-200-2882 ■ *Web:* www.hstg.org

Bushline Inc
707 Industrial Pk Rd ... New Tazewell TN 37825 423-626-5246 319-2
Web: bushline.com

Bushnell Corp 9200 Cody St ... Overland Park KS 66214 913-752-3400 752-3550 544
TF: 800-423-3537 ■ *Web:* www.bushnell.com

Bushnell Ctr for the Performing Arts
166 Capitol Ave ... Hartford CT 06106 860-987-6000 987-6070 572
TF: 888-824-2874 ■ *Web:* www.bushnell.org

Bushnell Illinois Tank Co
650 W Davis St ... Bushnell IL 61422 309-772-3106 772-2045 273
Web: www.schuldbushnell.com

Bushwacker Inc 6710 N Catlin Ave ... Portland OR 97203 503-283-4335 283-3007 60
TF: 800-234-8920 ■ *Web:* www.bushwacker.com

Bushwick Metals LLC
560 N Washington Ave ... Bridgeport CT 06604 888-399-4070 723
TF: 888-399-4070 ■ *Web:* www.bushwickmetals.com

Business & Institutional Furniture Manufacturers Assn (BIFMA)
678 Front Ave NW Ste 150 ... Grand Rapids MI 49504 616-285-3963 49-13

Business & Legal Reports Inc (BLR)
141 Mill Rock Rd E ... Old Saybrook CT 06475 860-510-0100 510-7225 637-9
TF: 800-727-5257 ■ *Web:* www.blr.com

	Phone	Fax	Class
Business Advancement Inc 178 Sycamore Terr .... Glen Rock NJ 07452 *Web:* www.businessadvance.com	201-612-1228		194
Business Card Service Inc 3200 143rd Cir .... Burnsville MN 55306 *TF:* 800-405-8860 ■ *Web:* www.bcsinet.com	952-895-6750		627
Business Cards Tomorrow Inc 3000 NE 30th Pl 5th Fl .... Fort Lauderdale FL 33306 *Web:* www.bctonline.net	954-563-1224		535
Business Computer Design International Inc 1333 Burr Ridge Pkwy Ste 200 .... Burr Ridge IL 60527 *Web:* www.bcdsoftware.com	630-986-0800	986-0926	178-1
Business Consumer Alliance 315 N La Cadena Dr .... Colton CA 92324	909-825-7280		79
Business Council for International Understanding (BCIU) 1212 Ave of the Americas 10th Fl .... New York NY 10036 *Web:* www.bciu.org	212-490-0460	697-8526	49-12
Business Council of Alabama 2 N Jackson St Ste 501 .... Montgomery AL 36101 *TF:* 800-665-9647 ■ *Web:* www.bcatoday.org	334-834-6000		140
Business Council of Fairfield County (SACIA) 1 Landmark Sq Ste 300 .... Stamford CT 06901 *Web:* www.businessfairfield.com	203-359-3220	967-8294	139
Business Council of New York State Inc 152 Washington Ave .... Albany NY 12210 *TF:* 800-358-1202 ■ *Web:* www.bcnys.org	518-465-7511	465-4389	140
Business Council of Westchester 108 Corporate Pk Dr Ste 101 .... White Plains NY 10604 *Web:* thebcw.org	914-948-2110	948-0122	139
Business Direct Inc 5620 Old Bullard Rd Ste 128 .... Tyler TX 75703 *TF:* 888-580-7799	888-580-7799		7
Business Efficacy 6130 Blue Cir Dr Ste 100 .... Minneapolis MN 55343 *Web:* www.businessefficacy.com	952-217-0425		195
Business Executives for National Security (BENS) 1030 15th St NW Ste 200 .... Washington DC 20005 *Web:* www.bens.org	202-296-2125	296-2490	49-12
Business Facilities Magazine 44 Apple St Ste 3 .... Tinton Falls NJ 07724 *TF:* 800-524-0337 ■ *Web:* www.businessfacilities.com	732-842-7433	758-6634	457-5
Business First 465 Main St .... Buffalo NY 14203 *Web:* www.bizjournals.com	716-854-5822	854-3394	457-5
Business First 455 S Fourth St Ste 278 .... Louisville KY 40202 *Web:* www.bizjournals.com	502-583-1731	587-1703	457-5
Business Forms Management Assn (BFMA) 3800 Old Cheney Rd Ste 101-285 .... Lincoln NE 68516 **Fax Area Code:* 877 ■ *TF:* 888-367-3078 ■ *Web:* www.bfma.org	402-216-0479	204-5979*	49-12
Business Furniture Corp 8421 Bearing Dr Ste 200 .... Indianapolis IN 46278 *TF:* 800-774-5544 ■ *Web:* businessfurniture.net	317-216-1600	216-1602	320
Business Furniture Inc 10 Lanidex Ctr W .... Parsippany NJ 07054 *Web:* www.bfionline.com	973-503-0730	503-1565	320
Business Impact Group LLC 2411 Galpin Ct Ste 120 .... Chanhassen MN 55317 *Web:* www.impactgroup.us	952-278-7000		549
Business Inn 180 MacLaren St .... Ottawa ON K2P0L3 *TF:* 800-363-1777 ■ *Web:* thebusinessinn.com	613-232-1121	232-8143	379
Business Insurance Magazine 711 Third Ave .... New York NY 10017 **Fax Area Code:* 312 ■ *TF:* 877-812-1587 ■ *Web:* www.businessinsurance.com	212-210-0100	280-3174*	457-5
Business Intelligence Advisor 37 Broadway Ste 1 .... Arlington MA 02474 *Web:* www.cutter.com	781-648-8700	648-8707	531-3
Business Interiors 1111 Valley View Ln .... Irving TX 75061 *TF:* 800-568-9281 ■ *Web:* www.bijackson.com	800-568-9281		321
Business Journal of Milwaukee 825 N Jefferson St Ste 200 .... Milwaukee WI 53202 *Web:* www.bizjournals.com/milwaukee	414-278-7788	278-7028	457-5
Business Journal of Phoenix 101 N First Ave Ste 2300 .... Phoenix AZ 85003 *Web:* www.bizjournals.com	602-230-8400	230-0955	457-5
Business Journal of Portland 851 SW Sixth Ave Ste 500 .... Portland OR 97204 *TF:* 800-377-2671 ■ *Web:* www.bizjournals.com	503-274-8733	219-3450	457-5
Business Journal of Tampa Bay 4890 W Kennedy Blvd Ste 850 .... Tampa FL 33609 *Web:* www.bizjournals.com/tampabay	813-873-8225	876-1827	457-5
Business Journal, The 25 E Boardman St .... Youngstown OH 44501 *TF:* 800-837-6397 ■ *Web:* businessjournaldaily.com	330-744-5023	744-5838	457-5
Business Leaders for Michigan 600 Renaissance Ctr Ste 1760 .... Detroit MI 48243 *Web:* www.businessleadersformichigan.com	313-259-5400		194
Business Marketing Assn (BMA) 708 Third Ave 33rd Fl .... New York NY 10017 *Web:* www.marketing.org	212-697-5950	687-7310	49-18
Business News Network (BNN) 299 Queen St W .... Toronto ON M5V2Z5 *TF:* 855-326-6266 ■ *Web:* www.bnn.ca	416-384-6600		740
Business News Publishing Co 2401 W Big Beaver Rd Ste 700 .... Troy MI 48084 *TF:* 800-837-7370 ■ *Web:* www.bnpmedia.com	248-362-3700	362-0317	637-9
Business Professionals of America 5454 Cleveland Ave .... Columbus OH 43231 *TF:* 800-334-2007 ■ *Web:* www.bpa.org	614-895-7277	895-1165	49-5
Business Protection Specialists Inc 1296 E Victor Rd .... Victor NY 14564 *TF:* 800-560-2199 ■ *Web:* www.securingpeople.com	800-560-2199		693
Business Resource Group (BRG) 10440 N Central Expy Ste 1150 .... Dallas TX 75231 *TF:* 888-391-9166 ■ *Web:* www.brg.com	214-777-5100		194
Business Roundtable (BR) 300 New Jersey Ave NW Ste 800 .... Washington DC 20001 *Web:* businessroundtable.org	202-872-1260	466-3509	49-12
Business Stationery LLC 4944 Commerce Pkwy .... Cleveland OH 44128 *TF:* 800-234-9954 ■ *Web:* www.identitygroup.com/bps/business-stationery	216-514-1277		534
Business Strategy Inc 944 52nd St SE .... Grand Rapids MI 49508	616-261-2200		2
Business Systems & Consultants Inc 113 Little Vly Ct .... Birmingham AL 35244 *Web:* bscsolutions.com	205-988-3300		45
Business Technology Assn (BTA) 12411 Wornall Rd Ste 200 .... Kansas City MO 64145 *TF:* 800-325-7219 ■ *Web:* www.bta.org	816-941-3100	941-2829	49-18
Business Training Library Inc 285 Chesterfield Business Pkwy .... Chesterfield MO 63005 *Web:* www.bizlibrary.com	636-534-1000	534-1001	194
Business Valuation Center LLC 560 Herndon Pkwy Ste 1025 .... Washington DC 20006 *TF:* 800-856-6780 ■ *Web:* businessvaluationcenter.com	703-787-0012		463
Business Wire 44 Montgomery St 20th Fl .... San Francisco CA 94111 *Web:* www.businesswire.com	415-986-4422	788-5335	530
Business Wise Inc 6190 Powers Ferry Rd NW .... Atlanta GA 30339 *Web:* www.businesswise.com	770-956-1955		627
BusinessBroker Network LLC 375 Northridge Rd Ste 475 .... Atlanta GA 30350 *Web:* www.businessbroker.net	770-391-5061		194
BusinessEdge Solutions Inc 1 Tower Ctr Blvd .... East Brunswick NJ 08816 *Web:* emc.com/domains/businessedge/index.htm	732-828-3200	839-3600	225
BusinessGenetics Inc 9605 S Kingston Ct Ste 290 .... Englewood CO 80112 *Web:* www.businessgenetics.net	720-266-1024		196
Business-Higher Education Forum 2025 M St NW Ste 800 .... Washington DC 20036 *Web:* www.bhef.com	202-367-1189	367-2269	49-5
Business-Industry Political Action Committee (BIPAC) 1707 L St NW Ste 350 .... Washington DC 20036 *Web:* www.bipac.org	202-833-1880	833-2338	615
Businesspersons Between Jobs Inc 601 Claymont Dr .... Ballwin MO 63011 *Web:* bbj.org	636-394-1440		194
BusinessPlans Inc 432 E Pearl St .... Miamisburg OH 45342 *TF:* 800-659-3035 ■ *Web:* www.businessplansinc.com	937-865-6501		463
Business-to-Business Marketing Communications Inc 900 Ridgefield Dr Ste 270 .... Raleigh NC 27609 *Web:* www.btbmarketing.com	919-872-8172	872-8875	195
Busken Bakery Inc 2675 Madison Rd .... Cincinnati OH 45208 *Web:* www.busken.com	513-871-5330		68
Buskirk Lumber Co 319 Oak St .... Freeport MI 49325 *TF:* 800-860-9663 ■ *Web:* www.buskirklumber.com	616-765-5103	765-3380	683
Busler Enterprises Inc 2601 N St Joseph Ave .... Evansville IN 47720 *TF:* 800-457-3232 ■ *Web:* buslerlubricants.com	812-424-7511		324
BUSlink Media 440 Cloverleaf Dr .... Baldwin Park CA 91706 *Web:* www.buslink.com	626-336-1888		194
BUSPAC 700 13th St NW Ste 575 .... Washington DC 20005 *TF:* 800-283-2877 ■ *Web:* buses.org	202-842-1645	842-0850	615
Buss Mechanical Services Inc 4471 Henry St .... Boise ID 83709 *Web:* bussmechanical.com	208-562-0600		612
Busse Design USA Inc 5857 Chabot Ct .... Oakland CA 94618 *Web:* www.bussedesign.com	510-596-9422		344
Busse/SJI Corp 124 N Columbus St .... Randolph WI 53956 **Fax Area Code:* 920 ■ *TF:* 800-882-4995 ■ *Web:* www.arrowheadsystems.com	800-882-4995	326-3134*	470
Busseto Foods Inc 1351 N Crystal Ave .... Fresno CA 93728 *Web:* www.busseto.com	559-485-9882		296-26
Bustin Industrial Products Inc 401 Oak St .... East Stroudsburg PA 18301 *Web:* www.bustin-usa.com	570-424-6500		480
Bustos Cheri (Rep D - IL) 1009 Longworth Bldg .... Washington DC 20515 *Web:* bustos.house.gov	202-225-5905		342-2
Busy Beaver Bldg Centers 2940 Library Rd .... Pittsburgh PA 15234 *TF:* 800-732-0999 ■ *Web:* www.busybeaver.com	412-882-6633	882-6833	364
Busy Bee Cleaning Company Inc 18 Wilson Ave .... West Chester PA 19382 *Web:* busybeecleaningcompany.com	610-430-6888		104
Busy Body Home Fitness 9990 Empire St .... San Diego CA 92126 *Web:* www.busybody.com	949-261-6363	258-5744	711
Butano State Park 1500 Cloverdale Rd .... Pescadero CA 94060 *Web:* www.parks.ca.gov/default.asp?page_id=536	650-879-2040		565
Butch Quinn Rosemurgy Jardis Burkhart Lewandowski & Miller PC 816 Ludington St .... Escanaba MI 49829 *Web:* www.bqrlaw.com	906-786-4422		428
Butchart Gardens, The 800 Benvenuto Ave .... Brentwood Bay BC V8M1J8 *TF:* 866-652-4422 ■ *Web:* www.butchartgardens.com	250-652-4422	652-7751	97
Butcher Air Conditioning Company Inc 101 Boyce St .... Broussard LA 70518 *Web:* butcherac.com	337-837-2000		189-10
Butcher Block 15 Booth Dr .... Plattsburgh NY 12901 *Web:* www.butcherblockrestaurant.com	518-563-0920		671
Butcher Distributors Inc 101 Boyce Rd .... Broussard LA 70518 *TF:* 800-960-0008 ■ *Web:* www.butcherdistributors.com	337-837-2088	837-2069	612
Butcher Shop, The 552 Tremont St .... Boston MA 02118 *Web:* www.thebutchershopboston.com	617-423-4800		671
Butier Engineering Inc 17782 17th St Ste 107 .... Tustin CA 92780 *Web:* www.butier.com	714-832-7222		256
Butler Automatic Inc 41 Leona Dr .... Middleboro MA 02346 *Web:* www.butlerautomatic.com	508-923-0544		547
Butler Brothers Supply Division Inc 2001 Lisbon St .... Lewiston ME 04240 *TF:* 888-784-6875 ■ *Web:* www.butlerbros.com	207-784-6875		186

				Phone	Fax	Class
Butler Capital Investments LLC 222 Court Sq Second Fl Ste 3 *Web:* www.butlercap.com	Charlottesville	VA	22902	434-295-5888		690
Butler Carpet Mart Inc Dba Bob'S Carpet Mart 10815 US Hwy 19 N	Clearwater	FL	33764	727-571-9998		290
Butler Color Press Inc 119 Bonnie Dr *Web:* www.butlercp.com	Butler	PA	16002	724-283-9132		627
Butler Community College 901 S Haverhill Rd **Fax:* Admissions ■ *TF:* 800-782-4732 ■ *Web:* www.butlercc.edu	El Dorado	KS	67042	316-321-2222	322-3316*	162
Butler County 428 Sixth St *Web:* www.butlercoiowa.org	Allison	IA	50602	319-267-2487	267-2488	338
Butler County 124 W Diamond St PO Box 1208 *Web:* www.co.butler.pa.us	Butler	PA	16003	724-284-5233	284-5244	338
Butler County 451 N Fifth St *Web:* www.co.butler.ne.us	David City	NE	68632	402-367-7430	367-3329	338
Butler County 205 W Central Ave *TF:* 800-822-6104 ■ *Web:* www.bucoks.com	El Dorado	KS	67042	316-322-4300	322-4387	338
Butler County 315 High St *TF:* 800-582-4267 ■ *Web:* www.butlercountyohio.org	Hamilton	OH	45011	513-887-3278	887-3966	338
Butler County PO Box 449 *Web:* www.revenue.ky.gov	Morgantown	KY	42261	270-526-5676	526-2658	338
Butler County 100 N Main St Rm 202 *Web:* butler.countyportal.net	Poplar Bluff	MO	63901	573-686-8050	686-8066	338
Butler County Board of Education 215 Administrative Dr *Web:* www.butlerco.k12.al.us	Greenville	AL	36037	334-382-2665		685
Butler County Chamber of Commerce 101 E Diamond St Ste 116 *Web:* www.butlercountychamber.com	Butler	PA	16001	724-283-2222	283-0224	139
Butler County Community College 107 College Dr *TF:* 888-826-2829 ■ *Web:* www.bc3.edu	Butler	PA	16002	724-287-8711	285-6047	162
Butler County Ford 400 S Main St *Web:* www.butlercountyford.net	Butler	PA	16001	724-287-2766		57
Butler County REC 521 N Main PO Box 98 *TF:* 888-267-2726 ■ *Web:* www.butlerrec.coop	Allison	IA	50602	319-267-2726	267-2566	245
Butler County Revenue Commission 700 Ct Sq *Web:* butlercountyal.com	Greenville	AL	36037	334-382-3221	382-0385	338
Butler County Rural Public Power District 1331 N Fourth St *TF:* 800-230-0569 ■ *Web:* www.butlerppd.com	David City	NE	68632	402-367-3081	367-6114	245
Butler Eagle 114 W Diamond St *TF:* 800-842-8098 ■ *Web:* www.butlereagle.com	Butler	PA	16001	724-282-8000	282-4180	532-2
Butler Fairman & Seufert Inc 8450 Wfield Blvd Ste 300 *Web:* bfsengr.com	Indianapolis	IN	46240	317-713-4615		261
Butler Health System 1 Hospital Way *TF:* 800-368-1019 ■ *Web:* butlerhealthsystem.org	Butler	PA	16001	724-283-6666		374-3
Butler Home Products LLC 237 Cedar Hill St *TF:* 888-318-8521 ■ *Web:* www.cleanerhomeliving.com	Marlborough	MA	01752	508-597-8000	597-8010	508
Butler Hospital 345 Blackstone Blvd *Web:* www.butler.org	Providence	RI	02906	401-455-6200		374-5
Butler Institute of American Art 524 Wick Ave *TF:* 800-745-3000 ■ *Web:* www.butlerart.com	Youngstown	OH	44502	330-743-1711	743-9567	520
Butler Library 535 W 114th St *Web:* library.columbia.edu	New York	NY	10027	212-854-7309	854-9099	434-6
Butler Manufacturing Co 1540 Genessee St *Web:* www.butlermfg.com	Kansas City	MO	64102	816-968-3000		105
Butler Motor Transit 210 S Monroe St PO Box 1602 *TF:* 800-222-8750 ■ *Web:* web.coachusa.com/butler	Butler	PA	16003	724-282-1000		107
Butler National Corp 19920 W 161st St *OTC:* BUKS ■ *Web:* www.butlernational.com	Olathe	KS	66062	913-780-9595	780-5088	529
Butler Pappas Weihmuller Katz Craig LLP 80 SW Eighth St Ste 3300 *Web:* www.butler.legal	Miami	FL	33130	305-416-9998		466
Butler Real Estate 1540 Genessee St *Web:* www.butlermfg.com	Kansas City	MO	64102	816-968-3000		653
Butler Rural Electric Co-op Assn Inc 216 S Vine St PO Box 1242 *TF:* 800-464-0060 ■ *Web:* www.butler.coop	El Dorado	KS	67042	316-321-9600	321-9980	245
Butler Rural Electric Co-op Inc (BREC) 3888 Still-Beckett Rd *TF:* 800-255-2732 ■ *Web:* www.butlerrural.coop	Oxford	OH	45056	513-867-4400		245
Butler Shine Stern & Partners 20 Liberty Ship Way *Web:* bssp.com	Sausalito	CA	94965	415-331-6049		7
Butler Supply Inc 965 Horan Dr *TF:* 800-850-9949 ■ *Web:* www.butlersupply.com	Fenton	MO	63026	636-349-9000	349-7877	246
Butler Technologies Inc 231 W Wayne St *TF:* 800-494-6656 ■ *Web:* www.butlertechnologies.com	Butler	PA	16001	724-283-6656		174
Butler Transport Inc 347 N James St *TF:* 800-345-8158 ■ *Web:* www.butlertransport.com	Kansas City	KS	66118	913-321-0047	342-5725	780
Butler University 4600 Sunset Ave **Fax:* Admissions ■ *TF:* 800-368-6852 ■ *Web:* www.butler.edu	Indianapolis	IN	46208	317-940-8100	940-8150*	166
Butler Winery 1022 N College Ave *Web:* www.butlerwinery.com	Bloomington	IN	47404	812-339-7233		50-7
Butler/Newco Printing & Laminating Inc 250 Hamburg Tpke *TF:* 800-524-0786 ■ *Web:* www.butlerprinting.com	Butler	NJ	07405	973-838-8550	838-1767	802
Butler-Dearden Paper Service Inc PO Box 1069 *TF:* 800-634-7070 ■ *Web:* www.butlerdearden.com	Boylston	MA	01505	508-869-9000	869-0211	559
Butte College 3536 Butte Campus Dr **Fax:* Admissions ■ *TF Hum Res:* 800-933-8322 ■ *Web:* www.butte.edu	Oroville	CA	95965	530-895-2511	879-4313*	162
Butte County 248 W Grand Ave	Arco	ID	83213	208-527-3047		338
Butte County 25 County Ctr Dr *Web:* www.buttecounty.net	Oroville	CA	95965	530-538-7691	538-7975	338
Butte County Extension Office 849 Fifth Ave *Web:* butte.sdcounties.org	Belle Fourche	SD	57717	605-892-3371	892-9064	338
Butte County Library 1820 Mitchell Ave *Web:* www.buttecounty.net/bclibrary	Oroville	CA	95966	530-538-7641	538-7235	434-3
Butte Electric Co-op 109 Dartmouth Ave *TF:* 800-928-8839 ■ *Web:* www.butteelectric.com	Newell	SD	57760	605-456-2494		245
Butterball Farms Inc 1435 Buchanan Ave SW *Web:* www.butterballfarms.com	Grand Rapids	MI	49507	616-243-0105		296-25
Butterfield Foods Co 225 Hubbard Ave	Butterfield	MN	56120	507-956-5103		619
Butterfield GK (Rep D - NC) 2080 Rayburn HOB *Web:* butterfield.house.gov	Washington	DC	20515	202-225-3101		342-2
Butterfield Trail Village 1923 E Joyce Blvd *Web:* www.butterfieldtrailvillage.com	Fayetteville	AR	72703	479-442-7220		672
Butterfly House 11455 Obee Rd *Web:* www.wheelerfarms.com	Whitehouse	OH	43571	419-877-2733		50-5
Butterfly House - Faust Park, The 15193 Olive Blvd *TF:* 800-642-8842 ■ *Web:* www.missouribotanicalgarden.org	Chesterfield	MO	63017	636-530-0076	530-1516	50-5
Butterfly Pavilion & Insect Ctr 6252 W 104th Ave *Web:* www.butterflies.org	Westminster	CO	80020	303-469-5441	657-5944	823
Butterfly World 3600 W Sample Rd *Web:* www.butterflyworld.com	Coconut Creek	FL	33073	954-977-4400	977-4501	50-5
Butterkrust Bakery Inc 3355 W Memorial Blvd *Web:* flowersfoods.com	Lakeland	FL	33815	863-682-1155		68
Buttermilk Falls State Park 112 E Buttermilk Falls Rd 105 Enfield Falls Rd *Web:* parks.ny.gov/parks/151	Ithaca	NY	14850	607-273-5761		565
Butters Construction & Development Inc 6820 Lyons Technology Ctr Ste 100 *Web:* www.butters.com	Coconut Creek	FL	33073	954-312-2415	570-8844	186
Butters-Fetting Company Inc 1669 S First St *TF:* 800-361-6154 ■ *Web:* www.buttersfetting.com	Milwaukee	WI	53204	414-645-1535	645-7622	189-10
Butte-Silver Bow Chamber of Commerce 1000 George St *TF:* 800-735-6814 ■ *Web:* www.buttechambersite.org	Butte	MT	59701	406-723-3177		139
Butte-Silver Bow Public Library 226 W Broadway *TF:* 800-794-4061 ■ *Web:* www.buttepubliclibrary.info	Butte	MT	59701	406-723-3361		434-3
Butt-Holdsworth Memorial Library 505 Water St *Web:* www.kerrvilletx.gov	Kerrville	TX	78028	830-257-8422	792-5552	434-3
Button Bay State Park 5 Button Bay State Pk Rd *Web:* www.vtstateparks.com	Vergennes	VT	05491	802-475-2377		565
Buttonwood Park Zoo 425 Hawthorn St *Web:* www.bpzoo.org	New Bedford	MA	02740	508-991-6178		823
Butts County 625 W Third St # 4 Ste 4 *Web:* buttscountyga.com	Jackson	GA	30233	770-775-8200	775-8211	338
Butts County Board of Education 181 N Mulberry St *Web:* www.butts.k12.ga.us	Jackson	GA	30233	770-504-2300	504-2305	685
Butts Foods Inc 2596 Bransford Ave *TF:* 800-962-8570 ■ *Web:* www.buttsfoods.com	Nashville	TN	37204	615-674-2030		297-10
Butzel Long PC 150 W Jefferson Ste 900 *Web:* www.butzel.com	Detroit	MI	48226	313-225-7000		41
Buurma Farms Inc 3909 Kok Rd *TF:* 888-428-8762 ■ *Web:* www.buurmafarms.com	Willard	OH	44890	419-935-6411	935-1918	10-11
Buursma Agency 238 Hoover Blvd Ste 4 *Web:* buursmaagency.com	Holland	MI	49423	616-392-2105		390
Buxton Co 245 Cadwell Dr *TF:* 800-426-3638 ■ *Web:* www.buxton.co	Springfield	MA	01104	413-734-5900	785-1367	430
Buxton Co 2651 S Polaris Dr *Web:* www.buxtonco.com	Fort Worth	TX	76137	817-332-3681		656
Buxy's Salty Dog 2707 Philadelphia Ave *Web:* buxys.com	Ocean City	MD	21842	410-289-0973	289-0038	671
Buy Gitomer 310 Arlington Ave *TF:* 800-748-3746 ■ *Web:* www.gitomer.com	Charlotte	NC	28203	704-333-1112		463
Buy Me Beauty 4221 NE 12th Terr *Web:* www.buymebeauty.com	Oakland Park	FL	33334	954-568-7150		77
Buy Owner Inc 1192 E Newport Ctr Dr Ste 200 *Web:* www.buyowner.com	Deerfield Beach	FL	33442-7749	954-202-7777		5
Buy Rite Liquidators 1076 Park Rd *Web:* buyriteliquidators.com	Blandon	PA	19510	610-926-4444		41
BUYandHOLD.com Securities Corp *c/o Freedom Investments, Inc* 375 Raritan Ctr Pkwy Ste D *TF:* 800-646-8212 ■ *Web:* www.buyandhold.com	Edison	NJ	08837	800-646-8212		690
Buyatab Online Inc B1 - 788 Beatty St *TF:* 888-267-0447 ■ *Web:* www.buyatab.com	Vancouver	BC	V6B2M1	888-267-0447		224
Buyer Advertising Inc 189 Wells Ave *TF:* 800-908-5395 ■ *Web:* www.buyerads.com	Newton	MA	02459	617-969-4646		193
Buyer Group, The 950 Celebration Blvd Ste 208 *Web:* www.thebuyergroup.com	Celebration	FL	34747	954-354-1411		5
Buyers Best Friend Inc 38 Lyon St *Web:* www.bbfdirect.com	San Francisco	CA	94117	415-375-0439		387
BUZ'N 102.9 625 Second Ave S *Web:* buzn1029.cbslocal.com	Minneapolis	MN	55402	612-370-0611		645-101
Buzas Greenhouses 3927 Newburg Rd *Web:* www.buzasgreenhouses.com	Easton	PA	18045	610-252-5289		192
Buzz Co, The 62 W Huron St Ste 2W *Web:* www.buzzco.com	Chicago	IL	60654	312-255-0808		260

Name / Address	City	State	Zip	Phone	Fax	Class
Buzz Marketing Group						
1018 Laurel Oak Rd Ste 1	Voorhees	NJ	08043	856-346-3456		195
Web: buzzmg.com						
Buzz Oates Construction LP						
8615 Elder Creek Rd	Sacramento	CA	95828	916-379-3800		653
Web: www.buzzoates.com						
Buzzwire Inc 1123 Auraria Pkwy	Denver	CO	80204	720-259-0100	557-0668*	387
**Fax Area Code:* 303						
BV Cornerstone Ventures LP						
385 Interlocken Crescent Ste 250	Broomfield	CO	80021	303-410-2510	466-9316	792
Web: www.bvcv.com						
BVI (National Eye Institute)						
Vision Council, The						
225 Reinekers Ln Ste 700	Alexandria	VA	22314	703-548-4560		48-17
TF: 800-372-3937						
BVK Inc 250 W Coventry Ct Ste 300	Milwaukee	WI	53217	414-228-1990		7
TF: 800-888-4848 ■ *Web:* www.bvk.com						
BVM Corp 430 S Navajo St	Denver	CO	80223	303-975-1402		537
TF: 800-521-8800 ■ *Web:* www.bvmcorp.com						
Bvs Performance Systems Inc						
4060 glass rd NE	Cedar rapids	IA	52402	319-378-1807		463
Web: www.bvs.com						
BVT Equity Holdings Inc						
400 Interstate N Pkwy Ste 700	Atlanta	GA	30339	770-618-3500	618-3578	655
Web: www.bvt.com						
BW Container Systems						
1305 Lakeview Dr	Romeoville	IL	60446	630-759-6800	759-2299	207
TF: 800-527-0494 ■ *Web:* www.bwcontainersystems.com						
B-W Graphics Inc 101 Westview St	Versailles	MO	65084	573-378-6363		627
Web: www.bwgraphics.com						
BW Rogers Co 195 S Main St Ste 400	Akron	OH	44308	330-315-3100		295
Web: www.bwrogers.com						
B&W Tek Inc 19 Shea Way Ste 301	Newark	DE	19713	302-368-7824		407
Web: www.bwtek.com						
BWAY (Brockway-Smith Co) 146 Dascomb Rd	Andover	MA	01810	978-475-7100	820-0000*	499
**Fax Area Code:* 732 ■ *TF:* 800-225-7912 ■ *Web:* www.brosco.com						
BWAY Corp 8607 Roberts Dr Ste 250	Atlanta	GA	30350	770-645-4800	645-4810	124
TF: 800-527-2267 ■ *Web:* www.bwaycorp.com						
Bwb Properties Inc 1384 N 450 E	Orem	UT	84097	801-222-3600		652
Bwbacon Group 621 kalamath st	Denver	CO	80204	303-593-1425		260
Web: www.bwbacon.com						
BWD Group LLC 45 Executive Dr	Plainview	NY	11803	516-327-2700	327-2800	390
Web: www.bwd.us						
BWI (Baltimore/Washington International Thurgood Marshall Airport)						
PO Box 8766	Baltimore	MD	21240	410-859-7111	768-9452	27
TF: 800-435-9294 ■ *Web:* www.bwiairport.com						
BWX Technologies Inc						
13024 Ballantyne Corporate Pl Ste 700	Charlotte	NC	28277	704-625-4900		143
Web: www.babcock.com						
Byard F Brogan Inc PO Box 0369	Glenside	PA	19038	215-885-3550	885-1366	409
TF: 800 232 7642 ■ *Web:* www.bfbrogan.com						
Bybee Stone Company Inc						
6293 N Matthews Dr	Ellettsville	IN	47429	812-876-2215		724
TF: 800-457-4530 ■ *Web:* www.bybeestonc.com						
Bybel Rutledge LLP 1017 Mumma Rd	Lemoyne	PA	17043	717-731-1700		428
TF: 800-425-8609 ■ *Web:* www.bybelrutledge.com						
Byblos 3218 Magazine St	New Orleans	LA	70115	504-894-1233	894-1239	671
Web: www.byblosrestaurants.com						
Byblos Byblos Lebanese Restaurant						
1406 N Main St	Fort Worth	TX	76106	817-625-9667		671
Web: www.byblostx.com						
Byblos Cafe 2832 S MacDill Ave	Tampa	FL	33629	813-805-7977		671
Web: www.bybloscafe.com						
Byblos Restaurant 3332 S Mill Ave	Tempe	AZ	85282	480-894-1945		671
Web: www.amdest.com						
Byce & Associates Inc						
487 Portage St	Kalamazoo	MI	49007	269-381-6170		261
Web: www.byce.com						
Bycor General Contractors Inc						
6490 Marindustry Pl	San Diego	CA	92121	858-587-1901		186
Web: www.bycor.com						
By-Crete 517 King St	Lebanon	PA	17042	717-866-7690		183
Web: www.bycrete.com						
Byer California 66 Potrero Ave	San Francisco	CA	94103	415-626-7844		155-4
TF: 844-628-4498 ■ *Web:* byerca.com						
Byerly Aviation 6100 EM Dirkson Pkwy	Peoria	IL	61607	309-697-6300		24
TF: 800 315 1095 ■ *Web:* www.byerlyaviation.com						
Byerly Ford 4041 Dixie Hwy	Louisville	KY	40216	502-448-1661		57
TF: 888-436-0819 ■ *Web:* www.byerlyford.com						
Byers Choice Ltd 4355 County Line Rd	Chalfont	PA	18914	215-822-6700		362
Web: www.byerschoice.com						
Byers Engineering Co 6285 Barfield Rd	Atlanta	GA	30328	404-843-1000	843-2000	261
TF: 800-241-4042 ■ *Web:* www.byers.com						
Byers-Evans House Museum						
1310 Bannock St	Denver	CO	80204	303-620-4933		520
TF: 800-824-0150 ■ *Web:* www.historycolorado.org						
Bygone Designs PO Box 229	Newport	MN	55055	651-451-6737		593
Web: www.bygones.com						
Byline Bank 3639 N Broadway St	Chicago	IL	60613	773-244-7000		70
TF: 866-957-7700 ■ *Web:* www.bylinebank.com						
Byline Bank 180 N LaSalle St	Chicago	IL	60601	773-244-7000		70
Web: www.bylinebank.com						
Byram Healthcare Centers Inc						
120 Bloomingdale Rd	White Plains	NY	10605	914-286-2000		475
TF: 800-354-4054 ■ *Web:* www.byramhealthcare.com						
Byram Laboratories Inc						
1 Columbia Rd	Branchburg	NJ	08876	800-766-1212		246
TF: 800-766-1212 ■ *Web:* www.byramlabs.com						
Byran Company Inc, The						
779 Avery Blvd N	Ridgeland	MS	39157	601-956-1533		757
Web: thebryancompany.com						
Byrd Cookie Company Inc						
6700 Waters Ave	Savannah	GA	31406	912-355-1716		345
TF: 800-291-2973 ■ *Web:* www.byrdcookiecompany.com						
Byrd Maintenance Services Inc						
3172 Hwy 20 West	Decatur	AL	35601	256-355-1627		393
Web: www.bmsi1.com						
Byrne Bradley (Rep R - AL)						
119 Cannon HOB	Washington	DC	20515	202-225-4931	225-0562	342-2
Web: byrne.house.gov						
Byrne Software Technologies Inc						
16091 Swingley Ridge Rd Ste 200	Chesterfield	MO	63017	636-537-2505		177
TF: 800-573-1874 ■ *Web:* www.byrnesoftware.com						
Byrne's Northpoint Travel						
1213 Sheridan Rd	Winthrop Harbor	IL	60096	847-872-9223		775
Web: byrnestravel.com						
Byrnes & Kiefer Co 131 Kline Ave	Callery	PA	16024	724-538-5200		296-1
Web: www.bkcompany.com						
Byrnes Agency Inc 394 Lake Rd	Dayville	CT	06241	860-774-8549		390
Web: byrnesagency.com						
Byron Originals Fuel Sales						
119 E State Hwy 175 PO Box 279	Ida Grove	IA	51445	800-594-9421		579
TF: 800-594-9421 ■ *Web:* byronfuels.com						
Byron Products Inc						
3781 Port Union Rd	Fairfield	OH	45014	513-870-9111		484
Web: www.byronproducts.com						
Bystronic Inc 200 Airport Rd	Elgin	IL	60123	847-214-0300		454
Web: www.bystronic.com						
Byte Right Support Inc						
335 N Charles St	Baltimore	MD	21201	410-347-2983		175
TF: 800-573-1874 ■ *Web:* byterightsupport.com						
Bytemobile Inc						
4988 Great America Pkwy	Santa Clara	CA	95054	408-790-8000		681
TF: 800-424-8749 ■ *Web:* www.citrix.com						
Bytespeed LLC 3131 24th Ave S	Moorhead	MN	56560	218-227-0445		173-2
TF: 877-553-0777 ■ *Web:* www.bytespeed.com						
Bytewyze 120 Iowa Ln Ste 101	Cary	NC	27511	919-465-1916		177
TF: 800-446-0744 ■ *Web:* www.bytewyze.com						
Bytown Museum						
1 Canal Ln PO Box 523 Stn B	Ottawa	ON	K1P5P6	613-234-4570	234-4846	520
Web: www.bytownmuseum.com						
BYU Museum of Peoples and Cultures						
2201 N Canyon Rd	Provo	UT	84602	801-422-0020	422-0026	520
Web: mpc.byu.edu						
Byzantine Catholic Seminary of SS Cyril & Methodius						
3605 Perrysville Ave	Pittsburgh	PA	15214	412-321-8383	321-9936	167-3
Web: www.bcs.edu						
BZ Media LLC						
225 BroadHollow Rd Ste 211 E	Melville	NY	11747	631-421-4158		532-3
Web: www.bzmedia.com						

C

Name / Address	City	State	Zip	Phone	Fax	Class
C & A Financial Group 2111 Rte 34 S	Wall	NJ	07719	732-528-4800		390
Web: www.ca-strategy.com						
C & A Industries Inc						
13609 California St	Omaha	NE	68154	402-891-0009	891-9461	721
TF: 800-574-9829 ■ *Web:* www.ca-industries.com						
C & b Consulting Engineers						
449 Tenth St	San Francisco	CA	94103	415-437-7330		256
Web: www.cbengineers.com						
C & B Piping Inc 8804 Parkway Dr	Leeds	AL	35094	205-699-0455		480
Web: www.cbpiping.com						
C & C Boiler Sales & Service Inc						
3401 Rotary Dr	Charlotte	NC	28269	704-597-0003		610
Web: www.ccboiler.com						
C & C Market Research Inc						
1115 S Waldron Rd Ste 207	Fort Smith	AR	72903	479-785-5637		668
Web: www.ccmarketresearch.com						
C & C Reservoirs Inc						
13831 NW Fwy Ste 450	Houston	TX	77040	713-776-3872		194
Web: www.ccreservoirs.com						
C & C Technologies Inc						
730 E Kaliste Saloom Rd	Lafayette	LA	70508	337-210-0000		256
Web: www.cctechnol.com						
C & D Technologies Inc						
1400 Union Meeting Rd PO Box 3053	Blue Bell	PA	19422	215-619-2700	619-7899	74
TF: 800-543-8630 ■ *Web:* www.cdtechno.com						
C & D Zodiac Inc						
5701 Bolsa Ave	Huntington Beach	CA	92647	714-934-0000		529
C & e Computers						
165 Ramona Ave	South San Francisco	CA	94080	650-872-6543		175
Web: cdgrp.com						
C & E Specialities 2530 Laude Dr	Rockford	IL	61109	815-229-9230		627
Web: www.cespecialties.com						
C & F Enterprises Inc						
819 Bluecrab Rd	Newport News	VA	23606	757-873-5688		361
TF: 888-889-9868 ■ *Web:* www.cnfei.com						
C & F Financial Corp						
1313 E Main St Ste 400	Richmond	VA	23181	804-843-4584	843-3017	360-2
NASDAQ: CFFI ■ *TF:* 800-583-3863 ■ *Web:* cffc.com						
C & F Foods Inc						
15620 E Valley Blvd	City of Industry	CA	91744	626-723-1000	723-1212	275
Web: www.cnf-foods.com						
C & F Packing Company Inc						
515 Park Ave	Lake Villa	IL	60046	847-245-2000		473
Web: www.cfpacking.com						
C & F Tool & Die Co						
7206 Eckhert Rd	San Antonio	TX	78238	210-522-9310		454
Web: www.c-ftool.com						
C & G Boat Works Inc						
401 Cochran Bridge Causeway Hwy 98 Hwy 98	Mobile	AL	36603	251-694-1300	694-1306	698
Web: www.cgboatworks.com						
C & H Bus Lines Inc 448 Pine St	Macon	GA	31201	478-746-6441		107
C & H International						
4751 Wilshire Blvd Ste 201	Los Angeles	CA	90010	323-933-2288	939-2286	16
TF: 800-833-8888 ■ *Web:* www.cnhintl.com						
C & H Machine Inc						
943 S Andreasen Dr	Escondido	CA	92029	760-746-6459		757
Web: www.c-hmachine.com						

Company / Address	City	State	Zip	Phone	Fax	Class
C & H Stone Company Inc 4000 S Rockport Rd *Web:* chstoneinc.com	Bloomington	IN	47403	812-336-2560	331-7292	724
C & H Sugar Co Inc 2300 Contra Costa Blvd Ste 600 *TF:* 800-773-1803 ■ *Web:* www.chsugar.com	Pleasant Hill	CA	94523	925-688-1731		296-38
C & J Clark America Inc 156 Oak St *TF Cust Svc:* 800-211-5461 ■ *Web:* www.clarksusa.com	Newton Upper Falls	MA	02464	800-211-5461		301
C & J Industries 760 Water St *TF:* 800-226-3696 ■ *Web:* www.cjindustries.com	Meadville	PA	16335	814-724-4950	724-4959	604
C & J Jewelry Company Inc 100 Dupont Dr *TF:* 888-527-4268 ■ *Web:* www.candjjewelry.com	Providence	RI	02907	401-944-2200		408
C & K Components Inc 15 Riverdale Ave *Web:* www.ck-components.com	Newton	MA	02458	617-969-3700		729
C & K Industrial Services Inc 5617 Schaaf Rd *Web:* www.ckindustrial.com	Independence	OH	44131	216-642-0055		553
C & K Johnson Industries Inc 1061 Samoa Blvd *Web:* www.ckjohnsonind.com	Arcata	CA	95521	707-822-7687		492
C & K Markets Inc 615 Fifth St *Web:* www.ckmarket.com	Brookings	OR	97415	541-469-3113	469-6717	345
C & L Bus Company Inc 12200 W Broward Blvd *Web:* www.ahschool.com	Plantation	FL	33325	954-472-7800		108
C & L Electric Co-op Corp 900 Church St PO Box 9 *Web:* www.clelectric.com	Star City	AR	71667	870-628-4221	628-4676	245
C & L Supply Co PO Box 578 *TF:* 800-256-6411 ■ *Web:* www.clsupplyinc.com	Vinita	OK	74301	800-256-6411		38
C & I Value Advisors LLC 4805 W Laurel St Ste 100 *TF:* 800-521-5730 ■ *Web:* clvalue.com	Tampa	FL	33607	813-286-7373		2
C & M Conveyor 4598 SR 37 *TF:* 800-551-3195 ■ *Web:* www.cmconveyor.com	Mitchell	IN	47446	812-849-5647		207
C & M Corp 349 Lake Rd *Web:* www.cmcorporation.com	Dayville	CT	06241	860-774-4812		814
C & M Food Distributing Inc 7935 Sugar Pine Ct *Web:* www.c-m-foods.com	Reno	NV	89523	775-787-3020		805
C & R Distributing Inc 8528 Alameda Ave *Web:* www.candrdistributing.com	El Paso	TX	79907	915-860-4205		579
C & R Mechanical 12825 Pennridge Dr *TF:* 800-524-3828 ■ *Web:* www.crmechanical.com	Bridgeton	MO	63044	314-739-1800	739-1721	189-10
C & R Racing Inc 6950 Guion Rd *Web:* www.crracing.com	Indianapolis	IN	46268	317-293-4100		54
C & R Research Services Inc 500 N Michigan Ave Ste 1200 *TF:* 800-543-9393 ■ *Web:* crresearch.com	Chicago	IL	60611	312-828-9200	527-3113	466
C & S Companies (CSCOS) 499 Col Eileen Collins Blvd *TF:* 877-277-6583 ■ *Web:* www.cscos.com	Syracuse	NY	13212	315-455-2000	455-9667	261
C & S Engineering Corp 956 Old Colony Rd *Web:* www.cscos.com	Meriden	CT	06451	203-235-5727		75
C & S Sales Inc 12947 Chadron Ave *Web:* www.cssales.com	Hawthorne	CA	90250	310-538-1219	538-2814	534
C & S Wholesale Grocers Inc 47 Old Ferry Rd PO Box 821 *Web:* www.cswg.com	Brattleboro	VT	05301	802-464-6333		297-8
C Bennett Building Supply Inc 1700 W Terra Ln *Web:* www.cbennett.net	O'Fallon	MO	63366	636-379-9886		361
C Burgett & Assoc Inc 1462 N FM 2199 Rd	Scottsville	TX	75688	903-938-6638		91
C C Tatham & Assoc Ltd 115 Sandford Fleming Dr Ste 200 *Web:* www.cctatham.com	Collingwood	ON	L9Y5A6	705-444-2565		256
C Cowles & Co Inc 83 Water St *TF:* 800-624-4483 ■ *Web:* www.ccowles.com	New Haven	CT	06511	203-865-3117		489
C Cretors & Co 3243 N California Ave *TF:* 800-228-1885 ■ *Web:* www.cretors.com	Chicago	IL	60618	773-588-1690	588-7141	298
C d Barnes Associates Inc 3437 Eastern Ave SE *TF:* 800-481-0164 ■ *Web:* cdbarnes.com	Grand Rapids	MI	49508	616-241-4491		463
C D Henderson Construction Services Ltd 1985 Forest Ln *Web:* www.cdhenderson.com	Garland	TX	75042	972-272-5466		360-3
C Dental X Ray 1050 Northgate Dr Ste 110 *TF:* 800-561-3357 ■ *Web:* www.cdental.com	San Rafael	CA	94903	415-472-1323		415
C E Oil Tools & Supply Inc 104 Ridona St *Web:* www.ceoiltool.com	Lafayette	LA	70508	337-237-4941		539
C Enterprises LP 2445 Cades Way *Web:* www.copierdepot.com	Vista	CA	92081	760-599-5111		174
C Erickson & Sons Inc 2200 ARCH St Ste 200 *Web:* www.cerickson.com	Philadelphia	PA	19103	215-568-3120	496-9460	186
C f a Staffing 543 W N St *Web:* www.cfainc.us	Lima	OH	45801	419-224-0035		193
C F Evans & Company Inc 125 Regional Pkwy *Web:* www.cfevans.com	Orangeburg	SC	29118	803-536-6443		186
C H Garmong & Son Inc 3050 Poplar St *TF:* 800-894-2962 ■ *Web:* www.garmong.net	Terre Haute	IN	47803	812-234-3714		610
C I Thornburg Company Inc, The 4034 Altizer Ave *Web:* www.cithornburg.com	Huntington	WV	25705	304-523-3484		595
C J Nolte Co, The 49 Village Ct *Web:* cjnolte.com	Hazlet	NJ	07730	732-739-1800	739-1814	112
C J Schlosser & Company LLC 233 E Ctr Dr PO Box 416 *Web:* www.cjsco.com	Alton	IL	62002	618-465-7717		2
C L Graphics Inc 134 Virginia Rd Ste A *Web:* www.clgraphics.com	Crystal Lake	IL	60014	815-455-0900		7
C Lazy U Ranch 3640 Colorado Hwy 125 PO Box 379 *TF:* 800-228-9792 ■ *Web:* www.clazyu.com	Granby	CO	80446	970-887-3344	887-3917	239
C m Buck & Associates Inc 6850 Guion Rd *TF:* 800-382-3961 ■ *Web:* www.cmbuck.com	Indianapolis	IN	46268	317-293-5704		393
C M S North America 4095 Korona Ct SE *TF:* 800-931-6083 ■ *Web:* www.cmsna.com	Caledonia	MI	49316	616-698-9970		358
C M School Supply Inc 940 N Central Ave *TF:* 800-464-6681 ■ *Web:* www.cmschoolsupply.com	Upland	CA	91786	909-982-9695		535
C Myers Corp 8222 S 48th St Ste 275 *TF:* 800-238-7475 ■ *Web:* www.cmyers.com	Phoenix	AZ	85044	602-840-0606		194
C Na Insurance 100 Centerview Dr	Nashville	TN	37214	615-871-1400		391-4
C Overaa & Company Inc 200 Parr Blvd *Web:* www.overaa.com	Richmond	CA	94801	510-234-0926	237-2435	186
C P Environmental Group Inc 1092 Fifth Ave	New Kensington	PA	15068	724-594-1900		196
C P H & Assoc 711 S Dearborn St Unit 205 *TF:* 800-875-1911 ■ *Web:* www.cphins.com	Chicago	IL	60605	312-987-9823		390
C R & A Custom Inc 312 W Pico Blvd *Web:* www.cracustom.com	Los Angeles	CA	90015	213-749-4440		627
C R Hipp Construction Inc 4981 Dorchester Rd Ste *TF:* 800-678-3940 ■ *Web:* www.crhippconstruction.com	North Charleston	SC	29418	843-744-4477		261
C R International Inc 9105 Whiskey Bottom Rd Ste J *Web:* www.cri-inc.net	Laurel	MD	20723	301-210-1540		246
C R T & Associates Inc 806 Hastings St Ste 8 *Web:* www.crt-a.com	Traverse City	MI	49686	231-946-1680		387
C Restaurant 1600 Howe St Ste 2	Vancouver	BC	V6Z2L9	604-681-1164		671
C S Davidson Inc 38 N Duke St *Web:* csdavidson.com	York	PA	17401	717-846-4805		261
C s Precision Manufacturing Inc 140028 Lockwood Rd *TF:* 800-841-7954 ■ *Web:* csprecisionmfg.com	Gering	NE	69341	308-436-2099		358
C Spire 1018 Highland Colony Pkwy Ste 300 *TF:* 855-277-4735 ■ *Web:* www.cspire.com	Ridgeland	MS	39157	855-277-4735		387
C Steinweg Inc 1201 Wallace St *Web:* www.steinweg.com	Baltimore	MD	21230	410-752-8254		581
C Stuart Inc Dba Columbia Pharmacy 2840 Long Beach Blvd	Long Beach	CA	90806	562-426-0303		237
C T Earle Maintenance Co 7001 Gibsonton Dr	Gibsonton	FL	33534	813-677-7803		186
C T S Services Inc 260 Maple St *Web:* www.ctsservices.com	Bellingham	MA	02019	508-528-7720		175
C W I Inc 650 Three Springs Raod *TF:* 888-626-7576 ■ *Web:* www.campingworld.com	Bowling Green	KY	42104	888-626-7576		711
C W Rod Tool Company Inc 15050 Northgreen Dr *Web:* www.cwrodtool.com	Houston	TX	77032	281-449-0881		791
C W Thomas Inc 8000 State Rd *Web:* www.cwthomas.com	Philadelphia	PA	19136	215-335-0200		596
C Walters Intercoastal Corp Inc 20081 Ellipse *Web:* www.destinationwater.com	Foothill Ranch	CA	92610	949-448-9940		711
C'mon Inn Grand Forks 3051 32nd Ave S *TF:* 800-255-2323 ■ *Web:* www.cmoninn.com	Grand Forks	ND	58201	701-775-3320		379
C. E. Bradley Laboratories Inc PO Box 8238 *Web:* www.cebradley.com	Brattleboro	VT	05304	802-257-7971	257-7070	550
C. F. Bean LLC 619 Engineers Rd *Web:* www.cfbean.com	Belle Chasse	LA	70037	504-587-8700		192
C. L. Smith Co 1311 S 39th St *TF:* 800-264-1202 ■ *Web:* www.clsmith.com	Saint Louis	MO	63110	314-771-1202		608
C. Martin Company Inc 3395 W Cheyenne Ave *Web:* www.cmartin.com	North Las Vegas	NV	89032	702-656-8080		186
C. P. Richards Construction Company Inc 2654 Dekalb Medical Pkwy **Fax Area Code: 770*	Lithonia	GA	30058	678-244-1450	981-5776*	261
C.A Rasmussen Inc 28548 Livingston Ave *TF:* 800-303-8629 ■ *Web:* www.carasmussen.com	Valencia	CA	91355	661-367-9040	367-9099	188-4
C.a. Murren & Sons Co Inc 2275 Loganville Hwy *TF:* 866-912-8906 ■ *Web:* www.camurren.com	Grayson	GA	30017	770-682-2940		186
C.B.S. Boring & Machine Company Inc 33750 Riviera Dr *Web:* www.cbsboring.com	Fraser	MI	48026	586-294-7540		757
C.J. Driscoll & Associates 2636 Via Carrillo *Web:* www.cjdriscoll.com	Palos Verdes Estates	CA	90274	310-544-5046		195
C.K. Smith & Company Inc 99 Crescent St *TF:* 800-922-8341 ■ *Web:* www.cksmithsuperior.com	Worcester	MA	01605	508-753-1475		581
C.S. McKee LP 1 Gateway Ctr 8th Fl *Web:* www.csmckee.com	Pittsburgh	PA	15222	412-566-1234		528
C.t. Wilson Construction Co PO Box 2011 *Web:* www.ctwilson.com	Durham	NC	27702	919-383-2535		186
C.W. Brown Inc 1 Labriola Ct *Web:* www.cwbrown.net	Armonk	NY	10504	914-741-1212		186
CúSuite Communications 401 N Cattlemen Rd *Web:* www.c-suitecomms.com	Sarasota	FL	34232	941-365-2710		466
C12 Energy LLC 2054 University Ave Ste 400	Berkeley	CA	94704	617-674-2478		192

Name / Address	City	State	Zip	Phone	Fax	Class
C12 Group LLC, The 4101 Piedmont Pkwy *Web:* www.c12group.com	Greensboro	NC	27410	336-841-7100		317
C14 Consulting Group LLC 1307 Summerhill Dr *Web:* www.c14consultinggroup.com	Malvern	PA	19355	610-644-2243		261
C1S Group Inc 4231 Sigma Rd Ste 110 *Web:* www.c1sinc.com	Dallas	TX	75244	972-386-7005		186
C2 Group LLC 325 Seventh St NW Ste 400 Liberty Pl *Web:* www.thec2group.com	Washington	DC	20004	202-567-2900		463
C2 Imaging 274 Fillmore Ave E *Web:* www.c2imagingllc.com	Saint Paul	MN	55107	646-557-6300		7
C28 1180 Galleria At Tyler	Riverside	CA	92503	951-354-9777		157-6
C2AE 106 W Allegan St Ste 500 *TF:* 866-454-3923 ■ *Web:* www.c2ae.com	Lansing	MI	48933	866-454-3923		261
C2ER (Council for Community and Economic Research) *C2ER* 1700 N Moore St Ste 2225 **Fax Area Code:* 480 ■ *Web:* www.c2er.org	Arlington	VA	22209	703-522-4980	393-5098*	49-12
C2F Inc 6600 SW 111th Ave *TF:* 800-544-8825 ■ *Web:* www.c2f.com	Beaverton	OR	97008	503-643-9050		96
C2I LLC Po Box C *Web:* www.c2invest.net	The Plains	VA	20198	540-253-2500		192
C2it Consulting Inc 9107 state Rd 142 *Web:* www.c2itconsulting.net	Martinsville	IN	46151	317-721-2248		463
C2k 10555 Jefferson Blvd	Culver City	CA	90232	310-279-5530		177
C3 Consulting 2975 Sidco Dr *Web:* www.c3-consult.com	Nashville	TN	37204	615-371-8612		463
C3 Corp 3300 E Venture Dr *Web:* www.c3ingenuity.com	Appleton	WI	54911	920-749-9944		261
C3LS 941 Clint Moore Rd *Web:* c3ls.com	Boca Raton	FL	33487	561-995-9004		177
C-4 Analytics LLC 999 Broadway Ste 500 *Web:* www.c-4analytics.com	Saugus	MA	01906	617-250-8888		195
C4 Planning Solutions LLC 4914 Deans Bridge Rd *Web:* www.c4plans.com	Blythe	GA	30805	706-592-1520		194
C5 Group Inc 1329 Bay St *Web:* www.c5groupinc.com	Toronto	ON	M5R2C4	416-927-0718		224
C5 Insight Inc 9319 Robert D Snyder Rd Ste 348 *Web:* www.c5insight.com	Charlotte	NC	28223	704-895-2500		463
C7 Data Centers Inc 14870 S Pony Express Rd Ste 200 *Web:* www.c7.com	Bluffdale	UT	84065	801-822-5300		225
CA (Cocaine Anonymous World Services Inc) PO Box 492000 *TF:* 800-347-8998 ■ *Web:* www.ca.org	Los Angeles	CA	90049	310-559-5833	559-2554	48-21
CA Inc 1 CA Plaza *NASDAQ: CA* ■ **Fax Area Code:* 631 ■ *TF:* 800-225-5224 ■ *Web:* www.ca.com	Islandia	NY	11749	800-225-5224	342-6800*	178-1
CA Lawton Company Inc 1950 Enterprise Way *Web:* www.calawton.com	De Pere	WI	54115	920-337-2470		456
Ca Lindman Inc 10401 Guilford Rd *TF:* 877-737-8675 ■ *Web:* www.calindman.com	Jessup	MD	20794	301-470-4700	470-4708	186
CA Spalding Co 1011 Cedar Ave *Web:* www.caspalding.com	Croydon	PA	19021	267-550-9000		757
C&A Tool Engineering Inc 4100 N US 33 PO Box 94 *Web:* www.catool.com	Churubusco	IN	46723	260-693-2167	693-3633	757
CA Walker Research Solutions Inc 100 W Broadway Ste 1170 *Web:* www.cawalker.com	Glendale	CA	91210	626-584-8180	584-8199	466
Ca'Brea 3900 Wilshire Blvd *Web:* www.cabreala.com	Los Angeles	CA	90010	323-938-2863	938-8659	671
Ca'del Sole 4100 Cahuenga Blvd *Web:* www.cadelsole.com	Toluka Lake	CA	91602	818-985-4669		671
CAA (Canadian Automobile Assn) 2151 Thurston Dr *TF:* 800-267-8713 ■ *Web:* www.caa.ca	Ottawa	ON	K1G6C9	613-820-1890	247-0118	48-23
CAA (Creative Artists Agency Inc) 2000 Ave of the Stars *Web:* www.caa.com	Los Angeles	CA	90067	424-288-2000	288-2900	731
CAA (Council on Aviation Accreditation) *Aviation Accreditation Board International* 3410 Skyway Dr *TF:* 800-767-4767 ■ *Web:* www.aabi.aero	Auburn	AL	36830	334-844-2431	844-2432	48-1
CAA Central Ontario 60 Commerce Valley Dr E *TF:* 800-268-3750 ■ *Web:* www.caasco.com	Thornhill	ON	L3T7P9	905-771-3000	771-3101	53
CAA Manitoba 870 Empress St *TF:* 800-222-4357 ■ *Web:* www.caamanitoba.com	Winnipeg	MB	R3C2Z3	204-262-6166		53
CAA Maritimes Ltd 378 Westmorland Rd *TF:* 800-471-1611 ■ *Web:* ww2.aaa.com	Saint John	NB	E2J2G4	506-634-1400	653-9500	53
Caa Niagara 155 Main St E *TF:* 800-263-7272 ■ *Web:* www.caaniagara.ca	Grimsby	ON	L3M1P2	905-945-5555		775
CAA North & East Ontario PO Box 8350 *TF:* 800-267-8713 ■ *Web:* caaneo.ca	Ottawa	ON	K1G3T2	613-820-1890	820-4646	53
CAA Quebec 444 Bouvier St *TF:* 800-222-4357 ■ *Web:* www.caaquebec.com	Quebec	QC	G2J1E3	418-624-8222		53
CAA Saskatchewan 200 N Albert St *Web:* www.caasask.sk.ca	Regina	SK	S4R5E2	306-791-4314		390
CAA Sports 2000 Ave of the Stars *Web:* sports.caa.com	Los Angeles	CA	90067	424-288-2000	288-2900	731
CAA Stoney Creek 163 Centennial Pkwy N *TF:* 800-992-8143 ■ *Web:* www.caasco.com	Hamilton	ON	L8E1H8	905-664-8000	664-8080	53
CAAHEP (Commission on Accreditation of Allied Health Education Programs) 1361 Pk St *TF:* 800-228-2262 ■ *Web:* www.caahep.org	Clearwater	FL	33756	727-210-2350	210-2354	48-1
Caasco Signs 2719 Texas Ave **Fax Area Code:* 281 ■ *Web:* creativesigntc.com	Texas City	TX	77590	409-945-4929	332-1503*	701
CAB (Video Advertising Bureau) 830 Third Ave 2nd Fl *Web:* www.thevab.com	New York	NY	10022	212-508-1200	832-3268	49-18
Cab Signs 38 Livonia Ave *TF:* 800-394-1690 ■ *Web:* www.cab-signs.com	Brooklyn	NY	11212	718-385-1600		627
Caballo Blanco Restaurante 5604 Franklin Blvd	Sacramento	CA	95824	916-428-6706		671
Caballo Energy LLC 2007 E 15th St	Tulsa	OK	74104	918-794-8800		580
Cabana 533 Clematis St *Web:* www.cabanarestaurant.com	West Palm Beach	FL	33401	561-833-4773		671
Cabaniss, Johnston, Gardner, Dumas & O'Neal LLP Park Pl Tower 2001 Park Pl N Ste 700 *Web:* www.cabaniss.com	Birmingham	AL	35203	205-716-5200		428
Cabaret Systems Inc 8848 Red Oak Blvd *Web:* cabaretsystems.com	Charlotte	NC	28217	704-333-1100		174
Cabarrus County 65 Church St S *TF:* 800-777-9898 ■ *Web:* www.cabarruscounty.us	Concord	NC	28025	704-920-2100	920-2820	338
Cabarrus County Convention & Visitors Bureau 3003 Dale Earnhardt Blvd *TF:* 800-848-3740 ■ *Web:* www.visitcabarrus.com	Kannapolis	NC	28083	704-782-4340	782-4333	206
Cabarrus County School District 4401 Old Airport Rd *Web:* www.cabarrus.k12.nc.us	Concord	NC	28025	704-786-6191		685
Cabarrus Plastics Inc 2845 Armentrout Dr *TF:* 800-459-7328	Concord	NC	28025	800-459-7328		596
Cabarrus Regional Chamber of Commerce 3003 Dale Earnhardt Blvd *TF:* 800-264-6823 ■ *Web:* www.cabarrus.biz	Kannapolis	NC	28083	704-782-4000	782-4050	139
Cabedge Design 1310 Clinton St Ste 200 *Web:* www.cabedge.com	Nashville	TN	37212	615-942-9937	942-9976	631
Cabela's Inc 1 Cabela Dr *NYSE: CAB* ■ *TF:* 800-237-8888 ■ *Web:* www.cabelas.com	Sidney	NE	69160	308-254-5505		711
Cabell County 750 Fifth Ave Ste 300 *Web:* www.cabellcounty.org	Huntington	WV	25701	304-526-8625	526-8632	338
Cabell County Public Library 455 Ninth St Plaza *TF:* 800-368-8808 ■ *Web:* www.cabell.lib.wv.us	Huntington	WV	25701	304-528-5700	528-5701	434-3
Cabell Huntington Hospital 1340 Hal Greer Blvd *TF:* 800-941-8140 ■ *Web:* www.cabellhuntington.org	Huntington	WV	25701	304-526-2000		374-3
Cabell-Huntington Convention & Visitors Bureau PO Box 347 *TF:* 800-635-6329 ■ *Web:* www.wvvisit.org	Huntington	WV	25708	304-525-7333	525-7345	206
Cabello Assoc 8340 Little Eagle Ct Ste 200 *TF:* 800-280-1179 ■ *Web:* www.cabelloassociates.com	Indianapolis	IN	46234	317-209-9991		7
CabelTel International Corp 1603 Lyndon B Johnson Fwy **Fax Area Code:* 469 ■ *TF:* 800-400-6407 ■ *Web:* www.newconceptenergy.com	Dallas	TX	75234	972-407-8400	522-4240*	451
Cabem Technologies LLC 90 Oak St Ste 302 Ste 201 *Web:* www.cabem.com	Newton Upper Falls	MA	02464	508-541-3123		261
Caber Sure Fit Inc 25A E Pearce St Unit 2 *Web:* www.cabersurefit.com	Richmond Hill	ON	L4B2M9	905-886-5849	886-5917	361
Cabinet Components & Distribution Inc 760 Beltline Rd *Web:* www.cabinetcomponents.com	Sauk Centre	MN	56378	320-352-5404		115
Cabinet Discounters Inc 9500 Berger Rd *Web:* www.cabinetdiscounters.com	Columbia	MD	21046	410-793-1265		321
Cabinet Outlet Inc 1168 N 50th Pl *Web:* milwaukeecabinetry.com	Milwaukee	WI	53208	414-771-1960	771-3638	362
Cabinet Press Inc, The 17 Executive Dr *TF:* 800-681-6248 ■ *Web:* www.cabinet.com	Hudson	NH	03051	603-673-3100		532-3
Cabinet Tronix 280 Trousdale Dr Ste A *TF:* 866-876-6199 ■ *Web:* www.cabinet-tronix.com	Chula Vista	CA	91910	866-876-6199		819
Cabinetry By Karman Inc 6000 Stratler St *TF:* 800-255-3581 ■ *Web:* www.cabinetrybykarman.com	Salt Lake City	UT	84107	801-281-6400		115
Cabinetry Concepts Inc 14410 Azurite St NW *Web:* www.cabinetryconcepts.com	Anoka	MN	55303	763-427-4600		115
Cabinets 2000 Inc 11100 Firestone Blvd *Web:* www.cabinets2000.com	Norwalk	CA	90650	562-868-0909		115
Cabinets By Michael 4301 Murray Ave *Web:* www.cabinetsbymichael.com	Ft. Worth	TX	76117	817-485-1962		115
Cabinets To Go LLC 6901 Crestwood Blvd *Web:* www.cabinetstogo.com	Birmingham	AL	35210	205-623-2209		690
Cabins Usa Gatlinburg Llc 510 Ski Mountain Rd Ste 6 *Web:* cabinsusagatlinburg.com	Gatlinburg	TN	37738	865-436-5031		377
CABLCF (Creditors Adjustment Bureau-LC Financial) 14226 Ventura Blvd *TF:* 800-800-4523 ■ *Web:* www.cab-lcf.com	Sherman Oaks	CA	91423	818-990-4800	780-3112	160
Cable Aml Inc 2271 W 205th St Ste 101 *Web:* cableaml.com	Torrance	CA	90501	310-222-5599		261
Cable Center, The 2000 Buchtel Blvd *Web:* www.cablecenter.org	Denver	CO	80210	720-502-7500		116
Cable Com Inc 12115 Roxie Dr *TF:* 800-880-2468 ■ *Web:* www.cablecominc.com	Austin	TX	78729	512-250-5901		116
Cable Connection, The 52 Heppner Dr *TF:* 800-851-2961 ■ *Web:* www.thecableconnection.com	Carson City	NV	89706	775-885-1443	885-2734	116
Cable Coop 27 E College St *TF:* 800-890-9471 ■ *Web:* www.oberlin.net	Oberlin	OH	44074	440-775-4001		116
Cable Form Inc 8845 Three Notch Rd *Web:* www.cableform.com	Troy	VA	22974	434-589-8224		203
Cable Huston Benedic 1001 SW Fifth Ave Ste 2000 *TF:* 800-314-0746 ■ *Web:* www.cablehuston.com	Portland	OR	97204	503-224-3092		428
Cable Line Inc 239 Main St Ste 102 *Web:* www.cable-line.com	East Greenville	PA	18041	215-258-1380		116

Phone | Fax | Class

Cable Manufacturing & Assembly Co
10896 Industrial Pkwy NW Bolivar OH 44612 330-874-2900 203
Web: www.cmacable.com

Cable Markers Company Inc
13805-C Alton Pkwy Irvine CA 92618 800-746-7655 699-1642* 467
**Fax Area Code:* 949 ■ *TF:* 800-746-7655 ■ *Web:* www.cablemarkers.com

Cable One Inc 210 E Earll Dr Phoenix AZ 85012 602-364-6000 364-6010 116
TF: 877-692-2253 ■ *Web:* www.cableone.net

Cable Public Affairs Channel (CPAC)
PO Box 81099 Ottawa ON K1P1B1 877-287-2722 567-2749* 740
**Fax Area Code:* 613 ■ *TF:* 877-287-2722 ■ *Web:* www.cpac.ca

Cable Satellite Public Affairs Network (C-SPAN)
400 N Capitol St NW Ste 650 Washington DC 20001 202-737-3220 740
Web: www.c-span.org

Cable Television Laboratories Inc
858 Coal Creek Cir Louisville CO 80027 303-661-9100 661-9199 49-14
Web: www.cablelabs.com

Cable USA LLC 2584 S Horseshoe Dr Naples FL 34104 239-643-6400 643-4230 814
Web: cableusallc.com

CableAmerica Corp 7822 E Gray Rd Scottsdale AZ 85260 866-871-4492 116
TF: 866-871-4492 ■ *Web:* www.cableamerica.com

CableCom LLC 6070 N Flint Rd Glendale WI 53209 414-226-2205 116
Web: cablecomllc.com

Cable-Comm Technologies Inc
800 Enterprise Ct Naperville IL 60563 630-717-7179 116
Web: www.cable-comm.com

Cablecraft Motion Controls LLC
2110 Summit St New Haven IN 46774 260-749-5105 493-2387 620
Web: www.cablecraft.com

Cable-Dahmer Chevrolet Inc
1834 S Noland Rd Independence MO 64055 816-256-2118 57
TF: 866-618-1320 ■ *Web:* www.cabledahmer.com

Cables to Go Inc 3599 Dayton Pk Dr Dayton OH 45414 937-224-8646 814
TF: 800-826-7904 ■ *Web:* www.cablestogo.com

CableTest Systems Inc 400 Alden Rd Markham ON L3R4C1 905-475-2607 776
Web: www.cabletest.com

Cablevision Systems Corp
1111 Stewart Ave Bethpage NY 11714 516-803-2300 116
NYSE: CVC ■ *Web:* www.cablevision.com

Cableworks Communications Inc
3112 Main St Unit #3 Salisbury NB E4J2L6 506-372-9542 681
Web: www.cableworkscommunications.com

Cabo Drilling (Ontario) Corp
20 Sixth St New Westminster BC V3L2Y8 705-567-9311 540
Web: www.cabo.ca

Cabo Seafood Grill & Cantina
1041 S Oxnard Blvd Oxnard CA 93030 805-487-6933 487-6954 671
Web: www.caboseafoodgrill.com

Cabo's Island Grill & Bar
1221 Apalachee Pkwy Tallahassee FL 32301 850-878-7707 671
Web: www.cabosgrill.com

Cabot Advisory Group LLC, The
90 Washington Valley Rd Bedminster NJ 07921 908-719-8966 194

Cabot Coach Builders Inc
99 Newark St Haverhill MA 01832 978-374-4530 647
TF: 800-544-5587 ■ *Web:* www.royalelimo.com

Cabot Corp 2 Seaport Ln Ste 1300 Boston MA 02210 617-345-0100 342-6103 145
NYSE: CBT ■ *TF:* 800-322-1236 ■ *Web:* www.cabotcorp.com

Cabot Creamery 193 Home Farm Way Waitsfield VT 05673 802-229-9361 296-5
TF: 888-792-2268 ■ *Web:* www.cabotcheese.coop

Cabot House Inc 10 Industrial Way Amesbury MA 01913 978-834-9280 321
Web: www.cabothouse.com

Cabot Microelectronics Corp
870 N Commons Dr Aurora IL 60504 630-375-6631 375-5539 145
NASDAQ: CCMP ■ *TF:* 800-811-2756 ■ *Web:* www.cabotcmp.com

Cabot Oil & Gas Corp
840 Gessner Rd Ste 1200 Houston TX 77024 281-848-2799 787
NYSE: COG ■ *TF:* 800-434-3985 ■ *Web:* cabotog.com

Cabot Specialty Fluids Inc
Waterway Plaza Two 10001 Woodlock Forest Dr
Ste 275 The Woodlands TX 77380 281-298-9955 298-6190 145
TF: 800-322-1236 ■ *Web:* www.cabotcorp.com

Cabot Supermetals
1095 Windward Ridge Pkwy Ste 200 Alpharetta GA 30005 610-367-1500 485
Web: www.cabotcorp.com

Cabot Wealth Management Inc
216 Essex St Salem MA 01970 978-745-9233 528
TF: 800-888-6468 ■ *Web:* www.ecabot.com

Cabot Wealth Network
176 N St PO Box 2049 Salem MA 01970 800-326-8826 745-1283* 531-9
**Fax Area Code:* 978 ■ *TF Orders:* 800-326-8826 ■ *Web:* www.cabot.net

Cabot's Pueblo Museum
67-616 E Desert View Ave Desert Hot Springs CA 92240 760-329-7610 520
TF: 800-475-7300 ■ *Web:* www.cabotsmuseum.org

CabotWrenn 405 Rink Dam Rd PO Box 1767 Hickory NC 28603 828-495-4607 495-1294 319-1
Web: www.cabotwrenn.com

Cabrera Capital Markets LLC
10 S La Salle St Ste 1050 Chicago IL 60603 312-236-8888 236-8936 690
Web: www.cabreracapital.com

Cabrillo Advisors LLC
1200 Prospect St Ste 550 La Jolla CA 92037 858-452-9500 70
Web: www.cabrilloadvisors.com

Cabrillo College 6500 Soquel Dr Aptos CA 95003 831-479-6100 479-5782* 162
**Fax:* Admitting ■ *TF:* 888-442-4551 ■ *Web:* www.cabrillo.edu

Cabrillo Marine Aquarium
3720 Stephen M White Dr San Pedro CA 90731 310-548-7562 548-2649 40
Web: www.cabrillomarineaquarium.org

Cabrillo National Monument
1800 Cabrillo Memorial Dr San Diego CA 92106 619-557-5450 226-6311 564
TF: 800-236-7916 ■ *Web:* www.nps.gov

Cabrillo Unified School District
498 Kelly Ave Half Moon Bay CA 94019 650-712-7100 726-0279 685
Web: www.cabrillo.k12.ca.us

Cabrini College 610 King of Prussia Rd Radnor PA 19087 610-902-8552 902-8508* 166
**Fax:* Acctg ■ *TF:* 800-848-1003 ■ *Web:* www.cabrini.edu

CABT (Coalition Against Bigger Trucks)
1001 N Fairfax St Ste 515 Alexandria VA 22314 703-535-3131 49-21
Web: www.cabt.org

Cabwaylingo State Forest
4279 Cabwaylingo Pk Rd Dunlow WV 25511 304-385-4255 565
Web: www.cabwaylingo.com

CAC (Contemporary Art Ctr of Virginia)
2200 Parks Ave Virginia Beach VA 23451 757-425-0000 50-2
Web: www.cacv.org

CAC (Cement Assn of Canada)
502-350 Sparks St Ottawa ON K1R7S8 613-236-9471 563-4498 49-3
TF: 800-221-5105 ■ *Web:* www.cement.ca

CAC (Coating & Adhesive Corp)
1901 Popular St PO Box 1080 Leland NC 28451 910-371-3184 371-5580 550
TF: 800-410-2999 ■ *Web:* www.cacoatings.com

CAC China 30 Camptown Rd Irvington NJ 07111 973-371-4300 361
Web: www.chinacac.com

Cacapon Resort State Park
818 Cacapon Lodge Dr Berkeley Springs WV 25411 304-258-1022 565
Web: www.cacaponresort.com

CACC (Charleston Area Convention Ctr Complex)
5001 Coliseum Dr Charleston SC 29418 843-725-1307 205
Web: www.charlestonconventioncenter.com

Cacharel Restaurant & Grand Ballroom
2221 E Lamar Blvd Arlington TX 76006 817-640-9981 671
Web: www.cacharel.net

Cache Cache Bistro 205 S Mill St Aspen CO 81611 970-925-3835 671
Web: www.cachecache.com

Cache Chamber of Commerce 160 N Main St Logan UT 84321 435-752-2161 753-5825 139
TF: 800-233-6510 ■ *Web:* www.cachechamber.com

Cache County School District
2063 N 1200 E North Logan UT 84341 435-752-3925 753-2168 685
Web: www.ccsdut.org

Cache Creek Casino Resort 14455 Hwy 16 Brooks CA 95606 530-796-3118 133
Web: cachecreek.com

Cache Creek Foods LLC
411 Pioneer Ave Woodland CA 95776 530-662-1764 345
Web: www.cachecreekfoods.com

Cache River State Natural Area
930 Sunflower Ln Belknap IL 62908 618-657-2064 565
Web: www.dnr.illinois.gov/parks/pages/cacheriver.aspx

Cache Valley Electric Inc 875 N 1000 W Logan UT 84321 435-752-6405 752-9111 189-4
TF: 888-558-0600 ■ *Web:* www.cve.com

Cachet Financial Services
175 S Lake Ave Ste 200 Pasadena CA 91101 855-591-9865 2
TF: 855-591-9865 ■ *Web:* www.cachetbanq.com

CACi 4121 Union Rd Ste 201 St. Louis MO 63129 800-777-7971 160
TF: 800-777-7971 ■ *Web:* www.cacionline.net

CACI International Inc
1100 N Glebe Rd Arlington VA 22201 703-841-7800 841-7882 180
NYSE: CACI ■ *TF:* 866-606-3471 ■ *Web:* www.caci.com

CACI MTL Systems Inc
2685 Hibiscus Way Beavercreek OH 45431 937-426-3111 703
Web: www.caci.com

Cacique Inc 14923 Procter Ave La Puente CA 91746 626-961-3399 369-8083* 296-5
**Fax:* Sales ■ *TF:* 800-521-6987 ■ *Web:* caciqueinc.com

Caco-Pacific Corp 813 N Cummings Rd Covina CA 91724 626-331-3361 966-4219 757
TF: 800-422-4002 ■ *Web:* www.cacopacific.com

Cactus 4220 E Madison Seattle WA 98112 206-324-4140 671
Web: www.cactusrestaurants.com

Cactus Cantina
3300 Wisconsin Ave NW Washington DC 20016 202-686-7222 671
Web: www.cactuscantina.com

Cactus Feeders Inc
2209 W Seventh Ave Amarillo TX 79106 806-373-2333 371-4767 10-1
Web: www.cactusfeeders.com

Cactus Flower Florists
10822 N Scottsdale Rd Scottsdale AZ 85254 480-483-9200 483-9200* 292
**Fax:* Sales ■ *TF:* 800-922-2887 ■ *Web:* www.cactusflower.com

Cactus Jack's Casino
420 N Carson St Carson City NV 89701 775-882-8770 133

Cactus Jacks Southwest Grill
782 S Willow St Manchester NH 03103 603-627-8600 434-3200 671
Web: www.cactusjacksnh.com

Cactus Mailing Co
16121 N 78th St Ste 103 Scottsdale AZ 85260 480-443-1442 5
TF: 866-828-7794 ■ *Web:* www.cactusmailing.com

Cactus Punch Inc
1224 Heil Quaker Blvd LaVergne TN 37086 800-446-2333 635-4308* 344
**Fax Area Code:* 203 ■ *TF:* 800-446-2333 ■ *Web:* www.myembroideries.com

Cactus Ya Ya
15704 SE Mill Plain Blvd Vancouver WA 98684 360-944-9292 671

CACU (Community America Credit Union)
9777 Ridge Dr Lenexa KS 66219 913-905-7000 905-7111 219
TF: 800-892-7957 ■ *Web:* www.communityamerica.com

CAD (Cartridge Actuated Devices Inc)
51 Dwight Pl Fairfield NJ 07004 973-575-1312 268
Web: cartactdev.com

CAD & Graphic Supply Inc
2410 Luna Rd Ste 114 Carrollton TX 75006 972-409-7333 175
TF: 866-409-8211 ■ *Web:* www.cadgraphicsupply.com

Cad Control Systems
1017 Frenchman Dr Broussard LA 70518 337-369-3737 538
TF: 800-543-1968 ■ *Web:* cadoil.com

CAD Railway Industries Ltd
155 boul Montreal-Toronto (Hwy 2-20) Lachine QC H8S1B4 514-634-3131 650
Web: www.cadrail.ca

Cad Store Inc, The 15353 N 91st Ave Peoria AZ 85381 623-931-7936 557
TF: 800-576-6789 ■ *Web:* thecadstore.com

Cad Technology Center Inc
8101 Fourth Ave S Ste 100 Bloomington MN 55425 952-941-1181 180
TF: 866-941-1181 ■ *Web:* www.cadtechnologycenter.com

CAD Zone Inc, The 4790 SW Watson Beaverton OR 97005 503-641-1342 177
TF: 800-641-9077 ■ *Web:* www.cadzone.com

CAD/CAM Consulting Services Inc (CCCS)
1525 Rancho Conejo Blvd Ste 103 Newbury Park CA 91320 805-375-7676 375-7678 174
TF: 888-375-7676 ■ *Web:* www.cad-cam.com

Cadalog Inc 1448 King St Bellingham WA 98229 360-647-2426 647-2890 178-5
Web: www.cadalog-inc.com

Cadbury Retirement Community
51 Haddonfield Rd Ste 105 Cherry Hill NJ 08002 856-406-6229 672
Web: www.cadbury.org

				Phone	Fax	Class
CADCA (CPA Auto Dealer Consultants Assn) 1801 W End Ave Ste 800 *TF:* 800-231-2524 ■ *Web:* autodealercpas.com	Nashville	TN	37203	615-373-9880	377-7092	49-1
Cadco Ltd 145 Colebrook River Rd *Web:* www.cadco-ltd.com	Winsted	CT	06098	860-738-2500		362
Caddell Construction Co Inc 2700 Lagoon Pk Dr *Web:* www.caddell.com	Montgomery	AL	36109	334-272-7723	272-8844	186
Cadden & Fuller LLP 114 Pacifica Ste 450 *Web:* caddenfuller.com	Irvine	CA	92618	949-788-0827		445
Caddo County PO Box 68 *Web:* www.ok.gov	Anadarko	OK	73005	405-247-6609		338
Caddo Electric Co-op PO Box 70 *Web:* www.caddoelectric.com	Binger	OK	73009	405-656-2322	656-2327	245
Caddo Lake State Park 245 Pk Rd 2 *Web:* tpwd.texas.gov/state-parks/caddo-lake	Karnack	TX	75661	903-679-3351		565
Caddo Mills ISD 100 Fox Ln *TF:* 800-621-3900 ■ *Web:* www.caddomillsisd.org	Caddo Mills	TX	75135	903-527-6056		685
Caddo Parish School Board 1961 Midway Ave PO Box 32000 *Fax: Hum Res ■ *Web:* www.caddoschools.org	Shreveport	LA	71130	318-603-6300	603-6559*	685
Caddoan Mounds State Historic Site 1649 Texas 21 *Web:* www.thc.texas.gov	Alto	TX	75925	936-858-3218		565
Caddy Corp of America 509 Sharptown Rd *TF:* 800-800-4981 ■ *Web:* www.caddycorp.com	Bridgeport	NJ	08014	856-467-4222	467-5511	207
Caddy Printing & Graphics Inc 13701 Neutron Rd *Web:* www.caddyprinting.com	Dallas	TX	75244	972-991-1770		627
CADE (Commission on Accreditation for Dietetics Education) 120 S Riverside Plaza Ste 2000 *TF:* 800-877-1600 ■ *Web:* www.eatright.org	Chicago	IL	60606	312-899-0040		48-1
Cade & Assoc Adv Inc 1645 Metropolitan Blvd *Web:* www.cade1.com	Tallahassee	FL	32308	850-385-0300		4
Cadeau Express Inc 3494 E Sunset Rd *TF:* 800-240-0301 ■ *Web:* www.cadeauexpress.com	Las Vegas	NV	89120	702-433-1333		238
Cadence Aerospace 2600 94th St SW Bomarc Industrial Pk Ste 150 *Web:* www.cadenceaerospace.com	Everett	WA	98204	425-353-0405		454
Cadence Aerospace LLC 610 Newport Ctr Dr Ste 950 *Web:* www.prvaerospace.com	Newport Beach	CA	92660	949-877-3630		21
Cadence Capital Management 265 Franklin St 4th Fl *Web:* www.cadencecapital.com	Boston	MA	02110	617-624-3500	624-3591	401
Cadence Design Systems Inc 2655 Seely Ave *NASDAQ: CDNS* ■ *TF Cust Svc:* 800-746-6223 ■ *Web:* www.cadence.com	San Jose	CA	95134	408-943-1234	428-5001	178-5
Cadence Environmental Energy Inc 401 Cadence Park Plaza *Web:* www.cadencerecycling.com	Michigan City	IN	46360	219-879-0371		196
Cadence Group Inc 1095 Zonolite Rd Ste 105 *Web:* www.cadence-group.com	Atlanta	GA	30306	404-874-0544		225
Cadence Magazine Cadence Bldg *Web:* www.cadencebuilding.com	Redwood City	NY	13679	315-287-2852	287-2860	457-9
Cadence Marketing Llc 509 Lake Ct *Web:* www.cadencemarketingllc.com	Basalt	CO	81621	970-927-0377		195
Cadence Mcshane Corp 5057 Keller Springs Rd Ste 500 *Web:* www.cadencemcshane.com	Addison	TX	75001	972-239-2336		186
Cadence Research & Consulting 360 Via Las Brisas Ste 210 *Web:* www.cadenceresearch.com	Thousand Oaks	CA	91320	805-499-8603		466
Cadence Technologies Inc 1075 Windward Ridge Pkwy Ste 100 *TF:* 800-288-9288 ■ *Web:* www.cadencetechnologies.com	Alpharetta	GA	30005	770-667-6250		180
Cadet Mfg Company Inc 2500 W Fourth Plain Blvd *TF:* 800-442-2338 ■ *Web:* cadetheat.com	Vancouver	WA	98660	360-693-2505	694-6939	37
Cadex Electronics Inc 22000 Fraserwood Way *TF:* 800-565-5228 ■ *Web:* www.cadex.com	Richmond	BC	V6W1J6	604-231-7777	231-7755	246
Cadie Products Corp 151 E 11th St *TF:* 800-476-9944 ■ *Web:* www.cadie.com	Paterson	NJ	07524	973-278-8300	278-0303	508
Cadillac Area Chamber of Commerce 222 N Lake St *TF:* 800-634-7302 ■ *Web:* www.cadillac.org	Cadillac	MI	49601	231-775-9776	775-1440	139
Cadillac Area Public Schools 421 S Mitchell St *Web:* vikingnet.org	Cadillac	MI	49601	231-876-5000		685
Cadillac Area Visitors Bureau 201 N Mitchell St *TF:* 800-325-2525 ■ *Web:* www.cadillacmichigan.com	Cadillac	MI	49601	231-775-0657	779-5933	206
Cadillac Casting Inc 1500 Fourth Ave *Web:* cadillaccasting.com	Cadillac	MI	49601	231-779-9600		723
Cadillac Coffee Co 194 E Maple Rd *TF:* 800-438-6900 ■ *Web:* www.cadillaccoffee.com	Troy	MI	48083	248-545-2266		296-7
Cadillac Fairview Ltd 20 Queen St W 5th Fl *Web:* www.cadillacfairview.com	Toronto	ON	M5H3R4	416-598-8200		655
Cadillac Jack Inc 2450 Satellite Blvd *Web:* cadillacjack.com	Duluth	GA	30096	770-908-2094	908-1790	57
Cadillac Products Automotive Inc 5800 Crooks Rd *Web:* www.cadprod.com/cpac/index.shtml	Troy	MI	48098	248-813-8200		247
Cadillac-Wexford County Public Library 411 S Lake St *TF:* 800-625-9740 ■ *Web:* www.cadillaclibrary.org	Cadillac	MI	49601	231-775-6541		434-3
Cadiz Inc 550 S Hope St Ste 2850 *NASDAQ: CDZI* ■ *Web:* www.cadizinc.com	Los Angeles	CA	90071	213-271-1600	271-1614	787
Cadmium Cd LLC 19 Newport Dr Ste 101 *TF:* 877-426-6323 ■ *Web:* www.cadmiumcd.com	Forest Hill	MD	21050	410-638-9239		195
Cadmus Group Inc 100 Fifth Ave Ste 100 *Web:* www.cadmusgroup.com	Waltham	MA	02451	617-673-7000	673-7001	193
Cadnet Services 100 Carl Dr Ste 12 *Fax Area Code: 603 ■ *TF:* 866-522-3638 ■ *Web:* www.cadnetservices.com	Manchester	NH	03103	866-522-3638	296-2370*	180
Cadnetics Inc 10 Bedford Sq Ste 300 *Web:* www.cadnetics.com	Pittsburgh	PA	15203	412-642-2701		180
Cadre Computer Resources Co 201 E Fifth St Ste 1800 *TF:* 866-762-6700 ■ *Web:* www.cadre.net	Cincinnati	OH	45202	513-762-7350	762-6502	180
Cadsoft Consulting Inc 4578 N First Ave Ste 120 *Web:* cadsoft-consult.com	Tucson	AZ	85718	520-546-2233		180
Cadwell Laboratories Inc 909 N Kellogg St *TF:* 800-245-3001 ■ *Web:* www.cadwell.com	Kennewick	WA	99336	509-735-6481	783-6503	476
CAE (Center of the American Experiment) 8441 Wayzata Blvd Ste 350 *Web:* www.americanexperiment.org	Golden Valley	MN	55426	612-338-3605		634
CAE Inc 8585 Cote de Liesse *NYSE: CAE* ■ *TF:* 866-999-6223 ■ *Web:* www.cae.com	Saint Laurent	QC	H4T1G6	514-341-6780	341-7699	703
Caelum Research Corp 1700 Research Blvd Ste 250 *Web:* www.caelum.com	Rockville	MD	20850	301-424-8205	424-8183	668
Caen Engineering Inc 675 N Eckhoff St Ste G *Web:* www.caeneng.com	Orange	CA	92868	714-456-0800		256
CAEP (Canadian Assn of Emergency Physicians) 1785 Alta Vista Dr Ste 104 *TF:* 800-463-1158 ■ *Web:* www.caep.ca	Ottawa	ON	K1G3Y6	613-523-3343	523-0190	49-8
Caesar Creek State Park 8570 E State Rt 73 *Web:* www.caesarcreekstatepark.com	Waynesville	OH	45068	513-897-1092		565
Caesar's Entertainment Operating Company Inc 1 Caesars Palace Dr *Web:* www.caesars.com	Las Vegas	NV	89109	702-407-6000		378
Caesar's Palace 3570 Las Vegas Blvd S Caesar's Palace *TF:* 800-634-6001 ■ *Web:* www.caesars.com	Las Vegas	NV	89109	702-731-7110		671
Caesar's Steak House 512 Fourth Ave SW *TF:* 800-268-1133 ■ *Web:* caesarssteakhouse.com	Calgary	AB	T2P0J6	403-264-1222		671
Caesar, Rivise, Bernstein, Cohen & Pokotilow Ltd 12th Fl 1635 Market St *Web:* www.caesar.law	Philadelphia	PA	19103	215-567-2010		428
Caesars Atlantic City Hotel Casino 2100 Pacific Ave *TF:* 800-522-4700 ■ *Web:* www.totalrewards.com	Atlantic City	NJ	08401	609-348-4411		669
Caesars Head State Park 8155 Geer Hwy *TF:* 866-345-7275 ■ *Web:* www.southcarolinaparks.com	Cleveland	SC	29635	864-836-6115		565
Caesars License Company LLC 3655 Las Vegas Blvd S *TF:* 877-796-2096 ■ *Web:* www.caesars.com/paris-las-vegas	Las Vegas	NV	89109	702-946-7000		379
Caesars License Company LLC 377 Riverside Dr E *TF:* 800-991-7777 ■ *Web:* www.caesars.com/caesars-windsor	Windsor	ON	N9A7H7	519-258-7878		133
Cafa Corporate Finance 4269 Sainte-Catherine W Office 200 *Web:* www.cafa.ca	Westmount	QC	H3Z1P7	514-989-5508		401
Cafaro Co 2445 Belmont Ave *TF:* 800-747-5599 ■ *Web:* www.cafarocompany.com	Youngstown	OH	44504	330-747-2661	743-2902	653
Cafe 1217 1217 Malvern Ave *Web:* cafe1217.net	Hot Springs	AR	71901	501-318-1094		671
Cafe 1912 243 S Cooper at Peabody *Web:* cafe1912.com	Memphis	TN	38104	901-722-2700		671
Cafe 302 2700 Winchester Rd NE	Huntsville	AL	35811	256-852-3442		671
Cafe 615 615 Dauphin St *Web:* cafe615mobile.com	Mobile	AL	36602	251-432-8434		671
Cafe 668 885 Dundas St W *Web:* www.cafe668.com	Toronto	ON	M6J1V9	416-703-0668		671
Cafe Absinthe 1954 W N Ave *Web:* cafe-absinthe.com	Chicago	IL	60622	773-278-4488		671
Cafe Al Dente 412D Delaware *Web:* cafealdentekc.com	Kansas City	MO	64105	816-472-9444		671
Cafe Aladdin 530 Sixth Ave N *Web:* cafealaddinfargo.com	Fargo	ND	58102	701-298-0880		671
Cafe Amici 2301 Airport Thwy	Columbus	GA	31904	706-653-6361		671
Cafe Amici 1371 Main St *Web:* www.cafeamicisrq.com	Sarasota	FL	34236	941-951-6896		671
Cafe Asia 1550 Wilson Blvd *Web:* www.cafeasia.com	Arlington	VA	22209	703-741-0870		671
Cafe at Adele's 1112 N Carson St *Web:* www.adelesrestaurantandlounge.com	Carson City	NV	89701	775-882-3353		671
Cafe Atlantico 405 Figth St NW *Web:* www.cafeatlantico.com	Washington	DC	20004	202-393-0812	393-0555	671
Cafe Bacchus 76 High St *Web:* cafebacchus.net	Morgantown	WV	26505	304-296-9234		671
Cafe Baci 4001 S Tamiami Trl *Web:* www.cafebacisarasota.com	Sarasota	FL	34231	941-921-4848	923-8643	671
Cafe Bel Ami 229 E William St Ste 101 *Web:* www.cafebelami.biz	Wichita	KS	67202	316-267-3433		671
Cafe Boulud 20 E 76th St *Web:* www.danielnyc.com	New York	NY	10021	212-772-2600		671
Cafe Boulud 301 Australian Ave *Web:* www.danielnyc.com	Palm Beach	FL	33480	561-655-6060		671
Cafe Brazil 4408 Lowell Blvd *Web:* www.cafebrazildenver.com	Denver	CO	80211	303-480-1877		671
Cafe Capriccio 49 Grand St *Web:* www.cafecapriccio.com	Albany	NY	12207	518-465-0439	465-6822	671
Cafe Carlo 243 Lilac St *TF:* 800-723-3929 ■ *Web:* www.cafecarlo.com	Winnipeg	MB	R3M2S2	204-477-5544	477-1652	671
Cafe Castagna 1752 SE Hawthorne Blvd *Web:* www.castagnarestaurant.com	Portland	OR	97214	503-231-9959		671
Cafe Central 109 N Oregon St *Web:* www.cafecentral.com	El Paso	TX	79901	915-545-2233		671
Cafe Centro 200 Pk Ave *Web:* patinagroup.com	New York	NY	10166	212-818-1222		671
Cafe Chardonnay 4533 PGA Blvd *TF:* 800-524-7601 ■ *Web:* www.cafechardonnay.com	Palm Beach Gardens	FL	33418	561-627-2662		671

	City	State	ZIP	Phone	Fax	Class
Cafe de Thai 7499 Longly Ln *Web:* cafedethaireno.net	Reno	NV	89511	775-829-8424		671
Cafe Degas 3127 Esplanade Ave *Web:* www.cafedegas.com	New Orleans	LA	70119	504-945-5635	943-5255	671
Cafe du Berry 6439 SW MacAdam Ave *Web:* cafeduberry.ypguides.net	Portland	OR	97239	503-244-5551		671
Cafe du Jour 1107 E Carson St	Pittsburgh	PA	15203	412-488-9695		671
Cafe Express LLC 19443 Gulf Fwy *TF:* 800-550-1922 ■ *Web:* www.cafe-express.com	Webster	TX	77598	281-554-6999	554-5501	670
Cafe Fina 47 Fisherman's Wharf Ste 1 *TF:* 800-843-3462 ■ *Web:* www.cafefina.com	Monterey	CA	93940	831-372-5200	372-5209	671
Cafe Flora 2901 E Madison St *Web:* www.cafeflora.com	Seattle	WA	98112	206-325-9100		671
Cafe Giovanni 117 Rue Decatur St *Web:* www.cafegiovanni.com	New Orleans	LA	70118	504-529-2154		671
Cafe Istanbul 3983 Worth Ave *Web:* www.cafeistanbul.com	Columbus	OH	43219	614-473-9144		671
Cafe Istanbul 5450 W Lovers Ln *Web:* www.cafe-istanbul.net	Dallas	TX	75209	214-902-0919		671
Cafe Izmir 3711 Greenville Ave *Web:* www.cafeizmir.com	Dallas	TX	75206	214-826-7788		671
Cafe Japengo 8960 University Ctr Ln *Web:* www.cafejapengo.com	San Diego	CA	92122	858-450-3355		671
Cafe L'Europe 331 S County Rd *Web:* www.cafeleurope.com	Palm Beach	FL	33480	561-655-4020		671
Cafe Lago 2305 24th Ave E *Web:* www.cafelago.com	Seattle	WA	98112	206-329-8005		671
Cafe Lebanon 1390 Main St *Web:* www.cafelebanon.com	Springfield	MA	01103	413-737-7373		671
Cafe Lurcat 1624 Harmon Pl *Web:* www.cafelurcat.com	Minneapolis	MN	55403	612-486-5500		671
Cafe Madrid 5244 S Highland Dr *Web:* www.cafemadrid.net	Salt Lake City	UT	84117	801-273-0837		671
Cafe Madrid 4501 Travis St *Web:* www.cafemadrid-dallas.com	Dallas	TX	75205	214-528-1731		671
Cafe Marquesa 600 Fleming St *TF:* 800-869-4631 ■ *Web:* www.marquesa.com	Key West	FL	33040	305-292-1244		671
Cafe Martorano 3343 E Oakland Pk Blvd *Web:* www.cafemartorano.com	Fort Lauderdale	FL	33308	954-561-2554		671
Cafe Maxx 2601 E Atlantic Blvd *Web:* www.cafemaxx.com	Pompano Beach	FL	33062	954-782-0606	782-0648	671
Cafe Med Restaurant 4809 Scottdale Hwy *Web:* www.cafemedrestaurant.com	Bakersfield	CA	93309	661-834-4433		671
Cafe Modern 3200 Darnell St *TF:* 866-824-5566 ■ *Web:* www.themodern.org	Fort Worth	TX	76107	817-738-9215	735-1161	671
Cafe Mosaics 10844 82nd Ave *Web:* cafemosaics.com	Edmonton	AB	T6E2B3	780-433-9702		671
Cafe Normandie 185 Main St *TF:* 800-638-9192 ■ *Web:* www.cafenormandie.com	Annapolis	MD	21401	410-263-3382		671
Cafe on Park 3831 Pk Blvd *Web:* cafeonpark.com	San Diego	CA	92103	619-293-7275		671
Cafe One 11 111 Broyles St Ste 1 *Web:* www.cafeone11jc.com	Johnson City	TN	37601	423-283-4633		671
Cafe Pacific 24 Highland Pk Village *Web:* cafepacificdallas.com	Dallas	TX	75205	214-526-1170		671
Cafe Pacific 1033 W Oakland Ave *Web:* www.cafepacificjtn.com	Johnson City	TN	37604	423-610-0117		671
Cafe Parizade 2200 W Main St *Web:* www.parizadedurham.com	Durham	NC	27705	919-286-9712		671
Cafe Pasta 305 State St *Web:* www.cafepasta.com	Greensboro	NC	27408	336-272-1308		671
Cafe Piccolo 3222 E Broadway *Web:* www.cafepiccolo.com	Long Beach	CA	90803	562-438-1316		671
Cafe Pinot 700 W Fifth St *Web:* www.patinagroup.com	Los Angeles	CA	90071	213-239-6500		671
Cafe Poca Cosa 110 E Pennington St *Web:* cafepocacosatucson.com	Tucson	AZ	85701	520-622-6400		671
Cafe Prima Pasta 414 71st St *Web:* cafeprimapasta.com	Miami Beach	FL	33141	305-867-0106		671
Cafe Rabelais 2442 Times Blvd *Web:* www.caferabelais.com	Houston	TX	77005	713-520-8841		671
Cafe Rio 3025 East 3300 South *Web:* www.caferio.com	Salt Lake City	UT	84109	801-463-7250		671
Cafe Seville 2768 E Oakland Pk Blvd *TF:* 800-227-0560 ■ *Web:* www.cafeseville.com	Fort Lauderdale	FL	33306	954-565-1148		671
Cafe Society 212 N Evergreen St *Web:* cafesocietymemphis.com	Memphis	TN	38112	901-722-2177		671
Cafe Sole 1029 Southard St *Web:* cafesole.com	Key West	FL	33040	305-294-0230		671
Cafe Soriah 384 W 13th Ave *Web:* www.soriah.com	Eugene	OR	97401	541-342-4410		671
Cafe Stella 3932 W Sunset Blvd *Web:* www.cafestella.com	Los Angeles	CA	90029	323-666-0265	666-0258	671
Cafe Sunflower 2140 Peachtree Rd *Web:* www.cafesunflower.com	Atlanta	GA	30309	404-352-8859		671
Cafe Tandoor 2096 S Taylor Rd *Web:* cafetandoorcleveland.com	Cleveland Heights	OH	44118	216-371-8500	371-8560	671
Cafe Tu Tu Tango 8625 International Dr *Web:* www.cafetututango.com	Orlando	FL	32819	407-248-2222	352-3696	671
Cafe Twenty-Eight 2724 W 43rd St	Minneapolis	MN	55410	612-926-2800		671
Cafe Vermilionville 1304 W Pinhook Rd *Web:* www.cafev.com	Lafayette	LA	70503	337-237-0100		671
Cafe Vico 1125 N Federal Hwy *Web:* www.cafevicorestaurant.com	Fort Lauderdale	FL	33304	954-565-9681		671
Cafe Zucchero 1731 India St *Web:* www.cafezucchero.com	San Diego	CA	92101	619-531-1731		671
Cafe, The 3434 Peachtree Rd NE Ritz-Carlton Buckhead *TF:* 800-241-3333 ■ *Web:* www.ritzcarlton.com	Atlanta	GA	30326	404-237-2700		671
Cafefx 1130 E Clark Ave	Santa Maria	CA	93455	805-922-9479		512
Cafepress.com Inc 1850 Gateway Dr Ste 300 **Fax Area Code:* 650 ■ *TF:* 877-809-1659 ■ *Web:* www.cafepress.com	Foster City	CA	94404	877-809-1659	240-0260*	204
Caffe Boa 398 S Mill Ave *Web:* www.cafeboa.com	Tempe	AZ	85281	480-968-9112		671
Caffe Italia Ristorante 662 Central Ave	Albany	NY	12206	518-459-8029		671
Caffe La Strada 4716 E Second St *Web:* www.lastradalongbeach.com	Long Beach	CA	90803	562-433-8100		671
Caffe Luna 136 E Hargett St *Web:* www.cafeluna.com	Raleigh	NC	27601	919-832-6090		671
Caffe Mingo 807 NW 21st Ave *Web:* caffemingonw.com	Portland	OR	97209	503-226-4646		671
Caffe Molise 55 West 100 South *Web:* www.caffemolise.com	Salt Lake City	UT	84101	801-364-8833		671
Caffe Paridiso 4205 S MacDill Ave	Tampa	FL	33611	813-835-6622		671
Caffe Vialetto 4019 Le Jeune Rd *Web:* www.caffevialetto.com	Coral Gables	FL	33134	305-446-5659	446-3532	671
Cagan Management Group Inc 16554 Cagan Crossings Blvd Ste 4 *Web:* www.cagan.com	Clermont	FL	34714	352-242-2444		652
Cage Inc 6440 N Beltline Rd Ste 125 *Web:* www.cage-inc.com	Irving	TX	75063	972-550-1001		196
Cagle Steaks&BBQ 8732 Fourth St *Web:* www.caglesteaks.com	Lubbock	TX	79416	806-795-3879		671
Cagle's Farms Inc 1385 Collier Rd NW	Atlanta	GA	30318	404-355-2820		10-8
Cagles Mill Lake 1317 W Lieber Rd Ste 1 *Web:* www.in.gov	Cloverdale	IN	46120	765-795-4576		565
CAGW (Citizens Against Government Waste) 1301 Pennsylvania Ave NW Ste 1075 *TF:* 800-435-7352 ■ *Web:* www.cagw.org	Washington	DC	20004	202-467-5300	467-4253	48-7
Cagwin & Dorward Inc 1565 S Novato Blvd Ste B *TF:* 800-891-7710 ■ *Web:* www.cagwin.com	Novato	CA	94947	415-892-7710	897-7864	422
Cahaba Pressure Treated Forest Products Inc 12755 Montevallo Rd	Brierfield	AL	35035	205-926-9888		683
CAHI (Council for Affordable Health Insurance) 127 S Peyton St Ste 210	Alexandria	VA	22314	703-836-6200	836-6550	49-9
Cahill Contractors Inc 425 California St Ste 2200 *Web:* www.cahill-sf.com	San Francisco	CA	94104	415-986-0600		186
Cahokia Mounds State Historic Site 30 Ramey St *Web:* cahokiamounds.org	Collinsville	IL	62234	618-346-5160		565
CAI (Community Assns Institute) 6402 Arlington Blvd Ste 500 *TF:* 888-224-4321 ■ *Web:* www.caionline.org	Falls Church	VA	22042	703-970-9220	970-9558	48-7
CAI (Chrysler Aviation Inc) 7120 Hayvenhurst Ave Ste 309 *TF:* 800-995-0825 ■ *Web:* www.chrysleraviation.com	Van Nuys	CA	91406	818-989-7900		13
CAI (Computer Aid Inc) 1390 Ridgeview Dr *Web:* www.compaid.com	Allentown	PA	18104	610-530-5000	530-5298	177
CAI-CLAC 1809 S St Ste 101-245 *TF:* 888-909-7403 ■ *Web:* www.caiclac.com	Sacramento	CA	95811	916-791-4750		533
Cailor Fleming & Associates Inc 4610 Market St *TF:* 800-796-8495 ■ *Web:* cailorfleming.com	Youngstown	OH	44512	330-782-8068		390
Caiman Consulting Corp 15127 NE 24th St Ste 547 *Web:* www.caimanconsulting.com	Redmond	WA	98052	425-214-4598		196
Cain & Bultman Inc 2145 Dennis St *Web:* www.cainbultman.com	Jacksonville	FL	32204	904-356-4812		361
Cain Food Industries Inc 8401 Sovereign Row *Web:* www.cainfood.com	Dallas	TX	75247	214-630-4511		123
cain lamarre sengrl 630 boul Rene-Levesque Ouest Ste 2780 *Web:* www.clcw.ca	Montreal	QC	H3B1S6	514-393-4580		428
Cain Millwork Inc 1 Cain Pkwy *TF:* 800-417-3511 ■ *Web:* www.cainmillwork.com	Rochelle	IL	61068	815-561-9700		499
Cain Park Theatre 40 Severance Cir *TF:* 800-745-3000 ■ *Web:* cainpark.com	Cleveland Heights	OH	44118	216-371-3000	371-6995	572
Cain's Barber College Inc 365 E 51st St *Web:* www.cbcon51st.org	Chicago	IL	60615	773-536-4441		77
Cain's Foods Inc 114 E Main St *TF:* 800-225-0601 ■ *Web:* www.cainsfoods.com	Ayer	MA	01432	978-772-0300	772-0200	296-19
Caine Real Estate Group 111 Williams St *Web:* www.cbcaine.com	Greenville	SC	29601	864-250-2850		196
CAIR (Cair National) 453 New Jersey Ave SE *Web:* www.cair.com	Washington	DC	20003	202-488-8787	488-0833	48-7
Cair National (CAIR) 453 New Jersey Ave SE *Web:* www.cair.com	Washington	DC	20003	202-488-8787	488-0833	48-7
Cairncross & Hempelmann PS 524 Second Ave Ste 500 *Web:* www.cairncross.com	Seattle	WA	98104	206-587-0700		428
Cait Llc 799 Cromwell Park Dr Ste F *Web:* caitllc.net	Glen Burnie	MD	21061	410-863-4601		196
Caiterra International Energy Corp 900 Hastings St W Ste 500	Vancouver	BC	V6C1B5	778-839-7963		536
Caithness Corp 565 Fifth Ave 29Fl *Web:* www.caithnessenergy.com	New York	NY	10017	212-921-9099	921-9239	787
Cajahs Mountain Discount Drug Inc 2006 Connelly Springs Rd	Lenoir	NC	28645	828-726-8632		237
Cajun Boilers 2806 Albert Pike Rd *Web:* cajunboilers.com	Hot Springs	AR	71913	501-767-5695		671
Cajun Catfish House 6819 US Business 50 *TF:* 800-635-8210 ■ *Web:* www.cajuncatfishhouse.net	Jefferson City	MO	65109	573-893-4665		671

Company	Address	City	State	ZIP	Phone	Fax	Class	Notes
Cajun Chef Products Inc	519 Joseph Rd	Saint Martinville	LA	70582	337-394-7112		296-19	
Cajun Constructors Inc	15635 Airline Hwy	Baton Rouge	LA	70817	225-753-5857	751-9777	188-7	*TF:* 800-944-5857 ■ *Web:* cajunusa.com
Cajun Kettle Foods	698 Saint George Ave	New Orleans	LA	70121	504-733-8800		345	*Web:* www.kajunkettle.com
Cajun Queen	1800 E Seventh St	Charlotte	NC	28204	704-377-9017		671	*Web:* www.cajunqueen.net
Cajun Sugar Co-op Inc	2711 Northside Rd	New Iberia	LA	70563	337-365-3401	365-7820	296-38	*Web:* amscl.org
Cajun's Wharf	2400 Cantrell Rd	Little Rock	AR	72202	501-375-5351		671	*Web:* www.cajunswharf.com
Cajundome & Convention Ctr	444 Cajundome Blvd	Lafayette	LA	70506	337-265-2100	265-2311	205	*TF:* 800-745-3000 ■ *Web:* www.cajundome.com
Cake Development Corp	1785 E Sahara Ave Ste 490-423	Las Vegas	NV	89104	702-425-5085		177	*Web:* www.cakedc.com
Cakewalk Inc	268 Summer St 8th Fl	Boston	MA	02210	617-423-9004		174	*Web:* www.cakewalk.com
Cal Coast Telecom	886 Faulstich Ct	San Jose	CA	95112	408-275-8888		525	*TF:* 800-334-7663 ■ *Web:* www.cctcom.net
Cal Dive International Inc	Ste 2200 2500 City West Blvd	Houston	TX	77042	713-361-2600		539	
Cal Farley's Boys Ranch	600 W 11th St PO Box 1890	Amarillo	TX	79174	806-372-2341	372-6638	48-6	*TF:* 800-687-3722 ■ *Web:* www.calfarley.org
Cal Fasteners Inc	4300 E Miraloma Ave	Anaheim	CA	92807	714-854-1715		350	*Web:* www.cfi1.com
Cal Herbold Nursery	9403 E Ave	Hesperia	CA	92345	760-244-6125		323	
Cal Info	316 W Second St Ste 1102	Los Angeles	CA	90012	213-687-8710	687-8778	387	*TF:* 800-934-4448 ■ *Web:* www.calinfo.net
Cal Net Technology Group	9420 Topanga Canyon Blvd Ste 100	Chatsworth	CA	91311	818-701-5753		180	*TF:* 800-700-1000 ■ *Web:* www.calnettech.com
Cal Poly Pomona Foundation Inc	3801 W Temple Ave Bldg 55	Pomona	CA	91768	909-869-2950	869-3716	49-11	*Web:* foundation.cpp.edu
Cal Quality Electronics	2700 S Fairview St	Santa Ana	CA	92704	714-545-8886	545-4975	625	*Web:* www.calquality.com
Cal Spas Inc	1462 E Ninth St	Pomona	CA	91766	909-623-8781	629-0751	375	*TF:* 800-225-7727 ■ *Web:* www.calspas.com
Cal Tech Precision Inc	1830 N Lemon St	Anaheim	CA	92801	714-992-4130		57	*Web:* www.caltechprecision.com
Calabrese Management	2207 Forest Hills Dr	Harrisburg	PA	17112	717-238-9989	238-9985	47	*Web:* www.calabresemgt.com
Calabro Cheese Corp	580 Coe Ave	East Haven	CT	06512	203-469-1311	469-6929	296-5	*Web:* www.calabrocheese.com
Caladesi Island State Park	1 Cswy Blvd	Dunedin	FL	34698	727-469-5918		565	*Web:* www.floridastateparks.org/caladesiisland
Calamari's Squid Row	1317 State St	Erie	PA	16501	814-459-4276		671	*Web:* www.calamaris-squidrow.com
CALAMCO (California Ammonia Co)	1776 W March Ln Ste 420	Stockton	CA	95207	209-982-1000	983-0822	280	*TF:* 800-624-4200 ■ *Web:* www.calamco.com
Calamos Asset Management Inc	2020 Calamos Ct	Naperville	IL	60563	630-245-7200		401	*NASDAQ: CLMS* ■ *TF:* 800-582-6959 ■ *Web:* www.calamos.com
CalAmp Corp	1401 N Rice Ave	Oxnard	CA	93030	805-987-9000	419-8498	647	*NASDAQ: CAMP* ■ *Web:* www.calamp.com
Cal-ark Inc	PO Box 990	Mabelvale	AR	72103	501-455-3399		780	*TF:* 888-422-5275 ■ *Web:* www.calark.com
Calaveras Big Trees State Park	1170 State Hwy 4	Arnold	CA	95223	209-795-2334		565	*Web:* www.parks.ca.gov/default.asp?page_id=551
Calaveras County	891 Mountain Ranch Rd	San Andreas	CA	95249	209-754-6370	754-6733	338	*Web:* calaverasgov.us
Calaveras County Library	891 Mountain Ranch Rd	San Andreas	CA	95249	209-754-6510		434-3	*Web:* calaverasgov.us
Cal-a-Vie Spa	29402 Spa Havens Way	Vista	CA	92084	760-945-2055	630-0074	706	*TF:* 866-772-4283 ■ *Web:* www.cal-a-vie.com
Calavo Growers Inc	1141-A Cummings Rd	Santa Paula	CA	93060	805-525-1245	921-3287	315-4	*NASDAQ: CVGW* ■ *TF:* 800-654-8758 ■ *Web:* www.calavo.com
Calaway Systems Inc	32 Lindburgh St	Courtland	AL	35618	256-637-2736		687	*TF:* 800-552-8525 ■ *Web:* www.calawaysystems.com
Calbag Metals Co	2495 NW Nicolai St	Portland	OR	97210	503-226-3441		686	*TF:* 800-398-3441 ■ *Web:* www.calbag.com
Cal-Bay Systems Inc	3070 Kerner Blvd Ste B	San Rafael	CA	94901	415-258-9400		201	
CALC	235A E Ctr Dr	Alton	IL	62002	618-474-0616		463	*Web:* calc.edu
Calcasieu Parish	1000 Ryan St	Lake Charles	LA	70601	337-437-3550		338	*TF:* 800-542-7074 ■ *Web:* www.cppj.net
Calcasieu Parish Public Library System	301 W Claude St	Lake Charles	LA	70605	337-721-7116		434-3	*Web:* www.calcasieulibrary.org
Calcasieu Refining Co	4359 W Tank Farm Rd	Lake Charles	LA	70605	337-478-2130		580	*TF:* 800-272-3020 ■ *Web:* www.calcasieurefining.com
Cal-Chlor Corp	627 Jefferson St	Lafayette	LA	70501	337-264-1449	264-9359	146	*Web:* www.cal-chlor.com
Cal-Coast Dairy Systems Inc	424 S Tegner Rd	Turlock	CA	95380	209-634-9026	634-3458	273	*TF Cust Svc:* 800-732-6826 ■ *Web:* www.calcoastinc.com
Calcon Constructors Inc	2270 W Bates Ave	Englewood	CO	80110	303-762-1554		187	*Web:* www.calconci.com
Calcot Ltd	1900 E Brundage Ln	Bakersfield	CA	93307	661-327-5961		275	*Web:* www.calcot.net
Calculated Industries Inc	4840 Hytech Dr	Carson City	NV	89706	775-885-4900	885-4949	118	*TF:* 800-854-8075 ■ *Web:* www.calculated.com
Calder Bateman	10241 109 St NW	Edmonton	AB	T5J1N2	780-426-3610		196	*Web:* www.calderbateman.com
Calder Casino & Race Course	21001 NW 27th Ave	Miami	FL	33056	305-625-1311		642	*TF:* 800-522-4700 ■ *Web:* www.caldercasino.com
Calder Richards Consulting Engineers	634 South 400 West Ste 100	Salt Lake City	UT	84101	801-466-1699		261	*Web:* crceng.com
Caldera Corp	8290 W Sahara Ave Ste 186	Las Vegas	NV	89117	702-838-0716		536	
Caldera Engineering	695 S 320 W	Provo	UT	84601	801-356-2862		256	*Web:* www.calderaengineering.com
Caldwell Associates Architects Inc	116 N Tarragona St	Pensacola	FL	32502	850-432-9500		261	*Web:* www.caldwell-assoc.com
Caldwell Chamber of Commerce	704 Blaine St	Caldwell	ID	83605	208-459-7493	454-1284	139	*TF:* 866-206-6944 ■ *Web:* www.cityofcaldwell.com
Caldwell Community College & Technical Institute	2855 Hickory Blvd	Hudson	NC	28638	828-726-2200	726-2216*	162	**Fax:* Admissions ■ *Web:* www.cccti.edu/default.asp
Caldwell Consumer Health LLC	8 Elmer St	Madison	NJ	07940	973-360-1090		231	*Web:* bleedinggums.com
Caldwell County	49 E Main St PO Box 67	Kingston	MO	64650	816-586-2571	586-3001	338	*Web:* www.courts.mo.gov/page.jsp?id=1673
Caldwell County	905 W Ave NW	Lenoir	NC	28645	828-757-1300	757-1295	338	*Web:* www.caldwellcountync.org
Caldwell County	110 S Main St	Lockhart	TX	78644	512-398-1824		338	*Web:* www.co.caldwell.tx.us
Caldwell County Chamber of Commerce	1909 Hickory Blvd SE	Lenoir	NC	28645	828-726-0616	726-0385	139	*Web:* caldwellchambernc.com
Caldwell County Public Library	120 Hospital Ave	Lenoir	NC	28645	828-757-1270		434-3	*Web:* ccpl.libguides.com/main
Caldwell Hospice & Palliative Care	902 Kirkwood St NW	Lenoir	NC	28645	828-754-0101		371	*Web:* www.caldwellhospice.org
Caldwell Industries Inc	2351 New Millennium Dr	Louisville	KY	40216	502-778-6989		596	
Caldwell Manufacturing Inc	2605 Manitou Rd	Rochester	NY	14624	585-352-3790		743	*Web:* www.caldwellmfgco.com
Caldwell Memorial Hospital	321 Mulberry St SW	Lenoir	NC	28645	828-757-5100	757-5247	374-3	*TF:* 800-776-8383 ■ *Web:* www.caldwellmemorial.org
Caldwell Parish	PO Box 1737	Columbia	LA	71418	318-649-2681	649-5930	338	*TF:* 000 467 4357 ■ *Web:* lpgov.org
Caldwell Partners International Inc, The	165 Ave Rd	Toronto	ON	M5R3S4	416-920-7702		193	*Web:* www.caldwellpartners.com
Caldwell Richards Sorensen Inc	2060 East 2100 South	Salt Lake City	UT	84109	801-359-5565	359-4272	261	
Caldwell Securities Ltd	150 King St W Ste 1710	Toronto	ON	M5H1J9	416-862-7755		690	*TF:* 800-387-0859 ■ *Web:* www.caldwellsecurities.com
Caldwell Tanks Inc	4000 Tower Rd	Louisville	KY	40219	502-964-3361	966-8732	91	*Web:* www.caldwelltanks.com
Caldwell Travel Inc	5341 Virginia Way	Brentwood	TN	37027	615-327-2720		772	*Web:* www.travelcaldwell.com
Caldwell Trust Co	1400 Ctr Rd Ste Two	Venice	FL	34292	941-493-3600		401	*TF:* 800-338-9476 ■ *Web:* www.ctrust.com
Caldwell University	120 Bloomfield Ave	Caldwell	NJ	07006	973-618-3500	618-3600*	166	**Fax:* Admissions ■ *TF Admissions:* 888-864-9516 ■ *Web:* www.caldwell.edu
Caldwell Wholesale Company Inc	9630 Saint Vincent Ave	Shreveport	LA	71106	318-869-3101		756	
Caldwell Zoo	2203 ML King Blvd	Tyler	TX	75702	903-593-0121		823	*TF:* 800-235-5712 ■ *Web:* www.caldwellzoo.org
Cale Parking Systems USA Inc	13808 Monroes Business Pk	Tampa	FL	33635	813-405-3900		196	*Web:* www.caleparkingusa.com
CALEA (Commission on Accreditation for Law Enforcement Agencies)	13575 Heathcote Blvd Ste 320	Gainesville	VA	20155	703-352-4225	890-3126	49-7	*TF:* 877-789-6904 ■ *Web:* www.calea.org
Calea Ltd	2785 Skymark Ave Unit 2	Mississauga	ON	L4W4Y3	905-238-1234		363	*TF:* 888-909-3299 ■ *Web:* www.calea.ca
Caleb Smith State Park Preserve	581 W Jericho Tpke PO Box 963	Smithtown	NY	11787	631-265-1054		565	*Web:* parks.ny.gov/parks/124/details.aspx
Caled	550 Bercut Dr Ste G	Sacramento	CA	95811	916-448-8252		463	*Web:* www.caled.org
Caledon Chamber of Commerce	12598 Hwy S Ste 50	Bolton	ON	L7E1T6	905-857-7393	857-7405	137	*Web:* www.caledonchamber.com
Caledon Laboratories Ltd	40 Armstrong Ave	Georgetown	ON	L7G4R9	905-877-0101		226	*TF:* 877-225-3366 ■ *Web:* www.caledonlabs.com
Caledon State Park	11617 Caledon Rd	King George	VA	22485	540-663-3861		565	*TF:* 800-933-7275 ■ *Web:* www.dcr.virginia.gov
Caledonia County	1153 Main St Ste 4	Saint Johnsbury	VT	05819	802-748-6657	748-6659	338	*Web:* prosecutors.vermont.gov
Caledonia Haulers LLC	420 W Lincoln St PO Box 31	Caledonia	MN	55921	507-725-9000	725-9015	468	*TF:* 800-325-4728 ■ *Web:* www.caledoniahaulers.com
Caledonia State Park	101 Pine Grove Rd	Fayetteville	PA	17222	717-352-2161		565	*Web:* www.dcnr.state.pa.us

Name / Address	City	State	ZIP	Phone	Fax	Class
Calegari & Morris 123 Mission St 18th Fl *Web:* www.calegariandmorris.com	San Francisco	CA	94105	415-981-8766		2
Calendarscom LLC 6411 Burleson Rd *Web:* www.calendars.com	Austin	TX	78744	512-386-7220		292
Caler Group Inc, The 23337 Lago Mar Cir *Web:* www.calergroup.com	Boca Raton	FL	33433	561-394-8045		260
Calera Capital 580 California St Ste 2200 *Web:* www.caleracapital.com	San Francisco	CA	94104	415-632-5200		401
Calev Systems 333 S Miami Ave *Web:* www.cpmprint.com	Miami	FL	33130	305-672-2900	672-4044	627
Calex Express Inc 58 Pittston Ave *TF:* 800-292-2539 ■ *Web:* www.calexlogistics.com	Pittston	PA	18640	570-603-0180	603-0940	780
CALEX Manufacturing Co 2401 Stanwell Dr *TF:* 800-542-3355 ■ *Web:* www.calex.com	Concord	CA	94520	925-687-4411	687-3333	518
Calfrac Well Services Ltd 411 8 Ave SW *TF:* 866-770-3722 ■ *Web:* www.calfrac.com	Calgary	AB	T2P1E3	403-266-6000		539
Calgary Chamber of Commerce 237 Eighth Ave SE *Web:* www.calgarychamber.com	Calgary	AB	T2G5C3	403-750-0400	266-3413	137
Calgary City Hall 800 Macleod Trail SE PO Box 2100 *Web:* www.calgary.ca	Calgary	AB	T2P2M5	403-268-2489	538-6111	337
Calgary Co-Operative Association Ltd 110151 86th Ave SE Ste 110 *Web:* www.calgarycoop.com	Calgary	AB	T2H3A5	403-219-6025		237
Calgary Economic Development 731 First St SE *TF:* 888-222-5855 ■ *Web:* www.calgaryeconomicdevelopment.com	Calgary	AB	T2G2G9	403-221-7831		342
Calgary Exhibition & Stampede Ltd 1410 Olympic Way S E *TF:* 888-883-3828 ■ *Web:* www.calgarystampede.com	Calgary	AB	T2G2W1	403-261-0101		642
Calgary Handi-bus Assn 231 37 Ave NE *Web:* www.calgaryhandibus.com	Calgary	AB	T2E8J2	403-276-8028		108
Calgary Herald 215-16th St SE PO Box 2400 Stn M *TF:* 800-372-9219 ■ *Web:* www.calgaryherald.com	Calgary	AB	T2E7P5	403-235-7100	235-7379	532-1
Calgary International Airport 2000 Airport Rd NE *TF:* 877-254-7427 ■ *Web:* www.yyc.com	Calgary	AB	T2E6W5	403-735-1200	735-1281	27
Calgary Laboratory Services 3535 Research Rd NW *TF:* 800-661-3450 ■ *Web:* www.calgarylabservices.com	Calgary	AB	T2L2K8	403-770-3500		415
Calgary Philharmonic Orchestra 205 Eigth Ave SE *Web:* calgaryphil.com	Calgary	AB	T2G0K9	403-571-0270	294-7424	573-3
Calgary Stampeders 1817 Crowchild Trail NW McMahon Stadium *Web:* www.stampeders.com	Calgary	AB	T2M4R6	403-289-0205		715-2
Calgary Sun 2615 12th St NE *TF:* 877-624-1463 ■ *Web:* www.calgarysun.com	Calgary	AB	T2E7W9	403-410-1010		532-1
Calgary Winter Club 4611 14 St NW *Web:* www.calgarywinterclub.com	Calgary	AB	T2K1J7	403-289-5511		354
Calgary Zoo Botanical Garden & Prehistoric Park 1300 Zoo Rd NE *TF:* 800-588-9993 ■ *Web:* www.calgaryzoo.com	Calgary	AB	T2E7V6	403-232-9300	237-7582	823
Calgon Carbon Corp 3000 GSK Dr *NYSE: CCC* ■ *TF Cust Svc:* 800-422-7266 ■ *Web:* www.calgoncarbon.com	Moon Township	PA	15108	412-787-6700	787-6676	143
Calhoun & Company Communications LLC 3275 Sacramento St *Web:* calhounwine.com	San Francisco	CA	94115	415-346-2929		636
Calhoun City of Schools Superintendents Office 380 Barrett Rd *Web:* www.calhounschools.org	Calhoun	GA	30701	706-629-2900		685
Calhoun Community College PO Box 2216 *TF:* 800-626-3628 ■ *Web:* www.calhoun.edu	Decatur	AL	35609	256-306-2500	306-2941	162
Huntsville 102B Wynn Dr **Fax:* Admissions ■ *TF:* 800-626-3628 ■ *Web:* www.calhoun.edu	Huntsville	AL	35805	256-890-4701	890-4775*	162
Redstone Arsenal 6250 Hwy 31 N *TF:* 800-626-3628 ■ *Web:* www.calhoun.edu	Tanner	AL	35671	256-306-2500	306-2941	162
Calhoun Correctional Institution 19562 SE Institutional Dr Unit 1 *Web:* dc.state.fl.us	Blountstown	FL	32424	850-237-6500	237-6508	213
Calhoun County PO Box 230 *Web:* calhouncounty.wv.gov	Grantsville	WV	26147	304-354-6725	354-6725	338
Sheriff's Office 178 S Murphree St *Web:* www.calhounso.org	Pittsboro	MS	38951	662-412-3149	412-3199	338
Calhoun County Board of Education PO Box 2084 *Web:* www.calhoun.k12.al.us	Anniston	AL	36202	256-741-7400	237-5332	685
Calhoun County Chamber of Commerce 1330 Quintard Ave *Web:* www.calhounchamber.com	Anniston	AL	36201	256-237-3536	237-0126	139
Calhoun County Electric Co-op Assn 1015 Tonawanda St PO Box 312 *TF:* 800-821-4879 ■ *Web:* www.calhounrec.coop	Rockwell City	IA	50579	712-297-7112		245
Calhoun Enterprises 4155 Lomac St Ste G *TF:* 800-232-3179 ■ *Web:* calhounent.com	Montgomery	AL	36106	334-272-4400	272-7799	345
Calhoun Falls State Recreation Area 46 Maintenance Shop Rd *TF:* 866-345-7275 ■ *Web:* www.southcarolinaparks.com	Calhoun Falls	SC	29628	864-447-8267	447-8638	565
Calhoun School Inc, The 160 W 74th St *Web:* www.calhoun.org	New York	NY	10023	212-497-6500		685
Calhoun State Prison 27823 Main St *Web:* www.dcor.state.ga.us	Morgan	GA	39866	229-849-5000	849-5017	213
Calhoun's 10020 Kingston Pk *Web:* calhouns.com	Knoxville	TN	37922	865-673-3444		671
Calian Technology Ltd 340 Legget Dr Ste 101 *TSE: CTY* ■ *TF:* 877-225-4264 ■ *Web:* www.calian.com	Ottawa	ON	K2K1Y6	613-599-8600	599-8650	721
Caliber Advisors Inc 514 Via De La Valle Ste 210 *Web:* www.caliberadvisors.com	Solana Beach	CA	92075	858-792-8990		401

Name / Address	City	State	ZIP	Phone	Fax	Class
Caliber Construction Inc 240 N Orange Ave *Web:* www.caliberconstructioninc.com	Brea	CA	92821	714-255-2700		186
Calibre Computer Solutions LLC 405 W State St *Web:* www.calibreforhome.com	Princeton	IN	47670	812-386-8919		196
Calibre International LLC 6250 N Irwindale Ave *Web:* highcaliberline.com	Irwindale	CA	91702	626-969-4660		636
Calibre Systems Inc 6354 Walker Ln Ste 300 *TF:* 888-225-4273 ■ *Web:* www.calibresys.com	Alexandria	VA	22310-3252	703-797-8500	797-8501	180
Caliche Jr Sr. High School 301 Hagen St *Web:* www.re1valleyschools.org	Sterling	CO	80751	970-522-8200		685
CALICO (Computer Assisted Language Instruction Consortium) 214 Centennial Hall *Web:* www.calico.org	San Marcos	TX	78666	512-245-1417		48-9
Calico Building Services Inc 15550-C Rockfield Blvd *TF:* 800-576-7313 ■ *Web:* www.calicoweb.com	Irvine	CA	92618	800-576-7313		104
Calico Restaurant & Bar Teton Village Rd *Web:* www.calicorestaurant.com	Jackson	WY	83014	307-733-2460		671
Calient Technologies 25 Castilian Dr *Web:* www.calient.net	Goleta	CA	93117	805-562-5500		387
Caliente Resorts LLC 21240 Gran Via Blvd *Web:* www.calienteresorts.com	Land O Lakes	FL	34637	813-996-3700		239
Califone International Inc 9135 Alabama Ave Ste B *TF:* 800-722-0500 ■ *Web:* www.califone.com	Chatsworth	CA	91311	818-407-2400	407-2405	253
California						
Administrative Office of the Cts 455 Golden Gate Ave 3rd Fl *TF:* 800-900-5980 ■ *Web:* www.courtinfo.ca.gov	San Francisco	CA	94102	415-865-7740	865-4205	339-5
Aging Dept 1300 National Dr Ste 200 *Web:* www.aging.ca.gov	Sacramento	CA	95834	916-419-7500	928-2267	339-5
Arts Council 1300 'I' St Ste 930 *TF:* 800-201-6201 ■ *Web:* www.cac.ca.gov	Sacramento	CA	95814	916-322-6555	322-6575	339-5
Athletic Commission 1430 Howe Ave *Web:* www.dca.ca.gov	Sacramento	CA	95825	916-263-2195	263-2197	712
Attorney General 1300 I St *Web:* oag.ca.gov	Sacramento	CA	95814	916-445-9555		339-5
Bureau of Real Estate 1651 Exposition Blvd **Fax Area Code:* 916 ■ *TF:* 877-373-4542 ■ *Web:* www.dre.ca.gov	Sacramento	CA	95815	877-373-4542	263-8943*	339-5
Child Support Services Dept PO Box 419064 *TF:* 866-901-3212 ■ *Web:* www.childsup.ca.gov	Sacramento	CA	95741	916-464-5000		339-5
Conservation Dept 801 K St MS 24-01 *Web:* www.conservation.ca.gov	Sacramento	CA	95814	916-322-1080	445-0732	339-5
Consumer Affairs Dept 1625 N Market Blvd Ste N 112 *TF:* 800-952-5210 ■ *Web:* www.dca.ca.gov	Sacramento	CA	95834	916-445-1254		339-5
Corrections Dept PO Box 942883 *TF:* 877-256-6877 ■ *Web:* www.cdcr.ca.gov	Sacramento	CA	94283	916-324-7308		339-5
Economic Development Dept 915 I St 3rd Fl *Web:* portal.cityofsacramento.org	Sacramento	CA	95814	916-808-7223		339-5
Education Dept 1430 N St Ste 5602 *Web:* www.cde.ca.gov	Sacramento	CA	95814	916-319-0800		339-5
Emergency Services Office 3650 Schriever Ave *Web:* www.caloes.ca.gov	Mather	CA	95655	916-845-8510		339-5
Employment Development Dept 800 Capitol Mall MIC 83 *Web:* www.edd.ca.gov	Sacramento	CA	95814	916-654-8210	657-5294	259
Energy Commission 1516 Ninth St *Web:* www.energy.ca.gov	Sacramento	CA	95814	916-654-4287		339-5
Environmental Protection Agency 1001 I St *Web:* www.calepa.ca.gov	Sacramento	CA	95814	916-323-2514		339-5
Fair Political Practices Commission 428 J St Ste 620 *TF:* 866-275-3772 ■ *Web:* www.fppc.ca.gov	Sacramento	CA	95814	916-322-5660	322-0886	265
Finance Dept State Capitol Rm 1145 *Web:* www.dof.ca.gov	Sacramento	CA	95814	916-445-3878		339-5
Fish & Game Dept 1416 Ninth St 12th Fl *TF:* 888-334-2258 ■ *Web:* www.wildlife.ca.gov	Sacramento	CA	95814	916-445-0411	653-7387	339-5
Food & Agriculture Dept 1220 N St *Web:* www.cdfa.ca.gov	Sacramento	CA	95814	916-654-0466	657-4240	339-5
Health Care Services Dept PO Box 997413 MS 8502 *TF:* 800-735-2929 ■ *Web:* www.dhcs.ca.gov	Sacramento	CA	95899	800-735-2929		339-5
Historic Preservation Office PO Box 942896 *Web:* www.ohp.parks.ca.gov	Sacramento	CA	94296	916-445-7000		339-5
Horse Racing Board 1010 Hurley Way Rm 300 *Web:* www.chrb.ca.gov	Sacramento	CA	95825	916-263-6000	263-6042	339-5
Housing Finance Agency 500 Capitol Mall Ste 1400 *TF:* 877-922-5432 ■ *Web:* www.calhfa.ca.gov	Sacramento	CA	95814	877-922-5432		339-5
Industrial Relations Dept 455 Golden Gate Ave FL 2 *TF:* 800-736-7401 ■ *Web:* www.dir.ca.gov	San Francisco	CA	94102	415-703-5050	703-5058	339-5
Insurance Dept 300 Capitol Mall Ste 1700 *Web:* www.insurance.ca.gov	Sacramento	CA	95814	916-492-3500		339-5
Lieutenant Governor State Capitol Ste 1114 *Web:* www.ltg.ca.gov	Sacramento	CA	95814	916-445-8994		339-5
Medical Board 2005 Evergreen St Ste 1200 *TF:* 800-633-2322 ■ *Web:* www.mbc.ca.gov	Sacramento	CA	95815	916-263-2382	263-2944	339-5

Phone | Fax | Class

Mental Health Dept
1600 Ninth St PO Box 944202............Sacramento CA 94244 916-654-1690 339-5
TF: 800-273-8255 ■ *Web:* www.dds.ca.gov
Military Dept 9800 Goethe Rd..............Sacramento CA 95827 916-854-3000 339-5
Web: www.calguard.ca.gov
Motor Vehicles Dept 4700 Broadway.........Sacramento CA 95820 916-657-6437 339-5
TF: 800-777-0133 ■ *Web:* www.dmv.ca.gov
Office of the Governor
State Capitol Ste 1173..................Sacramento CA 95814 916-445-2841 558-3160 339-5
Web: www.gov.ca.gov
Office of Vital Records
PO Box 997410........................Sacramento CA 95899 916-445-2684 339-5
Web: www.cdph.ca.gov
Parks & Recreation Dept
PO Box 942896........................Sacramento CA 94296 916-653-6995 657-3903 339-5
TF: 800-777-0369 ■ *Web:* www.parks.ca.gov
Public Utilities Commission
505 Van Ness Ave ....San Francisco CA 94102 415-703-2782 703-1758 339-5
TF: 800-848-5580 ■ *Web:* www.cpuc.ca.gov
Rehabilitation Dept
721 Capitol Mall ....Sacramento CA 95814 916-324-1313 339-5
TF: 800-952-5544 ■ *Web:* www.rehab.cahwnet.gov
Secretary of State 1500 11th St.............Sacramento CA 95814 916-653-6814 653-4620 339-5
Web: www.sos.ca.gov
State Legislature State Capitol..............Sacramento CA 95814 916-324-4676 339-5
Web: www.leginfo.ca.gov
Supreme Court
333 W Santa Clara St Ste 1060.............San Jose CA 95113 408-277-1004 339-5
Web: www.courts.ca.gov
Teacher Credentialing Commission
1900 Capitol Ave......................Sacramento CA 95814 916-322-4974 339-5
Web: www.ctc.ca.gov
Transportation Dept 1120 N St..............Sacramento CA 95814 916-654-2852 339-5
Web: www.dot.ca.gov
Treasurer 915 Capitol Mall Rm 110 ....Sacramento CA 95814 916-653-2995 653-3125 339-5
Web: www.treasurer.ca.gov
Veterans Affairs Dept 1227 'O' St............Sacramento CA 95814 916-653-2573 339-5
TF: 800-952-5626 ■ *Web:* www.calvet.ca.gov
Victim Compensation Program
PO Box 3036..........................Sacramento CA 95812 800-777-9229 902-8669* 339-5
**Fax Area Code:* 866 ■ *TF:* 800-777-9229 ■ *Web:* www.vcgcb.ca.gov/victims
Workers' Compensation Div
PO Box 420603 ....San Francisco CA 94142 415-703-4600 339-5
Web: www.dir.ca.gov/dwc

California Academy of Sciences
55 Music Concourse Dr Golden Gate Pk ....San Francisco CA 94103 415-379-8000 520
Web: www.calacademy.org

California African American Museum
600 State Dr Exposition Pk..................Los Angeles CA 90037 213-744-7432 744-2050 520
Web: www.caamuseum.org

California Amforge Corp
750 N Vernon Ave.............................Azusa CA 91702 626-334-4931 21
Web: www.cal-amforge.com

California Ammonia Co (CALAMCO)
1776 W March Ln Ste 420 ....Stockton CA 95207 209-982-1000 983-0822 200
TF: 800-624-4200 ■ *Web:* www.calamco.com

California Analytical Instruments Inc
1312 W Grove Ave ....Orange CA 92865 714-974-5560 419
TF: 800-959-0949 ■ *Web:* www.gasanalyzers.com

California Assn of Realtors
525 S Virgil Ave ....Los Angeles CA 90020 213-739-8200 480-7724 656
Web: www.car.org

California Ballet Co (CBC)
4819 Ronson Ct ....San Diego CA 92111 858-560-5676 560-0072 573-1
Web: www.californiaballet.org

California Bank & Trust
11622 El Camino Real Ste 200................San Diego CA 92130 858-793-7400 793-7438 70
TF: 800-400-6080 ■ *Web:* www.calbanktrust.com

California Baptist University
8432 Magnolia Ave...........................Riverside CA 92504 951-689-5771 343-4525* 166
**Fax:* Admissions ■ *TF:* 877-228-8866 ■ *Web:* www.calbaptist.edu

California Bar Journal
180 Howard St ....San Francisco CA 94105 415-538-2000 457-15
Web: www.calbar.ca.gov

California Cafe Restaurants
Old Town 50 University Ave Ste 260...........Los Gatos CA 95030 408-354-8118 354-1400 670
Web: www.californiacafe.com

California Cartage Company Inc
2931 Redondo Ave ....Long Beach CA 90806 888-537-1432 780
TF: 888-537-1432 ■ *Web:* www.calcartage.com

California Cascade Industries
7512 14th Ave...........................Sacramento CA 95820 916-736-3353 683
Web: www.californiacascade.com

California Casualty Insurance Group
1900 Alameda De Las Pulgas................San Mateo CA 94403 650-574-4000 391-4
TF: 866-680-5143 ■ *Web:* www.calcas.com

California Cedar Products Co
2385 Arch Airport Rd Ste 500.................Stockton CA 95206 209-932-5001 571
Web: www.calcedar.com

California Chamber of Commerce
1215 K St Ste 1400 PO Box 1736............Sacramento CA 95812 916-444-6670 325-1272 140
TF: 800-649-4921 ■ *Web:* www.calchamber.com

California Christian College
5364 E Belmont Ave ....Fresno CA 93727 559-251-4215 385-2329 166
Web: www.calchristiancollege.edu

California Closet Co 1716 Fourth St ....Berkeley CA 94710 510-763-2033 256-8501* 189-11
**Fax Area Code:* 415 ■ *TF General:* 888-336-9707 ■ *Web:* www.californiaclosets.com

California College of the Arts
Oakland 5212 Broadway ....Oakland CA 94618 510-594-3600 164
TF: 800-447-1278 ■ *Web:* www.cca.edu
San Francisco 1111 Eigth St..............San Francisco CA 94107 415-703-9500 703-9539 164
TF: 800-447-1278 ■ *Web:* www.cca.edu

California Combining Corp
5607 S Santa Fe Ave.......................Los Angeles CA 90058 323-589-5727 585-8078 599
Web: www.californiacombining.com

California Community Foundation
445 S Figueroa St Ste 3400 ....Los Angeles CA 90071 213-413-4130 383-2046 303
Web: www.calfund.org

California Correctional Institution
24900 Hwy 202 PO Box 1031................ Tehachapi CA 93581 661-822-4402 213
Web: www.cdcr.ca.gov

California Cryobank Inc
11915 La Grange Ave ....Los Angeles CA 90025 310-443-5244 826-1605 545
TF: 866-927-9622 ■ *Web:* www.cryobank.com

California Cryobank Inc
950 Massachusetts Ave ....Cambridge MA 02139 617-497-8646 497-6531 545
TF: 888-810-2796 ■ *Web:* www.cryobank.com

California Cryobank Inc
700 Welch Rd Ste 103 .... Palo Alto CA 94304 650-324-1900 324-1946 545
Web: www.cryobank.com

California Ctr for the Arts
340 N Escondido Blvd ....Escondido CA 92025 760-839-4138 572
TF: 800-988-4253 ■ *Web:* www.artcenter.org

California Custom Fruits & Flavors Inc
15800 Tapia St .... Irwindale CA 91706 626-736-4130 123
Web: www.ccff.com

California Dairies Inc
2000 N Plaza Dr.............................Visalia CA 93291 559-625-2200 625-5433 296-27
TF: 800-722-3110 ■ *Web:* www.californiadairies.com

California Democratic Party
1401 21st St Ste 200 ....Sacramento CA 95811 916-442-5707 616-1
Web: www.cadem.org

California Dental Assn
1201 K St 14th Fl ....Sacramento CA 95814 916-443-0505 443-2943 227
TF: 800-736-7071 ■ *Web:* www.cda.org

California Department Of Veterans Affairs
1227 O St...............................Sacramento CA 94599 707-944-4600 793

California District Attorneys Association
921 11th St.............................Sacramento CA 95814 916-443-2017 41
Web: www.cdaa.org

California Dreaming
3241 Washington Rd ....Augusta GA 30907 706-860-6206 671
Web: www.centraarchy.com

California Dreaming
1 Ashley Pointe Dr ....Charleston SC 29407 843-766-1644 671
Web: www.centraarchy.com

California Eastern Laboratories Inc (CEL)
4590 Patrick Henry Dr .... Santa Clara CA 95054 408-988-3500 988-0279 246
TF: 800-390-3232 ■ *Web:* www.cel.com

California Educator Magazine
1705 Murchison Dr .... Burlingame CA 94010 650-697-1400 552-5002 457-8
Web: www.cta.org

California Exposition & State Fair
1600 Exposition Blvd ....Sacramento CA 95815 916-263-4041 31
Web: www.calexpo.com

California Flexrake Corp
9620 Gidley St .... Temple City CA 91780 626-443-4026 443-6887 429
TF: 800-266-4200 ■ *Web:* www.flexrake.com

California Gasket & Rubber Corp
533 W Collins Ave .... Orange CA 92867 310-323-4250 326
TF: 800-635-7084 ■ *Web:* www.calgasket.com

California Giant Inc 75 Sakata Ln .... Watsonville CA 95076 831-728-1773 728-0613 315-1
Web: www.calgiant.com

California Grill
Disney's Contemporary Resort
4600 N World Dr.....................Lake Buena Vista FL 32830 407-939-5277 671
Web: disneyworld.disney.go.com

California Grill
11999 Harbor Blvd......................Garden Grove CA 92840 714-740-6047 740-0465 671
TF: 800-233-1234 ■
Web: orangecounty.regency.hyatt.com/en/hotel/home.html

California Hospital Medical Ctr
1401 S Grand Ave.........................Los Angeles CA 90015 213-748-2411 374-3
Web: www.chmcla.org

California Hotel & Casino
12 E Ogden Ave .... Las Vegas NV 89101 702-385-1222 133
TF: 800-634-6505 ■ *Web:* www.thecal.com

California Institute of Technology
1200 E California Blvd ....Pasadena CA 91125 626-395-6811 683 3026* 166
**Fax:* Admissions ■ *TF:* 888-222-5832 ■ *Web:* www.caltech.edu

California Institute of Technology Library
1200 E California Blvd MC I-32 ....Pasadena CA 91125 626-395-3405 792-7540 434-6
Web: www.library.caltech.edu

California Institute of the Arts
24700 McBean Pkwy ....Valencia CA 91355 661-255-1050 253-7710 164
TF: 800-545-2787 ■ *Web:* www.calarts.edu

California International University
3130 Wilshire Blvd.......................Los Angeles CA 90010 213-381-3710 381-6990* 166
**Fax:* Admissions ■ *Web:* www.ciula.edu

California ISO
151 Blue Ravine Rd PO Box 639014............. Folsom CA 95630 916-351-4400 608-7222 787
TF: 800-220-4907 ■ *Web:* www.caiso.com

California Kitchen Cabinet Door Corp
400 Cochrane Cir........................Morgan Hill CA 95037 408-782-5700 782-9000 115
Web: www.caldoor.com

California Lawyer Magazine
44 Montgomery St Ste 250..............San Francisco CA 94104 415-296-2400 296-2400 457-15
Web: www.dailyjournal.com

California Lighting Sales Inc (CLS)
4900 Rivergrade Rd Ste D110................. Irwindale CA 91706 626-775-6000 775-6001 439
Web: www.californialightingsales.com

California Living Museum (CALM)
10500 Alfred Harrell Hwy ....Bakersfield CA 93306 661-872-2256 872-2205 520
Web: www.calmzoo.org

California Lutheran University
60 W Olsen Rd ....Thousand Oaks CA 91360 805-493-3135 493-3114 166
TF: 877-258-3678 ■ *Web:* www.callutheran.edu

California Lutheran University Pearson Library
60 W Olsen Rd ....Thousand Oaks CA 91360 805-493-3250 493-3842 434-6
TF: 877-258-3678 ■ *Web:* www.callutheran.edu

California Manufacturing Co
2270 Weldon Pkwy....................... Saint Louis MO 63146 314-567-4404 567-5062 155-3
Web: www.cmcbrands.com

California Maritime Academy
200 Maritime Academy Dr ....Vallejo CA 94590 707-654-1330 654-1336* 166
**Fax:* Admissions ■ *TF:* 800-561-1945 ■ *Web:* www.csum.edu

Name / Address	City	State	Zip	Phone	Fax	Class
California Market Ctr						
110 E Ninth St	Los Angeles	CA	90079	213-630-3600	630-3708	205
TF: 800-225-6278 ■ *Web:* www.californiamarketcenter.com						
California Medical Assn						
1201 J St Ste 200	Sacramento	CA	95814	916-444-5532		474
TF: 800-300-1506 ■ *Web:* www.cmanet.org						
California Men's Colony (CMC)						
Hwy 1 PO Box 8101	San Luis Obispo	CA	93409	805-547-7900		213
Web: www.cdcr.ca.gov						
California Military Museum						
1119 Second St	Sacramento	CA	95814	916-442-2883		520
Web: www.militarymuseum.org						
California Museum for History Women & the Arts						
1020 'O' St	Sacramento	CA	95814	916-653-7524	653-0314	520
Web: www.californiamuseum.org						
California Museum of Photography						
3824 Main St	Riverside	CA	92501	951-827-4787		520
Web: artsblock.ucr.edu						
California Neon Products Inc						
4530 Mission Gorge Pl	San Diego	CA	92120	619-283-2191	283-9503	701
TF: 800-822-6366 ■ *Web:* www.cnpsigns.com						
California Newspaper Service Bureau						
915 E First St	Los Angeles	CA	90012	213-229-5500	229-5481	530
TF: 800-788-7840 ■ *Web:* dailyjournal.com						
California Nurses Assn (CNA)						
2000 Franklin St	Oakland	CA	94612	510-273-2200	663-1625	533
Web: www.nationalnursesunited.org						
California Office Furniture						
3480 Industrial Blvd	Sacramento	CA	95811	916-442-6959	442-3480	320
TF: 877-442-6959 ■ *Web:* caloffice.com						
California Oregon Broadcasting Inc						
125 S Fir St	Medford	OR	97501	541-779-5555	779-5564	738
Web: www.kobi5.com						
California Pacific Homes						
38 Executive Pk Ste 200	Irvine	CA	92614	949-833-6000	833-6133	653
Web: www.calpacifichomes.com						
California Pacific Medical Ctr						
3700 California St	San Francisco	CA	94118	415-600-6000		374-3
TF: 800-478-8837 ■ *Web:* www.cpmc.org						
California Pacific Medical Ctr Davies Campus						
Castro & Duboce Sts	San Francisco	CA	94114	415-600-6000		374-3
TF: 800-478-8837 ■ *Web:* www.cpmc.org						
California Pacific Medical Ctr Pacific Campus						
2333 Buchanan St	San Francisco	CA	94115	415-600-6000		374-3
TF: 800-478-8837 ■ *Web:* www.cpmc.org						
California Pacific Medical Ctr Research Institute						
475 Brannan St Ste 220	San Francisco	CA	94107	415-600-1600	600-1753	668
TF: 855-354-2778 ■ *Web:* www.cpmc.org/professionals/research						
California Pacific University						
1017 E Grand Ave	Escondido	CA	92025	760-739-7730		166
TF: 800-458-9667						
California Pajarosa						
133 Hughes Rd PO Box 684	Watsonville	CA	95077	831-722-6374	722-1316	369
Web: www.pajarosa.com						
California Panel & Veneer Co						
14055 Artesia Blvd	Cerritos	CA	90703	562-926-5834	926-3139	613
TF: 800-451-1745 ■ *Web:* www.calpanel.com						
California Parlor Car Tours						
500 Sutter St Ste 401	San Francisco	CA	94102	415-474-7500	673-1539	760
TF: 800-227-4250 ■ *Web:* www.calpartours.com						
California Pharmacists Assn (CPhA)						
4030 Lennane Dr	Sacramento	CA	95834	916-779-1400	779-1401	585
TF: 866-365-7472 ■ *Web:* www.cpha.com						
California Philharmonic Orchestra						
600 Playhouse Alley	Pasadena	CA	91101	626-300-8200		573-3
Web: calphil.com/home						
California Pizza Kitchen Inc						
18601 Airport Way Ste 135	Santa Ana	CA	92707	949-252-6125		670
NASDAQ: CPKI ■ *Web:* www.cpk.com						
California Polytechnic State University						
1 Grand Ave	San Luis Obispo	CA	93407	805-756-1111	756-5400	166
TF: 800-424-6723 ■ *Web:* www.calpoly.edu						
California Polytechnic State University Kennedy Library						
1 Grand Ave Bldg 35	San Luis Obispo	CA	93407	805-756-2305	756-5770	434-6
Web: www.lib.calpoly.edu						
California Portland Cement Co						
2025 E Financial Way	Glendora	CA	91741	626-852-6200		135
TF Cust Svc: 800-272-1891 ■ *Web:* www.calportland.com						
California Precision Products Inc						
6790 Flanders Dr	San Diego	CA	92121	858-638-7300		697
Web: www.cal-precision.com						
California Primary Care Assn						
1231 I St Ste 400	Sacramento	CA	95814	916-440-8170		194
Web: www.cpca.org						
California Prison Industry Authority						
560 E Natoma St	Folsom	CA	95630	916-358-2733	358-2660*	630
**Fax:* Cust Svc ■ *TF:* 800-732-9253 ■ *Web:* www.pia.ca.gov						
California Products Corp						
150 Dascomb Rd	Andover	MA	01810	978-623-9980	533-6788*	550
**Fax Area Code:* 800 ■ *TF:* 800-225-1141 ■ *Web:* www.californiapaints.com						
California Public Interest Research Group (CAPIRG)						
1107 Ninth St Ste 601	Sacramento	CA	95814	916-448-4516		633
Web: www.calpirg.org						
California Public Radio						
4100 Vachell Ln	San Luis Obispo	CA	93401	805-549-8855		632
TF: 800-549-8855 ■ *Web:* www.kcbx.org						
California Real Estate Magazine						
525 S Virgil Ave	Los Angeles	CA	90020	213-739-8200	480-7724	457-5
TF: 888-811-5281 ■ *Web:* www.car.org						
California Regional Multiple Listing Service Inc						
180 Via Verde Ste 200	San Dimas	CA	91773	909-859-2040		387
Web: go.crmls.org						
California Republican Party						
1903 W Magnolia Blvd	Burbank	CA	91506	818-841-5210		616-2
Web: www.cagop.org						
California Rollin II						
274 N Goodman St	Rochester	NY	14607	585-271-8990		671
Web: californiarollin.com						
California Saw & Knife Works						
721 Brannan St	San Francisco	CA	94103	415-861-0644	861-0406	682
TF: 888-729-6533 ■ *Web:* www.calsaw.com						
California Science Ctr						
700 Exposition Park Dr	Los Angeles	CA	90037	213-744-7400		520
Web: californiasciencecenter.org						
California Shellfish Co						
505 Beach St Ste 200	San Francisco	CA	94133	415-923-7400		297-5
California Sidecar Inc						
100 Motorcycle Run	Arrington	VA	22922	434-263-6500		82
Web: www.californiasidecar.com						
California Southern Baptist Convention						
678 E Shaw Ave	Fresno	CA	93710	559-229-9533	229-2824	48-20
Web: www.csbc.com						
California Sports Inc						
555 N Nash St	El Segundo	CA	90245	310-426-6000		360-3
California State Archives						
1020 'O' St	Sacramento	CA	95814	916-653-7715	653-7134	520
TF: 800-633-5155 ■ *Web:* www.sos.ca.gov						
California State Library 900 N St	Sacramento	CA	95814	916-654-0261	654-0241	434-5
TF: 800-952-5666 ■ *Web:* www.library.ca.gov						
California State Mining & Mineral Museum						
5005 Fairgrounds Rd	Mariposa	CA	95338	209-742-7625	966-3597	565
Web: www.parks.ca.gov/default.asp?page_id=588						
California State Polytechnic University Pomona						
3801 W Temple Ave	Pomona	CA	91768	909-869-7659	869-4555*	166
**Fax:* Admissions ■ *Web:* www.cpp.edu						
California State Prison Corcoran						
4001 King Ave PO Box 8800	Corcoran	CA	93212	559-992-8800	386-7461	213
Web: www.cdcr.ca.gov						
California State Prison Los Angeles County						
44750 60th St W	Lancaster	CA	93536	661-729-2000		213
Web: cdcr.ca.gov						
California State Prison Solano						
2100 Peabody Rd PO Box 4000	Vacaville	CA	95696	707-451-0182		213
Web: www.cdcr.ca.gov						
California State Railroad Museum						
125 "I" St 111 'I' St	Sacramento	CA	95814	916-323-9280	327-5655	565
Web: www.californiarailroad.museum						
California State University						
401 Golden Shore	Long Beach	CA	90802	562-951-4000		786
TF: 800-325-4000 ■ *Web:* www.calstate.edu						
Bakersfield 9001 Stockdale Hwy	Bakersfield	CA	93311	661-654-2011		166
Web: auxiliary.calstate.edu						
Channel Islands 1 University Dr	Camarillo	CA	93012	805-437-8400		166
Web: www.csuci.edu						
Chico CSU Chico	Chico	CA	95929	530-898-6321	898-6456*	166
**Fax:* Admissions ■ *TF Admissions:* 800-542-4426 ■ *Web:* www.csuchico.edu						
Dominguez Hills 1000 E Victoria St	Carson	CA	90747	310-243-3300		166
TF: 888-545-6512 ■ *Web:* www.csudh.edu						
East Bay 25800 Carlos Bee Blvd	Hayward	CA	94542	510-885-3000	885-4059	166
TF: 800-884-1684 ■ *Web:* www.csueastbay.edu						
Fresno 5241 N Maple Ave	Fresno	CA	93740	559-278-4240	278-4812*	166
**Fax:* Admissions ■ *TF:* 800-700-2320 ■ *Web:* www.fresnostate.edu						
Fullerton 800 N State College Blvd	Fullerton	CA	92834	657-278-2011	278-2300*	166
**Fax Area Code:* 714 ■ *TF:* 888-433-9406 ■ *Web:* www.fullerton.edu						
Long Beach 1250 Bellflower Blvd	Long Beach	CA	90840	562-985-4111	985-4973*	166
**Fax:* Admissions ■ *TF:* 800-663-1144 ■ *Web:* www.csulb.edu						
Los Angeles						
5151 State University Dr	Los Angeles	CA	90032	323-343-3000	343-6306*	166
**Fax:* Admissions ■ *Web:* www.calstatela.edu						
Monterey Bay 100 Campus Ctr	Seaside	CA	93955	831-582-3000	582-3738*	166
**Fax:* Admissions ■ *Web:* www.csumb.edu						
Northridge 18111 Nordhoff St	Northridge	CA	91330	818-677-1200	677-3766	166
TF: 800-399-4529 ■ *Web:* www.csun.edu						
Sacramento 6000 J St	Sacramento	CA	95819	916-278-3901	278-7473	166
TF: 800-667-7531 ■ *Web:* www.csus.edu						
San Bernardino						
5500 University Pkwy	San Bernardino	CA	92407	909-537-5188	537-7034	166
TF: 866-275-3772 ■ *Web:* www.csusb.edu						
San Marcos						
333 S Twin Oaks Valley Rd	San Marcos	CA	92096	760-750-4000	750-3248*	166
**Fax:* Admissions ■ *TF:* 888-225-5427 ■ *Web:* www.csusm.edu						
Stanislaus 1 University Cir	Turlock	CA	95382	209-667-3152	667-3788	166
TF: 800-235-9292 ■ *Web:* www.csustan.edu						
California State University Chico						
Meriam Library 400 W First St	Chico	CA	95929	530-898-6502	898-4443	434-6
Web: www.csuchico.edu/library						
California State University Long Beach						
University Library						
1250 Bellflower Blvd	Long Beach	CA	90840	562-985-4047	985-1703	434-6
Web: www.csulb.edu/library						
California State University Los Angeles						
Kennedy Memorial Library						
5151 State University Dr	Los Angeles	CA	90032	323-343-3988	343-6401	434-6
Web: www.calstatela.edu/library						
California State University Northridge						
Oviatt Library 18111 Nordhoff St	Northridge	CA	91330	818-677-2285	677-2676	434-6
Web: library.csun.edu						
California State University Sacramento						
Library 2000 State University Dr E	Sacramento	CA	95819	916-278-5679	278-4160	434-6
Web: www.library.csus.edu						
California State University San Bernardino						
Pfau Library						
5500 University Pkwy	San Bernardino	CA	92407	909-537-3447		434-6
Web: www.lib.csusb.edu						
California State University San Marcos						
Library 333 S Twin Oaks Valley Rd	San Marcos	CA	92096	760-750-4340		434-6
Web: www.csusm.edu						
California State University Stanislaus						
Library 1 University Cir	Turlock	CA	95382	209-667-3234	667-3164	434-6
Web: library.csustan.edu						
Stockton Ctr 612 E Magnolia St	Stockton	CA	95202	209-467-5300	467-5333	166
Web: www.csustan.edu						
California Steel & Tube						
16049 Stephens St	City of Industry	CA	91745	626-968-5511		490
TF: 800-338-8823 ■ *Web:* californiasteelandtube.com						

	Phone	Fax	Class

California Steel Industries Inc
14000 San Bernardino Ave .... Fontana CA 92335 909-350-6300 480
Web: www.californiasteel.com

California Steel Services Inc
1212 S Mtn View Ave .... San Bernardino CA 92408 909-796-2222 492
Web: www.calsteel.com

California Supermarket
127 E Second St .... Calexico CA 92231 760-357-4061 345
Web: www.superbikeschool.com

California Technology Ventures LLC
670 N Rosemead Blvd Ste 201 .... Pasadena CA 91107 626-351-3700 401
Web: www.ctventures.com

California Theatre of Performing Arts
562 W Fourth St .... San Bernardino CA 92401 909-885-5152 885-8948 572
TF: 800-745-3000 ■ *Web:* www.californiatheatre.net

California TrusFrame 23665 Cajalco Rd .... Perris CA 92570 951-657-7491 817
Web: caltrusframe.com

California University of Pennsylvania
250 University Ave .... California PA 15419 724-938-4000 938-4564 166
TF: 888-412-0479 ■ *Web:* calu.edu

California University of Pennsylvania Louis L Manderino Library
250 University Ave .... California PA 15419 724-938-4091 938-5901 434-6
Web: www.library.calu.edu

California Water Service Group
1720 N First St .... San Jose CA 95112 408-367-8200 367-8430 787
NYSE: CWT ■ *TF:* 866-734-0743 ■ *Web:* www.calwater.com

California Wellness Foundation (CWF)
6320 Canoga Ave Ste 1700 .... Woodland Hills CA 91367 818-702-1900 702-1999 303
Web: www.calwellness.org

California Western School of Law
225 Cedar St .... San Diego CA 92101 619-239-0391 167-1
TF: 800-255-4252 ■ *Web:* www.cwsl.edu

California's Great America
4701 Great America Pkwy .... Santa Clara CA 95054 408-988-1776 32
Web: www.cagreatamerica.com

Californian, The 123 W Alisal St .... Salinas CA 93901 831-424-2221 754-4293 532-2
Web: www.thecalifornian.com

Californos 4124 Pennsylvania Ave .... Kansas City MO 64111 816-531-7878 671
Web: www.californos.com

Calipatria State Prison
7018 Blair Rd .... Calipatria CA 92233 760-348-7000 213
Web: cdcr.ca.gov

Caliper Corporation Inc
506 Carnegie Ctr Ste 300 .... Princeton NJ 08543 609-524-1400 193
Web: www.calipercorp.com

Caliper Life Sciences Inc 68 Elm St .... Hopkinton MA 01748 508-435-9500 435-3439 419
TF: 800-762-4000 ■ *Web:* www.perkinelmer.com

Calise & Sons Bakery Inc 2 Quality Dr .... Lincoln RI 02865 401-334-3444 334-0938 296-1
TF: 800-225-4737 ■ *Web:* www.calisebakery.com

Calista Corp 301 Calista Ct Ste A .... Anchorage AK 99518 907-279-5516 272-5060 655
TF: 800-277-5516 ■ *Web:* www.calistacorp.com

Calistoga Beverage Co
865 Silverado Trl .... Calistoga CA 94515 800-365-4446 805
TF: 800-365-4446

Calistoga Ranch 580 Lommel Rd .... Calistoga CA 94515 707-254-2800 669
TF: 800-942-4220 ■ *Web:* calistogaranch.aubergeresorts.com

Calistoga Spa Hot Springs
1006 Washington St .... Calistoga CA 94515 707-942-6269 942-4214 706
TF: 866-822-5772 ■ *Web:* www.calistogaspa.com

Calix Society, The
3881 Highland Ave Ste 201 .... St Paul MN 55110 651-773-3117 48-21
TF: 800-398-0524 ■ *Web:* www.calixsociety.org

Call for Action
11820 Parklawn Dr Ste 340 .... Rockville MD 20852 240-747-0225 48-10
Web: www.callforaction.org

Call One Inc
400 Imperial Blvd PO Box 9002 .... Cape Canaveral FL 32920 321-783-2400 799-9222 735
TF: 800-749-3160 ■ *Web:* www.calloneonline.com

Callaghan Tire 1511 38th Ave E .... Bradenton FL 34208 941-746-6188 754
Web: www.callaghantire.com

Callahan Chemical Co
Broad St & Filmore Ave .... Palmyra NJ 08065 800-257-7967 336-2283* 146
**Fax Area Code: 936* ■ *TF:* 800-257-7967 ■ *Web:* www.calchem.com

Callahan County 100 W Fourth St .... Baird TX 79504 325-854-5873 338
Web: www.co.callahan.tx.us

Callahan Eye Foundation Hospital
1720 University Blvd .... Birmingham AL 35233 205-325-8100 374-7
TF: 800-292-8166 ■ *Web:* uabmedicine.org

Callahan Financial Planning Co
3157 Farnam St Ste 7112 .... Omaha NE 68131 402-341-2000 194
Web: callahanplanning.com

Callahan Inc 80 First St .... Bridgewater MA 02324 508-279-0012 186
TF: 800-876-8420 ■ *Web:* www.callahan-inc.com

Call-A-Head Corp
304 Crossbay Blvd .... Broad Channel NY 11693 718-318-5762 610
Web: www.callahead.com

Callan & Woodworth Moving & Storage
900 Hwy 212 .... Michigan City IN 46360 269-447-1578 519
TF: 800-584-0551 ■ *Web:* www.callanmoving.com

Callan Associates Inc
600 Montgomery St Ste 800 .... San Francisco CA 94111 415-974-5060 291-4014 401
TF: 800-227-3288 ■ *Web:* www.callan.com

Callanwolde Fine Arts Ctr
980 Briarcliff Rd NE .... Atlanta GA 30306 404-872-5338 872-5175 50-2
TF: 800-979-3370 ■ *Web:* www.callanwolde.org

Callas Contractors Inc
10549 Downsville Pk .... Hagerstown MD 21740 301-739-8400 188-10
Web: www.callascontractors.com

Callaway Cars Inc 3 High St .... Old Lyme CT 06371 860-434-9002 57
TF: 866-927-9400 ■ *Web:* www.callawaycars.com

Callaway County Clerk 10 E Fifth St .... Fulton MO 65251 573-642-0730 642-7181 338
Web: callawaycountyclerk.com

Callaway Electric Co-op
1313 Co-op Dr PO Box 250 .... Fulton MO 65251 573-642-3326 245
TF: 888-642-4840 ■ *Web:* www.callawayelectric.com

Callaway Gardens 17800 Hwy 27 .... Pine Mountain GA 31822 706-663-2281 663-5122 669
TF: 800-225-5292 ■ *Web:* www.callawaygardens.com

Callaway Golf Co 2180 Rutherford Rd .... Carlsbad CA 92008 760-931-1771 931-8013 710
NYSE: ELY ■ *TF:* 800-588-9836 ■ *Web:* www.callawaygolf.com

Callaway Partners LLC
600 Galleria Pkwy SE Ste 1400 .... Atlanta GA 30339 404-496-5230 252-9078 292
Web: www.warbirdconsulting.com

Callbright Corp 6700 Hollister .... Houston TX 77040 877-462-2552 390
TF: 877-462-2552 ■ *Web:* www.callbright.com

CallDirek 4770 Biscayne Blvd Ste 1480 .... Miami FL 33137 866-673-4735 387
TF: 866-673-4735

Callenor Company Inc
N 60 W 15725 Kohler Ln .... Menomonee Falls WI 53051 262-252-3343 252-3873 125
TF: 800-813-7429 ■ *Web:* www.callenor.com

Callero & Callero LLP
7800 N Milwaukee Ave .... Niles IL 60714 847-966-2040 2
Web: www.callero.com

Caller-Times
820 N Lower Broadway .... Corpus Christi TX 78401 361-884-2011 886-3732* 532-2
**Fax: Edit* ■ *TF:* 800-827-2011 ■ *Web:* www.caller.com

Callidus Technologies Inc
7130 S Lewis St Ste 335 .... Tulsa OK 74136 918-496-7599 488-9450 318
Web: www.callidus.com

Calling Solutions By Phone Power Inc
2200 McCullough Ave .... San Antonio TX 78212 210-801-9630 737
TF Cust Svc: 800-683-5500 ■ *Web:* www.callingsolutions.org

Calliope Learning 1581H Hillside Ave .... Victoria BC V8T2C1 250-213-6239 194
Web: www.calliopelearning.com

Callister & Reynolds
823 Las Vegas Blvd S .... Las Vegas NV 89101 702-333-3334 445
Web: reynoldslawyers.com

Callisto Integration
635 Fourth Line Ste 16 .... Oakville ON L6L5B3 905-339-0059 194
TF: 800-387-0467 ■ *Web:* www.aseco.net

Callisto Pharmaceuticals Inc
420 Lexington Ave Ste 2012 .... New York NY 10170 212-297-0010 297-0019 85
AMEX: KAL ■ *Web:* www.synergypharma.com

Callon Petroleum Co 200 N Canal St .... Natchez MS 39120 601-442-1601 446-1410 540
NYSE: CPE ■ *TF:* 800-451-1294 ■ *Web:* www.callon.com

Callos & Associates
1375 S Main St Ste 101 .... North Canton OH 44720 614-575-4900 260
TF: 800-422-5567 ■ *Web:* www.callos.com

Calloway County 101 S Fifth St Ste 5 .... Murray KY 42071 270-753-3923 759-9611 338
TF: 800-479-2082 ■ *Web:* calloway.clerkinfo.net

Calloway Laboratories Inc
12 Gill St Ste 4000 .... Woburn MA 01801 781-224-9899 415

Calloway's Nursery Inc
4200 Airport Fwy Ste 200 .... Fort Worth TX 76117 817-222-1122 323
OTC: CLWY ■ *TF:* 800-243-6550 ■ *Web:* www.calloways.com

Callware Technologies Inc 9100 S 500 W .... Sandy UT 84070 801-988-6800 178-7
TF: 800-888-4226 ■ *Web:* www.callware.com

CALM (California Living Museum)
10500 Alfred Harrell Hwy .... Bakersfield CA 93306 661-872-2256 872-2205 520
Web: www.calmzoo.org

CALMAC Manufacturing Corp
3-00 Banta Pl .... Fair Lawn NJ 07410 201-797-1511 194
Web: www.calmac.com

Calmare Therapeutics Inc
1375 Kings Hwy .... Fairfield CT 06824 203-368-6044 368-5399 195
Web: calmaretherapeutics.com

Calmark Inc 1400 W 44th St .... Chicago IL 60609 773-247-7200 5

Calmax Technology Inc
526 Laurelwood Rd .... Santa Clara CA 95054 408-748-8660 757
Web: www.calmaxtechnology.com

CalMet Services Inc
7230 Petterson Lane Paramount .... Downey CA 90723 562-259-1239 529-7958 804
Web: www.calmetservices.com

Calmetto 883 NE Main St Ste 2 .... Simpsonville SC 29681 864-962-2201 195
Web: www.siia.org

Calmont Leasing Ltd
14610 Yellowhead Trail NW .... Edmonton AB T5L3C5 855-474-2568 778
TF: 855-474-2568 ■ *Web:* www.calmont.ca

Calmoseptine Inc
16602 Burke Ln .... Huntington Beach CA 92647 714-840-3405 231
TF: 800-800-3405 ■ *Web:* www.calmoseptine.com

Calnet Inc 12359 Sunrise Vly Dr Ste 270 .... Reston VA 20191 703-547-6800 547-6806 194
TF General: 877-322-5638 ■ *Web:* www.calnet.com

Calnetix Technologies LLC
16323 Shoemaker Ave .... Cerritos CA 90703 562-293-1660 518
Web: www.calnetix.com

Calolympic Glove & Safety Company Inc
1720 Delilah St .... Corona CA 92879 951-340-2229 340-3337 679
TF: 800-421-6630 ■ *Web:* www.caloly-safety.com

Caloris Engineering LLC
8649 Commerce Dr .... Easton MD 21601 410-822-6900 261
Web: caloris.com

Cal-Pac Chemical Company Inc
6231 Maywood Ave .... Huntington Park CA 90255 323-585-2178 145
Web: www.calpacchem.com

Cal-Partitions Inc
23814 President Ave .... Harbor City CA 90710 310-539-1911 286

Calphalon Corp PO Box 583 .... Toledo OH 43697 800-809-7267 666-2859* 486
**Fax Area Code: 419* ■ **Fax: Sales* ■ *TF:* 800-809-7267 ■ *Web:* www.calphalon.com

Calpico Inc
1387 San Mateo Ave .... South San Francisco CA 94080 650-588-2241 326
TF: 800-998-9115 ■ *Web:* www.calpicoinc.com

Calpine Containers Inc
9499 N Ford Wahington Rd Ste 103 .... Fresno CA 93730 559-519-7199 101
Web: www.calpinecontainers.com

Calpine Corp 717 Texas Ave Ste 1000 .... Houston TX 77002 713-830-2000 787
NYSE: CPN ■ *TF:* 800-367-5690 ■ *Web:* www.calpine.com

Calpop Com Inc 600 W Seventh St .... Los Angeles CA 90017 866-467-8846 224
TF: 866-467-8846

CalPortland 5975 E Marginal Way S .... Seattle WA 98134 206-764-3000 182
TF: 800-750-0123 ■ *Web:* www.calportland.com

Cal-Royal Products Inc
6605 Flotilla St .... City Of Commerce CA 90040 323-888-6601 350
TF: 800-876-9258 ■ *Web:* www.cal-royal.com

CalSAE 717 13th St Lwr Level .... Sacramento CA 95814 916-443-8980 260
Web: www.calsae.org

Calsak Corp 1411 W 190th St Ste 400 .... Gardena CA 90248 310-719-9500 719-1300 603
TF: 888-663-6005 ■ *Web:* www.calsak.com

Name / Address	City	State	Zip	Phone	Fax	Class
Cal-Sierra Pipe LLC 3033 S 99 Hwy W Frontage Rd *Web:* www.calsierrapipe.com	Stockton	CA	95215	209-466-0988		690
CalsonicKansei North America Inc 1 Calsonic Way *TF:* 800-442-1162 ■ *Web:* www.calsonic.com	Shelbyville	TN	37160	931-684-4490	684-2724	15
Calstrip Steel Corp 7140 Bandini Blvd *Web:* calstripsteel.com	Los Angeles	CA	90040	323-726-1345	722-8269	723
CalSurance 681 S Parker St Ste 300 *TF:* 800-762-7800 ■ *Web:* www.calsurance.com	Orange	CA	92868	714-939-0800	939-1641	390
Calton & Assoc Inc 2701 N Rocky Point Dr Ste 1000 *TF:* 800-942-0262 ■ *Web:* calton.com	Tampa	FL	33607	813-264-0440		690
Calumet Armature & Electric Company Inc 1050 W 134th St *Web:* www.calumetarmature.com	Riverdale	IL	60827	708-841-6880		518
Calumet City Chamber of Commerce 80 River Oaks Ctr PO Box 2406 *Web:* www.calumetcitychamber.com	Calumet City	IL	60409	708-891-5888		139
Calumet City Public Library 660 Manistee Ave *Web:* calumetcitypl.org	Calumet City	IL	60409	708-862-6220	862-0872	434-3
Calumet College of Saint Joseph 2400 New York Ave **Fax:* Admissions ■ *TF:* 877-700-9100 ■ *Web:* www.ccsj.edu	Whiting	IN	46394	219-473-4215	473-4336*	166
Calumet County 206 Ct St *Web:* www.co.calumet.wi.us	Chilton	WI	53014	920-849-2361	849-1469	338
Calumet Diversified Meats Inc 10000 80th Ave *TF:* 800-752-7427 ■ *Web:* www.porkchops.com	Pleasant Prairie	WI	53158	262-947-7200	947-7209	297-9
Calumet Specialty Products Partners LP 2780 Waterfront Pkwy E Dr Ste 200 *NASDAQ: CLMT* ■ *TF:* 800-437-3188 ■ *Web:* www.calumetspecialty.com	Indianapolis	IN	46214	317-328-5660	328-5668	580
Cal-Van Tools 7918 Industrial Village Rd *TF:* 800-537-1077 ■ *Web:* www.cal-vantools.com	Greensboro	NC	27409	800-537-1077	537-1717	758
Calvary Baptist Christian Academy 543 Randolph St *Web:* calvarymeadville.com	Meadville	PA	16335	814-724-8099		48-20
Calvary Bible College & Theological Seminary 15800 Calvary Rd **Fax:* Admissions ■ *TF:* 800-326-3960 ■ *Web:* www.calvary.edu	Kansas City	MO	64147	816-322-3960	331-4474*	161
Calvary Chapel 13500 Philmont Ave *Web:* www.ccphilly.org	Philadelphia	PA	19116	215-969-1520		48-20
Calvary Chapel of Costa Mesa Inc 3800 S Fairview St *Web:* www.calvarychapelcostamesa.com	Santa Ana	CA	92704	714-979-4422		48-20
Calvary Church of Pacific 701 Palisades Dr *Web:* www.calvarypalisades.org	Pacific Palisades	CA	90272	310-454-6537		685
Calvert Cliffs State Park 10540 H G Trueman Rd *Web:* dnr2.maryland.gov	Lusby	MD	20657	301-743-7613		565
Calvert Company Inc 3559 S Truman Rd *Web:* calvertglulam.com	Washougal	WA	98671	360-835-3110		817
Calvert County 175 Main St *TF:* 800-492-7122 ■ *Web:* www.co.cal.md.us	Prince Frederick	MD	20678	410-535-1600		338
Calvert County Chamber of Commerce PO Box 9 **Fax Area Code:* 443 ■ *TF:* 800-972-4389 ■ *Web:* www.calvertchamber.org	Prince Frederick	MD	20678	410-535-2577	295-7213*	139
Calvert County Nursing Center Inc 85 Hospital Rd *TF:* 800-327-2879 ■ *Web:* calvertcountynursingcenter.org	Prince Frederick	MD	20678	410-535-2300		371
Calvert County Public Library 850 Costley Way *Web:* www.calvert.lib.md.us	Prince Frederick	MD	20678	410-535-0291		434-3
Calvert Investment Counsel LLC 4 N Park Dr Ste 201 *Web:* www.calvertinvestmentcounsel.com	Hunt Valley	MD	21030	410-435-3270		401
Calvert Investments Inc 4550 Montgomery Ave Ste 1000N *TF:* 800-368-2748 ■ *Web:* www.calvert.com	Bethesda	MD	20814	301-951-4800		528
Calvert Ken (Rep R - CA) 2205 Rayburn Bldg *Web:* calvert.house.gov	Washington	DC	20515	202-225-1986	225-2004	342-2
Calvert Labs 1225 Crescent Green Ste 115 *TF:* 800-300-8114 ■ *Web:* www.calvertlabs.com	Cary	NC	27518	919-854-4453		418
Calvert Marine Museum 14200 Solomons Island Rd PO Box 97 *TF:* 800-735-2258 ■ *Web:* www.calvertmarinemuseum.com	Solomons	MD	20688	410-326-2042	326-6691	520
Calvert Plumbing & Heating Company Inc 5806 York Rd *Web:* calvertinc.com	Baltimore	MD	21212	410-323-5400		189-10
Calvert Retail LP 100 W Rockland Rd Ste A PO Box 302 *Web:* www.calvertretail.com	Montchanin	DE	19710	302-622-8811	622-8602	362
Calvert's Restaurant 475 Highland Ave *Web:* www.calvertsrestaurant.com	Augusta	GA	30909	706-738-4514		671
Calverton National Cemetery 210 Princeton Blvd *Web:* www.cem.va.gov	Calverton	NY	11933	631-727-5410	369-4397	136
Calvin B Taylor House Museum 208 N Main St *TF:* 800-235-4045 ■ *Web:* www.taylorhousemuseum.org	Berlin	MD	21811	410-641-1019		520
Calvin College 3201 Burton St SE **Fax:* Admissions ■ *TF:* 800-688-0122 ■ *Web:* www.calvin.edu	Grand Rapids	MI	49546	616-526-6000	526-6777*	166
Calvin Giordano & Assoc Inc 1800 Eller Dr Ste 600 *Web:* cgasolutions.com	Fort Lauderdale	FL	33316	954-921-7781		261
Calvin Theological Seminary 3233 Burton St SE *TF:* 800-388-6034 ■ *Web:* www.calvinseminary.edu	Grand Rapids	MI	49546	616-957-6036	957-8621	167-3
Calvo Eddie Baza (R) PO Box 2950 PO Box 2950 *Web:* governor.guam.gov	Agana	GU	96932	671-472-8931	477-4826	343
Calypso Technology Inc 595 Market St Ste 1800 *Web:* www.calypso.com	San Francisco	CA	94105	415-817-2400	284-1222	178
Calypte Biomedical Corp 15875 SW 72nd Ave *OTC: CBMC* ■ *TF:* 800-424-6723 ■ *Web:* www.calypte.com	Portland	OR	97224	503-726-2227	601-6299	231
Calyx Transportation Group Inc 107 Alfred Kuehne Blvd	Brampton	ON	L6T4K3	905-494-4747		314
Calzone Case Co 225 Black Rock Ave *TF Cust Svc:* 800-243-5152 ■ *Web:* www.calzonecase.com	Bridgeport	CT	06605	203-367-5766	336-4406	453
CAM (CAM Raleigh) 409 W Martin St *Web:* camraleigh.org	Raleigh	NC	27603	919-261-5920		520
CAM Administrative Services Inc 25800 Northwestern Hwy Ste 700 *Web:* www.camads.com	Southfield	MI	48075	248-827-1050		390
CAM Commerce Solutions Inc 17075 Newhope St Ste A *TF:* 800-726-3282 ■ *Web:* www.camcommerce.com	Fountain Valley	CA	92708	714-241-9241	241-9893	178-10
Cam Consulting Group Llc 10 Tudor Ct *TF:* 800-416-4861 ■ *Web:* cam4consulting.com	Chesterfield	NJ	08515	609-291-1937		196
CAM Innovation Inc 215 Philadelphia St *TF:* 800-367-7629 ■ *Web:* www.caminnovation.com	Hanover	PA	17331	717-637-5988		295
CAM International LLC 503 Space Park S *TF:* 800-251-8544 ■ *Web:* www.caminternational.com	Nashville	TN	37211	800-251-8544		61
CAM Raleigh (CAM) 409 W Martin St *Web:* camraleigh.org	Raleigh	NC	27603	919-261-5920		520
Cam Services Inc 5664 Selmaraine Dr *TF:* 800-576-3050 ■ *Web:* www.camservices.com	Culver City	CA	90230	310-390-3552		256
Cam Superline Inc 4763 Zane A Miller Dr *Web:* www.camsuperline.com	Waynesboro	PA	17268	717-749-3369		120
Cam Tran Company Ltd 203 Purdy Rd *Web:* www.camtran.com	Colborne	ON	K0K1S0	905-355-3224		767
Cama Inc 31 Audubon St *TF:* 800-660-5360 ■ *Web:* www.camainc.com	New Haven	CT	06511	203-777-9921		393
CAMAC Inc 1330 Post Oak Blvd Ste 2200 *Web:* www.camac.com	Houston	TX	77056	713-965-5100	965-5128	538
CAMACOL (Latin Chamber of Commerce of the US) 1417 W Flagler St *Web:* www.camacol.org	Miami	FL	33135	305-642-3870		138
Camadro Inc 508 Mohawk St Ste A *Web:* freearcade.com	Tecumseh	MI	49286	517-423-0523		180
Camag Scientific Inc 515 Cornelius Harnett Dr *Web:* www.camagusa.com	Wilmington	NC	28401	910-343-1830		250
Camalloy Inc 1960 N Main St *Web:* www.camalloy.com	Washington	PA	15301	724-222-2022		492
Camano Island State Park 2269 S Lowell Pt Rd *Web:* parks.wa.gov	Camano Island	WA	98282	360-387-3031		565
Camar Aircraft Parts Co 743 Flynn Rd *Web:* www.camarac.com	Camarillo	CA	93012	805-389-8944		57
Camarillo Chamber of Commerce 2400 Ventura Blvd *TF:* 800-664-3489 ■ *Web:* camarillochamber.org	Camarillo	CA	93010	805-484-4383	484-1395	139
Camarillo Premium Outlets 740 E Ventura Blvd *Web:* www.premiumoutlets.com	Camarillo	CA	93010	805-445-8520		460
Camas County 501 Soldier Rd *TF:* 800-815-2666 ■ *Web:* www.idaho.gov/aboutidaho/county/camas.html	Fairfield	ID	83327	208-764-2242	764-2349	338
Camas-Washougal Chamber of Commerce 422 NE Fourth Ave *TF:* 844-262-1100 ■ *Web:* www.cwchamber.com	Camas	WA	98607	360-834-2472	834-9171	139
Cambay Group Inc, The 2999 Oak Rd Ste 400 *Web:* www.cambaygroup.com	Walnut Creek	CA	94597	925-933-1405		194
Cambelt International Corp 2820 West 1100 South *TF:* 855-226-2358 ■ *Web:* www.cambelt.com	Salt Lake City	UT	84104	801-972-5511	972-5522	207
Camber Corp 670 Discovery Dr *TF:* 800-998-7988 ■ *Web:* www.camber.com	Huntsville	AL	35806	256-922-0200	922-3599	180
Cambex Corp 337 Tpke Rd *OTC: CBEX* ■ *TF:* 800-325-5565 ■ *Web:* www.cambex.com	Southborough	MA	01772	508-281-0209	281-0214	176
Cambey & West Inc 120 N Route 9W *Web:* www.cambeywest.com	Congers	NY	10920	845-267-3490		225
Cambiar Investors Inc 2401 E Second Ave Ste 500 *TF:* 888-673-9950 ■ *Web:* www.cambiar.com	Denver	CO	80206	888-673-9950		401
Cambium Learning Group Inc 17855 Dallas Pkwy Ste 400 *TF:* 800-225-5800 ■ *Web:* www.cambiumlearning.com	Dallas	TX	75287	214-932-9500		242
Cambodia Embassy 4530 16th St NW *Web:* www.embassyofcambodia.org	Washington	DC	20011	202-726-7742	726-8381	257
Cambrex Charles City Inc 1205 11th St *Web:* www.cambrex.com	Charles City	IA	50616	641-257-1000	228-4152	479
Cambrex Corp 1 Meadowlands Plaza *NYSE: CBM* ■ *TF:* 866-286-9133 ■ *Web:* www.cambrex.com	East Rutherford	NJ	07073	201-804-3000	804-9852	479
Cambria Bicycle Outfitter 1645 Commerce Way *Web:* www.cambriabike.com	Paso Robles	CA	93446	805-221-2602		711
Cambria Capital LLC 488 E Winchester St Ste 200 *TF:* 877-226-0477 ■ *Web:* www.cambriacapital.com	Salt Lake City	UT	84107	801-320-9606		401
Cambria Consulting Inc 1 Bowdoin Sq *Web:* www.cambriaconsulting.com	Boston	MA	02114	617-523-7500		194
Cambria Corp 3723 Haven Ave Ste 130 *Web:* www.cambria.com	Menlo Park	CA	94025	650-328-9270		809
Cambria County 200 S Ctr St *TF:* 800-492-9292 ■ *Web:* www.cambriacountypa.gov	Ebensburg	PA	15931	814-472-1540	472-0761	338
Cambria County Library System 248 Main St *Web:* www.cclsys.org	Johnstown	PA	15901	814-536-5131	536-6905	434-3

Phone | Fax | Class

Cambria Inc 31496 Cambria Ave Ste 220 ... Le Sueur MN 56058 507-665-5003 115
Web: www.cambriausa.com
Cambria Music PO Box 374 ... Lomita CA 90717 310-831-1322 833-7442 657
Web: www.cambriamus.com
Cambria Pines Realty Inc
746-A Main St ... Cambria CA 93428 805-927-8616 652
TF: 800-676-8616 ■ *Web:* cambriapinesrealty.com
Cambria Solutions Inc
1050 20th St Ste 275 ... Sacramento CA 95811 916-326-4446 194
Web: www.cambriasolutions.com
Cambrian Management 2398 W 44th St ... Odessa TX 79764 432-550-5245 540
Cambridge Area Chamber of Commerce
607 Wheeling Ave ... Cambridge OH 43725 740-439-6688 439-6689 139
Web: www.cambridgeohiochamber.com
Cambridge Associates LLC 125 High St ... Boston MA 02110 617-457-7500 401
Web: www.cambridgeassociates.com
Cambridge BioMarketing Group LLC
245 First St 12th Fl ... Cambridge MA 02142 617-225-0001 4
Web: www.cambridgebmg.com
Cambridge Chamber of Commerce
859 Massachusetts Ave ... Cambridge MA 02139 617-876-4100 139
Web: www.cambridgechamber.org
Cambridge Chamber of Commerce
750 Hespeler Rd ... Cambridge ON N3H5L8 519-622-2221 622-0177 137
TF General: 800-749-7560 ■ *Web:* www.cambridgechamber.com
Cambridge College Inc
360 Merrimack St 4th fl ... Lawrence MA 01843 617-868-1000 800
TF: 800-829-4723 ■ *Web:* www.cambridgecollege.edu
Cambridge Credit Counseling Corp
67 Hunt St ... Agawam MA 01001 413-821-8900 226
Web: www.cambridge-credit.org
Cambridge Engineering Inc
PO Box 1010 ... Chesterfield MO 63006 636-532-2233 530-6133 318
TF: 800-899-1989 ■ *Web:* www.cambridge-eng.com
Cambridge Financial Group Inc
4100 Horizons Dr Ste 200 ... Columbus OH 43220 614 457 1530 401
Web: www.cfginc.net
Cambridge Hospital
1493 Cambridge St ... Cambridge MA 02139 617-665-1000 374-3
TF: 800-439-2370 ■ *Web:* www.challiance.org
Cambridge Innovations Inc
Cambridge Innovation Ctr
1 Broadway 14th Fl ... Cambridge MA 02142 617-758-4200 792
Web: cic.us
Cambridge International
105 Goodwill Rd ... Cambridge MD 21613 410-901-4979 901-4979 207
TF: 800-638-9560 ■ *Web:* www.cambridge-intl.com
Cambridge Isotope Laboratories Inc
3 Highwood Dr ... Tewksbury MA 01876 978-749-8000 749-2768 145
TF: 800-322-1174 ■ *Web:* www.isotope.com
Cambridge Lasers Inc 853 Brown Rd ... Fremont CA 94539 510-651-0110 535
Web: www.cambridgelasers.com
Cambridge Medical Ctr (CMC)
701 S Dellwood St ... Cambridge MN 55008 763-689-7700 374-3
TF: 800-252-4133 ■ *Web:* www.allinahealth.org
Cambridge Memorial Hospital
700 Coronation Blvd ... Cambridge ON N1R3G2 519-621-2330 740-4938 374-2
Web: www.cmh.org
Cambridge Meridian Group Inc
50 Church St Ste 50 ... Cambridge MA 02138 617-876-7400 194
Web: www.cambridgemeridian.com
Cambridge Metals & Plastics
500 S Cleveland ... Cambridge MN 55008 763-689-4800 697
Web: www.cmp-wwm.com
Cambridge Office for Tourism Inc
4 Brattle St Ste 208 ... Cambridge MA 02138 617-441-2884 206
Web: www.cambridgeusa.org
Cambridge Packing Company Inc
41-43 Foodmart Rd ... Boston MA 02118 617-269-6700 297-9
TF: 800-722-6726 ■ *Web:* www.cambridgepacking.com
Cambridge Pro Fab Inc
470 Franklin Blvd ... Cambridge ON N1R8G6 519-740-6033 518
Web: www.cambridgeprofab.com
Cambridge Public Library
449 Broadway ... Cambridge MA 02138 617-349-4040 434-3
TF: 800-327-5050 ■ *Web:* www.cambridgema.gov/cpl
Cambridge Realty Capital LLC
125 S Wacker Dr Ste 1800 ... Chicago IL 60606 312-357-1601 652
Web: www.cambridgecap.com
Cambridge Resources Corp
960 Alabama Ave ... Brooklyn NY 11207 718-927-0009 605-2
Web: www.cambridgeresources.com
Cambridge Savings Bank
1374 Massachusetts Ave ... Cambridge MA 02138 617-441-4155 520-5306* 70
**Fax:* Cust Svc ■ *TF:* 888-418-5626 ■ *Web:* cambridgesavings.com
Cambridge School of Culinary Arts
2020 Massachusetts Ave ... Cambridge MA 02140 617-354-2020 576-1963 163
Web: www.cambridgeculinary.com
Cambridge School of Weston
45 Georgian Rd ... Weston MA 02493 781-642-8650 622
Web: www.csw.org
Cambridge Silversmith Ltd
116 Lehigh Dr ... Fairfield NJ 07004 973-227-4400 227-5600 361
TF: 800-890-3366 ■ *Web:* www.cambridgesilversmiths.com
Cambridge Street Metal Corp (CSM)
82 Stevens St ... East Taunton MA 02718 508-822-2278 822-4667 492
TF: 800-254-7580 ■ *Web:* www.csmetal.net
Cambridge Suites Hotel Halifax
1583 Brunswick St ... Halifax NS B3J3P5 902-420-0555 420-9379 379
TF: 800-565-1263 ■ *Web:* www.cambridgesuiteshalifax.com
Cambridge Suites Hotel Toronto
15 Richmond St E ... Toronto ON M5C1N2 416-368-1990 601-3751 379
TF: 800-463-1990 ■ *Web:* www.cambridgesuitestoronto.com
Cambridge Technology Inc
25 Hartwell Ave ... Lexington MA 02421 781-541-1600 541-1601 472
TF: 800-342-3757 ■ *Web:* www.cambridgetechnology.com
Cambridge Trust Co
1336 Massachusetts Ave ... Cambridge MA 02138 617-876-5500 70
Web: cambridgetrust.com

Cambridge Valley Machining Inc
28 Perry Ln ... Cambridge NY 12816 518-677-5617 454
TF: 000-313-1021 ■ *Web:* www.cvmusa.com
Cambridge Viscosity Inc
101 Stn Landing ... Medford MA 02155 781-393-6500 203
Web: www.cambridgeviscosity.com
Cambridge Whos Who Publishing Inc
498 RXR Plaza ... Uniondale NY 11556 516-535-1515 535-1514 637-9
TF: 866-933-1555 ■ *Web:* cambridgewhoswho.com
Cambridgeport Air Systems
8 Fanaras Dr ... Salisbury MA 01952 978-465-8481 610
TF: 877-648-2872 ■ *Web:* www.cambridgeport.net
CambridgeSoft Corp
100 CambridgePark Dr ... Cambridge MA 02140 617-588-9100 588-9190 178-5
TF: 800-315-7300 ■ *Web:* www.cambridgesoft.com
CambridgeWorld 34 Franklin Ave ... Brooklyn NY 11205 718-858-5002 858-5437 119
TF: 800-221-2253 ■ *Web:* www.cambridgeworld.com
Cambro Manufacturing Co
5801 Skylab Rd ... Huntington Beach CA 92647 714-848-1555 842-3430* 300
**Fax:* Cust Svc ■ *TF:* 800-833-3003 ■ *Web:* www.cambro.com
CAMC Health System Inc
501 Morris St ... Charleston WV 25301 304-388-5432 353
Web: www.camc.org
Camcad Technologies Inc
5840 Red Bug Lake Rd Ste 175 ... Winter Springs FL 32708 407-327-4975 177
Web: www.camcadtech.com
Camco Chemical Co 8145 Holton Dr ... Florence KY 41042 859-727-3200 727-1508 151
TF Cust Svc: 800-354-1001 ■ *Web:* www.camco-chem.com
Camco Manufacturing Inc
121 Landmark Dr ... Greensboro NC 27409 800-334-2004 247
TF: 800-334-2004 ■ *Web:* www.camco.net
Camco Pacific Construction Company Inc
19712 MacArthur Blvd Ste 200 ... Irvine CA 92612 949-251-1300 186
Web: www.camcopacific.com
Camcor Partners Inc
525 Eigth Ave S W Ste 4080 ... Calgary AB T2P1G1 403-508-2950 401
Web: www.camcorpartners.com
Camcraft Inc 1080 Muirfield Dr ... Hanover Park IL 60133 630-582-6000 582-6019 621
Web: www.camcraft.com
Camden Central School District
51 Third St ... Camden NY 13316 315-245-2500 685
Web: www.camdenschools.org
Camden Children's Garden
3 Riverside Dr ... Camden NJ 08103 856-365-8733 365-8733 97
Web: www.camdenchildrensgarden.org
Camden County 117 N NC 343 PO Box 190 ... Camden NC 27921 252-338-1919 333-1603 338
Web: camdencountync.gov
Camden County 520 Market St Rm 102 ... Camden NJ 08102 856-225-5300 338
TF: 866-226-3362 ■ *Web:* www.camdencounty.com
Camden County 1 Court Cir Ste 3 ... Camdenton MO 65020 573-346-4440 338
TF: 800-781-0157 ■ *Web:* www.camdenmo.org
Camden County 200 E Fourth St ... Woodbine GA 31569 912-576-7395 576-5647 338
Web: www.co.camden.ga.us
Camden County Chamber of Commerce
2603 Osborne Rd Unit CC ... Saint Marys GA 31558 912-673-3101 673-3109 139
Web: www.camdenchamber.com
Camden County College
200 College Dr ... Blackwood NJ 08012 856-227-7200 374-4917 162
Web: www.camdencc.edu
Camden City 200 N Broadway PO Box 200 ... Camden NJ 08102 856-338-1817 162
Web: www.camdencc.edu
Camden County Health Services Ctr
425 Woodbury Turnersville Rd ... Blackwood NJ 08012 856-374-6600 450
Web: www.cchsc.com
Camden County Library 203 Laurel Rd ... Voorhees NJ 08043 856-772-1636 772-6105 434-3
TF: 877-222-3737 ■ *Web:* www.camdencountylibrary.org
Camden County Library District
89 Rodeo Rd PO Box 1320 ... Camdenton MO 65020 573-346-5954 346-1263 434-3
Web: www.ccld.us
Camden County Regional Chamber of Commerce
295 Rte 70 W ... Cherry Hill NJ 08002 856-667-1600 667-1464 139
Camden Hills State Park 280 Belfast Rd ... Camden ME 04843 207-236-3109 565
Web: www.maine.gov
Camden National Corp 2 Elm St ... Camden ME 04843 207-236-8821 236-6256 360-2
NYSE: CAC ■ *TF:* 800-860-8821 ■ *Web:* www.camdennational.com
Camden Property Trust
11 Greenway Plaza Ste 2400 ... Houston TX 77046 713-354-2500 354-2700* 655
NYSE: CPT ■ **Fax:* Mktg ■ *TF:* 800-922-6336 ■ *Web:* www.camdenliving.com
Camden Public Library (CPL) 55 Main St ... Camden ME 04843 207-236-3440 236-6673 434-3
TF: 800-562-2529 ■ *Web:* www.librarycamden.org
Camden Publications 331 E Bell St ... Camden MI 49232 517-368-0365 368-5131 532-4
TF: 800-222-6336 ■ *Web:* www.farmersadvance.com
Camden State Park 1897 County Rd ... Lynd MN 56157 507-865-4530 865-4608 565
Web: www.dnr.state.mn.us
Came Americas Automation LLC
11345 NW 122nd St ... Medley FL 33178 305-433-3307 358
Web: www.came-americas.com
Cameco Corp 2121 11th St W ... Saskatoon SK S7M1J3 306-956-6200 502
NYSE: CCO ■ *Web:* www.cameco.com
Camel Grinding Wheels 7525 N Oak Pk Ave ... Niles IL 60714 847-647-5994 1
Web: www.cgwheels.com
Camel Rock Casino 17486A Hwy 84/285 ... Santa Fe NM 87506 505-983-2667 982-2331 133
TF: 800-483-1040 ■ *Web:* www.camelrockcasino.com
Camelback Inn JW Marriott Resort Golf Club & Spa
5402 E Lincoln Dr ... Scottsdale AZ 85253 480-948-1700 669
TF: 800-242-2635 ■ *Web:* www.marriott.com
CAMELBACK MOUNTAIN 301 Resort Dr ... Tannersville PA 18372 570-629-1661 31
Web: www.skicamelback.com
Camelbeach Mountain Waterpark
309 Resort Dr ... Tannersville PA 18372 570-629-1662 32
Web: www.camelbeach.com
Camellia Foods
1300 Diamond Springs Rd ... Virginia Beach VA 23455 757-855-3371 345
Camellia Symphony Orchestra
1731 Howe Ave Ste 499 ... Sacramento CA 95825 916-929-6655 573-3
TF: 800-838-3006 ■ *Web:* www.camelliasymphony.org
Camelot Carpet Mills Inc
17111 Red Hill Ave ... Irvine CA 92614 949-474-4000 477-9218 131
Web: www.camelotcarpetmills.com

Phone | Fax | Class

Camelot Cleaners Co 8590 Frederick St ... Omaha NE 68124 402-393-5257 426
Web: camelotcleanersomaha.com

Camelot Community Care Inc
4910 D Creekside Dr ... Clearwater FL 33760 727-593-0003 595-0735 48-6
TF: 800-435-7352 ■ *Web:* www.camelotcommunitycare.org

Camelot Entertainment Group
300 Spectrum Center Dr Ste 400 ... Irvine CA 92618 949-754-3030 514
Web: www.camelotfilms.com

Camelot Homes
6607 N Scottsdale Rd Ste H100 ... Scottsdale AZ 85250 480-367-4300 652
Web: www.camelothomes.com

Cameo Personnel Systems Inc
440 S Main St ... Milltown NJ 08850 732-613-0088 260
Web: www.crsco.com

Camera Corner Inc PO Box 1899 ... Burlington NC 27216 336-228-0251 222-8011 119
TF: 800-868-2462 ■ *Web:* www.camcor.com

Camerican International Inc
45 Eisenhower Dr ... Paramus NJ 07652 201-587-0101 587-2040* 297-11
*Fax: Hum Res ■ *Web:* camerican.com

Cameron 1333 W Loop S Ste 1700 ... Houston TX 77027 713-513-3300 513-3320 537
NYSE: CAM ■ *Web:* cameron.slb.com

Cameron & Mittleman LLP
301 Promenade St ... Providence RI 02903 401-331-5700 445
Web: www.cm-law.com

Cameron Accounting & Financial Service
121 W Third St ... Cameron MO 64429 816-632-3786 251
Web: www.cameron-mo.com

Cameron Balloons US PO Box 3672 ... Ann Arbor MI 48106 734-426-5525 426-5026 28
TF: 866-423-6178 ■ *Web:* www.cameronballoons.com

Cameron Christopher Thomas Adv Inc
2901 Walnut St ... Denver CO 80205 303-531-7180 4

Cameron Construction
573 West 3560 South Ste 1 ... Salt Lake City UT 84115 801-268-3584 261
Web: www.cameronconst.com

Cameron County 20 E Fifth St ... Emporium PA 15834 814-486-2315 338
TF: 800-672-9435 ■ *Web:* www.pacourts.us

Cameron Engineering & Associates LLP
100 Sunnyside Blvd Ste 100 ... Woodbury NY 11797 516-827-4900 256
Web: www.cameronengineering.com

Cameron Glass Inc
3550 W Tacoma St ... Broken Arrow OK 74012 918-254-6000 252-4665 329
Web: www.camglass.com

Cameron Holdings Corp
1200 Prospect St ... La Jolla CA 92037 858-551-1335 551-1343 360-3
Web: www.cameron-holdings.com

Cameron Instruments Inc
173 Woolwich St ... Guelph ON N1H3V4 519-824-7111 358
TF: 888-863-8010 ■ *Web:* cameroninstruments.com

Cameron Mitchell Restaurants
390 W Nationwide Blvd ... Columbus OH 43215 614-621-3663 671
Web: www.cameronmitchell.com

Cameron Parish
148 Smith Cir PO Box 1280 ... Cameron LA 70631 337-775-5718 775-5567 338
Web: www.parishofcameron.net

Cameron Park Zoo 1701 N Fourth St ... Waco TX 76707 254-750-8400 750-8430 823
TF: 800-521-2660 ■ *Web:* www.cameronparkzoo.com

Cameron Smith & Associates Inc
3350 S Pinnacle Hills Pkwy Ste 101 ... Rogers AR 72758 479-271-6042 260
TF: 800-253-0750 ■ *Web:* www.csarecruiters.com

Cameron Thomson Group Ltd
390 Bay St Ste 1706 ... Toronto ON M5H2Y2 416-350-5009 350-5005 401
TF: 800-395-9943 ■ *Web:* www.cameronthomson.com

Cameron University 2800 W Gore Blvd ... Lawton OK 73505 580-581-2289 581-5514* 166
*Fax: Admissions ■ *TF Admissions:* 888-454-7600 ■ *Web:* www.cameron.edu

Cameron, Hodges, Coleman, LaPointe & Wright PA
111 N Magnolia Ave Ste 1350 ... Orlando FL 32801 407-841-5030 428
TF: 888-841-5030 ■ *Web:* www.cameronhodges.com

Cameron-cole LLC
200 E Government St Ste 100 ... Pensacola FL 32502 850-434-1011 196
Web: www.cameron-cole.com

Cameroon 22 E 73rd St ... New York NY 10021 212-794-2295 249-0533 784
Web: www.delecam.us

Cameroon Embassy
3400 International Dr NW ... Washington DC 20008 202-265-8790 387-3826 257
Web: www.cameroonembassyusa.org

Camesa Inc 1615 Spur 529 ... Rosenberg TX 77471 281-342-4494 253
TF: 800-866-0001 ■ *Web:* www.camesainc.com

Camex Equipment Sales & Rental Inc
1806 Second St ... Nisku AB T9E0W8 780-955-2770 539
TF: 877-955-2770 ■ *Web:* www.camex.ca

Camfour Inc
65 Wfield Industrial Park Rd ... Westfield MA 01085 413-564-2300 690

CAM-I (Consortium for Advanced Mfg International)
6836 Bee Cave Ste 256 ... Austin TX 78746 512-296-6872 49-13
Web: www.cam-i.org

Camie Campbell Inc
9225 Watson Ind Pk ... St. Louis MO 63126 314-968-3222 3
Web: www.camie.com

Camille Lightner Playhouse
1 Dean Porter Pk ... Brownsville TX 78520 956-542-8900 572
Web: camilleplayhouse.org

Camille's 1202 Simonton St ... Key West FL 33040 305-296-4811 671
TF: 800-869-4631 ■ *Web:* www.camilleskeywest.com

Camilles Restaurant 71 Bradford St ... Providence RI 02903 401-751-4812 671
Web: www.camillesonthehill.com

Camillus Octagon House
5420 W Genesee St ... Camillus NY 13031 315-488-7800 50-3
Web: octagonhouseofcamillus.org

Camin Cargo Control Inc 230 Marion Ave ... Linden NJ 07036 908-862-1899 523-0616* 743
*Fax: Hum Res ■ *Web:* www.camincargo.com

Camino Agave Inc 672 W FM 468 ... Cotulla TX 78014 830-393-1051 539
Web: www.caminoagave.com

Camino Modular Systems Inc
3175 Airway Dr ... Mississauga ON L4V1C2 416-936-5900 675-2424 360-3
Web: www.caminomodular.com

Camino Real El Paso 101 S El Paso St ... El Paso TX 79901 915-534-3050 534-3024 379
TF: 800-769-4300 ■ *Web:* www.caminoreal.com

Camino Real Foods Inc
2638 E Vernon Ave ... Vernon CA 90058 323-585-6599 585-5420 296-36
TF: 800-421-6201 ■ *Web:* www.caminorealkitchens.com

Camino Real Hotel LLC
2856 E Main St ... Eagle Pass TX 78852 830-757-8111 379

Cammenga Company LLC 2011 Bailey St ... Dearborn MI 48124 313-914-7160 807
Web: www.cammenga.com

Camnet Inc 3201 Fourth St NW ... Albuquerque NM 87107 505-761-4500 4
Web: camnet.us

Camosun College 3100 Foul Bay Rd ... Victoria BC V8P5J2 250-370-3018 162
Web: camosun.ca

Camosy Construction Inc
43451 N US Hwy 41 ... Zion IL 60099 847-395-6800 395-6891 186
Web: www.camosy.com

Camp Arrowhead 20 Arrowhead Rd ... Pittsford NY 14534 585-383-4590 239
Web: www.rochesterymca.org

Camp Butler National Cemetery
5063 Camp Butler Rd ... Springfield IL 62707 217-492-4070 492-4072 136
TF: 877-907-8585 ■ *Web:* www.cem.va.gov/cems/nchp/campbutler.asp

Camp Chewonki 485 Chewonki Neck Rd ... Wiscasset ME 04578 207-882-7323 239
Web: www.chewonki.org

CAMP Conferences Inc
540 W Frntage Rd Ste 2205 ... Northfield IL 60093 312-527-2800 239
Web: www.campconferences.com

Camp County 126 Church St ... Pittsburg TX 75686 903-856-2731 856-2309 338
Web: www.co.camp.tx.us

Camp Creek State Park
2390 Camp Creek Rd ... Camp Creek WV 25820 304-425-9481 565
Web: www.campcreekstatepark.com

Camp Drugstore 600 Ferguson ... Wood River IL 62095 618-254-6223 238

Camp Florence 4859 S Jetty Rd ... Florence OR 97439 541-997-2076 412
TF: 800-588-9003 ■ *Web:* oregon.gov

Camp Floyd/Stagecoach Inn State Park & Museum
18035 W 1540 N ... Fairfield UT 84013 801-768-8932 565
Web: www.stateparks.utah.gov

Camp Georgetown Correctional Facility
3191 Crumbhill Rd ... Georgetown NY 13072 315-837-4446 213

Camp Helen State Park
23937 Panama City Beach Pkwy ... Panama City Beach FL 32413 850-233-5059 236-3204 565
Web: www.floridastateparks.org

Camp Hilbert 5403 Monument Ave ... Richmond VA 23226 804-285-6500 239
Web: www.weinsteinjcc.org

Camp Hill Presbyterian Church
101 N 23rd St ... Camp Hill PA 17011 717-737-0488 48-20
Web: www.thechpc.org

Camp Lebanon 1205 Acorn Rd ... Burtrum MN 56318 320-573-2125 239
TF: 800-816-1502 ■ *Web:* camplebanon.org

Camp Moring & Cannon LLC
1418 Laurel St ... Columbia SC 29201 803-252-9375 2
Web: cmccpas.net

Camp Nelson National Cemetery
6980 Danville Rd ... Nicholasville KY 40356 859-885-5727 887-4860 136
TF: 800-827-1000 ■ *Web:* www.cem.va.gov

Camp Ocean Pines Inc 1473 Randall Dr ... Cambria CA 93428 805-927-0254 239
Web: campoceanpines.org

Camp Olympia 723 Olympia Dr ... Trinity TX 75862 936-594-2541 594-8143 297-8
TF: 800-735-6190 ■ *Web:* www.campolympia.com

Camp Oty'okwa
24799 Purcell Rd ... South Bloomingville OH 43152 740-385-5279 239
Web: campotyokwalodging.com

Camp Plymouth State Park
2008 Scout Camp Rd ... Ludlow VT 05149 802-228-2025 565
Web: www.vtstateparks.com

Camp Randall Stadium 1440 Monroe St ... Madison WI 53711 608-262-1866 720
Web: www.uwbadgers.com

Camp Rocky Point 1586 Hanna Dr ... Denison TX 75020 903-465-5270 239
Web: gsnetx.org

Camp Simcha 430 White Rd ... Glen Spey NY 12737 845-856-1432 239
TF: 888-756-1432 ■ *Web:* campsimcha.org

Camp Summit Boot Camp 2407 N 500 W ... La Porte IN 46350 219-874-9898 326-9218 412
Web: in.gov

Camp Sunshine 35 Acadia Rd ... Casco ME 04015 207-655-3800 239
Web: campsunshine.org

Camp Tawonga
131 Steuart St Ste 460 ... San Francisco CA 94105 415-543-2267 239
TF: 800-447-4475 ■ *Web:* tawonga.org

Camp Tillamook 6820 Barracks Cir ... Tillamook OR 97141 503-842-4243 842-1476 412
Web: www.oregon.gov

Camp Ventures LLC
280 Second St Ste 280 ... Los Altos CA 94022 650-949-0804 618-1719 792
Web: www.campventures.com

Campagne 1600 Post Alley ... Seattle WA 98101 206-728-2233 671
Web: cafecampagne.com

Campagnia 1185 E Champlain Dr ... Fresno CA 93720 559-433-3300 433-3066 671
Web: www.campagnia.net

Campaign Consultation Inc
2819 Saint Paul St ... Baltimore MD 21218 410-243-7979 194
Web: www.campaignconsultation.com

Campaign for Tobacco-Free Kids
1400 'I' St NW Ste 1200 ... Washington DC 20005 202-296-5469 296-5427 48-17
Web: www.tobaccofreekids.org

Campaign for Working Families (CWF)
PO Box 1222 ... Arlington VA 22206 703-671-8800 615
Web: www.cwfpac.com

Campaign Legal Ctr
1411 K St NW Ste 1400 ... Washington DC 20005 202-736-2200 736-2222 48-7
TF: 877-855-5007 ■ *Web:* www.campaignlegalcenter.org

Campaign Services Inc
117 N Saint Asaph St ... Alexandria VA 22314 703-684-3435 196
Web: campaignsolutions.com

Campania International
2452 Quakertown Rd ... Pennsburg PA 18073 215-541-4627 183
Web: www.campaniainternational.com

Campbell & Associates Inc
1923 Bailey Rd Ste A ... Cuyahoga Falls OH 44221 330-945-4117 727
TF: 800-233-4117 ■ *Web:* www.campbellsurvey.com

				Phone	Fax	Class
Campbell & George Co 1100 Industrial Rd Ste 12 — *TF:* 800-682-4224 ■ *Web:* cgco.com	San Carlos	CA	94070	650-654-5000		253
Campbell | Guin 2711 University Blvd — *Web:* www.campbellguin.com	Tuscaloosa	AL	35401	205-633-0200	633-0290	428
Campbell Blueprint & Supply Company Inc 3124 Broad Ave — *Web:* memphisreprographics.com	Memphis	TN	38112	901-327-7385		240
Campbell Chamber of Commerce 1628 W Campbell Ave — *Web:* campbellchamber.net	Campbell	CA	95008	408-378-6252	378-0192	139
Campbell Christian Schools 1075 E Campbell Ave — *TF:* 800-264-7955 ■ *Web:* www.campbellchristian.org	Campbell	CA	95008	408-370-4900		685
Campbell County 1635 Reata Dr — *TF:* 800-457-9312 ■ *Web:* www.ccgov.net	Gillette	WY	82718	307-682-0552	682-8418	338
Campbell County 570 Main St Ste A21 — *TF:* 800-238-1443 ■ *Web:* campbellcountytn.gov	Jacksboro	TN	37757	423-562-4985	566-3852	338
Campbell County 1098 Monmouth St Ste 204 — *TF:* 800-947-5161 ■ *Web:* www.campbellcountyky.org	Newport	KY	41071	859-292-3845		338
Campbell County 732 Village Hwy — *Web:* www.co.campbell.va.us	Rustburg	VA	24588	434-332-9517	332-9518	338
Campbell County Board of Education 101 Orchard Ln — *TF:* 800-942-3767 ■ *Web:* campbell.k12.ky.us	Alexandria	KY	41001	859-635-2173	448-2428	685
Campbell County Chamber of Commerce 314 S Gillette Ave — *TF:* 800-448-7801 ■ *Web:* www.gillettechamber.com	Gillette	WY	82716	307-682-3673	682-0538	139
Campbell County Dept of Education 172 Valley St — *Web:* www.campbell.k12.tn.us	Jacksboro	TN	37757	423-562-8377	566-7562	685
Campbell County Memorial Hospital 501 S Burma PO Box 3011 — **Fax:* Hum Res ■ *Web:* www.cchwyo.org	Gillette	WY	82717	307-688-1000	688-1516*	374-3
Campbell County Public Library 2101 S 4-J Rd — *Web:* ccgov.net/384/library	Gillette	WY	82718	307-682-3223	686-4009	434-3
Campbell County Public Library 684 Village Hwy PO Box 310 — *Web:* campbellcountylibraries.org	Rustburg	VA	24588	434-332-9560		434-3
Campbell Earl Construction Co 6060 Armour Dr	Houston	TX	77020	713-673-6208		188-8
Campbell Foundry Co 800 Bergen St — *Web:* www.campbellfoundry.com	Harrison	NJ	07029	973-483-5480	483-1843	307
Campbell Galt & Newlands Inc 700 NE Multnomah St Ste 1300 — *Web:* usinw.usi.biz	Portland	OR	97232	503-299-3403		390
Campbell Grinder Co 1226 Pontaluna Rd — *Web:* www.campbellgrinder.com	Spring Lake	MI	49456	231-798-6464	798-6466	261
Campbell Hausfeld A Scott Fetzer Co 100 Production Dr — *Web:* www.chpower.com	Harrison	OH	45030	513-367-4811		172
Campbell Historical Museum 51 N Central Ave — *Web:* www.ci.campbell.ca.us	Campbell	CA	95008	408-866-2757		520
Campbell Manufacturing Inc 127 E Spring St — *TF:* 800-523-0224 ■ *Web:* www.bakerwatersystems.com	Bechtelsville	PA	19505	610-367-2107	369-3580	595
Campbell Marketing & Communications 3200 Greenfield St Ste 280 — *Web:* www.campbellmarketing.com	Dearborn	MI	48120	313-336-9000		636
Campbell Printing Co 2017 Cleveland Hwy — *TF:* 866-828-5240 ■ *Web:* www.campbellprintingco.com	Dalton	GA	30721	706-259-3344		627
Campbell Rappold & Yurasits LLP 1033 S Cedar Crest Blvd — *Web:* crycpas.com	Allentown	PA	18103	610-435-7489		2
Campbell River & District Chamber of Commerce 900 Alder St Enterprise Ctr — *Web:* www.campbellriverchamber.ca	Campbell River	BC	V9W2P6	250-287-4636	286-6490	137
Campbell River Hospital 375 Second Ave — *Web:* www.viha.ca	Campbell River	BC	V9W3V1	250-850-2141		374-2
Campbell Scientific Inc 815 W 1800 N — *Web:* www.campbellsci.com	Logan	UT	84321	435-753-2342	750-9540	201
Campbell Sevey Inc 15350 Minnetonka Blvd — *Web:* www.campbell-sevey.com	Minnetonka	MN	55345	952-935-2345		789
Campbell Soup Co 1 Campbell Pl — *NYSE:* CPB ■ *TF:* 800-257-8443 ■ *Web:* www.campbellsoupcompany.com	Camden	NJ	08103	856-342-4800	342-3878	296-36
Campbell Union High School District 3235 Union Ave — *Web:* www.cuhsd.org	San Jose	CA	95124	408-371-0960		685
Campbell Union School District 155 N Third St — *Web:* www.campbellusd.org	Campbell	CA	95008	408-364-4200		685
Campbell University 450 Leslie Campbell Ave PO Box 546 — **Fax:* Admissions ■ *TF:* 800-334-4111 ■ *Web:* www.campbell.edu	Buies Creek	NC	27506	910-893-1290	893-1288*	166
Campbell University Norman Adrian Wiggins School of Law 113 Main St — *TF:* 800-334-4111	Buies Creek	NC	27506	910-893-1200		167-1
Campbell Wrapper Corp 1415 Fortune Ave — *TF:* 800-727-4210 ■ *Web:* www.campbellwrapper.com	De Pere	WI	54115	920-983-7100		547
Campbell's Resort 104 W Woodin Ave PO Box 278 — *TF:* 800-553-8225 ■ *Web:* www.campbellsresort.com	Chelan	WA	98816	509-682-2561	682-2177	669
Campbell-Ewald 2000 Brush St Ste 601 — *TF:* 800-438-7325 ■ *Web:* www.c-e.com	Detroit	MI	48226	586-574-3400		4
Campbellsport Bldg Supply Inc 227 W Main St PO Box 510 — *Web:* www.drexelteam.com	Campbellsport	WI	53010	920-533-4412	533-4333	191-3
Campbellsville University 1 University Dr — **Fax:* Admissions ■ *TF Admissions:* 800-264-6014 ■ *Web:* www.campbellsville.edu	Campbellsville	KY	42718	270-789-5000	789-5071*	166
Camperoo Inc 148 Townsend St — *TF:* 888-538-8809 ■ *Web:* www.camperoo.com	San Francisco	TX	94107	888-538-8809		387
Camperos Grill & Bar 2500 N Expy 77/83 — *Web:* camperosgrillandbar.com	Brownsville	TX	78521	956-546-8172		671
Campers Inn Inc 35 Robert Milligan Pkwy — *TF:* 800-524-8978 ■ *Web:* www.campersinn.com	Merrimack	NH	03054	603-883-1082		360-3
Campfire 40 Fulton St — *Web:* www.campfirenyc.com	New York	NY	10038	212-612-9600		121
Camphill Special School Inc 1784 Fairview Rd — *Web:* camphillspecialschool.org	Glenmoore	PA	19343	610-469-9236		685
Camphor Technologies Inc 1584 Independence Blvd — *Web:* www.camphortech.com	Sarasota	FL	34234	941-360-0025	360-0035	238
Campiello 1177 Third St S — *Web:* www.campiello.damico.com	Naples	FL	34102	239-435-1166		671
Camping Investigations 4427 N 27th Ave — *TF:* 800-862-8458 ■ *Web:* www.campingcompanies.com	Phoenix	AZ	85017	602-864-7860		400
Camping World RV Sales 8155 Rivers Ave — *TF:* 888-586-5446 ■ *Web:* rv.campingworld.com	Charleston	SC	29406	888-586-5446		791
Campino Restaurant 70 Jabez St	Newark	NJ	07105	973-589-4004		671
Campion College at the University of Regina 3737 Wascana Pkwy — *TF:* 800-667-7282 ■ *Web:* www.campioncollege.sk.ca	Regina	SK	S4S0A2	306-586-4242	359-1200	785
Campion Renewal Ctr 319 Concord Rd — *Web:* www.campioncenter.org	Weston	MA	02493	781-419-1337	894-5864	673
Campito Plumbing & Heating Inc 3 Hemlock St	Latham	NY	12110	518-785-0994		189-10
Campmor Inc 400 Corporate Dr PO Box 680 — *Web:* campmor.com	Mahwah	NJ	07430	201-335-9064		711
Campo do Fiori 205 S Mill St — *Web:* www.campodefiori.net	Aspen	CO	81611	970-920-7717		671
Campora Inc 2525 E Mariposa Rd — *Web:* www.campora.com	Stockton	CA	95213	209-466-8611		316
Campos Creative Works 1715 14th St — *Web:* www.ccwla.com	Santa Monica	CA	90404	310-453-1511		514
Campos Engineering Inc 7430 Greenville Ave — *Web:* www.camposengineering.com	Dallas	TX	75231	214-696-6291		256
Campos Market Research 216 Blvd Of The Allies — *Web:* www.campos.com	Pittsburgh	PA	15222	412-471-8484		196
Campton Place Restaurant 340 Stockton St — *Web:* www.camptonplacesf.com	San Francisco	CA	94108	415-955-5555		671
Campus Crusade for Christ International 100 Lake Hart Dr — *TF:* 888-278-7233 ■ *Web:* www.cru.org	Orlando	FL	32832	407-826-2500		48-20
Campus Federal Credit Union PO Box 98036 — **Fax Area Code:* 602 ■ *TF:* 888-769-8841 ■ *Web:* www.campusfederal.org	Baton Rouge	LA	70898	225-769-8841	659-2197*	219
Campus Inn & Suites 390 E Broadway	Eugene	OR	97401	541-343-3376	485-9392	379
Campus Media Group Inc 2 Appletree Sq 4th Fl — *Web:* www.campusmediagroup.com	Bloomington	MN	55425	952-854-3100		7
Campus Outreach 2200 Briarwood Way — *Web:* www.campusoutreach.org	Birmingham	AL	35243	205-776-5500		48-20
Campus Special LLC, The 3575 Koger Blvd Ste 300 — *TF:* 800-365-8520 ■ *Web:* www.campusspecial.com	Duluth	GA	30096	800-365-8520		195
Campus Televideo Inc 100 First Stamford Pl — *TF:* 866-615-8674 ■ *Web:* www.campustelevideo.com	Stamford	CT	06902	203-983-5400		116
Campus Text Inc 107 Forrest Ave — *Web:* campustext.com	Narberth	PA	19072	610-664-6900		96
Campus USA Credit Union PO Box 147029 — *TF:* 800-367-6440 ■ *Web:* www.campuscu.com	Gainesville	FL	32614	352-335-9090		219
Campus2careers Inc 4700 Guadalupe St Ste A342 — *TF:* 800-826-9972 ■ *Web:* www.campus2careers.com	Austin	TX	78751	512-354-7690		260
CampusCareerCenter Inc 110 Rockview St Ste 1 — *Web:* www.campuscareercenter.com	Boston	MA	02130	617-661-2613		260
Camron-Stanford House 1418 Lakeside Dr — *TF:* 800-545-2433 ■ *Web:* www.cshouse.org	Oakland	CA	94612	510-874-7802	874-7803	50-3
Camshaft Machine Co 717 Woodworth Rd — *Web:* www.camshaftmachine.com	Jackson	MI	49202	517-787-2040		247
Cam-Wal Electric Co-op Inc 404 W Scranton St PO Box 135 — *TF:* 800-269-7676 ■ *Web:* www.cam-walnet.com	Selby	SD	57472	800-269-7676		245
Can Corp of America Inc 326 June Ave — *Web:* www.cancorpam.com	Blandon	PA	19510	610-926-3044		124
Can Lines Engineering 9839 Downey Norwalk Rd PO Box 7039 — *TF:* 800-486-6074 ■ *Web:* www.canlines.com	Downey	CA	90241	562-861-2996	869-5293	207
Can Manufacturers Institute (CMI) 1730 Rhode Island Ave NW Ste 1000 — *Web:* www.cancentral.com	Washington	DC	20036	202-232-4677	232-5756	49-13
CANA (Cremation Assn of North America) 499 Northgate Pkwy — *TF:* 800-765-0107 ■ *Web:* www.cremationassociation.org	Wheeling	IL	60090	312-245-1077	321-4098	49-4
Canaan Printing Inc 4820 Jefferson Davis Hwy — *TF:* 800-332-3580 ■ *Web:* www.canaanprinting.net	Richmond	VA	23234	804-271-4820		627
Canaan Valley Resort & Conference Ctr 230 Main Lodge Rd — *TF:* 800-622-4121 ■ *Web:* www.canaanresort.com	Davis	WV	26260	304-866-4121		669
CANAC Inc 6505 Trans-Canada Hwy Ste 405 — *TF:* 800-588-4387 ■ *Web:* www.canac.com	St Laurent	QC	H4T1S3	514-734-4700	734-4850	650

	Phone	Fax	Class
Canaccord Genuity, Research Division Pacific Centre 609 Granville St Ste 2200 PO Box 10337 .... Vancouver BC V7Y1H2 *Web:* www.canaccordgenuity.com	604-643-7300		401
Canad Inns - Club Regent Casino Hotel 1415 Regent Ave W........................ Winnipeg MB R2C3B2 *TF:* 888-332-2623 ■ *Web:* www.canadinns.com	204-667-5560	667-5913	379
Canad Inns Fort Garry 1824 Pembina Hwy........................ Winnipeg MB R3T2G2 *TF:* 888-332-2623 ■ *Web:* www.canadinns.com	204-261-7450	261-5433	379
Canad Inns Garden City 2100 McPhillips St........................ Winnipeg MB R2V3T9 *TF:* 888-332-2623 ■ *Web:* www.canadinns.com	204-633-0024	697-3377	379
Canad Inns Polo Park 1405 St Matthews Ave .... Winnipeg MB R3G0K5 *TF:* 888-332-2623 ■ *Web:* www.canadinns.com	204-775-8791	783-4039	379
Canada 885 Second Ave 14th Fl................ New York NY 10017 *TF:* 800-267-8376 ■ *Web:* www.canadainternational.gc.ca	212-848-1100	848-1195	784
Consulate General 200 S Biscayne Blvd Ste 1600................ Miami FL 33131 *Web:* canadainternational.gc.ca	305-579-1600	346-2767	257
Consulate General 500 N Akard St Ste 2900..................... Dallas TX 75201 *TF:* 800-267-8376 ■ *Web:* www.canadainternational.gc.ca	214-922-9806		257
Consulate General 1251 Ave of the Americas Concourse Level.... New York NY 10020 *TF:* 800-267-8376 ■ *Web:* www.canadainternational.gc.ca	212-596-1628	596-1790	257
Consulate General 180 N Stetson Ave Ste 2400 .... Chicago IL 60601 *Web:* www.can-am.gc.ca/chicago	312-616-1860	616-1877	257
Consulate General 701 Fourth Ave S 9th Fl................. Minneapolis MN 55415 *Web:* www.canadainternational.gc.ca	612-333-4641	332-4061	257
Consulate General 1175 Peachtree St NE Ste 1700............... Atlanta GA 30361 *Web:* can-am.gc.ca	404-532-2000	532-2050	257
Embassy 501 Pennsylvania Ave NW .... Washington DC 20001 *TF:* 800-567-6868 ■ *Web:* can-am.gc.ca	202-682-1740	682-7726	257
Canada Agriculture Museum 901 Prince of Wales Dr.......................... Ottawa ON K2C3K1 *TF:* 866-442-4416 ■ *Web:* cafmuseum.techno-science.ca	613-991-3044	993-7923	520
Canada Alloy Casting Co 529 Manitou Dr .... Kitchener ON N2C1S2 *TF:* 800-276-6075 ■ *Web:* www.cac.ca	519-895-1161	895-1169	307
Canada Aviation Museum & Space Museum 11 Aviation Pkwy .... Ottawa ON K1K2X5 *Web:* casmuseum.techno-science.ca	613-993-2010	990-3655	520
Canada College 4200 Farm Hill Blvd .... Redwood City CA 94061 **Fax:* Admissions ■ *Web:* www.canadacollege.edu	650-306-3100	306-3113*	162
Canada Colors & Chemicals Ltd 175 Bloor St E Ste 1300 N Twr .... Toronto ON M4W3R8 *TF:* 800-461-1638 ■ *Web:* www.ccc-group.com	416-443-5500	449-9039	146
Canada Deposit Insurance Corp 50 O'Connor St 17th Fl.................... Ottawa ON K1P6L2 *TF:* 800-461-2342 ■ *Web:* www.cdic.ca	613-996-2081		509
Canada Economic Development 1255 Peel St Ste 900 .... Montreal QC H3B2T9 *Web:* www.dec-ced.gc.ca	514-283-2500		627
Canada Energy Partners Inc 595 Burrard St Ste 3123.................... Vancouver BC V6C3L6 *Web:* www.canadaenergypartners.com	604-909-1154		539
Canada Flowers 4073 Longhurst Ave..................... Niagara Falls ON L2E6G5 *TF:* 888-705-9999 ■ *Web:* www.canadaflowers.ca	905-354-2713		292
Canada Forgings Inc 130 Hagar St .... Welland ON L3B5P8 *TF:* 800-263-0440 ■ *Web:* www.canforge.com	905-735-1220		541
Canada Labour Congress 2841 Riverside Dr............................ Ottawa ON K1V8X7 *Web:* canadianlabour.ca	613-521-3400		414
Canada Life Assurance Co, The 330 University Ave .... Toronto ON M5G1R8 *TF:* 888-252-1847 ■ *Web:* www.canadalife.com	416-597-1456		391-4
Canada Media Fund 50 Wellington St E Ste 202.................... Toronto ON M5E1C8 *TF:* 877-975-0766 ■ *Web:* www.cmf-fmc.ca	416-214-4400		393
Canada Mortgage & Housing Corp 700 Montreal Rd.............................. Ottawa ON K1A0P7 *Web:* www.cmhc-schl.gc.ca	613-748-2000		509
Canada Olympic Hall of Fame & Museum 88 Canada Olympic Rd SW.................... Calgary AB T3B5R5 *Web:* www.winsport.ca	403-247-5452	286-7213	522
Canada Pipe Co 1757 Burlington St E PO Box 2849............ Hamilton ON L8H3L5 *Web:* www.canadapipe.com	905-547-3251	547-7369	492
Canada School of Public Service 373 Sussex Dr .... Ottawa ON K1N6Z2 *TF:* 866-703-9598 ■ *Web:* www.csps-efpc.gc.ca	819-953-5400		623
Canada Science & Technology Museum 2421 Lancaster Rd .... Ottawa ON K1G5A3 *TF:* 866-442-4416 ■ *Web:* cstmuseum.techno-science.ca/en	613-991-3044	990-3654	520
Canada Sportswear Corp 230 Barmac Dr.............................. North York ON M9L2Z3 *Web:* www.canadasportswear.com	416-740-8020		157-6
Canada's Sports Hall of Fame 169 Canada Olympic Rd SW................... Calgary AB T3B6B7 *Web:* www.sportshall.ca	403-776-1040		522
Canada-Israel Industrial Research & Development Foundation 371A Richmond Rd........................... Ottawa ON K2A0E7 *Web:* www.ciirdf.ca	972-971-0900		305
Canadel Furniture Inc 700 Canadel Ave........................... Louiseville QC J5V2L6 *Web:* www.canadel.com	819-228-8471	228-8389	319-2
Canadian Academy of Sport Medicine (CASM) 55 Metcalfe St Ste 300........................ Ottawa ON K1P6L5 *TF:* 877-585-2394 ■ *Web:* casem-acmse.org	613-748-5851	912-0128	49-8
Canadian Advanced Technology Alliance 388 Albert St................................ Ottawa ON K1R5B2 *Web:* www.cata.ca	613-236-6550		138

	Phone	Fax	Class
Canadian American Restoration Supplies 2600 Bond St .... Rochester Hills MI 48309 *Web:* www.catsfastferry.com	248-227-7462		54
Canadian Architectural Certification Board 1 Nicholas St Ste 710............................ Ottawa ON K1N7B7 *Web:* cacb.ca/en/home	613-241-8399	241-7991	48-1
Canadian Assn of Emergency Physicians (CAEP) 1785 Alta Vista Dr Ste 104 .... Ottawa ON K1G3Y6 *TF:* 800-463-1158 ■ *Web:* www.caep.ca	613-523-3343	523-0190	49-8
Canadian Association of Petroleum Producers 350 - Seventh Ave S W Ste 2100 .... Calgary AB T2P3N9 *Web:* www.capp.ca	403-267-1100		78
Canadian Automobile Assn (CAA) 2151 Thurston Dr.............................. Ottawa ON K1G6C9 *TF:* 800-267-8713 ■ *Web:* www.caa.ca	613-820-1890	247-0118	48-23
Canadian Bank Note Company Ltd (CBNC) 145 Richmond Rd............................ Ottawa ON K1Z1A1 *Web:* www.cbnco.com	613-722-3421		627
Canadian Bar Assn 500-865 Carling Ave.......... Ottawa ON K1S5S8 *TF:* 800-267-8860 ■ *Web:* www.cba.org	613-237-2925	237-0185	138
Canadian Bearings Ltd 1600 Drew Rd......................... Mississauga ON L5S1S5 *TF:* 800-229-2327 ■ *Web:* www.canadianbearings.com	905-670-6700	670-0459	385
Canadian Breast Cancer Foundation 375 University Ave Ste 301.................... Toronto ON M5G2J5 *TF:* 800-387-9816 ■ *Web:* www.cbcf.org	416-815-1313		303
Canadian Broadcasting Corp (CBC) PO Box 3220 .... Ottawa ON K1Y1E4 *Web:* www.cbc.radio-canada.ca	514-597-6000		643
Canadian Cancer Society 55 St Clair Ave W Ste 300 .... Toronto ON M4V2Y7 *Web:* www.cancer.ca	416-961-7223		138
Canadian Centre for Architecture 1920 Baile St .... Montreal QC H3H2S6 *Web:* cca.qc.ca	514-939-7000	939-7020	520
Canadian Chamber of Commerce 360 Albert St Ste 420.......................... Ottawa ON K1R7X7 *Web:* www.chamber.ca	613-238-4000	238-7643	137
Canadian Chamber of Commerce Montreal Office 1155 University St Ste 709.................. Montreal QC H3B3A7 *Web:* www.chamber.ca	514-866-4334	866-7296	137
Canadian Chamber of Commerce Toronto Office 55 University Ave Ste 901.................... Toronto ON M5J2H7 *Web:* www.chamber.ca	416-868-6415	868-0189	137
Canadian College of Naturopathic Medicine 1255 Sheppard Ave E.......................... Toronto ON M2K1E2 *TF:* 866-241-2266 ■ *Web:* www.ccnm.edu	416-498-1255		785
Canadian Council for International Co-op (CCIC) 450 Rideau St Ste 200 .... Ottawa ON K1N5Z4 *Web:* www.ccic.ca	613-241-7007	241-5302	48-5
Canadian County 201 N Choctaw St............. El Reno OK 73036 *Web:* www.canadiancounty.org	405-262-1070	422-2411	338
Canadian Dental Association 1815 Alta Vista Dr.............................. Ottawa ON K1G3Y6 *TF:* 866-521-2322 ■ *Web:* www.cda-adc.ca	613-523-7114	523-7736	48-1
Canadian Electricity Association 66 Slater St................................... Ottawa ON K1P5H1 *Web:* www.electricity.ca	613-230-9263		138
Canadian Enerdata Ltd 86 Ringwood Dr Ste 201.................... Stouffville ON L4A1C3 *Web:* www.enerdata.com	905-642-8167		194
Canadian Federation of Humane Societies (CFHS) 30 Concourse Gate Ste 102 .... Ottawa ON K2E7V7 *TF:* 888-678-2347 ■ *Web:* cfhs.ca	613-224-8072		48-3
Canadian Finance & Leasing Association 15 Toronto St .... Toronto ON M5C2E3 *TF:* 877-213-7373 ■ *Web:* www.cfla-acfl.ca	416-860-1133		138
Canadian Fishing Co Foot of Gore Ave.......................... Vancouver BC V6A2Y7 *Web:* www.canfisco.com	604-681-0211	681-3277	285
Canadian Football Hall of Fame & Museum 58 Jackson St W.......................... Hamilton ON L8P1H4 *Web:* www.cfhof.ca	905-528-7566	528-9781	522
Canadian Football League 50 Wellington St E 3rd Fl .... Toronto ON M5E1C8 *TF:* 855-264-4242 ■ *Web:* www.cfl.ca	416-322-9650	322-9651	715-2
Canadian Forest Products Ltd 5162 Northwood Pulp Mill Rd PO Box 9000 .... Prince George BC V2L4W2 **Fax Area Code:* 250 ■ **Fax:* Acctg ■ *Web:* www.canfor.com	604-661-5241	962-3473*	638
Canadian Forestry Accreditation Board 18 Pommel Crescent .... Kanata ON K2M1A2 *Web:* www.cfab.ca	613-599-7259	599-8107	48-1
Canadian Golf Hall of Fame & Museum 1333 Dorval Dr Ste 1 .... Oakville ON L6M4X7 *TF:* 800-263-0009 ■ *Web:* www.rcga.org	905-849-9700	845-7040	522
Canadian Health Libraries Assn (CHLA) 39 River St .... Toronto ON M5A3P1 *TF:* 800-321-1433 ■ *Web:* www.chla-absc.ca	416-646-1600	646-9460	49-11
Canadian Home Income Plan Corp 1090 Pender St W......................... Vancouver BC V6E2N7 *Web:* www.chip.ca	604-685-2447		403
Canadian Honker 1203 Second St SW .... Rochester MN 55902 *TF:* 800-634-8277 ■ *Web:* canadianhonker.com	507-282-6572		671
Canadian Hospital Specialties ULC 2810 Coventry Rd.......................... Oakville ON L6H6R1 *TF:* 800-461-1423 ■ *Web:* www.chsltd.com	905-825-9300		475
Canadian Imperial Bank of Commerce (CIBC) 199 Bay St Commerce Ct W .... Toronto ON M5L1A2 *NYSE:* CM ■ *TF:* 800-465-2422 ■ *Web:* www.cibc.com	800-465-2422		70
Canadian Industrial Distributors Inc 175 Sun Pac Blvd.......................... Brampton ON L6S5Z6	905-595-0411		96

Name / Address	City	State	Postal	Phone	Fax	Class
Canadian Information Processing Society (CIPS) 5090 Explorer Dr Ste 001 — TF: 877-275-2477 ■ Web: www.cips.ca	Mississauga	ON	L4W4T9	905-602-1370	602-7884	48-1
Canadian Institute, The 1329 Bay St — Web: www.canadianinstitute.com	Toronto	ON	M5R2C4	416-927-7936		387
Canadian Kennel Club (CKC) 200 Ronson Dr Ste 400 — TF: 800-250-8040 ■ Web: www.ckc.ca	Etobicoke	ON	M9W5Z9	416-675-5511	675-6506	48-3
Canadian Library Assn (CLA) 328 Frank St	Ottawa	ON	K2P0X8	613-232-9625	563-9895	49-11
Canadian Livestock Insurance 480 University Ave Ste 412 — TF: 800-727-1502 ■ Web: www.cdnlivestock.ca	Toronto	ON	M5G1V2	416-510-8191	510-8186	391-1
Canadian Living Magazine 25 Sheppard Ave W Ste 100 — TF: 800-387-6332 ■ Web: www.canadianliving.com	Toronto	ON	M2N6S7	416-733-7600		457-11
Canadian Manufacturers & Exporters 1 Nicholas St Ste 1500 — Web: www.cme-mec.ca	Ottawa	BC	K1N7B7	613-238-8888		138
Canadian Medical Assn (CMA) 1867 Alta Vista Dr — TF: 800-663-7336 ■ Web: www.cma.ca	Ottawa	ON	K1G5W8	613-731-9331		49-8
Canadian Memorial Chiropractic College 6100 Leslie St — TF: 800-463-2923 ■ Web: www.cmcc.ca	Toronto	ON	M2H3J1	416-482-2340		785
Canadian Mental Health Association 8 King St E Ste 810 — TF: 800-616-8816 ■ Web: www.cmha.ca	Toronto	ON	M5C1B5	416-484-7750		138
Canadian Museum of Civilization 100 Laurier St — TF: 800-555-5621 ■ Web: historymuseum.ca	Gatineau	QC	K1A0M8	819-776-7000	776-8300	520
Canadian Museum of Flight 5333 216th St Hngr Ste 3 — Web: www.canadianflight.org	Langley	BC	V2Y2N3	604-532-0035	532-0056	520
Canadian Museum of Nature 240 McLeod St — *Fax: Mktg ■ TF: 800-263-4433 ■ Web: www.nature.ca	Ottawa	ON	K2P2R1	613-566-4700	364-4021*	520
Canadian Museum of Rail Travel 57 Van Horne St S PO Box 400 — Web: www.crowsnest.bc.ca/cmrt	Cranbrook	BC	V1C4H9	250-489-3918	489-5744	520
Canadian Musical Reproduction Rights Agency Ltd The 56 Wellesley St W Ste 320 — Web: www.cmrra.ca	Toronto	ON	M5S2S3	416-926-1966		138
Canadian Musician CM 4056 Dorchester Rd Ste 202 — *Fax Area Code: 888 ■ TF: 800-363-6336 ■ Web: www.canadianmusician.com	Niagara Falls	ON	L2E6M9	905-374-8878	665-1307*	457-9
Canadian National Railway Co 935 Rue de la Gauchetiere O — TSE: CNR ■ TF: 888-668-4626 ■ Web: www.cn.ca	Montreal	QC	H3B2M9	888-888-5909		648
Canadian Natural Resources Ltd (CNRL) 855 Second St SW Ste 2500 — NYSE: CNQ ■ TF: 888-878-3700 ■ Web: www.cnrl.com	Calgary	AB	T2P4J8	403-517-6700	517-7350	536
Canadian Pacific Railway Co 401 9 Ave SW Ste 500 — *Fax Area Code: 800 ■ *Fax: Hum Res ■ TF: 888-333-6370 ■ Web: www.cpr.ca	Calgary	AB	T2P4Z4	403-319-7000	704-3000*	648
Canadian Parks & Recreation Assn (CPRA) 1180 Walkley Rd PO Box 83069 — Web: www.cpra.ca	Ottawa	ON	K1V2M5	613-523-5315		48-23
Canadian Parks & Wilderness Society (CPAWS) 250 City Ctr Ave Ste 506 — TF: 800-333-9453 ■ Web: www.cpaws.org	Ottawa	ON	K1R6K7	613-569-7226	569-7098	48-13
Canadian Payroll Association 250 Bloor St E — TF: 800-387-4693 ■ Web: www.payroll.ca	Toronto	ON	M4W1E6	416-487-3380		138
Canadian Peregrine Foundation 25 Crouse Rd Unit 20 — TF: 888-709-3944 ■ Web: www.peregrine-foundation.ca	Toronto	ON	M1R5P8	416-481-1233	481-7158	48-3
Canadian Press Ltd, The 36 King St E — Web: www.thecanadianpress.com	Toronto	ON	M5C2L9	416-364-0321		532-3
Canadian Professional Sales Association 310 Front St W Ste 800 — TF: 888-267-2772 ■ Web: www.cpsa.com	Toronto	ON	M5V3B5	416-408-2685		196
Canadian Real Estate Investment Trust (CREIT) 175 Bloor St E Ste 500 — TSE: REF.UN ■ Web: www.creit.ca	Toronto	ON	M4W3R8	416-628-7771	628-7777	654
Canadian Seed Growers' Association 240 Catherine St — Web: www.seedgrowers.ca	Ottawa	ON	K2P2G8	613-236-0497		138
Canadian Society of Customs Brokers 55 Murray St Ste 320 — TF: 800-668-6870 ■ Web: cscb.ca	Ottawa	ON	K1N5M3	613-562-3543		138
Canadian Solar Solutions Inc 545 Speedvale Ave W — Web: canadiansolar.com	Guelph	ON	N1K1E6	519-954-2057		253
Canadian Southern Baptist Seminary 200 Seminary View — TF: 877-922-2727 ■ Web: www.csbs.ca	Cochrane	AB	T4C2G1	403-932-6622	932-7049	167-3
Canadian Tire Corp Ltd 2180 Yonge St PO Box 770 Stn K — TSE: CTC ■ TF: 800-387-8803 ■ Web: www.corp.canadiantire.ca	Toronto	ON	M4P2V8	416-480-3000	544-7715	185
Canadian Tool & Die Ltd 1331 Chevrier Blvd — TF: 800-204-4150 ■ Web: www.canadiantool.com	Winnipeg	MB	R3T1Y4	204-453-6833		757
Canadian Urban Institute 555 Richmond St W — Web: www.canurb.org	Toronto	ON	M5T3A3	416-365-0816		194
Canadian Utilities Ltd 1400 909 - 11th Ave SW — TSE: CU ■ Web: www.canadianutilities.com	Calgary	AB	T2R1N6	403-292-7500	292-7532	787
Canadian Valley Electric Co-op 11277 S 356 PO Box 751 — TF: 877-382-3680 ■ Web: www.canadianvalley.org	Seminole	OK	74868	405-382-3680		245
Canadian Valley Technology Ctr 6505 E US Hwy 66 — Web: www.cvtech.edu	El Reno	OK	73036	405-262-2629		507
Canadian Veterinary Medical Assn (CVMA) 339 Booth St — TF: 800-567-2862 ■ Web: canadianveterinarians.net	Ottawa	ON	K1R7K1	613-236-1162	236-9681	49-8
Canadian Warplane Heritage Museum 9280 Airport Rd — TF: 800-555-8775 ■ Web: www.warplane.com	Mount Hope	ON	L0R1W0	905-679-4183		522
Canadian Water Resources Assn (CWRA) 9 Corvus Ct — Web: www.cwra.org	Ottawa	ON	K2E7Z4	613-237-9363		48-13
Canadian Western Bank 10303 Jasper Ave Ste 3000 — TSE: CWB ■ Web: www.cwbank.com	Edmonton	AB	T5J3X6	780-423-8888		70
Canadian Wildlife Federation (CWF) 350 Michael Cowpland Dr — TF: 800-563-9453 ■ Web: www.cwf-fcf.org	Kanata	ON	K2M2W1	613-599-9594	599-4428	48-13
CanaDream Corp 2510 27 St NE — TF: 800-461-7368 ■ Web: www.canadream.com	Calgary	AB	T1Y7G1	403-291-1000		121
Canal Barge Company Inc 835 Union St — TF: 800-467-6941 ■ Web: www.canalbarge.com	New Orleans	LA	70112	504-581-2424	584-1505	314
Canal Insurance Co 400 E Stone Ave PO Box 7 — TF: 800-452-6911 ■ Web: canalinsurance.com	Greenville	SC	29601	800-452-6911		391-4
Canal Park Lodge 250 Canal Pk Dr — TF: 800-777-8560 ■ Web: www.canalparklodge.com	Duluth	MN	55802	218-279-6000		379
Canal Park Stadium 300 S Main St — TF: 888-223-6000 ■ Web: www.milb.com	Akron	OH	44308	330-253-5151		720
Canal Wood LLC 2430 Main St — TF: 866-587-1460 ■ Web: www.canalwood.com	Conway	SC	29526	843-488-9663		448
Canaletto 3355 Las Vegas Blvd S — TF: 866-659-9643 ■ Web: www.venetian.com	Las Vegas	NV	89109	702-414-1000	414-1100	671
CanAm Coal Corp 1201-5th St SW Ste 202 — Web: www.canamcoal.com	Calgary	AB	T2R0Y6	403-262-3797		501
Canam Group Inc 11535 First Ave Bureau 500 — TSE: CAM ■ TF: 877-499-6049 ■ Web: groupecanam.com/en	Saint-Georges	QC	G5Y7H5	418-228-8031		723
Can-am Plumbing Inc 151 Wyoming St — TF: 800-786-9797 ■ Web: www.canamplumbing.com	Pleasanton	CA	94566	925-846-1833		610
Canamax Energy Ltd 324 - Eighth Ave SW Ste 610 — Web: www.canamaxenergy.ca	Calgary	AB	T2P2Z2	587-349-5186		536
Canamould Extrusions Inc 101a Roytec Rd — TF: 866-874-6762 ■ Web: www.canamould.com	Woodbridge	ON	L4L8A9	905-264-4436		499
Canandaigua City School District 143 N Pearl St — Web: www.canandaiguaschools.org	Canandaigua	NY	14424	585-396-3700		685
Canandaigua Inn on the Lake 770 S Main St — TF: 800-228-2801 ■ Web: www.theinnonthelake.com	Canandaigua	NY	14424	585-394-7800	394-5003	379
Canandaigua Lake State Marine Park 620 S Main St — Web: parks.ny.gov/parks/3/details.aspx	Canandaigua	NY	14424	315-789-2331		565
Canandaigua National Corp 72 S Main St — OTC: CNND ■ Web: www.cnbank.com	Canandaigua	NY	14424	585-394-4260		70
Canandaigua Wine Company Inc 235 N Bloomfield Rd — TF: 888-659-7900 ■ Web: www.cbrands.com	Canandaigua	NY	14424	585-396-7600		80-3
Canara Inc 2077 Convention Center Concourse Ste 425 — Web: www.canara.com	Atlanta	GA	30337	415-462-8950	532-2384	253
Canard Aerospace Corp 250 Fuller St S Ste 201 — Web: www.canardaero.com	Shakopee	MN	55379	952-944-7990		256
Canarie 45 O'Connor St Ste 500 — TF: 800-959-5525 ■ Web: www.canarie.ca	Ottawa	ON	K1P1A4	613-943-5454	943-5443	48-9
Canary Hotel 31 W Carrillo — TF: 866-999-5401 ■ Web: www.canarysantabarbara.com	Santa Barbara	CA	93101	805-884-0300	884-8153	379
Canary Marketing Inc 600 San Ramon Vly Blvd Ste 200 — Web: www.canarymarketing.com	Danville	CA	94526	925-314-1888		195
Canatal Industries Inc 2885 Boul Frontenac E — Web: www.canatal.com	Thetford Mines	QC	G6G6P6	418-338-6044		105
Canaudit Inc 2139 Tapo St Ste 206 — Web: www.canaudit.com	Simi Valley	CA	93063	805-583-3723		194
Canaveral National Seashore 212 S Washington Ave — Web: www.nps.gov/cana	Titusville	FL	32796	321-267-1110	264-2906	564
Canberra Corp 3610 Holland Sylvania Rd — TF: 800-832-8992 ■ Web: www.canberracorp.com	Toledo	OH	43615	419-841-6616	841-7597	151
Canberra Industries Inc 800 Research Pkwy — TF Sales: 800-243-3955 ■ Web: www.canberra.com	Meriden	CT	06450	203-238-2351	235-1347	472
Can-Blast Inc 755 Wallace Rd Unit 3 — Web: www.can-blast.com	North Bay	ON	P1B8K4	705-474-3431	476-7643	268
Canby School District 1130 S Ivy — Web: www.canby.k12.or.us	Canby	OR	97013	503-266-7861	266-0022	685
Cancap Pharmaceutical Ltd 13111 Vanier Pl Unit 180 — TF: 877-998-2378 ■ Web: www.cancappharma.com	Richmond	BC	V6V2J1	604-278-2188	278-2210	231
Cancer Care Inc 275 Seventh Ave 22nd Fl — TF: 800-813-4673 ■ Web: www.cancercare.org	New York	NY	10001	212-712-8400	712-8495	48-17
Cancer Care Ontario 620 University Ave — Web: www.cancercare.on.ca	Toronto	ON	M5G2L7	416-971-9800		743
Cancer Genetics Inc Meadows Office Complex 201 Rt 17 N 2nd Fl — TF: 888-334-4988 ■ Web: www.cancergenetics.com	Rutherford	NJ	07070	201-528-9200		231
Cancer Letter PO Box 9905 — Web: www.cancerletter.com	Washington	DC	20016	202-362-1809	379-1787	531-8
Cancer Research Ctr of Hawaii University of Hawaii 1236 Lauhala St — Web: www.uhcancercenter.org	Honolulu	HI	96813	808-586-3010		668

Name / Address	City	State	Zip	Phone	Fax	Class
Cancun Grill 15406 NW 77th Ct. Web: cancungrillmiamilakes.com	Miami	FL	33016	305-826-8571		671
Cancun Mexican Restaurant 201 N Gloster St. Web: cancunmexicantupelo.com	Tupelo	MS	38804	662-842-9557		671
Candela Controls Inc 751 Business Park Blvd Ste 101. Web: www.candelacontrols.com	Winter Garden	FL	34787	407-654-2420		362
Candela Corp 530 Boston Post Rd. NASDAQ: CLZR ■ TF: 800-733-8550 ■ Web: syneron-candela.com	Wayland	MA	01778	508-358-7400	358-5602	424
Candelas 416 Third Ave Web: www.candelas-sd.com	San Diego	CA	92101	619-702-4455		671
Candelis Inc 18821 Bardeen Ave. Web: www.candelis.com	Irvine	CA	92612	949-852-1000		415
Candid Color Systems Inc 1300 Metropolitan Ave TF: 800-336-4550 ■ Web: www.candid.com	Oklahoma City	OK	73108	405-947-8747	951-7353	588
Candid Litho Printing Ltd 25-11 Hunters Point Web: www.candidlitho.com	Long Island	NY	11101	212-431-3800		344
Candlelight Cabinetry Inc 24 Michigan St Web: www.candlelightcab.com	Lockport	NY	14094	716-434-6543	434-6748	115
Candlelighters Childhood Cancer Foundation 10920 Connecticut Ave Suuite A PO Box 498 TF: 800-366-2223 ■ Web: www.acco.org	Kensington	MD	20895	301-962-3520	962-3521	48-17
Candler County 705 N Lewis St.	Metter	GA	30439	912-685-2835	685-4823	338
Candler Hospital 5353 Reynolds St TF: 800-622-6877 ■ Web: www.sjchs.org	Savannah	GA	31405	912-819-6000		374-3
Candlesticks Inc 112 W 34th St Ste 901	New York	NY	10120	212-947-8900		155-4
Candlewest Systems Group Ltd 4400 Dominion St Unit 100 Web: www.encorebusiness.com	Burnaby	BC	V5G4G3	604-737-8570		525
Candlewick Press Inc 99 Dover St Web: www.candlewick.com	Somerville	MA	02144	617-661-3330	661-0565	637-2
Can-do Promotions Inc 6517 Wise Ave NW. TF: 800-325-7981 ■ Web: www.candopromo.com	North Canton	OH	44720	800-325-7981		184
Cando Railway Services Ltd 740 Rosser Ave Fl 4 TF: 866-989-5310 ■ Web: www.candoltd.com	Brandon	MB	R7A0K9	204-725-2627		650
Candoris Technologies LLC 9 E Main St. Web: www.candoris.com	Annville	PA	17003	717-228-1600		196
Candy & Schonwald Pllc 3116 Live Oak St Web: cscpa.com	Dallas	TX	75204	214-826-6660		2
Candy Bouquet International Inc 510 Mclean St TF: 877-226-3901 ■ Web: www.candybouquet.com	Little Rock	AR	72202	501-375-9990	375-9998	123
Candy Express 3320 Greencastle Rd. Web: candyexpress.com	Burtonsville	MD	20866	301-384-5889		123
Cane Creek Cycling Components 355 Cane Creek Rd. TF: 800-234-2725 ■ Web: www.canecreek.com	Fletcher	NC	28732	828-684-3551	684-1057	82
Cane Creek State Park 50 State Pk Rd TF: 888-287-2757 ■ Web: www.arkansasstateparks.com	Star City	AR	71667	870-628-4714		565
Cane River Creole National Historical Park 400 Rapides Dr. Web: www.nps.gov/cari	Natchitoches	LA	71457	318-356-8441	352-4549	564
Caneel Bay Inc North Shore Rd. Web: www.caneelbay.com	Cruz Bay	VI	00831	340-776-6111		378
Can-Eng Furnaces International Ltd 6800 Montrose Rd PO Box 628 Web: www.can-eng.com	Niagara Falls	ON	L2E6V5	905-356-1327		610
Canerector Inc 1 Sparks Ave. Web: www.canerector.com	North York	ON	M2H2W1	416-225-6240		490
Caney Fork Electric Co-op Inc 920 Smithville Hwy PO Box 272. TF: 888-505-3030 ■ Web: www.caneyforkec.com	McMinnville	TN	37110	931-473-3116	473-4939	245
Caney Valley Electric Co-op Assn Inc, The 401 Lawrence St PO Box 308 TF: 800-310-8911 ■ Web: www.caneyvalley.com	Cedar Vale	KS	67024	620-758-2262	758-2926	245
Canfield & Tack Inc 925 Exchange St TF General: 800-836-0861 ■ Web: www.canfieldtack.com	Rochester	NY	14608	585-235-7710		627
Canfield Connector Div 8510 Foxwood Ct TF: 800-554-5071 ■ Web: www.canfieldconnector.com	Youngstown	OH	44514	800-554-5071		201
Canfield Equipment Service 21533 Mound Rd TF: 800-637-3956 ■ Web: www.canfieldequipment.com	Warren	MI	48091	586-757-2020		57
Canfield Scientific Inc 253 Passaic Ave Web: www.canfieldsci.com	Fairfield	NJ	07004	973-276-0336		179
Cangene Corp 155 Innovation Dr. TSE: CNJ ■ Web: www.cangene.com	Winnipeg	MB	R3T5Y3	204-275-4200		85
Cangro Industries Long Island Transmission Co 495 Smith St. TF: 800-422-9210 ■ Web: www.cangroindustries.com	Farmingdale	NY	11735	631-454-9000	454-9155	620
Canidium LLC 3801 Kirby Dr, S456 TF: 877-651-1837 ■ Web: www.canidium.com	Houston	TX	77024	877-651-1837		196
Caniglia's Venice Inn 6920 Pacific St Web: canigliasveniceinn.com	Omaha	NE	68106	402-556-3111		671
Canine Companions for Independence Inc (CCI) 2965 Dutton Ave PO Box 446 TF: 800-572-2275 ■ Web: www.cci.org	Santa Rosa	CA	95402	707-577-1700		48-17
Canine Country Club Kennel & Pet Resort, The 33306 Tract 43 Rd. Web: www.caninecountryclub.com	Los Fresnos	TX	78566	505-898-0725		794
Canisius College 2001 Main St *Fax: Admissions ■ TF: 800-843-1517 ■ Web: www.canisius.edu	Buffalo	NY	14208	716-888-2200	888-3230*	166
Cankdeska Cikana Community College PO Box 269 TF: 888-783-1463 ■ Web: www.littlehoop.edu	Fort Totten	ND	58335	701-766-4415	766-4077	165
Canlan Ice Sports Corp 6501 Sprott st TF: 800-709-1838 ■ Web: www.icesports.com	Burnaby	BC	V5B3B8	604-736-9152		354
Canlis Restaurant 2576 Aurora Ave N Web: www.canlis.com	Seattle	WA	98109	206-283-3313		671
CAN-med Healthcare 200 Bluewater Rd. TF: 800-565-7553 ■ Web: www.canmedhealthcare.com	Bedford	NS	B4B1G9	902-455-4649		475
Cannagrow Holdings Inc 8101 E Prentice Ave Ste 500. Web: cannagrowholdings.com	Greenwood Village	CO	80111	720-486-5309		45
Cannella Response Television LLC 492 N Pine St Web: www.drtv.com	Burlington	WI	53105	262-763-4810		195
Cannery Casino & Hotel, The Cannery Casino Resorts LLC 2121 E Craig Rd. TF: 866-999-4899 ■ Web: www.cannerycasino.com	North Las Vegas	NV	89030	702-507-5700		379
Cannon & Co 5605 Murray Ave Web: www.cannoncpa.com	Memphis	TN	38119	901-761-1710		734
Cannon & Dunphy Sc 595 N Barker Rd. Web: www.cannon-dunphy.com	Brookfield	WI	53045	262-780-7188		428
Cannon & Wendt Electric Co 4020 N 16th St Web: www.cannon-wendt.com	Phoenix	AZ	85016	602-279-1681	230-8464	189-4
Cannon Air Force Base 110 Alison Ave Ste 1150 TF: 877-283-3858 ■ Web: www.cannon.af.mil	Cannon AFB	NM	88103	575-784-4131	784-8101	497-1
Cannon Building Svc Inc 1640 Sierra Madre Cir Web: www.cannonbuilding.com	Placentia	CA	92870	714-630-9570		256
Cannon Cochran Management Services Inc 2 E Main St Towne Centre Bldg Ste 208 TF: 800-252-5059 ■ Web: www.ccmsi.com	Danville	IL	61832	217-446-1089		463
Cannon Constructors Inc 17000 Ventura Blvd Ste 301 Web: www.cannongroup.com	Encino	CA	91316	818-906-6200	906-6220	189-9
Cannon County 200 W Main St Web: www.cannontn.com	Woodbury	TN	37190	615-563-4278		338
Cannon Design 2170 Whitehaven Rd. Web: www.cannondesign.com	Grand Island	NY	14072	716-773-6800	773-5909	261
Cannon Equipment Co 15100 Business Pkwy. Web: www.cannonequipment.com	Rosemount	MN	55068	651-322-6300		233
Cannon Instrument Co 2139 High Tech Rd Web: www.cannoninstrument.com	State College	PA	16803	814-353-8000		653
Cannon IV Inc 950 Dorman St Web: www.cannon4.com	Indianapolis	IN	46202	317-951-0500		179
Cannon Marketing Inc 4684 US Hwy 70 W. TF: 800-952-5913 ■ Web: www.1cmi.com	Kinston	NC	28504	252-527-3361		665
Cannon Muskegon Corp 2875 Lincoln St TF: 800-253-0371 ■ Web: cannonmuskegon.com	Muskegon	MI	49441	231-755-1681	755-4975	485
Cannon Sports Inc 11614 Pendleton St TF: 800-929-0959 ■ Web: www.cannonsports.com	Sun Valley	CA	91352	818-683-1000		711
Cannon Wright Blount Pllc 756 Ridge Lake Blvd Ste 100 Web: www.cannonwrightblount.com	Memphis	TN	38120	901-685-7500		2
Cannonball Advertising & Promotion 8251 Maryland Ave Ste 200 Web: www.cannonballagency.com	Saint Louis	MO	63105	314-445-6400		7
Canny Bowen Inc 400 Madison Ave Ste 11-D. Web: www.cannybowen.com	New York	NY	10017	212-949-6611		266
Cano Container Corp 3920 Enterprise Ct Web: www.canocontainer.com	Aurora	IL	60504	630-585-7500		100
Cano Corp 225 Industrial Rd. TF: 800-447-3462 ■ Web: www.canocorp.com	Fitchburg	MA	01420	978-342-0953		286
Cano Petroleum Inc 6500 N Belt Line Rd Ste 200. OTC: CANOQ	Irving	TX	75063	214-687-0030		536
Canoe 4199 Paces Ferry Rd NW Web: www.canoeatl.com	Atlanta	GA	30339	770-432-2663		671
Canoe Bay PO Box 28 Web: www.canoebay.com	Chetek	WI	54728	715-924-4594		379
Canoe Creek State Park 205 Canoe Creek Rd. Web: www.dcnr.state.pa.us	Hollidaysburg	PA	16648	814-695-6807		565
Canoe Island Lodge 3820 Lakeshore Dr TF: 800-234-0265 ■ Web: www.canoeislandlodge.com	Diamond Point	NY	12824	518-668-5592	668-2012	669
Canoe-Picnic Point State Park 36661 Cedar Pt State Pk Dr Web: parks.ny.gov/parks/64/details.aspx	Clayton	NY	13624	315-654-2522		565
Canoga Park/West Hills Chamber of Commerce 7248 Owensmouth Ave. TF: 800-843-5678 ■ Web: www.cpwhchambcr.org	Canoga Park	CA	91303	818-884-4222		139
Canoga Perkins Corp 20600 Prairie St TF Tech Supp: 800-360-6642 ■ Web: www.canoga.com	Chatsworth	CA	91311	818-718-6300	718-6312	173-3
Canon Business Solutions-Central 425 N Martingale Rd Ste 100 TF: 844-443-4636 ■ Web: csa.canon.com	Schaumburg	IL	60173	847-706-3400		112
Canon City Chamber of Commerce 403 Royal Gorge Blvd. TF: 800-876-7922 ■ Web: www.canoncity.com	Canon City	CO	81212	719-275-2331		139
Canon Information Technology Services Inc 850 Greenbrier Cir Web: www.cits.canon.com	Chesapeake	VA	23320	757-579-7100		196
Canon Law Society of America (CLSA) 3025 Fourth St NE Ste 111. TF: 800-452-5110 ■ Web: www.clsa.org	Washington	DC	20017	202-832-2350	832-2331	48-20
Canon Recruiting Group LLC 26531 Summit Cir Web: www.canonrecruiting.com	Santa Clarita	CA	91350	661-252-7400		260
Canonsburg General Hospital 100 Medical Blvd Web: ahn.org	Canonsburg	PA	15317	724-745-6100	873-5876	374-3
Canoochee Electric Membership Corp 342 E Brazell St TF: 800-342-0134 ■ Web: www.canoocheeemc.com	Reidsville	GA	30453	800-342-0134		245

Name / Address	City	State	Zip	Phone	Fax	Class
Canopach Inc 48 Wall St 11th Fl *Web:* www.canopach.com	New York	NY	10005	347-694-7809		463
Canopies Party Rental 7234 N 60th St *Web:* canopiesevents.com	Milwaukee	WI	53223	414-760-0770		62
Canplas Industries Ltd 500 Veterans Dr *TF:* 800-461-1771 ■ *Web:* www.canplas.com	Barrie	ON	L4M4V3	705-726-3361		605-2
Canpotex Ltd 111 Second Ave S Ste 400 PO Box 1600 *Web:* www.canpotex.com	Saskatoon	SK	S7K3R7	306-931-2200	653-5505	146
Canron Construction Inc 4600 NE 138th Ave *Web:* supremegroup.com	Portland	OR	97230	503-255-8634	253-3907	189-14
Cansec Systems Ltd 3105 Unit 9 *TF:* 877-545-7755 ■ *Web:* www.cansec.com	Mississauga	ON	L5L4L2	905-820-2404		693
Canso Islands National Historic Site 1465 Union St *Web:* www.pc.gc.ca/eng/lhn-nhs/ns/canso/index.aspx	Canso	NS	B0E1B0	902-366-3136	295-3496	563
Canson Inc 21 Industrial Dr *Web:* www.cansonstudio.com	South Hadley	MA	01075	413-538-9250		43
CanTalk (Canada) Inc 70 Arthur St Ste 250 *TF:* 800-480-9686 ■ *Web:* www.cantalk.com	Winnipeg	MB	R3B1G7	800-480-9686		768
Canteen Service Co 712 Industrial Dr *TF:* 800-467-2471 ■ *Web:* www.canteenatyourservice.com	Owensboro	KY	42301	270-683-2471		299
Canteen Vending Services *Compass Group* 2400 Yorkmont Rd *TF:* 800-357-0012 ■ *Web:* www.compass-usa.com	Charlotte	NC	28217	704-328-4000		299
Cantel Medical Corp 150 Clove Rd 9th Fl *NYSE: CMN* ■ *TF:* 800-714-4152 ■ *Web:* www.cantelmedical.com	Little Falls	NJ	07424	973-890-7220	890-7270	476
Cantella & Company Inc 28 State St 40th Fl *Web:* www.cantella.com	Boston	MA	02109	617-521-8630		390
Canter & Assoc LLC 12975 Coral Tree Pl *TF Cust Svc:* 800-669-9011 ■ *Web:* www.canter.net	Los Angeles	CA	90066	310-578-4700	301-7512	766
Canterbury Designs 5632 W Washington Blvd *TF:* 800-935-7111 ■ *Web:* www.canterburyintl.com	Los Angeles	CA	90016	323-936-7111	936-7115	153
Canterbury Health Facility 1720 Knowles Rd	Phenix City	AL	36869	334-291-0485		450
Canterbury Park Holding Corp 1100 Canterbury Rd *NASDAQ: CPHC* ■ *TF:* 800-340-6361 ■ *Web:* www.canterburypark.com	Shakopee	MN	55379	952-445-7223		642
Canterbury School 101 Aspetuck Ave *Web:* www.cbury.org	New Milford	CT	06776	860-210-3800		622
Canterbury Shaker Village 288 Shaker Rd *Web:* www.shakers.org	Canterbury	NH	03224	603-783-9511		520
CANTEX Inc 202 Progress Rd *TF:* 800-257-5288 ■ *Web:* www.cantexinc.com	Auburndale	FL	33823	817-215-7000	215-7001	596
Cantey Hanger LLP 600 W Sixth St Ste 300 *Web:* www.canteyhanger.com	Fort Worth	TX	76102	817-877-2863		226
Cantina Italiana 346 Hanover St *Web:* www.cantinaitaliana.com	Boston	MA	02113	617-723-4577	723-6357	671
Cantler's Riverside Inn 458 Forest Beach Rd *Web:* www.cantlers.com	Annapolis	MD	21409	410-757-1311	757-6784	671
Canton Chamber of Commerce 45525 Hanford Rd *Web:* www.cantonchamber.com	Canton	MI	48187	734-453-4040	453-4503	139
Canton Chinese Buffet 1118 NE 78th St	Vancouver	WA	98665	360-576-8699		671
Canton Drop Forge Inc 4575 Southway St SW *TF:* 800-446-7404 ■ *Web:* www.cantondropforge.com	Canton	OH	44706	330-477-4511	477-2046	483
Canton Food Co 750 S Alameda St *Web:* www.cantonfoodco.com	Los Angeles	CA	90021	213-688-7707		297-8
Canton Grill 2610 SE 82nd Ave *Web:* canton-grill.com	Portland	OR	97266	503-774-1135		671
Canton Group, The 2920 Odonnell St *Web:* cantongroup.com	Baltimore	MD	21224	410-675-5708		177
Canton Inn Restaurant 947 N Pk Dr *Web:* cantoninnevansville.com	Evansville	IN	47710	812-428-6611		671
Canton Palace Theatre 605 Market Ave N *Web:* www.cantonpalacetheatre.org	Canton	OH	44702	330-454-8172	454-8171	572
Canton Public Library 1200 S Canton Ctr Rd *TF:* 888-988-6300 ■ *Web:* www.cantonpl.org	Canton	MI	48188	734-397-0999	397-1130	434-3
Canton Public School District 403 Lincoln St *Web:* www.cantonschools.net	Canton	MS	39046	601-859-4110		685
Canton Regional Chamber of Commerce 222 Market Ave N *TF:* 800-533-4302 ■ *Web:* www.cantonchamber.org	Canton	OH	44702	330-456-7253	452-7786	139
Canton Symphony Orchestra 1001 Market Ave N *Web:* www.cantonsymphony.org	Canton	OH	44702	330-452-3434	452-4429	573-3
Canton Twp Historical Museum 1022 N Canton Ctr Rd *Web:* www.cantonhistoricalsociety.org	Canton	MI	48187	734-397-0088		522
Canton/Stark County Convention & Visitors Bureau 222 Market Ave N *TF:* 800-552-6051 ■ *Web:* www.visitcanton.com	Canton	OH	44702	330-454-1439	456-3600	206
Cantor & Cantor CPA'S 31550 Northwestern Hwy	Farmington Hills	MI	48334	248-851-0664		2
Cantor Colburn LLP 22nd Fl 20 Church St *Web:* www.cantorcolburn.com	Hartford	CT	06103	860-286-2929		428
Cantor Fitzgerald Canada Corp 181 University Ave Ste 1500 *Web:* www.cantor.com	Toronto	ON	M5H3M7	416-350-5212		401
Cantor Fitzgerald LP 499 Pk Ave *Web:* www.cantor.com	New York	NY	10022	212-938-5000		690
Cantrell 1400 S Bradford St *Web:* www.cantrell.com	Gainesville	GA	30503	770-536-3611		296
Cantu Pest Control 323 Industrial Blvd Ste C *Web:* cantupestcontrol.com	Mckinney	TX	75069	972-562-9999		192
Cantwell Maria (Sen D - WA) 511 Hart Senate Office Bldg *Web:* www.cantwell.senate.gov	Washington	DC	20510	202-224-3441	228-0514	342-2
Canusa Hershman Recycling Co 45 NE Industrial Rd *Web:* www.chrecycling.com	Branford	CT	06405	203-488-0887		660
Canvas Products Co 274 S Waterman St *TF:* 877-293-1669 ■ *Web:* www.canvaspc.com	Detroit	MI	48209	313-496-1000		733
Canvas Specialty PO Box 22268 *TF:* 800-894-3801 ■ *Web:* www.can-spec.com	Los Angeles	CA	90040	323-722-1156		733
Canweb Internet Services 1086 Modeland Rd *TF:* 877-422-6932 ■ *Web:* www.canweb.ca	Sarnia	ON	N7S6L2	519-332-6900		180
CanWel Building Materials Group Ltd 609 Granville St Ste 1100 *Web:* www.canwel.com	Vancouver	BC	V7Y1G6	604-432-1400		364
CanWest DHI 660 Speedvale Ave W *TF:* 800-549-4373 ■ *Web:* www.canwestdhi.com	Guelph	ON	N1K1E5	519-824-2320		743
Canwest Propane Partnership 1700 440 - Second Ave SW *Web:* www.canwestpropane.com	Calgary	AB	T2P5E9	403-206-4100		580
Canyon Air Service Inc 416 S Vermont Ave *Web:* canyonair.com	Glendora	CA	91741	626-335-1116	914-1088	610
Canyon Casino 131 Main St *Web:* www.canyoncasino.com	Black Hawk	CO	80422	303-777-1111		133
Canyon Chamber of Commerce 1518 Fifth Ave *TF:* 800-999-9481 ■ *Web:* www.canyonchamber.org	Canyon	TX	79015	806-655-7815	655-4608	139
Canyon Concert Ballet 1031 Conifer St *Web:* www.ccballet.org	Fort Collins	CO	80524	970-472-4156		573-1
Canyon County 1115 Albany St *Web:* www.canyonco.org	Caldwell	ID	83605	208-454-7300	454-7525	338
Canyon Creek Cabinet Co 16726 Tye St SE *TF:* 800-228-1830 ■ *Web:* www.canyoncreek.com	Monroe	WA	98272	360-348-4973	348-4810	115
Canyon Creek Travel Inc 333 W Campbell Rd Ste 440 *TF:* 800-952-1998 ■ *Web:* www.canyoncreektravel.com	Richardson	TX	75080	972-238-1998		775
Canyon de Chelly National Monument PO Box 588 *Web:* www.nps.gov	Chinle	AZ	86503	928-674-5500	674-5507	564
Canyon Explorations Inc 675 W Clay Ave *TF:* 800-654-0723 ■ *Web:* www.canyonexplorations.com	Flagstaff	AZ	86001	928-774-4559	774-4655	536
Canyon Graphics Inc 6680 Cobra Way *TF:* 800-435-5544 ■ *Web:* www.canyongraphics.com	San Diego	CA	92121	858-646-0444		344
Canyon Marketing and Media POBox 2223 *Web:* www.canyoninternational.com	Folsom	CA	95763	916-933-3026		5
Canyon Ranch 165 Kemble St *TF Resv:* 800-742-9000 ■ *Web:* www.canyonranch.com	Lenox	MA	01240	413-637-4100	637-0057	669
Canyon Ranch SpaClub at the Venetian 3355 Las Vegas Blvd S Ste 1159 *TF:* 877-220-2688 ■ *Web:* www.canyonranch.com	Las Vegas	NV	89109	702-414-3606		707
Canyon Ranch Tucson 8600 E Rockcliff Rd *TF:* 800-742-9000 ■ *Web:* www.canyonranch.com	Tucson	AZ	85750	520-749-9000	749-1646	669
Canyon Ridge Christian Church 6200 W Lone Mtn Rd *Web:* www.canyonridge.org	Las Vegas	NV	89130	702-658-2722		48-20
Canyon Specialty Foods Inc 11035 Switzer Ave	Dallas	TX	75238	214-352-1771		297-8
Canyon State Wireless 8 Corral Rd	Sierra Vista	AZ	85635	520-458-4772		647
Canyon Tax & Bookkeeping Service 22342 Avenida Empresa Ste 280 *Web:* canyontax.com	Rancho Santa Margarita	CA	92688	949-888-2829		734
Canyonlands National Park 2282 SW Resource Blvd *TF:* 800-394-9978 ■ *Web:* www.nps.gov/cany	Moab	UT	84532	435-719-2313	719-2300	564
Canyonville Christian Academy 250 E First St *Web:* www.canyonville.net	Canyonville	OR	97417	541-839-4401	839-6228	622
CAO Group Inc 4628 Skyhawk Dr *TF:* 877-877-9778 ■ *Web:* www.caogroup.com	West Jordan	UT	84084	801-256-9282	256-9287	419
CAOT (Canadian Assn of Occupational Therapists) 1125 Colonel By Dr *TF:* 800-434-2268 ■ *Web:* www.caot.ca	Ottawa	ON	K1S5R1	613-523-2268		48-1
CAP (College of American Pathologists) 325 Waukegan Rd *TF:* 800-323-4040 ■ *Web:* www.cap.org	Northfield	IL	60093	847-832-7000	832-8168	49-8
CAP (Children Awaiting Parents Inc) 595 Blossom Rd Ste 306 *TF:* 888-835-8802 ■ *Web:* www.capbook.org	Rochester	NY	14610	585-232-5110	232-2634	48-6
CAP Barbell Inc 10820 Westpark *Web:* www.capbarbell.com	Houston	TX	77042	713-977-3090		711
CAP Index Inc 150 John Robert Thomas Dr The Commons at Lincoln C *TF:* 800-378-6777 ■ *Web:* capindex.com	Exton	PA	19341	610-903-3000		196
Cap n Cork 1031 Broadway *Web:* www.capncork.com	Fort Wayne	IN	46802	260-423-1496		443
Cap Rock Telephone Co-op Inc PO Box 300 *Web:* www.caprock-spur.com	Spur	TX	79370	806-271-3336		736
Cap's 4325 Myrtle St *Web:* www.capsonthewater.com	Saint Augustine	FL	32084	904-824-8794		671
Cap's Place Island Restaurant 2765 NE 28th Ct *Web:* www.capsplace.com	Lighthouse Point	FL	33064	954-941-0418		671
Cap*Rock Winery 408 E Woodrow Rd *TF:* 800-687-5236 ■ *Web:* www.caprockwinery.com	Lubbock	TX	79423	806-686-4452		50-7

Phone | Fax | Class

Capax Global LLC
590 Headquarters Plaza ... Morristown NJ 07960 | 973-401-0660 | | 225
TF: 888-682-8900 ■ *Web:* www.capaxglobal.com

Capco Inc 1328 Winters Ave ... Grand Junction CO 81501 | 970-243-8750 | | 268
Web: www.capcoinc.com

Capco LLC 1349 Arcadia Dr ... Columbus IN 47201 | 812-375-1700 | | 488

Capcom USA Inc 800 Concar Dr Ste 300 ... San Mateo CA 94402 | 650-350-6500 | 350-6657 | 178-6
Web: www.capcom.com

Capdevila at Lateresita
3248 W Columbus Dr ... Tampa FL 33607 | 813-879-9704 | | 671
Web: www.lateresitarestaurant.com

Cape & Island Kitchens Inc
99 State Rd Rte 3A ... Sagamore Beach MA 02562 | 508-888-4762 | | 362
Web: capekitchens.com

Cape Air 660 Barnstable Rd ... Hyannis MA 02601 | 508-771-6944 | 227-3247* | 25
**Fax Area Code:* 800 ■ *TF:* 800-227-3247 ■ *Web:* www.capeair.com

Cape Ann Chamber of Commerce
33 Commercial St ... Gloucester MA 01930 | 978-283-1601 | 283-4740 | 139
Web: capeannchamber.com

Cape Arago State Park Cape Arago Hwy ... Coos Bay OR 97420 | 541-888-3778 | | 565
TF: 800-551-6949 ■ *Web:* www.oregonstateparks.org

Cape Blanco State Park
39745 S Hwy 101 ... Port Orford OR 97465 | 541-332-6774 | | 565
Web: www.oregonstateparks.org

Cape Breton Post
255 George St PO Box 1500 ... Sydney NS B1P6K6 | 902-564-5451 | 564-6280 | 532-1
Web: www.capebretonpost.com

Cape Breton Regional Library
50 Falmouth St ... Sydney NS B1P6X9 | 902-562-3279 | 564-0765 | 436
TF: 800-565-8161 ■ *Web:* cbrl.ca

Cape Breton University
1250 Grand Lake Rd ... Sydney NS B1P6L2 | 902-539-5300 | 562-0119 | 785
TF: 888-959-9995 ■ *Web:* www.cbu.ca

Cape Christian Academy
10 Oyster Rd ... Cape May Court House NJ 08210 | 609-465-4132 | | 148
Web: capechristianacademy.com

Cape Cod Canal Regional Chamber of Commerce
70 Main St ... Buzzards Bay MA 02532 | 508-759-6000 | 759-6965 | 139
TF: 888-332-2732 ■ *Web:* www.capecodcanalchamber.org

Cape Cod Chamber of Commerce
5 Shoot Flying Hill Rd ... Centerville MA 02632 | 508-362-3225 | 362-3698 | 139
TF: 888-332-2732 ■ *Web:* www.capecodchamber.org

Cape Cod Children's Museum
577 Great Neck Rd S ... Mashpee MA 02649 | 508-539-8788 | | 521
Web: www.capecodchildrensmuseum.org

Cape Cod Coast Guard Air Station
2300 Wilson Blvd Ste 500 ... Arlington VA 20598 | 202-372-4620 | | 158
TF: 877-669-8724 ■ *Web:* uscg.mil/d1/airstacapecod

Cape Cod Community College
2240 Iyanough Rd ... West Barnstable MA 02668 | 508-362-2131 | 375-4089* | 162
**Fax:* Admissions ■ *TF:* 877-846-3672 ■ *Web:* www.capecod.edu

Cape Cod Five Cents Savings Bank
532 Rte 28 PO Box 20 ... Harwich Port MA 02646 | 508-430-0400 | 430-0403 | 70
TF: 800-678-1855 ■ *Web:* www.capecodfive.com

Cape Cod Hospital 27 Pk St ... Hyannis MA 02601 | 508-771-1800 | | 374-3
TF: 800-545-5014 ■ *Web:* www.capecodhealth.org/capecodhospital

Cape Cod Irish Village 822 Rt 28 ... S.Yarmouth MA 02664 | 508-771-0100 | | 379
Web: www.capecod-irishvillage.com

Cape Cod Life Magazine
13 Steeple St Ste 204 PO Box 1439 ... Mashpee MA 02649 | 508-419-7381 | 477-1225 | 457-22
TF: 800-698-1717 ■ *Web:* www.capecodlife.com

Cape Cod Lumber Co Inc
225 Groveland St ... Abington MA 02351 | 781-878-0715 | 871-6726 | 364
Web: capecodlumber.com

Cape Cod Maritime Museum
135 S St PO Box 443 ... Hyannis MA 02601 | 508-775-1723 | 775-1706 | 520
Web: www.capecodmaritimemuseum.org

Cape Cod Museum of Natural History
869 Main St ... Brewster MA 02631 | 508-896-3867 | 896-8844 | 520
Web: www.ccmnh.org

Cape Cod Potato Chip Co
100 Breed's Hill Rd ... Hyannis MA 02601 | 508-775-3358 | | 296-35
TF: 888-881-2447 ■ *Web:* www.capecodchips.com

Cape Cod Regional Transit Authority (CCRTA)
215 Iyannough Rd PO Box 1988 ... Hyannis MA 02601 | 508-775-8504 | 775-8513 | 468
TF: 800-352-7155 ■ *Web:* www.capecodtransit.org

Cape Cod Shipbuilding Co
7 Narrows Rd PO Box 152 ... Wareham MA 02571 | 508-295-3550 | 295-3551 | 90
Web: www.capecodshipbuilding.com

Cape Cod Times 319 Main St ... Hyannis MA 02601 | 508-775-1200 | 771-3292* | 532-2
**Fax:* Edit ■ *TF:* 800-451-7887 ■ *Web:* www.capecodonline.com

Cape Codder Resort & Spa
1225 Iyanough Rd Rt 132 Bearse's Way ... Hyannis MA 02601 | 508-771-3000 | | 669
TF: 888-297-2200 ■ *Web:* www.capecodderresort.com

Cape Coral Plumbing Inc
5812 Enterprise Pkwy ... Fort Myers FL 33905 | 239-693-4714 | | 189-10
Web: capecoralplumbing.com

Cape Design Engineering Co
191 Center St Ste 201 ... Cape Canaveral FL 32920 | 321-799-2970 | | 256
Web: www.cdeco.com

Cape Disappointment State Park
PO Box 488 ... Ilwaco WA 98624 | 360-642-3078 | | 565
Web: capedisappointment.org

Cape Electronics 19 Dupont Ave ... South Yarmouth MA 02664 | 508-394-2405 | | 54
Web: capeelectronics.com

Cape Fear Botanical Garden
536 N Eastern Blvd PO Box 53485 ... Fayetteville NC 28301 | 910-486-0221 | 486-4209 | 97
Web: capefearbg.org

Cape Fear Community College
411 N Front St ... Wilmington NC 28401 | 910-362-7000 | 362-7080* | 162
**Fax:* Admissions ■ *Web:* www.cfcc.edu

Cape Fear Hospital
5301 Wrightsville Ave ... Wilmington NC 28403 | 910-452-8100 | | 374-3
Web: www.nhrmc.org

Cape Fear Valley Medical Ctr (CFVMC)
1638 Owen Dr PO Box 2000 ... Fayetteville NC 28304 | 910-609-4000 | | 374-3
Web: www.capefearvalley.com

Cape Fox Corp PO Box 8558 ... Ketchikan AK 99901 | 907-225-5163 | | 194
Web: www.capefoxcorp.com

Cape Gazette
17585 Nassau Commons Blvd PO Box 213 ... Lewes DE 19958 | 302-645-7700 | 645-1664 | 532-4
Web: capegazette.villagesoup.com

Cape Girardeau Area Chamber of Commerce
1267 N Mt Auburn Rd ... Cape Girardeau MO 63701 | 573-335-3312 | 335-4686 | 139
Web: www.capechamber.com

Cape Girardeau Convention & Visitors Bureau
400 Broadway Ste 100 ... Cape Girardeau MO 63701 | 573-335-1631 | 334-6702 | 206
TF: 800-777-0068 ■ *Web:* www.visitcape.com

Cape Girardeau County
1 Barton Sq Ste 301 ... Jackson MO 63755 | 573-243-3547 | 204-2418 | 338
TF: 800-392-8222 ■ *Web:* www.capecounty.us

Cape Girardeau Public Library
711 N Clark St ... Cape Girardeau MO 63701 | 573-334-5279 | 334-8334 | 434-3
TF: 800-800-5123 ■ *Web:* www.capelibrary.org

Cape Hatteras Electric Co-op
47109 Light Plant Rd PO Box 9 ... Buxton NC 27920 | 252-995-5616 | 995-4088 | 245
TF: 800-454-5616 ■ *Web:* www.chec.coop

Cape Hatteras National Seashore
1401 National Pk Dr ... Manteo NC 27954 | 252-473-2111 | 473-2595 | 564
Web: www.nps.gov/caha

Cape Henlopen State Park
42 Cape Henlopen Dr ... Lewes DE 19958 | 302-645-8983 | | 565
Web: www.destateparks.com

Cape Henry Associates Inc
1206 Laskin Rd Ste 100 ... Virginia Beach VA 23451 | 757-502-7424 | | 463
Web: www.cape-henry.com

Cape Henry Lighthouse
583 Atlantic Ave ... Fort Story VA 23459 | 757-422-9421 | | 50-3

Cape Jourimain Nature Centre Inc
5039 Route 16 ... Bayfield NB E4M3Z8 | 506-538-2220 | | 138
Web: www.capejourimain.ca

Cape Krusenstern National Monument
PO Box 1029 ... Kotzebue AK 99752 | 907-442-3890 | 442-8316 | 564
Web: www.nps.gov/cakr

Cape Lookout National Seashore
131 Charles St ... Harkers Island NC 28531 | 252-728-2250 | 728-2160 | 564
Web: www.nps.gov

Cape Lookout State Park
13000 Whiskey Creek Rd W ... Tillamook OR 97141 | 503-842-4981 | | 565
Web: oregonstateparks.org

Cape May County
7 N Main St PO Box 5000 ... Cape May Court House NJ 08210 | 609-465-1010 | 465-8625 | 338
TF: 800-621-5388 ■ *Web:* capemaycountynj.gov

Cape May County Chamber of Commerce
13 Crest Haven Rd PO Box 74 ... Cape May Court House NJ 08210 | 609-465-7181 | 465-5017 | 139
Web: www.capemaycountychamber.com

Cape May County Herald 1508 Rt 47 ... Rio Grande NJ 08242 | 609-886-8600 | | 532-4

Cape May County Library (CMCL)
30 Mechanic St ... Cape May Court House NJ 08210 | 609-463-6350 | | 434-3
TF: 800-207-1675 ■ *Web:* www.cmclibrary.org

Cape May Point State Park
PO Box 107 ... Cape May Point NJ 08212 | 609-884-2159 | | 565
Web: www.njparksandforests.org

Cape Regional Medical Ctr Inc (CRMC)
2 Stone Harbor Blvd ... Cape May Court House NJ 08210 | 609-463-2000 | | 374-3
TF: 800-222-1222 ■ *Web:* www.caperegional.com

Cape Securities Inc
2005 Pennsylvania Ave ... Mcdonough GA 30253 | 678-583-1120 | | 691
Web: www.capesecurities.com

Embassy 3415 Massachusetts Ave NW ... Washington DC 20007 | 202-965-6820 | | 257
Web: www.embcv-usa.gov.cv

Cape Vincent Correctional Facility
36560 New York 12E ... Cape Vincent NY 13618 | 315-654-4100 | | 213

Capel Inc 831 N Main St ... Troy NC 27371 | 800-382-6574 | 572-7040* | 131
**Fax Area Code:* 910 ■ *TF:* 800-334-3711 ■ *Web:* www.capelrugs.com

Capell & Howard PC 150 S Perry St ... Montgomery AL 36104 | 334-241-8000 | | 428
Web: capellhoward.com

Capella Education Co
225 S Sixth St 9th Fl ... Minneapolis MN 55402 | 612-339-8650 | | 242
NASDAQ: CPLA ■ *TF Cust Svc:* 888-227-3552 ■ *Web:* www.capella.edu

Capella Hotel Group
3384 Peachtree Rd Ste 375 ... Atlanta GA 30326 | 404-842-7280 | | 379
Web: www.capellahotelgroup.com

Capella Hotels & Resorts
3384 Peachtree Rd Ste 375 ... Atlanta GA 30326 | 404-842-7280 | | 707
Web: www.capellahotels.com

Capellon Pharmaceuticals Ltd
7509 Flagstone St ... Fort Worth TX 76118 | 817-595-5820 | | 238
Web: www.capellon.com

Capen Hill Nature Sanctuary
56 Capen Rd PO Box 218 ... Charlton City MA 01508 | 508-248-5516 | 248-5516 | 50-5
TF: 800-597-8194 ■ *Web:* www.capenhill.org

Capers 14502 Cantrell Rd ... Little Rock AR 72223 | 501-868-7600 | | 671
Web: www.capersrestaurant.com

Capezio/Ballet Makers Inc 1 Campus Rd ... Totowa NJ 07512 | 973-595-9000 | 595-9120 | 301
TF Acctg: 800-533-1887 ■ *Web:* www.capezio.com

CapFinancial Partners LLC
4208 Six Forks Rd Ste 1700 ... Raleigh NC 27609 | 919-870-6822 | | 401
TF: 800-216-0645 ■ *Web:* www.captrustadvisors.com

Capgemini US LLC 623 Fifth Ave # 33 ... New York NY 10022 | 212-314-8000 | | 180
Web: www.capgemini.com

CapGen Financial Group
120 W 45th St Ste 1010 ... New York NY 10036 | 212-542-6868 | | 194
Web: www.capgen.com

Capilano University
2055 Purcell Way ... North Vancouver BC V7J3H5 | 604-986-1911 | | 162
TF: 800-371-8111 ■ *Web:* www.capilanou.ca

Capintec Inc 6 Arrow Rd ... Ramsey NJ 07446 | 201-825-9500 | | 153
Web: www.capintec.com

CAPIRG (California Public Interest Research Group)
1107 Ninth St Ste 601 ... Sacramento CA 95814 | 916-448-4516 | | 633
Web: www.calpirg.org

Capital 5110 N 40th St Ste 242 ... Phoenix AZ 85018 | 602-381-0709 | | 613

Capital Access Group
150 California St Ste 250 ... San Francisco CA 94111 | 415-217-7600 | | 217
Web: www.capitalaccess.com

Phone | Fax | Class

Capital Advisors Group Inc
Chatham Ctr 29 Crafts St Ste 270 .... Newton MA 02458 617-630-8100 401
Web: www.capitaladvisors.com

Capital Advisors Inc
2200 S Utica Pl Ste 150 .... Tulsa OK 74114 918-599-0045 401
Web: www.capitaladv.com

Capital Advisors Limited LLC
20600 Chagrin Blvd .... Shaker Heights OH 44122 216-295-7900 194
TF: 888-295-7908 ■ *Web:* www.capitaladvisorsltd.com

Capital Agricultural Property Services Inc
801 Warrenville Rd Ste 150 .... Lisle IL 60532 630-434-9150 434-9343 315-3
TF: 800-243-2060 ■ *Web:* www.capitalag.com

Capital Ale House 623 E Main St .... Richmond VA 23219 804-780-2537 671
Web: www.capitalalehouse.com

Capital Alliance Corp
2777 N Stemmons Fwy Ste 1220 .... Dallas TX 75207 214-638-8280 638-8009 70
Web: www.cadallas.com

Capital Alpha Partners LLC
600 Pennsylvania Ave SE Ste 220 .... Washington DC 20003 202-548-0111 401
Web: www.capalphadc.com

Capital Analysts Inc 218 Glenside Ave .... Wyncote PA 19095 800-242-1421 390
TF: 800-242-1421 ■ *Web:* www.capitalanalysts.com

Capital Area District Library
401 S Capitol Ave .... Lansing MI 48933 517-367-6300 374-1068 434-3
TF: 800-625-9740 ■ *Web:* www.cadl.org

Capital Automobile Co
2210 Cobb Pkwy SE .... Smyrna GA 30080 770-952-2277 989-8439 57
Web: www.capitalcadillac.com

Capital Automotive Real Estate Services Inc
8270 Greensboro Dr Ste 950 .... McLean VA 22102 703-288-3075 654
Web: www.capitalautomotive.com

Capital Brewery 7734 Terr Ave .... Middleton WI 53562 608-836-7100 102
TF: 800-598-6352 ■ *Web:* www.capital-brewery.com

Capital Christian Ctr
9470 Micron Ave .... Sacramento CA 95827 916-856-5683 48-20
Web: capitalonline.cc

Capital City Bank
2111 N Monroe St PO Box 900 .... Tallahassee FL 32302 850-402-7500 70
TF: 888-671-0400 ■ *Web:* www.ccbg.com

Capital City Bank Group Inc
PO Box 900 .... Tallahassee FL 32302 850-402-7500 360-2
NASDAQ: CCBG ■ *TF:* 888-671-0400 ■ *Web:* www.ccbg.com

Capital City Club Inc
7 John Portman Blvd .... Atlanta GA 30303 404-523-8221 354
Web: www.capitalcityclub.org

Capital City Press Inc PO Box 588 .... Baton Rouge LA 70821 225-383-1111 637-8
TF: 800-960-6397 ■ *Web:* theadvocate.com

Capital Community College
950 Main St .... Hartford CT 06103 860-906-5000 906-5129 162
TF: 800-894-6126 ■ *Web:* www.capitalcc.edu

Capital Concepts Group Inc
1030 4720 Kingsway .... Burnaby BC V5H4N2 604-432-7743 401

Capital Consulting Corp
2810 Old Lee Hwy Ste 304 .... Fairfax VA 22031 703-876-0400 194
Web: www.capconcorp.com

Capital Corrugated Inc
8333 24th Ave .... Sacramento CA 95826 916-388-7848 100
Web: www.capitalcorrugated.com

Capital Culinary Institute of Keiser College
Melbourne 900 S Babcock St .... Melbourne FL 32901 321-409-4800 725-3766 163
TF: 877-636-3618 ■ *Web:* www.keiseruniversity.edu/melbourne

Capital Datacorp
3600 Madison Ave Ste 65 .... North Highlands CA 95660 916-529-4063 180
TF: 800-474-9514 ■ *Web:* www.capdata.com

Capital Directions Inc
322 S Jefferson St .... Mason MI 48854 517-676-0500 360-2

Capital District Physicians' Health Plan
500 Patroon Creek Blvd .... Albany NY 12206 518-641-3000 641-3507 391-3
TF: 888-258-0477 ■ *Web:* www.cdphp.com

Capital District Psychiatric Ctr
75 New Scotland Ave .... Albany NY 12208 518-447-9611 434-0041 374-5
Web: www.omh.ny.gov/omhweb/facilities/cdpc

Capital District Transportation Authority (CDTA)
110 Watervliet Ave .... Albany NY 12206 518-482-8822 437-8318 468
Web: www.cdta.org

Capital Electric Construction Company Inc
600 Broadway Ste 600 .... Kansas City MO 64105 816-472-9500 421-4244 189-4
Web: www.capitalelectric.com

Capital Electric Co-op Inc
4111 State St .... Bismarck ND 58503 701-223-1513 223-1557 245
TF: 888-223-1513 ■ *Web:* www.capitalelec.com

Capital Engineering LLC
6933 Indianpolis Blvd .... Hammond IN 46324 219-844-1984 256
Web: www.capital-eng.com

Capital Equipment & Handling Inc
1100 Cottonwood Ave .... Hartland WI 53029 262-369-5500 358
Web: www.cehwi.com

Capital Excavation Co
2967 Business Park Dr .... Buda TX 78610 512-440-1717 261
Web: capitalexcavation.com

Capital Farm Credit Aca 7000 Woodway Dr .... Waco TX 76712 254-776-7506 776-8112 69
TF: 877-944-5500 ■ *Web:* www.capitalfarmcredit.com

Capital Ford Inc 4900 Capital Blvd .... Raleigh NC 27616 919-790-4600 57
TF: 877-659-2496 ■ *Web:* www.capitalford.com

Capital Gallery of Contemporary Art
314 Lewis St .... Frankfort KY 40601 502-223-2649 50-2
TF: 800-355-9192 ■ *Web:* ellenglasgow.com

Capital Gazette Communications LLC
2000 Capital Dr .... Annapolis MD 21401 410-268-5000 637-8
Web: www.capitalgazette.com

Capital Grille 1 Union Stn .... Providence RI 02903 401-521-5600 671
Web: www.thecapitalgrille.com

Capital Grille 900 Boylston St .... Boston MA 02115 866-518-9113 671
TF: 866-518-9113 ■ *Web:* www.thecapitalgrille.com

Capital Grille 444 Brickell Ave .... Miami FL 33131 305-374-4500 671
Web: www.thecapitalgrille.com

Capital Grille 1450 Larimer St .... Denver CO 80202 303-539-2500 671
Web: www.thecapitalgrille.com

Capital Grille 633 N St Clair St .... Chicago IL 60611 312-337-9400 671
Web: www.thecapitalgrille.com

Capital Grille Offices, The
1000 Darden Ctr Dr .... Orlando FL 32837 202-737-6200 671
Web: www.thecapitalgrille.com

Capital Grille, The
255 E Paces Ferry Rd .... Atlanta GA 30305 404-262-1162 671
Web: www.thecapitalgrille.com

Capital Grille, The 500 Crescent Ct .... Dallas TX 75201 214-303-0500 671
Web: www.thecapitalgrille.com

Capital Grille, The
1338 Chestnut St .... Philadelphia PA 19107 215-545-9588 671
Web: www.thecapitalgrille.com

Capital Group Cos Inc
333 S Hope St .... Los Angeles CA 90071 213-615-0514 401
TF: 800-421-8511 ■ *Web:* thecapitalgroup.com

Capital Growth Management LP
1 International Pl .... Boston MA 02110 617-737-3225 401
TF: 800-345-4048 ■ *Web:* www.cgmfunds.com

Capital Growth Planning Inc
405 E Lexington Ave Ste 201 .... El Cajon CA 92020 619-440-7023 691
Web: www.capplan.com

Capital Guardian Holding LLC
1355 Greenwood Cliff Ste 250 .... Charlotte NC 28204 704-705-1860 691
Web: www.capitalguardianllc.com

Capital Health Plan PO Box 15349 .... Tallahassee FL 32317 850-383-3333 383-3339 391-3
TF: 800-390-1434 ■ *Web:* www.capitalhealth.com

Capital Health System at Fuld
750 Brunswick Ave .... Trenton NJ 08638 609-394-6000 374-3
Web: www.capitalhealth.org

Capital Health System at Mercer
446 Bellevue Ave .... Trenton NJ 08618 609-394-4000 374-3
Web: www.capitalhealth.org

Capital High School
1500 Greenbrier St .... Charleston WV 25311 304-348-6500 685
Web: chs.kana.k12.wv.us

Capital Hill Group
45 O'Connor St Ste 1540 .... Ottawa ON K1P1A4 613-235-0221 196
TF: 800-463-7705 ■ *Web:* capitalhillgroup.ca

Capital Hill Hotel & Suites
88 Albert St .... Ottawa ON K1P5E9 613-235-1413 235-6047 379
TF: 800-463-7705 ■ *Web:* www.capitalhill.com

Capital Hospice Inc
2900 Telestar Ct .... Falls Church VA 22042 703-538-2065 371
TF: 855-571-5700 ■ *Web:* www.capitalcaring.org

Capital Hotel 111 W Markham St .... Little Rock AR 72201 501-374-7474 370-7091 379
TF: 877-637-0037 ■ *Web:* www.capitalhotel.com/site

Capital Imaging Inc
2521 E Michigan Ave .... Lansing MI 48912 517-482-2292 627
TF: 800-787-8111 ■ *Web:* www.capital-imaging.com

Capital Innovations LLC
325 Forest Grove Dr Ste 100 .... Pewaukee WI 53072 262-746-3100 401
Web: www.capinnovations.com

Capital Institutional Services Inc
1601 Elm St Ste 3900 .... Dallas TX 75201 214-720-0055 954-0040 401
TF: 800-247-6729 ■ *Web:* www.capis.com

Capital Investment Advisors Inc
200 Sandy Springs Pl NE Ste 300 .... Atlanta GA 30328 404-531-0018 194
TF: 800-531-0018 ■ *Web:* www.yourwealth.com

Capital Journal 333 W Dakota Ave .... Pierre SD 57501 605-224-7301 224-9210 532-2
TF: 800-537-0025 ■ *Web:* www.capjournal.com

Capital Link Inc
230 Park Ave Ste 1536 .... New York NY 10169 212-661-7566 401
Web: www.capitallink.com

Capital Lumber Company Inc
5110 N 40th St Ste 242 .... Phoenix AZ 85018 602-381-0709 690
Web: www.capital-lumber.com

Capital Machine Company Inc
2801 Roosevelt Ave .... Indianapolis IN 46218 317-638-6661 636-5122 821
Web: www.capitalmachineco.com

Capital Management Corp, The
4101 Cox Rd Ste 110 .... Glen Allen VA 23060 804-270-4000 401
TF: 800-283-1153 ■ *Web:* www.the-cmc.com

Capital Management Enterprises Inc
1111 W Dekalb Pk .... Wayne PA 19087 610-265-9600 391-3
Web: www.cms-advisors.com

Capital Manor 1955 Dallas Hwy NW .... Salem OR 97304 503-967-3086 672
Web: www.capitalmanor.com

Capital Markets Advisors LLC
1 Great Neck Rd Ste 1 .... Great Neck NY 11021 516-487-9815 345
Web: www.capmark.org

Capital Markets Cooperative LLC
814 A1A N Ste 303 .... Ponte Vedra Beach FL 32082 904-543-0052 345
Web: www.capmkts.org

Capital Medical Ctr
3900 Capital Mall Dr SW .... Olympia WA 98502 360-754-5858 956-2574 374-3
TF: 888-677-9757 ■ *Web:* www.capitalmedical.com

Capital Merchant Solutions Inc
3005 Gill St Ste 2 .... Bloomington IL 61704 877-495-2419 251
TF: 877-495-2419 ■ *Web:* holyprocessing.com

Capital Mercury Apparel
1359 Broadway 19th Fl .... New York NY 10018 212-704-4800 704-4830 155-12

Capital Network Inc, The
281 Summer St 2nd Fl .... Boston MA 02210 781-591-0291 792
Web: www.thecapitalnetwork.org

Capital Newspapers
1901 Fish Hatchery Rd .... Madison WI 53713 920-887-0321 887-8790* 637-8
**Fax: Cust Svc* ■ *TF:* 888-798-4468 ■ *Web:* www.wiscnews.com

Capital Office Systems
3201 Industrial Ave .... Fairbanks AK 99701 907-777-1500 321
Web: www.capital-office.com

Capital One Auto Finance Inc
PO Box 60511 .... City of Industry CA 91716 800-946-0332 70
TF: 800-946-0332 ■ *Web:* www.capitalone.com

Capital One Financial Corp
1680 Capital One Dr .... McLean VA 22102 800-926-1000 290-7335* 215
NYSE: COF ■ **Fax Area Code: 877* ■ *TF:* 800-655-2265 ■ *Web:* www.capitalone.com

Company	Phone	Fax	Class
Capital One FSB *Capital One Bank* 15000 Capital One Dr .... Richmond VA 23238 *TF:* 877-383-4802 ■ *Web:* www.capitalone.com	877-383-4802		70
Capital Premium Financing Inc 12235 S 800 E .... Draper UT 84020 *Web:* www.capitalpremium.net	801-571-0775		401
Capital Printing Corp 420 South Ave. .... Middlesex NJ 08846 *TF:* 800-575-4238 ■ *Web:* www.capitalprintingcorp.com	732-560-1515		627
Capital Properties Management LTD 12929 Shaker Blvd .... Cleveland OH 44120 *Web:* cpm-ltd.com	216-991-3057		260
Capital Public Radio Inc 7055 Folsom Blvd .... Sacramento CA 95826 *TF:* 877-480-5900 ■ *Web:* www.capradio.org	916-278-8900	278-8989	645-140
Capital Realty Advisors Inc 600 Sandtree Dr Ste 109........... Palm Beach Gardens FL 33403 *TF:* 800-940-1088 ■ *Web:* www.capitalrealtyadvisors.com	561-624-5888		463
Capital Region International Airport 4100 Capital City Blvd .... Lansing MI 48906 *TF:* 866-841-4900 ■ *Web:* www.flylansing.com	517-321-6121	321-6197	27
Capital Region Medical Ctr 1125 Madison St .... Jefferson City MO 65101 *Web:* www.crmc.org	573-632-5000	632-5880	374-3
Capital Regional Medical Ctr (CRMC) 2626 Capital Medical Blvd .... Tallahassee FL 32308 *TF:* 800-994-6610 ■ *Web:* www.capitalregionalmedicalcenter.com	850-325-5000	325-5198	374-3
Capital Repertory Theatre 432 State St .... Schenectady NY 12305 *Web:* www.capitalrep.org	518-462-4531	881-1823	749
Capital Research & Management Co (CRMC) 333 S Hope St .... Los Angeles CA 90071 *TF:* 800-421-4225 ■ *Web:* thecapitalgroup.com	213-486-9200		401
Capital Research Ctr 1513 16th St NW .... Washington DC 20036 *TF:* 800-459-3950 ■ *Web:* www.capitalresearch.org	202-483-6900		634
Capital Resin Corp 324 Dering Ave .... Columbus OH 43207 *Web:* www.capitalresin.com	614-445-7177	445-7290	605-2
Capital Resource Partners 31 State St 6th Fl .... Boston MA 02109 *TF:* 800-623-2880 ■ *Web:* www.crp.com	617-478-9600	478-9605	792
Capital Restaurant Concepts Ltd (CRC) 1305 Wisconsin Ave NW .... Washington DC 20007 *Web:* www.capitalrestaurants.com	202-339-6800	339-6801	670
Capital Review Group 1430 E Missouri Ave Ste B-165 .... Phoenix AZ 85014 *Web:* www.capitalreviewgroup.com	602-741-7776		463
Capital Senior Living Corp 14160 Dallas Pkwy Ste 300 .... Dallas TX 75254 *NYSE: CSU* ■ *TF:* 800-635-1232 ■ *Web:* www.capitalsenior.com	972-770-5600	770-5666	672
Capital Southwest Corp 5400 Lyndon B Johnson Fwy Ste 1300........... Dallas TX 75240 *NASDAQ: CSWC* ■ *TF:* 800-937-5449 ■ *Web:* www.capitalsouthwest.com	214-238-5700	238-5701	792
Capital Spectrum Inc 6800 Burleson Rd Ste 180 .... Austin TX 78744 *Web:* csiprinting.com/services	512-443-0088	443-2196	92
Capital Springs 3101 Lake Farm Rd .... Madison WI 53711 *Web:* friendsofcapitalsprings.org	608-224-3606		565
Capital Strategies Group Inc 850 Shades Creek Pkwy Ste 300 .... Birmingham AL 35209 *Web:* capitalstrategies.net	205-263-2400		390
Capital Times 1901 Fish Hatchery Rd........... Madison WI 53713 *TF:* 800-362-8333 ■ *Web:* host.madison.com	608-252-6400		532-2
Capital Tower & Communications Inc 13330 Amberly Rd .... Waverly NE 68462 *TF:* 800-767-5435 ■ *Web:* www.capitaltower.com	402-786-3333		480
Capital Transportation Solutions LLC 1915 Vaughn Rd.......................... Kennesaw GA 30144 *Web:* shipwithcts.com	770-690-8684		311
Capital University College & Main St.......... Columbus OH 43209 **Fax:* Admissions ■ *TF:* 866-544-6175 ■ *Web:* www.capital.edu	614-236-6101	236-6926*	166
Capital University Law School 303 E Broad St .... Columbus OH 43215 *TF:* 800-362-2779 ■ *Web:* www.law.capital.edu	614-236-6500	236-6972	167-1
Capital Valuation Group Inc 1 N Pinckney St Ste 200..................... Madison WI 53703 *Web:* www.capvalgroup.com	608-257-2757		41
Capital Veneer Works Inc 2550 Jackson Ferry Rd.................. Montgomery AL 36104 *TF:* 800-734-4667 ■ *Web:* capitalmat.com	334-264-1401	264-6923	613
Capital Well Service LLC 1437 E St .... Jourdanton TX 78026	830-767-2036	769-3468	536
Capital Workforce Partners 1 Union Pl 3rd Fl.............................. Hartford CT 06103 *TF:* 800-894-6126 ■ *Web:* www.capitalworkforce.org	860-522-1111		260
Capital X-Ray Inc 2189 Notasulga Rd .... Tallassee AL 36078 *Web:* www.capitalxray.com	334-283-8410		475
Capital, The 2000 Capital Dr................. Annapolis MD 21401 *TF:* 800-557-2068 ■ *Web:* www.capitalgazette.com	410-268-5000	268-4643	532-2
Capital-Plus Inc (CPI) 3250 W Henderson Rd Ste 201.............. Columbus OH 43220 *Web:* www.capplus.com	614-848-7620		272
CapitalSoft Inc 1702 N Collins Blvd Ste 211 .... Richardson TX 75080 *Web:* www.capitalsoft.com	972-220-1560		180
CapitalSource Inc 5404 Wisconsin Ave..................... Chevy Chase MD 20815 *NYSE: CSE* ■ *Web:* www.capitalsource.com	301-841-2700		509
Capito, Shelley Moore (Sen R - WV) 172 Russell Senate Office Bldg............. Washington DC 20510 *Web:* www.capito.senate.gov/contact/contact-shelley	202-224-6472		342-2
Capitol Aggregates Ltd 12625 Wetmore Rd Ste 301 .... San Antonio TX 78247 *TF:* 800-292-5315 ■ *Web:* www.capitolaggregates.com	210-871-6100		46
Capitol Aluminum & Glass Corp 1276 W Main St........................... Bellevue OH 44811 *TF:* 800-331-8268 ■ *Web:* www.capitol-windows.com	419-483-7050		330
Capitol Archives & Record Storage Inc 133 Laurel St .... Hartford CT 06106 *TF:* 800-381-2277 ■ *Web:* www.capitolarchives.com	860-951-8981		194

Company	Phone	Fax	Class
Capitol Bancorp Ltd 200 N Washington Sq........................ Lansing MI 48933 *OTC: CBCRQ* ■ *Web:* www.capitolbancorp.com	517-487-6555		360-2
Capitol Broadcasting Co Inc 2619 Western Blvd .... Raleigh NC 27606 *TF:* 800-234-4857 ■ *Web:* capitolbroadcasting.com	919-890-6000	890-6095	738
Capitol Chevrolet Montgomery 711 Eastern Blvd........................ Montgomery AL 36117 *TF Sales:* 800-410-1137 ■ *Web:* www.capitolchevrolet.com	334-272-8700		57
Capitol Chophouse 9 E Wilson St............. Madison WI 53703 *Web:* chophouse411.com/chophouse_location_cch.asp	608-255-0165		671
Capitol City Container Corp 8240 Zionsville Rd .... Indianapolis IN 46268 *TF:* 800-233-5145 ■ *Web:* www.capcitycont.com	317-875-0290		100
Capitol City Produce 16550 Commercial Ave.................. Baton Rouge LA 70816 *TF:* 800-349-1583 ■ *Web:* www.capitolcityproduce.com	225-272-8153	272-8152	296-21
Capitol City Speakers Bureau 1620 S Fifth St .... Springfield IL 62703 *TF:* 800-397-3183 ■ *Web:* www.capcityspeakers.com	217-544-8552	544-1496	708
Capitol Computers Inc 151 Water St........... Augusta ME 04330 *TF:* 800-370-4267 ■ *Web:* www.capcomp.com	207-623-2700		180
Capitol Connection 4400 University Dr MS 1D2 .... Fairfax VA 22030 *TF:* 844-504-7161 ■ *Web:* capitolconnection.org	703-993-3100		116
Capitol Construction Services Inc 11051 Village Square Ln Ste 100................ Fishers IN 46038 *Web:* www.capitolconstruct.com	317-574-5488		186
Capitol Copy Service 116 W State St............ Trenton NJ 08608 *Web:* capitol-copy.com	609-989-8776		113
Capitol Creag LLC 1300 Penn Ave NW........ Washington DC 20004	202-355-1028		463
Capitol Ctr for the Arts 44 S Main St .... Concord NH 03301 *TF:* 800-698-4468 ■ *Web:* www.ccanh.com	603-225-1111	224-3408	572
Capitol Detective Agency 2922 N 18th Pl............................ Phoenix AZ 85016	602-265-3462		400
Capitol Distributing Inc 3500 E Commercial Ct .... Meridian ID 83642 *Web:* www.capitoldist.com	208-888-5112	888-5989	345
Capitol Employee Benefits Inc 224 Web Foot Ln .... Stevensville MD 21666 *Web:* capitolbenefits.com	410-604-6488		193
Capitol Federal Financial 700 Kansas Ave .... Topeka KS 66603 *NASDAQ: CFFN* ■ *TF:* 888-822-7333 ■ *Web:* www.capfed.com	785-235-1341		360-2
Capitol Fiber Inc 6610 Electronics Dr .... Springfield VA 22151 *Web:* capitolfiber.com	703-245-6171	658-0212	96
Capitol FSB 700 S Kansas Ave.................. Topeka KS 66603 *TF:* 888-822-7333 ■ *Web:* www.capfed.com	785-235-1341		70
Capitol Granite & Marble 1700 Oak Lake Blvd .... Midlothian VA 23112 *Web:* www.capitolgraniteandmarble.com	804-379-2641		115
Capitol Hill Hotel 200 C St SE .... Washington DC 20003 *TF:* 800-491-2525 ■ *Web:* capitolhillhotel-dc.com	202-543-6000	547-2608	379
Capitol Hill Publishing Corp 1625 K St NW Ste 900 .... Washington DC 20006 *Web:* www.thehill.com	202-628-8500		532-3
Capitol Hill Times 4000 Aurora Ave N Ste 100 .... Seattle WA 98103 *TF:* 800-658-2510 ■ *Web:* www.pacificpublishingcompany.com	206-461-1300		532-4
Capitol Indemnity Corp 1600 Aspen Commons..................... Middleton WI 53562 *TF:* 800-475-4450 ■ *Web:* www.capspecialty.com	608-829-4200	829-7408	391-4
Capitol Insurance Cos 1600 Aspen Commons PO Box 5900.......... Middleton WI 53562 *TF:* 800-475-4450 ■ *Web:* www.capspecialty.com	608-829-4200	829-7408	391-4
Capitol Lien Records & Research Inc 1010 N Dale St.......................... Saint Paul MN 55117 *TF:* 800-845-4077 ■ *Web:* www.capitollien.com	651-488-0100	488-0200	635
Capitol Petroleum Equipment Inc 11319 Old Baltimore Pk .... Beltsville MD 20705 *TF:* 800-735-2258 ■ *Web:* www.cpe123.com	301-931-9090		539
Capitol Plaza Hotel 415 W McCarty St .... Jefferson City MO 65101 *TF:* 800-338-8088 ■ *Web:* capitolplazajeffersoncity.com	573-635-1234	635-4565	671
Capitol Plaza Hotel & Conference Ctr 100 State St .... Montpelier VT 05602 *TF:* 800-274-5252 ■ *Web:* www.capitolplaza.com	802-223-5252		379
Capitol Plaza Hotel Jefferson City 415 W McCarty St .... Jefferson City MO 65101 *TF:* 800-338-8088 ■ *Web:* www.capitolplazajeffersoncity.com	573-635-1234	635-4565	379
Capitol Press 5306 Beethoven St .... Los Angeles CA 90066 *Web:* www.capitolpress.com	310-577-6606		627
Capitol Reef National Park PO Box 15............ Torrey UT 84775 *Web:* www.nps.gov	435-425-3791	425-3026	564
Capitol Reservations 1730 Rhode Island Ave NW .... Washington DC 20036 *TF:* 800-847-4832 ■ *Web:* www.visitdc.com	202-452-1270	452-0537	376
Capitol Saddlery 8121 N Research Blvd........... Austin TX 78758	512-478-9300		431
Capitol Securities Management Inc 100 Concourse Blvd...................... Glen Allen VA 23059 *Web:* www.capitolsecurities.com	804-612-9700		690
Capitol Security Police Inc 730 Puerto Rico 704 Calle Victor L¢pez......... San Juan PR 00906 *Web:* www.capitolsecuritypr.com	787-727-1700		393
Capitol Services Inc 206 E Ninth St Ste 1300....................... Austin TX 78701 *TF:* 800-345-4647 ■ *Web:* www.capitolservices.com	800-345-4647	432-3622	635
Capitol Stampings Corp 2700 W N Ave........ Milwaukee WI 53208 *TF:* 800-532-2252 ■ *Web:* www.capitolstampings.com	414-372-3500	372-3535	488
Capitol Steel & Iron LLC 1726 S Agnew .... Oklahoma City OK 73108	405-632-7710		492
Capitol Steps Productions Inc 210 N Washington St..................... Alexandria VA 22314 *TF:* 800-733-7837 ■ *Web:* www.capsteps.com	703-683-8330		632
Capitol Technology University 11301 Springfield Rd .... Laurel MD 20708 **Fax:* Admissions ■ *TF:* 800-950-1992 ■ *Web:* www.captechu.edu	301-369-2800	953-1442*	166

	Phone	Fax	Class
Capitol Theatre 50 W 200 S Salt Lake City UT 84101 *Web:* artsaltlake.org	801-355-2787		572
Capitol Theatre 149 Westchester Ave. Port Chester NY 10573 *Web:* www.thecapitoltheatre.com	914-937-4126		572
Capitol Transamerica Corp 1600 Aspen Commons Middleton WI 53562 **Fax:* Hum Res ■ *TF:* 800-475-4450 ■ *Web:* www.capspecialty.com	608-829-4200	829-7409*	360-4
Capitol Tunneling Inc 2216 Refugee Rd Columbus OH 43207 *TF:* 800-303-8629 ■ *Web:* www.capitoltunneling.com	614-444-0255		188
Capitol Uniform & Linen Service 195 Commerce Way Dover DE 19904 *TF:* 800-822-7352 ■ *Web:* www.capitollinen.com	302-674-1511		442
Capitol Wholesale Meatsinc 8751 W 50th St. Mccook IL 60525 *Web:* www.fontanini.com	708-485-4800		473
Capitol-Husting Company Inc 12001 W Carmen Ave. Milwaukee WI 53225 *TF:* 800-242-2231 ■ *Web:* www.capitol-husting.com	414-353-1000	353-0768	81-3
CapitolWatch 7526 Diplomat Dr Manassas VA 20109 *Web:* www.capitolwatch.org	202-544-2600		48-7
CapitolWorks Inc 2000 P St NW. Washington DC 20036 *TF:* 800-210-6113 ■ *Web:* www.capitolworks.com	202-785-2020		260
Caplan and Earnest LLC 1800 Broadway Ste 200 Boulder CO 80302 *TF:* 800-973-1177 ■ *Web:* www.celaw.com	303-443-8010		445
Caplan's Mens Shops Inc 916 Third St Alexandria LA 71301 *TF:* 800-346-1958 ■ *Web:* www.shopcaplans.com	318-427-7700		157-3
Caplugs LLC 2150 Elmwood Ave Buffalo NY 14207 *TF Cust Svc:* 888-227-5847 ■ *Web:* www.caplugs.com	716-876-9855	874-1680	154
Capone's 1701 Woodroffe Ave Nepean ON K2G1W2 *Web:* www.capones.com	613-226-6947		671
Capone's Cucina 19688 Beach Blvd Ste 10 Huntington Beach CA 92646 *Web:* www.caponescucina.com	714-593-2888		671
CAPP/USA Inc 201 Marple Ave Clifton Heights PA 19018 **Fax Area Code:* 800 ■ **Fax:* Sales ■ *TF:* 800-356-8000 ■ *Web:* www.cappusa.com	610-394-1100	237-3292*	202
Cappa & Graham Inc 401 Terry A Francois Blvd Ste 128 San Francisco CA 94158 *Web:* www.cappa-graham.com	415-512-6967		184
Cappelli Enterprises Inc 115 E Stevens Ave Valhalla NY 10595 *Web:* www.cappelli-inc.com	914-769-6500		653
Cappello Capital Corp 100 Wilshire Blvd Ste 1200 Santa Monica CA 90401 *Web:* www.cappellocorp.com	310-393-6632		401
Capps Manufacturing Inc 2121 S Edwards Wichita KS 67213 *Web:* www.cappsmfg.com	316-942-9351		22
Cappy's 5011 Broadway St San Antonio TX 78209 *Web:* www.cappysrestaurant.com	210-828-9669		671
CAPREIT 11200 Rockville Pk Ste 100 Rockville MD 20852 *Web:* www.capreit.com	301-231-8700		655
Capri 313 E State St. Rockford IL 61104 *Web:* caprirockford.com	815-965-6341		671
Capri Capital Partners LLC 875 N Michigan Ave Ste 3430 Chicago IL 60611 *Web:* www.capricap.com	312-573-5300		194
Capri IGA Foodliner 224 E Harris Ave. Greenville IL 62246	618-664-0022		345
Capriccio 2 Pine St Providence RI 02903	401-421-1320		671
Capriccio 2424 N University Dr Pembroke Pines FL 33024 *Web:* www.capriccios.net	954-432-7001		671
Capricorn Coffees Inc 353 Tenth St San Francisco CA 94103 *TF:* 800-541-0758 ■ *Web:* www.capricorncoffees.com	415-621-8500	621-9875	297-2
Capricorn Management LLC 30 E Elm St. Greenwich CT 06830 *Web:* www.capricornholdings.com	203-861-6600		403
Capricorn Pharma Inc 6900 English Muffin Way Frederick MD 21703	301-696-8520		583
Capricorn Products LLC 12 Rice St. Portland ME 04103 *Web:* www.capricornproducts.com	207-321-0014		231
Capricorn Systems Inc 3569 Habersham At N. Tucker GA 30084 *Web:* www.capricornsys.com	678-514-1080	514-1081	225
Capris Furniture Industries Inc 1401 NW 27th Ave Ocala FL 34475 *Web:* www.caprisfurniture.com	352-629-8889		319-2
Caprock Canyons State Park & Trailway 850 Caprock Canyon Pk Rd Quitaque TX 79255 *Web:* tpwd.texas.gov/state-parks/caprock-canyons	806-455-1492		565
CapRock Communications Inc 4400 S Sam Houston Pkwy E Houston TX 77048 *TF:* 888-482-0289 ■ *Web:* www.harriscaprock.com	832-668-2300		681
Caprock Mfg 2303 120th St. Lubbock TX 79423 *Web:* www.caprock-mfg.com	806-745-6454		596
Capron Company Inc 411 N Stonestreet Ave. Rockville MD 20850 *Web:* capron.com	301-424-9500		189-10
Capron Park Zoo 201 County St Attleboro MA 02703 **Fax Area Code:* 508 ■ *Web:* www.capronparkzoo.com	774-203-1840	223-2208*	823
CAPS LLC 10600 Virginia Ave. Culver City CA 90232 *Web:* www.capspayroll.com	310-280-0755		734
Capsmith Inc 2240 Old Lake Mary Rd Sanford FL 32771 *TF:* 800-228-3889 ■ *Web:* capsmith.com	407-328-7660		157-6
Capsonic Group 460 Second St. Elgin IL 60123 *Web:* www.capsonic.com	847-888-7300		604
CapSouth Partners 2216 W Main St. Dothan AL 36301 *TF:* 800-929-1001 ■ *Web:* www.capsouthpartners.com	334-673-8600		463
Capstead Mortgage Corp 8401 N Central Expy Ste 800 Dallas TX 75225 *NYSE:* CMO ■ *TF:* 800-358-2323 ■ *Web:* www.capstead.com	214-874-2323	874-2398	654
Capstone Development LLC 1200 G St, NW Ste 800. Washington DC 20005 *Web:* www.capstonedevco.com/#about	202-661-3536	434-8707	377
Capstone Hotel Ltd 320 Paul W Bryant Dr Tuscaloosa AL 35401 *Web:* www.hotelcapstone.com	205-752-3200		378
Capstone Investments Research Div 12760 High Bluff Dr Ste 120. San Diego CA 92130 *Web:* www.capstoneinvestments.com	858-875-4500		690
Capstone Metering LLC 1600 Capital Ave Ste 200 Plano TX 75074 *Web:* capstonemetering.com	214-469-1065		407
Capstone Natural Resources LLC 2250 E 73rd St Tulsa OK 74136 *Web:* capstonenr.com	918-236-3800		536
Capstone Production Group 1638 S Saunders St Raleigh NC 27603 *TF:* 800-951-4005 ■ *Web:* capstoneproductiongroup.com	919-838-8030		344
Capstone Real Estate Investments LLC 431 Office Park Dr Birmingham AL 35223 *Web:* www.capstonecompanies.com	205-414-6400		655
Capstone Technology Corp 14300 SE First St Vancouver WA 98684 *Web:* www.capstonetechnology.com	360-619-5010		177
Capstone Therapeutics Corp 1275 W Washington St Ste 101 Tempe AZ 85281 *OTC:* CAPS ■ *TF:* 800-937-5520 ■ *Web:* www.capstonethx.com	602-286-5520		477
Capstone Turbine Corp 21211 Nordhoff St Chatsworth CA 91311 *NASDAQ:* CPST ■ *TF:* 866-422-7786 ■ *Web:* www.capstoneturbine.com	818-734-5300	734-5320	262
Capstrat Inc 1201 Edwards Mill Rd 4th Fl Raleigh NC 27607 *Web:* capstrat.com	919-828-0806		194
CAPT (Celina Aluminum Precision Technology Inc) 7059 Staeger Rd Celina OH 45822 *Web:* www.capt-celina.com	419-586-2278	586-6474	621
Capt Harrys Fishing Supply Company Inc 8501 NW Seventh Ave Miami FL 33150 *TF:* 800-327-4000 ■ *Web:* www.captharry.com	305-374-4661		711
Capt Hirams Resort 1606 Indian River Dr. Sebastian FL 32958 *Web:* www.hirams.com	772-589-4345		379
Captain Bangs Hallett House 11 Strawberry Ln PO Box 11. Yarmouth Port MA 02675 *Web:* www.hsoy.org	508-362-3021		50-3
Captain Bill's Seafood Co 2701 Century Harbor Rd. Middleton WI 53562 *Web:* www.capbills.com	608-831-7327		671
Captain Brian's Seafood Market & Restaurant 8421 N Tamiami Trl. Sarasota FL 34243 *Web:* www.captainbriansseafood.com	941-351-4492		671
Captain D's LLC 624 Grassmere Park Dr Ste 30 Nashville TN 37211 *TF:* 800-314-4819 ■ *Web:* www.captainds.com	615-391-5461	231-2309	670
Captain Daniel Stone Inn 10 Water St. Brunswick ME 04011 *Web:* thedanielhotel.com	207-373-1824		379
Captain George's 1401 29th Ave Myrtle Beach SC 29577 *Web:* www.captaingeorges.com	843-916-2278		671
Captain George's Seafood 1956 Laskin Rd. Virginia Beach VA 23454 *Web:* www.captaingeorges.com	757-428-3494		671
Captain George's Seafood Restaurant 5363 Richmond Rd. Williamsburg VA 23188 *TF:* 800-786-6932 ■ *Web:* www.captaingeorges.com	757-565-2323		671
Captain Gosnold Village 230 Gosnold St. Hyannis MA 02601 *TF:* 800-287-2071 ■ *Web:* www.captaingosnold.com	508-775-9111		669
Captain Kens Foods Inc 344 Robert St S Saint Paul MN 55107 *Web:* www.captainkens.com	651-298-0071		297-8
Captain Linnell House 137 Skaket Beach Rd Orleans MA 02653 *Web:* www.linnell.com	508-255-3400		671
Captain Merry Guesthouse & Fine Dining 399 Sinsinawa Ave East Dubuque IL 61025 *Web:* www.privatestay.com	815-747-3644		671
Captain's Cove Seaport 1 Bostwick Ave Bridgeport CT 06605 *Web:* www.captainscoveseaport.com	203-335-7104		671
Captain's Tavern Restaurant Inc 9625 S Dixie Hwy Miami FL 33156 *Web:* www.captainstavernmiami.com	305-666-5979		671
CaptainU LLC 5807 S Woodlawn Dr Ste 207. Chicago IL 60637 *Web:* www.captainu.com	773-834-9097		387
CAPTE (Commission on Accreditation in Physical Therapy Education) 1111 N Fairfax St Alexandria VA 22314 *TF:* 800-999-2782 ■ *Web:* www.capteonline.org/home.aspx	703-706-3245	838-8910	48-1
Captec Engineering Inc 301 NW Flagler Ave Stuart FL 34994 *Web:* gocaptec.com	772-692-4344		261
Captek Softgel Int'l Inc 16218 Arthur St Cerritos CA 90703 *Web:* www.capteksoftgel.com	562-921-9511		583
CaptionMax Inc 2438 27th Ave S Minneapolis MN 55406 *Web:* www.captionmax.com	612-341-3566		116
Captiv 8 102 W 38th St 5th Fl. New York NY 10018 *Web:* www.captiv8promos.com	212-473-2440		129
Captive Fastener Corp 19 Thornton Rd. Oakland NJ 07436 *TF:* 800-526-4430 ■ *Web:* www.captive-fastener.com	201-337-6800	337-1012	278
Captive-aire Systems Inc 4641 Paragon Pk Rd. Raleigh NC 27616 *TF:* 800-334-9256 ■ *Web:* www.captiveaire.com	919-882-2410	882-5204	697
Captree State Park PO Box 247. Babylon NY 11702 *Web:* parks.ny.gov/parks/65/details.aspx	631-669-0449		565
CapTrust Advisors LLC 102 W Whiting St Ste 400 Tampa FL 33602 *Web:* www.captrustadv.com	813-218-5000		401
Capuano Michael E (Rep D - MA) 1414 Longworth Bldg Washington DC 20515 *Web:* www.house.gov/capuano	202-225-5111	225-9322	342-2

				Phone	Fax	Class
Capulin Volcano National Monument 46 Volcano Rd *Web:* www.nps.gov/cavo	Capulin	NM	88414	505-278-2201		564
CapWealth Advisors LLC 3000 Meridian Blvd Ste 250 *TF:* 800-281-6574 ■ *Web:* capwealthadvisors.com	Franklin	TN	37067	615-778-0740		463
Car Care Council 7101 Wisconsin Ave **Fax Area Code:* 301 ■ *Web:* www.carcare.org	Bethesda	MD	20814	240-333-1088	654-3299*	49-21
Car Charging Group Inc 1691 Michigan Ave Ste 425 *Web:* www.carcharging.com	Miami Beach	FL	33139	305-521-0200		253
Car City Motor Company Inc 3100 S US Hwy 169 *TF:* 800-525-7008 ■ *Web:* www.carcitymotors.com	Saint Joseph	MO	64503	816-233-9149		57
Car Clinic Productions 5675 N Davis Hwy *TF:* 888-227-2546 ■ *Web:* www.carclinicnetwork.com	Pensacola	FL	32503	850-478-3139	477-0862	646
Car Parts Warehouse Inc 5200 W 130th St *Web:* www.carpartswarehouse.net	Akron	OH	44311	216-676-5100		60
Car People Marketing Inc 3818 S Nova Rd ste C *Web:* www.carpeoplemarketing.com	Port Orange	FL	32127	386-761-3131		195
Car Rentals Inc 1570 S Washington Ave *Web:* www.avisnj.com	Piscataway	NJ	08854	732-752-6800		126
Car Toys Inc 400 Fairview Ave N Ste 900 *TF:* 888-227-8697 ■ *Web:* www.cartoys.com	Seattle	WA	98109	206-443-0980	443-2525	52
CARA Group Inc, The Drake Oak Brook Plaza 2215 York Rd Ste 300 *TF:* 866-401-2272 ■ *Web:* www.caracorp.com	Oak Brook	IL	60523	630-574-2272		180
Cara Operations Ltd 199 Four Valley Dr *TF:* 800-860-4082 ■ *Web:* www.cara.com	Vaughan	ON	L4K0B8	905-760-2244		299
Carahsoft Technology Corp 12369 Sunrise Vly Dr Ste D2 *TF:* 888-662-2724 ■ *Web:* www.carahsoft.com	Reston	VA	20191	703-871-8500	871-8505	225
Caramagno Foods Co 14255 Dequindre St *Web:* www.caramagnofoods.com	Detroit	MI	48212	313-869-8200		345
Caramba 5421 W Glendale Ave *Web:* carambamex.com	Glendale	AZ	85301	623-934-8888		671
Caramoor Center for Music and The Arts Inc 149 Girdle Ridge Rd *Web:* www.caramoor.org	Katonah	NY	10536	914-232-5035		522
Carana Corp 4350 Fairfax Dr Ste 900 *Web:* www.carana.com	Arlington	VA	22203	703-243-1700		194
Carando Inc 20 Carando Dr *Web:* carando.com	Springfield	MA	01104	413-781-5620		296-26
Caraustar Industries Inc 5000 Austell-Powder Springs Rd Ste 300 *TF:* 800-858-1438 ■ *Web:* www.caraustar.com	Austell	GA	30106	770-948-3100		554
Caravan Facilities Management LLC 1400 Weiss St *TF:* 855-211-7450 ■ *Web:* www.caravanfm.com	Saginaw	MI	48602	855-211-7450		192
Caravelle Resort Hotel & Villas 6900 N Ocean Blvd *TF:* 800-297-3413 ■ *Web:* www.thecaravelle.com	Myrtle Beach	SC	29572	843-918-8000		669
Caraway Watson 307 W Seventh St Ste 1000 *TF:* 800-900-4250 ■ *Web:* watsoncaraway.com	Fort Worth	TX	76102	817-870-1717		445
Carbajal Salud (Rep D-CA) 212 Cannon HOB *Web:* carbajal.house.gov	Washington	DC	20515	202-225-3601		342-2
Carbide Industries LLC 4400 Bells Ln *Web:* www.carbidellc.com	Louisville	KY	40211	502-775-4100		440
Carbide Probes Inc 1328 Research Park Dr *Web:* www.carbideprobes.com	Dayton	OH	45432	937-429-1235	429-2103	815
Carbis Walker LLP 2599 Wilmington Rd *Web:* carbis.com	New Castle	PA	16105	724-658-1565		2
Carbite Golf Inc 5816 Dryden Pl	Carlsbad	CA	92008	760-929-1410	929-1360	711
Carbo Ceramics Inc 575 N Dairy Ashford Rd Ste 300 *NYSE:* CRR ■ *TF:* 800-551-3247 ■ *Web:* www.carboceramics.com	Houston	TX	77079	281-921-6400		537
Carboline Co 350 Hanley Industrial Ct *TF:* 800-848-4645 ■ *Web:* www.carboline.com	Saint Louis	MO	63144	314-644-1000	644-4617	550
Carbon County 2 Hazard Sq PO Box 129 *TF:* 800-441-1315 ■ *Web:* www.carboncounty.com	Jim Thorpe	PA	18229	570-325-3611	325-3622	338
Carbon County PO Box 1017 *TF:* 800-228-3547 ■ *Web:* www.wyomingcarboncounty.com	Rawlins	WY	82301	800-228-3547		338
Carbon County 17 W 11th St PO Box 887 *Web:* co.carbon.mt.us	Red Lodge	MT	59068	406-446-1220	446-2640	338
Carbon Credit Capital LLC 561 Broadway Ste 6A *Web:* www.carboncreditcapital.com	New York	NY	10012	212-925-5697		251
Carbon Design Systems Inc 125 Nagog Pk *Web:* www.carbondesignsystems.com	Acton	MA	01720	978-264-7300		226
Carbon Power & Light Inc 100 E Willow Ave PO Box 579 *TF:* 800-359-0249 ■ *Web:* www.carbonpower.com	Saratoga	WY	82331	307-326-5206		245
Carbon Resources of Florida Inc 11023 Gatewood Dr Ste 103 *Web:* www.carbonresourcesofflorida.com	Bradenton	FL	34211	941-747-2630		311
Carbon Sciences Inc 5511C Ekwill St *Web:* www.carbonsciences.com	Santa Barbara	CA	93111	805-456-7000		539
Carbondale Chamber of Commerce 131 S Illinois Ave *Web:* www.carbondalechamber.com	Carbondale	IL	62901	618-549-2146	529-5063	139
Carbondale Elementary School District 95 925 S Giant City Rd *Web:* www.ces95.org	Carbondale	IL	62902	618-457-3591		186
Carbondale Public Library 405 W Main St *Web:* carbondalepubliclibrary.org	Carbondale	IL	62901	618-457-0354	457-0353	434-3
Carbone Metal Fabricator Inc 240 Marginal St *Web:* www.cmfi.com	Chelsea	MA	02150	617-884-0237		697
Carbone's Ristorante 588 Franklin Ave *TF:* 800-435-3285 ■ *Web:* www.carbonesct.com	Hartford	CT	06114	860-296-9646		671
CarbonWrap Solutions LLC 2820 E Ft Lowell Rd *TF:* 866-380-1269 ■ *Web:* www.carbonwrapsolutions.com	Tucson	AZ	85716	520-292-3109		539
Carbonyx International USA Inc 1255 W 15th St Ste 320 *Web:* www.carbonyx.com	Plano	TX	75025	972-943-3355		127
Carbro Corp 15724 Condon Ave PO Box 278 *TF:* 888-738-4400 ■ *Web:* www.carbrocorp.com	Lawndale	CA	90260	310-643-8400	643-9703	493
Carcinoid Cancer Foundation Inc 333 Mamaroneck Ave Ste 492 *TF:* 888-722-3132 ■ *Web:* www.carcinoid.org	White Plains	NY	10605	888-722-3132		48-17
Carco Inc 10333 Shoemaker PO Box 13859 *TF:* 800-255-3924 ■ *Web:* www.carcousa.com	Detroit	MI	48213	313-925-9000	925-9602	467
Carco International Inc 2721 Midland Blvd *TF:* 800-824-3215 ■ *Web:* www.carcoint.com	Fort Smith	AR	72904	479-441-3270		274
Carco National Lease Inc 2905 N 32nd St *TF:* 800-643-2596 ■ *Web:* carcotrans.com	Fort Smith	AR	72904	479-441-3200		778
Carcoustics USA Inc 1400 Durant Dr *Web:* www.carcoustics.com	Howell	MI	48843	517-548-6700		52
Card Player Media LLC 6940 O'Bannon Dr Ste 8 *Web:* www.cardplayer.com	Las Vegas	NV	89117	702-871-1720		637-9
Card USA Inc 2500 Hollywood Blvd Ste 212 *TF:* 800-764-7600 ■ *Web:* www.cardusa.com	Hollywood	FL	33020	954-862-1300		344
Cardagin Networks Inc 120 Buckingham Rd	Charlottesville	NC	22903	703-963-7576		5
Cardell Cabinetry 3215 N Panam Expy *Web:* www.cardell.com	San Antonio	TX	78219	210-225-0290		115
Cardenas Marketing Network Inc 1459 W Hubbard St *Web:* www.cmnevents.com	Chicago	IL	60642	312-492-6424		5
Cardenas Markets Inc 2501 E Guasti Rd *Web:* cardenasmarkets.com	Ontario	CA	91761	909-923-7426		345
Cardenas Tony (Rep D - CA) 1510 Longworth HOB FL 5 *Web:* cardenas.house.gov	Washington	DC	20515	202-225-6131	225-0819	342-2
Cardero's 1583 Coal Harbour Quay *Web:* www.vancouverdine.com/carderos	Vancouver	BC	V6G3E7	604-669-7666		671
Carderock Capital Management Inc 2 Wisconsin Cir Ste 510 *Web:* www.carderockcapital.com	Chevy Chase	MD	20815	301-951-5288		401
Cardi Corp 400 Lincoln Ave *Web:* www.cardi.com	Warwick	RI	02888	401-739-8300		188-4
Cardi's Furniture 1 Furniture Way *TF:* 866-419-4096 ■ *Web:* www.cardis.com	Swansea	MA	02777	508-379-7510		321
Cardiac Dimensions Inc 5540 Lake Washington Blvd NE *TF:* 800-270-6702 ■ *Web:* www.cardiacdimensions.com	Kirkland	WA	98033	425-605-5900		475
Cardiac Pacemakers Inc 4100 Hamline Ave N	Saint Paul	MN	55112	651-638-4000		250
Cardiac Science Corp 3303 Monte Villa Pkwy **Fax:* Cust Svc ■ *TF Cust Svc:* 800-426-0337 ■ *Web:* www.cardiacscience.com	Bothell	WA	98021	425-402-2000	402-2001*	250
CardiacAssist Inc 240 Alpha Dr *TF:* 800-373-1607 ■ *Web:* www.tandemlife.com	Pittsburgh	PA	15238	412-963-7770		476
Cardiff Park Advisors 2257 Vista La Nisa *TF:* 888-332-2238 ■ *Web:* www.cardiffpark.com	Carlsbad	CA	92009	760-635-7526		196
Cardigan Mountain School 62 Alumni Dr *Web:* www.cardigan.org	Canaan	NH	03741	603-523-4321		622
Cardigan State Park 658 Cardigan Mtn Rd *Web:* www.nhstateparks.org	Orange	NH	03741	603-227-8745		565
Cardin Benjamin L (Sen D - MD) 509 Hart Bldg *Web:* www.cardin.senate.gov	Washington	DC	20510	202-224-4524	224-1651	342-2
Cardinal Aluminum Co 6910 Preston Hwy *TF Cust Svc:* 800-398-7833 ■ *Web:* cardinalaluminum.com	Louisville	KY	40219	502-969-9302		485
Cardinal Building Maintenance 4952 W 128th Pl	Alsip	IL	60803	708-385-3575		256
Cardinal Capital Management LLC 4 Greenwich Office Pk *Web:* www.cardcap.com	Greenwich	CT	06831	203-863-8990		401
Cardinal Carryor Inc 1055 Grade Ln *Web:* www.cardinalcarryor.com	Louisville	KY	40213	502-363-6641		770
Cardinal Color Inc 50 First Ave *Web:* www.cardinalcolor.com	Paterson	NJ	07524	973-684-1919	684-0865	146
Cardinal Construction Inc 531 Commercial St PO Box 897 *Web:* www.cardinalconst.com	Waterloo	IA	50704	319-232-5400		186
Cardinal Detecto Scale Manufacturing Co 203 E Daugherty St *TF:* 800-441-4237 ■ *Web:* www.cardet.com	Webb City	MO	64870	417-673-4631	673-5001	684
Cardinal Distributing Company LLC 269 Jackrabbit Ln *Web:* www.cardinaldistributing.com	Bozeman	MT	59718	406-586-0241	587-1156	81-3
Cardinal Gates 79 Amlajack Way *TF:* 800-318-3380 ■ *Web:* www.cardinalgates.com	Newnan	GA	30265	770-252-4200		64
Cardinal Glass Industries 775 Prairie Center Dr *Web:* www.cardinalcorp.com	Eden Prairie	MN	55344	952-229-2600	935-5538	329
Cardinal Group Inc, The 406 King St E *Web:* www.cardinalgroup.ca	Toronto	ON	M5A1L4	416-971-4494		192

				Phone	Fax	Class
Cardinal Hayes High School 650 grand concourse	Bronx	NY	10451	718-292-6100		685
Cardinal Health Distribution 7000 Cardinal Pl *TF:* 800-926-0834 ■ *Web:* www.cardinalhealth.com/en.html	Dublin	OH	43017	614-757-5000	757-6000	238
Cardinal Health Inc 7000 Cardinal Pl *NYSE: CAH* ■ *TF:* 800-926-0834 ■ *Web:* www.cardinalhealth.com/en.html	Dublin	OH	43017	614-757-5000	757-6000	360-3
Cardinal Health Nuclear Pharmacy Services 7000 Cardinal Pl *TF:* 800-326-6457 ■ *Web:* www.cardinalhealth.com	Dublin	OH	43017	614-757-5000	757-6000	238
Cardinal Hill Healthcare System 2050 Versailles Rd *Web:* www.cardinalhill.org	Lexington	KY	40504	859-254-5701		374-6
Cardinal Homes Inc 525 Barnesville Hwy *Web:* www.cardinalhomes.com	Wylliesburg	VA	23976	434-735-8111	735-8824	106
Cardinal Honda 531 Rt 12 *Web:* www.cardinalhonda.com	Groton	CT	06340	860-449-0411		57
Cardinal Ice Equipment Inc 3311 Gilmore Industrial B *Web:* iceguys.com	Louisville	KY	40213	502-966-4579		665
Cardinal Industries Inc 21-01 51st Ave *TF:* 800-622-8339 ■ *Web:* www.cardinalgames.com	Long Island	NY	11101	718-784-3000	482-7877	762
Cardinal International 30 Corporate Dr *Web:* www.cardinalglass.com	Wayne	NJ	07470	973-628-0900		361
Cardinal Logistics Management Corp 5333 Davidson Hwy *Web:* www.cardlog.com	Concord	NC	28027	704-786-6125		449
Cardinal Machinery Inc 7535 Appling Ctr Dr *TF:* 800-239-5250 ■ *Web:* www.cardinalmachinery.com	Memphis	TN	38133	901-377-3107		358
Cardinal Management Group 3704 Golf Trl Ln *Web:* cardinalmanagementgroup.com	Fairfax	VA	22033	703-591-1818		652
Cardinal Meat Specialists Ltd 155 Hedgedale Rd *TF:* 800-363-1439 ■ *Web:* www.cardinalmeats.com	Brampton	ON	L6T5P3	905-459-4436		297-9
Cardinal Mfg Company Inc 225 Eiler Ave PO Box 14127 *Web:* www.cardinalmfg.com	Louisville	KY	40214	502-363-2661		490
Cardinal O'hara High School 39 Ohara Rd *Web:* www.cardinalohara.com	Tonawanda	NY	14150	716-695-2600		685
Cardinal Office Products Inc 576 E Main St **Fax Area Code:* 800 ■ *TF:* 800-589-5886 ■ *Web:* cardinaloffice.com	Frankfort	KY	40601	502-875-3300	539-4325*	534
Cardinal Pacific Escrow Inc 6615 E Pacific Coast Hwy Ste 240 *Web:* www.cardinalpacific.com	Long Beach	CA	90803	562-493-9393		652
Cardinal Partners 230 Nassau St *Web:* www.cardinalpartners.com	Princeton	NJ	08542	609-924-6452	683-0174	792
Cardinal Path LLC 301 W Warner Rd Ste 136 *Web:* www.cardinalpath.com	Tempe	AZ	85284	480-285-1622		631
Cardinal Point Solutions LLC 935 N Third Ave	St. Charles	IL	60174	630-584-7851		196
Cardinal Ritter Senior Services 7601 Watson Rd *Web:* www.ccstl.org	Saint Louis	MO	63119	314-961-8000		451
Cardinal Scale Manufacturing Company Inc 203 E Daugherty St PO Box 151 *Web:* www.cardinalscale.com	Webb City	MO	64870	417-673-4631		362
Cardinal Services Inc 1721 Indian Wood Cir A *TF:* 800-579-7967 ■ *Web:* www.cardinalstaffing.com	Maumee	OH	43537	419-893-5400		260
Cardinal Shoe Corp 468 Canal St *Web:* cardinalshoe.com	Lawrence	MA	01840	603-401-7557		301
Cardinal Stritch University 6801 N Yates Rd *TF:* 800-347-8822 ■ *Web:* www.stritch.edu	Milwaukee	WI	53217	414-410-4000		166
Cardinal Transport Inc 7180 E Reed Rd *TF:* 800-435-9302 ■ *Web:* www.cardinaltransport.com	Coal City	IL	60416	815-634-4443	634-8267	780
Cardinal Venture Capital 325 Sharon Pk Dr Ste 107 *Web:* www.cardinalvc.com	Menlo Park	CA	94025	650-289-4700		792
Cardiogenesis Corp 11 Musick *Web:* www.cryolife.com/products/cardiogenesis	Irvine	CA	92618	949-420-1800		250
CardioGenics Holdings Inc 6295 Northam Dr Unit 8 *Web:* www.cardiogenics.com	Mississauga	ON	L4V1W8	905-673-8501		419
CardioGrip Corp 12554 W Bridger St Ste 108 *Web:* www.zona.com	Boise	ID	83713	208-322-9399		475
CardioKinetix Inc 925 Hamilton Ave *Web:* www.cardiokinetix.com	Menlo Park	CA	94025	650-364-7016		668
Cardiome Pharma Corp 1441 Creekside Dr 6th Fl *NASDAQ: CRME* ■ *TF:* 800-330-9928 ■ *Web:* www.cardiome.com	Vancouver	BC	V6J4S7	604-677-6905	677-6915	85
CardioMed Supplies Inc 199 Saint David St *TF:* 800-387-9757 ■ *Web:* www.cardiomed.com	Lindsay	ON	K9V5K7	705-328-2518	328-9747	475
CardioNexus Corp 710 N Post Oak Rd Ste 103 *TF:* 800-969-6601 ■ *Web:* www.cardionexus.com	Houston	TX	77024	281-769-4201		743
Cardiosolutions Inc 75 Mill St *Web:* www.cardiosolutionsinc.com	Stoughton	MA	02072	781-344-0801		194
Cardiovascular Consultants PC 4330 Wornall Rd Ste 2000 *Web:* saintlukeshealthsystem.org	Kansas City	MO	64111	816-931-1883		582
Cardiovascular Research Foundation 111 E 59th St *TF:* 800-248-8558 ■ *Web:* www.crf.org	New York	NY	10022	646-434-4500		743
Cardiovascular Systems Inc 1225 Old H 8 NW *TF:* 877-274-0360 ■ *Web:* www.csi360.com	St Paul	MN	55112	651-259-1600		476
CardLogix 16 Hughes Ste 100 *TF:* 866-392-8326 ■ *Web:* www.cardlogix.com	Irvine	CA	92618	949-380-1312	380-1428	704
Cardlytics Inc 675 Ponce de Leon Ave NE Ste 6000 *TF:* 888-798-5802 ■ *Web:* www.cardlytics.com	Atlanta	GA	30308	888-798-5802		5
Cardno ChemRisk 101 Second St Ste 700 *Web:* www.cardnochemrisk.com	San Francisco	CA	94105	415-896-2400		463
Cardo Systems Inc 1204 Parkway View Dr *TF:* 800-488-0363 ■ *Web:* cardosystems.com	Pittsburgh	PA	15205	412-788-4533	788-0270	454
Cardolite Corp 500 Doremus Ave **Fax Area Code:* 973 ■ *Web:* www.cardolite.com	Newark	NJ	07105	201-344-5015	344-1197*	144
Cardon & Assoc Inc 2749 E Covenanter Dr *Web:* cardon.us	Bloomington	IN	47401	812-332-2265		463
Cardone Industries Inc 5501 Whitaker Ave *TF Cust Svc:* 800-777-4780 ■ *Web:* www.cardone.com	Philadelphia	PA	19124	215-912-3000	912-3700	60
CardScan Inc 25 First St Ste 107 *TF:* 800-942-6739 ■ *Web:* www.cardscan.com	Cambridge	MA	02141	617-492-4200		173-7
CardSmart Retail Corp 11 Executive Ave **Fax Area Code:* 401 ■ *TF:* 888-782-7050 ■ *Web:* www.cardsmart.com	Edison	NJ	08817	888-782-7050	726-2384*	310
CardTrak LLC 4055 Tamiami Trail *TF:* 800-344-7714 ■ *Web:* www.cardtrak.com	Port Charlotte	FL	33952	800-344-7714	741-2140	393
Cardtronics GP Inc 3110 Hayes Rd Ste 300 *Web:* www.cardtronics.com	Houston	TX	77082	281-596-9988		225
Cardwell Distributing Inc 8137 S State St *TF:* 800-561-0051 ■ *Web:* www.cardwelldist.com	Midvale	UT	84047	801-561-4251		579
Cardwell Group 24481 Detroit Rd Ste 300 *Web:* www.connectionsonline.net	Cleveland	OH	44145	440-892-1410		196
Cardwell Printing & Advertising 15470 Warwick Blvd *Web:* cardwellprinting.com	Newport News	VA	23608	757-888-0674		627
Cardwell Westinghouse Co 8400 S Stewart Ave *TF:* 800-821-2376 ■ *Web:* www.wabtec.com	Chicago	IL	60620	773-483-7575		650
CARE (Coalition for Auto Repair Equality) 105 Oronoco St Ste 115 *TF:* 800-229-5380 ■ *Web:* www.careauto.org	Alexandria	VA	22314	703-519-7555	519-7747	49-21
Care Acctg Inc 110 Central Sq Dr	Beaver Falls	PA	15010	724-843-1400		2
Care Finders Inc 191 Main St *Web:* carefinders.org	Hackensack	NJ	07601	201-342-5122		260
Care Fusion 1100 Bird Ctr Dr	Palm Springs	CA	92262	760-778-7200		250
Care Industries Inc 27312-68 Twp Rd 394 *Web:* www.careindustries.ca	Blackfalds	AB	T0M0J0	403-347-7337		538
Care Medical Systems 1840 S Central St	Visalia	CA	93277	559-741-9005		475
Care of Trees Inc 2371 Foster Ave *TF:* 888-661-8268 ■ *Web:* www.thecareoftrees.com	Wheeling	IL	60090	888-661-8268		776
Care Partners 68 Sweeten Creek Rd *TF:* 800-627-1533 ■ *Web:* www.carepartners.org	Asheville	NC	28803	828-252-2255		363
Care Resources Inc 1026 Cromwell Bridge Rd *Web:* www.careresourcesinc.com	Baltimore	MD	21286	410-583-1515		260
CARE USA 151 Ellis St NE **Fax:* Hum Res ■ *TF:* 800-521-2273 ■ *Web:* www.care.org	Atlanta	GA	30303	404-681-2552	577-5977*	48-5
Care Wise LabLogic Systems Inc 1040 E Brandon Blvd *Web:* www.carewise.com	Brandon	FL	33511	408-779-5531		45
Care Zone Inc 1463 East Republican St Ste 198 *TF:* 888-407-7785 ■ *Web:* carezone.com	Seattle	WA	98112	888-407-7785		387
Careage Development 4411 Point Fosdick Dr NW Ste 203 *TF:* 800-863-2318 ■ *Web:* www.careage.com	Gig Harbor	WA	98335	253-853-4457	853-5280	186
CareCentric Inc 20 Church St 12th Fl *TF:* 866-467-8263 ■ *Web:* www.carecentrix.com	Hartford	CT	06103	800-808-1902		178-10
Carecycle Solutions LLC 3406 Main St *Web:* carecyclesolutions.net	Dallas	TX	75226	214-698-0600		363
Career Co 15880 Rose Ave *Web:* www.siliconvalleycareercounselor.com	Los Gatos	CA	95030	408-354-1964		193
Career College Assn (CCA) 1101 Connecticut Ave NW Ste 900 *Web:* www.career.org	Washington	DC	20036	202-336-6700	336-6828	49-5
Career College of Northern Nevada 1421 Pullman Dr *Web:* www.ccnn.edu	Sparks	NV	89434	775-856-2266		166
Career Education Corp (CEC) 2895 Greenspoint Pkwy Ste 600 *NASDAQ: CECO* ■ *Web:* www.careered.com	Hoffman Estates	IL	60196	847-781-3600	781-3610	242
Career Exposure Inc 805 SW Broadway	Portland	OR	97205	503-221-7779		260
Career Foundations Inc 4011 Westchase Blvd Ste 200 *TF:* 800-264-1170 ■ *Web:* www.careerfoundations.com	Raleigh	NC	27607	919-828-1000		260
Career Path Training Corp 11300 Fourth St N Ste 200 *Web:* www.careerpathtraining.com	St Petersburg	FL	33716	727-342-6420		360-2
Career Solutions International Inc 400 Lexington Green Ln *Web:* www.csigroup.net	Sanford	FL	32771	407-688-6727		260
Career Step LLC 4692 N 300 W Ste 150 *TF:* 800-246-7837 ■ *Web:* www.careerstep.com	Provo	UT	84604	801-489-9393		764
Career Team LLC 3580 Main St *Web:* www.careerteam.com	Hartford	CT	06120	203-407-8800		41
CareerBoard LLC 23245 Mercantile Rd *Web:* www.careerboard.com	Beachwood	OH	44122	216-595-1632	595-3688	260
CareerBuilder Inc 200 N LaSalle St Ste 1100 *TF:* 800-638-4212 ■ *Web:* www.careerbuilder.com	Chicago	IL	60601	773-527-3600		395
CareerCurve LLC 5005 Rockside Rd Ste 600 *TF:* 800-314-8230 ■ *Web:* www.careercurve.com	Cleveland	OH	44131	800-314-8230		41
CareerPlanners Inc 19037 Raines Dr *Web:* www.careerplanners.com	Rockville	MD	20855	301-216-9597		260

				Phone	Fax	Class
Careerpros LLC 3392 Hillcrest Rd *TF:* 800-383-7641 ■ *Web:* www.careerpros.com	Dubuque	IA	52002	563-556-3040		41
Careers Express 234 Mall Blvd Ste 120 *TF:* 800-264-1170 ■ *Web:* careersexpress.com	Kng Of Prussa	PA	19406	610-768-1788		631
Careers Inc 208 Ave Ponce De Leon Ste 1100 *TF:* 800-955-6443 ■ *Web:* www.careersincpr.com	San Juan	PR	00918	787-764-2298		463
Careers The Next Generation Foundation 10470 176 St NW *TF:* 888-757-7172 ■ *Web:* nextgen.org	Edmonton	AB	T5S1L3	780-426-3414		305
careerSMITH Inc 537 Newport Ctr Dr Ste 364 *TF:* 800-875-1292 ■ *Web:* www.careersmith.com	Newport Beach	CA	92660	949-760-8666		260
CareerSource Polk 500 E Lake Howard Dr *Web:* www.careersourcepolk.com	Winter Haven	FL	33881	863-508-1100		260
CareerStaff Unlimited Inc 6363 N State Hwy 161 Ste 525 *TF:* 888-993-4599 ■ *Web:* www.therapistsunlimited.com	Irving	TX	75038	888-993-4599		721
CareEvolution Inc 320 Miller Ave Ste 195 *Web:* careevolution.com	Ann Arbor	MI	48104	734-678-4788		177
CareFirst BlueCross BlueShield 10455 Mill Run Cir *TF:* 800-638-6756 ■ *Web:* www.carefirst.com	Owings Mills	MD	21117	410-581-3000		391-3
Carefirst Seniors & Community Services Association 3601 Victoria Park Ave *TF:* 800-268-7708 ■ *Web:* www.carefirstseniors.com	Scarborough	ON	M1W3Y3	416-502-2323		138
CareFlite 3110 S Great SW Pkwy *Web:* www.careflite.org	Grand Prairie	TX	75052	972-339-4200		30
Carefree of Colorado 2145 W Sixth Ave *TF:* 800-223-4583 ■ *Web:* www.carefreeofcolorado.com	Broomfield	CO	80020	303-469-3324		733
Carefree Resort & Conference Ctr 37220 Mule Train Rd *TF:* 888-692-4343 ■ *Web:* www.carefree-resort.com	Carefree	AZ	85377	888-692-4343		707
Carefree Vacations Inc 11885 Carmel Mountain Rd Ste 906 *TF:* 800-266-3476 ■ *Web:* www.carefreevacations.com	San Diego	CA	92128	800-795-0720		771
Careful Courier Service Inc PO Box 51118 **Fax Area Code:* 628 ■ *Web:* www.carefulcourier.com	Palo Alto	CA	94306	650-903-9393	239-0194*	546
CareFusion Corp 3750 Torrey View Ct *NYSE:* CFN ■ *TF:* 888-876-4287 ■ *Web:* www.carefusion.com	San Diego	CA	92130	858-617-2000		476
CareGo Holdings Inc 3600 Dundas St Ste 300 *Web:* carego.com	Burlington	ON	L7M4B8	905-592-4900		314
CareGroup Inc 330 Brookline Ave *Web:* www.caregroup.org	Boston	MA	02215	617-667-3700	975-5450	353
Careline Medical Equipment & Supply Company LLC 89 - 54th St SW *Web:* www.carelincmed.com	Grand Rapids	MI	49548	616-249-2273		363
Carelink Health Plans 500 Virginia St E Ste 400 *TF:* 800-348-2922 ■ *Web:* coventryhealthcare.com	Charleston	WV	25301	304-348-2900		391-3
Carelli's of Boulder 645 30th St *Web:* www.carellis.com	Boulder	CO	80303	303-938-9300		671
Caremark Rx Inc PO Box 832407 *TF:* 877-460-7766 ■ *Web:* www.caremark.com	Richardson	TX	75083	877-460-7766		586
Carenbauer Distributing Corp 1900 Jacob St *Web:* www.abwholesaler.com	Wheeling	WV	26003	304-232-3000		81-1
Carenet Healthcare Services 11845 I-10 W Ste 400 *TF:* 800-809-7000 ■ *Web:* www.callcarenet.com	San Antonio	TX	78230	800-809-7000		393
CareOne At Valley 300 Old Hook Rd *Web:* www.care-one.com	Westwood	NJ	07675	201-664-8888		450
CarePartners Mountain Area Hospice PO Box 5779 *TF:* 800-627-1533 ■ *Web:* www.carepartners.org	Asheville	NC	28813	828-255-0231	255-2944	371
Carepoint Inc 215 E Bay St Ste 304 *TF:* 800-296-1825 ■ *Web:* carepoint.com	Charleston	SC	29401	843-853-6999		237
Carepoint Partners LLC 8280 Montgomery Rd Ste 101 *Web:* carepointpartners.com	Cincinnati	OH	45236	513-891-6666		363
Carepro Health Services 1014 Fifth Ave SE *TF:* 800-575-8810 ■ *Web:* www.careprohs.com	Cedar Rapids	IA	52403	800-575-8810		194
CareSource 230 N Main St *TF:* 800-488-0134 ■ *Web:* www.caresource.com	Dayton	OH	45402	937-224-3300		352
Caresource Health Plan 740 SE Seventh St *TF:* 888-460-0185 ■ *Web:* www.mripa.org	Grants Pass	OR	97526	541-471-4106		363
CareSource Home Health & Hospice LLC 1624 East 4500 South *TF:* 800-488-1901 ■ *Web:* caresourcehealthcare.com	Salt Lake City	UT	84117	801-266-7200		260
Carestar Inc 5566 Cheviot Rd *TF:* 866-834-4712 ■ *Web:* carestar.com	Cincinnati	OH	45247	513-618-8300		363
Carestream Health 150 Verona St *TF:* 888-777-2072 ■ *Web:* www.carestream.com	Rochester	NY	14608	585-627-1800		476
CAREstream Medical Ltd 20133 102 Ave Units 1 **Fax Area Code:* 888 ■ *Web:* www.carestreammedical.com	Langley	BC	V1M4B4	604-552-5486	310-2187*	475
Care-Tech Laboratories Inc 3224 S KingsHwy Blvd *TF:* 800-325-9681 ■ *Web:* www.caretechlabs.com	Saint Louis	MO	63139	314-772-4610	772-4613	582
Caretel Inns of America Inc 910 S Washington Ave	Royal Oak	MI	48067	248-850-7138		379
Caretti Inc 4590 Industrial Pk Rd PO Box 1301 *Web:* www.carettimasonry.com	Camp Hill	PA	17011	717-737-6759	737-6880	189-7
CareWatch Inc 3483 Satellite Blvd Ste 211 S *TF:* 800-901-2454 ■ *Web:* www.carewatch.com	Duluth	GA	30096	770-409-0244		177
Carewest 10301 Southport Ln SW Southport Twr *Web:* www.albertahealthservices.ca	Calgary	AB	T2W1S7	403-943-8140		371
CareWorks Technologies Ltd 5555 Glendon Ct *TF:* 800-669-9623 ■ *Web:* www.careworkstech.com	Dublin	OH	43016	800-669-9623		196
Carey Color Inc 6835 Ridge Rd *TF:* 800-555-3142 ■ *Web:* careyweb.com	Wadsworth	OH	44281	330-239-1835		195
Carey Digital 1718 Central Pkwy *TF:* 800-767-6071 ■ *Web:* www.careydigital.com	Cincinnati	OH	45214	513-241-5210	241-2205	781
Carey Executive Limousine 245 University Ave *TF:* 800-241-3943 ■ *Web:* www.careyatlanta.com	Atlanta	GA	30315	404-223-2000		441
Carey Hilliard's Restaurants 11111 Abercom St *Web:* careyhilliards.com	Savannah	GA	31419	912-925-3225		670
Carey International Inc 4530 Wisconsin Ave NW *TF:* 800-336-4646 ■ *Web:* www.carey.com	Washington	DC	20016	202-895-1200		441
Carey Sales & Services Inc 3141-47 Frederick Ave *TF:* 800-848-7748 ■ *Web:* www.careysales.com	Baltimore	MD	21229	410-945-7878		35
Carey Theological College 5920 Iona Dr *TF:* 844-862-2739 ■ *Web:* www.carey-edu.ca	Vancouver	BC	V6T1J6	604-224-4308	224-5014	167-3
CARF (Commission on Accreditation of Rehabilitation Facilities International) 6951 E Southpoint Rd *TF:* 888-281-6531 ■ *Web:* www.carf.org	Tucson	AZ	85756	520-325-1044	318-1129	48-1
Carfaro Inc 2075 E State St *Web:* www.carfaro.com	Trenton	NJ	08619	609-890-6600		492
Cargill Assoc Inc 4701 Altamesa Blvd *TF:* 800-433-2233 ■ *Web:* www.cargillassociates.com	Fort Worth	TX	76133	817-292-9374		317
Cargill Energy PO Box 9300 *TF:* 800-227-4455 ■ *Web:* www.cargill.com	Minneapolis	MN	55440	800-227-4455		579
Cargill Foundation 15407 McGinty Rd W Ste 46 **Fax Area Code:* 952 ■ *TF:* 800-227-4455 ■ *Web:* www.cargill.com	Wayzata	MN	55391	877-765-8867	742-1087*	304
Cargill Inc 15407 McGinty Rd W *TF:* 800-227-4455 ■ *Web:* www.cargill.com	Wayzata	MN	55391	800-227-4455		275
Cargill Ltd 300-240 Graham Ave PO Box 5900 *TF:* 888-855-8558 ■ *Web:* www.cargill.ca	Winnipeg	MB	R3C4C5	204-947-0141	947-6444	275
Cargill Meat Solutions 151 N Main PO Box 2519 *Web:* cargill.com	Wichita	KS	67201	316-291-2500		473
Cargill Salt Inc PO Box 5621 *TF:* 888-385-7258 ■ *Web:* www.cargill.com	Minneapolis	MN	55440	888-385-7258		680
Cargille-Sacher Laboratories Inc 55 Commerce Rd *Web:* www.cargille.com	Cedar Grove	NJ	07009	973-239-6633	239-6096	419
Cargo Airline Assn 1620 L St NW Ste 610 *Web:* cargoair.org	Washington	DC	20036	202-293-1030		49-21
Cargo Control USA Inc 911 Fields Dr *TF:* 888-775-5059 ■ *Web:* www.cargocontrolusa.com	Sanford	NC	27330	919-775-5059		366
Cargo Equipment Corp 640 Church Rd *TF:* 888-557-8727 ■ *Web:* www.cargoequipmentcorp.com	Elgin	IL	60123	847-741-7272		770
Cargo Express Inc 1790 Yardley Stn Dr	Yardley	PA	19067	215-493-2662	493-4430	465
Cargo Management Systems Llc 827 E Main St *TF:* 855-484-9235 ■ *Web:* www.cmscargo.com	Richmond	KY	40475	855-484-9235		195
Cargo Pacific Logistics 800 Mark St *Web:* www.cargopacificlogistics.com	Elk Grove Village	IL	60007	847-750-1230		314
Cargo Solution Express Inc 14589 Valley Blvd *Web:* www.cargosolutionexpress.com	Fontana	CA	92335	909-350-1644		449
Cargo Transporters Inc 3390 N Oxford St PO Box 850 *Web:* www.cargotransporters.com	Claremont	NC	28610	828-459-3282		780
Carhartt Inc 5750 Mercury Dr *TF:* 800-833-3118 ■ *Web:* www.carhartt.com	Dearborn	MI	48126	313-271-8460		155-19
Caribbean Cove Hotel & Water Park 3850 Depauw Blvd *Web:* www.caribbeancovewaterpark.com	Indianapolis	IN	46268	317-872-9790		379
Caribbean Gardens 1590 Goodlette-Frank Rd *Web:* napleszoo.org	Naples	FL	34102	239-262-5409	262-6866	823
Caribbean Grill 5183 Lee Hwy	Arlington	VA	22207	703-241-8947		671
Caribbean Jack's 721 Ballough Rd *Web:* www.caribbeanjacks.com	Daytona Beach	FL	32114	386-523-3000	252-7362	671
Caribbean Products Ltd 3624 Falls Rd *TF:* 888-689-5068	Baltimore	MD	21211	888-689-5068		296-26
Caribbean Resort & Villas 3000 N Ocean Blvd *TF:* 800-552-8509 ■ *Web:* www.caribbeanresort.com	Myrtle Beach	SC	29577	800-552-8509		669
Caribbean Tourism Organization 80 Broad St 32nd Fl *Web:* www.onecaribbean.org	New York	NY	10004	212-635-9530	635-9511	775
Caribbean Travel & Life Magazine 460 N Orlando Ave Ste 200 *Web:* www.bonniercorp.com	Winter Park	FL	32789	407-628-4802	628-7061	457-22
Caribe Federal Credit Union 195 Oneil St *Web:* caribefederal.com	San Juan	PR	00918	787-474-5147		219
Caribe Hilton 1 San Geronimo St *Web:* www.caribehilton.com	San Juan	PR	00901	787-721-0303	725-8849	669
Caribe Royale 8203 World Ctr Dr *TF Resv:* 800-823-8000 ■ *Web:* www.thecaribehotelsorlando.com	Orlando	FL	32821	407-238-8000		379
Caribe Royale Orlando All-Suites Hotel & Convention Ctr 8101 World Ctr Dr *TF Resv:* 800-823-8300 ■ *Web:* www.thecaribehotelsorlando.com	Orlando	FL	32821	407-238-8000	238-8050	379
Cariboo Regional District 180 N Third Ave Ste D *Web:* cariboord.bc.ca	Williams Lake	BC	V2G2A4	250-392-3351		435
Caribou Coffee Company Inc 3900 Lakebreeze Ave N *NASDAQ:* CBOU ■ *TF Cust Svc:* 888-227-4268 ■ *Web:* www.cariboucoffee.com	Minneapolis	MN	55429	763-592-2200	592-2300	159

	Phone	Fax	Class
Caribou County 159 S Main . . . . Soda Springs ID 83276 *TF:* 800-972-7660 ■ *Web:* www.cariboucounty.us	208-547-4324	547-4759	338
Caribou Highlands Lodge 371 Ski Hill Rd PO Box 99 . . . . Lutsen MN 55612 *TF:* 800-642-6036 ■ *Web:* www.caribouhighlands.com	218-663-7241		669
Caribou Road Services Ltd 5110 52nd Ave . . . . Pouce Coupe BC V0C2C0 *TF:* 800-667-2322 ■ *Web:* www.caribouroads.com	250-786-5440		261
Caridad & Louie's Restaurant 187 S Broadway . . . . Yonkers NY 10701	914-375-9777		671
Carilion New River Valley Medical Ctr 2900 Lamb Cir . . . . Christiansburg VA 24073 *TF:* 800-432-7874 ■ *Web:* www.carilionclinic.org	540-731-2000		374-3
Carilion Roanoke Community Hospital (CRCH) 101 Elm Ave SE . . . . Roanoke VA 24013 *TF:* 800-422-8482 ■ *Web:* carilionclinic.org	540-985-8000		374-3
Carilion Roanoke Memorial Hospital 1906 Belleview Ave . . . . Roanoke VA 24014 *TF:* 800-422-8482 ■ *Web:* www.carilionclinic.org	540-981-7000		374-3
Carillion Canada Inc 7077 Keele St . . . . Concord ON L4K0B6 *Web:* www.carillion.ca	905-532-5200		256
Carillon Financials Corp 13601 Preston Rd Ste 550 . . . . Dallas TX 75240 *Web:* www.carillon.us	972-437-2230		177
Carillon Historical Park 1000 Carillon Blvd . . . . Dayton OH 45409 *Web:* www.daytonhistory.org	937-293-2841		520
Carina Technology Inc 1300 Meridian St Ste A-13 . . . . Huntsville AL 35801 *TF:* 866-915-5464 ■ *Web:* www.carinatek.com	256-704-0422		177
Carinet 8929 Complex Dr . . . . San Diego CA 92123 *Web:* www.cari.net	858-974-5080		396
Caring Hands Animal Hospital of Arlington LLC 5659 Stone Rd . . . . Centreville VA 20120 *Web:* caringhandsvet.com	703-830-5700		794
Caring House Inc 2625 Pickett Rd . . . . Durham NC 27705 *Web:* www.caringhouse.com	919-490-5449		372
Carino's Italian 150 Cascade Mall Dr . . . . Burlington WA 98233 *Web:* www.carinos.com	360-757-4535		670
CARIS-Universal Systems Ltd 115 Waggoners Ln . . . . Fredericton NB E3B2L4 *Web:* www.caris.com	506-458-8533		387
Carithers Wallace Courtenay Co 4343 NE Expy . . . . Atlanta GA 30340 *TF:* 800-292-8220 ■ *Web:* www.c-w-c.com	770-493-8200	491-6374	320
Carl Albert State College 1507 S McKenna St . . . . Poteau OK 74953 *TF:* 800-256-7511 ■ *Web:* www.carlalbert.edu	918-647-1300		162
Carl Belt Inc 11521 Milnor Ave PO Box 1210 . . . . Cumberland MD 21502 *TF:* 888-729-1616 ■ *Web:* www.thebeltgroup.com	301-729-8900		186
Carl Bloom Assoc Inc 81 Main St Ste 126 . . . . White Plains NY 10601 *Web:* www.carlbloom.com	914-761-2800	761-2744	5
Carl Bolander & Sons Company Inc 251 Starkey St . . . . Saint Paul MN 55107 *Web:* www.bolander.com	651-224-6299		189-5
Carl Buddig & Co 950 176th St . . . . Homewood IL 60430 *TF:* 888-633-5684 ■ *Web:* www.buddig.com	708-798-0900	798-1284	296-26
Carl Diebold Lumber Co 725 NW Dunbar Ave . . . . Troutdale OR 97060 *TF:* 800-548-2500 ■ *Web:* dieboldlumber.com	503-669-8226		683
Carl Domino Inc 515 N Flagler Dr Ste 702 . . . . West Palm Beach FL 33401 *Web:* www.carldomino.com	561-833-2882		401
Carl E Mellen & Co 601 W Greenwood Ave . . . . Waukegan IL 60087 *Web:* carlmellen.com	847-244-3500		390
Carl Elliott Regional Library 98 E 18th St . . . . Jasper AL 35501	205-221-2568		434-3
Carl Fischer Inc 48 Wall St 28th Fl . . . . New York NY 10005 *TF:* 800-762-2328 ■ *Web:* www.carlfischer.com	212-777-0900	477-6996	637-7
Carl Nelson Insurance Agency I 1519 N 11th Ave . . . . Hanford CA 93230 *TF:* 800-582-4264 ■ *Web:* carlnelsonins.com	559-584-4495		390
Carl R Bieber Tourways Inc 320 Fair St PO Box 180 . . . . Kutztown PA 19530 *TF:* 800-243-2374 ■ *Web:* www.biebertourways.com	610-683-7333		107
Carl Sandburg College 2400 Tom L Wilson Blvd . . . . Galesburg IL 61401 *TF:* 877-236-1862 ■ *Web:* www.sandburg.edu	309-344-2518	344-3291	162
Carl Sandburg Home National Historic Site 81 Carl Sadburg Ln . . . . Flat Rock NC 28731 *TF:* 877-642-4743 ■ *Web:* www.nps.gov	828-693-4178	693-4179	564
Carl Sandburg Jr High School 2600 Martin Ln . . . . Rolling Meadows IL 60008 *Web:* www.ccsd15.net	847-963-7800		685
Carl Schaedel & Company Inc 4 Sperry Rd Ste 4 . . . . Fairfield NJ 07004	973-244-1311		38
Carl Vinson Veterans Affairs Medical Ctr 1826 Veterans Blvd . . . . Dublin GA 31021 *TF:* 800-595-5229 ■ *Web:* va.gov	478-272-1210		374-8
Carl Walker Inc 5136 Lovers Ln . . . . Portage MI 49002 *Web:* www.carlwalker.com	269-381-2222		261
Carl Warren & Company Inc 17862 E 17th St Ste 111 . . . . Tustin CA 92870 *Web:* www.carlwarren.com	657-622-4200		390
Carl Zeiss Canada Ltd 45 Valleybrook D . . . . Toronto ON M3B2S6 *Web:* www.zeiss.ca	416-449-4523	449-0641	475
Carl Zeiss Inc 1 Zeiss Dr . . . . Thornwood NY 10594 *TF:* 800-233-2343 ■ *Web:* www.zeiss.com	914-747-1800	681-7446	544
Carl Zeiss Industrial Metrology 6250 Sycamore Ln N . . . . Maple Grove MN 55369 *TF:* 800-327-9735 ■ *Web:* www.zeiss.com	763-744-2400		493
Carl's Golfland Inc 1976 S Telegraph Rd . . . . Bloomfield Hills MI 48302 *TF:* 877-412-2757 ■ *Web:* www.carlsgolfland.com	248-335-8095		711
Carla's Pasta Inc 50 Talbot Ln . . . . South Windsor CT 06074 *Web:* www.carlaspasta.com	860-436-4042		296-31
Carlbrook School LLC, The 3046 Carlbrook Rd . . . . South Boston VA 24592 *TF:* 800-244-1113 ■ *Web:* www.carlbrook.org	434-476-2406		685
Carle Foundation Hospital 611 W Pk St . . . . Urbana IL 61801 *Web:* www.carle.org	217-383-3311	383-3137	374-3
Carle Hospice 611 W Park St . . . . Urbana IL 61801 *TF:* 800-239-3620 ■ *Web:* www.carle.org	217-383-3311		371
Carleen Bright Arboretum 9001 Bosque Blvd . . . . Woodway TX 76712 *Web:* www.woodway-texas.com	254-399-9204		97
Carlen Enterprises Inc 1760 Apollo Ct . . . . Seal Beach CA 90740	562-296-1055	296-1052	157-5
Car-Lene Research Inc 430 Lake Cook Rd Ste B . . . . Deerfield IL 60015 *Web:* www.carleneresearch.com	847-940-2000		466
Carleton College 100 S College St . . . . Northfield MN 55057 **Fax:* Admissions ■ *TF Admissions:* 800-995-2275 ■ *Web:* www.carleton.edu	507-646-4000	646-4526*	166
Carleton Insurance Agency 383 Kings Hwy N . . . . Cherry Hill NJ 08034 *Web:* www.carletoninsurance.com	856-482-6200		390
Carleton Life Support Systems Inc 2734 Hickory Grove Rd . . . . Davenport IA 52804 *Web:* www.cobham.com	563-383-6000	383-6430	22
Carleton Martello Tower National Historic Site 454 Whipple St . . . . St John NB E2M2R3 *Web:* www.pc.gc.ca/eng/lhn-nhs/nb/carleton/index.aspx	506-636-4011	887-6011	563
Carleton Technologies Inc 10 Cobham Dr . . . . Orchard Park NY 14127 *Web:* resources.carltech.com	716-662-0006	662-0747	576
Carleton University 1125 Colonel By Dr . . . . Ottawa ON K1S5B6 *TF:* 888-354-4414 ■ *Web:* www.carleton.ca	613-520-7400	520-3847	785
Carleton-Willard Village (CWV) 100 Old Billerica Rd . . . . Bedford MA 01730 *Web:* www.cwvillage.org	781-275-8700	275-5787	672
Carlex Glass Co 77 Excellence Way . . . . Vonore TN 37885 *Web:* www.carlex.com	423-884-1105		330
Carley Foundry Inc 8301 Coral Sea St NE . . . . Blaine MN 55449 *Web:* www.carleyfoundry.com	763-780-5123		492
Carley Lamps Inc 1502 W 228th St . . . . Torrance CA 90501 *Web:* www.carleylamps.com	310-325-8474	534-2912	437
Carley State Park 19041 Hwy 74 . . . . Altura MN 55910 *TF:* 888-646-6367 ■ *Web:* www.stateparks.com/carley.html	507-932-3007		565
Carlie C's IGA Inc 10 Carlie C'S Dr . . . . Dunn NC 28334 *Web:* www.carliecs.com	910-892-4124		297-8
Carlile Macy Inc 15 Third St . . . . Santa Rosa CA 95401 *Web:* www.carlilemacy.com	707-542-6451		256
Carlile Patchen & Murphy LLP 366 E Broad St . . . . Columbus OH 43215 *Web:* www.cpmlaw.com	614-228-6135	221-0216	428
Carling Technologies Inc 60 Johnson Ave . . . . Plainville CT 06062 *TF:* 800-243-8556 ■ *Web:* www.carlingtech.com	860-793-9281	793-9231	815
Carlinville Primary School 18456 Shipman Rd . . . . Carlinville IL 62626 *Web:* www.carlinvilleschools.net	217-854-9823		685
Carlisle & Company Inc 30 Monument Sq Ste 225 . . . . Concord MA 01742 *Web:* www.carlisle-co.com	978-318-0500		194
Carlisle & Finch Co 4562 W Mitchell Ave . . . . Cincinnati OH 45232 *TF:* 800-828-3186 ■ *Web:* www.carlislefinch.com	513-681-6080	681-6226	439
Carlisle Corp 263 Wagner Pl . . . . Memphis TN 38103 *Web:* www.carlislecorp.com	901-526-5000		653
Carlisle Cos Inc 13925 Ballantyne Corporate Pl Ste 400 . . . . Charlotte NC 28277 *NYSE: CSL* ■ *TF:* 800-248-5995 ■ *Web:* www.carlisle.com	704-501-1100	501-1190	60
Carlisle County PO Box 176 . . . . Bardwell KY 42023 *Web:* carlislecountyclerk.com/printable-forms	270-628-3233	628-0191	338
Carlisle Finishing 3863 Carlisle Chester Hwy . . . . Carlisle SC 29031 *Web:* www.itg-global.com	864-466-4100		745-7
Carlisle FoodService Products Inc 4711 E Hefner Rd . . . . Oklahoma City OK 73131 *TF:* 800-654-8210 ■ *Web:* www.carlislefsp.com	405-475-5600	475-5607	300
Carlisle Industrial Brake 1031 E Hillside Dr . . . . Bloomington IN 47401 *TF:* 800-873-6361 ■ *Web:* www.carlislebrake.com	812-336-3811	334-8775	60
Carlisle Plastics Co 320 S Ohio Ave . . . . New Carlisle OH 45344 *Web:* www.carlisleplastics.com	937-845-9411		596
Carlisle Power Transmission Products Inc 2601 W Battlefield . . . . Springfield MO 65807	417-881-7440		370
Carlisle Productions Inc 1000 Bryn Mawr Rd . . . . Carlisle PA 17013 *TF:* 800-245-8118 ■ *Web:* www.carlisleevents.com	717-243-7855		184
Carlisle Regional Medical Ctr 361 Alexander Spring Rd . . . . Carlisle PA 17015 *Web:* carlislermc.com	717-249-1212		374-3
Carlisle Sanitary Maintenance Products 402 S Black River St . . . . Sparta WI 54656 **Fax Area Code:* 800 ■ *TF:* 800-654-8210 ■ *Web:* www.carlislefsp.com	608-269-2151	872-4701*	103
Carlisle SynTec 1285 Ritner Hwy PO Box 7000 . . . . Carlisle PA 17013 *TF:* 800-479-6832 ■ *Web:* www.carlislesyntec.com	717-245-7000	245-7053	191-4
Carlisle Tax Credit Advisors 263 Summer St 6th Fl . . . . Boston MA 02210 *Web:* www.carlisletaxcredits.com	617-500-8620	500-9920	734
Carlisle Wide Plank Floors Inc 1676 Route 9 . . . . Stoddard NH 03464 *TF:* 800-595-9663 ■ *Web:* www.wideplankflooring.com	603-446-3937		364
Carlith LLC 250 Carpenter Blvd . . . . Carpentersville IL 60110	847-426-3488		627
Carlitos Gardel 7963 Melrose Ave . . . . Los Angeles CA 90046 *Web:* www.carlitosgardel.com	323-655-0891		671
Carlo Doria Plumbing & Heating 23 Waterhouse Rd . . . . Cape Elizabeth ME 04107	207-799-0066		610

Phone | Fax | Class

Carlo Gavazzi Inc
750 Hastings Ln........Buffalo Grove IL 60089 847-465-6100 261
TF: 800-222-2659 ■ *Web:* www.gavazzionline.com

Carlos & Pepe's 1420 Peel St........Montreal QC H3A1S8 514-288-3090 671
Web: carlospepes.com

Carlos Brazilian International Cuisine
4167 Electric Rd SW........Roanoke VA 24018 540-776-1117 671
Web: carlosbrazilian.com

Carlow University 3333 Fifth Ave........Pittsburgh PA 15213 412-578-6000 578-6689 166
TF: 800-333-2275 ■ *Web:* www.carlow.edu

Carlsbad Chamber of Commerce
5934 Priestly Dr........Carlsbad CA 92008 760-931-8400 931-9153 139
Web: www.carlsbad.org

Carlsbad Chamber of Commerce
302 S Canal St........Carlsbad NM 88220 575-887-6516 885-1455 139
Web: www.carlsbadchamber.com

Carlsbad Convention & Visitors Bureau
400 Carlsbad Village Dr........Carlsbad CA 92008 760-434-6093 206
Web: www.visitcarlsbad.com

Carlsbad Current-Argus 620 S Main St........Carlsbad NM 88220 575-887-5501 532-2
Web: www.currentargus.com

Carlsbad Medical Ctr
2430 W Pierce St........Carlsbad NM 88220 575-887-4100 374-3
Web: www.carlsbadmedicalcenter.com

Carlsbad Premium Outlets
5620 Paseo del Norte........Carlsbad CA 92008 760-804-9000 460
Web: www.premiumoutlets.com

Carlsbad State Beach
c/o San Diego Coast District Office
4477 Pacific Hwy........San Diego CA 92110 760-438-3143 565
TF: 800-777-0369 ■ *Web:* www.parks.ca.gov/default.asp?page_id=653

Carlsbad Technology Inc
5922 Farnsworth Ct........Carlsbad CA 92008 760-431-8284 231
Web: carlsbadtech.com

Carlsen & Assoc 1439 Grove St........Healdsburg CA 95448 707-431-2000 297
Web: carlsenassociates.com

Carlsen Resources
312 W Riverwoods Dr........New Hope PA 18938 215-862-5610 193
TF: 800-264-1170 ■ *Web:* www.carlsenresources.com

Carlsmith Ball LLP
1001 Bishop St Ste 2100........Honolulu HI 96813 808-523-2500 523-0842 428
Web: www.carlsmith.com

Carlson
Radisson Hotels & Resorts
701 Carlson Pkwy........Minnetonka MN 55305 763-762-2222 379
Web: www.carlson.com

Carlson & Messer LLP
5959 W Century Blvd Ste 1214........Los Angeles CA 90045 310-242-2200 41
Web: www.cmtlaw.com

Carlson Capital Management Inc
11 Bridge Sq........Northfield MN 55057 507-645-8887 194
Web: carlsoncap.com

Carlson Cos Inc 701 Carlson Pkwy........Minnetonka MN 55305 763-212-5000 185
TF: 800-328-9680 ■ *Web:* www.carlson.com

Carlson Craft Inc
1750 Tower Blvd........North Mankato MN 56003 800-774-6848 627
TF: 800-774-6848 ■ *Web:* www.carlsoncraft.com

Carlson Ctr 2010 Second Ave........Fairbanks AK 99701 907-451-7800 451-1195 205
Web: www.carlson-center.com

Carlson Group Inc
34 Executive Pk Ste 250........Irvine CA 92614 949-251-0455 251-0465 256
Web: www.carlson-dc.com

Carlson Hotels Worldwide
701 Carlson Pkwy........Minneapolis MN 55305 763-212-5000 379
Web: www.carlson.com

Carlson Paving Products Inc
18425 50th Ave E........Tacoma WA 98446 253-875-8000 190
Web: www.carlsonpavingproducts.com

Carlson Real Estate Company Inc
301 Carlson Pkwy Ste 100........Minnetonka MN 55305 952-404-5000 652
Web: carlsonrealestate.biz

Carlson Software Inc
102 W Second St........Maysville KY 41056 606-564-5028 177
TF: 800-989-5028 ■ *Web:* www.carlsonsw.com

Carlson Systems Holdings Inc
10840 Harney St........Omaha NE 68154 402-593-5300 385
Web: www.csystems.com

Carlson Testing Inc 8430 SW Hunziker........Tigard OR 97223 503-684-3460 743
Web: www.carlsontesting.com

Carlson Tool & Machine Co 2300 Gary Ln........Geneva IL 60134 630-232-2460 232-2016 455
Web: www.carlson-tool.com

Carlson Tool & Manufacturing Corp
W57 N14386 Doerr Way PO Box 85........Cedarburg WI 53012 262-377-2020 757
TF: 800-532-2252 ■ *Web:* www.carlsontool.com

Carlson Wagonlit Travel Inc
701 Carlson Pkwy........Minnetonka MN 55305 800-213-7295 212-2409* 772
*Fax Area Code: 763 ■ *TF:* 800-213-7295 ■ *Web:* www.carlsonwagonlit.com

Carlson, Brigance & Doering Inc
5501 W William Cannon Dr........Austin TX 78749 512-280-5160 261
Web: cbdeng.com

Carlson, Caspers, Vandenburgh & Lindquist
225 S Sixth St Ste 4200........Minneapolis MN 55402 612-436-9600 428
TF: 800-973-1177 ■ *Web:* carlsoncaspers.com

Carlson, Gaskey & Olds A Professional Corp
400 W Maple Rd Ste 350........Birmingham MI 48009 248-988-8360 428
Web: www.cgolaw.com

Carlstar Group LLC, The
725 Cool Springs Blvd Ste 500........Franklin TN 37067 615-503-0220 503-0228 370
TF: 800-889-7367 ■ *Web:* www.carlstargroup.com

Carlthorp School
438 San Vicente Blvd........Santa Monica CA 90402 310-451-1332 685
Web: carlthorp.org

Carlton Arms 160 E 25th St........New York NY 10010 212-679-0680 379
Web: www.carltonarms.com

Carlton Bates Co 3600 W 69th St........Little Rock AR 72209 501-562-9100 246
TF: 866-600-6040 ■ *Web:* www.carltonbates.com

Carlton Co 3901 SE Naef Rd........Milwaukie OR 97267 503-659-8911 682
Web: carltonproducts.com

Carlton County PO Box 130........Carlton MN 55718 218-384-9166 384-9182 338
Web: www.co.carlton.mn.us

Carlton Fields PA
4221 W Boy Scout Blvd Corporate Ctr Three
Ste 1000........Tampa FL 33607 813-223-7000 428
Web: www.carltonfields.com

Carlton Foods Corp 880 Texas 46........New Braunfels TX 78130 830-625-7583 296-26
TF: 800-628-9849 ■ *Web:* www.carltonfoods.com

Carlton Forge Works Inc
7743 E Adams St........Paramount CA 90723 562-633-1131 483
Web: carltonforgeworks.com

Carlton Group Inc 120 Landmark Dr........Greensboro NC 27409 336-668-7677 361
TF: 800-722-7824 ■ *Web:* www.carltonscale.com

Carlton on Madison Ave
88 Madison Ave........New York NY 10016 212-532-4100 696-9758 379
TF Resv: 800-601-8500 ■ *Web:* www.carltonhotelny.com

Carlton Restaurant, The
500 Grant St BNY Mellon Ctr........Pittsburgh PA 15219 412-391-4099 281-1704 671
Web: www.thecarltonrestaurant.com

Carlton Scale 196 Industrial Dr........Roanoke VA 24019 540-992-6095 361
Web: carltonscale.com

Carluccio, Leone, Dimon, Doyle & Sacks LLC
9 Robbins St........Toms River NJ 08753 732-797-1600 428
TF: 800-529-3161 ■ *Web:* cldds.com

Carlyle 4000 Campbell Ave........Arlington VA 22206 703-931-0777 931-9420 671
Web: www.greatamericanrestaurants.com

Carlyle Capital Markets Inc
14755 Preston Rd Ste510........Dallas TX 75254 972-404-8686 690
Web: www.carlylecapitalmarkets.com

Carlyle Hotel, The
1731 New Hampshire Ave NW........Washington DC 20009 202-234-3200 379
TF: 877-301-0019 ■ *Web:* www.carlylehoteldc.com

Carlyle House Historic Park
121 N Fairfax St........Alexandria VA 22314 703-549-2997 549-5738 520
TF: 800-877-0954 ■ *Web:* www.novaparks.com

Carlyle Johnson Machine Co (CJM)
291 Boston Tpke........Bolton CT 06043 860-643-1531 646-2645 620
TF: 888-629-4867 ■ *Web:* www.cjmco.com

Carlyle Lake State Fish & Wildlife Area
RR 2........Vandalia IL 62471 618-425-3533 565
Web: www.stateparks.com

Carlynton School District
435 Kings Hwy........Carnegie PA 15106 412-429-8400 685
Web: www.carlynton.k12.pa.us

Carma Laboratories Inc
5801 W Airways Ave........Franklin WI 53132 414-421-7707 231
Web: www.mycarmex.com

Carman Callahan & Ingham LLP
Carman Bldg 280 Main St........Farmingdale NY 11735 516-249-3450 428
Web: www.carmancallahan.com

CARMANAH Design & Manufacturing Inc
15050 - 54A Ave Unit 8 Unit 8........Surrey BC V3S5X7 604-299-3431 454

Carman-Dunne PC 2 Lakeview Ave........Lynbrook NY 11563 516-599-5563 261

CarMax Inc 12800 Tuckahoe Creek Pkwy........Richmond VA 23238 800-519-1511 57
NYSE: KMX ■ *TF:* 800-519-1511 ■ *Web:* www.carmax.com

Carmel Clay Public Library
55 Fourth Ave SE........Carmel IN 46032 317-844-3361 434-3
TF: 800-908-4490 ■ *Web:* www.carmel.lib.in.us

Carmel Contractors Inc
8030 England St........Charlotte NC 28273 704-552-2338 186
Web: www.carmelcontractors.com

Carmel Mission 3080 Rio Rd........Carmel CA 93923 831-624-1271 50-1
Web: www.carmelmission.org

Carmel Mission Inn 3665 Rio Rd........Carmel CA 93923 831-624-1841 378
Web: www.carmelmissioninn.com

Carmel River Inn 26600 Oliver Rd........Carmel CA 93923 831-624-1575 379
TF: 800-882-8142 ■ *Web:* www.carmelriverinn.com

Carmel Valley Manor
8545 Carmel Valley Rd........Carmel CA 93923 831-624-1281 622-4543 672
TF: 800-544-5546 ■ *Web:* www.cvmanor.com

Carmel Valley Ranch Resort
1 Old Ranch Rd........Carmel CA 93923 831-625-9500 669
TF: 866-405-5037 ■ *Web:* www.carmelvalleyranch.com

Carmell Therapeutics Corp
3636 Boulevard of the Allies........Pittsburgh PA 15213 412-894-8248 668
Web: www.carmellrx.com

Carmelo's 14795 Memorial Dr........Houston TX 77079 281-531-0696 671
Web: www.carmelosrestaurant.com

Carmen & Family Bar-B-Q
41986 Fremont Blvd........Fremont CA 94538 510-657-5464 671
Web: carmenandfamilybbq.com

Carmen Anthony Steakhouse
660 State St........New Haven CT 06511 203-773-1444 671

Carmeuse North America
11 Stanwix St 11th Fl........Pittsburgh PA 15222 412-995-5500 995-5570 440
TF: 866-243-0965 ■ *Web:* www.carmeusena.com

Carmichael Brasher Tuvell & Co
1647 Mt Vernon Rd........Atlanta GA 30338 678-443-9200 2
Web: www.cbtcpa.com

Carmichael Chamber of Commerce
6825 Fair Oaks Blvd Ste 100........Carmichael CA 95608 916-481-1002 481-1003 139
TF: 800-991-6147 ■ *Web:* carmichaelchamber.com

Carmichael Lynch Relate
110 N Fifth St........Minneapolis MN 55403 612-334-6000 334-6090 636
Web: spongpr.com

Carmike Cinemas Inc 1301 First Ave........Columbus GA 31901 706-576-3400 748
NASDAQ: CKEC ■ *Web:* www.carmike.com

Carmine's on Penn 92 S Pennsylvania........Denver CO 80209 303-777-6443 777-4129 671
Web: www.carminescolorado.com

Carmine's Steak House
20 S Fourth St........Saint Louis MO 63102 314-241-1631 671
Web: www.lombardosrestaurants.com

Carmine's Tuscan Grill Ristorante
1500 Whalley Ave........New Haven CT 06515 203-389-2805 671
Web: www.carminestuscangrill.com

Carmines Gourmet Market
2401 Pga Blvd........Palm Beach Gardens FL 33410 561-775-0105 345
Web: www.carmines.com

	Phone	Fax	Class
Carmody Torrance Sandak & Hennessey LLP 50 Leavenworth St .... Waterbury CT 06721 TF: 800-529-6275 ■ Web: carmodylaw.com	203-573-1200		428
Carnahan Group Inc 5005 W Laurel St Ste 204........ Tampa FL 33607 Web: www.carnahangroup.com	813-289-2588		463
Carnahan Proctor & Cross Inc 604 Courtland St Ste 101........ Orlando FL 32804 Web: www.carnahan-proctor.com	954-972-3959		256
Carnations Home Fashions Inc 53 Jeanne Dr .... Newburgh NY 12550 TF: 800-866-8949 ■ Web: www.carnationhomefashions.com	212-679-6017		361
Carneghi-Nakasako & Assoc 1602 The Alameda Ste 103........ San Jose CA 95126 Web: cbpappraisal.com	408-535-0900	535-0909	655
Carnegie Art Museum 424 S 'C' St .... Oxnard CA 93030 Web: www.carnegieam.org	805-385-8158	483-3654	520
Carnegie Corp of New York 437 Madison Ave .... New York NY 10022 TF: 800-336-7323 ■ Web: www.carnegie.org	212-371-3200	754-4073	305
Carnegie Council for Ethics in International Affairs (CCEIA) Merrill House 170 E 64th St........ New York NY 10065 Web: www.carnegiecouncil.org	212-838-4120	752-2432	634
Carnegie East House For Seniors 1844 Second Ave .... New York NY 10128 TF: 888-410-0033 ■ Web: carnegieeast.org	212-410-0033		196
Carnegie Endowment for International Peace 1779 Massachusetts Ave NW .... Washington DC 20036 Web: www.carnegieendowment.org	202-483-7600	483-1840	634
Carnegie Fabrics Inc 110 N Centre Ave .... Rockville Centre NY 11570 Web: www.carnegiefabrics.com	516-678-6770	678-6875	87
Carnegie Hall 881 Seventh Ave........ New York NY 10019 TF: 800-728-3843 ■ Web: www.carnegiehall.org	212-247-7800	581-6539	572
Carnegie Hotel 1216 W State of Franklin Rd........ Johnson City TN 37604 TF: 866-757-8277 ■ Web: www.carnegiehotel.com	423-979-6400	979-6424	379
Carnegie Institute 4400 Forbes Ave........ Pittsburgh PA 15213 Web: www.carnegiemuseums.org	412-622-3114		520
Carnegie Institution of Washington 1530 P St NW........ Washington DC 20005 Web: www.carnegiescience.edu	202-387-6400	387-8092	668
Carnegie Learning Inc 437 Grant St .... Pittsburgh PA 15219 TF: 888-851-7094 ■ Web: www.carnegielearning.com	412-690-6284	690-2444	177
Carnegie Library of Pittsburgh 4400 Forbes Ave........ Pittsburgh PA 15213 Web: carnegielibrary.org	412-622-3114		434-3
Carnegie Mellon University 5000 Forbes Ave........ Pittsburgh PA 15213 *Fax: Admissions ■ TF: 844-625-4600 ■ Web: www.cmu.edu	412-268-2000	268-7838*	166
Carnegie Museum of Art 4400 Forbes Ave........ Pittsburgh PA 15213 Web: www.cmoa.org	412-622-3131	622-3112	520
Carnegie Observatories 813 Santa Barbara St .... Pasadena CA 91101 Web: obs.carnegiescience.edu	626-577-1122		466
Carnegie Public Library 127 S N St .... Washington Court House OH 43160 Web: www.cplwcho.org	740-335-2540	335-2928	434-3
Carnegie Regional Library 630 Griggs Ave........ Grafton ND 58237	701-352-2754	352-2757	434-3
Carnegie Science Ctr 1 Allegheny Ave .... Pittsburgh PA 15212 Web: www.carnegiesciencecenter.org	412-237-3400	237-3375	520
Carnegie-Stout Public Library 360 W 11th St........ Dubuque IA 52001 Web: www.dubuque.lib.ia.us	563-589-4225	589-4217	434-3
Carneros Inn, The 4048 Sonoma Hwy .... Napa CA 94559 TF: 888-400-9000 ■ Web: www.thecarnerosinn.com	707-299-4900	299-4950	707
Carnes Co 448 S Main St........ Verona WI 53593 Web: www.carnes.com	608-845-6411	845-6470	14
Carney Group, The 925 Harvest Dr Ste 240........ Blue Bell PA 19422 Web: www.carneyjobs.com	215-646-6200		260
Carney John (D) Legislative Hall .... Dover DE 19901 Web: governor.delaware.gov	302-744-4101	739-2775	343
Carney, Sandoe & Associates, Limited Partnersh 44 Bromfield St........ Boston MA 02108 TF: 800-225-7986 ■ Web: www.carneysandoe.com	617-542-0260		242
Carnicerias Jimenez 4204 W N Ave........ Chicago IL 60639 Web: www.carniceriasjimenez.com	773-486-5805		297-8
Carnifex Ferry Battlefield State Park 1194 Carnifex Ferry Rd........ Summersville WV 26651 Web: www.carnifexferrybattlefieldstatepark.com	304-872-0825		565
Carnival Cruise Lines 3655 NW 87th Ave .... Miami FL 33178 TF: 800-764-7419 ■ Web: carnival.com	305-599-2600		220
Carnow Conibear & Associates Ltd 600 W Van Buren Ste 500........ Chicago IL 60607 TF: 800-860-4486 ■ Web: www.ccaltd.com	312-782-4486	782-5145	193
Caro Ctr 2000 Chambers Rd........ Caro MI 48723 Web: michigan.gov	989-673-3191	673-6749	374-5
Caro Foods Inc 2324 Bayou Blue Rd........ Houma LA 70364 TF: 800-395-2276 ■ Web: www.performancefoodservice.com/Caro	985-872-1483	876-0825	297-7
Carol Drake 1913 N Green Vly Pkwy .... Henderson NV 89074 Web: caroldrake.com	702-361-0300		390
Carol Fox & Associates 1412 W Belmont Ave .... Chicago IL 60657 Web: www.carolfoxassociates.com	773-327-3830		636
Carol H Williams Advertising 1625 Clay St Ste 800 .... Oakland CA 94612 Web: www.carolhwilliams.com	510-763-5200	763-9266	4
Carol House Furniture Co 2332 Millpark Dr .... Maryland Heights MO 63043 TF: 800-969-4337 ■ Web: www.carolhouse.com	314-427-4200		321
Carol Stream Public Library 616 Hiawatha Dr........ Carol Stream IL 60188 Web: www.cslibrary.org	630-653-0755	653-6809	434-3

	Phone	Fax	Class
Carol Woods Retirement Community 750 Weaver Dairy Rd .... Chapel Hill NC 27514 TF: 800-518-9333 ■ Web: carolwoods.org	919-968-4511		672
Carol'S Carpet Inc 1640 NE Blvd........ Montgomery AL 36117 Web: carolscarpetmontgomery.com	334-603-8713		290
Carol's Corner Cafe 7800 NE St Johns Blvd........ Vancouver WA 98665	360-573-6357		671
Carolace Embroidery Company Inc 2147 Hudson Terr........ Fort Lee NJ 07024 Web: www.trimplace.com	608-709-8746		258
Carole Fabrics Inc PO Box 1436 .... Augusta GA 30903 TF: 800-241-0920 ■ Web: carolefabrics.com	706-863-4742		746
Carole Joy Creations Inc 1087 Federal Rd Unit 8........ Brookfield CT 06804	203-740-4490		130
Carole Wren Inc 30-30 47th Ave........ Long Island NY 11101 Web: www.carolewren.com	718-552-3800		155-21
Carolina Advanced Digital Inc 133 Triangle Trade Dr........ Cary NC 27513 TF: 800-435-2212 ■ Web: www.cadinc.com	919-663-2211		463
Carolina Apothecary Inc 726 S Scales St .... Reidsville NC 27320 TF: 800-633-1447 ■ Web: www.carolinaapothecary.com	336-342-0071		475
Carolina Ballet Inc 3401-131 Atlantic Ave .... Raleigh NC 27604 Web: www.carolinaballet.com	919-719-0800	719-0910	573-1
Carolina Bank Holdings Inc 101 N Spring St .... Greensboro NC 27401 NASDAQ: CLBH ■ Web: www.carolinabank.com	336-288-1898	387-4359	360-2
Carolina Beach State Park 1010 State Park Rd PO Box 475........ Carolina Beach NC 28428 Web: www.ncparks.gov	910-458-8206		565
Carolina Biological Supply Co 2700 York Rd .... Burlington NC 27215 TF: 800-334-5551 ■ Web: www.carolina.com	336-584-0381	584-7686	243
Carolina Brush Manufacturing Company Inc 3093 Northwest Blvd .... Gastonia NC 28052 TF: 800-881-5101 ■ Web: www.carolinabrush.com	704-867-0286		362
Carolina Business Furniture LLC 535 Archdale Blvd .... Archdale NC 27263 TF: 800-763-0212 ■ Web: www.carolinabusinessfurniture.com	336-431-9400	431-9511	319-1
Carolina Cabinet Co 3363 Hwy 301 N........ Wilson NC 27893 Web: www.3c-inc.net	252-291-5181	291-8039	286
Carolina Canners Inc PO Box 1628........ Cheraw SC 29520 Web: carolinacanners.com	843-537-5281	537-6743	81-2
Carolina Carports Inc 187 Cardinal Ridge Trl .... Dobson NC 27017 TF: 800-670-4262 ■ Web: www.carolinacarportsinc.com	800-670-4262		487
Carolina Casualty Insurance Co 5011 Gate Pkwy Ste 200........ Jacksonville FL 32256 TF: 800-874-8053 ■ Web: www.carolinacas.com	904-363-0900	363-8098	391-4
Carolina Classic Boats Inc 109 Anchors Way Dr........ Edenton NC 27932 Web: www.carolinaclassicboats.com	252-482-3699		90
Carolina Color Corp 100 E 17th St........ Salisbury NC 28144 Web: www.carocolor.com	704-637-7000		596
Carolina Computer Training Inc 33 Villa Rd Ste 100........ Greenville SC 29615 Web: www.cctbusiness.com	864-527-8100		180
Carolina Container Co 909 Prospect St .... High Point NC 27260 TF: 800-627-0825 ■ Web: www.carolinacontainer.com	336-883-7146	883-7570	100
Carolina Designs Realty Inc 1197 Duck Rd........ Kitty Hawk NC 27949 TF: 800-368-3825 ■ Web: www.carolinadesigns.com	252-261-3934		656
Carolina Dragway 302 Dragstrip Rd........ Aiken SC 29803 TF: 877-471-7223 ■ Web: www.houseofhook.com	803-471-2285		515
Carolina Eye Assoc PA 2170 Midland Rd .... Southern Pines NC 28387 TF: 800-733-5357 ■ Web: www.carolinaeye.com	910-295-2100	295-5339	798
Carolina Eyecare Physicians 2060 Charlie Hall Blvd Ste 201........ Charleston SC 29414 Web: www.carolinaeyecare.com	843-722-2010		543
Carolina Fabricators Inc 3831 Hwy 321 .... West Columbia SC 29172 Web: www.carolinafab.net	803-794-4906		124
Carolina Farms Real Estate 547 S Main St........ King NC 27021 Web: www.carolinafarms.com	336-983-5263		652
Carolina Filters Inc 109 E Newberry Ave .... Sumter SC 29150 TF: 800-849-5646 ■ Web: www.carolinafilters.com	803-773-6842		806
Carolina Financial Group 185 W Main St .... Brevard NC 28712 Web: www.carofin.com	828-393-0088		194
Carolina Foods Inc 1807 S Tryon St........ Charlotte NC 28203 TF: 800-234-0441 ■ Web: carolinafoodsinc.com	704-333-9812		296-1
Carolina Foothills Chamber of Commerce 2753 Lynn Rd Ste A .... Tryon NC 28782 Web: www.carolinafoothillschamber.com	828-859-6236		139
Carolina Forge Co LLC 2401 Stantonsburg Rd .... Wilson NC 27893 Web: www.carolinaforgeco.com	252-237-8181		75
Carolina Glove Co 116 Mclin Creek Rd PO Box 999 .... Conover NC 28613 TF: 800-335-1918 ■ Web: www.carolinaglove.com	828-464-1132	485-2416	155-8
Carolina Group 2405 Westwood Ave Ste 101 .... Richmond VA 23230	804-349-4796		756
Carolina Herrera 501 Seventh Ave 17th Fl........ New York NY 10018 Web: www.carolinaherrera.com	212-944-5757	944-7996	277
Carolina Hosiery Mills Inc 710 Plantation Dr .... Burlington NC 27215	336-226-5581		155-10
Carolina Hurricanes 1400 EdwaRds Mill Rd .... Raleigh NC 27607 Web: hurricanes.nhl.com	919-467-7825	462-7030	716
Carolina Inn 211 Pittsboro St........ Chapel Hill NC 27516 TF: 800-962-8519 ■ Web: www.carolinainn.com	919-933-2001		379
Carolina International Trucks Inc 1619 Bluff Rd .... Columbia SC 29201 TF: 800-868-4923 ■ Web: www.carolinainternational.com	803-799-4923		57

	Phone	Fax	Class
Carolina Material Handling Services Inc PO Box 6 ....Columbia SC 29202 *TF:* 800-922-6709 ■ *Web:* www.cmhservices.net	803-695-0149	783-1659	385
Carolina Mattress Guild Inc 385 N Dr # Business......................Thomasville NC 27360	336-476-1333		321
Carolina Meadows 100 Carolina Meadows....................Chapel Hill NC 27517 *TF:* 800-458-6756 ■ *Web:* www.carolinameadows.org	919-942-4014		672
Carolina Medical Lab 1815 Back Creek Dr .... Charlotte NC 28213 *TF:* 800-963-3522 ■ *Web:* www.cmedlab.com	704-598-8818		415
Carolina Medical Products Company Inc 8026 US Hwy 264A .... Farmville NC 27828 *Web:* www.carolinamedical.com	252-753-7111		238
Carolina Mfg 7025 Augusta Rd................ Greenville SC 29605 *TF:* 800-845-2744 ■ *Web:* thebandannacompany.com	864-299-0600	299-0603	155-13
Carolina Mills Inc 618 N Carolina Ave........... Maiden NC 28650 **Fax Area Code:* 848 ■ *Web:* www.carolinamills.com	828-428-9911	428-6254*	745-9
Carolina Narrow Fabric Co 1100 N Patterson Ave.................. Winston-Salem NC 27101 *TF:* 800-914-3538 ■ *Web:* www.carolinanarrowfabric.com	336-631-3000	631-3060	745-5
Carolina Opry 8901 Hwy 17 N.............. Myrtle Beach SC 29572 *TF:* 800-843-6779 ■ *Web:* thecarolinaopry.com	800-843-6779		572
Carolina Packers Inc 2999 S Bright Leaf Blvd .... Smithfield NC 27577 *TF:* 800-682-7675 ■ *Web:* www.carolinapackers.com	919-934-2181	989-6794	473
Carolina Panthers Bank of America Stadium 800 S Mint St......... Charlotte NC 28202 *TF:* 888-297-8673 ■ *Web:* www.panthers.com	704-358-7000	358-7618	715-3
Carolina Pines Regional Medical Ctr 1304 W Bobo Newsome Hwy .... Hartsville SC 29550 *Web:* www.cprmc.com	843-339-2100		374-3
Carolina Place Mall 11025 Carolina Pl Pkwy ....Pineville NC 28134 *Web:* www.carolinaplace.com	704-543-9300		460
Carolina Precision Plastics LLC 405 Commerce Pl..........................Asheboro NC 27203 *Web:* cppglobal.com	336-498-2654		596
Carolina Premier Bank 13024 Ballantyne Corporate Pl Ste 100 .... Charlotte NC 28277 *Web:* www.carolinapremierbank.com	704-752-9292		70
Carolina Pride Foods Inc 1 Packer Ave............................ Greenwood SC 29646 *Web:* carolinapride.publishpath.com	864-229-5611		296-26
Carolina Raptor Ctr 6000 Sample Rd..........................Huntersville NC 28078 *Web:* carolinaraptorcenter.org	704-875-6521		522
Carolina Rim & Wheel Co 1308 Upper Asbury Ave .... Charlotte NC 28206 *TF:* 800-247-4337 ■ *Web:* www.truckpro.com	704-334-7276		61
Carolina Scales Inc 929 N Lucas St.......................... West Columbia SC 29169 *Web:* www.carolinascales.com	803-739-4360		361
Carolina Skiff Inc 3231 Fulford Rd............Waycross GA 31503 *TF:* 800-422-7282 ■ *Web:* www.carolinaskiff.com	912-287-0547		90
Carolina Stair Supply Inc 316 Herrick St...........................Uhrichsville OH 44683 *Web:* www.carolinastair.com	740-922-3333		499
Carolina Supplyhouse Inc 218 Second Loop Rd ....Florence SC 29504 *Web:* www.thesupplyhouse.com	843-662-0702		362
Carolina Theatre 310 S Greene St .... Greensboro NC 27401 *TF:* 800-344-2282 ■ *Web:* www.carolinatheatre.com	336-333-2600		572
Carolina Trust Bank 901 E Main St .... Lincolnton NC 28092 *NASDAQ: CART* ■ *TF:* 877-983-5537 ■ *Web:* www.carolinatrust.com	704-735-1104	735-1104	70
Carolina Veterinary Specialists 2225 Township Rd .... Charlotte NC 28273 *Web:* www.carolinavet.com	704-504-9608		794
Carolina Village 600 Carolina Village Rd ....Hendersonville NC 28792 *Web:* www.carolinavillage.com	828-692-6275		672
Carolina Wholesale Office Machine Company Inc 425 E Arrowhead Dr .... Charlotte NC 28213 *Web:* www.cwholesale.com	704-598-8101		320
Carolina's 12045 Chapman Ave.............Garden Grove CA 92840 *Web:* carolinasitalianrestaurant.com	714-971-5551		671
Carolina's 10 Exchange St ....Charleston SC 29401 *Web:* www.carolinasrestaurant.com	843-724-3800		671
Carolina, Theatre of Durham, The 309 W Morgan St ....Durham NC 27701 *TF:* 800-745-3000 ■ *Web:* www.carolinatheatre.org	919-560-3040	560-3065	572
CarolinaEast Health System 2000 Neuse Blvd ....New Bern NC 28561 *Web:* www.carolinaeasthealth.com	252-633-8111		374-3
Carolinas Auto Supply House Inc 2135 Tipton Dr........................... Charlotte NC 28206 **Fax Area Code:* 800 ■ *TF:* 800-438-4070 ■ *Web:* www.autosupplyhouse.com	704-334-4646	377-7016*	61
Carolinas HealthCare System 1000 Blythe Blvd PO Box 32861.............. Charlotte NC 28232 *Web:* www.carolinashealthcare.org	704-355-2000		353
Carolinas Hospital System 805 Pamplico Hwy ....Florence SC 29505 *TF:* 800-922-0742 ■ *Web:* www.carolinashospital.com	843-674-5000		374-3
Carolinas Investment Consulting LLC 5605 Carnegie Blvd Ste 400................... Charlotte NC 28209 *TF:* 800-255-2904 ■ *Web:* www.carolinasinvest.com	704-643-2455		401
Carolinas Medical Center-NorthEast 920 Church St N...........................Concord NC 28025 *TF:* 800-575-1275 ■ *Web:* www.carolinashealthcare.org	704-403-1275	403-3000	374-3
Carolinas Medical Center-University 8800 N Tryon St .... Charlotte NC 28262 *TF:* 800-821-1535 ■ *Web:* www.carolinashealthcare.org	704-863-6000	863-6236	374-3
Carolinas Medical Ctr 1000 Blythe Blvd .... Charlotte NC 28203 *Web:* www.carolinashealthcare.org	704-355-2000		374-3
Carolinas Medical Ctr Mercy 2001 Vail Ave .... Charlotte NC 28207 *TF:* 800-821-1535 ■ *Web:* www.carolinashealthcare.org	800-821-1535		374-3
Carolinas Medical Ctr Union (CMCU) 600 Hospital Dr .... Monroe NC 28112 *TF:* 800-994-6610 ■ *Web:* www.carolinashealthcare.org	704-283-3100		374-3
Caroline County 117 Ennis St............Bowling Green VA 22427 *Web:* www.co.caroline.va.us	804-633-5380	633-4970	338
Caroline County 109 Market St.................Denton MD 21629 *Web:* www.carolinemd.org	410-479-0660	479-4060	338
Caroline County Chamber of Commerce 9194 Legion Rd Ste 1.........................Denton MD 21629 *Web:* www.carolinechamber.org	410-479-4638	479-4862	139
Caroline County Public Library 100 Market St...............................Denton MD 21629 *TF:* 800-832-3277 ■ *Web:* www.carolib.org	410-479-1343	479-1443	434-3
Caroline Distribution 150 Fifth Ave ....New York NY 10011 *Web:* www.caroline.com	212-886-7500		523
Carollo Engineers 2700 Ygnacio Valley Rd Ste 300............Walnut Creek CA 94598 *TF:* 800-523-5826 ■ *Web:* www.carollo.com	925-932-1710	930-0208	261
Carolyn Dorfman Dance Co (CDDC) 2780 Morris Ave Ste 1-A ....Union NJ 07083 *Web:* carolyndorfman.dance	908-687-8855	686-5245	573-1
Caron Compactor Co 1204 Ullrey Ave .... Escalon CA 95320 *TF:* 800-542-2766 ■ *Web:* www.caroncompactor.com	209-838-2062		190
Caron Engineering Inc 1931 Sanford Rd.......... Wells ME 04090 *TF:* 800-325-3670 ■ *Web:* www.caroneng.com	207-646-6071		180
Carondelet Saint Joseph's Hospital 350 N Wilmot Rd ....Tucson AZ 85711 *Web:* www.carondelet.org	520-873-3000		374-3
Carondelet St. Mary's Hospital 1601 W St Mary's Rd ....Tucson AZ 85745 *Web:* www.carondelet.org	520-872-3000		374-3
Caroplast Inc PO Box 668405............. Charlotte NC 28266 *TF:* 800-327-5797 ■ *Web:* www.caroplast.com	704-394-4191		612
Carotek Inc 700 Sam Newell Rd PO Box 1395.............Matthews NC 28106 *Web:* www.carotek.com	704-844-1100		358
Carothers & Vlasman CPA'S PC 3555 Stanford Rd Ste 104................. Fort Collins CO 80525	970-223-7471		2
Carousel Beachfront Hotel & Suites 11700 Coastal Hwy.........................Ocean City MD 21842 *TF:* 800-641-0011 ■ *Web:* www.carouselhotel.com	410-524-1000	524-7766	379
Carousel Industries of North America Inc 659 S County Trl.............................Exeter RI 02822 *TF:* 800-401-0760 ■ *Web:* www.carouselindustries.com	800-401-0760		224
Carousel Inn & Suites 1530 S Harbor Blvd .... Anaheim CA 92802 *TF:* 800-854-6767 ■ *Web:* www.carouselinnandsuites.com	714-758-0444	772-9960	379
Carousel Mall 295 Carousel Mall .... San Bernardino CA 92401 *Web:* carouselmall.net	909-884-0106		460
Carousel Restaurant 304 N Brand Blvd......... Glendale CA 91203 *Web:* www.carouselrestaurant.com	818-246-7775	246-6627	671
Carousel Signs & Designs Inc 2312 Commerce Ctr Dr Ste B.................. Rockville VA 23146 *Web:* www.carouselsigns.com	804-620-3200		701
Carousel30 500 Montgomery St Ste 650................. Alexandria VA 22314 *Web:* www.carousel30.com	703-260-1180		5
Carpe Diem 1535 Elizabeth Ave .... Charlotte NC 28204 *Web:* www.carpediemrestaurant.com	704-377-7976		671
Carpedia International Ltd 75 Navy St .... Oakville ON L6J2Z1 *TF:* 877-445-8288 ■ *Web:* www.carpedia.com	877-445-8288		463
Carpenter Co 5016 Monument Ave .... Richmond VA 23230 *TF:* 800-288-3830 ■ *Web:* www.carpenter.com	804-359-0800	353-0694	601
Carpenter Contractors of America Inc 3900 Ave D NW ....Winter Haven FL 33880 *TF:* 800-959-8806 ■ *Web:* www.carpentercontractors.com	863-294-6449	299-9940	189-2
Carpenter Industries Inc 4140 Concord Pkwy S ....Concord NC 28027 *Web:* www.denniscarpenter.net	704-786-8139		247
Carpenter Lipps & Leland LLP 280 N High St Ste 1300 .... Columbus OH 43215 *TF:* 800-355-6446 ■ *Web:* carpenterlipps.com	614-365-4100		428
Carpenter Powder Products 600 Mayer St ....Bridgeville PA 15017 *TF:* 866-790-9092 ■ *Web:* www.cartech.com	412-257-5102	257-5058	595
Carpenter Specialty Alloys Operations 101 W Bern St ....Reading PA 19601 *TF:* 800-654-6543 ■ *Web:* www.cartech.com/contact.aspx?id=3858	610-208-2000	208-3716	723
Carpenter Technology Corp PO Box 14662 ....Reading PA 19612 *NYSE: CRS* ■ *TF:* 800-654-6543 ■ *Web:* www.cartech.com	610-208-2000	208-3716	723
Carpenter Technology Corporation - Latrobe Operations (PA) 2626 Ligonier St.............................. Latrobe PA 15650 **Fax Area Code:* 302 ■ *TF:* 800-241-8527 ■ *Web:* www.cartech.com	724-537-7711	636-5454*	492
Carpenters' Hall 320 Chestnut St............Philadelphia PA 19106 *Web:* www.ushistory.org/carpentershall	215-925-0167		50-3
Carpentree Inc 2724 N Sheridan Rd.............. Tulsa OK 74115 *Web:* carpentree.com	918-582-3600		361
Carper Thomas R (Sen D - DE) 513 Hart Bldg .... Washington DC 20510 *Web:* www.carper.senate.gov	202-224-2441	228-2190	342-2
Carpet & Rug Institute (CRI) 100 S Hamilton St PO Box 2048............... Dalton GA 30720 *TF:* 800-653-8338 ■ *Web:* www.carpet-rug.org	706-278-3176	278-8835	49-4
Carpet Cushions & Supplies Inc 1520 Pratt Blvd......................Elk Grove Village IL 60007 *Web:* www.carpetcushions.com	847-364-6760	364-6785	131
Carpet Exchange 1133 S Platte River Dr.......... Denver CO 80223 *Web:* www.carpetexchangeonline.com	303-744-3300		131
Carpet House 1320 Woodlawn .... Lincoln IL 62656	217-735-2531		290
Carpet King Inc 1815 W River Rd N ....Minneapolis MN 55411 *TF:* 800-375-3608 ■ *Web:* www.carpet-king.com	612-588-7600		290
Carpet Tech 6613 19th St ....Lubbock TX 79407 *TF:* 800-789-1331 ■ *Web:* www.callcarpettech.com	806-795-5142		290
Carpetile Co 8 W Main St ....Plano IL 60545	630-552-3400		290
Carpets Plus by Design 330 Lockwood.........Woodville WI 54028 *Web:* stpaulflooring.us	715-698-2200		131

Name	Address	City	State	ZIP	Phone	Fax	Class	Other
Carpin Manufacturing Inc	411 Austin Rd	Waterbury	CT	06705	203-574-2556	753-8771	154	*Web:* www.carpin.com
Carr & Assoc	5251 W 116th Pl Ste 200	Leawood	KS	66211	913-451-9220	451-9228	393	*Web:* www.carrassessments.com
Carr & Co	2556 Piney Rd	Morganton	NC	28655	828-433-5200		321	*TF:* 800-514-6963 ■ *Web:* www.carr.com
Carr & Ferrell LLP	120 Constitution Dr	Menlo Park	CA	94025	650-812-3400		428	*Web:* www.carrferrell.com
Carr Auto Group	11635 SW Canyon Rd	Beaverton	OR	97005	503-644-2161		57	*Web:* www.carrauto.com
Carr Business Systems	130 Spagnoli Rd	Melville	NY	11747	631-249-9880		112	*TF:* 800-720-2277 ■ *Web:* www.carr-global.com
Carr Concrete Corp	Waverly Rd	Waverly	WV	26184	304-464-4013		183	*TF:* 800-837-8918 ■ *Web:* www.carrconcrete.com
Carr Corp	1547 11th St	Santa Monica	CA	90401	310-587-1113	395-9751	591	*TF:* 800-952-2398 ■ *Web:* www.carrcorporation.com
Carr Creek State Park	Hwy 15	Sassafras	KY	41759	606-642-4050		565	*Web:* www.parks.ky.gov
Carr Engineering Inc	12500 Castlebridge Dr	Houston	TX	77065	281-894-8955		256	*Web:* carrengineeringinc.com
Carr Environmental Group Inc	504 Spring Hill Dr Ste 300 Spring	Houston	TX	77386	281-872-9300	872-4521	192	*Web:* www.ceg-group.com
Carr Lane Mfg	4200 Carr Ln Ct	Saint Louis	MO	63119	314-647-6200	647-5736	757	*TF:* 800-622-4824 ■ *Web:* www.carrlane.com
Carr McClellan Ingersall Thompson	216 Park Rd	Burlingame	CA	94010	650-342-9600		428	*Web:* www.carr-mcclellan.com
Carr Riggs & Ingram LLC	1117 Boll Weevil Cir	Enterprise	AL	36330	334-347-0088		2	*Web:* www.cricpa.com
Carr's Restaurant	50 W Grant St	Lancaster	PA	17603	717-299-7090		671	*Web:* www.carrsrestaurant.com
Carreno Group Inc	714 Parker St	Houston	TX	77007	713-426-4300		636	
Carrera & Partners Inc	388 SW 12th Ave	Deerfield Beach	FL	33442	954-360-9111		7	*TF:* 800-842-1342 ■ *Web:* www.carreraadvertising.com
Carreta's Grill	2320 Veterans Memorial Blvd	Metairie	LA	70002	504-837-6696		671	*Web:* carretasgrillrestaurant.com
Carriage House	24460 Adams Rd	South Bend	IN	46628	574-272-9220		671	*Web:* www.carriagehousedining.com
Carriage House Cos Inc, The	196 Newton St	Fredonia	NY	14063	716-673-1000	673-8443*	296-20	*Fax: Sales
Carriage Services Inc	3040 Post Oak Blvd Ste 300	Houston	TX	77056	713-332-8400		510	*NYSE: CSV* ■ *TF:* 866-332-8400 ■ *Web:* www.carriageservices.com
Carriage Works Inc	1877 Mallard Ln	Klamath Falls	OR	97601	541-882-0700		820	*TF:* 800-257-7855 ■ *Web:* www.carriageworks.com
Carrico Implement Company Inc	3160 US 24 Hwy	Beloit	KS	67420	785-738-5744	738-2648	274	*TF:* 877-542-4099 ■ *Web:* www.carricoimplement.com
Carrier Clinic	252 County Rd 601	Belle Mead	NJ	08502	908-281-1000		374-5	*TF:* 800-933-3579 ■ *Web:* carrierclinic.org
Carrier Coach Inc	271 Buffalo St	Gowanda	NY	14070	716-532-2600		30	*Web:* www.coach.com
Carrier Interamerica	10801 NW 103rd St Ste 1	Medley	FL	33178	305-590-1000		610	*Web:* www.carrierca.com
Carrier IQ Inc	640 W California Ave Ste 100	Sunnyvale	CA	94086	650-625-5400		179	
Carrier Lumber Ltd	4722 Continental Way	Prince George	BC	V2N5S5	250-563-9271		683	*Web:* www.carrierlumber.bc.ca
Carrier Services of Tennessee Inc	2534 N Mt Juliet Rd	Mount Juliet	TN	37122	615-758-9757		478	*TF:* 800-825-7508 ■ *Web:* www.carrierservtn.com
Carrier Vibrating Equipment Inc	3400 Fern Valley Rd	Louisville	KY	40213	502-969-3171	969-3172	207	*TF:* 800-547-7278 ■ *Web:* www.carriervibrating.com
Carriercom Lp	200 s Tenth st	McAllen	TX	78501	956-682-3656		387	*Web:* www.carriercom.net
Carriere Bernier Ltee	25 Petit Bernier CP 548	Saint-jean-sur-richelieu	QC	J3B6Z8	450-545-2000		135	*Web:* www.carrierebernier.com
Carrillo Business Technologies Inc	750 The City Dr S Ste 225	Orange	CA	92868	888-241-7585		179	*TF:* 888-241-7585 ■ *Web:* www.cbtechinc.com
Carrington Convention & Visitors Bureau	City Hall 103 Tenth Ave N PO Box 501	Carrington	ND	58421	701-652-2524	652-2391	206	*TF:* 800-641-9668 ■ *Web:* www.cgtn-nd.com
Carrington Foods Company Inc	200 Jacintoport Blvd # D	Saraland	AL	36571	251-675-9700		297-8	*Web:* www.carringtonfoods.com
Carris Reels Inc	46 Ripley Rd	Rutland	VT	05701	802-773-9111		279	*Web:* www.carris.com
Carrizo Oil & Gas Inc	1000 Louisiana Ste 1500	Houston	TX	77002	713-328-1000	328-1035	536	*NASDAQ: CRZO* ■ *Web:* carrizo.com
Carroll & Blackman Inc	3120 Fannin St	Beaumont	TX	77701	409-833-3363	833-0317	256	*Web:* www.cbieng.com
Carroll & Co	425 N Canon Dr	Beverly Hills	CA	90210	310-273-9060	273-7974	157-3	*TF:* 800-238-9400 ■ *Web:* www.carrollandco.com
Carroll Co	2900 W Kingsley Rd	Garland	TX	75041	972-278-1304	840-0678	151	*TF:* 800-527-5722 ■ *Web:* www.carrollco.com
Carroll College	1601 N Benton Ave	Helena	MT	59625	406-447-4300	447-4533	166	*TF:* 800-992-3648 ■ *Web:* www.carroll.edu
Carroll Community College	1601 Washington Rd	Westminster	MD	21157	410-386-8000		162	*TF:* 888-221-9748 ■ *Web:* www.carrollcc.edu
Carroll Cos Inc	1640 Old Hwy 421 S	Boone	NC	28607	828-264-2521	264-2633	431	*TF:* 800-884-2521 ■ *Web:* www.clgco.com
Carroll County	114 E Sixth St	Carroll	IA	51401	712-792-4923		338	*Web:* www.co.carroll.ia.us
Carroll County	423 College St Rm 408 PO Box 338	Carrollton	GA	30112	770-830-5800	830-5992	338	*Web:* www.carrollcountyga.com
Carroll County	440 Main St Courthouse	Carrollton	KY	41008	502-732-7005		338	*Web:* www.carrollcountyky.com
Carroll County	8 S Main Ste 6	Carrollton	MO	64633	660-542-0615		338	
Carroll County	105 B E Washington St PO Box 59	Carrollton	MS	38917	662-237-4413		338	*Web:* carrollcountyms.org
Carroll County	119 S Lisbon St Ste 201	Carrollton	OH	44615	330-627-4869	627-6656	338	*TF:* 800-750-0750 ■ *Web:* www.carrollcountyohio.net
Carroll County	114 E Main St Ste C PO Box 175	Delphi	IN	46923	765-564-6757	564-2207	338	*TF:* 866-374-6813 ■ *Web:* www.carrollcountyindiana.com
Carroll County	605-1 Pine St	Hillsville	VA	24343	276-730-3070	730-3071	338	*Web:* carrollcountyva.org
Carroll County	20740 East Main St PO Box 726	Huntingdon	TN	38344	731-986-1936	986-1935	338	*Web:* www.carrollcounty-tn-chamber.com
Carroll County	8215 Black Oak Rd	Mount Carroll	IL	61053	815-244-2035		338	*TF:* 800-485-0145 ■ *Web:* www.gocarrollcounty.com
Carroll County	225 N Ctr St	Westminster	MD	21157	410-386-2011	840-8932	338	*TF:* 800-735-2258 ■ *Web:* www.ccgovernment.carr.org
Carroll County Board of Ed	125 N Court St Ste 101	Westminster	MD	21157	410-751-3000		685	*Web:* www.carrollk12.org
Carroll County Chamber of Commerce	700 Corporate Ctr Ct # L	Westminster	MD	21157	410-848-9050	876-1023	139	*Web:* www.carrollcountychamber.org
Carroll County Chamber of Commerce	200 Northside Dr	Carrollton	GA	30117	770-832-2446	832-1300	139	*Web:* www.carroll-ga.org
Carroll County Chamber of Commerce	20740 Main St E	Huntingdon	TN	38344	731-986-4664	986-2029	139	*Web:* www.carrollcounty-tn-chamber.com
Carroll County Chamber of Commerce & Economic Development	61 N Lisbon St PO Box 277	Carrollton	OH	44615	330-627-4811	627-3674	139	*TF:* 877-727-0103 ■ *Web:* www.carrollohchamber.com
Carroll County District Library	70 Second St NE	Carrollton	OH	44615	330-627-2613	627-2523	434-3	*Web:* carrolllibrary.org
Carroll County Economic Development	111 N Mason St	Carrollton	MO	64633	660-542-0922		194	
Carroll County Public Library	1100 Green Valley Rd New	Windsor	MD	21776	410-386-4500	386-4509	434-3	*Web:* www.library.carr.org
Carroll County School District	605 9 Pine St	Hillsville	VA	24343	276-730-3200	728-3195	186	*Web:* www.ccpsd.k12.va.us
Carroll County Sheriff's Office	95 Water Village Rd PO Box 190	Ossipee	NH	03864	603-539-2204		330	*TF:* 800-552-8960 ■ *Web:* carrollcountynh.net
Carroll County Times	115 Airport Dr Ste 170	Westminster	MD	21157	410-848-4400		532-2	*TF:* 877-228-4637 ■ *Web:* www.carrollcountytimes.com
Carroll CountyClerk	210 W Church St	Berryville	AR	72616	870-423-2022		338	
Carroll Electric Co-op Corp	920 Hwy 62 Spur	Berryville	AR	72616	870-423-2161	423-4815	245	*TF:* 800-432-9720 ■ *Web:* www.carrollecc.com
Carroll Electric Co-op Inc	350 Canton Rd NW	Carrollton	OH	44615	330-627-2116		245	*TF:* 800-232-7697 ■ *Web:* cecpower.coop
Carroll Electric Membership Corp	155 N Hwy 113	Carrollton	GA	30117	770-832-3552	832-0240	245	*TF:* 800-822-4563 ■ *Web:* www.cemc.com
Carroll Engineering Corp	949 Easton Rd	Warrington	PA	18976	215-343-5700	343-0875	261	*Web:* www.carrollengineering.com
Carroll Fulmer Logistics Corp	8340 American Way	Groveland	FL	34736	352-429-5000		780	*Web:* www.cfulmer.com
Carroll Hospice	292 Stoner Ave	Westminster	MD	21157	410-871-8000		371	*TF:* 800-966-3877 ■ *Web:* carrollcountytimes.com
Carroll Hospital Ctr	200 Memorial Ave	Westminster	MD	21157	410-848-3000		374-3	*Web:* carrollhospitalcenter.org
Carroll Independent Fuel Co	2700 Loch Raven Rd	Baltimore	MD	21218	410-235-9911		316	*Web:* www.carrollhomeservices.com
Carroll Lutheran Village	300 St Luke Cir	Westminster	MD	21158	410-848-0090		672	*TF:* 877-848-0095 ■ *Web:* www.carrolllutheranvillage.org
Carroll Properties Partnership	12734 Kenwood Ln Ste 35	Fort Myers	FL	33907	239-278-5900		379	*Web:* carroll-properties.com
Carroll Publishing Co	4701 Sangamore Rd Ste S-155	Bethesda	MD	20816	301-263-9800	263-9801	637-2	*TF:* 800-336-4240 ■ *Web:* www.carrollpublishing.com
Carroll Seating Company Inc	10 Lincoln St	Kansas City	KS	66103	816-471-2929	471-3001	320	*TF:* 800-972-3779 ■ *Web:* www.carrollseating.com
Carroll Service Co	505 W Illinois Rt 64	Lanark	IL	61046	815-493-2181	493-6173	276	*Web:* carrollsvc.com
Carroll University	100 NE Ave	Waukesha	WI	53186	262-547-1211	951-3037*	166	*Fax: Admissions ■ *TF:* 800-227-7655 ■ *Web:* www.carrollu.edu
Carroll Valley Golf Resort	78 Country Club Trail	Carroll Valley	PA	17320	717-642-8282		669	*TF:* 855-784-0330 ■ *Web:* libertymountainresort.com
Carrollton Public Library	4220 N Josey Ln	Carrollton	TX	75010	972-466-4800	466-4722	434-3	*TF:* 888-727-2978 ■ *Web:* www.cityofcarrollton.com/library
Carrollwood News	5625 W Waters Ave G	Tampa	FL	33634	813-259-8295		532-4	

	Phone	Fax	Class
Carrols Restaurant Group Inc 968 James St .... Syracuse NY 13203 *NASDAQ: TAST* ■ *TF:* 800-348-1074 ■ *Web:* www.carrols.com	315-424-0513		670
Carrom 218 E Dowland St.......... Ludington MI 49431 *TF:* 800-223-6047 ■ *Web:* www.carrom.com	231-845-1263	843-9276	319-2
Carron Net Company Inc 1623 17th St PO Box 177.......... Two Rivers WI 54241 *TF:* 800-558-7768 ■ *Web:* www.carronnet.com	920-793-2217	793-2122	208
Carrot & Stick Inc 115 New St Ste A.......... Decatur GA 30030 *Web:* www.carrotandstick.com	404-371-1891		636
Carrot Medical LLC 22122 20th Ave SE Ste H-166.......... Bothell WA 98021 *TF:* 866-492-3533 ■ *Web:* carrotmedical.com	425-318-8089		743
Cars & Trucks r Us 7676 Happy Valley Rd.......... Cave City KY 42127 *Web:* ucarsandtrucks.com	270-773-2886		57
Cars.com 175 W Jackson Blvd Ste 800.......... Chicago IL 60604 *TF:* 888-246-6298 ■ *Web:* www.cars.com	312-601-5000	601-5755	58
Carsan Engineering Inc 221 Corporate Cir Ste H.......... Golden CO 80401	303-237-9608		256
CarsDirect.com Inc 909 N Sepulveda Blvd 11th Fl.......... El Segundo CA 90245 *TF Cust Svc:* 888-227-7347 ■ *Web:* www.carsdirect.com	888-227-7347		58
Carsey-Werner LLC 16027 Ventura Blvd Ste 600.......... Encino CA 91436 *Web:* www.carseywerner.com	818-464-9600		511
Carskadden Optical Co 1525 Highpoint Ct.......... Zanesville OH 43701	740-452-9306		542
CarSmart 18872 MacArthur Blvd Ste 200.......... Irvine CA 92612 *Web:* www.autobytel.com	949-225-4500		58
Carson 3125 NW 35th Ave.......... Portland OR 97210 *TF:* 800-998-7767 ■ *Web:* www.carsonoil.com	503-224-8500		579
Carson Andre (Rep D - IN) 2135 Rayburn HOB.......... Washington DC 20515 *Web:* carson.house.gov	202-225-4011	225-5633	342-2
Carson Boxberger LLP 301 W Jefferson Blvd Ste 200.......... Fort Wayne IN 46802 *TF:* 800-900-4250 ■ *Web:* www.carsonboxberger.com	260-423-9411		445
Carson Chamber of Commerce 530 E Del Amo Blvd.......... Carson CA 90746 *Web:* www.carsonchamber.com	310-217-4590	217-4591	139
Carson City Area Chamber of Commerce 1900 S Carson St Ste 200.......... Carson City NV 89701 *Web:* www.carsoncitychamber.com	775-882-1565	882-4179	139
Carson City City Hall 201 N Carson St.......... Carson City NV 89701 *Web:* carson.org	775-887-2100	887-2139	337
Carson City Correctional Facility 10274 Boyer Rd.......... Carson City MI 48811 *Web:* www.michigan.gov/corrections	989-584-3941		213
Carson City (Independent City) 201 N Carson St.......... Carson City NV 89701 *Web:* carson.org	775-887-2100	887-2286	338
Carson City Library 900 N Roop St.......... Carson City NV 89701 *Web:* carsoncitylibrary.org	775-887-2244	887-2273	434-3
Carson City Nugget 507 N Carson St.......... Carson City NV 89701 *TF:* 800-426-5239 ■ *Web:* www.ccnugget.com	775-882-1626		133
Carson City Symphony PO Box 2001 PO Box 2001.......... Carson City NV 89702 *Web:* www.ccsymphony.com	775-883-4154	883-4371	573-3
Carson County PO Box 487.......... Panhandle TX 79068 *TF:* 800-275-8777 ■ *Web:* www.co.carson.tx.us	806-537-3873	537-3623	338
Carson Ctr 801 E Carson St.......... Carson CA 90745 *Web:* www.carsoncenter.com	310-835-0212	835-0160	205
Carson Doubletree Hotel Civic Plaza, The 2 Civic Plaza.......... Carson CA 90745 *Web:* www.carsondoubletree.com	310-830-9200		378
Carson Dunlop Home Inspections 407-120 Carlton St.......... Toronto ON M5A4K2 *Web:* www.carsondunlop.com	416-964-9415		652
Carson Group Advertising, The 1708 Hwy 6 S.......... Houston TX 77077 *TF:* 800-331-3282 ■ *Web:* www.carsongroupadvertising.com	281-496-2600		7
Carson Helicopters 952 Blooming Glen Rd.......... Perkasie PA 18944 *Web:* www.carsonhelicopters.com	215-249-3535	249-1352	359
Carson Hot Springs 1500 Hot Springs Rd.......... Carson City NV 89706 *TF:* 888-917-3711 ■ *Web:* carsonhotsprings.com	775-885-8844		50-5
Carson Long Military Institute 200 N Carlisle St.......... New Bloomfield PA 17068 *Web:* www.carsonlong.org	717-582-2121		622
Carson Tahoe Hospital 1600 Medical Pkwy.......... Carson City NV 89703 *Web:* www.carsontahoe.com/regional-medical-center	775-445-8000		374-3
Carson Valley Chamber of Commerce & Visitors Authority 1477 Hwy 395 N Ste A.......... Gardnerville NV 89410 *TF:* 800-727-7677 ■ *Web:* www.carsonvalleynv.org	775-782-8144	782-1025	139
Carson Valley Inn Inc 1627 US Hwy 395 N.......... Minden NV 89423 *TF:* 866-284-7766 ■ *Web:* www.cvinn.com	775-782-9711		121
Carson Valley Museum & Cultural Ctr 1477 old US Hwy 395 S.......... Gardnerville NV 89410	775-782-2555		520
Carson's Inc PO Box 14186.......... Archdale NC 27263 *Web:* www.carsonsofhp.com	336-397-4339		319-2
Carson's Nut-Bolt & Tool Co 301 Hammett St Ext.......... Greenville SC 29609 *Web:* www.carsons-nbt.com	864-242-4720		351
Carson-Dellosa Publishing Company Inc 7027 Albert Pick Rd.......... Greensboro NC 27409 *TF:* 800-321-0943 ■ *Web:* www.carsondellosa.com	336-632-0084		243
Carsonite Composites LLC 19845 US Hwy 76.......... Newberry SC 29108 *TF:* 800-648-7916 ■ *Web:* www.carsonite.com	803-321-1185	276-8940	678
Carson-Newman College 1646 Russell Ave.......... Jefferson City TN 37760 *Fax: Admissions ■ *TF:* 800-678-9061 ■ *Web:* www.cn.edu	865-471-2000	471-3502*	166
CARSTAR Quality Collision Service 8400 W 110th St Ste 200.......... Overland Park KS 66210 *TF Cust Svc:* 800-227-7827 ■ *Web:* www.carstar.com	913-451-1294		62-4
Carstens Industries Inc 733 W Main St.......... Melrose MN 56352 *Web:* www.carstensindustries.com	320-256-3919	256-4052	710
Carswell Distributing Co 3750 N Liberty St.......... Winston-Salem NC 27105 *TF:* 800-929-1948 ■ *Web:* www.carswelldist.com	336-767-7700		429
CARTA (Charleston Area Regional Transportation Authority) 1362 McMillan Ave Ste 100.......... North Charleston SC 29405 *Web:* www.ridecarta.com	843-724-7420		468
Cartec International Inc 106 Powder Mill Rd.......... Canton CT 06019 *TF:* 800-821-4434 ■ *Web:* www.cartec.com	860-693-9395		605-2
Carten Controls 604 W Johnson Ave.......... Cheshire CT 06410 *Web:* www.cartenus.com	203-699-2100		790
Carter & Holmes N3150 Iris Rd.......... Lake Geneva WI 53147 *Web:* www.carterholmes.com	262-215-5494	203-7111	155-13
Carter & Sloope Inc 6310 Peake Rd.......... Macon GA 31210 *Web:* cartersloope.com	478-477-3923		261
Carter Bank & Trust 1300 Kings Mtn Rd.......... Martinsville VA 24112 *Web:* carterbankandtrust.com	276-656-1776		70
Carter Barron Amphitheatre 4850 Colorado Ave NW.......... Washington DC 20008 *Web:* www.nps.gov/rocr/planyourvisit/cbarron.htm	202-426-0486		572
Carter BloodCare 2205 Hwy 121.......... Bedford TX 76021 *TF:* 800-366-2834 ■ *Web:* www.carterbloodcare.org	817-412-5000		89
Carter Bros LLC 3015 RN Martin St.......... East Point GA 30344 *TF:* 888-818-0152 ■ *Web:* carterbrothers.com	888-818-0152		692
Carter Buddy (Rep R - GA) 432 Cannon HOB.......... Washington DC 20515 *Web:* buddycarter.house.gov	202-225-5831	226-2269	342-2
Carter Business Service Inc 150A Andover St.......... Danvers MA 01923 *Web:* carterbusiness.com	781-246-4300		160
Carter Composition Corp 2007 N Hamilton St.......... Richmond VA 23230 *TF:* 800-882-1844 ■ *Web:* www.carterprinting.com	804-359-9206		627
Carter County 101 1St Ave SW.......... Ardmore OK 73401 *TF:* 800-231-8668 ■ *Web:* cartercountyok.us	580-223-8162		338
Carter County 214 Pk St PO Box 315.......... Ekalaka MT 59324 *Web:* www.cartercountymt.info	406-775-8749	775-8750	338
Carter County 500 Veterans Memorial Pkwy PO Box 190.......... Elizabethton TN 37643 *Web:* tourcartercounty.com	423-547-3850	547-3854	338
Carter County 300 W Main St Rm 227.......... Grayson KY 41143 *Web:* www.cartercountyclerksoffice.com	606-474-5366	474-6991	338
Carter County 105 Main St.......... Van Buren MO 63965	573-323-4513		338
Carter Ctr 1 Copenhill Ave 453 Freedom Pkwy.......... Atlanta GA 30307 *TF:* 800-550-3560 ■ *Web:* www.cartercenter.org	404-420-5100	331-0283	634
Carter Day International Inc 500 73rd Ave NE.......... Minneapolis MN 55432 *Web:* www.carterday.com	763-571-1000	571-3012	273
Carter Enterprises Inc 119 W Main St.......... Arcadia IN 46030 *Web:* www.carterent.com	317-984-1497		295
Carter Express Inc 4020 W 73rd St.......... Anderson IN 46011 *TF:* 800-738-7705 ■ *Web:* www.carter-express.com	800-738-7705		194
Carter Group LLC, The 1621 University Blvd S.......... Mobile AL 36609 *Web:* www.thecartergroup.com	251-342-0999		260
Carter Healthcare 3105 S Meridian Ave.......... Oklahoma City OK 73119 *TF:* 888-951-1112 ■ *Web:* www.carterhealthcare.com	405-947-7700	947-7300	363
Carter John (Rep R - TX) 2110 Rayburn HOB.......... Washington DC 20515 *Web:* carter.house.gov	202-225-3864	225-5866	342-2
Carter Ledyard & Milburn LLP 2 Wall St Fl 13.......... New York NY 10005 *Web:* www.clm.com	212-732-3200	732-3232	428
Carter Lumber Co Inc 601 Tallmadge Rd.......... Kent OH 44240 *Web:* www.carterlumber.com	330-673-6100		364
Carter Machinery Company Inc 1330 Lynchburg Tpk.......... Salem VA 24153 *Web:* www.cartermachinery.com	540-387-1111		190
Carter Mario Injury Lawyers 176 Wethersfield Ave.......... Hartford CT 06114 *TF:* 844-634-5656 ■ *Web:* cartermario.com	844-634-5656		428
Carter Motor Co 400 S Railroad St.......... Warren IL 61087 *Web:* www.cartermotor.com	815-745-2100		57
Carter Printing Company Inc 1739 E Grand Ave.......... Des Moines IA 50316 *Web:* carterprinting.net	515-265-6139		627
CarterBaldwin Inc 200 Mansell Ct E Ste 450.......... Roswell GA 30076 *Web:* www.carterbaldwin.com	678-448-0000		193
CarterEnergy Corp 6000 Metcalf Ave.......... Overland Park KS 66202 *TF:* 800-444-8672 ■ *Web:* www.carterenergy.com	913-643-2300		581
Carteret Community College 3505 Arendell St.......... Morehead City NC 28557 *Web:* www.carteret.edu	252-222-6000	222-6265	162
Carteret Correctional Center 1084 Orange St PO Box 220.......... Newport NC 28570 *Web:* www.doc.state.nc.us	252-223-5100	223-3069	213
Carteret County Courthouse Sq.......... Beaufort NC 28516 *Web:* carteretcountync.gov	252-728-8450	728-2092	338
Carteret County Chamber of Commerce 801 Arendell St Ste 1.......... Morehead City NC 28557 *TF:* 800-622-6278 ■ *Web:* www.nccoastchamber.com	252-726-6350	726-3505	139
Carteret General Hospital 3500 Arendell St PO Box 1619.......... Morehead City NC 28557 *Web:* www.carterethealth.org	252-808-6000		374-3
Carteret-Craven Electric Co-op (CCEC) 1300 Hwy 24 W PO Box 1490.......... Newport NC 28570 *TF:* 800-682-2217 ■ *Web:* www.carteretcravenelectric.coop	252-247-3107		245

				Phone	Fax	Class
Carter-Hoffmann Corp 1551 Mccormick Ave *Web:* www.carter-hoffmann.com	Mundelein	IL	60060	847-362-5500		427
Carter-lambert Divisions Llc 3023 Hubbard Rd Ste 210 *Web:* www.carterlambert.com	Landover	MD	20785	703-286-0826		396
Carter-Lee ProBuild 1717 W Washington St *TF:* 800-344-9242 ■ *Web:* probuildindy.com	Indianapolis	IN	46222	317-639-5431	639-6982	499
Cartersville City Schools 15 Nelson St PO Box 3310 *Web:* cartersvilleschools.org	Cartersville	GA	30120	770-382-5880	387-7476	685
Cartersville-Bartow County Chamber of Commerce 122 W Main St PO Box 307 *TF:* 800-527-9395 ■ *Web:* www.cartersvillechamber.com	Cartersville	GA	30120	770-382-1466	382-2704	139
Carthage College 2001 Alford Pk Dr **Fax:* Admissions ■ *TF Admissions:* 800-351-4058 ■ *Web:* www.carthage.edu	Kenosha	WI	53140	262-551-8500	551-5762*	166
Carthage Mills 4243 Hunt Rd *TF Sales:* 800-543-4430 ■ *Web:* www.carthagemills.com	Cincinnati	OH	45242	513-794-1600	794-3434	745-3
Carthage Veterinary Service Ltd 34 W Main St *Web:* www.hogvet.com	Carthage	IL	62321	217-357-2811		794
Carthage Water & Electric Plant PO Box 611 *Web:* cwep.com	Carthage	MO	64836	417-237-7300	237-7306	787
Cartier Place Suite Hotel 180 Cooper St *TF:* 800-236-8399 ■ *Web:* www.suitedreams.com	Ottawa	ON	K2P2L5	613-236-5000	238-3842	379
CarTika Medical Inc 6550 Wedgwood Rd N Ste 300 *TF:* 800-678-2737 ■ *Web:* www.cartikamedical.com	Maple Grove	MN	55311	763-545-5188		477
Cartis Group 3011 N Lamar *Web:* carterstrategy.com	Austin	TX	78705	512-476-2600		7
Cartmell Home for Aged Inc 2212 W Reagan St *Web:* cartmellhome.org	Palestine	TX	75801	903-727-8500		371
Cartner Glass Systems Inc 2508 Westinghouse Blvd	Charlotte	NC	28273	704-588-1976		189-6
Carton Donofrio Partners Inc 100 N Charles St *Web:* www.cartondonofrio.com	Baltimore	MD	21201	410-576-9000		4
Carton Service Inc First Quality Dr PO Box 702 *TF General:* 800-533-7744 ■ *Web:* www.cartonservice.com	Shelby	OH	44875	419-342-5010	342-4804	101
Cartoon Art Museum 655 Mission St *Web:* www.cartoonart.org	San Francisco	CA	94105	415-227-8666	243-8666	520
Cartoon Cuts LP 927 N University Dr *Web:* www.cartooncuts.com	Coral Springs	FL	33071	954-341-4221		77
Cartoon Network Inc, The 1015 Techwood Dr *Web:* www.cartoonnetwork.com	Atlanta	GA	30318	404-878-0694		740
Cartridge Actuated Devices Inc (CAD) 51 Dwight Pl *Web:* cartactdev.com	Fairfield	NJ	07004	973-575-1312		268
Cartus Corp 40 Apple Ridge Rd *TF:* 800-817-1928 ■ *Web:* www.cartus.com	Danbury	CT	06810	203-205-3400	205-6575	666
Cartwright Cos, The 11901 Cartwright Ave **Fax Area Code:* 816 ■ *TF:* 800-821-2334 ■ *Web:* www.cartwrightcompanies.com	Grandview	MO	64030	800-821-2334	442-6360*	519
Cartwright Matthew (Rep D - PA) 1034 Longworth Bldg *Web:* cartwright.house.gov	Washington	DC	20515	202-225-5546	226-0996	342-2
Carty & Company Inc 6263 Poplar Ave Ste 800 *Web:* www.cartyco.com	Memphis	TN	38119	901-767-8940		401
Carus Corp 315 Fifth St *TF:* 800-435-6856 ■ *Web:* www.caruscorporation.com	Peru	IL	61354	815-223-1500	224-6697	143
Caruso Affiliated Holdings LLC 101 The Grove Dr *Web:* caruso.com	Los Angeles	CA	90036	323-900-8100		360-2
Caruso Inc 3465 Hauck Rd *TF:* 800-759-7659 ■ *Web:* www.carusologistics.com	Cincinnati	OH	45241	513-860-9200		10-11
Caruso Turley Scott Inc 1215 W Rio Salado Pkwy Ste 200 *Web:* www.ctsaz.com	Tempe	AZ	85281	480-774-1700		256
Caruthers Raisin Packing Company Inc 12797 S Elm Ave	Caruthers	CA	93609	559-864-9448		297-8
CarVal Investors LLC 9320 Excelsior Blvd 7th Fl *TF:* 800-638-2479 ■ *Web:* www.carvalinvestors.com	Hopkins	MN	55343	952-984-3774		401
Carvel Express 200 Glenridge Pt Pkwy Ste 200 *TF:* 800-322-4848 ■ *Web:* www.carvel.com	Atlanta	GA	30342	800-322-4848		381
Carver & Associates Inc 4177 Northeast Expy *Web:* www.carverassoc.com	Atlanta	GA	30340	770-446-2677		317
Carver Bancorp Inc 75 W 125th St *NASDAQ: CARV* ■ *Web:* www.carverbank.com	New York	NY	10027	718-230-2900		360-2
Carver Bible College 3870 Cascade Rd *Web:* www.carver.edu	Atlanta	GA	30331	404-527-4520	527-4524	166
Carver Boat Corp LLC 790 Markham Dr PO Box 1010 *Web:* www.carveryachts.com	Pulaski	WI	54162	920-822-3214		90
Carver Brewing Co 1022 Main Ave *Web:* www.carverbrewing.com	Durango	CO	81301	970-259-2545		671
Carver Community Cultural Ctr 226 N Hackberry St *Web:* www.thecarver.org	San Antonio	TX	78202	210-207-7211		50-2
Carver County 606 E Fourth St *Web:* www.co.carver.mn.us	Chaska	MN	55318	952-361-1500		338
Carver County Library 4 City Hall Plaza *Web:* www.carverlib.org	Chaska	MN	55318	952-448-9395	448-9392	434-3
Carver Florek & James LLC 2246 University Park Blvd *Web:* cfjcpa.com	Layton	UT	84041	801-926-1177		2
Carver FSB 75 W 125th St *Web:* www.carverbank.com	New York	NY	10027	718-230-2900		70
Carver Machine Works 129 Christian Service Camp Rd *Web:* www.cmwglobal.com	Washington	NC	27889	252-975-3101		454
Carver Pump Co 2415 Pk Ave *Web:* www.carverpump.com	Muscatine	IA	52761	563-263-3410	262-7688	641
Carver's Steakhouse 2620 32nd Ave NE	Calgary	AB	T1Y6B8	403-250-6327		671
Carvers Steak & Chops 11940 Bernardo Plaza Dr *TF:* 800-561-3357 ■ *Web:* www.carverssteak.com	San Diego	CA	92128	858-485-1262		670
Carville National Leather Corp 10 Knox Ave PO Box 40	Johnstown	NY	12095	518-762-1634	762-8973	432
Carvin Corp 12340 World Trade Dr *TF:* 800-854-2235 ■ *Web:* www.carvin.com	San Diego	CA	92128	858-487-8700		527
Carvin French Jewelers Inc 515 Madison Ave Ste 1605	New York	NY	10022	212-755-6474		409
Car-X Assoc Corp 1375 E Woodfield Rd Ste 500 *Web:* www.carx.com	Schaumburg	IL	60173	847-273-8920		310
Cary Academy 1500 N Harrison Ave *TF:* 800-948-2557 ■ *Web:* www.caryacademy.org	Cary	NC	27513	919-677-3873		685
Cary Chamber of Commerce 307 N Academy St *Web:* www.carychamber.com	Cary	NC	27513	919-467-1016	469-2375	139
Cary Concrete Products Inc 211 Dean St Ste 1D *TF:* 800-634-9091 ■ *Web:* www.caryconcrete.com	Woodstock	IL	60098	815-338-2301	337-5801	183
Cary Kopczynski & Company Inc PS Bellevue Pl 10500 Eighth St Ste 800 *Web:* www.ckcps.com	Bellevue	WA	98004	425-455-2144		256
Cary Memorial Library 1874 Massachusetts Ave *Web:* www.carylibrary.org	Lexington	MA	02420	781-862-6288	862-7355	434-3
Cary Oil Company Inc 110 Mackenan Dr *TF:* 800-227-9645 ■ *Web:* www.caryoil.com	Cary	NC	27511	919-462-1100	481-6862	581
Cary Pharmaceuticals Inc 9903 Windy Hollow Rd *Web:* www.carypharma.com	Great Falls	VA	22066	703-759-7460		582
Cary Towne Ctr 1105 Walnut St *Web:* www.shopcarytownecentermall.com	Cary	NC	27511	919-467-0145		460
Carylon Corp 2500 W Arthington St *TF:* 800-621-4342 ■ *Web:* www.caryloncorp.com	Chicago	IL	60612	312-666-7700	666-5810	667
CAS (Center for Auto Safety) 1825 Connecticut Ave NW Ste 330 *Web:* www.autosafety.org	Washington	DC	20009	202-328-7700		49-21
CAS (Chemical Abstracts Service) 2540 Olentangy River Rd *TF:* 800-848-6538 ■ *Web:* cas.org	Columbus	OH	43202	614-447-3600	447-3713	387
CAS (Casualty Actuarial Society) 4350 Fairfax Dr # 250 *TF:* 800-766-0070 ■ *Web:* www.casact.org	Arlington	VA	22203	703-276-3100	276-3108	49-9
CAS Inc 345 Bob Health *TF:* 800-729-8686 ■ *Web:* cascares.cas-inc.com	Huntsville	AL	35806	256-971-6126	922-4207	261
CAS Medical Systems Inc 44 E Industrial Rd *NASDAQ: CASM* ■ *TF:* 800-227-4414 ■ *Web:* www.fore-sight.com	Branford	CT	06405	203-488-6056	488-9438	476
CASA (National CASA Assn) 100 W Harrison St North Tower Ste 500 *TF:* 800-628-3233 ■ *Web:* www.casaforchildren.org	Seattle	WA	98119	206-270-0072	270-0078	48-6
Casa Alvarez 106 Dawson Pl *Web:* www.casaalvarezfoods.com	Longmont	CO	80504	720-491-1985		671
Casa Baez 1292 Lancaster Dr NE	Salem	OR	97301	503-371-3867		671
Casa Bonita 6715 W Colfax Ave *Web:* www.casabonitadenver.com	Lakewood	CO	80214	303-232-5115		671
Casa Colina Ctr for Rehabilitation 255 E Bonita Ave *TF:* 800-926-5462 ■ *Web:* www.casacolina.org	Pomona	CA	91769	909-596-7733	596-7845	450
Casa D'Amici 485 High St *Web:* www.casadamici.com	Morgantown	WV	26507	304-292-4400		671
Casa D'Angelo 1201 N Federal Hwy *TF:* 800-430-8903 ■ *Web:* casa-d-angelo.com	Fort Lauderdale	FL	33304	954-564-1234		671
Casa Dante 737 Newark Ave *TF:* 800-934-7673 ■ *Web:* www.casadante.com	Jersey City	NJ	07306	201-795-2750	795-1225	671
Casa de Luz 1701 Toomey Rd *Web:* www.casadeluz.org	Austin	TX	78704	512-476-2535		671
Casa De Nana 995 Boston Rd *Web:* www.casadenana.com	Springfield	MA	01119	413-783-1549		671
Casa De Soto 8562 Garden Grove Blvd *Web:* www.casadesoto.com	Garden Grove	CA	92844	714-530-4200		671
Casa de Trujillo 122 W Sixth St	Cheyenne	WY	82007	307-635-1227		671
Casa del Herrero 1387 E Valley Rd *Web:* www.casadelherrero.com	Santa Barbara	CA	93108	805-565-5653	969-2371	97
Casa Del Rey 901 W Russell St *Web:* www.casadelrey.com	Sioux Falls	SD	57104	605-338-6078		671
Casa Di Copani 3414 Burnet Ave *Web:* casadicopani.com	Syracuse	NY	13206	315-463-1031		671
Casa Di Mir Montessori School 90 E Latimer Ave *Web:* www.casadimir.org	Campbell	CA	95008	408-370-3073		685
Casa Dorinda 300 Hot Springs Rd *TF:* 800-311-3412 ■ *Web:* casadorinda.org	Santa Barbara	CA	93108	805-969-8011	969-8686	672
Casa Esperanza 1005 Yale NE *TF:* 866-654-1338 ■ *Web:* casanm.org	Albuquerque	NM	87106	505-246-2700	277-9876	372
CASA Exploration LLC 1800 Post Oak Blvd Ste 380 *Web:* www.casaexploration.com	Houston	TX	77056	832-325-2300		536
Casa Fiesta 801 Louisville Rd *Web:* links2frankfort.com	Frankfort	KY	40601	502-226-5010		671
Casa Fuentes 1107 W Hwy 76 *Web:* www.casafuentes.com	Branson	MO	65616	417-339-3888		671
Casa Garcia 8814 Veterans Memorial Blvd *Web:* casa-garcia.com	Metairie	LA	70003	504-464-0354		671

	Phone	Fax	Class
Casa Grande Regional Medical Ctr (CGRMC) 1800 E Florence Blvd .... Casa Grande AZ 85122 *Web:* bannerhealth.com/casagrande	520-381-6300	381-6435	374-3
Casa Grande Ruins National Monument 1100 W Ruins Dr .... Coolidge AZ 85128 *TF:* 877-642-4743 ■ *Web:* www.nps.gov	520-723-3172	723-7209	564
Casa Grande Suite Hotel 834 Ocean Dr .... Miami Beach FL 33139 *Web:* www.casagrandesuitehotel.com	305-672-7003		379
Casa Grande Valley Newspaper Inc 200 W Second St .... Casa Grande AZ 85122 *TF:* 877-326-2056 ■ *Web:* www.pinalcentral.com	520-836-7461	836-0343	637-8
Casa Herrerra Inc 2655 N Pine St .... Pomona CA 91767 *TF:* 800-624-3916 ■ *Web:* www.casaherrera.com	909-392-3930	392-0231	298
Casa Juancho 2436 SW Eigth St................. Miami FL 33135 *Web:* www.casajuancho.com	305-642-2452	642-2524	671
Casa Linda Furniture Inc 4815 Whittier Blvd ....Los Angeles CA 90022 *Web:* www.furniturecasalinda.com	323-263-3851		321
Casa Madrona Hotel 801 Bridgeway .... Sausalito CA 94965 *TF General:* 800-288-0502 ■ *Web:* www.casamadrona.com	415-332-0502	331-3125	379
Casa Manana Theatre 3101 W Lancaster Ave .... Fort Worth TX 76107 *Web:* www.casamanana.org	817-332-2272		572
Casa Marina Hotel & Restaurant 691 First St N .... Jacksonville Beach FL 32250 *TF:* 800-780-5733 ■ *Web:* www.casamarinahotel.com	904-270-0025		707
Casa Marina Resort & Beach Club 1500 Reynolds St.............................Key West FL 33040 *TF:* 888-303-5719 ■ *Web:* www.casamarinaresort.com	305-296-3535	296-4633	669
Casa Mia 716 Plum St..............................Olympia WA 98501 *Web:* www.casamiarestaurants.com	360-352-0440		671
Casa Molina 6225 E Speedway ....Tucson AZ 85712	520-886-5468		671
Casa Monica Hotel 95 Cordova St....................... Saint Augustine FL 32084 *TF Help Line:* 800-648-1888 ■ *Web:* www.casamonica.com	904-827-1888	819-6065	379
Casa Mono 52 Irving Pl .... New York NY 10003 *Web:* casamononyc.com	212-253-2773		671
Casa Munras Hotel 700 Munras Ave .... Monterey CA 93940 *TF:* 800-222-2446 ■ *Web:* www.hotelcasamunras.com	831-375-2411	375-1365	379
Casa Navarro State Historic Site 228 S Laredo St ....San Antonio TX 78207 *Web:* www.thc.texas.gov	210-226-4801	226-4801	565
Casa Palmero 1518 Cypress Dr............Pebble Beach CA 93953 *TF:* 800-654-9300 ■ *Web:* pebblebeach.com	831-622-6650	622-6655	669
CASA Payroll Service LLC 3120 Fire Rd.................... Egg Harbor Township NJ 08234 *Web:* www.casapayroll.com	609-383-0677	383-0907	734
Casa Ristoranti 7539 W Jefferson Blvd .... Fort Wayne IN 46825 *Web:* www.casarestaurants.com	260-399-2455		671
Casa Romero 30 Gloucester St .... Boston MA 02115 *Web:* www.casaromero.com	617-536-4341		671
Casa Rondena Winery 733 Chavez Rd NW...................... Albuquerque NM 87107 *Web:* www.casarondena.com	505-344-5911	343-1823	50-7
Casa Vasca 141 Elm St ....Newark NJ 07105 *TF:* 800-828-9241 ■ *Web:* casavascarestaurant.com	973-465-1350		671
Casa Via Mar Inn & Tennis Club 377 W Ch Islands Blvd.................. Port Hueneme CA 93041 *Web:* www.casaviamar.com	805-984-6222	984-9490	379
Casa Ybel Resort 2255 W Gulf Dr............................ Sanibel Island FL 33957 *TF:* 800-276-4753 ■ *Web:* www.casaybelresort.com	239-472-3145		669
Casablanca 3516 Fair Oaks Blvd............. Sacramento CA 95864	916-979-1160		671
Casablanca Cafe 3049 Alhambra St..................... Fort Lauderdale FL 33304 *TF:* 800-442-1162 ■ *Web:* www.casablancacafeonline.com	954-764-3500		671
Casablanca Fan Co 761 Corporate Ctr Dr ....Pomona CA 91768 *TF:* 888-227-2178 ■ *Web:* www.casablancafanco.com	909-689-1477		37
Casablanca Hotel 147 W 43rd St.............New York NY 10036 *TF:* 888-922-7225 ■ *Web:* www.casablancahotel.com	212-869-1212	391-7585	379
Casablanca Resort 950 W Mesquite Blvd .... Mesquite NV 89027 *TF:* 800-459-7529 ■ *Web:* www.casablancaresort.com	702-346-7529		669
Casanova 5th Ave..................................Carmel CA 93923 *Web:* www.casanovacarmel.com	831-625-0501		671
Casavant Freres Inc 900 rue Girouard est.....................St. Hyacinthe QC J2S2Y2 *Web:* www.casavant.ca	450-773-5001		526
Casbah 229 S Highland Ave .... Pittsburgh PA 15206 *Web:* casbahpgh.com	412-661-5656		671
Casbah 20 E Broughton St .... Savannah GA 31401 *Web:* www.casbahrestaurant.com	912-234-6168		671
Cascade Autocenter 148 Easy St............Wenatchee WA 98801 *Web:* www.cascadeautocenter.com	509-663-0011		57
Cascade Bancorp 1100 NW Wall St.............. Bend OR 97701 *NASDAQ: CACB* ■ *TF Cust Svc:* 877-617-3400 ■ *Web:* www.botc.com	541-385-6205		360-2
Cascade Bicycle Club 7400 Sand Point Way NE Ste 101s............... Seattle WA 98115 *Web:* www.cascade.org	206-522-3222		711
Cascade Caverns 226 Cascade Caverns Rd........Boerne TX 78015 *Web:* www.cascadecaverns.com	830-755-8080		50-5
Cascade Computer Maintenance Inc 750 Front St NE .... Salem OR 97302 *Web:* www.ccmaint.com	503-581-0081		175
Cascade Controls Northwest 19785 NE San Raffael St......................Portland OR 97230 *Web:* www.cascade-nw.com	503-252-3116		358
Cascade Corp 2201 NE 201st Ave..............Fairview OR 97024 *NYSE: CASC* ■ *TF:* 800-227-2233 ■ *Web:* www.cascorp.com	503-669-6300		470
Cascade County 325 Second Ave N .... Great Falls MT 59401 *Web:* www.cascadecountymt.gov	406-454-6795	454-6797	338
Cascade Credit Services Inc 1635 SE Malden St Ste D.......................Portland OR 97202 *Web:* cascadecredit.com	503-722-2009		70
Cascade Culinary Institute 2600 NW College Way .... Bend OR 97701 *Web:* www.cocc.edu	541-383-7700		163
Cascade Dafo Inc 1360 Sunset Ave ....Ferndale WA 98248 *Web:* www.cascadedafo.com	360-543-9306		475
Cascade Designs Inc 4000 First Ave S .... Seattle WA 98134 *TF Cust Svc:* 800-531-9531 ■ *Web:* www.cascadedesigns.com	206-505-9500	505-9525	710
Cascade Earth Sciences Ltd 4900 California Blvd Tower B-210 ....Bakersfield CA 93309 *Web:* www.cascade-earth.com	661-324-2668		538
Cascade Federal Credit Union 18020 80th Ave S..............................Kent WA 98032 *TF:* 800-562-2853 ■ *Web:* www.cascadefcu.org	425-251-8888	251-0299	216
Cascade Financial Management Inc 950 17th St Ste 950 ....Denver CO 80202 *TF:* 800-353-0008 ■ *Web:* www.cascade-inc.com	800-353-0008		194
Cascade Hardwoods Inc 158 Ribelin Rd........ Chehalis WA 98532 *Web:* www.cascadehardwood.com	360-748-3317		683
Cascade Lodge 3719 W Hwy 61 .... Lutsen MN 55612 *TF:* 800-322-9543 ■ *Web:* www.cascadelodgemn.com	218-387-1112		669
Cascade Lumber Co 1000 First Ave E ....Cascade IA 52033 *Web:* www.caslbr.com	563-852-3232		817
Cascade Machinery & Electric Inc 4600 E Marginal Way S .... Seattle WA 98134 *TF:* 800-289-0500 ■ *Web:* www.cascade-machinery.com	206-762-0500	767-5122	385
Cascade Microtech Inc 2430 NW 206th Ave ....Beaverton OR 97006 *NASDAQ: CSCD* ■ *TF:* 800-854-8400 ■ *Web:* www.cascademicrotech.com	503-601-1000	601-1010	248
Cascade Natural Gas Corp (CNGC) 8113 W Grandridge Blvd ....Kennewick WA 99336 *TF:* 888-522-1130 ■ *Web:* www.cngc.com	206-624-3900		787
Cascade Networks Inc 1111 - 11th Ave PO Box 887 ....Longview WA 98632 *TF:* 800-967-8107 ■ *Web:* www.cni.net	360-414-5990		180
Cascade Orthopedic Supply Inc 2638 Aztec Dr......................................Chico CA 95928 *Web:* www.cascade-usa.com	530-879-1500		475
Cascade Pacific Pulp LLC 30480 American Dr.............................. Halsey OR 97348 *Web:* www.cascadepulp.com	541-369-2841		638
Cascade Plastics Co Inc 7009 45th St Ct E.................................. Fife WA 98424	253-922-3460		499
Cascade Policy Institute 4850 SW Scholls Ferry Rd Ste 103.............Portland OR 97225 *Web:* www.cascadepolicy.org	503-242-0900	242-3822	634
Cascade Pump Co 10107 Norwalk Blvd..................Santa Fe Springs CA 90670 *Web:* www.cascadepump.com	562-946-1414		641
Cascade Regional Blood Services 220 S 'I' St .... Tacoma WA 98405 *TF:* 877-242-5663 ■ *Web:* www.crbs.net	253-383-2553		89
Cascade River State Park 3481 W Hwy 61........ Lutsen MN 55612 *Web:* www.dnr.state.mn.us	218-387-3053	387-3054	565
Cascade Rubber Products Inc 1828 NW Quimby St.............................Portland OR 97209 *TF:* 800-468-4285 ■ *Web:* cascaderubber.com	503-248-1992		326
Cascade Steel Rolling Mills Inc (CSRM) 3200 N Hwy 99 W PO Box 687............ McMinnville OR 97128 *TF:* 800-283-2776 ■ *Web:* www.cascadesteel.com	503-472-4181	434-5739	723
Cascade Timber Consulting Inc 3210 Hwy 20 ....Sweet Home OR 97386 *TF:* 800-783-6818 ■ *Web:* cascadetimber.com	541-367-2111	367-2117	302
Cascade Waterworks Manufacturing 1213 Badger St...................................Yorkville IL 60560 *Web:* www.cascademfg.com	630-553-0840		595
Cascade Wholesale Hardware Inc 5650 NW .... Hillsboro OR 97124 *TF General:* 800-877-9987 ■ *Web:* www.cascade.com	503-614-2600	629-5793	351
Cascade Wood Products Inc PO Box 2429 .... White City OR 97503 *TF:* 800-423-3311 ■ *Web:* www.cascadewood.com	541-826-2911		499
Cascade365 1670 Corporate Cir Ste 202......... Petaluma CA 94954 *TF:* 888-417-1531 ■ *Web:* www.cascadereceivables.com	707-981-4002		393
Cascades Inc 404 Marie-Victorin Blvd ....Kingsey Falls QC J0A1B0 *TSE: CAS* ■ *TF:* 800-361-4070 ■ *Web:* www.cascades.com	819-363-5100	363-5155	561
Cascadia Managing Brands 1109 First Ave Ste 400........................ Seattle WA 98101 *TF:* 800-572-8585 ■ *Web:* www.cascadiaconsulting.com	206-343-9759		463
Cascadia Motivation Inc 4646 Riverside Dr Ste 14 .... Red Deer AB T4N6Y5 *Web:* www.cascadiamotivation.com	403-340-8687	342-5644	772
Cascadia State Park 725 Summer St NE Ste C .... Salem OR 97301 *Web:* www.oregonstateparks.org	503-986-0707		565
Cascadian Building Maintenance Ltd 1331 118th Ave SE ste 100.........................Bellevue WA 98056 *Web:* www.cascadian.org	425-455-8404	454-7978	256
Cascio Interstate Music 13819 W National Ave .... New Berlin WI 53151 *TF:* 800-462-2263 ■ *Web:* www.interstatemusic.com	262-789-7600		526
Cascio's Steak House 1620 S Tenth St ....Omaha NE 68108 *Web:* www.casciossteakhouse.com	402-345-8313		671
Casco Bay Engineering Inc 424 Fore St..Portland ME 04101 *TF:* 800-892-8707 ■ *Web:* cascobayengineering.com	207-842-2800		261
Casco Equipment Corp 4141 Flat Rock Dr.............................. Riverside CA 92505 *TF:* 800-628-0076 ■ *Web:* www.cascoequip.com	951-324-8500		358
CASCO International Inc 4205 E Dixon Blvd ....Shelby NC 28152 *TF:* 800-535-5690 ■ *Web:* www.cashort.com	800-535-5690		260
Cascone's 3737 N Oak Trafficway............. Kansas City MO 64116 *Web:* www.cascones.com	816-454-7977		671
Casden Properties LLC 9090 Wilshire Blvd...................... Beverly Hills CA 90211	310-274-5553		653

Phone *Fax* *Class*

CASE (Council of Administrators of Special Education)
Osigian Office Centre 101 Katelyn Cir
Ste E .... Warner Robins GA 31000 470-333-6092 333-2453 49-5
TF: 800-585-1753 ■ *Web:* www.casecec.org
CASE (Council for Advancement & Support of Education)
1307 New York Ave NW Ste 1000 .... Washington DC 20005 202-328-5900 387-4973 49-5
TF Orders: 800-554-8536 ■ *Web:* www.case.org
Case Construction LLC
56 Midtown Park W Ste A .... Mobile AL 36606 251-338-2400 338-2405 186
Case Contracting Co
2311 Turkey Creek Rd .... Plant City FL 33566 813-754-3477 186
TF: 800-790-6202 ■ *Web:* www.casecontracting.com
Case Crating & Packing
3340A Greens Rd Ste 900 .... Houston TX 77032 713-862-7283 200
Web: www.casecratingandpacking.com
Case Design Corp 333 School Ln .... Telford PA 18969 215-703-0130 703-0139 199
TF: 800-847-4176 ■ *Web:* www.casedesigncorp.com
Case Farms Inc 121 Rand St .... Morganton NC 28655 828-438-6900 619
Web: www.casefarms.com
Case Foundation Co 1325 West Lake St .... Roselle IL 60172 630-529-2911 188-2
TF: 800-999-4087 ■ *Web:* www.casefoundation.com
Case Logic Inc 6303 Dry Creek Pkwy .... Longmont CO 80503 303-652-1000 534
TF: 800-925-8111 ■ *Web:* www.caselogic.com
Case Management Society of America (CMSA)
6301 Ranch Dr .... Little Rock AR 72223 501-225-2229 221-9068 49-8
TF: 800-216-2672 ■ *Web:* www.cmsa.org
Case Medical Inc 65 Railroad Ave .... Ridgefield NJ 07657 201-313-1999 488
Web: www.casemed.com
Case Paper Company Inc
500 Mamaroneck Ave .... Harrison NY 10528 914-899-3500 777-1028 554
TF: 800-222-2922 ■ *Web:* www.casepaper.com
Case Pomeroy & Co Inc 529 Fifth Ave .... New York NY 10017 212-867-2211 536
Case Sabatini & Co
470 Sts Run Rd Ste 1 .... Pittsburgh PA 15236 412-881-4411 2
Web: www.casesabatini.com
Case Systems Inc 2700 James Savage Rd .... Midland MI 48642 080 406 0610 803-1
Web: www.casesystems.com
Case Western Reserve University
2061 Cornell Rd .... Cleveland OH 44106 216-368-2000 368-5111 166
TF: 800-967-8898 ■ *Web:* www.case.edu
Case Western Reserve University kelvin Smith Library
11055 Euclid Ave .... Cleveland OH 44106 216-368-3506 368-3669 434-6
Web: library.case.edu
Case Western Reserve University School of Law
11075 E Blvd .... Cleveland OH 44106 216-368-3600 167-1
TF: 800-756-0036 ■ *Web:* law.case.edu
Case Western Reserve University School of Medicine (CWRU)
2109 Adelbert Rd .... Cleveland OH 44106 216-368-3450 368-6011 167-2
Web: case.edu/medicine
Casella Waste Systems Inc
25 Greens Hill Ln .... Rutland VT 05701 802-775-0325 804
NASDAQ: CWST ■ *TF:* 800-227-3552 ■ *Web:* www.casella.com
Caselle Inc
1656 South East Bay Blvd Ste 100 .... Provo UT 84606 801-850-5000 179
Web: www.caselle.com
Casepro Inc
21738 Hardy Oak Blvd Ste 105 .... San Antonio TX 78258 210-496-0050 363
Cases By Source Inc 215 Island Rd .... Mahwah NJ 07430 201-831-0005 557
Web: www.casesbysource.com
CaseSoft Div
5000 Sawgrass Village Cir Ste 21 .... Ponte Vedra Beach FL 32082 904-273-5000 273-5001 178-11
TF: 800-368-6955 ■ *Web:* www.casesoft.com
Casey Communications Inc
8301 Maryland Ave Ste 350 .... St. Louis MO 63105 314-721-2828 636
Web: www.caseycomm.com
Casey Gerry Schenk Francavilla Blatt & Penfield LLP
110 Laurel St .... San Diego CA 92101 619-238-1811 428
TF: 800-292-5865 ■ *Web:* www.caseygerry.com
Casey Moore's Oyster House
850 S Ash Ave .... Tempe AZ 85281 480-968-9935 671
TF: 800-946-4452 ■ *Web:* caseymoores.com
Casey Neilon & Assoc LLC
503 N Division St .... Carson City NV 89703 775-283-5555 2
Web: caseyneilon.com
Casey Printing Inc
398 E San Antonio Dr .... King City CA 93930 831-385-3222 627
Web: www.caseyconnect.com/home
Casey Products
11230 Katherine Crossing .... Woodridge IL 60517 630-960-3360 351
Web: www.caseyproducts.com
Casey Research LLC
55 NE Fifth Ave .... Delray Beach FL 33483 602-445-2736 401
TF: 888-512-2739 ■ *Web:* www.caseyresearch.com
Casey Robert P Jr (Sen D - PA)
393 Russell Bldg .... Washington DC 20510 202-224-6324 228-0604 342-2
Web: www.casey.senate.gov
Casey State Bank 305-307 N Central Ave .... Casey IL 62420 217-932-2136 932-4370 70
TF: 866-666-2754 ■ *Web:* www.caseystatebank.com
Casey's Foods 124 W Gartner Rd .... Naperville IL 60540 630-369-1686 345
Web: www.caseysfoods.com
Casey's General Stores
1 SE Convenience Blvd .... Ankeny IA 50021 515-965-6100 204
NASDAQ: CASY ■ *Web:* www.caseys.com
Casey, Quirk & Associates LLC
17 Old King's Hwy S Ste 200 .... Darien CT 06820 203-899-3000 196
Web: www.caseyquirk.com
Caseys Furniture Inc 11 S Second St .... Temple TX 76501 254-773-5555 321
Casgrain & Company Ltd
1200 Mcgill College Ave 21st Fl .... Montreal QC H3B4G7 514-871-8080 401
Web: www.casgrain.ca
Cash Acme Inc
2727 Paces Ferry Rd SE Ste 1800 .... Atlanta GA 30339 877-700-4242 789
TF: 877-700-4242 ■ *Web:* www.cashacme.com
Cash Control Business Systems
9101 Lackland Rd .... Overland MO 63114 314-427-6143 535
Web: www.cashcontrolbiz.com
Cash Flow Solutions Inc
5166 College Corner Pk .... Oxford OH 45056 800-736-5123 196
TF: 800-736-5123 ■ *Web:* www.followthefrog.com

Phone *Fax* *Class*

Cash Management Solutions Inc
13921 Icot Blvd Ste 710 .... Clearwater FL 33760 727-524-1103 174
TF: 800-345-7243 ■ *Web:* www.cashmgmt.com
Cash Plus Inc 3002 Dow Ave Ste 120 .... Tustin CA 92780 714-731-2274 731-2099 141
Web: www.cashplusinc.com
Cashco Inc 607 W 15th St .... Ellsworth KS 67439 785-472-4461 472-3539 790
Web: www.cashco.com
Casher Assoc Inc 110 Pond Brook Rd .... Newton MA 02467 617-527-3927 225
Web: www.casherassociates.com
Cashiers Historical Society
1940 Hwy 107 S .... Cashiers NC 28717 828-743-7710 743-7169 50-3
Web: www.cashiershistoricalsociety.org
Cashin Assoc PC
1200 Veterans Memorial Hwy Ste 200 .... Hauppauge NY 11788 631-348-7600 261
Web: cashinassociates.com
Cashion's Eat Place
1819 Columbia Rd NW .... Washington DC 20009 202-797-1819 671
Web: www.cashionseatplace.com
Cashman & Katz LLC
76 Eastern Blvd .... Glastonbury CT 06033 860-652-0300 344
Web: www.cashman-katz.com
Cashman Equipment Co
3300 St Rose Pkwy .... Henderson NV 89052 702-649-8777 45
TF: 800-937-2326 ■ *Web:* www.cashmanequipment.com
Cashmere Molding
20004 144th Ave NE .... Woodinville WA 98072 425-485-6515 608
Cashtown Inn Restaurant
1325 Old Rt 30 PO Box 103 .... Cashtown PA 17310 717-334-9722 334-4679 671
TF: 800-367-1797 ■ *Web:* cashtowninn.com
Cash-Wa Distributing Co
401 W Fourth St .... Kearney NE 68845 308-237-3151 234-6018 297-8
TF: 800-652-0010 ■ *Web:* www.cashwa.com
CASI (Computer Analytical Service)
1418 S Third St .... Louisville KY 40208 502-635-2019 180
Casiano Communications Inc
1700 Fernandez Juncos Ave .... San Juan PR 00909 787-728-3000 268-1001 637-8
Casino Arizona at Salt River
524 N 92nd St .... Scottsdale AZ 85256 480-850-7777 133
TF General: 866-877-9897 ■ *Web:* www.casinoarizona.com
Casino Aztar 421 NW Riverside Dr .... Evansville IN 47708 812-433-4000 133
TF: 800-342-5386 ■ *Web:* www.tropevansville.com
Casino City Inc
95 Wells Ave Ste 125 .... Newton Center MA 02459 617-332-2850 637-10
Web: www.casinocitypress.com
Casino Factory Shoppes LLC
13118 Hwy 61 N .... Robinsonville MS 38664 662-363-1940 460
Casino Fandango 3800 S Carson St .... Carson City NV 89701 775-885-7000 133
Web: www.casinofandango.com
Casino New Brunswick LP 21 Casino Dr .... Moncton NB E1G0R7 506-859-7770 133
TF: 877-859-7775 ■ *Web:* www.casinonb.ca
Casino Niagara 5705 Falls Ave .... Niagara Falls ON L2E6T3 888-325-5788 133
TF: 888-325-5788 ■ *Web:* www.casinoniagara.com
Casino Nova Scotia
1983 Upper Water St .... Halifax NS B3J3Y5 902-425-7777 133
TF: 888-642-6376 ■ *Web:* www.casinonovascotia.com
Casino One Corp 999 N Second St .... St. Louis MO 63102 341-881-7777 132
Web: www.lumiereplace.com
Casino Pauma
777 Pauma Reservation Rd PO Box 1067 .... Pauma Valley CA 92061 760-742-2177 31
Web: www.casinopauma.com
Casino Pier & Water Works
800 Ocean Terr .... Seaside Heights NJ 08751 732-793-6488 32
Web: www.casinopiernj.com
Casino Queen 200 S Front St .... East Saint Louis IL 62201 618-874-5000 133
TF: 800-777-0777 ■ *Web:* www.casinoqueen.com
Casino Royale Hotel
3411 Las Vegas Blvd S .... Las Vegas NV 89109 702-737-3500 379
TF: 800-854-7666 ■ *Web:* www.casinoroyalehotel.com
Casino San Pablo of Lytton Rancheria
13255 San Pablo Ave .... San Pablo CA 94806 510-215-7888 452
Web: www.sanpablolytton.com
Casio Computer Company Ltd
570 Mt Pleasant Ave .... Dover NJ 07801 973-361-5400 537-8964* 591
**Fax:* Hum Res ■ *Web:* www.casio.com
Cask 'n' Cleaver
8689 Ninth St .... Rancho Cucamonga CA 91730 909-981-5771 981-9734 670
TF: 800-995-4452 ■ *Web:* www.caskncleaver.com
Cask LLC 9350 Waxie Way Ste 210 .... San Diego CA 92123 866-535-8915 196
TF: 866-535-8915 ■ *Web:* www.caskllc.com
CASLPA (Speech-Language and Audiology Canada)
1 Nicholas St Ste 1000 .... Ottawa ON K1N7B7 613-567-9968 567-2859 48-1
TF: 800-259-8519 ■ *Web:* sac-conference.ca
CASM (Canadian Academy of Sport Medicine)
55 Metcalfe St Ste 300 .... Ottawa ON K1P6L5 613-748-5851 912-0128 49-8
TF: 877-585-2394 ■ *Web:* casem-acmse.org
Casne Engineering Inc
10604 NE 38th Pl Ste 205 .... Kirkland WA 98033 425-522-1000 256
Web: www.casne.com
Casner & Edwards LLP 303 Congress St .... Boston MA 02210 617-426-5900 428
Web: www.casneredwards.com
Casnet 947 W Waterloo Rd .... Akron OH 44314 330-848-8800 317
Web: gotocasnet.com
Casper Area Chamber of Commerce
500 N Ctr St .... Casper WY 82601 307-234-5311 265-2643 139
TF: 866-234-5311 ■ *Web:* www.casperwyoming.org
Casper Area Convention & Visitors Bureau
139 W Second St Ste 1B .... Casper WY 82601 307-234-5362 206
TF: 800-852-1882 ■ *Web:* visitcasper.com
Casper City Hall 200 N David St .... Casper WY 82601 307-235-8400 235-7575 337
Web: www.casperwy.gov
Casper College 125 College Dr .... Casper WY 82601 307-268-2100 268-2611* 162
**Fax:* Admissions ■ *TF:* 800-442-2963 ■ *Web:* www.caspercollege.edu
Casper Events Ctr 1 Events Dr .... Casper WY 82601 307-235-8441 205
TF: 800-442-2256 ■ *Web:* www.casperwy.gov
Casper Planetarium 904 N Poplar St .... Casper WY 82601 307-577-0310 598
Web: casperplanetarium.com
Caspian Energy Inc
649 Varsity Estates Crescent NW .... Calgary AB T2R0C5 403-252-2462 536
Web: www.caspianenergyinc.com

Name	City	State	ZIP	Phone	Fax	Class
Cass 1810 Water Pl SE Ste 180 *Web:* www.cassecurity.com	Atlanta	GA	30339	770-916-0060	916-0080	693
Cass Cable Tv Inc 100 Redbud Rd *TF:* 800-252-1799 ■ *Web:* www.casscomm.com	Virginia	IL	62691	217-452-7725		116
Cass Construction Inc 1100 Wagner Dr *Web:* www.cassconstruction.com	El Cajon	CA	92020	619-590-0929		261
Cass County 5 W Seventh St *Web:* www.atlanticiowa.com/county	Atlantic	IA	50022	712-243-5503		338
Cass County 120 N Broadway *Web:* casscountymi.org	Cassopolis	MI	49031	269-445-4420		338
Cass County 211 Ninth St S *Web:* www.casscountynd.gov	Fargo	ND	58103	701-241-5600	241-5728	338
Cass County PO Box 449 *Web:* www.co.cass.tx.us	Linden	TX	75563	903-756-5071	756-8057	338
Cass County 200 Ct Pk *TF:* 800-859-5553 ■ *Web:* co.cass.in.us	Logansport	IN	46947	574-753-7740	722-1556	338
Cass County 346 Main St *TF:* 800-256-2777 ■ *Web:* www.cassne.org	Plattsmouth	NE	68048	402-296-9300	296-9332	338
Cass County 100 E Springfield St PO Box 203 *Web:* www.illinoiscourts.gov	Virginia	IL	62691	217-452-7225	452-7219	338
Cass County Electric Co-op Inc 4100 32nd Ave SW *TF:* 800-248-3292 ■ *Web:* www.kwh.com	Fargo	ND	58104	701-356-4400		245
Cass County Public Library 400 E Mechanic St *Web:* www.casscolibrary.org	Harrisonville	MO	64701	816-380-4600	884-2301	434-3
Cass County Publishing Company Inc 301 S Lexington *Web:* www.demo-mo.com	Harrisonville	MO	64701	816-380-3228		532-3
Cass Data & Mailing Services Inc 26 Eglin Pkwy SE Ste 4 *Web:* cassdata.com	Fort Walton Beach	FL	32548	850-862-5110		5
Cass Information Systems Inc 13001 Hollenberg Dr *NASDAQ: CASS* ■ *TF:* 888-569-4707 ■ *Web:* www.cassinfo.com	Bridgeton	MO	63044	314-506-5500	506-5560	225
Cass Scenic Railroad State Park 242 Main St *Web:* www.cassrailroad.com	Cass	WV	24927	304-456-4300		565
Cass Screw Machine Products Co 4800 N Lilac Dr *Web:* www.csmp.com	Brooklyn Center	MN	55429	763-535-0501	535-9238	621
Cass Tours 2621 Green River Rd Ste 105-222 *TF:* 800-593-6510 ■ *Web:* www.casstours.com	Corona	CA	92882	951-371-3511		771
Cassandra Ballet of Toledo 3157 Sylvania Ave *Web:* cassandraballet.com	Toledo	OH	43613	419-475-0458		573-1
Cassara Management Group Inc 125 Canal Landing Blvd Ste 120 *Web:* www.cassaramgi.com	Rochester	NY	14626	585-720-1700		463
Cassarino's Restaurant 177 Atwells Ave *Web:* www.cassarinosri.com	Providence	RI	02903	401-751-3333		671
Casselman River Bridge State Park 580 Taylor Ave *TF:* 877-620-8367 ■ *Web:* dnr2.maryland.gov	Annapolis	MD	21401	877-620-8367		565
Cassels Brock & Blackwell LLP 2100 Scotia Plaza 40 King St W *Web:* www.casselsbrock.com	Toronto	ON	M5H3C2	416-869-5300		428
Cassens Transport Co 145 N Kansas St *Web:* www.cassens.com/transport	Edwardsville	IL	62025	618-656-3006	692-7316	780
Cassia County 1459 Overland Ave *Web:* www.cassiacounty.org	Burley	ID	83318	208-878-7302	878-9109	338
Cassia County Fairgrounds 1101 Elba Ave *Web:* cassiacountyfair.com	Burley	ID	83318	208-678-9150		642
Cassidy & Assoc 733 Tenth St NW Ste 400 *Web:* www.cassidy.com	Washington	DC	20001	202-347-0773	347-0785	636
Cassidy Bill (Sen R - LA) 520 Hart Senate Office Bldg *Web:* www.cassidy.senate.gov	Washington	DC	20510	202-224-5824	224-9735	342-2
Cassidy Fine Foods 3657 Old Getwell Rd	Memphis	TN	38118	901-542-5100		297-5
Cassidy-Tricker Industrial Sales 1608 Hwy 13 W *Web:* cassidytricker.com	Burnsville	MN	55337	952-882-6338		350
Cassin & Cassin LLP 711 Third Ave 20th Fl *Web:* www.cassinllp.com	New York	NY	10017	212-972-6161		428
Cassling Diagnostic Imaging Inc 13808 F St *Web:* www.cassling.com	Omaha	NE	68137	402-334-5000		475
Casson-Mark Corp 10515 Markison Rd *Web:* www.cmarkcorp.com	Dallas	TX	75238	214-340-0880		196
Cassville Area Chamber of Commerce 504 Main St *Web:* www.cassville.com	Cassville	MO	65625	417-847-2814		139
Casswood Insurance Agency Ltd 5 Executive Pk Dr *TF:* 800-972-2242 ■ *Web:* www.casswood.com	Clifton Park	NY	12065	518-373-8700	373-8799	390
Cast & Crew Entertainment Services LLC 2300 Empire Ave *Web:* www.castandcrew.com	Burbank	CA	91504	818-848-6022		2
Cast Products Inc 4200 N Nordica Ave *Web:* castproducts.com	Norridge	IL	60706	708-457-1500		358
Cast Specialties Inc 26711 Miles Ave *Web:* www.diecastingusa.net	Warrensville Hts	OH	44128	216-292-7393		308
Cast Systems LLC 19400 Peachland Blvd *TF:* 800-754-3641 ■ *Web:* www.castsystemsllc.com	Port Charlotte	FL	33948	941-625-3474		183
Cast Technologies Inc 1100 SW Washington St *Web:* casttechnologies.net	Peoria	IL	61602	309-676-2157	676-2167	308
Castagna 1752 SE Hawthorne Blvd *Web:* www.castagnarestaurant.com	Portland	OR	97214	503-231-7373		671
Castalloy Inc 1701 Industrial Ln PO Box 827 *TF:* 800-211-0900 ■ *Web:* www.castalloycorp.com	Waukesha	WI	53189	262-547-0070	547-2215	307
Cast-Crete Corp 6324 County Rd 579 *TF:* 800-999-4641 ■ *Web:* www.castcrete.com	Seffner	FL	33584	813-621-4641		183
Castellan Inc 16255 Ventura Blvd Ste 930 *TF:* 800-497-9764 ■ *Web:* www.castellan.net	Encino	CA	91436	818-789-0088		177
Castelli Marble Inc 3958 Superior Ave E *Web:* castellimarbleinc.com	Cleveland	OH	44114	216-361-1222	361-1797	191-1
Caster Concepts Inc 16000 E Michigan Ave *TF:* 800-800-0036 ■ *Web:* www.casterconcepts.com	Albion	MI	49224	517-629-8838		358
Caster Technology Corp 11552 Markon Dr *TF:* 866-547-8090 ■ *Web:* www.castertech.com	Garden Grove	CA	92841	714-893-6886		351
Castile Ventures 65 William St Ste 205 *Web:* www.castileventures.com	Wellesley	MA	02481	781-890-0060		792
Castilleja School Foundation 1310 Bryant St *Web:* www.castilleja.org	Palo Alto	CA	94301	650-328-3160		685
Castillo de San Marcos National Monument 1 S Castillo Dr *Web:* www.nps.gov/casa	Saint Augustine	FL	32084	904-829-6506	823-9388	564
Castine Moving & Storage 1235 Chestnut St *TF:* 800-225-8068 ■ *Web:* www.castinemovers.com	Athol	MA	01331	978-249-9105	249-5337	519
Casting Solutions LLC 2345 Licking Rd *Web:* www.burnhamfoundry.com	Zanesville	OH	43701	740-452-9371		307
Castle & Cooke Inc 10900 Wilshire Blvd Ste 1600 *Web:* www.castlecooke.com	Los Angeles	CA	90024	310-208-3636		653
Castle Branch Inc 1845 Sir Tyler Dr *TF:* 800-772-6270 ■ *Web:* www.castlebranch.com	Wilmington	NC	28405	910-815-3880		435
Castle Brands Inc 122 E 42nd St Ste 4700 *NYSE: ROX* ■ *TF:* 800-882-8140 ■ *Web:* www.castlebrandsinc.com	New York	NY	10168	646-356-0200	356-0222	81-3
Castle Breckenridge Management 5185 Comanche Dr Ste D *Web:* www.cbmgmt.com	La Mesa	CA	91942	619-697-3191		256
Castle Contracting LLC 760 S Second St *Web:* www.castlecontracting.com	St. Louis	MO	63102	314-421-0042		188
Castle Creek Capital LLC 6051 El Tordo *Web:* www.castlecreek.com	Rancho Santa Fe	CA	92067	858-756-8300		401
Castle Harlan Inc 150 E 58th St *Web:* www.castleharlan.com	New York	NY	10155	212-644-8600	207-8042	403
Castle High School 3344 State Rt 261 *Web:* www.warrickschools.com	Newburgh	IN	47630	812-853-3331		685
Castle Hill Inn & Resort 590 Ocean Dr *TF:* 888-466-1355 ■ *Web:* www.castlehillinn.com	Newport	RI	02840	401-849-3800	849-3838	669
Castle Hill Retirement Village 3575 N Moorpark Rd	Thousand Oaks	CA	91360	805-492-2471		672
Castle In The Clouds Rt 171 **Fax Area Code: 903* ■ *Web:* www.castleintheclouds.org	Moultonborough	NH	03254	603-476-5900	628-6729*	671
Castle in the Sand Hotel 3701 Atlantic Ave *TF:* 800-552-7263 ■ *Web:* www.castleinthesand.com	Ocean City	MD	21842	410-289-6846	289-9446	379
Castle Inn & Suites 1734 S Harbor Blvd *TF:* 800-227-8530 ■ *Web:* www.castleinn.com	Anaheim	CA	92802	714-774-8111	956-4736	379
Castle Keepers of Charleston Inc 2030 Harley St *Web:* www.castle-keepers.com	North Charleston	SC	29406	843-569-4400		104
Castle Lake Insurance LLC 3385 S Holmes Ave *Web:* castlelakeinsurance.com	Idaho Falls	ID	83404	208-522-7778		390
Castle McCulloch 3925 Kivett Dr *Web:* www.castlemcculloch.com	Jamestown	NC	27282	336-887-5413		50-3
Castle Medical Ctr 640 Ulukahiki St *Web:* www.adventisthealth.org	Kailua	HI	96734	808-263-5500		374-3
Castle Park 3500 Polk St *TF:* 800-899-9841 ■ *Web:* www.castlepark.com	Riverside	CA	92505	951-785-3000		32
Castle Rock State Park 1365 W Castle Rd *Web:* www.dnr.illinois.gov/parks/pages/castlerock.aspx	Oregon	IL	61061	815-732-7329		565
Castle Sprinkler & Alalarm 5117 College Ave *Web:* www.csafire.com	College Park	MD	20740	301-927-7300		406
Castle Worldwide Inc 900 Perimeter Pk Rd Ste G *TF:* 800-655-4845 ■ *Web:* www.castleworldwide.com	Morrisville	NC	27560	919-572-6880	361-2426	244
Castlebay Irish Pub 193-A Main St	Annapolis	MD	21401	410-626-0165		671
Castlegarde Inc 4911 S W Shore Blvd *TF:* 866-751-3203 ■ *Web:* www.castlegarde.com	Tampa	FL	33611	813-872-4844		693
Castle-Pierce Printing Co 2247 Ryf Rd *TF:* 800-816-2640 ■ *Web:* www.castlepierce.com	Oshkosh	WI	54903	920-235-2020		627
Castles Information Network 301 Alamo Dr *Web:* www.castles.com	Vacaville	CA	95688	707-455-3401		225
Castles n Coasters 9445 N Metro Pkwy E *Web:* www.castlesncoasters.com	Phoenix	AZ	85051	602-997-7575		31
Castleton Square Mall 6020 E 82nd St *Web:* www.simon.com	Indianapolis	IN	46250	317-849-9993	849-4689	460
Castleton State College 86 Seminary St **Fax: Admissions* ■ *TF:* 800-639-8521 ■ *Web:* www.csc.vsc.edu	Castleton	VT	05735	802-468-5611	468-1476*	166
Castletop Capital 3600 N Capital of Texas Hwy Bldg B Ste 320 *Web:* www.castletopcapital.com	Austin	TX	78746	512-329-6600		528

Phone Fax Class

Castlewood Canyon State Park
2989 S Hwy 83 .... Franktown CO 80116 303-688-5242 565
Web: cpw.state.co.us
Castlewood State Park
1401 Kiefer Creek Rd .... Ballwin MO 63021 636-227-4433 565
Web: www.mostateparks.com
Castlewood Surgical Inc
91 Main St Ste 302 .... Concord MA 01742 978-610-6321 610-6315 475
Casto 250 Civic Center Dr Ste 500 .... Columbus OH 43215 614-228-5331 469-8376 655
Web: www.castoinfo.com
Casto Technical Services Inc
540 Leon Sullivan Way .... Charleston WV 25301 304-346-0549 610
TF: 800-232-2221 ■ *Web:* castotech.com
Casto Travel Inc
2560 N First St Ste 150 .... San Jose CA 95131 800-832-3445 984-7007* 771
**Fax Area Code:* 408 ■ *TF:* 800-832-3445 ■ *Web:* www.casto.com
Castor Kathy (Rep D - FL)
2052 Rayburn HOB .... Washington DC 20515 202-225-3376 225-5652 342-2
Web: castor.house.gov
Cast-Rite Corp 515 E Airline Way .... Gardena CA 90248 310-532-2080 532-0605 308
Web: www.cast-rite.com
Castro County 100 E Bedford St .... Dimmitt TX 79027 806-647-3338 647-5438 338
TF: 800-252-9229 ■ *Web:* www.co.castro.tx.us
Castro Joaquin (Rep D - TX)
1221 Longworth HOB .... Washington DC 20515 202-225-3236 225-1915 342-2
Web: castro.house.gov
Castro Valley Chamber of Commerce
3467 Castro Vly Blvd .... Castro Valley CA 94546 510-537-5300 537-5335 139
Web: www.edenareachamber.com
Castrol Industrial North America Inc
150 W Warrenville Rd .... Naperville IL 60563 877-641-1600 648-9801 541
TF: 877-641-1600 ■ *Web:* www.castrol.com
Casual Apparel Inc 139 S Main St .... Sparta TN 38583 931-836-3004 750
Casual Cushion Corp
1686 Overview Dr .... Rock Hill SC 29730 803-329-2932 361
Web: www.casualcushion.com
Casual Designs Furniture Inc
36523 Lighthouse Rd .... Selbyville DE 19975 302-436-8224 321
TF: 888-629-1717 ■ *Web:* www.casualdesignsfurniture.com
Casual Male Retail Group Inc
555 Tpke St .... Canton MA 02021 781-828-9300 157-3
NASDAQ: DXLG ■ *Web:* casual-male-big-and-tall.destinationxl.com
Casualty Actuarial Society (CAS)
4350 Fairfax Dr # 250 .... Arlington VA 22203 703-276-3100 276-3108 49-9
TF: 800-766-0070 ■ *Web:* www.casact.org
Caswell Developmental Ctr
2415 W Vernon Ave .... Kinston NC 28504 252-208-4000 230
Web: caswellcenter.org
Caswood Group Inc, The
811 Ayrault Rd Ste 2 .... Fairport NY 14450 585-425-0332 463
Web: www.caswood.com
Cat Doctor, The 535 N 22nd St .... Philadelphia PA 19130 215-561-7668 794
Web: www.thecatdr.com
Cat Pumps 1681 94th Ln NE .... Minneapolis MN 55449 763-780-5440 780-2958 641
Web: www.catpumps.com
Cat Tales Zoological Park
17020 Newport Hwy .... Mead WA 99021 509-238-4126 238-4126 823
Web: www.cattales.org
CAT Technology Inc
411 Hackensack Ave 7th Fl .... Hackensack NJ 07601 201-727-9299 463
Web: www.catamerica.com
Catahoula Correctional Ctr
499 Columbia Rd .... Harrisonburg LA 71340 318-744-2121 744-2126 213
TF: 800-443-7681 ■ *Web:* lasallecorrections.com
Catahoula Parish
301 Bushley St PO Box 654 .... Harrisonburg LA 71340 318-744-5497 744-5488 338
Web: www.laclerksofcourt.org
Catal Restaurant & Uva Bar
1510 Disneyland Dr .... Anaheim CA 92802 714-774-4442 671
Web: www.patinagroup.com
Cataldo Ambulance Service Inc
137 Washington St .... Somerville MA 02143 617-625-0126 30
Web: www.cataldoambulance.com
Catalent Pharma Solutions Inc
14 Schoolhouse Rd .... Somerset NJ 08873 732-537-6200 231
Web: www.catalent.com
Catalina Canyon Resort & Spa
888 Country Club Dr .... Avalon CA 90704 310-510-0325 510-0900 669
Web: www.hiresortcatalina.com
Catalina Care Ctr 2611 N Warren Ave .... Tucson AZ 85719 520-795-9574 450
Web: catalinacare.com
Catalina Express Berth 95 .... San Pedro CA 90731 310-519-7971 468
TF: 800-481-3470 ■ *Web:* www.catalinaexpress.com
Catalina Graphic Films Inc
27001 Agoura Rd Ste 100 .... Calabasas Hills CA 91301 818-880-8060 880-1144 600
TF: 800-333-3136 ■ *Web:* www.catalinagraphicfilms.com
Catalina High School 3645 E Pima St .... Tucson AZ 85716 520-232-8400 685
TF: 800-992-0112 ■ *Web:* www.catalinahighschoolfoundation.org
Catalina Island Visitors Bureau
1 Green Pier PO Box 217 .... Avalon CA 90704 310-510-1520 510-7607 206
TF: 877-854-1125 ■ *Web:* www.catalinachamber.com
Catalina Marketing Corp
200 Carillon Pkwy .... Saint Petersburg FL 33716 727-579-5000 556-2700 5
Web: www.catalina.com
Catalina Mechanical Contracting Inc
2702 S Alvernon Way .... Tucson AZ 85713 520-745-3000 610
Web: www.btucson.com
Catalina Restaurant Group Inc
2200 Faraday Ave Ste 250 .... Carlsbad CA 92008 760-804-5750 670
Web: www.catalinarestaurantgroup.com
Catalina State Park 11570 N Oracle Rd .... Tucson AZ 85737 520-628-5798 565
Catalina Yachts Inc
21200 Victory Blvd .... Woodland Hills CA 91367 818-884-7700 884-3810 90
Web: www.catalinayachts.com
Catalog.com Inc
14000 Quail Springs Pkwy Ste 3600 .... Oklahoma City OK 73134 405-753-9300 753-9353 808
TF: 888-932-4376 ■ *Web:* www.webhero.com

Phone Fax Class

Catalpa Systems Inc
53 W Jackson Blvd # 552 .... Chicago IL 60604 312-663-3658 177
TF: 000-914-2259 ■ *Web:* www.catalpa-systems.com
Catalpha Advertising & Design Inc
6801 Loch Raven Blvd .... Towson MD 21286 410-337-0066 7
TF: 888-337-0066 ■ *Web:* www.catalpha.com
Catalyst 109 N Orlando Ave .... Cocoa Beach FL 32931 321-783-1530 710
Catalyst Awareness Inc
355 Elmira Rd N Ste 127 .... Guelph ON N1K1S5 866-749-3697 260
TF: 866-749-3697 ■ *Web:* catalystawareness.com
Catalyst Biosciences Inc
260 Littlefield Ave .... South San Francisco CA 94080 650-871-0761 743
Web: www.catalystbiosciences.com
Catalyst Communications Technologies Inc
2107 Graves Mill Rd Mail Stop D .... Forest VA 24551 434-582-6146 224
Web: www.catcomtec.com
Catalyst Direct Inc 110 Marina Dr .... Rochester NY 14626 585-453-8300 7
Web: www.catalystinc.com
Catalyst Energy Inc
424 S 27th St Ste 304 .... Pittsburgh PA 15203 412-325-4350 536
Web: www.catalystenergyinc.com
Catalyst House Inc
32545 Golden Lantern St .... Dana Point CA 92629 949-443-0096 463
Web: www.catalysthouse.net
Catalyst IT Services Inc
502 S Sharp St .... Baltimore MD 21201 410-385-2500 196
Web: catalystdevworks.com
Catalyst Mktg Design Inc
930 S Calhoun St .... Fort Wayne IN 46802 260-422-4888 194
Web: catalystgetsit.com
Catalyst Paper Corp
3600 Lysander Ln 2nd Fl .... Richmond BC V7B1C3 604-247-4400 247-0512 557
TSE: CTL ■ *Web:* www.catalystpaper.com
Catalyst Pharmaceutical Research LLC
1111 S Arroyo Pkwy Ste 200 .... Pasadena CA 91105 626-568-8645 587
Catalytic Combustion Corp
709 21st Ave .... Bloomer WI 54724 715-568-2882 194
Web: www.catalyticcombustion.com
Catalytic Products International Inc
980 Ensell Rd .... Lake Zurich IL 60047 847-438-0334 804
Web: www.cpilink.com
Catamount Constructors Inc
1250 Bergen Pkwy Ste B200 .... Evergreen CO 80439 303-679-0087 186
Web: www.catamountinc.com
Catamount Energy Corp
71 Allen St Ste 101 .... Rutland VT 05701 802-773-6684 196
Catamount Ventures
400 Pacific Ave 3rd Fl .... San Francisco CA 94133 415-277-0300 277-0301 792
Web: www.catamountventures.com
Catanese Group PC 307 State St .... Johnstown PA 15905 814-255-8400 2
Web: catanesegroup.com
Catania-Spagna Corp 1 Nemco Way .... Ayer MA 01432 978-772-7900 297-8
Web: cataniaoils.com
Catapult Systems Inc
1221 S MoPac Expwy Ste 350 .... Austin TX 78746 512-328-8181 180
TF: 800-528-6248 ■ *Web:* www.catapultsystems.com
Catapult Technology
11 Canal Center Plaza Fl 2 .... Alexandria VA 22314 703-880-2333 405-8047* 463
**Fax Area Code:* 888 ■ *Web:* catapult.sc3.com
CatapultWorks Demand Group
300 Orchard City Dr Ste 131 .... Campbell CA 95008 408-369-8111 194
Web: www.r2integrated.com
Cataract Elementary School
6070 State Hwy 27 .... Sparta WI 54656 608-272-3111 685
Web: www.sparta.org
Catawba College 2300 W Innes St .... Salisbury NC 28144 704-637-4111 637-4222* 166
**Fax:* Admissions ■ *TF:* 800-228-2922 ■ *Web:* www.catawba.edu
Catawba Correctional Ctr
1347 Prison Camp Rd .... Newton NC 28658 828-466-5521 213
Catawba County PO Box 389 .... Newton NC 28658 828-465-8201 465-8392 338
Web: www.catawbacountync.gov/depts/servicemain.asp
Catawba County Chamber of Commerce
1055 Southgate Corporate Pk SW .... Hickory NC 28603 828-328-6111 328-1175 139
Web: www.catawbachamber.org
Catawba County Library 115 W C St .... Newton NC 28658 828-465-8664 434-3
Web: www.catawbacountync.gov/library
Catawba Hospital
5525 Catawba Hospital Dr .... Catawba VA 24070 540-375-4200 374-5
TF: 800-451-5544 ■ *Web:* www.catawba.dbhds.virginia.gov
Catawba Island State Park
4049 E Moores Dock Rd .... Port Clinton OH 43452 419-797-4530 565
Web: www.ohiodnr.com
Catawba Print & Mail Inc
1215 15th St Dr NE .... Hickory NC 28601 828-324-2021 5
Web: www.imagemarkonline.com
Catawba Valley Community College
2550 US Hwy 70 SE .... Hickory NC 28602 828-327-7000 327-7276 162
TF: 800-433-3243 ■ *Web:* www.cvcc.edu
Catawba Valley Medical Ctr
810 Fairgrove Church Rd SE .... Hickory NC 28602 828-326-3000 374-3
Web: www.catawbavalleymedical.org
Catawissa Wood & Components Inc
1015 W Valley Ave .... Elysburg PA 17824 570-644-1928 486-2800 683
Web: www.catlmbr.com
Catch Oyster Bar/Seafood Restaurant
100 Eigth Ave SE .... Calgary AB T2G0K6 403-206-0000 206-0005 671
Web: hyatt.com
Catch, The 2100 E Katella Ave Ste 104 .... Anaheim CA 92806 714-935-0101 671
Web: www.catchanaheim.com
Catchpole PO Box 812007 .... Wellesley MA 02482 781-775-8795 463
TF: 866-431-2666 ■ *Web:* www.catchpole.com
Cate School 1960 Cate Mesa Rd .... Carpinteria CA 93013 805-684-4127 622
Web: www.cate.org
CaTECH Systems Ltd
201 Whitehall Dr Unit 4 .... Markham ON L3R9Y3 905-944-0000 224
Web: catech-systems.com
Caterina's Ristorante
9104 W Oklahoma Ave .... Milwaukee WI 53227 414-541-4200 671
Web: www.caterinasristorante.com

				Phone	Fax	Class
Caterpillar Engine Systems Inc 100 NE Adams St	Peoria	IL	61629	309-675-1000		190
Caterpillar Financial Services Corp 2120 W End Ave *Web:* www.catfinancial.com	Nashville	TN	37203	615-341-1000		390
Caterpillar Inc 100 NE Adams St *NYSE: CAT* ■ *Web:* www.cat.com	Peoria	IL	61629	309-675-1000		190
Caterpillar Inc Employees PAC 100 NE Adams St *TF:* 800-437-4228 ■ *Web:* caterpillar.com	Peoria	IL	61629	309-675-2337		615
Caterpillar Logistics Services Inc 500 N Morton Ave *Web:* www.caterpillar.com	Morton	IL	61550	309-266-3591		449
Caterpillar Paving Products Inc 9401 85th Ave N	Brooklyn Park	MN	55445	763-425-4100		190
Caterpillar Remanufacturing 751 International Dr	Franklin	IN	46131	317-738-2117		262
Cates Engineering Ltd 7500 Iron Bar Ln Ste 209 *Web:* www.cateseng.com	Gainesville	VA	20155	571-261-9280		261
Catfish Bend Casinos II LLC 3001 Winegard Dr *TF:* 866-792-9948 ■ *Web:* www.thepzazz.com	Burlington	IA	52601	319-753-2946		452
Catfish Corner 780 S Treadaway Blvd	Abilene	TX	79602	325-672-3620		671
Catfish Cove 1615 Phoenix Ave	Fort Smith	AR	72901	479-646-8835		671
Cathay General Bancorp Inc 777 N Broadway *NASDAQ: CATY* ■ *TF:* 800-922-8429 ■ *Web:* www.cathaybank.com	Los Angeles	CA	90012	213-625-4700	625-1368	360-2
Cathay Inn 3714 N Div St *Web:* www.cathayinn.com	Spokane	WA	99207	509-326-2226		671
Cathay Pacific Cargo 6040 Avion Dr Ste 338 *TF:* 800-628-6960 ■ *Web:* www.cathaypacificcargo.com	Los Angeles	CA	90045	310-417-0052	348-9789	12
Cathedral Basilica of Saint Joseph 80 S Market St *TF:* 800-745-3000 ■ *Web:* www.stjosephcathedral.org	San Jose	CA	95113	408-283-8100		50-1
Cathedral Basilica of Saint Louis (New Cathedral) 4431 Lindell Blvd *Web:* www.cathedralstl.org	Saint Louis	MO	63108	314-373-8200	373-8290	50-1
Cathedral Basilica of the Sacred Heart 89 Ridge St *Web:* www.cathedralbasilica.org	Newark	NJ	07104	973-484-4600	483-8253	50-1
Cathedral Caverns State Park 637 Cave Rd *TF:* 800-252-7275 ■ *Web:* www.alapark.com	Woodville	AL	35776	256-728-8193	728-8193	565
Cathedral Church of All Saints Martello St & University Ave *TF:* 800-341-7981 ■ *Web:* www.cathedralchurchofallsaints.com	Halifax	NS	B3H4Z1	902-423-6002	423-1437	50-1
Cathedral Church of Saint John the Divine 1047 Amsterdam Ave *Web:* www.stjohndivine.org	New York	NY	10025	212-316-7490	932-7347	50-1
Cathedral Church of Saint Mark 231 East 100 South	Salt Lake City	UT	84111	801-322-3400		50-1
Cathedral City Chamber of Commerce 68950 E Palm Canyon Dr *TF:* 800-427-2200 ■ *Web:* www.cathedralcitycc.com	Cathedral City	CA	92234	760-328-1213	321-0659	139
Cathedral Corp 632 Ellsworth Rd Griffis Technology Pk *TF:* 800-698-0299 ■ *Web:* www.cathedralcorporation.com	Rome	NY	13441	315-338-0021		627
Cathedral Energy Services Ltd 6030 3 St SE *Web:* www.cathedralenergyservices.com	Calgary	AB	T2H1K2	403-265-2560		540
Cathedral Gorge State Park PO Box 176 *Web:* www.parks.nv.gov	Panaca	NV	89042	775-728-4460		565
Cathedral High School 1253 Bishops Rd	Los Angeles	CA	90012	323-225-2438		685
Cathedral of Christ the King 299 Colony Blvd *Web:* cathedralctk.org	Lexington	KY	40502	859-268-2861	268-8061	50-1
Cathedral of Our Lady of the Angels 555 W Temple St *TF:* 877-680-5277 ■ *Web:* www.olacathedral.org	Los Angeles	CA	90012	213-680-5200	620-1982	50-1
Cathedral of Saint John the Evangelist Museum 515 Cathedral St *TF:* 800-393-9954 ■ *Web:* www.saintjohncathedral.org/welcome.html	Lafayette	LA	70501	337-232-1322	232-1379	520
Cathedral of Saint Paul 239 Selby Ave *Web:* www.cathedralsaintpaul.org	Saint Paul	MN	55102	651-228-1766		50-1
Cathedral of Saints Peter & Paul 30 Fenner St	Providence	RI	02903	401-331-2434		50-1
Cathedral of the Blessed Sacrament 1017 11th St *Web:* www.blessedsaccathedral.org	Sacramento	CA	95814	916-444-3071		50-1
Cathedral of the Immaculate Conception 2 S Claiborne St *TF:* 800-247-8420 ■ *Web:* www.mobilecathedral.org	Mobile	AL	36602	251-434-1565	434-1588	50-1
Cathedral of the Immaculate Conception 125 Eagle St *Web:* www.cathedralic.com	Albany	NY	12202	518-463-4447	436-5177	50-1
Cathedral of the Madeleine 331 E S Temple St *Web:* www.utcotm.org	Salt Lake City	UT	84111	801-328-8941	364-6504	50-1
Cathedral Press Inc 600 NE Sixth St *TF Cust Svc:* 800-874-8332 ■ *Web:* www.cathedralpress.com	Long Prairie	MN	56347	320-732-6143	732-3457	637-10
Cathedral School for Boys 1275 Sacramento St *Web:* www.cathedralschool.net	San Francisco	CA	94108	415-771-6600		48-20
Cathedral State Park Rt 1 12 Cathedral Way *Web:* www.cathedralstatepark.com	Aurora	WV	26705	304-735-3771		565
Cathedral Village 600 E Cathedral Rd *TF:* 800-382-1385 ■ *Web:* www.presbyterianseniorliving.org	Philadelphia	PA	19128	215-487-1300		393
Catholic Biblical Assn of America 433 Caldwell Hall *Web:* www.catholicbiblical.org	Washington	DC	20064	202-319-5519	319-4799	48-20
Catholic Charities of Buffalo New York Inc 741 Delaware Ave *Web:* www.ccwny.org	Buffalo	NY	14209	716-218-1400		49-15
Catholic Charities USA 2050 Ballenger Ave Ste 400 *TF:* 800-919-9338 ■ *Web:* www.catholiccharitiesusa.org	Alexandria	VA	22314	703-549-1390	549-1656	48-5
Catholic Digest PO Box 6015 *TF:* 800-678-2836 ■ *Web:* www.catholicdigest.com	New London	CT	06320	800-678-2836		457-18
Catholic Diocese of Buffalo 795 Main St *Web:* www.buffalodiocese.org	Buffalo	NY	14203	716-847-8700		673
Catholic Diocese of Peoria, The 607 NE Madison Ave *Web:* www.cdop.org	Peoria	IL	61603	309-682-5823		50-1
Catholic Extension 150 S Wacker Dr Ste 2000 **Fax Area Code: 312* ■ *TF:* 800-842-7804 ■ *Web:* www.catholicextension.org	Chicago	IL	60606	800-842-7804	236-5276*	48-20
Catholic Health Assn of the US (CHA) 4455 Woodson Rd *TF:* 800-230-7823 ■ *Web:* www.chausa.org	Saint Louis	MO	63134	314-427-2500	427-0029	49-8
Catholic Health Initiatives 1999 Broadway Ste 2600 *Web:* catholichealthinitiatives.net	Denver	CO	80202	303-298-9100		353
Catholic Health System 2157 Main St *Web:* www.chsli.org	Buffalo	NY	14214	716-862-1170		592
Catholic Healthcare West 185 Berry St Ste 300 *Web:* www.dignityhealth.org	San Francisco	CA	94107	415-438-5500	438-5724	353
Catholic High School 855 HEARTHSTONE DR *Web:* catholichigh.org	Baton Rouge	LA	70806	225-383-0397		685
Catholic Hospice Inc 14875 NW 77th Ave Ste 100 *TF:* 800-464-3904 ■ *Web:* www.catholichealthservices.org	Miami Lakes	FL	33014	305-822-2380	824-0665	371
Catholic Medical Ctr (CMC) 100 McGregor St *TF:* 800-437-9666 ■ *Web:* www.catholicmedicalcenter.org	Manchester	NH	03102	603-668-3545		374-3
Catholic Medical Mission Board (CMMB) 10 W 17th St *TF:* 800-678-5659 ■ *Web:* www.cmmb.org	New York	NY	10011	212-242-7757		48-5
Catholic Memorial High School 235 Baker St *Web:* www.catholicmemorial.org	West Roxbury	MA	02132	617-469-8000		713
Catholic Mutual Group 10843 Old Mill Rd *TF:* 800-228-6108 ■ *Web:* www.catholicmutual.org	Omaha	NE	68154	402-551-8765	551-2943	391-5
Catholic News Publishing Company Inc 210 N Ave *Web:* catholicguides.com	New Rochelle	NY	10801	914-632-1220		637-2
Catholic Order of Foresters 355 Shuman Blvd *TF:* 800-617-4176 ■ *Web:* catholicforester.org	Naperville	IL	60563	630-983-4900		391-2
Catholic Press Assn (CPA) 205 W Monroe St Ste 470 *TF:* 800-777-7432 ■ *Web:* www.catholicpress.org	Chicago	IL	60606	312-380-6789	361-0256	49-14
Catholic Relief Services (CRS) 228 W Lexington St *TF:* 800-235-2772 ■ *Web:* www.crs.org	Baltimore	MD	21201	410-625-2220	685-1635	48-5
Catholic Social Services 12431 Stony Plain Rd *Web:* www.cssalberta.ca	Edmonton	AB	T5N3N3	780-432-1137	439-3154	48-20
Catholic Supply of st Louis Inc 6759 Chippewa St *TF:* 800-325-9026 ■ *Web:* www.catholicsupply.com	Saint Louis	MO	63109	314-644-0643		48-20
Catholic Theological Union 5416 S Cornell Ave *Web:* www.ctu.edu	Chicago	IL	60615	773-324-8000	324-4360	167-3
Catholic Transcript Inc, The 467 Bloomfield Ave *TF:* 800-726-2381 ■ *Web:* www.catholictranscript.org	Bloomfield	CT	06002	860-286-2828		48-20
Catholic United Financial 3499 Lexington Ave N *Web:* www.catholicunitedfinancial.org	St Paul	MN	55126	651-490-0170		390
Catholic University of America 620 Michigan Ave NE *TF:* 800-673-2772 ■ *Web:* www.cua.edu	Washington	DC	20064	202-319-5000	319-6533	166
Catholic University of America Columbus School of Law 3600 John McCormack Rd NE *Web:* www.law.edu	Washington	DC	20064	202-319-5140	319-4459	167-1
Catholic University of America, The 620 Michigan Ave NE *TF:* 800-537-5487 ■ *Web:* www.cua.edu	Washington	DC	20064	202-319-5052	319-4985	637-4
CatholicMatch LLC PO Box 154 *TF:* 888-605-3977 ■ *Web:* www.catholicmatch.com	Zelienople	PA	16063	888-605-3977		387
Cathy's Concepts Inc 6900 E 30th St *Web:* www.cathysconcepts.com	Indianapolis	IN	46219	317-860-1700		292
Catlow Inc 2750 US Rt 40 *Web:* catlow.com	Tipp City	OH	45371	937-898-3236		295
Cato Corp, The 8100 Denmark Rd *TF:* 800-526-9169 ■ *Web:* www.catofashions.com	Charlotte	NC	28273	704-554-8510		157-6
Cato Institute 1000 Massachusetts Ave NW *Web:* www.cato.org	Washington	DC	20001	202-842-0200	842-3490	634
Cato Research Ltd 4364 S Alston Ave *Web:* www.cato.com	Durham	NC	27713	919-361-2286	361-2290	194
Catoctin Mountain Park 6602 Foxville Rd *Web:* www.nps.gov	Thurmont	MD	21788	301-663-9330		564
Caton Connector Corp 26 Wapping Rd *Web:* www.caton.com	Kingston	MA	02364	781-585-4315		815
Catoosa County 875 Lafayette St *Web:* www.catoosa.com	Ringgold	GA	30736	706-965-2500		338
Catoosa County Area Chamber of Commerce 264 Catoosa Cir *TF:* 800-961-3119 ■ *Web:* www.catoosachamberofcommerce.com	Ringgold	GA	30736	706-965-5201	965-8224	139
Cator Ruma & Assoc Co 896 Tabor St *Web:* catorruma.com	Lakewood	CO	80401	303-232-6200		256

				Phone	Fax	Class
Catral Doyle Creative Co 231 E Buffalo St Ste 301 *Web:* www.cdcreative.com	Milwaukee	WI	53202	414-276-3075		7
Catriona Jeffries Gallery 274 E First Ave *TF:* 800-665-4287 ■ *Web:* www.catrionajeffries.com	Vancouver	BC	V5T1A6	604-736-1554	736-1054	42
Cats Co 1607 E Big Beaver Rd Ste 110 *Web:* www.catscompany.com	Troy	MI	48083	248-816-2287		177
Catskill Area Hospice & Palliative Care Inc 1 Birchwood Dr *TF:* 800-306-3870 ■ *Web:* www.cahpc.org	Oneonta	NY	13820	607-432-6773		371
Catskill Regional Medical Ctr 68 Harris-Bushville Rd PO Box 800 *TF:* 888-846-5945 ■ *Web:* www.crmcny.org	Harris	NY	12742	845-794-3300	794-3240	374-3
Cattan Services Group Inc 1006 Haywood Dr *Web:* www.cattan.com	College Station	TX	77845	979-260-7200		463
Cattaneo Bros Inc 769 Caudill St *TF:* 800-243-8537 ■ *Web:* www.cattaneobros.com	San Luis Obispo	CA	93401	805-543-7188	543-4698	296-26
Cattaraugus County 303 Ct St *Web:* www.cattco.org	Little Valley	NY	14755	716-938-9111		338
Cattle Baron Restaurants Inc 901 S Main St *Web:* www.cattlebaron.com	Roswell	NM	88203	575-622-3311		671
Cattle Empire LLC 1174 Empire Cir *Web:* www.cattle-empire.net	Satanta	KS	67870	620-649-2235		446
Cattle Raisers Museum 1600 Gendy St *Web:* www.cattleraisersmuseum.org	Fort Worth	TX	76107	817-332-8551	336-2470	520
CattleLog 10305 102nd Terr *TF:* 866-239-2665 ■ *Web:* www.cattlelog.com	Sebastian	FL	32958	866-239-2665		466
Cattleman's Club Steakhouse & Lounge 29608 SD Hwy 34 *Web:* cattlemansclubsteakhouse.com	Pierre	SD	57501	605-224-9774		671
Cattleman's Steakhouse 3450 S Fabens Carlsbad Rd *Web:* www.cattlemanssteakhouse.com	Fabens	TX	79838	915-544-3200		671
Cattlemen's Cut Supper Club 369 Vaughn Frontage Rd S *Web:* cattlemenscut.com	Great Falls	MT	59404	406-452-0702		671
Cattrell Cos Inc 906 Franklin St *Web:* cattrell.com	Toronto	OH	43964	740-537-2481		189-10
Cattron Group International 58 W Shenango St *Web:* www.cattron.com	Sharpsville	PA	16150	724-962-3571	962-4310	647
Catty Corp 6111 White Oaks Rd *Web:* www.cattycorp.com	Harvard	IL	60033	815-943-2288	943-4473	548
Catylist Inc 2360 E Stadium Blvd Ste 16 *TF:* 877-595-5478	Chicago	IL	48104	877-595-5478		225
CAU (Community Assn Underwriters of America) 2 Caufield Pl *Web:* www.cauinsure.com	Newtown	PA	18940	267-757-7100		391-4
Caufield & Flood 407 E Congress Pkwy Ste A *TF:* 800-201-3187 ■ *Web:* www.cfcpas.com	Crystal Lake	IL	60014	847-669-5950		2
Cauldwell Wingate Company LLC 380 Lexington Ave *Web:* www.cauldwellwingate.com	New York	NY	10168	212-983-7150		41
Caumsett State Historic Park Preserve 25 Lloyd Harbor Rd *Web:* www.nysparks.com	Huntington	NY	11743	631-423-1770		565
Causeit Inc 1631 NE Broadway Ste 249 *Web:* causeit.org	Portland	OR	97232	503-493-7332		466
Causeway Lumber Co 3318 SW Second Ave *TF:* 800-322-1500 ■ *Web:* www.causewaylumber.com	Fort Lauderdale	FL	33315	954-763-1224		191-3
Cautela-Solutions Ltd 201 Lawrence Dr PMB 104 *Web:* www.cautela-solutions.com	Heath	TX	75032	972-772-8020		196
Cauthorne Paper Co 12124 S Washington Hwy *TF:* 800-552-3011 ■ *Web:* www.cauthornepaper.com	Ashland	VA	23005	804-798-6999	798-6466	557
Cauttrell Enterprises Inc 7618 N Broadway *Web:* www.cauttrellenterprises.com	St. Louis	MO	63147	314-385-4270		480
CAV Distributing Corp 253 Utah Ave *Web:* www.cavd.com	South San Francisco	CA	94080	650-588-2228		514
CAV Restaurant 14 Imperial Pl *TF:* 800-294-7709 ■ *Web:* www.cavrestaurant.com	Providence	RI	02903	401-751-9164	274-9107	671
Cavadeas Engineering Corp 10045 N State Rd 27 Ste 200	Hayward	WI	54843	715-634-4176		261
Cavalier County Job Development Authority 901 Third St Ste 5 *Web:* www.ccjda.org	Langdon	ND	58249	701-256-3475	256-3536	338
Cavalier Energy Inc 5 Ave SW Ste 2500-255 *Web:* cavalierenergy.com	Calgary	AB	T2P3G6	403-268-3940		579
Cavalier Home Builders LLC 32 Wilson Blvd Ste 100 PO Box 300	Addison	AL	35540	256-747-1575	747-2344	505
Cavalier Homes Alabama 32 Wilson Blvd PO Box 300 *TF:* 800-465-7923 ■ *Web:* cavalierhomebuilders.net	Addison	AL	35540	800-465-7923		505
Cavalier Hotel 4201 Atlantic Ave *Web:* www.cavalierhotel.com	Virginia Beach	VA	23451	757-425-8555		669
Cavalier Logistics Management Inc 45085 Old Ox Rd *Web:* www.cavlog.com	Dulles	VA	20166	703-733-4010		194
Cavalier Telephone LLC 2134 W Laburnum Ave *TF:* 800-683-3944	Richmond	VA	23227	804-565-7500	422-4392	736
Cavallino LLC 599 Bridgeway *Web:* www.cavallinollc.com	Sausalito	CA	94965	415-285-9300		401
Cavanagh Law Firm, The 1850 N Central Ave *TF:* 888-824-3476 ■ *Web:* www.cavanaghlaw.com	Phoenix	AZ	85004	602-322-4000	322-4100	428
Cavanal Hill Investment Management Inc 1 Williams Ctr 15th Fl *Web:* cavanalhillfunds.com	Tulsa	OK	74172	918-588-8688		401
Cavanaugh Flight Museum 4572 Claire Chennault Addison Airport *Web:* www.cavanaughflightmuseum.com	Addison	TX	75001	972-380-8800		520
Cavanaugh Press Inc 8960 Yellow Brick Rd *Web:* www.cavanaughpress.com	Baltimore	MD	21237	410-391-1900		627
Cavanaugh Tocci Associates Inc 327 Boston Post Rd *Web:* cavtocci.com	Sudbury	MA	01776	978-443-7871		463
Cavco Industries Inc 1001 N Central Ave 8th Fl *NASDAQ: CVCO* ■ *TF:* 800-790-9111 ■ *Web:* www.cavco.com	Phoenix	AZ	85004	602-256-6263	256-6189	505
Cave City Convention Ctr 502 Mammoth Cave St *Web:* cavecity.com	Cave City	KY	42127	270-773-3131		232
Cave Hill Cemetery & Arboretum 701 Baxter Ave *Web:* www.cavehillcemetery.com	Louisville	KY	40204	502-451-5630	451-5655	97
Cave Lake State Park PO Box 151761 *Web:* parks.nv.gov/parks/cave-lake-state-park	Ely	NV	89315	775-867-3001		565
Cave of the Mounds 2975 CAve of the Mounds Rd PO Box 148 *Web:* www.caveofthemounds.com	Blue Mounds	WI	53517	608-437-3038	437-4181	50-5
Cave of the Winds 100 Cave of the Winds Rd *TF:* 800-525-2250 ■ *Web:* www.caveofthewinds.com	Manitou Springs	CO	80829	719-685-5444	685-1712	50-5
Cave Vin 5555 Xerxes Ave S *Web:* cave-vin.net	Minneapolis	MN	55410	612-922-0100		671
Cave-In-Rock State Park 1 New State Park Rd	Cave-In-Rock	IL	62919	618-289-4325		565
Cavender Cadillac Co 7625 N Loop 1604 E *Web:* www.cavendercadillac.com	San Antonio	TX	78233	210-226-7221		57
Cavender's 2025 SW Loop 323 *Web:* www.cavenders.com	Tyler	TX	75701	903-561-2510		157-5
Caveon LLC 6905 S 1300 E Ste 468 *Web:* www.caveon.com	Midvale	UT	84047	801-208-0103		693
Cavetown Planing Mill Co 12032 Mapleville Rd *Web:* www.cavetown.com	Cavetown	MD	21783	301-733-7940		683
Cavey's 45 E Ctr St *Web:* www.caveysrestaurant.com	Manchester	CT	06040	860-643-2751		671
Caviar Russe 538 Madison Ave *Web:* www.caviarrusse.com	New York	NY	10022	212-980-5908		671
Cavico Corp 17011 Beach Blvd Ste 1230 *OTC: CAVO* ■ **Fax Area Code: 302* ■ *Web:* www.cavicocorp.com	Huntington Beach	CA	92647	714-843-5456	996-5818*	186
Caviness Beef Packers Ltd 3255 US Hwy 60 *Web:* www.cavinessbeefpackers.com	Hereford	TX	79045	806-357-2443		473
Caviness Lambert Engineering LLC 508 E N St Ste 202 *Web:* www.cl-e.com	Greenville	SC	29601	864-242-5844		261
Cavium Inc 2315 N First St *Web:* investor.caviumnetworks.com	San Jose	CA	95131	408-943-7100		696
C-Axis Inc 800 Tower Dr *Web:* c-axis.com	Hamel	MN	55340	763-478-8982		454
Caxton Growth Partners 5755 Granger Rd Ste 100	Independence	OH	44131	216-867-9780		194
Caxy Consulting LLC 212 W Van Buren Ste 100 *TF:* 800-835-4603 ■ *Web:* www.caxy.com	Chicago	IL	60607	312-207-6200		395
Cayce Historical Museum 1800 12th St *TF:* 800-922-0983 ■ *Web:* www.caycesc.net	Cayce	SC	29033	803-796-9020	796-9072	520
Caye Home Furnishings LLC 1201 W Bankhead St *Web:* www.cayefurniture.com	New Albany	MS	38652	662-534-4762		361
Cayenta Canada Corp 4200 N Fraser Way Ste 201 *TF:* 866-229-3682 ■ *Web:* www.cayenta.com	Burnaby	BC	V5J5K7	604-570-4300	291-0742	39
Caylor Industrial Sales Inc PO Box 4659 *Web:* www.caylorindustrial.com	Dalton	GA	30721	706-226-3198	278-4104	612
Cayman Airways Cargo Services 6103 NW 72nd Ave *TF:* 800-252-2746 ■ *Web:* www.caymanairways.com	Miami	FL	33166	305-526-3190	455-5616	12
Cayman Airways Ltd 91 Owen Roberts Dr *TF:* 800-422-9626 ■ *Web:* www.caymanairways.com	Grand Cayman	KY	10092	345-949-8200	949-7607	25
Cayman Islands Dept of Tourism 350 Fifth Ave *TF:* 800-235-5888 ■ *Web:* www.caymanislands.ky	New York	NY	10118	212-889-9009	889-9125	775
Cayman Islands Dept of Tourism 8300 NW 53rd St Ste 103 *TF:* 800-553-4939 ■ *Web:* www.caymanislands.ky	Miami	FL	33166	305-599-9033	599-3766	775
Cayman Technologies Inc 12954 Stonecreek Dr Ste E *TF:* 877-370-9470 ■ *Web:* www.caymantech.com	Pickerington	OH	43147	614-759-9461		180
Cayo Costa State Park PO Box 1150 *Web:* www.floridastateparks.org/cayocosta	Boca Grande	FL	33921	941-964-0375		565
Cayuga Community College 197 Franklin St *TF:* 866-598-8883 ■ *Web:* www.cayuga-cc.edu	Auburn	NY	13021	315-255-1743	255-2117	162
Cayuga Correctional Facility 2202 State Rt 38A PO Box 1150 *Web:* www.doccs.ny.gov	Moravia	NY	13118	315-497-1110		213
Cayuga County 160 Genesee St *TF:* 800-771-7755 ■ *Web:* www.cayugacounty.us	Auburn	NY	13021	315-253-1271		338
Cayuga County Chamber of Commerce 2 State St *Web:* www.cayugacountychamber.com	Auburn	NY	13021	315-252-7291	255-3077	139
Cayuga Lake State Park 2678 Lower Lake Rd *Web:* parks.ny.gov/parks/123/hunting.aspx	Seneca Falls	NY	13148	315-568-5163	568-5336	565
Cayuga Medical Ctr 101 Dates Dr *Web:* www.cayugamed.org	Ithaca	NY	14850	607-274-4011	274-4527	374-3

Name / Address	City	State	Zip	Phone	Fax	Class
Cayuse Technologies LLC 72632 Coyote Rd *Web:* www.cayusetechnologies.com	Pendleton	OR	97801	541-278-8200		177
Caza Oil & Gas Inc Ste 200 10077 Grogan's Mill Rd *Web:* www.cazapetro.com	The Woodlands	TX	77380	281-363-4442		536
Cazarin Web Group 7064 E Fish Lake Rd *TF:* 800-258-8579 ■ *Web:* www.cazarin.com	Minneapolis	MN	55311	763-420-9992		180
Cazenovia College 8 Sullivan St *TF:* 800-654-3210 ■ *Web:* cazenovia.edu	Cazenovia	NY	13035	315-655-7208		166
Cazenovia Equipment Company Inc 2 Remington Park Dr *TF:* 800-932-0607 ■ *Web:* www.cazenoviaequipment.com	Cazenovia	NY	13035	315-655-8620		45
CB Displays International 5141 S Procyon *Web:* www.cbdisplays.com	Las Vegas	NV	89118	702-739-9301		232
CB Engineering Pacific Inc 909 Seventh Ave Ste 201 *Web:* www.cb-pacific.com	Kirkland	WA	98033	425-822-1702		256
CB Fleet Co Inc 4615 Murray Pl PO Box 11349 *TF:* 866-255-6960 ■ *Web:* www.cbfleet.com	Lynchburg	VA	24506	866-255-6960		582
CB Information Services Inc 160 Varick St Fl 12 *Web:* www.cbinsights.com	New York	NY	10013	212-292-3148		387
CB Kaupp & Sons Inc 6-10 Newark Way *Web:* kaupp-kihm.com	Maplewood	NJ	07040	973-761-4000		483
CB Ragland Co 2720 Eugenia Ave *Web:* www.cbragland.com	Nashville	TN	37211	615-254-2841		297-8
Cbaia 1125 Jefferson Davis Hwy Ste 380 *TF:* 800-455-5600 ■ *Web:* www.cbaia.com	Fredericksburg	VA	22401	540-604-9731		475
CBAN (Community Banking Advisory Network) 1801 W End Ave Ste 800 *TF:* 800-231-2524 ■ *Web:* www.bankingcpas.com	Nashville	TN	37203	615-373-9880	377-7092	49-2
CBB (Citizens Business Bank) 701 N Haven Ave *TF Cust Svc:* 888-222-5432 ■ *Web:* www.cbbank.com	Ontario	CA	91764	909-980-4030	481-2130	70
CBC (California Ballet Co) 4819 Ronson Ct *Web:* www.californiaballet.org	San Diego	CA	92111	858-560-5676	560-0072	573-1
CBC (Children's Book Council) 54 W 39th St 14th Fl *Web:* www.cbcbooks.org	New York	NY	10018	212-966-1990		49-16
CBC (Coors Distributing Co) 5400 N Pecos St *Web:* www.coors.com	Denver	CO	80221	303-433-6541		81-1
CBC 1724 Westmount Blvd NW *Web:* www.cbc.ca	Calgary	AB	T2N3G7	403-521-6000	521-6079	741-21
CBC (Canadian Broadcasting Corp) PO Box 3220 *Web:* www.cbc.radio-canada.ca	Ottawa	ON	K1Y1E4	514-597-6000		643
CBC (Crawford Broadcasting Co) 2821 S Parker Rd Ste 1205 *Web:* www.crawfordbroadcasting.com	Denver	CO	80014	303-433-5500	433-1555	643
CBC Manitoba 541 Portage Ave *TF:* 877-666-6292 ■ *Web:* cbc.ca/news/canada/manitoba	Winnipeg	MB	R3C2H1	204-788-3222		645-177
CBC National Bank 1891 S 14th St *Web:* www.cbcnationalbankmortgage.com	Fernandina Beach	FL	32034	904-321-0400	277-0167	70
CBC Radio 1724 Westmount Blvd NW **Fax:* News Rm ■ *Web:* cbc.ca/news/canada/calgary	Calgary	AB	T2N3G7	403-521-6000	521-6262*	645-27
CBC Radio Canada 181 Queen St PO Box 3220 *Web:* www.cbc.ca	Ottawa	ON	K1P1K9	613-288-6000		644
CBCInnovis Inc 250 E Town St *TF:* 877-284-8322 ■ *Web:* www.cbcinnovis.com	Columbus	OH	43215	877-284-8322		218
CBCL Ltd 1489 Hollis St *Web:* www.cbcl.ca	Halifax	NS	B3J2R7	902-421-7241		256
CBD (Cincinnati Bell Directory) 312 Plum St Ste 600 *TF:* 800-877-0475 ■ *Web:* vivial.net	Cincinnati	OH	45202	800-877-0475		637-6
CBE (Center for Biofilm Engineering) Montana State University PO Box 173980 *Web:* www.biofilm.montana.edu	Bozeman	MT	59717	406-994-4770	994-6098	668
CBE Companies Inc 1309 Technology Pkwy *TF:* 800-925-6686 ■ *Web:* www.cbecompanies.com	Cedar Falls	IA	50613	800-925-6686		393
CBE Technologies Inc 215 N Brow St *Web:* www.cbetech.com	East Providence	RI	02914	401-453-1234		225
CBET-TV Ch 9 (CBC) 825 Riverside Dr W *Web:* cbc.ca/news/canada/windsor	Windsor	ON	N9A5K9	519-255-3411		741
CBG Corp 4616 W Howard Ln Ste 900 *Web:* www.cbgcorp.com	Austin	TX	78758	512-491-7541		538
CBH Homes 1977 E Overland Rd *Web:* www.cbhhomes.com	Meridian	ID	83642	208-288-5560		655
CBI 600 Unicorn Park Dr *TF:* 800-817-8601 ■ *Web:* www.cbinet.com	Woburn	MA	01801	339-298-2100		194
CBI Group LLC Casho Mill Professional Ctr 1501 Casho Mill Rd Ste 9 *Web:* www.thecbigroup.com	Newark	DE	19711	302-266-0860		194
CBI Laboratories 4201 Diplomacy Rd **Fax Area Code:* 800 ■ *TF:* 800-822-7546 ■ *Web:* www.cbiskincare.com	Fort Worth	TX	76155	972-241-7546	352-1094*	214
CBI Services Inc 14105 S Route 59 *TF:* 866-235-5687 ■ *Web:* www.cbi.com	Plainfield	IL	60544	815-439-6668	439-6001	189-14
CBIZ Benefits & Insurance Services of Maryland Inc 44 Baltimore St **Fax:* Sales ■ *TF Cust Svc:* 800-615-8418 ■ *Web:* www.cbiz.com	Cumberland	MD	21502	301-777-1500	951-0425*	390
CBIZ Tofias PC 500 Boylston St *Web:* www.cbiz.com	Boston	MA	02116	617-761-0600	761-0601	2
CBLPath Inc 2100 SE 17th St *Web:* www.cblpath.com	Ocala	FL	34471	352-732-9990		415
CBM (Christian Blind Mission) 450 E Pk Ave *TF:* 800-937-2264 ■ *Web:* www.cbmus.org	Greenville	SC	29601	864-239-0065	239-0069	48-5
Cbm 2614 Hickory St *Web:* www.cbme.net	Santa Ana	CA	92707	714-424-9250		693
Cbm Chartered Accountants 152 Jackson St E Ste 200 *Web:* www.cbmca.com	Hamilton	ON	L8N1L3	905-572-7220		2
CBM of America Inc 1455 W Newport Ctr Dr *TF:* 800-881-8202 ■ *Web:* www.cbmusa.com	Deerfield Beach	FL	33442	954-698-9104		180
CBM Systems Inc 13515 SW Millikan Way	Beaverton	OR	97005	503-520-1660		104
CBMC (Christian Business Men's Connection) 5746 Marlin Rd Ste 602 Osborne Ctr *TF:* 800-566-2262 ■ *Web:* www.cbmc.com	Chattanooga	TN	37411	423-698-4444	629-4434	48-20
CBMR (Crested Butte Mountain Resort) 12 Snowmass Rd PO Box 5700 *TF:* 877-547-5143 ■ *Web:* www.skicb.com/cbmr	Crested Butte	CO	81225	877-547-5143		669
CBN (Christian Broadcasting Network) 977 Centerville Tpke *TF:* 800-823-6053 ■ *Web:* www.cbn.com	Virginia Beach	VA	23463	800-823-6053		740
CBNC (Canadian Bank Note Company Ltd) 145 Richmond Rd *Web:* www.cbnco.com	Ottawa	ON	K1Z1A1	613-722-3421		627
CBOE (Chicago Board Options Exchange) 400 S La Salle St *Web:* www.cboe.com	Chicago	IL	60605	312-786-5600	786-8818	691
CBOE Stock Exchange LLC 400 S LaSalle St *Web:* www.cboe.com/aboutcboe/legal/cbsx-regulatory.aspx	Chicago	IL	60605	312-786-7449		691
Cbol Corp 19850 Plummer St *Web:* www.cbol.com	Chatsworth	CA	91311	818-704-8200	704-4336	21
Cbord Group Inc, The 950 Danby Rd Ste 100C *TF:* 844-462-2673 ■ *Web:* www.cbord.com	Ithaca	NY	14850	844-462-2673		180
CBOSS Inc 7332 Southern Blvd Sutton Ctr Plaza *Web:* www.cboss.com	Boardman	OH	44512	330-726-0429		224
CBR International Corp 2905 Wilderness Pl Ste 202 *Web:* www.cbrintl.com	Boulder	CO	80301	720-746-1190		466
CBR Laser Inc 340 Rt 116 W *Web:* www.cbrlaser.com	Plessisville	QC	G6L2Y2	819-362-9339		295
CBRL Group Inc PO Box 787 *TF:* 800-333-9566 ■ *Web:* www.crackerbarrel.com	Lebanon	TN	37088	800-333-9566		360-3
CBR-Technology Corp 15581 Sunburst Ln *TF:* 800-227-0700 ■ *Web:* www.cbrtechnology.com	Huntington Beach	CA	92647	714-901-5740		463
CBS Broadcasting Inc 51 W 52nd St *Web:* www.cbs.com	New York	NY	10019	212-975-4321		739
CBS Builders Supply Inc 1000 Carroll St *Web:* www.cbsbuilderssupply.com	Clermont	FL	34711	352-394-2116		791
CBS Construction Ltd 150 MacKay Crescent *TF:* 800-582-3273 ■ *Web:* www.cbsconstruction.ca	Fort Mcmurray	AB	T9H4W8	780-743-1810		186
CBS Corp 51 W 52nd St *NYSE: CBS* ■ *Web:* www.cbscorporation.com	New York	NY	10019	212-975-4321		739
CBS Denver 1044 Lincoln St *Web:* denver.cbslocal.com	Denver	CO	80203	303-861-4444	830-6380	741-39
CBS Interactive Inc 235 Second St *Web:* www.cbsinteractive.com	San Francisco	CA	94105	415-344-2000		808
CBS Manufacturing Co, The 35 Kripes Rd *Web:* www.cbsmfg.com	East Granby	CT	06026	860-653-8100		21
CBS Miami 194 NW 187th St *Web:* miami.cbslocal.com/category/sports	Miami	FL	33169	305-654-1700		645
CBS News 524 W 57th St *Web:* www.cbsnews.com	New York	NY	10019	212-975-3247		514
CBS Newspath 524 W 57th St	New York	NY	10019	212-975-6121		742
CBS Radio 1271 Ave of the Americas Fl 44 *Web:* www.cbsradio.com	New York	NY	10020	248-855-5100		645
CBS Radio Network 524 W 57th St *TF:* 800-798-2510 ■ *Web:* www.cbsnews.com	New York	NY	10019	212-975-3247		644
CBS Studio Ctr 4024 Radford Ave *Web:* www.cbssc.com	Studio City	CA	91604	818-655-5000		514
CBS Television Distribution 2450 Colorado Ave Ste 500E *TF:* 800-495-7713 ■ *Web:* www.cbstvd.com	Santa Monica	CA	90404	310-264-3300	264-3301	514
CBS Television Stations Group 51 W 52nd St *Web:* www.cbs.com	New York	NY	10019	212-975-4321		738
CBSE (Center for Biophysical Sciences & Engineering) University of Alabama CBSE 100 1720 2nd Ave S *Web:* www.uab.edu	Birmingham	AL	35294	205-934-5329	934-0480	668
CBSL Transportation Services Inc 4750 S Merrimac Ave *Web:* www.cbsltrans.com	Chicago	IL	60638	708-496-1100		311
CBT Bank 11 N Second St PO Box 171 *TF:* 888-765-7551 ■ *Web:* www.cbtbank.bank	Clearfield	PA	16830	814-765-7551	765-2943	70
CBT Sports LLC 12 Cadillac Dr Ste 230 *Web:* 247sports.com	Brentwood	TN	37027	615-879-3786		387
CBV Collections 1200-100 Sheppard Ave E *TF:* 866-877-9323 ■ *Web:* www.cbvcollections.com	Toronto	ON	M2N6N5	416-482-9323		160
CBVE-FM 104.7 (CBC) PO Box 3220 Station C *TF:* 866-306-4636 ■ *Web:* www.cbc.radio-canada.ca	Ottawa	ON	K1Y1E4	866-306-4636		645-130
CBV-FM 106.3 (CBC) 888 Rue Saint-Jean *TF:* 866-306-4636 ■ *Web:* www.cbc.radio-canada.ca	Quebec	QC	G1R5H6	418-654-1341		645
Cbw Automation 3939 automation way *TF:* 800-229-9500 ■ *Web:* www.cbwautomation.com	Fort collins	CO	80525	970-229-9500		757
CBY Systems Inc 33 S Duke St *Web:* www.cby.com	York	PA	17401	717-843-8685		160

				Phone	Fax	Class
Cc Coaching & Consulting Inc 5595 S Sycamore St *Web:* www.cccandc.com	Littleton	CO	80120	303-984-9000		196
Cc Columbia Collectors Inc 1104 Main St Ste 311 *TF:* 800-694-7585 ■ *Web:* columbiacollectors.com	Vancouver	WA	98660	360-694-7585		160
C&C Fabrication Company Inc 30 Fabrication Dr *TF:* 888-485-5130 ■ *Web:* www.ccfab.com	Lacey's Spring	AL	35754	256-881-7300		198
C&C Metal Products Corp 456 Nordhoff Pl *Web:* www.ccmetal.com	Englewood	NJ	07631	201-569-7300		295
CC Myers Inc 3286 Fitzgerald Rd *Web:* www.ccmyers.com	Rancho Cordova	CA	95742	916-635-9370		188-4
Cc Pollen Co 3627 E Indian School Rd Ste 209 *TF:* 800-875-0096 ■ *Web:* www.beepollen.com	Phoenix	AZ	85018	800-875-0096		799
CCA (Career College Assn) 1101 Connecticut Ave NW Ste 900 *Web:* www.career.org	Washington	DC	20036	202-336-6700	336-6828	49-5
CCA (Coastal Conservation Assn) 6919 Portwest Dr Ste 100 *TF:* 800-201-3474 ■ *Web:* www.joincca.org	Houston	TX	77024	713-626-4234	626-5852	48-13
CCA Global Partners 4301 Earth City Expy **Fax Area Code:* 603 ■ *TF:* 800-466-6984 ■ *Web:* www.ccaglobalpartners.com	Earth City	MO	63045	314-506-0000	626-3444*	361
CCA Industries Inc 200 Murray Hill Pkwy *NYSE:* CAW ■ *TF Cust Svc:* 800-524-2720 ■ *Web:* www.ccaindustries.com	East Rutherford	NJ	07073	201-935-3232		214
Cca Medical Inc 6 Southridge Ct *TF:* 800-775-2556 ■ *Web:* www.ccamedical.com	Greenville	SC	29607	864-233-2700		180
CCAII (Computer Consulting Assoc International) 200 Pequot Ave *Web:* www.ccaii.com	Southport	CT	06890	203-255-8966		721
CCAR (CCAR) University of Colorado ECNT 320 UCB 431 *Web:* ccar.colorado.edu	Boulder	CO	80309	303-492-3105	492-2825	668
CCAR (Central Conference of American Rabbis) 355 Lexington Ave *Web:* www.ccarnet.org	New York	NY	10017	212-972-3636		48-20
CCAS (Cross Country Automotive Services) 1 Cabot Rd *Web:* www.agero.com	Medford	MA	02155	781-393-9300	395-6706	53
CCB Community Bank 225 E Three Notch St *Web:* bankccb.com	Andalusia	AL	36420	334-222-2561		70
CCC (Center for Community Change) 1536 U St NW *TF:* 800-233-1200 ■ *Web:* www.communitychange.org	Washington	DC	20009	202-339-9300	387-4891	48-5
CCC (Copyright Clearance Ctr Inc) 222 Rosewood Dr *TF:* 855-239-3415 ■ *Web:* www.copyright.com	Danvers	MA	01923	978-750-8400	646-8600	49-16
CCC (Consolidated Container Co) 3101 Towercreek Pkwy Ste 300 *TF Sales:* 888-831-2184 ■ *Web:* www.cccllc.com	Atlanta	GA	30339	678-742-4600	742-4750	548
CCC (Clovis Community College) 417 Schepps Blvd **Fax:* Admissions ■ *TF:* 800-769-1409 ■ *Web:* www.clovis.edu	Clovis	NM	88101	575-769-2811	769-4190*	162
CCC Group Inc 5797 Dietrich Rd *Web:* www.cccgroupinc.com	San Antonio	TX	78219	210-661-4251	661-6060	188-7
CCC Information Services Inc 222 Merchandise Mart Plaza *TF:* 800-621-8070 ■ *Web:* www.cccis.com	Chicago	IL	60654	800-621-8070		225
CCC Investment Banking 155 Wellington St W Ste 3720 *Web:* www.cccinvestmentbanking.com	Toronto	ON	M5V3H1	416-599-4206		70
CCCC (Conference on College Composition & Communication) 1111 W Kenyon Rd *TF:* 877-369-6283 ■ *Web:* www.ncte.org/cccc	Urbana	IL	61801	217-328-3870		49-5
CCCC (Cherokee County Chamber of Commerce) 805 W US 64 Hwy *TF:* 800-633-7655 ■ *Web:* www.cherokeecountychamber.com	Murphy	NC	28906	828-837-2242	837-6012	139
CCCS (CAD/CAM Consulting Services Inc) 1525 Rancho Conejo Blvd Ste 103 *TF:* 888-375-7676 ■ *Web:* www.cad-cam.com	Newbury Park	CA	91320	805-375-7676	375-7678	174
CCCS (Community Counseling & Correctional Service) 471 E Mercury St *Web:* www.cccscorp.com	Butte	MT	59701	406-782-0417		48-15
CCCU (Council for Christian Colleges & Universities) 321 Eigth St NE *Web:* www.cccu.org	Washington	DC	20002	202-546-8713	546-8913	49-5
CCCVB (Clermont County Convention & Visitors Bureau) 410 E Main St PO Box 100 *TF:* 800-796-4282 ■ *Web:* www.visitclermontohio.com	Batavia	OH	45103	513-732-3600		206
CCD (Consortium for Citizens with Disabilities) 1660 L St NW Ste 701 *Web:* www.c-c-d.org	Washington	DC	20036	202-783-2229		48-6
CCDNCVB (Crescent City-Del Norte County Chamber of Commerce) 1001 Front St *TF:* 800-343-8300 ■ *Web:* delnorte.org	Crescent City	CA	95531	707-464-3174	464-3561	206
CCEC (Carteret-Craven Electric Co-op) 1300 Hwy 24 W PO Box 1490 *TF:* 800-682-2217 ■ *Web:* www.carteretcravenelectric.coop	Newport	NC	28570	252-247-3107		245
CCEIA (Carnegie Council for Ethics in International Affairs) Merrill House 170 E 64th St *Web:* www.carnegiecouncil.org	New York	NY	10065	212-838-4120	752-2432	634
CCF (Clarity Coverdale Fury) 120 S Sixth St 1 Financial Plz Ste 1300 *Web:* www.claritycoverdalefury.com	Minneapolis	MN	55402	612-339-3902		4
CCFA (Crohn's & Colitis Foundation of America) 733 Third Ave Ste 510 **Fax Area Code:* 212 ■ *TF:* 800-932-2423 ■ *Web:* www.crohnscolitisfoundation.org	New York	NY	10017	800-932-2423	679-3567*	48-17
Ccg Automation Inc 3868 congress pkwy *Web:* www.ccgautomation.com	Richfield	OH	44286	330-659-5082		463
CCG Facilities Integration Inc 1500 S Edgewood St *Web:* www.ccgfacilities.com	Baltimore	MD	21227	410-525-0010		194
CCG Investor Relations Inc 10960 Wilshire Blvd Ste 2050	Los Angeles	CA	90024	310-477-9800		387
CCGA (Chicago Council on Global Affairs, The) 332 S Michigan Ave Ste 1100 *Web:* www.thechicagocouncil.org	Chicago	IL	60604	312-726-3860	821-7555	634
CCH (Covenant Children's Hospital) 4015 22nd Pl *Web:* covenanthealth.org	Lubbock	TX	79410	806-725-0000		374-1
CCH Small Firm Services 225 Chastain Meadows Ct NW Ste 200 *TF Sales:* 866-345-4171 ■ *Web:* www.cchsfs.com	Kennesaw	GA	30144	866-345-4171		178-10
CCH Washington Service Bureau Inc 1015 15th St NW 10th Fl *TF:* 800-955-5219 ■ *Web:* www.wsb.com	Washington	DC	20005	202-312-6600		635
CCHC Southern Gastroenterology Associates 3100 Wellons Blvd *Web:* www.cchchealthcare.com	New Bern	NC	28562	252-634-9000		543
CCI (Canine Companions for Independence Inc) 2965 Dutton Ave PO Box 446 *TF:* 800-572-2275 ■ *Web:* www.cci.org	Santa Rosa	CA	95402	707-577-1700		48-17
CCI (Charlestown Retirement Community) 715 Maiden Choice Ln *TF:* 800-917-8649 ■ *Web:* ericksonliving.com	Catonsville	MD	21228	410-242-2880		672
CCI (Columbus Cir Investors Inc) 1 Stn Pl Metro Ctr *Web:* www.columbuscircle.com	Stamford	CT	06902	203-353-6000		401
CCI Communications Inc 155 North 400 West Ste 100 *Web:* www.ccicom.com	Salt Lake City	UT	84103	801-994-4100		387
CCI Mechanical Inc 2345 S CCI Way PO Box 25788 *Web:* ccimechanical.com	Salt Lake City	UT	84119	801-973-9000	975-7204	189-10
CCI Thermal Technologies Inc 5918 Roper Rd *TF Cust Svc:* 800-661-8529 ■ *Web:* www.ccithermal.com	Edmonton	AB	T6B3E1	780-466-3178	468-5904	318
CCIA (Computer & Communications Industry Assn) 666 11th St NW *Web:* www.ccianet.org	Washington	DC	20001	202-783-0070	783-0534	49-20
CCIA (Consumer Credit Industry Assn) 6300 Powers Ferry Rd Ste 600-286 *Web:* www.cciaonline.com	Atlanta	GA	30339	678-858-4001		49-9
CCIC (Canadian Council for International Co-op) 450 Rideau St Ste 200 *Web:* www.ccic.ca	Ottawa	ON	K1N5Z4	613-241-7007	241-5302	48-5
CCIM Institute 430 N Michigan Ave Ste 800 *TF:* 800-621-7027 ■ *Web:* www.ccim.com	Chicago	IL	60611	312-321-4460	321-4530	49-17
CCL Container Corp 1 Llodio Dr *Web:* www.cclcontainer.com	Hermitage	PA	16148	724-981-4420		124
CCL Industries Inc 105 Gordon Baker Rd Ste 500 *TSE:* CCL/B ■ *Web:* www.cclind.com	Toronto	ON	M2H3P8	416-756-8500		548
CCL Label Inc 161 Worcester Rd Ste 502 *Web:* www.cclind.com	Framingham	MA	01701	508-872-4511	872-7671	413
CCM (Comprehensive Care Management Corp) 1250 Waters Pl Tower 1 Ste 602 *TF:* 877-226-8500 ■ *Web:* www.centerlighthealthcare.org	Bronx	NY	10461	877-226-8500		450
CCMC (Crozer-Chester Medical Ctr) 1 Medical Ctr Blvd *Web:* www.crozerkeystone.org	Upland	PA	19013	610-447-2000		374-3
CCMcD (Clark-Cutler-McDermott Co) 5 Fisher St	Franklin	MA	02038	508-528-1200	528-1406	745-6
CCMG (Clark Capital Management Group Inc) 1650 Market St 1 Liberty Pl 53rd Fl *TF:* 800-766-2264 ■ *Web:* www.ccmg.com	Philadelphia	PA	19103	215-569-2224	569-3639	401
CCON (Columbia College of Nursing) 4425 N Port Washington Rd *TF:* 800-221-5573 ■ *Web:* www.ccon.edu	Glendale	WI	53212	414-326-2330	326-2331	166
Ccp Global Inc 6825 Hobson Valley Dr Ste 302 *Web:* www.ccpglobal.com	Woodridge	IL	60517	312-543-5030		809
CCPL (Collier County Public Library) 2385 Orange Blossom Dr *Web:* www.colliergov.net	Naples	FL	34109	239-593-0177		434-3
CCPL (Cecil County Public Library) 301 Newark Ave *TF:* 800-232-4595 ■ *Web:* www.cecil.ebranch.info	Elkton	MD	21921	410-996-1055	996-5604	434-3
CCPS (Center for Chemical Process Safety) 120 Wall St *TF:* 800-242-4363 ■ *Web:* www.aiche.org/CCPS	New York	NY	10005	646-495-1371	495-1504	49-19
CCR (Council for Chemical Research Inc) 1730 Rhode Island Ave NW Ste 302 *Web:* www.ccrhq.org	Washington	DC	20036	202-429-3971	429-3976	49-19
CCR (Communications Credit & Recovery) 20 Broad Hollow Rd Ste 1002 *TF:* 800-327-3648 ■ *Web:* www.ccrcollect.com	Melville	NY	11747	631-923-2200	923-2784	160
CCRA Travel Commerce Network 320 Hemphill St *Web:* www.ccra.com	Fort Worth	TX	76104	682-233-0909		393
CCRKBA (Citizens Committee for the Right to Keep & Bear Arms) 12500 NE Tenth Pl *TF:* 800-426-4302 ■ *Web:* www.ccrkba.org	Bellevue	WA	98005	425-454-4911	451-3959	48-7
CCRLLP (Grant Thornton) 1400 Computer Dr *Web:* www.grantthornton.com	Westborough	MA	01581	508-926-2200		2
CCRTA (Cape Cod Regional Transit Authority) 215 Iyannough Rd PO Box 1988 *TF:* 800-352-7155 ■ *Web:* www.capecodtransit.org	Hyannis	MA	02601	508-775-8504	775-8513	468
CCS (Cleveland Chamber Symphony, The) 11125 Magnolia Dr The Music School Settlement *Web:* www.clevelandchambersymphony.org	Cleveland	OH	44106	216-202-4227		573-3
CCS (Credit Control Services Inc) 2 Wells Ave Ste 1 *TF:* 800-526-0532 ■ *Web:* gsaadvantage.gov	Newton	MA	02459	617-965-2000	762-3035	160
CCS (Custom Computer Specialists Inc) 70 Suffolk Ct *TF:* 800-598-8989 ■ *Web:* www.customtech.com	Hauppauge	NY	11788	631-864-6699	543-2512	180

	City	State	ZIP	Phone	Fax	Class
CCS (Check Cashing Store) 6340 NW Fifth Way *TF:* 800-361-1407 ■ *Web:* www.thecheckcashingstore.com	Fort Lauderdale	FL	33309	800-361-1407		141
CCS (Continental Currency Services Inc) PO Box 10970 *Web:* www.ccurr.com	Santa Ana	CA	92711	714-667-6699	569-0882	217
CCS (Craven County School) 3600 Trent Rd *Web:* www.craven.k12.nc.us	New Bern	NC	28562	252-514-6300	514-6351	685
CCS Medical Inc 1505 LBJ Fwy Ste 600 *TF:* 800-726-9811 ■ *Web:* www.ccsmed.com	Farmers Branch	TX	75234	800-260-8193		475
CCS of South Carolina Inc 2325 Prosperity Way Ste 8 *TF:* 800-449-8045 ■ *Web:* www.cleanworldusa.com	Florence	SC	29501	843-669-2273		104
CCS Presentation Systems Inc 17350 N Hartford Dr *TF:* 800-742-5036 ■ *Web:* www.ccsprojects.com	Scottsdale	AZ	85255	480-348-0100		196
CCSAA (Cross Country Ski Areas Assn) 259 Bolton Rd *TF:* 877-779-2754 ■ *Web:* www.xcski.org	Winchester	NH	03470	603-239-4341	239-6387	48-22
CCSD (Charleston County School District) 75 Calhoun St *TF:* 800-241-8898 ■ *Web:* www.ccsdschools.com	Charleston	SC	29401	843-937-6300	937-6307	685
CCSD (Clark County School District) 5100 W Sahara Ave *TF:* 866-799-8997 ■ *Web:* www.ccsd.net	Las Vegas	NV	89146	702-799-5000	799-5125	685
CCSNH (Community College System of New Hampshire) 26 College Dr *TF:* 866-945-2255 ■ *Web:* www.ccsnh.edu	Concord	NH	03301	603-271-2722	271-2725	162
CCSSO (Council of Chief State School Officers) 1 Massachusetts Ave NW Ste 700 *Web:* www.ccsso.org	Washington	DC	20001	202-336-7000	408-8072	49-5
CCT (Chesapeake Conventions & Tourism Bureau) 860 Greenbrier Cir Ste 101 *TF:* 888-889-5551 ■ *Web:* www.visitchesapeake.com	Chesapeake	VA	23320	757-502-4898	502-8016	206
CCT Technologies Inc 482 W San Carlos St *TF:* 800-997-9250 ■ *Web:* www.cland.com	San Jose	CA	95110	408-519-3200		174
CCT Telecomm 1106 E Turner Rd *Web:* www.4cct.com	Lodi	CA	95240	209-365-9500		387
CCTF Corp 5407 - 53 Ave NW *TF:* 800-661-3633 ■ *Web:* www.cctf.com	Edmonton	AB	T6B3G2	780-463-8700		111
CCTI (Composite Can & Tube Institute) 50 S Pickett St *Web:* www.cctiwdc.org	Alexandria	VA	22304	703-823-7234	823-7237	49-13
C-cube Consulting Inc 1238 Ridge Oak Ct *Web:* ccubeconsulting.net	San Jose	CA	95120	408-268-4886		180
CCUSD (Culver City Unified School District) 4034 Irving Pl *TF:* 855-446-2673 ■ *Web:* www.ccusd.org	Culver City	CA	90232	310-842-4220	842-4205	685
CCVS (Veterinary Specialists of the Southeast) 3163 W Montague Ave *Web:* www.ccvsllc.com	North Charleston	SC	29418	843-747-1507	747-7920	794
CCW Products Inc 5861 Tennyson St *Web:* www.ccwproducts.com	Arvada	CO	80003	303-427-9663		98
CCWF (Central California Women's Facility) 23370 Rd 22 PO Box 1501 *Web:* www.cdcr.ca.gov/facilities_locator/ccwf.html	Chowchilla	CA	93610	559-665-5531		213
CCX Corp 1399 Horizon Ave *Web:* www.ccxcorp.com	Lafayette	CO	80026	303-666-5206		111
CD Diagnostics Inc 650 Naamans Rd Ste 100 *Web:* cddiagnostics.com	Claymont	DE	19703	302-367-7770		743
CD Ford & Sons Inc PO Box 300 *TF:* 800-383-4661 ■ *Web:* www.cdford.com	Geneseo	IL	61254	309-944-4661	944-3703	369
CD Group Inc 5550 Triangle Pkwy *Web:* www.cdgroup.com	Norcross	GA	30092	678-268-2000	268-2001	180
CD Hartnett Co 302 N Main St *Web:* esite.cd-hartnett.com	Weatherford	TX	76086	817-594-3813	594-9714	297-8
CD Moody Construction Company Inc 6017 Redan Rd *Web:* www.cdmoodyconstruction.com	Lithonia	GA	30058	770-482-7778	482-7727	186
CD Publications 8204 Fenton St *TF:* 800-666-6380 ■ *Web:* cdpublications.com	Silver Spring	MD	20910	301-588-6380	588-6385	531-2
CD Smith Construction Inc 889 E Johnson St *Web:* www.cd-smith.com	Fond du Lac	WI	54935	920-924-2900		186
C&D Technologies 11 Cabot Blvd *TF:* 800-233-2765 ■ *Web:* www.murata-ps.com	Mansfield	MA	02048	508-339-3000	339-6356	253
CD Universe 101 N Plains Industrial Rd *TF:* 800-231-7937 ■ *Web:* www.cduniverse.com	Wallingford	CT	06492	203-294-1648	294-0391	525
C&D Valve Manufacturing Co 201 NW 67th St *TF:* 800-654-9233 ■ *Web:* www.cdvalve.com	Oklahoma City	OK	73116	405-843-5621		789
C&D Zodiac 7330 Lincoln Way *Web:* www.cdzodiac.com	Garden Grove	CA	92841	714-891-1906		22
CDA (Chemically Dependent Anonymous) PO Box 423 *TF:* 888-232-4673 ■ *Web:* cdawebsitedev.com	Severna Park	MD	21146	888-232-4673		48-21
CDA 8500 S Tryon St *Web:* www.cda.us/en/site__2	Charlotte	NC	28273	704-504-1877		311
CDC (Centers for Disease Control & Prevention) 1600 Clifton Rd NE *Web:* www.cdc.gov	Atlanta	GA	30333	404-639-7000	639-7111	340-10
CDC Distributors 10511 Medallion Dr *TF:* 800-678-2321 ■ *Web:* cdcdist.com	Cincinnati	OH	45241	513-771-3100	771-2920	361
CDC Small Business Finance Corp 2448 Historic Decatur Rd Ste 200 *TF:* 800-611-5170 ■ *Web:* cdcloans.com	San Diego	CA	92106	619-291-3594		216
CDCHY (Chambre de Commerce Haute-Yamaska Region) 90 Rue Robinson S Ste 102 *Web:* cchyr.ca	Granby	QC	J2G7L4	450-372-6100	372-3161	137
CDD 11603 Crosswinds Way Ste 100 *TF:* 888-858-8663 ■ *Web:* www.cddmedical.com	San Antonio	TX	78233	210-590-3033		415
CDDC (Carolyn Dorfman Dance Co) 2780 Morris Ave Ste 1-A *Web:* carolyndorfman.dance	Union	NJ	07083	908-687-8855	686-5245	573-1
CDEC (Continental Divide ElectricCo-op Inc) 200 E High St PO Box 1087 *Web:* www.cdec.coop	Grants	NM	87020	505-285-6656		245
CDEX Inc 4555 S Palo Verde Ste 123 *Web:* www.cdex-inc.com	Tucson	AZ	85714	520-745-5172		407
CDF (Children's Defense Fund) 25 E St NW *TF:* 800-233-1200 ■ *Web:* www.childrensdefense.org	Washington	DC	20001	202-628-8787	662-3510	48-6
CDF Corp 77 Industrial Park Rd *TF:* 800-443-1920 ■ *Web:* www.cdf1.com	Plymouth	MA	02360	508-747-5858		601
CDGRA (Colorado Dude & Guest Ranch Assn) PO Box D *TF:* 866-942-3472 ■ *Web:* www.coloradoranch.com	Shawnee	CO	80475	866-942-3472		48-23
Cdh 15 Ionia Ave SW *Web:* www.cdh.com	Grand Rapids	MI	49503	616-776-1600		317
CDH Energy Corp 2695 Bingley Rd PO Box 641 *Web:* www.cdhenergy.com	Cazenovia	NY	13035	315-655-1063		261
CDI (Consolidated Devices Inc) 19220 San Jose Ave *TF:* 800-525-6319 ■ *Web:* www.cditorque.com	City of Industry	CA	91748	626-965-0668	810-2759	758
CDI Contractors LLC 3000 Cantrell Rd *Web:* www.cdicon.com	Little Rock	AR	72202	501-666-4300	666-4741	186
CDI Corp 1735 Market St Ste 200 *TF:* 866-472-2203 ■ *Web:* www.cdicorp.com	Philadelphia	PA	19103	215-282-8300		261
CDI Credit Inc 6160 Peachtree Dunwoody Rd NE Ste B-210 *TF:* 800-633-3961 ■ *Web:* www.cdicredit.com	Atlanta	GA	30328	770-350-5070	394-2197	635
CDIA (Consumer Data Industry Assn) 1090 Vermont Ave NW Ste 200 *Web:* www.cdiaonline.org	Washington	DC	20005	202-371-0910	371-0134	49-2
CdLS (Cornelia de Lange Syndrome Foundation Inc) 302 W Main St Ste 100 *TF:* 800-753-2357 ■ *Web:* www.cdlsusa.org	Avon	CT	06001	860-676-8166	676-8337	48-17
CDM (Cline Davis & Mann Inc) 220 E 42nd St *Web:* www.clinedavis.com	New York	NY	10017	212-907-4300		4
CDM Smith Inc 75 State St Ste 701 **Fax Area Code:* 615 ■ *Web:* cdmsmith.com	Boston	MA	02109	617-452-6000	345-3901*	261
CDM Technologies Inc 2975 McMillan Ave Ste 272	San Luis Obispo	CA	93401	805-541-3750		177
CDMA (Chain Drug Marketing Assn) 43157 W Nine-Mile Rd PO Box 995 *TF:* 800-935-2362 ■ *Web:* www.chaindrug.com	Novi	MI	48376	248-449-9300	449-9396	49-18
CDMS Inc 550 Sherbrooke W West Tower Ste 250 *TF:* 866-337-2367 ■ *Web:* www.cdmsfirst.com	Montreal	QC	H3A1B9	514-286-2367		180
CDNetworks Inc 1919 S Bascom Ave Ste 600 *Web:* www.cdnetworks.com	Campbell	CA	95008	408-228-3700		387
Cdo Technologies Inc 5200 Sprngfeld St Ste 320 *TF:* 866-307-6616 ■ *Web:* www.cdotech.com	Dayton	OH	45431	937-258-0022	258-1614	449
C-Double Web Development 5201 College Ave *TF:* 800-441-2816 ■ *Web:* c-double.com	Bakersfield	CA	93306	661-872-2738		180
Cdr Assessment Group Inc 1644 S Denver Ave *TF:* 888-406-0100 ■ *Web:* cdrassessmentgroup.com	Tulsa	OK	74119	918-488-0722		195
CDR Data 1028 N Lake Ave Ste 105 *Web:* www.cdrdata.com	Pasadena	CA	91104	626-791-9700		116
CDR Fundraising Group 16900 Science Dr Ste 210 *Web:* www.cdrfg.com	Bowie	MD	20715	301-858-1500		393
CDR Maguire 8669 NW 36 St Ste 340 *Web:* www.cdrmaguire.com	Doral	FL	33166	786-235-8534		261
CDRI (Chihuahuan Desert Research Institute) 43869 State Hwy 118 PO Box 905 *Web:* cdri.org	Fort Davis	TX	79734	432-364-2499		97
Cds - Networks & Services Inc 672 Stratford Blvd *Web:* www.cdsnetworks.com	Kinston	NC	28504	252-523-6664		175
CDS Analytical Inc 465 Limestone Rd PO Box 277 *TF:* 800-541-6593 ■ *Web:* www.cdsanalytical.com	Oxford	PA	19363	610-932-3636	932-4158	419
Cds Engineering Inc 40725 Encyclopedia Cir *Web:* www.cdsengineeringinc.com	Fremont	CA	94538	510-252-2100		454
CDS Logistics Management Inc 1225 Bengies Rd Ste A *TF:* 866 640 9550 ■ *Web:* www.cdslogistics.net	Baltimore	MD	21220	410-314-8000		311
CDS-John Blue Co 290 Pinehurst Dr *TF:* 800-253-2583 ■ *Web:* www.cds-johnblue.com	Huntsville	AL	35806	256-721-9090		641
Cdspi 155 Lesmill Rd *TF:* 800-561-9401 ■ *Web:* cdspi.com	Toronto	ON	M3B2T8	416-296-9401		391-3
CDT (Center for Democracy & Technology) 1401 K St NW Ste 200 *TF:* 800-869-4499 ■ *Web:* www.cdt.org	Washington	DC	20005	202-637-9800	637-0968	48-7
CDT (Community Development Trust) 1350 Broadway Ste 700 *Web:* www.cdt.biz	New York	NY	10018	212-271-5080	271-5079	655
CDT (Continental Divide Trail Society) 3704 N Charles St Ste 601 *Web:* www.cdtsociety.org	Baltimore	MD	21218	410-235-9610		48-23
CDT Micrographics Inc 137 Water St *Web:* www.cdtmicrographics.com	Exeter	NH	03833	603-778-6140		180
CDTA (Capital District Transportation Authority) 110 Watervliet Ave *Web:* www.cdta.org	Albany	NY	12206	518-482-8822	437-8318	468
CDW Corp 200 N Milwaukee Ave *TF:* 800-800-4239 ■ *Web:* www.cdw.com	Vernon Hills	IL	60061	847-465-6000	465-6800	179
CE Conover & Company Inc 4106 Blanche Rd *TF:* 800-266-6837 ■ *Web:* conoverseals.com	Bensalem	PA	19020	215-639-6666	639-1799	326

Phone | Fax | Class

CE Holden Inc 938 Rt 910 .... Cheswick PA 15024 412-767-5050 767-9922 621
Web: www.ceholden.com
C-E Minerals Inc
901 E Eigth Ave. .... King of Prussia PA 19406 610-265-6880 663
Web: www.ceminerals.com
CE National Inc
1003 Presidential Dr. .... Winona Lake IN 46590 574-267-6622 48-20
Web: cenational.org
CE Niehoff & Co 2021 Lee St .... Evanston IL 60202 847-866-6030 492-1242 247
TF Tech Supp: 800-643-4633 ■ *Web:* www.ceniehoff.com
Ce Ready Mix 185 N Washington Rd. .... Apollo PA 15613 724-727-3331 182
Web: www.cticoordinators.com/ceready.htm
CE Resource Inc
1482 Stone Point Dr Ste 100 .... Roseville CA 95661 800-707-5644 463
TF: 800-707-5644 ■ *Web:* www.paragoncet.com
CE Thurston & Sons Inc 3335 Croft St .... Norfolk VA 23513 757-855-7700 189-9
TF: 800-444-7713 ■ *Web:* www.cethurston.com
CE Toland & Son 5300 Industrial Way............ Benicia CA 94510 707-747-1000 747-5300 189-14
TF: 800-242-5175 ■ *Web:* cetoland.com
CEA (Cultural Experiences Abroad)
2999 N 44th St Ste 200 .... Phoenix AZ 85018 480-557-7900 557-7926 760
TF: 800-266-4441 ■ *Web:* www.ceastudyabroad.com
CEA (Commission on English Language Program Accreditation)
801 N Fairfax St Ste 402A.................. Alexandria VA 22314 703-665-3400 519-2071 48-1
Web: www.cea-accredit.org
CEA-HOW (Compulsive Eaters Anonymous - HOW)
5500 E Atherton St Ste 227B .... Long Beach CA 90815 562-342-9344 48-21
Web: www.ceahow.org
Ceavco Audio-visual Co 6240 W 54th Ave .... Arvada CO 80002 303-539-3500 38
Web: www.ceavco.com
CEBOS Ltd 5936 Ford Court Ste 203 .... Brighton MI 48116 810-534-2222 463
Web: www.cebos.com
CEC (Career Education Corp)
2895 Greenspoint Pkwy Ste 600.......... Hoffman Estates IL 60196 847-781-3600 781-3610 242
NASDAQ: CECO ■ *Web:* www.careerco.com
CEC (Central Electric Co-op Inc)
2098 Hwy 97 N............................ Redmond OR 97756 541-548-2144 245
Cec Controls Co Inc 14555 Barber Ave .... Warren MI 48088 586-779-0222 779-0266 201
TF: 877-924-0303 ■ *Web:* www.ceccontrols.com
CEC Entertainment Inc
3903 W Airport Frwy. .... Irving TX 75062 972-258-8507 670
NYSE: CEC ■ *TF:* 888-778-7193 ■ *Web:* www.chuckecheese.com
CEC Industries Ltd 599 Bond St............ Lincolnshire IL 60069 847-821-1199 54
TF: 800-572-4168 ■ *Web:* cecindustries.com
Cecchin Plumbing & Heating Inc
4N275 Cavalry Dr..................... Bloomingdale IL 60108 630-529-4046 610
Web: cecchin-inc.com
Cecconi Simone Inc 1335 Dundas St W .... Toronto ON M6J1Y3 416-588-5900 393
TF: 800 463 2566 ■ *Web:* www.cecconisimone.com
Cecelia Packing Corp
24780 E South Ave..................... Orange Cove CA 93646 559-626-5000 11-1
Web: ceceliapack.com
Ceci New York 130 W 23rd St Fl 2 .... New York NY 10011 212-989-0695 627
Web: cecinewyork.com
Cecil Community College
1 Seahawk Dr............................ North East MD 21901 410-287-6060 287-1001* 162
**Fax:* Admissions ■ *TF:* 866-966-1001 ■ *Web:* www.cecil.edu
Cecil County 129 E Main St Rm 108............. Elkton MD 21921 410-996-5375 338
Web: www.ccgov.org
Cecil County Chamber of Commerce
106 E Main St Ste 101 .... Elkton MD 21921 410-392-3833 139
Web: www.cecilchamber.com
Cecil County Public Library (CCPL)
301 Newark Ave .... Elkton MD 21921 410-996-1055 996-5604 434-3
TF: 800-232-4595 ■ *Web:* www.cecil.ebranch.info
Cecil M. Harden Lake
1588 S Raccoon Pkwy .... Rockville IN 47872 765-344-1412 565
Web: www.in.gov
CECO (Compressor Engineering Corp)
5440 Alder Dr............................. Houston TX 77081 713-664-7333 664-6444 172
TF: 800-879-2326 ■ *Web:* www.tryceco.com
Ceco Bldg Systems 2400 Hwy 45 N.......... Columbus MS 39705 662-328-6722 105
TF: 800-282-2260 ■ *Web:* www.cecobuildings.com
Ceco Concrete Construction LLC
9135 Barton .... Overland Park KS 66214 913-362-1855 189-3
TF: 800-221-0323 ■ *Web:* www.cecoconcrete.com
Ceco Door 9159 Telecom Dr.......................... Milan TN 38358 731-686-8345 686-4211 234
Web: www.cecodoor.com
CED (Committee for Economic Development)
1530 Wilson Blvd Ste 400 .... Arlington VA 22209 202-296-5860 223-0776 634
TF: 800-676-7353 ■ *Web:* www.ced.org
CED (Consolidated Electrical Distributors Inc)
9201 J St .... Omaha NE 68127 402-592-7500 246
Web: www.ced-aec.com
Cedar Bluff State Park 32001 147 Hwy .... Ellis KS 67637 785-726-3212 565
Web: ksoutdoors.com
Cedar Breaks National Monument
2390 W Hwy 56 Ste 11................... Cedar City UT 84720 435-586-9451 586-3813 564
TF: 877-642-4743 ■ *Web:* www.nps.gov
Cedar Brook Financial Partners LLC
5885 Landerbrook Dr Ste 200............. Cleveland OH 44124 440-683-9200 401
Web: cedarbrookfinancial.com
Cedar City-Brian Head Tourism & Convention Bureau
581 N Main St .... Cedar City UT 84721 435-586-5124 586-4022 206
TF: 800-354-4849 ■ *Web:* www.visitcedarcity.com
Cedar County 101 S Broadway .... Hartington NE 68739 402-254-7411 254-7410 338
Web: www.co.cedar.ne.us
Cedar County 400 Cedar St..................... Tipton IA 52772 563-886-2101 886-3594 338
TF: 800-735-3942 ■ *Web:* www.cedarcounty.org
Cedar Creek & Belle Grove National Historical Park
7718 1/2 Main St .... Middletown VA 22645 540-868-9176 869-4527 564
Web: www.nps.gov
Cedar Creek Correctional Ctr
12200 Bordeaux Rd PO Box 37 .... Littlerock WA 98556 360-359-4100 213
Web: www.doc.wa.gov/facilities/prison/cccc
Cedar Creek Lake Area Chamber of Commerce
604 S Third St Ste E .... Mabank TX 75147 903-887-3152 887-3695 139
Web: www.cedarcreeklakechamber.com

Phone | Fax | Class

Cedar Creek State Park
2947 Cedar Creek Rd .... Glenville WV 26351 304-462-7158 565
Web: www.cedarcreeksp.com
Cedar Crest College 100 College Dr .... Allentown PA 18104 610-437-4471 606-4647* 166
**Fax:* Admissions ■ *TF Admissions:* 800-360-1222 ■ *Web:* www.cedarcrest.edu
Cedar Crest Specialties Inc
7269 Hwy 60 PO Box 260................... Cedarburg WI 53012 262-377-7252 377-5554 296-25
TF Hotline: 800-877-8341 ■ *Web:* www.cedarcresticecream.com
Cedar Fair LP 1 Cedar Pt Dr .... Sandusky OH 44870 419-627-2233 627-2260 31
NYSE: FUN ■ *Web:* www.cedarfair.com
Cedar Fair Parks
14523 Carowinds Blvd .... Charlotte NC 28273 704-588-2600 32
TF: 800-888-4386 ■ *Web:* www.carowinds.com
Cedar Falls Public Library
524 Main St .... Cedar Falls IA 50613 319-273-8643 434-3
Web: www.cedarfallspubliclibrary.org
Cedar Farms 2100 Hornig Rd .... Philadelphia PA 19116 215-934-7100 297-6
TF: 800-220-2217 ■ *Web:* www.cedarfarms.com
Cedar Financial Advisors Inc
3853 SW Hall Blvd .... Beaverton OR 97005 503-512-5890 401
Web: www.cedaradvisors.com
Cedar Graphics Inc 311 Parsons Dr........... Hiawatha IA 52233 319-395-6900 238-0467* 393
**Fax Area Code:* 866 ■ *TF:* 800-393-2399 ■ *Web:* www.cedargraphicsinc.com
Cedar Grove Composting Inc
7343 E Marginal Way S .... Seattle WA 98108 877-764-5748 832-3030* 186
**Fax Area Code:* 206 ■ *TF:* 888-832-3008 ■ *Web:* www.cedar-grove.com
Cedar Hill Associates LLC
120 S LaSalle St Ste 1750 .... Chicago IL 60603 312-445-2900 690
Web: www.cedhill.com
Cedar Hill State Park
1570 W FM 1382 .... Cedar Hill TX 75104 972-291-3900 565
Web: tpwd.texas.gov/state-parks/cedar-hill
Cedar Island State Park County Rt 93 .... Hammond NY 13646 315-482-3331 565
Web: parks.ny.gov/parks/25/details.aspx
Cedar Key Museum State Park
12231 SW 166 Ct.......................... Cedar Key FL 32625 352-543-5350 565
Web: www.floridastateparks.org
Cedar Lake Nursing Home
1611 W Royall Blvd .... Malakoff TX 75148 903-489-1702 371
TF: 800-252-2412 ■ *Web:* cedarlakenursing.com
Cedar Management Consulting International LLC
250 Park Ave 7th Fl .... New York NY 10177 212-572-6314 194
Web: www.cedar-consulting.com
Cedar Petrochemicals Inc
110 Wall St Ste 700 .... New York NY 10005 212-288-4320 169
Cedar Point Amusement Park
1 Cedar Point Dr........................... Sandusky OH 44870 419-627-2350 32
Web: www.cedarpoint.com
Cedar Point State Park
36661 Cedar Pt State Pk Dr .... Clayton NY 13624 315-654-2522 565
Web: parks.ny.gov/parks/21/details.aspx
Cedar Rapids & Iowa City Railway Co
2330 12th St SW .... Cedar Rapids IA 52404 319-786-3098 640
Web: www.crandic.com
Cedar Rapids Area Chamber of Commerce
424 First Ave NE....................... Cedar Rapids IA 52401 319-398-5317 398-5228 139
Web: www.cedarrapids.org
Cedar Rapids Area Convention & Visitors Bureau
87 16th Ave Ste 200..................... Cedar Rapids IA 52404 319-398-5009 398-5089 206
TF: 800-735-5557 ■ *Web:* www.gocedarrapids.com
Cedar Rapids City Hall
3851 River Ridge Dr NE .... Cedar Rapids IA 52402 319-286-5670 286-5130 337
Web: www.cedar-rapids.org
Cedar Rapids Museum of Art
410 Third Ave SE .... Cedar Rapids IA 52401 319-366-7503 366-4111 520
Web: www.crma.org
Cedar Rapids Public Library
2600 Edgewood Rd SW Ste 330........... Cedar Rapids IA 52404 319-398-5123 398-0476 434-3
Web: www.crlibrary.org
Cedar Rock
2611 Quasqueton Diagonal Blvd
Buch Co Hwy W-35 .... Independence IA 50644 319-934-3572 565
Web: www.iowadnr.gov
Cedar Shake & Shingle Bureau
7101 Horne St Ste 2 .... Mission BC V2V7A2 604-820-7700 820-0266 49-3
Web: www.cedarbureau.org
Cedar Shopping Centers Inc
44 S Bayles Ave Ste 304............... Port Washington NY 11050 516-767-6492 655
NYSE: CDR ■ *Web:* www.cedarrealtytrust.com
Cedar Springs Behavioral Health System
2135 Southgate Rd................. Colorado Springs CO 80906 719-633-4114 578-0857 374-5
TF: 800-888-1088 ■ *Web:* cedarspringsbhs.com
Cedar Springs Post
36 E Maple PO Box 370 .... Cedar Springs MI 49319 616-696-3655 696-9010 532-4
TF: 888-937-4514 ■ *Web:* www.cedarspringspost.com
Cedar Valley Arboretum & Botanic Gardens
1927 E Orange Rd........................ Waterloo IA 50701 319-226-4966 226-4966 97
Web: www.cedarvalleyarboretum.org
Cedar Valley College
3030 N Dallas Ave .... Lancaster TX 75134 972-860-8201 162
Web: www.dcccd.edu
Cedar Valley Hospice
2101 Kimball Ave Ste 401 .... Waterloo IA 50702 319-272-2002 272-2071 371
TF: 800-617-1972 ■ *Web:* www.cvhospice.org
Cedar Ventures LLC
2870 Peachtree Rd Ste 493.......................... Atlanta GA 30305 404-239-8416 691
Web: cedarventures.com
Cedara Software Corp
6303 Airport Rd Ste 500................. Mississauga ON L4V1R8 905-364-8000 364-8100 178-10
TF: 800-724-5970 ■ *Web:* www.merge.com
Cedarburg Cultural Center
W62 N546 Washington Ave .... Cedarburg WI 53012 262-375-3676 520
TF: 800 657 6775 ■ *Web:* www.cedarburgculturalcenter.org
Cedar-Knox Public Power District
56272 W Hwy 84 PO Box 947 .... Hartington NE 68739 402-254-6291 245
Web: www.cedarknoxppd.com
Cedarlane Laboratories Inc
4410 Paletta Ct............................ Burlington ON L7L5R2 905-878-8891 288-0020* 231
**Fax Area Code:* 289 ■ *TF:* 800-268-5058 ■ *Web:* www.cedarlanelabs.com

				Phone	Fax	Class
Cedarome Canada Inc 21 Rue Paul-Gauguin Ste E-22 *Web:* www.cedarome.com	Candiac	QC	J5R3X8	450-659-8000	659-8010	296-37
Cedars Business Services LLC 5230 Las Virgenes Rd *TF:* 800-804-3353 ■ *Web:* www.cedarfinancial.com	Calabasas	CA	91302	818-224-3800		160
Cedars Mediterranean Foods Inc 50 Foundation Ave *Web:* www.cedarsfoods.com	Ward Hill	MA	01835	978-372-8010		805
Cedars of Lebanon State Park 328 Cedar Forest Rd *TF:* 800-713-5180 ■ *Web:* www.state.tn.us	Lebanon	TN	37090	615-443-2769		565
Cedars-Sinai Medical Ctr (CSMC) 8700 Beverly Blvd *TF:* 800-233-2771 ■ *Web:* cedars-sinai.edu	Los Angeles	CA	90048	310-423-3277		374-3
Cedarstone 209 E Liberty Dr *Web:* www.cedarstonepartners.com	Wheaton	IL	60187	630-580-5750		193
CedarStone Bank 900 W Main St *Web:* www.cedarstonebank.com	Lebanon	TN	37087	615-443-1411		70
Cedarstore.com 5410 Rt 8 *TF:* 888-885-3806 ■ *Web:* www.cedarstore.com	Gibsonia	PA	15044	724-444-5300		106
Cedarville State Forest 10201 Bee Oak Rd *Web:* dnr2.maryland.gov	Brandywine	MD	20613	301-888-1410		565
Cedarville University 251 N Main St **Fax:* Admissions ■ *TF:* 800-233-2784 ■ *Web:* www.cedarville.edu	Cedarville	OH	45314	937-766-7700	766-7575*	166
Cedarwood Plaza 12504 Cedar Rd *Web:* www.lhshealth.com	Cleveland Heights	OH	44106	216-371-3600	371-4661	450
CEDC (Central European Distribution Corp) 3000 Atrium Way Ste 265 *NASDAQ: CEDC* ■ *Web:* www.cedc.com	Mount Laurel	NJ	08054	856-273-6980		81-1
Cedco 3201 Tremont Ave *Web:* www.cedco.net	North Bend	OR	97459	541-756-0662		452
Ceder's Restaurant 7732 W Sand Lake Rd *Web:* www.orlandocedars.com	Orlando	FL	32819	407-351-6000		671
CEDIA (Custom Electronic Design & Installation Assn) 7150 Winton Dr Ste 300 *TF:* 800-669-5329 ■ *Web:* www.cedia.net	Indianapolis	IN	46268	317-328-4336	735-4012	49-19
CEE (Coalition for Employment Through Exports) 1625 K St NW Ste 200 *Web:* www.usaexport.org	Washington	DC	20006	202-296-6107	296-9709	49-18
Cee Kay Supply Co 5835 Manchester Ave *Web:* www.ceekay.com	Saint Louis	MO	63110	314-644-3500	644-4336	385
CEEMCO Inc 3330 E Kemper Rd *Web:* www.ceemco.com	Cincinnati	OH	45241	513-563-8822		697
Ceeva Inc 643 First Ave Ste 300 *TF:* 866-233-8248 ■ *Web:* www.ceeva.com	Pittsburgh	PA	15219	412-690-2300		194
CEF (Committee for Education Funding) 1800 M St NW Ste 500 *Web:* www.cef.org	Washington	DC	20036	202-383-0083		48-11
CEF Industries Inc 320 S Church St *TF:* 800-888-6419 ■ *Web:* www.cefindustries.com	Addison	IL	60101	630-628-2299	628-1386	22
Cefco Convenience Stores 6261 Central Pointe Pkwy *Web:* www.cefcostores.com	Temple	TX	76504	254-791-0009	791-0018	345
CeFO Inc 88 Inverness Cir E Ste L107 *Web:* www.cefo.net	Englewood	CO	80112	720-506-4105		734
Cegep Andre Laurendeau 1111 Rue Lapierre *Web:* www.claurendeau.qc.ca	Lasalle	QC	H8N2J4	514-364-3320		165
Cegep De L'outaouais 333 Boul De La Cite-des-jeunes	Gatineau	QC	J8Y6M4	819-770-4012		165
Cegep De Matane 616 Ave Holy Redeemer *TF:* 800-463-4299 ■ *Web:* www.cegep-matane.qc.ca	Matane	QC	G4W1L1	418-562-1240	566-2115	167
Cegep De Sainte-Foy 2410 Ch Sainte-Foy *Web:* www.cegep-ste-foy.qc.ca	Sainte-foy	QC	G1V1T3	418-659-6600		162
Cegep De Thetford 671 Boul Frontenac O *Web:* www.cegepthetford.ca	Thetford Mines	QC	G6G1N1	418-338-8591		162
Cegep Marie-Victorin 7000 rue Marie-Victorin *Web:* www.collegemv.qc.ca	Montreal	QC	H1G2J6	514-325-0150		165
CEI (Computer Enterprises Inc) 1000 Omega Dr Ste 1150 *Web:* www.ceiamerica.com	Pittsburgh	PA	15205	412-341-3541	341-0519	721
CEI (Construction Enterprises Inc) 2179 Edward Curd Ln Ste 100 *Web:* www.constructionenterprises.com	Franklin	TN	37067	615-332-8880	771-0818	187
CEI Enterprises Inc 245 WoodwaRd Rd SE **Fax Area Code:* 505 ■ *TF:* 800-545-4034 ■ *Web:* www.ceienterprises.com	Albuquerque	NM	87102	800-545-4034	243-1422*	14
Ceia USA Ltd 9155 Dutton Dr *Web:* www.ceia-usa.com	Twinsburg	OH	44087	330-405-3190		691
Ceiba 701 14th St NW *Web:* www.ceibarestaurant.com	Washington	DC	20005	202-393-3983		671
Ceilings & Interior Systems Construction Assn (CISCA) 1010 Jorie Blvd Ste 30 **Fax Area Code:* 866 ■ *TF:* 866-560-8537 ■ *Web:* cisca.org	Oak Brook	IL	60523	630-584-1919	560-8537*	49-3
CEIR (Center for Exhibition Industry Research) 12700 Park Central Dr Ste 308 *Web:* www.ceir.org	Dallas	TX	75251	972-687-9242	692-6020	49-18
Ceis Review Inc 8 Tannery Ln *Web:* ceisreview.com	Camden	ME	04843	207-230-2515		652
Ceiva Logic Inc 214 E Magnolia Blvd *TF Tech Supp:* 877-693-7263 ■ *Web:* www.ceiva.com	Burbank	CA	91502	818-562-1495	562-1491	591
Cejka Search Inc 4 Cityplace Dr Ste 300 *TF:* 800-678-7858 ■ *Web:* www.cejkasearch.com	Saint Louis	MO	63141	314-726-1603	726-0026	721
CEL (California Eastern Laboratories Inc) 4590 Patrick Henry Dr *TF:* 800-390-3232 ■ *Web:* www.cel.com	Santa Clara	CA	95054	408-988-3500	988-0279	246
Cel Oil Products Corp 5402 Dutton Ave *Web:* www.celoil.com/carolina-fuel-services	Charleston	SC	29406	843-744-2525		539

				Phone	Fax	Class
CELA (National Research Ctr on English Learning & Achievement) School of Education University of Albany B9 1400 Washington Ave *Web:* www.albany.edu	Albany	NY	12222	518-442-5026	442-5933	668
Celaborelle Phoenician Buffet 2257 Hemphill St	Fort Worth	TX	76110	817-922-8118		671
CelAccess Systems Inc 13619 Inwood Rd Ste 360 *Web:* cell-gate.com	Dallas	TX	75244	972-231-1999		693
Celadon Spa 1180 F St NW Frnt 1 *TF:* 800-424-9280 ■ *Web:* www.celadonspa.com	Washington	DC	20004	202-347-3333		77
Celadon Trucking Services Inc 9503 E 33rd St *TF:* 800-235-2366 ■ *Web:* www.celadontrucking.com	Indianapolis	IN	46235	317-972-7000		780
Celanese Corp 1601 W LBJ Fwy *NYSE: CE* ■ *TF:* 800-627-9581 ■ *Web:* www.celanese.com	Dallas	TX	75234	972-443-4000		144
Celator Pharmaceuticals Inc 303B College Rd E *Web:* celatorpharma.com	Princeton	NJ	08540	609-243-0123		668
Celdara Medical LLC 16 Cavendish Ct *Web:* www.celdaramedical.com	Lebanon	NH	03766	617-320-8521		415
Celebration Restaurant & Catering 4503 W Lovers Ln *Web:* www.celebrationrestaurant.com	Dallas	TX	75206	214-351-5681	904-1716	671
Celebration Town Hall 851 Celebration Ave *Web:* www.celebration.fl.us	Kissimmee	FL	34747	407-566-1200		50-6
Celebration! Cinema 2121 Celebration Ave *Web:* www.celebrationcinema.com	Grand Rapids	MI	49525	616-530-7469		748
Celebritees Inc 1014 Atlantic Ave *TF:* 877-831-1005 ■ *Web:* www.celebritees.net	Savannah	GA	31401	912-233-9941		184
Celebrity Hotel Inc 629 Main St *Web:* www.celebritycasinos.com	Deadwood	SD	57732	605-578-1909		370
Celebrity Theatre 440 N 32nd St *Web:* celebritytheatre.com	Phoenix	AZ	85008	602-267-1600		572
Celenia 7887 E Belleview Ave Ste 150 *Web:* www.celenia.com	Marietta	GA	30062	303-469-2346		463
Celergo LLC 750 Estate Dr Ste 110 *TF:* 800-234-1840 ■ *Web:* www.celergo.com	Deerfield	IL	60015	847-512-2600		570
Celerity Consulting Group Inc 2 Gough St Ste 300 *TF:* 866-224-4333 ■ *Web:* www.celerityconsulting.net	San Francisco	CA	94103	415-986-8850		196
Celerity Staffing Solutions 6273 University Ave *TF:* 800-888-5894 ■ *Web:* www.celeritystaffing.com	Middleton	WI	53562	608-238-3410		260
Celerity Systems Inc 8401 Greensboro Dr Ste 500 *TF:* 800-213-4817 ■ *Web:* www.celerity.com	McLean	VA	22102	703-848-1900	848-2139	647
Celestial Restaurant 1071 Celestial St *Web:* www.thecelestial.com	Cincinnati	OH	45202	513-241-4455	241-4855	671
Celestial Seasonings Inc 4600 Sleepytime Dr *TF:* 800-351-8175 ■ *Web:* www.celestialseasonings.com	Boulder	CO	80301	800-351-8175		296-40
Celestica Inc 844 Don Mills Rd *NYSE: CLS* ■ *TF:* 888-899-9998 ■ *Web:* www.celestica.com	Toronto	ON	M3C1V7	416-448-5800	448-4810	253
Celex Laboratories Inc 21600 Westminster Hwy Ste 115 *Web:* www.celexlaboratories.com	Richmond	BC	V6V0A2	604-231-6077	231-6078	799
Celgard LLC 13800 S Lakes Dr *Web:* www.celgard.com	Charlotte	NC	28273	704-588-5310		600
Celgene Corp 86 Morris Ave *NASDAQ: CELG* ■ *TF:* 888-771-0141 ■ *Web:* www.celgene.com	Summit	NJ	07901	908-673-9000	673-9001	85
Celigo LLC 230 Twin Dolphin Dr Ste A *Web:* www.celigo.com	Redwood City	CA	94065	650-579-0210		196
Celina Aluminum Precision Technology Inc (CAPT) 7059 Staeger Rd *Web:* www.capt-celina.com	Celina	OH	45822	419-586-2278	586-6474	621
Celina-Mercer County Chamber of Commerce 226 N Main St *TF:* 800-239-5042 ■ *Web:* www.celinamercer.com	Celina	OH	45822	419-586-2219	586-8645	139
Celis Semiconductor Corp 5475 Mark Dabling Blvd Ste 102	Colorado Springs	CO	80918	719-260-9133		696
Cell Marque Corp 6600 Sierra College Blvd *Web:* www.cellmarque.com	Rocklin	CA	95677	916-746-8900		479
Cell Point Systems Inc 44931 Industrial Dr *Web:* www.cellpointsystems.com	San Francisco	CA	94538	510-270-2280		261
Cell Resin Technologies 1789 Buerkle Cir *Web:* www.cellresin.com	Saint Paul	MN	55110	651-770-9161		466
Cell Response Formulation LLC 4115 S Pub Pl *TF:* 888-364-7839 ■ *Web:* www.mulliganstewpetfood.com	Jackson	WY	83002	307-734-7839		297-9
Cell Signaling Technology Inc 3 Trask Ln *TF:* 877-678-8324 ■ *Web:* www.cellsignal.com	Danvers	MA	01923	978-867-2300	867-2400	418
Cella Consulting LLC 4350 E W Hwy Ste 307 *Web:* www.cellaconsulting.com	Bethesda	MD	20814	301-280-0313		196
CellAegis Devices Inc 139 Mulock Ave 1st Fl *Web:* www.cellaegisdevices.com	Toronto	ON	M6N1G9	647-722-9601		475
Cellar Restaurant, The 220 Magnolia Ave *Web:* www.thecellarrestaurant.com	Daytona Beach	FL	32114	386-258-0011		671
Cellcom Services Inc 11301 W 218th St	Peculiar	MO	64078	816-779-5660		188-1
Cell-con Inc 305 Commerce Dr Ste 300 *TF:* 800-771-7139 ■ *Web:* www.cell-con.com	Exton	PA	19341	610-280-7630	280-7685	74
Cellectar Biosciences 3301 Agriculture Dr *Web:* cellectarbiosciences.com	Madison	WI	53716	608-441-8120		231
Cellhire USA LLC 3520 W Miller Rd Ste 100 *TF:* 877-244-7242 ■ *Web:* www.cellhire.com	Garland	TX	75041	214-355-5200		736

Phone | Fax | Class

Cellino & Barnes PC
2500 Main Pl Tower 350 Main St ... Buffalo NY 14202 716-854-2020 428
TF: 800-888-8888 ■ Web: www.cellinoandbarnes.com
Cello & Maudru Construction Company Inc
2505 Oak St ... Napa CA 94559 707-257-0454 186
Web: www.cello-maudru.com
Cello Professional Products
1354 Old Post Rd ... Havre de Grace MD 21078 410-939-1234 939-3028 151
TF: 800-638-4850 ■ Web: www.cello-online.com
Cellofoam North America Inc
1917 Rockdale Industrial Blvd ... Conyers GA 30012 770-929-3688 929-3608 601
TF: 800-241-3634 ■ Web: www.cellofoam.com
Cellotape Inc 47623 Fremont Blvd ... Fremont CA 94538 510-651-5551 651-8091 413
TF: 800-231-0608 ■ Web: www.cellotape.com
Cellox Corp 1200 Industrial St ... Reedsburg WI 53959 608-524-2316 524-2362 601
TF: 800-382-9102 ■ Web: www.cellox.com
Cell-Tel Government Systems Inc
8226-B Phillips Hwy Ste 290 ... Jacksonville FL 32256 904-363-1111 363-0032 246
TF: 800-737-7545 ■ Web: www.cell-tel.com
Celltron Inc 1110 W Seventh St ... Galena KS 66739 620-783-1333 61
Web: www.celltron.com
CellTrust Corp
14822 N 73rd St Bldg B Ste 113 ... Scottsdale AZ 85260 480-515-5200 195
Web: www.celltrust.com
CellularOne 1500 S White Mtn Rd Ste 3 ... Show Low AZ 85901 928-537-0690 387
Web: www.cellularoneonline.com
Cellunet Mfg Co
1006 Jacksonville Rd ... Burlington Township NJ 08016 609-386-1147 745-4
Cellusuede Products Inc
500 N Madison St ... Rockford IL 61107 815-964-8619 964-7949 745-2
Web: www.cellusuede.com
Cels Enterprises Inc
3485 S La Cienega Blvd ... Los Angeles CA 90016 310-838-2103 301
Web: www.chineselaundry.com
CEL-SCI Corp 8229 Boone Blvd Ste 802 ... Vienna VA 22182 703-506-9460 506-9471 85
NYSE: CVM ■ Web: www.cel-sci.com
Celsion Corp 10220-L Old Columbia Rd ... Columbia MD 21046 410-290-5390 290-5394 476
NASDAQ: CLSN ■ TF: 888-504-7965 ■ Web: www.celsion.com
Celt Corp
65 Boston Post Rd W Ste 200 ... Marlborough MA 01752 508-624-4474 177
Web: celtcorp.com
Celt Inc 3462 Clemmons Rd ... Clemmons NC 27012 336-712-9906 507
Web: www.celt-inc.com
Celtech Corp 1300 Terminal Dr ... Carlsbad NM 88220 575-887-2044 201
Web: www.aseholdings.com
Celtic Commercial Finance
4 Pk Plaza Ste 300 ... Irvine CA 92614 949-263-3880 263-1331 264-2
Web: www.celticfinance.com
Celtic Crossing Irish Pub & Restaurant
903 S Cooper St ... Memphis TN 38104 901-274-5151 671
Web: www.celticcrossingmemphis.com
Celtic Financial Group LLC
60 Cutter Mill Rd Ste 600 ... Great Neck NY 11021 516-466-0550 215
Celtic Healthcare 150 Scharberry Ln ... Mars PA 16046 800-355-8894 931-4288 371
TF: 800-355-8894 ■ Web: www.celtichealthcare.com
Celtic House Venture Partners Inc
239 Argyle Ave Ste 100 ... Ottawa ON K2P1B8 613-569-7200 569-7209 528
Web: www.celtic-house.com
Celtic Inc
316 N Milwaukee St Ste 350 ... Milwaukee WI 53202 262-789-7630 4
Web: www.celticinc.com
Celtic Marine Corp
3888 S Sherwood Forest Blvd
Celtic Ctr Bldg 1 ... Baton Rouge LA 70816 225-752-2490 752-2582 314
TF: 800-899-7195 ■ Web: www.celticmarine.com
Celtic Tavern, The 1801 Blake St ... Denver CO 80202 303-308-1795 308-1576 671
Web: www.theceltictavern.com
Celtrade Canada Inc 7566 Bath Rd ... Mississauga ON L4T1L2 905-678-1322 296-37
Web: www.celtradecanada.ca
Celula Inc
11011 Torreyana Rd Ste 200 ... San Diego CA 92121 858-875-8800 406
Web: www.celula-inc.com
CEM Corp 3100 Smith Farm Rd ... Matthews NC 28104 704-821-7015 821-7894 419
TF: 800-726-3331 ■ Web: www.cem.com
Cembell Industries Inc
740 CCC Rd (Hwy 628) ... Montz LA 70068 985-652-1188 14
Web: www.cembell.com
CEMCO 263 N Covina Ln ... City Of Industry CA 91744 800-775-2362 330-7598* 105
*Fax Area Code: 626 ■ TF: 800-775-2362 ■ Web: www.cemcosteel.com
Cemco Partitions Inc
5340 US Hwy 220 N ... Summerfield NC 27358 336-643-6316 321
Web: www.cemcopartitions.com
Cemcon Ltd 2280 White Oak Cir Ste 100 ... Aurora IL 60502 630-862-2100 256
Web: www.cemcon.com
Cemen Tech Inc 1700 N 14th St ... Indianola IA 50125 515-961-7407 190
TF: 800-247-2464 ■ Web: www.cementech.com
Cement Assn of Canada (CAC)
502-350 Sparks St ... Ottawa ON K1R7S8 613-236-9471 563-4498 49-3
TF: 800-221-5105 ■ Web: www.cement.ca
Cement Industries Inc
2925 Hanson St PO Box 823 ... Fort Myers FL 33902 239-332-1440 332-0370 183
TF: 800-332-1440 ■ Web: www.cementindustries.com
Cement Products & Supply Co Inc
516 W Main St ... Lakeland FL 33815 863-686-5141 183
Web: cementproducts.us
Cemex USA 929 Gessner Rd Ste 1900 ... Houston TX 77024 713-650-6200 317-6047* 135
NYSE: CX ■ *Fax Area Code: 212 ■ TF: 888-292-0070 ■ Web: www.cemex.com
Cemline Corp PO Box 55 ... Cheswick PA 15024 724-274-5430 274-5448 36
TF: 800-245-6268 ■ Web: www.cemline.com
Cemline Corp 808 Freeport Rd ... Cheswick PA 15024 724-275-1168 427
Web: www.cemline.com
Cempazuchi 1205 E Brady St ... Milwaukee WI 53202 414-291-5233 671
Web: www.cempazuchi.com
Cemstone Products Co
2025 Centre Pt Blvd Ste 300 ... Mendota Heights MN 55120 651-688-9292 688-0124 182
TF: 800-236-7866 ■ Web: www.cemstone.com
Cemtrol Inc 3035 E La Jolla St ... Anaheim CA 92806 714-666-6606 666-6616 173-2
Web: www.cemtrol.com

Cen-Cal Fire Systems Inc PO Box 1284 ... Lodi CA 95240 209-334-9119 45
Web: cen-calfire.com
Cencor Realty Services Inc
3102 Maple Ave Ste 500 ... Dallas TX 75201 214-954-0300 953-0860 655
Web: www.weitzmangroup.com
Cendec Systems Inc
Ste 315 1615 Tenth Ave SW ... Calgary AB T3C0J7 403-215-9936 179
Web: cendec.com
Cendrex Inc 11303 26th Ave ... Montreal QC H1E6N6 514-493-1489 198
Web: www.cendrex.com
Cenergistic Inc 5950 Sherry Ln Ste 900 ... Dallas TX 75225 214-273-2814 194
TF: 888-782-7937 ■ Web: www.cenergistic.com
Cengage Learning 10650 Tobben Dr ... Independence KY 41051 800-544-0550 647-4599* 637-2
*Fax Area Code: 859 ■ TF: 800-544-0550 ■ Web: www.cengage.com
Cengage Learning PO Box 6904 ... Florence KY 41022 800-354-9706 487-8488 637-2
TF: 800-354-9706 ■ Web: www.cengage.com/highered
Cengea Solutions Inc
330 St Mary Ave Ste 1160 ... Winnipeg MB R3C3Z5 204-957-7566 463
TF: 800-668-7722 ■ Web: www.cengea.com
Cenoplex LLC 5121 Bee Cave Rd Ste 106 ... Austin TX 78746 512-843-0036 843-0037 5
Cenovus Energy Inc
500 Centre St SE PO Box 766 ... Calgary AB T2P0M5 403-766-2000 536
Web: www.cenovus.com
Centaur Capital Partners LP
Southlake Town Sq 1460 Main St Ste 234 ... Southlake TX 76092 817-488-9632 401
Web: www.centaurcapital.com
Centaur Pharmaceuticals Inc
1220 Memorex Dr ... Santa Clara CA 95050 408-822-1600 231
Web: www.centpharm.com
Centaur Products Inc 6855 Antrim Ave ... Burnaby BC V5J4M5 604-430-3088 711
Web: www.centaurproducts.com
Centaurus Financial
2300 E Katella Ave Ste 200 ... Anaheim CA 92806 714-456-1790 690
Web: centaurusfinancial.com
Centegra Memorial Medical Ctr
3701 Doty Rd ... Woodstock IL 60098 815-338-2500 374-3
TF: 877-236-8347 ■ Web: www.centegra.org
Centegra Northern Illinois Medical Ctr
4201 Medical Ctr Dr ... McHenry IL 60050 815-344-5000 374-3
TF: 800-222-1222 ■ Web: www.centegra.org
Centenary College
400 Jefferson St ... Hackettstown NJ 07840 908-852-1400 852-3454* 166
*Fax: Admissions ■ TF Admissions: 800-236-8679 ■ Web: www.centenaryuniversity.edu
Centenary College of Louisiana
2911 Centenary Blvd ... Shreveport LA 71104 318-869-5131 869-5005* 166
*Fax: Admissions ■ TF Admissions: 800-234-4448 ■ Web: www.centenary.edu
Centenary State Historic Site
3522 College St ... Jackson LA 70748 225-634-7925 565
TF: 888-677-2364 ■ Web: www.crt.state.la.us
Centene Corp 7700 Forsyth Blvd ... Saint Louis MO 63105 314-725-4477 391-3
NYSE: CNC ■ TF General: 800-293-0056 ■ Web: www.centene.com
Centennial Broadcasting LLC
6201 Town Ctr Dr Ste 210 ... Clemmons NC 27012 336-766-2828 645-10
Web: www.centennialbroadcasting.com
Centennial Conferences
908 Main St Ste 350 ... Louisville CO 80027 303-499-2299 499-2599 184
Web: www.centennialconferences.com
Centennial Hall Convention Ctr
101 Egan Dr ... Juneau AK 99801 907-586-5283 586-1135 205
TF: 800-478-4170 ■ Web: www.juneau.org
Centennial Hotel 96 Pleasant St ... Concord NH 03301 603-227-9000 225-5031 379
Web: www.thecentennialhotel.com
Centennial Independent School District No 12
4757 N Rd ... Circle Pines MN 55014 763-792-5000 685
Centennial Medical Ctr
2300 Patterson St ... Nashville TN 37203 615-342-1000 374-3
Web: tristarcentennial.com
Centennial Olympic Park
265 Pk Ave W NW ... Atlanta GA 30313 404-223-4412 223-4499 50-5
Web: www.centennialpark.com
Centennial Optical Ltd
158 Norfinch Dr ... Toronto ON M3N1X6 416-739-8539 475
TF: 800-494-4171 ■ Web: www.centennialoptical.com
Centennial School District
18135 SE Brooklyn ... Portland OR 97236 503-760-7990 762-3689 685
Web: csd28j.org
Centennial School District
433 Centennial Rd ... Warminster PA 18974 215-441-6000 441-5105 685
Web: www.centennialsd.org
Centennial Travelers
311 S College Ave ... Fort Collins CO 80524 970-484-4988 760
TF: 800-223-0675 ■ Web: www.centennialtravel.com
Centennial Windows Ltd
687 Sovereign Rd ... London ON N5V4K8 519-451-0508 499
TF: 800-265-1995 ■ Web: www.centennialwindows.com
Center BMW 5201 Van Nuys Blvd ... Sherman Oaks CA 91401 818-907-9995 364
Web: centerbmw.com
Center Church 60 Gold St ... Hartford CT 06103 860-249-5631 246-3915 50-1
Web: www.centerchurchhartford.org
Center City Film & Video
1503 Walnut St ... Philadelphia PA 19102 215-568-4134 514
Web: www.ccfv.com
Center Coast Capital Advisors LP
1600 Smith Ste 3800 ... Houston TX 77002 713-759-1400 528
Web: www.centercoastcap.com
Center Court Key West 916 Center St ... Key West FL 33040 305-295-7313 379
Center Enterprises Inc
30 Shield St ... West Hartford CT 06110 860-953-4423 953-2948 243
TF Orders: 800-542-2214 ■ Web: www.centerenterprises.com
Center Financial Corp
651 Pennsylvania Ave SE ... Washington DC 20003 202-546-8500 360-2
Web: taxpayer.net
Center for Action & Contempla
1823 Five Points Rd SW ... Albuquerque NM 87105 505-242-9588 48-20
Web: www.cac.org
Center for Advanced Biotechnology & Medicine
Rutgers The State University of New Jersey
679 Hoes Ln ... Piscataway NJ 08854 848-445-9898 235-5318* 668
*Fax Area Code: 732 ■ Web: www3.cabm.rutgers.edu

Organization	City	State	Zip	Phone	Fax	Class
Center for American Progress 1333 H St NW 10th Fl *Web:* www.americanprogress.org	Washington	DC	20005	202-682-1611	682-1867	634
Center for Animals & Public Policy Cummings School of Veterinary Medicine at Tufts University 200 Westboro Rd *Web:* vet.tufts.edu	North Grafton	MA	01536	508-839-7991	839-3337	634
Center for Art & Education 104 N 13th St *TF:* 800-745-3000 ■ *Web:* www.art-ed.org	Van Buren	AR	72956	479-474-7767	474-4411	50-2
Center for Assn Growth 1926 Waukegan Rd Ste 1 *TF:* 800-492-6462 ■ *Web:* tcag.us	Glenview	IL	60025	847-657-6700	657-6819	47
Center for Assn Resources Inc 1901 N Roselle Rd Ste 920 **Fax Area Code:* 847 ■ *TF:* 888-705-1434 ■ *Web:* www.association-resources.com	Schaumburg	IL	60195	888-705-1434	885-8393*	47
Center for Auto Safety (CAS) 1825 Connecticut Ave NW Ste 330 *Web:* www.autosafety.org	Washington	DC	20009	202-328-7700		49-21
Center for Automation Research University of Maryland AV Williams Bldg 115 Rm 4413 *TF:* 800-868-0094 ■ *Web:* www.cfar.umd.edu	College Park	MD	20742	301-405-4526	314-9115	668
Center for Beethoven Studies & Museum 150 E San Fernando St 5th Fl Rm 580 *Web:* www.sjsu.edu	San Jose	CA	95112	408-808-2058	808-2060	520
Center for Behavioral Health Inc, The 175 Cedar Ln Ste A *Web:* www.njpsychologist.com	Teaneck	NJ	07666	201-692-9500		543
Center for Biofilm Engineering (CBE) Montana State University PO Box 173980 *Web:* www.biofilm.montana.edu	Bozeman	MT	59717	406-994-4770	994-6098	668
Center for Biophysical Sciences & Engineering (CBSE) University of Alabama CBSE 100 1720 2nd Ave S *Web:* www.uab.edu	Birmingham	AL	35294	205-934-5329	934-0480	668
Center for Chemical Process Safety (CCPS) 120 Wall St *TF:* 800-242-4363 ■ *Web:* www.aiche.org/CCPS	New York	NY	10005	646-495-1371	495-1504	49-19
Center for Civic Education 5145 Douglas Fir Rd *TF:* 800-350-4223 ■ *Web:* www.civiced.org	Calabasas	CA	91302	818-591-9321		194
Center for Cognitive Liberty & Ethics PO Box 73481 *TF:* 888-950-6463 ■ *Web:* www.cognitiveliberty.org	Davis	CA	95617	530-750-7912		634
Center for Collaborative 33 Harrison Ave # 6 *Web:* cce.org	Boston	MA	02111	617-421-0134		194
Center for Community Change (CCC) 1536 U St NW *TF:* 800-233-1200 ■ *Web:* www.communitychange.org	Washington	DC	20009	202-339-9300	387-4891	48-5
Center for Contemporary Arts, The 220 Cypress St *Web:* www.center-arts.com	Abilene	TX	79601	325-677-8389	677-1171	50-2
Center for Creative Leadership 1 Leadership Pl PO Box 26300 *Web:* www.ccl.org	Greensboro	NC	27438	336-545-2810	282-3284	765
Center for Creative Photography 1030 N Olive Rd *TF:* 888-472-4732 ■ *Web:* www.creativephotography.org	Tucson	AZ	85721	520-621-7968	621-9444	520
Center for Crops Utilization Research Iowa State University 1041 Food Sciences Bldg 536 Farm House Lane *Web:* www.ccur.iastate.edu	Ames	IA	50011	515-294-0160	294-6261	668
Center for Cuban Studies 231 W 29th St Ste 401 *Web:* centerforcubanstudies.org	New York	NY	10001	212-242-0559	242-1937	48-14
Center for Cultural Interchange 746 N La Salle Dr *TF:* 866-224-0061 ■ *Web:* www.cci-exchange.com	Chicago	IL	60654	312-944-2544		194
Center for Democracy & Technology (CDT) 1401 K St NW Ste 200 *TF:* 800-869-4499 ■ *Web:* www.cdt.org	Washington	DC	20005	202-637-9800	637-0968	48-7
Center for Diagnostic Imaging 5775 Wayzata Blvd Ste 190 *TF:* 800-537-0005 ■ *Web:* mycdi.com	Saint Louis Park	MN	55416	952-541-1840	847-1152	383
Center for Education Rice University 320 IBC Bldg PO Box 1892 *Web:* www.centerforeducation.rice.edu	Houston	TX	77251	713-348-4827	348-4229	668
Center for Electromechanics University of Texas at Austin 10100 Burnet Rd Bldg 133 *Web:* www.utexas.edu/research/cem	Austin	TX	78758	512-471-4496	471-0781	668
Center for Engineering Logistics & Distribution University of Arkansas Dept of Industrial Engineer 4207 Bell Engineering Ctr *Web:* celdi.org	Fayetteville	AR	72701	479-575-2124		668
Center for Equal Opportunity (CEO) 14 Pidgeon Hill Dr Ste 500 *Web:* www.ceousa.org	Sterling	VA	20165	703-421-5443	421-6401	634
Center for Exhibition Industry Research (CEIR) 12700 Park Central Dr Ste 308 *Web:* www.ceir.org	Dallas	TX	75251	972-687-9242	692-6020	49-18
Center for Genetic Testing at Saint Francis 6465 S Yale Ave *TF:* 877-789-6001 ■ *Web:* www.saintfrancis.com	Tulsa	OK	74136	918-502-1720		417
Center for Global Change Science 77 Massachusetts Ave 54-1312 77 Massachusetts Ave *Web:* cgcs.mit.edu	Cambridge	MA	02139	617-253-4902	253-0354	668
Center for Grain & Animal Health Research 1515 College Ave **Fax Area Code:* 785 ■ *TF:* 800-627-0388 ■ *Web:* www.ars.usda.gov	Manhattan	KS	66502	800-627-0388	776-2789*	668
Center for High Performance Software Research (HiPerSoft) Rice University 6100 Main St MS-41 *Web:* www.hipersoft.rice.edu	Houston	TX	77005	713-348-5186	348-3111	668
Center for Hope 1900 Raritan Rd *Web:* www.centerforhope.com	Scotch Plains	NJ	07076	908-889-7780	889-5172	371
Center for Hospice Care Inc 111 Sunnybrook Ct *TF:* 800-413-9083 ■ *Web:* www.cfhcare.org	South Bend	IN	46637	574-243-3100	243-3134	371
Center for Human Services 7200 Wisconsin Ave Ste 600 *Web:* www.chs-urc.org	Bethesda	MD	20814	301-654-8338	941-8427	48-5
Center for Immigration Studies 1522 K St NW Ste 820 *Web:* www.cis.org	Washington	DC	20005	202-466-8185	466-8076	634
Center for Individual Rights (CIR) 1233 20th St NW Ste 300 *TF:* 877-426-2665 ■ *Web:* www.cir-usa.org	Washington	DC	20036	202-833-8400	833-8410	48-8
Center for Information Systems Research (CISR) Massachusetts Institute of Technology 245 First St, E94-15th Floor *Web:* cisr.mit.edu	Cambridge	MA	02142	617-253-2348	253-4424	668
Center for Innovation University of N Dakota *Web:* www.innovators.net	Grand Forks	ND	58202	701-777-3132	777-2339	402
Center for Integrative Toxicology 1129 Farm Ln Rm 165 *Web:* iit.msu.edu	East Lansing	MI	48824	517-353-6469	355-4603	668
Center for International Development at Harvard University (CID) Rubenstein Bldg 79 JFK St 1 Eliot St Bldg 79 JFK St *Web:* www.hks.harvard.edu/centers/cid	Cambridge	MA	02138	617-495-4112	496-8753	634
Center for International Private Enterprise 1155 15th St NW Ste 700 *Web:* www.cipe.org	Washington	DC	20005	202-721-9200	721-9250	634
Center for International Trade in Forest Products (CINTRAFOR) University of Washington PO Box 352100 *Web:* www.cintrafor.org	Seattle	WA	98195	206-543-8684	685-0790	668
Center for Lasik Ophthalmology Consultants, The 5800 Colonial Dr Ste 103 *Web:* www.bestvision.com	Margate	FL	33063	954-969-0090		798
Center for Law & Social Policy (CLASP) 1015 15th St NW Ste 400 *TF:* 800-821-4367 ■ *Web:* www.clasp.org	Washington	DC	20005	202-906-8000	842-2885	634
Center for Lesbian & Gay Studies (CLAGS) *University of New York* 365 Fifth Ave Rm 7115 *Web:* www.clags.org	New York	NY	10016	212-817-1955	817-1567	668
Center for Mathematical Studies in Economics & Management Sciences 580 Leverone Hall 2001 Sheridan Rd *Web:* www.kellogg.northwestern.edu/research/math	Evanston	IL	60208	847-491-3527	491-2530	634
Center for Media Literacy 23852 Pacific Coast Hwy Ste 472 *Web:* www.medialit.org	Malibu	CA	90265	310-456-1225		49-14
Center for Medical Agricultural & Veterinary Entomology (CMAVE) 1700 SW 23rd Dr *Web:* www.ars.usda.gov/saa/cmave	Gainesville	FL	32608	352-374-5901	374-5852	668
Center for Migration Studies of New York Inc *Archives Intern* 307 E 60th St 4th Fl **Fax Area Code:* 646 ■ *Web:* cmsny.org/archives	New York	NY	10022	212-337-3080	998-4625*	434-4
Center for Nanophysics & Advanced Materials University of Maryland *Web:* cnam.umd.edu	College Park	MD	20742	301-405-8285	405-3779	668
Center for Neighborhood Technology 2125 W N Ave *Web:* www.cnt.org	Chicago	IL	60647	773-278-4800	278-3840	634
Center for Nutrition Policy & Promotion (CNPP) 3101 Pk Ctr Dr 10th Fl *Web:* www.cnpp.usda.gov	Alexandria	VA	22302-1594	703-305-7600	305-3300	340-1
Center for Organ Recovery & Education (CORE) 204 Sigma Dr RIDC Pk *TF:* 800-366-6777 ■ *Web:* www.core.org	Pittsburgh	PA	15238	412-963-3550		269
Center for Policy Research Syracuse University 426 Eggers Hall *TF:* 800-325-3535 ■ *Web:* www.maxwell.syr.edu	Syracuse	NY	13244	315-443-3114	443-1081	634
Center for Practical Bioethics 1111 Main St Ste 500 *TF:* 800-344-3829 ■ *Web:* www.practicalbioethics.org	Kansas City	MO	64105	816-221-1100	221-2002	48-17
Center for Professional 1 Liberty Blvd *Web:* www.cfpie.com	Malvern	PA	19355	610-648-7550		194
Center for Public Integrity 910 17th St NW 7th Fl *Web:* www.publicintegrity.org	Washington	DC	20006	202-466-1300	466-1101	634
Center for Public Leadership Harvard Univ John F Kennedy School of Government 79 JFK St *Web:* cpl.hks.harvard.edu	Cambridge	MA	02138	617-496-8866	496-3337	634
Center for Puppetry Arts 1404 Spring St NW *TF:* 800-642-3629 ■ *Web:* www.puppet.org	Atlanta	GA	30309	404-873-3089	873-9907	50-2
Center for Radiophysics & Space Research Cornell University 616A Space Science Bldg *Web:* www.astro.cornell.edu	Ithaca	NY	14853	607-255-1955	255-3433	668
Center for Real Estate Education & Research 210 S Poplar St	New Washington	IN	47162	812-333-2299		652
Center for Reproductive Rights 120 Wall St 14th Fl *Web:* www.reproductiverights.org	New York	NY	10005	917-637-3600	637-3666	48-8
Center for Research in Mathematics & Science Education San Diego State University 6475 Alvarado Rd Ste 206 *TF:* 800-573-8804 ■ *Web:* www.sci.sdsu.edu	San Diego	CA	92120	619-594-7933	594-1581	668
Center for Responsive Politics 1101 14th St NW Ste 1030 *TF:* 800-733-6440 ■ *Web:* www.opensecrets.org	Washington	DC	20005	202-857-0044	857-7809	634
Center for Science in the Public Interest (CSPI) 1875 Connecticut Ave NW Ste 300 *Web:* www.cspinet.org	Washington	DC	20009	202-332-9110	265-4954	49-19
Center for Security Policy 1920 L St NW *Web:* centerforsecuritypolicy.org	Washington	DC	20036	202-835-9077		634

Phone | Fax | Class

Center for Southern Folklore
119 S Main St .... Memphis TN 38103 901-525-3655 520
TF: 800-478-3160 ■ *Web:* www.southernfolklore.com

Center for Space Plasma & Aeronomic Research
University of Alabama Huntsville .... Huntsville AL 35899 256-961-7403 961-7730 668
TF: 800-824-2255 ■ *Web:* www.uah.edu

Center for Space Research
University of Texas at Austin
University of Texas Ste 200 .... Austin TX 78759 512-471-5573 471-3570 668
Web: www.csr.utexas.edu

Center for Strategic & International Studies
1800 K St NW Ste 400 .... Washington DC 20006 202-887-0200 775-3199 634
Web: www.csis.org

Center for Sustainable Environmental Technologies
Iowa State University
1140 Biorenewables Research Lab .... Ames IA 50011 515-294-6302 294-3091 668
Web: www.cset.iastate.edu

Center for the Arts
103 Ctr for the Arts .... Buffalo NY 14260 716-645-2787 645-6973 572
TF: 800-745-3000 ■ *Web:* www.ubcfa.org

Center for the Study of Language & Information
Stanford University
Cordura Hall 210 Panama St .... Stanford CA 94305 650-725-3286 723-0758 668
Web: www-csli.stanford.edu

Center for the Study of Teaching & Policy (CTP)
University of Washington
100 Gerberding Hall PO Box 351265 .... Seattle WA 98195 206-221-4114 616-8158 668
Web: www.depts.washington.edu

Center for Visual Arts - Greensboro
200 N Davie St PO Box 13 .... Greensboro NC 27401 336-333-7475 333-7477 50-2
Web: www.greensboroart.org

Center for Western Studies
2101 S Summit Ave Augustana College .... Sioux Falls SD 57197 605-274-4007 274-4999 520
TF: 800-727-2844 ■ *Web:* www.augie.edu

Center for Women Policy Studies
1776 Masachusetts Ave NW Ste 450 .... Washington DC 20036 202-872-1770 296-8962 48-24
Web: www.centerwomenpolicy.org

Center for Wooden Boats
1010 Valley St. .... Seattle WA 98109 206-382-2628 382-2699 520
Web: www.cwb.org

Center in the Square 1 Market Sq SE .... Roanoke VA 24011 540-342-5700 50-6
Web: www.centerinthesquare.org

Center Independent School Dist
404 Mosby St .... Center TX 75935 936-598-5642 685
Web: www.centerisd.org

Center Industries Corp 2505 S Custer .... Wichita KS 67217 316-942-8255 697
Web: www.centerindustries.com

Center Line Electric Inc
26554 Lawrence .... Center Line MI 48015 586-757-5505 759-2453 189-4
Web: www.centerline-elec.com

Center Mfg Inc 990 84th St. .... Byron Center MI 49315 920-387-4500 489
Web: www.mecinc.com

Center Municipal Revenue Collection
PO Box 195387 .... San Juan PR 00926 787-625-2746 535
Web: www.crimpr.net

Center of Contemporary Arts
524 Trinity Ave .... Saint Louis MO 63130 314-725-6555 725 6222 50-2
TF: 800-530-5930 ■ *Web:* www.cocastl.org

Center of Southwest Studies
1000 Rim Dr. .... Durango CO 81301 970-247-7456 247-7422 520
Web: swcenter.fortlewis.edu

Center of the American Experiment (CAE)
8441 Wayzata Blvd Ste 350 .... Golden Valley MN 55426 612-338-3605 634
Web: www.americanexperiment.org

Center of Vocational Alternative For Men
3770 N High St .... Columbus OH 43214 614-294-7117 242
TF: 877-521-2682 ■ *Web:* www.cova.org

Center of Workforce Innovations Inc, The
2804 Boilermaker Ct Ste E .... Valparaiso IN 46383 219-462-2940 463
TF: 800-743-3333 ■ *Web:* www.innovativeworkforce.com

Center Oil Co
600 Mason Ridge Ctr Dr. .... Saint Louis MO 63141 314-682-3501 579
Web: www.centeroil.com

Center on Budget & Policy Priorities
820 First St NE Ste 510 .... Washington DC 20002 202-408-1080 408-1056 634
Web: www.cbpp.org

Center on Education & Training for Employment
Ohio State University 1900 Kenny Rd .... Columbus OH 43210 614-292-6869 292-3742 668
TF: 800-848-4815 ■ *Web:* cete.osu.edu

Center on Human Development & Disability
University of Washington 1701 NE Columbia Rd
PO Box 357920 .... Seattle WA 98195 206-543-2832 543-3561 668
TF: 800-636-1089 ■ *Web:* www.depts.washington.edu/chdd

Center on Human Policy
805 S Crouse Ave. .... Syracuse NY 13244 315-443-3851 48-17
Web: thechp.syr.edu

Center Partners Inc
4401 Innovation Dr. .... Fort Collins CO 80525 970-206-9000 317
TF: 800-835-3466 ■ *Web:* www.qualfon.com

Center Rock Inc 118 Schrock Dr .... Berlin PA 15530 814-267-7100 480
Web: www.centerrock.com

Center Stage 700 N Calvert St. .... Baltimore MD 21202 410-986-4000 749
Web: www.centerstage.org

Center Stage Productions Inc
20-10 Maple Ave .... Fair Lawn NJ 07410 973-423-5000 393
TF: 800-955-1663 ■ *Web:* www.cspdisplay.com

Center Theatre Group
601 W Temple St. .... Los Angeles CA 90012 213-628-2772 573-4
Web: centertheatregroup.org

Center to Support Excellence in Teaching
520 Galvez Mall 5th Fl Ste 531 .... Stanford CA 94305 650-721-1660 723-3654 668
Web: cset.stanford.edu

Center Township Trustee of Marion Company Indiana
863 Massachusetts Ave .... Indianapolis IN 46204 317-633-3610 305
Web: www.centergov.org

CenterCal Properties LLC
7455 SW Bridgeport Rd .... Tigard OR 97224 503-968-8940 653
Web: www.centercal.com

Centerchem Inc
20 Glover Ave Merritt On The River. .... Norwalk CT 06850 203-822-9800 146
Web: www.centerchem.com

Centered Networks Inc
1527 Stockton St 2nd Fl .... San Francisco CA 94133 415-294-7776 174
Web: www.centerednetworks.com

CenterGate Research Group LLC
420 S Smith Rd .... Tempe AZ 85281 480-804-8100 179
TF: 800-430-9818 ■ *Web:* www.centergate.com

Centerless Rebuilders Inc
57877 Main St .... New Haven MI 48048 586-749-6529 454
Web: www.centerless.net

Centerplate 2187 Atlantic St .... Stamford CT 06902 203-975-5900 299
TF: 800-698-6992 ■ *Web:* www.centerplate.com

CenterPoint Energy Inc
1111 Louisiana St. .... Houston TX 77002 713-207-1111 360-5
NYSE: CNP ■ *TF Cust Svc:* 800-495-9880 ■ *Web:* www.centerpointenergy.com

Centerpoint Medical Ctr
19600 E 39th St .... Independence MO 64057 816-698-7000 374-3
Web: www.centerpointmedical.com

CenterPoint Properties Trust
1808 Swift Dr .... Oak Brook IL 60523 630-586-8000 586-8010 655
Web: centerpoint.com

CenterPoint Ventures
6300 Bridge Pt Pkwy Bldg 1 Ste 500 .... Austin TX 78730 512-795-5800 795-5849 792
Web: www.cpventures.com

CenterPointe Inc 2633 P St .... Lincoln NE 68503 402-475-8717 726
Web: www.centerpointe.org

Centers for Disease Control & Prevention (CDC)
1600 Clifton Rd NE. .... Atlanta GA 30333 404-639-7000 639-7111 340-10
Web: www.cdc.gov
National Center for Chronic Disease Prevention & H
4770 Buford Hwy NE .... Atlanta GA 30341 800-232-4636 340-10
TF: 800-232-4636 ■ *Web:* www.cdc.gov/nccdphp
National Center for Emerging & Zoonotic Infectious
1600 Clifton Rd .... Atlanta GA 30333 404-639-3311 340-10
TF: 800-232-4636 ■ *Web:* cdc.gov
National Center for Environmental Health
4770 Buford Hwy Bldg 101 .... Atlanta GA 30341 404-639-3311 340-10
TF: 800-232-4636 ■ *Web:* www.cdc.gov
National Center for Health Marketing
1600 Clifton Rd NE .... Atlanta GA 30333 404-639-3311 340-10
TF: 800-311-3435 ■ *Web:* cdc.gov/healthcommunication
National Center for Health Statistics
6525 Belcrest Rd .... Hyattsville MD 20782 301-458-4000 340-10
Web: www.cdc.gov
National Center for HIV/AIDS Viral Hepatitis STD &
1600 Clifton Rd .... Atlanta GA 30333 800-232-4636 340-10
TF: 800-232-4636 ■ *Web:* www.cdc.gov/NCHHSTP
National Center for Immunization & Respiratory Dis
1600 Clifton Rd NE MS E-05 .... Atlanta GA 30333 800-232-4636 340-10
TF: 800-232-4636 ■ *Web:* www.cdc.gov/vaccines
National Center for Injury Prevention & Control (N
4770 Buford Hwy NE .... Atlanta GA 30341 800-232-4636 340-10
TF: 800-232-4636 ■ *Web:* www.cdc.gov/injury
National Center for Public Health Informatics
1600 Clifton Rd NE .... Atlanta GA 30333 800-232-4636 718-2093* 340-10
**Fax Area Code:* 404 ■ *TF:* 800-232-4636 ■ *Web:* www.cdc.gov/ncphi
National Center on Birth Defects & Developmental D
1600 Clifton Rd .... Atlanta GA 30329 404-639-3311 340-10
TF: 800-232-4636 ■ *Web:* www.cdc.gov/ncbddd
National Institute for Occupational Safety & Healt
200 Independence Ave SW .... Washington DC 20201 404-639-3286 340-10
TF: 800-356-4674 ■ *Web:* www.cdc.gov/niosh
National Office of Public Health Genomics
4770 Buford Hwy MS K-89 .... Atlanta GA 30341 770-488-8510 340-10
TF: 877-442-9719 ■ *Web:* www.cdc.gov/genomics
Travelers Health 1600 Clifton Rd NE .... Atlanta GA 30333 800-232-4636 340-10
TF: 800-232-4636 ■ *Web:* wwwnc.cdc.gov/travel

Centers for Medicare & Medicaid Services (CMS)
7500 Security Blvd .... Baltimore MD 21244 800-633-4227 340-10
TF: 800-633-4227 ■ *Web:* www.cms.gov
Medicare.gov 7500 Security Blvd .... Baltimore MD 21244 800-633-4227 340-10
TF: 800-633-4227 ■ *Web:* www.medicare.gov
New York Regional Office
26 Federal Plaza Rm 3812 .... New York NY 10278 212-616-2439 380-8855* 340-10
**Fax Area Code:* 443 ■ *Web:* cms.gov/regionaloffices

Centers for Medicare & Medicaid Services Regional Offices
Region I JFK Federal Bldg Rm 2325 .... Boston MA 02203 617-565-1188 565 1339 340-10
TF: 800-382-8387 ■ *Web:* www.cms.gov
Region III
150 S Independence Mall W Ste 216 .... Philadelphia PA 19106 215-861-4140 861-4240 340-10
Web: www.cms.gov
Region IV 61 Forsyth St SW Ste 4T20 .... Atlanta GA 30303 404-562-1738 380-8945* 340-10
**Fax Area Code:* 443 ■ *TF:* 800-382-8387 ■ *Web:* www.cms.gov
Region IX
90 Seventh St Ste 5-300 .... San Francisco CA 94105 415-744-3502 744-3517 340-10
TF: 800-296-1217 ■ *Web:* www.cms.gov
Region V 233 N Michigan Ave Ste 600 .... Chicago IL 60601 312-886-5344 353-0252 340-10
Web: cms.gov/regionaloffices
Region VI 1301 Young St Ste 714 .... Dallas TX 75202 214-767-6427 340-10
Web: www.cms.gov
Region VII
Richard Bolling Federal Bldg
601 E 12th St Ste 235 .... Kansas City MO 64106 303-844-7481 340-10
Web: www.cms.gov
Region VIII 1600 Broadway Ste 700 .... Denver CO 80202 303-844-7035 844-3753 340-10
Web: www.cms.gov
Region X 2201 Sixth Ave Ste 801 .... Seattle WA 98121 206-615-2306 340-10
TF: 800-382-8387 ■ *Web:* www.cms.gov

CenterStaging Corp 3407 Winona Ave. .... Burbank CA 91504 818-559-4333 514
Web: www.centerstaging.com

Centerstate Banks Inc
42725 US Hwy 27 .... Davenport FL 33837 855-863-2265 70
TF: 855-863-2265 ■ *Web:* centerstatebank.com

Centerville Public Library
585 Main St .... Centerville MA 02632 508-790-6220 790-6218 434-3
Web: www.centervillelibrary.org

Name / Address	City	State	Zip	Phone	Fax	Class
CenTex House Leveling 1120 E 52nd St *TF:* 888-425-5438 ■ *Web:* www.centexhouseleveling.com	Austin	TX	78723	512-444-5438		186
Centex Materials Inc 3019 Alvin Devane Blvd Ste 100 *Web:* eaglematerials.com	Austin	TX	78741	512-460-3003		182
Centice 215 Southport Dr Ste 1000 *Web:* www.centice.com	Morrisville	NC	27560	919-674-4000	653-0428	231
Centimark Corp 12 Grandview Cir *TF:* 800-558-4100 ■ *Web:* www.centimark.com	Canonsburg	PA	15317	800-558-4100		189-12
Centinela Elementary School 1123 Marlborough Ave *TF:* 800-942-2761 ■ *Web:* inglewood.k12.ca.us	Inglewood	CA	90302	310-680-5440		685
Centinela Hospital Medical Ctr 555 E Hardy St *Web:* www.centinelamed.com	Inglewood	CA	90301	310-673-4660		374-3
Centinela State Prison 2302 Brown Rd PO Box 731 *Web:* cdcr.ca.gov	Imperial	CA	92251	760-337-7900	337-7665	213
Cento Fine Foods Inc 100 Cento Blvd *Web:* www.cento.com	West Deptford	NJ	08086	856-853-7800		296-25
Centon Electronics Inc 27412 Aliso Viejo Pkwy *TF:* 800-234-9292 ■ *Web:* www.centon.com	Aliso Viejo	CA	92656	949-855-9111		625
Centra Consulting Inc 413 W Idaho St Ste 302	Boise	ID	83702	208-338-9400		196
Centra Financial Holdings Inc 101 Venture Dra *Web:* www.bankwithunited.com	Morgantown	WV	26508	304-598-2000		780
Centra Health Inc 1920 Atherholt Rd *TF:* 800-947-5442 ■ *Web:* www.centrahealth.com	Lynchburg	VA	24501	434-947-3000		353
Centra Industries Inc 24 Cherry Blossom Rd *Web:* www.centra-ind.com	Cambridge	ON	N3H4R7	519-650-2828	650-7474	21
Centra Technology Inc 25 Burlington Mall Rd *Web:* www.centratechnology.com	Burlington	MA	01803	781-272-7887	272-7836	261
CenTrak 125 Pheasant Run *Web:* www.centrak.com	Newtown	PA	18940	215-860-2928		475
Central Address Systems Inc 10303 Crown Point Ave *TF:* 800-482-7705 ■ *Web:* www.cas-online.com	Omaha	NE	68134	402-964-9998		7
Central AG Services 325 North St E	Eagle Bend	MN	56446	218-738-2552		447
Central Air Conditioning Inc 3435 W Harry St *Web:* www.centralairco.com	Wichita	KS	67213	316-945-0797		189-10
Central Airlines Inc 411 NW Lou Holland Dr *Web:* www.centralairsouthwest.com	Kansas City	MO	64116	816-472-7711	472-1682	12
Central Alabama Community College 1675 Cherokee Rd *TF:* 800-643-2657 ■ *Web:* www.cacc.edu	Alexander City	AL	35010	256-234-6346	215-4244	162
Childersburg 34091 US Hwy 280 *Web:* www.cacc.edu	Childersburg	AL	35044	256-378-5576	378-2027	162
Central Alabama Electric Co-op 1802 Hwy 31 N *TF:* 800-545-5735 ■ *Web:* caec.coop	Prattville	AL	36067	334-365-6762		245
Central Allied Enterprises Inc 1243 Raff Rd SW *TF:* 800-862-6011 ■ *Web:* www.central-allied.com	Canton	OH	44710	330-477-6751	477-1660	188-4
Central Aluminum Co 2045 Broehm Rd *Web:* www.centralaluminum.com	Columbus	OH	43207	614-491-5700		480
Central Arizona College 8470 N Overfield Rd **Fax:* Admissions ■ *TF:* 800-237-9814 ■ *Web:* www.centralaz.edu	Coolidge	AZ	85228	520-494-5444	494-5083*	162
Central Arizona Supply 208 S Country Club Dr *TF:* 800-416-6490 ■ *Web:* www.centralazsupply.com	Mesa	AZ	85210	480-834-5817		612
Central Bank 238 Madison St *Web:* www.centralbancompany.com	Jefferson City	MO	65101	573-634-1155		70
Central Bank 101 W Commercial St *Web:* www.fscb.com	Lebanon	MO	65536	417-532-2151		360-2
Central Bank of Kansas City 2301 Independence Ave *Web:* www.centralbankkc.com	Kansas City	MO	64124	816-483-1210	483-2586	70
Central Baptist College 1501 College Ave *TF:* 800-205-6872 ■ *Web:* www.cbc.edu	Conway	AR	72034	501-329-6872		166
Central Baptist Theological Seminary 6601 Monticello Rd **Fax Area Code:* 412 ■ *Web:* www.cbts.edu	Shawnee	KS	66226	913-667-5700	788-6510*	167-3
Central Baptist Village 4747 N Canfield Ave *Web:* www.cbvillage.org	Norridge	IL	60706	708-583-8500		48-20
Central BBQ 2249 Central Ave *Web:* cbqmemphis.com	Memphis	TN	38104	901-272-9377		671
Central Beef Industry LLC 571 W Kings Hwy	Center Hill	FL	33514	352-793-3671		473
Central Boiler Inc 20502 160th St *Web:* www.centralboiler.com	Greenbush	MN	56726	218-782-2575		362
Central Boston Elder Services Inc 2315 Washington St *TF:* 800-922-2275 ■ *Web:* www.centralboston.org	Boston	MA	02119	617-277-7416	277-2005	450
Central Brevard Library 308 Forest Ave *Web:* www.brevardfl.gov	Cocoa	FL	32922	321-633-1792		434-3
Central Bucks Chamber of Commerce 252 W Swamp Rd Ste 23 *Web:* www.centralbuckschamber.com	Doylestown	PA	18901	215-348-3913	348-7154	139
Central Builders Supply Company Inc 125 Bridge Ave PO Box 152 *TF:* 800-326-9361 ■ *Web:* centralbuilderssupply.com	Sunbury	PA	17801	570-286-6461	286-5108	182
Central California Blood Ctr 4343 W Herndon Ave *TF:* 800-649-5399 ■ *Web:* donateblood.org	Fresno	CA	93722	559-389-5433	225-1602	89
Central California Traction Co 2201 W Washington St Ste 12 *Web:* www.cctrailroad.com	Stockton	CA	95203	209-466-6927		651
Central California Women's Facility (CCWF) 23370 Rd 22 PO Box 1501 *Web:* www.cdcr.ca.gov/facilities_locator/ccwf.html	Chowchilla	CA	93610	559-665-5531		213
Central Carolina Community College 1105 Kelly Dr **Fax:* Admissions ■ *TF:* 800-682-8353 ■ *Web:* www.cccc.edu	Sanford	NC	27330	919-775-5401	718-7380*	162
Central Carolina Hospital 1135 Carthage St *TF:* 800-292-2262 ■ *Web:* www.centralcarolinahosp.com	Sanford	NC	27330	919-774-2100	774-2295	374-3
Central Carolina Products Inc 250 W Old Glencoe Rd *Web:* www.ccair.com	Burlington	NC	27217	336-226-0005		596
Central Carolina Technical College 506 N Guignard Dr *TF:* 800-221-8711 ■ *Web:* www.cctech.edu	Sumter	SC	29150	803-778-1961	778-6696	800
Central Ceilings Inc 36 Norfolk Ave *TF:* 800-354-6996 ■ *Web:* www.centralceilings.com	South Easton	MA	02375	508-238-6985	238-2191	189-9
Central Christian College PO Box 1403 **Fax:* Admissions ■ *TF:* 800-835-0078 ■ *Web:* www.centralchristian.edu	McPherson	KS	67460	620-241-0723	241-6032*	166
Central Christian College of the Bible 911 E Urbandale Dr *TF:* 888-263-3900 ■ *Web:* www.cccb.edu	Moberly	MO	65270	660-263-3900	263-3936	161
Central City Integrated Health 10 Peterboro St *Web:* www.dcccmh.org	Detroit	MI	48201	313-831-3160		726
Central City Opera 400 S Colorado Blvd Ste 530 *Web:* www.centralcityopera.org	Denver	CO	80246	303-292-6500	292-4958	573-2
Central Coast Pathology Consultants Inc 3701 S Higuera St Ste 200 *Web:* www.ccpathology.com	San Luis Obispo	CA	93401	805-541-6033		415
Central Coast Pharmacy Specialists 590A Main St *Web:* www.ccpsrx.com	Templeton	CA	93465	805-434-5999		584
Central College 812 University St **Fax:* Admissions ■ *TF:* 877-462-3687 ■ *Web:* www.central.edu	Pella	IA	50219	641-628-5285	628-5983*	166
Central Communications & Electronics Inc 1413 Cline St *Web:* www.centralcomwireless.com	Knoxville	TN	37921	865-525-2308		246
Central Community College *Columbus* 4500 63rd St PO Box 1027 **Fax:* Admissions ■ *Web:* www.cccneb.edu	Columbus	NE	68602	402-564-7132	562-1201*	162
Grand Island 3134 W Hwy 34 PO Box 4903 **Fax:* Admissions ■ *TF:* 877-222-0780 ■ *Web:* www.cccneb.edu	Grand Island	NE	68802	308-398-4222	398-7399*	162
Hastings 550 Technical Blvd *Web:* www.cccneb.edu	Hastings	NE	68901	402-463-9811	461-2454	162
Central Concrete Supermix Inc 4300 SW 74th Ave *Web:* www.supermix.com	Miami	FL	33155	305-262-3250	267-0698	182
Central Concrete Supply Company Inc 755 Stockton Ave *TF:* 866-404-1000 ■ *Web:* www.centralconcrete.com	San Jose	CA	95126	408-293-6272	294-3162	182
Central Conference of American Rabbis (CCAR) 355 Lexington Ave *Web:* www.ccarnet.org	New York	NY	10017	212-972-3636		48-20
Central Connecticut State University 1615 Stanley St *TF:* 800-894-6126 ■ *Web:* www.ccsu.edu	New Britain	CT	06050	860-832-2278	832-2295	166
Central Container Corp 3901 85th Ave N *Web:* www.centralcontainer.com	Minneapolis	MN	55443	763-425-7444		100
Central Credit Services Inc 9550 Regency Sq Blvd Ste 602 *Web:* www.ccscollect.com	Jacksonville	FL	32225	904-724-1800		393
Central Crude Inc 4187 Hwy 3059 PO Box 1863 *TF:* 800-245-8408 ■ *Web:* www.centralcrude.com	Lake Charles	LA	70602	337-436-1000	436-9602	581
Central Defense Security 50 Vantage Way Ste 251 *Web:* www.centdef.com	Nashville	TN	37228	615-256-0300		693
Central Distributors Inc 15 Foss Rd *Web:* www.centraldistributors.com	Lewiston	ME	04240	207-784-4026		81-1
Central Electric Co-op Inc (CEC) 2098 Hwy 97 N	Redmond	OR	97756	541-548-2144		245
Central Electric Membership Corp 128 Wilson Rd *TF:* 800-446-7752 ■ *Web:* www.centralelectriconline.com	Sanford	NC	27331	919-774-4900		245
Central Electric Power Assn 104 E Main St *TF:* 866-846-5671 ■ *Web:* www.centralepa.com	Carthage	MS	39051	601-267-5671		245
Central European Distribution Corp (CEDC) 3000 Atrium Way Ste 265 *NASDAQ: CEDC* ■ *Web:* www.cedc.com	Mount Laurel	NJ	08054	856-273-6980		81-1
Central Fairfax Chamber of Commerce 11166 Fairfax Blvd Ste 407 *Web:* www.cfcc.org	Fairfax	VA	22030	703-591-2450	591-2820	139
Central Florida Box Corp 2950 Lake Emma Rd *Web:* www.centralfloridabox.com	Lake Mary	FL	32746	407-936-1277		100
Central Florida Community College *Citrus County* 3800 S Lecanto Hwy *Web:* www.cf.edu	Lecanto	FL	34461	352-746-6721	249-1218	162
Levy County 114 Rodgers Blvd *Web:* www.cf.edu	Chiefland	FL	32626	352-493-9533	493-9994	162
Ocala 3001 SW College Rd *Web:* cf.edu	Ocala	FL	34474	352-237-2111	291-4450	162
Central Florida Electric Co-op Inc 1124 N Young Blvd *TF:* 800-227-1302 ■ *Web:* www.cfec.com	Chiefland	FL	32626	352-493-2511	493-4499	245
Central Florida Investments Inc 5601 Windhover Dr *Web:* www.westgateresorts.com	Orlando	FL	32819	407-351-3351		753
Central Florida Press Inc 4560 L B Mcleod Rd *Web:* www.printcfp.com	Orlando	FL	32811	407-843-5811		174

Name / Address	City	State	ZIP	Phone	Fax	Class
Central Florida Regional Hospital						
1401 W Seminole Blvd	Sanford	FL	32771	407-321-4500		374-3
Web: www.centralfloridaregional.com						
Central Florida Regional Transportation Authority (Inc)						
455 N Garland Ave	Orlando	FL	32801	407-841-2279		468
Web: www.golynx.com						
Central Florida Visitors & Convention Bureau						
101 Adventure Ct	Davenport	FL	33837	863-420-2586	420-2593	206
TF: 800-828-7655 ■ *Web:* www.visitcentralflorida.org						
Central Florida Zoological Park						
3755 NW Hwy 17-92 & I-4 PO Box 470309	Lake Monroe	FL	32747	407-323-4450	321-0900	823
TF: 800-435-7352 ■ *Web:* www.centralfloridazoo.org						
Central Flying Service Inc						
1501 Bond St	Little Rock	AR	72202	501-375-3245		63
TF: 800-888-5387 ■ *Web:* www.flycfs.com						
Central Freight Lines Inc PO Box 2638	Waco	TX	76702	800-782-5036	741-5370*	780
**Fax Area Code:* 254 ■ *TF:* 800-782-5036 ■ *Web:* www.centralfreight.com						
Central Garden & Pet Co						
1340 Treat Blvd Ste 600	Walnut Creek	CA	94597	925-948-4000		293
NASDAQ: CENT ■ *TF:* 800-356-2017 ■ *Web:* www.central.com						
Central Georgia Electric Membership Corp						
923 S Mulberry St	Jackson	GA	30233	770-775-7857	504-7877*	245
**Fax:* Cust Svc ■ *TF:* 800-222-4877 ■ *Web:* www.cgemc.com						
Central Georgia Technical College						
3300 Macon Tech Dr.	Macon	GA	31206	478-757-3400	757-3454	800
TF: 866-430-0135 ■ *Web:* centralgatech.edu						
Central Graphics & Container Group Ltd						
5526 Timberlea Blvd.	Mississauga	ON	L4W2T7	905-238-8400	238-8127	100
Web: www.centralgraphics.ca						
Central Grocers Co-op Inc						
2600 W Haven Ave	Joliet	IL	60433	815-553-8800		297-8
Web: www.central-grocers.com						
Central Heating And 2317 Nc Hwy 11 N	Kinston	NC	28501	252-527-6676		189-10
Web: centralheatairconditioning.com						
Central Home Health Care Inc						
20245 W 12 Mile Rd Ste 100	Southfield	MI	48076	248-569-5410		363
Web: centralhomecare.com						
Central Hudson Gas & Electric Corp						
284 S Ave.	Poughkeepsie	NY	12601	845-452-2700		787
TF: 800-527-2714						
Central Illinois Community Blood Ctr						
1999 Wabash Ave	Springfield	IL	62703	217-753-1530	753-8116	89
TF Help Line: 866-448-3253 ■ *Web:* bloodcenter.org/home.aspx?region=104&sap=1						
Central Illinois Tourism Development Office						
700 E Adams St	Springfield	IL	62701	217-525-7980		206
Web: www.visitcentralillinois.com						
Central Indiana Hardware Company Inc						
9190 Corporation Dr.	Indianapolis	IN	46256	317-558-5700		350
Web: www.cih-indy.com						
Central Industries Inc						
11438 Cronridge Dr Ste W	Owings Mills	MD	21117	800-304-8484	932-1222	539
TF: 800-304-8484 ■ *Web:* www.centralindustriesusa.com						
Central Ink Corp						
1100 Harvester Rd	West Chicago	IL	60185	630-231-6500	231-6554	388
TF: 800-345-2541 ■ *Web:* www.cicink.com						
Central Insulation Systems Inc						
300 Murray Rd	Cincinnati	OH	45217	513-242-0600		607
TF: 800-544-7502 ■ *Web:* www.centralinsulation.com						
Central Insurance Cos						
800 S Washington St	Van Wert	OH	45891	419-238-1010	238-7626*	391-4
**Fax:* Claims ■ *TF:* 800-736-7000 ■ *Web:* www.central-insurance.com						
Central Intelligence Agency (CIA)						
Office of Public Affairs	Washington	DC	20505	703-482-0623	482-1739	340-20
Web: www.cia.gov						
Central Iowa Co-op						
2829 Westown Pkwy Ste 350	West Des Moines	IA	50266	515-225-1334	225-8511	275
TF: 800-513-3938 ■ *Web:* www.heartlandcoop.com						
Central Iowa Power Cooperative						
1400 Hwy 13 SE	Cedar Rapids	IA	52403	319-366-8011		787
TF: 800-766-7912 ■ *Web:* www.cipco.net						
Central IQ Inc 14527 Cotswolds Dr.	Tampa	FL	33626	813-920-4001		463
Web: www.centraliq.com						
Central Jersey Blood Ctr						
494 Sycamore Ave	Shrewsbury	NJ	07702	732-842-5750		89
TF: 888-712-5663 ■ *Web:* www.cjbcblood.org						
Central Jersey Supply Company Inc						
201 Second St	Perth Amboy	NJ	08861	732-826-7400		612
Central Lakes College						
Brainerd 501 W College Dr	Brainerd	MN	56401	218-855-8199	855-8057*	162
**Fax:* Admissions ■ *TF:* 800-933-0346 ■ *Web:* www.clcmn.edu						
Staples 1830 Airport Rd.	Staples	MN	56479	218-894-5100	894-5185	162
TF: 800-247-6836 ■ *Web:* www.clcmn.edu						
Central Library of Rochester & Monroe County						
115 S Ave.	Rochester	NY	14604	585-428-7300	428-8353	434-3
Web: www3.libraryweb.org/home2.aspx						
Central Louisiana Chamber of Commerce						
1118 Third St PO Box 992	Alexandria	LA	71309	318-442-6671	442-6734	139
Web: www.cenlachamber.org						
Central Louisiana State Hospital						
242 W Shamrock St	Pineville	LA	71360	318-484-6200	484-6501	374-5
TF: 888-342-6207 ■ *Web:* www.dhh.louisiana.gov						
Central Maine Community College						
1250 Turner St	Auburn	ME	04210	207-755-5100	755-5493	800
TF Admissions: 800-891-2002 ■ *Web:* www.cmcc.edu						
Central Maine Medical Ctr						
300 Main St	Lewiston	ME	04240	207-795-0111		374-3
Web: www.cmmc.org						
Central Maine Medical Ctr School of Nursing						
70 Middle St.	Lewiston	ME	04240	207-795-2840	795-2849	800
TF: 800-228-3734 ■ *Web:* mchp.edu						
Central Maine Power Co 83 Edison Dr	Augusta	ME	04336	207-623-3521	621-4778	787
TF: 800-565-0121 ■ *Web:* www.cmpco.com						
Central Maintenance & Welding Inc (CMW)						
2620 E Keysville Rd	Lithia	FL	33547	813-737-1402	737-1820	189-14
TF: 877-704-7411 ■ *Web:* www.cmw.cc						
Central Management Inc (CMI)						
820 Gessner Rd Ste 1525	Houston	TX	77024	713-961-9777		652
Web: www.cmirealestate.com						
Central Mass Web Design Inc						
70 Snake Pond Rd	Gardner	MA	01440	978-632-5300		179
Web: www.centralmasswebdesign.com						
Central Mechanical Construction Company Inc						
631 Pecan Cir	Manhattan	KS	66502	785-537-2437	537-2491	189-10
TF: 800-631-6999 ■ *Web:* www.centralmechanical.com						
Central Medical Equipment Rentals Inc						
2850 Douglas Rd 3rd Fl	Coral Gables	FL	33134	305-441-0156	441-1095	475
Web: www.empmed.com						
Central Metal Fabricators Inc						
900 SW 70th Ave	Miami	FL	33144	305-261-6262		492
Web: www.centralmetalfab.com						
Central Metal Finishing Inc						
80 Flagship Dr	North Andover	MA	01845	978-685-4811		481
Web: www.cenmet.com						
Central Metals Inc 1054 S Second St	Camden	NJ	08103	856-963-5844		492
Web: www.centralmetals.com						
Central Methodist University						
411 Central Methodist Sq.	Fayette	MO	65248	660-248-3391	248-1872*	166
**Fax:* Admissions ■ *TF:* 877-268-1854 ■ *Web:* www.centralmethodist.edu						
Central Michigan Correctional Facility						
320 N Hubbard	Saint Louis	MI	48880	989-681-6668		213
Web: www.michigan.gov/corrections						
Central Michigan University						
102 Warriner Hall	Mount Pleasant	MI	48859	989-774-4000	774-7267*	166
**Fax:* Admissions ■ *TF Admissions:* 888-292-5366 ■ *Web:* www.cmich.edu						
Central Mine Equipment Company Inc						
4215 Rider Trl N	Earth City	MO	63045	314-291-7700	291-4880	190
TF: 800-325-8827 ■ *Web:* www.cmeco.com						
Central Minnesota Fabricating Inc						
2725 W Gorton Ave.	Willmar	MN	56201	320-235-4181		480
TF: 800-839-8857 ■ *Web:* www.cmf-inc.com						
Central Mississippi Correctional Facility						
3794 Hwy 468	Pearl	MS	39208	601-932-2880	932-6202	213
Web: www.mdoc.ms.gov/Pages/Facility-Locations.aspx						
Central Mississippi Medical Ctr						
1850 Chadwick Dr	Jackson	MS	39204	601-376-1000		374-3
TF: 800-459-2222 ■ *Web:* www.merithealthcentral.com						
Central Missouri Correctional Ctr						
2600 Hwy 179	Jefferson City	MO	65109	573-751-2053		213
Central Missouri ElectricCo-op Inc						
22702 Hwy 65 PO Box 939	Sedalia	MO	65302	660-826-2900		245
TF: 855-875-7165 ■ *Web:* www.cmecinc.com						
Central Moloney Inc						
2400 W Sixth Ave	Pine Bluff	AR	71601	870-534-5332	536-4002	767
Web: www.centralmoloneyinc.com						
Central Montcalm Public School						
1480 S Sheridan Rd	Stanton	MI	48888	989-831-5243		685
Web: www.central-montcalm.org						
Central National Bank 800 SE Quincy St	Topeka	KS	66612	785-234-2265	234-9660	70
Web: centralnational.com						
Central Nebraska Packing Inc						
2800 E Eigth St PO Box 550	North Platte	NE	69103	308-532-1250	532-2744	473
TF Cust Svc: 800-445-2881 ■ *Web:* www.nebraskabrand.com						
Central New Mexico Community College						
10549 Universe Blvd NW	Albuquerque	NM	87114	505-224-3000	224-3237	800
TF: 888-453-1304 ■ *Web:* www.cnm.edu						
Central New Mexico Correctional Facility						
1525 Morris Rd	Los Lunas	NM	87031	505-865-1622		213
Central New York Business Journal, The						
269 W Jefferson St	Syracuse	NY	13202	315-579-3919		457-5
TF: 800-836-3539 ■ *Web:* www.cnybj.com						
Central New York Regional Transportation Authority						
200 Cortland Ave	Syracuse	NY	13205	315-442-3400	442-3337	468
Web: www.centro.org						
Central Ohio Lions Eye Bank						
262 Neil Ave Ste 140	Columbus	OH	43215	614-545-2057		269
Web: www.coleb.org						
Central Ohio Printing Co 55 W High St.	London	OH	43140	740-852-1616		532-3
TF: 800-335-2620 ■ *Web:* www.madison-press.com						
Central Ohio Technical College						
1179 University Dr	Newark	OH	43055	740-366-9494		800
TF: 800-963-9275 ■ *Web:* www.cotc.edu						
Central Ohio Transit Authority (COTA)						
33 N High St.	Columbus	OH	43215	614-228-1776	275-5933	468
TF: 800-638-6338 ■ *Web:* www.cota.com						
Central Oil & Supply Corp						
2300 Booth St.	Monroe	LA	71201	318-388-2602		581
TF: 800-489-6634 ■ *Web:* www.central-oil.com						
Central Oklahoma Detention Juvenile Ctr						
700 S Ninth St	Tecumseh	OK	74873	405-598-2135	598-8713	412
Web: www.ok.gov						
Central Ontario Healthcare Procurement Alliance						
95 Mural St.	Richmond Hill	ON	L4B3G2	905-886-5319		317
TF: 866-897-8812 ■ *Web:* www.cohpa.ca						
Central Oregon Community College						
2600 NW College Way	Bend	OR	97701	541-383-7700	383-7506*	162
**Fax:* Admissions ■ *Web:* www.cocc.edu						
Central Oregon Mall on The Internet, The						
25 NW Minnesota Ave Ste 8	Bend	OR	97701	541-317-3963		396
Web: www.centraloregonmall.com						
Central Oregon Visitors Assn						
57100 Beaver Dr Bldg 6 Ste 130	Sunriver	OR	97707	800-800-8334		206
TF: 800-800-8334 ■ *Web:* www.visitcentraloregon.com						
Central Pacific Financial Corp						
PO Box 3590	Honolulu	HI	96811	808-544-0500	544-0500	360-2
NYSE: CPF ■ *TF:* 800-342-8422 ■ *Web:* www.centralpacificbank.com						
Central Paper Products Co Inc						
350 Gay St John C. Mongan Industrial Park	Manchester	NH	03103	603-624-4065	624-8795	559
TF: 800-339-4065 ■ *Web:* www.centralpaper.com						
Central Park 830 Fifth Ave.	New York	NY	10065	212-360-1461		50-5
TF: 800-991-7088 ■ *Web:* www.centralparknyc.org						
Central Park Group LLC						
805 Third Ave 18th Fl	New York	NY	10022	212-317-9200		401
Web: www.centralparkgroup.com						
Central Park Zoo Fifth Ave & 64th St	New York	NY	10065	212-439-6500		823
Web: centralparkzoo.com						

Phone | Fax | Class

Central Pasco Chamber of Commerce
2810 Land O' Lakes Blvd ....Land O Lakes FL 34639 813-909-2722 909-0827 139
TF: 800-435-7352 ■ *Web:* www.centralpascochamber.com

Central Pattern Co 8830 Pershall Rd..........Hazelwood MO 63042 314-524-3626 522-8399 567
Web: www.centralpattern.com

Central Pennsylvania Blood Bank
8167 Adams Dr...........................Hummelstown PA 17036 717-566-6161 89
TF: 800-771-0059 ■ *Web:* www.cpbb.org

Central Pennsylvania College
600 Valley Rd PO Box 309 .... Summerdale PA 17093 717-732-0702 732-5254 800
TF: 800-759-2727 ■ *Web:* www.centralpenn.edu

Central Petroleum Transport Inc (CPT)
6115 Mitchell St.......................... Sioux City IA 51111 712-258-6357 258-8592 780
TF: 800-798-6357 ■ *Web:* www.cptrans.com

Central Piedmont Community College
1201 Elizabeth Ave......................... Charlotte NC 28204 704-330-2722 330-6136* 162
**Fax:* Admissions ■ *TF:* 877-530-8815 ■ *Web:* www.cpcc.edu
Cato 8120 Grier Rd PO Box 35009 .... Charlotte NC 28235 704-330-4801 330-4884* 162
**Fax:* Admissions ■ *Web:* www.cpcc.edu
Harper 315 W Hebron St.................... Charlotte NC 28273 704-330-4400 330-4444 162
Web: www.cpcc.edu
Levine 2800 Campus Ridge Rd................Matthews NC 28105 704-330-4200 330-4210 162
Web: cpcc.edu
North 11930 Verhoeff Dr.................Huntersville NC 28078 704-330-4100 330-4113* 162
**Fax:* Admissions ■ *Web:* www.cpcc.edu/campuses/north

Central Pinellas Chamber of Commerce
151 Third St NW.............................Largo FL 33770 727-584-2321 586-3112 139
Web: www.centralchamber.biz

Central Pipe Supply Inc
101 Ware Rd PO Box 5470.......................... Pearl MS 39288 601-939-3322 932-8944 595
TF: 800-844-7700 ■ *Web:* www.centralpipe.com

Central Power Electric Co-op
525 20th Ave SW ....Minot ND 58701 701-852-4407 245
Web: www.centralpwr.com

Central Power Systems & Services
9200 W Liberty Dr ....Liberty MO 64068 816-781-8070 781-2207* 385
**Fax:* Sales ■ *TF:* 800-444-0442 ■ *Web:* www.cpower.com

Central Pre-Mix Concrete Co
5111 E Broadway ....Spokane WA 99212 509-534-6221 183
Web: www.centralpremix.com

Central Prison 1300 Western Blvd .... Raleigh NC 27606 919-733-0800 715-2645 213
Web: www.ncdps.gov

Central Products LLC
7750 Georgetown Rd ....Indianapolis IN 46268 317-876-1010 14
Web: www.centralrestaurant.com

Central Puget Sound Regional Transit Authority
401 S Jackson St .... Seattle WA 98104 206-398-5000 689-3360* 468
**Fax:* Hum Res ■ *TF:* 800-201-4900 ■ *Web:* www.soundtransit.org

Central Record PO Box 1027 ....Medford NJ 08055 609-654-5000 532-4
TF: 800-825-7653 ■ *Web:* southjerseylocalnews.com

Central Refrigerated Service Inc
5175 W 2100 S......................West Valley City UT 84120 801-924-7000 924-7142 780

Central Reservation Service of New England Inc
300 Terminal C
Logan International Airport.................East Boston MA 02128 617-569-3800 376

Central Resources Inc
1775 Sherman St Ste 2600....................Denver CO 80203 303-830-0100 830-9297 538
Web: www.centralresources.com

Central Rhode Island Chamber of Commerce
3288 Post Rd ....Warwick RI 02886 401-732-1100 732-1107 139
TF: 800-221-1939 ■ *Web:* www.centralrichamber.com

Central Rubber & Plastics
17416 County Rd 34........................ Goshen IN 46528 574-534-6411 677
Web: www.centralrubbercompany.com

Central Rural Electric Co-op
3304 S Boomer Rd PO Box 1809.............. Stillwater OK 74076 405-372-2884 372-8559 245
TF: 800-375-2884 ■ *Web:* www.crec.coop

Central Sales & Service Inc
110 Industrial Ct............................ Waverly TN 37185 931-296-1940 650
Web: www.centralsales-service.com

Central Securities Corp
630 Fifth Ave Ste 820.......................New York NY 10111 212-698-2020 405
NYSE: CET ■ *TF:* 866-593-2507 ■ *Web:* www.centralsecurities.com

Central Security Life Insurance Co
PO Box 833879 PO Box 833879............ Richardson TX 75083 972-699-2770 699-2788 391-2
Web: www.cslic.com

Central Service Assn 93 S Coley Rd .... Tupelo MS 38801 662-842-5962 840-1329 225
TF: 877-842-5962 ■ *Web:* www.csa1.com

Central Signaling 2033 Hamilton Rd .... Columbus GA 31904 706-322-3756 692
TF: 800-554-1101 ■ *Web:* www.censignal.com

Central Specialties Ltd
220 Exchange Dr ....Crystal Lake IL 60014 815-459-6000 459-6562 64
TF: 800-873-4370 ■ *Web:* www.csltd.com

Central State Hospital
26317 W Washington St....................Petersburg VA 23803 804-524-7000 374-5
Web: www.csh.dbhds.virginia.gov

Central State Hospital
10510 LaGrange Rd ....Louisville KY 40223 502-253-7000 374-5
Web: kentucky.gov

Central State University
1400 Brush Row Rd PO Box 1004 .... Wilberforce OH 45384 937-376-6011 376-6648* 166
**Fax:* Admissions ■ *TF:* 800-388-2781 ■ *Web:* www.centralstate.edu

Central States Bus Sales Inc
2450 Cassens Dr .... Fenton MO 63026 636-343-6050 59
Web: www.centralstatesbus.com

Central States Business Forms Inc
2500 Industrial Pkwy .... Dewey OK 74029 800-331-0920 534-3470* 110
**Fax Area Code:* 918 ■ *TF:* 800-331-0920 ■ *Web:* www.centralstates.net

Central States Coach Repairs
3426 Gilbert Rd ....Grand Prairie TX 75050 972-399-1059 107
TF: 800-533-1939 ■ *Web:* www.bus-charter.com

Central States Health & Life Company of Omaha
1212 N 96th St.............................Omaha NE 68114 402-397-1111 391-2
TF: 800-826-6587 ■ *Web:* www.cso.com

Central States Indemnity Company of Omaha (CSI)
1212 N 96th St.............................Omaha NE 68114 402-997-8000 391-5
TF: 800-321-0102 ■ *Web:* www.csi-omaha.com

Central States Industrial Supply Inc
8720 S 137th Cir ....Omaha NE 68138 402-894-1003 492
Web: www.centralstatesgroup.com

Central Station Alarm Assn (CSAA)
8150 Leesburg Pk Ste 700 ....Vienna VA 22180 703-242-4670 242-4675 49-3
Web: www.csaaintl.org

Central Steel Fabricators Inc
1843 S 54th Ave............................. Cicero IL 60804 708-652-2037 480
TF: 855-652-7010 ■ *Web:* www.centralsteelfab.com

Central Street Health Ctr
26 Central St.............................Somerville MA 02143 617-591-6033 591-6452 726
Web: www.challiance.org

Central Systems Htg & A/C Inc
2857 Wbound 40 Hwy ....Blue Springs MO 64015 816-228-2022 189-10

Central Tax Inc 534 Notre-Dame St ....Repentigny QC J6A2T8 450-585-8293 734
Web: www.centraletaxes.com

Central Texas College PO Box 1800 .... Killeen TX 76540 254-526-7161 162
TF: 800-792-3348 ■ *Web:* www.online.ctcd.edu

Central Texas Corrugated LP 7200 Mars Dr .... Waco TX 76712 254-776-6902 548
Web: www.ctcwaco.com

Central Texas Electric Co-op Inc (CTEC)
386 Friendship Ln PO Box 553............Fredericksburg TX 78624 830-997-2126 245
TF General: 800-900-2832 ■ *Web:* www.ctec.coop

Central Texas Iron Works
1000 Winchell Dr ....Waco TX 76712 254-776-8000 772-5811 480
Web: www.ctiw.com

Central Texas Medical Ctr (CTMC)
1301 Wonder World Dr..................San Marcos TX 78666 512-353-8979 374-3
TF: 800-927-9004 ■ *Web:* www.ctmc.org

Central Texas Veterans Health Care System
1901 Veterans Memorial Dr ....Temple TX 76504 254-778-4811 374-8
TF: 800-423-2111 ■ *Web:* www.centraltexas.va.gov

Central Textiles Inc 237 Mill Ave................Central SC 29630 864-639-2491 639-4513 745-1
Web: ctextiles.com

Central Transportation Systems Inc
4105 Rio Bravo Ste 100 .... El Paso TX 79902 800-283-3106 449
TF: 800-283-3106 ■ *Web:* www.centralsystems.com

Central Union High School District
351 W Ross Ave........................... El Centro CA 92243 760-336-4500 353-3606 685
Web: www.cuhsd.net

Central Utah Correctional Facility
255 East 300 North........................Gunnison UT 84634 435-528-6000 213
Web: corrections.utah.gov

Central Valley Broadband LLC
1624 Santa Clara Dr Ste 250 .... Roseville CA 95661 530-852-0318 225
Web: www.calwisp.com

Central Valley Community Bancorp
7100 N Financial Dr Ste 101.................. Fresno CA 93720 559-298-1775 360-2
NASDAQ: CVCY ■ *TF:* 866-294-9588 ■ *Web:* www.cvcb.com

Central Valley Electric Co-op Inc
1505 N 13th St PO Box 230 .... Artesia NM 88211 575-746-3571 245
Web: www.cvecoop.org

Central Vermont Chamber of Commerce
33 Stewart Rd.............................Berlin VT 05602 802-229-5711 229-5713 139
TF: 877-887-3678 ■ *Web:* www.centralvt.com

Central Vermont Home Health & Hospice
600 Granger Rd .... Barre VT 05641 802-223-1878 363
TF: 800-286-1219 ■ *Web:* www.cvhhh.org

Central Vermont Medical Ctr (CVMC)
130 Fisher Rd..............................Berlin VT 05602 802-371-4100 374-3
Web: www.cvmc.org

Central Virginia Community College
3506 WaRds Rd ....Lynchburg VA 24502 434-832-7600 832-7793* 162
**Fax:* Admissions ■ *Web:* centralvirginia.edu

Central Virginia Electric Co-op
800 Co-op Way PO Box 247................Lovingston VA 22949 434-263-8336 263-8339 245
TF: 800-367-2832 ■ *Web:* www.mycvec.com

Central Virginia Training Ctr
521 Colony Rd ....Madison Heights VA 24572 434-947-6000 230
TF: 866-897-6095 ■ *Web:* www.cvtc.dbhds.virginia.gov

Central Washington Comprehensive Mental Health
PO Box 959 ....Yakima WA 98907 509-575-4084 352
Web: www.cwcmh.org

Central Washington Hospital
1201 S Miller St.........................Wenatchee WA 98801 509-662-1511 374-5
TF: 800-365-6428 ■ *Web:* www.cwhs.com

Central Washington University
400 E University Way ....Ellensburg WA 98926 509-963-1111 963-3022* 166
**Fax:* Admissions ■ *TF Admissions:* 866-298-4968 ■ *Web:* www.cwu.edu

Central Washington University Brooks Library
400 E University Way ....Ellensburg WA 98926 509-963-3682 963-3684 434-6
TF: 800-290-3327 ■ *Web:* www.lib.cwu.edu

Central West Ballet Co (CWB)
5039 Pendecost Dr Ste B2 .... Modesto CA 95356 209-576-8957 576-1308 573-1
Web: cwballet.org

Central Wholesale Electrical Distributors Inc
6611 Preston Ave .... Livermore CA 94551 925-245-9310 246
TF: 800-847-4430 ■ *Web:* cwed.com

Central Woodwork Inc
870 Keough Rd...........................Collierville TN 38017 901-363-4141 499
TF: 800-788-3775 ■ *Web:* www.centralwoodwork.com

Central Wyoming College
2660 Peck Ave ....Riverton WY 82501 307-855-2000 855-2092 162
TF: 800-735-8418 ■ *Web:* www.cwc.edu

Central Wyoming Fairgrounds
1700 Fairgrounds Rd ....Casper WY 82604 307-235-5775 266-4224 642
TF: 800-227-5122 ■ *Web:* www.centralwyomingfair.com

Central Wyoming Hospice Program
319 S Wilson St............................Casper WY 82601 307-577-4832 577-4841 371
Web: www.cwhp.org

Central Yavapai Fire District
8555 E Yavapai Rd ....Prescott Valley AZ 86314 928-772-7711 302
Web: centralyavapaifire.org

Centralia College 600 W Locust St .... Centralia WA 98531 360-736-9391 330-7503* 162
**Fax:* Admissions ■ *Web:* www.centralia.edu

Centralia Correctional Ctr
9330 Shattuc Rd PO Box 1266 .... Centralia IL 62801 618-533-4111 533-4112 213
Web: www2.illinois.gov

				Phone	Fax	Class
Centralia Sentinel 232 E Broadway	Centralia	IL	62801	618-532-5604	532-1212	532-2
TF: 800-371-9892 ■ *Web:* www.morningsentinel.com						
Centralia Square 201 S Pearl	Centralia	WA	98531	360-736-6406		460
Web: www.myantiquemall.com/centraliasquare.html						
Centralia-Chehalis Chamber of Commerce						
500 NW Chamber of Commerce Way	Chehalis	WA	98532	360-748-8885	748-8763	139
TF: 800-525-3323 ■ *Web:* chamberway.com						
Centralized Supply Chain Services LLC						
8140 Ward Pkwy	Kansas City	MO	64114	913-438-5552		466
Web: www.cscscoop.com						
CentralVac International						
23455 Hellman Ave PO Box 259	Dollar Bay	MI	49922	800-666-3133		788
TF: 800-666-3133 ■ *Web:* www.centralvac.com						
CentraState Medical Ctr						
901 W Main St	Freehold	NJ	07728	732-431-2000		374-3
Web: www.centrastate.com						
Centratel LLC						
141 NW Greenwood Ave Ste 200	Bend	OR	97701	541-385-2616	388-2351	246
Web: www.centratel.com						
Centrav Inc 511 E Travelers Trl	Burnsville	MN	55337	952-886-7650	886-7640	16
TF: 800-874-2033 ■ *Web:* www.centrav.com						
Centre at Salisbury						
2300 N Salisbury Blvd	Salisbury	MD	21801	410-548-1600		460
Web: www.centreatsalisbury.com						
Centre College 600 W Walnut St	Danville	KY	40422	859-238-5350	238-5373	166
TF: 800-423-6236 ■ *Web:* www.centre.edu						
Centre County						
420 Holmes St Willowbank Office Bldg	Bellefonte	PA	16823	814-355-6700	355-6980	338
TF: 800-637-2757 ■ *Web:* centrecountypa.gov						
Centre County Convention & Visitors Bureau						
800 E Pk Ave	State College	PA	16803	814-231-1400	231-8123	206
TF: 800-358-5466 ■ *Web:* www.visitpennstate.org						
Centre Daily Times						
3400 E College Ave	State College	PA	16801	814-238-5000		532-2
TF: 800-327-5500 ■ *Web:* www.centredaily.com						
Centre de sant et de services sociaux d'Argenteuil						
145 boul Providence	Lachute	QC	J8H4C7	450-562-3761	566-3316	374-2
Web: csssargenteuil.qc.ca						
Centre for Addiction & Mental Health Foundation						
901 King St W Ste 502	Toronto	ON	M5V3H5	416-979-6909		305
TF: 800-414-0471 ■ *Web:* www.supportcamh.ca						
Centre for Skills Development & Training, The						
3350 S Service Rd	Burlington	ON	L7N3M6	905-333-3499		148
TF: 888-315-5521 ■ *Web:* thecentre.on.ca						
Centre for Well-Being at the Phoenician						
6000 E Camelback Rd	Scottsdale	AZ	85251	800-843-2392		707
TF: 800-843-2392 ■ *Web:* www.thephoenician.com						
Centre Hospitalier d'Amqui						
135 Rue de l'Hopital	Amqui	QC	G5J2K5	418-629-2211	629-4498	374-2
TF: 800-808-6352 ■ *Web:* www.chamqui.com						
Centre Hospitalier Hotel-Dieu d'Amos						
622 4e Rue O	Amos	QC	J9T2S2	819-732-3341		374-2
Web: csssea.ca						
Centre Hospitalier Mount Sinai						
5690 Cavendish Blvd	Montreal	QC	H4W1S7	514-369-2222	369-2225	374-2
Web: sinaimontreal.ca						
Centre Hospitalier Regional du Grand Portage						
75 Rue St Henri	Riviere-du-Loup	QC	G5R2A4	418-868-1010		374-2
Web: csssriviereduloup.qc.ca						
Centre Hospitalier Regional du Suroit						
150 Rue St Thomas	Salaberry-de-Valleyfield	QC	J6T6C1	450-371-9920	371-7454	374-2
Web: centrejeunessemonteregie.qc.ca						
Centre in the Square 101 Queen St N	Kitchener	ON	N2H6P7	519-578-1570		572
TF: 800-265-8977 ■ *Web:* centreinthesquare.com						
Centre Lane Partners LLC						
1 Grand Central Pl 60 E 42nd St Ste 1250	New York	NY	10165	646-843-0710		528
Web: www.centrelanepartners.com						
Centre Regional de Services Aux Bibliotheques Publiques de la Monteregie Inc						
275 Rue Conrad-Pelletier	La Prairie	QC	J5R4V1	450-444-5433	659-3364	436
Web: www.reseaubiblioduquebec.qc.ca						
Centre Regional de Services Aux Bibliotheques Publiques des Laurentides Inc						
29 Rue Brissette	Sainte-Agathe-des-Monts	QC	J8C3L1	819-326-6440	326-0885	436
Web: www.reseaubiblioduquebec.qc.ca						
Centre Street United Methodist Church						
217 N Centre St	Cumberland	MD	21502	301-722-5370		48-20
Web: centrestreetumc.com						
Centreville Savings Bank						
1218 Main St	West Warwick	RI	02893	401-821-9100		70
Web: www.centrevillebank.com						
CENTRIA 1005 Beaver Grade Rd	Moon Township	PA	15108	412-299-8000	299-8051*	480
**Fax:* Hum Res ■ *TF:* 800-759-7474 ■ *Web:* www.centria.com						
Centric Business Systems Inc						
10702 Red Run Blvd	Owings Mills	MD	21117	410-902-3300		179
TF: 800-677-1997 ■ *Web:* www.centricbiz.com						
Centric Health Resources Inc						
17877 Chesterfield Airport Rd	Chesterfield	MO	63005	636-519-2400		237
Web: www.centrichealthresources.com						
Centric Parts Inc						
14528 Bonelli St	City Of Industry	CA	91746	626-961-5775		57
Web: centricparts.com						
Centric Software Inc						
655 Campbell Technology Pkwy Ste 200	Campbell	CA	95008	408-574-7802	866-5869	39
Web: www.centricsoftware.com						
Centrilogy Consulting						
3201 Walker Pl	Grapevine	TX	76051	817-416-9722		463
Centriq University						
8700 State Line Rd Ste 200	Leawood	KS	66206	913-322-7000		177
Web: www.centriq.com						
Centris Consulting Inc 800 James Ave	Scranton	PA	18510	570-963-1136		194
Web: www.centrisconsulting.com						
Centrix Builders Inc						
160 S Linden Ave						
Ste 100 S San Francisco	San Francisco	CA	94080	650-876-9400		186
Web: www.centrixbuilders.com						
Centrix Inc 770 River Rd	Shelton	CT	06484	203-929-5582		228
TF: 800-235-5862 ■ *Web:* www.centrixdental.com						
Centrix Pharmaceutical Inc						
31 Inverness Ctr Pkwy Ste 270	Birmingham	AL	35242	205-991-9870		231
Web: www.cenrx.com						
Centro De Servicios & Viajes Inc						
525 "H" st	Union City	CA	94587	510-675-5620		775
Web: centrodeservicios.org						
Centro Inc 950 N Bend Dr	North Liberty	IA	52317	319-626-3200	626-3203	604
Web: www.centroinc.com						
Centro Ybor 1600 E Eigth Ave	Tampa	FL	33605	813-242-4660		50-6
Web: www.centroybor.com						
Centron Data Services Inc						
1175 Devin Dr	Norton Shores	MI	49441	800-732-8787	799-0092*	5
**Fax Area Code:* 231 ■ *TF Cust Svc:* 800-732-8787 ■ *Web:* www.centrondata.com						
Centron Industries Inc						
20760 Leapwood Ave	Carson	CA	90746	310-324-6443		246
Web: www.centronind.com						
Centronia 1420 Columbia Rd NW Fl 1	Washington	DC	20009	202-332-4200		685
Web: www.centronia.org						
Centrose LLC 918 Deming Way	Madison	WI	53717	608-836-0207		668
Web: www.centrosepharma.com						
CENTROSOLAR America Inc						
8350 E Evans Rd Ste E-1	Scottsdale	AZ	85260	480-348-2555		253
Web: www.centrosolaramerica.com						
Centrus Energy Corp						
6903 Rockledge Dr Ste 800	Bethesda	MD	20817	301-564-3200	564-3201	143
NYSE: USU ■ *TF:* 800-273-7754 ■ *Web:* www.centrusenergy.com						
Centrus Group Inc						
1653 Merriman Rd Ste 211	Akron	OH	44313	330-864-5800		195
Web: centrusgroup.com						
Centura Home Care & Hospice						
1391 Speer Blvd Ste 600	Denver	CO	80204	303-561-5000		371
Web: www.centurahealthathome.org						
Centuria Corp						
1851 Alexander Bell Dr Ste 440	Reston	VA	20191	703-435-4600	435-9974	463
Web: www.centuria.com						
Centurion Cargo 4500 NW36th St	Miami	FL	33166	305-871-0130		12
Web: www.centurioncargo.com						
Centurion Counsel Inc						
1282 Pacific Oaks Pl	Escondido	CA	92029	760-471-8536		690
Web: www.centurioncounsel.com						
Centurion Data Systems						
N27w23957 Paul Rd Ste 102	Pewaukee	WI	53072	262-524-9290		180
TF: 800-215-9040 ■ *Web:* www.cendatsys.com						
Centurion Industries Inc						
1107 N Taylor Rd	Garrett	IN	46738	260-357-6665	357-6761	190
TF: 888-832-4466 ■ *Web:* www.centurionind.com						
Centurion Investments Inc						
18377 Edison Ave	Chesterfield	MO	63005	636-532-2674		770
Web: www.avmats.com						
Centurion Medical Products						
100 Centurion Way	Williamston	MI	48895	517-546-5400	546-9388	477
TF: 800-248-4058 ■ *Web:* www.centurionmp.com						
Centurion Products Inc						
50 Van Buren St	Nashville	TN	37208	615-256-6694		183
Web: www.centurionstone.com						
Centurion Service Group LLC						
3325 Mt Prospect Rd	Franklin Park	IL	60131	708-761-6655		225
Web: www.centurionservice.com						
Century 21 A Property Shoppe						
2033 N Main St	Salinas	CA	93906	831-443-2121	443-9436	652
Web: www.c21aps.com						
Century 21 Consolidated Real Estate						
2820 Flamingo Rd	Las Vegas	NV	89121	702-732-7282		652
Century 21 Dept Stores						
22 Cortlandt St	New York	NY	10007	212-227-9092		229
Web: www.c21stores.com						
Century 21 Percy Fulton Ltd						
2911 Kennedy Rd	Toronto	ON	M1V1S8	416-298-8200		652
Web: www.century21toronto.com						
CENTURY 21 Salvadori Realty						
3500 N G St	Merced	CA	95340	209-383-6475		652
TF: 800-557-6033 ■ *Web:* c21salvadori.com						
CENTURY 21 Sweyer & Assoc						
1630 Military Cutoff Rd	Wilmington	NC	28403	910-256-0021		652
Web: www.century21sweyer.com						
Century 3-Plus LLC						
2410 W Aero Park Ct	Traverse City	MI	49686	231-946-7500		295
Web: www.centinc.com						
Century Aluminum						
1 S Wacker Dr Ste 1000	Chicago	IL	60606	312-696-3101	696-3102	485
Web: centuryaluminum.com						
Century Aluminum Co						
2511 Garden Rd Ste 200 Bldg A	Monterey	CA	93940	831-642-9300		485
NASDAQ: CENX ■ *Web:* www.centuryaluminum.com						
Century Bancorp Inc 400 Mystic Ave	Medford	MA	02155	781-393-4160		360-2
NASDAQ: CNBKA ■ *TF:* 866-823-6887 ■ *Web:* www.centurybank.com						
Century Capital Management LLC						
100 Federal St 29th Fl	Boston	MA	02110	617-482-3060		796
Web: www.centurycap.com						
Century Casinos Inc						
2860 S Cir Dr Ste 350	Colorado Springs	CO	80906	719-527-8300		132
NASDAQ: CNTY ■ *TF:* 888-966-2257 ■ *Web:* www.cnty.com						
Century City Chamber of Commerce						
2029 Century Pk E	Los Angeles	CA	90067	310-553-2222	553-4623	139
TF: 800-462-7899 ■ *Web:* www.centurycitycc.com						
Century City Fitness Club & Spa						
10250 Santa Monica	Century City	CA	90067	310-552-0420		707
Web: www.equinox.com						
Century City Flower Mart						
9551 W Pico Blvd	Los Angeles	CA	90035	310-277-6737		292
Web: www.centurycityflowermarket.com						
Century College						
3300 Century Ave N	White Bear Lake	MN	55115	651-779-3300	773-1796*	162
**Fax:* Admissions ■ *TF:* 800-228-1978 ■ *Web:* www.century.edu						
Century Concrete Inc						
1364 Air Rail Ave	Virginia Beach	VA	23455	757-460-5366	460-3296	186
Web: www.centuryconcreteinc.com						
Century Ctr 120 S St Joseph St	South Bend	IN	46601	574-235-9711	235-9185	205
TF: 800-272-2054 ■ *Web:* www.centurycenter.org						
Century Direct LLC 15 Enter Ln	Islandia	NY	11749	212-763-0600	349-9528*	5
**Fax Area Code:* 718 ■ *Web:* www.centurydirect.net						

	Phone	Fax	Class
Century Distributors Inc 15710 Crabbs Branch Way ... Rockville MD 20855 *Web:* www.centurydist.com	301-212-9100	212-9681	335
Century Engineering Inc 10710 Gilroy Rd ... Hunt Valley MD 21031 *TF:* 800-318-6867 ■ *Web:* www.centuryeng.com	443-589-2400		261
Century Equipment Inc 5959 Angola Rd PO Box 352889 ... Toledo OH 43615 *Web:* www.centuryequip.com	419-865-7400	865-8215	472
Century Fasteners Corp 50-20 Ireland St ... Elmhurst NY 11373 *TF:* 800-221-0769 ■ *Web:* www.centuryfasteners.com	718-446-5000	426-8119	246
Century Foods International 400 Century Ct ... Sparta WI 54656 *Web:* www.centuryfoods.com	608-269-1900		296-27
Century Foundation, The 1 Whitehall St 15th Fl ... New York NY 10004 *Web:* www.tcf.org	212-535-4441		634
Century Foundry Inc 339 W Hovey Ave ... Muskegon MI 49444 *Web:* www.centuryfoundry.com	231-733-1572		492
Century Furniture LLC 401 11th St NW ... Hickory NC 28601 *TF:* 800-852-5552 ■ *Web:* www.centuryfurniture.com	828-328-1851	328-2176	319-2
Century Graphics & Metals Inc 550 S N Lake Blvd Ste 1000 ... Altamonte Springs FL 32701 **Fax Area Code:* 407 ■ *TF:* 800-327-5664 ■ *Web:* www.centurygraphics.com	800-327-5664	262-8291*	701
Century Group Inc, The 1106 W Napoleon St PO Box 228 ... Sulphur LA 70664 *TF:* 800-527-5232 ■ *Web:* www.centurygrp.com	337-527-5266	527-8028	183
Century Health Solutions Inc 2951 SW Woodside Dr ... Topeka KS 66614 *TF:* 800-227-0089 ■ *Web:* www.centuryinsuranceagencyks.com	785-233-1816		194
Century Hotel South Beach 140 Ocean Dr ... Miami Beach FL 33139 *Web:* centurymiamibeach.com	305-674-8855		379
Century II Performing Arts & Convention Ctr 225 W Douglas Ave ... Wichita KS 67202 *Web:* www.century2.org	316-264-9121		205
Century II Staffing Inc 278 Franklin Rd Ste 350 ... Brentwood TN 37027 *Web:* www.centuryii.net	615-665-9060		631
Century III Mall 3075 Clairton Rd ... West Mifflin PA 15123 *Web:* www.simon.com	412-653-1222		460
Century Industries Inc 2300 E 145th St ... Little Rock AR 72206 *Web:* www.century-inc.com	501-897-5253		499
Century Insurance Group 550 Polaris Pkwy Ste 300 ... Westerville OH 43082 **Fax Area Code:* 800 ■ *TF:* 877-855-8462 ■ *Web:* www.meadowbrook.com	614-895-2000	832-8793*	391-5
Century Junior High School 10801 W 159th St ... Orland Park IL 60467 *Web:* www.orland135.org	708-364-3500		685
Century Kitchen Inc Rt 309 And Railroad Crossing ... Colmar PA 18915 *Web:* www.centurykitchens.com	215-822-1300		286
Century Manufacturing Inc 9750 E 50TH St N ... Bel Aire KS 09750 *Web:* www.centurymfg.com	316-636-5423		608
Century Marketing Solutions LLC 3000 Cameron St ... Monroe LA 71201 *TF:* 800-256-6000 ■ *Web:* www.centurymarketingsolutions.com	800-256-6000		627
Century Martial Art Supply Inc 1000 Century Blvd ... Oklahoma City OK 73110 *TF Sales:* 800-626-2787 ■ *Web:* www.centurymartialarts.com	405-732-2226		711
Century Mechanical Contractors Inc 3008 Wichita Ct ... Fort Worth TX 76140 *Web:* www.centurymech.com	817-293-3803		610
Century Media 2323 W El Segundo Blvd ... Hawthorne CA 90250 *Web:* www.centurymedia.com	323-418-1400	418-0118	657
Century Metal Spinning Company Inc 430 Meyer Rd ... Bensenville IL 60106 *Web:* www.centurymetalspinning.com	630-595-3900		483
Century Mold Company Inc 25 Vantage Point Dr ... Rochester NY 14624 *Web:* www.centurymold.com	585-352-8600		596
Century National Bank 14 S Fifth St ... Zanesville OH 43701 *TF Cust Svc:* 800-548-3557 ■ *Web:* www.centurynationalbank.com	740-454-2521		70
Century Packaging Inc 42 Edgeboro Rd ... East Brunswick NJ 08816 *Web:* www.centurypackaginginc.com	732-249-6600		561
Century Plaza Hotel & Spa 1015 Burrard St ... Vancouver BC V6Z1Y5 *TF:* 800-663-1818 ■ *Web:* www.century-plaza.com	604-687-0575		379
Century Plumbing Inc 901 SW 69th Ave ... Miami FL 33144 *Web:* www.centuryplumbing.com	305-261-4731		612
Century Precision Machine Inc 1130 W Grove Ave ... Orange CA 92865 *TF:* 800-704-1078 ■ *Web:* www.centuryindustriesinc.com	714-637-3691		454
Century Ready-Mix Corp 3250 Armand St PO Box 4420 ... Monroe LA 71211 *TF:* 800-732-3969 ■ *Web:* centuryreadymix.com	318-322-4444	322-7299	182
Century Roof Tile 23135 Saklan Rd ... Hayward CA 94545 *TF:* 888-233-7548 ■ *Web:* www.centuryrooftile.com	510-780-9489		191-1
Century Snacks 5560 E Slauson Ave ... Commerce CA 90040 *Web:* www.newcenturysnacks.com	323-278-9578		297-8
Century Spring Corp 222 E 16th St ... Los Angeles CA 90015 *TF:* 800-237-5225 ■ *Web:* www.centuryspring.com	213-749-1466	749-3802	719
Century Steel Erectors Co 210 Washington Ave ... Dravosburg PA 15034 *TF:* 888-601-8801 ■ *Web:* www.centurysteel.com	412-469-8800	469-0813	189-14
Century Suites Hotel 300 SR-446 ... Bloomington IN 47401 *TF:* 800-766-5446 ■ *Web:* www.centurysuites.com	812-336-7777		379
Century Tile Supply Co 747 E Roosevelt Rd ... Lombard IL 60148 **Fax Area Code:* 773 ■ *TF:* 888-845-3968 ■ *Web:* www.century-tile.com	630-495-2300	237-8257*	290
Century Tool & Gage Co 200 S Alloy Dr ... Fenton MI 48430 *Web:* www.centurytool.com	810-629-0784		711
Century Tool & Mfg 90 McMillen Rd ... Antioch IL 60002 **Fax Area Code:* 847 ■ *TF:* 800-635-3831 ■ *Web:* www.centurycamping.com	800-635-3831	395-3305*	710
Century Tool Inc 21495 147th Ave N ... Rogers MN 55374 *Web:* www.century-tool.com	763-428-2168		454
Century Village 14653 E Pk St ... Burton OH 44021 *TF:* 800-642-0388 ■ *Web:* centuryvillagemuseum.org	440-834-1492		520
Century Wealth Management LLC 1770 Kirby Pkwy Ste 117 ... Memphis TN 38138 *TF:* 855-850-5532 ■ *Web:* www.centurywealth.com	901-850-5532		401
Century Wireline Services 1223 S 71st E Ave ... Tulsa OK 74112 *Web:* www.centurywirelineservices.com	918-838-9811		536
Century-National Insurance Co 16650 Sherman Way PO Box 3999 ... Van Nuys CA 91406-3782 *TF Cust Svc:* 800-894-8384 ■ *Web:* www.centurynational.com	818-760-0880		391-4
CenturyTel Inc 100 Centurylink Dr PO Box 4065 ... Monroe LA 71211 *NYSE: CTL* ■ *TF:* 877-290-5458 ■ *Web:* www.centurylink.com	318-388-9000		360-3
Cenveo Inc 200 First Stamford Pl 2nd Fl ... Stamford CT 06902 *NYSE: CVO* ■ *Web:* www.cenveo.com	203-595-3000		263
Cenvill Recreation Inc 1601 Forum Pl Ste 500 W Palm Beach ... West Palm Beach FL 33401 *Web:* www.cenrec.com	561-640-3133		463
CEO (Center for Equal Opportunity) 14 Pidgeon Hill Dr Ste 500 ... Sterling VA 20165 *Web:* www.ceousa.org	703-421-5443	421-6401	634
CEO Inc 412 Louise Ave ... Charlotte NC 28204 *Web:* ceoinc.com	704-372-4701		193
CEOExpress Co 1 Broadway 14th Fl ... Cambridge MA 02142 *TF:* 800-333-7680 ■ *Web:* www.ceoexpress.com	617-482-1200	225-4440	397
Cepeda Systems & Software Analysis Inc 2225 Drake Ave SW Ste 8 ... Huntsville AL 35805 *Web:* www.cepedasystems.com	256-428-8186		179
Cephasonics Inc 160 Saratoga Ave Ste 180 ... Santa Clara CA 95051 *Web:* www.cephasonics.com	408-249-4629		201
Cepheid 904 E Caribbean Dr ... Sunnyvale CA 94089 *NASDAQ: CPHD* ■ *TF:* 888-838-3222 ■ *Web:* www.cepheid.com	408-541-4191	541-4192	419
Cepstral LLC 1801 E Carson St 2nd Fl ... Pittsburgh PA 15203 *Web:* www.cepstral.com	412-432-0400		177
Ceptaris Therapeutics Inc 101 Lindenwood Dr Ste 400 ... Malvern PA 19355	610-975-9290		231
Cequence Energy Ltd 215 Ninth Ave SW Ste 1400 ... Calgary AB T2P1K3 *Web:* www.cequence-energy.com	403-229-3050		536
Cequent Towing Products 47774 Anchor Ct W ... Plymouth MI 48170 **Fax Area Code:* 734 ■ *TF:* 800-521-0510 ■ *Web:* www.draw-tite.com	800-521-0510	656-3009*	763
Cequent Trailer Products 1050 Indianhead Dr ... Mosinee WI 54455 *TF:* 800-604-9466 ■ *Web:* www.fultonperformance.com	715-693-1700	693-1799	763
CERAGEM Co Inc 3699 Wilshire Blvd Ste 930 ... Los Angeles CA 90010 *TF:* 800-903-9333 ■ *Web:* www.ceragem.com	213-480-7070	480-7071	475
Ceragon Networks Ltd 5916 Stone Creek Dr Ste 110 ... The Colony TX 75056 *NASDAQ: CRNT* ■ **Fax Area Code:* 214 ■ *Web:* www.ceragon.com	201-845-6955	494-6080*	735
Cerami & Associates Inc 404 Fifth Ave ... New York NY 10018 *Web:* www.ceramiassociates.com	212-370-1776		261
Ceramic Technology Inc 606 Wardell Industrial Pk ... Cedar Bluff VA 24609 *TF:* 800-437-1142 ■ *Web:* ceramictech.net	800-437-1142		567
Ceramo Company Inc 681 Kasten Dr ... Jackson MO 63755 *TF:* 800-325-8303 ■ *Web:* www.ceramousa.com	573-243-3138	243-3130	334
CeramTec North America Corp Technology Pl ... Laurens SC 29360 *TF:* 800-752-7325 ■ *Web:* www.ceramtec.com	864-682-3215	682-1140	249
CERATECH Inc 1500 N Beauregard St Ste 320 ... Alexandria VA 22311 *Web:* www.ceratechinc.com	703-894-1130		183
Cerberus Capital Management LP 875 Third Ave ... New York NY 10022 *Web:* www.cerberuscapital.com	212-891-2100		405
CERC (Columbia Environmental Research Ctr) 4200 New Haven Rd ... Columbia MO 65201 *TF:* 888-283-7626 ■ *Web:* www.cerc.usgs.gov	573-875-5399	876-1896	668
Cereal Food Processors Inc 2001 Shawnee Mission Pkwy ... Mission Woods KS 66205 *TF:* 800-728-7511 ■ *Web:* www.cerealfood.com	913-890-6300		296-23
Ceredo-Kenova Public Library 1200 Oak St ... Kenova WV 25530 *Web:* www.wcpl.lib.wv.us	304-453-2462	453-2462	434-3
Ceregenics Inc 999 18th St Ste 3000 ... Denver CO 80202 **Fax Area Code:* 855 ■ *Web:* www.ceregenics.com	303-274-9101	237-3436*	463
Ceres Chamber of Commerce 2491 Lawrence St ... Ceres CA 95307 *Web:* www.cereschamber.com	209-537-2601		139
Ceres Consulting LLC 3808 Cookson Rd E St Louis ... St Louis IL 62201 *Web:* www.ceresbarge.com	618-271-7903		313
Ceres Courier 138 S Center St ... Turlock CA 95380 *Web:* cerescourier.com	209-537-5032	537-0543	532-4
Ceres Environmental 3825 85th Ave N ... Minneapolis MN 55443 *Web:* www.ceresenvironmental.com	763-488-5621		683
Ceres Solutions LLP 2112 Indianapolis Rd PO Box 432 ... Crawfordsville IN 47933 *TF General:* 800-878-0952 ■ *Web:* ceresllp.com	765-362-6700	362-7010	275
Ceres Technology Group Inc 2985 Sterling Court Ste A ... Boulder CO 80301 *Web:* www.boulderpcs.com	303-440-6963		180
Ceres Terminals Inc 2 Tower Ctr Blvd ... East Brunswick NJ 08816 *Web:* www.ceresglobal.com	201-974-3800	974-3850	465

Phone | Fax | Class

Cereus Graphics Printing Co
2950-2 E Broadway Rd........................Phoenix AZ 85040 602-445-0681 627
Web: cereusgraphics.com
Cerex Advanced Fabrics Inc
610 Chemstrand Rd......................Cantonment FL 32533 850-968-0100 745-6
TF: 800-572-3739 ■ *Web:* www.cerex.com
Ceri Linden LLC 180 Linden St................Wellesley MA 02482 781-416-0900 157-6
Web: ceriboutique.com
Ceridian Benefits Services Inc
3201 34th St S........................St. Petersburg FL 33711 727-864-3300 195
Web: www.ceridian.com
Cermetek Microelectronics Inc
374 Turquoise St...........................Milpitas CA 95035 408-752-5000 942-1346 173-3
TF: 800-882-6271 ■ *Web:* www.cermetek.com
Cernan Earth & Space Ctr
2000 N Fifth Ave Triton College.............River Grove IL 60171 708-456-0300 598
TF: 800-972-7000 ■ *Web:* www.triton.edu
Cerner Corp
2800 Rockcreek Pkwy................North Kansas City MO 64117 816-221-1024 178-11
NASDAQ: CERN ■ *TF:* 888-827-7220 ■ *Web:* www.cerner.com
Ceros Financial Services Inc
1445 Research Blvd Ste 530..................Rockville MD 20850 866-842-3356 690
TF: 866-842-3356 ■ *Web:* www.cerosfs.com
Cerow & Company CPA'S PA
1801 Sarno Rd Ste 3......................Melbourne FL 32935 321-242-2511 2
Cerrell Assoc Inc
320 N Larchmont Blvd....................Los Angeles CA 90004 323-466-3445 466-8653 636
Web: www.cerrell.com
Cerritos Chamber of Commerce
13259 S St...............................Cerritos CA 90703 562-467-0800 467-0840 139
Web: www.cerritos.org
Cerritos Civic Ctr
18025 Bloomfield Ave........................Cerritos CA 90703 562-916-1350 916-1375 434-3
TF: 866-402-7433 ■ *Web:* www.cerritos.us
Cerritos College 11110 Alondra Blvd............Norwalk CA 90650 562-860-2451 467-5068* 162
**Fax:* Admitting ■ *TF:* 800-829-1040 ■ *Web:* www.cerritos.edu
Cerritos Ctr for the Performing Arts
12700 Ctr Ct Dr...........................Cerritos CA 90703 562-916-8501 916-8514 572
TF: 800-300-4345 ■ *Web:* www.cerritoscenter.com
Cerro Coso Community College
Bishop 4090 W Line St..........................Bishop CA 93514 760-872-1565 872-5319* 162
**Fax:* Admissions ■ *TF:* 888-537-6932 ■ *Web:* www.cerrocoso.edu
Indian Wells Valley
3000 College Heights Blvd...............Ridgecrest CA 93555 760-384-6100 384-6377* 162
**Fax:* Admissions ■ *TF:* 888-537-6932 ■ *Web:* www.cerrocoso.edu
Kern River Valley
5520 Lake Isabella Blvd................Lake Isabella CA 93240 760-379-5501 379-5547* 162
**Fax:* Admissions ■ *TF:* 888-537-6932 ■ *Web:* www.cerrocoso.edu
Mammoth
101 College Pkwy PO Box 1865......Mammoth Lakes CA 93546 760-934-2875 924-1613* 162
**Fax:* Admissions ■ *TF:* 888-537-6932 ■ *Web:* www.cerrocoso.edu
South Kern 140 Methusa Ave.................Edwards AFB CA 93524 661-258-8644 258-0651* 162
**Fax:* Admissions ■ *TF:* 888-537-6932 ■ *Web:* www.cerrocoso.edu/sk
Cerro Fabricated Products Inc
300 Triangle Dr.........................Weyers Cave VA 24486 540-234-9252 234-8416 482
Web: www.cerrofabricated.com
Cerro Flow Products Inc
PO Box 66800..........................Saint Louis MO 63166 618-337-6000 337-6958 490
TF: 888-237-7611 ■ *Web:* www.cerroflow.com
Cerro Gordo County
220 N Washington Ave...................Mason City IA 50401 641-421-3065 421-3072 338
Web: co.cerro-gordo.ia.us
Cerro Wire & Cable Company Inc
1099 Thompson Rd SE.....................Hartselle AL 35640 256-773-2522 013
TF: 800-523-3869 ■ *Web:* www.cerrowire.com
Cersosimo Lumber Co Inc
1103 Vernon St...........................Brattleboro VT 05301 802-254-4508 477-6585* 683
**Fax Area Code:* 413 ■ *TF:* 800-326-5647 ■ *Web:* www.cersosimolumber.com
CERT (Computer Emergency Response Team)
4500 Fifth Ave 4500 Fifth Ave.............Pittsburgh PA 15213 412-268-7090 268-6989 668
TF: 800-598-6831 ■ *Web:* www.cert.org
Certain Affinity Inc 7620 Guadalupe St...........Austin TX 78752 512-524-8510 225
Web: www.certainaffinity.com
CertainTeed Corp
750 E Swedesford Rd...................Valley Forge PA 19482 610-341-7000 389
TF Prod Info: 800-782-8777 ■ *Web:* www.certainteed.com
CertainTeed Gypsum
2424 Lakeshore Rd W...................Mississauga ON L5J1K4 905-823-9881 823-4860 347
TF: 800-233-8990 ■ *Web:* www.certainteed.com
CertaPro Painters Ltd
150 Green Tree Rd Ste 1003....................Oaks PA 19456 800-689-7271 189-8
TF: 800-689-7271 ■ *Web:* www.certapro.com
Certec Consulting Inc
4037 N Harvard Ave.................Arlington Heights IL 60004 847-253-8968 180
Web: www.certecconsulting.com
Certex USA Inc 1721 W Culver St...............Phoenix AZ 85007 602-271-9048 492
TF: 800-225-2103 ■ *Web:* www.certex.com
Certicom Corp
4701 Tahoe Blvd Bldg A................Mississauga ON L4W0B5 905-507-4220 507-4230 178-12
TF: 800-561-6100 ■ *Web:* www.certicom.com
Certif-a-gift Company the
1625 E Algonquin Rd................Arlington Heights IL 60005 847-718-0300 459
Web: certif-a-gift.com
Certified Alloy Products Inc
3245 Cherry Ave PO Box 90.................Long Beach CA 90801 562-595-6621 485
TF: 800-421-3763 ■ *Web:* doncasters.com
Certified Business Brokers Ltd
12141 Wickchester Ln Ste 200................Houston TX 77092 713-680-1200 41
Web: www.certifiedbb.com
Certified Enameling Inc
3342 Emery St............................Los Angeles CA 90023 323-264-4403 481
Web: www.certifiedenameling.com
Certified Financial Planner Board of Standards Inc
1425 K St NW Ste 500...................Washington DC 20005 202-379-2200 379-2299 49-2
TF: 800-487-1497 ■ *Web:* www.cfp.net
Certified Freight Logistics Inc
1344 White Ct..........................Santa Maria CA 93458 805-925-9900 311
Web: driveforcfl.com
Certified Horsemanship Assn (CHA)
1795 Alysheba Way Ste 7102.................Lexington KY 40509 859-259-3399 255-0726 48-3
TF: 800-399-0138 ■ *Web:* www.cha-ahse.org
Certified Languages International LLC
4800 SW Macadam Ave Ste 400................Portland OR 97239 800-362-3241 768
TF: 800-362-3241 ■ *Web:* www.certifiedlanguages.com
Certified Metal Finishing Inc
1420 SW 28th Ave....................Pompano Beach FL 33069 954-979-0707 481
Web: certifiedmetalfinishing.com
Certified Oil Corp 949 King Ave.............Columbus OH 43212 614-421-7500 68
Web: certifiedoil.com
Certified Plumbing of Brevard
1401 Pennykamp St NE.....................Palm Bay FL 32907 321-676-0812 610
Web: www.certpah.com
Certified Power Inc 970 Campus Dr..........Mundelein IL 60060 847-573-3800 573-3832 620
TF: 888-905-7411 ■ *Web:* www.certifiedpower.com
Certified Restoration DryCleaning Network LLC
2060 Coolidge Hwy............................Berkley MI 48072 800-963-2736 246-7868* 310
**Fax Area Code:* 248 ■ *TF:* 800-963-2736 ■ *Web:* crdn.com
Certified Safety Manufacturing Inc
1400 Chestnut Ave......................Kansas City MO 64127 816-483-9090 476
TF: 800-854-9091 ■ *Web:* www.certifiedsafetymfg.com
Certified Semen Services
401 Bernadette Dr PO Box 1033..............Columbia MO 65203 573-445-4406 446-2279 11-2
Web: www.naab-css.org
Certified Slings & Supply Inc
PO Box 180127..........................Casselberry FL 32718 407-331-6677 260-9196 385
Web: www.certifiedslings.com
Certified Stainless Service Inc
2704 Railroad Ave.............................Ceres CA 95307 209-537-4747 480
Web: www.west-mark.com
Certified Transmission Rebuilders Inc
1801 S 54th St..............................Omaha NE 68106 402-558-2117 62-6
Web: www.certifiedtransmission.com
Certipay 199 Ave B NW Ste 270..........Winter Haven FL 33881 863-299-2400 299-2131 2
TF: 000-422-3702 ■ *Web:* www.certipay.com
Certis USA LLC
9145 Guilford Rd Ste 175....................Columbia MD 21046 800-250-5024 604-7015* 280
**Fax Area Code:* 301 ■ *TF:* 800-250-5024 ■ *Web:* www.certisusa.com
Certus International Inc
9 Cedarwood Dr Ste 8.........................Bedford NH 03110 603-627-1212 193
TF: 800-969-3218 ■ *Web:* www.certusintl.com
Cerus Corp 2550 Stanwell Dr..................Concord CA 94520 925-288-6000 288-6001 85
NASDAQ: CERS ■ *TF:* 800-401-1957 ■ *Web:* www.cerus.com
Cervantes 3318 S Mill Ave......................Tempe AZ 85282 480-921-9113 671
Web: cervantesrestaurant.com
Cerwin-Vega Inc 3000 SW 42nd St...........Hollywood FL 33312 954-316-1501 316-1590 52
Web: www.cerwinvega.com
CES (IEEE Consumer Electronics Society)
445 Hoes Ln.............................Piscataway NJ 08854 732-562-3844 981-9019 49-19
Web: cesoc.ieee.org
Ces Machine Products Inc
8880 Double Diamond Pkwy....................Reno NV 89521 775-852-0900 454
Web: www.cesmachine.com
Ces Mail Communications Inc
2319 Atlantic Ave............................Raleigh NC 27604 919-833-5785 5
Web: www.cesmail.com
Ces Network Services Inc
920 County Rd 376.........................Barksdale TX 78828 972-241-3683 261
TF: 800-873-4161 ■ *Web:* www.cesnetser.com
CES USA Inc
235 Remington Blvd Ste H.................Bolingbrook IL 60440 630-296-8939 463
Web: www.cesltd.com
Cesare Inc 7108 S Alton Way Bldg B...........Centennial CO 80112 303-220-0300 261
Web: cesareinc.com
CESD Talent Agency Inc
10635 Santa Monica Blvd Ste 130........Los Angeles CA 90025 310-475-2111 731
Web: www.cesdtalent.com
Cesium Telecom Inc 5798 Ferrier..............Montreal QC H4P1M7 514-798-8686 736
TF: 877-798-8686 ■ *Web:* www.cesiumonline.com
Ceso Inc 8534 Yankee St Ste 2B.................Dayton OH 45458 937-435-8584 261
Web: cesoinc.com
Cessco Fabrication & Engineering Ltd
7310-99 St..............................Edmonton AB T6E3R8 780-433-9531 432-7899 480
TF: 800-272-9698 ■ *Web:* www.cessco.ca
Cessford Construction Co
3808 Old Hwy 61.........................Burlington IA 52601 319-753-2297 753-0926 503-5
Web: www.omgmidwest.com
Cessna Aircraft Co 1 Cessna Blvd..............Wichita KS 67215 316-517-6000 517-7250 20
Web: cessna.txtav.com
CET Engineering Services
1240 N Mountain Rd......................Harrisburg PA 17112 717-541-0622 261
Web: ghd.com
Cetac Technologies Inc
14306 Industrial Rd..........................Omaha NE 68144 402-733-2829 733-5292 419
TF: 800-369-2822 ■ *Web:* www.teledynecetac.com
CETCO (Colloid Environmental Technologies Co)
2870 Forbs Ave.......................Hoffman Estates IL 60192 847-851-1899 527-9948* 3
**Fax Area Code:* 800 ■ *TF:* 800-527-9948 ■ *Web:* www.cetco.com
CETCO Energy Services Company LLC
1001 Ochsner Blvd Ste 425.................Covington LA 70433 985-871-4700 538
Web: cetcoenergyservices.com
Cetera Financial Group Inc
200 N Sepulveda Blvd Ste 1200.............El Segundo CA 90245 866-489-3100 690
TF: 866-489-3100 ■ *Web:* www.cetera.com
Cetylite Industries 9051 River Rd..........Pennsauken NJ 08110 856-665-6111 231
Web: www.cetylite.com
Cev Multimedia Ltd 1020 SE Loop 289..........Lubbock TX 79404 806-745-8820 514
TF: 877-610-5017 ■ *Web:* www.cevmultimedia.com
CEVA Ground US LP 15390 Vickery Dr...........Houston TX 77032 281-227-5000 311
Web: www.selectscg.com
CEVA Inc 1174 Castro St Ste 210...........Mountain View CA 94040 650-417-7900 696
Web: www.ceva-dsp.com
Ceva Logistics US Holdings Inc
10751 Deerwood Park Blvd 201.............Jacksonville FL 32256 904-928-1400 311
Web: cevalogistics.com
CExchange Inc
1100 Venture Ct Ste 120...................Carrollton TX 75006 972-695-2060 695-2079 393

	Phone	Fax	Class
CF Industries Inc 4 Pkwy N Ste 400 Deerfield IL 60015 *TF:* 800-462-8565 ■ *Web:* www.cfindustries.com	847-405-2400	405-2711	280
CF Jordan Construction LLC 7700 CF Jordan Dr El Paso TX 79912 *Web:* jordanfosterconstruction.com	915-877-3333	877-3999	186
CF Martin & Company Inc 510 Sycamore St PO Box 329 Nazareth PA 18064 *TF:* 888-433-9177 ■ *Web:* www.martinguitar.com	610-759-2837	759-5757	527
CF Napa 2787 Napa Valley Coporate Dr Napa CA 94558 *Web:* www.cfnapa.com	707-265-1891	265-1899	393
CF Roark Welding & Engineering Company Inc 136 N Green St Brownsburg IN 46112 *Web:* www.roarkfab.com	317-852-3163		256
CFA (Consumer Federation of America) 1620 I St NW Ste 200 Washington DC 20006 *TF:* 877-382-4357 ■ *Web:* www.consumerfed.org	202-387-6121	265-7989	48-10
CFA Institute 915 E High St Charlottesville VA 22902 *TF:* 800-247-8132 ■ *Web:* www.cfainstitute.org	434-951-5499	951-5262	49-2
Cfan Co 1000 Technology Way San Marcos TX 78666 *Web:* www.cfan.com	512-353-2832		22
CFBank 565 Main St Wellsville OH 14895 *NASDAQ: CFBK* ■ *TF:* 866-668-4606 ■ *Web:* www.cfbankonline.com	330-666-7979	666-7959	360-2
CFBR-FM 100.3 (CR) 18520 Stony Plain Rd Ste 100 Edmonton AB T5S2E2 *Web:* www.iheartradio.ca/100-3-the-bear	780-486-2800		645-52
CFC Canadoil Inc 8000 Market St Ste 100 Houston TX 77029 *Web:* www.cfcfittings.com	713-676-0077		492
CFC Farm & Home Ctr 15172 Brandy Rd PO Box 2002 Culpeper VA 22701 *TF:* 800-284-2667 ■ *Web:* www.cfcfarmhome.com/Locations/culpeper.aspx	540-825-2200	825-2200	280
CFC Inc 320 W Eigth St Ste 200 Bloomington IN 47402 *Web:* www.cfcproperties.com	812-332-0053	333-4680	653
CFC International Inc 500 State St Chicago Heights IL 60411 *TF:* 800-393-4505 ■ *Web:* www.cfcintl.com	708-891-3456	758-5989	3
CFC Technology 7100 Northland Cir Ste 305 Brooklyn Park MN 55428 *Web:* www.cfctechnology.com	763-235-5300		196
CFCA (Christian Foundation for Children & Aging) 1 Elmwood Ave Kansas City KS 66103 *TF:* 800-875-6564 ■ *Web:* unbound.org	913-384-6500	384-2211	48-6
CFCC (Cuyahoga Falls Chamber of Commerce) 151 Portage Trl Ste 1 Cuyahoga Falls OH 44221 *TF:* 800-248-4040 ■ *Web:* cfchamber.com	330-929-6756	929-4278	139
CFCU Community Credit Union 1030 Craft Rd Ithaca NY 14850 *TF:* 800-428-8340 ■ *Web:* mycfcu.com	607-257-8500		219
CFE Equipment Corp 818 Widgeon Rd Norfolk VA 23513 *Web:* www.cfeequipment.com	757-858-2660		358
CFG (Creative Financial Group) 16 Campus Blvd Newtown Square PA 19073 *TF:* 800-893-4824 ■ *Web:* creativefinancialgroup.com	610-325-6100	325-6240	401
CFG Community Bank 1422 Clarkview Rd Baltimore MD 21209 *TF:* 866-619-1417 ■ *Web:* www.cfgcommunitybank.com	410-823-0500	823-6685	70
CFHS (Canadian Federation of Humane Societies) 30 Concourse Gate Ste 102 Ottawa ON K2E7V7 *TF:* 888-678-2347 ■ *Web:* cfhs.ca	613-224-8072		48-3
CFI Group 625 Avis Dr Ann Arbor MI 48108 *Web:* www.cfigroup.com	734-930-9090		194
CFI Manufacturing Inc 2150 Whitfield Ave Sarasota FL 34243	941-751-1000		319-4
Cfi Mechanical Inc 6109 Brittmoore Rd Houston TX 77041 *Web:* cfimechanical.com	832-467-8200	467-8203	610
CFI Tire Service 1520 E S Omaha Bridge Rd Council Bluffs IA 51503 *Web:* cfitirecb.com	712-388-9744		57
Cfj Manufacturing 5001 N Fwy Ste E Fort Worth TX 76106 *TF:* 800-527-6938 ■ *Web:* www.cfjmanufacturinglp.com	817-625-9559		226
CFM Partners Inc 4435 Macomb St NW Washington DC 20016 *Web:* www.cfmpartners.com	202-364-2380		194
CFMA (Construction Financial Management Assn) 100 Village Blvd Ste 200A Princeton NJ 08540 *TF:* 877-462-7827 ■ *Web:* www.cfma.org	609-452-8000	452-0474	49-1
CFNY-FM 102.1 (Alt) 25 Dock Side Dr Toronto ON M5A0B5 *TF:* 800-242-0100 ■ *Web:* www.edge.ca	416-870-3343		645-165
CFO Connection LLC, The 15 Oakland St Newburyport MA 01950 *Web:* www.thecfoconnection.com	978-255-1236		41
CFO Magazine 253 Summer St Boston MA 02210 *TF:* 800-772-1119 ■ *Web:* ww2.cfo.com	617-345-9700		457-5
CFO Selections LLC 310 120th Ave NE Ste 101 Bellevue WA 98005 *Web:* www.cfoselections.com	206-686-4480		260
CFO Strategies LLC 2221 Arbutus St Newport Beach CA 92660	949-338-9394		194
Cfocus Software Inc 10536 joyceton dr Largo MD 20774 *TF:* 800-883-2055 ■ *Web:* www.cfocussoftware.com	301-499-2650		396
CFOs 2Go Inc 500 Ygnacio Valley Rd Ste 410 Walnut Creek CA 94596 *Web:* www.2gocompanies.com	925-299-4450		463
CFRA-AM 580 (N/T) 87 George St Ottawa ON K1N9H7 *TF:* 800-580-2372 ■ *Web:* www.iheartradio.ca/580-cfra	613-789-2486		645-117
CFS Bancorp Inc 707 Ridge Rd Munster IN 46321 *NASDAQ: CITZ* ■ **Fax Area Code: 317* ■ *Web:* www.firstmerchants.com	219-513-5123	770-7572*	360-2
CFS II Inc 2488 E 81st St Ste 500 Tulsa OK 74137 *Web:* www.cfstwo.com	918-394-3950		393
CFS Investment Advisory Services LLC 97 Lackawanna Ave Ste 101 Totowa NJ 07512 *Web:* www.cfsias.com	973-826-8800		401
CFU (Croatian Fraternal Union of America) 100 Delaney Dr Pittsburgh PA 15235 *Web:* www.croatianfraternalunion.org	412-843-0380	823-1594	48-14
CFVMC (Cape Fear Valley Medical Ctr) 1638 Owen Dr PO Box 2000 Fayetteville NC 28304 *Web:* www.capefearvalley.com	910-609-4000		374-3
CFW Associated Engineers Inc 9200 Leesgate Rd Ste 200 Louisville KY 40222 *Web:* cfwengineers.com	502-423-0805		256
CFX Inc 55 Broadway Ste 2608 New York NY 10006 *Web:* www.cfx.com	212-431-5800		463
CG Automation 60 Fadem Rd Springfield NJ 07081 *Web:* www.qeiinc.com	973-379-7400	379-2138	173-2
Cg Design Concepts 1150 N Highland Ave Ste 3 Fullerton CA 92835 *Web:* www.cgdesignconcepts.com	714-871-7342		344
CG Life 657 West Lake St 5th Fl Chicago IL 60661 *Web:* cglife.com	860-226-6000	226-5400	7
CG Power Systems USA Inc 1 Pauwels Dr Washington MO 63090 *Web:* cgglobal.com	636-239-9300		767
CG Schmidt Inc 11777 West Lake Pk Dr Milwaukee WI 53224 *TF:* 800-248-1254 ■ *Web:* www.cgschmidt.com	414-577-1177	577-1155	186
C&G Systems Corp 320 E Main St Lake Zurich IL 60047 *Web:* www.cgsystems.com	847-816-9700		480
CGA (Compressed Gas Assn) 4221 Walney Rd 5th Fl Chantilly VA 20151 *TF:* 800-783-7890 ■ *Web:* www.cganet.com	703-788-2700	961-1831	49-13
CGA Engineers Inc 8179 E 41st St Tulsa OK 74145 *Web:* cgaengineers.com	918-749-5800		256
Cga Law Firm 106 Harrisburg St East Berlin PA 17316 *TF:* 800-447-5375 ■ *Web:* www.cgalaw.com	717-848-4900		428
CGF Industries Inc 2420 N Woodlawn Bldg 100 Ste A Wichita KS 67220 *Web:* www.cgcpi.com	316-691-4500		360-3
CGH (Coral Gables Hospital Inc) 3100 Douglas Rd Coral Gables FL 33134 *TF:* 866-728-3677 ■ *Web:* www.coralgableshospital.com	305-445-8461	441-6879	374-3
CGH Medical Ctr (CGHMC) 100 E LeFevre Rd Sterling IL 61081 *TF:* 800-625-4790 ■ *Web:* www.cghmc.com	815-625-0400	625-4825	374-3
CGHMC (CGH Medical Ctr) 100 E LeFevre Rd Sterling IL 61081 *TF:* 800-625-4790 ■ *Web:* www.cghmc.com	815-625-0400	625-4825	374-3
CGI Communications Inc 130 E Main St Rochester NY 14604 *TF:* 800-398-3029 ■ *Web:* www.cgicommunications.com	585-427-0020		514
CGI Federal Inc 12601 Fair Lks Cir Fairfax VA 22033 *Web:* www.cgi.com/en/us-federal/services-solutions	703-227-6000		196
CGI Group Inc 1130 Sherbrooke St W 7th Fl Montreal QC H3A2M8 *TSE: GIB/A* ■ *TF:* 800-828-8377 ■ *Web:* www.cgi.com	514-841-3200	841-3299	180
Cgi Interactive Communications Inc 76 Otis St Westborough MA 01581 *Web:* www.cgiinteractive.com	508-898-2500		809
CGLA Infrastructure Inc 1827 Jefferson Pl NW Washington DC 20036 *Web:* www.cg-la.com	202-776-0990		194
CGM (China Grill Management Inc) 60 W 53rd St New York NY 10019 *Web:* www.chinagrillmgt.com	212-333-7788		670
CGM Funds 38 Newbury St Ste 8 Boston MA 02116 *TF:* 800-345-4048 ■ *Web:* www.cgmfunds.com	617-859-7714		528
CGM Inc 1445 Ford Rd Bensalem PA 19020 *TF:* 800-523-6570 ■ *Web:* www.cgmbuildingproducts.com	215-638-4400	638-7949	135
Cgn & Assoc Inc 415 SW Washington St Peoria IL 61602 *TF:* 888-746-4246 ■ *Web:* www.cgnglobal.com	309-495-2100		194
CGNAD (Compass Group North American Div) 2400 Yorkmont Rd Charlotte NC 28217 *TF:* 800-357-0012 ■ *Web:* www.compass-usa.com	704-328-4000		299
CGR Products Inc 4655 US Hwy 29 N Greensboro NC 27405 *TF:* 877-313-6785 ■ *Web:* www.cgrproducts.com	336-621-4568	375-5324	326
CGRMC (Casa Grande Regional Medical Ctr) 1800 E Florence Blvd Casa Grande AZ 85122 *Web:* bannerhealth.com/casagrande	520-381-6300	381-6435	374-3
CGS (Council of Graduate Schools) 1 Dupont Cir NW Ste 230 Washington DC 20036 *TF:* 800-297-3775 ■ *Web:* www.cgsnet.org	202-223-3791	331-7157	49-5
Cgs Motorsports 3227 Producer Way Ste 134 Pomona CA 91768 *Web:* www.cgsmotorsports.com	909-444-5536		393
CGS Technology Associates Inc 242 Old New Brunswick Rd Ste 420 Piscataway NJ 08854 *Web:* www.cgsonline.com	732-750-4141		180
CGX Energy Inc 333 Bay St Ste 1100 Toronto ON M5H2R2 *Web:* www.cgxenergy.com	416-364-5569		536
CH (Clarion Hospital) 1 Hospital Dr Clarion PA 16214 *TF:* 800-522-0505 ■ *Web:* www.clarionhospital.org	814-226-9500	226-1224	374-3
CH Briggs Hardware Company Inc 2047 Kutztown Rd Reading PA 19605 *Web:* www.chbriggs.com	610-929-6969		350
CH Ellis Co Inc 2432 SE Ave Indianapolis IN 46201 *TF Sales:* 800-466-3351 ■ *Web:* www.chellis.com	317-636-3351	635-5140	453
CH Energy Group Inc 284 S Ave Poughkeepsie NY 12601 *NYSE: CHG* ■ *TF:* 800-527-2714 ■ *Web:* www.chenergygroup.com	845-452-2000		360-5
CH Evans Brewing Co at the Albany Pump Station 19 Quackenbush Sq Albany NY 12207 *Web:* www.evansale.com	518-447-9000		671
CH Fenstermaker & Associates LLC 135 Regency Sq Lafayette LA 70508 *Web:* www.fenstermaker.com	337-237-2200		302
CH Guernsey & Co 5555 N Grand Blvd Oklahoma City OK 73112 *Web:* www.guernsey.us	405-416-8100	416-8111	261
CH Hanson Co 2000 N Aurora Rd Naperville IL 60563 *TF:* 800-827-3398 ■ *Web:* www.chhanson.com	630-848-2000	848-2515	467
CH Perez & Assoc Consulting Engineers in 9594 NW 41st St Ste 201 Doral FL 33178 *Web:* p-a.cc	305-592-1070		256
CH Powell Co 75 Shawmut Rd Canton MA 02021 *Web:* chpowell.com	781-302-7300		311
CH Products 970 Pk Ctr Dr Vista CA 92081 *Web:* www.chproducts.com	760-598-2518	598-2524	173-1

Phone | Fax | Class

CH Robinson Worldwide Inc
14701 Charlson Rd ... Eden Prairie MN 55347 952-683-3950 449
NASDAQ: CHRW ■ *TF Cust Svc:* 855 229 6128 ■ *Web:* www.chrobinson.com

CH Technologies (USA) Inc
263 Center Ave Ste 1 ... Westwood NJ 07675 201-666-2335 419
Web: www.envmed.com

CH2M Hill Cos Ltd 9191 S Jamica St ... Englewood CO 80112 303-771-0900 286-9250* 192
**Fax Area Code:* 720 ■ *TF:* 800-585-8367 ■ *Web:* www.ch2m.com

CHA (Certified Horsemanship Assn)
1795 Alysheba Way Ste 7102 ... Lexington KY 40509 859-259-3399 255-0726 48-3
TF: 800-399-0138 ■ *Web:* www.cha-ahse.org

CHA (Catholic Health Assn of the US)
4455 Woodson Rd ... Saint Louis MO 63134 314-427-2500 427-0029 49-8
TF: 800-230-7823 ■ *Web:* www.chausa.org

CHA (Craft & Hobby Assn)
319 E 54th St ... Elmwood Park NJ 07407 201-835-1200 797-0657 48-18
TF: 800-822-0494 ■ *Web:* www.craftandhobby.org

CHA (Community Hospital Anderson)
1515 N Madison Ave ... Anderson IN 46011 765-298-4242 374-3
TF: 800-777-7775 ■ *Web:* www.communityanderson.com

Cha Cha Cha 656 N Virgil Ave ... Los Angeles CA 90004 323-664-7723 664-7769 671
Web: www.theoriginalchachacha.com

CHA Industries 4201 Business Ctr Dr ... Fremont CA 94538 510-683-8554 683-3848* 386
**Fax:* Sales ■ *Web:* www.chaindustries.com

Cha! Cha! Cha! 1208 NW Glisan St ... Portland OR 97209 503-221-2111 671
Web: chachachapdx.com

ChaatCafe.com 1902 University Ave ... Berkeley CA 94704 510-845-1431 671
Web: www.chaatcafes.com

Chabot College 25555 Hesperian Blvd ... Hayward CA 94545 925-485-5215 162
Web: www.chabotcollege.edu

Chabot Space & Science Ctr
10000 Skyline Blvd ... Oakland CA 94619 510-336-7300 336-7491 520
TF: 800-704-9804 ■ *Web:* www.chabotspace.org

Chabot Steve (Rep R - OH)
2371 Rayburn HOB ... Washington DC 20515 202-225-2216 225-3012 342-2
Web: chabot.house.gov

Chace Ruttenberg & Freedman LLP
Wayland Bldg 1 Park Row Ste 300 ... Providence RI 02903 401-453-6400 445
Web: www.crfllp.com

Chaco Culture National Historical Park
PO Box 220 ... Nageezi NM 87037 505-786-7014 786-7061 564
TF: 877-642-4743 ■ *Web:* www.nps.gov/chcu

Chad Mission 129 E 36th St ... New York NY 10016 212-986-0980 784

Chad Stephens Inc Dba Comfort Solutions
1470 Wall Ave ... Ogden UT 84404 801-393-2206 189-10

Cha-Da Thai 420-J Jonestown Rd ... Winston-Salem NC 27104 336-659-8466 671
Web: chadathai-nc.com

Chadbourne & Parke Llp
30 Rockefeller Plaza ... New York NY 10112 212-408-5100 41
Web: www.chadbourne.com

CHADD (Children & Adults with Attention-Deficit/Hyperactivity Disorder)
8181 Professional Pl Ste 150 ... Landover MD 20785 301-306-7070 306-7090 48-17
TF: 800 233 4050 ■ *Web:* www.chadd.org

Chadderton Trucking Inc 40 Stewart Way ... Sharon PA 16146 724-981-5050 981-1615 780
TF: 800-327-6868 ■ *Web:* www.chaddertontrucking.com

Chaddsford Winery
632 Baltimore Pk ... Chadds Ford PA 19317 610-388-6221 50-7
Web: www.chaddsford.com

Chadick Ellig Inc 300 Pk Ave ... New York NY 10022 212-688-8671 266
Web: www.chadickellig.com

Chadron State College 1000 Main St ... Chadron NE 69337 308-432-6000 432-6229 166
TF: 800-242-3766 ■ *Web:* www.csc.edu

Chadron State Park 15951 Hwy 385 ... Chadron NE 69337 308-432-6167 565
Web: outdoornebraska.gov

Chadwick Martin Bailey Inc
179 S St 3rd Fl ... Boston MA 02111 617-350-8922 466
Web: www.cmbinfo.com

Chadwick's of Boston 500 Bic Dr Bldg 4 ... Milford CT 06461 877-330-3393 459
TF: 877-330-3393 ■ *Web:* www.chadwicks.com

Chaffee County 104 Crestone Ave ... Salida CO 81201 719-539-4004 539-8588 338
TF: 800-423-1108 ■ *Web:* www.chaffeecounty.org

Chaffetz Jason (Rep R - UT)
2236 Rayburn HOB ... Washington DC 20515 202-225-7751 225-5629 342-2
Web: chaffetz.house.gov

Chaffetz Lindsey LLP
1700 BRdway 33rd Fl ... New York NY 10019 212-257-6960 428
Web: www.chaffetzlindsey.com

Chaffey College
5885 Haven Ave ... Rancho Cucamonga CA 91737 909-652-6000 162
TF: 800-535-2421 ■ *Web:* www.chaffey.edu

Chagrin Consulting Services
24800 Chagrin Blvd Ste 207 ... Beachwood OH 44122 216-514-3301 463
Web: www.chagrinconsulting.com

Chagrin Valley Chamber of Commerce
83 N Main St ... Chagrin Falls OH 44022 440-247-6607 139
Web: www.cvcc.org

Chahinkapa Zoo Park & Carousel
1004 RJ Hughes Dr ... Wahpeton ND 58075 701-642-8709 642-9285 823
TF: 800-342-4671 ■ *Web:* www.wahpetonpark.com

Chain Drug Marketing Assn (CDMA)
43157 W Nine-Mile Rd PO Box 995 ... Novi MI 48376 248-449-9300 449-9396 49-18
TF: 800-935-2362 ■ *Web:* www.chaindrug.com

Chain O'Lakes State Park
8916 Wilmot Rd ... Spring Grove IL 60081 847-587-5512 565
Web: www.dnr.illinois.gov/Parks/Pages/ChainOLakes.aspx

Chain O'Lakes State Park 2355 E 75 S ... Albion IN 46701 260-636-2654 565
Web: www.in.gov

Chain Store Guide
10117 Princess Palm Ave Ste 375 ... Tampa FL 33610 800-927-9292 627-6888* 637-6
**Fax Area Code:* 813 ■ *TF:* 800-927-9292 ■ *Web:* www.chainstoreguide.com

Chainsaw Inc
1017 N Las Palmas Ave ... Los Angeles CA 90038 323-785-1550 514
Web: www.chainsawedit.com

Chair King Inc, The
5405 W Sam Houston Pkwy N ... Houston TX 77041 713-690-1919 321
Web: www.chairking.com

Chairish 1657 Defoor Ave NW ... Atlanta GA 30318 404-351-5717 321

Chair-man Mills Inc 501 Consumers Rd ... Toronto ON M2J5E2 416-391-0400 205
Web: www.chairmanmills.com

Chakeres Theatres Inc
200 N Murray St ... Springfield OH 45503 937-323-6447 748
Web: www.chakerestheatres.com

Chakra Communications Inc
80 W Drullard Ave ... Lancaster NY 14086 716-505-7300 627
Web: www.chakracentral.com

Chalet Basque 200 Oak St ... Bakersfield CA 93304 661-327-2915 671

Chalfant Manufacturing Company
50 Pearl Rd Ste 212 ... Brunswick OH 44212 330-273-3510 273-8149 816
Web: www.chalfant-obo.com/docs/frmHome.aspx

Chalk & Vermilion Fine Arts Inc
55 Old Post Rd Ste 2 ... Greenwich CT 06830 203-869-9500 637-10
TF: 800-877-2250 ■ *Web:* www.chalk-vermilion.com

Chalkboard, The 1324 S Main St ... Tulsa OK 74119 918-582-1964 671
Web: chalkboardtulsa.com

Chalker Flores LLP
14951 N Dallas Pkwy Ste 400 ... Dallas TX 75254 214-866-0001 866-0010 428
Web: www.chalkerflores.com

Challenge Dairy Products Inc
11875 Dublin Blvd Ste B230 ... Dublin CA 94568 925-828-6160 551-7591 296-3
Web: www.challengedairy.com

Challenge Enterprises of North Florida Inc
3530 Enterprise Way ... Green Cove Springs FL 32043 904-284-9859 631
TF: 800-226-6356 ■ *Web:* www.ccar.org

Challenge Graphics Corp
16611 Roscoe Pl ... North Hills CA 91343 818-892-0123 532-3
Web: www.challenge-graphics.com

Challenge Management Inc (CMI)
4230 LBJ Fwy Ste 414 ... Dallas TX 75244 972-755-2560 755-2561 47
Web: www.challenge-management.com

Challenge Printing Co, The
2 Bridewell Pl ... Clifton NJ 07014 973-471-4700 627
TF: 800-654-1234 ■ *Web:* www.challengeprintingco.com

Challenge Publications Inc
9509 Vassar Ave Ste A ... Chatsworth CA 91311 818-700-6868 700-6282 637-9
TF: 800-562-9182 ■ *Web:* www.challengeweb.com

Challenged Athletes Foundation
9591 Waples St ... San Diego CA 92121 858-866-0959 305
Web: www.challengedathletes.org

Challenger Ctr for Space Science Education
422 First St SE 3rd Fl ... Washington DC 20003 202-827-1580 969-5747* 48-11
**Fax Area Code:* 800 ■ *TF General:* 800-969-5747 ■ *Web:* www.challenger.org

Challenger Gray & Christmas Inc
150 S Wacker Dr Ste 2800 ... Chicago IL 60606 312-332-5790 193
TF: 855-242-3424 ■ *Web:* www.challengergray.com

Challenger Industries Inc 743 Hill Rd ... Dalton GA 30721 706-278-7707 131

Challenger Learning Ctr (CLC)
316 Washington Ave
Wheeling Jesuit University ... Wheeling WV 26003 304-243-2279 243-4397 520
TF: 800-624-6992 ■ *Web:* www.wju.edu/clc

Challenger Learning Ctr
701 Front Ave Coca-Cola Space Science Ctr ... Columbus GA 31901 706-649-1470 649-1478 520
Web: www.ccssc.org

Challenger Learning Ctr
2600-A Barhamville Rd ... Columbia SC 29204 803-929-3951 520
Web: www.richlandone.org

Challenger Lighting Company Inc
2475 Alft Ln ... Elgin IL 60124 847-717-4700 362
Web: challengerlighting.com

Chally Group Worldwide Inc
3123 Research Blvd ... Dayton OH 45420 937-259-1200 463
TF: 800-254-5995 ■ *Web:* chally.com

Chalmers & Kubeck Inc 150 Commerce Dr ... Aston PA 19014 610-494-4300 485-1484 454
TF: 800-242-5637 ■ *Web:* www.candk.com

Chalmers Group 6400 Northam Dr ... Mississauga ON L4V1J1 905-362-6400 61
Web: www.chalmersgroup.com

Chalmette Refining LLC
500 W Saint Bernard Hwy ... Chalmette LA 70043 504-281-1212 500
Web: www.chalmetterefining.com

Chama River Brewing Co
4939 Pan American Fwy ... Albuquerque NM 87109 505-342-1800 671
Web: www.chamariverbrewery.com

Chambar 562 Beatty St ... Vancouver BC V6B2L3 604-879-7119 671
Web: www.chambar.com

Chamber Discoveries Inc
1300 E Shaw Ave Ste 127 ... Fresno CA 93710 559-244-6600 772
Web: www.chamberdiscoveries.com

Chamber Music America (CMA)
305 Seventh Ave 5th Fl ... New York NY 10001 212-242-2022 242-7955 48-4
TF: 888-221-9836 ■ *Web:* www.chamber-music.org

Chamber Music Society of Lincoln Ctr
70 Lincoln Ctr Plaza ... New York NY 10023 212-875-5788 42
TF: 800-838-3006 ■ *Web:* www.chambermusicsociety.org

Chamber of Business & Industry of Centre County
200 Innovation Blvd Ste 150 ... State College PA 16803 814-234-1829 234-5869 139
TF: 877-234-5050 ■ *Web:* www.cbicc.org

Chamber of Commerce
200 Pocasset St ... Fall River MA 02721 508-676-8226 675-5932 139
Web: www.fallriverchamber.com

Chamber of Commerce
101 Bill Smith Blvd ... King of Prussia PA 19406 610-265-1776 265-0473 139
TF: 800-841-4141 ■ *Web:* montgomerycountychamber.org

Chamber of Commerce 195 Water St ... Naugatuck CT 06770 203-729-4511 729-4512 139
Web: www.waterburychamber.com

Chamber of Commerce - Grand Haven-Spring Lake-Ferrysburg
1 S Harbor Dr ... Grand Haven MI 49417 616-842-4910 842-0379 139
TF: 800-764-2836 ■ *Web:* www.grandhavenchamber.org

Chamber of Commerce - Murray-Calloway County, The
805 N 12th St ... Murray KY 42071 270-753-5171 139
Web: www.mymurray.com

Chamber of Commerce Mountain View
580 Castro St ... Mountain View CA 94041 650-968-8378 968-5668 139
Web: www.chambermv.org

Chamber of Commerce of Eastern Connecticut Inc
914 Hartford Tpke ... Waterford CT 06385 860-701-9113 139
Web: www.chamberect.com

Chamber of Commerce of Fargo Moorhead
202 First Ave N ... Moorhead MN 56560 218-233-1100 233-1200 139
Web: www.fmchamber.com

Name / Address	Phone	Fax	Class
Chamber of Commerce of Harrison County 111 W Walnut St. Corydon IN 47112 *Web:* www.harrisonchamber.org	812-738-0120	738-0500	139
Chamber of Commerce of Huntsville/Madison County 225 Church St. Huntsville AL 35801 *Web:* hsvchamber.org	256-535-2000	535-2015	139
Chamber of Commerce of Kitchener & Waterloo 80 Queen St N PO Box 2367. Kitchener ON N2H6L4 *Web:* www.greaterkwchamber.com	519-576-5000	742-4760	137
Chamber of Commerce of New Rochelle 459 Main St. New Rochelle NY 10801 *TF:* 800-841-4000 ■ *Web:* www.newrochellechamber.org	914-632-5700		139
Chamber of Commerce of Northwest Connecticut 333 Kennedy Dr Ste R101 PO Box 59. Torrington CT 06790 *TF:* 800-795-3272 ■ *Web:* www.nwctchamberofcommerce.org	860-482-6586	489-8851	139
Chamber of Commerce of Sandusky County 215 Croghan St. Fremont OH 43420 *TF:* 800-334-3886 ■ *Web:* www.scchamber.org	419-332-1591	332-8666	139
Chamber of Commerce of Smyth County 214 W Main St. Marion VA 24354 *Web:* www.smythchamber.org	276-783-3161		139
Chamber of Commerce of Southern New Jersey 4015 Main St. Voorhees NJ 08043 *TF:* 800-642-3780 ■ *Web:* www.chambersnj.com	856-424-7776	424-8180	139
Chamber of Commerce of Southwest Indiana 318 Main St Ste 401. Evansville IN 47708 *TF:* 800-317-8518 ■ *Web:* swinchamber.com	812-425-8147	421-5883	139
Chamber of Commerce of Southwestern Madison County 3600 Nameoki Rd Ste 202. Granite City IL 62040 *Web:* www.chamberswmadisoncounty.com	618-876-6400	876-6448	139
Chamber of Commerce of the Massapequas Inc 674 Broadway. Massapequa NY 11758 *TF:* 800-951-9774 ■ *Web:* massapequachamber.org	516-541-1443	541-8625	139
Chamber of Commerce of the Palm Beaches 401 N Flagler Dr. West Palm Beach FL 33401 *TF:* 800-275-8777 ■ *Web:* www.palmbeaches.org	561-833-3711	833-5582	139
Chamber of Commerce of the Tonawandas 254 Sweeney St. North Tonawanda NY 14120 *Web:* www.the-tonawandas.com	716-692-5120	692-1867	139
Chamber of Commerce of Ulster County 55 Albany Ave. Kingston NY 12401 *Web:* www.ulsterchamber.org	845-338-5100	338-0968	139
Chamber of Commerce of West Alabama 2200 University Blvd. Tuscaloosa AL 35401 *Web:* www.tuscaloosachamber.com	205-758-7588	391-0565	139
Chamber of Commerce serving Middletown Monroe & Trenton 1500 Central Ave. Middletown OH 45044 *TF:* 800-837-3200 ■ *Web:* thechamberofcommerce.org	513-422-4551	422-6831	139
Chamber of Medford/Jackson County 101 E Eigth St. Medford OR 97501 *Web:* www.medfordchamber.com	541-779-4847	776-4808	139
Chamber of Schenectady County 1473 Erie Blvd. Schenectady NY 12305 *Web:* www.schenectadychamber.org	518-372-5656		139
Chamber of Southern Saratoga County 58 Clifton Country Rd Ste 102. Clifton Park NY 12065 *TF:* 800-766-9001 ■ *Web:* www.southernsaratoga.org	518-371-7748	371-5025	139
Chamber of Southwest Florida 5621 Banner Dr Ste 114. Fort Myers FL 33912 *Web:* chamberswfl.com	239-433-4111	275-2103	139
Chamber Orchestra of Philadelphia 1520 Locust St Ste 500. Philadelphia PA 19102 *TF:* 800-732-0999 ■ *Web:* www.chamberorchestra.org	215-545-5451	545-3868	573-3
Chamber South 6410 SW 80th St. South Miami FL 33143 *TF:* 800-206-3715 ■ *Web:* www.chambersouth.com	305-661-1621	666-0508	139
Chamber/Southwest Louisiana 120 W Pujo St. Lake Charles LA 70601 *TF:* 800-829-3676 ■ *Web:* allianceswla.org	337-433-3632	436-3727	139
Chamberlain College of Nursing 11830 Westline Industrial Ste 106. Saint Louis MO 63146 *TF:* 888-556-8226 ■ *Web:* www.chamberlain.edu	314-991-6200		166
Chamberlain Group 845 Larch Ave. Elmhurst IL 60126 *Web:* www.chamberlaingroup.com	630-279-3600	530-6091	350
Chamberlain West Hollywood 1000 Westmount Dr. West Hollywood CA 90069 *TF:* 877-686-2082 ■ *Web:* www.chamberlainwesthollywood.com	310-657-7400	854-6744	379
Chamberlin Insurance Group Inc 485 Devon Park Dr. Wayne PA 19087	610-674-0999		390
Chamberlin Rubber Co 3333 Brighton-Henrietta Townline Rd. Rochester NY 14623 *Web:* www.chamberlinrubber.com	585-427-7780		370
Chambers County 404 Washington Ave. Anahuac TX 77514 *Web:* www.co.chambers.tx.us	409-267-8309	267-8315	338
Chambers Gasket & Manufacturing Co 4701 W Rice St. Chicago IL 60651 *TF:* 800-572-2479 ■ *Web:* www.chambersgasket.com	773-626-8800	626-1430	326
Chambers Group Inc 5 Hutton Centre Dr Ste 750. Santa Ana CA 92707 *Web:* www.chambersgroupinc.com	949-261-5414		194
Chambers Hotel 15 W 56th St. New York NY 10019 *Web:* www.chambershotel.com	212-974-5656	974-5657	379
Chambers of Commerce / Tourism 106 E Jefferson St. Tallahassee FL 32301 *TF:* 800-628-2866 ■ *Web:* www.visittallahassee.com	850-606-2305	606-2301	206
Chambersburg Hospital 112 N Seventh St. Chambersburg PA 17201 *Web:* www.summithealth.org	717-267-3000		374-3
ChamberWest 1241 W Village Main Dr Ste B. West Valley City UT 84119 *TF:* 800-448-2327 ■ *Web:* chamberwest.com	801-977-8755	977-8329	139
Chambre de Commerce de la Region Sherbrookoise 9 Rue Wellington S. Sherbrooke QC J1H5C8 *Web:* www.ccsherbrooke.com	819-822-6151	822-6156	137
Chambre de Commerce du Quebec 555 boul Ren,-L,vesque W Ste 1100. Montreal QC H2Z1B1 **Fax Area Code:* 514 ■ *Web:* www.fccq.ca	418-692-3853	844-0226*	137
Chambre de Commerce et d'Industrie du Quebec Metropolitain 17 rue Saint-Louis. Quebec QC G1R3Y8 *Web:* www.cciquebec.ca	418-692-3853	694-2286	137
Chambre de Commerce Haute-Yamaska Region (CDCHY) 90 Rue Robinson S Ste 102. Granby QC J2G7L4 *Web:* cchyr.ca	450-372-6100	372-3161	137
Chameleon Consulting Inc 89 Falmouth Rd W. Arlington MA 02474 *TF:* 866-903-7912 ■ *Web:* www.chamcon.com	781-646-2272		180
Chameleon Group LLC 951 Islington St. Portsmouth NH 03801 *TF:* 800-773-9182 ■ *Web:* www.chameleonsales.com	603-570-4300		196
Chameleon Like Inc 345 Kishimura Dr. Gilroy CA 95020 *TF:* 800-561-3357 ■ *Web:* www.chameleonlike.com	408-847-3661		627
Chameleon Technologies Inc 520 Kirkland Way Ste 101. Kirkland WA 98033 *Web:* www.chameleontechinc.com	425-827-1173		260
Chaminade 1 Chaminade Ln. Santa Cruz CA 95065 *TF:* 800-283-6569 ■ *Web:* www.chaminade.com	831-475-5600	476-4798	377
Chaminade College Preparatory School 425 S Lindbergh Blvd. Saint Louis MO 63131 *TF:* 877-378-6847 ■ *Web:* chaminade-stl.org	314-993-4400		622
Chaminade University 3140 Waialae Ave. Honolulu HI 96816 *TF:* 800-735-3733 ■ *Web:* www.chaminade.edu	808-735-4711		166
Chamizal National Memorial 800 S San Marcial St. El Paso TX 79905 *TF:* 877-642-4743 ■ *Web:* www.nps.gov	915-532-7273	532-7240	564
Chamlin & Assoc Inc 3017 Fifth St. Peru IL 61354 *Web:* chamlin.com	815-223-3344		261
Chamness Technology Inc 2255 Little Wall Lake Rd. Blairsburg IA 50034 *Web:* www.chamnesstechnology.com	515-325-6133		196
Champaign County 1776 E Washington St. Urbana IL 61802 *Web:* www.co.champaign.il.us	217-384-3776	384-3896	338
Champaign County 1512 S US Hwy 68 Ste A100. Urbana OH 43078 *Web:* www.co.champaign.oh.us	937 484 1611	484-1609	338
Champaign County Chamber of Commerce 1817 S Neil St Ste 201. Champaign IL 61820 *TF:* 800-328-1627 ■ *Web:* champaigncounty.org	217-359-1791	359-1809	139
Champaign County Chamber of Commerce 113 Miami St. Urbana OH 43078 *TF:* 877-873-5764 ■ *Web:* www.champaignohio.com	937-653-5764	652-1599	139
Champaign County Convention & Visitors Bureau 108 S Neil St. Champaign IL 61820 *TF:* 800-369-6151 ■ *Web:* www.visitchampaigncounty.org	217-351-4133		206
Champaign-Urbana Mass Transit District 1101 E University Ave. Urbana IL 61802 *Web:* www.cumtd.com	217-384-8188	384-8215	468
Champaign-Urbana Symphony Orchestra (CUSO) 701 Devonshire Dr Ste C-24. Champaign IL 61820 *Web:* www.cusymphony.org	217-351-9139		573-3
Champion A Gardner Denver Inc 1301 N Euclid Ave. Princeton IL 61356 *Web:* www.gardnerdenver.com	815-875-3321		172
Champion Aerospace LLC 1230 Old Norris Rd. Liberty SC 29657 *Web:* www.championaerospace.com	864-843-1162		22
Champion Aluminum Corp 140 Eileen Way. Syosset NY 11791 *Web:* www.championwindows.com	516-921-6200		234
Champion Awards and Apparel Inc 3649 Winplace Rd. Memphis TN 38118 *Web:* www.gochampion.net	901-365-4830		344
Champion Bus Inc 331 Graham Rd. Imlay City MI 48444 *TF:* 800-776-4943 ■ *Web:* www.championbus.com	810-724-6474		516
Champion Chemical Co 8319 S Greenleaf Ave. Whittier CA 90602 *TF:* 800-424-9300 ■ *Web:* www.championchemical.com	800-424-9300	898-8064	151
Champion Chevrolet Cadillac of Johnson City LLC 3606 Bristol Hwy. Johnson City TN 37601 *Web:* www.championjc.com	423-218-0317		57
Champion Cleaners 2548 Rocky Ridge Rd. Vestavia AL 35243 *Web:* www.championcleaners.com	205-824-7737		426
Champion Co 400 Harrison St. Springfield OH 45505 *Web:* www.thechampioncompany.com	937-324-5681	324-2397	198
Champion College Services Inc 7776 S Pointe Pkwy W Ste 250. Tempe AZ 85044 *TF:* 800-761-7376 ■ *Web:* www.championcollegeservices.com	480-947-7375		194
Champion Construction Corp 941 Forest Ave. Staten Island NY 10310 *Web:* www.championcc.homestead.com	718-818-8202	818-8238	685
Champion Container Corp 180 Essex Ave E. Avenel NJ 07001 *Web:* www.championcontainer.com	732-636-6700	855-8663	199
Champion Electric Inc 3950 Garner Rd. Riverside CA 92501 *TF:* 800-214-6438 ■ *Web:* www.championelec.com	951-276-9619		121
Champion Energy Corporation 175 Sunnyside Blvd. Plainview NY 11803 *Web:* www.championenergy.com	914-576-6190	576-6126	14
Champion Enterprises Management Co 755 W Big Beaver Rd Ste 1000. Troy MI 48084 *Web:* www.championhomes.com	910-814-4256		505
Champion Foods LLC 23900 Bell Rd. New Boston MI 48164 *Web:* www.championfoods.com	734-753-3663		296-36
Champion Graphics 3901 Virginia Ave. Cincinnati OH 45227 *TF:* 800-989-3901 ■ *Web:* champion-graphics.com	513-271-3800	271-5963	627
Champion Hotels LLC 3048 N Grand Blvd. Oklahoma City OK 73107 *Web:* www.championhotels.com	405-606-7400		378
Champion Industrial Contractors Inc 1420 Coldwell Ave PO Box 4399. Modesto CA 95350 *TF:* 800-431-2584 ■ *Web:* championindustrial.com	209-524-6601	524-6931	189-10
Champion Industries Inc PO Box 2968 PO Box 2968. Huntington WV 25728 *OTC:* CHMP ■ *TF:* 800-624-3431 ■ *Web:* champion-industries.com	304-528-2791	528-2746	627
Champion Laboratories Inc 200 S Fourth St. Albion IL 62806 *Web:* www.champlabs.com	618-445-6011		60

Phone | Fax | Class

Champion Lumber Co
1313 Chicago Ave Ste 100 .... Riverside CA 92507 951-684-5670 275-0825 191-3
Web: www.championlumber.net

Champion Mfg Industries Inc
6021 N Galena Rd .... Peoria IL 61614 309-685-1031 595

Champion Mill State Historical Park
73122 338 Ave .... Enders NE 69027 308-737-6577 565
Web: outdoornebraska.gov

Champion Photochemistry
7895 Tranmere Dr .... Mississauga ON L5S1V9 905-670-7900 670-2581 591
TF: 800-387-3430 ■ Web: www.championphotochemistry.com

Champion Power Equipment Inc
10006 Santa Fe Springs Rd .... Santa Fe Springs CA 90670 562-236-9422 61
TF: 877-338-0999 ■ Web: www.championpowerequipment.com

Champion Precast Inc 2441 N Hwy 61 .... Troy MO 63379 573-384-5855 183
Web: www.championprecast.com

Champion Preferred Automotive
2020 Lexington Rd .... Nicholasville KY 40356 859-269-4141 57
Web: www.championautos.com

Champion Safe Co Inc 2055 S Larsen Pkwy .... Provo UT 84606 801-377-7199 377-7195 361
Web: www.championsafe.com

Champion Shuffleboard Ltd
7216 Burns St .... Richland Hills TX 76118 972-595-5312 710
TF: 800-826-7856 ■ Web: www.championshuffleboard.com

Champion Site Prep LP
455-A Highway 195 .... Georgetown TX 78633 512-863-3453 863-3463 186
Web: www.idigdirt.com

Champion Solutions Group
791 Pk of Commerce Blvd Ste 200 .... Boca Raton FL 33487 561-997-2900 997-4043 174
TF: 800-771-7000 ■ Web: www.championsg.com

Champion Technologies Inc
845 Mckinley St .... Eugene OR 97402 800-547-6180 247
TF: 800-547-6180 ■ Web: www.stillchampion.com

Champion Window Mfg Inc
12121 Champion Way Cincinnati OH 45241 513-346-4600 346-4614 235
TF: 877-424-2674 ■ Web: www.championwindow.com

Champion-Arrowhead LLC
5147 Alhambra Ave .... Los Angeles CA 90032 323-221-9137 221-2579 609
TF: 800-332-4267 ■ Web: www.arrowheadbrass.com

Champions for Life Sports Ctr
453 Grant Ave Rd .... Auburn NY 13021 315-252-9305 711
Web: championsforlife.org

Champions Pipe & Supply Inc
2 NorthPoint Dr Ste 800 .... Houston TX 77060 713-468-6555 468-7936 612
TF: 800-299-6555 ■ Web: www.championspipe.com

Champions Real Estate Group LLC
6117 Richmond Ave Ste 120 .... Houston TX 77057 713-785-6666 652
Web: creg1.com

Champions Way Enterprises Inc
980 First St W .... North Vancouver BC V7P3N4 877-774-5425 809
TF: 877-774-5425 ■ Web: www.championsway.com

Champlain Cable Corp
175 Hercules Dr .... Colchester VT 05446 800-451-5162 814
TF: 800-451-5162 ■ Web: www.champcable.com

Champlain College 163 S Willard St .... Burlington VT 05401 802-860-2700 860-2767 166
TF: 800-570-5858 ■ Web: www.champlain.edu

Champlain Oil Company Inc
45 San Remo Dr .... South Burlington VT 05403 802-864-5380 579
Web: www.champlainoil.com

Champlain Valley Educational Services
PO Box 455 .... Plattsburgh NY 12901 518-561-0100 800
Web: www.cves.org

Champlain Valley Equipment Inc
453 Exchange St .... Middlebury VT 05753 802-388-4967 323
Web: www.champlainvalleyequipment.com

Champlain Valley Exposition
105 Pearl St .... Essex Junction VT 05452 802-878-5545 32
Web: www.cvph.org

Champlin Foundations, The
2000 Chapel View Blvd .... Cranston RI 02920 212-620-4230 305
TF: 800-424-9836 ■ Web: foundationcenter.org

Champps Americana
3100 Dodge St Best Western Midway .... Dubuque IA 52003 563-690-2040 671
Web: www.champpsdubuque.com

Champps Entertainment Inc
19111 Dallas Pkwy Ste 370 .... Dallas TX 75287 972-581-1171 670
Web: www.champps.com

Champs Sports 311 Manatee Ave W .... Bradenton FL 34205 715-261-9706 261-9550* 711
*Fax: Mktg ■ TF: 800-991-6813

Chance Rides Manufacturing Inc
4219 Irving .... Wichita KS 67209 316-945-6555 454
Web: www.chancerides.com

Chancellor Hotel on Union Square
433 Powell St .... San Francisco CA 94102 415-362-2004 362-1403 379
TF: 800-428-4748 ■ Web: www.chancellorhotel.com

Chand LLC 157 Hwy 654 .... Mathews LA 70375 985-532-2512 532-3262 770
TF: 800-777-5211 ■ Web: www.chand.com

Chandler Asset Management Inc
6225 Lusk Blvd .... San Diego CA 92121 858-546-3737 528
TF: 800-317-4747 ■ Web: www.chandlerasset.com

Chandler Chamber of Commerce
25 S Arizona Pl Ste 201 .... Chandler AZ 85225 480-963-4571 963-0188 139
TF: 800-963-4571 ■ Web: www.chandlerchamber.com

Chandler Chicco Agency
450 W 15th St 7th Fl .... New York NY 10011 212-229-8400 636
Web: www.ccapr.com

Chandler Concrete Company Inc
1006 S Church St PO Box 131 .... Burlington NC 27216 336-226-1181 226-2969 182
Web: www.chandlerconcrete.com

Chandler Ctr for the Arts
250 N Arizona Ave .... Chandler AZ 85225 480-782-2680 782-2684 572
TF: 800-946-4452 ■ Web: www.chandlercenter.org

Chandler Group Executive Search Inc
4165 Shoreline Dr Ste 220 .... Spring Park MN 55384 952-471-3000 260
TF: 800-642-9940 ■ Web: www.chandgroup.com

Chandler Hall Hospice 99 Barclay St .... Newtown PA 18940 215-860-4000 371
TF: 888-603-1973 ■ Web: ch.kendal.org

Chandler Industries Inc
1654 N Ninth St .... Montevideo MN 56265 320-269-8893 269-5827 482
TF: 800-269-5527 ■ Web: www.chandlerindustries.com

Chandler Inn 26 Chandler St .... Boston MA 02116 617-482-3450 542-3428 379
TF: 800-842-3450 ■ Web: www.chandlerinn.com

Chandler Instruments Company LLC
2001 N Indianwood Ave .... Broken Arrow OK 74012 918-250-7200 358
Web: www.chandlereng.com

Chandler Medical Ctr Library
500 S Limestone St .... Lexington KY 40506 859-323-5300 323-1040 434-1
Web: libraries.uky.edu

Chandler Packaging Inc
7595 Raytheon Rd .... San Diego CA 92111 858-292-9094 549
Web: www.chanpack.com

Chandler Properties
2799 California St .... San Francisco CA 94115 415-921-5733 652
Web: chandlerproperties.com

Chandler Public Library
22 S Delaware St .... Chandler AZ 85225 480-782-2800 782-2823 434-3
Web: www.chandlerlibrary.org

Chandler Regional Medical Center
1955 W Frye Rd .... Chandler AZ 85224 480-728-3000 374-3
TF: 844-803-9002 ■ Web: hospitals.dignityhealth.org

Chandler's Crabhouse
901 Fairview Ave N .... Seattle WA 98109 206-223-2722 671
Web: www.schwartzbros.com/chandlers-crabhouse

Chandler-Gilbert Community College
Pecos 2626 E Pecos Rd .... Chandler AZ 85225 480-732-7000 732-7099* 162
*Fax: Admissions ■ Web: www.cgc.maricopa.edu
Williams 7360 E Tahoe Ave .... Mesa AZ 85212 480-988-8000 988-8993 162
Web: www.cgc.maricopa.edu

Chandlers Plywood Products Inc
3716 Waverly Rd .... Huntington WV 25704 304-429-1311 115
Web: www.chandlerkitchens.com

Chanel Inc 15 E 57th St .... New York NY 10022 212-355-5050 574
TF: 800-550-0005 ■ Web: www.chanel.com

Chanen Construction Company Inc
3300 N Third Ave .... Phoenix AZ 85013 602-266-3600 186
TF: 800-458-6253 ■ Web: www.srchanen.com

Chaney & Associates
230 Highview Ave .... Pittsburgh PA 15238 412-767-0307 196
Web: www.chaneyassociates.com

Chaney Enterprises
12480 Mattawoman Dr PO Box 548 .... Waldorf MD 20604 301-932-5000 183
TF: 888-244-0411 ■ Web: www.chaneyenterprises.com

Chaney Instrument Co 965 Wells St .... Lake Geneva WI 53147 877-221-1252 201
TF: 877-221-1252 ■ Web: www.chaneyinstrument.com

Chaney Systems Inc
5100 S Calhoun Rd .... New Berlin WI 53151 262-679-6000 180
Web: www.chaney.net

Chaney's Music Exchange
1501 N Main St .... Walnut Creek CA 94596 925-933-6310 526
Web: www.listentocds.com

Chang & Boos 1305 11th St Ste 301 .... Bellingham WA 98225 360-671-5945 428
TF: 800-925-1875 ■ Web: www.americanlaw.com

Change Companies, The
5221 Sigstrom Dr .... Carson City NV 89706 775-885-2610 196
TF: 888-889-8866 ■ Web: www.changecompanies.net

Changes Salon & Day Spa Inc
1475 N Broadway .... Walnut Creek CA 94596 925-947-1814 77
Web: changessalon.com

Changfeng Energy Inc
32 S Unionville Ave Ste 2036 .... Markham ON L3R9S6 647-313-0066 313-0088 536
Web: www.changfengenergy.com

Changing Hands Bookstore
6428 S McClintock Dr .... Tempe AZ 85283 480-730-0205 730-1196 95
Web: www.changinghands.com

Changing Our World Inc
220 E 42nd St 5th Fl .... New York NY 10017 212-499-0866 317
Web: www.changingourworld.com

Channahon State Park PO Box 54 .... Channahon IL 60410 815-467-4271 565
Web: www.dnr.illinois.gov/parks/pages/channahon.aspx

Channel 45 WHFT TV 3324 Pembroke Rd ...... Hollywood FL 33021 954-962-1700 741
TF: 800-447-7235 ■ Web: tbn.org

Channel 96.1 801 Wood Ridge Ctr Dr .... Charlotte NC 28217 704-714-9444 645-33
Web: 1029thelake.iheart.com

Channel Building Company Inc
355 Middlesex Ave .... Wilmington MA 01887 978-657-7300 186
TF: 800-786-1210 ■ Web: www.channelbuilding.com

Channel Islands Aviation
305 Durley Ave Camarillo Airport .... Camarillo CA 93010 805-987-1301 987-8301 63
TF: 800-947-4228 ■ Web: www.flycia.com

Channel Islands National Park
1901 Spinnaker Dr .... Ventura CA 93001 805-658-5730 658-5799 564
Web: www.nps.gov

Channel Islands Surfboards Inc
36 Anacapa St .... Santa Barbara CA 93101 805-966-7213 711
Web: www.cisurfboards.com

Channel Partners LLC 10 Holland Dr .... Irvine CA 92618 949-472-6711 597-2278 195

Channel Products Inc
7100 Wilson Mills Rd .... Chesterland OH 44026 440-423-0113 423-1502 202
Web: www.channelproducts.com

Channel Solutions LLC
3145 E Chandler Blvd Ste 110 .... Phoenix AZ 85048 866-501-9690 196
TF: 866-501-9690 ■ Web: www.cscorp-us.com

Channel Systems Inc 74 98th Ave .... Oakland CA 94603 510-568-7170 186
Web: www.channelsystems.com

Channell 26040 Ynez Rd .... Temecula CA 92591 951-719-2600 296-2322 647
OTC: CHNL ■ Web: www.channell.com

Channellock Inc 1306 S Main St .... Meadville PA 16335 800-724-3018 962-2583 758
TF Cust Svc: 800-724-3018 ■ Web: www.channellock.com

ChannelMeter Inc
1061 Market St Ste 508 .... San Francisco CA 94103 415-578-0714 387
Web: channelmeter.com

Channelnet 3 Harbor Dr Ste 206 .... Sausalito CA 94965 415-332-4704 332-1635 177
Web: www.channelnet.com

Channing Bete Co
1 Community Pl .... South Deerfield MA 01373 413-665-7611 499-6464* 637-10
*Fax Area Code: 800 ■ *Fax: Cust Svc ■ TF: 800-477-4776 ■ Web: www.channing-bete.com

Name / Address	City	State	Zip	Phone	Fax	Class
Channing House 850 Webster St. *Web:* www.channinghouse.org	Palo Alto	CA	94301	650-327-0950		672
Chant Engineering 59 Industrial Dr. *TF:* 888-567-0983 ■ *Web:* www.chantengineering.com	New Britain	PA	18901	215-230-4260		454
Chanterelle 2 Harrison St	New York	NY	10013	212-966-6143		671
Chanticleer Garden 786 Church Rd. *Web:* www.chanticleergarden.org	Wayne	PA	19087	610-687-4163	293-0149	97
Chanticleer Inn 1458 E Dollar Lake Rd *TF:* 800-752-9193 ■ *Web:* www.chanticleerinn.com	Eagle River	WI	54521	715-479-4486	479-0004	669
Chantiers Chibougamau Ltd 521 Chemin Merrill PO 216 *Web:* www.chibou.com	Chibougamau	QC	G8P2K7	418-748-6481		817
Chantland-MHS 502 Seventh St N. *Web:* www.chantland.com	Dakota City	IA	50529	515-332-4045		697
Chantland-Pvs Co, The PO Box 69 *Web:* www.chantlandpulley.com	Humboldt	IA	50548	515-332-4040	332-4923	207
Chao & Company Ltd 8460 Tyco Rd Ste E *Web:* www.chaoco.com	Vienna	VA	22182	703-847-4380		194
Chao Pra Ya Thai Cuisine 580 Adams St	Eugene	OR	97402	541-344-1706		671
CHAP (Community Health Accreditation Program Inc) 1275 K St NW Ste 800 *TF:* 800-656-9656 ■ *Web:* www.chapinc.org	Washington	DC	20005	202-862-3413	862-3419	48-1
Chapa Elementary School 5670 N Doffing Rd *Web:* lajoyaisd.com	Mission	TX	78574	956-580-6150		685
Chapala 136 Oakway ctr *Web:* chapalamex.com	Eugene	OR	97401	541-434-6113		671
Chaparral Boats Inc 300 Industrial park Blvd *Web:* www.chaparralboats.com	Nashville	GA	31639	229-686-7481	686-3660	90
Chaparral Communications Inc 950 S Bascom Ave Ste 3111 *Web:* www.chaparral.net	San Jose	CA	95128	408-294-2900	294-6969	647
Chaparral Elementary School 451 Chaparral Dr	Claremont	CA	91711	909-398-0305		685
Chaparral Energy Inc 701 Cedar Lake Blvd. *TF:* 866-478-8770 ■ *Web:* www.chaparralenergy.com	Oklahoma City	OK	73114	405-478-8770		538
Chaparral Gold Corp 7950 E Acoma Dr Ste 211 *TSE: IMZ*	Scottsdale	AZ	85260	480-483-9932	483-9926	502
Chaparral High School 1600 N Cuyamaca St *Web:* chaparral.guhsd.net	El Cajon	CA	92020	619-956-4600		685
Chapco Inc 10 Denlar Dr *Web:* www.chapcoinc.com	Chester	CT	06412	860-526-9535		697
Chapel Hill Public Library 100 Library Dr *Web:* chapelhillpubliclibrary.org	Chapel Hill	NC	27514	919-968-2777		434-3
Chapel Hill/Orange County Visitors Bureau 501 W Franklin St. **Fax Area Code:* 919 ■ *TF:* 888-968-2060 ■ *Web:* www.visitchapelhill.org	Chapel Hill	NC	27516	888-968-2060	968-2062*	206
Chapel Hill-Carrboro Chamber of Commerce 104 S Estes Dr *TF:* 800-694-9784 ■ *Web:* www.carolinachamber.org	Chapel Hill	NC	27515	919-967-7075	968-6874	139
Chapel Hills Mall 1710 Briargate Blvd *Web:* www.chapelhillsmall.com	Colorado Springs	CO	80920	719-594-0111		460
Chapel Steel Co 590 N Bethlehem Pk *TF:* 800-570-7674 ■ *Web:* www.chapelsteel.com	Lower Gwynedd	PA	19002	215-793-0899	793-0919	454
Chapel Valley Landscape Co 3275 Jennings Chapel Rd. *Web:* www.chapelvalley.com	Woodbine	MD	21797	301-924-5400		422
Chapelwood United Methodist Church 11140 Greenbay St. *TF:* 800-317-0787 ■ *Web:* www.chapelwood.org	Houston	TX	77024	713-465-3467		366
Chapin & Bangs Co, The 165 River St *Web:* www.cbsteel.com	Bridgeport	CT	06604	203-333-4183		492
Chapin Davis Investments 2 Village Sq Ste 200 *Web:* www.chapindavis.com	Baltimore	MD	21210	410-435-3200		691
Chapin Hall Center For Children 1313 E 60th St *Web:* www.chapinhall.org	Chicago	IL	60637	773-753-5900		652
Chapin International Inc 700 Ellicott St. *Web:* www.chapinmfg.com	Batavia	NY	14021	585-343-3140		172
Chapin Memorial Library 400 14th Ave N. *Web:* www.cityofmyrtlebeach.com	Myrtle Beach	SC	29577	843-918-1275	918-1288	434-3
Chapin School 100 E End Ave *Web:* www.chapin.edu	New York	NY	10028	212-744-2335		623
Chaplaincy Health Care 2108 W Entiat Ave. *Web:* www.tricitieschaplaincy.org	Kennewick	WA	99336	509-783-7416	735-7850	371
Chaplins Bellevue Subaru-volkswagen 15000 SE Eastgate Way *Web:* www.chaplins.com	Bellevue	WA	98007	425-641-2002		57
Chapman & Intrieri LLP 2236 Mariner Sq Dr Ste 300. *Web:* chapmanandintrieri.com	Alameda	CA	94501	510-864-3600		428
Chapman Associates 16 E Schaumburg Rd Ste 3. *Web:* www.chapman-usa.com	Schaumburg	IL	60194	847-884-0010		41
Chapman Corp 331 S Main St. *Web:* www.chapmancorporation.com	Washington	PA	15301	724-228-1900		189-10
Chapman Cubine Adams + Hussey 2000 15th St N Ste 550 *TF:* 800-222-2962 ■ *Web:* www.ccah.com	Arlington	VA	22201	703-248-0025	248-0029	317
Chapman Engineering Corp 2321 Cape Cod Way. *TF:* 800-511-9300 ■ *Web:* www.chapmanengineering.com	Santa Ana	CA	92703	714-542-1942		697
Chapman Medical Ctr 2601 E Chapman Ave. *Web:* www.chapman-gmc.com	Orange	CA	92869	714-633-0011		374-3

Name / Address	City	State	Zip	Phone	Fax	Class
Chapman Mfg Company Inc PO Box 359 *Web:* www.chapmanco.com	Avon	MA	02322	508-588-3200	587-7592	439
Chapman State Park 4790 Chapman Dam Rd *Web:* www.dcnr.state.pa.us	Clarendon	PA	16313	814-723-0250		565
Chapman University 1 University Dr **Fax:* Admissions ■ *TF:* 888-282-7759 ■ *Web:* www.chapman.edu	Orange	CA	92866	714-997-6815	997-6713*	166
Chapman/Leonard Studio Equipment Inc 12950 Raymer St *TF:* 888-883-6559 ■ *Web:* www.chapman-leonard.com	North Hollywood	CA	91605	818-764-6726	764-6730	722
Chappell Farms Inc 166 Boiling Springs Rd *TF:* 800-438-4834 ■ *Web:* www.chappellfarms.com	Barnwell	SC	29812	803-584-2565	584-3676	315-3
Chappell's Restaurant & Sports Museum 323 Armour Rd. *Web:* chappellsrestaurant.com	North Kansas City	MO	64116	816-421-0002		671
Chapter IV Investors 301 S Tryon St Ste 1850. *Web:* www.chapterivinvestors.com	Charlotte	NC	28202	704-644-4070		317
Chapters Health System west 12470 Telecom Dr Ste 100 *TF:* 866-204-8611 ■ *Web:* www.chaptershealth.org	Temple Terrace	FL	33637	813-871-8111		371
Char Thai 5039 Fifth St.	Tucson	AZ	85711	520-795-1715		671
CharacTell Ltd 34 Wessex Rd *Web:* www.charactell.com	Newton Center	MA	02459	617-965-1014		41
Characters 10257 105th St *Web:* www.characters.ca	Edmonton	AB	T5J1E3	780-421-4100	425-1550	671
Charbon Steakhouse 450 Gare du Palais (old port) *Web:* charbonsteakhouse.com	Quebec	QC	G1K3X2	418-522-0133		671
Char-Broil 1442 Belfast Ave *TF:* 800-241-7548 ■ *Web:* www.charbroil.com	Columbus	GA	31902	800-241-7548		36
Chardon Laboratories Inc 7300 Tussing Rd. *TF:* 888-660-1724 ■ *Web:* chardonlabs.com	Reynoldsburg	OH	43068	888-660-1724		743
CHARGED.fm 10 Jay St *TF:* 800-346-0538 ■ *Web:* www.charged.fm	Brooklyn	NY	11201	646-490-2700		224
Chargeurs Wool USA 178 Wool Rd.	Jamestown	SC	29453	843-257-2212		745-9
Chariho Regional School District 455 Switch Rd *Web:* www.chariho.k12.ri.us	Wood River Junction	RI	02894	401-364-7575	415-6076	685
Chariot Eagle Inc 931 NW 37th Ave *Web:* www.charioteagle.com	Ocala	FL	34475	352-629-7007	629-6920	505
Charisma Magazine 600 Rinehart Rd. *TF:* 800-749-6500 ■ *Web:* www.charismamag.com	Lake Mary	FL	32746	407-333-0600	333-7100	457-18
Chariton County 306 S Cherry St *Web:* www.rootsweb.ancestry.com	Keytesville	MO	65261	660-288-3273		338
Chariton Valley Electric Co-op 2090 Hwy 5 PO Box 486. *TF:* 800-475-1702 ■ *Web:* www.cvrec.com	Albia	IA	52531	641-932-7126		245
Charity Home Health Services Inc 500 Carson Plaza Ste 228. *Web:* charityhhs.com	Carson	CA	90746	310-527-4339		363
CharityUSA.com LLC 600 University St Ste 1000 One Union Square *TF:* 888-811-5271 ■ *Web:* www.charityusa.com	Seattle	WA	98101	206-268-5400	264-8448	387
Charivari 2521 Bagby St. *Web:* www.charivarirest.com	Houston	TX	77006	713-521-7231		671
Charkit Chemical Corp 32 Haviland St Unit 1 *TF:* 800-424-9300 ■ *Web:* www.charkit.com	Norwalk	CT	06854	203-299-3220	299-1355	146
Charles & Colvard Ltd 170 Southport Dr *NASDAQ: CTHR* ■ *TF:* 800-210-4367 ■ *Web:* www.moissanite.com	Morrisville	NC	27560	919-468-0399		411
Charles & Emma Frye Free Public Art Museum 704 Terry Ave *TF:* 800-758-7459 ■ *Web:* www.fryemuseum.org	Seattle	WA	98104	206-622-9250		520
Charles & Helen Schwab Foundation 1650 S Amphlett Blvd Ste 300 *Web:* www.schwabfoundation.org	San Mateo	CA	94402	650-655-2410	655-2411	305
Charles A & Anne Morrow Lindbergh Foundation 2150 Third Ave N Ste 310. *Web:* www.lindberghfoundation.org	Anoka	MN	55303	763-576-1596		48-13
Charles A Hones Inc 355 Rte 49 PO Box 405 *Web:* www.charlesahones.com	Cleveland	NY	13042	631-842-8886	842-9300	357
Charles A. Lindbergh State Park 1615 Lindbergh Dr S *TF:* 888-646-6367 ■ *Web:* www.dnr.state.mn.us	Little Falls	MN	56345	320-616-2525	616-2526	565
Charles Agapiou Ltd 9017 Santa Monica Blvd. *Web:* www.rollsandbentley.com	West Hollywood	CA	90069	310-274-6201		62
Charles Allis Art Museum 1801 N Prospect Ave *Web:* www.cavtmuseums.org	Milwaukee	WI	53202	414-278-8295		520
Charles Bond Company 11 Green St PO Box 105. **Fax Area Code:* 888 ■ *TF:* 800-922-0125 ■ *Web:* www.bondgear.com	Christiana	PA	17509	610-593-5171	922-0125*	709
Charles Bowman & Company Inc 3328 John F Donnelly Dr *Web:* www.charlesbowman.com	Holland	MI	49424	616-786-4000	786-2864	238
Charles C Brandt Construction Co 1505 N Sherman Dr *Web:* www.ccbrandt.com	Indianapolis	IN	46201	317-375-1111	375-4321	186
Charles C Thomas Publisher 2600 S First St *TF Sales:* 800-258-8980 ■ *Web:* www.ccthomas.com	Springfield	IL	62704	217-789-8980	789-9130	637-2
Charles C. Parks Co 500 Belvedere Dr. *TF:* 800-873-2406 ■ *Web:* www.charlescparks.com	Gallatin	TN	37066	615-452-2406	451-4212	297-11
Charles City Forest Products 2200 Barnetts Rd *Web:* ccforestproducts.com	Providence Forge	VA	23140	804-966-2336		683
Charles Cole Memorial Hospital 1001 E Second St. *Web:* www.colememorial.org	Coudersport	PA	16915	814-274-9300		374-3
Charles County 200 Baltimore St *Web:* www.charlescountymd.gov	La Plata	MD	20646	301-645-0600	645-0560	338

Phone | Fax | Class

Charles County Chamber of Commerce
101 Centennial St Ste A...La Plata MD 20646 301-932-6500 932-3945 139
TF: 800-992-3194 ■ Web: www.charlescountychamber.org

Charles Craft Inc
21381 Charles Craft Ln...Laurinburg NC 28352 910-844-3521 844-9333 745-9
Web: www.charlescraftinc.com/contactus.html

Charles d Hankey Law Office PC
434 E New York St...Indianapolis IN 46202 317-634-8565 428
TF: 800-520-3633 ■ Web: www.hankeylawoffice.com

Charles David of California
5731 Buckingham Pkwy...Culver City CA 90230 310-348-5050 301

Charles DeWeese Construction Inc
765 Industrial By Pass PO Box 504...Franklin KY 42135 270-586-9122 186
TF: 800-404-6064 ■ Web: www.charlesdeweeseconstruction.com

Charles Dunn Co Inc
800 W Sixth St 6th Fl...Los Angeles CA 90017 213-683-0500 652
Web: www.charlesdunn.com

Charles E Egeler Correctional Facility
3855 Cooper St...Jackson MI 49201 517-780-5600 780-5814 213
TF: 855-444-3911 ■ Web: www.michigan.gov/corrections

Charles E Gillman Co
907 E Frontage Rd...Rio Rico AZ 85648 520-281-1141 281-1372 815
TF: 800-783-2589 ■ Web: www.gillman.com

Charles E Jarrell Contracting
4208 Rider Trail N...Earth City MO 63045 314-291-0100 697
Web: www.jarrellcontracting.com

Charles E Lakin Enterprises
8990 W Dodge Rd Ste 225...Omaha NE 68114 402-393-5550 655

Charles E Reed & AssocPC
3636 Professional Dr...Port Arthur TX 77642 409-983-3277 2

Charles Eisen & Assoc Inc
595 S Broadway Ste 110E...Denver CO 80209 303-744-3200 321
Web: www.egg-and-dart.com

Charles F Evans Company Inc
800 Canal St...Elmira NY 14901 607-734-8161 733-5422 189-12
Web: evansroofingcompany.com

Charles F Kettering Memorial Hospital
3535 Southern Blvd...Kettering OH 45429 937-298-4331 374-3
TF: 800-250-4511 ■ Web: www.ketteringhealth.org

Charles G Lawson Trucking
7815 Mobile Hwy...Hope Hull AL 36043 334-284-3220 780

Charles Gabus Ford Inc
4545 Merle Hay Rd...Des Moines IA 50310 515-270-0707 57
TF Sales: 800-934-2287 ■ Web: charlesgabusford.com

Charles GG Schmidt & Company Inc
301 W Grand Ave...Montvale NJ 07645 201-391-5300 391-3565 758
TF: 800-724-6438 ■ Web: www.cggschmidt.com

Charles Gojer & Associates Inc
11615 Forest Central Dr...Dallas TX 75243 214-340-1199 261
TF: 800-544-4576 ■ Web: www.cgojer.com

Charles H West Farms Inc
2953 Tub Mill Pond Rd...Milford DE 19963 302-335-3936 10-11

Charles H Wright Museum of African American History
315 E Warren Ave...Detroit MI 48201 313-494-5800 494-5855 520
Web: thewright.org

Charles Hayden Foundation
140 Broadway...New York NY 10005 212-785-3677 305
Web: foundationcenter.org

Charles Hayden Planetarium
1 Science Pk...Boston MA 02114 617-723-2500 589-0362 598
Web: www.mos.org

Charles Hosmer Morse Museum of American Art
445 N Pk Ave...Winter Park FL 32789 407-645-5311 647-1284 520
Web: www.morsemuseum.org

Charles Hotel Harvard Square
1 Bennett St...Cambridge MA 02138 617-864-1200 864-5715 379
TF: 800-882-1818 ■ Web: www.charleshotel.com

Charles Industries Ltd
5600 Apollo Dr...Rolling Meadows IL 60008 847-806-6300 806-6231 735
TF: 800-458-4747 ■ Web: www.charlesindustries.com

Charles Inn, The 20 Broad St...Bangor ME 04401 207-992-2820 379
Web: www.thecharlesinn.com

Charles Jones LLC PO Box 8488...Trenton NJ 08650 800-792-8888 883-0677 635
TF: 800-792-8888 ■ Web: www.charlesjones.com

Charles L Crane Agency Co
100 N Broadway Ste 900...Saint Louis MO 63102 314-241-8700 444-4970 390
TF: 800-264-8722 ■ Web: www.craneagency.com

Charles Leonard Inc 145 Kennedy Dr...Hauppauge NY 11788 631-273-6700 273-6777 350
TF: 800-999-7202 ■ Web: www.charlesleonard.com

Charles Leonard Western Inc
235 W 140th St...Los Angeles CA 90061 310-715-7464 350
Web: clnational.com

Charles Machine Works Inc PO Box 66...Perry OK 73077 580-336-4402 190
TF Cust Svc: 800-654-6481 ■ Web: www.ditchwitch.com

Charles Machine Works Inc, The
1959 W First...Perry OK 73077 580-336-4402 190
Web: charlesmachine.works

Charles Mcmurray Co 2520 N Argyle Ave...Fresno CA 93727 559-292-5751 350
Web: www.charlesmcmurray.com

Charles Mears State Park
400 W Lowell St...Pentwater MI 49449 231-869-2051 565
Web: www.michigandnr.com

Charles Mix County PO Box 490...Lake Andes SD 57356 605-487-7131 487-7221 338
Web: charlesmix.sdcounties.org

Charles Mix Electric Assn Inc
440 Lake St...Lake Andes SD 57356 605-487-7321 245
TF: 800-208-8587 ■ Web: www.cme.coop

Charles N. White Construction Company Inc
613 Crescent Cir Ste 100...Ridgeland MS 39157 601-898-5180 186
Web: www.whiteconst.com

Charles P. Blouin Inc
203 New Zealand Rd...Seabrook NH 03874 603-474-3400 474-7118 189-10
Web: www.cpblouin.com

Charles Paddock Zoo 9305 Pismo Ave...Atascadero CA 93422 805-461-5080 823
TF: 800-832-3474 ■ Web: www.charlespaddockzoo.org

Charles Pankow Builders Ltd
199 SLos Robles Ave Ste 300...Pasadena CA 91101 626-304-1190 696-1782 186
TF: 800-326-8373 ■ Web: www.pankow.com

Phone | Fax | Class

Charles Penzone Inc 1480 Manning Pkwy...Powell OH 43065 614-898-1200 77
Web: www.charlespenzone.com

Charles Pinckney National Historic Site
1214 Middle St...Sullivans Island SC 29482 843-881-5516 881-7070 564
Web: www.nps.gov/chpi

Charles Playhouse 74 Warrenton St...Boston MA 02116 617-426-6912 572
Web: www.blueman.com

Charles R Drew University of Medicine & Science
1731 E 120th St...Los Angeles CA 90059 323-563-4800 563-4957* 166
*Fax: Admissions ■ Web: www.cdrewu.edu

Charles River Analytics Inc
625 Mt Auburn St Ste 3...Cambridge MA 02138 617-491-3474 177
TF: 877-547-4600 ■ Web: www.cra.com

Charles River Development Inc
700 District Ave...Burlington MA 01803 781-238-0099 238-0088 178-10
Web: www.crd.com

Charles River Laboratories Inc
251 Ballardvale St...Wilmington MA 01887 781-222-6000 658-7132* 668
NYSE: CRL ■ *Fax Area Code: 978 ■ TF: 800-772-3271 ■ Web: www.criver.com

Charles River Ventures
1 Broadway 15th Fl...Cambridge MA 02142 781-768-6000 792
Web: www.crv.com

Charles Ross & Son Co
710 Old Willets Path...Hauppauge NY 11788 631-234-0500 234-0691 386
TF: 800-243-7677 ■ Web: www.mixers.com

Charles Ryan Assoc Inc
601 Morris St Ste 301...Charleston WV 25301 877-342-0161 636
TF: 877-342-0161 ■ Web: www.charlesryan.com

Charles Schwab & Co Inc
211 Main St...San Francisco CA 94105 415-667-1009 690
TF Cust Svc: 800-648-5300 ■ Web: www.schwab.com

Charles Stark Draper Laboratory Inc
555 Technology Sq...Cambridge MA 02139 617-258-1000 668
Web: www.draper.com

Charles Stewart Mott Community College
1401 E Ct St...Flint MI 48503 810-762-0200 762-5611 162
Web: www.mcc.edu

Charles Stewart Mott Foundation
503 S Saginaw St Ste 1200...Flint MI 48502 810-238-5651 766-1753 305
TF: 800-421-9512 ■ Web: www.mott.org

Charles Tombras Adv Inc
630 Concord St...Knoxville TN 37919 865-524-5376 4
Web: www.tombras.com

Charles Towne Landing State Historic Site
1500 Old Towne Rd...Charleston SC 29407 843-852-4200 852-4205 565
TF: 866-345-7275 ■ Web: www.southcarolinaparks.com

Charles W Carter Co Hawaii Inc
1299 Kaumualii St...Honolulu HI 96817 808-832-6292 54
Web: www.cwcarterco.com

Charles Wolf Couture
579 Fifth Ave Ste 1518...New York NY 10017 212-371-6130 411

Charleston 1000 Lancaster St...Baltimore MD 21202 410-332-7373 671
Web: www.charlestonrestaurant.com

Charleston Area Chamber of Commerce
501 Jackson Ave...Charleston IL 61920 217-345-7041 345-7042 139
Web: www.charlestonchamber.com

Charleston Area Convention & Visitors Bureau
423 King St...Charleston SC 29403 843-853-8000 853-0444 206
TF: 800-868-8118 ■ Web: www.charlestoncvb.com

Charleston Area Convention Ctr Complex (CACC)
5001 Coliseum Dr...Charleston SC 29418 843-725-1307 205
Web: www.charlestonconventioncenter.com

Charleston Area Medical Ctr
501 Morris St...Charleston WV 25301 304-388-5432 374-3
Web: www.camc.org

Charleston Area Regional Transportation Authority (CARTA)
1362 McMillan Ave Ste 100...North Charleston SC 29405 843-724-7420 468
Web: www.ridecarta.com

Charleston Ballet
100 Capitol St Ste 302...Charleston WV 25301 304-342-6541 573-1
Web: www.thecharlestonballet.com

Charleston City Paper
1049 Morrison Dr # B...Charleston SC 29403 843-577-5304 532-5
Web: www.charlestoncitypaper.com

Charleston Civic Ctr & Coliseum
200 Civic Ctr Dr...Charleston WV 25301 304-345-1500 345-3492 205
Web: www.charlestonwvciviccenter.com

Charleston Coast Guard Base
196 Tradd St...Charleston SC 29401 843-724-7600 158
TF: 800-424-8802 ■ Web: www.uscg.mil

Charleston Convention & Visitors Bureau
601 Morris St Ste 204...Charleston WV 25301 304-344-5075 206
Web: www.charlestonwv.com

Charleston County 4045 Bridge View...Charleston SC 29405 843-958-4030 958-4035 338
TF: 800-735-2905 ■ Web: www.charlestoncounty.org

Charleston County Public Library
68 Calhoun St...Charleston SC 29401 843-805-6930 727-3741 434-3
TF: 800-768-3676 ■ Web: www.ccpl.org

Charleston County School District (CCSD)
75 Calhoun St...Charleston SC 29401 843-937-6300 937-6307 685
TF: 800-241-8898 ■ Web: www.ccsdschools.com

Charleston Crab House
145 Wappoo Creek Dr...Charleston SC 29412 843-795-1963 671
Web: www.charlestoncrabhouse.com

Charleston Gazette
1001 Virginia St E...Charleston WV 25301 304-348-5140 348-1233 532-2
TF: 800-982-6397 ■ Web: www.wvgazettemail.com

Charleston Grill 224 King St...Charleston SC 29401 843-577-4522 671
Web: www.charlestongrill.com

Charleston International Airport
5500 International Blvd Ste 101...Charleston SC 29418 843-767-7000 760-3020 27
Web: www.chs airport.com

Charleston Light Opera Guild
411 Tennessee Ave...Charleston WV 25302 304-343-2287 573-2
Web: charlestonwv.com

Charleston Metal Products Inc
350 Grant St...Waterloo IN 46793 260-837-8211 837-8101 621
Web: www.charlestonmetal.com

Phone | Fax | Class

Charleston Metro Chamber of Commerce
4500 Leeds Ave Ste 100 .... North Charleston SC 29405 843-577-2510 723-4853 139
Web: www.charlestonchamber.net

Charleston Museum 360 Meeting St .... Charleston SC 29403 843-722-2996 722-1784 520
TF: 800-782-3608 ■ *Web:* www.charlestonmuseum.org

Charleston Naval Hospital
110 NNPTC Cir. .... Goose Creek SC 29445 843-794-6221 374-4
Web: www.med.navy.mil/sites/chas/pages/default.aspx

Charleston Newspapers Ltd
1001 Virginia St E. .... Charleston WV 25301 304-348-4848 532-3
TF: 800-982-6397 ■ *Web:* www.cnpapers.com

Charleston Place 205 Meeting St. .... Charleston SC 29401 843-722-4900 722-0728 379
TF: 888-635-2350 ■ *Web:* belmond.com/charleston-place

Charleston Regional Chamber of Commerce
1116 Smith St. .... Charleston WV 25301 304-340-4253 340-4275 139
TF: 800-792-4326 ■ *Web:* www.charlestonareaalliance.org

Charleston (SC) City Hall
50 Broad St. .... Charleston SC 29401 843-577-6970 720-3959 337
Web: www.charleston-sc.gov

Charleston School of Law LLC, The
81 Mary St .... Charleston SC 29403 843-329-1000 685
Web: www.charlestonlaw.edu

Charleston Southern University
9200 University Blvd .... Charleston SC 29423 843-863-7050 863-7070 166
TF: 800-947-7474 ■ *Web:* www.csuniv.edu

Charleston Steel & Metal Co
3038 Hwy 52 .... Mt. Holly SC 29461 843-722-2278 723
Web: www.charlestonsteelandmetal.com

Charleston Symphony Orchestra
756 St Andrews Blvd .... Charleston SC 29407 843-723-7528 573-3
TF: 800-892-3298 ■ *Web:* www.charlestonsymphony.com

Charleston (WV) City Hall
200 Civic Ctr Dr .... Charleston WV 25301 304-348-8000 348-8157 337
Web: www.cityofcharleston.org

Charleston's 5907 NW Expy St .... Oklahoma City OK 73132 405-721-0060 671
Web: charlestons.com

Charlestown Breachway
Charlestown Beach Rd .... Charlestown RI 02813 401-364-7000 322-3083 565
Web: riparks.com

Charlestown Clark County Public Library
51 Clark Rd. .... Charlestown IN 47111 812-256-3337 434-3
Web: www.clarkco.lib.in.us

Charlestown Retirement Community (CCI)
715 Maiden Choice Ln. .... Catonsville MD 21228 410-242-2880 672
TF: 800-917-8649 ■ *Web:* ericksonliving.com

Charlestown State Park
12500 Indiana 62 .... Charlestown IN 47111 812-256-5600 565
Web: www.in.gov

Charlestowne Mall
3800 E Main St. .... Saint Charles IL 60174 630-513-1120 460
Web: www.charlestownemall.com

Charlevoix County 203 Antrim St .... Charlevoix MI 49720 231-547-7200 547-7217 338
TF: 800-548-9157 ■ *Web:* www.charlevoixcounty.org

Charlevoix Public Schools
104 E St Marys Dr .... Charlevoix MI 49720 231-547-3200 547-0556 685
Web: www.rayder.net

Charley G's Seafood Grill
3809 Ambassador Caffery Pkwy .... Lafayette LA 70503 337-981-0108 671
Web: www.charleygs.com

Charley's Concrete Co
11801 Katy Rd .... Fort Worth TX 76244 817-431-3515 182
Web: www.charleysconcrete.com

Charley's Crab Restaurant
63 Market St SW. .... Grand Rapids MI 49503 616-459-2500 459-8142 671
TF: 800-528-8989 ■ *Web:* www.muer.com

Charley's Steak House
8255 International Dr .... Orlando FL 32819 407-363-0228 671
Web: www.talkofthetownrestaurants.com

Charleys Philly Steaks
2500 Farmers Dr Ste 140 .... Columbus OH 43235 614-336-9960 670
TF: 800-437-8325 ■ *Web:* www.charleys.com

Charlie Bravo Aviation Llc
160 Terminal Rd .... Georgetown TX 78628 512-868-9000 261
Web: www.wepushtin.com

Charlie Palmer Steak
101 Constitution Ave NW .... Washington DC 20001 202-547-8100 671

Charlie's L'Etoile Verte
8 New Orleans Rd. .... Hilton Head Island SC 29928 843-785-9277 671
Web: www.charliesgreenstar.com

Charlie's on the Lake 4150 S 144th St .... Omaha NE 68137 402-894-9411 671
Web: www.charliesonthelake.net

Charlie's Steak-Ribs-Ale
3009 W State Hwy 76 .... Branson MO 65616 417-334-6090 671

Charlotte Anodizing Products Inc
591 E Packard Hwy. .... Charlotte MI 48813 517-543-1911 481
TF: 800-818-6945 ■ *Web:* www.charlotte-anodizing.com

Charlotte Appliances Inc
3200 Lake Ave .... Rochester NY 14612 585-663-5050 321
TF: 800-244-0405 ■ *Web:* www.charlotteappliance.com

Charlotte Bobcats 333 E Trade St .... Charlotte NC 28202 704-688-8600 714-1
Web: www.nba.com/bobcats

Charlotte Business Journal
1100 S Tryon St Ste 100. .... Charlotte NC 28203 704-973-1100 457-5
Web: www.bizjournals.com

Charlotte Chamber of Commerce
330 S Tryon St PO Box 32785 .... Charlotte NC 28202 704-378-1300 374-1903 139
Web: www.charlottechamber.com

Charlotte City Hall
Charlotte-Mecklenburg Government Ctr
600 E 4th St .... Charlotte NC 28202 704-336-2241 336-6644 337
TF: 800-418-2065 ■ *Web:* charmeck.org

Charlotte Convention & Visitors Bureau
500 S College St Ste 300. .... Charlotte NC 28202 704-334-2282 342-3972 206
TF: 800-722-1994 ■ *Web:* www.charlottesgotalot.com

Charlotte Convention Ctr
501 S College St. .... Charlotte NC 28202 704-339-6000 339-6024 205
TF: 800-224-6422 ■ *Web:* www.charlotteconventionctr.com

Phone | Fax | Class

Charlotte Correctional Institution
33123 Oil Well Rd. .... Punta Gorda FL 33955 941-833-2300 575-5747 213
TF: 800-543-5353 ■ *Web:* dc.state.fl.us

Charlotte County
250 LeGrande Ave Ste A
PO Box 608 .... Charlotte Court House VA 23923 434-542-5117 542-5248 338
Web: www.charlotteva.com

Charlotte County
18500 Murdoch Cir .... Port Charlotte FL 33948 941-743-1300 338
Web: www.charlottecountyfl.gov

Charlotte County Chamber of Commerce
311 W Retta Esplanade .... Punta Gorda FL 33950 941-639-6330 639-6330 139
TF: 800-554-4375 ■ *Web:* www.charlottecountychamber.org

Charlotte Hall Veterans Home
29449 Charlotte Hall Rd .... Charlotte Hall MD 20622 301-884-8171 793
Web: charhall.org

Charlotte Hawkins Brown Museum
6136 Burlington Rd PO Box B .... Sedalia NC 27342 336-449-4846 449-0176 520
TF: 800-767-1560 ■ *Web:* www.nchistoricsites.org

Charlotte Hungerford Hospital (CHH)
540 Litchfield St .... Torrington CT 06790 860-496-6666 482-8627 374-3
Web: charlottehungerford.org

Charlotte Institute of Rehabilitation
1100 Blythe Blvd .... Charlotte NC 28203 704-355-4300 374-6
TF: 800-634-2256 ■ *Web:* www.carolinashealthcare.org

Charlotte Latin Schools Inc
9502 Providence Rd .... Charlotte NC 28277 704-846-1100 685
Web: www.charlottelatin.org

Charlotte Mecklenburg Library
310 N Tryon St .... Charlotte NC 28202 704-416-0100 434-3
Web: cmlibrary.org

Charlotte Motor Speedway
5555 Concord Pkwy S .... Concord NC 28027 704-455-3200 455-2547 642
TF: 800-455-3267 ■ *Web:* www.charlottemotorspeedway.com

Charlotte Museum of History & Hezekiah Alexander Homesite
3500 Shamrock Dr .... Charlotte NC 28215 704-568-1774 520
Web: www.charlottemuseum.org

Charlotte Observer, The
600 S Tryon St .... Charlotte NC 28202 704-358-5000 358-5036 532-2
TF: 800-332-0686 ■ *Web:* www.charlotteobserver.com

Charlotte Pipe & Foundry Co
2109 Randolph Rd .... Charlotte NC 28207 704-372-5030 348-6450 490
TF: 800-438-6091 ■ *Web:* www.charlottepipe.com

Charlotte Pipe & Foundry Co
2109 Randolph Rd .... Charlotte NC 28207 704-289-2531 596
Web: www.charlottepipe.com

Charlotte Radiological P.A
1701 East Blvd .... Charlotte NC 28203 704-334-7800 418
Web: www.charlotteradiology.com

Charlotte Russe Inc
5910 Pacific Center Blvd .... San Diego CA 92121 888-211-7271 157-6
TF: 888-211-7271 ■ *Web:* www.charlotterusse.com

Charlotte Soccer Academy
901 Sam Newell Rd E .... Matthews NC 28105 704-708-4166 713

Charlotte Street Grill & Pub
157 Charlotte St .... Asheville NC 28801 828-252-2948 671
TF: 800-232-7238 ■ *Web:* charlottestreetpub.com

Charlotte-Mecklenburg Schools
701 E ML King Jr Blvd .... Charlotte NC 28202 980-343-3000 343-5661 685
TF: 800-244-6224 ■ *Web:* www.cms.k12.nc.us

Charlottesville (Independent City)
605 E Main St. .... Charlottesville VA 22902 434-970-3101 970-3890 338
TF: 800-552-7001 ■ *Web:* www.charlottesville.org

Charlottesville Regional Chamber of Commerce
209 Fifth St NE .... Charlottesville VA 22902 434-295-3141 295-3144 139
TF: 800-321-6742 ■ *Web:* www.cvillechamber.com

Charlton County 68 Kingsland Ste B. .... Folkston GA 31537 912-496-2549 338
Web: georgia.gov/cities-counties/charlton-county

Charlton Memorial Hospital
363 Highland Ave .... Fall River MA 02720 508-679-3131 374-3
TF: 800-276-0103 ■ *Web:* www.southcoast.org

Charm City Concierge Inc
1437 E Ft Ave .... Baltimore MD 21230 410-727-4569 260
Web: www.charmcityconcierge.com

Charm Jewelry Ltd 140 Portland St .... Dartmouth NS B2Y1J1 902-463-7177 410
Web: charmdiamondcentres.com

Charm Sciences Inc 659 Andover St .... Lawrence MA 01843 978-687-9200 687-9216 479
TF: 800-343-2170 ■ *Web:* www.charm.com

Charmer Sunbelt Group, The
60 E 42nd St Ste 1915 .... New York NY 10165 212-699-7000 699-7099 81-3
TF: 888-262-9787 ■ *Web:* www.charmer-sunbelt.com

Charming Shoppes Inc
933 MacArthur Blvd .... Mahwah NJ 07430 551-777-6700 157-6
NASDAQ: ASNA ■ *Web:* www.ascenaretail.com

Charms Co 7401 S Cicero Ave .... Chicago IL 60629 773-838-3400 401-0087* 296-8
**Fax Area Code:* 415 ■ *TF:* 800-267-0037 ■ *Web:* tootsie.com

Charnstrom 5391 12th Ave E .... Shakopee MN 55379 800-328-2962 916-3215 470
TF Cust Svc: 800-328-2962 ■ *Web:* www.charnstrom.com

Chart House 5700 SW Terwilliger Blvd .... Portland OR 97239 503-246-6963 671
Web: www.chart-house.com

Chart House 1501 River Pl Blvd. .... Jacksonville FL 32207 904-398-3353 671
Web: www.chart-house.com

Chart House
201 Gulf of Mexico Dr .... Longboat Key FL 34228 941-383-5593 671
Web: www.chart-house.com

Chart House Restaurant
1 Cameron St .... Alexandria VA 22314 703-684-5080 671
Web: www.chart-house.com

Chart Industries Inc
1 Infinity Corporate Centre Dr
Ste 300 .... Garfield Heights OH 44125 440-753-1490 753-1491 91
TF: 800-422-2790 ■ *Web:* www.chartindustries.com

Chartbeat Inc
826 Broadway 12th St 6th Fl. .... New York NY 10003 646-786-8472 387
Web: www.chartbeat.com

Charter at Beaver Creek
120 Offerson Rd .... Beaver Creek CO 81620 970-949-6660 379
TF: 800-525-6660 ■ *Web:* www.wyndhamvacationrentals.com

Name / Address	City	State	ZIP	Phone	Fax	Class
Charter Brokerage LLC 383 Main Ave Ste 506 *Web:* charterbrokerage.net	Norwalk	CT	06851	203-840-7500		690
Charter Communications Inc 12405 Powerscourt Dr Ste 100 *NASDAQ: CHTR* ■ *TF:* 888-438-2427 ■ *Web:* www.spectrum.com	Saint Louis	MO	63131	314-965-0555	965-9745	116
Charter Dura-Bar 2100 West Lake Shore Dr *TF:* 800-437-8789 ■ *Web:* charterdura-bar.com	Woodstock	IL	60098	815-338-3900		307
Charter Enterprises LLC 1255 Corporate Ctr Dr Ste PH402 *Web:* www.charterbbq.com	Monterey Park	CA	91754	323-269-6868		360-2
Charter Films Inc 1901 Winter St PO Box 277 *TF:* 877-411-3456 ■ *Web:* www.charternex.com	Superior	WI	54880	715-395-8258		548
Charter Flight Inc 1928 S Blvd. *TF:* 800-521-3148 ■ *Web:* www.charterflightinc.com	Charlotte	NC	28208	704-359-9124		13
Charter Industries 2255 29th St S E *TF:* 800-538-9088 ■ *Web:* www.charterindustries.com	Grand Rapids	MI	49508	616-245-3388		351
Charter Medical Ltd 3948-A Westpoint Blvd *Web:* www.chartermedical.com	Winston-Salem	NC	27103	336-768-6447		475
Charter Mfg Company Inc 1212 W Glen Oaks Ln *TF:* 800-437-8789 ■ *Web:* www.chartermfg.com	Mequon	WI	53092	262-243-4700		723
Charter Oak Cultural Ctr 21 Charter Oak Ave *Web:* www.charteroakcenter.org	Hartford	CT	06106	860-310-2580		50-2
Charter Oak State College 55 Paul J Manafort Dr *TF:* 800-235-6559 ■ *Web:* www.charteroak.edu	New Britain	CT	06053	860-832-3800		166
Charter One Hotels & Resorts Inc 6731 Professional Pkwy W Ste 100 *Web:* www.charteronehotels.com	Sarasota	FL	34239	941-907-9017	907-9854	379
Charter Plastics 221 S Perry St *Web:* www.charterplastics.com	Titusville	PA	16354	814-827-9665		608
Charter Schools USA 6245 N Federal Hwy 5th Fl *Web:* www.charterschoolsusa.com	Fort Lauderdale	FL	33308	954-202-3500	202-3512	242
Charter Services Inc 8400 Airport Rd W *Web:* www.csijets.com	Mobile	AL	36608	251-633-6090		13
Charter Steel Trading Company Inc 4401 W Roosevelt Rd *Web:* www.chartersteeltrading.com	Chicago	IL	60624	773-522-3100		492
Charter Trust Co 90 N Main St *TF:* 800-281-5772 ■ *Web:* www.chartertrust.com	Concord	NH	03301	603-224-1350		194
Charter Wire 3700 W Milwaukee Rd *TF:* 800-436-9074 ■ *Web:* www.charterwire.com	Milwaukee	WI	53208	414-390-3000	390-3031	813
CharterBank 1233 OG Skinner Dr *TF:* 800-763-4444 ■ *Web:* www.charterbk.com	West Point	GA	31833	706-645-1391	645-1370	70
Chartered Business Valuators 277 Wellington St W Ste 710 *TF:* 866-770-7315 ■ *Web:* www.cicbv.ca	Toronto	ON	M5V3H2	416-977-1117		772
Chartis Group LLC 220 W Kinzie St 3rd Fl *TF:* 877-667-4700 ■ *Web:* www.chartis.com	Chicago	IL	60654	877-667-4700		463
Chartist Newsletter PO Box 758 *TF:* 800-942-4278 ■ *Web:* thechartist.com	Seal Beach	CA	90740	562-596-2385		531-9
Charton Management Inc 373 Timberline Pkwy *Web:* charton.biz	Vienna	WV	26105	304-865-2222		463
Chartpak Inc 1 River Rd *TF:* 800-628-1910 ■ *Web:* www.chartpak.com	Leeds	MA	01053	413-584-5446	584-6781	43
Chartway Federal Credit Union 160 Newtown Rd **Fax:* Hum Res ■ *TF:* 800-678-8765 ■ *Web:* www.chartway.com	Virginia Beach	VA	23462	757-552-1000	671-7601*	219
Chartwell Hospitality LLC 2000 Meridian Blvd Ste 200 *Web:* www.chartwellhospitality.com	Franklin	TN	37067	615-550-1270		379
Chartwell Master Care LP 100 Milverton Dr Ste 700 *Web:* chartwell.com	Mississauga	ON	L5R4H1	905-501-9219		371
Chas G Allen Company Inc 25 Williamsville Rd *TF:* 800-861-7228 ■ *Web:* www.chasgallen.com	Barre	MA	01005	978-355-2911	355-2917	455
Chas Roberts Heating & Air Conditioning Inc 9828 N 19th Ave *Web:* www.chasroberts.com	Phoenix	AZ	85021	602-331-2686		189-10
Chasan Leyner & Lamparello A Professional Corp 300 Harmon Meadow Blvd *Web:* www.chasanlaw.com	Secaucus	NJ	07094	201-348-6000		428
Chasco Constructors Ltd LLP 2801 E Old Settlers Blvd *Web:* www.chasco.com	Round Rock	TX	78665	512-244-0600		186
Chase & Associates Cpas PC 9293 Corporate Cir *Web:* www.chaseadvisors.com	Manassas	VA	20110	703-361-7114		196
Chase & Sons Inc 295 University Ave *TF:* 800-323-4182 ■ *Web:* www.chasecorp.com	Westwood	MA	02090	781-332-0700		816
Chase Bank 28 Liberty St *TF:* 800-935-9935 ■ *Web:* www.chase.com	New York	NY	10005	800-935-9935		70
Chase Brass & Copper Co 14212 Selwyn Dr **Fax:* Mail Rm ■ *TF:* 800-537-4291 ■ *Web:* www.chasebrass.com	Montpelier	OH	43543	419-485-3193	485-5945*	485
Chase Brexton Health Services Inc 1111 N Charles St *Web:* www.chasebrexton.org	Baltimore	MD	21201	410-837-2050		353
Chase Collegiate School 565 Chase Pkwy *Web:* www.smmct.org	Waterbury	CT	06708	203-236-9500		148
Chase Corp 26 Summer St *NYSE: CCF* ■ **Fax Area Code:* 508 ■ *TF:* 800-323-4182 ■ *Web:* www.chasecorp.com	Bridgewater	MA	02324	781-332-0700	697-6419*	3
Chase County 300 Pearl St *Web:* chasecountychamber.org/county-government	Cottonwood Falls	KS	66845	620-273-6423		338
Chase County 32804 741 Rd PO Box 1299 *Web:* www.co.chase.ne.us	Imperial	NE	69033	308-882-7500	882-7552	338
Chase Enterprises Inc 6509 W Reno Ave *TF:* 800-525-4970 ■ *Web:* www.chappellsupply.com	Oklahoma City	OK	73127	405-495-1722		196
Chase Field 401 E Jefferson St *Web:* azchasefield.com	Phoenix	AZ	85004	602-462-6500		720
Chase Home Museum of Utah Folk Art 617 East South Temple *Web:* heritage.utah.gov	Salt Lake City	UT	84102	801-533-5760	533-4202	520
Chase Hotel at Palm Springs 200 W Arenas Rd *TF:* 877-532-4273 ■ *Web:* www.chasehotelpalmsprings.com	Palm Springs	CA	92262	760-320-8866	323-1501	379
Chase Industries Inc 10021 Commerce Park Dr *TF:* 800-543-4455 ■ *Web:* www.chasedoors.com	Cincinnati	OH	45246	513-860-5565		480
Chase Park Plaza Royal Sonesta St Louis, The 212 N KingsHwy Blvd *Web:* www.chaseparkplaza.com	Saint Louis	MO	63108	314-633-3000	633-3077	379
Chase Paymentech Solutions LLC 14221 Dallas Pkwy *TF Cust Svc:* 800-708-3740 ■ *Web:* www.chasepaymentech.com	Dallas	TX	75254	800-708-3740		255
Chase Plastic Services Inc 6467 Waldon Ctr Dr *TF:* 800-232-4273 ■ *Web:* www.chaseplastics.com	Clarkston	MI	48346	248-620-2120		690
Chase-Lloyd House 22 Maryland Ave	Annapolis	MD	21401	410-263-2723		50-3
Chase-Logeman Corp 303 Friendship Dr *Web:* www.chaselogeman.com	Greensboro	NC	27409	336-665-0754		358
ChaseSource LP 3311 W Alabama *Web:* www.chasesource.com	Houston	TX	77098	713-874-5800		260
Chastain Homer L & Associates LLP 5 N Country Club Rd *Web:* www.chastainengineers.com	Decatur	IL	62521	217-422-8544		727
Chastain-Skillman Inc 4705 Old Rd 37 *TF:* 800-651-2960 ■ *Web:* www.chastainskillman.com	Lakeland	FL	33813	863-646-1402	647-3806	261
Chateau du Sureau 48688 Victoria Ln *Web:* www.chateausureau.com	Oakhurst	CA	93644	559-683-6860	683-0800	379
Chateau Dupre Hotel 131 Rue Decatur *Web:* www.bestneworleanshotels.com	New Orleans	LA	70130	504-569-0600		379
Chateau Elan Resort & Conference Ctr 100 Rue Charlemagne *TF:* 800-233-9463 ■ *Web:* www.chateauelan.com	Braselton	GA	30517	678-425-0900		377
Chateau Elan Winery 100 Tour de France *TF:* 800-233-9463 ■ *Web:* www.chateauelan.com	Braselton	GA	30517	678-425-0900		50-7
Chateau Grille 415 N State Hwy 265 *TF:* 888-333-5253 ■ *Web:* www.chateauonthelake.com	Branson	MO	65616	417-334-1161	339-5566	671
Chateau Hotel & Conference Ctr, The 1601 Jumer Dr *Web:* www.chateauhotel.biz	Bloomington	IL	61704	309-662-2020		379
Chateau Julien Wine Estate 8940 Carmel Valley Rd *Web:* www.greatamericanwinegroup.com	Carmel	CA	93923	831-920-4736	624-6138	50-7
Chateau Louis Hotel & Conference Ctr 11727 Kingsway *TF:* 800-661-9843 ■ *Web:* www.chateaulouis.com	Edmonton	AB	T5G3A1	780-452-7770	454-3436	379
Chateau Marmont Hotel 8221 Sunset Blvd *Web:* www.chateaumarmont.com	Los Angeles	CA	90046	323-656-1010	655-5311	379
Chateau Montelena Winery 1429 Tubbs Ln *Web:* www.montelena.com	Calistoga	CA	94515	707-942-5105	942-4221	80-3
Chateau Morrisette Winery 287 Winery Rd SW *TF:* 866-695-2001 ■ *Web:* thedogs.com	Floyd	VA	24091	540-593-2865	593-2868	50-7
Chateau on the Lake 415 N State Hwy 265 *TF:* 888-333-5253 ■ *Web:* www.chateauonthelake.com	Branson	MO	65616	417-334-1161	339-5566	379
Chateau Resort & Conference Center, The 300 Camelback Rd *TF:* 800-245-5900 ■ *Web:* chateauresort.com	Tannersville	PA	18372	570-629-5900		707
Chateau Restaurant 201 Hanover St	Manchester	NH	03104	603-606-3026		671
Chateau Rouge 1505 S Broadway Ave *TF:* 800-926-1601 ■ *Web:* www.chateaurouge.com	Red Lodge	MT	59068	406-446-1601		707
Chateau Saint Jean 8555 Sonoma Hwy *Web:* www.chateaustjean.com	Kenwood	CA	95452	707-257-5784		50-7
Chateau Ste Michelle Winery 14111 NE 145th St *TF:* 800-267-6793 ■ *Web:* www.ste-michelle.com	Woodinville	WA	98072	425-415-3300		50-7
Chateau Vaudreuil Suites Hotel 21700 Rt Transcanada Hwy *TF:* 800-363-7896 ■ *Web:* chateauvaudreuil.ca	Vaudreuil-Dorion	QC	J7V8P3	450-455-0955	455-6617	379
Chateau Versailles 1659 Sherbrooke St W *TF:* 888-933-8111 ■ *Web:* www.chateauversaillesmontreal.com	Montreal	QC	H3H1E3	514-933-3611		379
Chateaugay Correctional Facility 7874 US-11 *Web:* doccs.ny.gov	Chateaugay	NY	12920	518-497-3300		213
Chateau-Sur-Mer 474 Bellevue Ave *TF:* 800-326-6030 ■ *Web:* www.newportmansions.org	Newport	RI	02840	401-847-1000	847-1361	50-3
Chatfield Hollow State Park 381 Rt 80 *Web:* www.ct.gov	Killingworth	CT	06419	860-663-2030		565
Chatfield State Park 11500 N Roxborough Pk Rd *Web:* cpw.state.co.us	Littleton	CO	80125	303-791-7275		565
Chatham Bars Inn 297 Shore Rd *TF:* 800-527-4884 ■ *Web:* www.chathambarsinn.com	Chatham	MA	02633	508-945-0096		669
Chatham Central School District 50 Woodbridge Ave *Web:* www.chathamcentralschools.com	Chatham	NY	12037	518-392-2400		685
Chatham Chamber of Commerce 531 E Third St *TF:* 800-329-7466 ■ *Web:* www.ccucc.net	Siler City	NC	27344	919-742-3333	742-1333	139
Chatham County 124 Bull St *Web:* www.chathamcounty.org	Savannah	GA	31401	912-652-7869	652-7874	338
Chatham Daily News 138 King St W *Web:* www.chathamdailynews.ca	Chatham	ON	N7M1E3	519-354-2000		532-1

				Phone	Fax	Class
Chatham Financial Corp 235 Whitehorse Ln *Web:* www.chathamfinancial.com	Kennett Square	PA	19348	610-925-3120		403
Chatham Hall 800 Chatham Hall Cir *TF:* 877-644-2941 ■ *Web:* www.chathamhall.org	Chatham	VA	24531	434-432-2941	432-2405	622
Chatham Imports Inc 245 Fifth Ave *Web:* www.chathamimports.com	New York	NY	10016	212-473-1100		80-3
Chatham Lodging Trust 50 Cocoanut Row Ste 200 *TF:* 800-546-7866 ■ *Web:* www.chathamlodgingtrust.com	Palm Beach	FL	33480	561-802-4477		403
Chatham Search International Inc 3 Lion Gardiner *Web:* www.chathamct.com	Cromwell	CT	06416	860-635-5538		260
Chatham Steel Corp 501 W Boundary St *TF:* 800-800-1337 ■ *Web:* www.chathamsteel.com	Savannah	GA	31401	912-233-5751	944-0236	492
Chatham University 1 Woodland Rd *TF:* 800-837-1290 ■ *Web:* www.chatham.edu	Pittsburgh	PA	15232	412-365-1100	365-1609	166
Chatham's Place Restaurant 7575 Doctor Philips Blvd *Web:* www.chathamsplace.com	Orlando	FL	32819	407-345-2992	345-0307	671
Chatham-Kent Chamber of Commerce 54 Fourth St *Web:* www.chatham-kentchamber.ca	Chatham	ON	N7M2G2	519-352-7540	352-8741	137
Chatham-Kent Health Alliance 80 Grand Ave W PO Box 2030 *Web:* www.ckha.on.ca	Chatham	ON	N7M5L9	519-352-6400	436-2522	374-2
ChatID Inc 900 Broadway Ste 706 *Web:* www.chatid.com	New York	NY	10003	646-494-5678		387
Chatillon-DeMenil Mansion & Museum 3352 DeMenil Pl *Web:* www.demenil.org	Saint Louis	MO	63118	314-771-5828		520
Chatlos Foundation PO Box 915048 *Web:* www.chatlos.org	Longwood	FL	32791	407-862-5077		305
Chatr Mobile 333 Bloor St E 8th Fl *TF:* 800-485-9745 ■ *Web:* www.chatrwireless.com	Toronto	ON	M4W1G9	800-485-9745		224
Chatsworth Chamber of Commerce 10038 Old Depot Plaza Rd *TF:* 800-613-5903 ■ *Web:* www.chatsworthchamber.com	Chatsworth	CA	91311	818-341-2428	341-4930	139
Chatsworth Data Corp 9735 Lurline Ave **Fax Area Code:* 877 ■ *TF:* 877-380-6855 ■ *Web:* www.chatsworthdata.com	Chatsworth	CA	91311	818-350-5072	380-6855*	248
Chatsworth Products Inc 31425 Agoura Rd *TF:* 800-834-4969 ■ *Web:* www.chatsworth.com	Westlake Village	CA	91361	818-735-6100	735-6199	176
Chatsworth Securities LLC 95 East Putnam Ave *Web:* www.chatsworthgroup.com	Greenwich	CT	06830	203-629-2612	629-2375	690
Chatsworth-Murray County Chamber of Commerce PO Box 516 *TF:* 800-969-9490 ■ *Web:* www.murraycountychamber.org	Chatsworth	GA	30705	706-695-2834	517-1623	139
Chattahoochee Nature Ctr 9135 Willeo Rd *TF:* 800-241-4113 ■ *Web:* chattnaturecenter.org	Roswell	GA	30075	770-992-2055	552-0926	50-5
Chattahoochee River National Recreation Area 1978 Island Ford Pkwy **Fax Area Code:* 770 ■ *TF:* 877-874-2478 ■ *Web:* www.nps.gov/chat	Atlanta	GA	30350	678-538-1200	399-8087*	564
Chattahoochee Valley Community College 2602 College Dr **Fax:* Admissions ■ *Web:* www.cv.edu	Phenix City	AL	36869	334-291-4900	291-4994*	162
Chattanooga Area Chamber of Commerce 811 Broad St *TF:* 877-756-1684 ■ *Web:* www.chattanoogachamber.com	Chattanooga	TN	37402	423-756-2121	267-7242	139
Chattanooga Area Convention & Visitors Bureau 215 Broad St *TF:* 800-322-3344 ■ *Web:* www.chattanoogafun.com	Chattanooga	TN	37402	423-756-8687	265-1630	206
Chattanooga City Hall 101 E 11th St Ste 100 *TF:* 800-251-9202 ■ *Web:* www.chattanooga.gov	Chattanooga	TN	37402	423-757-5152		337
Chattanooga Convention Ctr 1150 Carter St *TF:* 800-962-5213 ■ *Web:* www.chattconvention.org	Chattanooga	TN	37402	423-756-0001		205
Chattanooga Group 4717 Adams Rd *TF:* 800-592-7329 ■ *Web:* www.djoglobal.com	Hixson	TN	37343	423-870-2281	875-5497	477
Chattanooga Metropolitan Airport 1001 Airport Rd Ste 14 *Web:* www.chattairport.com	Chattanooga	TN	37421	423-855-2202	855-2212	27
Chattanooga National Cemetery 1200 Bailey Ave *TF:* 877-907-8585 ■ *Web:* www.cem.va.gov	Chattanooga	TN	37404	423-855-6590	855-6597	136
Chattanooga public Library 1001 Broad St *Web:* www.lib.chattanooga.gov	Chattanooga	TN	37402	423-757-5310		434-3
Chattanooga State Technical Community College 4501 Amnicola Hwy **Fax:* Admissions ■ *TF:* 866-547-3733 ■ *Web:* www.chattanoogastate.edu	Chattanooga	TN	37406	423-697-4400	697-4709*	162
Chattanooga Symphony & Opera (CSO) 701 Broad St *Web:* chattanoogasymphony.org	Chattanooga	TN	37402	423-267-8583	265-6520	573-3
Chattanooga Theatre Centre 400 River St *Web:* www.theatrecentre.com	Chattanooga	TN	37405	423-267-8534		572
Chattanooga Times Free Press 400 E 11th St *Web:* www.timesfreepress.com	Chattanooga	TN	37403	423-756-6900	757-6383	532-2
Chattanooga Zoo 301 N Holltzclaw Ave *TF:* 800-238-2000 ■ *Web:* chattzoo.org	Chattanooga	TN	37404	423-697-1322	697-1329	823
Chattanoogan, The 1201 Broad St *TF:* 877-756-1684 ■ *Web:* www.chattanooganhotel.com	Chattanooga	TN	37402	423-756-3400		377
Chattaway 358 22nd Ave S	Saint Petersburg	FL	33705	727-823-1594		671
Chattem Inc 1715 W 38th St PO Box 2219 *Web:* www.chattem.com	Chattanooga	TN	37409	423-821-4571	821-0395	214
Chattooga County PO Box 211 *Web:* www.georgia.gov	Summerville	GA	30747	706-857-0700	857-0742	338
Chaucer's Books 3321 State St *Web:* www.chaucersbooks.com	Santa Barbara	CA	93105	805-682-6787		95
Chaudhary & Assoc Inc 211 Gateway Rd W Ste 204 *Web:* chaudhary.com	Napa	CA	94558	707-255-2729		261
Chauncey Conference Ctr 1 Chauncey Rd *Web:* www.acc-chaunceyconferencecenter.com	Princeton	NJ	08541	609-921-3600	683-4958	377
Chautauqua County 3 N Erie St *TF:* 800-252-8748 ■ *Web:* www.co.chautauqua.ny.us	Mayville	NY	14757	716-753-4211	753-4756	338
Chautauqua County 215 N Chautauqua St *Web:* chautauquacountyks.com	Sedan	KS	67361	620-725-5800	725-5801	338
Chautauqua County Chamber of Commerce 512 Falconer St *Web:* www.chautauquachamber.org	Jamestown	NY	14701	716-484-1101	487-0785	139
Chautauqua County Chamber of Commerce 10785 Bennett Rd *Web:* www.chautauquachamber.org	Dunkirk	NY	14048	716-366-6200	366-4276	139
Chautauqua County Visitors Bureau Chautauqua Main Gate Rt 394 PO Box 1441 *TF:* 800-242-4569 ■ *Web:* www.tourchautauqua.com	Chautauqua	NY	14722	716-357-4569	357-2284	206
Chautauqua Dining Hall 900 Baseline Rd *Web:* www.chautauqua.com	Boulder	CO	80302	303-440-3776		671
Chautauqua Region Community Foundation Inc 418 Spring St *TF:* 800-245-5681 ■ *Web:* crcfonline.org	Jamestown	NY	14701	716-661-3390		305
Chautauqua-Cattaraugus Library System 106 W Fifth St *Web:* cclslib.ent.sirsi.net/client/en_US/default	Jamestown	NY	14701	716-484-7135	483-6880	434-3
Chauvin Arnoux Inc 15 Faraday Dr *TF:* 800-343-1391 ■ *Web:* www.aemc.com	Dover	NH	03820	603-749-6434		407
Chavez Grieves Consulting Engrs Inc 4700 Lincoln Rd NE *Web:* www.cg-engrs.com	Albuquerque	NM	87109	505-344-4080		261
Chavigny 365 Rue Chavigny *Web:* www.chavigny.qc.ca	Trois-RiviŠres	QC	G9B1A7	819-840-0400		623
Chaya Brasserie 110 Navy St *Web:* www.thechaya.com	Venice	CA	90291	310-396-1179		671
Chaya Brasserie 132 The Embarcadero *Web:* www.thechaya.com	San Francisco	CA	94105	415-777-8688		671
Chazen Museum of Art 800 University Ave University of Wisconsin *Web:* www.chazen.wisc.edu	Madison	WI	53706	608-263-2246	263-8188	520
CHC Consulting 1845 W Orangewood Ave Ste 300 *Web:* chcconsulting.com	Orange	CA	92868	949-250-0004		194
CHC Helicopter Corp 4740 Agar Dr *Web:* www.chc.ca	Richmond	BC	V7B1A3	604-276-7500		359
CHCBC (Community Health Ctr of Branch County) 274 E Chicago St *TF:* 800-994-6610 ■ *Web:* www.chcbc.com	Coldwater	MI	49036	517-279-5400	279-8830	374-3
CHEA (Council for Higher Education Accreditation) 1 Dupont Cir NW Ste 510 *Web:* www.chea.org	Washington	DC	20036	202-955-6126	955-6129	48-1
Cheaha Regional Library 935 Coleman St *Web:* www.cheaharegionallibrary.org	Heflin	AL	36264	256-463-7125	463-7125	434-3
Cheaha Resort State Park 19644 Hwy 281 *TF:* 800-610-5801 ■ *Web:* www.alapark.com	Delta	AL	36258	256-488-5111	488-5885	565
Cheap Joe's Art Stuff Inc 374 Industrial Park Dr *TF:* 800-227-2788 ■ *Web:* www.cheapjoes.com	Boone	NC	28607	828-263-5472		522
Cheapside Bar & Grill 131 Cheapside St *TF:* 800-233-1234 ■ *Web:* www.cheapsidebarandgrill.com	Lexington	KY	40507	859-254-0046		671
Cheatham County 100 Public Sq *Web:* www.cheathamcountytn.gov	Ashland City	TN	37015	615-792-4316		338
Cheatham County Chamber of Commerce 108 N Main St PO Box 354 *Web:* www.cheathamchamber.org	Ashland City	TN	37015	615-792-6722	792-5001	139
Cheatham County Public Library 188 County Services Dr Ste 200	Ashland City	TN	37015	615-792-4828		434-3
Cheboygan County 870 S Main St *TF:* 800-521-9772 ■ *Web:* www.cheboygancounty.net	Cheboygan	MI	49721	231-627-8808		338
Cheboygan State Park 4490 Beach Rd *Web:* www.michigandnr.com	Cheboygan	MI	49721	231-627-2811		565
Checchi & Company Consulting Inc 1899 L St NW Ste 800 *Web:* www.checchiconsulting.com	Washington	DC	20036	202-452-9700	466-9070	194
Checchi Capital Advisors LLC 190 N Canon Dr Ste 402 *Web:* www.goodnewschannel.net	Beverly Hills	CA	90210	310-432-0010		514
Check Cashing Place Inc, The 945 Fifth Ave *Web:* thecheckcashingplaceinc.com	San Diego	CA	92101	619-239-6151		251
Check Cashing Store (CCS) 6340 NW Fifth Way *TF:* 800-361-1407 ■ *Web:* www.thecheckcashingstore.com	Fort Lauderdale	FL	33309	800-361-1407		141
Check Cashing USA Inc 899 NW 37th Ave *TF:* 800-786-9666 ■ *Web:* www.checkcashingusa.com	Miami	FL	33125	305-644-1840		141
Check Point Software Technologies Ltd 800 Bridge Pkwy *NASDAQ:* CHKP ■ *TF:* 800-429-4391 ■ *Web:* www.checkpoint.com	Redwood City	CA	94065	650-628-2000	654-4233	178-12
Check Printers Inc 1530 Antioch Pike **Fax Area Code:* 615 ■ *TF:* 800-766-1217 ■ *Web:* www.check-printers.com	Antioch	TN	37013	800-766-1217	324-3323*	142
Checker Industrial Ltd 3345 Wyandotte St *Web:* www.checkerindustrial.com	East Windsor	ON	N8Y4S2	519-258-2022		111
Checker Machine Inc 2701 Nevada Ave N *Web:* www.checkermachine.com	New Hope	MN	55427	763-544-5000		454
Checkerboard Ltd 216 W Boylston St *Web:* checkernet.com	West Boylston	MA	01583	508-835-2475		130
Checkered Flag Motor Car Corp 5225 Virginia Beach Blvd *TF:* 866-414-7820 ■ *Web:* www.checkeredflag.com	Virginia Beach	VA	23462	757-687-3486		57
Checkers Drive-In Restaurants Inc 4300 W Cypress St Ste 600 *TF:* 800-800-8072 ■ *Web:* www.checkers.com	Tampa	FL	33607	813-283-7000		670

Company	City	ST	ZIP	Phone	Fax	Class
CheckPoint HR 2035 Lincoln Hwy Ste 1080 *TF:* 800 385 0331 ■ *Web:* www.checkpointhr.com	Edison	NJ	08817	732-287-8270	287-2297	570
Checkpoint Systems Inc 101 Wolf Dr *NYSE: CKP* ■ *TF:* 800-257-5540 ■ *Web:* www.checkpointsystems.com	Thorofare	NJ	08086	856-848-1800	848-0937	692
Checks In The Mail Inc 2435 Goodwin Ln *TF:* 800-733-4443 ■ *Web:* www.secure.checksinthemail.com	New Braunfels	TX	78135	800-733-4443		142
Checks Unlimited 8245 N Union Blvd *TF:* 800-210-0468 ■ *Web:* www.checksunlimited.com	Colorado Springs	CO	80920	719-531-3900		142
Checkview Corp 8180 upland cir *Web:* www.checkview.com	Chanhassen	MN	55317	952-227-5853		693
Checon Corp 30 Larsen Way *TF:* 800-730-2557 ■ *Web:* www.checon.com	North Attleboro	MA	02763	508-809-5100	809-5163	815
CHED-AM 630 (N/T) 5204 84th St *Web:* globalnews.ca/radio/630ched/?gref=630ched	Edmonton	AB	T6E5N8	780-440-6300		645-52
Cheddar's Casual Cafe 700 I- 635 Service Rd *Web:* cheddars.com	Irving	TX	75063	972-409-0300		670
Cheeca Lodge & Spa 81801 Overseas Hwy Mile Marker 82 *TF:* 800-327-2888 ■ *Web:* www.cheeca.com	Islamorada	FL	33036	305-664-4651		707
Cheektowaga Chamber of Commerce 2875 Union Rd Ste 50 *Web:* www.cheektowaga.org	Cheektowaga	NY	14227	716-684-5838	684-5571	139
Cheekwood estate and gardens 1200 Forrest Pk Dr *Web:* www.cheekwood.org	Nashville	TN	37205	615-356-8000		97
Cheer Inc 546 S Bedford St *Web:* cheerde.com	Georgetown	DE	19947	302-856-5187		363
Cheers 17 Depot St *Web:* www.cheersnh.com	Concord	NH	03301	603-228-0180	226-3459	671
Cheers Liquor Mart 1105 N Circle Dr *TF:* 800-879-5225 ■ *Web:* www.cheersliquormart.com	Colorado Springs	CO	80909	719-574-2244		443
Cheeseburger in Paradise 10562 US Hwy 98W *Web:* www.cheeseburgerinparadise.com	Miramar Beach	FL	32550	850-837-0197	837-0866	671
Cheesecake Factory 4200 Conroy Rd *Web:* www.thecheesecakefactory.com	Orlando	FL	32839	407-226-0333		671
Cheesecake Factory 8701 Keystone Xing Ste 4A *Web:* www.thecheesecakefactory.com	Indianapolis	IN	46240	317-566-0100		671
Cheesecake Factory 321 W Katella Ave *Web:* www.thecheesecakefactory.com	Anaheim	CA	92802	714-533-7500		671
Cheesecake Factory 11800 W Broad St *Web:* www.thecheesecakefactory.com	Richmond	VA	23233	804-364-4300		671
Cheesecake Factory Inc 26901 Malibu Hills Rd *NASDAQ: CAKE* ■ *TF:* 800-962-4284 ■ *Web:* www.thecheesecakefactory.com	Calabasas Hills	CA	91301	818-871-3000	871-3001	670
Cheesecake Factory South San Jose 925 Blossom Hill Rd *Web:* www.thecheesecakefactory.com	San Jose	CA	95123	408-225-6948		671
Cheesequake State Park 300 Gordon Rd *Web:* www.njparkandforests.org	Matawan	NJ	07747	732-566-2161		565
Cheevers & Company Inc 440 S LaSalle St Ste 710 *TF:* 866-928-7643 ■ *Web:* www.cheeversco.com	Chicago	IL	60605	312-224-7922		690
Chef Allen's 19088 NE 29th Ave *Web:* www.chefallens.com	Aventura	FL	33180	305-935-2900		671
Chef John Folse & Company Inc 2517 S Philippe Ave *Web:* www.jfolse.com	Gonzales	LA	70737	225-644-6000		296-14
Chef John Folse Culinary Institute PO Box 2099 *Web:* www.nicholls.edu	Thibodaux	LA	70310	985-449-7100		163
Chef Mavro 1969 S King St *Web:* www.chefmavro.com	Honolulu	HI	96826	808-944-4714		671
Chef Wayne's Big Mamou 63 Liberty St *Web:* www.chefwaynes-bigmamou.com	Springfield	MA	01103	413-732-1011		671
Chef's Requested Foods Inc 2600 Exchange Ave *Web:* www.chefsrequested.com	Oklahoma City	OK	73108	405-239-2610		297-8
Chef's Table 118 Main St *Web:* neci.edu	Montpelier	VT	05602	802-229-9202		671
Chefs International Inc 62 Broadway *Web:* www.lobster.com	Point Pleasant Beach	NJ	08742	732-295-0350		670
Chefs' Warehouse Holdings LLC 100 E Ridge Rd *Web:* www.chefswarehouse.com	Ridgefield	CT	06877	718-842-8700		299
Chehayeb & Assoc Inc 3702 W Azeele St *Web:* chehayeb.com	Tampa	FL	33609	813-876-1415		261
Cheim & Read 547 W 25th St *Web:* www.cheimread.com	New York	NY	10001	212-242-7727	242-7737	42
Chelan County 350 Orondo Ave *Web:* www.co.chelan.wa.us	Wenatchee	WA	98801	509-667-6380	667-6611	338
Chelan Fruit Marketing 5 Howser Rd *TF:* 800-634-6533 ■ *Web:* www.chelanfresh.com	Chelan	WA	98816	509-682-4252	682-2651	315-3
Cheley Colorado Camps Inc 601 Steele St *TF:* 800-359-7200 ■ *Web:* www.cheley.com	Denver	CO	80206	303-377-3616		239
Chella Professional Skin Care 507 Calle San Pablo *TF:* 877-424-3552 ■ *Web:* www.chella.com	Camarillo	CA	93012	805-383-7711		77
Chelmsford Public Library 25 Boston Rd *TF:* 800-867-3281 ■ *Web:* www.chelmsfordlibrary.org	Chelmsford	MA	01824	978-256-5521	256-8511	434-3
Chelo's Inc 1725 Mendon Rd Ste 209 *Web:* www.chelos.com	Cumberland	RI	02864	401-312-6500	312-6501	670
Chelsea Bldg Products 565 Cedar Way *TF:* 800-424-3573 ■ *Web:* www.chelseabuildingproducts.com	Oakmont	PA	15139	800-424-3573		235
Chelsea District Library 221 S Main St *Web:* chelseadistrictlibrary.org	Chelsea	MI	48118	734-475-8732		434-3
Chelsea Green Publishing Co 85 N Main St *Web:* chelseagreen.com	White River Junction	VT	05001	802-295-6300		637-2
Chelsea Investment Corp 5993 Avenida Encinas Ste 101 *Web:* www.chelseainvestco.com	Carlsbad	CA	92008	760-456-6000		653
Chelsea Lumber Co 1 Old Barn Cir *TF:* 800-875-9126 ■ *Web:* www.chelsealumber.com	Chelsea	MI	48118	734-475-9126	475-7320	191-3
Chelsea Milling Co 201 W N St PO Box 460 *TF:* 800-727-2460 ■ *Web:* www.jiffymix.com	Chelsea	MI	48118	734-475-1361	475-4630	296-23
Chelsea Pictures Inc 33 Bond St Unit 1 *Web:* www.chelsea.com	New York	NY	10012	212-431-3434		514
Chelsea Piers Sports & Entertainment Complex 23rd St & Hudson River *Web:* www.chelseapiers.com	New York	NY	10011	212-336-6400	336-6130	354
Chelsea Savoy Hotel 204 W 23rd St *TF:* 866-929-9353 ■ *Web:* www.chelseasavoynyc.com	New York	NY	10011	212-929-9353	741-6309	379
Chelsea Soldiers Home 91 Crest Ave *Web:* mass.gov	Chelsea	MA	02150	617-884-5660	884-1162	793
Chelsio Communications Inc 370 San Aleso Ave Ste 100 *Web:* www.chelsio.com	Sunnyvale	CA	94085	408-962-3600		225
Chelten House Products Inc 607 Heron Dr *Web:* www.cheltenhouse.com	Swedesboro	NJ	08085	856-467-1600	467-4769	296-33
Chem Nut Inc 800 Business Pk Dr	Leesburg	GA	31763	229-883-7050		276
Chem Processing Inc 3910 Linden Oaks Dr *TF:* 800-262-2119 ■ *Web:* www.chemprocessing.com	Rockford	IL	61109	815-874-8118		481
CHEM Rx 750 Park Pl *Web:* www.chemrx.net	Long Beach	NY	11561	516-889-8770		237
Chem Space Assoc Inc 655 William Pitt Way *Web:* www.lcms.com	Pittsburgh	PA	15238	412-828-3191		194
Chem USA Corp 38507 Cherry St *TF:* 800-866-2436 ■ *Web:* www.chemusa.com	Newark	CA	94560	510-608-8818	608-8828	173-2
ChemADVISOR Inc 811 Camp Horne Rd Stone Quarry Crossing Ste 220 *Web:* www.chemadvisor.com	Pittsburgh	PA	15237	412-847-2000		194
Chemart Co 15 New England Way *Web:* www.chemart.com	Lincoln	RI	02865	401-333-9200	333-9200	481
Chematics Inc PO Box 293 *TF:* 800-348-5174 ■ *Web:* www.chematics.com	North Webster	IN	46555	574-834-2406	834-7427	231
Chembio Diagnostics Inc 3661 Horseblock Rd *NASDAQ: CEMI* ■ *TF:* 844-243-6246 ■ *Web:* www.chembio.com	Medford	NY	11763	631-924-1135		582
Chemed Corp 255 E Fifth St Ste 2600 *NYSE: CHE* ■ *TF General:* 800-224-3633 ■ *Web:* www.chemed.com	Cincinnati	OH	45202	513-762-6900		185
Chemeketa Community College 4000 Lancaster Dr NE PO Box 14007 **Fax:* Admissions ■ *Web:* www.chemeketa.edu	Salem	OR	97305	503-399-5006	399-3918*	162
Chemence Inc 185 Bluegrass Valley Pkwy *Web:* www.chemence.com	Alpharetta	GA	30005	770-664-6624	664-6620	3
Chemetal 39 O'Neil St *TF:* 800-807-7341 ■ *Web:* www.chmetal.com	EastHampton	MA	01027	413-529-0718	529-9898	295
Chemetrics Inc 4295 Catlett Rd *Web:* www.chemetrics.com	Calverton	VA	20138	540-788-9026	788-4856	419
ChemGenes Corp 33 Industrial Way *Web:* www.chemgenes.com	Wilmington	MA	01887	978-694-4500		231
Chemgrout Inc 805 E 31st St *Web:* www.chemgrout.com	La Grange Park	IL	60526	708-354-7112	354-3881	190
Chemguard Inc 204 S Sixth Ave *Web:* www.chemguard.com	Mansfield	TX	76063	817-473-9964		52
Chemic Engineers & Constructors Inc 4820 Fm 2004 Rd *Web:* chemic.com	Hitchcock	TX	77563	409-986-6504		261
Chemical & Industrial Engineering Inc 1930 Bishop Ln Ste 800 *Web:* www.cieng.com	Louisville	KY	40218	502-451-4977	451-9574	261
Chemical Abstracts Service (CAS) 2540 Olentangy River Rd *TF:* 800-848-6538 ■ *Web:* cas.org	Columbus	OH	43202	614-447-3600	447-3713	387
Chemical Bank 333 E Main St *NASDAQ: CHFC* ■ *TF:* 800-867-9757 ■ *Web:* www.chemicalbankmi.com	Midland	MI	48640	989-839-5350		360-2
Chemical Processing Magazine 1501 E Woodfield Rd Ste 400N *TF:* 800-343-4048 ■ *Web:* www.chemicalprocessing.com	Schaumburg	IL	60173	630-467-1300		457-21
Chemical Products Corp 102 Old Mill Rd *TF Cust Svc:* 877-210-9814 ■ *Web:* www.chemicalproductscorp.com	Cartersville	GA	30120	770-382-2144		143
Chemical Regulation Reporter 1801 S Bell St *TF:* 800-372-1033	Arlington	VA	22202	703-341-5777		531-5
Chemical Safety Corp 5901 Christie Ave *TF:* 888-594-1100 ■ *Web:* www.chemicalsafety.com	Emeryville	CA	94608	510-594-1000	594-1100	39
Chemical Solvents Inc 3751 Jennings Rd *Web:* www.chemicalsolvents.com	Cleveland	OH	44109	216-741-9310		541
Chemical Waste Management Inc 1001 Fannin St Ste 4000 *TF:* 800-633-7871 ■ *Web:* www.wm.com	Houston	TX	77002	713-512-6200		667
Chemical Week 140 E 45th St 2 Grand Central Tower,40th Fl *TF Cust Svc:* 866-501-7540 ■ *Web:* www.chemweek.com	New York	NY	10017	212-884-9528	884-9514	457-21
Chemically Dependent Anonymous (CDA) PO Box 423 *TF:* 888-232-4673 ■ *Web:* cdawebsitedev.com	Severna Park	MD	21146	888-232-4673		48-21
Chemin-A-Haut State Park 14656 State Pk Rd *TF:* 888-677-2436 ■ *Web:* www.crt.state.la.us	Bastrop	LA	71220	318-283-0812		565
Chemineer Inc 5870 Poe Ave **Fax:* Sales ■ *TF:* 800-643-0641 ■ *Web:* www.chemineer.com	Dayton	OH	45414	937-454-3200	454-3379*	386
Chemi-Source Inc 2665 Vista Pacific Dr *Web:* www.mrm-usa.com	Oceanside	CA	92056	760-477-8177		256
Chemithon Corp 5430 W Marginal Way SW *Web:* www.chemithon.com	Seattle	WA	98106	206-937-9954	932-3786	386

				Phone	Fax	Class
Chemline Inc 5151 Natural Bridge Rd *Web:* www.chemline.net	Saint Louis	MO	63115	314-664-2230		481
Chemlink Laboratories Inc 3960 Royal Dr. *Web:* chemlinklabs.com	Kennesaw	GA	30144	770-499-8008		476
Chemoil Corp 4 Embarcadero Ctr 34thFl. *Web:* www.chemoil.com	San Francisco	CA	94111	656-880-8200		579
Chemonics International Inc 1717 H St NW. *Web:* www.chemonics.com	Washington	DC	20006	202-955-3300		194
Chempacific Corp 6200 Freeport Ctr *Web:* www.chempacific.com	Baltimore	MD	21224	410-633-5771		146
Chem-pak Inc 242 Corning Way *TF:* 800-336-9828 ■ *Web:* www.chem-pak.com	Martinsburg	WV	25405	304-262-1880		295
Chem-plate Industries Inc 1800 Touhy Ave *Web:* www.chemplateindustries.com	Elk Grove Village	IL	60007	847-640-1600	640-1699	484
Chemprene Inc 483 Fishkill Ave *TF:* 800-431-9981 ■ *Web:* www.chemprene.com	Beacon	NY	12508	845-831-2800	831-4639	370
ChemQuest Group Inc, The 8150 Corporate Dr Ste 250. *Web:* www.chemquest.com	Cincinnati	OH	45242	513-469-7555		463
Chemready Filter Corp 9594 Velvetleaf Cir	San Ramon	CA	94582	925-735-0414		366
Chemresearch Company Inc 1101 W Hilton Ave *Web:* chemresearchco.com	Phoenix	AZ	85007	602-253-4175		481
ChemRite CoPac 19725 W Edgewood Dr Bldg A101 *Web:* www.chemritecopac.com	Lannon	WI	53046	262-255-3880		393
Chemroy Canada Inc 106 Summerlea Rd. *Web:* www.chemroy.com	Brampton	ON	L6T4X3	905-789-0701	789-7170	146
Chemsolv Inc 1140 Industry Ave SE *Web:* www.chemsolv.com	Roanoke	VA	24013	540-427-4000	427-3207	146
Chemstar Products Co 3915 Hiawatha Ave *TF:* 800-328-5037 ■ *Web:* www.chemstar.com	Minneapolis	MN	55406	612-722-0079	722-2473	144
Chemstress Consultant Co 39 S Main St *TF:* 800-676-1170 ■ *Web:* www.chemstress.com	Akron	OH	44308	330-535-5591	535-1431	261
Chem-Tainer Industries Inc 361 Neptune Ave. *TF:* 800-275-2436 ■ *Web:* www.chemtainer.com	West Babylon	NY	11704	631-661-8300	661-8209	199
ChemTech Consultants Inc 1370 Washington Pk. *Web:* www.chemtech88.com	Bridgeville	PA	15017	412-221-1360		261
Chemtex International Inc 1979 Eastwood Rd *Web:* www.chemtex.com	Wilmington	NC	28403	910-509-4400	509-4567	261
Chemtex Print Usa Inc 3061 E Maria St *Web:* chemtexprint.com	Rancho Dominguez	CA	90221	310-900-1818		258
Chemtool Inc 801 W Rockton Rd. *TF:* 800-535-5053 ■ *Web:* www.chemtool.com	Rockton	IL	61072	815-459-1250		145
Chem-Trend LP 1445 McPherson Pk Dr *TF:* 800-727-7730 ■ *Web:* www.chemtrend.com	Howell	MI	48843	517-546-4520		541
Chemtrol Div NIBCO Inc 1516 Middlebury St *TF:* 800-234-0227 ■ *Web:* nibco.com/industrial-plastics/chemtrol	Elkhart	IN	46516	574-295-3000	295-3307	596
Chemtron Corp 35850 Schneider Ct *TF:* 800-676-5091 ■ *Web:* www.chemtron-corp.com	Avon	OH	44011	440-937-6348		660
Chemtronics Inc 8125 Cobb Centre Dr. *TF:* 800-645-5244 ■ *Web:* www.chemtronics.com	Kennesaw	GA	30152	770-424-4888		145
Chemtura USA Corp 199 Benson Rd. *Web:* chemtura.com	Middlebury	CT	06749	203-573-2000		146
Chemung County 210 Lake St PO Box 588 *Web:* www.chemungcounty.com	Elmira	NY	14902	607-737-2920		338
Chemung County Chamber of Commerce 400 E Church St *TF General:* 800-627-5892 ■ *Web:* www.chemungchamber.org	Elmira	NY	14901	607-734-5137	734-4490	139
Chemung Supply Corp PO Box 527 *TF:* 800-733-5508 ■ *Web:* www.chemungsupply.com	Elmira	NY	14903	607-733-5506	732-5379	191-2
ChemWerth Inc 1764 Litchfield Tpke *Web:* www.chemwerth.com	Woodbridge	CT	06525	203-387-7794	397-8132	479
Chen Dance Ctr 70 Mulberry St 2nd Fl *Web:* www.chendancecenter.org	New York	NY	10013	212-349-0126	349-0494	573-1
Chen Ling Palace 9856 Magnolia Ave *Web:* chenlingpalace.com	Riverside	CA	92503	951-351-8511		671
CHEN PR Inc Reservoir Pl 1601 Trapelo Rd Ste 360 *Web:* www.chenpr.com	Waltham	MA	02451	781-466-8282		636
Chena Hot Springs Resort LLC PO Box 58740 *Web:* www.chenahotsprings.com	Fairbanks	AK	99711	907-451-8104		378
Chena River State Recreation Area c/o Northern Area Office 3700 Airport Way *Web:* www.dnr.alaska.gov/parks/units/chena	Fairbanks	AK	99709	907-451-2705		565
Chenango County 5 Ct St *Web:* www.co.chenango.ny.us	Norwich	NY	13815	607-337-1450	337-1455	338
Chenango Valley State Park 153 State Pk Rd *Web:* parks.ny.gov/parks/41/details.aspx	Chenango Forks	NY	13746	607-648-5251		565
Cheney Liz (Rep R - WY) 416 Cannon HOB *Web:* cheney.house.gov	Washington	DC	20515	202-225-2311	225-3057	342-2
Cheney Pulp & Paper Company Inc 1000 Anderson St. *Web:* www.cheneypulp.com	Franklin	OH	45005	937-746-9991		638
Cheney State Park 16000 NE 50th St. *Web:* ksoutdoors.com	Cheney	KS	67025	316-542-3664		565
Cheng Cohen LLC 311 N Aberdeen Ste 400 *TF:* 800-543-7362 ■ *Web:* www.chengcohen.com	Chicago	IL	60607	312-243-1701		428
Chengdu 179 Pk Rd *Web:* chengduwesthartford.com	West Hartford	CT	06119	860-232-6455	232-3002	671
Cheniere Energy Inc 700 Milam St Ste 800. *NYSE:* LNG ■ *TF:* 877-375-5002 ■ *Web:* www.cheniere.com	Houston	TX	77002	713-375-5000	375-6000	325
Chenomx Inc 10230 Jasper Ave Ste 4350 *Web:* www.chenomx.com	Edmonton	AB	T5J4P6	780-432-0033		179
Chenoweth Ford Inc 1564 E Pike St. *TF:* 888-461-4540 ■ *Web:* www.chenford.com	Clarksburg	WV	26301	888-461-4540		57
CHEP USA 8517 S Pk Cir *TF Cust Svc:* 866-855-2437 ■ *Web:* www.chep.com	Orlando	FL	32819	407-370-2437		648
Chepenik Financial Services 1010 Orange Ave *Web:* www.chepenikfinancial.com	Winter Park	FL	32789	407-660-1010		251
Cheraw State Park 100 State Pk Rd. *TF:* 800-868-9630 ■ *Web:* www.southcarolinaparks.com	Cheraw	SC	29520	843-537-9656		565
Cher-Make Sausage Co 2915 Calumet Ave. **Fax Area Code:* 920 ■ *TF:* 800-242-7679 ■ *Web:* www.cher-make.com	Manitowoc	WI	54220	800-242-7679	683-5990*	296-26
Cherney Microbiological Services Ltd 1110 S Huron Rd *Web:* cherneymicro.com	Green Bay	WI	54311	920-406-8300		743
Chernoff Diamond & Company LLC 725 RXR Plaza E Tower *Web:* www.chernoffdiamond.com	Uniondale	NY	11556	516-683-6100		193
Cherokee Brick & Tile Co Inc 3250 Waterville Rd *TF:* 800-277-2745 ■ *Web:* www.cherokeebrick.com	Macon	GA	31206	800-277-2745		150
Cherokee Consulting LLC 5057 Bear Mtn Dr *TF:* 800-573-1874 ■ *Web:* www.cherokeeconsultingllc.com	Evergreen	CO	80439	303-674-4857		180
Cherokee County 90 N St Ste 310 *TF:* 800-338-6745 ■ *Web:* www.cherokeega.com	Canton	GA	30114	678-493-6511	493-6013	338
Cherokee County 260 Cedar Bluff Rd Ste 103 *Web:* www.cherokee-county-al.com	Centre	AL	35960	256-927-3668		338
Cherokee County 520 W Main St *Web:* www.cherokeecountyiowa.com	Cherokee	IA	51012	712-225-6744		338
Cherokee County 110 W Maple *Web:* cherokeecountyks.gov	Columbus	KS	66725	620-429-2042		338
Cherokee County 210 N Limestone St	Gaffney	SC	29340	864-487-2560		338
Cherokee County 75 Peachtree St. *Web:* cherokeecounty-nc.gov	Murphy	NC	28906	828-837-5527	837-9684	338
Cherokee County 165 E Sixth St Ste 203 Ste 203 *TF:* 800-541-2524 ■ *Web:* www.co.cherokee.tx.us	Rusk	TX	75785	903-683-6540	683-5953	338
Cherokee County 213 W Delaware St *Web:* oklahomacounty.org	Tahlequah	OK	74464	918-456-0691		338
Cherokee County Chamber of Commerce 3605 Marietta Hwy *Web:* www.cherokee-chamber.com	Canton	GA	30114	770-345-0400		139
Cherokee County Chamber of Commerce (CCCC) 805 W US 64 Hwy *TF:* 800-633-7655 ■ *Web:* www.cherokeecountychamber.com	Murphy	NC	28906	828-837-2242	837-6012	139
Cherokee County Chamber of Commerce 225 S Limestone St *Web:* www.cherokeechamber.org	Gaffney	SC	29340	864-489-5721		139
Cherokee County Public Library 300 E Rutledge Ave.	Gaffney	SC	29340	864-487-2711		434-3
Cherokee County School District 1205 Bluffs Pkwy *Web:* cherokeek12.net	Canton	GA	30114	770-479-1871		685
Cherokee County School District 1 141 Twin Lake Rd *Web:* www.cherokee1.k12.sc.us	Gaffney	SC	29341	864-206-2201		685
Cherokee Distributing Company Inc 200 Miller Main Cir *TF:* 800-362-9459 ■ *Web:* cherokeedistributing.com	Knoxville	TN	37919	865-588-7641	558-8941	81-1
Cherokee Electric Co-op 1550 Clarence Chestnut Bypass PO Box O *TF:* 800-952-2667 ■ *Web:* www.cherokee.coop	Centre	AL	35960	256-927-5524	927-2278	245
Cherokee Enterprises Inc 14474 Commerce Way *TF:* 800-861-8314 ■ *Web:* www.cherokeecorp.com	Miami Lakes	FL	33016	305-828-3353		463
Cherokee Heritage Ctr & National Museum 21192 S Keeler Dr *TF:* 888-999-6007 ■ *Web:* www.cherokeeheritage.org	Park Hill	OK	74451	918-456-6007		520
Cherokee Inc 5990 Sepulveda Blvd Ste 600. *NASDAQ:* CHKE ■ *TF:* 800-446-2377 ■ *Web:* www.thecherokeegroup.com	Sherman Oaks	CA	91411	818-908-9868		301
Cherokee Information Services Inc 2850 Eisenhower Ave Ste 210 *Web:* www.cherokee-inc.com	Alexandria	VA	22314	703-416-0720	416-1045	180
Cherokee Investment Partners LLC 111 E Hargett St Ste 300. *Web:* www.cherokeefund.com	Raleigh	NC	27601	919-743-2500		401
Cherokee Landing State Park 28610 Pk 20. *Web:* www.travelok.com	Park Hill	OK	74451	918-457-5716	457-4871	565
Cherokee Ledger News, The 521 E Main St. *Web:* www.ledgernews.com	Canton	GA	30114	770-479-1441	479-3505	532-3
Cherokee Metals Company Inc 5883 Glenridge Dr NE.	Atlanta	GA	30328	770-449-1444		491
Cherokee Nation Businesses 10838 E Marshall St Ste 220 *Web:* cherokee-crc.com	Tulsa	OK	74116	918-582-9110		196
Cherokee Nation Entertainment 16489 Hwy 62 *Web:* www.cherokeecasino.com	Tahlequah	OK	74464	918-207-3600		132
Cherokee Park Ranch 436 Cherokee Hills Dr *Web:* www.cherokeeparkranch.com	Livermore	CO	80536	970-493-6522	493-5802	239
Cherokee State Park N 4475 Rd *TF:* 866-602-4653 ■ *Web:* www.travelok.com	Langley	OK	74350	918-435-8066		565
Cherokee Steel Supply 196 Leroy Anderson Dr. *TF:* 800-729-0334 ■ *Web:* www.cherokeesteel.com	Monroe	GA	30655	770-207-4621		492
Cherokee Tribal Travel & Promotions 498 Tsali Blvd. *TF:* 877-440-9990	Cherokee	NC	28719	828-359-6492	554-6475	206
Cherry Aerospace LLC 1224 E Warner Ave *Web:* www.cherryaerospace.com	Santa Ana	CA	92705	714-545-5511		621

	Phone	Fax	Class
Cherry Bekaert & Holland LLP 200 S Tenth St Ste 900 Richmond VA 23219 *Web:* www.cbh.com	804-673-5700	673-4290	2
Cherry Brook Zoo Inc 901 Foster Thurston Dr Saint John NB E2K5H9 *TF:* 800-321-1433 ■ *Web:* www.cherrybrookzoo.com	506-634-1440	634-0717	823
Cherry Corp 11200 88th Ave Pleasant Prairie WI 53158 *TF:* 800-510-1689 ■ *Web:* cherryamericas.com	262-942-6500		815
Cherry County PO Box 120 Valentine NE 69201 *Web:* www.co.cherry.ne.us	402-376-2771	376-3095	338
Cherry Creek Dodge 2727 S Havana St Denver CO 80014 *TF Sales:* 888-891-7522 ■ *Web:* www.cherrycreekdodge.com	303-751-1104		57
Cherry Creek Grill 3104 E 26th St Sioux Falls SD 57103 *Web:* cherrycreek-grill.com	605-336-2333		671
Cherry Creek Media 501 S Cherry St Ste 480 Denver CO 80246 *Web:* www.cherrycreekradio.com	303-468-6500	468-6555	643
Cherry Creek Shopping Ctr 3000 E First Ave Denver CO 80206 *TF:* 800-247-2336 ■ *Web:* www.shopcherrycreek.com	303-388-3900		460
Cherry Creek State Park 4201 S Parker Rd Aurora CO 80014 *TF:* 866-265-6447 ■ *Web:* cpw.state.co.us	303-699-3860	699-3864	565
Cherry Demolition 6131 Selinsky Rd Houston TX 77048 *TF:* 800-444-1123 ■ *Web:* www.cherrycompanies.com	713-987-0000	987-0629	189-16
Cherry Growers Inc 6331 US Hwy 31 Grawn MI 49637 *Web:* www.cherrygrowers.net	231-276-9241	276-7075	296-21
Cherry Hill Construction Inc 8211 Washington Blvd Jessup MD 20794 *Web:* www.cherryhillconstruction.com	410-799-3577	799-5483	188-4
Cherry Hill Photo Enterprises Inc 4 East Stow Rd Marlton NJ 08003 *TF:* 800-969-2440 ■ *Web:* www.cherryhillphoto.com	856-663-1616	663-0880	590
Cherry Hill Winery 7867 Crowley Rd PO Box 80 Rickreall OR 97371 *Web:* www.cherryhillwinery.com	503-623-7867	623-7878	50-7
Cherry Hospital 201 Stevens Mill Rd Goldsboro NC 27530 *Web:* www.ncdhhs.gov/dsohf/cherry	919-731-3200		374-5
Cherry Lake Tree Farm 7836 Cherry Lake Rd Groveland FL 34736 *Web:* www.cherrylake.com	352-429-2171		752
Cherry Meat Packers Inc 4750 S California Ave Chicago IL 60632	773-927-1200		473
Cherry Plain State Park 10 State Park Rd Petersburg NY 12138	518-733-5400		565
Cherry Springs State Park c/o Lyman Run State Pk 4639 Cherry Springs Rd Coudersport PA 16915 *Web:* www.dcnr.state.pa.us	814-435-5010		565
Cherry Systems Inc 2270 Northwest Pkwy Ste 125 Marietta GA 30067 *TF:* 800-500-2840 ■ *Web:* www.cherrysystems.com	770-955-2395		624
Cherry Tree Design 320 Pronghorn Trl Bozeman MT 59718 *TF:* 800-634-3268 ■ *Web:* www.cherrytreedesign.com	406-582-8800		279
Cherry Tree Investment Co 301 Carlson Pkwy Ste 103 Minnetonka MN 55305 *Web:* www.cherrytree.com	952-893-9012	893-9036	792
Cherry's Industrial Equipment 600 Morse Ave Elk Grove Village IL 60007 *TF:* 800-350-0011 ■ *Web:* cherrysind.com	800-350-0011		360
Cherrydale Farms Fundraising 707 N Vly Forge Rd Lansdale PA 19446 *TF:* 877-619-4822 ■ *Web:* www.cherrydale.com	877-619-4822		296-8
Cherryfield Foods Inc 320 Ridge Rd Cherryfield ME 04622 *Web:* www.oxfordfrozenfoods.com	207-546-7573	546-2713	315-1
Cherryland Electric Co-op 5930 US 31 S PO Box 298 Grawn MI 49637 *TF:* 800-442-8616 ■ *Web:* cherrylandelectric.coop	231-486-9200		245
Cherryman Industries 5690 Lindbergh Ln Bell CA 90201 *Web:* cherrymanindustries.com	323-780-0859		321
Cherryroad Technologies Inc 301 Gibraltar Dr Ste 2C Morris Plains NJ 07950 *TF:* 877-402-7804 ■ *Web:* www.cherryroad.com	973-402-7802		177
Cherry-Todd Electric Co-op Inc 625 W Second St Mission SD 57555 *TF:* 800-856-4417 ■ *Web:* cherry-todd.com	605-856-4416		245
Cherubini Metal Works Ltd 570 Wilkinson Ave Dartmouth NS B3B0J4	902-468-5630		480
Cheryl & Co 646 McCorkle Blvd Westerville OH 43082 **Fax Area Code:* 614 ■ *TF:* 800-443-8124 ■ *Web:* www.cheryls.com	800-443-8124	891-8699*	68
Cheryl Andrews Marketing Communications 331 Almeria Ave Coral Gables FL 33134 *TF:* 800-771-4711 ■ *Web:* www.cam-pr.com	305-444-4033		7
Chesapeake & Ohio Canal National Historical Park 1850 Dual Hwy Ste 100 Hagerstown MD 21740 *TF:* 800-999-3613 ■ *Web:* www.nps.gov/choh	301-739-4200	739-5275	564
Chesapeake Arboretum 624 Oak Grove Rd Chesapeake VA 23320 *Web:* www.cityofchesapeake.net	757-382-7060		97
Chesapeake Arts Ctr 194 Hammonds Ln Brooklyn Park MD 21225 *Web:* www.chesapeakearts.org	410-636-6597		572
Chesapeake Bank of Maryland 2001 E Joppa Rd Baltimore MD 21234 *Web:* chesapeakebank.com	410-661-1141	665-8604	70
Chesapeake Bay Magazine 1819 Bay Ridge Ave Ste 180 Annapolis MD 21403 *TF:* 800-283-2883 ■ *Web:* www.chesapeakeboating.net	410-263-2662	267-6924	457-22
Chesapeake Bay Maritime Museum 213 N Talbot St Saint Michaels MD 21663 *Web:* www.cbmm.org	410-745-2916	745-6088	520
Chesapeake Bay Packing LLC 800 Terminal Ave Newport News VA 23607 *Web:* www.chesapeakebaypacking.com	757-244-8440	244-8500	296-14
Chesapeake Bay Seafood House Assoc LLC 1960 Gallows Rd Ste 200 Vienna VA 22182 *Web:* www.chesapeakerestaurants.com	703-827-0320	893-1536	670
Chesapeake Children's Museum 25 Silopanna Rd Annapolis MD 21403 *Web:* www.theccm.org	410-990-1993		521
Chesapeake City Hall 306 Cedar Rd Chesapeake VA 23322 *Web:* cityofchesapeake.net	757-382-6151	382-6678	338
Chesapeake College PO Box 8 Wye Mills MD 21679 **Fax:* Admissions ■ *Web:* www.chesapeake.edu	410-758-1537	827-5878*	162
Chesapeake Conventions & Tourism Bureau (CCT) 860 Greenbrier Cir Ste 101 Chesapeake VA 23320 *TF:* 888-889-5551 ■ *Web:* www.visitchesapeake.com	757-502-4898	502-8016	206
Chesapeake Energy Corp 6100 N Western Ave Oklahoma City OK 73118 *NYSE:* CHK ■ *Web:* chk.com	405-848-3000		536
Chesapeake Lodging Trust (CLT) 1997 Annapolis Exchange Pkwy Ste 410 Annapolis MD 21401 *NYSE:* CHSP ■ *TF:* 800-698-2820 ■ *Web:* www.chesapeakelodgingtrust.com	800-698-2820		654
Chesapeake Medical Systems Inc 118 Cedar St Cambridge MD 21613 *Web:* chesapeakemedicalsystems.com	410-228-0221	228-4561	353
Chesapeake Planetarium 312 Cedar Rd Chesapeake VA 23322 *Web:* virginia.org	757-547-0153		598
Chesapeake Public Library 298 Cedar Rd Chesapeake VA 23322 *Web:* www.chesapeake.lib.va.us	757-410-7100		434-3
Chesapeake Regional Medical Ctr 736 Battlefield Blvd N Chesapeake VA 23320 *TF:* 800-456-8121 ■ *Web:* www.chesapeakeregional.com	757-312-8121		374-3
Chesapeake Seafood House 3045 Clear Lake Ave Springfield IL 62702 *Web:* www.chesapeakeseafoodhouse.com	217-522-5220		671
Chesapeake Spice Co LLC 4613 Mercedes Dr Belcamp MD 21017 *Web:* www.chesapeakespice.com	410-272-6100		123
Chesapeake Structural Systems Inc 2401 Roxbury Rd Charles City VA 23030 *Web:* www.chestruc.com	804-559-1711		817
Chesapeake Utilities Corp 909 Silver Lake Blvd Dover DE 19904 *NYSE:* CPK ■ *TF:* 800-732-0330 ■ *Web:* www.chpk.com	302-734-6799	734-6750	787
Chesapeake Woodworking Inc 125 N Kresson St Baltimore MD 21224 *Web:* www.chesapeakewoodworking.net	410-276-1060		200
Chesapeake's 600 Union Ave Knoxville TN 37902 *Web:* www.chesapeakes.com	865-673-3400		671
Chesbro Music Company Inc 327 Broadway St Idaho Falls ID 83402 *Web:* www.chesbromusic.com	208-522-8691		527
Cheshire Academy 10 Main St Cheshire CT 06410 *Web:* www.cheshireacademy.org	203-272-5396	250-7209	622
Cheshire Center Pediatric Comm 2500 N Church St Greensboro NC 27405 *TF:* 800-360-1099 ■ *Web:* www.cheshirecenter.net	336-375-2240		7
Cheshire Chamber of Commerce 195 S Main St Cheshire CT 06410 *TF:* 800-953-4467 ■ *Web:* www.cheshirechamber.org	203-272-2345	271-3044	139
Cheshire County 12 Ct St Keene NH 03431 *Web:* www.co.cheshire.nh.us	603-352-6902		338
Cheshire Marketing Inc 3209 Guess Rd Ste 100 Durham NC 27705 *TF:* 800-495-4633 ■ *Web:* www.cheshiremarketing.com	800-495-4633		195
Cheshire Medical Ctr 580 Ct St Keene NH 03431 *Web:* www.cheshire-med.com	603-354-5400		374-3
Cheshire Oil Company Inc 678 Marlborough St PO Box 586 Keene NH 03431 *TF:* 800-286-6363 ■ *Web:* www.cheshireoil.com	603-352-0001		316
Cheshire Public Library 104 Main St Cheshire CT 06410 *TF:* 800-275-2273 ■ *Web:* cheshirelibrary.com	203-272-2245	272-7714	434-3
Cheshire, The 6300 Clayton Rd Saint Louis MO 63117 *Web:* www.cheshirestl.com	314-647-7300	647-0442	379
Chester Bross Construction Co 6739 CR 423 Palmyra MO 63461 *Web:* www.cbrossgroup.com	573-221-5958	221-1892	780
Chester County 140 Main St PO Box 580 Chester SC 29706 *Web:* www.chestercounty.org	803-385-2605		338
Chester County 313 W Market St Ste 6202 PO Box 2748 West Chester PA 19380 *TF:* 800-692-1100 ■ *Web:* www.chesco.org	610-344-6100	344-5995	338
Chester County Bar Association, The 15 W Gay St 2nd Fl West Chester PA 19380 *TF:* 800-701-5161 ■ *Web:* chescobar.org	610-692-1889		533
Chester County Chamber of Commerce 109 Gadsden St Chester SC 29706 *Web:* www.chesterchamber.com	803-581-4142	581-2431	139
Chester County Historical Society 225 N High St West Chester PA 19380 *Web:* www.chestercohistorical.org	610-692-4800		520
Chester County Hospital 701 E Marshall St West Chester PA 19380 **Fax:* Admitting ■ *Web:* www.cchosp.com	610-431-5000	430-2958*	374-3
Chester County Library 450 Exton Sq Pkwy Exton PA 19341 *Web:* www.ccls.org	610-280-2600		434-3
Chester County Library 100 Ctr St Chester SC 29706 *Web:* www.chesterlibsc.org	803-377-8145	377-8146	434-3
Chester County School District 109 Hinton St Chester SC 29706 *Web:* www.chester.k12.sc.us	803-385-6122		685
Chester County Tourist Bureau 300 Greenwood Rd Kennett Square PA 19348 *Web:* www.brandywinevalley.com	484-770-8550	770-8557	206
Chester Engineers Inc 1555 Coraopolis Heights Rd Moon Township PA 15108 *Web:* www.chester-engineers.com	412-809-6600		256
Chester Fritz Auditorium 3475 University Ave Grand Forks ND 58202 *TF:* 800-375-4068 ■ *Web:* und.edu	701-777-3076	777-4710	572
Chester Inc 555 Eastport Ctr Dr Valparaiso IN 46383 *TF:* 800-778-1131 ■ *Web:* chesterinc.com	219-465-7555		296-35

Name / Address	City	State	Zip	Phone	Fax	Class
Chester Mental Health Ctr 1315 Lehman Dr. *TF:* 800-843-6154 ■ *Web:* www.dhs.state.il.us	Chester	IL	62233	618-826-4571		374-5
Chester State Park 759 State Pk Dr *TF:* 866-345-7275 ■ *Web:* www.southcarolinaparks.com	Chester	SC	29706	803-385-2680		565
Chester Valley Engineers Inc 83 Chestnut Rd. *TF:* 800-878-2202 ■ *Web:* www.chesterv.com	Paoli	PA	19301	610-644-4623		261
Chester Water Authority PO Box 467 *TF:* 800-793-2323 ■ *Web:* www.chesterwater.com	Chester	PA	19016	610-876-8185		805
Chester's International LLC 3500 Colonnade Pkwy Ste 325 *TF:* 800-554-4537 ■ *Web:* www.chestersinternational.com	Birmingham	AL	35243	205-949-4690		310
Chesterfield Chamber of Commerce 101 Chesterfield Business Pkwy *Web:* www.chesterfieldmochamber.com	Chesterfield	MO	63005	636-532-3399	532-7446	139
Chesterfield County PO Box 70 *TF:* 800-468-3382 ■ *Web:* www.chesterfield.gov	Chesterfield	VA	23832	804-748-1201	751-4993	338
Chesterfield County Library 119 Main St *Web:* chesterfield.lib.sc.us	Chesterfield	SC	29709	843-623-7489	623-3295	434-3
Chesterfield Gorge Natural Area 1823 Route 9 *Web:* www.nhstateparks.org	Chesterfield	NH	03443	603-363-8373		565
Chesterfield Hotel 363 Cocoanut Row *TF:* 800-243-7871 ■ *Web:* www.chesterfieldpb.com	Palm Beach	FL	33480	561-659-5800		379
Chesterfield Yarn Mills Inc 201 N Maple St. *Web:* www.chesterfieldwraps.com	Pageland	SC	29728	843-672-7211		745-9
Chester-Jensen Company Inc PO Box 908 *TF:* 800-685-3750 ■ *Web:* www.chester-jensen.com	Chester	PA	19016	610-876-6276	876-0485	298
Chesterton Tribune 193 S Calumet Rd *TF:* 800-589-3331 ■ *Web:* www.chestertontribune.com	Chesterton	IN	46304	219-926-1131		532-3
Chestnut Hill College 9601 Germantown Ave **Fax:* Admissions ■ *TF:* 800-248-0052 ■ *Web:* www.chc.edu	Philadelphia	PA	19118	215-248-7001	248-7082*	166
Chestnut Hill Hospital 8835 Germantown Ave *Web:* www.chestnuthillhealth.com	Philadelphia	PA	19118	215-248-8200		374-3
Chestnut Hill Hotel 8229 Germantown Ave *TF:* 800-628-9744 ■ *Web:* www.chestnuthillhotel.com	Philadelphia	PA	19118	215-242-5905	242-8778	379
Chestnut Investment Advisory 402 Bethlehem Pk. *TF:* 800-232-4782 ■ *Web:* www.regardingyourmoney.com	Erdenheim	PA	19038	215-836-4880		796
Chestnut Mountain Resort 8700 Chestnut Dr. *TF:* 800-397-1320 ■ *Web:* www.chestnutmtn.com	Galena	IL	61036	800-397-1320		378
Chestnut Ridge Foam Inc PO Box 781 *Web:* www.chestnutridgefoam.com	Latrobe	PA	15650	724-537-9000		601
Chet Morrison Contractors LLC 9 Bayou Dularge Rd *TF:* 800-600-5751 ■ *Web:* www.chetmorrison.com	Houma	LA	70363	985-868-1950		188
Chet Nichols Inc 1904 S M139 *Web:* www.chetnichols.com	Benton Harbor	MI	49022	269-925-1183		54
Chetan Sharma Consulting LLC 1778 12th Ave NE **Fax Area Code:* 703 ■ *Web:* www.chetansharma.com	Issaquah	WA	98029	425-657-0555	848-2981*	196
Chettinaad Palace 2205 N Central Expy *Web:* www.chettinaadpalace.com	Plano	TX	75075	469-229-9100		671
Cheverus High School 267 Ocean Ave *Web:* www.cheverus.org	Portland	ME	04103	207-774-6238		685
Chevo Consulting LLC 2275 Research Blvd Ste 100 *Web:* www.chevoconsulting.com	Rockville	MD	20850	301-309-0040		196
Chevrolet of Naperville 1515 W Ogden Ave *Web:* www.chevroletofnaperville.com	Naperville	IL	60540	630-596-1189		57
Chevron Canada Ltd 1200 - 1050 W Pender St *TF:* 800-663-1650 ■ *Web:* www.chevron.ca	Vancouver	BC	V6E3T4	604-668-5300		580
Chevron Corp 6001 Bollinger Canyon Rd *NYSE: CVX* ■ *TF Cust Svc:* 800-368-8357 ■ *Web:* www.chevron.com	San Ramon	CA	94583	925-842-1000		536
Chevron Global Marine Products LLC 9401 Williamsburg Plaza Ste 201 *TF:* 800-283-9582 ■ *Web:* www.chevronmarineproducts.com	Louisville	KY	40222	914-285-7390		580
Chevron Phillips Chemical Company LP 10001 Six Pines Dr. *TF:* 800-231-1212 ■ *Web:* www.cpchem.com	The Woodlands	TX	77380	832-813-4100		144
Chevron Phillips Chemical Company Performance Pipe Division 5085 W Pk Blvd Ste 500 *TF:* 800-527-0662 ■ *Web:* www.performancepipe.com	Plano	TX	75093	972-599-6600		596
Chevron Pipe Line Co 4800 Fournace Pl *TF:* 877-596-2800 ■ *Web:* www.chevron.com/prodserv/cpl	Bellaire	TX	77401	877-596-2800		597
Chevron Technology Ventures (CTV) 6001 Bollinger Canyon Rd *NYSE: CVX* ■ *Web:* www.chevron.com/technologyventures	San Ramon	CA	94583	925-842-1000		792
Chevron Texaco Credit Card Ctr PO Box P **Fax Area Code:* 925 ■ *TF:* 800-243-8766 ■ *Web:* www.chevrontexacocards.com	Concord	CA	94524	800-243-8766	827-6367*	215
Chevy Chase Trust Co 7501 Wisconsin Ave W Tower Ste 1500W *Web:* www.chevychasetrust.com	Bethesda	MD	20814	240-497-5000		401
Chevys Inc 31100 Courthouse Dr. *Web:* www.chevys.com	Union City	CA	94587	858-205-1123		670
Chewacla State Park 124 Shell Toomer Pkwy *TF:* 800-252-7275 ■ *Web:* www.alapark.com	Auburn	AL	36830	334-887-5621	821-2439	565
Cheyenne Area Convention & Visitors Bureau 121 W 15th St Ste 202 *TF:* 800-426-5009 ■ *Web:* www.cheyenne.org	Cheyenne	WY	82001	307-778-3133	778-3190	206
Cheyenne Botanic Gardens 710 S Lions Pk Dr *Web:* www.botanic.org	Cheyenne	WY	82001	307-637-6458		97
Cheyenne City Hall 2101 O'Neil Ave *TF:* 855-491-1859 ■ *Web:* www.cheyennecity.org	Cheyenne	WY	82001	307-637-6200	637-6454	337
Cheyenne Civic Ctr 510 W 20th St. *TF:* 877-691-2787 ■ *Web:* www.cheyennecity.org	Cheyenne	WY	82001	307-637-6364	637-6365	572
Cheyenne County PO Box 567 *Web:* www.co.cheyenne.co.us	Cheyenne Wells	CO	80810	719-767-5685	767-8730	338
Cheyenne County 212 E Washington *Web:* www.cheyennecounty.org	Saint Francis	KS	67756	785-332-8850		338
Cheyenne County 2473 Craig Ave PO Box 217 **Fax:* Hum Res ■ *Web:* www.cheyennecountyne.ne	Sidney	NE	69162	308-254-2141	254-5049*	338
Cheyenne Depot Museum 121 W 15th St Ste 300 *Web:* www.cheyennedepotmuseum.org	Cheyenne	WY	82001	307-632-3905	632-0614	520
Cheyenne Frontier Days Old West Museum 4610 N Carey Ave PO Box 2720 *Web:* www.oldwestmuseum.org	Cheyenne	WY	82001	307-778-7290	778-7288	520
Cheyenne Little Theatre Players PO Box 20087 *Web:* www.cheyennelittletheatre.org	Cheyenne	WY	82003	307-638-6543		572
Cheyenne Mountain Conference Resort 3225 Broadmoor Valley Rd. *TF:* 800-428-8886 ■ *Web:* www.cheyennemountain.com	Colorado Springs	CO	80906	719-538-4000		377
Cheyenne Mountain State Park 4255 Sinton Rd. *Web:* cpw.state.co.us	Colorado Springs	CO	80907	719-227-5256		565
Cheyenne Mountain Zoological Park 4250 Cheyenne Mtn Zoo Rd *Web:* www.cmzoo.org	Colorado Springs	CO	80906	719-633-9925	633-2254	823
Cheyenne Newspaper Inc 702 W Lincolnway *TF:* 800-561-6268 ■ *Web:* www.wyomingnews.com	Cheyenne	WY	82001	307-634-3361	633-3189	637-8
Cheyenne Regional Airport 4000 Airport Pkwy PO Box 2210 *Web:* www.cheyenneairport.com	Cheyenne	WY	82001	307-634-7071	632-1206	27
Cheyenne Regional Medical Ctr (CRMC) 214 E 23rd St *Web:* www.crmcwy.org	Cheyenne	WY	82001	307-634-2273		374-3
Cheyenne State Recreation Area I-80 Exit 300 PO Box 944 *Web:* outdoornebraska.gov	Wood River	NE	68883	308-385-6210		565
Cheyenne Symphony Orchestra (CSO) 1904 Thomes Ave *Web:* www.cheyennesymphony.org	Cheyenne	WY	82001	307-778-8561	634-7512	573-3
Cheyney University of Pennsylvania 1837 University Cir PO Box 200 **Fax:* Admissions ■ *TF:* 800-243-9639 ■ *Web:* www.cheyney.edu	Cheyney	PA	19319	610-399-2275	399-2099*	166
Chez Jean-Pierre Bistro 132 N County Rd *Web:* chezjean-pierre.com	Palm Beach	FL	33480	561-833-1171		671
Chez la Mere Michel 1209 Rue Guy *Web:* www.chezlameremichel.ca	Montreal	QC	H3H2L3	514-934-0473		671
Chez Leveque 1030 Laurier Ave W *Web:* www.chezleveque.ca	Outremont	QC	H2V2K8	514-279-7355		671
Chez Nous 510 Neches St. *Web:* cheznousaustin.com	Austin	TX	78701	512-473-2413		671
Chez Papa Bistrot 1401 18th St	San Francisco	CA	94107	415-824-8205		671
Chez Pascal 960 Hope St. *Web:* www.chez-pascal.com	Providence	RI	02906	401-421-4422		671
Chez Spencer 82 14th St *Web:* www.chezspencer.net	San Francisco	CA	94103	415-864-2191		671
Chez Thuy Restaurant 2655 28th St *Web:* www.chezthuy.com	Boulder	CO	80301	303-442-1700		671
Chez Zee American Bistro 5406 Balcones Dr *Web:* www.chez-zee.com	Austin	TX	78731	512-454-2666		671
CHEZ-FM 106.1 (CR) 2001 Thurston Dr *Web:* www.1061chez.ca	Ottawa	ON	K1G6C9	613-736-2001		645-117
Chezgal Merchandising Creations 8936 W 25th St. *TF:* 800-293-4232 ■ *Web:* www.cmc-promotional-merchandising.com	Los Angeles	CA	90034	310-841-5893		241
CHF Home Furnishings 104 S Orchard St *Web:* www.shopchf.com	Boise	ID	83705	208-343-7769		362
CHF Industries Inc 1 Pk Ave 9th Fl *TF Cust Svc:* 800-243-7090 ■ *Web:* www.chfindustries.com	New York	NY	10016	212-951-7800		746
CHFM-FM 95.9 (AC) 535 Seventh Ave SW *Web:* kiss959.com	San Francisco	AB	T2P0Y4	403-246-9696		645-27
CHH (Charlotte Hungerford Hospital) 540 Litchfield St *Web:* charlottehungerford.org	Torrington	CT	06790	860-496-6666	482-8627	374-3
CHI (Children's Hospice International) 500 Montgomery St Ste 400 *Web:* www.chionline.org	Alexandria	VA	22314	703-684-0330		49-8
Chi Alpha Campus Ministries USA 1445 Booneville Ave *Web:* www.chialpha.com	Springfield	MO	65802	417-862-2781	865-9947	48-16
Chi Corp 5265 Naiman Pkwy *TF:* 800-828-0599 ■ *Web:* www.chicorporation.com	Cleveland	OH	44139	440-498-2300		180
Chi Dynasty 1813 Hillhurst Ave *Web:* www.chidynasty.com	Los Angeles	CA	90027	323-667-3388	667-3393	671
Chi Engineering Services Inc 430 W Rd *Web:* www.chiengineering.com	Portsmouth	NH	03801	603-433-5654		256
CHI Health Wellness Center at Immanuel 7105 Newport Ave.	Omaha	NE	68152	402-572-2900		372
Chi Omega Fraternity 3395 Players Club Pkwy *Web:* www.chiomega.com	Memphis	TN	38125	901-748-8600	748-8686	48-16
CHI Overhead Doors Inc 1485 Sunrise Dr *Web:* www.chiohd.com	Arthur	IL	61911	217-543-2135		480
Chi Phi Fraternity 1160 Satellite Blvd *TF:* 800-849-1824 ■ *Web:* www.chiphi.org	Suwanee	GA	30024	404-231-1824		48-16
Chi Psi Fraternity 45 Rutledge St *Web:* www.chipsi.org	Nashville	TN	37210	615-736-2520	736-2366	48-16

Phone | Fax | Class

CHI Solutions Inc
801 W Ellsworth Rd Ste 202 ... Ann Arbor MI 48108 734-662-6363 668
Web: www.chisolutionsinc.com
CHI St Joseph Health 2801 Franciscan Dr ... Bryan TX 77802 979-776-3777 374-3
Web: www.st-joseph.org
CHI St. Vincent 2 St Vincent Cir ... Little Rock AR 72205 501-552-3000 374-3
Web: www.stvincenthealth.com
Chia Shiang 2016 Packard St ... Ann Arbor MI 48104 734-741-0778 671
Chiado 864 College St ... Toronto ON M6H1A3 416-538-1910 588-8383 671
Web: www.chiadorestaurant.com
Chiampou Travis Besaw & Kershner LLP
45 Bryant Woods N ... Amherst NY 14228 716-630-2400 2
Web: ctbk.com
Chiang Patel & Yerby
1820 Regal Row Ste 200 ... Dallas TX 75235 214-638-0500 638-3723 261
Web: www.cpyi.com
Chiante Cafe & Restaurant
2805 - 32 Ave NE ... Calgary AB T1Y6J1 403-291-2707 291-1615 671
Web: chianticafe.ca
Chianti Cafe 1438 17th Ave SW ... Calgary AB T2T0C8 403-229-1600 671
Web: www.chianticafe.ca
Chianti Restaurant 6535 Line Ave ... Shreveport LA 71106 318-868-8866 671
Web: chiantirestaurant.net
Chiba Bank Ltd
1133 Ave of the Americas 15th Fl ... New York NY 10036 212-354-7777 354-8575 70
Web: www.chibabank.co.jp/english/corporate/profile
Chicago Architecture Foundation
224 S Michigan Ave ... Chicago IL 60604 312-922-3432 95
TF: 800-680-7345 ■ *Web:* www.architecture.org
Chicago Automobile Trade Assn
18 W 200 Butterfield Rd ... Oakbrook Terrace IL 60181 630-495-2282 138
Web: cata.info
Chicago Bears 1000 Football Dr ... Lake Forest IL 60045 847-295-6600 715-3
Web: www.chicagobears.com
Chicago Blackhawks 1901 W Madison St ... Chicago IL 60612 312-455-7000 455-7041* 716
**Fax:* PR ■ *TF:* 800-843-2827 ■ *Web:* blackhawks.nhl.com
Chicago Board of Education
125 S Clark St ... Chicago IL 60603 773-553-1600 553-3543 685
Web: www.cps.edu/about_cps/pages/aboutcps.aspx
Chicago Board Options Exchange (CBOE)
400 S La Salle St ... Chicago IL 60605 312-786-5600 786-8818 691
Web: www.cboe.com
Chicago Boiler Co 1300 NW Ave ... Gurnee IL 60031 847-662-4000 662-4003 91
TF Cust Svc: 800-522-7343 ■ *Web:* cbmills.com
Chicago Botanic Garden
1000 Lake Cook Rd ... Glencoe IL 60022 847-835-5440 835-4484 97
TF: 877-829-5500 ■ *Web:* www.chicagobotanic.org
Chicago Bridge & Iron Co
6001 Rogerdale Rd ... Houston TX 77072 713-485-1000 189-14
NYSE: CBI ■ *TF General:* 866-235-5687 ■ *Web:* www.cbi.com
Chicago Bulls 1001 W Madison St ... Chicago IL 60612 312-455-4000 714-1
Web: www.nba.com
Chicago Children's Museum
700 E Grand Ave ... Chicago IL 60611 312-527-1000 527-9082 521
Web: chicagochildrensmuseum.org
Chicago Chop House 60 W Ontario St ... Chicago IL 60654 312-787-7100 671
Web: www.chicagochophouse.com
Chicago City Hall 121 N La Salle St ... Chicago IL 60602 312-744-4000 337
TF: 800-832-6352 ■ *Web:* cityofchicago.org
Chicago Community Trust & Affiliates
111 E Wacker Dr Ste 1400 ... Chicago IL 60601 312-616-8000 616-7955 303
Web: www.cct.org
Chicago Convention & Tourism Bureau
2301 S Lake Shore Dr
McCormick Complex Lakeside Ctr ... Chicago IL 60616 312-567-8500 206
Web: www.choosechicago.com
Chicago Cornea Consultants Ltd
806 S Central Ave Ste 300 ... Highland Park IL 60035 847-882-5900 882-6028 798
Web: www.chicagocornea.com
Chicago Council on Global Affairs, The (CCGA)
332 S Michigan Ave Ste 1100 ... Chicago IL 60604 312-726-3860 821-7555 634
Web: www.thechicagocouncil.org
Chicago Cubs 1060 W Addison St Ste 1 ... Chicago IL 60613 773-404-2827 404-4129* 713
**Fax:* PR ■ *Web:* chicago.cubs.mlb.com
Chicago Cutting Die Co
3555 Woodhead Dr ... Northbrook IL 60062 847-509-5800 509-0355 757
Web: www.chicagocuttingdie.com
Chicago Defender 4445 S King Dr ... Chicago IL 60653 312-225-2400 532-2
TF: 800-270-7721 ■ *Web:* www.chicagodefender.com
Chicago Display Marketing Corp
2021 W St ... River Grove IL 60171 708-842-0001 681-0010* 233
**Fax Area Code:* 800 ■ *TF:* 800-681-4340 ■ *Web:* www.chicagodisplay.com
Chicago Dowel Company Inc
4700 W Grand Ave ... Chicago IL 60639 773-622-2000 622-2047 820
TF: 800-333-6935 ■ *Web:* www.chicagodowel.com
Chicago Dryer Co 2200 N Pulaski Rd ... Chicago IL 60639 773-235-4430 235-4439 427
Web: www.chidry.com
Chicago Elevator Co 3260 W Grand Ave ... Chicago IL 60651 773-227-0737 189-1
Chicago Equity Partners LLC
180 N LaSalle St Ste 3800 ... Chicago IL 60601 312-629-8200 528
Web: www.chicagoequity.com
Chicago Executive Airport
1020 Plant Rd ... Wheeling IL 60090 847-537-2580 63
Web: chiexec.com
Chicago Extruded Metals Co (CXM)
1601 S 54th Ave ... Cicero IL 60804 800-323-8102 780-3479* 485
**Fax Area Code:* 708 ■ *TF Cust Svc:* 800-323-8102 ■ *Web:* www.cxm.com
Chicago Faucets A Geberit Co
2100 S Clearwater Dr ... Des Plaines IL 60018 847-803-5000 298-3101* 609
**Fax:* Sales ■ *TF:* 800-323-5060 ■ *Web:* www.chicagofaucets.com
Chicago Fire 7000 S Harlem Ave ... Bridgeview IL 60455 708-594-7200 496-6050 717
TF: 888-657-3473 ■ *Web:* www.chicago-fire.com
Chicago Flame Hardening Company Inc
5200 Railroad Ave ... East Chicago IN 46312 219-397-6475 484
Web: www.cflame.com
Chicago Gasket Co 1285 W N Ave ... Chicago IL 60622 773-486-3060 486-3784 326
TF: 800-833-5666 ■ *Web:* www.chicagogasket.com

Chicago Gear-DO James Corp
2823 W Fulton St ... Chicago IL 60612 773-638-0508 638-7161 709
Web: www.oc gear.com
Chicago Hardware & Fixture Co
9100 Parklane Ave ... Franklin Park IL 60131 847-455-6609 455-0012 350
TF: 800-424-9473 ■ *Web:* www.chicagohardware.com
Chicago Heights Steel Acquisition Corp
211 E Main St ... Chicago Heights IL 60411 708-756-5648 723
Web: chs.com
Chicago History Museum
1601 N Clark St ... Chicago IL 60614 312-642-4600 266-2077 520
Web: www.chicagohistory.org
Chicago International Film Festival
Cinema Chicago 30 E Adams St Ste 800 ... Chicago IL 60603 312-683-0121 683-0122 282
TF: 800-982-2787 ■ *Web:* www.chicagofilmfestival.com
Chicago Joe's 820 S Fourth St ... Las Vegas NV 89101 702-382-5637 671
Web: www.chicagojoesrestaurant.com
Chicago Lakeshore Hospital
4840 N Marine Dr ... Chicago IL 60640 773-878-9700 374-5
TF Cust Svc: 800-888-0560 ■ *Web:* www.chicagolakeshorehospital.com
Chicago Legal Search Ltd
180 N LaSalle St ... Chicago IL 60601 312-251-2580 251-0223 266
TF: 800-973-1177 ■ *Web:* www.chicagolegalsearch.com
Chicago Life Magazine PO Box 11311 ... Chicago IL 60611 773-549-1523 457-22
TF: 800-896-9095 ■ *Web:* www.chicagolife.net
Chicago Lighthouse, The
1850 W Roosevelt Rd ... Chicago IL 60608 312-666-1331 242
Chicago Magazine
435 N Michigan Ave Ste 1100 ... Chicago IL 60611 312-222-8999 457-22
TF: 800-999-0879 ■ *Web:* www.chicagomag.com
Chicago Mailing Tube Co
400 N Leavitt St ... Chicago IL 60612 312-243-6050 243-6545 125
TF: 800-882-9002 ■ *Web:* www.mailing-tube.com
Chicago Meat Authority Inc (CMA)
1120 W 47th Pl ... Chicago IL 60609 773-254-3811 254-5851 296-26
TF: 800-383-3811 ■ *Web:* www.chicagomeat.com
Chicago Metal Fabricators Inc
3724 S Rockwell St ... Chicago IL 60632 773-523-5755 523-8680 482
TF: 877-400-5995 ■ *Web:* www.chicagometal.com
Chicago Metallic Corp
4849 S Austin Ave ... Chicago IL 60638 708-563-4600 222-3744* 491
**Fax Area Code:* 800 ■ *Web:* www.chicago-metallic.com
Chicago Midway Airport
5700 S Cicero Ave ... Chicago IL 60638 773-838-0600 27
TF: 800-832-6352 ■ *Web:* www.flychicago.com
Chicago Mold Engineering Co
615 Stetson Ave ... Saint Charles IL 60174 630-584-1311 584-8695 757
TF: 800-394-2460 ■ *Web:* www.chicagomold.com
Chicago Nannies Inc
101 N Marion St Ste 300 ... Oak Park IL 60301 708-524-2101 260
TF: 866-900-9605 ■ *Web:* www.chicagonanniesinc.com
Chicago Nut & Bolt Inc
150 Covington Dr ... Bloomingdale IL 60108 630-529-8600 350
TF: 888-529-8600 ■ *Web:* www.cnb-inc.com
Chicago Oakbrook Financial Group
903 Commerce Dr Ste 300 ... Oak Brook IL 60523 630-954-5572 403
Web: www.cofgroup.com
Chicago Office of Tourism & Culture
78 E Washington St 4th Fl ... Chicago IL 60602 312-744-2400 206
TF: 888-871-5311 ■ *Web:* www.choosechicago.com
Chicago Opera Theater
70 E Lake St Ste 815 ... Chicago IL 60601 312-704-8420 573-2
Web: www.chicagooperatheater.org
Chicago Parking Meters LLC
2735 N Ashland Ave ... Chicago IL 60614 773-935-2178 192
Web: www.chicagometers.com
Chicago Patrolmen'S Federal Credit Union
1407 W Washington Blvd ... Chicago IL 60607 312-726-8814 219
Web: cpdfcu.com
Chicago Pneumatic Tool Co
1800 Overview Dr ... Rock Hill SC 29730 803-817-7000 228-9096* 759
**Fax Area Code:* 800 ■ **Fax:* Hum Res ■ *TF:* 800-624-4735 ■ *Web:* www.cp.com
Chicago Powdered Metal Products Co
9700 Waveland Ave ... Franklin Park IL 60131 847-678-2836 295
TF: 800-783-2420 ■ *Web:* www.chipm.com
Chicago Premium Outlets
1650 Premium Outlets Blvd ... Aurora IL 60502 630-585-2200 460
Web: www.premiumoutlets.com
Chicago Public Library 400 S State St ... Chicago IL 60605 312-747-4300 434-3
TF: 800-472-4643 ■ *Web:* www.chipublib.org
Chicago Public Radio 848 E Grand Ave ... Chicago IL 60611 312-948-4600 645-10
TF: 800-252-8951 ■ *Web:* www.chicagopublicradio.org
Chicago Reader 11 E Illinois St ... Chicago IL 60611 312-828-0350 828-9926 532-5
TF: 888-473-5362 ■ *Web:* www.chicagoreader.com
Chicago Records Management Inc
3815 Carnation St ... Franklin Park IL 60131 847-678-0002 186
TF: 800-568-9300 ■ *Web:* www.chicagorecords.com
Chicago Rivet & Machine Co
901 Frontenac Rd ... Naperville IL 60563 630-357-8500 983-9314 278
AMEX: CVR ■ *TF:* 800-289-7483 ■ *Web:* www.chicagorivet.com
Chicago Scenic Studios Inc
1315 N Branch St ... Chicago IL 60642 312-274-9900 8
TF: 800-634-4873 ■ *Web:* www.chicagoscenic.com
Chicago Shakespeare Theater
800 E Grand Ave Navy Pier ... Chicago IL 60611 312-595-5600 595-5644 572
Web: www.chicagoshakes.com
Chicago Sinfonietta
70 E Lake St Ste 226 ... Chicago IL 60601 312-236-3681 236-5429 573-3
TF: 800-838-3006 ■ *Web:* www.chicagosinfonietta.org
Chicago Sky 20 W Kinzie St Ste 1000 ... Chicago IL 60610 312-828-9550 714-2
TF: 877-329-9622 ■ *Web:* www.wnba.com
Chicago Slitter Company Inc, The
1025 W Thorndale Ave ... Itasca IL 60143 630-875-9800 190
Web: www.therdigroup.com
Chicago South Loop Hotel 11 W 26th St ... Chicago IL 60616 312-225-7000 378
Web: www.chicagosouthloophotel.com
Chicago Southland Chamber of Commerce
920 W 175th St ... Homewood IL 60430 708-957-6950 957-6968 139
Web: www.chicagosouthlandchamber.com

Name / Address	City	State	Zip	Phone	Fax	Class
Chicago Southland CVB 2304 173rd St. *TF:* 888-895-8233 ■ *Web:* www.cscvb.com	Lansing	IL	60438	708-895-8200	895-8288	206
Chicago Southshore & South Bend Railroad 505 N Carroll Ave *TF:* 800-356-2079 ■ *Web:* www.anacostia.com/railroads/css	Michigan City	IN	46360	219-874-9000	879-3754	648
Chicago State University 9501 S King Dr **Fax:* Admissions ■ *TF:* 800-937-3898 ■ *Web:* www.csu.edu	Chicago	IL	60628	773-995-2513	995-3820*	166
Chicago Steel Container Corp 1846 S Kilbourn Ave *TF:* 800-633-4933 ■ *Web:* chicagosteelcontainer.com	Chicago	IL	60623	773-277-2244	277-1585	198
Chicago Stock Exchange 440 S LaSalle St *Web:* chx.com	Chicago	IL	60605	312-663-2222		691
Chicago Style SEO Inc 4619 N Ravenswood Ave Ste 104 *Web:* www.chicagostyleseo.com	Chicago	IL	60640	773-809-5002		5
Chicago Sun-Times 350 N Orleans St *Web:* www.suntimes.com	Chicago	IL	60654	312-321-3000		532-2
Chicago Supernatural Tours PO Box 557544 *Web:* www.ghosttours.com	Chicago	IL	60655	708-499-0300		760
Chicago Symphony Orchestra 220 S Michigan Ave *TF:* 800-223-7114 ■ *Web:* www.cso.org	Chicago	IL	60604	312-294-3000	294-3035	573-3
Chicago Teachers Union 222 Merchandise Mart Plaza Ste 400 *Web:* www.ctunet.com	Chicago	IL	60654	312-329-9100	329-6200	414
Chicago Title & Trust Co 171 N Clark St *TF:* 800-621-1919 ■ *Web:* www.ctic.com	Chicago	IL	60601	312-223-2000		391-6
Chicago Title Company of Oregon 10135 SE Sunnyside Rd Ste 300 *Web:* www.chicagotitleoregon.com	Clackamas	OR	97015	503-794-5860		391-6
Chicago Transit Authority (CTA) 567 West Lake St *Web:* www.transitchicago.com	Chicago	IL	60661	312-664-7200		468
Chicago Tribune 5400 N Lakewood Ave *TF:* 800-874-2863 ■ *Web:* www.chicagotribune.com	Chicago	IL	60640	312-222-3232		532-4
Chicago Tube & Iron Co 1 Chicago Tube Dr *TF Cust Svc:* 800-972-0217 ■ *Web:* www.chicagotube.com	Romeoville	IL	60446	815-834-2500	588-3958	492
Chicago White Metal Casting Inc 649 N Rt 83 *Web:* www.cwmdiecast.com	Bensenville	IL	60106	630-595-4424	595-4474	308
Chicago White Sox US Cellular Field 333 W 35th St *Web:* chicago.whitesox.mlb.com	Chicago	IL	60616	312-674-1000		713
Chicago Wilcox Mfg Co Inc 16928 State St **Fax Area Code:* 708 ■ *TF:* 800-323-5282 ■ *Web:* www.chicagowilcox.com	South Holland	IL	60473	800-323-5282	339-9876*	326
Chicago Wine Co 835 N Central Ave *TF:* 800-344-0763 ■ *Web:* www.tcwc.com	Wood Dale	IL	60191	630-594-2972		443
Chicago's wshe 100.3 130 E Randolph St Ste 2780 *Web:* wshechicago.com	Chicago	IL	60601	312-297-5100	297-5155	645-36
Chicago-Kent College of Law Illinois Institute of Technology 565 W Adams St *Web:* www.kentlaw.iit.edu	Chicago	IL	60661	312-906-5000	906-5280	167-1
Chicagoland Bicycle Federation 9 W Hubbard St Ste 402 *Web:* www.activetrans.org	Chicago	IL	60654	312-427-3325		711
Chicagoland Chamber of Commerce 410 N Michigan Ave Ste 900 *Web:* www.chicagolandchamber.org	Chicago	IL	60611	312-494-6700	861-0660	139
Chicagoland Speedway 500 Speedway Blvd *TF:* 888-629-7223 ■ *Web:* www.chicagolandspeedway.com	Joliet	IL	60433	815-722-5500	727-7895	515
Chicago-Read Mental Health Ctr 4200 N Oak Pk Ave *TF:* 800-322-7143 ■ *Web:* www.dhs.state.il.us	Chicago	IL	60634	773-794-4000	794-4046	374-5
Chicanos Por La Causa Inc 1112 E Buckeye Rd *Web:* www.cplc.org	Phoenix	AZ	85034	602-257-0700	256-2740	192
Chick Master Incubator Co 945 Lafayette Rd PO Box 704 *TF:* 800-727-8726 ■ *Web:* www.chickmaster.com	Medina	OH	44256	330-722-5591	723-0233	273
Chick's 18011 S Dupont Hwy *TF:* 800-444-2441 ■ *Web:* chicksaddlery.com	Harrington	DE	19952	302-398-4630		711
Chickamauga & Chattanooga National Military Park 3370 Lafayette Rd **Fax Area Code:* 423 ■ *Web:* www.nps.gov/chch	Fort Oglethorpe	GA	30742	706-866-9241	752-5215*	564
Chickasaw County 1 Pinson Sq *Web:* chickasaw.msghn.org	Houston	MS	38851	662-456-2513		338
Chickasaw Distributors Inc 800 Bering Dr Ste 330 *Web:* www.chickasawdistributors.com	Houston	TX	77057	713-974-2905	974-3109	492
Chickasaw Electric Co-op 17970 US Hwy 64 E PO Box 459 *Web:* chickasaw.coop	Somerville	TN	38068	901-465-3591	465-5392	245
Chickasaw Holding Co 124 W Vinita *Web:* www.chickasawholding.com	Sulphur	OK	73086	580-622-2111		787
Chickasaw Nation, The 520 Arlington St PO Box 1548 *TF:* 866-466-1481 ■ *Web:* www.chickasaw.net	Ada	OK	74821	580-436-2603	436-7297	48-11
Chickasaw National Recreation Area 1008 W Second St *Web:* www.nps.gov	Sulphur	OK	73086	580-622-7234	622-6931	564
Chickasaw State Park 26955 US Hwy 43 *TF:* 800-760-4089 ■ *Web:* www.alapark.com	Gallion	AL	36742	334-295-8230	295-8230	565
Chickasaw State Park 20 Cabin Ln *Web:* www.state.tn.us	Henderson	TN	38340	731-989-5141		565
Chickasaw Telecommunications Services Inc 5 N McCormick *Web:* stillwater.brightok.net	Oklahoma City	OK	73127	405-946-1200		393
Chickasaw Voting Information 8 E Prospect St *Web:* www.chickasawcoia.org	New Hampton	IA	50659	641-394-2100	394-5541	338
Chick-fil-A Inc 5200 Buffington Rd *TF:* 800-232-2677 ■ *Web:* www.chick-fil-a.com	Atlanta	GA	30349	404-765-8000		670
Chico Chamber of Commerce 441 Main St *TF:* 800-852-8570 ■ *Web:* www.chicochamber.com	Chico	CA	95928	530-891-5556	891-3613	139
Chico Enterprise Record 400 E Pk Ave PO Box 9 *TF:* 877-229-8655 ■ *Web:* www.chicoer.com	Chico	CA	95927	530-891-1234	342-3617	532-2
Chico News & Review 353 E Second St *TF:* 866-703-3873 ■ *Web:* www.newsreview.com	Chico	CA	95928	530-894-2300	894-0143	532-5
Chico Produce Inc 70 Pepsi Way PO Box 1069 *TF:* 888-232-0908 ■ *Web:* www.propacificfresh.com	Durham	CA	95938	530-893-0596	893-5973	297-7
Chico Unified School District 1163 E Seventh St *Web:* www.bcoe.org	Chico	CA	95928	530-891-3000		685
Chico's FAS Inc 11215 Metro Pkwy *NYSE:* CHS ■ *TF:* 800-690-6903 ■ *Web:* www.chicosfas.com	Fort Myers	FL	33966	888-855-4986		157-6
Chicony America Inc 53 Parker *Web:* www.chicony.com.tw	Irvine	CA	92618	949-380-0928		173-1
Chicopee Chamber of Commerce 264 Exchange St *Web:* www.chicopeechamber.org	Chicopee	MA	01013	413-594-2101	594-2103	139
Chicopee Memorial State Park 570 Burnett Rd *Web:* www.mass.gov	Chicopee Falls	MA	01020	413-594-9416		565
Chicopee Provision Co Inc 19 Sitarz St *TF:* 800-924-6328 ■ *Web:* www.bluesealkielbasa.com	Chicopee	MA	01013	413-594-4765		296-26
Chicopee Public Library 449 Front St *TF:* 800-824-6548 ■ *Web:* www.chicopeepubliclibrary.org	Chicopee	MA	01013	413-594-1800	594-1819	434-3
Chicora Alley 608B S Main St *Web:* www.chicoraalley.com	Greenville	SC	29601	864-232-4100		671
Chicot County 108 Main St *Web:* chicotcounty.arkansas.gov	Lake Village	AR	71653	870-265-8040	265-8018	338
Chicot State Park 3469 Chicot Pk Rd *TF:* 888-677-2442 ■ *Web:* www.crt.state.la.us	Ville Platte	LA	70586	337-363-2403		565
Chief Architect Inc 6500 N Mineral Dr *Web:* www.chiefarchitect.com	Coeur D'Alene	ID	83815	208-292-3400		174
Chief Automotive Systems Inc 1924 E Fourth St **Fax:* Mktg ■ *TF:* 800-445-9262 ■ *Web:* www.chiefautomotive.com	Grand Island	NE	68802	308-384-9747	384-8966*	386
Chief Custom Homes 111 Grant St PO Box 127 *Web:* bonnavilla.com	Aurora	NE	68818	402-694-5250	694-5873	505
Chief Dull Knife College PO Box 98 *Web:* www.cdkc.edu	Lame Deer	MT	59043	406-477-6215	477-6219	165
Chief Executive Magazine 1 Sound Shore Dr Ste 100 *TF:* 800-869-6882 ■ *Web:* www.chiefexecutive.net	Greenwich	CT	06830	203-930-2700	930-2701	457-5
Chief Executives Organization 7920 Norfolk Ave Ste 400 *Web:* www.ceo.org	Bethesda	MD	20814	301-656-9220		49-12
Chief Logan State Park 376 Little Buffalo Creek Rd *Web:* www.chiefloganstatepark.com	Logan	WV	25601	304-792-7125		565
Chief Manufacturing Inc 6436 City W Pkwy Ste 700 *Web:* www.chiefmfg.com	Prairie	MN	55378	952-894-6280		194
Chief Plenty Coups State Park 1 Edgar/Pryor Rd *Web:* www.fwp.mt.gov	Pryor	MT	59066	406-252-1289		565
Chief Super Market Inc 1340 W High St Ste E *Web:* chiefmarkets.com	Defiance	OH	43512	419-782-0950		345
Chief Vann House State Historic Site 82 Georgia 225 *Web:* www.gastateparks.org	Chatsworth	GA	30705	706-695-2598		565
Chief White Crane Recreation Area 31323 Toe Rd *Web:* www.gfp.sd.gov	Yankton	SD	57078	605-668-2985		565
Chieftain Wild Rice Co 1210 Basswood Ave *Web:* www.chieftainwildrice.com	Spooner	WI	54801	715-635-6401		123
Chignecto-central Regional 60 Lorne St *TF:* 800-770-0008 ■ *Web:* www.ccrsb.ca	Truro	NS	B2N3K3	902-897-8923		685
Chihuahuan Desert Research Institute (CDRI) 43869 State Hwy 118 PO Box 905 *Web:* cdri.org	Fort Davis	TX	79734	432-364-2499		97
Chilangos 447 Manton Ave	Providence	RI	02909	401-383-4877		671
Child Care Links 6601 Owens Dr Ste 100 *Web:* www.childcarelinks.org	Pleasanton	CA	94588	925-417-8733	730-4942	148
Child Development Assoc Inc 678 Third Ave Ste 201 *TF:* 888-755-2445 ■ *Web:* www.cdasandiego.com	Chula Vista	CA	91910	619-427-4411		148
Child Evangelism Fellowship Inc 17482 Hwy M *TF:* 800-748-7710 ■ *Web:* www.cefonline.com	Warrenton	MO	63383	636-456-4321		48-20
Child Find Canada 212-2211 McPhillips St *TF:* 800-387-7962 ■ *Web:* www.childfind.ca	Winnipeg	MB	R2V3M5	204-339 5584	339-5587	48-6
Child Guidance Resource Centers 2000 Old W Chester Pk *Web:* www.cgrc.org	Havertown	PA	19083	484-454-8700		726
Child Health Foundation 110 E Ridgely Rd *Web:* www.childhealthfoundation.org	Timonium	MD	21093	410-992-5512	992-5641	48-5
Child Lures Prevention 5166 Shelburne Rd *TF:* 800-552-2197 ■ *Web:* www.childluresprevention.com	Shelburne	VT	05482	802-985-8458	985-8418	48-6
Child Trends 4301 Connecticut Ave NW Ste 350 *Web:* www.childtrends.org	Washington	DC	20008	240-223-9200	200-1238	48-6
Child Welfare Information Gateway Children's Bureau/ACYF 330 C St SW *TF:* 800-394-3366 ■ *Web:* www.childwelfare.gov	Washington	DC	20201	703-385-7565	385-3206	340-10
Child Welfare League of America (CWLA) 2345 Crystal Dr Ste 250 *Web:* www.cwla.org	Arlington	VA	22202	202-688-4200		48-6

	Phone	Fax	Class
Childcare Network 3009 University Ave .... Columbus GA 31909 *TF:* 866-521-5437 ■ *Web:* www.childcarenetwork.com	706-562-8600		148
Childcraft Education Corp 1156 Four Star Dr........ Mount Joy PA 17552 **Fax Area Code:* 888 ■ *TF:* 800-631-5652	800-631-5652	532-4453*	459
Childers Oil Co 51 Hwy 2034 .... Whitesburg KY 41858 *Web:* www.doublekwik.com	606-633-2525		581
Childhaven 316 Broadway .... Seattle WA 98122 *Web:* www.childhaven.org	206-624-6477	621-8374	353
Childhelp USA 4350 E Camelback Rd Bldg F250........ Phoenix AZ 85018 *TF:* 800-422-4453 ■ *Web:* www.childhelp.org	480-922-8212	922-7061	48-6
Children & Adults with Attention-Deficit/Hyperactivity Disorder (CHADD) 8181 Professional Pl Ste 150........ Landover MD 20785 *TF:* 800-233-4050 ■ *Web:* www.chadd.org	301-306-7070	306-7090	48-17
Children & Youth Funding Report 8204 Fenton St........ Silver Spring MD 20910 *TF:* 800-666-6380 ■ *Web:* www.cdpublications.com/cyf	301-588-6380	588-6385	531-8
Children Awaiting Parents Inc (CAP) 595 Blossom Rd Ste 306 .... Rochester NY 14610 *TF:* 888-835-8802 ■ *Web:* www.capbook.org	585-232-5110	232-2634	48-6
Children First Home Healthcare Service 4448 Edgewater Dr........ Orlando FL 32804 *TF:* 800-207-0802 ■ *Web:* www.childrenfirsthomecare.com	407-513-3000		260
Children Inc 4205 Dover Rd........ Richmond VA 23221 *TF:* 800-538-5381 ■ *Web:* childrenincorporated.org	804-359-4562		48-6
Children International 2000 E Red Bridge Rd........ Kansas City MO 64131 *TF:* 800-888-3089 ■ *Web:* www.children.org	816-942-2000	942-3714	48-5
Children of Deaf Adults Inc (CODA) 3131 Calle Mariposa .... Santa Barbara CA 93105 *Web:* coda-international.wildapricot.org	805-682-0997		48-6
Children of Lesbians & Gays Everywhere (COLAGE) 3815 S Othello St Ste 100 .... Seattle WA 98118 *TF:* 800-657-3717 ■ *Web:* www.colage.org	415-861-5437		48-21
Children of the Night 14530 Sylvan St........ Van Nuys CA 91411 *TF:* 800-551-1300 ■ *Web:* www.childrenofthenight.org	818-908-4474	908-1468	48-6
Children's Book Council (CBC) 54 W 39th St 14th Fl........ New York NY 10018 *Web:* www.cbcbooks.org	212-966-1990		49-16
Children's Book Insider 901 Columbia Rd........ Fort Collins CO 80525 *Web:* cbiclubhouse.com/clubhouse	970-495-0056		531-11
Children's Bureau of Southern California 1910 Magnolia Ave........ Los Angeles CA 90004 *TF:* 800-730-3933 ■ *Web:* www.all4kids.org	213-342-0100		352
Children's Defense Fund (CDF) 25 E St NW........ Washington DC 20001 *TF:* 800-233-1200 ■ *Web:* www.childrensdefense.org	202-628-8787	662-3510	48-6
Children's Discovery Museum of San Jose 180 Woz Way .... San Jose CA 95110 *Web:* www.cdm.org	408-298-5437	298-6826	521
Children's Discovery Museum of the Desert 71701 Gerald Ford Dr........ Rancho Mirage CA 92270 *Web:* www.cdmod.org	760-321-0602	321-1605	521
Children's Educational Network Inc 283 S Escondido Blvd .... Escondido CA 92025 *Web:* www.childrenseducationalnetwork.com	760-233-2863		194
Children's Eye Foundation 1631 Lancaster Dr Ste 200........ Grapevine TX 76051 *TF:* 800-788-2020 ■ *Web:* www.childrenseyefoundation.org	817-310-2641		48-17
Children's Fairyland Theme Park 699 Bellevue Ave .... Oakland CA 94610 *TF:* 800-421-1180 ■ *Web:* www.fairyland.org	510-452-2259	452-2261	32
Children's Hands-On Museum 2213 University Blvd .... Tuscaloosa AL 35401 *Web:* www.chomonline.org	205-349-4235	349-4276	521
Children's Healthcare of Atlanta at Egleston 1405 Clifton Rd NE........ Atlanta GA 30322 *TF:* 888-785-7778 ■ *Web:* www.choa.org	404-785-6000		374-1
Children's Healthcare of Atlanta at Scottish Rite 1001 Johnson Ferry Rd NE........ Atlanta GA 30342 *TF:* 888-785-7778 ■ *Web:* www.choa.org	404-785-5252		374-1
Children's Home + Aid 125 S Wacker Dr 14th Fl........ Chicago IL 60606 *Web:* www.childrenshomeandaid.org	312-424-0200		148
Children's Hope House 7922 W Jefferson Blvd .... Fort Wayne IN 46804 *Web:* childrenshopefw.org	260-459-8550		372
Children's Hospice International (CHI) 500 Montgomery St Ste 400........ Alexandria VA 22314 *Web:* www.chionline.org	703-684-0330		49-8
Children's Hospital 200 Henry Clay Ave .... New Orleans LA 70118 *TF:* 800-299-9511 ■ *Web:* www.chnola.org	504-899-9511		374-1
Children's Hospital & Medical Ctr 8200 Dodge St........ Omaha NE 68114 **Fax:* Admitting ■ *Web:* childrensomaha.org	402-955-5400	955-4046*	374-1
Children's Hospital & Research Ctr at Oakland 747 52nd St .... Oakland CA 94609 **Fax:* Admitting ■ *Web:* www.childrenshospitaloakland.org	510-428-3000	658-1923*	374-1
Children's Hospital at OU Medical Ctr, The 1200 N Everett Dr........ Oklahoma City OK 73104 *Web:* www.oumedicine.com	405-271-5656		374-3
Children's Hospital Bone Marrow Transplant Program LSU Health Science Ctr 200 Henry Clay Ave .... New Orleans LA 70118 *Web:* www.chnola.org	504-896-9740		769
Children's Hospital Boston 300 Longwood Ave........ Boston MA 02115 *TF:* 800-355-7944 ■ *Web:* www.childrenshospital.org	617-355-6000		374-1
Children's Hospital Medical Ctr of Akron 1 Perkins Sq........ Akron OH 44308 **Fax:* Admitting ■ *TF:* 800-262-0333 ■ *Web:* www.akronchildrens.org	330-543-1000	543-3146*	374-1
Children's Hospital of Alabama 1600 Seventh Ave S .... Birmingham AL 35233 *TF:* 800-504-9768 ■ *Web:* childrensal.org	205-939-9100		374-1
Children's Hospital of Eastern Ontario 401 Smyth Rd........ Ottawa ON K1H8L1 *TF:* 800-797-0007 ■ *Web:* www.cheo.on.ca	613-737-7600	738-4866	374-2
Children's Hospital of Michigan 3901 Beaubien Blvd .... Detroit MI 48201 *Web:* www.dmc.org	313-745-5437		374-1
Children's Hospital of Orange County 455 S Main St........ Orange CA 92868 *Web:* www.choc.org	714-997-3000		374-1
Children's Hospital of Orange County Blood & Donor Services 505 S Main St........ Orange CA 92868 *TF:* 800-228-5234 ■ *Web:* www.choc.org	714-509-8339		769
Children's Hospital of Philadelphia 3400 Civic Ctr Blvd .... Philadelphia PA 19104 *Web:* www.chop.edu	215-590-1000		374-1
Children's Hospital of Philadelphia Stem Cell Transplant Program 3401 Civic Ctr Blvd .... Philadelphia PA 19104 **Fax Area Code:* 215 ■ *TF:* 800-879-2467 ■ *Web:* www.chop.edu	800-879-2467	590-4744*	769
Children's Hospital of Pittsburgh 4401 Penn Ave........ Pittsburgh PA 15224 *Web:* www.chp.edu	412-692-5325		374-1
Children's Hospital of the King's Daughters 601 Children's Ln........ Norfolk VA 23507 *TF:* 800-395-2453 ■ *Web:* www.chkd.org	757-668-7000		374-1
Children's Hospital of Wisconsin 9000 W Wisconsin Ave........ Milwaukee WI 53226 **Fax:* Admitting ■ *TF:* 800-266-0366 ■ *Web:* www.chw.org	414-266-2000	266-2547*	374-1
Children's Hospitals & Clinics Minneapolis 2525 Chicago Ave........ Minneapolis MN 55404 *TF:* 866-225-3251 ■ *Web:* childrensmn.org	612-813-6000	813-6807	374-1
Children's House at Johns Hopkins 1915 McElderry St........ Baltimore MD 21205 *TF:* 800-933-5470 ■ *Web:* believeintomorrow.org	410-614-2560	614-2568	372
Children's Institute of Pittsburgh 1405 Shady Ave........ Pittsburgh PA 15217 *TF:* 877-433-1109 ■ *Web:* www.amazingkids.org	412-420-2400	420-2200	374-1
Children's Leukemia Research Assn 585 Stewart Ave Ste 18........ Garden City NY 11530 *TF:* 800-955-4572 ■ *Web:* www.childrensleukemia.org	516-222-1944	222-0457	48-17
Children's Medical Ctr 1 Children's Plaza........ Dayton OH 45404 **Fax:* Admitting ■ *TF:* 800-228-4055 ■ *Web:* www.childrensdayton.org	937-641-3000	641-3326*	374-1
Children's Medical Ctr of Dallas 1935 Medical District Dr........ Dallas TX 75235 *Web:* www.childrens.com	214-456-7000		374-1
Children's Memorial Hospital 2300 Children's Plaza........ Chicago IL 60614 *TF:* 800-526-0844 ■ *Web:* www.luriechildrens.org	312-227-4000		374-1
Children's Mercy Hospital & Clinics 2401 Gillham Rd........ Kansas City MO 64108 *TF:* 866-512-2168 ■ *Web:* www.childrensmercy.org	816-234-3000		374-1
Children's Miracle Network 4220 Steeles Ave W Ste C18 .... Woodbridge ON L4L3S8 *Web:* www.childrensmiraclenetwork.ca	905-265-9750	265-9749	48-5
Children's Museum 498 Crawford Blvd .... Boca Raton FL 33432 *Web:* www.cmboca.org	561-368-6875		521
Children's Museum of Acadiana 201 E Congress St .... Lafayette LA 70501 *TF:* 800-962-9133 ■ *Web:* www.childrensmuseumofacadiana.com/home	337-232-8500	232-8167	521
Children's Museum of Atlanta, The 275 Centennial Olympic Pk Dr NW........ Atlanta GA 30313 *Web:* www.childrensmuseumatlanta.org	404-659-5437	223-3675	521
Children's Museum of Cleveland 3813 Euclid Ave .... Cleveland OH 44115 *Web:* www.clevelandchildrensmuseum.org	216-791-7114	791-8838	521
Children's Museum of Denver 2121 Children's Museum Dr........ Denver CO 80211 *Web:* www.mychildsmuseum.org	303-433-7444	433-9520	521
Children's Museum of History Natural History Science & Technology 311 Main St .... Utica NY 13501 *Web:* www.museum4kids.net	315-724-6129	724-6120	521
Children's Museum of Houston 1500 Binz St........ Houston TX 77004 *Web:* www.cmhouston.org	713-522-1138	522-5747	521
Children's Museum of Indianapolis 3000 N Meridian St .... Indianapolis IN 46208 *TF:* 800-820-6214 ■ *Web:* www.childrensmuseum.org	317-334-3322	920-2001	520
Children's Museum of Lake Charles 327 Broad St........ Lake Charles LA 70601 *Web:* www.swlakids.org	337-433-9420		521
Children's Museum of Maine 142 Free St PO Box 4041........ Portland ME 04101 *TF:* 800-838-3006 ■ *Web:* www.kitetails.org	207-828-1234	828-5726	521
Children's Museum of Manhattan 212 W 83rd St .... New York NY 10024 *TF:* 800-838-3006 ■ *Web:* www.cmom.org	212-721-1223	721-1127	521
Children's Museum of Memphis 2525 Central Ave .... Memphis TN 38104 *TF:* 800-979-3370 ■ *Web:* www.cmom.com	901-458-2678	458-4033	521
Children's Museum of Montana 22 Railroad Sq .... Great Falls MT 59401	406-452-6661		520
Children's Museum of New Hampshire 6 Washington St........ Dover NH 03820 *TF:* 800-625-7738 ■ *Web:* www.childrens-museum.org	603-742-2002		521
Children's Museum of Northern Nevada 813 N Carson St........ Carson City NV 89701 *TF:* 800-992-3598 ■ *Web:* www.cmnn.org	775-884-2226	884-2179	521
Children's Museum of Oak Ridge 461 W Outer Dr........ Oak Ridge TN 37830 *TF:* 877-524-1223 ■ *Web:* www.childrensmuseumofoakridge.org	865-482-1074	481-4889	521
Children's Museum of Pittsburgh 10 Children's Way........ Pittsburgh PA 15212 *TF:* 800-732-0999 ■ *Web:* www.pittsburghkids.org	412-322-5058		521
Children's Museum of Science & Technology 250 Jordan Rd .... Troy NY 12180 *Web:* www.cmost.org	518-235-2120	235-6836	520

Name / Address	Phone	Fax	Class
Children's Museum of South Carolina 2204 N Oak St .... Myrtle Beach SC 29577 *Web:* www.cmsckids.org	843-946-9469	946-7011	521
Children's Museum of Stockton 402 W Weber Ave .... Stockton CA 95202 *Web:* www.stocktongov.com	209-465-4386		521
Children's Museum of Tacoma 936 Broadway .... Tacoma WA 98402 *Web:* www.playtacoma.org	253-627-6031	627-2436	521
Children's Museum of the Arts 103 Charlton St .... New York NY 10014 *TF:* 800-376-5850 ■ *Web:* www.cmany.org	212-274-0986	274-1776	521
Children's Museum of the Lowcountry 25 Ann St .... Charleston SC 29403 *Web:* www.explorecml.org	843-853-8962	853-1042	521
Children's Museum of Virginia 221 High St .... Portsmouth VA 23704 *Web:* childrensmuseumvirginia.com	757-393-5258		521
Children's Museum Seattle 305 Harrison St .... Seattle WA 98109 *Web:* www.thechildrensmuseum.org	206-441-1768	448-0910	521
Children's Musical Theater San Jose (CMTS) 1401 Parkmoor Ave Ste 100 .... San Jose CA 95126 *Web:* www.cmtsj.org	408-288-5437		573-4
Children's National Medical Ctr (CNMC) 111 Michigan Ave NW .... Washington DC 20010 *TF:* 800-884-5433 ■ *Web:* www.childrensnational.org	202-476-5000		374-1
Children's Nutrition Research Center 1100 Bates St .... Houston TX 77030 *Web:* www.bcm.edu/cnrc	713-798-6767	798-7098	668
Children's Organ Transplant Assn (COTA) 2501 W Cota Dr .... Bloomington IN 47403 *TF:* 800-366-2682 ■ *Web:* www.cota.org	812-336-8872	336-8885	48-17
Children's Place Retail Stores Inc 500 Plaza Dr .... Secaucus NJ 07094 *NASDAQ: PLCE* ■ *TF:* 877-752-2387 ■ *Web:* www.childrensplace.com	201-558-2400		157-1
Children's Press 557 Broadway .... New York NY 10012 *TF:* 800-724-6527 ■ *Web:* scholastic.co.in	800-724-6527		637-2
Children's Research Institute Children's National Medical Ctr 111 Michigan Ave NW .... Washington DC 20010 *TF:* 888-884-2327 ■ *Web:* www.childrensnational.org	202-476-5000		668
Children's Science Explorium 300 S Military Trl .... Boca Raton FL 33486 *TF:* 800-319-0884 ■ *Web:* www.scienceexplorium.org	561-347-3912	347-3910	521
Children's Specialized Hospital 150 New Providence Rd .... Mountainside NJ 07092 *TF:* 888-244-5373 ■ *Web:* www.childrens-specialized.org	908-233-3720	233-4967	374-1
Children's Tumor Foundation 95 Pine St 16th Fl .... New York NY 10005 *TF:* 800-323-7938 ■ *Web:* www.ctf.org	212-344-6633	747-0004	48-17
Children's Wish Foundation International 8615 Roswell Rd .... Atlanta GA 30350 *TF:* 800-323-9474 ■ *Web:* www.childrenswish.org	770-393-9474	393-0683	48-17
Childrens Discovery Museum, The 177 Main St .... Acton MA 01720 *TF:* 800-544-6666 ■ *Web:* www.discoverymuseums.org	978-264-4200		520
Childrens Education Connection Inc 6301 Hwy 39 .... Meridian MS 39305 *Web:* childrenseducationconnection.com	601-485-2856		194
Childrens Hopechest PO Box 63842 .... Colorado Springs CO 80962 *Web:* www.hopechest.org	719-487-7800		48-20
Childrens Plus Inc 1387 Dutch American Way .... Beecher IL 60401 *TF:* 800-230-1279 ■ *Web:* www.childrensplusinc.com	800-230-1279		95
Childress County 1710 Ave F NW .... Childress TX 79201 *Web:* www.childresscad.org	940-937-6062	937-3386	338
Childress Directional Drilling 6429 cunningham rd .... Houston TX 77041 *TF:* 800-460-8070 ■ *Web:* www.childressdrilling.com	713-466-7979		540
Childs Company LLC 3438 Peachtree Raod Phipps Tower Ste 1400-B ..... Atlanta GA 30326 *Web:* www.childscompany.com	404-751-3049		401
Childventures Early Learning Academy Inc Burlington Campus 2180 Itabashi Way .... Burlington ON L7M5A5 *TF:* 800-263-6480 ■ *Web:* www.childventures.ca	905-637-8481		685
Chile			
Consulate General 866 UN Plaza Ste 601 .... New York NY 10017 *Web:* chile.gob.cl/es	212-980-3366	888-5288	257
Consulate General 870 Market St Ste 1058 .... San Francisco CA 94102 *Web:* chile.gob.cl/san-francisco/en	415-982-7662		257
Embassy 1732 Massachusetts Ave NW .... Washington DC 20036 *TF:* 855-310-8471	202-785-1746	887-5579	257
Chile Mission 885 Second Ave 40th Fl .... New York NY 10017 *Web:* chile.gob.cl/onu/en	917-322-6800	322-6890	784
Chile-US Chamber of Commerce 8333 NW 53rd St Ste 450 .... Doral FL 33166 *Web:* www.chileus.org	786-499-0635		138
Chili Public Library 3333 Chili Ave .... Rochester NY 14624 *Web:* www.libraryweb.org/chili	585-889-2200		434-3
Chilito's 2405 S Valley Dr .... Las Cruces NM 88005 *Web:* chilitos.net	575-526-4184		671
Chilivis, Cochran, Larkins & Bever LLP 3127 Maple Dr NE .... Atlanta GA 30305 *TF:* 800-900-4250 ■ *Web:* www.cclblawyers.com	404-233-4171		428
Chilkoot Lake State Recreation Site 10 Mile Lutak Rd .... Haines AK 99827 *Web:* www.dnr.alaska.gov	907-465-4563		565
Chiller Solutions LLC 101 Alexander Ave .... Pompton Plains NJ 07444 *TF:* 800-526-5201 ■ *Web:* www.edwards-eng.com	973-835-2800		14
Chillicothe & Ross County Public Library 140 S Paint St .... Chillicothe OH 45601 *Web:* crcpl.org	740-702-4145		434-3
Chillicothe Correctional Ctr 3151 Litton Rd .... Chillicothe MO 64601 *TF:* 800-392-8486 ■ *Web:* doc.mo.gov	660-646-4032	646-1217	213
Chillicothe Gazette 50 W Main St .... Chillicothe OH 45601 *TF:* 877-424-0215 ■ *Web:* www.chillicothegazette.com	740-773-2111	772-9505	532-2
Chillicothe-Ross Chamber of Commerce 45 E Main St .... Chillicothe OH 45601 *Web:* www.chillicotheohio.com	740-702-2722	702-2727	139
Chillingsworth 2449 Main St .... Brewster MA 02631 *Web:* www.chillingsworth.com	508-896-3640		671
Chilliwack Chamber of Commerce 46093 Yale Rd Ste 201 .... Chilliwack BC V2P2L8 *Web:* www.chilliwackchamber.com	604-793-4323	793-4303	137
Chilliwack General Hospital 45600 Menholm Rd .... Chilliwack BC V2P1P7 *TF:* 800-331-1533 ■ *Web:* www.fraserhealth.ca	604-795-4141	795-4110	374-2
Chillybears 6 Brook Rd .... Needham MA 02494 *Web:* www.chillybears.com	781-455-6321		5
Chilmar Corp 5724 Belair Rd .... Baltimore MD 21206 *Web:* chilmar.com	410-426-5482		189-10
Chiltern Inn 11 Cromwell Harbor Rd .... Bar Harbor ME 04609 *TF:* 800-709-0114 ■ *Web:* www.chilterninnbarharbor.com	207-288-3371		379
Chilton County PO Box 1948 .... Clanton AL 35046 *TF:* 800-545-5735 ■ *Web:* www.chiltoncounty.org	205-755-1551	280-7204	338
Chilton Hospital 97 W Pkwy .... Pompton Plains NJ 07444 *Web:* www.chiltonhealth.org	973-831-5000		374-3
Chime Education Foundation 710 Avis Dr Ste 200 .... Ann Arbor MI 48108 *Web:* chimecentral.org	734-665-0000	665-4922	166
Chime Master Systems PO Box 936 .... Lancaster OH 43130 **Fax Area Code: 740* ■ *TF:* 800-344-7464 ■ *Web:* www.chimemaster.com	800-344-7464	746-9566*	527
Chimes Inc, The 4815 Seton Dr .... Baltimore MD 21215 *Web:* www.chimes.org	410-358-6400		687
Chimes Restaurant & Tap Room 3357 Highland Rd .... Baton Rouge LA 70802 *Web:* www.thechimes.com	225-383-1754		671
Chimi's 1304 E 15th St .... Tulsa OK 74120 *Web:* chimismexican.com	918-587-4411		671
Chimney Rock Inn 800 Thompson Ave .... Bound Brook NJ 08805 *Web:* www.chimneyrockinn.com	732-469-4600		378
Chimney Rock Park 431 Main St .... Chimney Rock NC 28720 *TF:* 800-277-9611 ■ *Web:* www.chimneyrockpark.com	828-625-9611	625-9610	97
Chimney Rock Public Power District 128 Eighth St PO Box 608 .... Bayard NE 69334 *TF:* 877-773-6300 ■ *Web:* www.crppd.com	308-586-1824		245
China 350 E 35th St .... New York NY 10016 *Web:* www.china-un.org	212-655-6100	634-7626	784
Consulate General 1450 Laguna St .... San Francisco CA 94115 *Web:* www.chinaconsulatesf.org	415-852-5941		257
Consulate General 100 W Erie St .... Chicago IL 60654 *TF:* 800-860-8610 ■ *Web:* www.chinaconsulatechicago.org	312-803-0095	803-0110	257
Consulate General 3417 Montrose Blvd .... Houston TX 77006 *Web:* houston.china-consulate.org	713-520-1462	521-3064	257
Consulate General 443 Shatto Pl .... Los Angeles CA 90020 *Web:* losangeles.china-consulate.org	213-807-8088	807-8091	257
Embassy 2201 Wisconsin Ave NW Ste 110 .... Washington DC 20007 *Web:* www.china-embassy.org	202-337-1956	588-9760	257
China Airlines Cargo Sales & Service 11201 Aviation Blvd .... Los Angeles CA 90045 **Fax Area Code: 907* ■ *TF:* 800-778-4838 ■ *Web:* www.china-airlines.com	310-646-4293	248-4176*	12
China Buffet 1300 US Hwy 127 S .... Frankfort KY 40601	502-226-3400		671
China Camp State Park 101 Peacock Gap Trl .... San Rafael CA 94901 *Web:* www.parks.ca.gov/default.asp?page_id=466	415-456-0766		565
China Capital 530 N Gloster St .... Tupelo MS 38804	662-841-0484		671
China Chef 4335 Lake Michigan Dr NW .... Grand Rapids MI 49534 *Web:* chinachef49534.com	616-791-4488		671
China Chef Restaurant 5010 SW Ninth St .... Des Moines IA 50315	515-256-8005		671
China Chili 39116 State St .... Fremont CA 94538	510-791-1688		671
China Cooks 215 Northwood Dr .... Atlanta GA 30342	404-252-6611		671
China Daily Press 2121 W Mission Rd .... Alhambra CA 91803 *Web:* usqiaobao.com	626-281-8500		532-2
China Dragon 27 E Queen Ave .... Spokane WA 99207 *Web:* chinadragonspokane.com	509-483-5209		671
China Dynasty 1689 W Ln Ave .... Upper Arlington OH 43221 *Web:* www.chinadynasty-cmh.com	614-486-7126	486-4131	671
China East 1810 Hwy 50 E .... Carson City NV 89701	775-885-6996		671
China East Restaurant 1086 S Virginia St .... Reno NV 89502	775-348-7020		671
China Garden 2550 32nd Ave S .... Grand Forks ND 58201	701-772-0660		671
China Garden 1929 N Washington St .... Bismarck ND 58501	701-224-0698		671
China Garden 1100 Wilson Blvd Twin Towers - Mall Level .... Rossyln VA 22209 *Web:* chinagardenva.com	703-525-5317	525-5568	671
China Gourmet 3340 Erie Ave .... Cincinnati OH 45208 *Web:* thechinagourmet.com	513-871-6612		671
China Grill Management Inc (CGM) 60 W 53rd St .... New York NY 10019 *Web:* www.chinagrillmgt.com	212-333-7788		670
China Institute in America 125 E 65th St .... New York NY 10065 *Web:* www.chinainstitute.org	212-744-8181	628-4159	48-14
China Jade 2190 Brookpark Rd .... Cleveland OH 44134 *Web:* www.chinajadecleveland.com	216-749-4720		671
China Light 571 Broadway .... Bangor ME 04401 *Web:* chinalightbangor.com	207-947-6759		671
China Moon 5600 Brainerd Rd .... Chattanooga TN 37411 *Web:* chinamoontn.com	423-893-8088	855-5288	671
China National Tourist Office 370 Lexington Ave Ste 912 .... New York NY 10017 *Web:* www.cnto.org	212-760-8218	760-8809	775
China Ocean Shipping Co Americas Inc (COSCO) 100 Lighting Way .... Secaucus NJ 07094 *TF:* 800-242-7354 ■ *Web:* www.cosco-usa.com	201-422-0500	422-8956	220

Name / Address	City	State	ZIP	Phone	Fax	Class
China Palace 213 N Washington St. *Web:* chinapalacogreenbay.com	Green Bay	WI	54301	920-433-0688		671
China Rose Restaurant 228 28th St SE *TF:* 800-667-4980 ■ *Web:* www.chinarose.ca	Calgary	AB	T2A6J9	403-248-2711	248-6810	671
China Star 2425 W Walnut St. *Web:* garlandchinastar.com	Garland	TX	75042	972-487-8311		671
China Star 1444 E Republic Rd	Springfield	MO	65804	417-887-9779		671
China Star Chinese Restaurant 11-15 Main St *Web:* www.chinastarvt.com	Montpelier	VT	05602	802-223-0808		671
China Town 326 S Nevada Ave. *Web:* chinatown-restaurant.com	Colorado Springs	CO	80903	719-632-5151		671
China Travel Service Chicago Inc 2145b S China Pl *TF:* 800-793-8856 ■ *Web:* www.nexusholidays.com	Chicago	IL	60616	312-328-0688		775
China Wok 111 E Wood Shopping Ctr *Web:* www.chinawokky.com	Frankfort	KY	40601	502-695-9388		671
CHIN-AM 1540 (Ethnic) 622 College St *Web:* www.chinradio.com	Toronto	ON	M6G1B6	416-531-9991	531-5274	645-165
Chinati Foundation PO Box 1135. *TF:* 800-667-9464 ■ *Web:* www.chinati.org	Marfa	TX	79843	432-729-4362	729-4597	95
Chinatown 3900 Hillsboro Pk *Web:* nashvillechinatown.com	Nashville	TN	37215	615-269-3275		671
Chinatown 850 W Broadway	Jackson	WY	83001	307-733-8856		671
Chinatrust Bank USA 801 S Figueroa St Ste 2300 *TF:* 888-308-0986 ■ *Web:* www.chinatrustusa.com	Los Angeles	CA	90017	310-791-2828		70
Chincoteague Seafood Company Inc 7056 Forest Grove Rd. *Web:* www.chincoteagueseafood.com	Parsonsburg	MD	21849	410-260-4800		805
Chinese Chamber of Commerce of Hawaii 8 S King St *TF:* 877-533-2444 ■ *Web:* www.chinesechamber.com	Honolulu	HI	96817	808-533-3181		138
Chinese Chamber of Commerce of Los Angeles 977 N Broadway Ground Fl Ste E *Web:* www.lachinesechamber.org	Los Angeles	CA	90012	213-617-0396	617-2128	138
Chinese Chamber of Commerce of San Francisco 730 Sacramento St	San Francisco	CA	94108	415-982-3000		138
Chinese Dragon 108 E Superior St	Duluth	MN	55802	218-723-4036		671
Chinese Laundry Shoes 3485 S La Cienega Blvd *TF:* 888-935-8825 ■ *Web:* www.chineselaundry.com	Los Angeles	CA	90016	310-838-2103		301
CHIN-FM 100.7 (Ethnic) 622 College St *Web:* www.chinradio.com	Toronto	ON	M6G1B6	416-531-9991	531-5274	645-165
Chinn Exploration Co 4601 Mccann Rd *Web:* www.chinnexploration.com	Longview	TX	75605	903-663-4260		539
Chino Champion PO Box 607 *Web:* www.championnewspapers.com	Chino	CA	91708	909-628-5501	590-1217	532-4
Chino Hills Ford 4480 Chino Hills Pkwy *TF:* 866-261-0153 ■ *Web:* chinohillsford.com	Chino	CA	91710	866-261-0153		57
Chino Hills High School 16150 Pomona Rincon Rd *Web:* chino.k12.ca.us	Chino Hills	CA	91709	909-606-7540		605
Chino Valley Chamber of Commerce 13150 Seventh St *Web:* chinovalleychamberofcommerce.com	Chino	CA	91710	909-627-6177	627-4180	139
Chino Valley Ranchers 5611 Peck Rd *TF:* 800-354-4503 ■ *Web:* www.chinovalleyranchers.com	Arcadia	CA	91006	800-354-4503		297-10
Chinois on Main 2709 Main St *TF:* 888-646-3387 ■ *Web:* www.wolfgangpuck.com	Santa Monica	CA	90405	310-392-9025	396-5102	671
Chinook Lumber Inc 17606 SR- 9 SE. *Web:* www.chinooklumber.com	Snohomish	WA	98296	360-668-8800		364
Chinook Winds Casino Resort 1777 NW 44th St *TF:* 888-244-6665 ■ *Web:* www.chinookwindscasino.com	Lincoln City	OR	97367	541-996-5825		452
Chinook's at Salmon Bay 1900 W Nickerson St Ste 103. *Web:* anthonys.com	Seattle	WA	98119	206-283-4665		671
Chintz & Co 1720 Store St *TF:* 800-263-8575 ■ *Web:* www.chintz.com	Victoria	BC	V8W1V5	250-381-2404		362
Chip Steak & Provision Co 232 Dewey St **Fax Area Code:* 507	Mankato	MN	56001	416-236-1163	388-6279*	473
Chipola College 3094 Indian Cir. **Fax:* Admissions ■ *Web:* www.chipola.edu	Marianna	FL	32446	850-526-2761	718-2287*	166
Chipotle Mexican Grill Inc 1401 Wynkoop St *NYSE:* CMG ■ *TF:* 800-732-0330 ■ *Web:* www.chipotle.com	Denver	CO	80202	303-595-4000		670
Chippendales USA LLC 4 ExpressWay Plaza Ste 218. *TF:* 866-244-7999 ■ *Web:* www.chippendales.com	Roslyn Heights	NY	11577	516-454-0981		149
Chippewa Correctional Facility 4269 W M-80 *Web:* www.michigan.gov/corrections	Kincheloe	MI	49784	906-495-2275		213
Chippewa County 711 N Bridge St *Web:* www.co.chippewa.wi.us	Chippewa Falls	WI	54729	715-726-7980	726-7987	338
Chippewa County 629 N 11th St. **Fax:* Acctg ■ *TF:* 800-450-8608 ■ *Web:* www.co.chippewa.mn.us	Montevideo	MN	56265	320-269-7447	269-7412*	338
Chippewa Falls Area Chamber of Commerce 10 S Bridge St *TF:* 888-723-0024 ■ *Web:* www.chippewachamber.org	Chippewa Falls	WI	54729	715-723-0331	723-0332	139
Chippewa Falls Public Library 105 W Central St *Web:* www.chippewafallslibrary.org	Chippewa Falls	WI	54729	715-723-1146		434-3
Chippewa Moraine Ice Age State Recreation Area 13394 County Hwy M. *Web:* dnr.wi.gov	New Auburn	WI	54757	715-967-2800	967-2801	565
Chippewa Trucking 510 E S Ave *TF:* 866-777-1399	Chippewa Falls	WI	54729	715-726-2457	726-2455	107
Chippewa Valley Electric Co-op 317 S Eigth St. *TF:* 800-300-6800 ■ *Web:* www.cvecoop.com	Cornell	WI	54732	715-239-6800	239-6160	245
Chippewa Valley Ethanol Company LLC 270 20th St NW *Web:* www.cvec.com	Benson	MN	56215	320-843-4813	843-4800	145
Chippewa Valley Technical College 620 W Clairemont Ave *TF:* 800-547-2882 ■ *Web:* www.cvtc.edu	Eau Claire	WI	54701	715-833-6200	833-6470	800
Chippokes Plantation State Park 695 Chippokes Pk Rd *Web:* www.dcr.virginia.gov	Surry	VA	23883	757-294-3728		565
Chips Computer Services 14491 Forest Blvd N Apt 1b *Web:* www.chipscs.com	Hugo	MN	55038	651-407-8555		175
CHIPS Technology Group LLC 5 Aerial Way Ste 400 *Web:* www.chipstechnologygroup.com	Syosset	NY	11791	516-377-6585		174
Chipton-ross Inc 343 Main St. *TF:* 800-927-9318 ■ *Web:* www.chiptonross.com	El Segundo	CA	90245	310-414-7800		631
Chiquita Brands International Inc 250 E Fifth St *NYSE:* CQB ■ *TF:* 800-242-5472 ■ *Web:* chiquita.com	Cincinnati	OH	45202	513-784-8000		315-4
Chiral Quest Inc 7 Deer Park Dr Ste C1. *Web:* www.chiralquest.com	Monmouth Junction	NJ	08852	732-274-0399		231
Chirch Global Mfg LLC 1150 Ridgeview Dr *Web:* www.chirchmfg.com	Mchenry	IL	60050	815-385-5600		697
ChiRhoClin Inc 4000 Blackburn Ln Ste 270 *Web:* www.chirhoclin.com	Burtonsville	MD	20866	301-476-8388		231
Chiricahua National Monument 12856 E Rhyolite Creek Rd *TF:* 877-444-6777 ■ *Web:* www.nps.gov/chir	Willcox	AZ	85643	520-824-3560	824-3421	564
Chiro Inc 2260 S Vista Ave. *Web:* www.mrcleansystems.com	Bloomington	CA	92316	909-879-1160		291
Chiro. Advance Services Inc W5240 Oak Hill Rd *Web:* chiroadvance.com	Trego	WI	54888	715-635-5211		463
Chiron Data Systems Inc 1802 Regent Ct *Web:* www.chirondata.com	Corinth	TX	76210	940-497-3134		396
Chiropractic Health Plan of California PO Box 190 **Fax Area Code:* 925 ■ *TF:* 800-995-2442 ■ *Web:* www.chpc.com	Clayton	CA	94517	800-995-2442	844-3124*	391-3
Chirpify Inc 317 SW Alder St Ste 1100 *Web:* www.chirpify.com	Portland	OR	97204	503-208-3068		387
Chisago County 313 N Main St. *TF:* 888-234-1246 ■ *Web:* www.co.chisago.mn.us	Center City	MN	55012	651-257-1300	213-8876	338
Chisesi Bros Meat Packing Co 5221 Jefferson Hwy *TF:* 800-966-3550 ■ *Web:* www.chisesibros.com	New Orleans	LA	70123	504-822-3550		473
Chisholm Fleming & Assoc 317 Renfrew Dr Ste 301 *TF:* 888-241-4149 ■ *Web:* www.chisholmfleming.com	Markham	ON	L3R9S8	905-474-1458		256
Chisholm Trail Broadcasting Co 316 E Willow Rd	Enid	OK	73701	580-237-1390		116
Chiso Restaurant 3520 Fremont Ave N. *Web:* www.chisoseattle.com	Seattle	WA	98103	206-632-3430		671
Chisum High School 3250 S Church St *Web:* www.chisumisd.org	Paris	TX	75462	903-737-2800		685
Chitiva's Salsa & Sports Bar & Grille 445 W Weber Ave *Web:* www.chitiva.net	Stockton	CA	95203	209-941-8605		671
Chitresh Das Dance Co 2325 Third St Ste 320. *Web:* www.kathak.org	San Francisco	CA	94107	415-333-9000		573-1
Chittenango Falls State Park 2300 Rathbun Rd *Web:* parks.ny.gov/parks/130	Cazenovia	NY	13035	315-637-6111		565
Chittenden County 175 Main St. *Web:* www.ccrpcvt.org	Burlington	VT	05401	802-846-4490		338
Chittenden Regional Correctional Facility 7 Farrell St *Web:* www.doc.state.vt.us	South Burlington	VT	05403	802-863-7356	863-7473	213
Chives Canadian Bistro 1537 Barrington St *Web:* www.chives.ca	Halifax	NS	B3J1Z4	902-420-9626		671
CHL Medical Partners 1055 Washington Blvd 6th Fl *Web:* www.chlmedical.com	Stamford	CT	06901	203-324-7700	324-3636	792
CHL Systems 476 Meetinghouse Rd. *Web:* www.chlsystems.com	Souderton	PA	18964	215-723-7284	723-9115	261
CHLA (Canadian Health Libraries Assn) 39 River St *TF:* 800-321-1433 ■ *Web:* www.chla-absc.ca	Toronto	ON	M5A3P1	416-646-1600	646-9460	49-11
Chloe 232 Arch St *Web:* www.chloebyob.com	Philadelphia	PA	19106	215-629-2337		671
Chlorine Institute Inc 1300 Wilson Blvd. *TF:* 800-424-9300 ■ *Web:* www.chlorineinstitute.org	Arlington	VA	22209	703-894-4140	894-4130	49-13
CHME Inc 289 Foster City Blvd Ste A *Web:* www.chme.org	Foster City	CA	94404	650-357-8550		475
CHMWarnick 548 Cabot St *Web:* www.chmhotel.com	Beverly	MA	01915	978-522-7000		379
CHN (Coalition on Human Needs) 1120 Connecticut Ave NW *Web:* www.chn.org	Washington	DC	20036	202-223-2532	223-2538	48-5
Choate Construction Co 8200 Roberts Dr Ste 600 *Web:* www.choateco.com	Atlanta	GA	30350	678-892-1200	892-1202	186
Choate Rosemary Hall 333 Christian St *Web:* www.choate.edu	Wallingford	CT	06492	203-697-2239	697-2629	622
Chocolate Factory Theater 549 49th Ave. *Web:* chocolatefactorytheater.org	Long Island	NY	11101	718-482-7069		297
Chocolates a la Carte 24836 Ave Rockefeller **Fax Area Code:* 661 ■ **Fax:* Sales ■ *TF Cust Svc:* 800-818-2462 ■ *Web:* www.chocolatesalacarte.com	Valencia	CA	91355	800-818-2462	257-4999*	296-8
Choctaw Casino Resorts 3735 Choctaw Rd *TF:* 888-652-4628 ■ *Web:* www.choctawcasinos.com	Durant	OK	74701	580-920-0160		452

Phone | Fax | Class

Choctaw County
55 E Quinn St PO Box 737 — Ackerman MS 39735 — 662-285-3778 285-2440 338
TF: 800-821-9157 ■ *Web:* choctawcountyms.com

Choctaw County 117 S Mulberry St Ste 9 — Butler AL 36904 — 205-459-2155 338
Web: Www.alabama.gov

Choctaw County Public Library
124 N Academy Ave — Butler AL 36904 — 205-459-2542 434-3

Choctaw Electric Co-op Inc
1033 N 4250 Rd — Hugo OK 74743 — 580-326-6486 245
TF: 800-780-6486 ■ *Web:* www.choctawelectric.coop

Choctaw Management Services Enterprise
2101 W Arkansas St — Durant OK 74701 — 866-326-1000 260
TF: 866-326-1000 ■ *Web:* www.cmse.net

Choctaw Transportation Co Inc
1311 E Ct — Dyersburg TN 38025 — 731-286-0012 188-5
Web: choctawtrans.com

Choctawhatchee Electric Co-op Inc
1350 W Baldwin Ave — DeFuniak Springs FL 32435 — 850-892-2111 892-9243 245
TF: 800-342-0990 ■ *Web:* www.chelco.com

Choctaw-Kaul Distribution Co
3540 Vinewood Ave — Detroit MI 48208 — 313-894-9494 894-7977 576
Web: www.choctawkaul.com

Choi & Burns LLC
156 W 56th St 18th Fl — New York NY 10019 — 212-755-7051 355-2610 266
Web: www.choiburns.com

Choi Bros Inc 3401 W Div St — Chicago IL 60651 — 773-489-2800 489-3030 155-1
TF: 800-524-2464 ■ *Web:* www.choibrothers.com

Choice Books LLC
2387 Grace Chapel Rd — Harrisonburg VA 22801 — 540-434-1827 434-9894 96
TF: 800-827-1894 ■ *Web:* www.choicebooks.org

Choice Exploration Inc 2221 Ave J — Arlington TX 76006 — 817-633-7777 539
Web: www.choiceexploration.com

Choice Financial Group 645 Hill Ave — Grafton ND 58237 — 701-352-0242 70
Web: choicefinancialgroup.com

Choice Genetics
1415 28th St Ste 400 — West Des Moines IA 50266 — 515-225-9420 11-2
Web: choice-genetics.com

Choice Group 755 W Big Beaver Rd — Troy MI 48084 — 248-362-4150 362-4154 654
Web: www.choiceproperties.com

Choice Hotels Canada Inc
5090 Explorer Dr Ste 500 — Mississauga ON L4W4T9 — 905-602-2222 378
TF: 800-859-7459 ■ *Web:* www.choicehotels.ca

Choice Hotels International Inc
10750 Columbia Pk — Silver Spring MD 20901 — 301-592-5000 379
NYSE: CHH ■ *TF:* 800-424-6423 ■ *Web:* www.choicehotels.com

Choice Hotels International Inc
621 S Atlantic Ave — Ormond Beach FL 32176 — 386-672-4550 669
Web: www.choicehotels.com/ascend

Choice Hotels International Inc
1 Choice Hotels Cir Ste 400 — Rockville MD 20850 — 301-592-5000 379
TF: 800-424-6423 ■ *Web:* www.choicehotels.com

Choice Hotels International Inc
9655 Grove Cir N — Maple Grove MN 55369 — 763-494-5556 379
Web: www.choicehotels.com

Choice Hotelsÿ
1 Choice Hotels Cir Ste 400 — Rockville MD 20850 — 301-592-5000 379
Web: www.choicehotels.com

Choice One Engineering Corp
440 E Hoewisher Rd — Sidney OH 45365 — 937-497-0200 256
Web: choiceoneengineering.com

Choice Precision Machine Inc
4380 Commerce Dr — Whitehall PA 18052 — 610-502-1111 454
Web: www.choiceprecision.com

Choice Solutions Inc
420 Lakeside Ave — Marlborough MA 01752 — 508-229-0044 242

Choice Telecommunications Inc
7640 Dixie Hwy Ste 150 — Clarkston MI 48346 — 248-922-1150 196
Web: www.choicetel.com

Choice Translating Inc
112 S Tryon St Ste 1500 — Charlotte NC 28284 — 704-717-0043 393
TF: 800-534-0722 ■ *Web:* www.choicetranslating.com

ChoiceStream Inc 25 Drydock Ave 5th Fl — Boston MA 02210 — 617-498-7800 7
Web: www.choicestream.com

Choke Canyon State Park PO Box 2 — Calliham TX 78007 — 361-786-3868 565
Web: tpwd.texas.gov/state-parks/choke-canyon

Cholestech Corp
9975 Summers Ridge Rd — San Diego CA 92121 — 510-732-7200 231
TF: 866-284-3684 ■ *Web:* www.alere.com

Cholla Custom Cabinets Inc
1727 E Deer Valley Rd — Phoenix AZ 85024 — 623-322-9949 321

CHOMP (Community Hospital of the Monterey Peninsula)
23625 Holman Hwy — Monterey CA 93940 — 831-624-5311 625-4948 374-3
TF: 888-452-4667 ■ *Web:* www.chomp.org

Choo Choo Build-it Mart
1600 McIntosh St — Vidalia GA 30474 — 912-537-4108 364

Choochai Thai Cuisine 2330 19th St — Lubbock TX 79401 — 806-747-1767 671

Chooljian Bros Packing Company Inc
3192 S Indianola St — Sanger CA 93657 — 559-875-5501 875-1582 11-1
TF: 800-555-5211 ■ *Web:* www.chooljianbrothers.com

Choose Digital Inc
4040 Aurora St — Coral Gables FL 33146 — 305-443-5981 387

Chop House 262 S Palm Canyon Dr — Palm Springs CA 92262 — 760-320-4500 671

Chop House 9700 Kingston Pk — Knoxville TN 37922 — 865-531-2467 693-4814 671
Web: thechophouse.com

Chop House Ann Arbor, The
322 S Main St — Ann Arbor MI 48104 — 734-669-9977 671
Web: thechophouseannarbor.com

Chop House, The 2011 Gunbarrel Rd — Chattanooga TN 37421 — 423-892-1222 671
Web: www.thechophouse.com

Chop's City Grill 837 Fifth Ave S — Naples FL 34102 — 239-262-4677 671
Web: www.chopscitygrill.com

Chophouse '47 36 Beacon Dr — Greenville SC 29615 — 864-286-8700 671
Web: www.centraarchy.com/chophouse47.php

Chopper Trading
141 W Jackson Blvd Ste 2201A — Chicago IL 60604 — 312-628-3500 690
Web: www.choppertrading.com

Chopra Ctr at La Costa Resort & Spa
2013 Costa del Mar Rd — Carlsbad CA 92009 — 760-494-1600 494-1608 673
TF: 888-424-6772 ■ *Web:* www.chopra.com

Chops/Lobster Bar
70 W Paces Ferry Rd NW — Atlanta GA 30305 — 404-262-2675 240-6645 671
Web: www.buckheadrestaurants.com

Chopstick House 5412 E Indiana St — Evansville IN 47715 — 812-473-5551 671
Web: www.chopstickhouserestaurant.net

Chopsticks 4783 E Olive Ave — Fresno CA 93702 — 559-255-0489 671

Choptank Electric Co-op Inc
24820 Meeting House Rd PO Box 430 — Denton MD 21629 — 877-892-0001 479-3516* 245
**Fax Area Code: 410* ■ *TF:* 877-892-0001 ■ *Web:* www.choptankelectric.com

Choristers Guild 2834 W Kingsley Rd — Garland TX 75041 — 972-271-1521 48-4
TF: 800-246-7478 ■ *Web:* www.choristersguild.org

Chorus America
1156 15th St NW Ste 310 — Washington DC 20005 — 202-331-7577 331-7599 48-4
Web: www.chorusamerica.org

Chorus Aviation Inc
3 Spectacle Lake Dr — Dartmouth NS B3B1W8 — 902-873-5000 787
TF: 800-963-9611 ■ *Web:* www.flyjazz.ca

Chouteau County Courthouse
1308 Franklin St — Fort Benton MT 59442 — 406-622-5151 622-3012 338
Web: www.co.chouteau.mt.us

Chow's Contemporary Chinese Food
720 St Michaels Dr — Santa Fe NM 87505 — 505-471-7120 671
Web: www.mychows.com

Chowan County 113 E King St — Edenton NC 27932 — 252-482-8431 338
Web: www.chowancounty-nc.gov

Chowan University
1 University Pl — Murfreesboro NC 27855 — 252-398-6439 166
TF Admissions: 888-424-6926 ■ *Web:* www.chowan.edu

CHP & Assoc Consulting Engineers Inc
7660 Woodway Dr Ste 400 — Houston TX 77063 — 713-977-3430 194
Web: buryinc.com

CHP International Inc
1040 N Blvd Ste 220 — Oak Park IL 60301 — 708-848-9650 196
TF: 800 449-2614 ■ *Web:* www.chpinternational.com

CHPA (Consumer Healthcare Products Assn)
1150 Connecticut Ave NW # 700 — Washington DC 20036 — 202-429-9260 223-6835 49-4
TF: 800-222-1222 ■ *Web:* www.chpa.org

CHQM-FM 103.5 (AC)
969 Robson St Ste 500 — Vancouver BC V6Z1X5 — 604-871-9000 871-2901 645-171
Web: www.iheartradio.ca/qmfm

CHQR-AM 770 (N/T)
200 Barclay Parade SW — Calgary AB T2P4R5 — 403-716-6500 645-27
Web: globalnews.ca/radio/newstalk770/?gref=newstalk770

CHR Solutions Inc
9700 Bissonnet Ste 2800 — Houston TX 77036 — 713-995-4778 196
Web: www.chrsolutions.com

CHRIE (International Council on Hotel Restaurant & Institutional Education)
2810 N Parham Rd Ste 230 — Richmond VA 23294 — 804-346-4800 346-5009 49-5
Web: www.chrie.org

Chris Alston Chassisworks Inc
8661 Younger Creek Dr — Sacramento CA 95828 — 916-388-0288 54
TF: 800-722-2269 ■ *Web:* www.cachassisworks.com

Chris Madrid's 1900 Blanco Rd — San Antonio TX 78212 — 210-735-3552 671
Web: chrismadrids.com

Chris Smith Realty 1204 Third Ave — Spring Lake NJ 07762 — 732-449-3777 449-7790 652
Web: chrissmithrealty.com

Chris Woods Construction Company Inc
8068 US Hwy 70 — Memphis TN 38133 — 901-386-3182 186
TF: 800-983-0152 ■ *Web:* www.chriswoodsconstruction.com

Chris Young Consulting Co
83 N 64th St — Harrisburg PA 17111 — 717-561-9742 180
Web: chrisyoungconsulting.com

Chrisad Inc
11 Professional Ctr Pkwy — San Rafael CA 94903 — 415-924-8575 7
TF: 800-505-4150 ■ *Web:* www.chrisad.com

Chrisanntha Construction Corp
4661 Dewey Ave PO Box 165 — Gorham NY 14461 — 585-526-6376 187
Web: www.chrisanntha.com

Chris-Craft Boats 8161 15th St E — Sarasota FL 34243 — 941-351-4900 358-3717 90
Web: chriscraft.com

Chrisian Inc 17561 Hillside Ave — Jamaica NY 11432 — 718-465-9151 225
Web: www.chrisian.com

Chrisken Property Management LLC
345 N Canal St Ste 201 — Chicago IL 60606 — 312-454-1626 454-1627 655
Web: www.chrisken.com

Christ & Grace Episcopal Church
1545 S Sycamore St — Petersburg VA 23805 — 804-733-7202 48-20
Web: christandgrace.org

Christ Church Cathedral
125 Monument Cir — Indianapolis IN 46204 — 317-636-4577 50-1
TF: 800-669-5786 ■ *Web:* www.cccindy.org

Christ Church Cathedral 45 Church St — Hartford CT 06103 — 860-527-7231 50-1
Web: www.cccathedral.org

Christ Church Cathedral
1210 Locust St — Saint Louis MO 63103 — 314 231-3454 231-3142 50-1
Web: www.christchurchcathedral.us

Christ Church Cathedral
690 Burrard St — Vancouver BC V6C2L1 — 604-682-3848 50-1
Web: thecathedral.ca

Christ Church Episcopal
10 N Church St — Greenville SC 29601 — 864-271-8773 242-0879 50-1
Web: www.ccgsc.org

Christ Church in Philadelphia
20 N American St — Philadelphia PA 19106 — 215-922-1695 922-3578 50-1
Web: www.christchurchphila.org

Christ Church of Universal Love, The
11699 130th Ave — Largo FL 33778 — 727-585-5088 48-20

Christ Church Xp 8800 Vaughn Rd — Montgomery AL 36117 — 334-387-0566 48-20
Web: christchurchxp.net

Christ Episcopal Church
State & Water Sts PO Box 1374 — Dover DE 19903 — 302-734-5731 50-1
Web: www.christchurchdover.org

Christ Hospital 176 Palisade Ave — Jersey City NJ 07306 — 201-795-8200 374-3
Web: www.carepointhealth.org

Christ Hospital Health Network, The
2139 Auburn Ave — Cincinnati OH 45219 — 513-585-2000 585-3200 374-3
Web: www.thechristhospital.com

Christ in Youth Inc PO Box B — Joplin MO 64801 — 417-781-2273 781-5958 48-20
TF: 855-999-7238 ■ *Web:* ciy.com

Name / Address	City	State	ZIP	Phone	Fax	Class
Christ School 500 Christ School Rd *TF:* 800-422-3212 ■ *Web:* www.christschool.org	Arden	NC	28704	828-684-6232	684-4869	622
Christ the King Retreat Ctr 621 First Ave S *Web:* www.kingshouse.com	Buffalo	MN	55313	763-682-1394	682-3453	673
Christ The King School Mothers Club Inc 4100 Colgate Ave *TF:* 800-465-0561 ■ *Web:* www.cks.org	Dallas	TX	75225	214-365-1234		685
Christ The King Seminary 711 Knox Rd *Web:* www.cks.edu	East Aurora	NY	14052	716-652-8900	652-8903	167-3
Christ Universal Temple 11901 S Ashland Ave Apt S *Web:* www.cutemple.org	Chicago	IL	60643	773-568-2282		48-20
Christa Construction LLC 119 Victor Heights Pkwy *Web:* www.christa.com	Victor	NY	14564	585-924-3050		186
Christa McAuliffe Planetarium 2 Institute Dr *Web:* www.starhop.com	Concord	NH	03301	603-271-7827	271-7832	598
Christchurch School 49 Seahorse Ln *TF:* 800-296-2306 ■ *Web:* www.christchurchschool.org	Christchurch	VA	23031	804-758-2306	758-0721	622
Christel DeHaan Fine Arts Ctr 1400 E Hanna Ave University of Indianapolis *TF:* 800-232-8634 ■ *Web:* www.uindy.edu/arts	Indianapolis	IN	46227	317-788-3566	788-3383	572
Christendom College 134 Christendom Dr **Fax:* Admissions ■ *TF:* 800-877-5456 ■ *Web:* www.christendom.edu	Front Royal	VA	22630	540-636-2900	636-1655*	166
Christensen Farms 23971 County Rd 10 *Web:* www.christensenfarms.com	Sleepy Eye	MN	56085	507-794-5310		10-6
Christensen Industries 2990 S Main St *Web:* www.christensenindustries.com	Salt Lake City	UT	84115	801-466-3334	466-1441	697
Christensen O'Connor Johnson & Kindness PLLC 1201 Third Ave Ste 3600 *Web:* www.cojk.com	Seattle	WA	98101	206-682-8100		428
Christensen Roberts Solutions 60 Pond St *Web:* www.crsol.com	Milford	CT	06460	203-389-4440		194
Christensen Shipyards Ltd 4400 SE Columbia Way *Web:* www.christensenyachts.com	Vancouver	WA	98661	360-695-3238		770
Christenson Transportation Inc 2001 W Old Rt 66 *TF:* 800-980-2493 ■ *Web:* www.christensontrans.com	Strafford	MO	65757	417-866-5993		780
Christian & Missionary Alliance 8595 Explorer Dr *TF:* 800-700-2651 ■ *Web:* www.cmalliance.org	Colorado Springs	CO	80920	719-599-5999		48-20
Christian Aid Ministries PO Box 360 *Web:* christianaidministries.org	Berlin	OH	44610	330-893-2428	893-2305	48-20
Christian Alliance for Humanitarian Aid Inc 4401 Rice Dyer Rd *Web:* christian-alliance.org	Pearland	TX	77581	281-412-2285		743
Christian Appalachian Project 6550 S KY Rt 321 PO Box 459 *TF:* 800-755-5322 ■ *Web:* www.christianapp.org	Hagerhill	KY	41222	800-755-5322		48-5
Christian Blind Mission (CBM) 450 E Pk Ave *TF:* 800-937-2264 ■ *Web:* www.cbmus.org	Greenville	SC	29601	864-239-0065	239-0069	48-5
Christian Broadcasting Network (CBN) 977 Centerville Tpke *TF:* 800-823-6053 ■ *Web:* www.cbn.com	Virginia Beach	VA	23463	800-823-6053		740
Christian Bros University 650 E Pkwy S **Fax:* Admissions ■ *TF Admissions:* 800-288-7576 ■ *Web:* www.cbu.edu	Memphis	TN	38104	901-321-3000	321-3494*	166
Christian Brothers Retreat 4401 Redwood Rd *Web:* www.christianbrosretreat.com	Napa	CA	94558	707-252-3810		378
Christian Business Men's Connection (CBMC) 5746 Marlin Rd Ste 602 Osborne Ctr *TF:* 800-566-2262 ■ *Web:* www.cbmc.com	Chattanooga	TN	37411	423-698-4444	629-4434	48-20
Christian Church (Disciples of Christ) 130 E Washington St *TF:* 800-668-8016 ■ *Web:* www.disciples.org	Indianapolis	IN	46204	317-635-3100	635-3700	48-20
Christian Coalition of America PO Box 37030 **Fax Area Code:* 808 ■ *TF:* 888-999-6778 ■ *Web:* www.cc.org	Washington	DC	20013	202-479-6900	586-0006*	48-7
Christian County 511 S Main St *Web:* www.christiancountyky.gov/county-clerk	Hopkinsville	KY	42240	270-887-4100		338
Christian County 100 W Church St Rm 206 *Web:* www.christiancountymo.gov	Ozark	MO	65721	417-582-4300	581-8331	338
Christian County 101 S Main St PO Box 647 *TF:* 800-368-8683 ■ *Web:* christiancountyil.com	Taylorville	IL	62568	217-824-4969	824-5105	338
Christian County Library 1005 N Fourth Ave *Web:* christiancountylibrary.org	Ozark	MO	65721	417-581-2432	581-8855	434-3
Christian County Public Schools 200 Glass Ave *TF:* 800-274-7374 ■ *Web:* www.christian.kyschools.us	Hopkinsville	KY	42240	270-887-7000	887-1316	685
Christian Dior 712 Fifth Ave 37th Fl *TF:* 800-929-3467 ■ *Web:* dior.com	New York	NY	10019	212-582-0500	582-1063	277
Christian Disaster Response International PO Box 3339 *TF:* 800-919-9338 ■ *Web:* www.cdresponse.org	Winter Haven	FL	33885	863-967-4357		48-5
Christian Fellowship Church Foundation 21673 Beaumeade Cir *Web:* www.cfellowshipc.org	Ashburn	VA	20147	703-729-3900		48-20
Christian Foundation for Children & Aging (CFCA) 1 Elmwood Ave *TF:* 800-875-6564 ■ *Web:* unbound.org	Kansas City	KS	66103	913-384-6500	384-2211	48-6
Christian Horizons 200 N Postville Dr *TF:* 800-535-8717 ■ *Web:* www.christianhomes.org	Lincoln	IL	62656	217-732-9651	732-8686	363
Christian Leadership Alliance (CLA) 635 Camino De Los Mares Ste 216 *TF:* 800-263-6317 ■ *Web:* www.christianleadershipalliance.org	San Clemente	CA	92673	949-487-0900	487-0927	49-12
Christian Legal Society (CLS) 8001 Braddock Rd Ste 300 *TF:* 800-225-4008 ■ *Web:* www.clsnet.org	Springfield	VA	22151	703-642-1070	642-1075	49-10
Christian Medical & Dental Assn (CMDA) 2604 Hwy 421 PO Box 7500 *TF:* 888-231-2637 ■ *Web:* www.cmda.org	Bristol	TN	37620	423-844-1000	844-1005	49-8
Christian Reformed Church in North America (CRC) 2850 Kalamazoo Ave SE *TF:* 800-272-5125 ■ *Web:* www.crcna.org	Grand Rapids	MI	49560	616-241-1691	224-0834	48-20
Christian Reformed World Relief Committee (CRWRC) 2850 Kalamazoo Ave SE *TF:* 800-552-7972 ■ *Web:* www.worldrenew.net	Grand Rapids	MI	49560	616-241-1691	224-0806	48-5
Christian Schools International (CSI) 3350 E Paris Ave SE *TF:* 800-635-8288 ■ *Web:* www.csionline.org	Grand Rapids	MI	49512	616-957-1070	957-5022	49-5
Christian Science Monitor 210 Massachusetts Ave *Web:* www.csmonitor.com	Boston	MA	02115	617-450-2000		532-3
Christian Science Publishing Society 210 Massachusetts Ave P02-15 *TF:* 800-456-2220 ■ *Web:* www.csmonitor.com	Boston	MA	02115	617-450-2300		637-8
Christian Television Network Inc (CTN) 6922 142nd Ave N *TF:* 800-716-7729 ■ *Web:* www.ctnonline.com	Largo	FL	33771	727-535-5622	531-2497	738
Christian Theological Seminary 1000 W 42nd St *TF:* 800-585-0108 ■ *Web:* www.cts.edu	Indianapolis	IN	46208	317-924-1331		167-3
Christian Witness Theological Seminary 1975 Concourse Dr *Web:* www.cwts.edu	San Jose	CA	95131	408-433-2280		167-3
Christiana Care Health System 501 W 14th St *TF:* 855-250-9594 ■ *Web:* www.christianacare.org	Wilmington	DE	19801	302-366-1929		353
Christiana Hospital 4755 Ogletown-Stanton Rd *Web:* www.christianacare.org	Newark	DE	19718	302-733-1000		374-3
Christiana Mall 132 Christiana Mal *TF:* 800-433-7300 ■ *Web:* www.christianamall.com	Newark	DE	19702	302-731-9815		400
Christianity Today 465 Gundersen Dr *TF Cust Svc:* 800-222-1840 ■ *Web:* christianitytoday.com/iyf	Carol Stream	IL	60188	630-260-6200	260-0114	457-11
Christianity Today International 465 Gundersen Dr *TF:* 800-222-1840 ■ *Web:* www.christianitytoday.com	Carol Stream	IL	60188	630-260-6200	260-0114	637-9
Christianity Today Magazine 465 Gundersen Dr *TF:* 800-999-1704 ■ *Web:* www.christianitytoday.com	Carol Stream	IL	60188	630-260-6200	260-0114	457-10
Christiansen Aviation Inc 200 Lear Jet Ln *Web:* www.christiansenaviation.com	Tulsa	OK	74132	918-298-6650	298-6656	24
Christianson Air Conditioning & Plumbing 1950 Louis Henna Blvd *TF:* 000-406-0614 ■ *Web:* www.christiansonco.com	Round Rock	TX	78664	512-246-5200	246-5201	189-10
Christianson Systems Inc 20421 15th St SE PO Box 138 *TF:* 800-328-0090 ■ *Web:* www.christianson.com	Blomkest	MN	56216	320-995-6141	995-6145	207
Christie Christopher (R) The State Houseÿ PO Box 001 **Fax Area Code:* 6.0 ■ *Web:* www.state.nj.us/governor	Trenton	NJ	08625	.51-201-e+009	977-7e1009*	343
Christie Cookie Co 1205 Third Ave N *TF:* 800-458-2447 ■ *Web:* www.christiecookies.com	Nashville	TN	37208	615-242-3817	242-5572	296-9
Christie Lodge PO Box 1196 *TF:* 888-325-6343 ■ *Web:* www.christielodge.com	Avon	CO	81620	970-845-4504		378
Christie's Bistro 925 S Creyts Rd *Web:* www.ihg.com	Lansing	MI	48917	517-323-4190	323-2100	671
Christie's of Newport 14 Perry Mill Wharf *TF:* 800-936-0277 ■ *Web:* www.41north.com	Newport	RI	02840	401-847-5400		671
Christina Cultural Arts Ctr 705 N Market St *Web:* ccacde.org	Wilmington	DE	19801	302-652-0101	652-7480	572
Christina's Grill & Bar 21382 Hwy 160 W	Durango	CO	81303	970-382-3844		671
Christini's 7600 Dr Phillips Blvd *Web:* www.christinis.com	Orlando	FL	32819	407-345-8770	345-8700	671
Christman Company Inc 208 N Capitol Ave *TF:* 800-253-9751 ■ *Web:* www.christmanco.com	Lansing	MI	48933	517-482-1488	482-3520	186
Christmas Decor Inc 709 E 44th St *Web:* www.christmasdecor.net	Lubbock	TX	79404	806-722-1225		310
Christo's 2632 Nicollet Ave *Web:* www.christos.com	Minneapolis	MN	55408	612-871-2111	871-8129	671
Christopher & Banks Corp 2400 Xenium Ln N *NYSE:* CBK ■ *Web:* www.christopherandbanks.com	Plymouth	MN	55441	763-551-5000	551-5198	157-6
Christopher Cutts Gallery 21 Morrow Ave *TF:* 800-442-2787 ■ *Web:* www.cuttsgallery.com	Toronto	ON	M6R2H9	416-532-5566	532-7272	42
Christopher Enterprises 155 W 2050 N **Fax Area Code:* 801 ■ *TF:* 800-453-1406 ■ *Web:* www.drchristopher.com	Spanish Fork	UT	84660	800-453-1406	794-6801*	355
Christopher Guy 12670 World Plaza Ln Bldg 62 Ste 2 *Web:* www.christopherguy.com	Fort Myers	FL	33907	239-939-9838		361
Christopher Martin's 860 State St *Web:* www.christophermartins.com	New Haven	CT	06511	203-776-8835		671
Christopher Newport University 1 University Pl **Fax:* Admissions ■ *TF Admissions:* 800-333-4268 ■ *Web:* www.cnu.edu	Newport News	VA	23606	757-594-7015	594-7333*	166
Christopher Newport University Smith Library 1 University Pl *Web:* cnu.edu	Newport News	VA	23606	757-594-7133		434-6
Christopher Ranch 305 Bloomfield Ave *TF:* 800-779-1156 ■ *Web:* primuslabs.com	Gilroy	CA	95020	408-847-1100	847-5488	10-11
Christopher Reeve Foundation 636 Morris Tpke Ste 3A *TF:* 800-225-0292 ■ *Web:* www.christopherreeve.org	Short Hills	NJ	07078	973-379-2690		48-17

Phone | Fax | Class

Christopher Smith Leonard Bristow Stanell & Wells PA
Suntrust Bank Bldg 1001 Third Ave W
Ste 700 .... Bradenton FL 34205 941-748-1040 734
Web: www.cslcpa.com

Christopher's Crush
2502 E Camelback Rd .... Phoenix AZ 85016 602-522-2344 671
Web: www.christophersaz.com

Christopher's Seafood & Steak House
134 W Pierpont Ave .... Salt Lake City UT 84101 801-519-8515 671
Web: www.christophersteakhouse.com

Christophers, The
5 Hanover Sq 11th Fl .... New York NY 10004 212-759-4050 838-5073 48-20
TF: 888-298-4050 ■ *Web:* www.christophers.org

Christopherson Homes Inc
1315 Airport Blvd .... Santa Rosa CA 95403 707-524-8222 360-6208 653

Christos Mediterranean Grille
130 Sixth St .... Pittsburgh PA 15222 412-261-6442 671
Web: christosmediterraneangrille.com

Christown Spectrum Mall
1703 W Bethany Home Rd .... Phoenix AZ 85015 602-249-0670 460
Web: www.christownspectrum.com

CHRISTUS Bossier Medical Ctr
4241 Woodcock Dr Ste A-100 .... San Antonio TX 78228 210-785-5200 374-3
TF: 800-263-4795 ■ *Web:* www.christushealth.org

CHRISTUS Health
919 Hidden Ridge Ste 450 .... Irving TX 75038 469-282-2000 353
Web: www.christushealth.org

CHRISTUS Health
4241 Woodcock Dr # A100 .... San Antonio TX 78228 210-785-5200 371
Web: www.christushomecare.org

CHRISTUS Health
2606 Hospital Blvd .... Corpus Christi TX 78405 361-902-4000 374-3
Web: www.christusspohn.org

CHRISTUS Saint Michael Health System
2600 St Michael Dr .... Texarkana TX 75503 903-614-1000 614-2212 374-3
Web: www.christushealth.org/St-Michael

CHRISTUS Santa Rosa Health System
333 N Santa Rosa St .... San Antonio TX 78207 210-704-2011 704-3632 374-3
Web: www.christussantarosa.org

CHRISTUS Schumpert Health System
1453 E Bert Kouns Industrial Loop .... Shreveport LA 71101 318-681-4500 353

CHRISTUS Shreveport-Bossier Health System
1453 E Bert Kouns .... Shreveport LA 71105 318-681-4500 374-3
TF: 888-681-4138 ■ *Web:* christushealthsb.org

CHRISTUS Southeast Texas Health System
2830 Calder St .... Beaumont TX 77702 409-892-7171 924-3959 374-3
TF: 866-683-3627 ■ *Web:* christussetx.org

CHRISTUS Southeast Texas Health System
3600 Gates Blvd PO Box 3696 .... Port Arthur TX 77642 409-985-7431 989-1033 374-3
TF: 866-683-3627 ■ *Web:* christussetx.org

CHRISTUS Spohn Health System
1702 Santa Fe St .... Corpus Christi TX 78404 361-881-3000 881-3755 353
Web: www.christushealth.org/spohn

CHRISTUS Spohn Health system
5950 Saratoga Blvd .... Corpus Christi TX 78414 361-985-5000 374-3
Web: www.christusspohn.org

CHRISTUS Spohn Hospital Corpus Christi Shoreline
600 Elizabeth St .... Corpus Christi TX 78404 361-881-3640 374-3
Web: www.christushealth.org

CHRISTUS Spohn Hospital Kleberg
1311 General Cavazos Blvd .... Kingsville TX 78363 361-595-1661 374-3
Web: www.christushealth.org/spohn

CHRISTUS St. Patrick Health System
524 Dr Michael DeBakey Dr .... Lake Charles LA 70601 337-436-2511 491-7157 374-3
Web: christusstpatrick.org

CHRISTUS St. Vincent
455 St Michael's Dr .... Santa Fe NM 87505 505-983-3361 913-5210 374-3
Web: www.stvin.org

Christus Victor Lutheran Church Inc of Knox County Tennessee
4110 Central Ave Pike .... Knoxville TN 37912 865-687-6622 48-20
Web: christusvictorknoxville.org

Christy Capital Management Inc
2939 Mcmanus Rd .... Macon GA 31220 478-314-2160 765
TF: 866-331-7749 ■ *Web:* www.christycapital.com

Christy Refractories Co
4641 McRee Ave .... Saint Louis MO 63110 314-773-7500 773-8371 500
Web: www.christyco.com

Christy Sports LLC 875 Parfet St .... Lakewood CO 80215 303-237-6321 711
Web: www.christysports.com

Christy's
3101 Ponce de Leon Blvd .... Coral Gables FL 33134 305-446-1400 446-3257 671
Web: www.christysrestaurant.com

Chrom Tech Inc
5995 149th St W Ste 102 .... Apple Valley MN 55124 952-431-6000 419
TF: 800-822-5242 ■ *Web:* www.chromtech.com

Chroma Technology Corp
10 Imtec Ln .... Bellows Falls VT 05101 802-428-2500 544
Web: www.chroma.com

ChromaGen Vision LLC
326 W Cedar St Ste 1 .... Kennett Square PA 19348 855-473-2323 544
TF: 855-473-2323 ■ *Web:* www.ireadbetternow.com

Chromaline Corp 4832 Grand Ave .... Duluth MN 55807 218-628-2217 628-3245 628
TF: 800-328-4261 ■ *Web:* www.chromaline.com

Chromalloy Gas Turbine LLC
330 Blaisdell Rd .... Orangeburg NY 10962 845-359-4700 21
TF: 800-937-2376 ■ *Web:* www.chromalloy.com

Chromalloy Nevada
3636 Arrowhead Dr .... Carson City NV 89706 775-687-8833 21
Web: chromalloy.com

Chromalox Inc 103 Gamma Dr Ext .... Pittsburgh PA 15238 412-967-3800 14
Web: www.chromalox.com

Chromaprobe Inc 10 Kimler Dr .... Maryland Heights MO 63043 314-738-0001 738-0001 231
TF: 888-964-1400 ■ *Web:* www.chromaprobe.com

Chromatin Inc 10 S Lasalle St Ste 2100 .... Chicago IL 60603 312-292-5400 652
Web: www.chromatininc.com

Chromcraft Revington Inc
1330 Win Hentschel Blvd .... West Lafayette IN 47906 765-807-2640 319-2
OTC: CRCV ■ *TF:* 800-732-0330 ■ *Web:* www.chromcraft-revington.com

Chromium Corp 14911 Quorum Dr Ste 600 .... Dallas TX 75254 216-271-4910 262
TF: 888-346-4747 ■ *Web:* www.chromcorp.com

Chronicle Books 680 Second St .... San Francisco CA 94107 415-537-4200 537-4460 637-2
TF: 800-722-6657 ■ *Web:* www.chroniclebooks.com

Chronicle Herald, The PO Box 610 .... Halifax NS B3J2T2 902-426-2811 426-1158 532-1
TF: 800-563-1187 ■ *Web:* thechronicleherald.ca

Chronicle Independent 909 W Dekalb St .... Camden SC 29020 803-432-6157 432-7609 532-4
TF General: 800-922-5431 ■ *Web:* www.chronicle-independent.com

Chronicle of Higher Education, The
1255 23rd St NW Ste 700 .... Washington DC 20037 202-466-1000 452-1033 457-8
TF: 800-728-2803 ■ *Web:* www.chronicle.com

Chronicle, The 225 E Ave .... Elyria OH 44035 440-329-7000 329-7282 532-2
Web: chronicle.northcoastnow.com

Chronicle, The 15 Ridge St .... Glens Falls NY 12801 518-792-1126 793-1587 532-4
Web: glensfallschronicle.com

Chronicle-Journal, The
75 S Cumberland St .... Thunder Bay ON P7B1A3 807-343-6200 532-1
Web: www.chroniclejournal.com

Chronicle-Tribune 610 S Adams St .... Marion IN 46953 765-664-5111 668-4256 532-2
TF: 800-955-7888 ■ *Web:* www.chronicle-tribune.com

Chronister Oil Co
2026 N Republic St .... Springfield IL 62702 217-523-5050 579

Chrysalis Consulting LLC
11711 N Pennsylvania St .... Carmel IN 46032 317-844-1400 194
Web: www.chrysalisglobal.com

Chrysalis Inn & Spa 804 Tenth St .... Bellingham WA 98225 360-756-1005 379
TF: 888-808-0005 ■ *Web:* www.thechrysalisinn.com

Chrysalis Packaging & Assembly Corp
130 W Edgerton Ave Ste 130 .... Milwaukee WI 53207 414-744-8550 88
Web: www.chryspac.com

Chrysalis Ventures
101 S Fifth St Ste 1650 .... Louisville KY 40202 502-583-7644 792
Web: www.chrysalisventures.com

Chrysler Aviation Inc (CAI)
7120 Hayvenhurst Ave Ste 309 .... Van Nuys CA 91406 818-989-7900 13
TF: 800-995-0825 ■ *Web:* www.chrysleraviation.com

Chrysler Group LLC
1000 Chrysler Dr .... Auburn Hills MI 48326 800-423-6343 59
TF Cust Svc: 800-423-6343 ■ *Web:* www.dodge.com

Chrysler Museum of Art 245 W Olney Rd .... Norfolk VA 23510 757-664-6200 664-6201 520
Web: www.chrysler.org

Chs Engineers Inc
12507 Bel Red Rd Ste 101 .... Bellevue WA 98005 425-637-3693 261
Web: www.chsengineers.com

CHS Inc 5500 Cenex Dr .... Inver Grove Heights MN 55077 651-355-6000 276
NASDAQ: CHSCP ■ *TF:* 800-232-3639 ■ *Web:* www.chsinc.com

CHSB (Community Hospital of San Bernardino)
1805 Medical Ctr Dr .... San Bernardino CA 92411 909-887-6333 887-6468 374-3
Web: www.chsb.org

CHSI (Comprehensive Health Services Inc)
10701 Parkridge Blvd Ste 200 .... Reston VA 20191 703-760-0700 391-3
TF: 800-638-8083 ■ *Web:* www.chsmedical.com

CHSL (Cleveland Health Sciences Library)
Case Western Reserve University Robbins Bldg
2109 Adelbert Rd .... Cleveland OH 44106 216-368-4540 434-1
Web: www.case.edu/chsl/library/index.html

CHT Global Corp
2107 N First St Ste 580 .... San Jose CA 95131 408-988-1898 387
Web: www.chtglobal.com

CHT R Beitlich Corp
5046 Old Pineville Rd .... Charlotte NC 28217 704-523-4242 145

CHU de Quebec 1050 Ch Sainte-Foy .... Quebec QC G1S4L8 418-682-7511 682-7877* 374-2
**Fax:* Admissions ■ *Web:* www.cha.quebec.qc.ca

Chu Judy (Rep D - CA)
2423 Rayburn HOB .... Washington DC 20515 202-225-5464 225-5467 342-2
Web: chu.house.gov

Chu Ring & Hazel 241 A St Ste 300 .... Boston MA 02210 617-443-9800 445
Web: www.chu-ring.com

CHU Sainte-Justine
3175 Ch de la Cote-Sainte-Catherine .... Montreal QC H3T1C5 514-345-4931 345-4760 374-2
TF: 888-235-3667 ■ *Web:* www.chusj.org/fr/accueil

Chubb & Son 15 Mountain View Rd .... Warren NJ 07059 908-903-2000 391-4
TF: 800-252-4670 ■ *Web:* www.chubb.com

Chubb Corp 15 Mountain View Rd .... Warren NJ 07059 908-903-2000 360-4
NYSE: CB ■ *TF:* 800-252-4670 ■ *Web:* www.chubb.com

Chubb Group of Insurance Cos
15 Mtn View Rd .... Warren NJ 07059 908-903-2000 391-4
Web: www.chubb.com

Chubb Specialty Insurance
82 Hopmeadow St .... Simsbury CT 06070 860-408-2000 408-2002 391-5
TF: 800-252-4670 ■ *Web:* www.chubb.com

Chubu Electric Power Co Inc
900 17th St NW Ste 1220 .... Washington DC 20006 202-775-1960 331-9256 787
Web: www.chuden.co.jp

Chuck Patterson Inc 200 E Ave .... Chico CA 95926 530-895-1771 57
Web: www.chuckpattersontoyota.net

Chuck Schubert & Associates
17197 N Laurel Park Dr Ste 114 .... Livonia MI 48152 734-953-5600 196
TF: 800-914-2259 ■ *Web:* csasoftware.com

Chuck's Restaurant 3610 Sixth Ave .... Des Moines IA 50313 515-244-4104 671
Web: www.chucksdesmoines.com

Chuck's Steak House
2335 Kalakaua Ave .... Honolulu HI 96815 808-923-1228 671
Web: www.chuckshawaii.com

Chuck's Steak House Inc 20 Segar St .... Danbury CT 06810 203-792-5555 670
Web: www.chuckssteakhouse.com

Chuckawalla Valley State Prison (CVSP)
19025 Wiley's Well Rd PO Box 2289 .... Blythe CA 92226 760-922-5300 922-6855 213
Web: cdcr.ca.gov

CHUDNOW Mfg Company Inc
3055 New St PO Box 10 .... Oceanside NY 11572 516-593-4222 593-4156 300
Web: www.chudnowmfg.com

Chugach Electric Assn Inc
5601 Electron Dr .... Anchorage AK 99518 907-563-7494 562-0027 245
TF: 800-478-7494 ■ *Web:* www.chugachelectric.com

Chugach Management Services Inc
3800 Centerpoint Dr Ste 601 .... Anchorage AK 99503 907-563-8866 463
Web: www.chugach.com

Name / Address	City	State	Zip	Phone	Fax	Class
Chugach State Park 18620 Seward Hwy *TF:* 800-478-6196 ■ *Web:* dnr.alaska.gov	Anchorage	AK	99516	907-345-5014	345-6982	565
Chukchansi Gold Resort & Casino 711 Lucky Ln *TF:* 866-794-6946 ■ *Web:* chukchansigold.com	Coarsegold	CA	93614	866-794-6946		378
Chula Vista Chamber of Commerce 233 Fourth Ave *Web:* www.chulavistachamber.org	Chula Vista	CA	91910	619-420-6603	420-1269	139
Chula Vista Convention & Visitors Bureau 233 Fourth Ave *Web:* www.chulavistaconvis.com	Chula Vista	CA	91910	619-426-2882	420-1269	206
Chula Vista Heritage Museum 360 Third Ave *TF:* 800-490-0591 ■ *Web:* www.chulavistaca.gov	Chula Vista	CA	91910	619-427-8092		520
Chula Vista Public Library 365 F St *TF:* 800-984-4636 ■ *Web:* www.chulavistaca.gov/departments/library	Chula Vista	CA	91910	619-691-5069	427-4246	434-3
Chula Vista Resort 2501 River Rd *TF:* 800-388-4782 ■ *Web:* www.chulavistaresort.com	Wisconsin Dells	WI	53965	608-254-8366	254-7653	669
Chuma Holdings Inc 20945 Devonshire St Ste 208	Chatsworth	CA	91311	702-751-8455		536
Chumash Casino Resort 3400 E Hwy 246 *TF:* 800-248-6274 ■ *Web:* chumashcasino.com	Santa Ynez	CA	93460	805-686-0855		452
Chumney & Associates 660 US-1 Ste 2 *Web:* chumneyads.com	North Palm Beach	FL	33408	561-882-0066		7
Chung Oak 15320 A & B Warwick Blvd	Newport News	VA	23608	757-874-3505		671
Chungs Gourmet Foods 3907 Dennis St *Web:* www.chungsfoods.com	Houston	TX	77004	713-741-2118		296-36
Church & Chapel Metal Arts Inc 2616 W Grand Ave *TF:* 800-992-1234 ■ *Web:* www.church-chapel.com	Chicago	IL	60612	800-992-1234	626-3299	510
Church & Dwight Canada Corp 635 Secretariat Ct *Web:* www.churchdwight.ca	Mississauga	ON	L5S2A5	905-696-6570	564-0356	583
Church & Dwight Company Inc 469 N Harrison St *NYSE: CHD* ■ *TF:* 800-617-4220 ■ *Web:* www.churchdwight.com	Princeton	NJ	08543	800-617-4220		214
Church & Murdock Electric Inc 5709 Wattsburg Rd *TF:* 800-679-9567 ■ *Web:* www.churchandmurdock.com	Erie	PA	16509	814-825-3456	825-4043	189-4
Church & Stagg Office Supply Company Inc 3421 Sixth Ave	Birmingham	AL	35222	205-251-2951		535
Church Brew Works 3525 Liberty Ave *Web:* www.churchbrew.com	Pittsburgh	PA	15201	412-688-8200		671
Church Creek 1250 W Central Rd *Web:* www.sunriseseniorliving.com	Arlington Heights	IL	60005	847-506-3200		672
Church Divinity School of the Pacific 2451 Ridge Rd *Web:* www.cdsp.edu	Berkeley	CA	94709	510-204-0700	644-0712	167-3
Church Metal Spinning Co 5050 N 124th St *Web:* www.churchmetal.com	Milwaukee	WI	53225	414-461-6460		757
Church Mutual Insurance Co 3000 Schuster Ln *TF:* 800-554-2642 ■ *Web:* www.churchmutual.com	Merrill	WI	54452	715-536-5577	539-4650	391-4
Church of God in Christ Inc 930 Mason St *TF:* 877-746-8578 ■ *Web:* www.cogic.org	Memphis	TN	38126	901-947-9300		48-20
Church of God Ministries 1201 E Fifth St *TF:* 800-848-2464 ■ *Web:* jesusisthesubject.org	Anderson	IN	46012	765-642-0256	642-5652	48-20
Church of God World Missions (COGWM) 2490 Keith St PO Box 8016 *TF:* 800-345-7492 ■ *Web:* www.cogwm.org	Cleveland	TN	37320	423-478-7190		48-20
Church of Jesus Christ of Latter-Day Saints 50 E N Temple St *TF:* 800-453-3860 ■ *Web:* www.lds.org	Salt Lake City	UT	84150	801-240-1000		48-20
Church of Our Lady of Lourdes 901 Atwells Ave *Web:* parishesonline.com	Providence	RI	02909	401-272-8127		48-20
Church of Scientology Flag Service Organization 500 Cleveland St *Web:* scientology-fso.org	Clearwater	FL	33755	727-467-5000		48-20
Church of the Brethren 1451 Dundee Ave *TF:* 800-323-8039 ■ *Web:* www.brethren.org	Elgin	IL	60120	847-742-5100	742-1407	48-20
Church of The Holy Communion 218 Ashley Ave *Web:* www.holycomm.org	Charleston	SC	29403	843-722-2024		48-20
Church of the Nazarene 17001 Prairie Star Pkwy *Web:* www.nazarene.org	Lenexa	KS	66220	913-577-0500		48-20
Church of the Transfiguration 1 E 29th St *TF:* 800-253-7521 ■ *Web:* www.littlechurch.org	New York	NY	10016	212-684-6770		50-1
Church Women United (CWU) 475 Riverside Dr Ste 243 *TF:* 800-298-5551 ■ *Web:* www.churchwomen.org	New York	NY	10115	212-870-2347	870-2338	48-20
Church World Service 28606 Phillips St PO Box 968 *TF:* 800-297-1516 ■ *Web:* www.cwsglobal.org	Elkhart	IN	46515	574-264-3102	262-0966	48-5
Church World Service Emergency Response Program 475 Riverside Dr Ste 700 *TF:* 888-297-2767 ■ *Web:* www.cwserp.org	New York	NY	10115	212-870-2061	870-3220	48-5
Churchill & Harriman LLC 239 Wall St *Web:* chus.com	Princeton	NJ	08540	609-921-3551		225
Churchill Cabinet Co 4616 W 19th St *TF Sales:* 800-379-9776 ■ *Web:* www.chicago gaming.com	Cicero	IL	60804	708-780-0070	780-9762	286
Churchill Corporate Services 56 Utter Ave *TF:* 800-941-7458 ■ *Web:* www.furnishedhousing.com	Hawthorne	NJ	07506	973-636-9400	636-0179	210
Churchill County 155 N Taylor St Ste 110 *Web:* nv-churchillcounty.civicplus.com	Fallon	NV	89406	775-423-6028		338
Churchill County Museum & Archives 1050 S Maine St *Web:* www.ccmuseum.org	Fallon	NV	89406	775-423-3677	423-3662	520
Churchill County School District 545 E Richards St *Web:* www.churchill.k12.nv.us	Fallon	NV	89406	775-423-5184	423-2959	685
Churchill Development Corp 5 Choke Cherry Rd Ste 360 *Web:* www.churchillbuilders.com	Rockville	MD	20850	240-243-1000		187
Churchill Downs Inc 700 Central Ave *NASDAQ: CHDN* ■ *TF:* 800-994-9909 ■ *Web:* www.churchilldowns.com	Louisville	KY	40208	502-636-4400		642
Churchill Hotel 1914 Connecticut Ave NW *TF:* 800-424-2464 ■ *Web:* www.thechurchillhotel.com	Washington	DC	20009	202-797-2000	462-0944	379
Churchill Nature Tours PO Box 429 *TF:* 877-636-2968 ■ *Web:* www.churchillnaturetours.com	Erickson	MB	R0J0P0	204-636-2968	636-2557	760
Churchill School & Center, The 301 E 29th St *Web:* www.churchillschool.com	New York	NY	10016	212-722-0610		148
Churchill's Food & Spirits 340 S Saginaw St *Web:* churchillsflint.com	Flint	MI	48502	810-238-3800		671
Churchville Fire Equipment Corp 340 Sanford Rd S *Web:* www.churchvillefire.com	Churchville	NY	14428	585-293-1688		791
Churchwell Co 814 S Edgewood Ave *TF:* 877-537-6166 ■ *Web:* www.churchwellcompany.com	Jacksonville	FL	32205	904-356-5721		9
Churrascaria Plataforma 316 W 49th St *Web:* plataformaonline.com	New York	NY	10019	212-245-0505	974-8250	671
Churrasco's 2055 Westheimer Rd *Web:* www.cordua.com	Houston	TX	77098	713-527-8300	527-0847	671
Chutney's Etc 1944 Hillview St *Web:* www.chutneysetc.com	Sarasota	FL	34239	941-954-4444		671
Chuy's Mesquite Broiler 2500 New Stine Rd *Web:* bajachuys.com	Bakersfield	CA	93309	661-833-3469		671
CHWC (Bryan Hospital) 433 W High St *Web:* www.chwchospital.org	Bryan	OH	43506	419-636-1131	630-2155	374-3
Chyron Corp 5 Hub Dr *NASDAQ: CHYR* ■ *Web:* chyronhego.com	Melville	NY	11747	631-845-2000		178-8
CI (Conservation International) 2011 Crystal Dr Ste 500 *TF:* 800-406-2306 ■ *Web:* www.conservation.org	Arlington	VA	22202	703-341-2400	553-0654	48-13
CI Financial Corp Twentieth 2 Queen St E Fl *TF:* 800-268-9374 ■ *Web:* www.theglobeandmail.com/globe-investor	Toronto	ON	M5C3G7	800-268-9374		787
CI Hayes 33 Fwy Dr *Web:* www.cihayes.com	Cranston	RI	02920	401-467-5200	467-2108	318
Ci Metal Fabrication 6205 St Louis St *Web:* www.cimetalfab.com	Meridian	MS	39307	601-483-6281	693-6529	697
Ci Radar LLC 4046 Wetherburn Way Ste 1 *TF:* 800-421-0617 ■ *Web:* www.ciradar.com	Norcross	GA	30092	678-680-2103		393
CIA (Central Intelligence Agency) Office of Public Affairs *Web:* www.cia.gov	Washington	DC	20505	703-482-0623	482-1739	340-20
Cianbro Corp 335 Hunnewell Ave *TF:* 866-242-6276 ■ *Web:* www.cianbro.com	Pittsfield	ME	04967	866-242-6276		188-4
CIANJ (Commerce & Industry Assn of New Jersey) 61 S Paramus Rd *Web:* www.cianj.org	Paramus	NJ	07652	201-368-2100	368-3438	139
Ciao Italia 6149 Westwood Blvd *Web:* www.ciaoitaliaonline.com	Orlando	FL	32821	407-354-0770		671
Ciao Systems Inc 4326 Lorcom Ln *Web:* www.ciaosoftware.com	Arlington	VA	22207	703-524-9356		225
CIBA Vision Corp 11460 Johns Creek Pkwy *TF:* 800-875-3001 ■ *Web:* www.alcon.com	Duluth	GA	30097	678-415-3937	415-4260	542
CIBC (Canadian Imperial Bank of Commerce) 199 Bay St Commerce Ct W *NYSE: CM* ■ *TF:* 800-465-2422 ■ *Web:* www.cibc.com	Toronto	ON	M5L1A2	800-465-2422		70
CIBC Mellon Global Securities Services Co 320 Bay St PO Box 1 *TF:* 888-439-2457 ■ *Web:* www.cibcmellon.com	Toronto	ON	M5H4A6	416-643-5000		528
CIBC Wood Gundy Capital 425 Lexington Ave *TF:* 800-999-6726 ■ *Web:* www.cibcwm.com	New York	NY	10017	212-856-4000		792
CIBER Inc 6363 S Fiddler's Green Cir Ste 1400 *NYSE: CBR* ■ *TF:* 800-242-3799 ■ *Web:* www.ciber.com	Greenwood Village	CO	80111	303-220-0100	220-7100	180
CIBO (Council of Industrial Boiler Owners) 6801 Kennedy Rd Ste 102 *Web:* www.cibo.org	Warrenton	VA	20187	540-349-9043		49-13
Cibo Global LLC 1000 Sansome Ste 200 *Web:* www.cibosf.com	San Francisco	CA	94111	415-233-6606		195
Cibola County 515 W High Ave *Web:* www.co.cibola.nm.us	Grants	NM	87020	505-285-2510		338
Cibola Systems Corp 180 S Cypress St *Web:* www.cibolasystems.com	Orange	CA	92866	714-480-0272		196
Cibus Global 6455 Nancy Ridge Dr Ste 100 *Web:* www.cibus.com	San Diego	CA	92121	858-450-0008		668
CIC Energy Consulting 150 S Wacker Dr Ste 2400	Chicago	IL	60606	312-466-0500		463
CIC Group Inc 530 Maryville Centre Dr Ste 100 *Web:* www.cicgroup.com	Saint Louis	MO	63141	314-682-2900		360-3
CIC Photonics Inc 9000 Washington St *Web:* www.cicp.com	Albuquerque	NM	87113	505-343-9500		711
Cic Plus Inc 7321 ridgeway ave *Web:* www.cicplus.com	Skokie	IL	60076	847-677-9800		138
Cicada 617 S Olive St *Web:* www.cicadarestaurant.com	Los Angeles	CA	90014	213-488-9488	488-9546	671

				Phone	Fax	Class
Cicatelli Associates Inc-ccd 505 Eighth Ave Ste 1900 *Web:* www.caiglobal.org	New York	NY	10018	212-594-7741	629-3321	305
CICA-TV Ch 19 (Ind) 2180 Yonge St Stn Q PO Box 200 *TF:* 800-613-0513 ■ *Web:* tvo.org	Toronto	ON	M4T2T1	416-484-2600	484-4234	741-136
Ciccio Cafe 875 Claire-Fontaine	Quebec	QC	G1R3A8	418-525-6161		671
Cicero Group 35 N Rio Grande St *Web:* cicerogroup.com	Salt Lake City	UT	84101	801-456-6700		463
Cicero Inc 8000 Regency Pkwy Ste 542 *TF:* 866-538-3588 ■ *Web:* www.ciceroinc.com	Cary	NC	27518	919-380-5000		178-1
Cicero Public Library 5225 W Cermak Rd *TF:* 800-447-4278 ■ *Web:* cicerolibrary.org	Cicero	IL	60804	708-652-8084	652-8095	434-3
Ciceron Inc 126 N Third St Ste 200 *Web:* www.ciceron.com	Minneapolis	MN	55401	612-204-1919		4
CiCi Enterprises LP 1080 W Bethel Rd	Coppell	TX	75019	972-745-4200		670
Cicilline David (Rep D - RI) 2244 Rayburn HOB *Web:* cicilline.house.gov	Washington	DC	20515	202-225-4911	225-3290	342-2
Cicinelli & Dippolito CPAs PC 1858 Commerce St *Web:* cdcpas.com	Yorktown Heights	NY	10598	914-302-2290		2
Cicoil Corp 24960 Ave Tibbitts *Web:* www.cicoil.com	Valencia	CA	91355	661-295-1295	295-0813	814
Cicon Engineering 6633 Odessa Ave *Web:* www.cicon.com	Van Nuys	CA	91406	818-909-6060		529
CID (Center for International Development at Harvard University) Rubenstein Bldg 79 JFK St 1 Eliot St Bldg 79 JFK St *Web:* www.hks.harvard.edu/centers/cid	Cambridge	MA	02138	617-495-4112	496-8753	634
CID Bio-Science Inc 4845 NW Camas Meadows Dr *TF:* 800-767-0119 ■ *Web:* www.cid-inc.com	Camas	WA	98607	360-833-8835		639
CID Capital Inc 201 W 103rd St Ste 200 *Web:* www.cidcap.com	Indianapolis	IN	46290	317-818-5030	644-2914	792
CID Performance Tooling Inc 6 Willey Rd *TF:* 800-964-2331 ■ *Web:* www.cidtools.com	Saco	ME	04072	207-286-3319		697
CIDA (Council for Interior Design Accreditation) 206 Grandville Ave Ste 350 *Web:* www.accredit-id.org	Grand Rapids	MI	49503	616-458-0400	458-0460	48-1
CiDRA Corp 50 Barnes Pk N *TF:* 877-243-7277 ■ *Web:* www.cidra.com	Wallingford	CT	06492	203-265-0035	294-4211	735
CIEE (Council on International Educational Exchange) 300 Fore St *TF Cust Svc:* 888-268-6245 ■ *Web:* www.ciee.org	Portland	ME	04101	207-553-4000	553-5272	49-5
Cielito Lindo Mexicano 2953 S National Ave	Springfield	MO	65804	417-886-3320		671
Cielo Vista Mall 8401 Gateway Blvd W *TF:* 800-333-5032 ■ *Web:* www.simon.com	El Paso	TX	79925	915-779-7071	772-4926	460
CIENA Corp 1201 Winterson Rd *NASDAQ: CIEN* ■ *TF:* 800-921-1144 ■ *Web:* www.ciena.com	Linthicum	MD	21090	410-694-5700	694-5750	735
CIENA Corp Metro Transport Div 1185 Sanctuary Pkwy *Web:* www.ciena.com	Alpharetta	GA	30009	678-867-5100	867-5101	176
CIES (Council for International Exchange of Scholars) 1400 K St NW Ste 700 *Web:* www.cies.org	Washington	DC	20005	202-686-4000		49-5
CIG (CIG) 888 Seventh Ave 17th Floor *Web:* www.cig.com	New York	NY	10019	212-897-6635	897-6640	637-11
Cigar.com Inc 1911 Spillman Dr **Fax Area Code: 877* ■ *TF:* 800-357-9800 ■ *Web:* www.cigar.com	Bethlehem	PA	18015	800-357-9800	464-2872*	756
Cigarette Racing Team LLC 4355 NW 128th St *Web:* www.cigaretteracing.com	Opa Locka	FL	33054	305-931-4564	769-4355	90
CIGNA 900 Cottage Grove Rd **Fax Area Code: 800* ■ *TF:* 800-244-6224 ■ *Web:* www.cigna.com	Hartford	CT	06002	860-226-6000	351-3616*	391-2
CIGNA Behavioral Health Inc 11095 Viking Dr Ste 350 *TF:* 800-753-0540 ■ *Web:* www.cignabehavioral.com	Eden Prairie	MN	55344	800-433-5768		462
CIGNA Corp 1601 Chestnut St *NYSE: CI* ■ *Web:* www.cigna.com	Philadelphia	PA	19192	215-761-1000		360-4
CIGNA Foundation 900 Cottage Grove Rd *NYSE: CI* ■ *TF:* 866-438-2446 ■ *Web:* cigna.com/index.html	Bloomfield	CT	06002	866-438-2446		304
CIGNA Healthcare 900 Cottage Grove Rd *TF:* 800-997-1654 ■ *Web:* www.cigna.com/health	Hartford	CT	06152	860-226-6000		391-3
CIGNA Healthcare of North Carolina Inc 701 Corporate Ctr Dr *TF:* 800-942-1654 ■ *Web:* www.cigna.com	Raleigh	NC	27607	919-854-7000		391-3
Cigniti Inc 433 E Las Colinas Blvd Ste 1300 *Web:* www.cigniti.com	Irving	TX	75039	972-756-0622		180
CIGNYS 68 Williamson St	Saginaw	MI	48601	989-753-1411		207
Cilantro 338 17th Ave SW *Web:* cilantrocalgary.com	Calgary	AB	T2S0A8	403-229-1177	245-5239	671
CIM (Inter-American Commission of Women) 1889 F St NW *Web:* www.oas.org/cim	Washington	DC	20006	202-458-6084	458-6094	48-24
CIM Concepts Inc 100 W Commons Blvd Ste 101 *Web:* cimconcepts.com	New Castle	DE	19720	302-613-5400		180
Cima Labs Inc 7325 Aspen Ln *Web:* www.cimalabs.com	Brooklyn Park	MN	55428	763-488-4700	488-4800	85
CIMA Technologies 1035 Eastside Rd *Web:* cima-technologies.com	El Paso	TX	79915	915-775-1919		261
Cimarron Correctional Facility 3200 S Kings Hwy *TF:* 800-656-4673 ■ *Web:* www.cca.com	Cushing	OK	74023	918-225-3336	225-3363	213
Cimarron County PO Box 145 *Web:* www.ok.gov/tax	Boise City	OK	73933	580-544-2251		338
Cimarron Electric Co-op PO Box 299 *TF:* 800-375-4121 ■ *Web:* www.cimarronelectric.com	Kingfisher	OK	73750	405-375-4121	375-4209	245
Cimarron Energy Inc 1012 24th Ave NW Ste 100 PO Box 722110 *TF:* 800-822-8755 ■ *Web:* www.cimarronenergy.com	Norman	OK	73070	405-928-7373		539
Cimarron Software Services Inc 1115 Gemini *Web:* www.cimarroninc.com	Houston	TX	77058	281-226-5100	226-5190	177
CIMCO Communications Inc 1901 S Meyers Rd 7th Fl *Web:* www.cimco.net	Oakbrook Terrace	IL	60181	630-691-8080		387
CIMCO Refrigeration 65 Villiers St *TF:* 800-267-1418 ■ *Web:* www.cimcorefrigeration.com	Toronto	ON	M5A3S1	416-465-7581		664
CIMdata Inc 3909 Research Park Dr *Web:* www.cimdata.com	Ann Arbor	MI	48108	734-668-9922		194
Ciment Quebec Inc 145 Blvd du Centenaire *Web:* www.bcr.cc	St. Basile De Portneuf	QC	G0A3G0	418-329-2100		183
Cimetrics Inc 141 Tremont St Fl 11 *Web:* www.cimetrics.com	Boston	MA	02111	617-350-7550		177
Cimmaron Field Services Inc 303 W Wall St Bank of America Tower Ste 600 *TF:* 877-944-2705 ■ *Web:* www.cimmaron.com	Midland	TX	79701	877-944-2705		536
Cimro of Nebraska 1230 O St Ste 120 *TF:* 800-300-8190 ■ *Web:* www.cimronebraska.org	Lincoln	NE	68508	402-476-1399		463
CIMS (Courant Institute of Mathematical Sciences) *New York University* 251 Mercer St *Web:* www.cims.nyu.edu	New York	NY	10012	212-998-1212	995-4121	668
Cinchseal Associates Inc 731 Hylton Rd *TF:* 800-699-9277 ■ *Web:* www.cinchseal.com	Pennsauken	NJ	08110	856-662-5162		326
CinCin Ristorante 1154 Robson St *Web:* www.cincin.net	Vancouver	BC	V6E1B2	604-688-7338	688-7339	671
Cincinnati Art Museum 953 Eden Pk Dr *TF:* 877-472-4226 ■ *Web:* www.cincinnatiartmuseum.org	Cincinnati	OH	45202	513-721-2787		520
Cincinnati Asset Management Inc 4350 Glndl Milford Rd 1 *Web:* www.cambonds.com	Cincinnati	OH	45242	513-554-8500		401
Cincinnati Ballet 1555 Central Pkwy *Web:* www.cballet.org	Cincinnati	OH	45214	513-621-5219	621-4844	573-1
Cincinnati Bell Directory (CBD) 312 Plum St Ste 600 *TF:* 800-877-0475 ■ *Web:* vivial.net	Cincinnati	OH	45202	800-877-0475		637-6
Cincinnati Bell Inc 221 E Fourth St *NYSE: CBB* ■ *TF:* 800-387-3638 ■ *Web:* www.cincinnatibell.com	Cincinnati	OH	45202	513-397-9900		736
Cincinnati Bengals 1 Paul Brown Stadium *TF:* 866-621-8383 ■ *Web:* www.bengals.com	Cincinnati	OH	45202	513-621-3550	621-3570	715-3
Cincinnati Business Courier 101 W Seventh St *Web:* www.bizjournals.com	Cincinnati	OH	45202	513-621-6665	621-2462	457-5
Cincinnati Casualty Co 6200 S Gilmore Rd	Fairfield	OH	45014	513-870-2000		391-5
Cincinnati Children's Hospital Medical Ctr 3333 Burnet Ave *TF:* 800-344-2462 ■ *Web:* www.cincinnatichildrens.org	Cincinnati	OH	45229	513-636-4200		374-1
Cincinnati Christian University 2700 Glenway Ave *TF:* 800-949-4228 ■ *Web:* www.ccuniversity.edu	Cincinnati	OH	45204	513-244-8100	244-8140	161
Cincinnati City Hall 801 Plum St *Web:* www.cincinnati-oh.gov	Cincinnati	OH	45202	513-352-3000		337
Cincinnati CityBeat 811 Race St	Cincinnati	OH	45202	513-665-4700		532-5
Cincinnati College of Mortuary Science 645 W N Bend Rd *TF:* 888-377-8433 ■ *Web:* www.ccms.edu	Cincinnati	OH	45224	513-761-2020	761-3333	800
Cincinnati Enquirer 312 Elm St *TF:* 800-876-4500 ■ *Web:* www.cincinnati.com	Cincinnati	OH	45202	513-721-2700	768-8340	532-2
Cincinnati Eye Bank for Sight Restoration Inc 4015 Executive Pk Dr Ste 330 *Web:* www.cintieb.org	Cincinnati	OH	45241	513-861-3716	483-3984	269
Cincinnati Fan & Ventilator 7697 Snider Rd *Web:* www.cincinnatifan.com	Mason	OH	45040	513-573-0600	573-0640	18
Cincinnati Financial Corp 6200 S Gilmore Rd *NASDAQ: CINF* ■ *TF:* 800-364-3400 ■ *Web:* cinfin.com	Fairfield	OH	45014	513-870-2000		360-4
Cincinnati Fire Museum 315 W Court St Ste 1 *Web:* www.cincyfiremuseum.com	Cincinnati	OH	45202	513-621-5553		521
Cincinnati Floor Company Inc 5162 Broerman Ave *TF:* 800-886-4501 ■ *Web:* www.cincifloor.com	Cincinnati	OH	45217	513-641-4500	482-4204	189-2
Cincinnati Gardens 2250 Seymour Ave *Web:* www.cincygardens.com	Cincinnati	OH	45212	513-631-7793	351-5898	720
Cincinnati Gasket Packing & Manufacturing Inc 40 Illinois Ave *TF:* 800-833-1121 ■ *Web:* www.cgindustrialglass.com	Cincinnati	OH	45215	513-761-3458	761-2994	326
Cincinnati Gilbert Machine Tool Company LLC 3366 Beekman St *Web:* www.cincinnatigilbert.com	Cincinnati	OH	45223	513-541-4815	541-4885	493
Cincinnati History Museum 1301 Western Ave Cincinnati Museum Ctr *TF:* 800-733-2077 ■ *Web:* www.cincymuseum.org	Cincinnati	OH	45203	513-287-7000		520
Cincinnati Inc 7420 Kilby Rd *Web:* www.e-ci.com	Harrison	OH	45030	513-367-7100	367-7552	456
Cincinnati Insurance Co 6200 S Gilmore Rd *TF:* 800-888-0616 ■ *Web:* cinfin.com	Fairfield	OH	45014	513-870-2000		391-4
Cincinnati Magazine 441 Vine St Ste 200 *Web:* www.cincinnatimagazine.com	Cincinnati	OH	45202	513-421-4300		457-22
Cincinnati Metropolitan Housing Authority 1627 Western Ave *Web:* www.cintimha.com	Cincinnati	OH	45214	513-421-2642		210
Cincinnati Music Hall 650 Walnut St *Web:* www.cincinnatiarts.org	Cincinnati	OH	45202	513-744-3344	744-3345	572
Cincinnati Opera 1243 Elm St *Web:* www.cincinnatiopera.org	Cincinnati	OH	45202	513-768-5500	768-5553	573-2

Phone | Fax | Class

Cincinnati Playhouse in the Park
962 Mt Adams Cir .... Cincinnati OH 45202 513-345-2242 345-2250 572
TF: 800-582-3208 ■ *Web:* www.cincyplay.com

Cincinnati Preserving Company Inc
3015 E Kemper Rd .... Cincinnati OH 45241 513-771-2000 771-8381 296-20
TF Cust Svc: 800-222-9966 ■ *Web:* www.clearbrookfarms.com

Cincinnati Reds
100 Joe Nuxhall Way .... Cincinnati OH 45202 513-381-7337 765-7342 713
TF: 877-647-7337 ■ *Web:* cincinnati.reds.mlb.com

Cincinnati State Technical & Community College
3520 Central Pkwy .... Cincinnati OH 45223 513-569-1500 569-1562* 162
**Fax:* Admissions ■ *TF:* 877-569-0115 ■ *Web:* www.cincinnatistate.edu

Cincinnati Symphony Orchestra
1241 Elm St Music Hall .... Cincinnati OH 45202 513-621-1919 744-3535 573-3
Web: www.cincinnatisymphony.org

Cincinnati USA Regional Chamber
441 Vine St Ste 300 .... Cincinnati OH 45202 513-579-3100 579-3102 139
Web: www.cincinnatichamber.com

Cincinnati Ventilating Company Inc
7410 Industrial Rd .... Florence KY 41042 859-371-1320 697
Web: www.cvc-fab.com

Cincinnati Zoo & Botanical Garden
3400 Vine St........ Cincinnati OH 45220 513-281-4700 559-7790 823
TF: 800-944-4776 ■ *Web:* www.cincinnatizoo.org

Cincinnatian Hotel 601 Vine St .... Cincinnati OH 45202 513-381-3000 651-0256 379
TF: 800-942-9000 ■ *Web:* www.cincinnatianhotel.com

Cincinnati-Northern Kentucky International Airport
PO Box 752000 .... Cincinnati OH 45275 859-767-3151 27
TF: 800-990-8841 ■ *Web:* www.cvgairport.com

Cincinnatus Consulting LLC
1721 Spruce St........ Philadelphia PA 19103 267-872-0313 693
Web: www.cincinnatus-consulting.com

Cinco Energy Land Services
9235 Katy Fwy Ste 400........ Houston TX 77024 713-463-6009 690
Web: cincoland.com

Cincom Systems Inc 55 Merchant St........ Cincinnati OH 45246 513-612-2300 612-2000 178-1
TF: 800-224-6266 ■ *Web:* www.cincom.com

Cinder & Concrete Block Corp
10111 Beaver Dam Rd .... Cockeysville MD 21030 410-666-2350 183
Web: cinderblockonline.com

Cind-R-Lite Block Co
4745 Mitchell St........ North Las Vegas NV 89081 702-651-1550 183
Web: www.cind-r-lite.com

Cindus Corp 515 Stn Ave........ Cincinnati OH 45215 800-543-4691 948-8805* 554
**Fax Area Code:* 513 ■ *TF:* 800-543-4691 ■ *Web:* www.cindus.com

Cine Magnetics Inc 100 Business Pk Dr........ Armonk NY 10504 914-273-7500 273-7575 658
TF: 800-431-1102 ■ *Web:* www.cminyla.com

Cinecraft Productions Inc
2515 Franklin Blvd........ Cleveland OH 44113 216-781-2300 514
Web: www.cinecraft.com

Cineflix Media Inc
3510 Saint Laurent Blvd Ste 202 .... Montreal QC H2X2V2 514-278-3140 514
Web: www.cineflix.com

Cinema Libre Studio
120 S Victory Blvd........ Burbank CA 91502 818-588-3033 349-9922 512
Web: www.cinemalibrestudio.com

Cinemark USA Inc
3900 Dallas Pkwy Ste 500 .... Plano TX 75093 972-665-1000 665-1004 748
TF: 800-246-3627 ■ *Web:* www.cinemark.com

Cinemavault Releasing Inc
1240 Bay St Ste 307........ Toronto ON M5R2A7 416-363-6060 514
Web: www.cinemavault.com

Cinemax 1100 Ave of the Americas........ New York NY 10036 212-512-1002 740
Web: www.cinemax.com

Cinemotion Inc 9062 General Dr........ Plymouth MI 48170 734-454-4433 514
Web: cinemotioninc.com

Cineplex Digital Networks
369 York St Ste 2C .... London ON N6B3R4 519-438-0111 8
TF: 866-353-8324 ■ *Web:* ok3.com

Cineplex Entertainment LP
1303 Yonge St .... Toronto ON M4T2Y9 416-323-6600 748
TF: 800-333-0061 ■ *Web:* www.cineplex.com

Cinergy Children's Museum
1301 Western Ave Cincinnati Museum Ctr...... Cincinnati OH 45203 513-287-7000 521
TF: 800-733-2077 ■ *Web:* www.cincymuseum.org

Cinespace Film Studios
2621 W 15th Pl Ste 100........ Chicago IL 60608 773-521-8000 514
Web: www.cinespace.com

Cine-tal Systems Inc
8383 Craig St Ste 130 .... Indianapolis IN 46250 317-576-0091 576-0117 33

Cinetel Films
8255 W Sunset Blvd........ West Hollywood CA 90046 323-654-4000 514
Web: cinetelfilms.com

Cinetic Media Inc
555 W 25th St 4th Fl........ New York NY 10001 212-204-7979 194
Web: www.cineticmedia.com

Cinfab Mechanical Inc
5240 Lester Rd........ Cincinnati OH 45213 513-396-6100 396-7574 189-10
TF: 800-543-4020 ■ *Web:* www.cinfab.com

Cinmar LLC 5566 W Chester Rd........ West Chester OH 45069 888-263-9850 603-1492* 459
**Fax Area Code:* 513 ■ *TF:* 888-263-9850 ■ *Web:* www.frontgate.com

Cinnabar California Inc
4571 Electronics Pl........ Los Angeles CA 90039 818-842-8190 842-0563 181
Web: www.cinnabar.com

Cinque Terre 10 Dana St........ Portland ME 04101 207-772-1330 671
Web: www.vignolamaine.com

Cinram International Inc
2255 Markham Rd .... Scarborough ON M1B2W3 416-298-8190 658

Cinta Salon 23 Grant Ave........ San Francisco CA 94108 415-989-1000 77
Web: cinta.com

Cintas Canada Ltd 6300 Kennedy Rd........ Mississauga ON L5T2X5 905-670-4409 393
TF: 800-342-1015 ■ *Web:* www.cintas.ca

Cintas Corp PO Box 625737 .... Cincinnati OH 45262 513-459-1200 442
NASDAQ: CTAS ■ *TF:* 800-786-4367 ■ *Web:* www.cintas.com

CINTRAFOR (Center for International Trade in Forest Products)
University of Washington PO Box 352100 .... Seattle WA 98195 206-543-8684 685-0790 668
Web: www.cintrafor.org

Cintrex Audio Visual 656 Axminister Dr .... Fenton MO 63026 636-343-0178 514
TF: 800-325-9541 ■ *Web:* www.cintrexav.com

CIO Association of Canada
7270 Woodbine Ave Ste 204........ Markham ON L3R4B9 905-752-1899 138
TF: 800-228-3000 ■ *Web:* www.ciocan.ca

CIO Magazine
492 Old Connecticut Path PO Box 9208...... Framingham MA 01701 508-872-0080 879-7784 457-5
Web: www.cio.com

CIO Solutions
5425 Hollister Ave Ste 150........ Santa Barbara CA 93111 805-692-6700 180
TF: 800-467-4448 ■ *Web:* www.ciosolutions.com

Cioppino's Mediterranean Grill & Enoteca
1133 Hamilton St........ Vancouver BC V6B5P6 604-688-7466 671
Web: cioppinosyaletown.com

Ciorba Group Inc
5507 N Cumberland Ave Ste 402........ Chicago IL 60656 773-775-4009 261
TF: 800-321-6607 ■ *Web:* www.ciorba.com

CIP Group, The 799 Cambridge St .... Cambridge MA 02141 617-354-0866 463
Web: www.askcip.com

Cip Real Estate Property Services Inc
19762 Macarthur Blvd Ste 300........ Irvine CA 92612 949-474-7030 652
Web: www.ciprealestate.com

Cipher Systems LLC
2661 Riva Rd Ste 1000........ Annapolis MD 21401 410-412-3326 194
TF: 888-899-1523 ■ *Web:* www.cipher-sys.com

CipherMax Inc 3 Results Way........ Cupertino CA 95014 408-861-3697 194

Cipherspace LLC 376 Main St Ste 100........ Bedminster NJ 07921 973-630-1050 177
Web: www.cipherspace.com

Ciplex
475 Washington Blvd Ste A .... Marina Del Rey CA 90292 310-461-0330 5
Web: www.ciplex.com

Ciproms Inc 3600 Woodview Trce .... Indianapolis IN 46268 317-870-0480 463
Web: www.ciproms.com

CIPS (Canadian Information Processing Society)
5090 Explorer Dr Ste 801........ Mississauga ON L4W4T9 905-602-1370 602-7884 48-1
TF: 877-275-2477 ■ *Web:* www.cips.ca

CIR (Center for Individual Rights)
1233 20th St NW Ste 300........ Washington DC 20036 202-833-8400 833-8410 48-8
TF: 877-426-2665 ■ *Web:* www.cir-usa.org

CIR Law Offices LLP
8665 Gibbs Dr Ste 150........ San Diego CA 92123 800-496-8909 41
TF: 800-496-8909 ■ *Web:* www.cirlaw.com

Ciranda Inc 221 Vine St........ Hudson WI 54016 715-386-1737 297-8
Web: www.ciranda.com

Circa 1801 1 Jacquard Dr........ Connelly Springs NC 28612 828-397-7003 745-1

Circa 1886 149 Wentworth St........ Charleston SC 29401 843-853-7828 671
Web: www.circa1886.com

Circa Corp 1330 Fitzgerald Ave .... San Francisco CA 94124 415-822-1600 155-2

Circa Enterprises Inc
206-5 Richard Way SW........ Calgary AB T2G4M6 403-258-2011 736
Web: www.circaent.com

Circa Inc 415 Madison Ave 19th Fl .... New York NY 10017 212-486-6013 411
TF: 877-876-5493 ■ *Web:* circajewels.com

Circa Information Technology
12001 Woodruff Ave........ Downey CA 90241 562-803-1594 178-10
Web: www.circausa.com

Circa39 Hotel 3900 Collins Ave .... Miami Beach FL 33140 305-538-4900 538-4998 379
Web: www.circa39.com

Circadian Technologies Inc
2 Main St Ste 310........ Stoneham MA 02180 781-439-6300 439-6399 194
TF: 800-284-5001 ■ *Web:* www.circadian.com

Circle 1 Network Inc
131 W Seeboth St........ Milwaukee WI 53204 414-271-5437 387
Web: www.circle1network.com

Circle B Company Inc
5636 S Meridian St........ Indianapolis IN 46217 317-787-5746 780-2654 109-9
TF: 800-886-8077 ■ *Web:* circlebco.com

Circle Bolt & Nut Company Inc
158 Pringle St........ Kingston PA 18704 570-718-6001 350
TF: 800-548-2658 ■ *Web:* circlebolt.com

Circle Buick Gmc Inc 2440 45th St........ Highland IN 46322 219-865-4400 57
Web: circleautomotive.com

Circle City Bar & Grille
350 W Maryland St........ Indianapolis IN 46225 317-405-6100 671
TF: 877-640-7666 ■ *Web:* indymarriott.com

Circle Family Care 3919 N Albany Ave .... Chicago IL 60618 773-478-4747 726
TF: 800-514-1224 ■ *Web:* www.cfhcn.org

Circle Floors Inc
1911 Revere Beach Pkwy .... Everett MA 02149 617-381-6600 290
Web: jzaino.powweb.com/circlefloors

Circle Foods LLC
8411 Siempre Viva Rd .... San Diego CA 92154 619-671-3900 296-37
Web: www.circlefoods.com

Circle Furniture Inc 19 Craig Rd........ Acton MA 01720 978-263-4509 321
Web: outlet.circlefurniture.com

Circle Graphics LLC 120 Ninth Ave .... Longmont CO 80501 303-532-2370 627
TF: 800-367-2472 ■ *Web:* www.circlegraphicsonline.com

Circle Group, The 1275 Alderman Dr........ Alpharetta GA 30005 678-356-1000 189-9
Web: www.thecirclegroup.com

Circle in the Square Theatre
1633 Broadway........ New York NY 10019 212-239-6200 747
Web: www.telecharge.com

Circle J Trailers 312 W Simplot Blvd .... Caldwell ID 83065 208-459-0842 459-0106 779
TF: 800-247-2535 ■ *Web:* www.circlejtrailers.com

Circle Media Inc 5817 Old Leeds Rd .... Irondale AL 35210 800-356-9916 532-3
TF: 800-356-9916 ■ *Web:* www.ncregister.com

Circle S Ranch Inc 1604 Cir S Ranch Rd........ Monroe NC 28112 704-764-7414 447

Circle s Studio LLC 201 W Seventh St........ Richmond VA 23224 804-232-2908 7
TF: 800-261-1537 ■ *Web:* www.circlesstudio.com

Circle Seal Controls Inc
2301 Wardlow Cir........ Corona CA 92880 951-270-6200 270-6201 789
TF: 800-991-2726 ■ *Web:* www.circle-seal.com

Circle Star Energy Corp
7065 Confederate Park Rd Ste 102........ Fort Worth TX 76108 817-744-8502 536

Circle Theatre 230 W Fourth St .... Fort Worth TX 76102 817-877-3040 877-3536 572
Web: www.circletheatre.com

Circle Theatre
1607 Robinson Rd SE........ Grand Rapids MI 49506 616-632-1980 456-8540 573-4
TF: 800-782-4607 ■ *Web:* www.circletheatre.org

Phone | Fax | Class

Circle X Land & Cattle Company Ltd
3131 Briarcrest Dr Ste 220 ... Bryan TX 77802 979-776-5760 776-4818 446
Web: www.bre.com
Circle Z Ranch PO Box 194 ... Patagonia AZ 85624 888-854-2525 239
TF: 888-854-2525 ■ *Web:* www.circlez.com
Circle-Prosco Inc 401 N Gates Dr ... Bloomington IN 47404 812-339-3653 143
Web: www.circleprosco.com
Circleville City School District
388 Clark Dr ... Circleville OH 43113 740-474-4340 474-6600 685
TF: 800-418-6423 ■ *Web:* www.circlevillecityschools.org
Circor Aerospace Inc 2301 Wardlow Cir ... Corona CA 92880 951-270-6200 350
TF: 800-344-8724 ■ *Web:* www.circoraerospace.com
CIRCOR Energy 1500 SE 89th St ... Oklahoma City OK 73149 405-631-1533 778-1072* 789
**Fax Area Code:* 845 ■ *TF:* 800-398-2493 ■ *Web:* circorenergy.com
CIRCOR International Inc
30 Corporate Dr Ste 200 ... Burlington MA 01803 781-270-1200 270-1299 641
NYSE: CIR ■ *Web:* www.circor.com
Circuit Assembly Corp 18 Thomas St ... Irvine CA 92618 949-855-7887 855-4298 253
Web: www.circuitassembly.com
Circuit Express Inc 229 S Clark Dr ... Tempe AZ 85281 800-979-4722 625
TF: 800-979-4722 ■ *Web:* www.4pcb.com
Circular Congregational Church
150 Meeting St ... Charleston SC 29401 843-577-6400 50-1
Web: www.circularchurch.org
Circular Technologies
3275 Prairie Ave ... Boulder CO 80301 303-443-8512 820
TF: 800-215-1831 ■ *Web:* www.circulartech.com
Circus Circus Hotel & Casino Reno
500 N Sierra St ... Reno NV 89503 775-329-0711 328-9652 133
TF: 800-648-5010 ■ *Web:* www.circusreno.com
Circus Circus Hotel Casino & Theme Park Las Vegas
2880 Las Vegas Blvd S ... Las Vegas NV 89109 702-734-0410 133
TF Resv: 800-634-3450 ■ *Web:* www.circuscircus.com
Circus World Museum 550 Water St ... Baraboo WI 53913 608-356-8341 356-1800 520
TF: 866-693-1500 ■ *Web:* circusworldbaraboo.org
Cirm Corp 109 Long Hill Terr ... New Haven CT 06515 914-298-7024 539
Ciro's Cote Sud 7918 Maple St ... New Orleans LA 70118 504-866-9551 671
Web: www.cotesudrestaurant.com
Cirque Corp
2463 South 3850 West ... Salt Lake City UT 84120 801-467-1100 467-0208 173-1
TF: 800-454-3375 ■ *Web:* www.cirque.com
Cirque du Soleil Inc 8400 Second Ave ... Montreal QC H1Z4M6 514-722-2324 722-3692 149
TF: 800-678-2119 ■ *Web:* www.cirquedusoleil.com
Cirrascale Corp 12140 Community Rd ... Poway CA 92064 858-874-3800 874-3838 173-8
TF: 888-942-3800 ■ *Web:* www.cirrascale.com
Cirro Energy Services Inc
2745 Dallas Pkwy Ste 200 ... Plano TX 75093 866-791-1911 463
TF: 866-691-1911 ■ *Web:* www.cirroenergy.com
Cirro Inc
31920 Del Obispo Ste 260 ... San Juan Capistrano CA 92675 949-900-4567 196
Web: www.cirro.com
Cirrus Assoc LLC
11757 Katy Fwy Ste 1300 ... Houston TX 77079 281-854-2383 194
Web: www.cirrusassociates.com
Cirrus Design Corp 4515 Taylor Cir ... Hermantown MN 55811 218-727-2737 20
Web: www.cirrusaircraft.com
Cirrus Healthcare Products LLC
60 Main St PO Box 220 ... Cold Spring Harbor NY 11724 631-692-7600 582
Web: www.cirrushealthcare.com
Cirrus Logic Inc 2901 Via Fortuna ... Austin TX 78746 512-851-4000 851-4977 696
NASDAQ: CRUS ■ *TF:* 800-888-5016 ■ *Web:* www.cirrus.com
Cirrus Research LLC
303 S Broadway Ste 212 Tarrytown ... New York NY 10591 914-289-1400 401
Web: www.cirrus-res.com
Cirrus9 Inc 15 Market Sq ... Saint John NB E2L1E8 855-643-6691 224
TF: 855-643-6691 ■ *Web:* www.cirrus9.net
Cirtec Medical Systems LLC
9200 Xylon Ave N ... Brooklyn Park MN 55445 763-493-8556 261
Web: cirtecmed.com
CIS (Clinical Immunology Society)
555 E Wells St Ste 1100 ... Milwaukee WI 53202 414-224-8095 272-6070 49-8
TF: 800-472-6930 ■ *Web:* www.clinimmsoc.org
CIS (IEEE Computational Intelligence Society)
IEEE CIS 445 Hoes Ln ... Piscataway NJ 08855 732-465-5892 455-1560* 49-19
**Fax Area Code:* 858 ■ *Web:* cis.ieee.org
CIS Biotech Inc 2701 N Decatur Rd ... Decatur GA 30033 404-576-8856 418
Web: www.cisbiotech.com
CIS Group Ltd
55 Castonguay St Ste 301 ... St-jerome QC J7Y2H9 450-432-1550 2
Web: www.cis-group.com
CISCA (Ceilings & Interior Systems Construction Assn)
1010 Jorie Blvd Ste 30 ... Oak Brook IL 60523 630-584-1919 560-8537* 49-3
**Fax Area Code:* 866 ■ *TF:* 866-560-8537 ■ *Web:* cisca.org
Cisco Air Systems Inc 214 27th St ... Sacramento CA 95816 916-444-2525 358
TF: 800-813-6763 ■ *Web:* www.ciscoair.com
CISCO Inc 1702 Townhurst Ste 2811 ... Houston TX 77043 713-461-9407 393
Web: www.ciscocollect.com
Cisco Junior College
101 College Heights ... Cisco TX 76437 254-442-5000 162
Web: cisco.edu
Abilene 717 E Industrial Blvd ... Abilene TX 79602 325-794-4400 442-5100* 162
**Fax Area Code:* 254 ■ *Web:* cisco.edu
Cisco Systems Inc 170 W Tasman Dr ... San Jose CA 95134 408-526-4000 526-4100 176
NASDAQ: CSCO ■ *TF:* 800-553-6387 ■ *Web:* www.cisco.com
Cisco-Eagle 2120 Valley View Ln ... Dallas TX 75234 972-406-9330 406-9577 385
TF: 888-877-3861 ■ *Web:* www.cisco-eagle.com
Cision US Inc
130 East Randolph St 7th Fl ... Chicago IL 60601 312-922-2400 637-6
TF: 800-588-3827 ■ *Web:* www.cision.com
Cision US Inc
12051 Indian Creek Ct ... Beltsville MD 20705 312-922-2400 39
NASDAQ: VOCS ■ *TF:* 866-639-5087 ■ *Web:* www.vocus.com
CISR (Center for Information Systems Research)
Massachusetts Institute of Technology
245 First St, E94-15th Floor ... Cambridge MA 02142 617-253-2348 253-4424 668
Web: cisr.mit.edu
Cistera Networks Inc
6509 Windcrest Dr Ste 160 ... Plano TX 75024 972-381-4699 177
Web: web.cistera.com

Cisys Inc 8386 Six Forks Rd ... Raleigh NC 27615 844-494-9236 177
TF: 844-494-9236 ■ *Web:* www.cisys.com
CIT Group Inc 505 Fifth Ave ... New York NY 10017 212-771-0505 216
NYSE: CIT ■ *Web:* www.cit.com
CIT Group Inc 1 CIT Dr ... Livingston NJ 07039 973-740-5000 216
NYSE: CIT ■ *Web:* www.cit.com
Citadel Federal Credit Union
520 Eagleview Blvd ... Exton PA 19341 610-380-6000 380-6070 219
TF: 800-666-0191
Citadel Information Services
4 Cornwall Dr Ste 225 ... East Brunswick NJ 08816 732-238-0072 180
Web: www.citadelinc.com
Citadel Mall
2070 Sam Rittenberg Blvd Ste 200 ... Charleston SC 29407 843-766-8321 460
Web: www.citadelmall.net
Citadel Mall, The
750 Citadel Dr E ... Colorado Springs CO 80909 719-591-2900 460
Web: www.shopthecitadel.com
Citadel, The 171 Moultrie St ... Charleston SC 29409 843-953-5230 953-7036 166
TF: 800-868-1842 ■ *Web:* www.citadel.edu
Citagenix Inc 1111 Autoroute Chomedy ... Laval QC H7W5J8 450-688-8699 475
Web: www.citagenix.com
Citarella 2135 Broadway ... New York NY 10023 212-874-0383 297-8
Web: www.citarella.com
Citation Communications Inc
1855 Indian Rd Ste 207 ... West Palm Beach FL 33409 561-688-0330 387
TF: 800-286-5109 ■ *Web:* citation2way.com
Citation Crude Marketing Inc
14077 Cutten Rd ... Houston TX 77069 281-891-1000 579
Web: www.cogc.com
Citation Oil & Gas Corp
14077 Cutten Rd ... Houston TX 77069 281-891-1000 536
Web: www.cogc.com
Citation Solutions Inc
5450 NW Central Dr ... Houston TX 77092 713-895-8261 396
Web: www.citationsolutions.com
Citco Fund Services San Francisco Inc
560 Mission St Fl 26 ... San Francisco CA 94105 415-228-0390 401
Web: www.citco.com
Citent Inc 600 Anton Blvd ... Costa Mesa CA 92626 714-436-6100 463
Web: www.citent.com
CITGO Petroleum Corp
1293 Eldridge Pkwy ... Houston TX 77077 832-486-4700 580
TF: 800-424-9300 ■ *Web:* www.citgo.com
CITGO Pipeline Co 1293 Eldridge Pkwy ... Houston TX 77077 832-486-4000 597
TF: 800-756-2484 ■ *Web:* www.citgo.com
CITI (Columbia Institute for Tele-Information)
3022 Broadway Uris Hall ... New York NY 10027 212-854-4222 854-1471 668
Web: www8.gsb.columbia.edu/citi
Citi Habitats 250 Park Ave S 4th fl ... New York NY 10016 212-685-7777 652
Web: www.citihabitats.com
Citi Trends Inc 104 Coleman Blvd ... Savannah GA 31408 912-236-1561 157-2
NASDAQ: CTRN ■ *TF:* 800-732-0330 ■ *Web:* www.cititrends.com
Citibank (Delaware)
4500 New Linden Hill Rd ... Sioux Falls SD 57117 210-677-3789 70
TF: 800-374-9700 ■ *Web:* online.citi.com
Citibank NA 399 Pk Ave ... New York NY 10022 800-627-3999 70
TF: 800-627-3999 ■ *Web:* citigroup.com
Citibank (South Dakota) NA
701 E 60th St N ... Sioux Falls SD 57104 605-331-2626 70
TF: 800-627-3999 ■ *Web:* online.citi.com/us/welcome.c
Cities of Gold Casino
10-B Cities of Gold Rd ... Santa Fe NM 87506 505-455-3313 133
TF: 800-455-3313 ■ *Web:* www.citiesofgold.com
CITI-FM 92.1 (CR) 4-166 Osborne St ... Winnipeg MB R3L1Y8 204-788-3400 645-177
Web: www.921citi.ca
Citigroup Inc 399 Pk Ave ... New York NY 10043 212-559-1000 360-3
NYSE: C ■ *Web:* citigroup.com
Citilites 138 N Main St ... Dayton OH 45402 937-222-0623 671
Web: victoriatheatre.com
CitiMortgage Inc 1000 Technology Dr ... O'Fallon MO 63368 800-283-7918 509
TF Cust Svc: 800-283-7918 ■ *Web:* www.citimortgage.com
CitiusTech Inc 2 Research Way ... Princeton NJ 08540 877-248-4871 225
TF: 877-248-4871 ■ *Web:* www.citiustech.com
Citizant Inc
5180 Parkstone Dr Ste 100 ... Chantilly VA 20151 703-667-9420 177
TF: 877-248-4926 ■ *Web:* citizant.com
Citizen Auto Stage Co
3594 E Lincoln St ... Tucson AZ 85714 520-622-8811 107
TF: 800-276-1528 ■ *Web:* graylinearizona.com
Citizen National Bank Of Bluffton, The
102 S Main St PO Box 88 ... Bluffton OH 45817 419-358-8040 70
TF: 800-262-4663 ■ *Web:* www.cnbohio.com
Citizen Publishing Company Inc
260 Tenth St ... Windom MN 56101 507-831-3455 831-3740 637-8
Web: www.windomnews.com
Citizen Systems America Corp
363 Van Ness Way Ste 404 ... Torrance CA 90501 310-781-1460 781-9152 173-6
TF: 800-421-6516 ■ *Web:* www.citizen-systems.com
Citizen Tribune
1609 W First N St PO Box 625 ... Morristown TN 37815 423-581-5630 581-8863 532-2
TF: 800-624-0281 ■ *Web:* www.citizentribune.com
Citizen Watch Co of America Inc
1000 W 190th St ... Torrance CA 90502 800-321-1023 153
TF: 800-321-1023 ■ *Web:* www.citizenwatch.com
Citizens & Northern Corp
90-92 Main St ... Wellsboro PA 16901 570-724-3411 724-6395 360-2
NASDAQ: CZNC ■ *Web:* cnbankpa.com
Citizens Against Government Waste (CAGW)
1301 Pennsylvania Ave NW Ste 1075 ... Washington DC 20004 202-467-5300 467-4253 48-7
TF: 800-435-7352 ■ *Web:* www.cagw.org
Citizens Bank of Clovis 420 Wheeler ... Texico NM 88135 575-482-3381 762-7259 70
TF: 844-657-3553 ■ *Web:* www.citizensbankofclovis.com
Citizens Bank of Las Cruces
505 S Main St ... Las Cruces NM 88004 575-647-4100 70
Web: www.citizenslc.com
Citizens Bank of Massachusetts
28 State St ... Boston MA 02109 800-610-7300 70
TF: 800-610-7300 ■ *Web:* www.citizensbank.com

Phone | Fax | Class

Citizens Bank of Mukwonago
301 N Rochester St PO Box 223 .... Mukwonago WI 53149 262-363-6500 363-6515 70
TF: 877-546-5868 ■ *Web:* www.citizenbank.com

Citizens Bank of Rhode Island
1 Citizens Plaza .... Providence RI 02903 401-456-7000 362-6343* 70
**Fax Area Code:* 877 ■ *TF Cust Svc:* 800-922-9999 ■ *Web:* www.citizensbank.com

Citizens Business Bank (CBB)
701 N Haven Ave .... Ontario CA 91764 909-980-4030 481-2130 70
TF Cust Svc: 888-222-5432 ■ *Web:* www.cbbank.com

Citizens Committee for the Right to Keep & Bear Arms (CCRKBA)
12500 NE Tenth Pl .... Bellevue WA 98005 425-454-4911 451-3959 48-7
TF: 800-426-4302 ■ *Web:* www.ccrkba.org

Citizens Equity First Credit Union
5401 W Dirksen Pkwy .... Peoria IL 61607 309-633-7000 219
TF Cust Svc: 800-633-7077 ■ *Web:* www.cefcu.com

Citizens Federal Savings & Loan Assn
110 N Main St PO Box 9 .... Bellefontaine OH 43311 937-593-0015 593-6577 69
TF: 800-436-5177 ■ *Web:* www.citizensfederalsl.com

Citizens Financial Corp
12910 Shelbyville Rd Ste 300 .... Louisville KY 40243 502-244-2420 360-4
OTC: CFIN ■ *TF:* 800-843-7752 ■ *Web:* www.citizensfinancialcorp.com

Citizens Financial Group Inc
1 Citizens Dr .... Riverside RI 02915 401-456-7000 360-2
TF: 800-922-9999 ■ *Web:* www.citizensbank.com

Citizens Financial Services
707 Ridge Rd .... Munster IN 46321 219-836-5500 70
TF: 800-205-3464 ■ *Web:* www.firstmerchants.com

Citizens For Citizens Inc
264 Griffin St .... Fall River MA 02724 508-679-0041 324-7503 48-15
Web: www.cfcinc.org

Citizens for Tax Justice (CTJ)
1616 P St NW Ste 200-B .... Washington DC 20036 202-299-1066 299-1065 48-7
TF: 888-626-2622 ■ *Web:* www.ctj.org

Citizens Gas & Coke Utility
2020 N Meridian St .... Indianapolis IN 46202 317-924-3311 927-4395 787
TF: 800-427-4217 ■ *Web:* www.citizensenergygroup.com

Citizens Gas Fuel Co 127 N Main St .... Adrian MI 49221 517-265-2144 536
TF: 800-482-7171 ■ *Web:* www.citizensgasfuel.com

Citizens Holding Co
521 Main St PO Box 209 .... Philadelphia MS 39350 601-656-4692 360-2
NASDAQ: CIZN ■ *Web:* www.thecitizensbankphila.com

Citizens Insurance Company of America
400 E Anderson Ln .... Austin TX 78752 512-837-7100 836-9785 391-2
TF: 800-880-5044 ■ *Web:* www.citizensinc.com

Citizens Medical Ctr
2701 Hospital Dr .... Victoria TX 77901 361-573-9181 374-3
Web: citizensmedicalcenter.org

Citizens Network for Foreign Affairs (CNFA)
1020 L St NW Ste 710 .... Washington DC 20036 202-296-3920 48-5
TF: 800-392-3532 ■ *Web:* www.cnfa.org

Citizens Network for Sustainable Development (CitNet)
PO Box 7458 .... Silver Spring MD 20907 301-588-5550 48-13
Web: www.citnet.org

Citizens News 71 Weid Dr .... Naugatuck CT 06770 203-729-2228 729-9099 532-2
Web: mycitizensnews.com

Citizens of Humanity Inc
5715 Bickett St .... Huntington Park CA 90255 323-923-1240 157-6
Web: www.citizensofhumanity.com

Citizens Property Insurance Corp
6676 Corporate Ctr Pkwy .... Jacksonville FL 32216 904-296-6105 390
Web: www.citizensfla.com

Citizens Security Life Insurance Co
12910 Shelbyville Rd Ste 300 .... Louisville KY 40243 502-244-2420 254-4059 391-2
TF: 800-843-7752 ■ *Web:* www.citizenssecuritylife.com

Citizens South Banking Corp
519 S New Hope Rd PO Box 2249 .... Gastonia NC 28054 704-868-5200 360-2
NASDAQ: CSBC ■ *Web:* www.parksterlingbank.com

Citizens State Bank
1300 W Hildebrand Ave PO Box 5970 .... San Antonio TX 78201 210-785-2300 785-2301 70
Web: Www.csbsa.com

Citizens Telephone Co 26 S Main St .... Hammond NY 13646 315-324-5911 116
Web: www.cit-tele.com

Citizens Telephone Co-op PO Box 137 .... Floyd VA 24091 540-745-2111 745-3791 736
TF: 800-941-0426 ■ *Web:* www.citizens.coop

Citizens Trust Bank
1700 Third Ave N .... Birmingham AL 35203 205-328-2041 70
TF: 888-214-3099 ■ *Web:* www.ctbconnect.com

Citizens' Electric Co
1775 Industrial Blvd PO Box 551 .... Lewisburg PA 17837 570-524-2231 524-5887 245
TF: 877-487-9384 ■ *Web:* www.citizenselectric.com

Citizens' Voice, The
75 N Washington St .... Wilkes-Barre PA 18701 570-821-2000 821-2247* 532-2
**Fax:* News Rm ■ *Web:* www.citizensvoice.com

CitNet (Citizens Network for Sustainable Development)
PO Box 7458 .... Silver Spring MD 20907 301-588-5550 48-13
Web: www.citnet.org

Citrin Cooperman & Company LLP
529 Fifth Ave .... New York NY 10017 212-697-1000 697-1004 2
TF: 800-538-6525 ■ *Web:* www.citrincooperman.com

Citris Grill
2991 East 3300 South .... Salt Lake City UT 84109 801-466-1202 671
Web: www.citrisgrill.com

Citrix Systems Inc
851 W Cypress Creek Rd .... Fort Lauderdale FL 33309 954-267-3000 267-9319 178-12
NASDAQ: CTXS ■ *TF:* 800-393-1888 ■ *Web:* www.citrix.com

Citrus & Allied Essences Ltd
3000 Marcus Ave Ste 3E11 .... Lake Success NY 11042 516-354-1200 354-1262 145
TF: 800-424-9300 ■ *Web:* www.citrusandallied.com

Citrus College 1000 W Foothill Blvd .... Glendora CA 91741 626-963-0323 914-8613* 162
**Fax:* Admissions ■ *Web:* www.citruscollege.edu

Citrus County 110 N Apopka Ave .... Inverness FL 34450 352-341-6400 341-6491 338
Web: www.clerk.citrus.fl.us

Citrus County Chamber of Commerce
401 Tompkins St .... Inverness FL 34450 352-726-2801 637-1921 139
TF: 800-275-6614 ■ *Web:* www.citruscountychamber.com

Citrus County Chamber of Commerce
28 NW US Hwy 19 .... Crystal River FL 34428 352-795-3149 139
TF: 800-665-6701 ■ *Web:* www.citruscountychamber.com

Citrus County Chronicle
1624 N Meadowcrest Blvd .... Crystal River FL 34429 352-563-6363 532-2
Web: www.chronicleonline.com

Citrus County Library System
425 W Roosevelt Blvd .... Beverly Hills FL 34465 352-746-9077 746-9493 434-3
Web: www.citruslibraries.org

Citrus County School District
1007 W Main St .... Inverness FL 34450 352-726-1931 685
Web: www.citrus.k12.fl.us

Citrus Heights Chamber
7920 Alta Sunrise Dr Ste 100 .... Citrus Heights CA 95610 916-722-4545 722-4543 139
Web: www.chchamber.com

Citrus Memorial Hospital
502 W Highland Blvd .... Inverness FL 34452 352-726-1551 374-3
TF: 800-437-2672 ■ *Web:* www.citrusmh.com

Citrus Systems Inc 415 11th Ave S .... Hopkins MN 55343 952-935-0410 296-20
Web: www.citrussystems.com

Citrus Valley Hospice
820 N Phillips Ave .... West Covina CA 91791 626-859-2263 371
TF: 800-227-2345 ■ *Web:* www.cvhp.org

Citrus Valley Medical Ctr Inter-Community Campus
210 W San BernaRdino Rd .... Covina CA 91723 626-331-7331 374-3
Web: www.cvhp.org

Citterio USA Corp 2008 SR- 940 .... Freeland PA 18224 570-636-3171 636-5340 296-26
TF: 800-435-8888 ■ *Web:* www.citteriousa.com

City 33 Dundas St E .... Toronto ON M5B1B8 416-764-3003 741-136
TF: 888-336-9978 ■ *Web:* www.citytv.com/toronto

City Water, Light & Power
800 E Monroe St
4th Fl Municipal Center E .... Springfield IL 62701 217-789-2116 789-2136 539
Web: www.cwlp.com

City and County of Butte-Silver Bow
155 W Granite St .... Butte MT 59701 406-497-6200 497-6328 338
Web: www.co.silverbow.mt.us

City Auto Glass Inc
116 S Concord Exchange .... South Saint Paul MN 55075 651-552-1000 62-2
TF: 888-552-4272 ■ *Web:* www.cityautoglass.com

City Auto Sales 4932 Elmore Rd .... Memphis TN 38128 901-377-9502 57
Web: www.cityauto.com

City Barbeque Inc 6175 Emerald Pkwy .... Dublin OH 43016 614-583-0999 670
Web: citybbq.com

City Beverages of Orlando
10928 Florida Crown Dr .... Orlando FL 32824 407-251-4049 851-7100 81-1
TF: 800-331-2829 ■ *Web:* www.abwholesaler.com

City Bikes
8401 Connecticut Ave Ste 111 .... Chevy Chase MD 20815 301-652-1777 711
Web: www.citybikes.com

City Brewing Company LLC
925 S Third St .... La Crosse WI 54601 608-785-4200 785-4300 80-1
Web: www.citybrewery.com

City Cafe 5757 W Lovers Ln .... Dallas TX 75209 214-351-2233 671
TF: 800-442-1162 ■ *Web:* www.thecitycafedallas.com

City Cellar Wine Bar & Grill
700 S Rosemary Ave .... West Palm Beach FL 33401 561-366-0071 671
Web: bigtimerestaurants.com

City Center Parking Inc
514 SW Sixth Ave Ste 223 .... Portland OR 97204 503-221-1666 562
Web: www.citycenterparking.com

City College of New York
138th St & Convent Ave .... New York NY 10031 212-650-6448 650-6417* 100
**Fax:* Admissions ■ *TF Admissions:* 800-286-9937 ■ *Web:* www.ccny.cuny.edu

City College of New York Cohen Library
160 Convent Ave .... New York NY 10031 212-650-7155 650-7604 434-6
Web: www.ccny.cuny.edu/library

City College of San Francisco
50 Phelan Ave .... San Francisco CA 94112 415-239-3000 239-3936* 162
**Fax:* Admissions ■ *TF:* 800-433-3243 ■ *Web:* www.ccsf.edu

City Colleges of Chicago
226 W Jackson .... Chicago IL 60606 312-553-2500 553-3075* 162
**Fax:* Admissions ■ *TF:* 866-908-7582 ■ *Web:* www.ccc.edu

City Cuisine 2586 Main St .... Riverside CA 92501 951-682-9566 671

City Dash 949 Laidlaw Ave .... Cincinnati OH 45237 513-562-2000 187
Web: www.citydash.com

City Escape Holidays
13470 Washington Blvd Ste 101 .... Marina del Rey CA 90292 800-222-0022 827-5575* 771
**Fax Area Code:* 310 ■ *TF:* 800-222-0022 ■ *Web:* www.cityescapeholidays.com

City Florist of Redlands
122 Cajon St .... Redlands CA 92373 909-793-4141 292
Web: cityfloristofredlands.com

City Foods Inc 4230 S Racine Ave .... Chicago, IL 60609 773-523-1566 473
Web: www.beasbest.com

City Furniture Inc 6701 N Hiatus Rd .... Tamarac FL 33321 954-597-2200 718-3360 321
TF: 866-930-4233 ■ *Web:* www.cityfurniture.com

City Glass Co 8037 H St .... Omaha NE 68127 402-593-1242 329
Web: www.cityglasscompany.com

City Glass Company of Colorado Springs
414 W Colorado Ave .... Colorado Springs CO 80905 719-634-2891 330
TF: 800-561-3357 ■ *Web:* www.cityglasscompany.net

City Holding Co 25 Gatewater Rd .... Charleston WV 25313 304-769-1100 360-2
NASDAQ: CHCO ■ *TF:* 800-528-2273 ■ *Web:* www.bankatcity.com

City Lights Booksellers
261 Columbus Ave .... San Francisco CA 94133 415-362-8193 95
Web: www.citylights.com

City Lights of China
1731 Connecticut Ave NW .... Washington DC 20009 202-265-6688 265-1369 671
Web: www.citylightsofchina.com

City Lights Theatre 529 S Second St .... San Jose CA 95112 408-295-4200 295-8318 573-4
TF: 800-220-0182 ■ *Web:* www.cltc.org

City Line Distributers
20 Industry Dr .... West Haven CT 06516 203-931-3707 186
Web: www.citylinefoods.com

City Market 219 W Bryan St Ste 207 .... Savannah GA 31401 912-232-4903 50-6
TF: 800-523-3373 ■ *Web:* www.savannahcitymarket.com

City Market 555 Sandhill Ln .... Grand Junction CO 81505 970-241-0750 345
Web: www.citymarket.com

City Mattress Inc
12660 Bonita Beach Rd .... Bonita Springs FL 34135 239-908-2700 321
Web: www.citymattress.com

Name / Address	City	State	ZIP	Phone	Fax	Class
City Mill Company Ltd 660 N Nimitz Hwy TF: 800-488-4888 ■ Web: www.citymill.com	Honolulu	HI	96817	808-533-3811		364
City Motors of Cartersville 352 N Tennessee St	Cartersville	GA	30120	770-382-5780		57
City National Bank 400 N Roxbury Dr TF Cust Svc: 800-773-7100 ■ Web: www.cnb.com	Beverly Hills	CA	90210	310-888-6000		70
City National Bank of Florida 450 E Las Olas Blvd TF: 800-762-2489 ■ Web: www.citynationalcm.com	Fort Lauderdale	FL	33301	954-467-6667		70
City National Bank of New Jersey (CNB) 900 Broad St TF: 877-350-3524 ■ Web: www.citynatbank.com	Newark	NJ	07102	973-624-0865		70
City National Bank of Sulphur Springs, The 201 Connally	Sulphur Springs	TX	75482	903-885-7523		70
City National Bank of West Virginia 3601 McCorckle Ave TF: 888-816-8064 ■ Web: www.bankatcity.com	Charleston	WV	25304	304-926-3324	925-8073	70
City Newspaper 250 N Goodman St Web: www.rochestercitynewspaper.com	Rochester	NY	14607	585-244-3329		532-5
city of Asheville, The 87 Haywood St Web: www.ashevillenc.gov	Asheville	NC	28801	828-251-1122		205
City of Austin Employees' Retirement System 418 E Highland Mall Blvd TF: 800-336-8264 ■ Web: www.coaers.org	Austin	TX	78752	512-458-2551		528
City of Bay Village Ohio 350 Dover Ctr Rd Web: www.cityofbayvillage.com	Bay Village	OH	44140	440-899-3412		734
City of Birmingham, Alabama 331 Cotton Ave SW Web: www.informationbirmingham.com	Birmingham	AL	35211	205-780-5656		520
City of Buena Vista 2039 Sycamore Ave Web: www.bvcity.org	Buena Vista	VA	24416	540-261-6121		338
City of Carlsbad Library 1250 Carlsbad Village Dr TF: 866-275-3772 ■ Web: carlsbadca.gov	Carlsbad	CA	92008	760-434-2870	929-0256	434-3
City of Champaign 102 N Neil St Web: www.ci.champaign.il.us	Champaign	IL	61820	217-403-8700	403-8980	337
City of Chicago 121 N LaSalle St Web: www.cityofchicago.org	Chicago	IL	60602	312-744-5000		50-2
City of Chula Vista 276 Fourth Ave TF: 877-478-5478 ■ Web: chulavistaca.gov	Chula Vista	CA	91910	619-691-5047		52
City of Clarksville 199 Tenth St TF: 800-342-1003 ■ Web: www.cityofclarksville.com	Clarksville	TN	37040	931-645-7464		256
City of Clinton Sheriff Department 184 Detention Dr PO Box 451 TF: 800-830-8015 ■ Web: www.vbcso.com	Clinton	AR	72031	501-745-2112		338
City of Com, The 1559 S Brownlee Blvd TF: 888-785-0500 ■ Web: cityof.com	Corpus Christi	TX	78404	888-785-0500		7
City of Dayton 40 S Edwin C Moses Blvd Web: www.daytonohio.gov	Dayton	OH	45402	937-333-2489		50-2
City of Dearborn 1300 S Telegraph Rd Web: www.cityofdearborn.org	Dearborn	MI	48124	313-563-4653		31
City of Fargo 200 Third St N Web: fargond.gov	Fargo	ND	58102	701-241-1310		434-3
City of Farmers Branch 13000 William Dodson Pkwy Web: www.farmersbranchtx.gov	Farmers Branch	TX	75234	972-247-3131		434-3
City of Great Falls PO Box 5021 Web: www.greatfallsmt.net	Great Falls	MT	59403	406-771-0885		205
City of Hope National Medical Ctr Hematology & Hematopoietic Cell Transplantation Div 1500 E Duarte Rd TF: 800-826-4673 ■ Web: cityofhope.org	Duarte	CA	91010	626-256-4673		769
City of Jackson, The 219 S President St Web: www.jacksonms.gov	Jackson	MS	39201	601-960-1084	960-2193	337
City of Kamloops 105 Seymour St Web: www.kamloops.ca	Kamloops	BC	V2C2C6	250-828-3439		354
City of Kodiak Alaska City of Kodiak 710 Mill Bay Rd Web: city.kodiak.ak.us	Kodiak	AK	99615	907-486-8640	486-8014	618
City of Leawood, Kansas 4800 Town Ctr Dr Web: www.leawood.org	Leawood	KS	66211	913-339-6700		393
City of Logan Recreation Ctr 195 S 100 W Web: loganutah.org	Logan	UT	84321	435-716-9250		564
City of Naples 735 Eigth St S Web: www.naplesgov.com	Naples	FL	34102	239-213-1015	213-1025	337
City of New Westminster 511 Royal Ave Web: www.newwestcity.ca	New Westminster	BC	V3L1H9	604-527-4605		194
City of Newark 920 Broad St Web: www.ci.newark.nj.us	Newark	NJ	07102	973-733-8004	733-5352	337
City of Palm Springs 300 S Sunrise Way TF: 800-611-1911 ■ Web: www.palmspringsca.gov	Palm Springs	CA	92262	760-322-7323		434-3
City of Pendleton 500 SW Dorion Ave TF: 800-238-5355 ■ Web: www.pendleton.or.us	Pendleton	OR	97801	541-966-0201	966-0251	205
City of Piedmont Recreation Department 358 Hillside Ave Web: www.ci.piedmont.ca.us/recreation	Piedmont	CA	94611	510-420-3070		564
City of Quebec 2 Rue des Jardins Web: www.ville.quebec.qc.ca	Quebec	QC	G1R4S9	418-641-6651		337
City of Rancho Cucamonga califonia 7368 Archibald Ave Web: www.rcpl.lib.ca.us	Rancho Cucamonga	CA	91730	909-477-2720	477-2849	434-3
City of Rocks National Reserve PO Box 169 Web: www.nps.gov/ciro	Almo	ID	83312	208-824-5910	824-5563	564
City Of Salem 101 S Broadway TF: 800-755-5000 ■ Web: www.salemil.us	Salem	IL	62881	618-548-2222	548-5330	206
City of San Leandro Public Library, The 835 E 14th St Web: www.sanleandro.org	San Leandro	CA	94577	510-577-3351	278-3095	434-3
City of Saskatoon Parks Branch 222 Third Ave N Web: www.city.saskatoon.sk.ca	Saskatoon	SK	S7K0J5	306-975-2476		564
City of Spokane 808 W Spokane Falls Blvd Web: my.spokanecity.org/parksrec	Spokane	WA	99201	509-625-6677		50-2
City of St. Petersburg PO Box 2842 Web: www.stpete.org	Saint Petersburg	FL	33731	727-893-7111	892-5102	337
City of Sterling Heights Library 40255 Dodge Pk Rd Web: www.shpl.net	Sterling Heights	MI	48313	586-446-2665		434-3
City of Thomasville Tourism Authority 144 E Jackson St TF: 800-533-4587 ■ Web: www.thomasvillega.com	Thomasville	GA	31792	229-226-3424	228-4188	206
City of Truth or Consequences 685 Marie St Web: www.torcnm.org	Truth Or Consequences	NM	87901	575-894-2603		48-20
City of Vacaville Inc, The 650 Merchant St TF: 800-759-7159 ■ Web: www.ci.vacaville.ca.us	Vacaville	CA	95688	707-449-5100		256
City of Wetaskiwin Recreation 4705-50 Ave TF: 800-419-2913 ■ Web: www.wetaskiwin.ca	Wetaskiwin	AB	T9A2E9	780-361-4444		706
City Pages 300 Third St PO Box 942 Web: www.thecitypages.com	Wausau	WI	54402	715-845-5171	848-5887	532-5
City Paper, The 210 12th Ave S Ste 100 Web: www.nashvillecitypaper.com	Nashville	TN	37203	615-244-7989	244-8578	532-2
City Pipe & Supply Corp PO Box 2112 TF: 844-307-4044 ■ Web: www.citypipe.com	Odessa	TX	79760	432-332-1541	333-2300	492
City Plumbing & Electric Supply Co 730 EE Butler Pkwy TF: 800-260-2024 ■ Web: www.cpesupply.com	Gainesville	GA	30501	770-532-4123		612
City Point National Cemetery 10th Ave & Davis St Web: www.cem.va.gov/cems/nchp/citypoint.asp	Hopewell	VA	23860	804-795-2031	795-1064	136
City Press Inc W238 N1650 Rockwood Dr Web: www.citypressinc.com	Waukesha	WI	53188	262-523-3000		174
City Printing Company Inc 122 Oak Hill Ave Web: www.cityprinting.com	Youngstown	OH	44502	330-747-5691		627
City Property Management Co 4645 E Cotton Gin Loop Web: cityproperty.com	Phoenix	AZ	85040	602-437-4777		652
City Public Service Board PO Box 1771 TF: 800-870-1006 ■ Web: www.cpsenergy.com	San Antonio	TX	78296	210-353-2222		787
City Savings Bank & Trust 301 N Pine St TF: 800-920-8661 ■ Web: citysavingsbank.com	Deridder	LA	70634	337-463-8661		70
City Shirt Company Inc 10 City Shirt Rd	Frackville	PA	17931	570-874-4251		155-19
City Steam Brewery Cafe 942 Main St TF: 800-707-3530 ■ Web: www.citysteambrewerycafe.com	Hartford	CT	06103	860-525-1600		671
City Suites Hotel 933 W Belmont Ave Web: www.chicagocitysuites.com	Chicago	IL	60657	773-404-3400		379
City Supply Corp 2326 Bell Ave TF: 800-400-2377 ■ Web: www.citysupplycorp.com	Des Moines	IA	50321	515-288-3211		612
City Theatre Co 1300 Bingham St Web: www.citytheatrecompany.org	Pittsburgh	PA	15203	412-431-4400	431-5535	749
City Thermo Pane Ltd 420 Industrielle St TF: 800-552-5408 ■ Web: www.citythermopane.com	Beresford	NB	E8K2C2	506-542-1130	542-1139	499
City Union Mission Inc 1100 E 11th St Web: cityunionmission.org	Kansas City	MO	64106	816-474-9380		48-20
City University 11900 NE First St TF Admissions: 800-426-5596 ■ Web: www.cityu.edu	Bellevue	WA	98005	425-637-1010		166
City University of New York (CUNY) 535 E 80th St TF: 800-286-9937 ■ Web: www.cuny.edu	New York	NY	10075	212-997-2869	794-5397	786
City University of New York School of Law 65-21 Main St *Fax: Admissions ■ Web: www.law.cuny.edu	Flushing	NY	11367	718-340-4200	340-4435*	167-1
Cityfeetcom Inc 443 Park Ave S Ste 3A Web: www.cityfeet.com	New York	NY	10016	212-924-6450		652
Cityfone 3991 Henning Dr Ste 101 Web: www.cityfone.net	Burnaby	BC	V5C6N5	604-298-5900		387
Citygate GIS LLC 125 Cathedral St Web: www.citygategis.com	Annapolis	MD	21401	410-295-3333		261
CityKids Foundation 601 W 26th St Ste 325 TF: 800-897-0089 ■ Web: www.citykids.com	New York	NY	10001	212-925-3320		48-6
CityPlace 700 S Rosemary Ave Web: www.cityplace.com	West Palm Beach	FL	33401	561-366-1000	366-1001	50-6
CityScan Inc 222 Merchandise Mart Plaza Ste 1212 Web: cityscan.com	Chicago	IL	60654	312-218-0688		463
Cityside Subaru 790 Pleasant St Web: citysidesubaru.com	Belmont	MA	02478	617-826-5000		57
Cityspan Technologies Inc 2437 Durant Ave Ste 206 TF: 800-821-0887 ■ Web: www.cityspan.com	Berkeley	CA	94704	510-665-1700		809
Citystaff Inc 1701 K St NW Ste 500 Web: www.citystaffdc.com	Washington	DC	20006	202-861-4200		193
Cityview 414 61st St Web: www.dmcityview.com	Des Moines	IA	50312	515-953-4822	953-1394	532-5
Civacon 4304 N Mattox Rd TF Sales: 888-526-5657 ■ Web: www.opwglobal.com/civacon	Kansas City	MO	64150	816-741-6600	741-1061	790
CIVC Partners 191 N Wacker Dr Ste 1100 Web: www.civc.com	Chicago	IL	60606	312-873-7300	873-7300	792
CIVCO Medical Instruments 102 First St TF: 877-329-2482 ■ Web: www.civcomedical.com	Kalona	IA	52247	319-248-6757	248-6660	382

Name / Address	City	State	Zip	Phone	Fax	Class
Cives Corp 1825 Old Alabama Rd Ste 200 *Web:* www.cives.com	Roswell	GA	30076	770-993-4424	998-2361	188-10
Cives Steel Co 210 Cives Ln *Web:* www.cives.com	Winchester	VA	22603	540-667-3480		480
Civic Ctr Music Hall 201 N Walker St *TF:* 800-364-7111 ■ *Web:* www.okcciviccenter.org	Oklahoma City	OK	73102	405-297-2584		572
Civic Ctr of Greater Des Moines 221 Walnut St *TF:* 800-745-3000 ■ *Web:* www.desmoinesperformingarts.org	Des Moines	IA	50309	515-246-2300	246-2305	572
Civic Opera House 20 N Wacker Dr *Web:* www.lyricopera.org	Chicago	IL	60606	312-332-2244	332-8120	572
Civic Orchestra of Tucson (COT) PO Box 42764 *TF:* 800-352-8404 ■ *Web:* www.cotmusic.org	Tucson	AZ	85733	520-730-3371		573-3
Civic Plaza Hotel 505 Pine St	Abilene	TX	79601	325-676-0222		379
Civic Resource Group LLC 915 Wilshire Blvd Ste 1680 *TF:* 800-771-0026 ■ *Web:* civicconnect.com	Los Angeles	CA	90017	213-225-1170	225-1175	196
Civic Theatre of Allentown 527 N 19th St *Web:* www.civictheatre.com	Allentown	PA	18104	610-432-8943		572
Civil & Environmental Consultants Inc 333 Baldwin Rd *TF:* 800-365-2324 ■ *Web:* www.cecinc.com	Pittsburgh	PA	15205	412-429-2324	429-2114	261
Civil Constructors Inc 2283 US Hwy 20 E *TF:* 800-500-2011 ■ *Web:* www.helmgroup.com	Freeport	IL	61032	815-235-2200		188-4
Civil Consulting Group Pllc 1515 Heritage Dr *Web:* civilgroup.net	Mckinney	TX	75069	972-569-9193		261
Civil Dynamics Inc 109a Route 515 *Web:* www.civildynamics.com	Stockholm	NJ	07460	973-697-3496		261
Civil Engineering Magazine 1801 Alexander Bell Dr *Fax: Edit ■ *TF:* 800-548-2723 ■ *Web:* asce.org	Heston	VA	20191	703-295-6300	295-6300*	457-21
Civil Service Employees Insurance Co 2121 N California Blvd Ste 989 *TF:* 800-282-6848 ■ *Web:* www.cseinsurance.com	Walnut Creek	CA	94596	800-282-6848		391-4
Civil Site Design Group PLLC 630 Southgate Ave Ste A *Web:* www.civil-site.com	Nashville	TN	37203	615-248-9999		261
Civil War Trust (CWPT) 1331 H St NW Ste 1001 *TF:* 888-606-1400 ■ *Web:* www.civilwar.org	Washington	DC	20005	202-367-1861	367-1865	48-13
Civil Works Engineers Inc 3151 Airway Ave *Web:* civilworksengineers.com	Costa Mesa	CA	92626	714-966-9060		261
Civilian Police International LLC 18980 Upper Belmont Pl W 4th Fl	West Leesburg	VA	20176	703-724-5788		507
Civiltec Engineering Inc 118 W Lime Ave *Web:* www.civiltec.com	Monrovia	CA	91016	626-357-0588		261
Civiltech Engineering Inc 450 E Devon Ave Ste 300 *Web:* civiltechinc.com	Itasca	IL	60143	630 773 3900		261
Civista Bank 100 E Water St *TF:* 888-645-4121 ■ *Web:* www.civistabank.com	Sandusky	OH	44870	419-625-4121		69
Civitan International PO Box 130744 *TF:* 800-248-4826 ■ *Web:* www.civitan.org	Birmingham	AL	35213	205-591-8910	591-8910	48-15
Civtech Designs Inc 11012 Rhodenda Pl *Web:* civtechdesigns.com	Upper Marlboro	MD	20772	240-244-5517		261
CJ & Associates Inc 16915 W Victor Rd *Web:* www.cjassociatesinc.com	New Berlin	WI	53151	262-786-1772		321
CJ Brown Energy PC 4245 Union Rd Ste 204b *Web:* www.cjbrownenergy.com	Buffalo	NY	14225	716-565-9190		196
CJ Erickson Plumbing Co 4141 W 124th Pl *Web:* www.cjerickson.com	Alsip	IL	60803	708-371-4900		610
CJ Grand Hotel & Spa 67585 Hacienda Ave *Web:* cjmineralspa.com	Desert Hot Springs	CA	92240	760-329-4488		379
CJ Horner Company Inc 105 W Grand Ave *TF:* 800-426-4261 ■ *Web:* cjhornerinc.com	Hot Springs	AR	71901	501-321-9600		182
CJ Mahan Construction Co 3400 SW Blvd *TF:* 800-808-3868 ■ *Web:* www.cjmahan.com	Grove City	OH	43123	614-875-8200	875-1175	188-4
CJ Vitner & Co 4202 W 45th St *Web:* www.vitners.com	Chicago	IL	60632	773-523-7900	523-9143	296-35
CJ's in Tiger Country 704 E Broadway *Web:* www.cjsintigercountry.com	Columbia	MO	65201	573-442-7777		671
CJAY 92 ROCKS 1110 Ctr St NE Ste 300 *Web:* www.cjay92.com	Calgary	AB	T2E2R2	403-240-5800		645-27
CJBS LLC 2100 Sanders Rd Ste 200 *Web:* www.cjbs.com	Northbrook	IL	60062	847-945-2888		2
CJE SeniorLife 3003 W Touhy Ave *Web:* www.cje.net	Chicago	IL	60645	773-508-1000	508-1028	48-17
CJK 3962 Virginia Ave *TF:* 800-598-7808 ■ *Web:* www.cjkusa.com	Cincinnati	OH	45227	513-271-6035	271-6082	626
CJL Engineering Inc 1550 Coraopolis Heights Rd Ste 340 *Web:* www.cjlengineering.com	Moon Township	PA	15108	412-262-1220		261
CJM (Carlyle Johnson Machine Co) 291 Boston Tpke *TF:* 888-629-4867 ■ *Web:* www.cjmco.com	Bolton	CT	06043	860-643-1531	646-2645	620
CJOB-AM 680 (N/T) 1440 Jack Blick Ave *Web:* globalnews.ca/radio/cjob/?gref=cjob	Winnipeg	MB	R3G0L4	204-786-2471	783-4512	645-177
CJOH-TV Ch 13 (CTV) 87 George St *Web:* ottawa.ctvnews.ca	Ottawa	ON	K1N9H7	613-224-1313		741-96
CJRW 303 W Capitol Ave *Web:* www.cjrw.com	Little Rock	AR	72201	501-975-6251	975-4241	4
CJS Securities Inc Westchester Financial Ctr 50 Main St Ste 325 *Web:* www.cjssecurities.com	White Plains	NY	10606	914-287-7600		690
CJT Koolcarb Inc 494 Mission St *TF:* 800-323-2299 ■ *Web:* www.cjtkoolcarb.com	Carol Stream	IL	60188	630-690-5933	690-6355	493
CJW Medical Ctr 7101 Jahnke Rd *TF:* 800-468-6620 ■ *Web:* hcavirginia.com	Richmond	VA	23225	804-320-3911		374-3
C-K Composites Inc 361 Bridgeport Rd *TF:* 800-974-4669 ■ *Web:* www.ckcomposites.com	Mount Pleasant	PA	15666	724-547-4581	547-2890	599
CK Technologies Inc 3629 Vista Mercado *Web:* www.ckt.com	Camarillo	CA	93012	805-987-4801		246
CK Technologies LLC 1701 Magda Dr *Web:* www.cktech.biz	Montpelier	OH	43543	419-485-1110		62-4
CK Worldwide Inc 3501 C St NE *TF:* 800-426-0877 ■ *Web:* www.ckworldwide.com	Auburn	WA	98002	253-854-5820	939-1746	811
CKC (Canadian Kennel Club) 200 Ronson Dr Ste 400 *TF:* 800-250-8040 ■ *Web:* www.ckc.ca	Etobicoke	ON	M9W5Z9	416-675-5511	675-6506	48-3
Ckc Laboratories Inc 5046 Sierra Pines Dr *Web:* www.ckc.com	Mariposa	CA	95338	209-966-5240		180
Ckgp/Pw & Assoc Inc 989 Chicago Rd *Web:* www.ckgppw.com	Troy	MI	48083	248-577-0400		261
CKHS (Crozer-Keystone Health System) 190 W Sproul Rd *TF:* 800-254-3258 ■ *Web:* www.crozerkeystone.org	Springfield	PA	19064	610-328-8700	328-8725	353
CKLW-AM 800 (N/T) 1640 Ouellette Ave *TF:* 800-263-2559 ■ *Web:* www.iheartradio.ca/am800	Windsor	ON	N8X1L1	519-258-8888	258-0182	645
CKM Staffing 500 Giuseppe Ct Ste 1 *Web:* www.ckmstaffing.com	Roseville	CA	95678	916-297-6815		41
CKMX-AM 1060 (Ctry) 1110 Ctr St NE Ste 300 *Web:* www.classiccountryam1060.com	Calgary	AB	T2E2R2	403-240-4100	262-3645	645-27
CKR Interactive Inc 399 NThird St *TF:* 800-263-5257 ■ *Web:* www.ckrinteractive.com	Campbell	CA	95008	408-517-1400		7
CKS Packaging Inc 445 Great SW Pkwy *Web:* www.ckspackaging.com	Atlanta	GA	30336	404-691-8900		601
CL Hauthaway & Sons Corp 638 Summer St *TF:* 800-541-6752 ■ *Web:* www.hauthaway.com	Lynn	MA	01905	781-592-6444	599-9565	605-2
CL King & Associates Inc 9 Elk St *Web:* clking.com	Albany	NY	12207	518-431-3555		690
CL Services Inc 600 S Central Ave Ste 300 *Web:* www.clservicesinc.com	Atlanta	GA	30354	678-686-0933		194
CL Swanson Corp 1133 Pennsylvania St *Web:* www.swansons.net	Denver	CO	80203	303-832-3920	832-7795	299
CLA (Christian Leadership Alliance) 635 Camino De Los Mares Ste 216 *TF:* 800-263-6317 ■ *Web:* www.christianleadershipalliance.org	San Clemente	CA	92673	949-487-0900	487-0927	49-12
CLA (Canadian Library Assn) 328 Frank St	Ottawa	ON	K2P0X8	613-232-9625	563-9895	49-11
CLA (Coin Laundry Assn) 1s660 Midwest Rd Ste 205 *TF:* 800-570-5629 ■ *Web:* www.coinlaundry.org	Oakbrook Terrace	IL	60181	630-953-7920		49-4
CLAAS of America Inc 8401 S 132nd St *Web:* www.claasofamerica.com	Omaha	NE	68138	402 861 1000	861 1003	273
Clack Corp 4462 Duraform Ln *TF:* 800-755-3010 ■ *Web:* www.clackcorp.com	Windsor	WI	53598	608-846-3010	846-2586	806
Clackamas County 2051 Kaen Rd *TF:* 800-488-8280 ■ *Web:* www.clackamas.us	Oregon City	OR	97045	503-655-8551	650-5688	338
Clackamas County Library 16201 SE McLoughlin Blvd *Web:* www.clackamas.us/lib/hours.html	Oak Grove	OR	97267	503-655-8543		434-3
Clackamas Town Ctr 12000 SE 82nd Ave *Web:* www.clackamastowncenter.com	Happy Valley	OR	97086	503-653-6913		460
Clad Metal Specialities Inc 1516 Fifth Industrial Ct *Web:* www.cladmetal.com	Bay Shore	NY	11706	631-666-7750		488
CLAdirect Inc 8600 NW 17th St Ste 140 *Web:* cladirect.com	Miami	FL	33126	305-418-4253		180
Claflin University 400 Magnolia St *TF:* 800-922-1276 ■ *Web:* www.claflin.edu	Orangeburg	SC	29115	803-535-5000	535-5385	166
CLAGS (Center for Lesbian & Gay Studies) *University of New York* 365 Fifth Ave Rm 7115 *Web:* www.clags.org	New York	NY	10016	212-817-1955	817-1567	668
Claiborne County 404 Market St *Web:* www.claiborne.k12.ms.us	Port Gibson	MS	39150	601-437-4232	437-4409	338
Claiborne County 1740 Main St *Web:* www.clairbornepartnership.com	Tazewell	TN	37879	423-626-9270		338
Claiborne County Chamber of Commerce 3222 Hwy 25 E Ste 1	Tazewell	TN	37879	423-626-4149		139
Claiborne County Hospital & Nursing Home 1850 Old Knoxville Rd *Web:* www.claibornehospital.org	Tazewell	TN	37879	423-626-4211		374-3
Claiborne Electric Co-Op Inc 12525 Hwy 9 PO Box 719 *Web:* www.our.coop	Homer	LA	71040	318-927-3504		245
Claiborne Farm 703 Winchester Rd *Web:* www.claibornefarm.com	Paris	KY	40361	859-233-4252	987-0008	368
Claiborne Parish 512 E Main St *Web:* www.claiborneone.org	Homer	LA	71040	318-927-9601		338
Claim Technologies Inc 100 Court Ave Ste 306 *Web:* www.claimtechnologies.com	Des Moines	IA	50309	515-244-7322		390
ClaimReturn Inc 3004 Irving Blvd *Web:* claimreturn.com	Dallas	TX	75247	817-953-2424		260
Claims Verification Inc 6700 N Andrews Ave Ste 200 *TF:* 888-284-2000 ■ *Web:* www.cvi.com	Ft. Lauderdale	FL	33309	888-284-2000		400
Claimsnet.com Inc 14860 Montfort Dr Ste 250 *TF:* 800-356-1511 ■ *Web:* www.claimsnet.com	Dallas	TX	75254	972-458-1701	458-1737	225
Claimsource One Services Group Inc 490 Sun Vly Dr Ste 103	Roswell	GA	30076	404-252-1771		652

Name / Address	City	State	Zip	Phone	Fax	Class
Claire Manufacturing Co 1005 S Westgate Ave *TF Sales:* 800-252-4731 ■ *Web:* www.clairemfg.com	Addison	IL	60101	630-543-7600	543-4310	145
Claire's Accessories 2400 W Central Rd *TF:* 800-252-4737 ■ *Web:* www.claires.co.uk	Hoffman Estates	IL	60192	847-765-1100	765-4676	157-6
Claire's Corner Copia 1000 Chapel St *Web:* www.clairescornercopia.com	New Haven	CT	06510	203-562-3888		671
Clairmont Place 2100 Clairmont Lake *TF:* 800-284-0311 ■ *Web:* clairmontplace.com	Decatur	GA	30033	404-633-8875	633-9417	672
Clairmount Group Plc 18424 Mack Ave *Web:* clairmount.com	Grosse Pointe Farms	MI	48236	313-642-1102		734
Clairon Metals Corp 11194 Alcovy Rd *Web:* www.claironmetals.com	Covington	GA	30014	770-786-9681	786-4183	488
Clairvia Inc 2525 Meridian Pkwy Ste 100	Durham	NC	27713	919-382-8282		177
Claitor's Law Books & Publishing Division PO Box 261333 *TF:* 800-274-1403 ■ *Web:* www.claitors.com	Baton Rouge	LA	70826	225-344-0476	344-0480	626
Clallam Bay Corrections Ctr 1830 Eagle Crest Way *Web:* doc.wa.gov	Clallam Bay	WA	98326	360-963-2000		213
Clallam County 223 E Fourth St Ste 2 *TF:* 800-424-5555 ■ *Web:* www.clallam.net	Port Angeles	WA	98362	360-417-2318	417-2493	338
Clam Gulch State Recreation Area PO Box 1247 *Web:* dnr.alaska.gov/parks/units/clamglch.htm	Soldotna	AK	99669	907-262-5581		565
Clamp Swing Pricing Company Inc 8386 Capwell Dr *TF:* 800-227-7615 ■ *Web:* clampswing.com	Oakland	CA	94621	510-567-1600		413
Clampco Products Inc 1743 Wall Rd *Web:* clampco.com	Wadsworth	OH	44281	330-336-8857		350
Clampitt Paper Company of Dallas 9207 Ambassador Row *Web:* www.clampitt.com	Dallas	TX	75247	214-638-3300		553
Clamshell Structures Inc 1101 Maulhardt Ave *TF:* 800-360-8853 ■ *Web:* www.clamshell.com	Oxnard	CA	93030	805-988-1340	988-2266	733
Clancy & Theys Construction Co 516 W Cabarrus St *Web:* www.clancytheys.com	Raleigh	NC	27603	919-834-3601	834-2439	186
Clancy's 6100 Annunciation St *Web:* clancysneworleans.com	New Orleans	LA	70118	504-895-1111		671
Clara Barton National Historic Site 5801 Oxford Rd *TF:* 800-514-3849 ■ *Web:* www.nps.gov/clba	Glen Echo	MD	20812	301-320-1410		564
Clara Maass Medical Ctr 1 Clara Maass Dr *TF:* 800-300-0628 ■ *Web:* www.barnabashealth.org	Belleville	NJ	07109	973-450-2000		374-3
Clara's 637 E Michigan Ave *Web:* www.claras.com	Lansing	MI	48912	517-372-7120		671
Clarcor Inc 840 Crescent Ctr Dr Ste 600 *NYSE:* CLC ■ *TF:* 800-252-7267 ■ *Web:* www.clarcor.com	Franklin	TN	37067	615-771-3100	771-5616	18
Clare County 225 W Main PO Box 438 *Web:* www.clareco.net	Harrison	MI	48625	989-539-2510	539-6616	338
Clare Inc 78 Cherry Hill Dr *TF:* 800-272-5273 ■ *Web:* www.ixysic.com	Beverly	MA	01915	978-524-6700	524-4700	696
Clare Oaks 825 Carillon Dr *TF:* 866-523-9510 ■ *Web:* www.clareoaks.com	Bartlett	IL	60103	630-372-1983		371
Clare Rose Inc 100 Rose Executive Blvd *Web:* www.clarerose.com/agecheck.aspx	East Yaphank	NY	11967	631-475-1840		81-1
Claremont Animal Hospital Inc 446 Charlestown Rd *Web:* www.claremontanimalhospital.com	Claremont	NH	03743	603-543-0117		794
Claremont Chamber of Commerce 205 Yale Ave *TF:* 800-321-2752 ■ *Web:* www.claremontchamber.org	Claremont	CA	91711	909-624-1681	624-6629	139
Claremont Companies Inc 1 Lakeshore Ctr *TF:* 800-848-9077 ■ *Web:* www.claremontcorp.com	Bridgewater	MA	02324	508-279-4300		528
Claremont Flock LLC 107 Scott Dr *TF:* 800-297-6306 ■ *Web:* www.claremontflock.com	Leominster	MA	01453	978-534-6191	534-7352	745-8
Claremont Institute 937 W Foothill Blvd Ste E *Web:* www.claremont.org	Claremont	CA	91711	909-621-6825		634
Claremont McKenna College 500 E Ninth St *Web:* www.cmc.edu	Claremont	CA	91711	909-621-8088	621-8516	166
Claremont Resort & Spa 41 Tunnel Rd *TF:* 800-551-7266 ■ *Web:* www.fairmont.com/claremont-berkeley	Berkeley	CA	94705	510-843-3000		669
Claremont Sales Corp 35 Winsome Dr PO Box 430 *TF:* 800-222-4448 ■ *Web:* claremontcorporation.com	Durham	CT	06422	860-349-4499	349-7977	389
Claremont School of Theology 1325 N College Ave **Fax:* Admissions ■ *Web:* www.cst.edu	Claremont	CA	91711	909-447-2500	447-6389*	167-3
Claremore Regional Hospital LLC 1202 N Muskogee Pl *Web:* hillcrestclaremore.com	Claremore	OK	74017	918-341-2556		374-3
Clarence Brown Theatre *University of Tennessee* 206 McClung Tower *Web:* www.clarencebrowntheatre.com	Knoxville	TN	37996	865-974-5161	974-4867	572
Clarence Fahnestock State Park 1498 Rt 301 *Web:* parks.ny.gov/parks/133	Carmel	NY	10512	845-225-7207		565
Clarendon College 1122 College Dr PO Box 968 **Fax:* Admissions ■ *TF:* 800-687-9737 ■ *Web:* www.clarendoncollege.edu	Clarendon	TX	79226	806-874-3571	874-5080*	162
Clarendon County 19 N Brooks St *TF:* 800-556-0110 ■ *Web:* www.clarendoncounty.com	Manning	SC	29102	803-435-4405		338
Clarendon Grill 1101 N Highland St *Web:* www.cgrill.com	Arlington	VA	22201	703-524-7455	524-9598	671
Clarendon Hall School 1140 S Dukes St	Summerton	SC	29148	803-485-3550		685
Clarendon Hotel & Suites 401 W Clarendon Ave *Web:* goclarendon.com	Phoenix	AZ	85013	602-252-7363		379
Claret Canada Inc 1400 Rue Joliot-curie *TF:* 800-567-7442 ■ *Web:* claretnet.com	Boucherville	QC	J4B7L9	450-449-5774		757
Claret Medical Inc 1745 Copperhill Pkwy Ste 1 *Web:* www.claretmedical.com	Santa Rosa	CA	95403	707-528-9300		723
Claricent Inc 22 Preserve way *TF:* 888-325-6496 ■ *Web:* www.claricent.com	Sturbridge	MA	01566	888-325-6496		177
Claridge Products & Equipment Inc 601 Hwy 62 65 PO Box 910 *TF:* 800-434-4610 ■ *Web:* www.claridgeproducts.com	Harrison	AR	72602	870-743-2200	743-1908	243
Clarinda Correctional Facility 1800 N 16th St Ste 1 *Web:* www.doc.state.ia.us	Clarinda	IA	51632	712-542-5634	542-4844	213
Clarion Area Chamber of Business & Industry 650 Main St *Web:* www.clarionpa.com	Clarion	PA	16214	814-226-9161	226-4903	139
Clarion Associates Inc 30W Monore St Ste 810 *Web:* clarionassociates.com	Chicago	IL	60603	312-630-9400		449
Clarion Bathware Inc 44 Amsler Ave *Web:* www.clarionbathware.com	Shippenville	PA	16254	814-226-5374		362
Clarion Books 215 Pk Ave S *TF:* 800-767-8420 ■ *Web:* www.hmhco.com	New York	NY	10003	212-420-5800		637-2
Clarion Construction Inc 21067 Commerce Pointe Dr *Web:* www.clarionconst.com	Walnut	CA	91789	909-598-4060		186
Clarion Corp of America 6200 Gateway Dr *TF:* 800-347-8667 ■ *Web:* www.clarion.com	Cypress	CA	90630	310-327-9100	327-1999	52
Clarion County 421 Main St Courthouse *Web:* www.co.clarion.pa.us	Clarion	PA	16214	814-226-4000		338
Clarion Hospital (CH) 1 Hospital Dr *TF:* 800-522-0505 ■ *Web:* www.clarionhospital.org	Clarion	PA	16214	814-226-9500	226-1224	374-3
Clarion Hotel & Conference Ctr Antietam Creek 901 Dual Hwy *Web:* www.clarionhagerstown.com	Hagerstown	MD	21740	301-733-5100	733-9192	377
Clarion Laminates LLC 301 Fiberboard Rd *Web:* www.clarionindustries.com/laminates.php	Shippenville	PA	16254	814-226-8032		499
Clarion Medical Technologies Inc 125 Fleming Dr *Web:* www.clarionmedical.com	Cambridge	ON	N1T2B8	519-620-3900		475
Clarion Technologies Inc 170 College Ave Ste 300 *Web:* www.clariontechnologies.com	Holland	MI	49423	616-698-7277		256
Clarion University of Pennsylvania 840 Wood St **Fax:* Admissions ■ *TF:* 800-672-7171 ■ *Web:* www.clarion.edu	Clarion	PA	16214	814-393-2306	393-2030*	166
Venango 1801 W First St *TF:* 800-672-7171 ■ *Web:* www.clarion.edu	Oil City	PA	16301	814-676-6591	676-1348	166
Clarion-Ledger, The 201 S Congress St *TF:* 877-850-5343 ■ *Web:* www.clarionledger.com	Jackson	MS	39201	601-961-7000	961-7211	532-2
ClariPhy Communications Inc 7585 Irvine Ctr Dr Ste 100 *TF:* 800-767-3652 ■ *Web:* www.clariphy.com	Irvine	CA	92618	949-861-3074		186
Claris Construction Inc 153 S Main St *Web:* www.clarisconstruction.com	Newtown	CT	06470	203-364-9460		186
Claris Networks LLC 6100 Lonas Dr *Web:* clarisnetworks.com	Knoxville	TN	37909	865-251-5555		225
Clarite Consulting 20 Tower Hill Rd *Web:* www.clariteconsulting.com	Mountain Lakes	NJ	07046	973-541-0051		196
Claritee Group LLC 196 W Ashland St *Web:* www.clariteegroup.com	Doylestown	PA	18901	267-338-3300		194
Clarity Coverdale Fury (CCF) 120 S Sixth St 1 Financial Plz Ste 1300 *Web:* www.claritycoverdalefury.com	Minneapolis	MN	55402	612-339-3902		4
Clarity Innovations Inc 1001 SE Water Ave Ste 400 *TF:* 877-683-3187 ■ *Web:* www.clarity-innovations.com	Portland	OR	97214	503-248-4300		256
Clarity Partners LLC 20 N Clark St Ste 3600 *Web:* www.claritypartners.com	Chicago	IL	60602	312-920-0550		463
Clarity Software Solutions Inc 92 Wall St Ste 1 *Web:* www.clarityssi.com	Madison	CT	06443	203-453-3999		177
Clark & Sullivan Constructors Inc 905 Industrial Way Ste 26 *Web:* www.clarksullivan.com	Sparks	NV	89431	775-355-8500		186
Clark & Wamberg LLC 102 S Wynstone Park Dr	North Barrington	IL	60010	847-304-5800		194
Clark Atlanta University 223 James P Brawley Dr SW **Fax:* Admissions ■ *TF Admissions:* 800-688-3228 ■ *Web:* www.cau.edu	Atlanta	GA	30314	404-880-8000	880-6174*	166
Clark Brothers Instrument Company Inc 56680 Mound Rd *Web:* www.clarkbrothers.net	Shelby Township	MI	48316	586-781-7000		54
Clark Builders Ltd 4703 - 52 Ave *TF:* 800-794-5325 ■ *Web:* www.clarkbuilders.com	Edmonton	AB	T6B3R6	780-395-3300		261
Clark Capital Management Group Inc (CCMG) 1650 Market St 1 Liberty Pl 53rd Fl *TF:* 800-766-2264 ■ *Web:* www.ccmg.com	Philadelphia	PA	19103	215-569-2224	569-3639	401
Clark College 1800 E McLoughlin Blvd **Fax:* Admissions ■ *TF:* 800-275-2471 ■ *Web:* www.clark.edu	Vancouver	WA	98663	360-992-2000	992-2876*	162
Clark Construction Co 3535 Moores River Dr *Web:* www.clarkcc.com	Lansing	MI	48911	517-372-0940	372-0668	188-7
Clark Construction Group LLC 7500 Old Georgetown Rd *TF:* 800-655-1330 ■ *Web:* www.clarkconstruction.com	Bethesda	MD	20814	301-272-8100		186

Phone | Fax | Class

Clark Contractors Inc
19651 Descartes . . . . . Foothill Ranch CA 92610 949-581-6577 256
Web: www.clarkcontractors.com
Clark County 401 Clay St. . . . . Arkadelphia AR 71923 870-246-4491 246-6505 338
TF: 800-434-4800 ■ *Web:* www.clarkcountyarkansas.com
Clark County 913 Highland St. . . . . Ashland KS 67831 620-635-2813 635-2051 338
TF: 800-829-0922 ■ *Web:* www.clarkcountyks.com
Clark County 320 W Main St. . . . . Grangeville ID 83530 208-983-2751 983-1428 338
TF: 800-252-0233 ■ *Web:* www.idaho.gov
Clark County 501 E Ct Ave. . . . . Jeffersonville IN 47130 812-285-6275 285-6366 338
Web: www.co.clark.in.us
Clark County 252 N Morgan St . . . . . Kahoka MO 63445 660-727-1072 338
Web: www.mogenclark.com
Clark County
500 S Grand Central Pkwy . . . . . Las Vegas NV 89155 702-455-0000 338
Web: www.clarkcountynv.gov
Clark County
501 Archer Ave County Courthouse . . . . . Marshall IL 62441 217-826-8311 338
Web: www.clarkcountyil.org
Clark County 517 Court St Rm 301 . . . . . Neillsville WI 54456 715-743-5148 743-5154 338
Web: www.co.clark.wi.us
Clark County
101 N Limestone St Ste 112 . . . . . Springfield OH 45502 937-521-1680 328-2436 338
Web: www.clarkcountyohio.gov
Clark County PO Box 5000 . . . . . Vancouver WA 98666 360-397-2000 397-6099 338
Web: www.clark.wa.gov
Clark County 34 S Main St . . . . . Winchester KY 40391 859-745-0200 737-5678 338
Web: www.clarkcoky.com
Clark County Event Center at The Fairgrounds
17402 NE Delfel Rd . . . . . Ridgefield WA 98642 360-397-6180 720
Web: www.clarkcofair.com
Clark County Historical Museum
1511 Main St . . . . . Vancouver WA 98660 360-993-5679 993-5683 520
Web: cchmuseum.org
Clark County Museum
1830 S Boulder Hwy. . . . . Henderson NV 89002 702-455-7955 455-7948 520
Web: clarkcountynv.gov
Clark County Public Library
201 S Fountain Ave. . . . . Springfield OH 45501 937-328-6903 328-6908 434-3
Web: ccplohio.org
Clark County REMC
7810 State Rd 60 PO Box 411 . . . . . Sellersburg IN 47172 812-246-3316 245
TF: 800-462-6988 ■ *Web:* www.theremc.com
Clark County School District (CCSD)
5100 W Sahara Ave. . . . . Las Vegas NV 89146 702-799-5000 799-5125 685
TF: 866-799-8997 ■ *Web:* www.ccsd.net
Clark Dietz Inc 125 W Church St . . . . . Champaign IL 61820 217-373-8900 256
Web: www.clark-dietz.com
Clark Distributing Co Inc
1300 Highway 51 S . . . . . Dyersburg TN 38024 731-285-1500 443
TF: 800-382-9851 ■ *Web:* www.clarkdistributingco.com
Clark Dodge Asset Management
2 Gannett Dr 2nd Fl . . . . . White Plains NY 10604 914-694-2390 528
Web: www.clarkdodgewealth.com
Clark Electric Co-op
124 N Main St PO Box 190. . . . . Greenwood WI 54437 715-267-6188 245
TF: 800-272-6188 ■ *Web:* www.cecoop.com
Clark Energy Co-op Inc
2640 Ironworks Rd . . . . . Winchester KY 40391 859-744-4251 245
TF: 800-992-3269 ■ *Web:* www.clarkenergy.com
Clark Engineering Corp
621 Lilac Dr N . . . . . Minneapolis MN 55422 763-545-9196 261
TF: 877-246-9196 ■ *Web:* www.clark-eng.com
Clark Filter Inc 3649 Hempland Rd . . . . . Lancaster PA 17601 717-285-5941 650
TF: 800-252-4647 ■ *Web:* www.clarkfilter.com
Clark Foam Products Corp
655 Remington Blvd . . . . . Bolingbrook IL 60440 630-226-5900 226-5959 601
TF: 888-284-2290 ■ *Web:* www.clarkfoam.net
Clark Food Service Equipment
2209 Old Philadelphia Pk. . . . . Lancaster PA 17602 717-392-7363 690
Web: www.clarkfoodserviceequipment.biz
Clark Freight Lines Inc
5129 Pine Ave. . . . . Pasadena TX 77503 281-487-3160 314
Web: www.clarkfreight.com
Clark Grave Vault Co, The
375 E Fifth Ave . . . . . Columbus OH 43201 614-294-3761 134
Web: www.clarkvault.com
Clark Insurance 2385 Congress St . . . . . Portland ME 04102 207-774-6257 774-2994 390
Web: clarkinsurance.com
Clark Katherine (Rep D - MA)
1415 Longworth HOB . . . . . Washington DC 20515 202-225-2836 342-2
Web: katherineclark.house.gov
Clark Martire & Bartolomeo
375 Sylvan Ave. . . . . Englewood Cliffs NJ 07632 201-568-0011 668
Web: www.cmbinc.com
Clark Material Handling Co
700 Enterprise Dr . . . . . Lexington KY 40510 859-422-6400 470
TF: 866-252-5275 ■ *Web:* www.clarkmhc.com
Clark Mc Dowall 404 E 11th St. . . . . New York NY 10009 212-473-3737 463
Web: www.clarkmcdowall.com
Clark Memorial Hospital (CMH)
1220 Missouri Ave . . . . . Jeffersonville IN 47130 812-282-6631 283-6330 374-3
Web: www.clarkmemorial.org
Clark Metal Products Co
100 Serrell Dr . . . . . Blairsville PA 15717 724-459-7550 459-0207 489
Web: www.clark-metal.com
Clark Nuber PS
10900 NE Fourth St Ste 1700. . . . . Bellevue WA 98004 425-454-4919 2
TF General: 800-504-8747 ■ *Web:* www.clarknuber.com
Clark Oil Company Inc
720 Station St. . . . . Waynesboro MS 39367 601-735-4847 706
Web: www.clark oil.com
Clark Patterson Engineers Surveyor & Architects PC
205 St Paul St Ste 500 . . . . . Rochester NY 14604 585-454-4570 256
Web: www.clarkpattersonlee.com
Clark Personnel Service
1180 Montlimar Dr . . . . . Mobile AL 36609 251-471-6777 260
TF: 800-826-9947 ■ *Web:* www.clarkpersonnel.com

Phone | Fax | Class

Clark Planetarium 110 S 400 W. . . . . Salt Lake City UT 84101 385-468-7827 598
TF: 800-501-2885 ■ *Web:* www.clarkplanetarium.net
Clark Precision Machined Components LLC
320 Fourth St . . . . . Blawnox PA 15238 412-828-1210 490
Web: www.clarkprecision.com
Clark Public Library 303 Westfield Ave . . . . . Clark NJ 07066 732-388-5999 434-3
Clark Regional Medical Ctr Inc
175 Hospital Dr . . . . . Winchester KY 40391 859-745-3500 374-3
Web: www.clarkregional.org
Clark Reservation State Park
6105 E Seneca Tpke . . . . . Jamesville NY 13078 315-492-1590 565
Web: parks.ny.gov/parks/126/details.aspx
Clark Schaefer Hackett & Co
1 E Fourth St Ste 1200 . . . . . Cincinnati OH 45202 513-241-3111 2
TF: 800-772-8144 ■ *Web:* www.cshco.com
Clark Specialty Co Inc
6824 Industrial Park Rd . . . . . Bath NY 14810 607-776-3193 776-3190 697
Web: www.clarkspecialty.com
Clark State Community College
570 E Leffel Ln . . . . . Springfield OH 45506 937-325-0691 328-6097 162
Web: www.clarkstate.edu
Clark Steel Fabricators Inc
12610 Vigilante Rd . . . . . Lakeside CA 92040 619-390-1502 480
TF: 800-564-3110 ■ *Web:* www.clarksteelfab.com
Clark Street Grill 811 Spruce St. . . . . Saint Louis MO 63102 314-552-5850 671
Web: www.clarkstreetgrill.com
Clark Technology Systems Inc
159 Harveys Ln. . . . . Milton PA 17847 570-742-1819 295
Web: www.clarkts.com
Clark Transfer Inc 800A Paxton St. . . . . Harrisburg PA 17104 717-238-0801 186
TF: 800-488-7585 ■ *Web:* www.clarktransfer.com
Clark University 950 Main St . . . . . Worcester MA 01610 508-793-7711 793-8821 166
TF: 800-462-5275 ■ *Web:* www.clarku.edu
Clark Wilson LLP
900 885 W Georgia St . . . . . Vancouver BC V6C3H1 604-687-5700 687-6314 41
Web: www.cwilson.com
Clark's Lookout State Park
4200 Bannack Rd 4200 Bannack Rd. . . . . Dillon MT 59725 406-834-3413 565
Web: stateparks.mt.gov
Clark, Gagliardi & Miller PC
99 Court St. . . . . White Plains NY 10601 800-734-5694 428
TF: 800-734-5694 ■ *Web:* www.cgmlaw.com
Clarkco State Park 386 Clarkco Rd . . . . . Quitman MS 39355 601-776-6651 565
Web: www.mdwfp.com/parkview/parks.asp?id=4842
Clark-Cutler-McDermott Co (CCMcD)
5 Fisher St . . . . . Franklin MA 02038 508-528-1200 528-1406 745-6
Clark-Dunbar Flooring Superstore
3232 Empire Dr . . . . . Alexandria LA 71301 318-445-0262 290
TF: 800-256-1467 ■ *Web:* www.clarkdunbarsuperstore.com
Clarke & Rush Mechanical Inc
4411 Auburn Blvd. . . . . Sacramento CA 95841 916-609-2665 610
Web: clarke-rush.com
Clarke College 1550 Clarke Dr . . . . . Dubuque IA 52001 563-588-6300 588-6789* 166
**Fax:* Admissions ■ *TF:* 888-825-2753 ■ *Web:* www.clarke.edu
Clarke Cooke House
1 Bannister's Wharf. . . . . Newport RI 02840 401-849-4500 849-8750 671
Web: www.bannistersnewport.com
Clarke County 101 N Church Ct Ste B. . . . . Berryville VA 22611 540-955-5100 338
Web: www.clarkecounty.gov
Clarke County PO Box 548 . . . . . Grove Hill AL 36451 251-275-3507 275-8517 338
Web: clarkecountyal.com
Clarke County 100 S Main . . . . . Osceola IA 50213 641-342-3315 338
Web: www.clarkecountyia.org
Clarke Historical Museum 240 E St . . . . . Eureka CA 95501 707-443-1947 520
Web: www.clarkemuseum.org
Clarke House Museum
1827 S Indiana Ave . . . . . Chicago IL 60616 312-326-1480 520
TF: 800-798-0988 ■ *Web:* www.cityofchicago.org
Clarke Power Services Inc
3133 E Kemper Rd . . . . . Cincinnati OH 45241 513-771-2200 358
TF: 800-513-9591 ■ *Web:* www.clarkepowerservices.com
Clarke Silverglate PA
799 Brickell Plaza Ste 900 . . . . . Miami FL 33131 305-377-0700 428
Web: www.cspalaw.com
Clarke Yvette D (Rep D - NY)
2058 Rayburn HOB. . . . . Washington DC 20515 202-225-6231 226-0112 342-2
Web: clarke.house.gov
Clark-Floyd Counties Convention & Tourism Bureau
315 Southern Indiana Ave. . . . . Jeffersonville IN 47130 812-282-6654 282-1904 206
TF: 800-552-3842 ■ *Web:* www.gosoin.com
Clark-Lindsey Village 101 W Windsor Rd. . . . . Urbana IL 61802 217-344-2144 672
TF: 800-998-2581 ■ *Web:* www.clark-lindsey.com
Clark-Pacific Corp
1980 S River Rd . . . . . West Sacramento CA 95691 916-371-0305 372-0323 187
Web: www.clarkpacific.com
Clark-Reliance Corp
16633 Foltz Pkwy . . . . . Strongsville OH 44149 440-572-1500 572-1500 495
TF: 800-238-4027 ■ *Web:* www.clarkreliance.com
Clarks Summit State Hospital
1451 Hillside Dr. . . . . Clarks Summit PA 18411 570-586-2011 587-7415 374-5
Clarksburg Exponent Telegram
324 Hewes Ave . . . . . Clarksburg WV 26301 304-626-1400 624-4188 532-2
TF: 800-982-6034 ■ *Web:* theet.com
Clarksburg State Park
1199 Middle Rd . . . . . Clarksburg MA 01247 413-664-8345 565
Web: www.mass.gov
Clarksdale Municipal School District
135 Washington Ave PO Box 1088. . . . . Clarksdale MS 38614 662-627-8500 624-9405 186
TF: 877-820-7831 ■ *Web:* www.cmsd.k12.ms.us
Clarksdale-Coahoma County Chamber of Commerce & Industrial Foundation
1540 DeSoto Ave . . . . . Clarksdale MS 38614 662-627-7337 627-1313 139
TF: 800-626-3764 ■ *Web:* www.clarksdale.com
Clarkson College 101 S 42nd St. . . . . Omaha NE 68131 402-552-3100 552-6057* 166
**Fax:* Admissions ■ *TF:* 800-647-5500 ■ *Web:* www.clarksoncollege.edu
Clarkson Construction Co
4133 Gardner Ave. . . . . Kansas City MO 64120 816-483-8800 241-6823 188-4
Web: clarksonconstruction.com
Clarkson University 10 Clarkson Ave. . . . . Potsdam NY 13699 315-268-6480 268-7647* 166
**Fax:* Admissions ■ *TF Admissions:* 800-527-6577 ■ *Web:* www.clarkson.edu

Name / Address	City	State	ZIP	Phone	Fax	Class
Clarkston Area Chamber of Commerce 5856 S Main St. *Web:* www.clarkston.org	Clarkston	MI	48346	248-625-8055	625-8041	139
Clarkston Consulting 2655 Meridian Pkwy Ste 400 *TF:* 800-652-4274 ■ *Web:* www.clarkstonconsulting.com	Durham	NC	27713	919-484-4400	484-4450	180
Clarkston Specialty Healthcare Ctr 4800 Clintonville Rd *Web:* savaseniorcare.com	Clarkston	MI	48346	248-674-0903		450
Clarksville Area Chamber of Commerce 25 Jefferson St Ste 300 *TF:* 800-530-2487 ■ *Web:* www.clarksvillechamber.com	Clarksville	TN	37040	931-647-2331	645-1574	139
Clarksville Foundry Inc 1140 Red River St *Web:* www.clarksvillefoundry.com	Clarksville	TN	37040	931-647-1538		480
Clarksville Montgomery County Public Library 350 Pageant Ln *TF:* 877-239-6635 ■ *Web:* www.mcgtn.org/library	Clarksville	TN	37040	931-648-8826	648-8831	434-3
Clarksville/Montgomery County Tourist Commission 25 Jefferson St Ste 300 *TF:* 800-530-2487 ■ *Web:* www.clarksvillepartnership.com	Clarksville	TN	37040	931-647-2331	645-1574	206
ClarkWestern Dietrich Building Systems LLC 9100 Centre Pointe Dr Ste 210 *Web:* www.clarkdietrich.com	West Chester	OH	45069	513-870-1100		191-1
Clarus Mktg Group LLC 500 Enterprise Dr 2nd Fl *TF:* 855-226-7047 ■ *Web:* www.claruscommerce.com	Rocky Hill	CT	06067	860-358-9198		194
Clarus Therapeutics Inc 555 Skokie Blvd Ste 340 *Web:* www.clarustherapeutics.com	Northbrook	IL	60062	847-562-4300		231
Clary Corp 150 E Huntington Dr *TF:* 800-551-6111 ■ *Web:* www.clary.com	Monrovia	CA	91016	626-359-4486	305-0254	253
CLASP (Center for Law & Social Policy) 1015 15th St NW Ste 400 *TF:* 800-821-4367 ■ *Web:* www.clasp.org	Washington	DC	20005	202-906-8000	842-2885	634
Class 1 Controls Inc 1720 Elmview Dr *Web:* www.class1controls.com	Houston	TX	77080	713-467-8397		261
Class Act Federal Credit Union 3620 Fern Valley Rd *TF:* 800-292-2960 ■ *Web:* www.classact.org	Louisville	KY	40219	502-964-7575	966-2061	219
Class Action Litigation Report 1801 S Bell St *TF:* 800-372-1033 ■ *Web:* www.bna.com/class-action-litigation-p5442	Arlington	VA	22202	800-372-1033		531-7
Classic Arts Showcase PO Box 828 *Web:* www.classicartsshowcase.org	Burbank	CA	91503	323-878-0283	878-0329	740
Classic Blind Ltd 2801 Brasher Ln Ste 100	Bedford	TX	76021	817-540-9300		361
Classic Brands LLC 8214 Wellmoor Ct *TF:* 877-707-7533 ■ *Web:* www.classicmattress.com	Jessup	MD	20794	410-904-0006		471
Classic Brass Inc 2051 Stoneman Cir *TF:* 800-869-3173 ■ *Web:* www.classic-brass.com	Lakewood	NY	14750	716-763-1400		350
Classic Cafe 865 Westminster St *Web:* classiccaferi.com	Providence	RI	02903	401-273-0707		671
Classic Care Pharmacy Corp 1320 Heine Ct *Web:* www.classiccare.ca	Burlington	ON	L7L6L9	905-631-9027		237
Classic Cinemas 603 Rogers St *Web:* www.classiccinemas.com	Downers Grove	IL	60515	630-968-1600	968-1626	748
Classic City Beverages LLC 530 Calhoun Dr *Web:* jandlventuresllc.com	Athens	GA	30601	706-353-1650	353-1655	81-1
Classic Components Corp 23605 Telo Ave *Web:* www.class-ic.com	Torrance	CA	90505	310-539-5500		246
Classic Containers Inc 1700 S Hellman Ave *Web:* www.classiccontainers.com	Ontario	CA	91761	909-930-3610		362
Classic Custom Vacations 5893 Rue Ferrari *TF:* 800-635-1333 ■ *Web:* www.classicvacations.com	San Jose	CA	95138	800-635-1333		771
Classic Die Services Inc 6926 Trafalgar Dr Ste D *Web:* www.classicdieservices.com	Fort Wayne	IN	46803	260-748-6907		41
Classic Display Inc 80 Fountain St Ste 1 *Web:* www.classicdisplay.com	Pawtucket	RI	02860	401-721-2240		344
Classic Distributing & Beverage Group Inc 120 N Puente Ave *Web:* www.cdbginc.com	City Of Industry	CA	91746	626-934-3700		80-2
Classic Floors Inc 13725 S Mur Len Rd *Web:* www.classicfloors.com	Olathe	KS	66062	913-780-2171		291
Classic Golf Management Inc 2295 Towne Lake Pkwy Ste 116 *Web:* www.cgmgolf.com	Woodstock	GA	30189	770-928-1600		706
Classic Hostess Inc 2 Skillman St Ste 313 *TF:* 888-280-6539 ■ *Web:* www.classichostess.com	Brooklyn	NY	11205	888-280-6539		393
Classic Industrial Services Inc 6748 Complex Dr *Web:* www.classicindustrial.com	Baton Rouge	LA	70809	225-756-4450		261
Classic Leather Inc PO Box 2404 *Web:* www.classic-leather.com	Hickory	NC	28603	828-328-2046	324 6212	319-2
Classic Medallics Inc 520 S Fulton Ave *TF:* 800-221-1348 ■ *Web:* www.classic-medallics.com	Mount Vernon	NY	10550	914-530-6259	530-6258	777
Classic Optical Laboratories Inc 3710 Belmont Ave *Web:* www.classicoptical.com	Youngstown	OH	44505	330-759-8245		237
Classic Packaging Co 5570 Bethania Rd *Web:* www.classicpackaging.com	Pfafftown	NC	27040	336-922-4224		601
Classic Parking Inc 3208 Royal St *TF:* 800-547-0263 ■ *Web:* classicparking.com	Los Angeles	CA	90007	213-742-1238		562
Classic Party Rentals 901 W Hillcrest Blvd *TF:* 800-678-3854 ■ *Web:* www.classicpartyrentals.com	Inglewood	CA	90301	310-535-3660		264-2
Classic Sheet Metal Inc 1065 Sesame St *Web:* www.classic-sheet-metal.com	Franklin Park	IL	60131	630-694-0300		492
Classic Student Tours 75 Rhoads Ctr Dr *TF:* 800-860-0246 ■ *Web:* classicstudenttours.com	Dayton	OH	45458	937-439-0032	439-0041	760
Classic Touch Limousine Inc 908 N Walnut St *TF:* 800-319-0082 ■ *Web:* www.classictouchlimo.com	Bloomington	IN	47404	812-339-7269		441
Classic Trains Magazine 21027 Crossroads Cir PO Box 1612 *TF:* 800-533-6644 ■ *Web:* ctr.trains.com	Waukesha	WI	53187	262-796-8776	796-1615	457-14
Classic Travel Inc 4767 Okemos Rd *TF:* 800-643-3449 ■ *Web:* www.classictravelusa.com	Okemos	MI	48864	517-349-6200		772
Classic Tube 80 Rotech Dr *TF:* 800-882-3711 ■ *Web:* www.classictube.com	Lancaster	NY	14086	716-759-1800		595
Classic Turning Inc 3000 E S St *Web:* www.classicturning.com	Jackson	MI	49201	517-764-1335		757
Classic Wines LLC 6489 E 39th Ave *Web:* www.classicwines.net	Denver	CO	80207	303-825-1360		80-3
Classic Worldwide Productions 5001 E Royalton Rd *TF:* 800-838-5377 ■ *Web:* classicworldwide.com	Cleveland	OH	44147	440-838-5377		513
Classical 95.5 KHFM 4125 Carlisle Blvd NE *Web:* www.classicalkhfm.com	Albuquerque	NM	87107	505-878-0980	878-0098	645-4
Classical Academy 975 Stout Rd *Web:* www.tcatitans.org	Colorado Springs	CO	80921	719-484-0091		449
Classical Marketing LLC 150 N Martingale Rd Ste 800 *TF:* 800-613-3489 ■ *Web:* classicalmarketing.com	Schaumburg	IL	60173	847-969-1696		195
Classroom Inc 245 Fifth Ave 20th Fl *Web:* www.classroominc.org	New York	NY	10016	212-545-8400		194
Classy 100 471 Robison Rd *Web:* www.classy100.com	Erie	PA	16509	814-868-5355	868-1876	645-54
Classy Llama Studios LLC 4064 S Lone Pine *Web:* www.classyllama.com	Springfield	MO	65804	417-866-8887		180
Clatsop Community College 1653 Jerome Ave *TF:* 855-252-8767 ■ *Web:* www.clatsopcc.edu	Astoria	OR	97103	503-325-0910	325-5738	162
Clatsop County 820 Exchange St Ste 100 *Web:* www.co.clatsop.or.us	Astoria	OR	97103	503-325-8511	325-9307	338
Claude Howard Lumber Company Inc 600 Pk Ave *Web:* sbcontract.com	Statesboro	GA	30458	912-764-5407	764-6279	683
Clausing Industrial Inc 1819 N Pitcher St *Web:* www.clausing-industrial.com	Kalamazoo	MI	49007	269-345-7155		358
Clausman & Assoc PC 1980 E 116th St	Carmel	IN	46032	317-844-3110		2
Claverack Rural Electric Co-op Inc 32750 W US 6 *TF:* 800-326-9799 ■ *Web:* www.claverack.com	Wysox	PA	18854	570-265-2167	265-6019	245
Claws 'n' Paws Wild Animal Park 1475 Ledgedale Rd *Web:* www.clawsnpaws.com	Lake Ariel	PA	18436	570-698-6154		823
Clawson Tank Co 4701 White Lake Rd *TF:* 800-272-1367 ■ *Web:* www.clawsontank.com	Clarkston	MI	48346	248-625-8700	625-3066	91
Claxton Poultry Farms 8816 Hwy 301 N *TF:* 888-739-3181 ■ *Web:* www.claxtonpoultry.com	Claxton	GA	30417	912-739-3181		619
Claxton Printing Co Inc 1118 Culpepper Dr SW *Web:* www.claxtonprinting.com	Conyers	GA	30094	404-521-0933		627
Claxton-Hepburn Medical Ctr 214 King St **Fax:* Hum Res ■ *TF:* 888-220-0042 ■ *Web:* www.claxtonhepburn.org	Ogdensburg	NY	13669	315-393-3600	393-8506*	374-3
Clay County 25 Court Sq *Web:* claycountyprobate.com	Ashland	AL	36251	256-354-2198	354-4778	338
Clay County 609 E National Ave Rm 211 *Web:* www.claycountyin.gov	Brazil	IN	47834	812-448-9023	446-9602	338
Clay County 424 Brown St *TF:* 800-264-3161 ■ *Web:* www.dalehollowlake.org	Celina	TN	38551	931-243-3338	243-6809	338
Clay County 712 Fifth St *TF:* 800-368-8683 ■ *Web:* claycountykansas.org	Clay Center	KS	67432	785-632-2552	632-5856	338
Clay County PO Box 519 *Web:* www.georgia.gov	Fort Gaines	GA	39851	229-768-3238	768-3672	338
Clay County 477 Houston St *Web:* www.claycountygov.com	Green Cove Springs	FL	32043	904-284-6376	284-9780	338
Clay County 33 Main St *TF:* 800-849-0496 ■ *Web:* www.clayconc.com	Hayesville	NC	28904	828-389-0089	389-9749	338
Clay County PO Box 548 *TF:* 800-388-8075 ■ *Web:* www.co.clay.tx.us	Henrietta	TX	76365	940-538-4631	538-5597	338
Clay County 1 Courthouse Sq *TF:* 800-552-7583 ■ *Web:* claycoelections.com	Liberty	MO	64068	816-407-3600		338
Clay County PO Box 160 *Web:* www.claycountyillinois.org	Louisville	IL	62858	618-665-3626	665-3607	338
Clay County 807 11th St N *Web:* claycountymn.gov	Moorhead	MN	56560	218-299-5012	299-5195	338
Clay County 215 W Fourth St *Web:* www.co.clay.ia.us	Spencer	IA	51301	712-262-9438		338
Clay County 211 W Main St Ste 200 *Web:* www.claycountysd.org	Vermillion	SD	57069	605 677 7120	677 7104	338
Clay County PO Box 815 *Web:* www.claycountyms.com	West Point	MS	39773	662-494-3124	492-4059	338
Clay County Chamber of Commerce 1734 Kingsley Ave *TF:* 800-435-7352 ■ *Web:* www.claychamber.com	Orange Park	FL	32073	904-264-2651	264-0070	139
Clay County Electric Co-op Corp 3111 US-67 *TF:* 800-521-2450 ■ *Web:* www.claycountyelectric.com	Corning	AR	72422	870-857-3521	857-3523	245
Clay County Savings Bank 1178 W Kansas St PO Box 277 *Web:* www.claycountysavings.com	Liberty	MO	64069	816-781-4500	781-1668	70
Clay Ctr for the Arts & Sciences 1 Clay Sq *Web:* www.theclaycenter.org	Charleston	WV	25301	304-561-3570		572
Clay Dunn Enterprises Inc 1606 E Carson St *TF:* 800-605-2247 ■ *Web:* www.airtecperforms.com	Carson	CA	90745	310-549-1698		35

	Phone	Fax	Class
Clay Electric Co-op Inc 225 W Walker Dr SR100 PO Box 308 . . . . . Keystone Heights FL 32656 *TF:* 800-224-4917 ■ *Web:* www.clayelectric.com	352-473-8000	473-1403	245
Clay Herman Realtor Inc 251 Park Rd Ste 710 . . . . . Burlingame CA 94010 *Web:* clayherman.com	650-342-1141		652
Clay Ingels Company LLC 914 Delaware Ave . . . . . Lexington KY 40505 *Web:* www.clay-ingels.com	859-252-0836		191-1
Clay Lacy Aviation 7435 Valjean Ave . . . . . Van Nuys CA 91406 *TF:* 800-423-2904 ■ *Web:* www.claylacy.com	818-989-2900	904-3450	13
Clay Pit 1601 Guadalupe St . . . . . Austin TX 78701 *Web:* www.claypit.com	512-322-5131		671
Clay Pit Ponds State Park Preserve 83 Nielsen Ave . . . . . Staten Island NY 10309 *Web:* parks.ny.gov/parks/166/details.aspx	718-967-1976	966-5294	565
Clay Pit State Vehicular Recreation Area 400 Glen Dr . . . . . Oroville CA 95966 *Web:* www.parks.ca.gov	530-538-2200		565
Clay Today 3513 US Hwy 17 . . . . . Fleming Island FL 32003 *TF:* 888-434-9844 ■ *Web:* www.claytodayonline.com	904-264-3200		532-4
Clay William "Lacy" Jr (Rep D - MO) 2428 Rayburn HOB . . . . . Washington DC 20515 *Web:* lacyclay.house.gov	202-225-2406	226-3717	342-2
Claybar Constracting Inc 424 Macnab St . . . . . Dundas ON L9H2L3 *TF:* 866-801-9305 ■ *Web:* www.claybar.ca	905-627-8000		610
Clayton & Mckervey PC 2000 Town Ctr Ste 1800 . . . . . Southfield MI 48075 *Web:* www.claytonmckervey.com	248-208-8860		2
Clayton Block Co PO Box 3015 . . . . . Lakewood NJ 08701 **Fax Area Code:* 732 ■ *TF:* 800-662-3044 ■ *Web:* www.claytonco.com	800-662-3044	751-7618*	183
Clayton Capital Partners 8112 Maryland Ave Ste 250 . . . . . St. Louis MO 63105 *TF:* 800-383-8000 ■ *Web:* claytoncapitalpartners.com	314-725-9939		317
Clayton Corp 866 Horan Dr . . . . . Fenton MO 63026 *TF Cust Svc:* 800-729-8220 ■ *Web:* www.claytoncorp.com	636-349-5333	349-5335	601
Clayton Cos, The PO Box 3015 . . . . . Lakewood NJ 08701 *TF:* 800-662-3044 ■ *Web:* www.claytonco.com	800-662-3044		183
Clayton County 111 High St NE . . . . . Elkader IA 52043 *Web:* www.claytoncountyiowa.net	563-245-2204		338
Clayton County 112 Smith St . . . . . Jonesboro GA 30236 *Web:* www.co.clayton.ga.us	770-477-3211	477-3217	338
Clayton County Chamber of Commerce 2270 Mt Zion Rd . . . . . Jonesboro GA 30236 *Web:* www.claytonchamber.org	678-610-4021	610-4025	139
Clayton County Library System 865 Battle Creek Rd . . . . . Jonesboro GA 30236 *Web:* claytonpl.org	770-473-3850		434-3
Clayton Dubilier & Rice Inc 375 Pk Ave 18th Fl . . . . . New York NY 10152 *Web:* www.cdr-inc.com	212-407-5200	407-5252	403
Clayton Environmental Services Inc 808 Walker St . . . . . Columbia TN 38401 *Web:* www.vendorbit.com/cms/claytonenvironmental	931-388-6806		445
Clayton Holdings LLC 100 BeaRd Sawmill Rd Ste 200 . . . . . Shelton CT 06484 *TF:* 877-291-5301 ■ *Web:* www.clayton.com	203-926-5600		360-3
Clayton Industries 17477 Hurley St . . . . . City of Industry CA 01744 *TF:* 800-423-4585 ■ *Web:* www.claytonindustries.com	626-435-1200	435-0180	472
Clayton Lake State Park Hwy 271 . . . . . Clayton OK 74536 *Web:* www.travelok.com	918-569-7981		565
Clayton Levy & Little Architects 1001 E Eighth St . . . . . Austin TX 78702 *Web:* www.claytonlevylittle.com	512-477-1727		41
Clayton Metals Inc 546 Clayton Ct . . . . . Wood Dale IL 60191 **Fax Area Code:* 630 ■ *TF:* 800-323-7628 ■ *Web:* www.claytonmetals.com	800-323-7628	860-1053*	492
Clayton Neighbor 5442 Frontage Rd Ste 130 . . . . . Forest Park GA 30297 *Web:* www.mdjonline.com/neighbor_newspapers	404-363-8484		532-4
Clayton on the Park 7343 Scottsdale Mall . . . . . Scottsdale AZ 85251 *Web:* www.theclaytononthepark.com	480-990-7300		379
Clayton State University 2000 Clayton State Blvd . . . . . Morrow GA 30260 **Fax:* Admissions ■ *TF:* 800-533-2062 ■ *Web:* www.clayton.edu	678-466-4000	466-4149*	166
Clayton Tile Distributing Company Inc 535 Woodruff Rd . . . . . Greenville SC 29607 *Web:* claytontileco.com	864-288-6290		290
Clayton Williams Energy Inc 6 Desta Dr . . . . . Midland TX 79705 *NASDAQ: CWEI* ■ *TF:* 800-690-6903 ■ *Web:* www.claytonwilliams.com	432-682-6324		536
Claytor Lake State Park 6620 Ben H Boden Dr . . . . . Dublin VA 24084 *Web:* www.dcr.virginia.gov	540-643-2500		565
Clay-Union Electric Corp 1410 E Cherry St PO Box 317 . . . . . Vermillion SD 57069 *TF:* 800-696-2832 ■ *Web:* www.clayunionelectric.coop	605-624-2673		245
Clayworks Ltd 629 Bedford Hwy . . . . . Halifax NS B3M2L6 *Web:* clayworks.ca	902-445-4453		361
CLC (Challenger Learning Ctr) 316 Washington Ave Wheeling Jesuit University . . . . . Wheeling WV 26003 *TF:* 800-624-6992 ■ *Web:* www.wju.edu/clc	304-243-2279	243-4397	520
CLC Inc 3001 Lava Ridge Ct . . . . . Roseville CA 95661 *Web:* www.clcincorporated.com	916-789-7600		2
CLC Networks 2275 Northwest Pkwy SE Ste 110 . . . . . Marietta GA 30067 *Web:* www.clcnetworks.com	678-564-0522		529
Clean Air Engineering Inc 500 W Wood St . . . . . Palatine IL 60067 *TF:* 800-553-5511 ■ *Web:* www.cleanair.com	847-991-3300		41
Clean Air Report 1919 S Eads St Ste 201 . . . . . Arlington VA 22202 *TF:* 800-424-9068 ■ *Web:* www.insideepa.com	703-416-8505	416-8543	531-5
Clean Air Solutions Inc 826 Bayridge Pl . . . . . Fairfield CA 94534 *Web:* www.cleanroomspecialists.com	707-864-9499		246

	Phone	Fax	Class
Clean Air Technology Inc 41105 Capital Dr . . . . . Canton MI 48187 **Fax Area Code:* 734 ■ *TF:* 800-459-6320 ■ *Web:* www.cleanairtechnology.com	800-459-6320	459-9437*	449
Clean Coal Technologies Inc 12th Fl 295 Madison Ave . . . . . New York NY 10017 *Web:* www.cleancoaltechnologiesinc.com	646-710-3549		202
Clean Design Inc 6601 Six Forks Rd Ste 400 . . . . . Raleigh NC 27615 *Web:* www.cleandesign.com	919-544-2193		4
Clean Diesel Technologies Inc 4567 Telephone Rd Ste 206 . . . . . Ventura CA 93003 *NASDAQ: CDTI* ■ *TF:* 800-661-9963 ■ *Web:* www.cdti.com	805-639-9458		386
Clean Earth of North Jersey Inc 115 Jacobus Ave . . . . . South Kearny NJ 07032 *TF:* 877-445-3478 ■ *Web:* cleanearthinc.com	973-344-4004	344-8652	660
Clean Foods Inc 760 E Santa Maria St . . . . . Santa Paula CA 93060 *Web:* cafealtura.com	805-933-3027		297-8
Clean Fuels Ohio 530 W Spring St Ste 250 . . . . . Columbus OH 43215 *Web:* cleanfuelsohio.org	614-884-7336		580
Clean Harbors Inc 42 Longwater Dr PO Box 9149 . . . . . Norwell MA 02061 *NYSE: CLH* ■ *TF:* 800-282-0058 ■ *Web:* www.cleanharbors.com	781-792-5000		667
Clean Master 2201 Park Ave . . . . . Chico CA 95928 *Web:* www.onlyforpc.com	530-343-0123		577
Clean Ones Corp PO Box 40008 . . . . . Portland OR 97240 *TF:* 800-367-4587 ■ *Web:* www.cleanones.com	800-367-4587		256
Clean Power LLC 124 N 121st St . . . . . Milwaukee WI 53226 *TF:* 800-588-1608 ■ *Web:* www.cleanpower1.com	414-302-3000		152
Clean Rooms West Inc 1392 Industrial Dr . . . . . Tustin CA 92780 *Web:* www.cleanroomswest.com	714-258-7700		385
Clean Street Inc 1937 W 169th St . . . . . Gardena CA 90247 **Fax Area Code:* 310 ■ *TF:* 800-225-7316 ■ *Web:* www.cleanstreet.com	800-225-7316	538-8015*	667
Clean Tech Inc 500 Dunham St . . . . . Dundee MI 48131 *Web:* www.cleantechrestoration.com	734-529-2475		506
Clean Uniform Co 1316 S Seventh St . . . . . St. Louis MO 63104 *Web:* www.cleanuniform.com	314-421-1220		393
Clean Water Action 4455 Connecticut Ave NW . . . . . Washington DC 20008 *TF:* 800-657-3864 ■ *Web:* www.cleanwateraction.org	202-895-0420	895-0438	48-13
Cleaning Authority 7230 Lee DeForest Dr . . . . . Columbia MD 21046 *TF:* 888-658-0659 ■ *Web:* www.thecleaningauthority.com	888-658-0659		310
CleanNet USA 9861 Brokenland Pkwy Ste 208 . . . . . Columbia MD 21046 *TF:* 800-735-8838 ■ *Web:* www.cleannetusa.com	410-720-6444	720-5307	152
Cleanroom Systems 7000 Performance Dr . . . . . North Syracuse NY 13212 *TF:* 800-825-3268 ■ *Web:* www.cleanroomsystems.com	315-452-7400	452-7420	18
Clean-Tech Co 211 S Jefferson Ave . . . . . Saint Louis MO 63103 *Web:* www.cleantechcompany.com	314-652-2388		152
Cleantech Open, The 425 Broadway . . . . . Redwood City CA 94063 *TF:* 888-989-6736 ■ *Web:* www.cleantechopen.com	888-989-6736		463
Cleanwise Inc 1100 E Woodfield Rd Ste 200 . . . . . Schaumburg IL 60173 *TF:* 877-790-2497 ■ *Web:* www.cleanwise.com	877-255-5230		393
CLEAR (Council on Licensure Enforcement & Regulation) 403 Marquis Ave . . . . . Lexington KY 40502 *Web:* www.clearhq.org	859-269-1289		49-7
Clear Align LLC 2550 Blvd Of The Generals Ste 280 . . . . . Eagleville PA 19403 *Web:* www.clearalign.com	484-956-0510		256
Clear Blue Skies Communications 2 Thatcher St . . . . . Hyde Park MA 02136	617-361-3229		194
Clear Brook Manor 1100 E Northampton St . . . . . Laurel Run PA 18706 *TF:* 800-582-6241 ■ *Web:* clearbrookinc.com	800-582-6241		726
Clear Ch Outdoor Inc 2325 E Camelback Rd Ste 400 . . . . . Phoenix AZ 85016 *Web:* www.clearchanneloutdoor.com	602-381-5700		8
Clear Comfort Water 3063 Sterling Cir Unit 8 . . . . . Boulder CO 80301 *Web:* clearcomfort.com	303-872-4477		192
Clear Creek Baptist Bible College 300 Clear Creek Rd . . . . . Pineville KY 40977 *TF:* 866-340-3196 ■ *Web:* www.ccbbc.edu	606-337-3196	337-2372	161
Clear Creek County 405 Argentine St . . . . . Georgetown CO 80444 *Web:* www.co.clear-creek.co.us	303-679-2312	679-2440	338
Clear Creek State Park 38 Clear Creek State Pk Rd . . . . . Sigel PA 15860 *Web:* www.dcnr.state.pa.us	814-752-2368		565
Clear Edge Technical Fabrics 7160 Northland Cir N . . . . . Minneapolis MN 55428 *TF:* 800-328-3036 ■ *Web:* www.clear-edge.com/products/technical-fabrics	763-535-3220	535-6040	745-3
Clear Government Solutions Inc 11850 Baltimore Ave . . . . . Beltsville MD 20705 *Web:* www.cleargovsolutions.com	301-289-3000		225
Clear Image Printing Inc 731 W Wilson Ave . . . . . Glendale CA 91203 *Web:* clearimageprinting.com	818-547-4684		627
Clear Labs 2529 Central Ave Ste 203 . . . . . St. Petersburg FL 33713 *Web:* www.theclearagency.com	727-289-7204		7
Clear Lake Area Chamber of Commerce 1201 NASA Pkwy . . . . . Houston TX 77058 *TF:* 800-877-8339 ■ *Web:* www.clearlakearea.com	281-488-7676	488-8981	139
Clear Lake Convention & Visitors Bureau 205 Main Ave PO Box 188 . . . . . Clear Lake IA 50428 *TF:* 800-285-5338 ■ *Web:* www.clearlakeiowa.com	641-357-2159	357-8141	206
Clear Lake Regional Medical Ctr 500 W Medical Ctr Blvd . . . . . Webster TX 77598 *Web:* www.clearlakermc.com	281-332-2511		374-3
Clear Lake State Park 2730 S Lakeview Dr . . . . . Clear Lake IA 50428 *Web:* www.iowadnr.gov	641-357-4212		565

	Phone	Fax	Class
Clear Lake State Park 20500 M-33 N. Atlanta MI 49709	989-785-4388		565
Web: www.michigandnr.com			
Clear Lam Packaging Inc			
1950 Pratt Blvd. Elk Grove Village IL 60007	847-439-8570	439-8589	548
Web: www.clearlam.com			
Clear Link Technologies LLC			
5202 W Douglas Corrigan Way Ste 300 Salt Lake City UT 84116	801-424-0018		195
Web: www.clearlink.com			
Clear Pack Co			
11610 Copenhagen Ct Franklin Park IL 60131	847-957-6282		596
Clear Resolution Consulting LLC			
5523 Research Park Dr Ste 240 Baltimore MD 21228	443-543-5260		196
Web: www.crctoday.com			
Clear Seas Research 2401 W Big Beaver Rd. Troy MI 48084	248-786-1683		466
TF: 800-811-6640 ■ *Web:* clearseas.mobi			
Clear Technologies Inc			
16650 Westgrove Rd Ste 400 Addison TX 75001	972-906-7500		525
Web: www.cleartechnologies.net			
Clear View Bag Co 5 Burdick Dr. Albany NY 12205	518-458-7153	458-1401	66
TF: 800-458-7153 ■ *Web:* www.clearviewbag.com			
Clear View Sanitarium & Convalescent Ctr			
15823 S Western Ave Gardena CA 90247	310-538-2323	538-3509	450
TF: 800-321-1245 ■ *Web:* clearviewcare.com			
Clear Water Outdoor LLC			
744 W Main St Lake Geneva WI 53147	262-348-2420		711
Web: www.clearwateroutdoor.com			
ClearBridge Compensation Group LLC			
515 Madison Ave 32nd Fl. New York NY 10022	212-886-1022		194
Web: www.clearbridgecomp.com			
Clearbridge Technology Group			
6 Fortune Dr Billerica MA 01821	781-916-2284		260
TF: 877-808-2284 ■ *Web:* www.clearbridgetech.com			
Clear-Com USA 850 Marina Village Pkwy Alameda CA 94501	510-337-6600		392
TF: 800-462-4357 ■ *Web:* www.clearcom.com			
ClearConnex Inc			
1021 Main Campus Rd Ste 300 Raleigh NC 27606	760-845-4028		196
ClearCreek Partners			
1165 Delaware St Ste 130. Denver CO 80204	303-383-1100		194
Web: www.clearcreekpartners.com			
ClearEdge IT Solutions LLC			
10620 Guilford Rd Ste 200. Jessup MD 20794	443-212-4700		196
Web: www.clearedgeit.com			
Clearedge Mktg LLC			
415 N Lasalle St Ste 202 Chicago Il 60654	312-731-3149		194
Web: www.clearedgemarketing.com			
ClearEdge Partners Inc			
8 Pleasant St Ste E-2 South Natick MA 01760	508-655-1022		631
Web: www.clearedgepartners.com			
CLEAResult 4301 Westbank Dr Ste 300 Austin TX 78746	512-327-9200		194
Web: www.clearesult.com			
Clearfield County 230 E Market St Clearfield PA 16830	814-765-2641	765-2640	338
Web: www.clearfieldco.org			
Clearfield Hospital			
809 Tpke Ave PO Box 992 Clearfield PA 16830	814-765-5341		374-3
TF: 800-281-8000 ■ *Web:* phhealthcare.org			
ClearFreight Inc			
880 Apollo St Ste 101. El Segundo CA 90245	310-726-0400		345
Web: www.clearfreight.com			
Clearinghouse Community Development Financial Institution			
23861 El Toro Rd Ste 401. Lake Forest CA 92630	949-859-3600		41
Web: www.clearinghousecdfi.com			
Clearlight Glass & Mirror Inc			
1318 Shields Rd Kernersville NC 27284	336-993-7300		362
TF: 800-420-2337 ■ *Web:* www.clearlightglass.com			
ClearOne Communications Inc			
5225 Wiley Post Way Salt Lake City UT 84116	801-975-7200	977-0087	735
TF: 800-945-7730 ■ *Web:* www.clearone.com			
Clearpath Capital Partners			
222 Front St 3rd Fl San Francisco CA 94111	415-682-6900		627
Web: clearpathcapital.com			
ClearPath Diagnostics			
600 E Genesee St Ste 305. Syracuse NY 13202	315-234-3300		418
Web: www.clearpathdiagnostics.com			
ClearPoint Inc 89 Willow Ave Unit 1R. Hoboken NJ 07030	201-683-9944		177
Web: www.clearpointlearning.com			
ClearSail Communications LLC			
3950 Braxton Houston TX 77063	713-230-2800		398
TF: 888-905-0888 ■ *Web:* www.clearsail.net			
ClearShot Communications LLC			
5 Great Vly Pkwy Ste 333 Malvern PA 19355	610-648-3895		387
Clearsign Combustion Corp			
12870 Interurban Ave S Seattle WA 98168	206-673-4848		201
Web: www.clearsign.com			
Clearspan Components Inc			
6110 Old Hwy 80 W Meridian MS 39307	601-483-3941	483-3941	105
TF: 800-478-0258 ■ *Web:* merchantcircle.com			
Clearspring Capital Group			
11000 Richmond Ste 550. Houston TX 77042	713-339-1903		401
Web: www.clearspringcapitalgroup.com			
ClearStaff Inc			
251 N Bolingbrook Dr. Bolingbrook IL 60440	630-759-2900	759-2919	260
Web: www.clearstaff.net			
Clearstone Venture Partners			
725 Arizona Ave Ste 304. Santa Monica CA 90401	310-460-7900		792
Web: www.clearstone.com			
ClearStream Energy Services LP			
2112 Premier Way Sherwood Park AB T8H2G4	780-410-9835		536
TF: 855-410-9835 ■ *Web:* www.clearstreamenergy.ca			
ClearTech Industries Inc			
2302 Hanselman Ave Saskatoon SK S7L5Z3	306-664-2522		146
Web: www.cleartech.ca			
ClearTrade Inc			
5415 N Sheridan Rd Ste 5512 Chicago IL 60640	773-561-9777		169
Web: www.cleartrade.com			
Clearview Cleaning Service			
1804 Windermere Ave. Wilmington DE 19804	302-994-5215		256
Clear-view Technologies Inc			
1722 Ringwood Ave Ste 200. San Jose CA 95131	408-512-3549		463

	Phone	Fax	Class
Clear-Vu Products Inc			
29 New York Ave. Westbury NY 11590	516-333-8880		601
Web: www.clear-vu.com			
Clearwater Christian College			
3400 Gulf to Bay Blvd. Clearwater FL 33759	727-726-1153		166
Web: www.clearwater.edu			
Clearwater County 213 Main Ave N. Bagley MN 56621	218-694-6520	694-6244*	338
**Fax:* Acctg ■ *TF:* 800-368-8683 ■ *Web:* www.co.clearwater.mn.us			
Clearwater County 150 Michigan Ave Orofino ID 83544	208-476-3615		338
TF: 800-632-0905 ■ *Web:* www.clearwatercounty.org			
Clearwater Marine Aquarium			
249 Windward Passage Clearwater FL 33767	727-441-1790		40
Web: www.seewinter.com			
Clearwater Power Co			
4230 Hatwai Rd PO Box 997. Lewiston ID 83501	208-743-1501	746-3902	245
TF: 888-743-1501 ■ *Web:* www.clearwaterpower.com			
Clearwater Public Library			
100 N Osceola Ave Clearwater FL 33755	727-562-4970	562-4977	434-3
TF: 800-342-8060 ■ *Web:* www.myclearwater.com/cpl			
Clearwater Regional Chamber of Commerce			
401 Cleveland St Clearwater FL 33755	727-461-0011	449-2889	139
TF: 877-447-7356 ■ *Web:* www.clearwaterflorida.org			
Clearwater Spas			
18800 Woodinville Snohomish Rd Woodinville WA 98072	425-481-1918		610
Web: www.clearwaterspas.com			
Clearwater State Recreation Site			
3700 Airport Way Fairbanks AK 99709	907-451-2695		565
Web: www.dnr.alaska.gov			
Clearwater-Polk Electric Co-op			
315 Main Ave N Bagley MN 56621	218-694-6241		245
TF: 888-694-3833 ■ *Web:* www.clearwater-polk.com			
Cleary Building Corp 190 Paoli St Verona WI 53593	608-845-9700		186
TF: 800-373-5550 ■ *Web:* clearybuilding.com			
Cleary Gottlieb Steen & Hamilton			
1 Liberty Plaza New York NY 10006	212-225-2000		41
Web: www.cgsh.com			
Cleary Millwork Company Inc			
235 Dividend Rd. Rocky Hill CT 06067	800-486-7600		191-3
TF: 800-486-7600 ■ *Web:* www.clearymillwork.com			
Cleary University 3601 Plymouth Rd Ann Arbor MI 48105	734-332-4477	332-4646	800
TF: 800-686-1883 ■ *Web:* www.cleary.edu			
Livingston 3750 Cleary Dr. Howell MI 48843	517-548-3670	552-7805	800
TF: 800-686-1883 ■ *Web:* www.cleary.edu			
Cleary Zimmermann Engineers Inc			
1344 S Flores St. San Antonio TX 78204	210-447-6100		261
Web: www.clearyzimmermann.com			
Cleaveland Price Inc 14000 Rt 993. Trafford PA 15085	724-864-4177		729
Web: www.cleavelandprice.com			
Cleaver Brooks 221 Law St. Thomasville GA 31792	229-226-3024	226-3027	91
TF: 800-250-5883 ■ *Web:* www.cleaver-brooks.com			
Cleaver Brooks			
11950 West Lake Pk Dr. Milwaukee WI 53224	414-359-0600		91
Web: www.cleaverbrooks.com			
Cleaver Emanuel (Rep D - MO)			
2335 Rayburn Bldg. Washington DC 20515	202-225-4535	225-4403	342-2
Web: cleaver.house.gov			
Cleburne Chamber of Commerce			
1511 W Henderson St. Cleburne TX 76033	817-645-2455	641-3069	139
TF: 800-621-8566 ■ *Web:* www.cleburnechamber.com			
Cleburne County 300 W Main St. Heber Springs AR 72543	501-362-8402	362-4605	338
Web: www.cleburnecountyar.com			
Cleburne County 120 Vickery St Rm 202 Heflin AL 36264	256-463-2651		338
Web: cleburnecounty.us			
Cleburne State Park 5800 Pk Rd 21 Cleburne TX 76033	817-645-4215		565
Web: tpwd.texas.gov/state-parks/cleburne			
Cleco Corp 2030 Donahue Ferry Rd. Pineville LA 71361	318-484-7400		787
TF Cust Svc: 800-622-6537 ■ *Web:* cleco.com			
Cleft Palate Foundation (CPF)			
1504 E Franklin St Ste 102. Chapel Hill NC 27514	919-933-9044	933-9604	48-17
TF: 800-242-5338 ■ *Web:* www.cleftline.org			
Cleftstone Manor 92 Eden St. Bar Harbor ME 04609	207-288-8086		379
TF: 888-288-4951 ■ *Web:* www.cleftstone.com			
Clegg's Termite and Pest Control LLC			
2401 Reichard St Durham NC 27705	919-477-2134		577
Web: www.cleggs.com			
Cleland Site Prep Inc PO Box 3822. Bluffton SC 29910	843-987-0500		261
Web: www.clelandsiteprep.com			
Clemco Industries Corp			
l Cable Car Dr. Washington MO 63090	636-239-0300	726-7559*	386
**Fax Area Code:* 800 ■ *Web:* www.clemcoindustries.com			
Clemens Construction Company Inc			
1435 Walnut St 2nd Fl Philadelphia PA 19102	215-567-5757		186
Web: www.clemensconstruction.com			
Clement Communications Inc			
3 Creek Pkwy Upper Chichester PA 19061	610-459-4200		637-10
TF: 800-253-6368 ■ *Web:* www.clement.com			
Clement Industries Inc PO Box 914 Minden LA 71058	318-377-2776	377-2776	779
TF Cust Svc: 800-562-5948 ■ *Web:* www.clementind.com			
Clement Manor 3939 S 92nd St Greenfield WI 53228	414-321-1800		450
Web: www.clementmanor.com			
Clement Support Services Inc			
480 Vandell Way. Campbell CA 95008	408-227-1171		612
Clementia			
4150 Ste-Catherine St W Ste 550. Montreal QC H3Z2Y5	514-940-3600		476
Web: clementiapharma.com			
Clementon Amusement Park & Splash World Waterpark			
144 Berlin Rd Clementon NJ 08021	856-783-0263		31
Web: www.clementonpark.com			
Clements Marketplace Inc			
2575 E Main Rd Portsmouth RI 02871	401-683-0180		345
Web: www.clementsmarket.com			
Clements National Co			
6650 S Narragansett Ave. Chicago IL 60638	708-594-5890	594-2481	18
TF: 800-966-0016 ■ *Web:* www.cadillacproducts.com			
Clemson Univ Service			
605 W Main St Ste 109. Lexington SC 29072	803-785-8515		794
Clemson University 105 Sikes Hall Clemson SC 29634	864-656-3311	656-2464*	166
**Fax:* Admissions ■ *TF:* 800-640-2657 ■ *Web:* www.clemson.edu			

	Phone	Fax	Class
Clemson University 201 Sikes Hall PO Box 343001................Clemson SC 29634 *Web:* www.clemson.edu	864-656-5186		434-6
Cleo Parker Robinson Dance 119 Pk Ave W................................Denver CO 80205 *Web:* www.cleoparkerdance.org	303-295-1759		573-1
Clermont Chamber of Commerce 4355 Ferguson Dr Ste 150..................Cincinnati OH 45245 *Web:* www.clermontchamber.com	513-576-5000	576-5001	139
Clermont County 101 E Main St.................Batavia OH 45103 *Web:* www.clermontcountyohio.gov	513-732-7300	732-7921	338
Clermont County Convention & Visitors Bureau (CCCVB) 410 E Main St PO Box 100....................Batavia OH 45103 *TF:* 800-796-4282 ■ *Web:* www.visitclermontohio.com	513-732-3600		206
Clermont County Public Library System 326 Broadway St.............................Batavia OH 45103 *Web:* clermontlibrary.org	513-732-2736	732-3177	434-3
Clermont Mercy Hospital 3000 Hospital Dr............................Batavia OH 45103	513-732-8200		374-3
Clermont State Historic Site 1 Clermont Ave..........................Germantown NY 12526 *TF:* 800-456-2267 ■ *Web:* parks.ny.gov/historic-sites/16/hunting.aspx	518-537-4240	537-6240	565
Clermont Steel Fabricators LLC 2565 Old SR 32.............................Batavia OH 45103 *Web:* www.clermontsteel.com	513-732-6033	732-5344	480
Clerysys Inc 30 S Wacker Dr Ste 2200...........Chicago IL 60606 *Web:* www.clerysys.com	312-466-7500		809
Cleveland Biolabs Inc 73 High St...............Buffalo NY 14203 *NASDAQ: CBLI* ■ *Web:* www.cbiolabs.com	716-849-6810		668
Cleveland Botanical Garden 11030 E Blvd.............................Cleveland OH 44106 *Web:* www.cbgarden.org	216-721-1600	721-2056	97
Cleveland Bradley County Public Library 795 N Church St NE........................Cleveland TN 37311 *TF:* 800-342-3262 ■ *Web:* www.clevelandlibrary.org	423-472-2163		434-3
Cleveland Bros Equipment Company Inc 5300 Paxton St...........................Harrisburg PA 17111 *TF:* 866-551-4602 ■ *Web:* www.clevelandbrothers.com	717-564-2121		358
Cleveland Browns 76 Lou Groza Blvd.............Berea OH 44017 *Web:* www.clevelandbrowns.com	440-891-5000		715-3
Cleveland Cavaliers Quicken Loans Arena 1 Ctr Ct................Cleveland OH 44115 **Fax:* PR ■ *TF:* 800-332-2287 ■ *Web:* www.nba.com	216-420-2000	420-2298*	714-1
Cleveland Cement Contractors Inc 4823 Van Epps Rd.........................Cleveland OH 44131 *TF:* 800-221-0323 ■ *Web:* www.clevelandcement.com	216-741-3954	741-9278	189-3
Cleveland Chamber Symphony, The (CCS) 11125 Magnolia Dr The Music School Settlement.................Cleveland OH 44106 *Web:* www.clevelandchambersymphony.org	216-202-4227		573-3
Cleveland Chiropractic College of Los Angeles Inc 590 N Vermont Ave......................Los Angeles CA 90004 *Web:* www.cleveland.edu	913-234-0600		166
Cleveland City Hall 601 Lakeside Ave..........................Cleveland OH 44114 *TF:* 800-589-3101 ■ *Web:* www.cleveland-oh.gov	216-664-2000		337
Cleveland Clinic 2049 E 100th St.............Cleveland OH 44195 *Web:* my.clevelandclinic.org	216-444-2200		374-3
Cleveland Clinic 9500 Euclid Ave.............Cleveland OH 44195 *TF:* 800-223-2273 ■ *Web:* my.clevelandclinic.org	216-444-2200		374-3
Cleveland Clinic Hospital 2950 Cleveland Clinic Blvd..................Weston FL 33331 *TF:* 866-293-7866 ■ *Web:* my.clevelandclinic.org	954-689-5000		374-3
Cleveland Community College 137 S Post Rd..............................Shelby NC 28152 *Web:* clevelandcc.edu	704-484-4000		162
Cleveland Construction Inc 8620 Tyler Blvd.............................Mentor OH 44060 *Web:* www.clevelandconstruction.com	440-255-8000	205-1138	189-9
Cleveland Corp 42810 N Green Bay Rd.............Zion IL 60099 *TF:* 800-281-3464 ■ *Web:* www.clevelandcorp.com	847-872-7200		686
Cleveland Costume & Display 1271 Pearl Rd...........................Brunswick OH 44212 *Web:* clevelandcostume.com	440-846-9292		155-6
Cleveland County 2550 W Franklin Rd...........Norman OK 73069 *Web:* www.clevelandcountyok.com	405-701-8888		338
Cleveland County PO Box 368...................Rison AR 71665 *Web:* www.argenweb.net/cleveland	870-325-6214		338
Cleveland County 311 E Marion St..............Shelby NC 28150 *Web:* www.clevelandcounty.com	704-484-4800	484-4930	338
Cleveland County Chamber of Commerce 200 S Lafayette St..........................Shelby NC 28150 *Web:* www.clevelandchamber.org	704-487-8521	487-7458	139
Cleveland Die & Manufacturing Co 20303 First Ave...................Middleburg Heights OH 44130 *Web:* www.clevelanddie.com	440-243-3404		483
Cleveland Electric Labortories 1776 Enterprise Pkwy.....................Twinsburg OH 44087 *Web:* www.clevelandelectriclabs.com	330-425-4747		201
Cleveland Foundation 1422 Euclid Ave Ste 1300...................Cleveland OH 44115 *TF:* 877-554-5054 ■ *Web:* www.clevelandfoundation.org	216-861-3810		303
Cleveland Gear Co 3249 E 80th St............Cleveland OH 44104 *TF:* 800-423-3169 ■ *Web:* www.clevelandgear.com	216-641-9000	641-2731	709
Cleveland Golf Co 5601 Skylab Rd....................Huntington Beach CA 92647 *TF Cust Svc:* 800-999-6263 ■ *Web:* www.clevelandgolf.com	800-999-6263		710
Cleveland Group Inc 1281 Fulton Industrial Blvd...................Atlanta GA 30336 *Web:* www.clevelandelectric.com	404-696-4550		189-4
Cleveland Health Sciences Library (CHSL) *Case Western Reserve University Robbins Bldg* 2109 Adelbert Rd..........................Cleveland OH 44106 *Web:* www.case.edu/chsl/library/index.html	216-368-4540		434-1
Cleveland HeartLab Inc 6701 Carnegie Ave Ste 500.................Cleveland OH 44103 *TF:* 866-358-9828 ■ *Web:* www.clevelandheartlab.com	866-358-9828		415
Cleveland Heights-University Heights Public Library 2345 Lee Rd......................Cleveland Heights OH 44118 *Web:* www.heightslibrary.org	216-932-3600	932-0932	434-3
Cleveland Hopkins International Airport 5300 Riverside Dr.........................Cleveland OH 44135 *Web:* www.clevelandairport.com	216-265-6000	265-6021	27
Cleveland Indians 2401 Ontario St............Cleveland OH 44115 *Web:* cleveland.indians.mlb.com	216-420-4487		713
Cleveland Institute of Art 11141 E Blvd..............................Cleveland OH 44106 **Fax Area Code:* 216 ■ *TF:* 800-223-4700 ■ *Web:* www.cia.edu	800-223-4700	754-3634*	164
Cleveland Institute of Electronics 1776 E 17th St............................Cleveland OH 44114 *TF:* 800-243-6446 ■ *Web:* www.cie-wc.edu	216-781-9400	781-0331	800
Cleveland Institute of Music 11021 E Blvd..............................Cleveland OH 44106 *TF:* 800-686-1141 ■ *Web:* www.cim.edu	216-791-5000	791-3063	166
Cleveland International Film Festival 2510 Market Ave...........................Cleveland OH 44113 *Web:* www.clevelandfilm.org	216-623-3456	623-0103	282
Cleveland Magazine 1422 Euclid Ave Ste 730....................Cleveland OH 44115 *TF:* 800-210-7293 ■ *Web:* www.clevelandmagazine.com	216-771-2833	781-6318	457-22
Cleveland Metroparks Zoo 3900 Wildlife Way.........................Cleveland OH 44109 *Web:* clevelandmetroparks.com/zoo/zoo.aspx	216-661-6500		823
Cleveland Motion Controls Inc 7550 Hub Pkwy.............................Cleveland OH 44125 *TF:* 800-321-8072 ■ *Web:* www.cmccontrols.com	216-524-8800	642-2199	203
Cleveland Municipal School District (CMSD) 1380 E Sixth St...........................Cleveland OH 44114 **Fax:* Hum Res ■ *Web:* www.clevelandmetroschools.org	216-838-0000	361-2018*	685
Cleveland Museum of Art 11150 E Blvd..............................Cleveland OH 44106 *TF Sales:* 800-469-4449 ■ *Web:* www.clevelandart.org	216-421-7340	707-6679	520
Cleveland Museum of Natural History 1 Wade Oval Dr............................Cleveland OH 44106 *TF:* 800-317-9155 ■ *Web:* www.cmnh.org	216-231-4600	231-5919	520
Cleveland Orchestra, The 11001 Euclid Ave Severance Hall.............Cleveland OH 44106 *TF:* 800-686-1141 ■ *Web:* www.clevelandorchestra.com	216-231-1111	231-4029	573-3
Cleveland Plant & Flower Co 12920 Corporate Dr........................Cleveland OH 44130 *TF:* 888-231-7569 ■ *Web:* www.cpfco.com	216-898-3500		293
Cleveland Plumbing Supply Company Inc 143 E Washington St....................Chagrin Falls OH 44022 *TF:* 800-331-1078 ■ *Web:* www.clevelandplumbing.com	440-247-2555	247-2116	612
Cleveland Pops Orchestra 24000 Mercantile Rd Ste 11.................Cleveland OH 44122 *Web:* www.clevelandpops.com	216-765-7677		573-3
Cleveland Public Library 325 Superior Ave..........................Cleveland OH 44114 *TF:* 800-362-1262 ■ *Web:* www.cpl.org	216-623-2800	623-7015	434-3
Cleveland Public Theatre 6415 Detroit Ave..........................Cleveland OH 44102 *TF:* 800-995-5222 ■ *Web:* www.cptonline.org	216-631-2727	631-2575	573-4
Cleveland Punch & Die Co 666 Pratt St PO Box 769.....................Ravenna OH 44266 *TF:* 888-451-4342 ■ *Web:* www.clevelandpunch.com	888-451-4342	451-6877	757
Cleveland Range Co 1333 E 179th St..........Cleveland OH 44110 *TF:* 800-338-2204 ■ *Web:* www.clevelandrange.com	216-481-4900	481-3782	298
Cleveland Regional Medical Ctr 300 E Crockett St.........................Cleveland TX 77327 *Web:* www.clevelandregionalmedicalcenter.com	281-593-1811		374-3
Cleveland Research Co 1375 East Ninth St Ste 2700.................Cleveland OH 44114 *Web:* www.cleveland-research.com	216-649-7250		401
Cleveland Scene 1468 W Ninth St Ste 805....................Cleveland OH 44113 *Web:* www.clevescene.com	216-241-7550	802-7212	532-5
Cleveland State Community College 3535 Adkisson Dr..........................Cleveland TN 37312 *TF:* 800-604-2722 ■ *Web:* clevelandstatecc.edu	423-472-7141	478-6255	162
Cleveland State University 2121 Euclid Ave...........................Cleveland OH 44115 **Fax:* Admissions ■ *TF:* 888-278-6446 ■ *Web:* www.csuohio.edu	216-687-2000	687-9210*	166
Cleveland State University Cleveland-Marshall College of Law 1801 Euclid Ave LB 138.....................Cleveland OH 44115 *TF:* 866-687-2304 ■ *Web:* www.law.csuohio.edu	216-687-2344	687-6881	167-1
Cleveland Steel Container Corp 30310 Emerald Valley Pkwy ste #400..........Glenwillow OH 44139 *Web:* www.cscpails.com	440-349-8000	349-8101	492
Cleveland Tool & Machine 5240 Smith Rd..........................Brook Park OH 44142 *TF:* 800-253-4502 ■ *Web:* www.clevtool.com	216-267-6010		454
Cleveland Track Material Inc 7000 Central Ave..........................Cleveland OH 44104 *Web:* www.clevelandtrack.com	216-881-8800		567
Cleveland Wire Cloth & Manufacturing Co 3573 E 78th St............................Cleveland OH 44105 *TF:* 800-321-3234 ■ *Web:* www.wirecloth.com	216-341-1832	341-1876	688
Cleveland/Bradley Chamber of Commerce 225 Keith St..............................Cleveland TN 37311 *TF:* 800-533-9930 ■ *Web:* www.clevelandchamber.com	423-472-6587	472-2019	139
Cleveland-Bolivar County Chamber of Commerce 600 Third St..............................Cleveland MS 38732 *TF:* 800-256-8444 ■ *Web:* clevelandmschamber.com	662-843-2712	843-2718	139
Cleveland-Cuyahoga County Port Authority 1375 E Ninth St Ste 2300....................Cleveland OH 44114 *Web:* portofcleveland.com	216-241-8004		618
Clever Devices Ltd 300 Crossways Pk Dr.......................Woodbury NY 11797 *TF:* 800-872-6129 ■ *Web:* www.cleverdevices.com	516-433-6100		180
Clevest Solutions Inc 13911 Wireless Way Ste 100................Richmond BC V6V3B9 *TF:* 866-915-0088 ■ *Web:* www.clevest.com	604-214-9700		224
ClevrU Corp 1-564 Weber St N...............Waterloo ON N2L5C8 *Web:* www.clevru.com	519-746-1898		242

Phone | Fax | Class

Clewiston Public Library System
120 W Osceola Ave. Clewiston FL 33440 863-983-1493 983-9194 434-3
Web: www.hendrylibraries.org

CLIA (Cruise Lines International Assn)
1201 F St NW Ste 250 Washington DC 20004 754-224-2200 48-23
TF: 855-444-2542 ■ *Web:* www.cruising.org

Click Model Management
129 W 27th St PH New York NY 10001 212-206-1717 206-6228* 506
*Fax: Resv ■ *Web:* www.clickmodel.com

Click2mail 3103 Tenth St N Ste 201 Arlington VA 22201 703-521-9029 627
TF: 866-665-2787 ■ *Web:* click2mail.com

ClickAway Corp
457 E McGlincy Ln Ste 1 Campbell CA 95008 408-626-9400 175
Web: www.clickaway.com

ClickCulture Inc
9121 Anson Way Ste 200 Raleigh NC 27615 919-420-7736 7
TF: 800-421-9668 ■ *Web:* www.clickculture.com

ClickGen LLC 1613 NW 136th Ave Ste 100 Sunrise FL 33323 954-653-9200 5

CLICK-into Inc
8300 Woodbine Ave Ste 301 Markham ON L3R9Y7 905-477-8853 180
Web: www.click-into.com

Clicks Billiards
3100 Monticello Ave Ste 350 Dallas TX 75205 214-521-7001 659
Web: clicks.com

ClickSafety.com Inc
2185 N California Blvd Ste 425 Walnut Creek CA 94596 800-971-1080 765
TF: 800-971-1080 ■ *Web:* www.clicksafety.com

ClickSoftware Inc
35 Corporate Dr Ste 400 Burlington MA 01803 781-272-5903 272-6409 178-7
NASDAQ: CKSW ■ *TF:* 888-438-3308 ■ *Web:* www.clicksoftware.com

clickworker.com Inc PO Box 601 Penfield NY 14526 585-210-3912 387
Web: www.clickworker.com

Client Focused Media Inc
1611 San Marco Blvd Jacksonville FL 32207 904-232-3001 195
Web: cfmedia.net

Client Mktg Systems Inc
880 Price St Pismo Beach CA 93449 805-773-7981 194

Client Services Inc
3451 Harry S Truman Blvd St Charles MO 63301 636-947-2321 160

Client Solution Architects
52 Gettysburg Pk Mechanicsburg PA 17055 717-795-9104 113
Web: www.csaassociates.com

Client Success Group Inc
5166 Sunny Creek Dr San Jose CA 95135 408-531-1907 194
Web: www.clientsuccessgroup.com

Clientize com Inc
160 W Camino Real Ste 250 Boca Raton FL 33432 561-417-5533 195
Web: www.clientize.com

Clients First Business Solutions LLC
670 N Beers St Bldg 4 Holmdel NJ 07733 866-677-6290 177
TF: 866-677-6290 ■ *Web:* www.clientsfirst-us.com

Cliff Castle Casino
555 W Middle Verde Rd Camp Verde AZ 86322 928-567-7999 452
TF: 800-381-7568 ■ *Web:* www.cliffcastlecasinohotel.com

Cliff Findlay Auto Ctr Inc
3730 Stockton Hill Rd Kingman AZ 86409 928-757-4041 757-9701 57

Cliff House at Pikes Peak
306 Canyon Ave Manitou Springs CO 80829 888-212-7000 379
TF: 888-212-7000 ■ *Web:* www.thecliffhouse.com

Cliff House Resort & Spa
591 Shore Rd Cape Neddick ME 03902 207-361-1000 669
Web: www.destinationhotels.com/cliff-house

Cliff Spa at Snowbird
Hwy 210 PO Box 929000 Snowbird UT 84092 801-933-2225 707
TF: 800-453-3000 ■ *Web:* www.snowbird.com

Cliff Viessman Inc
215 First Ave PO Box 175 Gary SD 57237 605-272-5241 468
TF: 800-328-2408 ■ *Web:* www.viessmantrucking.com

Cliff Weil Inc
8043 Industrial Pk Rd Mechanicsville VA 23116 804-746-1321 746-2595 543
TF: 800-446-9345 ■ *Web:* www.cliffweil.com

Cliff's Amusement Park Inc
4800 Osuna Rd NE Albuquerque NM 87109 505-881-9373 31
Web: www.cliffsamusementpark.com

Cliffbreakers River Restaurant
700 W Riverside Blvd Rockford IL 61103 815-282-3033 671
Web: www.cliffbreakers.com

Clifford & Rano Insurance Agency Inc
57 Cedar St Worcester MA 01609 508-752-8284 390
TF: 800-660-8284 ■ *Web:* cliffordrano.com

Clifford Chance LLP 31 W 52nd St New York NY 10019 212-878-8000 878-8375 428
Web: www.cliffordchance.com

Clifford Paper Inc
600 E Crescent Ave Upper Saddle River NJ 07458 201-934-5115 934-5188 553
Web: www.cliffordpaper.com

Clifford-Jacobs Forging Co
2410 N Fifth St PO Box 830 Champaign IL 61822 217-352-5172 352-4629 483
Web: www.clifford-jacobs.com

Cliffs Natural Resources
200 Public Sq Ste 3300 Cleveland OH 44114 216-694-5700 502
TF: 800-732-0330 ■ *Web:* www.cliffsnaturalresources.com

Cliffs of the Neuse State Park
240 Park Entrance Rd Seven Springs NC 28578 919-778-6234 565
Web: www.ncparks.gov/visit/parks/clne/main.php

Cliffwater LLC
4640 Admiralty Way
Ste 1101 Marina Twr Marina Del Rey CA 90292 310-448-5000 194
Web: www.cliffwater.com

Clift, The 495 Geary St San Francisco CA 94102 415-775-4700 379
Web: morganshotelgroup.com

Clifton Assoc Ltd 340 Maxwell Cres Regina SK S4N5Y5 306-721-7611 256
Web: www.clifton.ca

Clifton Public Library 292 Piaget Ave Clifton NJ 07011 973-772-5500 434-3
TF: 800-227-2345 ■ *Web:* www.cliftonpl.org

Clifton Savings Bancorp Inc
1433 Van Houten Ave Clifton NJ 07013 973-473-2200 360-2
NASDAQ: CSBK ■ *TF:* 888-562-6727 ■ *Web:* www.cliftonsavings.com

Clifton Square 3700 E Douglas Wichita KS 67208 316-686-2177 460
Web: www.cliftonsquare.com

Clifton T Perkins Hospital Ctr
8450 Dorsey Run Rd Jessup MD 20794 410-724-3000 724-3009 374-5
TF: 877-463-3464 ■ *Web:* dhmh.maryland.gov

CliftonLarsonAllen - CLA
301 SW Adams St Ste 1000 Peoria IL 61602 309-671-4500 671-4508 2
TF: 888-529-2648 ■ *Web:* www.claconnect.com

Clifty Engineering & Tool Company Inc
2949 Clifty Dr Madison IN 47250 812-273-3272 273-3272 757
Web: www.cliftyengineering.com

Clifty Falls State Park 1501 Green Rd Madison IN 47250 812-273-8885 565
Web: www.in.gov

ClimaCool Corp 15 S Virginia Oklahoma City OK 73106 405-815-3000 14
Web: www.climacoolcorp.com

Climate Design Air Conditioningln
12530 47th Way N Clearwater FL 33762 888-572-7245 189-10
TF: 888-572-7245 ■ *Web:* climatedesign.com

Climate Engineers Inc 3005 Robins Rd Hiawatha IA 52233 319-364-1569 189-10
Web: climate-engr.com

Climate Registry, The
PO Box 811488 Los Angeles CA 90081 866-523-0764 192
TF: 866-523-0764 ■ *Web:* www.theclimateregistry.org

Climatec Inc 2851 W Kathleen Rd Phoenix AZ 85053 602-944-3330 186
Web: www.climatec.com

Clima-Tech 200 Bilmar Dr Ste 180 Pittsburgh PA 15205 208-377-9755 189-10
Web: clima-tech.com

ClimateCraft Inc
518 N Indiana Ave Oklahoma City OK 73106 405-415-9230 610
Web: www.climatecraft.com

ClimateMaster Inc
7300 SW 44th St Oklahoma City OK 73179 405-745-6000 745-2006* 14
*Fax: Cust Svc ■ *TF:* 800-299-9747 ■ *Web:* www.climatemaster.com

Climatronics Corp 140 Wilbur Pl Bohemia NY 11716 631-567-7300 668
Web: www.climatronics.com

Climax Manufacturing Co 7840 SR 26 Lowville NY 13367 315-376-8000 376-2034 557
TF: 800-225-4629 ■ *Web:* www.climaxpkg.com

Climax Molybdenum Co PO Box 220 Fort Madison IA 52627 602-366-8100 366-7318* 502
*Fax: Hum Res ■ *Web:* www.climaxmolybdenum.com

Climbing Magazine 5720 Flatiron Pkwy Boulder CO 80301 800-829-5895 457-20
TF: 800-829-5895 ■ *Web:* www.climbing.com

Clinch County 46 S College St Homerville GA 31634 912-487-5321 487-5068 338
Web: www.clinchcounty.com

Clinch-Tite Corp
5264 Lake St PO Box 456 Sandy Lake PA 16145 724-376-7315 376-2785 551
TF General: 800-241-0900 ■ *Web:* www.clinchtite.com

Cline Davis & Mann Inc (CDM)
220 E 42nd St New York NY 10017 212-907-4300 4
Web: www.clinedavis.com

Cline Design Assoc of Wilmington Pllc
125 N Harrington St Raleigh NC 27603 919-833-6413 314
Web: www.clinedesignassoc.com

Cline Falls State Scenic Viewpoint
7100 OR-126 Redmond OR 97756 800-551-6949 565
TF: 800-551-6949 ■ *Web:* www.oregonstateparks.org

Cline Mining Corp
Heritage Bldg 181 Bay St Brookfield Pl
3rd Fl Toronto ON M5J2T3 416-504-7600 501
Web: www.clinemining.com

C-Line Products Inc
1100 E Business Ctr Dr Mount Prospect IL 60056 847-827-6661 827-3329 534
TF: 800-323-6084 ■ *Web:* www.c-lineproducts.com

Cline Resource & Development Co
430 Harper Park Dr Beckley WV 25801 304-255-7458 194
Web: www.clineres.com

Cline Tool & Service Co PO Box 866 Newton IA 50208 641-792-7081 792-0309 493
TF: 866-561-3022 ■ *Web:* www.clinetool.com

Cline Williams Wright Johnson & Oldfather L L P
1900 USBank Bldg 233 S 13th St Lincoln NE 68508 402-474-6900 445
Web: www.clinewilliams.com

Cling's Aerospace LLC 700 W 22nd St Tempe AZ 85282 480-968-1778 968-0576 454
Web: www.clingsaz.com

ClingZ Inc 541 Laser Rd NE Rio Rancho NM 87124 505-892-2500 601
Web: www.clingz.com

Clinic of Distinctive 638 11 Ave SW Calgary AB T2R0E2 403-294-0036 226
TF: 800-664-2561 ■ *Web:* distinctivetherapy.com

Clinic Service Corp 3464 S Willow St Denver CO 80231 303-755-2900 2
TF: 800-929-5395 ■ *Web:* www.clinicservice.com

Clinical & Laboratory Standards Institute (CLSI)
950 W Valley Rd Ste 2500 Wayne PA 19087 610-688-0100 688-0700 49-8
Web: www.clsi.org

Clinical Immunology Society (CIS)
555 E Wells St Ste 1100 Milwaukee WI 53202 414-224-8095 272-6070 49-8
TF: 800-472-6930 ■ *Web:* www.clinimmsoc.org

Clinical Information Network Inc
8283 N Hayden Rd Hayden Corporate Ctr
Ste 270 Scottsdale AZ 85258 480-422-1811 415

Clinical Laboratories of Hawaii LLP
91-2135 Ft Weaver Rd Ste 300 Ewa Beach HI 96706 808-677-7999 415
Web: www.clinicallabs.com

Clinical Laboratory Management Assn (CLMA)
401 N Michigan Ave Ste 2000 Chicago IL 60611 312-321-5111 673-6927 49-19
Web: www.clma.org

Clinical Laboratory Partners LLC
129 Patricia M Genova Dr Newington CT 06111 860-545-2299 415
TF: 800-286-9800 ■ *Web:* www.clinicallaboratorypartners.com

Clinical Meeting Management Inc
313 Cedar St Bastrop TX 78602 512-303-6610 196
Web: www.cmmglobal.com

Clinical Pathology Laboratories Inc
9200 Wall St Austin TX 78754 512-339-1275 415
TF: 800-595-1275 ■ *Web:* www.cpllabs.com

Clinical Research Advantage Inc
2141 E Broadway Rd Tempe AZ 85282 480-820-5656 466
Web: www.radiantresearch.com

Clinical Science Laboratory Inc
51 Francis Ave Mansfield MA 02048 508-339-6106 415
Web: clinicalsciencelab.com

Clinicient Inc
708 SW Third Ave Ste 400 Portland OR 97204 503-525-0275 177
Web: www.clinicient.com

Phone | Fax | Class

CliniComp International
9655 Towne Ctr Dr San Diego CA 92121 858-546-8202 546-1801 178-10
TF: 800-350-8202 ■ *Web:* www.clinicomp.com

Clinilabs Inc 423 W 55th St 4th Fl New York NY 10019 646-215-6400 231
Web: www.clinilabs.com

CLINIQA Corp 288 Distribution St San Marcos CA 92078 760-744-1900 231
Web: www.cliniqa.com

Clinique Laboratories Inc
767 Fifth Ave New York NY 10153 212-572-3983 214
TF: 800-419-4041 ■ *Web:* www.clinique.com

Clink Events LLC
4201 Marathon Blvd Ste 301 Austin TX 78756 512-236-0264 226
Web: www.clinkevents.com

Clinkerdagger 621 W Mallon Ave Spokane WA 99201 509-328-5965 671
Web: www.clinkerdagger.com

Clinton Area Chamber of Commerce
721 S Second St Clinton IA 52732 563-242-5702 242-5803 139
Web: www.clintonia.com

Clinton Community College
1000 Lincoln Blvd Clinton IA 52732 563-244-7001 244-7107* 162
**Fax:* Library ■ *TF:* 877-495-3320 ■ *Web:* www.eicc.edu

Clinton Community College
136 Clinton Pt Dr Plattsburgh NY 12901 518-562-4200 562-4158 162
TF: 800-552-1160 ■ *Web:* www.clinton.edu

Clinton Correctional Facility
1156 Cook St Dannemora NY 12929 518-492-2511 213
Web: www.doccs.ny.gov/faclist.html

Clinton County 46 S S St Wilmington OH 45177 937-382-2316 383-3455 338
Web: www.co.clinton.oh.us
Fiscal Court 100 S Cross St Albany KY 42602 606-387-5234 387-7651 338
Web: clintoncounty.ky.gov

Clinton County Economic Partnership
212 N Jay St Lock Haven PA 17745 570-748-5782 893-0433 139
TF: 888-388-6991 ■ *Web:* www.clintoncountyinfo.com

Clinton County Electric Co-op Inc
475 N Main St PO Box 40 Breese IL 62230 618-526-7282 526-4561 245
TF: 800-526-7282 ■ *Web:* cceci.com

Clinton County Regional Educatonal Service Agency Resa
1013 S US Hwy 27 Saint Johns MI 48879 989-224-6831 244
TF: 800-562-7618 ■ *Web:* www.ccresa.org

Clinton Electronics Corp
6701 Clinton Rd Loves Park IL 61111 815-633-1444 253
TF: 800-549-6393 ■ *Web:* www.clintonelectronics.com

Clinton Family Ford Lincoln Mercury of Rock Hill Inc
1884 Canterbury Glen Ln Rock Hill SC 29730 803-366-3181 57
Web: clintonfamilyford.com

Clinton Fences Company Inc
2630 Old Washington Rd Waldorf MD 20601 301-645-8808 186
TF: 800-323-6869 ■ *Web:* fencesouthernmd.com

Clinton House State Historic Site
549 Main St PO Box 88 Poughkeepsie NY 12602 845-471-1630 565
Web: parks.ny.gov/historic-sites/1/details.aspx

Clinton Inn Hotel 145 Dean Dr Tenafly NJ 07670 201-871-3200 871-3435 379
TF: 800-275-4411 ■ *Web:* www.clinton-inn.com

Clinton Junior College
1029 Crawford Rd Rock Hill SC 29730 803-327-7402 327-3261* 162
**Fax:* Admissions ■ *TF:* 877-837-9645

Clinton Lake State Recreation Area
7251 Ranger Rd DeWitt IL 61735 217-935-8722 565
Web: www.dnr.illinois.gov/Parks/Pages/ClintonLake.aspx

Clinton Memorial Hospital (CMH)
610 W Main St Wilmington OH 45177 937-382-6611 374-3
TF: 800-803-9648 ■ *Web:* www.cmhregional.com

Clinton Public Library 118 S Hicks St Clinton TN 37716 865-457-0519 434-3
Web: clintonpubliclibrary.org

Clinton Public Library
306 Eigth Ave S Clinton IA 52732 563-242-8441 242-8162 434-3
Web: clintonpubliclibrary.us

Clinton Public School District
PO Box 300 Clinton MS 39060 601-924-7533 685
Web: www.clintonpublicschools.com

Clinton Rubin LLC
Five Neshaminy Interplex Ste 205 Trevose PA 19053 215-245-2212 180
Web: clintonrubin.com

Clinton State Park 798 N 1415 Rd Lawrence KS 66049 785-842-8562 565
Web: ksoutdoors.com

Clintondale Aviation Inc
652 Rt Highland Ste 201 New York NY 12528 845-883-9657 883-5277 13
Web: www.clintondale.com

Clinton-Essex-Franklin Library System
33 Oak St Plattsburgh NY 12901 518-563-5190 563-0421 434-3
Web: www.cefls.org

Clintrak Clinical Labeling Services LLC
2800 Veterans Hwy Bohemia NY 11716 631-467-3900 627
Web: www.fisherclinicalservices.com

Clio Area School District 430 N Mill St Clio MI 48420 810-591-0500 685
Web: www.clioschools.org

Clio Awards Inc
825 Eighth Ave 29th Fl New York NY 10019 212-683-4300 683-4796 49-18
Web: clios.com/awards

ClioSoft Inc
39500 Stevenson Pl Ste 110 Fremont CA 94539 510-790-4732 177
Web: www.cliosoft.com

Clippard Instrument Lab
7390 Colerain Ave Cincinnati OH 45239 513-521-4261 521-4464 223
TF: 877-245-6247 ■ *Web:* www.clippard.com

Clipper Americas Inc
2500 City W Blvd Ste 500 Houston TX 77042 713-953-2200 953-2201 780
Web: www.clipper-group.com

Clipper Exxpress Inc
9014 Heritage Pkwy Ste 300 Woodridge IL 60517 630-739-0700 739-1817 449
TF: 800-678-2547 ■ *Web:* www.clippergroup.com

Clipper Fund 2949 E Elvira Rd Ste 101 Tucson AZ 85756 800-432-2504 528
TF: 800-432-2504 ■ *Web:* www.clipperfund.com

Clipper Magazine LLC
3708 Hempland Rd Mountville PA 17554 717-569-5100 532-3
Web: www.clippermagazine.com

Clipper Navigation Inc
2701 Alaskan Way Pier 69 Seattle WA 98121 206-443-2560 771
TF: 800-888-2535 ■ *Web:* www.clippervacations.com

Clipper Oil Co
2040 Harbor Island Dr Ste 203 San Diego CA 92101 619-692-9701 580
Web: www.clipperoil.com

Clips & Clamps Industries
15050 Keel St Plymouth MI 48170 734-455-0880 488
Web: www.clipsclamps.com

Clixo LLC 222 Milwaukee St Ste 307 Denver CO 80206 303-632-8722 5
Web: www.clixosearch.com

CLLA (Commercial Law League of America)
70 E Lake St Ste 630 Chicago IL 60601 312-781-2000 781-2010 49-10
TF: 800-978-2552 ■ *Web:* www.clla.org

Clm Equipment Company Inc
3135 Hwy 90 E Broussard LA 70518 337-837-6693 190
TF: 800-256-0490 ■ *Web:* www.clmequipment.com

CLMA (Clinical Laboratory Management Assn)
401 N Michigan Ave Ste 2000 Chicago IL 60611 312-321-5111 673-6927 49-19
Web: www.clma.org

Clock Family Restaurant 8409 Dyer St El Paso TX 79904 915-751-6367 671

Clock Mobility 6700 Clay Ave Grand Rapids MI 49548 616-698-9400 698-9495 62-7
TF: 800-732-5625 ■ *Web:* www.clockmobility.com

Clock Restaurants
902 Clint Moore Rd Ste 126 Boca Raton FL 33487 561-994-3440 670

Clocktower Inn Hotel
181 E Santa Clara St Ventura CA 93001 805-652-0141 643-1432 379
Web: www.clocktowerinn.com

Clocktower Technology Services Inc
308 W Central St Ste B Franklin MA 02038 508-541-6143 525
Web: www.clocktowertech.com

Clockwork 4120 Yonge St North York ON M2P2B8 416-222-8990 180
Web: www.clockwork.ca

Clockwork Marketing Services Inc
10245 Centurion Pkwy N Ste 315 Jacksonville FL 32256 904-280-7960 636
Web: www.clockworkmarketing.com

Cloeren Inc 401 16th St Orange TX 77630 409-886-5820 454
Web: www.cloeren.com

Clofine Dairy Products Inc
1407 New Rd Linwood NJ 08221 609-653-1000 653-0127 297-4
TF: 800-441-1001 ■ *Web:* www.clofinedairy.com

Cloisters Museum Fort Tryon Pk New York NY 10040 212-923-3700 795-3640 520
TF: 800-662-3397 ■ *Web:* www.metmuseum.org

Cloneys Pharmacy Inc 525 Fifth St Eureka CA 95501 707-443-1614 237
Web: cloneys.com

Clopay Bldg Products Inc 8585 Duke Blvd Mason OH 45040 800-225-6729 234
TF: 800-225-6729 ■ *Web:* www.clopaydoor.com

Clopay Plastic Products Co
8585 Duke Blvd Mason OH 45040 513-770-4800 600
TF: 800-282-2260 ■ *Web:* www.clopayplastics.com

Cloppert, Latanick, Sauter & Washburn LLP
225 E Broad St Fl 4 Columbus OH 43215 614-461-4455 428
Web: www.cloppertlaw.com

Cloquet Area Chamber of Commerce
225 Sunnyside Dr Cloquet MN 55720 218-879-1551 878-0223 139
TF: 800-554-4350 ■ *Web:* www.cloquet.com

Clore Automotive
8600 NE Underground Dr Pillar 240 Kansas City MO 64161 816-459-2200 811
Web: www.cloreautomotive.com

Clorox Co 1221 Broadway Oakland CA 94612 510-271-7000 185
NYSE: CLX ■ *TF Cust Svc:* 800-424-9300 ■ *Web:* www.thecloroxcompany.com

Clos du Bois
19410 Geyserville Ave Geyserville CA 95441 707-857-1651 80-3
TF Sales: 800-222-3189 ■ *Web:* www.closduboisͅ.com

Close Jensen & Miller PC
1137 Silas Deane Hwy Wethersfield CT 06109 860-563-9375 261

Close To My Heart 1199 W 700 S Pleasant Grove UT 84062 888-655-6552 157-6
TF: 888-655-6552 ■ *Web:* www.closetomyheart.com

Close Up Foundation
1330 Braddock Pl Ste 400 Alexandria VA 22314 703-706-3300 48-7
TF: 800-256-7387 ■ *Web:* www.closeup.org

closerlook Inc
212 W Superior St Ste 300 Chicago IL 60654 312-640-3700 463
Web: www.closerlook.com

Closet Factory 12800 S Broadway Los Angeles CA 90061 310-516-7000 189-11
TF: 800-838-7995 ■ *Web:* www.closetfactory.com

Closing USA LLC 903 Elmgrove Rd Rochester NY 14624 585-454-1730 652
Web: www.closingusa.com

ClosingCorp Inc
6165 Greenwich Dr Ste 300 San Diego CA 92122 858-551-1500 772
Web: www.closing.com

Closure Medical Corp
5250 Greens Dairy Rd Raleigh NC 27616 919-876-7800 228
Web: www.closuremed.com

Clothes Minded Inc 1160 Sandhill Ave Carson CA 90746 310-638-9931 157-6

Clothing Cove, The 414 N Main St Milford MI 48381 248-685-2500 157-6

Clothworks 6301 W Marginal Way SW Seattle WA 98106 206-762-7886 258
TF: 800-874-0541 ■ *Web:* www.clothworks.com

Cloud 10 Corp
6786 S Revere Pkwy Ste 100 Centennial CO 80112 303-952-3215 393
Web: www.cloud10corp.com

Cloud 9 Living
4999 Pearl E Cir Ste 102 Boulder CO 80301 866-525-6839 196
TF: 866-525-6839 ■ *Web:* www.cloud9living.com

Cloud Cap Technology Inc
205 N Wasco Loop Ste 103 Hood River OR 97031 541-387-2120 387-2030 529
Web: www.cloudcaptech.com

Cloud County 811 Washington St Concordia KS 66901 785-243-8110 338
TF: 800-432-2484 ■ *Web:* www.cloudcountyks.org

Cloud County Community College
2221 Campus Dr Concordia KS 66901 785-243-1435 162
TF: 800-729-5101 ■ *Web:* www.cloud.edu

Cloud Creek Systems Inc
31255 Cedar Vly Dr Ste 319 Westlake Village CA 91362 818-865-2800 180
Web: www.cloudcreek.com

Cloud Packaging Solutions LLC
424 Howard Ave Des Plaines IL 60018 847-390-9410 123
Web: www.cloudeg.com

Phone | Fax | Class

Cloud Peak Energy Inc (RTEA)
505 S Gillette Ave PO Box 3009 .... Gillette WY 82717 307-687-6000 262-0604* 501
*Fax Area Code: 303 ■ TF: 866-470-4300 ■ Web: www.cloudpeakenergy.com

Cloud Strategy Partners LLC
129 Lauren Cir .... Scotts Valley CA 95066 408-857-9872 463
Web: www.cloudstrategypartners.com

Cloud9 Wine Bar 25 E Tenth St .... Erie PA 16501 814-870-9007 671
Web: bertrandsbistro.com

CloudCheckr Inc
339 East Ave Ste 202-1 .... Rochester NY 14604 585-413-0869 387
Web: cloudcheckr.com

Cloudland Canyon State Park
122 Cloudland Canyon Pk .... Rising Fawn GA 30738 706-657-4050 565
Web: www.gastateparks.org

Cloud-rider Designs Ltd
1260 Eighth Ave .... Regina SK S4R1C9 306-761-2119 350
TF: 800-632-1255 ■ Web: www.cloud-rider.com

CloudSway LLC 711 Pacific Ave .... Tacoma WA 98402 855-212-5683 387
TF: 855-212-5683 ■ Web: www.cloudsway.com

Cloudwerx Data Solutions Inc
1440 28th St NE Ste 2 .... Calgary AB T2A7W6 403-538-6659 396
Web: www.cloudwerx.com

Clough State Park 455 Clough Pk Rd .... Weare NH 03281 603-529-7112 565
Web: www.nhstateparks.org

Clougherty Packing Co
3049 E Vernon Ave .... Los Angeles CA 90058 800-846-7635 473
TF Sales: 800-846-7635 ■ Web: www.farmerjohn.com

Clouse Engineering Inc
5010 E Shea Blvd .... Phoenix AZ 85020 602-395-9300 256
Web: clouseaz.com

Clove Lakes Health Care & Rehabilitation Ctr
25 Fanning St .... Staten Island NY 10314 718-289-7900 450
Web: www.clovelakes.com

Clover Farms Dairy PO Box 14627 .... Reading PA 19612 610-921-9111 296-27
TF: 800-323-0123 ■ Web: www.cloverfarms.com

Clover Global Group
2431 W Irving Park Rd .... Chicago IL 60618 773-267-6767 463

Clover Knits Inc 1075 Jackson Heights .... Clover SC 29710 803-222-3021 745-4

Clover Park Technical College
4500 Steilacoom Blvd SW .... Lakewood WA 98499 253-589-5800 162
Web: www.cptc.edu

Clover Technologies Group
4200 Columbus Dr .... Ottawa IL 61350 815-431-8100 591
Web: www.clovertech.com

Clover Wireless LLC
2700 W Higgins Rd ste 100 .... Hoffman Estates CA 60169 815-431-8100 393
Web: www.cloverwireless.com

Clover Yarns Inc
1030 Tanyard Branch Trl .... Clover VA 24534 434-454-7151 745-9

Cloverdale Equipment Co
13133 Cloverdale St .... Oak Park MI 48237 248-399-6600 399-7730 264-3
TF: 888-388-9182 ■ Web: www.cloverdale-equip.com

Cloverdale Foods Co 3015 34th St NW .... Mandan ND 58554 800-669-9511 663-0690* 296-26
*Fax Area Code: 701 ■ TF: 800-669-9511 ■ Web: www.cloverdalefoods.com

Cloverhill Bakery Inc
2035 N Narragansett Ave .... Chicago IL 60639 773-745-9800 745-1647 296-1
Web: www.cloverhill.com

Cloverland Green Spring Dairy Inc
2701 Loch Raven Rd .... Baltimore MD 21218 410-235-4477 296-27
TF Orders: 800-492-0094 ■ Web: www.cloverlanddairy.com

CloverLeaf Digital LLC
20 Jay St Ste 213 .... Brooklyn NY 11201 718-438-6448 514
Web: www.cloverleafdigital.com

Clover-Stornetta Farms Inc
PO Box 750369 .... Petaluma CA 94975 707-778-8448 297-4
TF: 800-237-3315 ■ Web: cloversonoma.com

Clovis Botanical Garden
945 N Clovis Ave .... Clovis CA 93611 559-298-3091 97
Web: clovisbotanicalgarden.org

Clovis Chamber of Commerce
325 Pollasky Ave .... Clovis CA 93612 559-299-7363 299-2969 139
Web: www.clovischamber.com

Clovis Community College (CCC)
417 Schepps Blvd .... Clovis NM 88101 575-769-2811 769-4190* 162
*Fax: Admissions ■ TF: 800-769-1409 ■ Web: www.clovis.edu

Clovis Unified School District
1450 Herndon Ave .... Clovis CA 93611 559-327-9300 327-9339 685
TF: 877-544-6664 ■ Web: www.cusd.com

Clovis/Curry County Chamber of Commerce
105 E Third St .... Clovis NM 88101 575-763-3435 763-7266 139
TF: 800-261-7656 ■ Web: www.clovisnm.org

Clow Stamping Co 23103 County Rd 3 .... Merrifield MN 56465 218-765-3111 488
Web: www.clowstamping.com

Clow Valve Co 902 S Second St .... Oskaloosa IA 52577 641-673-8611 673-8269 789
TF: 800-829-2569 ■ Web: www.clowvalve.com

Cloward H2o 2696 N University Ave .... Provo UT 84604 801-375-1223 261
TF: 800-950-1132 ■ Web: www.clowardh2o.com

Clowns of America International (COAI)
PO Box 122 .... Eustis FL 32727 352-357-1676 48-4
TF: 877-816-6941 ■ Web: www.coai.org

CLP (Cutter Lumber Products)
10 Rickenbacker Cir .... Livermore CA 94551 925-443-5959 443-0648 551
TF: 800-433-3827 ■ Web: cutterlumber.com

CLR Group Ltd 8 Eagle Ctr Ste 5 .... Ofallon IL 62269 618-624-6799 624-6795 809

CLS (Christian Legal Society)
8001 Braddock Rd Ste 300 .... Springfield VA 22151 703-642-1070 642-1075 49-10
TF: 800-225-4008 ■ Web: www.clsnet.org

CLS (California Lighting Sales Inc)
4900 Rivergrade Rd Ste D110 .... Irwindale CA 91706 626-775-6000 775-6001 439
Web: www.californialightingsales.com

CLS Group 609 S Kelly Ave Ste D .... Edmond OK 73003 405-348-5460 551-8270 188-1
TF: 800-445-3950 ■ Web: www.clsgroup.com

CLS Investments LLC 17605 Wright St .... Omaha NE 68130 402-493-3313 690
TF: 888-455-4244 ■ Web: www.clsinvest.com

CLS Lexi-tech Ltd 10 Dawson Ave .... Dieppe NB E1A6C8 506-859-5200 393
Web: www.cls-lexitech.com/index.php?/en/home

CLS Strategies
1850 M St, NW Ste 550 .... Washington DC 20036 202-289-5900 196
Web: www.clsdc.com

CLSA (Canon Law Society of America)
3025 Fourth St NE Ste 111 .... Washington DC 20017 202-832-2350 832-2331 48-20
TF: 800-452-5110 ■ Web: www.clsa.org

CLSI (Clinical & Laboratory Standards Institute)
950 W Valley Rd Ste 2500 .... Wayne PA 19087 610-688-0100 688-0700 49-8
Web: www.clsi.org

CLT (Chesapeake Lodging Trust)
1997 Annapolis Exchange Pkwy Ste 410 .... Annapolis MD 21401 800-698-2820 654
NYSE: CHSP ■ TF: 800-698-2820 ■ Web: www.chesapeakelodgingtrust.com

Club Cal Neva Hotel Casino, The
38 E Second St PO Box 2071 .... Reno NV 89501 775-323-1046 669
TF: 877-777-7303 ■ Web: www.clubcalneva.com

Club Colors Inc 420 E State Pkwy .... Schaumburg IL 60173 847-490-3636 701
Web: www.clubcolors.com

Club Cruise 1509 Grass Vly Hwy .... Auburn CA 95603 530-889-2582 772
Web: clubcruise.com

Club Europa 802 W Oregon St .... Urbana IL 61801 217-344-5863 344-4072 760
TF: 800-331-1882 ■ Web: www.clubeuropatravel.com

Club Holdings LLC
11101 W 120th Ave Ste 300 .... Broomfield CO 80021 800-550-0324 377
TF: 800-550-0324 ■ Web: www.quintess.com

Club Managers Assn of America (CMAA)
1733 King St .... Alexandria VA 22314 703-739-9500 739-0124 49-12
TF: 800-409-7755 ■ Web: www.cmaa.org

Club Marketing Services Inc
101 W Central .... Bentonville AR 72712 479-696-3100 5
TF: 800-821-2799 ■ Web: www.clubmarketing.com

Club Med Sandpiper
4500 SE Pine Vly St .... Port Saint Lucie FL 34952 772-398-5100 669
TF: 888-932-2582 ■ Web: clubmed.co.in

Club One Casino 1033 Van Ness Ave .... Fresno CA 93721 559-497-3000 133
Web: www.clubonecasino.com

Club Paris 417 W Fifth Ave .... Anchorage AK 99501 907-277-6332 671
TF: 800-330-0326 ■ Web: www.clubparisrestaurant.com

Club Quarters Hotels 49 W 45th St .... New York NY 10036 203-905-2100 377
Web: clubquarters.com

Club Soda 235 E Superior St .... Fort Wayne IN 46802 260-426-3442 426-4214 671
Web: www.clubsodafortwayne.com

ClubCorp Inc
3030 Lyndon B Johnson Fwy Ste 600 .... Dallas TX 75234 972-243-6191 655
TF: 800-433-5079 ■ Web: www.clubcorp.com

Clubfurniture.com
11535 Carmel Commons Blvd Ste 202 .... Charlotte NC 28226 888-378-8383 791
TF: 888-378-8383 ■ Web: www.clubfurniture.com

ClubHouse Hotel & Suites Sioux Falls
2320 S Louise Ave .... Sioux Falls SD 57106 605-361-8700 361-5950 379
TF: 866-534-8700 ■ Web: siouxfalls.clubhouseinn.com

ClubLink Corp 15675 Dufferin St .... King City ON L7B1K5 905-841-3730 841-1134 655
TF: 800-661-1818 ■ Web: en.clublink.ca

Clubsport of San Ramon
350 Bollinger Canyon Ln .... San Ramon CA 94582 925-735-8500 735-7916 354
TF: 800-561-3357 ■ Web: www.clubsportsr.com

Clusters & Hops 707 N Monroe St .... Tallahassee FL 32303 850-222-2669 222-0469 671
Web: www.winencheese.com

Clustrix Inc 201 Mission St .... San Francisco CA 94105 415-501-9560 387
Web: www.clustrix.com

CLUW (Coalition of Labor Union Women)
815 16th St NW 2nd Fl .... Washington DC 20006 202-508-6969 508-6968 48-24
TF: 800-981-9495 ■ Web: www.cluw.org

CLV Group Inc 485 Bank St Ste 200 .... Ottawa ON K2P1Z2 613-728-2000 390
Web: www.clvgroup.com

CLX Logistics LLC
1777 Sentry Pkwy W Abington Hall Ste 300 .... Blue Bell PA 19422 215-461-3805 194
Web: www.clxlogistics.com

Clyburn James E (Rep D - SC)
242 Cannon HOB .... Washington DC 20515 202-225-3315 225-2313 342-2
Web: clyburn.house.gov

Clyde Bergemann Bachmann Inc
416 Lewiston Junction Rd .... Auburn ME 04210 207-784-1903 261
Web: www.cbpg.com

Clyde Cooper's BBQ
327 S Wilmington St .... Raleigh NC 27601 919-832-7614 671
Web: clydecoopersbbq.com

Clyde Cos Inc 730 N 1500 W .... Orem UT 84057 801-802-6900 191-2
Web: www.clydeinc.com

Clyde Duneier Inc
415 Madison Ave Fl 6 .... New York NY 10017 212-398-1122 411
Web: www.clydeduneier.com

Clyde Industrial 36445 S Reserve Cir .... Avon OH 44011 440-653-1062 463
Web: www.clydeindustrial.com

Clyde Machines Inc
1150 State Hwy 55 N PO Box 194 .... Glenwood MN 56334 320-634-4503 634-4506 470
TF: 800-704-1078 ■ Web: www.clydemachines.com

Clyde Peeling's Reptiland
18628 US Rt 15 .... Allenwood PA 17810 800-737-8452 823
TF: 800-737-8452 ■ Web: www.reptiland.com

CLYDE UNION Pumps
4600 W Dickman Rd .... Battle Creek MI 49037 269-966-4600 962-7549 641

Clyde's Restaurant Group
3236 M St NW .... Washington DC 20007 202-333-9180 625-7429 670
Web: www.clydes.com

Clyde's Transfer Inc
8015 Industrial Pk Rd .... Mechanicsville VA 23116 804-746-1135 746-8898 685
TF: 800-342-8758 ■ Web: clydestransfer.com

Cly-Del Mfg Co 151 Sharon Rd .... Waterbury CT 06721 203-574-2100 753-3326 488

Clyfford Still Museum 1250 Bannock St .... Denver CO 80204 720-354-4880 522
Web: www.clyffordstillmuseum.org

CM Almy Inc 1 Ruth Rd .... Pittsfield ME 04967 207-487-3232 155-14
TF: 800-225-2569 ■ Web: www.almy.com

CM Artists New York
127 W 96th St Ste 13 B .... New York NY 10025 212-864-1005 864-1066 731
Web: www.cmartists.com

CM Bidwell & Associates Ltd
20 Old Pali Pl .... Honolulu HI 96817 808-595-1099 401
Web: www.cmbidwellandassociates.com

CM Company Inc 431 W McGregor Ct .... Boise ID 83705 208-384-0800 186
Web: www.cmcompany.com

Phone | Fax | Class

Cm Construction Company Inc
12215 Nicollet Ave .... Burnsville MN 55337 952-895-8223 186
Web: www.cmconstructionco.com

CM Paula Co 6049 Hi-Tek Ct .... Mason OH 45040 800-543-4464 327
TF: 800-543-4464 ■ *Web:* www.cmpaula.com

CM Ranch
167 Fish Hatchery Rd PO Box 217 .... Dubois WY 82513 307-455-2331 239
TF: 800-455-0721 ■ *Web:* www.cmranch.com

CM Reprographics Inc
4445 S Valley View Ste #1 .... Las Vegas NV 89103 702-222-1757 627
Web: www.cmrepro.com

CM Russell Museum 400 13th St N .... Great Falls MT 59401 406-727-8787 727-2402 520
Web: www.cmrussell.org

CM Services Inc
800 Roosevelt Rd Bldg C Ste 312 .... Glen Ellyn IL 60137 630-858-7337 790-3095 47
TF: 800-613-6672 ■ *Web:* www.cmservices.com

CM Solutions Inc 2674 S Harper Rd .... Corinth MS 38834 662-287-8810 625
Web: www.cm-solutions.biz

CM Trailers Inc
200 County Rd PO Box 680 .... Madill OK 73446 580-795-5536 779
TF: 888-268-7577 ■ *Web:* www.cmtrailers.com

CMA (Chicago Meat Authority Inc)
1120 W 47th Pl .... Chicago IL 60609 773-254-3811 254-5851 296-26
TF: 800-383-3811 ■ *Web:* www.chicagomeat.com

CMA (Chamber Music America)
305 Seventh Ave 5th Fl .... New York NY 10001 212-242-2022 242-7955 48-4
TF: 888-221-9836 ■ *Web:* www.chamber-music.org

CMA (Canadian Medical Assn)
1867 Alta Vista Dr .... Ottawa ON K1G5W8 613-731-9331 49-8
TF: 800-663-7336 ■ *Web:* www.cma.ca

CMA (Country Music Assn Inc)
1 Music Cir S .... Nashville TN 37203 615-244-2840 726-0314 48-4
TF: 800-788-3045 ■ *Web:* cmaworld.com

CMA (Crystal Meth Anonymous)
4470 W Sunset Blvd Ste 107 PO Box 555 ..... Los Angeles CA 90027 877-262-6691 48-21
TF: 877-262-6691 ■ *Web:* www.crystalmeth.org

CMA Consulting Services Inc
700 Troy Schenectady Rd .... Latham NY 12110 518-783-9003 783-5093 177
TF: 800-276-6101 ■ *Web:* www.cma.com

CMA Dishmachines 12700 Knott St .... Garden Grove CA 92841 714-898-8781 386
TF: 800-854-6417 ■ *Web:* www.cmadishmachines.com

Cma Engineers 35 Bow St .... Portsmouth NH 03801 603-431-6196 261
Web: cmaengineers.com

CMAA (Crane Manufacturers Assn of America)
8720 Red Oak Blvd Ste 201 .... Charlotte NC 28217 704-676-1190 676-1199 49-13
TF: 800-345-1815 ■ *Web:* www.mhi.org

CMAA (Club Managers Assn of America)
1733 King St .... Alexandria VA 22314 703-739-9500 739-0124 49-12
TF: 800-409-7755 ■ *Web:* www.cmaa.org

CMAVE (Center for Medical Agricultural & Veterinary Entomology)
1700 SW 23rd Dr .... Gainesville FL 32608 352-374-5901 374-5852 668
Web: www.ars.usda.gov/saa/cmave

Cmbs Medical Business Services
223 N First Ave Ste 201 .... Arcadia CA 91006 626-821-1411 113
TF: 800-540-2627 ■ *Web:* cmbsllc.net

CMC (Catholic Medical Ctr)
100 McGregor St .... Manchester NH 03102 603-668-3545 374-3
TF: 800-437-9666 ■ *Web:* www.catholicmedicalcenter.org

CMC (Commercial Metals Co)
6565 N MacArthur Blvd Ste 800 .... Irving TX 75039 214-689-4300 689-4300 723
NYSE: CMC ■ *Web:* www.cmc.com

CMC (Communications Manufacturing Co)
2234 Colby Ave .... Los Angeles CA 90064 310-828-3200 248
TF Orders: 800-462-5532 ■ *Web:* www.gotocmc.com

CMC (Geisinger Health System)
1800 Mulberry St .... Scranton PA 18510 570-703-8000 374-3
TF: 800-230-4565 ■ *Web:* www.geisinger.org

CMC (Community Medical Ctr)
99 Hwy 37 W .... Toms River NJ 08755 732-557-8000 374-3
TF: 888-724-7123 ■ *Web:* www.barnabashealth.org

CMC (Concrete Materials Corp)
106 Industry Rd .... Richmond KY 40475 859-623-4238 623-4255 182
Web: www.concretematerialscompany.net

CMC (California Men's Colony)
Hwy 1 PO Box 8101 .... San Luis Obispo CA 93409 805-547-7900 213
Web: www.cdcr.ca.gov

CMC (Cambridge Medical Ctr)
701 S Dellwood St .... Cambridge MN 55008 763-689-7700 374-3
TF: 800-252-4133 ■ *Web:* www.allinahealth.org

CMC (Colleton Medical Ctr)
501 Robertson Blvd .... Walterboro SC 29488 843-782-2000 374-3
TF: 866-492-9083 ■ *Web:* www.colletonmedical.com

CMC (Cumberland Medical Ctr)
421 S Main St .... Crossville TN 38555 931-484-9511 374-3
Web: www.cmchealthcare.org

CMC America Corp 210 S Center St .... Joliet IL 60436 815-726-4336 362
TF: 800-713-0462 ■ *Web:* cmc-america.com

CMC Biologics 22021 20th Ave SE .... Bothell WA 98021 425-485-1900 486-0300 85
TF: 800-845-6973 ■ *Web:* www.cmcbio.com

CMC Capitol City Steel 14501 S IH 35 .... Buda TX 78610 512-282-8820 480
TF: 888-682-7337 ■ *Web:* www.cmc.com

CMC Commercial Metal 2784 Old Dallas Rd .... Waco TX 76705 254-799-2471 799-6227 480
Web: www.cmc.com

CMC Construction Services
9103 E Almeda Rd .... Houston TX 77054 713-799-1150 799-8431 385
TF: 877-297-9111 ■ *Web:* www.cmcconstructionservices.com

CMC Rebar 4846 Singleton Blvd .... Dallas TX 75212 214-428-2861 492
Web: www.cmc.com

CMC Rebar Carolinas
2528 N Chester St .... Gastonia NC 28052 704-865-8571 480
Web: www.cmc.com

CMC Rebar Georgia 251 Hosea Rd .... Lawrenceville GA 30046 770-963-6251 339-6623 480
TF: 888-682-7337 ■ *Web:* www.cmc.com

CMC Rescue Inc 41 Aero Camino .... Goleta CA 93117 805-562-9120 711
Web: www.cmcrescue.com

CMC-KUHNKE 1060 Broadway .... Albany NY 12204 518-694-3310 41
Web: www.cmc-kuhnke.com

CMCL (Cape May County Library)
30 Mechanic St .... Cape May Court House NJ 08210 609-463-6350 434-3
TF: 800-207-1675 ■ *Web:* www.cmclibrary.org

CMCU (Carolinas Medical Ctr Union)
600 Hospital Dr .... Monroe NC 28112 704-283-3100 374-3
TF: 800-994-6610 ■ *Web:* www.carolinashealthcare.org

CMD 1631 NW Thurman St .... Portland OR 97209 503-223-6794 223-2430 4
Web: www.cmdpdx.com

CMD Corp
2901-3005 E Pershing St PO Box 1279 .... Appleton WI 54912 920-730-6888 111
Web: www.cmd-corp.com

CMD Outsourcing Solutions Inc
729 E Pratt St Ste 700 .... Baltimore MD 21202 410-347-5544 393
Web: www.cmdosi.com

CMD Products 1410 Flightline Dr Ste D .... Lincoln CA 95648 916-434-0228 429
TF: 800-210-9949 ■ *Web:* www.cmdproducts.com

CMDA (Christian Medical & Dental Assn)
2604 Hwy 421 PO Box 7500 .... Bristol TN 37620 423-844-1000 844-1005 49-8
TF: 888-231-2637 ■ *Web:* www.cmda.org

CME Assoc 439 N Pearl St .... Albany NY 12204 518-432-5820 743
Web: www.cmeassociates.com

Cme Assoc Inc 32 Crabtree Ln .... Woodstock CT 06281 860-928-7848 256
TF: 888-291-3227 ■ *Web:* www.cmeengineering.com

CME Group Inc 20 S Wacker Dr .... Chicago IL 60606 312-930-1000 466-4410 691
NASDAQ: CME ■ *TF:* 866-716-7274 ■ *Web:* www.cmegroup.com

Cme Printing Inc
8181 Commerce Park Dr .... Houston TX 77036 713-271-7700 627
TF: 800-331-3282 ■ *Web:* cmeprinting.com

CMF Associates LLC
325 Chestnut St Ste 410 .... Philadelphia PA 19106 215-531-7500 194
Web: www.cmfassociates.com

CMG (Color Marketing Group)
1908 Mt Vernon Ave .... Alexandria VA 22301 703-329-8500 535-3190 49-18
Web: www.colormarketing.org

CMG (Computer Measurement Group)
3501 Rt 42 Ste 130 & 121 .... Turnersville NJ 08012 856-401-1700 48-9

CMG Environmental 67 Hall Rd .... Sturbridge MA 01566 774-241-0901 261

CMG Surety LLC
1016 Collier Ctr Way Ste 100 .... Naples FL 34110 239-597-0128 796
Web: www.cmgsurety.com

CMG Worldwide Inc
10500 Crosspoint Blvd .... Indianapolis IN 46256 317-570-5000 7
Web: www.cmgworldwide.com

CMH (Clark Memorial Hospital)
1220 Missouri Ave .... Jeffersonville IN 47130 812-282-6631 283-6330 374-3
Web: www.clarkmemorial.org

CMH (Clinton Memorial Hospital)
610 W Main St .... Wilmington OH 45177 937-382-6611 374-3
TF: 800-803-9648 ■ *Web:* www.cmhregional.com

CMH (Community Memorial Hospital)
W 180 N 8085 Town Hall Rd .... Menomonee Falls WI 53051 262-251-1000 374-3
Web: froedtert.com

CMH Space Flooring Products Inc
6950 Aviation Blvd .... Glen Burnie MD 21061 800-922-9248 131
TF: 800-922-9248 ■ *Web:* www.cmhspace.com

CMHIFL (Colorado Mental Health Institute at Fort Logan)
3520 W Oxford Ave .... Denver CO 80236 303-866-7066 374-5

CMHIP (Colorado Mental Health Institute at Pueblo)
1600 W 24th St .... Pueblo CO 81003 719-546-4000 374-5
Web: www.colorado.gov

CMI (Can Manufacturers Institute)
1730 Rhode Island Ave NW Ste 1000 .... Washington DC 20036 202-232-4677 232-5756 49-13
Web: www.cancentral.com

CMI (Challenge Management Inc)
4230 LBJ Fwy Ste 414 .... Dallas TX 75244 972-755-2560 755-2561 47
Web: www.challenge-management.com

CMI (Central Management Inc)
820 Gessner Rd Ste 1525 .... Houston TX 77024 713-961-9777 652
Web: www.cmirealestate.com

Cmi 6704 Guada Coma Dr .... Schertz TX 78154 210-967-6169 967-9233 418
TF: 800-840-1070 ■ *Web:* www.cmi-satx.com

CMI Credit Mediators Inc
414 Sansom St .... Upper Darby PA 19082 610-352-5151 160
TF: 800-456-3328 ■ *Web:* www.cmiweb.com

CMI EFCO Inc 435 W Wilson St .... Salem OH 44460 330-332-4661 332-4661 318
TF: 877-225-2674 ■ *Web:* www.cmigroupe.com

CMI Inc 316 E Ninth St .... Owensboro KY 42303 270-685-6545 685-6678 529
TF: 866-835-0690 ■ *Web:* www.alcoholtest.com

CMI Plastics Inc 222 Pepsi Way .... Ayden NC 28513 252-746-2171 608
TF: 877-395-1920 ■ *Web:* www.cmiplastics.com

CMIC (Connecticut Medical Insurance Co)
80 Glastonbury Blvd 3rd Fl .... Glastonbury CT 06033 860-633-7788 391-5

Cmj Engineering & Testing Inc
7636 Pebble Dr .... Fort Worth TX 76118 817-284-9400 261
Web: www.cmjengr.com

CMLS Financial Ltd
Oceanic Plaza Bldg
2110 - 1066 W Hastings St .... Vancouver BC V6E3X2 604-687-2118 509
Web: m.cmls.ca

CMMB (Catholic Medical Mission Board)
10 W 17th St .... New York NY 10011 212-242-7757 48-5
TF: 800-678-5659 ■ *Web:* www.cmmb.org

CMMG Inc 620 County Rd 118 .... Fayette MO 65248 660-248-2293 711
Web: www.cmmginc.com

C-MOR LLC 2626 W Broad St .... Richmond VA 23220 804-474-7000 474-7099 521
Web: c-mor.org

CMP Industries LLC 413 N Pearl St .... Albany NY 12207-1311 518-434-3147 434-1288 476
Web: cmpindustries.com

CMRG Interactive 2401 Trinity Ln .... Mckinney TX 75070 888-828-8097 226
TF: 888-828-8097 ■ *Web:* www.cmrgsolutions.com

CMS (College Music Society)
312 E Pine St .... Missoula MT 59802 406-721-9616 721-9419 49-5
TF: 800-729-0235 ■ *Web:* www.music.org

CMS (Centers for Medicare & Medicaid Services)
7500 Security Blvd .... Baltimore MD 21244 800-633-4227 340-10
TF: 800-633-4227 ■ *Web:* www.cms.gov

Name / Address	City	State	Zip	Phone	Fax	Class
Cms Communications Inc 722 Goddard Ave *TF:* 800-755-9169 ■ *Web:* www.cmsc.com	Chesterfield	MO	63005	800-755-9169		246
CMS Electric Co-op Inc 509 E Carthage St *TF:* 800-794-2353 ■ *Web:* www.cmselectric.com	Meade	KS	67864	620-873-2184		245
CMS Energy Corp 1 Energy Plaza *NYSE: CMS* ■ *TF:* 800-477-5050 ■ *Web:* www.cmsenergy.com	Jackson	MI	49201	517-788-0550		360-5
CMS Innovative Consultants 8 Fletcher Pl *Web:* www.cmsav.com	Melville	NY	11747	631-425-3000		194
CMS Mechanical Services Inc 609 Technology Cir Ste A *Web:* mechanicalservicesco.com	Windsor	CO	80550	970-686-6800		610
CMS Mid-Atlantic Inc 295 Totowa Rd *TF:* 800-267-1981 ■ *Web:* www.cmsmidatlantic.com	Totowa	NJ	07512	800-267-1981		393
CMS Peripherals Inc 12 Mauchly Unit E *TF:* 800-327-5773 ■ *Web:* www.cmsproducts.com	Irvine	CA	92618	714-424-5520		173-8
CMSA (Case Management Society of America) 6301 Ranch Dr *TF:* 800-216-2672 ■ *Web:* www.cmsa.org	Little Rock	AR	72223	501-225-2229	221-9068	49-8
Cmsa Inc 2142 Alt 19 St A *TF:* 800-438-7325 ■ *Web:* www.cmsa.com	Palm Harbor	FL	34683	727-447-3396		7
CMSD (Cleveland Municipal School District) 1380 E Sixth St **Fax:* Hum Res ■ *Web:* www.clevelandmetroschools.org	Cleveland	OH	44114	216-838-0000	361-2018*	685
CMT (Country Music Television) 330 Commerce St *Web:* www.cmt.com	Nashville	TN	37201	615-335-8400		740
CMT (Core Molding Technologies Inc) 800 Manor Pk Dr *NYSE: CMT* ■ *Web:* www.coremt.com	Columbus	OH	43228	614-870-5000		604
CMTS (Children's Musical Theater San Jose) 1401 Parkmoor Ave Ste 100 *Web:* www.cmtsj.org	San Jose	CA	95126	408-288-5437		573-4
CMW (Central Maintenance & Welding Inc) 2620 E Keysville Rd *TF:* 877-704-7411 ■ *Web:* www.cmw.cc	Lithia	FL	33547	813-737-1402	737-1820	189-14
CMW Inc 70 S Gray St *Web:* www.cmwinc.com	Indianapolis	IN	46201	317-634-8884		482
Cn Staffing Inc 1201 Richardson Dr Ste 150 *Web:* www.cnstaffing.com	Richardson	TX	75080	972-484-3922		260
CNA (California Nurses Assn) 2000 Franklin St *Web:* www.nationalnursesunited.org	Oakland	CA	94612	510-273-2200	663-1625	533
CNA (Colorado Nurses Assn) 2851 S Parker Rd Ste 1210 *Web:* coloradonurses.org	Aurora	CO	80014	720-457-1194		533
CNA (Connecticut Nurses Assn) 377 Research Pkwy Ste 2D *Web:* www.ctnurses.org	Meriden	CT	06450	203-238-1207	238-3437	533
CNA Corp 4825 Mark Ctr Dr *TF:* 800-344-0007 ■ *Web:* www.cna.org	Alexandria	VA	22311	703-824-2000	824-2949	668
CNA Financial Corp 333 S Wabash Ave *NYSE: CNA* ■ *TF:* 800-262-4357 ■ *Web:* www.cna.com	Chicago	IL	60604	312-822-5000		360-4
Cna National Warranty Corp 4150 N Drinkwater Blvd Ste 400 *Web:* cnanational.com	Scottsdale	AZ	85251	480-941-1626		390
CNA Surety Corp 333 S Wabash Ave *NYSE: L* ■ *TF:* 877-672-6115 ■ *Web:* www.cnasurety.com	Chicago	IL	60604	312-822-5000		391-5
CNB (City National Bank of New Jersey) 900 Broad St *TF:* 877-350-3524 ■ *Web:* www.citynatbank.com	Newark	NJ	07102	973-624-0865		70
CNB Financial Corp 1 S Second St PO Box 42 *NASDAQ: CCNE* ■ *TF:* 800-492-3221 ■ *Web:* www.cnbbank.bank	Clearfield	PA	16830	814-765-9621	765-8294	360-2
CNB Technology USA Inc 2310 E Artesia Blvd *TF:* 800-375-5283 ■ *Web:* www.cnbusa.com	Long Beach	CA	90805	562-728-8500		693
CNBC Inc 900 Sylvan Ave *Web:* www.cnbc.com	Englewood Cliffs	NJ	07632	201-735-2622		740
CNBS Inc 7200 W 132nd St Ste 240 *TF:* 800-222-0978 ■ *Web:* www.cnbsnet.com	Overland Park	KS	66213	800-222-0978		690
CNC Assoc Ny Inc 101 Kentile Rd *Web:* www.cncassociates.com	South Plainfield	NJ	07080	718-416-3853		191-3
Cnc Consulting Inc 50 E Palisade Ave Ste 410 *Web:* www.cncconsult.com	Englewood	NJ	07631	201-541-9121		180
CNC Engineering Inc 19 Bacon Rd *Web:* www.cnc1.com	Enfield	CT	06082	860-749-1780		256
CNC Industries Inc 3810 Fourier Dr *Web:* www.cncind.com	Fort Wayne	IN	46818	260-490-5700		111
CNC Industries Ltd 9331 39 Ave *TF:* 877-262-2343 ■ *Web:* www.cncindustries.com	Edmonton	AB	T6E5T3	780-469-2346		454
CNC Machine Products Inc 1709 W 20th St *Web:* www.cncmp.com	Joplin	MO	64804	417-782-2627		757
CNC Software Inc 671 Old Post Rd *TF:* 800-228-2877 ■ *Web:* www.mastercam.com	Tolland	CT	06084	860-875-5006		225
CNF (Cornell NanoScale Science & Technology Facility) Cornell University 250 Duffield Hall *Web:* www.cnf.cornell.edu	Ithaca	NY	14853	607-255-2329	255-8601	668
CNFA (Citizens Network for Foreign Affairs) 1828 L St NW Ste 710 *TF:* 800-392-3532 ■ *Web:* www.cnfa.org	Washington	DC	20036	202-296-3920		48-5
CNG (Connecticut Natural Gas Corp) 76 Meadow St *Web:* www.cngcorp.com	East Hartford	CT	06108	860-727-3000		787
Cng Engineering PLLC 1917 N New Braunfels Ave Ste 201 *Web:* cngengineering.com	San Antonio	TX	78208	210-224-8841		261
CNGC (Cascade Natural Gas Corp) 8113 W Grandridge Blvd *TF:* 888-522-1130 ■ *Web:* www.cngc.com	Kennewick	WA	99336	206-624-3900		787
Cnic Inc 4418 Monroe Rd E *TF:* 800-566-2320 ■ *Web:* www.cnic-inc.com	Charlotte	NC	28205	704-344-0090		175
CNMC (Children's National Medical Ctr) 111 Michigan Ave NW *TF:* 800-884-5433 ■ *Web:* www.childrensnational.org	Washington	DC	20010	202-476-5000		374-1
CNN Radio Network 190 Marietta St Ste 1 *Web:* cnnradio.cnn.com	Atlanta	GA	30303	404-827-2750		644
CNP Technologies LLC 806 Tyvola Rd Ste 102 *TF:* 800-767-3263 ■ *Web:* www.cnp.net	Charlotte	NC	28217	704-927-6600		180
CNPP (Center for Nutrition Policy & Promotion) 3101 Pk Ctr Dr 10th Fl *Web:* www.cnpp.usda.gov	Alexandria	VA	22302-1594	703-305-7600	305-3300	340-1
CNRL (Canadian Natural Resources Ltd) 855 Second St SW Ste 2500 *NYSE: CNQ* ■ *TF:* 888-878-3700 ■ *Web:* www.cnrl.com	Calgary	AB	T2P4J8	403-517-6700	517-7350	536
CNS Home Health & Hospice 690 E N Ave Ste 100 *TF:* 800-942-9412 ■ *Web:* www.cnshomehealth.org	Carol Stream	IL	60188	630-665-7000		371
CNS Response Inc 85 Enterprise Ste 410 *TF:* 888-545-2677 ■ *Web:* www.cnsresponse.com	Aliso Viejo	CA	92656	949-420-4400		250
CNS Therapeutics Inc 332 Minnesota St W1750 *Web:* www.gablofen.com	St Paul	MN	55101	651-207-6959		231
CNW Inc 4710 Madison Rd	Cincinnati	OH	45227	513-321-2775		621
Co Do Vietnamese Restaurant 1411 17th Ave SW	Calgary	AB	T2T0C3	403-228-7798		671
Co/op Optical Vision Designs 2424 E Eight-Mile *Web:* www.coopoptical.com	Detroit	MI	48234	313-366-5100	366-7313	543
COA (Council on Accreditation) 45 Broadway 29th Fl *TF:* 866-262-8088 ■ *Web:* www.coanet.org	New York	NY	10006	212-797-3000	797-1428	48-1
Coach & Equipment Manufacturing Corp 130 Horizon Pk Dr PO Box 36 *TF:* 800-724-8464 ■ *Web:* www.coachandequipment.com	Penn Yan	NY	14527	800-724-8464		516
Coach & Four Restaurant 5206 Williamson Rd *Web:* www.coachandfour.com	Roanoke	VA	24012	540-362-4220		671
Coach Canada's Health Informatics Association 250 Consumers Rd *TF:* 888-253-8554 ■ *Web:* coachorgnew.com	North York	ON	M2J4V6	416-494-9324		138
Coach House Inc 3480 Technology Dr *TF:* 800-235-0984 ■ *Web:* www.coachhouserv.com	Nokomis	FL	34275	941-485-0984		120
Coach House Theatre 732 W Exchange St *TF:* 800-686-1141 ■ *Web:* www.coachhousetheatre.org	Akron	OH	44302	330-434-7741		572
Coach Inc 342 Madison Ave *NYSE: COH* ■ *TF:* 800-444-3611 ■ *Web:* world.coach.com	New York	NY	10173	212-594-1850	594-1682	430
Coach Stop Inn, The 715 State Hwy 3 Bar Harbor *Web:* www.coachstopinn.com	Maine	PA	16901	207-288-9886		378
Coach Tours Ltd 475 Federal Rd *TF:* 800-822-6224 ■ *Web:* www.coachtour.com	Brookfield	CT	06804	203-740-1118		760
Coachella Valley History Museum 82616 Miles Ave *TF:* 800-476-7506 ■ *Web:* www.cvhm.org	Indio	CA	92201	760-342-6651	863-5232	520
Coachella Valley Unified School District 87-225 Church St	Thermal	CA	92274	760-399-5137		685
Coachman Inn 32959 SR-Hwy 20 *Web:* www.thecoachmaninn.com	Oak Harbor	WA	98277	360-675-0727		379
Coact Associates Ltd 2748 Centennial Rd *TF:* 866-646-4400 ■ *Web:* teamcoact.com	Toledo	OH	43617	866-646-4400		196
COACT Inc 9140 Guilford Rd Ste N *Web:* www.coact.com	Columbia	MD	21046	301-498-0150		261
CoAdna Photonics Inc 733 Palomar Ave *Web:* www.coadna.com	Sunnyvale	CA	94085	408-736-1100		735
Co-Advantage Resources 3350 Buschwood Park Dr Ste 200 *TF:* 800-868-1016 ■ *Web:* www.coadvantage.com	Tampa	FL	33618	813-935-2000		631
CoAEMSP 8301 Lakeview Pkwy Ste 111-312 *Web:* www.coaemsp.org	Rowlett	TX	75088	817-330-0080		48-1
Coahoma County PO Box 98 *Web:* www.coahomacounty.net	Clarksdale	MS	38614	662-624-3000	624-3040	338
Coahoma Electric Power Assn 340 Hopson St *Web:* coahomaepa.com	Lyon	MS	38645	662-624-8321		245
COAI (Clowns of America International) PO Box 122 *TF:* 877-816-6941 ■ *Web:* www.coai.org	Eustis	FL	32727	352-357-1676		48-4
Coair Inc 85 Rue Des Buissons *Web:* www.coair.qc.ca	Levis	QC	G6V5B6	418-835-0141		358
Coakley & Williams Construction Inc 7475 Wisconsin Ave Ste 900 *Web:* www.coakleywilliams.com	Bethesda	MD	20814	301-963-5000		187
Coal County 4 N Main St	Coalgate	OK	74538	580-927-2103	927-4003	338
Coal Outlook 1200 G St NW Ste 1100 *TF:* 800-752-8878 ■ *Web:* www.platts.com	Washington	DC	20005	212-904-3070	904-4209	531-5
Coal Valley News 350 Main St *Web:* www.coalvalleynews.com	Madison	WV	25130	304-369-1165	369-1166	532-4
Coalesce Corp 447 Miller Ave Ste E *Web:* www.coalesce.com	Mill Valley	CA	94941	415-384-3040		195
Coalesce Mktg & Design Inc 4321 W College Ave Ste 250 *Web:* www.coalescemarketing.com	Appleton	WI	54914	920-380-4444		194
Coalfire Systems Inc 361 Centennial Pkwy Ste 150 *Web:* www.coalfire.com	Louisville	CO	80027	303-554-6333		180
Coalition Against Bigger Trucks (CABT) 1001 N Fairfax St Ste 515 *Web:* www.cabt.org	Alexandria	VA	22314	703-535-3131		49-21
Coalition Against Insurance Fraud 1012 14th St NW Ste 200 *TF:* 800-835-6422 ■ *Web:* www.insurancefraud.org	Washington	DC	20005	202-393-7330	318-9189	49-9
Coalition for Auto Repair Equality (CARE) 105 Oronoco St Ste 115 *TF:* 800-229-5380 ■ *Web:* www.careauto.org	Alexandria	VA	22314	703-519-7555	519-7747	49-21

Name / Address	City	State	Zip	Phone	Fax	Class
Coalition for Buzzards Bay Inc, The 114 Front St *TF:* 800-776-0188 ■ *Web:* www.savebuzzardsbay.org	New Dedford	MA	02740	508-999-6363		804
Coalition for Employment Through Exports (CEE) 1625 K St NW Ste 200 *Web:* www.usaexport.org	Washington	DC	20006	202-296-6107	296-9709	49-18
Coalition for Government Procurement 1990 M St NW Ste 450 *Web:* thecgp.org	Washington	DC	20036	202-331-0975	822-9788	49-18
Coalition for Networked Information 21 Dupont Cir Ste 800 *Web:* www.cni.org	Washington	DC	20036	202-296-5098	872-0884	48-9
Coalition for Responsible Waste Incineration (CRWI) 1615 L St NW Ste 1350 *Web:* www.crwi.org	Washington	DC	20036	202-452-1241		48-13
Coalition of Health Services Inc 301 S Polk St Ste 740 *TF:* 800-442-7893 ■ *Web:* cohs.net	Amarillo	TX	79101	806-337-1700		463
Coalition of Labor Union Women (CLUW) 815 16th St NW 2nd Fl *TF:* 800-981-9495 ■ *Web:* www.cluw.org	Washington	DC	20006	202-508-6969	508-6968	48-24
Coalition on Human Needs (CHN) 1120 Connecticut Ave NW *Web:* www.chn.org	Washington	DC	20036	202-223-2532	223-2538	48-5
Coalition to Stop Gun Violence 805 15th St NW Ste 700 *TF:* 800-486-6963 ■ *Web:* www.csgv.org	Washington	DC	20005	202-408-0061		48-7
Co-Alliance LLP 5250 E US Hwy 36 Bldg 1000 *TF:* 800-525-0272 ■ *Web:* www.co-alliance.com	Avon	IN	46123	317-745-4491	718-1850	275
CoaLogix Inc 11707 Steele Creek Rd	Charlotte	NC	28273	704-827-8933		192
Coan Construction Company Inc 1481 E Grand Ave *Web:* www.coanconstruction.com	Pomona	CA	91766	909-868-6812		121
Coan Engineering LLC 2277 E North St *Web:* www.coanracing.com	Kokomo	IN	46901	765-456-3957		54
Co-Anon Family Groups PO Box 3664 *TF:* 800-898-9985 ■ *Web:* www.co-anon.org	Gilbert	AZ	85299	480-442-3869		48-21
Coast 39 John St *Web:* www.holycityhospitality.com	Charleston	SC	29403	843-722-8838	722-8835	671
Coast 931 E Wisconsin Ave *Web:* www.coastrestaurant.com	Milwaukee	WI	53202	414-727-5555	727-0777	671
Coast 1054 Alberni St *Web:* www.glowbalgroup.com	Vancouver	BC	V6E1A3	604-685-5010		671
Coast 2 Coast 7704 Basswood Dr *Web:* www.c2csurveys.com	Chattanooga	TN	37416	423-296-9000		701
Coast Aluminum & Architectural Inc 30551 Huntwood Ave *Web:* www.coastaluminum.com	Hayward	CA	94544	510-441-6600		492
Coast Capital Savings 645 Tyee Rd Ste 400 *TF:* 888-517-7000 ■ *Web:* www.coastcapitalsavings.com	Victoria	BC	V9A6X5	250-483-7000		70
Coast Central Credit Union Inc 2650 Harrison Ave *TF:* 800-974-9727 ■ *Web:* www.coastccu.org	Eureka	CA	95501	707-445-8801		219
Coast Coatings LLC 227 Calle Pintoresco *Web:* www.coastpowdercoating.com	San Clemente	CA	92672	949-492-9037		481
Coast Communications Company Inc 349 Damon Rd *Web:* www.coastaccess.com	Ocean Shores	WA	98569	360-289-2252		116
Coast Composites Inc 1395 S Lyon St *Web:* www.coastcomposites.com	Santa Ana	CA	92705	949-455-0665		757
Coast Dental Services Inc 4010 W Boy Scout Blvd Ste 1100 *TF:* 800-327-6453 ■ *Web:* www.coastdental.com	Tampa	FL	33607	813-288-1999	289-4500	463
Coast Edmonton House Suite Hotel 1090 W Georgia S Ste 900 *TF:* 800-716-6199 ■ *Web:* www.coasthotels.com	Vancouver	BC	V6E3V7	604-682-7982		379
Coast Electric Power Assn 18020 Hwy Ste 603 *TF Cust Svc:* 800-624-3348 ■ *Web:* www.coastepa.com	Kiln	MS	39556	228-363-7000		245
Coast Guard Exchange System 510 Independence Pkwy Ste 500 *TF:* 800-572-0230 ■ *Web:* shopcgx.com	Chesapeake	VA	23320	800-572-0230		791
Coast Guard Sector Detroit 110 Mt Elliott Ave *Web:* www.uscg.mil	Detroit	MI	48207	313-568-9525	568-9469	158
Coast Guard Sector Sault Sainte Marie 337 Water St *Web:* www.uscg.mil/d9/sectSaultSteMarie	Sault Sainte Marie	MI	49783	906-635-3217		158
Coast Hotels & Resorts Canada 1090 W Georgia St *Web:* www.coasthotels.com	Vancouver	BC	V6E3V7	604-682-7982	682-8942	379
Coast Hotels & Resorts USA 2003 Western Ave Ste 500 *Web:* www.coasthotels.com	Seattle	WA	98121	206-826-2700	826-2701	379
Coast Oil Co 4250 Williams Rd *Web:* www.coastoil.com	San Jose	CA	95129	408-252-7720		540
Coast Packing Co 3275 E Vernon Ave	Vernon	CA	90058	323-277-7700		296-12
Coast Personnel 2295 De La Cruz Blvd *Web:* www.coastjobs.com	Santa Clara	CA	95050	408-653-2100		260
Coast Plating Inc 128 W 154th St *Web:* www.coastplating.com	Gardena	CA	90248	323-770-0240		481
Coast Plaza Doctors Hospital Inc 13100 Studebaker Rd *Web:* avantihospitals.com	Norwalk	CA	90650	562-868-3751		374-3
Coast Plaza Hotel 1316 33 St NE *TF:* 800-661-1464 ■ *Web:* www.calgaryplaza.com	Calgary	AB	T2A6B6	403-248-8888		379
Coast Pneumatics 8055 E Crystal Dr *TF:* 800-696-6165 ■ *Web:* coastpneumatics.com	Anaheim	CA	92807	714-921-2255		358
Coast Produce Co 1791 Bay St *Web:* www.coastproduce.com	Los Angeles	CA	90021	213-955-4900	955-4949	10-11
COAST Products Inc 8033 NE Holman St *TF:* 800-426-5858 ■ *Web:* www.coastportland.com	Portland	OR	97218	503-234-4545		362
Coast Professional Inc 214 Expo Cir Ste 7 *Web:* www.coastprofessional.net	West Monroe	LA	71292	318-807-4500		160

Name / Address	City	State	Zip	Phone	Fax	Class
Coast Pump Water Technologies Inc 610 Groveland Ave *Web:* www.coastpumpwatertechnology.com	Venice	FL	34285	941-484-3738		429
Coast Seafoods Co 14711 NE 29th Pl Ste 111 *Web:* coastseafoods.com	Bellevue	WA	98007	425-702-8800		296-14
Coast Surveying Inc 15031 Pkwy Loop Ste B *Web:* coastsurvey.com	Tustin	CA	92780	714-918-6266		727
Coast to Coast Business Equipment Inc 8 Vanderbilt *TF:* 800-854-4641 ■ *Web:* www.ctcbe.com	Irvine	CA	92619	949-457-7300	457-7365	589
Coast To Coast Construction 12th St & Winchester Ave *Web:* www.coast-to-coast-inc.com	Washington	DC	20004	202-681-8242		186
Coast to Coast Corporate Housing 10773 Los Alamitos Blvd *TF:* 800-451-9466 ■ *Web:* www.ctchousing.com	Los Alamitos	CA	90720	562-795-0250	795-0251	210
Coast to Coast Moving & Storage Co 136 41st St *TF:* 800-872-6683 ■ *Web:* www.ctcvanlines.com	Brooklyn	NY	11232	718-443-5800		519
Coast Tool Co 2099 edison ave *TF:* 888-675-3737 ■ *Web:* www.coasttool.com	San leandro	CA	94577	510-569-1945		350
Coast2Coast Diagnostics Inc 600 N Tustin Ave Ste 110 *TF:* 800-730-9263 ■ *Web:* www.c2cdiagnostics.net	Santa Ana	CA	92705	800-730-9263		415
Coastal & Marine Institute San Diego State University 4165 Spruance Rd *Web:* www.sci.sdsu.edu/cmi	San Diego	CA	92101	619-594-1308		668
Coastal Administrative Services 103 E Holly Ste 214 **Fax Area Code:* 360 ■ *TF:* 800-870-1831 ■ *Web:* www.coastaladmin.com	Bellingham	WA	98225	800-870-1831	746-8386*	260
Coastal Agrobusiness Inc 3702 Evans St PO Box 856 *TF:* 800-758-1828 ■ *Web:* www.coastalagro.com	Greenville	NC	27835	252-756-1126	756-3282	280
Coastal Automotive Service Garage 2006 Cottonwood Ave *Web:* www.awesomenet.net	Bay City	TX	77414	979-245-8361		54
Coastal Bend Blood Ctr 209 N Padre Island Dr *TF:* 800-299-4943 ■ *Web:* www.coastalbendbloodcenter.org	Corpus Christi	TX	78406	361-855-4943	855-2641	89
Coastal Bend College *Beeville* 3800 Charco Rd **Fax:* Admissions ■ *TF:* 866-722-2030 ■ *Web:* coastalbend.edu	Beeville	TX	78102	361-358-2838	354-2254*	162
Coastal Beverage Co Inc 301 Harley Rd *TF:* 800-273-0555 ■ *Web:* www.coastalbev.com	Wilmington	NC	28405	910-799-3011	392-3674	81-1
Coastal Bridge Company LLC 4825 Jamestown Ave PO Box 14715 *Web:* www.coastalbridge.com	Baton Rouge	LA	70898	225-766-0244	766-0423	46
Coastal Building Maintenance 15405 NW Seventh Ave *TF:* 800-357-7790 ■ *Web:* www.cbmflorida.com	Miami	FL	33169	305-681-6100		104
Coastal Carolina Community College 444 Western Blvd **Fax:* Admissions ■ *TF:* 800-908-9946 ■ *Web:* coastalcarolina.edu	Jacksonville	NC	28546	910-455-1221	455-7027*	162
Coastal Carolina University PO Box 261954 *TF:* 800-277-7000 ■ *Web:* www.coastal.edu	Conway	SC	29528	843-349-2170	349-2127	166
Coastal Casting Service Inc 2903 Gano St *TF:* 800-433-6223 ■ *Web:* coastalcasting.com	Houston	TX	77009	713-223-4439		757
Coastal Cement Corp 36 Drydock Ave	Boston	MA	02210	617-350-0183		135
Coastal Conservation Assn (CCA) 6919 Portwest Dr Ste 100 *TF:* 800-201-3474 ■ *Web:* www.joincca.org	Houston	TX	77024	713-626-4234	626-5852	48-13
Coastal Corrosion Control Surveys LLC 10172 Mammoth Ave *TF:* 800-894-2120 ■ *Web:* www.coastalcorrosion.com	Baton Rouge	LA	70814	225-275-6131		492
Coastal Credit LLC 3852 Virginia Beach Boulvard *Web:* www.coastalcreditllc.com	Virginia Beach	VA	23452	757-340-6000		401
Coastal Electric Co-op 1265 S Coastal Hwy *TF:* 800-421-2343 ■ *Web:* coastalelectriccooperative.com	Midway	GA	31320-0109	912-884-3311		245
Coastal Electric Co-op Inc 2269 Jefferies Hwy *Web:* www.coastal.coop	Walterboro	SC	29488	843-538-5700		245
Coastal Environmental Systems Inc 820 First Ave S *Web:* www.coastalenvironmental.com	Seattle	WA	98134	206-682-6048		407
Coastal Federal Credit Union 1000 St Albans Dr *TF:* 800-868-4262 ■ *Web:* www.coastal24.com	Raleigh	NC	27609	919-420-8000		219
Coastal Foods Inc 14212 Interdr W	Houston	TX	77032	281-987-8985		297-8
Coastal Harbor Treatment Ctr 1150 Cornell Ave *TF:* 844-657-2638 ■ *Web:* coastalharbor.com	Savannah	GA	31406	912-354-3911		374-5
Coastal Healthcare Consulting Inc 6808 220th St SW Ste 204 *Web:* www.coastalhealthcare.com	Mountlake Terrace	WA	98043	206-324-6540		196
Coastal Helicopters Inc 8995 Yandukin Dr *TF:* 800-789-5610 ■ *Web:* www.coastalhelicopters.com	Juneau	AK	99801	907-789-5600		359
Coastal Hospice & Palliative Care 2604 Old Ocean City Rd PO Box 1733 *TF:* 800-780-7886 ■ *Web:* www.coastalhospice.org	Salisbury	MD	21804	410-742-8732		371
Coastal Hotel Group Inc 6501 Railroad Ave SE *Web:* www.coastalhotel.com	Snoqualmie	WA	98065	425-888-2556		378
Coastal Inn Concorde 379 Windmill Rd *TF:* 800-565-1565 ■ *Web:* coastalinns.com	Dartmouth	NS	B3A1J6	902-465-7777		379
Coastal Inns Inc 111 Warwick St Box 280 *TF:* 800-665-7829 ■ *Web:* www.coastalinns.com	Digby	NS	B0V1A0	800-401-1155		379
Coastal Journal 97 Commercial St *TF:* 800-649-6241 ■ *Web:* www.coastaljournal.com	Bath	ME	04530	207-443-6241		532-4

Company / Address	City	State	ZIP	Phone	Fax	Class
Coastal Logistics Group Inc 50 Sonny Perdue Dr *Web:* www.clg-sav.com	Garden City	GA	31408	912-964-0707		194
Coastal Maine Botanical Gardens PO Box 234 *Web:* www.mainegardens.org	Boothbay	ME	04537	207-633-4333	633-2366	97
Coastal Mechanical Services LLC 394 E Dr *TF:* 866-584-9528 ■ *Web:* www.coastalmechanical.com	Melbourne	FL	32904	321-725-3061	984-0718	189-10
Coastal Mountain Fuels 501 Industrial Pk Pl *Web:* www.cmfuels.ca	Gold River	BC	V0P2G0	250-283-2514		536
Coastal Pacific Food Distributors Inc (CPFD) 1015 Performance Dr *TF:* 800-500-2611 ■ *Web:* www.cpfd.com	Stockton	CA	95206	209-983-2454		297-8
Coastal Palms Hotel 120th St Coastal Hwy *TF:* 800-641-0011 ■ *Web:* www.coastalpalmshotel.com	Ocean City	MD	21842	800-641-0011		379
Coastal Plain Ventures LLC 211 Broad Hollow Rd *Web:* www.amsteelpro.com	Swainsboro	GA	30401	706-413-3806		234
Coastal Planning & Engineering Inc 2481 NW Boca Raton Blvd *Web:* cbi.com/markets/infrastructure/maritime	Boca Raton	FL	33431	561-391-8102		256
Coastal Plumbing Supply Company Inc 480 Bay St *Web:* www.coastalsupplygroup.com.	Staten Island	NY	10304	718-447-2692		612
Coastal Printing Inc of Sarasota 1730 Independence Blvd Ste 34234 *Web:* www.coastalprint.com	Sarasota	FL	34234	941-351-1515		627
Coastal Reprographics Services 880 Via Esteban Ste B *Web:* gocrs.com	San Luis Obispo	CA	93401	805-543-5247		113
Coastal Software & Consulting Inc PO Box 872106 *Web:* www.coastalsoftware.com	Vancouver	WA	98687-2106	360-891-6174		177
Coastal Steel Construction Inc 950 31st St S	St. Petersburg	FL	33712	727-327-7123		480
Coastal Steel Inc 870 Cidco Rd *Web:* www.coastalsteel.com	Cocoa	FL	32923	321-632-8228		480
Coastal Tag & Label Inc 13233 Barton Cir *Web:* www.coastaltag.com	Santa Fe Springs	CA	90670	562-946-4318		627
Coastal Timbers Inc 1310 Jane St *Web:* www.coastaltimbers.com	New Iberia	LA	70563	337-369-3017	365-0003	683
Coastal Tractor Inc 10 Harris Pl *Web:* www.coastaltractor.com	Salinas	CA	93901	831-757-4101		57
Coastal Training Technologies Corp 500 Studio Dr *TF:* 866-333-6888 ■ *Web:* www.coastal.com	Virginia Beach	VA	23452	757-498-9014		513
Coastal Transport Co Inc 1603 Ackerman Rd *TF:* 800-523-8612 ■ *Web:* coastaltransport.com	San Antonio	TX	78219	210-661-4287		780
Coastal Transportation Inc 4025 13th Ave W *TF:* 800-544-2580 ■ *Web:* www.coastaltransportation.com	Seattle	WA	98119	206-282-9979	283-9121	312
Coastline Community College 11460 Warner Ave **Fax:* Admissions ■ *TF:* 866-422-2645 ■ *Web:* www.coastline.edu	Fountain Valley	CA	92708	714-546-7600	241-6288*	162
Coastline Equipment 1930 Lockwood St *Web:* www.coastlineequipment.com	Oxnard	CA	93036	805-485-2106		57
Coastline Metal Finishing Corp 7061 Patterson Dr *Web:* www.coastlinemetalfinishing.com	Garden Grove	CA	92841	714-895-9099		481
Coates Field Service Inc 4800 N Santa Fe *Web:* www.coatesfieldservice.com	Oklahoma City	OK	73118	405-528-5676		194
Coating & Adhesive Corp (CAC) 1901 Popular St PO Box 1080 *TF:* 800-410-2999 ■ *Web:* www.cacoatings.com	Leland	NC	28451	910-371-3184	371-5580	550
Coating Place Inc 200 Paoli St *Web:* www.coatingplace.com	Verona	WI	53593	608-845-9521	845-9526	582
Coatings Resource Corp 15541 Commerce Ln *Web:* www.coatingsresource.com	Huntington Beach	CA	92649	714-894-5252	893-2322	550
Coats North America 3430 Toringdon Way Ste 301 *TF:* 800-631-0965 ■ *Web:* www.coats.com	Charlotte	NC	28277	704-329-5800		745-9
Coaxial Dynamics 6800 Lake Abrams Dr *TF:* 800-262-9425 ■ *Web:* www.coaxial.com	Middleburg Heights	OH	44130	440-243-1100	243-1101	647
Coaxis Inc 1515 SE Water Ave Ste 300 *TF:* 800-333-3197 ■ *Web:* viewpoint.com	Portland	OR	97214	800-333-3197		177
Coaxis International 1816 Old St Augustine Rd *Web:* www.coaxis-asp.net	Tallahassee	FL	32301	850-391-1022	391-1023	180
COBA/Select Sires Inc 1224 Alton Darby Creek Rd *TF:* 800-837-2621 ■ *Web:* www.cobaselect.com	Columbus	OH	43228	614-878-5333	870-2622	11-2
Cobalt Boats LLC 1715 N Eigth St *TF:* 800-468-5764 ■ *Web:* www.cobaltboats.com	Neodesha	KS	66757	620-325-2653	325-2361	90
Cobalt Digital Inc 2506 Galen Dr *TF:* 800-669-1691 ■ *Web:* www.cobaltdigital.com	Urbana	IL	61802	217-344-1243		647
Cobalt Pharmaceuticals Inc 6500 Kitimat Rd *TF:* 866-254-6111 ■ *Web:* actavis.ca	Mississauga	ON	L5N2B8	905-814-1820		231
Cobalt Technologies Inc 500 Clyde Ave *Web:* cobalttech.com	Mountain View	CA	94043	650-230-0760		668
Cobalt Truck Equipment 4620 E Trent Ave *Web:* www.critzer.com	Spokane	WA	99212	509-534-0446		57
Cobb & Cole 149 S Ridgewood Ave Ste 700 *Web:* www.cobbcole.com	Daytona Beach	FL	32114	386-255-8171		428
Cobb Architects LLC 67 Washtington St *Web:* www.cobbarchitecture.com	Charleston	SC	29403	843-856-7333		256
Cobb Chamber of Commerce 240 I- N Pkwy *Web:* www.cobbchamber.org	Atlanta	GA	30339	770-980-2000	980-9510	139
Cobb County 100 Cherokee St Ste 300 *TF:* 800-772-1213 ■ *Web:* www.cobbcounty.org	Marietta	GA	30090	770-528-1000	528-2606	338
Cobb County Public Library System 266 Roswell St *TF:* 800-521-0600 ■ *Web:* www.cobbcat.org	Marietta	GA	30060	770-528-2320		434-3
Cobb EMC 1000 EMC Pkwy PO Box 369 **Fax Area Code:* 678 ■ **Fax:* Hum Res ■ *Web:* www.cobbemc.com	Marietta	GA	30061	770-429-2100	355-3363*	245
Cobb Fendley & Assoc Inc 13430 Northwest Fwy Ste 1100 *Web:* www.cobfen.com	Houston	TX	77040	713-462-3242	462-3262	256
Cobb Galleria Centre 2 Galleria Pkwy *Web:* www.cobbgalleria.com	Atlanta	GA	30339	770-955-8000		205
Cobb Mechanical Contractors 2906 W Morrison *Web:* www.cobbmechanical.com	Colorado Springs	CO	80904	719-471-8958	389-0127	189-10
Cobb Planning Group 1206 N Broadway *TF:* 800-560-1988 ■ *Web:* www.cobbplanninggroup.com	Santa Ana	CA	92701	714-550-7242		528
Cobb Strecker Dunphy & Zimmermann Inc 150 S Fifth St Ste 2800 *Web:* www.csdz.com	Minneapolis	MN	55402	612-349-2400		390
Cobb Theatres LLC 2000-B Southbridge Pkwy Ste 100 *Web:* www.cobbtheatres.com	Birmingham	AL	35209	205-802-7766		748
Cobb Travel & Tourism 1 Galleria Pkwy *TF:* 800-451-3480 ■ *Web:* www.travelcobb.org	Atlanta	GA	30339	678-303-2622		206
Cobbleheads Bar & Grill 3154 Central Blvd *Web:* www.cobbleheads.com	Brownsville	TX	78520	956-546-6224		671
Cobblestone Capital Advisors LLC 140 Allens Creek Rd *TF:* 800-264-2769 ■ *Web:* cobblestonecap.com	Rochester	NY	14618	585-473-3333		690
Cobb-Vantress Inc PO Box 1030 *TF:* 800-748-9719 ■ *Web:* www.cobb-vantress.com	Siloam Springs	AR	72761	479-524-3166	524-3043	11-2
Cober Evolving Solutions 1351 Strasburg Rd *TF:* 800-263-7136 ■ *Web:* www.cobersolutions.com	Kitchener	ON	N2R1H2	519-745-7136		627
Cobham Electronic Systems Inc 1001 Pawtucket Blvd	Lowell	MA	01854	978-442-4700		21
Cobian International Group Inc The Major Bldg at Universal Studios 5728 Major Blv Ste 601	Orlando	FL	32819	407-447-1140	447-1184	393
Coblentz Patch Duffy & Bass LLP 1 Ferry Bldg Ste 200 *Web:* www.coblentzlaw.com	San Francisco	CA	94111	415-391-4800		41
Cobleskill-Richmondville Central School District 155 Washington Ave *Web:* www.crcs.k12.ny.us	Cobleskill	NY	12043	518-234-4032		685
Cobo Conference & Exhibition Ctr 1 Washington Blvd *Web:* www.cobocenter.com	Detroit	MI	48226	313-877-8777	877-8577	205
Cobon Plastics Corp 90 S St *TF:* 800-360-1324 ■ *Web:* www.cobonplastics.com	Newark	NJ	07114	973-344-6330		370
Coborn's Inc 1921 Coborn Blvd *Web:* www.cobornsinc.com	Saint Cloud	MN	56301	320-252-4222	252-0014	345
Cobra Anchors Corp 504 Mount-Laurel Ave *TF:* 800-423-6587 ■ *Web:* www.cobraanchors.com	Temple	PA	19560	610-929-5764		350
Cobra Electronics Corp 6500 W Cortland St *NASDAQ: COBR* ■ *TF:* 800-448-2244 ■ *Web:* www.cobra.com	Chicago	IL	60707	773-889-8870	889-8870	647
Cobra Engineering Inc 23801 La Palma Ave *Web:* www.cobrausa.com	Yorba Linda	CA	92887	714-692-8180	692-5019	256
Cobra Metal Works Inc 1140 Jansen Farm Dr *Web:* www.cobrametalworks.com	Elgin	IL	60123	847-214-8400		454
Cobra Mfg Co Inc 7909 E 148th St S *TF:* 800-352-6272 ■ *Web:* www.cobraarchery.com	Bixby	OK	74008	800-352-6272		710
Cobra Oil & Gas Corp 2201 Kell Blvd PO Box 8206 *Web:* www.cobraogc.com	Wichita Falls	TX	76308	940-716-5100	716-5190	536
COBRA Solutions Inc 4500 S Lakeshore Dr *Web:* www.cobra-solutions.com	Tempe	AZ	85282	480-831-6078		734
Cobra Wire & Cable Inc 2930 Turnpike Dr *Web:* www.cobrawire.com	Hatboro	PA	19040	215-674-8773		253
Cobscook Bay State Park 40 S Edmunds Rd *Web:* www.maine.gov	Dennysville	ME	04628	207-726-4412		565
Coburn Co, The 834 E Milwaukee St *TF:* 800-776-7042 ■ *Web:* coburn.com	Whitewater	WI	53190	262-473-2822	473-3522	600
Coburn Supply Company Inc 390 Pk St Ste 100 *TF:* 800-832-8492 ■ *Web:* www.coburns.com	Beaumont	TX	77701	409-838-6363	838-1920	612
Coca-Cola Bottling Co 725 E Erie Ave	Philadelphia	PA	19134	215-427-4500		81-2
Coca-Cola Bottling Co Consolidated 4100 Coca-Cola Plaza *NASDAQ: COKE* ■ *TF:* 800-777-2653 ■ *Web:* www.cokeconsolidated.com	Charlotte	NC	28211	704-557-4000		81-2
Coca-Cola Enterprises Inc 2500 Windy Ridge Pkwy *NYSE: CCE* ■ *Web:* www.ccep.com	Atlanta	GA	30339	678-260-3246		81-2
Coca-Cola Enterprises (Mid-America) 9000 Marshall Dr *Web:* www.cokecce.com	Lenexa	KS	66215	913-492-8100		805
Coca-Cola Export Corp, The 1 Coca Cola Plaza NW *Web:* www.coca-colacompany.com	Atlanta	GA	30313	404-676-2121		805
Coca-Cola Foundation Inc PO Box 1734 *TF:* 800-438-2653 ■ *Web:* www.coca-colacompany.com	Atlanta	GA	30301	800-438-2653		304
Coca-Cola Nonpartisan Committee for Good Government PO Box 1734 *TF:* 800-438-2653 ■ *Web:* www.coca-colacompany.com	Atlanta	GA	30301	800-438-2653		615
Coca-Cola Space Science Ctr 701 Front Ave *Web:* www.ccssc.org	Columbus	GA	31901	706-649-1470	649-1478	520

Phone Fax Class

Cocaine Anonymous World Services Inc (CA)
PO Box 492000 ....Los Angeles CA 90049 310-559-5833 559-2554 48-21
TF: 800-347-8998 ■ *Web:* www.ca.org
CoCal Landscape Services Inc
333 E 76th Ave ....Denver CO 80229 303-531-6930 776
Web: www.cocal.com
COCAT LLC 4905 Lima St ....Denver CO 80239 303-565-3800 192
Web: www.cocat.com
Cocca's Inn & Suites
Corner of Wolf Rd & Central Ave ....Albany NY 12205 518-459-2240 459-9758 379
TF: 888-426-2227 ■ *Web:* www.coccas.com
Cocciardi & Associates Inc
4 Kacey Ct ....Mechanicsburg PA 17055 717-766-4500 428
TF: 800-377-3024 ■ *Web:* www.cocciardi.com
Cochise College 4190 W Hwy 80 ....Douglas AZ 85607 520-364-7943 417-4006* 162
**Fax:* Admissions ■ *TF:* 800-966-7943 ■ *Web:* cochise.edu
Sierra Vista 901 N Colombo Ave ....Sierra Vista AZ 85635 520-515-0500 515-5452* 162
**Fax:* Admissions ■ *TF:* 800-966-7943 ■ *Web:* cochise.edu
Cochise County
100 Quality Hill Rd PO Box CK ....Bisbee AZ 85603 520-432-9200 432-5016 338
Web: cochise.az.gov
Cochise County Library District
100 Quality Hill Rd ....Bisbee AZ 85603 520-432-8930 432-7339 434-3
Web: cochise.az.gov
Cochon Dingue Le 46 Champlain Blvd ....Quebec QC G1K4E8 418-692-2013 671
Web: www.cochondingue.com
Cochran County 100 N Main St ....Morton TX 79346 806-266-5508 266-9027 338
TF: 800-360-6025 ■ *Web:* www.co.cochran.tx.us
Cochran Davis & Associates P C
36 Malaga Cove Plaza Palos Verdes Estates
Ste 206 ....California CA 90274 310-373-0900 445
Web: cochranlaw1.com
Cochran Electric Company Inc
12500 Aurora Ave N ....Seattle WA 98133 206-367-1900 189-4
TF: 800-418-1818 ■ *Web:* www.cochraninc.com
Cochran Firm LLC 111 E Main St ....Dothan AL 36301 334-793-1555 428
TF: 800-843-3476 ■ *Web:* www.cochranfirm.com
Cochran Foley & Assoc
15510 Farmington Rd ....Livonia MI 48154 734-425-2400 445
Web: www.cochranlaw.com
Cochran Forest Products Inc
702 NE Okinawa St ....Lake City FL 32055 386-752-0335 755-5561 820
Web: www.cochranforestproducts.com
Cochran School of Nursing
967 N Broadway ....Yonkers NY 10701 914-964-4444 800
Web: www.riversidehealth.org
Cochran Thad (Sen R - MS)
113 Dirksen Bldg ....Washington DC 20510 202-224-5054 342-2
Web: www.cochran.senate.gov
Cochran, Cochran & Yale LLC
955 E Henrietta Rd ....Rochester NY 14623 585-424-6060 463
Web: www.ccy.com
Cochrane Technologies Inc
PO Box 81276 ....Lafayette LA 70598 337-837-3334 837-7134 727
TF: 800-346-3745 ■ *Web:* www.cochranetech.com
Cocina Superior
587 Brookwood Village ....Homewood AL 35209 205-259-1980 259-1987 671
Web: www.thecocinasuperior.com
Cock of the Walk 2624 Music Vly Dr ....Nashville TN 37214 615-889-1930 671
Web: www.cockofthewalkrestaurant.com
Cockburn Enterprises Inc
334 East Washington Dr ....Muscle Shoals AL 35661 256-381-3620 757
Cocke County Tourism
433 B Prospect Ave ....Newport TN 37821 423-625-9675 338
Web: www.cockecounty.com
Cockrell Investment Group
6138 Orange Ave ....Long Beach CA 90805 562-984-7176 796
Coco Pazzo 300 W Hubbard St ....Chicago IL 60654 312-836-0900 671
Web: www.cocopazzochicago.com
Coco Rico 3907 St-Laurent Blvd ....Montreal QC H2W1X9 514-849-5554 671
Cocoa Beach Area Chamber of Commerce
400 Fortenberry Rd ....Merritt Island FL 32952 321-459-2200 459-2232 139
TF: 800-248-5955 ■ *Web:* www.cocoabeachchamber.com
Coconino Community College
Lonetree 2800 S Lone Tree Rd ....Flagstaff AZ 86001 928-527-1222 226-4110* 162
**Fax:* Admissions ■ *TF:* 800-350-7122 ■ *Web:* www.coconino.edu
Coconino County 219 E Cherry Ave ....Flagstaff AZ 86001 928-774-5011 338
TF: 800-559-9289 ■ *Web:* www.coconino.az.gov
Coconut Mallory Resort & Marina
1445 S Roosevelt Blvd ....Key West FL 33040 305-292-0017 377
TF: 800-640-6886 ■ *Web:* mallorykeywest.com
Coconut Malorie Resort 200 59th St ....Ocean City MD 21842 410-723-6100 669
TF: 855-826-6361 ■
Web: vacationcondos.com/coconut-malorie-festiva-resort
Cocoro Bistro & Sushi Bar
2105 Pacific Ave ....Stockton CA 95204 209-941-6053 671
Web: cocorobistro.com
CocoWalk 3015 Grand Ave ....Coconut Grove FL 33133 305-444-0777 441-8936 50-6
Web: www.cocowalk.net
CODA (Co-Dependents Anonymous Inc)
PO Box 33577 ....Phoenix AZ 85067 602-277-7991 48-21
TF: 888-444-2359 ■ *Web:* www.codependents.org
CODA (Children of Deaf Adults Inc)
3131 Calle Mariposa ....Santa Barbara CA 93105 805-682-0997 48-6
Web: coda-international.wildapricot.org
CODA Inc 30 Industrial Ave ....Mahwah NJ 07430 201-825-7400 825-8133 629
Web: www.codamount.com
CoDa Therapeutics Inc
10505 Sorrento Valley Rd Ste 395 ....San Diego CA 92121 858-677-0474 231
Web: codatherapeutics.com
Codale Electric Supply Inc
5225 West 2400 South PO Box 702070 ....Salt Lake City UT 84120 801-975-7300 977-8833 246
TF: 800-300-6634 ■ *Web:* www.codale.com
CODAN US Corp 3511 W Sunflower Ave ....Santa Ana CA 92704 714-545-2111 166
Web: www.codanusa.com
Codan US Inc 8430 Kao Cir ....Manassas VA 20110 703-361-2721 246
Web: www.codan.com.au

Phone Fax Class

Codding Enterprises
1400 Valley House Dr Ste 100 ....Rohnert Park CA 94928 707-795-3550 655
Web: www.codding.com
Coddington Group LLC, The
115 W St Ste 300 ....Annapolis MD 21401 410-263-6200 260
TF: 800-264-1170 ■ *Web:* www.coddingtongroup.com
Code and Theory Inc
575 Broadway 5th Fl ....New York NY 10012 212-358-0717 5
Web: www.codeandtheory.com
Code Blue Corp 259 Hedcor St ....Holland MI 49423 616-392-8296 693
Web: www.codeblue.com
Code Environmental Services Inc
400 Middlesex Ave ....Carteret NJ 07008 732-969-2700 261
Web: www.codeenvironmental.com
Code for America Labs Inc
155 Ninth St ....San Francisco CA 94103 510-645-9626 196
Web: www.codeforamerica.org
Code Green Networks Inc
385 Moffett Park Dr Ste 105 ....Sunnyvale CA 94089 408-716-4200 177
Web: www.codegreennetworks.com
Code Hennessy & Simmons Inc
10 S Wacker Dr Ste 3300 ....Chicago IL 60606 312-876-1840 893-2132 792
Web: www.chsonline.com
CodeExcellence.com Inc 3553 31 St NW ....Calgary AB T2L2K7 403-800-2071 224
Web: www.codeexcellence.com
Co-Dependents Anonymous Inc (CODA)
PO Box 33577 ....Phoenix AZ 85067 602-277-7991 48-21
TF: 888-444-2359 ■ *Web:* www.codependents.org
Codilis & Associates PC
15W030 N Frontage Rd ....Burr Ridge IL 60527 630-794-5300 428
Web: www.codilis.com
Codington County 14 First Ave SE ....Watertown SD 57201 605-882-6288 338
Web: www.codington.org
Codington-Clark Electric Co-op
3520 Ninth Ave SW PO Box 880 ....Watertown SD 57201 605-886-5848 245
TF: 800-463-8938 ■ *Web:* www.codingtonclarkelectric.coop
Cody Company Inc 4200 N I-45 ....Ennis TX 75119 972-875-5884 875-0308 697
Web: www.codycompany.com
Cody Laboratories Inc
601 Yellowstone Ave ....Cody WY 82414 307-587-7099 231
Web: www.codylabs.com
Cody Pools Inc 2300 W Parmer Ln ....Austin TX 78727 512-835-4966 45
TF: 800-678-8742 ■ *Web:* www.codypools.com
Coe & Van Loo Consultants Inc
4550 N 12th St ....Phoenix AZ 85014 602-264-6831 261
TF: 800-431-2584 ■ *Web:* www.cvlci.com
Coe Capital Management LLC
9 Pkwy N Ste 325 ....Deerfield IL 60015 847-597-1700 528
Web: www.coecapital.com
Coe College 1220 First Ave NE ....Cedar Rapids IA 52402 319-399-8500 399-8816 166
TF: 877-225-5263 ■ *Web:* www.coe.edu
COECO Office Systems Co
2521 N Church St ....Rocky Mount NC 27804 252-977-1121 320
TF: 800-682-6844 ■ *Web:* www.coeco.com
Coen Co Inc 11920 East Apache St ....Tulsa CA 74116 918-234-1800 91
Web: www.coen.com
Coen Oil Co 1045 W Chestnut St ....Washington PA 15301 724-223-5500 579
Web: www.coenoil.com
Coeur Business Group Inc
18 Hawk Ridge Dr Ste 150 ....Lake Saint Louis MO 63367 636-561-2455 190
Web: www.coeurgroup.com
Coeur d Alene 810 Coeur D Alene Ave ....Venice CA 90291 310-821-7813 623
Web: coeurdalene.org
Coeur d'Alene Area Chamber of Commerce
105 N First St Ste 100 ....Coeur d'Alene ID 83814 208-664-3194 667-9338 139
TF: 877-782-9232 ■ *Web:* www.cdachamber.com
Coeur d'Alene Press
201 N Second St ....Coeur d'Alene ID 83814 208-664-8176 664-0212 532-2
Web: www.cdapress.com
Coeur d'Alene Public Library
702 E Front ....Coeur d'Alene ID 83814 208-769-2315 769-2381 434-3
TF: 800-829-1040 ■ *Web:* www.cdalibrary.org
Coeur d'Alene Resort
115 S Second St ....Coeur d'Alene ID 83814 208-765-4000 664-7276 669
TF: 800-688-5253 ■ *Web:* www.cdaresort.com
Coeur de Lion
926 Massachusetts Ave NW ....Washington DC 20001 202-414-0500 414-0513 671
Web: www.henleypark.com
Coeur Inc 209 Creekside Dr ....Washington NC 27889 252-946-1963 608
Web: coeurinc.com
Cofa Media Inc
2544 Gateway Rd Ste 201 ....Carlsbad CA 92009 619-602-2529 463
TF: 800-399-2001 ■ *Web:* www.cofamedia.com
Coface Services North America Inc
50 Millstone Rd ....East Windsor NJ 08520 609-469-0400 490-1582 218
TF: 877-626-3223 ■ *Web:* www.coface-usa.com
Coffee Bean International
9120 NE Alderwood Rd ....Portland OR 97220 503-227-4490 225-9604 297-2
TF: 800-877-0474 ■ *Web:* www.coffeebeanintl.com
Coffee Beanery Ltd, The
3429 Pierson Pl ....Flushing MI 48433 800-441-2255 733-1536* 159
**Fax Area Code:* 810 ■ *TF:* 800-441-2255 ■ *Web:* www.coffeebeanery.com
Coffee County 101 S Peterson Ave ....Douglas GA 31533 912-384-4799 384-0291 338
TF: 800-436-7442 ■ *Web:* www.coffeecountygov.com
Coffee County 2 County Complex ....New Brockton AL 36351 334-894-5556 338
Web: www.coffeecounty.us
Coffee County 1329 McArthur Dr ....Manchester TN 37355 931-723-5106 723-8248 338
Web: www.coffeecountytn.org
Coffee Creek Correctional Facility
24499 SW Grahams Ferry Rd ....Wilsonville OR 97070 503-570-6400 570-6417 213
Web: www.oregon.gov
Coffee Exchange 207 Wickenden St ....Providence RI 02903 401-273-1198 379
TF: 877-263-3334 ■ *Web:* www.coffeexchange.com
Coffee Holding Company Inc
3475 Victory Blvd ....Staten Island NY 10314 718-832-0800 832-0892 296-7
NASDAQ: JVA ■ *TF:* 800-458-2233 ■ *Web:* www.coffeeholding.com
Coffee Masters Inc
7606 Industrial Ct ....Spring Grove IL 60081 815-675-0088 675-3166 297-2
TF: 800-334-6485 ■ *Web:* www.coffeemasters.com

Phone | Fax | Class

Coffee Memorial Blood Ctr
7500 Wallace Dr — Amarillo TX 79124 — 806-358-4563 — 89
TF: 800-421-9529 ■ *Web:* www.thegiftoflife.org

Coffee Regional Medical Ctr (CRMC)
1101 Ocilla Rd — Douglas GA 31533 — 912-384-1900 — 374-3
TF: 800-555-4444 ■ *Web:* www.coffeeregional.org

Coffee Solutions Inc
2B Airport Dr Ext. — Hopedale MA 01747 — 508-422-9233 — 463
Web: www.coffeesolutions.net

Coffeen Lake State Fish & Wildlife Area
15084 N Fourth Ave — Coffeen IL 62017 — 217-537-3351 — 565
Web: www.dnr.illinois.gov/parks/pages/coffeenlake.aspx

Coffey Communications Inc
1505 Business One Cir. — Walla Walla WA 99362 — 509-525-0101 — 637-9
Web: coffeycomm.com

Coffey County 110 S Sixth St — Burlington KS 66389 — 620-364-2191 — 364-8975 — 338
Web: www.coffeycountyks.org

Coffeyville Community College
400 W 11th St. — Coffeyville KS 67337 — 620-251-7700 — 162

Coffeyville Regional Medical Ctr
1400 W Fourth St — Coffeyville KS 67337 — 620-251-1200 — 374-3
TF: 800-540-2762 ■ *Web:* www.crmcinc.com

Coffin Turbo Pump Inc 326 S Dean St — Englewood NJ 07631 — 201-568-4700 — 568-4716 — 641
TF: 800-568-9798 ■ *Web:* www.coffinturbopump.com

Coffman Mike (Rep R - CO)
2443 Rayburn Bldg Rm 2443 — Washington DC 20515 — 202-225-7882 — 226-4623 — 342-2
Web: coffman.house.gov

Coffman Truck Sales
1149 West Lake St Rt 31 — Aurora IL 60506 — 630-892-7093 — 892-1080 — 57
TF: 800-255-7641 ■ *Web:* www.coffmantrucks.com

Cogeco Cable Inc
5 Pl Ville-Marie Office 1700 — Montreal QC H3B0B3 — 514-874-2600 — 874-2625 — 116
TF: 800-855-0511 ■ *Web:* www.cogeco.ca

Cogeco Peer 1 413 Horner Ave — Etobicoke ON M8W4W3 — 877-504-0091 — 225
TF: 877-720-2228 ■ *Web:* www.cogecopeer1.com/en

Cogency Software Inc
500 Airport Blvd Ste 152 — Burlingame CA 94010 — 650-685-2500 — 39
Web: www.cogencysoftware.com

Cogenix Consulting Ltd
50 Burnhamthorpe Rd W — Mississauga ON L5B3C2 — 905-803-9132 — 194

Cogent Communications Group Inc
1015 31st St NW — Washington DC 20007 — 202-295-4200 — 338-8798 — 394
NASDAQ: CCOI ■ *TF:* 877-875-4432 ■ *Web:* www.cogentco.com

Cogent Industrial Technologies
13091 Vanier Pl Ste 180 — Richmond BC V6V2J1 — 604-207-8878 — 261
TF: 800-424-3996 ■ *Web:* www.cogentind.com

Cogentic LLC 1834 Collins St Ste E — Tarzana CA 91356 — 818-578-6930 — 463
Web: www.cogentic.com

Cogentrix Energy Inc
9405 Arrowpoint Blvd — Charlotte NC 28273 — 704-525-3800 — 245
Web: www.cogentrix.com

Coghlan's Ltd 121 Irene St — Winnipeg MB R3T4C7 — 204-284-9550 — 711
TF: 877-264-4526 ■ *Web:* www.coghlans.com

Cogistics Inc 2485 Drane Field Rd — Lakeland FL 33811 — 863-647-9389 — 194
Web: www.cogistics.com

Cognify PO Box 69337 — Oro Valley AZ 85737 — 888-264-6439 — 224
TF: 888-264-6439 ■ *Web:* www.cognify.com

CogniTech Corp
1060 East 100 South Ste 306 — Salt Lake City UT 84102 — 801-322-0101 — 177
Web: www.cognitech-ut.com

Cognitim Inc
455 N Whisman Rd Ste 400 — Mountain View CA 94043 — 650-404-8000 — 177
Web: www.cognitim.com

Cognitive Technologies Inc
16333 S Great Oaks Dr Ste 201 — Round Rock TX 78681 — 703-562-0600 — 180
Web: www.cog-ps.com

Cognizant Technology Solutions Corp
500 Frank W Burr Blvd — Teaneck NJ 07666 — 201-801-0233 — 801-0243* — 180
NASDAQ: CTSH ■ **Fax:* Mktg ■ *TF:* 888-937-3277 ■ *Web:* www.cognizant.com

Cogo's Co 2589 Boyce Plaza Rd — Pittsburgh PA 15241 — 412-257-1550 — 345
Web: www.cogos.com

Cogswell Polytechnical College
1175 Bordeaux Dr — Sunnyvale CA 94089 — 408-541-0100 — 747-0764* — 166
**Fax:* Admissions ■ *TF:* 800-264-7955 ■ *Web:* www.cogswell.edu

COGWM (Church of God World Missions)
2490 Keith St PO Box 8016 — Cleveland TN 37320 — 423-478-7190 — 48-20
TF: 800-345-7492 ■ *Web:* www.cogwm.org

Cohasset Assoc Inc
505 N Lake Shore Dr Apt 3806 — Chicago IL 60611 — 312-527-1550 — 194
Web: www.cohasset.com

Cohasset Harbor Inn 124 Elm St — Cohasset MA 02025 — 781-383-6650 — 379
TF: 800-252-5287 ■ *Web:* cohassetharborresort.com

Cohber Press PO Box 93100 — Rochester NY 14692 — 585-475-9100 — 475-9406 — 781
TF: 800-724-3032 ■ *Web:* www.cohber.com

Cohen & Co 1350 Euclid Ave Ste 800 — Cleveland OH 44115 — 216-579-1040 — 734
Web: www.cohencpa.com

Cohen & Company Creative Inc
12002 Miramar Pkwy Ste C — Miramar FL 33025 — 954-923-8133 — 5
Web: www.cohenadv.com

Cohen & Gresser LLP 800 Third Ave — New York NY 10022 — 212-957-7600 — 428
Web: www.cohengresser.com

Cohen & Grigsby Pc 625 Liberty Ave — Pittsburgh PA 15222 — 412-297-4900 — 209-0672 — 428
Web: www.cohenlaw.com

Cohen & Steers Inc 280 Pk Ave 10th Fl — New York NY 10017 — 212-832-3232 — 401
NYSE: CNS ■ *TF:* 800-330-7348 ■ *Web:* www.cohenandsteers.com

Cohen Asset Management Inc
1900 Ave of the Stars Ste 500 — Los Angeles CA 90067 — 310-860-0598 — 194
Web: www.cohenasset.com

Cohen Bros Inc 1723 Woodlawn Ave — Middletown OH 45044 — 513-422-3696 — 422-9018 — 686
Web: www.cohenbrothersinc.com

Cohen Brown Management Group
11835 Olympic Blvd Ste 920 — Los Angeles CA 90064 — 310-966-1001 — 631
Web: cohenbrown.com

Cohen Financial LP
227 W Monroe St Ste 1000 — Chicago IL 60606 — 312-346-5680 — 346-6669 — 652
Web: www.cohenfinancial.com

Cohen Group, The
500 Eighth St NW Ste 200 — Washington DC 20004 — 202-863-7200 — 317
Web: www.cohengroup.net

Cohen Highley LLP 255 Queens Ave — London ON N6A5R8 — 519-672-9330 — 428
TF: 800-563-1020 ■ *Web:* www.cohenhighley.com

Cohen Placitella & Roth P C
2001 Market St Ste 2900 — Philadelphia PA 19103 — 215-567-3500 — 445
Web: www.cprlaw.com

Cohen Seglias Pallas Greenhall & Furman PC
30 S 17th St 19th Fl United Plz — Philadelphia PA 19103 — 215-564-1700 — 428
Web: cohenseglias.com

Cohen Steve (Rep D - TN)
2404 Rayburn HOB — Washington DC 20515 — 202-225-3265 — 225-5663 — 342-2
Web: cohen.house.gov

Cohen, Hurkin, Ehrenfeld, Pomerantz & Tenenbaum
25 Chapel St Ste 705 — Brooklyn NY 11201 — 718-596-9000 — 428
TF: 800-820-4877 ■ *Web:* www.cohenhurkin.com

Cohen-Esrey Real Estate Services LLC
6800 W 64th St — Overland Park KS 66202 — 913-671-3300 — 671-3301 — 652
Web: www.cohenesrey.com

Coherent Inc
5100 Patrick Henry Dr — Santa Clara CA 95054 — 408-764-4000 — 764-4000 — 425
NASDAQ: COHR ■ *TF Sales:* 800-527-3786 ■ *Web:* www.coherent.com

Coherent Solutions Inc
1600 Utica Ave S Ste 120 — Minneapolis MN 55416 — 612-279-6262 — 177
Web: www.coherentsolutions.com

Coherex Medical Inc
3598 West 1820 South — Salt Lake City UT 84104 — 801-433-9900 — 743
Web: www.coherex.com

Cohesion Corp
5151 Pfeiffer Rd Ste 105 — Cincinnati OH 45242 — 513-587-7700 — 196
Web: www.cohesion.com

Cohesionforce Inc 360C Quality Cir. — Huntsville AL 35806 — 256-562-0600 — 261
Web: cohesionforce.com

Cohn 2434 W Caithness Pl — Denver CO 80211 — 303-839-1415 — 195
TF: 800-816-6710 ■ *Web:* www.cohnmarketing.com

Cohn & Gregory Inc 5450 Midway Rd — Fort Worth TX 76117 — 817-831-9998 — 385
Web: www.cgsupply.com

Cohn & Wolfe 200 Fifth Ave — New York NY 10010 — 212-798-9700 — 329-9900 — 636
TF: 800-898-4475 ■ *Web:* www.cohnwolfe.com

Cohn Restaurant Group
2225 Hancock St — San Diego CA 92110 — 619-236-1299 — 236-1300 — 671
Web: www.cohnrestaurants.com

Cohn Wholesale Fruit & Grocery
3511 Camino Del Rio S Ste 306 — San Diego CA 92108 — 619-528-1113 — 345

Coho Partners Ltd
300 Berwyn Park 801 Cassatt Rd Ste 100 — Berwyn PA 19312 — 484-318-7575 — 401
Web: www.cohopartners.com

Cohoes Fashions Inc
156 Hillside Rd Garden City Ctr — Cranston RI 02920 — 401-946-7740 — 157-4
Web: www.cohoesfashions.com

Cohu Inc 12367 Crosthwaite Cir — Poway CA 92064 — 858-848-8100 — 848-8185 — 248
NASDAQ: COHU ■ *TF:* 800-685-5050 ■ *Web:* www.cohu.com

Coil Construction Inc 209 E Broadway — Columbia MO 65203 — 573-874-1444 — 443-3039 — 685
Web: www.coilconstruction.com

Coil Tubing Technology Holding Inc
19511 Wied Rd Ste E — Spring TX 77388 — 281-651-0200 — 539
Web: www.coiltubingtechnology.com

Coilcraft Inc 1102 Silver Lake Rd — Cary IL 60013 — 847-639-2361 — 639-1469 — 253
TF: 800-322-2645 ■ *Web:* www.coilcraft.com

Coilhose Pneumatics Inc
19 Kimberly Rd — East Brunswick NJ 08816 — 732-390-8480 — 390-9693 — 370
TF: 800-424-9300 ■ *Web:* www.coilhose.com

Coiling Technologies Inc
7777 Wright Rd — Houston TX 77041 — 713-849-4000 — 718
Web: www.coilingtech.com

Coilmaster Corp 440 Industrial Dr — Moscow TN 38057 — 901-877-3333 — 35
Web: coilmastercorp.com

Coilplus Ohio Inc
4801 Gateway Blvd — Springfield OH 45502 — 937-322-4455 — 492
Web: coilplusohio.com

Coilplus Pennsylvania Inc
5135 Bleigh St — Philadelphia PA 19136 — 215-331-5200 — 331-9538 — 492
Web: www.coilplus.com

Coils Inc 11716 Algonquin Rd — Huntley IL 60142 — 847-669-5115 — 669-5150 — 253

Coin Acceptors Inc 300 Hunter Ave — Saint Louis MO 63124 — 314-725-0100 — 725-2896 — 55
TF: 800-325-2646 ■ *Web:* www.coinco.com

Coin Laundry Assn (CLA)
1s660 Midwest Rd Ste 205 — Oakbrook Terrace IL 60181 — 630-953-7920 — 49-4
TF: 800-570-5629 ■ *Web:* www.coinlaundry.org

Coin World Magazine 911 S Vandemark Rd — Sidney OH 45365 — 937-498-0800 — 457-14
Web: www.coinworld.com

COINage Magazine 3585 Maple St Ste 232 — Ventura CA 93003 — 800-764-6278 — 457-14
TF: 800-764-6278 ■ *Web:* coinagemag.com

Coining Technologies Inc
400 Kuller Rd — Clifton NJ 07011 — 973-253-0500 — 483
Web: www.coining.com

CoinLab Inc 71 Columbia St Ste 300 — Seattle WA 98104 — 855-522-2646 — 393
TF: 855-522-2646 ■ *Web:* coinlab.com

Coinmach Service Corp
303 Sunnyside Blvd Ste 70 — Plainview NY 11803 — 516-349-8555 — 349-9125 — 426
TF: 877-264-6622 ■ *Web:* www.cscsw.com

Coinstar Inc 1800 114th Ave SE — Bellevue WA 98004 — 425-943-8000 — 55
TF: 800-928-2274 ■ *Web:* www.coinstar.com

Coke County 13 E Seventh St — Robert Lee TX 76945 — 325-453-2631 — 453-2650 — 338
Web: co.coke.tx.us

Coker & Palmer Inc 1667 Lelia Dr — Jackson MS 39216 — 601-354-0860 — 691
Web: www.cokerpalmer.com

Coker College 300 E College Ave — Hartsville SC 29550 — 843-383-8000 — 383-8056* — 166
**Fax:* Admissions ■ *TF:* 800-950-1908 ■ *Web:* www.coker.edu

Coker Consulting
2400 Lakeview Pkwy Ste 400 — Alpharetta GA 30009 — 800-345-5829 — 463
TF: 800-345-5829 ■ *Web:* www.cokergroup.com

Coker Tire Co 1317 Chestnut St — Chattanooga TN 37402 — 423-265-6368 — 754
Web: www.cokertire.com

Cokesbury Village 726 Loveville Rd — Hockessin DE 19707 — 302-235-6000 — 672
TF: 800-530-2377 ■ *Web:* actsretirement.org

Cokeva Inc 9000 Foothills Blvd — Roseville CA 95747 — 916-462-6000 — 196
Web: www.cokeva.com

COKINOS | YOUNG 1221 Lamar 16th Fl — Houston TX 77010 — 713-535-5500 — 428
Web: www.cbylaw.com

Phone | Fax | Class

Col Pump Company Inc
131 E Railroad St ... Columbiana OH 44408 330-482-1029 492
Web: www.col-pump.net

COLA 9881 Broken Land Pkwy Ste 200 ... Columbia MD 21046 410-381-6581 381-8611* 49-8
**Fax:* Hum Res ■ *TF:* 800-981-9883 ■ *Web:* www.cola.org

COLA (ABA Commission on Law & Aging)
1050 Connecticut Ave NW Ste 400 ... Washington DC 20036 202-662-1000 662-8698 49-10
Web: www.americanbar.org/groups/law_aging.html

Colad Group 801 Exchange St ... Buffalo NY 14210 716-961-1776 961-1753 555
TF: 800-950-1755 ■ *Web:* www.colad.com

COLAGE (Children of Lesbians & Gays Everywhere)
3815 S Othello St Ste 100 ... Seattle WA 98118 415-861-5437 48-21
TF: 800-657-3717 ■ *Web:* www.colage.org

Colaianni Construction Inc
2141 State Rt 150 ... Dillonvale OH 43917 740-769-2362 186
TF: 800-854-8485 ■ *Web:* www.colaianniconst.com

Colangelo Synergy Marketing Inc
120 Tokeneke Rd ... Darien CT 06820 203-662-6600 662-6601 7
Web: www.colangelo-sm.com

Colao's Ristorante 2826 Plum St ... Erie PA 16508 814-866-9621 671
Web: colaos.com

Colautti Group 2575 Sheffield Rd ... Ottawa ON K1B3V6 613-822-1440 463
Web: www.colauttigroup.com

Colba.Net Telecom Inc
6465 TransCanada Hwy Ville St-Laurent ... Montreal QC H4T1S3 514-856-3500 224
TF: 888-477-7189 ■ *Web:* www.colba.net

Colbert County 201 N Main St ... Tuscumbia AL 35674 256-386-8500 386-8510 338
Web: www.colbertcounty.org

Colbert Packaging Corp
28355 N Bradley Rd ... Lake Forest IL 60045 847-367-5990 367-4403 101
Web: www.colbertpkg.com

Colbert, Matz, Rosenfelt Inc
2835 Smith Ave Ste G ... Baltimore MD 21209 410-653-3838 261
TF: 800-820-7154 ■ *Web:* www.cmrengineers.com

Colborne Corp 28495 N Ballard Dr ... Lake Forest IL 60045 847-371-0101 371-0101 298
TF: 800-626-9501 ■ *Web:* www.colbornefoodbotics.com

Colburn Earth Science Museum
2 S Pack Sq ... Asheville NC 28801 828-254-7162 257-4505 520
Web: colburnmuseum.org

Colby Attorneys Service Company Inc
111 Washington Ave Ste 703 ... Albany NY 12210 800-832-1220 635
TF: 800-832-1220 ■ *Web:* www.colbyservice.com

Colby College 4800 Mayflower Hill ... Waterville ME 04901 207-859-4800 859-4828* 166
**Fax:* Admissions ■ *TF Admissions:* 800-723-3032 ■ *Web:* www.colby.edu

Colby College Miller Library
4000 Mayflower Hill ... Waterville ME 04901 207-859-4000 859-4055 434-6
Web: www.colby.edu

Colby College Museum of Art
5600 Mayflower Hill ... Waterville ME 04901 207-859-5600 859-5606 520
Web: www.colby.edu

Colby Community College
1255 S Range Ave ... Colby KS 67701 785-462-3984 460-4691* 162
**Fax:* Admissions ■ *TF:* 888-634-9350 ■ *Web:* www.colbycc.edu

Colby Convention & Visitors Bureau
350 S Range Ste 10 ... Colby KS 67701 785-460-7643 460-4509 206
TF: 800-499-7928 ■ *Web:* www.oasisontheplains.com

Colby Equipment Company Inc
3048 Ridgeview Dr ... Indianapolis IN 46226 317-545-4221 358
TF: 800-443-2081 ■ *Web:* www.colbyequipment.com

Colby Hill Inn 33 The Oaks PO Box 779 ... Henniker NH 03242 603-428-3281 428-9218 379
TF: 800-531-0330 ■ *Web:* www.colbyhillinn.com

Colby Metal Inc 701 Industrial Dr ... Colby WI 54421 715-223-2334 492
Web: www.colbymetal.com

Colby-Sawyer College 541 Main St ... New London NH 03257 603-526-3700 526-3452* 166
**Fax:* Admissions ■ *TF Admissions:* 800-272-1015 ■ *Web:* www.colby-sawyer.edu

Colchester Christian Academy 15 Elm St ... Truro NS B2N3H5 902-895-6520 623
Web: colchesterchristianacademy.ca

Colchester Regional Hospital
207 Willow St ... Truro NS B2N5A1 902-893-4321 893-5559 374-2
TF: 800-460-2110 ■ *Web:* www.cehha.nshealth.ca

Colcord Hotel 15 N Robinson Ave ... Oklahoma City OK 73102 405-601-4300 379
Web: www.colcordhotel.com

Cold Air Distributors Warehouse of Florida Inc
3053 Industrial 31st St ... Fort Pierce FL 34946 772-466-3036 61
Web: www.coldairdistributors.com

Cold Bore Technology Inc
5970 Centre St SE Ste 200 ... Calgary AB T2H0C1 403-991-7295 538
Web: coldboretechnology.com

Cold Heading Co 21777 Hoover Rd ... Warren MI 48089 586-497-7000 278
Web: www.coldheading.com

Cold Open Inc 1313 Innes Pl ... Venice CA 90291 310-399-3307 7
TF: 800-438-7325 ■ *Web:* www.coldopen.com

Cold Shot Chillers 14020 InterDr W ... Houston TX 77032 281-227-8400 14
TF: 800-473-9178 ■ *Web:* www.waterchillers.com

Cold Spring Brewing Co
219 Red River Ave N ... Cold Spring MN 56320 320-685-8686 685-8318 102
Web: www.coldspringbrewery.com

Cold Spring Granite Inc
17482 Granite W Rd ... Cold Spring MN 56320 320-685-3621 685-8490 724
TF: 800-328-5040 ■ *Web:* www.coldspringusa.com

Cold Spring Harbor Laboratory (CSHL)
1 Bungtown Rd ... Cold Spring Harbor NY 11724 516-367-8800 367-8455 668
Web: www.cshl.edu

Cold Spring Harbor State Park
25 Lloyd Harbor Rd ... Huntington NY 11743 631-423-1770 565
Web: parks.ny.gov/parks/115

Cold Stone Creamery Inc
9311 E Via De Ventura ... Scottsdale AZ 85258 480-362-4800 362-4812 381
TF Cust Svc: 866-452-4252 ■ *Web:* www.coldstonecreamery.com

Cold Water Area Chamber of Commerce
20 Div St ... Coldwater MI 49036 517-278-5985 139
Web: coldwaterchamber.com

Coldebt Collection Systems
8 S Michigan Ave Ste 618 ... Chicago IL 60603 312-759-3804 160
Web: www.coldebtcollections.com

Colder Products Co 1001 Westgate Dr ... St Paul MN 55114 651-645-0091 596
Web: www.colder.com

Colder's Inc 333 S 108th St ... West Allis WI 53214 414-476-1574 321
Web: www.colders.com

Coldiron Companies Inc 200 N Sooner Rd ... Edmond OK 73034 405-562-2910 311
TF: 800-293-4369 ■ *Web:* www.coldironcompanies.com

Coldmatic 8500 Keele St ... Concord ON L4K2A6 905-326-7600 664
Web: www.coldmatic.com

Coldspring 17482 Granite W Rd ... Cold Spring MN 56320 800-328-5040 473-4881 724
TF: 800-328-5040 ■ *Web:* www.coldspringusa.com

ColdStar Solutions Inc
1015 Henry Eng Pl ... Victoria BC V9B6B2 250-381-3399 311
TF: 800-201-1277 ■ *Web:* www.coldstarfreight.com

Coldwater Community Schools
401 Sauk River Dr ... Coldwater MI 49036 517-279-5910 279-7651 685
Web: www.coldwaterschools.org

Coldwater Lake State Park
Copeland Rd ... Coldwater MI 49036 517-780-7866 565
Web: www.michigandnr.com

Coldwell Banker 950 Essington Rd ... Joliet IL 60435 815-744-1000 652
Web: www.cbhonig-bell.com

Coldwell Banker Gundaker
2458 Old Dorsett Rd Ste 300 ... Maryland Heights MO 63043 314-298-5000 652
Web: www.coldwellbankerhomes.com/st-louis

Coldwell Banker Howard Perry & Walston
1001 Wade Ave ... Raleigh NC 27605 919-782-5600 652
Web: www.hpw.com

Coldwell Banker Platinum Partners
6349 Abercorn St ... Savannah GA 31405 912-352-1222 652

Coldwell Banker Residential Brokerage
600 Grant St Ste 925 ... Denver CO 80203 303-409-1500 409-6336 652
TF All: 800-552-6787 ■ *Web:* www.coldwellbankerhomes.com/colorado

Coldwell Banker Residential Real Estate
5951 Cattleridge Ave ... Sarasota FL 34232 941-487-1400 652
Web: www.coldwellbankerhomes.com/florida

Coldwell Banker Schmidt Realtors
402 E Front St ... Traverse City MI 49686 231-922-2350 652
Web: www.cbgreatlakes.com

Coldwell Banker Select Professionals
1000 N Prince St ... Lancaster PA 17603 717-569-0608 652

Cole & Reed PC 531 Couch Dr ... Oklahoma City OK 73102 405-239-7961 2
Web: rsmus.com/who-we-are/welcome-cole-reed.html

Cole & Weber United
221 Yale Ave N Ste 600 ... Seattle WA 98109 206-447-9595 233-0178 4
Web: www.coleweber.com

Cole Carbide Industries Inc
4930 S Lapeer Rd ... Orion Twp MI 48359 586-757-8700 757-8701 493
Web: www.colecarbide.com

Cole Chemical & Distributing Inc
1500 S Dairy Ashford St Ste 450 ... Houston TX 77077 713-465-2653 461-3462 146
Web: www.colechem.com

Cole County
301 E High St Ste 100 ... Jefferson City MO 65101 573-634-9100 634-8031 338
Web: www.colecounty.org

Cole County Historical Museum
109 Madison St ... Jefferson City MO 65101 573-635-1850 520
TF: 800-769-4183 ■ *Web:* www.colecohistsoc.org

Cole Hersee Co 20 Old Colony Ave ... Boston MA 02127 617-268-2100 815
Web: www.colehersee.com

Cole Home Healthcare of Houston Inc
16835 Deer Creek Dr Ste 220 ... Spring TX 77379 281-379-7052 363
Web: colehealthcare.com

Cole Industrial Inc 5924 203rd St SW ... Lynnwood WA 98036 425-774-6602 610
TF: 800-627-2653 ■ *Web:* www.coleindust.com

Cole Information Services
3401 NW 39th St ... Lincoln NE 68524 402-555-5678 637-6
TF: 800-800-3271 ■ *Web:* www.coleinformation.com

Cole Instrument Corp
2650 S Croddy Way ... Santa Ana CA 92704 714-556-3100 241-9061* 729
**Fax:* Sales ■ *Web:* www.cole-switches.com

Cole International Inc
3033 - 34th Ave NE ... Calgary AB T1Y6X2 403-262-2771 314
TF: 800-813-4281 ■ *Web:* www.coleintl.com

Cole Kepro International LLC
4170-103 Distribution Cir ... North Las Vegas NV 89030 702-633-4270 115
Web: colekepro.com

Cole Land Transportation Museum
405 Perry Rd ... Bangor ME 04401 207-990-3600 990-2653 520
TF: 800-377-3987 ■ *Web:* www.colemuseum.org

Cole Martinez Curtis & Assoc
4040 Del Rey Ave # 7 ... Marina del Rey CA 90292 310-827-7200 393
Web: www.cmcadesign.com

Cole Papers Inc 1300 N 38th St ... Fargo ND 58102 701-282-5311 282-5513 553
TF: 800-800-8090 ■ *Web:* www.colepapers.com

Cole Scott & Kissane pa
617 Whitehead St ... Key West FL 33040 305-294-4440 428
Web: www.csklegal.com

Cole Screw Machine Products Inc
36 Nettleton Ave PO Box 1007 ... North Haven CT 06473 203-772-6675 621
Web: colescrew.com

Cole Sport Inc 1615 Park Ave ... Park City UT 84060 435-649-4800 711
TF: 800-345-2938 ■ *Web:* www.colesport.com

Cole State Jail 3801 Silo Rd ... Bonham TX 75418 903-583-1100 583-7903 213
Web: tdcj.state.tx.us

Cole Tom (Rep R - OK)
2467 Rayburn HOB ... Washington DC 20515 202-225-6165 225-3512 342-2
Web: cole.house.gov

Cole Tool & Die Co 241 Ashland Rd ... Mansfield OH 44905 419-522-1272 522-5506 757
TF: 800-837-2653 ■ *Web:* www.coletool.com

Cole Warren & Long Inc
2 Penn Ctr Ste 312 ... Philadelphia PA 19102 215-563-0701 563-2907 266
Web: www.cwl-inc.com

Cole-Haan 8701 Keystone Crossing ... Indianapolis IN 46240 317-810-0160 301
TF: 800-695-8945 ■ *Web:* www.colehaan.com

Colehour & Cohen 1011 Wern Ave Ste 702 ... Seattle WA 98104 206-262-0363 636
Web: www.cplusc.com

Coleman A Young International Airport
11499 Conner ... Detroit MI 48213 313-628-2146 372-2448 27
TF: 800-874-9426 ■ *Web:* www.detroitmi.gov

Coleman American Moving Services Inc
PO Box 960 ... Midland City AL 36350 866-929-1482 780
TF: 877-693-7060 ■ *Web:* www.colemanallied.com

Name / Address	City	State	Zip	Phone	Fax	Class
Coleman College 8888 Balboa Ave. *TF:* 800-430-2030 ■ *Web:* www.coleman.edu	San Diego	CA	92123	858-499-0202	499-0233	166
Coleman Company Inc 3600 N Hydraulic *TF Cust Svc:* 800-835-3278 ■ *Web:* www.coleman.com	Wichita	KS	67219	800-835-3278		710
Coleman County 100 W Live Oak *Web:* www.co.coleman.tx.us	Coleman	TX	76834	325-625-2889		338
Coleman County Electric Co-op Inc 3300 N Hwy 84 PO Box 860 *TF:* 800-560-2128 ■ *Web:* www.colemanelectric.org	Coleman	TX	76834	325-625-2128	625-4600	245
Coleman Dairy Inc 6901 I-30 *TF:* 800-365-1551 ■ *Web:* hilanddairy.com	Little Rock	AR	72209	501-748-1700		296-27
Coleman E Adler & Sons Inc 722 Canal St *TF:* 800-925-7912 ■ *Web:* www.adlersjewelry.com	New Orleans	LA	70130	504-523-5292	568-0610	410
Coleman Equipment Inc 24000 W 43rd St *Web:* www.colemanequip.com	Bonner Springs	KS	66012	913-422-3040	422-3044	274
Coleman Floor Company 2777 Jefferson Davis Hwy Unit 2777-103 *Web:* www.colemanfloor.com	Stafford	VA	22554	410-796-7204		290
Coleman Instrument Co 11575 Goldcoast Dr *TF:* 800-899-5745 ■ *Web:* www.colemaninstrument.com	Cincinnati	OH	45249	513-489-5745		358
Coleman Isd 2400 S Concho St *Web:* www.colemanisd.net	Coleman	TX	76834	325-625-4369		685
Coleman Lew & Associates Inc 326 W Tenth St *TF:* 800-533-9523 ■ *Web:* www.colemanlew.com	Charlotte	NC	28202	704-377-0362		193
Coleman Oil Co 335 Mill Rd *Web:* www.colemanoil.com	Lewiston	ID	83501	208-799-2000		581
Coleman Professional Services 3920 Lovers Ln *TF:* 800-673-1347 ■ *Web:* www.colemanservices.org	Ravenna	OH	44266	330-296-3555		726
Coleman Research Inc 909 Aviation Pkwy Ste 400 *Web:* www.colemaninsights.com	Morrisville	NC	27560	919-571-0000		466
Coleman State Park 1155 Diamond Pond Rd *Web:* www.nhstateparks.org	Stewartstown	NH	03597	603-237-5382		565
Coleman Sudol Sapone P C 714 Colorado Ave *Web:* www.patentassets.com	Bridgeport	CT	06605	203-366-3560		445
Coleman's Fish Market 2226 Centre Market	Wheeling	WV	26003	304-232-8510		671
Coleman-Adams Construction Inc 1031 Performance Rd *Web:* www.coleman-adams.com	Forest	VA	24551	434-525-4700		186
Cole-Parmer Instrument Co 625 E Bunker Ct *TF:* 800-323-4340 ■ *Web:* www.coleparmer.com	Vernon Hills	IL	60061	847-549-7600	247-2929	420
Coler & Colantonio Inc 101 Accord Pk Dr *Web:* www.col-col.com	Norwell	MA	02061	781-982-5400		261
Coler-Goldwater Specialty Hospital & Nursing Facility 900 Main St *Web:* nychealthandhospitals.org	New York	NY	10044	212-848-6000		374-7
Coles County 651 Jackson Ave Rm 122 *Web:* www.co.coles.il.us	Charleston	IL	61920	217-348-0501	348-7337	338
Coles Creek State Park 13003 NY-37	Waddington	NY	13694	315-388-5636		565
Coles Mktg Communications Inc 3950 Priority Way S Dr Ste 106 *Web:* www.colesmarketing.com	Indianapolis	IN	46240	317-571-0051		194
Coles Quality Foods Inc 25 Ottawa SW 4th Fl *Web:* www.coles.com	Grand Rapids	MI	49503	616-975-0081		68
Coles-Moultrie Electric Co-op 104 DeWitt Ave E PO Box 709 *Web:* www.cmec.coop	Mattoon	IL	61938	217-235-0341		245
Colette Phillips Communications 1 Mckinley Sq Fl 6 *TF:* 800-763-0703 ■ *Web:* cpcglobal.com	Boston	MA	02109	617-357-5777		636
Coley & Associates Inc 140 Heimer Rd Ste 400 *Web:* www.coleyinc.com	San Antonio	TX	78232	210-402-6766		396
Colfax Corp 8730 Stony Pt Pkwy Ste 150 *TF:* 800-777-7401 ■ *Web:* www.colfaxcorp.com	Richmond	VA	23235	804-560-4070	560-4076	641
Colfax County 230 N Third St PO Box 1498 *Web:* www.co.colfax.nm.us	Raton	NM	87740	575-445-9661	445-2902	338
Colfax County 411 E 11th St *Web:* www.colfaxne.com	Schuyler	NE	68661	402-352-8504		338
Colfax Elementary School 24825 Ben Taylor Rd *Web:* www.colfax.k12.ca.us	Colfax	CA	95713	530-346-2202		685
Colgate Inn One Payne St *Web:* www.colgateinn.com	Hamilton	NY	13346	315-824-2300	824-4500	379
Colgate Rochester Crozer Divinity School 1100 S Goodman St *TF:* 888-937-3732 ■ *Web:* www.crcds.edu	Rochester	NY	14620	585-271-1320	271-8013	167-3
Colgate University 13 Oak Dr **Fax:* Admissions ■ *Web:* www.colgate.edu	Hamilton	NY	13346	315-228-1000	228-7544*	166
Colibri Ltd 419 E Crossville Rd Ste 102 *Web:* www.colibrilimited.com	Roswell	GA	30075	678-352-1001		180
Colima 130 N Fairview St *Web:* www.colimarest.com	Santa Ana	CA	92703	714-836-1254		671
Coliseum Medical Ctr 350 Hospital Dr *Web:* www.coliseumhealthsystem.com	Macon	GA	31217	478-765-7000		374-3
Colite International Ltd 5 Technology Cir *TF:* 800-760-7926 ■ *Web:* www.colite.com	Columbia	SC	29203	803-926-7926		610
CollabNet Inc 8000 Marina Blvd Ste 600 *TF:* 888-532-6823 ■ *Web:* www.collab.net	Brisbane	CA	94005	650-228-2500	228-2501	177
Collabrus Inc 111 Sutter St Ste 900 *Web:* www.collabrus.com	San Francisco	CA	94104	415-288-1826		734
CollabWorks 650 El Camino Real Ste O *Web:* collabworks.com	Redwood City	CA	94063	650-368-2523		393
Collarini Corp 11111 Richmond Ave Ste 126 *Web:* www.collarini.com	Houston	TX	77082	504-887-7127		539
Colle & McVoy Inc 400 First Ave N Ste 700 *Web:* www.collemcvoy.com	Minneapolis	MN	55401	612-305-6000		4
Collectcents Inc 1450 Meyerside Dr 2nd Fl *TF:* 800-256-8964 ■ *Web:* www.collectcents.com	Mississauga	ON	L5T2N5	905-670-7575		160
Collectcorp Corp 400 E Van Buren St	Phoenix	AZ	85004	602-443-2920		160
Collective Digital Studio LLC 8383 Wilshire Blvd Ste 1050 *Web:* www.studio71.com/us?showpopover=true	Beverly Hills	CA	90211	323-370-1500		514
Collective Technologies LLC 9433 Bee Caves Rd Bldg III Ste 200 *Web:* www.colltech.com	Austin	TX	78733	512-263-5500	263-0606	225
Collective[i] 130 Madison Ave *TF:* 888-890-0020 ■ *Web:* www.collectivei.com	New York	NY	10016	888-890-0020		466
Collectiveview Inc 3333 S Bannock St Ste 425 *Web:* completenetwork.com	Englewood	CO	80110	303-268-3800		180
Collector Books 5801 Kentucky Dam Rd *TF:* 800-626-5420 ■ *Web:* www.collectorbooks.com	Paducah	KY	42003	270-898-6211		95
Collector Car Network Inc 1345 E Chandler Blvd Ste 101 *Web:* classiccars.com	Phoenix	AZ	85048	480-285-1600		387
Collectors Alliance Inc 1942 Swarthmore Ave *Web:* www.collectorsalliance.com	Lakewood	NJ	08701	732-730-3580		292
Collectors Universe Inc PO Box 6280 *NASDAQ: CLCT* ■ *TF:* 800-325-1121 ■ *Web:* www.collectors.com	Newport Beach	CA	92658	949-567-1234	833-7955	51
College & University Professional Assn for Hum Res (CUPA-HR) 1811 Commons Pt Dr *TF:* 877-287-2474 ■ *Web:* www.cupahr.org	Knoxville	TN	37932	865-637-7673	637-7674	49-5
College Board 45 Columbus Ave *TF:* 800-927-4302 ■ *Web:* www.collegeboard.org	New York	NY	10023	212-713-8000		244
College De Maisonneuve 3800 Rue Sherbrooke E *Web:* www.cmaisonneuve.qc.ca	Montreal	QC	H1X2A2	514-251-1444		165
College De Rosemont 6400 16e Ave *Web:* www.crosemont.qc.ca	Montreal	QC	H1X2S9	514-376-1620		162
College De Valleyfield (cegep) 169 Rue Champlain *Web:* www.colval.qc.ca	Salaberry-de-valleyfield	QC	J6T1X6	450-373-9441		165
College Health Services LLC 144 Turnpike Rd Ste 240 *TF:* 866-636-8336 ■ *Web:* www.studenthealth101.com	Southborough	MA	01772	866-636-8336		177
College Hospital 10802 College Pl *TF:* 800-352-3301 ■ *Web:* www.collegehospitals.com	Cerritos	CA	90703	562-924-9581	809-0981	374-5
College Hospital Costa Mesa 301 Victoria St *TF:* 800-773-8001 ■ *Web:* www.collegehospitals.com	Costa Mesa	CA	92627	949-642-2734		374-5
College Houses Co-ops 1906 Pearl St Ofc 101 *Web:* collegehouses.org	Austin	TX	78705	512-476-5678		379
College Internship Program Inc 18 Park St *Web:* www.cipworldwide.org	Lee	MA	01238	413-243-0710		148
College Jacques-prevert 12349 Rue De Serres *Web:* collegejacquesprevert.ca	Montreal	QC	H4J2H1	514-336-2330		623
College Jean De Brebeuf 3200 Ch De La Cote-sainte-catherine *Web:* www.brebeuf.qc.ca	Montreal	QC	H3T1C1	514-342-1320		685
College Merici 755 Ch St-Louis *TF:* 800-208-1463 ■ *Web:* www.merici.ca	Quebec	QC	G1S1C1	418-683-1591	682-8938	162
College Music Society (CMS) 312 E Pine St *TF:* 800-729-0235 ■ *Web:* www.music.org	Missoula	MT	59802	406-721-9616	721-9419	49-5
College Nannies & Tutors Inc 850 Mill St *Web:* www.collegenanniesandtutors.com/nanny	Wayzata	MN	55391	952-285-7667		260
College Notre Dame, Quebec 3791 chemin Queen Mary *Web:* www.collegenotre-dame.qc.ca	Montreal	QC	H3V1A8	514-739-3371		685
College of Alameda 555 Ralph Appezzato Meml Pkwy *Web:* www.alameda.peralta.edu	Alameda	CA	94501	510-522-7221	769-6019	162
College of American Pathologists (CAP) 325 Waukegan Rd *TF:* 800-323-4040 ■ *Web:* www.cap.org	Northfield	IL	60093	847-832-7000	832-8168	49-8
College of American Pathologists PAC 1350 I St NW Ste 590 *TF:* 800-392-9994 ■ *Web:* www.cap.org	Washington	DC	20005	202-354-7100	354-7155	615
College of Biblical Studies-Houston 7000 Regency Sq Blvd Ste 110 *TF:* 844-227-9673 ■ *Web:* www.cbshouston.edu	Houston	TX	77036	713-785-5995		161
College of Charleston 66 George St *TF:* 866-327-2400 ■ *Web:* www.cofc.edu	Charleston	SC	29424	843-805-5507	953-6322	166
College of Court Reporting Inc 111 W Tenth St Ste 111 *TF:* 866-294-3974 ■ *Web:* www.ccr.edu	Hobart	IN	46342	219-942-1459	942-1631	800
College of DuPage 425 Fawell Blvd **Fax:* Admissions ■ *Web:* www.cod.edu	Glen Ellyn	IL	60137	630-942-2380	790-2686*	162
College of Eastern Utah 451 E 400 N **Fax:* Admissions ■ *TF:* 800-336-2381 ■ *Web:* usueastern.edu	Price	UT	84501	435-613-5000	613-5814*	162
San Juan 639 W 100 S **Fax:* Admissions ■ *TF:* 800-395-2969 ■ *Web:* usueastern.edu	Blanding	UT	84511	435-678-2201	678-2220*	162
College of Family Physicians of Canada The 2630 Skymark Ave *Web:* www.cfpc.ca	Mississauga	ON	L4W5A4	905-629-0900		167
College of Idaho 2112 Cleveland Blvd **Fax:* Admissions ■ *TF Admissions:* 800-224-3246 ■ *Web:* www.collegeofidaho.edu	Caldwell	ID	83605	208-459-5011	459-5757*	166
College of Lake County *Grayslake* 19351 W Washington St **Fax:* Admissions ■ *Web:* www.clcillinois.edu	Grayslake	IL	60030	847-223-6601	543-3061*	162

	Phone	Fax	Class
Lakeshore 33 N Genessee St . . . . Waukegan IL 60085 **Fax:* Admissions ■ *Web:* www.clcillinois.edu	847-623-8686	543-2170*	162
College of Marin 835 College Ave . . . . Kentfield CA 94904 *Web:* www.marin.edu	415-457-8811		162
Indian Valley 1800 Ignacio Blvd . . . . Novato CA 94949 **Fax:* Admissions ■ *TF:* 800-579-2878 ■ *Web:* www.marin.edu	415-883-2211	884-0429*	162
College of Menominee Nation PO Box 1179 . . . . Keshena WI 54135 **Fax:* Admissions ■ *TF:* 800-567-2344 ■ *Web:* www.menominee.edu	715-799-5600	799-4392*	165
College of Mount Saint Joseph 5701 Delhi Rd. . . . . Cincinnati OH 45233 *TF:* 800-654-9314 ■ *Web:* www.msj.edu	513-244-4200	244-4601	166
College of Mount Saint Vincent 6301 Riverdale Ave. . . . . Riverdale NY 10471 *TF:* 800-722-4867 ■ *Web:* www.mountsaintvincent.edu	718-405-3304		166
College of New Rochelle 29 Castle Pl . . . . New Rochelle NY 10805 *TF:* 800-933-5923 ■ *Web:* www.cnr.edu	914-654-5000		166
College of Nurses of Ontario 101 Davenport Rd. . . . . Toronto ON M5R3P1 *TF:* 800-387-5526 ■ *Web:* www.cno.org	416-928-0900		162
College of Registered Nurses of Manitoba 890 Pembina Hwy. . . . . Winnipeg MB R3M2M8 *TF:* 800-665-2027 ■ *Web:* www.crnm.mb.ca	204-774-3477		165
College of Saint Catherine 2004 Randolph Ave. . . . . Saint Paul MN 55105 *TF:* 800-945-4599 ■ *Web:* www.stkate.edu	651-690-6000		166
Minneapolis 601 25th Ave S . . . . Minneapolis MN 55454 **Fax:* Admissions ■ *TF:* 800-945-4599 ■ *Web:* www.stkate.edu	651-690-7700	690-7849*	166
College of Saint Elizabeth 2 Convent Rd . . . . Morristown NJ 07960 **Fax:* Admissions ■ *TF Admissions:* 800-210-7900 ■ *Web:* www.cse.edu	973-290-4700	290-4710*	166
College of Saint Joseph in Vermont 71 Clement Rd . . . . Rutland VT 05701 *TF Admissions:* 877-270-9998 ■ *Web:* www.csj.edu	802-773-5900		166
College of Saint Mary 7000 Mercy Rd . . . . Omaha NE 68106 **Fax:* Admissions ■ *TF:* 800-926-5534 ■ *Web:* www.csm.edu	402-399-2400	399-2412*	166
College of Saint Rose 432 Western Ave . . . . Albany NY 12203 **Fax:* Admissions ■ *TF:* 800-637-8556 ■ *Web:* www.strose.edu	518-454-5150	454-2013*	166
College of Saint Scholastica 1200 Kenwood Ave. . . . . Duluth MN 55811 **Fax:* Admissions ■ *TF:* 800-447-5444 ■ *Web:* www.css.edu	218-723-6046	723-5991*	166
College of San Mateo 1700 W Hillsdale Blvd . . . . San Mateo CA 94402 **Fax:* Admissions ■ *Web:* www.collegeofsanmateo.edu	650-574-6161	574-6506*	162
College of Santa Fe 1600 St Michaels Dr. . . . . Santa Fe NM 87505 *TF:* 800-862-7759 ■ *Web:* mycollegeoptions.org	505-424-5050		166
College of Southern Idaho PO Box 1238 . . . . Twin Falls ID 83303 **Fax:* Admissions ■ *TF:* 800-680-0274 ■ *Web:* www.csi.edu	208-733-9554	736-3014*	162
College of Southern Maryland *La Plata* 8730 Mitchell Rd PO Box 910 . . . . La Plata MD 20646 *Web:* www.csmd.edu	301-934-2251	870-3008	162
Leonardtown 22950 Hollywood Rd . . . . Leonardtown MD 20650 **Fax:* Admissions ■ *TF:* 800-933-9177 ■ *Web:* www.csmd.edu	240-725-5300	725-5400*	162
Prince Frederick 115 J W Williams Rd . . . . Prince Frederick MD 20678 *TF:* 800-933-9177 ■ *Web:* www.csmd.edu	443-550-6000	550-6100	162
College of Southern Nevada *Cheyenne* 3200 E Cheyenne Ave . . . . North Las Vegas NV 89030 *Web:* www.csn.edu	702-651-4000		162
College of Staten Island 2800 Victory Blvd. . . . . Staten Island NY 10314 *TF:* 888-442-4551 ■ *Web:* www.csi.cuny.edu	718-982-2000	982-2500	166
College of the Albemarle PO Box 2327 . . . . Elizabeth City NC 27906 **Fax:* Admissions ■ *TF:* 800-335-9050 ■ *Web:* www.albemarle.edu	252-335-0821	335-2011*	162
College of the Atlantic 105 Eden St . . . . Bar Harbor ME 04609 **Fax:* Admissions ■ *TF Admissions:* 800-528-0025 ■ *Web:* www.coa.edu	207-288-5015	288-4126*	166
College of the Canyons 26455 Rockwell Canyon Rd . . . . Santa Clarita CA 91355 **Fax:* Admissions ■ *TF:* 800-695-4858 ■ *Web:* www.canyons.edu	661-259-7800	362-5566*	162
College of the Desert 43-500 Monterey Ave. . . . . Palm Desert CA 92260 **Fax:* Admissions ■ *Web:* www.collegeofthedesert.edu	760-346-8041	862-1379*	162
College of the Holy Cross 1 College St . . . . Worcester MA 01610 *TF:* 800-442-2421 ■ *Web:* www.holycross.edu	508-793-2011	793-3888	166
College of the Holy Cross Dinand Library 1 College St . . . . Worcester MA 01610 *TF:* 877-433-1843 ■ *Web:* www.holycross.edu	508-793-2642	793-2372	434-6
College of the Mainland 1200 N Amburn Rd. . . . . Texas City TX 77591 *TF:* 888-258-8859 ■ *Web:* www.com.edu	409-938-1211		162
College of the Ozarks 1 Industrial Dr PO Box 17. . . . . Point Lookout MO 65726 **Fax:* Admissions ■ *TF Admissions:* 800-222-0525 ■ *Web:* www.cofo.edu	417-334-6411	335-2618*	166
College of the Redwoods 7351 Tompkins Hill Rd. . . . . Eureka CA 95501 **Fax:* Admissions ■ *TF:* 800-641-0400 ■ *Web:* www.redwoods.edu	707-476-4100	476-4406*	162
Del Norte 883 W Washington Blvd . . . . Crescent City CA 95531 **Fax:* Admissions ■ *TF:* 800-641-0400 ■ *Web:* www.redwoods.edu	707-465-2300	464-6867*	162
Mendocino Coast 440 Alger St . . . . Fort Bragg CA 95437 *TF:* 800-641-0400 ■ *Web:* www.redwoods.edu	707-962-2600	961-0943	162
College of the Sequoias 915 S Mooney Blvd . . . . Visalia CA 93277 *Web:* www.cos.edu	559-730-3700		162
College of the Siskiyous 800 College Ave . . . . Weed CA 96094 **Fax:* Admissions ■ *TF:* 888-397-4339 ■ *Web:* www.siskiyous.edu	530-938-4461	938-5367*	162
College of the Southwest 6610 N Lovington Hwy. . . . . Hobbs NM 88240 **Fax Area Code:* 505 ■ **Fax:* Admissions ■ *TF:* 800-530-4400 ■ *Web:* www.usw.edu	575-392-6561	392-6006*	166
College of Westchester (CW) 325 Central Ave . . . . White Plains NY 10606 **Fax Area Code:* 914 ■ **Fax:* Admissions ■ *TF:* 800-660-7093 ■ *Web:* www.cw.edu	800-660-7093	948-5441*	800

	Phone	Fax	Class
College of William & Mary PO Box 8795 . . . . Williamsburg VA 23187 **Fax:* Admissions ■ *Web:* www.wm.edu	757-221-4000	221-1242*	166
College of Wooster 1189 Beall Ave . . . . Wooster OH 44691 *TF:* 800-877-9905 ■ *Web:* www.wooster.edu	330-263-2000	263-2621	166
College Outlook & Career Opportunities Magazine 20 E Gregory Blvd. . . . . Kansas City MO 64114 *TF:* 800-274-8867 ■ *Web:* www.mymajors.com	816-361-0616		457-11
College Parents of America (CPA) 2200 Wilson Blvd Ste 102-396. . . . . Arlington VA 22201 *TF:* 888-761-6702 ■ *Web:* www.collegeparents.org	888-761-6702		48-11
College Regina Assumpta 1750 Rue Sauriol E. . . . . Montreal QC H2C1X4 *Web:* www.reginaassumpta.qc.ca	514-382-4121		685
College Savings Bank PO Box 3769 . . . . Princeton NJ 08543 **Fax Area Code:* 609 ■ *TF:* 800-888-2723 ■ *Web:* www.collegesavings.com	800-888-2723	987-3760*	70
College Station Ford 1351 Earl Rudder Fwy S. . . . . College Station TX 77845 *TF:* 888-508-0241 ■ *Web:* www.collegestationford.com	888-508-0241		57
College Station Medical Ctr 1604 Rock Prairie Rd . . . . College Station TX 77845 *Web:* www.csmedcenter.com	979-764-5100		374-3
CollegeBound Network 1200 S Ave Ste 202 . . . . Staten Island NY 10314 *Web:* www.collegebound.net	718-761-4800	761-3300	637-9
CollegeDegrees.com LLC 1001 McKinney St Ste 650. . . . . Houston TX 77002 *Web:* www.collegedegrees.com	713-534-1948		387
Colleges Ontario 20 Bay St Ste 1600 . . . . Toronto ON M5J2N8 *Web:* www.collegesontario.org	647-258-7670	258-7699	242
Collegiate Funding Services LLC 10304 Spotsylvania Ave . . . . Fredericksburg VA 22408 *Web:* htyp.org	540-374-1600		217
Collegium Pharmaceutical Inc 400 Highland Corporate Dr. . . . . Cumberland RI 02864 *Web:* collegiumpharma.com	401-762-2000		231
Collen IP Intellectual Property Law P C 80 S Highland Ave . . . . Ossining NY 10562 *Web:* collenip.com	914-941-5484		445
Colleton County 31 Klein St . . . . Walterboro SC 29488 *TF:* 800-922-6081 ■ *Web:* www.colletoncounty.org	843-549-1725	549-7215	338
Colleton County Memorial Library 600 Hampton St . . . . Walterboro SC 29488 *Web:* www.colletonlibrary.org	843-549-5621	549-5122	434-3
Colleton Medical Ctr (CMC) 501 Robertson Blvd . . . . Walterboro SC 29488 *TF:* 866-492-9083 ■ *Web:* www.colletonmedical.com	843-782-2000		374-3
Colleton State Park 147 Wayside Ln . . . . Walterboro SC 29488 *Web:* www.southcarolinaparks.com	843-538-8206		565
Collett & Assoc LLC 1111 Metropolitan Ave Ste 700 . . . . Charlotte NC 28204 *Web:* www.collettre.com/home	704-206-8300		652
Colletti-fiss Llc 8423 E Charter Oak Dr . . . . Scottsdale AZ 85260 *Web:* collettifiss.com	480-483-1480		195
Collicutt Energy Services Ltd 8133 Edgar Industrial Close . . . . Red Deer AB T4P3R4 *Web:* collicutt.com	403-309-9250		112
Collier County Museum 3331 Tamiami Trl E. . . . . Naples FL 34112 *Web:* www.colliermuseums.com	239-252-8476		520
Collier County Public Library (CCPL) 2385 Orange Blossom Dr . . . . Naples FL 34109 *Web:* www.colliergov.net	239-593-0177		434-3
Collier County School Board 5775 Osceola Trl. . . . . Naples FL 34109 *TF:* 800-950-6264 ■ *Web:* www.collierschools.com/site/default.aspx?pageid=1	239-377-0001	377-0336	685
Collier Enterprises Management Inc 2550 Goodlette Rd N Ste 100 . . . . Naples FL 34103 *Web:* www.collierenterprises.com	239-261-4455		652
Collier Insurance 606 S Mendenhall Rd Ste 200 . . . . Memphis TN 38117 *TF General:* 866-600-2655 ■ *Web:* www.collierinsurance.com	901-529-2900	529-2916	390
Collier Memorial State Park 46000 Hwy 97 N. . . . . Chiloquin OR 97624 *Web:* www.oregonstateparks.org	541-783-2471		565
Colliers International 7200 Glen Forest Dr Ste 200 . . . . Richmond VA 23226 *Web:* www.colliers.com	804-788-1000	782-1746	652
Colliers Parrish International Inc 1 Almaden Blvd Ste 300 . . . . San Jose CA 95113 *Web:* www.collierparrish.com	408-282-4000		652
Colliers Pinkard 7172 Columbia Gateway Dr Ste 400. . . . . Columbia MD 21046 *Web:* www.colliers.com/en-gb	443-297-9000	543-0191	652
Collier-Seminole State Park 20200 E Tamiami Trl . . . . Naples FL 34114 *Web:* www.floridastateparks.org/collierseminole	239-394-3397	394-5113	565
Collierville Chamber of Commerce 485 Halle Pk Dr . . . . Collierville TN 38017 *Web:* www.colliervillechamber.com	901-853-1949	853-2399	139
Colliflower Inc 9320 Pulaski Hwy . . . . Baltimore MD 21220 *Web:* www.colliflower.com	410-686-1200		295
Colligo Networks Inc 400-1152 Mainland St. . . . . Vancouver BC V6B4X2 *TF:* 866-685-7962 ■ *Web:* www.colligo.com	604-685-7962		179
Collin County 2300 Bloomdale Rd Ste 2106. . . . . McKinney TX 75071 *TF:* 800-974-2437 ■ *Web:* www.collincountytx.gov/pages/default.aspx	972-548-4185	547-5731	338
Collin County Community College *Central Park* 2200 W University Dr . . . . McKinney TX 75070 **Fax:* Admissions ■ *Web:* collin.edu	972-548-6790	548-6702*	162
Preston Ridge 9700 Wade Blvd. . . . . Frisco TX 75035 **Fax:* Admissions ■ *Web:* collin.edu	972-377-1582	377-1723*	162
Spring Creek 2800 E Spring Creek Pkwy. . . . . Plano TX 75074 **Fax:* Admissions ■ *Web:* collin.edu	972-881-5790	881-5174*	162
Collin Creek Mall 811 N Central Expy . . . . Plano TX 75075 *Web:* www.collincreekmall.com	972-543-0369		460

Phone | Fax | Class

Collin Street Bakery Inc
401 W Seventh Ave ... Corsicana TX 75151 800-267-4657 872-6879* 68
**Fax Area Code:* 903 ■ *TF Sales:* 800-267-4657 ■ *Web:* www.collinstreet.com

Collingswood Nursing Facilities Inc
299 Hurley Ave ... Rockville MD 20850 301-762-8900 371
TF: 800-321-1245 ■ *Web:* www.collingswoodnursing.com

Collingsworth County 800 W Ave ... Wellington TX 79095 806-447-5408 447-5418 338
Web: co.collingsworth.tx.us

Collington Episcopal Community
10450 Lottsford Rd ... Mitchellville MD 20721 888-257-9468 541-5044* 672
**Fax Area Code:* 301 ■ *TF:* 888-257-9468 ■ *Web:* collington.kendal.org

Collingwood Events
45 Saint Paul St ... Collingwood ON L9Y3P1 705-445-4811 342
TF: 800-465-9077 ■ *Web:* www.collingwood.ca

Collins & Hermann Inc 1215 Dunn Rd ... St. Louis MO 63138 314-869-8000 492
Web: www.collinsandhermann.com

Collins & Lacy PC 1330 Lady St 6th Fl ... Columbia SC 29201 803-256-2660 428
TF: 888-648-0526 ■ *Web:* www.collinsandlacy.com

Collins Barrow Calgary LLP
1400 First Alberta Pl 777 - Eighth Ave SW ... Calgary AB T2P3R5 403-298-1500 2
Web: www.collinsbarrow.com

Collins Barrow Ottawa LLP
400-301 Moodie Dr ... Ottawa ON K2H9C4 613-820-8010 401
Web: www.collinsbarrowottawa.com

Collins Bowling Centers Inc
750 E New Cir Rd ... Lexington KY 40505 859-252-3429 99
Web: www.collinsbowling.com

Collins Bus Corp
415 W Sixth Ave PO Box 2946 ... Hutchinson KS 67504 620-662-9000 662-3838 59
Web: www.collinsbus.com

Collins Capital Management Inc
7077 Bonneval Rd Ste 340 ... Jacksonville FL 32216 904-493-7500 401
Web: www.collinscmi.com

Collins Chris (Rep R - NY)
1117 Longworth Bldg ... Washington DC 20515 202-225-5265 225-5910 342-2
Web: chriscollins.house.gov

Collins Community Credit Union
1150 42nd St NE ... Cedar Rapids IA 52402 319-393-9000 219
Web: www.collinscu.org

Collins Computing Inc
26050 Acero St ... Mission Viejo CA 92691 949-457-0500 177
Web: www.collinscomputing.com

Collins Consulting 630 Woofter Ave ... Colby KS 67701 785-462-8352 194
Web: collins.net

Collins Correctional Facility
Middle Rd PO Box 490 ... Collins NY 14034 716-532-4588 213
Web: www.doccs.ny.gov

Collins Cos 1618 SW First Ave Ste 500 ... Portland OR 97201 800-329-1219 227-5349* 683
**Fax Area Code:* 503 ■ *TF:* 800-329-1219 ■ *Web:* www.collinsco.com

Collins Doug (Rep R - GA)
1504 Longworth HOB ... Washington DC 20515 202-225-9893 226-1224 342-2
Web: dougcollins.house.gov

Collins Electric Co Inc
53 Second Ave ... Chicopee MA 01020 413-592-9221 592-4157 189-4
TF: 877-553-2810 ■ *Web:* www.collinselectricco.com

Collins Industries Ltd 3740-73 Ave ... Edmonton AB T6B2Z2 780-440-1414 480
TF: 800-831-9252 ■ *Web:* www.collins-industries-ltd.com

Collins Irish Pub 2 N Laroux St ... Flagstaff AZ 86001 928-214-7363 671
Web: www.collinsirishpub.com

Collins Law Firm P C, The
1770 N Park St Ste 202 ... Naperville IL 60563 630-527-1595 445
TF: 800-715-3582 ■ *Web:* www.collinslaw.com

Collins Manufacturing Co
2000 Bowser Rd ... Cookeville TN 38506 931-528-5151 528-5472 76
TF: 800-292-6450 ■ *Web:* www.collinsmfgco.com

Collins Pipeline Co
355 Mississippi 588 ... Collins MS 39428 601-765-6593 597

Collins Plumbing Inc
8130 Commercial St ... La Mesa CA 91942 619-469-0800 189-10
Web: collinsplumbing.com

Collins Susan M (Sen R - ME)
413 Dirksen Bldg ... Washington DC 20510 202-224-2523 224-2693 342-2
Web: www.collins.senate.gov

Collinsville Chamber of Commerce
221 W Main St ... Collinsville IL 62234 618-344-2884 344-7499 139
Web: www.discovercollinsville.com

Collinsville Community
240 Regency Ctr ... Collinsville IL 62234 618-343-2878 148
Web: kahoks.org

Colloid Environmental Technologies Co (CETCO)
2870 Forbs Ave ... Hoffman Estates IL 60192 847-851-1899 527-9948* 3
**Fax Area Code:* 800 ■ *TF:* 800-527-9948 ■ *Web:* www.cetco.com

Colloidal Dynamics Pty Ltd
5150 Palm Valley Rd Ste 303 ... Ponte Vedra Beach FL 32082 904-686-1536 201
Web: www.colloidal-dynamics.com

Collum's Lumber Products LLC
1723 Barnwell Hwy ... Allendale SC 29810 803-584-3451 683
Web: www.collumlumber.com

Colmac Coil Manufacturing Inc
370 N Lincoln St PO Box 571 ... Colville WA 99114 509-684-2595 684-8331 14
TF: 800-845-6778 ■ *Web:* www.colmaccoil.com

Colmac Industries Inc PO Box 72 ... Colville WA 99114 509-684-4505 684-4500 427
TF: 800-926-5622 ■ *Web:* www.colmacind.com

Colman Wolf Sanitary Supply Co
15201 E 11-Mile Rd ... Roseville MI 48066 586-779-5500 508
Web: www.theprofgroup.com

Colmery-O'Neil Veterans Affairs Medical Ctr
2200 SW Gage Blvd ... Topeka KS 66622 785-350-3111 374-8
TF: 800-574-8387 ■ *Web:* www.topeka.va.gov

Col-Met Spray Booths Inc
1635 Innovation Dr ... Rockwall TX 75032 972-772-1919 111
TF: 800-280-0780 ■ *Web:* www.colmetsb.com

Cologix Inc 2300 15th St Ste 300 ... Denver CO 80202 720-230-7000 224
TF: 800-638-6336 ■ *Web:* www.cologix.com

Coloma Frozen Foods Inc 4145 Coloma Rd ... Coloma MI 49038 269-849-0500 849-0886 296-21
TF: 800-642-2723 ■ *Web:* www.colomafrozen.com

Colombia 140 E 57th St ... New York NY 10022 212-355-7776 371-2813 784
Web: nuevayork-onu.mision.gov.co

Phone | Fax | Class

Consulate General
500 N Michigan Ave Ste 2040 ... Chicago IL 60611 312-923-1196 923-1197 257
Web: www.chicago.consulado.gov.co/en

Consulate General
5851 San Felipe Ste 300 ... Houston TX 77057 713-527-8919 529-3395 257
Web: www.colhouston.org

Embassy 1724 Massachusetts Ave, NW ... Washington DC 20036 202-387-8338 232-8643 257
TF: 800-395-2872 ■ *Web:* www.colombiaemb.org

Colombia Energy Resources Inc
1 Embarcadero Ctr Ste 500 ... San Francisco CA 94111 415-460-1165 501

Colombian American Chamber of Commerce
2305 NW 107 Ave Ste 1m14 box 105 ... Miami FL 33172 305-446-2542 138
Web: www.colombiachamber.com

Colonel Denning State Park
1599 Doubling Gap Rd ... Newville PA 17241 717-776-5272 565
Web: www.dcnr.state.pa.us

Colonel Florence A Blanchfield Army Community Hospital
650 Joel Dr ... Fort Campbell KY 42223 270-798-8400 374-4

Colonial Air 1605 Airport Rd ... New Bedford MA 02746 508-997-0620 990-2582 63
Web: www.colonial-air.com

Colonial Bag Corp
205 E Fullerton Ave ... Carol Stream IL 60188 630-690-3999 690-1571 66
TF: 800-445-7496 ■ *Web:* www.colonialbag.com

Colonial Bronze Co 511 Winsted Rd ... Torrington CT 06790 860-489-9233 355-7903* 350
**Fax Area Code:* 800 ■ *TF All:* 800-355-7903 ■ *Web:* www.colonialbronze.com

Colonial Commercial Corp
275 Wagaraw Rd ... Hawthorne NJ 07506 973-427-8224 14
OTC: CCOM ■ *Web:* www.colonialcomm.com

Colonial Country Club Inc
3735 Country Club Cir ... Fort Worth TX 76109 817-927-4200 711
Web: www.colonialfw.com

Colonial Diversified Polymer Products LLC
2055 Forrest St Ext PO Box 930 ... Dyersburg TN 38025 731-287-3636 677
Web: www.colonialdpp.com

Colonial Dorchester State Historic Site
300 State Pk Rd ... Summerville SC 29485 843-873-1740 565
Web: www.southcarolinaparks.com

Colonial Engineering Inc
6400 Corporate Ave ... Portage MI 49002 269-323-2495 323-0630 595
TF: 800-374-0234 ■ *Web:* www.colonialengineering.com

Colonial Farm Credit Aca
7104 Mechanicsville Tpke ... Mechanicsville VA 23111 804-746-1252 216
TF: 800-777-8908 ■ *Web:* www.colonialfarmcredit.com

Colonial Freight Systems Inc
10924 McBride Ln ... Knoxville TN 37932 865-966-9711 966-3649 780
TF: 800-826-1402 ■ *Web:* www.cfsi.com

Colonial Garage & Distributors Ltd
59 Majors Path ... St John'S NL A1A4Z9 709-579-4015 61
Web: www.colonialautoparts.ca

Colonial Group Inc 101 N Lathrop Ave ... Savannah GA 31415 912-236-1331 235-3881 324
Web: colonialgroupinc.com

Colonial Heights (Independent City)
201 James Ave PO Box 3401 ... Colonial Heights VA 23834 804-520-9265 520-9207 338
Web: www.colonialheightsva.gov

Colonial Hills Baptist Church
5375 W Mt Morris Rd ... Mount Morris MI 48458 810-687-1570 48-20

Colonial House 2315 Mt Rushmore Rd ... Rapid City SD 57701 605-342-4640 671
Web: www.colonialhousernb.com

Colonial House Inn
277 Main St Rt 6A ... Yarmouth Port MA 02675 508-362-4348 362-8034 671
Web: www.colonialhousecapecod.com/dine.html

Colonial Inn (Reno) 250 N Arlington Ave ... Reno NV 89501 775-322-3838 377
Web: www.colonialgardencourt.com

Colonial Intermediate Unit 20
6 Danforth Rd ... Easton PA 18045 610-252-5550 252-5740 148
Web: www.ciu20.org

Colonial Life & Accident Insurance Co
1200 Colonial Life Blvd ... Columbia SC 29210 800-325-4368 391-2
TF: 800-325-4368 ■ *Web:* www.coloniallife.com

Colonial Machine Co 1041 Mogadore Rd ... Kent OH 44240 330-673-5859 673-5859 757
Web: www.colonial-machine.com

Colonial Materials of Fayetteville Inc
570 Belt Blvd ... Fayetteville NC 28301 910-485-5099 191-1
Web: colonialmaterials.com

Colonial Metal Products Inc
2350 Quality Ln ... Hermitage PA 16148 724-346-6379 492
Web: www.colonialmetalproducts.com

Colonial Metals Co
217 Linden St PO Box 311 ... Columbia PA 17512 717-684-2311 684-9555 485
Web: www.colonialmetalsco.com

Colonial Mills Inc
560 Mineral Spring Ave ... Pawtucket RI 02860 401-724-6279 364
Web: www.colonialmills.com

Colonial Millwork Ltd RR 219 ... Beverly WV 26253 800-833-7612 499
TF: 800-833-7612 ■ *Web:* www.colonialmillwork.com

Colonial National Historical Park
PO Box 210 ... Yorktown VA 23690 757-898-3400 898-6346 564
TF: 866-945-7920 ■ *Web:* www.nps.gov/colo

Colonial Nursing & Rehabilitation Inc
125 Broad St ... Weymouth MA 02188 781-337-3121 450
TF: 800-245-8389 ■ *Web:* welchhrg.com

Colonial Opticians 4942 St Elmo Ave ... Bethesda MD 20814 301-657-3332 543
Web: colonialopticians.com

Colonial Parking Inc
1050 Thomas Jefferson St NW Ste 100 ... Washington DC 20007 202-295-8100 295-8111 562
TF: 877-777-4778 ■ *Web:* www.ecolonial.com

Colonial Pemaquid State Historic Site
PO Box 304 ... New Harbor ME 04554 207-677-2423 565
Web: www.maine.gov

Colonial Penn Life Insurance Co
399 Market St ... Philadelphia PA 19181 877-877-8052 391-2
TF: 800-523-9100 ■ *Web:* www.colonialpenn.com

Colonial Pipeline Co
1185 Sanctuary Pkwy Ste 100 ... Alpharetta GA 30009 678-762-2200 762-2883 597
TF: 800-275-3004 ■ *Web:* www.colpipe.com

Colonial Press Inc, The
10607 Harrison St ... Omaha NE 68128 402-593-0580 627
Web: www.thecolonialpress.net

	Phone	Fax	Class
Colonial Properties Trust 6584 Poplar Ave .... Memphis TN 38138 *NYSE: CLP* ■ **Fax Area Code:* 901 ■ *TF:* 866-620-1130 ■ *Web:* www.maac.com	866-620-1130	248-4188*	655
Colonial Saw Company Inc 122 Pembroke St .... Kingston NY 02364 *Web:* www.csaw.com	781-585-4364		358
Colonial Spanish Quarter Museum 33 St George St .... Saint Augustine FL 32084 *TF:* 888-991-0933 ■ *Web:* colonialquarter.com	888-991-0933		520
Colonial Spirits, The 87 Great Rd .... Acton MA 01720 *Web:* colonialspirits.com	978-263-7775		443
Colonial Systems Inc 326 Ballardvale St Ste 200 .... Wilmington MA 01887 *TF:* 800-966-3375 ■ *Web:* colonialsystems.com	978-657-6508		179
Colonial Theatre 106 Boylston St........ Boston MA 02116 *Web:* boston.broadway.com	212-307-2166		572
Colonial Truck Co 1833 Commerce Rd........ Richmond VA 23224 *TF:* 800-234-8782 ■ *Web:* www.colonialtruckofrichmond.com	804-232-3492		780
Colonial Williamsburg Foundation PO Box 1776 .... Williamsburg VA 23187 *TF:* 800-447-8679 ■ *Web:* www.history.org	757-229-1000		305
Colonial Williamsburg Reservation Ctr PO Box 1776 .... Williamsburg VA 23187 *TF:* 800-447-8679 ■ *Web:* www.history.org	757-229-1000		376
ColonialWebb Contractors Co 2820 Ackley Ave........ Richmond VA 23228 *TF:* 877-208-3894 ■ *Web:* www.colonialwebb.com	804-916-1400		189-10
Colonie Center 131 Colonie Ctr .... Albany NY 12205 *Web:* www.shopatcoloniecenter.com	518-459-9020		460
Colonna Bros Inc PO Box 808 .... North Bergen NJ 07047 *TF:* 800-697-9925 ■ *Web:* www.colonnabrothers.com	201-864-1115		296-5
Colonna's Shipyard Inc 400 E Indian River Rd........ Norfolk VA 23523 *TF:* 800-265-6627 ■ *Web:* www.colonnaship.com	757-545-2414	543-2480	698
Colonnade Hotel 120 Huntington Ave .... Boston MA 02116 *TF:* 800-962-3030 ■ *Web:* www.colonnadehotel.com	617-424-7000	424-1717	379
Colonnades, The 2600 Barracks Rd........ Charlottesville VA 22901 *Web:* www.sunriseseniorliving.com	434-963-4198		672
Colony Brands Inc 1112 Seventh Ave........ Monroe WI 53566 *Web:* www.theswisscolony.net	608-328-8400	328-8457	459
Colony Capital Management 3050 Peachtree Rd NW Ste 200 .... Atlanta GA 30305 *Web:* www.colonycapital.com	404-365-5050	523-7877	401
Colony Group LLC, The 2 Atlantic Ave........ Boston MA 02110 *Web:* www.thecolonygroup.com	617-723-8200		194
Colony Hotel 140 Ocean Ave........ Kennebunkport ME 04046 *TF:* 800-552-2363 ■ *Web:* www.thecolonyhotel.com	207-967-3331		669
Colony Hotel & Cabana Club 525 E Atlantic Ave........ Delray Beach FL 33483 *TF:* 800-552-2363 ■ *Web:* www.thecolonyhotel.com	561-276-4123		379
Colony Inc 2500 Galvin Dr .... Elgin IL 60123 *TF:* 800-735-1300 ■ *Web:* www.colonydisplay.com	847-426-5300		233
Colony Palms Hotel 572 N Indian Canyon Dr........ Palm Springs CA 92262 *TF:* 800-557-2187 ■ *Web:* www.colonypalmshotel.com	760-969-1800		132
Colony Pub & Grille 2670 W Eigth St........ Erie PA 16505 *Web:* colonypub.com	814-838-2162		671
Colony Public Library, The 6800 Main St .... The Colony TX 75056 *Web:* thecolonytx.gov	972-625-1900		434-3
Colony South Hotel 7401 Surratts Rd........ Clinton MD 20735 *Web:* www.colonysouth.com	301-856-4500	856-4500	379
Color Ad Inc 18601 S Santa Fe Ave........ Rancho Dominguez CA 90221 *TF:* 888-264-6991 ■ *Web:* www.gocolorad.com	888-264-6991		627
Color Art Integrated Interiors 1325 N Warson Rd .... St. Louis MO 63132 *Web:* www.color-art.com	314-432-3000		320
Color Communication Inc 4000 W Fillmore St........ Chicago IL 60624 **Fax Area Code:* 773 ■ *TF:* 800-458-5743 ■ *Web:* www.ccicolor.com	800-458-5743	638-0887*	781
Color Craft Label Co 158 Vance Ave .... Memphis TN 38103 *Web:* www.colorcraftlabel.com	901-525-4762		638
Color House Graphics Inc 3505 Eastern Ave SE........ Grand Rapids MI 49508 *TF:* 800-454-1916 ■ *Web:* www.colorhousegraphics.com	616-241-1916		781
Color Imaging Inc 4350 Peachtree Industrial Blvd Ste 100 .... Norcross GA 30071 **Fax Area Code:* 800 ■ *TF:* 800-783-1090 ■ *Web:* www.colorimaging.com	770-840-1090	783-9010*	628
Color Ink Inc W250 N6681 Hwy 164 PO Box 360 .... Sussex WI 53089 *TF:* 800-348-2686 ■ *Web:* www.colorink.com	262-246-5000		627
Color Kinetics Distribution Inc 1247 Norwood Ave........ Itasca IL 60143 *Web:* www.colorkinetics.com	630-285-9772		253
Color Marketing Group (CMG) 1908 Mt Vernon Ave........ Alexandria VA 22301 *Web:* www.colormarketing.org	703-329-8500	535-3190	49-18
Color Me Beautiful 7000 Infantry Ridge Rd Ste 200 .... Manassas VA 20109 *TF:* 800-265-6763 ■ *Web:* www.colormebeautiful.com	800-265-6763		366
Color Me Mine Enterprises Inc 3722 San Fernando Rd........ Glendale CA 91204 **Fax Area Code:* 858 ■ *Web:* www.colormemine.com	818-291-5900	312-5501*	310
Color Merchants 6 E 45th St Rm 1704........ New York NY 10017 *TF:* 800-356-3851 ■ *Web:* www.colormerchants.com	212-682-4788		410
Color Optics 40 Green Pond Rd........ Rockaway NJ 07866 *Web:* www.coloroptics.com	973-664-3100		92
Color Pigments Manufacturers Assn Inc 300 N Washington St Ste 105........ Alexandria VA 22314 *TF:* 800-926-4404 ■ *Web:* www.pigments.org	703-684-4044	684-1795	49-13
Color Place, The 1330 Conant St........ Dallas TX 75207 *Web:* www.thecolorplace.com	214-631-7174		627
Color Putty Company Inc PO Box 738 .... Monroe WI 53566 *Web:* www.colorputty.com	608-325-6033	325-6397	550
Color Reflections 10795 Rockley Rd .... Houston TX 77099 *TF:* 800-328-7154 ■ *Web:* www.colorreflections.com	713-626-4045		113

	Phone	Fax	Class
Color Resolutions International 575 Quality Blvd........ Fairfield OH 45014 *TF:* 800-346-8570 ■ *Web:* new.colorresolutions.com	513-552-7200		388
Color Spot Nurseries Inc 2575 Olive Hill Rd .... Fallbrook CA 92028 **Fax Area Code:* 800 ■ *TF:* 800-554-4065 ■ *Web:* www.colorspot.com	760-695-1480	250-5135*	369
Color Technology 2455 NW Nicolai St........ Portland OR 97210 *Web:* www.colortechnology.com	503-294-0393		781
Color Web Printers Inc 4700 Bowling St SW........ Cedar Rapids IA 52404 *TF:* 888-265-1511 ■ *Web:* www.colorwebprinters.com	888-265-1511		627
Color West Inc 3405 W Pacific Ave........ Burbank CA 91505	818-840-8881		627
Colorado			
Aging & Adult Services Div 1575 Sherman St 10th Fl........ Denver CO 80203 *TF:* 800-773-1366 ■ *Web:* www.colorado.gov	303-866-2636	866-2696	339-6
Agriculture Dept 305 Interlocken Pkwy........ Broomfield CO 80021 *Web:* www.colorado.gov/ag	303-869-9000		339-6
Arts Council 1625 Broadway Ste 2700 .... Denver CO 80202 *Web:* www.coloradocreativeindustries.org	303-892-3840	892-3848	339-6
Attorney General 1300 Broadway 10th Fl........ Denver CO 80203 *Web:* www.coloradoattorneygeneral.gov	720-508-6000	508-6030	339-6
Banking Div 1560 Broadway St Ste 975 .... Denver CO 80202 *Web:* colorado.gov/cs	303-894-7575		339-6
Child Support Enforcement Div 1575 Sherman St 5th Fl........ Denver CO 80203 *Web:* www.childsupport.state.co.us	303-866-4300	866-4360	339-6
Children Youth & Families Office 1575 Sherman St........ Denver CO 80203 *TF:* 800-799-5876 ■ *Web:* www.colorado.gov	800-799-5876		339-6
CollegeInvest 1560 Broadway Ste 1700 .... Denver CO 80202 *TF:* 800-448-2424 ■ *Web:* collegeinvest.org	303-376-8800	296-4811	725
Corrections Dept 2862 S Cir Dr........ Colorado Springs CO 80906 *Web:* www.doc.state.co.us	719-579-9580		339-6
Economic Development Commission 1625 Broadway Ste 2700........ Denver CO 80202 *Web:* www.advancecolorado.com	303-892-3840	892-3848	339-6
Education Dept 201 E Colfax Ave........ Denver CO 80203 *Web:* www.cde.state.co.us	303-866-6600	830-0793	339-6
Educator Licensing Unit 201 E Colfax Ave .... Denver CO 80203 *Web:* www.cde.state.co.us	303-866-6600	830-0793	339-6
Emergency Management Office 9195 E Mineral Ave Ste 200........ Centennial CO 80112 *TF:* 877-820-7831 ■ *Web:* www.coemergency.com	720-279-0026	852-6750	339-6
General Assembly 200 E Colfax Ave .... Denver CO 80203 *Web:* www.leg.state.co.us	303-866-3521		339-6
Governor 136 State Capitol Bldg........ Denver CO 30203 *Web:* www.colorado.gov/governor	303-866-2471	866-2003	339-6
Higher Education Commission 1380 Lawrence St .... Denver CO 80202 *Web:* www.state.co.us	303-862-3001	996-1329	339-6
Historical Society 1300 Broadway........ Denver CO 80203 *Web:* www.historycolorado.org	303-866-3682		339-6
Housing & Finance Authority 1313 Sherman St Rm 500 .... Denver CO 80203 *Web:* www.colorado.gov	303-864-7810	864-7856	339-6
Human Services Dept 1575 Sherman St 8th Fl........ Denver CO 80204 *Web:* www.colorado.gov	303-866-5700	866-5563	339-6
Insurance Div 1560 Broadway Ste 850 .... Denver CO 80202 *TF:* 800-930-3745 ■ *Web:* www.colorado.gov	303-894-7499	894-7455	339-6
Labor & Employment Dept 633 17th St Ste 201........ Denver CO 80203 *TF:* 800-388-5515 ■ *Web:* www.coworkforce.com	303-318-8000		259
Lieutenant Governor 130 State Capitol Bldg........ Denver CO 80203 *Web:* colorado.gov	303-866-2087		339-6
Lottery 225 N Main St........ Pueblo CO 81003 *TF:* 800-999-2959 ■ *Web:* www.coloradolottery.com	719-546-2400	546-5208	452
Measurements Standards Section 3125 Wyandot St .... Denver CO 80211 *Web:* www.colorado.gov/ag	303-477-4220	477-4248	339-6
Medical Examiners Board 1560 Broadway Ste 1350........ Denver CO 80202 *Web:* colorado.gov/cs	303-894-7690	894-7692	339-6
Motor Vehicle Div 1881 Pierce St .... Lakewood CO 80214 *Web:* www.colorado.gov/revenue/dmv	303-205-5600		339-6
Natural Resources Dept 1313 Sherman St Rm 718 .... Denver CO 80203 *TF:* 800-536-5308 ■ *Web:* www.dnr.state.co.us	303-866-3311		339-6
Office of Information Technology 601 E 18th Ave Ste 250 .... Denver CO 80203 *Web:* www.colorado.gov	303-764-7700		339-6
Parks & Outdoor Recreation Div 1313 Sherman St Rm 618 .... Denver CO 80203 *TF Campground Resv:* 800-678-2267 ■ *Web:* cpw.state.co.us	303-866-3437		339-6
Parole Board 1600 W 24th St Bldg 54........ Pueblo CO 81003 *Web:* www.ccjrc.org/resources.shtml	719-583-5800		339-6
Public Health & Environment Dept (CDPHE) 4300 Cherry Creek Dr S........ Denver CO 80246 *Web:* www.colorado.gov	303-692-2000		339-6
Public Utilities Commission 1560 Broadway Ste 250........ Denver CO 80203 *TF:* 800-888-0170 ■ *Web:* www.colorado.gov	303-894-2000	894-2065	339-6
Real Estate Commission 1560 Broadway Ste 925........ Denver CO 80202 *Web:* www.colorado.gov/pacific/dora/division-real-estate	303-894-2166	894-2683	339-6
Regulatory Agencies Dept 1560 Broadway Ste 110........ Denver CO 80202 *TF:* 800-886-7675 ■ *Web:* cdn.colorado.gov	303-894-7855	894-7885	339-6
Secretary of State 1700 Broadway 2nd Fl .... Denver CO 80290 *Web:* www.sos.state.co.us	303-894-2200		339-6
Securities Div 1560 Broadway Ste 900 .... Denver CO 80202 *Web:* cdn.colorado.gov	303-894-2320	861-2126	339-6

	Phone	Fax	Class
State Court Administrator			
1301 Pennsylvania St Ste 300 ... Denver CO 80203	720-625-5000		339-6
TF: 800-888-0001 ■ *Web:* www.courts.state.co.us			
State Government Information			
1525 Sherman St 4th Fl ... Denver CO 80203	303-866-2000	866-5909	339-6
Web: www.colorado.gov			
State Patrol 700 Kipling St ... Lakewood CO 80215	303-239-4500		339-6
Web: www.colorado.gov			
Supreme Court 1300 Broadway Ste 500 ... Denver CO 80203	303-457-5800		339-6
TF: 877-888-1370 ■ *Web:* www.coloradosupremecourt.com			
Tourism Office 1625 Broadway Ste 1700 ... Denver CO 80202	303-892-3840	892-3848	339-6
Web: www.colorado.com			
Transportation Dept			
4201 E Arkansas Ave ... Denver CO 80222	303-757-9228		339-6
Web: www.coloradodot.info			
Treasurer			
200 E Colfax Ave State Capitol Ste 140 ... Denver CO 80203	303-866-2441	866-2123	339-6
Web: www.colorado.gov			
Victims Programs Office			
700 Kipling St Ste 1000 ... Denver CO 80215	303-239-4442	239-4491	339-6
TF: 888-282-1080 ■ *Web:* dcj.state.co.us/ovp			
Vital Records Section			
4300 Cherry Creek Dr S ... Denver CO 80246	303-692-2200		339-6
Web: www.cdc.gov/nchs/w2w.htm			
Vocational Rehabilitation Div			
2211 W Evans ... Denver CO 80223	303-866-4150		339-6
Web: www.colorado.gov/pacific/dvr			
Wildlife Div 6060 Broadway ... Denver CO 80216	303-297-1192		339-6
Web: cpw.state.co.us			
Workers Compensation Div			
633 17th St Ste 400 ... Denver CO 80202	303-318-8700		339-6
Web: www.colorado.gov			
Colorado Academy 3800 S Pierce St ... Denver CO 80235	303-986-1501		685
Web: www.coloradoacademy.org			
Colorado Asphalt Services Inc			
3700 E 56th Ave ... Commerce CO 80022	303-292-3434	292-6267	189-3
Web: www.coloradoasphalt.com			
Colorado Assn of Commerce & Industry			
1600 Broadway Ste 1000 ... Denver CO 80202	303-831-7411	860-1439	140
Web: www.cochamber.com			
Colorado Assn of Realtors			
309 Inverness Way S ... Englewood CO 80112	303-790-7099	790-7299	656
TF: 800-944-6550 ■ *Web:* www.coloradorealtors.com			
Colorado Avalanche			
Pepsi Ctr 1000 Chopper Cir ... Denver CO 80204	303-405-1100		716
TF: 800-979-3370 ■ *Web:* avalanche.nhl.com			
Colorado Ballet 1278 Lincoln St ... Denver CO 80203	303-837-8888	861-7174	573-1
Web: www.coloradoballet.org			
Colorado Bar Assn 1900 Grant St Ste 900 ... Denver CO 80203	303-860-1115	894-0821	72
TF: 800-332-6736 ■ *Web:* www.cobar.org			
Colorado Belle Hotel & Casino			
2100 S Casino Dr ... Laughlin NV 89029	702-298-4000		133
TF Resv: 877-460-0777 ■ *Web:* www.coloradobelle.com			
Colorado Bend State Park			
6031 Colorado Pk Rd ... Bend TX 76824	325-628-3240		565
Web: tpwd.texas.gov/state-parks/colorado-bend			
Colorado Boxed Beef Co			
302 Progress Rd ... Auburndale FL 33823	863-967-0636		297-9
Web: www.coloradoboxedbeef.com			
Colorado Business Bank 821 17th St ... Denver CO 80202	303-293-2265		360-2
TF: 800-574-4714 ■ *Web:* cobizbank.com			
Colorado Cattle Company & Guest Ranch			
70008 County Rd 132 ... New Raymer CO 80742	970-437-5345		239
Web: www.coloradocattlecompany.com			
Colorado Charter Lines			
4960 Locust St ... Commerce CO 80022	303-287-0239	287-2819	107
TF: 800-821-7491 ■ *Web:* www.bus-charter.com/coloradocharter.htm			
Colorado Christian University			
8787 W Alameda Ave ... Lakewood CO 80226	303-963-3200	963-3201	166
TF: 800-443-2484 ■ *Web:* www.ccu.edu			
Loveland 3553 Clydesdale Pkwy Ste 300 ... Loveland CO 80538	970-669-8700	669-8701*	166
*Fax: Admissions ■ *TF:* 800-443-2484 ■ *Web:* www.ccu.edu			
Colorado College			
14 E Cache La Poudre St ... Colorado Springs CO 80903	719-389-6344	389-6816*	166
*Fax: Admissions ■ *TF:* 800-542-7214 ■ *Web:* www.coloradocollege.edu			
Colorado Container Corp 4221 Monaco St ... Denver CO 80216	303-331-0400	331-9455	100
Web: www.packagingcorp.com			
Colorado Convention Ctr 700 14th St ... Denver CO 80202	303-228-8000	228-8103	205
Web: www.denverconvention.com			
Colorado Correctional Industries			
4999 Oakland St ... Denver CO 80239	719-226-4206	226-4220	211
TF Cust Svc: 800-685-7891 ■ *Web:* www.coloradoci.com			
Colorado County			
318 Springs St Ste 103 ... Columbus TX 78934	979-732-2155	732-8852	338
Web: www.co.colorado.tx.us			
Colorado Daily 5450 Western Ave ... Boulder CO 80301	303-473-1111		532-2
Web: www.coloradodaily.com			
Colorado Data Mail Inc			
2525 W Fourth Ave ... Denver CO 80219	303-629-6155		5
Web: www.coloradodatamail.com			
Colorado Democratic Party			
789 Sherman St ... Denver CO 80204	303-623-4762	623-2443	616-1
TF: 800-995-3386 ■ *Web:* www.coloradodems.org			
Colorado Dental Assn			
8301 E Prentice Ave Ste 400 ... Greenwood Village CO 80111	303-740-6900	740-7989	227
TF: 866-777-4771 ■ *Web:* www.cdaonline.org			
Colorado Dude & Guest Ranch Assn (CDGRA)			
PO Box D ... Shawnee CO 80475	866-942-3472		48-23
TF: 866-942-3472 ■ *Web:* www.coloradoranch.com			
Colorado Energy Management LLC			
2575 Park Ln Ste 200 ... Lafayette CO 80026	303-442-5112		256
Web: www.coloradoenergy.com			
Colorado Farm Bureau Mutual Insurance Co			
PO Box 5647 ... Denver CO 80217	303-749-7500	660-1694	391-4
TF: 800-315-5998 ■ *Web:* www.cfbmic.com			
Colorado Fasteners and Specialty Tools Inc			
570 Turner Dr Ste C ... Durango CO 81303	970-749-2992		351
Web: www.coloradofasteners.com			
Colorado Fsb			
8400 E Prentice Ave Ste 545 ... Greenwood Village CO 80111	303-793-3555	793-3560	70
TF: 877-484-2372 ■ *Web:* www.coloradofederalbank.com			
Colorado Lawyer Magazine			
1900 Grant St 9th Fl ... Denver CO 80203	303-860-1115	830-3990	457-15
TF: 800-332-6736 ■ *Web:* www.cobar.org/tcl/index.cfm			
Colorado Medical Society			
7351 Lowry Blvd ... Denver CO 80230	720-859-1001	859-7509	474
TF: 800-654-5653 ■ *Web:* www.cms.org			
Colorado Mental Health Institute at Fort Logan (CMHIFL)			
3520 W Oxford Ave ... Denver CO 80236	303-866-7066		374-5
Colorado Mental Health Institute at Pueblo (CMHIP)			
1600 W 24th St ... Pueblo CO 81003	719-546-4000		374-5
Web: www.colorado.gov			
Colorado Mountain College			
Alpine 1330 Bob Adams Dr ... Steamboat Springs CO 80487	970-870-4444	870-4535*	162
*Fax: Admissions ■ *TF:* 800-621-8559 ■ *Web:* www.coloradomtn.edu			
Aspen 0255 Sage Way ... Aspen CO 81611	970-925-7740	925-6045	162
TF: 800-621-8559 ■ *Web:* www.coloradomtn.edu			
Spring Valley			
3000 County Rd 114 ... Glenwood Springs CO 81601	970-945-7481	928-9668	162
TF: 800-621-8559 ■ *Web:* www.coloradomtn.edu			
Colorado National Monument			
1750 Rim Rock Dr ... Fruita CO 81521	970-858-3617	858-0372	564
TF: 866-945-7920 ■ *Web:* www.nps.gov			
Colorado National Speedway			
4281 Graden Blvd ... Dacono CO 80514	303-665-4173	828-2403	515
Web: www.coloradospeedway.com			
Colorado Network Staffing Inc			
8787 TurnPk Dr ... Westminster CO 80031	303-430-1441		396
TF: 800-511-5010 ■ *Web:* www.conetstaff.com			
Colorado Northwestern Community College			
500 Kennedy Dr ... Rangely CO 81648	970-675-3335	675-3343*	162
*Fax: Admissions ■ *TF:* 800-562-1105 ■ *Web:* www.cncc.edu			
Craig 50 College Dr ... Craig CO 81625	800-562-1105	824-1134*	162
*Fax Area Code: 970 ■ *Fax: Admissions ■ *TF:* 800-562-1105 ■ *Web:* www.cncc.edu			
Colorado Nurses Assn (CNA)			
2851 S Parker Rd Ste 1210 ... Aurora CO 80014	720-457-1194		533
Web: coloradonurses.org			
Colorado Passport Agency			
Colorado Agency			
3151 S Vaughn Way Ste 600 ... Aurora CO 80014	877-487-2778		340-16
TF: 888-874-7793 ■ *Web:* travel.state.gov			
Colorado Petroleum Products Co			
4080 Globeville Rd ... Denver CO 80216	303-294-0302		541
TF: 800-424-9300 ■ *Web:* www.colopetro.com			
Colorado Pharmacists Society			
6825 E Tennessee Ave Ste 440 ... Denver CO 80224	303-756-3069		585
Web: www.copharm.org			
Colorado Precast Concrete Inc			
1820 14th St SE ... Loveland CO 80537	970-669-0535		183
Web: www.coloprecast.com			
Colorado Press Clipping Service			
1336 Glenarm Pl ... Denver CO 80204	303-571-5117	571-1803	624
Web: www.coloradopressassociation.com			
Colorado Prime Foods			
500 Bi-County Blvd Ste 400 ... Farmingdale NY 11735	631-694-1111		366
TF: 800-365-2404 ■ *Web:* www.reordermenu.com			
Colorado Public Interest Research Group (COPIRG)			
1543 Wazee St Ste 330 ... Denver CO 80202	303-573-7474		633
Web: www.copirg.org			
Colorado Railroad Museum			
17155 W 44th Ave ... Golden CO 80403	303-279-4591	279-4229	520
TF: 800-365-6263 ■ *Web:* coloradorailroadmuseum.org			
Colorado Rapids 6000 Victory Way ... Commerce CO 80022	303-727-3500	727-3536	717
TF: 800-979-3370 ■ *Web:* www.coloradorapids.com			
Colorado Republican Party			
5950 S Willow Dr Ste 210 ... Greenwood Village CO 80111	303-758-3333		616-2
Web: www.cologop.org			
Colorado River Animal Medical Center Inc			
2079 Hwy 95 ... Bullhead City AZ 86442	928-763-7387		794
TF: 800-275-8777 ■ *Web:* www.cramcvet.com			
Colorado Rockies			
Coors Field 2001 Blake St ... Denver CO 80205	303-292-0200	312-2115*	713
*Fax: PR ■ *Web:* colorado.rockies.mlb.com			
Colorado Rocky Mountain School			
1493 County Rd 106 ... Carbondale CO 81623	970-963-2562	963-9865	622
Web: www.crms.org			
Colorado School of English 331 14th St ... Denver CO 80202	720-932-8900	932-0315	423
TF: 877-234-0654 ■ *Web:* www.englishamerica.com			
Colorado School of Mines 1600 Maple St ... Golden CO 80401	303-273-3000	273-3509	166
TF: 800-446-9488 ■ *Web:* www.mines.edu			
Colorado School of Mines Foundation			
1812 Illinois St ... Golden CO 80401	303-273-3275	273-3165	305
TF: 800-446-9488 ■ *Web:* giving.mines.edu/s/840/start_foundation.aspx			
Colorado Serum Co			
4950 York St PO Box 16428 ... Denver CO 80216	303-295-7527	295-1923	85
TF Orders: 800-525-2065 ■ *Web:* www.colorado-serum.com			
Colorado Ski Country USA Inc			
1444 Wazee S Ste 320 ... Denver CO 80202	303-837-0793		711
Web: www.coloradoski.com			
Colorado Sports Hall of Fame			
1701 Mile High Stadium ... Denver CO 80204	720-258-3888		522
Web: www.coloradosports.org			
Colorado Springs Chamber and EDC			
102 S Tejon St Ste 430 ... Colorado Springs CO 80903	719-471-8183		139
Web: www.coloradospringsbusinessalliance.com			
Colorado Springs City Auditorium			
221 E Kiowa St ... Colorado Springs CO 80903	719-385-5969	385-6584	205
TF: 800-888-4748 ■ *Web:* www.springsgov.com			
Colorado Springs City Hall			
107 N Nevada Ave Ste 205 ... Colorado Springs CO 80903	719-385-5900	385-5488	337
Web: www.springsgov.com			
Colorado Springs Convention & Visitors Bureau			
515 S Cascade Ave ... Colorado Springs CO 80903	719-635-7506	635-4968	206
TF: 800-888-4748 ■ *Web:* www.visitcos.com			
Colorado Springs Fine Arts Ctr			
30 W Dale St ... Colorado Springs CO 80903	719-634-5581		520
Web: colorado.com			

Name / Address	City	State	Zip	Phone	Fax	Class
Colorado Springs Independent 235 S Nevada Ave — *Web:* www.csindy.com	Colorado Springs	CO	80903	719-577-4545	577-4107	532-5
Colorado Springs Marriott 5580 Tech Center Dr	Colorado Springs	CO	80919	719-260-1800		378
Colorado Springs Municipal Airport 7770 Milton E Proby Pkwy — *Web:* www.springsgov.com	Colorado Springs	CO	80916	719-550-1900	550-1901	27
Colorado Springs Philharmonic PO Box 1266 — *TF:* 800-525-9623 ■ *Web:* www.csphilharmonic.org	Colorado Springs	CO	80901	719-575-9632	575-9656	573-3
Colorado Springs Pioneers Museum 215 S Tejon St — *Web:* www.springsgov.com	Colorado Springs	CO	80903	719-385-5990	385-5645	520
Colorado Springs School District #11 1115 N El Paso St — *TF:* 800-273-8255 ■ *Web:* d11.org	Colorado Springs	CO	80903	719-520-2000	577-4546	685
Colorado Springs Utilities 111 S Cascade Ave — *TF:* 800-238-5434 ■ *Web:* www.csu.org	Colorado Springs	CO	80903	719-448-4800	668-7288	787
Colorado State Bank & Trust NA PO Box 2300 — *Web:* www.csbt.com	Tulsa	OK	74192	303-861-2111		70
Colorado State Library 201 E Colfax Ave Rm 309 — *Web:* www.cde.state.co.us	Denver	CO	80203	303-866-6900	866-6940	434-5
Colorado State University 200 West Lake St — **Fax:* Admissions ■ *TF:* 800-491-4366 ■ *Web:* www.colostate.edu	Fort Collins	CO	80523	970-491-1101	491-7799*	166
Morgan Library 1201 Center Ave Mall, 1019 Campus Delivery — *Web:* www.lib.colostate.edu	Fort Collins	CO	80523	970-491-1833	491-1195	434-6
Pueblo 2200 Bonforte Blvd	Pueblo	CO	81001	719-549-2462	442-2605	166
Colorado State University System 410 17th St Ste 2440 — *Web:* www.csusystem.edu	Denver	CO	80202	303-534-6290	534-6298	786
Colorado State Veterans Nursing Home-Rifle 851 E Fifth St — *Web:* colorado.gov	Rifle	CO	81650	970-625-0842	625-3706	793
Colorado Storm Soccer Assoc 7002 S Revere Pkwy Ste 60 — *Web:* www.shippertmedical.com	Centennial	CO	80112	303-799-0151		717
Colorado Symphony Orchestra 1000 14th St Unit 15 — *TF:* 877-292-7979 ■ *Web:* www.coloradosymphony.org	Denver	CO	80202	303-623-7876	293-2649	573-3
Colorado Technical University 4435 N Chestnut St — *TF:* 855-230-0555 ■ *Web:* www.coloradotech.edu	Colorado Springs	CO	80907	719-598-0200		166
Colorado Technical University Denver 1865 W 121st Ave Bldg C Ste 100 — *TF:* 877-250-9372 ■ *Web:* www.coloradotech.edu/denver	Westminster	CO	80234	303-362-2900		800
Colorado Time Systems 1551 E 11th St — *TF:* 800-279-0111 ■ *Web:* www.coloradotime.com	Loveland	CO	80537	970-667-1000	667-5876	701
Colorado Trails Ranch 12161 County Rd 240 — *TF:* 800-323-3833 ■ *Web:* www.coloradotrails.com	Durango	CO	81301	970-247-5055	385-7372	239
Colorado Trust 1600 Sherman St — *TF:* 888-847-9140 ■ *Web:* www.coloradotrust.org	Denver	CO	80203	303-837-1200	839-9034	303
Colorado Valley Transit Inc 108 Cardinal Ln PO Box 940 — *TF:* 800-548-1068 ■ *Web:* www.gotransit.org	Columbus	TX	78934	979-732-6281	732-6283	108
Colorado Veterinary Medical Assn 191 Yuma St — *TF:* 800-228-5429 ■ *Web:* colovma.org	Denver	CO	80223	303-318-0447	318-0450	795
Colorado West Investments Inc 1731 E Niagara Rd — *TF:* 888-249-9882 ■ *Web:* cowestinvest.com	Montrose	CO	81401	970-249-9882		690
Coloradoan, The 1300 Riverside Ave — *TF:* 877-424-0063 ■ *Web:* www.coloradoan.com	Fort Collins	CO	80524	970-493-6397		532-2
Colorama Wholesale Nursery 1025 N Todd Ave — *TF:* 800-736-5608 ■ *Web:* coloramanursery.com	Azusa	CA	91702	626-969-3585		369
ColorCentric Corp 100 Carlson Rd — *Web:* www.colorcentriccorp.com	Rochester	NY	14610	585-288-1240		627
Colorcon Inc 415 Moyer Blvd — *Web:* www.colorcon.com	West Point	PA	19486	215-699-7733	661-2605	144
ColorDynamics 200 E Bethany Dr — *Web:* www.colordynamics.com	Allen	TX	75002	972-390-6500		627
Coloredge, Inc 132 W 31st St — *TF:* 800-321-8864 ■ *Web:* www.merisel.com	New York	NY	10001	212-594-4800		174
Color-Fi Inc 320 Neeley St — *TF:* 800-483-6382 ■ *Web:* www.colorfi.com	Sumter	SC	29150	803-436-4200	436-4220	605-1
Colorfx Inc 10776 Aurora Ave — *TF:* 800-348-9044 ■ *Web:* www.colorfxprint.com	Des Moines	IA	50322	800-348-9044		174
Color-Glo International 7111 Ohms Ln — *TF:* 800-333-8523 ■ *Web:* colorglo.com	Minneapolis	MN	55439	952-835-1338		62-1
ColorGraphics Inc 150 N Myers St — *Web:* www.colorgraphics.com	Los Angeles	CA	90033	323-261-7171	261-7077	627
Colorid LLC 20480 Chartwls Ctr Dr — *TF:* 888-682-6567 ■ *Web:* www.colorid.com	Cornelius	NC	28031	704-987-2238		358
Colorite Plastics Co 460 E Swedesford Rd Suite 3000 — *Web:* tekni-plex.com	Wayne	NJ	19087	484-690-1520		370
Colormark LC 1840 Hutton Dr Bldg 208 — *Web:* www.colormark-lc.com	Carrollton	TX	75006	972-243-1919		627
Colors By Design 7723 Densmore Ave — *TF:* 800-832-8436	Van Nuys	CA	91406	800-832-8436	824-2530	130
Colors of The West LLC 201 W Rt 66 — *Web:* colorsofthewestusa.com	Williams	AZ	86046	928-635-9559		327
Colors on Parade 125 Daytona St PO Box 50940 — *TF Cust Svc:* 866-756-4207 ■ *Web:* www.colorsonparade.com	Conway	SC	29526	843-347-8818		62-4
Colortech Graphics Inc 28700 Hayes Rd — *TF:* 800-801-8324 ■ *Web:* www.colortechgraphics.com	Roseville	MI	48066	586-779-7800		627
Colosseum Online Inc 800 Petrolia Rd — *TF:* 877-739-7873 ■ *Web:* www.colosseum.com	Toronto	ON	M3J3K4	416-739-7873		225
Colourbox Hairdressing 305 Cordova St W — *Web:* colourboxhair.com	Vancouver	BC	V6B1E5	604-669-6354		77
Colpitts World Travel 875 Providence Hwy — *TF:* 800-550-4650 ■ *Web:* www.colpittswt.com	Dedham	MA	02026	781-326-7800		772
Colquitt County PO Box 517 — *Web:* www.ccboc.com	Moultrie	GA	31776	229-616-7056	616-7498	338
Colquitt Regional Medical Ctr (CRMC) 3131 S Main St PO Box 40 — *TF:* 888-262-2762 ■ *Web:* www.colquittregional.com	Moultrie	GA	31768	229-985-3420		374-3
COLSA Corp 6728 Odyssey Dr — *Web:* www.colsa.com	Huntsville	AL	35806	256-964-5555		180
Colsky Media Inc 2740 Van Ness Ave Ste 220	San Francisco	CA	94109	415-673-5400		7
Colson & Colson Construction Co 2260 McGilchrist St SE — *Web:* www.colson-colson.com	Salem	OR	97302	503-586-7401		187
Colson Associates Inc 1 N Franklin St Site 2420 — *Web:* www.colsongroup.com	Chicago	IL	60606	312-980-1100		475
Colson Caster Corp 3700 Airport Rd — *Web:* www.colsoncaster.com	Jonesboro	AR	72401	870-932-4501		596
Colt Defense LLC 547 New Pk Ave — *Web:* www.colt.com	West Hartford	CT	06110	860-232-4489	244-1442	807
Colt International Inc 300 Flint Ridge Rd — *Web:* www.coltinternational.com	Webster	TX	77598	281-280-2100		194
Colt State Park Hope St — *Web:* www.riparks.com	Bristol	RI	02809	401-253-7482	253-6766	565
Colt's Plastics Co 969 N Main St PO Box 429 — *TF:* 800-222-2658 ■ *Web:* www.coltsplastics.com	Dayville	CT	06241	860-774-2301	779-0782	98
Colten Cummins Watson & Vincent PO 3959 Pender Dr Ste 200 — *Web:* www.coltenlaw.com	Fairfax	VA	22030	703-277-9700		428
Coltene/Whaledent Inc 235 Ascot Pkwy — *TF:* 800-221-3046 ■ *Web:* www.coltene.com	Cuyahoga Falls	OH	44223	330-916-8800	916-7077	228
Colton Chamber of Commerce 655 N La Cadena Dr — *TF:* 800-444-5865 ■ *Web:* coltonchamber.org	Colton	CA	92324	909-825-2222	824-1650	139
Colton Hall Museum 570 Pacific St Monterey City Hall — *Web:* www.monterey.org/museum	Monterey	CA	93940	831-646-5648	646-3917	520
Colton Point State Park c/o Leonard Harrison State Pk 4797 Rt 660 — *Web:* www.dcnr.state.pa.us	Wellsboro	PA	16901	570-724-3061		565
Colton Public Library 656 N Ninth St — *Web:* ci.colton.ca.us	Colton	CA	92324	909-370-5083		434-3
Colts Neck High School 59 Five Points Rd — *Web:* www.frhsd.com	Colts Neck	NJ	07722	732-761-0190		685
Coltwell Industries Inc 55 Winans Ave — *Web:* www.coltwell.com	Cranford	NJ	07016	908-276-7600		697
Colucci & Umans Inc 218 E 50th St — *Web:* www.colucci-umans.com	New York	NY	10022	212-935-5700		428
Columbia 411 St Armands Cir — *Web:* www.columbiarestaurant.com	Sarasota	FL	34236	941-388-3987		671
Columbia Air Services 175 Tower Ave Groton-New London Airport — *TF:* 800-787-5001 ■ *Web:* columbiaaironline.com	Groton	CT	06340	860-449-1400	405-7269	63
Columbia Analytical Services Inc 1317 S 13th Ave — *Web:* www.caslab.com	Kelso	WA	98626	360-577-7222		743
Columbia Artists Management LLC 1790 Broadway — *Web:* www.cami.com	New York	NY	10019	212-841-9500	841-9744	731
Columbia Athletic Clubs 2930 228th Ave SE — *Web:* www.columbiaathletic.com	Sammamish	WA	98075	425-313-0123		354
Columbia Bank 1301 A St Ste 800 — *NASDAQ: COLB* ■ *TF:* 800-305-1905 ■ *Web:* www.columbiabank.com	Tacoma	WA	98402	253-305-1900		360-2
Columbia Bank, The 7168 Columbia Gateway Dr — *TF:* 888-822-2265 ■ *Web:* www.thecolumbiabank.com	Columbia	MD	21046	888-822-2265		70
Columbia Basin College 2600 N 20th Ave — *Web:* www.columbiabasin.edu	Pasco	WA	99301	509-547-0511	546-0401	162
Columbia Basin Electric Co-op 171 W Linden Way — *Web:* cbec.cc	Heppner	OR	97036	541 676 9146		245
Columbia Bible College 2940 Clearbrook Rd — *TF:* 800-283-0881 ■ *Web:* www.columbiabc.edu	Abbotsford	BC	V2T2Z8	604-853-3358	853-3063	785
Columbia Boiler Co 390 Old Reading Pk PO Box 1070 — *Web:* www.columbiaboiler.com	Pottstown	PA	19464	610-323-2700	323-7292	91
Columbia Capital 204 S Union St — *Web:* www.colcap.com	Alexandria	VA	22314	703-519-2000	519-5870	792
Columbia Cascade Co 1300 SW Sixth Ave Ste 310 — *TF:* 800-547-1940 ■ *Web:* www.timberform.com	Portland	OR	97201	503-223-1157	223-4530	346
Columbia Chamber of Commerce 300 S Providence Rd — *TF:* 800-361-4827 ■ *Web:* www.columbiamochamber.com	Columbia	MO	65203	573-874-1132	443-3986	139
Columbia City Ballet 1545 Main St — *TF:* 800-899-7408 ■ *Web:* www.columbiacityballet.com	Columbia	SC	29201	803-799-7605		573-1
Columbia College 1001 Rogers St — **Fax:* Admissions ■ *TF:* 800-231-2391 ■ *Web:* www.ccis.edu	Columbia	MO	65216	573-875-8700	875-7209*	166
Columbia College 1301 Columbia College Dr — *TF:* 800-277-1301 ■ *Web:* www.columbiasc.edu	Columbia	SC	29203	803-786-3871	786-3674	166
Columbia College 11600 Columbia College Dr — *TF:* 888-722-2873 ■ *Web:* www.gocolumbia.edu	Sonora	CA	95370	209-588-5100	588-5104	162

	Phone	Fax	Class
Columbia College Chicago 600 S Michigan Ave .... Chicago IL 60605 *Fax: Admissions ■ TF: 866-705-0200 ■ Web: www.colum.edu	312-663-1600	344-8024*	166
Columbia College Hollywood 18618 Oxnard St. .... Tarzana CA 91356 TF: 800-785-0585 ■ Web: www.columbiacollege.edu	818-345-8414	345-9053	166
Columbia College Jefferson City 3314 Emerald Ln .... Jefferson City MO 65109 TF: 800-231-2391 ■ Web: ccis.edu/jeffcity	573-634-3250	634-8507	166
Columbia College Lake of the Ozarks 900 College Blvd .... Osage Beach MO 65065 TF: 800-231-2391 ■ Web: www.ccis.edu	573-348-6463	348-1791	166
Columbia College of Nursing (CCON) 4425 N Port Washington Rd .... Glendale WI 53212 TF: 800-221-5573 ■ Web: www.ccon.edu	414-326-2330	326-2331	166
Columbia College Orlando 2600 Technology Dr Ste 100 .... Orlando FL 32804 *Fax: Admissions ■ TF: 800-231-2391 ■ Web: www.ccis.edu	407-293-9911	293-8530*	166
Columbia Community Mental Health 58646 McNulty Way .... Saint Helens OR 97051 TF: 800-294-5211 ■ Web: www.ccmh1.com	503-397-5211		726
Columbia Convention & Visitors Bureau 300 S Providence Rd .... Columbia MO 65203 TF: 800-652-0987 ■ Web: www.visitcolumbiamo.com	573-875-1231	443-3986	206
Columbia Correctional Institution 2925 Columbia Dr .... Portage WI 53901 Web: doc.wi.gov	608-742-9100	742-9111	213
Columbia Corrugated Box Company Inc 12777 SW Tualatin Sherwood Rd .... Tualatin OR 97062 Web: www.ccbox.com	503-692-3344		100
Columbia County 35 W Main St .... Bloomsburg PA 17815 Web: www.columbiapa.org	570-389-5600	784-0257	338
Columbia County 341 E Main St .... Dayton WA 99328 Web: www.columbiaco.com	509-382-4542	382-2490	338
Columbia County PO Box 498 .... Evans GA 30809 Web: www.columbiacountyga.gov	706-868-3379	868-3348	338
Columbia County 560 Warren St .... Hudson NY 12534 Web: columbiacountyny.com	518-828-3339		338
Columbia County 135 NE Hernando Ave # 203 .... Lake City FL 32055 TF: 800-342-8170 ■ Web: www.columbiacountyfla.com	386-755-4100		338
Columbia County 112 E Edgewater St .... Portage WI 53901 Web: www.co.columbia.wi.us	608-742-9654	742-9602	338
Columbia County 230 Strand St .... Saint Helens OR 97051 TF: 800-735-2900 ■ Web: www.co.columbia.or.us	503-397-3796	397-7266	338
Columbia County Chamber of Commerce 507 Warren St .... Hudson NY 12534 TF: 800-951-9774 ■ Web: columbiachamber-ny.com	518-828-4417	822-9539	139
Columbia County Public Library 308 NW Columbia Ave .... Lake City FL 32055 Web: www.columbiacountyfla.com/default.asp	386-758-2101	758-2135	434-3
Columbia Crest Winery 178810 State Rt 221 PO Box 231 .... Paterson WA 99345 *Fax Area Code: 425 ■ TF: 888-309-9463 ■ Web: www.columbiacrest.com	509-875-4227	415-3657*	80-3
Columbia Daily Tribune 101 N Fourth St .... Columbia MO 65201 TF: 800-333-6799 ■ Web: www.columbiatribune.com	573-815-1700	815-1701	532-2
Columbia Data Products Inc 925 Sunshine Ln Ste 1080 .... Altamonte Springs FL 32714 TF Sales: 800-613-6288 ■ Web: cdp.com	407-869-6700	862-4725	178-12
Columbia Distributing Co 6840 N Cutter Cir .... Portland OR 97217 TF: 888-417-5001 ■ Web: www.coldist.com	503-289-9600		81-1
Columbia Elevator Products Company Inc 380 Horace St .... Bridgeport NY 06610 TF: 888-858-1558 ■ Web: www.columbiaelevator.com	888-858-1558		189-1
Columbia Empire Farms 31461 NE Bell Rd .... Sherwood OR 97140 TF: 800-910-5377 ■ Web: www.columbiaempirefarms.com	503-538-2156		10-10
Columbia Energy & Environmental Services Inc 1806 Terminal Dr .... Richland WA 99354 Web: columbia-energy.com	509-946-7111		256
Columbia Environmental Research Ctr (CERC) 4200 New Haven Rd .... Columbia MO 65201 TF: 888-283-7626 ■ Web: www.cerc.usgs.gov	573-875-5399	876-1896	668
Columbia Forest Products Inc Columbia Plywood Div 7900 Triad Ctr Dr Ste 200 .... Greensboro NC 27409 TF: 800-637-1609 ■ Web: columbiaforestproducts.com	800-637-1609		613
Columbia Fruit Packers Inc 2575 Euclid Ave PO Box 920 .... Wenatchee WA 98801 Web: www.columbiafruit.com	509-662-7153	662-0933	546
Columbia Gas of Ohio Inc 200 Civic Ctr Dr .... Columbus OH 43215 TF: 800-807-9781 ■ Web: columbiagasohio.com	800-344-4077		787
Columbia Gas of Virginia Inc 1809 Coyote Dr .... Chester VA 23836 TF Cust Svc: 800-544-5606 ■ Web: www.columbiagasva.com	800-543-8911		787
Columbia Gear Corp 530 County Rd 50 .... Avon MN 56310 TF: 800-323-9838 ■ Web: www.columbiagear.com	320-356-7301	356-2131	709
Columbia Gorge Hotel 4000 Westcliff Dr .... Hood River OR 97031 Web: www.columbiagorgehotel.com	541-386-5566		379
Columbia Gorge Premium Outlets 450 NW 257th Way Ste 110 .... Troutdale OR 97060 Web: www.premiumoutlets.com	503-669-8060		460
Columbia Helicopters Inc 14452 Arndt Rd NE .... Aurora OR 97002 Web: www.colheli.com	503-678-1222	678-1222	359
Columbia Hills State Park PO Box 426 .... Dallesport WA 98617 Web: www.parks.wa.gov	509-767-1159		565
Columbia Hospitality 2223 Alaskan Way Ste 200 .... Seattle WA 98121 Web: www.columbiahospitality.com	206-239-1800	239-1801	379
Columbia Industries Inc PO Box 746 .... Hopkinsville KY 42240 TF: 800-531-5920 ■ Web: www.columbia300.com	270-881-1200		710
Columbia Institute for Tele-Information (CITI) 3022 Broadway Uris Hall .... New York NY 10027 Web: www8.gsb.columbia.edu/citi	212-854-4222	854-1471	668
Columbia International University 7435 Monticello Rd .... Columbia SC 29203 TF: 800-777-2227 ■ Web: www.ciu.edu	803-754-4100	786-4209	161
Columbia Lakes Resort & Conference Ctr 188 Freeman Blvd .... West Columbia TX 77486 TF: 800-231-1030 ■ Web: www.columbialakesgolf.com	979-345-5151		669
Columbia Legal Services 6 S Second St Ste 510 .... Yakima WA 98901 TF: 800-562-6025 ■ Web: www.columbialegal.org	509-575-5593		445
Columbia Lutheran Home 4700 Phinney Ave N .... Seattle WA 98103 Web: www.columbialutheranhome.com	206-632-7400		48-20
Columbia Magazine 1 Columbus Plaza .... New Haven CT 06510 TF: 800-380-9995 ■ Web: www.kofc.org	203-752-4000	752-4000	457-10
Columbia Manufacturing Inc 165 Route 66 E .... Columbia CT 06237 Web: www.columbiamfginc.com	860-228-2259		21
Columbia Memorial Hospital 71 Prospect Ave .... Hudson NY 12534 TF: 866-539-1370 ■ Web: www.columbiamemorialhealth.org	518-828-7601	828-9980	374-3
Columbia Metal Spinning Company Inc 4351 N Normandy Ave .... Chicago IL 60634 Web: www.cmspinning.com	773-685-2800		198
Columbia Metropolitan Airport 3000 Aviation Way W .... Columbia SC 29170 Web: www.columbiaairport.com	803-822-5010		27
Columbia Metropolitan Convention & Visitors Bureau 1101 Lincoln St PO Box 15 .... Columbia SC 29202 TF: 800-264-4884 ■ Web: www.columbiacvb.com	803-545-0000	545-0013	206
Columbia Mfg Corp 14400 S San Pedro St .... Gardena CA 90248 TF: 800-729-3667 ■ Web: www.columbiamfg.com	310-327-9300	323-9862	234
Columbia Mfg Inc 1 Cycle St .... Westfield MA 01085 TF: 800-346-1126 ■ Web: www.columbiamfginc.com	413-562-3664	568-5345	319-3
Columbia Missourian 221 S Eigth St .... Columbia MO 65201 *Fax: News Rm ■ TF: 855-270-6572 ■ Web: columbiamissourian.com	573-882-5700	882-5702*	532-2
Columbia (MO) City Hall 701 E Broadway PO Box 6015 .... Columbia MO 65205 Web: www.como.gov	573-874-7111		337
Columbia Montour chamber of Commerce, The 238 Market St .... Bloomsburg PA 17815 TF: 800-342-5775 ■ Web: www.columbiamontourchamber.com	570-784-2522	784-2661	139
Columbia Museum of Art 1515 Main St .... Columbia SC 29201 TF: 800-222-7270 ■ Web: columbiamuseum.org	803-799-2810		520
Columbia Northwest Engineering 249 N Elder St .... Moses Lake WA 98837 Web: www.cnweng.com	509-766-1226		256
Columbia Okura LLC 301 Grove St # A .... Vancouver WA 98661 Web: www.columbiaokura.com	360-735-1952		207
Columbia Omnicorp 14 W 33rd St .... New York NY 10001 Web: columbiaomni.com	212-279-6161		535
Columbia Packing Company Inc 2807 E 11th St .... Dallas TX 75203 Web: www.columbiapacking.com	214-946-8171		473
Columbia Panel Manufacturing Co 100 Giles St .... High Point NC 27263	336-861-4100		613
Columbia ParCar Corp 1115 Commercial Ave .... Reedsburg WI 53959 *Fax Area Code: 608 ■ TF: 800-222-4653 ■ Web: www.parcar.com	800-222-4653	524-8380*	516
Columbia Pipe & Supply Co 1120 W Pershing Rd .... Chicago IL 60609 TF: 888-429-4635 ■ Web: www.columbiapipe.com	773-927-6600	927-8415	492
Columbia Place 7201 Two Notch Rd .... Columbia SC 29223 Web: columbiaplacemall.com	803-788-4678	736-9168	460
Columbia Power Co-op Assn 311 Wilson St .... Monument OR 97864	541-934-2311		245
Columbia Regional Airport 11300 S Airport Dr .... Columbia MO 65201 Web: www.flycou.com	573-874-7508		27
Columbia Restaurant 2025 E Seventh Ave .... Tampa FL 33605 TF: 800-940-6256 ■ Web: www.columbiarestaurant.com	904-824-3341		671
Columbia River Correctional Institution 2575 Ctr St NE .... Salem OR 97301 Web: www.oregon.gov	503-280-6646	280-6012	213
Columbia River Knife & Tool Inc 18348 SW 126th Pl .... Tualatin OR 97062 TF: 800-891-3100 ■ Web: www.crkt.com	503-685-5015		350
Columbia River Log Scaling & Grading Bureau 260 Oakway Ctr .... Eugene OR 97401 Web: www.crls.com	541-342-6007		302
Columbia River Maritime Museum 1792 Marine Dr .... Astoria OR 97103 TF: 800-875-6807 ■ Web: www.crmm.org	503-325-2323	325-2331	520
Columbia Room Inc 1108 E Marina Way .... Hood River OR 97031 TF: 800-828-7873 ■ Web: www.hoodriverinn.com	541-386-2200		707
Columbia Rural Electric Assn Inc 115 E Main St .... Dayton WA 99328 TF: 800-642-1231 ■ Web: www.columbiarea.com	509-382-2578		245
Columbia Saint Mary's Hospital 2025 E Newport Ave .... Milwaukee WI 53211 Web: www.columbia-stmarys.org	414-961-3300		374-3
Columbia Saint Mary's Hospital 2323 N Lake Dr .... Milwaukee WI 53211 TF: 800-994-6610 ■ Web: www.columbia-stmarys.org	414-291-1000		374-3
Columbia Saint Mary's Hospital Ozaukee 13111 N Port Washington Rd .... Mequon WI 53097 TF: 800-457-6004 ■ Web: www.columbia-stmarys.org	262-243-7300		374-3
Columbia Savings Bank 19-01 Rt 208 .... Fair Lawn NJ 07410 TF Cust Svc: 800-747-4428 ■ Web: www.columbiabankonline.com	800-522-4167		70
Columbia Scholastic Press Assn (CSPA) Columbia University 90 Morningside Dr Ste B01 .... New York NY 10027 Web: cspa.columbia.edu	212-854-9400	854-9401	48-11

Name / Address	City	State	Zip	Phone	Fax	Class
Columbia Showcase & Cabinet Co 11034 Sherman Way	Sun Valley	CA	91352	818-765-9710		364
Web: www.columbiashowcase.com						
Columbia Specialty Company Inc 5875 Obispo Ave	Long Beach	CA	90805	562-634-6425		358
Web: www.columbiaspecialty.com						
Columbia Sportswear Co 14375 NW Science Pk Dr	Portland	OR	97229	503-985-4000	985-5800	155-1
NASDAQ: COLM ■ *TF:* 800-622-6953 ■ *Web:* www.columbia.com						
Columbia Star PO Box 5955	Columbia	SC	29250	803-771-0219		637-8
Web: www.thecolumbiastar.com						
Columbia State Bank PO Box 2156	Tacoma	WA	98401	253-305-1900		70
TF: 800-305-1905 ■ *Web:* www.columbiabank.com						
Columbia State Community College 1665 Hampshire Pk	Columbia	TN	38401	931-540-2722	540-2830*	162
**Fax:* Admissions ■ *TF:* 800-848-0298 ■ *Web:* www.columbiastate.edu						
Clifton 795 Main St	Clifton	TN	38425	931-676-6966	676-6941	162
Web: columbiastate.edu						
Columbia State Historic Park 11255 Jackson St	Columbia	CA	95310	209-588-9128		565
Web: www.parks.ca.gov						
Columbia Steel Casting Co Inc 10425 N Bloss Ave	Portland	OR	97203	503-286-0685	286-1743	307
TF: 800-547-9471 ■ *Web:* www.columbiasteel.com						
Columbia Steel Inc 2175 N Linden Ave	Rialto	CA	92377	909-874-8840		492
Web: www.columbiasteelinc.com						
Columbia Sussex Corp 740 Centre View Blvd	Crestview Hills	KY	41017	859-578-1100	578-1154	379
Web: www.columbiasussex.com						
Columbia Telecommunications Corp 10613 Concord St	Kensington	MD	20895	301-933-1488		261
Web: www.ctcnet.us						
Columbia Theological Seminary 701 S Columbia Dr	Decatur	GA	30030	404-378-8821	377-9696	167-3
TF: 888-601-8916 ■ *Web:* www.ctsnet.edu						
Columbia Threadneedle Investments 1 Financial Ctr	Boston	MA	02111	800-426-3750		401
TF: 800-426-3750 ■ *Web:* www.columbiathreadneedleus.com						
Columbia University 2960 Broadway	New York	NY	10027	212-854-1754		166
Web: www.columbia.edu						
Columbia University Press 61 W 62nd St 3rd Fl	New York	NY	10023	212-459-0600	459-3677	637-4
TF: 800-944-8648 ■ *Web:* www.columbia.edu						
Columbia University School of Law 435 W 116th St	New York	NY	10027	212-854-2640	854-1109	167-1
Web: www.law.columbia.edu						
Columbia Utilities Heating Corp 8751 18th Ave	Brooklyn	NY	11214	877-726-5862	851-2427*	316
**Fax Area Code:* 718 ■ *TF:* 877-726-5862 ■ *Web:* www.columbiautilities.com						
Columbia Ventures Corp (CVC) 14301 SE First St Ste 110	Vancouver	WA	98684	360-816-1840		405
Web: www.colventures.com						
Columbia Vista Corp PO Box 489	Vancouver	WA	98666	360-892-0770	944-8229	683
Web: www.columbiavistacorp.com						
Columbia West Capital LLC 14624 N Scottsdale Rd Ste 124	Scottsdale	AZ	85254	480-664-3949		690
Web: www.columbiawestcap.com						
Columbia Winery 14030 NE 145th St	Woodinville	WA	98072	425-482-7490		50-7
TF: 800-488-2347 ■ *Web:* www.columbiawinery.com						
Columbia Woodworking Inc 935 Brentwood Rd NE	Washington	DC	20018	202-526-2387	526-5163	499
Columbia-Greene Community College 4400 Rt 23	Hudson	NY	12534	518-828-4181	822-2015	162
TF: 888-668-4293 ■ *Web:* www.sunycgcc.edu						
Columbia-Montour Visitors Bureau 121 Papermill Rd	Bloomsburg	PA	17815	570-784-8279		206
TF: 800-847-4810 ■ *Web:* www.itourcolumbiamontour.com						
Columbian 701 W Eigth St PO Box 180	Vancouver	WA	98660	360-694-3391		532-2
TF: 800-743-3391 ■ *Web:* www.columbian.com						
Columbian Chemicals Co 1800 W Oak Commons Ct	Marietta	GA	30062	770-792-9400		145
TF: 800-235-4003 ■ *Web:* www.birlacarbon.com						
Columbian Mutual Life Insurance Co Vestal Pkwy E	Binghamton	NY	13902	607-724-2472		390
Web: www.cfglife.com						
Columbian Park Zoo 1915 Scott St	Lafayette	IN	47904	765-807-1540	807-1547	823
TF: 800-438-9926 ■ *Web:* www.lafayette.in.gov						
Columbian Tectank 2101 S 21st St	Parsons	KS	67357	620-421-0200	421-9122	91
Web: www.cstindustries.com						
Columbiana Centre Mall 100 Columbiana Cir	Columbia	SC	29212	803-732-6255		460
Web: www.columbianacentre.com						
Columbiana County 105 S Market St	Lisbon	OH	44432	330-424-9519		338
Web: www.columbianacounty.org						
Columbiana Hi Tech LLC 1802 Fairfax Rd	Greensboro	NC	27407	336-497-3600		295
Web: www.chtnuclear.com						
Columbus Air Force Base 555 Seventh St	Columbus AFB	MS	39710	662-434-7068	434-7009	497-1
Web: www.columbus.af.mil						
Columbus Alive 34 S Third St	Columbus	OH	43215	614-221-2449	461-8746	532-5
Web: www.columbusalive.com						
Columbus Area Chamber of Commerce 500 Franklin St	Columbus	IN	47201	812-379-4457		139
TF: 800-404-6642 ■ *Web:* www.columbusareachamber.com						
Columbus Area Visitors Ctr 506 Fifth St	Columbus	IN	47201	812-378-2622		206
TF: 800-468-6564 ■ *Web:* www.columbus.in.us						
Columbus Bank & Trust Co 1148 Broadway	Columbus	GA	31901	706-649-4900		70
TF: 800-334-9007 ■ *Web:* www.synovus.com						
Columbus Blue Jackets Nationwide Arena 200 W Nationwide Blvd Ste Level	Columbus	OH	43215	614-246-4625	246-4007	716
Web: bluejackets.nhl.com						
Columbus Business First 303 W Nationwide Blvd	Columbus	OH	43215	614-461-4040	365-2980	457-5
TF: 800-486-3289 ■ *Web:* www.bizjournals.com						

Name / Address	City	State	Zip	Phone	Fax	Class
Columbus Castings 2211 Parsons Ave	Columbus	OH	43207	614-444-2121		307
TF: 800-422-0550 ■ *Web:* www.columbuscastings.com						
Columbus Chamber of Commerce 150 S Front St Ste 200	Columbus	OH	43215	614-221-1321	221-1408	139
TF: 877-771-5202 ■ *Web:* www.columbus.org						
Columbus Cir Investors Inc (CCI) 1 Stn Pl Metro Ctr	Stamford	CT	06902	203-353-6000		401
Web: www.columbuscircle.com						
Columbus City Schools 270 E State St	Columbus	OH	43215	614-365-5000	365-5652	685
Web: www.columbus.k12.oh.us						
Columbus Civic Ctr 400 Fourth St	Columbus	GA	31901	706-653-4482		720
Web: www.columbuscivicenter.org						
Columbus College of Art & Design 60 Cleveland Ave	Columbus	OH	43215	614-224-9101	222-4040	164
TF: 877-997-2223 ■ *Web:* www.ccad.edu						
Columbus Consolidated Government Ctr 100 Tenth St	Columbus	GA	31901	706-653-4000		337
Web: www.columbusga.org						
Columbus Container Inc 3460 Commerce Dr	Columbus	IN	47201	812-376-9301		100
Web: www.columbuscontainer.com						
Columbus Convention & Visitors Bureau 900 Front Ave	Columbus	GA	31901	706-322-1613	322-0701	206
TF: 800-999-1613 ■ *Web:* www.visitcolumbusga.com						
Columbus Convention & Visitors Bureau PO Box 789	Columbus	MS	39703	662-329-1191	329-8969	206
TF: 800-327-2686 ■ *Web:* visitcolumbusms.org						
Columbus County PO Box 1587	Whiteville	NC	28472	910-641-3000		338
TF: 800-553-9759 ■ *Web:* www.columbusco.org						
Columbus County Schools PO Box 729	Whiteville	NC	28472	910-642-5168	640-1010	685
Web: www.columbus.k12.nc.us						
Columbus Dispatch 62 E Broad St	Columbus	OH	43215	614-461-5000		532-2
Web: www.dispatch.com						
Columbus Door Company Inc 1884 Elmwood Ave	Warwick	RI	02888	401-781-7792		234
Web: www.columbusdoor.com						
Columbus Electric Co-op Inc 900 N Gold St PO Box 631	Deming	NM	88031	505-546-8838		245
TF: 800-950-2667 ■ *Web:* www.columbusco-op.org						
Columbus Engineering Consultants Ltd 840 Michigan Ave	Columbus	OH	43215	614-228-3500		261
Web: ceceng.net						
Columbus Fish Market 1245 Olentangy River Rd	Columbus	OH	43212	614-291-3474		671
Web: mitchellsfishmarket.com						
Columbus Foundation, The 1234 E Broad St	Columbus	OH	43205	614-251-4000	251-4009	303
Web: www.columbusfoundation.org						
Columbus Georgia Convention & Trade Ctr 801 Front Ave	Columbus	GA	31901	706-327-4522		205
Web: www.columbusga.org/tradecenter						
Columbus Hospice 7020 Moon Rd	Columbus	GA	31909	706-569-7992		371
Web: www.columbushospice.com						
Columbus Hospital 495 N 13th St	Newark	NJ	07107	973-587-7777	587-7829	374-3
TF: 800-772-1213 ■ *Web:* www.columbusltach.org						
Columbus Humanities Arts & Technology Academy 1333 Morse Rd	Columbus	OH	43229	614-261-1200		685
TF: 000-656-6763 ■ *Web:* columbushumanitiesata.org						
Columbus Hydraulics Co PO Box 250	Columbus	NE	68601	402-564-8544	564-0129	223
Web: www.columbushydraulics.com						
Columbus Industries Inc 2938 SR-752 PO Box 257	Ashville	OH	43103	740-983-2552	983-4622	18
Web: www.colind.com						
Columbus Jack Corp 2222 S Third St	Columbus	OH	43207	614-443-7492		454
Web: www.columbusjack.com						
Columbus Jewish Foundation 1175 College Ave	Columbus	OH	43209	614-237-7686		305
Web: www.jewishcolumbus.org						
Columbus Ledger-Enquirer 17 W 12th St	Columbus	GA	31901	706-324-5526	576-6290	532-2
TF: 800-282-7859 ■ *Web:* www.ledger-enquirer.com						
Columbus Life Insurance Co 400 E Fourth St PO Box 5737	Cincinnati	OH	45202	800-677-9595		391-2
TF: 800-677-9595 ■ *Web:* www.columbuslife.com						
Columbus Marble Works Corp 2415 Hwy 45 N	Columbus	MS	39705	662-328-1477		724
TF Cust Svc: 800-647-1055 ■ *Web:* www.columbusmarbleworks.net						
Columbus McKinnon Corp 140 John James Audubon Pkwy	Amherst	NY	14228	716-689-5400		470
NASDAQ: CMCO ■ *TF:* 800-888-0985 ■ *Web:* www.cmworks.com						
Columbus Metropolitan Airport 3250 W Britt David Rd	Columbus	GA	31909	706-324-2449		27
Web: flycolumbusga.com						
Columbus Metropolitan Library 96 S Grant Ave	Columbus	OH	43215	614-645-2275		434-3
Web: www.columbuslibrary.org						
Columbus Monthly Magazine 34 S Third St	Columbus	OH	43215	614-888-4567		457-22
Web: www.columbusmonthly.com						
Columbus Motor Speedway Inc 1841 Williams Rd	Columbus	OH	43207	614-491-1047		515
Web: www.columbusspeedway.com						
Columbus Museum 1251 Wynnton Rd	Columbus	GA	31906	706-748-2562	748-2570	520
TF: 800-272-3900 ■ *Web:* www.columbusmuseum.com						
Columbus Museum of Art 480 E Broad St	Columbus	OH	43215	614-221-6801	221-0226	520
Web: www.columbusmuseum.org						
Columbus Park Trattoria 205 Main St	Stamford	CT	06901	203-967-9191		671
Web: www.columbusparktrattoria.com						
Columbus Pipe & Equipment Co 773 E Markison Ave	Columbus	OH	43207	614-444-7871		492
Web: www.columbuspipe.com						
Columbus Productions Inc 4580 Cargo Dr	Columbus	GA	31907	706-644-1595		174
Web: www.columbusproductionsinc.com						
Columbus Public Library 3000 Macon Rd	Columbus	GA	31906	706-243-2669		434-3
TF: 800-652-0782 ■ *Web:* www.cvlga.org/branches/columbus						

Name / Address	City	State	Zip	Phone	Fax	Class
Columbus Public Library 2504 14th St *Web:* www.columbusne.us/library	Columbus	NE	68601	402-564-7116		434-3
Columbus Races 822 15th St *Web:* www.agpark.com	Columbus	NE	68601	402-564-0133		642
Columbus Regional Healthcare System 500 Jefferson St *Web:* www.crhealthcare.org	Whiteville	NC	28472	910-642-8011	642-9305	374-3
Columbus Regional Hospital 2400 E 17th St *TF:* 800-841-4938 ■ *Web:* www.crh.org	Columbus	IN	47201	812-379-4441		374-3
Columbus Rehabilitation & Subacute Institute 44 S Souder Ave *TF:* 800-284-0311 ■ *Web:* columbusrehabskillednursing.com	Columbus	OH	43222	614-228-5900		450
Columbus State Community College 550 E Spring St *Fax: Admissions ■ *TF:* 800-621-6407 ■ *Web:* www.cscc.edu	Columbus	OH	43215	614-287-2400	287-6019*	162
Columbus State University 4225 University Ave *TF:* 866-264-2035 ■ *Web:* columbusstate.edu	Columbus	GA	31907	706-507-8800		166
Columbus Symphony Orchestra 935 First Ave *TF:* 800-999-1613 ■ *Web:* www.csoga.org	Columbus	GA	31901	706-323-5059	323-7051	573-3
Columbus Symphony Orchestra 55 E State St *TF:* 800-653-8000 ■ *Web:* www.columbussymphony.com	Columbus	OH	43215	614-228-9600	224-7273	573-3
Columbus Technical College 928 Manchester Expy *Web:* www.columbustech.edu	Columbus	GA	31904	706-649-1800		800
Columbus Zoo & Aquarium 4850 W Powell Rd *TF:* 800-666-5397 ■ *Web:* columbuszoo.org	Powell	OH	43065	614-645-3400	645-3465	823
Columbus-Belmont State Park 350 Pk Rd *Web:* www.parks.ky.gov	Columbus	KY	42032	270-677-2327		565
Columbus-Lowndes County Library 314 N Seventh St	Columbus	MS	39701	662-329-5300		434-3
Columbus-Muscogee County 100 Tenth St *Web:* www.columbusga.com	Columbus	GA	31901	706-653-4000		338
Column Technologies Inc 10 E 22nd St Ste 110 *TF:* 866-265-8665 ■ *Web:* www.columnit.com	Downers Grove	IL	60515	630-515-6660	271-1508	174
Columns, The 3811 St Charles Ave *TF:* 800-445-9308 ■ *Web:* www.thecolumns.com	New Orleans	LA	70115	504-899-9308	899-8170	379
Colusa Casino & Bingo 3770 Hwy 45 *Web:* www.colusacasino.com	Colusa	CA	95932	530-458-8844		2
Colusa County 546 Jay St *Web:* countyofcolusa.org	Colusa	CA	95932	530-458-0500	458-0512	338
Colusa County Office of Education 345 Fifth St	Colusa	CA	95932	530-458-0350		685
Colusa Elevator Co 2531 N County Rd *Web:* www.colusaelevator.com	Colusa	IL	62329	217-755-4221		10-5
Colussy Chevrolet 3073 Washington Pike *Web:* colussy.com	Bridgeville	PA	15017	412-564-4132		57
Colville Tribal Casinos 729 Jackson St *Web:* www.colvillecasinos.com	Omak	WA	98841	509-422-8590		452
Colvin Engineering Assoc Inc 244 West 300 North *Web:* cea-ut.com	Salt Lake City	UT	84103	801-322-2400		261
Colwell Flower Shop & Wedding Boutique 2448 Brightwood Rd SE *TF:* 800-297-1661 ■ *Web:* www.colwellflowershop.com	New Philadelphia	OH	44663	330-339-1661		292
Colwell Industries Inc 123 N Third St *Web:* www.colwellindustries.com	Minneapolis	MN	55401	612-340-0365		86
Colwell North America 2605 Marian Dr PO Box 308 *Web:* www.colwellcolour.com	Kendallville	IN	46755	260-347-1981		627
Colwill Engineering Mep & Fp 4750 E Adamo Dr *Web:* www.colwillengineering.com	Tampa	FL	33605	813-241-2525		256
COM DEV International Ltd 155 Sheldon Dr *TSE: CDV* ■ *Web:* www.comdevinternational.com	Cambridge	ON	N1R7H6	519-622-2300	622-1691	735
Comag Marketing Group LLC 155 Village Blvd Ste 300 *TF:* 866-790-9353 ■ *Web:* www.i-cmg.com	Princeton	NJ	08540	609-524-1800	524-1629	96
Comaintel Inc 121 Second Ave Ste 100 *Web:* www.comaintel.com	Grand-mere	QC	G9T7G1	819-538-6583		196
Comal County 199 Main Plaza *TF:* 877-724-9475 ■ *Web:* www.co.comal.tx.us	New Braunfels	TX	78130	830-221-1100	620-5506	338
Coman & Anderson PC 650 Warrenville Rd Ste 500	Lisle	IL	60532	630-428-2660		428
Comanche Chamber of Commerce & Agriculture 304 S Austin St *Web:* comanchechamber.org	Comanche	TX	76442	325-356-3233		338
Comanche County 315 SW Fifth St Ste 304 *Web:* www.comanchecounty.us	Lawton	OK	73501	580-355-5214		338
Comanche County Memorial Hospital 3401 NW Gore Blvd *TF:* 800-561-3357 ■ *Web:* www.ccmhonline.com	Lawton	OK	73505	580-355-8620		374-3
Comanche Electric Co-op Assn 201 W Wrights Ave *TF:* 800-915-2533 ■ *Web:* www.ceca.coop	Comanche	TX	76442	325-356-2533		245
Comanco 4301 Sterling Commerce Dr *Web:* comanco.com	Plant City	FL	33566	813-988-8829	988-8779	186
Co-Mar Aviation 1020 Woodhurst St *TF:* 800-845-1308 ■ *Web:* www.comaraviation.com	Bowling Green	KY	42103	270-781-9797	793-0525	63
Comar Inc 1 Comar Pl *TF:* 800-962-6627 ■ *Web:* www.comar.com	Buena	NJ	08310	856-692-6100	692-9251	199
Comarco Inc 25541 Commerce Ctr Dr *OTC: CMRO* ■ *TF:* 800-638-2772 ■ *Web:* www.comarco.com	Lake Forest	CA	92630	949-599-7400		735
Comarco Products Inc 501 Jackson St *Web:* www.comarco.net	Camden	NJ	08104	856-342-7557		123
Comarco Wireless Technologies Inc 25541 Commerce Ctr Dr	Lake Forest	CA	92630	949-599-7400	599-1430	735
COMARK Communications 104 Feeding Hills Rd *TF:* 800-288-8364 ■ *Web:* www.comarktv.com	Southwick	MA	01077	413-998-1100		647
Comark Corp 93 W St *TF:* 800-280-8522 ■ *Web:* www.comarkcorp.com	Medfield	MA	02052	508-359-8161	359-2267	173-2
Comark Direct 507 S Main St *TF:* 888-742-0405 ■ *Web:* comarkdirect.com	Ft. Worth	TX	76104	888-742-0405		5
Comark Instruments Inc Bldg 50-209 PO Box 500 *Web:* www.comarkinstruments.net	Beaverton	OR	97077	503-643-5204	644-5859	407
Combat Air Museum 7016 SE Forbes Ave Forbes Field *Web:* www.combatairmuseum.org	Topeka	KS	66619	785-862-3303	862-3304	520
Combe Inc 1101 Westchester Ave *TF:* 800-431-2610 ■ *Web:* www.combe.com	White Plains	NY	10604	914-694-5454		214
CombiMatrix Corp 300 Goddard Ste 100 *NASDAQ: CBMX* ■ *TF:* 800-710-0624 ■ *Web:* www.combimatrix.com	Irvine	CA	92618	949-753-0624	753-1504	85
Combination Door Co 1000 Morris St *Web:* www.combinationdoor.com	Fond du Lac	WI	54935	920-922-2050	922-2917	236
Combine International Inc 354 Indusco Ct *Web:* www.combine.com/#!/pageHome	Troy	MI	48083	248-585-9900		411
Combined Express Inc 3685 Marshall Ln *TF:* 800-777-0458 ■ *Web:* www.combinedexpress.com	Bensalem	PA	19020	800-777-0458		311
Combined Properties Inc 300 Commercial St *Web:* www.combinedproperties.com	Malden	MA	02148	781-321-7800	321-5144	655
Combined Refrigeration Resources Inc 1118 First St *Web:* www.combinedrefrigeration.com	Humble	TX	77338	281-540-7552		610
Combined Specialities International Inc 205 San Marin Dr Ste 5 *Web:* combinedspecialties.com	Novato	CA	94945	415-209-0012		390
Combined Systems Inc 388 Kinsman Rd *Web:* www.combinedsystems.com	Jamestown	PA	16134	724-932-2177		268
Combined Technologies Inc 13970 W Polo Trl Dr *TF:* 877-968-4855 ■ *Web:* ctipack.com	Lake Forest	IL	60045	847-968-4855		561
Combined Transport Inc 5656 Crater Lake Ave *TF:* 800-547-2870 ■ *Web:* www.combinedtransport.com	Central Point	OR	97502	541-734-7418	826-2001	780
Combs Insurance Agency Inc 341 S Alaska St *Web:* combsinsurance.com	Palmer	AK	99645	907-745-2144		390
CoMc LLC 13423 F St *Web:* www.snapstone.com	Omaha	NE	68137	402-505-7627		364
ComCanada Communications Inc 232-1027 Davie St *Web:* www.comcanada.ca	Vancouver	BC	V6E4L2	604-998-4500		224
Comcar Industries Inc 502 E Bridgers Ave *TF Cust Svc:* 877-426-6227 ■ *Web:* www.joincomcar.com	Auburndale	FL	33823	863-967-1101	965-1620	780
Comcast Cable Communications LLC 1701 John F Kennedy Blvd *TF:* 800-624-0331 ■ *Web:* www.xfinity.com	Philadelphia	PA	19103	215-665-1700	981-7790	116
Comcast Corp 1701 JFK Blvd *NASDAQ: CMCSA* ■ *TF:* 800-266-2278 ■ *Web:* www.xfinity.com	Philadelphia	PA	19103	215-665-1700	981-7790	360-3
Comcast SPORTSNET Bay Area LP 360 Third St 2nd Fl *TF:* 800-945-2288 ■ *Web:* www.csnbayarea.com	San Francisco	CA	94107	415-296-8900		116
Comcast Technology Solutions 1899 Wynkoop St Ste 550 *Web:* www.comcastwholesale.com	Denver	CO	80202	206-436-7900	257-6060	116
Comcentric Inc 10463 Park Meadows Dr Ste 208 *Web:* www.comcentric.com	Lone Tree	CO	80124	303-805-4700		193
Comco Inc 2151 N Lincoln St *TF:* 800-796-6626 ■ *Web:* www.comcoinc.com	Burbank	CA	91504	818-841-5500	955-8365	1
Comco Plastics Inc 98-31 Jamaica Ave *TF:* 800-221-9555 ■ *Web:* www.comcoplastics.com	Woodhaven	NY	11421	718-849-9000		602
Comcor Environmental Ltd 320 Pinebush Rd Ste 12 *Web:* www.comcor.com	Cambridge	ON	N1T1Z6	519-621-6669		668
COMCOR Event & Meeting Production 1040 Bayview Dr Ste 407 *TF:* 800-835-6770 ■ *Web:* www.comcorevents.com	Fort Lauderdale	FL	33304	954-491-3233		184
Comdata Corp 5301 Maryland Way *TF:* 800-266-3282 ■ *Web:* www.comdata.com	Brentwood	TN	37027	615-370-7000		69
Comdel Inc 11 Kondelin Rd *TF:* 800-468-3144 ■ *Web:* www.comdel.com	Gloucester	MA	01930	978-282-0620	282-4980	253
Come Back in 508 E Wilson St *Web:* comebackintavern.com	Madison	WI	53703	608-258-8619		379
Comedical Inc 7100 Roosevelt Way NE *Web:* www.comedical.com	Seattle	WA	98115	206-524-7424		475
Comedy Central 1775 Broadway *TF:* 800-723-4763 ■ *Web:* cc.com	New York	NY	10019	212-767-8600	767-8592	740
Comedy Central 345 Hudson St *TF:* 800-523-0823 ■ *Web:* cc.com	New York	NY	10014	212-767-8600		395
Comedy Works Inc 1226 15th St *Web:* www.comedyworks.com	Denver	CO	80202	303-595-3637		749
CoMentis Inc 280 Utah Ave Ste 275 *Web:* www.athenagen.com	South San Francisco	CA	94080	650-869-7600		231
Comer Holdings LLC 21624 Melrose Ave *Web:* www.comerholdings.com	Southfield	MI	48075	248-663-5700		247
Comer Industries Inc 12730 Virkler Dr *Web:* www.comerindustries.com	Charlotte	NC	28273	704-588-8400		188
Comer James (Rep R - KY) 1513 Longworth HOB *Web:* comer.house.gov	Washington	DC	20515	202-225-3115		342-2
Comerica Bank 411 W Lafayette *TF:* 800-292-1300 ■ *Web:* www.comerica.com	Detroit	MI	48226	313-222-4000		70
Comerica Bank-California 333 W Santa Clara St *TF:* 800-522-2265 ■ *Web:* www.comerica.com	San Jose	CA	95113	408-556-5300		70

Phone | Fax | Class

Comerica Bank-Texas 1717 Main St............. Dallas TX 75201 800-925-2160 70
TF: 800-925-2160 ■ *Web:* www.comerica.com
Comerica Theatre 400 W Washington St......... Phoenix AZ 85003 602-379-2800 572
Web: www.comericatheatre.com
Comet Die & Engraving Co
909 Larch Ave............................. Elmhurst IL 60126 630-833-5600 833-2644 757
TF: 800-684-7831 ■ *Web:* www.cometdie.com
Comet Micro System Inc
390 Swift Ave Ste 24.............. South San Francisco CA 94080 650-615-9123 180
TF: 800-787-6707 ■ *Web:* www.cometmicro.com
Comet Technologies Inc
3400 Gilchrist Rd............................Akron OH 44260 330-798-4800 420
Web: www.yxlon.com
Cometic Gasket Inc 8090 Auburn Rd...........Concord OH 44077 440-354-0777 326
TF: 800-752-9850 ■ *Web:* www.cometic.com
Com-Fab Inc
4657 Price HilliaRds Rd....................Plain City OH 43064 740-857-1107 857-1757 763
TF: 866-522-1794 ■ *Web:* www.comfab-inc.com
ComForcare Senior Services Inc
2520 Telegraph Rd Ste 100.............Bloomfield Hills MI 48302 248-745-9700 745-9763 310
TF: 800-886-4044 ■ *Web:* www.comforcare.com
Comfort - Air Engineering Inc
11403 Jones Maltsberger Rd..............San Antonio TX 78216 210-494-1691 256
Web: www.comfort-air.com
Comfort Caregivers Inc
6501 E Greenway Pkwy Ste 103............. Scottsdale AZ 85254 602-482-7777 363
TF: 800-272-3900 ■ *Web:* www.comfortcaregivers.com
Comfort Group Inc, The
659 Thompson Ln......................... Nashville TN 37204 615-263-2900 189-10
Web: www.thecomfortgroup.com
Comfort Inn & Suites
2485 Hotel Circle Pl....................... San Diego CA 92108 619-881-6200 297-6179 378
Web: www.choicehotels.com
Comfort Inn & Suites Milwaukee
916 E State St............................Milwaukee WI 53202 414-276-8800 442-1100* 379
**Fax Area Code:* 916 ■ *TF:* 800-424-6423 ■ *Web:* www.choicehotels.com
Comfort Products Distributing LLC
13202 I St.................................Omaha NE 68137 402-334-7777 612
TF: 800-779-8299 ■ *Web:* www.comfortproducts.com
Comfort Research
3860 Roger B Chaffee SE.................Grand Rapids MI 49548 616-475-5000 601
Web: www.comfortresearch.com
Comfort Systems USA 9745 Bent Oak Dr.........Houston TX 77040 832-590-5700 189-10
Comfort Systems USA Inc
675 Bering Ste 400..........................Houston TX 77057 713-830-9600 830-9696 189-10
NYSE: FIX ■ *TF:* 800-723-8431 ■ *Web:* www.comfortsystemsusa.com
Comfortex Inc 1680 Wilkie Dr.................. Winona MN 55987 507-454-6579 454-6581 471
TF: 800-445-4007 ■ *Web:* www.comfortexinc.com
Comfortex Window Fashions Inc
21 Elm St.............................. Maplewood NY 12189 518-273-3333 336-4580* 87
**Fax Area Code:* 800 ■ *TF Cust Svc:* 800-843-4151 ■ *Web:* www.comfortex.com
Comgraphics Inc 329 W 18th St 10th Fl........ Chicago IL 60616 312-226-0900 496
Web: ww3.cgichicago.com
COMHAR Inc 100 W Lehigh Ave.............Philadelphia PA 19133 215-203-3000 726
TF: 800-848-3367 ■ *Web:* comhar.org
Comic Strip Live
1568 Second Ave Frnt......................New York NY 10028 212-861-9386 95
Web: www.comicstriplive.com
Coming Attractions Theatres
1644 Ashland St Unit 5...................... Ashland OR 97520 541-488-1021 748
Web: www.catheatres.com
Comint Apparel Group LLC
463 Seventh Ave 11th Fl...................New York NY 10018 212-947-7474 96
Web: www.comintapparel.com
Comit Technologies
1325 Eraste Landry Rd...................... Lafayette LA 70506 337-326-5479 180
Web: www.comittechnologies.com
Comlink Network Services
4009 S Meridian St......................Indianapolis IN 46217 317-786-3496 180
TF: 800-875-8118 ■ *Web:* comlinkns.com
COMM Group Inc
2003 S Easton Rd Ste 100................ Doylestown PA 18901 215-348-8775 376
Web: www.cheapcaribbean.com
Comm Source Data Inc
200 Waler Way Unit 2..................Saint Augustine FL 32086 904-829-8922 180
TF: 800-718-4199 ■ *Web:* www.comm-source-data.com
Command Alkon Inc
1800 International Pk Dr Ste 400...........Birmingham AL 35243 205-879-3282 178-10
TF: 800-624-1872 ■ *Web:* www.commandalkon.com
Command Consulting Group LLC
1919 M St NW STE 200..................Washington DC 20036 202-207-2930 194
Web: www.commandcg.com
Command Ctr Inc
3609 S Wadsworth Blvd Ste 250............. Lakewood ID 80235 866-464-5844 721
OTC: CCNI ■ *TF:* 866-464-5844 ■ *Web:* www.commandonline.com
Command Financial Press Corp
345 Hudson St...........................New York NY 10014 212-274-0070 626
Web: www.commandfinancial.com
Command Medical Products Inc
15 Signal Ave.........................Ormond Beach FL 32174 386-672-8116 476
Web: www.commandmedical.com
Command Plastic Corp 124 W Ave........... Tallmadge OH 44278 330-434-3497 434-8316 548
TF: 800-321-8001 ■ *Web:* www.commandplastic.com
Command Post Technologies Inc
1039 Champions Way........................Suffolk VA 23435 757-394-1311 256
Web: commandposttech.com
Command Security Corp
388 Westchester Ave Ste 1J/H.............Port Chester NY 10573 914-937-2969 693
Web: www.commandsecurity.com
Command Spanish Inc PO Box 1091............. Petal MS 39465 601-582-8378 582-5177 96
TF: 800-250-8637 ■ *Web:* www.commandspanish.com
Command Web Offset Inc 100 Castle Rd.......Secaucus NJ 07094 201-863-8100 863-5443 626
Web: www.commandweb.com
Commander Buildings Inc
22223 Highway 38 N....................Monticello IA 52310 319-465-5961 480
Web: www.commanderbuildings.com
Commander Electric Inc
500 Johnson Ave PO Box 526................ Bohemia NY 11716 631-563-3223 563-8322 189-4
Web: www.commanderelectric.com

Commander Hotel 1401 Atlantic Ave.........Ocean City MD 21842 888-289-6166 379
TF: 888-289-6166 ■ *Web:* www.commanderhotel.com
Commando Products Inc
420A Blue Ridge Ext......................Grandview MO 64030 816-966-8889 351
Web: www.commandoproducts.com
CommCare Corp
601 Poydras St 2755 Pan American Life Ctr
....................................New Orleans LA 70130 504-324-8950 371
TF: 877-792-5434 ■ *Web:* www.commcare.com
Commemorative Brands Inc 7211 Cir S Rd....... Austin TX 78745 800-225-3687 637-2
TF: 800-225-3687 ■ *Web:* www.balfour.com
Commenco Inc 4901 Bristol Ave............Kansas City MO 64129 816-753-2166 736
TF: 800-292-9725 ■ *Web:* www.commenco.com
Commentary Magazine
561 Seventh Ave 16th Fl....................New York NY 10018 212-891-1400 457-10
TF: 800-829-6270 ■ *Web:* www.commentarymagazine.com
Commerce & Industry Assn of New Jersey (CIANJ)
61 S Paramus Rd.......................... Paramus NJ 07652 201-368-2100 368-3438 139
Web: www.cianj.org
Commerce Bank & Trust Co
386 Main St............................ Worcester MA 01608 508-797-6842 797-6836 70
TF: 800-698-2265 ■ *Web:* www.bankatcommerce.com
Commerce Casino 6131 Telegraph Rd.........Commerce CA 90040 323-721-2100 133
Web: www.commercecasino.com
Commerce Chenango 15 S Broad St...........Norwich NY 13815 607-334-1400 139
Web: www.chenangony.org
Commerce Corp 7603 Energy Pkwy...........Baltimore MD 21226 410-255-3500 429
TF: 800-883-0234 ■ *Web:* bfgsupply.com
Commerce Insurance Co 211 Main St.......... Webster MA 01570 508-943-9000 391-4
TF: 800-221-1605 ■ *Web:* www.commerceinsurance.com
Commerce Printing Service
322 N 12th St.........................Sacramento CA 95811 916-442-8100 627
Web: www.commerceprinting.com
Commerce Solutions Inc
7 Fourth St Ste 46.........................Petaluma CA 94952 707-773-1198 525
Web: www.commercesolutions.com
Commercewest Bank NA
2111 Business Ctr Dr..........................Irvine CA 92612 949-251-6959 70
OTC: CWBK ■ *Web:* www.cwbk.com
Commercial & Architectural Products Inc
PO Box 250.................................Dover OH 44622 330-343-6621 343-7296 499
TF: 800-377-1221 ■ *Web:* www.marlite.com
Commercial Air 601 Ransdell Rd..............Lebanon IN 46052 765-482-8121 186
Web: www.commercialair.com
Commercial Appeal 495 Union Ave............Memphis TN 38103 901-529-2345 532-2
TF: 800-444-6397 ■ *Web:* www.commercialappeal.com
Commercial Bank 301 N State St PO Box 638....... Alma MI 48801 989-463-2185 70
OTC: CEFC ■ *TF:* 800-547-8531 ■ *Web:* www.commercial-bank.com
Commercial Computer Service Inc
2916 W Sixth St...................... Fort Worth TX 76107 817-335-6411 225
Web: minimaxgolf.com
Commercial Contracting Corp
4260 N Atlantic Blvd.................... Auburn Hills MI 48326 248-209-0500 209-0501 109-1
Web: www.cccnetwork.com
Commercial Contractors Inc
4900 Fairbanks St........................Anchorage AK 99503 907-563-1911 290
Web: www.aphome.com
Commercial Cutting & Graphics LLC
208 Central Ave..........................Mansfield OH 44905 419-526-4800 554
TF: 800-995-2251 ■ *Web:* www.commercialcutting.com
Commercial Distributing Co Inc
46 S Broad St..........................Westfield MA 01085 413-562-9691 562-7302 81-1
Web: commercialdist.com
Commercial Driver Training
600 Patton Ave.......................West Babylon NY 11704 631-249-1330 800
TF: 800-649-7447 ■ *Web:* www.cdtschool.com
Commercial Furniture Interiors Inc
1154 Rt 22 W.........................Mountainside NJ 07092 908-518-1670 654-8436 393
Web: www.cfioffice.com
Commercial Honing Co Inc
8608 Sultana Ave.......................... Fontana CA 92335 909-829-1211 829-7631 223
TF: 800-310-7915 ■ *Web:* www.commercialhoning.com
Commercial Interior Resources Inc
1761 Reynolds Ave...........................Irvine CA 92614 949-752-1470 290
Web: www.cir-resource.com
Commercial Jet Inc
4600 NW 36 St Miami International Airport
Bldg 896................................. Miami FL 33166 305-341-5150 454
Web: www.commercialjet.com
Commercial Law League of America (CLLA)
70 E Lake St Ste 630........................Chicago IL 60601 312-781-2000 781-2010 49-10
TF: 800-978-2552 ■ *Web:* www.clla.org
Commercial Lighting Industries
81161 Indio Blvd............................ Indio CA 92201 760-343-2704 439
TF: 800-755-0155 ■ *Web:* www.commercial-lighting.net
Commercial Lumber & Pallet Co
135 Long Ln.......................City Of Industry CA 91746 800-252-4968 200
TF: 800-252-4968 ■ *Web:* www.clcpallets.com
Commercial Mailing Accessories Inc
28220 Playmor Beach Rd.................Rocky Mount MO 65072 800-325-7303 4
TF: 800-325-7303 ■ *Web:* www.dispensamatic.com
Commercial Manufacturing & Assembly Inc
17087 Hayes St........................ Grand Haven MI 49417 616-847-9980 488
Web: www.callcma.com
Commercial Metal Fabricators Company Inc
150 Commerce Park Dr.......................Dayton OH 45404 937-233-4911 480
Web: Www.Cmfcu.Com
Commercial Metals Co (CMC)
6565 N MacArthur Blvd Ste 800.................Irving TX 75039 214-689-4300 689-4300 723
NYSE: CMC ■ *Web:* www.cmc.com
Commercial Millwork Solutions Inc
15051 Biscayne Ave W.................. Rosemount MN 55068 651-322-5353 115
Web: www.commercialmillworksolutions.com
Commercial National Financial Corp
900 Ligonier St...................... Latrobe PA 15650 724-539-3501 360-2
OTC: CNAF ■ *TF:* 800-803-2265 ■ *Web:* www.cnbthebankonline.com
Commercial Plastics Co (CPC)
800 Allanson Rd........................Mundelein IL 60060 847-566-1700 604
Web: www.ecommercialplastics.com

Name / Address	Phone	Fax	Class
Commercial Programming Systems Inc 4400 Coldwater Canyon Ave Studio City CA 91604 *Fax Area Code: 818 ■ TF: 888-277-4562 ■ Web: www.cpsinc.com	323-851-2681	301-1996*	177
Commercial Properties Realty Trust 100 North St Baton Rouge LA 70802 TF: 800-648-9064 ■ Web: www.cprt.com	225-924-7206	924-1235	654
Commercial Ready Mix Products Inc PO Box 189 Winton NC 27986 Web: www.crmpinc.com	252-358-5461	358-4912	191-1
Commercial Realty & Resources Corp 1415 Wyckoff Rd PO Box 1468 Wall NJ 07719 Web: njresources.com	732-938-1111		652
Commercial Refrigerator Door Company Inc 6200 Porter Rd Sarasota FL 34240 Web: www.styleline.com	941-371-8110		234
Commercial Resins Company Inc 8100 E 96th Ave Henderson CO 80640 Web: commercialresins.com	303-288-3914		480
Commercial Siding & Maintenance Co, The 8059 Crile Rd Painesville OH 44077 TF: 800-229-4276 ■ Web: www.commercialsiding.com	440-352-7800	352-7048	189-12
Commercial Steel Treating Corp 31440 Stephenson Hwy Madison Heights MI 48071 Web: www.commercialsteel.com	248-588-3300	588-3534	484
Commercial Storage & Distribution Co 432 Richmond Rd Texarkana TX 75503	903-794-2202		780
Commercial Turf Products Ltd 1777 Miller Pkwy Streetsboro OH 44241	330-995-7000		429
Commercial Vehicle Group Inc 7800 Walton Pkwy New Albany OH 43054 NASDAQ: CVGI ■ Web: www.cvgrp.com	614-289-5360		60
Commercial Wood Products Co 10019 Yucca Rd Adelanto CA 92301	760-246-4530		115
Commercial-News 17 W N St Danville IL 61832 *Fax: News Rm ■ TF: 877-732-8258 ■ Web: www.commercial-news.com	217-446-1000	446-6648*	532-2
Commerx Computer Systems Inc 2880 Argentia Rd Unit 1 Mississauga ON L5N7X8 Web: www.commerx.ca	905-542-9400		224
Commerzbank AG 2 World Financial Ctr New York NY 10281 Web: www.corporates.commerzbank.com	212-266-7200		70
Commission for Economic Development in Orem 56 N State St Rm 101 Orem UT 84057 Web: econdev.orem.org	801-229-7172	229-7031	139
Commission Junction Inc 530 E Montecito St Santa Barbara CA 93103 TF: 800-761-1072 ■ Web: www.cj.com	805-730-8000	730-8001	7
Commission of Fine Arts 401 F St NW Ste 312 Washington DC 20001 Web: www.cfa.gov	202-504-2200	504-2195	340-20
Commission on Accreditation for Dietetics Education (CADE) 120 S Riverside Plaza Ste 2000 Chicago IL 60606 TF: 800-877-1600 ■ Web: www.eatright.org	312-899-0040		48-1
Commission on Accreditation for Law Enforcement Agencies (CALEA) 13575 Heathcote Blvd Ste 320 Gainesville VA 20155 TF: 877-789-6904 ■ Web: www.calea.org	703-352-4225	890-3126	49-7
Commission on Accreditation in Physical Therapy Education (CAPTE) 1111 N Fairfax St Alexandria VA 22314 TF: 800-999-2782 ■ Web: www.capteonline.org/home.aspx	703-706-3245	838-8910	48-1
Commission on Accreditation of Allied Health Education Programs (CAAHEP) 1361 Pk St Clearwater FL 33756 TF: 800-228-2262 ■ Web: www.caahep.org	727-210-2350	210-2354	48-1
Commission on Accreditation of Healthcare Management Education 6110 Executive Blvd Ste 614 Rockville MD 20852 Web: www.cahme.org	301-298-1820		48-1
Commission on Accreditation of Rehabilitation Facilities International (CARF) 6951 E Southpoint Rd Tucson AZ 85756 TF: 888-281-6531 ■ Web: www.carf.org	520-325-1044	318-1129	48-1
Commission on English Language Program Accreditation (CEA) 801 N Fairfax St Ste 402A Alexandria VA 22314 Web: www.cea-accredit.org	703-665-3400	519-2071	48-1
Commission on Massage Therapy Accreditation (COMTA) 5335 Wisconsin Ave NW Ste 440 Washington DC 20015 Web: www.comta.org	202-895-1518		48-1
Commission on Presidential Scholars *US Presidential Scholars Program* 400 Maryland Ave SW Department of Education Bldg Washington DC 20202 Web: www2.ed.gov/programs/psp/commission.html	202-401-0961	260-7464	340-20
Commission on Professionals in Science & Technology (CPST) 1200 New York Ave NW Ste 113 Washington DC 20005	202-326-7080		49-19
Commission on Security & Cooperation in Europe 234 Ford House Office Bldg 3rd & D Sts SW Washington DC 20515 Web: www.csce.gov	202-225-1901	226-4199	340-20
Commissioners of Public Works 121 W Ct Ave Greenwood SC 29646 Web: www.greenwoodcpw.com	864-942-8100	942-8114	787
Committee for Economic Development (CED) 1530 Wilson Blvd Ste 400 Arlington VA 22209 TF: 800-676-7353 ■ Web: www.ced.org	202-296-5860	223-0776	634
Committee for Education Funding (CEF) 1800 M St NW Ste 500 Washington DC 20036 Web: www.cef.org	202-383-0083		48-11
Committee for Purchase from People Who Are Blind or Severely Disabled, The 1421 Jefferson Davis Hwy Jefferson Plaza 2 Ste 10800 Arlington VA 22202 Web: www.abilityone.gov	703-603-7740		340-20
Committee on Foreign Investments in the US *Department of the Treasury Office* 1500 Pennsylvania Ave NW Washington DC 20220 Web: www.treasury.gov	202-622-2000	622-2000	340-20
Commnet Wireless LLC 400 Northridge Rd Ste 325 Atlanta GA 30350 Web: www.commnetwireless.com	678-338-5960		387
Commodity Components International Inc 100 Summit St Peabody MA 01960 Web: www.cci-inc.com	978-538-0020	538-3633	246
Commodity Futures Trading Commission 1155 21 St NW Washington DC 20581 TF: 866-366-2382 ■ Web: www.cftc.gov	202-418-5000	418-5521	340-20
Commodity Futures Trading Commission Regional Offices			
Central Region 525 W Monroe St Chicago IL 60661 TF: 800-621-3570 ■ Web: www.cftc.gov	312-596-0700	596-0713	340-20
Eastern Region 140 Broadway 19th Fl New York NY 10005 Web: www.cftc.gov	646-746-9700	746-9938	340-20
Southwestern Region 2 Emanuel Cleaver II Blvd Ste 300 Kansas City MO 64112 Web: www.cftc.gov	816-960-7700	960-7750	340-20
Commodity Information Systems Inc 3030 NW Expy Ste 725 Oklahoma City OK 73112 TF: 800-231-0477 ■ Web: www.cis-okc.com	405-604-8726	604-8726	637-9
Commodity Research Bureau 330 S Wells St Ste 612 Chicago IL 60606 TF: 800-621-5271 ■ Web: www.crbtrader.com	312-554-8456	939-4135	531-9
Commodity Sourcing Group (CSG) 19730 Ralston St Detroit MI 48203	313-366-0660		463
Commodity Systems Inc 200 W Palmetto Park Rd Ste 200 Boca Raton FL 33432 TF: 800-274-4727 ■ Web: www.csidata.com	561-392-8663		224
Commodore Builders 80 Bridge St Newton MA 02458 Web: www.commodorebuilders.com	617-614-3500		186
Commodore Corp 1423 Lincolnway E Goshen IN 46526 Web: www.commodorehomes.com	574-533-7100		505
Commodore Plastics LLC 26 Maple Ave Bloomfield NY 14469 Web: www.commodoresolutions.com	585-657-7777		599
Common Cause 1133 19th St NW 9th Fl Washington DC 20036 Web: www.commoncause.org	202-833-1200	659-3716	48-7
Common Census Inc 90 Bridge St FL 105 Westbrook ME 04092 Web: www.commoncensus.com	207-854-5454		390
Common Interest Management Services Inc 315 Diablo Rd Ste 221 Danville CA 94526 Web: www.commoninterest.com	925-743-3080		195
Common Man, The 25 Water St Concord NH 03301 Web: www.thecman.com	603-228-3463		671
Common Sense Advisory Inc 100 Merrimack St Lowell MA 01852 Web: commonsenseadvisory.com	978-275-0500		256
Common Source LP, The 14500 N Fwy Houston TX 77090 Web: www.commonsource.com	281-260-9220		445
Commonfund Inc 15 Old Danbury Rd Wilton CT 06897 Web: www.commonfund.org	203-563-5000		401
Commongood Careers 31 St James Ave Boston MA 02116 Web: commongoodcareers.org	617-542-1404		463
Commons at Orlando Lutheran Towers, The 300 E Church St Orlando FL 32801 TF: 800-859-1033 ■ Web: orlandoseniorhealth.org	407-422-4103		48-20
Commons Capital LP 320 Washington St 4th Fl Brookline MA 02445 Web: www.commonscapital.com	617-739-3500		792
Commons, The 1928 S Commons Federal Way WA 98003 Web: www.shopthecommonsmall.com	253-839-6150	946-1413	460
Commonweal Magazine 475 Riverside Dr Rm 405 New York NY 10115 Web: www.commonwealmagazine.org	212-662-4200	662-4183	457-17
Commonwealth Altadis Inc 5900 N Andrews Ave Ste 1000 Fort Lauderdale FL 33309 Web: www.altadisusa.com	954-772-9000		756
Commonwealth Assoc Inc PO Box 1124 Jackson MI 49204 Web: www.cai-engr.com	517-788-3000		261
Commonwealth Bank of Australia 599 Lexington Ave 17th Fl New York NY 10022 Web: www.commbank.com.au	212-848-9200		70
Commonwealth Biotechnologies Inc 601 Biotech Dr Richmond VA 23235 TF: 800-735-9224 ■ Web: cbi-biotech.com	804-648-3820	648-2641	417
Commonwealth Canvas Inc 5 Perkins Way Newburyport MA 01950 TF: 877-922-6827 ■ Web: www.commonwealthcanvas.com	978-499-3900	499-3933	733
Commonwealth Capital Advisors LLC 30 S Wacker Dr 22nd Fl Chicago IL 60606	808-744-9713		401
Commonwealth Capital Ventures 400 Cummings Park Dr Ste 1725 Woburn MA 01801 Web: www.commonwealthvc.com	781-890-5554		792
Commonwealth Club, The 555 Post St San Francisco CA 94102 TF: 800-847-7730 ■ Web: www.commonwealthclub.org	415-597-6700	597-6729	632
Commonwealth Credit Union PO Box 978 Frankfort KY 40602 TF: 800-228-6420 ■ Web: www.ccuky.org	502-564-4775		219
Commonwealth Electric Co of Midwest PO Box 80638 Lincoln NE 68501 TF: 800-773-4480 ■ Web: www.commonwealthelectric.com	402-474-1341	474-0114	189-4
Commonwealth Financial Network 29 Sawyer Rd Waltham MA 02453 *Fax Area Code: 866 ■ TF: 800-237-0081 ■ Web: www.commonwealth.com	781-736-0700	316-8357*	401
Commonwealth Fund 1 E 75th St New York NY 10021 Web: www.commonwealthfund.org	212-606-3800	606-3500	305
Commonwealth Health Corporation Inc 800 Park St Bowling Green KY 42101 TF: 800-786-1581 ■ Web: www.chc.net	270-745-1500		363
Commonwealth Hosiery Mills Inc 4964 Island Ford Rd Randleman NC 27317 TF: 800-561-3357 ■ Web: commonwealthhosiery.com	336-498-2621		155-10
Commonwealth Hotels LLC 100 E Rivercenter Blvd Ste 1050 Covington KY 41011 Web: www.commonwealthhotels.com	859-261-5522		378
Commonwealth Institute 186 Hampshire St Cambridge MA 02139 Web: comw.org	617-547-4474	868-1267	634
Commonwealth Laminating & Coating Inc 345 Beaver Creek Dr Martinsville VA 24112 TF General: 888-321-5111 ■ Web: www.suntekfilms.com	276-632-4991	632-0173	699
Commonwealth Land Title Insurance Co 601 Riverside Ave Jacksonville FL 32204 TF: 888-866-3684 ■ Web: www.cltic.com	888-866-3684		391-6

Phone | Fax | Class

Commonwealth National Bank
2214 St Stephens Rd .... Mobile AL 36617 251-476-5938 70
Web: ecommonwealthbank.com

Commonwealth Park Suites Hotel
901 Bank St .... Richmond VA 23219 804-343-7300 379
TF: 888-343-7301 ■ *Web:* www.commonwealthparksuites.com

Commonwealth Public Broadcasting
23 Sesame St .... Richmond VA 23235 804-320-1301 632
Web: www.ideastations.org

Commonwealth Telephone Co
1 Newbury St Ste 103 .... Peabody MA 01960 978-536-9500 736
TF: 800-439-7170 ■ *Web:* www.commonwealthtel.com

Commonwealth Toy & Novelty Co
45 W 25th St 7th Fl .... New York NY 10010 212-242-4070 645-4279 762
TF: 800-572-1519 ■ *Web:* commonwealthtoy.com

CommScope Inc
1100 Commscope Pl SE PO Box 339 .... Hickory NC 28603 828-324-2200 328-3400* 814
**Fax:* Cust Svc ■ *TF:* 800-982-1708 ■ *Web:* www.commscope.com

CommStructures Inc 101 E Roberts Rd .... Pensacola FL 32534 850-968-9293 968-9283 188-1
Web: www.commstructures.com

Communauto Inc
335 rue St-Joseph Est Ste 310 .... Quebec QC G1K3B4 418-523-1788 126
Web: www.communauto.com

Communca Inc 31 N Erie St .... Toledo OH 43604 800-800-7890 514
TF: 800-800-7890 ■ *Web:* www.communica.world

Communi Care At Waterford
955 Garden Lake Pkwy .... Toledo OH 43614 419-382-2200 450
TF: 800-321-8383 ■ *Web:* www.communicarehealth.com

Communication Data Services
1901 Bell Ave .... Des Moines IA 50315 515-246-6837 246-6687 225
TF: 866-897-7987 ■ *Web:* www.cds-global.com

Communication Services Inc
2151 E Broadway Rd .... Tempe AZ 85282 480-905-8689 736
Web: www.com-serv.com

Communication Technologies Inc
14151 Newbrook Dr Ste 400 .... Chantilly VA 20151 703-961-9080 961-1330 735
TF: 888-266-8358 ■ *Web:* www.comtechnologies.com

Communication Wiring Specialists Inc
8909 Complex Dr Ste F .... San Diego CA 92123 858-278-4545 387
TF: 800-600-6998 ■ *Web:* www.cwssandiego.com

Communications & Power Industries Inc Beverly Microwave Div (CPI-BMD)
150 Sohier Rd .... Beverly MA 01915 978-922-6000 922-2736 647
Web: cpii.com/division.cfm/8

Communications & Power Industries LLC
607 Hansen Way .... Palo Alto CA 94303 650-846-2900 846-3276* 253
**Fax:* PR ■ *TF:* 800-231-4818 ■ *Web:* www.cpii.com

Communications Corp of America
700 St John St Ste 300 .... Lafayette LA 70501 337-237-1142 738

Communications Credit & Recovery (CCR)
20 Broad Hollow Rd Ste 1002 .... Melville NY 11747 631-923-2200 923-2784 160
TF: 800-327-3648 ■ *Web:* www.ccrcollect.com

Communications Daily
2115 Ward Ct NW .... Washington DC 20037 202-872-9200 531-11
TF: 800-771-9202 ■ *Web:* www.warren-news.com

Communications Manufacturing Co (CMC)
2234 Colby Ave .... Los Angeles CA 90064 310-828-3200 248
TF Orders: 800-462-5532 ■ *Web:* www.gotocmc.com

Communications Media Inc
2200 Renaissance Blvd .... King Of Prussia PA 19406 484-322-0880 4
Web: www.cmimedia.com

Communications News PO Box 866 .... Osprey FL 34229 941-539-7579 457-5
TF: 800-827-9715 ■ *Web:* www.comnews.com

Communications Resource Inc
8280 Greensboro Dr Ste 500 .... Mc Lean VA 22102 703-245-4120 356-4860 177
TF: 888-900-9757 ■ *Web:* www.cri-solutions.com

Communications Supply Service Assn (CSSA)
5700 Murray St .... Little Rock AR 72209 501-562-7666 562-7616 49-20
TF: 800-252-2772 ■ *Web:* www.cssa.net

Communications Systems Inc
10900 Red Cir Dr .... Minnetonka MN 55343 952-996-1674 735
NASDAQ: JCS ■ *TF:* 800-268-5130 ■ *Web:* www.commsystems.com

Communications Test Design Inc
1339 Enterprise Dr .... West Chester PA 19380 610-436-5203 735
TF: 800-223-3910 ■ *Web:* www.ctdi.com

Communications Workers of America (CWA)
501 Third St NW .... Washington DC 20001 202-434-1100 414
Web: www.cwa-union.org

Communico Ltd 19 Ludlow Rd .... Westport CT 06880 203-226-7117 463
Web: www.communicoltd.com

Communicorp Inc 1001 Lockwood Ave .... Columbus GA 31999 706-324-1182 321-3100 627
Web: communicorp.com

CommuniGate Systems Inc
655 Redwood Hwy Ste 275 .... Mill Valley CA 94941 415-383-7164 383-7461 178-12
TF: 800-262-4722 ■ *Web:* www.stalker.com

Communispond Inc 12 Barns Ln .... East Hampton NY 11937 631-907-8010 194
TF: 800-529-5925 ■ *Web:* www.communispond.com

Communist Party USA
235 W 23rd St 8th Fl .... New York NY 10011 212-989-4994 229-1713 616
Web: www.cpusa.org

Communities Foundation of Texas Inc
5500 Caruth Haven Ln .... Dallas TX 75225 214-750-4222 750-4210 303
Web: www.cftexas.org

Community Action Partnership
1140 Connecticut Ave NW Ste 1210 .... Washington DC 20036 202-265-7546 265-5048 48-5
TF: 800-639-4065 ■ *Web:* www.communityactionpartnership.com

Community America Credit Union (CACU)
9777 Ridge Dr .... Lenexa KS 66219 913-905-7000 905-7111 219
TF: 800-892-7957 ■ *Web:* www.communityamerica.com

Community Asphalt Corp
9675 NW 117 Ave Ste 108 .... Miami FL 33178 305-884-9444 884-9448 46
TF General: 800-736-4255 ■ *Web:* www.cacorp.net

Community Assn Underwriters of America (CAU)
2 Caufield Pl .... Newtown PA 18940 267-757-7100 391-4
Web: www.cauinsure.com

Community Assns Institute (CAI)
6402 Arlington Blvd Ste 500 .... Falls Church VA 22042 703-970-9220 970-9558 48-7
TF: 888-224-4321 ■ *Web:* www.caionline.org

Phone | Fax | Class

Community Banc Investments Inc
26 E Main St .... New Concord OH 43762 740-826-7601 690
Web: www.cbibankstocks.com

Community Bank 505 E Colorado Blvd .... Pasadena CA 91101 800-788-9999 69
TF: 800-788-9999 ■ *Web:* www.cbank.com

Community Bank of Midwest
2220 Broadway Ave .... Great Bend KS 67530 620-792-5111 70
Web: www.communitybankmidwest.com

Community Bank of Raymore PO Box 200 .... Raymore MO 64083 816-322-2100 322-5915 70
TF: 800-523-4175 ■ *Web:* www.cbronline.net

Community Bank Shares of Indiana Inc
101 W Spring St .... New Albany IN 47150 812-944-2224 360-2
NASDAQ: YCB ■ *TF:* 866-944-2004 ■ *Web:* www.yourcommunitybank.com

Community Bank System Inc
5790 Widewaters Pkwy .... Syracuse NY 13214 315-445-2282 360-2
NYSE: CBU ■ *TF:* 866-764-8638 ■ *Web:* www.communitybankna.com

Community Bankers Merchant Services Inc
908 S Old Missouri Rd .... Springdale AZ 72764 479-725-1000 218
Web: www.merchantprocessing.com

Community Banking Advisory Network (CBAN)
1801 W End Ave Ste 800 .... Nashville TN 37203 615-373-9880 377-7092 49-2
TF: 800-231-2524 ■ *Web:* www.bankingcpas.com

Community Bankshares Inc
5570 DTC Pkwy .... Greenwood Village CO 80111 720-529-3336 360-2
Web: www.cobnks.com

Community Blood Bank of Northwest Pennsylvania
2646 Peach St .... Erie PA 16508 814-456-4206 452-3966 89
TF: 877-842-0631 ■ *Web:* www.fourhearts.org

Community Blood Ctr 349 S Main St .... Dayton OH 45402 937-461-3450 461-9217 89
TF: 800-388-4483 ■ *Web:* www.cbccts.org
Gladstone Ctr 7265 N Oak Trafficway .... Gladstone MO 64118 816-468-9813 89
TF: 877-468-6844 ■ *Web:* www.savealifenow.org

Community Blood Ctr Inc
4406 W Spencer St .... Appleton WI 54914 920-738-3131 89
TF: 800-280-4102 ■ *Web:* www.communityblood.org

Community Blood Ctr of the Ozarks
220 W Plainview Rd .... Springfield MO 65810 417-227-5000 89
TF: 800-280-5337 ■ *Web:* www.cbco.org

Community Blood Services
970 Linwood Ave W PO Box 39 .... Paramus NJ 07653 201-444-3900 670-6174 89
TF: 866-228-1500 ■ *Web:* www.communitybloodservices.org

Community Blood Services of Illinois
1408 W University Ave .... Urbana IL 61801 217-367-2202 89
TF: 800-217-4483 ■ *Web:* bloodcenter.org/home.aspx?region=134&sap=2

Community Broadcasters LLC
199 Wealtha Ave .... Watertown NY 13601 315-782-1240 645-10
Web: www.commbroadcasters.com

Community Care 218 W Sixth St .... Tulsa OK 74119 918-594-5200 391-3
TF: 800-278-7563 ■ *Web:* www.ccok.com

Community Care Inc
1555 S Layton Blvd .... Milwaukee WI 53215 414-385-6600 194
TF: 866-992-6600 ■ *Web:* www.communitycareinc.org

Community Coffee Co
3332 Partridge Ln Bldg A .... Baton Rouge LA 70809 800-884-5282 643-8199 296-7
TF: 800-688-0990 ■ *Web:* www.communitycoffee.com

Community College Foundation, The
1901 Royal Oaks Dr Ste 100 .... Sacramento CA 95815 916-418-5115 305
Web: www.communitycollege.org

Community College of Allegheny County
Allegheny 808 Ridge Ave .... Pittsburgh PA 15212 412-237-2525 237-4581* 162
**Fax:* Admissions ■ *Web:* www.ccac.edu
Boyce 595 Beatty Rd .... Monroeville PA 15146 724-325-6614 162
Web: www.ccac.edu
North 8701 Perry Hwy .... Pittsburgh PA 15237 412-366-7000 162
Web: www.ccac.edu
South 1750 Clairton Rd Rt 885 .... West Mifflin PA 15122 412-469-1100 469-6291* 162
**Fax:* Admissions ■ *TF:* 800-273-8439 ■ *Web:* www.ccac.edu

Community College of Aurora
16000 E Centretech Pkwy .... Aurora CO 80011 303-360-4700 361-7432* 162
**Fax:* Admissions ■ *TF:* 844 493 8255 ■ *Web:* www.ccaurora.edu

Community College of Baltimore County
Catonsville 800 S Rolling Rd .... Catonsville MD 21228 410-455-6050 719-6546* 162
**Fax:* Admissions ■ *Web:* www.ccbcmd.edu
Dundalk 7200 Sollers Pt Rd .... Baltimore MD 21222 410-282-6700 285-9903 162
Web: www.ccbcmd.edu
Essex 7201 Rossville Blvd .... Baltimore MD 21237 410-682-6000 840-2824* 162
**Fax Area Code:* 443 ■ **Fax:* Admissions ■ *TF:* 877-557-2575 ■ *Web:* ccbcmd.edu
Hunt Valley 11101 McCormick Rd .... Hunt Valley MD 21031 410-771-6835 162
Web: www.ccbcmd.edu

Community College of Beaver County
1 Campus Dr .... Monaca PA 15061 724-775-8561 728-7599* 162
**Fax:* Admissions ■ *TF:* 800-335-0222 ■ *Web:* www.ccbc.edu

Community College of Denver
1111 E Colfax Ave .... Denver CO 80204 303-556-2600 556-2431 162
TF: 800-621-7440 ■ *Web:* www.ccd.edu

Community College of Philadelphia
1700 Spring Garden St .... Philadelphia PA 19130 215-751-8000 751-8001* 162
**Fax:* Admissions ■ *Web:* www.ccp.edu

Community College of Rhode Island
Flanagan 1762 Louisquisset Pk .... Lincoln RI 02865 401-333-7000 333-7122* 162
**Fax:* Admissions ■ *TF:* 800-494-8100 ■ *Web:* www.ccri.edu
Knight 400 E Ave .... Warwick RI 02886 401-825-1000 825-2394* 162
**Fax:* Admissions ■ *Web:* www.ccri.edu
Liston 1 Hilton St .... Providence RI 02905 401-455-6000 162
TF: 800-494-8100 ■ *Web:* www.ccri.edu

Community College of Southern Nevada Planetarium
3200 E Cheyenne Ave .... North Las Vegas NV 89030 702-651-4759 651-4825 598
TF: 800-630-7563 ■ *Web:* www.csn.edu/planetarium

Community College of Vermont
Bennington 324 Main St .... Bennington VT 05201 802-447-2361 447-3246* 162
**Fax:* Admissions ■ *TF:* 800-431-0025 ■ *Web:* ccv.edu
Brattleboro
70 Landmark Hill Ste 101 .... Brattleboro VT 05301 802-254-6370 257-2593 162
TF: 800-431-0025 ■
Web: ccv.edu/documents/2014/07/brattleboro-parking.pdf
Middlebury 10 Merchants Row Ste 223 .... Middlebury VT 05753 802-388-3032 388-4686* 162
**Fax:* Admissions ■ *TF:* 800-431-0025 ■ *Web:* www.ccv.edu
Montpelier PO Box 489 .... Montpelier VT 05602 802-828-4060 162
TF: 800-228-6686 ■ *Web:* www.ccv.edu

Phone Fax Class

Morrisville 197 Harrell St Ste 2 .... Morrisville VT 05661 802-888-4258 888-2554* 162
*Fax: Admissions ■ TF: 800-431-0025 ■ Web: www.ccv.edu
Newport 100 Main St Ste 150 .... Newport VT 05855 802-334-3387 334-5373* 162
*Fax: Admissions ■ TF: 800-431-0025 ■ Web: ccv.edu/event/newport-open-house
Rutland 60 W St. .... Rutland VT 05701 802-786-6996 786-4980* 162
*Fax: Admissions ■ TF: 800-228-6686 ■ Web: www.ccv.edu
Saint Albans 142 S Main St Ste 2 .... Saint Albans VT 05478 802-524-6541 524-5216* 162
*Fax: Admissions ■ Web: www.ccv.edu
Saint Johnsbury
1197 Main St Ste 3 .... Saint Johnsbury VT 05819 802-748-6673 748-5014* 162
*Fax: Admissions ■ TF: 800-228-6686 ■ Web: www.ccv.edu
Springfield 307 S St .... Springfield VT 05156 802-885-8360 885-8373 162
Web: www.ccv.edu
Upper Valley
145 Billings Farm Rd .... White River Junction VT 05001 802-295-8822 295-8862* 162
*Fax: Admissions ■ TF: 800-431-0025 ■ Web: www.ccv.edu

Community College System of New Hampshire (CCSNH)
26 College Dr .... Concord NH 03301 603-271-2722 271-2725 162
TF: 866-945-2255 ■ Web: www.ccsnh.edu

Community Computer Service Inc
PO Box 980 .... Auburn NY 13021 315-255-1751 178-10

Community Counseling & Correctional Service (CCCS)
471 E Mercury St .... Butte MT 59701 406-782-0417 48-15
Web: www.cccscorp.com

Community Development Digest
8204 Fenton St .... Silver Spring MD 20910 301-588-6380 588-6385 531-7
TF: 800-666-6380 ■ Web: www.cdpublications.com

Community Development Partnership
256 W Beacon Str 256 W Beacon .... Philadelphia MS 39350 601-656-1000 656-1066 139
TF: 877-752-2643 ■ Web: www.neshoba.org

Community Development Trust (CDT)
1350 Broadway Ste 700 .... New York NY 10018 212-271-5080 271-5079 655
Web: www.cdt.biz

Community Educational Television
10902 S Wilcrest Dr .... Houston TX 77099 281-561-5828 738
Web: myedutv.org

Community Eldercare Services LLC
2844 Traceland Dr. .... Tupelo MS 38801 662-680-3148 463

Community Electric Co-op
52 W Windsor Blvd. .... Windsor VA 23487 757-242-6181 245
TF: 855-700-2667 ■ Web: www.comelec.coop

Community First Bank
925 Wisconsin Ave .... Boscobel WI 53805 608-375-4117 375-4119 70
Web: www.cfbank.com

Community First Bank Na PO Box 39 .... Forest OH 45843 419-273-2595 360-2
Web: www.com1stbank.com

Community Food Bank of New Jersey Inc
31 Evans Terminal .... Hillside NJ 07205 908-355-3663 355-0270 48-5
TF: 866-527-1087 ■ Web: www.cfbnj.org

Community Food Coop 908 W Main St .... Bozeman MT 59715 406-587-4039 345
TF: 800-847-4868 ■ Web: www.bozo.coop

Community Foundation for Greater Atlanta Inc
191 Peachtree St NE Ste 1000, 10th Fl .... Atlanta GA 30303 404-688-5525 688-3060 303
Web: www.cfgreateratlanta.org

Community Foundation for Greater New Haven
70 Audubon St .... New Haven CT 06510 203-777-2386 787-6584 303
TF: 877-829-5500 ■ Web: www.cfgnh.org

Community Foundation for the National Capital Region
1201 15th St NW Ste 420 .... Washington DC 20005 202-955-5890 955-8084 303
Web: www.thecommunityfoundation.org

Community Foundation of Greater Memphis
1900 Union Ave .... Memphis TN 38104 901-728-4600 303
Web: www.cfgm.org

Community Foundation Serving Richmond & Central Virginia, The
7501 Boulders View Dr Ste 110 .... Richmond VA 23225 804-330-7400 330-5992 303
Web: www.tcfrichmond.org

Community Foundation Silicon Valley
60 S Market St Ste 1000 .... San Jose CA 95113 408-278-2200 303
Web: www.siliconvalleycf.org

Community Health Accreditation Program Inc (CHAP)
1275 K St NW Ste 800 .... Washington DC 20005 202-862-3413 862-3419 48-1
TF: 800-656-9656 ■ Web: www.chapinc.org

Community Health Charities
1199 N Fairfax St .... Alexandria VA 22314 703-528-1007 838-5975 48-5
TF: 800-654-0845 ■ Web: www.healthcharities.org

Community Health Ctr of Branch County (CHCBC)
274 E Chicago St .... Coldwater MI 49036 517-279-5400 279-8830 374-3
TF: 800-994-6610 ■ Web: www.chcbc.com

Community Health Funding Week
8204 Fenton St .... Silver Spring MD 20910 301-588-6380 531-7
TF: 800-666-6380 ■ Web: www.cdpublications.com

Community Health Systems Inc
4000 Meridian Blvd .... Franklin TN 37067 615-465-7000 353
NYSE: CYH ■ TF: 888-373-9600 ■ Web: www.chs.net

Community High School District 99
6301 Springside Ave. .... Downers Grove IL 60516 630-795-7100 685
Web: csd99.org

Community Hospice 1480 Carter Ave .... Ashland KY 41101 606-329-1890 329-0018 371
TF: 800-926-6184 ■ Web: www.chospice.org

Community Hospice Inc 4368 Spyres Way ...... Modesto CA 95356 209-578-6300 371
TF: 866-645-4567 ■ Web: www.hospiceheart.org

Community Hospice of Albany
445 New Karner Rd .... Albany NY 12205 518-724-0200 724-0299 371
Web: communityhospice.org

Community Hospice of Northeast Florida
4266 Sunbeam Rd .... Jacksonville FL 32257 904-268-5200 371
TF: 800-274-6614 ■ Web: www.communityhospice.com

Community Hospice of Texas
6100 Western Pl Ste 150 .... Fort Worth TX 76107 817-870-2795 371
TF: 800-226-0373 ■ Web: www.chot.org

Community Hospital
5637 Marine Pkwy .... New Port Richey FL 34652 727-848-1733 374-3
TF: 800-749-0933 ■ Web: medicalcentertrinity.com

Community Hospital 2615 E High St .... Springfield OH 45505 937-325-0531 374-3
Web: www.community-mercy.org

Community Hospital 901 Macarthur Blvd. .... Munster IN 46321 219-836-1600 374-3
Web: www.comhs.org

Phone Fax Class

Community Hospital Anderson (CHA)
1515 N Madison Ave .... Anderson IN 46011 765-298-4242 374-3
TF: 800-777-7775 ■ Web: www.communityanderson.com

Community Hospital East
1500 N Ritter Ave .... Indianapolis IN 46219 317-355-1411 374-3
Web: ecommunity.com

Community Hospital of Long Beach
1720 Termino Ave. .... Long Beach CA 90804 562-933-9000 498-4443 374-3
TF: 800-994-6610

Community Hospital of San Bernardino (CHSB)
1805 Medical Ctr Dr .... San Bernardino CA 92411 909-887-6333 887-6468 374-3
Web: www.chsb.org

Community Hospital of the Monterey Peninsula (CHOMP)
23625 Holman Hwy .... Monterey CA 93940 831-624-5311 625-4948 374-3
TF: 888-452-4667 ■ Web: www.chomp.org

Community Hospitals and Wellness Centers
433 W High St .... Bryan OH 43506 419-636-1131 636-3100 2
NYSE: CBZ ■ Web: www.cbizinc.com

Community Imports Inc
8340 W 159th St. .... Orland Park IL 60462 708-364-2600 755
Web: www.communityhonda.com

Community Investors Bancorp Inc
119 S Sandusky Ave. .... Bucyrus OH 44820 419-562-7055 562-5516 360-2
OTC: CIBN ■ TF: 800-222-4955 ■ Web: www.ffcb.com

Community Life 372 Kinderkamack Rd .... Westwood NJ 07675 201-664-2501 532-4

Community Link Inc 1665 N Fourth St .... Breese IL 62230 618-526-8800 242
Web: www.commlink.org

Community Medical Ctr (CMC)
99 Hwy 37 W .... Toms River NJ 08755 732-557-8000 374-3
TF: 888-724-7123 ■ Web: www.barnabashealth.org

Community Medical Ctr
2827 Ft Missoula Rd .... Missoula MT 59804 406-728-4100 374-3
TF: 800-994-6610 ■ Web: www.communitymed.org

Community Memorial Healthcenter
412 Bracey Ln. .... South Hill VA 23970 434-447-3151 374-3
Web: vcu-cmh.org

Community Memorial Hospital
147 N Brent St .... Ventura CA 93003 805-652-5011 667-2895 374-3
Web: www.cmhshealth.org/cmh/index.shtml

Community Memorial Hospital (CMH)
W 180 N 8085 Town Hall Rd. .... Menomonee Falls WI 53051 262-251-1000 374-3
Web: froedtert.com

Community Mortgage Corp
142 Timber Creek Dr. .... Cordova TN 38018 901-759-4400 403
Web: www.communitymtg.com

Community National Bank
4811 Highway 5 .... Newport VT 05855 802-334-7915 70
Web: www.communitynationalbank.com

Community New Life Hospice
5054 Waterford Dr .... Sheffield Village OH 44035 440-934-1458 371
Web: mercyonline.org

Community Newspaper Co Inc
72 Cherry Hill Dr .... Beverly MA 01915 978-739-1300 739-8501 637-8
Web: www.wickedlocal.com

Community Newspapers Inc
6605 SE Lake Rd .... Portland OR 97222 503-684-0360 620-3433 637-8
Web: www.portlandtribune.com

Community Nursing & Rehabilitation Ctr
1136 N Mill St .... Naperville IL 60563 630-355-3300 450

Community of Christ
1001 W Walnut St. .... Independence MO 64050 816-833-1000 521-3085* 48-20
*Fax: Hum Res ■ TF: 800-825-2806 ■ Web: www.cofchrist.org

Community Options Inc 16 Farber Rd .... Princeton NJ 08540 609-951-9900 951-9112 48-6
Web: www.comop.org

Community Oriented Policing Services (COPS)
145 N St NE .... Washington DC 20530 202-514-5328 340-14
TF: 800-421-6770 ■ Web: www.cops.usdoj.gov

Community Partnership of The Ozarks Inc
330 N Jefferson Ave Ste A .... Springfield MO 65806 417-888-2020 726
Web: www.commpartnership.org

Community Pharmacies
16 Commerce Dr Ste 1 PO Box 528 .... Augusta ME 04332 800-730-4840 622-3264* 237
*Fax Area Code: 207 ■ TF: 800-730-4840 ■ Web: www.communityrx.com

Community Preservation Corp, The (CPC)
28 E 28th St 9Fl .... New York NY 10016 212-869-5300 509
Web: www.communityp.com

Community Press Newspapers
394 Wards Corner Rd .... Loveland OH 45140 513-242-4300 637-8

Community Professional Loudspeakers
333 E Fifth St .... Chester PA 19013 610-876-3400 874-0190 52
TF: 800-523-4934 ■ Web: www.communitypro.com

Community Regional Medical Ctr
2823 Fresno St .... Fresno CA 93721 559-459-6000 374-3
TF: 800-431-8455 ■ Web: www.communitymedical.org

Community Renewal Team Inc
555 Windsor St. .... Hartford CT 06120 860-560-5600 48-5
Web: www.crtct.org

Community Resource Federal Credit Union
20 Wade Rd .... Latham NY 12110 518-783-2211 783-2266 219
TF: 888-783-2211 ■ Web: communityresourcefcu.com

Community Services Group (CSG)
320 Highland Dr PO Box 597 .... Mountville PA 17554 717-285-7121 285-2658 353
TF: 877-907-7970 ■ Web: csgonline.org

Community Shores Bank Corp
1030 W Norton Ave. .... Muskegon MI 49441 231-780-1800 360-2
OTC: CSHB ■ TF: 888-853-6633 ■ Web: www.communityshores.com

Community State Bank 208 N Ctr .... Shelbina MO 63468 573-588-4101 588-4408 360-2
Web: www.commbankonline.com

Community State Bank
1414 W 11th St PO Box 219 .... Coffeyville KS 67337 620-251-1313 70

Community Suffolk Inc 304 Second St .... Everett MA 02149 617-389-5200 389-6680 297-7
Web: community-suffolk.com

Community Surgical Supply Inc
1390 Rt 37 W .... Toms River NJ 08755 732-349-2990 477
TF: 800-349-2990 ■ Web: www.communitysurgical.com

Community Teamwork Inc
155 Merrimack St .... Lowell MA 01852 978-459-0551 48-21
Web: www.commteam.org

	Phone	Fax	Class
Community Theater 100 S St ... Morristown NJ 07960 *TF:* 888-278-7769 ■ *Web:* www.mayoarts.org	973-455-1607		748
Community Tissue Services 2900 College Dr ... Kettering OH 45420 **Fax Area Code: 937* ■ *TF:* 800-684-7783 ■ *Web:* www.communitytissue.org	800-684-7783	461-4237*	545
Community Tissue Services 3573 Bristol Pike Ste 201 ... Bensalem PA 19020 *TF:* 800-684-7783 ■ *Web:* www.communitytissue.org	215-245-4506		545
Community Title & Escrow Ltd 2600 State St Bldg D ... Alton IL 62002 *TF:* 800-854-4049 ■ *Web:* communitytitle.net	618-466-7755	466-7782	391-6
Community Transportation Assn of America (CTAA) 1341 G St NW 10th Fl ... Washington DC 20005 *TF:* 800-891-0590 ■ *Web:* www.ctaa.org	202-628-1480	737-9197	49-21
Community Trust Bank NA 346 N Mayo Trl PO Box 2947 ... Pikeville KY 41501 *TF:* 800-422-1090 ■ *Web:* www.ctbi.com	606-432-1414		70
Community Unit School District 200 130 W Pk Ave ... Wheaton IL 60189 *Web:* www.cusd200.org	630-682-2000	682-2227	685
Community VNA 10 Emory St ... Attleboro MA 02703 *TF:* 800-220-0110 ■ *Web:* www.communityvna.com	508-222-0118	226-8939	371
Community Voice PO Box 2038 ... Rohnert Park CA 94927 *TF:* 800-231-3236 ■ *Web:* www.thecommunityvoice.com	707-584-2222		532-4
Community Waste Disposal Inc 2010 California Crossing ... Dallas TX 75220 *Web:* www.communitywastedisposal.com	972-392-9300	392-9301	804
Community West Bancshares 445 Pine Ave ... Goleta CA 93117 *NASDAQ: CWBC* ■ *Web:* www.communitywest.com	805-692-5821		360-2
Communitywide Federal Credit Union 1555 W Western Ave ... South Bend IN 46619 *Web:* www.comwide.com	574-239-2700		219
Commutair Inc 24950 Country Club Blvd Ste 300 ... North Olmsted OH 44070 *Web:* www.commutair.com	440-779-4588	779-4688	25
Comm-Works Holdings LLC 1405 Xenium Ln N Ste 120 ... Minneapolis MN 55441 *TF:* 800-853-8090 ■ *Web:* www.comm-works.com	763-258-5800	475-6656	252
Com-Net Services 7786 S Commerce Ave ... Baton Rouge LA 70815 *TF:* 800-676-2137 ■ *Web:* www.comnetserv.com	225-928-1231	928-1249	224
Comnexia Corp 590 W Crssvlle Rd ... Roswell GA 30075 *Web:* www.comnexia.com	678-323-5000		196
Co-Mo Electric Co-op Inc 29868 Hwy 5 PO Box 220 ... Tipton MO 65081 *TF:* 800-781-0157 ■ *Web:* www.co-mo.coop	660-433-5521		245
Como Textile Prints Inc 193 E Railway Ave ... Paterson NJ 07503	973-279-2950		745-7
Como Zoo & Conservatory 1225 Estabrook Dr ... Saint Paul MN 55103 *Web:* comozooconservatory.org	651-487-8200		97
Comoros 866 UN Plaza Ste 418 ... New York NY 10017 *Web:* www.un.int	212-750-1637	750-1657	781
Comox Air Force Museum 19 Wing comex PO Box 1000 Stn Forces ... Lazo BC V0R2K0 *Web:* www.comoxairforcemuseum.ca	250-339-8102	339-0162	520
Comox Valley Chamber of Commerce 2040 Cliffe Ave ... Courtenay BC V9N2L3 *TF:* 888-357-4471 ■ *Web:* www.comoxvalleychamber.com	250-334-3234	334-4908	137
Com-Pac International Inc 800 W Industrial Park Rd ... Carbondale IL 62901 *Web:* com-pac.com	618-529-2421		553
Compact Information Systems Inc 7120 185th Ave NE Ste 150 ... Redmond WA 98052 *TF:* 800-561-3357 ■ *Web:* www.compactlists.com	425-869-1379		225
Compact Membrane Systems Inc 335 Water St ... Newport DE 19804 *Web:* www.compactmembrane.com	302-999-7996		743
Compact Power Equipment Centers LLC 3326 Hwy 51 ... Fort Mill SC 29715 *Web:* compactpowerrents.com	803-548-4348	548-2762	23
Compaction America 2000 Kentville Rd ... Kewanee IL 61443 *Web:* www.cafcu-il.com	309-853-3571		190
Compaction Technologies Inc 1171 Northland Dr Ste 121 ... Mendota Heights MN 55120 *TF:* 877-860-6900 ■ *Web:* www.compactiontechnologies.com	877-860-6900		192
Compadre LLC 2105 Donley Dr Ste 100 ... Austin TX 78758 *Web:* compadre.com	512-334-1000		393
Compagnie Beaulieu Canada 335 Ch Roxton ... Acton Vale QC J0H1A0	450-546-5000		131
Compak Asset Management 1801 Dove St ... Newport Beach CA 92660 *TF:* 800-388-9700 ■ *Web:* www.compak.com	800-388-9700		401
COMPanion Corp 1831 Ft Union Blvd ... Salt Lake City UT 84121 *TF:* 800-347-6439 ■ *Web:* www.companioncorp.com	801-943-7277		177
Companion Health Services Inc PO Box 1095 ... Guthrie OK 02113 *Web:* www.companionhealth.net	405-282-6288		475
Companion Life Insurance Co 7909 Parklane Rd Ste 200 ... Columbia SC 29223 *TF:* 800-753-0404 ■ *Web:* www.companionlife.com	803-735-1251	735-0736	391-2
Companion Pets Inc (CPI) 2001 N Black Canyon Hwy ... Phoenix AZ 85009 *TF:* 800-646-3611 ■ *Web:* www.cpipets.com	602-255-0166	255-0841	578
Companion Professional Services LLC 1301 Gervais St Ste 1700 ... Columbia SC 29201 *TF:* 800-780-1170 ■ *Web:* www.tmfloyd.com	803-765-1310	765-1431	177
Companions & Homemakers Inc 613 New Britain Ave ... Farmington CT 06032 *TF:* 800-348-4663 ■ *Web:* www.companionsandhomemakers.com	860-677-4948		810
Company C Inc 102 Old Tpke Rd ... Concord NH 03301 *Web:* www.companyc.com	603-226-4460		361
Company Car Chauffeured Transportation 7138 Envoy Ct ... Dallas TX 75247 *TF:* 888-559-0708 ■ *Web:* www.limodfw.com	214-824-0011	827-0136	441
Company of the Cauldron 5 India St ... Nantucket MA 02554 *Web:* www.companyofthecauldron.com	508-228-4016		671

	Phone	Fax	Class
Company Voice LLC 930 Harvest Dr Union Meeting Corporate Ctr Ste 100 ... Blue Bell PA 19422 *Web:* companyvoice.com	610-636-7656		393
Compare Foods 1050 E Main St ... Bridgeport CT 06608 *Web:* www.comparesupermarkets.com	203-366-9060		345
Compas Inc 4300 Haddonfield Rd Ste 200 ... Pennsauken NJ 08109 *Web:* www.compasonline.com	856-667-8577		4
Compass Animal Health Inc 16703 - 116 Ave NW ... Edmonton AB T5M3V1 *Web:* www.compass-ah.com	780-451-6517		476
Compass Bancshares Inc 15 S 20th St ... Birmingham AL 35233 *TF:* 800-266-7277 ■ *Web:* www.bbvacompass.com	205-297-1986	297-7836	360-2
Compass Capital Management Inc 400 Baker Bldg 706 Second Ave S ... Minneapolis MN 55402 *Web:* www.compasscap.com	612-338-4051		528
Compass Career Management Solutions LLC 8509 Crown Crescent Ct ... Charlotte NC 28227 *Web:* www.compasscareer.com	704-849-2500		194
Compass Collective 2150 Button Gwinnett Dr ... Atlanta GA 30340 *Web:* www.compasscollective.com	404-875-6543		8
Compass Computer Group Inc 9408 Ravenna Rd ... Twinsburg OH 44087 *Web:* www.compasscomputergroup.com	330-963-0800		196
Compass Cove Ocean Resort 2311 S Ocean Blvd ... Myrtle Beach SC 29577 *TF:* 800-331-0934 ■ *Web:* www.compasscove.com	843-448-8373	448-5444	669
Compass Enterprise Solutions Inc 223 E State St ... Geneva IL 60134 *Web:* www.compass-solutions.com	630-208-0200		631
Compass Group North American Div (CGNAD) 2400 Yorkmont Rd ... Charlotte NC 28217 *TF:* 800-357-0012 ■ *Web:* www.compass-usa.com	704-328-4000		299
Compass Health Inc 200 S 13th St Ste 208 ... Grover Beach CA 93433 *TF:* 800-213-0154 ■ *Web:* www.compass-health.com	805-474-7010		371
Compass Healthcare Marketers 200 princeton S corporate ctr ... Ewing NJ 08628	609-688-8440		387
Compass iTech LLC 7601 N Federal Hwy Ste 215 A ... Boca Raton FL 33487	561-756-8285		317
Compass Marketing Inc 222 Severn Ave ... Annapolis MD 21403 *Web:* www.compassmarketinginc.com	410-268-0030		7
Compass Minerals International 9900 W 109th St Ste 100 ... Overland Park KS 66210 *NYSE: CMP* ■ *TF Cust Svc:* 866-755-1743 ■ *Web:* www.compassminerals.com	913-344-9200		680
Compass Mktg Solutions LLC 808 P St Ste 300 ... Lincoln NE 68508 *Web:* compassventures.com	402-438-3222		194
Compass Office Solutions LLC 3320 Enterprise Way ... Miramar FL 33025 *Web:* www.compass-office.com	954-430-4590		321
Compass Point Research & Trading LLC 1055 Thomas Jefferson St NW Ste 303 ... Washington DC 20007 *Web:* www.compasspointllc.com	202-540-7300		690
Compass Rose Media 1101 Pacific Ave Ste 230 ... Santa Cruz CA 95060 *Web:* www.compassrosemedia.com	831-457-3533		514
Compass Systems Inc 21471 Great Mills Rd ... Lexington Park MD 20653 *Web:* www.compass-sys-inc.com	301-737-4640		261
Compassion & Choices PO Box 101810 ... Denver CO 80250 **Fax Area Code: 866* ■ *TF:* 800-247-7421 ■ *Web:* www.compassionandchoices.org	303-639-1202	312-2690*	48-17
Compassion Canada 985 Adelaide St S ... London ON N6E4A3 *TF:* 800-563-5437 ■ *Web:* compassion.ca	519-668-0224		48-20
Compassion International 12290 Voyager Pkwy ... Colorado Springs CO 80921 **Fax: Hum Res* ■ *TF:* 800-336-7676 ■ *Web:* www.compassion.com	719-487-7000	481-1893*	48-5
Compassionate Care Hospice 3331 St Rd Ste 410 ... Bensalem PA 19020 *TF:* 800-584-8165 ■ *Web:* www.cchnet.net	215-245-3525	245-3540	371
Compassionate Care Hospice 21-00 Rt 208 S ... Fair Lawn NJ 07410 *TF:* 800-844-4774 ■ *Web:* cchnet.net	201-796-5600		371
Compassionate Care Hospice of Delaware 702 Wilmington Ave ... Wilmington DE 19805 *TF General:* 800-219-0092 ■ *Web:* www.cchnet.net	302-993-9090	993-9094	371
Compassionate Friends PO Box 3696 ... Oak Brook IL 60522 *TF:* 877-969-0010 ■ *Web:* www.compassionatefriends.org	630-990-0010	990-0246	48-21
Compassionate Passages Inc 29869 White Hall Dr ... Farmington Hills MI 48331 *Web:* compassionatepassages.org	248-592-9390		636
CompassLearning Inc 203 Colorado St ... Austin TX 78701 *TF:* 800-232-9556 ■ *Web:* www.edgenuity.com/edgenuity-and-compass	512-478-9600		178-3
Compatico Inc 4710 44th St SE ... Grand Rapids MI 49512 *TF:* 800-336-1772 ■ *Web:* www.compatico.com	616-940-1772		351
Compax Inc 1210 N Blue Gum St ... Anaheim CA 92806 *TF:* 800-783-2420 ■ *Web:* www.compaxinc.com	714-630-3670	632-1344	482
CompBenefits Corp 100 Mansell Ct E Ste 400 ... Roswell GA 30076 **Fax: Cust Svc* ■ *TF:* 800-633-1262 ■ *Web:* www.compbenefits.com	770-552-7101	998-6871*	391-3
Compciti Business Solutions Inc 261 W 35th St Ste 603 ... New York NY 10001 *TF:* 800-331-5114 ■ *Web:* www.compciti.com	212-594-4374		175
Compensation Resources Inc 310 Rt 17 N ... Upper Saddle River NJ 07458 *TF:* 877-934-0505 ■ *Web:* www.compensationresources.com	201-934-0505	934-0737	194
Compensia Inc 1731 Technology Dr Ste 810 ... San Jose CA 95110 *Web:* www.compensia.com	408-876-4025		194
Competency & Credentialing Institute 2170 S Parker Rd Ste 295 ... Denver CO 80231 *TF:* 888-257-2667 ■ *Web:* www.cc-institute.org	303-369-9566		148
Competition Bureau Canada 50 Victoria St ... Gatineau QC K1A0C9 *TF:* 800-348-5358 ■ *Web:* www.competitionbureau.gc.ca	819-997-4282		393

	Phone	Fax	Class
Competition Cams Inc 3406 Democrat Rd. Memphis TN 38118 — *TF:* 800-999-0853 ■ *Web:* www.compcams.com	901-795-2400	366-1807	60
Competitive Cyclist 2222 Cantrell Rd. Little Rock AR 72202 — *Web:* www.competitivecyclist.com	501-663-8796		517
Competitive Engineering Inc 3371 E Hemisphere Loop Tucson AZ 85706 — *Web:* www.ceiglobal.com	520-746-0270		454
Competitive Innovations LLC 2724 Dorr Ave Ste 100G Fairfax VA 22031 — *TF:* 800-642-9240 ■ *Web:* www.cillc.com	703-698-5000		177
CompetitivEdge 196 S Main St. Colchester CT 06415	860-537-6731		624
Competitor Magazine 9477 Waples St Ste 150 San Diego CA 92121 — *TF:* 800-311-1255 ■ *Web:* running.competitor.com	800-311-1255		457-20
Compex 110 Second St. Silverton OR 97381 — *Fax Area Code: 866 ■ *Fax: Sales ■ *Web:* compextech.com	503-873-0188	746-0634*	176
Compex Legal Services Inc 325 S Maple Ave. Torrance CA 90503 — *TF Cust Svc:* 800-426-6739 ■ *Web:* www.cpxlegal.com	800-426-6739	479-3365	445
CompHealth Inc 7259 S Bingham Junction Blvd Midvale UT 84047 — *TF:* 800-453-3030 ■ *Web:* www.chghealthcare.com	800-466-0637		721
Complemar Partners 500 Lee Rd Ste 200 Rochester NY 14606 — *TF:* 800-388-7254 ■ *Web:* www.complemar.com	585-647-5800	647-5800	555
Complete Business Consultants 1901 Jefferson Ave Ste 105 Tacoma WA 98402	253-383-3700		2
Complete Data Solutions LLC 7115 Leesburg Pk Ste 317 Falls Church VA 22043 — *Web:* know-your-data.com	703-536-3282		225
Complete Healthcare Communications Inc 1 Dickinson Dr Ste 200. Chadds Ford PA 19317 — *Web:* www.thechcgroup.com	610-358-3600		194
Complete Home Concepts Inc 4380 Beljoum Blvd Riverside MO 64150 — *TF:* 800-473-0619 ■ *Web:* www.completehomeconcepts.com	816-471-4663		183
Complete Innovations Inc 475 Cochrane Dr Ste 8 Markham ON L3R9R5 — *TF:* 800-565-9931 ■ *Web:* www.fleetcomplete.com	905-944-0863		177
Complete Network Management 649 Enterprise Dr Houma LA 70360 — *TF:* 800-462-8848 ■ *Web:* completenetwork.com	985-580-3040		196
Complete Payroll Processing Inc 7488 SR- 39 Po Box 190 Perry NY 14530 — *TF:* 888-237-5800 ■ *Web:* www.completepayroll.com	585-237-5800		2
Complete Pharmacy Care Inc 4206 Dalrock Rd. Rowlett TX 75088 — *TF:* 866-804-6937 ■ *Web:* www.completepharmacycare.com	972-675-3300		238
Complete Property Services Inc 140 Pine Ave S Oldsmar FL 34677 — *Web:* www.completeproperty.com	727-793-9777		186
Complete Prototype Services Inc 44783 Morley Dr Clinton Township MI 48036 — *Web:* www.completeprototype.com	586-469-9155		454
Complete Pump Service 461 S Irmen Dr. Addison IL 60101 — *TF:* 800-752-0888 ■ *Web:* www.completepump.com	630-628-1600		641
Complete Rx Ltd 3100 S Gessner Rd Ste 640 Houston TX 77063 — *Web:* completerx.com	713-355-1196	355-5404	237
Complete Systems Support 2 Rosemar Cir Ste A Parkersburg WV 26104 — *Web:* www.cssiwv.com	304-428-2143		177
Complete Travel Services 3841 Nostrand Ave. Brooklyn NY 11235	718-934-9400		760
Completech Inc 5960 Stoneridge Dr Ste 204 Pleasanton CA 94588 — *Web:* www.completech.com	925-462-9600		260
Complex Steel & Wire Corp 36254 Annapolis St Wayne MI 48184 — *TF:* 800-521-0666 ■ *Web:* www.complexsteel.com	734-326-1600	326-7421	307
Complex Technologies Corp 518 Old Post Rd Ste 7 Edison NJ 08817 — *Web:* www.complextech.com	732-709-5180		180
Complexe Les Ailes 677 Sainte-Catherine St W Montreal QC H3A3T2 — *Web:* www.complexelesailes.com	514-288-3759		460
Compli 610 SW Broadway Ste 600 Portland OR 97205 — *TF:* 800-481-8309 ■ *Web:* www.compli.com	503-294-2020		177
Complia Health 1827 Walden Office Sq Ste 104 Schaumburg IL 60173 — *TF:* 866-802-7704 ■ *Web:* www.sncoast.com	866-802-7704		525
Compliance Corp 21617 S Essex Dr Ste 34 Lexington Park MD 20653 — *Web:* www.compliancecorporation.com	301-863-8070	863-8290	194
Compliance Professional Resources LLC 11 Hanover Sq Ste 501 New York NY 10005 — *Web:* www.complianceprofessionalresources.com	212-257-6500		194
Compliance Services Group Inc 7619 University Ave Lubbock TX 79423	806-748-0040	748-0030	194
Compmanagement Inc PO Box 884 Dublin OH 43017 — *TF:* 800-825-6755 ■ *Web:* www.compmgt.com	614-376-5300	766-6888	463
Compo Steel Products Inc 3637 N Holton St Milwaukee WI 53212 — *Web:* www.composteel.com	414-962-6800		480
Component Control Inc 1731 Kettner Blvd San Diego CA 92101 — *TF:* 800-558-6327 ■ *Web:* www.componentcontrol.com	619-696-5400		177
Component Design Northwest Inc 2355 NW Vaughn St Portland OR 97210 — *Web:* www.cdn-timeandtemp.com	503-225-0900		361
Component Engineers Inc 108 N Plains Industrial Rd Wallingford CT 06492 — *Web:* ceiprecision.com	203-269-0557	269-1357	454
Component Enterprises Co Inc 235 E Penn St PO Box 189 Norristown PA 19401 — *Fax Area Code: 610 ■ *TF:* 877-232-7253 ■ *Web:* www.componententerprises.com	877-232-7253	272-7040*	815
Component Hardware Group Inc 1890 Swarthmore Ave. Lakewood NJ 08701 — *TF:* 800-526-3694 ■ *Web:* www.componenthardware.com	732-363-4700	364-8110	350
Component InterTechnologies Inc 2426 Perry Hwy Hadley PA 16130 — *Web:* www.cit-hadley.com	724-253-3161		246
Component Repair Technologies Inc 8507 Tyler Blvd. Mentor OH 44060 — *Web:* componentrepair.com	440-255-1793		57
ComponentArt Inc 222 Bay St Ste 1201 Toronto ON M5K1E7	416-622-2923		179
ComponentOne LLC 201 S Highland Ave Third Fl 3rd Fl Pittsburgh PA 15206 — *TF:* 800-858-2739 ■ *Web:* www.componentone.com	412-681-4343	681-4384	178-12
Components Corp of America 5950 Berkshire Ln # 1550 Dallas TX 75225 — *Web:* www.ccoadallas.com	214-969-0166	969-5905	729
Components Distributors Inc 2601 Blake St Ste 200 Denver CO 80205 — *TF:* 800-777-7334 ■ *Web:* www.cdiweb.com	800-777-7334		246
Comporium Communications 332 E Main St. Rock Hill SC 29730 — *TF:* 888-403-2667 ■ *Web:* www.comporium.com	803-326-6064	326-5708	736
Comport Consulting Corp 78 Orchard St. Ramsey NJ 07446 — *Web:* www.comport.com	201-236-0505		180
Composidie Inc 1295 Rt 380. Apollo PA 15613 — *Web:* www.composidie.com	724-727-3466	727-3788	757
Composiflex Inc 8100 Hawthorne Dr. Erie PA 16509 — *Web:* www.composiflex.com	814-866-8616		596
Composite Can & Tube Institute (CCTI) 50 S Pickett St Alexandria VA 22304 — *Web:* www.cctiwdc.org	703-823-7234	823-7237	49-13
Composite Engineering Inc 5381 Raley Blvd Sacramento CA 95838 — *Web:* www.kratosusd.com/about-kusd/about-cei	916-991-1990		610
Composite Manufacturing Inc 970 Calle Amanecer Ste B San Clemente CA 92673 — *Web:* www.carbonfiber.com	949-361-7580		476
Composite Motors Acquisition Inc 15460 Aviation Loop Dr Brooksville FL 34604 — *Web:* compositemotors.com	352-799-2599		518
Composite Panel Assn 19465 Deerfield Ave Ste 306 Leesburg VA 20176 — *TF:* 866-426-6767 ■ *Web:* compositepanel.org	703-724-1128		49-3
Composite Resources Inc 485 Lakeshore Pkwy. Rock Hill SC 29730 — *Web:* www.composite-resources.com	803-366-9700		20
Composite Solutions Corp 1820 W Vly Hwy N Auburn WA 98001 — *Web:* www.compositesolutions.com	253-833-1878		57
Composite Technologies Co LLC 401 N Keowee St Dayton OH 45404 — *Web:* www.ctcplastics.com	937-228-2880		596
Composite Technology Development Inc 2600 Campus Dr Lafayette CO 80026 — *Web:* www.ctd-materials.com	303-664-0394		261
Compositech Inc 5315 Walt Pl Indianapolis IN 46254 — *TF:* 800-447-8372 ■ *Web:* www.zipp.com	317-481-1120		517
Composites Horizons Inc 1471 Industrial Pk St Covina CA 91722 — *Web:* aipaerospace.com/composites-home	626-331-0861	339-3220	113
Composites Innovation Centre 158 Commerce Dr Winnipeg MB R3P0Z6 — *TF:* 800-870-1044 ■ *Web:* www.compositesinnovation.ca	204-262-3400		261
Composites Unlimited Inc 53770 Airport Rd Scappoose OR 97056 — *Web:* www.compositesunlimited.com	503-543-7031		20
Composition Materials Company Inc 249 Pepes Farm Rd Milford CT 06460 — *TF:* 800-262-7763 ■ *Web:* compomat.com	203-874-6500	874-6505	1
Compounding Solutions LLC 258 Goddard Rd Lewiston ME 04240 — *Web:* www.compoundingsolutions.net	207-777-1122		596
Compqsoft Inc 505N Sam Houston Pkwy E Ste 682 Houston TX 77060 — *Web:* www.compqsoft.com	281-914-4428		196
Comprehensive Care Management Corp (CCM) 1250 Waters Pl Tower 1 Ste 602 Bronx NY 10461 — *TF:* 877-226-8500 ■ *Web:* www.centerlighthealthcare.org	877-226-8500		450
Comprehensive Consulting Group 1800 Walt Whitman Rd. Melville NY 11747 — *Web:* www.ccg1800.com	631-249-0500		194
Comprehensive EAP 4 Mt Royal Ave Marlborough MA 01752 — *TF:* 800-344-1011 ■ *Web:* www.compeap.com	800-344-1011		462
Comprehensive Energy Services Inc 777 Bennett Dr Longwood FL 32750 — *Web:* www.cesmechanical.com	407-682-1313		610
Comprehensive Financial Planning Inc 1075 Main Ave Ste 216 Durango CO 81301 — *TF:* 877-901-5227 ■ *Web:* www.compfinancial.com	970-385-5227		194
Comprehensive Health Service 8810 Astronaut Blvd Cape Canaveral FL 32920 — *Web:* www.chef.org	321-783-2720		592
Comprehensive Health Services Inc (CHSI) 10701 Parkridge Blvd Ste 200 Reston VA 20191 — *TF:* 800-638-8083 ■ *Web:* www.chsmedical.com	703-760-0700		391-3
Comprehensive Loss Management Inc 15800 32nd Ave N Ste 106 Minneapolis MN 55447 — *Web:* www.clmi-training.com	763-551-1022		194
Comprehensive Pharmacy Services Inc (CPS) 6409 N Quail Hollow Rd Memphis TN 38120 — *TF:* 800-968-6962 ■ *Web:* www.cpspharm.com	901-748-0470		194
Comprehensive Systems Inc 1700 Clark St Charles City IA 50616 — *Web:* comprehensivesystems.org	641-228-4842	228-4675	451
Comprehensive Tissue Ctr 11402 University Ave Rm 7415 Edmonton AB T6G2J3 — *TF:* 866-407-1970 ■ *Web:* albertahealthservices.ca/pagenotfound.htm	780-407-7510		545

				Phone	Fax	Class
Comprehensive Traffic Systems Inc 4300 Harlan St *Web:* cts-worldwide.net	Wheat Ridge	CO	80033	303-867-4039		174
Compressed Air Systems Inc 9303 Stannum St *TF:* 800-626-8177 ■ *Web:* www.compressedairsystems.com	Tampa	FL	33619	813-626-8177	628-0187	172
Compressed Gas Assn (CGA) 4221 Walney Rd 5th Fl *TF:* 800-783-7890 ■ *Web:* www.cganet.com	Chantilly	VA	20151	703-788-2700	961-1831	49-13
Compression Leasing Services Inc 1935 N Loop Ave *Web:* www.compressionleasing.com	Casper	WY	82601	307-265-3242		172
Compressor Controls Corp 4725 121st St *Web:* www.cccglobal.com	Des Moines	IA	50323	515-270-0857	270-1331	201
Compressor Engineering Corp (CECO) 5440 Alder Dr *TF:* 800-879-2326 ■ *Web:* www.tryceco.com	Houston	TX	77081	713-664-7333	664-6444	172
Compressor Products International 4410 Greenbriar Dr *TF:* 800-675-6646 ■ *Web:* www.c-p-i.com	Stafford	TX	77477	281-207-4600	207-4612	128
Compro Computer Services Inc 105 E Dr *Web:* www.compro.net	Melbourne	FL	32904	321-725-3624		175
ComPsych Corp 455 N City Front Plaza Dr NBC Tower 13th Fl *TF:* 800-851-1714 ■ *Web:* www.compsych.com	Chicago	IL	60611	312-595-4000		462
Compsys Inc 800 Wilcrest Ste 260	Houston	TX	77042	713-961-3999		180
CompTIA (Computing Technology Industry Assn) 3500 Lacey Rd Ste 100 *Web:* www.comptia.org	Downers Grove	IL	60515	630-678-8300	678-8384	48-9
Compton Engineering 156 Nixon St *Web:* www.comptonengineering.com	Biloxi	MS	39530	228-432-2133		256
Comptroller of the Currency 250 E St SW *TF Cust Svc:* 800-613-6743 ■ *Web:* www.occ.treas.gov	Washington	DC	20219	202-874-5000	874-5221	340-18
Comptron Data Inc 6164 S Hwy 92 *Web:* www.comptekinc.com	Hereford	AZ	85615	520-803-0800		180
Compu- Vision Consulting Inc 2050 SR- 27 Ste 202 *Web:* www.compuvis.com	North Brunswick	NJ	08902	732-422-1500		194
Compu-Aire Inc 8167 Byron Rd *Web:* www.compu-aire.com	Whittier	CA	90606	562-945-8971		664
Compucolor Associates Inc 2200 Marcus Ave *Web:* www.compucolor.com	New Hyde Park	NY	11042	516-358-0000		627
CompuCom Systems Inc 7171 Forest Ln *TF Cust Svc:* 800-597-0555 ■ *Web:* www.compucom.com	Dallas	TX	75230	972-856-3600		176
Compu-Cure New Orleans Inc 3528 Holiday Dr *Web:* compucure.com	New Orleans	LA	70114	504-486-7741		180
CompuCycle Inc 7700 Kempwood Dr *Web:* www.compucycle.net	Houston	TX	77055	713-869-6700		175
Compu-data International LLC 431 Nursery Rd Ste A300 *TF:* 866-936-6069 ■ *Web:* www.cdlac.com	Spring	TX	77380	281-292-1333		177
Compudent Systems Inc 10345 Keele St Ste 6 *Web:* compudentinc.com	Maple	ON	L6A3Y9	905-417-9345		175
CompuDyne Corp 2530 Riva Rd Ste 201 *Web:* www.compudyne.com	Annapolis	MD	21401	410-224-4415		692
Compugen Inc 100 Via Renzo Dr *TF:* 800-387-5045 ■ *Web:* www.compugen.com	Richmond Hill	ON	L4S0B8	905-707-2000		395
Compulink Inc 1205 Gandy Blvd N *TF:* 800-231-6685 ■ *Web:* www.compulink.com	Saint Petersburg	FL	33702	727-579-1500	578-8420	814
Compulsive Eaters Anonymous - HOW (CEA-HOW) 5500 E Atherton St Ste 227B *Web:* www.ceahow.org	Long Beach	CA	90815	562-342-9344		48-21
Compu-Mail LLC 3235 Grand Island Blvd *TF:* 800-275-8777 ■ *Web:* compu-mail.com	Grand Island	NY	14072	716-775-8001		195
Compumation Inc 205 W Grand Ave *TF:* 800-860-1921 ■ *Web:* www.compumation.com	Bensenville	IL	60106	630-860-1921		261
CompuMed Inc 5777 W Century Blvd Ste 360 *Web:* compumedinc.com	Los Angeles	CA	90045	310-258-5000		419
CompuNet Consulting Group Inc 6535 Shiloh Rd Ste 300 *Web:* www.ccgi.net	Alpharetta	GA	30005	678-965-6500		180
Compunetics Inc 700 Seco Rd *Web:* www.compunetics.com	Monroeville	PA	15146	412-373-8110	373-8060	625
Compunetix Inc 2420 Mosside Blvd *TF:* 800-879-4266 ■ *Web:* www.compunetix.com	Monroeville	PA	15146	412-373-8110	373-2720	735
Compunite Computers Inc 39 US Hwy 46 Ste 803 *Web:* www.champion-workflow.com	Pine Brook	NJ	07058	973-227-6008		180
Compunnel Software Group Inc 103 Morgan Ln Ste 102 *TF:* 800-696-8128 ■ *Web:* www.compunnel.com	Plainsboro	NJ	08536	800-696-8128		721
CompuOne Corp 9888 Carroll Centre Rd Ste 201 *TF:* 888-226-6781 ■ *Web:* www.compuone.com	San Diego	CA	92126	858-404-7000		196
CompuPros Ltd 2 Bent Tree Twr 16479 Dallas Pkwy Ste 800 *Web:* www.compupros.com	Addison	TX	75001	972-250-4504		177
Compusearch Software Systems Inc 21251 Ridgetop Cir **Fax Area Code:* 703 ■ *TF:* 855-817-2720 ■ *Web:* www.compusearch.com	Dulles	VA	20166	571-449-4000	481-3442*	177
Compusoft Integrated Solutions Inc 31500 W 13 Mile Rd Ste 200 *Web:* www.compusoft-is.com	Farmington Hills	MI	48334	248-538-9494		196
Comp-u-sultants Inc 131 Waterford Rd *Web:* www.comp-u-sultants.com	Island Park	NY	11558	516-897-8477		175
Computac Inc 162 N Main St *Web:* www.computac.com	West Lebanon	NH	03784	603-298-5721	298-6189	178-10
Computan 3350 Merrittville Hwy *Web:* www.computan.com	Thorold	ON	L2V4Y6	905-984-8388		180

				Phone	Fax	Class
Computech Business Solutions 118 N Conistor Ln, Ste B, #321 *Web:* www.ctbsonline.com	Liberty	MO	64068	816-880-0988		180
Computech Consulting Inc 707 W 700 S Ste 201 *Web:* www.i4.net	Woods Cross	UT	84087	801-294-6400		194
Computech Corp 100 W Kirby St Ste 101 *Web:* www.computechcorp.com	Detroit	MI	48202	248-594-6500		177
Computech International Inc 525 Northern Blvd *Web:* www.cti-intl.com	Great Neck	NY	11021	516-487-0101		174
Computech Systems Inc 400 C SouthLk Blvd *Web:* computechsystemsinc.com	North Chesterfield	VA	23236	804-897-7917		195
Computechnique 407 Stonebrook Dr *Web:* computechnique.com	Benton	IL	62812	618-439-4000		175
Computek 9580 Commerce Center Dr *Web:* www.computek.com	Rancho Cucamonga	CA	91730	909-987-8515		180
Computek Inc 355 Crawford St Ste 214 *Web:* www.e-computek.com	Portsmouth	VA	23704	757-399-0320		177
Computer & Communications Industry Assn (CCIA) 666 11th St NW *Web:* www.ccianet.org	Washington	DC	20001	202-783-0070	783-0534	49-20
Computer Age Engineering Inc 867 E 38th St *Web:* www.caeweb.com	Marion	IN	46953	765-674-8551		256
Computer Aid Inc (CAI) 1390 Ridgeview Dr *Web:* www.compaid.com	Allentown	PA	18104	610-530-5000	530-5298	177
Computer Aided Technology Inc 165 N Arlington Heights Rd Ste 101 *TF:* 888-308-2284 ■ *Web:* www.cati.com	Buffalo Grove	IL	60089	888-308-2284		174
Computer Analyst Service & Support 28110 Orchard Lake Rd *Web:* www.cass-tech.com	Farmington Hills	MI	48334	248-538-7374		177
Computer Analytical Service (CASI) 1418 S Third St	Louisville	KY	40208	502-635-2019		180
Computer Arts Inc 320 SW Fifth Ave *TF:* 800-365-9335 ■ *Web:* www.gocai.com	Meridian	ID	83642	208-385-9335		177
Computer Assisted Language Instruction Consortium (CALICO) 214 Centennial Hall *Web:* www.calico.org	San Marcos	TX	78666	512-245-1417		48-9
Computer Business Applications Inc 507 N Mulberry St *Web:* www.cbatech.com	Elizabethtown	KY	42701	270-737-1888		2
Computer Centerline 1500 Broad St *Web:* www.cclprotech.com	Greensburg	PA	15601	724-838-0852		175
Computer Clinic Center Inc 4427 Wisconsin Ave NW *Web:* www.cccits.com	Washington	DC	20016	202-362-9702		175
Computer Components Corp 2751 S Hampton Rd *Web:* compcomp.com	Philadelphia	PA	19154	215-676-7600	464-7876	697
Computer Composition Corp 1401 W Girard Ave *Web:* www.computercomposition.com	Madison Heights	MI	48071	248-545-4330	544-1611	781
Computer Connection of Central New York Inc 11206 Cosby Manor Rd	Utica	NY	13502	315-724-2209		174
Computer Consulting Assoc International (CCAII) 200 Pequot Ave *Web:* www.ccaii.com	Southport	CT	06890	203-255-8966		721
Computer Consulting Operations Specialists Inc 600 Corporate Pointe *Web:* www.ccops.com	Culver City	CA	90230	310-568-5000		736
Computer Crafts Inc 57 Thomas Rd *Web:* www.computer-crafts.com	Hawthorne	NJ	07506	973-423-3500		174
Computer Credit Inc 470 W Hanes Mill Rd Ste 200 *TF:* 800-942-2995	Winston-Salem	NC	27105	336-761-1524	201-0590	160
Computer Designs Inc 5235 W Coplay Rd *Web:* www.computer-designs.com	Whitehall	PA	18052	610-261-2100		535
Computer Dynamics Inc 3030 Whitehall Pk Dr **Fax Area Code:* 704 ■ *TF:* 866-599-6512 ■ *Web:* www.cdynamics.com	Charlotte	NC	28273	866-599-6512	583-9671*	174
Computer Economics Inc 2082 Business Ctr Dr Ste 240 *Web:* www.computereconomics.com	Irvine	CA	92612	949-831-8700	442-7688	637-9
Computer Economics Report, The 2082 Business Ctr Dr Ste 240 *TF:* 800-326-8100 ■ *Web:* www.computereconomics.com	Irvine	CA	92612	949-831-8700	442-7688	531-3
Computer Emergency Response Team (CERT) 4500 Fifth Ave 4500 Fifth Ave *TF:* 800-598-6831 ■ *Web:* www.cert.org	Pittsburgh	PA	15213	412-268-7090	268-6989	668
Computer Engineering 509 NW Fifth St *TF:* 800-473-1976 ■ *Web:* www.thinkcei.com	Blue Springs	MO	64014	816-228-2976		225
Computer Enterprises Inc (CEI) 1000 Omega Dr Ste 1150 *Web:* www.ceiamerica.com	Pittsburgh	PA	15205	412-341-3541	341-0519	721
Computer Equip Svces 261 W Main St *TF:* 800-337-3808 ■ *Web:* netces.com	Bay Shore	NY	11706	631-666-1234		175
Computer Explorers 12715 Telge Rd *TF:* 800-531-5053 ■ *Web:* www.computerexplorers.com	Cypress	TX	77429	800-531-5053		148
Computer Frontiers Inc 5970 Frederick Crossing Ln Ste 101 *Web:* www.computer-frontiers.com	Frederick	MD	21704	301-601-0624		177
Computer Fulfillment 24 Cook St *Web:* www.computerfulfillment.com	Billerica	MA	01821	978-671-0440	671-0450	225
Computer Generated Solutions Inc 200 Vesey St Three World Financial Ctr 27th Fl *Web:* www.cgsinc.com	New York	NY	10281	212-408-3800		180
Computer Guidance Corp 15035 N 75th St *TF:* 888-361-4551 ■ *Web:* www.computerguidance.com	Scottsdale	AZ	85260	480-444-7000		177

Name / Address	City	State	ZIP	Phone	Fax	Class
Computer Heaven 577 Oak Villa Blvd *TF:* 800-548-4128 ■ *Web:* computerheaven.com	Baton Rouge	LA	70815	225-923-0999		175
Computer History Museum, The 1401 N Shoreline Blvd *Web:* www.computerhistory.org	Mountain View	CA	94043	650-810-1010		520
Computer Magazine 10662 Los Vaqueros Cir *TF Orders:* 800-272-6657 ■ *Web:* www.computer.org	Los Alamitos	CA	90720	714-821-8380	821-4010	457-7
Computer Management Technologies Inc 731 Gratiot Ave *Web:* www.cmtonline.com	Saginaw	MI	48602	989-791-4860	791-4928	194
Computer Measurement Group (CMG) 3501 Rt 42 Ste 130 & 121	Turnersville	NJ	08012	856-401-1700		48-9
Computer Modelling Group Ltd 200 1824 Crowchild Trl NW *Web:* www.cmgl.ca	Calgary	AB	T2M3Y7	403-531-1300		539
Computer Modules Inc 11409 W Bernardo Ct *Web:* www.dveo.com	San Diego	CA	92127	858-613-1818	613-1815	625
Computer Office Solutions 7266 SW 48th St *Web:* www.snappydsl.com	Miami	FL	33155	305-663-8620		177
Computer Parts Warehouse 4681 Calle Bolero *Web:* www.thecpw.com	Camarillo	CA	93012	805-987-5882		177
Computer Power Solutions Inc 4644 Katella Ave *TF:* 800-444-1938 ■ *Web:* www.computerpowersolutions.com	Los Alamitos	CA	90720	562-493-4487		180
Computer Programs & Systems Inc (CPSI) 6600 Wall St *NASDAQ: CPSI* ■ *Web:* www.cpsi.com	Mobile	AL	36695	251-639-8100	639-8214	39
Computer Pundits Corp 6515 Cecilia Cir *TF:* 888-786-3487 ■ *Web:* www.computerpundits.com	Bloomington	MN	55439	952-854-2422		180
Computer Repair & Sales 2930 W Main St *Web:* www.computerrepair.org	Rapid City	SD	57702	605-399-0278	342-6141	175
Computer Rescue 2434 Brockton St *Web:* www.computerrescuesa.com	San Antonio	TX	78217	210-366-4811		175
Computer Resource Solutions 1 Pierce Pl *Web:* www.crscorp.com	Itasca	IL	60143	630-467-1010		194
Computer Science & Artificial Intelligence Laboratory (CSAIL) 32 Vassar St Bldg 32 *Web:* www.csail.mit.edu	Cambridge	MA	02139	617-253-5851	258-8682	668
Computer Services Inc 3901 Technology Dr *OTC: CSVI* ■ *TF:* 800-545-4274 ■ *Web:* www.csiweb.com	Paducah	KY	42001	270-442-7361		225
Computer Solutions Inc 4217 S 84th St *Web:* www.csimicro.com	Omaha	NE	68127	402-339-7441		246
Computer Specialists Inc 2101 Gaither Rd Ste 175	Rockville	MD	20850	301-921-2111		175
Computer Spectrum Inc 200 Distillery Commons Ste 250 *Web:* www.computerspectrum.com	Louisville	KY	40206	502-585-8866		180
Computer Task Group Inc (CTG) 800 Delaware Ave *OTC: CTG* ■ *TF:* 800-992-5350 ■ *Web:* www.ctg.com	Buffalo	NY	14209	716-882-8000	887-7464	180
Computer Team Inc 1049 State St *TF:* 800-355-0450 ■ *Web:* www.computerteam.com	Bettendorf	IA	52722	563-355-0426		177
Computer Technology Law Report 1801 S Bell St *TF:* 800-372-1033 ■ *Web:* www.bna.com/computer-technology-law-p6795	Arlington	VA	22202	800-372-1033		531-7
Computer Training Systems 200 W Douglas Ave Ste 230 *Web:* www.ctsys.com	Wichita	KS	67202	316-265-1585		194
Computer Troubleshooters USA 7100 E Pleasant Valley Rd Ste 300 *TF:* 877-704-1702 ■ *Web:* www.technology-solved.com	Independence	OH	44131	800-905-4335		310
Computer Workshop Inc, The 5131 Post Rd Ste 102 *TF:* 800-639-3535 ■ *Web:* www.tcworkshop.com	Dublin	OH	43017	614-798-9505		764
Computer Wrangler On-site Service 4937 320th St *TF:* 800-245-0187 ■ *Web:* www.computerwrangler.net	Stacy	MN	55079	651-462-8809		809
Computerized Assessments & Learning LLC 1202 E 23rd St Ste B *Web:* www.caltesting.org	Lawrence	KS	66046	785-856-3850		194
Computerized Screening Inc 9550 Gateway Dr *Web:* www.computerizedscreening.com	Reno	NV	89521	775-359-1191		476
ComputerJobs.com Inc 1995 N Pk Pl SE *TF:* 800-850-0045 ■ *Web:* www.computerjobs.com	Atlanta	GA	30339	770-850-0045		260
ComputerLogic Inc 4951 Forsyth Rd *TF:* 800-933-6564 ■ *Web:* www.computerlogic.com	Macon	GA	31210	478-474-5593		177
ComputerPlus Sales & Service Inc 5 Northway Ct *TF:* 800-849-4426 ■ *Web:* www.computer-plus.com	Greer	SC	29651	800-849-4426		175
Computers 4 Kids 19 E Broadway St *Web:* www.computers4kids.us	Oviedo	FL	32765	407-796-5111		764
Computers in Libraries Magazine 143 Old Marlton Pk *TF:* 800-300-9868 ■ *Web:* www.infotoday.com/cilmag	Medford	NJ	08055	609-654-6266	654-4309	457-7
Computers Unlimited 2407 Montana Ave *TF:* 800-763-0308 ■ *Web:* www.cu.net	Billings	MT	59101	406-255-9500	255-9595	178-10
Computers Visionaries Inc 1075 Oak St Ste 2 *Web:* computervisionaries.com	Pittston	PA	18640	570-891-0220		180
ComputerSearch Corp 331 Audubon Pkwy	Amherst	NY	14228	716-689-0511		2
ComputerSmith Inc 457 Lazelle Rd *Web:* computersmith.com	Westerville	OH	43081	614-436-0131		177
Computerway Food Systems 635 SW St *Web:* www.mycfs.com	High Point	NC	27260	336-841-7289		296
Computerwise Inc 302 N Winchester Ln *TF:* 800-255-3739 ■ *Web:* www.computerwise.com	Olathe	KS	66062	913-829-0600	829-0810	173-7
Computerworks of Chicago Inc 5153 N Clark St *TF:* 800-977-8212 ■ *Web:* www.booklog.com	Chicago	IL	60640	773-275-4437		177
Computerworks Technologies 711 S Victory Blvd *Web:* www.computerworkstech.com	Burbank	CA	91502	818-244-4484		610
Computerworld Magazine 1 Speen St *TF:* 800-343-6474 ■ *Web:* www.computerworld.com	Framingham	MA	01701	508-879-0700		457-7
Computing Integrity Inc 60 Belvedere Ave *TF:* 800-237-4968 ■ *Web:* cintegrity.com	Richmond	CA	94801	510-233-5400		177
Computing Research Assn 1828 L St NW *Web:* www.cra.org	Washington	DC	20036	202-234-2111	667-1066	48-9
Computing Technologies Inc 3028 Javier Rd Ste 400 *Web:* www.cots.com	Fairfax	VA	22031	703-280-8800	280-8804	178-1
Computing Technology Industry Assn (CompTIA) 3500 Lacey Rd Ste 100 *Web:* www.comptia.org	Downers Grove	IL	60515	630-678-8300	678-8384	48-9
Computrition Inc 19808 Nordhoff Pl *TF:* 800-222-4488 ■ *Web:* www.computrition.com	Chatsworth	CA	91311	800-222-4488		177
Computype Inc 2285 W County Rd C *TF:* 800-328-0852 ■ *Web:* www.computype.com	St. Paul	MN	55113	651-633-0633		627
Compuware Corp 1 Campus Martius St *NASDAQ: CPWR* ■ *Web:* www.compuware.com	Detroit	MI	48226	313-227-7300		178-1
Compuweigh Corp 50 Middle Quarter Rd *Web:* www.compuweigh.com	Woodbury	CT	06798	203-262-9400		684
CompX International Inc 5430 LBJ Fwy Ste 1700 *NYSE: CIX* ■ *Web:* www.compx.com	Dallas	TX	75240	972-448-1400	448-1408	350
Compx Security Products Inc 200 Old Mill Rd *Web:* www.compxnet.com	Mauldin	SC	29662	864-297-6655		295
Comres Telecom 424 SW 12th Ave *Web:* www.comresusa.com	Deerfield Beach	FL	33442	954-462-9600		179
ComResource Inc 1159 Dublin Rd Ste 200 *Web:* www.comresource.com	Columbus	OH	43215	614-221-6348		180
Com-Sal Inc 11723 Northline Industrial Dr *TF:* 800-333-1422 ■ *Web:* www.comsal.com	Maryland Heights	MO	63043	800-333-1422		246
ComSci LLC 485B Rt 1 S Ste 100 *Web:* uplandsoftware.com/comsci	Iselin	NJ	08830	732-632-8000		196
comScore Inc 11950 Democracy Dr # 600 *TF:* 866-276-6972 ■ *Web:* www.comscore.com	Reston	VA	20190	703-438-2000	438-2051	466
Comsearch 19700 Janelia Farm Blvd *Web:* www.comsearch.com	Ashburn	VA	20147	703-726-5500	726-5600	261
Comservco U S A Inc 141 Central Ave Ste W *Web:* www.comservcousa.com	Farmingdale	NY	11735	631-753-2000		175
COMSO Inc 6303 Ivy Ln Ste 300 *Web:* www.comso.com	Greenbelt	MD	20770	301-345-0046		177
ComSonics Inc 1350 Port Republic Rd PO Box 1106 *TF:* 800-336-9681 ■ *Web:* www.comsonics.com	Harrisonburg	VA	22801	540-434-5965	432-9794	639
ComSouth Telecommunications Inc 99 Broad St PO Box 1298 *Web:* www.comsouth.net	Hawkinsville	AK	31036	478-783-4001		116
Comspark International Inc 3265 W Sarazens Cir Ste 201 *Web:* www.comsparkint.com	Memphis	TN	38125	901-758-0261		177
Comspec Corp 822 N Elm St *Web:* www.comspeccorp.com	Greensboro	NC	27401	336-370-1456		194
Comstar Enterprises Inc PO Box 6698 *TF:* 800-533-2343 ■ *Web:* comstar-inc.com	Springdale	AR	72766	479-361-2111	361-1069	48-11
ComStar Networks LLC 1820 NE Jensen Beach Blvd Ste 564 *TF:* 800-516-1595 ■ *Web:* www.comstarnetwork.net	Jensen Beach	FL	34957	800-516-1595		195
Comstock Barbara (Rep R - VA) 226 Cannon HOB *Web:* comstock.house.gov	Washington	DC	20515	202-225-5136	225-0437	342-2
Comstock Historic House 506 Eigth St S *TF:* 800-657-3773 ■ *Web:* mnhs.org/visit	Moorhead	MN	56560	218-291-4211		50-3
Comstock Holding Companies Inc 1886 Metro Ctr Dr 4th Fl *NASDAQ: CHCI* ■ *Web:* comstockhomes.com	Reston	VA	20190	703-883-1700	760-1520	653
Comstock Resources Inc 5300 Town & Country Blvd Ste 500 *NYSE: CRK* ■ *TF:* 800-929-4884 ■ *Web:* crkfrisco.com	Frisco	TX	75034	972-668-8800	668-8812	536
Comstock Telcom 5445 Equity Ave *Web:* www.comstocktel.com	Reno	NV	89502	775-856-2227		246
Comstor Inc 14850 Conference Ctr Dr Ste 200 *TF:* 800-955-9590 ■ *Web:* www.comstor.com	Chantilly	VA	20151	703-345-5100		174
Comstor Productivity Ctr Inc 441 W Sharp Ave *TF:* 800-776-2451 ■ *Web:* www.comstorinc.com	Spokane	WA	99201	509-534-5080	536-0281	496
COMTA (Commission on Massage Therapy Accreditation) 5335 Wisconsin Ave NW Ste 440 *Web:* www.comta.org	Washington	DC	20015	202-895-1518		48-1
Comtec Manufacturing Inc 1012 Delaum Rd *Web:* www.comtecmfg.com	Saint Marys	PA	15857	814-834-9300		295
Comtech EF Data Corp 2114 W Seventh St *Web:* www.comtechefdata.com	Tempe	AZ	85281	480-333-2200	333-2540	173-3
Comtech Mobile Datacom Corp 20430 Century Blvd *Web:* www.comtechmobile.com	Germantown	MD	20874	240-686-3300		225
Comtech Network Systems Inc 1320 Lincoln Ave Ste 4 *Web:* www.comtechnetworks.com	Holbrook	NY	11741	631-981-2694		180
Comtech PST Corp 105 Baylis Rd *Web:* www.comtechpst.com	Melville	NY	11747	631-777-8900		647
Com-Tech Service Group Inc 17827 Commerce Dr *Web:* www.comtechservices.net	Westfield	IN	46074	317-867-4486		480

Name / Address	City	State	Zip	Phone	Fax	Class
Comtech Systems Inc 2900 Titan Row Ste 142 — *TF:* 800-732-0330 ■ *Web:* www.comtechsystems.com	Orlando	FL	32809	407-854-1950	851-6960	647
Comtech Telecommunications Corp 68 S Service Rd Ste 230 — *NASDAQ: CMTL* ■ *Web:* www.comtechtel.com	Melville	NY	11747	631-962-7000		647
Comtel 750 Ensminger Rd Ste 100 — *Web:* www.comtel.us	Tonawanda	NY	14150	716-874-5500		194
Comtel Corp 39810 Grand River Ave Ste 180 — *TF:* 800-335-2505 ■ *Web:* www.comtel.com	Novi	MI	48375	248-888-4730	888-4743	246
Comtrac Services Inc 2250 Lithonia Industrial Blvd — *Web:* comtracinc.com	Stone Mountain	GA	30083	770-934-9595		261
Comtran Corp 330A Turner St — *Web:* comtrancorp.com	Attleboro	MA	02703	508-399-7004		814
Comtrans 2336 E Magnolia St — *Web:* www.gocomtrans.com	Phoenix	AZ	85034	602-231-0102		478
Comtrex Systems Corp 1827 Powers Ferry Rd SE Ste 200 — *Web:* comtrex.co.uk	Atlanta	GA	30339	856-778-0090		614
Comtrol Corp 100 Fifth Ave NW — *TF:* 800-926-6876 ■ *Web:* www.comtrol.com	Maple Grove	MN	55112	763-494-4100	494-4199	176
Comus International Inc 454 Allwood Rd — *Web:* www.comus-intl.com	Clifton	NJ	07012	973-777-6900		729
Comvox Systems LLC 5570-403 Florida Mining Blvd S — *Web:* www.comvox.com	Jacksonville	FL	32257	904-309-6300		196
Comware Technical Services Inc 17922 Sky Park Cir Ste E — *TF:* 800-460-1970 ■ *Web:* comwaretech.com	Irvine	CA	92614	949-851-9600		175
Comwave Networks Inc 61 Wildcat Rd — *TF:* 877-474-6638 ■ *Web:* www.comwave.net	Toronto	ON	M3J2P5	416-663-9700		387
Comworks Multi Media 2192 Yorkshire Rd — *Web:* www.comworksonline.com	Birmingham	MI	48009	248-649-5454		463
Comyns, Smith, McCleary & Deaver LLP 3470 Mt Diablo Blvd Ste A110 — *Web:* csmllp.com	Lafayette	CA	94549	925-299-1040		2
Con Cast Pipe LP 299 Brock Rd S RR#3 — *TF:* 800-668-7473 ■ *Web:* www.concastpipe.com	Guelph	ON	N1H6H9	800-668-7473		183
Con Forms 777 Maritime Dr — *TF:* 800-223-3676 ■ *Web:* www.conforms.com	Port Washington	WI	53074	262-284-7800	284-7878	183
Conagra Brands Inc 215 W Field Rd — *TF:* 877-266-2472 ■ *Web:* www.conagrafoods.com	Naperville	IL	60563	630-857-1000		473
Conagra Brands Inc 1 ConAgra Dr — *NYSE: CAG* ■ **Fax:* Hum Res ■ *TF:* 877-266-2472 ■ *Web:* www.conagrafoods.com	Omaha	NE	68102	402-240-4000	595-4707*	360-3
ConAgra Foods Foodservice Co 5 ConAgra Dr — *TF:* 800-357-6543 ■ *Web:* www.conagrafoodservice.com	Omaha	NE	68102	800-357-6543		297-6
Conair Corp 1 Cummings Point Rd — *OTC: CNGA* ■ *TF:* 800-326-6247 ■ *Web:* www.conair.com	Stamford	CT	06902	203-351-9000		37
Conair Group Inc 1510 Tower St — *Web:* conair.ca	Abbotsford	BC	V2T6H5	604-855-1171		20
ConAm Management Corp 3990 Ruffin Rd Ste 100 — *Web:* www.conam.com	San Diego	CA	92123	858-614-7200		652
Conant Auto Retail Group 18900 Studebaker Rd — *TF:* 888-318-5001 ■ *Web:* www.thecargroup.com	Cerritos	CA	90703	888-318-5001		57
Conaway K Michael (Rep R - TX) 2430 Rayburn HOB — *Web:* conaway.house.gov	Washington	DC	20515	202-225-3605	225-1783	342-2
Conax Buffalo Technologies LLC 2300 Walden Ave — *TF:* 800-223-2389 ■ *Web:* www.conaxtechnologies.com	Buffalo	NY	14225	716-684-4500	684-7433	201
Conbraco Industries Inc 701 Matthew-Mint Hill Rd Ste A — *Web:* www.apollovalves.com	Matthews	NC	28105	704-841-6000		609
Concast Inc 1010 N Star Dr — *Web:* www.concastinc.com	Zumbrota	MN	55992	507-732-4095		183
Concast Metal Products Co 131 Myoma Rd PO Box 816 — *Web:* www.concast.com	Mars	PA	16046	724-538-4000		295
Concensus Consulting LLC 103 Fox Trot Dr — *Web:* concensus.com	Mars	PA	16046	724-898-1888		194
Concentra Inc 5080 Spectrum Dr Ste 1200 W — *TF:* 866-944-6046 ■ *Web:* www.concentra.com	Addison	TX	75001	866-944-6046		463
Concentric Energy Advisors Inc 293 Boston Post Rd W Ste 500 — *Web:* www.ceadvisors.com	Marlborough	MA	01752	508-263-6200		194
Concentrix Corp 3750 Monroe Ave — *TF:* 800-747-0583 ■ *Web:* www.concentrix.com	Pittsford	NY	14534	585-218-5300		113
Concept Art House Inc 785 Market St Ste 1100 — *Web:* www.conceptarthouse.com	San Francisco	CA	94103	415-707-1500		514
Concept Boats Corp 2410 NW 147th St — *TF:* 888-635-8712 ■ *Web:* www.conceptboats.com	Opa Locka	FL	33054	305-635-8712	635-9543	90
Concept Display & Packaging Corp 20 River Terr — *Web:* www.conceptdisplaycorp.com	New York	NY	10282	212-566-2359		233
Concept Dynamics Ltd 1101 State Rd 2nd Fl — *Web:* cdlweb.net	New Glarus	WI	60050	608-422-4860		177
Concept Electronics Inc 6243 Renoir Ave — *Web:* www.ceibr.com	Baton Rouge	LA	70806	225-927-8614		351
Concept Group Inc 332 Minnesota St Ste N10 — *Web:* conceptgroup.com	Saint Paul	MN	55101	651-221-9710		4
Concept Molds Inc 12273 N Us 131 — *Web:* www.conceptmolds.com	Schoolcraft	MI	49087	269-679-2100	679-2157	711
Concept Plastics Inc (CPI) PO Box 847 — *Web:* www.cpico.com	High Point	NC	27261	336-889-2001	889-5752	608
Concept Services Ltd 230 Quadral Dr Ste A — *Web:* www.conceptservicesltd.com	Wadsworth	OH	44281	330-336-2571		737
Concept Studio LLC, The 165 Kings Hwy N — *Web:* www.tcspromo.com	Westport	CT	06880	203-227-7444		195
Concept Systems Inc 1957 Fescue St SE — *Web:* conceptsystemsinc.com	Albany	OR	97322	541-791-8140		261
Conception Abbey PO Box 501 — *TF:* 800-621-7440 ■ *Web:* www.conceptionabbey.org	Conception	MO	64433	660-944-3100	944-2811	673
Conception To Reality Inc 6020 W 91 Ave — *Web:* ctr-inc.com	Westminster	CO	80031	303-225-0230		463
Conceptronic Inc 1860 Smithtown Ave — *TF:* 800-835-0606 ■ *Web:* www.conceptronic.com	Ronkonkoma	NY	11779	631-981-7081	981-7095	695
Concepts 3 Marketing and Management Inc 309 N Waterview Dr — *Web:* www.concepts3inc.com	Richardson	TX	75080	972-690-8412		193
Concepts Av Integration 3712 S 132nd St — *TF:* 877-422-3933 ■ *Web:* www.conceptsav.com	Omaha	NE	68144	402-298-5011		610
Concepts Diversified 2509 Kesslersville Rd	Easton	PA	18040	610-250-9996		390
Concepts NREC 217 Billings Farm Rd — *Web:* www.conceptsnrec.com	White River Junction	VT	05001	802-296-2321	296-2325	261
Concepts of Independence Inc 120 Wall St 9th Fl — *TF:* 800-818-2402 ■ *Web:* www.coiny.org	New York	NY	10005	212-293-9999		196
Concepts to Operations Inc 12502 Trelawn Terr — *Web:* www.concepts2ops.com	Bowie	MD	20721	301-249-2007		196
Concepts Tv Production 53 Indian Ln E — *Web:* www.conceptstv.com	Towaco	NJ	07082	973-331-1500	331-1550	514
ConceptShare Inc 130 Slater St — *TF:* 844-227-7848 ■ *Web:* www.conceptshare.com	Ottawa	ON	K1P6E2	613-903-4431		387
Conceptual Financial Planning Inc 3962 N Richmond St Ste B — *TF:* 800-300-9500 ■ *Web:* www.viainsurance.com	Appleton	WI	54913	920-731-9500		690
Concern America 2015 N Broadway — *TF:* 800-266-2376 ■ *Web:* www.concernamerica.org	Santa Ana	CA	92706	714-953-8575	953-1242	48-5
Concerned United Birthparents Inc (CUB) PO Box 503475 — **Fax Area Code:* 858 ■ *TF:* 800-822-2777 ■ *Web:* www.cubirthparents.org	San Diego	CA	92150	800-822-2777	712-3317*	48-21
Concerns of Police Survivors Inc (COPS) 846 Old S 5 PO Box 3199 — *TF:* 800-784-2677 ■ *Web:* www.nationalcops.org	Camdenton	MO	65020	573-346-4911	346-1414	48-21
Concero Inc 10220 SW Greenburg Rd	Portland	OR	97223	971-222-1900		390
Concerto Marketing Group Inc 128 Hastings St W — *TF:* 877-873-2738 ■ *Web:* www.concertomarketing.com	Vancouver	BC	V6B1G8	604-684-8933		7
Conch House Heritage Inn 625 Truman Ave — *TF:* 800-207-5806 ■ *Web:* www.conchhouse.com	Key West	FL	33040	305-293-0020		379
Conch House Marina Resort 57 Comares Ave — *TF:* 800-940-6256 ■ *Web:* www.conch-house.com	Saint Augustine	FL	32080	904-829-0646	829-5414	379
Conchita Foods Inc 10051 NW 99th Ave Ste 3 — *Web:* www.conchita-foods.com	Miami	FL	33178	305-888-9703	888-1020	296
Concho County PO Box 98 — *Web:* www.co.concho.tx.us	Paint Rock	TX	76866	325-732-4322		338
Concho Resources Inc 600 W Illinois Ave — *NYSE: CXO* ■ *Web:* www.concho.com	Midland	TX	79701	432-683-7443	683-7441	538
Concho Valley Electric Co-op Inc 2530 Pulliam St PO Box 3388 — *Web:* www.cvec.coop	San Angelo	TX	76902	325-655-6957	655-6950	245
Concierge Core Services LLC 4001 S Lkshore Dr Ste 106 — *TF:* 888-624-2643 ■ *Web:* www.conciergecom.com	Tempe	AZ	85282	888-624-2643		116
Concklin Insurance Agency Inc 240 S Wmore Ave — *Web:* concklin.com	Lombard	IL	60148	630-268-1600		390
Conco Inc 4000 Oaklawn Dr — *Web:* www.concocontainers.com	Louisville	KY	40219	502-969-1333	962-2190	198
Conconully State Park 119 W Broadway Ave — *Web:* www.parks.wa.gov	Conconully	WA	98819	509-826-7408		565
Concord Academy 166 Main St — *Web:* www.concordacademy.org	Concord	MA	01742	978-402-2200	402-2210	622
Concord Care Center of Toledo Inc 3121 Glanzman Rd	Toledo	OH	43614	419-385-6616		371
Concord City Hall 41 Green St — *TF:* 800-852-3345 ■ *Web:* www.concordnh.gov	Concord	NH	03301	603-225-8500	225-8592	337
Concord Coalition 1011 Arlington Blvd Ste 300 — *TF:* 888-333-4248 ■ *Web:* www.concordcoalition.org	Arlington	VA	22209	703-894-6222	894-6231	48-7
Concord Confections Ltd 345 Courtland Ave — *TF:* 800-267-0037 ■ *Web:* ic.gc.ca/eic/site/icgc.nsf/eng/home	Concord	ON	L4K5A6	905-660-8989	660-8979	296-6
Concord Cos Inc 4215 E McDowell Rd Ste 201 — *Web:* www.concordinc.com	Mesa	AZ	85215	480-962-8080	962-0707	186
Concord Custom Cleaners 1303 US 127 Byp S Ste A — *Web:* www.concordcustomcleaners.com	Frankfort	KY	40601	859-422-4800		426
Concord Document Services Inc 1321 W 12th St — *TF:* 800-246-7881 ■ *Web:* www.copying.la	Los Angeles	CA	90015	213-745-3175		225
Concord Engineering & Surveying Inc 45 Spring St — *Web:* www.concordengineering.com	Concord	NC	28025	704-786-5404		727
Concord Engineering Group 520 S Burnt Mill Rd — *TF:* 800-938-5760 ■ *Web:* www.concord-engineering.com	Voorhees	NJ	08043	856-427-0200		256
Concord Foods Inc 10 Minuteman Way — *Web:* www.concordfoods.com	Brockton	MA	02301	508-580-1700		296-18
Concord Group Insurance Cos 4 Bouton St — *TF:* 800-852-3380 ■ *Web:* www.concordgroupinsurance.com	Concord	NH	03301	800-852-3380		391-4

	Phone	Fax	Class
Concord Hospital 250 Pleasant St, Concord NH 03301 *Web:* www.concordhospital.org	603-225-2711		374-3
Concord International Investments Group LP 610 Fifth Ave 6th Fl, New York NY 10022 *Web:* www.concordus.com	212-759-2375		690
Concord Iron Works Inc 1501 Loveridge Rd Ste 15, Pittsburg CA 94565 *Web:* www.concordiron.com	925-432-0136		480
Concord Litho Group 92 Old Tpke Rd, Concord NH 03301 *TF:* 800-258-3662 ■ *Web:* www.concordlitho.com	603-225-3328	225-6120	627
Concord Mall 4737 Concord Pk, Wilmington DE 19803 *Web:* www.concordmall.com	302-478-9271	479-8314	460
Concord Mills 8111 Concord Mills Blvd, Concord NC 28027 *Web:* simon.com/default.aspx	704-979-3000		460
Concord Monitor 1 Monitor Dr PO Box 1177, Concord NH 03302 *Web:* www.concordmonitor.com	603-224-5301	224-8120	532-2
Concord Oil Company Inc 147 Lowell Rd, Concord MA 01742 *Web:* concordoilco.com	978-369-3333	287-0157	579
Concord Promotions Inc 2000 Bloomingdale Rd, Glendale Heights IL 60139 *TF:* 800-648-8588 ■ *Web:* store.concordms.com/concordms/index.html	630-893-6453		463
Concord Public Library 45 Green St, Concord NH 03301 *TF:* 800-852-3345 ■ *Web:* www.concordnh.gov	603-225-8670		434-3
Concord Regional Visiting Nurse Assoc Hospice Program 30 Pillsbury St, Concord NH 03301 *TF:* 800-924-8620 ■ *Web:* www.crvna.org	603-224-4093	227-7525	371
Concord Road Equipment Manufacturing Inc 348 Chester St, Painesville OH 44077 *TF:* 800-942-7623 ■ *Web:* www.concordroadequipment.com	440-357-5344		57
Concord Servicing Corp 4150 N Drinkwater Blvd, Scottsdale AZ 85251 *TF:* 866-493-6393 ■ *Web:* www.concordservicing.com	866-493-6393		317
Concord Speedway 7940 US Hwy 601, South Concord NC 28025 *Web:* www.concordspeedway.net	704-782-4221	782-4420	515
Concord Steel Centre Ltd 147 Ashbridge Cir, Woodbridge ON L4L3R5 *TF:* 800-669-2931 ■ *Web:* www.concordsteel.com	905-856-1717		295
Concord Tool & Mfg 118 N Groesbeck Hwy, Mount Clemens MI 48043 *Web:* www.concordtool.com	586-465-6537	465-7301	489
Concord University PO Box 1000, Athens WV 24712 **Fax:* Admissions ■ *TF:* 800-344-6679 ■ *Web:* www.concord.edu	304-384-3115	384-3218*	166
Concorde Asset Management LLC 1120 E Long Lake Rd Ste 250, Troy MI 48085 *Web:* www.concordefinancial.com	248-740-8500		401
Concorde Battery Corp 2009 W San Bernardino Rd, West Covina CA 91790 *Web:* www.concordebattery.com	626-813-1234		20
Concorde Career Colleges 5800 Foxridge Dr Ste 500, Mission KS 66202 *TF:* 800-693-7010 ■ *Web:* www.concorde.edu	913-831-9977	831-6556	800
Concorde Career Colleges Inc *San Bernardino* 201 E Airport Dr, San Bernardino CA 92408 *TF:* 800-852-8434 ■ *Web:* www.concorde.edu	909-884-8891	384-1768	800
San Diego 4393 Imperial Ave Ste 100, San Diego CA 92113 *TF:* 800-693-7010 ■ *Web:* www.concorde.edu	619-688-0800	220-4177	800
Concorde Career Colleges Inc Denver 111 N Havana St, Aurora CO 80010 *Web:* www.concorde.edu	303-861-1151	839-5478	800
Concorde Career Colleges inc Kansas City 3239 Broadway, Kansas City MO 64111 *Web:* www.concorde.edu	816-531-5223	756-3231	800
Concorde Career Colleges inc Miramar 10933 Marks Way, Miramar FL 33025 *TF:* 800-693-7010 ■ *Web:* www.concorde.edu	954-731-8880		800
Concorde Inc 1835 Market St Fl 12, Philadelphia PA 19103 *Web:* www.concorde2000.com	215-563-5555		592
Concordia College 901 Eigth St S, Moorhead MN 56562 *TF:* 800-699-9897 ■ *Web:* www.concordiacollege.edu	218-299-4000	299-4720	166
Concordia College New York 171 White Plains Rd, Bronxville NY 10708 **Fax:* Admissions ■ *TF Admissions:* 800-937-2655 ■ *Web:* www.concordia-ny.edu	914-337-9300	395-4636*	166
Concordia College Selma 1712 Broad St, Selma AL 36701	334-874-5700		166
Concordia Electric Co-op Inc 1865 Hwy 84 W PO Box 98, Jonesville LA 71343 *TF:* 800-617-6282 ■ *Web:* www.concordiaelectric.com	318-339-7969	339-7462	245
Concordia Historical Institute 804 Seminary Pl, Saint Louis MO 63105 *TF:* 800-759-9192 ■ *Web:* www.lutheranhistory.org	314-505-7900	505-7901	520
Concordia Hospital 1095 Concordia Ave, Winnipeg MB R2K3S8 *TF:* 888-315-9257 ■ *Web:* www.concordiahospital.mb.ca	204-667-1560	667-1049	374-2
Concordia International Forwarding Inc 70 E Sunrise Hwy Ste 605, Valley Stream NY 11581 *Web:* www.concordiafreight.com	516-561-1100	561-1323	311
Concordia Language Villages 8659 Thorsonveien Rd, Bemidji MN 56601 *TF:* 800-450-2214 ■ *Web:* concordialanguagevillages.org	218-586-8600		239
Concordia Lutheran Seminary 7040 Ada Blvd, Edmonton AB T5B4E3 *Web:* www.concordiasem.ab.ca	780-474-1468	479-3067	167-3
Concordia Parish PO Box 790, Vidalia LA 71373 *Web:* www.concordiaclerk.org	318-336-4204	336-8777	338
Concordia Publishing House Inc 3558 S Jefferson Ave, Saint Louis MO 63118 *TF Cust Svc:* 800-325-3040 ■ *Web:* www.cph.org	314-268-1000	268-1329	637-3
Concordia Seminary 801 Seminary Pl, Saint Louis MO 63105 *TF:* 800-822-9545 ■ *Web:* www.csl.edu	314-505-7000		167-3
Concordia Theological Seminary 6600 N Clinton St, Fort Wayne IN 46825 *TF:* 800-481-2155 ■ *Web:* www.ctsfw.edu	260-452-2100	452-2121	167-3
Concordia University 1455 de Maisonneuve Blvd W, Montreal QC H3G1M8 *TF:* 866-333-2271 ■ *Web:* www.concordia.ca	514-848-2424	848-2621	785
Concordia University Ann Arbor 4090 Geddes Rd, Ann Arbor MI 48105 *TF:* 888-282-2338 ■ *Web:* www.cuaa.edu	734-995-7300	995-4610	166
Concordia University Austin 3400 IH-35 N, Austin TX 78705 *TF:* 800-865-4282 ■ *Web:* www.concordia.edu	512-486-2000		166
Concordia University Chicago 7400 Augusta St, River Forest IL 60305 *TF:* 888-258-6773 ■ *Web:* www.cuchicago.edu	708-771-8300		166
Concordia University College of Alberta 7128 Ada Blvd NW, Edmonton AB T5B4E4 *TF:* 866-479-5200 ■ *Web:* www.concordia.ab.ca	780-479-9220	378-8460	785
Concordia University Irvine 1530 Concordia W, Irvine CA 92612 *TF:* 800-229-1200 ■ *Web:* www.cui.edu	949-854-8002	854-6894	166
Concordia University Nebraska 800 N Columbia Ave, Seward NE 68434 **Fax:* Admissions ■ *TF:* 800-535-5494 ■ *Web:* www.cune.edu	402-643-3651	643-4073*	166
Concordia University Portland 2811 NE Holman St, Portland OR 97211 **Fax:* Admissions ■ *TF:* 800-321-9371 ■ *Web:* www.cu-portland.edu	503-288-9371	280-8531*	166
Concordia University Wisconsin 12800 N Lake Shore Dr, Mequon WI 53097 *TF Admissions:* 888-628-9472 ■ *Web:* www.cuw.edu	262-243-5700		166
Conco-west Inc 322 E Wetmore St, Manteca CA 95337 *TF:* 800-794-7961 ■ *Web:* www.concowestinc.com	209-239-2110		261
Concrete Company of Springfield 510 N Sherman Pkwy, Springfield MO 65802	417-862-9336		182
Concrete Contractors Interstate 12599 Stotler Ct, Poway CA 92064 *TF:* 800-454-2446 ■ *Web:* seicci.com	858-679-5550		377
Concrete Equipment Company Inc 237 N 13th St, Blair NE 68008 *Web:* con-e-co.com	402-426-4181		183
Concrete General Inc 8000 Beechcraft Ave, Gaithersburg MD 20879 *Web:* www.concretegeneral.com	301-948-4450	948-8273	188-4
Concrete Materials Corp (CMC) 106 Industry Rd, Richmond KY 40475 *Web:* www.concretematerialscompany.net	859-623-4238	623-4255	182
Concrete Materials Inc 3000 W Madison St, Sioux Falls SD 57118 *Web:* www.concretematerialscompany.com	605-357-6000	334-6221	188-4
Concrete Reinforcing Steel Institute (CRSI) 933 N Plum Grove Rd, Schaumburg IL 60173 *Web:* www.crsi.org	847-517-1200	517-1206	49-3
Concrete Sealants Inc 9325 SR- 201, Tipp City OH 45371 *Web:* www.conseal.com	937-845-8776		3
Concrete Structures Inc 12100 NW 58 St, Miami FL 33178 *Web:* www.concretestructures.net	305-597-9393		183
Concrete Supply Co 215 Industrial Blvd, Mocksville NC 27028 *Web:* www.concretesupplyco.net	336-751-9128		182
Concrete Systems Inc 15 Independence Dr, Londonderry NH 03053 *Web:* www.csigroup.com/csi/html/index2.shtml	603-432-1840		183
Concrete Technology Corp 1123 Port of Tacoma Rd PO Box 2259, Tacoma WA 98401 *Web:* www.concretetech.com	253-383-3545		183
Concrete Tie Corp 130 E Oris St, Compton CA 90222 *TF:* 800-531-3355 ■ *Web:* www.concretetie.net	310-886-1000	638-8363	183
Concurrent 4375 River Green Pkwy Ste 100, Duluth GA 30096 *NASDAQ: CCUR* ■ *TF:* 866-978-7363 ■ *Web:* www.concurrent.com	678-258-4000	258-4300	178-8
Concurrent EDA LLC 5001 Baum Blvd Ste 640, Pittsburgh PA 15213 *Web:* www.concurrenteda.com	412-687-8800		177
Condado Vanderbilt Hotel Towers 1055 Ashford Ave, San Juan PR 00907 *Web:* www.condadovanderbilt.com	787-721-5500		707
Condal Distributors 531 Dupont St, Bronx NY 10474	718-589-1100		297-11
Conde Group Inc 4141 Jutland Dr Ste 130, San Diego CA 92117 *TF:* 800-838-0819 ■ *Web:* www.condegroup.com	800-838-0819		196
Conde-Charlotte Museum House 104 Theatre St, Mobile AL 36602	251-432-4722		50-3
Conder Flag Co 4705 Dwight Evans Rd, Charlotte NC 28217 *TF:* 855-344-1500 ■ *Web:* www.conderflags.com	855-344-1500		557
Condit Exhibits LLC 5151 Bannock St, Denver CO 80216 *Web:* www.condit.com	303-744-7167		232
Condley & Co LLP 993 N Third St, Abilene TX 79601 *Web:* www.condley.com	325-677-6251	677-0006	2
Condo Control Central 10 St Mary Stÿ Ste 200, Toronto ON M5X1C7 *TF:* 888-762-6636 ■ *Web:* www.condocontrolcentral.com	888-762-6636		224
Condon & Forsyth Llp 7 Times Sq 18th Fl, New York NY 10036 *Web:* www.condonlaw.com	212-490-9100		445
Condon Oil Co 126 E Jackson St, Ripon WI 54971 *TF:* 800-452-1212 ■ *Web:* www.condoncompanies.com	800-452-1212		579
Condon-Johnson & Assoc 480 Roland Way Ste 200, Oakland CA 94621 *Web:* www.condonjohnson.com	510-636-2100	568-9316	186
Condor Capital Management Inc 1973 Washington Valley Rd, Martinsville NJ 08836 *Web:* www.condorcapital.com	732-356-7323		194
Condor Earth Technologies Inc 21663 Brian Ln, Sonora CA 95370 *TF:* 800-800-0490 ■ *Web:* www.condorearth.com	209-532-0361		194
Condor Outdoor Products 5268 Rivergrade Rd, Irwindale CA 91706 *TF:* 800-552-2554 ■ *Web:* www.condoroutdoor.com	800-552-2554		711
Condor Reliability Services Inc 3400 De La Cruz Blvd Unit R, Santa Clara CA 95054 *Web:* www.crsigroup.com	408-486-9600		45
Condortech Services Inc 6621-A Electronic Dr, Springfield VA 22151 *TF:* 800-842-9171 ■ *Web:* www.condortech.com	703-916-9200		180

Name / Address	City	State	Zip	Phone	Fax	Class
Condotte America Inc 10790 NW 127th St	Medley	FL	33178	305-670-7585		186
Web: www.condottiamerica.com						
Conduant Corp 1501 S Sunset St Ste C	Longmont	CO	80501	303-485-2721		658
Web: www.conduant.com						
Conducive Consulting Inc 3445 Executive Ctr Dr Ste 216	Austin	TX	78731	512-551-0660		463
Web: www.conducivesi.com						
Conductix 10102 F St	Omaha	NE	68127	402-339-9300	339-9627	117
TF: 800-521-4888 ■ *Web:* www.conductix.us						
Conductors Guild 719 Twinridge Ln	Richmond	VA	23235	804-553-1378	553-1876	48-4
Web: www.conductorsguild.org						
Conduit Corp 3212 W End Ave Ste 500	Nashville	TN	37203	615-269-5710		180
Web: www.conduitcorporation.com						
Conduit Pipe Products Co 1501 W Main St	West Jefferson	OH	43162	614-879-9114	879-5185	816
TF: 800-848-6125 ■ *Web:* www.conduitpipe.com						
Condusiv Technologies 7590 N Glenoaks Blvd	Burbank	CA	91504	818-771-1600	252-5512	178-12
TF Sales: 800-829-6468						
Condustrial Inc 105 East N St	Greenville	SC	29601	864-235-3619		260
TF: 888-794-7798 ■ *Web:* www.condustrial.com						
Condux International 145 Kingswood Rd	Mankato	MN	56001	507-387-6576		190
Web: www.condux.com						
Cone & Smith PC 3421 Rainbow Pkwy	Rainbow City	AL	35906	256-413-3057		2
Cone Denim LLC 804 Green Valley Rd Ste 300	Greensboro	NC	27408	336-379-6220	379-6287	745-1
Web: www.conedenim.com						
Cone Drive Operations Inc - A Textron Co 240 E 12th St	Traverse City	MI	49685	231-946-8410	907-2663*	709
**Fax Area Code:* 888 ■ *TF Sales:* 888-994-2663 ■ *Web:* www.conedrive.com						
Cone Inc 855 Boylston St	Boston	MA	02116	617-227-2111	227-2111	636
Web: www.conecomm.com						
Cone Solvents, Inc. 6185 Cockrill Bend Cir	Nashville	TN	37209	615-350-6166		324
Web: conesolvents.com						
Coneco Engineers & Scientists Inc 4 First St	Bridgewater	MA	02324	508-697-3191		261
TF: 800-548-3355 ■ *Web:* www.coneco.com						
Conejos County 6683 County Rd 13	Conejos	CO	81129	719-376-2014		338
Web: www.conejoscounty.org						
Conelec of Florida LLC 3045 Tech Park Way	Deland	FL	32724	386-873-3800		253
Web: www.conelec.net						
Conenza Inc 810 Third Ave Ste 220	Seattle	WA	98104	206-792-4247		225
Web: www.conenza.com						
Conergy Inc 2460 W 26th Ave Ste 280C	Denver	CO	80211	720-305-0700		787
Web: www.conergy.com						
ConEst Software Systems Inc 592 Harvey Rd	Manchester	NH	03103	603-437-9353		177
Web: www.conest.com						
Conestoga Capital Advisors LLC 259 N Radnor Chester Rd Radnor Ct Ste 120	Radnor	PA	19087	484-654-1380		401
TF: 800-320-7790 ■ *Web:* www.conestogacapital.com						
Conestoga Energy Partners LLC 1701 N Kansas Ave PO Box 1178	Liberal	KS	67905	620-624-2901		41
Conestoga State Recreation Area 3800 NW 105th St	Lincoln	NE	68524	402-796-2362		565
Web: outdoornebraska.gov						
Conestoga Supply Corp 11011 Sheldon Rd	Houston	TX	77044	832-391-9431	456-7574*	492
**Fax Area Code:* 281 ■ *Web:* www.conestogasupply.com						
Conestoga Tours Inc 1619 Manheim Pike Ste A	Lancaster	PA	17601	717-569-1111		107
TF: 800-538-2222 ■ *Web:* www.conestogatours.com						
Conestoga Valley School District 2110 Horseshoe Rd	Lancaster	PA	17601	717-397-2421	397-0442	685
TF: 800-732-0025 ■ *Web:* www.cvsd.k12.pa.us						
Conestoga Wood Specialties Inc 245 Reading Rd	East Earl	PA	17519	800-964-3667		115
TF: 800-964-3667 ■ *Web:* www.conestogawood.com						
Conesys Inc 2280 208th St	Torrance	CA	90501	310-618-3737		253
Web: www.conesys.com						
CoNetrix LLC 5214 68th St Ste 200	Lubbock	TX	79424	806-687-8600		177
TF: 800-356-6568 ■ *Web:* www.conetrix.com						
Conewago Enterprises Inc 660 Edgegrove Rd	Hanover	PA	17331	717-632-7722		261
Web: www.conewago.com						
Conexant Systems Inc 1901 Main St Ste 300	Irvine	CA	92614	949-483-4600	370-8990*	696
**Fax Area Code:* 781 ■ *TF:* 888-855-4562 ■ *Web:* www.conexant.com						
Conexess Group LLC 4336 Kenilwood Dr	Nashville	TN	37204	615-242-1014		260
TF: 800-432-7008 ■ *Web:* www.conexess.com						
Conexnet Corp 1020 S Wabash Ave Apt 5d	Chicago	IL	60605	312-692-0898		525
Web: conexnet.com						
Conexus Financial Partners LP 721 Rt 202/206	Bridgewater	NJ	08807	908-231-9101		401
Web: www.conexuscapital.com						
Coney Island Hospital 2601 Ocean Pkwy	Brooklyn	NY	11235	718-616-3000		374-3
Web: www.nyc.gov						
Coney Island Park 6201 Kellogg Ave	Cincinnati	OH	45230	513-232-8230	231-1352	32
TF: 800-788-8008 ■ *Web:* www.coneyislandpark.com						
Confederate Memorial Hall 3148 Kingston Pk	Knoxville	TN	37919	865-522-2371		50-3
Web: www.knoxvillecmh.org						
Confederate Memorial State Historic Site 211 W First St	Higginsville	MO	64037	660-584-2853		565
Web: www.mostateparks.com						
Confederate Museum 929 Camp St	New Orleans	LA	70130	504-523-4522		520
TF: 800-568-6968 ■ *Web:* www.confederatemuseum.com						
Confederate Reunion Grounds State Historic Site 1738 FM 2705	Mexia	TX	76667	254-472-0959		565
Web: www.thc.texas.gov						
Confer Plastics Inc (CPI) 97 Witmer Rd	North Tonawanda	NY	14120	716-693-2056	694-3102	604
TF: 800-635-3213 ■ *Web:* www.conferplastics.com						
Conference & Logistics Consultants Inc 31 Old Solomans Island Rd	Annapolis	MD	21401	410-571-0590	571-0592	184
Web: www.gomeeting.com						
Conference & Travel 5655 Coventry Ln	Fort Wayne	IN	46804	260-434-6600		184
TF: 800-346-9807 ■ *Web:* www.conftvl.com						
Conference & Visitors Bureau of Montgomery County MD Inc 111 Rockville Pk Ste 800	Rockville	MD	20850	240-777-2060	777-2065	206
TF: 877-789-6904 ■ *Web:* www.visitmontgomery.com						
Conference Board Inc 845 Third Ave	New York	NY	10022	212-759-0900	980-7014	49-12
Web: www.conference-board.org						
Conference Consultants 445 El Escarpado	Stanford	CA	94305	650-324-1653		184
Conference Ctr at NorthPointe 100 Green Meadows Dr S	Lewis Center	OH	43035	614-880-4300		377
TF: 844-475-5045 ■ *Web:* www.nwhotelandconferencecenter.com						
Conference Group Inc 1580 Fishinger Rd	Columbus	OH	43221	614-488-2030		184
Conference Group LLC, The 254 Chapman Rd Topkis Bldg Ste 102	Newark	DE	19702	302-224-8255		179
Web: conferencegroup.com						
Conference Hotels Unlimited 51 Harborview Rd	Hull	MA	02045	781-925-4000	925-2474	184
Web: conferencehotels.com						
Conference Management Assoc Inc 45 Lyme Rd Ste 304	Hanover	NH	03755	603-643-2325		184
Conference Management Services PO Box 2506	Monterey	CA	93942	831-622-7772	622-0711	184
Web: www.conferencemanagement.net						
Conference of Radiation Control Program Directors (CRCPD) 1030 Burlington Ln # 4B	Frankfort	KY	40601	502-227-4543	227-7862	49-7
TF: 800-251-3331 ■ *Web:* www.crcpd.org						
Conference of State Bank Supervisors (CSBS) 1129 20th St NW 9th Fl	Washington	DC	20036	202-296-2840	296-1928	49-7
Web: www.csbs.org						
Conference on College Composition & Communication (CCCC) 1111 W Kenyon Rd	Urbana	IL	61801	217-328-3870		49-5
TF: 877-369-6283 ■ *Web:* www.ncte.org/cccc						
Conference Plus Inc 1051 E Woodfield Rd	Schaumburg	IL	60173	847-619-6100		736
Web: conferenceplus.com						
Conference Solutions Inc 520 SW Yamhill St Ste 430	Portland	OR	97204	503-244-4294	244-2401	184
Web: www.conferencesolutionsinc.com						
Conference Technologies Inc 11653 Adie Rd	Maryland Heights	MO	63043	314-993-1400		41
Web: www.conferencetech.com						
Confident Care Corp 3 University Plaza Dr Ste 340	Hackensack	NJ	07601	201-498-9400	498-1556	363
TF: 066-839-2273 ■ *Web:* www.confidentcarecorp.com						
Configure Inc 1800 Hamilton Ave Ste 200	San Jose	CA	95123	408-269-1122		174
Web: www.configureinc.com						
Configure One Inc 900 Jorie Blvd Ste 190	Oak Brook	IL	60523	630-368-9950		261
Web: www.configureone.com						
Confluence Advisors LLC 200 Wallace Rd	Wexford	PA	15090	724-940-1900		70
Web: www.confluenceadvisorsllc.com						
Confluence Energy LLC 1809 Hwy 9	Kremmling	CO	80459	970-724-9839		020
Web: www.confluenceenergy.com						
Confluent Translations LLC 340 Mansfield Ave	Pittsburgh	PA	15220	412-539-1410		7
TF: 888-539-9077 ■ *Web:* www.confluenttranslations.com						
Conforce International Inc 51A Caldari Rd 2nd Fl	Concord	ON	L4K4G3	416-234-0266		499
Conforma Clad Inc 501 Park E Blvd	New Albany	IN	47150	812-948-2118		481
Web: www.conformaclad.com						
Conforma Laboratories Inc 4705 Colley Ave	Norfolk	VA	23508	757-321-0200	321-0201	542
TF: 800-426-1700 ■ *Web:* www.conforma.com						
Confrerie de la Chaine des Rotisseurs 285 Madison Ave	Madison	NJ	07940	973-360-9200	360-9330	49-6
Web: www.chaineus.org						
Confucius Asian Bistro 558 Washington Blvd	Jersey City	NJ	07310	201-386-8898	386-8896	671
Web: confucius558.com						
Congaree National Park 100 National Pk Rd	Hopkins	SC	29061	803-776-4396	783-4241	564
Web: www.nps.gov						
Congdon's Aids To Daily Living Ltd 100 A Ave Ste 15830	Edmonton	AB	T5P0L8	780-483-1762		45
Web: congdons.ca						
Conger & Elsea Inc 9870 Hwy 92	Woodstock	GA	30188	770-926-1131		463
TF: 800-875-8709 ■ *Web:* www.conger-elsea.com						
Congleton Hacker Co PO Box 22640	Lexington	KY	40522	859-254-6481		186
Web: www.congleton-hacker.com						
Conglom Inc 2600 Marie-Curie Ave	Saint-Laurent	QC	H4S2C3	514-333-6666		601
TF: 877-333-0098 ■ *Web:* www.conglom.com						
Congoleum Corp 3500 Quakerridge Rd PO Box 3127	Mercerville	NJ	08619	609-584-3000		291
TF: 800-274-3266 ■ *Web:* www.congoleum.com						
Congregation Beth Elohim 90 Hasell St	Charleston	SC	29401	843-723-1090	723-0537	50-1
Web: www.kkbe.org						
Congregation Mikveh Israel 44 N Fourth St	Philadelphia	PA	19106	215-922-5446	922-1550	50-1
Web: www.mikvehisrael.org						
Congregation Rodeph Sholom 7 W 83rd St	New York	NY	10024	212-362-8800		48-20
Web: www.rodephsholom.org						
Congress Daily 600 New Hampshire Ave The Watergate	Washington	DC	20037	202-266-7000		531-7
Web: nationaljournal.com						
Congress of Racial Equality (CORE) 730 W Cheyenne Ave Ste 150	North Las Vegas	NV	89030	702-637-7968	637-7953	48-8
Web: www.congressofracialequality.org						

				Phone	Fax	Class
Congress of Russian-Americans						
2460 Sutter St.	San Francisco	CA	94115	415-928-5841		48-14
Web: www.russian-americans.org						
Congress Plaza Hotel & Convention Ctr						
520 S Michigan Ave	Chicago	IL	60605	312-427-3800	427-2919	379
TF: 800-635-1666 ■ *Web:* www.congressplazahotel.com						
Congress Watch						
215 Pennsylvania Ave SE	Washington	DC	20003	202-546-4996	547-7392	48-7
TF: 800-289-3787 ■ *Web:* www.citizen.org/congress						
Congress.Org 77 K St NE	Washington	DC	20002	202-650-6500		397
Web: www.congress.org						
Congressional Budget Office						
Ford House Office Bldg 4th Fl 2D St	Washington	DC	20515	202-226-2602		342
Web: www.cbo.gov						
Congressional Quarterly House Action Reports						
77 K St NE	Washington	DC	20002	202-650-6500		531-7
Web: cqrollcall.com						
Congruent Investment Partners LLC						
3400 Carlisle Sty Ste 430	Dallas	TX	75204	214-760-7411		528
Web: www.congruentinv.com						
Conifer Park 79 Glenridge Rd	Schenectady	NY	12302	518-399-6446	952-8228	726
TF: 800-989-6446 ■ *Web:* www.coniferpark.com						
Conifex Timber Inc						
980 700 W Georgia St PO Box 10070	Vancouver	BC	V7Y1B6	604-688-9090		279
TF: 866-301-2949 ■ *Web:* www.conifex.com						
Conimar Corp 1724 NE 22nd Ave	Ocala	FL	34470	352-732-7235		596
Web: www.conimar.com						
Conine Clubhouse						
1005 Joe DiMaggio Dr	Hollywood	FL	33021	954-265-5324		372
TF: 866-532-4362 ■ *Web:* www.jdch.com						
Coni-Seal Inc 1980 Swarthmore Ave	Lakewood	NJ	08701	732-363-2550		247
Web: www.coni-seal.com						
Conitex-Sonoco Usainc						
1302 Industrial Pike	Gastonia	NC	28052	704-864-5406		125
Web: www.conitex.com						
CONIX Systems Inc						
7252 Main St	Manchester Center	VT	05255	800-332-1899		177
TF: 800-332-1899 ■ *Web:* conix.com						
Conjur Inc 460 Totten Pond Rd	Waltham	MA	02451	855-648-5919		387
TF: 855-648-5919 ■ *Web:* www.conjur.net						
Conklin & de Decker 62B Cranberry Hwy	Orleans	MA	02653	508-255-5975		463
Web: www.conklindd.com						
Conklin Company Inc 551 Valley Pk Dr	Shakopee	MN	55379	952-445-6010		366
TF: 800-888-8838 ■ *Web:* www.conklin.com						
Conklin Metal Industries						
236 Moore St, SE	Atlanta	GA	30312	404-688-4510		697
Web: www.conklinmetal.com						
Conklin Office Furniture						
56 N Canal St	Holyoke	MA	01040	413-315-6777		320
Web: www.conklinoffice.com						
Conlan Co, The 1800 Pkwy Pl Ste 1010	Marietta	GA	30067	770-423-8000	423-8010	186
Web: www.conlancompany.com						
Conley Publishing Group Ltd						
119 Monroe St	Beaver Dam	WI	53916	920-885-7800		627
Conley Transport Ii Inc						
2104 Eastline Rd	Searcy	AR	72143	800-338-8700	268-6810*	449
**Fax Area Code:* 501 ■ *TF:* 800-338-8700 ■ *Web:* www.conleytransport.com						
Conlin Travel Inc						
3270 Washtenaw Ave	Ann Arbor	MI	48104	734-677-0900	677-0901	771
TF: 800-426-6546 ■ *Web:* www.conlintravel.com						
Conlin's Digital Print & Copy Ctr						
52 W Lancaster Ave	Malvern	PA	19355	610-647-6100		113
Web: www.conlinscopy.com						
Conlin's Furniture Inc						
739 S 20th St W	Billings	MT	59102	406-656-4900		321
Web: www.conlins.com						
Conlon Construction Company Inc						
1100 Rockdale Rd	Dubuque	IA	52003	563-583-1724		186
Web: www.conlonco.com						
Conmaco/Rector LP						
1602 Engineers Rd	Belle Chasse	LA	70037	504-394-7330	393-8715	358
Web: www.conmaco.com						
Conmed Corp 525 French Rd	Utica	NY	13502	315-797-8375	438-3051*	476
NASDAQ: CNMD ■ **Fax Area Code:* 800 ■ **Fax:* Cust Svc ■ *TF:* 800-448-6506 ■ *Web:* www.conmed.com						
ConMed Endoscopic Technologie						
525 French Rd	Utica	NY	13502	315-797-8375	797-0321	476
TF: 800-225-1332 ■ *Web:* www.conmed.com						
CONMED Linvatec 11311 Concept Blvd	Largo	FL	33773	727-392-6464	399-5256*	476
**Fax:* Cust Svc ■ *TF Cust Svc:* 800-448-6506 ■ *Web:* www.conmed.com						
Conn's Inc 3295 College St	Beaumont	TX	77701	409-832-1696		35
NASDAQ: CONN ■ *TF Cust Svc:* 800-511-5750 ■ *Web:* www.conns.com						
Connacher Oil & Gas Ltd						
640 Fifth Ave SW	Calgary	AB	T2P0B2	403-538-6201		536
Web: www.connacheroil.com						
Conneaut Lake Park						
12382 Center St	Conneaut Lake	PA	16316	814-382-5115		32
Web: www.conneautlakepark.com						
Conneaut Savings Bank						
305 Main St PO Box 740	Conneaut	OH	44030	440-599-8121	593-6446	70
TF: 888-453-2311 ■ *Web:* www.conneautsavings.com						
Conneaut School District						
219 W School Dr	Linesville	PA	16424	814-683-5900		685
Web: www.conneautsd.org						
Connect America LLC 816 Pkwy	Broomall	PA	19008	800-654-6100	353-1350*	475
**Fax Area Code:* 610 ■ *TF:* 800-654-6100 ■ *Web:* connectamerica.com						
Connect PR 1 Market St 36th Fl	San Francisco	CA	94105	415-222-9691		636
TF: 800-455-8855 ■ *Web:* www.connectmarketing.com						
Connect Public Relations						
80 East 100 North	Provo	UT	84606	801-373-7888		636
Web: www.connectmarketing.com						
Connect Tech Inc 42 Arrow Rd	Guelph	ON	N1K1S6	519-836-1291		180
TF: 800-426-8979 ■ *Web:* www.connecttech.com						
CONNECT: The Knowledge Network Corp						
5602 S Nevada St	Littleton	CO	80120	303-730-7171		180
Web: www.xtivia.com						
Connect802 Corp						
111 Deerwood Rd Ste 200	San Ramon	CA	94583	925-552-0802		116
Web: www.connect802.com						

				Phone	Fax	Class
Connect-Air International Inc						
4240 'B' St NW	Auburn	WA	98001	253-813-5599		492
TF: 800-247-1978 ■ *Web:* www.connect-air.com						
ConnectEd 2150 Shattuck Ste 1200	Berkeley	CA	94704	510-849-4945		305
Web: www.connectedcalifornia.org						
Connected Nation						
444 N Capitol St, NW	Bowling Green	KY	20001	877-846-7710		466
TF: 877-846-7710 ■ *Web:* www.connectednation.com						
ConnectiCare Inc						
175 Scott Swamp Rd	Farmington	CT	06032	860-674-5700	674-5728	391-3
TF Cust Svc: 800-251-7722 ■ *Web:* www.connecticare.com						
Connecticut						
Accountancy Board 30 Trinity St	Hartford	CT	06106	860-509-6179	509-6247	339-7
Web: www.sots.ct.gov						
Administrative Services Dept						
165 Capitol Ave 4th Fl	Hartford	CT	06106	860-713-5172	713-7479	339-7
Web: www.das.state.ct.us						
Aging Commission						
55 Farmington Ave Ste 508	Hartford	CT	06106	860-424-5274	424-5301	339-7
TF: 866-218-6631 ■ *Web:* www.cga.ct.gov						
Agriculture Dept						
450 Columbus Blvd Ste 701	Hartford	CT	06103	860-713-2500	713-2515	339-7
Web: www.ct.gov/doag						
Attorney General 55 Elm St	Hartford	CT	06106	860-808-5318	808-5387	339-7
Web: www.ct.gov						
Banking Dept 260 Constitution Plaza	Hartford	CT	06103	860-240-8230	240-8295	339-7
TF: 800-831-7225 ■ *Web:* www.ct.gov						
Chief Medical Examiner						
11 Shuttle Rd	Farmington	CT	06032	860-679-3980	679-1257	339-7
TF: 800-842-8820 ■ *Web:* www.ct.gov						
Child Support Assistance						
55 Farmington Ave	Hartford	CT	06106	800-228-5437		339-7
TF: 800-228-5437 ■ *Web:* www.ct.gov						
Commission on Culture & Tourism						
1 Constitution Plaza	Hartford	CT	06103	860-256-2800	256-2811	339-7
Web: www.cultureandtourism.org						
Consumer Protection Dept						
450 ColumbusyBlvd Ste 901	Hartford	CT	06106	860-713-6100	707-1966	339-7
TF: 800-842-2649 ■ *Web:* www.ct.gov						
Correction Dept						
24 Wolcott Hill Rd	Wethersfield	CT	06109	860-692-7780	692-7783	339-7
Web: www.ct.gov/doc						
Department of Administrative Services, The						
101 E River Dr Rm 1002	East Hartford	CT	06108	860-713-5100		339-7
Web: www.das.ct.gov						
Department of Education						
PO Box 150471	Hartford	CT	06115	860-713-6969	713-7017	339-7
Web: www.ct.gov						
Department of Energy and Environmental Protection						
79 Elm St	Hartford	CT	06106	860-424-3000	424-4070	339-7
Web: www.ct.gov						
Economic & Community Development Dept						
505 Hudson St	Hartford	CT	06106	860-270-8000	270-8188	339-7
Web: www.ct.gov						
Emergency Management and Homeland Security Div						
25 Sigourney St Fl 6	Hartford	CT	06106	203-525-6959	256-0815*	339-7
**Fax Area Code:* 860 ■ *TF:* 800-397-8876 ■ *Web:* www.ct.gov/hls						
Environmental and Energy Protection Dept						
79 Elm St	Hartford	CT	06106	860-424-3000		339-7
Web: www.ct.gov/deep						
Ethics Commission						
18-20 Trinity St Ste 205	Hartford	CT	06106	860-263-2400	263-2402	265
Web: www.ct.gov/ethics/site/default.asp						
General Assembly						
300 Capitol Ave Rm 5100	Hartford	CT	06106	860-240-0100		339-7
Web: www.cga.ct.gov						
Governor 210 Capitol Ave	Hartford	CT	06106	860-240-0222	240-8627	339-7
Web: www.ct.gov						
Higher Education Dept						
450 Columbus Blvd Ste 510	Hartford	CT	06105	860-947-1800	947-1310	339-7
TF: 800-842-0229 ■ *Web:* www.ctdhe.org						
Housing Finance Authority 999 W St	Rocky Hill	CT	06067	860-721-9501		339-7
Web: www.chfa.org						
Insurance Dept 153 Market St	Hartford	CT	06103	860-297-3800	566-7410	339-7
TF: 800-203-3447 ■ *Web:* www.ct.gov						
Judicial Branch 231 Capitol Ave	Hartford	CT	06106	860-757-2100	757-2130	339-7
Web: www.jud.state.ct.us						
Labor Dept 200 Folly Brook Blvd	Wethersfield	CT	06109	860-263-6000		259
Web: www.ctdol.state.ct.us						
Lieutenant Governor						
210 Capitol Ave Rm 304	Hartford	CT	06106	860-524-7384		339-7
Web: www.ct.gov						
Motor Vehicles Dept 60 State St	Wethersfield	CT	06161	860-263-5700	524-4898	339-7
Web: www.ct.gov						
Parole Board 55 W Main St Ste 520	Waterbury	CT	06702	203-805-6605	805-6652	339-7
Web: www.ct.gov						
Public Health Dept 410 Capitol Ave	Hartford	CT	06134	860-509-8000	509-7111	339-7
Web: www.ct.gov						
Public Utility Control Dept						
10 Franklin Sq	New Britain	CT	06051	860-827-1553		339-7
TF: 800-382-4586 ■ *Web:* www.ct.gov						
Real Estate & Professional Trades Div						
165 Capitol Ave	Hartford	CT	06106	860-713-6100		339-7
TF: 800-842-2649 ■ *Web:* www.ct.gov						
Rehabilitation Services Bureau						
55 Farmington Ave Fl 12	Hartford	CT	06105	860-424-4844	424-4850	339-7
TF: 800-537-2549 ■ *Web:* www.ct.gov/brs/site/default.asp						
Secretary of State 30 Trinity St	Hartford	CT	06106	860-509-6200	509-6209	339-7
Web: www.sots.ct.gov						
State Police Div						
1111 Country Club Rd	Middletown	CT	06457	860-685-8000	685-8354	339-7
Web: ct.gov						
Supreme Court 231 Capitol Ave	Hartford	CT	06106	860-757-2200		339-7
Web: www.jud.state.ct.us/external/supapp						
Transportation Dept						
2800 Berlin Tpke	Newington	CT	06111	860-594-2000		339-7
Web: www.ct.gov						
Treasurer 55 Elm St	Hartford	CT	06106	860-702-3000		339-7
TF: 800-618-3404 ■ *Web:* www.ott.ct.gov						

Name / Address	City	State	Zip	Phone	Fax	Class
Veterans Affairs Dept 287 W St	Rocky Hill	CT	06067	860-721-5891	721-5904	339-7
TF: 800-447-0961 ■ *Web:* www.ct.gov/ctva						
Victim Services Office 225 Spring St 4th Fl	Wethersfield	CT	06109	800-822-8428		339-7
TF: 800-822-8428 ■ *Web:* www.jud.state.ct.us						
Weights & Measures Div 450 Columbus Blvd	Hartford	CT	06103	860-713-6100		339-7
TF: 800-842-2649 ■ *Web:* www.ct.gov						
Workers' Compensation Commission 21 Oak St 4th Fl	Hartford	CT	06106	860-493-1500	247-1361	339-7
TF: 800-223-9675 ■ *Web:* www.wcc.state.ct.us						
Connecticut Assn of Realtors 111 Founders Plaza Ste 1101	East Hartford	CT	06108	860-290-6601	290-6615	656
TF: 800-335-4862 ■ *Web:* www.ctrealtor.com						
Connecticut Audubon Society Birdcraft Museum & Sanctuary 314 Unquowa Rd	Fairfield	CT	06824	203-259-0416		520
Web: www.ctaudubon.org						
Connecticut Audubon Society Nature Ctr 2325 Burr St	Fairfield	CT	06824	203-259-6305	254-7365	50-5
Web: www.ctaudubon.org						
Connecticut Ballet 20 Acosta St	Stamford	CT	06902	203-964-1211		573-1
Web: connecticutballet.org						
Connecticut Bank & Trust Co 58 State House Sq	Hartford	CT	06103	860-246-5200		360-2
Web: www.berkshirebank.com						
Connecticut Bar Assn 30 Bank St PO Box 350	New Britain	CT	06050	860-223-4400	223-4400	72
Web: www.ctbar.org						
Connecticut Business & Industry Assn 350 Church St	Hartford	CT	06103	860-244-1900	278-8562	140
TF: 800-599-4816 ■ *Web:* www.cbia.com						
Connecticut Children's Medical Ctr 282 Washington St	Hartford	CT	06106	860-545-9000		374-1
Web: www.connecticutchildrens.org						
Connecticut Children's Museum 22 Wall St	New Haven	CT	06511	203-562-5437	787-9414	521
Web: www.childrensbuilding.org						
Connecticut College 270 Mohegan Ave	New London	CT	06320	860-439-2000	439-4301*	166
**Fax:* Admissions ■ *TF:* 800-892-3363 ■ *Web:* www.conncoll.edu						
Connecticut College Arboretum 270 Mohegan Ave PO Box 5201	New London	CT	06320	860-447-1911	439-5482	97
Web: www.conncoll.edu						
Connecticut Democratic Party 30 Arbor St	Hartford	CT	06106	860-560-1775	387-0147	616-1
TF: 800-995-3386 ■ *Web:* www.ctdems.org						
Connecticut Historical Society Museum 1 Elizabeth St	Hartford	CT	06105	860-236-5621	236-2664	520
Web: www.chs.org						
Connecticut Hospice 100 Double Beach Rd	Branford	CT	06405	203-315-7500	315-7561*	371
**Fax:* Hum Res ■ *Web:* www.hospice.com						
Connecticut Hypodermics Inc 519 Main St	Yalesville	CT	06492	203-265-4881	284-1520	477
Web: www.connhypo.com						
Connecticut Innovations Inc 865 Brook St 3rd Fl	Rocky Hill	CT	06067	860-563-5851	563-4877	792
TF: 800-733-4763 ■ *Web:* www.ctinnovations.com						
Connecticut Juvenile Training School 1225 Silver St	Middletown	CT	06457	860-638-2400		412
Connecticut Laminating Company Inc 162 James St	New Haven	CT	06513	203-787-2184	787-4073	599
TF: 800-753-9119 ■ *Web:* www.ctlaminating.com						
Connecticut Lawyer Magazine 30 Bank St PO Box 350	New Britain	CT	06050	860-223-4400	223-4488	457-15
Web: www.ctbar.org						
Connecticut Magazine 100 Gando Dr	New Haven	CT	06513	203-789-5300	789-5255	457-22
TF: 877-396-8937 ■ *Web:* www.connecticutmag.com						
Connecticut Medical Insurance Co (CMIC) 80 Glastonbury Blvd 3rd Fl	Glastonbury	CT	06033	860-633-7788		391-5
Connecticut Medicine Magazine 160 St Ronan St	New Haven	CT	06511	203-865-0587	865-4997	457-16
TF: 800-406-1527 ■ *Web:* www.csms.org						
Connecticut Natural Gas Corp (CNG) 76 Meadow St	East Hartford	CT	06108	860-727-3000		787
Web: www.cngcorp.com						
Connecticut Nurses Assn (CNA) 377 Research Pkwy Ste 2D	Meriden	CT	06450	203-238-1207	238-3437	533
Web: www.ctnurses.org						
Connecticut On-Line Computer Ctr Inc 100 Executive Blvd	Southington	CT	06489	860-678-0444	677-1169	225
Web: www.cocc.com						
Connecticut Pharmacists Assn 35 Cold Spring Rd Ste 121	Rocky Hill	CT	06067	860-563-4619	257-8241	585
Web: www.ctpharmacists.org						
Connecticut Post 410 State St	Bridgeport	CT	06604	203-333-0161	367-8158	532-2
TF Edit: 800-542-3354 ■ *Web:* www.ctpost.com						
Connecticut Public Broadcasting Inc (CPBI) 1049 Asylum Ave	Hartford	CT	06105	860-278-5310		632
TF: 877-444-4485 ■ *Web:* www.cpbn.org						
Connecticut Public Interest Research Group (CONNPIRG) 2074 Park St	Hartford	CT	06106	860-233-7554	233-7574	633
Web: www.connpirg.org						
Connecticut Radio Holding LLC 1208 Cromwell Ave Ste C	Rocky Hill	CT	06067	860-563-4867		647
Web: connradio.com						
Connecticut Republican Party 31 Pratt St	Hartford	CT	06103	860-422-8211	422-8175	616-2
Web: ct.gop						
Connecticut River Greenway State Park 136 Damon Rd	NorthHampton	MA	01060	413-586-8706		565
Web: mass.gov						
Connecticut Science Center Inc 250 Columbus Blvd	Hartford	CT	06103	860-724-3623		520
TF: 800-411-9671 ■ *Web:* www.ctsciencecenter.org						
Connecticut Spring & Stamping Corp 48 Spring Ln	Farmington	CT	06034	860-677-1341	677-7199*	719
**Fax:* Cust Svc ■ *TF:* 800-556-7620 ■ *Web:* ctspring.com						
Connecticut State Library 231 Capitol Ave	Hartford	CT	06106	860-757-6510	757-6503	434-5
TF: 866-886-4478 ■ *Web:* www.ctstatelibrary.org						
Connecticut State Medical Society 160 St Ronan St	New Haven	CT	06511	203-865-0587		474
TF: 800-406-1527 ■ *Web:* www.csms.org						
Connecticut State Museum of Natural History UConn Unit 4023	Storrs	CT	06269	860-486-4460	486-0827	520
Web: www.mnh.uconn.edu						
Connecticut State University System 39 Woodland St	Hartford	CT	06105	860-493-0000		786
Web: www.ct.edu						
Connecticut Transit 100 Leibert Rd	Hartford	CT	06141	860-522-8101	247-1810	468
Web: www.cttransit.com						
Connecticut Valley Arms (CVA) 1685 Boggs Rd Ste 300	Duluth	GA	30096	770-449-4687	242-8546	284
TF: 800-320-8767 ■ *Web:* www.cva.com						
Connecticut Valley Hospital 1000 Silver St	Middletown	CT	06457	860-262-5000	262-5989	374-5
Web: ct.gov						
Connecticut Valley Railroad State Park 1 Railroad Ave PO Box 452	Essex	CT	06426	860-767-0103	767-0104	565
TF: 866-526-2014 ■ *Web:* www.essexsteamtrain.com						
Connecticut Veterinary Medical Assn PO Box 107	Glastonbury	CT	06033	860-635-7770		795
Web: www.ctvet.org						
Connecticut Water Service Inc 93 W Main St	Clinton	CT	06413	800-286-5700	664-8081*	360-5
NASDAQ: CTWS ■ **Fax Area Code:* 860 ■ **Fax:* Cust Svc ■ *TF:* 800-286-5700 ■ *Web:* www.ctwater.com						
Connecting Generations 100 W Tenth St Ste 1115	Wilmington	DE	19801	302-656-2122	656-2123	48-6
TF: 877-202-9050 ■ *Web:* www.connecting-generations.org						
Connection Pointe Christian Church of Brownsburg 1800 N Green St	Brownsburg	IN	46112	317-852-2221		48-20
Web: www.connectionpointe.org						
Connection, The 11351 Hupp Dr	Burnsville	MN	55337	952-940-5400		737
TF Sales: 800-883-5777 ■ *Web:* www.theconnectioncc.com						
Connectit Networks Inc 4603 NE St Johns Rd Ste B	Vancouver	WA	98661	360-450-0860		393
Web: www.connectitnetworks.com						
Connective Capital Management LLC 385 Homer Ave	Palo Alto	CA	94301	650-321-4826		528
Web: connectcap.com						
ConnectOne Bank 301 Sylvan Ave	Englewood Cliffs	NJ	07632	201-816-4460		360-2
NASDAQ: CNBC ■ *Web:* connectonebank.com						
Connector Manufacturing Co 3501 Symmes Rd	Hamilton	OH	45015	513-860-4455		815
Web: www.cmclugs.com						
Connector Specialists Inc 175 James Dr E	St Rose	LA	70087	504-469-1659		492
Web: www.connectorspecialists.com						
Connectria Hosting 10845 Olive Blvd Ste 300	Saint Louis	MO	63141	314-587-7000	587-7090	39
TF: 800 781 7820 ■ *Web:* www.connectria.com						
Connectronics Corp 2745 Avondale Ave	Toledo	OH	43607	419-537-0020		815
Web: www.connectronicscorp.com						
Connecture Inc 18500 W Corporate Dr Ste 250	Brookfield	WI	53045	262-432-8282		390
Web: www.connecture.com						
ConnectWise Inc 4110 George Rd Ste 200	Tampa	FL	33634	813-463-4700		179
TF: 800-671-6898 ■ *Web:* www.connectwise.com						
Connell Bros Co Ltd 345 California St 27th Fl	San Francisco	CA	94104	415-772-4000	772-4100	146
TF: 800-210-9839 ■ *Web:* www.connellbrothers.com						
Connell Finance Company Inc 200 Connell Dr	Berkeley Heights	NJ	07922	908-673-3700	673-3800	216
Web: www.connellfinance.com						
Connell Foley LLP 85 Livingston Ave	Roseland	NJ	07068	973-535-0500		428
Web: www.connellfoley.com						
Connell Limited Partnership 1 International Pl 31st Fl	Boston	MA	02110	617-391-5577	737-1617	686
Web: www.connell-lp.com						
Connell Oil Incorporated Co *CO-Energy* 1015 N Oregon Ave	Pasco	WA	99301	509-547-3326		581
Web: www.connelloil.com						
Connell Realty & Development Co 200 Connell Dr	Berkeley Heights	NJ	07922	908-673-3700		653
Web: www.connell-realestate.com						
Connell's Map Lee Flowers & Gifts 3014 E Broad St	Columbus	OH	43209	614-237-8653		292
TF: 000-790-8980 ■ *Web:* www.cmlflowers.com						
Connelly Baker Wotring LLP 700 JPMorgan Chase Tower 600 Travis St	Houston	TX	77002	713-980-1700	980-1701	428
Connelly Partners LLC 46 Waltham St 4th Fl	Boston	MA	02118	617-521-5400		4
Web: www.connellypartners.com						
Connelly Skis Inc 20621 52nd Ave W	Lynnwood	WA	98036	425-775-5416	778-9590	710
Web: www.connellyskis.com						
Conner & Winters 1700 One Leadership Sq 211 N Robinson	Oklahoma City	OK	73102	405-272-5711		445
Web: www.cwlaw.com						
Conner Ash PC 12101 Woodcrest Exec Dr 300	Saint Louis	MO	63141	314-205-2510		2
TF: 877-366-1690 ■ *Web:* www.connerash.com						
Conner Homes Co 12600 SE 38th St	Bellevue	WA	98006	425-455-9280		653
Web: www.connerhomes.com						
Conner Industries Inc 3800 Sandshell Dr Ste 235	Fort Worth	TX	76137	817-847-0361		683
Web: www.connerindustries.com						
Conner Prairie Living History Museum 13400 Allisonville Rd	Fishers	IN	46038	317-776-6000	776-6014	520
TF: 800-966-1836 ■ *Web:* www.connerprairie.org						
Conner Rosenkranz LLC 19 E 74th St	New York	NY	10021	212-517-3710		42
TF: 800-270-7951 ■ *Web:* www.crsculpture.com						
Connetics Corp 3160 Porter Dr	Palo Alto	CA	94304	650-843-2800		238
Web: www.olux.com						

Phone | Fax | Class

Connetquot River State Park Preserve
PO Box 505 .... Oakdale NY 11769 631-581-1005 565
Web: parks.ny.gov/parks/8

Connexio Media 904 Fournie Ln .... Collinsville IL 62234 618-628-8888 5
Web: connexiomedia.com

Connexsys Engineering Inc
3075 Research Dr .... Richmond CA 94806 510-243-2050 261

Connexus Energy Co-op
14601 Ramsey Blvd .... Ramsey MN 55303 763-323-2650 323-2603 245
TF: 877-382-4357 ■ *Web:* www.connexusenergy.com

Connexus Inc 10000 N Central Expy .... Dallas TX 75231 214-443-2600 443-2620 390
Web: www.idontwanttotravel.com

Conney Safety Products LLC
3202 Latham Dr .... Madison WI 53744 608-271-3300 535
Web: www.conney.com

Conning Asset Management Co
1 Financial Plaza .... Hartford CT 06103 860-299-2000 401
Web: www.conning.com

Connolly Consulting Associates Inc
50 Danbury Rd .... Wilton CT 06897 203-529-2000 734
Web: www.cotiviti.com/healthcare

Connolly Gerald E "Gerry" (Rep D - VA)
2238 Rayburn HOB .... Washington DC 20515 202-225-1492 225-3071 342-2
Web: connolly.house.gov

Connor Battlefield State Historic Site
55 US-14 .... Ranchester WY 82839 307-684-7629 565
Web: wyoparks.state.wy.us/site/siteinfo.aspx?siteid=15

Connor Co 2800 N E Adams .... Peoria IL 61603 309-688-1068 612
Web: www.connorco.com

Connor Corp
10633 Coldwater Rd Ste 200 .... Fort Wayne IN 46845 260-424-1601 604
Web: www.connorcorp.com

Connors Investor Services Inc
1210 Broadcasting Rd Ste 200 .... Wyomissing PA 19610 610-376-7418 401
TF: 877-376-7418 ■ *Web:* www.connorsinvestor.com

Connors State College 700 College Rd .... Warner OK 74469 918-463-2931 463-6324 162
Web: connorsstate.edu

Connor-Winfield Corp
2111 Comprehensive Dr .... Aurora IL 60505 630-851-4722 203
Web: www.conwin.com

CONNPIRG (Connecticut Public Interest Research Group)
2074 Park St .... Hartford CT 06106 860-233-7554 233-7574 633
Web: www.connpirg.org

Conn-Selmer Inc 600 Industrial Pkwy .... Elkhart IN 46516 574-522-1675 527
TF: 800-348-7426 ■ *Web:* www.bachbrass.com

ConnXus Inc 5155 Financial Way .... Mason OH 45040 513-204-2873 387
Web: connxus.com

ConocoPhillips 600 N Dairy Ashford Rd .... Houston TX 77079 281-293-1000 536
NYSE: COP ■ *TF:* 800-264-8026 ■ *Web:* www.conocophillips.com

ConocoPhillips Alaska Co
600 N Dairy Ashford PO Box 2197 .... Houston TX 77079 281-293-1000 325
Web: www.conocophillips.com

Conolog Corp 5 Columbia Rd .... Somerville NJ 08876 908-722-8081 647
OTC: CNLG ■ *TF:* 800-526-3984 ■ *Web:* iniven.com

Conopco Project Management
5448 Prairie Stone Pkwy .... Hoffman Estates IL 60192 847-645-5000 645-5050 652
Web: www.conopco.com

Conoptics International Sales Corp
19 Eagle Rd .... Danbury CT 06810 203-743-3349 790-6145 544
TF: 800-748-3349 ■ *Web:* www.conoptics.com

Conproco Corp 17 Production Dr .... Dover NH 03820 800-258-3500 182
TF: 800-258-3500 ■ *Web:* www.conproco.com

Conquest Technologies Inc
9250 Rumsey Rd Ste B .... Columbia MD 21045 410-740-4448 463
Web: www.conquesttechnologies.com

Conquip Inc 11255 Pyrites Way .... Rancho Cordova CA 95670 916-379-8200 454
Web: www.conquip.com

Conrac Inc 5124 Commerce Dr .... Baldwin Park CA 91706 626-480-0095 480-0077 173-4
TF: 800-451-5288 ■ *Web:* www.conrac.us

Conrad & Bischoff Inc
2251 N Holmes Ave .... Idaho Falls ID 83401 208-522-4217 581
Web: www.conradbischoff.com

Conrad & Scherer LLP
633 S Federal Hwy .... Fort Lauderdale FL 33301 954-462-5500 428
Web: www.conradscherer.com

Conrad Acceptance Corp
476 W Vermont Ave .... Escondido CA 92025 760-735-5000 160
TF: 800-824-6623 ■ *Web:* www.payconrad.com

Conrad Bros Inc
800 Industrial Ave .... Chesapeake VA 23324 757-543-3521 187
Web: www.conradbrothersinc.com

Conrad Caldwell House Museum, The
1402 St James Ct .... Louisville KY 40208 502-636-5023 520
TF: 800-976-8986 ■ *Web:* www.conrad-caldwell.org

Conrad Capital Management Inc
1377 Motor Pkwy Ste 406 .... Islandia NY 11749 631-439-7878 439-7879 401
Web: www.conradcapital.com

Conrad Chicago 101 E Erie St .... Chicago IL 60611 312-667-6700 378
Web: conradhotels3.hilton.com

Conrad Co, The 1304 Farmville Rd .... Memphis TN 38122 901-323-5926 22
TF: 800-815-3343 ■ *Web:* www.theconradcompany.com

Conrad Forest Products
68765 Wildwood Dr .... North Bend OR 97459 800-356-7146 756-0131* 818
*Fax Area Code: 541 ■ *TF:* 800-356-7146 ■ *Web:* www.conradfp.com

Conrad Industries Inc
1501 Front St .... Morgan City LA 70380 985-384-3060 385-4090 698
Web: www.conradindustries.com

Conrad Motel 100 Conrad Ct .... Glenville WV 26351 304-462-7316 379

Conrad N Hilton Foundation
100 W Liberty St Ste 840 .... Reno NV 89501 775-323-4221 305
Web: www.hiltonfoundation.org

Conrad Schmitt Studios Inc
2405 S 162nd St .... New Berlin WI 53151 262-786-3030 186
TF: 800-969-3033 ■ *Web:* www.conradschmitt.com

Conrad, Trosch & Kemmy PA
301 S McDowell St Ste 809 .... Charlotte NC 28204 704-553-8221 428
Web: www.ctklawyers.com

Conrad-American Inc PO Box 2000 .... Houghton IA 52631 319-469-4141 469-6012 273
TF General: 800-553-1791 ■ *Web:* www.conradamerican.com

Conrad-Jarvis Corp 217 Conant St .... Pawtucket RI 02860 401-722-8700 726-8860* 745-5
*Fax: Orders ■ *Web:* conrad-jarvis.com

Con-Real Support Group LP
1900 Ballpark Way Ste 110 .... Arlington TX 76006 817-640-4420 186
Web: www.con-real.com

CONREC (Contaminant Recovery Systems)
9 Rocky Hill Rd .... Smithfield RI 02917 401-231-3770 667
Web: www.conrec.net

Conroe Regional Medical Ctr
504 Medical Ctr Blvd .... Conroe TX 77304 936-539-1111 374-3
TF: 888-633-2687 ■ *Web:* www.conroeregional.com

Conroy & Knowlton Inc
320 S Montebello Blvd .... Montebello CA 90640 323-665-5288 722-4670 602
Web: www.conroyknowlton.com

Conroy Media Ltd 6713 Kingery Hwy .... Willowbrook IL 60527 630-920-7800 7
Web: conroymedialtd.squarespace.com

Conroy, Simberg, Krevans, Abel, Lurvey, Morrow, Kraft, Klein, Goldberg PA
3440 Hollywood Blvd 2nd Fl .... Hollywood FL 33021 954-961-1400 428
Web: www.conroysimberg.com

Consarc Corp 100 Indel Ave .... Rancocas NJ 08073 609-267-8000 267-1366* 318
*Fax: Sales ■ *Web:* www.consarc.com

Conseco Inc 11825 N Pennsylvania St .... Carmel IN 46032 866-595-2255 360-4
NYSE: CNO ■ *TF:* 866-595-2255 ■ *Web:* www.conseco.com

Conseco Senior Health Insurance Co
11825 N Pennsylvania St .... Carmel IN 46032 866-595-2255 391-2
TF: 866-595-2255 ■ *Web:* www.conseco.com

Conseil Des Ecoles Publique De L'est De L'ontario
2445 St Laurent Blvd .... Ottawa ON K1G6C3 613-742-8960 685
Web: www.cepeo.on.ca

Consensus Advisors LLC 73 Newbury St .... Boston MA 02116 617-437-6500 41
TF: 800-289-9999 ■ *Web:* www.consensusadvisors.com

Consensus International LLC
10640 NW 27th St Ste A-102 .... Doral FL 33172 786-206-0034 809
Web: www.consensusintl.com

Consensus Orthopedics Inc
1115 Windfield Way Ste 100 .... El Dorado Hills CA 95762 916-355-7100 477
Web: www.consensusortho.com

Conserv FS Inc 1110 McConnell Rd .... Woodstock IL 60098 815-334-5950 791
Web: www.conservfs.com

Conservancy Oil Company of Grand Junction Inc
825 First Ave .... Grand Junction CO 81501 970-243-6934 579
Web: www.conservancyoil.com

Conservation & Production Research Laboratory (CPRL)
USDA/ARS PO Box 10 .... Bushland TX 79012 806-356-5724 356-5750 668
Web: www.ars.usda.gov

Conservation Fund
1655 N Fort Myer Dr Ste 1300 .... Arlington VA 22209 703-525-6300 525-4610 48-13
Web: www.conservationfund.org

Conservation International (CI)
2011 Crystal Dr Ste 500 .... Arlington VA 22202 703-341-2400 553-0654 48-13
TF: 800-406-2306 ■ *Web:* www.conservation.org

Conservation Treaty Fund (CTSF)
3705 CaRdiff Rd .... Chevy Chase MD 20815 301-652-6390 48-13

Conservatory Garden
14 E 60th St Central Pk .... New York NY 10022 212-310-6600 97
Web: www.centralparknyc.org

Conservatory of Flowers
100 John F Kennedy Dr .... San Francisco CA 94118 415-831-2090 97
Web: www.conservatoryofflowers.org

Conservatory of Recording Arts & Sciences
2300 E Broadway Rd .... Tempe AZ 85282 480-858-9400 166
Web: www.audiorecordingschool.com

Conservco Water Conservation Products LLC
550 W Plumb Ln Ste B-147 .... Reno NV 89509 775-747-3333 326
TF: 800-253-2467 ■ *Web:* www.dripstop.com

Considine & Considine
1501 Fifth Ave Ste 400 .... San Diego CA 92101 619-231-1977 2
Web: www.cccpa.com

Consiglio's 165 Wooster St .... New Haven CT 06511 203-865-4489 671
Web: www.consiglios.com

CONSOL Energy Inc
1000 Consol Energy Dr .... Canonsburg PA 15317 724-485-4000 360-3
NYSE: CNX ■ *TF:* 800-544-8024 ■ *Web:* www.consolenergy.com

ConSol Inc
7407 Tam O'Shanter Dr Ste 200 .... Stockton CA 95210 209-473-5000 463
Web: www.consol.ws

Consolidated Beverages Inc
12 St Mark St .... Auburn MA 01501 508-832-5311 81-1
TF: 800-922-8128 ■ *Web:* consolidatedbeverages.com

Consolidated Bottle Corp 77 Union St .... Toronto ON M6N3N2 416-656-7777 454
TF: 800-561-1354 ■ *Web:* www.consbottle.com

Consolidated Brick & Bldg Supls Inc
127 W 24th St Fl 3 .... New York NY 10011 212-645-6700 191-1
Web: www.consolidatedbrick.com

Consolidated Carpet Assoc LLC
45 W 25th St 8th Fl .... New York NY 10010 212-226-4600 131
Web: www.consolidatedcarpet.com

Consolidated Casting Corp
1501 S I-45 RG .... Hutchins TX 75141 972-225-7305 225-2970 306
Web: www.consolicast.com

Consolidated Catfish Cos LLC
299 S St PO Box 271 .... Isola MS 38754 662-962-3101 962-0114 296-14
TF: 800-228-3474 ■ *Web:* countryselect.com

Consolidated Ceramic Products Inc
838 Cherry St .... Blanchester OH 45107 937-783-2476 783-2539 500
TF: 800-669-1799 ■ *Web:* www.ccpi-inc.com

Consolidated Chassis Management LLC
500 International Dr .... Budd Lake NJ 07828 973-298-8900 194
Web: www.ccmpool.com

Consolidated Communications Holdings Inc
121 S 17th St .... Mattoon IL 61938 217-235-3311 360-3
NASDAQ: CNSL ■ *Web:* consolidated.com

Consolidated Construction Management Services Inc
9 Professional Cir Ste 204 .... Colts Neck NJ 07722 732-303-1997 194
TF: 800-225-3813 ■ *Web:* www.ccmscorp.com

Consolidated Container Co (CCC)
3101 Towercreek Pkwy Ste 300 .... Atlanta GA 30339 678-742-4600 742-4750 548
TF Sales: 888-831-2184 ■ *Web:* www.cccllc.com

	Phone	Fax	Class
Consolidated Devices Inc (CDI) 19220 San Jose Ave .... City of Industry CA 91748 *TF:* 800-525-6319 ■ *Web:* www.cditorque.com	626-965-0668	810-2759	758
Consolidated Disposal Services Inc 12949 Telegraph Rd .... Santa Fe Springs CA 90670 *TF:* 800-299-4898 ■ *Web:* republicservices.com	800-299-4898		804
Consolidated Distribution Corp 1285 101st St .... Lemont IL 60439 *Web:* www.cdcsupply.com	630-972-9800		186
Consolidated Edison Inc 4 Irving Pl .... New York NY 10003 *NYSE: ED* ■ *TF:* 800-752-6633 ■ *Web:* coned.com	212-460-4600		360-5
Consolidated Electric Co-op 3940 E Liberty St .... Mexico MO 65265 *TF:* 800-621-0091 ■ *Web:* www.consolidatedelectric.com	573-581-3630	581-0990	245
Consolidated Electrical Distributors Inc (CED) 9201 J St .... Omaha NE 68127 *Web:* www.ced-aec.com	402-592-7500		246
Consolidated Electronic Wire & Cable Co 11044 King St .... Franklin Park IL 60131 *TF:* 800-621-4278 ■ *Web:* www.conwire.com	847-455-8830	455-8837	814
Consolidated Energy Co 910 Main St .... Jesup IA 50648 **Fax Area Code:* 319 ■ *TF:* 800-338-3021 ■ *Web:* www.cecgas.com	800-338-3021	827-3154*	579
Consolidated Engineering Company Inc 1971 Mccollum Pkwy NW .... Kennesaw GA 30144 *Web:* www.cec-intl.com	770-422-5100		256
Consolidated Fabricators Corp 14620 Arminta St .... Van Nuys CA 91402 *Web:* www.con-fab.com	818-901-1005		124
Consolidated Fiberglass Products Co 3801 Standard St .... Bakersfield CA 93308 *Web:* www.conglas.com	661-323-6026		46
Consolidated Fibers 8100 S Blvd .... Charlotte NC 28273 *TF:* 800-243-8621 ■ *Web:* www.consolidatedfibers.com	800-243-8621		605-1
Consolidated Graphics Group Inc 1014 E 40th St .... Cleveland OH 44103 *Web:* csinc.com	216-881-9191		627
Consolidated Graphics Inc 5858 Westheimer Rd Ste 200 .... Houston TX 77057 *NYSE: CGX*	713-787-0977	787-5013	627
Consolidated Industries Inc 677 Mixville Rd .... Cheshire CT 06410 *Web:* www.forgemetal.com	203-272-5371	272-5672	483
Consolidated Metal Products Inc 1028 Depot St .... Cincinnati OH 45204 *Web:* www.cmpubolt.com	513-251-2624		455
Consolidated Metco Inc 5701 SE Columbia Way .... Vancouver WA 98661 *TF Sales:* 800-547-9473 ■ *Web:* www.conmet.com	800-547-9473		60
Consolidated Pipe & Supply Inc 1205 Hilltop Pkwy .... Birmingham AL 35204 *Web:* www.consolidatedpipe.com	205-323-7261	251-7838	492
Consolidated Precision Products 8333 Wilcox Ave .... Cudahy CA 90201 *Web:* cppcorp.com	323-773-2363	562-3174	308
Consolidated Printers Inc 2630 Eigth St .... Berkeley CA 94710 *Web:* www.consoprinters.com	510-843-8524	486-0580	626
Consolidated Publishing Co 4305 McClellan Blvd PO Box 189 .... Anniston AL 36206 *TF:* 866-814-9253 ■ *Web:* www.annistonstar.com	256-236-1551	241-1991	637-0
Consolidated Rail Corp 1717 Arch St Ste 3210 .... Philadelphia PA 19103 *TF:* 800-272-0911 ■ *Web:* www.conrail.com	215-209-2000		648
Consolidated Shoe Company Inc 22290 Timberlake Rd .... Lynchburg VA 24502 *TF:* 800-368-7463 ■ *Web:* www.consolidatedshoe.com	434-239-0391		301
Consolidated Steel Services Inc 632 Glendale Vly Blvd .... Fallentimber PA 16639 *TF:* 800-237-8783 ■ *Web:* www.csteel.com	814-944-5890	943-8278	492
Consolidated Storage Cos 225 Main St .... Tatamy PA 18085 **Fax Area Code:* 888 ■ *TF Cust Svc:* 800-323-0801 ■ *Web:* www.equipto.com	610-253-2775	859-2121*	286
Consolidated Supply Co 7337 SW Kable Ln .... Tigard OR 97224 *TF:* 800-929-5810 ■ *Web:* www.consolidatedsupply.com	503-620-7050	684-3254	612
Consolidated Systems Inc 650 Rosewood Dr .... Columbia SC 29201 *Web:* www.csisteel.com	803-771-7920		697
CONSOR Inc 7342 Girard Ave Ste 8 .... La Jolla CA 92037 *Web:* www.consor.com	858-454-9091		463
Consortia Consulting Inc 233 S 13th St Ste 1225 .... Lincoln NE 68508 *Web:* www.consortiaconsulting.com	402-441-4315		194
Consortium Book Sales & Distribution Inc The Keg House 34 Thirteenth Ave NE Ste 101 .... Minneapolis MN 55413 *Web:* www.cbsd.com	612-746-2600		96
Consortium for Advanced Mfg International (CAM-I) 6836 Bee Cave Ste 256 .... Austin TX 78746 *Web:* www.cam-i.org	512-296-6872		49-13
Consortium for Citizens with Disabilities (CCD) 1660 L St NW Ste 701 .... Washington DC 20036 *Web:* www.c-c-d.org	202-783-2229		48-6
Consortium for Policy Research in Education (CPRE) University of Pennsylvania 3440 Market St Ste 560 .... Philadelphia PA 19104 *Web:* www.cpre.org	215-573-0700	573-7914	634
Consortium for School Networking (CoSN) 1025 Vermont Ave NW Ste 1010 .... Washington DC 20005 *TF:* 866-267-8747 ■ *Web:* www.cosn.org	202-861-2676	393-2011	48-9
ConSova Corp 1536 Cole Blvd Ste 350 .... Lakewood CO 80401 *TF:* 866-529-9107 ■ *Web:* www.consova.com	866-529-9107		196
Conspectus Inc 2231 Route 50 PO Box 248 .... Tuckahoe NJ 08250 *Web:* www.conspectusinc.com	609-628-2390		193
Constable Commercial Real Estate Services 2845 Moorpark Ave Ste 112 .... San Jose CA 95128 *Web:* www.constablecommercial.com	408-984-3700		652
Constangy, Brooks & Smith LLC 230 Peachtree St N W Ste 2400 .... Atlanta GA 30303 *Web:* constangy.com	404-525-8622		428
Constantine's Wood Ctr 1040 E Oakland Pk Blvd .... Fort Lauderdale FL 33334 *TF:* 800-443-9667 ■ *Web:* www.constantines.com	954-561-1716	565-8149	613
Constat Corp 1860 Blake St Ste 650 .... Denver CO 80202 *Web:* constat.com	303-572-1051		194
Constellation Brands Inc 207 High Pt Dr Bldg 100 .... Victor NY 14564 *NYSE: STZ* ■ *TF:* 888-724-2169 ■ *Web:* www.cbrands.com	888-724-2169		81-3
Constellation Technology Corp 7887 Bryan Dairy Rd Ste 100 .... Largo FL 33777 *TF:* 800-335-7355 ■ *Web:* www.contech.com	727-547-0600		218
Constellium Automotive USA LLC 46555 Magellan Dr .... Novi MI 48377 *Web:* www.constellium.com	248-668-3211		492
Constitution Convention Museum State Park 200 Allen Memorial Way .... Port Saint Joe FL 32456 *Web:* www.floridastateparks.org	850-229-8029		565
Constitution Gardens 900 Ohio Dr SW .... Washington DC 20024 *Web:* www.nps.gov/coga	202-426-6841	724-0764	564
Constitution Square State Historic Site 134 S Second St .... Danville KY 40422 *Web:* www.parks.ky.gov	859-239-7089		565
Constitutional Rights Foundation 601 S Kingsley Dr .... Los Angeles CA 90005 *TF:* 800-488-4273 ■ *Web:* www.crf usa.org	213-487-5590	386-0459	48-7
Construct Two Group 30 S Ivey Ln .... Orlando FL 32811 *Web:* www.constructtwo.com	407-295-9812		186
Construction Albert Jean Ltd 4045 Parthenais St .... Montreal QC H2K3T8 *Web:* www.albertjean.com	514-522-2121		186
Construction Book Express Inc 401 S Wright Rd .... Janesville WI 53546 *Web:* www.constructionbook.com	608-743-8031		090
Construction Claims Monthly 2222 Sedwick Rd .... Durham NC 27713 *TF:* 800-223-8720 ■ *Web:* www.constructionclaimsmonthly.org	800-223-8720	508-2592	531-13
Construction Enterprises Inc (CEI) 2179 Edward Curd Ln Ste 100 .... Franklin TN 37067 *Web:* www.constructionenterprises.com	615-332-8880	771-0818	187
Construction Financial Management Assn (CFMA) 100 Village Blvd Ste 200A .... Princeton NJ 08540 *TF:* 877-462-7827 ■ *Web:* www.cfma.org	609-452-8000	452-0474	49-1
Construction Labor Report 1801 S Bell St .... Arlington VA 22202 *TF:* 800-372-1033 ■ *Web:* www.bna.com/construction-labor-report-p6002	800-372-1033		531-13
Construction Metals LLC 13169 B Slover Ave .... Fontana CA 92337 *TF:* 800-576-9810 ■ *Web:* www.constructionmetals.com	909-390-9880		236
Construction Outfitters International Inc 37450 I-10 W Ste 101 .... Boerne TX 78006 *Web:* www.coiworld.com	830-816-2104	816-2464	186
Construction Process Solutions Ltd 4327 Red Bank Rd .... Cincinnati OH 45227 *TF:* 877-295-9876 ■ *Web:* www.cpsconsult.com	513-271-9020		530
Construction Products Inc 1631 Ashport Rd .... Jackson TN 38305 *TF:* 800-238-8226 ■ *Web:* www.cpi-tn.com	731-668-7305	668-1361	183
Construction Services Inc 2214 S Lincoln St .... Amarillo TX 79109	806-373-1732		189-12
Construction Software Technologies Inc 4500 W Lake Forest Dr Ste 502 .... Cincinnati OH 45242 *TF:* 800-364-2059 ■ *Web:* www.isqft.com	513-645-8004	645-8005	178-10
Construction Specialties Inc 3 Werner Way .... Lebanon NJ 08833 *TF:* 800-972-7214 ■ *Web:* c-sgroup.com	908-236-0800	236-0801	491
Construction Systems Software Inc PO Box 203184 .... Austin TX 78720 *TF:* 800-531-1035 ■ *Web:* www.cssisw.com	800-531-1035		178-10
Construction Testing & Engineering Inc 1441 Montiel Rd Ste 115 .... Escondido CA 92026 **Fax Area Code:* 209 ■ *TF:* 800-576-4955 ■ *Web:* www.cte-inc.net	760-746-4955	839-2895*	743
Construction Trailer Specialists Inc 2535 Rose Pkwy .... Sikeston MO 63801 *Web:* www.constructiontrailerspecialists.com	573-481-0941		779
Constructors Association of Western Pennsylvania 800 Cranberry Woods Dr Ste 110 ...... Cranberry Township PA 16066 *TF:* 877-343-2297 ■ *Web:* www.cawp.org	412-343-8000		138
Constructors Inc 1815 Y St .... Lincoln NE 68508 *Web:* www.constructorslincoln.com	402-434-1764	434-1799	188-4
Construx Software 11820 Northup Way Ste E-200 .... Bellevue WA 98005 *TF:* 866-296-6300 ■ *Web:* www.construx.com	425-636-0100	636-0159	177
Consulate General 870 Market St Ste 1067 .... San Francisco CA 94102 *TF:* 877-714-7378 ■ *Web:* www.consuladoperu.com	415-362-5185	362-2836	257
Consulate General 100 Hamilton Plaza .... Paterson NJ 07505 *Web:* www.consuladoperu.com	973-278-3324	278-0254	257
Consulate General 150 S Independence Mall W 1026 Public Ledger Bldg .... Philadelphia PA 19106 *TF:* 800-531-0840 ■ *Web:* www.consfiladelfia.esteri.it	215-592-7329	592-9808	257
Consulate General of El Salvador 46 Pk Ave .... New York NY 10016 *Web:* www.consuladonuevayork.rree.gob.sv	212-889-3608		784
Consulate General of Honduras *Consulate General* 365 Canal St .... New Orleans LA 70130	504-522-3118		257
Consulate General of Liberia 866 UN Plaza Ste 249 .... New York NY 10017 *Web:* www.liberianconsulate-ny.com	212-687-1033		784
Consulate General of Paraguay 801 Second Ave Ste 600 .... New York NY 10017 *Web:* www.mre.gov.py/Sitios/Home/Index/consulpar-ny	212-682-9441	682-9443	257

				Phone	Fax	Class
Consulate General of Romania *Consulate General* 11766 Wilshire Blvd Ste 560 *TF:* 800-780-5733 ■ *Web:* www.consulateromania.org	Los Angeles	CA	90025	310-444-0043		257
Consulate General of Switzerland 633 Third Ave 30th Fl *Web:* www.eda.admin.ch/newyork	New York	NY	10017	212-599-5700		257
Consulate General of the Republic of Liberia in New York, The *Consulate General* 866 United Nations Plaza Ste 249 *Web:* liberianconsulate-ny.com	New York	NY	10017	212-687-1025	599-3189	257
Consulate General of the Republic of Suriname 7205 Corporate Dr Ste 302 *Web:* www.scgmia.com	Miami	FL	33126	305-463-0694	463-0694	257
Consulate Health Care at Lake Parker 2020 West Lake Parker Dr *Web:* www.consulatemgt.com	Lakeland	FL	33805	863-682-7580		450
Consulate Health Care of Brandon 701 Victoria St *Web:* consulatehealthcare.com	Brandon	FL	33510	813-681-4220		450
Consulate Health Care of Tallahassee 800 Concourse Pkwy S Ste 200 *Web:* www.consulatehealthcare.com	Maitland	FL	32751	407-571-1550	571-1599	450
Consult Dynamics Inc 1016 Delaware Ave *TF:* 800-784-4788 ■ *Web:* www.dca.net	Wilmington	DE	19806	302-654-1019		180
Consult Usa Inc 634 Alpha Dr *TF:* 866-963-8621 ■ *Web:* consultusa.com	Pittsburgh	PA	15238	412-963-8621		177
Consultant Engineering Service Inc 811 W Fifth St 101 *Web:* www.ceseng.net	Winston Salem	NC	27101	336-724-0139		261
Consultants & Builders Inc 3850 Peachtree Industrial Blvd *Web:* www.consultantsandbuilders.com	Duluth	GA	30096	770-729-8183		194
Consultants in Laboratory Medicine 3170 W Central Ave *Web:* www.clm-pml.com	Toledo	OH	43606	419-534-3500		415
ConsultKAP Inc 3115 Woodchuck Way SW Dept 101 *Web:* www.consultkap.com	Conyers	GA	30094	770-918-9390		317
Consultnet LLC 10813 S River Front Pkwy Ste 150 *TF:* 888-215-9675 ■ *Web:* consultnet.com	South Jordan	UT	84095	801-208-3700	208-3643	721
Consumer Attorneys of California 770 L St Ste 1200 *TF:* 800-424-2725 ■ *Web:* www.caoc.org	Sacramento	CA	95814	916-442-6902		428
Consumer Brands LLC 4600 Campus Dr Ste 107 *Web:* www.consumerbrands.com	Newport Beach	CA	92660	949-267-4117		366
Consumer Credit Industry Assn (CCIA) 6300 Powers Ferry Rd Ste 600-286 *Web:* www.cciaonline.com	Atlanta	GA	30339	678-858-4001		49-9
Consumer Data Industry Assn (CDIA) 1090 Vermont Ave NW Ste 200 *Web:* www.cdiaonline.org	Washington	DC	20005	202-371-0910	371-0134	49-2
Consumer Federation of America (CFA) 1620 I St NW Ste 200 *TF:* 877-382-4357 ■ *Web:* www.consumerfed.org	Washington	DC	20006	202-387-6121	265-7989	48-10
Consumer Healthcare Products Assn (CHPA) 1150 Connecticut Ave NW # 700 *TF:* 800-222-1222 ■ *Web:* www.chpa.org	Washington	DC	20036	202-429-9260	223-6835	49-4
Consumer Marine Supply 88 Royal Dr *Web:* www.consumermarinesupply.com	Brick	NJ	08723	732-477-0119		196
Consumer Oil & Supply Co 100 Railroad St	Braymer	MO	64624	660-645-2215		316
Consumer Product Safety Commission (CPSC) 4340 E W Hwy Ste 502 *TF:* 800-638-2772 ■ *Web:* www.cpsc.gov	Bethesda	MD	20814	301-504-7923	504-0051	340-20
Consumer Reports Magazine 101 Truman Ave *TF Orders:* 800-333-0663 ■ *Web:* www.consumerreports.org	Yonkers	NY	10703	914-378-2000		457-11
Consumer Reports On Health 101 Truman Ave *TF:* 800-234-1645 ■ *Web:* www.consumerreports.org	Yonkers	NY	10703	914-378-2000		531-8
Consumer Safety Technology Inc 10520 Hickman Rd Ste F *Web:* www.intoxalock.com	Des Moines	IA	50325	515-331-7643		57
Consumer Sales Solutions 537 Douglas Ave *Web:* bk.com	Dunedin	FL	34698	727-733-8700		194
Consumer Specialty Products Assn PAC 1667 K St NW Ste 300 *Web:* www.cspa.org	Washington	DC	20006	202-872-8110	223-2636	615
Consumer Textile Corp 123 N 4Th	Clinton	OK	73601	580-323-3111		426
Consumer'S Beverages Company Inc 2765 Genesee St *Web:* consumersbeverages.com	Buffalo	NY	14225	716-893-7040		443
ConsumerMetrics Inc 2299 Perimeter Park Dr *Web:* www.cmiresearch.com	Atlanta	GA	30341	678-805-4000		605-2
Consumers Energy 2074 242nd St *TF:* 800-696-6552 ■ *Web:* www.consumersenergy.net	Marshalltown	IA	50158	641-752-1593	752-5738	245
Consumers Energy Co 1 Energy Plaza *TF Cust Svc:* 800-477-5050 ■ *Web:* www.consumersenergy.com	Jackson	MI	49201	517-788-0550		787
Consumers Petroleum of Ct 204 Spring Hill Rd *Web:* www.cameca.com	Trumbull	CT	06611	203-261-3123		579
Consumers Pipe & Supply Co 13424 Arrow Blvd *TF:* 800-338-7473 ■ *Web:* www.consumerspipe.com	Fontana	CA	92335	909-728-4828	728-4829	492
Consumers Power Inc (CPI) 6990 W Hills Rd *TF:* 800-872-9036	Philomath	OR	97370	541-929-3124	929-8673	245
Consumers Produce Co 1 21st St *Web:* www.consumersproduce.com	Pittsburgh	PA	15222	412-281-0722	281-6541	297-7
Consumers Union of US Inc 101 Truman Ave *TF:* 800-927-4357 ■ *Web:* www.consumersunion.org	Yonkers	NY	10703	914-378-2000		637-9

				Phone	Fax	Class
Consumers Vinegar & Spice Company Inc 4723 S Washtenaw Ave *TF:* 800-580-3477 ■ *Web:* cvsco.com	Chicago	IL	60632	773-376-4100	376-6224	296-41
Consumers' Research Council of America (CRCA) 2020 Pennsylvania Ave NW Ste 300-A *TF:* 877-774-6337 ■ *Web:* www.consumersresearchcncl.org	Washington	DC	20006	202-835-9698	835-9739	48-10
Consutech Systems LLC PO Box 15119 *Web:* www.consutech.com	Richmond	VA	23227	804-746-4120	730-9056	318
Contact 101 Inc 777 N Rainbow Blvd Ste 250 **Fax Area Code: 720* ■ *TF:* 888-731-2397	Las Vegas	NV	89107	888-731-2397	269-1890*	466
Contact America Inc 2325 Maryland Rd Ste 150 *Web:* www.contact-america.com	Willow Grove	PA	19090	858-459-8438		393
Contact Castle Hotel & Spa 400 Benedict Ave *Web:* castlehotelandspa.com	Tarrytown	NY	10591	914-631-1980		379
Contact Industries Inc 9200 SE Sunnybrook Blvd Ste 200 *TF:* 800-547-1038 ■ *Web:* www.contactind.com	Clackamas	OR	97015	503-228-7361	221-1340	499
Contact International Inc 8001 Lincoln Ave Ste 201	Skokie	IL	60077	847-324-4411		463
Contact Lens Manufacturers Assn PO Box 29398 *TF:* 800-344-9060 ■ *Web:* www.clma.net	Lincoln	NE	68529	402-465-4122	465-4187	49-4
Contact Systems Inc 50 Miry Brook Rd *Web:* www.contactsystems.com	Danbury	CT	06810	203-743-3837		695
Contactpointe of Pittsburgh 2593 Wexford Bayne Rd Ste 200 *TF:* 877-255-4916 ■ *Web:* contactpointe.com	Sewickley	PA	15143	412-788-0680		379
Container Consulting Service Inc 455 Mayock Rd *Web:* www.ccs-packaging.com	Gilroy	CA	95020	408-842-1919		194
Container Graphics Corp 114 Edinburgh S Dr Ste 104 *Web:* www.containergraphics.com	Cary	NC	27511	919-481-4200	469-4897	781
Container Manufacturing Inc 50 Baekeland Ave *Web:* www.containermanufacturing.com	Middlesex	NJ	08846	732-563-0100		333
Container Port Group 1340 Depot St Ste 103 *Web:* www.containerport.com	Cleveland	OH	44116	440-333-1330	333-1520	780
Container Products Corp 112 N College Rd *Web:* www.c-p-c.com	Wilmington	NC	28405	910-392-6100		124
Container Research Corp (CRC) 2 New Rd *TF:* 844-220-9574 ■ *Web:* www.crc-flex.com	Aston	PA	19014	610-459-2160		198
Container Store, The 500 Freeport Pkwy *TF:* 800-733-3532 ■ *Web:* www.containerstore.com	Coppell	TX	75019	972-538-6000		362
Container Supply Company Inc 12571 Western Ave *Web:* containersupplycompany.com	Garden Grove	CA	92841	714-892-8321	892-3824	124
ContainerWorld Forwarding Services Inc 16133 Blundell Rd *TF:* 877-838-8880 ■ *Web:* www.containerworld.com	Richmond	BC	V6W0A3	604-276-1300		311
Containment Solutions Inc 5150 Jefferson Chemical Rd *Web:* www.containmentsolutions.com	Conroe	TX	77301	936-756-7731		600
Contaminant Recovery Systems (CONREC) 9 Rocky Hill Rd *Web:* www.conrec.net	Smithfield	RI	02917	401-231-3770		667
Contango Oil & Gas Co 3700 Buffalo Speedway Ste 960 *NYSE: MCF* ■ *Web:* www.contango.com	Houston	TX	77098	713-960-1901	960-1065	536
Contava Inc 4103 97 St NW *Web:* www.contava.com	Edmonton	AB	T6E6E9	780-434-7564		196
CONTAX Inc 893 Yonge St *TF:* 800-741-9206 ■ *Web:* www.contax.com	Toronto	ON	M4W2H2	416-927-1913		193
Contec Systems Industrial Corp 1566 Medical Dr Ste 310 *Web:* contecsystems.com	Pottstown	PA	19464	610-326-3235		180
Con-Tech Carpentry LLC 366 W Fourth St *TF:* 800-561-3357 ■ *Web:* www.contechcarpentry.com	Eureka	MO	63025	636-938-4748		261
Contech Construction Products Inc 9025 Centre Pt Dr Ste 400 *TF:* 800-338-1122 ■ *Web:* www.conteches.com	West Chester	OH	45069	513-645-7000	645-7993	697
Con-Tech Lighting 2783 Shermer Rd *TF:* 800-728-0312 ■ *Web:* www.con-techlighting.com	Northbrook	IL	60062	847-559-5500	559-5505	439
Contecture International Ltd 17252 Armstrong Ave Ste A *Web:* www.contextureintl.com	Irvine	CA	92614	949-250-0811		514
Con-tek Machine Inc 3575 Hoffman Rd E *TF:* 800-968-9801 ■ *Web:* www.con-tek.com	Saint Paul	MN	55110	651-779-6058		111
Contemar Silo Systems Inc 30 Pennsylvania Ave Unit 8 *TF:* 800-567-2741 ■ *Web:* www.contemar.com	Concord	ON	L4K4A5	905-669-3604		296
Contempo Ceramic Tile Corp 3732 South 300 West *Web:* contempotile.com	Salt Lake City	UT	84115	801-262-1717		191-1
Contempora Fabrics Inc 351 Contempora Dr *Web:* www.contemporafabrics.com	Lumberton	NC	28358	910-738-7131	738-9575	745-4
Contemporary Art Ctr of Virginia (CAC) 2200 Parks Ave *Web:* www.cacv.org	Virginia Beach	VA	23451	757-425-0000		50-2
Contemporary Art Museum Saint Louis 3750 Washington Blvd *Web:* camstl.org	Saint Louis	MO	63108	314-535-4660	535-1226	520
Contemporary Arts Ctr 44 E Sixth St *TF:* 800-644-6862 ■ *Web:* www.contemporaryartscenter.org	Cincinnati	OH	45202	513-345-8400		50-2
Contemporary Arts Ctr 900 Camp St *TF:* 800-568-6968 ■ *Web:* www.cacno.org	New Orleans	LA	70130	504-528-3805	528-3828	572
Contemporary Arts Museum 5216 Montrose Blvd *TF:* 800-982-2787 ■ *Web:* www.camh.org	Houston	TX	77006	713-284-8250	284-8275	520

Phone | Fax | Class

Contemporary Benefits Design Inc
1956 Wellness Blvd Monroe NC 28110 704-296-0900 194
Contemporary Control Systems Inc
2431 Curtiss St. Downers Grove IL 60515 630-963-7070 963-0109 176
TF: 800-375-3363 ■ *Web:* www.ccontrols.com
Contemporary Dance Theatre
1805 Larch Ave. Cincinnati OH 45224 513-591-1222 573-1
TF: 800-901-4216 ■ *Web:* www.cdt-dance.org
Contemporary Electrical Services Inc
1954 Isaac Newton Sq W Reston VA 20190 703-255-9226 189-4
Web: www.cont-elec.com
Contemporary Productions LLC
190 Carondelet Plaza Ste 1111 Saint Louis MO 63105 314-721-9090 181
Web: www.contemporaryproductions.com
Contemporary Software Concepts Inc
455 Pennsylvania Ave Ste 205 Fort Washington PA 19034 610-687-6000 177
TF: 800-764-1066 ■ *Web:* www.consoftware.com
Contemporary Tours
1400 Old Country Rd Ste 100 Westbury NY 11590 516-484-5032 760
TF: 800-627-8873 ■ *Web:* www.contemporarytours.com
Content Firm LLC, The
26 Academy Dr E Whippany NJ 07981 973-993-8098 195
Web: evanschuman.com
Content Management Corp
37900 Central Ct Newark CA 94560 510-505-1100 627
TF: 877-495-3720 ■ *Web:* www.cmcondemand.com
Content Solutions 1413 E Mckinney St Denton TX 76209 940-384-9407 317
Web: www.yourcontentsolutions.com
Conterra Ultra Broadband LLC
2101 Rexford Rd Ste 200E Charlotte NC 28211 704-365-6701 652
TF: 800-634-1374 ■ *Web:* www.conterra.com
Con-Test Analytical Laboratory
39 Spruce St 2 East Longmeadow MA 01028 413-525-2332 743
TF: 800-244-8378 ■ *Web:* www.contestlabs.com
Contex Americas Inc
15737 Crabbs Branch Way Derwood MD 20855 240-399-5600 268-1118 196
Web: www.contex.com
Context Creative Inc
317 Adelaide St W Toronto ON M5V1P9 416-972-1439 180
Web: contextcreative.com
Contigo Systems Inc
2700 Production Way Vancouver BC V5A4X1 604-683-3106 525
Web: www.contigo.com
Contiki Holidays
801 E Katella Ave 3rd Fl Anaheim CA 92805 714-935-0808 760
TF: 800-944-5708 ■ *Web:* www.contiki.com
Continental Airlines Inc
900 Grand Plaza Dr. Houston TX 77067 713-952-1630 26
TF: 800-621-7467 ■ *Web:* www.united.com
Continental American Insurance Company Inc
2801 Devine St Columbia SC 29205 803-256-6265 390
Continental Art Supplies
7041 Reseda Blvd. Reseda CA 91335 818-345-1044 45
Web: www.continentalart.com
Continental Assurance Co
333 S Wabash Ave Chicago IL 60604 312-822-5000 391-2
Web: www.cna.com
Continental Battery Corp
4919 Woodall St. Dallas TX 75247 214-631-5701 634-7846 74
TF: 800-442-0081 ■ *Web:* www.continentalbattery.com
Continental Bayside Hotel
146 Biscayne Blvd Miami FL 33132 305-358-4555 379
Web: www.crshotels.com
Continental Binder & Specialty Corp
407 W Compton Blvd Gardena CA 90248 310-324-8227 715-6740 86
TF: 800-872-2897 ■ *Web:* www.continentalbinder.com
Continental Bindery Corp
700 Fargo Ave. Elk Grove Village IL 60007 847-439-6811 92
Continental Biomass Industries Inc
22 Whittier St Newton NH 03858 603-382-0556 190
Web: www.cbi-inc.com
Continental Cabinet Inc 2841 Pierce St Dallas TX 75233 214-467-4444 115
Web: www.continentalcabinet.com
Continental Cast Stone Manufacturing Inc
22001 W 83rd St Shawnee KS 66227 800-989-7866 422-7272* 724
*Fax Area Code: 913 ■ *TF:* 800-989-7866 ■ *Web:* www.continentalcaststone.com
Continental Casting LLC
801 Second St Monroe City MO 63456 573-735-4577 492
Web: www.continentalcasting.com
Continental Casualty Co
333 S Wabash Ave Chicago IL 60604 312-822-5000 822-6419 391-4
TF: 800-262-2000 ■ *Web:* www.cna.com
Continental Cement Company LLC
16100 Swingley Ridge Rd Ste 230 Chesterfield MO 63017 636-532-7440 532-7445 135
TF: 800-625-1144 ■ *Web:* www.continentalcement.com
Continental Coin Corp
5627 Sepulveda Blvd Van Nuys CA 91411 818-781-4232 782-6779 411
TF: 800-552-6467 ■ *Web:* continentalcoin.com
Continental Colorcraft
1166 W Garvey Ave Monterey Park CA 91754 323-283-3000 283-3206 781
Web: www.continentalcolorcraft.com
Continental Concession Supplies Inc
575 Jericho Tpke Ste 300 Jericho NY 11753 516-739-8777 739-8750 297-3
TF: 800-516-0090 ■ *Web:* www.ccsicandy.com
Continental Currency Services Inc (CCS)
PO Box 10970 Santa Ana CA 92711 714-667-6699 569-0882 217
Web: www.ccurr.com
Continental Design & Engineering Inc
1524 Jackson St Anderson IN 46016 765-778-9999 302
TF: 800-875-4557 ■ *Web:* continental-design.com
Continental Development Corp
2041 Rosecrans Ave Ste 200 Ste 200 El Segundo CA 90245 310-640-1520 414-9279 685
Web: www.continentaldevelopment.com
Continental Disc Corp
3160 W Heartland Dr Liberty MO 64068 816-792-1500 792-2277 789
Web: www.contdisc.com
Continental Divide ElectricCo-op Inc (CDEC)
200 E High St PO Box 1087 Grants NM 87020 505-285-6656 245
Web: www.cdec.coop
Continental Divide Trail Society (CDT)
3704 N Charles St Ste 601 Baltimore MD 21218 410-235-9610 48-23
Web: www.cdtsociety.org
Continental Electric Company Inc
9501 E Fifth Ave PO Box 2710 Gary IN 46403 219-938-3460 938-3469 189-4
Web: www.continentalelectric.com
Continental Electric Motors Inc
23 Sebago St Clifton NJ 07013 800-335-6718 518
TF: 800-335-6718 ■ *Web:* www.cecoinc.com
Continental Electronics Corp
4212 S Buckner Blvd Dallas TX 75227 214-381-7161 381-4949 647
TF: 800-733-5011 ■ *Web:* www.contelec.com
Continental Fire Sprinkler Co
4518 S 133rd St Omaha NE 68137 402-330-5170 610
TF: 800-543-5170 ■ *Web:* www.continental-fire.com
Continental Flowers Inc 8101 NW 21 St Miami FL 33122 305-594-4214 292
TF: 800-327-2715 ■ *Web:* www.continentalflowers.com
Continental Forge Company Inc
412 E El Segundo Blvd Compton CA 90222 310-603-1014 483
Web: www.cforge.com
Continental Glass Systems Inc
325 W 74th Pl. Hialeah FL 33014 305-231-1101 256
Web: www.cgsfl.com
Continental Graphics Corp
4060 N Lakewood Blvd Bldg 801 5th Fl Long Beach CA 90808 714-503-4200 827-5111 225
TF: 800-862-5691 ■ *Web:* www.cdgnow.com
Continental Linen Services
4200 Manchester Rd. Kalamazoo MI 49001 800-878-4357 442
TF: 800-878-4357 ■ *Web:* www.clsimage.com
Continental Loose Leaf Inc
1122 16th Ave. Minneapolis MN 55414 612-378-4800 378-7680 86
TF: 888-719-5013 ■ *Web:* www.continentallooseleaf.com
Continental Machines Inc
5505 W 123rd St Savage MN 55378 952-895-6400 455
TF: 800-463-8134 ■ *Web:* continentalhydraulics.com
Continental Manufacturing Co
305 Rock Industrial Pk Dr. Bridgeton MO 63044 314-656-4301 770-9938 508
TF: 800-325-1051 ■ *Web:* www.continentalcommercialproducts.com
Continental Maritime of San Diego Inc
1995 Bay Front St San Diego CA 92113 619-234-8851 696-7358 698
TF: 877-631-0020 ■ *Web:* www.continentalmaritime.com
Continental Metal Products Co
35 Olympia Ave. Woburn MA 01888 781-935-4400 427
Web: www.continentalmetal.com
Continental Mineral Processing Corp
11817 Mosteller Rd Cincinnati OH 45241 513-771-7190 771-9153 500
Web: www.continentalmineral.com
Continental Motors Inc 2039 Broad St Mobile AL 36615 251-438-3411 432-7352 21
TF: 800-718-3411 ■ *Web:* www.tcmlink.com
Continental Office Furniture & Supply Corp
2601 Silver Dr Columbus OH 43211 614-262-5010 320
Web: www.continentaloffice.com
Continental Paper Grading Company Inc
1623 S Lumber St Chicago IL 60616 312-226-2010 226-2025 660
Web: www.cpgco.com
Continental Precision Corp
230 Saint Nicholas Ave. South Plainfield NJ 07080 908-754-7063 131
Web: www.montrosemolders.com
Continental Resources Inc
175 Middlesex Tpke Bedford MA 01730 781-275-0850 176
TF: 800-937-4688 ■ *Web:* www.conres.com
Continental Safety Equipment
2935 Waters Rd Ste 140 Eagan MN 55121 651-454-7233 454-3217 679
TF: 800-844-7003 ■ *Web:* www.csesafety.com
Continental Service Group Inc
200 Cross Keys Office Pk Fairport NY 14450 585-421-1000 160
TF: 800-724-7500 ■ *Web:* www.conserve-arm.com
Continental Shelf Assoc Inc
8502 SW Kansas Ave Stuart FL 34997 772-219-3000 219-3010 194
Web: www.conshelf.com
Continental Stock Transfer & Trust Company Inc
17 Battery Pl New York NY 10004 212-509-4000 690
Web: www.continentalstock.com
Continental Studwelding Ltd
35 Devon Rd. Brampton ON L6T5B6 905-792-3650 792-3711 481
TF: 800-848-9442 ■ *Web:* www.constud.ca
Continental Tire North America Inc
1800 Continental Blvd Charlotte NC 28273 704-583-3900 754
TF: 877-235-0102 ■ *Web:* www.conti-online.com
Continental Traffic Service Inc (CTSI)
5100 Poplar Ave 15th Fl Memphis TN 38137 901-766-1500 766-1520 311
TF: 888-836-5135 ■ *Web:* www.ctsi-global.com
Continental Web Press Inc
1430 Industrial Dr. Itasca IL 60143 630-773-1903 773-1903 627
TF: 800-558-8724 ■ *Web:* www.continentalweb.com
Continental Western Group
11201 Douglas Ave. Urbandale IA 50322 515-473-3000 473-3015* 391-4
*Fax: Hum Res ■ *TF:* 800-235-2942 ■ *Web:* www.cwgins.com
Continental, The 138 Market St Philadelphia PA 19106 215-923-6069 671
Web: www.continentalmartinibar.com
Continental-Capri Inc
250 Jackson St Englewood NJ 07631 201-568-7100 296-26
Contingent Network Services LLC
4400 Port Union Rd West Chester OH 45011 513-860-2573 387
Web: www.contingent.com
Contingent Workforce Solutions Inc
2430 Meadowpine Blvd Ste 101 Mississauga ON L5N6S2 866-837-8630 2
TF: 866-837-8630 ■ *Web:* cwsolutions.ca
Continucare Corp
7200 Corporate Ctr Dr Ste 600 Miami FL 33126 305-500-2000 500-2080 363
TF: 866-312-7154 ■ *Web:* www.continucare.com
Continuing Education of The Bar Sute 410
300 Frank H Ogawa Plaza Ste 410 Oakland CA 94612 510-302-2000 166
TF: 800-232-3444 ■ *Web:* www.ceb.com
Continuous Learning Group Inc, The
500 Cherrington Pkwy Ste 350 Pittsburgh PA 15108 412-269-7240 463
Web: www.clg.com

Phone | Fax | Class

Continuous Metal Technology
439 W Main St . . . Ridgway PA 15853 814-772-9274 697
Web: www.powdered-metal.com

Continuum 3150 Central Expy . . . Santa Clara CA 95051 408-727-3240 727-3550 425
TF: 888-532-1064 ■ *Web:* www.continuumlasers.com

Continuum Legal
1651 Old Meadow Rd Ste 600 . . . McLean VA 22102 703-734-7474 721
Web: www.continuumlegal.com

CONTMID Group 24000 Western Ave . . . Park Forest IL 60466 708-747-1200 747-9373 278
Web: www.contmid.com

Contour Saws Inc
900 Graceland Ave . . . Des Plaines IL 60016 800-259-6834 682
TF: 800-259-6834 ■ *Web:* contoursawsinc.com

Contour Tool Inc
38830 Taylor Pkwy . . . North Ridgeville OH 44039 440-365-7333 365-7335 621
Web: contourprecisionmilling.com

Contoural Inc
5150 El Camino Real Ste D-30 . . . Los Altos CA 94022 650-390-0800 194
Web: www.contoural.com

Contours Express Inc
156 Imperial Way . . . Nicholasville KY 40356 855-589-9662 241-2234* 354
**Fax Area Code:* 859 ■ *TF:* 855-589-9662 ■ *Web:* www.contoursexpress.com

Contra Costa College
2600 Mission Bell . . . San Pablo CA 94806 510-235-7800 412-0769 162
Web: www.contracosta.edu

Contra Costa County
651 Pine St 10th Fl . . . Martinez CA 94553 925-335-1080 335-1098 338
Web: www.co.contra-costa.ca.us

Contra Costa County Library
75 Santa Barbara Rd . . . Pleasant Hill CA 94523 925-646-6423 646-6461 434-3
TF: 800-984-4636 ■ *Web:* www.ccclib.org

Contra Costa Health Services
2500 Alhambra Ave . . . Martinez CA 94553 925-370-5000 370-5138 374-3
TF: 877-661-6230 ■ *Web:* www.cchealth.org/medical_center

Contract Converting LLC PO Box 247 . . . Greenville WI 54942 920-757-4000 92
Web: www.contractconverting.com

Contract Design Magazine
770 Broadway . . . New York NY 10004 800-697-8859 654-7205* 457-5
**Fax Area Code:* 646 ■ *TF:* 800-697-8859 ■ *Web:* www.contractdesign.com

Contract Environments Inc
1020 W 18th St . . . Wilmington DE 19802 302-658-0668 393
Web: contractenvironments.net

Contract Fabrication & Design LLC
5427 Fm 546 . . . Princeton TX 75407 972-736-2260 529
Web: cfdintl.com

Contract Fabricators Inc
105 Rolfing Rd . . . Holly Springs MS 38635 662-252-6330 480
Web: www.contractfab.com

Contract Furnishings Mart
22230 84th Ave S Ste 110 . . . Kent WA 98032 503-542-8900 290
Web: www.cfmfloors.com

Contract Land Staff LLC
2245 Texas Dr Ste 200 . . . Sugar Land TX 77479 281-240-3370 194
TF: 800-874-4519 ■ *Web:* www.contractlandstaff.com

Contract Manufacturers Inc
729 N Fleishel Ave . . . Tyler TX 75702 903-597-8297 664
Web: www.cmitx.net

Contract Office Group Inc
1731 Technology Dr . . . San Jose CA 95110 408-213-1790 321
Web: www.cog.com

Contract Packaging Resources Inc
8009 Industrial Village Rd . . . Greensboro NC 27409 336-665-1300 582
Web: www.cprwebsite.com

Contract Pharmacal Corp
135 Adams Ave . . . Hauppauge NY 11788 631-231-4610 231-4610 479
Web: www.cpc.com

Contract Pharmacy Services Inc
125 Titus Ave . . . Warrington PA 18976 267-487-9000 487-9050 238
Web: www.contractpharmacy.com

Contract Resource Group LLC
7108 Old Katy Rd Ste 150 . . . Houston TX 77024 713-803-0100 321
Web: www.crgoffice.com

Contractors Cargo Co 500 S Alameda St . . . Compton CA 90221 310-609-1957 358
Web: contractorscargo.com

Contractors Equipment Supply Company Inc
2000 E Overland Rd . . . Meridian ID 83642 208-888-3337 888-3088 190

Contractors Material Co
10320 S Medallion Dr . . . Cincinnati OH 45241 513-733-3000 480
Web: www.cmcmmi.com

Contractors Northwest Inc
3731 N Ramsey Rd . . . Coeur d'Alene ID 83815 208-667-2456 667-6388 188-10
Web: www.contractorsnorthwest.com

Contractors Register Inc
800 E Main St . . . Jefferson Valley NY 10535 800-431-2584 243-0287* 637-6
**Fax Area Code:* 914 ■ *TF:* 800-431-2584

Contractors Steel Co 36555 Amrhein Rd . . . Livonia MI 48150 734-464-4000 452-3939* 492
**Fax:* Sales ■ *TF:* 800-521-3946 ■ *Web:* www.contractorssteel.com

Contrans Corp 1179 Ridgeway Rd . . . Woodstock ON N4V1E3 519-421-4600 360-2
Web: www.contrans.ca

Contrast Creative 2598 Highstone Rd . . . Cary NC 27519 919-469-9151 514
Web: www.contrastcreative.com

Contrex Inc 8900 Zachary Ln N . . . Maple Grove MN 55369 763-424-7800 203
TF: 800-342-4411 ■ *Web:* www.contrexinc.com

Control Alt Design Ltd
1760 Britannia Dr Ste 8 . . . Elgin IL 60124 847-695-4050 454
Web: www.controlalt.com

Control Dynamics Corp 960 Louis Dr . . . Warminster PA 18974 215-956-0700 647

Control Engineering Magazine
2000 Clearwater Dr . . . Oak Brook IL 60523 630-288-8000 288-8580 457-21
Web: www.controleng.com

Control Flow Inc
9201 Fairbanks N Houston Rd . . . Houston TX 77064 281-890-8300 890-3947 790
TF: 800-231-9922 ■ *Web:* www.controlflow.com

Control Gaging Inc 5200 Venture Dr . . . Ann Arbor MI 48108 734-668-6750 201
Web: www.controlgaging.com

Control Line Equipment Inc
14750 Industrial Pkwy . . . Cleveland OH 44135 216-433-7766 223
TF: 888-895-1440 ■ *Web:* www.control-line.com

Phone | Fax | Class

Control Logistics Inc 1213 Pope Ln . . . Lake Worth FL 33460 561-641-2031 57
Web: www.aerowindows.com

Control Masters Inc
5235 Katrine Ave . . . Downers Grove IL 60515 630-968-2390 968-3260 203
Web: www.controlmasters.com

Control Module Inc 89 Phoenix Ave . . . Enfield CT 06082 860-745-2433 407
Web: www.controlmod.com

Control Point Corp
110 Castilian Dr Ste 200 . . . Goleta CA 93117 805-882-1884 261
Web: control-pt.com

Control Printing Group Inc
4212 S Hocker Dr Ste 150 . . . Independence MO 64055 816-350-8100 627
TF: 800-333-2820 ■ *Web:* www.controlprinting.com

Control Resources Inc
11 Beaver Brook Rd . . . Littleton MA 01460 978-486-4160 203
Web: controlresources.com

Control Southern Inc
3850 Lakefield Dr . . . Suwanee GA 30024 770-495-3100 358
TF: 800-749-0215 ■ *Web:* www.controlsouthern.com

Control Systems International Inc
8040 Nieman Rd . . . Lenexa KS 66214 913-599-5010 177

Control Techniques Americas
12005 Technology Dr . . . Eden Prairie MN 55344 952-995-8000 709
Web: www.emersonindustrial.com/en-US/controltechniques/Pages/home.aspx

Control Technology Inc
5734 Middlebrook Pike . . . Knoxville TN 37921 865-584-0440 203
Web: www.controltechnology.com

Controlled Access Inc
1515 W 130th St . . . Hinckley OH 44233 330-273-6185 639
TF: 800-942-0829 ■ *Web:* www.controlledaccess.com

Controlled Automation Inc
15421 Stony Creek Way B . . . Noblesville IN 46060 317-770-3870 729
Web: www.controlledautomationinc.com

Controlled Contamination Services LLC
6150 Lusk Blvd Ste B205 . . . San Diego CA 92121 888-979-9608 256
TF: 888-979-9608 ■ *Web:* www.cleanroomcleaning.com

Controlled Kinematics Inc
46740 Lakeview Blvd . . . Fremont CA 94538 408-945-1616 350
Web: www.ckinematics.com

Controlled Power Co 1955 Stephenson Hwy . . . Troy MI 48083 248-528-3700 528-0411 767
TF: 800-521-4792 ■ *Web:* www.controlledpwr.com

Controllers Group Inc
1818 The Alameda . . . San Jose CA 95126 408-294-0004 260
TF: 800-992-4647 ■ *Web:* www.controllersgroup.net

Controls Corporation of America
1501 Harpers Rd . . . Virginia Beach VA 23454 757-422-8330 45
TF: 800-225-0473 ■ *Web:* www.concoa.com

Controls Southeast Inc PO Box 7500 . . . Charlotte NC 28241 704-588-3030 644-5100 595
TF: 877-788-3030 ■ *Web:* www.csiheat.com

Conval Inc 265 Field Rd . . . Somers CT 06071 860-749-0761 763-3557 789
Web: www.conval.com

Convalescent Center of Honolulu
1900 Bachelot St . . . Honolulu HI 96817 808-531-5302 371
Web: ccoh.us

Convenience Retailers LLC
80980 US Hwy 111 . . . Indio CA 92201 760-347-2900 297-8

Convenient Food Mart
123 Gateway Blvd N . . . Elyria OH 44035 440-322-6301 345
Web: myconvenient.com

Convention & Visitors Bureau of Marion County
1000 Cole St Ste A . . . Fairmont WV 26554 304-368-1123 206
TF: 800-834-7365 ■ *Web:* www.marioncvb.com

Convention & Visitors Bureau-Village of Pinehurst Southern Pines Aberdeen Area
10677 Hwy 15-501 . . . Southern Pines NC 28387 910-692-3330 692-2493 206
TF: 800-346-5362 ■ *Web:* www.homeofgolf.com

Convention Consultants Historic Savannah Foundation
117 W Perry St . . . Savannah GA 31401 912-234-4088 184
TF: 800-559-6627 ■ *Web:* www.conventionconsultants.net

Conventus 516 N Ogden Ave Ste 115 . . . Chicago IL 60642 312-421-3270 180
Web: www.conventus-sei.com

Conventus Orthopaedics Inc
10200 73rd Ave N Ste 122 . . . Maple Grove MN 55369 763-515-5000 477
TF: 855-418-6466 ■ *Web:* www.conventusortho.com

Convergence LLC 6 Journey Ste 160 . . . Aliso Viejo CA 92656 949-716-8322 225
Web: www.convergence.net

Convergent Laser Technologies
1660 S Loop Rd . . . Alameda CA 94502 510-832-2130 832-1600 424
Web: www.convergentlaser.com

Convergent Media Systems Corp
190 Bluegrass Valley Pkwy
1 Convergent Ctr . . . Alpharetta GA 30005 770-369-9000 369-9100 736
TF: 800-331-5997 ■ *Web:* www.convergent.com

Convergent Wealth Advisors LLC
12505 Park Potomac Ave Ste 400 . . . Potomac MD 20854 301-770-6300 691
TF: 888-444-6347

ConvergeOne LLC 3344 Hwy 149 . . . Eagan MN 55121 888-321-6227 387
TF: 888-321-6227 ■ *Web:* convergeone.com

Convergint Technologies LLC
1651 Wilkening Rd . . . Schaumburg IL 60173 847-229-0222 693
Web: www.convergint.com

Convergys Corp 201 E Fourth St . . . Cincinnati OH 45202 513-723-7000 737
NYSE: CVG ■ *TF:* 888-284-9900 ■ *Web:* www.convergys.com

Converse College 580 E Main St . . . Spartanburg SC 29302 864-596-9000 596-9225* 166
**Fax:* Admissions ■ *TF Admissions:* 800-766-1125 ■ *Web:* www.converse.edu

Converse Consultants
717 S Myrtle Ave . . . Monrovia CA 91016 626-930-1200 930-1212 261
TF: 800-355-3969 ■ *Web:* www.converseconsultants.com

Converse County 107 N Fifth St Ste 114 . . . Douglas WY 82633 307-358-2244 770-3590* 338
**Fax Area Code:* 866 ■ *TF:* 800-460-5657 ■ *Web:* www.conversecounty.org

Converse International School of Languages
636 Broadway Ste 210 . . . San Diego CA 92101 619-239-3363 239-3778 423
TF: 800-818-9128 ■ *Web:* www.cisl.edu

Converteam Inc 610 Epsilon Dr . . . Pittsburgh PA 15238 412-967-0765 203
Web: www.gepowerconversion.com

Convertech Inc 353 Richard Mine Rd . . . Wharton NJ 07885 973-328-1850 628
Web: www.convertech.com

Convexx 6865 S Ea Ste 101 . . . Las Vegas NV 89119 702-450-7662 760
Web: www.convexx.com

Phone Fax Class

Con-Vey Keystone
526 NE Chestnut Roseburg ... Roseburg OR 97470 541-672-5506 672-2513 207
TF: 800-766-6705 ■ *Web:* www.con-vey.com

Convey Technology Inc 2 Campbell Dr ... Somers NY 10589 914-277-7502 180
Web: www.conveytechnology.com

Conveyco Technologies Inc PO Box 1000 ... Bristol CT 06011 860-589-8215 583-1384 385
TF: 800-229-8215 ■ *Web:* www.conveyco.com

Conveyer & Caster Corp
3501 Detroit Ave ... Cleveland OH 44113 216-631-4448 351
TF: 800-777-0600 ■ *Web:* www.cc-efi.com

Conveyor Components Co
130 Seltzer Rd ... Croswell MI 48422 810-679-4211 679-4510 207
TF Cust Svc: 800-233-3233 ■ *Web:* www.conveyorcomponents.com

Conveyor Dynamics Inc
1111 W Holly St Ste A ... Bellingham WA 98225 360-671-2200 256
Web: www.conveyor-dynamics.com

Conveyor Engineering & Manufacturing Co
1345 76th Ave SW ... Cedar Rapids IA 52404 319-364-5600 207
Web: www.conveyoreng.com

Conveyor Handling Company Inc
6715 Santa Barbara Ct ... Elkridge MD 21075 410-379-2700 358
Web: www.conveyorhandling.com

Conveyor Technologies Inc
5313 Womack Rd ... Sanford NC 27330 919-776-7227 207
Web: www.conveyor-technologies.com

Conveyors Inc 620 S Fourth Ave ... Mansfield TX 76063 817-473-4645 473-3024 207
TF: 800-243-9327 ■ *Web:* www.conveyorsinc.net

Convince & Convert
4463 Forest Hill Dr ... Bloomington IN 47401 602-616-1895 393
Web: www.convinceandconvert.com

Convio Inc 11501 Domain Dr Ste 200 ... Austin TX 78758 512-652-2600 180
TF: 888-528-9501 ■ *Web:* www.convio.com

Convoy Servicing Company Inc
3323 Jane Ln ... Dallas TX 75247 214-638-3050 610
TF: 800-592-3295 ■ *Web:* www.convoyservicing.com

Conway & Greenwood Inc
766 E Whitaker Mill Rd Ste 310 ... Raleigh NC 27608 984-444-2125 260
Web: www.conwaygreenwood.com

Conway & Owen Inc
1455 Bluegrass Lakes Pkwy ... Alpharetta GA 30004 678-350-9000 256
Web: www.conway-owen.com

Conway Area Chamber of Commerce
900 Oak St ... Conway AR 72032 501-327-7788 327-7790 139
TF: 800-750-8155 ■ *Web:* www.conwaychamber.org

Conway Area Chamber of Commerce
203 Main St ... Conway SC 29526 843-248-2273 248-0003 139
TF: 800-356-3016 ■ *Web:* www.conwayscchamber.com

Conway Cemetery State Park
One Capitol Mall 1 Capitol Mall ... Little Rock AR 72201 888-287-2757 565
TF: 888-287-2757 ■ *Web:* www.arkansasstateparks.com/conwaycemetery

Conway County 117 S Moose St ... Morrilton AR 72110 501-354-9640 338

Conway Daily Sun 64 Seavey St ... North Conway NH 03860 603-356-3456 532-3
TF: 800-526-5426 ■ *Web:* badgerrealty.com

Con-Way Freight 2211 Old Earhart Rd ... Ann Arbor MI 48105 734-994-6600 780
TF: 800-755-2728

Conway Glass Tinting Plus 701 Sixth St ... Conway AR 72032 501-450-7587 362
Web: conwayglasstinting.net

Conway Import Co Inc
11051 W Addison St ... Franklin Park IL 60131 847-455-5600 304-4021* 296-19
**Fax Area Code:* 800 ■ *TF:* 800-323-8801 ■ *Web:* conwaydressings.com

Conway MacKenzie Inc
401 S Old Woodward Ave Ste 340 ... Birmingham MI 48009 248-433-3100 194
Web: www.conwaymackenzie.com

Conway Management Co
547 Amherst St Ste 106 ... Nashua NH 03063 603-889-1130 463
TF: 800-359-0099 ■ *Web:* www.conwaymgmt.com

Conway Marketing Communications
6400 Baum Dr ... Knoxville TN 37919 865-588-5731 7
TF: 800-882-7875 ■ *Web:* www.conwaymktg.com

Conway Medical Ctr
300 Singleton Ridge Rd ... Conway SC 29526 843-347-7111 374-3
TF: 800-922-5431 ■ *Web:* www.conwaymedicalcenter.com

Conway Regional Hospital
2302 College Ave ... Conway AR 72032 501-329-3831 374-3
TF: 800-245-3314 ■ *Web:* www.conwayregional.org

Conway Services LLC
1220 Big Orange Rd ... Cordova TN 38018 901-384-3511 610
Web: www.conwayservices.net

Conway, Olejniczak & Jerry SC
231 S Adams St ... Green Bay WI 54301 920-437-0476 428
Web: www.lcojlaw.com

Conxxus LLC 330 W Ottawa ... Paxton IL 60957 217-379-2026 224
TF: 800-448-4320 ■ *Web:* www.conxxus.com

Conyers Jr John (Rep D - MI)
2426 Rayburn Bldg ... Washington DC 20515 202-225-5126 225-0072 342-2
Web: conyers.house.gov

Conyers-Rockdale Chamber of Commerce
1186 Scott St ... Conyers GA 30012 770-483-7049 922-8415 139
Web: www.conyers-rockdale.com

Cooch & Taylor
1000 W St The Brandywine Bldg 10th Fl ... Wilmington DE 19801 302-984-3800 428
Web: www.coochtaylor.com

Cook & Boardman Inc
9347 D Ducks Ln Ste A ... Charlotte NC 28273 704-334-8683 334-9366 234
Web: www.cookandboardman.com

Cook & Co 12 Masterton Rd ... Bronxville NY 10708 914-779-4838 194
Web: www.cook-co.com

Cook Assoc Inc 212 W Kinzie St ... Chicago IL 60654 312-329-0900 266
Web: www.cookassociates.com

Cook Aviation Inc 970 S Kirby Rd ... Bloomington IN 47403 812-825-2392 825-3701 63
TF: 800-880-3499 ■ *Web:* www.cookaviation.com

Cook Biotech Inc
1425 Innovation Pl ... West Lafayette IN 47906 765-497-3355 85
TF: 888-299-4224 ■ *Web:* www.cookbiotech.com

Cook Brothers Inc 1740 N Kostner Ave ... Chicago IL 60639 773-770-1200 321
TF: 800-334-7661 ■ *Web:* www.cookbrothers.com

Cook Children's Medical Ctr
801 Seventh Ave ... Fort Worth TX 76104 682-885-4000 374-1
Web: cookchildrens.org

Cook Coggin Engineers Inc
703 Crossover Rd ... Tupelo MS 38802 662-842-7381 261
Web: cookcoggin.com

Cook Communications Ministries
4050 Lee Vance View ... Colorado Springs CO 80918 800-323-7543 637-9
TF: 800-323-7543 ■ *Web:* www.davidccook.com

Cook Concrete Products Inc
5461 Eastside Rd ... Redding CA 96001 530-243-2562 243-6881 183
TF: 800-367-2020 ■ *Web:* www.cookconcreteproducts.com

Cook County 69 W Washington Ste 500 ... Chicago IL 60602 312-603-5656 603-6767 338
Web: www.cookcountyclerk.com

Cook County 411 W Second St ... Grand Marais MN 55604 218-387-3647 387-3007 338
Web: www.co.cook.mn.us

Cook Flatt & Strobel Engineers
2930 SW Woodside Dr ... Topeka KS 66614 785-272-4706 261
Web: cfse.com

Cook Forest State Park PO Box 120 ... Cooksburg PA 16217 814-744-8407 565
Web: www.dcnr.state.pa.us

Cook Gm Super Store 1193 W Saginaw Rd ... Vassar MI 48768 989-882-4074 57
Web: cookgm.com

Cook Hotel & Conference Ctr
3848 West Lakeshore Dr ... Baton Rouge LA 70808 225-383-2665 377
TF: 866-610-2665 ■ *Web:* www.thecookhotel.com

Cook Inc PO Box 4195 ... Bloomington IN 47402 812-339-2235 339-2235 476
TF: 800-457-4500 ■ *Web:* www.cookmedical.com

Cook Inlet Region Inc
2525 C St Ste 500 ... Anchorage AK 99503 907-274-8638 760
Web: www.ciri.com

Cook Medical Inc
1186 Montgomery Ln ... Vandergrift PA 15690 724-845-8621 476
TF General: 800-457-4500 ■ *Web:* www.cookmedical.com

Cook Medical Inc
4900 Bethania Stn Rd ... Winston-Salem NC 27105 336-744-0157 476
TF: 800-457-4500 ■ *Web:* www.cookmedical.com

Cook Medical Inc PO Box 4195 ... Bloomington IN 47402 812-339-2235 554-8335* 476
**Fax Area Code:* 800 ■ *TF:* 800-457-4500 ■ *Web:* www.cookmedical.com

Cook Memorial Public Library District
413-n Milwaukee Ave ... Libertyville IL 60048 847-362-2330 434-3
Web: www.cooklib.org

Cook Moving Systems Inc 1845 Dale Rd ... Buffalo NY 14225 800-828-7144 519
TF: 800-828-7144 ■ *Web:* www.cookmoving.com

Cook Paul (Rep R - CA)
1222 Longworth Bldg ... Washington DC 20515 202-225-5861 342-2
Web: cook.house.gov

Cook Pine Capital LLC
73 Arch St Greenwich 2nd Fl ... Greenwich CT 06830 203-861-2930 401
Web: www.cookpinecapital.com

Cook Security Group Inc
5841 SE International Way ... Milwaukie OR 97222 503-786-5173 693
Web: www.cooksecuritygroup.com

Cook Street School of Fine Cooking
1937 Market St ... Denver CO 80202 303-308-9300 308-9400 163
Web: www.cookstreet.com

Cook Systems International Inc
6799 Great Oaks Rd Atrium II Ste 200 ... Memphis TN 38138 901-757-8877 180
TF: 800-266-5185 ■ *Web:* www.cooksys.com

Cook Truck Equipment & Tools
3701 Harlee Ave ... Charlotte NC 28208 704-392-4138 57
TF: 800-241-4210 ■ *Web:* www.cooktruck.com

Cook Urological Inc PO Box 4195 ... Bloomington IN 47402 812-339-2235 476
TF: 800-457-4500 ■ *Web:* www.cookmedical.com

Cook's Corner
19152 Santiago Canyon Rd ... Trabuco Canyon CA 92679 949-858-0266 361
Web: cookscorners.com

Cook's Ham Inc 200 S Second St ... Lincoln NE 68508 402-475-6700 296-20
TF: 800-332-8400 ■ *Web:* www.mycooksham.com

Cook's Illustrated Magazine
PO Box 470739 ... Brookline MA 02447 617-232-1000 457-11
TF Circ: 800-526-8442 ■ *Web:* www.cooksillustrated.com

Cook's Pest Control Inc
1741 Fifth Ave SE ... Decatur AL 35601 256-355-3285 577
TF: 800-616-5299 ■ *Web:* www.cookspest.com

Cookbook Publishers Inc 9825 Widmer Rd ... Lenexa KS 66215 913-492-5900 492-5947 626
TF: 800-227-7282 ■ *Web:* www.cookbookpublishers.com

Cooke & Bieler LP
1700 Market St Ste 3222 ... Philadelphia PA 19103 215-567-1101 567-1681 401
TF: 800-541-7774 ■ *Web:* www.cooke-bieler.com

Cooke County 101S Dixon ... Gainesville TX 76240 940-668-5420 668-5522 338
Web: www.co.cooke.tx.us

Cooke County Electric Co-op
11799 W US Hwy 82 PO Box 530 ... Muenster TX 76252 940-759-2211 759-4122* 245
**Fax:* Cust Svc ■ *TF:* 800-962-0296 ■ *Web:* www.cceca.com

Cooke Sales & Service Company Inc
1422 Washington St ... Chillicothe MO 64601 660-646-1166 358

Cooke Trucking Co Inc
1759 S Andy Griffith Pkwy ... Mount Airy NC 27030 336-786-5181 789-7132 780
TF: 800-888-9502 ■ *Web:* www.cooketrucking.com

Cooke's Crating Inc
3124 E 11th St ... Los Angeles CA 90023 323-268-5101 262-2001 549
Web: www.cookescrating.com

Cooke's Seafood 1120 Iyannough Rd ... Hyannis MA 02601 508-775-0450 671
Web: www.cookesseafood.com

Cookeville Area-Putnam County Chamber of Commerce
1 W First St ... Cookeville TN 38501 931-526-2211 526-4023 139
TF: 800-264-5541 ■ *Web:* www.cookevillechamber.com

Cookeville Newspapers Inc
1300 Neal St ... Cookeville TN 38501 931-526-9715 532-3
Web: www.herald-citizen.com

Cookeville Regional Medical Ctr (CRMC)
1 Medical Ctr Blvd ... Cookeville TN 38501 931-528-2541 374-3
TF: 800-897-1898 ■ *Web:* www.crmchealth.org

Cookie Jar 1006 Cadillac Ct ... Fairbanks AK 99701 907-479-8319 671
Web: www.cookiejarfairbanks.com

Cookies By Design Inc
1865 Summit Ave Ste 605 ... Plano TX 75074 972-398-9536 398-9542 310
TF: 800-945-2665 ■ *Web:* www.cookiesbydesign.com

Cookies From Home Inc
1605 W University Dr Ste 106 ... Tempe AZ 85281 480-894-1944 68
Web: www.cookiesfromhome.com

Phone | Fax | Class

Cookies The Kids Department Store
510 Fulton St ... Brooklyn NY 11201 718-797-3300 229
TF: 877-942-6654 ■ *Web:* www.cookieskids.com

Cook-Illinois Corp
2100 Clearwater Dr ... Oak Brook IL 60523 708-560-9840 560-0661 109
Web: cookillinois.com

Cooking & Hospitality Institute of Chicago
361 W Chestnut St ... Chicago IL 60610 312-944-0882 944-8557 163
TF Admissions: 877-828-7772 ■ *Web:* www.chefs.edu

Cooking Light Magazine
2100 Lakeshore Dr ... Birmingham AL 35209 205-445-6000 445-6600 457-13
TF: 800-366-4712 ■ *Web:* www.cookinglight.com

Cookshack 2304 N Ash St ... Ponca City OK 74601 580-765-3669 361
TF: 800-423-0698 ■ *Web:* cookshack.com

Cookson Co 2417 S 50th Ave ... Phoenix AZ 85043 602-272-4244 234
TF: 800-294-4358 ■ *Web:* www.cooksondoor.com

Cookson Hills Electric Co-op Inc
1002 E Main St ... Stigler OK 74462 918-967-4614 245
TF: 800-328-2368 ■ *Web:* www.cooksonhills.com

Cookson Peirce & Company Inc
555 Grant St Ste 380 ... Pittsburgh PA 15219 412-471-5320 401
Web: www.cooksonpeirce.com

CookTek LLC 156 N Jefferson St Ste 300 ... Chicago IL 60661 312-563-9600 36
TF: 888-266-5835 ■ *Web:* www.cooktek.com

Cool Amphibious Manufacturers International LLC
714 Okeetee Rd ... Ridgeland SC 29936 843-717-2444 717-2424 120
Web: www.camillc.com

Cool Check Air Conditioning
25 Coronet Rd Ste 4 ... Etobicoke ON M8Z2L8 416-236-1000 236-4323 610
Web: coolcheck.ca

Cool Earth Solar Inc
4659 Las Positas Rd Ste C ... Livermore CA 94551 925-454-8506 357
Web: www.coolearthsolar.com

Cool Energy Inc
5541 Central Ave Ste 172 ... Boulder CO 80301 303-442-2121 357
Web: coolenergy.com

Cool Gear International LLC
10 Cordage Park Cir ... Plymouth MA 02360 855-393-2665 361
TF: 855-393-2665 ■ *Web:* www.coolgearinc.com

Cool River Cafe 1045 Hidden Ridge ... Irving TX 75038 972-871-8881 871-8882 671
Web: www.coolrivercafe.com

Coolant Control Inc
5353 Spring Grove Ave ... Cincinnati OH 45217 513-471-8770 146
TF: 800-535-3885 ■ *Web:* www.coolantcontrol.com

Cooley Dickinson Hospital
30 Locust St ... NorthHampton MA 01060 413-582-2000 582-2952 374-3
Web: www.cooleydickinson.org

Cooley Dickinson VNA & Hospice
168 Industrial Dr ... NorthHampton MA 01060 413-584-1060 371
Web: www.vnaandhospice.org

Cooley Group 50 Esten Ave ... Pawtucket RI 02860 401-724-9000 745-2
TF Cust Svc: 800-992-0072 ■ *Web:* www.cooleygroup.com

Cooley LLP 3000 El Camino Real ... Palo Alto CA 94306 650-843-5000 849-7400 428
Web: www.cooley.com

Cooley Motors Corp
401 N Greenbush Rd ... Rensselaer NY 12144 518-283-2902 57
TF: 888-518-0245 ■ *Web:* www.cooleyvw.com

Coolidge State Park
855 Coolidge State Pk Rd ... Plymouth VT 05056 802-672-3612 565
Web: www.vtstateparks.com

Cooling Technology Institute (CTI)
2611 FM 1960 Rd W Ste A-101 ... Houston TX 77068 281-583-4087 537-1721 48-12
TF: 800-344-4866 ■ *Web:* www.cti.org

Cooling Tower Technologies Inc
52410 Clark Rd ... White Castle LA 70788 225-545-3040 596
Web: www.crownctti.com

CoolSprings Galleria
1800 Galleria Blvd ... Franklin TN 37067 615-771-2050 460
TF: 800-336-3335 ■ *Web:* www.coolspringsgalleria.com

CoolTronics 220 E Madison St Ste 1220 ... Tampa FL 33602 813-259-4407 791
Web: www.cooltronics.com

Coon Brent & Associates Law Firm Pc
215 Orleans St ... Beaumont TX 77701 409-835-2666 428
TF: 866-335-2666 ■ *Web:* bcoonlaw.com

Coon Memorial Home Health
1411 Denver Ave ... Dalhart TX 79022 806-244-8738 363
Web: www.dhchd.org

Coon Valley Telecommunications
105 Central Ave ... Coon Valley WI 54623 608-452-3101 225
TF: 800-242-8511 ■ *Web:* www.coonvalleytel.com

Cooner Wire Co 9265 Owensmouth Ave ... Chatsworth CA 91311 818-882-8311 709-8281 813
Web: www.coonerwire.com

Cooney State Park PO Box 254 ... Joliet MT 59041 406-445-2326 565
Web: www.fwp.mt.gov

Coons Christopher A (Sen D - DE)
127A Russell Bldg ... Washington DC 20510 202-224-5042 342-2
Web: www.coons.senate.gov

Coontail Corner 5466 Park St ... Boulder Junction WI 54512 888-874-0885 711
TF: 888-874-0885 ■ *Web:* coontailsports.com

Co-op America 1612 K St NW Ste 600 ... Washington DC 20006 202-872-5307 331-8166 48-13
TF: 800-584-7336 ■ *Web:* www.greenamerica.org

Co-op Communciations Inc
412 Washington Ave ... Belleville NJ 07109 800-833-2700 736
TF: 800-833-2700 ■ *Web:* www.cooperativenet.com

Co-Op Country Farmers Elevator
340 Dupont Ave NE ... Renville MN 56284 320-329-8377 207
Web: www.coopcountry.com

Co-op Elevator Co 7211 E Michigan Ave ... Pigeon MI 48755 989-453-4500 453-3942 275
TF: 800-968-0601 ■ *Web:* www.coopelev.com

Co-op Feed Dealers Inc
380 Broome Corporate Pkwy PO Box 670 ... Conklin NY 13748 607-651-9078 651-9078 276
TF Cust Svc: 800-333-0895 ■ *Web:* www.cfd.coop

Co-op Finance Assn Inc, The
10100 N Ambassador Dr Ste 315
PO Box 901532 ... Kansas City MO 64153 816-214-4200 214-4221 216
TF: 877-835-5232 ■ *Web:* www.cfafs.com

CO-OP Financial Services Inc
9692 Haven Ave ... Rancho Cucamonga CA 91730 800-782-9042 393
TF: 800-782-9042 ■ *Web:* www.co-opfs.org

Co-op Gas Inc 4395 Hwy 56 ... Pauline SC 29374 864-583-6546 316
Web: www.ballooncountry.com

Coop Purdel LA
155 Rue Saint-Jean-Baptiste ... Le Bic QC G0L1B0 418-736-4363 111
Web: www.purdel.qc.ca

Co-op State Research Education & Extension Service
1400 Independence Ave SW Ste 2201 ... Washington DC 20250 202-401-4952 720-6486 340-1
Web: nifa.usda.gov

Cooper & Company Inc
10179 Commerce Park Dr ... Cincinnati OH 45246 513-671-6067 410
Web: www.dakotawatchsales.com

Cooper Aerial Survey Co
1692 W Grant Rd ... Tucson AZ 85745 520-884-7580 727
TF: 800-229-2279 ■ *Web:* cooperaerial.com

Cooper Atkins Corp
33 Reeds Gap Rd ... Middlefield CT 06455 860-349-3473 349-8994 201
TF Sales: 800-835-5011 ■ *Web:* cooper-atkins.com/default.asp

Cooper B-Line Inc 509 W Monroe St ... Highland IL 62249 618-654-2184 356-1438* 816
*Fax Area Code: 800 ■ *TF:* 800-851-7415 ■ *Web:* www.cooperindustries.com

Cooper Brothers Construction Company Inc
3005 Citizens Pkwy ... Selma AL 36701 334-874-8267 186
Web: cooperbrothersconstruction.com

Cooper Bussmann Inc
114 Old State Rd ... Ellisville MO 63021 636-394-2877 394-2877* 815
*Fax: Cust Svc ■ *TF:* 855-287-7626 ■ *Web:* www.cooperindustries.com

Cooper Carry Inc
191 Peachtree St NE Ste 2400 ... Atlanta GA 30303 404-237-2000 237-0276 261
Web: www.coopercarry.com

Cooper Communities Inc 903 N 47th St ... Rogers AR 72756 479-246-6500 653
TF: 800-648-6401 ■ *Web:* www.cooper-communities.com

Cooper Cos Inc
6140 Stoneridge Mall Rd Ste 590 ... Pleasanton CA 94588 925-460-3600 542
NYSE: COO ■ *TF:* 888-822-2660 ■ *Web:* www.coopercos.com

Cooper County 200 Main St ... Boonville MO 65233 660-882-2114 882-5645 338
Web: www.coopercountymo.gov

Cooper Crouse-Hinds 1201 Wolf St ... Syracuse NY 13208 315-477-5531 477-5531 815
TF: 866-764-5454 ■ *Web:* www.cooperindustries.com

Cooper Engineering Co Inc
2600 College Dr ... Rice Lake WI 54868 715-234-7008 261
Web: www.cooperengineering.net

Cooper Farms
22348 County Rd 140 PO Box 547 ... Oakwood OH 45873 419-594-3325 594-3372 10-8
TF: 800-423-2765 ■ *Web:* www.cooperfarms.com

Cooper Green Hospital
1515 Sixth Ave S ... Birmingham AL 35233 205-930-3200 374-3

Cooper Hand Tools Inc
3535 Glenwood Ave ... Raleigh NC 27612 919-781-7200 350

Cooper High School 3639 Sayles Blvd ... Abilene TX 79605 325-691-1000 685
Web: abileneisd.org

Cooper Hosiery Mills Inc
4005 Gault Ave N ... Fort Payne AL 35967 256-845-1491 155-10

Cooper Hotel & Conference Ctr
12230 Preston Rd ... Dallas TX 75230 972-386-0306 379
TF: 800-444-5187 ■ *Web:* www.cooperaerobics.com

Cooper Hotels
1661 Arrion Brainner Dr Ste 200 ... Memphis TN 38120 901-322-1400 322-1403 379
Web: www.cooperhotels.com

Cooper Industries
600 Travis St Ste 5400 ... Houston TX 77002 713-209-8400 209-8995 815
NYSE: ETN ■ *TF:* 866-853-4293 ■ *Web:* www.cooperindustries.com

Cooper Jim (Rep D - TN)
1536 Longworth Bldg ... Washington DC 20515 202-225-4311 226-1035 342-2
Web: www.cooper.house.gov

Cooper Lake State Park
1664 Farm Rd 1529 S ... Cooper TX 75432 903-395-3100 565
Web: tpwd.texas.gov/state-parks/cooper-lake

Cooper Legal Services Dwayne E Cooper Attorney at Law
718 S Washinton St ... Marion IN 46953 765-573-3133 428
TF: 800-959-1825 ■ *Web:* cooperlegalservices.com

Cooper Lighting Inc
1121 Hwy 74 S ... Peachtree City GA 30269 770-486-4800 486-4801 439
Web: www.cooperindustries.com

Cooper Motors Inc 985 York St ... Hanover PA 17331 866-414-2809 57
TF: 866-414-2809 ■ *Web:* coopermotors.com

Cooper Perkins Inc 10 Maguire Rd ... Lexington MA 02421 781-538-5536 463
Web: www.cooperperkins.com

Cooper Power Systems Inc
2300 Badger Dr ... Waukesha WI 53187 262-896-2400 896-2313 767
TF: 800-223-5227 ■ *Web:* www.cooperindustries.com

Cooper Pugeda Management Inc
65 Mccoppin St ... San Francisco CA 94103 415-543-6515 186
TF: 800-733-0660 ■ *Web:* www.cpmservices.com

Cooper Ray (D)
Office of the Governor
20301 Mail Service Ctr ... Raleigh NC 27699 919-814-2000 733-2120 343
Web: governor.nc.gov

Cooper Split Roller Bearing Corp, The
5365 Robin Hood Rd Ste B ... Norfolk VA 23513 757-460-0925 75
Web: www.cooperbearings.com

Cooper STEEL Inc
503 N Hillcrest Dr ... Shelbyville TN 37160 931-684-7962 480
Web: www.coopersteel.com

Cooper Street Correctional Facility
3100 Cooper St ... Jackson MI 49201 517-780-6175 213
Web: www.michigan.gov/corrections

Cooper Thomas LLC 923 V St NW ... Washington DC 20001 202-387-8366 195
Web: cooperthomas.com

Cooper Tire & Rubber Co 701 Lima Ave ... Findlay OH 45840 419-423-1321 754
NYSE: CTB ■ *TF:* 800-854-6288 ■ *Web:* www.coopertire.com

Cooper Union for the Advancement of Science & Art
30 Cooper Sq ... New York NY 10003 212-353-4100 353-4327* 166
*Fax: Admissions ■ *TF:* 800-872-2777 ■ *Web:* www.cooper.edu

Cooper University Hospital
3 Cooper Plaza ... Camden NJ 08103 856-342-2000 374-3
TF: 800-826-6737 ■ *Web:* www.cooperhealth.org

Cooper Wellness Program
12230 Preston Rd ... Dallas TX 75230 972-386-4777 706
TF: 800-444-5192 ■ *Web:* cooperaerobics.com

Phone | Fax | Class

Cooper Wiring Devices Inc
203 Cooper Cir. . . . Peachtree City GA 30269 770-631-2100 631-2100 815
TF Cust Svc: 866-853-4293 ■ *Web:* www.cooperindustries.com

Cooper Young Business Assn
2120 Young Ave . . . . Memphis TN 38104 901-276-7222 50-6
TF: 800-342-3308 ■ *Web:* lamplighter.cooperyoung.org

Cooper Zietz Engineers Inc
620 S W Fifth Ave Ste 1225 . . . . Portland OR 97204 503-253-5429 261

Cooper's Ale House
8065 Lake City Way NE. . . . Seattle WA 98115 206-522-2923 671
Web: www.coopersalehouse.com

Cooper's Seafood House
701 N Washington Ave. . . . Scranton PA 18509 570-346-6883 671
Web: www.coopers-seafood.com

Cooper, Travis & Company PLC
3008 Poston Ave. . . . Nashville TN 37203 615-329-4500 2
TF: 800-201-3187 ■ *Web:* www.coopertravis.com

Cooper/T Smith Stevedoring Co
118 N Royal St . . . . Mobile AL 36602 251-431-6100 465
Web: www.coopertsmith.com

Cooperative Forestiere Des Hautes-Laurentides
395 Boul Des Ruisseaux. . . . Mont-Laurier QC J9L0H6 819-623-4422 302
Web: www.cfhl.qc.ca

Cooperative Optical 2424 E 8 Mile Rd. . . . Detroit MI 48234 313-366-3290 542
Web: www.coopoptical.com

Cooper-Hewitt National Design Museum (Smithsonian Institution)
2 E 91st St . . . . New York NY 10128 212-849-8400 849-8401 520
Web: www.cooperhewitt.org

Coopers Creek Chemical Corp
884 River Rd. . . . West Conshohocken PA 19428 610-828-0375 828-9720 46
Web: www.cooperscreekchemical.com

Coopers Rock State Forest
61 County Line Dr . . . . Bruceton Mills WV 26525 304-594-1561 565
Web: www.coopersrockstateforest.com

Cooper-smith Adv LLC 4444 Bennett Rd . . . . Toledo OH 43612 419-470-5900 4
TF: 800-215-8812 ■ *Web:* cooper-smith.com

Cooper-Standard Automotive Fluid Systems Div
2110 Executive Hills Ct. . . . Auburn Hills MI 48326 248-836-9400 836-9116 60
Web: www.cooperstandard.com

Cooper-Standard Automotive Inc
39550 Orchard Hill Pl Dr . . . . Novi MI 48375 248-596-5900 60
Web: www.cooperstandard.com

CooperSurgical Inc 95 Corporate Dr . . . . Trumbull CT 06611 203-929-6321 262-0105* 476
**Fax Area Code:* 800 ■ **Fax:* Cust Svc ■ *TF:* 800-645-3760 ■ *Web:* www.coopersurgical.com

CooperVision Inc
209 High Point Dr Ste 200. . . . Victor NY 14564 585-385-6810 542
TF: 800-538-7850 ■ *Web:* www.coopercos.com

Cooptel 5521 Chemin de lAeroport. . . . Valcourt QC J0E2L0 450-532-2667 224
Web: www.cooptel.qc.ca

Coordinating Council on Juvenile Justice & Delinquency Prevention
810 Seventh St NW. . . . Washington DC 20531 202-307-5911 307-2093 340-20
Web: www.juvenilecouncil.gov

Coordinating Research Council Inc (CRC)
5755 N Point Pkwy Suite 265. . . . Alpharetta GA 30022 678-795-0506 795-0509 49-19
Web: www.crcao.com

Coors Credit Union 816 Washington Ave. . . . Golden CO 80401 303-279-6414 279-6336 219
TF: 800-770-6414

Coors Distributing Co (CBC)
5400 N Pecos St. . . . Denver CO 80221 303-433-6541 81-1
Web: www.coors.com

Coors Field 2001 Blake St . . . . Denver CO 80205 303-292-0200 312-2115 720
Web: colorado.rockies.mlb.com

CoorsTek Inc 600 Ninth St. . . . Golden CO 80401 303-278-4000 271-7009 249
TF: 800-821-6110 ■ *Web:* www.coorstek.com

Coos Bay Public Library
525 W Anderson Ave . . . . Coos Bay OR 97420 541-269-1101 434-3
Web: bay.cooslibraries.org

Coos Bay-North Bend Visitor & Convention Bureau
50 Central Ave . . . . Coos Bay OR 97420 541-269-0215 269-2861 206
TF: 800-824-8486 ■ *Web:* www.oregonsadventurecoast.com

Coos County 250 N Baxter St. . . . Coquille OR 97423 541-396-3121 396-4861 338
TF: 800-452-6010 ■ *Web:* www.co.coos.or.us

Coos County PO Box 10. . . . West Stewartstown NH 03597 603-246-3321 246-8117 338
TF: 800-637-0123 ■ *Web:* www.cooscountynh.us

Coosa County PO Box 10. . . . Rockford AL 35136 256-377-1350 377-2524 338
TF: 800-633-6282 ■ *Web:* www.coosacountyal.com

Coosa Pines Federal Credit Union
17591 Plant Rd. . . . Childersburg AL 35044 256-378-5559 378-3881 219
TF: 800-237-9789 ■ *Web:* www.coosapinesfcu.org

Coosa Valley HomeCare
209 W Spring St. . . . Sylacauga AL 35150 256 208-0087 374-3
Web: lhcgroup.com

Coos-Curry Electric Co-op Inc
43050 Hwy 101 PO Box 1268. . . . Port Orford OR 97465 541-332-3931 332-3501 245
Web: www.ccec.coop

COP Communications Inc 620 W Elk Ave . . . . Glendale CA 91204 818-291-1100 627
Web: www.copprints.com

COPA (American Postal Workers Union PAC)
1300 L St NW. . . . Washington DC 20005 202-842-4200 615
Web: apwu.org

COPE Inc 1120 G St NW Ste 550 . . . . Washington DC 20005 202-628-5100 628-5111 462
TF: 800-247-3054 ■ *Web:* www.cope-inc.com

Cope Plastics Inc 4441 Industrial Dr . . . . Godfrey IL 62002 618-466-0221 466-7975* 603
**Fax:* Acctg ■ *TF:* 800-851-5510 ■ *Web:* www.copeplastics.com

Cope's Knotty Pine Cafe
1530 Norris Rd. . . . Bakersfield CA 93308 661-399-0120 671

Copeland & Bieger P C
212 W Valley St . . . . Abingdon VA 24212 276-628-9525 445
Web: www.rcopelandlaw.com

Copeland Capital Management LLC
8 Tower Bridge 161 Washington St
Ste 1650. . . . Conshohocken PA 19428 484-530-4300 401
Web: www.copelandcapital.com

Copeland Industries 6841 Avenue U . . . . Houston TX 77011 713-926-7481 454
Web: www.copelandballvalves.com

Copeland's of New Orleans
1665 E Industrial Loop. . . . Shreveport LA 71106 318-797-0143 671
Web: www.copelandsofneworleans.com

Copelands of New Orleans
4957 Essen Ln . . . . Baton Rouge LA 70809 225-769-1800 671
Web: www.copelandsofneworleans.com

Copenhagen 1701 E Camelback Rd. . . . Phoenix AZ 85016 602-266-8060 321
Web: www.copenhagenliving.com

Copernicus Group Inc, The
1 Triangle Dr Ste 100 . . . . Durham NC 27713 919-465-4310 743
Web: www.cgirb.com

Copernicus Learning Ventures
250 W 50th St Fl L-29 . . . . New York NY 10019 646-215-9772 463

Copesan Services Inc
W175 N5711 Technology Dr. . . . Menomonee Falls WI 53051 800-267-3726 577
TF: 800-267-3726 ■ *Web:* www.copesan.com

Copia Creative Inc
3122 Santa Monica Blvd Ste 203 . . . . Santa Monica CA 90404 310-826-7422 7

Copia International Ltd
1220 Iroquois Dr Ste 180. . . . Naperville IL 60187 630-778-8898 778-8848* 173-3
**Fax:* Sales ■ *TF Sales:* 800-689-8898 ■ *Web:* www.copia.com

Copiah County
122 S Lowe St PO Box 507. . . . Hazlehurst MS 39083 601-894-1858 338
Web: www.copiahcounty.org

Copiah-Lincoln Community College
Natchez PO Box 649 . . . . Wesson MS 39191 601-442-9111 162
Web: www.colin.edu

Copic Insurance Co 7351 Lowry Blvd . . . . Denver CO 80230 720-858-6000 858-6001 391-5
TF: 800-421-1834 ■ *Web:* www.callcopic.com/cic

Copiers Northwest Inc
601 Dexter Ave N . . . . Seattle WA 98109 206-282-1200 282-2010 112
TF: 866-692-0700 ■ *Web:* www.copiersnw.com

COPIRG (Colorado Public Interest Research Group)
1543 Wazee St Ste 330. . . . Denver CO 80202 303-573-7474 633
Web: www.copirg.org

Copland Fabrics Inc
1714 Carolina Mill Rd . . . . Burlington NC 27217 336-226-0272 226-6452 745-1
Web: www.coplandfabrics.com

Copley Controls Corp 20 Dan Rd. . . . Canton MA 02021 781-828-0090 828-6547 472
Web: www.copleycontrols.com

Copley Hospital System
528 Washington Hwy . . . . Morrisville VT 05661 802-888-8888 374-3
TF: 800-564-1612 ■ *Web:* www.copleyvt.org

Copley Place 100 Huntington Ave Ste 100 . . . . Boston MA 02116 617-262-6600 460
TF: 877-746-6642 ■ *Web:* simon.com

Copley Square Hotel 47 Huntington Ave . . . . Boston MA 02116 617-536-9000 379
TF: 800-225-7062 ■ *Web:* www.copleysquarehotel.com

Coppel Corp 503 Scaroni Rd . . . . Calexico CA 92231 760-357-3707 96
Web: www.coppel.com

Coppell Chamber of Commerce
509 W Bethel Rd Ste 200 . . . . Coppell TX 75019 972-393-2829 393-0659 139
Web: www.coppellchamber.org

Copper Beech Inn, The 46 Main St. . . . Ivoryton CT 06442 860-767-0330 378
TF: 800-503-9624 ■ *Web:* www.copperbeechinn.com

Copper Breaks State Park 777 Pk Rd 62 . . . . Quanah TX 79252 940-839-4331 565
Web: tpwd.texas.gov/state-parks/copper-breaks

Copper Brite Inc
1482 E Valley Rd Ste 29 Ste 29 . . . . Santa Barbara CA 93108 805-565-1566 565-1394 151
Web: www.copperbrite.com

Copper Creek Canyon
3953 E 82nd St. . . . Indianapolis IN 46240 317-577-2990 321
Web: www.coppercreekcanyon.com

Copper Development Assn Inc
260 Madison Ave 16th Fl . . . . New York NY 10016 212-251-7200 251-7234 49-13
TF: 800-232-3282 ■ *Web:* www.copper.org

Copper Falls State Park
36764 Copper Falls Rd. . . . Mellen WI 54546 715-274-5123 565
Web: dnr.wi.gov

Copper Hills Youth Ctr
5899 Rivendell Dr. . . . West Jordan UT 84081 800 776 7116 569-2959* 374-1
**Fax Area Code:* 801 ■ *TF:* 800-776-7116 ■ *Web:* www.copperhillsyouthcenter.com

Copper Kettle Cafe
4004 Granny White Pk . . . . Nashville TN 37204 615-383-7242 383-7949 671
Web: copperkettlenashville.com

Copper Mountain College
6162 Rotary Way . . . . Joshua Tree CA 92252 760-366-3791 366-5255 162
TF: 866-366-3791 ■ *Web:* www.cmccd.edu

Copper Mountain Resort
209 Ten Mile Cir PO Box 3001. . . . Copper Mountain CO 80443 970-968-2882 669
TF: 888-219-2441 ■ *Web:* www.coppercolorado.com

Copper River Information Technology LLC
1577 C St Ste 201 . . . . Anchorage AK 99501 703-234-9000 631
Web: www.copperriverit.com

Copper State Rubber of Arizona Inc
750 S 59th Ave. . . . Phoenix AZ 85043 602-269-5927 370
Web: copperstaterubber.com

Copper Valley Electric Assn Inc (CVEA)
Mile 187 Glenn Hwy PO Box 45. . . . Glennallen AK 99588 907-822-3211 822-5586 245
TF: 866-835-2832 ■ *Web:* www.cvea.org

Copper Valley Telephone Cooperative Inc
329 Fairbanks Dr . . . . Valdez AK 99686 907-835-2231 224
Web: www.cvinternet.net

Copperas Cove Chamber of Commerce
204 E Robertson Ave. . . . Copperas Cove TX 76522 254-547-7571 547-5015 139
Web: www.copperascove.com

Copperas Cove Independent School District
703 W Ave D. . . . Copperas Cove TX 76522 254-547-1227 685
TF: 866-632-9992 ■ *Web:* www.ccisd.com

CopperLeaf Technologies Inc
4170 Still Creek Dr Ste 450 . . . . Burnaby BC V5C6C6 604-639-9700 179
TF: 800-627-3917 ■ *Web:* www.copperleaf.com

Copperstone Connect Inc
3308 Cindy Crescent Ste 200. . . . Mississauga ON L4Y3J6 416-849-2320 849-2316 196
Web: www.copperstoneconnect.com

CopperWynd Resort & Club
13225 N Eagle Ridge Dr. . . . Fountain Hills AZ 85268 480-333-1900 669
TF: 877-707-7760 ■ *Web:* www.copperwynd.com

Coppi 3363 Yonge St. . . . Toronto ON M4N2M6 416-484-4464 671
Web: www.coppi.ca

Coppin State University
2500 W N Ave. . . . Baltimore MD 21216 410-951-3600 523-7351* 166
**Fax:* Admissions ■ *TF Admissions:* 800-635-3674 ■ *Web:* www.coppin.edu

				Phone	Fax	Class
Copple, Rockey, Mckeever & Schlecht PC LLO 2425 Taylor Ave *TF:* 888-860-2425 ■ *Web:* www.greatadvocates.com	Norfolk	NE	68701	402-371-4300		428
COPS (Community Oriented Policing Services) 145 N St NE *TF:* 800-421-6770 ■ *Web:* www.cops.usdoj.gov	Washington	DC	20530	202-514-5328		340-14
COPS (Concerns of Police Survivors Inc) 846 Old S 5 PO Box 3199 *TF:* 800-784-2677 ■ *Web:* www.nationalcops.org	Camdenton	MO	65020	573-346-4911	346-1414	48-21
Copy Cat Printing 365 N Broadwell Ave *TF:* 800-400-8520 ■ *Web:* www.copycatprinting.com	Grand Island	NE	68803	308-384-8520		627
Copy Products Inc 2103 W Vista St *Web:* copyproductsinc.com	Springfield	MO	65807	417-889-5665		535
Copy Super Ctr 128 W Market St *Web:* www.totallypromotional.com	Celina	OH	45822	419-586-6620		627
Copy Systems Southwest 3201 Mercantile Ct *Web:* www.southwestcopy.com	Santa Fe	NM	87507	505-216-0124		627
Copy World 1728 Warwick Ave *TF:* 800-531-7404 ■ *Web:* copyworldri.com	Warwick	RI	02889	401-739-7400		627
Copylite Products Corp 4061 SW 47th Ave *Web:* www.copylite.com	Fort Lauderdale	FL	33314	954-581-2470		358
Copymat Digibranch 191 Battery St *Web:* www.copymat3.com	San Francisco	CA	94111	415-981-1300		113
CopyPage Inc 5418 McConnell Ave *Web:* www.copypage.com	Los Angeles	CA	90066	310-822-1620		627
Copyright Clearance Ctr Inc (CCC) 222 Rosewood Dr *TF:* 855-239-3415 ■ *Web:* www.copyright.com	Danvers	MA	01923	978-750-8400	646-8600	49-16
Copyright Society of the USA 1 E 53rd St *Web:* www.csusa.org	New York	NY	10022	212-354-6401	354-2847	49-16
Copyworks 4837 First Ave SE Ste 103 *Web:* copyworks.com	Cedar Rapids	IA	52402	319-373-5335		184
Coquette Cafe 316 N Milwaukee St *Web:* www.coquettecafe.com	Milwaukee	WI	53202	414-291-2655		671
Coquihalla Middle School 2975 Clapperton Ave *TF:* 800-667-4321 ■ *Web:* www.sd58.bc.ca	Merritt	BC	V1K1A3	250-378-6104		685
Coquille Myrtle Grove State Natural Site Powers Hwy *TF:* 800-551-6949 ■ *Web:* www.oregonstateparks.org	Myrtle Point	OR	97458	800-551-6949		565
Coquitlam Public Library 3001 Burlington Dr *Web:* coqlibrary.ca	Coquitlam	BC	V3B6X1	604-554-7323		434
Coradix Technology Consulting Ltd 151 Slater St *Web:* www.coradix.com	Ottawa	ON	K1P5H3	613-234-0800	234-0988	194
Coral Beach Resort & Suites 1105 S Ocean Blvd *TF:* 800-843-2684 ■ *Web:* www.coralbeachmyrtlebeachresort.com	Myrtle Beach	SC	29577	800-556-1754		669
Coral Chemical Co 1915 Industrial Ave *TF:* 800-228-4646 ■ *Web:* www.coral.com	Zion	IL	60099	847-246-6666	246-6667	145
Coral Color Process Ltd 50 Mall Dr *TF:* 800-564-7303 ■ *Web:* www.coralcolor.com	Commack	NY	11725	631-543-5200		627
Coral Dyeing & Finishing Corp 555 E 31st St	Paterson	NJ	07513	973-278-0272		745-7
Coral Gables Chamber of Commerce 224 Catalonia *TF:* 800-437-1009 ■ *Web:* coralgableschamber.org	Coral Gables	FL	33134	305-446-1657	446-9900	139
Coral Gables Hospital Inc (CGH) 3100 Douglas Rd *TF:* 866-728-3677 ■ *Web:* www.coralgableshospital.com	Coral Gables	FL	33134	305-445-8461	441-6879	374-3
Coral Hospitality LLC 9180 Galleria Ct Ste 600 *Web:* www.coralhospitality.com	Naples	FL	34109	239-449-1800		378
Coral Industries Inc 3010 Rice Mine Rd NE *Web:* www.coralind.com	Tuscaloosa	AL	35406	205-345-1013		610
Coral Kay Resort 2300 Caravelle Cir *TF:* 866-357-3682 ■ *Web:* www.staycoralcay.com	Kissimmee	FL	34746	407-787-0718		707
Coral Pink Sand Dunes State Park PO Box 95 *Web:* www.stateparks.utah.gov	Kanab	UT	84741	435-648-2800		565
Coral Productions Inc 100 Bickford St *TF:* 800-889-8662 ■ *Web:* www.coralproductions.com	Rochester	NY	14606	585-254-2580		129
Coral Reef Restaurant 1701 Atlantic Ave *TF:* 866-627-8483 ■ *Web:* ocmdhotels.com	Ocean City	MD	21842	410-289-2612	289-3381	671
Coral Ridge Mall 1451 Coral Ridge Ave *Web:* www.coralridgemall.com	Coralville	IA	52241	319-625-5522		460
Coral Ridge Presbyterian Church Inc 5555 N Federal Hwy *Web:* www.crpc.org	Fort Lauderdale	FL	33308	954-771-8840		48-20
Coral Springs Auto Mall 9400 W Atlantic Blvd *TF:* 800-353-8660 ■ *Web:* www.coralspringsautomall.com	Coral Springs	FL	33071	954-369-1016		57
Coral Springs Chamber of Commerce 11805 Heron Bay Blvd *TF:* 800-816-1256 ■ *Web:* www.cschamber.com	Coral Springs	FL	33076	954-752-4242	827-0543	139
Coral Springs Ctr for the Arts 2855 Coral Springs Dr *Web:* www.coralspringscenterforthearts.com	Coral Springs	FL	33065	954-344-5990	344-5980	572
Coral Springs Medical Ctr 3000 Coral Hills Dr *Web:* www.browardhealth.org	Coral Springs	FL	33065	954-344-3000		374-3
Coram Healthcare Corp 555 17th St Ste 1500 **Fax Area Code: 303* ■ *TF:* 800-267-2642 ■ *Web:* www.coramhc.com	Denver	CO	80202	800-267-2642	298-0043*	363
Coranet Corp 2 Washington St Ste 701 *TF:* 800-401-0760 ■ *Web:* coranet.com	New York	NY	10004	212-635-2770		224
Cora-Texas Mfg Company Inc 32505 Louisiana 1 PO Box 280 *Web:* www.coratexas.com	White Castle	LA	70788	225-545-3679	545-8360	296-38
Corban Onesource 235 Third St S Ste 300 *Web:* www.corbanone.com	St Petersburg	FL	33701	727-803-1800		251
Corban University 5000 Deer Pk Dr SE *Web:* www.corban.edu	Salem	OR	97317	503-581-8600		166
Corbett Duncan & Hubly PC 100 E Pierce Rd Ste 100 *Web:* www.cdhcpa.com	Itasca	IL	60143	630-285-0215		2
Corbett Lighting Inc 14508 Nelson Ave *TF:* 800-533-8769 ■ *Web:* www.corbettlighting.com	City of Industry	CA	91744	626-336-4511		439
Corbett Technology Solutions 4151 Lafeyette Ctr Dr Ste 700 *TF:* 800-572-7280 ■ *Web:* www.ctsi-usa.com	Chantilly	VA	20151	703-631-3377		180
Corbin 2360 Technology Pkwy *TF:* 800-538-7035 ■ *Web:* www.corbin.com	Hollister	CA	95023	831-634-1100	634-1059	517
Corbin Russwin Inc 225 Episcopal Rd *TF:* 800-438-1951 ■ *Web:* www.corbinrusswin.com	Berlin	CT	06037	860-225-7411		350
Corbin Turf & Ornamental Supply 1105 Old Buncombe Rd *Web:* corbinturf.com	Greenville	SC	29617	864-233-2113		366
Corbitt Manufacturing Co Inc 854 NW Guerdon St *Web:* www.cypress-mulch.com	Lake City	FL	32055	386-755-2555		323
Corbo Jewelers Inc 58 Pk Ave *Web:* www.corbojewelers.com	Rutherford	NJ	07070	201-438-4454	438-3108	410
Corby Industries Inc 1501 E Pennsylvania St *TF Sales:* 800-652-6729 ■ *Web:* www.corby.com	Allentown	PA	18109	610-433-1412	435-1963	692
Corbyn Investment Management Inc 2330 W Joppa Rd Ste 108 *Web:* corbyn.com	Lutherville	MD	21093	410-832-5500		401
Corcept Therapeutics Inc 149 Commonwealth Dr *NASDAQ: CORT* ■ *Web:* www.corcept.com	Menlo Park	CA	94025	650-327-3270	327-3218	85
Corchran Inc 1340 State St S *Web:* www.corchran.com	Waseca	MN	56093	507-835-3910	835-1382	697
Corcoran Ender & Assoc 4010 S California Av *Web:* cpa-chicago.com	Chicago	IL	60632	773-247-7132		2
Corcoran Group Inc, The 660 Madison Ave *TF:* 800-544-4055 ■ *Web:* www.corcoran.com	New York	NY	10021	212-355-3550		652
Corcoran Jennison Development Co 150 Mt Vernon St Bayside Ofc Ctr Ste 500 *Web:* www.corcoranjennison.com	Boston	MA	02125	617-822-7350	822-7352	653
Corcoran School of the Arts & Design 500 17th St NW *Web:* corcoran.gwu.edu	Washington	DC	20006	202-639-1800		164
Cord Camera Centers Inc 2030 Dividend Dr *Web:* www.cordcamera.com	Columbus	OH	43228	614-343-5000		525
Cord Moving & Storage 4101 Rider Trl N *Web:* www.cordmoving.com	Earth City	MO	63045	314-291-7440		449
Cord Sets Inc 1015 Fifth St N *TF:* 800-752-0580 ■ *Web:* www.cordsetsinc.com	Minneapolis	MN	55411	612-337-9700	337-0800	815
Cord Specialties Co 10632 Grand Ave *Web:* www.cordspecialties.com	Franklin Park	IL	60131	847-455-3503		815
Cordage Institute 994 Old Eagle School Rd Ste 1019 *Web:* www.ropecord.com	Wayne	PA	19087	610-971-4854	971-4859	49-13
Cordano Severson & Assoc Ltd 2321 Plainfield Rd *Web:* csatax.com	Crest Hill	IL	60403	815-744-1900		734
Cordell Hull Birthplace State Park 1300 Cordell Hull Memorial Dr *Web:* www.state.tn.us	Byrdstown	TN	38549	931-864-3247		565
Cordev Inc 146 B Hillwood Ave Ste 146 B *TF:* 800-257-1136 ■ *Web:* www.cordev.net	Falls Church	VA	22046	703-237-2802		196
Cordiant Capital Inc 1002 Sherbrooke St W Ste 2800 *Web:* cordiantcap.com	Montreal	QC	H3A2R7	514-286-1142		528
Cordillera Energy Partners III LLC 8450 E Crescent Pkwy Ste 400 *Web:* www.cordilleraep.com	Greenwood Village	CO	80111	303-290-0990		536
Cordis Corp 14201 NW 60th Ave *TF:* 800-327-7714 ■ *Web:* www.cordis.com	Miami Lakes	FL	33014	786-313-2000		476
Cordoba Corp 1401 N Broadway *Web:* www.cordobacorp.com	Los Angeles	CA	90012	213-895-0224		174
Cordova Bolt Inc 5601 Dolly Ave *Web:* www.cordovabolt.com	Buena Park	CA	90621	714-739-7500		350
Cordova Electric Co-op Inc 705 Second St PO Box 20 *Web:* www.cordovaelectric.com	Cordova	AK	99574	907-424-5555		245
Cordova High School 1800 Berryhill Rd *Web:* www.cadetsofcordova.org	Cordova	TN	38016	901-416-4540		685
Cordova Recreation & Park District 2197 Chase Dr *Web:* www.crpd.com	Rancho Cordova	CA	95670	916-362-1841		31
Cordova Ventures 70 Mansell Ct Ste 100	Roswell	GA	30076	678-942-0300	942-0301	792
Corduroy 1122 Ninth St NW *Web:* corduroydc.com	Washington	DC	20001	202-589-0699		671
Cordy Oilfield Services Inc 5366 55 St SE *Web:* www.cordy.ca	Calgary	AB	T2C3G9	403-266-2067		539
CORE (Congress of Racial Equality) 730 W Cheyenne Ave Ste 150 *Web:* www.congressofracialequality.org	North Las Vegas	NV	89030	702-637-7968	637-7953	48-8
CORE (Center for Organ Recovery & Education) 204 Sigma Dr RIDC Pk *TF:* 800-366-6777 ■ *Web:* www.core.org	Pittsburgh	PA	15238	412-963-3550		269

Company / Address	City	State	ZIP	Phone	Fax	Class
Core Bts Inc 10201 N Illinois St Ste 240 *TF:* 855-267-3287 ■ *Web:* www.corebts.com	Indianapolis	IN	46290	855 267 3287		113
Core Club, The 66 E 55th St *Web:* www.thecoreclub.com	New York	NY	10022	212-486-6600		354
CORE Construction Services of Arizona Inc 3036 E Greenway Rd *TF:* 800-364-2059 ■ *Web:* www.coreconstruction.com	Phoenix	AZ	85032	602-494-0800		186
Core Design Inc 14711 NE 29th Pl Ste 101 *Web:* www.coredesigninc.com	Bellevue	WA	98007	425-885-7877		727
Core Health & Fitness LLC 8000 NE Pkwy Dr Ste 220 *Web:* stairmaster.com	Vancouver	WA	98662	360-326-4090		706
Core Inc 6590 W Rogers Cir *Web:* www.core-aerospace.com	Boca Raton	FL	33487	561-241-4580		770
Core Laboratories 6316 Windfern Rd *NYSE: CLB* ■ *Web:* www.corelab.com	Houston	TX	77040	713-328-2673	328-2150	539
Core Management Resources Group Inc 515 Mulberry St *TF:* 888-741-2673 ■ *Web:* www.corehealthbenefits.com	Macon	GA	31201	478-741-3521		196
Core Medical Imaging Inc 6161 NE 175th St Ste 201 *TF:* 800-809-9729 ■ *Web:* www.coremedicalimaging.com	Kenmore	WA	98028	425-485-4330		475
Core Molding Technologies Inc (CMT) 800 Manor Pk Dr *NYSE: CMT* ■ *Web:* www.coremt.com	Columbus	OH	43228	614-870-5000		604
Core Partners LLC 320 Martin St Ste 140 *Web:* www.corepartners.net	Birmingham	MI	48009	248-399-9999		652
Core Pipe 170 Tubeway Dr *TF:* 800-222-3312 ■ *Web:* www.gerlin.com	Carol Stream	IL	60188	630-690-7000	690-9701	595
Core Power Services Inc 37428 Centralmont Pl *Web:* www.cpspower.com	Fremont	CA	94536	510-796-6682		767
Core Realty Holdings LLC 1600 Dove St Ste 450 *TF:* 800-478-4837 ■ *Web:* www.corerealtyholdings.com	Newport Beach	CA	92660	949-863-1031		403
Core Six Precision Glass 1737 Endeavor Dr *Web:* www.coresix.com	Williamsburg	VA	23185	757-888-1361		329
Core Twelve Inc 600 W Van Buren #1010 *Web:* www.core12.com	Chicago	IL	60607	312-274-1270		7
Core Vision IT Solutions 1266 NW Hwy *TF:* 855-788-5835 ■ *Web:* www.cvits.com	Palatine	IL	60067	855 788 5835		196
Coregistics 240 Northpoint Pkwy *Web:* www.coregistics.com	Acworth	GA	30102	678-453-5900		393
Corel Corp 1600 Carling Ave *TF Orders:* 800-772-6735 ■ *Web:* www.corel.com	Ottawa	ON	K1Z8R7	613-728-8200	761-9176	178-8
Corelis Inc Alondra Corporate Ctr 13100 Alondra Blvd *Web:* www.corelis.com	Cerritos	CA	90703	562-926-6727		201
CoreLogic SafeRent 7300 Westmore Rd Ste 3 *TF:* 866-873-3651 ■ *Web:* www.corelogic.com	Rockville	MD	20850	866-873-3651		635
CoreNet Global Inc 260 Peachtree St NW Ste 1500 *TF:* 800-726-8111 ■ *Web:* www.corenetglobal.org	Atlanta	GA	30303	404-589-3200	589-3201	49-17
Coresco Inc 1407 Airport Rd *TF:* 800-496-8727 ■ *Web:* www.coresco.com	Monroe	NC	28110	704-296-5600		5
Coreslab Structures Inc 150 W Placentia Ave *TF:* 800-291-9290 ■ *Web:* www.coreslab.com	Perris	CA	92571	951-943-9119	943-7571	183
CoreSource Inc 400 Field Dr *TF:* 800-832-3332 ■ *Web:* www.coresource.com	Lake Forest	IL	60045	847-604-9200		586
CORESTAFF Services 1775 St James Pl *TF:* 800-676-8326 ■ *Web:* www.corestaff.com	Houston	TX	77056	713-438-1400		721
Corestar International Corp 1044 Sandy Hill Rd *Web:* www.corestar-corp.com	Irwin	PA	15642	724-744-4094		180
Corestates Inc 3039 Premiere Pkwy	Duluth	GA	30097	770-242-9550		261
CoreTech 550 American Ave Ste 301 *TF:* 800-220-3337 ■ *Web:* xsellresources.com	King of Prussia	PA	19406	800-220-3337		194
Coretelligent LLC 75 Second Ave Ste 210 *TF:* 800-535-5198 ■ *Web:* coretelligent.com	Needham	MA	02494	781-247-4900		180
Core-Vens & Company Inc 2301 N Second St *Web:* www.corevensguninsurance.com	Clinton	IA	52732	563-242-5423		390
Corey Delta Inc 261 Arthur Rd PO Box 637 *Web:* www.coreydelta.com	Martinez	CA	94553	707-747-7500		188-5
Corey Steel Co 2800 S 61st Ct *TF:* 800-323-2750 ■ *Web:* www.coreysteel.com	Cicero	IL	60804	708-735-8000	735-8100	723
Corgan Assoc Inc 401 N Houston St *Web:* www.corgan.com	Dallas	TX	75202	214-748-2000		261
Coriander 282 Kent St *Web:* www.corianderthaiottawa.com	Ottawa	ON	K2P2A4	613-233-2828		671
Coriant 220 Mill Rd *Web:* www.coriant.com	Chelmsford	MA	01824	978-250-2900		176
Coridian Technologies Inc 1725 Lake Dr W *Web:* coridian.com	Chanhassen	MN	55317	952-361-9980		174
Coriell Institute for Medical Research 403 Haddon Ave *TF:* 800-752-3805 ■ *Web:* www.coriell.org	Camden	NJ	08103	856-966-7377		668
Corinth Area Convention & Visitors Bureau 215 N Fillmore St *Web:* www.corinth.net	Corinth	MS	38834	662-287-8300	286-0102	206
Corinth National Cemetery 1551 Horton St *TF:* 800-273-8255 ■ *Web:* www.cem.va.gov	Corinth	MS	38834	901-386-8311	382-0750	136
Corinthian Media 500 Eigth Ave 5th Fl *Web:* www.mediabuying.com	New York	NY	10018	212-279-5700		6
Corinthian Partners LLC 850 Third Ave Ste 16C *TF:* 800-899-8950 ■ *Web:* www.corinthianpartners.com	New York	NY	10022	212-287-1500		690
Corium International Inc 4558 50th St SE *Web:* www.coriumintl.com	Grand Rapids	MI	49512	616-656-4563		582
Corix Utilities (US) Inc 126 N Jefferson St Ste 300 *Web:* www.corix.com	Milwaukee	WI	53202	414-291-6520		393
Corizon 105 Westpark Dr Ste 200 *TF:* 800-729-0069 ■ *Web:* www.corizonhealth.com	Brentwood	TN	37027	800-729-0069		463
Cork Industries Inc 500 Kaiser Dr *Web:* www.corkind.com	Folcroft	PA	19032	610-522-9550		481
Cork Supply USA Inc 531 Stone Rd *Web:* corksupply.com	Benicia	CA	94510	707-746-0353		124
Cork'N Cleaver 221 E Washington Ctr Rd *Web:* corkncleaveronline.com	Fort Wayne	IN	46825	260-484-7772		671
Corken Inc 3805 NW 36th St *TF:* 800-631-4929 ■ *Web:* www.corken.com	Oklahoma City	OK	73112	405-946-5576	948-6664	641
Corker Bob (Sen R - TN) 425 Dirksen Bldg *Web:* www.corker.senate.gov	Washington	DC	20510	202-224-3344	228-0566	342-2
Corkin Shopland Gallery 55 Mill St Bldg 61 *Web:* www.corkingallery.com	Toronto	ON	M5A3C4	416-979-1980	979-7018	42
Corky's 100 Franklin Rd *TF:* 800-657-6910 ■ *Web:* corkysbbq.com	Brentwood	TN	37027	615-373-1020		671
Corland Co 327 s Isis Ave *Web:* www.coreland.com	Inglewood	CA	90301	310-670-3720		770
Corley Manufacturing Co PO Box 471 *Web:* www.corleymfg.com	Chattanooga	TN	37401	423-698-0284	622-3258	821
Corma Inc 10 McCleary Court Concord *Web:* www.corma.com	Toronto	ON	L4K2Z3	905-669-9397		111
Cormac Corp 13921 Park Ctr Rd Ste 180 *Web:* www.cormac-corp.com	Herndon	VA	20171	703-793-0931		396
Corman Bag Co 32 Arlington St *TF:* 800-772-7017 ■ *Web:* www.cormanbag.com	Chelsea	MA	02150	617-884-7600	437-7917	67
Cormark Securities Inc 200 Bay St Royal Bank Plaza S Tower Ste 2800 *Web:* www.cormark.com	Toronto	ON	M5J2J2	416-362-7485		4
Cormetech Inc 5000 International Dr *TF:* 800-424-9300 ■ *Web:* www.cormetech.com	Durham	NC	27712	919-620-3000	620-3001	143
Cormier Rice Milling Co Inc 501 W Third St	De Witt	AR	72042	870-946-3561		296-23
Corn Belt Energy Corp 1 Energy Way *TF:* 800-879-0339 ■ *Web:* www.cornbeltenergy.com	Bloomington	IL	61705	309-662-5330	663-4516	245
Corn Belt Power Co-op 1300 13th St N PO Box 508 *Web:* www.cbpower.coop	Humboldt	IA	50548	515-332-2571	332-1375	245
Corn Heritage Village 106 W Adams St Apt 1 *Web:* cornheritage.org	Corn	OK	73024	580-343-2295		672
Corn Palace 604 N Main St *TF:* 800-289-7469 ■ *Web:* www.cornpalace.org	Mitchell	SD	57301	605-995-8430		50-3
Corn Refiners Assn Inc (CRA) 1701 Pennsylvania Ave *Web:* www.corn.org	Washington	DC	20006	202-331-1634	331-2054	48-2
Corn Stock Theatre 1700 Pk Rd *Web:* www.cornstocktheatre.com	Peoria	IL	61604	309-676-2196		573-4
Corna/Kokosing Construction Co 6235 Westerville Rd *Web:* www.corna.com	Westerville	OH	43081	614-901-8844	212-5599	186
Cornelia Connelly School of The Holy Child 2323 W Broadway *TF:* 800-566-6150 ■ *Web:* connellyschoolanaheim.org	Anaheim	CA	92804	714-776-1717		685
Cornelia de Lange Syndrome Foundation Inc (CdLS) 302 W Main St Ste 100 *TF:* 800-753-2357 ■ *Web:* www.cdlsusa.org	Avon	CT	06001	860-676-8166	676-8337	48-17
Cornelius & Assoc Inc 631 Harden St Ste G	Columbia	SC	29205	803-779-3354	254-0183	194
Cornelius Seed Corn Co 14760 317th Ave *TF:* 800-218-1862 ■ *Web:* www.corneliusseed.com	Bellevue	IA	52031	563-672-3463		296-20
Cornell & Assoc Inc 2633 E Lake Ave Ste 307 *Web:* www.cornellandassociates.com	Seattle	WA	98102	206-329-0085		655
Cornell & Co Inc 224 Cornell Ln *Web:* www.cornellcraneandsteel.com	Westville	NJ	08093	856-742-1900	742-8186	264-3
Cornell Botanic Gardens 1 Plantations Rd *TF:* 800-269-8368 ■ *Web:* www.cornellplantations.org	Ithaca	NY	14850	607-255-2400		97
Cornell College 600 First St SW **Fax:* Admissions ■ *TF Admissions:* 800-747-1112 ■ *Web:* www.cornellcollege.edu	Mount Vernon	IA	52314	319-895-4215	895-4451*	166
Cornell Fine Arts Museum 1000 Holt Ave *Web:* www.rollins.edu/cfam	Winter Park	FL	32789	407-646-2526		520
Cornell Forge Co 6666 W 66th St *TF:* 800-954-6873 ■ *Web:* www.cornellforge.com	Chicago	IL	60638	708-458-1582	728-9883	483
Cornell Iron Works Inc 24 Elmwood Rd *TF:* 800-233-8366 ■ *Web:* www.cornelliron.com	Mountain Top	PA	18707	570-474-6773	474-9973	234
Cornell Law School 226 Myron Taylor Hall *Web:* www.lawschool.cornell.edu	Ithaca	NY	14853	607-255-5141	255-7193	167-1
Cornell Mayo Assoc Inc 600 Lanidex Plaza *Web:* www.cornell-mayo.com	Parsippany	NJ	07054	973-887-3069		174
Cornell NanoScale Science & Technology Facility (CNF) Cornell University 250 Duffield Hall *Web:* www.cnf.cornell.edu	Ithaca	NY	14853	607-255-2329	255-8601	668
Cornell Paper & Box Co 162 Van Dyke St *TF:* 800-288-1801 ■ *Web:* cornellpaper.com	Brooklyn	NY	11231	718-875-3202	875-3281	101
Cornell Pump Co 16261 SE 130th Ave *Web:* www.cornellpump.com	Clackamas	OR	97015	503-653-0330	653-0338	641
Cornell Roofing & Sheet Metal Co 901 S Northern *Web:* www.cornellroofingkansascity.com	Independence	MO	64053	816-252-8300		697

Phone | Fax | Class

Cornell School of Hotel Administration
Statler Hall Cornell University ... Ithaca NY 14853 607-255-8702 434-3
Web: sha.cornell.edu

Cornell Storefront Systems Inc
140 Maffet St ... Wilkes-barre PA 18705 570-706-2775 234
TF: 800-882-6772 ■ *Web:* www.cornellstorefronts.com

Cornell Technical Services LLC
9700 Patuxent Woods Dr Ste 140 ... Columbia MD 21046 301-560-2544 463
Web: www.cts-llc.com

Cornell University 410 Thurston Ave ... Ithaca NY 14850 607-255-5241 254-5175* 166
**Fax:* Admissions ■ *Web:* www.cornell.edu

Cornell University Olin Library
Olin & Uris Libraries ... Ithaca NY 14853 607-255-4144 255-6788 434-6
Web: olinuris.library.cornell.edu

Cornell University Press
750 Cascadilla St PO Box 6525 ... Ithaca NY 14850 607-277-2338 277-6292 637-4
TF Sales: 800-666-2211 ■ *Web:* www.cornellpress.cornell.edu

Corner Alliance Inc
1620 L St NW Ste 200 ... Washington DC 20036 202-754-8120 194
Web: www.corneralliance.com

Corner Bakery Cafe
5225 Beltline Rd Ste 58 ... Dallas TX 75254 469-547-0019 68
Web: www.cornerbakerycafe.com

Corner Bistro 3604 Silverside Rd ... Wilmington DE 19810 302-477-1778 671
Web: www.mybistro.com

Corner Music Inc 2705 12th Ave S ... Nashville TN 37204 615-297-9559 526
Web: cornermusicnashville.com

Corner View Restaurant 80 1/2 S St ... Concord NH 03301 603-229-4554 671

CornerCap Investment Counsel Inc
1355 Peachtree St NE The Peachtree Ste 1700 ... Atlanta GA 30309 404-870-0700 528
TF: 800-728-0670 ■ *Web:* www.cornercap.com

Cornerstar Inc 10145 NW Ash St ... Portland OR 97229 503-546-0500 226
Web: www.cornerstar.com

Cornerstone Advisors Asset Management Inc
74 W Broad St Ste 340 ... Bethlehem PA 18018 610-694-0900 401
TF: 800-923-0900 ■ *Web:* www.cornerstone-companies.com

Cornerstone Alliance Chamber Services
38 W Wall St ... Benton Harbor MI 49022 269-925-6100 925-4471 139
TF: 800-311-4634 ■ *Web:* www.cstonealliance.org

Cornerstone Commissioning Inc
11 Cold Spring Dr ... Boxford MA 01921 978-887-8177 256
Web: www.cornerstonecx.com

Cornerstone Consutling & Technology
44 Montgomery St Ste 3360 ... San Francisco CA 94104 415-705-7800 194
Web: www.cornerstoneconcilium.com

Cornerstone Equity Investors LLC
281 Tresser Blvd 12th Fl ... Stamford CT 06901 212-753-0901 826-6798 792
Web: www.cornerstone-equity.com

Cornerstone Group
2100 Hollywood Blvd ... Hollywood FL 33020 800-809-4099 653
TF: 800-809-4099 ■ *Web:* www.theapartmentcorner.com

Cornerstone Hospice and Palliative Care
2445 Ln Pk Rd ... Tavares FL 32778 352-343-1341 371
TF: 888-728-6234 ■ *Web:* cshospice.org

Cornerstone Hospital of Austin
4207 Burnet Rd ... Austin TX 78756 512-706-1900 374-7
TF: 800-338-7293 ■ *Web:* chghospitals.com

Cornerstone Medical Arts Ctr Hospital
159-05 Union Tpke ... Fresh Meadows NY 11366 718-906-6700 726
TF: 800-233-9999 ■ *Web:* www.cornerstoneny.com

Cornerstone National Insurance Co
3100 Falling Leaf Ct Ste 200 PO Box 6040 ... Columbia MO 65201 573-817-2481 390
Web: www.cornerstonenational.com

Cornerstone Services Inc 777 Joyce Rd ... Joliet IL 60436 815-741-7600 592
Web: www.cornerstoneservices.org

Cornerstone SMR Inc
4620 N State Rd 7 Ste 120 ... Fort Lauderdale FL 33309 954-714-7030 387
Web: www.cornerstonesmr.com

Cornerstone Systems Inc
3250 Players Club Pkwy ... Memphis TN 38125 901-842-0660 194
TF: 800-278-7677 ■ *Web:* www.cornerstone-systems.com

Cornerstone United Methodist Church Inc
8200 Immokalee Rd ... Naples FL 34119 239-354-9160 48-20
Web: cornerstonenaples.org

Cornerstone University
1001 E Beltline Ave NE ... Grand Rapids MI 49525 616-222-1426 222-1418* 166
**Fax:* Admissions ■ *TF Admissions:* 800-787-9778 ■ *Web:* www.cornerstone.edu

Cornet Technology Inc
6800 Versar Ctr Ste 216 ... Springfield VA 22151 703-658-3400 658-3440 52
Web: www.cornet.com

Cornhusker Bank 1101 Cornhusker Hwy ... Lincoln NE 68521 402-434-2265 70
TF: 877-837-4481 ■ *Web:* www.cornhuskerbank.com

Cornhusker Casualty Co PO Box 2048 ... Omaha NE 68103 888-495-8949 391-4
TF: 888-495-8949 ■ *Web:* www.bhhc.com

Cornhusker Hotel, The 333 S 13th St ... Lincoln NE 68508 402-474-7474 474-1847 379
TF: 866-706-7706 ■ *Web:* www.marriott.com

Cornhusker Public Power District
23169 235th Ave PO Box 9 ... Columbus NE 68602 402-564-2821 564-9907 245
TF: 800-955-2773 ■ *Web:* www.cornhusker-power.com

Cornhusker State Industries
800 Pioneers Blvd ... Lincoln NE 68502 402-471-4597 471-1236 630
TF: 800-348-7537 ■ *Web:* www.nebraska.gov

Corniche Furs Inc
345 Seventh Ave 20th Fl ... New York NY 10001 212-239-8655 155-7
Web: www.nycfur.com

Corniche Group Inc, The
8721 W Sunset Blvd Ste 200 ... West Hollywood CA 90069 310-854-6000 772

Corning Area Chamber of Commerce
1 W Market St Ste 302 ... Corning NY 14830 607-936-4686 936-4685 139
TF: 866-463-6264 ■ *Web:* www.corningny.com

Corning Cable Systems 800 17th St NW ... Hickory NC 28603 828-901-5000 325-5060 814
TF: 800-743-2671 ■ *Web:* www.corning.com

Corning Community College
1 Academic Dr ... Corning NY 14830 607-962-9251 962-9582* 162
**Fax:* Admissions ■ *Web:* www.corning-cc.edu

Corning Data Services Inc
139 Wardell St ... Corning NY 14830 800-455-5996 177
TF: 800-455-5996 ■ *Web:* corningdata.com

Corning Ford Inc 2280 Short Dr ... Corning CA 96021 530-824-5434 57
Web: www.corningford.com

Corning Gilbert Inc
5310 W Camelback Rd ... Glendale AZ 85301 623-245-1050 934-5160 253
Web: www.corning.com

Corning Hospital 176 Denison Pkwy E ... Corning NY 14830 607-937-7200 374-3
TF: 877-750-2042 ■ *Web:* www.guthrie.org

Corning Inc 1 Riverfront Plaza ... Corning NY 14831 607-974-9000 330
NYSE: GLW ■ *TF:* 800-503-4611 ■ *Web:* www.corning.com

Corning Inc Life Sciences Div
836 N St Bldg 300 Ste 3401 ... Tewksbury MA 01876 978-442-2200 635-2476 419
TF: 800-492-1110 ■ *Web:* www.corning.com/lifesciences

Corning Museum of Glass 1 Museum Way ... Corning NY 14830 607-937-5371 438-5410 520
TF Cust Svc: 800-732-6845 ■ *Web:* www.cmog.org

Cornish College of the Arts
710 E Roy St ... Seattle WA 98121 206-323-1400 720-1011 164
TF: 800-726-2787 ■ *Web:* www.cornish.edu

Cornucopia Tool & Plastics Inc
448 Sherwood Rd PO Box 1915 ... Paso Robles CA 93447 805-369-0030 369-0033 253
TF: 800-235-4144 ■ *Web:* www.cornucopiaplastics.com

Cornwall & Area Chamber of Commerce
113 Second St E ... Cornwall ON K6H1Y5 613-933-4004 933-8466 137
Web: www.cornwallchamber.com

Cornwall Community Hospital
840 McConnell Ave ... Cornwall ON K6H5S5 613-938-4240 930-4502 374-2
TF: 866-263-1560 ■ *Web:* www.cornwallhospital.ca

Cornwall Lebanon School District
105 E Evergreen Rd ... Lebanon PA 17042 717-272-2031 274-2786 685
Web: www.clsd.k12.pa.us

Cornwall Manor 1 Boyd St ... Cornwall PA 17016 717-273-2647 672
TF: 800-222-2476 ■ *Web:* www.cornwallmanor.org

Cornwall Standard Freeholder, The
1150 Montreal Rd ... Cornwall ON K6H1E2 613-933-3160 532-1
Web: www.standard-freeholder.com

Cornwell Data Services Inc
352 Evelyn St ... Paramus NJ 07652 201-261-1050 225
Web: cornwelldirect.com

Cornwell Quality Tools
667 Seville Rd ... Wadsworth OH 44281 330-336-3506 336-3337 758
TF: 800-321-8356 ■ *Web:* www.cornwelltools.com

Cornyn John (Sen R - TX)
517 Hart Bldg ... Washington DC 20510 202-224-2934 228-2856 342-2
Web: www.cornyn.senate.gov

Corona Brushes Inc 5065 Savarese Cir ... Tampa FL 33634 813-885-2525 882-9810 103
TF: 800-458-3483 ■ *Web:* www.coronabrushes.com

Corona Chamber of Commerce
904 E Sixth St ... Corona CA 92879 951-737-3350 737-3531 139
TF: 800-308-1422 ■ *Web:* www.mychamber.org

Corona Clipper Inc
22440 Tomasco Canyon Rd ... Corona CA 92883 951-737-6515 737-6515 429
TF: 800-234-2547 ■ *Web:* www.coronatoolsusa.com

Corona College Heights Orange & Lemon Assn
8000 Lincoln Ave ... Riverside CA 92504 951-688-1811 689-5115 315-2
Web: www.cchcitrus.com

Corona del Mar State Beach
3001 Ocean Blvd ... Corona Del Mar CA 92625 949-644-3151 565
Web: www.parks.ca.gov/default.asp?page_id=652

Corona Public Library 650 S Main St ... Corona CA 92882 951-736-2381 736-2499 434-3
TF: 800-735-2929 ■ *Web:* www.coronapubliclibrary.org

Coronado Care Ctr 11411 N 19th Ave ... Phoenix AZ 85029 602-256-7500 450
Web: www.coronadocare.com

Coronado Chamber of Commerce
875 Orange Ave Ste 102 ... Coronado CA 92118 619-435-9260 522-6577 139
Web: www.coronadochamber.com

Coronado Ctr
6600 Menaul Blvd NE Ste 1 ... Albuquerque NM 87110 505-881-2700 460
Web: www.coronadocenter.com

Coronado Manufacturing Inc
8991 Glenoaks Boulvard ... Sun Valley CA 91352 818-768-5010 22
Web: www.coronadomfg.com

Coronado National Memorial
4101 E Montezuma Canyon Rd ... Hereford AZ 85615 520-366-5515 366-5705 564
Web: www.nps.gov/coro

Coronado Public Library
640 Orange Ave ... Coronado CA 92118 619-522-7390 434-3
TF: 800-984-4636 ■ *Web:* www.coronado.ca.us

Coronado State Monument
485 Kuaua Rd ... Bernalillo NM 87004 505-867-5351 867-1733 50-3
Web: www.nmhistoricsites.org/coronado

Coronado Theatre 314 N Main St ... Rockford IL 61101 815-968-2722 968-1318 572
TF: 800-358-7666 ■ *Web:* www.coronadopac.org

Coronado Unified School District
201 Sixth St ... Coronado CA 92118 619-522-8900 808
Web: www.edline.net

Corona-Norco Unified School District
2820 Clark Ave ... Norco CA 92860 951-736-5000 685
Web: www.cnusd.k12.ca.us

Coronation Sheet Metal Company Inc
2198 Stanley Terr ... Union NJ 07083 908-686-0930 697
Web: www.coronationsheetmetal.com

Coronet Lighting 16210 S Avalon Blvd ... Carson CA 90746 310-593-9561 439
Web: www.coronetlighting.com

Corotec Corp 145 Hyde Rd ... Farmington CT 06032 860-678-0038 674-5229 386
TF: 800-423-0348 ■ *Web:* www.corotec.com

Corp for National & Community Service
AmeriCorps USA
1201 New York Ave NW ... Washington DC 20525 202-606-5000 340-20
TF: 800-833-3722 ■ *Web:* www.nationalservice.gov
Learn & Serve America
1201 New York Ave NW ... Washington DC 20525 202-606-5000 340-20
TF: 800-833-3722 ■ *Web:* www.nationalservice.gov
Senior Corps 1201 New York Ave NW ... Washington DC 20525 202-606-5000 340-20
TF: 800-833-3722 ■ *Web:* www.nationalservice.gov

CORPAC Steel Products Corp
20803 Biscayne Blvd Ste 502 ... Miami FL 33180 305-918-0540 492
Web: www.corpacsteel.com

Corpak Medsystems Inc
1001 Asbury Dr ... Buffalo Grove IL 60089 847-403-3400 476
TF: 800-323-6305 ■ *Web:* www.corpakmedsystems.com

	Phone	Fax	Class
CorpCare			
7000 Peachtree Dunwoody Rd Bldg 4 Ste 300 ...... Atlanta GA 30328	800-728-9444	396-9522*	462
*Fax Area Code: 770 ■ TF: 800-728-9444 ■ Web: www.corpcareeap.com			
Corpfinance International Ltd			
229 Niagara St .... Toronto ON M6J2L5	416-364-6191		217
Web: www.corpfinance.ca			
Corporate Accountability International			
10 Milk St Ste 610 .... Boston MA 02108	617-695-2525	695-2626	48-8
TF: 800-688-8797 ■ Web: www.stopcorporateabuse.org			
Corporate Air LLC			
15 Allegheny County Airport................West Mifflin PA 15122	412-469-6800		63
TF: 888-429-5377 ■ Web: www.travelredefined.com			
Corporate Air Technology			
1250 Aviation Ave Ste 125 .... San Jose CA 95110	408-977-0990		359
TF: 800-237-2359 ■ Web: corpairtech.com			
Corporate Business Solutions			
1523 Johnson Ferry Rd Ste 200................Marietta GA 30062	404-521-6030		570
TF: 800-239-8182 ■ Web: www.cbshro.com			
Corporate Care Works			
8649 Baypine Rd Ste 101..................Jacksonville FL 32256	904-296-9436	296-1511	462
Web: members.healthadvocate.com			
Corporate Chefs Inc 22 Parkridge Rd .... Haverhill MA 01835	978-372-7400		670
Web: www.corporatechefs.com			
Corporate Claims Management Inc			
782 Spirit 40 Pk.........................Chesterfield MO 63005	800-449-2264		390
TF: 800-449-2264 ■ Web: www.corporateclaims.com			
Corporate Compliance & Regulatory			
1617 JFK Blvd Ste 1750...................Philadelphia PA 19103	215-557-2300		531-7
TF: 877-256-2472 ■ Web: www.lawjournalnewsletters.com			
Corporate Construction Ltd			
8517 Excelsior Dr Ste 203 .... Madison WI 53717	608-827-6001	827-6066	186
Web: www.corporate-construction.com			
Corporate Development Associates Inc			
5335 Far Hills Ave Ste 304.....................Dayton OH 45429	937-439-4227		401
Web: www.cda-inc.net			
Corporate Disk Co 4610 Crime Pkwy........... McHenry IL 60050	800-634-3475		240
TF: 800-634-3475 ■ Web: www.disk.com			
Corporate Dynamics Inc			
1630 W Diehl Rd .... Naperville IL 60563	630-778-9991		194
Web: www.corpdyn.com			
Corporate Eagle Management Services Inc			
6320 Highland Rd...........................Waterford MI 48327	248-461-9000		21
Web: corporateeagle.com			
Corporate Environments 1636 NE Expwy .... Atlanta GA 30329	404-679-8999		320
Web: www.corporateenvironments.com			
Corporate Executive Board Co			
1919 N Lynn St........................... Arlington VA 22209	571-303-3000	303-3100	194
NYSE: CEB ■ TF: 866-913-2632 ■ Web: www.cebglobal.com			
Corporate Facilities Inc			
2129 Chestnut St ....Philadelphia PA 19103	215-279-9999		321
Web: www.cfi-knoll.com			
Corporate Finance Group Inc			
15 Broad St 5th Fl.............................. Boston MA 02109	617-531-8270		194
Web: www.cfgi.com			
Corporate Fitness Works Inc			
1200 16th St N.........................St Petersburg FL 33705	301-417-9697		354
TF: 855-417-9697 ■ Web: www.corporatefitnessworks.com			
Corporate Flight Inc			
6150 Highland Rd...........................Waterford MI 48327	248-666-8800		13
TF: 800-767-2473 ■ Web: corporateflight.com			
Corporate Graphics International Inc			
1885 Northway Dr......................North Mankato MN 56003	507-625-4400		627
Web: www.cgintl.com			
Corporate Healthcare Strategies LLC			
280 Granite Run Dr Ste 250 ....Lancaster PA 17601	717-581-8382		463
Web: www.stoudtadvisors.com			
Corporate Helicopters of San Diego			
3753 John J Montgomery Dr Ste 2............ San Diego CA 92123	858-505-5650	874-3038	359
TF: 800-345-6737 ■ Web: www.corporatehelicopters.com			
Corporate Image Maintenance			
2116 S Wright St .... Santa Ana CA 92705	714-966-5325		256
Corporate Incentive Travel Inc			
685 S Washington St .... Alexandria VA 22314	703-683-0123		772
Web: www.corporateincentivetravel.net			
Corporate Information Technologies Inc			
14 Brick Walk Ln......................... Farmington CT 06032	860-676-2720		174
Web: www.corpit.com			
Corporate Ink Public Relations Ltd			
90 Washington St........................... Newton MA 02458	617-969-9192		194
Web: www.corporateink.com			
Corporate Interior Systems			
3311 E Broadway Rd.........................Phoenix AZ 85040	602-304-0100		321
TF: 800-255-3847 ■ Web: www.cisinphx.com			
Corporate It Solutions Inc			
661 Pleasant St.............................Norwood MA 02062	888-521-2487		196
TF: 888-521-2487 ■ Web: www.corpitsol.com			
Corporate Jet Support Inc			
1 Graphic Pl ....Moonachie NJ 07074	201-807-0784		770
Web: www.corpjetsupport.com			
Corporate Mailing Services Inc			
1625 Knecht Ave.........................Halethorpe MD 21227	410-242-7356		5
Web: www.mailstreamsolutions.com			
Corporate Office Properties Trust			
6711 Columbia Gateway Dr Ste 300...........Columbia MD 21046	443-285-5400	285-7650	655
NYSE: OFC ■ Web: www.copt.com			
Corporate Payroll Services Inc			
1000 Miller Ct W .... Norcross GA 30071	770-446-7289		734
Web: www.corpay.com			
Corporate Synergies Group LLC			
5000 Dearborn Cir Ste 100................Mount Laurel NJ 08054	856-813-1500		390
Web: www.corpsyn.com			
Corporate Systems Engineering LLC			
1215 Brookville Way......................Indianapolis IN 46239	317-375-3600		177
Web: www.corporatesystems.com			
Corporate Telephone Services			
184 W Second St ....Boston MA 02127	617-625-1200		246
TF: 800-274-1211 ■ Web: corptelserv.com			
Corporate Traffic Inc			
2002 Southside Blvd ....Jacksonville FL 32216	904-727-0051	727-6804	311
Web: www.corporate-traffic.com			
Corporate Travel Management Group			
450 E 22nd St............................. Lombard IL 60148	630-691-8000		771
Web: www.corptrav.com			
Corporate Travel Service			
23420 Ford Rd Ste 1.................Dearborn Heights MI 48127	313-565-8888		772
Web: ctscentral.net			
Corporate University Xchange			
4900 Ritter Rd Ste 103 .... Mechanicsburg PA 17055	717-395-9267		463
Web: www.corpu.com			
Corporate Visions Inc			
1020 19th St NW Ste LL20.................Washington DC 20036	202-833-4333	833-4332	344
TF: 800-515-4577 ■ Web: www.corpvisions.com			
Corporate West Computer Systems			
1610 Dell Ave Ste F ....Campbell CA 95008	408-374-4655		196
TF: 800-700-5255 ■ Web: www.corpwest.com			
Corporate Writer & Editor			
111 E Wacker Dr Ste 500 ....Chicago IL 60601	312-960-4140		531-2
TF: 800-878-5331 ■ Web: www.ragan.com/main/home.aspx			
Corporation for Public Broadcasting (CPB)			
401 Ninth St NW.........................Washington DC 20004	202-879-9600	879-9700	305
TF: 800-272-2190 ■ Web: www.cpb.org			
Corporation Service Co			
2711 Centerville Rd Ste 400................. Wilmington DE 19808	302-636-5400	636-5454	113
TF: 866-403-5272 ■ Web: www.cscglobal.com			
Corps Network, The			
1275 K St NW Ste 1050 ....Washington DC 20005	202-737-6272	737-6277	48-6
Web: www.corpsnetwork.org			
Corps Solutions Llc			
235 Garrisonville Rd #202 .... Stafford VA 22554	540-300-1274	891-9570*	463
*Fax Area Code: 703 ■ Web: www.corps-solutions.com			
Corptax LLC			
1751 Lake Cook Rd Ste 100................. Deerfield IL 60015	800-966-1639	236-8011*	177
*Fax Area Code: 847 ■ TF: 800-966-1639 ■ Web: www.corptax.com			
Corpus Christi Ballet			
1621 N Mesquite St ....Corpus Christi TX 78401	361-882-4588	881-9291	573-1
TF: 800-745-3000 ■ Web: www.corpuschristiballet.com			
Corpus Christi City Hall			
1201 Leopard St PO Box 9277...........Corpus Christi TX 78469	361-826-2489		337
TF: 800-711-9112 ■ Web: www.cctexas.com			
Corpus Christi Coast Guard Air Station			
8930 Ocean Dr Hgr 41 ....Corpus Christi TX 78419	361-939-6212		158
Web: www.uscg.mil			
Corpus Christi Convention & Visitors Bureau			
101 N Shoreline Blvd Ste 430...........Corpus Christi TX 78401	361-881-1888	887-9023	206
TF: 800-678-6232 ■ Web: www.visitcorpuschristitx.org			
Corpus Christi Gasket & Fastener Inc			
PO Box 4074 ....Corpus Christi TX 78469	361-884-6366	884-0695	326
TF: 800-460-6366 ■ Web: www.ccgasket.com			
Corpus Christi International Airport			
1000 International Dr ....Corpus Christi TX 78406	361-289-0171	289-0251	27
TF: 800-352-0050 ■ Web: www.corpuschristiairport.com			
Corpus Christi Medical Ctr			
13725 NW Blvd ....Corpus Christi TX 78410	361-761-1000		374-3
TF: 800-994-6610 ■ Web: www.ccmedicalcenter.com			
Corpus Christi Medical Ctr Bay Area			
13725 NW Blvd ....Corpus Christi TX 78412	361-761-1000		374-3
TF: 800-994-6610 ■ Web: www.ccmedicalcenter.com			
Corpus Christi Museum of Science & History			
1900 N Chaparral St....................Corpus Christi TX 78401	361-826-4667		520
TF: 800-383-7677 ■ Web: ccmuseum.com			
Corpus Christi Public Libraries			
805 Comanche St.......................Corpus Christi TX 78401	361-826-7000		434-3
Web: www.cclibraries.com			
Corpus Christi Speedway			
241 Flato Rd..........................Corpus Christi TX 78405	361-289-8847		515
Web: www.ccspeedway.org			
Corpus Christi Symphony Orchestra			
555 N Carancahua St Tower II Ste 410			
Ste 410...............................Corpus Christi TX 78401	361-883-6683	882-4132	573-3
TF: 877-286-6683 ■ Web: www.ccsymphony.org			
Corr Tech Inc 4545 Homestead Rd ....Houston TX 77028	713-674-7887	674-0840	612
Web: www.corr-tech.com			
Corra Group			
13011 W Washington Blvd................Los Angeles CA 90066	310-822-7788		466
Web: www.corragroup.com			
Corradino Group 200 s Fifth st ....Louisville KY 40202	502-587-7221	587-2636	256
TF: 800-880-8241 ■ Web: www.corradino.com			
Correa J Luis (Rep D-CA)			
1039 Longworth HOB....................Washington DC 20515	202-225-2965		342-2
Web: correa.house.gov			
Correct Craft Inc			
14700 Aerospace Pkwy........................ Orlando FL 32832	407-855-4141	855-4141	90
TF: 800-346-2092 ■ Web: www.nautique.com			
Correct Rx Pharmacy Services Inc			
1352-C Charwood Rd........................Hanover MD 21076	800-636-0501		238
TF: 800-636-0501 ■ Web: www.correctrxpharmacy.com			
Correct Temp Inc 268 Hampstead Rd .... Methuen MA 01844	978-688-8700		189-10
Web: correcttemp.com			
Correctional Enterprises of Connecticut			
24 Wolcott Hill Rd.......................Wethersfield CT 06109	860-263-6839	263-6838	630
TF: 800-842-1146 ■ Web: www.ct.gov			
Corrections Corp of America			
10 Burton Hills Blvd .... Nashville TN 37215	615-263-3000	263-3000	211
NYSE: CXW ■ TF: 800-624-2931 ■ Web: www.cca.com			
Corrections Department			
16415 Spring Hill Dr ....Brooksville FL 34604	352-754-6715		213
Corrections Dept 1106 N Ave................ Bridgeport CT 06606	475-225-8000	225-8050	213
Web: ct.gov			
Correlated Products Inc			
5616 Progress Rd........................Indianapolis IN 46242	317-243-3248	244-8461	151
TF: 800-428-3266 ■ Web: cpiroadsolutions.com			
Correll Assoc PC			
26026 Telegraph Rd Ste 200................. Southfield MI 48033	248-355-5151		2
Web: correllcpa.com			

	Phone	Fax	Class
Corridor Capital LLC 12400 Wilshire Blvd Ste 645 .... Los Angeles CA 90025	310-442-7000		194
Web: www.corridorcapital.com			
Corridor Group Inc, The 6405 Metcalf Ste 108 .... Overland Park KS 66202	866-263-3795		194
TF: 866-263-3795 ■ *Web:* www.corridorgroup.com			
Corridor Resources Inc 5475 Spring Garden Rd .... Halifax NS B3J3T2	902-429-4511		536
TF: 888-429-4511 ■ *Web:* www.corridor.ca			
Corriente Resources Inc 5811 Cooney Rd Unit S209 .... Richmond BC V6X3M1	604-282-7212	282-7568	502
Web: www.corriente.com			
Corrigan Co 3545 Gratiot St................. Saint Louis MO 63103	314-771-6200	771-8537	189-10
Web: www.corriganco.com			
Corrigan Correctional Institution 986 Norwich-New London Tpke.............. Uncasville CT 06382	860-848-5700		213
Web: www.ct.gov			
Corrigan Moving Systems 23923 Research Dr................... Farmington Hills MI 48335	800-267-7442		519
TF: 800-267-7442 ■ *Web:* www.corriganmoving.com			
Corrosion Monitoring Services Inc 902 Equity Dr .... Saint Charles IL 60174	630-762-9300		481
Web: www.cmsinc.us			
Corrosion Probe Inc 12 Industrial Park Rd .... Centerbrook CT 06409	860-767-4402		261
TF: 800-245-6379 ■ *Web:* www.cpiengineering.com			
Corrpro Canada Inc 10848 - 214 St........... Edmonton AB T5S2A7	780-447-4565		256
TF: 800-661-8390 ■ *Web:* www.corrpro.ca			
Corrpro Cos Inc 1055 W Smith Rd .... Medina OH 44256	330-723-5082	722-7654	261
TF: 800-443-3516 ■ *Web:* www.corrpro.com			
Corrugated Container Corp 6405 Commonwealth Dr SW .... Roanoke VA 24018	540-774-0500		100
Web: www.cccbox.com			
Corrugated Gear & Services Inc 100 Anderson Rd .... Alpharetta GA 30004	770-475-8929	442-3371	547
TF: 800-969-0881 ■ *Web:* www.corrugatedgear.com			
Corry Contract Inc 21 Maple Ave................ Corry PA 16407	814-665-8221		320
Web: www.corrycontract.com			
Corry Forge Co 441 E Main St.................... Corry PA 16407	814-664-9664	664-9452	483
Web: www.ellwoodgroup.com			
Cors & Bassett 537 E Pete Rose Way Ste 400................ Cincinnati OH 45202	513-852-8200		428
Web: www.corsbassett.com			
Corsair Memory Inc 46221 Landing Pkwy .... Fremont CA 94538	510-657-8747	657-8748	173-5
TF: 888-222-4346 ■ *Web:* www.corsair.com			
Corsicana & Navarro County Chamber of Commerce 120 N 12th St............................ Corsicana TX 75110	903-874-4731	874-4187	139
Web: www.corsicana.org			
Corsicana Bedding Inc PO Box 1050 .... Corsicana TX 75151	903-872-2591		471
TF: 800-323-4349 ■ *Web:* www.corsicanabedding.com			
Corsicana Public Library 100 N 12th St............................ Corsicana TX 75110	903-654-4810		434-3
TF: 877-648-2836 ■ *Web:* www.cityofcorsicana.com			
CorsiTech 3200 SW Fwy Ste 2700.............. Houston TX 77027	281-431-3628		144
Web: www.corsicanatech.com			
Corson County 108 E First St PO Box 175 .... McIntosh SD 57641	605-273-4481	273-4481	338
Web: corson.sdcounties.org			
Corson's Inlet State Park 1304 Sloatsburg Rd County Rt 550 PO Box 450.. Ringwood NJ 07456	609-861-2404		565
Web: www.njparksandforests.org/parks/corsons.html			
Corstar Communications LLC 40 Saw Mill River Rd .... Hawthorne NY 10532	914-347-2700		180
TF: 800-433-5778 ■ *Web:* www.corstar.com			
Cortac Group Inc 29512 Baycrest Dr .... Rancho Palos Verdes CA 90275	310-377-2085		195
Web: www.cortacgroup.com			
Cortec Corp 4119 White Bear Pkwy............ Saint Paul MN 55110	651-429-1100	429-1122	145
TF: 800-426-7832 ■ *Web:* www.cortecvci.com			
Cortec Group 200 Park Ave 20th Fl............. New York NY 10017	212-370-5600		360-3
Web: www.cortecgroup.com			
Cortec Precision Sheet Metal Inc 2231 Will Wool Dr .... San Jose CA 95112	408-278-8540		697
Web: www.cortecprecision.com			
Cortech Engineering Inc 22785 Savi Ranch Pkwy.................. Yorba Linda CA 92887	714-779-0911		536
Web: cortecheng.com			
Cortech Solutions Inc 1409 Audubon Blvd Ste B1................ Wilmington NC 28403	910-362-1143		475
Web: www.cortechsolutions.com			
Cortek Inc 12 E V Hogan Dr.................... Hamlet NC 28345	910-582-0100		548
Web: www.cortek.us			
Cortelco Inc 1703 Sawyer Rd .... Corinth MS 38834	662-287-5281	287-3889	246
TF: 800-288-3132 ■ *Web:* www.cortelco.com			
Cortex Consultants Inc 1218 Langley St .... Victoria BC V8W1W2	250-360-1492		463
TF: 866-931-1192 ■ *Web:* www.cortex.ca			
Cortez Masto Catherine (Sen D - NV) 204 Russell Senate Office Bldg............ Washington DC 20510	202-224-3542		342-2
Web: www.cortezmasto.senate.gov/content/contact-senator			
Cortland County 46 Greenbush St Ste 101 .... Cortland NY 13045	607-753-5021	753-5378	338
TF: 800-772-1213 ■ *Web:* www.cortland-co.org			
Cortland Line Company Inc 3736 Kellogg Rd.............................. Cortland NY 13045	607-756-2851		710
Web: www.cortlandline.com			
Cortland Plastics International LLC 211 Main St .... Cortland NY 13045	607-662-0120		98
Web: www.cortlandplastics.com			
Cortland Regional Medical Ctr (CRMC) 134 Homer Ave.............................. Cortland NY 13045	607-756-3500		374-3
Web: www.cortlandregional.org			
Cortlandt Recreation Dept 1 Heady St .... Cortlandt Manor NY 10567	914-734-1050		564
TF: 800-836-6976 ■ *Web:* www.townofcortlandt.com			
Cortron Inc 59 Technology Dr .... Lowell MA 01851	978-975-5445	975-0357	173-1
Web: www.cortroninc.com			
CorTrust Bank 1801 S Marion Rd .... Sioux Falls SD 57106	605-361-8356		70
Web: www.cortrustbank.com			
Corum Group Ltd 19805 N Creek Pkwy Ste 300.................... Bothell WA 98011	425-455-8281		463
TF: 800-228-8281 ■ *Web:* www.corumgroup.com			
Corunna Public School District 124 N Shiawassee St .... Corunna MI 48817	989-743-6338	743-4474	685
TF: 866-632-9992 ■ *Web:* www.corunna.k12.mi.us			
Corus Group LLC 130 Technology Pkwy .... Norcross GA 30092	770-300-4700		180
TF: 800-937-4688 ■ *Web:* www.corus360.com			
Corus Realty Holdings Inc 6726 Curran St.............................. Mclean VA 22101	703-827-0075		652
Web: www.corushome.com			
Corvallis Area Chamber of Commerce 420 NW Second St......................... Corvallis OR 97330	541-757-1505		139
TF: 800-562-8526 ■ *Web:* www.corvallischamber.com			
Corvallis Microtechnology Inc 413 SW Jefferson Ave....................... Corvallis OR 97333	541-752-5456	752-4117	173-2
Web: www.cmtinc.com			
Corvallis Peter Productions 2200 N Interstate Ave .... Portland OR 97227	503-222-1665		226
TF: 800-528-1668 ■ *Web:* www.petercorvallis.com			
Corvallis School District 509 J 1555 SW 35th St PO Box 3509J............... Corvallis OR 97333	541-757-5811		780
Web: www.csd509j.net			
Corvallis Tourism 420 NW Second St........... Corvallis OR 97330	541-757-1544	753-2664	206
TF: 800-334-8118 ■ *Web:* www.visitcorvallis.com			
Corvallis-Benton County Library 645 NW Monroe Ave.......................... Corvallis OR 97330	541-766-6793	766-6915	434-3
Web: cbcpubliclibrary.net			
CorVel Corp 2010 Main St Ste 600 .... Irvine CA 92614	949-851-1473	851-1469	463
NASDAQ: CRVL ■ *TF:* 888-726-7835 ■ *Web:* www.corvel.com			
Corvette Diner 2965 Historic Decatur Rd .... San Diego CA 92103	619-542-1476		671
Web: cohnrestaurants.com			
Corvirtus LLC 1011 N Weber St.................... Colorado Springs CO 80903	800-322-5329		463
TF: 800-322-5329 ■ *Web:* www.corvirtus.com			
Corwin Press Inc 2455 Teller Rd.......... Thousand Oaks CA 91320	805-499-9734	499-0871	637-2
TF Orders: 800-233-9936 ■ *Web:* www.corwin.com			
Cory Watson Crowder & DeGaris 2131 Magnolia Ave....................... Birmingham AL 35205	205-328-2200		428
TF: 800-852-6299 ■ *Web:* www.cwcd.com			
Corybant PO Box 19136.......................... Boulder CO 80308	303-447-1988		194
Web: www.corybant.com			
Coryell County 620 E Main St PO Box 237.................... Gatesville TX 76528	254-865-5911	865-5064	338
Web: www.coryellcounty.org			
Corzo Castella Carballo Thompson Salman PA 901 Ponce De Leon Blvd Ste 900........... Coral Gables FL 33134	305-445-2900		256
Web: www.c3ts.com			
COSA Xentaur Corp 84G Horseblock Rd.......... Yaphank NY 11980	631-345-3434		407
Web: www.cosaxentaur.com			
Cosabella 12186 SW 128th St.................... Miami FL 33186	305-253-9904		157-6
Co-Sales Co 2700 N Third St Ste 1000 .... Phoenix AZ 85004	602-254-5555		194
Web: www.co-sales.com			
Cosanti Originals Inc 6433 Doubletree Ranch Rd.............. Paradise Valley AZ 85253	480-948-6145	998-4312	50-3
TF: 800-752-3187 ■ *Web:* www.cosanti.com			
Coscan Homes LLC 5555 Ravenswood Rd.................. Fort Lauderdale FL 33312	954-620-1000		653
COSCO (China Ocean Shipping Co Americas Inc) 100 Lighting Way .... Secaucus NJ 07094	201-422-0500	422-8956	220
TF: 800-242-7354 ■ *Web:* www.cosco-usa.com			
Cosco Fire Protection Inc 1075 W Lambert Rd Bldg D .... Brea CA 92821	714-989-1800	989-1801	189-13
TF: 800-485-3795 ■ *Web:* www.coscofire.com			
Cosco Industries Inc 7220 W Wilson Ave .... Harwood Heights IL 60706	708-867-5800		467
TF: 800-296-8970 ■ *Web:* www.coscoindustries.com			
Cosco International Inc 1633 Sands Pl SE Cumberland Business Pk ...... Marietta GA 30067	770-303-0797	303-0795	80-2
Web: www.coscous.com			
Cosentini Assoc Inc 2 Pennsylvania Plaza 3rd Fl .... New York NY 10121	212-615-3600		256
Web: www.cosentini.com			
CoServ Electric 7701 S Stemmons Fwy .... Corinth TX 76210	940-321-7800	270-6640	245
TF: 800-274-4014 ■ *Web:* coserv.com			
Cosfibel Inc 60 E 42nd St Ste 2301............. New York NY 10165	212-867-4133		711
Web: www.cosfibelgroup.com			
Cosgrove Aircraft Service Inc 70 Oser Ave .... Hauppauge NY 11788	631-231-6111		770
Web: www.cosgroveaircraft.com			
Cosgrove Associates Inc 747 Third Ave Fl 16 .... New York NY 10017	212-888-7202		344
TF: 000-413-9120 ■ *Web:* www.cosgroveny.com			
Coshocton County 401 1/2 Main St........... Coshocton OH 43812	740-622-1753		338
Coshocton County Chamber of Commerce 401 Main St .... Coshocton OH 43812	740-622-5411	622-9902	139
Web: www.coshoctoncounty.net			
Coshocton County Memorial Hospital Assn Inc 1460 Orange St........................... Coshocton OH 43812	740-622-6411		374-3
Web: www.ccmh.com			
COSI Columbus 333 W Broad St .... Columbus OH 43215	614-228-2674	228-6363	520
TF: 888-819-2674 ■ *Web:* www.cosi.org			
Cosi Cucina 1975 NW 86th St...................... Clive IA 50325	515-278-8148		671
Web: www.cosicucina.com			
Cosi Inc 1751 Lake Cook Rd Ste 600 .... Deerfield IL 60015	847-597-8800		670
NASDAQ: COSI ■ *Web:* www.getcosi.com			
COSI Toledo 1 Discovery Way .... Toledo OH 43604	419-244-2674	255-2674	520
TF: 800-590-9755 ■ *Web:* imaginationstationtoledo.org			
Coskata Inc 4575 Weaver Pkwy Ste 100 .... Warrenville IL 60555	630-657-5800	657-5801	194
Web: www.coskata.com			
Cosley Zoo 1356 N Gary Ave .... Wheaton IL 60187	630-665-5534	260-6408	823
TF: 800-226-3369 ■ *Web:* www.cosleyzoo.org			
Cosmed Group Inc 28 Narragansett Ave .... Jamestown RI 02835	401-423-2003		743
Web: www.cosmedgroup.com			

Phone | Fax | Class

COSMED USA Inc
2211 N Elton Ave Ste 305 Chicago IL 60614 773-645-8113 250
Web: www.cosmed.it
Cosmetic Essence Inc 2182 Hwy 35 Holmdel NJ 07733 732-888-7788 214
Web: www.cosmeticessence.com
Cosmetic Toiletry & Fragrance Assn PAC (CTFA PAC)
1101 17th St NW Ste 300 Washington DC 20036 202-331-1770 331-1969 615
TF: 800-227-5558 ■ *Web:* cir-safety.org
Cosmic Cafe 2912 Oak Lawn Dallas TX 75219 214-521-6157 521-9195 671
Web: www.cosmiccafedallas.com
Cosmic Cart Inc 521 Lansdowne Rd Charlotte NC 28270 704-651-8534 393
Web: cosmiccart.com
Cosmic Pictures Inc
1345 Major St Salt Lake City UT 84115 801-463-3880 514
Web: cosmicpictures.com
Cosmo 12 Kent Way Ste 201 PO Box 737 Byfield MA 01922 978-462-7311 465-6223 745-7
Web: www.cosmofabric.net
Cosmo Corp 30201 Aurora Rd Cleveland OH 44139 440-498-7500 498-7515 604
Web: www.cosmocorp.com
Cosmo Specialty Fibers Inc
1701 First St Cosmopolis WA 98537 360-500-4600 638
Web: www.cosmospecialtyfibers.com
Cosmoflex Inc 4142 Industrial Dr Hannibal MO 63401 573-221-0242 370
Cosmolab Inc 1100 Garrett Pkwy Lewisburg TN 37091 931-359-6253 214
Cosmopolitan Chamber of Commerce
30 E Adams St Ste 1050 Chicago IL 60603 312-499-0611 139
Cosmopolitan Hotel Toronto
8 Colborne St Toronto ON M5E1E1 416-350-2000 350-2460 379
TF: 800-958-3488 ■ *Web:* www.cosmotoronto.com
Cosmopolitan International
7341 W 80th St PO Box 4588 Lancaster PA 17604 913-648-4330 48-15
TF: 800-648-4331 ■ *Web:* www.cosmopolitan.org
Cosmopolitan Magazine 300 W 57th St New York NY 10019 212-649-2000 457-11
TF: 866-879-6636 ■ *Web:* www.cosmopolitan.com
Cosmopolitan Translation Bureau Inc
53 W Jackson Blvd Chicago IL 60604 312-726-2610 768
Web: www.cosmopolitantranslation.net
Cosmos Cafe 575 Grande Allee E Quebec QC G1R2K5 418-640-0606 671
Web: lecosmos.com
Cosmos Communications Inc
11-05 44th Dr Long Island NY 11101 718-482-1800 482-1968 627
TF: 800-223-5751 ■ *Web:* www.cosmoscommunications.com
Cosmos Consulting Group Inc
212 E Ohio St Chicago IL 60611 312-222-0700 194
Cosmos Sports 1690 Bonhill Rd Mississauga ON L5T1C8 905-564-4660 564-4881 194
Web: www.cosmossports.com
CoSN (Consortium for School Networking)
1025 Vermont Ave NW Ste 1010 Washington DC 20005 202-861-2676 393-2011 48-9
TF: 866-267-8747 ■ *Web:* www.cosn.org
Cosrich Group Inc
12243 Branford St Sun Valley CA 91352 818-686-2500 214
Web: www.ouchicsonline.com
Cossatot River State Park-Natural Area
1980 Hwy 278 W Wickes AR 71973 870-385-2201 565
TF: 877-665-6343 ■ *Web:* www.arkansasstateparks.com
COST (Council on State Taxation)
122 C St NW Ste 330 Washington DC 20001 202-484-5222 484-5229 49-12
Web: www.cost.org
Cost Control Associates Inc
310 Bay Rd Queensbury NY 12804 518-798-4437 196
TF: 800-836-3787 ■ *Web:* www.costcontrolassociates.com
Cost Plus Inc 200 Fourth St Oakland CA 94607 510-893-7300 893-3681 362
NASDAQ: CPWM ■ *TF:* 877-967-5362 ■ *Web:* www.worldmarket.com
Costa Cruise Lines
200 S Pk Rd Ste 200 Hollywood FL 33021 954-266-5600 220
TF: 800-462-6782 ■ *Web:* www.costacruise.com
Costa Del Mar
2361 Mason Ave Ste 100 Daytona Beach FL 32117 386-274-4000 274-4001 542
TF: 800-447-3700 ■ *Web:* www.costadelmar.com
Costa Fruit & Produce
18 Bunker Hill Industrial Pk Boston MA 02129 617-241-8007 241-8007 297-7
TF: 800-322-1374 ■ *Web:* www.freshideas.com
Costa Jim (Rep D - CA)
2081 Rayburn HOB Washington DC 20515 202-225-3341 342-2
Web: costa.house.gov
Costa Mesa Chamber of Commerce
1700 Adams Ave Ste 101 Costa Mesa CA 92626 714-885-9092 885-9094 139
Web: www.costamesachamber.com
Costa Nursery Farms Inc
21800 SW 162nd Ave Miami FL 33170 800-327-7074 369
TF: 800-327-7074 ■ *Web:* www.costafarms.com
Costa Rica 211 E 43rd St Rm 1002 New York NY 10017 212-986-6373 986-6842 784
Web: www.un.int
Consulate General
1605 W Olympic Blvd Ste 400 Los Angeles CA 90015 213-380-7915 380-5639 257
TF: 800-343-6332 ■ *Web:* www.costarica-embassy.org
Consulate General 2114 S St NW Washington DC 20008 202-499-2991 265-4795 257
Web: www.costarica-embassy.org
Consulate General
2730 SW Third Ave Ste 401 Miami FL 33129 305-871-7485 522-0119* 257
**Fax Area Code: 786* ■ *Web:* www.costarica-embassy.org
Embassy 2114 S St NW Washington DC 20008 202-499-2991 265-4795 257
TF: 800-556-9990 ■ *Web:* www.costarica-embassy.org
Costanoa Coastal Lodge & Camp
2001 Rossi Rd Pescadero CA 94060 650-879-1100 879-2275 669
TF: 877-262-7848 ■ *Web:* www.costanoa.com
CoStar Group Inc
2 Bethesda Metro Ctr 10th Fl Bethesda MD 20814 301-215-8300 178-10
NASDAQ: CSGP ■ *TF:* 800-613-1303 ■ *Web:* www.costar.com
Costar Video Systems LLC
101 Wrangler Dr Ste 201 Coppell TX 75019 469-635-6800 652
Web: www.costarvideo.com
Costco Wholesale Corp 999 Lake Dr Issaquah WA 98027 425-313-8100 812
NASDAQ: COST ■ *TF Cust Svc:* 800-774-2678 ■ *Web:* www.costco.com
Costello Inc 9990 Richmond Ave Ste 450 Houston TX 77042 713-783-7788 261
TF: 800-938-7272 ■ *Web:* www.costelloinc.com
Costello Ryan (Rep R - PA)
326 Cannon HOB Washington DC 20515 202-225-4315 342-2
Web: costello.house.gov

Costello, Porter, Hill, Heisterkamp, Bushnell & Carpenter LLP
Security Bldg 704 St Joseph St Rapid City SD 57709 605-343-2410 428
Web: www.costelloporter.com
Costich Engineering & Land Surveying PC
217 Lake Ave Rochester NY 14608 585-458-3020 261
Web: costich.com
Costilla County
233 Main St Ste C PO Box 99 San Luis CO 81152 719-672-3681 672-3856 338
Web: www.colorado.gov
Costume Gallery 4451 Rt 130 Burlington NJ 08016 609-386-6601 386-0677 155-6
TF: 800-222-8125 ■ *Web:* www.costumegallery.net
Costume Specialists Inc
211 N Fifth St Columbus OH 43215 614-464-2115 464-2114 155-6
TF: 800-596-9357 ■ *Web:* www.costumespecialists.com
Cosumnes River College
8401 Ctr Pkwy Sacramento CA 95823 916-691-7410 691-7467* 162
**Fax: Admissions* ■ *Web:* www.crc.losrios.edu
COT (Civic Orchestra of Tucson)
PO Box 42764 Tucson AZ 85733 520-730-3371 573-3
TF: 800-352-8404 ■ *Web:* www.cotmusic.org
COTA (Children's Organ Transplant Assn)
2501 W Cota Dr Bloomington IN 47403 812-336-8872 336-8885 48-17
TF: 800-366-2682 ■ *Web:* www.cota.org
COTA (Central Ohio Transit Authority)
33 N High St Columbus OH 43215 614-228-1776 275-5933 468
TF: 800-638-6338 ■ *Web:* www.cota.com
Cota & Cota Inc 4 Green St Bellows Falls VT 05101 802-463-0000 316
Web: www.cotaoil.com
Cotchett Pitre & McCarthy LLP
San Francisco Airport Office Ctr 840 Malcolm Rd
Ste 200 Burlingame CA 94010 650-697-6000 41
Web: www.cpmlegal.com
Coteau Properties Co 204 County Rd 15 Beulah ND 58523 701-873-2281 873-7226 501
TF: 800-334-7443 ■ *Web:* www.nacoal.com
Coterie, Theatre, The
2450 Grand Blvd Ste 144 Kansas City MO 64108 816-474-6785 474-7112 572
Web: thecoterie.org
Cothern Computer Systems Inc
1640 Lelia Dr Ste 200 Jackson MS 39216 601-969-1155 969-1184 178-7
TF: 800-844-1155 ■ *Web:* www.ccslink.com
Coto Technology USA
66 Whitecap Dr North Kingstown RI 02852 401-943-2686 942-0920 203
Web: www.cotorelay.com
Cott Corp 6525 Viscount Rd Mississauga ON L4V1H6 905-672-1900 881-1926* 80-2
NYSE: COT ■ **Fax Area Code:* 813 ■ *TF:* 800-564-6253 ■ *Web:* www.cott.com
Cott Systems Inc
2800 Corporate Exchange Dr Ste 300 Columbus OH 43231 614-847-4405 225
Web: www.cottsystems.com
Cotta Transmission Company LLC
1301 Prince Hall Dr Beloit WI 53511 608-368-5600 368-5605 709
Web: www.cotta.com
Cottage Grove Area Chamber of Commerce
7516 80th St S Ste 205 PO Box 16 Cottage Grove MN 55016 651-458-8334 458-8383 139
Web: www.cottagegrovechamber.org
Cottage Place 126 W Cottage Ave Flagstaff AZ 86001 928-774-8431 671
Web: www.cottageplace.com
Cotter High School 1115 W Broadway Winona MN 55987 507-453-5000 622
Web: www.cotterschools.org
Cotterman Co 130 Seltzer Rd Croswell MI 48422 810-679-4400 679-4510 421
TF: 800-552-3337 ■ *Web:* www.cotterman.com
Cottey College 1000 W Austin Blvd Nevada MO 64772 417-667-8181 667-8103* 162
**Fax: Admissions* ■ *TF:* 888-526-8839 ■ *Web:* www.cottey.edu
Cottle County PO Box 717 Paducah TX 79248 806-492-3823 492-2625 338
Web: www.co.cottle.tx.us
Cotton & Co 633 SE Fifth St Stuart FL 34994 772-287-6612 4
TF: 800-266-9076 ■ *Web:* www.thecottonsolution.com
Cotton Belt Inc 401 E Sater St Pinetops NC 27864 252-827-4192 827-5603 471
TF: 800-849-4192 ■ *Web:* www.edgecombe.com
Cotton City Antique Mall
2012 Airport Blvd Mobile AL 36606 251-479-9747 460
Web: antiquemalls.com
Cotton Council International
1521 New Hampshire Ave NW Washington DC 20036 202-745-7805 483-4040 48-2
Web: www.cottonusa.org
Cotton County 301 N Broadway Walters OK 73572 580-875-3029 338
Cotton Electric Co-op Inc
226 N Broadway Walters OK 73572 580-875-3351 245
TF: 800-522-3520 ■ *Web:* www.cottonelectric.com
Cotton Exchange Tavern
201 E River St Savannah GA 31401 912-232-7088 671
Cotton Goods Manufacturing Co
259 N California Ave Chicago IL 60612 773-265-0088 265-0096 746
TF: 800-747-9353 ■ *Web:* www.cottongoodsmfg.com
Cotton Inc 6399 Weston Pkwy Cary NC 27513 919-678-2220 678-2230 48-2
TF: 800-334-5868 ■ *Web:* www.cottoninc.com
Cotton Patch Cafe 3302 S Clack St Abilene TX 79606 325-691-0509 671
Web: www.cottonpatch.com
Cotton Tom (Sen R - AR)
124 Russell Senate Office Bldg Washington DC 20510 202-224-2353 342-2
Web: www.cotton.senate.gov
Cotton's Week
7193 Goodlett Farms Pkwy Cordova TN 38016 901-274-9030 725-0510 531-13
Web: www.cotton.org/news/cweek
Cottonimages.Com Inc 10481 NW 28th St Miami FL 33172 305-251-2560 344
TF: 888-642-7999 ■ *Web:* www.cottonimages.com
Cottonwood Chamber of Commerce
1010 S Main St Cottonwood AZ 86326 928-634-7593 634-7594 139
Web: www.cottonwoodchamberaz.org
Cottonwood County 900 Third Ave Windom MN 56101 507-831-1905 831-4553 338
TF: 800-967-1763 ■ *Web:* www.co.cottonwood.mn.us
Cottonwood Grille 913 W River St Boise ID 83702 208-333-9800 671
Web: www.cottonwoodgrille.com
Cottonwood Lake State Recreation Area
PO Box 38 Merriman NE 69218 308-684-3428 565
Web: outdoornebraska.gov
Cottonwood Public Library
100 S Sixth St Cottonwood AZ 86326 928-634-7559 634-0253 434-3
Web: ctwpl.info

	Phone	Fax	Class
Cottrell Inc 2125 Candler Rd.................Gainesville GA 30507 *TF Sales:* 800-827-0132 ■ *Web:* www.cottrelltrailers.com	770-532-7251	535-2831	779
Cottrell Paper Company Inc 1135 Rock City Rd PO Box 35 ....Rock City Falls NY 12863 *TF:* 800-948-3559 ■ *Web:* www.cottrellpaper.com	518-885-1702	885-1702	816
Coty Inc 350 Fifth Ave 17th Fl.................New York NY 10118 *Web:* www.coty.com	212-389-7300		574
Couch & Philippi Inc 10680 Fern Ave PO Box A ....Stanton CA 90680 *TF Orders:* 800-854-3360 ■ *Web:* www.couchandphilippi.com	714-527-2261	827-2077	701
Couch Distributing Company Inc 104 Lee Rd..............................Watsonville CA 95076 *Web:* www.couchdistributing.com	831-724-0649	724-4293	81-1
Couch White LLP 540 Broadway................Albany NY 12201 *TF:* 800-973-1177 ■ *Web:* www.couchwhite.com	518-426-4600		428
Cougar Drilling Solutions Inc 7319 - 17 St............................Edmonton AB T6P1P1 *Web:* www.cougards.com	780-440-2400		539
Cougar Helicopters Inc St John's International Airport 40 Craig Dobbins' Way...................Saint John's NL A1A4Y3 *Web:* www.cougar.ca	709-758-4800	758-4850	359
Cougar Mountain Zoo 19525 SE 54th St........ Issaquah WA 98027 *Web:* www.cougarmountainzoo.org	425-392-6278		823
Coughlin & Company Inc 140 E 19th Ave Ste 700 ....Denver CO 80203 *Web:* www.coughlinandcompany.com	303-863-1900		401
Coughlin Equipment Company Inc 2221 E Hwy 66............................El Reno OK 73036 *Web:* coughlinequipment.com	405-262-9101		358
Cougle Commission Co 345 N Aberdeen St.........................Chicago IL 60607 *TF:* 800-568-2240 ■ *Web:* www.couglefoods.com	312-666-7861		473
Coulson Group of Companies 4890 Cherry Creek Rd ....Port Alberni BC V9Y8E9 *TF:* 800-663-3456 ■ *Web:* www.coulsongroup.com	250-724-7600		787
Coulter & Justus PC 9717 Cogdill Rd Ste 201 ....Knoxville TN 37932 *Web:* cj-pc.com	865-637-4161		2
Coulter Cadillac Inc 1188 E Camelback Rd.......................Phoenix AZ 85014 *Web:* coulteroncamelback.com	602-714-3112		57
Coulter Forge Technology Inc 1494 67th St.............................Emeryville CA 94608 *TF:* 800-648-4884 ■ *Web:* www.coulter-forge.com	510-420-3500	420-3555	483
Coulter Lake Guest Ranch 80 County Rd 273...............................Rifle CO 81650 *TF:* 800-858-3046 ■ *Web:* www.coulterlake.com	970-625-1473		239
Coulter Press Inc 156 Church St...............Clinton MA 01510	978-368-0176		637-8
Coulter's Furniture 1324 Windsor Ave...........Windsor ON N8X3L9 *Web:* www.coulters.com	519-253-7422	253-3744	321
Councel for Secular Humanism & Csicop 3965 Rensch Rd...........................Amherst NY 14228 *Web:* www.centerforinquiry.net	716-636-4869		148
Council Bluffs Area Chamber of Commerce 149 W Broadway...........................Council Bluffs IA 51503 *TF:* 800-228-6878 ■ *Web:* www.councilbluffsiowa.com	712-325-1000	322-5698	139
Council Bluffs Public Library 400 Willow Ave..........................Council Bluffs IA 51503 *Web:* www.councilbluffslibrary.org	712-323-7553		434-3
Council for Advancement & Support of Education (CASE) 1307 New York Ave NW Ste 1000...........Washington DC 20005 *TF Orders:* 800-554-8536 ■ *Web:* www.case.org	202-328-5900	387-4973	49-5
Council for Affordable Health Insurance (CAHI) 127 S Peyton St Ste 210...................Alexandria VA 22314	703-836-6200	836-6550	49-9
Council for Chemical Research Inc (CCR) 1730 Rhode Island Ave NW Ste 302...........Washington DC 20036 *Web:* www.ccrhq.org	202-429-3971	429-3976	49-19
Council for Christian Colleges & Universities (CCCU) 321 Eigth St NE ....Washington DC 20002 *Web:* www.cccu.org	202-546-8713	546-8913	49-5
Council for Community and Economic Research (C2ER) *C2ER* 1700 N Moore St Ste 2225 ....Arlington VA 22209 **Fax Area Code:* 480 ■ *Web:* www.c2er.org	703-522-4980	393-5098*	49-12
Council For Economic Opportunities In Greater Cleveland 1228 Euclid Ave Ste 700....................Cleveland OH 44115 *Web:* www.ceogc.org	216-696-9077	696-0770	48-11
Council for Equal Rights in Adoption 444 E 76th St ....New York NY 10021 *Web:* www.adoptionhealing.com	212-988-0110	988-0291	48-6
Council for Higher Education Accreditation (CHEA) 1 Dupont Cir NW Ste 510.................Washington DC 20036 *Web:* www.chea.org	202-955-6126	955-6129	48-1
Council for Interior Design Accreditation (CIDA) 206 Grandville Ave Ste 350 ....Grand Rapids MI 49503 *Web:* www.accredit-id.org	616-458-0400	458-0460	48-1
Council for International Exchange of Scholars (CIES) 1400 K St NW Ste 700 ....Washington DC 20005 *Web:* www.cies.org	202-686-4000		49-5
Council for Opportunity in Education 1025 Vermont Ave NW Ste 900.............Washington DC 20005 *Web:* www.coenet.us	202-347-7430	347-0786	48-11
Council for Professional Recognition 2460 16th St NW ....Washington DC 20009 *TF:* 800-424-4310 ■ *Web:* www.cdacouncil.org	202-265-9090	265-9161	49-5
Council for Responsible Genetics (CRG) 5 Upland Rd Ste 3.......................Cambridge MA 02140 *TF:* 888-591-3911 ■ *Web:* www.councilforresponsiblegenetics.org	617-868-0870	491-5344	49-19
Council for Responsible Nutrition (CRN) 1828 L St NW Ste 900 ....Washington DC 20036 *Web:* www.crnusa.org	202-204-7700	204-7701	49-6
Council Grounds State Park N1895 Council Grounds Dr ....Merrill WI 54452 *Web:* reserveamerica.com	715-536-8773		565
Council Grove State Park 3201 Spurgin Rd FWP Reg 2 Ofc.............Missoula MT 59804 *Web:* stateparks.mt.gov	406-542-5500		565

	Phone	Fax	Class
Council Grove/Morris County Chamber of Commerce & Tourism 207 W Main St ....Council Grove KS 66846 *TF:* 800-835-8019 ■ *Web:* www.councilgrove.com	620-767-5413		206
Council of Administrators of Special Education (CASE) Osigian Office Centre 101 Katelyn Cir Ste E.....................................Warner Robins GA 31088 *TF:* 800-585-1753 ■ *Web:* www.casecec.org	478-333-6892	333-2453	49-5
Council of Better Business Bureaus Inc *Dispute Resolution Services & Mediation Training* 4200 Wilson Blvd Ste 800.................Arlington VA 22203 *TF:* 855-748-4600 ■ *Web:* www.bbb.org	703-276-0100	525-8277	41
Council of Better Business Bureaus Inc Wise Giving Alliance 4200 Wilson Blvd Ste 800 ....Arlington VA 22203 *TF:* 800-248-4040 ■ *Web:* www.bbb.org	703-276-0100	525-8277	48-10
Council of Canadians 170 Laurier Ave W Ste 700.................Ottawa ON K1P5V5 *TF:* 800-387-7177 ■ *Web:* www.canadians.org	613-233-2773		48-7
Council of Chief State School Officers (CCSSO) 1 Massachusetts Ave NW Ste 700 ....Washington DC 20001 *Web:* www.ccsso.org	202-336-7000	408-8072	49-5
Council of Economic Advisers 732 N Capitol St NW ....Washington DC 20401 *Web:* www.whitehouse.gov	202-512-1800		340
Council of Ethical Organizations 214 S Payne St...........................Alexandria VA 22314 *Web:* councilofethicalorganizations.com	703-683-7916		533
Council of Graduate Schools (CGS) 1 Dupont Cir NW Ste 230.................Washington DC 20036 *TF:* 800-297-3775 ■ *Web:* www.cgsnet.org	202-223-3791	331-7157	49-5
Council of Industrial Boiler Owners (CIBO) 6801 Kennedy Rd Ste 102 ....Warrenton VA 20187 *Web:* www.cibo.org	540-349-9043		49-13
Council of Institutional Investors 888 17th St NW Ste 500..................Washington DC 20006 *Web:* www.cii.org	202-822-0800		49-2
Council of Insurance Agents & Brokers 701 Pennsylvania Ave NW Ste 750...........Washington DC 20004 *TF:* 877-267-9855 ■ *Web:* www.ciab.com	202-783-4400	783-4410	49-9
Council of Real Estate Brokerage Managers (CRB) 430 N Michigan Ave.......................Chicago IL 60611 **Fax Area Code:* 312 ■ *TF:* 800-621-8738 ■ *Web:* www.crb.com	800-621-8738	329-8882*	49-17
Council of Residential Specialists 430 N Michigan Ave Ste 300 ....Chicago IL 60611 *TF:* 800-462-8841 ■ *Web:* www.crs.com	312-321-4400	329-8882	49-17
Council of State & Territorial Epidemiologists (CSTE) 2872 Woodcock Blvd Ste 303..................Atlanta GA 30341 *Web:* www.cste.org	770-458-3811	458-8516	49-7
Council of State Governments (CSG) 2760 Research Pk Dr ....Lexington KY 40511 *TF Sales:* 800-800-1910 ■ *Web:* www.csg.org	859-244-8000	244-8001	49-7
Council of Supply Chain Management Professionals 333 E Butterfield Rd Ste 140................. Lombard IL 60148 *Web:* www.cscmp.org	630-574-0985	574-0989	49-18
Council of the Americas 680 Pk Ave ....New York NY 10065 *Web:* as-coa.org	212-628-3200	249-5868	48-7
Council of the Great City Schools 1301 Pennsylvania Ave NW Ste 702.........Washington DC 20004 *TF:* 888-280-7903 ■ *Web:* www.cgcs.org	202-393-2427	393-2400	49-5
Council of the Section of Legal Education & Admissions to the Bar 321 N Clark St 21st Fl ....Chicago IL 60654 *TF:* 800-238-2667 ■ *Web:* www.americanbar.org	312-988-6738	988-5681	48-1
Council on Academic Accreditation in Audiology & Speech-Language Pathology 2200 Research Blvd ....Rockville MD 20850 *TF:* 800-498-2071 ■ *Web:* www.asha.org	301-296-5700		48-1
Council on Accreditation (COA) 45 Broadway 29th Fl.......................New York NY 10006 *TF:* 866-262-8088 ■ *Web:* www.coanet.org	212-797-3000	797-1428	48-1
Council on Accreditation of Nurse Anesthesia Educational Programs 222 S Prospect Ave.......................Park Ridge IL 60068 *TF:* 855-526-2262 ■ *Web:* www.aana.com	847-692-7050	692-6968	48-1
Council on Aviation Accreditation (CAA) *Aviation Accreditation Board International* 3410 Skyway Dr...........................Auburn AL 36830 *TF:* 800-767-4767 ■ *Web:* www.aabi.aero	334-844-2431	844-2432	48-1
Council on Chiropractic Education Commission on Accreditation 8049 N 85th Way ....Scottsdale AZ 85258 *TF:* 888-443-3506 ■ *Web:* www.cce-usa.org	480-443-8877	483-7333	48-1
Council on Education for Public Health 1010 Wayne Ave Ste 220 ....Silver Spring MD 20910 *Web:* www.ceph.org	202-789-1050	789-1895	48-1
Council on Environmental Quality 730 Jackson Pl NW ....Washington DC 20503 *Web:* www.whitehouse.gov/ceq	202-395-5750	456-0753	340
Council on Foundations 2121 Crystal Dr Ste 700...................Arlington VA 22202 *TF:* 800-673-9036 ■ *Web:* www.cof.org	703-879-0600	879-0800	48-5
Council on International Educational Exchange (CIEE) 300 Fore St................................Portland ME 04101 *TF Cust Svc:* 888-268-6245 ■ *Web:* www.ciee.org	207-553-4000	553-5272	49-5
Council on Licensure Enforcement & Regulation (CLEAR) 403 Marquis Ave...........................Lexington KY 40502 *Web:* www.clearhq.org	859-269-1289		49-7
Council on Naturopathic Medical Education 342 Main St .... Great Barrington MA 01230 *Web:* www.cnme.org	413-528-8877	528-8880	48-1
Council on Occupational Education 7840 Roswell Rd Bldg 300 Ste 325 ....Atlanta GA 30350 *TF:* 800-917-2081 ■ *Web:* www.council.org	770-396-3898	396-3790	48-1
Council on Quality & Leadership, The (CQL) 100 W Rd Ste 300.........................Towson MD 21204 *TF:* 800-628-2783 ■ *Web:* www.c-q-l.org	410-583-0060		48-1
Council on Size & Weight Discrimination (CSWD) PO Box 305 ....Mount Marion NY 12456 *Web:* www.cswd.org	845-679-1209	679-1206	48-17

Phone | Fax | Class

Council on Social Work Education (CSWE)
1701 Duke St Ste 200 ... Alexandria VA 22314 703-683-8080 683-8099 49-5
Web: www.cswe.org

Council on Social Work Education
1725 Duke St Ste 500 ... Alexandria VA 22314 703-683-8080 683-8099 48-1
Web: www.cswe.org

Council on State Taxation (COST)
122 C St NW Ste 330 ... Washington DC 20001 202-484-5222 484-5229 49-12
Web: www.cost.org

Council Rock School District
30 N Chancellor St ... Newtown PA 18940 215-944-1000 685
Web: www.crsd.org

Counsel Corp
1211 Ave of the Americas Ste 2902 ... New York NY 10036 212-696-0100 696-9809 405
NYSE: CXS ■ *TF:* 866-296-3743 ■ *Web:* www.snl.com

Counselors of Real Estate (CRE)
430 N Michigan Ave 2nd Fl ... Chicago IL 60611 312-329-8427 329-8881 49-17
Web: www.cre.org

Count Basie Theatre 99 Monmouth St ... Red Bank NJ 07701 732-842-9000 572
Web: www.countbasietheatre.org

Count Me In 5955 Edmond St ... Las Vegas NV 89118 866-514-5888 958-8779* 84
**Fax Area Code:* 800 ■ *TF:* 866-514-5888 ■ *Web:* www.countmeinllc.com

Counter Pro Inc 210 Lincoln St ... Manchester NH 03103 603-647-2444 191-3
TF: 800-899-2444 ■ *Web:* counterproincusa.com

Counterforce Inc
2740 Matheson Blvd E Unit 2A ... Mississauga ON L4W4X3 905-282-6200 693
TF: 800-591-7374 ■ *Web:* www.counterforce.com

Counterpane Montessori Inc
839 Hwy 314 ... Fayetteville GA 30214 770-461-2304 685
Web: www.counterpane.org

Counterparts LLC
2012 N 117th Ave Ste 105 ... Omaha NE 68164 402-932-2220 226
Web: www.mycounterparts.com

Counterstrike Corp
4956 Hayvenhurst Ave ... Encino CA 91316 818-906-7598 693
Web: www.counterstrike.com

Country 106.7 5026 Cliff Gookin Blvd ... Tupelo MS 38801 662-842-1067 844-2887 645-169
Web: wizard106.iheart.com

Country 96 KWWR 1705 E Liberty St ... Mexico MO 65265 573-581-5500 581-1801 645
Web: info.kwwr.com

Country 97.1 HANK FM
40 Monument Cir Ste 600 ... Indianapolis IN 46204 317-266-9700 684-2021 645-77
Web: www.hankfm.com

Country Aircheck
1102 17th Ave S Ste 205 ... Nashville TN 37212 615-320-1450 194
Web: countryaircheck.com

Country Bank for Savings 75 Main St ... Ware MA 01082 413-967-6221 967-3289 70
TF: 800-322-8233 ■ *Web:* www.countrybank.com

Country Cablevision Inc
9449 State Hwy 197 S ... Burnsville NC 28714 828-682-4074 116
TF: 800-722-4074 ■ *Web:* www.ccvn.com

Country Club Bank
2310 S Fourth St ... Leavenworth KS 66048 913-682-2300 360-2
Web: www.countryclubbank.com

Country Club Nissan 55 Oneida St ... Oneonta NY 13820 607-432-2800 57
Web: www.countryclubnissan.com

Country Court Nursing Center
1076 Coshocton Ave ... Mount Vernon OH 43050 740-397-4125 371
TF: 800-321-1245 ■ *Web:* countrycourt.com

Country Curtains
30 Main St PO Box 955 ... Stockbridge MA 01262 413-243-1474 243-1067 157-5
TF: 800-937-1237 ■ *Web:* www.countrycurtains.com

Country Floors Inc 15 E 16th St ... New York NY 10003 212-627-8300 291
Web: www.countryfloors.com

Country Fresh Mushroom Co
289 Chambers Rd PO Box 490 ... Toughkenamon PA 19374 610-268-3043 268-0479 297-7
Web: www.countryfreshmushrooms.com

Country Hearth 3450 S Clack St ... Abilene TX 79606 325-695-7700 379
Web: www.countryhearthabilene.com

Country Hearth Inn Inc
50 Glenlake Pkwy NE Ste 350 ... Atlanta GA 30328 770-393-2662 378
TF: 888-443-2784 ■ *Web:* www.redlion.com/country-hearth-inn-suites

Country Hills Health Care Inc
1580 Broadway ... El Cajon CA 92021 619-441-8745 371
Web: www.countryhills.com

Country Home Furniture LLC
1352 Main St ... East Earl PA 17519 717-354-2329 321
Web: www.chfs1.com

Country Home Products Inc
75 Meigs Rd ... Vergennes VT 05491 802-877-1200 459
Web: www.chp.com

Country House 4830 Kennett Pk ... Wilmington DE 19807 302-654-5101 672
TF: 800-976-7610 ■ *Web:* www.actsretirement.org

Country Inn at the Mall
936 Stillwater Ave ... Bangor ME 04401 207-941-0200 379
TF Resv: 800-244-3961 ■ *Web:* www.countryinnatthemall.net

Country Inn Lake Resort
1332 Airport Rd ... Hot Springs AR 71913 501-767-3535 379
TF: 800-822-7402 ■ *Web:* www.countryinnlakeresort.com

COUNTRY Insurance & Financial Services
1705 Towanda Ave ... Bloomington IL 61701 866-268-6879 391-2
TF: 888-211-2555 ■ *Web:* www.countryfinancial.com

Country Lane Flower Shop
729 S Michigan Ave ... Howell MI 48843 517-546-1111 292
TF: 800-764-7673 ■ *Web:* www.countrylaneflowers.com

Country Life Farm 319 Old Joppa Rd ... Bel Air MD 21014 410-879-1952 879-6207 368
Web: www.countrylifefarm.com

Country Living Magazine
300 W 57th St ... New York NY 10019 212-649-3204 457-11
Web: www.countryliving.com

Country Maid Inc
1919 S Kinnickinnic Ave ... Milwaukee WI 53204 414-383-3970 123
Web: www.countrymaid.com

Country Mark Co-op
1200 Refinery Rd ... Mount Vernon IN 47620 800-832-5490 838-8196* 597
**Fax Area Code:* 812 ■ *TF:* 800-832-5490 ■ *Web:* www.countrymark.com

Country Music Assn Inc (CMA)
1 Music Cir S ... Nashville TN 37203 615-244-2840 726-0314 48-4
TF: 800-788-3045 ■ *Web:* cmaworld.com

Country Music Hall of Fame & Museum
222 Fifth Ave S ... Nashville TN 37203 615-416-2001 255-2245 520
TF: 800-852-6437 ■ *Web:* countrymusichalloffame.org

Country Music Television (CMT)
330 Commerce St ... Nashville TN 37201 615-335-8400 740
Web: www.cmt.com

Country Mutual Insurance Co
1701 Towanda Ave ... Bloomington IL 61701 866-268-6879 821-5160* 391-4
**Fax Area Code:* 309 ■ *TF Cust Svc:* 888-211-2555 ■ *Web:* www.countryfinancial.com

Country Oven Bakery Inc
2840 Pioneer Dr ... Bowling Green KY 42101 270-782-3200 296-2

Country Pride Co-op (CPC)
201 S Monroe PO Box 529 ... Winner SD 57580 605-842-2711 10-5
TF: 888-325-7743 ■ *Web:* www.countrypridecoop.com

Country Pure Foods Inc
681 W Waterloo Rd ... Akron OH 44314 330-753-2293 848-4287 296-20
Web: www.juice4u.com

Country Radio Broadcasters Inc (CRB)
819 18th Ave S ... Nashville TN 37203 615-327-4487 329-4492 49-14
TF: 800-659-9889 ■ *Web:* countryradioseminar.com

Country Sampler Magazine
707 Kautz Rd ... Saint Charles IL 60174 630-377-8000 457-14
Web: www.countrysampler.com

Country Silk Inc
100 S Washington Ave ... Dunellen NJ 08812 732-752-5556 752-7550 293
Web: www.countrysilk.com

Country Springs Hotel & Conference Ctr
2810 Golf Rd ... Pewaukee WI 53072 262-547-0201 377
TF: 800-247-6640 ■ *Web:* www.countryspringshotel.com

Country Today 701 S Farwell St ... Eau Claire WI 54701 715-833-9270 532-4
Web: www.thecountrytoday.com

Country Way 5325 Mowry Ave ... Fremont CA 94536 510-797-3188 671

Country's Barbecue 2016 12th Ave ... Columbus GA 31901 706-327-7702 671
TF General: 800-285-4267 ■ *Web:* www.countrysbarbecue.com

Countryside Asset Management Corp
7490 Clubhouse Rd Ste 201 ... Boulder CO 80301 303-530-0700 656

Countryside Bank (SBC)
6734 Joliet Rd ... Countryside IL 60525 708-485-3100 485-3106 70
Web: www.bankcountryside.com

Countryside Co-op 514 E Main St ... Durand WI 54736 715-672-8947 672-5131 276
TF: 800-236-7585 ■ *Web:* www.countrysidecoop.com

Countryside Vineyards Winery
658 Henry Harr Rd ... Blountville TN 37617 423-323-1660 50-7
TF: 800-237-2591 ■ *Web:* cvwineryandsupply.com

CountryTyme Inc
3451 Cincinnati-Zanesville Rd SW ... Lancaster OH 43130 740-475-6001 653
TF: 800-213-8365 ■ *Web:* www.countrytyme.com

Countrywide Tire & Rubber Inc
17200 Medina Rd Ste 100 ... Plymouth MN 55447 763-546-1636 755
Web: www.countrywidetire.com

Counts Sausage Company Inc
222 Church St ... Prosperity SC 29127 803-364-2392 296-26

County & Circuit Clerk 206 W Third St ... Fordyce AR 71742 870-352-2307 338

County Beverage Company Inc
1290 SE Hamblen Rd ... Lees Summit MO 64081 816-525-4550 297-8

County Clare 1234 N Astor St ... Milwaukee WI 53202 414-272-5273 290-6300 671
TF: 800-942-5273 ■ *Web:* www.countyclare-inn.com

County College of Morris
214 Ctr Grove Rd ... Randolph NJ 07869 973-328-5000 162
TF: 888-726-3260 ■ *Web:* www.ccm.edu

County Concrete Corp 50 Railroad Ave ... Kenvil NJ 07847 973-584-7122 182
Web: www.countyconcretenj.com

County Engineers Assn of Ohio
6500 Busch Blvd Ste 100 ... Columbus OH 43229 614-221-0707 256
Web: www.ceao.org

County Library 1304 Old Knoxville Rd ... Tazewell TN 37879 423-626-5414 434-3

County Line 9600 Tramway Blvd NE ... Albuquerque NM 87122 505-856-7477 671
Web: www.countyline.com

County of Bedford Virginia
122 E Main St Ste 202 ... Bedford VA 24523 540-586-7601 586-0406 338
Web: www.co.bedford.va.us

County of Greene 93 E High St ... Waynesburg PA 15370 724-852-5210 852-5327 338
TF: 888-852-5399 ■ *Web:* www.co.greene.pa.us

County of San Bernardino
2024 Orange Tree Ln ... Redlands CA 92374 909-307-2669 307-0539 520
Web: sbcounty.gov

County Press
1521 Imlay City Rd PO Box 220 ... Lapeer MI 48446 810-664-0811 664-5852 532-4
Web: thecountypress.mihomepaper.com

County Regional Vocational Sch
147 Pond St ... Franklin MA 02038 508-528-5400 162
Web: www.tri-county.tc

County Rescue Services
1765 Allouez Ave ... Green Bay WI 54311 920-469-9779 30
TF: 800-550-3214 ■ *Web:* www.countyrescue.com

Coup des Tartes 1725 E Osborn Rd ... Phoenix AZ 85016 602-212-1082 671
Web: nicetartes.com

Coup, The 924 17th Ave SW ... Calgary AB T2T0A2 403-541-1041 671
Web: www.thecoup.ca

Coupland-Moran Engineers Inc
6001 Indian School Rd NE Ste 200 ... Albuquerque NM 87110 505-884-8868 48-20
Web: www.cmenm.com

CouponMom Inc, The 4686 Scribner Ct ... Marietta GA 30062 770-649-0447 393
Web: www.couponmom.com

Courant Institute of Mathematical Sciences (CIMS)
New York University 251 Mercer St ... New York NY 10012 212-998-1212 995-4121 668
Web: www.cims.nyu.edu

Courier Cafe 111 N Race St ... Urbana IL 61801 217-328-1811 671
Web: couriercafe.squarespace.com

Courier Capital Corp
1114 Delaware Ave ... Buffalo NY 14209 716-883-9595 401
TF: 800-783-1086 ■ *Web:* www.couriercapital.com

Courier Graphics Corp 2621 S 37th St ... Phoenix AZ 85034 602-437-9700 627
TF: 800-454-6381 ■ *Web:* www.couriergraphics.com

Courier Journal 1828 Darby Dr ... Florence AL 35630 256-764-4268 760-9618 532-4
Web: www.courierjournal.net

Courier Printing 1 Courier Pl ... Smyrna TN 37167 615-355-4000 627
TF: 800-467-0444 ■ *Web:* www.courierprinting.com

Phone | Fax | Class

Courier, The
701 W Sandusky St PO Box 609 Findlay OH 45839 419-422-5151 422-2937 532-2
Web: www.thecourier.com

Courier, The 3030 Barrow St Houma LA 70360 985-879-1557 857-2244 532-2
Web: www.houmatoday.com

Courier-Journal
525 W Broadway PO Box 740031 Louisville KY 40201 502-582-4011 532-2
TF: 800-765-4011 ■ *Web:* www.courier-journal.com

Courier-Life Inc
1 Metrotech Ctr Ste 1001 Brooklyn NY 11201 718-260-2500 360-3
Web: www.brooklyndaily.com

Courier-Post 301 Cuthbert Blvd Cherry Hill NJ 08002 856-663-6000 532-2
TF: 800-677-6289 ■ *Web:* www.courierpostonline.com

Courier-Tribune 500 Sunset Ave Asheboro NC 27203 336-625-2101 532-2
TF: 800-488-0444 ■ *Web:* www.courier-tribune.com

Courion Industries 3044 Lambdin Ave St. Louis MO 63115 314-533-5700 647
Web: www.couriondoors.com

Court Avenue Brewing Co 309 Ct Ave Des Moines IA 50309 515-282-2739 282-3789 671
TF: 800-372-2946 ■ *Web:* www.courtavebrew.com

Court House Cafe
350 S Battlefield Blvd Chesapeake VA 23322 757-482-7077 671
Web: gbcourthousecafe.com

Court Reporting Institute of Houston
13101 NW Fwy Ste 100 Houston TX 77040 713-996-8300 800
TF: 866-996-8300 ■ *Web:* www.cri.edu

Court Services & Offender Supervision Agency for the District of Columbia
633 Indiana Ave NW Washington DC 20004 202-220-5300 220-5350 340-20
Web: www.csosa.gov

Court Square Ventures
455 Second St SE Ste 401 Charlottesville VA 22902 434-817-3300 792
Web: courtsquareventures.com

Court Street Ford Inc
558 William Latham Dr Bourbonnais IL 60914 815-939-9600 57
Web: courtstreetford.com

Court Theatre 5535 S Ellis Ave Chicago IL 60637 773-702-7005 749
Web: www.courttheatre.org

Court Thomas Wingert
11800 Monarch St PO Box 6207 Garden Grove CA 92841 714-379-5519 379-5549 806
TF: 800-359-7337 ■ *Web:* www.jlwingert.com

Courtemanche and Assoc
4475 Morris Park Dr Ste B Charlotte NC 28227 704-573-4535 463
Web: www.courtemanche-assocs.com

Courtesy Assoc 2025 M St NW Ste 800 Washington DC 20036 800-647-4689 184
TF: 800-647-4689 ■ *Web:* www.courtesyassociates.com

Courtesy Building Services Inc
2154 W Northwest Hwy Ste 214 Dallas TX 75220 972-831-1444 104
TF: 800-479-3853 ■ *Web:* www.courtesybldgservices.com

Courtesy Chevrolet
1233 E Camelback Rd Phoenix AZ 85014 602-235-0255 57
TF: 877-295-4648 ■ *Web:* www.houseofcourtesy.com

Courtesy Chevrolet Ctr
750 Camino Del Rio N San Diego CA 92108 619-297-4321 516
Web: www.courtesysandiego.com

Courtesy Chrysler Jeep Dodge
9207 Adamo Dr E Tampa FL 33619 813-620-4300 57
TF: 866-343-9730 ■ *Web:* www.courtesychryslerjeepdodge.com

Courtesy Insurance Agency
324 W Hefner Rd Oklahoma City OK 73114 405-755-4571 390
Web: ciaokc.com

Courthouse Fitness
451 Division St Ste 200 Salem OR 97301 503-588-2582 354
TF: 800-452-5687 ■ *Web:* courthousefit.com

Courtland Associates Inc
22500 Orchard Lake Rd Farmington MI 48336 248-888-3535 193

Courtney Honda 767 Bridgeport Ave Milford CT 06460 203-877-2888 57
Web: courtneyhonda.com

Courtney Joe (Rep D - CT)
2348 Rayburn Bldg Washington DC 20515 202-225-2076 225-4977 342-2
Web: courtney.house.gov

Courtroom Sciences Inc
4950 N O'Connor Rd Irving TX 75062 972-717-1773 717-3985 445
TF: 800-514-5879 ■ *Web:* www.courtroomsciences.com

Courts Plus Fitness Ctr
3491 University Dr S Fargo ND 58104 701-237-4805 42
Web: www.courtsplus.org

Courtyard Anaheim at Disneyland, The
2045 S Harbor Blvd Anaheim CA 92802 714-740-2645 378
Web: www.marriott.com

Courtyard by Marriott Waikiki Beach
400 Royal Hawaiian Ave Honolulu HI 96815 808-954-4000 954-4047 379
Web: marriott.com

Courtyard Cafe 18 St Thomas St Toronto ON M5S3E7 416-971-9666 921-9121 671
TF Cust Svc: 877-999-2767 ■ *Web:* www.windsorarmshotel.com

Courtyard Fort Lauderdale Beach
440 Seabreeze Blvd Fort Lauderdale FL 33316 954-524-8733 525-8145 379
TF: 888-236-2427 ■ *Web:* www.marriott.com/courtyard/travel.mi

Courtyard San Diego Oceanside
3501 Seagate Way Oceanside CA 92056 760-966-1000 379
Web: marriott.com

Coushatta Casino Resort
777 Coushatta Dr PO Box 1510 Kinder LA 70648 800-584-7263 133
TF: 800-584-7263 ■ *Web:* coushattacasinoresort.com

Cousin Corp of America
12333 Enterprise Blvd Largo FL 33773 727-536-3568 96
Web: www.cousin.com

Cousin's Restaurant 3545 Robie St Halifax NS B3K4S7 902-455-8931 671
Web: www.cousinsrestaurant.webs.com

Cousineau Inc
3 Valley Rd PO Box 58 North Anson ME 04958 207-635-4445 448
TF: 877-268-7463 ■ *Web:* www.cousineaus.com

Cousino's Steak House
1842 Woodville Rd Oregon OH 43616 419-693-0862 671

Cousins Properties Inc
191 Peachtree St NE Ste 500 Atlanta GA 30303 404-407-1000 655
NYSE: CUZ ■ *Web:* www.cousinsproperties.com

Cousins Submarines Inc
N83 W13400 Leon Rd Menomonee Falls WI 53051 262-253-7700 253-7710 670
TF: 800-238-9736 ■ *Web:* www.cousinssubs.com

Couts Heating & Cooling Inc
1693 Rimpau Ave Corona CA 92881 951-278-5560 610
Web: www.couts.com

Couturier Iron Craft Inc
5050 W River Dr NE Comstock Park MI 49321 616-784-6780 492
TF: 800-281-4404 ■ *Web:* www.couturierironcraft.com

Couvrette Building Systems
8665 Argent St Ste D Santee CA 92071 619-938-8000 186

Couzens Lansky Fealk Ellis & Lazar P C
39395 Twelve Mile Rd Ste 200 Farmington Hills MI 48331 248-489-8600 445
Web: www.couzens.com

Cova Hotel 655 Ellis St San Francisco CA 94109 415-771-3000 393
Web: www.covahotel.com

Covalent Medical Inc
4750 S State St Ste 301 Ann Arbor MI 48108 734-429-2451 3
Web: www.covamed.com

Covalent Partners LLC
Reservoir Woods 930 Winter St Ste 2800 Waltham MA 02451 617-658-5500 528
Web: www.covalentpartnersllc.com

Covalon Technologies Ltd
405 Britannia Rd E Ste 106 Mississauga ON L4Z3E6 905-568-8400 582
TF: 877-711-6055 ■ *Web:* www.covalon.com

Covance Inc 210 Carnegie Ctr Princeton NJ 08540 609-419-2240 85
NYSE: CVD ■ *TF:* 888-268-2623 ■ *Web:* www.covance.com

Covanta Energy Corp 445 South St Morristown NJ 07960 862-345-5000 787
NYSE: CVA ■ *TF:* 800-950-8749 ■ *Web:* covanta.com

Cove Haven Pocono Palace
5222 Milford Rd East Stroudsburg PA 18302 800-432-9932 669
TF: 877-822-3333 ■ *Web:* www.covepoconoresorts.com

Cove Inn 900 Broad Ave S Naples FL 34102 239-262-7161 261-6905 379
TF: 800-255-4365 ■ *Web:* www.coveinnnaples.com

Cove Lake State Park
110 Cove Lake Ln Caryville TN 37714 423-566-9701 565
TF: 800-250-8615

Cove Palisades State Park
7300 Jordan Rd Culver OR 97734 541-546-3412 565
Web: www.oregonstateparks.org

Cove West 335 S Hale Ave Fullerton CA 92831 714-525-2930 525-2928 813
Web: covewestusa.com

Cove, The 606 W Cypress St San Antonio TX 78212 210-227-2683 671
Web: thecove.us

COVELLO GROUP Inc, The
1660 Olympic Blvd Ste 300 Walnut Creek CA 94596 925-933-2300 194
Web: www.covellogroup.com

Covenant Aviation Security LLC
400 Quadrangle Dr Ste A Bolingbrook IL 60440 630-771-0800 693
Web: www.covenantsecurity.com

Covenant Care Home
600 Mt Moriah Church Rd Lumberton NC 28360 910-738-7777 371
TF: 877-708-7689 ■ *Web:* www.covenantcareathome.org

Covenant Children's Hospital (CCH)
4015 22nd Pl Lubbock TX 79410 806-725-0000 374-1
Web: covenanthealth.org

Covenant College
14049 Scenic Hwy Lookout Mountain GA 30750 706-820-1560 820-0893* 166
**Fax:* Admissions ■ *TF:* 888-451-2683 ■ *Web:* www.covenant.edu

Covenant Health System 3615 19th St Lubbock TX 79410 806-725-0000 725-0324 353
Web: www.covenanthealth.org

Covenant Health Systems Inc
100 Ames Pond Dr Ste 102 Tewksbury MA 01876 781-861-3535 851-0828* 353
**Fax Area Code:* 978 ■ *Web:* www.covenanthealth.net

Covenant Hospice 5041 N 12th Ave Pensacola FL 32504 850-433-2155 371
TF: 800-541-3072 ■ *Web:* www.choosecovenant.org/hospice

Covenant House 5 Penn Plaza Ste 2 New York NY 10001 212-727-4000 48-6
TF: 800-999-9999 ■ *Web:* www.covenanthouse.org

Covenant Medical Ctr 3421 W Ninth St Waterloo IA 50702 319-272-8000 374-3
Web: www.wheatoniowa.org

Covenant Medical Ctr 3615 19th St Lubbock TX 79410 806-725-0000 374-3
Web: www.covenanthealth.org

Covenant Medical Ctr Cooper
700 Cooper Ave Saginaw MI 48602 989-583-0000 374-3
Web: www.covenanthealthcare.com

Covenant Retirement Communities Inc
5700 Old OrchaRd Rd Skokie IL 60077 773-878-2294 672
Web: www.covenantretirement.org

Covenant Transport Inc
400 Birmingham Hwy Chattanooga TN 37419 423-821-1212 821-5442 780
NASDAQ: CVTI ■ *TF:* 800-334-9686 ■ *Web:* www.covenanttransport.com

Covenant United Methodist Church
6824 Tuckaseegee Rd Charlotte NC 28214 704-392-3925 48-20
Web: www.gbgm-umc.org

Covenant Village 1351 Robinwood Rd Gastonia NC 28054 704-867-2319 672

Covenant Village of Cromwell & Pilgrim Manor
52 Missionary Rd Cromwell CT 06416 860-635-2690 632-2407 672
TF: 800-255-8989 ■ *Web:* www.covenantvillageofcromwell.org

Covenant Village of Florida
9215 W Broward Blvd Plantation FL 33324 954-472-2860 672
TF: 800-910-2442 ■ *Web:* www.covenantretirement.org

Covenant Village of Golden Valley
5800 St Croix Ave Minneapolis MN 55422 763-546-6125 565-3809* 672
**Fax Area Code:* 617 ■ *TF:* 877-825-9763 ■ *Web:* www.covenantvillageofgoldenvalley.org

Covenant Village of Turlock
2125 N Olive Ave Turlock CA 95382 209-216-5610 565-3809* 672
**Fax Area Code:* 617 ■ *Web:* www.covenantvillageofturlock.org

Covenant Woods
7090 Covenant Woods Dr Mechanicsville VA 23111 804-569-8000 672
Web: www.covenantwoods.com

Coventry First LLC
7111 Vly Green Rd Fort Washington PA 19034 877-836-8300 233-3201* 796
**Fax Area Code:* 215 ■ *TF:* 877-836-8300 ■ *Web:* www.coventry.com

Coventry Health Care Inc
6705 Rockledge Dr Ste 900 Bethesda MD 20817 301-581-0600 581-0600* 391-3
NYSE: CVH ■ **Fax:* Hum Res ■ *TF:* 866-667-3062 ■ *Web:* www.coventryhealthcare.com

Coventry Health Care of Delaware Inc
750 Prides Crossing Ste 200 Newark DE 19713 800-833-7423 391-3
TF: 800-833-7423 ■ *Web:* coventryhealthcare.com

Coventry Health Care of Georgia Inc
1100 Cir 75 Pkwy Ste 1400 Atlanta GA 30339 678-202-2100 391-3
TF: 800-470-2004 ■ *Web:* chcgeorgia.coventryhealthcare.com

Phone | Fax | Class

Coventry Health Care of Iowa Inc
4320 114th St. Urbandale IA 50322 515-225-1234 391-3
TF: 800-470-6352 ■ *Web:* chciowa.coventryhealthcare.com

Coventry Health Care of Kansas Inc
8320 Ward Pkwy. Kansas City MO 64114 800-969-3343 391-3
TF: 800-969-3343 ■ *Web:* chckansas.coventryhealthcare.com

Coventry Health Care of Louisiana Inc
1720 S Sykes Dr. Bismarck ND 58504 800-341-6613 391-3
TF Sales: 800-341-6613 ■ *Web:* chclouisiana.coventryhealthcare.com

Coventry Health Care of Nebraska Inc
15950 W Dodge Rd Omaha NE 68118-4030 402-498-9030 391-3
TF: 855-449-2889 ■ *Web:* chcnebraska.coventryhealthcare.com

Coventry Lumber Inc
2030 Nooseneck Hill Rd. Coventry RI 02816 401-821-2800 191-3
TF: 800-390-0919 ■ *Web:* www.coventrylumber.com

Coventry Public Library
1672 Flat River Rd Coventry RI 02816 401-822-9100 822-9133 434-3
Web: www.coventrylibrary.org

Covera Solutions Inc
1021 Watervliet-Shaker Rd PO Box 13539 Albany NY 12205 866-526-8372 437-8286* 255
**Fax Area Code:* 518 ■ *TF:* 866-526-8372 ■ *Web:* www.coverasolutions.com

Covera Ventures
6836 Bee Caves Rd Ste275. Austin TX 78746 512-795-5870 792
Web: www.coveraventures.com

Coverage Inc 14130-J Sullyfield Cir Chantilly VA 20151 703-631-8000 390
Web: coverageinc.com

Coverall Cleaning Concepts
5201 Congress Ave Ste 275 Boca Raton FL 33487 866-296-8944 922-2423* 152
**Fax Area Code:* 561 ■ *TF:* 800-537-3371 ■ *Web:* www.coverall.com

Coverbind Corp 3200 Corporate Dr. Wilmington NC 28405 910-799-4116 799-3935 608
TF: 800-366-6060 ■ *Web:* www.coverbind.com

Covered Wagon Tours LLC
158 Thacher St Hornell NY 14843 607-324-3900 107
Web: www.coveredwagontours.net

Covert Manufacturing Inc 328 S East St Galion OH 44833 419-468-1761 454
Web: www.covertmfg.com

Covestic Inc 5555 Lakeview Dr Ste 100 Kirkland WA 98033 425-803-9889 180
Web: www.covestic.com

Covetrix It Consulting Group
18333 Preston Rd Ste 550 Dallas TX 75252 214-575-9583 196

Covina Chamber of Commerce
935 W Badillo St Ste 100 Covina CA 91722 626-967-4191 966-9660 139
Web: www.covina.org

Covina Public Library 234 N Second Ave Covina CA 91723 626-384-5300 434-3
TF: 800-984-4636 ■ *Web:* covinaca.gov

Covington & Burling LLP
1 City Ctr 850 Tenth St NW. Washington DC 20001 202-662-6000 662-6291 428
Web: www.cov.com

Covington Capital Management
601 S Figueroa St Ste 2000 Los Angeles CA 90017 213-629-7500 401
Web: www.covingtoncapitalmanagement.com

Covington County
260 Hillcrest Dr PO Box 188. Andalusia AL 36420 334-428-2540 428-2606 338
TF: 800-634-8001 ■ *Web:* www.covcounty.com

Covington County PO Box 1679 Collins MS 39428 601-765-4242 338
Web: www.msgw.org

Covington Electric Co-op Inc
18836 US Hwy 84. Andalusia AL 36421 334-222-4121 245
TF: 800-239-4121 ■ *Web:* www.cov-elect.com

Covington Flooring Co Inc
709 First Ave N. Birmingham AL 35203 205-328-2330 328-2496 189-2
TF: 800-824-1229 ■ *Web:* www.covington.com

Covington Foods Inc 419 Fourth St Covington IN 47932 765-793-2470 793-0209 345
Web: www.covingtonfoods.com

Covington House 4201 Main St Vancouver WA 98663 360-695-6750 50-3
Web: www.clark.wa.gov

Covington (Independent City)
333 W Locust St. Covington VA 24426 540-965-6300 965-6303 338
Web: www.covington.va.us

Covington Industries Inc
470 Seventh Ave Ste 900 New York NY 10018 212-689-2200 745-1
Web: covingtonfabric.com

Covington Leader, The 2001 Hwy 51 S. Covington TN 38019 901-476-7116 532-3
Web: www.covingtonleader.com

Covington Patrick Hagins Stern & Lewis PA
211 Pettigru St Greenville SC 29601 864-242-9000 428
Web: covpatlaw.com

Covington Planter Co 410 Hodges Ave Albany GA 31701 229-888-2032 888-0448 273
Web: www.covingtonplanter.com

Covington Travel
4800 Cox Rd Ste 200 Glen Allen VA 23060 804-747-7077 747-5170 771
TF: 800-922-9218 ■ *Web:* www.covingtontravel.com

Covington-Tipton County Chamber of Commerce
PO Box 683 Covington TN 38019 901-476-9727 476-0056 139
Web: www.covington-tiptoncochamber.com

Covino's 3265 Independence Pkwy. Plano TX 75075 972-519-0345 671
Web: covinos.com

Cow Palace 2600 Geneva Ave Daly City CA 94014 415-404-4100 404-4111 205
Web: www.cowpalace.com

Cowan Bolduc Doherty CPAs & Advisors
231 Sutton St North Andover MA 01845 978-620-2000 2
Web: www.cbdcpa.com

Cowan Graphics Inc 9253 48 St NW Edmonton AB T6B2R9 780-577-5700 627
TF: 800-661-6996 ■ *Web:* www.cowan.ca

Cowan Lake State Park
1750 Osborn Rd Wilmington OH 45177 937-382-1096 565
Web: www.ohiodnr.com

Cowans Gap State Park
6235 Aughwick Rd Fort Loudon PA 17224 717-485-3948 565
Web: www.dcnr.state.pa.us

Cowboy Ciao Wine Bar & Grill
7133 E Stetson Dr. Scottsdale AZ 85251 480-946-3111 671
Web: www.cowboyciao.com

Cowboy Maloney's Electric City
1313 Harding St Jackson MS 39202 601-948-5600 38
Web: cowboy-maloney.com

Cowboy Village Resort
120 S Flat Creek Dr PO Box 38. Jackson WY 83001 307-733-3121 379
TF: 800-962-4988 ■ *Web:* www.townsquareinns.com/cowboy-village

Cowelco a California Corp
1634 W 14th St. Long Beach CA 90813 562-432-5766 480
Web: www.cowelco.com

Coweta County 22 E Broad St Newnan GA 30263 770-254-2601 254-2606 338
TF: 800-282-5804 ■ *Web:* www.coweta.ga.us

Coweta-Fayette Electric Membership Corp
807 Collinsworth Rd. Palmetto GA 30268 770-502-0226 251-9788 245
TF: 877-746-4362 ■ *Web:* www.utility.org

Cowiche Growers Inc
251 Cowiche City Rd Cowiche WA 98923 509-678-4168 315-3
Web: www.cowichegrowers.com

Cowin & Company Inc
301 Industrial Dr. Birmingham AL 35219 205-945-1300 194
TF: 800-228-0429 ■ *Web:* www.cowin-co.com

Cowles & Thompson A Professional Corp
901 Main St Ste 3900. Dallas TX 75202 214-672-2000 672-2020 428
Web: www.cowlesthompson.com

Cowles Publishing Co
999 W Riverside Ave. Spokane WA 99201 509-459-5000 532-3
Web: www.spokesman.com

Cowley County 311 E Ninth Ave Winfield KS 67156 620-221-5400 221-5498 338
TF: 800-876-3469 ■ *Web:* www.cowleycounty.org

Cowley County Community College & Area Vocational-Technical School
PO Box 1147 Arkansas City KS 67005 620-442-0430 441-5350 162
TF: 800-593-2222 ■ *Web:* www.cowley.edu

Cowlitz County 312 SW First Ave Kelso WA 98626 360-577-3016 338
TF: 800-562-6000 ■ *Web:* www.co.cowlitz.wa.us

Cowlitz County Tourism
1900 Seventh Ave. Longview WA 98632 360-577-3137 206
TF: 800-833-6388 ■ *Web:* www.visitmtsthelens.com

CoWorx Staffing Services LLC
1375 Plainfield Ave. Watchung NJ 07069 908-757-5300 260
TF: 800-754-7000 ■ *Web:* www.coworxstaffing.com

Cowpens National Battlefield
4001 Chesnee Hwy PO Box 308. Gaffney SC 29341 864-461-2828 461-7795 564
Web: www.nps.gov/cowp

Cowtown Boots 11401 Gateway Blvd W El Paso TX 79936 915-593-2929 593-2249 301
TF: 800-580-2698 ■ *Web:* store.cowtownboots.com

Cowtown Bus Charters Inc
5504 Forest Hill Dr. Fort Worth TX 76119 817-531-3287 107
TF: 877-287-4897 ■ *Web:* www.cowtowncharters.com

Cowtown Coliseum
121 E Exchange Ave Fort Worth TX 76164 817-625-1025 720
TF: 888-269-8696 ■ *Web:* stockyardsrodeo.com

Cox & Company Inc
1664 Old Country Rd Plainview NY 11803 212-366-0200 22
Web: www.coxandco.com

Cox & Dinkins Inc 724 Beltline Blvd. Columbia SC 29205 803-254-0518 261
Web: coxanddinkins.com

Cox & Palmer LLP
1100-1959 Upper Water St Purdy's Wharf Tower I Halifax NS B3J3N2 902-421-6262 41
Web: www.coxandpalmerlaw.com

Cox Arboretum MetroPark
6733 Springboro Pike. Dayton OH 45449 937-275-7275 97
TF: 800-865-6543 ■ *Web:* www.metroparks.org/Parks/CoxArboretum

Cox Business Services Convention Ctr
1 Myriad Gardens Oklahoma City OK 73102 405-602-8500 602-8505 205
Web: www.coxconventioncenter.com

Cox Communications Inc
1400 Lake Hearn Dr Atlanta GA 30319 404-843-5000 843-5000 116
TF: 866-961-0027 ■ *Web:* cox.com

Cox Elearning Consultants Llc
3848 Macgregor Cmn. Livermore CA 94551 925-373-6558 721
TF: 866-240-3540 ■ *Web:* www.coxec.com

Cox Engineering Co 35 Industrial Dr Canton MA 02021 781-302-3300 302-3444 189-10
Web: coxengineering.com

Cox Hospital North
1423 N Jefferson Ave Springfield MO 65802 417-269-3000 374-3
TF: 800-711-9455 ■ *Web:* www.coxhealth.com

Cox Industries Inc
860 Cannon Bridge Rd PO Box 1124 Orangeburg SC 29116 803-534-7467 534-1410 818
TF: 800-476-4401 ■ *Web:* www.coxwood.com

Cox Interior Inc
1751 Old Columbia Rd. Campbellsville KY 42718 800-733-1751 465-7977* 499
**Fax Area Code:* 270 ■ *TF:* 800-733-1751 ■ *Web:* www.coxinterior.com

Cox Manufacturing Co
5500 N Loop 1604 E. San Antonio TX 78247 210-657-7731 657-2345 621
TF: 800-900-7981 ■ *Web:* www.coxmanufacturing.com

Cox Matthews & Associates Inc
10520 Warwick Ave Ste B-8 Fairfax VA 22030 703-385-2981 514
Web: www.diverseeducation.com

Cox Mclain Environmental Consulting Inc
6010 Balcones Dr Ste 210 Austin TX 78731 512-338-2223 192
TF: 800-477-6990 ■ *Web:* www.coxmclain.com

Cox Media Group
6205 Peachtree Dunwoody Rd Atlanta GA 30328 678-645-0000 645-5002 637-8
Web: www.coxmediagroup.com

Cox Media Group Tampa
11300 Fourth St N Ste 300. Saint Petersburg FL 33716 727-579-2000 645-162
TF: 888-723-9388 ■ *Web:* www.wduv.com

Cox Medical Center South
3801 S National Ave. Springfield MO 65807 417-269-6000 374-3
TF: 800-711-9455 ■ *Web:* www.coxhealth.com

Cox North America Inc 8181 Coleman Rd. Haslett MI 48840 517-339-3330 317
TF: 800-822-8114 ■ *Web:* www.cox-applicators.com

Cox Sales Co 2035 Cook Dr. Salem VA 24153 540-345-2636 711
TF: 800-382-6108 ■ *Web:* www.glue4you.com

Cox Schepp Construction Inc
2410 Dunavant St. Charlotte NC 28203 704-716-2100 186
TF: 800-954-0823 ■ *Web:* www.coxschepp.com

Cox Smith Matthews Inc
112 E Pecan St Ste 1800 San Antonio TX 78205 210-554-5500 428

Cox Transportation Services Inc
10448 Dow Gil Rd Ashland VA 23005 804-798-1477 798-1299 780
TF: 800-288-8118 ■ *Web:* www.truckingforamerica.com

Phone | Fax | Class

Coxsackie Correctional Facility
11260 Rt 9W PO Box 200 .... Coxsackie NY 12051 | 518-731-2781 | | 213
Web: www.doccs.ny.gov

Coy C Carpenter Library
Wake Forest Baptist Medical Center
Medical Ctr Blvd .... Winston-Salem NC 27157 | 336-716-2011 | 716-2186 | 434-1
Web: www.wakehealth.edu/library

Coyle Carpet One Inc
250 W Beltline Hwy .... Madison WI 53713 | 608-257-0291 | | 290
Web: www.coylecarpet.com

Coyle Hospitality Group
244 Madison Ave Ste 369 .... New York NY 10016 | 212-629-2083 | | 463
TF: 800-891-9292 ■ *Web:* www.coylehospitality.com

Coyle Reproductions Inc
14949 Firestone Blvd .... La Mirada CA 90638 | 866-269-5373 | | 627
TF: 866-269-5373 ■ *Web:* www.coylerepro.com

Coyne College Inc 330 N Green St .... Chicago IL 60607 | 773-577-8100 | | 764
TF: 800-707-1922 ■ *Web:* www.coynecollege.edu

Coyne Public Relations LLC
5 Wood Hollow Rd .... Parsippany NJ 07054 | 973-588-2000 | | 636
Web: www.coynepr.com

Coyne Textile Services Inc
140 Cortland Ave .... Syracuse NY 13202 | 315-475-1626 | | 442

Coyote Bluff Cafe 2417 S Grand St .... Amarillo TX 79103 | 806-373-4640 | | 671
Web: coyotebluffcafe.com

Coyote Cafe 132 W Water St .... Santa Fe NM 87501 | 505-983-1615 | | 671
Web: www.coyotecafe.com

Coyote Creek State Park
Hwy 434 Mile Marker 17 .... Guadalupita NM 87722 | 575-387-2328 | | 565
Web: www.emnrd.state.nm.us

Coyote Flaco 635 New Britain Ave. .... Hartford CT 06106 | 860-953-1299 | | 671
Web: www.mycoyoteflaco.com

Coyote Lake Feedyard Inc
1287 FM 1731 .... Muleshoe TX 79347 | 806-946-3321 | | 10-1
TF: 800-299-3321 ■ *Web:* www.coyotelakefeedyard.com

Coyote Logistics LLC
2545 W Diversey Ave .... Chicago IL 60647 | 877-626-9683 | | 449
TF: 877-626-9683 ■ *Web:* www.coyote.com

Coyote Ridge Corrections Ctr
1301 N Ephrata St. .... Connell WA 99326 | 509-543-5800 | 543-5801 | 213
Web: www.doc.wa.gov

Coyote Software Corp
3425 Harvester Rd Ste 216 .... Burlington ON L7N3N1 | 905-639-8533 | | 177
Web: coyotecorp.com

Coyotes Ice LLC 9375 E Bell Rd .... Scottsdale AZ 85260 | 480-585-6354 | 585-9117 | 706
Web: www.coyotesice.com

Cozad Asset Management Inc
2501 Galen Dr .... Champaign IL 61821 | 217-356-8363 | | 528
TF: 800-437-1686 ■ *Web:* www.cozadassetmgmt.com

Cozen O'Connor 1900 Market St .... Philadelphia PA 19103 | 215-665-2000 | 665-2013 | 428
TF: 800-523-2900 ■ *Web:* www.cozen.com

Cozi 506 Second Ave Ste 800 .... Seattle WA 98104 | 206-957-8447 | | 387
Web: www.cozi.com

Cozymels Restaurant
2655 Grapevine Mills .... Grapevine TX 76051 | 972-724-0277 | | 670
Web: www.cozymels.com

Cozzini Inc 4300 W Bryn Mawr Ave .... Chicago IL 60646 | 773-478-9700 | 478-8689 | 470
Web: www.cozzini.com

CP Bourg Inc
50 Samuel Barnet Blvd .... New Bedford MA 02745 | 508-998-2171 | | 111
Web: www.cpbourg.com

CP Capital Securities Inc
3390 Mary St Ste116 .... Miami FL 33133 | 305-702-5500 | | 690
Web: www.cpcapital.com

CP Direct Inc 4600 Boston Way A .... Lanham MD 20706 | 301-918-4084 | | 627
Web: www.cpdirectinc.com

CP Federal Credit Union
1100 Clinton Rd .... Jackson MI 49202 | 517-784-7101 | | 219
Web: cpfederal.com

C-P Flexible Packaging 15 Grumbacher Rd .... York PA 17406 | 717-764-1193 | 764-2039 | 554
TF: 800-815-0667 ■ *Web:* www.cpconverters.com

CP Franchising LLC
3300 University Dr .... Coral Springs FL 33065 | 954-344-8060 | | 772
TF: 800-683-0206 ■ *Web:* www.cruiseplanners.com

CP Industries Inc (CPI)
2214 Walnut St. .... McKeesport PA 15132 | 412-664-6604 | 664-6653* | 91
**Fax:* Sales ■ *Web:* www.cp-industries.com

CP Industries Inc
12767 Industrial Dr PO Box 690 .... Granger IN 46530 | 574-273-3000 | 273-4000 | 91
Web: www.cpind.com

CP Medical Inc 803 NE 25th Ave .... Portland OR 97232 | 503-232-1555 | | 476
TF: 800-950-2763 ■ *Web:* www.cpmedical.com

CP Ward Inc PO Box 900 .... Scottsville NY 14546 | 585-889-8800 | | 189-5
Web: www.cpward.com

CPA (College Parents of America)
2200 Wilson Blvd Ste 102-396 .... Arlington VA 22201 | 888-761-6702 | | 48-11
TF: 888-761-6702 ■ *Web:* www.collegeparents.org

CPA (Catholic Press Assn)
205 W Monroe St Ste 470 .... Chicago IL 60606 | 312-380-6789 | 361-0256 | 49-14
TF: 800-777-7432 ■ *Web:* www.catholicpress.org

CPA Assoc International Inc
301 Rt 17 N .... Rutherford NJ 07070 | 201-804-8686 | | 49-1
Web: www.cpaai.com

CPA Auto Dealer Consultants Assn (CADCA)
1801 W End Ave Ste 800 .... Nashville TN 37203 | 615-373-9880 | 377-7092 | 49-1
TF: 800-231-2524 ■ *Web:* autodealercpas.com

CPA Tax Solutions LLC 375 Mather St .... Hamden CT 06514 | 203-248-8600 | | 2
Web: cpataxsolutionsllc.com

CPAC (Richard & Karen Carpenter Performing Arts Ctr)
6200 Atherton St. .... Long Beach CA 90815 | 562-985-7000 | 985-7023 | 572
Web: www.carpenterarts.org

CPAC (Cable Public Affairs Channel)
PO Box 81099 .... Ottawa ON K1P1B1 | 877-287-2722 | 567-2749* | 740
**Fax Area Code:* 613 ■ *TF:* 877-287-2722 ■ *Web:* www.cpac.ca

CPAmerica International
11801 Research Dr. .... Alachua FL 32615 | 386-418-4001 | 418-4002 | 49-1
TF: 800-992-2324 ■ *Web:* www.cpamerica.org

CPAWS (Canadian Parks & Wilderness Society)
250 City Ctr Ave Ste 506 .... Ottawa ON K1R6K7 | 613-569-7226 | 569-7098 | 48-13
TF: 800-333-9453 ■ *Web:* www.cpaws.org

CPB (Corporation for Public Broadcasting)
401 Ninth St NW. .... Washington DC 20004 | 202-879-9600 | 879-9700 | 305
TF: 800-272-2190 ■ *Web:* www.cpb.org

CPB (First NBC) 29092 Kretel Rd. .... Lacombe LA 70445 | 985-819-1200 | | 70
Web: www.firstnbcbank.com

CPBI (Connecticut Public Broadcasting Inc)
1049 Asylum Ave .... Hartford CT 06105 | 860-278-5310 | | 632
TF: 877-444-4485 ■ *Web:* www.cpbn.org

CPC (Commercial Plastics Co)
800 Allanson Rd .... Mundelein IL 60060 | 847-566-1700 | | 604
Web: www.ecommercialplastics.com

CPC (Community Preservation Corp, The)
28 E 28th St 9Fl .... New York NY 10016 | 212-869-5300 | | 509
Web: www.communityp.com

CPC (Country Pride Co-op)
201 S Monroe PO Box 529 .... Winner SD 57580 | 605-842-2711 | | 10-5
TF: 888-325-7743 ■ *Web:* www.countrypridecoop.com

CPC Laboratories Inc
9300 S Sangamon St .... Chicago IL 60620 | 312-532-9730 | 564-4858 | 393
Web: www.cpcpack.com

CPC Logistics Inc
14528 S Outer 40 Rd Ste 210 .... Chesterfield MO 63017 | 314-542-2266 | 542-0666 | 721
TF: 800-274-3746 ■ *Web:* www.callcpc.com

CPCU Society 720 Providence Rd .... Malvern PA 19355 | 800-932-2728 | 251-2780* | 49-9
**Fax Area Code:* 610 ■ *TF:* 800-932-2728 ■ *Web:* www.cpcusociety.org

CPE HR Inc
9000 Sunset Blvd Ste 900 .... West Hollywood CA 90064 | 310-270-9800 | | 193
Web: www.cpehr.com

CPF (Cleft Palate Foundation)
1504 E Franklin St Ste 102 .... Chapel Hill NC 27514 | 919-933-9044 | 933-9604 | 48-17
TF: 800-242-5338 ■ *Web:* www.cleftline.org

CPFD (Coastal Pacific Food Distributors Inc)
1015 Performance Dr .... Stockton CA 95206 | 209-983-2454 | | 297-8
TF: 800-500-2611 ■ *Web:* www.cpfd.com

CPH Engineers 500 W Fulton St .... Sanford FL 32771 | 866-609-0688 | 330-0639* | 261
**Fax Area Code:* 407 ■ *TF:* 866-609-0688 ■ *Web:* www.cphengineers.com

CPhA (California Pharmacists Assn)
4030 Lennane Dr .... Sacramento CA 95834 | 916-779-1400 | 779-1401 | 585
TF: 866-365-7472 ■ *Web:* www.cpha.com

CPI (Companion Pets Inc)
2001 N Black Canyon Hwy .... Phoenix AZ 85009 | 602-255-0166 | 255-0841 | 578
TF: 800-646-3611 ■ *Web:* www.cpipets.com

CPI (Capital-Plus Inc)
3250 W Henderson Rd Ste 201 .... Columbus OH 43220 | 614-848-7620 | | 272
Web: www.capplus.com

CPI (CP Industries Inc)
2214 Walnut St .... McKeesport PA 15132 | 412-664-6604 | 664-6653* | 91
**Fax:* Sales ■ *Web:* www.cp-industries.com

CPI (Consumers Power Inc)
6990 W Hills Rd .... Philomath OR 97370 | 541-929-3124 | 929-8673 | 245
TF: 800-872-9036

CPI (Confer Plastics Inc)
97 Witmer Rd .... North Tonawanda NY 14120 | 716-693-2056 | 694-3102 | 604
TF: 800-635-3213 ■ *Web:* www.conferplastics.com

CPI (Concept Plastics Inc) PO Box 847 .... High Point NC 27261 | 336-889-2001 | 889-5752 | 608
Web: www.cpico.com

CPI Aerostructures Inc
91 Heartland Blvd .... Edgewood NY 11717 | 631-586-5200 | 586-5840 | 621
NYSE: CVU ■ *Web:* www.cpiaero.com

CPI Corp 1706 Washington Ave .... Saint Louis MO 63103 | 314-231-1575 | | 590
OTC: CPIC ■ *Web:* www.cpicorp.com

CPI Daylighting Inc
28662 N Ballard Dr .... Lake Forest IL 60045 | 847-816-1060 | | 590
Web: www.cpidaylighting.com

CPI Group Inc, The 112 Fifth St N .... Columbus MS 39703 | 662-328-1042 | | 260
TF: 800-906-7107 ■ *Web:* www.cpi-group.com

Cpi Human Resources Solutions Inc
5203 Maverick Dr .... Austin TX 78727 | 512-335-9347 | | 317
Web: www.cpipartners.com

CPI International Inc
5580 Skylane Blvd .... Santa Rosa CA 95403 | 707-525-5788 | | 419
Web: www.cpiinternational.com

CPI Manufacturing LLC 108 Ledyard St .... Hartford CT 06114 | 860-296-7980 | | 20
Web: www.cpimanufacturing.com

CPI Wire Cloth & Screens Inc
2425 Roy Rd .... Pearland TX 77581 | 281-485-2300 | | 360-3
Web: cpiwirecloth.com

CPI-BMD (Communications & Power Industries Inc Beverly Microwave Div)
150 Sohier Rd .... Beverly MA 01915 | 978-922-6000 | 922-2736 | 647
Web: cpii.com/division.cfm/8

CPI-HR Inc 6830 Cochran Rd .... Solon OH 44139 | 440-542-7800 | | 390
Web: www.cpihr.com

CPL (Camden Public Library) 55 Main St .... Camden ME 04843 | 207-236-3440 | 236-6673 | 434-3
TF: 800-562-2529 ■ *Web:* www.librarycamden.org

CPM Constructors Inc
30 Bonney St PO Box B .... Freeport ME 04032 | 207-865-0000 | | 186
Web: www.cpmconstructors.com

CPM Group 168 Seventh St Ste 310 .... Brooklyn NY 11215 | 212-785-8320 | | 401
Web: www.cpmgroup.com

CPM Wolverine Proctor LLC
251 Gibraltar Rd .... Horsham PA 19044 | 215-443-5200 | 443-5206 | 298
TF: 800-428-0846 ■ *Web:* www.cpm.net

CPP Inc 185 N Wolfe Rd .... Sunnyvale CA 94086 | 650-969-8901 | | 637-2
TF: 800-624-1765 ■ *Web:* cpp.com

CPR Institute for Dispute Resolution
30 E 33rd St 6th Fl .... New York NY 10016 | 212-949-6490 | 949-8859 | 41
Web: www.cpradr.org

Cpr Savers & First Aid Supply
7904 E Chaparral Rdÿ Ste A110-242 .... Scottsdale AZ 85250 | 480-946-0971 | | 507
TF: 800-480-1277 ■ *Web:* www.cpr-savers.com

CPRA (Canadian Parks & Recreation Assn)
1180 Walkley Rd PO Box 83069 .... Ottawa ON K1V2M5 | 613-523-5315 | | 48-23
Web: www.cpra.ca

	Phone	Fax	Class
CPRE (Consortium for Policy Research in Education) University of Pennsylvania 3440 Market St Ste 560 Philadelphia PA 19104 *Web:* www.cpre.org	215-573-0700	573-7914	634
CPRL (Conservation & Production Research Laboratory) USDA/ARS PO Box 10 Bushland TX 79012 *Web:* www.ars.usda.gov	806-356-5724	356-5750	668
CPS (Comprehensive Pharmacy Services Inc) 6409 N Quail Hollow Rd Memphis TN 38120 *TF:* 800-968-6962 ■ *Web:* www.cpspharm.com	901-748-0470		194
CPS Cards 7520 Morris Ct Allentown PA 18106 *TF:* 888-817-8121 ■ *Web:* www.crdpersol.com	610-231-1860	231-1881	627
CPS Investment Advisors 1509 S Florida Ave Lakeland FL 33803 *Web:* www.cpalliance.com	863-688-1725		401
CPS Printing Inc 2304 Faraday Ave Carlsbad CA 92008 *TF:* 800-843-5325 ■ *Web:* www.cpsprinting.com	760-438-9411		627
CPS Technologies Corp 111 S Worcester St Norton MA 02766 *OTC: CPSH* ■ *Web:* www.alsic.com	508-222-0614		249
CPS Technology Group LLC 213 BEYNON DR South Abington Township PA 18411 *Web:* www.cpstechnologygroup.com	570-647-4206		393
CPSC (Consumer Product Safety Commission) 4340 E W Hwy Ste 502 Bethesda MD 20814 *TF:* 800-638-2772 ■ *Web:* www.cpsc.gov	301-504-7923	504-0051	340-20
CPSI (Computer Programs & Systems Inc) 6600 Wall St Mobile AL 36695 *NASDAQ: CPSI* ■ *Web:* www.cpsi.com	251-639-8100	639-8214	39
CPSI Consulting Inc 6760 Alexander Bell Dr Ste 120 Columbia MD 21046 *Web:* www.cpsiconsulting.com	410-455-0005		260
CPST (Commission on Professionals in Science & Technology) 1200 New York Ave NW Ste 113 Washington DC 20005	202-326-7080		49-19
CPT (Central Petroleum Transport Inc) 6115 Mitchell St Sioux City IA 51111 *TF:* 800-798-6357 ■ *Web:* www.cptrans.com	712-258-6357	258-8592	780
CPT Group Inc 16630 Aston St Irvine CA 92606 *Web:* www.cptgroup.com	949-852-8240		225
CPT of South Florida Inc 2699 Stirling Rd Ste A 101 Fort Lauderdale FL 33312 *Web:* www.cpt-florida.com	954-963-2775	963-5781	175
Cpu Venturetech 401 E Collins Dr Casper WY 82609 *Web:* www.cpuventuretech.com	307-235-6212		174
CPVH (CVPH Medical Ctr) 75 Beekman St Plattsburgh NY 12901 *Web:* www.cvph.org	518-561-2000	561-0881	374-3
CPX Inc 410 Kent St Kentland IN 47951 *Web:* www.cpxinc.com	812-718-5335		247
CQ's Restaurant 140-A Lighthouse Rd Harbour Town Hilton Head Island SC 29928 *TF:* 800-262-3458 ■ *Web:* www.cqsrestaurant.com	843-671-2779		671
CQL (Council on Quality & Leadership, The) 100 W Rd Ste 300 Towson MD 21204 *TF:* 800-628-2783 ■ *Web:* www.c-q-l.org	410-583-0060		48-1
CR Bard Inc 730 Central Ave Murray Hill NJ 07974 *NYSE: BCR* ■ *TF:* 800-556-6756 ■ *Web:* www.crbard.com	908-277-8000		476
CR Bard Inc Urological Div 8195 Industrial Blvd Covington GA 30014 *TF:* 800-526-4455 ■ *Web:* www.bardmedical.com	770-784-6100		476
CR Daniels Inc 3451 Ellicott Ctr Dr Ellicott City MD 21043 *TF:* 800-933-2638 ■ *Web:* www.crdaniels.com	410-461-2100	461-2987	733
CR England & Sons Inc 4701 West 2100 South Salt Lake City UT 84120 *TF:* 800-453-8826 ■ *Web:* www.crengland.com	801-972-2712		780
CR Laurence Company Inc 2503 E Vernon Ave PO Box 58923 Los Angeles CA 90058 **Fax Area Code:* 800 ■ *TF:* 800-421-6144 ■ *Web:* www.crlaurence.com	323-588-1281	262-3299*	191-2
CR Meyer & Sons Co 895 W 20th Ave Oshkosh WI 54902 *Web:* www.crmeyer.com	920-235-3350		186
CRA (Corn Refiners Assn Inc) 1701 Pennsylvania Ave Washington DC 20006 *Web:* www.corn.org	202-331-1634	331-2054	48-2
CRA International Inc 200 Clarendon St Ste T-33 Boston MA 02116 *NASDAQ: CRAI* ■ *Web:* www.crai.com	617-425-3000	425-3132	194
Crab Alley 9703 Golf Course Rd West Ocean City MD 21842 *Web:* craballeyoc.com	410-213-7800	213-1048	671
Crab Pot Restaurant & Bar, The 215 N Marina Dr Long Beach CA 90803 *Web:* www.crabpotlongbeach.com	562-430-0272		671
Crab Shell 46 Southfield Ave Stamford CT 06902 *Web:* www.crabshell.com	203-967-7229	967-7233	671
Crab Trap, The 1 Broadway Somers Point NJ 08244	609-927-7377		671
Crabby Mike's Calabash Seafood 290 Hwy 17 N Surfside Beach SC 29575 *Web:* www.crabbymikes.com	843-238-3524	238-3526	671
Crabtree & Evelyn Ltd 102 Peake Brook Rd Woodstock CT 06281 *TF:* 800-272-2873 ■ *Web:* www.crabtree-evelyn.com	860-928-2761		214
Crabtree Valley Mall 4325 Glenwood Ave Raleigh NC 27612 *TF:* 800-963-7467 ■ *Web:* www.crabtree-valley-mall.com	919-787-2506	787-7108	460
Cracker Barrel Convenience Stores Inc 11450 Airline Hwy Baton Rouge LA 70809	225-292-4344		204
Cracker Barrel Old Country Store Inc PO Box 787 Lebanon TN 37088 *NASDAQ: CBRL* ■ *TF:* 800-333-9566 ■ *Web:* www.crackerbarrel.com	615-444-5533	444-5533	670
Cracker Box, The 6682 Hwy 7 Bismarck AR 71929	501-865-2249		297-8
Craddock Finishing Corp 1400 W Illinois St Evansville IN 47710 *Web:* www.craddockfinishing.com	812-425-2691		481
Craden Peripherals Corp 7860 Airport Hwy Pennsauken NJ 08109 *TF:* 800-849-5300 ■ *Web:* www.craden.com	856-488-0700	488-0925	173-6

	Phone	Fax	Class
Cradlerock Group LLC, The 65 High St 402 Stamford CT 06905 *Web:* www.cradlerock.com	203-324-0088		194
Crafco Inc 420 N Roosevelt Ave Chandler AZ 85226 **Fax Area Code:* 480 ■ *TF:* 800-528-8242 ■ *Web:* www.crafco.com	602-276-0406	961-0513*	46
Craford Benefits Consultants 990 Fifth Ave San Rafael CA 94901 *TF:* 800-501-2920 ■ *Web:* www.craford.com	415-456-9790		463
Craft 43 E 19th St New York NY 10003 *Web:* www.craftrestaurantsinc.com	212-780-0880		671
Craft & Hobby Assn (CHA) 319 E 54th St Elmwood Park NJ 07407 *TF:* 800-822-0494 ■ *Web:* www.craftandhobby.org	201-835-1200	797-0657	48-18
Craft Brew Alliance 929 N Russell St Portland OR 97227 *NASDAQ: BREW* ■ *Web:* craftbrew.com	503-331-7270		102
Craft Emergency Relief Fund 535 Stone Cutters Way Ste 202 Montpelier VT 05602 *Web:* cerfplus.org	802-229-2306		522
Craft Inc 1929 County St PO Box 3049 South Attleboro MA 02703 *TF:* 800-827-2388 ■ *Web:* craft-inc.myshopify.com	508-761-7917	399-7240	350
Craft Machine Works Inc 2102 48th St Hampton VA 23661 *TF:* 800-208-6075 ■ *Web:* www.craftmachinc.com	757-380-8615	380-9120	454
Craft Manufacturing & Tooling Inc 7152 Central Ave Hot Springs AR 71913 *Web:* www.cmtair.com	501-525-0268		22
Craft Memorial Library 600 Commerce St Bluefield WV 24701 *Web:* craftmemorial.lib.wv.us	304-325-3943	325-3702	434-3
Craft Technologies Inc 4344 Frank Price Church Rd Wilson NC 27893 *TF:* 800-827-8478 ■ *Web:* www.crafttechnologies.com	252-206-7071		743
Craftcorps Inc 3401 Manor Rd Austin TX 78723 *Web:* www.craftcorps.com	512-476-8886		186
Craftech EDM Corp 2941 E La Jolla St Anaheim CA 92806 *Web:* www.craftechcorp.com	714-630-8117	630-7959	608
Craftech Metal Forming Inc 24100 Water Ave Ste B Perris CA 92570 *Web:* www.craftechmetal.com	951-940-6444		697
Craftmade International Inc 650 S Royal Ln Coppell TX 75019 *OTC: CRFT* ■ *TF:* 800-486-4892 ■ *Web:* www.craftmade.com	972-393-3800		37
Craftmaster Furniture Corp 221 Craftmaster Rd Hiddenite NC 28636 *Web:* www.cmfurniture.com	828-632-9786		319-2
Craftmaster Manufacturing Inc 680 Scattergood Dr Christiansburg VA 24073 *Web:* www.cmicompany.com	540-382-1721		499
Crafton Hills College 11711 Sand Canyon Rd Yucaipa CA 92399 **Fax:* Admissions ■ *TF:* 800-624-5561 ■ *Web:* www.craftonhills.edu	909-794-2161	389-9141*	162
Crafts 'n Things Magazine 911 Vandemark Rd PO Box 926 Sidney OH 45365-0926 *TF:* 866-222-3621 ■ *Web:* craftideas.com	937-498-0809	498-0876	457-14
Crafts Frames & Things 108 Owen Dr Fayetteville NC 28304 *TF:* 800-205-7819 ■ *Web:* www.craftsframesandthings.com	910-485-4833		45
Crafts Technology 91 Joey Dr Elk Grove Village IL 60007 *TF:* 800-323-6802 ■ *Web:* www.craftstech.net	847-750-0100	750-0102	455
Craftsman Custom Metals LLC 3838 N River Rd Schiller Park IL 60176 *Web:* www.ccm.com	847-655-0040		697
Craftsman Inn 7300 E Genesee St Fayetteville NY 13066 *Web:* www.craftsmaninn.com	315-637-8000		379
Craftsman Printing Inc 120 Citation Ct Birmingham AL 35209 *TF:* 800-543-1051 ■ *Web:* craftsmanprintinginc.com	205-942-3939		627
Craftsmen Machinery Co 1257 Worcester Rd Unit 167 Framingham MA 01701 *TF:* 800-490-6900 ■ *Web:* www.craftsmenmachinery.com	508-376-2001	376-2003	629
Craftsteak 3799 Las Vegas Blvd S Las Vegas NV 89109 *Web:* www.craftedhospitality.com	702-891-7318		671
Craftstones PO Box 847 Ramona CA 92065 *TF:* 800-588-5350 ■ *Web:* www.craftstones.com	760-789-1620	789-3432	407
CraftWorks Restaurants & Brewery Inc 201 W Main St Ste 301 Chattanooga TN 37408 *Web:* www.craftworksrestaurants.com	423-424-2000		360-3
Craggy Correctional Ctr 2992 Riverside Dr Asheville NC 28804 *Web:* ncdps.gov	828-645-5315	658-2183	213
Cragun's Conference & Golf Resort 11000 Cragun's Dr Brainerd MN 56401 **Fax Area Code:* 218 ■ *TF:* 800-272-4867 ■ *Web:* www.craguns.com	800-272-4867	829-9188*	669
CRAIC Technologies Inc 948 N Amelia Ave San Dimas CA 91773 *Web:* www.microspectra.com	310-573-8180		419
Craig County PO Box 308 New Castle VA 24127 *Web:* www.craigcountyva.gov	540-864-5010	864-5590	338
Craig Envelope Corp 12-01 44th Ave Long Island City NY 11101 *Web:* www.craigenvelope.com	718-786-4277		263
Craig Frames Inc 140 Industrial Pkwy Ithaca MI 48847 *Web:* www.craigframes.com	989-875-8600		200
Craig Hospital 3425 S Clarkson St Englewood CO 80113 *TF:* 800-247-0257 ■ *Web:* www.craighospital.org	303-789-8000	789-8219	374-6
Craig House State Historic Site 347 Freehold-Englishtown Rd Manalapan NJ 07726 *Web:* www.njparksandforests.org/historic/index.html	732-462-9616		565
Craig Lake State Park 851 County Rd AKE Champion MI 49814 *Web:* michigandnr.com	906-339-4461		565
Craig Manufacturing Ltd 96 Mclean Ave Hartland NB E7P2K5 *TF:* 800-565-5007 ■ *Web:* www.craig-mfg.com	800-565-5007		480
Craig Roberts Assoc Inc 4230 Avondale Ave Ste 202 Dallas TX 75219 *Web:* www.craigroberts.com	214-526-6470		196

Name / Address	City	State	ZIP	Phone	Fax	Class
Craig Test Boring Company Inc 5435 Harding Hwy PO Box 427 *Web:* craigtestboring.com	Mays Landing	NJ	08330	609-625-4862		261
Craig Thomas Pest Control Inc 1186 Route 9G *Web:* callcraig.com	Hyde Park	NY	12538	845-229-6833		577
Craig Transportation Co 26699 Eckel Rd *TF:* 800-521-9119 ■ *Web:* www.craigtransportation.com	Perrysburg	OH	43551	419-872-3333	874-9372	780
Craig-Botetourt Electric Co-op State Rt 615	New Castle	VA	24127	540-864-5121		245
Craige Brawley Liipfert & Walker LLP 110 Oakwood Dr Ste 300 *Web:* www.craigebrawley.com	Winston-Salem	NC	27103	336-725-0583		428
Craig-Hallum Capital Group LLC 222 S Ninth St Ste 350 *Web:* www.craig-hallum.com	Minneapolis	MN	55402	612-334-6300		401
Craighead County 511 S Main St *Web:* www.craigheadcounty.org	Jonesboro	AR	72401	870-933-4520	933-4514	338
Craighead Electric Co-op Corp 4314 Stadium Blvd PO Box 7503 *TF:* 800-794-5012 ■ *Web:* www.craigheadelectric.coop	Jonesboro	AR	72403	870-932-8301	972-5674	245
Crailo State Historic Site 9 1/2 Riverside Ave	Rensselaer	NY	12144	518-463-8738		565
Crain Bros Inc 300 Rita Dr *TF:* 800-525-6169 ■ *Web:* www.crainbrothers.com	Bell City	LA	70630	337-905-2411	905-2700	539
Crain Chemical Co 2624 Andjon Dr	Dallas	TX	75220	214-358-3301		151
Crain Communications Inc 1155 Gratiot Ave *TF:* 888-288-6954 ■ *Web:* www.crain.com	Detroit	MI	48207	313-446-6000		637-9
Crain's Chicago Business Magazine 150 N Michigan Ave 16th Fl *TF:* 877-812-1590 ■ *Web:* www.chicagobusiness.com	Chicago	IL	60601	312-649-5200	280-3150	457-5
Crain's Cleveland Business Magazine 700 W St Clair Ave Ste 310 *TF:* 888-909-9111 ■ *Web:* www.crainscleveland.com	Cleveland	OH	44113	216-522-1383	694-4264	457-5
Crain's Detroit Business Magazine 1155 Gratiot Ave *TF:* 888-909-9111 ■ *Web:* www.crainsdetroit.com	Detroit	MI	48207	313-446-6000	446-1687	457-5
Crain's New York Business Magazine 685 Third Ave 3rd Fl **Fax:* Edit ■ *TF:* 877-824-9379 ■ *Web:* www.crainsnewyork.com	New York	NY	10017	212-210-0100	210-0799*	457-5
Cramer 425 University Ave *Web:* www.cramer.com	Norwood	MA	02062	781-278-2300		4
Cramer & Assoc *Hodge Cramer & Assoc* 555 Metro Pl N Ste 500 *Web:* www.cramerfundraising.com	Dublin	OH	43017	614-766-4483		317
Cramer Fish Sciences 300 SE Arrow Creek Ln *Web:* www.fishsciences.net	Gresham	OR	97030	503-491-9577		192
Cramer Inc 1523 Grand Blvd *TF:* 800-366-6700 ■ *Web:* www.cramerinc.com	Kansas City	MO	64108	800-366-6700	607-2821	319-1
Cramer Johnson Wiggins & Assoc 1420 Edgewater Dr Ste 200 *Web:* cjw-assoc.com	Orlando	FL	32804	407-849-0044		390
Cramer Kevin (Rep R - ND) 1717 Longworth HOB *Web:* cramer.house.gov	Washington	DC	20515	202-225-2611		342-2
Cramer Products Inc 153 W Warren St *TF:* 800-345-2231 ■ *Web:* www.cramersportsmed.com	Gardner	KS	66030	913-856-7511		477
Cramer Rosenthal Mcglynn LLC 520 Madison Ave 20th Fl *Web:* www.crmllc.com	New York	NY	10022	212-838-3830		401
Cramer-Krasselt 246 E Chicago St *Web:* www.c-k.com	Milwaukee	WI	53202	414-227-3500		4
Cranberry Country Chamber of Commerce 40 N Main St *Web:* www.cranberrycountry.org	Middleboro	MA	02346	508-947-1499	947-1446	139
Cranberry Lumber Co 212 Resource Dr *Web:* www.cranberryhardwoods.com/clumber.html	Beckley	WV	25801	304-255-2268		683
Cranbrook Art Museum 39221 Woodward Ave *Web:* www.cranbrookart.edu/museum	Bloomfield Hills	MI	48303	248-645-3323	645-3324	520
Cranbrook Institute of Science 39221 Woodward Ave PO Box 801 *Web:* www.cranbrook.edu	Bloomfield Hills	MI	48303	248-645-3000		520
Cranbrook Schools 39221 Woodward Ave *Web:* www.schools.cranbrook.edu	Bloomfield Hills	MI	48304	248-645-3610	645-3025	622
Crandall Associates Inc 6 Litchfield Rd Ste 316 *Web:* www.crandallassociates.com	Port Washington	NY	11050	516-767-6800		260
Crandall Engineering Ltd 1077 St George Blvd *TF:* 866-857-2777 ■ *Web:* www.crandallnb.com	Moncton	NB	E1E4C9	506-857-2777	857-2753	194
Crandall Historical Printing Museum 275 E Ctr St *Web:* crandallmuseum.org	Provo	UT	84606	801-377-7777		520
Crandall Public Library 251 Glen St *Web:* www.crandalllibrary.org	Glens Falls	NY	12801	518-792-6508		434-3
Crandall University 333 Gorge Rd *TF:* 888-968-6228 ■ *Web:* crandallu.ca	Moncton	NB	E1G3H9	506-858-8970		785
Crane & Co Inc 30 S St *TF Cust Svc:* 800-268-2281 ■ *Web:* www.crane.com	Dalton	MA	01226	800-268-2281		552-2
Crane Aerospace & Electronics 3000 Winona Ave *Web:* www.craneae.com	Burbank	CA	91504	425-743-1313		22
Crane Cams Inc 530 Fentress Blvd *Web:* www.cranecams.com	Daytona Beach	FL	32114	386-310-4875		247
Crane Carrier (Canada) Ltd 11523 186 St *Web:* pacifictruck.com	Edmonton	AB	T5S2W6	780-443-2493		190
Crane Carrier Co 1925 N Sheridan Rd *TF:* 800-343-7357 ■ *Web:* www.cranecarrier.com	Tulsa	OK	74115	918-836-1651	832-7348	516
Crane ChemPharma Resistoflex 1 Quality Way *TF:* 800-407-3726 ■ *Web:* www.resistoflex.com	Marion	NC	28752	828-724-4000		596
Crane Co 100 First Stamford Pl 4th Fl *NYSE: CR* ■ *Web:* www.craneco.com	Stamford	CT	06902	203-363-7300		641
Crane Company Stockham Div 2129 Third Ave SE *TF:* 800-786-2542 ■ *Web:* www.cranecpe.com	Cullman	AL	35055	256-775-3800	775-3860	789
Crane Composites Inc 23525 W Eames St **Fax:* Hum Res ■ *TF:* 800-435-0080 ■ *Web:* www.cranecomposites.com	Channahon	IL	60410	815-467-8600	467-8666*	606
Crane Country Day School 1795 San Leandro Ln *Web:* www.craneschool.org	Santa Barbara	CA	93108	805-969-7732		685
Crane County 201 W Sixth St *Web:* www.co.crane.tx.us	Crane	TX	79731	432-558-3581	558-1185	338
Crane Creek State Park 2045 Morse Rd *Web:* www.ohiodnr.com	Columbus	OH	43229	614-265-6561		565
Crane Engineering Inc 707 Ford St *Web:* www.craneengineering.net	Kimberly	WI	54136	920-733-4425		385
Crane Hill Machine & Fabrication Inc 2476 E US Hwy 50 *Web:* www.cranehillmachine.com	Seymour	IN	47274	812-358-3534	358-2351	480
Crane Manufacturers Assn of America (CMAA) 8720 Red Oak Blvd Ste 201 *TF:* 800-345-1815 ■ *Web:* www.mhi.org	Charlotte	NC	28217	704-676-1190	676-1199	49-13
CRANE Merchandising Systems 2043 Woodland Pkwy Ste 102 *TF:* 800-628-8363 ■ *Web:* www.cranems.com	St. Louis	MO	63146	314-298-3500		111
Crane Metamarketing Ltd 831 Christopher Robin Rd *Web:* www.cranesnest.com	Alpharetta	GA	30005	770-642-2082		194
Crane Mills Inc 22938 S Ave	Corning	CA	96021	530-824-5427		448
Crane Nuclear Inc 2825 Cobb International Blvd *TF:* 800-795-8013 ■ *Web:* www.cranenuclear.com	Kennesaw	GA	30152	770-424-6343	429-4750	472
Crane Pest Control Inc 2700 Geary Blvd *Web:* www.cranepestcontrol.com	San Francisco	CA	94118	415-922-1666		577
Crane Pumps & Systems 420 Third St *Web:* www.cranepumps.com	Piqua	OH	45356	937-778-8947		641
Crane Tech Solutions LLC 2030 Ponderosa St *Web:* www.ct-sol.net	Portsmouth	VA	23701	757-405-0311	405-0313	470
Crane Worldwide Logistics LLC 1500 Rankin Rd *TF:* 888-870-2726 ■ *Web:* www.cranew.com	Houston	TX	77073	281-443-2777		449
Crane's Tavern & Steakhouse 26 New Orleans Rd *Web:* cranestavern.com	Hilton Head Island	SC	29928	843-341-2333		671
Cranel Inc 8999 Gemini Pkwy *TF General:* 800-288-3475 ■ *Web:* www.cranel.com	Columbus	OH	43240	614-431-8000	431-8388	174
Cranesmart Systems Inc 4908 97 St NW *TF:* 888-562-3222 ■ *Web:* cranesmart.com	Edmonton	AB	T6E5S1	780-437-2986		407
Cranesville Block Company Inc 1250 Riverfront Ctr *TF:* 800-347-5246 ■ *Web:* www.cranesville.com	Amsterdam	NY	12010	518-684-6000		183
Craneveyor Corp 1524 Potrero Ave **Fax Area Code:* 626 ■ *TF:* 888-501-0050 ■ *Web:* www.craneveyor.com	South El Monte	CA	91733	888-501-0050	442-7308*	470
Cranfill Sumner & Hartzog LLP 5420 Wade Park Blvd Ste 300	Raleigh	NC	27607	919-828-5100		428
Cranmore Mountain Resort 1 Skimobile Rd PO Box 1640 *TF:* 800-786-6754 ■ *Web:* www.cranmore.com	North Conway	NH	03860	603-356-5543	356-8526	669
Cranston Machinery Company Inc 2251 SE Oak Grove Blvd *TF:* 800-547-1012 ■ *Web:* www.cranston-machinery.com	Oak Grove	OR	97267	503-654-7751	654-7751	556
Cranston Print Works Co 1381 Cranston St *TF:* 800-876-2756 ■ *Web:* www.cpw.com	Cranston	RI	02920	401-943-4800		745-7
Cranston Public Library 140 Sockanosset Cross Rd *TF:* 800-359-3090 ■ *Web:* www.cranstonlibrary.org	Cranston	RI	02920	401-943-9080	946-5079	434-3
Cranwell Resort Spa & Golf Club 55 Lee Rd *TF:* 800-272-6935 ■ *Web:* www.cranwell.com	Lenox	MA	01240	413-637-1364	637-4364	669
Crapo Mike (Sen R - ID) 239 Dirksen Bldg *Web:* www.crapo.senate.gov	Washington	DC	20510	202-224-6142	228-1375	342-2
Crary Buchanan Attorneys At Law 759 SW Federal Hwy Ste 106 *Web:* www.crarybuchanan.com	Stuart	FL	34994	772-287-2600		445
Crary Co 237 12th St NW *Web:* www.crary.com	West Fargo	ND	58078	701-282-5520		429
CRAssoc Inc 8580 Cinderbed Rd Ste 2400 *TF:* 877-272-8960 ■ *Web:* www.crassoc.com	Newington	VA	22122	703-550-8145		463
Crater Lake National Park PO Box 7 *TF:* 800-367-2540 ■ *Web:* www.nps.gov	Crater Lake	OR	97604	541-594-3000	594-3010	564
Crater of Diamonds State Park 209 State Pk Rd *Web:* www.craterofdiamondsstatepark.com	Murfreesboro	AR	71958	870-285-3113		565
Craters & Freighters 331 Corporate Cir Ste J *TF:* 800-736-3335 ■ *Web:* www.cratersandfreighters.com	Golden	CO	80401	800-736-3335		310
Craters of the Moon National Monument & Preserve PO Box 29 *TF:* 800-562-3408 ■ *Web:* www.nps.gov/crmo	Arco	ID	83213	208-527-1335	527-3073	564
Cravath Swaine & Moore LLP 825 Eigth Ave Worldwide Plz *Web:* www.cravath.com	New York	NY	10019	212-474-1000	474-3700	428
Craven Community College 800 College Ct **Fax:* Admissions ■ *Web:* www.cravencc.edu	New Bern	NC	28562	252-638-4131	638-4649*	162
Craven County 406 Craven St *TF:* 800-437-5767 ■ *Web:* www.cravencountync.gov	New Bern	NC	28560	252-636-6600	637-0526	338

Phone | Fax | Class

Craven County Convention & Visitors Bureau
203 S Front St ....New Bern NC 28560 252-637-9400 637-0250 206
TF: 800-437-5767 ■ *Web:* www.visitnewbern.com

Craven County School (CCS)
3600 Trent Rd............................New Bern NC 28562 252-514-6300 514-6351 685
Web: www.craven.k12.nc.us

Craven Thompson & Associates Inc
3563 NW 53rd St ....Fort Lauderdale FL 33309 954-739-6400 261
TF: 800-581-7204 ■ *Web:* www.craventhompson.com

Cravetek Llc 24509 E Louisiana Cir ....Aurora CO 80018 303-364-8830 809

Crawdaddy's 414 Starr St ....Corpus Christi TX 78401 361-883-5432 671

Crawdaddy's
1025 S Moorland Rd Ste 400................Brookfield WI 53005 414-778-2228 671
TF: 800-727-9477 ■ *Web:* foodspot.com

Crawford Ausable School District
1135 N Old 27 ....Grayling MI 49738 989-344-3500 685
Web: www.casdk12.net

Crawford Auto-Aviation Museum
10825 E Blvd ....Cleveland OH 44106 216-721-5722 520
Web: wrhs.org

Crawford Broadcasting Co (CBC)
2821 S Parker Rd Ste 1205.....................Denver CO 80014 303-433-5500 433-1555 643
Web: www.crawfordbroadcasting.com

Crawford Central School District
11280 Mercer Pk ....Meadville PA 16335 814-724-3960 685
Web: www.craw.org

Crawford Consulting Services Inc
239 Highland Ave.....................East Pittsburgh PA 15112 412-823-0400 261
TF: 800-365-9010 ■ *Web:* www.crawfordconsultingservices.com

Crawford County 112 E Mansfield St ....Bucyrus OH 44820 419-562-5876 562-3491 338
Web: www.crawford-co.org

Crawford County 1202 Broadway Ste 5 ....Denison IA 51442 712-263-3045 263-8382 338
TF: 800-772-1213 ■ *Web:* www.crawfordcounty.org

Crawford County
715 Judicial Plaza Dr PO Box 375 ....English IN 47118 812-338-2565 338-2507 338
Web: www.in.gov/judiciary/2958.htm

Crawford County 111 E Forest Ave...............Girard KS 66743 620-724-6115 724-6007 338
Web: www.crawfordcountykansas.org

Crawford County 200 W Michigan Ave...........Grayling MI 49738 989-344-3206 344-3223 338
Web: www.crawfordco.org

Crawford County
1011 Hwy 341 N PO Box 1059.................Roberta GA 31078 478-836-3782 836-5818 338
TF: 800-436-7442 ■ *Web:* crawfordcountyga.org

Crawford County 903 Diamond Pk.............Meadville PA 16335 814-333-7400 337-0457 338
TF: 800-585-3737 ■ *Web:* crawfordcountyfairpa.com

Crawford County
225 N Beaumont Rd ....Prairie du Chien WI 53821 608-326-0200 338
TF: 877-794-2372 ■ *Web:* www.crawfordcountywi.org

Crawford County 100 Douglas St..............Robinson IL 62454 618-546-1212 546-0140 338
TF: 800-252-8980 ■ *Web:* www.crawfordcountycentral.com

Crawford County
302 Main St PO Box AS ....Steelville MO 65565 573-775-2376 775-3066 338
TF: 866-566-8267 ■ *Web:* crawfordcountymo.net

Crawford County 300 Main St Rm 7...........Van Buren AR 72956 479-474-1312 471-3236 338
Web: crawford-county.org

Crawford County School District
190 E Crusselle St ....Roberta GA 31078 478-836-3131 836-3114 685
Web: www.crawfordcounty.schoolinsites.com

Crawford County State Fish & Wildlife Area
12609 E 1700th Ave.......................Hutsonville IL 62433 618-563-4405 565
Web: dnr.illinois.gov/Lands/Landmgt/PARKS/R5/Crawford.htm

Crawford Electric Co-op Inc
10301 N Service Rd PO Box 10 ....Bourbon MO 65441 573-732-4415 245
TF: 800-677-2667 ■ *Web:* www.crawfordelec.com

Crawford Energy Inc
770 S Post Oak Ln Ste 520....................Houston TX 77056 713-626-2637 536
Web: www.crawfordenergy.com

Crawford Industries LLC
1414 Crawford Dr......................Crawfordsville IN 47933 800-428-0840 962-3343 548
TF: 800-428-0840 ■ *Web:* www.crawford-industries.com

Crawford Investment Counsel Inc
600 Galleria Pkwy Ste 1650 ....Atlanta GA 30339 770-859-0045 401
Web: www.crawfordinvestment.com

Crawford Merz Anderson Construction Co
2316 Fourth Ave S ....Minneapolis MN 55404 612-874-9011 186
Web: www.cmacco.com

Crawford Murphy & Tilly Inc
2750 W Washington St.....................Springfield IL 62702 217-787-8050 261
Web: www.cmtengr.com

Crawford Notch State Park
1464 US Rt 302 ....Harts Location NH 03812 603-374-2272 565
Web: www.nhstateparks.org

Crawford Rick (Rep R - AR)
2422 Rayburn HOB.......................Washington DC 20515 202-225-4076 225-5602 342-2
Web: crawford.house.gov

Crawford State Park 40468 CO-92 ....Crawford CO 81415 970-921-5721 565
Web: cpw.state.co.us

Crawford State Park 1 Lake Rd ....Farlington KS 66734 620-362-3671 565
Web: ksoutdoors.com

Crawford State Park 40468 Hwy 92 ....Crawford CO 81415 970-921-5721 565
Web: cpw.state.co.us/placestogo/parks/crawford

Crawford Strategy
200 E Camperdown Way......................Greenville SC 29601 864-232-2302 4
Web: www.crawfordstrategy.com

Crawford Supply Co
8150 Lehigh Ave.......................Morton Grove IL 60053 847-967-1414 612
Web: www.crawfordsupply.com

Crawford Technologies Inc
45 St Clair Ave W Ste 102 ....Toronto ON M4V1K9 416-923-0080 179
TF: 866-679-0864 ■ *Web:* www.crawfordtech.com

Crawfordsville Electric Light & Power
808 Lafayette Ave ....Crawfordsville IN 47933 765-362-1900 245
Web: metronetinc.com/crawfordsville

Crawfordsville-Montgomery County Chamber of Commerce
309 N Green St.......................Crawfordsville IN 47933 765-362-6800 362-6900 139
TF: 800-488-4414 ■ *Web:* www.crawfordsvillechamber.com

Crawley Petroleum Corp
105 N Hudson Ste 800...................Oklahoma City OK 73102 405-232-9700 536
Web: www.crawleypetroleum.com

Cray Inc 901 Fifth Ave Ste 1000.................Seattle WA 98164 206-701-2000 701-2500 173-2
NASDAQ: CRAY ■ *Web:* www.cray.com

Crazy Catfish 1410 W Buckingham Rd ....Garland TX 75042 972-487-2100 671

Crazy Crab
104 William Hilton Pkwy ....Hilton Head Island SC 29926 843-681-5021 671
TF: 800-686-3441 ■ *Web:* www.thecrazycrab.com

Crazy Horse 214 W Kirkwood Ave ....Bloomington IN 47404 812-336-8877 671
Web: www.crazyhorseindiana.com

Crazy Horse Gentlemen's Club
980 Market St.........................San Francisco CA 94102 415-658-9324 149
Web: www.crazyhorse-sf.com

Crazy Horse Memorial
Ave of the Chiefs.........................Crazy Horse SD 57730 605-673-4681 673-2185 50-4
Web: www.crazyhorsememorial.org

Crazy Shirts Inc 99-969 Iwaena St ....Aiea HI 96701 808-487-9919 155-3
TF: 800-771-2720 ■ *Web:* www.crazyshirts.com

Crazy Woman Creek Bancorp Inc
PO Box 1020 ....Buffalo WY 82834 307-684-5591 684-7854 360-2
TF: 877-684-2766 ■ *Web:* www.buffalofed.com

CRB (Council of Real Estate Brokerage Managers)
430 N Michigan Ave.........................Chicago IL 60611 800-621-8738 329-8882* 49-17
*Fax Area Code: 312 ■ *TF:* 800-621-8738 ■ *Web:* www.crb.com

CRB (Country Radio Broadcasters Inc)
819 18th Ave S...........................Nashville TN 37203 615-327-4487 329-4492 49-14
TF: 800-659-9889 ■ *Web:* countryradioseminar.com

CRC (Christian Reformed Church in North America)
2850 Kalamazoo Ave SE..................Grand Rapids MI 49560 616-241-1691 224-0834 48-20
TF: 800-272-5125 ■ *Web:* www.crcna.org

CRC (Container Research Corp) 2 New Rd ....Aston PA 19014 610-459-2160 198
TF: 844-220-9574 ■ *Web:* www.crc-flex.com

CRC (Coordinating Research Council Inc)
5755 N Point Pkwy Suite 265................Alpharetta GA 30022 678-795-0506 795-0509 49-19
Web: www.crcao.com

CRC (Capital Restaurant Concepts Ltd)
1305 Wisconsin Ave NW ....Washington DC 20007 202-339-6800 339-6801 670
Web: www.capitalrestaurants.com

CRC Evans Pipeline International Inc
10700 E Independence St..........................Tulsa OK 74116 918-438-2100 190
TF: 800-664-9224 ■ *Web:* www.crc-evans.com

CRC Industries Inc 885 Louis Dr ....Warminster PA 18974 215-674-4300 674-2196 541
TF Cust Svc: 800-556-5074 ■ *Web:* www.crcindustries.com

CRC Press LLC
6000 Broken Sound Pkwy NW Ste 300........Boca Raton FL 33487 561-994-0555 374-3401* 637-9
*Fax Area Code: 800 ■ *Fax: Cust Svc ■ *TF Cust Svc:* 800-272-7737 ■ *Web:* www.crcpress.com

CRC Sogema Inc
1111 Saint-Charles St W Saint-Charles Complex W To
Ste 700.................................Longueuil QC J4K5G4 450-651-2800 651-1681 463
Web: crcsogema.com

CRCA (Consumers' Research Council of America)
2020 Pennsylvania Ave NW Ste 300-A..........Washington DC 20006 202-835-9698 835-9739 48-10
TF: 877-774-6337 ■ *Web:* www.consumersresearchcncl.org

CRCH (Carilion Roanoke Community Hospital)
101 Elm Ave SE ....Roanoke VA 24013 540-985-8000 374-3
TF: 800-422-8482 ■ *Web:* carilionclinic.org

CRCPD (Conference of Radiation Control Program Directors)
1030 Burlington Ln # 4B ....Frankfort KY 40601 502-227-4543 227-7862 49-7
TF: 800-251-3331 ■ *Web:* www.crcpd.org

CRE (Counselors of Real Estate)
430 N Michigan Ave 2nd Fl ....Chicago IL 60611 312-329-8427 329-8881 49-17
Web: www.cre.org

Creagen Biosciences Inc 23 Rainin Rd ....Woburn MA 01801 781-938-1122 479
Web: www.creagenbio.com

Cream City Music
12505 W Bluemound Rd...................Brookfield WI 53005 262-860-1800 526
TF: 800-800-0087 ■ *Web:* www.warpdrivemusic.com

Creamer Metal Products Inc
77 S Madison Rd ....London OH 43140 740-852-1752 295
TF: 800-362-1603 ■ *Web:* creamermetal.com

Creamland Dairies Inc PO Box 961447..........El Paso TX 79996 505-247-0721 246-9696 296-25
TF: 800-395-7004 ■ *Web:* www.creamland.com

Cream-O-Land Dairy Inc 529 Cedar Ln ....Florence NJ 08518 609-499-3601 297-4
TF: 800-220-6455 ■ *Web:* www.creamoland.com

Creare Inc 16 Great Hollow Rd..................Hanover NH 03755 603-643-3800 643-4657 668
Web: www.creare.com

Create a Pack Foods Inc
W1344 Industrial Dr..........................Ixonia WI 53036 262-567-6069 297-8
Web: create-a-pack.com

Create Adv Group LLC
6022 Washington Blvd ....Culver City CA 90232 310-280-2999 4
Web: createadvertising.com

Create One for Me Inc
4416 NW 99th Ave ....Sunrise FL 33351 954-746-5199 344
Web: www.createoneforme.com

Create-a-card Inc 16 Brasswood Rd ....Saint James NY 11780 631-584-2273 535
TF: 800-753-6867 ■ *Web:* www.createacardinc.com

Createthe Group Inc
116 W Houston St 5th Fl ....New York NY 10012 212-375-7900 809
TF: 800-621-4841 ■ *Web:* www.createthegroup.com

Creatine Marketing
3840 Rosin Ct Ste 130 ....Sacramento CA 95834 916-302-4742 636
Web: creatinemarketing.com

Creating Keepsakes Magazine
14850 Pony Express Rd ....Bluffdale UT 84065 801-816-8300 816-8301 457-14
TF: 888-247-5282 ■ *Web:* www.creatingkeepsakes.com

Creation Engine
348 E Middlefield Rd ....Mountain View CA 94043 650-934-0176 180
TF: 800-431-8713 ■ *Web:* www.creationengine.com

Creation Ground Media
999 Clark Ave.........................Mountain View CA 94040 650-947-7779 514
Web: www.creationgroundmedia.com

Creative Advantage Inc
246 W End Ave Ste 9G ....New York NY 10023 212-475-9300 370-1636* 194
*Fax Area Code: 518

Creative Allies Inc
1204 Village Market Pl Ste 254 ....Morrisville NC 27560 828-252-6300 526

Creative Approaches
55 State St Ste 102.........................Bloomfield NY 14469 585-657-6379 196
Web: www.creativeapproachesinc.com

Company / Address	City	State	ZIP	Phone	Fax	Class
Creative Artists Agency Inc (CAA) 2000 Ave of the Stars *Web:* www.caa.com	Los Angeles	CA	90067	424-288-2000	288-2900	731
Creative Arts Theatre & School 602 E S St *Web:* www.creativearts.org	Arlington	TX	76010	817-861-2287	274-0793	572
Creative Assoc 1 Snoopy Pl	Santa Rosa	CA	95403	707-546-7121		344
Creative Assoc International Inc 5301 Wisconsin Ave NW Ste 700 *Web:* www.creativeassociatesinternational.com	Washington	DC	20015	202-966-5804		194
Creative Bath Products 250 Creative Dr *Web:* www.creativebath.com	Central Islip	NY	11722	631-582-8000	582-2020	746
Creative Breakthroughs Inc 2075 W Big Beaver Rd Ste 700 *Web:* cbisecure.com	Troy	MI	48084	248-519-4000	519-5555	225
Creative Broadcast Concepts 56 Industrial Park Rd *Web:* www.cbcads.com	Saco	ME	04072	207-283-9191		4
Creative Business Interiors 1535 S 101st St *TF:* 800-454-9796 ■ *Web:* www.creativebusinessinteriors.com	Milwaukee	WI	53214	414-545-8500		186
Creative Colors International Inc 19015 S Jodi Rd Ste E *TF:* 800-933-2656 ■ *Web:* www.wecanfixthat.com	Mokena	IL	60448	708-478-1437	478-1636	310
Creative Communications For The Parish Inc 1564 Fencorp Dr *TF:* 800-325-9414 ■ *Web:* www.creativecommunications.com	Fenton	MO	63026	636-305-9777	305-9333	637-2
Creative Contractors Inc 620 Drew St *Web:* www.creativecontractors.com	Clearwater	FL	33755	727-461-5522	447-4808	685
Creative Dining Services 1 Royal Pk Dr Ste 3 *Web:* www.creativedining.com	Zeeland	MI	49464	616-748-1700	748-1900	271
Creative Discovery Museum 321 Chestnut St *TF:* 800-964-8600 ■ *Web:* www.cdmfun.org	Chattanooga	TN	37402	423-756-2738	267-9344	521
Creative Dispute Resolutions LLC 211 Little Quarry Rd *Web:* creativedisputeresolutions.com	Gaithersburg	MD	20878	301-977-8002		445
Creative Door Services Ltd 14904 - 135 Ave *Web:* creativedoor.com	Edmonton	AB	T5V1R9	780-483-1789		480
Creative Educational Concepts 1792 Alysheba Way Ste 100	Lexington	KY	40509	859-260-1717		194
Creative Energy Options Inc 45 Country Pl Ln *Web:* www.retreatpa.com	White Haven	PA	18661	570-636-3858		194
Creative Engineering LLC 38 Milburn St *Web:* www.creativeengineering.com	Bronxville	NY	10708	914-771-5540		256
Creative Engineers Inc 15425 Elm Dr *Web:* www.creativeengineers.com	New Freedom	PA	17349	443-807-1202		256
Creative Environments 8920 S Hardy Dr *TF:* 855-777-9305 ■ *Web:* www.creativeenvironments.com	Tempe	AZ	85284	480-458-4100	777-9296	422
Creative Extrusion & Technologies Inc 230 Elliot St	Brockton	MA	02302	508-587-2290		432
Creative Film Management 430 W 14th St Fl 4 *TF:* 800-640-4884 ■ *Web:* www.crmmgt.com	New York	NY	10014	212-685-6070		514
Creative Financial Group (CFG) 16 Campus Blvd *TF:* 800-893-4824 ■ *Web:* creativefinancialgroup.com	Newtown Square	PA	19073	610-325-6100	325-6240	401
Creative Financial Group Ltd 1000 Abernathy Rd Bldg 400 Ste 1500 *Web:* www.cfgltd.com	Atlanta	GA	30328	770-913-9704		401
Creative Fire 313 Ontario Ave *Web:* creative-fire.com	Saskatoon	SK	S7K1S3	306-934-3337		4
Creative Foam Corp 300 N Alloy Dr *TF:* 800-529-4149 ■ *Web:* www.creativefoam.com	Fenton	MI	48430	810-629-4149		601
Creative Foods Corp 200 Garden City Plaza Ste 505 *Web:* www.creativefoodscorp.com	Garden City	NY	11530	516-746-6800		345
Creative Glass Center of America 1501 Glasstown Rd *TF:* 800-998-4552 ■ *Web:* www.wheatonarts.org	Millville	NJ	08332	856-825-6800		520
Creative Global Investments LLC Research Div 115 E 57th St 11th Fl *Web:* cg-inv.com	New York	NY	10022	212-939-7256		401
Creative Group Inc 619 N Lynndale Dr *Web:* www.creativegroupinc.com	Appleton	WI	54914	920-739-8850		193
Creative Health Capital LLC 351 Hubbard St Ste 312 *Web:* www.chcapital.com	Chicago	IL	60654	312-574-3740		70
Creative Hobbies Inc 900 Creek Rd *TF:* 800-843-5456 ■ *Web:* creativehobbies.com	Bellmawr	NJ	08031	856-933-2540		44
Creative HR Solutions Inc 13220 - 22Nd St N *Web:* www.creative-hr-solutions.com	Stillwater	MN	55082	651-260-1146		41
Creative Imaging Group 64 Mussey Rd *TF:* 800-882-1844 ■ *Web:* creative-ig.com	Scarborough	ME	04074	207-883-2999		627
Creative Impact Group Inc 801 Skokie Blvd Ste 108 *TF:* 800-445-2171 ■ *Web:* www.creativeimpactgroup.com	Northbrook	IL	60062	847-945-7401		184
Creative Kid Stuff 3939 E 46th St *TF:* 800-353-0710 ■ *Web:* www.creativekidstuff.com	Minneapolis	MN	55406	612-929-2431		761
Creative Kids Magazine PO Box 8813 *TF:* 800-998-2208 ■ *Web:* www.prufrock.com	Waco	TX	76714	254-756-3337		457-6
Creative Labs Inc 1901 McCarthy Blvd *Web:* www.us.creative.com	Milpitas	CA	95035	408-428-6600	428-6611	625
Creative Loafing Atlanta 115 Martin Luther King Jr Dr SW Ste 301 *Web:* www.creativeloafing.com	Atlanta	GA	30303	404-688-5623		532-5
Creative Loafing Tampa 1911 N 13th St Ste W200 *Web:* www.cltampa.com	Tampa	FL	33605	813-739-4800	739-4801	532-5
Creative Logistics Solutions Inc 980 Mercantile Dr Ste J *Web:* www.creativelogistics.com	Hanover	MD	21076	410-793-0708		180
Creative Management Services LLC 3 Alpine Ct *Web:* www.mc-2online.com	Chestnut Ridge	NY	10977	845-639-8600		194
Creative Marketing Alliance Inc 191 Clarksville Rd *Web:* www.cmasolutions.com	Princeton Junction	NJ	08550	609-799-6000	799-7032	4
Creative Mktg International Corp 11460 Tomahawk Creek Pkwy *TF:* 800-992-2642 ■ *Web:* www.creativeone.com	Leawood	KS	66211	913-814-0510		391-2
Creative Monograms 122 N 30th St *Web:* www.creativemonograms.com	Billings	MT	59101	406-259-9925		226
Creative Outdoor Advertising 2402 Stouffville Rd *TF:* 800-661-6088 ■ *Web:* www.creativeoutdoor.com	Gormley	ON	L0H1G0	800-661-6088		7
Creative Playthings Ltd 33 Loring Dr *Web:* www.creativeplaythings.com	Framingham	MA	01702	508-620-0900		710
Creative Producers Group Inc 1220 Olive St Ste 210 *Web:* www.creativeworks.com	Saint Louis	MO	63103	314-367-2255		4
Creative Pultrusions Inc 214 Industrial Ln *TF:* 888-274-7855 ■ *Web:* www.creativepultrusions.com	Alum Bank	PA	15521	814-839-4186	839-4276	191-3
Creative Security Company Inc 150 S Autumn St *Web:* www.creativesecurity.com	San Jose	CA	95110	408-295-2600		693
Creative Sign Designs 12801 Commodity Pl Ste 200 *TF:* 800-804-4809 ■ *Web:* www.creativesigndesigns.com	Tampa	FL	33626	813-818-7100		317
Creative Stage Lighting Company Inc 149 Rt 28 N PO Box 567 *Web:* www.creativestagelighting.com	North Creek	NY	12853	518-251-3302	251-2908	722
Creative Support Solutions 5508 W Hwy 290 Ste 203 *Web:* csssolutions.com	Austin	TX	78735	512-330-0701		463
Creative Teaching Press Inc 6262 Katella Ave *TF:* 800-444-4287 ■ *Web:* www.creativeteaching.com	Cypress	CA	90630	714-895-5047	895-6547	243
Creative Techniques Inc 200 Northpointe Dr *Web:* www.creativetechniques.com	Orion	MI	48359	248-373-3050		596
Creative Times Dayschool Inc 2878 Commerce Way	Ogden	UT	84401	801-334-7250		186
Creative Training Techniques International Inc 14530 Martin Dr *TF:* 800-383-9210 ■ *Web:* www.bobpikegroup.com	Eden Prairie	MN	55344	952-829-1954	829-0260	765
Creative Trust 2105 Elliston Pl *Web:* www.creativetrust.com	Brentwood	TN	37027	615-297-5010		506
creativeLIVE Inc 757 Thomas St *Web:* www.creativelive.com	Seattle	WA	98109	206-403-1395		387
Creativity for Kids 9450 Allen Dr *TF:* 800-311-8684 ■ *Web:* www.fabercastell.com	Cleveland	OH	44125	216-643-4660	643-4663	762
Creators Syndicate Inc 5777 W Century Blvd Ste 700 *Web:* www.creators.com	Los Angeles	CA	90045	310-337-7003		530
Credant Technologies Inc 15303 Dallas Pkwy Ste 1420 *TF:* 800-929-8331	Addison	TX	75001	972-458-5400	458-5454	177
Credent Technologies LLC 30 Brookfield St Ste A *Web:* www.credenttech.com	South Windsor	CT	06074	860-436-6391		196
Credigy Solutions Inc 3715 Davinci Court Ste 200 *Web:* www.credigy.net	Norcross	GA	30092	678-728-7310		393
Credit Acceptance Corp 25505 W 12 Mile Rd *TF:* 800-634-1506 ■ *Web:* www.creditacceptance.com	Southfield	MI	48034	248-353-2700		217
Credit Bureau of Connecticut Inc, The 600 Saw Mill Rd *Web:* www.avantus.com	West Haven	CT	06516	203-931-2000		218
Credit Card Systems Inc 180 Shepard Ave *TF:* 800-747-1269 ■ *Web:* www.ccsplastech.com	Wheeling	IL	60090	847-459-8320		704
Credit Consulting Services Inc 201 John St Ste E *TF:* 800-679-6888 ■ *Web:* www.creditconsultingservices.com	Salinas	CA	93901	831-424-0606		160
Credit Control Services Inc (CCS) 2 Wells Ave Ste 1 *TF:* 800-526-0532 ■ *Web:* gsaadvantage.gov	Newton	MA	02459	617-965-2000	762-3035	160
Credit Human Federal Credit Union PO Box 1356 *TF:* 800-234-7228 ■ *Web:* www.sacu.com	San Antonio	TX	78295	210-258-1234	258-1543	219
Credit Management LP 4200 International Pkwy *TF:* 800-377-7713 ■ *Web:* www.thecmigroup.com	Carrollton	TX	75007	800-377-7713		160
Credit Plus Inc 31550 WinterPl Pkwy *TF:* 800-258-3287 ■ *Web:* www.creditplus.com	Salisbury	MD	21804	410-742-9551		226
Credit Professionals International PO Box 220714 *Web:* www.creditprofessionals.org	Saint Louis	MO	63122	314-821-9393	821-7171	49-2
Credit Research Foundation (CRF) 8840 Columbia 100 Pkwy *TF:* 866-265-3298 ■ *Web:* www.crfonline.org	Columbia	MD	21045	410-740-5499	740-4620	49-2
Credit Suisse 11 Madison Ave *TF:* 800-222-8977 ■ *Web:* www.credit-suisse.com	New York	NY	10010	212-325-2000	325-6665	690
Credit Union Acceptance Company LLC 9601 Jones Rd Ste 108 *TF:* 866-970-2822 ■ *Web:* www.cuac.net	Houston	TX	77065	281-970-2822		219
Credit Union Directors Newsletter 5710 Mineral Pt Rd *Fax: Cust Svc ■ *TF:* 800-356-9655 ■ *Web:* www.cuna.org	Madison	WI	53705	608-231-4000	231-1869*	531-1
Credit Union Executives Society (CUES) 5510 Research Pk Dr *TF:* 800-252-2664 ■ *Web:* www.cues.org	Madison	WI	53711	608-271-2664	271-2303	49-2

	Phone	Fax	Class
Credit Union Legislative Action Council of CUNA (CULCAC) 601 Pennsylvania Ave NW S Bldg Ste 600 ..... Washington DC 20004 *Web:* cuna.org	202-638-5777	638-7734	615
Credit Union of Denver 9305 W Alameda Ave ..... Lakewood CO 80226 *TF:* 800-951-9014 ■ *Web:* www.cudenver.com	303-234-1700	239-1108	70
Credit Union of Southern California PO Box 200 ..... Whittier CA 90608 *Fax Area Code: 714 ■ *TF:* 866-287-6225 ■ *Web:* www.cusocal.org	562-698-8326	990-5492*	219
Credit Union of Texas PO Box 517028 ..... Dallas TX 75251 *TF:* 800-314-3828 ■ *Web:* www.cutx.org	972-263-9497	301-1980	219
Credit Valley Hospital 2200 Eglinton Ave W ..... Mississauga ON L5M2N1 *TF:* 877-292-4284 ■ *Web:* www.cvh.on.ca	905-813-2200	813-4168	374-2
Credit.com Inc 160 Spear St Ste 1020 ..... San Francisco CA 94105 *Web:* www.credit.com	415-901-1550		219
Creditors Adjustment Bureau-LC Financial (CABLCF) 14226 Ventura Blvd ..... Sherman Oaks CA 91423 *TF:* 800-800-4523 ■ *Web:* www.cab-lcf.com	818-990-4800	780-3112	160
Creditors Bureau Assoc 420 College St ..... Macon GA 31201 *TF:* 866-949-4213 ■ *Web:* www.cbamacon.com	478-750-1111		218
Creditors Financial Group LLC 3131 S Vaughn Way Ste 110 ..... Aurora CO 80014	303-369-2345		160
Creditors Service Bureau Inc 3410 SW Van Buren St Ste 101 ..... Topeka KS 66611 *Web:* tbcsoftware.com	785-266-4567		160
Cree Inc 4600 Silicon Dr ..... Durham NC 27703 *NASDAQ: CREE* ■ *TF:* 800-533-2583 ■ *Web:* www.cree.com	919-313-5300		696
Creed-Monarch Inc 1 Pucci Pk ..... New Britain CT 06051 *Web:* www.creedmonarch.com	860-826-4000		454
Creedmoor Psychiatric Ctr 79-25 Winchester Blvd ..... Queens Village NY 11427 *TF:* 800-597-8481 ■ *Web:* www.omh.ny.gov	718-464-7500	264-3636	374-5
Creek County 317 E Lee St Rm 100 ..... Sapulpa OK 74066 *Web:* www.okcountyrecords.com	918-224-4084		338
Creekside Cellars 28036 Hwy 74 ..... Evergreen CO 80439 *Web:* www.creeksidecellars.net	303-674-5460		443
Creekside Dinery 160 Nix Boat Yard Rd ..... Saint Augustine FL 32084 *Web:* creeksidedinery.com	904-829-6113		671
Creekside Inn 3400 El Camino Real ..... Palo Alto CA 94306 *TF:* 800-492-7335 ■ *Web:* www.greystonehotels.com	650-493-2411	493-6787	379
Creekstone Farms Premium Beef LLC 604 Goff Industrial Park Rd ..... Arkansas City KS 67005 *Web:* www.creekstonefarms.com	620-741-3100		473
Creel Printing LLC 6330 W Sunset Rd ..... Las Vegas NV 89118 *TF:* 800-882-1844 ■ *Web:* www.creelprint.com	702-735-8161		627
Creform Corp PO Box 830 ..... Greer SC 29652 *TF:* 800-839-8823 ■ *Web:* www.creform.com	864-989-1700	877-3863	723
Cregger Company Inc 629 12th St Extn ..... West Columbia SC 29169 *Web:* www.creggercompany.com	803-791-5195		610
Creighton Bros LLC PO Box 220 ..... Atwood IN 46502 *TF:* 800-864-2220 ■ *Web:* www.creightonbrothersllc.com	574-267-3101		10-8
Creighton University 2500 California Plaza ..... Omaha NE 68178 *Fax: Admissions ■ *TF:* 800-282-5835 ■ *Web:* www.creighton.edu	402-280-2700	280-2685*	166
Creighton University Medical Ctr 601 N 30th St ..... Omaha NE 68131 *TF:* 800-368-5097 ■ *Web:* www.creighton.edu	402-449-4000		374-3
CREIT (Canadian Real Estate Investment Trust) 175 Bloor St E Ste 500 ..... Toronto ON M4W3R8 *TSE: REF.UN* ■ *Web:* www.creit.ca	416-628-7771	628-7777	654
Cremac LLC 78 Delevan St ..... Brooklyn NY 11231 *Web:* www.cremac.com	718-222-4500		401
Cremach Tech Inc 369 Meyers Cir ..... Corona CA 92879 *Web:* www.cmtus.com	951-735-3194		454
Cremation Assn of North America (CANA) 499 Northgate Pkwy ..... Wheeling IL 60090 *TF:* 800-765-0107 ■ *Web:* www.cremationassociation.org	312-245-1077	321-4098	49-4
Creme Curls Bakery Inc 5292 Lawndale Ave ..... Hudsonville MI 49426 *Web:* www.cremecurls.com	616-669-6230		297-8
Crenlo LLC 1600 Fourth Ave NW ..... Rochester MN 55901 *Fax: Sales ■ *Web:* www.crenlo.com	507-289-3371	287-3405*	254
Crenshaw Consulting Engineers Inc 3516 Bush St Ste 200 ..... Raleigh NC 27609 *Web:* www.crenshawconsulting.com	919-871-1070		261
Crenshaw County PO Box 167 ..... Luverne AL 36049 *Web:* www.sos.alabama.gov	334-335-6575		338
Creole Fermentation Industries Inc 7331 Den Frederick Rd ..... Abbeville LA 70510	337-898-9377		296-41
Creor Group LLC Po Box 110398 ..... Campbell CA 95011 *TF:* 877-774-4312 ■ *Web:* creorgroup.com	408-248-4822		195
Creperie, The 10220 103rd St NW ..... Edmonton AB T5J4C9 *Web:* www.thecreperie.com	780-420-6656		671
Creps United Publications 1163 Water St ..... Indiana PA 15701 *TF:* 800-752-0555 ■ *Web:* www.crepsunited.com	724-463-8522		627
Crescendo Consulting Group 48 Free St Ste 206 ..... Portland ME 04101 *Web:* www.crescendocg.com	207-774-2345		194
Crescendo Designs 641 County Rd 39A ..... Southampton NY 11968 *Web:* crescendodesigns.com	631-283-2133		52
Crescendo Systems Corp 1600 Montgolfier ..... Laval QC H7T0A2 *TF:* 800-724-2930 ■ *Web:* www.crescendo.com	450-973-8029		177
Crescendo Ventures 600 Hansen Way ..... Palo Alto CA 94304 *Web:* www.crescendoventures.com	650-470-1200		792
Crescent Bank & Trust 1100 Poydras St Ste 100 ..... New Orleans LA 70163 *Web:* cbtno.com	504-556-5950		70
Crescent Cardboard Company LLC 100 W Willow Rd ..... Wheeling IL 60090 *TF:* 888-293-3956 ■ *Web:* www.crescentcardboard.com	847-537-3400	537-7153	560
Crescent City Consultants 1010 Common St Ste 3010 ..... New Orleans LA 70112 *Web:* www.ccc-nola.com	504-561-1191	568-0783	184
Crescent City-Del Norte County Chamber of Commerce (CCDNCVB) 1001 Front St ..... Crescent City CA 95531 *TF:* 800-343-8300 ■ *Web:* delnorte.org	707-464-3174	464-3561	206
Crescent Crown Distributing 5900 Almonaster Ave ..... New Orleans LA 70126 *TF:* 800-772-3971 ■ *Web:* crescentcrown.com	504-240-5900		81-1
Crescent Design Inc 9932 Mesa Rim Rd # B ..... San Diego CA 92121 *TF:* 800-735-9277 ■ *Web:* www.crescentdesign.com	858-452-3240		396
Crescent Directional Drilling LP 2040 Aldine Western Rd ..... Houston TX 77038 *Web:* crescentdirectional.com	281-668-9535		540
Crescent Electric Supply Co 7750 Dunleith Dr ..... East Dubuque IL 61025 *TF:* 800-858-8378 ■ *Web:* www.cesco.com	815-747-3145	747-7720	246
Crescent Energy Services LLC 1304 Engineers Rd ..... Belle Chasse LA 70037 *Web:* crescentes.com	504-433-4188		540
Crescent Ford Truck Sales 6121 Jefferson Hwy ..... Harahan LA 70123 *Web:* www.crescentfordtruckssharahan.com	504-818-1818		57
Crescent Hotel 403 N Crescent Dr ..... Beverly Hills CA 90210 *Web:* www.crescentbh.com	310-247-0505		379
Crescent Hotels & Resorts LLC 10306 Eaton Pl Ste 430 ..... Fairfax VA 22030	703-279-7820		379
Crescent Inc PO Box 669 ..... Niota TN 37826 *Web:* www.crescenthosiery.com	423-568-2101	568-2104	155-10
Crescent Industries Inc 70 E High St ..... New Freedom PA 17349 *Web:* www.crescentind.com	717-235-3844		596
Crescent Manufacturing Co 1310 Majestic Dr ..... Fremont OH 43420 *TF:* 800-537-1330 ■ *Web:* www.crescentblades.com	419-332-6484	332-6564	222
Crescent Marketing Inc 10285 Eagle Dr ..... North Collins NY 14111 *Web:* www.crescentmfg.net	716-337-0145		3
Crescent Plastics Inc 955 E Diamond Ave ..... Evansville IN 47711 *Web:* www.crescentplastics.com	812-428-9305		596
Crescent Point Energy Corp 585 Eighth Ave SW Ste 2000 ..... Calgary AB T2P1G1 *Web:* www.crescentpointenergy.com	403-693-0020		536
Crescent Real Estate 777 Main St Ste 2260 ..... Fort Worth TX 76102 *Web:* www.crescent.com	817-321-1566	321-2090	655
Crescent Resources Inc 227 W Trade St Ste 1000 ..... Charlotte NC 28202 *Web:* crescentcommunities.com	980-321-6000		653
Crescent Services LLC 5749 NW 132nd St ..... Oklahoma City OK 73142 *Web:* www.crescentservices.net	405-603-1200		196
Crescent Woolen Mills Co 1016 School St ..... Two Rivers WI 54241 *TF:* 800-220-5262 ■ *Web:* crescentwoolenmills.com	920-793-3331	793-3818	745-9
Crescenta Valley Chamber of Commerce 3131 Foothill Blvd Ste D ..... La Crescenta CA 91214 *TF:* 800-698-7698 ■ *Web:* www.crescentavalleychamber.org	818-248-4957	248-9625	139
Crescent News, The 624 W Second St ..... Defiance OH 43512 *Web:* www.crescent-news.com	419-784-5441		532-2
Cresco Lines Inc 15220 S Halsted St ..... Harvey IL 60426 *TF:* 800-323-4476 ■ *Web:* www.crescolines.com	708-339-1186	339-1186	780
Cres-Cor 5925 Heisley Rd ..... Mentor OH 44060 *TF:* 877-273-7267 ■ *Web:* www.crescor.com	440-350-1100	350-7267	286
Cresent Fine Furniture PO Box 1438 ..... Gallatin TN 37066 *TF:* 800-322-5100 ■ *Web:* www.cresent.com	615-452-1671		319-2
Cresleigh Homes Corp 433 California St Ste 700 ..... San Francisco CA 94104 *Web:* hotelpurchase.com	415-982-7777		186
Cresline-West Inc 600 Crosspointe Blvd ..... Evansville IN 47715 *Web:* www.cresline.com	812-428-9300	428-9353	596
Crespi Carmelite High School Inc 5031 Alonzo Ave ..... Encino CA 91316 *TF:* 800-540-4000 ■ *Web:* www.crespi.org	818-345-1672		685
Cress Photo PO Box 4262 ..... Wayne NJ 07474 *Web:* www.flashbulbs.com	973-694-1280	694-6965	119
Cressey Development Corp 555 W Eighth Ave Ste 200 ..... Vancouver BC V5Z1C6 *Web:* www.cressey.com	604-683-1256		186
Cressi-Sub Usa Inc 3 Rosol Ln ..... Saddle Brook NJ 07663 *Web:* www.cressi.com	201-594-1450		671
Cresskill Animal Hospital 39 Spring St ..... Cresskill NJ 07626 *TF:* 800-825-5391 ■ *Web:* www.cresskillanimalhosp.com	201-568-7700		794
Cressman Tubular Products Corp 3939 Beltline Rd Ste 460 ..... Addison TX 75001 *TF:* 800-259-5155 ■ *Web:* www.cressmantubular.com	214-352-5252		358
Crest Beverage Co 8870 Liquid Ct ..... San Diego CA 92121 *TF:* 800-555-5211 ■ *Web:* www.crestbeverage.com	858-452-2300		81-1
Crest Coating Inc 1361 S Allec St ..... Anaheim CA 92805 *Web:* www.crestcoating.com	714-635-7090	758-8752	481
Crest Craft Co 3860 Virginia Ave ..... Cincinnati OH 45227 *TF:* 800-860-1662 ■ *Web:* www.crestcraft.com	513-271-4858		627
Crest Electronics Inc 3706 Alliance Dr ..... Greensboro NC 27407 *TF:* 888-502-7378 ■ *Web:* www.crestelectronics.com	336-855-6422	855-6676	52
Crest Foam Industries Inc 100 Carol Pl ..... Moonachie NJ 07074 *Web:* www.inoacusa.com	201-807-0809	807-1113	601
Crest Foods Company Inc 905 Main St ..... Ashton IL 61006 *TF:* 877-273-7893 ■ *Web:* www.crestfoods.com	815-453-7411		296-17
Crest Foods Inc 101 W Renner Rd Ste 240 ..... Richardson TX 75082 *Web:* www.nestlecafe.com	214-495-9533		68
Crest Healthcare Supply 195 Third St ..... Dassel MN 55325 *TF:* 800-328-8908 ■ *Web:* www.cresthealthcare.com	320-275-3382	275-2306	392

	Phone	Fax	Class
Crest Industries Inc 231 Larkin Williams Industrial Ct................Fenton MO 63026 *Web:* www.crestmidwest.com	636-349-4800		690
Crest Manufacturing Co 5 Hood Dr .... Lincoln RI 02865 *TF:* 800-652-7378 ■ *Web:* www.crestmfg.com	401-333-1350	333-0821	488
Crest Semiconductors Inc 2001 Gateway Pl 610 W .... San Jose CA 95110 *Web:* www.slicex.com	408-441-0303		201
Crest Services 3015 Merle Hay Rd Ste 6 ....Des Moines IA 50310 *Web:* crestservices.org	515-331-1200		475
Crest Theater 1013 K St.................. Sacramento CA 95814 *Web:* www.thecrest.com	916-442-5189		748
Crest Ultrasonics Corp 18 Graphics Dr......................Ewing Township NJ 08628 *TF:* 800-992-7378 ■ *Web:* www.crest-ultrasonics.com	609-883-4000		782
Cresta Technology Corp 3900 Freedom Cir Ste 201 .... Santa Clara CA 95054 *Web:* www.crestatech.com	408-486-5610		201
Crestcom International Ltd 6900 E Belleview Ave ....Greenwood Village CO 80111 *TF:* 800-333-7680 ■ *Web:* www.crestcomleadership.com	303-267-8200		765
Crestec USA Inc 2410 Mira Mar Ave.......... Long Beach CA 90815 *Web:* www.crestecusa.com	310-327-9000	532-0361	627
Crested Butte Mountain Resort (CBMR) 12 Snowmass Rd PO Box 5700 ....Crested Butte CO 81225 *TF:* 877-547-5143 ■ *Web:* www.skicb.com/cbmr	877-547-5143		669
Cresthill Suites Hotel 1415 Washington Ave........................ Albany NY 12206 *Web:* www.cresthillsuites.com	518-454-0007		379
Cresting Wave 260 Harristown Rd............ Glen Rock NJ 07452 *Web:* www.crestingwave.com	201-444-0084		463
Crestline Hotels & Resorts 3950 University Dr Ste 301.................... Fairfax VA 22030 *Web:* www.crestlinehotels.com	571-529-6100	529-6095	379
Crestliner Inc 9040 Quaday Ave NE .... Ostego MN 55330 **Fax Area Code:* 320 ■ *TF:* 866-301-8544 ■ *Web:* www.crestliner.com	866-301-8544	256-4676*	90
Crestmark Bank 5480 Corporate Dr Ste 350.......... Troy MI 48098 **Fax Area Code:* 248 ■ *TF:* 888-999-8050 ■ *Web:* www.crestmark.com	888-999-8050	641-5101*	272
Crestmont Health Care Ctr 111 Trealout Dr.............................. Fenton MI 48430 *Web:* savaseniorcare.com	810-629-4105		450
Creststreet Asset Management Limited 70 University Ave Ste 1450................... Toronto ON M5J2M4	416-864-6330	862-8950	528
Crestview Area Chamber of Commerce 1447 Commerce Dr ....Crestview FL 32539 *Web:* www.crestviewchamber.com	850-682-3212	682-7413	139
Crestview Baptist Church Georgetown Texas 2300 Williams Dr........................Georgetown TX 78628 *Web:* crestviewbaptist.church	512-863-6576		48-20
Crestview Partners LP 667 Madison Ave 10th Fl...................New York NY 10065 *Web:* www.crestview.com	212-906-0700		360-3
Crestwood Advisors LLC 50 Federal St Ste 810..........................Boston MA 02110 *TF:* 877-273-7896 ■ *Web:* www.crestwoodadvisors.com	617-523-8880		401
Crestwood Energy Partners LP 700 Louisiana St Ste 2550.....................Houston TX 77002 *TF:* 800-642-1687 ■ *Web:* www.crestwoodlp.com	832-519-2200		579
Crestwood Manor 50 Lacey Rd................ Whiting NJ 08759 *TF General:* 877-467-1652 ■ *Web:* www.crestwoodmanoronline.org	732-849-4900		672
Crestwood Medical Ctr 1 Hospital Dr .... Huntsville AL 35801 *Web:* www.crestwoodmedcenter.com	256-429-4000		374-3
Crestwood Tubulars Inc 9962 Lin-Ferry Dr Ste 207 .... St. Louis MO 63123 *Web:* www.crestwoodtubulars.com	314-842-8604		492
Creswell-Richardson Supply 900 Appling St........................... Chattanooga TN 37406 *Web:* www.creswellrichardson.com	423-894-4117		253
Crete Area Chamber of Commerce 1182 Main St PO Box 263 .... Crete IL 60417 *Web:* www.cretechamber.com	708-672-9216	672-7640	139
Crete Carrier Corp 400 NW 56th St PO Box 81228 .... Lincoln NE 68528 **Fax:* Mktg ■ *TF Cust Svc:* 800-998-4095 ■ *Web:* www.cretecarrier.com	402-475-9521	479-2073*	780
Crete-Monee School District No 201-U 1500 S Sangamon St .... Crete IL 60417 *Web:* www.cm201u.org	708-367-8300		685
Creter Vault Corp 417 US Hwy 202 .... Flemington NJ 08822	908-782-7771		183
Cretex Concrete Products Wes 725 Bryan Stock Trail...........................Casper WY 82601 *Web:* www.cretexwest.com	307-265-3100	265-0013	183
Cretex Cos 311 Lowell Ave.................... Elk River MN 55330 *Web:* cretexcompanies.com	763-441-2121		183
Creutzfeldt-Jakob Disease Foundation Inc PO Box 5312 ....Akron OH 44334 **Fax Area Code:* 234 ■ *TF:* 800-659-1991 ■ *Web:* www.cjdfoundation.org	212-719-5900	466-7077*	48-17
Crew Energy Inc 250 5 St SW Ste 800 .... Calgary AB T2P0R4 *Web:* www.crewenergy.com	403-266-2088		536
Crew Engineers Inc 1250 Rt 23 N ....Butler NJ 07405 *Web:* crewengineers.com	973-492-3300		261
Crew Outfitters Inc 1001 Virginia Ave .... Atlanta GA 30354 *TF:* 888-345-5353 ■ *Web:* www.crewoutfitters.com	888-345-5353		156
Crexendo Inc 1615 S 52nd St .... Tempe AZ 85281 *OTC:* CXDO ■ *TF:* 866-621-6111 ■ *Web:* crexendo.com	801-431-4695		39
CRF (Credit Research Foundation) 8840 Columbia 100 Pkwy.....................Columbia MD 21045 *TF:* 866-265-3298 ■ *Web:* www.crfonline.org	410-740-5499	740-4620	49-2
CRG (Council for Responsible Genetics) 5 Upland Rd Ste 3.........................Cambridge MA 02140 *TF:* 888-591-3911 ■ *Web:* www.councilforresponsiblegenetics.org	617-868-0870	491-5344	49-19
CRG Consulting 301 Moodie Dr Ste 325........... Ottawa ON K2H9C4 *Web:* www.thecrg.com	613-596-2910	820-4718	194
CRG Gallery 195 Chrystie St .... New York NY 10002 *TF:* 800-524-2736 ■ *Web:* crggallery.com	212-229-2766	229-2788	42
CRG Global Inc 3 Signal Ave Ste A ....Ormond Beach FL 32174 *TF:* 800-831-1718 ■ *Web:* www.crgglobalinc.com	386-677-5644		668

	Phone	Fax	Class
CRH Medical Corp 999 Canada Pl Ste 578.....................Vancouver BC V6C3E1 *Web:* www.crhsystem.com	604-633-1440		476
CRI (Carpet & Rug Institute) 100 S Hamilton St PO Box 2048................. Dalton GA 30720 *TF:* 800-653-8338 ■ *Web:* www.carpet-rug.org	706-278-3176	278-8835	49-4
CRI 190 Godwin Ave.........................Midland Park NJ 07432 *Web:* www.cridps.com	201-857-1267		627
CRI Advantage Inc 6149 N Meeker Pl Ste 200 ....Boise ID 83713 *Web:* www.criadvantage.com	208-343-9192		180
Cricket Media Inc 7926 Jones Branch Dr Ste 870................. McLean VA 22102 **Fax Area Code:* 703 ■ *TF:* 800-821-0115 ■ *Web:* shop.cricketmedia.com	800-821-0115	885-3490*	457-6
Crier Newspapers LLC 5064 Nandina Ln Ste C....................Dunwoody GA 30338 *Web:* www.thecrier.net	770-451-4147	451-4223	532-4
Crime Alert Alarm Co 690 Lenfest Rd .... San Jose CA 95133 *Web:* www.crimealert.com	408-729-6200		45
Crimetek Security Services 3448 N Golden State Blvd.....................Turlock CA 95382 *Web:* www.crimetek.com	209-668-6208		693
Criminal Justice Department 3901 State Jail Rd.............................. El Paso TX 79938	915-856-0046		213
Criminal Law Reporter 1801 S Bell St.............................. Arlington VA 22202 *TF:* 800-372-1033 ■ *Web:* www.bna.com/criminal-law-reporter-p5446	800-372-1033		531-7
Crimson Consulting Group 4970 El Camino Real Ste 200................Los Altos CA 94022 *Web:* crimsonmarketing.com	650-960-3600		195
Crimson Resource Management Corp 410 17th St Ste 1010 ....Denver CO 80202 *Web:* www.crimsonrm.com	303-892-9333		536
Crisell & Assoc 2199 E Willow St............. Signal Hill CA 90755 *Web:* www.crisellcpas.com	562-595-0501		2
Crisp County 210 S Seventh St .... Cordele GA 31015 *Web:* www.crispcounty.com	229-276-2672	276-2675	338
Crisp County Board of Education PO Box 729 .... Cordele GA 31015 *Web:* www.crispschools.org	229-276-3400	276-3406	685
Crisp County Power Commission Inc PO Box 1218 .... Cordele GA 31010 *Web:* www.crispcountypower.com	229-273-3811		245
Crispin Corp 600 Wade Ave.................... Raleigh NC 27605 *Web:* www.crispincorp.com	919-845-7744		225
Crispin Porter & Bogusky LLC 3390 Mary St Ste 300 Coconut Grove .... Miami FL 33133 *Web:* www.cpbgroup.com	305-859-2070		5
Crisp-Ladew Fire Protection Co 5201 Saunders Rd ....Fort Worth TX 76119 *TF:* 800-550-2287 ■ *Web:* crisp-ladew.com	817-572-3663		189-13
Crissair Inc 28909 Avenue Williams ....Valencia CA 91355 *Web:* www.crissair.com	661-367-3300		790
Crissey Field State Recreation Site 1655 Hwy 101 N.......................... Brookings OR 97415 *TF:* 800-551-6949 ■ *Web:* www.oregonstateparks.org	541-469-2021		565
Crist Charlie (Rep D - FL) 427 Cannon HOB ....Washington DC 20515 *Web:* crist.house.gov	202-225-5961	225-9764	342-2
Crist Engineers Inc 1405 N Pierce St.......................... Little Rock AR 72207 *TF:* 800-950-5817 ■ *Web:* cristengineers.com	501-664-1552		261
Crist|Kolder Associates LLC 3250 Lacey Rd Ste 450................ Downers Grove IL 60515 *Web:* www.cristkolder.com	630-321-1110		260
CRISTA Ministries 19303 Fremont Ave N .... Seattle WA 98133 *TF Cust Svc:* 800-346-9140 ■ *Web:* www.crista.org	206-546-7200	546-7458	48-5
Cristek Interconnects Inc 5395 E Hunter Ave .... Anaheim CA 92807 *TF:* 888-265-9162 ■ *Web:* www.cristek.com	714-696-5200	696-5225	815
Cristi Cleaning Service Corp 77 Trinity Pl ....Hackensack NJ 07601 *TF:* 800-287-6173 ■ *Web:* www.cristicleaning.com	201-883-1717		104
Cristo Rey Jesuit High School 1852 W 22nd Pl ....Chicago IL 60608 *Web:* www.cristorey.net	773-890-6800		685
Criswell Automotive 503 Quince Orchard Rd .... Gaithersburg MD 20878 *TF:* 888-672-7559 ■ *Web:* www.criswellauto.com	888-672-7559		57
Criswell College 4010 Gaston Ave .... Dallas TX 75246 *TF:* 800-899-0012 ■ *Web:* www.criswell.edu	214-821-5433		166
Critchfield Mechanical Inc 1901 Junction Ave .... San Jose CA 95131 *TF:* 800-649-7803 ■ *Web:* www.cmihvac.com	408-437-7000	437-7199	189-10
Critchfield, Critchfield & Johnston Ltd 225 N Market St .... Wooster OH 44691 *TF:* 800-686-0440 ■ *Web:* www.ccj.com	330-264-4444		428
Criterion Catalysts & Technologies 16825 Northchase Dr Ste 1000.................Houston TX 77060 *Web:* www.criterioncatalysts.com	281-874-2600	874-2641	143
Criterion Laboratories Inc 3370 Progress Dr Ste J......................Bensalem PA 19020 *TF:* 800-677-1997 ■ *Web:* www.criterionlabs.com	215-244-1300		743
Criterion Technologies Inc 101 Mcintosh Pkwy ....Thomaston GA 30286 *Web:* criteriondomes.com	706-647-5082		608
Criterion Thread Company Inc 21744 98th Ave..........................Queens Village NY 11429 *TF General:* 800-695-0080 ■ *Web:* www.cthread.com	718-464-4200	464-3594	594
Critical Business Analysis Inc 134 W S Boundary St....................Perrysburg OH 43551 *Web:* cbainc.com	419-874-0800		463
Critical Care Services Inc 3010 Broadway St NE.....................Minneapolis MN 55413 *Web:* www.lifelinkiii.com	612-638-4900		30
Critical Mass Inc 1011 Ninth Ave SE Ste 300.................. Calgary AB T2G0H7 *Web:* www.criticalmass.com	403-262-3006		5

Phone Fax Class

Critical Mention Inc
521 Fifth Ave 16th Fl .... New York NY 10175 212-398-1141 225
Web: www.criticalmention.com
Critical Path Strategies Inc 33 Fm 474 .... Boerne TX 78006 830-249-1977 194
Web: criticalpathstrategies.com
Criticaledge Group Inc
2751 Dixwell Ave .... Hamden CT 06518 203-281-0006 2
Criticom Inc 4211 Forbes Blvd .... Lanham MD 20706 301-306-0600 736
TF: 800-449-3384 ■ *Web:* www.ultra-3eti.com
Criticom International Corp
715 W State Rd Ste 434 .... Longwood FL 32750 866-705-7705 818-1973* 693
**Fax Area Code:* 800 ■ *TF:* 866-705-7705 ■ *Web:* www.criticominternational.com
Critigen LLC
7604 Technology Way Ste 300 .... Denver CO 80237 303-706-0990 463
Web: www.critigen.com
CritiTech Inc 1849 E 1450 Rd .... Lawrence KS 66044 785-841-7120 238
Web: www.crititech.com
Crittenden County 100 Court St .... Marion AR 72364 870-739-3200 338
Web: crittendencounty.arkansas.gov
Crittenden County 107 S Main St .... Marion KY 42064 888-443-1610 338
TF: 888-443-1610 ■ *Web:* www.crittenden.clerkinfo.net
Crittenden Publishing Company Inc
1010 State Hwy 77 .... Marion AR 72364 870-735-2383 532-3
Web: www.theeveningtimes.com
Crittenden Regional Hospital
200 Tyler St .... West Memphis AR 72301 870-735-1500 374-3
Crittenton Children's Ctr
10918 Elm Ave .... Kansas City MO 64134 816-765-6600 374-1
Web: www.saintlukeshealthsystem.org
Crittenton Hospital
1101 W University Dr .... Rochester Hills MI 48307 248-652-5000 374-3
Web: www.crittenton.com
Critter Control Inc
9435 E Cherry Bend Rd .... Traverse City MI 49684 855-551-8814 310
TF: 800-451-6544 ■ *Web:* www.crittercontrol.com
Crivelli Chevrolet Buick Inc
1520 Route 31 .... Mt Pleasant PA 15666 724-547-2200 57
Crivelli Ford Inc 2085 Brodhead Rd .... Aliquippa PA 15001 724-857-0400 57
Web: crivelliford.com
Crivello Carlson Sc
710 N Plankinton Ave Ste 500 .... Milwaukee WI 53203 414-271-7722 428
TF: 800-236-9994 ■ *Web:* www.crivellocarlson.com
CRL Technologies Inc
5247 Brawner Pl .... Alexandria VA 22304 703-297-9900 256
Web: www.crltechnologies.com
CRM Co 15800 S Avalon Blvd .... Rancho Dominguez CA 90220 310-538-2222 755
Web: www.crmrubber.com
CRM Dynamics
5800 Ambler Dr Unit 106 .... Mississauga ON L5W4J4 866-740-2424 196
TF: 866-740-2424 ■ *Web:* www.crmdynamics.ca
CRM Innovation 8527 Bluejacket St .... Lenexa KS 66214 913-492-2764 177
Web: www.crminnovation.com
CRM Learning 2218 Faraday Ave Ste 110 .... Carlsbad CA 92008 760-431-9800 513
TF: 800-421-0833 ■ *Web:* www.crmlearning.com
CRMC (Cheyenne Regional Medical Ctr)
214 E 23rd St .... Cheyenne WY 82001 307-634-2273 374-3
Web: www.crmcwy.org
CRMC (Capital Research & Management Co)
333 S Hope St .... Los Angeles CA 90071 213-486-9200 401
TF: 800-421-4225 ■ *Web:* thecapitalgroup.com
CRMC (Cullman Regional Medical Ctr)
1912 Alabama Hwy 157 PO Box 1108 .... Cullman AL 35058 256-737-2000 737-2005 374-3
Web: cullmanregional.com
CRMC (Capital Regional Medical Ctr)
2626 Capital Medical Blvd .... Tallahassee FL 32308 850-325-5000 325-5198 374-3
TF: 800-994-6610 ■ *Web:* www.capitalregionalmedicalcenter.com
CRMC (Coffee Regional Medical Ctr)
1101 Ocilla Rd .... Douglas GA 31533 912-384-1900 374-3
TF: 800-555-4444 ■ *Web:* www.coffeeregional.org
CRMC (Colquitt Regional Medical Ctr)
3131 S Main St PO Box 40 .... Moultrie GA 31768 229-985-3420 374-3
TF: 888-262-2762 ■ *Web:* www.colquittregional.com
CRMC (Cape Regional Medical Ctr Inc)
2 Stone Harbor Blvd .... Cape May Court House NJ 08210 609-463-2000 374-3
TF: 800-222-1222 ■ *Web:* www.caperegional.com
CRMC (Cortland Regional Medical Ctr)
134 Homer Ave .... Cortland NY 13045 607-756-3500 374-3
Web: www.cortlandregional.org
CRMC (Cookeville Regional Medical Ctr)
1 Medical Ctr Blvd .... Cookeville TN 38501 931-528-2541 374-3
TF: 800-897-1898 ■ *Web:* www.crmchealth.org
CRMC (National Institute Child Health)
31 Center Dr Bldg 31 Rm 2A32 .... Bethesda MD 20892 800-370-2943 608
TF: 800-370-2943
CRMPlus Consulting Inc
11531 Meridian Point Dr .... Tampa FL 33626 813-343-2173 463
Web: www.crmplusconsulting.com
CRN (Council for Responsible Nutrition)
1828 L St NW Ste 900 .... Washington DC 20036 202-204-7700 204-7701 49-6
Web: www.crnusa.org
CRN Digital Talk Radio
10487 Sunland Blvd .... Sunland CA 91040 818-352-7152 352-3229 740
TF: 800-878-7529 ■ *Web:* www.crntalk.com
CRN International Inc 1 Circular Ave .... Hamden CT 06514 203-288-2002 6
Web: www.crnradio.com
CRO Analytics LLC
6139 Stoney Hill Rd .... New Hope PA 18938 571-436-4835 463
Web: croanalytics.com
Croatia 820 Second Ave 19th Fl .... New York NY 10017 212-986-1585 986-2011 784
Consulate General 369 Lexington Ave .... New York NY 10017 212-599-3066 599-3106 257
Consulate General
11766 Wilshire Blvd Ste 1250 .... Los Angeles CA 90025 310-477-1009 257
Web: www.croatiaemb.org
Consulate General
737 N Michigan Ave Ste 1030 .... Chicago IL 60611 312-482-9902 257
Web: www.croatiaemb.org
Croatian Fraternal Union of America (CFU)
100 Delaney Dr .... Pittsburgh PA 15235 412-843-0380 823-1594 48-14
Web: www.croatianfraternalunion.org

Croatian National Tourist Office
350 Fifth Ave Ste 4003 .... New York NY 10118 212-279-8672 279-8683 775
TF: 800-829-4416 ■ *Web:* www.croatia.hr
Crochet World Magazine 306 E Parr Rd .... Berne IN 46711 260-589-8741 457-14
Web: www.crochet-world.com
Crocker & Winsor Seafoods Inc
PO Box 51905 .... Boston MA 02205 617-269-3100 296-14
TF: 800-225-1597 ■ *Web:* www.crockerwinsor.com
Crocker Art Museum 216 'O' St .... Sacramento CA 95814 916-808-7000 520
Web: www.crockerartmuseum.org
Crocker Galleria
1 Montgomery St Ste 3220 .... San Francisco CA 94104 415-393-1505 460
Web: www.thecrockergalleria.com
Crocker Park 189 Crocker Pk Blvd .... Westlake OH 44145 440-871-6880 871-6889 50-6
Web: www.crockerpark.com
Crockett County 1301 Avenue AA .... Ozona TX 76943 325-392-2721 392-2723 338
Crockett Hotel 320 Bonham St .... San Antonio TX 78205 210-225-6500 225-6251 379
Web: www.crocketthotel.com
Crocs Inc 6328 Monarch Pk Pl .... Niwot CO 80503 303-848-7000 301
NASDAQ: CROX ■ *TF:* 866-306-3179 ■ *Web:* www.crocs.com
Croda Inc 300 Columbus Cir Ste A .... Edison NJ 08837 732-417-0800 417-0804 145
Web: www.croda.com
Croft LLC 107 Oliver Emmerich Dr .... McComb MS 39648 601-684-6121 485
TF: 800-437-8421 ■ *Web:* www.croftllc.com
Croft State Natural Area
450 Croft State Pk Rd .... Spartanburg SC 29302 864-585-1283 565
Web: www.southcarolinaparks.com
Crofutt & Smith Moving & Storage
1 Lenel Rd .... Landing NJ 07850 973-347-7200 360-2
Crohn's & Colitis Foundation of America (CCFA)
733 Third Ave Ste 510 .... New York NY 10017 800-932-2423 679-3567* 48-17
**Fax Area Code:* 212 ■ *TF:* 800-932-2423 ■ *Web:* www.crohnscolitisfoundation.org
CROM LLC 250 SW 36th Terr .... Gainesville FL 32607 352-372-3436 372-6209 183
Web: www.cromgnv.com
Croman Corp 801 Ave C .... White City OR 97503 541-826-4455 448
Web: www.croman.net
Crombie REIT 115 King St .... Stellarton NS B0K1S0 902-755-8100 755-6477 655
Web: crombiereit.ca
Cromer Material Handling Inc
4701 Oakport St .... Oakland CA 94601 510-534-6566 770
Web: www.cromer.com
Cromers Inc 1700 Huger St .... Columbia SC 29201 800-322-7688 296-36
TF: 800-322-7688 ■ *Web:* www.cromers.com
Crompco Corp
1815 Gallagher Rd .... Plymouth Meeting PA 19462 610-278-7203 466
Web: www.crompco.com
Cromwell Architect Engineers Inc
101 S Spring St .... Little Rock AR 72201 501-372-2900 261
Web: www.cromwell.com
Cromwell Group Inc
1824 Murfreesboro Rd 2nd Fl .... Nashville TN 37217 615-361-7560 366-4313 643
TF: 800-747-6278 ■ *Web:* www.cromwellradio.com
Cromwell Leather Company Inc
147 Palmer Ave .... Mamaroneck NY 10543 914-381-0100 381-0046 432
TF: 800-765-9278 ■ *Web:* www.cromwellgroup.com
Cromwell Morgan
244 Fifth Ave Ste 2400 .... New York NY 10001 212-726-2994 378
Crone Lumber Company Inc
501 N Park Ave .... Martinsville IN 46151 765-342-2259 683
TF: 800-933-0318 ■ *Web:* www.cronelbr.com
Croner Company Inc, The
1028 Sir Francis Drake Blvd .... Kentfield CA 94904 415-485-5530 463
TF: 800-225-6020 ■ *Web:* www.croner.biz
Cronin & Company Inc
800 Nicollet Mall Ste 2520 .... Minneapolis MN 55402 612-339-0561 690
Cronin & Company LLC 50 Nye Rd .... Glastonbury CT 06033 860-659-0514 7
Web: www.cronin-co.com
Cronin Business Solutions Inc
11720 SW 37th Ct Ste 300 .... Davie FL 33330 954-243-3101 180
Web: www.croninInc.com
Cronland Lumber Co PO Box 574 .... Lincolnton NC 28093 704-736-2691 735-8493 683
TF: 800-237-2428 ■ *Web:* www.cronlandlumber.com
Cronomagic Canada Inc
3333 boul Graham, Ste 700 Ste .... Mont-Royal QC H3R3L5 514-341-1579 180
TF: 800-427-6012 ■ *Web:* www.cronomagic.com
Crook County 300 NE Third St Rm 23 .... Prineville OR 97754 541-447-6553 416-2145 338
TF: 800-368-8683 ■ *Web:* www.co.crook.or.us
Crook County
309 Cleveland St PO Box 397 .... Sundance WY 82729 307-283-1323 283-3038 338
Web: www.crookcounty.wy.gov
Crook County School District 1
108 N Fourth St PO Box 830 .... Sundance WY 82729 307-283-2299 283-1810 780
Web: www.crook1.com
Crooked Creek State Recreation Site
PO Box 1247 .... Soldotna AK 99669 907-262-5581 565
Web: dnr.alaska.gov/parks/units/kasilof.htm
Crooked River State Park
6222 Charlie Smith Sr Hwy .... Saint Marys GA 31558 912-882-5256 565
Web: www.gastateparks.org
Crookham Company Inc PO Box 520 .... Caldwell ID 83606 208-459-7451 296-20
Web: www.crookham.com
Croop-LaFrance Inc
7647 Main St Fishers .... Victor NY 14564 585-869-6100 177
Web: www.croop-lafrance.com
Crop Quest Inc 1204 W Frntview ST, ... Dodge City KS 67801 620-225-2233 192
TF: 800-308-4842 ■ *Web:* www.cropquest.com
Crop Science Society of America (CSSA)
677 S Segoe Rd .... Madison WI 53711 608-273-8080 273-2021 48-2
TF: 800-755-2751 ■ *Web:* www.crops.org
CropKing Inc 134 W Dr .... Lodi OH 44254 330-302-4203 302-4204 276
TF: 800-321-5656 ■ *Web:* www.cropking.com
CropLife America 1156 15th St NW .... Washington DC 20005 202-296-1585 463-0474 48-2
TF: 800-266-9432 ■ *Web:* www.croplifeamerica.org
CROPP Co-op 1 Organic Way .... LaFarge WI 54639 888-444-6455 10-11
TF: 888-444-6455 ■ *Web:* www.organicvalley.coop

Name / Address	City	State	ZIP	Phone	Fax	Class
Crosbie & Company Inc 150 King St W Sun Life Financial Tower 15th Fl *TF:* 866-873-7002 ■ *Web:* www.crosbieco.com	Toronto	ON	M5H1J9	416-362-7726		317
Crosbie Foundry Company Inc 1600 Mishawaka St *Web:* www.crosbiefoundry.com	Elkhart	IN	46514	574-262-1502		308
Crosby & Overton Inc 1610 W 17th St *TF:* 800-827-6729 ■ *Web:* www.crosbyoverton.com	Long Beach	CA	90813	562-432-5445	436-7540	667
Crosby & Rowell Llp 299 Third St	Oakland	CA	94607	510-267-0300		445
Crosby Arboretum 370 Ridge Rd *Web:* www.msstate.edu	Picayune	MS	39466	601-799-2311	799-2372	97
Crosby County 201 W Aspen St Ste 102 *Web:* www.co.crosby.tx.us	Crosbyton	TX	79322	806-675-2334	675-2980	338
Crosby Group, The 2801 Dawson Rd *TF:* 800-772-1500 ■ *Web:* www.thecrosbygroup.com	Tulsa	OK	74110	918-834-4611	832-0940	470
Crosby Insurance Inc 8181 E Kaiser Blvd *Web:* crosbyinsurance.com	Anaheim	CA	92808	714-221-5200		390
Crosby Marketing Communications Inc The Crosby Bldg 705 Melvin Ave Ste 200 *Web:* www.crosbymarketing.com	Annapolis	MD	21401	410-626-0805		7
Crosby-brownlie Inc 100 Nassau St *Web:* crosbybrownlie.com	Rochester	NY	14605	585-325-1290		610
Crosbys Markets Inc 125 Canal St *TF:* 800-566-1088 ■ *Web:* www.crosbysmarkets.com	Salem	MA	01970	978-745-3571		345
Crosby-Wright 5907 N Rocking Rd *Web:* www.crosby-wright.com	Scottsdale	AZ	85250	480-367-1112		7
Crosman Corp 7629 Rt 5 & 20 *TF:* 800-724-7486 ■ *Web:* www.crosman.com	Bloomfield	NY	14469	585-657-6161	657-5405	284
Cross Agency, The 701 San Marco Blvd Ste 1603 *Web:* thecrossagency.com	Jacksonville	FL	32207	904-642-8902		7
Cross Atlantic Capital Partners 150 N Radnor Chester Rd Ste A225 *Web:* www.xacp.com	Radnor	PA	19087	610-995-2650	995-2650	792
Cross Automation Inc 2001 Oak Pkwy *Web:* www.cross-automation.com	Belmont	NC	28012	704-523-2222	523-6500	246
Cross Bros Inc 5255 Sheila St *TF:* 866-939-1057 ■ *Web:* www.crossbrothersinc.com	Los Angeles	CA	90040	323-266-2000	266-2106	482
Cross Circuit Electronics Inc 3020 Scott Blvd *Web:* www.cross-circuit.com	Santa Clara	CA	95054	408-654-9637		225
Cross City Corrections Dept 568 NE 255 St *TF:* 800-543-5353 ■ *Web:* dc.state.fl.us	Cross City	FL	32628	352-498-4444		213
Cross Co 4400 Piedmont Pkwy *TF:* 800-858-1737 ■ *Web:* www.crossco.com	Greensboro	NC	27410	336-856-6000	856-6999	385
Cross Country Automotive Services (CCAS) 1 Cabot Rd *Web:* www.agero.com	Medford	MA	02155	781-393-9300	395-6706	53
Cross Country Healthcare Inc 6551 Pk of Commerce Blvd *NASDAQ: CCRN* ■ *TF:* 800-347-2264 ■ *Web:* www.crosscountryhealthcare.com	Boca Raton	FL	33487	561-998-2232	998-8533	721
Cross Country Home Services 1625 NW 136th Ave Ste 200 *TF Cust Svc:* 800-778-8000 ■ *Web:* www.cchs.com	Sunrise	FL	33323	954-845-2468		367
Cross Country Ski Areas Assn (CCSAA) 259 Bolton Rd *TF:* 877-779-2754 ■ *Web:* www.xcski.org	Winchester	NH	03470	603-239-4341	239-6387	48-22
Cross County 705 E Union St Rm 8 *TF:* 800-247-3312 ■ *Web:* crosscountyar.org	Wynne	AR	72396	870-238-5735	238-5739	338
Cross County Shopping Ctr 8000 Mall Walk *Web:* www.crosscountycenter.com	Yonkers	NY	10704	914-968-9570		460
Cross Creek Resort 3815 Pennsylvania 8 *TF:* 800-461-3173 ■ *Web:* www.crosscreekresort.com	Titusville	PA	16354	814-827-9611		379
Cross Financial Corp 74 Gilman Rd PO Box 1388 *TF:* 800-999-7345 ■ *Web:* www.crossagency.com	Bangor	ME	04401	207-947-7345	941-0849	390
Cross Group Inc, The 1950 S Van Ave *TF:* 800-348-7247 ■ *Web:* www.thecrossgroup.com	Houma	LA	70363	985-868-3906		539
Cross Insurance Center 515 Main St *TF:* 800-745-3000 ■ *Web:* www.crossinsurancecenter.com	Bangor	ME	04401	207-561-8300		205
Cross Keys Village 2990 Carlisle Pk *TF Mktg:* 888-624-8242 ■ *Web:* www.crosskeysvillage.org	New Oxford	PA	17350	717-624-2161	624-5216	672
Cross Manufacturing Inc 11011 King St Ste 210 *TF:* 800-542-7677 ■ *Web:* www.crossmfg.com	Overland Park	KS	66210	913-451-1233	451-1235	640
Cross Match Technologies 3950 RCA Blvd Ste 5001 *Web:* www.crossmatch.com	Palm Beach Gardens	FL	33410	561-622-1650	622-9938	84
Cross Oil Refining & Marketing Inc 484 E Sixth St *TF:* 800-725-3066 ■ *Web:* www.crossoil.com	Smackover	AR	71762	870-881-8700	864-8656	580
Cross Petroleum Inc 6920 Lockheed Dr *TF:* 800-655-4427 ■ *Web:* www.crosspetroleum.com	Redding	CA	96002	530-221-2588		581
Cross Timbers State Park 144 Hwy 105 *Web:* ksoutdoors.com	Toronto	KS	66777	620-637-2213		565
Cross TV 370 W Camino Gardens Blvd Ste 300 *TF:* 877-276-7788 ■ *Web:* www.crosstv.com	Boca Raton	FL	33432	561-367-7454		740
Cross World Network 10 Van Winkle Rd *TF:* 800-572-0889 ■ *Web:* www.crossworldnetwork.com	Hudson	NY	12534	518-851-6688		463
Cross X Platform LLC 2570 Blvd Of The Generals Ste X *Web:* www.crossxplatform.com	Audubon	PA	19403	610-539-2297		194
Crossamerica Partners LP 515 Hamilton St Ste 200 *Web:* www.crossamericapartners.com	Allentown	PA	18101	610-625-8000		579
Crossbeam Capital 6919 Portwest Dr Ste 160 *Web:* www.crossbeamcapital.com	Houston	TX	77024	240-223-0821		251
Crosscheck Compliance LLC 810 W Washington Blvd *Web:* www.crosscheckcompliance.com	Chicago	IL	60607	312-346-4600		194
Crosscom National LLC 900 Deerfield Pkwy *Web:* www.crosscomnational.com	Buffalo Grove	IL	60089	847-520-9200		225
Crosscountry Courier Inc PO Box 4030 *TF:* 800-521-0287 ■ *Web:* www.crosscountrycourier.com	Bismarck	ND	58502	701-222-8498	223-5963	546
Crossed Sabres Ranch 829 N Fork Hwy *Web:* crossedsabresranch.com	Cody	WY	82414	307-587-3750		239
Crosset Company Inc 10295 Toebben Dr *TF:* 800-347-4902 ■ *Web:* crosset.com	Independence	KY	41051	859-283-5830	817-7634	297-7
Crossett Inc 201 S Carver St *TF General:* 800-876-2778 ■ *Web:* www.crossettinc.com	Warren	PA	16365	800-876-2778		780
Crossey Engineering Ltd 2255 Sheppard Ave E Ste E-331 *Web:* www.cel.ca	Toronto	ON	M2J4Y1	416-497-3111		261
Crossfield Products Corp 3000 E Harcourt St *Web:* www.crossfieldproducts.com	Rancho Dominguez	CA	90221	310-886-9100	886-9119	605-2
Crossfield Technology LLC 3445 Executive Center Dr Ste 125 *Web:* www.crossfieldtech.com	Austin	TX	78731	512-795-0220		696
Crossfire Media Inc 1940 Commerce St *Web:* www.crossfiremedia.com	Yorktown Heights	NY	10598	914-302-2900		195
Crossgates Baptist Church Inc 8 Crosswoods Rd *Web:* crossgates.org	Brandon	MS	39042	601-825-2562		48-20
Crossgates Inc 3555 Washington Rd *Web:* www.crossgatesinc.com	McMurray	PA	15317	724-941-9240	941-4339	187
Crossgates Mall 1 Crossgates Mall Rd *Web:* shopcrossgates.com	Albany	NY	12203	518-869-9565		460
Crossgates Recreation Inc 200 N Military Rd *TF:* 800-647-1689 ■ *Web:* www.crossgatesclub.com	Slidell	LA	70461	985-643-3500		354
CrossHarbor Capital Partners LLC 1 Boston Pl Ste 2300 *Web:* www.crossharborcapital.com	Boston	MA	02108	617-624-8300		401
Crossings Community Church 14600 N Portland Ave *Web:* crossings.church	Oklahoma City	OK	73134	405-755-2227		48-20
Crosslake Communications 35910 County Rd 66 PO Box 70 *TF:* 800-992-8220 ■ *Web:* www.crosslake.net	Crosslake	MN	56442	218-692-2777		387
Crossland Construction 833 S East Ave PO BOX 45 *Web:* www.crossland.com	Columbus	KS	66725	620-429-1414	429-1412	186
Crossland Mechanical Inc 237 W 37th St Rm 400 *Web:* www.crosslandmech.com	New York	NY	10018	212-719-5330		610
Crosslink Capital 2 Embarcadero Ctr Ste 2200 *Web:* www.crosslinkcapital.com	San Francisco	CA	94111	415-617-1800		792
Crossman Post Production LLC 35 Lone Hollow *TF:* 888-553-1958 ■ *Web:* www.crossmanpost.com	Sandy	UT	84092	801-553-1958	553-0953	512
Crossmark Graphics Inc 16100 W Overland Dr *TF:* 800-236-1994 ■ *Web:* www.crossmarkgraphicsinc.com	New Berlin	WI	53151	262-821-1343		627
Crossmark Inc 5100 Legacy Dr *TF:* 877-699-6275 ■ *Web:* www.crossmark.com	Plano	TX	75024	469-814-1000		195
Crossmatch 720 Bay Rd Ste 100 *Web:* www.crossmatch.com	Redwood City	CA	94063	650-474-4000	298-8313	84
Cross-Midwest Tire Co 401 S 42nd St *Web:* www.crossmidwest.com	Kansas City	KS	66106	913-321-3003		755
Crosspoint Realty Services Inc 260 California St Fl 4 *Web:* crosspointrealty.com	San Francisco	CA	94111	415-288-6888		652
Crosspoint Venture Partners 670 Woodside Rd	Redwood City	CA	94061	650-851-7600	851-7600	792
CrossRealms Inc 55 W Monroe St Ste 3330 *Web:* www.crossrealms.com	Chicago	IL	60603	312-278-4445		196
Crossroad Engineers 3417 Sherman Dr *TF:* 800-200-1820 ■ *Web:* www.crossroadengineers.com	Beech Grove	IN	46107	317-780-1555		261
Crossroad Farms Dairy 400 S Shortridge Rd	Indianapolis	IN	46219	317-229-7600		296-27
Crossroad Vintners 6429 Guion Rd *Web:* crossroadvintners.com	Indianapolis	IN	46268	317-471-1038		80-3
Crossroads Bible College 601 N Shortridge Rd *TF:* 800-822-3119 ■ *Web:* www.crossroads.edu	Indianapolis	IN	46219	317-789-8255		161
Crossroads College 920 Mayowood Rd SW *TF:* 800-456-7651 ■ *Web:* www.crossroadscollege.edu	Rochester	MN	55902	507-288-4563	288-9046	161
Crossroads For Youth 930 E Drahner PO Box 9 *Web:* www.crossroadsforyouth.org	Oxford	MI	48371	248-628-2561	628-3080	48-6
Crossroads Fuel Service Inc 1441 Fentress Rd *Web:* www.crossroadsfuel.com	Chesapeake	VA	23322	757-482-2179	482-7849	579
Crossroads Juvenile Ctr 17 Bristol St	Brooklyn	NY	11212	718-495-8160		412
Crossroads School For Arts & Sciences 1714 21st St *Web:* www.xrds.org	Santa Monica	CA	90404	310-829-7391		685
Crossroads Systems Inc 11000 N Mopac Expy *NASDAQ: CRDS* ■ *TF:* 800-643-7148 ■ *Web:* www.crossroads.com	Austin	TX	78759	512-349-0300		176
CrossRoadsNews Inc 2346 Candler Rd *Web:* www.crossroadsnews.com	Decatur	GA	30032	404-284-1888		532-3
Crosstex International Inc 10 Ranick Rd *Web:* www.crosstex.com	Hauppauge	NY	11788	631-582-6777		228
CrossUSA Inc 405 Becker Ave N	Sebeka	MN	56477	218-837-6114		175
Crossville Cumberland County Chamber of Commerce 34 S Main St *TF:* 877-465-3861 ■ *Web:* www.crossville-chamber.com	Crossville	TN	38555	931-484-8444	484-7511	139

	Phone	Fax	Class
Crossville Porcelain Stone/USA PO Box 1160 .... Crossville TN 38557 *TF:* 800-221-9093 ■ *Web:* www.crossvilleinc.com	931-484-2110	484-2110	751
Crosswater Digital Media LLC 695 Delaware Ave .... Buffalo NY 14209 *Web:* www.crosswater.net	716-884-8486		514
Crossway Community Church 13905 75th St .... Bristol WI 53104 *Web:* cwc.church	262-857-4488		48-20
Crossworld 306 Bala Ave .... Bala Cynwyd PA 19004 *TF:* 888-785-0087 ■ *Web:* www.crossworld.org	888-785-0087		48-20
Croswell Bus Lines Inc 975 W Main St .... Williamsburg OH 45176 *TF:* 800-782-8747 ■ *Web:* gocroswell.com	513-724-2206	724-3261	107
Crotched Mountain Rehabilitation Ctr 1 Verney Dr .... Greenfield NH 03047 *TF:* 800-433-2900 ■ *Web:* www.cmf.org	603-547-3311	547-3232	374-6
Crouch Group Inc, The 300 N Carroll Blvd Ste 103 .... Denton TX 76201 *TF:* 888-211-0273 ■ *Web:* thecrouchgroup.com	940-383-1990		7
Crounse Corp 400 Marine Way .... Paducah KY 42003 *Web:* www.crounse.com	270-444-9611	444-9615	314
Crouse Hospital 736 Irving Ave .... Syracuse NY 13210 *Web:* www.crouse.org	315-470-7111		374-3
Crow Executive Air Inc 28331 Lemoyne Rd Toledo Metcalf Airport .... Millbury OH 43447 *TF:* 800-972-2769 ■ *Web:* www.crowair.com	419-838-6921	838-6911	63
Crow Holdings Capital Partners LLC 3819 Maple Ave .... Dallas TX 75219 *Web:* www.crowholdingscapital.com	214-661-8000		528
Crow Wing Co-op Power & Light Co Hwy 371 N PO Box 507 .... Brainerd MN 56401 *TF:* 800-648-9401 ■ *Web:* www.cwpower.com	218-829-2827	825-2209	245
Crow Wing County 326 Laurel St .... Brainerd MN 56401 *TF:* 000-029-0C00 ■ *Web:* orowwing.uc	218-824-1067	824-1054	338
Crow Wing State Park 3124 State Pk Rd .... Brainerd MN 56401 *TF:* 888-646-6367 ■ *Web:* www.dnr.state.mn.us	218-825-3075	825-3077	565
Crow's Nest 939 W Fifth Ave Hotel Captain Cook .... Anchorage AK 99501 *Web:* captaincook.com/dining/crows-nest	907-276-6000		671
Crowded Ocean Inc PO Box 1676 .... Los Gatos CA 95031 *Web:* www.crowdedocean.com	408-355-0108		195
Crowder College 601 Laclede Ave .... Neosho MO 64850 **Fax:* Admissions ■ *TF:* 866-238-7788 ■ *Web:* www.crowder.edu	417-451-3223	455-5731*	162
Watley Ctr 601 Laclede .... Neosho MO 64850 *Web:* www.crowder.edu	417-847-1706	847-1367	162
Crowder Construction Company Inc PO Box 30007 .... Charlotte NC 28230 *TF:* 800-849-2966 ■ *Web:* www.crowdercc.com	704-372-3541	376-3573	188-4
Crowder State Park 76 Hwy 128 .... Trenton MO 64683 *Web:* www.mostateparks.com	660-359-6473		565
Crowders Mountain State Park 522 Pk Office Ln .... Kings Mountain NC 28086 *Web:* www.ncparks.gov	704-853-5375		565
CrowdFlower Inc 2111 Mission St Ste 302 .... San Francisco CA 94110 *Web:* www.crowdflower.com	415-471-1920		317
CrowdGather Inc 20300 Ventura Blvd Ste 330 .... Woodland Hills CA 91364 *Web:* www.crowdgather.com	818-435-2472		395
CrowdSource Solutions Inc 33 Bronze Pointe .... Swansea IL 62226 *TF:* 855-276-9376 ■ *Web:* www.crowdsource.com	855-276-9376		631
Crowdstar Inc 330 Primrose Rd Ste 306 .... Burlingame CA 94010 *Web:* crowdstar.com	650-347-4166		177
Crowe & Dunlevy 20 N Broadway Ave # 1800 20 N Broadway .... Oklahoma City OK 73102 *TF:* 800-337-4903 ■ *Web:* www.crowedunlevy.com	405-235-7700		445
Crowe Horwath International 488 Madison Ave Ste 202 .... New York NY 10022 *Web:* www.crowehorwath.net	212-808-2000		734
Crowe Horwath LLP 1 Mid America Plaza Ste 700 .... Oak Brook IL 60181 *Web:* www.crowehorwath.com	630-574-7878	574-1608	2
Crowe-Innes & Assoc 1120 Mar W Ste D .... Tiburon CA 94920 *Web:* www.croweinnes.com	415-435-6211		260
Crowell Weedon & Co 1 Wilshire Blvd 26th Fl .... Los Angeles CA 90017 *TF:* 800-227-0319 ■ *Web:* dadavidson.com	213-620-1850	244-9388	690
Crower Cams & Equipment 6180 Business Ctr Ct .... San Diego CA 92154 *Web:* www.crower.com	619-661-6477	661-6466	60
Crowes Mortuary & Chapel 118 US Hwy 74A .... Rutherfordton NC 28139 *Web:* crowemortuary.com	828-286-2304		48-20
Crowley Barrett & Karaba 20 S Clark St Ste 2310 .... Chicago IL 60603 *Web:* cbklaw.com	312-726-2468		41
Crowley County 631 Main St Ste 102 .... Ordway CO 81063 *TF:* 800-934-7128 ■ *Web:* www.colorado.gov	719-267-5225	267-4608	338
Crowley Fleck PLLP 490 N 31st St Ste 500 .... Billings MT 59101 *Web:* www.crowleyfleck.com	406-252-3441		428
Crowley Joseph (Rep D - NY) 1035 Longworth HOB .... Washington DC 20515 *Web:* crowley.house.gov	202-225-3965		342-2
Crowley Maritime Corp 9487 Regency Square Blvd .... Jacksonville FL 32225 *TF:* 800-276-9539 ■ *Web:* www.crowley.com	904-727-2200	727-2501	312
Crowley Museum & Nature Ctr 16405 Myakka Rd .... Sarasota FL 34240 *Web:* www.crowleymuseumnaturectr.org	941-322-1000		520
Crowley Ridge Regional Library 315 W Oak St .... Jonesboro AR 72401 *Web:* www.libraryinjonesboro.org	870-935-5133	935-7987	434-3
Crowley's Ridge College 100 College Dr .... Paragould AR 72450 **Fax:* Admissions ■ *TF:* 800-264-1096 ■ *Web:* www.crc.edu	870-236-6901	236-7748*	162
Crowley's Ridge State Park 2092 Hwy 168 N .... Paragould AR 72450 *Web:* www.arkansasstateparks.com	870-573-6751		565
Crown Advisors Inc 100 McKnight Park Dr Ste 110 .... Pittsburgh PA 15237 *Web:* www.crownsearch.com	412-348-1540		193
Crown American Hotels Co Pasquerilla Plaza .... Johnstown PA 15907 *TF:* 800-245-9295 ■ *Web:* www.crownamericanhotels.com	814-533-4600		379
Crown Asset Management LLC 3100 Breckinridge Blvd Ste 725 .... Duluth GA 30096 *Web:* www.crownasset.com	770-817-6700		463
Crown Audio Inc 1718 W Mishawaka Rd .... Elkhart IN 46517 *Web:* www.crownaudio.com	574-294-8000		52
Crown Auto Dealerships Inc 5237 34th St N .... St Petersburg FL 33714 *Web:* crowncars.com	727-527-7151		57
Crown Automotive Inc 83 Enterprise Dr .... Marshfield MA 02050 *Web:* www.crownautomotive.net	781-826-6200		54
Crown Battery Manufacturing Co 1445 Majestic Dr .... Fremont OH 43420 *TF:* 800-487-2879 ■ *Web:* www.crownbattery.com	419-334-7181	334-7416	74
Crown Castle International Corp 1220 Augusta Dr Ste 500 .... Houston TX 77057 *NYSE: CCI* ■ *TF:* 877-486-9377 ■ *Web:* www.crowncastle.com	713-570-3000		170
Crown Castle USA Inc 2000 Corporate Dr .... Canonsburg PA 15317 *TF:* 877-486-9377 ■ *Web:* crowncastle.com	724-416-2000	416-2200	170
Crown Central Petroleum Corp 1 N Charles St .... Baltimore MD 21201 *Web:* www.crowncentral.com	410-539-7400		580
Crown Coco Inc 1717 Broadway St .... Minneapolis MN 55413	612-378-9573		204
Crown College 8700 College View Dr .... Saint Bonifacius MN 55375 *TF:* 800-346-9252 ■ *Web:* www.crown.edu	952-446-4100	446-4149	161
Crown Column & Millwork Co LLC 3810 Pleasant Valley Rd .... Attalla AL 35954 *TF:* 888-862-0880 ■ *Web:* www.crowncolumn.com	888-862-0880		499
Crown Consulting Inc 1400 Key Blvd Ste 1100 .... Arlington VA 22209 *Web:* www.crownci.com	703-650-0663		317
Crown Corr Inc 7100 W 21st Ave .... Gary IN 46406 *TF:* 800-611-2907 ■ *Web:* www.crowncorr.com	219-949-8080	944-9922	189-12
Crown Crafts Inc 916 S Burnside .... Gonzales LA 70737 *NASDAQ: CRWS* ■ *TF:* 800-433-9560 ■ *Web:* www.crowncrafts.com	225-647-9100	647-8331	746
Crown Crafts Infant Products Inc 711 W Walnut St .... Compton CA 90220 *Web:* www.ccipInc.com	310-763-8100		64
Crown Energy Co 333 N Portland .... Oklahoma City OK 73107 *Web:* www.crownec.com	405-526-0111		536
Crown Enterprises Inc 145 Hutton Ranch Rd .... Kallspell MT 59901 *Web:* www.sportsmanskihaus.com	406-755-6484	758-7425	711
Crown Equipment Corp 44 S Washington St .... New Bremen OH 45809 *Web:* www.crown.com	419-029-2011	020 2000	470
Crown Extrusions Inc 122 Columbia Ct N .... Chaska MN 55318 *Web:* www.crownextrusions.com	952-448-3533		492
Crown Finonoial Minictries 601 Broad St SE .... Gainesville GA 30501 *TF:* 800-722-1976 ■ *Web:* www.crown.org	770-534-1000		401
Crown Gold Corp 970 Caughlin Crossing Ste 100 .... Reno NV 89519 *TSE: CWM* ■ *Web:* www.crowngoldcorp.com	775-284-7200		502
Crown Group Inc, The 2111 Walter Reuther Dr .... Warren MI 48091 *Web:* www.thecrowngrp.com	586-575-9800		360-3
Crown Hill National Cemetery 700 W 38th St .... Indianapolis IN 46208 *Web:* www.cem.va.gov	765-674-0284		136
Crown Holdings Inc 1 Crown Way .... Philadelphia PA 19154 *NYSE: CCK* ■ *TF:* 800-523-3644 ■ *Web:* www.crowncork.com	215-698-5100		124
Crown Industrial 213 Michelle Ct .... San Francisco CA 94080 *Web:* www.crown-industrial.com	650-952-5150		350
Crown Lift Trucks LLC 10685 Medallion Dr .... Cincinnati OH 45241 *Web:* www.okisys.com	513-874-2600		111
Crown Machine Inc 2707 N Main St .... Rockford IL 61103	815-877-7700		567
Crown Management Services Inc 1501 N Guillemard St .... Pensacola FL 32501 *TF:* 800-844-5280 ■ *Web:* crownlaundry.com	850-438-7578		426
Crown Manufacturing Co 8390 Wolf Lake Dr Ste 114 .... Bartlett TN 38133 *Web:* www.crown-plastics.com	901-371-8770		207
Crown Media Holdings Inc 12700 Ventura Blvd Ste 200 .... Studio City CA 91604 *NASDAQ: CRWN* ■ *TF:* 800-479-7328 ■ *Web:* www.hallmarkchannel.com	818-755-2400		740
Crown Metal Manufacturing Co 765 S SR 83 .... Elmhurst IL 60126 *Web:* www.crownmetal.com	630-279-9800	279-9807	286
Crown Micro Inc 48351 Fremont Blvd .... Fremont CA 94538 *Web:* www.crownmicro.com	510-490-8187		174
Crown Motors Ltd 196 Regent Blvd .... Holland MI 49423 *TF:* 800-466-7000 ■ *Web:* www.crownmotors.com	616-396-5268		57
Crown Nursing Home Associates Inc 3457 Nostrand Ave .... Brooklyn NY 11229 *Web:* www.crowncares.com	718-535-5100		371
Crown Packaging Corp 17854 Chesterfield Airport Rd .... Chesterfield MO 63005 **Fax Area Code:* 636 ■ *TF:* 888-880-0852 ■ *Web:* www.crownpack.com	314-731-4927	681-9600*	548
Crown Plastics Co 116 May Dr .... Harrison OH 45030 *TF:* 800-368-0238 ■ *Web:* www.crownplastics.com	513-367-0238		600

Name / Address	City	State	Zip	Phone	Fax	Class
Crown Point Press						
20 Hawthorne St	San Francisco	CA	94105	415-974-6273	495-4220	520
Web: www.crownpoint.com						
Crown Point State Historic Site						
21 Grandview Dr	Crown Point	NY	12928	518-597-4666	597-3666	565
TF: 800-456-2267 ■ *Web:* parks.ny.gov/historic-sites/34/details.aspx						
Crown Poly Inc						
5700 Bickett St	Huntington Park	CA	90255	323-585-5522		66
Web: www.crownpoly.com						
Crown Polymers LLC 11111 Kiley Dr	Huntley	IL	60142	847-659-0300		390
Web: www.crownpolymers.com						
Crown Products Company Inc						
6390 Phillips Hwy	Jacksonville	FL	32216	904-737-7144	737-3533	697
TF: 800-683-7144 ■ *Web:* www.crownproductsco.com						
Crown Products LLC 3107 Halls Mill Rd	Mobile	AL	36606	251-665-3600		9
Web: www.crownprod.com						
Crown Reef Resort						
2913 S Ocean Blvd	Myrtle Beach	SC	29577	843-626-8077	916-0735	379
TF: 800-291-6598 ■ *Web:* www.crownreef.com						
Crown Roll Leaf Inc 91 Illinois Ave	Paterson	NJ	07503	973-742-4000	742-0219	295
TF: 800-631-3831 ■ *Web:* www.crownrollleaf.com						
Crown Travel & Cruises						
240 Newton Rd Ste 106	Raleigh	NC	27615	919-870-1986	870-1666	771
TF: 800-869-7447 ■ *Web:* www.crowncruise.com						
Crown Trophy 529 N State Rd	Briarcliff Manor	NY	10510	914-941-0020		777
Web: www.crowntrophy.com						
Crown Tumbling Corp						
32571 Stephenson Hwy	Madison Heights	MI	48071	248-588-4990		481
Crown Valley Imaging LLC						
27401 Los Altos Ste 150	Mission Viejo	CA	92691	949-367-1010		418
TF: 800-720-6002 ■ *Web:* www.crownvalleyimaging.com						
Crown Vision Ctr 406 E Broadway	Alton	IL	62002	618-462-7611		543
Web: www.crownvisioncenter.com						
Crown Xpress Transport						
9931 Via De La Amistad	San Diego	CA	92154	619-671-9611		770
Web: www.crownxt.com						
Crowne Plaza Campbell House						
1375 S Broadway Rd	Lexington	KY	40504	859-255-4281	254-4368	379
Web: www.thecampbellhouse.com						
Crowne Plaza Chateau Lacombe						
10111 Bellamy Hill	Edmonton	AB	T5J1N7	780-428-6611		379
TF: 800-661-8801 ■ *Web:* www.chateaulacombe.com						
Crowne Plaza Hollywood Beach Resort						
4000 S Ocean Dr	Hollywood	FL	33019	954-454-4334		379
Web: cphollywoodbeach.com						
Crowne Plaza Hotel St Louis-Clayton						
7750 Carondelet Ave Clayton	Clayton	MO	63105	314-726-5400		378
Web: www.cpclayton.com						
Crowne Plaza Hotels & Resorts						
2701 Summer St	Stamford	CT	06905	203-359-1300		378
Web: www.ihg.com						
Crowne plaza Hotels & Resorts						
2270 Hotel Cir N	San Diego	CA	92108	619-297-1101		707
Web: www.ihg.com						
Crowne Plaza Minneapolis Airport West						
5401 Green Vly Dr	Bloomington	MN	55437	952-831-8000		378
Web: www.cpmsp.com						
Crowne Plaza Niagara Falls - Fallsview						
5685 Falls Ave	Niagara Falls	ON	L2E6W7	905-374-4447		378
TF: 800-263-7135 ■ *Web:* www.niagarafallscrowneplazahotel.com						
Crowne Plaza Ravinia						
4355 Ashford Dunwoody Rd	Atlanta	GA	30346	770-395-7700		378
Web: www.cpravinia.com						
Crowne Plaza St Paul Riverfront						
11 E Kellogg Blvd	St Paul	MN	55101	651-292-1900		379
Web: ihg.com						
Crowne Plaza Syracuse						
701 E Genesee St	Syracuse	NY	13210	315-479-7000	472-2700	379
TF: 888-227-6963 ■ *Web:* cpsyracuse.com						
Crowne Plaza Times Square Manhattan						
1605 Broadway	New York	NY	10019	212-977-4000		379
Crowned Grace International						
4415 Nicole Dr Ste F	Lanham	MD	20706	240-454-3624	842-1402	463
Web: www.crownedgrace.com						
Crownline Boats Inc						
11884 Country Club Rd	West Frankfort	IL	62896	618-937-6426		90
Web: www.crownline.com						
Crownover Lumber Company Inc						
501 Fairview Ave	Mc Arthur	OH	45651	740-596-5229		683
Web: www.crownoverlumber.com						
CrownQuest Operating LLC						
18 Desta Dr PO Box 53310	Midland	TX	79710	432-818-0300		540
Web: www.crownquest.com						
CrownTonka Inc						
15600 37th Ave N Ste 100	Plymouth	MN	55446	763-541-1410	541-1563	664
TF: 800-523-7337 ■ *Web:* www.crowntonka.com						
Crow-Segal Management Co						
341 N Maitland Ave Ste 130	Maitland	FL	32751	407-647-8839		47
Web: www.crowsegal.com						
Crozer-Chester Medical Ctr (CCMC)						
1 Medical Ctr Blvd	Upland	PA	19013	610-447-2000		374-3
Web: www.crozerkeystone.org						
Crozer-Keystone Health System (CKHS)						
190 W Sproul Rd	Springfield	PA	19064	610-328-8700	328-8725	353
TF: 800-254-3258 ■ *Web:* www.crozerkeystone.org						
CRP 4X4 Truck OutFitters						
2102 Ninth St Ste A	Greeley	CO	80631	970-351-8603		54
Web: crp4x4.com						
CRRG Inc PO Box 170904	Arlington	TX	76140	972-445-5990		624
Web: www.crrginc.com						
CRS (Catholic Relief Services)						
228 W Lexington St	Baltimore	MD	21201	410-625-2220	685-1635	48-5
TF: 800-235-2772 ■ *Web:* www.crs.org						
CRS Inc 4851 White Bear Pkwy	Saint Paul	MN	55110	651-294-2700	294-2900	112
TF: 800-333-4949 ■ *Web:* www.crs-usa.com						
CRS Jet Spares Inc						
6701 NW 12th Ave	Fort Lauderdale	FL	33309	954-972-2807	972-2708	22
TF: 800-338-5387 ■ *Web:* www.crsjetspares.com						
CRS Onesource						
2803 Tamarack Rd PO Box 1984	Owensboro	KY	42302	270-684-1469	685-5696	297-11
TF: 800-264-0710 ■ *Web:* www.crsonesource.com						
CRS Reprocessing LLC						
9780 Ormsby Station Rd Suite 2500	Louisville	KY	40223	502-778-3600	778-3606	579
Web: www.crs-reprocessing.com						
CRSI (Concrete Reinforcing Steel Institute)						
933 N Plum Grove Rd	Schaumburg	IL	60173	847-517-1200	517-1206	49-3
Web: www.crsi.org						
CRST International Inc						
3930 16th Ave SW PO Box 68	Cedar Rapids	IA	52406	800-736-2778		780
TF: 800-736-2778 ■ *Web:* www.crst.com						
CR-T 116 Mtn Way Dr	Orem	UT	84058	801-222-0930		180
Web: www.cr-t.com						
CRT Custom Products Inc						
7532 Hickory Hills Ct	Whites Creek	TN	37189	615-876-5490		761
TF: 800-453-2533 ■ *Web:* www.crtcustomproducts.com						
CRT Investment Banking LLC						
262 Harbor Dr	Stamford	CT	06902	203-569-6800	569-6499	70
TF: 866-410-5872 ■ *Web:* www.crtllc.com						
CRT Systems Inc 742 Anderson Rd N	Rock Hill	SC	29730	803-327-9030		177
CRU Acquisitions Group LLC						
1000 SE Tech Ctr Dr Ste 160	Vancouver	WA	98683	360-816-1800		173-8
TF: 800-260-9800 ■ *Web:* www.cru-inc.com						
Cru Cafe 18 Pinckney St	Charleston	SC	29401	843-534-2434		671
Web: www.crucafe.com						
Cru Solutions Inc						
7261 Engle Rd Ste 305	Cleveland	OH	44130	440-891-0330		175
Web: www.crusolutions.com						
Crucial Interactive Inc						
21 Camden St 5th Fl	Toronto	ON	M5V1V2	416-645-0135		195
TF: 877-244-6562 ■ *Web:* www.crucialinteractive.com						
Crucial Technology						
3475 E Commercial Ct	Meridian	ID	83642	208-363-5790	363-5501	625
TF: 800-336-8915 ■ *Web:* www.crucial.com						
Crucible Materials Corp						
575 State Fair Blvd	Syracuse	NY	13209	315-487-4111	470-9358*	723
**Fax:* Sales ■ *TF:* 800-365-1180 ■ *Web:* www.crucible.com						
Cruise & Travel Store						
5435 Scotts Vly Dr	Scotts Valley	CA	95066	831-438-8844		772
Cruise America 11 W Hampton Ave	Mesa	AZ	85210	480-464-7300	464-7321	120
TF: 800-671-8042 ■ *Web:* www.cruiseamerica.com						
Cruise Brokers 2803 W Busch Blvd Ste 100	Tampa	FL	33618	813-288-9597	932-9650	771
TF: 800-409-1919 ■ *Web:* www.cruisebrokers.com						
Cruise Brothers, The						
950 Wellington Ave	Cranston	RI	02910	800-827-7779		772
TF: 800-827-7779 ■ *Web:* www.cruisebrothers.com						
Cruise Concepts						
1329 Eniswood Pkwy	Palm Harbor	FL	34683	727-784-7245		771
TF: 800-752-7963 ■ *Web:* www.cruiseconcepts.com						
Cruise Connection LLC						
7932 N Oak Ste 210	Kansas City	MO	64118	816-420-8688	420-8667	771
TF: 800-572-0004 ■ *Web:* www.cruiseconnectionllc.com						
Cruise Connections Inc						
3411 Healy Dr Ste D	Winston-Salem	NC	27103	800-248-7447		771
TF: 800-248-7447 ■ *Web:* cruisedriveflystay.com						
Cruise Deals.com						
11111 Carmel Commons Blvd Ste 210	Charlotte	NC	28226	704-542-6414		772
TF: 800-668-6414 ■ *Web:* www.cruisedeals.com						
Cruise Industry News						
441 Lexington Ave Ste 809	New York	NY	10017	212-986-1025	986-1033	531-13
Web: www.cruiseindustrynews.com						
Cruise Lines International Assn (CLIA)						
1201 F St NW Ste 250	Washington	DC	20004	754-224-2200		48-23
TF: 855-444-2542 ■ *Web:* www.cruising.org						
Cruise People Inc						
10191 W Sample Rd Ste 215	Coral Springs	FL	33065	954-753-0069	340-1968	771
TF: 800-642-2469 ■ *Web:* www.cruisepeople.com						
Cruise People Ltd						
1252 Lawrence Ave E Ste 210	Don Mills	ON	M3A1C3	416-444-2410		771
TF: 800-268-6523 ■ *Web:* cruisepeople.com						
Cruise Shop, The						
700 Pasquinelli Dr Ste C	Westmont	IL	60559	630-325-7447	321-1669	771
TF: 800-622-6456 ■ *Web:* vikingtvl.com						
Cruise Specialists Inc						
221 First Ave W Ste 210	Seattle	WA	98119	206-285-5600		771
Web: cruisespecialists.com						
Cruise Travel Magazine						
990 Grove St Ste 400	Evanston	IL	60201	847-491-6440	491-0459	457-22
TF: 800-347-7707 ■ *Web:* cruisetravelmag.com						
Cruise Vacation Ctr						
2042 Central Pk Ave	Yonkers	NY	10710	800-803-7245	337-8672*	771
**Fax Area Code:* 914 ■ *TF:* 800-803-7245 ■ *Web:* www.cruisevacationcenter.com						
Cruise Web Inc						
3901 Calverton Blvd Ste 350	Calverton	MD	20705	240-487-0155		771
TF: 800-377-9383 ■ *Web:* www.cruiseweb.com						
Cruisecheapcom						
220 Congress Park Dr Ste 140	Delray Beach	FL	33445	561-243-2100		772
TF: 800-543-1915 ■ *Web:* www.cruisecheap.com						
CruiseOne Inc						
1201 W Cypress Creek Rd Ste 100	Fort Lauderdale	FL	33309	800-278-4731		772
TF: 800-278-4731 ■ *Web:* www.cruiseone.com						
Cruiser Rv LLC 7805 N State Rd 9	Howe	IN	46746	260-562-3500		120
Web: www.cruiserrv.com						
Cruises Inc						
1201 W Cypress Creek Rd Ste 100	Fort Lauderdale	FL	33309	888-282-1249		771
TF Cust Svc: 888-282-1249 ■ *Web:* www.cruisesinc.com						
Cruises.com 100 Fordham Rd Bldg C	Wilmington	MA	01887	800-288-6006		773
TF: 800-288-6006 ■ *Web:* www.cruises.com						
Cruising Gide Publications Inc						
1130 Pinehurst Rd Ste B	Dunedin	FL	34698	727-733-5322		5
TF: 800-330-9542 ■ *Web:* www.cruisingguides.com						
Cruising World Magazine						
55 Hammerlund Way	Middletown	RI	02842	401-845-5100	845-5180	457-4
Web: www.cruisingworld.com						
Crum & Forster Insurance Inc						
305 Madison Ave PO Box 1973	Morristown	NJ	07962	973-490-6600	490-6600*	391-4
**Fax:* Hum Res ■ *TF:* 800-690-5520 ■ *Web:* www.cfins.com						

	Phone	Fax	Class
Crum & Forster Pet Insurance Group 305 Madison Ave PO Box 1973 Morristown NJ 44706 *TF:* 800-807-6724 ■ *Web:* www.cfpetinsurance.com	800-807-6724		391-1
Crum Electric Supply Co 1165 W English Ave Casper WY 82601 *TF:* 800-726-2239 ■ *Web:* www.crum.com	307-266-1278	577-1312	246
Crump Insurance Services Inc 105 Eisenhower Pkwy Roseland NJ 07068 *TF:* 800-222-0087 ■ *Web:* crumplifeinsurance.com	973-461-2100		391-2
Crumpets 3920 Harry Wurzbach St San Antonio TX 78209 *Web:* www.crumpetsa.com	210-821-5600	821-5624	671
Crunch Brands 1 First Ave Bldg 34 Charlestown MA 02129 *Web:* crunchbrands.com	617-241-5553		195
Crunch Fitness International 220 W 19th St New York NY 10011 *TF:* 888-227-8624 ■ *Web:* www.crunch.com	212-370-0998		354
Crunchy Logistics 379 W Michigan St Ste 2000 Orlando FL 32801 *Web:* crunchy.co	407-476-2044		196
Crus Oil Inc 2260 SW Temple Salt Lake City UT 84115 *TF:* 800-658-8444 ■ *Web:* crusoil.com	801-466-8783		316
Crusader Paper Company Inc 350 Holt Rd North Andover MA 01845 **Fax Area Code:* 978 ■ *TF:* 800-421-0007 ■ *Web:* www.crusaderpaper.com	800-421-0007	794-1625*	554
Cruser & Mitchell LLP 275 Scientific Dr Norcross GA 30092 *Web:* cmlawfirm.com	404-881-2622		428
Crush Creative 1919 Empire Ave Burbank CA 91504 *Web:* www.crushcreative.com	818-842-1121		113
Crustacean 9646 Little Santa Monica Blvd Beverly Hills CA 90210 *Web:* houseofan.com	310-205-8990		671
Crustacean 1475 Polk St Ste 6 San Francisco CA 94109 *Web:* crustaceansf.com	415-776-2722		671
Crutchfield Corp 1 Crutchfield Pk Charlottesville VA 22911 *TF Sales:* 888-955 6000 ■ *Web:* www.crutchfield.com	434-817-1000		459
Crux, The 2216 E S St Anaheim CA 92806	714-563-2024		48-20
Cruz Ted (Sen R - TX) 404 Russell Bldg Washington DC 20510 *Web:* www.cruz.senate.gov	202-224-5922		342-2
CRV Inc 3407 Northeast Pkwy Ste 170 San Antonio TX 78218	210-828-8552	828-5042	175
CRW Assoc 16980 Via Tazon Ste 320 San Diego CA 92127	858-451-3030		256
Crw Engineering Group LLC 3940 Arctic Blvd Ste 300 Anchorage AK 99503 *Web:* www.crweng.com	907-562-3252		256
CRW Graphics Inc 9100 Pennsauken Hwy Pennsauken NJ 08110 *Web:* www.crwgraphics.com	856-662-9111		626
Crw Parts Inc 1211 68th St Baltimore MD 21237 *Web:* www.crwparts.com	410-866-3300		61
CRWI (Coalition for Responsible Waste Incineration) 1615 L St NW Ste 1350 Washington DC 20036 *Web:* www.crwi.org	202 452 1241		48-13
CRWRC (Christian Reformed World Relief Committee) 2850 Kalamazoo Ave SE Grand Rapids MI 49560 *TF:* 800-552-7972 ■ *Web:* www.worldrenew.net	616-241-1691	224-0806	48-5
Crydom Inc 2320 Paseo de las Americas Ste 201 San Diego CA 92154 *Web:* www.crydom.com	619-210-1550		203
Crye-Leike Inc 6525 N Quail Hollow Rd Memphis TN 38120 **Fax Area Code:* 901 ■ *TF:* 866-310-3102 ■ *Web:* www.crye-leike.com	866-310-3102	758-5641*	652
Cryobiology Inc 4830D Knightsbridge Blvd Columbus OH 43214 *TF:* 800-359-4375 ■ *Web:* www.cryobio.com	614-451-4375	451-5284	545
Cryogenic Experts Inc 531 Sandy Cir Oxnard CA 93036 *Web:* www.cexi.com	805-981-4500		743
Cryogenic Society of America Inc (CSA) 218 Lake St Oak Park IL 60302 *TF:* 800-426-2186 ■ *Web:* www.cryogenicsociety.org	708-383-6220	383-9337	49-19
Cryolife Inc 1655 Roberts Blvd NW Kennesaw GA 30144 *NYSE: CRY* ■ *TF:* 800-438-8285 ■ *Web:* www.cryolife.com	770-419-3355		85
Cryomagnetics Inc 1006 Alvin Weinberg Dr Oak Ridge TN 37830 *Web:* www.cryomagnetics.com	865-482-9551		295
Cryoquip Inc 25720 Jefferson Ave Murrieta CA 92562 *Web:* www.cryoquip.com	951-677-2060		357
Cryovac Food Packaging & Food Solutions 100 Rogers Bridge Rd Duncan SC 29334 *TF:* 800-391-5645 ■ *Web:* www.cryovac.com/en/default.aspx	800-391-5645		548
Crysler Animal Hospital 12440 E 40 Hwy Independence MO 64055 *Web:* www.crysleranimalhospital.com	816-358-2857		794
Crystal Beach Suites & Health Club 6985 Collins Ave Miami Beach FL 33141 *TF:* 888-643-4630 ■ *Web:* www.crystalbeachsuites.com	305-865-9555		379
Crystal Blanc 225 Gap Way Erlanger KY 41018 *TF:* 800-917-9173 ■ *Web:* www.jcharles.com	859-283-0039		362
Crystal Cabinet Works Inc 1100 Crystal Dr Princeton MN 55371 *Web:* www.ccworks.com	763-389-4187	389-5846	115
Crystal Communications Ltd 1525 Lakeville Dr Ste 230 Kingwood TX 77339 *TF:* 888-949-6603 ■ *Web:* www.crystalcomltd.com	281-361-5199		196
Crystal Cove State Park 8471 N Coast Hwy Laguna Beach CA 92651 *Web:* www.parks.ca.gov/default.asp?page_id=644	949-494-3539		565
Crystal Cruises Inc 11755 Wilshire Blvd Ste 900 Los Angeles CA 90025 *TF:* 800-446-6620 ■ *Web:* www.crystalcruises.com	310-785-9300		220
Crystal Engineering Solutions Inc 645 Executive Dr Troy MI 48083 *Web:* www.crystaleng.com	248-588-1390		261
Crystal Finishing Systems Inc 2610 Ross Ave Schofield WI 54476 *Web:* www.crystalfinishing.com	715-355-5351		481
Crystal Flash Limited Partnership 1754 Alpine Ave NW Grand Rapids MI 49504 *Web:* www.crystalflash.com	616-363-4851		579
Crystal Group Inc 850 Kacena Rd Hiawatha IA 52233 *TF:* 877-279-7863 ■ *Web:* www.crystalrugged.com	319-378-1636	393-2338	176
Crystal Inn 185 S State St Ste 1300 Salt Lake City UT 84111 *TF General:* 800-662-2525 ■ *Web:* www.crystalinns.com	801-320-7200	320-7201	379
Crystal Inn Salt Lake City Downtown 230 W 500 S Salt Lake City UT 84101 *TF:* 800-662-2525 ■ *Web:* crystalinns.com	801-328-4466	320-7201	379
Crystal Lake Chamber of Commerce 427 W Virginia St Crystal Lake IL 60014 *Web:* www.clchamber.com	815-459-1300	459-0243	139
Crystal Lake Public Library 126 W Paddock St Crystal Lake IL 60014 *TF:* 800-669-5556 ■ *Web:* www.crystallakelibrary.org	815-459-1687		434-3
Crystal Lake State Park 96 Bellwater Ave Barton VT 05822 *TF:* 888-409-7579 ■ *Web:* www.vtstateparks.com	802-525-6205		565
Crystal Lake State Recreation Area 7425 S US Hwy 281 Doniphan NE 68832 *Web:* outdoornebraska.gov	308-385-6210		565
Crystal McKenzie Inc 220 E 23rd St Ste 305 New York NY 10010 *Web:* www.cminyc.com	212-598-4567	598-4566	466
Crystal Media Networks 7201 Wisconsin Ave Ste 780 Bethesda MD 20814 *Web:* www.crystalmedianetworks.com	240-223-0850		644
Crystal Meth Anonymous (CMA) 4470 W Sunset Blvd Ste 107 PO Box 555 Los Angeles CA 90027 *TF:* 877-262-6691 ■ *Web:* www.crystalmeth.org	877-262-6691		48-21
Crystal Mountain Inc 33914 Crystal Mountain Blvd Enumclaw WA 98022 *Web:* crystalmountainresort.com	360-663-3050		378
Crystal Mountain Resort 12500 Crystal Mtn Dr Thompsonville MI 49683 *TF:* 800-968 7686 ■ *Web:* www.crystalmountain.com	231-378-2000	378-2998	669
Crystal River Archaeological State Park 3400 N Museum Pointe Crystal River FL 34428	352-795-3817		565
Crystal River Preserve State Park 3266 N Sailboat Ave Crystal River FL 34428 *TF:* 800-326-3521 ■ *Web:* www.floridastateparks.org/crystalriverpreserve	352-563-0450		565
Crystal Rock Holdings Inc 1050 Buckingham St Watertown CT 06795 *NYSE: AMEX* ■ *TF:* 800-525-0070 ■ *Web:* www.crystalrock.com	860-945-0661		80-2
Crystal Springs City Water Department 306 W Railroad Ave S Crystal Springs MS 39059 *Web:* www.crystalspringsmiss.com	601-892-4111		435
Crystal Steel Fabricators Inc 9317 Old Racetrack Rd Delmar DE 19940 *TF:* 800-310-5306 ■ *Web:* www.crystalsteel.com	302 846 0613		186
Crystal Technologies Group Inc 1566 Mcdaniel Dr West Chester PA 19380 *Web:* crystaltechnologies.com	610-430-2005		196
Crystal Thai 4819 First St N Arlington VA 22203 *Web:* www.crystalthai.com	703-522-1311		671
Crystal Valley Coop 721 W Humphrey PO Box 210 Lake Crystal MN 56055 *TF:* 800-622-2910 ■ *Web:* www.crystalvalley.coop	507-726-6455	726-6901	276
Crystal Wealth Management System Ltd 3385 Harvester Rd Ste 200 Burlington ON L7N3N2 *TF:* 877-299-2854 ■ *Web:* www.crystalwealth.com	905-332-4414		796
Crystallex International Corp 8 King St E Ste 1201 Toronto ON M5C1B5 *TF:* 800-738-1577 ■ *Web:* www.crystallex.com	416-203-2448	203-0099	502
Crystal-Like Plastics 21701 Plummer St Chatsworth CA 91311 *TF:* 800-554-6091 ■ *Web:* www.crystal-likeplastics.com	818-846-1818	846-0877	608
Crysteel Mfg Inc 52182 Ember Rd Lake Crystal MN 56055 *TF Orders:* 800-533-0494 ■ *Web:* www.crysteel.com	507-726-2728	726-2559	470
Crysteel Truck Equipment Inc 55248 Ember Rd Lake Crystal MN 56055 *TF General:* 800-722-0588 ■ *Web:* www.crysteeltruckequipment.com	800-722-0588		780
Crystek Crystals Corp 12730 Commonwealth Dr Fort Myers FL 33913 *TF:* 800-237-3061 ■ *Web:* www.crystek.com	239-561-3311	561-3311	253
Crystex Composites LLC 125 Clifton Blvd Clifton NJ 07011 *Web:* www.crystexllc.com	973-779-8866	779-2013	500
CS & P Technologies LP 18119 Telge Rd Cypress TX 77429 *TF:* 800-262-6103 ■ *Web:* www.csphouston.com	713-467-0869		641
CS Consulting Group LLC 11491 Raedene Way San Diego CA 92131 *Web:* www.csconsultinggroup.com	858-530-8250		196
Cs Illumination Inc 1210 Kestone Way Ste A&B Vista CA 92081 *TF:* 800-548-7533 ■ *Web:* csillumination.com	760-477-1244		362
CS Logistics Inc 11001 W Mitchell St Milwaukee WI 53214 *Web:* cslog.com	414-774-6322		546
CS McCrossan Inc PO Box 1240 Maple Grove MN 55311 *Web:* www.mccrossan.com	763-425-4167	425-1255	188-4
CS Mott Children's Hospital 1500 E Medical Ctr Dr Ann Arbor MI 48109 *TF:* 800-211-8181 ■ *Web:* www.mottchildren.org	734-936-4000	936-8571	374-1
CS Osborne & Company Inc 125 Jersey St Harrison NJ 07029 *TF:* 800-558-1033 ■ *Web:* www.csosborne.com	973-483-3232	484-3621	758
CS Packaging Inc 1620 Fullerton Ct Glendale Heights IL 60139 *Web:* cspackaging.com	630-690-1300		88
CS Solutions Inc 3440 Federal Dr Ste 100 Eagan MN 55122 *Web:* www.cssolutionsinc.com	651-603-8288		177
CS Wo & Sons Ltd 702 S Beretenia St Honolulu HI 96813 *Web:* www.cswo.com	808-543-5388		321
CS3 Technology 5272 S Lewis Ave Ste 100 Tulsa OK 74105 *Web:* www.crouchslavin.com	918-496-1600		174

	Phone	Fax	Class
CSA (Cryogenic Society of America Inc) 218 Lake St. .... Oak Park IL 60302 *TF:* 800-426-2186 ■ *Web:* www.cryogenicsociety.org	708-383-6220	383-9337	49-19
CSA Engineering Inc 2565 Leghorn St. .... Mountain View CA 94043 *Web:* www.csaengineering.com	650-210-9000		261
CSA Financial Corp 343 Commercial St. .... Boston MA 02109 *Web:* www.csafinancial.com	617-357-1700		216
CSA Group 178 Rexdale Blvd .... Toronto ON M9W1R3 *TF:* 800-463-6727 ■ *Web:* www.csagroup.org	416-747-4000		317
CSA Inc 2110 Powers Ferry Rd SE Ste 202 .... Atlanta GA 30339 *Web:* www.csaatl.com	770-955-3518	956-8748	178-5
CSAA (Central Station Alarm Assn) 8150 Leesburg Pk Ste 700 .... Vienna VA 22180 *Web:* www.csaaintl.org	703-242-4670	242-4675	49-3
CSAIL (Computer Science & Artificial Intelligence Laboratory) 32 Vassar St Bldg 32 .... Cambridge MA 02139 *Web:* www.csail.mit.edu	617-253-5851	258-8682	668
CSB Bancshares Inc 203 N Douglas .... Ellsworth KS 67439 *Web:* csbanc.com	785-472-3141		70
CSBA 1667 K St NW Ste 900 .... Washington DC 20006 *Web:* www.csbaonline.org	202-331-7990		194
CSBS (Conference of State Bank Supervisors) 1129 20th St NW 9th Fl .... Washington DC 20036 *Web:* www.csbs.org	202-296-2840	296-1928	49-7
Csbs Business Services Llc 200 Gary Rd .... Carrboro NC 27510 *Web:* www.csbsllc.com	919-932-7109		113
CSC (Curtis Steel Company) 6504 Hurst St .... Houston TX 77008 *TF:* 800-749-4621 ■ *Web:* www.curtissteelco.com	713-861-4621	861-9718	485
CSC Home & Hardware 1580 Earl L Core Rd .... Morgantown WV 26505 *Web:* www.wvcsc.com	304-292-1340		191-1
CSC Inc 1109 Court St .... Medford OR 97501 *Web:* www.medfab.com	541-779-1970		492
CSC Laboratories Inc 180 Westgate Dr .... Watsonville CA 95076 *Web:* www.csclabs.com	831-763-6931		544
CSCOS (C & S Companies) 499 Col Eileen Collins Blvd .... Syracuse NY 13212 *TF:* 877-277-6583 ■ *Web:* www.cscos.com	315-455-2000	455-9667	261
CSE Corp 600 Seco Rd .... Monroeville PA 15146 *TF:* 800-245-2224 ■ *Web:* www.csecorporation.com	412-856-9200	856-9203	678
CSE Inc 5400 S Wridge Dr .... New Berlin WI 53151 *Web:* www.csepromo.com	262-786-8400		5
CSF International Inc 1629 Barber Rd .... Sarasota FL 34240	941-379-0881		174
CSG (Council of State Governments) 2760 Research Pk Dr .... Lexington KY 40511 *TF Sales:* 800-800-1910 ■ *Web:* www.csg.org	859-244-8000	244-8001	49-7
CSG (Commodity Sourcing Group) 19730 Ralston St .... Detroit MI 48203	313-366-0660		463
CSG (Community Services Group) 320 Highland Dr PO Box 597 .... Mountville PA 17554 *TF:* 877-907-7970 ■ *Web:* csgonline.org	717-285-7121	285-2658	353
CSG Direct Inc 640 Maestro Dr Ste 100 .... Reno NV 89511 *Web:* www.csgdirect.com	775-852-9777		5
CSG Government Solutions Inc 180 N Stetson Ave Ste 3200 .... Chicago IL 60601 *Web:* www.csgdelivers.com	312-444-2760		463
CSG Professional Services Inc 734 NW 14th Ave .... Portland OR 97209 *Web:* csgpro.com	503-292-0859		177
CSG Systems International 9555 Maroon Cir .... Englewood CO 80112 *NASDAQ: CSGS* ■ *TF:* 800-579-1639 ■ *Web:* www.csgi.com	303-796-2850	200-3333	178-10
CSH Consulting Inc 18325 N Allied Way Ste 210 .... Phoenix AZ 85054 *TF:* 800-203-7981 ■ *Web:* go-impact.com	480-307-9000		260
C-Sharp Technologies Inc 4700 Coolbrook Dr .... Hilliard OH 43026 *Web:* www.c-sharp.com	614-668-7182		177
CSHL (Cold Spring Harbor Laboratory) 1 Bungtown Rd .... Cold Spring Harbor NY 11724 *Web:* www.cshl.edu	516-367-8800	367-8455	668
CSI (Christian Schools International) 3350 E Paris Ave SE .... Grand Rapids MI 49512 *TF:* 800-635-8288 ■ *Web:* www.csionline.org	616-957-1070	957-5022	49-5
CSI (Central States Indemnity Company of Omaha) 1212 N 96th St .... Omaha NE 68114 *TF:* 800-321-0102 ■ *Web:* www.csi-omaha.com	402-997-8000		391-5
CSI 2916 Annandale Rd .... Falls Church VA 22042 *Web:* csi2.com	703-205-0000		92
CSI Aviation Services Inc 3700 Rio Grand Blvd NW .... Albuquerque NM 87107 *TF:* 800-765-9464 ■ *Web:* csiaviation.com	505-761-9000		13
CSI Care Services Inc 432 First St PO Box 172 .... Eynon PA 18403 *Web:* www.casketshellsinc.com	570-876-2642	876-5613	134
CSI Compressor Systems Inc 3809 S FM 1788 .... Midland TX 79706 *Web:* www.csicompressco.com	432-563-1170		172
CSI Group Inc, The 11 Fairview Terr .... Paramus NJ 07652 *TF:* 800-461-3002 ■ *Web:* thecsigroup.com	201-587-1400		196
Csi Industries Inc 6910 W Ridge Rd .... Fairview PA 16415 *TF:* 800-937-9033 ■ *Web:* www.flo-bin.com	814-474-9353	474-5797	198
CSI International Inc 8120 State Rt 138 .... Williamsport OH 43164 *TF:* 800-795-4914 ■ *Web:* www.csi-international.com	740-420-5400	333-7335	178-12
CSI Latina Financial Inc 2100 Coral Way Ste 706 .... Miami FL 33145 *Web:* www.csilatina.com	305-860-1616		194
Csi Millwork 2800 Blacksmith Ln .... Kerrville TX 78028 *Web:* www.csimillwork.com	830-895-3800		115
Csi Recruiting 1905 Sherman St Ste 200 .... Denver CO 80203 *Web:* www.csirecruiting.com	303-996-0400		260
CSI Technologies LLC 2202 Oil Ctr Ct .... Houston TX 77073 *TF:* 800-259-5155 ■ *Web:* www.csi-tech.net	281-784-7990		261

	Phone	Fax	Class
CSI Worldwide Inc 40 Regency Plaza .... Glen Mills PA 19342 *TF:* 800-523-7118 ■ *Web:* www.csiworldwide.net	610-558-4500		184
CSJ Technologies Inc 7972 Tyler Blvd .... Mentor OH 44060 *Web:* www.csjtech.com	440-269-8915	269-8928	175
CSL Group 35 Village Rd ÿ3rd Fl .... Beverly MA 01949 *Web:* www.cslships.com/en	978-922-1300	922-1772	313
CSL Group Inc, The 759 Sq Victoria Sixth Fl .... Montreal QC H2Y2K3 *Web:* www.cslships.com/en/canada-steamship-lines	514-982-3800		312
Csl Plasma Inc 1100 N Miami Blvd Ste 613 .... Durham NC 27703 *Web:* www.cslplasma.com	919-530-1388		592
CSM (Cambridge Street Metal Corp) 82 Stevens St .... East Taunton MA 02718 *TF:* 800-254-7580 ■ *Web:* www.csmetal.net	508-822-2278	822-4667	492
CS&M Associates 500 Canal St .... New Orleans LA 70130 *Web:* www.sheratonneworleans.com	504-525-2500		378
CSM Capital Corp 625 Madison Ave 3rd Fl .... New York NY 10022 *Web:* www.csmcapitalcorp.com	212-400-9550		401
CSM Group Inc 444 W Michigan Ave Ste 100 .... Kalamazoo MI 49007 *Web:* www.csmgroup.com	269-746-5600		186
CSM Metal Fabricating & Engineering Inc 1800 S San Pedro St .... Los Angeles CA 90015 *TF:* 800-272-4806 ■ *Web:* www.csmworks.com	213-748-7321	749-5106	482
CSM Worldwide Inc 269 Sheffield St .... Mountainside NJ 07092 *Web:* www.csmworldwide.com	908-233-2882	233-1064	18
CSMC (Cedars-Sinai Medical Ctr) 8700 Beverly Blvd .... Los Angeles CA 90048 *TF:* 800-233-2771 ■ *Web:* cedars-sinai.edu	310-423-3277		374-3
CSN *West Charleston* 6375 W Charleston Blvd .... Las Vegas NV 89146 *Web:* www.csn.edu	702-651-5610		162
CSO (Chattanooga Symphony & Opera) 701 Broad St .... Chattanooga TN 37402 *Web:* chattanoogasymphony.org	423-267-8583	265-6520	573-3
CSO (Cheyenne Symphony Orchestra) 1904 Thomes Ave .... Cheyenne WY 82001 *Web:* www.cheyennesymphony.org	307-778-8561	634-7512	573-3
Cso Insights 36 Tamal Vista Blvd .... Corte Madera CA 94925 *Web:* www.csoinsights.com	415-924-3500		194
C-Solutions Inc 1900 Folsom St Ste 205 .... Boulder CO 80302 *Web:* www.gmsworks.com	303-786-9461		178-10
CSP Assoc Inc 55 Cambridge Pkwy Riverfront 2 .... Cambridge MA 02142 *Web:* www.cspassociates.com	617-225-2828		743
CSP Inc 43 Manning Rd .... Billerica MA 01821 *NASDAQ: CSPI* ■ *TF:* 800-325-3110 ■ *Web:* www.cspi.com	978-663-7598	663-0150	173-2
CSP Information Group Inc 300 S Riverside Plaza Ste 1600 .... Chicago IL 60606 *Web:* www.cspdailynews.com	312-876-0004		390
CSP Technologies 960 W Veterans Blvd .... Auburn AL 36832 *Web:* www.csptechnologies.com	334-887-8300		601
CSPA (Columbia Scholastic Press Assn) Columbia University 90 Morningside Dr Ste B01 .... New York NY 10027 *Web:* cspa.columbia.edu	212-854-9400	854-9401	48-11
C-SPAN (Cable Satellite Public Affairs Network) 400 N Capitol St NW Ste 650 .... Washington DC 20001 *Web:* www.c-span.org	202-737-3220		740
C-SPAN Extra 400 N Capitol St NW Ste 650 .... Washington DC 20001 *Web:* www.c-span.org	202-737-3220		740
C-SPAN3 400 N Capitol St NW Ste 650 .... Washington DC 20001 *Web:* www.c-span.org	202-737-3220		740
CSPI (Center for Science in the Public Interest) 1875 Connecticut Ave NW Ste 300 .... Washington DC 20009 *Web:* www.cspinet.org	202-332-9110	265-4954	49-19
CSR Enterprise Networks 155 Academy St .... Williamsport PA 17701 *Web:* www.csrinc.com	570-322-0590		180
CSRM (Cascade Steel Rolling Mills Inc) 3200 N Hwy 99 W PO Box 687 .... McMinnville OR 97128 *TF:* 800-283-2776 ■ *Web:* www.cascadesteel.com	503-472-4181	434-5739	723
CSRS (D+H CollateralGuard RC) 4126 Norland Ave Ste 200 .... Burnaby BC V5G3S8 *TF:* 866-873-9780 ■ *Web:* www.csrs.ca	604-637-4000	637-4001	635
Csrwire LLC 250 Albany St .... Springfield MA 01105 *Web:* csrwire.com	802-251-0110		530
CSS 10301 Democracy Ln Ste 300 .... Fairfax VA 22030 *TF:* 800-888-4612 ■ *Web:* www.css-dynamac.com	703-691-4612	691-4615	261
Cs&S Computer Systems Inc 1440 W University Dr .... Tempe AZ 85281 *TF:* 800-677-1997 ■ *Web:* www.css-computers.com	480-968-8585		196
CSS Industries Inc 1845 Walnut St Ste 800 .... Philadelphia PA 19103 *NYSE: CSS* ■ *Web:* www.cssindustries.com	215-569-9900	569-9979	637-10
CSS International Inc 115 River Landing Dr Daniel Island .... Charleston SC 29492 *TF:* 800-814-7705 ■ *Web:* www.cssus.com	800-814-7705		260
CSS Laboratories Inc 1641 McGaw Ave .... Irvine CA 92614 *TF:* 800-852-2680 ■ *Web:* www.csslabs.com	949-852-8161	852-0410	173-2
CSSA (Crop Science Society of America) 677 S Segoe Rd .... Madison WI 53711 *TF:* 800-755-2751 ■ *Web:* www.crops.org	608-273-8080	273-2021	48-2
CSSA (Communications Supply Service Assn) 5700 Murray St .... Little Rock AR 72209 *TF:* 800-252-2772 ■ *Web:* www.cssa.net	501-562-7666	562-7616	49-20
CSSC Inc 26 Mayfield Ave .... Edison NJ 08837	732-225-5555	626-6035	178-10
CSSI Inc 400 Virginia Ave SW Ste 210 .... Washington DC 20024 *Web:* www.cssiinc.com	202-863-2175		180
CSSS d'Antoine-Labelle 515 boul Dr Albiny-Paquette .... Mont-laurier QC J9L1K8 *Web:* www.csssal.org	819-623-6127		672

Phone | Fax | Class

CSSS du Lac des Deux-Montagnes
520 Boul Sauve .... Saint-Eustache QC J7R5B1 450-473-6811 473-6966 374-2
Web: www.moncsss.com

CST (Custom Sensors & Technologies)
14401 Princeton Ave....................... Moorpark CA 93021 805-552-3599 201
TF: 800-463-8134 ■ *Web:* www.cstsensors.com

Cst Data 10725 John Price Rd .... Charlotte NC 28273 704-927-3282 225
TF: 866-383-3282 ■ *Web:* cstdata.com

CST Technologies Inc
55 Northern Blvd Ste 200 .... Great Neck NY 11021 516-482-9001 482-0186 231
Web: www.cstti.com

CST/Berger Corp 255 W Fleming St .... Watseka IL 60970 815-432-5237 913-0049* 544
**Fax Area Code:* 800 ■ *TF:* 800-435-1859 ■ *Web:* www.cstberger.us

CSTE (Council of State & Territorial Epidemiologists)
2872 Woodcock Blvd Ste 303.................. Atlanta GA 30341 770-458-3811 458-8516 49-7
Web: www.cste.org

CSTM (Mexico Tourism Board)
225 N Michigan Ave Ste 1800 .... Chicago IL 60601 800-446-3942 775
TF General: 800-446-3942 ■ *Web:* www.visitmexico.com

Csubs 155 Chestnut Ridge Rd.................. Montvale NJ 07645 201-307-9900 96
Web: www.csubs.com

CSV Midstream Solutions Corp
Calgary Pl 2, 355 Fourth Ave SW Ste 700 .... Calgary AB T2P0J1 587-316-6900 316-6901 539
Web: www.csvmidstream.com

Csw Stuber Stroeh Engineering Group Inc
1310 Redwood Way Ste 220.................... Petaluma CA 94954 707-795-4764 256
Web: www.cswst2.com

CSWD (Council on Size & Weight Discrimination)
PO Box 305 .... Mount Marion NY 12456 845-679-1209 679-1206 48-17
Web: www.cswd.org

CSWE (Council on Social Work Education)
1701 Duke St Ste 200..................... Alexandria VA 22314 703-683-8080 683-8099 49-5
Web: www.cswe.org

CSX Corp 500 Water St 15th Fl.............. Jacksonville FL 32202 904-359-3200 185
NYSE: CSX ■ *TF:* 800 737-1663 ■ *Web:* csx.com

CSX Transportation Inc
500 Water St............................ Jacksonville FL 32202 904-359-3100 648
TF: 800-737-1663 ■ *Web:* www.csx.com

CT Consultants Inc 8150 Sterling Ct .... Mentor OH 44060 440-951-9000 951-7487 261
TF: 800-925-0988 ■ *Web:* www.ctconsultants.com

C&T Design & Equipment Company Inc
2750 Tobey Dr .... Indianapolis IN 46219 317-898-9602 406
TF: 800-966-3374 ■ *Web:* www.c-tdesign.com

Ct Gasket & Polymer Company Inc
12308 Cutten Rd........................... Houston TX 77066 800-299-1685 326
TF: 800-299-1685 ■ *Web:* www.ctgasket.com

CT Solutions Inc
12700 Fair Lakes Cir Ste 160.................. Fairfax VA 22033 703-289-1560 196
Web: www.ctsols.com

CTA (Chicago Transit Authority)
567 West Lake St .... Chicago IL 60661 312-664-7200 468
Web: www.transitchicago.com

CTA Acoustics Inc 100 CIA Blvd .... Corbin KY 40701 606-528-8050 528-0074 380
TF: 800-626-2930 ■ *Web:* www.ctaacoustics.com

CTA Architects Engineers
13 N 23rd St............................. Billings MT 59101 406-248-7455 261
Web: www.ctagroup.com

CTA Manufacturing Corp
263 Veterans Blvd.......................... Carlstadt NJ 07072 201-896-1000 896-1378 758
Web: www.ctatools.com

CTAA (Community Transportation Assn of America)
1341 G St NW 10th Fl.................... Washington DC 20005 202-628-1480 737-9197 49-21
TF: 800-891-0590 ■ *Web:* www.ctaa.org

CTAQ 1000 rue Raoul-Charette .... Joliette QC J6E8S6 450-755-4122 273
Web: www.intelia.com

CTB Corp 26327 Fallbrook Ave................. Wyoming MN 55092 651-462-3550 319-1
Web: www.ctbcorp.com

CTB Inc 611 N Higbee St PO Box 2000............ Milford IN 46542 574-658-4191 658-3471 273
TF: 800-261-8651 ■ *Web:* www.ctbinc.com

CTC International Group Inc
330 Clematis St Ste 220.............. West Palm Beach FL 33401 561-655-3111 693
Web: ctcintl.com

Cte Inc 30 Willow Springs Cir..................... York PA 17406 717-767-6636 488
Web: www.cte-inc.com

C-Team Systems Inc 38 Auriga Dr Unit 12......... Ottawa ON K2E8A5 613-727-8224 179
Web: www.cteam.ca

CTEC (Central Texas Electric Co-op Inc)
386 Friendship Ln PO Box 553............ Fredericksburg TX 78624 830-997-2126 245
TF General: 800-900-2832 ■ *Web:* www.ctec.coop

CTFA PAC (Cosmetic Toiletry & Fragrance Assn PAC)
1101 17th St NW Ste 300................. Washington DC 20036 202-331-1770 331-1969 615
TF: 800-227-5558 ■ *Web:* cir-safety.org

CTG (Computer Task Group Inc)
800 Delaware Ave........................... Buffalo NY 14209 716-882-8000 887-7464 180
OTC: CTG ■ *TF:* 800-992-5350 ■ *Web:* www.ctg.com

CTH Technologies Inc
18W 140 Butterfield Rd............... Oakbrook Terrace IL 60181 331-684-9700 177
Web: www.cthtech.com

CTI (Cooling Technology Institute)
2611 FM 1960 Rd W Ste A-101 .... Houston TX 77068 281-583-4087 537-1721 48-12
TF: 800-344-4866 ■ *Web:* www.cti.org

CTI & Assoc Inc 28001 Cabot Dr Ste 250............ Novi MI 48377 248-486-5100 256
Web: cticompanies.com

Cti Communication Technologies
18110 chesterfield airport rd.............. Chesterfield MO 63005 636-537-7200 224
Web: www.cti-stl.com

CTI Consultants Inc
13500 E Boundary Rd...................... Midlothian VA 23112 804-622-8630 256
Web: www.cti-consultants.com

CTI Consulting
9711 Washingtonian Blvd Ste 550 .... Gaithersburg MD 20878 301-528-8591 194
Web: www.countertech.com

CTI Inc 11105 Norrth Casa Grande Hwy .... Rillito AZ 85654 520-624-2348 682-3509 780
TF: 800-362-4952 ■ *Web:* www.cti-az.com

Cti Property Services
5916 Triangle Dr........................... Raleigh NC 27617 919-787-3789 776

CTJ (Citizens for Tax Justice)
1616 P St NW Ste 200-B .... Washington DC 20036 202-299-1066 299-1065 48-7
TF: 888-626-2622 ■ *Web:* www.ctj.org

CTL Aerospace Inc
5616 Spellmire Dr .... Cincinnati OH 45246 513-874-7900 874-2499 22
TF: 800 909-7616 ■ *Web:* www.ctlaerospace.com

Ctl Engineering Inc PO Box 44548 .... Columbus OH 43204 614-276-8123 261
Web: www.ctleng.com

CTL Inc 375 Bridgeport Ave..................... Shelton CT 06484 203-925-4266 177
Web: www.ctlinc.com

CTL/Thompson Inc 1971 W 12th Ave .... Denver CO 80204 303-825-0777 825-4252 261
Web: www.ctlthompson.com

CTLGroup 5400 Old OrchaRd Rd................. Skokie IL 60077 847-965-7500 965-6541 743
TF: 800-522-2285 ■ *Web:* www.ctlgroup.com

CTM Media Group Inc 11 Largo Dr S........... Stamford CT 06907 203-323-5161 5
Web: www.ctmmediagroup.com

CTMC (Central Texas Medical Ctr)
1301 Wonder World Dr.................... San Marcos TX 78666 512-353-8979 374-3
TF: 800-927-9004 ■ *Web:* www.ctmc.org

CTN (Christian Television Network Inc)
6922 142nd Ave N .... Largo FL 33771 727-535-5622 531-2497 738
TF: 800-716-7729 ■ *Web:* www.ctnonline.com

CTP (Center for the Study of Teaching & Policy)
University of Washington
100 Gerberding Hall PO Box 351265 .... Seattle WA 98195 206-221-4114 616-8158 668
Web: www.depts.washington.edu

CTP Corp 3750 Shelby St.................. Indianapolis IN 46227 317-787-1322 490
Web: www.tubeproc.com/ctp-corporation

CTRAC Computer Services Inc
16855 Foltz Pkwy .... Strongsville OH 44149 440-572-1000 572-3330 5

CTrends Inc 27142 Burbank.............. Foothill Ranch CA 92610 949-472-9050 179
TF: 800-437-7766 ■ *Web:* www.ctrends.com

CTS Capital Advisors LLC
7315 Wisconsin Ave Ste 500 E................ Bethesda MD 20814 240-482-3240 70
Web: www.ctsca.com

CTS Corp 905 W Blvd N .... Elkhart IN 46514 574-523-3800 293-6146 253
NYSE: CTS ■ *Web:* www.ctscorp.com

CTSF (Conservation Treaty Fund)
3705 CaRdiff Rd....................... Chevy Chase MD 20815 301-652-6390 48-13

CTSI (Continental Traffic Service Inc)
5100 Poplar Ave 15th Fl.................. Memphis TN 38137 901-766-1500 766-1520 311
TF: 888-836-5135 ■ *Web:* www.ctsi-global.com

CTV 80 Patina Rise SW .... Calgary AB T3H2W4 403-240-5600 240-5689 741-21
Web: calgary.ctvnews.ca

CTV 299 Queen St W .... Toronto ON M5V2Z5 416-384-5000 741
TF: 866-690-6179 ■ *Web:* www.ctv.ca

CTV (Chevron Technology Ventures)
6001 Bollinger Canyon Rd .... San Ramon CA 94583 925-842-1000 792
NYSE: CVX ■ *Web:* www.chevron.com/technologyventures

CTV Edmonton 18520 Stony Plain Rd NW....... Edmonton AB T5S1A8 780-483-3311 740

CTV-TV Ch 5 (CTV)
345 Graham Ave Ste 400 .... Winnipeg MB R3C5S6 204-788-3300 788-3399* 741-143
**Fax:* News Rm ■ *TF:* 800-461-1542 ■ *Web:* winnipeg.ctvnews.ca

CU America Financial Services
200 W 22nd St Ste 2800.................... Lombard IL 60148 630-620-5200 194
TF: 800-351-0449 ■ *Web:* www.cuamerica.com

CU Conferences
8711 Watson Rd Ste 200 .... St. Louis MO 63119 888-465-6010 387
TF: 888-465-6010 ■ *Web:* www.cuconferences.com

CU*Answers
6000 28th St SE Ste 100................. Grand Rapids MI 49546 616-285-5711 225
TF: 800-327-3478 ■ *Web:* www.cuanswers.com

CUB (Concerned United Birthparents Inc)
PO Box 503475 .... San Diego CA 92150 800-822-2777 712-3317* 48-21
**Fax Area Code:* 858 ■ *TF:* 800-822-2777 ■ *Web:* www.cubirthparents.org

CUD Energy Inc
5120 Woodway Dr Ste 10010.................. Houston TX 77056 713-677-0439 536
Web: www.cubenergyinc.com

Cub Foods 2612 S Broadway St.............. Alexandria MN 56308 320 762 1158 345
Web: www.cub.com/stores/view-store.1007697.html

Cub Foods Stores 421 S Third St............. Stillwater MN 55082 651-439-7200 345
Web: www.cub.com

Cuba 315 Lexington Ave .... New York NY 10016 212-689-7215 689-9073 784
TF General: 800-553-3210 ■ *Web:* un.org

Cuba Libre 2801 Pacific Ave.................. Atlantic City NJ 08401 609-348-6700 671
Web: www.cubalibrerestaurant.com

Cuba Libre Restaurant
10 S Second St......................... Philadelphia PA 19106 215-627-0666 627-6193 671
Web: www.cubalibrerestaurant.com

Cuba Rushford Central School 5476 Rt 305 .... Cuba NY 14727 585-968-2650 968-2651 685
Web: www.crcs.wnyric.org

Cuban American National Council
1223 SW Fourth St............................ Miami FL 33135 305-642-3484 642-9122 48-14
TF: 800-644-4223 ■ *Web:* www.cnc.org

Cubby's Inc 9230 Mormon Bridge Rd .... Omaha NE 68152 402-453-2468 453-4513 345
Web: www.cubbys.com

Cubeit Portable Storage Canada Inc
100 Canadian Rd .... Scarborough ON M1R4Z5 888-428-2348 111
TF: 888-428-2348 ■ *Web:* www.cubeit.ca

Cubex Inc 9794 Charlotte Hwy.................. Fort Mill SC 29707 803-547-0748 261
Web: cubexinc.com

Cubic Corp 9333 Balboa Ave .... San Diego CA 92123 858-277-6780 505-1523 703
NYSE: CUB ■ *TF:* 800-937-5449 ■ *Web:* www.cubic.com

Cubic Defense Systems
9333 Balboa Ave......................... San Diego CA 92123 858-277-6780 505-1524 703
TF: 800-937-5449 ■ *Web:* www.cubic.com

Cubic Designs Inc
5487 S Westridge Dr....................... New Berlin WI 53151 262-789-1966 480
Web: www.cubicdesigns.com

Cubic Energy Inc 9870 PLANO Rd .... Dallas TX 75238 972-686-0369 536
Web: www.cubicenergyinc.com

Cubic Transportation Systems Inc
5650 Kearny Mesa Rd...................... San Diego CA 92111 858-268-3100 292-9987 472
TF: 800-937-5449 ■ *Web:* www.cubic.com

Cubicles Office Environments
6221-A Yarrow Dr.......................... Carlsbad CA 92011 760-938-5572 597-0620 320
Web: www.coeoffice.com

Cubix Corp 2800 Lockheed Way............. Carson City NV 89706 775-888-1000 176
TF Sales: 800-829-0550 ■ *Web:* www.cubix.com

Phone | Fax | Class

Cubix Labs Inc
1875 K St NW Ste 453 4th FL. Washington DC 20006 866-978-2220 631
TF: 866-978-2220 ■ *Web:* www.socialcubix.com
Cubs' Ac 1950 S Industrial Hwy Ann Arbor MI 48104 734-665-4474 671
Cucina Forte 768 S Eigth St Philadelphia PA 19147 215-238-0778 671
Web: cucinaforte.com
Cudahy Patrick Inc
1 Sweet Apple-Wood Ln. Cudahy WI 53110 414-744-2000 744-4213 473
TF: 800-486-6900 ■ *Web:* www.patrickcudahy.com
Cudner & O'Connor Co 4035 W Kinzie St. Chicago IL 60624 773-826-0200 826-0477 388
Web: www.candocinks.com
CUE Inc 11 Leonberg Rd Cranberry Township PA 16066 724-772-5225 772-5280 600
TF: 800-283-4621 ■ *Web:* www.cue-inc.com
Cuellar Henry (Rep D - TX)
2209 Rayburn HOB. Washington DC 20515 202-225-1640 225-1641 342-2
Web: cuellar.house.gov
CUES (Credit Union Executives Society)
5510 Research Pk Dr Madison WI 53711 608-271-2664 271-2303 49-2
TF: 800-252-2664 ■ *Web:* www.cues.org
CUES Inc 3600 Rio Vista Ave Orlando FL 32805 407-849-0190 201
TF: 800-327-7791 ■ *Web:* www.cuesinc.com
Cuesta College PO Box 8106 San Luis Obispo CA 93403 805-546-3100 546-3975* 162
**Fax:* Admissions ■ *TF:* 877-732-0436 ■ *Web:* www.cuesta.edu
North County 2800 Buena Vista Dr Paso Robles CA 93446 805-591-6200 546-3152 162
Web: academic.cuesta.edu
CUI Global Inc 20050 SW 112th Ave. Tualatin OR 97062 503-612-2300 360-3
NASDAQ: CUI ■ *TF:* 800-275-4899 ■ *Web:* www.cuiglobal.com
Cuisinart 1 Cummings Pt Rd Stamford CT 06902 203-975-4609 975-4660 37
TF: 800-726-0190 ■ *Web:* www.cuisinart.com
Cuisine 670 Lothrop Rd Detroit MI 48202 313-872-5110 671
Web: www.cuisinerestaurant.com
Cuisine Magazine 2200 Grand Ave. Des Moines IA 50312 800-311-3995 457-11
TF: 800-311-3995 ■ *Web:* www.cuisineathome.com
Cuisine Solutions Inc
1501 Moran Rd Unit 100 Sterling VA 20166 703-270-2900 296-36
OTC: CUSI ■ *TF:* 888-285-4679 ■ *Web:* www.cuisinesolutions.com
Cuivre River Electric Co-op
1112 E Cherry St Troy MO 63379 636-528-8261 528-7696 245
TF: 800-392-3709 ■ *Web:* www.cuivre.com
Cuivre River State Park 678 State Rt 147 Troy MO 63379 636-528-7247 565
Web: www.mostateparks.com
Culberson Construction Inc
4500 Colony Rd Granbury TX 76048 817-573-3079 536
TF: 800-449-4366 ■ *Web:* www.ccincservices.com
Culberson County PO Box 158 Van Horn TX 79855 432-283-2058 283-9234 338
Web: www.co.culberson.tx.us
Culberson John (Rep R - TX)
2161 Rayburn HOB. Washington DC 20515 202-225-2571 225-4381 342-2
Web: culberson.house.gov
CULCAC (Credit Union Legislative Action Council of CUNA)
601 Pennsylvania Ave NW S Bldg Ste 600 Washington DC 20004 202-638-5777 638-7734 615
Web: cuna.org
Culinaire International
2100 Ross Ave Ste 3100. Dallas TX 75201 214-754-1880 299
Web: www.culinaireintl.com
Culinard-the Culinary Institute of Virginia College
436 Palisades Blvd Birmingham AL 35209 205-802-1200 163
Web: www.culinard.com
Culinarte Marketting Group LLC
808 Packerland Dr Green Bay WI 54303 920-498-3004 123
Web: www.bonewerksculinarte.com
Culinary Arts Museum at Johnson & Wales University
315 Harborside Blvd. Providence RI 02905 401-598-2805 520
TF: 800-745-5555 ■ *Web:* www.culinary.org
Culinary Depot Inc 2 Melnick Dr Monsey NY 10952 888-845-8200 406
TF: 888-845-8200 ■ *Web:* www.culinarydepotinc.com
Culinary Institute Alain & Marie LeNotre
7070 Allensby. Houston TX 77022 713-692-0077 163
TF: 888-536-6873 ■ *Web:* www.culinaryinstitute.edu
Culinary Institute of America
1946 Campus Dr Hyde Park NY 12538 845-452-9430 451-1068 163
TF Admissions: 800-285-4627 ■ *Web:* www.ciachef.edu
Culinary Institute of America at Greystone
2555 Main St Saint Helena CA 94574 707-967-1100 163
Web: www.ciachef.edu
Culinary Institute of Charleston
7000 Rivers Ave Charleston SC 29406 843-574-6111 163
TF: 877-349-7184 ■ *Web:* www.tridenttech.edu
Culinary Software Services Inc
1900 Folsom St Ste 210. Boulder CO 80302 303-447-3334 177
TF: 800-447-1466 ■ *Web:* www.culinarysoftware.com
Culinary Staffing Services
6363 Wilshire Blvd Ste 305 Los Angeles CA 90048 323-965-7582 260
Web: www.culinarystaffing.com
Cull Martin & Assoc Inc
320 N Jensen Rd Vestal NY 13850 607-722-3884 722-4264 317
Web: www.cullmartin.com
Cullen Coates & Assoc
173 Riviera Cir Larkspur CA 94939 415-945-9581 463
Web: www.cullencoates.com
Cullen/Frost Bankers Inc
100 W Houston St San Antonio TX 78205 210-220-4011 360-2
NYSE: CFR ■ *TF:* 800-562-6732 ■ *Web:* www.frostbank.com
Culligan International Co
9399 W Higgins Rd Ste 1100 Rosemont IL 60018 847-430-2800 806
TF: 800-285-5442 ■ *Web:* www.culligan.com
Cullinan Associates Inc
295 N Hubbards Ln 2nd Fl Louisville KY 40207 502-893-0300 401
TF: 800-611-4841 ■ *Web:* www.cullinan.com
Cullinan Properties Ltd
2020 W War Memorial Dr Ste 103 Peoria IL 61614 309-999-1700 653
Web: www.cullinanproperties.com
Cullman Area Chamber of Commerce
301 Second Ave SW Cullman AL 35055 256-734-0454 737-7443 139
TF: 800-313-5114 ■ *Web:* www.cullmanchamber.org
Cullman Cabinet & Supply Company Inc
1735 Childhaven Rd Cullman AL 35055 256-734-1540 115
Web: www.cullmancabinet.com

Phone | Fax | Class

Cullman Casting Corp
251 County Rd 490 Cullman AL 35055 256-735-0900 492
Web: www.cullmancasting.com
Cullman City School
301 First St NE Ste 100 Cullman AL 35055 256-734-2233 685
TF: 800-548-2547 ■ *Web:* www.cullmancats.net
Cullman County 500 Second Ave SW Cullman AL 35055 256-739-3530 338
Web: www.co.cullman.al.us
Cullman County Board of Education
PO Box 1590 Cullman AL 35056 256-734-2933 685
Web: www.ccboe.org
Cullman County Public Library System
200 Clark St NE Cullman AL 35055 256-734-1068 734-6902 434-3
TF: 800-648-3271 ■ *Web:* www.ccpls.com
Cullman Electric Cooperative
1749 Eva Rd NE Cullman AL 35055 256-737-3201 245
TF: 800-242-1806 ■ *Web:* www.cullmanec.com
Cullman Regional Medical Ctr (CRMC)
1912 Alabama Hwy 157 PO Box 1108 Cullman AL 35058 256-737-2000 737-2005 374-3
Web: cullmanregional.com
Cullum Mechanical Construction Inc
3325 Pacific Ave. North Charleston SC 29418 843-554-6645 189-10
TF: 800-251-6403 ■ *Web:* www.culluminc.com
Culp Construction Co
2320 S Main St. Salt Lake City UT 84115 801-486-2064 186
Web: www.culpco.com
Culp Inc 1823 Eastchester Dr High Point NC 27265 336-889-5161 745-1
NYSE: CFI ■ *Web:* www.culpinc.com
Culpeper Baptist Retirement Community
12425 Village Loop Culpeper VA 22701 540-825-2411 672
TF: 800-894-2411 ■ *Web:* culpeperretirement.org
Culpeper County 151 N Main St # 201 Culpeper VA 22701 540-727-3427 727-3460 338
Web: web.culpepercounty.gov
Culpeper County Library
271 Southgate Shopping Ctr Culpeper VA 22701 540-825-8691 434-3
Web: www2.youseemore.com/culpeper
Culpeper National Cemetery
305 US Ave. Culpeper VA 22701 540-825-0027 825-6684 136
TF: 800-827-1000 ■ *Web:* www.cem.va.gov/cems/nchp/culpeper.asp
Culpeper Wood Preservers Inc
15487 Braggs Corner Rd PO Box 1148 Culpeper VA 22701 800-817-6215 818
TF: 800-817-6215 ■ *Web:* www.culpeperwood.com
Culpepper & Company Inc 201 Haley Rd Ashland VA 23005 804-752-7171 345
Web: www.rrsfoodservice.com
Culpepper & Merriweather Circus
2588 E 2070 Rd Hugo OK 74743 580-326-8833 326-8866 149
Web: www.cmcircus.com
Culpepper & Terpening Inc
2980 S 25th St Fort Pierce FL 34981 772-464-3537 186
TF: 800-989-5525 ■ *Web:* www.ct-eng.com
Culpepper Investigations
Po Box 21594 El Sobrante CA 94820 510-243-9860 400
Cultural Ctr for Language School
3191 Coral Way Ste 114 Miami FL 33145 305-529-2257 443-8538 423
Web: www.cclsmiami.edu
Cultural Experiences Abroad (CEA)
2999 N 44th St Ste 200 Phoenix AZ 85018 480-557-7900 557-7926 760
TF: 800-266-4441 ■ *Web:* www.ceastudyabroad.com
Cultural Survival Inc
215 Prospect St Cambridge MA 02139 617-441-5400 441-5417 48-8
Web: www.culturalsurvival.org
Cultural Tourism DC
1250 H St NW Ste 1000 Washington DC 20005 202-661-7581 772
Web: www.culturaltourismdc.org
Culturalink Inc 922 E Wayne St South Bend IN 46617 574-233-3700 194
Culture Works 110 N Main St Ste 165 Dayton OH 45402 937-222-2787 181
Web: cultureworks.org
Culture22 Communications LLC
935B N Plum Grove Rd. Schaumburg IL 60173 847-517-9022 195
TF: 800-230-7429 ■ *Web:* www.culture22.com
Culver Academies 1300 Academy Rd. Culver IN 46511 574-842-7000 622
TF: 800-528-5837 ■ *Web:* www.culver.org
Culver Capital Group Inc
1600 Sunflower Ave Ste 120. Costa Mesa CA 92626 714-380-3000 691
Web: www.culvercapital.com
Culver City Chamber of Commerce
6000 Sepulveda Blvd Ste 1260. Culver City CA 90230 310-287-3850 139
Web: www.culvercitychamber.com
Culver City Unified School District (CCUSD)
4034 Irving Pl. Culver City CA 90232 310-842-4220 842-4205 685
TF: 855-446-2673 ■ *Web:* www.ccusd.org
Culver Duck Farms Inc PO Box 910 Middlebury IN 46540 574-825-9537 10-8
TF: 800-825-9225 ■ *Web:* www.culverduck.com
Culver Floor Covering Company Inc
2411 Ave X. Brooklyn NY 11235 718-332-3434 131
Web: www.culverfloors.org
Culver Franchising System Inc
1240 Water St. Prairie du Sac WI 53578 608-643-7980 643-7982 670
TF: 800-244-6227 ■ *Web:* www.culvers.com
Culver Glass Co
2619 NW Industrial St Portland OR 97210 503-226-2520 330
Web: www.culver-glass.com
Culver Studios
9336 W Washington Blvd Culver City CA 90232 310-202-1234 514
Web: www.theculverstudios.com
Culver-Newlin Inc Schl Furn
840 S Wanamaker Ave Ontario CA 91761 909-390-3715 320
TF: 800-564-3375 ■ *Web:* www.culver-newlin.com
Culwell & Son Inc 6319 Hillcrest Ave. Dallas TX 75205 214-522-7000 157-3
TF: 800-456-3412 ■ *Web:* www.culwell.com
Cumberland Architectural Millwork Inc
603 Davidson St. Nashville TN 37213 615-254-1710 499
Web: www.cumberlandmillwork.com
Cumberland Bay State Park
152 Cumberland Head Rd. Plattsburgh NY 12901 518-563-5240 565
Web: parks.ny.gov/parks/34
Cumberland Chrysler Ctr
1550 Interstate Dr Cookeville TN 38501 888-277-4902 57
TF: 888-277-4902 ■ *Web:* www.cumberlandchryslercenter.com

Name / Address	City	State	ZIP	Phone	Fax	Class
Cumberland County 164 W Broad St *Web:* www.co.cumberland.nj.us	Bridgeton	NJ	08302	856-453-2125		338
Cumberland County 601 Courthouse Sq PO Box 275 *Web:* cumberlandcountyclerk.com	Burkesville	KY	42717	270-864-3726	864-5884	338
Cumberland County 117 Dick St PO Box 1829 *Web:* www.co.cumberland.nc.us	Fayetteville	NC	28302	910-437-1921	678-7717	338
Cumberland County 142 Federal St Rm 102 *Web:* www.cumberlandcounty.org	Portland	ME	04101	207-871-8380	871-8292	338
Cumberland County 140 Courthouse Sq PO Box 146 *Web:* cumberlandco.org	Toledo	IL	62468	217-849-2631	849-2968	338
Cumberland County College 3322 College Dr *Fax: Admissions ■ *TF:* 800-792-8670 ■ *Web:* www.cccnj.net	Vineland	NJ	08360	856-691-8600	794-3368*	162
Cumberland County Library 800 E Commerce St *Web:* www.clueslibs.org	Bridgeton	NJ	08302	856-453-2210		434-3
Cumberland County Public Library 300 Maiden Ln *TF:* 866-488-7386 ■ *Web:* www.cumberland.lib.nc.us	Fayetteville	NC	28301	910-483-7727	486-5372	434-3
Cumberland Electric Membership Corp 1940 Madison St *TF:* 800-987-2362 ■ *Web:* www.cemc.org	Clarksville	TN	37043	931-645-2481		245
Cumberland Falls State Resort Park 7351 Hwy 90 *TF:* 800-325-0063 ■ *Web:* www.parks.ky.gov	Corbin	KY	40701	800-325-0063		565
Cumberland Furniture 321 Terminal St SW *TF:* 800-401-7877 ■ *Web:* www.cumberlandfurniture.com	Grand Rapids	MI	49548	800-401-7877		321
Cumberland Insurance Group 633 Shiloh Pike *Fax Area Code: 856 ■ *TF:* 800-232-6992 ■ *Web:* www.cumberlandgroup.com	Bridgeton	NJ	08302	800-232-6992	451-7564*	391-4
Cumberland Island National Seashore 101 Wheeler St *TF:* 877-860-6787 ■ *Web:* www.nps.gov	Saint Marys	GA	31558	912-882-4336	673-7747	564
Cumberland Lumber & Manufacturing Co 202 Red Rd	McMinnville	TN	37110	931-473-9542		683
Cumberland Mall 1000 Cumberland Mall *Web:* www.cumberlandmall.com	Atlanta	GA	30339	770-435-2206		460
Cumberland Medical Ctr (CMC) 421 S Main St *Web:* www.cmchealthcare.org	Crossville	TN	38555	931-484-9511		374-3
Cumberland Mountain State Park 24 Office Dr *Web:* www.state.tn.us	Crossville	TN	38555	931-484-6138		565
Cumberland Mutual Fire Insurance Co 633 Shiloh Pk *Fax Area Code: 856 ■ *TF:* 800-232-6992 ■ *Web:* www.cumberlandgroup.com	Bridgeton	NJ	08302	800-232-6992	451-7564*	391-4
Cumberland Optical Laboratory 806 Olympic St	Nashville	TN	37203	615-254-5868		542
Cumberland Packing Corp 2 Cumberland St *Web:* www.sweetnlow.com	Brooklyn	NY	11205	718-858-4200		296-38
Cumberland Private Wealth Management Inc 99 Yorkville Ave Ste 300 *TF:* 800-929-8296 ■ *Web:* www.cumberlandprivate.com	Toronto	ON	M5R3K5	416-929-1090		401
Cumberland Public Library 1464 Diamond Hill Rd *Web:* www.cumberlandlibrary.org	Cumberland	RI	02864	401-333-2552	334-0578	434-3
Cumberland Steel Div 4919 Grant Ave *Web:* www.cumberlandind.com	Cleveland	OH	44125	216-441-1800		492
Cumberland Times-News 19 Baltimore St *TF:* 800-742-8149 ■ *Web:* www.times-news.com	Cumberland	MD	21502	301-722-4600	722-5270	532-2
Cumberland Truck Parts 15 Sylmar Rd *TF:* 800-364-6995 ■ *Web:* www.cumberlandtruck.com	Nottingham	PA	19362	610-932-1152		54
Cumberland University 1 Cumberland Sq *TF:* 800-467-0562 ■ *Web:* www.cumberland.edu	Lebanon	TN	37087	615-444-2562	444-2569	166
Cumberland Valley Electric Inc 6219 N US Hwy 25 E *TF:* 800-513-2677 ■ *Web:* www.cumberlandvalley.coop	Gray	KY	40734	800-513-2677		245
Cumberland Wood Products Inc 275 Helenwood Detour Rd	Helenwood	TN	37755	423-569-6363		200
Cumbre Inc 3333 Concours Ste 5100 *TF:* 800-998-7986 ■ *Web:* www.cumbreinc.com	Ontario	CA	91764	909-484-2456	484-2491	390
Cuming Corp 225 Bodwell St *TF:* 800-432-6464 ■ *Web:* www.cumingcorp.com	Avon	MA	02322	508-580-2660		537
Cuming County 200 S Lincoln St Rm 202 *Web:* extension.unl.edu/statewide/cuming	West Point	NE	68788	402-372-6006		338
Cuming County Public Power District 500 S Main St *TF:* 877-572-2463 ■ *Web:* www.ccppd.com	West Point	NE	68788	402-372-2463	372-5832	245
Cummer Museum of Art & Gardens 829 Riverside Ave *Web:* www.cummermuseum.org	Jacksonville	FL	32204	904-356-6857	353-4101	520
Cumming-Forsyth County Chamber of Commerce 212 Kelly Mill Rd *Web:* www.cummingforsythchamber.org	Cumming	GA	30040	770-887-6461	781-8800	139
Cummings & Carroll PC 175 Great Neck Rd	Great Neck	NY	11021	516-482-3260		2
Cummings & Lockwood LLC 8000 Health Ctr Blvd Ste 300 *Web:* www.cl-law.com	Bonita Springs	FL	34135	239-947-8811		428
Cummings Co Inc 3500 Fairmount St Ste 504	Dallas	TX	75219	214-526-1772	665-9590	317
Cummings Elijah (Rep D - MD) 2163 Rayburn HOB *Web:* cummings.house.gov	Washington	DC	20515	202-225-4741	225-3178	342-2
Cummings Properties LLC 200 W Cummings Pk *Web:* www.meadowsestates.com	Woburn	MA	01801	781-935-8000		652
Cummings Signs 15 Century Blvd Ste 200 *TF:* 800-489-7446 ■ *Web:* www.cummingssigns.com	Nashville	TN	37214	800-489-7446		701

Name / Address	City	State	ZIP	Phone	Fax	Class
Cummings Veneers Inc 601 E Fourth St	New Albany	IN	47150	812-944-2269		613
Cummings Violich Inc 1750 Dayton Rd	Chico	CA	95928	530 894 6494		10-10
Cummins Aerospace 2200 E Orangethorpe Ave *Web:* www.cumminsaerospace.com	Anaheim	CA	92806	714-879-2800		529
Cummins Construction Company Inc 1420 W Chestnut Ave *TF:* 800-375-6001 ■ *Web:* www.cumminsasphalt.com	Enid	OK	73702	580-233-6000		188-4
Cummins Facility Services 5202 Marion Waldo Rd *TF:* 800-451-5629 ■ *Web:* www.cumminsfs.com	Prospect	OH	43342	740-726-9800		104
Cummins Family Produce Inc 2570 Eldridge Ave	Twin Falls	ID	83301	208-733-5371		11-1
Cummins Filtration 2931 Elm Hill Pike *Fax Area Code: 800 ■ *TF:* 800-777-7064 ■ *Web:* www.cumminsfiltration.com	Nashville	TN	37214	615-367-0040	999-8664*	60
Cummins Inc 500 Jackson St PO Box 3005 *NYSE: CMI* ■ *TF:* 800-343-7357 ■ *Web:* www.cummins.com	Columbus	IN	47201	812-377-5000	377-3334	262
Cummins Power Generation 1400 73rd Ave NE *Web:* www.cumminspower.com	Minneapolis	MN	55432	763-574-5000		518
Cummins-Allison Corp 852 Feehanville Dr *TF:* 800-786-5528 ■ *Web:* www.cumminsallison.com	Mount Prospect	IL	60056	847-299-9550	299-9550	111
Cumulus Media Inc 3280 Peachtree Rd NE Ste 2300 *TF:* 800-692-7753 ■ *Web:* www.cumulus.com	Atlanta	GA	30305	404-949-0700	949-0740	645-5
CUNA Mutual Group 5910 Mineral Pt Dr *TF:* 800-937-2644 ■ *Web:* www.cunamutual.com	Madison	WI	53705	608-238-5851		360-4
Cunard Line Ltd 24303 Town Ctr Dr Ste 200 *TF:* 800-728-6273 ■ *Web:* www.cunard.com	Valencia	CA	91355	661-753-1000		220
Cunetto House of Pasta 5453 Magnolia Ave *Web:* www.cunetto.com	Saint Louis	MO	63139	314-781-1135		671
Cunningham Brick Co Inc 701 N Main St *TF:* 800-672-6181	Lexington	NC	27292	336-248-8541	472-2404	150
Cunningham Distributing Inc 2015 Mills Ave	El Paso	TX	79901	915-533-6993		38
Cunningham Falls State Park 14039 Catoctin Hollow Rd *Web:* dnr.maryland.gov/publiclands/pages/western/cunningham.aspx	Thurmont	MD	21788	301-271-7574		565
Cunningham Lindsey Group Ltd 3030 Rocky Point Dr Ste 530 *Web:* www.cunninghamlindsey.com	Tampa	FL	33607	813-830-7100		390
Cunningham Manufacturing Co 318 S Webster St *TF:* 800-767-0038 ■ *Web:* www.cunninghamcylinders.com	Seattle	WA	98108	206-767-3713	762-3457	223
Cunningham Memorial Library 510 N 6 1/2 St *TF:* 800-851-4279 ■ *Web:* library.indstate.edu	Terre Haute	IN	47809	812-237-2580		434-6
Cunningham Pattern & Engineering Inc 4399 US 31 N PO Box 654 *Web:* server8.kproxy.com/servlet/redirect.srv/sruj/swytevqthgetbbjflmud/p1	Columbus	IN	47201	812-379-9571	379-9574	567
Cunningham-Limp 28970 Cabot Dr Ste 100 *Web:* www.cunninghamllmp.com	Novi	MI	48377	248 489 2300		685
CUNO Inc 400 Research Pkwy *TF:* 800-243-6894 ■ *Web:* www.3m.com	Meriden	CT	06450	203-237-5541	238-8701	386
CUNY (City University of New York) 535 E 80th St *TF:* 800-286-9937 ■ *Web:* www.cuny.edu	New York	NY	10075	212-997-2869	794-5397	786
Cuomo Andrew (D) NYS State Capitol Bldg *Web:* www.governor.ny.gov	Albany	NY	12224	518-474-8390		343
CUPA-HR (College & University Professional Assn for Hum Res) 1811 Commons Pt Dr *TF:* 877-287-2474 ■ *Web:* www.cupahr.org	Knoxville	TN	37932	865-637-7673	637-7674	49-5
Cupboard, The 1400 Union Ave *Web:* www.thecupboardrestaurant.com	Memphis	TN	38104	901-276-8015		671
Cupertino Chamber of Commerce 20455 Silverado Ave *TF:* 800-852-5711 ■ *Web:* cupertino-chamber.org	Cupertino	CA	95014	408-252-7054		139
Cupertino Courier 1095 The Alameda *Web:* www.mercurynews.com	San Jose	CA	95126	408-200-1000	200-1013	532-4
Cupertino Electric Inc 1132 N Seventh St *Web:* www.cei.com	San Jose	CA	95112	408-808-8000	275-8575	189-4
Cupertino Inn 10889 N De Anza Blvd *TF:* 800-222-4828 ■ *Web:* m.cupertinoinn.com	Cupertino	CA	95014	408-996-7700		707
Cupid Foundations Inc 475 Pk Ave S *TF:* 877-649-5283 ■ *Web:* cupidintimates.com	New York	NY	10016	212-686-6224	481-9357	155-18
Cupini's Fresh Pasta & Panini 1809 Westport Rd *Web:* www.cupinis.com	Kansas City	MO	64111	816-753-7662		671
Cupric Canyon Capital LLC 7373 E Doubletree Ranch Rd Ste A-180 *Web:* www.cupriccanyon.com	Scottsdale	AZ	85258	480-607-6771		787
Cura Hospitality Inc 2970 Corporate Court Ste 5 *TF:* 800-319-8862 ■ *Web:* www.curahospitality.com	Orefield	PA	18069	610-530-7300		196
CuraFlo British Columbia Ltd 7436 Fraser Park Dr *Web:* www.curaflobc.com	Burnaby	BC	V5J5B9	604-298-7278		481
Curatel LLC 1605 W Olympic Blvd Ste 800 *TF:* 866-287-2366 ■ *Web:* www.curatel.com	Los Angeles	CA	90015	866-287-2366		387
Curb Records 48 Music Sq E *TF:* 800-484-2038 ■ *Web:* www.curb.com	Nashville	TN	37203	615-321-5080		657
Curbell Inc 7 Cobham Dr *Web:* www.curbell.com	Orchard Park	NY	14127	716-667-3377		608
Curbelo Carlos (Rep R - FL) 1404 Longworth HOB *Web:* curbelo.house.gov	Washington	DC	20515	202-225-2778		342-2
Curbstone Financial Management Corp 741 Chestnut St *Web:* www.curbstonefinancial.com	Manchester	NH	03104	603-624-8462		194

	Phone	Fax	Class
Curecanti National Recreation Area 102 Elk Creek ... Gunnison CO 81230 *TF:* 866-713-9688 ■ *Web:* www.nps.gov/cure	970-641-2337	641-3127	564
CureSearch for Children's Cancer 4600 East-West Hwy Ste 600 ... Bethesda MD 20814 *TF:* 800-458-6223 ■ *Web:* www.curesearch.org	301-718-0047		668
Curian Capital LLC 7601 Technology Way ... Denver CO 80237 *Web:* www.curian.com	303-846-3800		528
Curie Metropolitan High School 4959 S Archer Ave ... Chicago IL 60632 *Web:* curiehs.org	773-535-2100		685
Curiosities Greeting Cards 21 Ashwood Ct ... Lancaster NY 14086 *Web:* www.curiosities.com	716-681-2801		130
Curious George Goes to WordsWorth 1 John F Kennedy St ... Cambridge MA 02138 *Web:* thecuriousgeorgestore.com	617-547-4500	547-4503	95
Curious Pictures Corp 440 Lafayette St Fl 5 ... New York NY 10003	212-674-1400		116
Curis Inc 4 Maguire Rd ... Lexington MA 02421 *NASDAQ: CRIS* ■ *Web:* www.curis.com	617-503-6500	503-6501	85
Curl Inc 201 Broadway 2nd Fl ... Cambridge MA 02142 *Web:* curl.com	617-761-1200		177
Curlew Lake Resources Inc 595 Howe St Ste 303 ... Vancouver BC V6C2T5 *Web:* www.curlew-lake.com	604-336-8613		536
Curlew Lake State Park 62 State Pk Rd ... Republic WA 99166 *Web:* www.parks.wa.gov	509-775-3592		565
Curra's Grill 614 E Oltorf St ... Austin TX 78704 *Web:* www.currasgrill.com	512-444-0012		671
Curran & Connors Inc 40 Adams Ave Ste 20 C ... Hauppauge NY 11788 *Web:* www.curran-connors.com	631-435-0400	435-0422	344
Curran Contracting Company Inc 286 Memorial Ct ... Crystal Lake IL 60014 *TF:* 800-229-9929 ■ *Web:* www.currancontracting.com	815-455-5100	455-7894	188-4
Curran Group Inc 286 Memorial Ct ... Crystal Lake IL 60014 *Web:* www.currangroup.com	815-455-5100	455-7894	188-4
Curran Investment Management 30 S Pearl St Omni Plaza 9th Fl ... Albany NY 12207 *TF:* 866-432-1246 ■ *Web:* www.curranllc.com	518-391-4246		401
Currenex Inc 1230 Ave of the Americas 18th Fl ... New York NY 10020 *Web:* www.currenex.com	212-340-1780		690
Current Analysis Inc 21335 Signal Hill Plaza Ste 200 ... Sterling VA 20164 *TF:* 877-787-8947 ■ *Web:* www.currentanalysis.com	703-404-9200	404-9300	178-1
Current Designs PO Box 247 ... Winona MN 55987 *Web:* www.cdkayak.com	507-454-5430	454-5448	710
Current House Productions LLC 3860 Via Del Rey ... Bonita Springs FL 34134 *Web:* chpadvertising.com	239-676-7658		511
Current Inc 30 Tyler St PO Box 120183 ... East Haven CT 06512 *TF:* 877-436-6542 ■ *Web:* www.currentcomposites.com	203-469-1337	467-8435	599
Current Medical Directions Inc 230 Pk Ave S ... New York NY 10003 *Web:* www.cmdny.com	212-614-6218	598-6909	94
Current Newspaper 6930 Carroll Ave Ste 350 ... Takoma Park MD 20912 *Web:* www.current.org	301-270-7240		532-3
Current USA Inc 1005 E Woodmen Rd ... Colorado Springs CO 80920 *TF Cust Svc:* 800-848-2848 ■ *Web:* www.currentcatalog.com	800-848-2848	993-3232	459
Current360 1324 E Washington St ... Louisville KY 40206 *Web:* current360.com	502-589-3567		5
Curriculum Assoc Inc 153 Rangeway Rd ... North Billerica MA 01862 *TF:* 800-225-0248 ■ *Web:* www.curriculumassociates.com	800-225-0248	225-0248	637-2
Curriculum Research & Development Group University of Hawaii 1776 University Ave ... Honolulu HI 96822 *Web:* manoa.hawaii.edu	808-956-7961	956-9486	668
Curriculum Technology LLC 3520 Seagate Way Ste 115 ... Oceanside CA 92056 *Web:* www.curriculumtechnology.com	760-295-0863		387
Currie Management Consultants Inc 292 Lincoln St ... Worcester MA 01605 *Web:* www.curriemanagement.com	508-752-9229		463
Currier Construction Inc 36 N 56th St ... Phoenix AZ 85034 *Web:* www.currierinc.com	602-274-4370		188
Currier Museum of Art 150 Ash St ... Manchester NH 03104 *TF:* 800-468-2553 ■ *Web:* www.currier.org	603-669-6144	669-7194	520
Curries Co 1502 12th St NW ... Mason City IA 50401 *Web:* www.curries.com	641-423-1334	424-8305	234
Currituck County 153 Courthouse Rd Ste 204 Ste 204 ... Currituck NC 27929 *Web:* www.co.currituck.nc.us	252-232-2075	232-3551	338
Currituck County Board of Education 2958 Caratoke Hwy ... Currituck NC 27929 *Web:* www.currituck.k12.nc.us	252-232-2223	232-3655	685
Curry College 1071 Blue Hill Ave ... Milton MA 02186 *TF:* 800-669-0686 ■ *Web:* www.curry.edu	617-333-2210	333-2114	166
Curry County 700 N Main St Ste 7 ... Clovis NM 88101 *TF:* 800-333-6438 ■ *Web:* currycounty.org	575-763-6016		338
Curry County 94235 Moore St Ste 125 ... Gold Beach OR 97444 *Web:* www.co.curry.or.us	541-247-3233	247-3436	338
Curt G Joa Inc 100 Crocker Ave PO Box 903 ... Sheboygan Falls WI 53085 *Web:* www.joa.com	920-467-6136	467-2924	556
Curt Manufacturing Inc 6208 Industrial Dr ... Eau Claire WI 54701 *Web:* www.curtmfg.com	715-831-8713		567
Curt Pringle & Associates LLC 1801 E Katella Ave Ste 1002 ... Anaheim CA 92805 *Web:* curtpringle.com	714-939-9070	939-9080	636
Curtain Call Costumes 333 E Seventh Ave ... York PA 17404 **Fax Area Code:* 800 ■ *TF:* 888-808-0801 ■ *Web:* www.curtaincallcostumes.com	717-852-6910	839-1039*	155-6
Curtain Wall Design & Consulting Inc 8070 Park Ln Ste 400 ... Dallas TX 75231 *Web:* cdc-usa.com	972-437-4200		261
Curtil 12 Betnr Industrial Dr ... Pittsfield MA 01201 *Web:* www.curtil.com	413-443-4481		604
Curtin & Heefner 250 N Pennsylvania ... Morrisville PA 19067 *TF:* 800-773-0680 ■ *Web:* www.curtinheefner.com	215-736-2521		428
Curtis 1105 Western Ave ... Cincinnati OH 45203 *Web:* www.curtisinc.com	513-621-8895		514
Curtis & Tompkins Ltd 2323 Fifth St ... Berkeley CA 94710 *TF:* 800-735-2929 ■ *Web:* curtisandtompkins.com	510-486-0900		743
Curtis 1000 Inc 1725 Breckinridge Pkwy Ste 500 ... Duluth GA 30096 **Fax Area Code:* 800 ■ *TF:* 877-287-8715 ■ *Web:* www.curtis1000.com	678-380-9095	944-8817*	263
Curtis Bay Energy 3200 Hawkins Pt Rd ... Baltimore MD 21226 *Web:* curtisbayenergy.com	410-354-3228	354-3591	804
Curtis Blakely & Company PC 2403 Judson Rd ... Longview TX 75605 *Web:* cbandco.com	903-758-0734		2
Curtis Circulation Company LLC 730 River Rd ... New Milford NJ 07646 *Web:* www.curtiscirc.com	201-634-7400		95
Curtis Contracting Inc 7481 Theron Rd ... West Point VA 23181 *Web:* www.curtiscontracting.net	804-843-4633		302
Curtis Dyna-Fog Ltd 135 Region S Dr ... Westfield IN 46074 **Fax Area Code:* 317 ■ *Web:* www.dynafog.com	678-688-5601	896-3788*	172
Curtis H Stout Inc 5110 Hollywood Ave ... Shreveport LA 71109 *Web:* www.colinx.com	318-636-7777		518
Curtis Industries Inc 2400 S 43rd St PO Box 343925 ... Milwaukee WI 53219 *TF:* 800-657-0853 ■ *Web:* www.curtisind.com	414-649-4200	649-4279	815
Curtis Industries LLC 111 Higgins St ... Worcester MA 01606 **Fax Area Code:* 508 ■ *TF:* 800-343-7676 ■ *Web:* curtisindustries.net	800-343-7676	854-3377*	516
Curtis Institute of Music 1726 Locust St ... Philadelphia PA 19103 *TF:* 800-640-4155 ■ *Web:* www.curtis.edu	215-893-5252	893-9065	166
Curtis Instruments Inc 200 Kisco Ave ... Mount Kisco NY 10549 *TF:* 800-777-3433 ■ *Web:* www.curtisinstruments.com	914-666-2971	666-2971	248
Curtis Liquor Stores Inc 790 Chief Justice Cushing Hwy ... Cohasset MA 02025 *Web:* www.curtisliquors.com	781-383-9800		443
Curtis M Phillips Ctr for the Performing Arts 3201 Hull Rd PO Box 112750 ... Gainesville FL 32611 *TF:* 800-905-2787 ■ *Web:* performingarts.ufl.edu	352-392-1900	392-3775	572
Curtis Machine Company Inc 2500 E Trl St ... Dodge City KS 67801 *TF:* 800-835-9166 ■ *Web:* www.curtismachine.com	620-227-7164		709
Curtis Media Group 3012 Highwoods Blvd Ste 200 ... Raleigh NC 27604	919-790-9392	882-1746	643
Curtis Metal Finishing Co 6645 Sims Dr ... Sterling Heights MI 48313 *Web:* www.curtismetal.com	586-939-2850		481
Curtis Miller Insurance Agency Inc 1800 Blizzard Dr ... Parkersburg WV 26101 *Web:* curtismillerins.com	304-485-6431		390
Curtis Packaging Corp 44 Berkshire Rd ... Sandy Hook CT 06482 *Web:* www.curtispackaging.com	203-426-5861	426-2684	101
Curtis Packing Co 2416 Randolph Ave ... Greensboro NC 27406 *TF:* 800-852-7890 ■ *Web:* www.curtispackingcompany.com	336-275-7684	275-1901	473
Curtis Restaurant Supply & Equipment Co 6577 E 40th St ... Tulsa OK 74145 *TF:* 800-766-2878 ■ *Web:* www.curtisequipment.com	918-622-7390	665-0990	300
Curtis Screw Company Inc 50 Thielman Dr ... Buffalo NY 14206	716-898-7800		621
Curtis Steel Company (CSC) 6504 Hurst St ... Houston TX 77008 *TF:* 800-749-4621 ■ *Web:* www.curtissteelco.com	713-861-4621	861-9718	485
Curtis, The 1405 Curtis St ... Denver CO 80202 *TF:* 800-525-6651 ■ *Web:* www.thecurtis.com	303-571-0300	825-4301	379
Curtiss Arlin Trucking Inc 582 SW First St Ste 1 ... Montevideo MN 56265	320-269-5581		780
Curtiss-Wright Corp 10 Waterview Blvd 2nd Fl ... Parsippany NJ 07054 *NYSE: CW* ■ *TF:* 855-449-0995 ■ *Web:* www.curtisswright.com	973-541-3700	541-3699	22
Curtiss-Wright Flight Systems 201 Old Boiling Springs Rd ... Shelby NC 28152 *Web:* www.curtisswright.com	704-481-1150		22
Curtiss-Wright Flow Control Corp 13925 Ballantyne Corporate Pl Ste 400 ... Charlotte NC 28277 *Web:* www.cwfc.com	704-869-4602		295
Curtiss-Wright Flow Control Target Rock Div 1966 Broadhollow Rd ... Farmingdale NY 11735 *Web:* www.curtisswright.com	631-293-3800		789
Curtis-Toledo Inc 1905 Kienlen Ave ... Saint Louis MO 63133 *TF:* 800-925-5431 ■ *Web:* us.fscurtis.com	314-383-1300	383-1300	172
Curved Glass Distributors Inc 72 Chapel St ... Derby CT 06418 *Web:* www.curvedglassdist.com	203-735-4665		54
Curwood Inc 2200 Badger Ave ... Oshkosh WI 54904	920-303-7300		599
Cusack Wholesale Meat Inc 301 SW 12th St ... Oklahoma City OK 73109 *TF:* 800-241-6328 ■ *Web:* www.cusackmeats.com	405-232-2114	232-2127	297-9
Cushing 420 W Huron St ... Chicago IL 60654 *Web:* www.cushingco.com	312-266-8228		627
Cushing Academy 39 School St PO Box 8000 ... Ashburnham MA 01430 *Web:* www.cushing.org	978-827-7000	827-6253	622
Cushing-Malloy Inc 1350 N Main St ... Ann Arbor MI 48104 *TF:* 888-295-7244 ■ *Web:* www.cushing-malloy.com	734-663-8554	663-5731	626

Name / Address	City	State	ZIP	Phone	Fax	Class
Cushman & Marden Inc 56 Pulaski St PO Box 3001 *Web:* www.cushmanandmarden.com	Peabody	MA	01960	978-532-1670	532-1670	34
Cushman & Wakefield Inc 1290 Ave of the Americas *Web:* www.cushmanwakefield.com	New York	NY	10014	212-841-7500	841-7867	652
Cushman School - Elementary School 592 NE 60th St *TF:* 800-435-7352 ■ *Web:* www.cushmanschool.org	Miami	FL	33137	305-757-1966		685
CUSO (Champaign-Urbana Symphony Orchestra) 701 Devonshire Dr Ste C-24 *Web:* www.cusymphony.org	Champaign	IL	61820	217-351-9139		573-3
Cusseta-Chattahoochee County Courthouse Annex 377 Broad St PO Box 299 *Web:* chattahoocheeclerkofcourt.com	Cusseta	GA	31805	706-989-3424	989-2005	338
Custer County PO Box 300 **Fax Area Code:* 580 ■ *Web:* custer.okcounties.org	Arapaho	OK	73620	405-522-0018	331-1131*	338
Custer County 431 S Tenth St *Web:* www.co.custer.ne.us	Broken Bow	NE	68822	308-872-5701		338
Custer County 801 E Main Ave *Web:* www.co.custer.id.us	Challis	ID	83226	208-879-2360	879-5246	338
Custer County 420 Mt Rushmore Rd Ste 6 *Web:* ujs.sd.gov	Custer	SD	57730	605-673-4816		338
Custer County 205 S Sixth St *Web:* www.custercountygov.com	Westcliffe	CO	81252	719-783-2441	783-2885	338
Custer Public Power District 625 E SE St PO Box 10 *TF:* 888-749-2453 ■ *Web:* www.custerpower.com	Broken Bow	NE	68822	308-872-2451	872-2378	245
Custer State Park 13329 US Hwy 16A *Web:* gfp.sd.gov	Custer	SD	57730	605-255-4515	255-4460	565
Custom Accents 1940 Lunt Ave *TF:* 888-553-6789 ■ *Web:* www.customaccents.com	Elk Grove Village	IL	60007	847-640-4725		608
Custom Air 5338 Pinkney Ave *TF:* 888-850-4507 ■ *Web:* www.customairinc.com	Sarasota	FL	34233	888-856-4507		610
Custom Air Products & Services Inc 35 Southbelt Industrial Dr *Web:* www.customairproducts.com	Houston	TX	77047	713-460-9009		454
Custom Aircraft Interiors 3701 Industry Ave *TF:* 800-423-2904 ■ *Web:* www.customaircraftinteriors.com	Lakewood	CA	90712	562-426-5098	490-0213	689
Custom Aluminum Products Inc 414 Div St **Fax Area Code:* 847 ■ *TF:* 800-745-6333 ■ *Web:* www.custom-aluminum.com	South Elgin	IL	60177	800-745-6333	741-2266*	485
Custom Automated Controls Inc 2019 Jefferson Terr *Web:* www.custautocont.com	New Iberia	LA	70560	337-369-1523		45
Custom Bldg Products 13001 Seal Beach Blvd *TF:* 800-272-8786 ■ *Web:* www.custombuildingproducts.com	Seal Beach	CA	90740	562-598-8808		3
Custom Bottle Inc 10 Great Hill Rd *Web:* www.custombottle.com	Naugatuck	CT	06770	203-723-6661		98
Custom Brackets 32 Alpha Pk *TF:* 800-530-2289 ■ *Web:* www.custombrackets.com	Cleveland	OH	44143	440-446-0819		454
Custom Builder Supply Company Inc PO Box 413 *Web:* www.custombuildersupply.com	Williamsburg	VA	23187	757-229-5150	253-7568	191-3
Custom Building Products Inc 8850 NW 79th Ave *Web:* www.custombuildingproducts.com	Medley	FL	33166	305-885-3444		182
Custom Business Forms Inc 210 Edge Pl *TF General:* 800-234-1221 ■ *Web:* www.cbfnet.com	Minneapolis	MN	55418	612-789-0002	789-6321	110
Custom Cable Corp 242 Butler St *TF:* 800-832-3600 ■ *Web:* www.customwireandcable.com	Westbury	NY	11590	516-334-3600		116
Custom Cable Industries Inc 3221 Cherry Palm Dr *TF:* 800-552-2232 ■ *Web:* www.inflightwave.com	Tampa	FL	33619	813-623-2232	623-3534	189-4
Custom Carbon Processing Inc 17310-106 Ave NW *Web:* www.customcarbonprocessing.com	Edmonton	AB	T5S1H9	780-443-4237	489-3935	580
Custom Chemicals Corp 30 Paul Kohner Pl	Elmwood Park	NJ	07407	201-791-2160		3
Custom Chrome Inc 155 E Main Ave Ste 150 *TF:* 800-729-3332 ■ *Web:* www.customchrome.com	Morgan Hill	CA	95037	408-778-0500		61
Custom Communications Inc 1661 Greenview Dr SW *Web:* www.custom-alarm.com	Rochester	MN	55902	507-288-5522		693
Custom Computer Specialists Inc (CCS) 70 Suffolk Ct *TF:* 800-598-8989 ■ *Web:* www.customtech.com	Hauppauge	NY	11788	631-864-6699	543-2512	180
Custom Consulting Associates LLC 1112 SW 118th Pl *Web:* www.cca-llc.net	Oklahoma City	OK	73170	405-691-3417		180
Custom Control Manufacturer of Kansas Inc 5601 Merriam Dr *Web:* www.customcontrolmfr.com	Merriam	KS	66203	913-722-0343		201
Custom Control Sensors Inc 21111 Plummer St *Web:* www.ccsdualsnap.com	Chatsworth	CA	91311	818-341-4610	709-0426	201
Custom Control Solutions Inc 8500 Fowler Ave *TF:* 800-219-9901 ■ *Web:* www.ccsinc-florida.com	Pensacola	FL	32534	850-473-8704		729
Custom Coolers LLC 5609 Azle Ave *TF:* 800-627-0488	Fort Worth	TX	76114	817-626-3737	626-1213	664
Custom Culinary 2505 S Finley Rd *Web:* www.customculinary.com	Lombard	IL	60148	630-928-4898		296-18
Custom Cylinders Inc 700 Industrial Dr Ste I *Web:* www.customcylinders.com	Cary	IL	60013	847-516-6467		641
Custom Direct Inc 715 E Irving Park Rd *Web:* www.customdirect.com	Roselle	IL	60172	630-529-1936		5
Custom Drapery Blinds & Shutters 3402 E T C Jester *TF:* 800-929-9211 ■ *Web:* www.cdbas.com	Houston	TX	77018	713-225-9211	227-0808	746
Custom Electronic Design & Installation Assn (CEDIA) 7150 Winton Dr Ste 300 *TF:* 800-669-5329 ■ *Web:* www.cedia.net	Indianapolis	IN	46268	317-328-4336	735-4012	49-19
Custom Engineering Co 2800 Mc Clelland Ave *Web:* www.customeng.com	Erie	PA	16510	814-898-2800		480
Custom Engineering Inc 12760 E US Hwy 40 *TF:* 800-795-1747 ■ *Web:* www.customengr.com	Independence	MO	64055	816-350-1473		261
Custom Environmental Services Inc 8041 N I 70 Frontage Rd Unit 11 *TF:* 800-310-7445 ■ *Web:* www.customsvcs.com	Arvada	CO	80002	303-423-9949		667
Custom Exhibits Corp 1830 N Indianwood Ave *TF:* 800-664-0309 ■ *Web:* www.customexhibits.com	Broken Arrow	OK	74012	918-250-2121		393
Custom Fiberglass Mfg Corp *Snugtop* 1711 Harbor Ave PO Box 121 *TF:* 800-768-4867 ■ *Web:* www.snugtop.com	Long Beach	CA	90813	562-432-5454	435-2992	120
Custom Global Logistics LLC 317 West Lake St *TF:* 800-446-8336 ■ *Web:* www.customgl.com	Northlake	IL	60164	800-446-8336		314
Custom Helicopters Ltd 401 Helicopter Dr *Web:* www.customheli.com	St. Andrews	MB	R1A3P7	204-338-7953		13
Custom Hotel 8639 Lincoln Blvd *TF:* 877-287-8601 ■ *Web:* www.jdvhotels.com	Los Angeles	CA	90045	310-645-0400		379
Custom Industries Inc 215 Aloe Rd	Greensboro	NC	27409	336-299-2885		744
Custom Learning Designs Inc 375 Concord Ave *TF:* 800-321-6607 ■ *Web:* www.cldinc.com	Belmont	MA	02478	617-489-1702		242
Custom Magnetics Inc 801 W Main St *Web:* www.custommag.com	North Manchester	IN	46962	260-982-8508		767
Custom Management Group LLC 154 Hansen Rd *Web:* www.custommanagement.com	Charlottesville	VA	22911	434-971-4788	977-1856	47
Custom Metal Crafters Inc 815 N Mountain Rd *Web:* www.custom-metal.com	Newington	CT	06111	860-953-4210	953-1746	594
Custom Metal Fabricators Inc 7601 Whitepine Rd Chesterfield Airport Ind Pk *TF:* 800-220-4084 ■ *Web:* www.custommetalfabricators.com	North Chesterfield	VA	23237	800-220-4084		697
Custom Metalcraft Inc 2332 E Division PO Box 10587 *Web:* www.custom-metalcraft.com	Springfield	MO	65808	417-862-0707		697
Custom Millwork Inc 2298 N Second St *Web:* www.custommillworkinc.com	North St Paul	MN	55109	651-770-2356		499
Custom Mold Engineering Inc 9780 S Franklin Dr *TF:* 800-448-2005 ■ *Web:* www.custommold.com	Franklin	WI	53132	414-421-5444		757
Custom Molded Products LLC 92 Grant St Ste A *Web:* www.custommolded.com	Wilmington	OH	45177	937-382-1070		596
Custom Pack Inc 662 Exton Cmns *TF:* 800-722-7005 ■ *Web:* www.custompackinc.com	Exton	PA	19341	610-321-2525	321-2526	601
Custom Packaging Inc 1315 W Baddour Pkwy *Web:* www.custompack.com	Lebanon	TN	37087	615-444-6025		100
Custom Paper Tubes Inc 15900 Industrial Pkwy *TF:* 800-343-8823 ■ *Web:* www.custompapertubes.com	Cleveland	OH	44135	216-362-2964	362-2980	125
Custom Pipe & Coupling Inc 10560 Fern St PO Box 978 *Web:* www.custompipe.com	Stanton	CA	90680	714-761-8801		595
Custom Plastics Inc 1940 Lunt Ave *Web:* www.customplasticsinc.com	Elk Grove Village	IL	60007	847-439-6770		596
Custom Poly Bag Inc 9465 Edison St NE *Web:* www.custompolybag.com	Alliance	OH	44601	330-935-2408		345
Custom Processing Services Inc 2 Birchmont Dr *TF:* 800-748-0563 ■ *Web:* www.customprocessingservices.com	Reading	PA	19606	610-779-7001		225
Custom Products of Litchfield Inc 1715 S Sibley Ave *TF:* 800-222-5463 ■ *Web:* www.cpcabs.com	Litchfield	MN	55355	320-693-3221		273
Custom Pultrusions Inc 1331 S Chillicothe Rd	Aurora	OH	44202	330-562-5201		599
Custom Roto Mold Inc 555 22nd St S *Web:* www.customrotomold.com	Benson	MN	56215	320-842-3357		596
Custom Sensors & Technologies (CST) 14401 Princeton Ave *TF:* 800-463-8134 ■ *Web:* www.cstsensors.com	Moorpark	CA	93021	805-552-3599		201
Custom Sensors & Technology 531 Axminister Dr *Web:* www.customsensors.com	Fenton	MO	63026	636-305-0666		419
Custom Stamping & Manufacturing Inc 4855 Hytech Dr	Carson City	NV	89706	503-238-3700		488
Custom Stone 2999 Teagarden St *Web:* www.customstoneusa.com	San Leandro	CA	94577	510-667-0099	667-0099	189-2
Custom Stud Inc 8415 220th St W *TF:* 800-394-9875 ■ *Web:* www.customstud.com	Lakeville	MN	55044	952-985-7000		351
Custom Systems & Controls 30 Main St Ste 6 *Web:* custom-sys.com	Ashland	MA	01721	508-879-4390		180
Custom Toll Free 10940 Wilshire Blvd 17th Fl *TF:* 800-287-8664 ■ *Web:* www.customtollfree.com	Los Angeles	CA	90024	800-933-3030		387
Custom Truck Accessories Inc 13408 Hwy 65 NE *TF:* 800-333-1282 ■ *Web:* www.customtruckaccess.com	Ham Lake	MN	55304	763-757-5326	757-5994	54
Custom Window Systems Inc 1900 SW 44th Ave *Web:* www.cws.cc	Ocala	FL	34474	352-368-6922		234
customedialabs 460 E Swedesford Rd Ste 2020 *Web:* www.customedialabs.com	Wayne	PA	19087	610-225-0350		7

	Phone	Fax	Class
Customer Communicator, The (TCC) 712 Main St Ste 187B........................Boonton NJ 07005 *TF:* 800-232-4317 ■ *Web:* www.customerservicegroup.com	973-265-2300	402-6056	531-2
Customer Elation Inc 9065 Lyndale Ave S ....Bloomington MN 55420 *Web:* www.customerelation.com	952-653-0801		195
Customer Group LLC, The 641 West Lake St ÿSuite 304 ....Chicago IL 60605 *TF:* 844-802-7867 ■ *Web:* www.customergroup.com	844-802-7867		463
Customer Insight Group Inc 6711 Secrest Cir.............................Arvada CO 80007 *Web:* www.customerinsightgroup.com	303-422-9758		449
Customer Magnetism Inc 2697 Intl Pkwy 1 Ste 201 ....Virginia Beach VA 23452 *TF:* 800-610-7265 ■ *Web:* www.customermagnetism.com	757-689-2875		7
Customer Paradigm Inc 5353 Manhattan Cir Ste 103....................Boulder CO 80303 *TF:* 888-772-0777 ■ *Web:* www.customerparadigm.com	303-499-9318		225
Customer Service Delivery Platform 15615 Alton Pkwy Ste 310......................Irvine CA 92618 *TF:* 888-741-2737 ■ *Web:* www.csdpcorp.com	888-741-2737		177
Customer Value Partners Inc 3701 Pender Dr Ste 200.......................Fairfax VA 22030 *Web:* www.cvpcorp.com	703-345-9100		317
CustomerVision Inc 515 N Second St ....Des Moines IA 50047	515-989-9900	989-2034	809
Customized Distribution Services Inc 20 Harry Shupe Blvd.........................Wharton NJ 07885 *Web:* www.cdslogistics.com	973-366-5090		803-1
Customized Energy Solutions Ltd 1528 Walnut St 22nd Fl ....Philadelphia PA 19102 *Web:* ces-ltd.com	215-875-9440		196
Customized Performance Inc 1342 Ridder Park Dr........................San Jose CA 95131 *TF:* 800-954-8258 ■ *Web:* www.custgroup.com	408-437-1720		104
Custom-Pak Inc 1131 Roosevelt St..............Clinton IA 52732 *Web:* www.custom-pak.com	563-242-1801	244-5362	199
Cut - to - Size Technology Inc 345 S Fairbank St...........................Addison IL 60101 *Web:* www.cuttosizetech.com	630-543-8328		683
Cut Flower Wholesale Inc 2122 Faulkner Rd NE ....Atlanta GA 30324 *Web:* www.cutflower.com	404-320-1619	634-7922	293
Cutco Corp 1116 E State St ....Olean NY 14760 *TF:* 800-828-0448 ■ *Web:* www.cutco.com	716-372-3111		222
Cutera Inc 3240 Bayshore Blvd .... Brisbane CA 94005 *NASDAQ: CUTR* ■ *TF:* 888-428-8372 ■ *Web:* www.cutera.com	415-657-5500	330-2444	476
Cuthbert Greenhouses Inc 4900 Hendron Rd.........................Groveport OH 43125 *TF:* 800-321-1939 ■ *Web:* www.cuthbertgreenhouse.com	614-836-3866	836-3767	369
Cut-Heal Animal Care Products Inc 923 S Cedar Hill Rd .... Cedar Hill TX 75104 **Fax Area Code:* 240 ■ *TF:* 800-288-4325	972-293-9700	597-2157*	584
Cutlass Capital LLC 229 Marlborough St..........Boston MA 02116 *Web:* www.cutlasscapital.com	617-867-0820		792
Cutler Associates Inc 43 Harvard St..........Worcester MA 01609 *Web:* cutlerdb.com	508-757-7500		186
Cutler Group LP 101 Montgomery St Ste 700............. San Francisco CA 94104 *Web:* www.cutlergrouplp.com	415-645-6745		690
Cutler Investment Counsel LLC 525 Bigham Knoll.......................Jacksonville OR 97530 *Web:* www.cutler.com	541-770-9000		401
Cutler Majestic Theatre at Emerson College 219 Tremont St.............................Boston MA 02116 *TF:* 888-627-7115 ■ *Web:* www.emerson.edu	617-824-8000	824-3209	572
Cutler Repaving Inc 921 E 27th St............Lawrence KS 66046 *Web:* www.cutlerrepaving.com	785-843-1524		188-4
Cutler-Dickerson Company Inc 507 College Ave.............................. Adrian MI 49221 *Web:* cutlerdickerson.com	517-265-5600		447
Cutlery & More LLC 135 Prairie Lake Rd ....East Dundee IL 60118 *TF:* 800-650-9866 ■ *Web:* www.cutleryandmore.com	800-650-9866		362
Cutten Realty Inc 2120 Campton Rd Ste C .... Eureka CA 95503 *TF:* 800-776-4458 ■ *Web:* cuttenrealty.com	707-445-8811		652
Cutter & Buck Inc 701 N 34th St Ste 400 .... Seattle WA 98103 *TF:* 800-713-7810 ■ *Web:* www.cutterbuck.com	888-338-9944		155-1
Cutter Aviation 2802 E Old Tower Rd ....Phoenix AZ 85034 *TF:* 800-234-5382 ■ *Web:* cutteraviation.com	602-273-1237	275-4010	24
Cutter Consortium 37 Broadway Ste 1.......... Arlington MA 02474 *Web:* www.cutter.com	781-648-8700	648-8707	531-3
Cutter Information Corp 37 Broadway Ste 1 .... Arlington MA 02474 *Web:* www.cutter.com	781-648-8700	648-8707	637-9
Cutter Lumber Products (CLP) 10 Rickenbacker Cir....................... Livermore CA 94551 *TF:* 800-433-3827 ■ *Web:* cutterlumber.com	925-443-5959	443-0648	551
Cutter's Crabhouse 2001 Western Ave............ Seattle WA 98121 *Web:* www.cuttersbayhouse.com	206-448-4884		671
Cutting Edge Countertops Inc 1300 Flagship Dr .... Perrysburg OH 43551 *TF:* 800-627-6115 ■ *Web:* www.cectops.com	419-873-9500		115
Cutting Edge Metal Fabrication Inc 220-A Tryon Rd .... Raleigh NC 27603 *Web:* www.cuttingedgemetal.com	919-865-1534		697
Cutting Edge Networked Storage 435 W Bradley Ave Ste C ....El Cajon CA 92020 *TF:* 800-257-1666 ■ *Web:* www.cuttedge.com	619-258-7800		177
Cutting Edge Products LLC 350 Turk Hill Pk .... Fairport NY 14450 *TF:* 800-889-4184 ■ *Web:* www.celasers.com	800-889-4184		476
Cuyahoga Community College *Eastern* 4250 Richmond Rd.............. Highland Hills OH 44122 **Fax:* Admissions ■ *TF:* 800-954-8742 ■ *Web:* www.tri-c.edu	216-987-2024	987-2214*	162
Metropolitan 2900 Community College Ave.............Cleveland OH 44115 *TF:* 800-954-8742 ■ *Web:* www.tri-c.edu	216-987-4200		162
Western 11000 Pleasant Valley Rd .... Parma OH 44130 **Fax:* Admissions ■ *TF:* 800-954-8742 ■ *Web:* www.tri-c.edu	216-987-2800	987-5071*	162
Cuyahoga County 1219 Ontario St ....Cleveland OH 44113 *TF:* 800-750-0750 ■ *Web:* www.cuyahogacounty.us	216-443-7010	443-5091	338
Cuyahoga County Public Library 2111 Snow Rd .... Parma OH 44134 *TF:* 800-749-5560 ■ *Web:* www.cuyahogalibrary.org	216-398-1800		434-3
Cuyahoga Falls Chamber of Commerce (CFCC) 151 Portage Trl Ste 1 .... Cuyahoga Falls OH 44221 *TF:* 800-248-4040 ■ *Web:* cfchamber.com	330-929-6756	929-4278	139
Cuyahoga Falls News-Press 1050 W Main St ....Kent OH 44240 *TF:* 800-560-9657 ■ *Web:* www.recordpub.com	330-541-9400		532-4
Cuyahoga Hills Juvenile Correctional Facility 4321 Green Rd .... Highland Hills OH 44128 *TF:* 800-872-3132 ■ *Web:* dys.ohio.gov	216-464-8200	464-3540	412
Cuyahoga Molded Plastics Corp 1265 Babbitt Rd ....Cleveland OH 44132 *TF:* 800-805-9549 ■ *Web:* www.cuyahogaplastics.com	216-261-2744	261-3537	604
Cuyahoga Valley National Park 15610 Vaughn Rd..........................Brecksville OH 44141 **Fax Area Code:* 440 ■ *TF:* 800-445-9667 ■ *Web:* www.nps.gov	216-524-1497	546-5989*	564
Cuyamaca College 900 Rancho San Diego Pkwy ....El Cajon CA 92019 **Fax:* Admissions ■ *TF:* 800-234-1597 ■ *Web:* www.cuyamaca.edu	619-660-4275	660-4575*	162
Cuyamaca Rancho State Park 13652 Hwy 79 ....Julian CA 92036 *TF:* 800-444-7275 ■ *Web:* www.parks.ca.gov/default.asp?page_id=667	760-765-0755	765-3021	565
Cuyuna Country State Recreation Area 307 Third St...............................Ironton MN 56455 *Web:* www.dnr.state.mn.us	218-546-5926	546-7369	565
Cv Holdings LLC 1030 Riverfront Ctr.......... Amsterdam NY 12010	518-627-0051		98
CV Ice Company Inc 83796 Date Ave............. Indio CA 92201	760-347-3529		380
CVA (Connecticut Valley Arms) 1685 Boggs Rd Ste 300 .... Duluth GA 30096 *TF:* 800-320-8767 ■ *Web:* www.cva.com	770-449-4687	242-8546	284
CVAC Systems Inc 43397 Business Park Dr D2 .... Temecula CA 92590 *TF:* 800-900-1713 ■ *Web:* www.cvacsystems.com	951-699-2086		250
CVB Financial Corp 701 N Haven Ave PO Box 51000 ....Ontario CA 91764 *NASDAQ: CVBF* ■ *TF:* 888-222-5432 ■ *Web:* www.cbbank.com	909-980-4030		360-2
CVC (Columbia Ventures Corp) 14301 SE First St Ste 110.................. Vancouver WA 98684 *Web:* www.colventures.com	360-816-1840		405
CVCertify Inc 1282 Auburn Grove Ln .... Reston VA 20194	703-662-1485		260
CVD Diamond Corp 2061 Piper Ln............. London ON N5V3S5 *TF:* 877-457-9903 ■ *Web:* www.cvddiamond.com	519-457-9903		481
CVD Equipment Corp 1860 Smithtown Ave................... Ronkonkoma NY 11779 *NASDAQ: CVV* ■ *Web:* www.cvdequipment.com	631-981-7081	981-7095	695
CVEA (Copper Valley Electric Assn Inc) Mile 187 Glenn Hwy PO Box 45.............Glennallen AK 99588 *TF:* 866-835-2832 ■ *Web:* www.cvea.org	907-822-3211	822-5586	245
Cvg International America Inc 7200 NW 19th St Ste 110.......................... Miami FL 33126	305-470-8100		385
Cvikota Company Inc, The 2031 32nd St S Ste 100 .... La Crosse WI 54601 *Web:* www.thebillingpros.com	608-788-8103		396
C-Ville Weekly 106 E Main St............. Charlottesville VA 22902 *Web:* www.c-ville.com	434-817-2749		532-5
CVMA (Canadian Veterinary Medical Assn) 339 Booth St.................................. Ottawa ON K1R7K1 *TF:* 800-567-2862 ■ *Web:* canadianveterinarians.net	613-236-1162	236-9681	49-8
CVMC (Central Vermont Medical Ctr) 130 Fisher Rd.................................Berlin VT 05602 *Web:* www.cvmc.org	802-371-4100		374-3
CVP Systems Inc 2518 Wisconsin Ave.................. Downers Grove IL 60515 *Web:* www.cvpsystems.com	630-852-1190		390
CVPH Medical Ctr (CPVH) 75 Beekman St .... Plattsburgh NY 12901 *Web:* www.cvph.org	518-561-2000	561-0881	374-3
CVS Corp 1 CVS Dr.......................Woonsocket RI 02895 **Fax:* Cust Svc ■ *TF Cust Svc:* 888-607-4287 ■ *Web:* www.cvs.com	401-765-1500	765-1500*	237
CVSP (Chuckawalla Valley State Prison) 19025 Wiley's Well Rd PO Box 2289 .... Blythe CA 92226 *Web:* cdcr.ca.gov	760-922-5300	922-6855	213
CW (College of Westchester) 325 Central Ave .... White Plains NY 10606 **Fax Area Code:* 914 ■ **Fax:* Admissions ■ *TF:* 800-660-7093 ■ *Web:* www.cw.edu	800-660-7093	948-5441*	800
CW Brabender Instruments Inc 50 E Wesley St ....South Hackensack NJ 07606 *Web:* www.cwbrabender.com	201-343-8425		407
CW Brower Inc 413 S Riverside Dr .... Modesto CA 95354	209-523-5447		345
CW Cole & Company Inc 2560 Rosemead Blvd .... South El Monte CA 91733 *Web:* www.colelighting.com	626-443-2473	443-9253	439
CW Driver General Contractors Inc 468 N Rosemead Blvd ....Pasadena CA 91107 *Web:* www.cwdriver.com	626-351-8800	351-8880	186
C&W Enterprises Inc 2522 SE Federal Hwy ....Stuart FL 34994 *TF:* 844-241-6442 ■ *Web:* www.cwnow.com	772-287-5215		175
CW Industries 130 James Way ....SoutHampton PA 18966 *Web:* www.cwind.com	215-355-7080	355-1088	729
CW Matthews Contracting Company Inc 1600 Kenview Dr .... Marietta GA 30061 *Web:* www.cwmatthews.com	770-422-7520		188-4
CW Network LLC, The 3300 Olive Ave........... Burbank CA 91505 *Web:* www.cwtv.com	818-977-2500		738
CW Ohio Inc 1209 Maple Ave.................Conneaut OH 44030 *TF:* 800-677-5801 ■ *Web:* www.cwohio.com	440-593-5800	593-4545	499
CW Plumbing & Design Inc 41683 Date St.................................Murrieta CA 92562	951-894-7703		189-10
CW Post Community Arboretum *Long Island University* 720 Northern Blvd .... Brookville NY 11548 *Web:* www.liu.edu	516-299-2000	299-3223	97

Company	Phone	Fax	Class
CW Seattle 1000 Dexter Ave N Ste 205 ... Seattle WA 98109 *TF:* 866-313-5789 ■ *Web:* cwseattle.cbslocal.com	206-441-1111	861-8915	741
CW Wright Construction Company Inc 11500 Iron Bridge Rd ... Chester VA 23831 *TF:* 800-769-6844 ■ *Web:* www.cwwright.com	804-768-1054	768-6057	188-10
CWA (Communications Workers of America) 501 Third St NW ... Washington DC 20001 *Web:* www.cwa-union.org	202-434-1100		414
CWB (Central West Ballet Co) 5039 Pendecost Dr Ste B2 ... Modesto CA 95356 *Web:* cwballet.org	209-576-8957	576-1308	573-1
CWB Maxium Financial 30 Vogell Rd Ste 1 ... Richmond Hill ON L4B3K6 *TF:* 800-379-5888 ■ *Web:* www.maxium.net	905-780-6150		569
CWB Property Management 5775 Perimeter Dr Ste 290 ... Dublin OH 43017 *Web:* www.cwbpm.com	614-793-2244		652
CWC Energy Services Corp 205 - Fifth Ave SW Bow Vly Sq II Ste 610 ... Calgary AB T2P2V7 *Web:* www.cwcenergyservices.com	403-264-2177		539
CWC Textron 1085 W Sherman Blvd ... Muskegon MI 49441 *TF:* 800-999-0853 ■ *Web:* www.cwctextron.com	231-733-1331		60
CWCVB (Wausau Central Wisconsin Convention & Visitors Bureau) 219 Jefferson St Ste B ... Wausau WI 54403 *TF:* 888-948-4748 ■ *Web:* www.visitwausau.com	715-355-8788	359-2306	206
CWF (Campaign for Working Families) PO Box 1222 ... Arlington VA 22206 *Web:* www.cwfpac.com	703-671-8800		615
CWF (Canadian Wildlife Federation) 350 Michael Cowpland Dr ... Kanata ON K2M2W1 *TF:* 800-563-9453 ■ *Web:* www.cwf-fcf.org	613-599-9594	599-4428	48-13
CWF (California Wellness Foundation) 6320 Canoga Ave Ste 1700 ... Woodland Hills CA 91367 *Web:* www.calwellness.org	818-702-1900	702-1999	303
CWI Gifts & Crafts 77 Cypress St SW ... Reynoldsburg OH 43068 *TF:* 800-666-5858 ■ *Web:* www.shopcwi.com	740-964-6210	964-6212	44
CWLA (Child Welfare League of America) 2345 Crystal Dr Ste 250 ... Arlington VA 22202 *Web:* www.cwla.org	202-688-4200		48-6
CWPS Inc 14120 A Sullyfield Cir ... Chantilly VA 20151 *TF:* 877-297-7472 ■ *Web:* www.cwps.com	877-297-7472		180
CWPT (Civil War Trust) 1331 H St NW Ste 1001 ... Washington DC 20005 *TF:* 888-606-1400 ■ *Web:* www.civilwar.org	202-367-1861	367-1865	48-13
CWR Mfg Corp 7000 Fly Rd ... Syracuse NY 13057 *TF:* 800-724-0311 ■ *Web:* www.cwronline.com	315-437-1032	437-1493	697
CWRA (Canadian Water Resources Assn) 9 Corvus Ct ... Ottawa ON K2E7Z4 *Web:* www.cwra.org	613-237-9363		48-13
CWRU (Case Western Reserve University School of Medicine) 2109 Adelbert Rd ... Cleveland OH 44106 *Web:* case.edu/medicine	216-368-3450	368-6011	167-2
CWS Consulting Group LLC 1005 Boylston St Ste 243 ... Newton Highlands MA 02461 *Web:* www.cwsgrp.com	617-314-6527	507-8560	463
CWU (Church Women United) 475 Riverside Dr Ste 243 ... New York NY 10115 *TF:* 800-298-5551 ■ *Web:* www.churchwomen.org	212-870-2347	870-2338	48-20
CWV (Carleton-Willard Village) 100 Old Billerica Rd ... Bedford MA 01730 *Web:* www.cwvillage.org	781-275-8700	275-5787	672
Cx Systems Inc 2381 Industrial Park Rd ... Lincolnton NC 28092 *Web:* www.cxsystemsinc.com	704-732-9432		567
CXM (Chicago Extruded Metals Co) 1601 S 54th Ave ... Cicero IL 60804 **Fax Area Code: 708* ■ *TF Cust Svc:* 800-323-8102 ■ *Web:* www.cxm.com	800-323-8102	780-3479*	485
CXR Larus Corp 894 Faulstich Ct ... San Jose CA 95112 *Web:* www.cxr.com	408-573-2700		248
CXT Inc 3808 N Sullivan Rd Bldg 7 ... Spokane WA 99216 *Web:* www.cxtinc.com	509-921-8766		183
CXtec 5404 S Bay Rd PO Box 4799 ... Syracuse NY 13212 *TF Orders:* 800-767-3282 ■ *Web:* www.cxtec.com	315-476-3000	455-1800	814
CYA Technologies Inc 4 Research Dr ... Shelton CT 06484	203-513-3111	513-3139	178-12
Cyan Worlds Inc 14617 N Newport Hwy ... Mead WA 99021 *Web:* cyan.com	509-468-0807	467-2209	178-6
Cyanotech Corp 73-4460 Queen Kaahumanu Hwy Ste 102 ... Kailua-Kona HI 96740 *NASDAQ: CYAN* ■ *TF Sales:* 800-453-1187 ■ *Web:* www.cyanotech.com	808-326-1353	329-4533	479
Cyber 360 Solutions Inc 1600 Providence Hwy Ste 15 ... Walpole MA 02081 *Web:* www.cyber360solutions.com	781-438-4380		631
Cyber Acoustics LLC 3109 NE 109th Ave ... Vancouver WA 98682 *Web:* www.cyberacoustics.com	360-883-0333		173-5
Cyber City Inc 224 W 30th St Rm 1100 ... New York NY 10001 *Web:* cybercityinc.com	212-633-0649		196
Cyber City Teleservices Ltd 401 Hackensack Ave ... Hackensack NJ 07601 *Web:* www.cctll.com	201-487-1616		393
Cyber Digital Inc 400 Oser Ave Ste 1650 ... Hauppauge NY 11788 *OTC: CYBD* ■ *Web:* www.cyberdigitalinc.com	631-231-1200	231-1446	735
Cyber Korp Inc 125 Fairfield Way Ste 380 ... Bloomingdale IL 60108 *TF:* 800-321-5586 ■ *Web:* www.cyberkorp.com	630-980-4416		180
Cyber Power Systems Inc 4241 12th Ave E Ste 400 ... Shakopee MN 55379 *TF:* 877-297-6937 ■ *Web:* www.cyberpowersystems.com	952-403-9500	403-0009	253
Cyber Press 3380 Viso Ct ... Santa Clara CA 95054	408-970-9200		627
Cyber Pro Systems Inc 1 World Trade Ctr Ste 2400 ... Long Beach CA 90831 *Web:* www.mdxnet.com	562-256-3800		225
Cyber Sytes 19981 Panama Cty Bch Pkwy ... Panama City Beach FL 32413 *TF:* 800-741-9519 ■ *Web:* www.cysy.com	850-233-5514		396
Cyber-Ark Software Inc 60 Wells Ave ... Newton MA 02459 *TF:* 888-808-9005 ■ *Web:* cyberark.com	617-965-1544		177
Cyberbest Technology Inc 604 Ctland St Ste 121 ... Orlando FL 32804 *TF:* 800-519-2983 ■ *Web:* www.cyberbesttech.com	407-732-6993		180
Cyberchrome Inc 3642 Main St ... Stone Ridge NY 12484 *Web:* cyberchromeusa.com	845-687-2671		177
CyberCoders Inc 6591 Irvine Ctr Dr Ste 200 ... Irvine CA 92618 *Web:* www.cybercoders.com	949-885-5151		193
CyberCore Technologies LLC 6605 Business Pkwy Meadowridge Business Pk ... Elkridge MD 21075 *Web:* www.cybercoretech.com	410-560-7177		180
Cyberdata Corp 3 Justin Ct ... Monterey CA 93940 *TF:* 800-363-8010 ■ *Web:* www.cyberdata.net	831-373-2601	373-4193	176
CyberData Inc 20 Max Ave ... Hicksville NY 11801 *Web:* cyberdata.com	516-942-8000	942-0800	39
Cybereason Inc 1 Broadway 15th Fl ... Cambridge MA 02142 *Web:* www.cybereason.com	781-768-6065		387
Cyberex 5900 Eastport Blvd ... Richmond VA 23231 *TF:* 800-238-5000 ■ *Web:* www.tnbpowersolutions.com	804-236-3300	236-3300	253
Cyberjaz Corp 2276 Todd Rd ... Aliquippa PA 15001 *Web:* www.cyberjaz.net	412-922-2000		180
CyberMark International Inc 2222 W Parkside Ln Ste 116 ... Phoenix AZ 85027 *TF:* 800-871-4130 ■ *Web:* www.cybermark.com	623-889-3380		177
Cybernetics Inc 111 Cybernetics Way ... Yorktown VA 23693 *Web:* www.cybernetics.com	757-833-9100	833-9300	173-8
Cyberonic Internet Communications Inc 544 Pleasant St ... Worcester MA 01602 *Web:* www.cyberonic.com	508-753-4545		225
Cyberonics Inc 100 Cyberonics Blvd The Cyberonics Bldg ... Houston TX 77058 *NASDAQ: CYBX* ■ *TF:* 800-332-1375 ■ *Web:* www.cyberonics.com	281-228-7262	218-9332	477
CyberOptics Corp 5900 Golden Hills Dr ... Minneapolis MN 55416 *NASDAQ: CYBE* ■ *TF Cust Svc:* 800-746-6315 ■ *Web:* www.cyberoptics.com	763-542-5000	542-5100	248
Cyber-Rain Inc 6345 Balboa Blvd Ste 230 ... Encino CA 91316 *TF:* 877-888-1452 ■ *Web:* www.cyber-rain.com	877-888-1452		407
Cybersearch Ltd 800 E Northwest Hwy Ste 950 ... Palatine IL 60074 *Web:* www.cybsearch.com	847-357-0200		196
Cybersoft 1958 Butler Pk Ste 100 ... Conshohocken PA 19428 *Web:* www.cybersoft.com	610-825-6785		180
Cybersoft North America Inc 1500 S Dairy Ashford St Ste 190 ... Houston TX 77077 *Web:* www.csnainc.com	281-752-0600		177
Cybersoft Technologies Inc 4422 Cypress Creek Pkwy Ste 400 ... Houston TX 77068 *Web:* www.cybersofttech.com	281-453-8500		180
Cyberspace Solutions LLC 12015 Lee Jackson Hwy Ste 400 ... Fairfax VA 22033 *Web:* www.cspacesol.com	703-574-4132	574-4964	225
CyberStaff America Ltd 253 W 35th St ... New York NY 10001	212-244-2300		721
Cybertech Systems & Software Inc 3401 Quebec St Ste 3600 ... Denver CO 80207 *Web:* www.cybertech.com	303-321-0592	321-0689	180
CyberThink Inc 1125 US Hwy 22 Ste 1 ... Bridgewater NJ 08807 *Web:* www.cyberthink.com	908-429-8008		177
Cybervillage Networkers 7773 Blueberry Hill Ln ... Ellicott City MD 21043 *TF:* 800-625-5468 ■ *Web:* www.cybernetworkers.com	410-579-1993		396
Cyberwolf Inc 1596 Pacheco St Ste 203 ... Santa Fe NM 87505 *Web:* www.cyberwolf.com	505-983-6463		177
Cyberwoven LLC 1523 Huger St Ste B ... Columbia SC 29201 *Web:* www.cyberwoven.com	803-376-8899		396
Cybex International Inc 10 Trotter Dr ... Medway MA 02053 *NASDAQ: CYBI* ■ *TF:* 888-462-9239 ■ *Web:* www.cybexintl.com	508-533-4300	533-5500	207
Cybrix Group 710 Oakfield Dr Ste 266 ... Brandon FL 33511 *Web:* www.cybrixgroup.com	813-630-2744		180
Cycle Country Access Corp 205 N Depot St PO Box 107 ... Fox Lake WI 53933 *TF Sales:* 800-841-2222 ■ *Web:* www.cyclecountry.com	800-841-2222		29
Cycle Shack Inc 1104 San Mateo Ave ... South San Francisco CA 94080	650-583-7014	583-9154	517
Cycle Systems Inc 2580 Broadway SW ... Roanoke VA 24014	540-981-1211		686
Cycle World Magazine 1499 Monrovia Ave ... Newport Beach CA 92663 *TF:* 800-456-3084 ■ *Web:* www.cycleworld.com	949-720-5300		457-3
Cycle-safe Inc 5211 Cascade Rd SE Ste 210 ... Grand Rapids MI 49546 *TF:* 888-950-6531 ■ *Web:* cyclesafe.com	616-954-9977		711
Cycle-Tex Inc 702 S Thornton Ave # 101 ... Dalton GA 30720 *TF:* 800-960-1116 ■ *Web:* www.cycletex.com	706-226-1116		660
Cyclics Corp 2135 Technology Dr ... Schenectady NY 12308 *Web:* www.cyclics.com	518-344-5359		601
Cyclonaire Corp 2922 N Division Ave ... York NE 68467 *TF:* 800-445-0730 ■ *Web:* www.cyclonaire.com	402-362-2000	362-2001	207
Cyclone Bicycle Supply 6500 SW Macadam Ave Ste 150 ... Portland OR 97239 *Web:* cyclonebicycle.com	503-226-0696		711
Cyclone Drilling Inc PO Box 908 ... Gillette WY 82717 *TF:* 800-318-3724 ■ *Web:* www.cyclonedrilling.com	307-682-4161	682-3158	540
Cyclone Interactive Multimedia Group Inc 535 Albany St Ste 402-A ... Boston MA 02118 *Web:* www.cycloneinteractive.com	617-350-8834		344
Cycom Canada Corp 31 Prince Andrew Pl Ste 1 ... North York ON M3C2H2 *TF:* 800-268-3171 ■ *Web:* www.cycom.com	416-494-5040		196
Cy-Fair Houston Chamber of Commerce 11734 Barker Cypress Ste 105 ... Cypress TX 77433 *TF:* 800-403-6120 ■ *Web:* www.cyfairchamber.com	281-373-1390	373-1394	139
CYGAM Energy Inc 340 - 12th Ave SW Ste 760 ... Calgary AB T2R1L5	403-802-6983	802-6984	538
Cygan Hayes Ltd 20635 Abbey Woods Ct N ... Frankfort IL 60423 *Web:* cyganhayes.com	815-534-5713	534-5523	2

	Phone	Fax	Class
Cygnus Corporation Inc 5640 Nicholson Ln Ste 300 .... Rockville MD 20852 *Web:* www.cygnusc.com	301-231-7537		196
Cygnus Inc 1701 Standish Ave.......... Petoskey MI 49770 *Web:* www.cygnusinc.net	231-347-5404		115
Cygnus Manufacturing Company LLC Victory Rd Business Park 491 Chantler Dr ...... Saxonburg PA 16056 *Web:* www.cmc-usa.com	724-352-8000		475
Cygnus Systems Inc 24700 Northwestern Hwy Ste 600.......... Southfield MI 48075 *TF:* 800-388-2280 ■ *Web:* www.cygnussystems.com	248-557-4600		196
CYIOS Corporation 1300 Pennsylvania Ave NW Ste 700.......... Washington DC 20004 *Web:* www.cyios.com	202-204-3006		180
Cykic Software Inc PO Box 3098.......... San Diego CA 92163 *TF:* 800-438-7325 ■ *Web:* www.cykic.com	619-459-8799		178-7
Cyl-tec Inc 971 W Industrial Dr.......... Aurora IL 60506 *TF:* 888-429-5832 ■ *Web:* cyl-tec.com	630-844-8800		743
Cyma Systems Inc 2330 W University Dr Ste 4 .... Tempe AZ 85281 **Fax Area Code:* 480 ■ *TF:* 800-292-2962 ■ *Web:* www.cyma.com	800-292-2962	303-2969*	178-1
Cymbel Corp 154 Wells Ave.......... Newton MA 02459 *Web:* www.cymbel.com	617-581-6633		177
Cymer Inc 17075 Thornmint Ct .... San Diego CA 92127 *NASDAQ: CYMI* ■ *Web:* www.cymer.com	858-385-7300	385-7100	425
Cyn Oil Corp 1771 Washington St .... Stoughton MA 02072 *TF:* 800-242-5818 ■ *Web:* www.cynenv.com	781-341-1777		667
Cynergy Solutions LLC 543 Country Club Dr Ste 538.......... Simi Valley CA 93065 *TF:* 877-296-3749 ■ *Web:* www.cynergysolutions.net	805-416-1610		196
Cynergy Systems Inc 1851 Chespark Dr .... Gastonia NC 28052 *Web:* www.cynergysystemsinc.com	704-864-2999		187
cynoSure Financial Inc 33490 Harper Ave.......... Clinton Township MI 48035 *TF:* 800-732-5569 ■ *Web:* www.cynosurefinancial.com	586-771-3334		390
Cynosure Inc 5 Carlisle Rd .... Westford MA 01886 *NASDAQ: CYNO* ■ *TF:* 800-886-2966 ■ *Web:* www.cynosure.com	978-256-4200		424
Cynthia C. & William E. Perry Pavilion 9400 Turkey Lake Rd.......... Orlando FL 32819 *TF:* 800-447-1435 ■ *Web:* www.orlandohealth.com/drpphillipshospital	321-842-8844	842-8871	372
Cynthia Rowley 376 Bleecker St.......... New York NY 10014 *Web:* www.cynthiarowley.com	212-242-3803		277
Cynthia Woods Mitchell Pavilion 2005 Lake Robbins Dr .... The Woodlands TX 77380 *TF:* 800-745-3000 ■ *Web:* www.woodlandscenter.org	281-363-3300	364-3011	572
Cyon Research Corp 8220 Stone Trail Dr.......... Bethesda MD 20817 *Web:* www.cyonresearch.com	301-365-9085	365-4586	194
Cyphers Agency Inc, The 53 Old Solomons Is Rd Ste G.......... Annapolis MD 21401 *TF:* 888-412-7469 ■ *Web:* thecyphersagency.com	888-412-7469		7
CypherWorX Inc 3349 Monroe Ave.......... Rochester NY 14618 *TF:* 888-685-4440 ■ *Web:* nptrainingworks.com	888-685-4440		387
Cypremort Point State Park 306 Beach Ln .... Cypremort Point LA 70538 *TF:* 888-867-4510 ■ *Web:* www.crt.state.la.us	337-867-4510		565
Cypress Asset Management Inc 4545 Post Oak Pl Dr Ste 205 .... Houston TX 77027 *Web:* cypressasset.com	713-512-2100		690
Cypress Bayou Casino 832 Martin Luther King Rd.......... Charenton LA 70523 *TF:* 800-284-4386 ■ *Web:* www.cypressbayou.com	800-284-4386		452
Cypress Capital Group Inc 251 Royal Palm Way Ste 500.......... Palm Beach FL 33480 *Web:* www.cypresscapitalgroup.com	561-659-5889		401
Cypress Care Inc 2736 Meadow Church Rd Ste 300 .... Duluth GA 30097 *TF:* 800-419-7191 ■ *Web:* www.cypresscare.com	800-419-7191		367
Cypress Chamber of Commerce 5550 Cerritos Ave Ste D.......... Cypress CA 90630 *Web:* www.cypresschamber.org	714-827-2430		139
Cypress College 9200 Vly View St .... Cypress CA 90630 **Fax:* Admissions ■ *TF:* 800-564-9979 ■ *Web:* www.cypresscollege.edu	714-484-7000	484-7446*	162
Cypress Energy Partners LP 5727 S Lewis Ave Ste 500 .... Tulsa OK 74105 *Web:* www.cypressenergy.com	918-748-3900		539
Cypress E&P Corp 8601 Ranch Rd 2222 Bldg III Ste 200.......... Austin TX 78730 *Web:* www.cypressep.com	512-342-6300		538
Cypress Fairbanks Medical Ctr 10655 Steepletop Dr.......... Houston TX 77065 *Web:* www.cyfairhospital.com	281-890-4285		374-3
Cypress Food Distributors Inc 3111 N University Dr Ste 612.......... Coral Springs FL 33065 *Web:* www.cypressfood.com	954-344-2900	344-3607	297-9
Cypress Gardens 3030 Cypress Gardens Rd .... Moncks Corner SC 29461 *Web:* www.cypressgardens.info	843-553-0515	569-0644	50-5
Cypress Grill 4404 W William Cannon Ste L .... Austin TX 78749 *Web:* www.cypressgrill.net	512-358-7474		671
Cypress Group LLC 437 Madison Ave 33rd Fl.......... New York NY 10022 *Web:* www.cypressgp.com	212-705-0150	705-0199	402
Cypress Hills National Cemetery 625 Jamaica Ave.......... Brooklyn NY 11208 *TF:* 800-535-1117 ■ *Web:* www.cem.va.gov/cems/nchp/cypresshills.asp	631-454-4949	694-5422	136
Cypress Hills Resource Corp 602-11th Ave SW Ste 416 .... Calgary AB V7X1J1 *Web:* www.cypresshillsresource.com	403-265-7663		536
Cypress Inn, The 501 Rice Mine Rd N .... Tuscaloosa AL 35406 *Web:* www.cypressinnrestaurant.com	205-345-6963	345-6997	671

	Phone	Fax	Class
Cypress Networks 4125 Walker Ave Ste C.......... Greensboro NC 27407 *TF:* 866-625-3502 ■ *Web:* www.cypressnetworks.net	336-841-3030		180
Cypress Operating Inc 330 Marshall St Ste 930.......... Shreveport LA 71101 *TF:* 800-654-6926 ■ *Web:* www.cypressop.com	318-424-2031		538
Cypress Regional Hospital 2004 Saskatchewan Dr.......... Swift Current SK S9H5M8 *TF:* 800-565-3559 ■ *Web:* www.cypressrha.ca	306-778-9400		374-2
Cypress Security LLC 478 Tehama St .... San Francisco CA 94103 *TF:* 866-345-1277 ■ *Web:* www.cypress-security.com	866-345-1277		693
Cypress Semiconductor Corp 198 Champion Ct.......... San Jose CA 95134 *NASDAQ: CY* ■ **Fax:* Mktg ■ *TF:* 800-541-4736 ■ *Web:* www.cypress.com	408-943-2600	943-4730*	696
Cypress Sharpridge Investments Inc (CYS) 890 Winter St .... Waltham MA 02451 *NYSE: CYS* ■ *Web:* www.cysinv.com	617-639-0440		403
Cypress Street Station 158 Cypress St.......... Abilene TX 79601 *TF:* 800-727-7704 ■ *Web:* www.cypress-street.com	325-676-3463	676-0715	671
Cypress Wealth Advisors LLC 101 California St Ste 1025.......... San Francisco CA 94111 *Web:* www.cypresswealth.com	415-489-2100		401
Cypress, The 320 E Tennessee St .... Tallahassee FL 32301 *Web:* www.cypressrestaurant.com	850-513-1100		671
Cypress-Fairbanks Independent School District PO Box 692003 .... Houston TX 77269 *Web:* www.cfisd.net	281-897-4000		685
Cyprus 13 E 40th St.......... New York NY 10016 *Web:* www.un.int	212-481-6023	685-7316	784
Consulate General 13 E 40th St.......... New York NY 10016 *Web:* cyprusembassy.net	212-686-6016	686-3660	257
Embassy 2211 R St NW.......... Washington DC 20008 *Web:* www.cyprusembassy.net	202-462-5772	483-6710	257
Cyprus Cafe 725 E Second Ave .... Durango CO 81301 *Web:* www.cypruscafe.com	970-385-6884		671
Cyprus Tourism Organization 13 E 40th St .... New York NY 10016 *TF:* 800-462-2748 ■ *Web:* www.visitcyprus.com	212-683-5280	683-5282	775
Cyquent Inc 5410 Edson Ln Ste 210C.......... Rockville MD 20852 *TF:* 866-509-0331 ■ *Web:* www.cyquent.com	240-292-0230		180
CYR Bus Lines 153 Gilman Falls Ave.......... Old Town ME 04468 *TF:* 800-244-2335 ■ *Web:* johntcyrandsons.com	207-827-2335	827-6763	107
Cyracom International Inc 5780 N Swan Rd.......... Tucson AZ 85718 *Web:* cyracom.com	520-745-9447		768
Cyril Bath Co 1610 Airport Rd.......... Monroe NC 28110 *Web:* www.cyrilbath.com	704-289-8531	289-3932	456
Cyril J Demeyere Ltd 261 Broadway .... Tillsonburg ON N4G4H8 *Web:* www.cjdleng.com	519-688-1000		261
Cyril Scott Company Inc, The 3950 State Rt 37 E .... Lancaster OH 43130	740-654-2271		627
CYS (Cypress Sharpridge Investments Inc) 890 Winter St.......... Waltham MA 02451 *NYSE: CYS* ■ *Web:* www.cysinv.com	617-639-0440		403
Cystic Fibrosis Foundation 6931 Arlington Rd Ste 200.......... Bethesda MD 20814 *TF:* 800-344-4823 ■ *Web:* www.cff.org	301-951-4422	951-6378	48-17
Cytak Inc 444 de Haro Ste 210.......... San Francisco CA 94107 *Web:* www.cytak.com	415-738-1650		734
Cytec Engineered Materials 2085 E Technology Cir Ste 300 .... Tempe AZ 85284 *Web:* www.cytec.com	480-730-2000	730-2088	605-2
Cytec Industries Inc 5 Garret Mtn Plaza .... West Paterson NJ 07424 *NYSE: CYT* ■ *TF:* 800-652-6013 ■ *Web:* www.cytec.com	973-357-3100		145
Cytokinetics Inc 280 E Grand Ave.......... South San Francisco CA 94080 *NASDAQ: CYTK* ■ *Web:* www.cytokinetics.com	650-624-3000	624-3010	85
Cytolab Pathology Services 6825 216th St SW .... Lynnwood WA 98036	425-712-8020		415
Cytori Therapeutics Inc 3020 Callan Rd.......... San Diego CA 92121 *NASDAQ: CYTX* ■ *Web:* www.cytori.com	858-458-0900		85
Cytosorbents Corp 7 Deer Park Dr Ste K.......... Monmouth Junction NJ 08852 *Web:* www.cytosorbents.com	732-329-8885		250
CytoSport Inc 1340 Treat Blvd Ste 350.......... Walnut Creek CA 94597 *TF:* 888-313-1922 ■ *Web:* www.cytosport.com	707-751-3942	748-5732	799
CytRx Corp 11726 San Vicente Blvd Ste 650.......... Los Angeles CA 90049 *NASDAQ: CYTR* ■ *TF:* 800-385-5790 ■ *Web:* www.cytrx.com	310-826-5648	826-6139	85
Czech Airlines 1 Penn Plaza Ste 1416.......... New York NY 10119 *TF:* 855-359-2932 ■ *Web:* www.csa.cz	855-359-2932		25
Czech Airlines OK Plus 147 W 35th St Ste 1505 .... New York NY 10001 **Fax Area Code:* 212 ■ *TF:* 855-359-2932 ■ *Web:* www.csa.cz	855-359-2932	279-6602*	26
Czech Republic 1109 Madison Ave.......... New York NY 10028 *TF:* 800-222-4357 ■ *Web:* www.mzv.cz/un.newyork	212-717-5643	717-5064	784
Consulate General 10990 Wilshire Blvd Ste 1100.......... Los Angeles CA 90024 *Web:* www.mzv.cz/losangeles	310-473-0889	473-9813	257
Consulate General 321 E 73rd St.......... New York NY 10021 *Web:* www.mzv.cz/consulate.newyork	646-422-3344	422-3311	257
Embassy 3900 Spring of Freedom St NW.......... Washington DC 20008 *Web:* www.mzv.cz	202-274-9100	966-8540	257
CZ-USA Inc 3327 N Seventh St.......... Kansas City KS 66117 *TF:* 800-955-4486 ■ *Web:* cz-usa.com	913-321-1811		711

D

Name / Address	Phone	Fax	Class
D & B 103 JFK Pkwy .... Short Hills NJ 07078 — *NYSE:* DNB ■ *TF:* 800-234-3867 ■ *Web:* www.dnb.com	973-921-5500		637-2
D & B Logistics 720 Washington St .... Hanover MA 02339 — *Web:* www.dblinc.net	781-829-4500		311
D & D Commodities Ltd PO Box 359 .... Stephen MN 56757 — *TF:* 800-543-3308 ■ *Web:* www.ddcommodities.com	800-543-3308		447
D & D Construction Services of Orlando Inc 2707 Rew Cir .... Ocoee FL 34761 — *Web:* www.ddconstructionservices.com	407-654-7545		186
D & D Distribution Services Inc 789 Kings Mill Rd. .... York PA 17403 — *TF:* 877-683-3358 ■ *Web:* www.dd-dist.com	717-845-1646		803-1
D & d Elevator Maintenance Inc 38 Hayes St .... Elmsford NY 10523 — *TF:* 800-654-8838 ■ *Web:* ddelevator.com	914-347-4344		104
D & D Equipment Rental Inc 10936 Shoemaker Ave .... Santa Fe Springs CA 90670 — *Web:* www.ddrental.com	562-595-4555	903-8881	264-3
D & D Foods Inc 9425 N 48th St .... Omaha NE 68152 — *TF:* 800-208-0364 ■ *Web:* hy-vee.com	402-571-4113		296-36
D & D Manufacturing Inc 500 Territorial Dr. .... Bolingbrook IL 60440 — *Fax Area Code: 630 ■ *TF:* 888-300-6869 ■ *Web:* www.ddmfg.com	888-300-6869	759-0043*	757
D & F Corp 42455 Merrill Rd .... Sterling Heights MI 48314 — *TF:* 800-322-1304 ■ *Web:* clientinfo.com/d-f	586-254-5300	254-5610	567
D & H Distributing Company Inc 2525 N Seventh St .... Harrisburg PA 17110 — *TF:* 800-340-1001 ■ *Web:* www.dandh.com	800-340-1001	340-1001	174
D & J Enterprises Inc 3495 Lee Rd 10 .... Auburn AL 36832 — *Web:* www.djenterprises.net	334-821-1249		188-4
D & J Oil Company Inc 4720 W Garriott .... Enid OK 73703 — *Web:* www.djoil.com	580-242-3636		539
D & L Entertainment Services Inc 4120 Main St .... Dallas TX 75226 — *Web:* dandlentertainment.com	214-634-0757		184
D & M Plastic Corp 150 French Rd PO Box 158 .... Burlington IL 60109 — *Web:* www.dmplastics.com	847-683-2054		604
D & m Tours Inc 117 E Seventh St .... Paterson NJ 07524	973-977-2001		760
D & R International Ltd 1100 Wayne Ave Ste 700 .... Silver Spring MD 20910 — *Web:* www.drintl.com	301-588-9387		256
D & R Sports Ctr Inc 8178 W Main St .... Kalamazoo MI 49009 — *Web:* www.dandrsports.com	269-372-2277	372-9072	711
D & S Cattle Co 2167 FL-66 .... Zolfo Springs FL 33890	863-735-1112		446
D & S Engineering Inc 1000 Golden Rd PO BOX 480 .... Millinocket ME 04462	207-723-6871		261
D & S Manufacturing Inc 301 E Main St .... Black River Falls WI 54615 — *Web:* www.dsmfg.com	715-284-5376	284-4084	482
D & S Mktg Systems Inc 1205 38th St .... Brooklyn NY 11218 — *Web:* dsmarketing.com	718-633-8383		194
D & W Fine Pack LLC 4162 Georgia Blvd .... San Bernardino CA 92407 — *Web:* www.dwfinepack.com	847-378-1200		590
D & W Inc 941 Oak St .... Elkhart IN 46514 — *TF:* 800-255-0829 ■ *Web:* www.dwincorp.com	574-264-9674	264-9859	329
D + R Lathian LLC 745 Hope Rd 2nd Fl .... Eatontown NJ 07724 — *Web:* www.drlathian.com	732-460-2500	460-2640	5
D A Crowley & Associates Inc 3 Overlook Dr .... Amherst NH 03031 — *Web:* www.dacrowley.com	603-673-7050		195
D B Western Inc 90418 Transpacific Ln .... North Bend OR 97459 — *Web:* www.dbwestern.com	541-756-0533		595
D Canale Beverages Inc 45 W EH Crump Blvd .... Memphis TN 38106 — *TF:* 800-331-2829 ■ *Web:* www.abwholesaler.com/dcanalebeverages	901-948-4543		81-1
D d Dunlap Companies Inc 16897 Algonquin St Ste A .... Huntington Beach CA 92649 — *TF:* 800-756-7047 ■ *Web:* dddunlap.com	714-840-6460		536
D Exposito & Partners LLC 875 Avenue of the Americas .... New York NY 10001 — *Web:* www.newamericanagency.com	646-747-8800		636
D F Richard Inc 124 Broadway .... Dover NH 03821 — *TF:* 800-649-6457 ■ *Web:* www.dfrichard.com	603-742-2020		316
D G Consulting 295 Blohm Ave .... Aromas CA 95004 — *Web:* dgconsult.com	831-726-7060		180
D Hilton Assoc Inc 9450 Grogans Mill Rd .... Spring TX 77380 — *TF:* 800-367-0433 ■ *Web:* www.dhilton.com	281-292-5088		194
D J Heating & Air Conditioning Inc 1409 Rt 9W .... Marlboro NY 12542	845-236-4436		189-10
D J Powers Company Inc 5000 Business Ctr Dr Ste 1000 .... Savannah GA 31405 — *Web:* www.djpowers.com	912-234-7241		311
D K Global 420 Missouri Ct .... Redlands CA 92373 — *TF:* 866-375-2214 ■ *Web:* dkglobal.net	909-747-0201		225
D L Evans Bank 397 N Overland PO Box 1188 .... Burley ID 83318 — *TF:* 888-873-9777 ■ *Web:* www.dlevans.com	208-678-9076	678-9093	70
D L s Electronic Systems Inc 1250 Peterson Dr .... Wheeling IL 60090 — *TF:* 800-345-0327 ■ *Web:* www.dlsemc.com	847-537-6400		743
D M Bowman Inc 10226 Governor Ln Blvd Ste 4009 .... Williamsport MD 21795 — *TF:* 800-326-3274 ■ *Web:* www.dmbowman.com	301-582-2784	223-5968	780
D m r International Inc 200 W Pk St Ste 104 .... Covington KY 41011 — *Web:* www.dmrinteractive.com	859-655-9200		466
D M Sales Engineering Inc 1325 Sunday Dr .... Indianapolis IN 46217 — *Web:* www.dmsales-eng.com	317-783-5493		596
D N Schwartz & Co 160 W 71st St Ste 12H .... New York NY 10023 — *Web:* www.dnschwartz.com	212-787-5017		260
D Net Internet Service 189 E Palmer St .... Franklin NC 28734 — *TF:* 877-601-3638 ■ *Web:* www.dnet.net	828-349-3638		225
D P Brown of Saginaw Inc 2845 Universal Dr .... Saginaw MI 48603 — *TF:* 877-799-9400 ■ *Web:* www.dpbrowntech.com	989-799-9400		393
D River State Recreation Site 725 Summer St NE Ste C .... Salem OR 97301 — *TF:* 800-551-6949 ■ *Web:* www.oregonstateparks.org	541-994-7341		565
D Samuel Gottesman Library 1300 Morris Park Ave Forchheimer Bldg Rm 132 .... Bronx NY 10461 — *Web:* library.einstein.yu.edu	718-430-3108	430-8795	434-1
D Side Advisors 12601 Easton Dr .... Saratoga CA 95070 — *Web:* dside.com	408-255-4620		195
D V Brown & Assoc Inc 567 Vickers St .... Tonawanda NY 14150 — *Web:* www.dvbrown.com	716-695-5533		610
D V O Enterprises Inc 620 Windsor Ct .... Alpine UT 84004 — *Web:* www.dvo.com	801-492-1290		180
D W Hammer & Company Inc 17480 Dallas Pkwy Ste 100 .... Dallas TX 75287 — *Web:* www.dwhammerco.com	972-250-2547		41
D W Smith Associates LLC 1450 SR-34 .... Wall Township NJ 07753 — *Web:* www.dwsmith.com	732-363-5850		727
D'Agostino Supermarkets Inc 1385 Boston Post Rd .... Larchmont NY 10538 — *Web:* www.dagnyc.com	914-833-4000		345
D'Ambra Construction Co Inc 800 Jefferson Blvd .... Warwick RI 02886 — *Web:* www.d-ambra.com	401-737-1300		188-4
D'Angelo Sandwich Shops 600 Providence Hwy .... Dedham MA 02026 — *TF:* 800-727-2446 ■ *Web:* www.dangelos.com	781-461-1200	461-1896	670
D'annunzio & Sons Inc 3730 Park Ave Ste 102 .... South Plainfield NJ 07080 — *Web:* www.dannunziocorp.com	732-574-1300	574-1244	186
D'Arcangelo & Co 510 Haight Ave .... Poughkeepsie NY 12603 — *Web:* www.darcangelo.com	845-473-7774		41
D'Arcy McGee's Irish Pub 199 Four Valley Dr .... Vaughan ON L4K0B8 — *TF:* 888-854-4402 ■ *Web:* darcymcgees.com	613-230-4433		671
D'Arrigo Bros Company of California Inc PO Box 850 .... Salinas CA 93902 — *TF Cust Svc:* 800-995-5939 ■ *Web:* www.andyboy.com	831-455-4500	455-4445	10-11
D'Arrigo Bros Company of New York Inc 315 Hunts Pt Terminal Market .... Bronx NY 10474 — *Web:* www.darrigony.com	718-991-5900	960-0544	297-7
D'Artagnan Inc 280 Wilson Ave Ste 1 .... Newark NJ 07105 — *TF:* 800-327-8246 ■ *Web:* www.dartagnan.com	973-344-0565	465-1870	296-26
D'Classico 58 Ellison St .... Paterson NJ 07505	973-569-4300		671
D'Huyvetter & Swichkow PC 519 Johnson Ferry Rd Ste A-100 .... Marietta GA 30068 — *Web:* www.dspccpa.com	404-231-3500		2
D'Onofrio General Contractors Corp 202 28th St .... Brooklyn NY 11232 — *Web:* donofrio.biz	718-832-5700		610
D'Orsay Restaurant Pub 65 Rue de Buade .... Vieux-Quebec QC G1R4A2 — *Web:* www.dorsayrestaurant.com	418-694-1582	694-1587	671
D'vontz 7208 E 38th St .... Tulsa OK 74145 — *TF:* 877-322-3600 ■ *Web:* www.dvontz.com	918-622-3600		610
D'Youville College 320 Porter Ave .... Buffalo NY 14201 — *Fax: Admissions ■ *TF:* 800-777-3921 ■ *Web:* www.dyc.edu	716-829-7600	829-7900*	166
D+H CollateralGuard RC (CSRS) 4126 Norland Ave Ste 200 .... Burnaby BC V5G3S8 — *TF:* 866-873-9780 ■ *Web:* www.csrs.ca	604-637-4000	637-4001	635
D. Crupi & Sons Ltd 85 Passmore Ave Agincourt .... Toronto ON M1V4S9 — *Web:* www.crupigroup.com	416-291-1986		261
D. P. Curtis Trucking Inc 1450 South Hwy 118 .... Richfield UT 84701 — *Fax Area Code: 435 ■ *TF:* 800-257-9151 ■ *Web:* www.dpcurtis.com	800-257-9151	896-6553*	780
D. Pagan Communications Inc 175 Pinelawn Rd Ste 215 .... Melville NY 11747 — *TF:* 800-253-7360 ■ *Web:* www.dpagan.com	631-659-2309		463
D. R. Payne & Associates Inc 119 N Robinson Ave Ste 400 .... Oklahoma City OK 73102 — *Web:* drpayne.com	405-272-0511		463
D.A.G. Construction Company Inc 4924 Winton Rd .... Cincinnati OH 45232 — *Web:* www.dag-cons.com	513-542-8597		186
D.A.R. State Park 6750 VT Rt 17 W .... Addison VT 05491 — *Web:* www.vtstateparks.com	802-759-2354		565
D.J. Simmons Inc 1009 Ridgeway Pl Ste 200 .... Farmington NM 87401 — *Web:* www.djsimmons.com	505-326-3753		536
D.M. Reid Associates Ltd 50 Grove St Ste 227 .... Salem MA 01970 — *Web:* www.dmreid.com	978-744-3818		636
D.Trio Marketing Group 401 N Third St Ste 480 .... Minneapolis MN 55401 — *Web:* www.dtrio.com	612-436-0323		195
D1 Sports Holdings LLC 7115 S Springs Dr .... Franklin TN 37067 — *TF:* 800-228-6635 ■ *Web:* www.d1sportstraining.com	615-778-1893		354
D2 Creative 28 World's Fair Dr .... Somerset NJ 08873 — *Web:* www.d2creative.com	732-507-7300		7
D2 Technologie 2119 Boul Marcel-laurin .... Saint-laurent QC H4R1K4 — *Web:* d2technologie.com	514-904-5888		736
D2M Inc 935 Benecia Ave .... Sunnyvale CA 94085 — *Web:* www.d2m-inc.com	650-567-9995		194
D3 Technical Services LLC 4600 W Kearney Ste 100 .... Springfield MO 65803 — *Web:* www.d3tech.net	417-831-7171		261

Company / Address	City	State	Zip	Phone	Fax	Class
D3Logic Inc 89 Commercial Way *Web:* www.d3logic.com	East Providence	RI	02914	401-435-4300		195
D4 Construction Services LLC 4121 Main St *Web:* www.d4cs.com	Rowlett	TX	75088	972-463-0390		186
d50 Media 1330 Boylston St Ste 200 *TF:* 800-582-9606 ■ *Web:* www.d50media.com	Chestnut Hill	MA	02461	800-582-9606		195
DA (Debtors Anonymous) PO Box 920888 *TF:* 800-421-2383 ■ *Web:* www.debtorsanonymous.org	Needham	MA	02492	781-453-2743	453-2745	48-21
D&A Building Services 321 Georgia Ave *Web:* www.dabuildingservices.com	Longwood	FL	32750	407-831-5388		41
Da Camera of Houston 1427 Branard St *Web:* www.dacamera.com	Houston	TX	77006	713-524-7601	524-4148	573-3
DA Collins Construction Co Inc 269 Ballard Rd *Web:* www.dacollins.com	Wilton	NY	12831	518-664-9855		188-4
DA Davidson & Company Inc 8 Third St N *TF:* 800-332-5915 ■ *Web:* dadavidson.com	Great Falls	MT	59401	406-727-4200	791-7238	690
DA Hoerr & Sons Inc 8020 N Shadetree Dr *TF:* 800-273-5436 ■ *Web:* www.hoerrnursery.com	Peoria	IL	61615	309-691-4561		323
DA Kreuter Assoc Inc 2250 Hickory Rd Ste 400 *Web:* www.dakassociates.com	Plymouth Meeting	PA	19462	610-834-1100		194
D-A Lubricant Co 1340 W 29th St *Fax: Cust Svc ■ *TF:* 800-645-5823 ■ *Web:* www.dalube.com	Indianapolis	IN	46208	317-923-5321	923-3884*	541
Da Marco 1520 Westheimer Rd *Web:* www.damarcohouston.com	Houston	TX	77006	713-807-8857		671
Da Maurizio *Fine Dining* 1496 Lower Water St *Web:* www.damaurizio.ca	Halifax	NS	B3J1R7	902-423-0859		671
Da Mimmo Italian Cuisine 217 S High St *Web:* www.damimmo.com	Baltimore	MD	21202	410-727-6876	727-1927	671
Da Pope Inc 1160 Chess Dr Ste 11 *TF:* 800-923-6255 ■ *Web:* www.dapope.com	Foster City	CA	94404	650-349-5086		186
Da Vinci Academy 37w080 Hopps Rd *Web:* www.dvacademy.org	Elgin	IL	60124	847-841-7532		148
Da Vinci Discovery Ctr of Science & Technology 3145 Hamilton Blvd Bypass *Web:* www.davincisciencecenter.org	Allentown	PA	18103	484-664-1002		520
Da/Pro Rubber Inc 601 N Poplar Ave *TF:* 800-264-2646 ■ *Web:* www.daprorubber.com	Broken Arrow	OK	74012	918-258-9386	258-3286	677
DAA Draexlmaier Automotive of America LLC 1751 E Main St	Duncan	SC	29334	864-433-8910		61
DAAD (German Academic Exchange Service) 871 United Nations Plaza *Web:* www.daad.org	New York	NY	10017	212-758-3223	755-5780	48-11
Dabko Industries Inc 50 Emmett St *Web:* www.rgdtech.com	Bristol	CT	06010	860-589-0756	585-0874	621
Dabney S Lancaster Community College 1000 Dabney Dr PO Box 1000 *Web:* dslcc.edu	Clifton Forge	VA	24422	540-863-2800		162
Dabney State Recreation Area 725 Summer St NE Ste C *TF:* 800-551-6949 ■ *Web:* www.oregonstateparks.org	Salem	OR	97301	503-695-2261		565
DAC (Dougherty Arts Ctr, The) 1110 Barton Springs Rd	Austin	TX	78704	512-974-4000	974-4039	50-2
DAC International Inc 6702 McNeil Dr *TF:* 800-527-2531 ■ *Web:* www.dacint.com	Austin	TX	78729	512-331-5323	331-4516	770
Dac Products Inc 625 Montroyal Rd *TF:* 800-431-1982 ■ *Web:* www.dacproducts.com	Rural Hall	NC	27045	800-431-1982		499
DAC Vision 3630 W Miller Ste 350 *TF:* 800-800-1550 ■ *Web:* www.dacvision.com	Garland	TX	75041	972-677-2700	677-2800	542
Dacallc 6550 McDonough Dr *Web:* dacaspecialtyservices.com	Norcross	GA	30093	770-451-6433		256
DACC (Dona Ana Branch Community College) 2800 N Sonoma Ranch Blvd *Fax: Admissions ■ *TF:* 800-903-7503 ■ *Web:* dacc.nmsu.edu	Las Cruces	NM	88011	575-528-7000	528-7300*	162
DACCO Transmission Parts 741 Dacco Dr PO Box 2789 *TF Cust Svc:* 866-645-1452 ■ *Web:* www.daccoinc.com	Cookeville	TN	38502	931-528-7581		60
Daco Inc 609 Airport Rd	North Aurora	IL	60542	630-897-8797		273
Dacon Corp 16 Huron Dr *Web:* www.dacon1.com	Natick	MA	01760	508-651-3600		610
Dacotah Paper Co 3940 15th Ave NW *TF:* 800-270-6352 ■ *Web:* www.dacotahpaper.com	Fargo	ND	58102	701-281-1734	281-9799	559
Dacra Glass 3333 N Commerce Dr *Web:* www.dacraglass.com	Muncie	IN	47303	765-286-3855		362
Dacro Industries Inc 9325-51 Ave *Web:* www.dacro.com	Edmonton	AB	T6E4W8	780-434-8900		106
Dadant & Sons Inc 51 S Second St *TF:* 888-922-1293 ■ *Web:* www.dadant.com	Hamilton	IL	62341	217-847-3324	847-3660	122
DADCO Inc 43850 Plymouth Oaks Blvd *Web:* www.dadco.net	Plymouth	MI	48170	734-207-1100		641
Daddies Board Shop LLC 7126 NE Sandy Blvd *Web:* www.daddiesboardshop.com	Portland	OR	97218	503-281-5123		711
Daddy Don'S Tax Service 8235 Santa Monica Blvd Ste 210 *Web:* daddydon.com	West Hollywood	CA	90046	323-656-7532		734
Dade Battlefield Historic State Park 3900 Commonwealth Blvd *Web:* www.floridastateparks.org	Tallahassee	FL	32399	352-793-4781		565
Dade County 71 Case Ave *TF:* 800-562-1239 ■ *Web:* www.dadecounty-ga.gov	Trenton	GA	30752	706-657-4625	657-8284	338
Dade Moeller & Assoc Inc 1835 Terminal Dr Ste 200 *Web:* www.dademoeller.com	Richland	WA	99354	509-946-0410		256
Dade Paper & Bag Co 9601 NW 112th Ave *Web:* www.dadepaper.com	Miami	FL	33178	305-805-2600		548
Dade Truss Company Inc 6401 NW 74th Ave *Web:* www.bcg.bz/miami.htm	Miami	FL	33166	305-592-8245		817
DadLabs Inc 4612 Burleson Rd Ste L *Web:* www.dadlabs.com	Austin	TX	78744	512-215-4026		387
Daedalus Books Inc 9645 Gerwig Ln *TF:* 800-395-2665 ■ *Web:* www.daedalusbooks.com	Columbia	MD	21046	410-309-2706		95
DaEdoardo Foxtown Grille 2203 Woodward Ave *Web:* daedoardo.net	Detroit	MI	48201	313-471-3500	471-3499	671
Daemar Inc 861 Cranberry Ct *TF:* 800-387-7115 ■ *Web:* www.daemar.com	Oakville	ON	L6L6J7	905-847-6500		350
Daemen College 4380 Main St *TF:* 800-462-7652 ■ *Web:* www.daemen.edu	Amherst	NY	14226	716-839-8225		166
Daewoo Motor America Inc 1055 W Victoria St	Placentia	CA	90220	562-313-1020		57
DAFCA Inc 10 Speen St *Fax Area Code: 508 ■ *Web:* dafca.com	Framingham	MA	04661	774-204-0020	875-9422*	809
Daffodil 163 Pearl St	Essex Junction	VT	05452	802-879-0212		157-6
DAG Media Inc 125-10 Queens Blvd Ste 14 *TF:* 800-261-2799 ■ *Web:* jewishyellow.com	Kew Gardens	NY	11415	718-263-8454	793-2522	637-6
Dage-MTI Inc 701 N Roeske Ave *Web:* www.dagemti.com	Michigan City	IN	46360	219-872-5514	872-5559	647
Daggett County 95 N First W *TF:* 800-764-0844 ■ *Web:* www.daggettcounty.org	Manila	UT	84046	435-784-3154	784-3335	338
Daggett Truck Line Inc 32717 County Rd 10 *TF:* 800-262-9393 ■ *Web:* daggetttruck.com	Frazee	MN	56544	218-334-3711	334-2566	780
Dagny Johnson Key Largo Hammock Botanical State Park 905 County Rd *Web:* www.floridastateparks.org/keylargohammock	Key Largo	FL	33037	305-451-1202		565
Dagom Gaden Tensung-Ling Monastery 2150 E Dolan Rd *Web:* www.ganden.org	Bloomington	IN	47404	812-334-3456		50-1
Dahab Assoc Inc 423 S Country Rd *Web:* www.dahab.com	Bay Shore	NY	11706	631-665-6181		401
Dahl Arts Ctr 713 Seventh St *TF:* 800-487-3223 ■ *Web:* www.thedahl.org	Rapid City	SD	57701	605-394-4101	394-6121	50-2
Dahl Bros Canada Ltd 2600 S Sheridan Way *TF:* 800-268-5355 ■ *Web:* dahlvalve.com	Mississauga	ON	L5J2M4	905-822-2330		350
Dahl Hatton Muir & Reese Ltd 217 S Birch Ave PO Box 698 *Web:* dhmrcpa.com	Hallock	MN	56728	218-843-2645		2
Dahl Morrow International 11260 Roger Bacon St Ste 204 *Web:* www.dahl-morrowintl.com	Reston	VA	20190	703-787-8117		266
Dahlak Restaurant inc 4708 Baltimore Ave *Web:* www.dahlakrestaurant.com	Philadelphia	PA	19143	215-726-6464		671
Dahle North America Inc 49 Vose Farm Rd Ste 110 *TF:* 800-243-8145 ■ *Web:* www.dahle.com	Peterborough	NH	03458	603-924-0003	924-1616	534
Dahlgren & Co Inc 1220 Sunflower St *Web:* www.sunflowerseed.com	Crookston	MN	56716	218-281-2985		296-28
Dahlgren Memorial Library Georgetown University Medical Ctr 3900 Reservoir R PO Box 571420 *Web:* dml.georgetown.edu	Washington	DC	20057-1420	202-687-1448		434-1
Dahlia Lounge 2001 Fourth Ave *Web:* www.tomdouglas.com	Seattle	WA	98121	206-682-4142		671
Dahlonega Gold Museum State Historic Site 1 Public Sq *Web:* www.gastateparks.org	Dahlonega	GA	30533	706-864-2257		565
Dahlsten Truck Line Inc 101 W Edgar PO Box 95 *TF:* 800-228-4313 ■ *Web:* www.dahlsten.com	Clay Center	NE	68933	402-762-3511	762-3592	780
Dahlstrom Display Inc 2875 S 25th Ave *Web:* dahlstromdisplay.com	Broadview	IL	60155	708-410-4500		627
DAI (Development Alternatives Inc) 7600 Wisconsin Ave Ste 200 *Web:* www.dai.com	Bethesda	MD	20814	301-771-7600		463
DAI (Denali Advance Integration) 17735 NE 65th St Ste 130 *TF:* 877-467-8008 ■ *Web:* www.denaliai.com	Redmond	WA	98052	425-885-4000		180
Dai Ceramics Inc 38240 Airport Pkwy *Web:* www.daiceramics.com	Willoughby	OH	44094	440-946-6964		751
Daido Corp of America 1031 Fred White Blvd *Web:* www.daidocorp.com	Portland	TN	37148	615-323-4020		620
Daidone Electric Inc 200 Raymond Blvd *Web:* daidoneelectric.com	Newark	NJ	07105	973-690-5216		189-4
Daifuku North American Holdings Co 6700 Tussing Rd *Web:* www.daifuku.com	Reynoldsburg	OH	43068	614-863-1888		207
Daiichi Sankyo Inc 2 Hilton Ct *Web:* www.dsi.com	Parsippany	NJ	07054	973-359-2600	944-2645	582
Daikichi Sushi Japanese Bistro 1400 N Battlefield Blvd *Web:* www.welovesushi.net	Chesapeake	VA	23320	757-549-0200	549-0200	671
Daikin America Inc 20 Olympic Dr *TF Cust Svc:* 800-365-9570 ■ *Web:* www.daikin-america.com	Orangeburg	NY	10962	845-365-9500		605-2
Dailey & Assoc 8687 Melrose Ave *Fax: Acctg ■ *Web:* www.daileyideas.com	West Hollywood	CA	90069	310-360-3100	360-3100*	4
Dailey Marketing Group Inc 29829 Santa Margarita Pkwy Ste 100 *TF:* 888-364-6584 ■ *Web:* www.daileymarketing.com	Rancho Santa Margarita	CA	92688	949-454-0751		7
Daily Advertiser, The 1100 Bertrand Dr *TF:* 800-259-8852 ■ *Web:* www.theadvertiser.com	Lafayette	LA	70506	337-289-6300		532-2
Daily American Republic 208 Poplar St PO Box 7 *TF:* 888-276-2242 ■ *Web:* darnews.com	Poplar Bluff	MO	63901	573-785-1414	785-2706	532-2
Daily Athenaeum 284 Prospect St *Web:* www.thedaonline.com	Morgantown	WV	26505	304-293-4141	293-6857	532-2

Name / Address	City	State	Zip	Phone	Fax	Class
Daily Breeze 5215 Torrance Blvd	Torrance	CA	90503	310-540-5511	540-6272*	532-2
**Fax:* Edit ■ *Web:* www.dailybreeze.com						
Daily Californian 600 Eshleman Hall	Berkeley	CA	94720	510-548-8300		532-3
Web: www.dailycal.org						
Daily Challenge 1195 Atlantic Ave	Brooklyn	NY	11216	718-636-9500		532-2
Web: www.challenge-group.com						
Daily Commerce 915 E First St	Los Angeles	CA	90012	213-229-5300		532-2
Web: www.dailyjournal.com						
Daily Commercial 212 E Main St	Leesburg	FL	34748	352-365-8200		532-2
Web: www.dailycommercial.com						
Daily Courier 1958 Commerce Ctr Cir	Prescott	AZ	86301	928-445-3333		532-2
TF: 800-273-8255 ■ *Web:* dcourier.com						
Daily Courier 550 Doyle Ave	Kelowna	BC	V1Y7V1	250-762-4445	762-3866	532-1
Web: www.kelownadailycourier.ca						
Daily Courier 409 SE Seventh St	Grants Pass	OR	97526	541-474-3700	474-3824	532-2
TF: 800-228-0457 ■ *Web:* www.thedailycourier.com						
Daily Environment Report						
1801 S Bell St	Arlington	VA	22202	800-372-1033		531-5
TF: 800-372-1033 ■ *Web:* www.bna.com/daily-environment-report-p4751						
Daily Express Inc 1072 Harrisburg Pk	Carlisle	PA	17013	717-243-5757	240-2103	780
TF: 800-735-3136 ■ *Web:* www.dailyexp.com						
Daily Freeman 79 Hurley Ave	Kingston	NY	12401	845-331-5000	331-3557	532-2
Web: www.dailyfreeman.com						
Daily Gazette						
2345 Maxon Rd Ext PO Box 1090	Schenectady	NY	12301	518-374-4141	395-3072	532-2
TF: 800-262-2211 ■ *Web:* www.dailygazette.com						
Daily Globe 37 W Main St	Shelby	OH	44875	419-342-3261		532-2
Web: www.sdgnewsgroup.com						
Daily Globe, The						
118 E McLeod Ave PO Box 548	Ironwood	MI	49938	906-932-2211	932-4211	637-8
TF: 800-236-2887 ■ *Web:* www.yourdailyglobe.com						
Daily Hampshire Gazette						
115 Conz St	NorthHampton	MA	01060	413-584-5000	585-5299	532-2
Web: www.gazettenet.com						
Daily Herald 1555 N Freedom Blvd	Provo	UT	84604	801-373-5050	344-2985	532-2
TF: 800-880-8075 ■ *Web:* www.heraldextra.com						
Daily Herald						
155 E Algonquin Rd	Arlington Heights	IL	60005	847-427-4300	427-1301	532-2
TF: 888-903-4070 ■ *Web:* www.dailyherald.com						
Daily Herald Co, The						
1213 California St	Everett	WA	98201	425-339-3000		532-3
Web: www.heraldnet.com						
Daily Instruments Inc						
5700 Hartsdale Dr	Houston	TX	77036	713-780-8600		639
Web: www.dailyinst.com						
Daily Inter Lake 727 E Idaho St	Kalispell	MT	59901	406-755-7000	752-6114	532-2
Web: www.dailyinterlake.com						
Daily Item, The 38 Exchange St PO Box 951	Lynn	MA	01903	781-593-7700		532-2
TF: 800-876-7060 ■ *Web:* www.itemlive.com						
Daily Item, The 200 Market St	Sunbury	PA	17801	570-286-5671		532-3
TF: 800-326-9608 ■ *Web:* www.dailyitem.com						
Daily Journal						
2575 N Morton St PO Box 699	Franklin	IN	46131	317-736-2777		532-2
TF: 888-736-7101 ■ *Web:* www.dailyjournal.net						
Daily Journal						
1513 St Joe Dr PO Box A	Park Hills	MO	63601	573-431-2010	431-7640	532-2
TF: 800-660-8166 ■ *Web:* dailyjournalonline.com						
Daily Journal 8 Dearborn Sq	Kankakee	IL	60901	815-937-3300	937-3876	532-2
NASDAQ: DJCO ■ *TF:* 866-299-9256 ■ *Web:* www.daily-journal.com						
Daily Journal 891 E Oak Rd	Vineland	NJ	08360	856-691-5000	563-5308	532-2
TF: 800-222-0104 ■ *Web:* www.thedailyjournal.com						
Daily Journal Corp 915 E First St	Los Angeles	CA	90012	213-229-5300	229-5481	637-8
NASDAQ: DJCO ■ *TF:* 800-640-4829 ■ *Web:* www.dailyjournal.com						
Daily Journal of Commerce						
921 SW Washington St Ste 210	Portland	OR	97205	503-226-1311	802-7239*	532-2
**Fax:* News Rm ■ *TF:* 800-451-9998 ■ *Web:* djcoregon.com						
Daily Juice Products 1 Daily Way	Verona	PA	15147	412-828-9020		296-20
TF: 800-984-0989 ■ *Web:* www.dailyscocktails.com						
Daily Labor Report 1801 S Bell St	Arlington	VA	22202	800-372-1033		531-7
TF: 800-372-1033 ■ *Web:* www.bna.com/daily-labor-report-p5449						
Daily Local News						
250 N Bradford Ave	West Chester	PA	19382	610-696-1775		532-2
TF: 800-568-7355 ■ *Web:* www.dailylocal.com						
Daily News						
813 College St PO Box 90012	Bowling Green	KY	42102	270-781-1700		532-2
Web: www.bgdailynews.com						
Daily News 724 Bell Fork Rd	Jacksonville	NC	28540	910-353-1171		532-2
Web: www.jdnews.com						
Daily News 770 11th Ave PO Box 189	Longview	WA	98632	360-577-2500	577-2538*	532-2
**Fax:* News Rm ■ *TF:* 800-341-4745 ■ *Web:* www.tdn.com						
Daily News Journal						
201 E Main St Ste 400	Murfreesboro	TN	37130	615-893-5860		532-2
Web: www.dnj.com						
Daily News of Los Angeles						
21221 Oxnard St	Woodland Hills	CA	91367	818-713-3000	713-0058	532-2
Web: www.dailynews.com						
Daily News Publishing Co						
193 Jefferson Ave	Memphis	TN	38103	901-523-1561		532-3
TF: 800-568-7625 ■ *Web:* www.memphisdailynews.com						
Daily News-Record						
231 S Liberty St	Harrisonburg	VA	22801	540-574-6200		532-2
TF: 800-248-5746 ■ *Web:* www.dnronline.com						
Daily News-Sun 10102 Santa Fe Dr	Sun City	AZ	85351	623-977-8351		532-2
Web: www.yourwestvalley.com						
Daily Nonpareil						
535 W Broadway Ste 300	Council Bluffs	IA	51503	712-328-1811	325-5776	532-2
TF: 800-283-1882 ■ *Web:* www.nonpareilonline.com						
Daily Pilot 1375 Sunflower Ave	Costa Mesa	CA	92626	714-966-4600		532-2
Web: www.latimes.com/socal/daily-pilot						
Daily Planet 15 Ctr St	Burlington	VT	05401	802-862-9647		671
Web: www.dailyplanet15.com						
Daily Press 7505 Warwick Blvd	Newport News	VA	23607	757-247-4600	245-8618	532-2
Web: www.dailypress.com						
Daily Press						
13891 Pk Ave PO Box 1389	Victorville	CA	92393	760-241-7744	241-1860	532-2
Web: www.vvdailypress.com						
Daily Printing Inc 2333 Niagara Ln	Plymouth	MN	55447	763-475-2333		627
Web: www.dailyprinting.com						

Name / Address	City	State	Zip	Phone	Fax	Class
Daily Progress 685 W Rio Rd	Charlottesville	VA	22902	434-978-7200	978-7252	637-8
TF: 866-469-4866 ■ *Web:* www.dailyprogress.com						
Daily Racing Form 100 Broadway 7th Fl	New York	NY	10005	212-366-7600		457-14
TF Cust Svc: 800-306-3676 ■ *Web:* www.drf.com						
Daily Record						
212 E Liberty St PO Box 918	Wooster	OH	44691	330-264-1125		532-2
TF: 800-686-2958 ■ *Web:* www.the-daily-record.com						
Daily Record 16 W Main St	Rochester	NY	14614	585-232-6920	232-2740	532-2
TF: 800-451-9998 ■ *Web:* www.nydailyrecord.com						
Daily Record Co, The 1414 Key Hwy	Baltimore	MD	21230	410-783-8153		532-3
Web: thedailyrecord.com						
Daily Record Inc 6 Century Dr	Parsippany	NJ	07054	973-428-6200	428-6666	637-8
Web: www.dailyrecord.com						
Daily Record, The 11 E Saratoga St	Baltimore	MD	21202	443-524-8100		637-8
Web: www.thedailyrecord.com						
Daily Report for Executives						
1801 S Bell St	Arlington	VA	22202	800-372-1033		531-2
TF: 800-372-1033 ■ *Web:* www.bna.com/daily-report-executives-p6093						
Daily Republic 1250 Texas St	Fairfield	CA	94533	707-425-4646	425-5924	532-2
TF: 800-438-7325 ■ *Web:* www.dailyrepublic.com						
Daily Sentinel PO Box 668	Grand Junction	CO	81502	970-242-5050	244-8578	532-2
TF: 800-332-5832 ■ *Web:* www.gjsentinel.com						
Daily Sentinel 111 Ct St	Pomeroy	OH	45769	740-992-2155	992-2157	532-2
Web: www.mydailysentinel.com						
Daily Sentinel 701 Veterans Dr	Scottsboro	AL	35768	256-259-1020	259-2709	532-2
TF: 877-985-9212 ■ *Web:* www.thedailysentinel.com						
Daily Southtown 6901 W 159th St	Tinley Park	IL	60477	708-633-6700	222-4674*	532-2
**Fax Area Code:* 312 ■ *Web:* www.chicagotribune.com/suburbs/daily-southtown						
Daily Star 102 Chestnut St PO Box 250	Oneonta	NY	13820	607-432-1000	432-5707	532-2
TF: 800-721-1000 ■ *Web:* www.thedailystar.com						
Daily Sun 1100 Main St	The Villages	FL	32159	352-753-1119		532-4
TF: 800-726-6592 ■ *Web:* www.thevillagesdailysun.com						
Daily Tax Report 1801 S Bell St	Arlington	VA	22202	800-372-1033		531-2
TF: 800-372-1033 ■ *Web:* www.bna.com/daily-tax-report-p7889						
Daily Telegram 133 N Winter St	Adrian	MI	49221	517-265-5111		532-2
TF: 800-968-5111 ■ *Web:* www.lenconnect.com						
Daily Times 618 Beam St	Salisbury	MD	21801	410-749-7171		532-2
TF: 877-335-6278 ■ *Web:* www.delmarvanow.com						
Daily Times 201 N Allen Ave	Farmington	NM	87401	505-325-4545	564-4630	532-2
TF: 877-599-3331 ■ *Web:* www.daily-times.com						
Daily Times 307 E Harper St	Maryville	TN	37804	865-981-1100	981-1175	532-2
Web: www.thedailytimes.com						
Daily Times-Call 350 Terry St	Longmont	CO	80501	303-776-2244		532-2
TF: 800-279-8537 ■ *Web:* www.timescall.com						
Daily World 315 S Michigan St	Aberdeen	WA	98520	360-532-4000	533-6039	532-2
Web: www.thedailyworld.com						
Dailybreak Inc 100 N Washington St	Boston	MA	02114	617-451-1790		387
Web: www.dailybreak.com						
DailyFeats Inc 22 Pearl St	Cambridge	MA	02139	617-714-3833		387
DailyFX 55 Water St 50th Fl	New York	NY	10041	212-897-7660		401
Web: www.dailyfx.com						
DailyMe Inc						
4000 Hollywood Blvd Ste 745-S	Hollywood	FL	33021	954-922-2999		237
Web: www.dailyme.com						
Daimler Vans Mfg LLC						
8501 Palmetto Commerce Pkwy	Ladson	SC	29456	843-695-5000		256
Web: daimler.com						
DaimlerChrysler Corp Jeep Div						
PO Box 21-8004	Auburn Hills	MI	48321	800-992-1997		59
TF Cust Svc: 800-992-1997 ■ *Web:* www.jeep.com						
Daines Steve (Sen R - MT)						
320 Hart Senate Office Bldg	Washington	DC	20510	202-224-2651		342-2
Web: www.daines.senate.gov						
Daingerfield State Park						
455 Pk Rd 17	Daingerfield	TX	75638	903-645-2921		565
Web: tpwd.texas.gov/state-parks/daingerfield						
Daired's Salon & Spa Pangea						
2400 W I-20	Arlington	TX	76017	817-465-9797		77
Web: daireds.com						
Dairiconcepts LP						
3253 E Chestnut Expy	Springfield	MO	65802	417-829-3400	829-3401	296-5
TF: 877-596-4374 ■ *Web:* www.dairiconcepts.com						
Dairy Barn Stores Inc						
544 Elwood Rd	East Northport	NY	11731	631-368-8050	266-2547	204
TF: 800-666-7667 ■ *Web:* www.dairybarn.com						
Dairy Conveyor Corp 38 Mt Ebo Dr S	Brewster	NY	10509	845-278-7878		207
Web: www.dairyconveyor.com						
Dairy Council Digest						
10255 W Higgins Rd Ste 900	Rosemont	IL	60018	847-627-3790		531-8
Web: www.nationaldairycouncil.org						
Dairy Ctr for the Arts 2590 Walnut St	Boulder	CO	80302	303-440-7826		50-2
Web: www.thedairy.org						
Dairy Farmers of America Inc						
10220 N Ambassador Dr	Kansas City	MO	64153	816-801-6455		296-5
TF: 888-332-6455 ■ *Web:* www.dfamilk.com						
Dairy Farmers of Ontario						
6780 Campobello Rd	Mississauga	ON	L5N2L8	905-821-8970		138
Web: www.milk.org						
Dairy Food USA Inc						
2819 County Rd F	Blue Mounds	WI	53517	608-437-5598		296-5
Web: www.dairyfoodusa.com						
Dairy Herd Management						
10901 W 84th Terr	Lenexa	KS	66214	913-438-8700	438-0695	457-1
TF: 800-255-5113 ■ *Web:* www.dairyherd.com						
Dairy Management Inc (DMI)						
10255 W Higgins Rd Ste 900	Rosemont	IL	60018	800-853-2479		48-2
TF: 800-853-2479 ■ *Web:* www.dairy.org						
Dairy One 730 Warren Rd	Ithaca	NY	14850	607-257-1272	257-6808	11-2
TF: 800-344-2697 ■ *Web:* www.dairyone.com						
Dairy Queen 7505 Metro Blvd	Minneapolis	MN	55439	952-830-0200		381
TF: 800-883-4279 ■ *Web:* www.dairyqueen.com						
Dairyamerica Inc						
7815 N Palm Ave Ste 250	Fresno	CA	93711	559-251-0992	251-1078	49-18
TF: 800-722-3110 ■ *Web:* www.dairyamerica.com						
Dairyland Greyhound Park						
5522 104th Ave	Kenosha	WI	53144	262-657-8200		133

Name / Address	City	State	Zip	Phone	Fax	Class
Dairyland Insurance Co 1800 N Pt Dr	Stevens Point	WI	54481	715-346-6000	999-4642*	391-4
*Fax Area Code: 800 ■ *Fax: Sales ■ TF Sales: 866-445-5364 ■ Web: www.sentry.com						
Dairyland Laboratories Inc 217 E Main St	Arcadia	WI	54612	608-323-2123		743
TF: 800-658-2481 ■ Web: www.dairylandlabs.net						
Dairyland Power Co-op 3200 E Ave S	La Crosse	WI	54601	608-788-4000		245
Web: www.dairylandpower.com						
Dairyland USA Corporation 1300 Viele Ave	Bronx	NY	10474	718-842-8700	378-2234	297-9
Dairymen's Feed & Supply Co 323 E Washington St	Petaluma	CA	94952	707-763-1585		447
Dais Analytic Corp 11552 Prosperous Dr	Odessa	FL	33556	727-375-8484		14
Web: www.daisanalytic.com						
Daishowa-Marubeni International Ltd 510 Burrard St Ste 700	Vancouver	BC	V6C3A8	604-684-4326		638
Web: www.dmi.ca						
Daisy Blue Naturals 2610 Yh Hanson Ave Ste 108	Albert Lea	MN	56007	507-373-0229		231
Web: daisybluenaturals.com						
Daisy Data Displays Inc 2850 Lewisberry Rd	York Haven	PA	17370	717-932-9999	932-8000	173-4
Web: www.makeitdaisy.com						
Daisy IT Supplies Sales & Service 8575 Red Oak Ave	Rancho Cucamonga	CA	91730	909-989-5585	989-5585	112
TF: 800-266-5585 ■ Web: daisyit.com						
Daisy Outdoor Products 400 W Stribling Dr	Rogers	AR	72756	479-636-1200		710
TF: 800-643-3458 ■ Web: www.daisy.com						
Daisy Rock Guitars 16320 Roscoe Blvd Ste 100	Van Nuys	CA	91410	877-693-2479		527
TF: 877-693-2479 ■ Web: www.daisyrock.com						
Daisy State Park 103 E Pk	Kirby	AR	71950	870-398-4487		565
Web: www.arkansasstateparks.com/daisy						
Daiwa Capital Markets America Inc Financial Sq 32 Old Slip	New York	NY	10005	212-612-7000		690
Web: www.us.daiwacm.com						
Daiwa Corp 11137 Warland Dr	Cypress	CA	90630	562-802-9589		710
TF: 800-736-4653 ■ Web: www.daiwa.com						
DAK Group Ltd, The 195 Rt 17 S	Rochelle Park	NJ	07662	201-712-9555		690
Web: www.dakgroup.com						
DAKE 724 Robbins Rd	Grand Haven	MI	49417	616-842-7110	842-0859	351
TF: 800-846-3253 ■ Web: www.dakecorp.com						
Dakkota Integrated Systems 1875 Holloway Dr	Holt	MI	48842	517-694-6500		247
Web: www.dakkotasystems.com						
Dakno 3101 Poplarwood Ct Ste 108	Raleigh	NC	27604	919-877-8511		463
Web: www.dakno.com						
Dako Services Inc 2966 Industrial Row	Troy	MI	48084	248-655-0100		260
Web: www.dakogroup.com						
Dakota Air Parts International Inc 1801 23rd Ave N Ste 119	Fargo	ND	58102	701-297-9999		21
Web: www.dakotaairparts.com						
Dakota Analytics Inc 205 Fifth Ave SW Ste 600	Calgary	AB	T2P2V7	403-264-6999		196
Web: www.dakotaanalytics.com						
Dakota Brands International Inc 2121 13th St NE	Jamestown	ND	58401	701-252-5073		296-1
TF: 800-844-5073 ■ Web: www.dakotabrands.com						
Dakota Central 630 Fifth St N	Carrington	ND	58421	701-652-3184		736
TF: 800-771-0974 ■ Web: www.daktel.com						
Dakota Communications 2999 Overland Ave Ste 210	Los Angeles	CA	90064	310-815-8444		636
Web: www.dakcomm.com						
Dakota Community Bank & Trust 1727 State St	Bismarck	ND	58501	701-255-9000		70
Web: dakotacommunitybank.com						
Dakota County 1601 Broadway	Dakota City	NE	68731	402-987-2126	987-2186	338
Web: www.dakotacountyne.org						
Dakota County 1560 Hwy 55	Hastings	MN	55033	651-438-8100	438-4405	338
Web: www.co.dakota.mn.us						
Dakota County Regional Chamber of Commerce 1121 Town Ctr Dr Ste 102	Eagan	MN	55123	651-452-9872	452-8978	139
Web: www.dcrchamber.com						
Dakota County Technical College 1300 E 145th St	Rosemount	MN	55068	651-423-8301	423-8775	800
TF: 877-937-3282 ■ Web: www.dctc.edu						
Dakota Creek Industries Inc 820 Fourth St PO Box 218	Anacortes	WA	98221	360-293-9575	293-6432	698
TF: 800-639-2715 ■ Web: www.dakotacreek.com						
Dakota Drug Inc 28 Main St N	Minot	ND	58703	701-852-2141		238
TF: 800-437-2018 ■ Web: www.dakdrug.com						
Dakota Electric Assn 4300 220th St W	Farmington	MN	55024	651-463-6144	463-6144	245
TF: 800-874-3409 ■ Web: www.dakotaelectric.com						
Dakota Energy Cooperative Inc PO Box 830	Huron	SD	57350	605-352-8591		245
TF: 800-353-8591 ■ Web: dakotaenergy.coop						
Dakota Fabricating Inc 12111 W Northern Ave	Glendale	AZ	85307	623-935-7805		207
Web: www.dakotafab.com						
Dakota Gasification Co PO Box 5540	Bismarck	ND	58506	701-221-4400	557-5336	787
TF: 866-747-3546 ■ Web: www.dakotagas.com						
Dakota Granite Co 48391 150th St PO Box 1351	Milbank	SD	57252	605-432-5580	432-6155	724
TF: 800-843-3333 ■ Web: dakotagranite.com						
Dakota Growers Pasta Company Inc 1 Pasta Ave	Carrington	ND	58421	701-652-2855		296-31
TF: 866-569-4411 ■ Web: www.viterra.com						
Dakota Homestead Title Insurance Co 315 S Phillips Ave	Sioux Falls	SD	57104	605-336-0388	996-3270	391-6
Web: www.tsptitle.com						
Dakota Jazz Club & Restaurant 1010 Nicollet Ave	Minneapolis	MN	55403	612-332-1010		671
Web: www.dakotacooks.com						
Dakota Line Inc PO Box 476	Vermillion	SD	57069	605-624-5228	624-5338	780
TF: 800-532-5682 ■ Web: www.dakotalines.com						
Dakota Lions Sight & Health 4501 W 61st St N	Sioux Falls	SD	57107	605-373-1008	373-1261	269
TF: 800-245-7846 ■ Web: www.dakotasight.org						
Dakota Marble Inc 902 W 19th St	Yankton	SD	57078	605-665-7241	665-7241	724
TF: 800-697-7241 ■ Web: www.dakotamarble.com						
Dakota Mfg Company Inc 1909 S Rowley St	Mitchell	SD	57301	605-996-5571	996-5572	779
TF: 800-232-5682 ■ Web: traileze.com						
Dakota Missouri Valley & Western Railroad Inc 3501 E Rosser Ave	Bismarck	ND	58501	701-223-9282		649
Web: www.dmvwrr.com						
Dakota Plains Co-op 151 Ninth Ave NW	Valley City	ND	58072	701-845-0812		324
Web: www.chsdakotaplainsag.com						
Dakota Riggers & Tool Supply Inc 704 E Benson Rd	Sioux Falls	SD	57104	605-335-0041		492
Web: www.dakotariggers.com						
Dakota State University 820 N Washington Ave	Madison	SD	57042	605-256-5139	256-5020	166
TF: 888-378-9988 ■ Web: www.dsu.edu						
Dakota Supply Group (DSG) 2601 Third Ave N	Fargo	ND	58102	701-237-9440	237-6504	246
TF: 800-437-4702 ■ Web: www.dakotasupplygroup.com						
Dakota Systems Inc 1057 Broadway Rd	Dracut	MA	01826	978-275-0600	275-0606	696
Web: www.dakotasystems.com						
Dakota Tube Inc 221 Airport Dr	Watertown	SD	57201	605-882-2156		454
Web: www.dakotatube.com						
Dakota Valley Electric Co-op 7296 Hwy 281	Edgeley	ND	58433	701-493-2281		245
TF: 800-342-4671 ■ Web: www.dakotavalley.com						
Dakota Vision Center LLC 5012 S Bur Oak Pl	Sioux Falls	SD	57108	605-361-1680		543
Web: dakotavisioncenter.com						
Dakota Wesleyan University 1200 W University Ave	Mitchell	SD	57301	605-995-2600	995-2699	166
TF: 800-333-8506 ■ Web: www.dwu.edu						
Dakota Zoo 602 Riverside Pk Rd	Bismarck	ND	58504	701-223-7543	258-8350	823
Web: www.dakotazoo.org						
Dakotacare 2600 W 49th St PO Box 7406	Sioux Falls	SD	57117	605-334-4000	334-8717	391-3
TF: 800-325-5598 ■ Web: www.dakotacare.com						
Daktronics Inc 201 Daktronics Dr	Brookings	SD	57006	605-692-0200	697-4700	173-4
NASDAQ: DAKT ■ TF: 800-325-8766 ■ Web: www.daktronics.com						
Dal Poggetto & Company LLP 149 Stony Cir	Santa Rosa	CA	95401	707-545-3311		2
Dalager Engineering Co 936 Railroad Ave	Bath	SD	57427	605-229-2412		256
Daland Corp 9313 Eat 34th St N Ste 100	Wichita	KS	67226	316-681-1081		194
Web: www.dalandcorp.com						
Dalat Restaurant 425 Pk Ave	Worcester	MA	01610	508-753-6036		671
DALB Inc 73 Industrial Blvd	Kearneysville	WV	25430	304-725-0300		627
Web: www.dalb.com						
Dalby, Wendland & Company PC 201 Centennial St Ste 300 PO Box 1150	Glenwood Springs	CO	81601	970-243-1921		196
TF: 800-332-7097 ■ Web: dalbycpa.com						
Dalco Metals Inc 857 Walworth St	Walworth	WI	53184	262-275-6175		295
Web: www.dalcometals.com						
Dale Barton Agency Inc 1100 East 6600 South	Salt Lake City	UT	84121	801-288-1600		390
TF: 866-288-1666 ■ Web: dalebarton.com						
Dale Carnegie & Assoc Inc 290 Motor Pkwy	Hauppauge	NY	11788	800-231-5800		765
TF: 800-231-5800 ■ Web: www.dalecarnegie.com						
Dale Corp 28091 Dequindre	Madison Heights	MI	48071	248-542-2400	542-6007	737
Web: www.dalecorp.com						
Dale County 202 Hwy 123 S Ste C	Ozark	AL	36360	334-774-6025	774-1841	338
Web: dalecountyal.org						
Dale Earnhardt Inc 1675 Dale Earnhardt Hwy 3	Mooresville	NC	28115	704-662-8000		642
Web: www.daleearnhardtinc.com						
Dale L Buchanan & Associates PC 1206 Pointe Centre Dr Ste 110	Chattanooga	TN	37421	800-945-4950		428
TF: 800-945-4950 ■ Web: dalebuchanan.com						
Dale Laboratories 2960 Simms St	Hollywood	FL	33020	954-925-0103	922-3008	588
TF: 800-327-1776 ■ Web: www.dalelabs.com						
Dale M Long PC CPA'S 5945 Ward Rd Ste 200	Arvada	CO	80004	303-431-2666		2
Web: dalelongpc.com						
Dale Medical Products Inc PO Box 1556	Plainville	MA	02762	800-343-3980	695-6587*	476
*Fax Area Code: 508 ■ TF: 800-343-3980 ■ Web: www.dalemed.com						
Dale Scott & Co 650 California St 8th Fl	San Francisco	CA	94108	415-956-1030		401
Web: www.dalescott.com						
Dale Tiffany Inc 14765 Firestone Blvd	La Mirada	CA	90638	714-739-2700		362
TF: 800-328-3253 ■ Web: www.daletiffany.com						
Dale Willey Automotive 2840 Iowa St	Lawrence	KS	66046	785-727-1124	843-4903	57
Web: dalewilleyauto.com						
Daler-Rowney USA Ltd 7 Corporate Dr	Cranbury	NJ	08512	609-655-5252	655-5852	43
Web: www.daler-rowney.com						
Dalesio's of Little Italy 829 Eastern Ave	Baltimore	MD	21202	410-539-1965		671
Web: www.dalesios.com						
Daley & Heft LLP 462 Stevens Ave Ste 201	Solana Beach	CA	92075	858-755-5666		428
Web: daleyheft.com						
Dalfen America Corp Westmount 4444 rue Sainte-Catherine W Ste 100	Montreal	QC	H3Z1R2	514-938-1050		528
Web: www.dalfen.com						
Dalhousie University 6299 S St Rm 125 Henry Hicks Academic Admin Bldg PO Box 15000	Halifax	NS	B3H4R2	902-494-3998	494-2839	785
Web: www.dal.ca						
Dalhousie University Faculty of Medicine 1459 Oxford St	Halifax	NS	B3H4R2	902-494-1874	494-6369*	167-2
*Fax: Admissions ■ Web: www.medicine.dal.ca						
Dali Restaurant 415 Washington St	Somerville	MA	02143	617-661-3254	661-2813	671
Web: www.dalirestaurant.com						

				Phone	Fax	Class
Dalia Kitchen Design Inc 1 Design Ctr Pl Ste 633	Boston	MA	02210	617-482-2566		115
Daliah Plastics Corp 134 W Wainman Ave. *Web:* www.daliahplastics.com	Asheboro	NC	27203	336-629-0551		600
Dall Bay State Marine Park 400 Willoughby Ave PO Box 111020 *Web:* www.dnr.alaska.gov	Juneau	AK	99811	907-465-4563		565
Dallago Corp 2411 E Aztec Ave	Gallup	NM	87301	505-722-6638		610
Dallam County PO Box 1352 *TF:* 800-433-0567 ■ *Web:* www.dallam.org	Dalhart	TX	79022	806-244-4751		338
Dallas Airmotive Inc 900 Nolen Dr Ste 100 *Web:* www.dallasairmotive.com	Grapevine	TX	76051	214-956-3001		20
Dallas Arboretum & Botanical Garden 8525 Garland Rd. *Web:* www.dallasarboretum.org	Dallas	TX	75218	214-515-6500	515-6522	97
Dallas Area Rapid Transit Authority (DART) 1401 Pacific Ave PO Box 660163 *TF:* 800-231-2222 ■ *Web:* www.dart.org	Dallas	TX	75202	214-749-3278		468
Dallas Athletic Club 4111 Dallas Athletic Club Dr *Web:* www.dallasathleticclub.org	Dallas	TX	75228	972-279-6517		711
Dallas Baptist University 3000 Mtn Creek Pkwy. **Fax:* Admissions ■ *TF:* 800-460-1328 ■ *Web:* www.dbu.edu	Dallas	TX	75211	214-333-7100	333-5447*	166
Dallas Bar Association 2101 Ross Ave. *Web:* www.dallasbar.org	Dallas	TX	75201	214-220-7400		95
Dallas Bias Fabrics Inc 1401 N Carroll Ave. *Web:* www.dallasbias.com	Dallas	TX	75204	214-824-2036	824-2036	34
Dallas Black Dance Theatre 2700 Flora St *Web:* www.dbdt.com	Dallas	TX	75201	214-871-2376	871-2842	573-1
Dallas Christian College 2700 Christian Pkwy. *TF:* 800-688-1029 ■ *Web:* www.dallas.edu	Dallas	TX	75234	972-241-3371	241-8021	161
Dallas City Hall 1500 Marilla St *Web:* www.dallascityhall.com	Dallas	TX	75201	214-670-4538	670-3946	337
Dallas City Packing Inc 3049 Morrell St	Dallas	TX	75203	214-948-3901		473
Dallas Container Corp 8330 Endicott Ln *Web:* www.dallascontainer.com	Dallas	TX	75227	214-381-7148		100
Dallas Convention & Visitors Bureau 325 N St Paul St Ste 700 *TF:* 800-232-5527 ■ *Web:* www.visitdallas.com	Dallas	TX	75201	214-571-1000	571-1000	206
Dallas Convention Ctr 650 S Griffin St *TF:* 877-850-2100 ■ *Web:* www.dallasconventioncenter.com	Dallas	TX	75202	214-939-2750	939-2700	205
Dallas County 801 Ct St *Web:* www.co.dallas.ia.us	Adel	IA	50003	515-993-5814		338
Dallas County 1201 Elm St *Web:* buffalococ.com	Dallas	TX	75202	214-653-7131		338
Dallas County 411 Elm St *TF:* 800-746-6110 ■ *Web:* www.dallascounty.org	Dallas	TX	75202	214-653-7361	653-7057	338
Dallas County 105 Lauderdale *Web:* www.dallascounty-al.org	Selma	AL	36702	334-874-2553	874-2587	338
Dallas County Hospital 610 Tenth St *TF:* 800-877-7541 ■ *Web:* www.dallascohospital.org	Perry	IA	50220	515-465-3547		374-3
Dallas County Medical Society 140 E 12th St *TF:* 800-252-3439 ■ *Web:* www.dallas-cms.org	Dallas	TX	75203	214-948-3622		633
Dallas Cowboys 1 Cowboys Pkwy. *Web:* www.dallascowboys.com	Irving	TX	75063	972-556-9900		715-3
Dallas Ctr - Grimes Community School District 1414 Walnut St Ste 200 *Web:* dcgschools.com	Dallas Center	IA	50063	515-992-3866		685
Dallas Ctr for Contemporary Art 161 Glass St *Web:* www.thecontemporary.net	Dallas	TX	75207	214-821-2522	821-9103	50-2
Dallas Data Center Inc 2636 Walnut Hill Ln Ste 202 *Web:* www.dallasdatacenter.com	Dallas	TX	75229	972-993-8888		393
Dallas Desk Inc 15207 Midway Rd *Web:* dallasdesk.com	Addison	TX	75001	972-788-1802		321
Dallas Digital Services LLC 5316 Bransford Rd *TF:* 800-808-4239 ■ *Web:* www.ddserv.com	Colleyville	TX	76034	817-577-8794		180
Dallas Fan Fares Inc 5485 Beltline Rd Ste 270 *TF:* 800-925-6979 ■ *Web:* www.fanfares.com	Dallas	TX	75254	972-239-9969		181
Dallas Firefighters Museum 3801 Parry Ave *Web:* dallasfiremuseum.com	Dallas	TX	75226	214-821-1500	821-1500	520
Dallas Galleria 13350 Dallas Pkwy *Web:* www.galleriadallas.com	Dallas	TX	75240	972-702-7100		460
Dallas Heritage Village 1515 S Harwood *Web:* www.dallasheritagevillage.org	Dallas	TX	75215	214-421-5141	428-6351	520
Dallas Holocaust Museum 211 N Record St Ste 100 *Web:* www.dallasholocaustmuseum.org	Dallas	TX	75202	214-741-7500	747-2270	520
Dallas Independent School District 3700 Ross Ave *TF:* 866-796-3682 ■ *Web:* www.dallasisd.org	Dallas	TX	75204	972-925-3700	925-4201	685
Dallas Institute of Funeral Service 3909 S Buckner Blvd *TF:* 800-235-5444 ■ *Web:* www.dallasinstitute.edu	Dallas	TX	75227	214-388-5466	388-0316	800
Dallas Johnson Greenhouse Inc 2802 Twin City Dr. *TF:* 800-445-4794 ■ *Web:* www.djgreenhouses.com	Council Bluffs	IA	51501	712-366-0407		369
Dallas Love Field 8008 Cedar Springs Rd LB 16 *TF:* 877-359-8474 ■ *Web:* www.dallas-lovefield.com	Dallas	TX	75235	214-670-5683	670-6051	27
Dallas Market Ctr 2100 Stemmons Fwy Ste 113 *TF:* 800-325-6587 ■ *Web:* www.dallasmarketcenter.com	Dallas	TX	75207	214-655-6100	749-5479	205
Dallas Mavericks 2909 Taylor St *Web:* www.nba.com	Dallas	TX	75226	214-747-6287	658-7121	714-1
Dallas Medical Ctr 7 Medical Pkwy *Web:* www.dallasmedcenter.com	Dallas	TX	75234	972-888-7000		374-3
Dallas Morning News 508 Young St *TF:* 800-925-1500 ■ *Web:* www.dallasnews.com	Dallas	TX	75202	214-977-8222	977-8319	532-2
Dallas Museum of Art 1717 N Harwood St **Fax Area Code:* 212 ■ *TF:* 800-745-3000 ■ *Web:* dma.org	Dallas	TX	75201	214-922-1200	736-6767*	520
Dallas Northeast Chamber of Commerce 9543 Losa Dr Ste 118 *Web:* www.eastdallaschamber.com	Dallas	TX	75218	214-328-4100		139
Dallas Observer 2501 Oak Lawn Ave Ste 700 PO Box 190289 *Web:* www.dallasobserver.com	Dallas	TX	75219	214-757-9000	757-8590	532-5
Dallas Opera 2403 Flora St Ste 500 *Web:* www.dallasopera.org	Dallas	TX	75201	214-443-1043	443-1060	573-2
Dallas Regional Chamber 700 N Pearl St Ste 1200 *Web:* www.dallaschamber.org	Dallas	TX	75201	214-746-6600	746-6799	139
Dallas Regional Medical Ctr (DRMC) 1011 N Galloway Ave **Fax Area Code:* 972 ■ *TF:* 800-562-6686 ■ *Web:* www.dallasregionalmedicalcenter.com	Mesquite	TX	75149	214-320-7000	289-9468*	374-3
Dallas Semiconductor Corp 4401 S Beltwood Pkwy **Fax:* Cust Svc ■ *Web:* www.maximintegrated.com	Dallas	TX	75244	972-371-3726	371-3715*	696
Dallas Stars 2601 Ave of the Stars *Web:* stars.nhl.com	Frisco	TX	75034	214-387-5500	387-5599	716
Dallas Symphony Orchestra 2301 Flora St *Web:* mydso.com	Dallas	TX	75201	214-849-4376		573-3
Dallas Theater Ctr 3636 Turtle Creek Blvd *Web:* www.dallastheatercenter.org	Dallas	TX	75219	214-526-8210	521-7666	749
Dallas Theological Seminary 3909 Swiss Ave *TF:* 800-992-0998 ■ *Web:* www.dts.edu	Dallas	TX	75204	800-387-9673		167-3
Dallas Waste Disposal & Recycling Inc 3303 Pluto St *Web:* www.dallasrecycling.net	Dallas	TX	75212	214-634-1831		660
Dallas World Aquarium 1801 N Griffin St. *TF:* 800-235-5712 ■ *Web:* www.dwazoo.com	Dallas	TX	75202	214-720-2224		40
Dallas-Fort Worth International Airport (DFW) 3200 E Airfield Dr PO Box 619428 *TF:* 800-252-7522 ■ *Web:* www.dfwairport.com	Dallas	TX	75261	972-973-8888	574-5509	27
Dallastown Area School District 700 New School Ln *TF:* 866-233-9796 ■ *Web:* www.dallastown.net	Dallastown	PA	17313	717-244-4021		685
Dallo Enterprises 5075 Federal Blvd *Web:* www.harvestranchmarkets.com	San Diego	CA	92102	619-527-3385		297-8
Dalmac Oilfield Services Inc 4934 - 89 St *TF:* 888-632-5622 ■ *Web:* www.dalmacenergy.com	Edmonton	AB	T6E5K1	780-988-8510		539
Dalmec Inc 409 Fox Ct. *TF:* 800-656-2140 ■ *Web:* www.dalmec.com	Bloomingdale	IL	60108	630-307-8426		295
Dalrymple Gravel & Contracting Company Inc 2105 S Broadway *TF:* 800-957-3130 ■ *Web:* www.dalrymplecompanies.com	Pine City	NY	14871	607-737-6200	737-1056	46
Dalsin Industries Inc 9111 Grand Ave S *Web:* www.dalsinind.com	Bloomington	MN	55420	952-881-2260		697
Dal-Tile International Inc 7834 Hawn Fwy *Web:* www.daltile.com	Dallas	TX	75217	214-398-1411	309-4140	751
Dalton & Finegold L L P 34 Essex St *TF:* 800-561-3357 ■ *Web:* www.dfllp.com	Andover	MA	01810	978-470-8400		445
Dalton Agency Inc, The 140 W Monroe St Ste 200 *Web:* www.daltonagency.com	Jacksonville	FL	32202	904-398-5222		4
Dalton Computer Services Inc 1612 Cleveland Hwy *Web:* www.daltoncomputer.com	Dalton	GA	30721	706-259-3327		175
Dalton Corp 310 Ellis St *Web:* www.daltonfoundries.com	Stryker	OH	43557	574-267-8111		203
Dalton Enterprises Inc 131 Willow St *TF:* 800-851-5606 ■ *Web:* www.latexite.com	Cheshire	CT	06410	203-272-3221	271-3396	46
Dalton Gear Co 212 Colfax Ave N *TF:* 800-328-7485 ■ *Web:* www.daltongear.com	Minneapolis	MN	55405	612-374-2150	374-2467	709
Dalton Greiner Hartman Maher & Company LLC 565 Fifth Ave Ste 2101 *TF:* 800-653-2839 ■ *Web:* www.dghm.com	New York	NY	10017	212-557-2445	557-4898	401
Dalton Investments LLC 1601 Cloverfield Blvd Ste 5050 N *Web:* www.daltoninvestments.com	Santa Monica	CA	90404	424-231-9100		401
Dalton Medical Corp 1435 Bradley Ln Ste 100 *Web:* www.daltonmedical.com	Carrollton	TX	75007	972-418-5129		475
Dalton Public Schools 300 W Waugh St PO Box 1408 *Web:* www.daltonpublicschools.com	Dalton	GA	30722	706-876-4000	226-4583	685
Dalton Schools Inc 108 E 89th St *Web:* www.dalton.org	New York	NY	10128	212-423-5200		685
Dalton State College 650 N College Dr *TF:* 800-829-4436 ■ *Web:* www.daltonstate.edu	Dalton	GA	30720	706-272-4436		166
Dalton-Whitfield Chamber of Commerce 890 College Dr *Web:* www.daltonchamber.org	Dalton	GA	30720	706-278-7373	226-8739	139
Daly City Public Library 40 Wembley Dr *TF:* 888-227-7669 ■ *Web:* www.dalycity.org	Daly City	CA	94015	650-991-8025	991-8225	434-3
Daly City-Colma Chamber of Commerce 355 Gellert Blvd Ste 138 *Web:* www.dalycity-colmachamber.org	Daly City	CA	94015	650-755-3900	755-5160	139
Daly Computers Inc 22521 Gateway Ctr Dr *TF:* 800-955-3259 ■ *Web:* www.daly.com	Clarksburg	MD	20871	301-670-0381	963-1516	176
Daly Seven Inc 4829 Riverside Dr *Web:* dalyseven.com	Danville	VA	24541	434-822-2161		379
Daman Consulting Inc 1250 S Capital Of Texas Hw *TF:* 800-875-8734 ■ *Web:* damaninc.com	Austin	TX	78746	512-329-6646		196

Name / Address	City	State	ZIP	Phone	Fax	Class
Daman Industrial Services Inc 754 Kittanning Hollow Rd PO Box 486 *Web:* www.damanindustrial.com	East Brady	PA	16028	724-526-5714	526-5277	454
Daman Products Co Inc 1811 N Home St *TF:* 800-959-7841 ■ *Web:* www.damanifolds.com	Mishawaka	IN	46545	574-259-7841	259-7665	790
Damar Services Inc 6067 Decatur Blvd *Web:* www.damar.org	Indianapolis	IN	46241	317-856-5201		672
Damariscotta Lake State Park 8 State Pk Rd *Web:* www.maine.gov	Jefferson	ME	04348	207-549-7600		565
Damascus 2276 S Colorado Blvd	Denver	CO	80222	303-757-3515		671
Damascus Bakery Inc 56 Gold St *Fax Area Code: 718 ■ *TF:* 800-367-7482 ■ *Web:* www.damascusbakery.com	Brooklyn	NY	11201	800-367-7482	403-0948*	68
Damascus Steel Casting Co Blockhouse Rd Run Extn *TF:* 800-920-2210 ■ *Web:* www.damascussteel.com	New Brighton	PA	15066	724-846-2770		492
Dameron Alloy Foundries Inc 927 S Santa Fe Ave *Web:* www.dameron.net	Compton	CA	90224	310-631-5165		492
Dameron Hospital Assn (DHA) 525 W Acacia St *Web:* www.dameronhospital.org	Stockton	CA	95203	209-944-5550		374-3
Damian's Cucina Italiana 3011 Smith St *TF:* 800-669-7061 ■ *Web:* www.damians.com	Houston	TX	77006	713-522-0439	522-4408	671
Damon G Douglas Co 26 Worlds Fair Dr Suite A *Fax Area Code: 732 ■ *Web:* www.dgdco.com	Somerset,	NJ	08873	908-272-0100	560-0305*	189-3
Damon Industries Inc 12435 Rockhill Ave NE *TF:* 800-362-9850 ■ *Web:* www.damonq.com	Alliance	OH	44601	330-821-5310	821-6355	151
Damon's Steak House 317 N Brand Blvd *Web:* www.damonsglendale.com	Glendale	CA	91203	818-507-1510		671
Damsky Paper Co 3501 First Ave N *Web:* www.damskypaper.com	Birmingham	AL	35222	205-521-9840	521-9840	554
Damuth Trane 1100 Cavalier Blvd *Web:* www.damuth.com	Chesapeake	VA	23323	757-558-0200	558-9715	187
Dan Bailey Fly Shop 209 W Park St *TF:* 800-356-4052 ■ *Web:* www.dan-bailey.com	Livingston	MT	59047	406-222-1673		711
Dan Dolan Printing Inc 2301 E Hennepin Ave *TF:* 800-847-5924 ■ *Web:* www.dolanprinting.com	Minneapolis	MN	55413	612-379-2311		627
Dan Klores Communications Inc (DKC) 261 Fifth Ave *Web:* www.dkcnews.com	New York	NY	10016	212-685-4300	685-9024	636
Dan Post Boot Co 1751 Alpine Dr *Web:* www.danpostboots.com	Clarksville	TN	37040	931-645-4466		301
Dan Schantz Farm & Greenhouses LLC 8025 Spinnerstown Rd *TF:* 800-451-3064 ■ *Web:* www.danschantz.com	Zionsville	PA	18092	610-967-2181		369
Dan Shing 15912 Stony Plain Rd	Edmonton	AB	T5P4A1	780-483-1143		671
Dan'l Webster Inn 149 Main St *TF:* 800-444-3566 ■ *Web:* www.danlwebsterinn.com	Sandwich	MA	02563	508-888-3622		379
Dan's Competition Inc 1 Competition Way *TF:* 888-888-3267 ■ *Web:* www.danscomp.com	Mount Vernon	IN	47620	888-888-3267		711
Dan's Excavating Inc 12955 23 Mile Rd *Web:* www.dansexc.com	Shelby	MI	48315	586-254-2040		196
Dan's Supermarket Inc 835 S Washington St Ste 4 *Web:* www.dansupermarket.com	Bismarck	ND	58504	701-258-2127		345
Dana B Kenyon Co 5772 Timuquana Rd *Web:* www.dbkenyon.com	Jacksonville	FL	32210	904-777-0833		652
Dana Biomedical Library Dartmouth College *Web:* www.dartmouth.edu	Hanover	NH	03755	603-650-1658	650-1354	434-1
Dana Communications Inc 2 E Broad St *Web:* www.danacommunications.com	Hopewell	NJ	08525	609-466-9187		4
Dana Group, The 6892 S Yosemite Ct *Web:* www.danainvestments.com	Centennial	CO	80112	303-694-7100		652
Dana Hall School 45 Dana Rd PO Box 9010 *Web:* www.danahall.org	Wellesley	MA	02482	781-235-3010		622
Dana Innovations 212 Avenida Fabricante *TF:* 800-582-7777 ■ *Web:* www.sonance.com	San Clemente	CA	92672	949-492-7777		52
Dana Kepner Company Inc 700 Alcott St *Web:* www.danakepner.com	Denver	CO	80204	303-623-6161		612
Dana Point Chamber of Commerce 24681 La Plaza Ste 115 *Web:* www.danapoint-chamber.com	Dana Point	CA	92629	949-496-1555		139
Dana Safety Supply Inc 5221 W Market St *Web:* www.danasafetysupply.com	Greensboro	NC	27409	336-854-5536		791
Dana Transport Inc 210 Essex Ave E *TF:* 800-733-3262 ■ *Web:* www.danacompanies.com	Avenel	NJ	07001	732-750-9100	636-7441	780
Dana-Farber Cancer Institute 44 Binney St *Fax: PR ■ *TF:* 866-408-3324 ■ *Web:* www.dana-farber.org	Boston	MA	02115	617-632-3000	632-5520*	374-7
Dana-Farber Cancer Institute Stem Cell/Bone Marrow Transplant Program 450 Brookline Ave Dana 2 *TF:* 866-408-3324 ■ *Web:* www.dana-farber.org	Boston	MA	02115	617-632-3591	632-4139	769
Danaher Corp 2200 Pennsylvania Ave NW Ste 800 *NYSE: DHR* ■ *TF:* 800-833-9200 ■ *Web:* www.danaher.com	Washington	DC	20037	202-828-0850	828-0860	472
Danal's Mexican Restaurant 508 N O'Connor Rd *Web:* danals-restaurant.com	Irving	TX	75061	972-254-2666		671
Danamark Watercare Ltd 2-90 Walker Dr *TF:* 888-326-2627 ■ *Web:* danamark.com	Brampton	ON	L6T4H6	888-326-2627		610
Dana-Thomas House (DTH) 301 E Lawrence Ave *TF:* 800-525-2660 ■ *Web:* www.dana-thomas.org	Springfield	IL	62703	217-782-6776		50-3
Danburg Management Corp 7700 Congress Ave Ste 3100 *Web:* www.danburg.com	Boca Raton	FL	33487	561-997-5777		509
Danbury Hospital (DH) 24 Hospital Ave *TF:* 800-516-3658 ■ *Web:* www.danburyhospital.org	Danbury	CT	06810	203-739-7000		374-3
Danbury Public Library 170 Main St *TF:* 800-445-2722 ■ *Web:* www.danburylibrary.org	Danbury	CT	06810	203-797-4505	796-1677	434-3
Danby Group LLP, The 3060-A Business Park Dr *TF:* 800-262-2629 ■ *Web:* www.danbygroup.com	Norcross	GA	30071	770-416-9844		535
Dancap Private Equity Inc 197 Sheppard Ave W *Web:* www.dancap.ca	Toronto	ON	M2N1M9	416-590-9444		528
Dance Bros Inc 825C Hammonds Ferry Rd *Web:* dancebrothers.com	Linthicum	MD	21090	410-789-8200	636-3663	189-3
Dance Magazine 333 Seventh Ave 11th Fl *TF:* 800-331-1750 ■ *Web:* www.dancemagazine.com	New York	NY	10001	212-979-4800		457-9
Dance Theatre of Harlem Inc 466 W 152nd St *TF:* 800-538-2538 ■ *Web:* www.dancetheatreofharlem.org	New York	NY	10031	212-690-2800	690-8736	573-1
Dance/USA 1111 16 St NW Ste 300 *TF:* 800-356-3754 ■ *Web:* www.danceusa.org	Washington	DC	20036	202-833-1717	833-2686	48-4
Dancing Deer Baking Company Inc 65 Sprague St W A *Web:* www.dancingdeer.com	Boston	MA	02136	617-442-7300		68
Dancker Sellew & Douglas 291 Evans Way	Somerville	NJ	08876	908-231-1600		320
Danco Inc 486 Lakewood Rd *Web:* www.danco-inc.com	Waterbury	CT	06704	203-753-5121		385
Danco Industrial Contractors Inc 1121 N Beverlye Rd *TF:* 800-622-2331 ■ *Web:* www.dancoindustrial.com	Dothan	AL	36303	334-792-3985		186
Danco Investors Group Lp 112 Second Ave N	Nashville	TN	37201	615-251-9521		238
Danco Metal Products Inc 760 Moore Rd *Web:* www.dancometal.com	Avon Lake	OH	44012	440-871-2300		697
Danco Precision Inc Wheatland & Mellon Sts *TF:* 800-886-7746 ■ *Web:* www.dancoprecision.com	Phoenixville	PA	19460	610-933-8981	935-2011	488
Dane County 210 ML King Jr Blvd Rm 106A *TF:* 800-398-7073 ■ *Web:* www.countyofdane.com	Madison	WI	53703	608-266-4121		338
Dane County Regional Airport 4000 International Ln *Web:* www.msnairport.com	Madison	WI	53704	608-246-3380	246-3385	27
Dane Holdings Inc 13529 W Camino del Sol *TF:* 800-653-2465 ■ *Web:* www.daneholdings.com	Sun City West	AZ	85375	623-825-3173		463
Dane Media LLC 385 Sylvan Ave Ste 24 *TF:* 888-233-2863 ■ *Web:* www.danemedia.com	Englewood Cliffs	NJ	07632	888-233-2863		195
Dane Street Congregational Church 10 Dane St *Web:* www.danestchurch.org	Beverly	MA	01915	978-922-4325		48-20
Danecraft Inc 1 Baker St *Web:* www.danecraft.com	Providence	RI	02905	401-941-7700		409
Danese 535 W 24th St 6th Fl *Web:* danesecorey.com	New York	NY	10011	212-223-2227		42
Danetracks Inc 7356 Santa Monica Blvd *Web:* www.danetracks.com	West Hollywood	CA	90046	323-512-8160		514
Danfords Hotel & Marina 25 E Broadway *TF:* 800-332-6367 ■ *Web:* www.danfords.com	Port Jefferson	NY	11777	800-332-6367		378
Danforth Pewterers Ltd 52 Seymour St *Web:* www.danforthpewter.com	Middlebury	VT	05753	802-388-8666		411
Danfoss 2800 E 13th St *NYSE: SHS* ■ *Web:* powersolutions.danfoss.com	Ames	IA	50010	515-239-6000	239-6318	640
Danfoss Scroll Technologies LLC 1 Scroll Dr *Web:* www.danfoss.com/home	Arkadelphia	AR	71923	870-246-0700		172
Dangerous Goods Advisory Council (DGAC) 7501 Greenway Ctr Dr Ste 760 *Web:* www.dgac.org	Greenbelt	MD	20770	202-289-4550	289-4074	49-21
Dangerous Music Inc 231 Stevens Rd *Web:* www.dangerousmusic.com	Edmeston	NY	13335	607-965-8011		52
DanHil Containers II Ltd 3715 Lucius McCelvey Dr *Web:* www.danhilcontainers.com	Temple	TX	76503	254-773-0704		100
Daniel 60 E 65th St *Web:* www.danielnyc.com	New York	NY	10065	212-288-0033		671
Daniel & Henry Co 1001 Highlands Plaza Dr W Ste 500 *TF:* 800-256-3462 ■ *Web:* www.danielandhenry.com	Saint Louis	MO	63110	314-421-1525	444-1990	390
Daniel & Stark Law Offices 100 W William Joel Bryan Pkwy *TF:* 800-474-1233 ■ *Web:* www.danielstarklaw.com	Bryan	TX	77803	979-846-8686		428
Daniel & Yeager (D&Y) 6767 Old Madison Pk Ste 690 *TF:* 800-955-1919 ■ *Web:* www.dystaffing.com	Huntsville	AL	35806	800-955-1919		266
Daniel B Stephens & Assoc Inc 6020 Academy NE Ste 100 *Web:* www.dbstephens.com	Albuquerque	NM	87109	505-822-9400		743
Daniel Boone Regional Library 100 W Broadway *TF:* 800-324-4806 ■ *Web:* www.dbrl.org	Columbia	MO	65203	573-443-3161	443-3281	434-3
Daniel Consultants Inc 8950 State Rt 108 229 *TF:* 800-677-1997 ■ *Web:* www.danielconsultants.com	Columbia	MD	21045	410-995-0090		261
Daniel Corp 3660 Grandview Pkwy *TF:* 800-991-4515 ■ *Web:* www.danielcorp.com	Birmingham	AL	35243	205-443-4500		655
Daniel d Stevens 7618 17th Ave *Web:* www.employeescreening.com	Brooklyn	NY	11214	718-234-0005		400

				Phone	Fax	Class
Daniel Defense Inc 101 War Fighter Way *Web:* www.danieldefense.com	Blackcreek	GA	31308	912-851-3238		807
Daniel F Young Inc 1235 Westlakes Dr Ste 255 *TF:* 866-407-0083 ■ *Web:* www.dfyoung.com	Berwyn	PA	19312	610-725-4000	725-0570	449
Daniel Forster Photography 57 High St *Web:* www.yachtphoto.com	Jamestown	RI	02835	401-423-1900		590
Daniel G Schuster LLC 3717 Crondall Ln *Web:* www.schusterconcrete.com	Owings Mills	MD	21117	410-363-3837		135
Daniel Gale Sotheby's International Realty 187 Park Ave *Web:* www.danielgale.com	Huntington	NY	11743	631-427-6600		652
Daniel George 2837 Culver Rd *Web:* www.birminghammenus.com/danielgeorge	Birmingham	AL	35223	205-871-3266		671
Daniel Group Ltd, The 400 Clarice Ave Ste 200 *TF:* 877-967-4242 ■ *Web:* thedanielgroup.com	Charlotte	NC	28204	877-967-4242		449
Daniel Measurement & Control Inc 11100 Brittmoore Park Dr *Web:* www.emerson.com/en-us/automation/daniel	Houston	TX	77041	713-827-6314	827-6312	201
Daniel Smith Artist Materials PO Box 84268 *TF:* 800-426-6740 ■ *Web:* www.danielsmith.com	Seattle	WA	98124	206-223-9599		459
Daniel Stowe Botanical Garden 6500 S New Hope Rd *Web:* www.dsbg.org	Belmont	NC	28012	704-825-4490	829-1240	97
Daniel Tanney Company Inc 3268 Clive Ave *Web:* dctanney.com	Bensalem	PA	19020	215-639-3131	638-3333	482
Daniel Webster Birthplace 131 N Rd *Web:* www.nhstateparks.org	Franklin	NH	03235	603-934-5057		565
Daniel Webster College 20 University Dr *TF:* 800-325-6876 ■ *Web:* www.dwc.edu	Nashua	NH	03063	603-577-6000	577-6001	166
Daniel's Broiler 809 Fairview Pl N *Web:* www.schwartzbros.com	Seattle	WA	98109	425-990-6310		671
Daniel's Group of Companies Inc, The 10520 Seven Mile Rd *TF:* 800-335-8747 ■ *Web:* www.meetings-incentives.com	Caledonia	WI	53108	262-835-3553		376
Daniele Inc PO Box 106 *TF:* 800-451-2535 ■ *Web:* www.danielefoods.com	Pascoag	RI	02859	401-568-6228	568-4788	296-26
Danielle House 160 Riverside Dr *Web:* www.daniellehouse.org	Binghamton	NY	13905	607-724-1540	724-1540	372
Daniels & Roberts Inc 209 N Seacrest Blvd Ste 2 *TF:* 800-488-0066 ■ *Web:* www.danielsandroberts.com	Boynton Beach	FL	33435	561-241-0066		7
Daniels Corp, The 20 Queen St W Ste 3400 *Web:* www.danielshomes.ca	Toronto	ON	M5H3R3	416-598-2129		186
Daniels County 120 Main St PO Box 91 *TF:* 800-638-3278 ■ *Web:* scobeymt.com	Scobey	MT	59263	406-487-2061		338
Daniels Home Ctr 255 S Euclid St *Web:* www.danielshomecenter.com	Anaheim	CA	92802	714-999-1285		321
Daniels Manufacturing Corp 526 Thorpe Rd *Web:* www.dmctools.com/default.html	Orlando	FL	32859	407-855-6161	855-6884	758
Daniels Porco & Lusardi LLP 1 Memorial Ave *Web:* www.danielsporco.com	Pawling	NY	12564	845-350-2837	855-5945	428
Danielson Designs Ltd 36750 Constitution Dr *Web:* www.danielsondesigns.com	Trinidad	CO	81082	719-846-4149		200
Danilo Black Inc 148 Madison Ave	New York	NY	10016	212-683-1177		344
Danis Bldg Construction Co 3233 Newmark Dr *Web:* www.danis.com	Miamisburg	OH	45342	937-228-1225	228-7443	186
Danisco US Inc Genencor Div 925 Page Mill Rd *Web:* biosciences.dupont.com	Palo Alto	CA	94304	650-846-7500		85
Danish-American Chamber of Commerce 885 Second Ave 18th Fl *Web:* www.daccny.com	New York	NY	10017	646-790-7169		138
DANK (German-American National Congress) 4740 N Western Ave Ste 206 *TF:* 888-872-3265 ■ *Web:* www.dank.org	Chicago	IL	60625	773-275-1100	275-4010	48-14
Danlaw Inc 41131 Vincenti Ct *Web:* www.danlawinc.com	Novi	MI	48375	248-476-5571		256
Danly IEM 6779 Engle Rd Ste A-F **Fax Area Code:* 440 ■ *TF:* 800-652-6462 ■ *Web:* www.danly.com	Cleveland	OH	44130	800-652-6462	239-7605*	757
Danmar Industries 2303 Oil Ctr Ct *Web:* www.danmarind.com	Houston	TX	77073	281-230-1000	230-1010	172
Danmark Energy L P 1907 E Old Hwy 80 *Web:* danmarkenergy.com	White Oak	TX	75693	903-297-5136	297-5122	536
Dann, Dorfman, Herrell & Skillman PC 1601 Market St Ste 2400 *Web:* www.ddhs.com	Philadelphia	PA	19103	215-563-4100		428
Dannemiller Inc 5711 NW Pkwy *TF:* 800-328-2308 ■ *Web:* www.dannemiller.com	San Antonio	TX	78249	800-328-2308		356
Dannenbaum Engineering Corp 3100 W Alabama *Web:* www.dannenbaum.com	Houston	TX	77098	713-520-9570		261
Danner Corp 307 Oravetz Pl SE *Web:* www.danner.net	Auburn	WA	98092	253-833-5333		599
Danner Manufacturing Inc 160 Oval Dr *Web:* www.dannermfg.com	Islandia	NY	11749	631-234-5261		608
Danner Shoe Manufacturing Co 17634 NE Airport *TF Cust Svc:* 800-345-0430 ■ *Web:* www.danner.com	Portland	OR	97230	503-251-1100	251-1119	301
Dannible & McKee LLP 221 S Warren St *Web:* www.dmconsulting.com	Syracuse	NY	13202	315-472-9127		2
Dannon Co 100 Hillside Ave *Web:* www.dannon.com	White Plains	NY	10603	914-872-8400		296-27
Danny Byrd Inc 1416 Sandersville Sharon Rd *TF:* 800-324-9353 ■ *Web:* www.dannybyrdinc.com	Laurel	MS	39443	601-649-2524		480
Danny Herman Trucking Inc PO Box 55 *TF:* 800-251-7500 ■ *Web:* www.dannyherman.com	Mountain City	TN	37683	423-727-9061		449
Danser Balaam & Frank 5 Independence Way	Princeton	NJ	08540	609-987-0300		2
Danson Decor Inc 3425 Douglas B Floreani *TF:* 800-363-1865 ■ *Web:* www.dansondecor.com	St Laurent	QC	H4S1Y6	514-335-2435		292
DANSR Inc 818 W Evergreen Ave *Web:* www.dansr.com	Chicago	IL	60642	312-475-0464		194
Dant Clayton Corp 1500 Bernheim Ln *Web:* www.stadiumbleachers.com	Louisville	KY	40210	502-634-3626		697
Dante's Creative Cuisine 1325 Eigth Ave N	Great Falls	MT	59401	406-453-9599		671
Danuser Machine Co 500 E Third St *Web:* www.danuser.com	Fulton	MO	65251	573-642-2246	642-2240	273
Danver 1 Grand St *TF:* 888-441-0537 ■ *Web:* www.danver.com	Wallingford	CT	06492	203-269-2300	265-6190	319-1
Danville Ambulance 12 A St *Web:* www.danvilleambulance.com	Danville	PA	17821	570-275-3031		30
Danville Area Community College 2000 E Main St **Fax:* Hum Res ■ *TF:* 877-342-3042 ■ *Web:* dacc.edu	Danville	IL	61832	217-443-3222	443-8560*	162
Danville Community College 1008 S Main St **Fax:* Admissions ■ *TF:* 800-560-4291 ■ *Web:* www.dcc.vccs.edu	Danville	VA	24541	434-797-2222	797-8541*	162
Danville Correctional Ctr 3820 E Main St *Web:* www2.illinois.gov	Danville	IL	61834	217-446-0441		213
Danville (Independent City) 401 Patton St PO Box 3300 *Web:* www.danville-va.gov	Danville	VA	24543	434-799-5168	799-6502	338
Danville Metal Stamping Company Inc 20 Oakwood Ave *Web:* www.danvillemetal.com	Danville	IL	61832	217-446-0647	446-0647	488
Danville National Cemetery 721 Lee St *Web:* www.cem.va.gov/cems/nchp/danvilleva.asp	Danville	VA	24541	704-636-2661	636-1115	136
Danville National Cemetery 1900 E Main St *TF:* 800-827-1000 ■ *Web:* www.cem.va.gov	Danville	IL	61832	217-554-4550	554-4803	136
Danville Pittsylvania County Chamber of Commerce 8653 US Hwy 29 PO Box 99 *TF:* 800-826-2355 ■ *Web:* www.dpchamber.org	Blairs	VA	24527	434-836-6990	836-6955	139
Danville Public Library 511 Patton St *Web:* readdanvilleva.org	Danville	VA	24541	434-799-5195		434-3
Danville Public Library 319 N Vermilion St *Web:* www.danville.lib.il.us	Danville	IL	61832	217-477-5220	477-5230	434-3
Danville Regional Medical Ctr 142 S Main St *TF:* 800-688-3762 ■ *Web:* danvilleregional.com	Danville	VA	24541	434-799-2100		374-3
Danville Signal Processing Inc 38570 100th Ave *TF:* 877-230-5629 ■ *Web:* www.danvillesignal.com	Cannon Falls	MN	55009	507-263-5854		194
Danville State Hospital 200 State Hospital Dr *Web:* dsh.thomas-industriesinc.com	Danville	PA	17821	570-271-4500		374-5
Danville-Boyle County Chamber of Commerce 105 East Walnut St *TF:* 800-548-4229 ■ *Web:* www.betterindanville.com	Danville	KY	40422	859-236-2805		139
Danya International Inc 8737 Colesville Rd Ste 1100 *Web:* www.danya.com	Silver Spring	MD	20910	301-565-2142		194
DAP Products Inc 2400 Boston St Ste 200 **Fax:* Cust Svc ■ *TF Cust Svc:* 800-543-3840 ■ *Web:* www.dap.com	Baltimore	MD	21224	410-675-2100	558-1068*	3
Dapco 2500 Bishop Cir E *Web:* www.dapcoind.com	Dexter	MI	48130	734-426-8900	426-2622	128
Dapper Tire Company Inc 4025 Lockridge St *TF:* 800-266-7172 ■ *Web:* www.dappertire.com	San Diego	CA	92102	619-266-1397	266-2384	755
Daprato Rigali Inc 6030 N NW Hwy *TF:* 800-288-0738 ■ *Web:* www.dapratorigali.com	Chicago	IL	60631	773-763-5511		724
Daq Electronics Inc 262B Old New Brunswick Rd *Web:* www.daq.net	Piscataway	NJ	08854	732-981-0050		625
DAR (National Society Daughters of the American Revolution) 1776 D St NW *TF:* 800-449-1776 ■ *Web:* www.dar.org	Washington	DC	20006	202-628-1776	879-3252	48-19
DAR Constitution Hall 1776 D St NW *TF:* 800-449-1776 ■ *Web:* dar.org/constitution-hall	Washington	DC	20006	202-628-1776		572
DAR Industrial Products Inc 2 Union Hill Bldg 1 *TF:* 800-903-1870 ■ *Web:* www.darindustrial.com	West Conshohocken	PA	19428	610-825-4900	825-4901	326
DAR Museum 1776 D St NW *TF:* 800-828-8218 ■ *Web:* www.dar.org/museum	Washington	DC	20006	202-879-3241	628-0820	520
DAR State Forest 78 Cape St Rt 112	Goshen	MA	01032	413-268-7098		565
Dara Thai 14 S San Francisco St *Web:* darathaiflagstaff.com	Flagstaff	AZ	86001	928-774-0047		671
Dara's Fast Lane 11130 Legion Dr *Web:* darascornermarket.com	St George	KS	66535	785-494-2400		297-8
Daramic Inc 5525 US Hwy 60 E *Web:* www.daramic.com	Owensboro	KY	42303	270-683-1561	686-9226	608
Darby Dan Farm 3225 Old Frankfort Pk *TF:* 888-321-0424 ■ *Web:* www.darbydan.com	Lexington	KY	40510	859-254-0424	281-6612	368
Darby Group Cos Inc 300 Jericho Quad	Jericho	NY	11753	516-683-1800		582
Darby Printing Co 6215 Purdue Dr	Atlanta	GA	30336	404-344-2665		626
DarCars Ltd 12210 Cherry Hill Rd *Web:* www.darcars.com	Silver Spring	MD	20904	301-622-0300		57
DARD 912 Custer Ave *Web:* www.tagmaster.net	Evanston	IL	60202	847-328-5000		9
Dardanelle & Russellville Railroad Co 4416 S Arkansas Ave *TF:* 888-877-7267 ■ *Web:* up.com	Russellville	AR	72802	479-968-6455	968-2634	648

	Phone	Fax	Class
Darden Restaurants Inc (DRI) 1000 Darden Center Dr. . . . . Orlando FL 32837 *NYSE:* DRI ■ *Web:* www.darden.com	407-245-4000		670
Dare 2 Share Ministries International PO Box 745323 . . . . Arvada CO 80006 *TF:* 800-462-8355 ■ *Web:* dare2share.org	303-425-1606		48-20
Dare County 954 Marshall Collins Dr . . . . Manteo NC 27954	252-475-5000		338
Dare Enterprices Inc 700 River Ave Ste 215 . . . . Pittsburgh PA 15212 *Web:* www.dareent.com	412-231-6100		256
Dare Foods Ltd 2481 Kingsway Dr . . . . Kitchener ON N2C1A6 *Web:* www.darefoods.com	519-893-5500		68
Dare Mighty Things Inc 1000 Market St Ste 102 . . . . Portsmouth NH 03801 *Web:* www.daremightythings.com	603-431-4331		256
Dare Products Inc 860 Betterly Rd PO Box 157. . . . . Battle Creek MI 49015 *TF:* 800-922-3273 ■ *Web:* www.dareproducts.com	269-965-2307	965-3261	279
Daret Inc 287 Margaret King Ave. . . . . Ringwood NJ 07456 *Web:* daret.com	973-962-6001		86
Darex 210 E Hersey St PO Box 730. . . . . Ashland OR 97520 *TF:* 800-597-6170 ■ *Web:* www.darex.com	541-488-2224	488-2229	455
Daria Metal Fabricators 1507 W Park Ave . . . . Perkasie PA 18944 *Web:* www.dariametalfabricators.com	215-453-2110		697
Darice Inc 13000 Darice Pkwy. . . . . Strongsville OH 44149 **Fax Area Code:* 440 ■ *TF:* 866-432-7423 ■ *Web:* www.darice.com	866-432-7423	238-1680*	44
Darien Lake Theme Park Resort 9993 Allegheny Rd PO Box 91 . . . . Darien Center NY 14040 *TF:* 866-640-0652 ■ *Web:* www.darienlake.com	585-599-4641	599-4053	32
Darien Lakes State Park 10475 Harlow Rd . . . . Darien Center NY 14040 *Web:* parks.ny.gov/parks/144/hunting.aspx	585-547-9242		565
Darien Nature Ctr Inc 120 Brookside Rd . . . . Darien CT 06820 *Web:* www.dariennaturecenter.org	203-655-7459		50-5
Darien Sport Shop Inc, The 1127 Post Rd . . . . Darien CT 06820 *TF:* 800-299-8864 ■ *Web:* dariensport.com	203-655-2575		711
Darigold 5601 Sixth Ave S Ste 300. . . . . Seattle WA 98108 *Web:* darigold.com	206-216-4283		296-27
Dari-Mart Stores Inc 125 E Sixth Ave. . . . . Junction City OR 97448 *Web:* www.darimart.com	541-998-2388		345
Dark Field Technologies Inc 70 Robinson Blvd. . . . . Orange CT 06477 *Web:* www.darkfield.com	203-298-0731		225
Dark Horse Comics Inc 10956 SE Main St. . . . . Milwaukie OR 97222 *TF:* 800-862-0052 ■ *Web:* www.darkhorse.com	503-652-8815	654-9440	637-5
Darke County 520 S Broadway St . . . . Greenville OH 45331 *Web:* www.co.darke.oh.us	937-547-7300	547-7367	338
Darke County Chamber of Commerce 622 S Broadway . . . . Greenville OH 45331 *TF:* 800-396-0787 ■ *Web:* www.darkecountyohio.com	937-548-2102		139
Darke Rural Electric Co-op Inc 1120 Fort Jefferson Rd . . . . Greenville OH 45331 *TF:* 800-776-5612 ■ *Web:* darkecountyohio.com	937-548-4114		245
Darkhorse Theater Ltd 4610 Charlotte Ave. . . . . Nashville-Davidson TN 37209 *Web:* darkhorsetheater.com	615-297-7113		572
Darkside Productions Inc 248 Third St Ste 644. . . . . Oakland CA 94607	510-208-2100		5
Darling Homes 2500 Legacy Dr Ste 100 . . . . Frisco TX 75034 *Web:* www.darlinghomes.com	469-252-2200		653
Darling International Inc 251 O'Connor Ridge Blvd Ste 300 . . . . Irving TX 75038 *NYSE:* DAR ■ *TF:* 800-800-4841 ■ *Web:* www.darlingii.com	972-717-0300		296-12
Darlington County 1 Public Sq. . . . . Darlington SC 29532 *TF:* 800-428-4322 ■ *Web:* www.darcosc.com	843-398-4100	393-8539	338
Darlington County Library 204 N Main St . . . . Darlington SC 29532 *Web:* www.darlington-lib.org	843-398-4940	398-4942	434-3
Darlington Fabrics Corp 36 Beach St . . . . Westerly RI 02891 *Web:* www.darlingtonfabrics.com	401-315-6279		745-4
Darlington Raceway 1301 Harry Bird Hwy . . . . Darlington SC 29532 **Fax Area Code:* 843 ■ *TF:* 866-459-7223 ■ *Web:* www.darlingtonraceway.com	866-459-7223	395-8920*	515
Darlington School 1014 Cave Spring Rd . . . . Rome GA 30161 *TF:* 800-368-4437 ■ *Web:* www.darlingtonschool.org	706-235-6051	232-3600	622
Darlington Veneer Company Inc 225 Fourth St . . . . Darlington SC 29532 *TF:* 800-845-2388 ■ *Web:* www.darlingtonveneer.com	843-393-3861	393-8243	613
Darlingtonia State Natural Site 84505 Hwy 101 S. . . . . Florence OR 97439 *TF:* 800-551-6949 ■ *Web:* www.oregonstateparks.org	541-997-3851		565
Darmody, Merlino & Company LLP 75 Federal St 15th Fl . . . . Boston MA 02110 *Web:* www.darmodymerlino.com	617-426-7300		2
Darnall Army Medical Ctr 36000 Darnall Loop . . . . Fort Hood TX 76544 *TF:* 800-305-6421 ■ *Web:* www.crdamc.amedd.army.mil	254-288-8000	286-7372	374-4
Daroff Design Inc 2121 Market St Ste 1 . . . . Philadelphia PA 19103 *Web:* www.daroffdesign.com	215-636-9900		393
Daroga State Park 1 S Daroga Park Rd . . . . Orondo WA 98843 *Web:* www.parks.wa.gov	509-784-0229		565
Daron Worldwide Trading Inc 24 Stewart Pl Unit 4 . . . . Fairfield NJ 07004 *TF:* 800-776-2324 ■ *Web:* www.daronwwt.com	973-882-0035		761
Daroth Capital Advisors LLC 130 E 59th St 12th Fl . . . . New York NY 10022 *Web:* www.daroth.com	212-687-2500		70
Darr & Collins LLC 1425 NW 150th St . . . . Edmond OK 73013 *Web:* darrcollins.com	405-285-2400		261
Darr Feedlot Inc 42826 Rd 759 . . . . Cozad NE 69130 *Web:* www.darrfeedlot.com	308-324-2363	324-2365	10-1
Dar-Ran Furniture Industries 2402 Shore St. . . . . High Point NC 27263 *TF:* 800-334-7891 ■ *Web:* www.darran.com	336-861-2400	861-6485	319-1
Darrell & King LLC 410 White Gables Ln . . . . Charlottesville VA 22903 *Web:* www.darrellandking.com	434-977-7010		401
Darrell Walker Personnel Systems 1976 Gadsden Hwy Ste 210 . . . . Birmingham AL 35235 *Web:* darrellwalkerworkforce.com	205-508-5511	508-5518	260
Darrow School 110 Darrow Rd . . . . New Lebanon NY 12125 *TF:* 877-432-7769 ■ *Web:* www.darrowschool.org	518-794-6000	794-7065	622
Darryl's Wood Fired Grill 3300 City Gate Blvd . . . . Greensboro NC 27407 *Web:* www.darrylswoodfiredgrill.com	336-294-1781		671
DART (Dallas Area Rapid Transit Authority) 1401 Pacific Ave PO Box 660163. . . . . Dallas TX 75202 *TF:* 800-231-2222 ■ *Web:* www.dart.org	214-749-3278		468
Dart Aerospace Ltd 1270 Aberdeen St. . . . . Hawkesbury ON K6A1K7 *TF:* 800-556-4166 ■ *Web:* www.dartaerospace.com	613-632-3336		21
Dart Appraisalcom 2600 W Big Beaver Rd Ste 540. Troy MI 48084 *TF:* 888-327-8123 ■ *Web:* dartappraisal.com	888-327-8123		652
Dart Container Corp 500 Hogsback Rd . . . . Mason MI 48854 **Fax Area Code:* 517 ■ *TF:* 800-248-5960 ■ *Web:* www.dartcontainer.com	800-248-5960	676-3883*	601
Dart Entities 1430 S Eastman Ave. . . . . Los Angeles CA 90023 *TF:* 800-285-0560 ■ *Web:* www.dartentities.com	323-264-1011	264-6925	803-1
Dart Manufacturing Co 3860 La Reunion Pkwy. . . . . Dallas TX 75212 *Web:* www.dartpromo.com	214-631-8024		534
Dart World Inc 140 Linwood St. Lynn MA 01905 *TF:* 800-225-2558 ■ *Web:* www.dartworld.com	781-581-6035		711
Dar-tech Inc 16485 Rockside Rd. . . . . Cleveland OH 44137 *TF:* 800-228-7347 ■ *Web:* www.dar-techinc.com	216-663-7600	663-8007	146
Dartmouth College 6016 McNutt Hall . . . . Hanover NH 03755 *TF:* 800-490-7010 ■ *Web:* www.dartmouth.edu	603-646-1110	646-1216	166
Dartmouth College Baker-Berry Library 6025 Baker-Berry Library . . . . Hanover NH 03755 *Web:* www.dartmouth.edu/~library/bakerberry	603-646-2704		434-6
Dartmouth Company Inc, The 351 Newbury St . . . . Boston MA 02115 *Web:* www.dartco.com	617-262-6620		652
Dartmouth General Hospital 325 Pleasant St. . . . . Dartmouth NS B2Y3S3 *Web:* www.cdha.nshealth.ca	902-465-8539		374-2
Dartmouth Public Libraries 732 Dartmouth St . . . . Dartmouth MA 02748 *Web:* www.town.dartmouth.ma.us/library	508-999-0726		434-3
Dartmouth-Hitchcock Medical Ctr 1 Medical Ctr Dr. . . . . Lebanon NH 03756 *TF:* 800-543-1624 ■ *Web:* www.dartmouth-hitchcock.org	603-650-5000	650-8765	374-3
Darue of California Inc 14102 S Broadway . . . . Los Angeles CA 90061 *Web:* www.darue.com	310-323-1350		155-21
Darvin Furniture 15400 S La Grange Rd . . . . Orland Park IL 60462 *TF:* 800-420-2337 ■ *Web:* darvin.com	708-460-4100		321
Darwill Inc 11900 Roosevelt Rd. . . . . Hillside IL 60162 *Web:* www.darwill.com	708-236-4900	236-5820	627
Darwin Martin House State Historic Site 125 Jewett Pkwy . . . . Buffalo NY 14214 *Web:* parks.ny.gov/historic-sites/35/details.aspx	716-856-3858		565
Darwood Manufacturing Co 620 W Railroad St S . . . . Pelham GA 31779 *Web:* www.darwoodmfg.com	229-294-4932	294-9323	155-20
Darya Restaurant 3800 S Plaza Dr. . . . . Santa Ana CA 92704 *TF:* 800-852-5046 ■ *Web:* daryasouthcoastplaza.com	714-557-6600		671
Daryl Flood Inc 450 Airline Dr Ste 100 . . . . Coppell TX 75019 *TF:* 800-325-9340 ■ *Web:* www.darylflood.com	972-471-1496		186
DAS Acquisition Company LLC 12140 Woodcrest Executive Dr Ste 150 . . . . St Louis MO 63141 *Web:* www.usa-mortgage.com	314-628-2000		217
DAS Inc 724 Lawn Rd . . . . Palmyra PA 17078 **Fax Area Code:* 800 ■ *TF:* 866-622-7979 ■ *Web:* www.das-roadpro.com	717-964-3642	437-3659*	38
Das Stein Haus 1436 Southridge Dr . . . . Jefferson City MO 65109 *TF:* 800-222-4734 ■ *Web:* www.dassteinhaus.com	573-634-3869		671
Das Waldcafe 12529 Warwick Blvd. . . . . Newport News VA 23606	757-930-1781		671
Dascenzo Intellectual Property Law PC 1000 S W Broadway Ste 1555 . . . . Portland OR 97205 *TF:* 800-905-4676 ■ *Web:* www.dascenzoiplaw.com	503-224-7529		428
Dasco Pro Inc 340 Blackhawk Pk Ave . . . . Rockford IL 61104 *TF:* 800-327-2690 ■ *Web:* dascopro.com	815-962-3727		758
Dash Inc W176 N9830 Rivercrest Dr. . . . . Germantown WI 53022 *Web:* dashdev.com	262-345-5600		225
Dash Point State Park 5700 SW Dash Pt Rd . . . . Federal Way WA 98023 *TF:* 888-226-7688 ■ *Web:* www.parks.wa.gov	253-661-4955		565
Dash Tours 1024 Winnipeg St . . . . Regina SK S4R8P8 *TF:* 800-265-0000 ■ *Web:* dashtours.com	306-352-2222	757-4126	760
DashGo Inc 1620 Broadway Ste C . . . . Santa Monica CA 90404 *Web:* www.dashgo.com	310-997-0675		387
Dashiell Corp 12301 Kurland Dr Ste 400. . . . . Houston TX 77034 *TF:* 800-872-0615 ■ *Web:* www.dashiell.com	713-558-6600	558-6694	189-4
Dashwood Industries Ltd 69323 Richmond St . . . . Centralia ON N0M1K0 *TF:* 800-265-4284 ■ *Web:* www.dashwood.com	519-228-6624		499
Dassault Falcon Jet Corp PO Box 2000 . . . . South Hackensack NJ 07606 **Fax Area Code:* 302 ■ **Fax:* Hum Res ■ *TF:* 800-527-2463 ■ *Web:* www.dassaultfalcon.com	201-440-6700	322-7221*	20
Dassault SystŠmes 166 Valley St. . . . . Providence RI 02909 *Web:* www.3ds.com/products-services/simulia	401-276-4400		178-8
Dassel-Cokato Public Schools PO Box 1700 . . . . Cokato MN 55321 *Web:* www.dc.k12.mn.us	320-286-4100		685
Dastmalchi Enterprises Inc 4490 Von Karman Ave Ste 150. . . . . Newport Beach CA 92660 *TF:* 888-358-0331 ■ *Web:* dastmalchi.com	888-358-0331		4
Data & Mailing Resources Inc 4929 Blalock Rd. . . . . Houston TX 77041 *TF:* 800-780-4707 ■ *Web:* www.dmr-inc.net	713-426-1550		5

Company / Address	City	State	Zip	Phone	Fax	Class
Data Access Corp 14000 SW 119th Ave *TF:* 800-451-3539 ■ *Web:* www.dataaccess.com	Miami	FL	33186	305-238-0012	238-0012	178-2
Data Advantage Group Inc 604 Mission St *Web:* www.dag.com	San Francisco	CA	94105	415-947-0400		177
Data Aire Inc 230 W BlueRidge Ave *Web:* www.dataaire.com	Orange	CA	92865	714-921-6000		14
Data Banque Ltd 5500 Brooktree Rd Ste 200 *Web:* www.databanque.com	Wexford	PA	15090	412-548-1030		195
Data Cable Technologies Inc 1306 Enterprise Dr *Web:* www.datacabletech.com	Romeoville	IL	60446	630-226-5600		111
Data Cell Systems Inc 250 Hwy 3201	Winnsboro	LA	71295	318-435-5800		116
Data Center West Inc 739 Welch St *Web:* www.datacenterwest.com	Medford	OR	97501	541-326-4212		387
Data Clean Corp 1033 Graceland Ave *Web:* www.dataclean.com	Des Plaines	IL	60016	847-296-3100		104
Data com Connect Two Waters Park Dr Ste 250 *Web:* connect.data.com	San Mateo	CA	94403	650-235-8400	655-2222	395
Data Communication Solutions Inc 10125 Crosstown Cir Ste 235 *Web:* www.dcs-is-edi.com	Eden Prairie	MN	55344	952-941-5466		194
Data Computer Corporation of America 5310 Dorsey Hall Dr *Web:* www.dcca.com	Ellicott City	MD	21042	410-992-3760		180
Data Concepts LLC 4405 Cox Rd *Web:* www.dataconcepts-inc.com	Glen Allen	VA	23060	804-968-4700		196
Data Connectors LLC 500 Chesterfield Ctr Ste 320 *Web:* www.dataconnectors.com	Chesterfield	MO	63017	636-778-9495	778-9496	206
Data Consulting Group Inc 965 E Jefferson Ave *TF:* 800-258-4343 ■ *Web:* www.dcgroupinc.com	Detroit	MI	48207	313-963-7771		180
Data Conversion Laboratory Inc 61-18 190th St Ste 205 *TF:* 800-321-2816 ■ *Web:* dclab.com	Fresh Meadows	NY	11365	718-357-8700		224
Data Dash Inc 3928 Delor St *TF:* 800-211-5988 ■ *Web:* www.datadash.com	Saint Louis	MO	63116	314-832-5788		225
Data Description Inc 840 Hanshaw Rd 2nd Fl *TF:* 800-573-5121 ■ *Web:* www.datadesk.com	Ithaca	NY	14850	607-257-1000		178-5
Data Device Corp 105 Wilbur Pl **Fax Area Code:* 414 ■ *TF Cust Svc:* 800-332-5757 ■ *Web:* www.ddc-web.com	Bohemia	NY	11716	631-567-5600	259-0240*	253
Data Dimensions Corp 400 Midland Ct *Web:* datadimensions.com	Janesville	WI	53546	608-757-1100		225
Data Direct Technologies 14100 SW Fwy	Sugar Land	TX	77478	281-491-4200		178-1
Data Electronic Devices Inc 32 NW Dr *Web:* www.dataed.com	Salem	NH	03079	603-893-2047	893-2956	518
Data Exchange Corp 3600 Via Pescador *TF:* 800-237-7911 ■ *Web:* www.dex.com	Camarillo	CA	93012	805-388-1711		175
Data Facts Inc 8520 Macon Rd Ste 2 *TF:* 800-785-5013 ■ *Web:* www.datafacts.com	Cordova	TN	38018	901-685-7599		218
Data Financial Inc 1100 Glen Oaks Ln *TF:* 800-334-8334 ■ *Web:* www.datafinancial.com	Mequon	WI	53092	262-243-5511		177
Data Flow Systems Inc 605 N John Rodes Blvd *Web:* dataflowsys.com	Melbourne	FL	32934	321-259-5009		647
Data Fusion Corp 10190 Bannock St *Web:* www.datafusion.com	Northglenn	CO	80260	720-872-2145		256
DATA Group (DBF) 9195 Torbram Rd *Web:* www.datacm.com	Brampton	ON	L6S6H2	905-791-3151	791-3277	110
Data Guardian 9136 Portage Industrial Dr *Web:* www.kalamazooxray.com	Portage	MI	49024	269-327-6296		317
Data I/O Corp 6464 185th Ave NE Ste 101 *NASDAQ: DAIO* ■ *TF:* 800-426-1045 ■ *Web:* dataio.com	Redmond	WA	98052	425-881-6444	881-6444	695
Data Impressions 17418 Studebaker Rd *TF:* 800-777-6488 ■ *Web:* dataimpressions.com	Cerritos	CA	90703	562-207-9050	207-9053	174
Data Inc 72 Summit Ave *Web:* www.datainc.biz	Montvale	NJ	07645	201-802-9800		177
Data Innovations Inc 120 Kimball Ave Ste 100 *Web:* www.datainnovations.com	South Burlington	VT	05403	802-658-2850		180
Data Integrity Inc 228 Highland Ave *Web:* www.dii2000.com	West Newton	MA	02465	617-964-1977		177
Data Interchange Standards Assn (DISA) 8300 Greensboro Dr Ste 800 *Web:* www.disa.org	McLean	VA	22043	703-970-4480	970-4488	48-9
Data Lab 7333 N Oak Pk Ave *Web:* www.data-lab.com	Niles	IL	60714	847-647-6678		225
Data Label Inc 1000 Spruce St *TF:* 800-457-0676 ■ *Web:* www.data-label.com	Terre Haute	IN	47807	812-232-0408	238-1847	413
Data Link Solutions LLC 350 Collins Rd NE *Web:* www.datalinksolutions.net	Cedar Rapids	IA	52498	319-295-4357		21
Data Mail Inc 240 Hartford Ave *Web:* www.data-mail.com	Newington	CT	06111	860-666-0399		5
Data Management Inc 537 New Britain Ave **Fax Area Code:* 800 ■ *TF Orders:* 800-243-1969 ■ *Web:* www.datamanage.com	Farmington	CT	06034	860-677-8586	428-1951*	86
Data Management Marketing 3225 Jordan Blvd *TF:* 888-266-4127 ■ *Web:* www.dmm-marketing.com	Malabar	FL	32950	321-725-8081		177
Data Panel Sales 7313 Washington Ave S *Web:* www.datapanel.com	Minneapolis	MN	55439	952-941-3511		246
Data Papers Inc 468 Industrial Pk Rd **Fax Area Code:* 888 ■ *TF:* 800-233-3032 ■ *Web:* www.datapapers.com	Muncy	PA	17756	800-233-3032	546-2366*	110
Data Paradigm Inc 2323 Bryan St Ste 2600 *Web:* dataparadigm.com	Dallas	TX	75201	214-468-0200	722-1860	177
Data Partners 12857 Banyan Creek Dr *TF:* 866-423-1818 ■ *Web:* www.datapartners.com	Fort Myers	FL	33908	866-423-1818		194
Data Path 318 McHenry Ave *TF:* 888-693-2827 ■ *Web:* mydatapath.com	Modesto	CA	95354	209-521-0055		196
Data Perceptions 174 Bridge St W *Web:* www.dataperceptions.com	Waterloo	ON	N2K1K9	519-749-9319		180
Data Physics Corp 2480 N 1ST ST Ste 100 *Web:* www.dataphysics.com	San Jose	CA	95131	408-437-0100		407
Data Pro Acctg Software Inc 111 Second Ave NE Ste 1200 *TF:* 800-237-6377 ■ *Web:* www.dpro.com	Saint Petersburg	FL	33701	727-803-1500	803-1535	178-1
Data Records Management Services Llc 1400 Husband Rd *TF:* 800-443-1610 ■ *Web:* www.drmsusa.com	Paducah	KY	42003	270-443-1255		463
Data Reduction Systems Corp 1323 Burnet Ave *Web:* www.drscorp.com	Union	NJ	07083	908-687-5636		225
Data Rx Management 305 W Woodard St *Web:* www.data-rx.com	Denison	TX	75020	903-465-0798		237
Data Sales Company Inc 3450 W Burnsville Pkwy *TF:* 800-328-2730 ■ *Web:* www.datasales.com	Burnsville	MN	55337	952-890-8838	895-3369	174
Data Science Automation Inc 375 Valleybrook Rd Ste 106 *Web:* www.dsautomation.com	Mc Murray	PA	15317	724-942-6330		256
Data Sciences International 119 14th St NW Ste 100 *TF:* 800-262-9687 ■ *Web:* datasci.com/buxco	St. Paul	MN	55112	800-262-9687		668
Data Select Systems Inc 2829 Townsgate Rd Ste 300 *TF:* 800-535-9978 ■ *Web:* www.clcsiii.com	Westlake Village	CA	91361	805-446-2090		177
Data Services Inc 31516 Winterplace Pkwy *TF:* 800-432-4066 ■ *Web:* www.dataservicesinc.com	Salisbury	MD	21804	410-546-2206		225
Data Source Inc 1400 Universal Ave *TF:* 877-846-9120 ■ *Web:* www.data-source.com	Kansas City	MO	64120	816-483-3282	483-3284	110
Data Square LLC 733 Summer St Ste 601 *Web:* www.datasquare.com	Stamford	CT	06901	203-964-9733		809
Data Storage Systems Ctr (DSSC) *Carnegie Mellon University* 5000 Forbes Ave *TF:* 800-864-0207 ■ *Web:* www.dssc.ece.cmu.edu	Pittsburgh	PA	15213	412-268-6600	268-3497	668
Data Stream Mobile Technologies 11531 Interchange Cir S *Web:* www.dswltech.net	Miramar	FL	33025	954-271-1240		194
Data Supplies Inc 11300 Lakefield Dr *Web:* datasuppliesinc.com	Duluth	GA	30097	770-476-4455		225
Data Systems Analysts Inc (DSA) Eigth Neshaminy Interplex Ste 209 *TF:* 877-422-4372 ■ *Web:* www.dsainc.com	Trevose	PA	19053	215-245-4800	245-4375	180
Data Technique Inc 3402 Airport Cir *Web:* www.datatechnique.com	Pittsburg	KS	66762	316-235-1000		809
Data Technology Inc 14225 Dayton Cir Ste 4 *TF General:* 888-334-9300 ■ *Web:* drtinc.com	Omaha	NE	68137	402-891-0711		547
Data Technology Services 1300 N Berard St *Web:* www.dtscom.com	Breaux Bridge	LA	70517	337-332-4347		194
Data Transformation Corp 1 Penn Plaza Ste 4515 *Web:* www.dtcss.com	New York	NY	10119	212-563-7565		697
Data Transmission Network Corp 9110 W Dodge Rd Ste 200 *TF:* 800-405-4000 ■ *Web:* www.dtn.com	Omaha	NE	68114	402-390-2328		387
Data Ventures 1475 Central Ave Ste 230 *TF:* 800-265-9201 ■ *Web:* www.dataventures.com	Los Alamos	NM	87544	505-662-6655		177
Data Vista Inc 122 Burrs Rd Ste A *Web:* datavista.com	Westampton	NJ	08060	609-702-9300		175
Data3 Corp 2448 E 81st St Ste 700 *Web:* www.datathree.com	Tulsa	OK	74137	918-237-4400		177
Databased Solutions Inc 1200 Route 22 *Web:* www.dbsiservices.com	Bridgewater	NJ	08807	908-314-0000		177
Databit Inc 200 Route 17 *TF:* 800-473-1577 ■ *Web:* www.databitinc.com	Mahwah	NJ	07430	201-529-8050		174
Databranch Inc 132 N Union St Ste 108 *Web:* www.databranch.com	Olean	NY	14760	716-373-4467		180
DataCan Services Corp 7485-45 Ave Close Ste 102 *Web:* www.datacan.ca	Red Deer	AB	T4P4C2	403-352-2245		253
DataCard Corp 11111 Bren Rd W *TF:* 800-328-8623 ■ *Web:* www.datacard.com	Minnetonka	MN	55343	952-933-1223	933-7971	704
Dataccount Inc 299 Broadway Ste 1016 *Web:* www.dataccount.com	New York	NY	10007	212-595-1044		463
DataCeutics Inc 1610 Medical Dr Ste 300 *Web:* www.dataceutics.com	Pottstown	PA	19464	610-970-2333		177
DataChambers LLC 3302 Old Lexington Rd *Web:* www.datachambers.com	Winston-Salem	NC	27107	336-499-6000		344
Dataclarity Corp 7200 Falls Of Neuse Rd Ste 202 *TF:* 800-963-5508 ■ *Web:* www.dataclaritycorp.com	Raleigh	NC	27615	919-256-6700		177
DataCo LLC 85 W Algonquin Rd Ste 360 *Web:* www.datacosolutions.com	Arlington Heights	IL	60005	847-290-0636		205
Datacolor 5 Princess Rd *TF General:* 800-340-1007 ■ *Web:* www.datacolor.com	Lawrenceville	NJ	08648	609-924-2189	895-7414	419
Datacom Inc 2517 S Santa Fe Ave *Web:* www.datacom.com	Vista	CA	92083	760-598-6000		116
Datacom Systems Inc 9 Adler Dr *Web:* www.datacomsystems.com	East Syracuse	NY	13057	315-463-9541		203
Datacomm Management Sciences Inc 25 Van Zant St Ste 2a	Norwalk	CT	06855	203-838-7183	838-1751	176

	City	State	ZIP	Phone	Fax	Class
DataComm Networks Inc 6801 N 54th St	Tampa	FL	33610	813-873-0674		180
Web: www.datacomm.com						
Datacon Inc 60 Blanchard Rd	Burlington	MA	01803	781-273-5800		625
Web: www.data-con.com						
Datacor Inc						
25 Hanover Rd Ste 300B	Florham Park	NJ	07932	973-822-1551		177
Web: www.datacor.com						
Datacore Consulting LLC						
5755 Granger Rd Ste 777	Independence	OH	44131	216-398-8499		631
TF: 800-244-4241 ■ *Web:* www.datacoreonline.com						
DataCore Software Corp						
6300 NW Fifth Way Corporate Pk	Fort Lauderdale	FL	33309	954-377-6000		387
Web: www.datacore.com						
Datacorp 200 W 17th St Ste 115	Cheyenne	WY	82001	307-634-1808		396
Web: www.mjdatacorp.com						
DataDirect Networks						
9351 Deering Ave	Chatsworth	CA	91311	818-700-7600	700-7601	173-8
TF: 800-837-2298 ■ *Web:* www.ddn.com						
Datadrill Communications Inc						
6701 Fairmount Dr SE	Calgary	AB	T2H0X6	403-269-7500		387
Web: www.datadrill.ca						
Datafirst Corp 2700 Sumner Blvd	Raleigh	NC	27616	919-876-6650		177
TF: 800-634-8504 ■ *Web:* www.datafirst.com						
Dataflo Corp 2722 S 87th Ave	Omaha	NE	68124	402-861-9454		225
Web: www.mydataflo.com						
Dataflux Corp 940 NW Cary Pkwy Ste 201	Cary	NC	27513	919-447-3000	677-4444	177
Dataforth Corp 3331 E Hemisphere Loop	Tucson	AZ	85706	520-741-1404	741-0762	173-3
TF: 800-444-7644 ■ *Web:* www.dataforth.com						
DataGardens Inc 14956 121 A Ave	Edmonton	AB	T5V1A3	780-784-5000	784-5001	396
Web: www.datagardens.com						
Datagenic Tool & Die Inc						
4280 Motor Ave	Culver City	CA	90232	310-253-9918		697
Data-Graphics Inc 240 Hartford Ave	Newington	CT	06111	860-667-0435		5
Web: www.datagraphicsinc.com						
DataGravity Inc						
100 Innovative Way Ste 3410	Nashua	NH	03062	603-943-8500		387
Web: www.datagravity.com						
Data-Linc Group						
3535 Factoria Blvd SE Ste 100	Bellevue	WA	98006	425-882-2206	867-0865	173-3
Web: www.data-linc.com						
Dataline LLC						
6703 Albunda Dr PO Box 50816	Knoxville	TN	37950	865-588-7740	558-0942	261
TF: 888-588-7740 ■ *Web:* www.datalinellc.com						
Dataline Systems Inc 2709 Pemberton Dr	Apopka	FL	32703	407-298-1234		396
TF: 800-225-5237 ■ *Web:* www.datalinesys.com						
Datalink Corp 8170 Upland Cir	Chanhassen	MN	55317	952-944-3462		173-8
NASDAQ: DTLK ■ *TF:* 800-448-6314 ■ *Web:* www.datalink.com						
DataLink Interactive Inc						
1120 Benfield Blvd Ste G	Millersville	MD	21108	410-729-0440		180
TF: 888-565-3279 ■ *Web:* www.datalinktech.com						
Datalink Software Consultants Inc						
4745 N Seventh St Ste 200	Phoenix	AZ	85014	602-279-7788		177
Web: www.datalinksc.com						
Datalog Technology Inc						
10707 - 50th St SE	Calgary	AB	T2C3E5	403-243-2024		539
Web: www.datalogtechnology.com						
Datalogic Scanning 959 Terry St	Eugene	OR	97402	541-683-5700	345-7140	173-7
TF: 800-695-5700 ■ *Web:* www.datalogic.com						
Datalogic Software Inc						
1501 S 77 Sunshinestrip	Harlingen	TX	78550	956-412-1424		177
TF: 800-544-7263 ■ *Web:* www.vesta.net						
Datalogics Inc						
101 N Wacker Dr Ste 1800	Chicago	IL	60606	312-853-8200	853-8282	178-1
Web: www.datalogics.com						
Datalok Co 5990 Malburg Way	Vernon	CA	90058	323-582-6100	581-8285	803-1
Datalux Corp 155 Aviation Dr	Winchester	VA	22602	540-662-1500	662-1682	173-2
TF: 800-328-2589 ■ *Web:* www.datalux.com						
Dataman Group Inc						
22594 Lemon Tree Ln	Boca Raton	FL	33428	561-451-9302		637-6
Web: datamangroup.com						
Datamann Inc 1994 Hartford Ave	Wilder	VT	05088	802-295-6600		178-11
TF: 800-451-4263 ■ *Web:* www.datamann.com						
DatamanUSA LLC						
6890 S Tucson Way Ste 100	Centennial	CO	80112	720-248-3121		463
TF: 800-677-1997 ■ *Web:* www.datamanusa.com						
Datamark Graphics Inc						
603 W Bailey St	Asheboro	NC	27203	888-629-6300		627
TF: 888-629-6300 ■ *Web:* www.datamarkgraphics.com						
Datamark Inc 123 W Mills Ave Ste 400	El Paso	TX	79901	800-477-1944		225
TF: 800-477-1944 ■ *Web:* www.datamark.net						
Datamart Direct Inc						
6405 Muirfield Dr	Hanover Park	IL	60133	630-307-7100		195
Datamatics Management Services Inc						
330 New Brunswick Ave	Fords	NJ	08863	732-738-9600	738-9603	178-1
TF: 800-673-0366 ■ *Web:* www.datamaticsinc.com						
Datamation Systems Inc						
125 Louis St	South Hackensack	NJ	07606	201-329-7200		697
Web: www.pc-security.com						
Data-Matique 2110 Sherwin St	Garland	TX	75041	972-272-3446		697
TF: 866-706-0981 ■ *Web:* www.data-matique.com						
Datamatrix Systems Inc						
505 Lincoln Hwy	East Mckeesport	PA	15035	412-825-3600		180
TF: 800-551-0224 ■ *Web:* www.getdatamatrix.com						
Datamax Corp 4501 Pkwy Commerce Blvd	Orlando	FL	32808	407-578-8007	578-8377	173-6
Web: www.datamaxcorp.com						
Datamax Office Systems Inc						
6717 Waldemar Ave	Saint Louis	MO	63139	314-633-1400		112
TF: 800-325-9299 ■ *Web:* www.datamaxstl.com						
Datamaxx Applied Technologies Inc						
2001 Drayton Dr	Tallahassee	FL	32311	850-558-8000		174
Web: www.datamaxx.com						
Datamine Internet Marketing Solutions Inc						
330 S Lake St	Gary	IN	46403	219-939-9987		7
TF: 877-328-2646 ■ *Web:* www.datamine.net						
Dataminr Inc 6 E 32nd St 2nd fl	New York	NY	10016	646-701-7826		387
Web: www.dataminr.com						

	City	State	ZIP	Phone	Fax	Class
DataMotion Inc						
35 Airport Rd Ste 120	Morristown	NJ	07960	973-455-1245	455-0750	178-7
TF: 800-672-7233 ■ *Web:* datamotion.com						
Datanomics 991 US Hwy 22 W Ste 301	Bridgewater	NJ	08807	908-707-8200		194
Web: www.datanomics.com						
DataPipe 10 Exchange Pl	Jersey City	NJ	07302	201-792-4847	749-5821*	808
**Fax Area Code: 888* ■ *TF:* 877-773-3306 ■ *Web:* www.datapipe.com						
Dataprise Inc						
9600 Blackwell Rd 4th Fl	Rockville	MD	20850	301-945-0700		177
TF: 800-653-6306 ■ *Web:* www.dataprise.com						
Datapro Inc						
770 Ponce De Leon Blvd 2nd Fl	Coral Gables	FL	33134	305-374-0606		180
Web: www.datapromiami.com						
Datapro Solutions Inc 6336 E Utah Ave	Spokane	WA	99212	509-532-3530		180
TF: 888-658-6881 ■ *Web:* datapronw.com						
Dataprobe Inc 1B Pearl Ct	Allendale	NJ	07401	201-934-9944		174
Web: www.dataprobe.com						
DataProfit Corp 330 Whitney Ave	Holyoke	MA	01040	413-536-2766	280-4646*	463
**Fax Area Code: 781*						
Data-Quest Inc						
4807 Jonestown Rd Ste 247	Harrisburg	PA	17109	717-545-2581		180
TF: 800-433-5778 ■ *Web:* www.dataquestinc.com						
Dataram Corp						
777 Alexander Rd Ste 100	Princeton	NJ	08540	609-799-0071	799-6734	625
NASDAQ: DRAM ■ *TF:* 800-328-2726 ■ *Web:* www.dataram.com						
Datarealm Internet Services Inc						
PO Box 1616	Hudson	WI	54016	877-227-3783	850-3660*	808
**Fax Area Code: 602* ■ *TF:* 877-227-3783 ■ *Web:* www.datarealm.com						
DataScan Field Services LLC						
5925 Cabot Pkwy	Alpharetta	GA	30005	770-754-6500	877-7226*	393
**Fax Area Code: 800* ■ *Web:* www.dsfs.com						
Datascan LP 2210 Hutton Dr Ste 100	Carrollton	TX	75006	866-441-4848		196
TF: 866-441-4848 ■ *Web:* www.datascan.com						
Dataserv Corp 8625 F St	Omaha	NE	68127	402-339-8700		175
TF: 888-901-8700 ■ *Web:* www.dataservcorp.com						
Datashield LLC						
455 E 200 S Ste 100	Salt Lake City	UT	84111	866-428-4567		196
TF: 866-428-4567 ■ *Web:* www.datashieldprotect.com						
Dataskill Inc 5675 Ruffin Rd Ste 100	San Diego	CA	92123	858-755-3800		180
TF: 800-481-3282 ■ *Web:* www.dataskill.com						
Datasoft Inc 700 Plaza Dr	Secaucus	NJ	07094	201-319-0494		225
Web: tradeblazer.com						
DataSphere Technologies Inc						
3350 161st Ave SE	Bellevue	WA	98008	866-912-7090		5
TF: 866-912-7090 ■ *Web:* www.secondspace.com						
Datassential						
1762 Westwood Blvd Ste 250	Los Angeles	CA	90024	877-886-3687		466
TF: 888-556-3687 ■ *Web:* www.datassential.com						
DataStarUSA Inc						
5904 Stonecreek Dr, Ste 120	The Colony	TX	75056	214-291-2000	291-0020	260
Datastrait Networks Inc						
3021 Harbor Ln N Ste 103	Minneapolis	MN	55447	763-746-4466		449
TF: 800-934-5432 ■ *Web:* datastrait.com						
Datasyst Engineering & Testing Services Inc						
S14W33511 Hwy 18	Delafield	WI	53018	262-968-4003		261
TF: 800-969-4050 ■ *Web:* www.datasysttest.com						
Datatech Depot Inc 4750 Ashley Dr	Hamilton	OH	45011	513-860-5651		175
Web: www.dtdi.com						
Datatech Labs 8000 e quincy ave	Denver	CO	80237	303-770-3282		624
TF: 888-288-3282 ■ *Web:* www.datatechlab.com						
Datatel Inc 4375 Fair Lakes Ct	Fairfax	VA	22033	800-223-7036		178-10
TF: 800-223-7036 ■ *Web:* www.ellucian.com						
Datatel Resources Corp						
1729 Pennsylvania Ave	Monaca	PA	15061	724-775-5300	775-0688	110
TF: 800-245-2688 ■ *Web:* www.datatelcorp.com						
Datatel Solutions Inc 875 Laurel Dr	Roseville	CA	95678	888-224-8647		196
TF: 888-224-8647 ■ *Web:* www.datatelsolutions.com						
DataTicket Inc						
4600 Campus Dr Ste 200	Newport Beach	CA	92660	888-752-0512		160
TF: 888-752-0512 ■ *Web:* www.dataticket.com						
Datatime Consulting 109 Forrest Ave	Narberth	PA	19072	610-668-9640		194
Web: www.datatimeconsult.com						
DataTrail Inc 6223 2 St SE Ste 205	Calgary	AB	T2H1J5	403-253-3651		387
Web: www.datatrail.com						
Datatrend Technologies Inc						
121 Cheshire Ln Ste 700	Minnetonka	MN	55305	952-931-1203		180
TF: 800-367-7472 ■ *Web:* www.datatrend.com						
DataTrends Publications Inc						
PO Box 3221	Leesburg	VA	20177	571-313-9916	771-9091*	637-9
**Fax Area Code: 703* ■ *Web:* www.datatrendspublications.com						
Datatronic Distribution Inc						
28151 Hwy 74	Romoland	CA	92585	951-928-7700		767
Web: www.datatronics.com						
Datavalet Technologies Inc						
5275 ch Queen-Mary	Montreal	QC	H3W1Y3	514-385-4448		225
Web: www.datavalet.com						
DataViz Inc 612 Wheelers Farms Rd	Milford	CT	06460	203-874-0085	874-4345	178-12
TF: 800-733-0030 ■ *Web:* www.dataviz.com						
Datawatch Corp 271 Mill Rd	Chelmsford	MA	01824	978-441-2200	441-1114	178-12
NASDAQ: DWCH ■ *TF:* 800-445-3311 ■ *Web:* www.datawatch.com						
Dataway Inc 255 Golden Gate Ave	San Francisco	CA	94102	415-882-8700		180
Web: www.dataway.com						
DataWorks Plus LLC						
728 N Pleasantburg Dr	Greenville	SC	29607	864-672-2780		177
TF: 866-632-2780 ■ *Web:* www.dataworksplus.com						
Dataxport 10950 Pellicano Dr Ste C4	El Paso	TX	79935	915-771-9090		225
Web: www.dataxport.net						
DA-TECH Corp 141 Railroad Dr	Ivyland	PA	18974	215-322-9410		518
Web: swemco.com						
Datel Systems Inc 5636 Ruffin Rd	San Diego	CA	92123	858-571-3100	571-0452	179
Web: www.datelsys.com						
Dates Weiser Furniture Corp						
1700 Broadway St	Buffalo	NY	14212	716-891-1700		321
TF: 800-466-7037 ■ *Web:* www.datesweiser.com						
Datex Billing Services Inc						
2333 N Sheridan Way	Mississauga	ON	L5K1A7	905-822-2300	766-2584	225
Web: www.datex.ca						

Phone | Fax | Class

Datonics LLC 84 Wooster St Ste 300............ New York NY 10012 646-867-0647 387
Web: datonics.com

Datotel LLC 710 N Tucker Ste 400.............. St. Louis MO 63101 314-241-0101 387
Web: www.datotel.com

Datron World Communications Inc
3030 Enterprise Ct............................ Vista CA 92081 760-597-1500 597-1510 647
Web: www.dtwc.com

Datroo Technologies LLC
1292 N First St Ste 707...................... Abilene TX 79601 325-675-8880 180
TF: 800-699-9503 ■ Web: www.datroo.com

Datrose Inc 660 Basket Rd..................... Webster NY 14580 585-265-1780 225
Web: datrose.com

DATTCO Inc 583 S St...................... New Britain CT 06051 860-229-4878 107
TF: 800-229-4879 ■ Web: dattco.com

Datum Engineers Inc
6516 Forest Park Rd.......................... Dallas TX 75235 214-358-0174 261
Web: datumengineers.com

Datum Filing Systems Inc
89 Church Rd............................ Emigsville PA 17318 717-764-6350 764-6656 286
TF: 800-828-8018 ■ Web: datumstorage.com

Datum Inspection Services Inc
21442 N 20th Ave........................... Phoenix AZ 85027 602-997-1340 261
Web: datum-inspection.com

Datum Technologies
6009 Business Blvd.......................... Sarasota FL 34240 941-256-8700 463
Web: www.datumcorporation.com

Dauenhauer & Son Plumbing & Piping Company Inc
3416 Robards Ct............................ Louisville KY 40218 502-451-2882 189-10
Web: www.dauenhauerplumbing.com

Daugaard Dennis (R)
500 East Capitol St............................ Pierre SD 57501 605-773-3212 773-4711 343
TF: 800-872-6190 ■ Web: sd.gov/governor

Daugherty Systems Inc
Three CityPl Ste 400...................... Saint Louis MO 63141 314-432-8200 180
Web: www.daugherty.com

Daughters of Miriam Ctr/Gallen Institute
155 Hazel St................................. Clifton NJ 07011 973-772-3700 450
TF: 800-627-0929 ■ Web: www.daughtersofmiriamcenter.org

Daughters of the Republic of Texas Library
PO Box 1401........................... San Antonio TX 78295 210-225-1071 434-3
Web: www.drtl.org

Daughters of Union Veterans of the Civil War
503 S Walnut St PO Box 211................ Springfield IL 62704 217-544-0616 520
Web: www.duvcw.org

Daughters of Utah Pioneers Museum
300 N Main St......................... Salt Lake City UT 84103 801-532-6479 532-4436 520
Web: www.dupinternational.org

Daum Commercial Real Estate Services
801 S Figueroa St Ste 600................ Los Angeles CA 90017 213-626-9101 652
Web: www.daumcommercial.com

Dauntless Molds 806 N Grand Ave............... Covina CA 91724 626-966-4494 966-4062 697
Web: www.dauntlessmolds.com

Dauphin County 2 S Second St 3rd Fl.......... Harrisburg PA 17101 717-780-6636 780-6468 338
TF: 800-328-0058 ■ Web: www.dauphincounty.org

Dauphin County Library System
101 Walnut St............................ Harrisburg PA 17101 717-234-4961 234-7479 434-3
Web: www.dcls.org

Dauphin Island Sea Lab Estuarium
101 Bienville Blvd..................... Dauphin Island AL 36528 251-861-2141 861-4646 40
Web: www.disl.org

Dauphin North America 300 Myrtle Ave.......... Boonton NJ 07005 973-263-1100 220-3044* 319-1
*Fax Area Code: 800 ■ TF Cust Svc: 800-631-1186 ■ Web: www.dauphin.com

Dauphine Orleans Hotel
415 Dauphine St....................... New Orleans LA 70112 504-586-1800 586-1409 379
TF: 800-521-7111 ■ Web: www.dauphineorleans.com

DAV (Disabled American Veterans)
3725 Alexandria Pike..................... Cold Spring KY 41076 859-441-7300 441-1416 48-19
TF: 877-426-2838 ■ Web: www.dav.org

Davalor Mold Corp
46480 Continental....................... Chesterfield MI 48047 586-598-0100 596
Web: www.davalor.com

Davanac Inc 1936 St Regis...................... Dorval QC H9P1H6 514-421-0177 421-0188 770
Web: www.davanac.com

Davanni's Inc 1100 Xenium Ln N............... Plymouth MN 55441 952-927-2300 670
Web: www.davannis.com

Davco Advertising Inc
89 N Kinzer Rd PO Box 288.................... Kinzers PA 17535 717-442-4155 7
TF: 800-283-2826 ■ Web: davcoadvertising.com

Davco Rest Home Resident
2526 W Tenth St......................... Owensboro KY 42301 270-684-1705 371
Web: www.fernterrace.com

DavCo Restaurants Inc
1657 Crofton Blvd.......................... Crofton MD 21114 410-721-3770 670
Web: www.wendavco.com

Davco Technology LLC
1600 Woodland Dr PO Box 487................. Saline MI 48176 734-429-5665 429-0741 60
TF: 800-328-2611 ■ Web: www.davcotec.com

Dave & Buster's 3000 Oakwood Blvd.......... Hollywood FL 33020 954-923-5505 671
TF: 888-300-1515 ■ Web: www.daveandbusters.com

Dave & Buster's
7025 Salisbury Rd....................... Jacksonville FL 32256 904-296-1525 671
Web: www.daveandbusters.com

Dave & Buster's Inc 2481 Manana Dr.......... Dallas TX 75220 214-357-9588 659
TF: 800-842-5369 ■ Web: www.daveandbusters.com

Dave Droegkamp Heating Air Conditioning & Sheet Metal Inc
540 Norton Dr.............................. Hartland WI 53029 262-367-2820 189-10
Web: davedroegkamp.com

Dave Sinclair Ford Inc
7466 S Lindbergh Blvd.................... Saint Louis MO 63125 314-892-2600 57
Web: www.davesinclairford.com

Dave Steel Company Inc 40 Meadow Rd........ Asheville NC 28803 828-252-2771 480
Web: www.davesteel.com

Dave Thomas Foundation for Adoption
716 Mt Airyshire Blvd Ste 100............... Columbus OH 43235 800-275-3832 305
TF: 800-275-3832 ■ Web: www.davethomasfoundation.org

Dave Walter 447 W Exchange St.................. Akron OH 44302 330-434-8989 57
Web: www.davewaltervw.com

Dave White Chevrolet Inc
5880 Monroe St............................ Sylvania OH 43560 419-885-4444 57
TF: 800-893-5217 ■ Web: www.davewhitechevy.com

Dave Wong's 2828 W March Ln................ Stockton CA 95219 209-951-4152 671
Web: davewongsrestaurant.com

Dave'S Pawn Shop 1576 N Main St........... Crossville TN 38555 931-484-8947 711
Web: davespawnshop.com

Dave's Place 210 Ctr St.................... Little Rock AR 72201 501-372-3283 671
Web: www.davesplacerestaurant.com

Davenport & Co LLC
901 E Cary St 1 James Center Ste 1100........ Richmond VA 23219 804-780-2000 690
TF: 800-846-6666 ■ Web: www.davenportllc.com

Davenport Cos, The
20 N Main St........................ South Yarmouth MA 02664 508-398-2293 186
TF: 800-822-3422 ■ Web: www.thedavenportcompanies.com

Davenport Hotel, The 10 S Post St............ Spokane WA 99201 509-455-8888 624-4455 379
TF: 800-899-1482 ■ Web: www.davenporthotelcollection.com

Davenport House Museum
324 E State St............................ Savannah GA 31401 912-236-8097 233-7938 520
TF: 800-496-7938 ■ Web: www.davenporthousemuseum.org

Davenport Insulation Inc
7400 Gateway Ct.......................... Manassas VA 20109 703-631-7744 189-9
TF: 855-626-6459 ■ Web: www.truteam.com/davenportmanassas

Davenport Machine Inc 167 Ames St.......... Rochester NY 14611 585-235-4545 235-6568 455
TF: 800-344-5748 ■ Web: www.davenportmachine.com

Davenport Public Library
321 Main St............................... Davenport IA 52801 563-326-7832 326-7809 434-3
Web: www.davenportlibrary.com

Davenport Theatrical Enterprises Inc
254 W 54th St 14th Fl...................... New York NY 10019 212-874-5348 514
Web: www.davenporttheatrical.com

Davenport University
Dearborn 4801 Oakman Blvd................ Dearborn MI 48126 313-581-4400 581-4480 166
TF: 800-585-1479 ■ Web: www.davenport.edu
Flint 4318 Miller Rd Ste A...................... Flint MI 48507 810-732-9977 732-9128* 166
*Fax: Admissions ■ TF: 800-727-1443 ■ Web: www.davenport.edu
Lansing 220 E Kalamazoo St.................. Lansing MI 48933 517-484-2000 484-1132* 166
*Fax: Admissions ■ TF: 800-686-1600 ■ Web: www.davenport.edu
Lettinga Campus
6191 Kraft Ave SE.................... Grand Rapids MI 49512 616-698-7111 554-5214 166
TF: 866-925-3884 ■ Web: www.davenport.edu
Saginaw 5300 Bay Rd....................... Saginaw MI 48604 989-799-7800 799-9696* 166
*Fax: Admissions ■ TF: 800-968-8133 ■ Web: www.davenport.edu
Warren 27650 Dequindre Rd................... Warren MI 48092 586-558-8700 558-7868* 166
*Fax: Admissions ■ TF: 800-724-7708 ■ Web: www.davenport.edu

Davenport, Evans, Hurwitz & Smith LLP
206 W 14th St.......................... Sioux Falls SD 57101 605-336-2880 428
TF: 800-272-3900 ■ Web: dehs.com

Davey Tree Expert Co 1500 N Mantua St............ Kent OH 44240 330-673-9511 673-7089* 776
*Fax: Hum Res ■ TF: 800-445-8733 ■ Web: www.davey.com

David A Bramble Inc
705 Morgnec Rd......................... Chestertown MD 21620 410-778-3023 778-3427 188-4
Web: www.davidabrambleinc.com

David A Noyes & Co 209 S LaSalle St........... Chicago IL 60604 312-782-0400 41
TF: 800-669-3732 ■ Web: www.danoyes.com

David A Smith Printing Inc
742 S 22nd St........................... Harrisburg PA 17104 717-564-3719 627
TF: 800-564-3117 ■ Web: www.dasprint.com

David A. Straz Jr Ctr for the Performing Arts
1010 N WC MacInnes Pl...................... Tampa FL 33602 813-222-1000 222-1057 572
TF: 800-955-1045 ■ Web: www.strazcenter.org

David Allen Co 407 Bryant Cir Ste H............... Ojai CA 93023 805-646-8432 194
Web: gettingthingsdone.com

David Aplin Group
700 Second St SW Ste 3050................. Edmonton AB T2P2W2 403-261-9000 273-7393* 260
*Fax Area Code: 855 ■ Web: www.aplin.com

David Berman Developments
340 Selby Ave.................................. Ottawa ON K2A3X6 613-728-6777 344
TF: 800-665-1809 ■ Web: www.davidberman.com

David Black Agency
335 Adams St Ste 2707...................... Brooklyn NY 11201 718-852-5500 852-5539 444
Web: www.davidblackagency.com

David Bohnett Foundation
245 S Beverly Dr....................... Beverly Hills CA 90212 310-276-0001 305
TF: 800-553-7326 ■ Web: www.bohnettfoundation.org

David Boland Inc
219 Indian River Ave Ste 201................ Titusville FL 32796 321-269-1345 610
Web: www.dboland.com

David Chapman Agency Inc
5700 W Mt Hope Rd......................... Lansing MI 48917 517-321-4600 390
Web: davidchapmanagency.com

David Chen Md Diagnostic Medical Group Inc
1129 S San Gabriel Blvd.................. San Gabriel CA 91776 626-287-6746 418
Web: www.dmg.net

David Clark Co 360 Franklin St................ Worcester MA 01604 508-751-5800 753-5827* 576
*Fax: Sales ■ TF Cust Svc: 800-298-6235 ■ Web: www.davidclark.com

David Crockett State Park
1400 W Gaines......................... Lawrenceburg TN 38464 931-762-9408 565
Web: tnstateparks.com

David Dobbs Enterprises Inc
4600 US Hwy 1 N..................... Saint Augustine FL 32095 904-824-6171 92
TF: 800-889-6368 ■ Web: www.menudesigns.com

David Evans & Assoc Inc (DEA)
2100 SW River Pkwy......................... Portland OR 97201 503-223-6663 223-2701 261
TF: 800-721-1916 ■ Web: www.deainc.com

David Findlay Jr Fine Art
724 Fifth Ave............................. New York NY 10019 212-486-7660 42
TF: 800-399-0929 ■ Web: www.davidfindlayjr.com

David Gooding Inc 173 Spark St............... Brockton MA 02302 508-894-2000 612
Web: www.goodingd.com

David Grant US Air Force Medical Ctr
101 Bodin Cir............................ Travis AFB CA 94535 707-423-3735 374-4
TF: 800-264-3462 ■ Web: www.travis.af.mil/units/dgmc

David H Fell & Company Inc
6009 Bandini Blvd........................ Commerce CA 90040 323-722-9992 722-6567 407
TF: 800-822-1996 ■ Web: www.dhfco.com

David Horowitz Freedom Ctr
14148 Magnolia Blvd Ste 103............ Sherman Oaks CA 91423 818-849-3470 196
Web: www.horowitzfreedomcenter.org

Name / Address	Phone	Fax	Class
David Hughes Custom Linen 14332 Wadkins Ave ... Gardena CA 90249 *Web:* customlinenservice.com	310-324-2465		442
David J Joseph Co (DJJ) 300 Pike St ... Cincinnati OH 45202 *Web:* www.djj.com	513-419-6200	419-6222	686
David J Thompson Mailing Corp 21 Naus Way PO Box 150 ... Bloomsburg PA 17815 *Web:* www.thompsonmailing.com	570-759-6690		5
David J. Frank Landscape Contracting Inc N120 W21350 Freistadt Rd ... Germantown WI 53022 *Web:* www.davidjfrank.com	262-255-4888		776
David Kucera Inc 42 Steves Ln ... Gardiner NY 12525 *TF:* 800-247-1727 ■ *Web:* davidkucerainc.com	845-255-1044		183
David L Adams Assoc Inc 1536 Ogden St ... Denver CO 80218	303-455-1900		261
David L Lawrence Convention Ctr 1000 Ft Duquesne Blvd ... Pittsburgh PA 15222 *TF:* 800-245-4500 ■ *Web:* www.pittsburghcc.com	412-565-6000	565-6008	205
David Mason & Assoc 800 S Vandeventer Ave ... Saint Louis MO 63110 *Web:* www.davidmason.com	314-534-1030		256
David Michael & Co Inc 10801 Decatur Rd ... Philadelphia PA 19154 *TF:* 800-363-5286 ■ *Web:* www.dmflavors.com	215-632-3100		296-15
David Monn LLC 135 W 27th St Ste 2 ... New York City NY 10001 *TF:* 800-442-1162 ■ *Web:* davidmonn.com	212-242-2009		232
David Naylor & Assoc Inc 3532 Hayden Ave ... Culver City CA 90232 *Web:* www.dnala.com	323-463-2826		514
David Nelson Construction Co 3483 Alternate 19 ... Palm Harbor FL 34683 *Web:* www.nelson-construction.com	727-784-7624		188-4
David Nolan Gallery 527 W 29th St ... New York NY 10001 *Web:* www.davidnolangallery.com	212-925-6190	334-9139	42
David Peyser Sportswear Inc 90 Spence St ... Bay Shore NY 11706	631-231-7788		155-12
David Plunkett Realty LLC 8832 Riverside Dr ... Parker AZ 85344 *Web:* davidplunkettrealty.com	928-667-1699		652
David Powell Inc 3190 Clearview Way Ste 100 ... San Mateo CA 94402 *Web:* www.davidpowell.com	650-357-6000		194
David Robert Ellis PA 275 Clearwater Largo Rd N ... Largo FL 33770 *Web:* davidellispa.com	727-518-6544		445
David S Palmer Arena 100 W Main St ... Danville IL 61832 *Web:* www.palmerarena.com	217-431-2424	431-6444	720
David Simpson Construction Company Inc 17177 Gillette Ave Unit A ... Irvine CA 92614 *Web:* www.davidsimpsonconstruction.com	949-250-1348		186
David Stires Assoc LLC 678 US Hwy 202/206 N ... Bridgewater NJ 08807 *Web:* dastires.com	908-252-7000		261
David Suzuki Foundation 219-2211 W Fourth Ave ... Vancouver BC V6K4S2 *TF:* 800-453-1533 ■ *Web:* www.davidsuzuki.org	604-732-4228		305
David Tate Insurance Agency Inc 2566 N Mcmullen Booth Rd Ste B ... Clearwater FL 33761 *Web:* www.davidtateinsurance.com	727-796-0408		390
David Taylor Cadillac Company Inc 10422 SW Fwy Bldg B ... Houston TX 77074 *Web:* www.davidtaylor.com	713-777-7151		57
David Textiles Inc 1920 S Tubeway Ave ... Commerce CA 90040 *TF:* 800-500-6120 ■ *Web:* www.davidtextiles.com	323-728-3231		258
David Traylor Zoo of Emporia 75 Soden Rd ... Emporia KS 66801 *Web:* www.emporiazoo.org	620-341-4365		823
David Wade Correctional Ctr 670 Bell Hill Rd ... Homer LA 71040	318-927-0400		213
David Weekley Homes Inc 1111 N Post Oak Rd ... Houston TX 77055 *TF:* 800-390-6774 ■ *Web:* www.davidweekleyhomes.com	713-963-0500	963-0322	653
David William Hotel Condo Assn 700 Biltmore Way ... Miami FL 33134 *Web:* davidwilliamcondo.com	305-903-1867		379
David Yurman Designs Inc 24 Vestry St ... New York NY 10013 *TF:* 888-398-7626 ■ *Web:* www.davidyurman.com	888-398-7626		409
David Zwirner Gallery 525 W 19th St ... New York NY 10011 *Web:* www.davidzwirner.com	212-727-2070	727-2072	42
David's Barbecue 5121 NW 39th Ave ... Gainesville FL 32606 *Web:* davidsbbq.com	352-373-2002		671
David's Bridal Inc 1001 Washington St ... Conshohocken PA 19428 *TF:* 844-400-3222 ■ *Web:* www.davidsbridal.com	610-943-5000		157-6
Davide 326 Commercial St ... Boston MA 02109 *Web:* www.daviderestaurant.com	617-227-5745		671
Davidge Data Systems Corp 20 Exchange Pl 39th Fl ... New York NY 10005	212-269-0901		690
Davids Clarence & Co 22901 S Ridgeland Ave ... Matteson IL 60443 *TF:* 800-462-2308 ■ *Web:* www.clarencedavids.com	708-720-4100	720-4200	422
Davidsmeyer Bus Service Inc 2513 E Higgins Rd ... Elk Grove Village IL 60007 *TF:* 800-323-0312 ■ *Web:* www.bus-charter.com/aboutus-dsm.htm	847-437-3767	437-4978	109
Davidson & Company LLP 1200 - 609 Granville St Pacific Centre ... Vancouver BC V7Y1G6 *Web:* www.davidson-co.com	604-687-0947		734
Davidson & Garrard Inc 810 Main St ... Lynchburg VA 24505 *Web:* dg-g.com	434-847-6600		401
Davidson & Jones Hotel Corp 1207 Front St ... Raleigh NC 27609 *Web:* davidsonandjones.com	919-828-0880		379
Davidson College PO Box 7156 ... Davidson NC 28035 **Fax:* Admissions ■ *TF:* 800-768-0380 ■ *Web:* www.davidson.edu	704-894-2000	894-2016*	166
Davidson Correctional Ctr 1400 Thomason St ... Lexington NC 27292 *Web:* www.doc.state.nc.us	336-249-7528		213

Name / Address	Phone	Fax	Class
Davidson Cos 8 Third St N PO Box 5015 ... Great Falls MT 59401 *TF:* 800-332-5915 ■ *Web:* dadavidson.com	406-727-4200		690
Davidson County 913 Greensboro St ... Lexington NC 27292 *Web:* www.co.davidson.nc.us	336-242-2000	248-8440	338
Davidson County 205 Metro Courthouse ... Nashville TN 37201 *Web:* www.nashville.gov	615-862-6770	862-6774	338
Davidson County Community College PO Box 1287 ... Lexington NC 27293 **Fax:* Admissions ■ *TF:* 800-233-4050 ■ *Web:* www.davidsonccc.edu	336-249-8186	224-0240*	162
Davidson Institute for Talent Development 9665 Gateway Dr ... Reno NV 89521 *Web:* www.davidsongifted.org	775-852-3483		196
Davidson Instruments Inc 9391 Grogan's Mill Rd ... The Woodlands TX 77380 *Web:* www.davidson-instruments.com	281-362-4900		201
Davidson Pipe Supply Company Inc 5002 Second Ave ... Brooklyn NY 11232	718-439-6300		360-2
Davidson Plyforms Inc 5505 33rd St SE ... Grand Rapids MI 49512 *Web:* lpworkfurniture.com	616-956-0033	956-0041	820
Davidson Technologies Inc 530 Discovery Dr Cummings Research Pk ... Huntsville AL 35806 *Web:* www.davidson-tech.com	256-922-0720	971-6861	21
Davidson Titles Inc 2345 Dr F E Wright Dr ... Jackson TN 38305 *Web:* www.davidsontitles.com	731-988-5333		96
Davidson's Inc 6100 Wilkinson Dr ... Prescott AZ 86301 *Web:* www.galleryofguns.com	928-776-8055		690
Davidson, Davidson & Kappel LLC 589 Eighth Ave 16th Fl ... New York NY 10018 *Web:* www.ddkpatent.com	212-736-1940		428
Davidson-Kennedy Co 800 Industrial Park Dr ... Marietta GA 30062 *TF:* 800-733-3434 ■ *Web:* www.equipmentinnovators.com	770-427-9467		120
Davidson-Peterson Associates Inc 201 Lafayette Ctr ... Kennebunk ME 04043 *Web:* digitalresearch.com	207-985-1790		466
Davie Brown Entertainment Inc 2225 S Carmelina Ave ... Los Angeles CA 90064 *Web:* www.daviebrown.com	310-979-1980		7
Davie County 123 S Main St ... Mocksville NC 27028 *Web:* www.daviecountync.gov	336-753-6040	751-7408	338
Davie County Chamber of Commerce 135 S Salisbury St ... Mocksville NC 27028 *Web:* www.daviechamber.com	336-751-3304	751-5697	139
Davie County Public Library 371 N Main St ... Mocksville NC 27028 *Web:* www.daviecountync.gov	336-753-6030	751-1370	434-3
Davie County Schools 220 Cherry St ... Mocksville NC 27028 *Web:* www.davie.k12.nc.us	336-751-5921	751-9013	685
Davie-Cooper City Chamber of Commerce 4185 Davie Rd ... Davie FL 33314 *Web:* www.davie-coopercity.org	954-581-0790	581-9684	139
Davies 808 State St ... Santa Barbara CA 93101 *Web:* www.daviespublicaffairs.com	805-963-5929		636
Davies Consulting Inc 6935 Wisconsin Ave Ste 600 ... Chevy Chase MD 20815 *TF:* 800-811-8336 ■ *Web:* www.daviescon.com	301-652-4535	907-9355	194
Davies Manor House 9336 Davies Plantation Rd ... Memphis TN 38133 *Web:* www.daviesmanorplantation.org	901-386-0715	388-4677	50-3
Davies Molding LLC 350 Kehoe Blvd ... Carol Stream IL 60188 *TF:* 800-554-9208 ■ *Web:* www.daviesmolding.com	630-510-8188	510-9944	621
Davies Park 10060 Jasper Ave NW ... Edmonton AB T5J3R8 *TF:* 800-446-3037 ■ *Web:* www.daviespark.com	780-420-9900		193
Davies Pearson PC 920 Fawcett Ave ... Tacoma WA 98401 *TF:* 800-439-1112 ■ *Web:* www.dpearson.com	253-620-1500		428
Davies Ward Phillips & Vineberg LLP 155 Wellington St W ... Toronto ON M5V3J7 *TF:* 800-668-7380 ■ *Web:* www.dwpv.com	416-863-0900		41
Daviess County 212 St Ann St ... Owensboro KY 42303 *Web:* www.daviessky.org	270-685-8434		338
Daviess County 200 E Walnut St ... Washington IN 47501 *Web:* www.daviesscounty.org	812-254-1091		338
Daviess County Clerk 102 N Main St ... Gallatin MO 64640 *Web:* daviesscountysheriff.com	660-663-2641		338
Daviess County Metal Sales Inc 9929 E US Hwy 50 ... Cannelburg IN 47519 *TF:* 800-279-4299 ■ *Web:* www.dcmetal.com	812-486-4299		697
Daviess County Public Library 2020 Frederica St ... Owensboro KY 42301 *Web:* www.dcplibrary.org	270-684-0211		434-3
Daviess-Martin County REMC 12628 E 75 N PO Box 430 ... Loogootee IN 47553 *TF:* 800-762-7362 ■ *Web:* www.dmremc.com	812-295-4200	295-4216	245
Davila Pharmacy Inc 1423 Guadalupe St ... San Antonio TX 78207 *TF:* 800-897-8428 ■ *Web:* www.davilapharmacy.com	210-226-5293	224-9257	237
Davinci Biosciences LLC 22667 Old Canal Rd ... Yorba Linda CA 92627 **Fax Area Code:* 877 ■ *TF:* 888-773-5959 ■ *Web:* www.dvbiologics.com	888-773-5959	773-5959*	743
Davinci Institute Inc 9191 Sheridan Blvd Ste 300 ... Westminster CO 80031 *Web:* davinciinstitute.com	303-666-4133		113
Davis & Assoc Inc 2852 N Webster Ave ... Indianapolis IN 46219 *Web:* www.davisassocindy.com	317-263-9947		186
Davis & Elkins College 100 Campus Dr ... Elkins WV 26241 **Fax:* Admissions ■ *TF:* 800-624-3157 ■ *Web:* dewv.edu	304-637-1900	637-1800*	166
Davis & Floyd Inc 1319 Hwy 72 221 E ... Greenwood SC 29649 *Web:* www.davisfloyd.com	864-229-5211	229-7844	261
Davis & Gilbert 1740 Broadway ... New York NY 10019 *TF:* 800-973-1177 ■ *Web:* www.dglaw.com	212-468-4800		428
Davis & Langdale Company Inc 231 E 60th St ... New York NY 10022 *Web:* www.davisandlangdale.com	212-838-0333	752-7764	42

Name / Address	City	State	Zip	Phone	Fax	Class
Davis & Wilkerson Pc 5113 SW Pk Ste 115	Austin	TX	78735	512-482-0614		428
Web: www.dwlaw.com						
Davis Aircraft Products Company Inc						
1150 Walnut Ave	Bohemia	NY	11716	631-563-1500		22
Web: www.davisaircraftproducts.com						
Davis Automotive Group Inc						
6135 Kruse Dr	Solon	OH	44139	440-542-0600		57
Web: www.davisautomotive.com						
Davis Beverage Group						
1530-A Bobali Dr	Harrisburg	PA	17104	717-914-1295		80-2
Davis Boat Works Inc						
99 Jefferson Ave	Newport News	VA	23607	757-247-0101		698
Web: www.davisboat.com						
Davis Brand Capital LLC						
1180 Peachtree St Ste 2605	Atlanta	GA	30309	404-347-7778		195
Web: davisbrandcapital.com						
Davis Calibration LLC						
4701 Mt Hope Dr Ste J	Baltimore	MD	21215	410-358-3900	358-0252	393
Web: www.inotek.com						
Davis Capital Corp						
200 S Wacker Dr 31st Fl	Chicago	IL	60606	312-623-4500		70
Web: www.daviscapital.com						
Davis Capital Partners LLC						
3 Harbor Dr Ste 301	Sausalito	CA	94965	415-362-3600		528
Web: www.daviscapitalpartners.com						
Davis Chamber of Commerce 604 3 St	Davis	CA	95616	530-756-5160	756-5190	139
Web: www.davischamber.com						
Davis Chamber of Commerce						
450 Simmons Way Ste 220	Kaysville	UT	84037	801-593-2200	593-2212	139
Web: www.davischamberofcommerce.com						
Davis College 400 Riverside Dr	Johnson City	NY	13790	607-729-1581	729-2962	161
TF: 800-331-4137 ■ *Web:* www.davisny.edu						
Davis College 4747 Monroe St	Toledo	OH	43623	419-473-2700	473-2472	800
TF: 800-477-7021 ■ *Web:* www.daviscollege.edu						
Davis Contractors Ltd 5206 Fm 236	Cuero	TX	77954	361-275-5721		189-10
Davis Correctional Facility						
6888 E 133Rd Rd	Holdenville	OK	74848	405-379-6400	379-6496	213
TF: 800-624-2931 ■ *Web:* cca.com						
Davis Cos 325 Donald J Lynch Blvd	Marlborough	MA	01752	763-231-0700	481-8519*	721
**Fax Area Code:* 508 ■ *TF:* 800-482-9494 ■ *Web:* www.daviscos.com						
Davis County						
28 E State St PO Box 618	Farmington	UT	84025	801-451-3324	451-3421	338
Web: www.co.davis.ut.us						
Davis County Clerk of Courts						
100 Courthouse Sq	Bloomfield	IA	52537	641-664-2011	664-2041	338
Web: www.daviscountyiowa.org						
Davis County Clipper Today						
1370 S 500 W	Woods Cross	UT	84010	801-295-2251		532-3
Web: davisclipper.com						
Davis County Library 61 S Main St	Farmington	UT	84025	801-444-2300	451-3281	434-3
Web: www.co.davis.ut.us						
Davis Danny K (Rep D - IL)						
2159 Rayburn Bldg	Washington	DC	20515	202-225-5006	225-5641	342-2
Web: www.davis.house.gov						
Davis Demographics & Planning Inc						
11850 Pierce St Ste 200	Riverside	CA	92505	951-270-5211		463
TF: 888-337-4471 ■ *Web:* www.davisdemographics.com						
Davis Direct Inc 1241 Newell Pkwy	Montgomery	AL	36110	334-277-0878		627
TF: 877-277-0878 ■ *Web:* davisdirect.net						
Davis Elementary School						
1050 Arlington Dr	Costa Mesa	CA	92626	714-424-7930		685
Web: davis.nmusd.us						
Davis Elen Adv						
865 S Figueroa St Ste 1200	Los Angeles	CA	90017	213-688-7000		4
TF: 800-908-5395 ■ *Web:* www.daviselen.com						
Davis Enterprise 315 G St	Davis	CA	95616	530-756-0800	756-6707	532-2
Web: www.davisenterprise.com						
Davis Ethical Pharmacy						
124 N Long Beach Rd	Rockville Centre	NY	11570	516-764-3200		237
Davis Express Inc PO Box 1276	Starke	FL	32091	800-874-4270		780
TF: 800-874-4270 ■ *Web:* www.davis-express.com						
Davis Funds 2949 E Elvira Rd Ste 101	Tucson	AR	85756	800-279-0279		528
TF: 800-279-0279 ■ *Web:* www.davisfunds.com						
Davis Furniture Industries Inc						
2401 S College Dr	High Point	NC	27261	336-889-2009	889-0031	319-1
Web: www.davis-furniture.com						
Davis Graham & Stubbs LLP						
1550 17th St Ste 500	Denver	CO	80202	303-892-9400	893-1379	428
Web: www.dgslaw.com						
Davis Hospital & Medical Ctr (DHMC)						
1600 W Antelope Dr	Layton	UT	84041	801-807-1000	807-7610	374-3
TF: 877-898-6080 ■ *Web:* www.davishospital.com						
Davis Industries Inc 9920 Richmond Hwy	Lorton	VA	22079	703-550-7402		686
Davis Instrument Corp 3465 Diablo Ave	Hayward	CA	94545	510-732-9229		472
TF: 800-678-3669 ■ *Web:* www.davisnet.com						
Davis Law Firm						
10500 Heitage Blvd Ste 102	San Antonio	TX	78216	210-444-4444		428
TF: 800-770-0127 ■ *Web:* www.jeffdavislawfirm.com						
Davis Memorial Hospital 812 Gorman Ave	Elkins	WV	26241	304-636-3300	637-3184	374-3
Web: www.davishealthsystem.org						
Davis Miles McGuire Gardner PLLC						
40 E Rio Salado Pkwy Ste 425	Tempe	AZ	85281	480-733-6800	733-9748	445
Web: www.davismiles.com						
Davis Mountains State Park						
State Hwy 118	Fort Davis	TX	79734	432-426-3337		565
Web: tpwd.texas.gov/state-parks/davis-mountains						
Davis Oil Co 904 Jernigan St	Perry	GA	31069	478-987-2443		316
TF: 800-277-4355 ■ *Web:* www.davis-company.com						
Davis Paint Company Inc						
1311 Iron St PO Box 7589	North Kansas City	MO	64116	816-471-4447	471-1460	550
TF: 800-821-2029 ■ *Web:* www.davispaint.com						
Davis Polk & Wardwell						
450 Lexington Ave	New York	NY	10017	212-450-4000	701-5800	428
Web: www.davispolk.com						
Davis Powers Inc						
640 N La Salle Dr Ste 565	Chicago	IL	60654	312-654-9239		177
Web: davispowers.com						
Davis Professional Services Inc						
820 Greenbrier Cir Ste 18	Chesapeake	VA	23320	757-431-1344		104
TF: 800-347-5444 ■ *Web:* www.davisproserv.com						
Davis Regional Medical Ctr						
218 Old Mocksville Rd PO Box 1823	Statesville	NC	28625	704-873-0281	838-7287	374-3
Web: www.davisregional.com						
Davis Rodney (Rep R - IL)						
1740 Longworth Bldg	Washington	DC	20515	202-225-2371	226-0791	342-2
Web: rodneydavis.house.gov						
Davis Smith Accounting Associates pa						
5582 Milford Harrington Hwy	Harrington	DE	19952	302-398-4020		2
Web: www.davis-smithaccounting.com						
Davis Susan (Rep D - CA)						
1214 Longworth HOB	Washington	DC	20515	202-225-2040	225-2948	342-2
Web: www.house.gov/susandavis						
Davis Theatre for the Performing Arts						
251 Montgomery St	Montgomery	AL	36104	334-241-9567		572
Web: trojan.troy.edu						
Davis Tool & Die Company Inc						
888 Bolger Ct	Fenton	MO	63026	636-343-0828		697
Web: www.davistool.com						
Davis Tool Inc 3740 NW Aloclek Pl	Hillsboro	OR	97124	503-648-0936		454
Web: www.davistl.com						
Davis Tuttle Venture Partners LP						
110 W Seventh St	Tulsa	OK	74103	918-584-7272	582-3404	792
Web: www.davistuttle.com						
Davis Vision Inc						
711 Troy-Schenectady Rd	Latham	NY	12110	800-999-5431	328-4761*	391-3
**Fax Area Code:* 888 ■ **Fax:* Claims ■ *TF:* 800-999-5431 ■ *Web:* www.davisvision.com						
Davis Wire Corp 5555 Irwindale Ave	Irwindale	CA	91706	626-969-7651		490
Web: www.daviswire.com						
Davis Wood Products Inc PO Box 604	Hudson	NC	28638	828-728-8444	728-4601	613
Web: www.daviswoodproducts.com						
Davis Wright Tremaine LLP						
1201 Third Ave #2200	Seattle	WA	98101	206-622-3150	757-7700	428
Web: www.dwt.com						
Davisco International Inc						
719 N Main St	Le Sueur	MN	56058	507-665-8811	665-3701	296-10
TF: 800-757-7611 ■ *Web:* www.daviscofoods.com						
Davis-Monthan Air Force Base						
5275 E Granite St	Davis-Monthan AFB	AZ	85707	520-228-3204	228-5299	497-1
Web: www.dm.af.mil						
Davison County Auditor						
200 E Fourth Ave	Mitchell	SD	57301	605-995-8608	995-8618	338
Web: www.davisoncounty.org						
Davison Fuels Inc						
8450 Tanner Williams Rd	Mobile	AL	36608	251-633-4444		579
Web: www.davisonoil.com						
Davissa Telephone Systems Inc						
23800 Commerce Pk	Cleveland	OH	44122	216-464-6633		225
Web: www.davissa.com						
Davis-Ulmer Sprinkler Company Inc						
1 Commerce Dr	Amherst	NY	14228	716-691-3200		386
TF: 877-691-3200 ■ *Web:* www.davisulmer.com						
DaVita Inc 1551 Wewatta St	Denver	CO	80202	303-405-2100		352
NYSE: DVA ■ *TF:* 800-310-4872 ■ *Web:* www.davita.com						
Davitt & Hanser Music Co						
3015 Kustom Dr	Hebron	KY	41048	859-817-7100	817-7150	527
TF: 800-999-5558 ■ *Web:* www.hansermusicgroup.com						
Davol Inc 100 Crossings Blvd	Warwick	RI	02886	800-556-6756		476
TF Cust Svc: 800-556-6756 ■ *Web:* www.davol.com						
Davroc						
2051 Williams Pkwy Units 20 and 21	Brampton	ON	L6S5T4	905-792-7792		261
Web: www.davroc.com						
Davy Crockett Birthplace State Park						
1245 Davy Crockett Pk Rd	Limestone	TN	37681	423-257-2167		565
TF: 888-250-8615 ■ *Web:* www.state.tn.us						
Daw Construction Group LLC						
12552 S 125 W	Draper	UT	84020	801-553-9111		186
TF: 800-748-4778 ■ *Web:* www.dawcg.com						
Daw Technologies Inc						
1600 West 2200 South Ste 201	Salt Lake City	UT	84119	801-977-3100		189-9
Web: www.dawtech.com						
Dawahares Inc 1845 Alexandria Dr	Lexington	KY	40504	859-278-0422	514-3299	157-2
TF: 800-677-9108 ■ *Web:* www.dawahares.com						
Dawat 210 E 58th St	New York	NY	10022	212-355-7555		671
Web: dawatny.com						
Dawda, Mann, Mulcahy & Sadler PLC						
39533 Woodward Ave Ste 200	Bloomfield Hills	MI	48304	248-642-3700		428
Web: dawdamann.com						
Dawe's Laboratories						
3355 N Arlington Heights Rd	Arlington Heights	IL	60004	847-577-2020	577-1898	584
Web: dawesnutrition.com						
Dawes Arboretum 7770 Jacksontown Rd SE	Newark	OH	43056	740-323-2355		97
TF: 800-443-2937 ■ *Web:* www.dawesarb.org						
Dawes County 451 Main St	Chadron	NE	69337	308-432-0100	432-5179	338
Web: dawes-county.com						
Dawn Enterprises Inc						
9155 Sweet Valley Dr	Valley View	OH	44125	216-447-1777		596
Web: www.dawn-ent.com						
Dawn Food Products Inc						
3333 Sargent Rd	Jackson	MI	49201	517-789-4400		296-16
TF Cust Svc: 800-292-1362 ■ *Web:* www.dawnfoods.com						
Dawnbreaker Inc 3161 Union St	North Chili	NY	14514	585-594-0025		194
Web: www.dawnbreaker.com						
Dawson & Assoc 3250 Mary St	Coconut Grove	FL	33133	305-443-1500		734
Web: www.flacpa.com						
Dawson Co 1681 W Second St	Pomona	CA	91766	626-797-9710		612
TF: 800-832-9766 ■ *Web:* www.dawsonco.com						
Dawson Community College						
300 College Dr	Glendive	MT	59330	406-377-3396		162
TF: 800-821-8320 ■ *Web:* www.dawson.edu						
Dawson Construction Inc						
PO Box 30920	Bellingham	WA	98225	360-756-1000	756-1001	186
Web: www.dawson.com						
Dawson County						
25 Justice Way Ste 2214	Dawsonville	GA	30534	706-344-3501	344-3504	338
TF: 800-843-9214 ■ *Web:* www.dawsoncounty.org						

Name / Address	City	State	Zip	Phone	Fax	Class
Dawson County 207 W Bell St *Web:* www.dawsoncountymontana.com	Glendive	MT	59330	406-377-3058	687-3563	338
Dawson County PO Box 1268 *Web:* www.co.dawson.tx.us	Lamesa	TX	79331	806-872-3778	872-2473	338
Dawson County 700 N Washington *Web:* dawsoncountyne.org	Lexington	NE	68850	308-324-2127	324-9832	338
Dawson County Board of Education, The 517 Allen St *TF:* 866-632-9992 ■ *Web:* www.dawsoncountyschools.org	Dawsonville	GA	30534	706-265-3246		685
Dawson Design Associates Inc 315 Second Ave S 300 *Web:* www.dawsondesignassociates.com	Seattle	WA	98104	206-932-3102		393
Dawson Geophysical Co 508 W Wall St Ste 800 *NASDAQ: DWSN* ■ *TF:* 800-332-9766 ■ *Web:* www.dawson3d.com	Midland	TX	79701	432-684-3000	684-3030	538
Dawson Insurance Agency Inc 721 First Ave N *Web:* dawsonins.com	Fargo	ND	58107	701-237-3311		390
Dawson Logistics Inc 431 N Vermilion *Web:* www.dawsonlogistics.com	Danville	IL	61832	217-442-7036		194
Dawson Metal Company Inc 825 Allen St *Web:* www.dawsonmetal.com	Jamestown	NY	14701	716-664-3815	664-3485	697
Dawson Mfg Co 1042 N Crystal Ave *Web:* www.dawsonmfg.com	Benton Harbor	MI	49022	269-925-0100	925-0997	676
Dawson Public Power District 75191 Rd 433 *TF:* 800-752-8305 ■ *Web:* www.dawsonpower.com	Lexington	NE	68850	308-324-2386		245
Dawson School 199 N School Ave *Web:* www.dawsonisd.net	Dawson	TX	76639	254-578-1031		393
Dawson's Kitchen 3360 Brookdale Ave *Web:* www.dawsonskitchen.com	Macon	GA	31204	478-742-9852		671
Dax Safety & Staffing Solutions LLC 307 NW 110th Terr *Web:* daxsafety.com	Kansas City	MO	64155	816-935-9137		260
Daxon Mktg 679 Buttonwood Dr	Brea	CA	92821	714-529-1218		4
Daxor Corp 350 Fifth Ave Ste 7120 *NYSE: DXR* ■ *Web:* www.daxor.com	New York	NY	10118	212-244-0555	244-0806	419
Day & Zimmermann Group Inc 1818 Market St *TF:* 877-319-0270 ■ *Web:* www.dayzim.com	Philadelphia	PA	19130	215-299-8000		727
Day Automation Systems Inc 7931 Rae Blvd *Web:* dayautomation.com	Victor	NY	14564	585-924-4630		256
Day Automotive Group 1600 Golden Mile Hwy *Web:* dayauto.com	Monroeville	PA	15146	724-327-0900		57
Day County 711 W First St *Web:* ujs.sd.gov	Webster	SD	57274	605-345-3771	345-3818	338
Day Enterprises Inc 1912 S Ridge Ave *Web:* www.carfare.com	Kannapolis	NC	28083	704-933-2218		194
Day Lumber Co 34 S Broad St *TF:* 800-975-6642 ■ *Web:* www.daylumber.com	Westfield	MA	01085	413-568-3511	568-6668	551
Day Motor Sports LLC 6100 Hwy 69 N *Web:* www.daymotorsports.com	Tyler	TX	75706	903-593-9815		54
Day Pitney LLP 242 Trumbull St *Web:* www.daypitney.com	Hartford	CT	06103	860-275-0100	275-0343	428
Day Pond State Park c/o Eastern District HQ 209 Hebron Rd *Web:* www.ct.gov	Marlborough	CT	06447	860-295-9523		565
Day Publishing Co 47 Eugene O'Neill Dr *TF:* 800-542-3354 ■ *Web:* www.theday.com	New London	CT	06320	860-442-2200		637-8
Day Vision Marketing 2222 S 12th St Ste D *TF:* 800-777-9684 ■ *Web:* www.dayvision.com	Allentown	PA	18103	610-403-3999		195
Day Wireless Systems Inc 4700 SE International Way *Web:* www.daywireless.com	Milwaukie	OR	97222	503-659-1240		480
Daybreak Express Inc 500 Ave P *TF:* 800-832-5660 ■ *Web:* www.daybreakexpress.com	Newark	NJ	07105	973-589-5931		311
Daybreak Oil & Gas Inc(NDA) 601 W Main Ave Ste 1012 *TF:* 800-962-4284 ■ *Web:* www.daybreakoilandgas.com	Spokane	WA	99201	509-232-7674		539
Daybreak Star Ctr 3801 W Government Way PO Box 99100 *TF:* 800-321-4321 ■ *Web:* www.unitedindians.org	Seattle	WA	98199	206-285-4425	282-3640	50-2
Daybreak Venture LLC 401 N Elm St *TF:* 800-345-5603 ■ *Web:* www.daybreakventure.com	Denton	TX	76201	940-387-4388		371
Day-Glo Color Corp 4515 St Clair Ave *TF:* 800-424-9300 ■ *Web:* www.dayglo.com	Cleveland	OH	44103	216-391-7070	391-7751	550
Dayhuff Group LLC, The 740 Lakeview Plaza Blvd Ste 300 *TF:* 800-426-9990 ■ *Web:* www.dayhuffgroup.com	Worthington	OH	43085	614-854-9999		180
Day-Lee Foods Inc 13055 Molette St *TF:* 800-329-5331 ■ *Web:* www.day-lee.com	Santa Fe Springs	CA	90670	562-903-3020		297-9
Daylight Donut Flour Company LLC 11707 E 11th St *TF:* 800-331-2245 ■ *Web:* www.daylightdonuts.com	Tulsa	OK	74128	918-438-0800		68
Daylight Transport 1501 Hughes Way Ste 200 *TF:* 800-468-9999 ■ *Web:* dylt.com	Long Beach	CA	90810	800-468-9999		780
Daylor Consulting Group Inc 10 Forbes Rd *Web:* www.daylor.com	Braintree	MA	02184	781-849-7070		256
Daymar College 3361 Buckland Sq *TF:* 800-456-3253 ■ *Web:* daymarcollege.edu	Owensboro	KY	42301	270-926-4040		800
Daymark Recovery Services Inc Stanly Center 1000 N First St Ste 1 *TF:* 866-275-9552 ■ *Web:* www.daymarkrecovery.org	Albemarle	NC	28001	704-983-2117		726
Daymark Solutions Inc 23 Third Ave *Web:* www.daymarksi.com	Burlington	MA	01803	781-359-3000		174
Daymon Assoc Inc 700 Fairfield Ave *Web:* www.daymon.com	Stamford	CT	06902	203-352-7500		195
Dayner Hall Marketing & Advertising 621 E Pine St *Web:* www.daynerhall.com	Orlando	FL	32801	407-428-5750		7
Days Inn Hinton-Jasper Hotel 358 Smith St *TF:* 800-259-4827 ■ *Web:* www.daysinnhinton.com	Hinton	AB	T7V2A1	780-817-1960		378
Days Inns Worldwide Inc 215 W 94th St Broadway *TF:* 800-225-3297 ■ *Web:* www.wyndhamhotels.com/days-inn	New York	NY	10025	212-866-6400		379
DaySpa Magazine 7628 Densmore Ave *TF:* 800-442-5667 ■ *Web:* www.dayspamagazine.com	Van Nuys	CA	91406	818-782-7328	782-7450	457-21
DaySpring Cards Inc 21154 Hwy 16 E *TF:* 800-944-8000 ■ *Web:* www.dayspring.com	Siloam Springs	AR	72761	479-524-9301		130
Daystar Television Network 3901 Hwy 121 PO Box 610546 *TF:* 800-329-0029 ■ *Web:* daystar.com	Bedford	TX	76021	817-571-1229	571-7458	740
Dayton Area Chamber of Commerce 1 Chamber Plaza Ste 200 *TF:* 800-621-9131 ■ *Web:* www.daytonchamber.org	Dayton	OH	45402	937-226-1444	226-8254	139
Dayton Art Institute 456 Belmonte Pk N *TF:* 800-272-8258 ■ *Web:* www.daytonartinstitute.org	Dayton	OH	45405	937-223-5277	223-3140	520
Dayton Aviation Heritage National Historical Park 16 S Williams St *TF:* 800-266-4767 ■ *Web:* www.nps.gov	Dayton	OH	45402	937-225-7705	222-4512	564
Dayton Ballet 140 N Main St *TF:* 800-745-3000 ■ *Web:* daytonperformingarts.org	Dayton	OH	45402	937-449-5060	223-9189	573-1
Dayton City Hall 101 W Third St PO Box 22 *Web:* www.daytonohio.gov	Dayton	OH	45401	937-333-3636	333-4297	337
Dayton City Paper 126 N Main St Ste 240 *TF:* 888-228-3630 ■ *Web:* www.daytoncitypaper.com	Dayton	OH	45402	937-222-8855	222-6113	532-5
Dayton City Schools 115 S Ludlow St *Web:* www.dps.k12.oh.us	Dayton	OH	45402	937-542-3000	542-3188	685
Dayton Contemporary Dance Co 840 Germantown St *TF:* 888-228-3630 ■ *Web:* www.dcdc.org	Dayton	OH	45402	937-228-3232	223-6156	573-1
Dayton Convention Ctr 22 E Fifth St *Web:* www.daytonconventioncenter.com	Dayton	OH	45402	937-333-4700	333-4711	205
Dayton Correctional Institution 4104 Germantown St PO Box 17399 *Web:* drc.ohio.gov/dci	Dayton	OH	45417	937-263-0060	263-1322	213
Dayton Daily News 1611 S Main St *TF:* 888-397-6397 ■ *Web:* www.daytondailynews.com	Dayton	OH	45409	937-225-2000	225-2489	532-2
Dayton Foundation 40 N Main St Ste 500 *TF:* 877-222-0410 ■ *Web:* www.daytonfoundation.org	Dayton	OH	45423	937-222-0410	222-0636	303
Dayton Freight Lines Inc 6450 Poe Ave *Web:* www.daytonfreight.com	Dayton	OH	45414	937-264-4060		314
Dayton International Airport 3600 Terminal Dr Ste 300 *TF:* 877-359-3291 ■ *Web:* www.flydayton.com	Vandalia	OH	45377	937-454-8200	454-8284	27
Dayton Machine Tool Co 1314 Webster St *Web:* www.dmtnet.com	Dayton	OH	45404	937-222-6444	222-6444	455
Dayton Mall 2700 Miamisburg Centerville Rd *Web:* www.daytonmall.com	Dayton	OH	45459	937-433-9834		460
Dayton Mark (D) 130 State Capitolÿ75 Rev Dr. Martin Luther KingÿJr. Blvd **Fax Area Code:* 6.5 ■ *Web:* www.governor.state.mn.us	St. Paul	MN	55155	.51-201-e+009	179-7e+009*	343
Dayton Metro Library 215 E Third St *Web:* www.daytonmetrolibrary.org	Dayton	OH	45402	937-463-2665		434-3
Dayton National Cemetery 4400 W Third St *TF:* 800-273-8255 ■ *Web:* www.cem.va.gov	Dayton	OH	45428	937-262-2115	268-2225	136
Dayton Newspapers Inc 116 S Main St *TF:* 800-643-6275 ■ *Web:* www.daytondailynews.com	Dayton	OH	45409	937-225-2000		637-8
Dayton Opera 126 N Main St Ste 210 *TF:* 800-272-3900 ■ *Web:* www.daytonperformingarts.org	Dayton	OH	45402	937-224-3521	223-9189	573-2
Dayton Parts LLC 3500 Industrial Rd PO Box 5795 *TF Cust Svc:* 800-225-2159 ■ *Web:* daytonparts.com	Harrisburg	PA	17110	717-255-8500	255-8500	60
Dayton Philharmonic Orchestra 126 N Main St Ste 210 *TF:* 888-228-3630 ■ *Web:* daytonperformingarts.org	Dayton	OH	45402	937-224-3521	223-9189	573-3
Dayton Power & Light Co PO Box 1247 *TF:* 800-433-8500 ■ *Web:* www.dpandl.com	Dayton	OH	45401	937-331-3900	331-3900	787
Dayton Progress Corp 500 Progress Rd *Web:* www.daytonprogress.com	Dayton	OH	45449	937-859-5111	859-5353	757
Dayton Rehabilitation Institute 1 Elizabeth Pl *TF:* 800-765-4772 ■ *Web:* reliantdayton.com	Dayton	OH	45417	937-424-8200		726
Dayton Reliable Air Filter Inc 2294 N Moraine Dr **Fax Area Code:* 937 ■ *TF Orders:* 800-699-0747 ■ *Web:* www.reliablefilter.com	Dayton	OH	45439	800-699-0747	293-3975*	17
Dayton Rogers Manufacturing Co 8401 W 35 W Service Dr *TF:* 800-677-8881 ■ *Web:* www.daytonrogers.com	Minneapolis	MN	55449	763-784-7714	784-7714	488
Dayton State Park PO Box 1478 *Web:* parks.nv.gov/parks/dayton	Dayton	NV	89403	775-687-5678		565
Dayton Superior Corp 1125 Byers Rd *TF:* 800-745-3700 ■ *Web:* www.daytonsuperior.com	Miamisburg	OH	45342	937-866-0711		350
Dayton T Brown Inc 1175 Church St *TF:* 800-232-6300 ■ *Web:* www.dtb.com	Bohemia	NY	11716	631-589-6300		743
Dayton Va Medical Ctr 4100 W Third St *TF:* 800-368-8262 ■ *Web:* dayton.va.gov	Dayton	OH	45428	937-268-6511		374-8
Dayton Visual Arts Ctr 118 N Jefferson St *Web:* www.daytonvisualarts.org	Dayton	OH	45402	937-224-3822		50-2
Dayton/Montgomery County Convention & Visitors Bureau 1 Chamber Plaza Ste A *TF:* 800-221-8235 ■ *Web:* daytoncvb.com	Dayton	OH	45402	937-226-8211	226-8294	206
Daytona Beach City Hall 301 S Ridgewood Ave Rm 210 *Web:* www.codb.us	Daytona Beach	FL	32114	386-671-8000	671-8115	337
Daytona Beach Community College 1200 W International Speedway Blvd *TF:* 877-822-6669 ■ *Web:* www.daytonastate.edu	Daytona Beach	FL	32114	386-506-3000	506-3940	162

	Phone	Fax	Class
Daytona Beach International Airport 700 Catalina Dr Ste 300 ... Daytona Beach FL 32114 *TF:* 800-255-2877 ■ *Web:* www.flydaytonafirst.com	386-248-8030		27
Daytona Beach News-Journal 901 Sixth St ... Daytona Beach FL 32117 *Web:* www.news-journalonline.com	386-252-1511	258-8465	532-2
Daytona Beach Resort & Conference Ctr 2700 N Atlantic Ave ... Daytona Beach FL 32118 *TF:* 800-654-6216 ■ *Web:* www.daytonabeachresort.com	386-672-3770		379
Daytona Beach Symphony Society PO Box 2 ... Daytona Beach FL 32115 *Web:* new.dbss.org	386-253-2901	253-5774	573-3
Daytona Flexible Packaging LLC 811 Fentress Ct ... Daytona Beach FL 32117 *Web:* www.pouchfill.com	386-274-4474		549
Daytona Inn Beach Resort 219 S Atlantic Ave ... Daytona Beach FL 32118 *TF General:* 800-874-1822 ■ *Web:* daytonainnbeachresort.com	386-252-3626	255-3680	379
Daytona International Speedway 1801 W International Speedway Blvd ... Daytona Beach FL 32114 *Web:* www.daytonainternationalspeedway.com	386-254-2700		515
Dayton-Granger Inc 3299 SW Ninth Ave ... Fort Lauderdale FL 33315 *TF:* 800-424-9300 ■ *Web:* www.daytongranger.com	954-463-3451	761-3172	647
Dayton-Phoenix Group Inc 1619 Kuntz Rd ... Dayton OH 45404 *TF:* 800-657-0707 ■ *Web:* www.dayton-phoenix.com	937-496-3974		650
Daytronic Corp 2566 Kohnle Dr ... Miamisburg OH 45342 *Web:* www.daytronic.com	937-293-2566		201
DAZ Productions Inc 12637 S 265 W Ste 300 ... Draper UT 84020 *Web:* www.daz3d.com	801-495-1777		225
DAZ Systems Inc 880 Apollo St Ste 201 ... El Segundo CA 90245 *Web:* www.dazsi.com	310-640-1300		177
Dazian LLC 10 Central Blvd ... South Hackensack NJ 07606 *TF:* 877-232-9426 ■ *Web:* www.dazian.com	201-549-1000	641-2728	745-2
Dazor Lighting Solutions 2079 Congressional ... Saint Louis MO 63146 *TF:* 800-345-9103 ■ *Web:* www.dazor.com	314-652-2400	652-2069	439
DB (Deutsche Bank Canada) 199 Bay St Commerce Ct W Ste 4700 ... Toronto ON M5L1E9 *TF:* 800-735-7777 ■ *Web:* www.db.com	416-682-8000	682-8383	70
DB & S Lumber Co 78 Accord Park Dr ... Norwell MA 02061 *TF:* 800-608-8701 ■ *Web:* www.dbslumber.com	781-878-3345		190
DB Aviation Inc 3550 N McAree Rd ... Waukegan IL 60087 *TF:* 888-362-6738 ■ *Web:* www.landmarkaviation.com	847-244-8504		63
DB Becker Company Inc 46 Leigh St ... Clinton NJ 08809 *TF:* 800-394-3991 ■ *Web:* www.dbbecker.com	908-730-6010	730-9118	146
db Bistro Moderne 55 W 44th St ... New York NY 10036 *Web:* www.danielnyc.com	212-391-2400		671
DB Consulting Group Inc 8403 Colesville Rd ... Silver Spring MD 20910 *Web:* www.dbconsultinggroup.com	301-589-4020		193
D&B Industrial Group 21649 Cedar Creek Ave ... Georgetown DE 19947 *Web:* www.dbindustrialgroup.com	302-855-0585		475
DB Root & Company Inc 436 Seventh Ave Ste 2800 ... Pittsburgh PA 15219 *TF:* 888-227-0913 ■ *Web:* www.dbroot.com	412-227-2800		194
D&B Sales & Marketing Solutions 460 Totten Pond Rd ... Waltham MA 02451 *TF:* 866-473-3932 ■ *Web:* www.hoovers.com	781-672-9200		178-1
DB Squared LLC 2928 N McKee Cir ... Fayetteville AR 72703	479-521-2976		41
Db Technologies Inc 3601 N First St PO Box 280 ... Bloomfield NM 87413 *Web:* dbtechnm.com	505-632-7900		179
DB5 202 N Ave 64 ... Los Angeles CA 90042 *Web:* www.dogsbollocks5.com	626-660-5484		5
DBA Engineering Ltd 401 Hanlan Rd ... Vaughan ON L4L3T1 *TF:* 800-819-8833 ■ *Web:* www.dbaeng.com	905-851-0090		256
dbaDIRECT Inc 7310 Turfway Rd Ste 300 ... Florence KY 41042 *Web:* www.dbadirect.com	859-283-2520		194
DBC (Diagnostics Biochem Canada Inc) 41 Byron Ave ... Dorchester ON N6M1A1 *Web:* www.dbc-labs.com	519-681-8731	268-7167	231
DBF (DATA Group) 9195 Torbram Rd ... Brampton ON L6S6H2 *Web:* www.datacm.com	905-791-3151	791-3277	110
DBG Partners Inc 940 S Kimball Ave Ste 100 ... Southlake TX 76092	817-442-1060	442-1052	631
DBI (Dee Brown Inc) 4101 S Shiloh Rd PO Box 570335 ... Dallas TX 75357 **Fax:* Tech Supp ■ *Web:* www.deebrowncompanies.com	214-321-6443	328-1039*	189-7
DBI (Delta Steel Technologies) 2204 Century Ctr Blvd ... Irving TX 75062 *Web:* www.dbimfg.com	972-438-7150	579-0100	494
DBI Beverage 245 S Spruce Ave Ste 900 ... San Francisco CA 94080 *TF:* 800-342-2350 ■ *Web:* www.dbibeverage.com	415-643-9900		81-1
DBI Inc 912 E Michigan Ave ... Lansing MI 48912 *TF:* 800-968-1324 ■ *Web:* www.dbiyes.com	517-485-3200	485-3202	535
DBK Concepts Inc 12905 SW 129 Ave ... Miami FL 33186 *TF:* 800-725-7226 ■ *Web:* www.dbk.com	305-596-7226	596-7222	175
Dbnet Systems Inc 3602 Keenland Dr ... Marietta GA 30062 *TF:* 800-319-8862 ■ *Web:* www.dbnetsystems.com	770-509-3638		225
dBrn Assoc Inc 189 Curtis Rd ... Hewlett Neck NY 11598 *Web:* www.dbrnassociates.com	516-569-4557		194
DBS Bank Ltd 725 S Figueroa St ... Los Angeles CA 90017 *TF:* 800-209-4555 ■ *Web:* www.dbs.com	213-627-0222		70
DBSA (Depression & Bipolar Support Alliance) 730 N Franklin St Ste 501 ... Chicago IL 60610 *TF:* 800-826-3632 ■ *Web:* www.dbsalliance.org	312-642-0049	642-7243	48-17
DBU (Duluth Business University) 4724 Mike Colalilo Dr ... Duluth MN 55807 *TF:* 800-777-8406 ■ *Web:* www.dbumn.edu	218-722-4000	628-2127	800
DC Connections 22650 Executive Dr Ste 125 ... Sterling VA 20166 *Web:* www.dcconnections.com	703-471-9757		116
DC Electronics 1870 Little Orchard St ... San Jose CA 95125 *Web:* www.dcelectronics.com	408-947-4500		814
DC Engineering PC 440 E Corporate Dr Ste 103 ... Meridian ID 83642 *Web:* www.dcengineering.net	208-288-2181		261
DC Equipment Inc 57 Old Mill Rd ... Geraldine AL 35974 *TF:* 800-720-3212 ■ *Web:* www.dcequipmentinc.com	256-659-4707		358
DC Group Inc 1977 W River Rd N ... Minneapolis MN 55411 *TF:* 800-838-7927 ■ *Web:* www.dc-group.com	800-838-7927		767
DC Humphrys Inc 5744 Woodland Ave ... Philadelphia PA 19143 *TF Sales:* 800-645-2059 ■ *Web:* www.sbcontract.com	215-724-8181	724-8706	733
DC Independent Film Festival (DCIFF) 701 Pennsylvania Ave NW ... Washington DC 20004 *Web:* dciff-indie.org	202-737-2300		282
DC Taylor Co 312 29th St NE ... Cedar Rapids IA 52402 *TF:* 800-876-6346 ■ *Web:* www.dctaylorco.com	319-363-2073	363-8311	189-12
DC United 2400 E Capitol St SE ... Washington DC 20003 *Web:* www.dcunited.com	202-587-5000	587-5400	717
DC101 1801 Rockville Pk ... Rockville MD 20852 *TF:* 866-913-2101 ■ *Web:* dc101.iheart.com	240-747-2700		645
DCA (Diamond Council of America) 3212 W End Ave Ste 202 ... Nashville TN 37203 *TF:* 877-283-5669 ■ *Web:* www.diamondcouncil.org	615-385-5301	385-4955	49-4
DCA (Distribution Contractors Assn) 101 W Renner Rd Ste 460 ... Richardson TX 75082 *Web:* www.dcaweb.org	972-680-0261	680-0461	49-3
DCAT (Drug Chemical & Associated Technologies Assn) 1 Washington Blvd Ste 7 ... Robbinsville NJ 08691 *TF:* 800-640-3228 ■ *Web:* www.dcat.org	609-448-1000		49-19
DCB (Denver Commercial Builders Inc) 909 E 62nd Ave ... Denver CO 80216 *Web:* www.dcb1.com	303-287-5525	287-3697	186
Dcc Lee Enterprises 12276 San Jose Blvd Ste 601 ... Jacksonville FL 32223 *Web:* www.mcdjax.com	904-288-6750		194
DCCC (Democratic Congressional Campaign Committee) 430 S Capitol St SE ... Washington DC 20003 *Web:* www.dccc.org	202-863-1500		48-7
DCCI (Dow Chemical Canada Inc) 450 First St SW Ste 2100 ... Calgary AB T2P5H1 *TF:* 800-447-4369 ■ *Web:* www.dow.com	403-267-3500	267-3597	144
DCEC (Delaware County Electric Co-op) 39 Elm St PO Box 471 ... Delhi NY 13753 *TF:* 866-436-1223 ■ *Web:* www.dce.coop	607-746-2341		245
DCG One 5501 Cass Ave ... Cleveland OH 44102 *Web:* www.directconnectgroup.com	216-281-2866	281-2824	7
DCG Precision Mfg 9 Trowbridge Dr ... Bethel CT 06801 *TF:* 800-848-7681 ■ *Web:* www.dcgprecision.com	203-743-5525	791-1737	621
DCH (Doctors Community Hospital) 8118 Good Luck Rd ... Lanham MD 20706 *Web:* www.dchweb.org	301-552-8118	552-8521	374-3
DCH (Delnor-Community Hospital) 300 Randall Rd ... Geneva IL 60134 *TF:* 800-223-9776 ■ *Web:* www.delnor.com	630-208-3000	718-2650	374-3
DCH (Douglas County Hospital) 111 17th Ave E ... Alexandria MN 56308 *Web:* www.dchospital.com	320-762-1511	762-6120	374-3
DCH Health System 809 University Blvd E ... Tuscaloosa AL 35401 *TF:* 800-266-4324 ■ *Web:* www.dchsystem.com	205-759-7111		353
DCH Honda of Nanuet 10 Rt 304 ... Nanuet NY 10954 *TF:* 888-495-0660 ■ *Web:* www.dchhondaofnanuet.com	845-623-1200		57
DCH Regional Medical Ctr 809 University Blvd E ... Tuscaloosa AL 35401 *TF:* 800-356-9596 ■ *Web:* dchsystem.com	205-759-7111		374-3
DCI (Dynamic Concepts Inc) 1730 17th St NE ... Washington DC 20002 *Web:* www.dcihq.com	202-944-8787	526-7233	735
DCI (Drum Corps International) PO Box 3129 ... Indianapolis IN 46206 *TF Orders:* 800-495-7469 ■ *Web:* www.dci.org	317-275-1212	713-0690	48-4
DCI (Development Counsellors International Ltd) 215 Pk Ave S 14th Fl ... New York NY 10003 *Web:* www.aboutdci.com	212-725-0707	725-2254	230
DCI (Discovery Ctr of Idaho) 131 Myrtle St ... Boise ID 83702 *Web:* www.dcidaho.com	208-343-9895		520
Dci Consulting Group Inc 1920 I St NW ... Washington DC 20006 *Web:* dciconsult.com	202-828-6900		463
DCI Inc 600 N 54th Ave ... Saint Cloud MN 56303 *TF:* 800-236-6603 ■ *Web:* www.dciinc.com	320-252-8200	252-0866	91
DCI International 305 N Springbrook Rd ... Newberg OR 97132 *Web:* www.dcionline.com	503-538-8343		228
DCI Marketing Inc 2727 W Good Hope Rd ... Milwaukee WI 53209 *Web:* www.dci-artform.com	414-228-7000		195
DCIFF (DC Independent Film Festival) 701 Pennsylvania Ave NW ... Washington DC 20004 *Web:* dciff-indie.org	202-737-2300		282
DCL (Door County Library) 107 S Fourth Ave ... Sturgeon Bay WI 54235 *TF:* 800-273-7877 ■ *Web:* www.doorcountylibrary.org	920-743-6578		434-3
DCL (Downey City Library) 11121 Brookshire Ave ... Downey CA 90241 *TF:* 877-846-3452 ■ *Web:* www.downeyca.org	562-904-7360	923-3763	434-3
DCL Corp 48641 Milmont Dr ... Fremont CA 94538 *Web:* www.dclcorp.com	510-651-5100		393
DCM (Distribution Center Management) 712 Main St Ste 187B ... Boonton NJ 07005 *TF:* 800-232-4317 ■ *Web:* www.distributiongroup.com	973-265-2300	402-6056	531-2
DCM Manufacturing Inc 4540 W 160th St ... Cleveland OH 44135 *Web:* www.dcm-mfg.com	216-265-8006		610
Dcm Tech Corp 4455 Theurer Blvd ... Winona MN 55987 *Web:* www.dcm-tech.com	507-452-4043		454

Name / Address	City	State	Zip	Phone	Fax	Class
DCNA (District of Columbia Nurses Assn) 5100 Wisconsin Ave NW Ste 306 *Web:* www.dcna.org	Washington	DC	20016	202-244-2705	362-8285	533
DCOR LLC 290 Maple Court Ste 290 *Web:* www.dcorusa.com	Ventura	CA	93003	805-535-2000		536
DCOTA (Design Ctr of the Americas) 1855 Griffin Rd *TF:* 877-992-9204 ■ *Web:* www.dcota.com	Dania Beach	FL	33004	954-920-7997		460
DCP (Dick Clark Productions Inc) 2900 Olympic Blvd *Web:* www.dickclark.com	Santa Monica	CA	90404	310-255-4600		514
DCP Midstream Partners LP 370 17th St Ste 2775 *NYSE:* DPM ■ *Web:* www.dcpmidstream.com	Denver	CO	80202	303-633-2900	605-2225	325
DCPS (District of Columbia Public Schools) 1200 First St NE *Web:* www.dcps.dc.gov	Washington	DC	20002	202-442-5885	442-5026	685
Dcr Business Solutions Inc PO Box 297 *Web:* www.dcrservices.com	Mulberry	FL	33860	863-904-1077	428-9027	188
DCR Workforce Inc 7795 NW Beacon Sq Blvd Ste 201 *TF:* 888-327-4867 ■ *Web:* www.dcrworkforce.com	Boca Raton	FL	33487	561-998-3737		196
DCS Corp 6909 Metro Park Dr Ste 500 dcscorp.com	Alexandria	VA	22310	571-227-6000		261
Dcs Netlink 1800 Macauley Ave *TF:* 877-327-6385 ■ *Web:* dcsnetlink.com	Rice Lake	WI	54868	715-236-7424		180
Dcse Inc 95 Argonaut Ste 260 *Web:* www.dcse.com	Aliso Viejo	CA	92656	949-465-3400		180
DCT (Diversified Chemical Technologies Inc) 15477 Woodrow Wilson St *TF:* 800-243-1424 ■ *Web:* www.dchem.com	Detroit	MI	48238	313-867-5444	867-3831	145
DCT Chambers Trucking Ltd 600 Waddington Dr *TF:* 800-575-2355 ■ *Web:* www.chambersgroup.co	Vernon	BC	V1T8T6	250-549-2157		478
DCU Ctr 50 Foster St *TF:* 800-745-3000 ■ *Web:* www.dcucenter.com	Worcester	MA	01608	508-755-6800	929-0111	720
dcVAST Inc 1319 Butterfield Rd Ste 504 *Web:* www.dcvast.com	Downers Grove	IL	60515	630-964-6060		196
Dcxcavation Inc 10641 Prospect Ave *Web:* dcxcavation.com	Santee	CA	92071	619-312-1550		362
DCX-CHOL Enterprises Inc 12831 S Figueroa St *Web:* www.dcxchol.com	Los Angeles	CA	90061	310-516-1692		625
DD Bean & Sons Co 207 Peterborough St **Fax:* Sales ■ *TF:* 800-326-8311 ■ *Web:* www.ddbean.com	Jaffrey	NH	03452	603-532-8311	532-6001*	469
DD Jones Transfer & Warehouse Co Inc 2121 Old Greenbrier Rd *TF:* 800-335-4787 ■ *Web:* www.ddjones.com	Chesapeake	VA	23320	757-494-0225	494-0291	803-1
D&D Sexton Inc PO Box 156 *TF:* 800-743-0265 ■ *Web:* www.ddsextoninc.com	Carthage	MO	64836	417-358-8727		780
DD Traders Inc Dba Demdaco 5000 W 134th St	Leawood	KS	66209	913-402-6800		362
DD Williamson & Company Inc 100 S Spring St *TF:* 800-227-2635 ■ *Web:* www.ddwcolor.com	Louisville	KY	40206	502-895-2438		296-15
DDA (Directory Distributing Assoc) 1602 Pk 370 Ct *TF General:* 800-325-1964	Hazelwood	MO	63042	314-592-8600	592-8790	96
DDAMC (Eisenhower Army Medical Ctr) 300 E Hospital Rd **Fax:* Admitting ■ *Web:* www.ddeamc.amedd.army.mil	Fort Gordon	GA	30905	706-787-5811	787-5342*	374-4
DDB Worldwide 437 Madison Ave *Web:* www.ddb.com	New York	NY	10022	212-415-2000	415-3414	4
DDC Group Inc, The 2 California Plaza 350 S Grand Ave Ste 1670 *Web:* ddcgroupinc.com	Los Angeles	CA	90071	213-334-4565		396
DDCF (Doris Duke Charitable Foundation) 650 Fifth Ave 19th Fl *Web:* www.ddcf.org	New York	NY	10019	212-974-7000	974-7590	305
DDC-I Inc 4600 E Shea Blvd Ste 102 *Web:* www.ddci.com	Phoenix	AZ	85028	602-275-7172	252-6054	178-2
DD&F Consulting Group 521 S Rock St *TF:* 800-498-8877 ■ *Web:* ddfconsulting.com	Little Rock	AR	72202	501-374-2600		463
DDF CPA Group 107A Edwards Rd *Web:* www.ddfcpa.com	Starke	FL	32091	904-964-7404		194
Ddh Enterprise Inc 2220 Oak Ridge Way *Web:* www.ddhent.com	Vista	CA	92081	760-599-0171	599-9397	815
Ddi System LLC 75 Glen Rd Ste 204 *TF:* 877-599-4334 ■ *Web:* www.ddisystem.com	Sandy Hook	CT	06482	877-599-4334		179
dDirect Inc 2707 Peachtree Sq *TF:* 800-257-5242 ■ *Web:* www.ddirect.com	Atlanta	GA	30360	678-530-0034		195
DDJ Capital Management LLC 130 Turner St Bldg 3 Ste 600 *Web:* www.ddjcap.com	Waltham	MA	02453	781-283-8500		401
Ddj Myers Ltd 4455 E Camelback Rd Ste C138 *Web:* ddjmyers.com	Phoenix	AZ	85018	602-840-9595		193
Ddl Business Systems 5321 Mulberry St *Web:* www.ddlbusiness.com	Stephens City	VA	22655	540-869-7855		535
DDL Inc 10200 Vly View Rd Ste 101 *TF:* 800-229-4235 ■ *Web:* www.testedandproven.com	Eden Prairie	MN	55344	952-941-9226		743
DDLC Energy 410 Bank St *Web:* ddlcenergy.com	New London	CT	06320	860-271-2020		316
DDM-Digital Imaging Data Processing and Mailing Services 1223 William St *Web:* www.ddmdirect.com	Buffalo	NY	14206	716-893-8671		393
DDV (Digital Datavoice Corp) 1210 Northland Dr Ste 160 *Web:* www.ddvc.com	Mendota Heights	MN	55120	651-994-2284	452-5470	387
De Anza Land & Leisure Corp 1615 Cordova St	Los Angeles	CA	90007	323-734-9951		748
De Beaubien Knight Simmons Mantzaris & Neal LLP 332 N Magnolia Ave *Web:* dsklawgroup.com	Orlando	FL	32801	407-422-2454		445
De Byle's Inc 20 N Brown St	Rhinelander	WI	54501	715-362-4406		157-2
De Cotiis Fitzpatrick Cole & Wisler LLP 500 Frank W Burr Blvd *Web:* www.decotiislaw.com	Teaneck	NJ	07666	201-928-1100		428
De Dietrich Process Systems Inc 244 Sheffield St *Web:* www.ddpsinc.com	Mountainside	NJ	07092	908-317-2585		454
De Forest Creative Group Ltd 300 West Lake St Ste A1 *Web:* www.deforestgroup.com	Elmhurst	IL	60126	630-834-7200		393
de gobierno PO Box 190759 *Web:* www.de.gobierno.pr	San Juan	PR	91900	787-759-8910		41
De Graff Memorial Hospital 445 Tremont St *TF:* 800-506-6480 ■ *Web:* www.kaleidahealth.org	North Tonawanda	NY	14120	716-694-4500		374-3
DE Harvey Builders Inc 3630 Westchase Dr *Web:* www.harveybuilders.com	Houston	TX	77242	713-783-8710		186
De Jager Construction Inc 75-60th St SW *Web:* www.dejagerconstruction.com	Wyoming	MI	49548	616-530-0060		186
De Kadt Marketing and Research Inc 162 Danbury Rd *TF:* 800-243-2991 ■ *Web:* dekadt.com	Ridgefield	CT	06877	203-431-1212		195
De Kalb Memorial Hospital Inc 1316 E Seventh St *Web:* dekalbhealth.com	Auburn	IN	46706	260-925-4600		374-3
De La Cruz & Assoc Metro Office Park, St 1 #9 *Web:* www.delacruz.com	Guyanabo	PR	00969	787-622-4141		7
De La Salle Collegiate 14600 Common Rd *Web:* www.delasallehs.com	Warren	MI	48093	586-778-2207		166
De La Torre's 1606 BaRdstown Rd *Web:* www.delatorres.com	Louisville	KY	40205	502-456-4955		671
De Leon Springs State Park 601 Ponce De Leon Blvd *Web:* www.floridastateparks.org	De Leon Springs	FL	32130	386-985-4212		565
D&E Machining LTD 150 Industrial Dr *Web:* www.demachining.com	Corry	PA	16407	814-664-3531		454
De Marque inc 400 Boul Jean-Lesage Bureau 540 *TF:* 888-458-9143 ■ *Web:* www.demarque.com	Quebec	QC	G1K8W1	418-658-9143		174
De Maximis Inc 450 Montbrook Ln *Web:* www.demaximis.com	Knoxville	TN	37919	865-691-5052	691-6485	463
De Medici 815 Fifth Ave *Web:* demedicisandiego.com	San Diego	CA	92101	619-702-7228		671
De Mores State Historic Site PO Box 106 *Web:* www.nd.gov	Medora	ND	58645	701-623-4355		565
De Rigo Rem 10941 La Tuna Canyon Rd *Web:* www.remeyewear.com	Sun Valley	CA	91352	818-504-3950		237
De Ronde Tire Supply Inc 95 Rapin Pl *TF:* 800-227-4647 ■ *Web:* www.etrucktire.com	Buffalo	NY	14211	716-897-6690	893-5716	755
De Ruijter int Usa 120 Harvest Dr *TF:* 800-328-1684 ■ *Web:* www.deruijterusa.com	Coldwater	OH	45828	419-678-3909		291
de Saisset Museum at Santa Clara University 500 El Camino Real *TF:* 866-554-6800 ■ *Web:* www.scu.edu/deSaisset	Santa Clara	CA	95053	408-554-4528		520
De Soto National Memorial 8300 Desoto Memorial Hwy *Web:* www.nps.gov	Bradenton	FL	34209	941-792-0458	792-5094	564
De Soto Public School District 73 610 Vineland School Rd *Web:* www.desoto.k12.mo.us	De Soto	MO	63020	636-586-1000		685
De Von's Jewelers Inc 1689 Arden Way *TF:* 800-928-2086 ■ *Web:* www.devonsjewelers.com	Sacramento	CA	95815	916-929-3991		410
De Wafelbakkers LLC 10000 Crystal Hill Rd *TF:* 800-924-3391 ■ *Web:* www.dewafelbakkers.com	North Little Rock	AR	72113	501-791-3320		296-1
De Well Container Shipping Corp 1 Cross Island Plaza Ste 302 *Web:* de-well.com	Rosedale	NY	11422	718-528-1888		314
De'Vons Optics Inc 10823 Bell Ct *Web:* coppermax.com	Rancho Cucamonga	CA	91730	909-466-4700		542
DEA (Drug Enforcement Administration) 700 Army-Navy Dr *Web:* www.justice.gov	Arlington	VA	22202	202-307-7596		340-14
DEA (David Evans & Assoc Inc) 2100 SW River Pkwy *TF:* 800-721-1916 ■ *Web:* www.deainc.com	Portland	OR	97201	503-223-6663	223-2701	261
Deacon Industrial Supply Co Inc 1510 Gehman Rd *Web:* www.deaconind.com	Harleysville	PA	19438	215-256-1715	256-1716	385
Deaconess Hospital 600 Mary St *TF:* 800-677-3422 ■ *Web:* www.deaconess.com	Evansville	IN	47747	812-450-5000		374-3
Deaconess Hospital 311 Straight St **Fax Area Code:* 937 ■ *TF:* 800-344-2462 ■ *Web:* www.deaconess-healthcare.com	Cincinnati	OH	45219	513-559-2100	783-5820*	374-3
Deaconess Long Term Care Inc (DLTC) 330 Straight St *Web:* www.deaconess-healthcare.com	Cincinnati	OH	45219	513-487-3600		450
Deaconess Medical Ctr 800 W Fifth Ave *Web:* www.deaconessspokane.com	Spokane	WA	99204	509-458-5800		374-3
Dead Horse Point State Park SR-313 *Web:* www.stateparks.utah.gov	Moab	UT	84532	435-259-2614		565
Dead Horse Ranch State Park 675 Dead Horse Ranch Rd	Cottonwood	AZ	86326	928-634-5283		565
Dead Ringer Putter Co 228 W Baltimore Ave	Clifton Heights	PA	19018	610-284-4653		292
Dead Timber State Recreation Area 227 County Rd & 12 Blvd *Web:* outdoornebraska.gov/deadtimber	Scribner	NE	68057	402-727-2922		565
Deaf Hearing Communication Centre Inc 630 Fairview Rd Ste 100 *Web:* www.dhcc.org	Swarthmore	PA	19081	610-604-0450		768

Phone | Fax | Class

Deaf Inter-link
100 Saint Francois St........................Florissant MO 63031 314-837-7757 138
TF: 800-330-7062 ■ *Web:* www.deafinterlink.com

Deaf Smith County 140 E Third St.............Hereford TX 79045 806-364-0625 364-6895 338
Web: deafsmithcad.org

Deaf Smith Electric Co-op Inc
1501 E First St PO Box 753..................Hereford TX 79045 806-364-1166 245
Web: www.deafsmith.coop

Deafness Research Foundation (DRF)
641 Lexington Ave 15th Fl...................New York NY 10022 212-328-9480 48-17
Web: hearinghealthfoundation.org

Deaf-Talk Inc 14 E Main St..................... Carnegie PA 15106 877-304-0004 768
TF: 877-304-0004 ■ *Web:* dtinterpreting.com

Deal LLC, The 20 Broad St....................New York NY 10005 212-313-9325 637-9
TF Cust Svc: 888-667-3325 ■ *Web:* www.thedeal.com

Deal Nathan (R) 203 State Capitol..............Atlanta GA 30334 404-656-1776 657-7332 343
Web: gov.georgia.gov

Dealer Impact Systems LLC
7733 Douglas Ave......................... Urbandale IA 50322 515-334-9638 4
Web: flickfusion.com

Dealer Media Group Inc
2201 W Plano Pkwy Ste 100.....................Plano TX 75075 972-881-1106 881-1526 5

Dealer Tire LLC 3711 Chester Ave.............Cleveland OH 44114 216-432-0088 755
TF: 800-933-2537 ■ *Web:* www.dealertire.com

Dealernet Inc
608 Matthews Mint Hill Rd Ste E..............Matthews NC 28105 704-321-3215 608
Web: www.dealernetinc.com

Dealers Truck Equipment Co
2460 Midway St..........................Shreveport LA 71108 318-635-7567 525-0903 516
TF: 800-259-7569 ■ *Web:* www.dealerstruck.com

DealersEdge PO Box 606.................Barnegat Light NJ 08006 609-879-4456 531-13
TF: 800-321-5312 ■ *Web:* www.dealersedge.com

Dealertrack CentralDispatch Inc
26387 Network Pl...........................Chicago IL 60673 858-259-6084 387
Web: www.centraldispatch.com

DealerTrack Holdings Inc
1111 Marcus Ave Ste M04................Lake Success NY 11042 516-734-3600 178-10
NASDAQ: TRAK ■ *TF:* 877-357-8725 ■ *Web:* www.dealertrack.com

DealFlow Analytics Inc
131 Jericho Tpke PH3........................Jericho NY 11753 516-876-8006 387
Web: dealflow.com

Dealmaker Media Inc
5 Lucerne St Ste 2..................... San Francisco CA 94103 415-864-2885 387
Web: www.dealmakermedia.com

DealNet Capital Corp
325 Milner Ave Ste 300...................... Toronto ON M1B5N1 855-912-3444 463
TF: 855-912-3444 ■ *Web:* www.dealnetcapital.com

Dealogic LLC 120 Broadway 8th Fl.............New York NY 10271 212-577-4400 177
Web: www.dealogic.com

Dealtaker Inc 5360 Legacy Dr Ste 115.............Plano TX 75024 214-234-9145 387
Web: www.dealtaker.com

Deam Lake State Recreation Area
1217 Deam Lake Rd..........................Borden IN 47106 812-246-5421 565
Web: www.in.gov

Dean & Co 8065 Leesburg Pk Ste 500............Vienna VA 22182 703-506-3900 506-3905 194
Web: www.dean.com

Dean & DeLuca Brands Inc
560 Broadway..............................New York NY 10012 212-226-6800 345
Web: www.deandeluca.com

Dean Baldwin Painting LP
2395 Bulverde Rd Ste 105................... Bulverde TX 78163 830-438-5340 529
Web: www.deanbaldwinpainting.com

Dean Cluck Feedyard Inc
105 Dean Cluck Ave...........................Gruver TX 79040 806-733-5021 733-2244 10-1
TF: 888-458-4787 ■ *Web:* deancluckfeedyard.com

Dean College 99 Main St.....................Franklin MA 02038 508-541-1508 541-8726* 162
**Fax:* Admissions ■ *TF:* 877-879-3326 ■ *Web:* www.dean.edu

Dean Custom Air LLC 120 Logan Rd............Bluffton SC 29909 843-706-2850 189-10
Web: deancustomair.com

Dean Foods 400 S Chamber Dr.................Decatur IN 46733 260-724-2136 296-25

Dean Foods Co
2711 N Haskell Ave Ste 3400................... Dallas TX 75204 214-303-3400 303-3499 296-27
NYSE: DF ■ *TF:* 800-395-7004 ■ *Web:* www.deanfoods.com

Dean Hardwoods Inc
9244 Industrial Blvd.........................Leland NC 28451 910-763-5409 290
Web: www.deanwood.com

Dean Health Insurance Inc
1277 Deming Way........................... Madison WI 53717 608-836-1400 827-4212 391-3
TF: 800-279-1301 ■ *Web:* www.deancare.com

Dean Institute of Technology
1501 W Liberty Ave........................ Pittsburgh PA 15226 412-531-4433 531-4435 800
TF: 800-575-9399 ■ *Web:* www.deantech.edu

Dean Kincaid Inc N2028 Hwy 106..............Palmyra WI 53156 262-495-3000 10-11

Dean Kurtz Construction
1651 Rand Rd............................Rapid City SD 57702 605-343-6665 186
TF: 800-843-3321 ■ *Web:* www.deankurtzconstruction.com

Dean Law Group, The
3990 Old Town Ave C-303.................. San Diego CA 92110 619-232-8377 428
Web: www.thedeanlawgroup.com

Dean Markley Strings Inc
3350 Scott Blvd Bldg 45.................. Santa Clara CA 95054 408-988-2456 527
Web: www.deanmarkley.com

Dean Sausage Company Inc
3750 Pleasant Valley Rd PO Box 750............. Attalla AL 35954 256-538-6082 296-26
Web: www.deansausage.com

Dean Snyder Construction Co
913 N 14th St............................Clear Lake IA 50428 641-357-2283 357-2232 186
Web: www.deansnyderconst.com

Dean Steel Buildings Inc
2929 Industrial Ave........................Fort Myers FL 33901 239-334-1051 334-2432 105
Web: www.deansteelbuildings.com

Dean Team Automotive Group Inc
15121 Manchester Rd.........................Ballwin MO 63011 636-227-0100 57
TF: 888-699-0663 ■ *Web:* www.deanteam.com

Dean Transportation Inc
4812 Aurelius Rd...........................Lansing MI 48910 517-319-8300 109
TF: 800-282-3326 ■ *Web:* deantransportation.com

Phone | Fax | Class

Dean Word Company Ltd
1245 River Rd.........................New Braunfels TX 78130 830-625-2365 606-5008 188-4
TF: 800-683-3926 ■ *Web:* www.deanword.com

Dean, Ringers, Morgan & Lawton PA
201 E Pine St Ste 1200....................... Orlando FL 32801 407-422-4310 428
Web: www.drml-law.com

Deangelis - Diamond Construction Inc
6635 Willow Park Dr.......................... Naples FL 34109 239-594-1994 186
Web: www.deangelisdiamond.com

Deanie's Seafood 1713 Lake Ave...............Metairie LA 70005 504-834-1225 671
Web: www.deanies.com

Deans Knight Capital Management Ltd
999 W Hastings St Ste 1500...............Vancouver BC V6C2W2 604-669-0212 401
Web: www.deansknight.com

Deans Mailing & List Services Inc
3015 W Weldon Ave.........................Phoenix AZ 85017 602-272-2100 5
Web: www.deansmailing.com

Deansteel Manufacturing Co
111 Merchant............................San Antonio TX 78204 210-226-8271 234
TF: 800-825-8271 ■ *Web:* www.deansteel.com

DeAnza College
21250 Stevens Creek Blvd...................Cupertino CA 95014 408-864-5678 864-8329* 162
**Fax:* Admissions ■ *TF:* 800-999-2782 ■ *Web:* www.deanza.edu

Dearborn Chamber of Commerce
22100 Michigan Ave........................ Dearborn MI 48124 313-584-6100 584-9818 139
Web: dearbornareachamber.org

Dearborn County 215 W High St........... Lawrenceburg IN 47025 812-537-8877 532-2021 338
Web: dearborncounty.org

Dearborn County Chamber of Commerce
320 Walnut St......................... Lawrenceburg IN 47025 812-537-0814 537-0845 139
TF: 800-322-8198 ■ *Web:* www.dearborncountychamber.org

Dearborn Federal Credit Union
400 Town Ctr Dr............................ Dearborn MI 48126 313-336-2700 336-2700 219
TF: 888-336-2700 ■ *Web:* www.dfcufinancial.com

Dearborn Heights Chamber of Commerce
22100 Michigan Ave Ste 2............Dearborn Heights MI 40124 313 274 7480 130
Web: www.dearbornareachamber.org

Dearborn Inn the - A Marriott Hotel
20301 Oakwood Blvd....................... Dearborn MI 48124 313-271-2700 271-2700 379
TF: 800-228-9290 ■ *Web:* www.marriott.com

Dearborn Mid-West Conveyor Co (DMWCC)
20334 Superior Rd...........................Taylor MI 48180 734-288-4400 207
Web: www.dmwcc.com

Dearborn Partners LLC
200 W Madison St Ste 1950..................Chicago IL 60606 312 795 1000 378
Web: www.dearbornpartners.com

Dearborn Sausage Co Inc
2450 Wyoming Ave.......................... Dearborn MI 48120 313-842-2375 842-2640 296-26
Web: dearbornbrand.com

Dearborn Times-Herald
13730 Michigan Ave......................... Dearborn MI 48126 313-584-4000 584-1357 532-4
TF: 866-468-7630 ■ *Web:* downriversundaytimes.com

Dearden's Furniture Co
700 S Main St...........................Los Angeles CA 90014 213-362-9600 321
TF: 800-545-5509 ■ *Web:* www.deardens.com

Deardorff Associates
319 E Lea Blvd......................... Wilmington DE 19802 302-764-7573 636
Web: www.deardorffassociates.com

Dearing Compressor & Pump Co
3974 Simon Rd.........................Youngstown OH 44512 330-783-2258 172
TF: 800-850-3440 ■ *Web:* www.dearingcomp.com

Dearth Chrysler Dodge Jeep Ram
520 Eigth St.............................. Monroe WI 53566 866-949-3653 57
TF: 877-495-5321 ■ *Web:* www.dearthmotorsinc.com

Death Valley Museum
Death Vly National Pk PO Box 579...........Death Valley CA 92328 760-786-2331 786-3283 520
TF: 800-544-0551 ■ *Web:* www.nps.gov/deva

Death Valley National Park
PO Box 579.............................Death Valley CA 92328 760-786-3200 786-3283 564
TF: 866-713-9688 ■ *Web:* www.nps.gov/deva

Deauville Beach Resort
6701 Collins Ave......................Miami Beach FL 33141 305-865-8511 669
TF: 800-327-6656 ■ *Web:* deauvillebeachresortmiami.com

Deaver Industries Inc 3120 Morgan Rd.........Bessemer AL 35022 205-426-4309 426-4364 439
Web: www.deaverind.com

DEB Inc
2815 Coliseum Centre Dr Ste 600........... Charlotte NC 28217 704-263-4240 263-9601 214
TF: 800-248-7190 ■ *Web:* www.debgroup.com

Debbie's Staffing Services Inc
4431 Cherry St Ste 50................. Winston-Salem NC 27105 336-744-2393 776-1661 721
Web: www.debbiesstaffing.com

Deb-El Food Products LLC
2 Papetti Plaza........................... Elizabeth NJ 07206 908-351-0330 297-8
TF: 800-421-3447 ■ *Web:* www.debelfoods.com

Debevoise & Plimpton LLP
919 Third Ave.............................New York NY 10022 212-909-6000 909-6836 428
Web: www.debevoise.com

Deboer Transportation Inc PO Box 145......... Blenker WI 54415 715-652-2911 780
Web: www.deboertrans.com

Deborah Heart & Lung Ctr
200 Trenton Rd........................Browns Mills NJ 08015 609-893-6611 893-1213 374-7
Web: www.deborah.org

Debos Diners Inc
7625 Hamilton Pk Dr Ste 26............... Chattanooga TN 37421 423-855-4650 670
Web: debosdiners.com

DeBourgh Manufacturing
27505 Otero Ave...........................La Junta CO 81050 800-328-8829 384-7713* 286
**Fax Area Code:* 719 ■ *TF:* 800-328-8829 ■ *Web:* www.debourgh.com

DeBra-Kuempel 3976 Southern Ave........... Cincinnati OH 45227 513-271-6500 271-4676 189-10
TF: 800-395-5741 ■ *Web:* www.debra-kuempel.com

Debt Buyers Inc
3080 S Durango Dr Ste 208................. Las Vegas NV 89117 702-946-8440 177
Web: www.srcnv.com

Debt Marketplace Inc, The
10440 Pioneer Blvd Ste 2..............Santa Fe Springs CA 90670 562-903-7220 708
TF: 800-713-0670 ■ *Web:* debtmarketplace.com

DebtFolio Inc
35 Braintree Hill Office Pk Ste 107............. Braintree MA 02184 866-876-3654 387
TF: 866-876-3654 ■ *Web:* www.geezeo.com

Phone | Fax | Class

Debtors Anonymous (DA) PO Box 920888 Needham MA 02492 781-453-2743 453-2745 48-21
TF: 800-421-2383 ■ *Web:* www.debtorsanonymous.org

DECA (Distributive Education Clubs of America)
1908 Assn Dr Reston VA 20191 703-860-5000 860-4013 49-5
Web: www.deca.org

Deca Aviation Engineering Ltd
7050 Telford Way Mississauga ON L5S1V7 905-405-1371 194
Web: deca-aviation.com

DECA Dimensions Magazine 1908 Assn Dr Reston VA 20191 703-860-5000 860-4013 457-6
Web: www.deca.org

Deca Technologies Inc
7855 S River Pkwy Ste 111 Tempe AZ 85284 480-345-9895 696
Web: www.decatechnologies.com

DeCarolis Truck Rental Inc
333 Colfax St Rochester NY 14606 585-254-1169 458-4072 778
TF: 800-666-1169 ■ *Web:* www.decarolis.com

Decatur Area Convention & Visitors Bureau
202 E N St Decatur IL 62523 217-423-7000 423-7455 206
TF: 800-331-4479 ■ *Web:* www.decaturcvb.com

Decatur Computers Inc
1234 N Water St Ste B Decatur IL 62521 217-475-0226 175
TF: 800-429-7140 ■ *Web:* decaturcomputers.com

Decatur Conference Center & Hotel
4191 W US Hwy 36 Wyckles Rd Decatur IL 62522 217-422-8800 378
Web: www.hoteldecatur.com

Decatur Co-op Assn 305 S York Ave Oberlin KS 67749 785-475-2234 475-3469 48-2
TF: 800-886-2293 ■ *Web:* www.decaturcoop.net

Decatur County PO Box 726 Bainbridge GA 39818 229-248-3030 246-2062 338
Web: decaturcountyga.org

Decatur County 22 W Main St Decaturville TN 38329 731-852-2131 338
TF: 800-525-6834 ■ *Web:* www.decaturcountytn.org

Decatur County
150 Courthouse Sq Ste 244 Greensburg IN 47240 812-663-8223 662-6627 338
TF: 800-622-4941 ■ *Web:* www.decaturcounty.in.gov

Decatur County 207 N Main St Leon IA 50144 641-446-4322 446-3616 338
Web: www.decaturcountyiowa.org

Decatur County Rural Electric Membership Corp
1430 W Main St PO Box 46 Greensburg IN 47240 812-663-3391 663-8572 245
TF: 800-844-7362 ■ *Web:* www.dcremc.com

Decatur Daily 201 First Ave SE Decatur AL 35601 256-353-4612 340-2392 532-2
TF: 888-353-4612 ■ *Web:* www.decaturdaily.com

Decatur General Hospital
1201 Seventh St SE Decatur AL 35601 256-341-2000 374-3
Web: decaturmorganhospital.net

Decatur Hotels LLC
317 Magazine St New Orleans LA 70130 504-539-9000 377

Decatur House Museum 1610 H St NW Washington DC 20006 202-218-4337 520
Web: www.whitehousehistory.org

Decatur Isd Education Foundation Inc
501 E Collins St Decatur TX 76234 940-393-7100 685
Web: www.decaturisd.us

Decatur Memorial Hospital
2300 N Edward St Decatur IL 62526 217-876-8121 876-2615 374-3
TF: 866-364-3600 ■ *Web:* www.dmhcares.com

Decatur Mold Tool & Engineering Inc
3330 N State Rd 7 North Vernon IN 47265 812-346-5188 346-7357 757
Web: www.decaturmold.com

Decatur Public Library
130 N Franklin St Decatur IL 62523 217-424-2900 233-4071 434-3
TF: 800-444-2801 ■ *Web:* decaturlibrary.org

Decatur Public Schools 110 Cedar St Decatur MI 49045 269-423-6800 685
Web: raiderpride.org

Decatur/Morgan County Convention & Visitors Bureau (DMCCVB)
719 Sixth Ave SE PO Box 2349 Decatur AL 35602 256-350-2028 206
TF: 800-232-5449 ■ *Web:* www.decaturcvb.org

Decatur-Morgan County Chamber of Commerce
515 Sixth Ave NE Decatur AL 35601 256-353-5312 353-2384 139
Web: www.dcc.org

Decca Design 476 S First St San Jose CA 95113 408-947-1411 194
Web: www.decdesign.com

Deccan International
5935 Cornerstone Ct W Ste 230 San Diego CA 92121 858-764-8400 174
Web: deccanintl.com

Deccofelt Corp 555 S Vermont Ave Glendora CA 91741 626-963-8511 745-2
TF Cust Svc: 800-543-3226 ■ *Web:* www.deccofelt.com

Decentrix Inc 1200 17th St Ste 770 Denver CO 80202 303-899-4000 225
TF: 800-763-4195 ■ *Web:* www.decentrix.net

Deception Pass State Park
41229 Washington 20 Oak Harbor WA 98277 360-675-2417 675-8991 565
Web: www.parks.wa.gov

Dechert Dynamics Corp 713 W Main St Palmyra PA 17078 717-838-1326 838-1525 454
Web: www.decherts.com

Dechert LLP 2929 Arch St Cira Ctr Philadelphia PA 19104 215-994-4000 994-2222 428
TF: 800-328-4880 ■ *Web:* www.dechert.com

Dechert-Hampe & Co (DHC)
33332 Valle Rd San Juan Capistrano CA 92675 949 429 1999 194
TF: 800-790-4788 ■ *Web:* www.dechert-hampe.com

Decibels Inc 1551 Center St Tacoma WA 98409 253-473-5855 116
Web: decibelsinc.com

Decimal Engineering Inc
2640 N Powerline Rd Pompano Beach FL 33069 954-975-7992 975-7994 256
Web: www.decimal.net

Decimal Technologies Inc
793 Jean-Paul-Vincent Blvd Ste 202 Longueuil QC J4G1R3 450-640-1222 463
Web: www.decimal.ca

Decision Academic Inc
411 Legget Dr Ste 501 Ottawa ON K2K3C9 613-254-9669 174
Web: www.decisionacademic.com

Decision Analyst Inc 604 Ave H E Arlington TX 76011 817-640-6166 640-6567 466
Web: www.decisionanalyst.com

Decision Counsel
2010 Crow Canyon Pl San Ramon CA 94583 510-859-3605 195
Web: decisioncounsel.com

Decision Diagnostics Corp
2660 Townsgate Rd Ste 300 Westlake Village CA 91361 805-446-1973 446-1983 475
Web: www.decisiondiagnostics.co

Decision Point State Marine Park
550 W Seventh Ave Ste 1230 Anchorage AK 99501 907-269-8400 269-8901 565
Web: dnr.alaska.gov/parks/units/pwssmp/smpwhit1.htm

Decision Software Inc 116 John St New York NY 10038 212-385-1662 690
Web: www.dsoftware.com

Decision Systems Plus Inc
248 Spring Lake Dr Ste 170 Itasca IL 60143 800-676-7374 180
TF: 800-676-7374 ■ *Web:* www.motherg.com

DecisionHR Inc
100 Carillon Pkwy Ste 350 St. Petersburg FL 33716 727-572-7331 631
Web: www.decisionhr.com

DecisionOne Corp 426 W Lancaster Ave Devon PA 19333 610-296-6000 296-2910 175
TF: 800-767-2876 ■ *Web:* decisionone.com

DecisionPoint Systems Inc
19655 Descartes Foothill Ranch CA 92610 949-465-0065 215-9642 177
OTC: DPSI ■ *TF:* 800-336-3670 ■ *Web:* www.decisionpt.com

DecisionQuest
21535 Hawthorne Blvd Ste 310 Torrance CA 90503 310-618-9600 618-1122 445
TF: 800-887-5696 ■ *Web:* www.decisionquest.com

Decisionwise Inc 1971 N State St Provo UT 84604 801-515-6500 196
Web: www.decision-wise.com

Decisive Business Systems Inc
7150 N Park Dr Ste 400 Pennsauken NJ 08109 856-910-0900 180
TF: 866-203-8948 ■ *Web:* www.decisivebiz.com

Decker Advertising 99 Citizens Dr Glastonbury CT 06033 860-659-1311 7
TF: 800-777-3677 ■ *Web:* www.deckerdoesit.com

Decker Electric Company Inc
1282 Folsom St San Francisco CA 94103 415-552-1622 189-4

Decker Manufacturing Corp
703 N Clark St Albion MI 49224 517-629-3955 629-3535 278
TF: 800-624-2019 ■ *Web:* www.deckernut.com

Decker Steel & Supply Inc
4500 Train Ave Cleveland OH 44102 216-281-7900 281-1441 492
Web: www.deckersteel.com

Decker Tape Products Inc
6 Stewart Pl Fairfield NJ 07004 973-227-5350 808-9418 732
TF: 800-227-5252 ■ *Web:* www.deckertape.com

Decker Truck Line Inc
4000 Fifth Ave S Fort Dodge IA 50501 515-576-4141 780
TF: 800-247-2537 ■ *Web:* www.deckertruckline.com

Decker Wright Corp
628 Shrewsbury Ave Red Bank NJ 07701 732-747-9373 177
Web: www.deckerwright.com

Deckers Outdoor Corp
495-A S Fairview Ave Goleta CA 93117 805-967-7611 967-9722 301
NYSE: DECK ■ *Web:* www.deckers.com

Decko Products Inc 2105 Superior St Sandusky OH 44870 419-626-5757 626-3135 296-8
TF General: 800-537-6143 ■ *Web:* www.decko.com

Declara Inc 977 Commercial St Palo Alto CA 94303 877-216-0604 387
TF: 877-216-0604 ■ *Web:* www.declara.com

Declaration House
599 S Seventh St Philadelphia PA 19106 215-965-7676 50-3
Web: www.nps.gov

Deco Chem Inc 3502 N Home St Mishawaka IN 46545 574-259-3787 388
TF: 888-332-6465 ■ *Web:* www.decochem.com

Deco Designs Systems Furniture Inc
1435 Koll Cir Ste 106 San Jose CA 95112 408-919-0234 321
Web: www.decodesigns.com

DECO Inc 11156 Zealand Ave N Champlin MN 55316 800-968-9114 245-0686* 693
**Fax Area Code:* 336 ■ *TF:* 800-968-9114 ■ *Web:* www.deco-inc.com

Deco Products Co 506 Sanford St Decorah IA 52101 563-382-4264 382-9845 308
TF: 800-327-9751 ■ *Web:* www.decoprod.com

DecoArt Inc 49 Cotton Ave Stanford KY 40484 606-365-3193 43
TF: 800-367-3047 ■ *Web:* www.decoart.com

Decoma International Inc
Magna Exteriors & Interiors
50 Casmir Ct Concord ON L4K4J5 905-669-2888 669-5075 489
TF: 888-348-2398 ■ *Web:* www.magna.com

Decor & You Inc 900 Main St S Southbury CT 06488 203-405-2126 310
Web: www.decorandyou.com

Decor Rest Furniture Ltd
208 Jacobs Pl High Point NC 27260 336-884-3420 321

Decorating Den Systems Inc
8659 Commerce Dr Easton MD 21601 410-822-9001 393
TF: 800-332-3367 ■ *Web:* www.decoratingden.com

Decorative Crafts Inc
50 Chestnut St Greenwich CT 06830 203-531-1500 531-1590 361
TF: 800-431-4455 ■ *Web:* www.decorativecrafts.com

Decorative Plant Service Inc
1150 Phelps St San Francisco CA 94124 415-826-8181 393
Web: www.decorative.com

Decore Hotels 10026 164 St NW Edmonton AB T5P4Y3 780-481-7578 377
Web: decorehotels.com

Decore-ative Specialties Inc
2772 S Peck Rd Monrovia CA 91016 626-254-9191 254-1515 115
TF: 800-729-7277 ■ *Web:* www.decore.com

Decotech Systems Inc
2151 Salvio St Ste 260 Concord CA 94520 925-954-1520 180
Web: www.decotech.com

DeCoty Coffee Company Inc
1920 Austin St San Angelo TX 76903 800-588-8001 655-6837* 296-7
**Fax Area Code:* 325 ■ *TF:* 800-588-8001 ■ *Web:* www.decoty.com

Dec-Tam Corp 50 Concord St North Reading MA 01864 978-470-2860 667
TF: 800-332-8261 ■ *Web:* www.dectam.com

Dectrader
3547 Old Conejo Rd Unit 101 Newbury Park CA 91320 805-498-4848 480-1898 174
Web: www.dectrader.com

Dectro International Inc
1000 Blvd du Parc-Technologique Quebec QC G1P4S3 418-650-0303 475
TF: 800-463-5566 ■ *Web:* www.dectro.com

Dectron 5685 Rue Cypihot Saint Laurent QC H4S1R3 514-336-3330 337-3336 360-3
TF: 888-332-8766

Decurion Corp, The
120 N Robertson Blvd Los Angeles CA 90048 310-659-9432 748
Web: www.decurion.com

Decurtis Corp 2314 Longmoore Ct Orlando FL 32835 407-522-8722 177
Web: www.decurtis.com

Decypher Technologies Ltd
200 Concord Plaza Dr San Antonio TX 78216 210-735-9900 196
Web: www.decypherpsigov.com

	Phone	Fax	Class
Dedham Country Day School 90 Sandy Valley Rd. . . . Dedham MA 02026 *Web:* www.dedhamcountryday.org	781-329-0850		239
Dedham Institution For Savings 55 Elm St PO Box 9107 . . . . Dedham MA 02026 *TF:* 888-289-0342 ■ *Web:* www.dedhamsavings.com	781-329-6700		70
Dedham Mall 300 Providence Hwy . . . . Dedham MA 02026 *Web:* www.dedham-mall.com	781-329-1210		460
Dedicated Computing N26 W23880 Commerce Cir. . . . . Waukesha WI 53188 *TF:* 877-333-4848 ■ *Web:* www.dedicatedcomputing.com	262-951-7200	523-2222	173-2
Dedicated Distribution Inc 640 Miami Ave . . . . Kansas City KS 66105 *TF:* 800-325-8367 ■ *Web:* www.dedicateddistribution.com	913-371-2200		475
Dedoes Industries Inc 1060 W Maple Rd. . . . . Walled Lake MI 48390 *TF:* 800-521-7086 ■ *Web:* www.dedoes.com	248-624-7710		111
Dee Brown Inc (DBI) 4101 S Shiloh Rd PO Box 570335 . . . . Dallas TX 75357 **Fax:* Tech Supp ■ *Web:* www.deebrowncompanies.com	214-321-6443	328-1039*	189-7
Dee Cramer Inc 4221 E Baldwin Rd . . . . Holly MI 48442 *TF:* 888-342-6995 ■ *Web:* www.deecramer.com	810-579-5000	579-2664	189-12
Dee Electronics Inc 2500 16th Ave SW . . . . Cedar Rapids IA 52404 *TF:* 800-747-3331 ■ *Web:* www.dee-inc.com	319-365-7551	365-8506	246
Dee J Wolfe CPA PC 818 NW 14th Ave . . . . Portland OR 97209 *Web:* deejwolfe.com	503-295-0366		2
Dee Paper Box Company Inc 100 Broomall St . . . . Chester PA 19013 *TF:* 800-359-0041 ■ *Web:* deepaperbox.com	610-876-9285	876-7040	101
Dee Plumbing Inc 3828 W 128th Pl . . . . Alsip IL 60803 *Web:* deeplumbing.com	708-389-8075		189-10
Dee Zee Inc 1572 NE 58th Ave. . . . . Des Moines IA 50313 *Web:* www.deezee.com	515-265-7331		489
Deegit 1900 E Golf Rd Ste 925 . . . . Schaumburg IL 60173 *Web:* www.deegit.com	847-330-1985		194
Deen Meats PO Box 4155 PO Box 4155. . . . Fort Worth TX 76164 *TF:* 800-333-3953 ■ *Web:* www.deenmeat.com	817-335-2257	338-9256	297-9
Deep Creek State Recreation Area PO Box 1247 . . . . Soldotna AK 99669 *Web:* dnr.alaska.gov/parks/units/deepck.htm	907-262-5581		565
Deep Dish TV 339 Lafayette St 3rd Fl. . . . . New York NY 10012 *Web:* www.deepdishtv.org	212-473-8933		740
Deep Down Inc 8827 W Sam Houston Pkwy N Ste 100. . . . . Houston TX 77040 *Web:* www.deepdowninc.com	281-517-5000		539
Deep East Texas Council of Governments 274 e lamar st. . . . . Jasper TX 75951 *TF:* 800-256-6848 ■ *Web:* www.detcog.org	409-384-5704		463
Deep East Texas Electric Co-op Inc 880 Texas Hwy 21 E PO Box 736 . . . . San Augustine TX 75972 *TF:* 800-392-5986 ■ *Web:* www.deepeast.com	936-275-2314	275-2135	245
Deep Foods Inc 1090 Springfield Rd. . . . . Union NJ 07083 *Web:* www.deepfoods.com	908-810-7500		296-9
Deep Fork Grill 5418 N Western Ave. . . . . Oklahoma City OK 73118 *Web:* www.deepforkgrill.com	405-848-7678		671
Deep Imaging Technologies Inc 990 Village Sq Dr . . . . Tomball TX 77375 *Web:* deepimaging.com	281-290-0492		253
Deep Meadow Correctional Ctr 3500 Woods Way . . . . State Farm VA 23160 *Web:* vadoc.virginia.gov	804-598-5503		213
Deep Mile Networks LLC 3100 Clarendon Blvd Ste 200 . . . . Arlington VA 22201 *Web:* www.deepmile.com	703-635-7983		396
Deep River Dyeing & Finishing Company Inc 225 Poplar St PO Box 217 . . . . Randleman NC 27317 *Web:* deepriverdyeing.com	336-498-4181	498-7252	745-7
Deep South Crane & Rigging 15324 Airline Hwy . . . . Baton Rouge LA 70817 *Web:* www.deepsouthcrane.com	225-753-4371		190
Deep Sushi 2624 Elm St. . . . . Dallas TX 75226 *TF:* 800-921-8498 ■ *Web:* www.deepsushi.com	214-651-1177		671
Deepwater Chemicals Inc 1210 Airpark Rd . . . . Woodward OK 73801 *TF:* 800-854-4064 ■ *Web:* www.deepwaterchemicals.com	580-256-0500	256-0575	806
Deepwell Services LLC 719 W New Castle St . . . . Zelienople PA 16063 *Web:* deepwellservices.com	724-473-0687		190
Deepwood Museum & Gardens 1116 Mission St SE . . . . Salem OR 97302 *TF:* 800-640-9653 ■ *Web:* oregonlink.com/sorry_notfound.html	503-363-1825		50-3
Deer Creek State Park 20635 State Park Rd 20 . . . . Mount Sterling OH 43143 *Web:* www.ohiodnr.com	740-869-3124		565
Deer Creek State Park PO Box 257. . . . . Midway UT 84049 *Web:* www.stateparks.utah.gov	435-654-0171		565
Deer Horn Aviation Ltd Co 8818 W Hwy 80 . . . . Midland TX 79706	432-561-9111		63
Deer Lake State Park 357 Main Pk Rd . . . . Santa Rosa Beach FL 32459 *Web:* www.floridastateparks.org/deerlake	850-267-8300		565
Deer Mountain Campground 5309 N Main St . . . . Pittsburg NH 03592 *Web:* www.nhstateparks.org	603-538-6965		565
Deer Park Chamber of Commerce 110 Ctr St. . . . . Deer Park TX 77536 *Web:* www.deerparkchamber.org	281-479-1559	476-4041	139
Deer Park Group Inc 21540 N Inglenook Ln . . . . Deer Park IL 60010 *Web:* www.deerparkinc.com	847-387-8002		463
Deer Park Public Library 3009 Ctr St. . . . . Deer Park TX 77536 *Web:* deerparktx.gov	281-478-7208	478-7212	434-3
Deer Path Inn 255 E Illinois Rd . . . . Lake Forest IL 60045 *Web:* thedeerpathinn.com	847-234-2280		379
Deer Valley Federal Credit Union 16215 N 28th Ave. . . . . Phoenix AZ 85053 *TF:* 800-579-5051 ■ *Web:* deervalleycu.org	602-375-7300	375-7333	219
Deer Valley Homebuilders Inc 205 Carriage St. . . . . Guin AL 35563 *Web:* www.deervalleyhb.com	205-468-8400		505
Deer Valley Ranch 16825 County Rd 162 . . . . Nathrop CO 81236 *TF:* 877-897-1297 ■ *Web:* www.deervalleyranch.com	719-395-2353		239
Deer Valley Resort Lodging PO Box 889 . . . . Park City UT 84060 *TF:* 800-558-3337 ■ *Web:* www.deervalley.com	435-645-6626	645-6538	669
Deer Valley Rock Art Ctr 3711 W Deer Valley Rd. . . . . Glendale AZ 85308 *TF:* 800-933-7890 ■ *Web:* www.asu.edu	623-582-8007	582-8831	50-2
Deerbrook Mall 20131 Hwy 59 N . . . . Humble TX 77338 *Web:* www.shopdeerbrookmall.com	281-446-5300		460
Deere & Co 1 John Deere Pl. . . . . Moline IL 61265 *NYSE:* DE ■ *TF:* 800-765-9588 ■ *Web:* www.deere.com	309-765-8000		185
Deere-Hitachi Construction Machinery Corp 1000 Deere Hitachi Rd . . . . Kernersville NC 27284	336-996-8100		190
Deerfield Academy 7 Boyden Ln . . . . Deerfield MA 01342 *Web:* www.deerfield.edu	413-772-0241	772-1100	622
Deerfield Bannockburn & Riverwoods Chamber of Commerce 601 Deerfield Rd Ste 200 . . . . Deerfield IL 60015 *Web:* www.dbrchamber.com	847-945-4660		139
Deerfield Communications Co 4241 Old US 27 S. . . . . Gaylord MI 49735 *Web:* www.deerfield.com	989-732-8856		178-7
Deerfield Construction Company Inc 8960 Glendale Milford Rd. . . . . Loveland OH 45140 *Web:* www.deerfieldconstruction.com	513-984-4096	984-4180	186
Deerfield Correctional Ctr 21360 Deerfield Dr. . . . . Capron VA 23829	434-658-4368		213
Deerfield Episcopal Retirement Community 1017 Hendersonville Rd . . . . Asheville NC 28803 *TF:* 800-284-1531 ■ *Web:* www.deerfieldwnc.org	828-274-1531	274-0238	672
Deerfield Public Library Inc 920 Waukegan Rd. . . . . Deerfield IL 60015 *TF:* 800-829-4059 ■ *Web:* deerfieldlibrary.org	847-945-3311		435
Deerfield Spa 650 Resica Falls Rd . . . . East Stroudsburg PA 18302 *TF:* 800-852-4494 ■ *Web:* www.deerfieldspa.com	570-223-0160		706
Deerfoot Inn & Casino 1000 11500 35th St SE. . . . . Calgary AB T2Z3W4 *TF:* 877-236-5225 ■ *Web:* www.deerfootinn.com	403-236-7529		379
Deerhurst Resort 1235 Deerhurst Dr . . . . Huntsville ON P1H2E8 *TF Sales:* 800-461-6522 ■ *Web:* www.deerhurstresort.com	705-789-6411		669
Deering Banjo Co 3733 Kenora Dr . . . . Spring Valley CA 91977 *TF:* 800-845-7791 ■ *Web:* www.deeringbanjos.com	619-464-8252		527
Deetken Group, The 1755 W Broadway Ste 501 . . . . Vancouver BC V6J4S5 *Web:* www.deetken.com	604-731-4424		463
Defabco Inc 3765 E Livingston Ave. . . . . Columbus OH 43227 *Web:* www.defabco.com	614-231-2700		697
DeFazio Peter (Rep D - OR) 2134 Rayburn Bldg. . . . . Washington DC 20515 *Web:* www.defazio.house.gov	202-225-6416		342-2
DeFehr Furniture Ltd 125 Furniture Pk. . . . . Winnipeg MB R2G1B9 *TF:* 877-333-3471 ■ *Web:* www.defehr.com	204-988-5630	663-4458	319-2
Defence Construction Canada Constitution Sq, 350 Albert St 19th Fl . . . . Ottawa ON K1A0K3 *Web:* www.dcc-cdc.gc.ca	613-998-9548		463
Defender Association of Philadelphia 1441 Sansom St 12th Fl. . . . . Philadelphia PA 19102 *Web:* www.philadefender.org	215-568-3190		445
Defender Inc 3750 Priority Way S Dr Ste 200 . . . . Indianapolis IN 46240 *Web:* www.homedefenders.com	317-810-4720	810-4723	116
Defender Industries Inc 42 Great Neck Rd . . . . Waterford CT 06385 *TF:* 800-628-8225 ■ *Web:* www.defender.com	860-701-3400	701-3424	770
Defender Resorts Inc 6301 N Kings Hwy . . . . Myrtle Beach SC 29572 *Web:* defenderresorts.com	843-449-1354		379
Defender Services Inc 9031 Garners Ferry Rd . . . . Hopkins SC 29061 *Web:* www.defenderservices.com	803-776-4220		104
Defenders of Wildlife 1130 17th St NW . . . . Washington DC 20036 *TF:* 800-385-9712 ■ *Web:* www.defenders.org	202-682-9400	682-1331	48-3
Defense Commissary Agency 1300 E Ave . . . . Fort Lee VA 23801 *TF:* 877-332-2471 ■ *Web:* www.commissaries.com	804-734-8000		340-3
Defense Contract Audit Agency 8725 John J Kingman Rd Ste 2135 . . . . Fort Belvoir VA 22060 *TF:* 855-414-5892 ■ *Web:* www.dcaa.mil	703-767-3265		340-3
Defense Contract Management Agency 6350 Walker Ln Ste 300 . . . . Alexandria VA 22310 *TF:* 888-576-3262 ■ *Web:* www.dcma.mil	888-576-3262		340-3
Defense Finance & Accounting Service 8899 E 56th St . . . . Indianapolis IN 46249 *TF:* 888-332-7411 ■ *Web:* www.dfas.mil	888-332-7411		734
Defense Information Systems Agency PO Box 4502 . . . . Arlington VA 22204 **Fax Area Code:* 703 ■ *TF:* 844-247-3457 ■ *Web:* www.disa.mil	844-247-3457	607-4344*	340-3
Defense Intelligence Agency 200 MacDill Blvd . . . . Washington DC 20340 *Web:* www.dia.mil	301-394-5587	394-5356	340-3
Defense Logistics Agency (DLA) 8725 John J Kingman Rd Ste 1644 . . . . Fort Belvoir VA 22060 *TF:* 800-565-3946 ■ *Web:* www.dla.mil/Pages/default.aspx	703-767-5200	767-6091	340-3
Defense Nuclear Facilities Safety Board 625 Indiana Ave NW Ste 700 . . . . Washington DC 20004 *TF:* 800-788-4016 ■ *Web:* www.dnfsb.gov	202-694-7000		340-20
Defense Office of Economic Adjustment 400 Army-Navy Dr Ste 200. . . . . Arlington VA 22202 *Web:* www.oea.gov	703-604-6020		340-3

Name	Address	City	State	ZIP	Phone	Fax	Class	Notes
Defense Prisoner of War/Missing Personnel Office (DPMO)	2600 Defense Pentagon	Washington	DC	20301	703-699-1169		340-3	*Web:* www.dpaa.mil
Defense Research Institute (DRI)	55 W Monroe St Ste 20	Chicago	IL	60603	312-795-1101	795-0749	49-10	*Web:* www.dri.org
Defense Security Service	27130 Telegraph Rd	Quantico	VA	22134	571-305-6562		340-3	*Web:* www.dss.mil
Defense Technical Information Center (DTIC)	8725 John J Kingman Rd Ste 0944	Fort Belvoir	VA	22060	800-225-3842		340-3	*TF:* 800-225-3842 ■ *Web:* www.dtic.mil
Defense Technology	*Safarland Group* 1855 S Loop Ave	Casper	WY	82601	307-235-2136	473-2713	284	*TF:* 877-248-3835 ■ *Web:* www.safariland.com/our-brands/defense-technology
Defense Threat Reduction Agency	8725 John T Kingman Rd MS 6201	Fort Belvoir	VA	22060	703-767-5870	767-4450	340-3	*TF:* 800-701-5096 ■ *Web:* www.dtra.mil
Defiance Area Chamber of Commerce	325 Clinton St	Defiance	OH	43512	419-782-7946	782-0111	139	*Web:* www.defiancechamber.com
Defiance College	701 N Clinton St	Defiance	OH	43512	419-784-4010	783-2468*	166	**Fax:* Admissions ■ *TF:* 800-520-4632 ■ *Web:* www.defiance.edu
Defiance County	500 Ct St	Defiance	OH	43512	419-782-4761	782-8449	338	*TF:* 800-675-3953 ■ *Web:* www.defiance-county.com
Defiance Metal Products	21 Seneca St	Defiance	OH	43512	419-784-5332	782-0148	488	*Web:* www.defiancemetal.com
Defiance Public Library	320 Ft St	Defiance	OH	43512	419-782-1456	782-6235	434-3	*TF:* 800-272-3900 ■ *Web:* www.defiancelibrary.org
Defiant Marine Inc	228 Redbud Ln	Bostic	NC	28018	828-245-2059	245-2079	90	*Web:* defiantmarine.net
Defibtech LLC	741 Boston Post Rd Ste 201	Guilford	CT	06437	203-453-4507		476	*TF:* 866-333-4248 ■ *Web:* www.defibtech.com
Defined Fitness	4930 Mcleod Rd NE	Albuquerque	NM	87109	505-888-7097		354	*Web:* www.defined.com
Defined Logic LLC	116 Chestnut St	Red Bank	NJ	07701	732-222-4310		177	*Web:* definedlogic.com
Definition 6 LLC	2115 Monroe Dr Ste 100	Atlanta	GA	30324	404-870-0323		7	*Web:* www.definition6.com
Definity Partners LLC	5474 Spellmire Dr Ste 420	West Chester	OH	45246	513-381-7200		463	*Web:* www.definitypartners.com
Deflect-O Corp	7035 E 86th St	Indianapolis	IN	46250	800-428-4328		534	*TF:* 800-428-4328 ■ *Web:* www.deflecto.com
DeFoe Corp	800 S Columbus Ave	Mount Vernon	NY	10550	914-699-7440		194	*Web:* www.defoecorp.com
Defta Partners	111 Pine St	San Francisco	CA	94111	415-433-2262		792	*Web:* www.deftapartners.com
Degan, Blanchard & Nash A Professional Law Corp	400 Poydras St Ste 2600	New Orleans	LA	70130	504-529-3333		428	*Web:* www.degan.com
Degenkolb	375 Beale St Ste 500	San Francisco	CA	94105	415-392-6952	981-3157	261	*Web:* www.degenkolb.com
Degesch America Inc	PO Box 116	Weyers Cave	VA	24486	540-234-9281		280	*TF:* 800-330-2525 ■ *Web:* www.degeschamerica.com
DeGette Diana (Rep D - CO)	2111 Rayburn HOB	Washington	DC	20515	202-225-4431	225-5657	342-2	*Web:* degette.house.gov
Degnon Assoc Inc	6728 Old McLean Village Dr	McLean	VA	22101	703-556-9222	556-8729	47	*Web:* degnon.org
DeGraaf Nature Ctr	600 Graafschap Rd	Holland	MI	49423	616-355-1057	355-1069	50-5	*TF:* 888-535-5792 ■ *Web:* cityofholland.com
DeGray Lake Resort State Park	2027 State Pk Entrance Rd	Bismarck	AR	71929	501-865-2801		565	*TF:* 800-737-8355 ■ *Web:* www.degray.com
DeGrazia Gallery in the Sun	6300 N Swan Rd	Tucson	AZ	85718	520-299-9191	299-1381	520	*TF:* 800-545-2185 ■ *Web:* www.degrazia.org
Degree Controls Inc	18 Meadowbrook Dr	Milford	NH	03055	603-672-8900		256	*TF:* 877-334-7332 ■ *Web:* www.degreec.com
Dehart & Company Public Relations LLC	1375 Lenoir Rhyne Blvd SE Ste 109	Hickory	NC	28602	828-325-4966		636	*Web:* www.dehartandcompany.com
Dehart Marine Electronics Inc	134 W Carolina Ave	Memphis	TN	38103	901-523-0945		179	*TF:* 800-523-4278 ■ *Web:* dehartmarine.com
Dehart Plumbing Heating & Air Inc	311 Bitritto Way	Modesto	CA	95356	209-523-4578		189-10	*Web:* dehartinc.com
DeHayes Consulting Group	2999 Douglas Blvd Ste 320	Roseville	CA	95661	916-782-8321		194	*Web:* www.dcgcorp.com
Dehco Inc	58263 Charlotte Ave	Elkhart	IN	46517	574-294-2684		3	*Web:* www.dehco.com
Dehli Palace Cuisine of India	2700 S Woodlands Village Blvd	Flagstaff	AZ	86001	928-556-0019		671	
Dehumidification Manufacturing Gp LLC	6609 Ave U	Houston	TX	77011	713-939-1166		14	*TF:* 866-736-8348 ■ *Web:* www.rentdh.com
DEI Holdings Inc	1 Viper Way	Vista	CA	92081	760-598-6200	598-6400	52	*OTC:* DEIX ■ *TF:* 800-876-0800 ■ *Web:* deiholdings.com
DEI Inc	1550 Kemper Meadow Dr	Cincinnati	OH	45240	513-825-5800		186	*Web:* www.dei-corp.com
Deig Bros Lumber & Construction Inc	2804 A St	Evansville	IN	47712	812-423-4201	421-5058	186	*Web:* www.deigbros.com
Deighton Associates Ltd	223 Brock St N Unit 7	Whitby	ON	L1N4H6	905-665-6605		261	*TF:* 888-219-6605 ■ *Web:* www.deighton.com
Deily Mooney & Glastetter LLP	8 Thurlow Terr	Albany	NY	12203	518-436-0344		428	*Web:* www.deilylawfirm.com
Dejana Industries Inc	30 Sagamore Hill Dr	Port Washington	NY	11050	516-944-3100		776	*Web:* www.dejanaindustries.com
Dejana Truck & Utility Equipment Company Inc	490 Pulaski Rd	Kings Park	NY	11754	631-544-9000	544-0942	780	*TF:* 877-335-2621 ■ *Web:* www.dejana.com
Dejour Energy Inc	598-999 Canada Pl	Vancouver	BC	V6C3E1	604-638-5050		536	*Web:* www.dxienergy.com
Dejuan Stroud Inc	348 W 36th St	New York	NJ	10018	212-431-9099		292	*Web:* www.dejuanstroud.com
DEKA Research & Development Corp	340 Commercial St	Manchester	NH	03101	603-669-5139		668	*Web:* www.dekaresearch.com
DeKalb Chamber of Commerce	125 Clairemont Ave Ste 235	Tucker	GA	30084	404-378-8000	378-3397	139	*Web:* www.dekalbchamber.org
DeKalb Chamber of Commerce	164 E Lincoln Hwy	DeKalb	IL	60115	815-756-6306	756-5164	139	*Web:* www.dekalb.org
DeKalb Convention & Visitors Bureau	1957 Lakeside Pkwy Ste 510	Tucker	GA	30084	770-492-5000		206	*TF:* 866-633-5252 ■ *Web:* www.visitatlantasdekalbcounty.com
DeKalb County	109 W Main St PO Box 248	Maysville	MO	64469	816-449-5402	449-2440	338	*TF:* 800-392-3738 ■ *Web:* dekalbcountymo.com
DeKalb County	556 N McDonough St	Decatur	GA	30030	404-371-2000		338	*Web:* www.dekalbcountyga.gov
DeKalb County	111 Grand Ave SW Ste 200	Fort Payne	AL	35967	256-845-8500		338	*Web:* www.dekalbcountyal.us
DeKalb County	732 S Congress Blvd	Smithville	TN	37166	615-597-5176		338	*Web:* www.dekalbtennessee.com
DeKalb County	110 E Sycamore St	Sycamore	IL	60178	815-895-7149	895-7148	338	*Web:* www.dekalbcounty.org
DeKalb County Public Library	215 Sycamore St	Decatur	GA	30030	404-370-3070	370-8469	434-3	*TF:* 800-677-1116 ■ *Web:* dekalblibrary.org
Dekalb Farmers Market	3000 E Ponce De Leon Ave	Decatur	GA	30030	404-377-6400		345	*Web:* www.dekalbfarmersmarket.com
DeKalb Feeds Inc	105 Dixon Ave	Rock Falls	IL	61071	815-625-4546		447	*TF:* 800-331-1465 ■ *Web:* dekalbfeeds.com
DeKalb Forge Co	1832 Pleasant St	DeKalb	IL	60115	815-758-6400	756-6958	483	*Web:* www.forgeresourcesgroup.com
DeKalb Public Library	309 Oak St	DeKalb	IL	60115	815-756-9568	756-7837	434-3	*TF:* 888-268-2824 ■ *Web:* www.dkpl.org
DeKalb Regional Medical Ctr	200 Medical Ctr Dr	Fort Payne	AL	35968	256-845-3150		374-3	*TF:* 800-373-6115 ■ *Web:* www.dekalbregional.com
DeKalb Symphony Orchestra (DSO)	PO Box 1313	Tucker	GA	30085	678-891-3565	891-3575	573-3	*Web:* www.dekalbsymphony.org
Dekatron Corp	5895 Allentown Rd	Camp Springs	MD	20746	301-702-1005		396	*TF:* 800-222-0400 ■ *Web:* www.dekatron.com
Dekker Bookbinding	2941 Clydon Ave SW	Grand Rapids	MI	49519	616-538-5160	538-0720	92	*Web:* www.dekkerbook.com
Dekker Ltd	3633 Inland Empire Blvd	Ontario	CA	91764	909-384-9000		177	
Dekko	2505 Dekko Dr	Garrett	IN	46738	260-357-3621	357-4293	815	*TF:* 800-829-3101 ■ *Web:* www.dekko.com
Dekoron Wire & Cable	1300 Industrial Blvd	Mount Pleasant	TX	75455	903-572-3475	572-6153*	814	**Fax:* Cust Svc ■ *Web:* www.dekoroncable.com
Dekra America Inc	3901 Roswell Rd Ste 120	Marietta	GA	30062	770-971-3788		393	*TF:* 800-831-6907 ■ *Web:* www.dekra-na.com
Del Amo Fashion Ctr	3525 Carson St	Torrance	CA	90503	310-542-8525	793-9235	460	*TF:* 877-746-6642 ■ *Web:* www.simon.com
Del Amo Hospital	23700 Camino Del Sol	Torrance	CA	90505	310-530-1151		374-5	*TF:* 800-533-5266 ■ *Web:* www.delamohospital.com
Del City Chamber of Commerce	PO Box 15643	Del City	OK	73155	405-677-1910		139	*TF:* 800-281-0446 ■ *Web:* www.delcitychamber.com
Del Conte's Landscaping Inc	41900 Boscell Rd	Fremont	CA	94538	510-353-6030		776	*Web:* www.visionrecycling.com
Del E Webb Memorial Library	Loma Linda University 11072 Anderson St	Loma Linda	CA	92350	909-558-4550		434-1	*Web:* www.llu.edu/llu/library
Del Frisco's Double Eagle Steak House	812 Main St	Fort Worth	TX	76102	817-877-3999		671	*Web:* www.delfriscos.com
Del Frisco's Double Eagle Steak House	3925 Paradise Rd	Las Vegas	NV	89169	702-796-0063		671	*Web:* www.delfriscos.com
Del Frisco's Restaurant Group, Inc.	1221 Ave of the Americas	New York	NY	10020	212-575-5129		671	*Web:* www.delfriscos.com
Del Mar Avionics	1601 Alton Pkwy Ste C	Irvine	CA	92606	949-250-3200	261-0529	529	*Web:* www.dma.com
Del Mar College	*East* 101 Baldwin Blvd	Corpus Christi	TX	78404	361-698-1200	698-1595*	162	**Fax:* Admissions ■ *TF:* 800-652-3357 ■ *Web:* www.delmar.edu
Del Mar Die Casting Co	12901 S Western Ave	Gardena	CA	90249	323-321-0600	327-1951*	308	**Fax Area Code:* 310
Del Mar Food Products Corp	1720 Beach Rd	Watsonville	CA	95076	831-722-3516	722-7690	296-21	*Web:* delmarfoods.com
Del Mar Scientific Acquisition Ltd	4951 Airport Pkwy Ste 803	Addison	TX	75001	972-661-5160		201	*TF:* 800-722-4270 ■ *Web:* www.delmarscientific.com
Del Mar Seafoods Inc	331 Ford St	Watsonville	CA	95076	831-763-3000		297-5	*Web:* www.delmarseafoods.com
Del Mar Thoroughbred Club	2260 Jimmy Durante Blvd	Del Mar	CA	92014	858-755-1141	755-1141	642	*TF:* 800-467-7385 ■ *Web:* www.dmtc.com
Del Monte Electric Company Inc	6998 Sierra Ct	Dublin	CA	94568	925-829-6000	829-6033	189-4	*TF:* 800-892-4784 ■ *Web:* www.delmonteelectric.com

	Phone	Fax	Class
Del Monte Foods Co 1 Maritime Plaza....................... San Francisco CA 94111 *TF Cust Svc:* 800-543-3090 ■ *Web:* www.delmonte.com	415-247-3000		296-20
Del Monte Fresh Produce Co 241 Sevilla Ave......................... Coral Gables FL 33134 *TF Cust Svc:* 800-950-3683 ■ *Web:* www.freshdelmonte.com	305-520-8400		297-7
Del Monte Lodge Renaissance Rochester Hotel & Spa, The 41 N Main St ....Pittsford NY 14534 *TF:* 866-237-5979 ■ *Web:* marriott.com/hotels/propertypage/rocdl	585-381-9900	381-9825	379
Del Norte Coast Redwoods State Park 1111 Second St ....Crescent City CA 95531 *Web:* www.parks.ca.gov/default.asp?page_id=414	707-465-7335		565
Del Norte County 981 H St Ste 200 ....Crescent City CA 95531 *Web:* www.co.del-norte.ca.us	707-464-7204		338
Del Posto 85 Tenth Ave...................... New York NY 10011 *Web:* www.delposto.com	212-497-8090		671
Del Real Foods LLC 11041 Inland Ave ....Mira Loma CA 91752 *Web:* delrealfoods.com	951-681-0395		345
Del Rey Beach State Recreation Site 100 Peter Iredale Rd...................... Hammond OR 97121 *TF:* 800-551-6949 ■ *Web:* www.oregonstateparks.org	800-551-6949		565
Del Rey Packing 5287 S Del Rey Ave .... Del Rey CA 93616 *Web:* delreypacking.com	559-888-2031	888-2715	315-5
Del Rio Chamber of Commerce (DRCoC) 1915 Veterans Blvd.........................Del Rio TX 78840 *TF General:* 877-218-5117 ■ *Web:* www.drchamber.com	830-775-3551	774-1813	139
Del Sol Medical Ctr 10301 Gateway W........... El Paso TX 79925 *TF:* 800-322-0712 ■ *Web:* www.laspalmasdelsolhealthcare.com	915-595-9000		374-3
Del Taco Inc 25521 Commercentre Dr Ste 200........... Lake Forest CA 92630 *TF Cust Svc:* 800-852-7204 ■ *Web:* www.deltaco.com	949-462-9300	462-7444	670
Del Tec Packaging Inc 4020 Pelham Ct .... Greenville SC 29606 *Web:* www.del-tec.com	864-288-7390		344
Del Toro Loan Servicing Inc 2300 Boswell Rd Ste 215 .... Chula Vista CA 91914 *Web:* www.deltoroloanservicing.com	619-474-5400		360-3
Dela Inc 175 Ward Hill Ave.................... Haverhill MA 01835	978-372-7783		3
Delaco Steel Corp 8111 Tireman Ave........... Dearborn MI 48126	313-491-1200		482
Delafield Hambrecht Inc 1301 Second Ave Ste 2850..................... Seattle WA 98101 *Web:* www.delafieldhambrecht.com	206-254-4100		528
DelaGet LLC 5320 W 23rd St Ste 140...................St Louis Park MN 55416 *TF:* 888-335-2438 ■ *Web:* www.delaget.com	888-335-2438		196
Delahousaye Angela Law Offices 1655 N Main St Ste 260...................Walnut Creek CA 94596 *Web:* www.delahousayelaw.com	925-944-3300		428
Delaine James Inc 10508C Boyer Blvd .... Austin TX 78758 **Fax Area Code:* 800 ■ *TF Claims:* 800-999-5333	512-835-5333	999-5555*	87
Delair Group LLC 8600 River Rd ....Delair NJ 08110 *Web:* jerith.com/delgard	215-676-4068		728
DELAMAR Greenwich Harbor 500 Steamboat Rd .... Greenwich CT 06830 *Web:* delamar.com/greenwich	203-661-9800		379
DeLand Area Chamber of Commerce 336 N Woodland Blvd.......................... DeLand FL 32720 *TF:* 800-611-5207 ■ *Web:* www.delandchamber.org	386-734-4331	734-4333	139
Delande Lighting 22 New Derby St............... Salem MA 01970 *Web:* delandelighting.com	978-744-2609		361
Delaney Automotive Group 626 Water St.........Indiana PA 15701 *Web:* www.delaneyauto.com	724-349-3000		57
Delaney Capital Management Ltd TD Bank Tower 4410-66 Wellington St W......... Toronto ON M5K1H1 *Web:* www.delaneycapital.com	416-361-0688		528
Delaney Computer Services 66 Orange Tpke ....Sloatsburg NY 10974 *Web:* dcsny.com	845-753-5800		180
Delaney Educational Enterprises Inc 1455 W Morena Blvd .... San Diego CA 92110 *Web:* deebooks.com	619-275-0063		366
Delaney House 500 Ehampton Rd..............Holyoke MA 01040 *Web:* logcabin-delaney.com	413-532-1800		671
Delaney John (Rep D - MD) 1632 Longworth Bldg....................Washington DC 20515 *Web:* delaney.house.gov	202-225-2721	225-2193	342-2
Delaney Meeting & Event Planning 1 Mill St Ste 315..........................Burlington VT 05401 *Web:* www.delaneymeetingevent.com	802-865-5202		195
Delaney, Wiles, Hayes, Gerety, Ellis & Young Inc 1007 W Third Ave Ste 400 ....Anchorage AK 99501 *TF:* 800-614-8005 ■ *Web:* www.delaneywiles.com	907-279-3581		428
Delano Union School District 1405 12th Ave..................................Delano CA 93215 *Web:* www.duesd.org	661-721-5000	725-2446	685
Delap LLP 5885 Meadows Rd Ste 200 ....Lake Oswego OR 97035 *Web:* delapcpa.com	503-697-4118		2
Delasoft Inc 630 Churchmans Rd Ste 108..........Newark DE 19702 *Web:* www.delasoft-inc.com	302-533-7913		809
DeLauro Rosa L (Rep D - CT) 2413 Rayburn Bldg.......................Washington DC 20515 *Web:* delauro.house.gov	202-225-3661	225-4890	342-2
Delavau LLC 10101 Roosevelt Blvd ....Philadelphia PA 19154 *Web:* www.delavau.com	215-671-1400		582
Delaware			
Administrative Office of the Courts The Renaissance Ctr 405 N King St Ste 507 . Wilmington DE 19801 *Web:* www.courts.delaware.gov	302-255-0090	255-2217	339-8
Aging & Adults with Physical Disabilites Services 1901 N DuPont Hwy ....New Castle DE 19720 *TF:* 800-223-9074 ■ *Web:* www.dhss.delaware.gov	800-223-9074		339-8
Agriculture Dept 2320 S Dupont Hwy ....Dover DE 19901 *TF:* 800-282-8685 ■ *Web:* dda.delaware.gov	302-698-4500		339-8
Arts Div 820 N French St 4th Fl............. Wilmington DE 19801 *Web:* www.artsdel.org	302-577-8278	577-6561	339-8
Attorney General 820 N French St........... Wilmington DE 19801 *Web:* attorneygeneral.delaware.gov	302-577-8400	577-6630	339-8

	Phone	Fax	Class
Bank Commissioner 555 E Loockerman St Ste 210 ....Dover DE 19901 *Web:* banking.delaware.gov	302-739-4235	739-3609	339-8
Chief Medical Examiner 200 S Adam St......................... Wilmington DE 19801 *Web:* dshs.delaware.gov/forensics/meUnit.shtml	302-577-3420	577-3416	339-8
Child Support Enforcement Div (DCSE) 84A Christiana Rd ....New Castle DE 19720 *Web:* www.dhss.delaware.gov/dhss/dcse	302-577-7171		339-8
Consumer Protection Unit 820 N French St 5th Fl.................. Wilmington DE 19801 *TF:* 800-220-5424 ■ *Web:* attorneygeneral.delaware.gov	302-577-8600	577-6499	339-8
Correction Dept 245 McKee Rd.................Dover DE 19904 *Web:* doc.delaware.gov	302-739-5601		339-8
Div of Motor Vehicles 303 Transportation Cir PO Box 698.............Dover DE 19903 *Web:* www.dmv.de.gov	302-744-2500		339-8
Economic Development Office 99 Kings Hwy.................................Dover DE 19901 *Web:* dedo.delaware.gov	302-739-4271	739-5749	339-8
Education Dept 401 Federal St Ste 2..............Dover DE 19901 *Web:* www.doe.state.de.us	302-735-4035	739-4654	339-8
Emergency Management Agency 165 Brick Store Landing Rd................. Smyrna DE 19977 *TF:* 877-729-3362 ■ *Web:* dema.delaware.gov	302-659-3362	659-6855	339-8
Finance Dept 820 N French St 8th Fl......... Wilmington DE 19801 *Web:* finance.delaware.gov	302-577-8987	577-8982	339-8
Fish & Wildlife Div 89 Kings Hwy ....Dover DE 19901 *Web:* www.dnrec.delaware.gov/fw/Pages/DFW-Portal.aspx	302-739-9910	739-6157	339-8
General Assembly Legislative Hall PO Box 1401 ....Dover DE 19903 *Web:* www.legis.delaware.gov	302-744-4162		339-8
Governor 150 Martin Luther King Jr Blvd S Tatnall Building .... Dover DE 19901 *Web:* governor.delaware.gov	302-744-4101	739-2775	339-8
Harness Racing Commission 2320 S Dupont Hwy.........................Dover DE 19901 *Web:* dda.delaware.gov	302-698-4599	697-6287	712
Health & Social Services Dept 1901 N DuPont Hwy ....New Castle DE 19720 *Web:* www.dhss.delaware.gov/dhss	302-255-9675		339-8
Higher Education Commission 401 Federal St Ste 2.............................Dover DE 19901 *Web:* www.doe.state.de.us	302-735-4000		339-8
Historical & Cultural Affairs Div 21 The Green ....Dover DE 19901 *Web:* www.history.delaware.gov/aboutagency.shtml	302-736-7400	739-5660	339-8
Housing Authority 18 The Green ....Dover DE 19901 *TF:* 888-363-8808 ■ *Web:* www.delaware.gov	302-739-4263		339-8
Lieutenant Governor 150 William Penn St 3rd Fl ....Dover DE 19901 *Web:* ltgov.delaware.gov	302-744-4333		339-8
Natural Resources & Environmental Control Dept 89 Kings Hwy.................................Dover DE 19901 *Web:* www.dnrec.state.de.us	302-739-9400	739-3106	339-8
Parks & Recreation Div 89 Kings Hwy ....Dover DE 19901 *TF Campground Resv:* 877-987-2757 ■ *Web:* www.destateparks.com	302-739-9220		339-8
Parole Board 820 N French St 5th Fl......... Wilmington DE 19801 *Web:* delaware.gov	302-577-5233	577-3501	339-8
Professional Regulation Div 861 Silver Lake Blvd Ste 203.................Dover DE 19904 *Web:* www.dpr.delaware.gov	302-744-4500	739-2711	339-8
Professional Standards Board 401 Federal St...................................Dover DE 19901 *Web:* www.doe.k12.de.us/csa/profstds/default.shtml	302-735-4000		339-8
Public Integrity Commission 410 Federal St Margaret O'Neill Bldg Ste 3 ....Dover DE 19901 *Web:* www.depic.delaware.gov	302-739-2399		265
Revenue Div 820 N French St Carvel State Office Bldg.... Wilmington DE 19801 *Web:* revenue.delaware.gov	302-577-8200	577-8202	339-8
Secretary of State 401 Federal St Ste 3 ....Dover DE 19901 *Web:* sos.delaware.gov	302-739-4111	739-3811	339-8
Securities Div 820 N French St 5th Fl.................. Wilmington DE 19801 *Web:* attorneygeneral.delaware.gov	302-577-8424	577-6987	339-8
Services for Children Youth & Their Families Dept 1825 Faulkland Rd.................... Wilmington DE 19805 *Web:* www.delaware.gov	302-633-2500		339-8
Technology & Information Dept 801 Silver Lake Blvd ....Dover DE 19904 *Web:* dti.delaware.gov	302-739-9500	677-7043	339-8
Thoroughbred Racing Commission 2320 S DuPont Hwy.............................Dover DE 19901 *TF:* 800-282-8685 ■ *Web:* dda.delaware.gov	302-698-4500		712
Tourism Office 99 Kings Hwy....................Dover DE 19901 *TF:* 866-284-7483 ■ *Web:* www.visitdelaware.com	302-739-4271	739-5749	339-8
Treasurer 820 Silver Lake Blvd Ste 100...........Dover DE 19904 *Web:* www.treasury.delaware.gov	302-672-6700	739-5635	339-8
Unemployment Insurance Div 4425 N Market St..................... Wilmington DE 19802 *Web:* uicc.delawareworks.com	302-761-8446		339-8
Veterans Affairs Commission 802 Silverlake Blvd Ste 100..................Dover DE 19904 *TF:* 800-344-9900 ■ *Web:* veteransaffairs.delaware.gov	302-739-2792	739-2794	339-8
Violent Crimes Compensation Board 240 N James St Ste 203 ....Newport DE 19804 *Web:* regulations.delaware.gov	302-995-8383		339-8
Vital Statistics Office PO Box 637 ....Dover DE 19903 *Web:* www.dhss.delaware.gov	302-283-7130		339-8
Vocational Rehabilitation Div (DVR) 4425 N Market St..................... Wilmington DE 19802 *Web:* dvr.delawareworks.com	302-761-8275		339-8
Weights & Measures Office 2320 S DuPont Hwy.............................Dover DE 19901 *TF:* 800-282-8685 ■ *Web:* dda.delaware.gov	302-698-4575	697-4483	339-8

Name / Address	City	State	Zip	Phone	Fax	Class
Delaware & Raritan Canal State Park						
145 Mapleton Rd	Princeton	NJ	08540	609-924-5705		565
Web: www.njparksandforests.org						
Delaware Agricultural Museum & Village						
866 N DuPont Hwy	Dover	DE	19901	302-734-1618	734-0457	520
TF: 800-276-3420 ■ *Web:* www.agriculturalmuseum.org						
Delaware Art Museum						
2301 Kentmere Pkwy	Wilmington	DE	19806	302-571-9590	571-0220	520
TF: 866-232-3714 ■ *Web:* www.delart.org						
Delaware Assn of Realtors						
134 E Water St	Dover	DE	19901	302-734-4444	734-1341	656
TF: 800-305-4445 ■ *Web:* www.delawarerealtor.com						
Delaware Canal State Park						
11 Lodi Hill Rd	Upper Black Eddy	PA	18972	610-982-5560		565
Web: www.dcnr.state.pa.us						
Delaware City School District						
248 N Washington St	Delaware	OH	43015	740-833-1100	833-1149	685
Web: www.dcs.k12.oh.us						
Delaware Company Christian School						
462 Malin Rd	Newtown Square	PA	19073	610-353-6522		685
Web: www.dccs.org						
Delaware Correctional Industries						
245 McKee Rd	Dover	DE	19904	302-739-5601	739-8220	630
Web: doc.delaware.gov						
Delaware County 101 N Sandusky St	Delaware	OH	43015	740-833-2100	833-2099	338
TF: 800-277-2177 ■ *Web:* www.co.delaware.oh.us						
Delaware County PO Box 426	Delhi	NY	13753	607-746-2123	746-6924	338
Web: www.co.delaware.ny.us						
Delaware County 301 E Main St	Manchester	IA	52057	563-927-4942	927-3074	338
TF: 800-735-2942 ■ *Web:* www.co.delaware.ia.us						
Delaware County 100 W Main St	Muncie	IN	47305	765-747-7730	747-7768	338
TF: 800-311-4634 ■ *Web:* www.co.delaware.in.us						
Delaware County Chamber of Commerce						
602 E Baltimore Pk	Media	PA	19063	610-565-3677		139
Web: www.delcochamber.org						
Delaware County Community College						
901 Media Line Rd	Media	PA	19063	610-359-5000	359-5343	162
TF: 800-908-9946 ■ *Web:* www.dccc.edu						
Downingtown 100 Bond Dr	Downingtown	PA	19335	484-237-6200		162
Web: dccc.edu						
Southeast 2000 Elmwood Ave	Sharon Hill	PA	19079	610-957-5700	957-5787	162
Web: www.dccc.edu						
Delaware County Daily Times						
500 Mildred Ave	Primos	PA	19018	610-622-8800		532-2
TF: 888-799-6299 ■ *Web:* www.delcotimes.com						
Delaware County District Library						
84 E Winter St	Delaware	OH	43015	740-362-3861	369-0196	434-3
TF: 866-862-7286 ■ *Web:* www.delawarelibrary.org						
Delaware County Electric Co-op (DCEC)						
39 Elm St PO Box 471	Delhi	NY	13753	607-746-2341		245
TF: 866-436-1223 ■ *Web:* www.dce.coop						
Delaware County Intermediate Unit						
200 Yale Ave	Morton	PA	19070	610-938-9000	938-9887	685
TF: 800-441-3215 ■ *Web:* www.dciu.org						
Delaware County Memorial Hospital						
501 N Lansdowne Ave	Drexel Hill	PA	19026	610-284-8100		374-3
TF: 877-884-1564 ■ *Web:* www.crozerkeystone.org						
Delaware Ctr for Horticulture						
1810 N DuPont St	Wilmington	DE	19806	302-658-6262	658-6267	97
Web: www.thedch.org						
Delaware Ctr for the Contemporary Arts						
200 S Madison St	Wilmington	DE	19801	302-656-6466	656-6944	50-2
Web: www.thedcca.org						
Delaware Democratic Party						
19 E Commons Blvd 2nd Fl	New Castle	DE	19720	302-328-9036	328-9386	616-1
TF: 800-685-5544 ■ *Web:* www.deldems.org						
Delaware Div of Libraries						
497 S Red Haven Ln	Dover	DE	19901	302-739-4748	739-6787	434-5
Web: www.lib.de.us						
Delaware Electric Co-op Inc						
PO Box 600	Greenwood	DE	19950	302-349-3147	349-3147	245
TF: 800-282-8595 ■ *Web:* www.delaware.coop						
Delaware Employment & Training Div						
4425 N Market St	Wilmington	DE	19802	302-761-8085		259
TF: 800-794-3032 ■ *Web:* www.delawareworks.com						
Delaware History Museum						
504 N Market St	Wilmington	DE	19801	302-656-0637	655-7844	520
Web: dehistory.org						
Delaware Hospice Inc						
3515 Silverside Rd	Wilmington	DE	19810	302-478-5707		363
TF: 800-838-9800 ■ *Web:* www.delawarehospice.org						
Delaware Hospital for the Chronically Ill						
100 Sunnyside Rd	Smyrna	DE	19977	302-223-1000		374-7
Web: dhss.delaware.gov						
Delaware Machinery & Tool						
700 S Mulberry St	Muncie	IN	47302	765-284-3335	289-7185	757
TF: 800-935-9935 ■ *Web:* www.delawaredynamics.com						
Delaware Mfg Industries Corp						
3776 Commerce Ct	Wheatfield	NY	14120	716-743-4360	743-4370	262
TF: 800-248-3642 ■ *Web:* www.dmic.com						
Delaware Museum of Natural History						
4840 Kennett Pk	Wilmington	DE	19807	302-658-9111	658-2610	520
Web: www.delmnh.org						
Delaware National Scenic River						
Delaware Water Gap National Recreation Area						
1978 River Rd	Bushkill	PA	18324	570-426-2435		564
TF: 800-543-4295 ■ *Web:* www.nps.gov/dewa						
Delaware North Cos Inc						
40 Fountain Plaza	Buffalo	NY	14202	716-858-5000		185
TF: 800-828-7240 ■ *Web:* www.delawarenorth.com						
Delaware Nurses Assn (DNA)						
4765 Ogletown-Stanton Rd Ste L10	Newark	DE	19713	302-733-5880		533
TF: 800-626-4081 ■ *Web:* www.denurses.org						
Delaware Pharmacists Society						
27 N Main St	Smyrna	DE	19977	302-659-3088		585
Web: www.dpsrx.org						
Delaware Power Systems Corp						
11782 Hammersmith Way Ste 118	Richmond	BC	V7A5E2	604-247-2800		196
Delaware Psychiatric Ctr						
1901 N Dupont Hwy	New Castle	DE	19720	302-255-2700	255-4428	374-5
TF: 800-652-2929 ■ *Web:* dhss.delaware.gov						
Delaware Racing Assn						
777 Delaware Pk Blvd	Wilmington	DE	19804	302-994-2521	994-3392	642
Web: www.delawarepark.com						
Delaware River Port Authority						
1 Port Center 2 Riverside Dr PO Box 1949	Camden	NJ	08101	856-968-2000	968-2242*	618
**Fax:* Hum Res ■ *Web:* www.drpa.org						
Delaware Seashore State Park						
130 Coastal Hwy	Rehoboth Beach	DE	19971	302-227-2800		565
Web: destateparks.com/park/delaware-seashore						
Delaware Sports Museum & Hall of Fame						
801 Shipyard Dr	Wilmington	DE	19801	302-425-3263	425-3713	522
Web: www.desports.org						
Delaware State Bar Assn						
405 N King St	Wilmington	DE	19801	302-658-5279		72
TF: 855-872-5911						
Delaware State Chamber of Commerce						
1201 N Orange St Ste 200 PO Box 671	Wilmington	DE	19899	302-655-7221	654-0691	140
TF: 800-292-9507 ■ *Web:* www.dscc.com						
Delaware State Dental Society						
200 Continental Dr Ste 111	Newark	DE	19713	302-368-7634	368-7669	227
Web: www.delawarestatedentalsociety.org						
Delaware State Lottery						
1575 McKee Rd Ste 102	Dover	DE	19904	302-739-5291	739-7586	452
Web: www.delottery.com						
Delaware State News 110 Galaxy Dr	Dover	DE	19901	302-674-3600		532-2
TF: 800-282-8586 ■ *Web:* www.delawarestatenews.net						
Delaware State Park 5202 US Rt 23 N	Delaware	OH	43015	740-548-4631		565
TF: 866-644-6727 ■ *Web:* www.dnr.state.oh.us						
Delaware State University						
1200 N DuPont Hwy	Dover	DE	19901	302-857-6351	857-6352*	166
**Fax:* Admissions ■ *TF Admissions:* 800-845-2544 ■ *Web:* www.desu.edu						
Delaware Symphony Orchestra, The						
818 N Market St	Wilmington	DE	19801	302-656-7442		573-3
Web: www.delawaresymphony.org						
Delaware Technical & Community College						
Owens 18800 Seashore Hwy PO Box 610	Georgetown	DE	19947	302-856-5400		800
Web: www.dtcc.edu						
Stanton 400 Stanton-Christiana Rd	Newark	DE	19713	302-454-3900	292-3816*	800
**Fax:* Admissions ■ *Web:* www.dtcc.edu						
Terry 100 Campus Dr	Dover	DE	19904	302-857-1000		800
Web: www.dtcc.edu/terry						
Delaware Theatre Co 200 Water St	Wilmington	DE	19801	302-594-1104	594-1107	749
Web: www.delawaretheatre.org						
Delaware This Week						
7801 N Central Dr	Lewis Center	OH	43035	740-888-6100	888-6006	532-4
Web: www.thisweeknews.com						
Delaware Transit Corp						
119 Lower Beach St Ste 100	Wilmington	DE	19805	302-576-6000		468
TF: 800-652-3278 ■ *Web:* www.dartfirststate.com						
Delaware Valley College						
700 E Butler Ave	Doylestown	PA	18901	215-489-2211		166
TF: 800-233-5825 ■ *Web:* www.delval.edu						
Delaware Valley Corp 500 Broadway	Lawrence	MA	01841	978-688-6995	688-5825	131
TF: 800-282-2260 ■ *Web:* www.dvc500.com						
Delaware Veterinary Medical Assn						
937 Monroe Terr	Dover	DE	19904	302-242-7014		795
Web: www.devma.org						
DelBene Suzan (Rep D - WA)						
2442 Rayburn HOB	Washington	DC	20515	202-225-6311	226-1606	342-2
Web: delbene.house.gov						
Delbridge Museum of Natural History						
805 S Kiwanis Ave	Sioux Falls	SD	57104	605-367-7003		520
Web: www.greatzoo.org						
Delcath Systems Inc						
1633 Broadway Ste C 22nd Fl	New York	NY	10019	212-489-2100		476
Web: www.delcath.com						
Delco Automation Inc						
3735 Thatcher Ave	Saskatoon	SK	S7R1B8	306-244-6449	665-7500	256
Web: www.delcoautomation.com						
Delco Diesel Services Inc						
1100 S Agnew Ave	Oklahoma City	OK	73108	405-232-3595		54
TF: 800-256-0395 ■ *Web:* www.delcodiesel.com						
Delco Electric Inc						
1 NW 132Nd St	Oklahoma City	OK	73114	405-302-0099		261
Web: www.delcoelectric.com						
Delco Office Systems Div Delco Assoc Inc						
55 Old Field Pt Rd	Greenwich	CT	06830	203-661-5101		319-1
Delcoline Inc 4919 Lawrence St	Hyattsville	MD	20781	301-864-4455		61
Web: www.delcoline.com						
Delcom Group LP						
2525B E SH 121 Ste 400	Lewisville	TX	75056	214-389-5500		196
TF: 800-308-9228 ■ *Web:* www.delcomgroup.com						
Delden Manufacturing Company Inc						
3530 N Kimball Dr	Kansas City	MO	64161	816-413-1600		499
TF: 800-821-3708 ■ *Web:* www.deldenmfg.com						
Delectables 533 N Fourth Ave	Tucson	AZ	85705	520-884-9289		671
Web: www.delectables.com						
Delek Refining Ltd 425 McMurrey Dr	Tyler	TX	75702	903-579-3400		580
Web: www.delekus.com						
DeLeon's Bromeliads Co						
13745 SW 216th St	Miami	FL	33170	305-238-6028	235-2354	369
TF: 800-448-8649 ■ *Web:* www.deleons4color.com						
Delex Systems Inc						
1953 Gallows Rd Ste 700	Vienna	VA	22182	703-734-8300	893-5338	261
Web: www.delex.com						
Delfield Co 980 S Isabella Rd	Mount Pleasant	MI	48858	989-773-7981	773-3210	298
TF: 800-733-8821 ■ *Web:* www.delfield.com						
Delfin Design & Manufacturing Inc						
23301 Antonio Pkwy	Rancho Santa Margarita	CA	92688	949-888-4644	354-7919*	362
**Fax Area Code:* 800 ■ *Web:* www.delfinfs.com						
Delfina 3621 18th St	San Francisco	CA	94110	415-552-4055		671
Web: www.delfinasf.com						
Delhi Palace 542 St Andrew Rd	Columbia	SC	29210	803-750-7760		671
Delhur Industries Inc						
4333 Tumwater Truck Rte	Port Angeles	WA	98363	360-457-1133		610
Web: delhur.com						

Company	City	State	ZIP	Phone	Fax	Class
Deli Express 16101 W 78th St *TF:* 800 328 8184 ■ *Web:* www.deliexpress.com	Eden Prairie	MN	55344	800-328-8184		296-36
Deli Management Inc 2400 Broadway *TF:* 800-444-3354 ■ *Web:* jasonsdeli.com	Beaumont	TX	77702	409-838-1976		670
Deli Partners LLC 1608 Rogers Rd	Fort Worth	TX	76107	817-738-9355		670
Delicious Living Magazine 1401 Pearl St Ste 200 *Web:* deliciousliving.com	Boulder	CO	80302	303-939-8440	998-9020	457-11
Delight Grecian Foods Inc 1201 Tonne Rd *TF:* 800-621-4387 ■ *Web:* www.greciandelight.com	Elk Grove Village	IL	60007	800-621-4387		296-1
DeLine Box & Display 3700 Lima St *Web:* www.delinebox.com	Denver	CO	80239	303-373-1430		100
Delisa Pallet Corp 91-97 Blanchard St *TF:* 800-255-2927 ■ *Web:* www.delisapallet.com	Newark	NJ	07105	973-344-8600		551
Delisi & Assoc PC 217 S Pennsylvania Ave *Web:* delisiassociates.com	Greensburg	PA	15601	724-832-8585		2
Delius Restaurant 2951 Cherry Ave *Web:* www.deliusrestaurant.com	Signal Hill	CA	90755	562-426-0694	426-0694	671
Delivery.com LLC 199 Water St Fl 23 *Web:* www.delivery.com	New York	NY	10038	212-294-7700		387
Delixus Inc 1160 Ridgemont Pl *Web:* www.delixus.com	Concord	CA	94521	925-672-2623		261
Delkin Devices Inc 13350 Kirkham Way *Web:* www.delkin.com	Poway	CA	92064	858-391-1234		174
Delkor Systems Inc 8700 Rendova St NE *TF:* 800-328-5558 ■ *Web:* www.delkorsystems.com	Circle Pines	MN	55014	800-328-5558		547
Dell 8270 Willow Oaks Corporate Dr Ste 300 *Web:* www.dell.com	Fairfax	VA	22031	703-289-8000		194
Dell Inc 1 Dell Way *NASDAQ: DELL* ■ *TF:* 800-879-3355 ■ *Web:* www.dell.com	Round Rock	TX	78682	512-338-4400	283-6161	173-2
Dell Perot Systems 370 Southpointe Blvd	Canonsburg	PA	15317	724-514-5000		180
Dell'Oro Group Inc 230 Redwood Shores Pkwy *Web:* www.delloro.com	Redwood City	CA	94065	650-622-9400		668
Dellas Graphics Inc 344 S Warren St *TF:* 800-246-0158 ■ *Web:* www.dellasgraphics.com	Syracuse	NY	13202	315-474-4641		174
DELLEMC 6801 Koll Ctr Pkwy *Web:* www.emc.com	Pleasanton	CA	94566	925-600-6800	600-6850	178-1
Dellenbach Motors 3111 S College Ave **Fax Area Code:* 970 ■ *TF:* 866-963-5689 ■ *Web:* www.dellenbach.com	Fort Collins	CO	80525	866-963-5689	226-0233*	57
Dellisart Lodging LLC 10800 Alpharetta Hwy Ste 208-776 **Fax Area Code:* 770 ■ *TF:* 877-606-0591 ■ *Web:* www.dellisart.com	Roswell	GA	30076	847-306-0954	558-4301*	377
Delmar Gardens of Lenexa Inc 9701 Monrovia St *Web:* www.delmargardens.com	Lenexa	KS	66215	913-492-1130		672
Delmar International Inc 10636 Cote de Liesse *TF:* 888-433-5627 ■ *Web:* www.delmarcargo.com	Montreal	QC	H8T1A5	514-636-8000		314
Delmar Products Inc 400 Christian Ln *Web:* www.delmarproducts.com	Berlin	CT	06037	860-828-6501		596
Delmar Systems Inc 8114 W Hwy 90 *Web:* www.delmarus.com	Broussard	LA	70518	337-365-0180		536
Delmarva Broadcasting Co PO Box 7492 *Web:* www.radiocenter.com	Wilmington	DE	19803	302-478-2700		643
Delmarva Broadcasting Company Inc 2727 Shipley Rd *Web:* www.delmarvabroadcasting.com	Wilmington	DE	19810	302-478-2700		645-10
Delmarva Collections Inc 820 E Main St *Web:* delmarvacollections.com	Salisbury	MD	21804	410-546-3742		160
Delmarva Foundation For Medical Care Inc (DFMC) 28464 Marlboro Ave *TF:* 800-999-3362 ■ *Web:* delmarvafoundation.org	Easton	MD	21601	410-822-0697		474
Delmarva Power PO Box 231 *TF Cust Svc:* 800-898-8042 ■ *Web:* www.delmarva.com	Wilmington	DE	19899	800-898-8042		787
Delmonico Steakhouse 3355 Las Vegas Blvd S Venetian Resort Hotel & Casino *Web:* www.emerils.com	Las Vegas	NV	89109	702-414-3737	414-3838	671
Delmonico's Italian Steakhouse Syracuse 2950 Erie Blvd E *Web:* www.delmonicositaliansteakhouse.com	Syracuse	NY	13224	315-445-1111	445-0257	671
Delmont Laboratories Inc 715 Harvard Ave PO Box 269 *TF:* 800-562-5541 ■ *Web:* www.delmontlabs.com	Swarthmore	PA	19081	610-543-2747	543-6298	584
Delnor-Community Hospital (DCH) 300 Randall Rd *TF:* 800-223-9776 ■ *Web:* www.delnor.com	Geneva	IL	60134	630-208-3000	718-2650	374-3
Delnor-Wiggins Pass State Park 11135 Gulfshore Dr *Web:* www.floridastateparks.org/park/Delnor-Wiggins	Naples	FL	34108	239-597-6196		565
Delo Screw Products Co 700 London Rd *TF:* 800-935-9935 ■ *Web:* www.deloscrew.com	Delaware	OH	43015	740-363-1971	363-0042	621
DeLoache Flowers 2927 Millwood Ave *Web:* deloacheflowershop.com	Columbia	SC	29205	803-256-1681		292
Deloitte & Touche USA LLP 1633 Broadway *Web:* www.deloitte.com	New York	NY	10019	212-489-1600		2
Deloitte Consulting LLP 30 Rockefeller Plaza *Web:* www.deloitte.com	New York	NY	10112	212-492-4000	489-1687	194
Deloitte Digital 837 N 34th St Ste 100 *Web:* www.deloittedigital.com/us	Seattle	WA	98103	206-633-1167		195
Deloitte Touche Tohmatsu 1633 Broadway *TF:* 800-752-5894 ■ *Web:* www.deloitte.com	New York	NY	10019	212-489-1600		2
Delon Hampton & Assoc Chartered 900 Seventh St NW Ste 800 *Web:* www.delonhampton.com	Washington	DC	20001	202-898-1999	371-2073	261
Delong's Inc 301 Dix Rd *Web:* www.delongsinc.com	Jefferson City	MO	65019	573-635-6121		480
DeLorme 2 DeLorme Dr PO Box 298 **Fax Area Code:* 800 ■ *TF Sales:* 800-561-5105	Yarmouth	ME	04096	207-846-7000	575-2244*	637-1
Delphax Technologies Inc 6100 W 110th St *OTC: DLPX* ■ *Web:* www.delphax.com	Bloomington	MN	55438	952-939-9000		629
Delphi Automotive LLP 5725 Delphi Dr *Web:* www.delphi.com	Troy	MI	48098	248-813-2334		60
Delphi Body Works Inc 313 S Washington St PO Box 30 *Web:* www.delphibodyworks.com	Delphi	IN	46923	765-564-2212	564-4255	516
Delphi Business Properties Inc 7100 Hayvenhurst Ave Ste 211 *Web:* go2delphi.com	Van Nuys	CA	91406	818-780-7878		652
Delphi Corp 5725 Delphi Dr *Web:* www.delphi.com	Troy	MI	48098	248-813-2334		60
Delphi Energy Corp 500 - Fourth Ave SW Ste 300 *TF:* 800-430-7207 ■ *Web:* www.delphienergy.ca	Calgary	AB	T2P2V6	403-265-6171		536
Delphi Engineering Group Inc 485 E 17th St Ste 400 *Web:* www.delphieng.com	Costa Mesa	CA	92627	949-515-1490		256
Delphi Financial Group Inc 1105 N Market St Ste 1230 *NYSE: DFG* ■ *TF:* 800-732-0330 ■ *Web:* www.delphifin.com	Wilmington	DE	19801	302-478-5142		360-4
Delphi Ventures 160 Bovet Rd Ste 408 *Web:* www.delphiventures.com	San Mateo	CA	94402	650-854-9650		792
Delphinus Engineering Inc 650 Baldwin Tower *Web:* www.delphinus.com	Eddystone	PA	19022	610-874-9160		261
Delphinus Medical Technologies LLC 45525 Grand River Ave *Web:* www.delphinusmt.com	Novi	MI	48374	248-522-9600		723
Delphos Herald Inc 405 N Main St *TF:* 800-589-6950 ■ *Web:* www.delphosherald.com	Delphos	OH	45833	419-695-0015		637-8
Delray Beach Library 100 W Atlantic Ave *Web:* www.delraylibrary.org	Delray Beach	FL	33444	561-266-0194		434-3
Delray Medical Ctr (DMC) 5352 Linton Blvd *Web:* www.delraymedicalctr.com	Delray Beach	FL	33484	561-498-4440	495-3103	374-3
Delsea Shop Rite PO Box 7812 **Fax Area Code:* 518 ■ *Web:* www.shoprite.com	Edison	NJ	08818	856-691-9395	713-4176*	345
Delsey Luggage 6735 Business Pkwy Ste A *TF:* 800-558-3344 ■ *Web:* www.delsey.com	Elkridge	MD	21075	410-796-5655		453
DelShah Capital LLC 114 E 13th St *Web:* www.delshah.com	New York	NY	10003	212-677-4506		652
DelStar Technologies Inc 220 E St Elmo Rd *TF:* 800-521-6713 ■ *Web:* www.delstarinc.com	Austin	TX	78745	512-447-7000	447-7444	608
Delsys Inc 23 Strathmore Rd *Web:* www.delsys.com	Natick	MA	01760	617-236-0599		250
Delta Air Lines Inc 1030 Delta Blvd *NYSE: DAL* ■ *TF:* 800-221-1212 ■ *Web:* www.delta.com	Atlanta	GA	30354	404-715-2600	773-2108	25
Delta Air Lines Inc PO Box 20559 Dept 670 **Fax Area Code:* 404 ■ *TF:* 800-352-2737 ■ *Web:* deltacargo.com	Atlanta	GA	30320	800-352-2737	714-5022*	12
Delta Apparel Inc 2750 Premier Pkwy Ste 100 *NYSE: DLA* ■ *TF:* 800-285-4456 ■ *Web:* www.deltaapparel.com	Duluth	GA	30097	678-775-6900	775-6992	155-3
Delta Area Chamber of Commerce 301 Main St *Web:* www.deltacolorado.org	Delta	CO	81416	970-874-8616	874-8618	139
Delta Area Hospice Care Ltd 522 Arnold Ave	Greenville	MS	38701	662-335-7040		371
Delta Bus Lines Inc 3107 Hwy 82E *Web:* deltabuslines.net	Greenville	MS	38701	662-335-2633	335-2634	107
Delta Carbona LP 376 Hollywood Ave Ste 208 *TF:* 888-746-5599 ■ *Web:* www.carbona.com	Fairfield	NJ	07004	973-808-6260		151
Delta Centrifugal Corp PO Box 1043 *TF Sales:* 888-433-3100 ■ *Web:* www.deltacentrifugal.com	Temple	TX	76503	254-773-9055		307
Delta Chamber of Commerce 6201 60th Ave *Web:* www.deltachamber.ca	Delta	BC	V4K4E2	604-946-4232	946-5285	137
Delta Chemical Corp 2601 Cannery Ave *TF:* 800-282-5322 ■ *Web:* www.usalco.com	Baltimore	MD	21226	410-354-0100	354-1021	145
Delta Chi Fraternity Inc 314 Church St	Iowa City	IA	52245	319-337-4811		48-16
Delta Children 114 W 26th St 8th Fl *TF:* 800-377-3777 ■ *Web:* www.deltachildren.com	New York	NY	10001	212-736-7000		64
Delta College 1961 Delta Rd **Fax:* Admissions ■ *Web:* www.delta.edu	University Center	MI	48710	989-686-9000	667-2202*	162
Delta College of Arts & Technology 7380 Exchange Pl *TF:* 800-858-0551 ■ *Web:* www.deltacollege.com	Baton Rouge	LA	70806	225-928-7770		162
Delta Compression & Equipment LLC 160 James Ln *TF:* 800-235-9142 ■ *Web:* www.deltacompression.com	Krotz Springs	LA	70750	337-566-8888		539
Delta Computer Group Inc 4 Dubon Ct *Web:* www.deltacomputergroup.com	Farmingdale	NY	11735	631-845-0400		174
Delta Concrete Products Co Inc 19431 W Piney Point Ave	Baton Rouge	LA	70817	225-665-6103		182
Delta Consolidated Industries Inc 4800 Krueger Dr *TF:* 800-643-0084 ■ *Web:* www.deltatruckstorage.com	Jonesboro	AR	72401	870-935-3711		488
Delta Controls Corp 585 Fortson St *Web:* www.deltacnt.com	Shreveport	LA	71107	318-424-8471		246
Delta Controls Inc 17850 - 56th Ave *Web:* www.deltacontrols.com	Surrey	BC	V3S1C7	604-574-9444	574-7793	407
Delta Cooling Towers Inc PO Box 315 *TF:* 800-289-3350 ■ *Web:* www.deltacooling.com	Rockaway	NJ	07866	973-586-2201	586-2243	472
Delta Corporate Services Inc 129 Littleton Rd *TF:* 800-335-8220 ■ *Web:* www.deltacorp.com	Parsippany	NJ	07054	973-334-6260	331-0144	180
Delta Correctional Ctr 11363 Lockhart Rd *Web:* www.colorado.gov	Delta	CO	81416	970-874-7614	874-5810	213

Name / Address	City	State	Zip	Phone	Fax	Class
Delta Corrugated Paper Products Corp W Ruby Ave *TF:* 800-466-9676 ■ *Web:* www.deltacorrugated.com	Palisades Park	NJ	07650	201-941-1910	941-9399	100
Delta Cos Inc 114 S Silver Springs Rd *Web:* www.deltacos.com	Cape Girardeau	MO	63703	573-334-5261	334-9576	188-4
Delta County 200 W Bonham St *Web:* www.deltacountytx.com/sheriff.html	Cooper	TX	75432	903-395-4118	395-4455	338
Delta County 501 Palmer St Ste 211 *Web:* www.deltacounty.com	Delta	CO	81416	970-874-2150	874-2161	338
Delta County 310 Ludington St *Web:* www.deltami.org	Escanaba	MI	49829	906-789-5105	789-5196	338
Delta County Area Chamber of Commerce 230 Ludington St *TF:* 888-335-8264 ■ *Web:* www.deltami.org	Escanaba	MI	49829	906-786-2192	786-8830	139
Delta Dallas Protech LP 15950 N Dallas Pkwy Ste 500 *Web:* www.deltadallas.com	Dallas	TX	75248	972-788-2300		260
Delta Data 1500 Sixth Ave Ste 1 *TF:* 800-723-8274 ■ *Web:* www.deltadatasoft.com	Columbus	GA	31901	706-324-0855		177
Delta Delta Delta Fraternity 2331 Brookhollow Plaza Dr *TF:* 877-746-7333 ■ *Web:* www.tridelta.org	Arlington	TX	76006	817-633-8001	652-0212	48-16
Delta Democrat Times 988 N Broadway St *Web:* www.ddtonline.com	Greenville	MS	38701	662-335-1155	335-2860	532-2
Delta Dental Insurance Company of Alaska PO Box 1809 *TF:* 800-521-2651 ■ *Web:* www.deltadentalins.com	Alpharetta	GA	30023	800-521-2651		391-3
Delta Dental of Arizona PO Box 43026 **Fax Area Code:* 602 ■ *TF:* 800-352-6132 ■ *Web:* www.deltadentalaz.com	Phoenix	AZ	85080	800-352-6132	588-3636*	391-3
Delta Dental of Arkansas 1513 Country Club Rd **Fax Area Code:* 877 ■ *TF:* 800-462-5410 ■ *Web:* www.deltadentalar.com	Sherwood	AR	72120	501-835-3400	992-1854*	391-3
Delta Dental of Colorado 4582 S Ulster St Ste 800 *TF:* 800-233-0860 ■ *Web:* www.deltadentalco.com	Denver	CO	80237	303-741-9300	741-9338	391-3
Delta Dental of Idaho 555 E Parkcenter Blvd PO Box 2870 *TF:* 800-356-7586 ■ *Web:* www.deltadentalid.com	Boise	ID	83706	208-489-3580	344-4649	391-3
Delta Dental of Indiana PO Box 30416 *TF:* 800-524-0149 ■ *Web:* www.deltadentalin.com	Lansing	MI	48909	800-524-0149		391-3
Delta Dental of Iowa 9000 Northpark Dr Ste 13 *TF Cust Svc:* 800-544-0718 ■ *Web:* www.deltadentalia.com	Johnston	IA	50131	515-261-5500		391-3
Delta Dental of Kansas 1619 N Waterfront Pkwy PO Box 789769 *TF:* 800-234-3375 ■ *Web:* www.deltadentalks.com	Wichita	KS	67278	316-264-4511	462-3392	391-3
Delta Dental of Kentucky 10100 Linn Station Rd *TF Cust Svc:* 800-955-2030 ■ *Web:* www.deltadentalky.com	Louisville	KY	40223	800-955-2030		391-3
Delta Dental of Louisiana PO Box 1803 *TF:* 800-422-4234 ■ *Web:* www.deltadentalins.com	Alpharetta	GA	30023	800-422-4234		391-3
Delta Dental of Maryland 1 Delta Dr *TF:* 800-932-0783 ■ *Web:* www.deltadentalins.com	Mechanicsburg	PA	17055	717-766-8500		391-3
Delta Dental of Massachusetts 465 Medford St *TF Cust Svc:* 800-872-0500 ■ *Web:* www.deltadentalma.com	Boston	MA	02129	617-886-1000	886-1199	391-3
Delta Dental of Michigan PO Box 30416 *TF:* 800-524-0149 ■ *Web:* www.deltadentalmi.com	Lansing	MI	48909	800-524-0149		391-3
Delta Dental of Minnesota PO Box 330 *TF:* 800-553-9536 ■ *Web:* www.deltadentalmn.org	Minneapolis	MN	55440	651-406-5900		391-3
Delta Dental of Missouri 12399 Gravois Rd Ste 2 *TF:* 800-392-1167 ■ *Web:* www.deltadentalmo.com	Saint Louis	MO	63127	314-656-3000	656-2900	391-3
Delta Dental of Montana PO Box 1803 *TF:* 800-422-4234 ■ *Web:* www.deltadentalins.com	Alpharetta	GA	30023	800-422-4234		391-3
Delta Dental of New Jersey 1639 State Rt 10 *TF:* 800-624-2633 ■ *Web:* deltadentalnj.com	Parsippany	NJ	07054	973-285-4000	285-4141	391-3
Delta Dental of New Jersey Inc PO Box 222 **Fax Area Code:* 973 ■ *TF:* 800-452-9310 ■ *Web:* deltadentalnj.com	Parsippany	NJ	07054	800-452-9310	285-4141*	391-3
Delta Dental of New Mexico 2500 Louisiana Blvd NE Ste 600 *TF:* 800-999-0963 ■ *Web:* www.deltadentalnm.com	Albuquerque	NM	87110	505-883-4777	883-7444	391-3
Delta Dental of New York 1 Delta Dr *TF:* 800-932-0783 ■ *Web:* www.deltadentalins.com	Mechanicsburg	PA	17055	717-766-8500		391-3
Delta Dental of Ohio PO Box 30416 *TF:* 800-524-0149 ■ *Web:* www.deltadentaloh.com	Lansing	MI	48909	800-524-0149		391-3
Delta Dental of Oklahoma 16 NW 63rd St Ste 201 *TF:* 800-522-0188 ■ *Web:* www.deltadentalok.org	Oklahoma City	OK	73116	405-607-2100	607-2190	391-3
Delta Dental of Pennsylvania 1 Delta Dr *TF:* 800-932-0783 ■ *Web:* www.deltadentalins.com	Mechanicsburg	PA	17055	800-932-0783		391-3
Delta Dental of Rhode Island 10 Charles St **Fax:* Cust Svc ■ *TF:* 800-598-6684 ■ *Web:* www.deltadentalri.com	Providence	RI	02904	401-752-6000	752-6060*	391-3
Delta Dental of South Dakota 720 N Euclid Ave PO Box 1157 *TF:* 800-627-3961 ■ *Web:* www.deltadentalsd.com	Pierre	SD	57501	605-224-7345	224-0909	391-3
Delta Dental of Tennessee 240 Venture Cir *TF Cust Svc:* 800-223-3104 ■ *Web:* www.deltadentaltn.com	Nashville	TN	37228	615-255-3175	244-8108	391-3
Delta Dental of Virginia 4818 Starkey Rd *TF:* 800-367-3531 ■ *Web:* www.deltadentalva.com	Roanoke	VA	24014	540-989-8000	725-3890	391-3
Delta Dental of West Virginia 1 Delta Dr *TF:* 800-932-0783 ■ *Web:* www.deltadentalins.com	Mechanicsburg	PA	17055	717-766-8500		391-3
Delta Dental of Wisconsin 2801 Hoover Rd PO Box 828 *TF:* 800-236-3713 ■ *Web:* www.deltadentalwi.com	Stevens Point	WI	54481	715-344-6087	344-9058	391-3
Delta Dental of Wyoming 6234 Yellowstone Rd PO Box 29 *TF:* 800-735-3379 ■ *Web:* www.deltadentalwy.org	Cheyenne	WY	82009	307-632-3313	632-7309	391-3
Delta Dental Plan of North Carolina 4242 Six Forks Rd Ste 970 *TF:* 800-587-9514 ■ *Web:* www.deltadentalnc.com	Raleigh	NC	27609	919-424-1046		391-3
Delta Downs Racetrack 2717 Delta Downs Dr *TF:* 800-589-7441 ■ *Web:* www.deltadowns.com	Vinton	LA	70668	800-589-7441		642
Delta Education LLC 80 NW Blvd *TF:* 800-258-1302 ■ *Web:* www.deltaeducation.com	Nashua	NH	03063	603-889-8899		243
Delta Electric Inc 911 Riverview Ave PO Box 1497 *Web:* www.deltaelectricwv.com	Logan	WV	25601	304-752-4625	752-0948	358
Delta Electric Power Assn 1700 Hwy 82 W *Web:* deltaepa.com	Greenwood	MS	38930	662-453-6352		245
Delta Electronics Manufacturing Corp 416 Cabot St *TF:* 800-444-6056 ■ *Web:* www.deltarf.com	Beverly	MA	01915	978-927-1060	922-6430	253
Delta Employees Credit Union 1025 Virginia Ave *TF:* 800-544-3328 ■ *Web:* www.deltacommunitycu.com	Atlanta	GA	30354	404-715-4725		219
Delta Engineers & Architects PC 184 Court St *Web:* delta-eas.com	Binghamton	NY	13901	607-231-6600		256
Delta Fastener Corp 7122 Old Katy Rd *Web:* www.deltafastener.com	Houston	TX	77024	713-868-2351		351
Delta Fine Arts Inc 2611 New Walkertown Rd *Web:* deltaartscenter.org	Winston-Salem	NC	27101	336-722-2625		50-2
Delta Fire Sprinklers Inc 111 Tech Dr *Web:* delta-fire.com	Sanford	FL	32771	407-328-3000		189-10
Delta Galil USA 1 Harmon Plaza 5th Fl *Web:* www.deltagalil.com	Secaucus	NJ	07094	201-902-0055	902-0070	155-18
Delta Gamma 3250 Riverside Dr Ste A-2 *TF:* 800-644-5414 ■ *Web:* www.deltagamma.org	Columbus	OH	43221	614-481-8169		48-16
Delta Group Inc 4801 Lincoln Rd NE *Web:* www.deltagroupinc.com	Albuquerque	NM	87109	505-883-7674		253
Delta Heritage Trail State Park PO Box 193 *Web:* www.arkansasstateparks.com	Watson	AR	71674	870-644-3474		565
Delta Hospital Foundation 5800 Mtn View Blvd *Web:* www.dhfoundation.ca	Delta	BC	V4K3V6	604-940-9695	940-9670	374-2
Delta Hotels 2685 Rue King O *TF:* 800-268-1133 ■ *Web:* www.deltahotels.com	Sherbrooke	QC	J1L1C1	819-822-1989	822-8990	377
Delta Industrial Services Inc 11501 Eagle St *Web:* www.deltaind.com	Minneapolis	MN	55448	763-755-7744		186
Delta Industries 39 Bradley Pk Rd *Web:* mbaerospace.com	East Granby	CT	06026	860-653-5041		21
Delta Kappa Epsilon Fraternity (DKE) 611 1/2 E William St *Web:* www.dke.org	Ann Arbor	MI	48104	734-302-4210		48-16
Delta King Riverboat Hotel 1000 Front St *TF:* 800-825-5464 ■ *Web:* www.deltaking.com	Sacramento	CA	95814	916-444-5464		379
Delta Lake State Park 8797 SR- 46 *Web:* parks.ny.gov/parks/66/hunting.aspx	Rome	NY	13440	315-337-4670		565
Delta M Corp 1003 Larsen Dr *TF:* 800-922-0083 ■ *Web:* www.deltamcorp.com	Oak Ridge	TN	37830	800-922-0083		407
Delta Machine & Ironworks Inc 5185 Adams Ave *Web:* www.deltamachineinc.com	Baton Rouge	LA	70806	225-356-2000		454
Delta Machining Inc 2361 Reum Rd *Web:* www.deltamach.com	Niles	MI	49120	269-683-7775		454
Delta Marketing Dynamics 205 S Salina St Ste 400 *TF:* 800-492-4516 ■ *Web:* deltamarketingdynamics.com	Syracuse	NY	13202	315-492-2905		195
Delta Materials Handling Inc 4676 Clarke Rd *Web:* www.deltamat.com	Memphis	TN	38141	901-795-7230		358
Delta Meadows 17645 State Hwy 160 *Web:* www.parks.ca.gov/default.asp?page_id=492	Rio Vista	CA	94571	916-777-7701		565
Delta Medical Ctr (DMC) 3000 Getwell Rd *TF:* 800-561-3357 ■ *Web:* www.deltamedcenter.com	Memphis	TN	38118	901-369-8100		374-3
Delta Medical Systems Inc 3280 Gateway Rd Suite 200 *TF:* 800-798-7574 ■ *Web:* www.deltamedicalsystems.com	Brookfield	WI	53045	800-798-7574	323-9321	475
Delta Metals Company Inc 1388 N Seventh St *Web:* www.delta-metals.com	Memphis	TN	38107	901-525-5000	575-3322	492
Delta Mold Inc 9415 Stockport Pl *Web:* www.deltamold.com	Charlotte	NC	28273	704-588-6600		711
Delta Montreal Hotel 475 President Kennedy Ave	Montreal	QC	H3A1J7	514-286-1986		707
Delta Natural Gas Co Inc 3617 Lexington Rd *NASDAQ:* DGAS ■ *TF:* 800-262-2012 ■ *Web:* www.deltagas.com	Winchester	KY	40391	859-744-6171		787
Delta Oil & Gas Inc 700 W Pender St Ste 604 *TF:* 866-355-3644 ■ *Web:* www.deltaoilandgas.com	Vancouver	BC	V6C1G8	604-602-1500		536
Delta Pacific Products Inc 33170 Central Ave *Web:* www.deltapacificinc.com	Union City	CA	94587	510-487-4411		608
Delta Packing Co 6021 E Kettleman Ln *Web:* www.deltapacking.com	Lodi	CA	95240	209-334-1023	334-0811	11-1
Delta Partners 32 Burrows Rd *Web:* www.deltapartners.ca	Ottawa	ON	K1J6E6	613-747-8121		463
Delta Pathology Group LLP 2915 Missouri Ave *Web:* www.deltapathology.com	Shreveport	LA	71109	318-621-8820		415
Delta Petroleum Co 10352 River Rd *Web:* ww1.deltapetro.com	Saint Rose	LA	70087	504-467-1399		541
Delta Phi Epsilon International Sorority 251 S Camac St *Web:* www.dphie.org	Philadelphia	PA	19107	215-732-5901	732-5906	48-16

	Phone	Fax	Class
Delta Pi Epsilon (DPE) 1914 Association Dr .... Reston VA 20191 *Web:* www.dpe.org	501-219-1866		48-16
Delta Polymers Midwest Inc 6685 Sterling Dr N .... Sterling Heights MI 48312 *TF:* 800-860-6848 ■ *Web:* www.deltapoly.com	586-795-2900		603
Delta Power Co 4484 Boeing Dr .... Rockford IL 61109 *Web:* www.delta-power.com	815-397-6628	397-2526	790
Delta Products Corporation 46101 Fremont Blvd .... Fremont CA 94538 *Web:* www.delta-americas.com	510-668-5100	668-0680	253
Delta Railroad Construction Inc 2648 W Prospect Rd PO Box 1398 .... Ashtabula OH 44004 *Web:* www.deltarr.com	440-992-2997	992-1311	188-4
Delta Regional Medical Ctr (DRMC) 1400 E Union St .... Greenville MS 38703 *Web:* www.deltaregional.com	662-378-3783		374-3
Delta Ridge Implement Inc 1150 US Hwy 425 .... Rayville LA 71269 *Web:* stihldealer.net	318-728-6423		274
Delta Risk LLC 106 S St Mary's St Ste 428 .... San Antonio TX 78205 *Web:* deltarisk.com	210-293-0707		196
Delta Rubber Co 39 Wauregan Rd PO Box 300 .... Danielson CT 06239 *Web:* nninc.com	860-779-0300		326
Delta Sales Yard Inc 700 W Fifth St .... Delta CO 81416 *TF:* 800-498-0767 ■ *Web:* www.deltasalesyard.com	970-874-4612	874-3087	446
Delta Scientific Corp 40355 Delta Ln .... Palmdale CA 93551 *Web:* www.deltascientific.com	661-575-1100	575-1109	678
Delta Sigma Phi Fraternity 2960 N Meridian St PO Box 88507 .... Indianapolis IN 46208 *Web:* www.deltasig.org	317-634-1899	634-1410	48-16
Delta Sigma Pi 330 S Campus Ave .... Oxford OH 45056 *TF:* 800-228-9290 ■ *Web:* www.deltasigmapi.org	513-523-1907	523-7292	48-16
Delta Sigma Theta Sorority Inc 1707 New Hampshire Ave NW .... Washington DC 20009 *TF:* 866 615 6464 ■ *Web:* www.deltasigmatheta.org	202-986-2400	986-2513	48-16
Delta Society 875 124th Ave NE Ste 101 .... Bellevue WA 98005 *TF:* 800-514-0301 ■ *Web:* www.petpartners.org	425-679-5500		48-17
Delta Solutions Inc 4 Parkway N .... Deerfield IL 60015	847-317-9544		525
Delta Staffing LLC 6100 Dixie Hwy Ste B .... Clarkston MI 48346 *TF:* 800-427-5100 ■ *Web:* www.delta-staffing.com	248-394-3940		260
Delta Star Inc 270 Industrial Rd .... San Carlos CA 94070 *TF:* 800-892-8673 ■ *Web:* www.deltastar.com	800-892-8673		767
Delta State Recreation Site Delta State Recreation Site Access Rd .... Delta Junction AK 99737 *Web:* www.dnr.alaska.gov	907-451-2695		565
Delta State University 1003 W Sunflower Rd .... Cleveland MS 38733 **Fax:* Admissions ■ *TF:* 800-468-6378 ■ *Web:* www.deltastate.edu	662-846-4020	846-4684*	166
Delta Steel Inc 7355 Roundhouse Ln .... Houston TX 77078 *TF:* 800-324-0220 ■ *Web:* deltasteel.com	713-635-1200	635-2060	492
Delta Steel Technologies (DBI) 2204 Century Ctr Blvd .... Irving TX 75062 *Web:* www.dbimfg.com	972-438-7150	579-0100	494
Delta SubSea LLC 550 Club Dr Ste 345 .... Montgomery TX 77316 *TF:* 800-591-7237 ■ *Web:* www.deltasubsea-rov.com	936-582-7237		539
Delta Systems Inc 1734 Frost Rd .... Streetsboro OH 44241 *Web:* phoenixtechnologyit.com	330-626-2811		729
Delta T Inc 8323 Loch Lomond Dr .... Pico Rivera CA 90660 *TF:* 800-928-5828 ■ *Web:* www.deltat.com	310-355-0355		612
Delta t Systems Inc 2171 State Rd 175 .... Richfield WI 53076 *TF:* 800 733 4204 ■ *Web:* deltatsys.com	262-628-0331		358
Delta Tau Data Systems Inc 21314 Lassen St .... Chatsworth CA 91311 *Web:* www.deltatau.com	818-998-2095		625
Delta Tau Delta Fraternity 10000 Allisonville Rd .... Fishers IN 46038 *TF:* 800-335-8795 ■ *Web:* www.delts.org	317-284-0203	284-0214	48-16
Delta Technology Corp 1223 Valentine Ave SE .... Pacific WA 98047	253-863-8415		189-10
Delta Theta Phi 225 Hillsborough St Ste 432 .... Raleigh NC 27603 *TF:* 800-783-2600 ■ *Web:* www.deltathetaphi.org	800 783 2600		48-16
Delta Tour & Travel Services Inc 3360 Flair Dr Ste 102 .... El Monte CA 91731 *Web:* deltatours.com	626-300-0033		760
Delta Training Partners Inc 4020 Oleander Dr .... Wilmington NC 28403 *Web:* deltatraining.com	910-790-1985		463
Delta Transformers Inc 1311-A rue Ampere .... Boucherville QC J4B5Z5 *Web:* www.delta.xfo.com	450-449-9774		767
Delta Upsilon International Fraternity 8705 Founders Rd .... Indianapolis IN 46268 *Web:* www.deltau.org	317-875-8900	876-1629	48-16
Delta Waterfowl Foundation PO Box 3128 .... Bismarck ND 58502 *TF:* 888-987-3695 ■ *Web:* www.deltawaterfowl.org	701-222-8857		48-3
Delta Western Inc 420 L St Ste 101 .... Anchorage AK 99501 *TF:* 800-478-2688 ■ *Web:* www.deltawestern.com	907-276-2688		316
Delta Whistler Village Suites 4308 Main St .... Whistler BC V0N1B4 *TF:* 888-299-3987	604-905-3987		669
Delta World Tire Co 203 Guilbeau Rd .... Lafayette LA 70506 *TF:* 800-887-9806 ■ *Web:* www.deltaworldtire.com	337-984-3098		54
Delta Zeta Sorority 202 E Church St .... Oxford OH 45056 *Web:* www.deltazeta.org	513-523-7597	523-1921	48-16
Deltacom Inc 7037 Old Madison Pike .... Huntsville AL 35806 *TF:* 800-239-3000 ■ *Web:* www.deltacom.com	800-239-3000		736
Deltagen Inc 1900 S Norfolk St Ste 105 .... San Mateo CA 94403 *Web:* www.deltagen.com	650-345-7602		178-10

	Phone	Fax	Class
Delta-Montrose Electric Assn 11925 6300 Rd .... Montrose CO 81401 *Web:* www.dmea.com	970-249-4572		245
Deltapac Packaging Inc 8200 de l'Industrie St .... Anjou QC H1J1S7 *TF:* 800-361-4177 ■ *Web:* www.deltapac.ca	514-352-5546	352-5703	601
DeltaSoft Inc 624 Courtyard Dr .... Hillsborough NJ 08844 *Web:* www.deltasoftinc.com	908-595-9777		177
deltathree Inc 75 Broad St .... New York NY 10004 *PINK: DDDC* ■ *TF:* 888-335-8230 ■ *Web:* deltathree.com	212-500-4850	500-4888	736
DeltaTRAK Inc PO Box 398 .... Pleasanton CA 94566 *TF:* 800-962-6776 ■ *Web:* www.deltatrak.com	925-249-2250	249-2251	202
Delta-Waseca 1400 Second St SE .... Waseca MN 56093 **Fax Area Code:* 507 ■ *Web:* www.deltawaseca.com	952-922-5569	835-1174*	516
Deltawrx 21700 Oxnard St Ste 530 .... Woodland Hills CA 91367 *Web:* www.deltawrx.com	818-227-9300		261
Deltec Asset Management LLC 623 Fifth Ave 28th Fl .... New York NY 10022 *Web:* www.deltec-ny.com	212-546-6200		401
Deltec Homes Inc 69 Bingham Rd .... Asheville NC 28806 *TF:* 800-642-2508 ■ *Web:* www.deltechomes.com	800-642-2508		186
Deltech Corp 11911 Scenic Hwy .... Baton Rouge LA 70807 *TF:* 800-424-9300 ■ *Web:* www.deltechcorp.com	225-775-0150	358-3149	605-1
Del-Tech Manufacturing Inc 9703 Penn Rd .... Prince George BC V2N5T6 *TF:* 800-736-7733 ■ *Web:* www.deltech.ca	250-564-3585		757
Deltek Inc 2291 Wood Oak Dr .... Herndon VA 20171 *NASDAQ: PROJ* ■ *TF:* 800-456-2009 ■ *Web:* www.deltek.com	703-734-8606	734-1146	178-1
Deltic Timber Corp PO Box 7200 .... El Dorado AR 71731 *NYSE: DEL* ■ *Web:* www.deltic.com	870-881-9400		752
Del-Tin Fiber LLC 757 Del-Tin Hwy .... El Dorado AR 71730 *Web:* www.deltinfiber.com	870-309-3100		820
Del-Ton Inc 330 Aviation Pkwy .... Elizabethtown NC 28337 *Web:* www.del-ton.com	910-645-2172		711
Deltona Corp 8014 SW 135th St Rd .... Ocala FL 34473 *TF:* 800-333-5866 ■ *Web:* www.deltona.com	352-347-2322		653
Deltrol Corp 2740 S 20th St .... Milwaukee WI 53215 *Web:* www.deltrol.com	414-671-6800		246
Deltrol Fluid Products 3001 Grant Ave .... Bellwood IL 60104 **Fax:* Sales ■ *TF:* 800-477-9772 ■ *Web:* www.deltrolfluid.com	708-547-0500	547-6881*	790
Del-tron Precision Inc 5 Trowbridge Dr .... Bethel CT 06801 *Web:* deltron.com	203-778-2727		75
Deltronic Corp 3900 W Segerstrom Ave .... Santa Ana CA 92704 *TF:* 800-451-6922 ■ *Web:* www.deltronic.com	714-545-5800	545-9548	493
Deltronic Crystal Industries Inc 64 Harding Ave .... Dover NJ 07801 *Web:* www.deltroniccrystal.com	973-328-7000		544
Deluca's Restaurant 2006 W Willow St .... Lansing MI 48917 *Web:* www.delucaspizza.com	517-487-6087		671
Delucchi Plus 1750 Pennsylvania Ave NW Ste 200 .... Washington DC 20006 *Web:* www.delucchiplus.com	202-349-4000		5
Deluxe Bldg Systems Inc 499 W Third St .... Berwick PA 18603 *TF:* 800-843-7372 ■ *Web:* deluxebuildingsystems.com	570-752-5914	752-1525	106
Deluxe Check Printing 1600 E Touhy Ave .... Des Plaines IL 60018 *TF:* 800-603-3000 ■ *Web:* www.deluxe.com	651-483-7111		627
Deluxe Corp 3680 N Victoria St .... Shoreview MN 55126 *NYSE: DLX* ■ *TF:* 800-328-7205 ■ *Web:* ww.deluxe.com	651-483-7111		360-3
Deluxe Digital Media Management Inc 29125 Ave Paine .... Valencia CA 91355 *Web:* www.bydeluxe.com	661-702-5000	775-2586	514
Deluxe Inn Odessa Hotel 1518 S Grant Ave .... Odessa TX 79761 *Web:* deluxeinnodessa.com	432-333-1486		379
Deluxe Plastics Inc 220 Industrial Ave .... Clintonville WI 54929 *Web:* www.deluxe-plastics.com	715-823-4200		596
Deluxe Stitcher Company Inc 3747 acorn ln .... Franklin Park IL 60131 *TF:* 800-634-0810 ■ *Web:* deluxestitcher.com	800-634-0810		757
Delva Tool & Machine Corp 1603 Industrial Hwy .... Cinnaminson NJ 08077 *Web:* www.delvatool.com	856-786-8700	786-8708	757
Delve Group Inc, The 21 W 46th St Ste 1103 .... New York NY 10036 *TF:* 800-659-7801 ■ *Web:* delvegroup.com	212-255-3870		463
Delvinia Inc 370 King St West 5th Fl .... Toronto ON M5V1J9 *TF:* 800-274-2985 ■ *Web:* www.delvinia.com	416-364-1455		225
Delaware *State Police Div* 1441 N DuPont Hwy PO Box 430 .... Dover DE 19903 *Web:* dsp.delaware.gov	302-739-5901		339-8
Delyse Inc 505 Reactor Way .... Reno NV 89502 *TF:* 800-441-6887 ■ *Web:* www.delyse.com	775-857-1811		296-9
Delzer Lithograph Co 510 S W Ave .... Waukesha WI 53186 *Web:* www.delzer.com	262-522-2600		627
DEMA (Diving Equipment & Marketing Assn) 3750 Convoy St Ste 310 .... San Diego CA 92111 *TF:* 800-862-3483 ■ *Web:* www.dema.org	858-616-6408	616-6495	49-4
Demae Japanese Restaurant 82 W Ctr St .... Provo UT 84601 *Web:* demae-japanese.com	801-374-0306		671
Demag Cranes & Components 29201 Aurora Rd .... Cleveland OH 44139 *Web:* www.demagcranes.us	440-248-2400		190
Demakes Enterprises Inc 37 Waterhill St .... Lynn MA 01905 *Web:* oldneighborhoodfoods.com	781-595-1557	595-7523	473
Demand Metric 562 Wellington St .... London ON N6A3R5 *TF:* 866 947 7744 ■ *Web:* www.demandmetric.com	519-495-9619		466
Demand Planning LLC 10g Roessler Rd Ste 508 .... Woburn MA 01801 *Web:* demandplanning.net	781-995-0685		193
Demand Printing Solutions Inc 3900 Rutledge Rd NE .... Albuquerque NM 87109 *Web:* www.dpsnm.com	505-881-2927		627

Phone | Fax | Class

Demar Direct Inc 1133 N Ridge Ave — Lombard IL 60148 — 630-873-1000 — 5
Web: www.demarinc.com

Demar Ltd 6200 Savoy Dr Ste 800 — Houston TX 77036 — 713-963-0930 963-0941 — 186
Web: www.demar-ltd.com

Demarest Lloyd State Park
115 Barneys Joy Rd — Dartmouth MA 02748 — 508-636-3298 — 565
Web: www.mass.gov

DeMaria Bldg Company Inc
3031 W Grand Blvd Ste 624 — Detroit MI 48202 — 313-870-2800 870-2810 — 186
Web: www.demariabuild.com

Dematic 507 Plymouth Ave NE — Grand Rapids MI 49505 — 877-725-7500 913-7701* — 470
**Fax Area Code:* 616 ■ *TF Cust Svc:* 877-725-7500 ■ *Web:* www.dematic.com

DeMatteo Monness LLC
780 Third Ave 45th Fl — New York NY 10017 — 212-833-9900 — 690
Web: www.dmllc.com

DEMCO (Dixie Electric Membership Corp)
PO Box 15659 — Baton Rouge LA 70895 — 225-261-1221 — 245
TF: 800-262-0221 ■ *Web:* www.demco.org

DEMCO (Dethmers Manufacturing Co)
4010 320th St — Boyden IA 51234 — 712-725-2311 725-2380 — 763
TF: 800-543-3626 ■ *Web:* www.demco-products.com

Demco Inc 4810 Forest Run Rd — Madison WI 53704 — 608-241-1201 241-1799 — 560
TF Orders: 800-356-1200 ■ *Web:* www.demco.com

Demello Mcauley Mcreynolds & Holland LLP
351 G St — Eureka CA 95501 — 707-445-0871 — 2
Web: dmmh-cpa.com

Dement Construction Co PO Box 1812 — Jackson TN 38302 — 731-424-6306 424-5308 — 188-4
Web: www.dementconstruction.com

DeMesy & Company Ltd
4514 Cole Ave Ste 808 — Dallas TX 75205 — 214-855-8777 871-6777 — 791
TF: 800-635-9006 ■ *Web:* www.demesy.com

Demeter Advisory Group LLC
220 Halleck St Ste 220 — San Francisco CA 94129 — 415-632-4400 — 690
Web: www.demetergroup.net

Demetrio's 4410 S Tamiami Trail — Sarasota FL 34231 — 941-922-1585 — 671
Web: www.demetriospizzeria.com

Demeure Operating Company Ltd
187 King St S Unit 202 — Waterloo ON N2J1R1 — 519-886-8881 — 387
Web: demeure.com

Deming Malone Livesay & Ostroff
9300 Shelbyville Rd Ste 1100 — Louisville KY 40222 — 502-426-9660 — 2
Web: www.dmlo.com

Demings Val (Rep D - FL)
238 Cannon HOB — Washington DC 20515 — 202-225-2176 — 342-2
Web: demings.house.gov

Demiurge Studios 130 Prospect St — Cambridge MA 02139 — 617-354-7772 354-7277 — 177
Web: demiurgestudios.com

Demler Egg Ranch 1455 N Warren Rd — San Jacinto CA 92582 — 951-654-8166 — 10-8

Demmer Corp 1600 N Larch St Ste 1 — Lansing MI 48906 — 517-321-3600 321-7449 — 757
TF: 800-968-0950 ■ *Web:* www.demmercorp.com

Demo's 2501 N St Mary's St — San Antonio TX 78212 — 210-732-7777 — 671
Web: www.demosgreekfood.com

Democracy 21 1825 I St NW — Washington DC 20006 — 202-429-2008 — 48-7
Web: www.democracy21.org

Democrat & Chronicle
55 Exchange Blvd — Rochester NY 14614 — 585-232-7100 258-2237* — 532-2
**Fax:* News Rm ■ *TF:* 800-790-9565 ■ *Web:* www.democratandchronicle.com

Democrat Printing & Lithographing Company Inc
6401 Lindsey Rd — Little Rock AR 72206 — 501-374-0271 — 344
Web: www.democratprinting.com

Democratic & Popular Republic of Algeria, The
Embassy - Consular Section
2118 Kalorama Rd NW — Washington DC 20008 — 202-265-2800 — 257
Web: www.embassy.org

Democratic Congressional Campaign Committee (DCCC)
430 S Capitol St SE — Washington DC 20003 — 202-863-1500 — 48-7
Web: www.dccc.org

Democratic Governors Assn (DGA)
1225 Eye St NW Ste 1100 — Washington DC 20005 — 202-772-5600 772-5602 — 48-7
Web: www.democraticgovernors.org

Democratic National Committee
430 S Capitol St SE — Washington DC 20003 — 202-863-8000 — 616
Web: www.democrats.org

Democratic People's Republic of Korea
820 Second Ave 13th Fl — New York NY 10017 — 212-972-3105 — 784
Web: www.un.org

Democratic Senatorial Campaign Committee (DSCC)
120 Maryland Ave NE — Washington DC 20002 — 202-224-2447 — 48-7
Web: www.dscc.org

Democratic Socialists of America
75 Maiden Ln Ste 505 — New York NY 10038 — 212-727-8610 — 616
Web: www.dsausa.org

DeMolay International
10200 NW Ambassador Dr — Kansas City MO 64153 — 816-891-8333 891-9062 — 48-15
TF Orders: 800-336-6529 ■ *Web:* www.demolay.org

Demonstrating To Win
7150 Campus Dr Ste 330 — Colorado Springs CO 80920 — 719-594-9959 — 195

DeMontrond 888 I- 45 S — Conroe TX 77304 — 281-443-2500 — 57
TF Sales: 888-843-6583 ■ *Web:* www.demontrond.com

DeMoulas Super Markets Inc 875 E St — Tewksbury MA 01876 — 978-851-8000 — 345
Web: mydemoulas.net

DeMoulin Bros & Company Inc
1025 S Fourth St — Greenville IL 62246 — 618-664-2000 664-1712 — 155-19
TF: 800-228-8134 ■ *Web:* www.demoulin.com

Dempewolf Ford Inc 2530 Us 41 N — Henderson KY 42420 — 270-827-3566 — 57
Web: dempewolfford.com

Dempsey Corp 47 Davies Ave — Toronto ON M4M2A9 — 416-461-0844 — 791
Web: www.dempseycorporation.com

Dempsey Insurance Agency Inc
145 Railroad Ave — Norwood MA 02062 — 781-762-0042 — 390
Web: demsure.com

Dempton Groupe Conseil
1255, University St Ste 450 — Montreal QC H3B3B6 — 514-657-3517 — 631
Web: www.dempton.com

Demptos Napa Cooperage
1050 Soscol Ferry Rd — Napa CA 94558 — 707-257-2628 — 200
Web: www.demptos.fr

Demsey Manufacturing Co
78 New Wood Rd — Watertown CT 06795 — 860-274-6209 274-6209 — 482
TF: 800-533-6739 ■ *Web:* www.demseymfg.com

Den Hartog Industries Inc
4010 Hospers Dr S PO Box 425 — Hospers IA 51238 — 712-752-8432 752-8222 — 608
TF: 800-342-3408 ■ *Web:* www.denhartogindustries.com

Denali Advance Integration (DAI)
17735 NE 65th St Ste 130 — Redmond WA 98052 — 425-885-4000 — 180
TF: 877-467-8008 ■ *Web:* www.denaliai.com

Denali Borough PO Box 480 — Healy AK 99743 — 907-683-1330 683-1340 — 338
Web: www.denaliborough.govoffice.com

Denali Commission 510 L St Ste 410 — Anchorage AK 99501 — 907-271-1414 271-1415 — 340-20
TF: 888-480-4321 ■ *Web:* www.denali.gov

Denali National Park & Preserve
PO Box 9 — Denali Park AK 99755 — 907-733-9119 683-9617 — 564
Web: www.nps.gov

Denali State Park 7278 E Bogard Rd — Wasilla AK 99654 — 907-745-3975 745-0938 — 565
TF: 800-478-6196 ■ *Web:* dnr.alaska.gov/parks/units/denali1.htm

Denark Construction Inc
1635 Western Ave Ste 105 — Knoxville TN 37921 — 865-637-1925 — 186
Web: www.denark.com

Denbury Resources Inc 5320 Legacy Dr — Plano TX 75024 — 972-673-2000 673-2430 — 536
NYSE: DNR ■ *TF General:* 800-348-9030 ■ *Web:* www.denbury.com

Denco Manufacturing Inc
2300 S 179th St — New Berlin WI 53146 — 262-782-2322 — 454
Web: www.dencomfg.com

Denco Security System LLC
4605 Clear Creek Pkwy — Northport AL 35475 — 205-333-9931 — 693

DenCol 4630 Washington St — Denver CO 80216 — 303-295-1683 295-1689 — 492
Web: www.dencol.com

Den-Con Tool Co 5354 S I-35 — Oklahoma City OK 73129 — 405-670-5942 — 358
Web: www.dencon.com

Dendreon Corp 301 Second Ave — Seattle WA 98101 — 206-256-4545 256-0571 — 85
OTC: DNDNQ ■ *TF:* 877-256-4545 ■ *Web:* www.dendreon.com

Denham Corp 567 W Shaw Ave Ste C1 — Fresno CA 93704 — 559-222-5284 — 260
Web: www.denham.net

Denham Jeff (Rep R - CA)
1730 Longworth Bldg — Washington DC 20515 — 202-225-4540 225-3402 — 342-2
Web: denham.house.gov

Denham-Blythe Company Inc
100 Trade St — Lexington KY 40511 — 859-255-7405 — 256
Web: www.denhamblythe.com

Denier Electric Co Inc 10891 SR- 128 — Harrison OH 45030 — 513-738-2641 738-5855 — 245
TF: 800-676-3282 ■ *Web:* www.denier.com

Denim Group Ltd
1354 N Loop 1604 E Ste 110 — San Antonio TX 78232 — 844-572-4400 — 177
TF: 844-572-4400 ■ *Web:* www.denimgroup.com

Deniro Marketing LLC
6777 Embarcadero Dr Ste 3 — Stockton CA 95219 — 209-477-7676 — 195
Web: www.deniromarketing.com

DENIS CIMAF Inc 188 de l'Eglise — Roxton Falls QC J0H1E0 — 450-548-7007 548-7008 — 190
TF: 800-282-6917 ■ *Web:* www.deniscimaf.com

Denise Resnik And Associates Inc
717 E Maryland Ave Ste 110 — Phoenix AZ 85014 — 602-956-8834 957-3159 — 636

Denison 400 W Loop — Granville OH 43023 — 740-587-6235 587-6285 — 434-6
TF: 800-336-4766 ■ *Web:* www.denison.edu/library

Denison Industries (DI) 22 Fielder Dr — Denison TX 75020 — 903-786-6500 786-6575 — 308
Web: denisonindustries.com

Denison Parking
36 S Pennsylvania St Ste 200 — Indianapolis IN 46204 — 317-633-4003 655-3101 — 562
TF: 800-745-3000 ■ *Web:* www.denisonparking.com

Denison Public Library 300 W Gandy St — Denison TX 75020 — 903-465-1797 — 434-3
Web: www.barr.org

Denison University 100 W College St — Granville OH 43023 — 740-587-6394 587-8321* — 166
**Fax:* Admissions ■ *TF:* 877-336-8648 ■ *Web:* www.denison.edu

Denison Yacht Sales
1535 SE 17th St Ste 119 — Fort Lauderdale FL 33316 — 954-763-3971 — 393
Web: www.denisonyachtsales.com

Denmar Correctional Ctr
HC 64 PO Box 125 — Hillsboro WV 24946 — 304-653-4201 653-4855 — 213
Web: wvdoc.com

Denmar Services Inc 605 SW B Ave Ste 2 — Lawton OK 73501 — 580-355-8900 — 463
Web: www.denmarservices.com

Denmark 6285 Barfield Rd NE Ste 200 — Atlanta GA 30328 — 404-256-3681 — 7
Web: www.denmarktheagency.com

Denmark
Consulate General
875 N Michigan Ave Ste 3950 — Chicago IL 60611 — 800-345-6541 787-8744* — 257
**Fax Area Code:* 312 ■ *TF:* 800-345-6541 ■ *Web:* denmark.visahq.com
Embassy 3200 Whitehaven St NW — Washington DC 20008 — 202-234-4300 328-1470 — 257
Web: usa.um.dk

Denmark Technical College
1126 Solomon Blatt Blvd PO Box 327 — Denmark SC 29042 — 803-793-5176 793-5942* — 800
**Fax:* Admissions ■ *Web:* www.denmarktech.edu

Den-Mat Corp 2727 Skyway Dr — Santa Maria CA 93455 — 805-922-8491 922-6933 — 228
TF: 800-433-6628 ■ *Web:* www.denmat.com

Dennen Steel Corp
3033 Fruit Ridge Ave NW — Grand Rapids MI 49544 — 616-784-2000 — 480
Web: www.dennensteel.com

Denney & Company Chtd
1096 N Eastland Dr Ste 200 — Twin Falls ID 83301 — 208-733-3223 — 2
Web: denneycpa.com

Denning & Company LLC
1 California St Ste 2800 — San Francisco CA 94111 — 415-399-3939 — 401
Web: www.denningandcompany.com

Dennis Hill State Park
c/o Burr Pond State Pk 385 Burr Mtn Rd — Torrington CT 06790 — 860-482-1817 — 565
Web: www.ct.gov

Dennis K Burke Inc 284 Eastern Ave — Chelsea MA 02150 — 617-884-7800 884-7638 — 449
TF: 800-289-2875 ■ *Web:* www.burkeoil.com

Dennis Paper Co 910 Acorn Dr — Nashville TN 37210 — 615-883-9010 885-2969 — 553
TF: 800-441-5684 ■ *Web:* www.dennispaper.com

Dennis PR Group 41 Crossroads — West Hartford CT 06117 — 860-778-3826 — 636
Web: www.dennispr.com

Dennis Steel Inc 1105 Leander Dr — Leander TX 78641 — 512-259-4001 — 492
Web: www.dennissteel.com

Dennis Supply Co PO Box 3376 — Sioux City IA 51102 — 712-255-7637 255-4913 — 665
TF: 800-352-4618 ■ *Web:* www.dennissupply.com

	Phone	Fax	Class
Dennis Uniform Mfg Company Inc 135 SE Hawthorne Blvd .... Portland OR 97214 *TF:* 800-854-6951 ■ *Web:* www.dennisuniform.com	800-854-6951		155-19
Dennis, Corry, Porter & Smith LLP 14 Piedmont Ctr 3535 Piedmont Rd NE Ste 900 .... Atlanta GA 30305 *TF:* 800-735-0838 ■ *Web:* www.dcplaw.com	404-365-0102		428
Dennis-Yarmouth Regional School District 296 Stn Ave .... South Yarmouth MA 02664 *Web:* www.dy-regional.k12.ma.us	508-398-7600	398-7622	685
Denny's Corp 203 E Main St .... Spartanburg SC 29319 *NASDAQ: DENN* ■ *TF Cust Svc:* 800-733-6697 ■ *Web:* www.dennys.com	864-597-8000		670
Denny's Inc 203 E Main St .... Spartanburg SC 29319 *Web:* www.dennys.com	864-597-8000		670
Denodo Technologies 530 Lytton Ave Ste 301 .... Palo Alto CA 94301 *Web:* www.denodo.com	650-566-8833		177
Denooyer Chevrolet Inc 127 Wolf Rd .... Albany NY 12205 *Web:* denooyerchevrolet.com	518-458-7700		57
Denovus Corporation Ltd PO Box 755 .... Ennis TX 75120 **Fax Area Code:* 972 ■ *TF:* 800-541-4994 ■ *Web:* www.denovus.com	214-789-5725	875-3554*	160
Denso International America Inc 24777 Denso Dr .... Southfield MI 48033 *Web:* www.densocorp-na.com	248-350-7500		60
Denso Manufacturing Tennessee Inc 1720 Robert C Jackson Dr .... Maryville TN 37801 *Web:* www.densocorp-na-dmtn.com	865-982-7000		247
Denso North America Inc 9747 Whithorn Dr .... Houston TX 77095 *TF:* 888-821-2300 ■ *Web:* www.densona.com	281-821-3355		146
Dent Charles W (Rep R - PA) 2082 Rayburn HOB .... Washington DC 20515 *Web:* dent.house.gov	202-225-6411	226-0778	342-2
Dent Clinic 711 48th Ave SE .... Calgary AB T2G2A7 *TF:* 888-722-3368 ■ *Web:* www.dentclinic.com	403-255-3111		62-4
Dent County 400 N Main St .... Salem MO 65560 *Web:* salemmo.com	573-729-4144		338
DENT Instruments Inc 925 SW Emkay Dr .... Bend OR 97702 *Web:* www.dentinstruments.com	541-388-4774		201
Dent Wizard International 4710 Earth City Expway .... Bridgeton MO 63044 *TF:* 800-267-9369 ■ *Web:* www.dentwizard.com	314-592-1800		62-4
Dental Care Alliance LLC 6240 Lake Osprey Dr .... Sarasota FL 34240 *Web:* dentalcarealliance.net	941-955-3150	914-9684	463
Dental Economics Magazine 1421 S Sheridan Rd .... Tulsa OK 74112 *TF:* 800-331-4463 ■ *Web:* www.dentaleconomics.com	800-331-4463		457-16
Dental Health Service 3833 Atlantic Blvd .... Long Beach CA 90807 *Web:* www.dentalhealthservices.com	562-595-6000		390
Dental Lifeline Network 1800 15th St Ste 100 .... Denver CO 80202 *TF:* 888 471 6334 ■ *Web:* dentallifeline.org	303-534-5360	534-5290	48-17
Dental Systems Inc PO Box 7331 .... Baytown TX 77522 *TF:* 800-683-2501 ■ *Web:* www.iaplus.com	281-943-7000	943-8000	180
Dental Technologies Inc (DTI) 5601 Arnold Rd .... Dublin CA 94568 *TF:* 800 229 0936 ■ *Web:* www.dtidental.com	925-829-3611		415
Dental Trade Alliance (DTA) 4350 N Fairfax Dr Ste 220 .... Arlington VA 22203 *Web:* www.dentaltradealliance.org	703-379-7755	931-9429	49-4
DEN-TAL-EZ Group Inc 2 W Liberty Blvd Ste 160 .... Malvern PA 19355 *TF:* 866-383-4636 ■ *Web:* dentalez.com	610-725-8004	725-9898	228
DEN-TAL-EZ Inc Equipment Div 2500 Hwy 31 S .... Bay Minette AL 36507 *TF:* 800-383-4636 ■ *Web:* dentalez.com	251-937-6781	937-0461	228
Dent-A-Med Inc 203 E Emma Ave .... Springdale AR 72764	479-750-6700		217
DENTCA Inc 357 Van Ness Way Ste 250 .... Torrance CA 90501 *Web:* www.dentca.com	424-558-8726	558-8738	228
DenTek Oral Care Inc 307 Excellence Way .... Maryville TN 37801 *TF:* 800-433-6835 ■ *Web:* www.dentek.com	800-433-6835		228
Dentists Insurance Co, The 1201 K St 17th Fl .... Sacramento CA 95814 **Fax Area Code:* 877 ■ *TF:* 800-733-0634 ■ *Web:* www.tdicinsurance.com	800-733-0633	498-6105*	391-5
Denton Chamber of Commerce 414 W Pkwy St .... Denton TX 76201 *Web:* www.denton-chamber.org	940-382-9693	382-0040	139
Denton County 1450 E McKinney .... Denton TX 76209 *TF:* 800-388-8477 ■ *Web:* dentoncounty.com	940-349-2012	349-2019	338
Denton Hill State Park c/o Lyman Run 454 Lyman Run Rd .... Galeton PA 16922 *Web:* www.dcnr.state.pa.us	814-435-2115		565
Denton Navarro Rocha & Bernal 2517 N Main Ave .... San Antonio TX 78212 *Web:* www.rampage-rgv.com	210-227-3243		445
Denton Plastics Inc 18811 NE San Rafael St .... Portland OR 97230 *Web:* www.denplas.com	503-257-9945		596
Denton Record-Chronicle 314 E Hickory St .... Denton TX 76201 *TF:* 800-275-1722 ■ *Web:* www.dentonrc.com	940-387-3811	566-6888	532-2
Dentsply International Inc Tulsa Dental Div 5100 E Skelly Dr Ste 300 .... Tulsa OK 74135 *TF:* 800-662-1202 ■ *Web:* www.dentsply.com	918-493-6598	493-6599	228
Dentsply Sirona 221 W Philadelphia St PO Box 872 .... York PA 17405 *NASDAQ: XRAY* ■ *TF:* 800-877-0020 ■ *Web:* www.dentsply.com	717-845-7511	849-4762	228
Dentsply Sirona 161 Vinyl Ct .... Woodbridge ON L4L4A3 *Web:* www.dentsply.com	905-851-6060		475
Dentsu Sports America Inc 32 Ave of the Americas 24th Fl .... New York NY 10013 *Web:* dentsusports.com	212-397-3333		4
Dentt Inc 10450 S State St .... Sandy UT 84070 *Web:* hammondtoy.com	801-561-3821		762
DeNuke Services Inc 702 S Illinois Ave Ste B-203 .... Oak Ridge TN 37830 *Web:* www.denuke.com	865-483-8620		393

	Phone	Fax	Class
Denver Academy of Court Reporting 9051 Harlan St Ste 20 .... Westminster CO 80031 *TF:* 866-712-2425 ■ *Web:* www.princeinstitute.edu	303-427-5292	427-5383	800
Denver Art Museum 100 W 14th Ave Pkwy .... Denver CO 80204 *TF:* 800-276-9253 ■ *Web:* www.denverartmuseum.org	720-865-5000	913-0001	520
Denver Athletic Club 1325 Glenarm Pl .... Denver CO 80204 *Web:* www.denverathleticclub.cc	303-534-1211		354
Denver Botanic Gardens 1005 York St .... Denver CO 80206 *Web:* www.botanicgardens.org	720-865-3500		97
Denver Broncos 13655 Broncos Pkwy .... Englewood CO 80112 *Web:* www.denverbroncos.com	303-649-9000		715-3
Denver Business Journal 1700 Broadway Ste 515 .... Denver CO 80290 *Web:* www.bizjournals.com/denver	303-837-3500		457-5
Denver City & County 201 W Colfax Ave 1st Fl .... Denver CO 80202 *Web:* www.denvergov.org	720-865-8400		338
Denver Coliseum 4600 Humboldt St .... Denver CO 80216 *TF:* 800-786-6210 ■ *Web:* www.denvercoliseum.com	720-865-2475		720
Denver Commercial Builders Inc (DCB) 909 E 62nd Ave .... Denver CO 80216 *Web:* www.dcb1.com	303-287-5525	287-3697	186
Denver Ctr for the Performing Arts 1101 13th St .... Denver CO 80204 *TF:* 800-641-1222 ■ *Web:* www.denvercenter.org	303-893-4000	595-9634	572
Denver Cyber Security 8100 E Union Ave Ste 2008 .... Denver CO 80237 *Web:* www.denvercybersecurity.com	303-997-5506		196
Denver Dermatology Consultants Pc 1551 Milky Way .... Thornton CO 80260 *Web:* www.denverderm.com	303-426-4525		77
Denver Film Society 1510 York 3rd Fl .... Denver CO 80206 *Web:* www.denverfilm.org	303-595-3456		282
Denver Fire Dept Federal Credit Union (DFDFCU) 2201 Federal Blvd .... Denver CO 80211 *TF:* 866-880-7770 ■ *Web:* www.dfdfcu.com	303-228-5300	228-5333	219
Denver Firefighters Museum 1326 Tremont Pl .... Denver CO 80204 *Web:* www.denverfirefightersmuseum.org	303-892-1436	892-1436	520
Denver Health Medical Ctr (DHMC) 777 Bannock St .... Denver CO 80204 *TF:* 800-222-1222 ■ *Web:* www.denverhealth.org	303-436-6000		374-3
Denver Hospice, The 501 S Cherry St Ste 700 .... Denver CO 80246 *Web:* www.thedenverhospice.org	303-321-2828	321-7171	371
Denver International Airport 8500 Pena Blvd .... Denver CO 80249 *TF:* 800-247-2336 ■ *Web:* www.flydenver.com	303-342-2000	342-2215	27
Denver Investments Republic Plaza 370 17th St Ste 5000 .... Denver CO 80202 *Web:* www.denvest.com	303-312-5000	312-4900	401
Denver Metro Chamber of Commerce 1445 Market St .... Denver CO 80202 *Web:* www.denverchamber.org	303 534 8500	534 3200	139
Denver Metro Convention & Visitors Bureau 1555 California St Ste 300 .... Denver CO 80202 *TF:* 800 480 2010 ■ *Web:* www.denver.org	303-892-1112		206
Denver Museum of Miniatures Dolls & Toys 1880 Gaylord St .... Denver CO 80206 *Web:* dmmdt.org	303-322-1053		520
Denver Museum of Nature & Science 2001 Colorado Blvd .... Denver CO 80205 *TF:* 800-925-3721 ■ *Web:* www.dmns.org	303-370-6000	331-6492	520
Denver Newspaper Agency 101 W Colfax Ave .... Denver CO 80202 *TF:* 800-336-7678 ■ *Web:* www.denverpost.com	303-954-1010	954-1010	637-8
Denver Nuggets 1000 Chopper Cir .... Denver CO 80204 *TF:* 800-745-3000 ■ *Web:* www.nba.com	303-405-1100	405-1315	714-1
Denver Performing Arts Complex 1400 Curtis St .... Denver CO 80204 *TF:* 800-745-3000 ■ *Web:* www.artscomplex.com	720-865-4220	865-4247	572
Denver Public Library 10 W 14th Ave Pkwy .... Denver CO 80204 *TF:* 800-842-7223 ■ *Web:* www.denverlibrary.org	720-865-1111		434-3
Denver Public Schools 900 Grant St .... Denver CO 80203 *TF:* 866-726-0033 ■ *Web:* dpsk12.org	720-423-3200		685
Denver Rescue Mission 6100 Smith Rd .... Denver CO 80216 *Web:* www.denverrescuemission.org	303-297-1815	295-1566	352
Denver Seminary 6399 S Santa Fe Dr .... Littleton CO 80120 *TF:* 800-922-3040 ■ *Web:* www.denverseminary.edu	303-761-2482	761-8060	167-3
Denver Veterans Affairs Medical Ctr 1055 Clermont St .... Denver CO 80220 **Fax:* Mail Rm ■ *TF:* 888-336-8262 ■ *Web:* Www.denver.va.gov	303-399-8020	393-2861*	374-8
Denver Wholesale Florists Co 4800 Dahlia St .... Denver CO 80216 *TF:* 800-829-8280 ■ *Web:* www.dwfwholesale.com	303-399-0970	376-3123	293
Denver Wire Rope & Supply Inc 4100 Dahlia St .... Denver CO 80216 *TF:* 800-873-3697 ■ *Web:* denverwirerope.com	303-377-5166		351
Denver Women's Correctional Facility 3600 Havana St .... Denver CO 80239	303-371-4804		213
Denver Zoo 2300 Steele St .... Denver CO 80205 *Web:* www.denverzoo.org	720-337-1400		823
DePalma Hotel Corp 700 Highlander Blvd Ste 400 .... Arlington TX 76015 *TF:* 800-980-6467 ■ *Web:* www.depalmahotels.com	817-557-1811	557-4333	379
DePalma's Italian Cafe 2300 University Blvd .... Tuscaloosa AL 35401 *Web:* depalmasdowntown.com	205-759-1879		671
Department of Agriculture (USDA) 1400 Independence Ave SW .... Washington DC 20250 *TF:* 844-433-2774 ■ *Web:* www.usda.gov	202-720-3631	720-2166	340-1
Department of Anthropology 211 Lafferty Hall .... Lexington KY 40506 *Web:* anthropology.as.uky.edu	859-257-2710	323-1968	520
Department of Commerce 1401 Constitution Ave NW Hoover Bldg .... Washington DC 20230 *TF:* 800-375-5283 ■ *Web:* www.commerce.gov	202-482-4883	482-5168	340-2

	City	State	Zip	Phone	Fax	Class
Department of Defense (DOD)						
The Pentagon	Washington	DC	20301	703-545-6700		340-3
Web: www.defense.gov						
Department of Education						
400 Maryland Ave SW	Washington	DC	20202	202-401-2000	401-0689	340-8
TF: 800-872-5327 ■ *Web:* www.ed.gov						
Inspector General's Fraud & Abuse Hotline						
400 Maryland Ave SW	Washington	DC	20202	800-647-8733		340-8
TF: 800-647-8733 ■ *Web:* www.ed.gov						
Office of Vocational & Adult Education						
550 12th St SW 11th Fl	Washington	DC	20202	202-245-7700		340-8
TF: 800-872-5327						
Region 2						
Financial Sq 32 Old Slip 25th Fl	New York	NY	10005	646-428-3906	428-3904	340-8
Web: www.ed.gov						
Region 3 100 Penn Sq E Ste 505	Philadelphia	PA	19107	215-656-6010	656-6020	340-8
Web: www.ed.gov						
Region 4						
Federal Ctr 61 Forsyth St SW Ste 19T40	Atlanta	GA	30303	404-974-9450	974-9459	340-8
Web: www.ed.gov						
Region 5 500 W Madison St Ste 1427	Chicago	IL	60661	312-730-1700	730-1704	340-8
Web: www.ed.gov						
Region 7 8930 Ward Pkwy Ste 2043	Kansas City	MO	64114	816-268-0400	268-0407	340-8
TF: 800-437-0833 ■ *Web:* www.ed.gov						
Region 8						
Cesar E Chavez Memorial Bldg						
1244 Speer Blvd Ste 310	Denver	CO	80204	303-844-3544	844-2524	340-8
Web: www.ed.gov						
Region 10						
400 Maryland Ave SW Jackson Federal Bldg	Washington	DC	20202	202-401-2000	872-5327*	340-8
**Fax Area Code: 800* ■ *Web:* www.ed.gov						
Office of Electricity Delivery & Energy Reliabilition						
1000 Independence Ave SW	Washington	DC	20585	202-586-1411		340-9
Web: www.energy.gov/oe						
Office of Fossil Energy						
1000 Independence Ave SW	Washington	DC	20585	202-586-6660	586-7847	340-9
Web: energy.gov						
Office of Legacy Management						
1000 Independence Ave SW						
Office of Stakeholder Relations LM-5	Washington	DC	20585	202-586-3559	586-1540	340-9
Web: energy.gov						
Department of Health & Human Services (HHS)						
330 Independence Ave SW	Washington	DC	20201	202-619-0150		340-10
TF: 877-696-6775 ■ *Web:* www.hhs.gov						
Region 2 26 Federal Plaza Rm 3835	New York	NY	10278	212-264-4600	264-3620	340-10
Web: hhs.gov						
Region 4						
1301 61 Forsyth St SW Ste 5B95	Atlanta	GA	30303	404-562-7889	562-7899	340-10
Web: www.hhs.gov						
Region 5 233 N Michigan Ave Ste 1300	Chicago	IL	60601	312-353-1385	353-0718	340-10
Web: www.hhs.gov						
Region 6 1301 Young St Ste 1124	Dallas	TX	75202	214-767-3879	767-3209	340-10
TF: 800-746-1554 ■ *Web:* www.hhs.gov						
Region 7 601 E 12th St	Kansas City	MO	64106	816-426-2821	426-2178	340-10
TF: 800-447-8477 ■ *Web:* hhs.gov						
Department of Health & Human Services Regional Offices						
Region 10 701 Fifth Ave Ste 1600	Seattle	WA	98121	206-615-2010	615-2087	340-10
TF: 800-422-6237 ■ *Web:* hhs.gov						
Department of Homeland Security (DHS)						
245 Murray Dr SW Bldg 410	Washington	DC	20528	202-282-8000	235-0443*	340-11
**Fax Area Code: 703* ■ *Web:* www.dhs.gov						
Ready Campaign 500 C St SW	Washington	DC	20472	800-621-3362	621-3362	340-11
TF: 800-621-3362 ■ *Web:* www.ready.gov						
Department of Housing & Urban Development (HUD)						
451 Seventh St SW	Washington	DC	20410	202-708-0685	619-8153	340-12
TF: 800-569-4287 ■ *Web:* www.hud.gov						
Public Affairs Office						
451 Seventh St SW	Washington	DC	20410	202-708-0980		340-12
TF: 800-333-4636 ■ *Web:* www.hud.gov						
Department of Housing & Urban Development Regional Offices						
Boston Regional Office						
Thomas P O'Neill Jr Federal Bldg						
10 Causeway St 3rd Fl	Boston	MA	02222	617-994-8200	565-6558	340-12
TF: 800-225-5342 ■ *Web:* portal.hud.gov						
Chicago Regional Office						
Ralph Metcalfe Federal Bldg						
77 W Jackson Blvd	Chicago	IL	60604	312-353-6236	353-5417	340-12
Web: portal.hud.gov						
Mid-Atlantic Region						
100 Penn Sq E	Philadelphia	PA	19107	215-656-0500	656-3445	340-12
TF: 800-225-5342 ■ *Web:* www.hud.gov						
New York City Regional Office						
26 Federal Plaza Ste 3541	New York	NY	10278	212-264-8000	264-3068	340-12
TF: 800-496-4294 ■ *Web:* portal.hud.gov						
Pacific/Hawaii Region						
600 Harrison St 3rd Fl	San Francisco	CA	94107	415-489-6524	436-8412	340-12
TF: 800-347-3739 ■ *Web:* portal.hud.gov						
Rocky Mountain Region						
1670 Broadway 25th Fl	Denver	CO	80202	303-672-5440	672-5004	340-12
TF: 800-955-2232 ■ *Web:* portal.hud.gov						
Seattle HUD Office						
909 First Ave Ste 200	Seattle	WA	98104	509-368-3200		340-12
Web: portal.hud.gov						
Southeast/Caribbean Region						
5 Points Plaza Bldg 40 Marietta St	Atlanta	GA	30303	404-331-5136	730-2392	340-12
Web: www.hud.gov						
Southwest Region						
801 N Cherry St Unit 45 Ste 2500	Fort Worth	TX	76102	817-978-5965	978-5569	340-12
TF: 800-877-8339 ■ *Web:* www.hud.gov						
Department of Justice (DOJ)						
950 Pennsylvania Ave NW	Washington	DC	20530	202-514-2007	514-5331	340-14
TF: 800-424-2980 ■ *Web:* www.justice.gov						
Antitrust Div						
950 Pennsylvania Ave NW	Washington	DC	20530	202-514-2401	616-2645	340-14
Web: www.justice.gov						
Civil Div 950 Pennsylvania Ave NW	Washington	DC	20530	202-514-3301	514-8071	340-14
Web: www.justice.gov						

	City	State	Zip	Phone	Fax	Class
Civil Rights Div						
950 Pennsylvania Ave NW	Washington	DC	20530	202-514-4609		340-14
Web: www.justice.gov						
Community Relations Service						
600 E St NW	Washington	DC	20530	202-305-2935	305-3009	340-14
Web: www.justice.gov						
Criminal Div 601 D St NW	Washington	DC	20530	202-514-0296		340-14
Web: www.justice.gov						
Environment & Natural Resources Div						
950 Pennsylvania Ave NW	Washington	DC	20530	202-514-2701	514-0557	340-14
Web: www.justice.gov						
National Security Div						
950 Pennsylvania Ave NW	Washington	DC	20530	202-514-1057		340-14
Web: www.justice.gov						
Office of Information & Privacy						
1425 New York Ave NW Ste 11050	Washington	DC	20530	202-514-3642	514-1009	340-14
Web: www.justice.gov						
Public Affairs Office						
950 Pennsylvania Ave NW	Washington	DC	20530	202-514-2000		340-14
Web: www.justice.gov						
Tax Div 950 Pennsylvania Ave NW	Washington	DC	20530	202-514-2901	514-5479	340-14
Web: www.justice.gov						
Department of Justice Antitrust Div Regional Office						
Atlanta Field Office						
Federal Bldg 75 Ted Turner Dr. SW Ste 600	Atlanta	GA	30303	404-331-7100	331-7110	340-14
Web: www.justice.gov/atr						
Chicago Field Office						
209 S LaSalle St Ste 600	Chicago	IL	60604	202-353-1555	353-1046*	340-14
**Fax Area Code: 312* ■ *Web:* www.justice.gov						
Cleveland Field Office						
55 Erieview Plaza Ste 700	Cleveland	OH	44114	216-522-4070	522-8332	340-14
Web: www.justice.gov						
Department of Justice Antitrust Div Regional Office						
Dallas Field Office						
1601 Elm St Ste 4950	Dallas	TX	75201	214-880-9401	353-8856*	340-14
**Fax Area Code: 202* ■ *Web:* www.justice.gov						
New York Field Office						
26 Federal Plaza Rm 3630	New York	NY	10278	202-514-2000	264-0678*	340-14
**Fax Area Code: 212* ■ *Web:* www.justice.gov/atr						
Philadelphia Field Office						
7th & Walnut St Ste 650	Philadelphia	PA	19106	215-597-7405	597-8838	340-14
Web: www.justice.gov						
San Francisco Field Office						
450 Golden Gate Ave Rm 10-0101						
PO Box 36046	San Francisco	CA	94102	415-436-6660	436-6687	340-14
Web: www.justice.gov/atr						
Department of Labor (DOL)						
200 Constitution Ave NW	Washington	DC	20210	202-693-4650		340-15
TF: 866-487-2365 ■ *Web:* www.dol.gov						
Job Corps						
200 Constitution Ave NW Ste N4463	Washington	DC	20210	202-693-3000	693-2767	340-15
TF: 800-733-5627 ■ *Web:* www.jobcorps.gov						
Office of Administrative Law Judges						
200 Constitution Ave NW Rm S-5220	Washington	DC	20210	202-693-6200	693-6220	340-15
TF: 866-487-2365 ■ *Web:* www.oalj.dol.gov						
Public Affairs Office						
200 Constitution Ave NW	Washington	DC	20210	202-693-4650	693-5057	340-15
TF: 866-487-2365 ■ *Web:* www.dol.gov						
Department of Labor Regional Offices						
Region 1 - Boston						
JFK Federal Bldg Ste 525	Boston	MA	02203	617-565-2072		340-15
TF: 800-347-8029 ■ *Web:* www.dol.gov						
Region 2 - New York						
201 Varick St Rm 983	New York	NY	10014	646-264-3650		340-15
Web: www.dol.gov						
Region 3 - Philadelphia						
170 S Independence Mall W Ste 631E West	Philadelphia	PA	19106	215-861-4860	861-4867	340-15
Web: www.dol.gov						
Region 3 Atlanta						
400 W Bay St Rm 63A	Jacksonville	FL	32202	904-351-0551	351-0560	340-15
Web: www.dol.gov						
Region 5 - Chicago 230 S Dearborn St	Chicago	IL	60604	312-596-5400	596-5401	340-15
TF: 800-285-9675 ■ *Web:* www.doleta.gov						
Region 6 Dallas						
Federal Bldg 525 S Griffin St Rm 407	Dallas	TX	75202	972-850-2409	850-2401	340-15
Web: www.dol.gov/owcp/contacts/dallas/arf.htm						
Region 8 - Denver						
1999 Broadway Ste 1620	Denver	CO	80202	303-844-1286	844-1283	340-15
TF: 800-827-5335 ■ *Web:* www.dol.gov						
Region 10-Seattle						
300 Fifth Ave Ste 1280	Seattle	WA	98104	206-757-6700	757-6705	340-15
Web: www.osha.gov						
Department of Natural Resources						
550 W Seventh Ave Ste 1260	Anchorage	AK	99501	907-269-8400		565
Web: dnr.alaska.gov/parks/units/haines.htm						
Department of State 2201 C St NW	Washington	DC	20520	202-647-4000	647-3344	340-16
TF: 800-877-8339 ■ *Web:* www.state.gov						
Department of the Air Force						
1670 Air Force Pentagon	Washington	DC	20330	703-695-9664	693-9601	340-4
Web: www.af.mil						
North American Aerospace Defense Command						
250 Vandenberg St Ste B-016	Peterson AFB	CO	80914	719-554-6889	554-3165	340-4
Web: www.norad.mil						
Department of the Army						
1500 Army Pentagon	Washington	DC	20310	703-697-5131		340-5
Web: www.army.mil						
US Army Center of Military History						
103 Third Ave SW Fort McNair Bldg 35	Washington	DC	20319	202-685-2727	512-2104	340-5
Web: www.history.army.mil						
Department of the Interior (DOI)						
1849 C St NW	Washington	DC	20240	202-208-3100		340-13
TF: 800-200-4853 ■ *Web:* www.doi.gov						
Department of the Navy						
1000 Navy Pentagon	Washington	DC	20350	703-695-8400		340-6
Web: www.navy.mil						
Bureau of Medicine and Surgery						
2300 E St NW	Washington	DC	20372	301-402-8878		340-6
Web: www.nlm.nih.gov						

Phone | Fax | Class

Judge Advocate General's Corps
1322 Patterson Ave Ste 3000 Washington Navy Yard DC 20374 202-685-5275 340-6
Web: www.jag.navy.mil
Office of Naval Intelligence
4251 Suitland Rd 4251 Suitland Rd. Washington DC 20395 301-669-3001 340-6
Web: www.oni.navy.mil
Office of Naval Research
1 Liberty Ctr 875 N Randolph St Ste 1425 Arlington VA 22203 703-696-5031 696-5940 340-6
Web: www.onr.navy.mil

Department of the Treasury
1500 Pennsylvania Ave NW Washington DC 20220 202-622-2000 622-6415 340-18
TF: 800-359-3898 ■ *Web:* www.treasury.gov

Department of Transportation (DOT)
1200 New Jersey Ave SE Washington DC 20590 202-366-4000 340-17
TF: 800-877-8339 ■ *Web:* www.transportation.gov

Department of Veterans Affairs (VA)
810 Vermont Ave NW Washington DC 20420 202-461-7600 340-19
TF Cust Svc: 800-827-1000 ■ *Web:* www.va.gov
National Center for Post-Traumatic Stress Disorder
215 N Main St White River Junction VT 05009 802-296-5132 296-5135 668
Web: www.ptsd.va.gov
Public & Intergovernmental Affairs Office
810 Vermont Ave NW Washington DC 20420 800-273-8255 340-19
TF: 800-273-8255 ■ *Web:* www1.va.gov/opa

Depaul Industries
4950 NE Martin Luther King Junior Blvd Portland OR 97211 503-281-1289 260
TF: 800-874-7917 ■ *Web:* www.depaulindustries.com

DePaul University
1 E Jackson Blvd Ste 9100 Chicago IL 60614 312-362-8300 362-5749 166
Web: www.depaul.edu

DePaul University College of Law
25 E Jackson Blvd Chicago IL 60604 312-362-8701 362-5280* 167-1
**Fax:* Admissions ■ *TF:* 800-445-8667 ■ *Web:* law.depaul.edu

DePaul University Library
2350 N Konmoro Avo Chicago IL 60614 312-362-8433 434-6
Web: library.depaul.edu/pages/default.aspx

DePauw University
101 E Seminary St Greencastle IN 46135 765-658-4006 658-4007* 166
**Fax:* Admissions ■ *TF:* 800-447-2495 ■ *Web:* www.depauw.edu

DePauw University West Library
11 E Larabee St Greencastle IN 46135 765-658-4420 658-4445 434-6
TF: 800-447-2495 ■ *Web:* depauw.edu/libraries

DePelchin Children's Ctr
4950 Memorial Dr Houston TX 77007 713-730-2335 802-3801 48-6
TF: 888-730-2335 ■ *Web:* www.depelchin.org

Dependable Clrs & Shirt Ldry
101 Adams St Denver CO 80206 303-322-8822 426
Web: www.dependablecleaners.com

Dependable Component Supply Corp
1003 E Newport Ctr Dr Deerfield Beach FL 33442 954-283-5800 283-5802 246
TF: 800-336-7100

Dependable Highway Express Inc
2440 S 48th Ave Phoenix AZ 85043 602-278-4401 278-4473 449
TF: 800-472-2037 ■ *Web:* www.godependable.com

Dependable Nurses of Phoenix Inc
1120 S Swan Rd Tucson AZ 85711 520-721-3822 363
Web: www.dependablehealth.com

Depersico Creative Group
1 Raymond Dr Havertown PA 19083 610-789-4400 344
TF: 800-279-3358 ■ *Web:* www.depersico.com

Depobook Reporting Services
1600 G St Ste 101 Modesto CA 95354 209-544-6466 544-6566 445
TF: 800-830-8885 ■ *Web:* www.depobook.com

Depoe Bay Whale Ctr
Oregon Parks and Recreation Department
119 US-101 Depoe Bay OR 97341 541 765 3304 565
TF: 800-551-6949 ■ *Web:* www.oregonstateparks.org

DepoMed Inc 7999 Gateway Blvd Ste 300 Newark CA 94560 510-744-8000 85
NASDAQ: DEPO ■ *Web:* depomed.com

Deposition Sciences Inc
3300 Coffey Ln Santa Rosa CA 95403 707-573-6700 573-6748 481
TF: 866-433-7724 ■ *Web:* www.depsci.com

Depository Trust Co 55 Water St New York NY 10041 212-855-1000 401
Web: www.dtcc.com

Depot Law Office Plc
222 W Apple St Ste 248 Hastings MI 49058 269-945-9557 445
Web: www.depotlawoffice.com

Depot, The
Saint Louis County Heritage & Arts Ctr
506 W Michigan St Duluth MN 55802 218-727-8025 520
Web: www.duluthdepot.org

Depotstar Inc 6180 140th Ave NW Ramsey MN 55303 763-506-9990 261
Web: www.depotstar.com

Depressed Anonymous PO Box 17414 Louisville KY 40217 502-569-1989 48-21
Web: www.depressedanon.com

Depression & Bipolar Support Alliance (DBSA)
730 N Franklin St Ste 501 Chicago IL 60610 312-642-0049 642-7243 48-17
TF: 800-826-3632 ■ *Web:* www.dbsalliance.org

Depression & Related Affective Disorders Assn (DRADA)
8201 Greensboro Dr Ste 300 McLean VA 22102 703-610-9026 49-15

Deprince Race & Zollo Inc
250 Park Ave S Ste 250 Ste 250 Winter Park FL 32789 407-420-9903 841-8778 194
Web: www.drz-inc.com

DEPTCOR 163 N Olden Ave Trenton NJ 08625 800-321-6524 633-2495* 630
**Fax Area Code:* 609 ■ *TF:* 800-321-6524 ■ *Web:* www.state.nj.us/deptcor

DeRaffele Mfg Company Inc
2525 Palmer Ave New Rochelle NY 10801 914-636-6850 105

Derby Academy 56 Burditt Ave Hingham MA 02043 781-749-0746 148
Web: derbyacademy.org

Derby Cellular Products Inc
150 Roosevelt Dr Derby CT 06418 203-735-4661 677

Derby City Antique Mall
3819 Bardstown Rd Louisville KY 40218 502-459-5151 460
Web: www.derbycityantiquemall.com

Derby Industries LLC
4451 Robards Ln Louisville KY 40218 502-451-7373 451-6330 803-1
TF: 800-569-4812 ■ *Web:* www.derbyllc.com

Derco Aerospace Inc
8000 W Tower Ave Milwaukee WI 53223 414-355-3066 770
Web: www.dercoaerospace.com

Derco Foods 2670 W Shaw Ln Fresno CA 93711 559-435-2664 435-8520 296-18
Web: www.dercofoods.com

Derecktor Shipyards Inc
311 E Boston Post Rd Mamaroneck NY 10543 914-698-5020 698
Web: www.derecktor.com

Derector Robert Assoc
19 W 44th St Fl 10 New York NY 10036 212-764-7272 256
Web: www.derector.com

Derek Engineering Inc
2800 Constant Comment Pl Louisville KY 40299 502-266-0041 261

Derek Witham Insurance Agency
685 Salem St Malden MA 02148 781-322-2886 390

Derfner & Altman 575 King St Ste B Charleston SC 29403 843-723-9804 445
Web: www.dawlegal.com

Derico of East Amherst Corp
18 Limestone Dr Williamsville NY 14221 716-810-0400 345

Dering Corp, The 1702 Hempstead Rd Lancaster PA 17601 717-394-4200 240
Web: www.echodatamedia.com

Deringer-Ney Inc
616 Atrium Dr Ste 100 Vernon Hills IL 60061 847-566-4100 367-6029 485
Web: www.deringerney.com

Derma Sciences Inc
214 Carnegie Ctr Ste 100 Princeton NJ 08540 609-514-4744 514-8554 475
TF: 800-825-4325 ■ *Web:* www.dermasciences.com

Dermatology Assoc of Atlanta
5555 Pchtrdnwyd Ste 190 Atlanta GA 30324 404-256-4457 374-7
TF: 800-233-0706 ■ *Web:* www.dermatlanta.com

Dermody, Burke & Brown CPAs LLC
443 N Franklin St Syracuse NY 13204 315-471-9171 2
Web: www.dbbllc.com

Dero Bike Racks Inc
504 Malcolm Ave SE Ste 100 Minneapolis MN 55414 612-359-0689 61
TF: 800-337-0729 ■ *Web:* www.dero.com

DeRoyal Industries Inc 200 DeBusk Ln Powell TN 37849 865-938-7828 477
TF: 800-251-9864 ■ *Web:* www.deroyal.com

DeRoyal Textiles 141 E York St Camden SC 29020 803-432-2403 424-5112 745-1
TF: 800-845-1062 ■ *Web:* www.deroyal.com

Derr & Gruenewald Construction Co (DGCC)
11100 E 108th Ave Brighton CO 80601 303-287-3456 190
Web: www.dgccsteel.com

Derr Flooring Company Inc
525 Davisville Rd PO Box 912 Willow Grove PA 19090 215-657-6300 361
TF: 800-523-3457 ■ *Web:* www.derrflooring.com

Derrel's Mini Storage 3502 W San Jose Fresno CA 93711 559-277-1452 224-1884 803-3
Web: www.derrels.com

Derrick Equipment Co
15630 Export Plaza Dr Houston TX 77032 281-590-3003 539
Web: derrick.com

Derrick Publishing Co
1510 W First St Oil City PA 16301 814-676-7444 677-8351 637-8
TF: 800-352-1002 ■ *Web:* www.thederrick.com

Derry Public Library 64 E Broadway Derry NH 03038 603-432-6140 432-6128 434-3
Web: derrypl.org

Derryfield Restaurant, The
625 Mammoth Rd Manchester NH 03104 603-623-2880 671
Web: www.thederryfield.com

Derse Exhibits Inc 3800 W Canal St Milwaukee WI 53208 414-257-2000 232
Web: www.derse.com

Der-Tex Corp 1 Lehner Rd Saco ME 04072 800-669-0364 745-2
TF: 800-669-0364 ■ *Web:* www.dertexcorp.com

DES (Directed Energy Solutions)
890 Elkton Dr Ste 101 Colorado Springs CO 80907 719-593-7848 593-7846 544

Des Moines Area Community College
Ankeny 2006 S Ankeny Blvd Ankeny IA 50021 515-964-6200 964-6391* 162
**Fax:* Admissions ■ *TF:* 800-362-2127 ■ *Web:* www.dmacc.edu/Pages/welcome.aspx
Boone 1125 Hancock Dr Boone IA 50036 515-432-7203 433-5033* 162
**Fax:* Admissions ■ *TF:* 800-362-2127 ■ *Web:* www.dmacc.edu/boone/Pages/welcome.aspx
Carroll 906 N Grant Rd Carroll IA 51401 712-792-1755 792-6358 162
TF: 800-622-3334 ■ *Web:* www.dmacc.edu/carroll/Pages/welcome.aspx
Urban/Des Moines 1100 Seventh St Des Moines IA 50314 515-244-4226 248-7253 162
TF: 800-622-3334 ■ *Web:* www.dmacc.edu/Pages/welcome.aspx

Des Moines Art Ctr 4700 Grand Ave Des Moines IA 50312 515-277-4405 271-0357 520
Web: www.desmoinesartcenter.org

Des Moines Botanical Ctr
909 Robert D Ray Dr Des Moines IA 50309 515-323-6290 97
Web: www.dmbotanicalgarden.com

Des Moines Business Record
100 Fourth St Des Moines IA 50309 515-288-3336 457-5
TF: 800-673-4763 ■ *Web:* www.businessrecord.com

Des Moines City Hall
400 Robert D Ray Dr Des Moines IA 50309 515-283-4500 237-1645 337
Web: www.dmgov.org

Des Moines County 513 N Main St Burlington IA 52601 319-753-8232 338
Web: www.dmcounty.com

Des Moines Golf & Country Club Educational Corp
1600 Jordan Creek Pkwy West Des Moines IA 50266 515-440-7500 226
TF: 800-879-1917 ■ *Web:* www.dmgcc.org

Des Moines Independent School District
901 Walnut St Des Moines IA 50309 515-242-7911 242-7579 685
TF: 800-452-1111 ■ *Web:* www.dmschools.org

Des Moines International Airport
5800 Fleur Dr Des Moines IA 50321 515-256-5050 256-5025 27
TF: 877-686-0029 ■ *Web:* www.dsmairport.com

Des Moines Metro Opera
106 W Boston Ave Indianola IA 50125 515-961-6221 961-6221 573-2
TF: 800-686-1141 ■ *Web:* www.desmoinesmetroopera.org

Des Moines Public Library
1000 Grand Ave Des Moines IA 50309 515-283-4152 237-1654 434-3
Web: dmpl.org

Des Moines Register 715 Locust St Des Moines IA 50309 515-284-8000 532-2
TF: 800-247-5346 ■ *Web:* www.desmoinesregister.com

Des Moines Symphony 221 Walnut St Des Moines IA 50309 515-280-4000 280-4005 573-3
Web: www.dmsymphony.org

Des Moines Unviersity
3200 Grand Ave Des Moines IA 50312 515-271-1400 800
Web: www.dmu.edu

Phone | Fax | Class

Des Plaines Chamber of Commerce & Industry
1401 E Oakton St . . . . . Des Plaines IL 60018 847-824-4200 824-7932 139
TF: 800-933-2412 ■ *Web:* www.dpchamber.com

Des Plaines Journal
622 Graceland Ave . . . . . Des Plaines IL 60016 847-299-5511 298-8549 532-4
TF: 800-719-4881 ■ *Web:* www.journal-topics.com

Des Plaines Park District
2222 Birch St . . . . . Des Plaines IL 60018 847-391-5700 31
Web: dpparks.org

Des Plaines Public Library
1501 Ellinwood Ave . . . . . Des Plaines IL 60016 847-827-5551 827-7974 434-3
TF: 800-829-1040 ■ *Web:* www.dppl.org

Des Plaines State Fish & Wildlife Area
24621 N River Rd . . . . . Wilmington IL 60481 815-423-5326 565
Web: www.dnr.illinois.gov/parks/pages/desplaines.aspx

Desai Nasr Consulting Engineers Inc
6765 Daly Rd . . . . . West Bloomfield MI 48322 248-932-2010 261
Web: www.desainasr.com

Desai Systems Inc
199 Oakwood Ave . . . . . West Hartford CT 06119 860-233-0011 463
Web: www.desai.com

DeSales University 2755 Stn Ave . . . . . Center Valley PA 18034 610-282-1100 282-0131 166
Web: www.desales.edu

Desane & Associates
310 Prospect Ave Apt 134 . . . . . Hackensack NJ 07601 201-342-0909 366
Web: www.desaneinc.com

DeSantis Breindel Inc 30 W 21 St . . . . . New York NY 10010 212-994-7680 7
TF: 800-727-6397 ■ *Web:* www.desantisbreindel.com

DeSantis Management Group
1950 Old Tustin Ave . . . . . Santa Ana CA 92705 714-550-9155 47
Web: www.desantisgroup.com

DeSantis Ron (Rep R - FL)
1524 Longworth HOB . . . . . Washington DC 20515 202-225-2706 226-6299 342-2
Web: desantis.house.gov

DeSaulnier Mark (Rep D - CA)
115 Cannon HOB . . . . . Washington DC 20515 202-225-2095 225-5609 342-2
Web: desaulnier.house.gov

Desbuild Inc 4744 Baltimore Ave . . . . . Hyattsville MD 20781 301-864-4095 186
TF: 800-347-9804 ■ *Web:* www.desbuild.com

Descanso Gardens 1418 Descanso Dr . . . . . La Canada CA 91011 818-949-4200 97
TF: 800-939-1293 ■ *Web:* www.descansogardens.org

Descartes Systems Group Inc
120 Randall Dr . . . . . Waterloo ON N2V1C6 519-746-8110 747-0082 178-12
TSE: DSG ■ *TF:* 800-419-8495 ■ *Web:* www.descartes.com

Des-Case Corp 675 N Main St . . . . . Goodlettsville TN 37072 615-672-8800 54
Web: descase.com

Desch Drive Technology Limited Partnership
240 Shearson Cres . . . . . Cambridge ON N1T1J6 519-621-4560 623-1169 350
Web: www.desch.de

Deschutes County 1300 NW Wall St Ste 200 . . . . . Bend OR 97701 541-330-4631 385-3202 338
TF: 800-237-3242 ■ *Web:* www.deschutes.org

Deschutes Public Library 507 NW Wall St . . . . . Bend OR 97701 541-312-1020 389-2982 434-3
TF: 855-268-3767 ■ *Web:* www.deschuteslibrary.org

Deschutes River State Recreation Area
89600 Biggs-Rufus Hwy . . . . . Wasco OR 97065 541-739-2322 565
Web: oregonstateparks.org

Desco Dental Systems LLC
5005 W Loomis Rd Ste 100 . . . . . Greenfield WI 53220 414-281-9192 177
TF: 800-392-7610 ■ *Web:* descodental.com

Desco Inc 1205 Lincolnton Rd . . . . . Salisbury NC 28147 704-633-6331 637-6966 246
Web: www.descoinc.com

Desco Industries Inc 3651 Walnut Ave . . . . . Chino CA 91710 909-627-8178 627-7449 248
Web: desco.descoindustries.com

Desco Plumbing & Heating Supply Inc
65 Worcester Rd . . . . . Etobicoke ON M9W5N7 416-213-1555 612
TF: 800-564-5146 ■ *Web:* www.desco.ca

Descor Builders
3164 Gold Camp Dr Ste 250 . . . . . Rancho Cordova CA 95670 916-463-0191 186
TF: 800-537-1339 ■ *Web:* www.descorbuilders.com

Deseret Book Co 45 W S Temple . . . . . Salt Lake City UT 84101 801-534-1515 637-3
TF: 800-453-4532 ■ *Web:* www.deseretbook.com

Deseret Management Corp
55 N 300 W Ste 800 . . . . . Salt Lake City UT 84101 801-538-0651 517-4600 185
Web: www.deseretmanagement.com

Deseret News
30 E 100 S Suite 400 PO Box 1257 . . . . . Salt Lake City UT 84110 801-236-6000 237-2121 532-2
TF: 800-999-7511 ■ *Web:* www.deseretnews.com

Desert Aire Corp
N120 W18485 Freistadt Rd . . . . . Germantown WI 53022 262-946-7400 14
Web: www.desert-aire.com

Desert Botanical Garden
1201 N Galvin Pkwy . . . . . Phoenix AZ 85008 480-941-1225 481-8124 97
TF: 888-314-9480 ■ *Web:* www.dbg.org

Desert Canyon Golf Resort
1030 Desert Canyon Blvd . . . . . Orondo WA 98843 509-784-1111 784-2701 669
TF: 800-258-4173 ■ *Web:* www.desertcanyon.com

Desert Dog Marketing LLC
4641 N 12th St Ste 200 . . . . . Phoenix AZ 85014 800-506-0398 225
TF: 800-506-0398 ■ *Web:* www.pinnaclecart.com

Desert Edge Brewery
273 Trolley Sq . . . . . Salt Lake City UT 84102 801-521-8917 671
Web: www.desertedgebrewery.com

Desert Hospital Hospice of the Desert Communities
1150 N Indian Canyon Dr . . . . . Palm Springs CA 92262 760-323-6642 371

Desert Hot Springs Spa Hotel
10805 Palm Dr . . . . . Desert Hot Springs CA 92240 760-329-6000 669
TF: 800-808-7727 ■ *Web:* www.dhsspa.com

Desert Island Films Inc
30 Portico Wy . . . . . Plymouth MA 02360 774-773-9223 511
Web: www.desertislandfilms.com

Desert Jade 3215 E Indian School Rd . . . . . Phoenix AZ 85018 602-954-0048 671
Web: www.desertjade68.com

Desert Mountain Properties LP
37700 Desert Mountain Pkwy . . . . . Scottsdale AZ 85262 480-488-2998 653
Web: www.desertmountain.com

Desert Paper & Envelope Company Inc
2700 Girard Blvd NE . . . . . Albuquerque NM 87107 505-884-0640 263
Web: www.desertenvelope.com

Desert Pipe & Supply
75200 Merle Dr . . . . . Palm Desert CA 92211 760-340-6322 612
Web: www.desertpipe.com

Desert Radio Group
1321 N Gene Autry Trl . . . . . Palm Springs CA 92262 760-322-7890 645-119

Desert Regional Medical Ctr
1150 N Indian Canyon Dr . . . . . Palm Springs CA 92262 760-323-6511 374-3
TF: 800-491-4990 ■ *Web:* www.desertregional.com

Desert Research Institute
2215 Raggio Pkwy . . . . . Reno NV 89512 775-673-7300 673-7397 668
Web: www.dri.edu

Desert Ridge Marketplace
21001 N Tatum Blvd . . . . . Phoenix AZ 85050 480-513-7586 563-1829 50-6
Web: www.shopdesertridge.com

Desert Riviera Hotel
610 E Palm Canyon Dr . . . . . Palm Springs CA 92264 760-327-5314 379
TF: 866-270-8322 ■ *Web:* www.desertrivierahotel.com

Desert Sands Charter High School
44130 20th St W . . . . . Lancaster CA 93534 877-360-5327 685
TF: 877-360-5327 ■ *Web:* www.dschs.org

Desert Schools Federal Credit Union
148 N 48th St . . . . . Phoenix AZ 85034 602-433-7000 634-2993 219
TF: 800-456-9171 ■ *Web:* www.desertschools.org

Desert Sky Mall 7611 W Thomas Rd . . . . . Phoenix AZ 85033 623-245-1404 460
Web: www.desertskymall.com

Desert Springs Hospital Medical Ctr
2075 E Flamingo Rd . . . . . Las Vegas NV 89119 702-733-8800 374-3
Web: www.desertspringshospital.com

Desert Springs Marriott Resort & Spa
74855 Country Club Dr . . . . . Palm Desert CA 92260 760-341-2211 341-1872 669
TF: 888-538-9459 ■ *Web:* www.marriott.com

Desert Sun 750 N Gene Autry Trl . . . . . Palm Springs CA 92263 760-322-8889 532-2
TF: 800-233-3741 ■ *Web:* desertsun.com

Desert Sun Motors Inc
2600 N White Sands Blvd . . . . . Alamogordo NM 88310 575-437-7530 57
Web: www.desertsunmotors.com

Desert Sun Publishing Co
PO Box 2734 . . . . . Palm Springs CA 92263 760-322-8889 322-8889 637-8
TF Advertising: 800-233-3741 ■ *Web:* desertsun.com

Desert Whale Jojoba Company Inc
2101 E Beverly Dr . . . . . Tucson AZ 85719 520-882-4195 194
Web: www.desertwhale.com

Desgraff Multimedia
779 rue Paul-Desruisseaux 2nd Fl . . . . . Sherbrooke QC J1J4L9 819-823-8024 396
TF: 800-527-2383 ■ *Web:* desgraff.com

Desha County
608 Robert S Moore Ave PO Box 188 . . . . . Arkansas City AR 71630 870-877-2426 338
Web: deshacounty.arkansas.gov

Desiccare Inc 3400 Pomona Blvd . . . . . Pomona CA 91768 909-444-8272 77
Web: www.desiccare.com

Design & Molding Services Inc
25 Howard St . . . . . Piscataway NJ 08854 732-752-0300 752-9672 604

Design & Production Inc
7110 Rainwater Pl . . . . . Lorton VA 22079 703-550-8640 339-0296 232
Web: www.d-and-p.com

Design 3 Engineering Inc
1211 24th St W Ste 7 . . . . . Billings MT 59102 406-245-5599 261

Design 446 Inc 2411 Atlantic Ave . . . . . Manasquan NJ 08736 732-292-2400 4
Web: www.design446.com

Design Alliance Inc
520 N Washington St . . . . . Alexandria VA 22314 703-838-9894 344
Web: www.designalliance.com

Design Compendium Inc, The
155 20th St . . . . . Brooklyn NY 11232 718-499-7722 195
TF: 800-995-2995 ■ *Web:* www.designcompendium.com

Design Concepts Inc
5301 Buttonwood Dr . . . . . Madison WI 53718 608-316-8400 261
Web: www.design-concepts.com

Design Ctr of the Americas (DCOTA)
1855 Griffin Rd . . . . . Dania Beach FL 33004 954-920-7997 460
TF: 877-992-9204 ■ *Web:* www.dcota.com

Design Design Inc 19 La Grave SE . . . . . Grand Rapids MI 49503 616-774-2448 130
TF: 800-334-3348 ■ *Web:* www.designdesign.us

Design Dimension Inc 901 N W St . . . . . Raleigh NC 27603 919-828-1485 463
TF: 800-447-0057 ■ *Web:* www.designdimension.com

Design Group Staffing Inc
10012 Jasper Ave . . . . . Edmonton AB T5J1R2 780-428-1505 428-7095 721
Web: dg.ca

Design Homes Inc
600 N Marquette Rd . . . . . Prairie du Chien WI 53821 608-326-6041 326-4233 106
TF: 800-627-9443 ■ *Web:* www.designhomes.com

Design Hub Inc 600 W Michigan Ave Ste C . . . . . Saline MI 48176 734-944-8705 177
Web: www.design-hub.com

Design Institute of San Diego
8555 Commerce Ave . . . . . San Diego CA 92121 858-566-1200 566-2711 166
TF: 800-619-4337 ■ *Web:* www.disd.edu

Design Integrity Inc
1155 W Fulton Market 2nd Fl . . . . . Chicago IL 60607 312-942-0602 261
Web: www.designintegrity.com

Design It Yourself Gift Baskets LLC
7999 Hansen Rd Ste 204 . . . . . Houston TX 77061 713-944-3440 129
TF: 800-589-7553 ■ *Web:* www.designityourselfgiftbaskets.com

Design Journal
23371 Mulholland Dr STE 253 . . . . . Woodland Hills CA 91364 310-394-4394 457-2
Web: www.designjournalmag.com

Design Management Institute (DMI)
38 Chauncy St Ste 800 . . . . . Boston MA 02111 617-338-6380 338-6570 48-4
Web: www.dmi.org

Design Masonry Inc
20703 Santa Clara St . . . . . Canyon Country CA 91351 661-298-1013 298-0117 189-7
Web: www.designmasonry.com

Design Molded Plastics
8220 Bavaria Rd . . . . . Macedonia OH 44056 330-963-4400 596
Web: www.designmolded.com

Design Net Technical Products Inc
341 Washington Hwy . . . . . Smithfield RI 02917 401-349-0695 463
Web: designnettech.com

Design News 225 Wyman St . . . . . Waltham MA 02451 763-746-2792 457-21
TF: 800-869-6882 ■ *Web:* www.designnews.com

	Phone	Fax	Class
Design Partners Inc 338 Main St, Racine WI 53403 *Web:* www.design-partners.com	262-637-2233		344
Design Partnership, The 1629 Telegraph Ave Ste 500, Oakland CA 94612 *Web:* www.dpsf.com	415-777-3737		186
Design Phase Inc 1771 S Lakeside Dr, Waukegan IL 60085 *TF:* 800-858-2352 ■ *Web:* dphase.com	847-473-0077		393
Design ProfessionalXL Group 2959 Salinas Hwy, Monterey CA 93940 *TF:* 800-227-4284 ■ *Web:* xlgroup.com	831-649-5522		401
Design Space Inc 91 Harvey Vickers Rd, Douglas GA 31535	912-384-9211		106
Design Space Mdlar Bldings Inc 29336 Airport Rd, Eugene OR 97402 *Web:* designspacemodular.com	541-461-9122		226
Design Specialties Inc 11100 W Heather Ave, Milwaukee WI 53224 *Web:* www.glassfireplacedoors.com	414-371-1200		362
Design Strategy Corp 805 Third Ave 11th Fl, New York NY 10022 *TF:* 800-331-8726 ■ *Web:* www.designstrategy.com	212-370-0000	949-3648	180
Design Systems Inc 38799 W 12 Mile Rd, Farmington Hills MI 48331	248-489-4300		261
Design Toscano Inc 1400 Morse Ave, Elk Grove Village IL 60007 *TF:* 800-525-5141 ■ *Web:* www.designtoscano.com	847-952-0100		459
Design Within Reach Inc 711 Canal St Third fl 3rd Fl, Stamford CT 06902 *OTC:* DWRI ■ *TF:* 800-944-2233 ■ *Web:* www.dwr.com	203-614-0600	614-0845	362
Design Workshops 486 Lesser St, Oakland CA 94601 *Web:* www.design-workshops.com	510-434-0727	434-0727	286
Design/Build Business Magazine 3030 Salt Creek Ln Ste 200, Arlington Heights IL 60005 *TF:* 800-547-7377 ■ *Web:* www.forresidentialpros.com	847-454-2714	454-2759	457-2
Design/Craft Fabrics Corp 2230 Ridge Dr, Glenview IL 60025 *Web:* www.design-craft.com	847-904-7000	904-7102	594
DESIGNASHIRT.COM 905 N Scottsdale Rd, Tempe AZ 85281 *TF:* 800-594-1206 ■ *Web:* www.designashirt.com	480-966-3500		627
Designatronics Inc 2101 Jericho Tpke, New Hyde Park NY 11040 *TF Orders:* 800-345-1144 ■ *Web:* www.sdp-si.com	516-328-3300	326-8827	709
Designed Business Interiors of Topeka Inc 107 W Sixth St, Topeka KS 66603 *Web:* dbi-topeka.com	785-233-2078		321
Designer Auto Sales 1304 Tenth Dr SE, Austin MN 55912	507-434-0123		57
Designer Blinds 4500 S 76th Cir, Omaha NE 68127	402-331-2283		361
Designer Decal Inc 1120 E First Ave, Spokane WA 99202 *TF:* 800-622-6333 ■ *Web:* www.designerdecal.com	509-535-0267	535-1476	687
Designer Floors of Texas 3841 Ranch Rd 620 S, Austin TX 78738 *Web:* austin.abbeycarpet.com	512-263-3333		290
Designers Choice Cabinetry Inc 100 TGK Cir, Rockledge FL 32955 *Web:* www.dccabinetry.com	321-632-0772		115
Designers Midwest 9563 Montgomery Rd Ste 104, Cincinnati OH 45242 *TF:* 800-940-6670 ■ *Web:* www.designeers.com	513-793-6670		261
Designers' Press Inc 6305 Chancellor Dr, Orlando FL 32809 *TF:* 800-334-9356 ■ *Web:* www.designerspressinc.com	407-843-3141		627
DesigneRx Pharmaceuticals Inc 4941 Allison Pkwy Ste B, Vacaville CA 95688 *Web:* www.drxpharma.com	707-451-0441		231
Designfax Magazine 2506 Tamiami Trail North, Nokomis FL 34275 *Web:* www.designfax.net	941-966-9521	966-2590	457-21
Designhammer Media Group LLC 1912 E Nc Hwy 54 Ste 201, Durham NC 27713 *TF:* 800-549-8628 ■ *Web:* dcsignhammer.com	919-544-0086		196
Designing Health Inc 28410 Witherspoon Pkwy, Valencia CA 91355 *TF:* 800-774-7387 ■ *Web:* www.missinglinkproducts.com	661-257-1705		479
Designs for Vision Inc 760 Koehler Ave, Ronkonkoma NY 11779 *Web:* www.designsforvision.com	631-585-3300		543
Designsensory Inc 1740 Commons Point Dr Centerpoint Commons Bldg 1, Knoxville TN 37932 *TF:* 800-583-0148 ■ *Web:* www.designsensory.com	865-690-2249		7
Designware Inc 54 Fieldstone-Bashan Dr, East Haddam CT 06423 *Web:* www.designwareinc.com	860-873-8938	873-9993	566
DesignworksUSA Inc 2201 Corporate Ctr Dr, Newbury Park CA 91320 *Web:* www.bmwgroupdesignworks.com	805-499-9590		261
DesignWrite Inc 175 Wall St, Princeton NJ 08540 *Web:* dwrite.com	609-924-1116		344
DeSilva Gates Construction Inc 11555 Dublin Blvd, Dublin CA 94568 *Web:* www.desilvagates.com	925-829-9220		188-5
Desire2Learn Inc 151 Charles SW Ste 400, Kitchener ON N2G1H6 *TF:* 888-772-0325 ■ *Web:* www.d2l.com	519-772-0325	772-0324	174
Desjardins Securities Inc 1170 Peel St Ste 300, Montreal QC H3B0A9 *TF:* 888-987-1749 ■ *Web:* www2.vmdconseil.ca	514-987-1749		401
DesJarlais Scott (Rep R - TN) 2301 Rayburn HOB, Washington DC 20515 *Web:* desjarlais.house.gov	202-225-6831	226-5172	342-2
Deskey 120 E Eighth St, Cincinnati OH 45202 *Web:* www.deskey.com	513-721-6800		195
DeskNet Inc 30 Montgomery St, Jersey City NJ 07302 *Web:* www.desknetinc.com	201-946-7080		178-1
Desks Inc Business Furniture 445 Bryant St Unit 8, Denver CO 80204 *Web:* www.desks-incorporated.com	303-777-7778		321
Desktop Consulting Services 43311 Joy Rd, Canton MI 48187 *TF:* 888-600-2731 ■ *Web:* dcs-mi.com	888-600-2731		175
DeskTop Labels 7277 Boone Ave N, Minneapolis MN 55428 *TF:* 800-241-9730 ■ *Web:* www.desktoplabels.com	800-241-9730		413
Desmond & Ahern Ltd 10827 S Western Ave, Chicago IL 60643 *Web:* www.desmondcpa.com	773-779-4720		2
Desmond Albany Hotel, The 660 Albany-Shaker Rd, Albany NY 12211 *TF:* 800-448-3500 ■ *Web:* www.desmondhotelsalbany.com	518-869-8100		671
Desmos Inc 1061 Market St, San Francisco CA 94103 *Web:* www.desmos.com	415-484-5342		387
DeSoto Chamber of Commerce 2010 N Hampton Rd Ste 200, DeSoto TX 75115 *Web:* www.desotochamber.org	972-224-3565	354-1022	139
Desoto Correctional Institution 13617 SE Hwy 70, Arcadia FL 34266 *Web:* dc.state.fl.us	863-494-3727	494-1740	213
DeSoto County 201 E Oak St, Arcadia FL 34266 *Web:* desotobocc.com	863-993-4800	993-4809	338
DeSoto County 365 Losher St, Hernando MS 38632 *TF:* 800-824-5061 ■ *Web:* www.desotocountyms.gov	662-429-1460		338
DeSoto County Chamber of Commerce 16 S Volusia Ave, Arcadia FL 34266 *Web:* www.desotochamberfl.com	863-494-4033	494-3312	139
DeSoto County Library 125 N Hillsboro Ave, Arcadia FL 34266 *Web:* www.myhlc.org	863-993-4851		434-3
DeSoto LLC 6751 N Sunset BLVD, Glendale AZ 85305	602-888-0341		151
DeSoto Memorial Hospital Inc 900 N Robert Ave, Arcadia FL 34266 *Web:* www.dmh.org	863-494-3535	494-8400	374-3
DeSoto Parish 101 Texas St PO Box 1206, Mansfield LA 71052 *Web:* desotoparishclerk.org	318-872-3110	872-4202	338
DeSoto Parish Chamber of Commerce 115 N Washington Ave, Mansfield LA 71052 *TF:* 800-844-4646 ■ *Web:* www.desotoparishchamber.net	318-872-1310	871-1875	139
DeSoto Parish Library 109 Crosby St, Mansfield LA 71052 *Web:* desotoparishlibrary.org	318-872-6100	872-6120	434-3
Desoto Parish School District 201 Crosby St, Mansfield LA 71052 *Web:* www.desotopsb.com	318-872-2836	872-1324	685
DeSoto Public Library 211 E Pleasant Run Rd Ste C, DeSoto TX 75115 *TF:* 800-886-9008 ■ *Web:* www.ci.desoto.tx.us	972-230-9656	230-5797	434-3
Desoto Sales Inc 20945 Osborne St, Canoga Park CA 91304 *TF:* 800-826-9779 ■ *Web:* www.desotosales.com	818-998-0853	998-7542	351
Despatch Industries Inc 8860 207th St W, Lakeville MN 55044 *TF:* 800-726-0110 ■ *Web:* www.despatch.com	952-469-5424	469-4513	318
DesPeres Hospital 2345 Dougherty Ferry Rd, Saint Louis MO 63122 *TF:* 888-457-5203 ■ *Web:* www.despereshospital.com	314-966-9100		374-3
Dessert Innovations Inc 25-B Enterprise Blvd, Atlanta GA 30336 *TF:* 800-359-7351 ■ *Web:* www.dessertinnovations.com	404-691-5000	691-5001	296-2
DE-STA-CO 1025 Doris Rd, Auburn Hills MI 48326 *TF:* 888 337-8226 ■ *Web:* www.destaco.com	248-836-6700		350
Destin Area Chamber of Commerce 4484 Legendary Dr Ste A, Destin FL 32541 *Web:* www.destinchamber.com	850-837-6241	654-5612	139
Destination America Inc 801 E Katella Ave, Anaheim CA 92805 *Web:* www.destamer.com	714-935-0040		48-20
Destination Canada 800 - 1045 Howe St, Vancouver BC V6Z2A9 *Web:* en.destinationcanada.com	604-638-8300		774
Destination Cinema Inc 4155 Harrison Blvd Ste 201, Ogden UT 84403 *Web:* www.destinationcinema.com	801-392-5881		514
Destination Hotels & Resorts Inc 10333 E Dry Creek Rd Ste 450, Englewood CO 80112 *TF:* 855-893-1011 ■ *Web:* www.destinationhotels.com	303-799-3830		379
Destination Maternity Corp 232 Strawbridge Dr, Moorestown NJ 08057 *NASDAQ:* DEST ■ *TF:* 800-466-6223 ■ *Web:* destinationmaternitycorp.com/home.asp	800-466-6223		157-6
Destination Resources 5435 Balboa Blvd Ste 106, Encino CA 91316 *TF:* 800-422-6524 ■ *Web:* www.destinationresources.com	818-995-7915	990-6129	184
Destination Services of Colorado Inc (DSC) PO Box 3660, Avon CO 81620 *TF:* 855-866-5290 ■ *Web:* www.dsc-co.com	970-476-6565		184
Destinations Unlimited Inc 5020 Council St NE, Cedar Rapids IA 52402 *TF:* 800-391-1359 ■ *Web:* www.duagency.com	319-393-1359		772
Destinta Theatres 215 Quassaick Ave, New Windsor NY 12553 *Web:* www.destinta.com	845-569-8181		685
Destiny Corp 2075 Silas Deane Hwy, Rocky Hill CT 06067 *Web:* www.destinycorp.com	860-721-1684		631
Destiny Industries LLC 250 R W Bryant Rd, Moultrie GA 31788 *TF:* 866-782-6600 ■ *Web:* www.destinyhomebuilders.com	866-782-6600		505
Destiny Mfg 2974 Interstate Pkwy, Brunswick OH 44212 *Web:* www.destinymfg.com	330-273-9000		488
Destiny Solutions Inc 40 Holly St, Toronto ON M4S3C3 *TF:* 866-403-0500 ■ *Web:* www.destinysolutions.com	416-480-0500		225
Destrehan Plantation 13034 River Rd, Destrehan LA 70047 *Web:* www.destrehanplantation.org	985-764-9315	725-1929	50-3
Destron Fearing 490 Villaume Ave, South Saint Paul MN 55075 *TF:* 800-328-0118 ■ *Web:* www.destronfearing.com	651-455-1621		647
DET Distributing Co 301 Great Cir Rd, Nashville TN 37228 *Web:* www.detdist.com	615-244-4113		81-1
Detail Drafting and Design Inc 1090 216th Ave, East Bethel MN 55011 *Web:* ddd-services.com	763-434-2110		180

Phone | Fax | Class

Detail Planners Llc
2629 Windguard Cir Ste 101 ... Wesley Chapel FL 33544 813-991-1348 317
Web: www.detailplanners.com
Details Magazine 4 Times Sq ... New York NY 10036 212-630-4000 457-11
Web: www.gq.com
Detar Hospital Navarro
506 E San Antonio St ... Victoria TX 77901 361-575-7441 374-3
Web: www.detar.com
Detar Hospital North 101 Medical Dr ... Victoria TX 77904 361-573-6100 374-3
Web: www.detar.com
DETC (Distance Education & Training Council)
1601 18th St NW Ste 2 ... Washington DC 20009 202-234-5100 332-1386 48-1
Web: www.deac.org
Detechtion Technologies
1100-8th Ave SW Ste 277 ... Calgary AB T2P3T8 403-250-9220 196
Web: www.detechtion.com
Detecto Scale Co
203 E Daugherty St PO Box 151 ... Webb City MO 64870 417-673-4631 673-4631 684
TF: 800-641-2008 ■ *Web:* www.detecto.com
Detector Electronics Corp
6901 W 110th St ... Minneapolis MN 55438 952-941-5665 692
Web: det-tronics.com
Deteq Services 1771 Westborough Dr ... Katy TX 77449 281-828-3030 261
Web: www.deteqservices.com
Detering Consulting Inc
306 Ferne Ave ... Palo Alto CA 94306 650-576-4516 260
Web: www.deteringconsulting.com
Deters Benzinger & LaVelle P S C
207 Thomas More Pkwy ... Crestview Hills KY 41017 859-341-1881 445
TF: 800-973-1177 ■ *Web:* www.dbllaw.com
Detex Corp 302 Detex Dr ... New Braunfels TX 78130 830-629-2900 620-6711 692
TF: 800-729-3839 ■ *Web:* www.detex.com
Dethmers Manufacturing Co (DEMCO)
4010 320th St ... Boyden IA 51234 712-725-2311 725-2380 763
TF: 800-543-3626 ■ *Web:* www.demco-products.com
Detmar Corp 2001 W Alexandrine Ave ... Detroit MI 48208 313-831-1155 350
Web: www.detmarcorp.com
Detrex Corp 24901 NW Hwy Ste 410 ... Southfield MI 48075 248-358-5800 145
Web: www.detrex.com
Detroit Athletic Club 241 Madison St ... Detroit MI 48226 313-963-9200 963-8891 354
Web: www.thedac.com
Detroit Bio-med Laboratories
23955 Fwy Park Dr ... Farmington Hills MI 48335 248-471-4111 415
TF: 800-338-3533 ■ *Web:* www.detroitbio.com
Detroit Chassis LLC 6501 Lynch Rd ... Detroit MI 48234 313-571-2100 59
Web: www.detroitchassis.com
Detroit City Hall
2 Woodward Ave Ste 200 ... Detroit MI 48226 313-224-3270 224-1466 337
Web: detroitmi.gov
Detroit Community High School
12675 Burt Rd ... Detroit MI 48228 313-537-3570 685
Web: www.detcomschools.org
Detroit Diesel Corp 13400 Outer Dr ... Detroit MI 48239 313-592-5000 262
Web: www.demanddetroit.com
Detroit Edge Tool Co 6570 E Nevada St ... Detroit MI 48234 313-366-4120 366-1890 493
TF: 800-404-2038 ■ *Web:* www.detroitedge.com
Detroit Engineered Products Inc
850 East Long Lake Rd Ste 103 ... Troy MI 48085 248-269-7130 180
Web: www.depusa.com
Detroit Free Press
615 W Lafayette Blvd ... Detroit MI 48226 313-222-6400 222-5981* 532-2
**Fax:* News Rm ■ *TF:* 800-395-3300 ■ *Web:* www.freep.com
Detroit Gallery-Contemporary
104 Fisher Rd Ste 104 ... Grosse Pointe Shores MI 48230 313-873-7888 50-2
Detroit Historical Museum
5401 Woodward Ave ... Detroit MI 48202 313-833-1805 833-5342 520
TF: 800-456-1701 ■ *Web:* www.detroithistorical.org
Detroit Hoist Co
6650 Sterling Dr N ... Sterling Heights MI 48312 586-268-2600 268-0044 470
TF: 800-521-9126 ■ *Web:* www.detroithoist.com
Detroit Institute of Arts
5200 Woodward Ave ... Detroit MI 48202 313-833-7900 520
Web: www.dia.org
Detroit Lake State Recreation Area
PO Box 549 ... Detroit OR 97342 503-854-3346 565
Web: www.oregonstateparks.org
Detroit Lakes Regional Chamber of Commerce
700 Summit Ave ... Detroit Lakes MN 56501 218-847-9202 847-9082 139
TF: 800-542-3992 ■ *Web:* www.visitdetroitlakes.com
Detroit Legal News Co 1409 Allen Rd Ste B ... Troy MI 48083 248-577-6100 577-6111 637-8
TF: 800-875-5275 ■ *Web:* www.legalnews.com
Detroit Lions 222 Republic Dr ... Allen Park MI 48101 313-216-4000 715-3
TF: 800-745-3000 ■ *Web:* www.detroitlions.com
Detroit Medical Ctr (DMC)
4707 St Antoine ... Detroit MI 48201 313-745-6035 353
Web: www.dmc.org
Detroit Metropolitan Airport
Smith Terminal - Mezzanine Level ... Detroit MI 48242 734-942-3550 27
Web: www.metroairport.com
Detroit Metropolitan Convention & Visitors Bureau
211 W Fort St Ste 1000 ... Detroit MI 48226 313-202-1800 206
TF: 877-424-5554 ■ *Web:* www.visitdetroit.com
Detroit News 615 W Lafayette Blvd ... Detroit MI 48226 313-222-2300 222-2335* 532-2
**Fax:* News Rm ■ *TF General:* 800-395-3300 ■ *Web:* www.detroitnews.com
Detroit Opera House 1526 Broadway ... Detroit MI 48226 313-961-3500 237-3412 572
Web: www.michiganopera.org
Detroit Pistons
Palace at Auburn Hills
6 Championship Dr ... Auburn Hills MI 48326 248-377-0100 377-4262 714-1
Web: www.nba.com
Detroit Public Library
5201 Woodward Ave ... Detroit MI 48202 313-481-1300 434-3
TF: 800-894-3592 ■ *Web:* www.detroitpubliclibrary.org
Detroit Public Schools
3031 W Grand Blvd ... Detroit MI 48202 313-873-7927 873-4564 685
Web: www.detroitk12.org
Detroit Pump & Mfg Co
450 Fair St Bldg D ... Ferndale MI 48220 248-544-4242 544-4141 385
TF: 800-686-1662 ■ *Web:* www.detroitpump.com

Detroit Quality Brush Mfg
32165 Schoolcraft Rd ... Livonia MI 48150 734-525-5660 525-0437 103
TF: 800-722-3037 ■ *Web:* www.dqb.com
Detroit Radiant Product Co
21400 Hoover Rd ... Warren MI 48089 586-756-0950 756-2626 318
TF: 800-222-1100 ■ *Web:* www.reverberray.com
Detroit Receiving Hospital & University Health Ctr
4201 St Antoine Blvd ... Detroit MI 48201 313-745-3000 374-3
Web: www.dmc.org/detroitreceiving
Detroit Red Wings
Joe Louis Arena 600 Civic Ctr Dr ... Detroit MI 48226 313-396-7444 567-0296* 716
**Fax:* PR ■ *Web:* redwings.nhl.com
Detroit Regional Chamber
1 Woodward Ave Ste 1900 ... Detroit MI 48226 313-964-4000 964-0183 139
TF: 800-427-5100 ■ *Web:* detroitchamber.com
Detroit Shock
5 Championship Dr
Palace at Auburn Hills ... Auburn Hills MI 48326 248-377-0100 377-0584 714-2
Detroit Stoker Co 1510 E First St ... Monroe MI 48161 734-241-9500 241-7126 318
TF: 800-786-5374 ■ *Web:* www.detroitstoker.com
Detroit Symphony Orchestra
3711 Woodward Ave ... Detroit MI 48201 313-576-5111 576-5109 573-3
TF: 800-434-6340 ■ *Web:* dso.org
Detroit Tigers
Comerica Pk 2100 Woodward Ave ... Detroit MI 48201 313-962-4000 471-2138* 713
**Fax:* PR ■ *TF:* 866-800-1275 ■ *Web:* detroit.tigers.mlb.com
Detroit Tool Metal Products Inc
949 Bethel Rd ... Lebanon MO 65536 312-374-4829 295
Web: www.ironform.com
Detroit Zoological Institute
8450 W Ten-Mile Rd ... Royal Oak MI 48067 248-541-5717 823
Web: www.detroitzoo.org
Detroit-Wayne County Port Authority
130 E Atwater St ... Detroit MI 48226 313-259-5091 259-5093 618
Web: www.portdetroit.com
Detronic Industries Inc
35800 Beattie Dr ... Sterling Heights MI 48312 586-977-5660 939-5340 697
TF: 800-772-7017 ■ *Web:* www.detronic.com
Detrow & Underwood Inc 12 W Main St ... Ashland OH 44805 419-289-0265 4
Web: www.detrowunderwood.com
Detyens Shipyards Inc
1670 Drydock Ave Bldg 236 Ste 200 ... North Charleston SC 29405 843-308-8000 308-8059 698
Web: www.detyens.com
Deublin Co 2050 Norman Dr W ... Waukegan IL 60085 847-689-8600 689-8690 620
Web: www.deublin.com
Deuel County 718 Third St PO Box 327 ... Chappell NE 69129 308-874-3308 874-3472 338
Web: www.co.deuel.ne.us
Deuel County 408 Fourth St W ... Clear Lake SD 57226 605-874-2312 874-1306 338
TF: 800-872-6190 ■ *Web:* www.deuelcountysd.com
Deutch Ted (Rep D - FL)
2447 Rayburn Bldg ... Washington DC 20515 202-225-3001 225-5974 342-2
Web: teddeutch.house.gov
Deutsch Design Works Inc
480 Gate 5 Rd Ste 100 ... Sausalito CA 94965 415-487-8520 344
Web: www.ddw.com
Deutsch Inc 330 W 34th St ... New York NY 10001 212-981-7600 4
Web: www.deutsch.com
Deutsch Williams Brooks DeRensis & Holland PC
1 Design Ctr Pl Ste 600 ... Boston MA 02210 617-951-2300 428
TF: 800-225-6201 ■ *Web:* www.dwboston.com
Deutsch, Kerrigan & Stiles LLP
755 Magazine St ... New Orleans LA 70130 504-581-5141 428
Web: www.deutschkerrigan.com
Deutsche Bank Americas Holding Corp
60 Wall St ... New York NY 10005 212-250-2500 360-4
Web: www.db.com
Deutsche Bank Canada (DB)
199 Bay St Commerce Ct W Ste 4700 ... Toronto ON M5L1E9 416-682-8000 682-8383 70
TF: 800-735-7777 ■ *Web:* www.db.com
Deutsche Steinzeug America Inc (DSA)
367 Curie Dr ... Alpharetta GA 30005 770-442-5500 751
Web: www.deutsche-steinzeug.de
Deutscher & Daughter Inc
10507 150th St ... Jamaica NY 11435 718-291-5600 351
TF: 800-605-7620 ■ *Web:* www.dddoors.com
DEVAR Inc 706 Bostwick Ave ... Bridgeport CT 06605 203-368-6751 407
Web: www.devarinc.com
Devault Foods 1 Devault Ln ... Devault PA 19432 610-644-2536 297-8
TF: 800-426-2874 ■ *Web:* www.devaultfoods.com
Devcare Solution Ltd
131 N High St Ste 640 ... Columbus OH 43215 614-221-2277 179
TF: 800-651-7142 ■ *Web:* www.devcare.com
Devcon Construction Inc
690 Gibraltar Dr ... Milpitas CA 95035 408-942-8200 942-8200 186
Web: www.devcon-const.com
Devcon Inc 30 Endicott St ... Danvers MA 01923 855-489-7262 774-0516* 3
**Fax Area Code:* 978 ■ *TF:* 800-626-7226 ■ *Web:* www.devcon.com
Develcon Inc
401 Magnetic Dr Units 15-17 ... Toronto ON M3J3H9 416-385-1390 736
Web: www.develcon.com
Developers Diversified Realty Corp
3300 Enterprise Pkwy ... Beachwood OH 44122 216-755-5500 755-1500 655
NYSE: DDR ■ *TF:* 877-225-5337 ■ *Web:* ddr.com
Developing World Markets Finance LLP
750 Washington Blvd Ste 500 ... Stamford CT 06901 203-655-5453 401
Web: www.dwmarkets.com
Development Alternatives Inc (DAI)
7600 Wisconsin Ave Ste 200 ... Bethesda MD 20814 301-771-7600 463
Web: www.dai.com
Development Counsellors International Ltd (DCI)
215 Pk Ave S 14th Fl ... New York NY 10003 212-725-0707 725-2254 230
Web: www.aboutdci.com
Development Dimensions International
1225 Washington Pike ... Bridgeville PA 15017 412-257-0600 220-2942 193
TF Mktg: 800-933-4463 ■ *Web:* www.ddiworld.com
Development Director's Letter
8204 Fenton St ... Silver Spring MD 20910 301-588-6380 588-6385 531-7
TF: 800-666-6380 ■ *Web:* cdpublications.com

	Phone	Fax	Class
Development Planning & Financing Group Inc 27127 Calle Arroyo Ste 1910 ... San Juan Capistrano CA 92675 *Web:* www.dpfg.com	949-388-9269		652
Development Services of America 16100 N 71st St Ste 520 ... Scottsdale AZ 85254 *Web:* www.developmentservicesofamerica.com	480-927-4892		653
Deveney Communication Consulting LLC 2406 Chartres St ... New Orleans LA 70117 *TF:* 800-925-0000 ■ *Web:* www.deveney.com	504-949-3999		636
Devereux 1291 Stanley Rd NW PO Box 1688 ... Kennesaw GA 30156 *TF:* 800-342-3357 ■ *Web:* www.devereux.org	678-303-5233		374-1
Devereux Advanced Behavioral Health 8000 Devereux Dr ... Viera FL 32940 *TF:* 800-338-3738 ■ *Web:* devereux.org	321-242-9100		374-1
Devereux Cleo Wallace 8405 Church Ranch Blvd ... Westminster CO 80021 **Fax:* Admitting ■ *TF:* 800-456-2536 ■ *Web:* www.devereux.org	303-466-7391	466-0904*	374-1
Devereux Glenholme School 81 Sabbaday Ln ... Washington CT 06793 *Web:* www.theglenholmeschool.org	860-868-7377	868-7894	622
DevFacto Technologies Inc 2250 Scotia Place Tower 1 10060 Jasper Ave ... Edmonton AB T5J3R8 *TF:* 877-323-3832 ■ *Web:* www.devfacto.com	587-520-9118		463
Devi 8 E 18th St ... New York NY 10003 *Web:* www.devinyc.com	212-691-1300		671
Device Engineering Inc 385 E Alamo Dr ... Chandler AZ 85225 *Web:* www.deiaz.com	480-303-0822		261
Devicenet USA Inc 4000 Moorpark Ave Ste 116 ... San Jose CA 95117 *Web:* www.devicenet-usa.com	408-557-0413		177
Devicix LLC 7680 Executive Dr ... Eden Prairie MN 55344 *Web:* www.devicix.com	952-368-0073		41
Devier Construction LLC 1932 Surgi Dr Ste F ... Mandeville LA 70448 *Web:* www.devierway.com	985-626-3184		186
deView Electronics USA Inc 1420 Lakeside Pkwy Ste 110 ... Lewisville TX 75057 *TF:* 877-433-8439 ■ *Web:* www.deviewelectronics.com	214-222-3332	222-3339	692
Devil Dog Mfg Company Inc 400 E Gannon Ave ... Zebulon NC 27597	919-269-7485		155-4
Devil's Den Preserve 33 Pent Rd ... Weston CT 06883 *TF:* 800-628-6860 ■ *Web:* www.nature.org	203-226-4991	226-4807	50-5
Devil's Den State Park 11333 W Arkansas Hwy 74 ... West Fork AR 72774 *TF:* 888-742-8701 ■ *Web:* www.arkansasstateparks.com	479-761-3325		565
Devil's Head Resort & Convention Ctr S 6330 Bluff Rd ... Merrimac WI 53561 *TF:* 800-472-6670 ■ *Web:* www.devilsheadresort.com	608-493-2251	493-2176	669
Devil's Hole State Park c/o Niagara Frontier Region PO Box 1132 ... Niagara Falls NY 14303 *Web:* parks.ny.gov/parks/42/details.aspx	716-284-5778		565
Devil's Hopyard State Park 366 Hopyard Rd ... East Haddam CT 06423 *Web:* www.ct.gov	860-424-3200		565
Devil's Lake State Park S5975 Pk Rd ... Baraboo WI 53913 *Web:* dnr.wi.gov	608-356-8301	356-4281	565
Devil's Lake State Recreation Area 198 NE 123rd St ... Lincoln City OR 97367 *TF:* 800-551-6949 ■ *Web:* www.oregonstateparks.org	800-551-6949		565
Devil's Millhopper Geological State Park 4732 Millhopper Rd ... Gainesville FL 32653 *Web:* www.floridastateparks.org/devilsmillhopper	352-955-2008		565
Devil's Sinkhole State Natural Area 101 N Sweeten St ... Rocksprings TX 78880 *Web:* tpwd.texas.gov	830-683-3762		565
Devils Fork State Park 161 Holcombe Cir ... Salem SC 29676 *TF:* 866-345-7275 ■ *Web:* www.southcarolinaparks.com	864-944-2639		565
Devils Postpile National Monument PO Box 3999 ... Mammoth Lakes CA 93546 *Web:* www.nps.gov/depo	760-934-2289	934-2289	564
Devils River State Natural Area HC 01 PO Box 513 ... Del Rio TX 78840 *Web:* tpwd.texas.gov/state-parks/devils-river	830-395-2133		565
Devils Tower National Monument Hwy 110 Bldg 170 PO Box 10 ... Devils Tower WY 82714 *Web:* www.nps.gov/deto	307-467-5283	467-5350	564
DEVIN International Inc 2545 SE Evangeline Thwy ... Lafayette LA 70508	337-233-3846		539
DeVinoenzi Metal Products Inc 1655 Rollins Rd ... Burlingame CA 94010 *Web:* www.devmetal.com	650-692-5800		610
Devine Bros Inc 38 Commerce St ... Norwalk CT 06850 *Web:* www.devinebi.com	203-866-4421		182
Devine Intermodal 3870 Ch Dr ... West Sacramento CA 95691 *TF:* 800-821-4635 ■ *Web:* www.devineintermodal.com	916-371-4430	371-0355	780
Devine Millimet 111 Amherst St ... Manchester NH 03101 *Web:* www.devinemillimet.com	603-669-1000		445
Devlin Video International LLC 1501 Broadway Ste 408 ... New York NY 10036 *Web:* www.devlinvideo.com	212-391-1313		514
Devlinhair Productions Inc 120 Wooster St 3 Ste ... New York NY 10012 *TF:* 800-928-1963 ■ *Web:* www.devlinhair.com	212-941-9009		627
Devon Bank 6445 N Western Ave ... Chicago IL 60645 *Web:* www.devonbank.com	773-465-2500	973-5647	70
Devon Energy Corp 20 N Broadway ... Oklahoma City OK 73102 *NYSE: DVN* ■ *TF:* 877-860-5820 ■ *Web:* www.devonenergy.com	405-235-3611		536
Devon Nicole House 21 Autumn St 5th Fl ... Boston MA 02215 *Web:* childrenshospital.org	617-355-8457		372
Devon Precision Industries Inc 251 Munson Rd ... Wolcott CT 06716 *TF:* 800-646-7584 ■ *Web:* www.devonprecision.com	203-879-1437	879-5556	621
Devon Self Storage Holdings LLC 2000 Powell St Ste 1240 ... Emeryville CA 94608 *Web:* www.devonselfstorage.com	510-450-1300		803-3

	Phone	Fax	Class
Devore & Johnson Inc 176 Forest Pkwy ... Forest Park GA 30297 *Web:* devoreandjohnson.com	404-366-4243		610
DeVore & Sons Inc 9020 E 35th St N ... Wichita KS 67226 *Web:* www.devoreandsons.com	316-267-3211		637-3
DeVos Place 303 Monroe Ave ... Grand Rapids MI 49503 *TF:* 800-822-6285 ■ *Web:* www.devosplace.org	616-742-6500	742-6590	205
DeVries Global 909 Third Ave ... New York NY 10022 *Web:* www.devriesglobal.com	212-546-8500		636
Devro Inc 785 Old Swamp Rd ... Swansea SC 29160	803-796-9730		473
DeVry University *Colorado Springs* 1175 Kelly Johnson Blvd ... Colorado Springs CO 80920 *TF Help Line:* 877-784-1997 ■ *Web:* www.devry.edu	719-632-3000		800
Denver 6312 S Fiddlers Green Cr Ste 150E ... Greenwood Village CO 80111 *TF:* 800-351-4040 ■ *Web:* www.wes.devry.edu	303-329-3000		800
DeVry University Addison 1221 N Swift Rd ... Addison IL 60101 *TF:* 800-346-5420 ■ *Web:* www.devry.edu	630-953-1300		800
DeVry University Chicago 3300 N Campbell Ave ... Chicago IL 60618 *Web:* www.chi.devry.edu	773-929-8500		800
DeVry University Crystal City 2450 Crystal Dr ... Arlington VA 22202 *Web:* www.devry.edu	703-414-4000		800
DeVry University Dayton 3610 Pentagon Blvd Ste 100 ... Dayton OH 45431 *Web:* www.devry.edu	937-320-3200		800
DeVry University Federal Way 3600 S 344th Way ... Federal Way WA 98001 *TF:* 800-533-3879 ■ *Web:* www.devry.edu	253-943-2800		800
DeVry University Fort Washington 1140 Virginia Dr ... Fort Washington PA 19034 *Web:* www.devry.edu	215-591-5700		800
DeVry University Fremont 6600 Dumbarton Cir ... Fremont CA 94555 **Fax:* Admissions ■ *TF:* 877-492-7903 ■ *Web:* www.fre.devry.edu	510-574-1200	742-0892*	800
DeVry University Houston 11125 Equity Dr ... Houston TX 77041 *TF:* 866-338-7934 ■ *Web:* www.devry.edu	713-973-3100		800
DeVry University Irving 4800 Regent Blvd Ste 200 ... Irving TX 75063 *TF:* 800-633-3879 ■ *Web:* www.devry.edu	972-929-6777		800
DeVry University Kansas City 1310 E 104th St 2nd Fl ... Kansas City MO 64131 *TF:* 800-821-3766 ■ *Web:* www.kc.devry.edu	816-941-0430	943-7551	800
DeVry University Long Beach 3880 Kilroy Airport Way ... Long Beach CA 90806 *TF:* 877-492-6903 ■ *Web:* www.lb.devry.edu	562-997-5300		800
DeVry University Long Island City 3020 Thomson Ave ... Long Island NY 11101 *TF:* 866-338-7934 ■ *Web:* www.devry.edu	718-361-0004		800
DeVry University Miramar 2300 SW 145th Ave ... Miramar FL 33027 *Web:* www.devry.edu	954-499-9800		800
DeVry University North Brunswick 630 US Hwy 1 ... North Brunswick NJ 08902 *TF:* 800-333-3879 ■ *Web:* www.nj.devry.edu	800-333-3879		800
DeVry University Orlando 4000 Millenia Blvd ... Orlando FL 32839 *TF:* 888-857-5757 ■ *Web:* www.devry.edu	407-345-2800		800
DeVry University Phoenix 2149 W Dunlap Ave ... Phoenix AZ 85021 *TF Cust Svc:* 800-528-0250 ■ *Web:* www.phx.devry.edu	602-870-9222		800
DeVry University Pomona 901 Corporate Ctr Dr ... Pomona CA 91768 *Web:* www.pom.devry.edu	909-622-8866		800
DeVry University Sherman Oaks 15301 Ventura Blvd Bldg D-100 ... Sherman Oaks CA 91403 *TF:* 866-338-7934 ■ *Web:* www.devry.edu	818-713-8111		800
DeVry University Tinley Park 18624 W Creek Dr ... Tinley Park IL 60477 *Web:* www.devry.edu	708-342-3300		800
DevTech Systems Inc 1700 N Moore St Ste 1720 ... Arlington VA 22209 *Web:* www.devtechsys.com	703-312-6038	312-6039	194
Devtopia Digital 220 King St W Ste 300 ... Toronto ON M5H1K4	416-239-4826		225
DEW Construction Corp 277 Blair Park Rd Ste 130 ... Williston VT 05495 *Web:* www.dewcorp.com	802-872-0505		186
Dew Distribution Services Inc 2201 Touhy Ave ... Elk Grove Village IL 60007 *TF:* 800-837-3391 ■ *Web:* www.dewdist.com	800-837-3391		649
Dew Software Inc 983 Corporate Way ... Fremont CA 94539 *TF:* 800-274-9185 ■ *Web:* www.dewsoftware.com	510-490-9995		180
DeWAL Industries Inc 15 Ray Trainor Dr ... Narragansett RI 02882 *TF:* 800-366-8356 ■ *Web:* www.dewal.com	401-789-9736		732
Dewalt Corp 1930 22nd St ... Bakersfield CA 93301 *TF:* 800-875-7921 ■ *Web:* dewaltcorp.com	661-323-4600		261
Dewberry & Davis 8401 Arlington Blvd ... Fairfax VA 22031 *Web:* www.dewberry.com	703-849-0100	849-0100	261
Dewey County PO Box 368 ... Taloga OK 73667	580-328-5521		338
Dewey County Clerk of Courts 710 C St ... Timber Lake SD 57656 *Web:* ujs.sd.gov	605-865-3566	865-3641	338
Dewey Ford Inc 3055 SE Delaware Ave ... Ankeny IA 50021 *TF:* 877-704-6793 ■ *Web:* www.deweyford.com	877-704-6793		126
Dewey Services Inc 939 E Union St ... Pasadena CA 91106 *TF:* 877-339-3973 ■ *Web:* deweypest.com	626-568-9248		577
Dewied International Inc 5010 IH-10 E ... San Antonio TX 78219 *TF:* 800-992-5600 ■ *Web:* www.dewied.com	210-661-6161	662-6112	296-26
Dewils Industries Inc 6307 NE 127th Ave ... Vancouver WA 98682 *TF:* 800-641-5641 ■ *Web:* www.dewils.com	360-892-0300		115

Phone | Fax | Class

DeWitt County
201 W Washington St PO Box 439 ... Clinton IL 61727 217-935-7780 338
Web: www.dewittcountyill.com

Dewitt Products Co 5860 Plumer Ave ... Detroit MI 48209 313-554-0575 554-2171 46
TF Cust Svc: 800-962-8599 ■ *Web:* www.dewittproducts.com

DeWitt Ross & Stevens SC
2 E Mifflin St Ste 600 ... Madison WI 53703 608-255-8891 428
TF: 800-900-4250 ■ *Web:* www.dewittross.com

DeWitt Wallace Decorative Arts Museum
326 Francis St W ... Williamsburg VA 23185 800-447-8679 520
TF: 800-447-8679 ■ *Web:* www.colonialwilliamsburg.com

Dewolf Point State Park
45920 County Rt 191 ... Fineview NY 13640 315-482-2012 565
Web: parks.ny.gov/parks/22/details.aspx

DeWys Manufacturing Inc 15300 Eigth Ave ... Marne MI 49435 616-677-5281 198
Web: www.dewysmfg.com

Dewz 1505 J St ... Modesto CA 95354 209-549-1101 671

DEX Products Inc
2019 E Monte Vista Ave Ste 500 ... Vacaville CA 95688 707-451-7864 561
Web: www.dexbaby.com

DexCom Inc 6340 Sequence Dr ... San Diego CA 92121 858-200-0200 85
NASDAQ: DXCM ■ *TF:* 888-738-3646 ■ *Web:* www.dexcom.com

Dexia 445 Pk Ave 7th Fl ... New York NY 10022 212-515-7000 70
Web: www.dexia.com

Dexisive Inc
1840 Michael Faraday Drý Ste 310a ... Reston VA 20190 703-935-0110 180
Web: www.dexisive.com

Dexmet Corp
22 Barnes Industrial Rd S ... Wallingford CT 06492 203-294-4440 295
TF: 800-714-8736 ■ *Web:* www.dexmet.com

Dexrex LLC 101 Rogers St Ste 200 ... Cambridge MA 02142 413-461-3031 590-7230* 225
**Fax Area Code:* 603

Dexta Corp 962 Kaiser Rd ... Napa CA 94558 707-255-2454 228
TF: 800-733-3982 ■ *Web:* www.dexta.com

Dexter & Chaney Inc
9700 Lake City Way NE ... Seattle WA 98115 206-364-1400 179
TF: 800-875-1400 ■ *Web:* www.dexterchaney.com

Dexter Avenue King Memorial Baptist Church
454 Dexter Ave ... Montgomery AL 36104 334-263-3970 50-1
Web: www.dexterkingmemorial.org

Dexter Axle 2900 Industrial Pkwy ... Elkhart IN 46516 574-295-7888 295-8666 60
TF: 800-522-7291 ■ *Web:* www.dexteraxle.com

Dexter Chassis Group
501 Miller Dr ... White Pigeon MI 49099 269-483-7681 120
Web: dexterchassisgroup.com

Dexter Co 2211 W Grimes Ave ... Fairfield IA 52556 641-472-5131 472-5131 427
Web: www.dexter.com

Dexter Magnetic Technologies Inc
1050 Morse Ave ... Elk Grove Village IL 60007 847-956-1140 458
Web: www.dextermag.com

Dexter Research Center Inc
7300 Huron River Dr ... Dexter MI 48130 734-426-3921 201
Web: www.dexterresearch.com

Dexter Solutions 3493 Lamar Ave ... Memphis TN 38118 800-641-3398 7
TF: 800-641-3398 ■ *Web:* dexterhospitality.com

Dexter State Recreation Site
725 Summer St NE Ste C ... Salem OR 97301 541-937-1173 565
Web: www.oregonstateparks.org

Dexter Wilson Engineering
2234 Faraday Ave ... Carlsbad CA 92008 760-438-4422 261
Web: www.dwilsoneng.com

Dexter-Russell Inc 44 River St ... Southbridge MA 01550 508-765-0201 764-2897 222
TF: 800-343-6042 ■ *Web:* www.dexter1818.com

Dey Mansion 199 Totowa Rd ... Wayne NJ 07470 973-696-1776 50-3

DeZurik Water Controls
250 Riverside Ave N ... Sartell MN 56377 320-259-2000 259-2227 789
Web: www.dezurik.com

Df Grafix Inc 5131 Santa Fe St Ste C ... San Diego CA 92109 858-866-0858 627
Web: www.dfgrafix.com

D&F Travel Inc 338 Central Ave Ste 320 ... Dunkirk NY 14048 800-832-3516 772
TF: 800-832-3516 ■ *Web:* www.dfbuses.com

DFC (Duke Diet & Fitness Ctr)
501 Douglas St ... Durham NC 27705 800-235-3853 706
TF: 800-235-3853 ■ *Web:* www.dukedietandfitness.org

DFDFCU (Denver Fire Dept Federal Credit Union)
2201 Federal Blvd ... Denver CO 80211 303-228-5300 228-5333 219
TF: 866-880-7770 ■ *Web:* www.dfdfcu.com

DFI 2404-51 Ave ... Edmonton AB T6P0E4 877-334-7453 536
TF: 877-334-7453 ■ *Web:* www.dfi.ca

DFJ (Draper Fisher Jurvetson)
2882 Sand Hill Rd Ste 150 ... Menlo Park CA 94025 650-233-9000 792
Web: www.dfj.com

DFMC (Delmarva Foundation For Medical Care Inc)
28464 Marlboro Ave ... Easton MD 21601 410-822-0697 474
TF: 800-999-3362 ■ *Web:* delmarvafoundation.org

DfR Solutions LLC
5110 Roanoke Pl Ste 101 ... College Park MD 20740 301-474-0607 261
Web: www.dfrsolutions.com

DFrank Plater Jr Prof Corp
610 Colcord Dr ... Oklahoma City OK 73102 405-236-3739 2

DFRC (US Dairy Forage Research Ctr)
1925 Linden Dr W ... Madison WI 53706 608-890-0050 668
Web: ars.usda.gov

DFS Flooring Inc 15651 Saticoy St ... Van Nuys CA 91406 818-374-5200 291
Web: www.dfsflooring.com

DFS Group 500 Main St ... Groton MA 01471 800-225-9528 110
TF General: 800-225-9528 ■ *Web:* www.dfsonline.com/dfsecat/loginservlet

DFT Communications 40 Temple St ... Fredonia NY 14063 716-673-3000 387
TF: 877-653-3100 ■ *Web:* www.dftcommunications.com

DFT Inc 140 Sheree Blvd ... Exton PA 19341 610-363-8903 789
TF: 800-206-4013 ■ *Web:* www.dft-valves.com

DFW (Dallas-Fort Worth International Airport)
3200 E Airfield Dr PO Box 619428 ... Dallas TX 75261 972-973-8888 574-5509 27
TF: 800-252-7522 ■ *Web:* www.dfwairport.com

Dfw Consulting Group Inc
1616 Corporate Ct ... Irving TX 75038 972-929-1199 261
Web: dfwcgi.com

DFW Furniture Warehouse
2500 Fairmont Ave ... Fairmont WV 26554 304-367-8980 321

DG Capital Management Inc
800 Boylston St 16th Fl ... Boston MA 02199 857-453-6705 194
Web: www.dgcap.com

D&G Machine Products Inc
50 Eisenhower Dr ... Westbrook ME 04092 207-854-1500 454
Web: www.dgmachine.com

DG Yuengling & Son Inc
5th & Mahantongo St ... Pottsville PA 17901 570-622-4141 102
Web: www.yuengling.com

DG3 North America Inc
100 Burma Rd ... Jersey City NJ 07305 201-793-5000 627
Web: www.dg3.com

DGA (Democratic Governors Assn)
1225 Eye St NW Ste 1100 ... Washington DC 20005 202-772-5600 772-5602 48-7
Web: www.democraticgovernors.org

DGAC (Dangerous Goods Advisory Council)
7501 Greenway Ctr Dr Ste 760 ... Greenbelt MD 20770 202-289-4550 289-4074 49-21
Web: www.dgac.org

DGA-PAC 7920 W Sunset Blvd ... Los Angeles CA 90046 310-289-2000 289-2029 615
TF: 800-421-4173 ■ *Web:* www.dga.org

DGCC (Derr & Gruenewald Construction Co)
11100 E 108th Ave ... Brighton CO 80601 303-287-3456 190
Web: www.dgccsteel.com

DGKR (DoubleTree Resort by Hilton Hotel Grand Key)
3990 S Roosevelt Blvd ... Key West FL 33040 305-293-1818 296-6962 669
TF: 800-444-5866 ■ *Web:* doubletree3.hilton.com

DGM Services Inc 1813 Greens Rd ... Houston TX 77032 281-821-0500 393
Web: www.dgm-usa.com

DGSE Cos Inc 11311 Reeder Rd ... Dallas TX 75229 972-484-3662 410
NYSE: DGSE ■ *TF:* 800-527-5307 ■ *Web:* www.dgse.com

DGWB Inc 217 N Main St Ste 200 ... Santa Ana CA 92701 714-881-2300 4
Web: www.dgwb.com

DH (Dominican Hospital)
1555 Soquel Dr ... Santa Cruz CA 95065 831-462-7700 374-3
TF: 866-466-1401 ■ *Web:* www.dominicanhospital.org

DH (Danbury Hospital) 24 Hospital Ave ... Danbury CT 06810 203-739-7000 374-3
TF: 800-516-3658 ■ *Web:* www.danburyhospital.org

DH Bader Management Services Inc
14435 Cherry Ln Ct Ste 210 ... Laurel MD 20707 301-953-1955 652
TF: 888-953-1955 ■ *Web:* dhbader.com

DH Blattner & Sons Inc 392 County Rd 50 ... Avon MN 56310 320-356-7351 356-7392 188-4
Web: www.dhblattner.com

DH Capital LLC
810 Seventh Ave Ste 2005 ... New York NY 10019 212-774-3720 690
Web: www.dhcapital.com

DH Corp 939 Eglinton Ave E ... Toronto ON M4G4H7 416-696-7700 401
Web: www.dh.com/cheques

Dh Web Inc 11377 Robinwood Dr Ste D ... Hagerstown MD 21742 301-733-7672 177
TF: 877-567-6599 ■ *Web:* www.dhwebsites.com

DHA (Dameron Hospital Assn)
525 W Acacia St ... Stockton CA 95203 209-944-5550 374-3
Web: www.dameronhospital.org

Dhaba 309 King St W ... Toronto ON M5V1J5 416-740-6622 740-4519 671
Web: www.dhaba.ca

Dharma Sushi 1576 Argyle St ... Halifax NS B3J2B3 902-425-7785 671

Dharma Trading Co 1604 Fourth St ... San Rafael CA 94901 415-456-1211 711
TF: 800-542-5227 ■ *Web:* dharmatrading.com

DHC (Dechert-Hampe & Co)
33332 Valle Rd ... San Juan Capistrano CA 92675 949-429-1999 194
TF: 800-790-4788 ■ *Web:* www.dechert-hampe.com

Dhc Communications Inc 607 Front St ... Nelson BC V1L4B6 250-352-0861 175
TF: 800-750-4662 ■ *Web:* www.dhc.bc.ca

DHI (Door & Hardware Institute)
14150 Newbrook Dr Ste 200 ... Chantilly VA 20151 703-222-2010 222-2410 49-3
Web: www.dhi.org

DHI Computing Service Inc 1525 W 820 N ... Provo UT 84601 800-453-9400 374-5316* 178-11
**Fax Area Code:* 801 ■ *TF:* 800-992-1344 ■ *Web:* www.dhiprovo.com

DHI Mortgage Co Ltd
10700 Pecan Park Blvd Ste 450 ... Austin TX 78750 512-502-0545 502-0031 217
TF: 800-315-8434 ■ *Web:* www.dhimortgage.com

DHI Services Inc
33502 State Hwy 249 ... Pinehurst TX 77362 281-201-4141 259-0260 536
Web: www.dhiservices.com

DHL Analytical
2300 Double Creek Dr ... Round Rock TX 78664 512-388-8222 743
Web: www.dhlanalytical.com

DHL Global Forwarding (Canada) Inc
6200 Edwards Blvd ... Mississauga ON L5T2V7 855-345-7447 311
TF: 855-345-7447

DHL Global Mail
2700 S Commerce Pkwy Ste 300 ... Weston FL 33331 954-903-6300 546
TF: 800-805-9306 ■ *Web:* www.dhl-usa.com

DHM Adhesives Inc 509 S Wall St Ste A ... Calhoun GA 30701 706-629-7960 711
Web: www.dhmadhesives.com

DHMC (Denver Health Medical Ctr)
777 Bannock St ... Denver CO 80204 303-436-6000 374-3
TF: 800-222-1222 ■ *Web:* www.denverhealth.org

DHMC (Davis Hospital & Medical Ctr)
1600 W Antelope Dr ... Layton UT 84041 801-807-1000 807-7610 374-3
TF: 877-898-6080 ■ *Web:* www.davishospital.com

DHR International
71 S Wacker Dr Ste 2700 ... Chicago IL 60606 312-782-1581 782-2096 266
Web: www.dhrinternational.com

DHS (Department of Homeland Security)
245 Murray Dr SW Bldg 410 ... Washington DC 20528 202-282-8000 235-0443* 340-11
**Fax Area Code:* 703 ■ *Web:* www.dhs.gov

DHS Drilling Co 1813 Coleman Cir ... Casper WY 82601 307-473-5377 540
Web: www.dhsdrilling.com

Dhx Advertising Inc
217 NE Eighth Ave ... Portland OR 97232 503-872-9616 7
Web: www.dhxadv.com

DI (Denison Industries) 22 Fielder Dr ... Denison TX 75020 903-786-6500 786-6575 308
Web: denisonindustries.com

Di Graphics Inc 4850 Ward Rd ... Wheat Ridge CO 80033 303-425-0510 627
TF: 800-433-2257 ■ *Web:* www.digraphics.com

Name / Address	City	State	ZIP	Phone	Fax	Class
Di Highway Sign & Structure Corp						
40 Grcenmon Avo	New York Mills	NY	13417	315-736-8312		701
Web: www.dihighway.com						
Di Paolo Cucina						
8560 Holcomb Bridge Rd	Alpharetta	GA	30022	770-587-1051		671
Web: www.dipaolorestaurant.com						
Diabetes Advisor Magazine						
1701 N Beauregard St	Alexandria	VA	22311	800-806-7801		457-16
TF: 800-342-2383 ■ *Web:* www.diabetesforecast.org						
Diabetes Forecast 8430 Peach St	Erie	PA	16509	814-864-5809		516
TF: 866-979-8132 ■ *Web:* www.bianchihonda.com						
Diabetes Forecast Magazine						
1701 N Beauregard St	Alexandria	VA	22311	703-549-1500		457-13
TF: 800-676-4065 ■ *Web:* www.diabetes.org						
Diabetes Research Institute						
1450 NW Tenth Ave	Miami	FL	33136	954-964-4040	243-4404*	668
**Fax Area Code: 305* ■ *TF:* 800-321-3437 ■ *Web:* www.diabetesresearch.org						
Diabetic Care Services & Pharmacy						
34099 Melinz Pkwy Unit F	Eastlake	OH	44095	440-954-7709		237
Diablo Media LLC 2641 Walnut St	Denver	CO	80205	303-305-4052		4
Web: www.diablomedia.com						
Diablo Mfg Company Inc						
900 Golden Gate Terr Ste B	Grass Valley	CA	95945	530-272-2241	272-2243	409
TF Cust Svc: 800-551-2233 ■ *Web:* www.diablosilver.com						
Diablo Valley College						
321 Golf Club Rd	Pleasant Hill	CA	94523	925-685-1230	609-8085	162
TF: 800-227-1060 ■ *Web:* www.dvc.edu						
Diacarb Tools Inc						
2525 Rue De Miniac	Saint-laurent	QC	H4S1E5	514-331-4360		358
Web: www.diacarb.com						
Diageo North America 801 Main Ave	Norwalk	CT	06851	203-229-2100		80-1
TF: 800-847-4109 ■ *Web:* www.diageo.com						
Diagnos Inc						
Ste 340 7005 Taschereau Blvd	Brossard	QC	J4Z1A7	450-678-8882		177
TF: 800 373 6303 ■ *Web:* www.diagnos.ca						
Diagnostic Imaging Inc						
4 Neshaminy Interplex Ste 209	Trevose	PA	19053	215-244-3070		415
Web: diiradiology.com						
Diagnostic Laboratory of Oklahoma LLC						
225 N East 97th St	Oklahoma City	OK	73114	405-608-6100		415
TF: 800-891-2917 ■ *Web:* www.dlolab.com						
Diagnostic Laboratory Services Inc						
99-859 Iwaiwa St	Aiea	HI	96701	808-589-5100		415
Web: www.dlslab.com						
Diagnostic Pathology Medical Group Inc						
3301 C St Ste 200e	Sacramento	CA	95816	916-446-0424		415
Web: www.dpmginc.com						
Diagnostics Biochem Canada Inc (DBC)						
41 Byron Ave	Dorchester	ON	N6M1A1	519-681-8731	268-7167	231
Web: www.dbc-labs.com						
Diagrind Inc 10491 164th Pl	Orland Park	IL	60467	708-460-4333	460-8842	1
TF: 800-790-4333 ■ *Web:* www.diagrind.com						
Dial Global Inc						
Candler Tower 220 W 42nd St	New York	NY	10036	212-967-2888		644
Web: www.westwoodone.com						
Dial Lighting Gallery						
2240 Kaluaopalena St	Honolulu	HI	96819	808-845-7811		361
Dial Security Inc						
760 W Ventura Blvd	Camarillo	CA	93010	805-389-6700		693
Web: www.dialcomm.com						
Dial Tool Industries Inc						
201 S Church St	Addison	IL	60101	630-543-3600		488
Web: www.dialtool.com						
Dial800 LLC						
9911 Pico Blvd Ste 1200	Los Angeles	CA	90035	800-342-5800		224
TF: 800 700 1987 ■ *Web:* www.dial800.com						
DialAmerica Marketing Inc						
960 MacArthur Blvd	Mahwah	NJ	07495	201-327-0200	327-4875	737
Web: www.dialamerica.com						
Dialight Corp 1501 SR 34	Farmingdale	NJ	07727	732-919-3119	751-5778	696
Web: www.dialight.com						
Dialink Corp						
1660 S Amphlett Blvd Ste 340	San Mateo	CA	94402	800-896-3425		387
TF: 800-896-3425 ■ *Web:* www.dialink.com						
Dialog						
2250 Perimeter Pk Dr Ste 300	Morrisville	NC	27560	919-804-6400	804-6410	387
TF: 800-334-2564 ■ *Web:* proquest.com						
Dialog Direct 13700 Oakland Ave Ste 400	Troy	MI	48083	313-957-5075		317
Web: www.dialogue-marketing.com						
Dialog One Llc						
2380 Wycliff St Ste 200	Saint Paul	MN	55114	651-379-8600		768
Web: www.dialog-one.com						
Dialog Wireline Services LLC						
3100 Maverick Dr	Kilgore	TX	75662	903-988-2311		539
TF: 800-409-8341 ■ *Web:* www.dialogwireline.com						
Dialog, The 1925 Delaware Ave	Wilmington	DE	19806	302-573-3109	573-6948	532-4
TF: 877-225-7870 ■ *Web:* www.cdow.org						
Dialogic Inc 1504 Mccarthy Blvd	Milpitas	CA	95035	408-750-9400		180
TF: 800-755-4444 ■ *Web:* www.dialogic.com						
Diamond Aircraft Industries Inc						
1560 Crumlin Sideroad	London	ON	N5V1S2	519-457-4000		20
TF: 888-359-3220 ■ *Web:* www.diamondaircraft.com						
Diamond Antenna & Microwave Corp						
59 Porter Rd	Littleton	MA	01460	978-486-0039	486-0079	253
TF: 800-638-2048 ■ *Web:* www.diamondantenna.com						
Diamond Attachments LLC						
2801A S Mississippi	Atoka	OK	74525	580-889-6202		791
TF: 800-445-1917 ■ *Web:* www.diamondattachments.com						
Diamond Bakery Co 756 Moowaa St	Honolulu	HI	96817	808-847-3551		297-3
Web: www.diamondbakery.com						
Diamond Bar High School						
21400 Pathfinder Rd	Diamond Bar	CA	91765	909-594-1405		685
Web: dbhs.wvusd.k12.ca.us						
Diamond Brand Canvas Products						
145 Cane Creek Industrial Pk Rd Ste 1	Fletcher	NC	28732	828-209-0322		733
Web: www.diamondbrandgear.com						
Diamond Cellar Inc 6280 Sawmill Rd	Dublin	OH	43017	614-336-4545		410
Web: www.diamondcellar.com						
Diamond Chain Co						
402 Kentucky Ave	Indianapolis	IN	46225	317-638-6431	638-6431	620
TF Cust Svc: 800-872-4246 ■ *Web:* www.diamondchain.com						
Diamond Chemical Company Inc						
Union Ave & Dubois St	East Rutherford	NJ	07073	201-935-4300	935-6997	151
Web: www.diamondchem.com						
Diamond Coach Corp						
2300 W Fourth St PO Box 489	Oswego	KS	67356	620-795-2191	795-2191	516
TF: 800-442-4645 ■ *Web:* www.diamondcoach.com						
Diamond Comic Distributors Inc						
1966 Greenspring Dr Ste 300	Timonium	MD	21093	410-560-7100	560-7148	637-5
TF: 800-452-6642 ■ *Web:* www.diamondcomics.com						
Diamond Council of America (DCA)						
3212 W End Ave Ste 202	Nashville	TN	37203	615-385-5301	385-4955	49-4
TF: 877-283-5669 ■ *Web:* www.diamondcouncil.org						
Diamond Creek Capital						
28 N Vista De Catalina	Laguna Beach	CA	92651	949-429-7707		528
Web: www.diamondcreekcap.com						
Diamond d General Engineering Inc						
32500 State Hwy 16	Woodland	CA	95695	530-662-2042		256
Web: www.ddge.net						
Diamond Die & Mold Co						
35401 Groesbeck Hwy	Clinton Township	MI	48035	586-791-0700	791-5419	757
Web: www.diamond-die.com						
Diamond Drugs Inc 645 Kolter Dr	Indiana	PA	15701	724-349-1111		231
TF: 800-882-6337 ■ *Web:* www.diamondpharmacy.com						
Diamond Edge Inc						
661 W State St Ste A	Pleasant Grove	UT	84062	801-785-8473		178-2
Web: www.diamondedge.com						
Diamond Energy Services Inc						
1521 N Service Rd W	Swift Current	SK	S9H3S9	306-778-6682		317
Web: www.diamondenergy.ca						
Diamond Equipment Inc						
1060 E Diamond Ave	Evansville	IN	47711	812-425-4428	421-1036	358
TF: 800-258-4428 ■ *Web:* www.diamondequipment.com						
Diamond Foods Inc 1050 S Diamond St	Stockton	CA	95205	209 467 6000		296-28
NASDAQ: DMND ■ *Web:* www.diamondfoods.com						
Diamond Fruit Growers Inc						
3515 Chevron Dr	Hood River	OR	97031	541-354-5300	354-5394	11-1
Web: www.diamondfruit.com						
Diamond Graphics Inc						
14350 Azurite St NW	Ramsey	MN	55303	763-235-4141		627
Web: www.dgiusa.net						
Diamond Group 13101 Preston Rd Ste 212	Dallas	TX	75240	972-788-1111		693
Web: www.thediamondgroup.ws						
Diamond H2O N1022 Quality Dr	Greenville	WI	54942	920-757-5440		104
TF: 800-236-8931 ■ *Web:* www.diamondh2o.com						
Diamond Head Inn 605 Diamond St	San Diego	CA	92109	858-273-1900	273-8532	379
TF: 888-478-7829 ■ *Web:* www.diamondheadinn.com						
Diamond Head State Monument						
PO Box 621	Honolulu	HI	96809	808-587-0404	587-0390	565
Web: www.hawaii.gov						
Diamond Hill Nursing & Rehabilitation						
100 New Tpke Rd	Troy	NY	12182	518-235-1410	426-4792	450
Web: news10.com						
Diamond Innovations Inc USA						
6325 Huntley Rd	Columbus	OH	43229	614-438-2000		1
Web: www.diamondinnovations.com						
Diamond Manufacturing Co						
243 W Eigth St	Wyoming	PA	18644	570-693-0300	693-3500	488
TF: 800-233-9601 ■ *Web:* www.diamondman.com						
Diamond Materials 924 S Heald St	Wilmington	DE	19801	302-658-6524		190
Web: www.diamondmaterials.com						
Diamond Mattress Company Inc						
3112 Las Hermanas St E	Compton	CA	90221	310-638-0363	638-2005	471
Web: www.diamondmattress.com						
Diamond Mktg Solutions Group Inc						
280 Madsen Dr	Bloomingdale	IL	60108	630-523-5250		637-6
Web: dmsolutions.com						
Diamond Motors/Mazda						
10968 Airline Hwy	Baton Rouge	LA	70816	225-295-3900		57
Web: diamondmazda.com						
Diamond Offshore Drilling Inc						
15415 Katy Fwy	Houston	TX	77094	281-492-5300	492-5316	540
NYSE: DO ■ *TF:* 800-848-1980 ■ *Web:* www.diamondoffshore.com						
Diamond Oil Well Drilling Company Inc						
2003 Commerce Dr	Midland	TX	79703	281-492-5300		539
TF: 800-848-1980 ■ *Web:* www.diamondoffshore.com						
Diamond Packaging Company Inc						
111 Commerce Dr PO Box 23620	Rochester	NY	14692	585-334-8030	334-9141	101
TF: 800-333-4079 ■ *Web:* www.diamondpackaging.com						
Diamond Parking Inc						
605 First Ave Ste 6000	Seattle	WA	98104	206-284-3100		562
Web: www.diamondparking.com						
Diamond Perforated Metals Inc						
7300 W Sunnyview Ave	Visalia	CA	93291	559-651-1889	651-1815	488
TF: 800-642-4334 ■ *Web:* www.diamondperf.com						
Diamond Personnel LLC						
352 Seventh Ave 3rd Fl	New York	NY	10001	212-631-7520		260
Web: www.diamondjob.com						
Diamond Plastics Corp						
1212 Johnstown Rd PO Box 1608	Grand Island	NE	68802	308-384-4400		596
TF: 800-782-7473 ■ *Web:* www.dpcpipe.com						
Diamond Products Inc 333 Prospect	Elyria	OH	44035	800-321-5336		1
TF: 800-321-5336 ■ *Web:* diamondproductsllc.com						
Diamond Realty Management Corp						
790 Watervliet Shaker Rd Ste 2	Latham	NY	12110	518-783-5000		652
Web: www.ambroselec.com						
Diamond Resorts International						
3745 Las Vegas Blvd S	Las Vegas	NV	89109	702-261-1000		753
Web: www.diamondresorts.com						
Diamond Saw Works Inc 12290 Olean Rd	Chaffee	NY	14030	716-496-7417		682
TF: 800-828-1180 ■ *Web:* www.diamondsaw.com						
Diamond Services Co						
4220 Oklahoma Ave	Woodward	OK	73801	580-256-3385		539
Web: diamond-services.com						
Diamond Services Corp						
503 S DeGravelle Rd	Amelia	LA	70340	985-631-2187	631-2442	539
TF: 800-879-1162 ■ *Web:* www.dscgom.com						

Name / Address	City	State	Zip	Phone	Fax	Class
Diamond Supply Co 447 N Fairfax Ave *Web:* www.diamondsupplyco.com	Los Angeles	CA	90036	323-966-5970		711
Diamond Technology Inc 567 Sutter St 3rd FL *Web:* www.diamondti.com	San Francisco	CA	94102	415-422-0074	727-3536	180
Diamond Tool & Die Inc 508 29th Ave *TF:* 800-227-1084 ■ *Web:* www.dtdjobshop.com	Oakland	CA	94601	510-534-7050	534-0454	757
Diamond Tour 203 E Lincoln Hwy *TF:* 800-826-5340 ■ *Web:* www.diamondtour.com	Dekalb	IL	60115	815-787-2649		711
Diamond Transportation System Inc 5021 21st St *TF:* 800-927-5702 ■ *Web:* diamondtrans.net	Racine	WI	53406	262-554-5400		780
Diamond Truck Body Manufacturing Inc 1908 E Fremont St *Web:* www.diamondtruckbody.com	Stockton	CA	95205	209-943-1655		57
Diamond V Mills Inc PO Box 74570 *TF:* 800-373-7234 ■ *Web:* www.diamondv.com	Cedar Rapids	IA	52407	319-366-0745		447
Diamond Vogel Paints 1110 Albany Pl SE PO Box 380 *TF:* 800-728-6435 ■ *Web:* www.diamondvogel.com	Orange City	IA	51041	712-737-4993	737-4998	550
Diamond Z Engineering Inc 5670 State Rd *Web:* diamondzengineering.com	Cleveland	OH	44134	440-842-6501		261
Diamond Z Manufacturing 11299 Bass Ln *TF:* 800-949-2383 ■ *Web:* www.diamondz.com	Caldwell	ID	83605	208-585-2929		295
Diamondback Energy Services LLC 14301 Caliber Dr Ste 200 *Web:* www.diamondbackenergy.com	Oklahoma City	OK	73134	405-242-4080		536
DiamondJacks Casino Resort 711 Diamond Jacks Blvd *TF:* 866-552-9629 ■ *Web:* diamondjacks.com	Bossier City	LA	71111	318-678-7777		133
DiamondRock Hospitality Co (DRHC) 3 Bethesda Metro Ctr Ste 1500 *NYSE: DRH* ■ *Web:* www.drhc.com	Bethesda	MD	20814	240-744-1150	744-1199	654
Dian Fossey Gorilla Fund International 800 Cherokee Ave SE *TF:* 800-851-0203 ■ *Web:* www.gorillafund.org	Atlanta	GA	30315	404-624-5881		48-3
Diana Fruit Company Inc 651 Mathew St	Santa Clara	CA	95050	408-727-9631	727-9890	296-20
Diana Wortham Theatre at Pack Place 2 S Pack Sq *TF:* 800-999-2160 ■ *Web:* www.dwtheatre.com	Asheville	NC	28801	828-257-4530	251-5652	572
Diana's Mexican Food Products Inc 16330 Pioneer Blvd *Web:* www.dianas.net	Norwalk	CA	90650	562-926-5802		123
Diane Von Furstenberg 440 W 14th St *TF:* 888-472-2383 ■ *Web:* world.dvf.com	New York	NY	10014	212-741-6607		277
DIANON Systems Inc 1 Forest Pkwy *TF:* 800-328-2666 ■ *Web:* www.dianon.com	Shelton	CT	06484	203-926-7100		418
Diario Las Americas 888 Brickell Ave 5th Fl *Web:* www.diariolasamericas.com	Miami	FL	33131	305-633-3341		532-2
Dias, Clifford Pe PC 7 Dey St *Web:* www.diaseng.com	New York	NY	10007	212-608-4811		261
DiaSorin Inc 1951 NW Ave *TF:* 855-677-0600 ■ *Web:* www.diasorin.com	Stillwater	MN	55082	651-439-9710		231
DIATHERIX Laboratories Inc 601 Genome Way Ste 4208 *Web:* www.diatherix.com	Huntsville	AL	35806	256-327-0699		415
Diaz Wholesale & Mfg Co Inc 5501 Fulton Industrial Blvd *Web:* www.diazfoods.com	Atlanta	GA	30336	404-344-5421		297-11
Diaz-Balart Mario (Rep R - FL) 440 Cannon HOB *Web:* mariodiazbalart.house.gov	Washington	DC	20515	202-225-4211	225-8576	342-2
DiAZiT Company Inc 941 US 1 Hwy *TF Cust Svc:* 800-334-6641 ■ *Web:* www.diazit.com	Youngsville	NC	27596	919-556-5188	556-3757	701
Diba Industries Inc 4 Precision Rd *Web:* www.dibaind.com	Danbury	CT	06810	203-744-0773		419
Dibble & Associates Consulting 7878 N 16th St Ste 200 *Web:* www.dibblecorp.com	Phoenix	AZ	85020	602-957-1155		261
Diboll Texas Independent School District 215 N Temple Dr *Web:* www.dibollisd.com	Diboll	TX	75941	936-829-4718		434-3
Dibrina Sure Benefits Consulting Inc 62 Frood Rd Ste 302 *Web:* dibrinasure.com	Sudbury	ON	P3C4Z3	705-688-9393		390
Dibuduo & Defendis 6873 N W Ave Ste 101 *Web:* dibu.com	Fresno	CA	93711	559-432-0222		390
Dicaliter / Dicaperlr Minerals, Inc 1 Bala Ave Ste 310 *TF:* 800-537-4415 ■ *Web:* dicalite.com	Bala Cynwyd	PA	19004	610-660-8820	660-8817	500
DiCarlo Distributors Inc 1630 N Ocean Ave *TF:* 800-342-2756 ■ *Web:* www.dicarlofood.com	Holtsville	NY	11742	631-758-6000	758-6096	297-8
Dice Inc 4101 NW Urbandale Dr *TF:* 877-386-3323 ■ *Web:* www.dice.com	Urbandale	IA	50322	515-280-1144	280-1452	260
dicentra 161 Bay St 27th Fl *TF:* 866-647-3279 ■ *Web:* www.dicentra.com	Toronto	ON	M5J2S1	416-361-3400		193
Dichello Distributors Inc 55 Marsh Hill Rd *Web:* www.dichello.com	Orange	CT	06477	203-891-2100		81-3
Dick & Jenny's 4501 Tchoupitoulas St *Web:* www.dickandjennys.com	New Orleans	LA	70115	504-894-9880		671
Dick Anderson Construction Inc 3424 Hwy 12 E *Web:* www.daconstruction.com	Helena	MT	59601	406-443-3225	443-1537	186
Dick Blick Co PO Box 1267 *TF Orders:* 800-447-8192 ■ *Web:* www.dickblick.com	Galesburg	IL	61402	309-343-6181		45
Dick Blick Holdings Inc 1849 Green Bay Rd Ste 310 *Web:* dickblick.com	Highland Park	IL	60035	847-681-6800		535
Dick Brantmeier Ford Inc 3624 Kohler Memorial Dr *TF:* 800-498-6111 ■ *Web:* dickbrantmeier.com	Sheboygan	WI	53082	920-458-6111		57
Dick Clark Productions Inc (DCP) 2900 Olympic Blvd *Web:* www.dickclark.com	Santa Monica	CA	90404	310-255-4600		514
Dick Gores Rv World 14590 Duval Pl W *TF:* 800-635-7008 ■ *Web:* www.dickgoresrvworld.com	Jacksonville	FL	32218	904-741-5100		516
Dick Lavy Trucking Inc 8848 State Rt 121 *TF:* 800-345-5289 ■ *Web:* www.dicklavytrucking.com	Bradford	OH	45308	937-448-2104		780
Dick Masheter Ford Inc 1090 S Hamilton Rd *TF:* 888-839-9646 ■ *Web:* masheterford.net	Columbus	OH	43227	888-839-9646		57
Dick's Last Resort 2211 N Lambar St *Web:* www.dickslastresort.com	Dallas	TX	75202	214-747-0001		670
Dick's Sporting Goods Inc 345 Ct St *Web:* www.dickssportinggoods.com	Coraopolis	PA	15108	724-273-3400		711
Dicke Safety Products 1201 Warren Ave *TF:* 877-891-0050 ■ *Web:* www.dicketool.com	Downers Grove	IL	60515	630-969-0050		360-3
Dickel George A Co 1950 Cascade Hollow Rd *Web:* www.georgedickel.com	Tullahoma	TN	37388	931-857-4110		80-1
Dickens Books Ltd 544 S First St **Fax Area Code:* 414 ■ *TF:* 800-236-7323	Milwaukee	WI	53202	800-236-7323	274-8690*	95
Dickens County 512 Montgomery St PO Box 120 *TF:* 800-385-8412 ■ *Web:* co.dickens.tx.us	Dickens	TX	79229	806-623-5531	623-5240	338
Dickenson County 293 Main St PO Box 1098 *Web:* www.dickensonva.org	Clintwood	VA	24228	276-926-1676	926-1649	338
Dickenson County School District 309 Volunteer Ave *TF:* 866-632-9992 ■ *Web:* www.dickenson.k12.va.us	Clintwood	VA	24228	276-926-4643	926-6374	685
Dickerson Engineering Inc 3343 N Ridge Ave *Web:* www.dei-pe.com	Arlington Heights	IL	60004	847-966-0290	966-0294	256
Dickerson Park Zoo 3043 N Ft *Web:* www.dickersonparkzoo.org	Springfield	MO	65803	417-833-1570	833-4459	823
Dickey County 205 15th St N PO Box 238 *Web:* www.dickeynd.com	Ellendale	ND	58436	701-349-4348	349-3277	338
Dickey Transport 401 E Fourth St *TF:* 800-247-1081 ■ *Web:* dickeytransport.com	Packwood	IA	52580	319-695-3601		579
DICKEY-John Corp 5200 Dickey-John Rd *TF:* 800-637-2952 ■ *Web:* www.dickey-john.com	Auburn	IL	62615	217-438-3371		639
Dickie McCamey & Chilcote PC 2 Ppg Pl Ste 400 *Web:* dmclaw.com	Pittsburgh	PA	15222	412-281-7272		445
Dickinson Area Partnership 600 S Stephenson Ave *Web:* www.dickinsonchamber.com	Iron Mountain	MI	49801	906-774-2002	774-2004	139
Dickinson Brands Inc 31 E High St *TF:* 800-424-9300 ■ *Web:* dickinsonbrands.com	East Hampton	CT	06424	860-267-2279		582
Dickinson Cameron Construction Company Inc 6184 Innovation Way *Web:* www.dickinsoncameron.com	Carlsbad	CA	92009	760-438-9114		186
Dickinson College PO Box 1773 **Fax:* Admissions ■ *TF:* 800-644-1773 ■ *Web:* www.dickinson.edu	Carlisle	PA	17013	717-243-5121	245-1442*	166
Dickinson College Waidner-Spahr Library PO Box 1773 *TF:* 800-543-3809 ■ *Web:* dickinson.edu	Carlisle	PA	17013	717-245-1397	245-1439	434-6
Dickinson Convention & Visitors Bureau 72 E Museum Dr *TF:* 800-279-7391 ■ *Web:* www.visitdickinson.com	Dickinson	ND	58601	701-483-4988	483-9261	206
Dickinson County PO Box 248 *Web:* www.dkcoks.org	Abilene	KS	67410	785-263-3774	263-2045	338
Dickinson County 705 S Stephenson Ave PO Box 609 *Web:* www.dickinsoncountymi.gov	Iron Mountain	MI	49801	906-774-0988	774-4660	338
Dickinson County 1802 Hill Ave *TF:* 800-368-8683 ■ *Web:* dickinsoncountyiowa.org	Spirit Lake	IA	51360	712-336-3356		338
Dickinson County Healthcare System 1721 S Stephenson Ave *Web:* www.dchs.org	Iron Mountain	MI	49801	906-774-1313		374-3
Dickinson County Library 401 Iron Mtn St *Web:* www.dcl-lib.org	Iron Mountain	MI	49801	906-774-1218		434-3
Dickinson Financial Corp 1111 Main St Ste 1600	Kansas City	MO	64105	816-472-5244		360-2
Dickinson Homes Inc 404 N Stephenson Ave Hwy US-2 PO Box 2245 *TF:* 800 438 4687 ■ *Web:* www.dickinsonhomes.com	Iron Mountain	MI	49801	906-774-2186	774-5207	106
Dickinson Press Inc 5100 33rd St SE *Web:* dickinsonpress.com	Grand Rapids	MI	49512	616-957-5100		637-2
Dickinson Roundell Inc 19 E 66th St *Web:* www.simondickinson.com	New York	NY	10065	212-772-8083	772-8186	42
Dickinson State University 291 Campus Dr **Fax:* Admissions ■ *TF:* 800-279-4295 ■ *Web:* www.dickinsonstate.edu	Dickinson	ND	58601	701-483-2507	483-9959*	166
Dickinson Theaters Inc 6801 W 107th St *Web:* www.dtmovies.com	Overland Park	KS	66211	913-432-2334		748
Dickman Directories Inc 6145 Columbus Pk *TF:* 877-836-4154 ■ *Web:* dickmandirectories.com	Lewis Center	OH	43035	740-548-6130	548-2217	637-6
Dickson Co 930 S Westwood Ave *TF:* 800-757-3747 ■ *Web:* www.dicksondata.com	Addison	IL	60101	630-543-3747	543-0498	201
Dickson Consulting 351 Old Babcock Trl *Web:* www.dicksonconsulting.biz	Gibsonia	PA	15044	724-272-1527		463
Dickson County PO Box 267 *TF:* 800-449-8366 ■ *Web:* www.dicksoncountytn.gov	Charlotte	TN	37036	615-789-7003	789-6075	338
Dickson County Chamber of Commerce 119 Hwy 70 E *TF:* 877-718-4967 ■ *Web:* www.dicksoncountychamber.com	Dickson	TN	37055	615-446-2349	441-3112	139

Name / Address	City	State	ZIP	Phone	Fax	Class
Dickson Herald PO Box 387 *Web:* www.tenncsocon.com	Ashland City	TN	37015	615-446-2811		532-4
Dickson Industries Inc 2425 Dean Ave *Web:* www.dicksonindustries.com	Des Moines	IA	50317	515-262-8061	262-1844	155-19
Dicksons Inc 709 B Ave E *Web:* www.dicksonsgifts.com	Seymour	IN	47274	812-522-1308		200
Dickstein Shapiro LLP 1825 Eye St NW *TF:* 800-203-3447 ■ *Web:* www.dicksteinshapiro.com	Washington	DC	20006	202-420-2200	420-2201	428
Dickten Masch Plastics LLC N44 W33341 Watertown Plank Rd *Web:* www.dicktenplastics.com	Nashotah	WI	53058	262-369-5555	367-5630	604
Diclaudio & Kramer LLC 50 Abele Rd Ste 1001	Bridgeville	PA	15017	412-220-7722		2
Dicom Inc 1650 Des Peres Rd Ste 100 *Web:* dicominc.com	St. Louis	MO	63131	314-909-0900		7
Didax Inc 395 Main St *TF:* 800-458-0024 ■ *Web:* www.didax.com	Rowley	MA	01969	800-458-0024	350-2345	243
Didier Aaron Inc 32 E 67th St *Web:* www.didieraaron.com	New York	NY	10065	212-988-5248		42
Die Services International 45000 Van Born Rd *TF:* 800-555-1212 ■ *Web:* www.dieservicesinternational.com	Belleville	MI	48111	734-699-3400	699-4081	757
Diebold & Assoc Ltd 1340 Remington Rd *Web:* dieboldcpa.com	Schaumburg	IL	60173	847-755-9000		2
Diebold Nixdorf Inc 5995 Mayfair Rd *NYSE: DBD* ■ *TF:* 800-999-3600 ■ *Web:* www.diebold.com	North Canton	OH	44720	330-490-4000		801
Dieckmann & Assoc 500 N Michigan Ave	Chicago	IL	60611	312-819-5900		266
Diecrafters Inc 1349 55th Ct *TF:* 800-632-4111 ■ *Web:* www.diecrafters.com	Cicero	IL	60804	708-656-3336	656-3386	555
Diederiks & Whitelaw Plc 13885 Hedgewood Dr Ste 317 *Web:* www.dwpatentlaw.com	Woodbridge	VA	22193	703 583 8300		428
Diedre Moire Corporation Inc 510 Horizon Ctr *Web:* www.diedremoire.com	Robbinsville	NJ	08691	609-584-9000		260
Dieffenbach's Potato Chips 51 Host Rd *Web:* www.dieffenbachs.com	Womelsdorf	PA	19567	610-589-2385		123
Diego & Son Printing Inc 2104 National Ave *TF:* 800-559-5529 ■ *Web:* www.diegoandson.com	San Diego	CA	92113	619 233 5373		627
Diehl Automotive Group Inc 258 Pittsburgh Rd *Web:* www.diehlauto.com	Butler	PA	16002	724-282-8898		57
Diehl Woodworking Mach Inc 981 S Wabash St PO Box 465 *TF:* 800-929-3070 ■ *Web:* diehlmachines.com	Wabash	IN	46992	260-563-2102	563-0206	821
Dielectric Communications Inc 22 Tower Rd *TF:* 800-341-9678 ■ *Web:* www.dielectric.com	Raymond	ME	04071	800-341-9678		647
Dielectric Corp W141 N9250 Fountain Blvd *Web:* www.dielectriccorp.com	Menomonee Falls	WI	53051	262-255-2600		596
Dielectric Laboratories Inc 2777 Route 20 E *Web:* www.knowlescapacitors.com	Cazenovia	NY	13035	315-655-8710	655-0445	250
Dielectric Sciences Inc 88 Turnpike Rd *Web:* www.dielectricsciences.com	Chelmsford	MA	01824	978-250-1507		815
Dielectrics Industries Inc 300 Burnett Rd *TF:* 800-472-7286 ■ *Web:* www.dielectrics.com	Chicopee	MA	01020	413-594-8111	594-2343	600
Diemasters Manufacturing Inc 2100 Touhy Ave *Web:* www.thediemasters.com	Elk Grove Village	IL	60007	847-640-9900	640-9900	757
Die-Matic Corp 201 Eastview Dr *Web:* www.die-matic.com	Brooklyn Hts	OH	44131	216-749-4656		488
Diemolding Corp 125 Rasbach St *Web:* www.diemolding.com	Canastota	NY	13032	315-697-2221		604
Dierbergs Markets Inc 16690 Swingley Ridge Rd *Web:* www.dierbergs.com	Chesterfield	MO	63017	636-532-8884	532-8759	345
Dieringer Research Group Inc, The 200 Bishops Way *Web:* www.thedrg.com	Brookfield	WI	53005	262-432-5200		466
Diesel Engine & Parts Co 8123 Hillsboro *Web:* www.depco.com	Houston	TX	77029	713-675-6100		358
Diesel Injection Service Company Inc 4710 Allmond Ave *Web:* www.dieselusa.com	Louisville	KY	40209	502-361-1181		247
Diesel Technology Forum Inc 5291 Corporate Dr Ste 102 *Web:* dieselforum.org	Frederick	MD	21703	301-668-7230		533
Dieselpoint Inc 117 N Jefferson St *Web:* www.dieselpoint.com	Chicago	IL	60661	773-528-1700		174
Dieste 1999 Bryan St Ste 2700 *Web:* www.dieste.com	Dallas	TX	75201	214-259-8000		4
Diestel Turkey Ranch 22200 Lyons Bald Mtn Rd *Web:* www.diestelturkey.com	Sonora	CA	95370	209-532-4950		10-8
Die-Tech Inc 295 Sipe Rd *Web:* www.die-tech.com	York Haven	PA	17370	717-938-6771		488
Dietech Industries Inc 102 Automation Dr *Web:* www.1dietech.com	Carrollton	GA	30117	770-836-1042		350
Dieterich-Post Co 616 Monterey Pass Rd *Fax Area Code: 800 ■ *TF:* 800-955-3729 ■ *Web:* www.dieterich-post.com	Monterey Park	CA	91754	626-289-5021	688-3729*	112
Dietz & Watson Inc 5701 Tacony St *TF:* 800-333-1974 ■ *Web:* www.dietzandwatson.com	Philadelphia	PA	19135	215-831-9000		296-26
Diffenbaugh Inc 6865 Airport Dr *TF:* 800-394-5334 ■ *Web:* www.diffenbaugh.com	Riverside	CA	92504	951-351-6865	351-6880	186
Differentiation Strategies Inc 3349 Southgate Ct SW	Cedar Rapids	IA	52404	319-365-3489		256
DiFrancesco, Bateman, Coley, Yospin, Kunzman, Davis, Lehrer & Flaum PC 15 Mountain Blvd *Web:* www.newjerseylaw.net	Warren	NJ	07059	908-757-7800		428
Difusion Technologies Inc 111 Cooperative Way Ste 250 *Web:* www.difusiontech.com	Georgetown	TX	78626	512-863-7777	626-3084	583
Dig Corp 1210 Activity Dr *TF:* 800-322-9146 ■ *Web:* www.digcorp.com	Vista	CA	92081	760-727-0914		273
Digalog Systems Inc 3180 S 166th St *Web:* www.digalogsystems.com	New Berlin	WI	53151	262-797-8000		201
Digennaro Communications 18 W 21st St 6th Fl *Web:* www.digennaro-usa.com	New York City	NY	10010	212-966-9525		636
Digerati Technologies Inc 3463 Magic Dr Ste 355 *OTC: DTGI* ■ *Web:* www.digerati-inc.com	San Antonio	TX	78229	210-614-7240		736
Digestive Care Inc 1120 Win Dr *TF:* 877-882-5950 ■ *Web:* www.digestivecare.com	Bethlehem	PA	18017	610-882-0349		231
Digett 105 Falls Court Ste 300 *Web:* digett.com	Boerne	TX	78006	210-853-5808		180
Dighton Rock State Park Bay View Ave *Web:* www.mass.gov	Berkley	MA	02779	508-822-7537		565
Digi International Inc 11001 Bren Rd E *NASDAQ: DGII* ■ *TF:* 877-912-3444 ■ *Web:* www.digi.com	Minnetonka	MN	55343	952-912-3444	912-4991	176
Digicomm Systems 106 Metairie Lawn Dr 307 *TF:* 800-737-7107 ■ *Web:* www.digicommsystems.com	Metairie	LA	70001	504-212-6770		396
Digicomp Research Corp 930 Danby Rd	Ithaca	NY	14850	607-273-5900		178-12
DIGICON Corp 7361 Calhoun Pl Ste 430 *Web:* www.digicon.com	Rockville	MD	20855	301-721-6300		196
Digicorp Inc 3315 N 124th St Ste E *Web:* digicorp-inc.com	Brookfield	WI	53005	262-402-6100		196
Digi-Key Corp 701 Brooks Ave S *TF:* 800-344-4539 ■ *Web:* www.digikey.com	Thief River Falls	MN	56701	218-681-6674	681-3380	246
Digilabs Inc 1032 Elwell Ct Ste 245 *Web:* www.digilabs.com	Palo Alto	CA	94303	650-390-9749		177
DigiLink Inc 840 S Pickett St *TF:* 877-806-3444 ■ *Web:* www.digilink-inc.com	Alexandria	VA	22304	703-340-1800		174
Digimap Data Services Inc 40 Kodiak Cres Unit 13 *TF:* 800-214-8524 ■ *Web:* www.digimap.com	Toronto	ON	M3J3G5	416-633-2213		226
Digimarc Corp 9405 SW Gemini Dr *NASDAQ: DMRC* ■ *TF:* 800-344-4627 ■ *Web:* www.digimarc.com	Beaverton	OR	97008	503-469-4800		178-12
Digineer 505 N Hwy 169 Ste 750 *Web:* www.digineer.com	Plymouth	MN	55441	763-210-2300	210-2301	178-10
DIGIOP Inc 9340 Priority Way W Dr Ste 200 *TF:* 800-968-3606 ■ *Web:* www.digiop.com	Indianapolis	IN	46240	800-968-3606		693
Digipen Institute of Technology 5001 150th Ave NE *TF:* 866-478-5236 ■ *Web:* www.digipen.edu	Redmond	WA	98052	425-558-0299		166
Digirad Corp 13950 Stowe Dr *NASDAQ: DRAD* ■ *TF:* 800-947-6134 ■ *Web:* www.digirad.com	Poway	CA	92064	858-726-1600	726-1700	382
Digirati Networks 9255 E River Rd NW *Web:* www.digirati-networks.com	Coon Rapids	MN	55433	763-784-3500		175
Digiscribe International LLC 150 Clearbrook Rd Ste 125 *TF:* 800-686-7577 ■ *Web:* www.digiscribe.info	Elmsford	NY	10523	800-686-7577		226
Digistream Investigation 417 mace blvd *TF:* 800-747-4329 ■ *Web:* www.digistream.com	Davis	CA	95618	800-747-4329		693
Digital Action Inc 8 E Germantown Pk *TF:* 800-823-5100 ■ *Web:* digital-action.com	Plymouth Meeting	PA	19462	610 941 0700		193
Digital Air Strike Co 6991 E Camelback Rd Ste B111 *TF:* 888-713-8958 ■ *Web:* digitalairstrike.com	Scottsdale	AZ	85251	888-713-8958		366
Digital Broadcast Inc 2731 NW 41 St Ste A *Web:* www.digitalbcast.com	Gainesville	FL	32606	352-377-8344		647
Digital Bungalow Inc 209 Essex St *TF:* 800-874-2458 ■ *Web:* www.digitalbungalow.com	Salem	MA	01970	978-565-0111		180
Digital Celerity LLC 548 Market St Ste 22067 *TF:* 888-963-8876 ■ *Web:* www.digitalcelerity.com	San Francisco	CA	94104	888-963-8876		180
Digital ChoreoGraphics PO Box 8268 *TF:* 800-548-1969 ■ *Web:* www.dcgfx.com	Newport Beach	CA	92658	949-548-1969		177
Digital Control Systems Inc 7401 SW Capitol Hwy *Web:* www.dcs-inc.net	Portland	OR	97219	503-246-8110		203
Digital Datavoice Corp (DDV) 1210 Northland Dr Ste 160 *Web:* www.ddvc.com	Mendota Heights	MN	55120	651-994-2284	452-5470	387
Digital Design Inc 67 Sand Pk Rd *TF:* 800-967-7746 ■ *Web:* www.genesisinkjet.com/ddiworldwide	Cedar Grove	NJ	07009	973-857-0900	857-9375	173-6
Digital Dialogue LLC 3252 University Dr Ste 165 *Fax Area Code: 248 ■ *TF:* 800-205-4268	Auburn Hills	MI	48326	800-205-4268	836-2601*	393
Digital Dogs 4727 E Bell Rd Ste 45 *Web:* www.digitaldogs.com	Phoenix	AZ	85032	480-451-3647		177
Digital Domain Productions Inc 300 Rose Ave *Web:* www.digitaldomain.com	Venice	CA	90291	310-314-2800		514
Digital Dot Systems Inc 13213 F St *Web:* www.ddsinc.com	Omaha	NE	68137	402-408-0115		175
Digital Employees' Federal Credit Union 220 Donald Lynch Blvd *TF:* 800-328-8797 ■ *Web:* www.dcu.org	Marlborough	MA	01752	508-263-6700	263-6392	219
Digital Engineering Systems 2450 Scott Blvd Ste 300 *TF:* 888-788-1898 ■ *Web:* www.digi-eng.com	Santa Clara	CA	95050	408-970-8551		761

Company / Address	Phone	Fax	Class
Digital Evidence Group Inc 1730 M St NW Ste 812....................Washington DC 20036 *Web:* www.digitalevidencegroup.com	202-232-0646		196
Digital Evolution Inc 139 Fulton St............New York NY 10038 *Web:* www.digitalevolution.com	212-732-2722		627
Digital Footprints International LLC 1142 Broadway Ste 400......................Tacoma WA 98402	253-590-4100		225
Digital Force Technologies LLC 9455 Waples St Ste 100....................San Diego CA 92121 *Web:* www.digitalforcetech.com	858-546-1244		256
Digital Foundry Inc 1707 Tiburon Blvd..................Belvedere Tiburon CA 94920 *Web:* www.digitalfoundry.com	415-789-1600		180
Digital FX Inc 6010 Perkins Rd Ste B...................Baton Rouge LA 70808 *Web:* www.digitalfx.tv	225-763-6010		514
Digital Harbor Inc 1934 Old Gallows Rd Ste 350..................Vienna VA 22182 *Web:* www.digitalharbor.com	703-635-3477		178-10
Digital Innovations 3436 N Kennicott Ste 200.............Arlington Heights IL 60004 *Web:* digitalinnovations.com	847-463-9000		52
Digital Inspections 804 NW Buchanan Ave Ste A.................Corvallis OR 97330 *TF:* 800-877-8783 ■ *Web:* www.digitalinspections.com	541-752-7233		365
Digital Intelligence Systems Corp 8270 Greensboro Dr.......................Chantilly VA 20151 *Web:* www.disys.com	703-752-7900		177
Digital I-Ollc 1424 30th St..................San Diego CA 92154 *TF:* 866-423-4433 ■ *Web:* www.digitalio.com	619-423-4433		177
Digital Kitchen LLC 1114 E Pk St 3rd Fl..........................Seattle WA 98122 *Web:* d-kitchen.com	206-267-0400		33
Digital Lagoon Inc 14685 W 105th..............Lenexa KS 66215 *TF:* 800-525-9395 ■ *Web:* www.lagoon.com	913-888-3468		33
Digital Light Innovations 3201 Industrial Terr Ste 120....................Austin TX 78758 *Web:* www.dlinnovations.com	512-617-4700		253
Digital Lightbridge LLC 11902 Little Rd......................New Port Richey FL 34654 *Web:* www.digitallightbridge.com	727-863-7806		7
Digital Machining Systems LLC 929 Ridge Rd...............................Duson LA 70529 *TF:* 800-530-8945 ■ *Web:* www.digitalmachining.com	337-984-6013		454
Digital Manga Inc 1487 W 178th St Ste 300....................Gardena CA 90248 *Web:* www.digitalmanga.com	310-817-8010		95
Digital Map Products Inc 18831 Von Karman Ave Ste 200..................Irvine CA 92612 *Web:* www.digitalmapproducts.com	949-333-5111		224
Digital Measures 301 N Broadway 4th Fl.....................Milwaukee WI 53202 *TF:* 866-348-5677 ■ *Web:* www.digitalmeasures.com	866-348-5677		180
Digital Monitoring Products Inc 2500 N Partnership Blvd....................Springfield MO 65803 *TF:* 800-641-4282 ■ *Web:* www.dmp.com	417-831-9362		668
Digital Networks Group Inc 100 Columbia Ste 100......................Aliso Viejo CA 92656 *Web:* www.digitalnetworksgroup.com	949-428-6333		224
Digital Ocean Corp 3701 Gillham Rd.........................Kansas City MO 64111 *Web:* www.digitaloceaninc.com	816-522-5764		180
Digital Operative 404 Camino del Rio S Ste 200...............San Diego CA 92108 *Web:* www.digitaloperative.com	619-795-0630		5
Digital Outpost 2772 Loker Ave W.............Carlsbad CA 92010 *Web:* www.digitaloutpost.com	760-431-3575		514
Digital Peach Web Design 1109 Russell Pkwy.....................Warner Robins GA 31088 *Web:* www.digitalpeach.com	478-922-1919		180
Digital Peripheral Solutions Inc 8015 E Crystal Dr.........................Anaheim CA 92807 *TF:* 877-998-3440 ■ *Web:* q-see.com	877-998-3440		173-8
Digital Photographer Magazine 12121 Wilshire Blvd 12th Fl................Los Angeles CA 90025 *TF:* 800-537-4619 ■ *Web:* www.dpmag.com	310-820-1500		457-14
Digital Pictures 212 N Second St...........Minneapolis MN 55401 *Web:* www.digitalpictures.com	612-371-4515		177
Digital Power Capital 411 W Putnam Ave.......................Greenwich CT 06830	203-862-7040		792
Digital Power Corp 41324 Christy St............Fremont CA 94538 *TF:* 866-344-7697 ■ *Web:* www.digipwr.com	510-353-4023	657-2635	253
Digital Pulp Inc 220 E 23rd St Ste 900.......................New York NY 10010 *Web:* www.digitalpulp.com	212-679-0676	679-6217	7
Digital Realty Trust Inc 4 Embarcadero Ctr Ste 3200..............San Francisco CA 94111 *NYSE: DLR* ■ *Web:* www.digitalrealty.com	415-738-6500		654
Digital Reef Inc 85 Swanson Rd Ste 310...................Boxborough MA 01719 *Web:* www.digitalreefinc.com	978-893-1000		387
Digital Rework Depot 1500 Soldiers Field Rd......................Brighton MA 02135 *Web:* digitalrework.com	617-562-1444		175
Digital River Inc 10380 Bren Rd W..........Minnetonka MN 55343 *NASDAQ: DRIV* ■ **Fax Area Code:* 952 ■ *TF:* 800-598-7450 ■ *Web:* www.digitalriver.com	800-598-7450	253-8497*	39
Digital Room Inc 8000 Haskell Ave..............Van Nuys CA 91406 *TF:* 866-266-5047 ■ *Web:* www.digitalroom.com	866-266-5047		627
Digital Security Controls (DSC) 3301 Langstaff Rd........................Concord ON L4K4L2 *TF:* 888-888-7838 ■ *Web:* www.dsc.com	905-760-3000		692
Digital Storage Inc 7611 Green Meadows Dr.................Lewis Center OH 43035 **Fax Area Code:* 800 ■ *TF:* 800-232-3475 ■ *Web:* www.digitalstorage.com	740-548-7179	803-8030*	174
Digital Street Inc 69550 Highway 111 Ste 201............Rancho Mirage CA 92270 *TF:* 866-464-5100 ■ *Web:* www.digitalstreets.tv	866-464-5100		463
Digital Surgeons LLC 1175 State St Ste 219.......................New Haven CT 06510 **Fax Area Code:* 617 ■ *Web:* www.digitalsurgeons.com	203-672-6201	812-8585*	809
Digital Technology International 1180 N Mountain Springs Pkwy..............Springville UT 84663 *Web:* newscyclesolutions.com	801-853-5000		178-10
Digital Traffic Systems Inc 6020 Academy Rd NE Ste 202.............Albuquerque NM 87109 *Web:* www.dtsits.com	505-881-4470		466
Digital Video Group Inc 8529 Meadowbridge Rd Ste 100...........Mechanicsville VA 23116 *Web:* www.digitalvideogroup.com	804-559-8850		647
Digital Video Networks LLC 9150 E Del Camino Ste 100................Scottsdale AZ 85258 *TF:* 800-234-4900 ■ *Web:* www.digitalvideonetworks.com	480-588-3511		180
Digital Video Services 401 Hall ST SW.........................Grand Rapids MI 49512 *TF:* 800-747-8273 ■ *Web:* www.dvs.com	616-975-9911		240
Digital Video Systems Inc (DVS) 357 Castro St Ste 5....................Mountain View CA 94041 *Web:* www.dvsystems.com	650-938-8815		52
Digital Voice Corp 1201 S Beltline Rd...........Coppell TX 75019	469-635-6507		735
Digital Watchdog Inc 5436 W Crenshaw St..........Tampa FL 33634 *TF:* 866-446-3595 ■ *Web:* digital-watchdog.com	813-888-9555		693
Digital West Media Inc 15011 Highland Valley Rd.................Escondido CA 92201 *Web:* www.dwmi.com	760-740-1787		809
DigitalOptics Corp 3025 Orchard Pkwy..........San Jose CA 95134	408-473-2500		253
DigitalSherpa 2 Sun Ct Ste 300................Norcross GA 30092	913-648-5757		5
DigitalTown Inc 11974 Portland Ave...........Burnsville MN 55337 *Web:* www.digitaltown.com	952-890-2362		395
DigitalWork Inc 14300 N Northsight Blvd Ste 206.............Scottsdale AZ 85260 **Fax Area Code:* 480 ■ *TF:* 877-496-7571 ■ *Web:* www.digitalwork.com	877-496-7571	272-6923*	39
Digitek Software Inc 650 Radio Dr 43035.....................Lewis Center OH 43035 *Web:* www.digiteksoftware.com	614-764-8875		196
Digi-Trax 650 Heathrow Dr...................Lincolnshire IL 60069 *TF:* 800-356-6126 ■ *Web:* www.digi-trax.com	847-613-2100	465-9055	351
Digium Inc 445 Jan Davis Dr NW.............Huntsville AL 35806 *Web:* www.digium.com	256-428-6000		180
Digiwaxx LLC 349 Fifth Ave 4th Fl..............New York NY 10016 *Web:* www.digiwaxx.com	212-665-8607		636
Dignity Memorial 1929 Allen Pkwy..............Houston TX 77019 *TF:* 800-894-2024 ■ *Web:* www.dignitymemorial.com	713-522-5141		510
DignityUSA Inc PO Box 376....................Medford MA 02155 **Fax Area Code:* 781 ■ *TF:* 800-877-8797 ■ *Web:* www.dignityusa.org	202-861-0017	397-0584*	48-21
DII (Doucette Industries Inc) 20 Leigh Dr..........York PA 17406 *TF:* 800-445-7511 ■ *Web:* www.doucetteindustries.com	717-845-8746	845-2864	14
Dii Computers Inc 2425 Blair Mill Rd......................Willow Grove PA 19090 *Web:* diicomputers.com	215-657-5055		246
Diji Integrated Press 4920 W Cypress St Ste 100....................Tampa FL 33607 *Web:* www.dijipress.com	813-289-1660		5
Dik Drug Company LLC 160 Tower Dr.........Burr Ridge IL 60527 *Web:* www.dikdrug.com	630-655-4000		231
Dileo Engineering LLC 2241 W Larkspur Dr.........................Phoenix AZ 85029	602-395-0756		256
Dileonardo International Inc 2348 Post Rd..............................Warwick RI 02886 *Web:* dileonardo.com	401-732-2900		261
Dillard Academy Charter School 504 W Elm St...........................Goldsboro NC 27530 *Web:* www.dillardacademy.org	919-581-0166		685
Dillard Mill State Historic Site 142 DillaRd Mill Rd........................Davisville MO 65456 *Web:* www.mostateparks.com	573-244-3120		565
Dillard University 2601 Gentilly Blvd.....................New Orleans LA 70122 *Web:* www.dillard.edu	504-283-8822		95
Dillard's Inc 1600 Cantrell Rd................Little Rock AR 72201 *NYSE: DDS* ■ *TF:* 800-643-8274 ■ *Web:* www.dillards.com	501-376-5200		229
Dilley Manufacturing Co 215 E Third St..........................Des Moines IA 50309 *TF:* 800-247-5087 ■ *Web:* www.dilleymfg.com	515-288-7289	288-4210	86
Dillin Engineered Systems Corp 8030 Broadstone Rd......................Perrysburg OH 43551 *Web:* www.dillinautomation.com	419-666-6789		111
Dillmeier Enterprises Inc 2903 Industrial Park Rd...................Van Buren AR 72956 *Web:* www.dillmeierglass.com	479-474-7733		321
Dillon Aero Inc 8009 E Dillons Way...........Scottsdale AZ 85260 *Web:* www.dillonaero.com	480-444-2919		807
Dillon Clarence Public Library 2336 Lamington Rd.....................Bedminster NJ 07921 *Web:* www.dillonlibrary.org	908-234-2325		434-3
Dillon County 109 S Third Ave PO Box 449....................Dillon SC 29536 *Web:* dilloncounty.sc.gov	843-774-1400	774-1443	338
Dillon County Chamber of Commerce 100 N MacArthur Ave.........................Dillon SC 29536 *Web:* www.cityofdillonsc.us	843-774-8551	774-0114	139
Dillon County Library 600 E Main St.............Dillon SC 29536 *Web:* dillon.lib.sc.us	843-774-0330	774-0733	434-3
Dillon Dennis Auto Park & Truck Ctr Inc 2777 S Orchard St............................Boise ID 83705 *Web:* www.dennisdillon.com	208-336-6000		57
Dillon State Park 5265 Dillon Hills Dr.....................Nashport OH 43830 *Web:* www.ohiodnr.com	740-453-4377		565
Dillon Video & Film Productions Inc 1552 SW Seventh Rd PO Box 82..................Ocala FL 34471 *Web:* www.dillonvideo.com	352-620-0686		514
Dillon Works! Inc 11775 Harbour Reach Dr....................Mukilteo WA 98275 *Web:* www.dillonworks.com	425-493-8309		4
Dillon Yarn Inc 1019 Titan Rd....................Dillon SC 29536 *Web:* dillonyarn.com	843-774-7353		745-9

Company	Phone	Fax	Class
Dilmar Oil Company Inc 1951 W Darlington St PO Box 5629............Florence SC 29501 *TF:* 800-922-5823 ■ *Web:* www.dilmar.com	800-922-5823		780
Dimar Manufacturing Corp 10123 Main St............................Clarence NY 14031 *Web:* www.dimarmfg.com	716-759-0351		697
DiMare Bros/New England Farms Packing Co 84 New England Produce Ctr..................Chelsea MA 02150 *Web:* dimarefresh.com	617-889-3800		297-7
DiMare Fresh Inc 4629 Diplomacy Rd.........Fort Worth TX 76155 *TF General:* 800-724-3307 ■ *Web:* www.dimarefresh.com	817-385-3000		297-7
Dimation Inc 505 W Travelers Trl..............Burnsville MN 55337 *Web:* www.dimation.com	952-746-3030		253
Dimco Gray Corp 900 Dimco Way............Centerville OH 45458 *Web:* www.dimcogray.com	937-433-7600		596
Dimco Steel Inc 3901 S Lamar St................Dallas TX 75215 *TF:* 877-428-8336 ■ *Web:* www.dimcosteel.com	214-428-8336	428-1929	686
Dime Bank, The 820 Church St PO Box 509..................Honesdale PA 18431 *TF:* 888-469-3463 ■ *Web:* www.thedimebank.com	570-253-1902		70
Dime Community Bancshares Inc 209 Havemeyer St..........................Brooklyn NY 11211 *NASDAQ: DCOM* ■ *TF:* 800-321-3463 ■ *Web:* www.dime.com	718-782-6200		360-2
Dimension Capital Management 1221 Brickell Ave Ste 2450.....................Miami FL 33131 *Web:* www.dimensioncapital.com	305-371-2776		194
Dimension Consulting Inc 501 W Broadway..........................San Diego CA 92101 *TF:* 855-222-6444 ■ *Web:* www.dimcon.com	703-636-0933		196
Dimension Development Co 769 Hwy 494..........................Natchitoches LA 71457 *Web:* www.dimdev.com	318-352-8238	352-8276	379
Dimension Energy Services 1 Fluor Daniel Dr Ste D1-7-50..............Sugar Land TX 77478 *Web:* www.dimensionenergyservices.com	832-564-4500		256
Dimension Engineering LLC 5171 Hudson Dr..............................Hudson OH 44236 *TF:* 800-349-5075 ■ *Web:* dimensionengineering.com	330-634-1430		261
Dimension Group I LP, The 10755 Sandhill Rd..........................Dallas TX 75238 *Web:* www.dimensiongrp.com	214-343-9400		261
Dimension One Spas 2070 Hacienda Dr Ste. H........................Vista CA 92081 *Web:* www.d1spas.com	760-297-4194		375
Dimensional Control Systems Inc 580 Kirts Blvd Ste 309..........................Troy MI 48084 *Web:* 3dcs.com	248-269-9777		256
Dimensional Insight Inc 60 Mall Rd Ste 210.......................Burlington MA 01803 *Web:* www.dimins.com	781-229-9111		387
Dimeo Construction Co 75 Chapman St...........................Providence RI 02905 *Web:* dimeo.com	401-781-9800	461-4580	186
Dimeo Schneider & Assoc LLC 500 W Madision St Ste 3855..................Chicago IL 60661 *Web:* www.dimeoschneider.com	312-853-1000	853-3352	401
Dimerco Express (USA) Corp 955 Dillon Dr............................Wood Dale IL 60191 *Web:* dimerco.com	630-595-7310		311
Dimex LLC 28305 SR-7........................Marietta OH 45750 *Web:* www.dimexcorp.com	740-374-3100		596
DiMillo's on the Water 25 Long Wharf..........Portland ME 04101 *Web:* www.dimillos.com	207-772-2216	772-1081	671
Dimitri J Ververelli Inc 211 N 13th St..........................Philadelphia PA 19107 *Web:* djvinc.com	215-496-0000		261
Dimmit County 103 N Fifth St............Carrizo Springs TX 78834 *Web:* www.dimmitcounty.org	830-876-3323		338
Dimock Gould & Co 190 22nd St................Moline IL 61265	309-797-0650		361
Din Ho's Chinese BBQ 8557 Research Blvd..........................Austin TX 78758 *Web:* www.dinhochinesebbq.com	512-832-8788		671
Dinah's Garden Hotel 4261 El Camino Real.....................Palo Alto CA 94306 *TF:* 800-227-8220 ■ *Web:* www.dinahshotel.com	650-493-2844		379
Dineen Construction Corp 70 Disco Rd Ste 300.........................Toronto ON M9W1L9 *Web:* www.dineen.com	416-675-7676		186
Diners Club International 8430 W Bryn Mawr Ave.....................Chicago IL 60631 *TF:* 800-234-6377 ■ *Web:* www.dinersclubus.com	773-380-5160	380-5337	215
Dingell Debbie (Rep D - MI) 116 Cannon HOB........................Washington DC 20515 *Web:* debbiedingell.house.gov	202-225-4071	226-0371	342-2
Dings Co 4740 W Electric Ave..............Milwaukee WI 53219 *TF:* 800-494-1918 ■ *Web:* www.dingsbrakes.com	414-672-7830	672-7830	386
Dini Communications 340 Campus Dr...........Edison NJ 08837 *Web:* dini.net	732-225-4514		180
Dini Group, The 7469 Draper Ave...............La Jolla CA 92037 *Web:* www.dinigroup.com	858-454-3419		225
Dining Alliance 307 Waverley Oaks Rd Ste 401.................Webster NY 02452 **Fax Area Code:* 585 ■ *Web:* www.diningalliance.com	617-275-8430	302-4447*	463
Dinkel r a & Associates Inc 4641 Willoughby Rd..............................Holt MI 48842 *Web:* ideasideas.com	517-699-7000		7
Dinkel's Bakery 3329 N Lincoln Ave............Chicago IL 60657 *TF Orders:* 800-822-8817 ■ *Web:* www.dinkels.com	773-281-7300	281-6169	296-1
Dinkes & Schwitzer 112 Madison Ave Fl 10....................New York NY 10016 *TF:* 800-933-1212 ■ *Web:* www.wsatlaw.com	212-683-3800		428
Dinklage Feedyards PO Box 274...................Sidney NE 69162 *TF:* 888-343-5940 ■ *Web:* www.dinklagefeedyards.com	308-254-5940	254-6260	10-1
Dino Software Corp PO Box 7105............Alexandria VA 22307 *TF:* 800-480-3466 ■ *Web:* www.dino-software.com	703-768-2610		177
Dino's 13 Lord St..........................Worcester MA 01604 *Web:* www.dineatdinos.com	508-753-9978		671
Dino's Trucking Inc 9615 Continental Indus Dr.................Saint Louis MO 63123 *TF:* 800-771-7805 ■ *Web:* www.dinoslogistics.com	314-631-3001	638-3562	780
Dinosaur National Monument 4545 E Hwy 40............................Dinosaur CO 81610 *TF:* 800-645-8465 ■ *Web:* www.nps.gov/dino	970-374-3000	374-3003	564
Dinosaur Securities LLC 470 Park Ave S 9th Fl.......................New York NY 10016 *Web:* www.dinogroup.com	212-448-9944		401
Dinosaur State Park 400 W St...............Rocky Hill CT 06067 *Web:* www.ct.gov	860-529-5816	257-7601	565
Dinova LLC 6455 E Johns Crossing Ste 220............Johns Creek GA 30097 *TF:* 888-346-6828 ■ *Web:* www.dinova.net	888-346-6828		393
Dinovite Inc 101 Miller Dr...................Crittenden KY 41030 *Web:* www.dinovite.com	859-428-1000		297-8
Dinwiddie County 14016 Boydton Plank Rd..................Dinwiddie VA 23841 *TF:* 800-755-0733 ■ *Web:* www.dinwiddieva.us	804-469-4500	469-4503	338
Dinwiddie County Public Schools 14016 Boydton Plank Rd..................Dinwiddie VA 23841 *Web:* www.dinwiddie.k12.va.us	804-469-4190	469-4197	685
Diocese of Davenport 2706 N Gaines St.........................Davenport IA 52804 *Web:* www.davenportdiocese.org	563-324-1911		48-20
Diocese of Greensburg 723 E Pittsburgh St......................Greensburg PA 15601 *TF:* 866-409-6455 ■ *Web:* www.dioceseofgreensburg.org	724-837-0901	837-0857	48-20
Diocese of Harrisburg 4800 Union Deposit Rd...................Harrisburg PA 17111 *Web:* hbgdiocese.org	717-657-4804		48-20
Diocese of La Crosse 3710 E Ave S...........La Crosse WI 54601 *Web:* diolc.org	608-788-7700		48-20
Diocese of Metuchen PO Box 191...........Metuchen NJ 08840 *Web:* www.diometuchen.org	732-562-1990		48-20
Diocese of Nashville 2400 21st Ave S..........................Nashville TN 37212 *Web:* www.dioceseofnashville.com	615-383-6393		48-20
Diocese of Phoenix 400 E Monroe St..........Phoenix AZ 85004 *Web:* dphx.org	602-257-0030		48-20
Diocese of Rochester 1150 Buffalo Rd............Roch NY 14624 *TF:* 800-388-7177 ■ *Web:* www.dor.org	585-328-3210		48-20
Diocese of San Bernardino Education & Welfare Corp 1201 E Highland Ave.................San Bernardino CA 92404 *Web:* sbdiocese.org	909-475-5300		48-20
Diocese of St. Augustine Inc 11625 Old St Augustine..................Jacksonville FL 32258 *TF:* 800-775-4659 ■ *Web:* www.dosafl.com	904-262-3200		48-20
Diocese of Steubenville Catholic Charities PO Box 969...........................Steubenville OH 43952 *TF:* 800-339-7890 ■ *Web:* www.diosteub.org	740-282-3631	282-3327	637-8
Diodes Inc 15660 N Dallas Pkwy Ste 850..........Dallas TX 75248 *NASDAQ: DIOD* ■ **Fax Area Code:* 805 ■ *Web:* www.diodes.com	972-385-2810	446-4850*	696
Diopsys Inc 16 Chapin Rd Ste 912.............Pine Brook NJ 07058 *TF:* 800-668-5236 ■ *Web:* www.diopsys.com	973-244-0622		476
Diosynth RTP Inc 101 J Morris Commons Ln.................Morrisville NC 27560 *Web:* www.fujifilmdiosynth.com	919-337-4477		479
Dipasa USA Inc 6600 Fm 802 Ste B..........Brownsville TX 78526 *Web:* dipasausa.com	956-831-4072	831-5893	297-8
Dipert Travel & Transportation Ltd PO Box 580..............................Arlington TX 76004 **Fax Area Code:* 017 ■ *TF:* 000-433-5335 ■ *Web:* www.dandipert.com	800-433-5335	543-3728*	760
Dipietro & Thornton 9550 Prototype Ct Ste 101......................Reno NV 89521 *Web:* dipietro-thornton.com	775-825-1040		2
Dipietro Todd Salon 177 Post St Fl 2.....................San Francisco CA 94108 *Web:* www.dipietrotodd.com	415-397-0177		77
Diplomatic Language Services LLC 1901 N Ft Myer Dr Ste 600.................Arlington VA 22209 *Web:* dlsdc.com	703-243-4855		423
Dircks Moving Services Inc 4340 W Mohave St...........................Phoenix AZ 85043 *TF:* 800-523-5038 ■ *Web:* www.dircks.com	602-267-9401	267-8188	780
Direct Answer Inc 106 Paul Mellon Ct Ste 200..................Waldorf MD 20602 *Web:* directanswer.com	301-932-9801		5
Direct Brands Inc 250 W 34th St 1 Penn Plz 4th Fl.............New York NY 10119	212-596-2116		93
Direct Choice 480 E Swedesford Rd Ste 210...................Wayne PA 19087 *Web:* www.directchoiceinc.com	610-995-8201		7
Direct Connection Printing & Mailing 1968 Yeager Ave.........................La Verne CA 91750 *TF:* 800-420-9937 ■ *Web:* www.directconnectionmail.com	909-392-2334		627
Direct Dimensions Inc 10310 S Dolfield Rd.....................Owings Mills MD 21117 *Web:* www.dirdim.com	410-998-0880		419
Direct Edge Media Inc 430 W Collins Ave...........................Orange CA 92867 *TF:* 800-556-5576 ■ *Web:* directedgemedia.com	714-221-8686		344
Direct Federal Credit Union PO Box 9123..............................Needham MA 02494 *Web:* www.direct.com	781-455-6500	455-9922	219
Direct Holdings Americas Inc 8280 Willow Oaks Corporate Dr..................Fairfax VA 22031 *TF:* 800-950-7887 ■ *Web:* www.timelife.com	800-950-7887		96
Direct Internet Access 141 Desiard St PO Box 7263..................Monroe LA 71201 **Fax Area Code:* 888 ■ *TF:* 800-296-2249 ■ *Web:* www.directinternet.net	800-296-2249	835-2121*	398
Direct Mail Processors Inc 1150 Conrad Ct........................Hagerstown MD 21740 *Web:* dmpinc.net	301-714-4700		5
Direct Marketing Assn Inc (DMA) 1120 Ave of the Americas.................New York NY 10036 *TF:* 855-422-0749 ■ *Web:* thedma.org	212-768-7277	302-6714	49-18

	Phone	Fax	Class
Direct Mktg Solutions Inc 8534 NE Alderwood Rd, Portland OR 97220 *Web:* www.resultsdm.com	503-281-1400		194
Direct Online Marketing 4727 Jacob St, Wheeling WV 26003 *TF:* 800-979-3177 ■ *Web:* www.directom.com	304-214-4850		225
Direct Optical Research Co 8725 115th Ave, Largo FL 33773 *Web:* www.dorc.com	727-319-9000		544
Direct Partners Inc 4755 Alla Rd, Marina Del Rey CA 90292 *Web:* www.directpartners.com	310-482-4200		7
Direct Relief International 27 S La Patera Ln, Goleta CA 93117 *TF:* 800-676-1638 ■ *Web:* www.directrelief.org	805-964-4767	681-4838	48-5
Direct Resource Solutions LLC 6912 N 97th Cir, Omaha NE 68122 *Web:* www.uaaclearinghouse.com	402-991-2810		5
Direct Response Insurance Administrative Services 7930 Century Blvd, Chanhassen MN 55317 *Web:* www.driasi.com	952-556-5600		390
Direct Selling Assn (DSA) 1667 K St NW Ste 1100, Washington DC 20006 *Web:* www.dsa.org	202-452-8866	452-9010	49-18
Direct Services Miami Inc 10390 Usa Today Way, Miramar FL 33025 *Web:* www.directservices.com	954-433-9810		180
Direct Source Inc 8176 Mallory Ct, Chanhassen MN 55317 *TF:* 800-934-8055 ■ *Web:* www.directsource.com	952-934-8000	934-8030	178-5
Direct Sports Inc 1720 Curve Rd, Pearisburg VA 24134 *TF:* 800-456-0072 ■ *Web:* directsports.com	800-456-0072		711
Direct Supply Inc 6767 N Industrial Rd, Milwaukee WI 53223 *Web:* www.directsupply.com	414-358-2805		192
Direct Tire & Auto Service 126 Galen St, Watertown MA 02472 *Web:* directtire.com	617-923-1800		57
Direct Travel 95 New Jersey 17, Paramus NJ 07652 *TF:* 800-831-1366 ■ *Web:* www.dt.com	201-847-9000		771
DirectBuy Inc 8450 Broadway, Merrillville IN 46410 *TF:* 800-320-3462 ■ *Web:* www.directbuy.com	219-736-1100		310
Directec Corp 1650 Lyndon Farm Ct Ste 202, Louisville KY 40223 *TF:* 800-588-7800 ■ *Web:* www.directec.com	502-357-5000		196
Directed Energy Solutions (DES) 890 Elkton Dr Ste 101, Colorado Springs CO 80907	719-593-7848	593-7846	544
DirectEmployers.com 9002 N Purdue Rd Quad III Ste 100, Indianapolis IN 46268 *TF:* 866-268-6206 ■ *Web:* www.directemployers.com	317-874-9000		393
Directions Research Inc 401 E Ct St, Cincinnati OH 45202 *Web:* www.directionsrsch.com	513-651-2990		466
DirectMailcom 201 Skipjack Rd, Prince Frederick MD 20678 *TF:* 866-284-5816 ■ *Web:* www.directmail.com	301-855-1700		5
Directors Guild of America 7920 W Sunset Blvd, Los Angeles CA 90046 *TF:* 800-421-4173 ■ *Web:* www.dga.org	310-289-2000	289-2029	414
Directory Distributing Assoc (DDA) 1602 Pk 370 Ct, Hazelwood MO 63042 *TF General:* 800-325-1964	314-592-8600	592-8790	96
Directory One Inc 9135 Katy Fwy Ste 204, Houston TX 77024 *TF:* 800-477-1324 ■ *Web:* www.directoryone.com	713-465-0051		225
DIRECTV Inc 2230 E Imperial Hwy, El Segundo CA 90245 *TF Cust Svc:* 800-531-5000 ■ *Web:* www.directv.com	800-531-5000		116
DirectWest Corp 2550 Sandra Schmirler Way Ste 200, Regina SK S4W1A1 *TF:* 800-667-8201 ■ *Web:* www.directwest.com	306-777-0333		225
Direxion Inc 2025 Kentucky Ave Ste A, Vestavia Hills AL 35216	205-823-7265		8
Dirks Group, The 3802 Hummingbird Rd, Wausau WI 54401 *TF:* 800-866-1486 ■ *Web:* www.dirksgroup.com	715-848-9865		180
Dirks, Van Essen & Murray 119 E Marcy St Ste 100, Santa Fe NM 87501 *TF:* 800-544-4450 ■ *Web:* www.dirksvanessen.com	505-820-2700		463
Dirksen Screw Products Co 14490 23-Mile Rd, Shelby Township MI 48315 *TF:* 800-732-5569 ■ *Web:* www.dirksenscrew.com	586-247-5400	247-9507	621
DIRTT Environmental Solutions Ltd 7303 - 30th St SE, Calgary AB T2C1N6 *Web:* www.dirtt.net	403-723-5000		236
Dirxion LLC 1859 Bowles Ave Ste 100, Fenton MO 63026 *TF:* 888-391-0202 ■ *Web:* www.dirxion.com	636-717-2300		174
DIS Corp 1315 Cornwall Ave, Bellingham WA 98225 *TF Cust Svc:* 800-426-8870 ■ *Web:* www.dis-corp.com	360-733-7610	647-6921	178-10
DISA (Data Interchange Standards Assn) 8300 Greensboro Dr Ste 800, McLean VA 22043 *Web:* www.disa.org	703-970-4480	970-4488	48-9
Disa Systems Inc 150 Transit Ave, Thomasville NC 27360 *TF:* 800-845-8508 ■ *Web:* www.disagroup.com	336-889-9187		18
Disability Funding Week 8204 Fenton St, Silver Spring MD 20910 **Fax Area Code:* 301 ■ *TF:* 800-666-6380 ■ *Web:* cdpublications.com	800-666-6380	588-6385*	531-8
Disability Law Compliance Report 610 Opperman Dr, Eagan MN 55123 *TF Cust Svc:* 800-328-4880 ■ *Web:* legalsolutions.thomsonreuters.com	651-687-7000	687-8722	531-7
Disability Rights Ctr Inc 18 Low Ave, Concord NH 03301 *TF:* 800-834-1721 ■ *Web:* www.drcnh.org	603-228-0432	225-2077	48-17
Disabled & Alone/Life Services for the Handicapped 1440 Broadway 23rd Floor, New York NY 10018 *TF:* 800-995-0066 ■ *Web:* www.disabledandalone.org	212-532-6740	532-6740	48-17
Disabled American Veterans (DAV) 3725 Alexandria Pike, Cold Spring KY 41076 *TF:* 877-426-2838 ■ *Web:* www.dav.org	859-441-7300	441-1416	48-19
Disabled Sports USA (DS/USA) 451 Hungerford Dr Ste 100, Rockville MD 20850 *TF:* 800-543-2754 ■ *Web:* www.disabledsportsusa.org	301-217-0960	217-0968	48-22
Disan Engineering Corp 101 Mohawk Dr, Nowata OK 74048 *Web:* www.disancorp.com	918-273-1636		22
DiSanto Technology Inc 10 Constitution Blvd S, Shelton CT 06484 *Web:* www.disanto.com	203-712-1030		295
Disaster News Network (DNN) PO Box 1746, Ellicott City MD 21041 *TF:* 888-384-3028 ■ *Web:* www.disasternews.net	443-393-3330	420-0085	530
Disc Graphics Inc 10 Gilpin Ave, Hauppauge NY 11788 *Web:* www.discgraphics.com	631-234-1400	234-1460	627
Disc Makers 7905 N Rt 130, Pennsauken NJ 08110 *TF:* 800-468-9353 ■ *Web:* www.discmakers.com	856-663-9030		173-8
Discera Inc 1961 Concourse Dr, San Jose CA 95131 *Web:* www.discera.com	408-432-8600		668
DISCERN Investment Analytics Inc 493 S El Camino, San Mateo CA 94402 *Web:* www.discern.com	415-817-9012		401
Discflo Corp 10850 Hartley Rd, Santee CA 92071 *Web:* www.discflo.com	619-596-3181		641
Discharge Resource Group 400 Oyster Point Blvd Ste 440, South San Francisco CA 94080 *TF:* 800-277-3727 ■ *Web:* drgstaffing.com	650-877-8111		582
Disciplined Growth Investors Inc Fifth St Towers 150 S Fifth St Ste 2550, Minneapolis MN 55402 *Web:* www.dginv.com	612-317-4100		401
Disco Inc 1895 Brannan Rd, McDonough GA 30253 *TF:* 800-325-1051 ■ *Web:* www.katyindustries.com	770-474-7575		508
DISCO International Inc 15 W 44th St 5th Fl, New York NY 10036 *Web:* www.discointer.com/en	212-382-0025		260
Discount Car & Truck Rentals Ltd 720 Arrow Rd, North York ON M9M2M1 *TF:* 866-742-5968 ■ *Web:* www.discountcar.com	866-742-5968		126
Discount Drug Mart Inc 211 Commerce Dr, Medina OH 44256 *TF:* 800-833-6278 ■ *Web:* www.discount-drugmart.com	330-725-2340	722-2990	237
Discount Labels Inc 4115 Profit Ct, New Albany IN 47150 *TF:* 800-995-9500 ■ *Web:* www.discountlabels.com	800-995-9500	995-9600	413
Discount RampsCom LLC 760 S Indiana Ave, West Bend WI 53095 *TF:* 888-651-3431 ■ *Web:* www.discountramps.com	262-338-3431		480
Discount School Supplies 2 Lower Ragsdale Rd Ste 125, Monterey CA 93940 *TF:* 800-919-5238 ■ *Web:* www.discountschoolsupply.com	800-919-5238	919-5235	761
DiscountMugs.com 12610 NW 115th Ave, Medley FL 33178 *TF:* 800-569-1980 ■ *Web:* www.discountmugs.com	800-569-1980		690
discover 2500 Lake Cook Rd, Riverwoods IL 60015 *Web:* www.discoverfinancial.com	224-405-0900		215
Discover Bank PO Box 30416, Salt Lake City UT 84130 *TF:* 800-347-7000 ■ *Web:* www.discover.com	302-323-7810		70
Discover Communications Inc 30 Victoria Crescent, Brampton ON L6T1E4 *TF:* 888-456-8989 ■ *Web:* www.getconnected.ca	905-455-5600		224
Discover Group Inc 2741 W 23rd St, Brooklyn NY 11224 *TF:* 866-456-6555 ■ *Web:* www.discovergroup.net	718-456-4500		535
Discover Klamath 205 Riverside Dr Ste B, Klamath Falls OR 97601 *TF:* 800-445-6728 ■ *Web:* www.meetmeinklamath.com	541-882-1501		206
Discover Mediaworks Inc 5236 Hwy 70 W, Eagle River WI 54521 *TF:* 800-644-7465 ■ *Web:* discovermediaworks.com	715-477-1500		7
Discover Reinsurance Company Inc 5 Batterson Pk, Farmington CT 06032	860-674-2660		463
Discover The Palm Beaches 1555 Palm Beach Lakes Blvd Ste 800, West Palm Beach FL 33401 *TF:* 800-554-7256 ■ *Web:* www.palmbeachfl.com	561-233-3000	233-3009	206
Discover The Palm Beaches 650 Okeechobee Blvd, West Palm Beach FL 33401 *Web:* www.palmbeachfl.com	561-366-3000	366-3001	205
Discovery Care Centre Corp 601 N Tenth St, Hamilton MT 59840 *TF:* 800-321-1245 ■ *Web:* www.discoverycare.com	406-363-2273		107
Discovery Communication Latin America 6505 Blue Lagoon Dr Ste 190, Miami FL 33126 *Web:* corporate.discovery.com	786-273-4700		740
Discovery Communications Inc 1 Discovery Pl, Silver Spring MD 20910 *NASDAQ: DISCA* ■ *TF:* 877-324-5850 ■ *Web:* corporate.discovery.com	240-662-2000		740
Discovery Cove 6000 Discovery Cove Way, Orlando FL 32821 *TF:* 877-434-7268 ■ *Web:* www.discoverycove.com	407-370-1280		823
Discovery Cruises Inc Port Everglades Terminal 1, Fort Lauderdale FL 33316	305-477-2867		220
Discovery Ctr (TDC) 1944 N Winery Ave, Fresno CA 93703 *TF:* 800-946-3039 ■ *Web:* www.thediscoverycenter.net	559-251-5533		521
Discovery Ctr Museum 711 N Main St, Rockford IL 61103 *Web:* www.discoverycentermuseum.org	815-963-6769		521
Discovery Ctr of Idaho (DCI) 131 Myrtle St, Boise ID 83702 *Web:* www.dcidaho.com	208-343-9895		520
Discovery Ctr of Springfield 438 E St Louis St, Springfield MO 65806 *TF:* 888-636-4395 ■ *Web:* www.discoverycenter.org	417-862-9910	862-6898	521
Discovery Ctr of the Southern Tier 60 Morgan Rd, Binghamton NY 13903 *Web:* www.thediscoverycenter.org	607-773-8661	773-8019	521
Discovery Gateway 444 West 100 South, Salt Lake City UT 84101 *TF:* 800-501-2885 ■ *Web:* www.discoverygateway.org	801-456-5437	456-5440	521
Discovery Green Conservancy 1500 Mckinney St, Houston TX 77010 *Web:* discoverygreen.com	713-400-7336		652
Discovery Information Technologies Inc 904 N Memorial Fwy, Nederland TX 77627 *TF:* 800-633-9876 ■ *Web:* www.discoveryit.com	409-727-7080		177
Discovery Inn Hotel 4701 Franklin Ave, Yellowknife NT X1A2N6 *TF:* 800-661-0454 ■ *Web:* www.discoveryinn.ca	867-873-4151		378
Discovery Institute 208 Columbia St, Seattle WA 98104 *Web:* www.discovery.org	206-292-0401	682-5320	634

Phone | Fax | Class

Discovery Life Cannel
8045 Kennett St .... Silver Spring MD 20910 240-662-0000 740
Web: www.discoverylife.com

Discovery Museum & Planetarium
4450 Pk Ave .... Bridgeport CT 06604 203-372-3521 374-1929 520
Web: www.discoverymuseum.org

Discovery Place 301 N Tryon St .... Charlotte NC 28202 704-372-6261 521
TF: 800-935-0553 ■ *Web:* www.discoveryplace.org

Discovery Research Group
6975 Union Pk Ctr Ste 150 .... Midvale UT 84047 800-678-3748 748-2784* 225
**Fax Area Code:* 801 ■ *TF:* 800-678-3748 ■ *Web:* www.discoveryresearchgroup.com

Discovery Science Ctr
2500 N Main St .... Santa Ana CA 92705 714-542-2823 520
TF: 800-810-3039 ■ *Web:* www.discoverycube.org

Discovery Theater
1100 Jefferson Dr SW .... Washington DC 20560 202-633-8700 343-1073 572
Web: www.discoverytheater.org

Discovery World 500 N Harbor Dr .... Milwaukee WI 53202 414-765-9966 765-0311 520
TF: 800-554-1448 ■ *Web:* www.discoveryworld.org

Discovery World Travel Inc
1045 Pennsylvania Ave .... Sheboygan WI 53081 920-459-2963 772
TF: 800-444-2963 ■ *Web:* www.tldiscovery.com

Discraft Inc 29592 Beck Rd .... Wixom MI 48393 248-624-2250 596
Web: discraft.com

Disguise 12120 Kear Pl .... Poway CA 92064 858-391-3600 391-3601 155-6
TF: 877-875-2557 ■ *Web:* www.disguise.com

DISH Network LLC
9601 S Meridian Blvd .... Englewood CO 80112 800-823-4929 116
NASDAQ: DISH ■ *TF:* 800-823-4929 ■ *Web:* www.dish.com

Dishman USA Inc 550 Union Ave Ste 9 .... Middlesex NJ 08846 732-560-4300 231
Web: www.wheelerjobin.com

Disk Software Inc 205 Ridgestone Dr .... Murphy TX 75094 972-423-7288 178-5
Web: www.disksoft.com

Dismas Distribution Services LLC
320-J Outerbelt St .... Columbus OH 43213 614-861-2525 631
Web: www.dismas.net

Dismex Food Inc 12255 SW 133rd Ct .... Miami FL 33186 305-238-6146 238-4032 297-8
Web: www.dismexfood.com

Disney
4401 Grand Floridian Way
Disney's Grand Floridian Resort .... Lake Buena Vista FL 32830 407-934-7639 671
Web: disneyworld.disney.go.com

Disney ABC Domestic Television
500 S Buena Vista St .... Burbank CA 91521 818-560-9300 742
Web: www.disneyabc.tv

Disney Consumer Products
500 S Buena Vista St .... Burbank CA 91521 818-560-1000 553-5402* 637-9
**Fax Area Code:* 215 ■ **Fax:* Cust Svc ■ *TF PR:* 855-553-4763 ■ *Web:* thewaltdisneycompany.com

Disney Vacation Club
1390 Celebration Blvd .... Celebration FL 34747 407-566-3100 753
TF: 800-500-3990 ■ *Web:* www.disneyvacationclub.disney.go.com

Disney's All-Star Movies Resort
1901 W Buena Vista Dr .... Lake Buena Vista FL 32830 407-939-7000 669
Web: disneyworld.disney.go.com

Disney's All-Star Music Resort
1801 W Buena Vista Dr .... Lake Buena Vista FL 32830 407-939-6000 669
Web: disneyworld.disney.go.com

Disney's All-Star Sports Resort
1701 W Buena Vista Dr .... Lake Buena Vista FL 32830 407-939-5000 669
Web: www.disneyworld.disney.go.com

Disney's Animal Kingdom
2901 Osceola Pkwy .... Lake Buena Vista FL 32830 407-938-3000 32
Web: disneyworld.disney.go.com/parks/animal-kingdom

Disney's Blizzard Beach
1534 Blizzard Beach Dr .... Lake Buena Vista FL 32830 407-560-3400 32
TF: 888-800-5447 ■ *Web:* www.disneyworld.disney.go.com

Disney's BoardWalk Inn
2101 N Epcot Resort Blvd .... Lake Buena Vista FL 32830 407-939-5100 669
Web: disneyworld.disney.go.com

Disney's California Adventure
1313 S Disneyland Dr .... Anaheim CA 92802 714-781-7290 32
TF: 800-225-2024 ■ *Web:* disneyland.disney.go.com

Disney's Caribbean Beach Resort
900 Cayman Way .... Lake Buena Vista FL 32830 407-934-3400 669
TF: 800-823-8300 ■ *Web:* disneyworld.disney.go.com

Disney's Contemporary Resort
4600 N World Dr .... Lake Buena Vista FL 32830 407-824-1000 669
Web: disneyworld.disney.go.com

Disney's Coronado Springs Resort
1000 W Buena Vista Dr .... Lake Buena Vista FL 32830 407-939-1000 669
Web: www.disneyworld.disney.go.com

Disney's Fort Wilderness Resort & Campground
4510 Ft Wilderness Trl .... Lake Buena Vista FL 32830 407-824-2900 669
Web: www.disneyworld.disney.go.com

Disney's Grand Floridian Resort & Spa
4401 Floridian Way .... Lake Buena Vista FL 32830 407-824-3000 669
Web: www.disneyworld.disney.go.com

Disney's Grand Floridian Spa
4401 Floridian Wy .... Lake Buena Vista FL 32830 407-824-2332 707
TF: 800-169-0730 ■ *Web:* disneyworld.disney.go.com

Disney's Hilton Head Island Resort
22 Harborside Ln .... Hilton Head Island SC 29928 843-341-4100 341-4130 669
Web: www.disneyvacationclub.disney.go.com

Disney's Hollywood Studios
351 S Studio Dr .... Lake Buena Vista FL 32830 407-939-5277 32
Web: disneyworld.disney.go.com/parks/hollywood-studios

Disney's Old Key West Resort
1510 N Cove Rd .... Lake Buena Vista FL 32830 407-827-7700 669
Web: disneyworld.disney.go.com

Disney's Paradise Pier Hotel
1717 S Disneyland Dr .... Anaheim CA 92802 714-999-0990 379
TF: 800-693-4344 ■ *Web:* www.disneyworld.disney.go.com

Disney's Polynesian Resort
1600 Seven Seas Dr .... Lake Buena Vista FL 32830 407-824-2000 669
Web: disneyworld.disney.go.com

Disney's Pop Century Resort
1050 Century Dr .... Lake Buena Vista FL 32830 407-938-4000 669
Web: disneyworld.disney.go.com

Disney's Port Orleans Resort-French Quarter
2201 Orleans Dr .... Lake Buena Vista FL 32830 407-934-5000 669
Web: www.disneyworld.disney.go.com

Disney's Port Orleans Resort-Riverside
1251 Riverside Dr .... Lake Buena Vista FL 32830 407-934-6000 669
Web: disneyworld.disney.go.com

Disney's Saratoga Springs Resort & Spa
1960 Broadway St .... Lake Buena Vista FL 32830 407-827-1100 379
Web: disneyworld.disney.go.com

Disney's Typhoon Lagoon
1145 E Buena Vista Blvd .... Lake Buena Vista FL 32830 407-560-4120 32
Web: disneyworld.disney.go.com

Disney's Wilderness Lodge
901 Timberline Dr .... Lake Buena Vista FL 32830 407-824-3200 669
Web: disneyworld.disney.go.com

Disney's Yacht Club Resort
1700 EPCOT Resorts Blvd .... Lake Buena Vista FL 32830 407-934-7000 669
Web: www.disneyworld.disney.go.com

Disney/Little Blue State Park Hwy 28 E .... Disney OK 74340 918-435-8066 435-2101 565
TF: 800-622-6317 ■ *Web:* www.travelok.com

Disneyland 1313 Disneyland Dr .... Anaheim CA 92802 714-781-4636 32
Web: www.disneyland.disney.go.com

Disneyland Hotel 1150 Magic Way .... Anaheim CA 92802 714-778-6600 956-6597 379
Web: disneyland.disney.go.com

Dispatch Publishing Company Inc, The
30 E First Ave .... Lexington NC 27293 336-249-3981 532-3
Web: www.the-dispatch.com

Dispatch, The 1720 Fifth Ave .... Moline IL 61265 309-764-4344 797-0317 532-2
Web: www.qconline.com

Dispatch, The 116 E Market St .... Blairsville PA 15717 724-459-6100 532-2
TF: 800-221-9282 ■ *Web:* triblive.com

Dispatch, The PO Box 248 .... Eatonville WA 98328 360-832-4411 532-4
Web: www.dispatchnews.com

Dispensers Optical Service Corp
1815 Plantside Dr
Bluegrass Industrial Park .... Louisville KY 40299 502-491-3440 491-3446 542

Dispensing Dynamics International
1020 Bixby Dr .... City of Industry CA 91745 626-961-3691 610
TF: 800-888-3698 ■ *Web:* www.dispensingdynamics.com

Display Connection Inc, The
131 W Commercial Ave .... Moonachie NJ 07074 201-438-1000 100
Web: www.displayconnection.com

Display Pack 1340 Monroe Ave NW .... Grand Rapids MI 49505 616-451-3061 451-8907 88
TF: 800-780-4707 ■ *Web:* www.displaypack.com

Display Producers Inc 1260 Zerega Ave .... Bronx NY 10462 718-904-1200 393
Web: www.displayproducersinc.com

Display Smart LLC 801 W 27th Terr .... Lawrence KS 66046 785-843-1869 233
TF: 888-843-1870 ■ *Web:* www.display-smart.com

Display Technologies LLC
1111 Marcus Ave Ste M68 .... Lake Success NY 11042 800-424-4220 233
TF: 800-424-4220 ■ *Web:* www.display-technologies.com

Display Works Inc
335 Gordons Corner Rd .... Manalapan NJ 07726 732-536-0800 8
Web: www.displayworks.com

DisplayLink Corp
480 S California Ave Ste 305 .... Palo Alto CA 94306 650-838-0481 668
Web: www.displaylink.com

Disposable Instrument Co
14248 Santa Fe Trl Dr .... Shawnee Mission KS 66215 913-492-6492 476
Web: www.disposableinstrument.com

Dispute Resolution Management Inc
770 E 9000 S Ste A2 .... Sandy UT 84094 801-355-1444 568-2410 463
Web: www.drmworld.com

Disqus Inc 301 Howard St Ste 300 .... San Francisco CA 94105 415-738-8848 387
Web: www.disqus.com

Dissolve Inc 425 78 Ave SW .... Calgary AB T2V5K5 800-518-6748 224
TF: 800-518-6748 ■ *Web:* www.dissolve.com

Disston Precision Inc
6795 State Rd .... Philadelphia PA 19135 215-338-1200 338-7060 682
TF Cust Svc: 800-238-1007 ■ *Web:* www.disstonprecision.com

Distance Education & Training Council (DETC)
1601 18th St NW Ste 2 .... Washington DC 20009 202-234-5100 332-1386 48-1
Web: www.deac.org

Distant Focus Corp
4114b Fieldstone Rd .... Champaign IL 61822 217-351-2655 196
Web: distantfocus.com

Distant Horizon PO Box 574 .... Frankfort IL 60423 773-932-7483 177
Web: www.distanthorizon.com

Distek Inc 121 N Ctr Dr .... North Brunswick NJ 08902 732-422-7585 111
Web: www.distekinc.com

Distek Integration Inc
1110 N County Rd 2350 .... Carthage IL 62321 217-357-3100 177
TF: 800-782-7318 ■ *Web:* www.distek.com

Distillata Co 1608 E 24th St .... Cleveland OH 44114 216-771-2900 771-1672 805
TF Cust Svc: 800-999-2906 ■ *Web:* www.distillata.com

Distilled Spirits Council of the US Inc
1250 'I' St NW Ste 400 .... Washington DC 20005 202-628-3544 682-8888 49-6
Web: www.discus.org

Distinct Corp
3315 Almaden Expy Ste 10 .... San Jose CA 95118 408-445-3270 445-3274 178-12
TF: 800-872-6265 ■ *Web:* www.distinct.com

Distinctive Dental Studio Ltd. Inc
1504 Wall St .... Naperville IL 60563 630-369-4600 415
TF: 800-552-7890 ■ *Web:* www.ddsltdlab.com

Distinctive Designs International Inc
120 Sibley Dr .... Russellville AL 35654 800-243-4787 293
TF: 800-243-4787 ■ *Web:* www.distinctivedesigns.com

Distinguished Programs Group LLC, The
1180 Ave Of The Americas 16th Fl .... New York NY 10036 212-297-3100 390
TF: 888-355-4626 ■ *Web:* www.distinguished.com

Dis-Tran Steel Fabrication LLC
529 Cenla Dr .... Pineville LA 71360 318-640-6892 480
Web: www.distran.com

Distribution Center Management (DCM)
712 Main St Ste 187B .... Boonton NJ 07005 973-265-2300 402-6056 531-2
TF: 800-232-4317 ■ *Web:* www.distributiongroup.com

Distribution Contractors Assn (DCA)
101 W Renner Rd Ste 460 .... Richardson TX 75082 972-680-0261 680-0461 49-3
Web: www.dcaweb.org

Phone | Fax | Class

Distribution Technology Inc
1701 Continental Blvd .... Charlotte NC 28273 704-587-5587 587-5591 803-1
TF: 800-758-3789 ■ *Web:* www.distributiontechnology.com

Distributive Education Clubs of America (DECA)
1908 Assn Dr .... Reston VA 20191 703-860-5000 860-4013 49-5
Web: www.deca.org

Distributors Solutions LLC PO Box 4030 ....Golden CO 80401 303-277-3359 277-2463 196
Web: www.distributorssolutions.com

Distributors Warehouse Inc
1900 Tenth St..............................Paducah KY 42001 270-442-8201 442-4914 61
Web: btbauto.com

District 1199 C Training & Upgrade Fund
100 S Broad St..........................Philadelphia PA 19110 215-568-2220 507
Web: www.1199ctraining.org

District Court of the Virgin Islands
US Virgin Islands
3013 Estate Golden Rock Ste 219 .... St. Croix VI 00802 340-774-0640 775-8075 341-2
Web: www.vid.uscourts.gov

District Creative Printing Inc
6350 Fallard Dr.......................Upper Marlboro MD 20772 301-868-8610 627
Web: www.dcpprint.com

District of Columbia (PSC)
Aging Office 500 K St NE Ste 900 S ....Washington DC 20002 202-724-5626 724-2008 339-9
Web: www.dcoa.dc.gov
Banking Bureau PO Box 96378.............Washington DC 20090 202-727-8000 535-1197 339-9
Web: disb.dc.gov
Bill Status
1350 Pennsylvania Ave NW.............Washington DC 20004 202-724-8026 724-8129 433
Web: dccouncil.us
Commission on the Arts & Humanities
200 I St SE..........................Washington DC 20003 202-724-5613 727-4135 339-9
Web: www.dcarts.dc.gov/dcarts
Consumer & Regulatory Affairs Dept
1100 Fourth St SW ....Washington DC 20024 202-442-4400 442-9445 339-9
Web: Www.dcra.dc.gov
Convention & Tourism Corp
901 Seventh St NW 4th Fl ....Washington DC 20001 202-789-7000 789-7037 339-9
TF: 800-422-8644 ■ *Web:* washington.org
Crime Victims Compensation Program
515 Fifth St NW Rm 109 Court Bldg A......Washington DC 20001 202-879-4216 879-4230 339-9
Web: www.dccourts.gov
Dept of Insurance Securities & Banking
810 First St NE Ste 701................Washington DC 20002 202-727-8000 339-9
Web: disb.dc.gov
Economic Development
1350 Pennsylvania Ave NW Ste 317 ....Washington DC 20004 202-727-6365 727-6703 339-9
Web: dmped.dc.gov
Government Information
920 Varnum St NE....................Washington DC 20017 202-727-1000 339-9
Web: dc.gov
Historic Preservation Office (HPO)
1100 Fourth St SW Ste E650............Washington DC 20024 202-442-8800 442-7638 339-9
Web: planning.dc.gov
Homeland Security & Emergency Management Agency
2720 Martin Luther King Jr Ave SE 8th Fl ... Washington DC 20032 202-727-6161 339-9
Web: hsema.dc.gov
Housing Finance Agency
815 Florida Ave NW....................Washington DC 20001 202-777-1600 339-9
Web: www.dchfa.org
Human Services Dept
64 New York Ave NE 6th Fl ....Washington DC 20002 202-671-4200 671-4326 339-9
Web: www.dhs.dc.gov
Lottery & Charitable Games Co
2235 Shannon Pl SE...................Washington DC 20020 202-645-8000 452
Web: www.dclottery.com
Paternity & Child Support Enforcement Office
441 Fourth St NW Ste 550N ....Washington DC 20001 202-442-9900 339-9
Web: cssd.dc.gov
Public Service Commission
1333 H St Ste 200 W Tower.............Washington DC 20005 202-626-5100 339-9
Web: www.dcpsc.org
Rehabilitation Services Administration (RSA)
250 East St SW ....Washington DC 20024 202-730-1700 339-9
Web: dds.dc.gov
Securities Bureau
810 First St NE Ste 701................Washington DC 20002 202-727-8000 535-1196 339-9
Web: disb.dc.gov
Tuition Assistance Grant Program
810 First St NE........................Washington DC 20001 202-727-2824 725
TF: 877-485-6751 ■ *Web:* www.osse.dc.gov
Vital Records Division
899 N Capitol St NE 1st Fl...............Washington DC 20002 202-442-5955 442-5955 339-9
Web: doh.dc.gov
Weights & Measures Office
1110 Fourth St SW ....Washington DC 20020 202-442-4400 442-9445 339-9
Web: dcra.dc.gov

District of Columbia Academy of Veterinary Medicine
PO Box 710477 ....Herndon VA 20171 703-733-0556 742-8745 795
Web: www.dcavm.org

District of Columbia Bar, The
1101 K St NW Ste 200 ....Washington DC 20005 202-737-4700 626-3453 72
TF: 877-333-2227 ■ *Web:* www.dcbar.org

District of Columbia Chamber of Commerce
506 Ninth St NW........................Washington DC 20004 202-347-7201 140
Web: www.dcchamber.org

District of Columbia Dental Society
2025 M St NW Ste 800...................Washington DC 20036 202-367-1163 227
Web: www.dcdental.org

District of Columbia Nurses Assn (DCNA)
5100 Wisconsin Ave NW Ste 306...........Washington DC 20016 202-244-2705 362-8285 533
Web: www.dcna.org

District of Columbia Public Schools (DCPS)
1200 First St NE.......................Washington DC 20002 202-442-5885 442-5026 685
Web: www.dcps.dc.gov

District Petroleum Products Inc
1814 River Rd Ste 100 .... Huron OH 44839 419-433-8373 579
Web: hymiler.com

District Photo Inc
10501 Rhode Island Ave..................... Beltsville MD 20705 301-937-5300 588
Web: www.districtphoto.com

District, The 11 S Tenth St ....Columbia MO 65201 573-442-6816 50-6
Web: www.discoverthedistrict.com

DIT-MCO International Corp
5612 Brighton Terr ....Kansas City MO 64130 816-444-9700 248
TF: 800-821-3487 ■ *Web:* www.ditmco.com

Ditta Meat Co PO Box 5623 ....Pasadena TX 77508 281-487-2010 297-9
Web: www.dittameat.com

Ditto 610 Smithfield St .... Pittsburgh PA 15222 412-434-6666 434-7276 113
Web: www.dittohq.com

Ditto Apparel of California Inc
229 Webb Smith Dr .... Colfax LA 71417 318-627-3264 155-11

Ditto Sales Inc 2332 Cathy Ln .... Jasper IN 47546 812-482-3043 482-9318 487
Web: www.dittosales.com

Dittoe Public Relations Inc
2815 E 62nd St Ste 300..................Indianapolis IN 46220 317-202-2280 636
Web: www.dittoepr.com

Div 15 Sales Inc 12026 Roberts Rd.............. La Vista NE 68128 402-597-6353 641
Web: www.division-15.com

Diva at the Met 645 Howe St .... Vancouver BC V6C2Y9 604-602-7788 671
TF: 800-667-2300 ■ *Web:* www.metropolitan.com/diva

Divane Bros Electric Co
2424 Rose St ....Franklin Park IL 60131 847-455-7143 189-4
Web: www.divanebros.com

Divcon EMS 4325 Elm St Ste 210 .... Dallas TX 75226 214-821-6958 463
Web: divconems.com

Dive N' Surf Inc 504 N Broadway ....Redondo Beach CA 90277 310-372-8423 711
Web: www.divensurf.com

Divergent Energy Services Corp
1170 800 - Sixth Ave SW...................... Calgary AB T2P3G3 403-543-0060 539
Web: www.divergentenergyservices.com

Divers Academy International
1500 Liberty Pl.................................Erial NJ 08081 800-238-3483 800
TF: 800-238-3483 ■ *Web:* www.diversacademy.edu

Divers Supply Inc
2396 Belle Chasse Hwy .... Gretna LA 70056 504-392-2800 711
Web: divers-supply.com

Diverse Power Inc 1400 S Davis Rd............LaGrange GA 30241 706-845-2000 245
TF: 800-845-8362 ■ *Web:* www.diversepower.com

Diverse Staffing Inc
6325 Digital Way Ste 100..................Indianapolis IN 46278 317-813-8000 734
Web: www.diversestaffing.com

Diverse Technology Solutions Inc
2949 Sunrise Hwy ....Islip Terrace NY 11752 631-224-1200 180
Web: www.diverse-technology.com

Diversegy LLC
2720 N Stemmons Fwy N Tower Tenth Fl Ste....... Dallas TX 75207 214-637-2400 393
Web: www.diversegy.com

Diversicare Healthcare Services Inc
537 Spring St.................................Dover TN 37058 931-232-6902 450
Web: diversicareofdover.com

Diversicare Healthcare Services Inc.
100 Elmhurst Dr .... Oak Ridge TN 37830 865-481-3367 450
Web: diversicareofoakridge.com

Diversicare Leasing Corp
1621 Galleria Blvd ....Brentwood TN 37027 615-771-7575 194
Web: www.advocat.com

Diversified Brokerage Services Inc
5501 Excelsior Blvd ....Minneapolis MN 55416 952-697-5000 390
Web: www.dbs-lifemark.com

Diversified Business Communications
121 Free St...............................Portland ME 04101 207-842-5500 637-9
Web: divcom.com

Diversified Chemical Technologies Inc (DCT)
15477 Woodrow Wilson St..................... Detroit MI 48238 313-867-5444 867-3831 145
TF: 800-243-1424 ■ *Web:* www.dchem.com

Diversified Collection Services Inc
1080 S Harlan Rd .... Lathrop CA 95330 209-858-3500 160

Diversified Contractors Inc
15915 Highland Dr.........................Mckenzie TN 38201 731-352-7996 480

Diversified Electronics Co Inc
PO Box 566 .... Forest Park GA 30298 404-361-4840 361-6327 246
TF: 800-646-7278 ■ *Web:* www.diversifiedelectronics.com

Diversified Funding Services Inc
125 Habersham Dr Ste C ....Fayetteville GA 30214 770-603-0055 272
TF: 888-603-0055 ■ *Web:* www.divfunding.com

Diversified Human Resources
3020 E Camelback Rd Ste 213.................Phoenix AZ 85016 480-941-5588 553-4684* 631
**Fax Area Code:* 602 ■ *TF:* 888-870-5588 ■ *Web:* www.dhr.net

Diversified International Sciences Corp
4550 Forbes Blvd Ste 300 .... Lanham MD 20706 301-731-9070 178-12

Diversified Labeling Solutions
1285 Hamilton Pkwy.......................... Itasca IL 60143 630-625-1225 552-1
TF: 800-397-3013 ■ *Web:* teamdls.com

Diversified Laboratories Inc
4150 Lafayette Ctr Dr .... Chantilly VA 20151 703-222-8700 668
Web: www.diversifiedlaboratories.com

Diversified Lenders Inc 5607 S Ave Q..........Lubbock TX 79412 800-288-3024 194
TF: 800-288-3024 ■ *Web:* www.diversifiedlenders.com

Diversified Machine Inc
28059 Ctr Oaks Ct ....Wixom MI 48393 248-277-4400 621

Diversified Maintenance Systems Inc
5110 Sunforest Dr Ste250 .... Tampa FL 33634 800-351-1557 152
TF: 800-351-1557 ■ *Web:* www.diversifiedm.com

Diversified Management Services
6919 Vista Dr W ....Des Moines IA 50266 515-282-8192 282-9117 47
Web: www.assoc-mgmt.com

Diversified Metal Fabricators Inc
665 Pylant St, NE........................... Atlanta GA 30306 404-875-1512 650
Web: www.dmfatlanta.com

Diversified Metal Products Inc
3710 N Yellowstone Hwy ....Idaho Falls ID 83401 208-529-9655 295
Web: www.diversifiedmetal.com

Diversified Plastics Corp
120 W Mt Vernon St............................Nixa MO 65714 417-725-2622 601
Web: www.dpcap.com

	Phone	Fax	Class
Diversified Products 3001 30th Ave S . . . Grand Forks ND 58201 *Web:* www.dps-us.com	701-746-0851		499
Diversified Search Cos 2005 Market St 33rd Fl . . . Philadelphia PA 19103 *TF:* 800-423-3932 ■ *Web:* www.divsearch.com	215-732-6666	568-8399	266
Diversified Systems Inc 556 Perry Ave . . . Greenville SC 29611 *Web:* diversifiedus.com	864-271-2668		744
Diversified Technology Consultants Inc (DTC) 2321 Whitney Ave Ste 301 . . . Hamden CT 06518 *Web:* www.teamdtc.com	203-239-4200		261
Diversified Technology Inc 476 Highland Colony Pkwy . . . Ridgeland MS 39157 *Web:* www.dtims.com	601-856-4121		625
Diversitec LLC 14321 Sommerville Ct . . . Midlothian VA 23113 *TF:* 800-229-6772 ■ *Web:* www.diversitec.com	804-379-6772		317
DiversiTech Inc 6650 Sugarloaf Pkwy Ste 100 . . . Duluth GA 30097 *TF:* 800-995-2222 ■ *Web:* www.diversitech.com	678-542-3600	542-3700	14
Diversity Advertising Inc 11271 Ventura Blvd Ste 151 . . . Studio City CA 91604 *Web:* www.hispanic-jobs.com	818-530-4852		260
Divide County 300 N Main . . . Crosby ND 58730 *Web:* www.ndaco.org	701-328-7300		338
Dividend Capital Trust 518 17th St Ste 1700 . . . Denver CO 80202 *TF:* 866-324-7348	303-228-2200	228-0128	654
Divine Brothers Co 200 Seward Ave . . . Utica NY 13502 *Web:* www.divinebrothers.com	315-797-0470		1
Divine Healthcare Network 856 Univerity Ave W . . . St Paul MN 55104 *Web:* divinecorporation.com	651-665-9795		363
Divine Providence Hospital 1100 Grampian Blvd . . . Williamsport PA 17701 *TF:* 800-433-0816 ■ *Web:* susquehannahealth.org	570-326-8000		374-3
Divine Redeemer United Presbyterian Church 407 N Calaveras . . . San Antonio TX 78207 *Web:* divineredeemersa.org	210-433-9551		48-20
Divine Word College 102 Jacoby Dr SW . . . Epworth IA 52045 **Fax:* Admissions ■ *TF:* 800-553-3321 ■ *Web:* www.dwci.edu	563-876-3353	876-3407*	166
Diving Equipment & Marketing Assn (DEMA) 3750 Convoy St Ste 310 . . . San Diego CA 92111 *TF:* 800-862-3483 ■ *Web:* www.dema.org	858-616-6408	616-6495	49-4
Division Laundry & Cleaners Inc 6649 Old Hwy 90 W . . . San Antonio TX 78227 *Web:* divisionlaundry.com	210-674-5110	673-8510	426
Division Scolaire Franco-Manitobaine No 49 1263 Dawson Rd . . . Lorette MB R0A0Y0 *Web:* www.dsfm.mb.ca	204-878-9399		685
Divisions Maintenance Group Inc 1 RiverFrnt Pl Ste 510 . . . Newport KY 41071 *TF:* 877-448-9730 ■ *Web:* www.divisionsinc.com	877-448-9730		192
DIVSYS International LLC 8110 Zionsville Rd . . . Indianapolis IN 46268 *Web:* www.divsys.com	317-405-9427		625
Divvies LLC 700 Oakridge Common . . . South Salem NY 10590 *Web:* www.divvies.com	914-533-0333		297-8
Diw Group Inc Dba Specialized Engineering 4845 International Blvd . . . Frederick MD 21703	301-607-4180		743
DIX (Alexander Communications Group Inc) 712 Main St Ste 187B . . . Boonton NJ 07005 *TF:* 800-232-4317 ■ *Web:* www.downtowndevelopment.com	973-265-2300	402-6056	531-2
Dix & Eaton Inc 200 Public Sq Ste 3900 . . . Cleveland OH 44114 *Web:* www.dix-eaton.com	216-241-0405		636
Dix Barrett & Stiltner Pc 5670 Greenwood Plaza Blvd Ste 505 . . . Greenwood Village CO 80111 *Web:* www.dbs-cpas.com	303-689-0844		2
Dix Corp 4024 S Grove Rd . . . Spokane WA 99224 *TF:* 800-827-8548 ■ *Web:* www.dixcorp.com	509-838-4455	838-4464	189-14
Dix Industries Inc 5500 RL Ostos Rd . . . Brownsville TX 78521 *Web:* www.dixshipping.com	956-831-4228	831-2559	465
Dixie Aerospace Inc 473 Dividend Dr . . . Peachtree City GA 30269 *Web:* www.dixieaerospace.com	678-490-0140		791
Dixie Barbecue Co 3301 N Roan St . . . Johnson City TN 37601 *Web:* dixiebarbeque.net	423-283-7447		671
Dixie Clay Co 305 Dixie Clay Rd . . . Bath SC 29816	803-593-2592		503-2
Dixie Construction Products Inc 970 Huff Rd NW . . . Atlanta GA 30318 *TF:* 800-992-1180 ■ *Web:* www.dixieconstruction.com	404-351-1100	350-2359	351
Dixie County 214 NE 351 Hwy PO Box 2600 . . . Cross City FL 32628 *Web:* dixie.fl.gov	352-498-1206	498-1207	338
Dixie Electric Co-op 9100 Atlanta Hwy . . . Montgomery AL 36117 *TF:* 888-349-4332 ■ *Web:* www.dixie.coop	334-288-1163		245
Dixie Electric Membership Corp (DEMCO) PO Box 15659 . . . Baton Rouge LA 70895 *TF:* 800-262-0221 ■ *Web:* www.demco.org	225-261-1221		245
Dixie Electric Power Assn 1863 US-184 PO Box 88 . . . Laurel MS 39443 *TF:* 888-465-9209 ■ *Web:* www.dixieepa.com	601-425-2535		245
Dixie Furniture Co 282 Richmond Hill . . . West Helena AR 72390	870-572-3493		321
Dixie Gas & Oil Corp 229 Lee Hwy P O Box 900 . . . Verona VA 24482 *Web:* www.dixiegas.com	540-248-6273		204
Dixie Graphics Co 636 Grassmere Pk . . . Nashville TN 37211 *Web:* www.dixiegraphics.com	615-832-7000	832-7621	781
Dixie Group Inc 104 Nowlin Ln Ste 101 . . . Chattanooga TN 37421 *NASDAQ:* DXYN ■ *TF:* 800-289-4811 ■ *Web:* www.thedixiegroup.com	423-510-7000		131
Dixie Gun Works Inc 1412 W Reelfoot Ave PO Box 130 . . . Union City TN 38281 *TF Orders:* 800-238-6785 ■ *Web:* dixiegunworks.com	731-885-0700	885-0440	711
Dixie House Cafe 6200 E Lancaster Ave . . . Fort Worth TX 76112 *Web:* www.dixiehousecafe.com	817-451-6180		671
Dixie Industries 3510 N Orchard Knob Ave . . . Chattanooga TN 37406 *TF:* 800-933-4943 ■ *Web:* cmforge.com	423-698-3323		350
Dixie Metal Products Inc 442 SW 54th Ct . . . Ocala FL 34474 *Web:* www.dixiemetals.com	352-873-2554		295
Dixie Outlet Mall 1250 S Service Rd . . . Mississauga ON L5E1V4 *Web:* www.dixieoutletmall.com	905-278-3494		460
Dixie Pipe Sales Inc 2407 Broiller . . . Houston TX 77054 *TF:* 800-733-3494 ■ *Web:* www.dixiepipe.com	713-796-2021	799-8628	490
Dixie Power 71 E Hwy 56 . . . Beryl UT 84714 *TF:* 800-874-0904 ■ *Web:* www.dixiepower.com	435-439-5311	439-5352	245
Dixie Restaurants Inc 1215 Rebsamen Pk Rd . . . Little Rock AR 72202 *Web:* www.dixiecafe.com	501-666-3494	666-8900	670
Dixie Southern Industrial Inc 1060 N Commonwealth Ave . . . Polk City FL 33868 *Web:* www.dsisteel.com	863-984-1900	984-1825	307
Dixie State University 225 S 700 E . . . Saint George UT 84770 *TF:* 855-628-8140 ■ *Web:* dixie.edu	435-652-7500		166
Dixie Store Fixtures & Sales Company Inc 2425 First Ave N . . . Birmingham AL 35203 *TF:* 800-323-4943 ■ *Web:* www.dixiestorefixtures.com	205-322-2442	322-2445	286
Dixieline Lumber Company Inc 3250 Sports Arena Blvd . . . San Diego CA 92110 *Web:* www.dixieline.com	619-224-4120	225-8192	364
Dixien 5286 Cir Dr . . . Lake City GA 30260 *Web:* www.dixien.com	404-366-7427		489
Dixie-Narco Inc 3330 Dixie-Narco Blvd . . . Williston SC 29853 *TF:* 800-688-9090 ■ *Web:* www.dixie-narco.com	803-266-5000	266-5000	55
Dixon Assoc Engineering LLC 313 E Jimmie Leeds Rd 2nd Fl . . . Galloway NJ 08205 *Web:* dixonassociates.com	609-652-7131		261
Dixon Blind & Awning Service 1800 Sunset Ave . . . Rocky Mount NC 27804	252-442-2145		87
Dixon Builders & Developers Inc 8050 Beckett Crt D Ste 213 . . . West Chester OH 45069 *Web:* www.dixonbuilders.com	513-887-6400	887-6643	653
Dixon Correctional Ctr 2600 N Brinton Ave . . . Dixon IL 61021	815-288-5561		213
Dixon Correctional Institute 5568 Hwy 68 . . . Jackson LA 70748 *Web:* doc.louisiana.gov	225-634-1200		213
Dixon County PO Box 395 . . . Ponca NE 68770 *Web:* www.co.dixon.ne.us	402-755-5604	755-5651	338
Dixon Gallery & Gardens 4339 Pk Ave . . . Memphis TN 38117 *Web:* www.dixon.org	901-761-5250	682-0943	520
Dixon Group Canada Ltd 2200 Logan Ave . . . Winnipeg MB R2R0J2 *Web:* canada.dixonvalve.com	204-633-5650		358
Dixon Howell Westmoreland & Newman Attys 924 Westwood Blvd Ste 850 . . . Los Angeles CA 90024 *TF:* 000-818-0382 ■ *Web:* dhwnlaw.com	310-208-4666		445
Dixon Hughes PLLC 6525 Morrison Blvd Ste 500 . . . Charlotte NC 28211 *Web:* www.dhgllp.com	704-367-7020	307-7760	2
Dixon Mitchell Investment Counsel Inc Ste 1680 1055 W Hastings St . . . Vancouver BC V6E2E9 *Web:* www.dixonmitchell.com	604-669-3136		528
Dixon Public Library 230 N First St . . . Dixon CA 95620 *Web:* www.dixonlibrary.com	707-678-5447	678-3515	434-3
Dixon Schwabl Advertising 1595 Moseley Rd . . . Victor NY 14564 *Web:* dixonschwabl.com	585-383-0380		636
Dixon Ticonderoga Co 195 International Pkwy . . . Heathrow FL 32746 **Fax:* Cust Svc ■ *TF:* 800-824-9430 ■ *Web:* www.dixonticonderoga.com	800-824-9430	232-9396*	571
Dixon Valve & Coupling Company Inc 800 High St . . . Chestertown MD 21620 *TF:* 877-963-4966 ■ *Web:* www.dixonvalve.com	877-963-4966		790
Dixville Notch State Park Rt 26 . . . Dixville NH 03576 *Web:* www.nhstateparks.org	603-538-6707		565
DIY Group Inc 2401 W 26th . . . Muncie IN 47302 *Web:* www.diygroup.com	765-284-9000		88
Dize Company Inc, The 1512 S Main St . . . Winston-salem NC 27127 *TF:* 800-583-8243 ■ *Web:* www.dizecompany.com	336-722-5181		350
DJ & A PC 3203 S Russell St . . . Missoula MT 59801 *TF:* 800-398-3522 ■ *Web:* www.djanda.com	406-721-4320		256
DJ Case & Assoc Inc 317 E Jefferson Blvd . . . Mishawaka IN 46545 *Web:* www.djcase.com	574-258-0100		636
DJ Jacobetti Home for Veterans 425 Fisher St . . . Marquette MI 49855 *TF:* 800-433-6760 ■ *Web:* michigan.gov	906-226-3576	226-2380	793
DJ Orthopedics Inc 1430 Decision St . . . Vista CA 92081 **Fax Area Code:* 800 ■ *TF:* 800-321-9549 ■ *Web:* www.djoglobal.com	760-727-1280	936-6569*	477
Djg Investigative Services Inc 1370 Briar Creek Rd . . . Charlotte NC 28205 *TF:* 800-927-0456 ■ *Web:* djginvestigativeservices.com	704-536-8025		693
DJJ (David J Joseph Co) 300 Pike St . . . Cincinnati OH 45202 *Web:* www.djj.com	513-419-6200	419-6222	686
DJL Construction Inc 1550 Ampere St Ste 200 . . . Boucherville QC J4B7L4	450-641-8000	655-1201	256
DJM Capital Partners Inc 60 S Market St Ste 1120 . . . San Jose CA 95113 *Web:* www.djmcapital.com	408-271-0366		652
DJS International Services Inc 4215 Gateway Dr Ste 100 . . . Colleyville TX 76034 *Web:* www.djsintl.com	972-929-8433		311
Djs Marketing Group Inc 2398 S Dixie Hwy . . . Miami FL 33133 *Web:* www.djs-marketing.com	305-640-5939		195

Company	Phone	Fax	Class
DK Consultants LLC 1307 Carpers Farm Way ... Vienna VA 22182 *Web:* www.dkconsult.net	703-438-3648		194
DK Manufacturing Lancaster Inc 2118 Commerce St ... Lancaster OH 43130 *Web:* dkmanufacturing.com	740-654-5566		608
Dk Security 5160 falcon view ave se ... Grand rapids MI 49512 *Web:* www.dksecurity.com	616-656-0123		693
D-K Trading Corp PO Box E ... Clarks Summit PA 18411 *Web:* www.dk-t.com	570-586-9662		559
Dka 5713 Corporate Way Ste 100 ... West Palm Beach FL 33407 *Web:* www.dkahome.com	561-640-9171		463
DKC (Dan Klores Communications Inc) 261 Fifth Ave ... New York NY 10016 *Web:* www.dkcnews.com	212-685-4300	685-9024	636
DKE (Delta Kappa Epsilon Fraternity) 611 1/2 E William St ... Ann Arbor MI 48104 *Web:* www.dke.org	734-302-4210		48-16
DKM (Dyson-Kissner-Moran Corp) 565 Fifth Ave 4th Fl ... New York NY 10017 *Web:* www.dkmcorp.com	212-661-4600		185
DKN Hotels LLC 42 Corporate Pk Ste 200 ... Irvine CA 92606 *Web:* www.dknhotels.com	714-427-4320		378
DKRW Advanced Fuels LLC 5444 Westheimer Ste 1560 ... Houston TX 77056 *Fax Area Code: 713 ■ *TF:* 855-876-4595	855-876-4595	355-3201*	536
Dky Inc 6009 Penn Ave S ... Minneapolis MN 55419 *Web:* dkyinc.com	612-798-4070		7
D&L Art Glass Supply 1440 W 52nd Ave ... Denver CO 80221 *TF:* 800-525-0940 ■ *Web:* www.dlartglass.com	303-449-8737		44
DL Blair Inc 400 Post Ave Ste 400 ... Westbury NY 11590 *TF:* 800-645-4710 ■ *Web:* www.dlblair.com	516-746-3700		5
DL Bliss State Park c/o Sierra District Office PO Box 266 ... Tahoma CA 96142 *Web:* www.parks.ca.gov/?page_id=505	530-525-7277		565
DL Carlson Investment Group Inc 101 N State St ... Concord NH 03301 *Web:* www.carlsoninvest.com	603-224-5977		401
D&L Energy Inc 2761 Salt Springs Rd ... Youngstown OH 44509	330-792-9524	792-9584	536
DL Geary Brewing Company Inc 38 Evergreen Dr ... Portland ME 04103 *TF:* 800-452-4633 ■ *Web:* www.gearybrewing.com	207-878-2337	878-2388	102
DL Lee & Sons Inc 927 Hwy 32 E ... Alma GA 31510 *TF:* 800-673-9339 ■ *Web:* www.dllee.com	912-632-4406	632-8298	473
DL Withers Construction LC 3220 E Harbour Dr ... Phoenix AZ 85034 *Web:* www.dlwithers.com	602-438-9500		186
DLA (Defense Logistics Agency) 8725 John J Kingman Rd Ste 1644 ... Fort Belvoir VA 22060 *TF:* 800-565-3946 ■ *Web:* www.dla.mil/Pages/default.aspx	703-767-5200	767-6091	340-3
DLA Piper 203 N LaSalle St Ste 1900 ... Chicago IL 60601 *Web:* www.dlapiper.com	312-368-4000		428
DLB Associates Consulting Engineers PC 265 Industrial Way W ... Eatontown NJ 07724 *Web:* www.dlbassociates.com	732-774-2000		256
Dld Lawyers 150 Alhambra Cir Ph ... Coral Gables FL 33134 *Web:* www.dldlawyers.com	305-443-4850		428
DLD State Recreation Area 7425 S US Hwy 281 ... Doniphan NE 68832 *Web:* outdoornebraska.gov	308-385-6211		565
DLGL Ltd 850 Bd Michele Bohec ... Blainville QC J7C5E2 *TF:* 800-387-4693 ■ *Web:* www.dlgl.com	450-979-4646		178-1
DLH Holdings Corp 1776 Peachtree St NW Ste 300S ... Atlanta GA 30309 *NASDAQ: DLHC* ■ *TF:* 800-743-1934 ■ *Web:* www.dlhcorp.com	770-554-3545		721
DLH Nordisk Inc 2307 W Cone Boulvard Ste 200 ... Greensboro NC 27408 *Web:* www.dlh.com/default.aspx	336-852-8341		683
D-Link Systems Inc 17595 Mt Herrmann St ... Fountain Valley CA 92708 *TF:* 800-326-1688 ■ *Web:* www.dlink.com	800-326-1688		176
DLL 1111 Old Eagle School Rd ... Wayne PA 19087 *TF:* 800-873-2474 ■ *Web:* www.dllgroup.com	610-386-5000		216
DLR Group Inc 6457 Frances Ste 200 ... Omaha NE 68106 *Web:* www.dlrgroup.com	402-393-4100		261
Dlt Solutions 13861 Sunrise Valley Dr Ste 400 ... Herndon VA 20171 *TF:* 800-262-4358 ■ *Web:* www.dlt.com	703-709-7172	709-8450	174
DLTC (Deaconess Long Term Care Inc) 330 Straight St ... Cincinnati OH 45219 *Web:* www.deaconess-healthcare.com	513-487-3600		450
DLZ Corp 6121 Huntley Rd ... Columbus OH 43229 *TF:* 800-336-5352 ■ *Web:* dlz.com	614-888-0040		261
DM Comp & Sons 31790 Merced Ave ... Bakersfield CA 93308 *TF:* 800-826-0200 ■ *Web:* www.dmcampandsons.com	661-399-5511		10-4
DM Contact Management 100-645 Tyee Rd ... Victoria BC V9A6X5 *Web:* www.dmcontact.com	250-383-8267		317
DM Figley Company Inc 10 Kelly Ct ... Menlo Park CA 94025 *TF:* 800-292-9919 ■ *Web:* www.dmfigley.com	650-329-8700	329-0601	146
DM Kelly & Co 3900 Ingersoll Ave Ste 300 ... Des Moines IA 50312 *Web:* www.dmkc.com	515-221-1133		690
DM Stamps & Specialties Inc 1101 N Riverfront Dr ... Mankato MN 56001 *Web:* www.dmstampsdiv.com	507-387-4444	387-4447	467
DM Transportation Management Services Inc 740 Reading Ave ... Boyertown PA 19512 *TF:* 888-399-0162 ■ *Web:* www.dmtrans.com	610-367-0162	369-0270	194
DMA (Direct Marketing Assn Inc) 1120 Ave of the Americas ... New York NY 10036 *TF:* 855-422-0749 ■ *Web:* thedma.org	212-768-7277	302-6714	49-18
DMC (Delta Medical Ctr) 3000 Getwell Rd ... Memphis TN 38118 *TF:* 800-561-3357 ■ *Web:* www.deltamedcenter.com	901-369-8100		374-3
DMC (Delray Medical Ctr) 5352 Linton Blvd ... Delray Beach FL 33484 *Web:* www.delraymedicalctr.com	561-498-4440	495-3103	374-3
DMC (Detroit Medical Ctr) 4707 St Antoine ... Detroit MI 48201 *Web:* www.dmc.org	313-745-6035		353
DMC Corp 10 Basin Dr Ste 130 ... Kearny NJ 07032 *Web:* www.dmc-usa.com	973-589-0606	589-8931	745-9
DMC Sinai-Grace Hospital 6071 W Outer Dr ... Detroit MI 48235 *TF:* 888-362-2500 ■ *Web:* www.sinaigrace.org	313-966-3300	966-3160	374-3
DMC Technology Group Inc 7657 King's Pointe Rd ... Toledo OH 43617 *Web:* dmctechgroup.com	419-535-2900		180
DMCCVB (Decatur/Morgan County Convention & Visitors Bureau) 719 Sixth Ave SE PO Box 2349 ... Decatur AL 35602 *TF:* 800-232-5449 ■ *Web:* www.decaturcvb.org	256-350-2028		206
D-M-E Co 29111 Stephenson Hwy ... Madison Heights MI 48071 *TF:* 800-626-6653 ■ *Web:* www.dme.net	248-398-6000	544-5705	604
DME-Direct Inc 28486 Westinghouse Pl Ste 120 ... Valencia CA 91355 *TF:* 877-721-7701 ■ *Web:* www.dme-direct.com	877-721-7701		194
DMG (Drohan Management Group) 11130 Sunrise Valley Dr Ste 350 ... Reston VA 20191 *Web:* www.drohanmgmt.com	703-437-4377	435-4390	47
DMG Events Inc 3 Stamford Landing Ste 400 46 Southfield Avenue ... Stamford CT 06902 *Web:* www.dmgevents.com	203-973-2940		387
DMI (Dairy Management Inc) 10255 W Higgins Rd Ste 900 ... Rosemont IL 60018 *TF:* 800-853-2479 ■ *Web:* www.dairy.org	800-853-2479		48-2
Dmi 235 W Jefferson Ave ... Naperville IL 60540 *Web:* www.dmihotels.com	630-428-1000		707
DMI (Design Management Institute) 38 Chauncy St Ste 800 ... Boston MA 02111 *Web:* www.dmi.org	617-338-6380	338-6570	48-4
Dmi Corp PO Box 53 ... Cedar Hill TX 75104 *Web:* www.deckermechanical.com	972-291-9907	299-6437	189-10
DMI Music & Media Solutions 35 W Dayton St ... Pasadena CA 91105 *Web:* www.dmimusic.com	626-795-0432		195
DMI Technology Group 406 Kays Dr ... Normal IL 61761 *Web:* www.dmitech.com	309-828-4439		177
DMJ Technologies LLC 140 Henley Ave Ste 5 ... New Milford NJ 07646 *Web:* www.dmjtechnologies.com	201-261-5560		179
DMK Associates 435 Commercial Ct ... Venice FL 34292	941-412-1293		261
DMNmedia 508 Young St ... Dallas TX 75202 *Web:* dmnmedia.com	214-842-6864		5
DMR Consulting Inc 7946 Front Beach Rd ... Panama City Beach FL 32407 *Web:* www.dmrcinc.com	850-230-3767		196
Dms 100 S Keowee St ... Dayton OH 45402 *Web:* www.daytonmailing.com	937-222-5056		5
DMS Facility Services 1040 Arroyo Dr ... South Pasadena CA 91030 *TF:* 800-443-8677 ■ *Web:* www.dmsfacilityservices.com	626-305-8500		104
DMS Laboratories Inc 2 Darts Mill Rd ... Flemington NJ 08822 *TF:* 800-567-4367 ■ *Web:* www.rapidvet.com	908-782-3353	782-0832	584
DMS Pharmaceutical Group Inc 810 Busse Hwy ... Park Ridge IL 60068 *TF:* 877-788-1100 ■ *Web:* www.dmspharma.com	847-518-1100		231
DMSI (DMSI) 2127 Ayrsley Town Blvd Ste 301 ... Charlotte NC 28273 *Web:* www.dmsi.net	704-587-3674		449
DMW Worldwide LLC 701 Lee Rd Ste 103 ... Chesterbrook PA 19087 *TF:* 800-888-7704 ■ *Web:* www.dmwdirect.com	610-407-0407	407-0410	5
DMWCC (Dearborn Mid-West Conveyor Co) 20334 Superior Rd ... Taylor MI 48180 *Web:* www.dmwcc.com	734-288-4400		207
DN Partners LLC 180 N LaSalle St Ste 2630 ... Chicago IL 60601 *Web:* www.dnpartners.com	312-332-7960		691
DN Tanks 351 Cypress Ln ... El Cajon CA 92020 *TF:* 800-227-8181 ■ *Web:* www.dntanks.com	619-440-8181		183
DNA (Delaware Nurses Assn) 4765 Ogletown-Stanton Rd Ste L10 ... Newark DE 19713 *TF:* 800-626-4081 ■ *Web:* www.denurses.org	302-733-5880		533
DNA Diagnostics Ctr 1 DDC Way ... Fairfield OH 45014 *TF:* 800-362-2368 ■ *Web:* www.dnacenter.com	513-881-7800	881-7803	417
DNA Genotek Inc 2 Beaverbrook Rd ... Kanata ON K2K1L1 *Web:* www.dnagenotek.com	613-723-5757		477
DNA Labs International Inc 240 SW Natura Ave ... Deerfield Beach FL 33441 *Web:* www.dnalabsinternational.com	954-426-5163		415
DNA LandMarks Inc 84 Richelieu St ... Saint Jean-Sur-Richelieu QC J3B6X3 *Web:* www.dnalandmarks.com	450-358-2621		10-3
DNA Model Management Inc 555 W 25th St ... New York NY 10001 *Web:* www.dnamodels.com	212-226-0080	226-7711	506
DNA Reference Lab Inc 5819 NW Loop 410 Ste 166 ... San Antonio TX 78238 *Web:* www.dnareferencelab.com	210-692-3800		418
DNB Engineering Inc 5969 Robinson Ave ... Riverside CA 92503 *Web:* www.dnbenginc.com	951-637-2630		256
DNC Parks & Resorts at KSC Inc State Rd 405 ... Titusville FL 32899 *TF:* 855-433-4210 ■ *Web:* www.kennedyspacecenter.com	855-433-4210		377
DND Fashion Inc 10434 Rush St ... South El Monte CA 91733	626-442-1423		157-6
DNE Systems Inc 50 Barnes Industrial Park N ... Wallingford CT 06492 *Web:* www.dne.com	203-265-7151		21
Dnfcontrols 12843 Foothill Blvd Ste D ... Sylmar CA 91342 *Web:* www.dnfcontrols.com	818-898-3380		647
DNN (Disaster News Network) PO Box 1746 ... Ellicott City MD 21041 *TF:* 888-384-3028 ■ *Web:* www.disasternews.net	443-393-3330	420-0085	530

Name / Address	City	State	ZIP	Phone	Fax	Class
DNP America LLC 335 Madison Ave 3rd Fl; *Web:* www.dnpamerica.com	New York	NY	10017	212-503-1060		360-3
Do All Travel Company Inc 4620 18th Ave; *Web:* www.doalltravel.com	Brooklyn	NY	11204	718-972-6000		772
Do it Best Corp 6502 Nelson Ave; *Web:* www.doitbest.com	Fort Wayne	IN	46803	260-748-5300		351
Do It Sports Inc 615 S Mansfield; *Web:* www.doitsports.com	Ypsilanti	MI	48197	734-544-7700		5
Do My Own Pest Control 4260 Communications Dr; *Web:* www.domyownpestcontrol.com	Norcross	GA	30093	770-840-8831		195
Do+Able Products Inc 5150 Edison Ave	Chino	CA	91710	909-465-0695		200
Doak House Museum Tusculum College Department of Museum Program & Studies, PO Box 5026; *Web:* www2.tusculum.edu	Greeneville	TN	37743	423-636-8554		520
Doane College 1014 Boswell Ave; *TF:* 800-333-6263 ■ *Web:* www.doane.edu	Crete	NE	68333	402-826-2161	826-8600	166
Grand Island 3180 W US Hwy 34; *TF:* 800-333-6263 ■ *Web:* www.doane.edu	Grand Island	NE	68801	308-398-0800	398-1726	166
Lincoln 303 N 52nd St; *TF:* 888-803-6263 ■ *Web:* www.doane.edu	Lincoln	NE	68504	402-466-4774	466-4228	166
DOAR Litigation Consulting 170 Earle Ave; *TF:* 800-875-8705 ■ *Web:* www.doar.com	Lynbrook	NY	11563	516-823-4000		445
Dobama Theater 2340 Lee Rd; *Web:* www.dobama.org	Cleveland Heights	OH	44118	216-932-6838	932-6838	572
Dobbin House Inc 89 Steinwehr Ave; *Web:* www.dobbinhouse.com/map.htm	Gettysburg	PA	17325	717-334-2100	334-6905	671
DOBER 11230 Katherine Crossing Ste 100; *TF:* 800-323-4983 ■ *Web:* www.dobergroup.com	Woodridge	IL	60517	630-410-7300	410-7444	145
Dobil Laboratories Inc 727 Butler St; *Web:* dobil.com	Pittsburgh	PA	15223	412-782-3399		261
Doble Engineering Co Inc 85 Walnut St; *TF:* 888-443-6253 ■ *Web:* www.doble.com	Watertown	MA	02472	617-926-4900	926-0528	248
Dobson's 956 Broadway Cir; *Web:* www.dobsonsrestaurant.com	San Diego	CA	92101	619-231-6771		671
Doc 2 E-file Inc 4500 S Wayside Dr Ste 102; *TF:* 888-649-2006 ■ *Web:* www.doc2e-file.com	Houston	TX	77087	713-649-2006		225
Doc Chey's Noodle House 37 Biltmore Ave; *Web:* www.doccheys.com	Asheville	NC	28801	828-252-8220		671
Doc's Drugs 230 Comet Dr; *Web:* www.docsdrugs.com	Braidwood	IL	60408	815-458-6104	458-6158	237
DocAuto Inc 3500 Pkwy Ln Ste 270; *TF:* 800-362-2886 ■ *Web:* www.docauto.com	Norcross	GA	30092	770-242-6747		387
Dock at Crayton Cove 845 12th Ave S; *Web:* www.dockcraytoncove.com	Naples	FL	34102	239-263-9940		671
Dock Street Asset Management 2 Spencer Pl; *Web:* www.dockstreet.net	Scarsdale	NY	10583	203-532-9470		194
Dock's Oyster House 2405 Atlantic Ave; *Web:* www.docksoysterhouse.com	Atlantic City	NJ	08401	609-345-0092		671
Docken & Co 900-800 6 Ave SW; *TF:* 877-269-3612 ■ *Web:* docken.com	Calgary	AB	T2P3G3	403-269-3612		428
Dockers Inn 3060 Green Mtn Dr; *TF:* 800-324-8748 ■ *Web:* www.dockersinn.com	Branson	MO	65616	417-334-3600		379
Dockweiler State Beach 12000 Vista del Mar; *Web:* www.parks.ca.gov	Playa del Rey	CA	90293	310-305-9503		565
DocMan Technologies 31300 Bainbridge Rd; *Web:* www.docmantech.com	Cleveland	OH	44122	440-542-9660		39
Doctor's Channel LLC, The 1133 Broadway 2nd Fl; *Web:* www.thedoctorschannel.com	New York	NY	10010	646-257-5739		387
Doctors Administrative Solutions LLC 1000 N Ashley Dr Ste 300; *Web:* dashealth.com	Tampa	FL	33602	813-774-9800		463
Doctors Community Hospital (DCH) 8118 Good Luck Rd; *Web:* www.dchweb.org	Lanham	MD	20706	301-552-8118	552-8521	374-3
Doctors Foster & Smith Inc 2253 Air Pk Rd PO Box 100; **Fax:* Cust Svc ■ *TF:* 800-826-7206 ■ *Web:* www.drsfostersmith.com	Rhinelander	WI	54501	800-381-7179	562-7169*	578
Doctors Hospital 5100 W Broad St; *TF:* 800-432-3309 ■ *Web:* www.ohiohealth.com/doctors	Columbus	OH	43228	614-544-1000		374-3
Doctors Hospital 3651 Wheeler Rd; *Web:* www.doctors-hospital.net	Augusta	GA	30909	706-651-3232		374-3
Doctors Hospital of Laredo 10700 McPherson Rd; *TF:* 844-244-4874 ■ *Web:* www.doctorshosplaredo.com	Laredo	TX	78045	956-523-2000	523-0444	374-3
Doctors Hospital Sarasota 5731 Bee Ridge Rd; *TF:* 800-523-5840 ■ *Web:* www.doctorsofsarasota.com	Sarasota	FL	34233	941-342-1100		374-3
Doctors Medical Ctr 1441 Florida Ave; *TF:* 800-827-4277 ■ *Web:* www.dmc-modesto.com	Modesto	CA	95350	209-578-1211	576-3680	374-3
Doctors Pathology Services 1253 College Park Dr; *Web:* dpspa.com	Dover	DE	19904	302-677-0000		418
Doctors Vision Ctr 413 Mill St PO Box 7396; *Web:* www.doctorsvisioncenter.com	Rocky Mount	NC	27804	252-442-0802		543
Doctors Without Borders USA Inc 333 Seventh Ave 2nd Fl; *TF:* 888-392-0392 ■ *Web:* www.doctorswithoutborders.org	New York	NY	10001	212-679-6800	679-7016	48-5
Doctors' Co, The 185 Greenwood Rd; *TF:* 800-421-2368 ■ *Web:* www.thedoctors.com	Napa	CA	94558	800-421-2368		391-5
Doctors' Hospital 5000 University Dr; *Web:* www.baptisthealth.net	Coral Gables	FL	33146	786-308-3000		374-3
DocuData Solutions LLC 7777 John Carpenter Fwy; *Web:* www.docudatasolutions.com	Dallas	TX	75247	214-678-9898		624
Docuforce 8343 E 32nd St N; *Web:* www.docuforce.biz	Wichita	KS	67226	316-636-5400		321
Documation LLC 1556 International Dr; *Web:* documation.com	Eau Claire	WI	54701	715-839-8899		174
Document Automation and Production Service 5450 Carlisle Pk Bldg 9	Mechanicsburg	PA	17050	717-605-2362		627
Document Imaging Systems Corp 1717 Olive St Ste 300; *Web:* disccorporation.com	Saint Louis	MO	63103	314-436-2800		396
Document Security Systems Inc 200 Canal View Blvd Ste 300; *NYSE: DSS* ■ *TF:* 877-407-8031 ■ *Web:* www.dsssecure.com	Rochester	NY	14623	585-325-3610	325-2977	178-10
Document Storage Systems Inc 12575 US Hwy 1 Ste 200-A; *Web:* www.dssinc.com	Juno Beach	FL	33408	561-284-7000		177
Documentation Strategies Inc 15 Second Ave; *TF:* 800-331-5114 ■ *Web:* www.docstrats.com	Rensselaer	NY	12144	518-432-1233		180
Docuplex Inc 725 E Bayley; *Web:* www.docuplex.com	Wichita	KS	67214	316-262-2662		627
Doc-U-Search Inc 63 Pleasant St PO Box 777; **Fax Area Code:* 603 ■ *TF:* 800-332-3034 ■ *Web:* www.docusearchinc.com	Concord	NH	03301	800-332-3034	224-2794*	635
DocuSource of North Carolina LLC 2800 Slater Rd; *Web:* www.docusourceofnc.com	Morrisville	NC	27560	919-459-5900		627
DOD (Department of Defense) The Pentagon; *Web:* www.defense.gov	Washington	DC	20301	703-545-6700		340-3
Dodd Camera 2077 E 30th St; *TF:* 855-544-1705 ■ *Web:* www.doddcamera.com	Cleveland	OH	44115	216-361-6800	361-6819	119
Dodd Creative Group Holding Company Inc 3720 Canton St Ste 100; *Web:* doddcreative.com	Dallas	TX	75226	214-821-6990		466
Dodd Technologies Inc 7979 W Fall Creek Dr; *Web:* doddtechnologies.com	Pendleton	IN	46064	317-485-4604		8
Doddridge County 118 E Ct St; *Web:* doddridgecounty.wv.gov	West Union	WV	26456	304-873-2631	873-1840	338
Dodds & Eder Inc 221 S St; *Web:* doddsandeder.com	Oyster Bay	NY	11771	516-922-4412		293
Dodge & Cox 555 California St 40th Fl; *TF:* 800-621-3979 ■ *Web:* www.dodgeandcoxworldwide.com	San Francisco	CA	94104	415-981-1710		401
Dodge & Cox Funds 30 Dan Rd PO Box 8422; *TF:* 800-621-3979 ■ *Web:* www.dodgeandcox.com	Canton	MA	02021	800-621-3979		528
Dodge #4 State Park 4250 Pkwy Dr; *Web:* www.michigandnr.com	Waterford	MI	48327	248-682-7323		565
Dodge City Area Chamber of Commerce 311 W Spruce St; *TF:* 800-963-5227 ■ *Web:* www.dodgechamber.com	Dodge City	KS	67801	620-227-3119	227-2957	139
Dodge City Community College 2501 N 14th Ave; **Fax:* Admissions ■ *TF:* 800-367-3222 ■ *Web:* www.dc3.edu	Dodge City	KS	67801	620-225-1321	227-9277*	162
Dodge Communications Inc 11675 Rainwater Dr Ste 300; *Web:* www.dodgecommunications.com	Alpharetta	GA	30009	770-998-0500		194
Dodge County PO Box 818; *TF:* 800-656-2298 ■ *Web:* www.dodgecountyga.com	Eastman	GA	31023	478-374-4361	374-8121	338
Dodge County 435 N Pk; *TF:* 800-331-5666 ■ *Web:* www.dodgecounty.ne.gov	Fremont	NE	68025	402-727-2767	727-2764	338
Dodge County 127 E Oak St; *Web:* www.co.dodge.wi.us	Juneau	WI	53039	920-386-3602	386-3928	338
Dodge County 22 Sixth St E Dept 91; *Web:* www.co.dodge.mn.us	Mantorville	MN	55955	507-635-6275	635-6323	338
Dodge County Convention & Visitors Bureau 338 N Main St; *Web:* www.fremontne.org	Fremont	NE	68025	402-753-6414	721-1511	206
Dodge County Hospital 901 Griffin Ave; *TF:* 800-999-5182 ■ *Web:* www.dodgecountyhospital.com	Eastman	GA	31023	478-448-4000		374-3
Dodge County Schools 720 College St; *Web:* www.dodge.k12.ga.us	Eastman	GA	31023	478-374-3783	374-6697	463
Dodge Nature Ctr 365 Marie Ave W; *TF:* 800-795-3272 ■ *Web:* www.dodgenaturecenter.org	West Saint Paul	MN	55118	651-455-4531	455-2575	50-5
Dodgen Aircraft 740 Grand St; *Web:* www.dodgenaircraft.com	Allegan	MI	49010	269-673-4157		63
Dodgen Industries Inc 1505 13th St N; *Web:* www.dodgen-bornfree.com	Humboldt	IA	50548	515-332-3755		120
Dodger Industries 2075 Stultz Rd PO Box 711; *TF Cust Svc:* 800-436-3437 ■ *Web:* www.dodgerindustries.com	Martinsville	VA	24112	800-436-3437		155-1
Dodger Stadium 1000 Elysian Pk Ave; *Web:* losangeles.dodgers.mlb.com/index.jsp?c_id=la	Los Angeles	CA	90012	323-224-1500		720
Dodson Aviation Inc 2110 Montana Rd; *Web:* www.dodson.com	Ottawa	KS	66067	785-242-4000		770
Dodson Bros Exterminating Company Inc 3712 Campbell Ave; *Web:* www.dodsonbros.com	Lynchburg	VA	24501	434-847-9051		577
DOE (US Department of Energy) 1000 Independence Ave SW; *TF:* 800-877-8339 ■ *Web:* www.energy.gov	Washington	DC	20585	202-586-5000	586-4403	340-9
Doe Anderson Inc 620 W Main St; *Web:* www.doeanderson.com	Louisville	KY	40202	502-589-1700		4
Doe Run Co, The 1801 Pk 270 Dr Ste 300; *TF:* 800-356-3786 ■ *Web:* www.doerun.com	Saint Louis	MO	63146	314-453-7100		485
Doe's Eat Place 1023 W Marckham St; *TF:* 800-522-4700 ■ *Web:* www.doeseatplace.net	Little Rock	AR	72201	501-376-1195		671
Doef's Greenhouses Ltd RR Site one Box 14 Ste 3; *Web:* www.doefsgreenhouses.com	Lacombe	AB	T4L2N3	403-782-2704		192

Company / Address	City	State	Zip	Phone	Fax	Class
Doepker Industries Ltd 300 Doepker Ave. TF: 800-535-5560 ■ Web: www.doepker.com	Annaheim	SK	S0K0G0	306-598-2171		120
Doeren Mayhew 305 W Big Beaver Rd Ste 200. Web: www.doeren.com	Troy	MI	48084	248-244-3000		2
Doerfer Engineering Corp PO Box 816. TF: 877-483-4700 ■ Web: www.doerfer.com	Waverly	IA	50677	877-483-4700		261
Doerle Food Services LLC 113 Kol Dr. Web: www.doerlefoods.com	Broussard	LA	70818	337-252-8551		805
Doerr Assoc 31 Church St TF: 800-438-7325 ■ Web: mdoerr.com	Winchester	MA	01890	781-729-9020		636
DOF Subsea USA Inc 5355 W Sam Houston Pkwy N Ste 390.	Houston	TX	77041	713-896-2500	984-1612	261
Dog & Duck Pub, The 2400 Webberville Rd Web: www.dogandduckpub.com	Austin	TX	78702	512-479-0598		671
Dog Fancy Magazine 3 Burroughs. TF Cust Svc: 800-546-7730	Irvine	CA	92618	949-855-8822	855-3045	457-14
Doggett Lloyd (Rep D - TX) 2307 Rayburn HOB. Web: doggett.house.gov	Washington	DC	20515	202-225-4865		342-2
doggyloot LLC 213 N Racine Ave. Web: www.doggyloot.com	Chicago	IL	60607	312-566-8122		387
DogLeggs LLC 2104 Thomas View Rd Web: www.dogleggs.com	Reston	VA	20191	703-715-0300		475
DogTime Media Inc 27 Maiden Ln Ste 700 Web: www.dogtime.com	San Francisco	CA	94108	415-830-9300		5
Dogwood Productions Inc 757 Government St. TF: 800-254-9903 ■ Web: www.dogwoodproductions.com	Mobile	AL	36602	251-476-0858		7
Doheny Eye Institute 1450 San Pablo St Web: www.doheny.org	Los Angeles	CA	90033	323-442-7100	442-7127	374-7
Doheny State Beach 25300 Dana Pt Harbor Dr Web: www.parks.ca.gov	Dana Point	CA	92629	949-496-6172		565
Doherty Enterprises Inc 7 Pearl Ct Web: www.dohertyinc.com	Allendale	NJ	07401	201-818-4669		194
Doherty Staffing Solutions Inc 7645 Metro Blvd Ste 1 Web: www.dohertystaffing.com	Edina	MN	55439	952-832-8300		260
Doherty Steel Inc 21110 W 311th St Web: www.dohertysteel.com	Paola	KS	66071	913-557-9200		492
Dohmen Research Inc PO Box 49-2433. Web: dohmencapital.com	Los Angeles	CA	90049	310-476-6933		531-9
Dohrn Transfer Co 625 Third Ave TF: 888-364-7621 ■ Web: www.dohrn.com	Rock Island	IL	61201	309-794-0723	794-1693	449
DOI (Department of the Interior) 1849 C St NW. TF: 800-200-4853 ■ Web: www.doi.gov	Washington	DC	20240	202-208-3100		340-13
DOJ (Department of Justice) 950 Pennsylvania Ave NW TF: 800-424-2980 ■ Web: www.justice.gov	Washington	DC	20530	202-514-2007	514-5331	340-14
Doka USA Ltd 214 Gates Rd. TF: 877-365-2872 ■ Web: www.doka.com	Little Ferry	NJ	07643	201-329-7839	641-6254	191-3
DOL (Department of Labor) 200 Constitution Ave NW TF: 866-487-2365 ■ Web: www.dol.gov	Washington	DC	20210	202-693-4650		340-15
Dolan Construction Inc 401 S 13th St. TF: 800-993-4416 ■ Web: www.dolanconstructioninc.com	Reading	PA	19602	610-372-4664		186
Dolby Laboratories Inc 100 Potrero Ave NYSE: DLB ■ Web: www.dolby.com/in/en/index.html	San Francisco	CA	94103	415-558-0200	645-4000	52
Dolce Europa 7520 Fullerton Rd	Springfield	VA	22153	703-451-9501		297-8
Dolce Hayes Mansion 200 Edenvale Ave TF: 866-981-3300 ■ Web: www.hayesmansion.com	San Jose	CA	95136	408-226-3200		377
Dolce Hotels and Resorts 201 Aberdeen Pkwy TF: 800-983-6523 ■ Web: www.dolce.com	Peachtree City	GA	30269	770-487-2666	631-4096	377
Dolce Hotels and Resorts 28 W Grand Ave Web: www.wyndhamhotels.com/dolce	Montvale	NJ	07645	201-307-8700		379
Dolce Printing Inc 29 Brook Ave TF: 800-882-1844 ■ Web: www.dolceprint.com	Maywood	NJ	07607	201-843-0400		627
Dolce Winery Inc PO Box 327 Web: www.dolcewine.com	Oakville	CA	94562	707-944-8868	944-2312	80-3
Dolcera Corp 3555 S El Camino Real Ste 305 TF: 800-816-6710 ■ Web: www.dolcera.com	San Mateo	CA	94403	650-425-6772		466
Dolden Wallace & Folick LLP 609 Granville St 18th Fl Web: www.dolden.com	Vancouver	BC	V7Y1G5	604-689-3222	689-3777	428
Dole Food Company Hawaii 802 Mapunapuna St TF: 800-697-9100 ■ Web: www.dolefruithawaii.com	Honolulu	HI	96819	808-861-8015	861-8020	297-7
Dole Food Company Inc 1 Dole Dr NYSE: DOLE ■ TF: 800-232-8888 ■ Web: www.dole.com	Westlake Village	CA	91362	818-879-6600		315-4
Dole Packaged Foods Co 1 Dole Dr Web: dole.com	Westlake Village	CA	91362	818-874-4000		296-20
Dole Refrigerating Co 1420 Higgs Rd. TF: 800-251-8990 ■ Web: www.doleref.com	Lewisburg	TN	37091	931-359-6211	359-8664	664
Dolese Bros Co 20 NW 13th St TF: 800-375-2311 ■ Web: dolese.com	Oklahoma City	OK	73103	405-235-2311		183
Doling Chang Ashmore CPA Inc 430 Sherman Ave Web: doling.com	Palo Alto	CA	94306	650-321-8744		2
Doll Capital Management 2420 Sand Hill Rd Ste 200. Web: www.dcm.com	Menlo Park	CA	94025	650-233-1400	854-9159	792
Dollamur LP 1734 E El Paso St Web: www.dollamur.com	Fort Worth	TX	76102	817-534-3344		711
Dollar Bank FSB 225 Forbes Ave TF: 800-828-5527 ■ Web: www.dollar.bank/personal	Pittsburgh	PA	15222	800-828-5527		70
Dollar Bill Copying 611 Church St Ste 4 Web: www.dollarbillcopying.com	Ann Arbor	MI	48104	734-665-9200		113
Dollar Financial Corp 1436 Lancaster Ave Ste 300 Web: www.dfcglobalcorp.com	Berwyn	PA	19312	610-296-3400	296-7844	141
Dollar General Corp 100 Mission Ridge NYSE: DG ■ TF: 800-777-1410 ■ Web: www.dollargeneral.com	Goodlettsville	TN	37072	615-855-4000		791
Dollar Loan Ctr LLC 6122 W Sahara Ave. TF: 866-550-4352 ■ Web: www.dontbebroke.com	Las Vegas	NV	89146	702-693-5626		217
Dollar Rent A Car Inc 5330 E 31st St. TF: 800-800-4000 ■ Web: www.dollar.com	Tulsa	OK	74135	918-669-3000		126
Dollar Thrifty Automotive Group Inc 5330 E 31st St PO Box 35985 TF: 800-334-1705 ■ Web: www.thrifty.com	Tulsa	OK	74135	918-660-7700		126
Dollar Tree Stores Inc 500 Volvo Pkwy NASDAQ: DLTR ■ TF: 877-530-8733 ■ Web: www.dollartree.com	Chesapeake	VA	23320	877-530-8733		791
Dolliver Memorial State Park 2757 Dolliver Pk Ave Web: www.iowadnr.gov	Lehigh	IA	50557	515-359-2539	359-2542	565
Dolly & Joe's 1045 S Reynolds St.	Toledo	OH	43615	419-385-2441		671
Dolly Packaging 320 N Fourth St	Tipp City	OH	45371	937-667-5414		64
Dolly's Pizza Franchising Inc 1097 Union Lake Rd TF: 800-442-1162 ■ Web: www.dollyspizza.com	White Lake	MI	48386	248-360-6440		670
Dollywood 2700 Dollywood Parks Blvd TF: 800-365-5996 ■ Web: www.dollywood.com	Pigeon Forge	TN	37863	800-365-5996		32
Dolomite Group Inc 1260 Jefferson Rd.	Rochester	NY	14623	585-424-6040		182
Dolores County 409 N Main St TF: 800-824-7842 ■ Web: www.dolorescounty.org	Dove Creek	CO	81324	970-677-2383	677-2815	338
Dolphin Aviation Inc 8191 N Tamiami Tr TF: 800-247-2433 ■ Web: dolphinaviation.com	Sarasota	FL	34243	941-355-2902		63
Dolphin Beach Resort 4900 Gulf Blvd TF: 800-237-8916 ■ Web: www.dolphinbeach.com	Saint Pete Beach	FL	33706	727-360-7011	367-5909	379
Dolphin Carpet & Tile 3550 NW 77th Ct TF: 800-639-3566 ■ Web: www.dolphincarpet.com	Miami	FL	33122	305-591-4141	378-1700	290
Dolphin Inc 740 S 59th Ave Web: www.dolphincasting.com	Phoenix	AZ	85043	602-272-6747	233-9570	306
Dolphin Inn 1705 Atlantic Ave Web: www.dolphininnhotel.com	Virginia Beach	VA	23451	757-491-1420		379
Dolphin Mall 11401 NW 12 St. Web: www.shopdolphinmall.com	Miami	FL	33172	305-365-7446	436-9000	460
Dolphin Shirt Co 757 Buckley Rd. TF: 800-377-3256 ■ Web: www.dolphinshirt.com	San Luis Obispo	CA	93401	805-541-2566		627
Dolphin Swim School Inc 1530 El Camino Ave TF: 800-436-5744 ■ Web: www.dolphinscuba.com	Sacramento	CA	95815	916-929-8188		711
Dolphin Technology Inc 2025 Gateway Pl Ste 270 Web: www.dolphin-ic.com	San Jose	CA	95110	408-392-0012		246
Dolphins Plus Inc 31 Corrine Pl TF: 866-860-7946 ■ Web: dolphinsplus.com	Key Largo	FL	33037	305-451-1993		804
Domaille Engineering LLC 7100 Dresser Dr NE Web: www.domailleengineering.com	Rochester	MN	55906	507-281-0275		697
Domain Assoc 1 Palmer Sq Ste 515 TF: 866-803-9204 ■ Web: www.domainvc.com	Princeton	NJ	08542	609-683-5656	683-9789	792
Domain Systems Inc 117 W 200 S. Web: www.domainsi.com	Farmington	UT	84025	801-447-3777		463
Domain, The 11410 Century Oaks Terr Web: www.simon.com	Austin	TX	78758	512-795-4230		460
Domain7 Solutions Inc 33820 S Fraser Way Unit 2A. Web: www.domain7.com	Abbotsford	BC	V2S2C5	604-855-3772		387
Domaine Chandon Inc 1 California Dr TF: 888-242-6366 ■ Web: www.chandon.com	Yountville	CA	94599	888-242-6366		80-3
Domaine Maizerets 2000 Montmorency Blvd Web: domainemaizerets.com	Quebec	QC	G1J5E7	418-666-3331	666-8122	50-5
Domaine Select Wine Estates LLC 105 Madison Ave Ste 2302. Web: www.domaineselect.com	New York	NY	10016	212-279-0799		80-3
Domain-It! 9891 Montgomery Rd. TF General: 866-269-2355 ■ Web: www.domainit.com	Cincinnati	OH	45242	513-351-4222		396
DomainPeople Inc 550 Burrard St Ste 200 Bentall 5 TF: 877-734-3667 ■ Web: www.domainpeople.com	Vancouver	BC	V6C2B5	604-639-1680	688-9013	396
DomainRegistry.com Inc 2301 E Evesham Rd Ste 204. Web: www.domainregistry.com	Voorhees	NJ	08043	856-335-5950		396
Dome Printing 340 Commerce Cir. TF: 800-343-3139 ■ Web: www.domeprinting.com	Sacramento	CA	95815	800-343-3139		627
DOmedia LLC 274 Marconi Blvd One Marconi Pl Ste 400. TF: 866-939-3663 ■ Web: domedia.com	Columbus	OH	43215	866-939-3663		225
Domengeaux Wright Roy & Edwards LLC 556 Jefferson St Ste 500. TF: 800-375-6186 ■ Web: www.wrightroy.com	Lafayette	LA	70501	337-233-3033		428
Domenico's on the Wharf 50 Fisherman's Wharf # 1 TF: 800-342-4295 ■ Web: www.domenicosmonterey.com	Monterey	CA	93940	831-372-3655	372-2073	671
Domestic Linen Supply & Laundry Co Inc 30555 NW Hwy. TF: 800-344-3555 ■ Web: www.domesticuniform.com	Farmington Hills	MI	48334	248-737-2000		442
Domestic Policy Council 1600 Pennsylvania Ave NW Web: whitehouse.gov/administration/eop/dpc	Washington	DC	20500	202-456-1111		340
Domestic Securities Inc 160 Summit Ave	Montvale	NJ	07645	201-505-9855		690
Domestic Tobacco Co 830 N Prince St	Lancaster	PA	17603	717-393-0613		756

	Phone	Fax	Class
Dometic Corp 2320 Industrial Pkwy. Elkhart IN 46516 *TF:* 800-544-4881 ■ *Web:* www.dometic.com	574-294-2511	293-9686	14
Dom-Ex LLC 109 Grant St. Hibbing MN 55746 *Web:* www.dom-ex.com	218-262-6116		386
Dominant Systems Corp 3850 Varsity Dr. Ann Arbor MI 48108 *TF:* 800-362-0883 ■ *Web:* domsys.com	734-971-1210		180
Dominguez State Jail 6535 Cagnon Rd. San Antonio TX 78252 *Web:* tdcj.state.tx.us	210-675-6620		213
Domini Social Investments PO Box 9785 Providence RI 02940 *TF:* 800-582-6757 ■ *Web:* www.domini.com	800-582-6757		528
Dominic's 5101 Wilson Ave South Saint Louis MO 63110 *Web:* www.dominicsrestaurant.com	314-771-1632		671
Dominic's 221 S Jefferson St Medina OH 44256 *Web:* www.dominicsitalianrestaurant.com	330-725-8424		671
Dominica *Embassy* 3216 New Mexico Ave NW Washington DC 20016	202-364-6781	364-6791	257
Dominican College 470 Western Hwy Orangeburg NY 10962 **Fax:* Admissions ■ *TF:* 866-432-4636 ■ *Web:* www.dc.edu	845-359-7800	365-3150*	166
Dominican Hospital (DH) 1555 Soquel Dr Santa Cruz CA 95065 *TF:* 866-466-1401 ■ *Web:* www.dominicanhospital.org	831-462-7700		374-3
Dominican House of Studies 487 Michigan Ave NE Washington DC 20017 *Web:* www.dhs.edu	202-529-5300		167-3
Dominican Republic 144 E 44th St 4th Fl New York NY 10017 *Web:* www.un.int	212-867-0833	297-2509	784
Consulate General 1038 Brickell Ave. Miami FL 33131 *Web:* www.domrep.org	305-358-3220	358-2318	257
Consulate General 1501 Broadway Ste 410 New York NY 10036 *Web:* www.domrep.org	212-768-2480	768-2677	257
Consulate General 500 N Brand Blvd Ste 960 Glendale CA 91203 *Web:* www.consulatedrwest.com	818-504-6605	504-6617	257
Consulate General 1715 22nd St NW Washington DC 20008 *Web:* www.domrep.org	202-332-6280	387-2459	257
Embassy 1715 22nd St NW Washington DC 20008 *Web:* www.domrep.org	202-332-6280	265-8057	257
Dominican Republic Tourist Board 136 E 57th St Ste 805 New York NY 10022 *Web:* www.dominicanrepublic.com	212-588-1012		775
Dominican School of Philosophy & Theology 2301 Vine St. Berkeley CA 94708 *TF:* 888-450-3778 ■ *Web:* www.dspt.edu	510-849-2030		167-3
Dominican Sisters of Mission San Jos 43326 Mission Blvd Fremont CA 94539 *Web:* www.msjdominicans.org	510-657-2468		162
Dominican University 7900 W Div St River Forest IL 60305 **Fax:* Admissions ■ *TF:* 800-828-8475 ■ *Web:* www.dom.edu	708-366-2490	524-5990*	166
Dominican University College 96 Empress Ave Ottawa ON K1R7G3 *Web:* udominicaine.ca	613-233-5696	233-6064	785
Dominican University of California 50 Acacia Ave San Rafael CA 94901 **Fax:* Admissions ■ *TF Admissions:* 888-323-6763 ■ *Web:* www.dominican.edu	415-457-4440	485-3214*	166
Dominick Abel Literary Agency Inc 146 W 82nd St Ste 1A New York NY 10024 *Web:* dalainc.com	212-877-0710		444
Dominion Aviation Services Inc 7511 Airfield Dr Richmond VA 23237 *TF:* 800-366-7793 ■ *Web:* dominionaviation.com	804-271-7793		579
Dominion Bldg Products 6949 Fairbanks N Houston Rd Houston TX 77040 *TF:* 800-826-2617 ■ *Web:* www.dominionproducts.com	800-826-2617		234
Dominion Blue Digital Reprographics 99 Sixth Ave W Vancouver BC V5Y1K2 *TF:* 800-906-6366 ■ *Web:* dominionblue.com	604-681-7504		627
Dominion Capital Inc 120 Tredegar St. Richmond VA 23219 *TF:* 888-366-8280	888-366-8280		509
Dominion Diagnostics LLC 211 Circuit Dr. North Kingstown RI 02852 *Web:* dominiondiagnostics.com	401-667-0800		743
Dominion Diamond Corp PO Box 4569 Sta A Toronto ON M5W4T9 *Web:* www.ddcorp.ca	416-362-2237	362-2230	411
Dominion Due Diligence Group 4121 Cox Rd Ste 200 Glen Allen VA 23060 *TF:* 800-272-7134 ■ *Web:* d3g.com	804-358-2020		104
Dominion Electric Supply Company Inc 5053 Lee Hwy. Arlington VA 22207 *TF:* 800-525-5006 ■ *Web:* www.dominionelectric.com	703-536-4400	741-0423	246
Dominion Energy 120 Tredegar St. Richmond VA 23219 *TF:* 888-216-3718 ■ *Web:* www.dom.com	888-216-3718		787
Dominion Energy Management 11250 Hopson Rd. Ashland VA 23005 *Web:* www.demiva.com	804-798-3189		610
Dominion Engineering Associates Inc 8511 Indian Hills Ct Ste 202 Fredericksburg VA 22407 *Web:* www.dea-inc.net	540-710-9339		261
Dominion Homes Inc 4900 Tuttle Crossing Blvd. Dublin OH 43016 *Web:* www.dominionhomes.com	614-356-5000		653
Dominion Hope 701 E Cary St. Richmond VA 23219 *TF:* 866-366-4357 ■ *Web:* www.dominionenergy.com	888-366-8280		787
Dominion Hospital 2960 Sleepy Hollow Rd Falls Church VA 22044 *TF:* 800-994-6610 ■ *Web:* www.dominionhospital.com	703-536-2000	533-9650	374-5
Dominion Lending Centres Inc 2215 Coquitlam Ave Port Coquitlam BC V3B1J6 *TF:* 866-928-6810 ■ *Web:* www.dominionlending.ca	866-928-6810		509
Dominion Lodging Inc 658 Roanoke Rd. Daleville VA 24083 *Web:* dominionlodging.com	540-992-4077		379
Dominion Mechanical Contractors Inc 12329 Braddock Rd Fairfax VA 22030 *Web:* dominion-mechanical.com	703-992-9588		610
Dominion North Carolina Power 701 E Cary St Richmond VA 23219 *TF:* 888-667-3000 ■ *Web:* www.dominionenergy.com	757-857-2112		787
Dominion Resources Inc 120 Tredegar St. Richmond VA 23219 *NYSE: D* ■ *TF:* 800-552-4034 ■ *Web:* www.dominionenergy.com	804-819-2000	819-2233	360-5
Dominion Technologies Inc 15736 Sturgeon St Roseville MI 48066 *Web:* www.dominiontec.com	586-773-3303		757
Dominion Ventures 1646 N California Blvd Walnut Creek CA 94596 *Web:* www.dominion.com	925-280-6338		792
Dominion Veterinary Laboratories Inc 1199 Sanford St Winnipeg MB R3E3A1 *TF:* 800-465-7122 ■ *Web:* www.domvet.com	204-589-7361	943-9612	584
Dominknow Learning Systems 40 Sunset Blvd Perth ON K7H2Y4 *Web:* www.dominknow.com	613-264-0096		225
Domino Machine Inc 4040 98 St NW Edmonton AB T6E3L3 *Web:* www.dominomachine.com	780-462-1354		757
Domino Recording Co 20 Jay St Ste 626 Brooklyn NY 11201 *Web:* www.dominorecordco.com	718-797-4229		657
Domino's Pizza Inc 30 Frank Lloyd Wright Dr Ann Arbor MI 48106 *NYSE: DPZ* ■ *TF:* 800-253-8182 ■ *Web:* dominos.com	734-930-3030		670
DOMOREGOOD 125 Ottawa Ave NW Ste 205 Grand Rapids MI 49503 *Web:* www.hanon-mckendry.com	616-776-1111		5
Doms Outdoor Outfitters 1870 First St. Livermore CA 94550 *TF:* 800-447-9629 ■ *Web:* www.domsoutdoor.com	925-447-9629		711
Domtar Corp 395 de Maisonneuve W. Montreal QC H3A1L6 *NYSE: UFS* ■ *TF:* 877-040-4466 ■ *Web:* www.domtar.com	514-848-5555		683
Domtar Paper Co LLC 200 N Grand Ave. Rothschild WI 54474 *Web:* www.domtar.com	715-359-3101		557
Domtech Inc 40 East Davis St Trenton ON K8V6S4 *TF:* 888-278-8258 ■ *Web:* www.domtech.net	613-394-4884		492
Domus Inc 123 Ave Of The Arts Ste 1980 Philadelphia PA 19109 *Web:* www.domusinc.com	215-772-2805		194
Don & Charlie's 7501 E Camelback Rd. Scottsdale AZ 85251 *Web:* www.donandcharlies.com	480-990-0900		671
Don Beyer Motors Inc 1231 W Broad St Falls Church VA 22046 *Web:* www.donbeyervolvo.com	703-237-5000		57
Don Buchwald & Assoc 6500 Wilshire Blvd Ste 2200 Los Angeles CA 90048 *Web:* www.buchwald.com	323-655-7400	655-7470	731
Don CeSar Beach Resort - A Loews Hotel 3400 Gulf Blvd Saint Pete Beach FL 33706 *TF:* 888-430-4999 ■ *Web:* www.loewshotels.com	727-360-1881		669
Don Chalmers Ford Inc 2500 Rio Rancho Blvd Rio Rancho NM 87124 *Web:* www.donchalmersford.com	505-897-2500		57
Don Chapin Company Inc, The 560 Crazy Horse Canyon Rd. Salinas CA 93907 *Web:* www.donchapin.com	831-449-4273	449-0700	186
Don Chucho's Mexican Restaurant 5770 Milgen Rd Columbus GA 31907	706-561-3040		671
Don Congdon Assoc Inc 110 William St Ste 2202 New York NY 10038 *Web:* www.doncongdon.com	212-727-2688	727-2688	444
Don Dye Company Inc 524 NW 20th Ave PO Box 107 Kingman KS 67068 *TF:* 800-794-2032 ■ *Web:* dondyeco.com	620-532-3131	532-2141	620
Don Farmer CPA Pa 508 Mulberry St PO Box 1858 Lenoir NC 28645 *Web:* donfarmercpa.com	828-754-1613		2
Don Ferderer Insurance 1930 Brea Canyon Rd. Diamond Bar CA 91765	909-396-1198		390
Don Garlits Museums 13700 SW 16th Ave Ocala FL 34473 *TF:* 877-271-3278 ■ *Web:* www.garlits.com	352-245-8661		522
Don Hall's Guesthouse 1313 W Washington Ctr Rd Fort Wayne IN 46825 *Web:* www.donhalls.com	260-489-2524		379
Don Hall's Restaurants 305 E Superior St Fort Wayne IN 46802 *Web:* www.donhalls.com	260-426-3411		671
Don Harrington Discovery Ctr 1200 Streit Dr. Amarillo TX 79106 *Web:* www.dhdc.org	806-355-9547		521
Don Herring Enterprises Ltd 4225 W Plano Pkwy Plano TX 75093 *Web:* www.donherring.com	972-387-8600		57
Don Hewlett Chevrolet Buick Inc 7601 S I-35 Georgetown TX 78626 *Web:* www.donhewlett.com	512-681-3000		57
Don Hummer Trucking Corp 1486 Hwy 6 NW PO Box 310 Oxford IA 52322 *TF:* 866-248-6637 ■ *Web:* www.donhummertrucking.com	319-828-2000	828-2105	780
Don Hutson Organization 516 Tennessee St Ste 219 Memphis TN 38103 *TF:* 800-647-9166 ■ *Web:* www.donhutson.com	901-767-0000		765
Don Jagoda Assoc Inc 100 Marcus Dr. Melville NY 11747 *Web:* www.dja.com	631-454-1800	454-1834	384
Don Jose Tequila's 351 Atwells Ave. Providence RI 02903 *Web:* donjosetequilas.com	401-454-8951		671
Don Jose's 2052 E Northern Lights Blvd. Anchorage AK 99508 *Web:* www.alaskadonjoses.com	907-279-5111	279-2053	671
Don Laughlin's Riverside Resort & Casino 1650 Casino Dr Laughlin NV 89029 *TF:* 800-227-3849 ■ *Web:* www.riversideresort.com	702-298-2535		133

	City	State	Zip	Phone	Fax	Class
Don Lee Farms 200 E Beach Ave *Web:* donleefarms.com	Inglewood	CA	90302	310-674-3180		296-2
Don Luis 15 N 26th St	Billings	MT	59101	406-256-3355		671
Don McGill Toyota Inc 11800 Katy Fwy *TF:* 866-938-0767 ■ *Web:* www.donmcgilltoyota.com	Houston	TX	77079	281-496-2000	977-3097	57
Don Pancho Authentic Mexican Foods Inc 3060 Industrial Way NE *Web:* www.donpancho.com	Salem	OR	97301	503-370-9710		123
Don Park LP 842 York Mills Rd *Web:* www.donpark.com	North York	ON	M3B3A8	416-449-7275		401
Don Pedro Island State Park 8450 Placida Rd PO Box 1150 *Web:* www.floridastateparks.org/donpedroisland	Boca Grande	FL	33921	941-964-0375		565
Don Pepe Restaurant & Catering 844 McCarter Hwy *Web:* www.donpeperestaurant.com	Newark	NJ	07102	973-623-4662		671
Don Pepino Sales Co 123 Railroad Ave *TF:* 888-281-6400 ■ *Web:* www.donpepino.com	Williamstown	NJ	08094	856-629-7429	629-6340	296-20
Don Quijote 362 Union St	Manchester	NH	03103	603-622-2246		671
Don Quijote USA Company Ltd 801 Kaheka St	Honolulu	HI	96814	808-973-4800		345
Don R Fruchey Inc 5608 Old Maumee Rd *Web:* www.donrfruchey.com	Fort Wayne	IN	46803	260-749-8502	749-6337	189-1
Don Rasmussen Co 720 NE Grand Ave *Web:* www.landroverportland.com	Portland	OR	97232	503-230-7700		57
Don Ray George & Assoc Inc 1604 Rio Grande St *Web:* drgainc.com	Austin	TX	78701	512-476-1245		261
Don Roberto Jewelers Inc 1020 Calle Recordo Ste 100 *Web:* www.donrobertojewelers.com	San Clemente	CA	92673	949-361-6700		410
Don Shula's Hotel & Golf Club 6842 Main St *Web:* www.donshulahotel.com	Miami Lakes	FL	33014	305-821-1150	820-8087	669
Don Small & Sons Oil Distributing Co Inc 112 Third St NW *TF:* 800-626-3213 ■ *Web:* www.smallandsonsoil.com	Auburn	WA	98002	253-833-0430		581
Don Stevens Inc 980 Discovery Rd *TF:* 800-444-2299 ■ *Web:* www.donstevens.com	Eagan	MN	55121	651-452-0872	452-4189	665
Don Young Co 8181 Ambassador Row *TF:* 800-367-0390 ■ *Web:* www.dycwindows.com	Dallas	TX	75247	214-630-0934	630-0406	480
Don's Lighthouse Grille 8905 Lake Ave *Web:* www.donslighthouse.com	Cleveland	OH	44102	216-961-6700		671
Don's Restaurants 8905 Lake Ave *Web:* www.strangcorp.com	Cleveland	OH	44102	216-961-6700	961-1966	670
Don's Seafood & Steakhouse 301 E Vermilion St	Lafayette	LA	70501	337-235-3551		671
Dona Ana Branch Community College (DACC) 2800 N Sonoma Ranch Blvd **Fax: Admissions* ■ *TF:* 800-903-7503 ■ *Web:* dacc.nmsu.edu	Las Cruces	NM	88011	575-528-7000	528-7300*	162
Dona Ana County 845 N Motel Blvd *TF:* 800-477-3632 ■ *Web:* donaanacounty.org	Las Cruces	NM	88007	575-647-7200	585-5538	338
Dona Lupe Cafe 2919 Pershing Dr	El Paso	TX	79903	915-566-9833		671
Donadio & Olsen Inc 40 W 27th St 5th Fl *TF:* 800-439-6687 ■ *Web:* donadio.com	New York	NY	10001	212-691-8077		444
Donahue Purohit Miller 1 Speedwell Ave *Web:* cpeducate.com	Morristown	NJ	07960	973-644-5055		7
Donahue Schriber Realty Group Inc 200 E Baker St Ste 100 *Web:* www.donahueschriber.com	Costa Mesa	CA	92626	714-545-1400	545-4222	655
Donahuefavret Contractors Inc 3030 E Causeway Approach *TF:* 800-626-4431 ■ *Web:* www.donahuefavret.com	Mandeville	LA	70448	985-626-4431		186
Donald Bruce & Co 3600 N Talman Ave	Chicago	IL	60618	773-477-8100		408
Donald E Graves CPA LLC 377 Main St Ste 400 *Web:* donaldegravescpa.com	Greenfield	MA	01301	413-774-6036		2
Donald E Stephens Convention Ctr 5555 N River Rd *TF:* 800-468-3571 ■ *Web:* www.rosemont.com	Rosemont	IL	60018	847-692-2220	696-9700	205
Donald Harris Law Firm 158 Columbus Ave Ste 302 *Web:* www.donaldharrislawfirm.com	Sandusky	OH	44870	419-621-9388		428
Donald Smith & Company Inc 152 W 57th St 22nd Fl *Web:* www.donaldsmithandco.com	New York	NY	10019	212-284-0990		401
Donald T Ostop & Company PC 790 Farmington Ave Bldg 2 *Web:* dtoco.com	Farmington	CT	06032	860-677-0779		2
Donald W Mcintosh Assoc 2200 N Park Ave *TF:* 800-597-7275 ■ *Web:* dwma.com	Winter Park	FL	32789	407-644-4068		261
Donald W Reynolds Foundation 1701 Village Ctr Cir *Web:* www.dwreynolds.org	Las Vegas	NV	89134	702-804-6000		305
Donald W Wyatt Detention Facility 950 High St *Web:* www.wyattdetention.com	Central Falls	RI	02863	401-729-1190	729-1194	213
Donaldson Capital Management LLC 20 NW First St 5th Fl *Web:* www.dcmol.com	Evansville	IN	47708	812-421-3211		401
Donaldson Company Inc 1400 W 94th St *NYSE: DCI* ■ *TF:* 800-365-1331 ■ *Web:* www.donaldson.com	Bloomington	MN	55431	952-887-3131		18
Donaldson Group Inc, The 88 Hopmeadow St *Web:* www.donaldson-group.com	Simsbury	CT	06089	860-658-9777		344
Donan Engineering Co Inc 11321 Plantside Dr *TF:* 800-482-5611 ■ *Web:* www.donan.com	Louisville	KY	40299	800-482-5611		400
Donanelle's Bar & Grill 4321 U S Hwy 49 *Web:* www.donanelles.com	Hattiesburg	MS	39401	601-545-3860		671
Donatech Corp 2094 185th St Ste 110 *TF:* 800-328-2133 ■ *Web:* www.donatech.com	Fairfield	IA	52556	641-472-7474		177
Donatelle Plastics Inc 501 County Rd E2 Ext *Web:* www.donatelle.net	New Brighton	MN	55112	651-633-4200		596
Donatello, The 501 Post St *TF:* 800-258-2366 ■ *Web:* www.clubdonatello.org	San Francisco	CA	94102	415-441-7100	441-7100	379
Donati Law Firm LLP 1545 Union Ave *Web:* www.donatilaw.com	Memphis	TN	38104	901-209-5500		428
Donatos Pizza 935 Taylor Stn Rd *TF:* 800-366-2867 ■ *Web:* www.donatos.com	Columbus	OH	43230	800-366-2867		670
Doncasters Inc 36 Spring Ln *Web:* www.doncasters.com	Farmington	CT	06032	860-677-1376		21
Doncasters Storms Forge Div 160 Cottage St *TF:* 800-453-1724 ■ *Web:* doncasters.com	Springfield	MA	01104	413-785-1801		483
Donco Paper Supply Co 2100 Losantiville Ave	Cincinnati	OH	45237	513-731-0208		638
Dondlinger & Sons Construction Company Inc 2656 S Sheridan *Web:* dondlinger.biz	Wichita	KS	67217	316-945-0555	945-9009	188-4
Donegal Group Inc 1195 River Rd *NASDAQ: DGICA* ■ *TF:* 800-877-0600 ■ *Web:* www.donegalgroup.com	Marietta	PA	17547	717-426-1931		360-4
Donegal Industries Inc 860 Anderson Ferry Rd	Mount Joy	PA	17552	717-653-4818		155-4
Donegal Mutual Insurance Co 1195 River Rd PO Box 302 *TF:* 800-877-0600 ■ *Web:* www.donegalgroup.com	Marietta	PA	17547	717-426-1931	426-7009	391-4
Donegal School District 1051 Koser Rd *Web:* www.donegal.k12.pa.us	Mount Joy	PA	17552	717-653-1447		685
Doneger Group, The 463 Seventh Ave *Web:* www.doneger.com	New York	NY	10018	212-564-1266		195
Donelans Super Mkt 248 Great Rd *TF:* 800-275-8777 ■ *Web:* www.donelans.com	Acton	MA	01720	978-635-9893		345
Donelson-Hermitage Chamber of Commerce 125 Donelson Pike PO Box 140200 *Web:* www.donelsonhermitagechamber.com	Nashville	TN	37214	615-883-7896		139
Doner Adv 25900 NW Hwy *Web:* doner.com	Southfield	MI	48075	248-354-9700		4
Doniphan County PO Box 278 *TF:* 800-232-0170 ■ *Web:* www.dpcountyks.com	Troy	KS	66087	785-985-3513	985-3723	338
Doniphan Electric Co-op Assn Inc 101 N Main PO Box 699 *Web:* www.donrec.org	Troy	KS	66087	785-985-3523		245
Donjon Marine Company Inc 100 Central Ave *Web:* www.donjon.com	Hillside	NJ	07205	908-964-8812	964-7426	465
Donlen Corp 2315 Sanders Rd *TF:* 800-323-1483 ■ *Web:* www.donlen.com	Northbrook	IL	60062	847-714-1400		289
Donlevy Laboratories Inc 11165 Delaware Pkwy *TF:* 800-551-5217 ■ *Web:* www.donlevylab.com	Crown Point	IN	46307	219-226-0001		418
Donley County 300 S Sully St PO Box 909 *TF:* 800-388-8075 ■ *Web:* www.co.donley.tx.us	Clarendon	TX	79226	806-874-3625	874-1181	338
Donley's Inc 5430 Warner Rd *Web:* www.donleyinc.com	Cleveland	OH	44125	216-524-6800	642-3216	189-3
Donna Karan International Inc 550 Seventh Ave *Web:* www.donnakaran.com	New York	NY	10018	212-789-1500	789-1820	155-21
Don-Nan Pump & Supply Co 3427 E Garden City Hwy *TF:* 800-348-7742 ■ *Web:* www.don-nan.com	Midland	TX	79706	432-682-7742		112
Donnell Systems Inc 130 S Main St Ste 375 *TF:* 800-232-3776 ■ *Web:* www.ocie.net	South Bend	IN	46601	574-232-3784		196
Donnelley/DePue State Fish & Wildlife Areas 1001 W Fourth St PO Box 52 *Web:* dnr.illinois.gov/Lands/Landmgt/PARKS/R1/Don.htm	DePue	IL	61322	815-447-2353		565
Donnelly College 608 N 18th St **Fax: Admissions* ■ *TF:* 800-908-9946 ■ *Web:* www.donnelly.edu	Kansas City	KS	66102	913-621-8700	621-8734*	162
Donnelly Creek State Recreation Site 3700 Airport Way *Web:* www.dnr.alaska.gov	Fairbanks	AK	99709	907-451-2705	451-2706	565
Donnelly Custom Manufacturing Co 105 Donovan *Web:* www.donnmfg.com	Alexandria	MN	56308	320-762-2396		596
Donnelly Joe (Sen D - IN) 720 Hart Bldg *Web:* www.donnelly.senate.gov	Washington	DC	20510	202-224-4814	224-5011	342-2
Donner Memorial State Park 12593 Donner Pass Rd *Web:* www.parks.ca.gov/default.asp?page_id=503	Truckee	CA	96161	530-582-7892		565
Donner Plumbing & Heating Inc 107 Candelaria Rd NW *Web:* donnerplumbing.com	Albuquerque	NM	87107	505-884-1017		610
Donofrio Kottke & Assoc Inc 7530 Wward Way *Web:* donofrio.cc	Madison	WI	53717	608-833-7530		261
Donohoe & Stapleton LLC 2781 Zelda Rd *TF:* 800-365-6896 ■ *Web:* donohoeandstapleton.com	Montgomery	AL	36106	334-269-3355		428
Donohoe Cos Inc 2101 Wisconsin Ave NW *Web:* www.donohoe.com	Washington	DC	20007	202-333-0880	342-3924	653
Donohue & Assoc Inc 3311 Weeden Creek Rd *Web:* www.donohue-associates.com	Sheboygan	WI	53081	920-208-0296		256
Donohue Brown Mathewson & Smyth LLC 140 S Dearborn St Ste 800 *Web:* www.dbmslaw.com	Chicago	IL	60603	312-422-0900		428
Donor Alliance Inc 720 S Colorado Blvd Ste 800-N *TF:* 888-868-4747 ■ *Web:* www.donoralliance.org	Denver	CO	80246	303-329-4747	321-1183	545
Donor Awareness Coalition 5323 Harry Hines Blvd	Dallas	TX	75390	214-648-2609		545

Phone | Fax | Class

Donor Network of Arizona
201 W Coolidge St . . . . . Phoenix AZ 85013 602-222-2200 222-2202 269
TF: 800-447-9477 ■ *Web:* www.dnaz.org

Donor Network West
12667 Alcosta Blvd Ste 600 . . . . . Oakland CA 94607 925-480-3101 545
TF: 888-570-9400 ■ *Web:* www.donornetworkwest.org

Donovan Advertising & Marketing Services
180 W Airport Rd . . . . . Lititz PA 17543 717-560-1333 560-2034 7
Web: www.donovanadv.com

Donovan Daniel (Rep R - NY)
1541 Longworth HOB . . . . . Washington DC 20515 202-225-3371 342-2
Web: donovan.house.gov

Donovan House 1155 14th St NW . . . . . Washington DC 20005 202-737-1200 378
Web: www.inndc.com

Donovan Marine Inc 6316 Humphreys St . . . . . Harahan LA 70123 504-488-5731 770
TF: 800-347-4464 ■ *Web:* www.donovanmarine.com

Donriver Inc
Images Tower B-27 Fourth Fl Jaypee Hospital Rd
B Block, Sector 132 . . . . . Dallas TX 20130 866-733-1684 196
TF: 866-733-1684 ■ *Web:* www.donriver.com

Dons Pharmacy 32 S Frederick Ave. . . . . Oelwein IA 50662 319-283-5254 237

Donsco Inc 124 N Front St. . . . . Wrightsville PA 17368 717-252-1561 307
Web: www.donsco.com

Dontech Inc
700 Airport Blvd, PO Box 889. . . . . Doylestown PA 18902 215-348-5010 596
Web: www.dontechinc.com

Dontino's La Vita Gardens
555 E Cuyahoga Falls Ave . . . . . Akron OH 44310 330-928-9530 671
Web: www.dontinos.com

Donzi Marine
1653 WhichaRds Beach Rd. . . . . Washington NC 27889 800-624-3304 90
TF: 800-624-3304 ■ *Web:* www.donzimarine.com

Doodad 7990 Second Flags Dr . . . . . Austell GA 30168 770-732-0321 627
Web: www.doodad.com

Doodles Campus Store 935 Main St . . . . . Montevallo AL 35115 205-665-1719 95
Web: www.doodlesbooks.com

Doody Mechanical Inc
7450 Flying Cloud Dr. . . . . Eden Prairie MN 55344 952-941-7010 189-10
TF: 800-322-9492 ■ *Web:* www.metromech.com

Dooley Enterprises Inc
1198 N Grove St Ste A . . . . . Anaheim CA 92806 714-630-6436 350
Web: www.dooleyenterprises.com

Dooley's Petroleum Inc 304 Main Ave . . . . . Murdock MN 56271 320-875-2641 581
TF: 800-520-2466 ■ *Web:* www.dooleypetro.com

Dooly County 110 E Union St PO Box 308. . . . . Vienna GA 31092 229-268-8275 268-8200 338
Web: www.doolychamber.com

Dooly State Prison
1412 Plunkett Rd PO Box 750 . . . . . Unadilla GA 31091 478-627-2000 213

Doon Technologies Inc
200 Middlesex-Essex Tpke Ste 309 . . . . . Iselin NJ 08830 732-404-1334 225
Web: www.doontec.com

Doonan Trailer Corp 36 NE Hwy 156 . . . . . Great Bend KS 67530 620-792-6222 792-3308 779
TF: 800-734-0608 ■ *Web:* www.doonan.com

Dooney & Bourke Inc 1 Regent St . . . . . East Norwalk CT 06855 203-853-7515 326-1496* 430
**Fax Area Code:* 800 ■ *TF Cust Svc:* 800-347-5000 ■ *Web:* www.dooney.com

Door & Hardware Institute (DHI)
14150 Newbrook Dr Ste 200. . . . . Chantilly VA 20151 703-222-2010 222-2410 49-3
Web: www.dhi.org

Door Components Inc 7980 Redwood Ave. . . . . Fontana CA 92336 909-770-5700 234
TF: 866-989-3667 ■ *Web:* www.dcihollowmetal.com

Door County 421 Nebraska St . . . . . Sturgeon Bay WI 54235 920-746-2200 746-2330 338
Web: www.co.door.wi.gov

Door County Library (DCL)
107 S Fourth Ave . . . . . Sturgeon Bay WI 54235 920-743-6578 434-3
TF: 800-273-7877 ■ *Web:* www.doorcountylibrary.org

Door Creek Church 6602 Dominion Dr. . . . . Madison WI 53718 608-222-8586 48-20
Web: www.doorcreekchurch.org

Door Engineering & Mfg LLC
400 Cherry St. . . . . Kasota MN 56050 507-931-6910 350
TF: 800-959-1352 ■ *Web:* www.doorengineering.com

Door Engineering Corp
1234 Ballentine Blvd. . . . . Norfolk VA 23504 757-622-5355 256
Web: www.dooreng.com

Door Systems Inc PO Box 511 . . . . . Framingham MA 01704 508-875-3508 191-3
TF: 800-545-3667 ■ *Web:* doorsys.com

Doormark Inc 430 Goolsby Blvd . . . . . Deerfield Beach FL 33442 954-418-4700 115
TF: 888-969-0124 ■ *Web:* www.doormark.com

Doorways, The 612 E Marshall St. . . . . Richmond VA 23219 804-828-6901 372
Web: www.thedoorways.org

Doostang Inc 129 W 29th St, 500s . . . . . New York NY 10001 650-561-3226 260
Web: www.doostang.com

Dopo/Adesso 4293 Piedmont Ave . . . . . Oakland CA 94611 510-652-3676 671
Web: www.dopoadesso.com/dopo

Dora Brothers Hospitality Corp
10734Sy Prairie st . . . . . Fishers IN 46038 317-578-9000 377
Web: www.dorahotels.com

Dora Hotel Company LLC
10734 Sky Prairie St. . . . . Fishers IN 46037 317-863-5700 379
Web: www.dorahotelco.com

Doral Arrowwood Conference Resort
975 Anderson Hill Rd . . . . . Rye Brook NY 10573 844-214-5500 323-5500* 377
**Fax Area Code:* 914 ■ *TF:* 844-211-0512 ■ *Web:* www.arrowwood.com

Doral Financial Corp
1441 F D Roosevelt Ave . . . . . San Juan PR 00920 787-749-4949 749-4191 360-2
NYSE: DRL ■ *TF:* 866-296-3743 ■ *Web:* www.snl.com

Doral Park Avenue Hotel 70 Park Ave. . . . . New York NY 10016 212-687-7050 377
Web: www.doralparkavenue.com

Doran Consulting LLC
3101 Magic Hollow Blvd . . . . . Virginia Beach VA 23453 757-368-2208 463
Web: doranconsulting.com

Doran Scales Inc 1315 Paramount Pkwy . . . . . Batavia IL 60510 630-879-1200 684
Web: www.doranscales.com

Dorchester Chamber of Commerce
528 Poplar St . . . . . Cambridge MD 21613 410-228-3575 228-6848 139
TF: 800-243-3425 ■ *Web:* www.dorchesterchamber.org

Dorchester County 101 Ridge St . . . . . Saint George SC 29477 843-563-0260 563-0288 338
Web: www.dorchestercounty.net

Dorchester County Council
501 Court Ln . . . . . Cambridge MD 21613 410-228-1700 228-9641 338
TF: 800-272-9829 ■ *Web:* www.docogonct.com

Dorchester County Library
506 N Parler Ave. . . . . Saint George SC 29477 843-563-9189 434-3
Web: www.dcl.lib.sc.us

Dorchester County Public Library
303 Gay St . . . . . Cambridge MD 21613 410-228-7331 228-6313 434-3
Web: www.dorchesterlibrary.org

Dorchester Minerals LP
3838 Oak Lawn Ave Ste 300. . . . . Dallas TX 75219 214-559-0300 559-0301 536
NASDAQ: DMLP ■ *TF:* 800-690-6903 ■ *Web:* www.dmlp.net

Dordick Law Corp
509 S Beverly Dr. . . . . Beverly Hills CA 90212 310-551-0949 445
Web: www.dordicklaw.com

Dordt College 498 Fourth Ave NE . . . . . Sioux Center IA 51250 712-722-6080 722-1198 166
TF: 800-343-6738 ■ *Web:* www.dordt.edu

Dorel Industries Inc
1255 Greene Ave Ste 300. . . . . Montreal QC H3Z2A4 514-934-3034 319-2
TSE: DII.B ■ *Web:* www.dorel.com

Dorel Juvenile Group USA
2525 State St . . . . . Columbus IN 47201 812-372-0141 372-0911 64
TF: 800-544-1108 ■ *Web:* na.doreljuvenile.com

Doremus 200 Varick St. . . . . New York NY 10014 212-366-3000 4
Web: www.doremus.com

Doremus Financial Printing
228 E 45th St 10th Fl . . . . . New York NY 10017 212-366-3800 627
Web: www.doremusfp.com

Dorey Electric Co PO Box 10158 . . . . . Norfolk VA 23513 757-855-3381 189-4
TF: 800-421-2584 ■ *Web:* www.doreyelectric.com

Dori Foods Inc 3410 Norfolk St. . . . . Richmond VA 23230 804-355-1600 805

Dorian Business Systems Inc
1985 Forest Ln . . . . . Garland TX 75042 972-485-1912 272-3927 177
Web: dorianbusinesssystems.com

Dorian Drake International Inc
2 Westchester Park Dr. . . . . White Plains NY 10604 914-697-9800 697-9683 61
Web: www.doriandrake.com

Dorignac's Food Ctr 725 Focis St . . . . . Metairie LA 70005 504-837-4650 832-8944 345
Web: dorignacs.com

Dorinco Reinsurance Co 1320 Waldo Ave. . . . . Midland MI 48642 989-636-0047 638-9963 391-4
TF: 800-514-9470 ■ *Web:* www.dorinco.com

Doris Duke Charitable Foundation (DDCF)
650 Fifth Ave 19th Fl . . . . . New York NY 10019 212-974-7000 974-7590 305
Web: www.ddcf.org

Dorling Kindersley Publishing
375 Hudson St . . . . . New York NY 10014 646-674-4047 674-4047 637-2
TF Cust Svc: 800-631-8571 ■ *Web:* www.dk.com/us

DORMA Architectural Hardware
DORMA Dr Drawer AC . . . . . Reamstown PA 17567 717-336-3881 336-2106 488
TF: 800-523-8483 ■ *Web:* www.dorma.com

DORMA Group North America Dorma Dr . . . . . Reamstown PA 17567 717-336-3881 336-2106 350
TF: 800-523-8483 ■ *Web:* www.dorma.com

Dorman Products Inc 3400 E Walnut St. . . . . Colmar PA 18915 215-997-1800 60
NASDAQ: DORM ■ *TF:* 800-523-2492 ■ *Web:* www.rblnc.com

Dormify Inc 10101 Molecular Dr . . . . . Rockville MD 20850 413-367-6439 361
Web: www.dormify.com

Dormont Manufacturing Co
6015 Enterprise Dr . . . . . Export PA 15632 800-367-6668 370
TF: 800-367-6668 ■ *Web:* www.dormont.com

Dorn Color Inc 11555 Berea Rd. . . . . Cleveland OH 44102 216-634-2252 561
TF: 800-310-2791 ■ *Web:* dorncolor.com

Dornbracht Americas Inc
1700 Executive Dr S Ste 600 . . . . . Duluth GA 30096 800-774-1181 610
TF: 800-774-1181 ■ *Web:* www.dornbracht.com

Dornerworks Ltd
3445 Lake Eastbrook Blvd SE. . . . . Grand Rapids MI 49546 616-245-8369 696
Web: www.dornerworks.com

Dorney Park & Wildwater Kingdom
3830 Dorney Pk Rd. . . . . Allentown PA 18104 610-395-3724 32
Web: dorneypark.com

Dornier MedTech America Inc
1155 Roberts Blvd . . . . . Kennesaw GA 30144 770-426-1315 426-6115 382
TF: 800-367-6437 ■ *Web:* www.dornier.com

Doron Precision Systems Inc
150 Corporate Dr PO Box 400 . . . . . Binghamton NY 13904 607-772-1610 772-6760 703
Web: www.doronprecision.com

Dorothea Dix Hospital
820 S Boylan Ave. . . . . Raleigh NC 27699 919-733-5540 374-5

Dorothy Bramlage Public Library Junction City
230 W Seventh St. . . . . Junction City KS 66441 785-238-4311 238-7873 434-3
TF: 800-727-2785 ■ *Web:* www.jclib.org

Dorothy Egg Farms LLC 271 Turkey Ln . . . . . Winthrop ME 04364 207-377-9927 10-8

Dorothy Lane Market Inc
2710 Far Hills Ave . . . . . Dayton OH 45419 937-299-3561 299-3568 345
Web: www.dorothylane.com

Dorr Street Cafe 5243 Dorr St . . . . . Toledo OH 43615 419-531-4446 671
Web: dorrstreetcafe.com

Dorris Lumber & Moulding Co, The
2601 Redding Ave. . . . . Sacramento CA 95820 916-452-7531 499
TF: 800-827-5823 ■ *Web:* www.dorrismoulding.com

Dorsett & Jackson Inc
3800 Noakes St . . . . . Los Angeles CA 90023 323-268-1815 268-9082 146
TF: 800-871-8365 ■ *Web:* www.dorsettandjackson.com

Dorsett Industries Inc
1304 May St PO Box 805 . . . . . Dalton GA 30721 706-278-1961 217-1775 131
TF: 800-241-4035 ■ *Web:* www.dorsettind.com

Dorsey & Whitney LLP
50 S Sixth St Ste 1500 . . . . . Minneapolis MN 55402 612-340-2600 340-2868 428
Web: www.dorsey.com

Dorst America Inc 64 S Commerce Way . . . . . Bethlehem PA 18017 610-317-2000 567

Dort Federal Credit Union Event Ctr
3501 Lapeer Rd . . . . . Flint MI 48503 810-744-0580 720
Web: www.dorteventcenter.com

Dortronics Systems Inc
1668 Sag Harbor Tpke . . . . . Sag Harbor NY 11963 631-725-0505 350
TF: 800-522-2940 ■ *Web:* www.dortronics.com

Dorvin D Leis Company Inc 202 Lalo St . . . . . Kahului HI 96732 808-877-3902 189-10
TF: 800-735-5272 ■ *Web:* www.leisinc.com

Name / Address	City	State	Zip	Phone	Fax	Class
Dos Locos 208 Rehoboth Ave *TF:* 800-285-0400 ■ *Web:* www.doslocos.com	Rehoboth Beach	DE	19971	302-227-3353		671
Dos Rios Partners 205 Wild Basin Rd S Bldg 3 Ste 100 *Web:* www.dosriospartners.com	Austin	TX	78746	512-298-0801		528
Dosha Salon & Spa 3490 SE Hawthorne Blvd *Web:* www.dosha.org	Portland	OR	97214	503-231-4993		77
Doss Aviation Inc 3670 Rebecca Ln *TF:* 888-803-4415 ■ *Web:* www.dossaviation.com	Colorado Springs	CO	80917	719-570-9804		579
Dossett Big 4 Buick Pontiac Cadillac Gmc Inc 628 S Gloster St *Web:* dossettbig4.com	Tupelo	MS	38801	662-842-4162		57
Dossin Great Lakes Museum 100 Strand Dr Belle Isle *TF:* 800-835-5237 ■ *Web:* www.detroithistorical.org	Detroit	MI	48207	313-833-5538	833-5342	520
Dostal Alley Casino 1 Dostal Alley *TF:* 888-949-2757 ■ *Web:* www.centralcitycolorado.com	Central City	CO	80427	303-582-1610	582-0143	133
Doster Construction Co 2100 International Pk Dr *Web:* www.dosterconstruction.com	Birmingham	AL	35243	205-443-3800	951-2612	186
DOT (Department of Transportation) 1200 New Jersey Ave SE *TF:* 800-877-8339 ■ *Web:* www.transportation.gov	Washington	DC	20590	202-366-4000		340-17
Dot Com Holdings of Buffalo Inc 1460 Military Rd *TF:* 877-636-3673 ■ *Web:* www.dotcomholdingsofbuffalo.com	Buffalo	NY	14217	877-636-3673		690
Dot Foods Inc 1 Dot Way PO Box 192 *TF:* 800-366-3687 ■ *Web:* www.dotfoods.com	Mount Sterling	IL	62353	217-773-4411	773-3321	297-6
Dot Generation Inc 16 Dyke Ln *Web:* www.dotgeneration.com	Stamford	CT	06902	203-967-8112		627
Dot Hill Systems Corp 1351 S Sunset St *NASDAQ:* HILL ■ *TF:* 800-872-2783 ■ *Web:* www.dothill.com	Longmont	CO	80501	303-845-3200	845-3655	176
Dot VN Inc 9449 Balboa Ave Ste 114 *TF:* 800-642-1687 ■ *Web:* www.dotvn.com	San Diego	CA	92123	858-571-2007		224
Dot Wo 6161 N May Ave *Web:* www.dot-wo.com	Oklahoma City	OK	73112	405-608-2388		671
Dothan Area Botanical Gardens 5130 Headland Ave *Web:* www.dabg.com	Dothan	AL	36303	334-793-3224		97
Dothan Area Chamber of Commerce 102 Jamestown Blvd *TF:* 800-221-1027 ■ *Web:* www.dothan.com	Dothan	AL	36301	334-792-5138	794-4796	139
Dothan Chrysler-Dodge Inc 4074 Ross Clark Cir NW *TF:* 877-674-9574 ■ *Web:* www.dothanchryslerdodge.net	Dothan	AL	36303	877-674-9574		57
Dothan Eagle PO Box 1968 *TF:* 800-811-1771 ■ *Web:* www.dothaneagle.com	Dothan	AL	36302	334-792-3141	712-7979	532-2
Dot-Line Transportation PO Box 8739 *TF:* 800-423-3780 ■ *Web:* www.dotline.net	Fountain Valley	CA	92728	323-780-9010		188-5
DotLoop LLC 700 W Pete Rose Way Ste 446 *Web:* www.dotloop.com	Cincinnati	OH	45203	513-257-0550		387
DOTmed.com Inc 29 Broadway Ste 2500 *Web:* www.dotmed.com/virtual-trade-show/booth/52638_DotmedCom,_Inc	New York	NY	10006	212-742-1200		387
dotPhoto Inc PO Box 92 *Web:* www.dotphoto.com	Titusville	NJ	08560	609-434-0340	434-0344	588
Dotronix Inc 160 First St SE *TF:* 800-720-7218 ■ *Web:* www.dotronix.com	New Brighton	MN	55112	651-633-1742	633-1065	173-4
Dotson Company Inc 200 W Rock St *TF:* 800-537-4237 ■ *Web:* www.dotson.com	Mankato	MN	56001	507-345-5018	345-1270	307
Dotster 8100 NE Pkwy Dr Ste 300 PO Box 821066 *TF:* 800-401-5250 ■ *Web:* www.dotster.com	Vancouver	WA	98682	360-449-5800	397-2699	396
Doty-Moore Tower Services Inc 1570 W Belt Line Rd	Cedar Hill	TX	75104	972-637-5000		480
Double Cola Company USA 537 Market St Ste 100 *Web:* double-cola.com	Chattanooga	TN	37402	423-267-5691		80-2
Double Diamond Co 5495 Belt Line Rd Ste 200 *TF:* 800-324-7438 ■ *Web:* www.ddresorts.com	Dallas	TX	75254	214-706-9801		653
Double Ditch State Historic Site N Dakota 1804 *Web:* www.history.nd.gov	Bismarck	ND	58503	701-328-2666	328-3710	565
Double Dragon 117 W Wayne St	Fort Wayne	IN	46802	260-422-6426		671
Double E Co 319 Manley St *Web:* ee-co.com	West Bridgewater	MA	02379	508-588-8099	580-2915	556
Double Eagle Capital Management LP 909 Lake Carolyn Pkwy Ste 1825 *TF:* 800-526-7249 ■ *Web:* www.doubleeaglecapital.com	Irving	TX	75039	972-869-6880		528
Double Eagle Hotel & Casino 442 E Bennett Ave *TF:* 800-711-7234 ■ *Web:* decasino.com	Cripple Creek	CO	80813	719-689-5000		133
Double Eagle Resort & Spa 5587 Hwy 158 *Web:* www.doubleeagle.com	June Lake	CA	93529	760-648-7004		669
Double Envelope Corp 7702 Plantation Rd *Web:* www.double-envelope.com	Roanoke	VA	24019	540-362-3311		263
Double H Plastics Inc 50 W St Rd *TF:* 800-523-3932 ■ *Web:* www.doublehplastics.com	Warminster	PA	18974	215-674-4100	674-5469	604
Double Infinity Inc 14414 Detroit Ave *Web:* www.doubleinfinity.com	Lakewood	OH	44107	216-228-7500		177
Double J Saddlery Inc 2243 US Hwy 77A S *Web:* www.doublejsaddlery.com	Yoakum	TX	77995	361-293-6364		711
Double Quick Printing Services Inc 2233 S Monaco Pkwy *Web:* www.dqprint.com	Denver	CO	80222	303-759-9999		627
Double R Productions 1621 Connecticut Ave NW Ste 400 *Web:* www.doublerproductions.com	Washington	DC	20009	202-797-7777		514
Double Trouble State Park 581 Pinewald Keswick Rd *Web:* www.state.nj.us	Bayville	NJ	08721	732-341-6662		565
Doublebees 111 Bill Foster Memorial Hwy *Web:* www.doublebees.com	Cabot	AR	72023	501-605-8989		297-8
DoubleCheck LLC 101 Gilbraltar Dr Ste 1E *TF:* 888-299-3980 ■ *Web:* www.doublechecksoftware.com	Morris Plains	NJ	07950	973-984-2229		177
Double-E Inc 1261 Profit Dr *Web:* www.doubleeinc.com	Dallas	TX	75247	214-631-2290		537
Doublehorn Communications 1601 Rio Grande St # 500 *TF:* 855-618-6423 ■ *Web:* www.doublehorn.com	Austin	TX	78701	512-637-5200		224
Doubleknot Inc 20665 Fourth St Ste 106 *Web:* www.doubleknot.com	Saratoga	CA	95070	408-971-9120		463
DoublePositive Marketing Group Inc 1501 S Clinton St Ste 1520 *Web:* www.doublepositive.com	Baltimore	MD	21224	410-332-0464		7
DoubleStar Inc 1161 Mcdermott Dr Ste 200 *Web:* www.doublestarinc.com	West Chester	PA	19380	610-719-1900		256
DoubleTree 2200 Fwy Blvd *TF:* 800-434-7894 ■ *Web:* doubletree3.hilton.com	Minneapolis	MN	55430	763-566-8000		378
DoubleTree by Hilton Baltimore - BWI Airport 890 Elkridge Landing Rd *Web:* doubletree3.hilton.com	Linthicum	MD	21090	410-859-8400		378
DoubleTree by Hilton Grand Rapids Airport Hotel 4747 28th St SE *Web:* doubletree3.hilton.com	Grand Rapids	MI	49512	616-957-0100	977-5632	671
DoubleTree by Hilton Hotel Bethesda - Washington DC 8120 Wisconsin Ave *Web:* doubletree3.hilton.com	Bethesda	MD	20814	301-652-2000		378
DoubleTree by Hilton Hotel Raleigh - Brownstone - University 1707 Hillsborough St *Web:* www.brownstonehotel.com	Raleigh	NC	27605	919-828-0811		378
Doubletree by Hilton Hotel Tucson-Reid Park 445 S Alvernon Way *Web:* www.dtreidpark.com	Tucson	AZ	85711	520-881-4200		378
Doubletree Claremont 555 W Foothill Blvd *TF:* 800-222-8733 ■ *Web:* www3.hilton.com	Claremont	CA	91711	909-626-2411	624-0756	379
Doubletree Hotel 2800 Via Cabrillo Marina *Web:* doubletree3.hilton.com	San Pedro	CA	90731	310-514-3344	514-8945	379
Doubletree Hotel Downtown Wilmington Legal District 700 N King St *TF:* 800-222-8733 ■ *Web:* www3.hilton.com	Wilmington	DE	19801	302-655-0400		379
Doubletree North Shore Hotel 9599 Skokie Blvd *TF:* 800-445-8667 ■ *Web:* www3.hilton.com	Skokie	IL	60077	847-679-7000		379
Doubletree Paradise Valley Resort 5401 N Scottsdale Rd *TF:* 800-222-8733 ■ *Web:* www3.hilton.com	Scottsdale	AZ	85250	480-947-5400	443-9702	669
DoubleTree Resort by Hilton Hotel Grand Key (DGKR) 3990 S Roosevelt Blvd *TF:* 800-444-5866 ■ *Web:* doubletree3.hilton.com	Key West	FL	33040	305-293-1818	296-6962	669
DoubleVerify Inc 233 Spring St *Web:* www.doubleverify.com	New York	NY	10013	212-631-2002		387
Doucet & Associates Inc 7401B Hwy 71 W Ste 160 *TF:* 800-527-4135 ■ *Web:* www.douceteengineers.com	Austin	TX	78735	512-583-2600		261
Doucette Industries Inc (DII) 20 Leigh Dr *TF:* 800-445-7511 ■ *Web:* www.doucetteindustries.com	York	PA	17406	717-845-8746	845-2864	14
Doug Ashy Building Materials Inc 1801 Rees St *Web:* www.dougashy.com	Breaux Bridge	LA	70517	337-332-5201	332-5226	364
Doug Hollyhand Construction Co 527 Main Ave *Web:* www.hollyhand.com	Northport	AL	35476	205-345-0955		186
Doug Mockett & Company Inc 1915 Abalone Ave *TF:* 800-523-1269 ■ *Web:* www.mockett.com	Torrance	CA	90501	310-318-2491		350
Doug Richert Pontiac Cadillac 1900 SW Topeka Blvd *Web:* www.dougrichert.com	Topeka	KS	66612	785-233-1361		54
Doug Varone & Dancers 37 W 32nd St *TF:* 800-366-2100 ■ *Web:* www.dougvaroneanddancers.org	New York	NY	10001	212-279-3344	279-3344	573-1
Doug's Hickory Pit Bar B Que 3313 S Georgia St	Amarillo	TX	79109	806-352-8471		671
Doug's Supermarket Inc 310 Main Ave NE *TF:* 800-280-2626 ■ *Web:* www.dougssupermarket.com	Warroad	MN	56763	218-386-1246		345
Dougherty & Company LLC 90 S Seventh St Ste 4300 *TF:* 800-328-4000 ■ *Web:* www.doughertymarkets.com	Minneapolis	MN	55402	612-376-4000		690
Dougherty Arts Ctr, The (DAC) 1110 Barton Springs Rd	Austin	TX	78704	512-974-4000	974-4039	50-2
Dougherty County 222 Pine Ave *Web:* www.albany.ga.us	Albany	GA	31701	229-431-2121	438-3967	338
Dougherty County Public Library 300 N Pine Ave *Web:* www.docolib.org	Albany	GA	31701	229-420-3200		434-3
Dougherty Hospice House 4509 Prince of Peace Pl *Web:* www.avera.org	Sioux Falls	SD	57103	605-322-7705		371
Dougherty Management Associates Inc 9 Meriam St Ste 4 *Web:* www.dmahealth.com	Lexington	MA	02420	781-863-1519		463
Dougherty Sprague Environmental Inc 3902 Industrial St Ste A *Web:* www.dsei.com	Rowlett	TX	75088	972-412-8666		256
Dougherty's Holdings Inc 16250 Dallas Pkwy Ste 102 *Web:* www.doughertys.com/corporate	Dallas	TX	75248	214-373-5300		237
Douglas & London P C 59 Maiden Ln Fl 6 *TF:* 800-963-4444 ■ *Web:* www.douglasandlondon.com	New York	NY	10038	212-566-7500	566-7501	445

	Phone	Fax	Class
Douglas & Sturgess Inc 1023 Factory St .... Richmond CA 94801 *TF:* 800-390-1000 ■ *Web:* www.artstuf.com	510-235-8411	235-4211	45
Douglas Allred Co 11452 El Camino Real Ste 200 .... San Diego CA 92130 *Web:* www.douglasallredco.com	858-793-0202	793-5363	655
Douglas Autotech Corp 300 Albers Rd .... Bronson MI 49028 *Web:* www.douglasautotech.com	517-369-2315	369-7217	60
Douglas Baldwin & Assoc PO Box 1249 .... La Canada CA 91012 *Web:* www.baldwinpi.com	818-952-4433	790-4622	400
Douglas Battery Manufacturing Co 500 Battery Dr .... Winston-Salem NC 27107 *TF:* 800-368-4527 ■ *Web:* www.douglasbattery.com	800-368-4527		74
Douglas Bros 423 Riverside Industrial Pkwy .... Portland ME 04103 *TF:* 800-341-0926 ■ *Web:* www.douglasbrothers.com	207-797-6771	797-8385	595
Douglas Corp 9650 Valley View Rd .... Eden Prairie MN 55344 *TF:* 800-806-6112 ■ *Web:* www.douglascorp.com	952-941-2944	942-3125	701
Douglas County 305 Eigth Ave W .... Alexandria MN 56308 *Web:* www.co.douglas.mn.us	320-762-3877		338
Douglas County 706 Braddock St PO Box 36 .... Armour SD 57313 *Web:* ujs.sd.gov	605-724-2585	724-2508	338
Douglas County 203 SE Second Ave PO Box 398 .... Ava MO 65608	417-683-6080		338
Douglas County 100 Third St .... Castle Rock CO 80104 *Web:* www.douglas.co.us	303-660-7401	688-1293	338
Douglas County 8700 Hospital Dr .... Douglasville GA 30134 *TF:* 800-822-5391 ■ *Web:* www.celebratedouglascounty.com	770-949-2000		338
Douglas County 1100 Massachusetts St First Level .... Lawrence KS 66044 *Web:* www.douglascountyks.org	785-832-5167		338
Douglas County 1616 Eighth St PO Box 218 .... Minden NV 89423 *Web:* cltr.douglasnv.us	775-782-9020	782-9016	338
Douglas County 1819 Farnam St .... Omaha NE 68183 *Web:* www.douglascounty-ne.gov	402-444-7025	444-6559	338
Douglas County 1036 SE Douglas St .... Roseburg OR 97470 *Web:* www.co.douglas.or.us	541-672-3311	440-4408	338
Douglas County 1313 Belknap St .... Superior WI 54880 *TF:* 800-422-7128 ■ *Web:* www.douglascountywi.org	715-395-1341	395-1421	338
Douglas County 401 S Ctr St PO Box 467 .... Tuscola IL 61953 *Web:* www.douglascountyil.com	217-253-2411	253-2233	338
Douglas County 213 Rainer St .... Waterville WA 98858 *Web:* www.douglascountywa.net	509-745-8537	745-9045	338
Douglas County Board of Education 9030 Hwy 5 .... Douglasville GA 30134 *Web:* www.douglas.k12.ga.us	770-651-2000		685
Douglas County Chamber of Commerce 6658 Church St .... Douglasville GA 30134 *TF:* 800-304-7056 ■ *Web:* www.douglascountygeorgia.com	770-942-5022	942-5876	139
Douglas County Hospital (DCH) 111 17th Ave E .... Alexandria MN 56308 *Web:* www.dchospital.com	320-762-1511	762-6120	374-3
Douglas County Libraries 100 S Wilcox .... Castle Rock CO 80104 *Web:* www.dcl.org	303-791-7323		431-3
Douglas County Library 1625 Library Ln .... Minden NV 89423 *Web:* douglas.lib.nv.us	775-782-9841		434-3
Douglas County Library 720 Fillmore St .... Alexandria MN 56308 *Web:* www.douglascountylibrary.org	320-762-3014		434-3
Douglas County Library System 1409 NE Diamond Lake Blvd .... Roseburg OR 97470 *TF:* 800-320-6306 ■ *Web:* www.dclibrary.us	541-440-4311		434-3
Douglas Cuddle Toys Company Inc 69 Krif Rd PO Box D .... Keene NH 03431 *TF:* 800-992-9002 ■ *Web:* www.douglascuddletoy.com	603-352-3414	352-1248	762
Douglas Daw CPA 1101 California Ave Ste 211 .... Corona CA 92881	951-582-9023		2
Douglas Electric Co-op Inc 400 Main Ave .... Armour SD 57313	605-724-2323		245
Douglas Elliman Property Management 675 Third Ave .... New York NY 10017 *Web:* www.ellimanpm.com	212-370-9200		655
Douglas Industries Co 3441 S 11th Ave .... Eldridge IA 52748 *TF:* 800-553-8907 ■ *Web:* www.douglas-sports.com	563-285-4162	285-4163	710
Douglas Laboratories Inc 600 Boyce Rd .... Pittsburgh PA 15205 *TF:* 800-245-4440 ■ *Web:* www.douglaslabs.com	800-245-4440		799
Douglas Machine Inc 3404 Iowa St .... Alexandria MN 56308 *Web:* www.douglas-machine.com	320-763-6587		547
Douglas Machines Corp 2101 Calumet St .... Clearwater FL 33765 *Web:* www.dougmac.com	727-461-3477		427
Douglas Orr Plumbing Inc 301 Flagler Dr .... Miami Springs FL 33166 *Web:* www.orrplumbing.com	305-887-1687		610
Douglas P Bates 144 Genesee St .... Auburn NY 13021	315-253-2782		690
Douglas Parking LLC 1721 Webster St .... Oakland CA 94612 *Web:* www.douglasparking.com	510-444-7412		562
Douglas Press Inc 2810 Madison St .... Bellwood IL 60104 *TF:* 800-323-0705 ■ *Web:* www.douglaspress.com	708-547-8400		322
Douglas State Forest 107 Wallum Lake Rd .... Douglas MA 01516 *Web:* www.mass.gov	508-476-7872		565
Douglas Steel Fabricating Corp 1312 S Waverly Rd .... Lansing MI 48917 *Web:* www.douglassteel.com	517-322-2050	322-0050	307
Douglas Steel Supply Co 5764 Alcoa Ave .... Los Angeles CA 90058 *Web:* www.douglassteelsupply.com	323-587-7676		492
Douglas Stewart Co, The 2402 Advance Rd .... Madison WI 53718 *TF:* 800-279-2795 ■ *Web:* www.dstewart.com	608-221-1155	221-5217	534
Douglas Udell Gallery 10332 124th St .... Edmonton AB T5N1R2 *TF:* 800-528-4278 ■ *Web:* www.douglasudellgallery.com	780-488-4445	488-8335	42
Douglas Wilson Cos Inc 450 B St Ste 1900 .... San Diego CA 92101 *Web:* www.douglaswilson.com	619-641-1141		194
Douglas/Quikut Co 118 E Douglas Rd .... Walnut Ridge AR 72476 **Fax Area Code:* 870 ■ *TF:* 800-982-5233 ■ *Web:* www.douglasquikut.com	800-982-5233	886-2911*	222
Douglas-Coffee County Chamber of Commerce 211 S Gaskin Ave .... Douglas GA 31533 *TF:* 888-426-3334 ■ *Web:* www.douglasga.org	912-384-1873	383-6304	139
Douglas-Guardian Services Corp 14800 St Mary's Ln .... Houston TX 77079 *TF:* 800-255-0552 ■ *Web:* www.douglasguardian.com	281-531-0500		399
Douglass College 100 George St .... New Brunswick NJ 08901 **Fax Area Code:* 732 ■ *Web:* douglass.rutgers.edu	848-932-9500	932-8877*	166
Douglass Colony Group Inc 5901 E 58th Ave .... Commerce CO 80022 *TF:* 877-288-0650 ■ *Web:* www.douglasscolony.com	303-288-2635		189-12
Douglass Distributing Co 325 E Forest Ave .... Sherman TX 75090 *TF:* 800-736-4316 ■ *Web:* www.douglassdist.com	903-893-1181		581
Douglass Industries Inc 412 Boston Ave .... Egg Harbor City NJ 08215 *Web:* www.dougind.com	609-965-6030		594
Douglass Theatre 355 ML King Jr Blvd .... Macon GA 31201 *TF:* 800-768-3401 ■ *Web:* www.douglasstheatre.org	478-742-2000		572
Douglass Truck Bodies Inc 231 21st St .... Bakersfield CA 93301 *TF:* 800-635-7641 ■ *Web:* www.douglasstruckbodies.com	661-327-0258	327-3894	516
Douthat State Park 14239 Douthat State Pk Rd .... Millboro VA 24460 *TF General:* 800-933-7275 ■ *Web:* www.dcr.virginia.gov/state-parks/douthat#general_information	540-862-8100	862-8104	565
Douthitt Corp 245 Adair St .... Detroit MI 48207 *TF:* 800-368-8448 ■ *Web:* www.douthittcorp.com	313-259-1565	259-6806	591
Dove Cleaners Inc 1560 Yonge St .... Toronto ON M4T2S9 *TF:* 866-999-3683 ■ *Web:* www.dovecleaners.com	416-413-7900		426
Dove Die & Stamping Co 15665 Brookpark Rd .... Cleveland OH 44142 *TF:* 800-365-0723 ■ *Web:* www.dovedie.com	216-267-3720	267-7250	488
Dove Equipment Company Inc 723 Sabrina Dr .... East Peoria IL 61611 *Web:* icafeinc.com/en_US/company/doveequipment	309-694-6228		358
Dove Lewis Emergency Animal Hospital Inc 1945 NW Pettygrove St .... Portland OR 97209 *Web:* www.dovelewis.org	503-228-7281		794
Dover Air Force Base 442 13th St .... Dover DE 19902 *Web:* www.dover.af.mil	302-677-3372	677-2901	497-1
Dover Chemical Corp 3676 Davis Rd NW .... Dover OH 44622 *TF General:* 800-321-8805 ■ *Web:* www.doverchem.com	330-343-7711	365-3927	145
Dover City Hall 15 ELoockerman St .... Dover DE 19901 *Web:* www.cityofdover.com	302-736-7008	736-7177	337
Dover Corp 3005 Highland Pkwy Ste 200 .... Downers Grove IL 60515 *NYSE: DOV* ■ *Web:* www.dovercorporation.com	630-541-1540	743-2671	185
Dover Downs Hotel & Casino 1131 N DuPont Hwy .... Dover DE 19901 *NYSE: DDE* ■ *TF:* 800-711-5882 ■ *Web:* www.doverdowns.com	302-674-4600		642
Dover Federal Credit Union 1075 Silver Lake Blvd .... Dover DE 19904 *Web:* doverfcu.com	302-678-8000		219
Dover Financial Research LLC 208 Dover Rd .... Westwood MA 02090 *Web:* www.doverfr.com	781-461-0922		401
Dover International Speedway 1131 N DuPont Hwy PO Box 843 .... Dover DE 19901 *TF:* 800-441-7223 ■ *Web:* www.doverspeedway.com	302-883-6500	672-0100	642
Dover Motorsports Inc 1131 N Dupont Hwy .... Dover DE 19901 *NYSE: DVD* ■ *Web:* www.dovermotorsportsinc.com	302-883-6500	672-0100	642
Dover Post 1196 S Little Creek Rd .... Dover DE 19901 *TF:* 800-942-1616 ■ *Web:* www.doverpost.com	302-678-3616		532-4
Dover Public Library 73 Locust St .... Dover NH 03820 *Web:* www.dover.nh.gov	603-516-6050	516-6053	434-3
Dover Publications Inc 31 E Second St .... Mineola NY 11501 *Web:* www.doverpublications.com	516-294-7000		532-3
Dover Saddlery Inc 525 Great Rd PO Box 1100 .... Littleton MA 01460 *NASDAQ: DOVR* ■ *TF:* 800-406-8204 ■ *Web:* www.doversaddlery.com	978-952-8062		710
Dover Tank & Plate Co, The 5725 Crown Rd NW .... Dover OH 44622 *Web:* www.dovertank.com	330-343-4443		480
Doverco Inc 2111 32e Ave .... Montreal QC H8T3J1 *Web:* www.doverco.ca	514-420-6060		358
Dovetail Communications Inc 30 E Beaver Creek Rd Ste 202 .... Richmond Hill ON L4B1J2 *TF:* 800-352-2282 ■ *Web:* dvtail.com	905-886-6640		224
Dovetail Internet Technologies LLC 40 Southbridge St Ste 210 .... Worcester MA 01608 *TF:* 800-561-3357 ■ *Web:* www.dovetailinternet.com	508-845-6465		225
Dovetail Public Relations 15951 Los Gatos Blvd Ste 16 .... Los Gatos CA 95032 *Web:* www.dovetailpr.com	408-395-3600		636
DOVICO Software Inc 236 St George St Ste 119 .... Moncton NB E1C1W1 *TF:* 800-618-8463 ■ *Web:* www.dovico.com	506-855-4477	384-0727	179
Dow AgroSciences LLC 9330 Zionsville Rd .... Indianapolis IN 46268 **Fax Area Code:* 800 ■ *TF:* 800-331-6451 ■ *Web:* www.dowagro.com	317-337-3000	905-7326*	280
Dow Chemical Canada Inc (DCCI) 450 First St SW Ste 2100 .... Calgary AB T2P5H1 *TF:* 800-447-4369 ■ *Web:* www.dow.com	403-267-3500	267-3597	144
Dow Chemical Co 2030 Dow Ctr .... Midland MI 48674 *NYSE: DOW* ■ *TF Cust Svc:* 800-422-8193 ■ *Web:* www.dow.com	989-636-1463	636-1830	144
Dow Chemical Co, The 100 Independence Mall W .... Philadelphia PA 19106 *Web:* www.dow.com	215-592-3000		605-2
Dow Chemical Company Foundation 2030 Dow Ctr .... Midland MI 48674 *TF:* 800-331-6451 ■ *Web:* www.dow.com/about/corp/social/social.htm	989-636-1000		304

	Phone	Fax	Class
Dow Chemical Company, The 1881 W Oak Pkwy. Marietta GA 30062 *TF:* 800-331-6451 ■ *Web:* www.dow.com	770-428-2684		601
Dow Chemical Employees' Credit Union 600 E Lyon Rd Midland MI 48640 *Web:* www.dcecu.org	989-835-7794		219
Dow Corning Corp PO Box 994 Midland MI 48686 *Fax: Hum Res ■ *TF Cust Svc:* 800-248-2481 ■ *Web:* www.dowcorning.com	989-496-4000	496-1886*	144
Dow Cover Co Inc 373 Lexington Ave New Haven CT 06513 *TF:* 800-735-8877 ■ *Web:* www.dowcover.com	203-469-5394	469-5394	349
Dow Electronics Inc 8603 E Adamo Dr Tampa FL 33619 *TF:* 800-627-2900 ■ *Web:* www.dowelectronics.com	813-626-5195	628-4990	246
Dow Event Ctr 303 Johnson St Saginaw MI 48607 *TF:* 800-745-3000 ■ *Web:* www.doweventcenter.com	989-759-1320	759-1322	572
Dow Gardens 1809 Eastman Ave Midland MI 48640 *Web:* www.dowgardens.org	989-631-2677		97
Dow Hotel Company LLC, The 16400 Southcenter Pkwy Ste 405 Seattle WA 98188 *Web:* www.dowhotelco.com	206-575-3600		378
Dow Jones & Company Inc 1211 Ave of the Americas New York NY 10281 *Web:* www.dowjones.com	212-416-2000		637-8
Dow Liquid Separations PO Box 1206 Midland MI 48642 *TF:* 800-447-4369 ■ *Web:* dow.com	989-636-1000	832-1465	806
Dow Screw Products 3810 Paule Ave Saint Louis MO 63125	314-638-5100		621
Dow Theory Forecasts 7412 Calumet Ave Hammond IN 46324 *TF:* 800-233-5922 ■ *Web:* www.dowtheory.com	800-233-5922		531-9
Dowagiac 217 N Fourth St Niles MI 49120 *TF:* 800-323-0390 ■ *Web:* www.leaderpub.com	269-683-2101		532-3
Dowding Industries Inc 449 Marilin St Eaton Rapids MI 48827 *Web:* www.dowdingindustries.com	517-663-5455		483
Dowdle Sports Inc 4415 Donelson Dr Eads TN 38028 *Web:* www.dowdlesports.com	901-466-7706		711
Dow-Key Microwave Corp 4822 McGrath St Ventura CA 93003 *TF:* 800-266-3695 ■ *Web:* www.dowkey.com	805-650-0260	650-1734	253
Dowl LLC 4041 B St Anchorage AK 99503 *Web:* www.dowl.com	907-562-2000		261
Dowley Inc 40 NE 46th St Oklahoma City OK 73105 *Web:* www.dowley.com	713-721-9732		246
Dowling & Yahnke Inc 12340 El Camino Real San Diego CA 92130 *Web:* dywealth.com	858-509-9500		690
Dowling Aaron Inc 8080 N Palm Ave 3rd Fl Fresno CA 93711 *Web:* bctconsulting.com	559-432-4500		445
Dowling College 150 Idle Hour Blvd Oakdale NY 11769 *Fax: Admissions ■ *TF:* 800-369-5464 ■ *Web:* www.dowling.edu	631-244-3000	244-1059*	166
Dowling Graphics Inc 12920 Automobile Blvd Clearwater FL 33762 *TF:* 800-749-6933 ■ *Web:* www.dowlinggraphics.com	727-573-5997		627
Dowlings Inc 91 Catamount Dr Milton VT 05468 *Web:* www.dowlingsinc.com	802-893-5100		805
Down Beat Magazine 102 N Haven Rd Elmhurst IL 60126 *Fax Area Code: 630 ■ *TF:* 800-554-7470 ■ *Web:* www.downbeat.com	651-251-9682	941-3210*	457-9
Down East 680 Commercial St Rockport ME 04856 *TF:* 800-766-1670 ■ *Web:* downeast.com	207-594-9544		457-22
Down to Earth 2525 S King St Honolulu HI 96826 *Web:* www.downtoearth.org	808-947-7678		479
Down To Earth Landscaping Inc 705 Wright-Debow Rd Jackson NJ 08527 *Web:* www.downtoearthlandscaping.com	732-833-7702		776
Down Under Linen & Bedding Ctr 5170 Dixie Rd Mississauga ON L4W1E3 *TF:* 888-624-6484 ■ *Web:* downunderbedding.com	905-624-5854		361
Downeast Correctional Dept 64 Base Rd Machiasport ME 04655	207-255-1100		213
Downeast Energy Corp 18 Spring St Brunswick ME 04011 *Web:* www.downeastenergy.com	207-729-9921		612
Downeast Graphics & Printing Inc 477 Washington Jct Rd Ellsworth ME 04605 *TF:* 800-427-5582 ■ *Web:* www.downeastgraphics.com	207-667-5582		627
Downers Grove Park District 2455 Warrenville Rd Downers Grove IL 60516 *Web:* www.dgparks.org	630-960-7500		31
Downers Grove Public Library 1050 Curtiss St Downers Grove IL 60515 *TF:* 800-227-0625 ■ *Web:* www.downersgrovelibrary.org	630-960-1200	960-9374	434-3
Downes Associates Inc 2129 Northwood Dr Salisbury MD 21801 *TF:* 800-775-3657 ■ *Web:* www.downesassociates.com	410-546-4422		261
Downey Brand LLP 621 Capitol Mall 18th Fl Sacramento CA 95814 *TF:* 800-973-1177 ■ *Web:* www.downeybrand.com	916-444-1000		428
Downey Chamber of Commerce 11131 Brookshire Ave Downey CA 90241 *Web:* www.downeychamber.com	562-923-2191	923-6388	139
Downey City Library (DCL) 11121 Brookshire Ave Downey CA 90241 *TF:* 877-846-3452 ■ *Web:* www.downeyca.org	562-904-7360	923-3763	434-3
Downey Grinding Co 12323 Bellflower Blvd Downey CA 90242 *TF:* 800-773-4504 ■ *Web:* www.downeygrinding.com	562-803-5556	803-3237	454
Downey High School 11040 Brookshire Ave Downey CA 90241 *Web:* www.dusd.net	562-869-7301		685
Downey Inc 2203 W Michigan St Milwaukee WI 53233	414-933-3123		189-10
Downey Mcgrath Group Inc 1225 I St NW Ste 600 Washington DC 20005	202-789-1110		636
Downey Publishing Inc 2545 E Southlake Blvd Southlake TX 76092 *Web:* downeypublishing.com	817-416-6661		637-6
Downey Regional Medical Ctr 11500 Brookshire Ave Downey CA 90241 *TF:* 800-954-8000 ■ *Web:* pihhealth.org	562-904-5000		374-3
Downing Displays Inc 550 Techne Ctr Dr Milford OH 45150 *TF:* 800-883-1800 ■ *Web:* www.downingdisplays.com	513-248-9800	248-2605	232
Downing Heating & Air Conditioning Inc 3070 Kerner Blvd Ste K San Rafael CA 94901 *Web:* downinghvac.com	415-485-1011		189-10
Downing Partners Inc 5150 E Yale Cir Denver CO 80222	303-830-6622		360-3
Downing Planetarium 5320 N Maple Ave MS DP132 California State University Fresno Fresno CA 93740 *Web:* www.fresnostate.edu	559-278-4121	278-4070	598
Downing Wellhead Equipment Inc 8528 S W Second St Oklahoma City OK 73128 *Web:* www.downingwell.com	405-789-8182		539
Down-Lite International Inc 8153 Duke Blvd Mason OH 45040 *Web:* www.downlite.com	513-229-3696		361
Downriver Grill 3315 W Northwest Blvd Spokane WA 99205 *Web:* www.downrivergrillspokane.com	509-323-1600		671
Downriver Refrigeration Supply Co 38170 N Executive Dr N Westland MI 48185 *Web:* www.downriversupply.com	734-728-0795		665
Downs Crane & Hoist Company Inc 8827 Juniper St Los Angeles CA 90002 *TF:* 800-748-5994 ■ *Web:* www.downscrane.com	323-589-6061	589-6066	470
Downs Tony Food Co 418 Benzel Ave SW Madelia MN 56062 *TF:* 800-967-2474 ■ *Web:* tonydownsfoods.com	507-642-3203		345
Downstream 1624 NW Johnson St Portland OR 97209 *Web:* www.downstream.com	503-226-1944		512
Downtown Aquarium 410 Bagby St & Memorial Dr Houston TX 77002 *Web:* www.aquariumrestaurants.com	713-223-3474		40
Downtown Aquarium - Denver 700 Water St Denver CO 80211 *Web:* www.aquariumrestaurants.com	303-561-4450		40
Downtown at the Gardens 11701 Lake Victoria Gardens Ave Ste 2203 Palm Beach Gardens FL 33410 *Web:* downtownatthegardens.com	561-340-1600		50-6
Downtown Athletic Store Inc 1180 Seminole Trail Ste 210 Charlottesville VA 22901 *TF:* 800-348-2649 ■ *Web:* www.downtownathletic.com	434-975-3696	975-2845	711
Downtown Austin Alliance 211 E Seventh St Ste 818 Austin TX 78701 *Web:* downtownaustin.com	512-469-1766		138
Downtown Cabaret Theatre 263 Golden Hill St Bridgeport CT 06604 *Web:* www.dtcab.com	203-576-1636		573-4
Downtown Digital Post 401 E Jefferson St Phoenix AZ 85004 *TF:* 800-275-8777 ■ *Web:* www.downtowndigitalpost.com	602-462-6464		514
Downtown Disney S Disneyland Dr Anaheim CA 92802 *Web:* disneyland.disney.go.com	714-781-4565		50-6
Downtown Erie Hotel 18 W 18th St Erie PA 16501 *TF:* 800-832-9101 ■ *Web:* www.downtownageriehotel.com	814-456-2961	456-7067	379
Downtown Grill 562 Mulberry St Ln Macon GA 31201 *Web:* www.macondowntowngrill.com	478-742-5999	742-9708	671
Downtown Grill & Brewery 424 S Gay St Knoxville TN 37902 *Web:* www.downtownbrewery.com	865-633-8111		671
Downtown Partners Chicago 200 E Randolph St Ste 3400 Chicago IL 60601 *Web:* www.downtownpartners.com	312-552-5800		7
Downtown Swimming Pool 324 Gold St Kingman AZ 86401 *Web:* www.downtowngrand.com	928-753-8155		706
Downtown Tempe Community 310 S Mill Ave Ste A-201 Tempe AZ 85281 *Web:* www.downtowntempe.com	480-355-6060	968-7882	460
Doxa Energy Ltd 777 Hornby St Ste 2080 Vancouver BC V6Z1S4 *Web:* www.doxaenergy.com	604-662-3692		536
DoxTek Inc 264 W Center St Orem UT 84057 *TF:* 877-705-7226 ■ *Web:* www.doxtek.com	877-705-7226		225
Doyle & Wachtstetter Inc 131 Commerce St Clute TX 77531 *Web:* www.dw-surveyor.com	979-265-3622		727
Doyle Mike (Rep D - PA) 239 Cannon Bldg Washington DC 20515 *Web:* doyle.house.gov	202-225-2135	225-3084	342-2
Doyle New York 175 E 87th St New York NY 10128 *Web:* doyle.com	212-427-2730	369-0892	520
Doyle Quane 571 Hartz Ave Danville CA 94526 *TF:* 800-785-9556 ■ *Web:* www.familylawgroup.com	925-314-2320		445
Doyle Security Systems Inc 792 Calkins Rd Rochester NY 14623 *TF:* 866-463-6953 ■ *Web:* godoyle.com	585-244-3400		692
Doyle Signs Inc 232 W IH- Rd Addison IL 60101 *Web:* www.doylesigns.com	630-543-9490	543-9493	701
Doylestown Hospital 595 W State St Doylestown PA 18901 *Web:* www.doylestownhealth.org	215-345-2200		374-3
Doyletech Corp 28 Thorncliff Pl Ste 201 Nepean ON K2H6L2	613-226-8900		463
Doyon Drilling Inc 11500 C St Ste 200 Anchorage AK 99515 *TF:* 800-478-9675 ■ *Web:* www.doyondrilling.com	907-563-5530		540
Doyon Ltd 1 Doyon Pl Ste 300 Fairbanks AK 99701 *TF:* 888-478-4755 ■ *Web:* www.doyon.com	907-459-2000		536
Dozens 2180 S Havana St Aurora CO 80014 *Web:* www.dozensrestaurant.com	303-337-6627		671
Dozier, Miller, Pollard & Murphy LLP Cameron Brown Bldg 301 S McDowell St Ste 700 Charlotte NC 28204 *TF:* 800-231-8707 ■ *Web:* doziermillerlaw.com	704-372-6373		428
Dp Guardian Inc 2270 W Chenango Ave Unit 300 Littleton CO 80120 *Web:* www.dpguardian.com	303-783-0191		180
Dp Murphy Company Inc 945 Grand Blvd Deer Park NY 11729 *TF:* 800-424-8724 ■ *Web:* dpmurphy.com	631-673-9400		5

Name / Address	City	State	Zip	Phone	Fax	Class
DP Products Inc 2015 Stone Ave *Web:* www.dpprod.com	San Jose	CA	95125	408-299-0190		454
DP Solutions Inc 1508 S First St. *TF:* 800-367-7472 ■ *Web:* www.dpsol.com	Lufkin	TX	75901	936-637-7977		175
DP Technology Corp 1150 Avenida Acaso *TF:* 800-627-8479 ■ *Web:* www.espritcam.com	Camarillo	CA	93012	805-388-6000		178-5
D-Patrick Motoplex Inc 200 N Green River Rd *Web:* www.dpat.com	Evansville	IN	47715	812-473-6500		57
DPC DATA Inc 103 Eisenhower Pkwy Ste 300 *TF:* 800-996-4747 ■ *Web:* www.dpcdata.com	Roseland	NJ	07068	201-346-0701		174
DPE (Delta Pi Epsilon) 1914 Association Dr *Web:* www.dpe.org	Reston	VA	20191	501-219-1866		48-16
DPE Systems Inc 425 Pontius Ave N Ste 430 *TF:* 800-541-6566 ■ *Web:* www.dpes.com	Seattle	WA	98109	206-223-3737	223-0859	180
DPEC Capital Inc 135 Fifth Ave. *TF:* 844-574-3577 ■ *Web:* finra.org	New York	NY	10010	301-590-6500		405
DPF Data Services Group Inc 1990 Swarthmore Ave. *TF:* 800-431-4416 ■ *Web:* www.dpfdata.com	Lakewood	NJ	08701	732-370-8840	370-1751	225
Dpi Labs Inc 1350 Arrow Hwy *Web:* www5.dpilabs.com	La Verne	CA	91750	909-392-5777		647
dPi Teleconnect LLC 1330 Capital Pkwy	Carrollton	TX	75006	972-488-5500		224
DPIS Engineering LLC 1600 E Hufsmith Rd *Web:* www.dpis.ws	Tomball	TX	77375	281-351-0048		261
dpiX LLC 1635 Aeroplaza Dr *TF:* 800-377-7765 ■ *Web:* www.dpix.com	Colorado Springs	CO	80916	719-457-7700		407
DPL Inc 1065 Woodman Dr. *NYSE:* DPL ■ *TF:* 800-433-8500 ■ *Web:* www.dplinc.com	Dayton	OH	45432	800-736-3001		360-5
DPL Wireless 53 Clark Rd *TF:* 800-561-8880 ■ *Web:* www.dpl.ca	Rothesay	NB	E2E2K9	506-847-2347	847-2348	387
Dployit Inc 14673 Midway Rd Ste 108 *Web:* www.dployit.com	Addison	TX	75001	214-550-6124		260
DPM Consulting Services Inc 507 E Maple Rd *Web:* www.dpmcs.com	Troy	MI	48083	248-740-8735		196
DPMO (Defense Prisoner of War/Missing Personnel Office) 2600 Defense Pentagon *Web:* www.dpaa.mil	Washington	DC	20301	703-699-1169		340-3
DPNM (New Mexico Democratic Party) 8214 Second St NW ste A *Web:* www.dpnm.net	Albuquerque	NM	87114	505-830-3650	830-3645	616-1
dPoint Technologies Inc 1455 E Georgia St Ste 330 *Web:* www.dpoint.ca	Vancouver	BC	V5L2A9	604-488-1132		610
DPR Construction Inc 1450 Veterans Blvd *TF:* 800-807-0336 ■ *Web:* www.dpr.com	Redwood City	CA	94063	650-474-1450	474-1451	186
DPRA Inc 200 Research Dr *Web:* www.dpra.com	Manhattan	KS	66503	785-539-3565		192
DPS Printing Service Inc 3500 S Blvd St 38c *TF:* 800-780-4707 ■ *Web:* www.dpsprinting.com	Edmond	OK	73013	405-340-0004		627
DPSI Inc 1801 Stanley Rd Ste 301 *TF:* 800-897-7233 ■ *Web:* www.dpsi.com	Greensboro	NC	27407	336-854-7700	854-7715	170-11
DPT Laboratories Ltd 318 McCullough *TF:* 866-225-5378 ■ *Web:* www.dptlabs.com	San Antonio	TX	78215	210-476-8150		582
Dr Delphinium Designs & Events 5806 W Lovers Ln & Tollway *TF:* 800-783-0790 ■ *Web:* www.drdelphinium.com	Dallas	TX	75225	214-522-9911	525-1240	292
Dr FirstCom Inc 9420 Key W Ave Ste 230 *Web:* drfirst.com	Rockville	MD	20850	301-231-9510		180
Dr Fresh Inc 6645 Caballero Blvd *TF:* 866-373-7371 ■ *Web:* www.drfreshdental.com	Buena Park	CA	90620	714-690-1573		475
Dr Georges L Dumont Regional Hospital 330 University Ave *TF:* 800-442-9799 ■ *Web:* vitalitenb.ca	Moncton	NB	E2A1A9	506-862-4000		374-2
DR Horton Inc 301 Commerce St Ste 500 *NYSE:* DHI ■ *TF:* 800-846-7866 ■ *Web:* www.drhorton.com	Fort Worth	TX	76102	817-390-8200		653
DR Johnson Lumber Co 1991 Pruner Rd PO Box 66 *Web:* www.drjlumber.com	Riddle	OR	97469	541-874-2231		683
Dr Pepper Museum & Free Enterprise Institute, The 300 S Fifth St *TF:* 800-745-3000 ■ *Web:* www.drpeppermuseum.com	Waco	TX	76701	254-757-1025		522
Dr Pepper/Seven-Up Inc 5301 Legacy Dr **Fax:* Hum Res ■ *TF:* 800-696-5891 ■ *Web:* www.drpeppersnapplegroup.com	Plano	TX	75024	972-673-7000	673-7000*	80-2
Dr Reddy's Laboratories Inc 200 Summerset Corporate Blvd *NYSE:* RDY ■ *Web:* www.drreddys.com	Bridgewater	NJ	08807	908-203-4900		582
DR Sperry & Co 623 Rathbone Ave *TF:* 888-997-9297 ■ *Web:* www.drsperry.com	Aurora	IL	60506	630-892-4361	892-1664	456
Dr Sun Yat-Sen Classical Chinese Garden 578 Carrall St *Web:* www.vancouverchinesegarden.com	Vancouver	BC	V6B5K2	604-662-3207	682-4008	97
Dr Tavel Optical Group 2839 Lafayette Rd *Web:* www.drtavel.com	Indianapolis	IN	46222	317-924-1300		543
Dr Thomas Walker State Historic Site 4929 KY 459 *Web:* www.parks.ky.gov	Barbourville	KY	40906	606-546-4400		565
Dr Vinyl & Assoc Ltd 1350 SE Hamblen Rd *TF General:* 800-531-6600 ■ *Web:* www.drvinyl.com	Lees Summit	MO	64081	816-525-6060		62-1
Dr Wilkinson's Hot Springs Resort 1507 Lincoln Ave *Web:* www.drwilkinson.com	Calistoga	CA	94515	707-942-4102	942-4412	669
Dr Willella Howe-Waffle House & Medical Museum 120 Civic Ctr Dr *Web:* www.santaanahistory.com	Santa Ana	CA	92701	714-547-9645		520
Dr. Denim Inc 1136 Market St *Web:* www.drdenimjeans.com/us	Philadelphia	PA	19107	215-564-5152	564-2984	157-3
Dr. Edmund A Babler Memorial State Park 800 Guy Pk Dr *Web:* www.mostateparks.com	Wildwood	MO	63005	636-458-3813		565
Dr. Sinatra 95 Old Shoals Rd *TF:* 800-304-1708 ■ *Web:* www.drsinatra.com	Arden	NC	28704	800-304-1708		531-8
Dr.King's by King Bio 3 Westside Dr **Fax Area Code:* 828 ■ *TF:* 800-237-4100 ■ *Web:* www.drkings.com/en	Asheville	NC	28806	800-725-9763	255-0940*	582
Drabinsky Gallery 114 Yorkville Ave.	Toronto	ON	M5R1B9	416-324-5766		42
DRADA (Depression & Related Affective Disorders Assn) 8201 Greensboro Dr Ste 300	McLean	VA	22102	703-610-9026		49-15
Draeger Medical Inc 3135 Quarry Rd **Fax Area Code:* 215 ■ *TF:* 800-437-2437 ■ *Web:* www.draeger.com	Telford	PA	18969	800-437-2437	723-5935*	250
Draeger's Super Markets Inc 222 E Fourth Ave *Web:* www.draegers.com	San Mateo	CA	94401	650-685-3715	244-6548	345
Drago Supply Co 740 Houston Ave **Fax:* Sales ■ *TF:* 877-609-7975 ■ *Web:* www.dragosupply.com	Port Arthur	TX	77640	409-983-4911	985-6542*	385
Drago's 3232 N Arnoult Rd *Web:* www.dragosrestaurant.com	Metairie	LA	70002	504-888-9254		671
Dragon Chinese Restaurant 3261 W Third St	Bloomington	IN	47404	812-332-6610		671
Dragon Claw USA Inc 16033 Arrow Hwy *TF:* 800-238-5296 ■ *Web:* www.dcamerica.net	Irwindale	CA	91706	626-480-0068	480-0018	276
Dragon King 1401 NE 78th St *Web:* dragonking78.com	Vancouver	WA	98665	360-574-6684		671
Dragon Products Co 960 Ocean Ave	Portland	ME	04103	207-879-2328		135
Dragonfly Capital Partners LLC The Packard Bldg 1310 S Tryon St Ste 109 *Web:* www.dragonflycapital.com	Charlotte	NC	28203	704-342-3491		401
Dragonfly Technologies 48 Wall St Ste 1100 *Web:* www.dragonflytech.com	New York	NY	10005	212-713-5250		113
Drahota Commercial LLC 4700 Innovation Dr Bldg C *Web:* www.drahota.com	Fort Collins	CO	80525	970-204-0100		186
Drain-All Inc 1170 Topside Rd *Web:* www.drain-all.com	Louisville	TN	37777	865-970-9290		789
Drais Pharmaceuticals Inc 520 US Hwy 22 Ste 201 *Web:* www.draispharma.com	Bridgewater	NJ	08807	908-895-1200		238
Drake Capital Advisors LLC 1 Fawcett Pl Ste 140 *Web:* www.drakeadvisors.com	Greenwich	CT	06830	203-861-7500		401
Drake College of Business 125 Broad St Fl 2	Elizabeth	NJ	07201	908-352-5509		166
Drake Commercial Lp 19310 Stone Oak Pkwy Ste 201 *Web:* drakecommercial.com	San Antonio	TX	78258	210-402-6363		652
Drake Corp 916 Jeffco Executive Dr *Web:* www.draketools.com	Imperial	MO	63052	636-464-5070		273
Drake Ctr 151 W Galbraith Rd *TF:* 800-948-0003 ■ *Web:* www.uchealth.com/danieldrakecenter	Cincinnati	OH	45216	513-418-2500		374-6
Drake Hotel, The 140 E Walton Pl *TF:* 800-553-7253 ■ *Web:* www.thedrakehotel.com	Chicago	IL	60611	312-787-2200	787-1431	379
Drake Petroleum Co Inc 221 Quinebaug Rd *TF:* 800-243-6366 ■ *Web:* www.drakepetro.com	North Grosvenordale	CT	06255	800-243-6366		579
Drake Software 235 E Palmer St. **Fax Area Code:* 828 ■ *TF:* 800-890-9500 ■ *Web:* www.drakesoftware.com	Franklin	NC	28734	800-890-9500	369-9928*	178-1
Drake University 2507 University Ave *TF:* 800-443-7253 ■ *Web:* www.drake.edu	Des Moines	IA	50311	515-271-3181	271-2831	166
Drake University Cowles Library 2507 University Ave *Web:* www.library.drake.edu	Des Moines	IA	50311	515-271-2111	271-3933	434-6
Drake University School of Law 2507 University Ave *TF:* 800-443-7253 ■ *Web:* www.law.drake.edu	Des Moines	IA	50311	515-271-2824	271-1958	167-1
Drake, Loeb, Heller, Kennedy, Gogerty, Gaba, Rodd PLLC 555 Hudson Vly Ave Ste 100 *Web:* www.drakeloeb.com	New Windsor	NY	12553	845-561-0550		428
Drake-Scruggs Equipment Inc 2000 S Dirksen Pkwy *TF:* 877-799-0398 ■ *Web:* www.drake-scruggs.com	Springfield	IL	62703	217-753-3871	753-2760	470
Drama Book Shop Inc 250 W 40th St. *TF:* 800-322-0595 ■ *Web:* www.dramabookshop.com	New York	NY	10018	212-944-0595	730-8739	95
Dramatics Magazine 2343 Auburn Ave *TF:* 800-848-2263 ■ *Web:* www.schooltheatre.org	Cincinnati	OH	45219	513-421-3900	421-7077	457-9
Dramatists Guild of America Inc 1501 Broadway Ste 701 *TF:* 800-289-9366 ■ *Web:* www.dramatistsguild.com	New York	NY	10036	212-398-9366	944-0420	48-4
Dramm & Echter Inc 1150 Quail Gardens Dr *TF:* 800-854-7021 ■ *Web:* www.drammechter.com	Encinitas	CA	92024	760-436-0188	436-2974	369
Dranetz-BMI 1000 New Durham Rd *TF:* 800-372-6832 ■ *Web:* www.dranetz.com	Edison	NJ	08818	732-287-3680	248-1834	248
Draper & Kramer Inc 55 E Monroe St Ste 3900 *Web:* www.draperandkramer.com	Chicago	IL	60603	312-346-8600	346-8600	655
Draper & Mcginley Pa 365 W Patrick St 1st Fl *Web:* www.drapermcginleypa.com	Frederick	MD	21701	301-694-7411	694-0954	2
Draper Aden Assoc Inc 2206 S Main St *Web:* www.daa.com	Blacksburg	VA	24060	540-552-0444	552-0291	192
Draper Fisher Jurvetson (DFJ) 2882 Sand Hill Rd Ste 150 *Web:* www.dfj.com	Menlo Park	CA	94025	650-233-9000		792
Draper Knitting Co 28 Draper Ln *TF:* 800-808-7707 ■ *Web:* www.draperknitting.com	Canton	MA	02021	781-828-0029	828-3034	745-4
Draper Shade & Screen Co 411 S Pearl St *TF:* 800-238-7999 ■ *Web:* www.draperinc.com	Spiceland	IN	47385	765-987-7999	987-7999	591
Draper Valley Farms Inc 1000 Jason Ln *Web:* www.drapervalleyfarms.com	Mount Vernon	WA	98273	360-424-7947		619

	Phone	Fax	Class
Drapers & Damons 9 Pasteur Ste 200............. Irvine CA 92618 *TF:* 800-843-1174 ■ *Web:* drapers.blair.com	800-843-1174		157-6
DRAXIMAGE Inc 16751 Transcanada Hwy........ Kirkland QC H9H4J4 *TF:* 888-633-5343 ■ *Web:* www.draximage.com	514-630-7080		238
Drayton Group 2295 N Opdyke Rd Ste D .... Auburn Hills MI 48326 *TF:* 888-655-4442 ■ *Web:* www.draytongroupinc.com	888-655-4442		104
Drayton, Drayton & Lamar Inc 616 Ponder Pl Dr Ste 2......................... Evans GA 30809 *TF:* 800-522-9226 ■ *Web:* www.ddlinc.com	706-854-1145		180
DRCoC (Del Rio Chamber of Commerce) 1915 Veterans Blvd.......................... Del Rio TX 78840 *TF General:* 877-218-5117 ■ *Web:* www.drchamber.com	830-775-3551	774-1813	139
DRE Inc 1800 Williamson Ct.................. Louisville KY 40223 *Web:* www.dremed.com	502-244-4444		475
Dream 210 W 55th St .... New York NY 10019 *Web:* www.dreamhotels.com	212-247-2000		379
Dream Local Digital LTD 463 Main St Rockland .... Thomaston ME 04841 **Fax Area Code:* 415 ■ *Web:* www.dreamlocal.com	207-593-7665	924-9993*	5
Dream Vision Studios Las Vegas LLC 4544 W Russell Rd Ste J .... Las Vegas NV 89118 *Web:* www.dreamvisionstudios.com	702-586-7335		514
Dreamentia Inc 453 S Spring St Ste 1101................. Los Angeles CA 90013 *Web:* www.dreamentia.com	213-347-6000		7
Dreamgear LLC 20001 S Western Ave........... Torrance CA 90501 *Web:* www.dreamgear.com	310-222-5522	222-5577	52
DreamJobs 6545 W Central Ave Ste 102 .... Toledo OH 43617 *Web:* www.dreamjobsna.com	567-455-5500		260
Dreamland Bar-B-que 5535 15th Ave E......................... Tuscaloosa AL 35405 *Web:* www.dreamlandbbq.com	205-758-8135		671
Dreamland Bar-B-Que Ribs 12 W Jefferson St...................... Montgomery AL 36104 *Web:* www.dreamlandbbq.com	334-273-7427		671
Dreamland Bar-B-Que Ribs 3855 University Dr .... Huntsville AL 35816 *Web:* www.dreamlandbbq.com	256-539-7427		671
Dreamland BBQ 1427 14th Ave S .... Birmingham AL 35205 *TF:* 800-752-0544 ■ *Web:* www.dreamlandbbq.com	205-933-2133		671
Dreamline Mfg Inc 1514 S Second St PO Box 1250.................. Cabot AR 72023 *TF:* 800-888-3585 ■ *Web:* www.dreamlinebedding.com	501-843-3585		471
DreamMaker Bath & Kitchen by Worldwide 510 N Valley Mills Dr Ste 304 .... Waco TX 76710 *TF:* 800-583-2133 ■ *Web:* www.dreammaker-remodel.com	800-583-2133		189-11
Dreamspan Product Innovation LLC 11645 N Cave Creek Rd .... Phoenix AZ 85020 *Web:* www.dreamspan.com	602-354-7640		195
Dreamstime LLC 1616 Wgate Cir .... Brentwood TN 37027 *Web:* www.dreamstime.com	615-771-5611		588
Dreamtime Inc 1115 Thompson Ave Ste 5 .... Santa Cruz CA 95062 *Web:* www.dreamtimeinc.com	831-464-6702		361
Dreamworks Animation LLC 1000 Flower St .... Glendale CA 91201 *Web:* www.dreamworks.com	818-695-5000		514
Dreamworld Backdrops 6450 Lusk Blvd Ste E-106 .... San Diego CA 92121 *TF:* 800-737-9869 ■ *Web:* www.dreamworldbackdrops.com	800-737-9869		722
Dreco Inc 7887 Root Rd................ North Ridgeville OH 44039 *Web:* www.drecoinc.com	440-327-6021		608
Drees Co 211 Grandview Dr .... Fort Mitchell KY 41017 *TF:* 866-265-2980 ■ *Web:* www.dreeshomes.com	859-578-4200	578-4200	187
Dreher Island State Recreation Area 3677 State Pk Rd .... Prosperity SC 29127 *TF:* 866-345-7275 ■ *Web:* www.southcarolinaparks.com	803-364-4152	364-0756	565
Dreher Langer & Tomkies LLP 41 S High St Ste 2250 .... Columbus OH 43215 *Web:* www.dltlaw.com	614-628-8000		428
Dreison International Inc 4540 W 160th St.......................... Cleveland OH 44135 *Web:* www.dreison.com	216-265-8006		60
Dremel Inc 4915 21st St....................... Racine WI 53406 *TF:* 800-437-3635 ■ *Web:* www.dremel.com	262-554-1390	554-7654	759
Drent Goebel North America Inc 2583 Chomedey Blvd .... Laval QC H7T2R2 *Web:* www.rdpmarathon.com	450-687-7262		628
Dresick Farms Inc PO Box 1260 .... Huron CA 93234	559-945-2513		10-11
Dresner Partners 20 N Clark St Ste 3550...................... Chicago IL 60602 *Web:* www.dresnerpartners.com	312-726-3600		690
Dress for Success Worldwide 32 E 31st St 7th Fl .... New York NY 10016 *Web:* www.dressforsuccess.org	212-532-1922		48-5
Dresser & Associates Inc 243 US Route 1 .... Scarborough ME 04074 *TF:* 866-885-7212 ■ *Web:* www.dresserassociates.com	207-885-0809		463
Dresser-Rand 10205 Westheimer Rd W 8 Twr Ste 1000 .... Houston TX 77042 *NYSE: DRC* ■ *TF:* 800-732-0330 ■ *Web:* www.dresser-rand.com	713-354-6100	354-6110	386
Dresser-Rand Co Paul Clark Dr PO Box 560......... Olean NY 14760 *Web:* www.dresser-rand.com	716-375-3000	375-3178	172
Dresser-Rand Co Reciprocating Products Div 100 Chemung St......................... Painted Post NY 14870 *Web:* www.dresser-rand.com	713-354-6100		172
Dresser-Rand Control Systems 1202 W Sam Houston Pkwy N................. Houston TX 77043 *Web:* www.dresser-rand.com/products/controls	713-365-2630		262
Dresser-Rand Steam Turbines 10205 Westheimer Rd......................... Houston TX 77042 *Web:* www.dresser-rand.com	713-354-6100	354-6110	262
Dressler Assoc 624 University Ave .... Palo Alto CA 94301	650-323-0456		721
Dreumex USA 3445 BoaRd Rd....................... York PA 17406 *TF:* 800-233-9382 ■ *Web:* www.dreumex.com/us	717-767-6881		151
Drew & Rogers Inc 30 Plymouth St .... Fairfield NJ 07004 *TF:* 800-610-6210 ■ *Web:* www.drewandrogers.com	973-575-6210		627
Drew County 210 S Main St................. Monticello AR 71655	870-460-6200		338

	Phone	Fax	Class
Drew Eckl & Farnham LLP 303 Peachtree St NE Ste 3500 .... Atlanta GA 30308 *Web:* www.deflaw.com	404-885-1400	876-0992	445
Drew Scientific Inc/ M W I Inc 4230 Shilling Way .... Dallas TX 75237 *Web:* www.drew-scientific.com	214-210-4900		153
Drew Shoe Corp 252 Quarry Rd................ Lancaster OH 43130 *TF:* 800-837-3739 ■ *Web:* www.drewshoe.com	740-653-4271		301
Drew University 36 Madison Ave .... Madison NJ 07940 **Fax:* Admissions ■ *Web:* www.drew.edu	973-408-3000	408-3068*	166
Drew University Theological School 36 Madison Ave .... Madison NJ 07940 *Web:* www.drew.edu	973-408-3258	408-3068	167-3
Drew Wireless 459 Collindale Ave NW.................... Grand Rapids MI 49504 *TF:* 800-322-1446 ■ *Web:* www.drewwireless.com	616-453-7200		194
Drexel Chemical Co 1700 Ch Ave PO Box 13327.................. Memphis TN 38113 *Web:* www.drexchem.com	901-774-4370	774-4666	280
Drexel University 3141 Chestnut St .... Philadelphia PA 19104 **Fax:* Admissions ■ *TF Admissions:* 866-358-1010 ■ *Web:* www.drexel.edu	215-895-2000	895-5939*	166
Drexel University College of Medicine 2900 Queen Ln........................... Philadelphia PA 19129 *Web:* www.drexel.edu/medicine	215-991-8202	843-1766	167-2
Drexel University Hagerty Library 33rd St & Market St .... Philadelphia PA 19104 *TF:* 888-278-8825 ■ *Web:* www.library.drexel.edu	215-895-2767	895-2070	434-6
Dreyco Inc 263 Veterans Blvd .... Carlstadt NJ 07072 *Web:* www.dreycoinc.com	201-896-9000		61
Dreyer's Grand Ice Cream Inc 5929 College Ave .... Oakland CA 94618 *Web:* dreyers.com	510-652-8187	601-4473	296-25
Dreyfus Ashby & Co 630 Third Ave 15th Fl .... New York NY 10017 *Web:* www.dreyfusashby.com	212-818-0770		80-3
Dreyfus Corp 200 Pk Ave.................... New York NY 10166 *Web:* public.dreyfus.com	212-495-1784		690
Dreyfus-Cortney & Lowery Bros Rigging 4400 N Galvez St .... New Orleans LA 70117 *TF:* 800-228-7660 ■ *Web:* www.dcl-usa.com	504-944-3366	947-8557	770
Dreyfuss Planetarium 49 Washington St.......... Newark NJ 07102 *TF:* 888-370-6765 ■ *Web:* www.newarkmuseum.org	973-596-6529	642-0459	598
DRF (Deafness Research Foundation) 641 Lexington Ave 15th Fl .... New York NY 10022 *Web:* hearinghealthfoundation.org	212-328-9480		48-17
DRG International Inc 841 Mountain Ave.......................... Springfield NJ 07081 *Web:* www.drg-international.com	973-564-7555		743
Drgreene.com 9000 Crow Canyon Rd Ste S220 .... Danville CA 94506 *Web:* www.drgreene.com	925-964-1793		356
DRHC (DiamondRock Hospitality Co) 3 Bethesda Metro Ctr Ste 1500............... Bethesda MD 20814 *NYSE: DRH* ■ *Web:* www.drhc.com	240-744-1150	744-1199	654
DRI (Defense Research Institute) 55 W Monroe St Ste 20 .... Chicago IL 60603 *Web:* www.dri.org	312-795-1101	795-0749	49-10
DRI (Darden Restaurants Inc) 1000 Darden Center Dr........................ Orlando FL 32837 *NYSE: DRI* ■ *Web:* www.darden.com	407-245-4000		670
DRI Consulting Inc 2 Otter Ln.............. North Oaks MN 55127 *Web:* www.dric.com	651-415-1400		463
Dri Mark Products Inc 999 S Oyster Bay Rd Ste 312 .... Bethpage NY 11714 *TF:* 800-645-9118 ■ *Web:* www.drimark.com	516-484-6200		571
Driehaus Capital Management Inc 25 E Erie St................................. Chicago IL 60611 *TF:* 800-688-8819 ■ *Web:* www.driehaus.com	312-587-3800		401
Driessen Water Inc 1690 Hwy 3 S .... Northfield MN 55057 *Web:* www.culliganiswater.com	507-645-6621		538
Driftwood Bay State Marine Park PO Box 1247 .... Soldotna AK 99669 *Web:* dnr.alaska.gov/parks/units/pwssmp/smpsewd.htm	907-262-5581		565
Driftwood Beach State Recreation Site 5580 S Coast Hwy .... Newport OR 97366 *TF:* 800-551-6949 ■ *Web:* www.oregonstateparks.org	800-551-6949		565
Driftwood Hospitality Management LLC 11770 US Hwy One Ste 202........... North Palm Beach FL 33408 *Web:* www.driftwoodhospitality.com	561-207-2700		379
Driftwood Hotel 435 Willoughby Ave .... Juneau AK 99801 *TF:* 800-544-2239 ■ *Web:* www.dhalaska.com	907-586-2280	586-1034	379
Driftwood Shores Resort 88416 First Ave............................ Florence OR 97439 *TF:* 800-422-5091 ■ *Web:* www.driftwoodshores.com	541-997-8263		379
Driggs Co LLC 8700 Ashwood Dr.......... Capitol Heights MD 20743 *Web:* www.driggs.net	301-350-4000		188-4
Drillers Service Inc 1792 Highland Ave NE .... Hickory NC 28601 *TF:* 800-334-2308 ■ *Web:* www.dsidsi.com	828-322-1100	322-7436	537
Drilling Structures International 2431 Kelly Ln............................... Houston TX 77066 *Web:* www.drillingstructuresintl.com	281-880-8833		537
Drilltec Technologies Inc 10875 Kempwood Ste 2 .... Houston TX 77043 *Web:* www.drilltec.com	713-895-9852		539
Dril-Quip Inc 13550 Hempstead Hwy............. Houston TX 77040 *NYSE: DRQ* ■ *TF:* 877-316-2631 ■ *Web:* www.dril-quip.com	713-939-7711	939-8063	537
Drink More Water Store 7595-A Rickenbacker Dr................ Gaithersburg MD 20879 *TF:* 800-697-2070 ■ *Web:* www.drinkmorewater.com	800-697-2070		14
Drinker Biddle & Reath LLP 1 Logan Sq Ste 2000 .... Philadelphia PA 19103 *Web:* www.drinkerbiddle.com	215-988-2700	988-2757	428
DRIP Investor 7412 Calumet Ave............. Hammond IN 46324 *TF:* 800-233-5922 ■ *Web:* www.dripinvestor.com	219-852-3200	931-6487	531-9
Dripping Springs State Park 16830 Dripping Springs Rd .... Okmulgee OK 74447 *TF:* 800-622-6317 ■ *Web:* www.travelok.com/listings/view.profile/id.2368	918-756-5971	759-9933	565

Phone | Fax | Class

Driptech Inc
2580 Wyandotte St Ste B ....Mountain View CA 94043 415-793-6735 273
Web: www.driptech.com

Dri-Rite Co
11600 S Ave O PO Box 170319 ....Chicago IL 60617 773-409-4127 221-2909 500
Web: www.dririte.com

Driscoll Children's Hospital
3533 S Alameda St......................Corpus Christi TX 78411 361-694-5000 374-1
TF: 800-324-5683 ■ *Web:* www.driscollchildrens.org

Driscoll Strawberry Assoc Inc
345 Westridge Dr........................Watsonville CA 95077 800-871-3333 315-1
TF: 800-871-3333 ■ *Web:* www.driscolls.com

Driskill Grill 604 Brazos St......................Austin TX 78701 512-391-7162 391-7059 671
Web: www.driskillgrill.com

Driskill Hotel 604 Brazos St......................Austin TX 78701 512-474-5911 474-2214 379
TF: 800-252-9367 ■ *Web:* www.driskillhotel.com

DRISTEEM Corp
14949 Technology Dr.....................Eden Prairie MN 55344 952-949-2415 229-3200 14
TF: 800-328-4447 ■ *Web:* www.dristeem.com

Drive Products Income Fund
1665 Shawson Dr.......................Mississauga ON L4W1T7 905-564-5800 61
Web: www.driveproducts.com

Drive Thru Technology Inc
1755 N Main St ....Los Angeles CA 90031 866-388-7877 173-2
TF: 800-933-8388 ■ *Web:* www.dttusa.com

Drive Train Industries Inc
5555 Joliet St...............................Denver CO 80239 303-292-5176 297-0473 61
TF: 800-525-6177 ■ *Web:* www.drivetrainindustries.com

Drivekore Inc 101 Wesley Dr.............Mechanicsburg PA 17055 717-697-7440 350
TF: 800-382-1311 ■ *Web:* www.drivekore.com

Driveline Holdings Inc
700 Freeport Pkwy Ste 100..................Coppell TX 75019 888-824-7505 195
TF: 888-824-7505 ■ *Web:* www.drivelineretail.com

DrivenBI LLC 221 E Walnut St Ste 229..........Pasadena CA 91101 626-795-2088 177
Web: www.drivenbi.com

DriverDO LLC
9393 W 110th St Ste 500................Overland Park KS 66210 844-366-6837 224
TF: 844-366-6837 ■ *Web:* www.driverdo.com

Drivers License Guide Co
1492 Oddstad Dr......................Redwood City CA 94063 650-369-4849 364-8740 637-10
TF: 800-227-8827 ■ *Web:* www.driverslicenseguide.com

Drivers Village 5885 E Cir Dr...................Cicero NY 13039 315-699-3846 57
Web: burdickdodgechryslerjeep.com

Drivestaff 114 N Hale St Ste 208..............Wheaton IL 60187 630-941-3748 260
Web: www.drivestaff.com

DriveTime Corp
4020 E Indian School Rd ....Phoenix AZ 85018 888-418-1212 57
TF: 888-418-1212 ■ *Web:* www.drivetime.com

Driving Force Inc, The 60 King Rd ....Inuvik NT X0E0T0 867-777-2346 126
Web: www.drivingforce.ca

Driving Records Facilities
PO Box 1086 ....Glen Burnie MD 21061 800-772-5510 635
TF: 800-772-5510 ■ *Web:* www.dr-rec-fac.com

DrivingSales LLC
8871 S Sandy Pkwy Ste 250....................Sandy UT 84070 866-943-8371 387
TF: 866-943-8371 ■ *Web:* www.drivingsales.com

Driv-Lok Inc 1140 Park Ave..................Sycamore IL 60178 815-895-8161 350
Web: www.driv-lok.com

DRM Inc 5324 N 134th Ave......................Omaha NE 68164 402-556-4098 573-0171 670
Web: www.drmarbys.com

DRM LLC 520 Crews St...................Lawrenceburg TN 38464 931-766-4500 610
Web: www.drmcontrols.com

DRMC (Delta Regional Medical Ctr)
1400 E Union St..........................Greenville MS 38703 662-378-3783 374-3
Web: www.deltaregional.com

DRMC (Dallas Regional Medical Ctr)
1011 N Galloway Ave.........................Mesquite TX 75149 214-320-7000 289-9468* 374-3
**Fax Area Code:* 972 ■ *TF:* 800-562-6686 ■ *Web:* www.dallasregionalmedicalcenter.com

DRMP (Dyer Riddle Mills & Precourt Inc)
941 Lake Baldwin Ln ....Orlando FL 32814 407-896-0594 896-4836 261
TF: 800-375-3767 ■ *Web:* www.drmp.com

Droege Computing Services Inc
20 W Colony Pl Ste 120......................Durham NC 27705 919-403-9459 177
Web: droegecomputing.com

Droga5 120 Wall St 11th Fl....................New York NY 10005 917-237-8888 5
Web: www.droga5.com

Drohan Management Group (DMG)
11130 Sunrise Valley Dr Ste 350 ....Reston VA 20191 703-437-4377 435-4390 47
Web: www.drohanmgmt.com

Droop Mountain Battlefield State Park
683 Droop Park Rd.........................Hillsboro WV 24946 304-653-4254 653-4254 565
Web: www.droopmountainbattlefield.com

Dropbox Inc 401 S Ninth St....................Ironton OH 45638 888-388-7768 480
TF: 888-388-7768 ■ *Web:* www.dropboxinc.com

DropThought Inc
2755 Great America Way Ste 425............Santa Clara CA 95054 855-437-6776 5
TF: 855-437-6776 ■ *Web:* www.dropthought.com

Droste Consultants Inc
140 Willow St........................North Andover MA 01845 978-686-5775 177
Web: www.droste1.com

Drowsy Water Ranch PO Box 147...............Granby CO 80446 970-725-3456 239
TF: 800-845-2292 ■ *Web:* www.drowsywater.com

Drs Mobile Environmental Systemsinc
4043 Mcmann Rd........................Cincinnati OH 45245 513-943-7189 779
Web: www.drs-mes.com

Drs Technologies-Marlo Coil
6060 Highway Pp.........................High Ridge MO 63049 636-677-6600 14
Web: www.drs.com

DRT Strategies Inc
4245 N Fairfax Dr Ste 800 ....Arlington VA 22203 571-482-2500 196
Web: www.drtstrategies.com

Drug Chemical & Associated Technologies Assn (DCAT)
1 Washington Blvd Ste 7 ....Robbinsville NJ 08691 609-448-1000 49-19
TF: 800-640-3228 ■ *Web:* www.dcat.org

Drug Detection Laboratories Inc
9700 Business Pk Dr Ste 407...............Sacramento CA 95827 916-366-3113 366-3917 416
Web: www.drugdetection.net

Drug Enforcement Administration (DEA)
700 Army-Navy Dr ....Arlington VA 22202 202-307-7596 340-14
Web: www.justice.gov
DEA Training Academy PO Box 1475...........Quantico VA 22134 202-353-1555 340-14
Web: justice.gov
El Paso Intelligence Ctr
11339 Simms St ....El Paso TX 79908 202-307-1000 340-14
Web: www.justice.gov

Drug Enforcement Administration Museum & Visitors Ctr
700 Army Navy Dr ....Arlington VA 22202 202-307-3463 307-8956 520
Web: www.deamuseum.org

Drug Enforcement Administration Regional Offices
Atlanta Div
Federal Bldg 75 Spring St SW................Atlanta GA 30303 404-893-7000 340-14
Web: www.justice.gov
Boston Div 15 New Sudbury St Rm E400 ....Boston MA 02203 617-557-2100 340-14
Web: www.justice.gov
Chicago Div
536 S Clark St 230 S Dearborn St............Chicago IL 60605 312-353-3640 340-14
Web: www.justice.gov
Dallas Div 10160 Technology Blvd E.............Dallas TX 75220 214-366-6900 340-14
TF: 800-882-9539 ■ *Web:* www.justice.gov
Detroit Div 431 Howard St....................Detroit MI 48226 313-234-4000 340-14
TF: 800-332-4288 ■ *Web:* www.justice.gov
Houston Div 1433 W Loop S Ste 600 ....Houston TX 77027 713-693-3000 340-14
TF: 800-332-4288 ■ *Web:* www.justice.gov
Los Angeles Div
255 E Temple St 17th Fl 17th Fl..........Los Angeles CA 90012 213-621-6700 340-14
Web: www.justice.gov
New Orleans Div
3838 N Cswy Blvd Ste 1800 ....Metairie LA 70002 504-840-1100 340-14
Web: www.justice.gov
New York Div 99 Tenth Ave ....New York NY 10011 212-337-3900 340-14
Web: www.justice.gov
Philadelphia Div
Federal Bldg 600 Arch St Rm 10224 ....Philadelphia PA 19106 215-861-3474 340-14
Web: www.justice.gov
Phoenix Div 3010 N Second St Ste 301 ....Phoenix AZ 85012 602-664-5600 340-14
Web: www.justice.gov
Saint Louis Div 317 S 16th St..............Saint Louis MO 63103 314-538-4600 340-14
Web: www.justice.gov
San Diego Div 4560 Viewridge Ave..........San Diego CA 92123 858-616-4100 340-14
TF: 800-332-4288 ■ *Web:* www.justice.gov
San Francisco Div
450 Golden Gate Ave.................San Francisco CA 94102 415-436-7900 340-14
Web: www.justice.gov
Seattle Div 400 Second Ave W..................Seattle WA 98119 206-553-5443 340-14
Web: www.justice.gov
Washington DC Div
800 K St NW Ste 500..................Washington DC 20001 202-305-8500 514-1009 340-14
TF: 800-488-3111 ■ *Web:* www.justice.gov

Drug Package Inc 901 Drug Package Ln ....O'Fallon MO 63366 800-325-6137 627
TF: 800-325-6137 ■ *Web:* www.drugpackage.com

Drug Plastics & Glass Company Inc
1 Bottle Dr ....Boyertown PA 19512 610-367-5000 367-9800 98
Web: www.drugplastics.com

Drug Policy Alliance
70 W 36th St 16th Fl........................New York NY 10018 212-613-8020 613-8021 48-8
Web: www.drugpolicy.org

Drug Topics Magazine
24950 Country Club Blvd Ste 200 ....North Olmsted OH 44070 440-891-2792 891-2735 457-5
TF Cust Svc: 877-922-2022 ■ *Web:* drugtopics.modernmedicine.com

DrugLogic Inc
11490 Commerce Park Dr Ste 540...............Reston VA 20191 703-821-3200 194
Web: www.druglogic.com

DrugScan Inc
200 Precision Rd Ste 200 PO Box 347..........Horsham PA 19044 800-235-4890 416
TF: 800-235-4890 ■ *Web:* www.drugscan.com

Druide informatique Inc
1435 rue Saint-Alexandre Bureau 1040 ....Montreal QC H3A2G4 514-484-4998 180
TF: 800-537-8433 ■ *Web:* www.druide.com

Druley Enterprises Inc
3305 N Anthony Blvd ....Fort Wayne IN 46805 260-424-4604 443
Web: www.belmontbev.com

Drum Corps International (DCI)
PO Box 3129 ....Indianapolis IN 46206 317-275-1212 713-0690 48-4
TF Orders: 800-495-7469 ■ *Web:* www.dci.org

Drum Creative 35 Cessna Ct.................Greenville SC 29607 864-254-6096 344
TF: 800-261-1537 ■ *Web:* drumcreative.com

Drummac Inc
1361 13th Ave S Ste 135 ....Jacksonville FL 32250 904-241-4999 393
Web: www.drummac.com

Drummer Online & Wright County Journal Press, The
108 Central Ave ....Buffalo MN 55313 763-682-1221 532-3
TF: 800-880-5047 ■ *Web:* www.thedrummer.com

Drummond Co Inc PO Box 10246............Birmingham AL 35202 205-945-6300 501
Web: www.drummondco.com

Drummond Press Inc, The
2472 Dennis St..........................Jacksonville FL 32204 904-354-2818 627

Drummond Printing Inc
2114 S Main St.............................Stuttgart AR 72160 870-673-2726 627
Web: www.drum-line.com

Drummond Woodsum LLP
84 Marginal Way Ste 600.....................Portland ME 04101 207-772-1941 428
Web: www.dwmlaw.com

Drumtech Inc 5200 Manchester Ave ....St. Louis MO 63110 314-647-3464 198
Web: www.drumtechus.com

Drury Capital Inc
47 Hulfish St Ste 340........................Princeton NJ 08542 609-252-1230 791
Web: www.drurycapital.com

Drury Co 4072 State Hwy K..............Cape Girardeau MO 63701 573-334-8271 186

Drury Design Dynamics Inc
49 W 27th St..............................New York NY 10001 212-213-4600 514
Web: www.drurydesign.com

Drury Hotels Company LLC
721 Emerson Rd Ste 400 ....Saint Louis MO 63141 314-429-2255 429-5166 379
TF: 800-378-7946 ■ *Web:* www.druryhotels.com

Drury University 900 N Benton Ave.............Springfield MO 65802 417-873-7879 866-3873 166
TF: 800-922-2274 ■ *Web:* www.drury.edu

	Phone	Fax	Class
Druva Software Inc 150 Mathilda Place, STE 450 ... Sunnyvale CA 94086 *TF:* 888-248-4976 ■ *Web:* www.druva.com	888-248-4976		387
DRW Trading Group 540 W Madison St Ste 2500 ... Chicago IL 60661 *Web:* www.drw.com	312-542-1000		690
Dry Cleaning Depot Inc 730 W Broward Blvd ... Fort Lauderdale FL 33312 *Web:* www.drycleaningdepot.com	954-522-3660		426
Dry Creek Products Inc 51 Edward St ... Arcade NY 14009 *Web:* www.drycreekproducts.com	585-492-2990		820
Dry Tortugas National Park PO Box 6208 ... Key West FL 33041 *TF:* 800-788-0511 ■ *Web:* www.nps.gov/drto	305-242-7700	242-7711	564
Dryclean USA Inc 290 NE 68th St ... Miami FL 33138 *Web:* www.drycleanusa.com	305-754-9966	754-8010	426
Drycleaning & Laundry Institute 14700 Sweitzer Ln ... Laurel MD 20707 **Fax Area Code:* 240 ■ *TF:* 800-638-2627 ■ *Web:* www.dlionline.org	301-622-1900	295-0685*	49-4
Dryden District Chamber of Commerce 284 Government St ... Dryden ON P8N2P3 *Web:* www.drydenchamber.ca	807-223-2622	223-2626	137
Dryden Municipal Telephone System 65 Princess St ... Dryden ON P8N1C8 *TF:* 800-668-6878 ■ *Web:* dmts.biz	807-223-1100		525
Dryhead Schively Ranch 1062 Rd 15 ... Lovell WY 82431 *Web:* www.dryheadranch.com	307-548-6688		239
Drymalla Construction Company Ltd 608 Harbert St PO Box 698 ... Columbus TX 78934 *Web:* www.drymalla.com	979-732-5731		186
Drysdales Inc 3220 S Memorial Dr ... Tulsa OK 74145 *TF:* 800-444-6481 ■ *Web:* www.drysdales.com	918-664-6481		328
Dryvit Systems Inc 1 Energy Way ... West Warwick RI 02893 *TF:* 800-556-7752 ■ *Web:* www.dryvit.com	401-822-4100	822-4510	389
Drywall Contractors Inc 2920 N Arlington Ave ... Indianapolis IN 46218 *Web:* www.drywallpartners.com	317-546-6605		189-9
DS & B Ltd 222 S Ninth St ... Minneapolis MN 55402 *Web:* dsb-cpa.com	612-359-9630		2
DS Brown Co 300 E Cherry St ... North Baltimore OH 45872 *TF:* 800-848-1730 ■ *Web:* www.dsbrown.com	419-257-3561	257-2200	191-2
D&S Communications Inc 1355 N Mclean Blvd ... Elgin IL 60123 *TF:* 800-227-8403 ■ *Web:* www.dscomm.com	847-468-8082		463
DS Containers Inc 1789 Hubbard Ave ... Batavia IL 60510 *Web:* www.dscontainers.com	630-406-9600		124
D&S Creative Communications Inc 140 Park Ave E ... Mansfield OH 44902 *Web:* www.blackriverdisplay.com	419-524-4312		7
DS Graphics Inc 120 Stedman St ... Lowell MA 01851 *Web:* www.dsgraphics.com	978-970-1359		627
D-S Pipe & Supply Company Inc 1301 Wicomico St Ste 3 ... Baltimore MD 21230 *TF:* 800-368-8880 ■ *Web:* www.dspipe.com	410-539-8000		612
D&S Pump & Supply Co 3784 Danbury Rd ... Brewster NY 10509 *Web:* www.dspumpco.com	845-279-3784		711
DS Services of America Inc 5660 New Northside Dr Ste 500 ... Atlanta GA 30328 *TF Cust Svc:* 800-201-6218 ■ *Web:* www.water.com	800-201-6218		805
DS/USA (Disabled Sports USA) 451 Hungerford Dr Ste 100 ... Rockville MD 20850 *TF:* 800-543-2754 ■ *Web:* www.disabledsportsusa.org	301-217-0960	217-0968	48-22
DSA (Deutsche Steinzeug America Inc) 367 Curie Dr ... Alpharetta GA 30005 *Web:* www.deutsche-steinzeug.de	770-442-5500		751
DSA (Data Systems Analysts Inc) Eigth Neshaminy Interplex Ste 209 ... Trevose PA 19053 *TF:* 877-422-4372 ■ *Web:* www.dsainc.com	215-245-4800	245-4375	180
DSA (Direct Selling Assn) 1667 K St NW Ste 1100 ... Washington DC 20006 *Web:* www.dsa.org	202-452-8866	452-9010	49-18
DSA Detection LLC 120 Water St Ste 211 ... North Andover MA 01845 *Web:* www.dsadetection.com	978-975-3200		693
DSA Encore LLC 50 Pocono Rd ... Brookfield CT 06804 *TF:* 800-529-9600 ■ *Web:* www.dsaencore.com	203-740-4200		253
DSA Factors 3126 N Lincoln Ave PO Box 577520 ... Chicago IL 60657 *Web:* www.dsafactors.com	773-248-9000	248-9005	272
DSC (Destination Services of Colorado Inc) PO Box 3660 ... Avon CO 81620 *TF:* 855-866-5290 ■ *Web:* www.dsc-co.com	970-476-6565		184
DSC (Digital Security Controls) 3301 Langstaff Rd ... Concord ON L4K4L2 *TF:* 888-888-7838 ■ *Web:* www.dsc.com	905-760-3000		692
DSC Logistics 1750 S Wolf Rd ... Des Plaines IL 60018 **Fax Area Code:* 847 ■ *TF:* 800-372-1960 ■ *Web:* www.dsclogistics.com	800-372-1960	390-7276*	449
DSCC (Democratic Senatorial Campaign Committee) 120 Maryland Ave NE ... Washington DC 20002 *Web:* www.dscc.org	202-224-2447		48-7
DSD Business Systems Inc 5120 Shoreham Pl Ste 280 ... San Diego CA 92122 *Web:* www.dsdinc.com	858-550-5900		177
DSG (Dakota Supply Group) 2601 Third Ave N ... Fargo ND 58102 *TF:* 800-437-4702 ■ *Web:* www.dakotasupplygroup.com	701-237-9440	237-6504	246
DSG Systems Inc 56 Inverness Dr E Ste 260 ... Englewood CO 80112 *Web:* www.dsgsys.com	303-790-0453	790-0866	177
DSG Tag Systems Inc 5455 152nd St Ste 214 ... Surrey BC V3S5A5 *TF:* 877-589-8806 ■ *Web:* www.dsgtag.com	877-589-8806		387
DSI Payroll Services 300 Atrium Dr ... Somerset NJ 08873 *Web:* businessfinder.lehighvalleylive.com	732-748-3200		570
DSI Underground Systems Inc 12427 S Pasture Rd Ste 201 ... Riverton UT 84096 *Web:* www.dsiunderground.com	385-557-5500		480
DS-IQ Inc 3326 160th Ave SE Ste 200 ... Bellevue WA 98008 *Web:* www.ds-iq.com	425-213-1400	974-1401	525
Dsj Printing Inc 3103 Pico Blvd ... Santa Monica CA 90405 *TF:* 800-700-8051 ■ *Web:* www.dsjprinting.com	310-828-8051		627
DSLextreme.com 21540 Plummer St Ste A ... Chatsworth CA 91311 **Fax Area Code:* 818 ■ *TF:* 866-243-8638 ■ *Web:* www.dslextreme.com	866-243-8638	206-0326*	398
DSM Chemicals North America Inc 1 Columbia Nitrogen Rd ... Augusta GA 30901 *TF:* 800-526-0189 ■ *Web:* www.dsm.com	706-849-6600		144
DSM Desotech Inc 1122 St Charles St ... Elgin IL 60120 **Fax:* Sales ■ *TF:* 800-222-7189 ■ *Web:* www.dsm.com	847-697-0400	468-7785*	145
DSM Engineering Plastics Inc 2267 W Mill Rd ... Evansville IN 47720 **Fax:* Cust Svc ■ *TF:* 800-333-4237 ■ *Web:* www.dsm.com	812-435-7500	435-7702*	605-2
DSM Food Specialties Inc 45 Waterview Blvd ... Parsippany NJ 07054 *TF:* 800-526-0189 ■ *Web:* www.dsm.com	973-257-1063	257-8420	296-42
DSM NeoResins Inc 730 Main St ... Wilmington MA 01887 *Web:* dsm.com	978-658-6600		605-2
DSN Group Inc 152 Lorraine Dr ... Lake Zurich IL 60047 *TF:* 888-445-2919 ■ *Web:* www.dsngroup.net	888-445-2919		525
DSO (DeKalb Symphony Orchestra) PO Box 1313 ... Tucker GA 30085 *Web:* www.dekalbsymphony.org	678-891-3565	891-3575	573-3
DS&O Electric Cooperative Inc 129 W Main St PO Box 286 ... Solomon KS 67480 *TF:* 800-376-3533 ■ *Web:* www.dsoelectric.com	785-655-2011	655-2805	245
DSP Builders Inc 12000 E 47th Ave Ste 201 ... Denver CO 80239 *Web:* www.dspbuilders.com	303-289-0666		186
DSP Group Inc 2580 N First St Ste 460 ... San Jose CA 95131 *NASDAQ: DSPG* ■ *TF:* 800-224-8377 ■ *Web:* www.dspg.com	408-986-4300	986-4323	696
DSSC (Data Storage Systems Ctr) *Carnegie Mellon University* 5000 Forbes Ave ... Pittsburgh PA 15213 *TF:* 800-864-8287 ■ *Web:* www.dssc.ece.cmu.edu	412-268-6600	268-3497	668
DST Controls 651 Stone Rd ... Benicia CA 94510 *TF:* 800-251-0773 ■ *Web:* www.dstcontrols.com	800-251-0773		203
DST Industries Inc 34364 Goddard Rd ... Romulus MI 48174 *Web:* www.dstindustries.com	734-941-0300		60
DST Output 5220 Robert J Mathews Pkwy ... El Dorado Hills CA 95762 *TF:* 800-441-7587 ■ *Web:* dstsystems.com	916-939-4960		496
DST Systems Inc 333 W 11th St ... Kansas City MO 64105 *NYSE: DST* ■ *Web:* www.dstsystems.com	816-435-1000	435-8630	178-1
DSX Access Systems Inc 10731 Rockwall Rd ... Dallas TX 75238 *TF:* 888-419-8353 ■ *Web:* www.dsxinc.com	214-553-6140	553-6147	693
DT Engineering 1107 Springfield Rd ... Lebanon MO 65536 *Web:* www.detroittool.com	417-532-2141		757
DTA (Dental Trade Alliance) 4350 N Fairfax Dr Ste 220 ... Arlington VA 22203 *Web:* www.dentaltradealliance.org	703-379-7755	931-9429	49-4
D-Ta Systems Inc 2500 Lancaster Rd ... Ottawa ON K1B4S5 *TF:* 877-382-3222 ■ *Web:* www.d-ta.com	613-745-8713		177
DTC (Diversified Technology Consultants Inc) 2321 Whitney Ave Ste 301 ... Hamden CT 06518 *Web:* www.teamdtc.com	203-239-4200		261
DTE Energy Co 1 Energy Plaza ... Detroit MI 48226 *NYSE: DTE* ■ *TF:* 800-477-4747 ■ *Web:* www.dteenergy.com	313-235-4000		360-5
DTE Energy Services 414 S Main St Ste 600 ... Ann Arbor MI 48104 *Web:* dtepowerandindustrial.com	734-302-4800		463
D-Tech Optoelectronics Inc USA 18007 Cortney Ct ... City Of Industry CA 91748 *Web:* www.dtechopto.com	626-956-1100		743
DTH (Dana-Thomas House) 301 E Lawrence Ave ... Springfield IL 62703 *TF:* 800-525-2660 ■ *Web:* www.dana-thomas.org	217-782-6776		50-3
DTI (Dental Technologies Inc) 5601 Arnold Rd ... Dublin CA 94568 *TF:* 800-229-0936 ■ *Web:* www.dtidental.com	925-829-3611		415
DTI Assoc Inc 2920 S Glebe Rd ... Arlington VA 22206	703-299-1600		449
DTI LLC 1196 FM 529 ... Houston TX 77041 *Web:* dtillc.com	713-856-8735		112
DTIC (Defense Technical Information Center) 8725 John J Kingman Rd Ste 0944 ... Fort Belvoir VA 22060 *TF:* 800-225-3842 ■ *Web:* www.dtic.mil	800-225-3842		340-3
DTLR Holding Inc 1300 Mercedes Dr ... Hanover MD 21076 *Web:* www.dtlr.com	410-850-5911		229
DTM Systems Inc 2323 Boundary Rd Unit 130 ... Vancouver BC V5M4V8 *TF:* 888-655-3282 ■ *Web:* www.dtm.ca	604-257-6700		179
DTN.IQ Inc 9110 W Dodge Rd Ste 200 ... Omaha NE 68114 *TF:* 800-475-4755 ■ *Web:* www.interquote.com	402-390-2328		407
Dtreds LLC 19980 Highland Vista Dr Ste 180-185 ... Ashburn VA 20147 *Web:* www.dtreds.com	571-313-1696		224
Dts Cos Inc 1640 Monad Rd ... Billings MT 59101 *TF:* 800-755-5855 ■ *Web:* www.dtsb.com	406-245-4695	245-5404	780
Dts Financial Group 5401 Tech Cir ... Moorpark CA 93021	805-532-9000		528
DTS Inc 5220 Las Virgenes Rd ... Calabasas CA 91302 *NASDAQ: DTSI* ■ *Web:* www.dts.com	818-436-1000		52
Du Hadaway Tool & Die Shop Inc 801 Dawson Dr ... Newark DE 19713 *Web:* duhadawaytool.com	302-366-0113		757
Du Page Airport Authority 2700 International Dr Ste 200 ... West Chicago IL 60185 *TF:* 800-208-5690 ■ *Web:* www.dupageairport.com	630-584-2211	584-3022	27
Dual Print & Mail LLC 340 Nagel Dr ... Cheektowaga NY 14225 *Web:* www.dualprinting.com	716-684-3825		627
Dualite Sales & Service Inc 1 Dualite Ln ... Williamsburg OH 45176 *TF:* 800-543-7271 ■ *Web:* www.dualite.com	513-724-7100	724-7100	701
Dual-Lite Inc 701 Millennium Blvd ... Greenville SC 29607 *TF:* 866-898-0131 ■ *Web:* www.dual-lite.com	864-678-1000	678-1415	439
Dualtone Music Group 3 Mcferrin Ave ... Nashville TN 37206 *Web:* www.dualtone.com	615-320-0620	320-0692	657

Name / Address	City	State	Zip	Phone	Fax	Class
Duane Morris Government Strategies LLC 605 Ninth St NW ste 1000 *Fax Area Code: 703 ■ Web: www.dmgs.com	Washington	DC	20004	202-776-7803	480-0488*	393
Duane Morris LLP 30 S 17th St. TF: 800-973-1177 ■ Web: www.duanemorris.com	Philadelphia	PA	19103	215-979-1000	979-1020	428
Duane Street Hotel 130 Duane St Web: www.duanestreethotel.com	New York	NY	10013	212-964-4600	964-4800	379
Duane's 3649 Mission Inn Ave TF: 800-843-7755 ■ Web: www.missioninn.com	Riverside	CA	92501	951-784-0300	683-1342	671
Duarte Unified School District 1620 Huntington Dr TF: 888-225-7377 ■ Web: www.duarte.k12.ca.us	Duarte	CA	91010	626-599-5000	599-5069	685
Dublin Chamber of Commerce 7080 Donlon Way Ste 110 TF: 800-310-2355 ■ Web: www.dublinchamberofcommerce.org	Dublin	CA	94568	925-828-6200	828-4247	139
Dublin Construction Company Inc 305 S Washington St Web: www.dublinconstruction.com	Dublin	GA	31021	478-272-0721		182
Dublin Convention & Visitors Bureau 9 S High St TF: 800-245-8387 ■ Web: www.visitdublinohio.com	Dublin	OH	43017	614-792-7666	760-1818	206
Dublin Pub 300 Wayne Ave Web: www.dubpub.com	Dayton	OH	45410	937-224-7822		671
Dublin School 18 Lehmann Way PO Box 522 Web: www.dublinschool.org	Dublin	NH	03444	603-563-8584		622
Dublin Unified School District 7471 Larkdale Ave Web: www.dublin.k12.ca.us	Dublin	CA	94568	925-828-2551	829-6532	685
Dublin Villager 7801 N Central Dr. TF: 888-837-4342 ■ Web: www.thisweeknews.com	Lewis Center	OH	43035	740-888-6100	888-6006	532-4
Dublin-Laurens County Chamber of Commerce 1200 Bellvue. TF: 800-829-4933 ■ Web: www.dublin-georgia.com	Dublin	GA	31021	478-272-5546	275-0811	139
Dubois & King Inc 28 N Main St. TF: 866-783-7101 ■ Web: www.dubois-king.com	Randolph	VT	05060	802-728-3376		261
DuBois Area School District Inc 500 Liberty Blvd Web: www.dasd.k12.pa.us	Du Bois	PA	15801	814-371-2700		187
Dubois Chemicals 3630 E Kemper Rd TF: 800-438-2647 ■ Web: www.duboischemicals.com	Cincinnati	OH	45241	800-438-2647	543-1720	151
DuBois Regional Medical Ctr 100 Hospital Ave. TF: 800-254-5164 ■ Web: phhealthcare.org	Du Bois	PA	15801	814-371-2200		374-3
Dubois Rural Electric Co-op Inc 1400 Energy Dr. Web: www.duboisrec.com	Jasper	IN	47547	812-482-5454		245
Dubois Wood Products Inc 707 E Sixth St. TF: 800-521-5381 ■ Web: www.duboiswood.com	Huntingburg	IN	47542	812-683-3613	683-3847	499
DuBois, Sheehan, Hamilton, Levin & Weissman LLC 511 Cooper St TF: 800-608-1350 ■ Web: www.duboislaw.com	Camden	NJ	08102	856-365-7665		428
Dubose National Energy Services Inc PO Box 499 Web: www.dubosenes.com	Clinton	NC	28329	910-590-2151	590-3555	492
Dubose Strapping Inc 906 Industrial Dr. Web: www.dubosestrapping.com	Clinton	NC	28328	910-590-1020		567
Dubuque Arboretum & Botanical Gardens 3800 Arboretum Dr. Web: www.dubuquearboretum.com	Dubuque	IA	52001	563-556-2100	556-2443	97
Dubuque Area Chamber of Commerce 300 Main St Ste 200. TF: 800-798-4748 ■ Web: www.dubuquechamber.com	Dubuque	IA	52001	563-557-9200	557-1591	139
Dubuque City Hall 50 W 13th St. TF: 800-426-4791 ■ Web: www.cityofdubuque.org	Dubuque	IA	52001	563-589-4100	589-0890	337
Dubuque County 720 Central Ave TF: 800-637-0128 ■ Web: www.dubuquecounty.org	Dubuque	IA	52001	563-589-4432		338
Dubuque Fairgrounds Speedway 14569 Old Hwy Rd Web: www.dbqfair.com	Dubuque	IA	52002	563-588-1406		515
Dubuque Museum of Art 701 Locust St. TF: 800-690-4006 ■ Web: www.dbqart.com	Dubuque	IA	52001	563-557-1851		520
Dubuque Regional Airport 11000 Airport Rd Web: www.flydbq.com	Dubuque	IA	52003	563-589-4128		27
Dubuque Stamping & Manufacturing Inc 3190 Jackson St. Web: www.dbqstamp.com	Dubuque	IA	52001	563-583-5716		488
Dubuque Symphony Orchestra 2728 Asbury Rd Ste 900. TF: 866-803-9280 ■ Web: www.dubuquesymphony.org	Dubuque	IA	52001	563-557-1677	557-9841	573-3
Duca Financial Services Credit Union Ltd 5290 Yonge St TF: 866-900-3822 ■ Web: duca.com	Toronto	ON	M2N5P9	416-223-8502		219
Ducci Electrical Contractors Inc 74 Scott Swamp Rd Web: duccielectrical.com	Farmington	CT	06032	860-489-9267	489-7980	189-4
Ducey Doug (R) State Capitoly 1700 W Washington Web: www.azgovernor.gov	Phoenix	AZ	85007	602-542-4331	542-7601	343
DuCharme McMillen & Assoc Inc 828 S Harrison St. Web: www.dmainc.com	Fort Wayne	IN	46802	260-484-8631	482-8152	734
Duchesnay Inc 950 Boul Mich'Le-Bohec Web: www.duchesnay.com	Blainville	QC	J7C5E2	450-433-7734	433-2211	238
Duchesne County 734 N Ctr St. Web: www.duchesne.utah.gov	Duchesne	UT	84021	435-738-1100	738-5522	338
Duchossois Industries Inc 845 Larch Ave. TF: 800-729-1959 ■ Web: duch.com	Elmhurst	IL	60126	630-279-3600		360-3
DUCK 2205 Stoner Ave	Los Angeles	CA	90064	310-478-0771	478-0773	33
Duck Co 5601 Gray St. Web: www.duckco.com	Arvada	CO	80002	303-423-5630		687
Duck Flats Pharma LLC 109 S St. Web: www.dfpharma.com	Elbridge	NY	13060	315-689-3407		463

Name / Address	City	State	Zip	Phone	Fax	Class
Duck Lake State Park 3560 Memorial Dr Web: www.michigandnr.com	North Muskegon	MI	49445	231-744-3480		565
Duck River Electric Membership Corp 305 Learning Way PO Box 89 TF: 800-325-8925 ■ Web: www.dremc.com	Shelbyville	TN	37160	931-684-4621	685-0013	245
Duck River Textile Inc 1000 New County Rd Ste 2 Web: www.duckrivertextile.com	Secaucus	NJ	07094	201-533-1000		258
Duckback 101 Prospect Ave. TF: 800-825-5382 ■ Web: www.superdeck.com	Cleveland	OH	44115	800-825-5382		550
Ducker Worldwide LLC 1250 Maplelawn Dr TF: 800-929-0086 ■ Web: www.ducker.com	Troy	MI	48084	248-644-0086		463
Duckfat 43 Middle St Web: www.duckfat.com	Portland	ME	04101	207-774-8080		671
Ducks Unlimited Magazine 1 Waterfowl Way TF: 800-453-8257 ■ Web: www.ducks.org	Memphis	TN	38120	901-758-3825	758-3850	457-20
Duckworth Pathology Group Inc 1211 Union Ave	Memphis	TN	38104	901-276-9192		415
Du-Co Ceramics Co 155 S Rebecca St PO Box 568 Web: www.du-co.com	Saxonburg	PA	16056	724-352-1511	352-1266	249
Ducommun AeroStructures Inc 268 E Gardena Blvd Web: www.ducommunaero.com	Gardena	CA	90248	310-380-5390		22
Ducommun Inc 268 E Gardena Blvd Web: www.ducommun.com	Gardena	CA	90248	310-380-5390		621
Ducommun Inc 23301 Wilmington Ave NYSE: DCO ■ TF: 800-522-6645 ■ Web: www.ducommun.com	Carson	CA	90745	310-513-7280	513-7279	203
Ducon Technologies Inc 19 Engineers Ln Web: www.ducon.com	Farmingdale	NY	11735	631-694-1700		18
Ductmate Industries Inc 210 Fifth St. Web: www.ductmate.com	Charleroi	PA	15022	724-258-0500		198
Duct-O-Wire Co 345 Adams Cir. TF: 800-752-6001 ■ Web: www.ductowire.com	Corona	CA	92882	951-735-8220	735-2372	203
Dude Girl LLC 11854 Kitzbuhel Rd Web: www.dudegirl.com	Truckee	CA	96161	530-550-3247	587-7635	772
Dude Rancher Lodge 415 N 29th St. TF: 800-221-3302 ■ Web: www.duderancherlodge.com	Billings	MT	59101	406-259-5561	259-0095	379
Dude Ranchers Assn 1122 12th St PO Box 2307 TF: 866-399-2339 ■ Web: www.duderanch.org	Cody	WY	82414	307-587-2339	587-2776	48-23
Dudek 605 Third St Web: dudek.com	Encinitas	CA	92024	760-942-5147		261
Dudek & Bock Spring Mfg Co 5100 W Roosevelt Rd Web: www.dudek-bock.com	Chicago	IL	60644	773-379-4100		719
Dudick Inc 1818 Miller Pkwy Web: www.dudick.com	Streetsboro	OH	44241	330-562-1970		596
Dudley & Smith PA 101 Fifth St E Ste 2602. Web: www.dudleyandsmith.com	Saint Paul	MN	55101	651-291-1717		428
Dudley Farm Historic State Park 18730 W Newberry Rd Web: www.floridastateparks.org	Newberry	FL	32669	352-472-1142		565
Dudley's 259 Westshort St Web: www.dudleysonshort.com	Lexington	KY	40507	859-252-1010	253-9383	671
Dudnyk 5 Walnut Grove Dr Ste 280. Web: www.dudnyk.com	Horsham	PA	19044	215-443-9406		4
Dudnyk Exchange 5 Walnut Grove Web: dudnyk.com	Horsham	PA	19044	215-443-9406		4
Due Amici 67 E Gay St Web: www.due-amici.com	Columbus	OH	43215	614-224-9373		671
Due North Consulting Inc 105 Owens Pkwy Ste C. TF: 800-899-2676 ■ Web: duenorthmedia.com	Birmingham	AL	35244	205-989-9394		196
Dueber's Inc 300 Industrial Blvd	Norwood Young America	MN	55397	952-467-3085	467-3001	791
Dueck Auto Group 12100 Featherstone Way. TF: 877-993-8325 ■ Web: www.dueckgm.com	Richmond	BC	V6W1K9	604-273-1311		57
Dueco N4 W22610 Bluemound Rd	Waukesha	WI	53186	262-547-8500	547-8407	385
Duerr Tool & Die Company Inc 1135 Springfield Rd	Union	NJ	07083	908-810-9035		596
Duff & Phelps Investment Management Co 200 S Wacker Dr Ste 500 TF: 800-338-8214 ■ Web: www.dpimc.com	Chicago	IL	60606	312-263-2610		401
Duff's 3651 Sheridan Dr Web: duffswings.com	Buffalo	NY	14226	716-834-6234		671
Duffel Financial & Construction Co 1430 Willow Pass Rd Ste 220.	Concord	CA	94520	925-603-8444		653
Dufferin Gate Productions Inc 20 Butterick Rd. Web: www.dufferingate.com	Toronto	ON	M8W3Z8	416-252-9998		514
Duffey Communications Inc 3379 Peachtree Rd NE Ste 300. Web: www.duffey.com	Atlanta	GA	30326	404-266-2600		636
Duffey Southeast Inc 7716 England St Ste A Web: duffeyse.com	Charlotte	NC	28273	704-527-3612		610
Duffield Aquatic 113 Metro Dr TF: 888-669-7551 ■ Web: www.duffieldaquatics.com	Anderson	SC	29625	888-669-7551		186
Duffield Assoc Inc 5400 Limestone Rd. TF: 877-732-9633 ■ Web: duffnet.com	Wilmington	DE	19808	302-239-6634	239-8485	186
Duffin Manufacturing Co 316 Warden Ave Web: www.duffinmfg.com	Elyria	OH	44035	440-323-4681	420-4004	621
Duffner Engineering 50 W Summit Dr. TF: 800-994-4991 ■ Web: duffnerengineering.com	Emerald Hills	CA	94062	650-701-1055		261
Duffy & Partners LLC 110 N Fifth St Ste 650 Web: www.duffy.com	Minneapolis	MN	55403	612-548-2333		195
Duffy & Shanley Inc 10 Charles St. Web: www.duffyshanley.com	Providence	RI	02904	401-274-0001		4

Name / Address	City	State	Zip	Phone	Fax	Class
Duffy Sean P (Rep R - WI) 2330 Rayburn Bldg *Web:* duffy.house.gov	Washington	DC	20515	202-225-3365	225-3240	342-2
Duffy's Collectible Cars 1195 Boyson Rd *Web:* www.duffys.com	Hiawatha	IA	52233	319-849-1400		520
Duffy's Restaurant 231 Darrow Rd *Web:* duffysrestaurantandgrill.com	Akron	OH	44305	330-784-5043		671
Duffy's Steak & Lobster House 1007 Simonton St *TF:* 800-492-1911 ■ *Web:* duffyskeywest.com	Key West	FL	33040	305-296-4900		671
DuffyGroup Inc 4727 E Union Hills Dr Ste 200 *Web:* www.duffygroup.com	Phoenix	AZ	85050	602-861-5840		193
Dufour Petroleum LP 1374 US 11	Petal	MS	39465	601-583-9991		685
Dufresne Furniture Ltd 116 Nature Pk Way *Web:* www.dufresne.ca	Winnipeg	MB	R3P0X8	204-989-9898	989-9885	321
Dufresne Manufacturing Co 1380 East County Rd E *Web:* www.dufresnemfg.com	St Paul	MN	55110	651-483-8130		480
Dufry 10300 NW 19th St Ste 114 *Web:* www.dufry.com	Doral	FL	33172	305-591-1763		443
Dugan & Meyers 11110 Kenwood Rd *Web:* www.dugan-meyers.com	Cincinnati	OH	45242	513-891-4300	891-0704	186
Dugan Production Corp 709 E Murray Dr *Web:* daily-times.com	Farmington	NM	87401	505-325-1821		536
Duggal Visual Solutions Inc 29 W 23th St *Web:* m.duggal.com	New York	NY	10010	212-924-8100		344
Duggan Joiner & Company PA 334 NW Third Ave *Web:* djcocpa.com	Ocala	FL	34475	352-732-0171		2
Duggan Manufacturing LLC 50150 Ryan Rd Ste 15 *Web:* www.dugganmfg.com	Shelby Township	MI	48317	586-254-7400		697
Dugway Proving Ground 5124 Kister Ave *Web:* www.dugway.army.mil	Dugway	UT	84022	435-831-2178		743
Duhig & Company Inc 5071 Telegraph Rd *Web:* www.duhig.com	Los Angeles	CA	90022	323-263-7161	263-7161	492
Duininck Inc 408 Sixth St PO Box 208 *TF General:* 800-328-8949 ■ *Web:* www.duininckcompanies.com	Prinsburg	MN	56281	800-328-8949		188-4
Dukal Corp 2 Flee2od Ct *Web:* www.dukal.com	Ronkonkoma	NY	11779	631-656-3800		475
Dukane 2900 Dukane Dr *Web:* www.dukane.com	Saint Charles	IL	60174	630-584-2300	584-2300	591
DuKane Precast Inc 1805 High Grove Ln *Web:* www.dukaneprecast.com	Naperville	IL	60540	630-355-8118		183
Duke Clinical Research & Treatment Ctr *Bone Marrow & Stem Cell Transplant Program* 2400 Pratt St *Web:* www.dukehealth.org	Durham	NC	27710	919-668-1002	668-1091	769
Duke Communications 1781 Jamestown Rd Ste 170 *Web:* www.widomaker.com	Williamsburg	VA	23185	757-253-9000		246
Duke Construction Inc 2600 Broad St Rd *TF:* 800-737-6099 ■ *Web:* www.dukeconstructioninc.net	Gum Spring	VA	23065	804-556-6992		390
Duke Diet & Fitness Ctr (DFC) 501 Douglas St *TF:* 800-235-3853 ■ *Web:* www.dukedietandfitness.org	Durham	NC	27705	800-235-3853		706
Duke Endowment 100 N Tryon St Ste 3500 *Web:* www.dukeendowment.org	Charlotte	NC	28202	704-376-0291	376-9336	305
Duke Energy Corp 550 S Tryon St *NYSE:* DUK ■ *TF:* 800-777-9898	Charlotte	NC	28202	800-777-9898		360-5
Duke Energy Ctr 525 Elm St *Web:* www.duke-energycenter.com	Cincinnati	OH	45202	513-419-7300	419-7327	205
Duke Farms 80 Rt 206 S *Web:* www.dukefarms.org	Hillsborough	NJ	08844	908-722-3700		97
Duke Health Raleigh Hospital 3400 Wake Forest Rd *Web:* www.dukehealth.org/hospitals/duke-raleigh-hospital/home	Raleigh	NC	27609	919-954-3000	954-3900	374-3
Duke Law 210 Science Dr PO Box 90362 *TF:* 888-529-2586 ■ *Web:* www.law.duke.edu	Durham	NC	27708	919-613-7006		167-1
Duke Law Firm Pc 1572 Montgomery Hwy Ste 205 *Web:* www.dukelawpc.com	Vestavia Hills	AL	35216	205-823-3900		445
Duke Manufacturing Co 2305 N Broadway *TF:* 800-735-3853 ■ *Web:* www.dukemfg.com	Saint Louis	MO	63102	314-231-1130	231-5074	298
Duke Memorial United Methodist Church 504 W Chapel Hill St *TF:* 800-913-6109 ■ *Web:* www.dukememorial.org	Durham	NC	27701	919-683-3467	682-3349	50-1
Duke Pediatric Blood and Marrow Transplant Program 1400 Morreene Rd PO Box 24-5176 *Fax Area Code: 520 ■ *TF:* 800-524-5928	Durham	NC	27705	919-668-1100	694-5009*	769
Duke Realty Corp 600 E 96th St Ste 100 *NYSE:* DRE-M.CL ■ *TF:* 800-875-3366 ■ *Web:* www.dukerealty.com	Indianapolis	IN	46240	317-808-6000	808-6794	655
Duke Towers- All Condominium Hotel 807 W Trinity Ave *TF:* 866-385-3869 ■ *Web:* www.duketower.com	Durham	NC	27701	919-687-4444	683-1215	379
Duke University 2138 Campus Dr PO Box 90586 *Fax: Admissions ■ *TF:* 800-443-3853 ■ *Web:* www.duke.edu	Durham	NC	27708	919-684-3214	681-8941*	166
Duke University Divinity School 407 Chapel Dr PO Box 90968 *TF:* 800-367-3853 ■ *Web:* www.divinity.duke.edu	Durham	NC	27708	919-660-3400	660-3473	167-3
Duke University Hospital 2301 Erwin Rd *Web:* www.dukehealth.org	Durham	NC	27710	919-684-8111		374-3
Duke University Medical Ctr Library 103 Seeley Mudd Bldg DUMC 3702 *Web:* www.mclibrary.duke.edu	Durham	NC	27710	919-660-1150	681-7599	434-1
Duke University Perkins Library 411 Chapel Dr *Web:* www.library.duke.edu	Durham	NC	27708	919-660-5870	660-5923	434-6
Duke University Press 905 W Main St Ste 18-B *Fax Area Code: 888 ■ *Fax: Cust Svc ■ *TF Cust Svc:* 888-651-0122 ■ *Web:* www.dukeupress.edu	Durham	NC	27701	919-687-3600	651-0124*	637-4
Duke University School of Medicine DUMC 3710 *TF:* 888-275-3853 ■ *Web:* medschool.duke.edu	Durham	NC	27710	919-684-2985		167-2
Duke's 8th Avenue Hotel 630 W Eigth Ave *TF:* 800-478-4837 ■ *Web:* www.dukesalaskahotel.com	Anchorage	AK	99501	907-274-6213		379
Duke's Huntington Beach 130 Kai Malina Pkwy *Web:* www.hulapie.com	Lahaina	HI	96761	808-667-4800		671
Duke's Source for Sports 3876 Bloor St W *TF:* 800-286-9003 ■ *Web:* www.sourceforsports.com	Etobicoke	ON	M9B1L3	416-233-2011		711
Dukem 1100 Maryland Ave *Web:* www.dukemrestaurant.com	Baltimore	MD	21201	410-385-0318		671
Dukes Aerospace 9060 Winnetka Ave *Web:* www.dukesaerospace.com	Northridge	CA	91324	818-350-1900		22
Dukes County PO Box 190 *TF:* 800-244-4630 ■ *Web:* www.dukescounty.org	Edgartown	MA	02539	508-696-3840	696-3841	338
Dukes Lumber Company Inc 28504 Dukes Lumber Rd *Web:* dukeslumber.com	Laurel	DE	19956	302-875-7551		364
Duley Hopkins & Assoc Inc 1200 Mtn Creek Rd *Web:* dha-us.com	Chattanooga	TN	37405	423-877-1220		177
Dulles Aviation Inc 10501 Observation Rd *TF:* 888-835-9324 ■ *Web:* www.dullesaviation.com	Manassas	VA	20110	703-361-2171		63
Dulles Expo & Conference Ctr 4320 Chantilly Shopping Ctr Dr *Web:* www.dullesexpo.com	Chantilly	VA	20151	703-378-0910		232
Dultmeier Sales LLC 13808 Industrial Rd *TF:* 888-677-5054 ■ *Web:* www.dultmeier.com	Omaha	NE	68137	402-333-1444		429
Duluth Area Chamber of Commerce 5 W First St Ste 101 *Web:* www.duluthchamber.com	Duluth	MN	55802	218-722-5501	722-3223	139
Duluth Business University (DBU) 4724 Mike Colalilo Dr *TF:* 800-777-8406 ■ *Web:* www.dbumn.edu	Duluth	MN	55807	218-722-4000	628-2127	800
Duluth City Hall 411 W First St *Web:* www.duluthmn.gov	Duluth	MN	55802	218-730-5500	730-5923	337
Duluth Entertainment Convention Ctr 350 Harbor Dr *TF:* 800-628-8385 ■ *Web:* www.decc.org	Duluth	MN	55802	218-722-5573	722-4247	205
Duluth International Airport 4701 Grinden Dr *TF:* 855-787-2227 ■ *Web:* www.duluthairport.com	Duluth	MN	55811	218-727-2968	727-2960	27
Duluth News-Tribune 424 W First St *TF Circ:* 800-456-8080 ■ *Web:* www.duluthnewstribune.com	Duluth	MN	55802	218-723-5281	720-4120	532-2
Duluth Pack 365 Canal Park Dr *TF:* 800-777-4439 ■ *Web:* www.duluthpack.com	Duluth	MN	55802	218-722-1707		711
Duluth Playhouse 506 W Michigan St *TF:* 800-982-2787 ■ *Web:* www.duluthplayhouse.org	Duluth	MN	55802	218-733-7555		572
Duluth Public Library 520 W Superior St *Web:* www.duluthlibrary.org	Duluth	MN	55802	218-730-4200		434-3
Dumbarton House 2715 Q St NW *TF:* 800-788-6455 ■ *Web:* www.dumbartonhouse.org	Washington	DC	20007	202-337-2288	337-0348	50-3
Dumbarton Oaks 1703 32nd St NW *Web:* www.doaks.org	Washington	DC	20007	202-339-6400		520
Dumbell Man Fitness Equipment, The 655 Hawaii Ave *TF:* 800-432-6266 ■ *Web:* www.dumbellman.com	Torrance	CA	90503	310-381-2900		354
Dumdum Nelida 5925 N Sacramento Ave	Chicago	IL	60659	773-561-6776		361
Du-Mont Co 7800 N Pioneer Ct	Peoria	IL	61615	309-692-7240		697
Dumont Ctr for Rehabilitation & Nursing Care 676 Pelham Rd *TF:* 800-282-5366 ■ *Web:* www.dumontcenter.com	New Rochelle	NY	10805	914-632-9600	632-9247	450
DuMor Inc PO Box 142 *TF:* 800-598-4018 ■ *Web:* www.dumor.com	Mifflintown	PA	17059	717-436-2106	436-9839	319-4
Dumore Corp 1030 Veterans St *TF:* 888-467-8288 ■ *Web:* www.dumorecorp.com	Mauston	WI	53948	608-847-6420		518
Dumouchelle Art Gallery 409 E Jefferson Ave *Web:* www.dumouchelles.com	Detroit	MI	48226	313-963-6255	963-8199	44
Dun & Bradstreet Receivable Management Services 103 JFK Pkwy *Web:* www.dnb.com.hk	Short Hills	NJ	07078	973-921-5500		160
Dun Transportation & Stringing Inc 304 Reynolds Ln *Web:* www.duntrans.com	Sherman	TX	75092	903-891-9660	891-9660	780
Dunaway's 351 SE St *Web:* www.dunaways.com	Indianapolis	IN	46204	317-638-7663		671
Dunbar Cave State Natural Area 401 Dunbar Cave Rd	Clarksville	TN	37043	931-648-5526		565
Dunbar Mechanical Inc 2806 N Reynolds Rd *TF:* 800-719-2201 ■ *Web:* www.dunbarmechanical.com	Toledo	OH	43615	419-537-1900	537-8840	189-10
Dunbarton Corp PO Box 8577 *TF:* 800-633-7553 ■ *Web:* www.dunbarton.com	Dothan	AL	36304	800-633-7553		234
Duncan & Son Lines Inc 23860 W US Hwy 85 *TF:* 800-528-4283 ■ *Web:* www.duncanandson.com	Buckeye	AZ	85326	623-386-4511	386-3656	780
Duncan Aviation Inc 3701 Aviation Rd *TF:* 800-228-4277 ■ *Web:* www.duncanaviation.aero	Lincoln	NE	68524	402-475-2611	475-5541	24
Duncan Cowichan Chamber of Commerce 2896 Drinkwater Rd *Web:* duncancc.bc.ca	Duncan	BC	V9L2C6	250-748-1111	746-8222	137
Duncan Disposal Co *Arlington* 1212 Harrison Ave *TF:* 800-766-1758 ■ *Web:* www.republicservices.com	Arlington	TX	76011	817-317-2000	860-0330	804
Duncan Enterprises 5673 E Shields Ave *TF:* 800-438-6226 ■ *Web:* www.ilovetocreate.com	Fresno	CA	93727	559-291-4444	291-4444	43

Name / Address	City	State	Zip	Phone	Fax	Class
Duncan Jeff (Rep R - SC) 2229 Rayburn HOB *Web:* jeffduncan.house.gov	Washington	DC	20515	202-225-5301	225-3216	342-2
Duncan John J Jr (Rep R - TN) 2207 Rayburn HOB *Web:* duncan.house.gov	Washington	DC	20515	202-225-5435	225-6444	342-2
Duncan Machinery Movers Inc 2004 Duncan Machinery Dr *Web:* www.dmmlex.com	Lexington	KY	40504	859-233-7333	233-7365	780
Duncan Mcintosh 18475 Bandilier *Web:* duncanmcintoshco.com	Fountain Valley	CA	92708	949-660-6150	660-6172	457-4
Duncan Oil Company Inc 849 Factory Rd *TF:* 800-527-2559 ■ *Web:* www.duncan-oil.com	Beavercreek	OH	45434	800-527-2559		579
Duncan Printing Co 619 S Fremont Ave Ste A *Web:* www.duncanprinting.com	Alhambra	CA	91803	626-281-2016		627
Duncan Regional Hospital 1407 Whisenant Dr *TF:* 800-579-7967 ■ *Web:* www.duncanregional.com	Duncan	OK	73533	580-252-5300	251-8829	374-3
Duncan Solutions Inc 633 W Wisconsin Ave Ste 1600 *TF:* 888-993-8622 ■ *Web:* www.duncansolutions.com	Milwaukee	WI	53203	888-993-8622		495
Duncan Supply Company Inc 910 N Illinois St *TF:* 800-382-5528 ■ *Web:* www.duncansupply.com	Indianapolis	IN	46204	317-634-1335	264-6689	612
Duncan Systems Inc 29391 Old US Hwy 33 *TF:* 800-551-9149 ■ *Web:* www.duncansys.com	Elkhart	IN	46516	800-551-9149		54
Duncan Valley Electric Co-op Inc PO Box 440 *TF:* 800-669-2503 ■ *Web:* www.dvec.org	Duncan	AZ	85534	928-359-2503		245
Duncan-Parnell Inc 900 S McDowell St *TF:* 800-849-7708 ■ *Web:* www.duncan-parnell.com	Charlotte	NC	28204	704-372-7766	333-3845	113
Duncanville Chamber of Commerce 300 E Wheatland Rd *Web:* www.duncanvillechamber.org	Duncanville	TX	75116	972-780-4990	298-9370	139
Duncanville Public Library 201 James Collins Blvd *TF:* 800-799-7233 ■ *Web:* duncanville.com	Duncanville	TX	75116	972-780-5050	780-6426	434-3
Duncan-Williams Inc 6750 Poplar Ave Ste 300 *TF:* 800-827-0827 ■ *Web:* www.duncanwilliams.com	Memphis	TN	38138	901-260-6800		690
Duncaster 40 Loeffler Rd *Web:* www.duncaster.org	Bloomfield	CT	06002	860-380-5006		672
Dundalk Eagle PO Box 8936 *Web:* www.dundalkeagle.com	Dundalk	MD	21222	410-288-6060		532-4
Dundee Citrus Growers Assn 111 First St N *Web:* www.dun-d.com	Dundee	FL	33838	863-439-1574	439-1535	11-1
Dundee Corp 1 Adelaide St E Ste 2100 *Web:* www.dundeecorp.com	Toronto	ON	M5C2V9	416-350-3388		360-3
Dundee Internet Service Inc 168 Riley St *TF:* 888-222-8485 ■ *Web:* dundee.net	Dundee	MI	48131	734-529-5331		225
Dundick Corp 4616 W 20th St *TF:* 800-322-4243 ■ *Web:* www.dundick.com	Cicero	IL	60804	708-656-6363	656-2359	493
Dundy County 102 Seventh Ave W PO Box 506 *Web:* www.co.dundy.ne.us	Benkelman	NE	69021	308-423-2058		338
Dunedin Chamber of Commerce 301 Main St *Web:* www.dunedinfl.com	Dunedin	FL	34698	727-733-3197	734-8942	139
Dunes Manor Hotel 2800 Baltimore Ave *TF:* 800-523-2888 ■ *Web:* www.dunesmanor.com	Ocean City	MD	21842	410-289-1100		379
Dungan Engineering pa 1574 Hwy 98 E *Web:* dunganeng.com	Columbia	MS	39429	601-731-2600		256
Dunham Price Inc 210 Mike Hooks Rd PO Box 760 *Web:* www.dunhamprice.com	Westlake	LA	70669	337-433-3900	433-8895	182
Dunham Tavern Museum 6709 Euclid Ave *TF:* 800-493-7655 ■ *Web:* www.dunhamtavern.org	Cleveland	OH	44103	216-431-1060		520
Dunham's Sports 5000 Dixie Hwy *TF:* 800-968-7845 ■ *Web:* www.dunhamssports.com	Waterford	MI	48329	248-674-4975		157-5
Dunhill Hotel 237 N Tryon St *TF:* 800-354-4141 ■ *Web:* www.dunhillhotel.com	Charlotte	NC	28202	704-332-4141		379
Dunkin' Donuts 130 Royall St *TF Cust Svc:* 800-859-5339 ■ *Web:* www.dunkindonuts.com	Canton	MA	02021	781-737-3000	737-4000	68
Dunkin' Donuts Ctr 1 LaSalle Sq *Web:* www.dunkindonutscenter.com	Providence	RI	02903	401-331-0700		720
Dunkin's Diamonds Inc 897 Hebron Rd *TF:* 877-343-4883 ■ *Web:* www.dunkinsdiamonds.com	Heath	OH	43056	877-343-4883		410
Dunkirk Aviation Sales & Service Inc 3389 Middle Rd *TF:* 800-947-4228 ■ *Web:* www.dkk.com	Dunkirk	NY	14048	716-366-6938	366-6986	63
Dunkirk Specialty Steel Corp 830 Brigham Rd *Web:* www.dunkirkspecialtysteel.com	Dunkirk	NY	14048	716-366-1000		723
Dunkley International Inc 1910 Lake St *Web:* www.dunkleyinternational.com	Kalamazoo	MI	49001	269-343-5583	343-5614	298
Dunklin County 35th Judicial Circuit 1175 Floyd St *Web:* www.courts.mo.gov	Kennett	MO	63857	573-888-2456		338
Dunlap & Company Inc 6325 E 100 S *Web:* www.dunlapinc.com	Columbus	IN	47202	812-376-3021		186
Dunlap Industries Inc 297 Industrial Park Rd **Fax Area Code: 423 ■ TF:* 800-251-7214 ■ *Web:* www.dunlapworld.com	Dunlap	TN	37327	800-251-7214	949-3648*	594
Dunlap Oil Company Inc 759 S Haskell Ave *TF:* 800-854-1646 ■ *Web:* www.dunlapoil.com	Willcox	AZ	85643	520-384-2248	384-5159	324
Dunlap's 90 Buford Ave *Web:* www.dunlapsrestaurant.com	Gettysburg	PA	17325	717-334-4816	334-2053	671
Dunlop Manufacturing Inc 150 Industrial Way *Web:* www.jimdunlop.com	Benicia	CA	94510	707-745-2722		527
Dunlop Tires 200 Innovation Way *TF:* 800-522-7458 ■ *Web:* www.dunloptires.com/en-US	Akron	OH	44316	800-522-7458		754
Dunmore Corp 145 Wharton Rd *TF:* 800-444-0242 ■ *Web:* www.dunmore.com	Bristol	PA	19007	215-781-8895	781-9293	600
Dunn & Company Inc 75 Green St *Web:* booktrauma.com	Clinton	MA	01510	978-368-8505		95
DUNN Capital Management LLC 309 SE Osceola St Dunn Bldg Ste 350 *Web:* www.dunncapital.com	Stuart	FL	34994	772-286-4777		401
Dunn Carney Allen Higgins & Tongue LLP 851 SW Sixth Ave Ste 1500 *Web:* www.dunncarney.com	Portland	OH	97204	503-224-6440		428
Dunn County 205 Owens St	Manning	ND	58642	701-573-4447		338
Dunn County 800 Wilson Ave *Web:* co.dunn.wi.us	Menomonie	WI	54751	715-232-1677	232-2534	338
Dunn Energy Co-op PO Box 220 *TF:* 800-924-0630 ■ *Web:* www.dunnenergy.com	Menomonie	WI	54751	715-232-6240		245
Dunn Group Inc, The 999 Riverview Dr Ste 386 *Web:* dunngrp.com	Totowa	NJ	07512	973-237-9500	237-9511	195
Dunn Hospitality Group LLC 300 SE Riverside Dr Ste 100 *Web:* www.dunnhospitalitygroup.com	Evansville	IN	47713	812-471-9300		379
Dunn Investment Co 3905 Messer Airport Hwy *Web:* dunnconstruction.com	Birmingham	AL	35222	205-592-8908		186
Dunn Lambert LLC E 80 Route 4 Ste 170 *Web:* www.njbizlawyer.com	Paramus	NJ	07652	201-957-0874	291-0140	428
Dunn Manufacturing Inc 1400 Goldmine Rd *TF:* 800-868-7111 ■ *Web:* facebook.com	Monroe	NC	28110	704-283-2147		9
Dunn Neal (Rep R - FL) 423 Cannon HOB *Web:* dunn.house.gov	Washington	DC	20515	202-225-5235	225-5615	342-2
Dunn Paper Inc 218 Riverview St *Web:* www.dunnpaper.com	Port Huron	MI	48060	810-984-5521		557
Dunn Roadbuilders LLC 411 W Oak St PO Box 6560 *Web:* www.dunnroadbuilders.com	Laurel	MS	39441	601-649-4111	425-4644	188-4
Dunn Safety Products Inc 37 S Sangamon St *TF:* 800-451-3866 ■ *Web:* www.dunnsafety.com	Chicago	IL	60607	312-666-5800		679
Dunn School 2555 Hwy 154 PO Box 98 *TF:* 800-287-9197 ■ *Web:* www.dunnschool.org	Los Olivos	CA	93441	805-688-6471	686-9715	622
Dunn Solutions Group Inc 5550 W Touhy Ave Ste 400 *Web:* www.dunnsolutions.com	Skokie	IL	60077	847-673-0900		177
Dunn State Park Rt 101 *Web:* www.mass.gov	Gardner	MA	01440	978-632-7897		565
Dunn-Edwards Corp 4885 E 52nd Pl *TF:* 800-537-4098 ■ *Web:* www.dunnedwards.com	Los Angeles	CA	90058	323-771-3330		550
Dunnellon Area Chamber of Commerce 20500 E Pennsylvania Ave	Dunnellon	FL	34432	352-489-2320		139
Dunnhumby USA LLC 444 W Third St *Web:* www.dunnhumby.com	Cincinnati	OH	45202	513-632-1020		466
Dunning Motors Inc 3745 Jackson Rd *Web:* www.dunningtoyota.com	Ann Arbor	MI	48103	734-997-7600		57
Dunnington Bartholow & Miller LLP 250 Park Ave *Web:* www.dunnington.com	New York	NY	10177	212-682-8811		428
Dunsmuir Hellman Historic Estate 2960 Peralta Oaks Ct *Web:* dunsmuir-hellman.com	Oakland	CA	94605	510-615-5555	562-8294	50-3
Dunthorpe Marketing Group Inc 8825 SE 11th Ave *Web:* www.dunthorpemarketing.com	Portland	OR	97202	503-236-4242		463
Dunwoody College of Technology 818 Dunwoody Blvd *TF:* 800-292-4625 ■ *Web:* www.dunwoody.edu	Minneapolis	MN	55403	612-374-5800	374-4128	800
Dunwoody Village 3500 W Chester Pk *Web:* www.dunwoody.org	Newtown Square	PA	19073	610-359-4400		77
Duo Consulting Inc 641 West Lake St Ste 301 *TF:* 800-555-0061 ■ *Web:* www.duoconsulting.com	Chicago	IL	60661	312-529-3000		177
Duo Fast Northeast 22 Tolland St *TF:* 888-399-5712	East Hartford	CT	06108	860-289-6861		350
Duo-Fast Carolinas Inc 1923 John Crossland Jr Dr *Web:* www.duofast.net	Charlotte	NC	28208	704-377-5721		385
Duo-Fast Construction 155 Harlem Ave *TF Cust Svc:* 877-489-2726 ■ *Web:* www.itwindfast.com	Glenview	IL	60025	847-783-5500	783-5500	758
Duoline Technologies 250 W Bluebird Rd *Web:* www.duoline.com	Gilmer	TX	75645	903-734-1371	734-1571	539
Duo-Safety Ladder Corp 513 W Ninth Ave *TF:* 877-386-5377 ■ *Web:* www.duosafety.com	Oshkosh	WI	54902	920-231-2740	231-2460	421
Dupaco Community Credit Union 3999 Pennsylvania Ave *TF:* 800-373-7600 ■ *Web:* dupaco.com	Dubuque	IA	52002	563-557-7600		219
DuPage Convention & Visitors Bureau 915 Harger Rd Ste 240 *TF:* 800-232-0502 ■ *Web:* www.discoverdupage.com	Oak Brook	IL	60523	630-575-8070	575-8078	206
DuPage County 421 N County Farm Rd *Web:* www.dupageco.org	Wheaton	IL	60187	630-407-5500	407-5501	338
DuPage Machine Products Inc 311 Longview Dr	Bloomingdale	IL	60108	630-690-5400		621
Duplan Construction Inc 390 Industrial St *TF:* 800-551-5602 ■ *Web:* duplanconstruction.com	Campbell	CA	95008	408-866-6682		186
Dupli Graphics Corp 6761 Thompson Rd N *TF:* 800-724-2477 ■ *Web:* www.duplionline.com	Syracuse	NY	13211	800-724-2477		627
Duplication Factory Inc 4275 Norex Dr	Chaska	MN	55318	952-227-8106		658

	Phone	Fax	Class
Duplin County 112 Duplin St Ste 101 .... Kenansville NC 28349 *TF:* 800-685-8916 ■ *Web:* www.duplincountync.com	910-296-2150	296-2156	338
Duplin County Library 107 Bowdens Rd.............................. Kenansville NC 28349 *Web:* www.duplincountync.com	910-296-2117		434-3
Dupli-Systems Inc 8260 Dow Cir .... Strongsville OH 44136 *TF:* 800-321-1610 ■ *Web:* www.dupli-systems.com	440-234-9415	234-2350	110
DuPont Advanced Fibers Systems 5401 Jefferson Davis Hwy .... Richmond VA 23234 *TF:* 800-441-7515 ■ *Web:* www.dupont.com	804-383-3845		605-1
DuPont Automotive 950 Stephenson Hwy PO Box 7013 .... Troy MI 48007 *TF:* 800-533-1313 ■ *Web:* www.dupont.com	248-583-8000		550
DuPont Chemical Solutions 1007 Market St.......................... Wilmington DE 19898 *TF:* 800-441-7515 ■ *Web:* www.dupont.com	302-774-1000	355-4013	145
DuPont Crop Protection PO Box 80705 .... Wilmington DE 19880 *TF:* 888-638-7668 ■ *Web:* www.dupont.com	302-774-1000	999-4399	280
DuPont Engineering Polymers Lancaster Pike Rt 141 Barley Mill Plz Bldg 22.................... Wilmington DE 19805 *TF:* 800-441-7515 ■ *Web:* www.dupont.com	302-999-4592		605-2
Dupont Fabros Technology Inc 1212 New York Ave NW Ste 900............ Washington DC 20005 *NYSE: DFT* ■ *Web:* www.dft.com	202-728-0044	728-0220	654
Dupont Grocery Inc 100 Barksdale Ave .... Du Pont WA 98327	253-964-5007		345
DuPont Historical Museum 207 Barksdale Ave ....Dupont WA 98327 *TF:* 800-804-0589 ■ *Web:* www.dupontmuseum.com	253-964-2399		520
DuPont Packaging & Industrial Polymers Barley Mill Plaza 26-2122 PO Box 80026...... Wilmington DE 19880 **Fax Area Code:* 302 ■ *TF:* 800-438-7225 ■ *Web:* www.dupont.com	703-305-7666	892-7390*	548
DuPont Performance Coatings 1007 Market St.......................... Wilmington DE 19898 *TF:* 800-441-7515 ■ *Web:* www.dupont.com	302-774-1000		550
Dupont Publishing Inc 3051 Tech Dr ....St Petersburg FL 33716 *Web:* dupontregistry.com	727-573-9339		637-9
DuPont Qualicon Henry Clay Rd Bldg 400 Rt 141 PO Box 80400 .... Wilmington DE 19880 *TF:* 800-863-6842 ■ *Web:* dupont.com	302-695-5300		231
DuPont Surfaces 4417 Lancaster Pk CRP 728/3105 .... Wilmington DE 19805 *TF:* 800-448-9835 ■ *Web:* www.dupont.com	302-774-1000		599
DuPont Theatre 1007 N Market St .... Wilmington DE 19801 *TF:* 800-338-0881 ■ *Web:* www.duponttheatre.com	302-656-4401		572
DuPont Titanium Technologies 1007 Market St.......................... Wilmington DE 19898 *TF:* 800-441-7515 ■ *Web:* www.dupont.com	302-774-1000		143
Dupps Co 548 N Cherry St .... Germantown OH 45327 *Web:* www.dupps.com	937-855-6555	855-6554	298
Dupre' Transport LLC 201 Energy Pkwy .... Lafayette LA 70508 *Web:* www.duprelogistics.com	337-237-8471		311
Dupree Plumbing Company Inc 869 Worley Dr............................... Marietta GA 30066 *Web:* www.dupreeplumbing.com	770-428-2291		189-10
Duquesne Light Holdings Inc 411 Seventh Ave........................... Pittsburgh PA 15219 *TF:* 888-393-7000 ■ *Web:* www.duquesnelight.com	412-393-7000	393-7000	360-5
Duquesne University 600 Forbes Ave .... Pittsburgh PA 15282 **Fax:* Admissions ■ *TF:* 800-456-0590 ■ *Web:* www.duq.edu	412-396-6000	396-5779*	166
DuQuoin State Fair 655 Executive Dr .... Du Quoin IL 62832 *Web:* www.illinois.gov/sites/dsf/Pages/default.aspx	618-542-1515	542-1541	642
DuQuoin Tourism Commission 20 N Chestnut St PO Box 1037................ Du Quoin IL 62832 *TF:* 800-455-9570 ■ *Web:* www.duquointourism.org	618-542-8338		206
Dura Automotive Systems Inc 1780 Pond Run......................... Auburn Hills MI 48326 **Fax Area Code:* 442 ■ *Web:* www.duraauto.com	248-299-7500	211-7544*	60
Dura Coat Products Inc 5361 Via Ricardo .... Riverside CA 92509 *Web:* www.duracoatproducts.com	951-341-6500		481
Dura Freight Inc 20405 E Business Pkwy.......... Walnut CA 91789 *Web:* www.durafreight.com	909-595-8100		313
Dura Medical Equipment Inc 7835 NW 148 St......................... Miami Lakes FL 33016 *Web:* www.bayshoreduramedical.com	305-821-1202		475
Dura Plastics Products Inc 533 E Third St............................ Beaumont CA 92223 *Web:* www.duraplastics.com	951-845-3161		596
Dura Supreme Inc 300 Dura Dr............. Howard Lake MN 55349 *Web:* www.durasupreme.com	320-543-3872		115
Dura Wax Co 4101 W Albany St................. McHenry IL 60050 *TF:* 800-435-5705 ■ *Web:* www.durawax.com	815-385-5000	344-8056	151
Durabac Inc 22 ch Milton ....Granby QC J2J0P2 *Web:* www.durabac.ca	450-378-1723		608
Dura-Bilt Products Inc PO Box 188........... Wellsburg NY 14894 *Web:* www.durabilt.com	570-596-2000		697
Durable Packaging International Inc 750 Northgate Pkwy .... Wheeling IL 60090 *Web:* www.durablepackaging.com	847-541-4400		295
Durable Products Inc PO Box 826............ Crossville TN 38557 *TF:* 800-373-3502 ■ *Web:* www.durableproductsinc.com	931-484-3502	456-7682	676
Dura-Bond Industries Inc 2658 Puckety Dr............................. Export PA 15632 *Web:* www.dura-bond.com	724-327-0782		480
Duracell 14 Research Dr....................... Bethel CT 06801 **Fax Area Code:* 866 ■ *TF:* 800-551-2355 ■ *Web:* www.duracell.com	800-544-5454	889-7911*	74
Duraclean International Inc 220 W Campus Dr .... Arlington Heights IL 60004 *TF:* 800-862-5326 ■ *Web:* www.duraclean.com	847-704-7100	704-7101	152
Duracote Corp 350 N Diamond St.............Ravenna OH 44266 *TF:* 800-321-2252 ■ *Web:* www.duracote.com	330-296-3487	296-5102	745-2

	Phone	Fax	Class
Duraflame Inc 2894 Mt Diablo Ave PO Box 1230 .... Stockton CA 95201 *TF:* 800-424-9300 ■ *Web:* www.duraflame.com	209-461-6600	462-9412	819
Dur-A-Flex Inc 95 Goodwin St.............. East Hartford CT 06108 *Web:* www.dur-a-flex.com	860-528-9838		683
Duralee Fabrics Ltd Inc 1775 Fifth Ave........................... Bay Shore NY 11706 **Fax Area Code:* 800 ■ **Fax:* Cust Svc ■ *TF Cust Svc:* 800-275-3872 ■ *Web:* www.duralee.com	631-273-8800	275-3297*	594
DuraLine Imaging Inc 578 Upward Rd Ste 11 .... Flat Rock NC 28731 *TF:* 800-982-3872 ■ *Web:* www.duralineimaging.com	828-692-1301		628
Duraloy Technologies Inc 120 Bridge St .... Scottdale PA 15683 **Fax:* Sales ■ *Web:* www.duraloy.com	724-887-5100	887-5224*	307
Duran Human Capital Partners Inc 300 Orchard City Dr Ste 142.................Campbell CA 95008 *TF:* 800-287-9682 ■ *Web:* www.duranhcp.com	408-540-0070	540-0073	721
Durand Chevrolet Inc 223 Washington St .... Hudson MA 01749 *Web:* durandchevrolet.com	978-562-7915		57
Durand Hedden House & Garden Assn 523 Ridgewood Rd .... Maplewood NJ 07040 *TF:* 800-245-1377 ■ *Web:* durandhedden.org	973-763-7712		50-3
Durango Area Tourism Office 111 S Camino del Rio.......................Durango CO 81301 *TF:* 800-525-8855 ■ *Web:* www.durango.org	970-247-3500		206
Durango Arts Ctr 802 E Second Ave............Durango CO 81301 *Web:* durangoarts.org	970-259-2606	259-6571	50-2
Durango Herald 1275 Main Ave ....Durango CO 81301 *TF:* 800-530-8318 ■ *Web:* www.durangoherald.com	970-247-3504	259-5011	532-2
Durango's 2121 Richmond Rd ....Lexington KY 40502	859-268-0723		671
Durant Area Chamber of Commerce 215 N Fourth St .... Durant OK 74701 *Web:* www.durantchamber.org	580-924-0848	924-0348	139
Durant Bancorp / First United Bank 1400 W Main .... Durant OK 74701 *TF:* 800-924-4427 ■ *Web:* firstunitedbank.com	580-924-2211		70
Durant's Restaurant 2611 N Central Ave.......................... Phoenix AZ 85004 *TF:* 800-313-0017 ■ *Web:* www.durantsaz.com	602-264-5967		671
Dura-Stress Inc 11325 County Rd 44 .... Leesburg FL 34788 *TF General:* 800-342-9239 ■ *Web:* www.durastress.com	352-787-1422	787-0080	183
DuraTech Industries International Inc PO Box 1940 .... Jamestown ND 58401 *TF:* 800-243-4601 ■ *Web:* www.duratechindustries.net	701-252-4601	252-0502	273
Duratrack Inc 950 Morse Ave .... Elk Grove Village IL 60007 *Web:* www.duratrack.com	847-806-0202		697
Dura-Vent Inc 877 Cotting Ct .... Vacaville CA 95688 *TF:* 800-835-4429 ■ *Web:* www.duravent.com	707-446-1786	446-4740	697
Duravit USA Inc 2205 Northmont Pkwy Ste 200................. Duluth GA 30096 *TF:* 888-387-2848 ■ *Web:* www.duravit.com	770-931-3575		612
Durawood Products Inc 18 Industrial Way ....Denver PA 17517 *Web:* www.durawood.com	717-336-0220		499
Durbin Richard J (Sen D - IL) 711 Hart Bldg ....Washington DC 20510 *Web:* www.durbin.senate.gov	202-224-2152	228-0400	342-2
Durbin Richard J (Sen D - IL) 711 Hart Senate Bldg ....Washington DC 20510 *Web:* www.durbin.senate.gov	202-224-2152	228-0400	342-2
Durcon Co 8464 Ronda Dr ....Canton MI 48187 *Web:* www.durcon.com	734-455-4520		420
DURECT Corp 2 Results Way ....Cupertino CA 95014 *NASDAQ: DRRX* ■ *Web:* www.durect.com	408-777-1417	777-3577	85
DureX Inc 5 Stahuber Ave.........................Union NJ 07083 *Web:* www.durexinc.com	908-688-0800	688-0718	488
Durex Industries Inc 190 Detroit St ....Cary IL 60013 *Web:* www.durexindustries.com	847-639-5600		203
Durham Academy Inc 3130 Pickett Rd........... Durham NC 27705 *TF:* 888-904-9149 ■ *Web:* www.da.org	919-489-9118		685
Durham Christian Homes Hair Styling 200 Glen Hill Dr ....Whitby ON L1N8R4 *Web:* durhamchristianhomes.salonpages.ca	905-430-1666		77
Durham City Hall 101 City Hall Plaza .... Durham NC 27701 *Web:* www.durhamnc.gov	919-560-1200	560-4835	337
Durham Co 722 Durham Rd ....Lebanon MO 65536 *Web:* www.durhamcompany.com	417-532-7121		816
Durham Convention & Visitors Bureau 101 E Morgan St.............................. Durham NC 27701 *TF:* 800-446-8604 ■ *Web:* durham-nc.com	919-687-0288	683-9555	206
Durham Correctional Ctr 3900 Guess Rd .... Durham NC 27705	919-477-2314		213
Durham Cos Inc 6300 Transit Rd................ Depew NY 14043 *TF:* 800-633-7724 ■ *Web:* www.durhamstaffing.com	716-684-3333	681-7408	721
Durham County 200 E Main St .... Durham NC 27701 *Web:* dconc.gov	919-560-0000	560-0020	338
Durham County Library 300 N Roxboro St......... Durham NC 27701 *Web:* www.durhamcountylibrary.org	919-560-0100		434-3
Durham Exchange Club Industries Inc 1717 E Lawson St............................ Durham NC 27703 *TF:* 800-510-9132 ■ *Web:* www.deci.org	919-596-1341	596-6380	721
Durham Furniture Inc 450 Lambton St W .... Durham ON N0G1R0 *TF:* 800-932-2006 ■ *Web:* durhamfurniture.com	519-369-2345	369-6515	319-2
Durham Jones & Pinegar 111 East Broadway Ste 2400 ....Salt Lake City UT 84111 *Web:* www.djplaw.com	801-415-3000	415-3500	428
Durham Manufacturing Co 201 Main St......... Durham CT 06422 *TF:* 800-243-3774 ■ *Web:* www.durhammfg.com	860-349-3427	349-8235	286
Durham Museum 801 S Tenth St..................Omaha NE 68108 *TF:* 800-745-3000 ■ *Web:* www.durhammuseum.org	402-444-5071	444-5397	520
Durham Symphony Orchestra PO Box 1993...... Durham NC 27702 *Web:* www.durhamsymphony.org	919-560-2736		573-3
Durham Technical Community College 1637 E Lawson St........................... Durham NC 27703 **Fax:* Admissions ■ *Web:* www.durhamtech.edu	919-536-7200	686-3669*	162
Durie Tangri LLP 217 Leidesdorff St .... San Francisco CA 94111 *Web:* www.durietangri.com	415-362-6666		466

Company	City	State	ZIP	Phone	Fax	Class
Durisol Inc 67 Frid St *Web:* www.armtcc.com	Hamilton	ON	L8P4M3	905-521-0999		192
Durkin Equipment Company Inc 2383 Chaffee Dr *TF:* 800-264-3875 ■ *Web:* www.durkininc.com	Saint Louis	MO	63146	314-432-2040		358
Duro Dyne Corp 81 Spence St *TF:* 800-899-3876 ■ *Web:* www.durodyne.com	Bay Shore	NY	11706	631-249-9000	249-9000	14
Duro Textiles LLC 110 Chace St *Web:* www.duroindustries.com	Fall River	MA	02724	508-675-0101		745-7
Durocher Auto Sales Inc 4651 Rt 9 *TF:* 877-215-8954 ■ *Web:* www.durocherauto.com	Plattsburgh	NY	12901	888-635-4599		57
Duro-Life Corp 2401 Huntington Dr N *Web:* www.duro-life.com	Algonquin	IL	60102	847-854-1044		454
Duron Plastics Ltd 965 Wilson Ave	Kitchener	ON	N2C1J1	519-884-8011		608
Durre Brothers Welding & Machine Shop Inc 405 S Chestnut *Web:* www.durrebros.com	Minonk	IL	61760	309-432-2512		757
Durst Corp Inc 129 Dermody St *Web:* www.durstcorp.com	Cranford	NJ	07016	908-653-1100		612
Durst Image Technology US LLC 50 Methodist Hill Dr Ste 100 *Web:* www.durstus.com	Rochester	NY	14623	585-486-0340		180
Dury's 701 Ewing Ave *TF:* 800-824-2379 ■ *Web:* www.durys.com	Nashville	TN	37203	615-255-3456	255-3506	119
DUSA Pharmaceuticals Inc 25 Upton Dr *NASDAQ: DUSA* ■ *TF:* 877-533-3872 ■ *Web:* www.dusapharma.com	Wilmington	MA	01887	978-657-7500	657-9193	85
DuSable Museum of African American History 740 E 56th Pl *Web:* www.dusablemuseum.org	Chicago	IL	60637	773-947-0600		520
Dusing Bros Ice Manufacturing Co 3607 Dixie Hwy	Elsmere	KY	41018	859-727-2720		380
Dustex Corp 100 Chastain Ctr Blvd Ste 195 *TF:* 800-647-6167 ■ *Web:* www.dustex.com	Kennesaw	GA	30144	770-429-5575	429-5556	18
Dustrol Inc 1200 E Main PO Box 309 *Web:* www.dustrol.com	Towanda	KS	67144	316-536-2262	536-2789	189-18
Dutailier Group Inc 299 Rue Chaput *TF:* 800-363-9817 ■ *Web:* www.dutailier.com	Sainte-Pie	QC	J0H1W0	450-772-2403	772-5055	319-2
Dutch Gold Honey Inc 2220 Dutch Gold Dr *TF:* 800-846-2753 ■ *Web:* www.dutchgoldhoney.com	Lancaster	PA	17601	717-393-1716	393-8687	296-24
Dutch Made Custom Cabinetry 10415 Roth Rd *TF:* 800-529-8970 ■ *Web:* www.dutchmade.com	Grabill	IN	46741	260-657-3311	657-5778	115
Dutch Maid Bakery Inc 50 Park St *Web:* www.dutchmaidbakery.com	Dorchester	MA	02122	617-265-5417		297-8
Dutch Oil Company Inc 730 Alabama St *Web:* www.dutchoil-victory.com	Columbus	MS	39702	662-327-5202		579
Dutch Quality Stone Inc 18012 Dover Rd *Web:* www.dutchqualitystone.com	Mount Eaton	OH	44659	330-359-7866		724
Dutch Square Center 421 Bush River Rd *Web:* www.dutchsquare.com	Columbia	SC	29210	803-772-3864	750-0036	460
Dutch Valley Bulk Food Distributors Inc 7615 Lancaster Ave *TF:* 800-733-4191 ■ *Web:* www.dutchvalleyfoods.com	Myerstown	PA	17067	717-933-4191	933-5466	297-8
Dutch Valley Supply Company Inc (DVS) 970 Progress Ctr Ave *TF:* 800-837-0904 ■ *Web:* www.dutchvalley.com	Lawrenceville	GA	30043	770-513-0612	513-0716	770
Dutch Wonderland Family Amusement Park 2249 Lincoln Hwy E *TF:* 866-386-2839 ■ *Web:* www.dutchwonderland.com	Lancaster	PA	17602	717-291-1888		32
Dutchess Beer Distributors Inc 5 Laurel St *Web:* dutchessbeer.com	Poughkeepsie	NY	12601	845-452-0940	452-0958	81-1
Dutchess Community College 53 Pendell Rd *TF:* 800-421-3481 ■ *Web:* www.sunydutchess.edu	Poughkeepsie	NY	12601	845-431-8010	431-8605	162
Dutchess County 22 Market St *Web:* www.co.dutchess.ny.us	Poughkeepsie	NY	12601	845-486-2120		338
Dutchess County Regional Chamber of Commerce 1 Civic Ctr Plaza Ste 400 *TF:* 800-817-2918 ■ *Web:* www.dcrcoc.org	Poughkeepsie	NY	12601	845-454-1700	454-1702	139
Dutchland Inc PO Box 549 *Web:* www.dutchlandinc.com	Gap	PA	17527	717-442-8282	442-9330	183
Dutchland Plastics Corp 54 Enterprise Ct *Web:* www.dutchland.com	Oostburg	WI	53070	920-564-3633	564-3337	608
Dutchland Plastics Southeast LLC 401 Furman Hall Rd *Web:* www.dutchlandplastics.com	Greenville	SC	29609	864-242-0790		596
Dutchman Hospitality Group 4985 Walnut St PO Box 158 *TF:* 800-824-2013 ■ *Web:* www.dhgroup.com	Walnut Creek	OH	44687	330-893-2926	893-2637	670
Dutchman Tree Farms 9689 W Walker Rd *TF:* 800-543-9828 ■ *Web:* www.dutchmantreefarms.com	Manton	MI	49663	231-839-7901		752
Dutchmen Mfg Inc 2164 Caragana Ct PO Box 2164 *TF:* 866-425-4369 ■ *Web:* www.dutchmen.com	Goshen	IN	46527	574-537-0600		120
Dutt & Wagner of Virginia Inc 1142 W Main St *TF:* 800-688-2116 ■ *Web:* duttandwagner.com	Abingdon	VA	24210	276-628-2116	628-4619	297-10
Dutton Family Theatre 3454 W 76 Country Blvd *TF:* 800-400-9343 ■ *Web:* www.theduttons.com	Branson	MO	65616	417-332-2772	339-4900	520
Dutton-Lainson Co 451 W Second St *Web:* www.dutton-lainson.com	Hastings	NE	68901	402-462-4141		612
Duty Free Americas Inc 6100 Hollywood Blvd 7th Fl *Web:* www.dutyfreeamericas.com	Hollywood	FL	33024	954-986-7700		241
Duval County 117 W Duval St *Web:* www.coj.net	Jacksonville	FL	32202	904-630-2409	630-2906	338
Duval County School System 1701 Prudential Dr *TF:* 800-238-3463 ■ *Web:* www.duvalschools.org	Jacksonville	FL	32207	904-390-2000	390-2586	685
Duval Regional Juvenile Detention Ctr 1241 E Eigth St	Jacksonville	FL	32206	904-798-4819		412
Duvinage Corp 60 W Oak Ridge Dr *TF:* 800-541-2645 ■ *Web:* www.duvinage.com	Hagerstown	MD	21740	301-733-8255	791-7240	491
DuVoice Corp 608 State St S Ste 100 *TF:* 800-888-1057 ■ *Web:* www.duvoice.com	Kirkland	WA	98033	425-889-9790		225
Duwest Tool & Die Inc 8400 Madison Ave *Web:* duwesttool.com	Cleveland	OH	44102	216-631-1060		697
DVD Empire 2140 Woodland Rd *TF:* 888-383-1880 ■ *Web:* www.dvdempire.com	Warrendale	PA	15086	888-383-1880		797
DVFG Advisors LLC 125 E Elm St Ste 300 *Web:* www.dvfgadvisors.com	Conshohocken	PA	19428	610-234-0500		466
DVFlora (DVWF) 520 Mantua Blvd N *TF:* 800-676-1212 ■ *Web:* www.dvwf.com	Sewell	NJ	08080	856-468-7000	464-2772	293
DVI Communications Inc 11 Park Pl Ste 906 *Web:* www.dvicomm.com	New York	NY	10007	212-267-2929		387
DVL Public Relations & Adv 700 12th Ave S Ste 400 *Web:* www.dvl.com	Nashville	TN	37203	615-244-1818		636
DVL Seigenthaler 700 12th Ave S *Web:* www.seig-pr.com	Nashville	TN	37203	615-244-1818		636
Dvp Technologies LLC 123 Hillcrest Dr *TF:* 800-572-2138 ■ *Web:* www.dvptech.com	Southbury	CT	06488	203-262-6005		196
DVS (Digital Video Systems Inc) 357 Castro St Ste 5 *Web:* www.dvsystems.com	Mountain View	CA	94041	650-938-8815		52
DVS (Dutch Valley Supply Company Inc) 970 Progress Ctr Ave *TF:* 800-837-0904 ■ *Web:* www.dutchvalley.com	Lawrenceville	GA	30043	770-513-0612	513-0716	770
DVWF (DVFlora) 520 Mantua Blvd N *TF:* 800-676-1212 ■ *Web:* www.dvwf.com	Sewell	NJ	08080	856-468-7000	464-2772	293
DW Clark Inc 692 N Bedford St *Web:* www.dwclark.com	East Bridgewater	MA	02333	508-378-4014		492
DW Green Co 8100 S Priest Dr *TF:* 800-253-7146 ■ *Web:* www.dwgreen.com	Tempe	AZ	85284	480-491-8483		4
DW Nicholson Corp 24747 Clawiter Rd *Web:* www.dwnicholson.com	Hayward	CA	94545	510-887-0900	783-9948	189-1
DW Turner Inc 400 Gold Ave SW 12th Fl *Web:* agenda-global.com	Albuquerque	NM	87102	505-888-5877		636
Dwellworks LLC 1317 Euclid Ave 2nd Fl *Web:* www.dwellworks.com	Cleveland	OH	44115	216-682-4200		393
Dwfritz Automation Inc 12100 SW Tualatin Rd *TF:* 800-763-4161 ■ *Web:* dwfritz.com	Wilsonville	OR	97070	503-598-9393		539
Dwight D Eisenhower Presidential Library & Museum 200 SE Fourth St *TF:* 877-746-4453 ■ *Web:* www.eisenhower.archives.gov	Abilene	KS	67410	785-263-6700	263-6715	434-2
Dwight D Eisenhower V A Medical Ctr 4101 S Fourth St *TF:* 800-952-8387 ■ *Web:* www.leavenworth.va.gov	Leavenworth	KS	66048	913-682-2000		374-8
Dwight G Lewis Lumber Company Inc 1895 Pennsylvania 87	Hillsgrove	PA	18619	570-924-3507		683
Dwight's Bistro 1527 Penman Rd *Web:* www.dwightsbistro.com	Jacksonville Beach	FL	32250	904-241-4496		671
Dworken-Hillman-LaMorte & Sterczala 4 Corporate Dr Ste 488 *TF:* 800-836-4340 ■ *Web:* dhls.com	Shelton	CT	06484	203-929-3535		2
Dworshak State Park 9934 Freeman Creek *TF:* 888-922-6743 ■ *Web:* parksandrecreation.idaho.gov/parks/dworshak	Lenore	ID	83541	208-476-5994		565
DWQ Assoc Ltd 38 N Ct St *Web:* www.dwqassociates.com	Providence	RI	02903	401-273-5220		194
DWS Inc 102 Kimball Ave Ste 2	South Burlington	VT	05403	802-861-6004		225
Dwyer Instruments Inc 102 Indiana Hwy 212 PO Box 373 *Web:* www.dwyer-inst.com	Michigan City	IN	46360	219-879-8000	872-9057	201
Dwyer Products Corp 1226 Michael Dr Ste F *TF:* 800-822-0092 ■ *Web:* www.dwyerproducts.com	Wood Dale	IL	60191	630-741-7900	741-7974	36
Dxm Productions 472 S Shoreline Blvd *Web:* www.dxm.com	Mountain View	CA	94041	650-969-6580		180
DxNA LLC 180 N 300 E *Web:* www.dxna.com	Saint George	UT	84770	435-628-0324		582
Dxo Communications Inc 1 Townline Cir *TF:* 800-463-3339 ■ *Web:* dxocom.com	Rochester	NY	14623	716-685-4395		5
DXP Enterprises Inc 7272 Pinemont Dr *NASDAQ: DXPE* ■ *TF:* 800-830-3973 ■ *Web:* www.dxpe.com	Houston	TX	77040	713-996-4700	996-4701	385
DXStorm.com Inc 824 Winston Churchill Blvd *TF:* 877-397-8676 ■ *Web:* www.dxstorm.com	Oakville	ON	L6J7X2	905-842-8262		224
D&Y (Daniel & Yeager) 6767 Old Madison Pk Ste 690 *TF:* 800-955-1919 ■ *Web:* www.dystaffing.com	Huntsville	AL	35806	800-955-1919		266
Dyadic International Inc 140 Intracoastal Pointe Dr Ste 404 *OTC: DYAI* ■ *Web:* www.dyadic.com	Jupiter	FL	33477	561-743-8333	743-8343	85
DyAnsys Inc 300 N Bayshore Blvd *TF:* 888-950-4321 ■ *Web:* www.dyansys.com	Burlingame	CA	94401	888-950-4321		743
Dyatech LLC 805 S Wheatley St Ste 600 *TF:* 866-651-4222 ■ *Web:* www.dyatech.com	Ridgeland	MS	39157	601-914-1004		390
Dybrook Products Inc 5232 Tod Ave Sw, Unit 23 *Web:* www.dybrook.com	Warren	OH	44481	330-392-7665		677
Dyck Arboretum of the Plains 177 W Hickory St *Web:* www.dyckarboretum.org	Hesston	KS	67062	620-327-8127		97
Dyckman Farmhouse Museum 4881 Broadway at 204th St *Web:* www.dyckmanfarmhouse.org	New York	NY	10034	212-304-9422		520

Company	Phone	Fax	Class
Dycom Industries Inc 11770 US Hwy 1 Ste 101 .... Palm Beach Gardens FL 33408 *NYSE:* DY ■ *TF:* 800-450-0786 ■ *Web:* www.dycomind.com	561-627-7171		189-4
Dycor Technologies Ltd 1851 94 St .... Edmonton AB T6N1E6 *TF:* 800-663-9267 ■ *Web:* www.dycor.com	780-486-0091		668
DYE Precision Inc 10637 Scripps Summit Ct .... San Diego CA 92131 *Web:* dyecnc.com	858-536-5183		454
Dyer County 115 Market St PO Box 1360 .... Dyersburg TN 38025 *TF:* 800-829-1040 ■ *Web:* tn.gov	731-286-7814	288-7719	338
Dyer Riddle Mills & Precourt Inc (DRMP) 941 Lake Baldwin Ln .... Orlando FL 32814 *TF:* 800-375-3767 ■ *Web:* www.drmp.com	407-896-0594	896-4836	261
Dyersburg Avionics of Caruthersville 2204 Airport Dr .... Caruthersville MO 63830	573-333-4296		63
Dyersburg Regional Medical Ctr 400 E Tickle St .... Dyersburg TN 38024 *TF:* 800-272-3900 ■ *Web:* www.tennova.com	731-285-2410		374-3
Dyersburg State Community College 1510 Lake Rd .... Dyersburg TN 38024 **Fax:* Admissions ■ *Web:* www.dscc.edu	731-286-3200	286-3325*	162
Dyersburg/Dyer County Chamber of Commerce 2000 Commerce Ave .... Dyersburg TN 38024 *Web:* dyerchamber.com	731-285-3433	286-4926	139
Dykes Library University of Kansas Medical Ctr 3901 Rainbow Blvd, Mail Stop 1050 .... Kansas City KS 66160 *Web:* library.kumc.edu	913-588-7166	588-8675	434-1
Dylan Hotel NYC 52 E 41st St .... New York NY 10017 *Web:* www.dylanhotel.com	212-338-0500	338-0569	379
Dymax Corp 318 Industrial Ln .... Torrington CT 06790 *TF:* 877-396-2963 ■ *Web:* www.dymax.com	860-482-1010	496-0608	3
Dymedix Corp 5985 Rice Creek Pkwy Ste 201 .... Shoreview MN 55126 *Web:* www.dymedix.com	763-789-8280		476
Dymun & Co 200 First Ave Ste 400 .... Pittsburgh PA 15222 *TF:* 800-558-4100 ■ *Web:* dymun.com	412-281-2345		195
Dyna Flex Ltd PO Box 99 .... Saint Ann MO 63074 *TF:* 800-489-4020 ■ *Web:* www.dynaflex.com	314-426-4020		743
Dyna Lync Corp 200 Consumer Rd Ste 604 .... Toronto ON M2J4R4 *Web:* www.dynalync.ca	416-398-2000		463
Dynabrade Inc 8989 Sheridan Dr .... Clarence NY 14031 *TF Cust Svc:* 800-828-7333 ■ *Web:* www.dynabrade.com	716-631-0100	631-2073	759
Dynacare Laboratories Inc 9200 W Wisconsin Ave .... Milwaukee WI 53226 *Web:* www.dynacaremilwaukee.com	414-805-7600		415
Dynacast Inc 14045 Ballantyne Corporate Pl .... Charlotte NC 28277 *Web:* www.dynacast.com	704-927-2790	927-2791	308
Dynaco Corp 3020 S Park Dr .... Tempe AZ 85282	602-437-8003	437-8015	625
Dynaco Inc 7050 N Fresno St Ste 210 .... Fresno CA 93720 *Web:* brg.co	559-485-8520		670
Dynacon Inc 831 Industrial Blvd .... Bryan TX 77803 *Web:* www.dynacon.com	979-823-2690		470
Dynacor Media 60 Ave Ste 9314 .... Edmonton AB T6E0C1 *Web:* dynacormedia.com	780-448-0093		180
Dynacraft Co 650 Milwaukee Ave N .... Algona WA 98001 *Web:* dynacraftnet.com	253-333-3000	333-3041	370
Dynadot LLC PO Box 345 .... San Mateo CA 94401 **Fax Area Code:* 415 ■ *TF Cust Svc:* 866-652-2039 ■ *Web:* www.dynadot.com	650-585-1961	869-2893*	396
Dyna-Empire Inc 1075 Stewart Ave .... Garden City NY 11530 *Web:* www.dyna-empire.com	516-222-2700		57
Dynaflair Corp 8147 Eagle Palm Dr .... Tampa FL 33605 *Web:* www.dynaflair.com	813-248-8100		234
Dynaflex Products 6466 Gayhart St .... Commerce CA 90040 *Web:* www.dynaflexproducts.com	323-724-1555		567
Dynagraphics Corp 4080 Norex Dr .... Chaska MN 55318 *TF:* 800-959-0108 ■ *Web:* www.dyna-graphics.com	800-959-0108		203
Dynalco 3690 NW 53rd St .... Fort Lauderdale FL 33309 *TF:* 800-368-6666 ■ *Web:* www.dynalco.com	954-739-4300	484-3376	201
Dynalec Corp 87 W Main St .... Sodus NY 14551 *Web:* www.dynalec.com	315-483-6923	483-6656	529
Dynalectric Corp 4462 Corporate Ctr Dr .... Los Alamitos CA 90720 **Fax Area Code:* 866 ■ **Fax:* Acctg ■ *TF:* 866-890-7794 ■ *Web:* www.kdc-systems.com	714-828-7000	890-7794*	189-4
DynaLifeDX Diagnostic Laboratory Services 10150 - 102 St Ste 200 .... Edmonton AB T5J5E2 *TF:* 800-661-9876 ■ *Web:* www.dynalifedx.com	780-451-3702		415
Dynalloy Inc 14762 Bentley Cir .... Tustin CA 92780 *Web:* www.dynalloy.com	714-436-1206	436-0511	253
Dynaloy LLC 6445 Olivia Ln .... Indianapolis IN 46226 *TF:* 800-669-5709 ■ *Web:* www.dynaloy.com	317-788-5694		145
Dynamation Research Inc 2301 Pontius Ave .... Los Angeles CA 90064 *TF:* 800-726-7997 ■ *Web:* www.dynamationresearch.com	310-477-1224		350
Dynamet Inc 195 Museum Rd .... Washington PA 15301 *TF:* 800-237-9655 ■ *Web:* www.cartech.com	724-228-1000	229-4195	485
DynaMetric Inc 717 S Myrtle Ave .... Monrovia CA 91016 *TF:* 800-525-6925 ■ *Web:* www.dynametric.com	626-358-2559	359-5701	735
Dynamic Air Engineering Inc 620 E Dyer Rd .... Santa Ana CA 92705 *Web:* www.dynamic-air.com	714-540-1000	545-9145	18
Dynamic Air Inc 1125 Willow Lake Blvd .... Saint Paul MN 55110 *Web:* www.dynamicair.com	651-484-2900	484-7015	207
Dynamic Automation 4525 Runway St .... Simi Valley CA 93063 *Web:* www.dynamicautomation.com	805-584-8476		358
Dynamic Business Solutions Inc 30100 Telegraph Rd Ste 322 .... Bingham Farms MI 48025 *TF:* 800-578-7880 ■ *Web:* www.qualitech.net	248-646-0093		179
Dynamic Civil Solutions Inc 2210 Second Ave N .... Birmingham AL 35203 *Web:* dcseng.com	205-358-7256		261
Dynamic Computer Corp 23400 Industrial Pk Ct .... Farmington Hills MI 48335 *TF:* 866-257-2111 ■ *Web:* www.dcc-online.com	248-473-2200		174
Dynamic Concepts Inc (DCI) 1730 17th St NE .... Washington DC 20002 *Web:* www.dcihq.com	202-944-8787	526-7233	735
Dynamic Cooking Systems 5800 Skylab Rd .... Huntington Beach CA 92647 *Web:* www.dcsappliances.com	714-372-7000		427
Dynamic Corporate Solutions Inc 1845 Town Ctr Blvd Ste 525 .... Fleming Island FL 32003 *Web:* www.dynamiccorp.com	904-278-5383		463
Dynamic Design & Manufacturing Inc 6321 Monarch Park Pl .... Niwot CO 80503 *Web:* www.dycoinc.com	303-652-0431		488
Dynamic Design Solutions Inc 3565 Centre Cir .... Fort Mill SC 29715 *TF:* 866-337-2010 ■ *Web:* www.dynamicdesignsolutionsinc.com	803-548-3609		256
Dynamic Devices 8 Lewis Cir .... Wilmington DE 19804 *TF:* 800-827-8478 ■ *Web:* dynamicdevices.com	302-994-2401		463
Dynamic Digital Adv 1265 Industrial Blvd .... Southampton PA 18966 *Web:* www.zeroonezero.com	215-355-6442		4
Dynamic Digital Depth Inc 2120 Colorado Ave Ste 100 .... Santa Monica CA 90404	310-566-3340	566-3380	174
Dynamic Direct Courier 57 Newkirk Rd .... Richmond Hill ON L4E1A4 *TF:* 800-567-0257 ■ *Web:* dynamicdirectcourier.com	905-884-4801		317
Dynamic Edge Inc 2245 S State St Ste 1200 .... Ann Arbor MI 48104 *Web:* www.dynedge.com	734-404-8061		180
Dynamic Energy Services International LLC 600 Jefferson St Ste 1400 .... Lafayette LA 70501 *Web:* www.morenogroupllc.com	337-237-1898	769-9615	536
Dynamic Engineering 221 Cessna St .... Watertown SD 57201 *Web:* www.dynamicengineering.net	605-886-5545		454
Dynamic Homes LLC 525 Roosevelt Ave .... Detroit Lakes MN 56501 **Fax:* Orders ■ *TF:* 800-492-4833 ■ *Web:* www.dynamichomes.com	218-847-2611	847-2617*	106
Dynamic Links International LLC 8286 Daleview Rd .... Cincinnati OH 45247 *Web:* dynamiclinksint.com	513-385-2600		463
Dynamic Manufacturing Inc 1930 N Mannheim Rd .... Melrose Park IL 60160 *Web:* www.dynamicmanufacturinginc.com	708-343-8753	343-8768	386
Dynamic Medical Systems Inc 2811 E Ana St .... Rancho Dominguez CA 90221 *Web:* www.godynamic.com	310-928-0251		475
Dynamic Mobile Data Systems Inc 285 Davidson Ave Ste 501 .... Somerset NJ 08873	732-302-1700	302-9558	224
Dynamic Motion Control Inc 1333 N Kingsbury St .... Chicago IL 60642 *Web:* www.dmcinfo.com	312-255-8757		180
Dynamic Network Factory Inc 21353 Cabot Blvd .... Hayward CA 94545 *TF:* 800-947-4742 ■ *Web:* www.dnfstorage.com	510-265-1122	265-1565	173-8
Dynamic Plastics Inc 29831 Commerce Blvd .... Chesterfield MI 48051 *Web:* www.dynamicplastics.com	586-749-6100		608
Dynamic Research Inc 355 Van Ness Ave Ste 200 .... Torrance CA 90501 *Web:* www.dynres.com	310-212-5211		261
Dynamic Sealing Technologies Inc 13829 Jay St NW .... Andover MN 55304 *Web:* www.dsti.com	763-786-3758		454
Dynamic Security Concepts Inc 1037 Morningside Dr Ste 10 6090 Danenhauer Ln .... Mays Landing NJ 08330 *Web:* www.dscinc.net	609-625-3942		256
Dynamic Security Inc 1102 Woodward Ave .... Muscle Shoals AL 35661 *Web:* www.dynamic.cc	256-383-5798		693
Dynamic Source Manufacturing Inc Unit 117 2765 - 48th Ave NE .... Calgary AB T3J5M9 *Web:* www.dynamicsourcemfg.com	403-516-1888		253
DYNAMIC SYSTEMS Inc 124 Maryland St .... El Segundo CA 90245 *Web:* www.dynamicsystemsinc.com	310-337-4400		174
Dynamic Test Solutions Inc 4360 W Chandler Blvd Ste 1 .... Chandler AZ 85226 *Web:* www.dynamic-test.com	480-632-0312		256
Dynamic Tool & Design Inc W133 N5180 Campbell Dr .... Menomonee Falls WI 53051 *TF:* 800-882-0886 ■ *Web:* www.dyntool.com	262-783-6340		711
Dynamic Tool Company Inc 1421 Vanderbilt Dr .... El Paso TX 79935 *Web:* dynamicdesignfabrication.com	915-598-2330		697
Dynamicard 332 S Juniper St Ste 101 .... Escondido CA 92025 *TF:* 800-928-7670 ■ *Web:* www.dynamicard.com	800-928-7670		5
Dynamics Edge Inc 2635 N First St Ste #148 .... San Jose CA 95134 *TF:* 800-453-5961 ■ *Web:* www.dynamicsedge.com	800-453-5961		196
Dynamis Inc 3707 Henson Rd .... Knoxville TN 37921 *TF:* 800-583-0148 ■ *Web:* dynamis-inc.com	865-588-5422		196
Dynamix Engineering Ltd 855 Grandview Ave .... Columbus OH 43215 *Web:* dynamix-ltd.com	614-443-1178		261
Dynanet Corp 8182 Lark Brown Rd Ste 300 .... Elkridge MD 21075 *TF:* 800-539-1992 ■ *Web:* www.dynanetcorp.com	443-661-1403		395
Dyna-Pak Corp 112 Helton Dr .... Lawrenceburg TN 38464 *Web:* www.dynapak.com	931-762-4016		557
Dynapar 1675 Delany Rd .... Gurnee IL 60031 *TF General:* 800-873-8731 ■ *Web:* www.dynapar.com	800-873-8731		801
Dynapower Corp 85 Meadowland Dr .... South Burlington VT 05403 *TF:* 800-332-1111 ■ *Web:* www.dynapower.com	802-860-7200		767
Dynaquip Controls 10 Harris Industrial Pk .... Saint Clair MO 63077 *TF:* 800-545-3636 ■ *Web:* www.dynaquip.com	636-629-3700	629-5528	790
Dynarex Corp 10 Glenshaw St .... Orangeburg NY 10962 *TF:* 888-335-7500 ■ *Web:* www.dynarex.com	845-365-8200	365-8201	477

Company / Address	City	State	ZIP	Phone	Fax	Class
Dynaric Inc 5740 Bayside Rd	Virginia Beach	VA	23455	800-526-0827		547
TF: 800-526-0827 ■ *Web:* www.dynaric.com						
Dynasign Corp 44040 Fremont Blvd	Fremont	CA	94538	510-405-5988		701
Web: www.dynasign.net						
Dynasplint Systems Inc						
770 Ritchie Hwy Ste W21	Severna Park	MD	21146	410-544-9530	380-3784*	264-4
**Fax Area Code:* 800 ■ *TF:* 800-638-6771 ■ *Web:* www.dynasplint.com						
Dynastar 1413 Crt Dr	Park City	UT	84098	435-252-3300		710
Web: www.dynastar.com						
Dynasteel Corp 4334 Old Millington Rd	Memphis	TN	38127	901-358-6231		91
Web: www.dynasteel.net						
Dynasty 5326 W 26th St	Sioux Falls	SD	57106	605-361-7788		671
Dynasty Import Co 2765 16th St	San Francisco	CA	94103	415-864-5084		787
TF: 800-227-3344 ■ *Web:* m.dynastygallery.com						
Dynasty Spas Inc 101 Dynasty Way	Athens	TN	37303	423-745-1972		610
Web: www.dynastyspas.com						
Dynasty Suites 1235 W Colton Ave	Redlands	CA	92374	909-793-6648	792-5219	379
TF General: 800-874-8958 ■ *Web:* www.dynastysuites.com						
Dynatect Mfg 2300 S Calhoun Rd	New Berlin	WI	53151	262-786-1500	786-3280	676
Web: www.dynatect.com						
Dynatem Inc 23263 Madero Ste C	Mission Viejo	CA	92691	949-855-3235	770-3481	625
TF: 800-543-3830 ■ *Web:* www.dynatem.com						
DynaTen Corp 4375 Diplomacy Rd	Fort Worth	TX	76155	817-616-2200		261
TF: 800-406-9614 ■ *Web:* www.dynaten.com						
Dynatronics Corp						
7030 Pk Centre Dr	Salt Lake City	UT	84121	801-568-7000	221-1919*	250
NASDAQ: DYNT ■ **Fax Area Code:* 800 ■ *TF:* 800-874-6251 ■ *Web:* www.dynatronics.com						
Dynavax Technologies Corp						
2929 Seventh St Ste 100	Berkeley	CA	94710	510-848-5100	848-1327	582
NASDAQ: DVAX ■ *TF:* 877-848-5100 ■ *Web:* www.dynavax.com						
Dynaxys LLC 11911 Tech Rd	Silver Spring	MD	20904	301-622-0900		177
Web: www.dynaxys.com						
Dyne Systems Company LLC						
W209N17391 Industrial Dr	Jackson	WI	53037	262-677-9300		639
Web: www.dynesystems.com						
Dynegy Inc 601 Travis St Ste 1400	Houston	TX	77002	713-507-6400		360-5
NYSE: DYN ■ *TF:* 800-633-4704 ■ *Web:* www.dynegy.com						
Dynetic Systems Inc						
19128 Industrial Blvd	Elk River	MN	55330	763-441-4300		518
Dynetics 1002 Explorer Blvd	Huntsville	AL	35806	256-964-4000		535
TF: 800-964-4291 ■ *Web:* www.dynetics.com						
Dynetics Engineering Corp						
515 Bond St	Lincolnshire	IL	60069	847-541-7300	541-7488	111
TF: 800-888-8110 ■ *Web:* www.dyneticsengineering.com						
Dynex Capital Inc						
4991 Lake Brook Dr Ste 100	Glen Allen	VA	23060	804-217-5800		654
NYSE: DX ■ *Web:* www.dynexcapital.com						
Dynex Rivett Inc 770 Capitol Dr	Pewaukee	WI	53072	262-691-0300	691-0312	789
Web: www.dynexhydraulics.com						
Dynfed Llc 6724 Wilson Ln	Bethesda	MD	20817	703-627-5950		396
Web: dynfed.com						
Dynisco LLC 38 Forge Pkwy	Franklin	MA	02038	508-541-9400	541-6206	472
TF General: 800-396-4726 ■ *Web:* www.dynisco.com						
Dyno Nobel Inc						
2795 E Cottonwood Pkwy Ste 500	Salt Lake City	UT	84121	801-364-4800	328-6452	268
TF: 800-473-2675 ■ *Web:* www.dynonobel.com						
Dynomax Inc 1535 Abbott Dr	Wheeling	IL	60090	847-680-8833		454
Web: www.dynomaxinc.com						
DynTek Inc						
4440 Von Karman Ste 200	Newport Beach	CA	92660	949-271-6700		178-10
Web: www.dyntek.com						
Dyonyx LP 1235 N Loop W	Houston	TX	77008	713-485-7000	830-5909	180
TF General: 855-749-6758 ■ *Web:* www.dyonyx.com						
Dyplast Products LLC						
12501 NW 38th Ave	Opa Locka	FL	33054	305-921-0110		601
Web: www.dyplastproducts.com						
Dyson-Kissner-Moran Corp (DKM)						
565 Fifth Ave 4th Fl	New York	NY	10017	212-661-4600		185
Web: www.dkmcorp.com						
Dystel & Goderich Literary Management						
1 Union Sq W Ste 904	New York	NY	10003	212-627-9100	627-9313	444
Web: www.dystel.com						
Dystonia Medical Research Foundation						
1 E Wacker Dr Ste 2810	Chicago	IL	60601	312-755-0198	803-0138	48-17
TF General: 800-377-3978 ■ *Web:* www.dystonia-foundation.org						
Dytech Group						
7201 Sandscove Ct Ste 4	Winter Park	FL	32792	407-678-8300		180
Web: www.dytech.com						
Dywidag Systems International						
320 Marmon Dr	Bolingbrook	IL	60440	630-739-1100	739-5517	189-3
TF: 800-457-7633 ■ *Web:* www.dywidag-systems.com						

E

Company / Address	City	State	ZIP	Phone	Fax	Class
E & a Consulting Group Inc						
330 N 117th St	Omaha	NE	68154	402-895-4700		256
Web: www.eacg.com						
E & A Industries Inc						
101 W Ohio St Ste 1350	Indianapolis	IN	46204	317-684-3150	681-5068	360-3
Web: ea-companies.com						
E & E It Consulting Services Inc						
5026 Arthur Ave	Mechanicsburg	PA	17050	717-975-1664		180
Web: ene-it-consulting.com						
E & M Bindery Inc 11 Peekay Dr	Clifton	NJ	07014	973-777-9300		626
TF: 800-736-2463 ■ *Web:* www.embindery.com						
E & O Mari Inc 256 Broadway	Newburgh	NY	12550	845-562-4400		527
Web: www.labella.com						
E & O Tool & Plastics Inc						
19178 Industrial Blvd NW	Elk River	MN	55330	763-441-6100	441-6452	608
Web: www.eoplastics.com						
E & S Ring Management Corp						
13900 Marquesas Wy	Marina Del Rey	CA	90292	310-337-5400		186
Web: www.esring.com						
E & T Plastic Manufacturing Co						
45-45 37th St	Long Island City	NY	11101	718-729-6226		596
Web: www.e-tplastics.com						
E & V Energy Corp 5700 State Rt 34	Auburn	NY	13021	315-253-6522		581
TF: 800-455-6522 ■ *Web:* www.eandvenergy.com						
E & V Restaurant 320 Chamberlain Ave	Paterson	NJ	07502	973-942-4664		671
Web: www.evrestaurant.com						
E Boyd & Associates Inc PO Box 99189	Raleigh	NC	27624	919-846-8000		360-3
Web: www.eboyd.com						
E C S 2741 S 21st Ave	Broadview	IL	60155	708-338-9700		256
TF: 800-621-0759 ■ *Web:* escalatorparts.com						
E C Wise Inc 101 Glacier Pt Ste D	San Rafael	CA	94901	415-355-9473		396
TF: 800-573-1874 ■ *Web:* www.ecwise.com						
E Caligari & Son Inc						
1333 Ingleside Rd	Norfolk	VA	23502	757-853-4511		189-8
TF: 800-421-2584 ■ *Web:* www.ecaligariandson.com						
E Commerce Partners Dotnet Corp						
59 Franklin St	New York	NY	10013	212-334-3390		225
TF: 866-431-6669 ■ *Web:* www.ecommercepartners.net						
E Dillon & Co						
2522 Swords Creek Rd PO Box 160	Swords Creek	VA	24649	276-873-6816	873-4208	183
TF: 800-234-8970 ■ *Web:* www.edillon.com						
E E Wine Inc 9108 Centreville Rd	Manassas	VA	20110	703-368-6568		316
Web: www.eewine.com						
E Gluck Corp						
60-15 Little Neck Pkwy	Little Neck	NY	11362	718-784-0700		153
TF: 800-840-2933 ■ *Web:* www.armitron.com						
E H Lynn Industries Inc						
524 Anderson Dr	Romeoville	IL	60446	815-328-8800		790
TF: 800-633-2948 ■ *Web:* www.ehlynn.com						
E H Publishing Inc PO Box 989	Framingham	MA	01701	508-663-1500	663-1599	637-9
Web: www.ehpub.com						
E Hofmann Plastics						
51 Centennial Rd	Orangeville	ON	L9W3R1	855-452-4014		603
TF: 855-452-4014 ■ *Web:* www.hofmannplastics.com						
E I Team Inc 2060 Sheridan Dr	Buffalo	NY	14223	716-870-4000		256
Web: www.eiteam.com						
E Ink Holdings Inc 733 Concord Ave	Cambridge	MA	02138	617-499-6000		225
Web: www.eink.com						
E Innovative Com Inc						
445 Poi Ct	Merritt Island	FL	32953	321-452-5905		180
Web: www.innovative-e.com						
E J Harrison & Sons PO Box 4009	Ventura	CA	93007	805-647-1414	644-7751	804
TF: 800-418-7274 ■ *Web:* www.ejharrison.com						
E John Schmitz & Sons Inc						
37 Loveton Cir	Sparks	MD	21152	410-329-3000		174
Web: www.schmitzpress.com						
E- Konomy Pool Service Inc						
3821 W Costco Dr Ste 115	Tucson	AZ	85711	520-325-6427		104
TF: 800-435-8599 ■ *Web:* www.e-konomy.com						
E L Hamm Assoc Inc						
4801 Columbus St Ste 400	Virginia Beach	VA	23462	757-497-5000		803-1
Web: www.elhamm.com						
e Learning Guild, The						
375 E St Ste 200	Santa Rosa	CA	95404	707-566-8990		196
Web: www.elearningguild.com						
E M J D Corp 4590 S Windermere St	Englewood	CO	80110	303-761-5236		483
Web: emjd.com						
E M Schroeder Agency Inc 294 Town Ctr Dr	Troy	MI	48084	248-689-1020		390
Web: emschroeder.com						
E Mitchell Inc 1580 Indiana St	San Francisco	CA	94107	415-826-2929		189-10
E Morris Communications Inc						
820 N Orleans	Chicago	IL	60610	312-943-2900		4
Web: www.emorris.com						
E P C Inc 2180 Bennett Rd	Philadelphia	PA	19116	215-464-1440		596
Web: www.plastx.com						
E p Radiological Services Inc						
8040 Remmet Ave Ste 1	Canoga Park	CA	91304	818-313-9729		177
Web: www.epradinc.com						
E P S 8845 Basil Western Rd	Canal Winchester	OH	43110	614-834-9126		693
Web: www.epsohio.com						
E Pi Bio Analytical						
9095 W Harristown Blvd	Niantic	IL	62551	217-963-2143		743
TF: 866-963-2143 ■ *Web:* www.epibas.com						
E Pluribus Partners Consultant						
104 Brookside Dr Fl 2	Greenwich	CT	06831	203-422-6511		196
Web: www.epluribuspartners.com						
E R O Resources Corp 1842 Clarkson St	Denver	CO	80218	303-830-1188		196
TF: 800-733-0660 ■ *Web:* www.eroresources.com						
E S Investments LLC						
14055 US Hwy 19 N	Clearwater	FL	33764	727-536-8822		488
Web: www.sunmicrostamping.com						
E S Kluft & Company LLC						
11096 Jersey Blvd Ste 101	Rancho Cucamonga	CA	91730	909-373-4211		321
Web: www.kluftmattress.com						
E S Robbins Corp						
2802 Avalon Ave	Muscle Shoals	AL	35661	256-248-2400	248-2410	600
TF: 866-934-6018 ■ *Web:* www.esrobbins.com						
E Sam Jones Distributor Inc						
4898 S Atlanta Rd	Smyrna	GA	30080	404-351-3250	351-4140	246
TF: 800-624-9849 ■ *Web:* www.esamjones.com						
E Sciences Inc 34 E Pine St	Orlando	FL	32801	407-481-9006		256
Web: www.esciencesinc.com						
E T & F Fastening Systems						
29019 Solon Rd	Solon	OH	44139	440-248-8655	248-0423	278
TF: 800-248-2376 ■ *Web:* www.etf-fastening.com						
E t Mktg. Solutions Ltd						
207-3833 Henning Dr	Burnaby	BC	V5C6N5	604-801-6168		7
Web: www.etmarketingsolutions.com						
E Tech Systems Inc						
1900 E Golf Rd Ste 950	Schaumburg	IL	60173	847-352-4770		41
TF: 800-963-1030 ■ *Web:* www.etechsys.com						
E Tour & Travel						
3626 Quadrangle Blvd Ste 400	Orlando	FL	32817	407-515-2400	658-1768	771
TF Sales: 800-339-5120 ■ *Web:* www.etourandtravel.com						
E Walker Consulting Inc						
4902 Crosspoint Dr	Doylestown	PA	18901	215-806-3537		809
TF: 800-573-1874 ■ *Web:* www.ewalkerconsulting.com						

Name / Address	City	State	ZIP	Phone	Fax	Class
E! Entertainment Television 5750 Wilshire Blvd *Web:* www.eonline.com	Los Angeles	CA	90036	323-954-2400		740
E*Trade Bank 671 N Glebe Rd *TF:* 800-387-2331 ■ *Web:* us.etrade.com	Arlington	VA	22203	877-800-1208		70
E*Trade Financial Corp 1271 Ave of the Americas 14th Fl *NASDAQ: ETFC* ■ *TF:* 800-387-2331 ■ *Web:* about.etrade.com	New York	NY	10020	800-387-2331		690
E*Trade Financial Corp Corporate Services 4500 Bohannon Dr *TF:* 800-387-2331 ■ *Web:* us.etrade.com	Menlo Park	CA	94025	650-331-6000		178-1
E. Boineau & Co 128 Beaufain St *TF:* 800-579-2628 ■ *Web:* www.eboineauandco.com	Charleston	SC	29401	843-723-1462		636
E. G. Ayers Distributing Inc 5819 S Broadway St *Web:* www.ayersdistributing.com	Eureka	CA	95503	707-445-2077		297-8
E. L. Farmer & Co 3800 E 42nd St Ste 417 *Web:* www.elfarmer.com	Odessa	TX	79762	432-366-2010		539
E. L. Robinson Engineering Co 5088 Washington St W *Web:* www.elrobinson.com	Charleston	WV	25313	304-776-7473		261
E.R. Stuebner Construction Inc 227 Blair Ave *Web:* www.ersconstruction.com	Reading	PA	19601	610-376-6625		186
E.S. Fox Ltd 9127 Montrose Rd *TF:* 866-233-8933 ■ *Web:* www.esfox.com	Niagara Falls	ON	L2E7J9	905-354-3700		261
E/g Electro-graph Inc 1491 Poinsettia Ave Ste 138 *Web:* plansee.com/en	Vista	CA	92081	760-438-9090		696
E/The Environmental Magazine 28 Knight St PO Box 5098 *TF:* 800-321-6742 ■ *Web:* www.emagazine.com	Norwalk	CT	06851	203-854-5559	866-0602	457-19
E1 Asset Management Inc 44 Wall St 9th Fl *Web:* e1am.com	New York	NY	10005	212-425-2670		690
E2 Consulting Engineers Inc 450 E 17th Ave Ste 200 *TF:* 888-835-9400 ■ *Web:* www.e2.com	Denver	CO	80203	303-232-9800		261
E3 Communications Inc 43 Ct St Ste 910 *Web:* www.e3communications.com	Buffalo	NY	14202	716-854-8182		445
E3 Consulting LLC 3333 S Bannock St Ste 740 *Web:* www.e3co.com	Englewood	CO	80110	303-762-7060		261
E3 Partners Ministry 16787 Bernardo Ctr Dr Ste 7 *Web:* e3partners.org	San Diego	CA	92128	858-485-9904		48-20
E3 Services Conseils Inc 19 Le Royer St W Ste 304 *TF:* 800-741-0696 ■ *Web:* e3sc.com	Montreal	QC	H2Y1W4	514-281-1737		193
e4e Inc 10720 Gilroy Rd *Web:* www.e4e.com	Hunt Valley	MD	21031	410-568-3075		113
e4Sciences LLC 27 Glen Rd N Entrance *Web:* www.e4sciences.com	Sandy Hook	CT	06482	203-270-8100		192
EA (Electronic Arts Inc) 209 Redwood Shores Pkwy *NASDAQ: EA* ■ *Web:* www.ea.com	Redwood City	CA	94065	650-628-1500		178-6
EA Consulting Inc 1024 Iron Point Rd *Web:* www.ea-inc.com	Folsom	CA	95630	916-357-6588	200-0368	180
EA Patten Co 303 Wetherell St *Web:* eapatten.com	Manchester	CT	06040	860-649-2851		790
EA Services Inc 13850 Gulf Fwy Ste 250 *Web:* www.easervices.com	Houston	TX	77034	281-922-4412	922-7917	41
EAA (Experimental Aircraft Assn) 3000 Poberezny Rd *TF:* 800-236-4800 ■ *Web:* www.eaa.org	Oshkosh	WI	54902	920-426-4800	426-4828	48-18
EAA AirVenture Museum 3000 Poberezny Rd *TF:* 888-322-3229 ■ *Web:* eaa.org/en/eaa-museum	Oshkosh	WI	54902	920-426-4800	426-6560	520
Eaa Environmental Abatement Associates Inc 239 Schuyler Ave Ste 125B *Web:* environmental-abatement.com	Kingston	PA	18704	570-283-0500		63
EAB (Edward A. Berg & Sons Inc) 75 W Century Rd *Web:* www.eaberg.com	Paramus	NJ	07652	201-845-8200	845-8201	297-3
eAcceleration Corp 1050 NE Hostmark St Ste 100-B *TF Sales:* 800-803-4588 ■ *Web:* www.eacceleration.com	Poulsbo	WA	98370	360-779-6301	598-2450	178-7
Eaccess Solutions Inc 407 N Quentin Rd *Web:* eaccess.com	Palatine	IL	60067	847-991-7190		366
EAD Motors Inc 1 Progress Dr *Web:* www.electrocraft.com	Dover	NH	03820	603-742-3330	742-3330	518
Eadie & Payne LLP 1839 W Redlands Blvd *TF:* 800-772-1213 ■ *Web:* eadiepaynellp.com	Redlands	CA	92373	909-793-2406		2
EADOC 180 Grand Ave Ste 995 *Web:* www.eadocsoftware.com	Oakland	CA	94612	510-903-9658		177
EADS Group 1126 Eigth Ave *TF:* 800-626-0904 ■ *Web:* www.eadsgroup.com	Altoona	PA	16602	814-944-5035	944-4862	261
Eagan Convention & Visitors Bureau 1501 Central Pkwy *TF:* 866-324-2620 ■ *Web:* www.eaganmn.com	Eagan	MN	55121	651-675-5546		206
Eagan Insurance Agency Inc 2629 N Cswy Blvd *TF:* 888-882-9600 ■ *Web:* www.eaganins.com	Metairie	LA	70002	504-836-9600	836-9621	390
Eagle 92.9, The 3800 Cornhusker Hwy *Web:* www.ktgl.com	Lincoln	NE	68504	402-466-1234		645-90
Eagle 96.9 5345 Madison Ave *Web:* www.eagle969.com	Sacramento	CA	95841	916-334-7777		645-140
eagle 96.9 classic hits, The 8000 Belfort Pkwy *TF:* 800-438-1601 ■ *Web:* www.969theeagle.com	Jacksonville	FL	32256	904-245-8500	245-8501	645-79
Eagle Affiliates Inc 1000 S Second St *TF:* 800-237-9255	Plainfield	NJ	07063	908-757-4464		607

Name / Address	City	State	ZIP	Phone	Fax	Class
Eagle Applied Sciences LLC 1826 N Loop 1604 W Ste 350 *Web:* www.eagle-app-sci.com	San Antonio	TX	78248	210-477-9242		177
Eagle Asset Management 880 Carillon Pkwy *TF:* 800-237-3101 ■ *Web:* www.eagleasset.com	Saint Petersburg	FL	33716	800-237-3101		401
Eagle Aviation 2861 Aviation Way Columbia Metropolitan Airport *TF:* 800-849-3245 ■ *Web:* www.eagle-aviation.com	West Columbia	SC	29170	803-822-5555	822-5529	63
Eagle Bancorp Inc 7815 Woodmont Ave *NASDAQ: EGBN* ■ **Fax Area Code:* 301 ■ *TF:* 800-364-8313 ■ *Web:* www.eaglebankcorp.com	Bethesda	MD	20814	240-497-2044	986-8529*	360-2
Eagle Beach State Recreation Area 400 Willoughby Ave 5th Fl *Web:* www.dnr.alaska.gov	Juneau	AK	99811	907-465-4563		565
Eagle Bend Manufacturing Inc 1000 Jd Yarnell Industrial Pkwy	Clinton	TN	37716	865-457-3800		247
Eagle Beverage Corp 1043 County Rt 25 *Web:* www.eaglebev.com	Oswego	NY	13126	315-343-5221		297-8
Eagle Brands Inc 3201 NW 72nd Ave *Web:* www.eaglebrands.com	Miami	FL	33122	305-599-2337		443
Eagle Bulk Shipping Inc 300 First Stamford Pl *Web:* www.eagleships.com	Stamford	CT	06902	212-785-2500		313
Eagle Burgmann Industries LP 10035 Brookriver Dr *Web:* www.eagleburgmann.com	Houston	TX	77040	713-939-9515	939-9091	326
Eagle Button Co Inc 700 Broadway *Web:* www.eaglebutton.com	Westwood	NJ	07675	201-652-4063		594
Eagle Cleaning Service Inc 525 Belview St *TF:* 877-864-5696 ■ *Web:* www.eaglecleaningservice.com	Bessemer	AL	35020	205-424-5252		104
Eagle Communications Inc 2703 Hall St Ste 15 Ste 15 *TF:* 877-613-2453 ■ *Web:* www.eaglecom.net	Hays	KS	67601	785-625-5910		643
Eagle Comtronics Inc 7665 Henry Clay Blvd *TF:* 800-448-7474 ■ *Web:* www.eaglecomtronics.com	Liverpool	NY	13088	315-622-3402	622-3800	647
Eagle Construction Services Inc 1624 Jacksonville Rd *Web:* www.eagle1construction.com	Burlington	NJ	08016	609-239-8000		463
Eagle Copters Ltd 823 Mctavish Rd NE *TF:* 800-564-6469 ■ *Web:* www.eaglecopters.com	Calgary	AB	T2E7G9	403-250-7370		359
Eagle Cornice Co Inc 89 Pettaconsett Ave *Web:* www.eaglecornice.com	Cranston	RI	02920	401-781-5978	781-6570	697
Eagle County PO Box 850 *TF:* 800-225-6136 ■ *Web:* www.eaglecounty.us	Eagle	CO	81631	970-328-8600	328-8716	338
Eagle Creek State Recreation Area 2341 Eagle Creek Rd *Web:* dnr.illinois.gov/Lands/Landmgt/PARKS/R3/EAGLECRK.HTM	Findlay	IL	62534	217-756-8260		565
Eagle Direct 1 Printer's Dr *TF:* 800-675-7669 ■ *Web:* www.eagledirects.com	Hermon	ME	04401	207-848-7300	848-7400	7
Eagle Distributing Co Inc 1100 S Bud Blvd	Fremont	NE	68025	402-721-0620		81-1
Eagle Distributing Company Inc 310 Radford Pl *TF:* 800-331-2829 ■ *Web:* eagledistributing.com	Knoxville	TN	37917	865-637-3311	525-9530	81-1
Eagle Energy Trust 500 4 Ave SW Ste 2710 *TF:* 855-531-1575 ■ *Web:* www.eagleenergytrust.com	Calgary	AB	T2P2V6	403-531-1575		536
Eagle Engineering Inc 2013 Van Bruen Ave *Web:* www.eagleonline.net	Indian Trail	NC	28079	704-882-4222		261
Eagle Environmental Inc 891 W Robinson Dr Ste 4 *TF:* 800-291-4367 ■ *Web:* www.cnnct.com	North Salt Lake	UT	84054	801-936-1155		186
Eagle Express Lines Inc 925 W 175th St *Web:* www.eagleexpresslines.com	Homewood	IL	60430	708-333-8400	333-7302	780
Eagle Family Foods Group LLC 1 Strawberry Ln **Fax Area Code:* 330 ■ *TF:* 888-550-9555 ■ *Web:* www.eaglebrand.com	Orrville	OH	44667	888-550-9555	684-6410*	296-27
Eagle Financial Management Services LLC 400 Travis St Ste 518 *Web:* www.eaglefms.net	Shreveport	LA	71101	318-675-0826		194
Eagle Flexible Packaging 1100 Kingsland Dr *TF:* 800-225-0180 ■ *Web:* www.eagleflexible.com	Batavia	IL	60510	630-406-1760		627
Eagle Ford Oil & Gas Corp 1110 Nasa Pkwy Ste 311	Houston	TX	77058	281-383-9648		536
Eagle Foundry Co Inc PO Box 250 *TF:* 800-789-3746 ■ *Web:* www.eaglefoundryco.com	Eagle Creek	OR	97022	503-637-3048	637-3091	307
Eagle Global Advisors LLC 5847 San Felipe Ste 930 *Web:* www.eagleglobal.com	Houston	TX	77057	713 952 3550		401
Eagle Graphics Inc 150 N Moyer St *Web:* www.eaglegraphic.com	Annville	PA	17003	717-867-5576	867-5579	110
Eagle Grinding Wheel Corp 2519 W Fulton St *TF:* 800-747-9353 ■ *Web:* www.eaglegrindingwheel.com	Chicago	IL	60612	312-733-1770	733-5949	1
Eagle Grips Inc 460 Randy Rd *TF:* 800-323-6144 ■ *Web:* eaglegrips.com	Carol Stream	IL	60188	630-260-0400		711
Eagle Group Inc 100 Industrial Blvd *TF:* 800-441-8440 ■ *Web:* www.eaglegrp.com	Clayton	DE	19938	302-653-3000	653-2065	300
Eagle Haven Computers Inc 5860 Clearfield Woodland Hwy *TF:* 800-832-6150 ■ *Web:* www.eaglehaven.com	Clearfield	PA	16830	814-765-5779		175
Eagle Helicopters Inc 4130 Heliport Dr *Web:* www.kachinaaviation.com	Nampa	ID	83687	208-318-0100		23
Eagle Herald Publishing 1809 Dunlap Ave *Web:* www.eagleherald.com	Marinette	WI	54143	715-735-6611		532-3
Eagle Hill School 242 Old Petersham Rd PO Box 116 *Web:* www.eaglehill.school/page	Hardwick	MA	01037	413-477-6000	477-6837	622
Eagle Investment Systems LLC 65 LaSalle Rd Ste 305 *Web:* www.eagleinvsys.com	West Hartford	CT	06107	860-561-4602		401

Company / Address	City	State	ZIP	Phone	Fax	Class
Eagle Iron Works 129 E Holcomb Ave *Web:* www.eagleironworks.com	Des Moines	IA	50313	515-243-1123	243-8214	190
Eagle Island State Park 4000 W Hatchery Rd *Web:* www.visitidaho.org	Eagle	ID	83616	208-939-0696	939-0696	565
Eagle Laboratories Inc 10201-A Trademark St *TF:* 800-867-8081 ■ *Web:* www.eaglelabs.com	Rancho Cucamonga	CA	91730	909-481-0011		475
Eagle Machine & Tool Corp 6060 Grand Haven Rd *Web:* www.eaglemachinetool.com	Norton Shores	MI	49441	231-798-8473		203
Eagle Magazine 1623 Gateway Cir S *TF:* 800-648-5080 ■ *Web:* www.foe.com	Grove City	OH	43123	614-883-2200	883-2201	457-10
Eagle Marine Industries Inc 1 Riverview Ave	Sauget	IL	62201	618-875-1153		465
Eagle Maritime Consultants Inc 1600 Space Park Dr *Web:* www.eaglemaritime.com	Houston	TX	77058	281-333-9880	333-9885	313
Eagle Marketing Inc Perfume Originals Products Div 2412 Sequoia Pk **Fax Area Code:* 405 ■ *TF:* 800-233-7424 ■ *Web:* www.eimi.com	Yukon	OK	73099	800-233-7424	354-7882*	574
Eagle Materials Inc 3811 Turtle Creek Blvd Ste 1100 *NYSE: EXP* ■ *TF:* 800-759-7625 ■ *Web:* www.eaglematerials.com	Dallas	TX	75219	214-432-2000	432-2100	135
Eagle Mfg Company Inc 2400 Charles St *Web:* www.eagle-mfg.com	Wellsburg	WV	26070	304-737-3171	737-3171	124
Eagle Microsystems Inc 366 Cir of Progress Dr *TF:* 800-524-5979 ■ *Web:* www.eaglemicrosystems.com	Pottstown	PA	19464	610-323-2250		362
Eagle Mountain Casino 681 S Tule Resv Rd *TF:* 800-903-3353 ■ *Web:* www.eaglemtncasino.com	Porterville	CA	93257	559-788-6220	788-6223	133
Eagle Mountain House 179 Carter Notch Rd PO Box 804 *TF:* 800-966-5779 ■ *Web:* www.eaglemt.com	Jackson	NH	03846	603-383-9111		379
Eagle Networks Inc 2738 W Bullard Ave *Web:* www.eaglenetworks.com	Fresno	CA	93711	559-448-8877		175
Eagle Newspapers Inc 4901 Indian School Rd NE PO Box 12008 *Web:* www.eaglenewspapers.com	Salem	OR	97305	503-393-1774		532-3
Eagle One Golf Products Inc 1340 N Jefferson St *TF:* 800-448-4409 ■ *Web:* www.eagleonegolf.com	Anaheim	CA	92807	714-983-0050		710
Eagle Ottawa Leather Company LLC 2930 W Auburn Rd *TF:* 800-839-1164 ■ *Web:* www.eagleottawa.com	Rochester Hills	MI	48309	248-853-3122		432
Eagle Parts & Products Inc 1411 Marvin Griffin Rd *TF:* 888-972-9911 ■ *Web:* www.eagleproducts.us	Augusta	GA	30906	706-790-6687	790-6066	61
Eagle Pass Chamber of Commerce 400 E Garrison St *TF:* 888-355-3224 ■ *Web:* eaglepasstexas.com	Eagle Pass	TX	78852	830-773-3224	773-8844	139
Eagle Pass Public Library 243 Bliss St *Web:* eaglepasstx.us	Eagle Pass	TX	78852	830-758-1361		434-3
Eagle Point National Cemetery 2763 Riley Rd *TF:* 800-535-1117 ■ *Web:* www.cem.va.gov	Eagle Point	OR	97524	541-826-2511	826-2888	136
Eagle Point Software Corp 600 Star Brewery Dr Ste 200 *TF:* 800-678-6565 ■ *Web:* www.eaglepoint.com	Dubuque	IA	52001	563-556-8392		178-10
Eagle Pointe Golf Resort 2250 E Pt Rd *Web:* www.eaglepointe.com	Bloomington	IN	47401	812-824-4040		669
Eagle Power & Equipment Corp 953 Bethlehem Pk *Web:* www.eaglepowerandequipment.com	Montgomeryville	PA	18936	215-699-5871		358
Eagle Professional Resources Inc 170 Laurier Ave W Ste 902 **Fax Area Code:* 416 ■ *TF:* 800-281-2339 ■ *Web:* www.eagleonline.com	Ottawa	ON	K1P5V5	613-234-1810	861-8401*	721
Eagle Publishing Co 75 S Church St *TF:* 800-245-0254 ■ *Web:* www.berkshireeagle.com	Pittsfield	MA	01201	413-447-7311	447-7311	637-8
Eagle Quest Golf Centers Inc 1001 United Blvd *Web:* www.eaglequestgolf.com	Coquitlam	BC	V3K4S8	604-523-6400		711
Eagle Raceway 617 S 238th St *Web:* eagleraceway.com	Eagle	NE	68347	402-238-2595	238-3768	515
Eagle Radio Inc 2703 Hall St Ste 15 *TF:* 877-613-2453 ■ *Web:* eaglecom.net	Hays	KS	67601	877-613-2453		643
Eagle Recognition 2706 Mtn Industrial Blvd *TF:* 888-287-4240 ■ *Web:* www.eaglerecognition.com	Tucker	GA	30084	770-985-0808		184
Eagle Ridge Hospital & Health Care Ctr 475 Guildford Way *TF:* 800-465-4911 ■ *Web:* www.fraserhealth.ca	Port Moody	BC	V3H3W9	604-461-2022	461-9972	374-2
Eagle Ridge Inn & Resort 444 Eagle Ridge Dr *TF:* 800-892-2269 ■ *Web:* www.eagleridge.com	Galena	IL	61036	815-777-2444	777-4502	669
Eagle River Homes LLC 21 S Groffdale Rd *Web:* www.eagleriverhomes.net	Leola	PA	17540	717-656-2381		186
Eagle River Nature Ctr 32750 Eagle River Rd *TF:* 800-642-0066 ■ *Web:* ernc.org	Eagle River	AK	99577	907-694-2108	694-2119	50-5
Eagle Rock Baptist Church 1499 Colorado Blvd *Web:* www.erockchurch.com	Los Angeles	CA	90041	323-255-4611		48-20
Eagle Rock Chamber of Commerce PO Box 41354 *TF:* 800-780-1230 ■ *Web:* www.eaglerockchamberofcommerce.com	Los Angeles	CA	90041	323-257-2197	257-4245	139
Eagle Rock Technologies Inc 1 Eagle Rock Dr *Web:* www.eaglerockonline.com	Bath	PA	18014	610-759-5200		757
Eagle Roller Mill Co 1101 Airport Rd *TF:* 800-223-9108 ■ *Web:* www.eaglerollermill.com	Shelby	NC	28150	704-487-5061	482-1263	447
Eagle Scaffolding Services Inc 67 Mill St *Web:* www.eaglescaffolding.com	Amityville	NY	11701	631-842-1700		358
Eagle Stainless Tube & Fabrication Inc 10 Discovery Way *Web:* www.eagletube.com	Franklin	MA	02038	508-528-8650		492
Eagle Steel Products Inc 3420 Collins Ln *Web:* www.eaglesteelproducts.com	Louisville	KY	40245	502-241-6004		492
Eagle Support Services Corp 2705 Artie St Bldg 400 Ste 30 *Web:* www.eaglesupport.com	Huntsville	AL	35805	256-534-2274	534-0606	449
Eagle Technologies Group 9850 Red Arrow Hwy *Web:* www.eagletechnologies.com	Bridgman	MI	49106	269-465-6986		494
Eagle Technology Inc 11019 N Towne Sq Rd *TF:* 800-388-3268 ■ *Web:* www.eaglecmms.com	Mequon	WI	53092	262-241-3845		177
Eagle Tool Co 101 Woodward Ave *Web:* eaglebroach.com	Iron Mountain	MI	49801	906-774-0284	774-0342	455
Eagle Trail State Recreation Site c/o Northern Area Office 3700 Airport Way *Web:* www.dnr.alaska.gov	Fairbanks	AK	99709	907-883-3686		565
Eagle Transport Corp 300 S Wesleyan Blvd Ste 202 *TF:* 800-776-9937 ■ *Web:* www.eagletransportcorp.com	Rocky Mount	NC	27804	252-937-2464		780
Eagle Valley Enterprise 108 W Second St *Web:* www.vaildaily.com	Eagle	CO	81631	970-328-6656		532-4
Eagle Van Lines Inc 5041 Beech Pl *Web:* www.eaglevanlines.com	Temple Hills	MD	20748	301-899-2022		313
Eagle Vision Pharmaceutical Corp 175 Krauser Rd	Downingtown	PA	19335	610-458-2346		238
Eagle Well Servicing Corp 8113-49 Ave Close *Web:* www.wesc.ca	Red Deer	AB	T4P2V5	403-346-7789		540
Eagle Wings Industries Inc (EWI) 400 Shellhouse Dr *Web:* www.ewiusa.com	Rantoul	IL	61866	217-892-4322		60
Eagle's Crest Grill 5301 S Columbia Rd *Web:* eaglescrestgrill.com	Grand Forks	ND	58201	701-787-3491		671
Eagle's Flight, Creative Training Excellence Inc 489 Clair Rd W *TF:* 800-567-8079 ■ *Web:* www.eaglesflight.com	Guelph	ON	N1L0H7	519-767-1747		463
Eagle's Nest Foundation 942 W Fourth St Ste 101 *TF:* 800-951-7442 ■ *Web:* www.enf.org	Winston Salem	NC	27101	336-761-1040		239
Eagle's Nest Resort 6103 Lavaque Rd *Web:* eaglesnestfishlake.com	Duluth	MN	55803	218-721-4147		669
Eagle:XM LLC 5105 E 41st Ave *TF:* 800-426-5376 ■ *Web:* www.eaglexm.com	Denver	CO	80216	303-320-5411		627
Eaglebrook School 271 Pine Nook Rd *Web:* www.eaglebrook.org	Deerfield	MA	01342	413-774-9111		622
EagleClaw Midstream Services LLC 414 W Texas Ave Ste 315 *Web:* www.eagleclawmidstream.com	Midland	TX	79701	432-789-1333		539
EAGLE-Net Alliance 295 Interlocken Blvd Ste 250 *Web:* www.co-eaglenet.net	Broomfield	CO	80021	720-210-9500		387
EagleOne Case Management Solutions Inc 80 Burr Ridge Pkwy Ste 121 *Web:* www.eagleonecms.com	Burr Ridge	IL	60527	630-655-0800		194
Eagle-Picher Minerals Inc 9785 Gateway Dr Ste 1000 *TF Cust Svc:* 800-228-3865 ■ *Web:* www.epminerals.com	Reno	NV	89521	775-824-7600	824-7601	500
EaglePicher Technologies LLC C & Porter St *TF:* 800-223-0425 ■ *Web:* www.eaglepicher.com	Joplin	MO	64801	417-623-8000		74
Eagleton, Eagleton & Harrison Inc 320 S Boston Ave Ste 1700 *Web:* www.eehlaw.com	Tulsa	OK	74103	918-584-0462		428
Eagle-Tribune 100 Tpke St *TF:* 800-927-9200 ■ *Web:* www.eagletribune.com	North Andover	MA	01845	978-946-2000	687-6045	532-2
Eagleville Elementary School S101w34511 County Rd Lo *Web:* www.masd.k12.wi.us/eves	LO Eagle	WI	53119	262-363-6258		685
Eagleville Hospital 100 Eagleville Rd *TF General:* 800-255-2019 ■ *Web:* www.eagleville.org	Eagleville	PA	19408	610-539-6000		726
Eaglewood Resort & Spa 1401 Nordic Rd *TF:* 877-285-6150 ■ *Web:* www.eaglewoodresort.com	Itasca	IL	60143	630-773-1400		669
EAI Inc Environmental Management Service 50 Prescott St *TF:* 800-886-3241 ■ *Web:* www.eaienviro.com	Jersey City	NJ	07304	201-395-0010		194
Eakas Corp 6251 Route 251 *Web:* www.eakas.com	Peru	IL	61354	815-223-8811		247
Eakes Office Plus 617 W Third St *TF:* 800-652-9396 ■ *Web:* www.eakes.com	Grand Island	NE	68801	308-382-8026	382-7401	535
Eakin Partners LLC Roundabout Plaza 1600 Division St Ste 600 *Web:* www.eakinpartners.com	Nashville	TN	37203	615-250-1800		652
EAM World 5502 NW 37th Ave *Web:* www.theraft.com	Miami	FL	33142	305-871-4050	637-8632	676
EANGUS (Enlisted Assn of the National Guard of the US) 3133 Mt Vernon Ave *TF:* 800-234-3264 ■ *Web:* www.memberconnections.com	Alexandria	VA	22305	703-519-3846	519-3849	48-19
EAP Systems 500 W Cummings Pk *TF:* 800-535-4841 ■ *Web:* www.theeap.com	Woburn	MA	01801	781-935-8850		462
EAPA (Employee Assistance Professionals Assn Inc) 4350 N Fairfax Dr Ste 740 *TF:* 800-937-8461 ■ *Web:* www.eapassn.org	Arlington	VA	22203	703-387-1000	522-4585	49-12
Earhart Petroleum Inc 1494 Lytle Rd *TF:* 800-686-2928 ■ *Web:* www.earhartpetroleum.com	Troy	OH	45373	937-335-2928		579
Earl & Brown Co Inc 5825 SW Arctic Dr **Fax Area Code:* 866 ■ *Web:* www.earlbrown.com	Beaverton	OR	97005	503-670-1170	432-9237*	246
Earl Burns Miller Japanese Garden 1250 Bellflower Blvd *TF:* 800-985-8880 ■ *Web:* www.csulb.edu/~jgarden	Long Beach	CA	90840	562-985-8885	985-5362	97

Name / Address	City	State	Zip	Phone	Fax	Class
Earl d Arnold Printing Co 630 Lunken Park Dr *Web:* www.arnoldprinting.com	Cincinnati	OH	45226	513-533-6900		627
Earl G Graves Ltd 130 Fifth Ave 10th Fl *TF Cust Svc:* 800-727-7777 ■ *Web:* www.blackenterprise.com	New York	NY	10011	212-242-8000		637-9
Earl Industries LLC 2 Harper Ave	Portsmouth	VA	23707	757-215-2500	215-2504	698
Earl K Long Medical Ctr 5825 Airline Hwy *Web:* legis.state.la.us	Baton Rouge	LA	70805	225-358-1000		374-3
Earl L Henderson Trucking Inc 206 W Main St *TF:* 800-447-8084 ■ *Web:* www.hendersontrucking.com	Salem	IL	62881	618-548-4667		780
Earl May Seed & Nursery 208 N Elm St *TF:* 800-843-9608 ■ *Web:* www.earlmay.com	Shenandoah	IA	51603	712-246-1020	246-2210	323
Earl W. Brydges Artpark State Park 450 S Fourth St *Web:* parks.ny.gov/parks/113/details.aspx	Lewiston	NY	14092	716-754-7766		565
Earl's Apparel Inc 908 S Fourth St *TF:* 800-527-3148 ■ *Web:* www.stanray.us	Crockett	TX	75835	936-544-5521	544-7973	155-19
Earl's Auction Co 5199 Lafayette Rd *Web:* www.earlsauction.com	Indianapolis	IN	46254	317-291-5843	291-5844	51
Earl's Rib Palace 6816 N Western Ave *TF:* 800-662-2580 ■ *Web:* www.earlsribpalace.com	Oklahoma City	OK	73116	405-843-9922		671
Earle Baum Center of The Blind 4539 Occidental Rd *Web:* www.earlebaum.org	Santa Rosa	CA	95401	707-523-3222		685
Earle Brown Heritage Ctr 6155 Earle Brown Dr *TF:* 800-524-0239 ■ *Web:* www.earlebrown.com	Minneapolis	MN	55430	763-569-6300		205
Earle M Jorgensen Co 10650 S Alameda St *TF Sales:* 800-336-5365 ■ *Web:* www.emjmetals.com	Lynwood	CA	90262	323-567-1122		490
Earle, The 121 W Washington St *Web:* www.theearle.com	Ann Arbor	MI	48104	734-994-0211		671
Earlham College 801 National Rd W **Fax:* Admissions ■ *TF:* 800-327-5426 ■ *Web:* www.earlham.edu	Richmond	IN	47374	765-983-1600	983-1560*	166
Earlham School of Religion 228 College Ave *TF:* 800-432-1377 ■ *Web:* www.esr.earlham.edu	Richmond	IN	47374	765-983-1423	983-1688	167-3
Earlimart School District PO Box 11970 *Web:* www.earlimart.org	Earlimart	CA	93219	661-849-3386		685
Early Advantage Llc 79 Sanford St *Web:* www.early-advantage.com	Fairfield	CT	06824	203-259-6480		5
Early Bird, The 5312 Sebring Warner Rd *TF:* 866-627-4557 ■ *Web:* earlybirdpaper.com	Greenville	OH	45331	937-548-3330		532-4
Early Childhood Report 360 Hiatt Dr *TF:* 800-621-5463 ■ *Web:* www.lrp.com	Palm Beach Gardens	FL	33418	561-622-6520	622-2423	531-4
Early Cochran & Olson LLC 1 E Upper Wacker Dr Ste 2510 *Web:* www.ecollc.com	Chicago	IL	60601	312-595-4200	595-4209	266
Early County PO Box 693 *Web:* georgia.gov/cities-counties/early-county	Blakely	GA	39823	229-723-4304	723-8684	338
Early County School District 11927 Columbia St *Web:* www.early.k12.ga.us	Blakely	GA	39823	229-723-4337		685
Early Express Services Inc 1333 E Second St *TF:* 800-822-3545 ■ *Web:* www.earlyexpress.com	Dayton	OH	45403	937-223-5801		5
Early Learning Coalition of Miami Dade & Monroe 2555 Ponce De Leon Blvd Ste 500 *TF:* 800-962-2873 ■ *Web:* www.elcmdm.org	Coral Gables	FL	33134	305-646-7220		242
EarlyWorks Children's Museum 404 Madison St *Web:* earlyworks.com	Huntsville	AL	35801	256-564-8100		521
Earmark LLC 1125 Dixwell Ave *TF:* 800-847-8366 ■ *Web:* www.earmark.com	Hamden	CT	06514	203-777-2130	777-2886	647
Earnest C Brooks Correctional Facility 2500 S Sheridan Dr *Web:* www.michigan.gov/corrections	Muskegon Heights	MI	49444	231-773-9200		213
Earnest Machine Products Co 12502 Plaza Dr *TF:* 800-327-6378 ■ *Web:* www.earnestmachine.com	Cleveland	OH	44130	216-362-1100	362-1694	351
Earnest Partners LLC 1180 Peachtree St Ste 2300 *TF:* 800-322-0068 ■ *Web:* www.earnestpartners.com	Atlanta	GA	30309	404-815-8772	815-8948	401
Earnhardt Auto Centers 7300 W Orchid Ln *TF:* 888-378-7711 ■ *Web:* www.earnhardt.com	Chandler	AZ	05220	480-920-4000		57
Earshot Jazz 3429 Fremont Pl Ste 309 *Web:* www.earshot.org	Seattle	WA	98103	206-547-6763	547-6286	48-4
Earth Day Network (EDN) 1616 P St NW Ste 340 *Web:* www.earthday.org	Washington	DC	20036	202-518-0044	518-8794	48-13
Earth Island 9201 Owensmouth Ave *TF:* 888-394-3949 ■ *Web:* followyourheart.com	Chatsworth	CA	91311	818-725-2820	725-2812	296-33
Earth Island Institute 2150 Allston Wy Ste 460 *Web:* www.earthisland.org	Berkeley	CA	94704	415-788-3666	788-7324	48-13
Earth Networks Inc 12410 Milestone Ctr Dr Ste 300 *TF:* 800-544-4429 ■ *Web:* www.earthnetworks.com	Germantown	MD	20876	301-250-4000		192
Earth Policy Institute 1350 Connecticut Ave NW Ste 403 *Web:* www.earth-policy.org	Washington	DC	20036	202-496-9290	496-9325	634
Earth Resource Systems LLC 805 Ashland Dr *Web:* www.earthresourcesystems.com	Tuscaloosa	AL	35406	404-513-5429		192
Earth Sciences & Resources Institute Sumwalt College Rm 333 Ste 301 *Web:* www.esri.sc.edu	Columbia	SC	29208	803-777-4243	777-2972	668
Earth Share 7735 Old Georgetown Rd Ste 900 *TF:* 800-875-3863 ■ *Web:* www.earthshare.org	Bethesda	MD	20814	240-333-0300	333-0301	48-13
Earth Sports LLC 746 W Algonquin Rd *Web:* www.erehwon.com	Arlington Heights	IL	60005	847-439-1400		711
Earth System Research Laboratory NOAA/ESRL 325 Broadway *Web:* www.esrl.noaa.gov	Boulder	CO	80305-3337	303-497-4104	497-6951	668
Earth Systems Services Inc 720 Aerovista Pl Ste 102 *TF:* 866-781-0112 ■ *Web:* www.earthsystems.com	San Luis Obispo	CA	93401	805-781-0112	781-0180	192
Earth Treks Rockville Climbing Center Llc 7125 Columbia Gateway Dr Ste C *Web:* www.earthtrekscIimbing.com	Columbia	MD	21046	410-872-0060		711
Earth, Ocean and Atmospheric Sciences 2020 - 2207 Main Mall *Web:* www.eoas.ubc.ca	Vancouver	BC	V6T1Z4	604-882-2449		165
Earthbalance Corp 2579 N Toledo Blade Blvd *Web:* www.earthbalance.com	North Port	FL	34289	941-426-7878		196
Earthbound Farm 1721 San Juan Hwy *TF:* 800-690-3200 ■ *Web:* www.earthboundfarm.com	San Juan Bautista	CA	95045	831-623-7880		10-11
EarthCam Inc 84 Kennedy St *Web:* www.earthcam.com	Hackensack	NJ	07601	201-488-1111	488-1119	397
Earthcon Consultants Inc 1880 W Oak Pkwy Bldg 100 Ste 106 *Web:* www.earthcon.com	Marietta	GA	30062	770-973-2100		192
EarthLink Inc 1375 Peachtree St NE *NASDAQ: ELNK* ■ **Fax:* Sales ■ *TF:* 866-383-3080 ■ *Web:* www.earthlink.net	Atlanta	GA	30309	404-815-0770	795-1034*	398
EarthLinked Technologies Inc 4151 S Pipkin Rd *TF:* 866-211-6102 ■ *Web:* earthlinked.com	Lakeland	FL	33811	863-701-0096		35
Earthplace 10 Woodside Ln *Web:* www.earthplace.org	Westport	CT	06880	203-227-7253	227-8909	50-5
Earthquake Engineering Research Institute (EERI) 499 14th St Ste 320 *Web:* www.eeri.org	Oakland	CA	94612	510-451-0905	451-5411	49-19
EarthRes Group Inc 6912 Old Easton Rd PO Box 468 *TF:* 800-264-4553 ■ *Web:* www.earthres.com	Pipersville	PA	18947	215-766-1211		261
EarthRights International 1612 K St NW Ste 401 *TF:* 888-224-9043 ■ *Web:* www.earthrights.org	Washington	DC	20006	202-466-5188	466-5189	48-13
Earthstone Energy Inc 633 17th St Ste 2320 *TF:* 800-732-0330 ■ *Web:* www.earthstoneenergy.com	Denver	CO	80202	303-296-3076		536
Earthwatch Institute 114 Western Ave *TF:* 800-776-0188 ■ *Web:* www.earthwatch.org	Boston	MA	02134	978-461-0081	461-2332	48-13
Earthwave Technologies Inc 710 E 64th St *Web:* www.earthwavetech.com	Indianapolis	IN	46220	317-257-8740		647
EarthWay Products Inc 1009 Maple St *TF:* 800-294-0671 ■ *Web:* www.earthway.com	Bristol	IN	46507	574-848-7491		429
EASA (Electrical Apparatus Service Assn) 1331 Baur Blvd *Web:* www.easa.com	Saint Louis	MO	63132	314-993-2220	993-1269	49-19
Ease Technologies Inc 10320 Little Patuxent Pkwy Ste 1104 *TF:* 888-327-3911 ■ *Web:* www.easetech.com	Columbia	MD	21044	301-854-0010		225
EASI LLC 7301 Parkway Dr **Fax Area Code:* 780 ■ *TF:* 888-963-7740 ■ *Web:* www.easi.com	Hanover	MI	21076	888-963-7740	514-3381*	463
eASIC Corp 2585 Augustine Dr Ste 100 *Web:* www.easic.com	Santa Clara	CA	95054	408-855-9200		246
Easley Winery 205 N College Ave *Web:* www.easleywinery.com	Indianapolis	IN	46202	317-636-4516	974-0128	50-7
Easom Automation Systems Inc 32471 Industrial Dr *Web:* www.easomeng.com	Madison Heights	MI	48071	248-307-0650	307-0701	386
East Air Corp 337 Second St *Web:* www.eastair.com	Hackensack	NJ	07601	201-487-6060	487-5938	770
East Alabama Medical Ctr 2000 Pepperell Pkwy *TF:* 800-381-3685 ■ *Web:* www.eamc.org	Opelika	AL	36801	334-749-3411		374-3
East Arkansas Community College 1700 Newcastle Rd **Fax:* Admissions ■ *TF:* 877-797-3222 ■ *Web:* www.eacc.edu	Forrest City	AR	72335	870-633-4480	633-3840*	162
East Balt Inc 1801 W 31st Pl *TF:* 800-621-8555 ■ *Web:* www.eastbalt.com	Chicago	IL	60608	773-376-4444		68
East Bank Club 500 N Kingsbury St *Web:* www.eastbankclub.com	Chicago	IL	60654	312-527-5800	644-3868	354
East Bank Community Theatro 630 Barksdale Blvd *Web:* bossierarts.org	Bossier City	LA	71111	318-741-8310		572
East Baton Rouge Parish 1755 Florida St *Web:* www.brgov.com	Baton Rouge	LA	70802	225-389-3129		338
East Baton Rouge Parish Library (EBRPL) 7711 Goodwood Blvd *Web:* www.ebrpl.com	Baton Rouge	LA	70806	225-231-3750		434-3
East Bay Chamber of Commerce 16 Cutler St *TF:* 877-797-9790 ■ *Web:* www.eastbaychamberri.org	Warren	RI	02885	401-245-0750	245-0110	139
East Bay Express 1335 Stanford Ave Ste 100 *Web:* www.eastbayexpress.com	Emeryville	CA	94608	510-879-3700	879-3794	532-5
East Bay Tire Co 2200 Huntington Dr Unit C *TF:* 800-831-8473 ■ *Web:* eastbaytire.com	Fairfield	CA	94533	707-437-4700	437-4800	755
East Beach 1 Burlingame State Pk *Web:* www.riparks.com	Charlestown	RI	02813	401-322-0450	322-3083	565
East Bernard Isd 723 College St *Web:* www.ebisd.org	East Bernard	TX	77435	979-335-7519		685
East Bonner County Library District 1407 W Cedar St *Web:* ebonnerlibrary.org	Sandpoint	ID	83864	208-263-6930		434-3

	Phone	Fax	Class
East Boston Savings Bank 10 Meridian St . . . . . Boston MA 02128 *TF:* 800-657-3272 ■ *Web:* www.ebsb.com	617-567-1500		70
East Brunswick Public Library 2 Jean Walling Civic Ctr . . . . . East Brunswick NJ 08816 *TF:* 800-829-1040 ■ *Web:* www.ebpl.org	732-390-6950	390-6869	434-3
East by Southwest 160 E College Dr . . . . . Durango CO 81301 *Web:* www.eastbysouthwest.com	970-247-5533		671
East Cafe Chinese Restaurant 15140 E Mississippi Ave . . . . . Aurora CO 80012	303-369-6103		671
East Canyon Hotel & Spa 288 E Camino Monte Vista . . . . . Palm Springs CA 92262 *TF:* 877-324-6835 ■ *Web:* www.eastcanyonps.com	760-320-1928		379
East Canyon State Park 5535 South Hwy 66 . . . . . Morgan UT 84050 *Web:* www.stateparks.utah.gov	801-829-6866		565
East Carolina University E Fifth St . . . . . Greenville NC 27858 *TF:* 800-328-0577 ■ *Web:* www.ecu.edu	252-328-6131	328-6640	166
East Carolina University Joyner Library E Fifth St . . . . . Greenville NC 27858 *Web:* www.ecu.edu/cs-lib	252-328-6518	328-4834	434-6
East Carroll Parish 400 First St PO Box 246 . . . . . Lake Providence LA 71254 *Web:* www.ecsheriff.com	318-559-2800	559-2567	338
East Central College 1964 Prairie Dell Rd . . . . . Union MO 63084 **Fax:* Admissions ■ *TF:* 800-392-6848 ■ *Web:* www.eastcentral.edu	636-583-5193	583-1897*	162
East Central Community College 15738 Highway 15 S PO Box 129 . . . . . Decatur MS 39327 **Fax:* Admissions ■ *TF:* 877-462-3222 ■ *Web:* www.eccc.edu/transcripts.html	601-635-2111	635-4011*	162
East Central Energy PO Box 39 . . . . . Braham MN 55006 *TF:* 800-254-7944 ■ *Web:* www.eastcentralenergy.com	800-254-7944		245
East Central Oklahoma Electric Co-op Inc 2001 S Wood Dr PO Box 1178 . . . . . Okmulgee OK 74447 *Web:* www.ecoec.com	918-756-0833	756-6539	245
East Central Regional Hospital *Augusta* 3405 Mike Padgett Hwy . . . . . Augusta GA 30906	706-790-2011		374-5
East Central Regional Library 244 S Birch St . . . . . Cambridge MN 55008	763-689-7390	689-7436	434-3
East Central University 1100 E 14th St . . . . . Ada OK 74820 *Web:* www.ecok.edu	580-332-8000		166
East Chicago Public Library (ECPL) 2401 E Columbus Dr . . . . . East Chicago IN 46312 *Web:* www.ecpl.org	219-397-2453		434-3
East Cleveland Board of Education 14305 Shaw Ave . . . . . Cleveland OH 44112 *Web:* www.east-cleveland.k12.oh.us	216-268-6600		685
East Coast Appliance Sales, Service & Parts Inc 2053 Laskin Rd . . . . . Virginia Beach VA 23454 *Web:* www.eastcoastappliance.com	757-425-2883		35
East Coast Datacom Inc 245 Gus Hipp Blvd Ste 3 . . . . . Rockledge FL 32955 *Web:* www.ecdata.com	321-637-9980		225
East Coast Graphics 125 Wireless Blvd . . . . . Hauppauge NY 11788 *Web:* www.ecoastgraphics.com	631-231-9300		393
East Coast Grill & Raw Bar 1271 Cambridge St . . . . . Cambridge MA 02139 *Web:* www.eastcoastgrill.net	617-714-4002		671
East Coast Lumber & Supply Co 308 Ave A . . . . . Fort Pierce FL 34950 *TF:* 800-658-7124 ■ *Web:* www.eastcoastlumber.com	321-636-0411		817
East Coast Metal Distributors, Inc 1313 S Briggs Ave . . . . . Durham NC 27703 *TF:* 844 227 9531 ■ *Web:* www.ecmdi.com	844-227-9531		612
East Coast Metals 171 Ruth Rd . . . . . Harleysville PA 19438 *TF:* 800-355-2060 ■ *Web:* eastcoastmetals.com	215-256-9550		492
East Coast Sales Company Inc 554 N State Rd . . . . . Briarcliff Manor NY 10510 *Web:* www.ecsceramics.com	914-923-5000		191-1
East Coast Security Services Inc 68 Stiles Rd . . . . . Salem NH 03079 *TF:* 800-639-2086 ■ *Web:* www.ecss.com	603-898-6823		693
East Cooper Medical Ctr 2000 Hospital Dr . . . . . Mount Pleasant SC 29464 *Web:* www.eastcoopermedctr.com	843-881-0100		374-3
East End Computers LLC 30 Long Island Ave . . . . . Sag Harbor NY 11963 *TF:* 800-592-2919 ■ *Web:* www.eastendcomputer.com	631-725-4000		179
East End Hospice 481 Westhampton-Riverhead Rd PO Box 1048 . . . . . WestHampton Beach NY 11978 *TF:* 877-513-0099 ■ *Web:* www.eeh.org	631-288-8400	288-8492	371
East Erie Commercial Railroad 1030 Lawrence Pkwy . . . . . Erie PA 16511	814-875-2188		651
East Fairfield Coal Co (EFCC) 10900 S Ave PO Box 217 . . . . . North Lima OH 44452 *TF:* 800-241-7074 ■ *Web:* www.eastfairfieldcoal.com	330-549-2165		501
East Feliciana Parish PO Box 427 . . . . . Jackson LA 70748 *Web:* www.felicianatourism.org	225-683-5145		338
East Fork State Park 3294 Elklick Rd . . . . . Bethel OH 45106 *Web:* www.ohiodnr.com	513-734-4323		565
East Gate Capital Management 5050 El Camino Real Ste 104 . . . . . Los Altos CA 94022	650-325-5077	325-5072	792
East Georgia College 131 College Cir . . . . . Swainsboro GA 30401 **Fax:* Admissions ■ *TF:* 800-715-4255 ■ *Web:* www.ega.edu	478-289-2000	289-2140*	162
East Georgia Regional Medical Ctr (EGRMC) 1499 Fair Rd . . . . . Statesboro GA 30458 *TF:* 844-455-8708 ■ *Web:* www.eastgeorgiaregional.com	912-486-1000		374-3
East Hampton Star Inc, The 153 Main St PO Box 5002 . . . . . East Hampton NY 11937 *TF:* 844-324-0777 ■ *Web:* www.easthamptonstar.com	631-324-0002	324-7943	637-8
East Harbor State Park 1169 N Buck Rd . . . . . Lakeside-Marblehead OH 43440 *Web:* eastharborstatepark.org	419-734-4424		565

	Phone	Fax	Class
East Harlem Tutorial Program 2050 Second Ave . . . . . New York NY 10029 *Web:* ehtp.org	212-831-0650		242
East Hartford Public Library 840 Main St . . . . . East Hartford CT 06108 *Web:* www.easthartfordct.gov/library	860-289-6429		434-3
East Hill Tire Inc 25239 104th Ave SE . . . . . Kent WA 98030 *Web:* www.easthilltire.com	253-852-3280		755
East Houston Regional Medical Ctr 13111 E Fwy . . . . . Houston TX 77015 *TF:* 800-979-3627 ■ *Web:* www.easthoustonrmc.com	713-393-2000		374-3
East India Co 349 York Ave . . . . . Winnipeg MB R3C3S9 *Web:* www.eastindiaco.com	204-947-3097	947-5019	671
East Jefferson General Hospital (EJGH) 4200 Houma Blvd . . . . . Metairie LA 70006 *TF:* 866-280-7737 ■ *Web:* www.ejgh.org	504-454-4000		374-3
East Jersey State Prison 1100 Woodbridge Ave Lock Bag R . . . . . Rahway NJ 07065 *Web:* state.nj.us	732-499-5010	499-5022	213
East Jordan Plastics Inc PO Box 575 . . . . . East Jordan MI 49727 **Fax Area Code:* 231 ■ *TF:* 800-353-1190 ■ *Web:* www.eastjordanplastics.com	800-353-1190	536-7090*	602
East Kansas Agri-Energy LLC 1304 S Main . . . . . Garnett KS 66032 *Web:* www.ekaellc.com	785-448-2888		580
East Kentucky Network LLC 101 Technology Trl . . . . . Ivel KY 41642 *Web:* www.appalachianwireless.com	606-477-2355		387
East Lansing Public Library 950 Abbott Rd . . . . . East Lansing MI 48823 *Web:* www.elpl.org	517-351-2420	351-9536	434-3
East Liberty Quarter Chamber of Commerce 5907 Penn Ave Ste 305 . . . . . Pittsburgh PA 15206 *Web:* www.eastlibertychamber.org	412-661-9660		139
East Lind Heat Treat Inc 32045 Dequindre Rd . . . . . Madison Heights MI 48071 *TF:* 800-521-3188 ■ *Web:* www.eastlind.com	248-585-1415		484
East Lion Corp 318 Brea Canyon Rd . . . . . City of Industry CA 91789 *TF:* 877-939-1818 ■ *Web:* www.eastlioncorp.com	626-912-1818	935-5858	301
East Liverpool City Hospital (ELCH) 425 W Fifth St . . . . . East Liverpool OH 43920 *Web:* www.elch.org	330-385-7200		374-3
East Los Angeles Chamber of Commerce 4716 E Cesar Chavez Ave . . . . . Los Angeles CA 90022 *TF:* 800-331-7593 ■ *Web:* www.eastlachamber.com	323-263-2005		139
East Los Angeles College 1301 Avenida Cesar Chavez . . . . . Monterey Park CA 91754 **Fax:* Admissions ■ *Web:* www.elac.edu	323-265-8650	265-8688*	162
East Louisiana State Hospital 4502 Hwy 951 . . . . . Jackson LA 70748 *Web:* new.dhh.louisiana.gov	225-634-0100		374-5
East Maine School District 63 (EMSD) 10150 Dee Rd . . . . . Des Plaines IL 60016 *TF:* 866-752-6850 ■ *Web:* www.emsd63.org	847-299-1900	299-9963	685
East Matunuck State Beach 950 Succotash Rd . . . . . South Kingstown RI 02881 *Web:* www.riparks.com	401-789-8585		565
East Meadow Public Library Front St & E Meadow Ave . . . . . East Meadow NY 11554 *Web:* eastmeadow.info	516-794-2570		434-3
East Mfg Corp 1871 State Rt 44 PO Box 277 . . . . . Randolph OH 44265 *TF:* 888-405-3278 ■ *Web:* www.eastmfg.com	330-325-9921	325-7851	779
East Mississippi Business Development Corp 1901 Front St PO Box 790 . . . . . Meridian MS 39302 *TF:* 800 748 7626 ■ *Web:* www.embdc.org	601-693-1306	693-5638	139
East Mississippi Community College (EMCC) 1512 Kemper St PO Box 158 . . . . . Scooba MS 39358	662-476-8442		162
East Mississippi Electric Power Assn (EMEPA) 2128 Hwy 39 N PO Box 5517 . . . . . Meridian MS 39302 *TF:* 800-532-1502 ■ *Web:* www.emepa.com	601-581-8600	482-0701	245
East Moline Correctional Ctr 100 Hillcrest Rd . . . . . East Moline IL 61244 *Web:* www.illinois.gov	309-755-4511		213
East Moline Metal Products Co 1201 Seventh St . . . . . East Moline IL 61244 *Web:* www.emmetal.com	309-752-1350	752-1380	488
East Ocean City 27 Beach St . . . . . Boston MA 02111 *Web:* www.eastoceancity.com	617 542 2504		671
East Orange Campus of the VA New Jersey Health Care System (NJHCS) 385 Tremont Ave . . . . . East Orange NJ 07018 **Fax Area Code:* 202 ■ **Fax:* Hum Res ■ *TF General:* 844-872-4681 ■ *Web:* www.usa.gov	844-872-4681	456-1414*	374-8
East Orange General Hospital 300 Central Ave . . . . . East Orange NJ 07018 *TF:* 800-772-1213 ■ *Web:* www.evh.org	973-672-8400		374-3
East Orange Public Library 21 S Arlington Ave . . . . . East Orange NJ 07018 *TF:* 800-573-8459 ■ *Web:* www.eopl.org	973-266-5600		434-3
East Penn Manufacturing Co 301 Fifth Ave . . . . . Oelwein IA 50662 *Web:* www.eastpenn-deka.com	319-283-7334		54
East Penn Mfg Co Inc PO Box 147 . . . . . Lyon Station PA 19536 *Web:* eastpennmanufacturing.com	610-682-6361	682-6361	60
East Penn School District 800 Pine St . . . . . Emmaus PA 18049 *Web:* www.eastpennsd.org	610-966-8300		685
East Providence Chamber of Commerce 1011 Waterman Ave . . . . . East Providence RI 02914 *Web:* www.eastprovidenceareachamber.com	401-438-1212	435-4581	139
East Providence Public Library 41 Grove Ave . . . . . East Providence RI 02914 *Web:* www.eastprovidencelibrary.org	401-434-2453		434-3
East Ramapo Central School District 105 S Madison Ave . . . . . Spring Valley NY 10977 *Web:* www.ercsd.org	845-577-6000		685
East Ridge Printing 1249 Ridgeway Ave Ste Y . . . . . Rochester NY 14615 *Web:* www.eastridgeprint.com	585-266-4911		627

Phone | Fax | Class

East Ridge Retirement Village
19301 SW 87th Ave, Miami FL 33157 — 786-842-4596 — 672
Web: www.eastridgeatcutlerbay.com

East River Energy Inc
401 Soundview Rd, Guilford CT 06437 — 203-453-1200 — 579
TF: 800-336-3762 ■ *Web:* www.eastriverenergy.com

East Rochester Public Library
317 Main St, East Rochester NY 14445 — 585-586-8302 — 434-3
Web: www.libraryweb.org

East Side Chamber of Commerce
3501 E 106th St Ste 200, Chicago IL 60617 — 773-721-7948 — 139
Web: www.eastsidechamber.com

East Side Clinical Laboratory Inc
10 Risho Ave, East Providence RI 02914 — 401-455-8400 — 415
Web: www.esclab.com

East Side House Inc 337 Alexander Ave, Bronx NY 10454 — 718-665-5250 — 242
TF: 800-282-3336 ■ *Web:* www.eastsidehouse.org

East Side Moving & Storage
4836 SE Powell Blvd, Portland OR 97206 — 503-777-4181 — 519
TF: 800-547-4600 ■ *Web:* www.move-northwest.com

East Side Plating Inc
8400 SE 26th Pl, Portland OR 97202 — 503-654-3774 — 481
TF: 800-394-8554 ■ *Web:* www.eastsideplating.com

East Side Union High School District
830 N Capitol Ave, San Jose CA 95133 — 408-347-5000 — 347-5045 — 685
Web: www.esuhsd.org

East St Tammany Chamber of Commerce
118 W Hall Ave, Slidell LA 70460 — 985-643-5678 — 649-2460 — 139
TF: 800-870-3673 ■ *Web:* estchamber.com

East Stroudsburg University
200 Prospect St, East Stroudsburg PA 18301 — 570-422-3542 — 422-3933* — 166
*Fax: Admissions ■ *TF Admissions:* 877-230-5547 ■ *Web:* www.esu.edu

East Stroudsburg University Kemp Library
200 Prospect St, East Stroudsburg PA 18301 — 570-422-3465 — 422-3151 — 434-6
TF: 877-422-1378 ■ *Web:* www.esu.edu/library

East Teak Trading Group Inc
1106 Drake Rd, Donalds SC 29638 — 864-379-2111 — 350
TF: 800-338-5636 ■ *Web:* www.eastteak.com

East Tennessee Children's Hospital
2018 Clinch Ave PO Box 15010, Knoxville TN 37901 — 865-541-8000 — 374-1
Web: www.etch.com

East Tennessee Historical Society
601 S Gay St PO Box 1629, Knoxville TN 37901 — 865-215-8824 — 215-8819 — 520
TF: 800-407-4324 ■ *Web:* www.easttnhistory.org

East Tennessee Human Resource Agency Inc
9111 Cross Park Dr Ste A-250, Knoxville TN 37923 — 865-691-2551 — 195
TF: 800-848-0298 ■ *Web:* www.ethra.org

East Tennessee Lions Eye Bank
1924 Alcoa Hwy U-26, Knoxville TN 37920 — 423-778-4000 — 269
Web: lionseyebanktn.com

East Tennessee Public Communications Corp
1611 E Magnolia Ave, Knoxville TN 37917 — 865-595-0220 — 595-0300 — 632
Web: www.easttennesseepbs.org

East Tennessee State University
PO Box 70731, Johnson City TN 37614 — 423-439-4213 — 439-4630 — 166
TF: 800-462-3878 ■ *Web:* www.etsu.edu

East Texas Arboretum (ETABS)
1601 Patterson Rd, Athens TX 75751 — 903-675-5630 — 97
Web: www.easttexasarboretum.org

East Texas Baptist University
1209 N Grove St, Marshall TX 75670 — 903-935-7963 — 923-2001* — 166
*Fax: Admissions ■ *TF:* 800-804-3828 ■ *Web:* www.etbu.edu

East Texas Medical Ctr Athens
2000 S Palestine St, Athens TX 75751 — 903-676-1000 — 374-3
Web: www.etmc.org

East Texas Medical Ctr Tyler
1000 S Beckham Ave, Tyler TX 75701 — 903-597-0351 — 374-3
Web: www.etmc.org

East Town 770 N Jefferson St, Milwaukee WI 53202 — 414-271-1416 — 271-6401 — 50-6
Web: www.easttown.com

East Towne Mall 89 E Towne Mall, Madison WI 53704 — 608-244-1387 — 460
Web: www.shopeasttowne-mall.com

East Valley School District 361
12325 E Grace Ave, Spokane WA 99216 — 509-924-1830 — 927-9500 — 685
Web: www.evsd.org

East Valley Tribune 120 W First Ave, Mesa AZ 85210 — 480-898-6500 — 898-6362 — 532-2
TF: 877-728-5414 ■ *Web:* www.eastvalleytribune.com

East Valley Water District
3654 E Highland Ave Ste 18, Highland CA 92346 — 909-889-9501 — 806
TF: 866-275-3772 ■ *Web:* www.eastvalley.org

East West Bancorp Inc 1881 W Main St, Alhambra CA 91801 — 626-308-2012 — 360-2
NASDAQ: EWBC ■ *TF:* 888-895-5650 ■ *Web:* www.eastwestbank.com

East West Bookshop of Palo Alto
324 Castro St, Mountain View CA 94041 — 650-988-9800 — 95
TF: 800-909-6161 ■ *Web:* www.eastwest.com

East West Label Co
1000 E Hector St, Conshohocken PA 19428 — 610-825-0410 — 413
TF: 800-441-7333 ■ *Web:* www.ewlabel.com

Eastaboga Tackle Mfg Co Inc
261 Mudd St, Eastaboga AL 36260 — 256-831-9682 — 710
Web: www.eastabogatackle.com

Eastbourne Capital Management LLC
1101 Fifth Ave Ste 370, San Rafael CA 94901 — 415-448-1200 — 401

East-Central Iowa Rural Electric Co-op
2400 Bing Miller Ln, Urbana IA 52345 — 319-443-4343 — 443-4359 — 245
TF: 877-850-4343 ■ *Web:* www.ecirec.com

Eastco Multi Media Solutions Inc
3646 California Rd, Orchard Park NY 14127 — 716-662-0536 — 514
TF: 800-365-8273 ■ *Web:* www.eastcomultimedia.com

Eastconn 376 Hartford Tpke, Hampton CT 06247 — 860-455-0707 — 685
Web: www.eastconn.org

Easter & Stoney Ps 206 E First St, Aberdeen WA 98520 — 360-533-7272 — 2

Easter Owens Electric Co 6692 Fig St, Arvada CO 80004 — 303-431-0111 — 203
TF: 866-204-3707 ■ *Web:* www.easter-owens.com

Easter Seals 230 W Monroe St Ste 1800, Chicago IL 60606 — 312-726-6200 — 726-1494 — 48-17
TF: 800-221-6827 ■ *Web:* www.easterseals.com

Easterly & Co PO Box 541791 Ste 950, Houston TX 77254 — 832-330-8120 — 4
Web: www.easterly.com

Eastern Alloys Inc
11 Henry Henning Dr PO Box 317, Maybrook NY 12543 — 845-427-2151 — 427-5185 — 485
Web: www.eazall.com

Eastern Analytical Inc 25 chenell dr, Concord NH 03301 — 603-228-0525 — 743
Web: easternanalytical.com

Eastern Arizona College
615 N Stadium Ave, Thatcher AZ 85552 — 928-428-8472 — 428-2578 — 162
TF: 800-678-3808 ■ *Web:* www.eac.edu

Eastern Aviation Fuels Inc
601 Mccarthy Blvd, New Bern NC 28562 — 252-633-0066 — 579
Web: www.easternaviationfuels.com

Eastern Awning Systems Inc
843 Echo Lake Rd, Watertown CT 06795 — 860-274-9218 — 567
Web: www.easternawning.com

Eastern Bank 1 Eastern Pl, Lynn MA 01901 — 781-599-2100 — 598-7697 — 70
TF: 800-327-8376 ■ *Web:* www.easternbank.com

Eastern Bank Corp 265 Franklin St, Boston MA 02110 — 617-897-1008 — 360-2
TF Cust Svc: 800-327-8376 ■ *Web:* www.easternbank.com

Eastern Business Forms Inc PO Box 10, Mauldin SC 29662 — 800-387-2648 — 110
TF: 800-387-2648 ■ *Web:* www.ebf-inc.com

Eastern Carolina Nissan
3315 Hwy 70 E, New Bern NC 28560 — 252-636-1000 — 57
Web: ecnissan.com

Eastern Co, The
112 Bridge St PO Box 460, Naugatuck CT 06770 — 203-729-2255 — 723-8653 — 350
NASDAQ: EML ■ *TF:* 800-221-0982 ■ *Web:* www.easterncompany.com

Eastern Computer Exchange Inc
105 Cascade Blvd, Milford CT 06460 — 203-877-4334 — 174
Web: www.ecei.com

Eastern Concrete Materials Inc
475 Market St, Elmwood Park NJ 07407 — 201-797-7979 — 182
TF: 800-822-7242 ■ *Web:* www.us-concrete.com

Eastern Connecticut State University
83 Windham St, Willimantic CT 06226 — 860-465-5000 — 465-5544* — 166
*Fax: Admissions ■ *TF Admissions:* 877-353-3278 ■ *Web:* www.easternct.edu

Eastern Connecticut State University Smith Library
83 Windham St, Willimantic CT 06226 — 860-465-4506 — 465-5522 — 434-6
TF: 800-578-1449 ■ *Web:* www.easternct.edu

Eastern Connecticut Symphony Orchestra
289 State St, New London CT 06320 — 860-443-2876 — 573-3
Web: www.ectsymphony.com

Eastern Construction Company Ltd
505 Consumers Rd Ste 1100, Toronto ON M2J5G2 — 416-497-7110 — 186
Web: www.easternconstruction.com

Eastern Correctional Facility
30 Institution Rd PO Box 338, Napanoch NY 12458 — 845-647-7400 — 213
Web: www.doccs.ny.gov/faclist.html

Eastern Correctional Institution
30420 Revells Neck Rd, Westover MD 21890 — 410-845-4000 — 213

Eastern Correctional Institution
2821 Hwy 903 N PO Box 215, Maury NC 28554 — 252-747-8101 — 747-8260 — 213
Web: www.ncdps.gov

Eastern Data Inc 4386 Park Dr, Norcross GA 30093 — 770-279-8888 — 174
Web: www.ediatlanta.com

Eastern Design Services
PO Box 17606, Greenville SC 29606 — 864-271-1228 — 260
Web: www.easterndesign.com

Eastern Exterior Wall Systems
3400 High Point Blvd, Bethlehem PA 18017 — 610-868-5522 — 106
Web: www.eews.com

Eastern Federal Corp 901 E Blvd, Charlotte NC 28203 — 704-377-3495 — 748
Web: easternfederal.com

Eastern Fisheries Inc
14 Hervey Tichon Ave, New Bedford MA 02740 — 508-993-5300 — 991-2226 — 296-14
Web: easternfisheries.com

Eastern Floral & Gift Shop
818 Butterworth St SW, Grand Rapids MI 49504 — 616-949-2200 — 292
TF: 800-494-2202 ■ *Web:* www.easternfloral.com

Eastern Foods Inc
1000 Naturally Fresh Blvd, Atlanta GA 30349 — 800-765-1950 — 296-19
TF: 800-765-1950 ■ *Web:* www.naturallyfresh.com

Eastern Fuels Inc 386 NC Hwy 42 W, Ahoskie NC 27910 — 252-332-5021 — 581
Web: www.easternfuels.com

Eastern Gateway Community College
4000 Sunset Blvd, Steubenville OH 43952 — 740-264-5591 — 264-1338 — 800
TF: 800-682-6553 ■ *Web:* egcc.edu

Eastern Idaho Regional Medical Ctr (EIRMC)
3100 Channing Way, Idaho Falls ID 83404 — 208-529-6111 — 529-7021 — 374-3
Web: www.eirmc.com

Eastern Idaho Technical College
1600 S 25th E, Idaho Falls ID 83404 — 208-524-3000 — 525-7026 — 800
TF: 800-662-0261 ■ *Web:* www.eitc.edu

Eastern Illini Electric Co-op
330 W Ottawa PO Box 96, Paxton IL 60957 — 217-379-2131 — 379-2936 — 245
TF: 800-824-5102 ■ *Web:* eiec.org

Eastern Illinois University
600 Lincoln Ave, Charleston IL 61920 — 217-581-2223 — 581-7060* — 166
*Fax: Admissions ■ *TF Admissions:* 800-252-5711 ■ *Web:* www.eiu.edu

Eastern Industries Inc
3912 Brumbaugh Rd, New Enterprise PA 16664 — 814-766-2211 — 867-1886* — 503-5
*Fax Area Code: 610 ■ *Web:* www.eastern-ind.com

Eastern Iowa Airport, The
2515 Arthur Collins PkwySW, Cedar Rapids IA 52404 — 319-362-8336 — 362-1670 — 27
Web: www.eiairport.org

Eastern Iowa Light & Power Co-op
600 E Fifth St PO Box 3003, Wilton IA 52778 — 563-732-2211 — 245
TF: 800-728-1242 ■ *Web:* www.easterniowa.com

Eastern Janitorial Services Inc
23 N Michigan Ave, Kenilworth NJ 07033 — 908-298-8120 — 192
Web: www.easternjs.com

Eastern Kentucky Correctional Complex
200 Rd to Justice, West Liberty KY 41472 — 606-743-2800 — 743-2811 — 213
TF: 800-325-6000 ■ *Web:* www.corrections.ky.gov

Eastern Kentucky University
521 Lancaster Ave, Richmond KY 40475 — 859-622-2106 — 622-8024 — 166
TF: 800-465-9191 ■ *Web:* www.eku.edu

Eastern Lift Truck Company Inc
549 E Linwood Ave, Maple Shade NJ 08052 — 856-779-8880 — 482-8804 — 385
TF: 866-980-7175 ■ *Web:* www.easternlifttruck.com

	Phone	Fax	Class
Eastern Light Capital Inc 100 Pine St Ste 560 San Francisco CA 94111 *OTC: ELCI*	415-693-9500		509
Eastern Long Island Hospital Assn, The 201 Manor Pl Greenport NY 11944 *Web:* www.elih.org	631-477-1000		374-3
Eastern Louisiana Mental Health System Greenwell Springs Campus 628 N Fourth St PO Box 629 Baton Rouge LA 70802 *Web:* dhh.louisiana.gov/index.cfm/directory/detail/219	225-634-0100		374-5
Eastern Maine Community College 354 Hogan Rd Bangor ME 04401 *TF:* 800-286-9357 ■ *Web:* www.emcc.edu	207-974-4600		800
Eastern Maine Electric Co-op Inc 21 Union St Calais ME 04619 *TF:* 800-696-7444 ■ *Web:* www.emec.com	207-454-7555		245
Eastern Maine Healthcare Systems (EMHS) 43 Whiting Hill Rd Brewer ME 04412 *TF:* 877-366-3662 ■ *Web:* www.emhs.org	207-973-7050	973-7139	353
Eastern Maine Medical Ctr 489 State St Bangor ME 04401 *Web:* www.emmc.org	207-973-7000		374-3
Eastern Manufacturing Inc 2151 Cabot Blvd W Langhorne PA 19047 *Web:* www.easterncatalytic.com	215-702-3600		247
Eastern Maumee Bay Chamber of Commerce 2460 Navaree Ave Oregon OH 43616 *TF:* 800-837-3200 ■ *Web:* www.embchamber.org	419-693-5580	693-9990	139
Eastern Mechanical Services Inc 3 Starr St Danbury CT 06810 *Web:* emsinc.us	203-792-7668	748-0385	189-10
Eastern Mennonite University 1200 Pk Rd Harrisonburg VA 22802 **Fax:* Admissions ■ *TF Admissions:* 800-368-2665 ■ *Web:* www.emu.edu	540-432-4118	432-4444*	166
Eastern Metal Supply Inc 3600 23rd Ave S Lake Worth FL 33461 *Web:* www.easternmetal.com	561-533-6061		492
Eastern Metal/USA-SIGN 1430 Sullivan St Elmira NY 14901 *TF Sales:* 800-872-7446 ■ *Web:* www.usa-sign.com	607-734-2295	734-8783	701
Eastern Michigan University 900 Oakwood St Ypsilanti MI 48197 *TF:* 800-468-6368 ■ *Web:* www.emich.edu	734-487-1849		166
Eastern Michigan University Halle Library 955 W Cir Dr Ypsilanti MI 48197 *TF:* 888-888-3465 ■ *Web:* emich.edu/library/index.php	734-487-0020	487-8861	434-6
Eastern Millwork Co 3222 Oley Tpke Rd Reading PA 19606	610-779-3550		499
Eastern Mountain Sports 1 Vose Farm Rd Peterborough NH 03458 *TF:* 888-463-6367 ■ *Web:* www.ems.com	603-924-7231		711
Eastern Museum of Motor Racing 100 Baltimore Rd York Springs PA 17372 *Web:* www.emmr.org	717-528-8279		522
Eastern National 470 Maryland Dr Ste 1 Fort Washington PA 19034 *Web:* www.easternnational.org	215-283-6900		95
Eastern Nazarene College 23 E Elm Ave Quincy MA 02170 *TF:* 800-883-6288 ■ *Web:* www.enc.edu	617-745-3000	745-3929	166
Eastern Nc School for The Deaf 1311 US Hwy 301 N Wilson NC 27893 *Web:* encsd.net	252-237-2450		685
Eastern Nebraska Veterans Home 12505 S 40th St Bellevue NE 68123 *Web:* dhhs.ne.gov	402-595-2180		793
Eastern New Mexico Medical Ctr 405 W Country Club Rd Roswell NM 88201 *TF:* 800-222-1222 ■ *Web:* www.enmmc.com	575-622-8170		374-3
Eastern New Mexico University 1500 S Ave K Portales NM 88130 *TF:* 800-367-3668 ■ *Web:* www.enmu.edu	575-562-1011		166
Eastern New Mexico University Roswell 52 University Blvd Roswell NM 88203 *TF:* 800-243-6687 ■ *Web:* www.roswell.enmu.edu	800-243-6687		162
Eastern New Mexico University-ruidoso 709 Mechem Dr Ruidoso NM 88345 *TF:* 800-934-3668 ■ *Web:* www.ruidoso.enmu.edu	575-257-2120		166
Eastern Oil Co 590 S Paddock St Pontiac MI 48341 *TF:* 800-550-3645 ■ *Web:* www.easternoil.com	248-333-1333		579
Eastern Oklahoma District Library System 801 W Okmulgee Ave Muskogee OK 74401 *TF:* 888-291-8152 ■ *Web:* www.eodls.lib.ok.us	918-682-6657	683-0436	434-3
Eastern Oklahoma State College 1301 W Main St Wilburton OK 74578 *Web:* www.cosc.edu	918-465-2361	465-4417	162
Eastern Oregon University 1 University Blvd La Grande OR 97850 **Fax:* Admissions ■ *TF:* 800-452-8639 ■ *Web:* www.eou.edu	541-962-3393	962-3418*	166
Eastern Oregon University Pierce Library 1 University Blvd La Grande OR 97850 *Web:* library.eou.edu	541-962-3579	962-3335	434-6
Eastern Oregon Youth Correctional Facility 1800 W Monroe St Burns OR 97720 *Web:* oregon.gov	541-573-3133	573-3665	412
Eastern Pennsylvania Supply Co 700 Scott St Wilkes-Barre PA 18705 *TF:* 800-432-8075 ■ *Web:* www.easternpenn.com	570-823-1181	824-2514	612
Eastern Pierce County Chamber of Commerce 323 N Meridian PO Box 1298 Puyallup WA 98371 *TF:* 800-272-2662 ■ *Web:* www.puyallupsumnerchamber.com	253-845-6755		139
Eastern Regional Research Ctr (ERRC) 600 E Mermaid Ln Wyndmoor PA 19038 *Web:* www.ars.usda.gov	215-233-6400	233-6559	668
Eastern Sanitation Ltd 17 Adam St Antigonish NS B2G2G1 *Web:* easternsanitation.com	902-863-1744		660
Eastern Sheet Metal LLC 8959 Blue Ash Rd Blue Ash OH 45242 *Web:* www.easternsheetmetal.com	513-793-3440		697
Eastern Shipbuilding Group Inc 2200 Nelson St Panama City FL 32401 *Web:* www.easternshipbuilding.com	850-763-1900		698
Eastern Shore Centre 30500 State Hwy 181 Spanish Fort AL 36527 *Web:* easternshorecentre.com	251-625-0060	625-0039	460
Eastern Shore Chamber of Commerce 29750 Larry Dee Cawyer Dr PO Box 310 Daphne AL 36526 *Web:* www.eschamber.com	251-621-8222	621-8001	139
Eastern Shore Community College 29300 Lankford Hwy Melfa VA 23410 **Fax:* Admissions ■ *TF:* 800-639-8521 ■ *Web:* www.es.vccs.edu	757-789-1789	789-1737*	162
Eastern Shore Foods LLC 13249 Lankford Hwy Mappsville VA 23407	757-824-5651		296-14
Eastern Shore Natural Gas Co 1110 Forest Ave Ste 201 Dover DE 19904 *TF:* 877-650-1257 ■ *Web:* www.esng.com	302-734-6720		787
Eastern Shore of Virginia Chamber of Commerce 19056 Pkwy Rd Melfa VA 23410 *Web:* www.esvachamber.org	757-787-2460	787-8687	139
Eastern Skateboard Supply Inc 6612 Amsterdam Way Wilmington NC 28405 *TF:* 800-358-7588 ■ *Web:* www.easternskatesupply.com	910-791-8240		711
Eastern Star Church 5750 E 30th St Indianapolis IN 46218 *Web:* www.easternstarchurch.org	317-591-5050		48-20
Eastern State Hospital (ESH) 4601 Ironbound Rd Williamsburg VA 23188 *TF:* 800-994-6610 ■ *Web:* esh.dbhds.virginia.gov	757-253-5161		374-5
Eastern State Penitentiary Historic Site 22nd St & Fairmount Ave Philadelphia PA 19130 *TF:* 800-537-7676 ■ *Web:* www.easternstate.org	215-236-3300	236-5289	50-3
Eastern Steel Corp 1946 Pitkin Ave Brooklyn NY 11207 *Web:* www.easternsteel.com	718-495-5300		492
Eastern Tea Corp 1 Engelhard Dr Monroe Township NJ 08831 *Web:* www.easterntea.com	609-860-1100		296-40
Eastern University 1300 Eagle Rd Wayne PA 19087 **Fax:* Admissions ■ *TF Admissions:* 800-452-0996 ■ *Web:* www.eastern.edu	610-341-5800	341-1723*	166
Eastern Virginia Bankshares Inc 330 Hospital Rd Tappahannock VA 22560 *NASDAQ: EVBS* ■ *TF General:* 866-296-3743 ■ *Web:* www.snl.com	804-443-8400	445-1047	360-2
Eastern Virginia Medical School 700 W Olney Rd PO Box 1980 Norfolk VA 23501 **Fax:* Admissions ■ *Web:* www.evms.edu	757-446-5812	446-5896*	167-2
Eastern Washington University 526 Fifth St Cheney WA 99004 **Fax:* Admissions ■ *TF:* 800-280-1256 ■ *Web:* www.ewu.edu	509-359-6200	359-6692*	166
Eastern West Virginia Community & Technical College 316 Eastern Dr Moorefield WV 26836 *TF:* 877-982-2322 ■ *Web:* www.easternwv.edu	304-434-8000	434-7000	162
Eastern Wholesale Fence Co Inc 274 Middle Island Rd Medford NY 11763 *TF:* 800-339-3362 ■ *Web:* www.easternfence.com	631-698-0900	698-6408	191-2
Eastern Winds 3740 Washington Blvd Ogden UT 84403 *Web:* easternwindsrestaurant.com	801-627-2739	627-2739	671
Eastern Wood Products Inc 2020 Mill Ln Williamsport PA 17701	570-326-1946		551
Eastern Wyoming College 3200 W 'C' St Torrington WY 82240 **Fax:* Admissions ■ *TF:* 800-658-3195 ■ *Web:* ewc.wy.edu	307-532-8200	532-8222*	162
Eastex Environmental Lab Inc 1119 S University Dr Nacogdoches TX 75961 *TF:* 800-525-0508	936-569-8879		196
Eastex Telephone Co-op Inc PO Box 150 Henderson TX 75653 *TF:* 800-232-7839 ■ *Web:* www.eastex.com	903-854-1000		736
Eastfield College 3737 Motley Dr Mesquite TX 75150 *Web:* eastfieldcollege.edu	972-860-7100	860-8306	162
Eastfield Mall 1655 Boston Rd Springfield MA 01129 *Web:* www.eastfieldmall.com	413-543-8000		460
Eastgate Mall 4601 Eastgate Blvd Cincinnati OH 45245 *Web:* www.shopeastgate-mall.com	513-752-2294		460
EastGroup Properties Inc 190 E Capitol St Ste 400 Jackson MS 39201 *NYSE: EGP* ■ *TF:* 800-695-1564 ■ *Web:* www.eastgroup.net	601-354-3555	352-1441	655
Eastham Drilling Inc 4710 Bellaire Blvd Ste 350 Bellaire TX 77401 *TF:* 800-460-8070 ■ *Web:* www.bigedrilling.com	713-661-6890		540
Eastham, Watson, Dale & Forney LLP The Niels Esperson Bldg 808 Travis Ste 1300 Houston TX 77002 *Web:* www.easthamlaw.com	713-225-0905		428
Eastland Center 18000 Vernier Rd Harper Woods MI 48225 *Web:* www.shopeastland.com	313-371-1501		460
Eastland County 100 W Main St Eastland TX 76448 *Web:* www.eastlandcountytexas.com	254-629-1583	629-8125	338
Eastland Food Corp 8305 Stayton Dr Jessup MD 20794 *Web:* www.eastlandfood.com	301-621-8140		297-8
Eastland Mall 800 N Green River Rd Evansville IN 47715 *Web:* www.shopeastlandmall.com	812-477-4848		460
Eastland Park Hotel 157 High St Portland ME 04101 *Web:* www.westinportlandharborview.com	207-775-5411		379
Eastland Shoe Mfg Corp 4 Meeting House Rd Freeport ME 04032 *TF:* 888-988-1998 ■ *Web:* www.eastlandshoe.com	207-865-6314	865-9261	301
Eastman & Beaudine Inc 7201 Bishop Rd Ste 220 Plano TX 75024 *TF:* 800-446-3037 ■ *Web:* www.eastman-beaudine.com	972-312-1012		266
Eastman & Smith Ltd 1 Seagate 24th Fl Toledo OH 43699 *Web:* www.eastmansmith.com	419-241-6000		428
Eastman Chemical Co 200 S Wilcox Dr Kingsport TN 37660 *NYSE: EMN* ■ *TF Cust Svc:* 800-327-8626 ■ *Web:* www.eastman.com	423-229-2000		144
Eastman Kodak Co 343 State St Rochester NY 14650 *OTC: EKDKQ* ■ *Web:* www.kodak.com	585-724-4000		591
Eastman Machine Co 779 Washington St Buffalo NY 14203 *TF:* 800-872-5571 ■ *Web:* www.eastmancuts.com	716-856-2200	856-1140	744
Eastman Theatre 26 Gibbs St Rochester NY 14604 *Web:* www.esm.rochester.edu	585-274-1110		572
Eastmont Towers 6315 O St Lincoln NE 68510 *Web:* www.eastmontliving.com	402-489-6591		672
Eastmont Town Center 7200 Bancroft Ave Ste 2 Oakland CA 94605	510-635-2966		460

Phone Fax Class

Easton Area School District Inc
1801 Bushkill Dr. Easton PA 18040 610-250-2400 685
Web: www.eastonsd.org
Easton Coach Co 1200 Conroy Pl. Easton PA 18040 610-253-4055 107
Web: eastoncoach.com
Easton Hospital 250 S 21st St Easton PA 18042 610-250-4000 374-3
TF: 866-800-3880 ■ *Web:* www.easton-hospital.com
Easton Tru-Flite LLC
2709 S Freeman Rd Monticello IN 47960 574-583-5131 710
Web: eastonarchery.com
Easton's Group of Hotels Inc
3100 Steeles Ave E Gateway Centre Ste 601 Markham ON L3R8T3 905-940-9409 378
Web: www.eastonsgroup.com
Eastover Hotel & Resort LLC 430 East St. Lenox MA 01240 413-637-0625 378
Web: www.eastover.com
Eastown Distributors Co
14400 Oakland Ave. Highland Park MI 48203 313-867-6900 81-1
TF: 800-498-4008 ■ *Web:* www.eastown.com
Eastpointe Memorial Library
15875 Oak St Eastpointe MI 48021 586-445-5096 434-3
TF: 800-649-7377 ■ *Web:* cityofeastpointe.net
Eastpointe Rehabilitation & Skilled Care Ctr
255 Central Ave Chelsea MA 02150 617-884-5700 450
Web: www.eastpointerehab.com
Eastport Port Authority 3 Madison St. Eastport ME 04631 207-853-4614 853-9584 618
Web: www.portofeastport.org
Eastridge Mall
2200 Eastridge Loop Ste 2062 San Jose CA 95122 408-238-3600 460
TF: 800-894-9908 ■ *Web:* www.eastridgecenter.com
Eastridge Workforce Solutions
2355 Northside Dr Ste 360 San Diego CA 92108 619-260-2100 734
TF: 877-862-2632 ■ *Web:* www.eastridge.com
Eastside Cafe 2113 Manor Rd. Austin TX 78722 512-476-5858 671
TF: 800-574-8897 ■ *Web:* www.eastsidecafeaustin.com
Eastside Medical Ctr
1700 Medical Way Snellville GA 30078 770-979-0200 374-3
Web: www.eastsidemedical.com
Eastside Retirement Assn
10901 17th Cir NE Redmond WA 98052 425-556-8100 672
Web: www.emeraldheights.com
Eastside Union School District
45006 30th St E Lancaster CA 93535 661-952-1200 952-1220 685
TF: 877-263-7995 ■ *Web:* www.eastside.k12.ca.us
Eastview Mall 7979 Pittsford-Victor Rd Victor NY 14564 585-223-4420 460
Web: www.eastviewmall.com
Eastway Supplies Inc
1561 Alum Creek Dr. Columbus OH 43209 614-252-0974 610
Web: www.eastwaysupplies.com
EastWest Institute (EWI)
1 E 26th St 20th Fl New York NY 10010 212-824-4100 824-4149 634
Web: www.eastwest.ngo
East-West University
816 S Michigan Ave Chicago IL 60605 312-939-0111 939-0083 166
Web: www.eastwest.edu
Eastwick Colleges Inc
10 S Franklin Tpke Ramsey NJ 07446 201-327-8877 162
Web: www.eastwickcollege.edu
Eastwood Mall 5555 Youngstown-Warren Rd Niles OH 44446 330-652-6980 544-5929 460
Web: eastwoodmall.com
Eastwood Towne Ctr 3003 Preyde Blvd Lansing MI 48912 517-316-9209 316-9214 460
Web: www.shopeastwoodtownecenter.com
Easy Analytic Software Inc
101 Haag Ave Bellmawr NJ 08031 856-931-5780 387
Web: www.easidemographics.com
Easy Automation Inc 102 Mill St. Welcome MN 56181 507-728-8214 358
Web: www.easy-automation.com
Easy Drive Stake Inc 4111 Todd Ln. Austin TX 78744 512-447-9879 279
Easy Dynamics Inc 2003 11th st nw. Washington DC 20001 202-558-7275 225
Web: www.easydynamics.com
Easy Ice LLC
925 W Washington St Ste 100 Marquette MI 49855 866-327-9423 791
TF: 866-327-9423 ■ *Web:* www.easyice.com
Easy Picker Golf Products Inc
415 Leonard Blvd N Lehigh Acres FL 33971 239-368-6600 711
Web: www.easypicker.com
Easy Rider Canoe & Kayak Co
PO Box 88108 Seattle WA 98138 425-228-3633 277-8778 710
Web: www.easyriderkayaks.com
Easy Way Food Stores Inc
814 Mt Moriah Rd Memphis TN 38117 901-683-8249 345
Easy-ad Inc 155 S Harvard St Hemet CA 92543 951-658-2244 532-3
Web: www.easyadlive.com
easyDNS 219 Dufferin St Ste 304A Toronto ON M6K3J1 416-535-8672 396
TF: 888-677-4741 ■ *Web:* easydns.com
Easylife Furniture Inc
6101 Knott Avo Buena Park CA 90620 714-367-1640 321
Easypak Llc 24 Jytek Dr. Leominster MA 01453 978-516-9155 344
Web: www.easypak.net
Easyriders Magazine
28210 Dorothy Dr. Agoura Hills CA 91301 818-889-8740 457-3
TF: 800-323-3484 ■ *Web:* www.paisanopub.com
EasyStreet Online Services Inc
9705 SW Sunshine Ct Beaverton OR 97005 503-646-8400 225
TF: 800-207-0740 ■ *Web:* www.easystreet.com
Easyturf 2750 La Mirada Dr Vista CA 92081 866-327-9887 608
TF: 866-353-3518 ■ *Web:* www.easyturf.com
Eat With Us PO Box 1368 Columbus MS 39703 662-327-6982 327-1672 671
TF: 888-222-9550 ■ *Web:* eatwithusrestaurants.com
Eat'n Park Hospitality Group
285 E Waterfront Dr Homestead PA 15120 412-461-2000 461-6000 670
TF: 800-947-4033 ■ *Web:* www.eatnpark.com
EATELCORP Inc 913 S Burnside Ave Gonzales LA 70737 225-621-4300 736
TF: 800-621-4211 ■ *Web:* eatel.com
Eaton & Berube Insurance Agency Inc
365 Nashua St Milford NH 03055 603-673-0500 390
Web: www.eatonberube.com
Eaton Aerospace LLC
9650 Jeronimo Rd Ste 1200 Irvine CA 92618 949-452-9500 21
Web: www.aerospace.eaton.com

Eaton Clothing & Furniture Ctr
116 E Lovett St Charlotte MI 48813 517-543-4334 321
Web: www.eatoncounty.org
Eaton Corp
1111 Superior Ave Eaton Ctr Cleveland OH 44114 216-523-5000 60
Web: www.eaton.com
Eaton County 1045 Independence Blvd Charlotte MI 48813 517-543-7500 541-0666 338
Web: eatoncounty.org
Eaton Fabricating CoInc
1009 McAlpin Ct Grafton OH 44044 440-926-3121 492
Web: www.eatonfabricating.com
Eaton Farm Confectioners Inc
30 Burbank Rd Sutton MA 01590 508-865-5235 865-7087 296-8
TF: 800-343-9300 ■ *Web:* www.eatonfarmcandies.com
Eaton Hydraulics 803 32nd Ave W Spencer IA 51301 712-264-3300 640
Web: www.eaton.com/Eaton/ProductsServices/Hydraulics/index.htm
Eaton Incentives Inc
271 Route 46W Ste H 212-215 Fairfield NJ 07004 973-882-7700 384
Eaton Metal Products Co 4803 York St Denver CO 80216 303-296-4800 296-4800 91
TF: 800-208-2657 ■ *Web:* www.eatonsalesservice.com
Eaton Office Supply Company Inc
180 John Glenn Dr Buffalo NY 14228 716-691-6100 691-0074 534
TF: 800-365-3237 ■ *Web:* www.eatonofficesupply.com
Eaton Oil Tools Inc 118 Rue DuPain Broussard LA 70518 337-856-8820 539
TF: 800-232-5317 ■ *Web:* www.eatonoiltools.com
Eaton Rapids Medical Ctr
1500 S Main St. Eaton Rapids MI 48827 517-663-2671 374-3
Web: www.eatonrapidsmedicalcenter.org
Eaton Steel Corp 10221 Capital Ave. Oak Park MI 48237 248-398-3434 398-3434 492
TF: 800-527-3851 ■ *Web:* www.eatonsteel.com
Eaton Vance Mutual Funds
2 International Pl Boston MA 02110 617-482-8260 528
TF: 800-225-6265 ■ *Web:* www.eatonvance.com
Eatons' Ranch 270 Eatons' Ranch Rd Wolf WY 82844 307-655-9285 239
TF: 800-210-1049 ■ *Web:* eatonsranch.com
EatStreet Inc
316 Washington Ave Ste 725 Madison WI 53703 866-654-8777 387
TF: 866-654-8777 ■ *Web:* eatstreet.com
Eau Claire Area Chamber of Commerce
101 N Farwell St Ste 101 Eau Claire WI 54703 715-834-1204 834-1956 139
Web: www.eauclairechamber.org
Eau Claire County 721 Oxford Ave Eau Claire WI 54703 715-839-4801 839-4854 338
Web: co.eau-claire.wi.us
Eau Claire Ford Lincoln Mercury
2909 Lorch Ave. Eau Claire WI 54701 715-852-1000 57
Web: www.eauclaireford.com
Eau Claire Press Co
701 S Farwell St. Eau Claire WI 54701 715-833-9200 637-8
TF: 800-236-8808 ■ *Web:* www.leadertelegram.com
EB Bradley Co 5080 S Alameda St. Los Angeles CA 90058 323-585-9201 585-5414 351
TF: 800-533-3030 ■ *Web:* www.ebbradley.com
EB Computing 32 Briarcliff Dr S. Ossining NY 10562 914-523-8142 196
Web: www.eb-computing.com
E&B Natural Resources Management Corp
1600 Norris Rd Bakersfield CA 93308 661-679-1700 536
Web: www.ebresources.com
EBA Engineering Consultants Ltd
14940-123 Ave Edmonton AB T5V1B4 780-451-2130 454-5688 194
Web: www.eba.ca
EBA Engineering Inc 4813 Seton Dr Baltimore MD 21215 410-358-7171 261
Web: ebaengineering.com
EBAA (Eye Bank Assn of America)
1015 18th St NW Ste 1010 Washington DC 20036 202-775-4999 429-6036 49-8
TF: 888-491-8833 ■ *Web:* www.restoresight.org
Ebara international corp
350 Salomon Cir Sparks NV 89434 775-356-2796 356-2884 641
Web: www.ebaraintl.com
Ebara Technologies Inc 51 Main Ave Sacramento CA 95838 916-920-5451 695
TF: 800-535-5376 ■ *Web:* www.ebaratech.com
eBay Inc 2065 Hamilton Ave. San Jose CA 95125 408-376-7400 376-7401 51
NASDAQ: EBAY ■ *TF:* 800-322-9266 ■ *Web:* www.ebay.com
EBB Associates Inc
1064 W Ocean View Ave Norfolk VA 23503 757-588-3939 256
Web: www.ebbweb.com
Ebbtide Corporation
2545 Jones Creek Rd White Bluff TN 37187 615-797-3193 797-4889 90
Web: www.ebbtideboats.com
EBC Inc 1095 Valets St L'ancienne-lorette QC G2E4M7 418-872-0600 186
Web: www.ebcinc.com
EBC Industries 1325 Liberty St Erie PA 16502 814-456-4287 350
Web: www.ebcind.com
EBCO General Contractor Ltd
305 W Gillis Cameron TX 76520 254-697-8516 186
Web: ebcogc.com
Ebco Industries Ltd
7851 Alderbridge Way Richmond BC V6X2A4 604-278-5578 454
Web: www.ebco.com
Ebel Inc 8270 Arlington Expy Jacksonville FL 32211 904-399-2777 320
TF: 800-835-3278 ■ *Web:* www.ebelinc.com
Ebenezer Baptist Church
407 Auburn Ave NE Atlanta GA 30312 404-688-7300 521-1129 50-1
Web: www.historicebenezer.org
Eberbach Corp 505 S Maple Rd Ann Arbor MI 48103 734-665-8877 419
TF: 800-422-2558 ■ *Web:* www.eberbachlabtools.com
Eberhard Hardware Manufacturing Ltd
1523 Bellmill Rd. Tillsonburg ON N4GOC9 519-688-3443 350
TF: 800-567-3344 ■ *Web:* www.eberhardcanada.com
Eberhard Mfg Co PO Box 368012 Cleveland OH 44149 440-238-9720 572-2732 350
TF: 800-334-6706 ■ *Web:* www.eberhard.com
Eberl Iron Works Inc 128 Sycamore St Buffalo NY 14204 716-854-7633 480
Web: www.eberliron.com
Eberline Services Inc
4520 Montgomery Blvd NE Ste 1A Albuquerque NM 87109 505-803-6373 463
Web: www.eberlineservices.com
Eberly Poultry Inc 1095 Mt Airy Rd Stevens PA 17578 717-336-6440 619
Web: www.eberlypoultry.com
Ebert Inc 23350 County Rd 10 Loretto MN 55357 763-498-7844 186
Web: www.ebertconst.com

Name / Address	City	State	ZIP	Phone	Fax	Class
Ebey's Landing National Historical Reserve 162 Cemetery Rd *Web:* www.nps.gov	Coupeville	WA	98239	360-678-6084	678-2246	564
EBG Consulting 419 Hudson Rd *Web:* www.ebgconsulting.com	Sudbury	MA	01776	978-261-5552		41
EBI Consulting Inc 21 B St *TF:* 800-786-2346 ■ *Web:* www.ebiconsulting.com	Burlington	MA	01803	781-273-2500		196
Ebisu 1283 Ninth Ave *Web:* www.ebisusushi.com	San Francisco	CA	94122	415-566-1770		671
Ebix BPO 151 N Lyon Ave *TF:* 800-996-9964 ■ *Web:* www.certsonline.com	Hemet	CA	92543	951-658-4000		225
Ebix Inc 5 Concourse Pkwy Ste 3200 *NASDAQ: EBIX* ■ *TF:* 800-755-2326 ■ *Web:* www.ebix.com	Atlanta	GA	30328	678-281-2020	281-2019	178-11
eBizdocs 85 Broadway *Web:* www.ebizdocs.net	Menands	NY	12204	518-456-1011		363
eBlox Inc 404 W 30th St Ste A *Web:* www.eblox.com	Austin	TX	78705	512-867-1001		225
EBM Industries Inc *EBM-papst Inc* 100 & 110 Hyde Rd *Web:* www.ebmpapst.us	Farmington	CT	06034	860-674-1515	674-8536	18
Ebner Furnaces Inc 224 Quadral Dr *TF:* 800-525-8173 ■ *Web:* ebner.cc/home	Wadsworth	OH	44281	330-335-1600	335-1605	357
Ebonite International Inc PO Box 746 *TF:* 800-326-6483 ■ *Web:* www.ebonite.com	Hopkinsville	KY	42241	270-881-1200	881-1201	710
Ebony Magazine 200 Michigan Ave *Web:* www.ebony.com	Chicago	IL	60605	312-322-9200		457-11
ebQuickstart 3000 S IH 35 Ste 320 *TF:* 800-566-3050 ■ *Web:* ebq.com	Austin	TX	78704	512-637-9696		195
EBR Systems Inc 686 W Maude Ave Ste 102 *Web:* www.ebrsystems.com	Sunnyvale	CA	94085	408-720-1906		250
EBRI (Employee Benefit Research Institute) 1100 13th St NW Ste 878 *Web:* www.ebri.org	Washington	DC	20005	202-659-0670	775-6312	634
Ebridge Consulting Llc 2275 E Continental Blvd Ste 120 *Web:* www.sibridge.com	Southlake	TX	76092	817-756-6231		463
Ebro Foods Inc 1330 W 43rd St *Web:* www.ebrofoods.com	Chicago	IL	60609	773-696-0150	696-0151	296-36
EBRPL (East Baton Rouge Parish Library) 7711 Goodwood Blvd *Web:* www.ebrpl.com	Baton Rouge	LA	70806	225-231-3750		434-3
EBS Associates Inc 7150 SW Hampton St Ste 200 *Web:* www.teachmequickbooks.com	Tigard	OR	97223	503-885-0776		734
EBSCO Creative Concepts 3500 Blue Lake Dr Ste 150 **Fax Area Code: 800* ■ *TF:* 800-756-7023 ■ *Web:* www.ebscocreativeconcepts.com	Birmingham	AL	35243	205-980-6789	505-7135*	9
EBSCO Industries Inc 5724 Hwy 280 *TF:* 800-653-2726 ■ *Web:* www.ebscoind.com	Birmingham	AL	35242	205-991-6600		185
EBSCO Industries Inc Vulcan Information Packaging Div PO Box 29 *TF:* 800-633-4526 ■ *Web:* www.binders.com	Vincent	AL	35178	800-633-4526	344-8939	86
EBSCO Information Services PO Box 1943 *TF:* 800 758 5995 ■ *Web:* www.ebsco.com	Birmingham	AL	35201	205-991-6600		387
EBSCO Publishing Inc 10 Estes St *TF:* 800-653-2726 ■ *Web:* www.ebscohost.com	Ipswich	MA	01938	978-356-6500	356-6500	637-10
EBSCO Subscription Services 110 Olmsted St Ste 100 *TF:* 800-653-2726 ■ *Web:* www.ebsco.com/home/about/ess.asp	Birmingham	AL	35242	205-995-1596	995-1518	96
EBSCO TeleServices 4150 Belden Village Ave NW Ste 401	Canton	OH	44718	330-492-5105		737
EBT Restaurant 1310 Carondelet Dr *Web:* www.ebtrestaurant.com	Kansas City	MO	64114	816-942-8870		671
Ebtec Corp 120 Shoemaker Ln *Web:* www.ebteccorp.com	Agawam	MA	01001	413-786-0393	789-2851	454
E-Builder Inc 1800 NW 69 Ave Ste 201 *TF:* 800-580-9322 ■ *Web:* www.e-builder.net	Plantation	FL	33313	954-556-6701		39
Ebus Inc 9250 Washburn Rd *TF:* 888-925-4263 ■ *Web:* www.ebus.com	Downey	CA	90242	562-904-3474		516
e-Business Express Inc 2208 E Enterprise Pkwy *Web:* e-businessexpress.com	Twinsburg	OH	44087	216-505-4400		396
Ebusiness Strategies Llc 18318 Fern Trl Ctr *TF:* 888-647-3249 ■ *Web:* askebiz.com	Houston	TX	77084	281-647-6183		463
eBusinessDesign 111 W St John St Ste 1100 *TF:* 800-573-1874 ■ *Web:* www.ebusinessdesign.com	San Jose	CA	95113	408-654-7900		196
eBX LLC 65 Franklin St Ste 201 *TF:* 800-958-4813 ■ *Web:* www.levelats.com	Boston	MA	02110	617-350-1600		690
Eby Co 4300 H St *TF:* 800-329-3430 ■ *Web:* www.ebycompany.com	Philadelphia	PA	19124	215-537-4700	537-4780	253
Eby-Brown Co 280 W Shuman Blvd Ste 280 *TF:* 800-553-8249 ■ *Web:* www.eby-brown.com	Naperville	IL	60563	630-778-2800	778-2830	756
EC & M Magazine 9800 Metcalf Ave *Web:* www.ecmweb.com	Overland Park	KS	66212	913-967-1782	514-6782	457-21
EC Boston 1 Faneuil Hall Sq *Web:* www.ecenglish.com	Boston	MA	02109	617-247-3033	247-2959	423
EC Co PO Box 10286 *TF:* 800-462-3370 ■ *Web:* ecpowerslife.com	Portland	OR	97296	800-659-3511		189-4
EC Council University Inc 6330 Riverside Plaza Ln NW Ste 210 *Web:* www.eccouncil.org	Albuquerque	NM	87120	505-341-3228		95
EC Ernst Inc 132 Log Canoe Cir *TF:* 800-683-7770 ■ *Web:* www.ecernst.com	Stevensville	MD	21666	301-350-7770	499-0933	189-4
EC Power International Inc 5120 Woodway Ste 5005	Houston	TX	77056	713-626-8700		321
EC Source Services LLC 6644 E Thomas Rd *Web:* ecsourceservices.com	Mesa	AZ	85215	480-245-7200		256
EC Suite LLC 2353 W University Dr *Web:* www.ecsuite.com	Tempe	AZ	85281	480-449-8817		387

Name / Address	City	State	ZIP	Phone	Fax	Class
ECA (Engineering Contractors' Assn) 2190 S Towne Centre Pl *Web:* www.ecaonline.net	Anaheim	CA	92806	714-937-5000	937-5030	49-19
ECA (Evangelical Church Alliance) 205 W Broadway St PO Box 9 *TF:* 888-855-6060 ■ *Web:* www.ecainternational.org	Bradley	IL	60915	815-937-0720	937-0720	48-20
ECA Edinburg Citrus Association PO Box 428 *Web:* www.txcitrus.com	Edinburg	TX	78541	956-383-2743		315-2
ECA Medical Instruments Inc 1107 Tourmaline Dr *Web:* www.ecamedical.com	Newbury Park	CA	91320	805-376-2509		350
Ecampusalberta 1301 16 Ave NW *TF:* 877-284-7248	Calgary	AB	T2M0L4	403-284-8777		685
eCapital Advisors LLC 7900 Xerxes Ave S Ste 1300 *Web:* www.ecapitaladvisors.com	Bloomington	MN	55431	952-947-9300	947-9301	463
ECAT (Escambia County Area Transit) 1515 W Fairfield Dr *Web:* www.goecat.com	Pensacola	FL	32501	850-595-3228	595-3222	468
ECC Capital Corp 2600 E Coast Hwy Ste 250 *OTC: ECRO* ■ *Web:* www.ecccapital.com	Corona Del Mar	CA	92625	949-954-7060		654
ECCB (Erie 2-Chautauqua Cattaraugus Boces) 8685 Erie Rd *TF:* 800-228-1184 ■ *Web:* www.e2ccb.org	Angola	NY	14006	716-549-4454		685
Eccles Community Art Ctr 2580 Jefferson Ave *Web:* www.ogden4arts.org	Ogden	UT	84401	801-392-6935	392-5295	50-2
Ecclesia College 9653 Nations Dr *TF:* 800-735-9926 ■ *Web:* ecollege.edu	Springdale	AR	72762	479-248-7236	248-1455	161
ECCO 833 W Diamond St *TF:* 800-635-5900 ■ *Web:* www.eccolink.com	Boise	ID	83705	800-635-5900	688-3226	700
ECCO III Enterprises Inc 201 Saw Mill River Rd *Web:* www.eccoiii.com	Yonkers	NY	10701	914-963-3600		188-4
ECCO Select Corp 4100 N Mulberry Dr Ste 400 *TF:* 800-804-4715 ■ *Web:* www.eccoselect.com	Kansas City	MO	64116	816-960-3800		177
Eccs Nationwide Mobile Laboratories 2525 Advance Rd *TF:* 800-972-4889 ■ *Web:* www.eccsmobilelab.com	Madison	WI	53718	608-221-8700		743
Ecd Systems Inc 2415 W Erie Dr *TF:* 800-547-9988 ■ *Web:* www.ecdsys.com	Tempe	AZ	85282	480-609-6300		177
ECDC (Ethiopian Community Development Council Inc) 901 S Highland St *Web:* www.ecdcus.org	Arlington	VA	22204	703-685-0510	685-0529	48-5
Ecessa Corp 13755 First Ave N Ste 100 *TF:* 800-669-6242 ■ *Web:* www.ecessa.com	Plymouth	MN	55441	763-694-9949	551-0664	735
ECFA (Evangelical Council for Financial Accountability) 440 W Jubal Early Dr Ste 130 *TF:* 800-323-9473 ■ *Web:* www.ecfa.org	Winchester	VA	22601	540-535-0103	535-0533	48-5
ECFC (Employers Council on Flexible Compensation) 927 15th St NW Ste 700 *Web:* www.ecfc.org	Washington	DC	20005	202-659-4300	216-9646	49-12
Ecg Consulting Group Inc 40 British American Blvd Ste 7 *Web:* www.ecgconsulting.com	Latham	NY	12110	518-220-9100		196
ECG Management Consultants Inc 1111 Third Ave Ste 2700 *TF:* 800-729-7635 ■ *Web:* www.ecgmc.com	Seattle	WA	98101	206-689-2200	689-2209	194
Echelon Corp 550 Meridian Ave *NASDAQ: ELON* ■ *TF:* 888-324-3566 ■ *Web:* www.echelon.com	San Jose	CA	95126	408-938-5200	790-3800	176
Echo Assoc Inc 933 Ridge Dr *Web:* callecho.com	Mclean	VA	22101	703-448-0633		177
Echo Bridge Entertainment LLC 3089 Airport Rd	La Crosse	WI	54603	608-784-6620		511
Echo Canyon Guest Ranch 12507 Echo Canyon Rd	La Veta	CO	81055	719-742-5261		239
Echo Canyon State Park HC 74 PO Box 295 *Web:* www.parks.nv.gov	Pioche	NV	89043	775-962-5103		565
Echo Design Group 10 E 40th St 16th Fl *TF General:* 800-327-3896 ■ *Web:* www.echodesign.com	New York	NY	10016	212-686-8771		155-13
Echo Digital Audio Corp 6450 Via Real Ste 1 *Web:* www.echoaudio.com	Carpinteria	CA	93013	805-684-4593		52
Echo Engineering & Production Supplies Inc 5406 W 78th St *Web:* www.echosupply.com	Indianapolis	IN	46268	317-876-8848		791
Echo Global Logistics Inc 600 W Chicago Ave Ste 725 *TF:* 800-354-7993 ■ *Web:* www.echo.com	Chicago	IL	60654	800-354-7993		194
Echo Group Inc, The 15 Washington St *TF:* 800-635-8209 ■ *Web:* www.echoman.com	Conway	NH	03818	603-447-8600		177
Echo Inc 400 Oakwood Rd *TF:* 800-673-1558 ■ *Web:* www.echo-usa.com	Lake Zurich	IL	60047	847-540-8400	540-9741	429
Echo Industrial Inc 1615 Ritner Hwy *Web:* www.echoindustrial.com	Carlisle	PA	17013	717-249-6319		454
Echo Lake Farm Produce Co PO Box 279 *TF:* 800-888-3447 ■ *Web:* www.echolakefoods.com	Burlington	WI	53105	800-888-3447		10-8
Echo Lake State Park 68 Echo Lake Rd *Web:* www.nhstateparks.org	Conway	NH	03818	603-356-2672		565
Echo Media Group 2842 E Walnut Ave Ste A *Web:* www.echomediapr.com	Tustin	CA	92780	714-573-0899		636
Echo Nest Corp, The 48 Grove St Davis Sq *Web:* the.echonest.com	Somerville	MA	02144	617-628-0233		809
Echo Rock Ventures 13620 Lincoln Way Ste 380	Auburn	CA	95603	530-823-9600	823-9650	183
Echo Technology Solutions 216 11th St *Web:* www.echots.com	San Francisco	CA	94103	415-857-3246		196
EchoData Services Inc 121 N Shirk Rd Ste 101 *TF:* 800-511-3870 ■ *Web:* www.echodata.com	New Holland	PA	17557	800-511-3870		393

	Phone	Fax	Class
Echols County 110 General Beloach St .... Statenville GA 31648 *Web:* echolscountyga.com	229-559-6538		338
Echometer Co 5001 Ditto Ln............... Wichita Falls TX 76302 *Web:* www.echometer.com	940-767-4334		639
Echomountain Llc 1483 Patriot Blvd .... Glenview IL 60026 *TF:* 877-311-1980 ■ *Web:* www.echomountain.com	877-311-1980		180
EchoPoint Media 409 Massachusetts Ave ....Indianapolis IN 46204 *Web:* echopointmedia.com	317-264-8400	264-8016	5
Echota Fabrics Inc 1394 US 41 N..............Calhoun GA 30701 *TF:* 800-763-9750 ■ *Web:* www.echotafabrics.com	706-629-9750	629-5229	746
Echota Technologies Corp 3286 Northpark Blvd Ste A......................Alcoa TN 37701	865-273-1270		180
Echoworx Corp 4101 Yonge St Ste 708........... Toronto ON M2P1N6 *TF:* 800-627-0861 ■ *Web:* www.echoworx.com	416-226-8600		179
ECI (Engine Components Inc) 9503 Middlex...................................San Antonio TX 78217 *TF:* 800-324-2359 ■ *Web:* eci.aero	210-820-8101	820-8102	21
ECI Technology Inc 60 Gordon Dr ....Totowa NJ 07512 *Web:* www.cvstechnology.com	973-890-1114		549
ECI Telecom Ltd 5100 NW 33rd Ave Ste 150 ....Fort Lauderdale FL 33309 *Web:* www.ecitele.com	954-772-3070	351-4404	735
ECII (Engineered Controls International Inc) 100 Rego Dr PO Box 247.............................Elon NC 27244 *TF:* 800-650-0061 ■ *Web:* www.regoproducts.com	336-449-7707	449-6594	789
Ecity Interactive Inc 136 S 15th St..........................Philadelphia PA 19102 *TF:* 800-559-4320 ■ *Web:* ecityinteractive.com	215-557-0767		195
eCivis Inc 418 N Fair Oaks Ave Ste 301 ....Pasadena CA 91103 *TF:* 877-232-4847 ■ *Web:* www.ecivis.com	877-232-4847		69
Eck Industries Inc 1602 N Eigth St PO Box 967................Manitowoc WI 54221 *Web:* www.eckindustries.com	920-682-4618	682-9298	308
Eck Supply Co 1405 W Main St.............. Richmond VA 23220 *Web:* www.ecksupply.com	804-359-5781		246
Eckards Home Improvement 2402 N Belt Hwy........................Saint Joseph MO 64506 *TF:* 800-264-2794 ■ *Web:* eckardsflooring.com	816-279-4522		290
Eckel Mfg Company Inc 8035 N County Rd W..........................Odessa TX 79764 *TF:* 800-654-4779 ■ *Web:* www.eckel.com	432-362-4336	362-1827	223
Eckell, Sparks, Levy, Auerbach, Monte, Sloane, Matthews & Auslander, PC 344 W Front St.............................. Media PA 19063 *TF:* 800-447-5375 ■ *Web:* www.eckellsparks.com	610-565-3700		428
Eckenrod Ford Lincoln Mercury of Cullman Inc 5255 Alabama Hwy 157 ....Cullman AL 35058 *TF:* 888-470-7346 ■ *Web:* eckenrodford.com	256-734-3361		57
Eckerd College 4200 54th Ave S.................... Saint Petersburg FL 33711 **Fax:* Admissions ■ *TF Admissions:* 800-456-9009 ■ *Web:* www.eckerd.edu	727-867-1166	866-2304*	166
Eckert & Ziegler Isotope Products Inc 24937 Ave Tibbitts ....Valencia CA 91355 *Web:* www.ezag.com/home	661-309-1010		419
Eckhart & Company Inc 4011 W 54th St.........................Indianapolis IN 46254 *TF:* 800-443-3791 ■ *Web:* www.eckhartandco.com	317-347-2665	347-2666	86
Eckhart Public Library 603 S Jackson St ....Auburn IN 46706 *TF:* 800-829-3676 ■ *Web:* www.epl.lib.in.us	260-925-2414		434-3
Eckhoff Accountancy Corp 145 N Redwood Dr....................... San Rafael CA 94903 *Web:* www.eckhoff.com	415-499-9400		2
Eckler Industries Inc 5200 S Washington Ave .... Titusville FL 32780 *Web:* www.ecklersautomotive.com	321-269-9680		247
Eckler Ltd 110 Sheppard Ave E Ste 900........... Toronto ON M2N7A3 *Web:* www.eckler.ca	416-429-3330		194
Eck-mundy Associates Inc 450 E 11th Ave ....Jasper IN 47546 *Web:* www.eck-mundy.com	812-634-8001		180
Eclectic Products Inc 1075 Arrowsmith St PO Box 2280 ....Eugene OR 97402 *TF:* 800-693-4667 ■ *Web:* www.eclecticproducts.com	800-693-4667		3
Eclectik Design, LLC 161 N Clark St Ste 1600.........................Chicago IL 60601 **Fax Area Code:* 773 ■ *Web:* www.eclectik.com	312-690-3181	751-2075*	130
Eclipse Advertising Inc 2255 N Ontario St Ste 230 ....Burbank CA 91504 *Web:* eclipsead.com	818-238-9388		708
Eclipse Bistro 1020 N Union St............. Wilmington DE 19805 *Web:* www.platinumdininggroup.com	302-658-1588		671
Eclipse Colour & Imaging Corp 875 Laurentian Dr........................ Burlington ON L7N3W7 *TF:* 800-668-6369 ■ *Web:* www.eclipseimaging.ca	905-634-1900		627
Eclipse Design Technologies Inc 33 W Higgins Rd Ste 650.............South Barrington IL 60010 *Web:* eclipsedt.com	847-844-8822		393
Eclipse di Luna 764 Miami Cir ....Atlanta GA 30324 *Web:* www.eclipsediluna.com	404-846-0449		671
Eclipse Energy Systems Inc 2345 Anvil St N .... Saint Petersburg FL 33710 *Web:* www.eclipsethinfilms.com	727-344-7300		196
Eclipse Foundation 102 Centrepointe Dr......... Nepean ON K2G6B1 *Web:* www.eclipse.org	613-224-9461		303
Eclipse Inc 1665 Elmwood Rd................. Rockford IL 61103 **Fax:* Cust Svc ■ *TF:* 888-826-3473 ■ *Web:* www.eclipsenet.com	815-877-3031	877-3336*	318
Eclipse Incentive Marketing Corp 1738 Lombard St ....Philadelphia PA 19146 *Web:* www.eimcorp.us	215-239-5794		463
Eclipse Marketing Services Inc 240 Cedar Knolls Rd Ste 100........... Cedar Knolls NJ 07927 *TF:* 800-837-4648 ■ *Web:* www.eclipsemarketingservices.com	800-837-4648		195
Ecliptic Enterprises Corp 398 W Washington Blvd Ste 100 ....Pasadena CA 91103 *Web:* www.eclipticenterprises.com	626-798-2436		387

	Phone	Fax	Class
ECM (Eliza Coffee Memorial Hospital) 205 Marengo St ....Florence AL 35630 *Web:* www.chgroup.org/ecm	256-768-9191		374-3
ECM Consultants Inc 4409 Utica St Ste 200........................ Metairie LA 70006 *Web:* ecmconsultants.com	504-885-4080		256
Ecm International 404 Executive Ctr Blvd .... El Paso TX 79902 *Web:* ecmintl.com	915-351-1900	351-1908	261
ECM Publishers Inc 4095 Coon Rapids Blvd .... Coon Rapids MN 55433 *Web:* www.ecm-inc.com	763-712-2400		637-8
ECMD Inc 2 Grandview St...............North Wilkesboro NC 28659 *TF:* 888-222-3961 ■ *Web:* www.ecmd.com	336-667-5976		690
ECO Building Products Inc 909 W Vista Way............................. Vista CA 92083	760-732-5826		683
ECO Canada 308 - 11th Ave SE Ste 200........... Calgary AB T2G0Y2 *TF:* 800-251-7773 ■ *Web:* www.eco.ca	403-233-0748		764
Eco Engineering LLC 11815 Hwy Dr Ste 600 .... Cincinnati OH 45241 *TF:* 800-301-2003 ■ *Web:* www.ecoengineering.com	513-985-8300		261
Eco Lips 329 Tenth Ave SE Ste 213...........Cedar Rapids IA 52401 *Web:* www.ecolips.com	319-364-2477		231
Eco Park Resort at Mt. St. Helens Inc 14000 Spirit Lake Hwy ....Toutle WA 98649 *Web:* www.ecoparkresort.com/tours.htm	360-274-7007		760
Eco Water Systems Inc 1890 Woodlane Dr .... Woodbury MN 55125 *TF:* 800-808-9899 ■ *Web:* www.ecowater.com	800-808-9899		427
eCoast Marketing Services 35E Industrial Way Ste 201...................Rochester NH 03867 *Web:* www.ecoastmarketing.com	603-516-7450		317
Ecodyne Ltd 4475 Corporate Dr.............. Burlington ON L7L5T9 *TF:* 888-326-3963 ■ *Web:* www.ecodyne.com	905-332-1404	332-6726	386
Ecodyne MRM 8203 Market St ....Houston TX 77029 *Web:* www.ecodynehx.com	713-675-3511	675-7922	91
ECOF (Eye Centers of Florida) 4101 Evans Ave ....Fort Myers FL 33901 *TF:* 888-393-2455 ■ *Web:* www.ecof.com	239-939-3456	936-8776	798
Ecojustice Canada 131 Water St Ste 214 .... Vancouver BC V6B4M3 *TF:* 800-926-7744 ■ *Web:* www.ecojustice.ca	604-685-5618	685-7813	48-13
Ecola State Park 84318 Ecola State Park Rd ....Cannon Beach OR 97110 *Web:* www.oregonstateparks.org	503-436-2844		565
Ecole De La Cle-des-champs 3858 Rue Principale ....Dunham QC J0E1M0 *Web:* cle-des-champs.csvdc.qc.ca	450-295-2722		685
Ecole Polytechnique de Montreal 2900 Boul Edouard-Montpetit .... Montreal QC H3T1J4 *Web:* www.polymtl.ca	514-340-4711		162
eCollect LLC PO Box 241548...................Mayfield OH 44124 *TF:* 888-569-6001 ■ *Web:* www.ecollectpayments.com	888-569-6001		393
Ecolo Odor Control Technologies Inc 59 Penn Dr .... Toronto ON M9L2A6 *TF:* 800-667-6355 ■ *Web:* www.ecolo.com	416-740-3900	740-3800	104
Ecological Fibers Inc 40 Pioneer Dr..........Lunenburg MA 01462 *TF:* 800-878-3878 ■ *Web:* www.ecofibers.com	978-537-0003	537-2238	557
Ecological Restoration & Management Inc (ER&M) 9475 Deereco Rd Ste 406.................. Timonium MD 21093 *Web:* www.er-m.com	410-337-4899	583-5678	186
Ecological Society of America (ESA) 1990 M St Ste 700 ....Washington DC 20036 *Web:* www.esa.org	202-833-8773	833-8775	49-19
Ecology & Environment Inc 368 Pleasant View Dr ....Lancaster NY 14086 *NASDAQ: EEI* ■ *Web:* www.ene.com	716-684-8060	684-0844	192
Ecology and Environment Inc 368 Pleasant View Dr ....Lancaster NY 14086 *Web:* www.ene.com	716-684-8060		193
Ecology Control Industries Inc 255 Parr Blvd .... Richmond CA 94801 *Web:* www.ecologycontrol.com	510-235-1393		667
Ecom Engineering Inc 1796 Tribute Rd Ste 100.................. Sacramento CA 95815 *Web:* www.ecomeng.com	916-641-5600		256
Ecom Enterprises Inc 1230 Oakmead Pkwy Ste 318 .... Sunnyvale CA 94085 *TF:* 877-955-3266 ■ *Web:* www.ecomenterprises.com	408-720-9194		180
Ecom Solutions 7326 Yellowstone Blvd .... Forest Hills NY 11375 *TF:* 800-219-8941 ■ *Web:* www.ecomsolutions.net	718-793-2828		180
Eco-Med Pharmaceuticals Inc 7050B Bramalea Rd Unit 58 .... Mississauga ON L5S1S9 *TF:* 800-624-9659 ■ *Web:* www.eco-med.com	905-405-1050	405-0775	582
EcoMedia LLC 919 Manhattan Ave Ste 100 ....Manhattan Beach CA 90266 *Web:* ecomedia.cbs.com	310-374-8212		530
e-Commerce Law & Strategy 120 Broadway 5th Fl.......................New York NY 10271 *TF:* 877-256-2472 ■ *Web:* www.lawjournalnewsletters.com	212-457-9400		531-7
E-Commerce Times (ECT) 16133 Ventura Blvd Ste 700...................Encino CA 91436 *TF:* 877-328-5500 ■ *Web:* www.ectnews.com	818-461-9700	461-9710	457-5
Ecomuseum 21125 Ch Sainte-Marie ....Sainte-Anne-de-Bellevue QC H9X3Y7 *Web:* www.zooecomuseum.ca	514-457-9449	457-0769	823
Econcordia 1250 Guy .... Montreal QC H3H2T4 *Web:* www.econcordia.com	514-848-8770		165
Econfina River State Park 4741 Econfina River Rd .... Lamont FL 32336 *Web:* www.floridastateparks.org	850-922-6007		565
Econo Foods 1600 Stephenson .... Iron Mountain MI 49801 *TF:* 877-295-4558 ■ *Web:* www.econotnc.com	906-774-1911		345
Econo Lodge 2934 Polynesian Isle Blvd ....Kissimmee FL 34746 *Web:* www.choicehotels.com/econo-lodge	407-787-4100		707
Econoco Corp 300 Karin Ln....................Hicksville NY 11801 **Fax Area Code:* 800 ■ *TF:* 800-645-7032 ■ *Web:* www.econoco.com	516-935-7700	505-8300*	286

Name / Address	City	State	Zip	Phone	Fax	Class
Econ-o-copy Inc 4437 Trenton St Ste A	Metairie	LA	70006	504-457-0032	457-0114	535
TF: 877-256-0310 ■ *Web:* www.econ-o-copy.com						
Econolite Control Products Inc						
3360 E La Palma Av	Anaheim	CA	92806	714-630-3700	630-6349	700
TF: 800-225-6480 ■ *Web:* www.econolite.com						
Econometric Society						
New York Univ Dept of Economics						
19 W Fourth St Sixth Fl	New York	NY	10012	212-998-3820	995-4487	49-5
Web: www.econometricsociety.org						
Economic Consulting Services LLC						
2001 L St NW	Washington	DC	20036	202-466-7720	466-2710	195
Web: www.economic-consulting.com						
Economic Development Administration						
1401 Constitution Ave NW	Washington	DC	20230	202-482-2900		340-2
Web: www.eda.gov						
Economic Development Administration Regional Office						
Atlanta 401 W Peachtree St NW Ste 1820	Atlanta	GA	30308	404-730-3002	730-3025	340-2
TF: 800-518-4726 ■ *Web:* www.eda.gov						
Austin 504 Lavaca St Ste 1100	Austin	TX	78701	512-381-8144	381-8177	340-2
Web: www.eda.gov						
Chicago 230 S Dearborn St	Chicago	IL	60606	312-353-8143		340-2
Web: www.eda.gov						
Denver 410 17th St Ste 250	Denver	CO	80202	303-844-4715	844-3968	340-2
Web: www.eda.gov/contacts.htm						
Philadelphia						
1401 Constitution Ave NW Ste 71014	Washington	DC	20230	202-482-5081		340-2
Web: www.eda.gov						
Seattle 915 Second Ave Rm 1890	Seattle	WA	98174	206-220-7660	220-7669	340-2
TF: 800-518-4726 ■ *Web:* www.eda.gov						
Economic Opportunity Board Of Clark County						
330 W Washington Ave Ste 7	Las Vegas	NV	89106	702-647-3307	647-3125	317
Web: www.eobccnv.org						
Economic Policy Institute						
1225 Eye St NW Ste 600	Washington	DC	20005	202-775-8810	775-0819	634
Web: www.epi.org						
Economic Research Service (ERS)						
US Dept of Agriculture						
1400 Independence Ave SW, Mail Stop 1800	Washington	DC	20250-0002	202-694-5050		340-1
Web: www.ers.usda.gov						
Economic Strategy Institute						
3050 K St NW Ste 220	Washington	DC	20007	202-965-9484	965-1104	634
Web: www.econstrat.org						
Economic Systems Inc						
3120 Frview Pk Dr Ste 500	Falls Church	VA	22042	703-642-5225		463
Web: www.econsys.com						
Economical Insurance						
111 Westmount Rd S PO Box 2000	Waterloo	ON	N2J4S4	519-570-8200	570-8389	391-4
TF: 800-265-2180 ■ *Web:* www.economical.com/en/home						
Economics & Statistics Administration						
1401 Constitution Ave NW	Washington	DC	20230	202-482-6607		340-2
Web: www.esa.doc.gov						
Economist Intelligence Unit						
750 Third Ave 5th Fl	New York	NY	10017	212-554-0600	586-1181	637-9
Web: www.eiu.com						
Economy Advertising Co, The						
2800 Hwy 6 E	Iowa City	IA	52240	319-354-1020		627
Web: www.bankersadvertising.com						
Economy Linen & Towel Service Inc						
80 Mead St	Dayton	OH	45402	937-222-4625		393
Web: www.economylinen.com						
Economy Lumber 720 Camden Ave	Campbell	CA	95008	408-378-5231	378-0258	364
Web: www.economylumber.com						
Economy Office Supply Co						
1725 Gardena Ave	Glendale	CA	91204	818-548-1525		535
TF: 800-844-0962 ■ *Web:* www.economyofficesupply.com						
Economy Paper Company of Rochester Inc						
1175 E Main St	Rochester	NY	14609	585-482-5340		557
Web: www.economypaper.com						
Economy Shoe Shop Cafe & Bar						
1663 Argyle St	Halifax	NS	B3J2B5	902-423-8845		671
Web: www.economyshoeshop.ca						
Economy Spring & Stamping Co						
29 DePaolo Dr	Southington	CT	06489	860-621-7358	621-7882	719
TF: 800-237-5225 ■ *Web:* www.mw-ind.com						
eContent Magazine						
143 Old Marlton Pike Ste 3	Medford	NJ	08055	609-654-6266	654-4309	457-7
TF: 800-300-9868 ■ *Web:* www.econtentmag.com						
EcoPower Hybrid Systems Inc						
9995 Ave de Catania Ste G	Brossard	QC	J4Z3V7	450-676-7755		112
Web: ecopowerhs.com						
eCornell 950 Danby Rd Ste 150	Ithaca	NY	14850	607-330-3200		242
TF: 866-326-7635 ■ *Web:* www.ecornell.com						
Eco-Site Inc 240 Leigh Farm Rd Ste 415	Durham	NC	27707	919-636-6810		647
Web: eco-site.com						
Ecosmart US LLC						
3315 NW 167th St	Miami Gardens	FL	33056	305-623-7900		36
Web: www.ecosmartus.com						
Ecosphere Environmental Services Inc						
776 E Second Ave	Durango	CO	81301	970-382-7256		463
Web: www.ecosphere-services.com						
EcoStrategy Group 195-B Bryant St	Palo Alto	CA	94301	650-321-6009		466
EcoTarium 222 Harrington Way	Worcester	MA	01604	508-929-2700	929-2701	521
TF: 800-625-7738 ■ *Web:* www.ecotarium.org						
ECPA (Evangelical Christian Publishers Assn)						
9633 S 48th St Ste 140	Phoenix	AZ	85044	480-966-3998	966-1944	49-16
Web: www.ecpa.org						
ECPI College of Technology						
5555 Greenwich Rd	Virginia Beach	VA	23462	757-490-9090		507
Web: www.ecpi.edu						
ECPL (East Chicago Public Library)						
2401 E Columbus Dr	East Chicago	IN	46312	219-397-2453		434-3
Web: www.ecpl.org						
Ecra Group 5600 N River Rd 14th Fl	Rosemont	IL	60018	847-318-0072		242
TF: 800-776-6644 ■ *Web:* www.ecragroup.com						
eCreative Group Inc						
2349 Jamestown Ave	Independence	IA	50644	319-334-5115		7
Web: www.ecreativegroup.com						
eCredit 777 Yamato Rd Ste 500	Boca Raton	FL	33431	561-226-9000		178-1
TF: 800-276-2321 ■ *Web:* www.cortera.com						
ECRI Institute						
5200 Butler Pike	Plymouth Meeting	PA	19462	610-825-6000	834-1275	48-17
TF: 866-247-3004 ■ *Web:* www.ecri.org						
ECRM Inc 554 Clark Rd	Tewksbury	MA	01876	978-851-0207	851-7016	111
TF: 800-537-3276 ■ *Web:* www.ecrm.com						
ECS (Electronic Cash Systems Inc)						
29883 Santa Margarita Pkwy	Rancho Santa Margarita	CA	92688	949-888-8580	888-8024	56
TF: 888-327-2860 ■ *Web:* www.ecspayments.com						
ECS (Education Commission of the States)						
700 Broadway Ste 810	Denver	CO	80203	303-299-3600	296-8332	49-5
Web: www.ecs.org						
ECS & R 3237 US Hwy 19	Cochranton	PA	16314	814-425-7773		196
TF: 866-815-0016 ■ *Web:* www.ecsr.net						
ECS Composites Inc						
3560 Rogue River Hwy	Grants Pass	OR	97527	541-476-8871	474-2479	199
Web: www.ecscase.com						
ECS Corporate Services LLC						
14026 Thunderbolt Pl Ste 300	Chantilly	VA	20151	571-299-6000		261
Web: www.ecslimited.com						
ECS Financial Services Inc						
3400 Dundee Rd	Northbrook	IL	60062	847-291-1333		2
TF: 800-826-7070 ■ *Web:* ecsfinancial.com						
ECSI International Inc						
790 Bloomfield Ave Bldg C-1	Clifton	NJ	07012	973-574-8555		693
Web: www.ecsiinternational.com						
ECSM Utility Contractors Inc						
1200 Walnut Bottom Rd Ste 101	Carlisle	PA	17015	717-258-8001		610
Web: ecsminc.com						
ECT (E-Commerce Times)						
16133 Ventura Blvd Ste 700	Encino	CA	91436	818-461-9700	461-9710	457-5
TF: 877-328-5500 ■ *Web:* www.ectnews.com						
ECT (Electric Coating Technologies)						
4407 Railroad Ave	East Chicago	IN	46312	219-378-1930	378-1933	481
Web: www.materialsciencescorp.com						
ECT (Everett Charles Technologies)						
700 E Harrison Ave	Pomona	CA	91767	909-625-5551		248
Web: www.ectinfo.com						
Ectaco Inc 31-21 31st St	Long Island	NY	11106	718-728-6110	728-4023	173-2
TF: 800-710-7920 ■ *Web:* www.ectaco.com						
Ector County 300 N Grant Ave Rm 111	Odessa	TX	79761	432-498-4130	498-4177	338
TF: 800-388-8075 ■ *Web:* www.co.ector.tx.us						
Ector County Library 321 W Fifth St	Odessa	TX	79761	432-332-0633	337-6502	434-3
Web: www.ector.lib.tx.us						
ECU (Educators Credit Union)						
1400 N Newman Rd PO Box 081040	Racine	WI	53406	262-886-5900	884-7233	219
TF: 800-236-5898 ■ *Web:* www.ecu.com						
ECU Staffing Inc						
2346 S Lynhurst Dr Ste 201A	Indianapolis	IN	46241	888-365-1440		260
TF: 888-365-1440 ■ *Web:* www.ecustaffing.com						
ECUA (Emerald Coast Utilities Authority)						
9255 Sturdevant St	Pensacola	FL	32514	850-476-0480		787
Web: www.ecua.fl.gov						
Ecuador 866 UN Plaza Ste 516	New York	NY	10017	212-935-1680	935-1835	784
Web: www.un.int/ecuador						
Ama la Vida 180 N Wabash Ave Ste 400	Chicago	IL	60603	312-338-1003	338-1004	257
Consulate General						
8484 Wilshire Blvd Ste 500	Beverly Hills	CA	90211	323-297-1150	297-1152	257
Web: cancilleria.gob.ec						
Consulate General 400 Market St 4th Fl	Newark	NJ	07105	973-344-8837		257
Web: www.consuladoecuadornj.com						
Consulate General						
4200 Westheimer Rd Ste 218	Houston	TX	77027	713-572-8731	572-8732	257
Web: www.cecunuevayork.com						
Consulate General						
1101 Brickell Ave Ste M102	Miami	FL	33131	305-373-8520	539-8313	257
Web: www.ecuador.org						
Consulate General						
800 Second Ave Ste 600	New York	NY	10017	212-808-0170	808-0188	257
Web: www.cecunuevayork.com						
Embassy 2535 15th St NW	Washington	DC	20009	202-234-7200	234-3429	257
Web: www.ecuador.org						
Ecuadorian-American Chamber of Commerce of Greater Miami						
1640 Town Center Cir Ste 210	Weston	FL	33326	305-539-0010		138
Ecuatours Travel Agency Inc						
154 Giralda Ave	Coral Gables	FL	33134	305-446-3999		772
Web: www.ecuatours.com						
E-cubed Media Synthesis Ltd						
3807 William St	Burnaby	BC	V5C3J1	604-294-1556		225
TF: 800-294-1556 ■ *Web:* www.e-cubed.net						
Ecumenical Theological Seminary (ETS)						
2930 Woodward Ave	Detroit	MI	48201	313-831-5200		167-3
Web: www.etseminary.org						
ECWA (Erie County Water Authority)						
295 Main St Rm 350	Buffalo	NY	14203	716-849-8484	849-8467	787
TF: 855-748-1076 ■ *Web:* www.ecwa.org						
eCycle Inc 7775 Walton Pkwy Ste 250	New Albany	OH	43054	610-939-0480		518
Web: www.e-cycle.com						
ED Etnyre & Co 1333 S Daysville Rd	Oregon	IL	61061	815-732-2116	732-7400	190
TF: 800-995-2116 ■ *Web:* www.etnyre.com						
Ed Fagan Inc						
769 Susquehanna Ave	Franklin Lakes	NJ	07417	201-891-4003	891-3207	492
TF: 800-335-6827 ■ *Web:* www.edfagan.com						
Ed Grush, General Contractor Inc						
3236 E Willow St	Signal Hill	CA	90755	562-426-9526		186
Web: www.edgrush.com						
Ed Levin Inc 52 W Main St	Cambridge	NY	12816	518-677-8595		410
Web: www.edlevinjewelry.com						
Ed Martin Inc 3800 E 96th St	Indianapolis	IN	46240	317-846-3800		57
TF: 800-211-5410 ■ *Web:* edmartinacura.com						
Ed Schmidt Automotive Group Inc						
26875 Dixie Hwy	Perrysburg	OH	43551	419-874-4331		57
Web: edschmidt.com						
Ed Smith Stadium 2700 12th St	Sarasota	FL	34237	941-954-4101	365-1587	720
Web: baltimore.orioles.mlb.com						
Ed Staub & Sons Petroleum Inc						
1301 Esplanade Ave	Klamath Falls	OR	97601	800-435-3835		316
TF: 800-435-3835 ■ *Web:* www.edstaub.com						

Company / Address	City	State	ZIP	Phone	Fax	Class
Ed Taylor Construction South Inc 2713 N Falkenburg Rd *Web:* www.edtaylor.net	Tampa	FL	33619	813-623-3724	621-1439	186
Ed's Restaurant 202 17th Ave SE *TF:* 800-661-1555 ■ *Web:* www.edsrestaurant.com	Calgary	AB	T2G1H4	403-262-3500		671
Eda Staffing Inc 371 Forest Ave Ste 2 *Web:* www.edastaffing.com	Portland	ME	04101	207-775-2577		193
EDAC Systems Inc 10970 Pierson Dr *Web:* www.edacsystems.com	Fredericksburg	VA	22408	540-361-1580		174
EDAC Technologies Corp 1806 New Britain Ave *NASDAQ: EDAC* ■ *Web:* www.edactechnologies.com	Farmington	CT	06032	860-678-8140	674-2718	248
EDAK Inc 630 Distribution Dr *Web:* www.edak.com	Melbourne	FL	32904	321-674-6804		697
eDaptive Systems 400 Red Brook Blvd Ste 120 *TF:* 800-760-8500 ■ *Web:* www.edaptivesys.com	Owings Mills	MD	21117	410-327-3366		225
EDAX Inc 91 McKee Dr *Web:* www.edax.com	Mahwah	NJ	07430	201-529-4880	529-3156	419
EDC (Education Development Ctr Inc) 55 Chapel St *TF:* 800-225-4276 ■ *Web:* www.edc.org	Newton	MA	02458	617-969-7100	969-5979	48-11
Edc Inc 950 Old Winston Rd *Web:* www.edcinc.com	Kernersville	NC	27284	336-993-0468		625
Edco & Arrowhead Products Inc 8700 Excelsior Blvd *TF:* 800-333-2580 ■ *Web:* www.edcoproducts.com	Hopkins	MN	55343	952-938-6313		697
Edco Disposal Corp 6670 Federal Blvd *Web:* www.edcodisposal.com	Lemon Grove	CA	91945	619-287-7555	287-4073	804
Edcomm Inc 1300 Virginia Dr Ste 1010 *TF:* 888-433-2666 ■ *Web:* edcomm.com	Fort Washington	PA	19034	888-433-2666		244
EDCON-PRJ Inc 171 S Van Gordon St Ste E *Web:* edcon-prj.com	Denver	CO	80228	303-980-6556		536
Edcor Data Services Corp 3310 W Big Beaver Ste 305 *TF:* 800-785-5585 ■ *Web:* www.edcor.com	Troy	MI	48084	248-530-4200		225
Edcouch-Elsa Independent School District PO Box 127 *Web:* www.eeisd.org	Edcouch	TX	78538	956-262-6000	262-6032	685
Eddie Bauer LLC PO Box 7001 *TF Orders:* 800-426-8020 ■ *Web:* www.eddiebauer.com	Groveport	OH	43125	800-426-8020		157-4
Eddie Johnson Private Contractor 5005 Creston St	Hyattsville	MD	20781	301-772-0466		610
Eddie Lee's 4700 Nantucket Dr	Toledo	OH	43623	419-882-0616		671
Eddie Martini's 8612 W Watertown Plank Rd *Web:* www.foodspot.com	Milwaukee	WI	53226	414-771-6680	771-5034	671
Eddie Merlot's 1502 Illinois Rd S *Web:* www.eddiemerlots.com	Fort Wayne	IN	46804	260-459-2222		671
Eddie's Tire Service Inc 3077 Valley Rd *TF:* 800-333-2104 ■ *Web:* www.eddiestireservice.com	Berkeley Springs	WV	25411	304-258-1368	258-1777	755
Eddington Thread Manufacturing Co PO Box 446 *TF:* 800-220-8901 ■ *Web:* www.edthread.com	Bensalem	PA	19020	215-639-8900	639-8900	745-9
Eddy County 101 W Greene St Ste 110 **Fax Area Code:* 575 ■ *Web:* www.co.eddy.nm.us	Carlsbad	NM	88220	505-887-9511	234-1835*	338
Eddy County 524 Central Ave *Web:* www.cityofnewrockford.com	New Rockford	ND	58356	701-947-2434	947-2279	338
Eddy Group Ltd 660 St Anne St *Web:* www.eddygroup.com	Bathurst	NB	E2A2N6	506-546-6631		652
Eddy Packing Company Inc 404 Airport Dr *TF:* 800-292-2361 ■ *Web:* www.eddypacking.com	Yoakum	TX	77995	361-293-2361	293-2254	473
Eddyline Kayaks 11977 Westar Ln *TF:* 800-635-5205 ■ *Web:* www.eddyline.com	Burlington	WA	98233	360-757-2300	757-2302	710
Edelbrock Corp 2700 California St *TF:* 800-739-3737 ■ *Web:* www.edelbrock.com	Torrance	CA	90503	310-781-2222	320-1187	60
Edelman Intelligence 1875 Eye St NW Ste 900 *Web:* edelmanintelligence.com	Washington	DC	20006	202-326-1772	312-1099	463
Edelman Public Relations Worldwide 200 E Randolph Dr 63rd Fl *Web:* www.edelman.com	Chicago	IL	60601	312-240-3000		636
Edelson Technology Partners 300 Tice Blvd *Web:* www.edelsontech.com	Woodcliff Lake	NJ	07677	201-930-9898	930-8899	792
Edelweiss 34 E Ramona Ave *TF:* 800-995-5974 ■ *Web:* www.restauranteur.com	Colorado Springs	CO	80905	719-633-2220		671
Edelweiss German Restaurant 3801 SW Blvd A *Web:* www.edelweissgermanrestaurant.com	Fort Worth	TX	76116	817-738-5934		671
Eden Foods Inc 701 Tecumseh Rd *TF Cust Svc:* 800-248-0320 ■ *Web:* www.edenfoods.com	Clinton	MI	49236	517-456-7424	456-6075	296-36
Eden Gardens State Park 181 Eden Gardens Rd *Web:* www.floridastateparks.org	Santa Rosa Beach	FL	32459	850-267-8320		565
Eden House 1015 Fleming St *TF:* 800-533-5397 ■ *Web:* www.edenhouse.com	Key West	FL	33040	800-533-5397		379
Eden i & r Inc 570 B St *TF:* 888-886-9660 ■ *Web:* www.edenir.org	Hayward	CA	94541	510-537-2710		138
Eden Labs LLC 1601 W Fifth St Ste 240 *TF:* 800-522-7556 ■ *Web:* edenlabs.com	Columbus	OH	43212	614-374-2455		333
Eden Medical Ctr (EMC) 20103 Lake Chabot Rd *Web:* www.edenmedicalcenter.org	Castro Valley	CA	94546	510-537-1234		374-3
Eden Prairie Chamber of Commerce 11455 Viking Dr Ste 270 *TF:* 800-932-8677 ■ *Web:* www.epchamber.org	Eden Prairie	MN	55344	952-944-2830	944-0229	139
Eden Roc - A Renaissance Beach Resort & Spa 4525 Collins Ave *TF:* 855-433-3676 ■ *Web:* edenrocmiami.com	Miami Beach	FL	33140	305-531-0000	674-5555	669
Eden Stone Company Inc W4520 Lime Rd *TF:* 800-472-2521 ■ *Web:* edenstone.net	Eden	WI	53019	920-477-2521		503-6
Eden Theological Seminary 475 E Lockwood Ave *TF:* 800-969-3627 ■ *Web:* www.eden.edu	Saint Louis	MO	63119	314-961-3627	918-2626	167-3
Edens & Avant 1221 Main St Ste 1000	Columbia	SC	29201	803-779-4420	765-0684	460
Edenwald 800 Southerly Rd *Web:* www.edenwald.org	Baltimore	MD	21286	410-339-6000	583-8786	672
Eder Flag Mfg Company Inc 1000 W Rawson Ave *TF:* 800-558-6044 ■ *Web:* www.ederflagnews.com	Oak Creek	WI	53154	414-764-3522		287
EDF Ventures 425 N Main St *Web:* www.edfvc.com	Ann Arbor	MI	48104	734-663-3213	663-7358	792
EDG Inc 3900 N Causeway Blvd Ste 700 *Web:* www.edg.net	Metairie	LA	70002	504-455-0858		463
Edgar Allan Poe Museum 1914-16 E Main St *Web:* www.poemuseum.org	Richmond	VA	23223	804-648-5523		520
Edgar Allan Poe National Historic Site 532 N Seventh St *Web:* www.nps.gov/edal	Philadelphia	PA	19123	215-597-8780	597-1901	564
Edgar Boettcher Mason Contractors Inc Yard 3803 N Euclid *TF:* 800-364-2059 ■ *Web:* www.boettchermasonry.com	Bay City	MI	48706	989-684-4807	684-4824	189-7
Edgar County 115 W Ct St *Web:* edgarcountyillinois.com	Paris	IL	61944	217-466-7433	466-7430	338
Edgar Dunn & Co 201 California St Ste 640 *Web:* www.edgardunn.com	San Francisco	CA	94111	415-977-1870		195
Edgar Evins State Park 1630 Edgar Evins State Pk Rd *TF:* 800-250-8619 ■ *Web:* www.state.tn.us	Silver Point	TN	38582	931-858-2446		565
Edgar Fabrics Inc 50 Commerce Dr	Hauppauge	NY	11788	631-435-9116	435-9151	594
Edgar Lomax Co 6564 Loisdale Ct Ste 310 *TF:* 866-205-0524 ■ *Web:* www.edgarlomax.com	Springfield	VA	22150	703-719-0026		401
EDGAR Online Inc 11200 Rockville Pk Ste 310 *NASDAQ: EDGR* ■ *TF:* 800-732-0330 ■ *Web:* edgar-online.com	Rockville	MD	20852	301-287-0300	287-0390	404
Edge Biosystems Inc 201 Perry Pkwy Ste 5 **Fax Area Code:* 800 ■ *Web:* www.edgebio.com	Gaithersburg	MD	20877	301-990-2685	326-2685*	194
Edge Communications Inc 17328 Ventura Blvd Ste 324 *Web:* www.edgecommunicationsinc.com	Encino	CA	91316	818-990-5001		636
Edge Electronics Inc 75 Orville Dr *TF:* 800-647-3343 ■ *Web:* www.edgeelectronics.com	Bohemia	NY	11716	631-471-3343	471-3405	173-8
Edge Information Management Inc 1682 W Hibiscus Blvd **Fax Area Code:* 800 ■ *TF:* 800-725-3343 ■ *Web:* www.edgeinformation.com	Melbourne	FL	32901	321-722-3343	780-3299*	635
EDge Interactive Inc 67 Mowat Ave Ste 533 *TF:* 800-211-5577 ■ *Web:* www.edgeip.com	Toronto	ON	M6K3E3	416-494-3343		224
Edge of Texas Steakhouse 8690 Edge of Texas *Web:* edgeoftexassteakhouse.com	El Paso	TX	79934	915-822-3343		671
Edge of the Cedars State Park Museum 660 W 400 N *Web:* stateparks.utah.gov	Blanding	UT	84511	435-678-2238		565
Edge Plastics Inc 449 Newman St *Web:* www.edgeplasticsinc.com	Mansfield	OH	44902	419-522-6696		596
Edge Products 1080 S Depot Dr *TF:* 888-360-3343 ■ *Web:* www.edgeproducts.com	Ogden	UT	84404	801-476-3343	476-3348	247
Edge Systems LLC 3S721 W Ave Ste 200 *TF Tech Supp:* 800-352-3343 ■ *Web:* www.edge.com	Warrenville	IL	60555	630-810-9669	810-9228	177
EDGE Tech Corp 9101 Harlan St Ste 260 *TF:* 800-259-6565 ■ *Web:* www.edgetechcorp.com	Westminster	CO	63122	800-259-6565		625
Edge Technologies Inc 3702 Pender Dr Ste 250 *TF:* 888-771-3343 ■ *Web:* www.edge-technologies.com	Fairfax	VA	22030	703-691-7900	691-4020	178-1
EDGE Technology Services Inc 116 Washington Ave 2nd Fl *Web:* edgets.com	North Haven	CT	06473	860-635-3342		225
Edge Training Systems 9710 Farrar Ct Ste P *Web:* www.edgetrainingsystems.com	North Chesterfield	VA	23236	804-272-0333		195
Edge Velocity Corp 68 Stiles Rd Ste G *Web:* www.edgevelocity.com	Salem	NH	03079	603-912-5618		647
Edgecombe County 201 St Andrew St PO Box 10 *Web:* www.edgecombecountync.gov	Tarboro	NC	27886	252-641-7852		338
Edgecombe County Memorial Library 909 N Main St *Web:* edgecombelibrary.libguides.com/homepage	Tarboro	NC	27886	252-823-1141		434-3
Edgecombe-Martin County Electric Membership Corp NC Hwy 33 E *TF:* 800-445-6486 ■ *Web:* www.ememc.com	Tarboro	NC	27886	252-823-2171		245
Edgefield County 129 Courthouse Sq PO Box 34 *Web:* www.edgefieldcounty.sc.gov	Edgefield	SC	29824	803-637-4080		338
EdgeLink LLC 115 SW Ash St Ste 321 *Web:* www.edgelink.com	Portland	OR	97204	503-246-3989	246-4375	193
Edgemark Partners 4510 cox rd Ste 305 *TF:* 800-488-0289 ■ *Web:* www.edgemarkpartners.com	Glen Allen	VA	23060	804-967-2000	967-2111	463
Edgemont Pharmaceuticals LLC 1250 Capital of Texas Hwy S Bldg 3 Ste 400 *TF:* 888-594-4332 ■ *Web:* www.edgemontpharma.com	Austin	TX	78746	512-550-8555		231
Edgen Corp 18444 Highland Rd *TF:* 866-334-3648 ■ *Web:* www.edgenmurray.com	Baton Rouge	LA	70809	225-756-9868	756-9868	385
Edgenet Inc 2948 Sidco Dr *TF:* 877-334-3638 ■ *Web:* www.edgenet.com	Atlanta	GA	30326	877-334-3638		177
EdgePoint Capital Advisors LLC 2000 Auburn Dr Ste 330 *Web:* www.edgepoint.com	Beachwood	OH	44122	216-831-2430		690
Edger Enterprises of Elmira Inc 330 E 14th St *Web:* www.edgerenterprises.com	Elmira Heights	NY	14903	607-733-9664		186

Phone | Fax | Class

Edgerton Contractors Inc
545 W Ryan Rd PO Box 901 ... Oak Creek WI 53154 414-764-4443 764-9788 189-16
TF: 800-345-2051 ■ *Web:* edgerton.us

EdgeStone Consulting Inc
Princeton Corporate Ctr 5 Independence Way
Ste 300 ... Princeton NJ 08540 609-514-5190 463
Web: www.edgestone.net

Edge-Sweets Co
2887 Three-Mile Rd NW ... Grand Rapids MI 49534 616-453-5458 453-5458 601
TF: 800-669-5709 ■ *Web:* www.edge-sweets.com

EdgeTheory LLC
800 Woodlands Pkwy Ste 210 ... Ridgeland MS 39157 650-830-5752 5
Web: www.edgetheory.com

Edgewater Automation LLC
481 Renaissance Dr ... St. Joseph MI 49085 269-983-1300 111
Web: www.edgewaterautomation.com

Edgewater Beach Hotel
1901 Gulf Shore Blvd N ... Naples FL 34102 239-403-2000 379
TF: 866-624-1695 ■ *Web:* www.edgewaternaples.com

Edgewater Beach Resort Management
11212 Front Beach Rd ... Panama City FL 32407 850-235-4044 378
TF: 800-693-0727 ■ *Web:* www.resortcollection.com

Edgewater Grill 861 W Harbor Dr ... San Diego CA 92101 619-232-7581 671
TF: 800-930-9721 ■ *Web:* www.edgewatergrill.com

Edgewater Hotel
2411 Alaskan Way Pier 67 ... Seattle WA 98121 206-728-7000 379
TF: 800-624-0670 ■ *Web:* www.edgewaterhotel.com

Edgewater Hotel & Casino
2020 S Casino Dr ... Laughlin NV 89029 702-298-2453 298-5606* 133
**Fax:* Mktg ■ *TF Resv:* 866-352-3553 ■ *Web:* www.edgewater-casino.com

Edgewater Pointe Estates
23315 Blue Water Cir ... Boca Raton FL 33433 561-391-6305 672
TF General: 888-339-2287 ■ *Web:* www.actsretirement.org

EdgeWater Power Boats 211 Dale St ... Edgewater FL 32132 386-426-5457 90
Web: www.ewboats.com

Edgewater Resort
200 Edgewater Cir ... Hot Springs AR 71913 501-767-3311 379
TF: 800-234-3687 ■ *Web:* www.ewresort.com

Edgewater Resort & Waterpark
2400 London Rd ... Duluth MN 55812 218-728-3601 379
TF: 800-777-7925 ■ *Web:* www.duluthwaterpark.com

EdgeWave Inc 15333 Ave of Science ... San Diego CA 92128 858-676-2277 177
TF: 800-782-3762 ■ *Web:* www.edgewave.com

Edgewood Building Supply Company Inc
1580 E Epler Ave ... Indianapolis IN 46227 317-786-9208 350
Web: www.edgewoodbuildingsupply.com

Edgewood College
1000 Edgewood College Dr ... Madison WI 53711 608-663-2294 663-2214 166
TF: 800-444-4861 ■ *Web:* www.edgewood.edu

Edgewood Convalescent Home Inc
513 S Bell St ... Edgewood IA 52042 563-928-6461 450

Edgewood Management LLC
535 Madison Ave 15th Fl ... New York NY 10022 212-652-9100 194
Web: www.edgewood.com

Edgewood Vista 214 Piper St ... Grand Island NE 68803 308-384-0717 371
Web: edgewoodseniorliving.com

EDI Specialists Inc 31 Bellows Rd ... Raynham MA 02767 800-821-4644 822-7375* 193
**Fax Area Code:* 508 ■ *TF:* 800-821-4644 ■ *Web:* www.edistaffing.com

Edible Arrangements LLC
95 Barnes Rd ... Wallingford CT 06492 304-894-8901 774-0531* 310
**Fax Area Code:* 203 ■ *TF Cust Svc:* 877-363-7848 ■ *Web:* www.ediblearrangements.com

Edibles Restaurant & Bar
704 University Ave ... Rochester NY 14607 585-271-4910 671
Web: www.ediblesrochester.com

EDIC College Inc
Ave Rafael Cordero Calle Gnova Urb Caguas Norte
... Caguas PR 00726 787-744-8519 166
Web: ediccollege.edu

Edifice Inc 1401 W Morehead St ... Charlotte NC 28208 704-332-0900 186
Web: www.edificeinc.com

Edify Technologies Inc
2200 S Main St Ste 306 ... Lombard IL 60148 630-932-9308 196
Web: www.edifytech.com

Edimer Pharmaceuticals Inc
55 Cambridge Pkwy Ste 102W ... Cambridge MA 02142 617-758-4300 231
TF: 866-334-4240 ■ *Web:* www.edimerpharma.com

Edina Realty Inc
6800 France Ave S Ste 600 ... Edina MN 55435 952-928-5563 652
Web: www.edinarealty.com

Edinboro University of Pennsylvania
200 E Normal St ... Edinboro PA 16444 814-732-2761 732-2420* 166
**Fax:* Admissions ■ *TF:* 888-846-2676 ■ *Web:* www.edinboro.edu

Edinboro University of Pennsylvania Baron-Forness Library (EUB)
200 Tartan Rd ... Edinboro PA 16444 814-732-2273 732-2883 434-6
TF: 888-845-2890 ■ *Web:* edinboro.edu/home/page_not_found.dot

Edinburg Chamber of Commerce
602 W University Dr ... Edinburg TX 78540 956-383-4974 383-6942 139
TF: 800-800-7214 ■ *Web:* www.edinburg.com

Edinburg Ctr Inc, The
1040 Waltham St ... Lexington MA 02421 781-862-3600 353
Web: www.edinburgcenter.org

Edinburg Public Library
1906 S Closner ... Edinburg TX 78539 956-383-6246 318-3446 434-3
Web: www.edinburg.lib.tx.us

Edinburg Regional Medical Ctr (ERMC)
1102 W Trenton Rd ... Edinburg TX 78539 956-388-6000 374-3
TF: 800-465-5585 ■ *Web:* www.southtexashealthsystem.com

eDirectory
7004 Little River Tpke Ste O ... Annandale VA 22003 703-914-0770 530
Web: www.edirectory.com

e-Discovery Law & Strategy
120 Broadway 5th Fl ... New York NY 10271 212-457-9400 531-7
TF: 877-256-2472 ■ *Web:* www.lawjournalnewsletters.com

Edison Biotechnology Institute
Ohio University
Konneker Research Laboratories The Ridges ... Athens OH 45701 740-593-4713 593-4795 668
TF: 800-444-2420 ■ *Web:* www.ohio.edu

Edison Carrier Solutions
2 Innovation Way 1st Fl ... Pomona CA 91768 800-634-7999 634-7999 387
TF: 800 634 7999 ■ *Web:* www.edisoncarriersolutions.com

Edison Chamber of Commerce
1028 Amboy Ave ... Edison NJ 08837 732-738-9482 738-9485 139
Web: www.edisonchamber.com

Edison Chouest Offshore
16201 E Main St ... Galliano LA 70354 985-601-4444 465
TF: 866-925-5161 ■ *Web:* www.chouest.com

Edison College
Charlotte 26300 Airport Rd ... Punta Gorda FL 33950 941-637-5629 637-3538* 162
**Fax:* Admissions ■ *TF:* 800-749-2322 ■ *Web:* fsw.edu

Edison Community College 1973 Edison Dr ... Piqua OH 45356 937-778-8600 778-1920 162
TF: 888-442-4551 ■ *Web:* www.edisonohio.edu

Edison Electric Institute (EEI)
701 Pennsylvania Ave NW ... Washington DC 20004 202-508-5000 508-5051 48-12
TF: 800-649-1202 ■ *Web:* www.eei.org

Edison International
2244 Walnut Grove Ave ... Rosemead CA 91770 626-302-1212 360-5
NYSE: EIX ■ *TF Cust Svc:* 800-655-4555 ■ *Web:* www.edison.com

Edison Lithograph & Printing Corp
3725 tonnelle ave ... North bergen NJ 07047 201-902-9191 627
Web: www.edisonlitho.com

Edison Price Lighting Inc (EPL)
41-50 22nd St ... Long Island NY 11101 718-685-0700 786-8530 439
TF: 800-929-3669 ■ *Web:* www.epl.com

Edison Properties LLC
100 Washington St ... Newark NJ 07102 973-643-0895 562
TF: 888-727-5327 ■ *Web:* www.parkfast.com

Edison School Elementary School
246 S Fair Ave ... Elmhurst IL 60126 630-834-4272 685
Web: edison.elmhurst205.org

Edison Township Free Public Library
340 Plainfield Ave ... Edison NJ 08817 732-287-2298 819-9134 434-3
TF: 800-275-4278 ■ *Web:* www.edisonpubliclibrary.net

Edison Venture Fund
281 Witherspoon St ... Lawrenceville NJ 08540 609-896-1900 792
TF: 800-899-3975 ■ *Web:* edisonpartners.com

Edison Welding Institute (EWI)
1250 Arthur E Adams Dr ... Columbus OH 43221 614-688-5000 688-5001 49-13
Web: www.ewi.org

EdisonLearning Inc
900 S Gay St Ste 1000 ... Knoxville TN 37902 865-329-3600 685
TF: 800-222-2811 ■ *Web:* www.edisonlearning.com

eDist 97 McKee Dr ... Mahwah NJ 07430 201-512-1400 391-5078* 692
**Fax Area Code:* 800 ■ *TF:* 800-800-6624 ■ *Web:* www.edist.com

Edisto Beach State Park
8377 State Cabin Rd ... Edisto Island SC 29438 843-869-2756 869-4428 565
TF: 866-345-7275 ■ *Web:* www.southcarolinaparks.com

Edisto Electric Co-op Inc
896 Calhoun St ... Bamberg SC 29003 803-245-5141 245-0188 245
TF: 800-433-3292 ■ *Web:* www.edistoelectric.com

Edit Bay 571 N Poplar Ste I ... Orange CA 92868 714-978-7878 512
Web: www.theeditbay.com

Edith Abbott Memorial Library
211 N Washington St ... Grand Island NE 68801 308-385-5333 385-5339 434-3
TF: 800-709-8814 ■ *Web:* www.grand-island.com

Edith J Carrier Arboretum & Botanical Gardens at James Madison University
780 University Blvd MSC 3705 ... Harrisonburg VA 22807 540-568-3194 568-5115 97
TF: 888-568-2586 ■ *Web:* www.jmu.edu

Edith Macy Conference Ctr
550 Chappaqua Rd ... Briarcliff Manor NY 10510 914-945-8000 377
Web: www.edithmacy.com

Edith Nourse Rogers Memorial Veterans Hospital
200 Springs Rd ... Bedford MA 01730 415-839-6885 882-0495 374-8
Web: en.wikipedia.org

Editor & Publisher Magazine
17782 Cowan Ste C ... Irvine CA 92614 949-660-6150 660-6172 457-5
TF: 855-896-7433 ■ *Web:* www.editorandpublisher.com

Editorial Freelancers Assn (EFA)
71 W 23rd St 4th Fl ... New York NY 10010 212-929-5400 929-5439 49-16
TF: 866-929-5400 ■ *Web:* www.the-efa.org

Editorial Projects in Education
6935 Arlington Rd Ste 100 ... Bethesda MD 20814 301-280-3100 280-3200 637-9
Web: www.edweek.org

EDJ Associates Inc
13873 Park Center Rd Ste 301 ... Herndon VA 20191 703-738-9150 463
Web: edjassociates.com

EDL Packaging Systems
1260 Parkview Rd ... Green Bay WI 54304 920-336-7744 547
Web: www.edlpackaging.com

Edlund Company Inc
159 Industrial Pkwy ... Burlington VT 05401 002-062-9661 862-4822 298
TF: 800-772-2126 ■ *Web:* www.edlundco.com

Edm Department Inc
1261 Humbracht Cir Ste A ... Bartlett IL 60103 630-736-0531 358
Web: edmdept.com

EDM International Inc
4001 Automation Way ... Fort Collins CO 80525 970-204-4001 256
Web: www.edmlink.com

Edm Services Inc 4100 Guardian St ... Simi Valley CA 93063 805-527-3300 261
Web: edmsvc.com

EDM Zap Parts Inc 1108 Front St Ste 2 ... Lisle IL 60532 630-852-1699 697
TF: 800-759-2839 ■ *Web:* www.edmzap.com

EDMC (Education Management Corp)
210 Sixth Ave 33rd Fl ... Pittsburgh PA 15222 412-562-0900 562-0598 242
NASDAQ: EDMC ■ *TF:* 800-275-2440 ■ *Web:* www.edmc.edu

Edminster Hinshaw Russ & Assoc Inc
10555 Woffice Dr ... Houston TX 77042 713-784-4500 256
Web: www.ehrainc.com

Edmo Distributors Inc
12830 E Mirabeau Pkwy ... Spokane Valley WA 99216 509-535-8280 535-8266 770
TF: 800-235-3300 ■ *Web:* www.edmo.com

Edmond A Swad P C 38701 Seven Mile Rd ... Livonia MI 48152 734-462-9333 2
Web: swadco.com

Edmond Area Chamber of Commerce
825 E Second St ... Edmond OK 73034 405-341-2808 340-5512 139
TF: 800-717-2601 ■ *Web:* www.edmondchamber.com

Name / Address	City	State	Zip	Phone	Fax	Class
Edmond Public Library 10 S Blvd *Web:* www.metrolibrary.org	Edmond	OK	73034	405-341-9282		434-3
Edmond Scientific Co 4229 Lafayette Center Dr Ste 1890 *Web:* www.edmondsci.com	Chantilly	VA	20151	703-955-7722		261
Edmond Sun PO Box 2470 *Web:* www.edmondsun.com	Edmond	OK	73083	405-341-2121	340-7363	532-2
Edmonds Community College 20000 68th Ave W *TF:* 866-886-4854 ■ *Web:* www.edcc.edu	Lynnwood	WA	98036	425-640-1500	640-1159	162
Edmonds Entertainment 1635 N Cahuenga Blvd *Web:* www.edmondsent.com	Los Angeles	CA	90028	323-860-1520		514
Edmonds Harbor Inn & Suites 130 W Dayton *TF:* 800-441-8033 ■ *Web:* www.bestwestern.com	Edmonds	WA	98020	425-771-5021	672-2880	379
Edmonson County PO Box 830 *TF:* 800-368-8683 ■ *Web:* edmonsoncountyclerk.com	Brownsville	KY	42210	270-597-2624	597-9714	338
Edmonton Chamber of Commerce 9990 Jasper Ave Ste 600 *Web:* www.edmontonchamber.com	Edmonton	AB	T5J1P7	780-426-4620	424-7946	137
Edmonton City Centre 10025-102A Ave *Web:* www.edmontoncitycentre.com	Edmonton	AB	T5J2Z2	780-426-8444		460
Edmonton City Hall 1 Sir Winston Churchill Sq 3rd Fl *Web:* www.edmonton.ca	Edmonton	AB	T5J2R7	780-442-5311	496-8210	337
Edmonton Eskimo Football Club, The 11000 Stadium Rd *Web:* www.esks.com	Edmonton	AB	T5H4E2	780-448-1525		713
Edmonton Exchanger Group of Cos 5545-89 St *Web:* www.edmontonexchanger.com	Edmonton	AB	T6E5W9	780-468-6722		295
Edmonton Folk Music Festival 10115 97a Ave NW *TF:* 800-485-1899 ■ *Web:* www.edmontonfolkfest.org	Edmonton	AB	T6E4T2	780-429-1899		138
Edmonton International Airport 8340 Sparrow Crescent *TF:* 800-854-9517 ■ *Web:* flyeia.com	Edmonton	AB	T9E8B7	780-800-0622		27
Edmonton Journal 10006 - 101 St *TF:* 800-232-9486 ■ *Web:* www.edmontonjournal.com	Edmonton	AB	T5J0S1	780-429-5100	498-5696	532-1
Edmonton Oilers 11230 110th St *TF:* 800-559-2333 ■ *Web:* oilers.nhl.com	Edmonton	AB	T5J0H6	780-414-4000	409-5890	716
Edmonton Public Library Office 7 Sir Winston Churchill Sq NW	Edmonton	AB	T5J2V4	780-496-7000		434
Edmonton Regional Airports Authority 1000 Airport Rd Edmonton International Airport *Web:* www.flyeia.com	Edmonton	AB	T9E0V3	780-890-8900		63
Edmonton Sun 10006 101 St Ste 250 *TF:* 888-786-7821 ■ *Web:* www.edmontonsun.com	Edmonton	AB	T5J0S1	780-468-5121		532-1
Edmonton Symphony Orchestra 9720 102nd Ave *TF:* 800-563-5081 ■ *Web:* www.edmontonsymphony.com	Edmonton	AB	T5J4B2	780-428-1108		573-3
Edmund Optics Inc 101 E Gloucester Pk *TF:* 800-363-1992 ■ *Web:* edmundoptics.com	Barrington	NJ	08007	856-547-3488	573-6295	544
Edmunds & Associates Inc 301 Tilton Rd **Fax Area Code:* 609 ■ *TF:* 888-336-6999 ■ *Web:* www.edmundsassoc.com	Northfield	NJ	08225	888-336-6999	645-3111*	5
Edmunds County PO Box 384 *Web:* www.edmunds.sdcounties.org	Ipswich	SD	57451	605-426-6671	426-6323	338
Edmunds Gages 45 Spring Ln *TF:* 800-878-1622 ■ *Web:* www.edmundsgages.com	Farmington	CT	06032	860-677-2813	677-4243	493
EDN (Earth Day Network) 1616 P St NW Ste 340 *Web:* www.earthday.org	Washington	DC	20036	202-518-0044	518-8794	48-13
EDN Aviation Inc 6720 Valjean Ave *Web:* www.ednaviation.com	Van Nuys	CA	91406	818-988-8826	904-6799	790
Edna McConnell Clark Foundation, The 415 Madison Ave 10th Fl *Web:* www.emcf.org	New York	NY	10017	212-551-9100	421-9325	305
Edo Japan International Inc 32 St SE Ste 4838 *TF:* 888-336-9888 ■ *Web:* www.edojapan.com	Calgary	AB	T2B2S6	403-215-8800	215-8801	670
EDO Sushi 484 Eglinton Ave W *Web:* edorestaurants.com	Toronto	ON	M5N1A5	416-322-3033		671
eDOC Communications 555 E Business Ctr Dr *Web:* www.edoccommunications.com	Mount Prospect	IL	60056	847-824-5610		627
Edo-ko 425 Spadina Rd *Web:* edorestaurants.com	Toronto	ON	M5P2W3	416-482-8973		671
Edom Laboratories Inc 100 E Jefryn Blvd Ste M *TF:* 800-723-3366 ■ *Web:* www.edomlaboratories.com	Deer Park	NY	11729	631-586-2266		799
Edon Farmers Co-op Assn Inc 205 S Michigan St PO Box 308 *TF:* 800-878-4093 ■ *Web:* www.edonfarmerscoop.com	Edon	OH	43518	419-272-2121		276
EDP Biotech Corp 6701 Baum Dr Ste 110 *Web:* www.edpbiotech.com	Knoxville	TN	37919	865-299-6250		231
EDP University 560 Ave Ponce De Leon	San Juan	PR	00918	787-765-3560		165
EDPA (Exhibit Designers & Producers Assn) 19 Compo Rd S *Web:* www.edpa.com	Westport	CT	06880	203-557-6321		49-18
Edro Corp 37 Commerce St *Web:* www.edrocorp.com	East Berlin	CT	06023	860-828-0311	828-5984	427
Edro Engineering Inc 20500 Carrey Rd *Web:* www.edro.com	Walnut	CA	91789	909-594-5751		596
EDS (IEEE Electron Devices Society) IEEE Operations Ctr 445 Hoes Ln *TF:* 800-678-4333 ■ *Web:* eds.ieee.org	Piscataway	NJ	08854	732-981-0060	562-6380	49-19
EDS Manufacturing Inc 765 N Target Range Rd *Web:* www.edsmanufacturing.com	Nogales	AZ	85621	520-287-9711		194
Edsal Mfg Company Inc 4400 S Packers Ave *Web:* www.edsal.com	Chicago	IL	60609	773-254-0600		286
Edsel & Eleanor Ford House 1100 Lake Shore Rd *Web:* www.fordhouse.org	Grosse Pointe Shores	MI	48236	313-884-4222	884-5977	50-3
Edstrom Industries Inc 819 Bakke Ave *TF:* 800-558-5913 ■ *Web:* www.edstrom.com	Waterford	WI	53185	262-534-5181	534-5184	420
Edsung Foodservice 1337 Mookaula St *Web:* edsung.com	Honolulu	HI	96817	808-845-3931		300
EDT (Engineering Design Technologies) 1705 Entp Way SE Ste 200 *Web:* www.edtinc.net	Marietta	GA	30067	770-988-0400	988-0300	685
EDT Corp 1006-J NE 146th St *Web:* www.edtcorp.com	Vancouver	WA	98685	360-574-7294		75
Edtec Central LLC 22932 Woodward Ave Ste C *Web:* edtec.net	Ferndale	MI	48220	248-582-8100		196
EdTek Services Inc 30 Wascana Ave **Fax Area Code:* 888 ■ *Web:* www.edtekservices.com	Toronto	ON	M5A1V5	647-435-7133	827-1184*	177
Eduardo de San Angel 2822 E Commercial Blvd *Web:* www.eduardodesanangel.com	Fort Lauderdale	FL	33308	954-772-4731	772-0794	671
Eduardo's Border Grill 1830 Westwood Blvd *Web:* www.eduardosbordergrill.com	Westwood	CA	90025	310-475-2410		671
Education Commission of the States (ECS) 700 Broadway Ste 810 *Web:* www.ecs.org	Denver	CO	80203	303-299-3600	296-8332	49-5
Education Ctr Inc 3515 W Market St Ste 200 *TF:* 800-714-7991 ■ *Web:* www.themailbox.com	Greensboro	NC	27403	336-854-0309		243
Education Development Ctr Inc (EDC) 55 Chapel St *TF:* 800-225-4276 ■ *Web:* www.edc.org	Newton	MA	02458	617-969-7100	969-5979	48-11
Education Grants Alert 360 Hiatt Dr *TF:* 800-621-5463 ■ *Web:* www.lrp.com	Palm Beach Gardens	FL	33418	561-622-6520	622-2423	531-4
Education Inc 2 Main St Ste 2A *Web:* www.educationinc.us	Plymouth	MA	02360	508-732-9101		148
Education Management Corp (EDMC) 210 Sixth Ave 33rd Fl *NASDAQ: EDMC* ■ *TF:* 800-275-2440 ■ *Web:* www.edmc.edu	Pittsburgh	PA	15222	412-562-0900	562-0598	242
Education Management Solutions Inc 436 Creamery Way Ste 300 **Fax Area Code:* 484 ■ *TF:* 877-367-5050 ■ *Web:* simulationiq.com	Exton	PA	19341	610-701-7002	653-1070*	178-7
Education Management Systems Inc 4110 Shipyard Blvd *TF:* 800-541-8999 ■ *Web:* www.mealsplus.com	Wilmington	NC	28403	910-799-0121		177
Education Online Services Corp 3303 W Commercial Blvd *Web:* www.educationonlineservices.com	Fort Lauderdale	FL	33309	954-606-5658		387
Education Realty Trust Inc 999 S Shady Grove Rd Ste 600 *NYSE: EDR* ■ *Web:* www.edrtrust.com	Memphis	TN	38120	901-259-2500		654
Education Resource Information Ctr (ERIC) 655 15th St NW Ste 500 *TF:* 800-538-3742 ■ *Web:* www.usa.gov	Washington	DC	20005	800-538-3742		197
Education Trust 1250 H St NW Ste 700 *Web:* www.edtrust.org	Washington	DC	20005	202-293-1217	293-2605	48-11
Education Week Magazine 6935 Arlington Rd *TF:* 800-346-1834 ■ *Web:* www.edweek.org	Bethesda	MD	20814	301-280-3100	280-3250	457-8
Education.com Inc 333 S B St Unit 101 *Web:* www.education.com	San Mateo	CA	94401	650-366-3380		387
Educational Communications Inc PO Box 351419 *Web:* www.ecoprojects.org	Los Angeles	CA	90035	310-559-9160	559-9160	48-13
Educational Development Corp 10302 E 55th Pl *NASDAQ: EDUC* ■ *TF:* 800-475-4522 ■ *Web:* www.edcpub.com	Tulsa	OK	74146	918-622-4522	665-7919	96
Educational Employees Credit Union PO Box 5242 *TF:* 800-538-3328 ■ *Web:* www.myeecu.org	Fresno	CA	93755	559-437-7700	451-0198	219
Educational Housing Services Inc 55 Clark St *TF:* 800-385-1689 ■ *Web:* www.studenthousing.org	Brooklyn	NY	11201	212-977-7622		49-5
Educational Insights Inc 380 N Fairway Dr *TF:* 800-995-4436 ■ *Web:* www.educationalinsights.com	Vernon Hills	IL	60061	800-995-4436		243
Educational Leadership Magazine 1703 N Beauregard St *TF:* 800-933-2723 ■ *Web:* www.ascd.org	Alexandria	VA	22311	703-578-9600	575-5400	457-8
Educational Marketer 60 Long Ridge Rd Ste 300 *Web:* educationalmarketer.net	Stamford	CT	06902	203-325-8193		531-10
Educational Media Foundation 5700 W Oaks Blvd *TF General:* 800-525-5683 ■ *Web:* www.klove.com	Rocklin	CA	95765	800-877-5600		643
Educational Research Newsletter PO Box 2347 **Fax Area Code:* 815 ■ *TF:* 800-321-7471 ■ *Web:* www.ernweb.com	South Portland	ME	04116	207-632-1954	461-5647*	531-4
Educational Supplies Inc 1506 S Salisbury Blvd *TF:* 800-772-7168 ■ *Web:* www.educationalsuppliesinc.com	Salisbury	MD	21801	410-543-2519	860-0584	243
Educational Testing Service Rosedale Rd *Web:* www.ets.org	Princeton	NJ	08541	609-921-9000	734-5410	244
Educational Theatre Assn 2343 Auburn Ave *TF:* 800-848-2263 ■ *Web:* www.schooltheatre.org	Cincinnati	OH	45219	513-421-3900	421-7077	48-4
Educational Tours 1123 Sterling Rd *TF:* 800-343-9003 ■ *Web:* www.edtours-us.com	Inverness	FL	34450	800-343-9003		760
Educational Travel Consultants (ETC) PO Box 1580 *TF:* 800-247-7969 ■ *Web:* www.educationaltravelconsultants.com	Hendersonville	NC	28793	828-693-0412	692-1591	760
Educational Travel Tours Inc PO Box 9028 *Web:* www.educationaltraveltours.com	Trenton	NJ	08650	609-587-1550	587-1550	760

Name / Address	City	State	ZIP	Phone	Fax	Class
Educationdynamics LLC						
5 Marine View Plaza Ste 212	Hoboken	NJ	07030	201-377-3000		4
Web: www.educationdynamics.com						
Educators Credit Union (ECU)						
1400 N Newman Rd PO Box 081040	Racine	WI	53406	262-886-5900	884-7233	219
TF: 800-236-5898 ■ *Web:* www.ecu.com						
Educators Mutual Insurance Assn Utah						
852 East Arrowhead Ln	Salt Lake City	UT	84107	801-262-7476		391-2
Web: emihealth.com						
Educators Publishing Service Inc (EPS)						
625 Mt Auburn St Third Fl PO Box 9031	Cambridge	MA	02139	800-225-5750		637-2
TF: 800-225-5750 ■ *Web:* eps.schoolspecialty.com						
Educators Resource Inc						
2575 Schillingers Rd	Semmes	AL	36575	800-868-2368	868-6212*	243
**Fax:* Cust Svc ■ *TF Cust Svc:* 800-868-2368 ■ *Web:* www.erdealer.com						
Educause 1150 18th St NW Ste 1010	Washington	DC	20036	202-872-4200	872-4318	48-9
Web: www.educause.edu						
Edufficient Inc 6 Forest Ave 2nd Fl	Paramus	NJ	07652	201-881-0030		195
TF: 888-648-1811 ■ *Web:* www.edufficient.com						
Edufii Inc 130 Buena Vista Ave	Mill Valley	CA	94941	888-414-7276		387
TF: 888-414-7276 ■ *Web:* edufii.com						
Eduplanet21 LLC						
5040 Louise Dr Ste 104	Mechanicsburg	PA	17055	717-884-9900		387
Web: www.eduplanet21.com						
Eduworks Corp						
136 SW Washington Ave Ste 203	Corvallis	OR	97333	541-753-0844		196
Web: eduworks.com						
EdVenture Children's Museum						
211 Gervais St	Columbia	SC	29201	803-779-3100	779-3144	521
TF: 888-236-2427 ■ *Web:* www.edventure.org						
Edvest College Savings Plan						
PO Box 55189	Boston	MA	02205	888-338-3789		725
TF: 888-338-3789 ■ *Web:* www.edvest.com						
Edward A Sherman Publishing Co						
101 Malbone Rd	Newport	RI	02840	401-849-3300	849-3306	637-8
TF: 800-320-2378 ■ *Web:* www.newportri.com						
Edward A. Berg & Sons Inc (EAB)						
75 W Century Rd	Paramus	NJ	07652	201-845-8200	845-8201	297-3
Web: www.eaberg.com						
Edward A. Williamson Law Firm Pllc, The						
509 S Church Ave	Philadelphia	MS	39350	601-656-5634		428
Web: www.eawlaw.com						
Edward Adams House Bed & Breakfast						
729 S Water St	Silverton	OR	97381	503-873-8868		377
TF: 800-551-6949 ■ *Web:* edwardadamshousebandb.com						
Edward B Howlin Inc 2880 Dunkirk Way	Dunkirk	MD	20754	301-855-8900		360-3
Web: ebhowlin.com						
Edward B O'reilly & Assoc Inc						
30 W Highland Ave	Philadelphia	PA	19118	215-242-8100		610
Web: www.eboreilly.com						
Edward Ball Wakulla Springs State Park						
465 Wakulla Park Dr	Wakulla Springs	FL	32327	850-561-7276		565
Web: www.floridastateparks.org						
Edward C Levy Co 9300 Dix Ave	Dearborn	MI	48120	313-843-7200	849-9441*	503-5
**Fax:* Sales ■ *TF:* 877-938-0007 ■ *Web:* www.edwclevy.com						
Edward D Astrin CPA A P C						
16633 Ventura Blvd Ste 1450	Encino	CA	91436	818-501-3022		2
Edward Day Gallery Inc 952 Queen St W	Toronto	ON	M6J1G8	416-921-6540		42
Web: www.edwarddaygallery.com						
Edward Don & Co						
2500 S Harlem Ave	North Riverside	IL	60546	800-777-4366		300
TF Cust Svc: 800-777-4366 ■ *Web:* www.don.com						
Edward Hines Jr Veterans Affairs Hospital						
5000 S Fifth Ave	Hines	IL	60141	708-202-8387		374-8
Web: www.hines.va.gov						
Edward Hospital						
801 S Washington St	Naperville	IL	60540	630-527-3000		374-3
Web: www.eehealth.org						
Edward J Darby & Son Inc						
2200 N Eigth St PO Box 50049	Philadelphia	PA	19133	215-236-2203	236-2203	688
TF: 800-875-6374 ■ *Web:* www.darbywiremesh.com						
Edward J Meloney Inc 22 Madison Ave	Lansdowne	PA	19050	610-626-4900		189-10
Edward Jones 12555 Manchester Rd	Saint Louis	MO	63131	314-515-2000	515-3269	690
TF: 800-441-2357 ■ *Web:* www.edwardjones.com						
Edward Joy Electric 905 Canal St	Syracuse	NY	13210	315-474-3361	479-8604	362
TF: 800-724-0664 ■ *Web:* www.edwardjoyelectric.com						
Edward King House 35 King St	Newport	RI	02840	401-846-7426		50-3
Web: www.edwardkinghouse.org						
Edward R. Madigan State Fish & Wildlife Area						
1366 1010th Ave	Lincoln	IL	62656	217-735-2424		565
Web: www.dnr.illinois.gov/parks/pages/edwardrmadigan.aspx						
Edward S Babcock & Sons Inc						
6100 Quail Vly Ct	Riverside	CA	92507	951-653-3351		743
Web: www.babcocklabs.com						
Edward Segal Inc						
360 Reynolds Bridge Rd	Thomaston	CT	06787	860-283-5821		454
TF: 800-869-9601 ■ *Web:* www.edwardsegalinc.com						
Edward Ted & Pat Jones- Confluence Point State Park						
1000 Riverlands Way	West Alton	MO	63386	636-899-1135		565
Web: www.mostateparks.com						
Edward Thomas Companies, The						
9950 Santa Monica Blvd	Beverly Hills	CA	90212	310-859-9366		707
Web: www.edwardthomasco.com						
Edward Tyler Nahem Fine Art Llc						
37 W 57th St Frnt 2	New York	NY	10019	212-517-2453		522
Web: www.edwardtylernahemfineart.com						
Edward W Powers Auditorium						
260 Federal Plaza W	Youngstown	OH	44503	330-744-4269		572
Web: www.youngstownsymphony.com/symphony_center.html						
Edward White Hospital						
2323 Ninth Ave N	Saint Petersburg	FL	33713	727-323-1111		374-3
Web: www.edwardwhitehospital.com						
Edwards Air Force Base						
305 E Popson Ave	Edwards AFB	CA	93524	661-277-1110	277-2732	497-1
Web: www.edwards.af.mil						
Edwards Bros Inc 2500 S State St	Ann Arbor	MI	48104	734-769-1000		626
Web: www.edwardsbrothersmalloy.com						
Edwards Company Inc						
41 Woodford Ave	Plainville	CT	06062	800-336-4206		693
TF: 800-336-4206 ■ *Web:* www.edwards-signals.com						
Edwards Construction & Development Inc						
Central Florida Community College	Ocala	FL	32674	352-854-6266		186
Web: www.edwardsconstruction.com						
Edwards County 50 E Main St Ste 7	Albion	IL	62806	618-445-2016		338
Web: www.sos.state.il.us						
Edwards County 721 Marsh Ave	Kinsley	KS	67547	620-659-2711	659-3613	338
TF: 800-696-0258 ■ *Web:* www.edwardscounty.org						
Edwards County PO Box 348	Rocksprings	TX	78880	830-683-6122		338
Web: www.edwardscountytexas.us						
Edwards Graphic Arts Inc						
2700 Bell Ave	Des Moines	IA	50321	515-280-9765		627
TF: 800-280-9765 ■ *Web:* www.ega.com						
Edwards Industries LLC						
6085 Marshalee Dr Ste 140	Elkridge	MD	21075	443-561-0180		196
TF: 800-556-2506 ■ *Web:* www.edwps.com						
Edwards Instrument Co 530 S Hwy H	Elkhorn	WI	53121	262-723-4221	723-4245	527
TF: 800-562-6838 ■ *Web:* www.edwards-instruments.com						
Edwards Jet Ctr 1691 Aviation Pl	Billings	MT	59105	406-252-0508	245-9491	63
TF: 866-353-8245 ■ *Web:* www.edwardsjetcenter.com						
Edwards John Bel (D) PO Box 94004	Baton Rouge	LA	70804	866-735-2001		343
TF: 866-735-2001 ■ *Web:* www.gov.louisiana.gov						
Edwards Label 2277 Knoll Dr	Ventura	CA	93003	805-658-2626		627
TF: 800-469-4176 ■ *Web:* www.edwardslabel.com						
Edwards Lifesciences Corp						
1 Edwards Way	Irvine	CA	92614	949-250-2500	250-2525*	582
NYSE: EW ■ **Fax:* Cust Svc ■ *TF:* 800-424-3278 ■ *Web:* www.edwards.com						
Edwards Lowell						
8712 Wilshire Blvd	Beverly Hills	CA	90211	310-360-0466		157-6
Edwards Manufacturing Co						
1107 Sykes St	Albert Lea	MN	56007	507-373-8206	373-9433	456
TF: 800-373-8206 ■ *Web:* www.edwardsironworkers.com						
Edwards Medical Supply						
495 Woodcreek Dr	Bolingbrook	IL	60440	630-370-0700		502
Web: www.edwardsmedical.com						
Edwards Publications Inc						
125 Eagles Nest Dr St A	Seneca	SC	29678	864-882-3272		532-3
Web: www.edwgroupinc.com						
Edwards Steel Structural Div						
1777 Mckinley Ave	Columbus	OH	43222	614-274-7015		492
Edwards Wood Products Inc						
2215 Old Lawyers Rd PO Box 219	Marshville	NC	28103	704-624-5098	624-6812	551
Web: www.ewpl.com						
Edwards, Kenny & Bray						
1900 - 1040 W Georgia St	Vancouver	BC	V6E4H3	604-689-1811		428
Web: www.ekb.com						
Edwardsburg Public Schools						
69410 Section St	Edwardsburg	MI	49112	269-663-1031		685
Web: www.edwardsburgpublicschools.org						
Edwards-Etherton Oil Company Inc						
411 N Fair St	Marion	IL	62959	618-993-6935		580
Web: www.edcospecialtyproducts.com						
Edwards-Freeman Inc						
441 E Hector St	Conshohocken	PA	19428	610-828-7440		296-32
Edwardsville Community School District 7						
708 St Louis St	Edwardsville	IL	62025	618-656-1182	692-7423	685
Web: www.ecusd7.org						
Edwin Gaynor Corp 200 Charles St	Stratford	CT	06615	203-378-5545	381-9019	815
TF: 800-342-9667 ■ *Web:* www.egaynor.com						
Edwin L Heim Co 1918 Greenwood St	Harrisburg	PA	17104	717-233-8711	233-8619	189-4
TF: 800-692-7316 ■ *Web:* www.edwinlheim.com						
Edwin Shaw Rehab 1621 Flickinger Rd	Akron	OH	44312	330-784-1271	948-8332	374-6
TF: 800-221-4601 ■ *Web:* www.akrongeneral.org						
Edwynn Houk Gallery						
745 Fifth Ave 4th Fl	New York	NY	10151	212-750-7070	688-4848	42
Web: www.houkgallery.com						
EE Cruz & Co Inc						
165 Ryan St The Cruz Bldg	South Plainfield	NJ	07080	908-462-9600		188-10
Web: eecruz.com						
EE Reed Construction LP						
333 Commerce Green Blvd	Sugar Land	TX	77478	281-933-4000	933-4852	186
Web: www.eereed.com						
EE Schenck Co 6000 N Cutter Cir	Portland	OR	97217	503-284-4124	288-4475	594
TF: 800-433-0722 ■ *Web:* www.eeschenck.com						
EECO Switch 1240 Pioneer St Ste A	Brea	CA	92821	714-835-6000		815
TF: 800-854-3808 ■ *Web:* www.eecoswitch.com						
Eegee's Inc 3360 E Ajo Way	Tucson	AZ	85713	520-294-3333	889-4340	670
TF: 800-442-1162 ■ *Web:* www.eegees.com						
EEI (Edison Electric Institute)						
701 Pennsylvania Ave NW	Washington	DC	20004	202-508-5000	508-5051	48-12
TF: 800-649-1202 ■ *Web:* www.eei.org						
EEI (Egizii Electric Inc)						
700 N MacArthur Blvd	Springfield	IL	62702	217-528-4001		189-4
EEI (Environmental Enterprises Inc)						
10163 Cincinnati Dayton Rd	Cincinnati	OH	45241	513-772-2818		667
TF: 800-722-2818 ■ *Web:* www.eeienv.com						
EEL River Fuels Inc 3371 N State St	Ukiah	CA	95482	707-462-5554		579
TF: 800-343-8354 ■ *Web:* www.erenergy.com						
EEOC (Equal Employment Opportunity Commission)						
1801 L St NW	Washington	DC	20507	202-663-4191		340-20
TF: 800-669-4000 ■ *Web:* www.eeoc.gov						
eeParts com Inc						
1505 Wallace Dr Ste 102	Carrollton	TX	75006	866-337-2787		396
TF: 866-337-2787 ■ *Web:* www.eeparts.com						
EERC (Energy & Environmental Research Ctr)						
University of N Dakota 15 N 23rd St S 9018	Grand Forks	ND	58202	701-777-5000	777-5181	668
Web: www.eerc.und.nodak.edu						
EERI (Earthquake Engineering Research Institute)						
499 14th St Ste 320	Oakland	CA	94612	510-451-0905	451-5411	49-19
Web: www.eeri.org						
EF Precision Design Inc						
2301 Computer Rd	Willow Grove	PA	19090	215-784-0861		757
TF: 800-536-3900 ■ *Web:* www.efgroup.com						
EF Tours 2 Education Cir	Cambridge	MA	02141	800-665-5364		760
TF: 800-872-8439 ■ *Web:* www.eftours.com						

Phone Fax Class

EFA (Editorial Freelancers Assn)
71 W 23rd St 4th Fl ... New York NY 10010 212-929-5400 929-5439 49-16
TF: 866-929-5400 ■ *Web:* www.the-efa.org

EFC (Evangelical Fellowship of Canada)
600 Alden Rd Markham Industrial Pk Ste 300 ... Markham ON L3R0E7 905-479-5885 479-4742 48-20
TF: 866-302-3362 ■ *Web:* www.evangelicalfellowship.ca

EFC Valve & Controls LLC
230 Progress Rd ... Longview TX 75604 903-759-0126 539

EFCC (East Fairfield Coal Co)
10900 S Ave PO Box 217 ... North Lima OH 44452 330-549-2165 501
TF: 800-241-7074 ■ *Web:* www.eastfairfieldcoal.com

EFCO Corp 1000 County Rd ... Monett MO 65708 417-235-3193 235-7313 234
TF: 800-221-4169 ■ *Web:* www.efcocorp.com

Efco Products Inc 130 Smith St ... Poughkeepsie NY 12601 845-452-4715 123
Web: efcoproducts.com

EFD Induction Inc
31511 Dequindre Rd ... Madison Heights MI 48071 248-658-0700 658-0701 386
Web: www.efd-induction.com

EFF (Electronic Frontier Foundation Inc)
454 Shotwell St ... San Francisco CA 94110 415-436-9333 436-9993 48-9
Web: www.eff.org

Effective Data Inc
1515 E Wdfield Rd ... Schaumburg IL 60173 847-969-9300 225
TF: 877-825-5233 ■ *Web:* effective-data.com

Effective Solar Products LLC
601 Crescent Ave ... Lockport LA 70374 985-532-0800 610
TF: 888-824-0090 ■ *Web:* www.effectivesolar.com

Effective Training Inc
14143 Farmington Rd ... Livonia MI 48154 734-744-5940 194
Web: www.etinews.com

Efficas Inc
7007 Winchester Cir Ste 120 ... Boulder CO 80301 303-381-2070 578
TF: 866-446-0388 ■ *Web:* www.efficas.com

Efficient Forms
10394 W Chatfield Ave Bldg 3 Ste 109 ... Littleton CO 80127 303-785-8600 225
Web: www.efficientforms.com

Efficient Machine Products
12133 Alameda Dr ... Strongsville OH 44149 440-268-0205 268-0215 621
Web: www.efficientm.com

Effigy Mounds National Monument
151 Hwy 76 ... Harpers Ferry IA 52146 563-873-3491 564
Web: www.nps.gov/efmo

Effingham Convention & Visitors Bureau
201 E Jefferson Ave ... Effingham IL 62401 217-342-5305 342-2746 206
TF: 800-772-0750 ■ *Web:* www.effinghamil.com

Effingham County 601 N Laurel St ... Springfield GA 31329 912-754-2123 754-4157 338
TF: 800-338-6745 ■ *Web:* www.effinghamcounty.org

Effingham County Chamber of Commerce
520 W Third St PO Box 1078 ... Springfield GA 31329 912-754-3301 754-1236 139
TF: 800-241-3333 ■ *Web:* www.effinghamcounty.com

Effingham County Illinois
101 N Fourth St
Effingham County Office bldg PO Box 628 ... Effingham IL 62401 217-342-6535 342-3577 338
Web: www.co.effingham.il.us

Effingham Equity Inc
201 W Roadway Ave ... Effingham IL 62401 217-342-4101 347-7601 275
TF: 800-223-1337 ■ *Web:* theequity.com

Effone Software Inc
1294 Kifer Rd Ste 709 ... Sunnyvale CA 94086 408-830-1010 177
Web: www.effone.com

Effort Foundry Inc 6980 Chrisphalt Dr ... Bath PA 18014 610-837-1837 492
TF: 800-446-8420 ■ *Web:* www.effortfoundry.com

Effox Inc
9759 Inter Ocean Dr ... West Chester Township OH 45246 513-874-8915 480
Web: www.effoxflextor.com

EFG Capital International Corp
701 Brickell Ave 9th Fl ... Miami FL 33131 305-482-8000 690
Web: www.efgcapital.com

E-filliate Inc
11321 White Rock Rd ... Rancho Cordova CA 95742 916-858-1000 459
TF: 800-592-7031 ■ *Web:* www.efilliate.com

EFILM LLC 1146 N Las Palmas Ave ... Hollywood CA 90038 323-463-7041 514
Web: www.efilm.com

EFJohnson Technologies
1440 Corporate Dr ... Irving TX 75038 972-819-0700 819-0639 647
TF: 800-328-3911 ■ *Web:* www.efjohnson.com

Efk Group LLC 1027 S Clinton Ave ... Trenton NJ 08611 609-393-5838 196
Web: www.efkgroup.com

Efonica FZ-LLC
420 Lexington Ave Ste 518 ... New York NY 10170 212-214-0642 387
Web: www.efonica.com

EFP Corp 223 Middleton Run Rd ... Elkhart IN 46516 574-295-4690 604
TF: 800-205-8537 ■ *Web:* www.efpcorp.com

EFR (Employee & Family Resources Inc)
505 Fifth Ave Ste 600 ... Des Moines IA 50309 515-288-9020 631
Web: www.efr.org

EFTEC North America LLC
20219 Northline Rd ... Taylor MI 48180 248-585-2200 374-2050* 3
**Fax Area Code:* 734 ■ *TF:* 800-621-0684 ■ *Web:* www.eftec.ch

eFulgent Datawarehousing Solutions
3404 W Cheryl Dr Ste A290 ... Phoenix AZ 85051 602-439-5503 196
Web: www.efulgent.com

EFX Media 2300 S Ninth St Ste 136 ... Arlington VA 22204 703-486-2303 6
Web: www.efxmedia.com

EG Capital Group LLC 39 W 54th St ... New York NY 10019 212-956-2600 77
Web: www.egcapitalgroup.com

EG Fisher Public Library
1289 Ingleside Ave ... Athens TN 37303 423-745-7782 745-1763 434-3
TF: 800-552-6843 ■ *Web:* fisherlibrary.org

E-G Gasket & Supply Inc
1011 Sentry Dr ... Waukesha WI 53186 262-549-8300 326
Web: www.eg-gasket.com

EG Penner Building Centres
200 Park Rd W ... Steinbach MB R5G1A1 204-326-1325 290
TF: 800-353-8733 ■ *Web:* www.egpenner.com

EG Systems LLC 6200 Village Pkwy ... Dublin CA 94568 408-528-3000 528-3562 695
TF: 800-538-5124 ■ *Web:* www.electroglas.com

Phone Fax Class

Eg Tax Service
2475 Niagara Falls Blvd ... Buffalo NY 14228 716-632-7886 393
Web: www.egtax.com

EGA (Embroiderers Guild of America)
426 W Jefferson St ... Louisville KY 40202 502-589-6956 584-7900 48-18
TF: 800-272-0152 ■ *Web:* www.egausa.org

eGain Communications Corp
1252 Borregas Ave ... Mountain View CA 94043 408-636-4500 230-7600* 39
NASDAQ: EGAN ■ **Fax Area Code:* 650 ■ *TF:* 888-603-4246 ■ *Web:* www.egain.com

Egan Bernard & Co
1900 Old Dixie Hwy ... Fort Pierce FL 34946 800-327-6676 465-1181* 315-2
**Fax Area Code:* 772 ■ *TF:* 800-327-6676 ■ *Web:* www.dneworld.com

Egan Printing, Co 1245 Elati St ... Denver CO 80204 303-534-0171 627
Web: eganprinting.com

Egan Visual Inc 300 Hanlan Rd ... Woodbridge ON L4L3P6 905-851-2826 320
TF: 888-609-8886 ■ *Web:* www.egan.com

EGC Group Inc, The
1175 Walt Whitman Rd Ste 200 ... Melville NY 11747 516-935-4944 5
Web: www.egcgroup.com

Ege Seramik America Inc
1721 Oakbrook Dr Ste C ... Norcross GA 30093 678-291-0888 291-0832 751
Web: www.egeseramik-usa.com

Egen Solutions Inc
40 Shuman Blvd Ste 302 ... Naperville IL 60563 630-870-1935 196
Web: egen.solutions

Egenera Inc 80 Central St ... Boxborough MA 01719 978-206-6300 206-6436 176
TF: 866-301-3117 ■ *Web:* www.egenera.com

Egg Harbor Yachts Inc
801 Philadelphia Ave PO Box 702 ... Egg Harbor City NJ 08215 609-965-2300 965-3517 90
Web: www.eggharboryachts.com

Egg, The
Empire State Plaza Concourse Level
Performing Arts Ctr ... Albany NY 12220 518-473-1845 473-1848 572
Web: www.theegg.org

Egge Machine Company Inc
11707 Slauson Ave ... Santa Fe Springs CA 90670 562-945-3419 454
TF: 800-866-3443 ■ *Web:* www.egge.com

Eggelhof Inc 1999 Kolfahl St ... Houston TX 77023 713-923-2101 358
Web: www.eggelhof.com

EGGers Consulting Company Inc
11272 Elm St Eggers Plaza ... Omaha NE 68144 402-333-3480 193
Web: www.eggersconsulting.com

Eggers Industries Inc 1 Eggers Dr ... Two Rivers WI 54241 920-793-1351 793-2958 613
TF: 800-255-7874 ■ *Web:* www.eggersindustries.com

Egging Co, The 12145 Rd 38 ... Gurley NE 69141 308-884-2233 273
Web: www.egging.com

Eggleston Services 6431 Tidewater Dr ... Norfolk VA 23509 757-625-2311 317
Web: egglestonservices.org

Egizii Electric Inc (EEI)
700 N MacArthur Blvd ... Springfield IL 62702 217-528-4001 189-4

EGL Holdings
3495 Piedmont Rd 11 Piedmont Ctr Ste 412 ... Atlanta GA 30305 404-949-8300 949-8311 792
Web: www.eglholdings.com

EGL Resources Inc
508 W Wall St Ste 1250 ... Midland TX 79701 432-687-6560 682-5852 540

Egli Machine Company Inc
240 State Hwy 7 ... Sidney NY 13838 607-563-3021 608
Web: www.eglimachine.com

Eglin Air Force Base Eglin Blvd ... Eglin AFB FL 32542 850-882-3931 497-1
Web: www.eglin.af.mil

Eglin Federal Credit Union
838 Eglin Pkwy NE ... Fort Walton Beach FL 32547 850-862-0111 862-0111 219
TF: 800-367-6159 ■ *Web:* eglinfcu.org

EGM LLC 3748 Industrial Park Dr ... Mobile AL 36693 251-662-1250 273
Web: www.egm-llc.com

Egmont Key State Park
3900 Commonwealth Blvd ... Tallahassee FL 32399 727-893-2627 565
Web: www.floridastateparks.org

Egon Zehnder International Inc
1 N Wacker Dr Ste 2300 ... Chicago IL 60606 312-260-8800 782-2846 266
TF: 800-800-5567 ■ *Web:* www.egonzehnder.com

eGov Strategies LLC
101 W Ohio St Ste 2250 ... Indianapolis IN 46225 877-634-3468 225
TF: 877-634-3468 ■ *Web:* www.egovstrategies.com

EGPI Firecreek Inc
6564 Smoke Tree Ln ... Scottsdale AZ 85253 480-948-6581 787
Web: www.egpifirecreek.com

EGR Inc 601 N Miller Blvd ... Oklahoma City OK 73107 405-943-0900 115
Web: egronline.com

EGRMC (East Georgia Regional Medical Ctr)
1499 Fair Rd ... Statesboro GA 30458 912-486-1000 374-3
TF: 844-455-8708 ■ *Web:* www.eastgeorgiaregional.com

Egroup Inc 482 Wando Park Blvd ... Mount Pleasant SC 29464 843-284-0146 196
Web: www.egroup-us.com

EGT Printing Solutions LLC
32031 Townley St ... Madison Heights MI 48071 248 583 2500 627
Web: www.egprint.com

eGumBall Inc 8687 Research Dr Ste 200 ... Irvine CA 92618 800-890-8940 195
TF: 800-890-8940 ■ *Web:* www.egumball.com

EGW.com Inc 4075 Papazian Way ... Fremont CA 94538 510-668-0268 668-0280 637-9
TF Cust Svc: 800-546-4754

Egypt 304 E 44th St ... New York NY 10017 212-503-0300 784
Web: egyptembassy.net
Consulate General
500 N Michigan Ave Ste 1900 ... Chicago IL 60611 312-828-9162 828-9167 257
Web: egypt.embassy-online.net
Embassy 3521 International Ct NW ... Washington DC 20008 202-895-5400 244-4319 257
Web: www.egyptembassy.net

EgyptAir 19 W 44th St Ste 1701 ... New York NY 10036 212-581-5600 25
Web: egyptair.com

Egyptian Electric Co-op Assn
PO Box 38 ... Steeleville IL 62288 800-606-1505 245
TF: 800-606-1505 ■ *Web:* www.eeca.coop

Egyptian Tourist Authority
45 Rockefeller Plaza Ste 2305 ... New York NY 10111 212-332-2570 775
Web: www.egypt.travel

Egyptian Workspace Partner
129 W Main St ... Belleville IL 62220 618-234-2323 234-0693 535
TF Cust Svc: 800-642-3949 ■ *Web:* www.egyptian-stationers.com

Phone | Fax | Class

EH Ashley & Company Inc
1 White Squadron Rd ... Riverside RI 02915 401-431-0950 411
TF: 800-735-7424 ■ *Web:* ehashley.com

Eh Krohl Consulting Inc
3704 Duxford Dr ... Raleigh NC 27614 919-676-4801 196
Web: www.fdacompliance.com

E&h Steel Corp 3635 Alabama 134 ... Midland City AL 36350 334-983-5636 983-6173 723
Web: www.ehsteel.com

EH Wachs Co
600 Knightsbridge Pkwy ... Lincolnshire IL 60069 847-537-8800 520-1147* 455
**Fax:* Sales ■ *TF:* 800-323-8185 ■ *Web:* www.ehwachs.com

Eharmony.com Inc
2401 Colorado Ave Ste A200 ... Santa Monica CA 90404 626-795-4814 585-4040 226
Web: www.eharmony.com

EHD Technologies LLC
1600 Westgate Cir ... Brentwood TN 37027 615-953-1907 180
Web: www.ehdtech.com

eHDL Inc 3106 Commerce Pkwy ... Miramar FL 33025 954-331-6500 194
Web: www.ehdl.com

eHire LLC 3565 Piedmont Rd NE Ste 300 ... Atlanta GA 30305 404-477-2680 177
Web: www.ehire.com

Ehlers & Assoc Inc
3060 Centre Pointe Dr ... Roseville MN 55113 651-697-8500 194
TF: 800-552-1171 ■ *Web:* www.ehlers-inc.com

Ehob Inc 250 N Belmont Ave ... Indianapolis IN 46222 317-972-4600 972-4601 477
TF: 800-899-5553 ■ *Web:* www.ehob.com

Ehresmann Engineering Inc
4400 W 31St St ... Yankton SD 57078 605-665-7532 480
Web: www.ehresmannengineering.com

Ehrhardt Keefe Steiner & Hottman PC
7979 E Tufts Ave Ste 400 ... Denver CO 80237 303-740-9400 740-9009 2
Web: www.eksh.com

Ehrhardt Tool & Machine Co
25 Central Industrial Dr ... Granite City IL 62040 314-436-6900 757
TF: 877-386-7856 ■ *Web:* www.ehrhardttool.com

EHRI (Employer's Hum Res Inc)
75899 State Hwy 16 ... Wagoner OK 74467 918-485-9404 631

EHS Support Inc 110 Kentzel Rd ... Pittsburgh PA 15237 412-855-3047 192
Web: www.ehs-support.com

Ehs-International Inc
13228 NE 20th St Ste 100 ... Bellevue WA 98005 425-455-2959 192
Web: www.ehsintl.com

EHT International Inc
1340 Gay Lussac Ste 10 ... Boucherville QC J4B7G4 450-906-0705 407
Web: www.ehtinternational.com

Ehvert Mission Critical
200 Adelaide St W Ste 201 ... Toronto ON M5H1W7 416-868-1933 261
Web: www.ehvert.com

EI Electronics LLC 1800 Shames Dr ... Westbury NY 11590 516-334-0870 338-4741 37
TF: 877-346-3837 ■ *Web:* www.electroind.com

EI Group Inc, The
2101 Gateway Centre Blvd Ste 200 ... Morrisville NC 27560 919-657-7500 186
TF: 800-717-3472 ■ *Web:* www.ei1.com

EI Microcircuits Inc 1651 Pohl Rd ... Mankato MN 56001 507-345-5786 345-7559 625
TF: 800-713-4015 ■ *Web:* www.eimicro.com

EIA (Environmental Information Assn)
6935 Wisconsin Ave Ste 306 ... Chevy Chase MD 20815 301-961-4999 961-3094 48-13
TF: 888-343-4342 ■ *Web:* www.eia-usa.org

EICC Inc 5100 W 41st St ... Cicero IL 60804 708-496-1170 366
Web: www.eiccoalition.org

Eichelberger Performing Arts Ctr
195 Stock St Ste 203 ... Hanover PA 17331 717-632-9356 637-4504 572
Web: theeich.org

Eichelbergers Inc 107 Texaco Rd ... Mechanicsburg PA 17050 717-766-4800 317
TF: 800-371-3313 ■ *Web:* www.eichelbergers.com

Eichen & Di Meglio 1 Dupont St ... Plainview NY 11803 516-576-3333 2
Web: eanddcpa.com

Eichleay Engineers Inc of California
1390 Willow Pass Rd Ste 600 ... Concord CA 94520 925-689-7000 689-7006 261
Web: www.eichleay.com

Eico Inc 1054 Yosemite Dr ... Milpitas CA 95035 408-945-9898 201
Web: www.eico.net

Eid-Co Homes 1701 32nd Ave S ... Fargo ND 58103 701-237-0510 187
Web: www.eid-co.com

Eide Bailly LLP 4310 17th Ave S ... Fargo ND 58103 701-239-8500 239-8600 2
TF: 800-547-6747 ■ *Web:* www.eidebailly.com

Eide Industries Inc 16215 Piuma Ave ... Cerritos CA 90703 562-402-8335 924-2233 733
TF: 800-422-6827 ■ *Web:* www.eideindustries.com

Eidelman Virant Capital
8000 Maryland Ave Ste 380 ... Saint Louis MO 63105 314-727-9686 401
Web: www.eidelmanvirant.com

Eielson Air Force Base
354 Broadway St Unit 2B ... Eielson AFB AK 99702 907-377-1110 377-1606 497-1
TF: 800-538-6647 ■ *Web:* www.eielson.af.mil

Eifel Mold & Engineering
31071 Fraser Dr ... Fraser MI 48026 586-296-9640 604
Web: eifelmoldandengineering.com

Eiffel Tower Restaurant
3655 Las Vegas Blvd S ... Las Vegas NV 89109 702-948-6937 942-0004 671
Web: www.eiffeltowerrestaurant.com

Eigen Video
13366 Grass Vly Ave Ste A ... Grass Valley CA 95945 530-274-1240 250
TF: 888-924-2020 ■ *Web:* www.eigen.com

Eikos Inc 2 Master Dr ... Franklin MA 02038 508-528-0300 668
TF: 888-345-6712 ■ *Web:* www.eikos.com

Eileen Koch & Co
9350 Wilshire Blvd Ste 323 ... Beverly Hills CA 90212 310-441-1000 636
Web: www.eileenkoch.com

Eimo Americas 14320 Portage Rd ... Vicksburg MI 49097 269-649-0545 608
Web: www.eimo.com

Einhorn, Harris, Ascher, Barbarito & Frost PC
165 E Main St ... Denville NJ 07834 973-627-7300 428
Web: www.einhornharris.com

Einstein at Elkins Park
60 E Township Line Rd ... Elkins Park PA 19027 215-663-6000 374-3
Web: einstein.edu

Einstein HR Inc
3805 Crestwood Pkwy Ste 100 ... Duluth GA 30096 770-962-1700 631
TF: 800-447-3237 ■ *Web:* www.einsteinhr.com

Einstein Noah Restaurant Group Inc
555 Zang St Ste 300 ... Lakewood CO 80228 303-568-8000 670
TF: 000-732-0330 ■ *Web:* www.einsteinbros.com

Eire Direct Marketing
720 N Franklin St Ste 310 ... Chicago IL 60654 312-640-4000 195
Web: www.eiredirect.com

EIRMC (Eastern Idaho Regional Medical Ctr)
3100 Channing Way ... Idaho Falls ID 83404 208-529-6111 529-7021 374-3
Web: www.eirmc.com

EIS Electro Imaging Systems
6553 Las Positas Rd ... Livermore CA 94551 800-207-4757 535
TF: 800-207-4757 ■ *Web:* www.eisonline.net

Eisai Inc 100 Tice Blvd ... Woodcliff Lake NJ 07677 201-692-1100 692-1804 582
TF: 866-613-4724 ■ *Web:* www.eisai.com

Eisbrenner Public Relations
2950 W Sq Lake Rd Ste 100 ... Troy MI 48098 248-641-1446 636
TF: 800-520-1140 ■ *Web:* www.eisbrenner.com

Eisenbach Consulting LLC
921 Shiloh Rd B-300 ... Tyler TX 75703 800-977-4020 463
TF: 800-977-4020 ■ *Web:* www.eisenbachconsulting.com

Eisenberg Group AC CPAs, The
2260 Avenida De La Playa ... La Jolla CA 92037 858-551-5500 2

Eisenhauer Manufacturing Co, The
409 Center St ... Van Wert OH 45891 419-238-0081 488
Web: www.eisenhauermfg.com

Eisenhower Army Medical Ctr (DDAMC)
300 E Hospital Rd ... Fort Gordon GA 30905 706-787-5811 787-5342* 374-4
**Fax:* Admitting ■ *Web:* www.ddeamc.amedd.army.mil

Eisenhower Birthplace State Historic Site
609 S Lamar Ave ... Denison TX 75021 903-465-8908 565
Web: www.thc.texas.gov

Eisenhower Inn & Conference Ctr
2634 Emmitsburg Rd ... Gettysburg PA 17325 717-334-8121 379
Web: www.eisenhower.com

Eisenhower Medical Ctr
39000 Bob Hope Dr ... Rancho Mirage CA 92270 760-340-3911 374-3
Web: www.emc.org

Eisenhower National Historic Site
1195 Baltimore Pk Ste 100 ... Gettysburg PA 17325 717-338-9114 338-0821 564
Web: www.nps.gov

Eisenhower State Park
29810 S Fairlawn Rd ... Osage City KS 66523 785-528-4102 565
Web: ksoutdoors.com

Eisenhower State Park 50 Pk Rd 20 ... Denison TX 75020 903-465-1956 565
Web: tpwd.texas.gov/state-parks/eisenhower

Eisenmann Corp 150 E Dartmoor Dr ... Crystal Lake IL 60014 815-455-4100 455-1018 318
TF: 800-251-3049 ■ *Web:* www.eisenmann.com

Eisman & Russo Inc
6455 Powers Ave ... Jacksonville FL 32217 904-733-1478 636-8828 261
Web: eismanandrusso.com

Eisner & Maglione CPA'S LLC
66 Commack Rd Ste 201 ... Commack NY 11725 631-499-4039 2
Web: emcpallc.com

Eisner LLP 750 Third Ave ... New York NY 10017 212-949-8700 2
Web: www.eisneramper.com

EIT (Electronic Instrumentation & Technology Inc)
108 Carpenter Dr ... Sterling VA 20164 703-478-0700 478-0291 253
Web: www.eit.com

eIT Professionals Corp
42180 Ford Rd Ste 275 ... Canton MI 48187 734-416-0059 260
Web: www.eitprofessionals.com

Eiteljorg Museum of American Indians & Western Art
500 W Washington St ... Indianapolis IN 46204 317-636-9378 275-1400 520
Web: www.eiteljorg.org

Eizo Nanao Technologies Inc
5710 Warland Dr ... Cypress CA 90630 562-431-5011 431-4811 173-4
TF: 800-800-5202 ■ *Web:* www.eizo.com

EJ Basler Co 9511 Ainslie St ... Schiller Park IL 60176 847-678-8880 678-8896 621
Web: www.ejbasler.com

EJ Del Monte Corp 909 Linden Ave ... Rochester NY 14625 585-586-3121 379
Web: delmontehotelgroup.com

E-J Electric Installation Co
46-41 Vernon Blvd ... Long Island NY 11101 718-786-9400 937-9120 189-4
TF: 800-421-0389 ■ *Web:* www.ej1899.com

E-J Enterprises Inc
7280 Baltimore Annapolis Blvd ... Glen Burnie MD 21061 410-625-8200 492

EJ Group Inc 301 Spring St ... East Jordan MI 49727 231-536-2261 536-4486 307
TF: 800-874-4100 ■ *Web:* americas.ejco.com

EJ Thomas Performing Arts Hall
198 Hill St University of Akron ... Akron OH 44325 330-972-7570 572
TF: 800-745-3000 ■ *Web:* www.uakron.edu/ej

EJ Welch Company Inc
13735 Lakefront Dr ... Earth City MO 63045 314-739-2273 361
Web: www.ejwelch.com

Ejcon Corp 5502 Shawland Rd ... Jacksonville FL 32254 904-786-0622 480
TF: 800-366-8356 ■ *Web:* www.ejcon.com

EJGH (East Jefferson General Hospital)
4200 Houma Blvd ... Metairie LA 70006 504-454-4000 374-3
TF: 866-280-7737 ■ *Web:* www.ejgh.org

Ejh Construction Inc
30896 W 8 Mile Rd ... Farmington Hills MI 48336 248-478-1400 186
TF: 800-854-4534 ■ *Web:* ejhconstruction.com

EJM Development Co
9061 Santa Monica Blvd ... Los Angeles CA 90069 310-278-1830 278-2965 653
Web: www.ejmdevelopment.com

EJM Engineering Inc
411 S Wells St Ste 1000 ... Chicago IL 60607 312-922-1700 261
Web: www.ejmengineering.com

Ejq Home Health Care Inc
800 Middle Ave ... Elyria OH 44035 440-323-7004 363
Web: ejqhomehealthcare.com

E&K Companies 343 Carol Ln ... Elmhurst IL 60126 630-530-9001 189-9
TF: 800-365-5760 ■ *Web:* www.e-kco.com

Ekahau Inc
1851 Alexander Bell Dr Ste 300 ... Reston VA 20191 866-435-2428 387
TF: 866-435-2428 ■ *Web:* www.ekahau.com

Eklind Tool Comany Inc
11040 King St ... Franklin Park IL 60131 847-994-8550 350
Web: www.eklindtool.net

Phone | Fax | Class

Eklund's Appliance & TV Co
1007 Central Ave W Great Falls MT 59404 406-761-3430 35
Web: www.eklundsappliance.com
Eklunds Inc 2860 Market Loop Southlake TX 76092 817-949-2030 186
Web: www.eklunds.com
Ekm Metering Inc 363 Berkeley Way Santa Cruz CA 95062 831-425-7371 196
Web: www.ekmmetering.com
Ekmanian Tax & Acctg A Professional Corp
404 East Branch St Ste 210 Pismo Beach CA 93449 805-556-4512 2
Web: ekmanianpa.com
Ekornes Inc 615 Pierce St Somerset NJ 08873 732-302-0097 361
Web: www.ekornes.com
EKRiley Investments LLC
1420 Fifth Ave Ste 3300 Seattle WA 98101 206-832-1520 690
Web: www.ekriley.com
Ekuber Ventures Inc
8300 Boone blvd Ste 512 Fl 5 Vienna VA 22182 703-624-1473 180
Web: ekuber.com
El Ad US Holding Inc
575 Madison Ave 22nd Fl New York NY 10022 212-213-8833 157-6
Web: www.eladgroup.com
El Al Israel Airlines Inc
15 E 26th St New York NY 10010 212-852-0600 25
TF: 800-223-6700 ■ *Web:* www.elal.com/en/usa/pages/default.aspx
El Alamo 1708 S Chambers Rd Aurora CO 80017 720-535-5309 671
Web: elalamogrande.comcastbiz.net
El Basha 424 Belmont St Worcester MA 01604 508-797-0884 671
TF: 800-822-5456 ■ *Web:* www.elbasharestaurant.com
El Burrito 550 Piikoi St Honolulu HI 96814 808-596-8225 671
El Cajon Motors D/B/A El Cajon Ford
1595 E Main St El Cajon CA 92021 619-579-8888 57
Web: www.elcajonmotors.com
El Camino College
16007 Crenshaw Blvd Torrance CA 90506 310-532-3670 660-3818 162
TF: 866-352-2646 ■ *Web:* www.elcamino.edu
Compton Ctr 1111 E Artesia Blvd Compton CA 90221 310-900-1600 162
Web: www.compton.edu
El Camino Real 2500 W Sylvania Ave Toledo OH 43613 419-472-0700 671
Web: elcaminorealtoledo.com
El Camino Store, The 420 Athena Dr Athens GA 30601 706-546-9217 57
TF: 888-685-5987 ■ *Web:* www.elcaminostore.com
El Campo Independent School District
700 W Norris St El Campo TX 77437 979-543-6771 685
Web: www.ecisd.org
El Canelo 2709 W 12th St Erie PA 16505 814-835-2290 671
Web: elcanelo.net
El Capitan Fresh Mexican Grill
1800 S Milton Rd Ste 21 Flagstaff AZ 86001 928-774-1083 671
Web: www.elcapitanfmg.com
El Caribe Resort
2125 S Atlantic Ave Daytona Beach FL 32118 386-252-1558 707
TF: 800-445-9889 ■ *Web:* elcaribe.com
El Centro Chamber of Commerce & Visitors Bureau
1095 S Fourth St El Centro CA 92243 760-352-3681 352-3246 139
Web: www.elcentrochamber.org
El Centro College 801 Main St Dallas TX 75202 214-860-2037 860-2233* 162
**Fax:* Admissions ■ *Web:* elcentrocollege.edu
El Centro Elementary School District
1256 Broadway St El Centro CA 92243 760-352-5712 685
Web: www.ecesd.org
El Centro Foods Inc
6930 1/2 Tujunga Ave North Hollywood CA 91605 818-766-4395 670
El Centro Public Library
539 State St El Centro CA 92243 760-337-4565 352-1384 434-3
TF: 877-482-5656 ■ *Web:* www.cityofelcentro.org/library
El Centro Regional Medical Ctr
1415 Ross Ave El Centro CA 92243 760-339-7100 374-3
TF: 800-879-4484 ■ *Web:* www.ecrmc.org
El Cerro Grande 108 S Kings Hwy Myrtle Beach SC 29577 843-946-9562 671
El Charro Cafe 311 N Ct Ave Tucson AZ 85701 520-622-1922 671
Web: www.elcharrocafe.com
El Chico 8409 I-30 Little Rock AR 72209 501-562-3762 671
Web: elchico.com
El Chorro Lodge
5550 E Lincoln Dr Paradise Valley AZ 85253 480-948-5170 671
Web: www.elchorro.com
El Comedor 1120 25th St S Great Falls MT 59405 406-761-5500 671
El Con Mall 3601 E Broadway Blvd Tucson AZ 85716 520-795-9958 460
El Conquistador Resort & Golden Door Spa
1000 El Conquistador Ave Fajardo PR 00738 787-863-1000 863-6500 669
TF Resv: 888-543-1282 ■ *Web:* www.elconresort.com
El Corral 2201 E River Rd Tucson AZ 85718 520-299-6092 671
Web: elcorraltucson.com
El Cortez Hotel & Casino
600 E Fremont St Las Vegas NV 89101 702-385-5200 133
TF: 800-634-6703 ■ *Web:* www.elcortezhotelcasino.com
El Coyote 7404 State Rd Cincinnati OH 45230 513-232-5757 671
Web: www.elcoyotecincy.com
El Dorado & Wesson Railway Co
900 SW Ave El Dorado AR 71730 870-863-7100 648
El Dorado Correctional Facility
1737 SE Hwy 54 PO Box 311 El Dorado KS 67042 316-321-7284 322-2018 213
Web: www.dc.state.ks.us
El Dorado County 360 Fair Ln Placerville CA 95667 530-621-5490 621-2147 338
Web: edcgov.us
El Dorado County Chamber of Commerce
542 Main St Placerville CA 95667 530-621-5885 642-1624 139
TF: 800-457-6279 ■ *Web:* www.eldoradocounty.org
El Dorado County Library
345 Fair Ln Placerville CA 95667 530-621-5540 434-3
TF: 800-984-4636 ■ *Web:* www.eldoradolibrary.org
El Dorado Engineering Inc
9089 S 1300 W Ste 150 West Jordan UT 84088 801-966-8288 966-8499 261
Web: www.eldoradoengineering.com
El Dorado Furniture Corp
4200 NW 167th St Miami FL 33054 305-624-2400 321
TF: 888-451-7800 ■ *Web:* www.eldoradofurniture.com

Phone | Fax | Class

El Dorado Molds Inc
2691 Mercantile Dr Rancho Cordova CA 95742 916-635-4558 697
Web: www.eldoradomolds.com
El Dorado Nature Ctr
7550 E Spring St Long Beach CA 90815 562-570-1745 570-8530 50-5
TF: 800-662-8887 ■ *Web:* longbeach.gov
El Dorado Savings Bank
4040 El Dorado Rd Placerville CA 95667 530-622-1492 70
TF: 800-874-9779 ■ *Web:* www.eldoradosavingsbank.com
El Dorado State Park
618 NE Bluestem Rd El Dorado KS 67042 316-321-7180 565
Web: ksoutdoors.com/state-parks/locations/el-dorado
El Dorado Trading Group Inc
760 San Antonio Rd Palo Alto CA 94303 800-227-8292 494-1995* 112
**Fax Area Code:* 650 ■ *TF:* 800-227-8292 ■ *Web:* www.edtg.com
El Dorado Ventures
702 Oak Grove Ave Menlo Park CA 94025 650-854-1200 792
TF: 800-854-8127 ■ *Web:* www.eldorado.com
El Encanto Inc
2001 Fourth St SW PO Box 293 Albuquerque NM 87103 505-243-2722 296-36
TF: 800-888-7336 ■ *Web:* www.buenofoods.com
El Farol 808 Canyon Rd Santa Fe NM 87501 505-983-9912 671
Web: www.elfarolsantafe.com
El Fenix Corp
1845 Woodall Rodgers Ste 1100 Dallas TX 75201 972-241-2171 241-3031 670
TF: 877-591-1918 ■ *Web:* www.elfenix.com
El Gallo Giro 1442 S Bristol St Santa Ana CA 92704 714-549-2011 671
Web: gallogiro.com
El Gaucho 319 SW Broadway Portland OR 97205 503-227-8794 227-3412 671
Web: www.elgaucho.com
El Gaucho 2505 First Ave Seattle WA 98121 206-728-1337 671
Web: www.elgaucho.com
El Gaucho 2119 Pacific Ave Tacoma WA 98402 253-272-1510 671
Web: www.elgaucho.com
El Gaucho-Aqua
2801 Alaskan Way Pier 70 Seattle WA 98121 206-956-9171 671
Web: elgaucho.com
EL Harvey & Sons Inc
68 Hopkinton Rd Westborough MA 01581 508-836-3000 836-3040 804
TF: 800-321-3002 ■ *Web:* www.elharvey.com
El Huarache Azteca
3842 International Blvd Oakland CA 94601 510-533-2395 671
Web: elhuaracheazteca.net
El Loco Mexican Cafe 465 Madison Ave Albany NY 12210 518-436-1855 671
Web: ellocomexicancafe.com
El Loro 801 Volvo Pkwy Ste 114 Chesapeake VA 23320 757-436-3415 671
Web: www.elloromexican.com
El Maguey 3738 S Noland Rd Independence MO 64055 816-252-6868 671
El Malpais National Monument
123 E Roosevelt Ave Grants NM 87020 505-285-4641 285-5661 564
Web: www.nps.gov
El Mar Plastics Inc 967 Sandhill Ave Carson CA 90746 310-327-3180 327-0491 603
El Mariachi 144 Washington Ave Albany NY 12210 518-432-7580 671
Web: elmariachisrestaurant.com
El Matador 2564 Ogden Ave Ogden UT 84401 801-393-3151 671
TF: 800-651-2105 ■ *Web:* elmatadorogden.com
El Matador Foods Inc 7201 Bayway Dr Baytown TX 77520 281-424-4555 838-1375 345
TF: 800-470-2447 ■ *Web:* www.elmatadorfoods.com
El Metate Mercado
125 N Rancho Santiago Blvd Orange CA 92869 714-771-5527 345
TF: 800-966-5199 ■ *Web:* www.elmetate.com
El Mexicano 5801 Rue Ferrari San Jose CA 95138 800-858-1119 532-2
TF: 800-858-1119 ■ *Web:* elmexicano.net/mexicano_wordpress
El Mexicano Inn 1215 30th Ave Gulfport MS 39501 228-863-3691 671
El Mirador 722 S St Mary St San Antonio TX 78205 210-225-9444 671
Web: www.elmiradorsatx.com
El Mirasol Regional Cuisines of Mexico
140 E Palm Canyon Dr Palm Springs CA 92264 760-323-0721 671
TF: 800-273-1194 ■ *Web:* elmirasolrestaurants.com
El Monte City School District
3540 Lexington Ave El Monte CA 91731 626-453-3700 685
Web: web.emcsd.org
El Monte Union High School District
3537 Johnson Ave El Monte CA 91731 626-444-9005 448-8419 685
Web: www.emuhsd.org
El Monte/South El Monte Chamber of Commerce
10505 Valley Blvd Ste 312 El Monte CA 91731 626-443-0180 139
Web: www.emsem.biz
El Morro National Monument
HC 61 PO Box 237 Ramah NM 87321 505-783-4226 783-4689 564
Web: www.nps.gov
El Mundo 2345 Frankfort Ave Louisville KY 40206 502-899-9930 671
Web: www.502elmundo.com
El Museo Latino 4701 S 25th St Omaha NE 68107 402-731-1137 733-7012 520
TF: 800-745-3000 ■ *Web:* www.elmuseolatino.org
El Mustee & Sons Inc
5431 W 164th St Brook Park OH 44142 216-267-3100 612
Web: www.mustee.com
El Novillero 4216 Franklin Blvd Sacramento CA 95820 916-456-4287 456-4149 671
Web: www.elnov.com
El Novillo Restaurant
15450 New Barn Rd Miami Lakes FL 33014 305-819-2755 671
Web: www.elnovillorestaurant.com
El Nuevo Herald 3511 NW 91st Ave Doral FL 33172 305-376-3535 532-2
TF: 866-949-6722 ■ *Web:* www.elnuevoherald.com
El Observador Publications Inc
99 N First St Ste 100 San Jose CA 95113 408-938-1700 532-3
Web: www.el-observador.com
El Paso Cafe 4235 N Pershing Dr Arlington VA 22203 703-243-9811 671
Web: elpasocafeva.com
El Paso Centennial Museum and Chihuahuan Desert Gardens
University Avenue & Wiggins Rd El Paso TX 79968 915-747-5565 747-5411 520
Web: www.utep.edu
El Paso City Hall 2 Civic Ctr Plaza El Paso TX 79901 915-541-4000 541-4501 337
TF: 800-252-9600 ■ *Web:* www.elpasotexas.gov
El Paso Community College
Mission Del Paso 10700 Gateway E El Paso TX 79927 915-831-7017 162
Web: www.epcc.edu

				Phone	Fax	Class
Northwest 6701 S Desert Blvd	El Paso	TX	79932	915-831-8848		162
Web: www.epcc.edu						
Valle Verde 919 Hunter Dr	El Paso	TX	79915	915-831-2000	831-2161*	162
*Fax: Admissions ■ TF: 800-531-8292 ■ Web: www.epcc.edu						
El Paso Convention & Performing Arts Ctr						
1 Civic Ctr Plaza	El Paso	TX	79901	915-534-0600	534-0687	205
TF: 800-351-6024 ■ Web: www.visitelpaso.com						
El Paso County						
200 S Cascade Ave	Colorado Springs	CO	80903	719-520-6200	520-6212	338
TF: 800-772-1213 ■ Web: www.elpasoco.com						
El Paso County 500 E San Antonio Ave	El Paso	TX	79901	915-546-2000		338
El Paso Electric Co						
100 N Stanton Stanton Tower	El Paso	TX	79901	915-543-5711	521-4766	787
NYSE: EE ■ TF: 800-351-1621 ■ Web: www.epelectric.com						
El Paso First Health Plans Inc						
1145 Westmoreland Dr	El Paso	TX	79925	915-532-3778	532-2877	48-17
TF: 877-532-3778 ■ Web: www.epfirst.com						
El Paso Independent School District						
6531 Boeing Dr	El Paso	TX	79925	915-779-3781	779-4280*	685
*Fax: Hum Res ■ Web: episd.org						
El Paso International Airport						
6701 Convair Rd	El Paso	TX	79925	915-780-4749		27
TF: 800-288-1784 ■ Web: www.elpasointernationalairport.com						
El Paso Museum of Art						
1 Art Festival Plaza	El Paso	TX	79901	915-532-1707	532-1010	520
Web: www.elpasoartmuseum.org						
El Paso Museum of History						
510 Santa Fe St	El Paso	TX	79901	915-351-3588	351-4345	520
Web: elpasotexas.gov						
El Paso Public Library						
501 N Oregon St	El Paso	TX	79901	915-543-5433		435
Web: elpasolibrary.org						
El Paso Speedway Park						
3590 W Picacho	Las Cruces	TX	88007	915-791-8749		515
Web: www.epspeedwaypark.com						
El Paso Symphony Orchestra						
1 Civic Ctr Plaza	El Paso	TX	79901	915-532-3776	533-8162	573-3
TF: 800-745-3000 ■ Web: www.epso.org						
El Paso Times						
300 N Campbell St Times Plz	El Paso	TX	79901	915-546-6100	546-6415*	532-2
*Fax: News Rm ■ Web: www.elpasotimes.com						
El Paso Zoo 4001 E Paisano Dr	El Paso	TX	79905	915-521-1850	521-1857	823
TF: 800-222-1222 ■ Web: www.elpasozoo.org						
El Patio Restaurant						
37311 Fremont Blvd	Fremont	CA	94536	510-796-1733		671
TF: 800-854-3684 ■ Web: elpatiooriginaldining.com						
El Periodico u s a Inc 801 E Fir Ave	Mcallen	TX	78501	956-631-5628		532-3
TF: 800-667-1962 ■ Web: www.elperiodicousa.com						
El Pinto 10500 Fourth St NW	Albuquerque	NM	87114	505-898-1771	890-0498	671
Web: www.elpinto.com						
El Pollo Loco						
3535 Harbor Blvd Ste 100	Costa Mesa	CA	92626	714-599-5000		670
TF: 877-375-4968 ■ Web: www.elpolloloco.com						
El Pollo Rico 932 N Kennmore St	Arlington	VA	22201	703-522-3220		671
Web: elpolloricorestaurant.com						
El Ran Furniture Ltd						
2751 Transcanada Hwy	Pointe-Claire	QC	H9R1B4	514-630-5656		319-2
TF: 800 361 6546 ■ Web: www.elran.com						
El Ranchero 131 W Second St	Oxnard	CA	93030	805-486-5665		671
El Rancho 2747 16th Ave SW	Cedar Rapids	IA	52404	319-298-8844		671
El Rancho de las Golondrinas Museum						
334 Los Pinos Rd	Santa Fe	NM	87507	505-471-2261	471-5623	520
Web: www.golondrinas.org						
El Rancho Inc 2600 McCree Rd Ste 100	Garland	TX	75041	972-526-7300		345
Web: www.elranchoinc.com						
El Rancho Inn-Steak & Lobster						
1457 E Mariposa Rd	Stockton	CA	95205	209-467-1529		671
El Rancho Supermercado						
22291 Redwood Rd	Castro Valley	CA	94546	510-728-1945		297-8
El Rey Inn 1862 Cerillos Rd	Santa Fe	NM	87505	505-982-1931		379
Web: www.elreycourt.com						
El Rincon 1485 S Arlington St	Akron	OH	44306	330-785-3724		671
El Rincon Community Clinic						
3809 W Grand Ave	Chicago	IL	60651	773-276-0200		726
Web: www.rinconfamilyservices.org						
El Rinconcitos						
4025 Prescott St	Corpus Christi	TX	78416	361-851-8020		671
El Rodeo 4659 Jonestown Rd	Harrisburg	PA	17109	717-652-5340		671
Web: elrodeopa.com						
El Rodeo 3404 Westgate Dr	Durham	NC	27707	919-402-9190		671
Web: elrodeodurhamnc.com						
El Rosal 3430 Tully Rd	Modesto	CA	95350	209-523-7071		671
Consulate General						
3450 Wilshire Blvd Ste 250	Los Angeles	CA	90010	213-234-9200		257
Web: www.elsalvador.org						
Consulate General						
1400 16th St Ste 100	Washington	DC	20036	202-595-7500	232-3763	257
Web: www.elsalvador.org						
Embassy 1400 16th St NW Ste 100	Washington	DC	20036	202-595-7500	232-3763	257
Web: www.elsalvador.org						
El Sarape 4043 Martin Way E	Olympia	WA	98506	360-459-5525		671
Web: www.elsarape.net						
El Serrano 2151 Columbia Ave	Lancaster	PA	17603	717-397-6191		671
Web: www.elserrano.com						
El Sol 1448 Danforth Ave	Toronto	ON	M4J1N4	416-405-8074		671
Web: elsol.ca						
El Sol Y La Luna 600 E Sixth St	Austin	TX	78701	512-444-7770		671
Web: elsolylalunaaustin.com						
El Sombrero 157 S Franklin St	Juneau	AK	99801	907-586-6770	586-6772	671
Web: elsombrerojuneau.com						
El Taco de Mexico 714 Santa Fe Dr	Denver	CO	80204	303-623-3926		671
Web: eltacodemexicodenver.com						
El Tapatio Markets Inc						
13635 Fwy Dr	Santa Fe Springs	CA	90670	562-293-4200		297-8
Web: www.eltapatiomarkets.com						
El Tiempo Cantina 3130 Richmond Ave	Houston	TX	77098	713-807-1600		671
Web: www.eltiempocantina.com						
El Toreo Mexican Restaurants						
3790 Peter's Creek	Roanoke	VA	24018	540-342-7060		671
Web: eltoreoroanoke.com						
El Torito Restaurants Inc						
5660 Katella Ave Ste 100	Cypress	CA	90630	562-346-1200		670
Web: www.eltorito.com						
El Toro 2600 S 48th St	Lincoln	NE	68506	402-488-3939		671
Web: facebook.com						
El Tovar Hotel 1 El Tovar Rd	Grand Canyon	AZ	86023	928-638-2631		379
TF: 888-297-2757 ■ Web: www.grandcanyonlodges.com						
El Vaquero 2195 Riverside Dr	Columbus	OH	43221	614-486-4547	486-4050	671
Web: vaquerorestaurant.com						
El Vez 121 S 13th St	Philadelphia	PA	19107	215-928-9800		671
Web: www.elvezrestaurant.com						
El ZOL 106.7 FM 7007 NW 77th Ave	Miami	FL	33166	305-444-9292	883-7701	645-99
Web: elzol.lamusica.com						
Ela Area Public Library District						
275 Mohawk Trl	Lake Zurich	IL	60047	847-438-3433	438-9290	434-3
TF: 800-436-0709 ■ Web: www.eapl.org						
Elad National Properties LLC						
1301 International Pkwy Ste 200	Sunrise	FL	33323	954-846-7800		4
Elaine P Nunez Community College						
3710 Paris Rd	Chalmette	LA	70043	504-278-7497	278-7480	162
TF: 800-256-3000 ■ Web: www.nunez.edu						
Elam Construction Inc						
556 Struthers Ave	Grand Junction	CO	81501	970-242-5370		188-4
TF: 800-675-4598 ■ Web: www.elamconstruction.com						
Elan Chemical Co 268 Doremus Ave	Newark	NJ	07105	973-344-8014	344-8014	144
Web: www.elan-chemical.com						
Elan Construction Ltd						
3639-27 St NE Ste 100	Calgary	AB	T1Y5E4	403-291-1165		187
Web: www.elanconstruction.com						
Elan Financial Services						
225 W Sta Sq Dr Ste 620	Pittsburgh	PA	15219	877-935-2637		401
TF: 877-935-2637 ■ Web: www.elanfinancialservices.com						
Elan Hotel 8435 Beverly Blvd	Los Angeles	CA	90048	323-658-6663	658-6640	379
TF: 866-203-2212 ■ Web: www.greystonehotels.com						
Elan Technologies						
400 E Royal Lny Ste260	Irving	TX	75039	972-501-9021		196
Web: elantech.net						
Elan Technology 169 Elan Ct	Midway	GA	31320	912-880-3526		332
Web: www.elantechnology.com						
Elanco Animal Health						
2500 Innovation Way	Greenfield	IN	46140	317-276-2000		584
TF: 877-352-6261 ■ Web: www.elanco.com						
Elangeni Consulting Inc						
115 Rt 46 W Bldg B Ste 13	Mountain Lakes	NJ	07046	973-541-1667		180
Web: www.elangeni.com						
Elant Inc 46 Harriman Dr	Goshen	NY	10924	800-501-3936		390
TF: 800-501-3936 ■ Web: www.elant.org						
Elantas PDG Inc 5200 N Second St	Saint Louis	MO	63147	314-621-5700	436-1030	145
TF: 800-325-7492 ■ Web: www.elantas.com						
ElanTech Inc 7852 Walker Dr Ste 425	Greenbelt	MD	20770	301-480-0000		177
Web: www.elantech inc.com						
Elara Systems						
2880 Sunrise Blvd Ste 200	Rancho Cordova	CA	95742	916-638-1658		180
TF: 000-313-0104 ■ Web: www.elarasystems.com						
Elarbee , Thompson , Sapp & Wilson LLP						
800 International Tower 229 Peachtree St NE	Atlanta	GA	30303	404-659-6700		428
Web: www.elarbeethompson.com						
Elastec Inc 1309 W Main	Carmi	IL	62821	618-382-2525		539
Web: www.elastec.com						
Elastic Creative 550 Bryant St	San Francisco	CA	94107	415-495-5595		512
Elastic Fabrics of America						
3112 Pleasant Garden Rd	Greensboro	NC	27406	336-275-9401		745-4
Web: www.elasticfabrics.com						
Elastic Therapy Inc						
718 Industrial Park Ave	Asheboro	NC	27205	336-625-0529		156
Web: www.elastictherapy.com						
Elasticity LLC						
1008 Locust Ave Ste 300	St. Louis	MO	63101	314-561-8253		636
Web: goelastic.com						
Elat Chayyim 116 Johnson Rd	Falls Village	CT	06031	800-398-2630		673
TF: 800-398-2630 ■ Web: hazon.org/isabella-freedman						
Elavon 2 Concourse Pkwy Ste 300	Atlanta	GA	30328	678-731-5000		178-4
TF: 800-725-1243 ■ Web: www.elavon.com						
eLawMarketing						
25 Robert Pitt Dr Ste 209G	Monsey	NY	10952	866-833-6245		317
TF: 866-833-6245 ■ Web: www.elawmarketing.com						
Elbar Duplicator Corp						
10526 Jamaica Ave	Richmond Hill	NY	11418	718-441-1123		113
TF: 800-540-1123 ■ Web: www.edcbizsolutions.com						
Elbeco Inc 4418 Pottsville Pk	Reading	PA	19605	610-921-0651	921-8651	155-19
TF: 800-468-4654 ■ Web: www.elbeco.com						
Elbert County 215 Comanche St PO Box 7	Kiowa	CO	80117	303-621-2131	621-2343	338
Web: www.elbertcounty-co.gov						
Elbert County Board of Education						
50 Laurel Dr	Elberton	GA	30635	706-213-4000		685
Web: www.elbert.k12.ga.us						
Elbert County Chamber Of Commerce						
104 Heard St	Elberton	GA	30635	706-283-5651	283-5722	338
Web: www.elbertga.com						
Elberta Crate & Box Co						
606 Dothan Hwy	Bainbridge	GA	39818	229-246-2266	246-0387	200
Web: www.elberta.net						
Elbit Systems of America						
4700 Marine Creek Pkwy	Fort Worth	TX	76179	817-234-6600		24
Web: www.elbitsystems-us.com						
Elbow River Casino (ERC) 218 18th Ave SE	Calgary	AB	T2G1L1	403-289-8880		379
Web: elbowrivercasino.com						
Elbow River Marketing Ltd						
1500 335 Eighth Ave SW	Calgary	AB	T2P1C9	403-232-6868		536
Web: www.elbowriver.com						
ELC (English Language Ctr Inc)						
10850 Wilshire Blvd Ste 210	Los Angeles	CA	90024	617-536-9788		423
Web: www.elc.edu						
ELC Industries LLC						
1439 Dave Lyle Blvd Ste 16-C	Rock Hill	SC	29730	803-980-7600	980-7676	745-5
Web: ricebraid.com						

Name / Address	City	State	ZIP	Phone	Fax	Class
ELCA (Evangelical Lutheran Church in America) 8765 W Higgins Rd *TF:* 800-638-3522 ■ *Web:* www.elca.org	Chicago	IL	60631	773-380-2700	380-1465	48-20
ELCH (East Liverpool City Hospital) 425 W Fifth St. *Web:* www.elch.org	East Liverpool	OH	43920	330-385-7200		374-3
ELCO Chevrolet Cadillac 15110 Manchester Rd. *Web:* www.elcochevrolet.com	Ballwin	MO	63011	636-227-5333		57
Elco Corp 1000 Belt Line St *TF:* 800-321-0467 ■ *Web:* www.elcocorp.com	Cleveland	OH	44109	216-749-2605	749-7462	541
Elco Laboratories Inc 2450 Horner Ave. *Web:* elcolabs.com	University Park	IL	60484	708-534-3000		151
ELCO Mutual Life & Annuity 916 Sherwood Dr *TF:* 888-872-7954 ■ *Web:* www.elcomutual.com	Lake Bluff	IL	60044	847-295-6000		391-2
Elcom International Inc 50 Braintree Hill Pk. *OTC: ELCO*	Braintree	MA	02184	781-501-4000		178-1
ELCON (Electricity Consumers Resource Council) 1101 K St NW Ste 700 *Web:* www.elcon.org	Washington	DC	20005	202-682-1390	289-6370	48-12
Elcon Assoc Inc 12670 NW Barnes Rd *Web:* www.elcon.com	Portland	OR	97229	503-644-2490		256
ELCON Inc 600 Twin Rail Dr *Web:* www.elconinc.net	Minooka	IL	60447	815-467-9500		203
ElDeCo Inc 5751 Augusta Rd *TF:* 800-777-9695 ■ *Web:* www.eldecoinc.com	Greenville	SC	29605	864-277-9088	277-2811	189-4
Elder Research Inc 300 W Main Ste 301 *Web:* www.elderresearch.com	Charlottesville	VA	22903	434-973-7673		466
Eldercare Locator 1730 Rhode Island Ave NW Ste 1200 **Fax Area Code: 202* ■ *TF:* 800-677-1116 ■ *Web:* www.eldercare.gov	Washington	DC	20036	800-677-1116	872-0057*	197
Elderhostel Inc 11 Ave de Lafayette **Fax Area Code: 877* ■ *TF:* 800-454-5768 ■ *Web:* www.roadscholar.org	Boston	MA	02111	800-454-5768	426-2166*	48-23
Elder-Jones Inc 1120 E 80th St Ste 211 *Web:* www.elderjones.com	Minneapolis	MN	55420	952-854-2854	854-2703	186
Elderkin, Martin, Kelly & Messina PC 150 E Eighth St Fl 2 *Web:* www.elderkinlaw.com	Erie	PA	16501	814-456-4000		428
Elderlee Inc 729 Cross Rd. *Web:* www.elderlee.com	Oak Corners	NY	14518	315-789-6670		183
Elderly Instruments 1100 N Washington Ave *TF:* 888-473-5810 ■ *Web:* www.elderly.com	Lansing	MI	48906	517-372-7890	372-5155	526
ElderWood Senior Care 5271 Main St *TF:* 888-826-9663 ■ *Web:* www.elderwood.com	Williamsville	NY	14221	716-565-9663		451
Eldon Hazlet State Recreation Area 20100 Hazlet Pk Rd *Web:* www.dnr.illinois.gov/Parks/Pages/EldonHazlet.aspx	Carlyle	IL	62231	618-594-3015		565
Eldon James Corp 10325 E 47th Ave *Web:* www.eldonjames.com	Denver	CO	80238	970-667-2728		601
Eldor Contracting Corp 30 Corporate Dr *Web:* www.eldor.com	Holtsville	NY	11742	631-218-0010		186
Eldorado Canyon State Park 9 Kneale Rd *TF:* 866-265-6447 ■ *Web:* cpw.state.co.us	Eldorado Springs	CO	80025	303-494-3943	499-2729	565
Eldorado Gold Corp 550 Burrard St *NYSE: ELD* ■ *TF:* 888-353-8166 ■ *Web:* www.eldoradogold.com	Vanouver	BC	V6C2B5	604-687-4018	687-4026	502
Eldorado Grill 744 Williamson St *Web:* eldoradogrillmadison.com	Madison	WI	53703	608-280-9378		671
Eldorado Hotel 309 W San Francisco St *TF:* 800-955-4455 ■ *Web:* www.eldoradohotel.com	Santa Fe	NM	87501	505-988-4455		379
Eldorado Hotel Casino 345 N Virginia St. *TF Resv:* 800-879-8879 ■ *Web:* www.eldoradoreno.com	Reno	NV	89501	775-786-5700		379
Eldorado National 1655 Wall St. *Web:* www.enconline.com	Salina	KS	67401	785-827-1033		59
Eldorado Resort Casino Shreveport 451 Clyde Fant Pkwy *TF:* 877-602-0711 ■ *Web:* www.eldoradoshreveport.com	Shreveport	LA	71101	318-220-0711		133
Eldridge Hotel 701 Massachusetts St *TF:* 800-527-0909 ■ *Web:* www.eldridgehotel.com	Lawrence	KS	66044	785-749-5011	749-4512	379
Eldridge Products Inc 2700 Garden Rd Bldg A *TF:* 800-321-3569 ■ *Web:* www.epiflow.com	Monterey	CA	93940	831-648-7777		201
Eleanor Roosevelt National Historic Site 4097 Albany Post Rd *TF:* 800-337-8474 ■ *Web:* www.nps.gov/elro	Hyde Park	NY	12538	845-229-9115	229-0739	564
Eleanor Slater Hospital 14 Harrington Rd *TF:* 800-438-8477 ■ *Web:* www.bhddh.ri.gov	Cranston	RI	02920	401-462-2339	462-3204	374-7
eLease Funding Inc 2820 Firstst Ave N *TF:* 800-499-2577 ■ *Web:* elease.com	St. Petersburg	FL	33713	727-209-1200	209-1201	23
Elec Tron Inc 2050 Northern *Web:* www.elec-troninc.com	Wichita	KS	67216	316-522-3401		729
Elecraft Inc Po Box 69. *Web:* www.elecraft.com	Aptos	CA	95001	831-763-4211		246
Elecsys Corp 846 N Mart-Way Ct *NASDAQ: ESYS* ■ *Web:* www.elecsyscorp.com	Olathe	KS	66061	913-647-0158	647-0132	360-3
Election Data Corp 29751 Vly Ctr Rd *Web:* www.electiondata.com	Valley Center	CA	92082	760-751-1131	751-1141	801
Election Services Corp 70 Trade Zone Ct. *Web:* electionservicescorp.com	Ronkonkoma	NY	11779	516-248-4200	248-4770	801
Election Systems & Software Inc 11208 John Galt Blvd *TF General:* 877-377-8683 ■ *Web:* essvote.com	Omaha	NE	68137	402-593-0101	593-8107	801
Elections USA Inc 1927 E Saw Mill Rd *TF:* 800-789-8683 ■ *Web:* www.electionsusainc.com	Quakertown	PA	18951	215-538-0779	538-3283	801
Electra Bicycle Company LLC 3270 Corporate View Ste A. *Web:* www.electrabike.com	Vista	CA	92081	760-607-2453		711
Electralloy Corp 175 Main St *TF:* 800-458-7273 ■ *Web:* www.electralloy.com	Oil City	PA	16301	814-678-4100	678-4100	723
Electra-med Corp 5332 Hill 23 Dr *TF:* 800-678-4856 ■ *Web:* www.electramed.com	Flint	MI	48507	810-232-4856		475
Electrex Inc 6 N Walnut St. **Fax Area Code: 620* ■ *TF:* 800-319-3676 ■ *Web:* www.electrexinc.com	Hutchinson	KS	67501	800-319-3676	669-9988*	253
Electric Apparatus Co 409 Roosevelt St *Web:* www.elecapp.net	Howell	MI	48843	517-546-0520	546-0547	518
Electric Cable Compounds Inc 108 Rado Dr *Web:* www.electriccablecompounds.com	Naugatuck	CT	06770	203-723-2590		116
Electric City Printing Co 730 Hampton Rd. *TF:* 800-277-1920 ■ *Web:* www.ecprint.com	Williamston	SC	29697	864-224-6331		627
Electric City Trolley Station & Museum 300 Cliff St *TF:* 800-732-0999 ■ *Web:* www.ectma.org	Scranton	PA	18503	570-963-6590	963-6447	520
Electric Coating Technologies (ECT) 4407 Railroad Ave. *Web:* www.materialsciencescorp.com	East Chicago	IN	46312	219-378-1930	378-1933	481
Electric Cooperatives of South Carolina Inc, The 808 Knox Abbott Dr *TF:* 800-459-2141 ■ *Web:* www.ecsc.org	Cayce	SC	29033	803-796-6060		138
Electric Golf Car Co 6150 Auburn Blvd. *Web:* www.electricgolfcarcompany.com	North Highlands	CA	95621	916-721-0507	721-0508	516
Electric Heater Co 45 Seymour St *TF:* 800-647-3165 ■ *Web:* www.hubbellheaters.com	Stratford	CT	06615	203-378-2659	378-3593	36
Electric Heating Equipment Co 1240 Oronoque Rd	Milford	CT	06461	203-882-0199		318
Electric Machinery Company Inc 800 Central Ave NE. *Web:* www.electricmachinery.com	Minneapolis	MN	55413	612-378-8000		518
Electric Materials Co 50 S Washington St *TF:* 800-356-2211 ■ *Web:* www.elecmat.com	North East	PA	16428	814-725-9621	725-3620	308
Electric Motor & Contracting Co Inc 3703 Cook Blvd *Web:* www.emc-co.com	Chesapeake	VA	23323	757-487-2121	487-5983	518
Electric Motors & Specialties Inc 701 W King St PO Box 180. *TF:* 800-474-0520 ■ *Web:* www.emsmotors.com	Garrett	IN	46738	260-357-4141	357-3888	518
Electric Power Door 522 W 27th St. *TF:* 800-346-5760 ■ *Web:* www.electricpowerdoor.com	Hibbing	MN	55746	218-263-8366		234
Electric Power Supply Assn (EPSA) 1401 New York Ave NW 11th Fl *Web:* www.epsa.org	Washington	DC	20005	202-628-8200	628-8260	48-12
Electric Power Systems Inc 3305 Arctic Blvd Ste 201 *TF:* 800-315-6338 ■ *Web:* www.epsinc.com	Anchorage	AK	99503	907-522-1953		261
Electric Pulp Inc 4901 S Isabel Pl Ste 200 *Web:* electricpulp.com	Sioux Falls	SD	57108	605-988-0177		225
Electric Rain 3100 Carbon Pl Ste 102. *Web:* www.erain.com	Boulder	CO	80301	303-543-8233		225
Electric Regulator Corp 6189 El Camino Real *TF:* 800-458-6566 ■ *Web:* www.electricregulator.com	Carlsbad	CA	92009	760-438-7873	438-0437	203
Electric Research & Mfg Co-op Inc PO Box 1228 *TF:* 800-238-5587 ■ *Web:* www.ermco-eci.com	Dyersburg	TN	38025	731-285-9121		767
Electric Resource Contractors Inc 4024 Washington Ave N *Web:* eganco.com	Minneapolis	MN	55412	612-522-6511		189-4
Electric Supply & Equipment Co 1812 E Wendover Ave. *TF:* 800-632-0268 ■ *Web:* www.ese-co.com	Greensboro	NC	27405	336-272-4123	274-4632	246
Electric Supply Inc 4407 N Manhattan Ave *TF:* 800-678-1894 ■ *Web:* www.electricsupplyinc.com	Tampa	FL	33614	813-872-1894	874-1680	246
Electric Utility Week 2 Penn Plaza 25th Fl. *TF:* 800-752-8878 ■ *Web:* www.platts.com	New York	NY	10121	212-904-3070		531-5
Electrical & Electronics 3881 Danbury Rd *Web:* www.eecontrols.com	Brewster	NY	10509	914-769-5000		203
Electrical Apparatus Service Assn (EASA) 1331 Baur Blvd. *Web:* www.easa.com	Saint Louis	MO	63132	314-993-2220	993-1269	49-19
Electrical Consultants Inc 3521 Gabel Rd *Web:* www.electricalconsultantsinc.com	Billings	MT	59102	406-259-9933		256
Electrical Contractors Inc 3510 Main St *Web:* www.ecincorporated.com	Hartford	CT	06120	860-549-2822	549-7948	189-4
Electrical Corp of America 7320 Arlington Ave. *Web:* www.ecahq.com	Raytown	MO	64133	816-737-3206		189-4
Electrical Distributing Inc 4600 NW St Helens Rd *TF:* 800-877-4229 ■ *Web:* www.edinw.com	Portland	OR	97210	503-226-4044	226-4040	38
Electrical Wholesale Supply Company of Utah 158 East 4500 South *TF:* 800-433-5331 ■ *Web:* www.borderstates.com	Salt Lake City	UT	84107	801-268-2555	268-2555	246
Electricity Consumers Resource Council (ELCON) 1101 K St NW Ste 700 *Web:* www.elcon.org	Washington	DC	20005	202-682-1390	289-6370	48-12
Electri-Cord Mfg Co Inc 312 E Main St. *Web:* www.electri-cord.com	Westfield	PA	16950	814-367-2265	367-2314	815
Electri-Flex Co 222 Central Ave *TF:* 800-323-6174 ■ *Web:* www.electriflex.com	Roselle	IL	60172	630-529-2920	529-0482	816
Electrix Inc 45 Spring St *Web:* www.electrixillumination.com	New Haven	CT	06519	203-776-5577	624-7545	439

Phone Fax Class

Electro Adapter Inc
20640 Nordhoff St .... Chatsworth CA 91311 818-998-1198 815
Web: www.electro-adapter.com

Electro Brand Inc
1127 S Mannheim Rd Ste 305 .... Westchester IL 60154 708-338-4400 246
TF: 800-982-3954 ■ *Web:* www.electrobrand-usa.com

Electro Dynamics Crystal Corp
9075 Cody St .... Overland Park KS 66214 913-888-1750 246
Web: www.electrodynamics.com

Electro Enterprises Inc
3601 N I-35 Service Rd .... Oklahoma City OK 73111 405-427-6591 57
TF: 800-324-6591 ■ *Web:* www.electroenterprises.com

Electro Impulse Laboratory Inc
1805 Rte 33 PO Box 278 .... Neptune NJ 07753 732-776-5800 776-6793 14
Web: www.electroimpulse.com

Electro Industries Inc
2150 W River St .... Monticello MN 55362 763-295-4138 37
Web: www.electromn.com

Electro Miniatures Corp
68 W Commercial Ave .... Moonachie NJ 07074 201-460-0510 518
Web: www.electro-miniatures.com

Electro National Corp 511 Matthew Dr .... Canton MS 39046 601-859-5511 815
Web: www.electronational.com

Electro Optical Industries Inc
859 Ward Dr .... Santa Barbara CA 93111 805-964-6701 967-8590 201
Web: www.electro-optical.com

Electro Prime Group LLC
4510 Lint Ave Ste B .... Toledo OH 43612 419-476-0100 295
Web: www.electroprime.com

Electro Rent Corp
6060 Sepulveda Blvd .... Van Nuys CA 91411 818-787-2100 786-4354 264-1
NASDAQ: ELRC ■ *TF Sales:* 800-688-1111 ■ *Web:* www.electrorent.com

Electro Sales Inc 100 Fellsway W .... Somerville MA 02145 617-666-0500 518

Electro Scientific Industries Inc
13900 NW Science Pk Dr .... Portland OR 97229 503-641-4141 425
NASDAQ: ESIO ■ *TF Cust Svc:* 800-331-4708 ■ *Web:* esi.com

Electro Standards Laboratories Inc
36 Western Industrial Dr .... Cranston RI 02921 401-943-1164 735
TF: 877-943-1164 ■ *Web:* www.electrostandards.com

Electro Static Technology
31 Winterbrook Rd .... Mechanic Falls ME 04256 207-998-5140 639
TF: 866-738-1857 ■ *Web:* www.est-static.com

Electro Steam Generator Corp
50 Indel Ave PO Box 438 .... Rancocas NJ 08073 609-288-9071 288-9078 262
TF: 866-617-0764 ■ *Web:* www.electrosteam.com

ElectroChem Inc 400 W Cummings Pk .... Woburn MA 01801 781-938-5300 194
Web: www.fuelcell.com

Electrochemical Society
65 S Main St Bldg D .... Pennington NJ 08534 609-737-1902 737-2743 49-19
Web: www.electrochem.org

Electrocon International Inc
405 Little Lake Dr .... Ann Arbor MI 48103 734-761-8612 177
TF: 888-240-4044 ■ *Web:* www.electrocon.com

Electrocube Inc 3366 Pomona Blvd .... Pomona CA 91768 909-595-4037 253
TF: 800-515-1112 ■ *Web:* www.electrocube.com

Electrocut-Pacific
993 E San Carlos Ave .... San Carlos CA 94070 650-591-8718 358
Web: electrocutpacific.com

Electro-Flex Heat Inc
5 Northwood Rd .... Bloomfield CT 06002 860-242-6287 242-7298 357
TF: 800-585-4213 ■ *Web:* www.electroflexheat.com

Electro-General Plastics Corp of Columbus
6200 Enterprise Pkwy .... Grove City OH 43123 614-871-2915 596
Web: www.electro-generalplastics.com

Electroid Co 45 Fadem Rd .... Springfield NJ 07081 973-467-8100 467-2606 203
Web: www.electroid.com

Electroimpact Inc
4413 Chennault Beach Rd .... Mukilteo WA 98275 425-348-8090 21
Web: www.electroimpact.com

Electrol Specialties Co
441 Clark St .... South Beloit IL 61080 815-389-2291 389-2294 254
TF: 800-325-0256 ■ *Web:* www.esc4cip.com

Electroline Data Communications Inc
N779 Communication Dr .... Appleton WI 54912 920-733-0303 196
Web: www.edci.com

Electrolux Appliances PO Box 212237 .... Augusta GA 30907 877-435-3287 36
TF: 877-435-3287 ■ *Web:* www.electroluxappliances.com

Electrolux Home Care Products Inc
PO Box 3900 .... Peoria IL 61612 800-282-2886 788
TF Cust Svc: 800-282-2886 ■ *Web:* www.eureka.com

Electro-Magnetic Products Inc
355 Crider Ave .... Moorestown NJ 08057 856-235-3011 722-0566 757
Web: www.empmags.com

Electro-Matic Products Co
2235 N Knox Ave .... Chicago IL 60639 773-235-4010 235-7317 203
Web: www.em-chicago.com

Electro-Matic Products Inc
23409 Industrial Pk Ct .... Farmington Hills MI 48335 248-478-1182 478-1472 246
TF: 888-879-1088 ■ *Web:* www.electro-matic.com

Electromech Technologies Inc
2600 S Custer .... Wichita KS 67217 316-941-0400 22
Web: www.electromech.com

Electro-Mechanical Corp 1 Goodson St .... Bristol VA 24201 276-669-4084 669-1869 253
Web: www.electro-mechanical.com

Electromek Diagnostic Systems Inc
412 W US Hwy 40 .... Troy IL 62294 618-667-6761 475
TF: 800-466-6761 ■ *Web:* www.electromek.com

Electromet Corp
879 Commonwealth Ave .... Hagerstown MD 21740 301-797-5900 697
Web: www.electromet.com

Electro-Methods Inc
330 Governors Hwy .... South Windsor CT 06074 860-289-8661 21
Web: electro-methods.com

Electro-Metrics Corp
231 Enterprise Rd .... Johnstown NY 12095 518-762-2600 762-2812 248
Web: www.electro-metrics.com

Electro-Motive Diesel Inc
9301 W 55th St .... La Grange IL 60525 708-387-6000 387-6626 650
TF: 800-255-5355 ■ *Web:* www.emdiesels.com

Electron Beam Technologies Inc
1275 Harvard Dr .... Kankakee IL 60901 815-935-2211 811
Web: www.electronbeam.com

Electron Energy Corp
924 Links Ave .... Landisville PA 17538 717-898-2294 898-0660 458
TF: 800-824-2735 ■ *Web:* www.electronenergy.com

Electronic Arts Inc (EA)
209 Redwood Shores Pkwy .... Redwood City CA 94065 650-628-1500 178-6
NASDAQ: EA ■ *Web:* www.ea.com

Electronic Cash Systems Inc (ECS)
29883 Santa Margarita Pkwy .... Rancho Santa Margarita CA 92688 949-888-8580 888-8024 56
TF: 888-327-2860 ■ *Web:* www.ecspayments.com

Electronic Commerce & Law Report
1801 S Bell St .... Arlington VA 22202 800-372-1033 531-1
TF: 800-372-1033 ■ *Web:* www.bna.com/electronic-commerce-law-p6796

Electronic Component News
100 Enterprise Dr Ste 600 .... Rockaway NJ 07866 973-920-7000 607-5488 457-21
Web: www.ecnmag.com

Electronic Contracting Co
6501 N 70th St .... Lincoln NE 68507 402-466-8274 466-0819 189-4
TF: 800-366-5320 ■ *Web:* www.eccoinc.com

Electronic Education Report
11200 Rockville Pk Ste 504 .... Rockville MD 20852 240-747-3096 747-3004* 531-4
**Fax:* Sales ■ *Web:* simbainformation.com

Electronic Entertainment Design & Research Inc
2075 Corte Del Nogal Ste B .... Carlsbad CA 92011 760-579-7100 401
Web: www.eedar.com

Electronic Environments Corp
410 Forest St .... Marlborough MA 01752 508-229-1400 303-0579 174
TF: 800-342-5332 ■ *Web:* www.eecnet.com

Electronic Frontier Foundation Inc (EFF)
454 Shotwell St .... San Francisco CA 94110 415-436-9333 436-9993 48-9
Web: www.eff.org

Electronic Information Report
11200 Rockville Pk Ste 504 .... Rockville MD 20852 240-747-3096 747-3004 531-3
Web: simbainformation.com

Electronic Instrumentation & Technology Inc (EIT)
108 Carpenter Dr .... Sterling VA 20164 703-478-0700 478-0291 253
Web: www.eit.com

Electronic Privacy Information Ctr (EPIC)
1718 Connecticut Ave NW Ste 200 .... Washington DC 20009 202-483-1140 483-1248 48-9
TF: 800-838-6554 ■ *Web:* www.epic.org

Electronic Security Assn Inc (ESA)
2300 Vly View Ln Ste 230 .... Irving TX 75062 214-260-5970 260-5979 49-3
TF: 888-447-1689 ■ *Web:* www.esaweb.org

Electronic Systems Packaging LLC (ESP)
1175 W Victoria St .... Rancho Dominguez CA 90220 310-639-2535 632-6666 815
Web: www.espbus.com

Electronic Systems Technology Inc
415 N Quay St Bldg B-1 .... Kennewick WA 99336 509-735-9092 783-5475 173-3
OTC: ELST ■ *Web:* www.estcom.com

Electronic Tele-Communications Inc
1915 MacArthur Rd .... Waukesha WI 53188 262-542-5600 542-1524 736
OTC: ETCIA ■ *TF:* 888-746-4382 ■ *Web:* www.etcia.com

Electronic Theatre Controls Inc
3031 Pleasantview Rd .... Middleton WI 53562 608-831-4116 836-1736 203
TF: 800-688-4116 ■ *Web:* www.etcconnect.com

Electronic Transactions Association, The
1101 16th St NW Ste 402 .... Washington DC 20036 202-828-2635 138
TF: 800-695-5509 ■ *Web:* www.electran.org

Electronic Warfare Assoc Inc (EWA Inc)
13873 Pk Ctr Rd Ste 500 .... Herndon VA 20171 703-904-5700 904-5779 180
TF General: 888-392-0002 ■ *Web:* www.ewa.com

Electronics for Imaging Inc
6750 Dumbarton Cir .... Fremont CA 94555 650-357-3500 357-3907 176
NASDAQ: EFII ■ *TF:* 888-334-8650 ■ *Web:* w3.efi.com

Electronics Representatives Assn (ERA)
1325 S Arlington Heights Rd
Ste 204 .... Elk Grove Village IL 60007 312-419-1432 419-1660 49-18
Web: www.era.org

Electronics Research 7777 Gardner Rd .... Chandler IN 47610 812-925-6000 647
Web: www.vwerl.com

Electronics Technicians Assn International (ETA)
5 Depot St .... Greencastle IN 46135 765-653-8262 653-4287 49-19
TF: 800-288-3824 ■ *Web:* www.eta-i.org

Electronique Mercier Ltee
162 Rue Fraser .... Riviere-du-loup QC G5R1C8 418-862-7269 736
Web: www.emercier.com

Electro-optical Imaging Inc
4300 Fortune Pl Ste C .... West Melbourne FL 32904 321-435-8722 544
Web: www.eoimaging.com

Electropac Company Inc
252 Willow St .... Manchester NH 03103 603-622-3711 625
TF: 800-400-5568 ■ *Web:* www.electropac.com

Electro-Petroleum Inc 8 Wistar Rd .... Villanova PA 19085 484-380-3456 538
Web: electropetroleum.com

Electro-Sensors Inc
6111 Blue Cir Dr .... Minnetonka MN 55343 952-930-0100 930-0130 495
NASDAQ: ELSE ■ *TF:* 800-328-6170 ■ *Web:* www.electro-sensors.com

Electrosonics 17150 15 Mile Rd .... Fraser MI 48026 586-415-5555 175
TF: 800-858-8448 ■ *Web:* www.electrosonics.net

Electro-Space Fabricators Inc
300 W High St .... Topton PA 19562 610-682-7181 697
Web: www.esfinc.com

Electro-spec Inc 1800 Commerce Pkwy .... Franklin IN 46131 317-738-9199 481
Web: www.electro-spec.com

Electrosteel USA LLC
270 Doug Baker Blvd .... Birmingham AL 35242 205-516-8154 492
Web: www.electrosteelusa.com

Electroswitch 2010 Yonkers Rd .... Raleigh NC 27604 919-833-0707 833-8016 815
TF: 888-768-2797 ■ *Web:* www.electro-nc.com

Electroswitch Corp 180 King Ave .... Weymouth MA 02188 781-335-5200 335-4253 729
TF: 800-572-0479 ■ *Web:* www.electroswitch.com

ElectroTech Inc
7101 Madison Ave W .... Minneapolis MN 55427 763-544-4288 246
TF: 800-544-4288 ■ *Web:* www.electrotech-inc.com

Electro-Tech Machining
2000 W Gaylord St .... Long Beach CA 90813 562-436-9281 436-9281 454
Web: www.etmgraphite.com

Name / Address	City	State	ZIP	Phone	Fax	Class
Electrovaya Inc 2645 Royal Windsor Dr *TSE:* EFL ■ *TF:* 800-388-2865 ■ *Web:* www.electrovaya.com	Mississauga	ON	L5J1K9	905-855-4610	822-7953	173-2
Electroworld Security Systems 867 E 26th St	Brooklyn	NY	11210	718-338-5831		693
ElectSolve Technology Solutions & Services Inc 4300 Youree Dr Bldg 1 Ste 520 *Web:* www.electsolve.com	Shreveport	LA	71105	318-221-2055		179
Elegant Illusions Inc 542 Lighthouse Ave Ste 5 *Web:* www.elegant-illusions.com	Pacific Grove	CA	93950	831-649-1814	649-1001	410
Elegant Voyages 1802 Keesling Ct *TF:* 800-555-3534 ■ *Web:* www.elegantvoyages.com	San Jose	CA	95125	408-239-0300	239-0304	771
Elektrisola Inc 126 High St *TF:* 800-325-2022 ■ *Web:* www.elektrisola.com	Boscawen	NH	03303	603-796-2114		813
Elektro Assemblies Inc 5140 Moundview Dr *TF:* 800-533-1558 ■ *Web:* elektroassemblies.com	Rochester	MN	55066	800-533-1558		743
Elemco Software Integration Group Ltd 245 Atlantic St *TF:* 800-978-3417 ■ *Web:* www.elemcosoftware.com	Central Islip	NY	11722	631-234-3099		180
Element Materials Technology 5405 E Schaaf Rd *TF:* 800-662-8378 ■ *Web:* www.element.com	Cleveland	OH	44131	216-524-1450	524-1459	743
Element Productions Inc 316 Stuart St 4th Fl *TF:* 800-690-0784 ■ *Web:* element.cc	Boston	MA	02116	617-779-8808		514
Elementa Group Inc 509 Glendale Ave E Ste 302	Niagara-on-the-lake	ON	L0S1J0	905-687-1900		580
Elementis Specialties Inc 469 Old Trenton Rd **Fax Area Code:* 609 ■ *TF:* 800-866-6800 ■ *Web:* www.elementis.com	East Windsor	NJ	08512	800-866-6800	443-2422*	143
Elementis Specialties Inc 329 Wyckoffs Mill Rd *Web:* www.elementis-specialties.com	Hightstown	NJ	08520	609-443-2000	443-2422	364
Elementum Solutions 2540 New Butler Rd *Web:* www.elementumsolutions.com	New Castle	PA	16101	724-656-8837		175
Elenbaas Co 421 Birch Bay Lynden Rd *TF:* 800-808-6954 ■ *Web:* www.elenbaasco.com	Lynden	WA	98264	360-354-3577		447
Elenco Electronics Inc 150 W Carpenter Ave *TF:* 800-533-2441 ■ *Web:* www.elenco.com	Wheeling	IL	60090	847-541-3800		242
Eleni's 205 E 42nd St **Fax Area Code:* 800 ■ *TF:* 888-435-3647 ■ *Web:* www.elenis.com	New York	NY	10017	888-435-3647	306-2101*	68
Elephant & Castle/Delta Winnipeg Hotel 350 St Mary Ave *Web:* www.elephantcastle.com	Winnipeg	MB	R3C3J2	204-942-5555		671
Elephant Bar Restaurant 10100 Stockdale Hwy *Web:* www.elephantbar.com	Bakersfield	CA	93311	661-663-3020		670
Elephant Productions Inc 3404 Guadalupe St *Web:* www.changs.com	Austin	TX	78705	512-302-3130		514
Elephant Ventures LLC 259 W 30th St Ste 403 **Fax Area Code:* 917 ■ *Web:* www.elephantventures.com	New York	NY	10001	212-730-6710	591-2809*	396
Elephant Walk 2067 Massachusetts Ave *Web:* elephantwalk.com/cambridge-directions	Cambridge	MA	02140	617-492-6900		671
Elerick & Elerick PA 265 N Wymore Rd *Web:* elerickandelerick.com	Winter Park	FL	32789	407-629-9995		2
Elert & Associates Telecommunications Consultants Inc 140 Third St S *TF:* 800-626-6234 ■ *Web:* www.elert.com	Stillwater	MN	55082	651-430-2772		449
Elevate Group Holdings LLC 615 Regal Row *Web:* www.elevate-group.com	Dallas	TX	75247	214-951-9502		4
Elevating Boats LLC 201 Dean Ct *TF:* 800-843-2895 ■ *Web:* www.ebi-inc.com	Houma	LA	70363	985-868-9655	868-9656	698
Elevation 905 Bernina Ave *Web:* thisiselevation.com	Atlanta	GA	30307	404-221-1705		512
Elevation B2B Marketing 1955 S Val Vista Dr Ste 101 *TF:* 800-456-0707 ■ *Web:* www.canyoncomm.com	Mesa	AZ	85204	480-775-8880		4
Elevation Ltd 1027 33rd St NW Ste 260 *Web:* www.elevation-us.com	Washington	DC	20007	202-380-3230		738
Elevation Resources LLC 200 N Loraine Ste 1010 *TF:* 800-270-7007 ■ *Web:* www.elevationres.com	Midland	TX	79701	432-686-7500		536
Elevator Doors Inc 15 Jane St *Web:* www.edi-eci.com	Paterson	NJ	07522	973-790-9100		234
Elevator Equipment Corp 4035 Goodwin Ave *TF:* 888-577-3326 ■ *Web:* www.elevatorequipment.com	Los Angeles	CA	90039	323-245-0147	245-9771	256
Elevator Research & Manufacturing Corp 1417 Elwood St *TF:* 800-252-1910 ■ *Web:* www.elevatorresearch.com	Los Angeles	CA	90021	213-746-1914		256
Eleven 1150 Smallman St *Web:* www.bigburrito.com	Pittsburgh	PA	15222	412-201-5656	201-5655	671
Eleven Engineering Inc 10150 - 100 St Ste 900 *Web:* elevenengineering.com	Edmonton	AB	T5J0P6	780-425-6511		256
Eleven Inc 445 Bush St *TF:* 800-438-7325 ■ *Web:* www.eleveninc.com	San Francisco	CA	94108	415-707-1111		7
Eleven Mile State Park 4229 County Rd 92 *Web:* cpw.state.co.us	Lake George	CO	80827	719-748-3401		565
Eleven Mile State Park c/o Eleven Mile State Pk 4229 County Rd 92 *Web:* cpw.state.co.us/placestogo/Parks/ElevenMile	Lake George	CO	80827	719-748-3401		565
Eleven South 216 11th Ave S *Web:* www.elevensouth.com	Jacksonville Beach	FL	32250	904-241-1112		671
Eleven Twenty Ltd 3700 Fairway Dr *Web:* www.eleventwenty.com	Woodbury	MN	55125	651-797-3070		463
Eleven Western Builders Inc 2862 Executive Pl *Web:* www.ewbinc.com	Escondido	CA	92029	760-796-6346		186
Eleven Wireless Inc 315 SW 11th Ave 3rd Fl *Web:* www.elevenwireless.com	Portland	OR	97205	503-222-4321		174
Elexco Land Service Inc 505 W Henley St *Web:* www.elexco.com	Olean	NY	14760	716-372-0788		538
ELFA (Equipment Leasing & Finance Assn) 1825 K St NW Ste 900 *Web:* www.elfaonline.org	Washington	DC	20006	202-238-3400	238-3401	49-18
Elfenworks Foundation 20 park rd *Web:* elfenworks.org	Burlingame	CA	94010	650-347-9700		305
Elfreth's Alley Museum 126 Elfreth's Alley *Web:* www.elfrethsalley.org	Philadelphia	PA	19106	215-574-0560		520
ELG Metals Inc 369 River Rd *Web:* www.elg.de	McKeesport	PA	15132	412-672-9200	672-0824	686
Elge Inc 1000 Cole Ave *Web:* www.elgeinc.com	Rosenberg	TX	77471	281-342-8228		479
Elgie Bus Lines Ltd 5137 Cobble Hills Rd *Web:* www.elgiebuslines.com	Thamesford	ON	N0M2M0	519-461-1227		108
Elgiloy Specialty Metals Ltd 1565 Fleetwood Dr *Web:* www.elgiloy.com	Elgin	IL	60123	847-695-1900		350
Elgin Academy 350 Park St *TF:* 800-276-2600 ■ *Web:* www.elginacademy.org	Elgin	IL	60120	847-695-0300		148
Elgin Area Chamber of Commerce 31 S Grove Ave *TF:* 800-621-3362 ■ *Web:* www.elginchamber.com	Elgin	IL	60120	847-741-5660	741-5677	139
Elgin Area Convention & Visitors Bureau 60 S Grove Ave *TF:* 800-217-5362 ■ *Web:* www.northernfoxrivervalley.com	Elgin	IL	60120	847-695-7540	695-7668	206
Elgin Community College 1700 Spartan Dr **Fax:* Admissions ■ *TF:* 855-850-2525 ■ *Web:* www.elgin.edu	Elgin	IL	60123	847-697-1000	608-5458*	162
Elgin Fastener Group 4 S Pk Ave Ste 203 *Web:* www.elginfasteners.com	Batesville	IN	47006	812-689-8917	689-6635	278
Elgin Industries Inc 1100 Jansen Farm Dr *Web:* www.elginind.com	Elgin	IL	60123	847-742-1720		247
Elgin Mental Health Ctr 750 S State St	Elgin	IL	60123	847-742-1040		374-5
Elgin Molded Plastics 909 Grace St **Fax Area Code:* 800 ■ *TF:* 800-548-5483 ■ *Web:* www.elginmolded.com	Elgin	IL	60120	847-931-2455	524-0087*	604
Elgin National Industries Inc 2001 Butterfield Rd *Web:* www.elginindustries.com	Downers Grove	IL	60515	630-434-7200	434-7272	190
Elgin Sweeper Co 1300 W Bartlett Rd *Web:* www.elginsweeper.com	Elgin	IL	60120	847-741-5370	742-3035	516
Elgin-Butler Brick Co 2601 McHale Crt *Web:* www.elginbutler.com	Austin	TX	78758	512-453-7366		150
ELI (Environmental Law Institute) 2000 L St NW Ste 620 *TF:* 800-433-5120 ■ *Web:* www.eli.org	Washington	DC	20036	202-939-3800	939-3868	49-10
ELI Inc 2675 Paces Ferry Rd SE Ste 470 *TF:* 800-497-7654 ■ *Web:* www.eliinc.com	Atlanta	GA	30339	770-319-7999		196
Eli Lilly & Co Lilly Corporate Ctr *NYSE:* LLY ■ *TF Prod Info:* 800-545-5979 ■ *Web:* www.lilly.com	Indianapolis	IN	46285	317-276-2000		582
Eli Lilly Canada Inc 3650 Danforth Ave **Fax:* Hum Res ■ *TF:* 888-545-5972 ■ *Web:* www.lilly.ca	Toronto	ON	M1N2E8	416-694-3221	699-7252*	582
Eli Whitney Museum 915 Whitney Ave *Web:* www.eliwhitney.org	Hamden	CT	06517	203-777-1833	777-1229	520
Eli's Cheesecake Co 6701 W Forest Preserve Dr *TF:* 800-999-8300 ■ *Web:* www.elicheesecake.com	Chicago	IL	60634	773-736-3417	205-3801	296-2
Elia 8611 Third Ave *Web:* www.eliarestaurant.com/elia	Brooklyn	NY	11209	718-748-9891		671
Elias Industries Inc 605 Epsilon Dr *TF:* 800-223-1067 ■ *Web:* tapcogenuinepartscenter.com	Pittsburgh	PA	15238	412-782-4300		609
Elias Matz Tiernan & Herrick The Walker Bldg 734 15th St NW 11th Fl	Washington	DC	20005	202-347-0300		445
Elias Sports Bureau Inc 500 Fifth Ave *Web:* www.esb.com	New York	NY	10110	212-869-1530		530
Elias Wilf Corp 10234 S Dolfield Rd *TF:* 800-289-6142 ■ *Web:* www.flooryou.com	Owings Mills	MD	21117	410-363-2400		290
Eliason Corp 9229 Shaver Rd *TF Cust Svc:* 800-828-3655 ■ *Web:* www.eliasoncorp.com	Portage	MI	49024	269-327-7003	327-7006	664
Eliassen Group LLC 30 Audubon Rd *TF:* 800-354-2773 ■ *Web:* www.eliassen.com	Wakefield	MA	01880	800-354-2773		260
Elijah Clark State Park 2959 McCormick Hwy *Web:* www.gastateparks.org	Lincolnton	GA	30817	706-359-3458		565
Elim Christian School 13020 S Central Ave *TF:* 877-935-4627 ■ *Web:* www.elimcs.org	Palos Heights	IL	60463	708-389-0555		685
Elim Park Place 140 Cook Hill Rd *TF:* 800-994-1776 ■ *Web:* www.elimpark.org	Cheshire	CT	06410	203-272-3547		672
Elimetal Inc 1515 Boul Pitfield *Web:* elimetal.com	St Laurent	QC	H4S1G3	514-956-7400	956-8110	697
eLine Technology 1070 W 124th Ave Ste B-100 *Web:* elinetechnology.com	Westminster	CO	80234	303-938-1133		693
Elinor Bedell State Park c/o Gull Pt State Pk 1500 Harpen St *Web:* www.iowabeautiful.com	Milford	IA	51351	712-337-3211		565
Elinvar Corp 1804 Hillsborough St *Web:* www.elinvar.com	Raleigh	NC	27605	919-622-5141		721
Eliot Hotel, The 370 Commonwealth Ave *TF:* 800-443-5468 ■ *Web:* www.eliothotel.com	Boston	MA	02215	617-267-1607	536-9114	379
Eliot Rose Asset Management LLC 1000 Chapel View Blvd Ste 240 *TF:* 866-585-5100 ■ *Web:* www.eliotrose.com	Cranston	RI	02920	401-588-5100		401

				Phone	Fax	Class
Elisa Act Biotechnologies 109 Carpenter Dr *TF:* 800-553-5472 ■ *Web:* www.elisaact.com	Sterling	VA	20165	800-553-5472		415
Elisabet Ney Museum 304 E 44th St *TF:* 800-680-7289 ■ *Web:* www.ci.austin.tx.us	Austin	TX	78751	512-458-2255		520
Elisabeth Morrow School, The 435 Lydecker St *Web:* elisabethmorrow.org	Englewood	NJ	07631	201-568-5566		685
Elitch Gardens 2000 Elitch Cir *Web:* www.elitchgardens.com	Denver	CO	80204	303-595-4386	629-0740	32
Elite PO Box 9630 **Fax Area Code:* 858 ■ *TF:* 800-204-3548 ■ *Web:* www.eliteworldwide.com	Rancho Santa Fe	CA	92067	800-204-3548	756-4781*	765
Elite Aluminum Corp 4650 Lyons Technology Pkwy *Web:* www.elitealuminum.com	Coconut Creek	FL	33073	954-949-3200		596
Elite Aviation LLC 7501 Hayvenhurst Pl *Web:* www.eliteaviation.com	Van Nuys	CA	91406	818-988-5387		13
Elite Coach 1685 W Main St *TF:* 800-722-6206 ■ *Web:* www.elitecoach.com	Ephrata	PA	17522	717-733-7710		107
Elite Electronic Engineering Inc 1516 Centre Cir *TF:* 800-354-8311 ■ *Web:* www.elitetest.com	Downers Grove	IL	60515	630-495-9770		261
Elite Floor Coverings Inc 3902 Auburn Way N *Web:* www.elitefloorcoverings.com	Auburn	WA	98002	253-735-2232		290
Elite Investigations Ltd 538 W 29th St *Web:* www.eliteinvestigation.com	New York	NY	10001	212-629-3131		693
Elite Island Resorts Inc 1065 SW 30th Ave *TF:* 800-771-4711 ■ *Web:* www.eliteislandresorts.com	Deerfield Beach	FL	33442	954-481-8787		707
Elite Lighting Company Inc 412 S Cypress St *Web:* www.elitelighting.com	Mullins	SC	29574	843-464-7681		362
Elite Limousine Service Inc 1059 12th Ave Ste E *TF:* 800-776-2098 ■ *Web:* www.elitelimohawaii.com	Honolulu	HI	96816	808-735-2431	735-5159	441
Elite Mktg Group 800 Bering Dr *Web:* www.elitemktg.net	Houston	TX	77057	713-507-1000		391-2
Elite Pharmaceuticals Inc 165 Ludlow Ave *OTC: ELTP* ■ *Web:* www.elitepharma.com	Northvale	NJ	07647	201-750-2646	750-2755	85
Elite Reprographics 363 Sixth St *Web:* www.eliterepro.com	San Francisco	CA	94103	415-957-1234		627
Elite Restaurant 141 E Capitol St	Jackson	MS	39201	601-352-5606		671
Elite Retails Services Inc PO Box 618 *Web:* www.elite construction.com	Lake Jackson	TX	77566	979-285-0712		186
Elite Show Services Inc 2878 Camino Del Rio S Ste 260 *Web:* www.eliteservicesusa.com	San Diego	CA	92108	619-574-1589	574-1588	271
Elite Spice Inc 7151 Montevideo Rd *Web:* www.elitespice.com	Jessup	MD	20794	410-796-1900		123
Elite Sportswear LP 2136 N 13th St *TF Cust Svc:* 800-345-4087 ■ *Web:* www.gkelite.com	Reading	PA	19604	610-921-1469		155-1
Elitexpo Cargo Systems 845 Commerce Dr *TF:* 800-543-5484 ■ *Web:* elitexpo.com	South Elgin	IL	60177	800-543-5484		463
Elixir Industries Inc 24800 Chrisanta Dr Ste 210 *TF:* 800-421-1942 ■ *Web:* www.elixirind.com	Mission Viejo	CA	92691	949-860-5000	860-5011	234
Eliza Bryant Village 7201 Wade Park Ave *Web:* www.elizabryant.org	Cleveland	OH	44103	216-361-6141		371
Eliza Coffee Memorial Hospital (ECM) 205 Marengo St *Web:* www.chgroup.org/ecm	Florence	AL	35630	256-768-9191		374-3
Elizabeth Arden Inc 880 SW 145th Ave Ste 200 *NASDAQ: RDEN* ■ *TF:* 800-326-7337 ■ *Web:* www.elizabetharden.com	Pembroke Pines	FL	33027	954-364-6900	364-6910	574
Elizabeth Arden Red Door Spa at Mystic Marriott Hotel & Spa 625 N Rd *TF:* 866-449-7390 ■ *Web:* www.marriott.com	Groton	CT	06340	860-446-2500	446-2696	707
Elizabeth Carbide Die Company Inc 601 Linden St *TF:* 800-637-3762 ■ *Web:* www.eliz.com	McKeesport	PA	15132	412-751-3000	754-0755	757
Elizabeth City Area Chamber of Commerce 502 E Ehringhaus St *Web:* www.elizabethcitychamber.org	Elizabeth City	NC	27909	252-335-4365	335-5732	139
Elizabeth City State University 1704 Weeksville Rd **Fax:* Admissions ■ *TF Admissions:* 800-347-3278 ■ *Web:* www.ecsu.edu	Elizabeth City	NC	27909	252-335-3400	335-3537*	166
Elizabeth Companies, The 601 Linden St **Fax Area Code:* 502 ■ *TF:* 800-325-4935 ■ *Web:* www.eliz.com	Mckeesport	PA	15132	412-751-3000	635-7850*	454
Elizabeth Gamble Garden 1431 Waverley St *Web:* www.gamblegarden.org	Palo Alto	CA	94301	650-329-1356		97
Elizabeth Glaser Pediatric AIDS Foundation 1140 Connecticut Ave NW Ste 200 *TF:* 888-499-4673 ■ *Web:* www.pedaids.org	Washington	DC	20036	202-296-9165	296-9185	48-17
Elizabeth Hospice 150 W Crest St *TF:* 800-797-2050 ■ *Web:* www.elizabethhospice.org	Escondido	CA	92025	760-737-2050		371
Elizabeth Myers Mitchell Art Gallery 60 College Ave	Annapolis	MD	21401	410-626-2556		50-2
Elizabeth on 37th 105 E 37th St *TF:* 800-517-9007 ■ *Web:* www.elizabethon37th.net	Savannah	GA	31401	912-236-5547		671
Elizabeth Park Rose Gardens 1561 Asylum Ave	West Hartford	CT	06117	860-231-9443		97
Elizabeth Public Library 11 S Broad St *Web:* www.elizpl.org	Elizabeth	NJ	07202	908-354-6060	354-5845	434-3
Elizabeth's 601 Gallier St *Web:* elizabethsrestaurantnola.com	New Orleans	LA	70117	504-944-9272		671
Elizabethan Gardens 1411 National Pk Dr *Web:* www.elizabethangardens.org	Manteo	NC	27954	252-473-3234	473-3244	97
Elizabethton/Carter County Chamber of Commerce Hwy 19 E *Web:* www.elizabethtonchamber.com	Elizabethton	TN	37644	423-547-3850	547-3854	139
Elizabethton-Carter County Public Library 201 N Sycamore St	Elizabethton	TN	37643	423-547-6360		434-3
Elizabethtown College 1 Alpha Dr **Fax:* Admissions ■ *TF:* 800-365-7402 ■ *Web:* www.etown.edu	Elizabethtown	PA	17022	717-361-1000	361-1365*	166
Elizabethtown Community & Technical College 600 College St Rd *TF:* 877-246-2322 ■ *Web:* www.elizabethtown.kctcs.edu	Elizabethtown	KY	42701	270-769-2371	769-0736	162
Elizabethtown Gas Co 1 Elizabethtown Plaza 1085 Morris Ave *TF:* 800-242-5830 ■ *Web:* www.elizabethtowngas.com	Union	NJ	07083	908-289-5000	289-1370	787
Elizabethtown-Hardin County Chamber of Commerce (HCCC) 111 W Dixie Ave *TF:* 800-437-0092 ■ *Web:* hardinchamber.com	Elizabethtown	KY	42701	270-765-4334	737-0690	139
Eljer Inc 1 Centennial Ave *TF:* 800-442-1902 ■ *Web:* www.eljer.com	Piscataway	NJ	08855	800-442-1902		611
Elk Brand Manufacturing Co 1601 County Hospital Rd PO Box 281287 *Web:* www.elkbrand.com	Nashville	TN	37228	615-254-4300		155-11
Elk City State Park 4825 Squaw Creek Rd *Web:* ksoutdoors.com/state-parks/locations/elk-city	Independence	KS	67301	620-331-6295		565
Elk Country Inn 480 W Pearl St PO Box 1255 *TF:* 800-483-8667 ■ *Web:* www.townsquareinns.com	Jackson	WY	83001	307-733-2364		379
Elk County PO Box 606 *TF:* 877-504-2490 ■ *Web:* elkcountyks.org	Howard	KS	67349	620-374-2490	374-2771	338
Elk County 250 Main St *TF:* 800-229-9983 ■ *Web:* www.co.elk.pa.us	Ridgway	PA	15853	814-776-1161	776-5379	338
Elk Environmental Services 1420 Clarion St *TF:* 800-851-7156 ■ *Web:* www.elkenv.com	Reading	PA	19601	610-372-4760		196
Elk Grove Citizen 8970 Elk Grove Blvd *Web:* www.egcitizen.com	Elk Grove	CA	95624	916-685-3945		532-4
Elk Grove Graphics Inc 1200 Chase Ave *TF:* 800-440-7861 ■ *Web:* elkgrovegraphics.com	Elk Grove Village	IL	60007	847-439-7834		627
Elk Grove Toyota 9640 W Stockton Blvd *Web:* www.elkgrovetoyota.com	Elk Grove	CA	95757	916-405-8000		57
Elk Grove Village Public Library 1001 Wellington Ave *TF:* 800-252-8980 ■ *Web:* www.egvpl.org	Elk Grove Village	IL	60007	847-439-0447	439-0475	434-3
ELK Lighting Creativity 12 Willow Ln **Fax Area Code:* 866 ■ *TF:* 800-613-3261 ■ *Web:* www.elklighting.com	Nesquehoning	PA	18240	800-613-3261	613-3264*	439
Elk Lighting Inc 12 Willow Ln **Fax Area Code:* 800 ■ *TF:* 866-203-1953 ■ *Web:* www.elkhospitality.com	Nesquehoning	PA	18240	866-283-1953	388-6052*	439
Elk Mountain Ranch PO Box 910 *TF:* 800-432-8812 ■ *Web:* elkmtn.com	Buena Vista	CO	81211	800-432-8812		239
Elk Neck State Park 4395 Turkey Pt Rd *Web:* dnr2.maryland.gov	North East	MD	21901	410-287-5333		565
ELK Products Inc 3266 US 70 W *TF:* 800-797-9355 ■ *Web:* www.elkproducts.com	Connelly Springs	NC	28612	828-397-4200		692
Elk Public House 1931 W Pacific Ave *Web:* wedonthaveone.com	Spokane	WA	99204	509-363-1973		671
Elk River Systems Inc 777 E Main Ste 108 *TF:* 888-771-0809 ■ *Web:* www.elkriversystems.com	Dozeman	MT	59715	406-632-4763		174
Elk Rock State Park 811 146th Ave *Web:* www.iowadnr.gov	Knoxville	IA	50138	641-842-6008		565
Elk State Park c/o Bendigo State Pk 533 State Pk Rd *Web:* www.dcnr.state.pa.us/stateparks/parks/elk.aspx	Johnsonburg	PA	15845	814-965-2646		565
Elk Valley Rancheria 2332 Howland Hill Rd *TF:* 866-464-4680 ■ *Web:* www.elk-valley.com	Crescent City	CA	95531	707-464-4680		708
Elkay Manufacturing Co 2222 Camden Ct *TF:* 800-476-4106 ■ *Web:* www.elkay.com	Oak Brook	IL	60523	630-574-8484	574-5012	609
Elkco Corp 50 Dangelo Dr Ste 5 *Web:* www.elkco.com	Marlborough	MA	01752	508-842-2111		177
Elkhart County 117 N Second St *Web:* www.elkhartcountyindiana.com	Goshen	IN	46526	574-535-6743		338
Elkhart County Convention & Visitors Bureau 219 Caravan Dr *TF:* 800-262-8161 ■ *Web:* www.amishcountry.org	Elkhart	IN	46514	574-262-8161	262-3925	206
Elkhart Products Corp 1255 Oak St *TF:* 800-284-4851 ■ *Web:* www.elkhartproducts.com	Elkhart	IN	46514	574-264-3181	264-4835	595
Elkhartnet 401 E Colfax Ave *Web:* www.elkhart.net	South Bend	IN	46617	574-524-1000		225
Elkhorn Bus Service Inc 511 S Lincoln St *Web:* www.jonestravel.com	Elkhorn	WI	53121	262-723-4309		772
Elkhorn Construction Inc 71 Allegiance Cir PO Box 809 *Web:* www.elkhornconstruction.com	Evanston	WY	82930	307-789-1595		188
Elkhorn Golf Club 1050 Elkhorn Dr *Web:* www.elkhorngc.com	Stockton	CA	95209	209-474-3900		669
Elkhorn Ranch Montana 33133 Gallatin Rd *Web:* www.elkhornranchmt.com	Gallatin Gateway	MT	59730	406-995-4291		239
Elkhorn Rural Public Power District 206 N Fourth St *TF:* 800-675-2185 ■ *Web:* www.erppd.com	Battle Creek	NE	68715	402-675-2185	675-6275	245
Elkhorn State Park 1420 E 6thAve c/o Helena Area Resource Office PO Box 200701 *Web:* stateparks.mt.gov	Helena	MT	59620	406-444-2535		565
Elkins Constructors Inc 6104 S Gazebo Pk *Web:* www.elkinsconstructors.com	Jacksonville	FL	32257	904-677-4610		188-10

Name / Address	City	State	Zip	Phone	Fax	Class
Elkins Retail Advertising Inc 6040 Hellyer Ave Ste 100 *Web:* elkinsadvertising.com	San Jose	CA	95138	408-249-1411		7
Elkins-Randolph County Chamber of Commerce (ERCCC) 200 Executive Plaza *Web:* www.erccc.com	Elkins	WV	26241	304-636-2717	636-8046	139
Elko Area Chamber of Commerce 1405 Idaho St *TF:* 800-428-7143 ■ *Web:* www.elkonevada.com	Elko	NV	89801	775-738-7135	738-7136	139
Elko Convention & Visitors Authority 700 Moren Way *TF:* 800-248-3556 ■ *Web:* www.elkocva.com	Elko	NV	89801	775-738-4091	738-2420	205
Elko County 569 Ct St *Web:* www.elkocountynv.net	Elko	NV	89801	775-738-5398	753-8535	338
Elko County Fairgrounds PO Box 2067 *Web:* www.elkocountyfair.com	Elko	NV	89803	775-738-3616	778-3468	642
Elko Speedway 26350 France Ave *Web:* www.goelkospeedway.com	Elko	MN	55020	952-461-7223		515
Elkon Gallery Inc 18 E 81st St Ste 2-A	New York	NY	10028	212-535-3940		42
Elks Magazine 2750 N Lakeview Ave *TF:* 800-892-8384 ■ *Web:* www.elks.org/elksmag	Chicago	IL	60614	773-755-4700	755-4745	457-10
Elkton Supply Company Inc 202 W Main St *Web:* www.elktonsupply.com	Elkton	MD	21921	410-398-1900		290
Ella Health 1 Lemoyne Sq Plaza Ste 102 (On Camp Hill Bypass Rd) *Web:* www.ellahealth.com	Lemoyne	PA	17043	717-695-9464		415
Elle K Associates Inc 11900 Castlegate Ct *Web:* ellekassociates.com	Rockville	MD	20852	301-984-4494		226
Ellen Trout Zoo 402 Zoo Cir *Web:* cityoflufkin.com/zoo	Lufkin	TX	75904	936-633-0399	633-0311	823
Ellenton Premium Outlets 5461 Factory Shops Blvd *Web:* www.premiumoutlets.com	Ellenton	FL	34222	941-723-1150		460
Eller-ITO Stevedoring Company LLC 1007 N America Way *Web:* www.ellerito.com	Miami	FL	33132	305-379-3700	371-9969	465
Ellery Queen Mystery Magazine (EQMM) 267 Broadway 4th Fl *TF:* 800-220-7443 ■ *Web:* www.themysteryplace.com/eqmm	New York	NY	10007	800-220-7443		457-11
Ellett Industries Ltd 1575 Kingsway Ave *Web:* www.ellett.ca	Port Coquitlam	BC	V3C4E5	604-941-8211		770
Ellicom Inc 905 Rue De Nemours *Web:* ellicom.com	Quebec	QC	G1H6Z5	418-623-8804		261
Ellie Fashion Group Inc 1447 Second St 3rd Fl *TF:* 844-338-5044	Santa Monica	CA	90401	888-926-9615		690
Ellie Mae Inc 4155 Hopyard Rd Ste 200 *TF:* 800-848-4904 ■ *Web:* elliemae.com	Pleasanton	CA	94588	925-227-7000		177
Ellington Elementary School 3001 Lindell Ave *TF:* 800-366-3687 ■ *Web:* www.qps.org	Quincy	IL	62301	217-222-5697		685
Elliot Companies, The 673 Blue Sky Pkwy *Web:* www.davishelliot.com	Lexington	KY	40509	859-263-5148	263-5486	189-4
Elliot Equipment Corp 1131 Country Club Rd *TF:* 800-823-7527 ■ *Web:* www.elliottequipment.com	Indianapolis	IN	46234	317-271-3065		111
Elliot Hospital 1 Elliot Way Ste 100 *TF:* 800-922-4999 ■ *Web:* www.elliothospital.org	Manchester	NH	03103	603-627-1669	624-2297	374-3
Elliot Rossen & Assoc 791 Apple Tree Ln *Web:* www.erossen.com	Highland Park	IL	60035	847-624-5752		463
Elliott & Bradley Plumbing Inc 10030 Windisch Rd *Web:* elliottandbradley.com	West Chester Township	OH	45069	513-772-0050		189-10
Elliott & Frantz Inc 450 E Church Rd *TF:* 800-220-3025 ■ *Web:* www.elliottfrantz.com	King Of Prussia	PA	19406	610-279-5200		358
Elliott Aviation Inc 6601 74th Ave PO Box 100 *TF:* 800-447-6711 ■ *Web:* www.elliottaviation.com	Milan	IL	61264	309-799-3183	799-2014	24
Elliott Bay Book Co 1521 Tenth Ave *TF:* 800-962-5311 ■ *Web:* www.elliottbaybook.com	Seattle	WA	98122	206-624-6600	903-1601	95
Elliott Bay Design Group LLC 5305 Shilshole Ave NW Ste 100 *Web:* www.ebdg.com	Seattle	WA	98107	206-782-3082		698
Elliott Community The 170 Metcalfe St *Web:* www.elliottcommunity.org	Guelph	ON	N1E4Y3	519-822-0491		371
Elliott Company of Indianapolis Inc 9200 Zionsville Rd *TF Orders:* 800-545-1213 ■ *Web:* www.elliottfoam.com	Indianapolis	IN	46268	317-291-1213	291-1213	601
Elliott County PO Box 710 *Web:* www.elliottcounty.ky.gov	Sandy Hook	KY	41171	606-738-5826	738-4509	338
Elliott Cove Capital Management 1000 Second Ave Ste 1440 *Web:* www.elliottcove.com	Seattle	WA	98104	206-267-2683		401
Elliott Davis Decosimo LLC 629 Market St Ste 100 *TF:* 800-782-8382 ■ *Web:* www.elliottdavis.com	Chattanooga	TN	37402	423-756-7100	756-2939	2
Elliott Davis LLC 200 E Broad St PO Box 6286 *TF:* 800-503-4721 ■ *Web:* www.elliottdavis.com	Greenville	SC	29606	864-242-3370		2
Elliott Electric Supply Co 2526 N Stallings Dr PO Box 630610 *TF:* 877-777-0242 ■ *Web:* www.elliottelectric.com	Nacogdoches	TX	75963	936-569-1184	569-1836	246
Elliott Group 901 N Fourth St *TF:* 888-352-7278 ■ *Web:* www.elliott-turbo.com	Jeannette	PA	15644	724-527-2811	600-8442	172
Elliott Homes 340 Palladio Pkwy Ste 521	Folsom	CA	95630	916-984-1300		653
Elliott Lewis Leiber & Stumpf Inc Certif 1611 e Fourth st *TF:* 800-821-5184 ■ *Web:* www.ellscpas.com	Santa Ana	CA	92701	714-569-1000		2

Name / Address	City	State	Zip	Phone	Fax	Class
Elliott Machine Works Inc 1351 Freese Works Pl *TF:* 800-299-0412 ■ *Web:* www.elliottmachine.com	Galion	OH	44833	419-468-4709		516
Elliott Management 40 W 57th St *Web:* www.elliottmgmt.com	New York	NY	10019	212-974-6000		402
Elliott Manufacturing Inc 11 Beckwith Ave *Web:* www.elliottmfg.com	Binghamton	NY	13901	607-772-0404		620
Elliott Mfg Company Inc 2664 Cherry Ave PO Box 11277 *Web:* www.elliott-mfg.com	Fresno	CA	93772	559-233-6235	233-6235	547
Elliott Tape Inc 1882 Pond Run *Web:* www.egitape.com	Auburn Hills	MI	48326	248-475-2000	475-5893	386
Elliott Wave International (EWI) PO Box 1618 *TF Cust Svc:* 800-336-1618 ■ *Web:* www.elliottwave.com	Gainesville	GA	30503	770-536-0309	536-2514	637-9
Elliott Wave Theorist PO Box 1618 *TF:* 800-336-1618 ■ *Web:* www.elliottwave.com	Gainesville	GA	30503	770-536-0309	536-2514	531-9
Elliott's Oyster House 1201 Alaskan Way Pier 56 *Web:* www.elliottsoysterhouse.com	Seattle	WA	98101	206-623-4340	224-0154	671
Elliott, Ostrander & Preston PC Union Bank Tower 707 SW Washington St Ste 1500 *TF:* 866-716-3410 ■ *Web:* www.eoplaw.com	Portland	OR	97205	503-224-7112		428
Elliott-Lewis Corp 2900 Black Lake Pl *Web:* www.elliottlewis.com	Philadelphia	PA	19154	215-698-4400	698-4436	14
Ellipse Arts Ctr 3700 S Four Mile Run Dr *Web:* www.arlingtonarts.org	Arlington	VA	22206	703-228-7710		50-2
Ellipse Communications Inc 14800 Quorum Dr Ste 420 *Web:* www.ellipseinc.com	Dallas	TX	75254	214-237-0199		387
ElliptiGO Inc 722 Genevieve St Ste O *Web:* www.elliptigo.com	Solana Beach	CA	92075	858-876-8677		517
elliquence LLC 2455 Grand Ave *Web:* www.elliquence.com	Baldwin	NY	11510	516-277-9000		475
Ellis & Associates Inc 7064 Davis Creek Rd *TF:* 800-273-0960 ■ *Web:* www.ellisassoc.com	Jacksonville	FL	32256	904-880-0960		743
Ellis & Associates Inc 508 Goldenmoss Loop *Web:* www.jellis.com	Ocoee	FL	34761	407-401-7136		45
Ellis & Watts Inc 4400 Glen Willow Lake Ln *Web:* www.elliswatts.com	Batavia	OH	45103	513-752-9000	752-4983	14
Ellis Coffee Co 2835 Bridge St *TF:* 800-822-3984 ■ *Web:* www.elliscoffee.com	Philadelphia	PA	19137	215-537-9500	535-5311	297-11
Ellis Corp 1400 W Bryn Mawr Ave *TF:* 800-611-6806 ■ *Web:* www.elliscorp.com	Itasca	IL	60143	630-250-9222	250-9241	427
Ellis County PO Box 176 *Web:* www.ellis.oklahoma.usassessor.com	Arnett	OK	73832	580-885-7975	885-7258	338
Ellis County 2700 Vine St *Web:* www.ellisco.org	Hays	KS	67601	785-628-3102		338
Ellis County 1201 N Hwy 77 Ste B *Web:* www.co.ellis.tx.us	Waxahachie	TX	75165	972-825-5000		338
Ellis Ged & Bodden pa 7171 N Federal Hwy *TF:* 888-342-3476 ■ *Web:* www.ellisandged.com	Boca Raton	FL	33487	561-995-1966		428
Ellis Hospital 1101 Nott St *TF:* 800-989-6446 ■ *Web:* www.ellismedicine.org/home/ellishospitalmain.aspx	Schenectady	NY	12308	518-243-4000		374-3
Ellis Law Group LLP 740 University Ave Ste 100 *Web:* www.womenlawyers-sacramento.org	Sacramento	CA	95825	916-283-8820		428
Ellis Management Services Inc 4324 N Beltine Rd *TF:* 888-988-3767 ■ *Web:* www.epmsonline.com	Irving	TX	75038	972-256-3767		196
Ellis Park Race Course LLC 3300 US 41 *Web:* www.ellisparkracing.com	Henderson	KY	42420	812-425-1456		642
Ellis Stone Construction 3201 Stanley St PO Box 366 *Web:* www.elliswi.com	Stevens Point	WI	54481	715-345-5000		186
Ellis, Li & McKinstry PLLC Market Pl Tower 2025 First Ave Ph A *Web:* www.elmlaw.com	Seattle	WA	98121	206-682-0565		428
EllisDon Corp 2045 Oxford St *Web:* www.ellisdon.com	London	ON	N5V2Z7	519-455-6770		186
Ellis-harper Advertising Inc 710 Stage Rd *Web:* www.ellisharper.com	Auburn	AL	36831	334-887-6536		463
Ellison Advertising 3410 SE 20th Ave *TF:* 800-561-3357 ■ *Web:* www.ellisonadvertising.com	Portland	OR	97202	503-236-8400		7
Ellison Bakery 4108 W Ferguson Rd *Web:* www.ebakery.com	Fort Wayne	IN	46809	260-747-6136		296-9
Ellison Educational Equipment Inc 25862 Commercentre Dr *TF:* 800-253-2240 ■ *Web:* www.ellison.com	Lake Forest	CA	92630	949-598-8822		358
Ellison Keith (Rep D - MN) 2263 Rayburn Bldg *Web:* ellison.house.gov	Washington	DC	20515	202-225-4755		342-2
Ellison Media Co 14804 N Cave Creek Rd *Web:* www.ellisonmedia.com	Phoenix	AZ	85032	602-404-4000		7
Ellison Medical Foundation 104 E Ridgeville Blvd *Web:* www.ellisonfoundation.org	Mount Airy	MD	21771	301-829-6410	657-1828	305
Ellison Technologies 9912 S Pioneer Blvd *Web:* www.ellisontechnologies.com	Santa Fe Springs	CA	90670	562-949-8311	949-9091	385
Ellison, Schneider, Harris & Donlan LLP 2600 Capitol Ave Ste 400 *Web:* www.eslawfirm.com	Sacramento	CA	95816	916-447-2166	447-3512	428
Ellisville Harbor State Park 198 Purgatory Rd *Web:* www.mass.gov	Sutton	MA	01590	508-234-3733		565

Phone | Fax | Class

Ellkay 259 Cedar Ln .... Teaneck NJ 07666 201-791-0606 177
Web: www.ellkay.com

Ellmaker State Wayside
198 NE 123rd St .... Newport OR 97365 800-551-6949 565
TF: 800-551-6949 ■ *Web:* www.oregonstateparks.org

Ellsworth Air Force Base
1958 Scott Dr .... Ellsworth AFB SD 57706 605-385-5056 385-4668 497-1
TF: 800-241-3005 ■ *Web:* www.ellsworth.af.mil

Ellsworth Area Chamber of Commerce
163 High St .... Ellsworth ME 04605 207-667-5584 667-2617 139
Web: www.ellsworthchamber.org

Ellsworth Community College
1100 College Ave .... Iowa Falls IA 50126 641-648-4611 648-3128* 162
**Fax:* Admissions ■ *TF:* 800-322-9235 ■ *Web:* ecc.iavalley.edu

Ellsworth Co-op Creamery Inc
232 N Wallace St .... Ellsworth WI 54011 715-273-4311 273-5318 296-5
TF: 800-200-6020 ■ *Web:* www.ellsworthcheese.com

Ellsworth Corp PO Box 1002 .... Germantown WI 53022 262-253-8600 146
TF: 877-454-9224 ■ *Web:* www.ellsworth.com

Ellsworth County 210 N Kansas St .... Ellsworth KS 67439 785-472-4161 472-3818 338
TF: 800-262-8683 ■ *Web:* www.ellsworthcounty.org

Ellucian 4375 Fair Lakes Ct .... Fairfax VA 22033 610-647-5930 178-10
TF: 800-223-7036 ■ *Web:* www.ellucian.com

Ellumen Inc
1401 Wilson Blvd Ste 1200 .... Arlington VA 22209 703-253-5555 196
Web: www.ellumen.com

Ellwood City Forge
800 Commercial Ave .... Ellwood City PA 16117 724-752-0055 752-3449 483
TF: 800-843-0166 ■ *Web:* www.ellwoodcityforge.com

Ellwood City Hospital
724 Pershing St .... Ellwood City PA 16117 724-752-0081 752-0966 374-3
TF: 800-720-2557 ■ *Web:* www.echospital.org

Ellwood Engineered Castings Co
7158 Hubbard Masury Rd .... Hubbard OH 44425 330-534-8668 723
Web: ellwoodengineeredcastings.com

Ellwood Thompson 10 S Thompson St .... Richmond VA 23221 804-359-7525 297-0
Web: www.ellwoodthompsons.com

Elm Chevrolet Co Inc 301 E Church St .... Elmira NY 14901 607-734-4141 57
TF: 877-265-6708 ■ *Web:* elmchevrolet.com

Elm Consulting
26741 Portola Pkwy Ste 1E#494 .... Foothill Ranch CA 92610 678-200-5220 196
Web: www.elmgroup.com

ELM Engineering Inc
900 Center Pike Dr .... Charlotte NC 28217 704-335-0396 261
Web: elmengr.com

Elm Press 16 Tremco Dr .... Terryville CT 06786 860-583-3600 627
Web: www.elmpress.com

ELM Resources
12950 Race Track Rd Ste 201 .... Tampa FL 33626 866-524-8198 387
TF: 866 524 8198 ■ *Web:* www.elmresources.com

Elm Street Oyster House 11 W Elm St .... Greenwich CT 06830 203-629-5795 671
Web: www.elmstreetoysterhouse.com

Elm Terrace Gardens 660 N Broad St .... Lansdale PA 19446 215-361-5600 672
Web: www.elmterracegardens.org

Elma Electronic Inc
44350 Grimmer Blvd .... Fremont CA 94538 510-656-3400 656-3783 253
Web: www.elma.com

Elmar Worldwide Inc
200 Gould Ave PO Box 245 .... Depew NY 14043 716-681-5650 681-5650 547
TF Cust Svc: 800-433-3562 ■ *Web:* www.elmarworldwide.com

Elmbrook Management Co
1908 12th Ave NW Ste E .... Ardmore OK 73401 580-226-3055 610
Web: www.elmbrookhomes.com

Elmbrook Memorial Hospital
19333 W N Ave .... Brookfield WI 53045 262-785-2000 374-3
Web: www.mywheaton.org/locations/elmbrook_memorial

Elmendorf Strategies LLC
900 Seventh St NW Ste 750 .... Washington DC 20001 202-737-1010 95
Web: www.elmendorfryan.com

Elmer Candy Corp 401 N Fifth St .... Ponchatoula LA 70454 985-386-6166 296-8
TF: 800-843-9537 ■ *Web:* elmerchocolate.com

Elmer Larson LLC 21218 Airport Rd .... Sycamore IL 60178 815-895-4837 503-4

Elmer's Products Inc 1 Easton Oval .... Columbus OH 43219 888-435-6377 3
TF: 888-435-6377 ■ *Web:* www.elmers.com

Elmet Technologies Inc
1560 Lisbon St .... Lewiston ME 04240 207-333-6100 786-8924 485
TF: 800-343-8008 ■ *Web:* www.elmettechnologies.com

Elmhurst Art Museum
150 S Cottage Hill Ave .... Elmhurst IL 60126 630-834-0202 522
Web: elmhurstartmuseum.org

Elmhurst Chamber of Commerce & Industry
300 A West Lake St Ste 201 .... Elmhurst IL 60126 630-834-6060 834-6002 139
Web: www.elmhurstchamber.org

Elmhurst College 190 Prospect Ave .... Elmhurst IL 60126 630-617-3400 166
TF: 800-697-1871 ■ *Web:* www.elmhurst.edu

Elmhurst Group, The
1 Bigelow Sq Ste 630 .... Pittsburgh PA 15219 412-281-8731 528
Web: www.elmhurstgroup.com

Elmhurst Hospital Ctr 79-01 Broadway .... Elmhurst NY 11373 718-334-4000 374-3
Web: nyc.gov

Elmhurst Inn, The 40 Holland Ave .... Bar Harbor ME 04609 207-288-3044 288-2719 379
Web: www.graycoteinn.com

Elmhurst Mutual Power & Light Co
120 132nd St S .... Tacoma WA 98444 253-531-4646 245
TF: 855-841-2178 ■ *Web:* www.elmhurstmutual.org

Elmhurst Public Library
125 S Prospect Ave .... Elmhurst IL 60126 630-279-8696 279-0636 434-3
Web: www.elmhurstpubliclibrary.org

Elmira Business Institute-elmira Campus
303 N Main St .... Elmira NY 14901 607-733-7177 166
Web: www.ebi.edu

Elmira College 1 Pk Pl .... Elmira NY 14901 607-735-1724 735-1718* 166
**Fax:* Admissions ■ *TF Admissions:* 800-935-6472 ■ *Web:* www.elmira.edu

Elmira Correctional Facility
1879 Davis St .... Elmira NY 14901 607-734-3901 213
Web: www.doccs.ny.gov/faclist.html

Elmira Psychiatric Ctr
100 Washington St .... Elmira NY 14901 607-737-4711 737-9080 374-5
TF: 800-597-8481 ■ *Web:* omh.ny.gov

Phone | Fax | Class

Elmira Savings Bank 333 E Water St .... Elmira NY 14901 607-734-3374 70
NASDAQ: ESBK ■ *TF:* 888-372-9299 ■ *Web:* www.elmirasavingsbank.com

Elmira Stamping & Mfg Corp
1704 Cedar St .... Elmira NY 14904 607-734-2058 732-0573 488
Web: www.elmirastamping.com

Elmont Union Free School District
135 Elmont Rd .... Elmont NY 11003 516-326-5500 326-5574 685
Web: www.elmontschools.org

Elmore Correctional Ctr
3520 Marion Spillway Rd .... Elmore AL 36025 334-567-1460 213
Web: www.doc.state.al.us

Elmore County
150 S Fourth E St Ste 5 .... Mountain Home ID 83647 208-587-2129 587-2134 338
Web: www.elmorecounty.org

Elmore County 100 E Commerce St .... Wetumpka AL 36092 334-567-1156 338
Web: www.elmoreco.org

Elmore County Public School System
100 H H Robison Dr PO Box 817 .... Wetumpka AL 36092 334-567-1200 685
Web: www.elmoreco.com

Elmore State Park 856 VT Rt 12 .... Lake Elmore VT 05657 802-888-2982 565
Web: www.vtstateparks.com

ELMS College 291 Springfield St .... Chicopee MA 01013 413-592-3189 166
TF Admissions: 800-255-3567 ■ *Web:* www.elms.edu

Elms Mansion & Gardens
3029 St Charles Ave .... New Orleans LA 70115 504-895-9200 50-3
Web: www.elmsmansion.com

Elmsford Sheet Metal Work Inc
23 Arlo Ln .... Cortlandt Manor NY 10567 914-739-6300 739-1285 189-12
Web: www.elmsfordsheetmetal.com

Elmwood Healthcare Ctr & Specialty Hospital (SFHCC)
401 N Broadway .... Green Springs OH 44836 419-639-2626 374-7
Web: elmwoodcommunities.com

Elmwood Inn, The 1256 Mt Hope Ave .... Rochester NY 14620 585-271-5195 671
Web: elmwoodinn.net

Elmwood Park Zoo 1661 Harding Blvd .... Norristown PA 19401 610-277-3825 292-0332 823
TF: 800-652-4143 ■ *Web:* www.elmwoodparkzoo.org

Elo Engineering Inc 7770 Ranchers Rd .... Fridley MN 55432 763-571-2820 697
Web: www.elo1.com

Elo TouchSystems Inc
301 Constitution Dr .... Menlo Park CA 94025 650-361-4700 361-4747 173-1
TF: 800-557-1458 ■ *Web:* www.elotouch.com

eLocal Listing
25240 Hancock Ave Ste 410 .... Murrieta CA 92563 800-285-0484 851-6822 5
TF: 800-285-0484 ■ *Web:* www.elocallisting.com

Elof Hansson Pulp Inc 565 Taxter Rd .... Elmsford NY 10523 914-345-8380 553
Web: www.elofhansson.com

Elon University 100 Campus Dr .... Elon NC 27244 336-278-2000 278-7699 166
TF: 800-334-8448 ■ *Web:* www.elon.edu

Elona Bio Technologies Inc
1040 Sierra Dr Ste 1000 .... Greenwood IN 46143 317-513-3138 582
Web: elonabiotech.wordpress.com

eLottery Inc
46 Southfield Ave
3 Stamford Landing Ste 310 .... Stamford CT 06902 203-388-1808 388-1809 322
Web: www.elottery.com

ElPaso Proud 801 N Oregon St .... El Paso TX 79902 915-532-5421 496-4590 741-43
Web: www.elpasoproud.com

Elrod's Cost Plus #2 2025 Ft Worth Ave .... Dallas TX 75208 214-942-0161 942-3376 320
Web: www.elrodscostplus.com

ELS Language Centers 7 Roszel Rd .... Princeton NJ 08540 609-759-5500 423
Web: www.els.edu

ELS Marketing Inc 3133 Orlando Dr .... Mississauga ON L4V1C5 905-612-1060 5
TF: 877-612-2673 ■ *Web:* www.corelogistics.net

Elsa's 3618 Linden Ave .... Dayton OH 45410 937-252-9635 671
Web: elsas.net

Elsa's on the Park
833 N Jefferson St .... Milwaukee WI 53202 414-765-0615 671
Web: www.elsas.com

ELSAG North America LLC 7 Sutton Pl .... Brewster NY 10509 336-379-7135 253
Web: www.elsag.com

ELSAL Inc 800 A St .... San Rafael CA 94901 415-472-8388 472-8389 309
Web: www2.elsal.com

Elsevier Science Ltd 360 Pk Ave S .... New York NY 10010 212-989-5800 633-3990 637-9
TF: 888-437-4636 ■ *Web:* www.elsevier.com

Elsing Museum 7777 S Lewis Ave .... Tulsa OK 74171 918-495-6262 520
Web: www.oru.edu

ElSohly Laboratories Inc
5 Industrial Pk Dr .... Oxford MS 38655 662-236-2609 234-0253 416
TF: 800-334-8571 ■ *Web:* www.elsohly.com

Elster American Meter Co
2221 Industrial Rd .... Nebraska City NE 68410 402-873-8200 873-7616 495
TF: 877-595-6254 ■ *Web:* www.elster-americanmeter.com

Elster Perfection Corp 436 N Eagle St .... Geneva OH 44041 440-415-1600 605-2
Web: www.elster-perfection.com

Elston-Richards Inc
5738 Eagle Dr SE Ste B .... Grand Rapids MI 49512 616-698-2698 698-8090 449
Web: www.elstonrichards.com

Elte 80 Ronald Ave .... Toronto ON M6E5A2 416-785-7885 290
TF: 888-276-3583 ■ *Web:* www.elte.com

Eltrex Industries 65 Sullivan St .... Rochester NY 14605 585-454-6100 194

Elusys Therapeutics Inc
25 Riverside Dr .... Pine Brook NJ 07058 973-808-0222 85
Web: www.elusys.com

Elvis Presley Birthplace & Museum
306 Elvis Presley Dr .... Tupelo MS 38801 662-841-1245 520
Web: www.elvispresleybirthplace.com

Elvis Presley Enterprises Inc
3734 Elvis Presley Blvd .... Memphis TN 38116 901-332-3322 344-3101 360-3
TF: 800-238-2000 ■ *Web:* www.elvis.com

Elward Construction Co 680 Harlan St .... Lakewood CO 80214 303-239-6303 189-1
TF: 800-933-5339 ■ *Web:* www.elward.com

Elwer Engineering Services
2202 Wolf Wy Ste 1110 .... West Des Moines IA 50265 515-276-2588 261
TF: 800-728-7511 ■ *Web:* www.eescompanies.com

Elwood Corp High Performance Motors Group
2701 N Green Bay Rd .... Racine WI 53404 262-637-6591 764-4298* 518
**Fax Area Code:* 414 ■ *TF:* 800-558-9489 ■ *Web:* www.elwood.com

Name / Address	City	State	Zip	Phone	Fax	Class
Ely State Prison 4569 NV-90	Ely	NV	89301	775-289-8800		213
Web: doc.nv.gov						
Ely Times 515 Murry St PO Box 150820	Ely	NV	89315	775-289-4491	289-4566	532-4
Web: www.elynews.com						
Elyria Foundry Co 120 Filbert St	Elyria	OH	44036	440-322-4657	323-1101	307
TF: 800-442-1162 ■ *Web:* www.elyriafoundry.com						
Elyria Mfg Corp						
145 Northrup St PO Box 479	Elyria	OH	44035	440-365-4171	365-4000	621
TF: 866-365-4171 ■ *Web:* www.emcprecision.com						
Elyria-Lorain Broadcasting Co						
538 Broad St 4th Fl	Elyria	OH	44035	440-322-3761		645-10
Web: elbc.northcoastnow.com						
Elyse Connolly Inc 23 W 16th St	New York	NY	10011	212-255-0886		393
Web: www.elyseconnolly.com						
Elysium Inc 3000 Town Ctr Ste 1330	Southfield	MI	48705	248-799-9800	281-0672	225
Web: www.elysiuminc.com						
Elzinga & Volkers 86 E Sixth St	Holland	MI	49423	616-392-2383	392-3752	685
TF General: 800-632-7734 ■ *Web:* www.elzinga-volkers.com						
Em Data Consultants Inc						
42 Queen St S Ste 201	Mississauga	ON	L5M1K4	905-858-8442	858-8408	180
Web: www.emdci.com						
EM Duggan Inc 140 Will Dr	Canton	MA	02021	781-828-2292	828-0991	189-10
Web: emduggan.com						
EM Microelectronic-US Inc						
5475 Mark Dabling Blvd Ste 200	Colorado Springs	CO	80918	719-593-2883		246
TF: 800-926-8926 ■ *Web:* www.emmicroelectronic.com						
EM Research Inc 1301 Corporate Blvd	Reno	NV	89502	775-345-2411		256
Web: www.emresearch.com						
Em's 271 N Ctr St	Salt Lake City	UT	84103	801-596-0566		671
Web: www.emsrestaurant.com						
EMA (Envelope Manufacturers Assn)						
500 Montgomery St Ste 550	Alexandria	VA	22314	703-739-2200	739-2209	49-4
Web: www.envelope.org						
EMA (Engine Manufacturers Assn)						
333 W Wacker Dr Ste 810	Chicago	IL	60606	312-929-1970	929-1975	49-13
Web: www.truckandenginemanufacturers.org						
Ema Brokerage LLC						
1300 Rt 73 Ste 306	Mount Laurel	NJ	08054	856-216-0211		690
TF: 855-267-5867 ■ *Web:* emabrokerage.com						
EMA Design Automation Inc						
225 Tech Park Dr	Rochester	NY	14623	585-334-6001		180
Web: www.ema-eda.com						
eMag Solutions LLC						
1120 Sanctuary Pkwy Ste 275	Alpharetta	GA	30009	404-995-6060		178-12
Web: www.emagsolutions.com						
eMagin Corp 3006 Northup Way Ste 103	Bellevue	WA	98004	425-284-5200	284-5201	173-4
NYSE: EMAN ■ *Web:* www.emagin.com						
eMagine 1082 Davol St	Fall River	MA	02720	877-530-7993		180
TF: 877-530-7993 ■ *Web:* www.emagine.com						
Email Co, The 15 Kainona Ave	Toronto	ON	M3H3H4	877-933-6245		366
TF: 877-933-6245 ■ *Web:* theemailcompany.com						
Emaint Enterprises LLC						
438 N Elmwood Rd	Marlton	NJ	08053	856-810-2700		177
Web: emaint.com						
Emanuel African Methodist Episcopal Church						
110 Calhoun St	Charleston	SC	29401	843-722-2561	722-1869	50-1
Web: www.emanuelamechurch.org						
Emanuel County 101 N Main St	Swainsboro	GA	30401	478-237-3881		338
TF: 800-436-7442 ■ *Web:* emanuelchamber.org						
Emanuel County Board of Education						
201 N Main St	Swainsboro	GA	30401	478-237-6674	419-1102	685
Web: www.emanuel.k12.ga.us						
Emanuel Medical Ctr (EMC) 825 Delbon Ave	Turlock	CA	95382	209-667-4200		374-3
Web: www.emanuelmedicalcenter.org						
Emarketingwerx Inc 5335 W 138th St	Hawthorne	CA	90250	310-686-2314		195
TF: 800-999-3103 ■ *Web:* www.emarketingwerx.com						
E-Markets Inc						
807 Mountain Ave Ste 200	Berthoud	CO	80513	877-674-7419		39
TF: 877-674-7419 ■ *Web:* www.e-markets.com						
emat Capital Management LLC						
7474 N Figueroa St Ste A	Los Angeles	CA	90041	323-255-1333		401
Web: www.ematcapital.com						
Emats Inc						
480 Claypool Hill Mall Rd	Cedar Bluff	VA	24609	276-963-8888		261
TF: 800-542-2990 ■ *Web:* www.emats-inc.com						
EMB Corp 1203 Hawkins Dr	Elizabethtown	KY	42701	270-737-1996	737-1909	247
Web: www.embcorp.com						
Emballages Jean Cartier Inc						
2325, Industriel Blvd	St-cesaire	QC	J0L1T0	450-469-3168		23
Web: www.cartierpackaging.com						
Embarcadero Resort Hotel & Marina						
1000 SE Bay Blvd	Newport	OR	97365	541-265-8521	265-7844	379
TF: 800-547-4779 ■ *Web:* embarcaderoresort.com						
Embarcadero Technologies Inc						
100 California St 12th Fl	San Francisco	CA	94111	415-834-3131	434-1721	178-2
Web: www.embarcadero.com						
Embark Corp 459 Broadway 4th Fl	New York	NY	10013	646-368-8394	962-4114*	387
**Fax Area Code:* 415 ■ *Web:* www.embark.com						
Embark Tree & Landscape Services						
2700 Palo Pinto	Houston	TX	77080	713-462-3261		776
Web: lmchouston.com						
Embassy CES 328 Seventh Ave 6th Fl	New York	NY	10001	212-629-7300		423
Web: embassyenglish.com						
Embassy Hotel 610 Polk St	San Francisco	CA	94102	415-673-1404	474-4188	379
Web: www.theembassyhotelsf.com						
Embassy Hotel & Suites 25 Cartier St	Ottawa	ON	K2P1J2	613-237-2111	563-1353	379
TF: 800-661-5495 ■ *Web:* www.ottawaembassy.com/default-en.html						
Embassy Industries Inc 315 Oser Ave	Hauppauge	NY	11788	631-694-1800	694-1832	357
Web: www.embassyind.com						
Embassy of Andorra in United States of America						
Two United Nations Plaza 27th Fl	New York	NY	10017	212-750-8064	750-6630	784
Embassy of Bosnia & Herzegovina						
Consulate General 2109 E St NW	Washington	DC	20037	202-337-1500	337-2909	257
Web: www.bhembassy.org						
Embassy of Gambia 5630 16th St NW	Washington	DC	20011	202-785-1379	342-0240	257
Web: www.gambiaembassy.us						
Embassy of Hungary						
3910 Shoemaker St NW	Washington	DC	20008	202-362-6730		257
Embassy of Israel						
Consulate General						
3514 International Dr	Washington	DC	20008	202-364-5500		257
Web: www.israelemb.org						
Embassy 2520 Massachusetts Ave NW	Washington	DC	20008	202-238-6700	328-2187	257
Web: www.us.emb-japan.go.jp/itprtop_ja/index.html						
Embassy of Seychelles						
Embassy 800 Second Ave Ste 400C	New York	NY	10017	212-972-1785		257
Embassy of Syria						
2215 Wyoming Ave NW	Washington	DC	20008	202-232-6313		257
Web: www.syrianembassy.us						
Embassy of the Kingdom of Bahrain						
Embassy 3502 International Dr NW	Washington	DC	20008	202-342-1111	362-2192	257
TF: 800-845-8968 ■ *Web:* www.bahrainembassy.org						
EMBASSY Products & Logistics						
PO Box 8066	Falls Church	VA	22041	703-845-0800	820-9385	449
Web: www.embassy-usa.com						
Embassy San Diego - Downtown #66378						
601 Pacific Hwy	San Diego	CA	92101	619-239-2400		707
Web: embassysuites3.hilton.com						
Embassy Suites Chicago Downtown Lakefront						
511 N Columbus Dr	Chicago	IL	60611	312-836-5900		379
Web: embassysuites3.hilton.com						
Embassy Suites Columbus-Dublin						
5100 Upper Metro Pl	Dublin	OH	43017	614-790-9000		379
Web: embassysuites3.hilton.com						
Embassy Suites Hotel & Casino-San Juan Puerto Rico						
8000 Tartak St Isla Verde Carolina	San Juan	PR	00979	787-791-0505		378
Web: embassysuites3.hilton.com						
Embassy Suites Hotel Orlando - International Drive South						
8978 International Dr	Orlando	FL	32819	407-352-1400		378
Web: embassysuites3.hilton.com						
Embassy Suites Memphis						
1022 S Shady Grove Rd	Memphis	TN	38120	901-684-1777		378
Web: www.indianaroof.com						
Embassy Suites Tysons Corner Hotel						
8517 Leesburg Pk	Vienna	VA	22182	703-883-0707		707
Web: embassysuites3.hilton.com/en/index.html						
Embassy Theatre						
125 W Jefferson Blvd	Fort Wayne	IN	46802	260-424-6287		572
Web: fwembassytheatre.org						
Embedded Data Systems LLC						
2019 Fortune Dr	Lawrenceburg	KY	40342	502-859-5490		177
Web: www.embeddeddatasystems.com						
Emberex Inc 220 E 11th Ave Ste 6	Eugene	OR	97401	541-687-5778		177
TF: 800-229-7526 ■ *Web:* www.emberex.com						
Embience Inc 6450 Lusk Blvd E202203	San Diego	CA	92121	858-366-0415		196
Web: www.embience.com						
EmblemHealth Co 55 Water St	New York	NY	10041	646-447-5000		391-3
TF: 800-447-8255 ■ *Web:* www.emblemhealth.com						
Embossed Graphics 1175 S Frontenac Rd	Aurora	IL	60504	630-236-4000		627
Web: embossedgraphics.com						
Embraer Aircraft Corp						
276 SW 34th St	Fort Lauderdale	FL	33315	954-359-3700	359-3701	20
Web: www.embraer.com.br						
Embraer Aircraft Maintenance Services Inc						
10 Airways Blvd	Nashville	TN	37217	615-367-2100		407
Web: www.embraerexecutivejets.com						
Embrey Partners Ltd						
1020 NE Loop 410 Ste 700	San Antonio	TX	78209	210-824-6044	824-7656	653
Web: www.embreydc.com						
Embroiderers Guild of America (EGA)						
426 W Jefferson St	Louisville	KY	40202	502-589-6956	584-7900	48-18
TF: 800-272-0152 ■ *Web:* www.egausa.org						
EmbroidMe Inc 2121 Vista Pkwy	West Palm Beach	FL	33411	561-640-7367		310
TF: 877-877-0234 ■ *Web:* www.embroidme.com						
Embry's 3361 Tates Creek Rd	Lexington	KY	40502	859-269-3390		157-6
TF: 800-236-2797 ■ *Web:* embrys.com						
Embryotech Laboratories Inc						
140 Hale St	Haverhill	MA	01830	978-373-7300		743
TF: 800-673-7500 ■ *Web:* www.embryotech.com						
Embry-Riddle Aeronautical University						
Daytona Beach						
600 S Clyde Morris Blvd	Daytona Beach	FL	32114	386-226-6000	226-7070*	166
**Fax:* Admissions ■ *TF:* 800-862-2416 ■ *Web:* www.erau.edu						
Embry-Riddle Aeronautical University Prescott						
3700 Willow Creek Rd	Prescott	AZ	86301	928-777-3728		166
TF: 800-888-3728 ■ *Web:* www.erau.edu						
EMC (Grady Electric Membership Corp)						
1499 US Hwy 84 W	Cairo	GA	39828	229-377-4182		245
TF: 877-757-6060 ■ *Web:* www.gradyemc.com						
EMC (IEEE Electromagnetic Compatibility Society)						
IEEE Operations Ctr 445 and 501 Hoes Ln	Piscataway	NJ	08854	732-981-0060	562-6380	49-19
TF: 800-678-4333 ■ *Web:* www.ewh.ieee.org/soc/emcs						
EMC (Eden Medical Ctr)						
20103 Lake Chabot Rd	Castro Valley	CA	94546	510-537-1234		374-3
Web: www.edenmedicalcenter.org						
EMC (Equipment Manufacturing Corp)						
14930 Marquardt Ave	Santa Fe Springs	CA	90670	562-623-9394		386
TF: 888-833-9000 ■ *Web:* www.equipmentmanufacturing.com						
EMC (Emanuel Medical Ctr) 825 Delbon Ave	Turlock	CA	95382	209-667-4200		374-3
Web: www.emanuelmedicalcenter.org						
EMC Corp						
2831 Mission College Blvd	Santa Clara	CA	95054	408-566-2000		178-12
TF Tech Supp: 877-534-2867 ■ *Web:* www.emc.com						
EMC Corp 176 S St	Hopkinton	MA	01748	508-435-1000		178-12
NYSE: EMC ■ *Web:* www.emc.com						
EMC Creative						
175 N California Blvd Ste 440	Walnut Creek	CA	94596	925-837-9380		195
Web: www.emccreative.com						
EMC Document Sciences Corp						
5958 Priestly Dr	Carlsbad	CA	92008	760-602-1400		178-1
Web: emc.com/domains/docscience/index.htm						
EMC Insurance Group Inc						
717 Mulberry St	Des Moines	IA	50309	515-280-2511		360-4
NASDAQ: EMCI ■ *TF:* 800-447-2295 ■ *Web:* www.emcins.com						
EMC Outdoor						
5074 W Chester Pike 2nd Fl	Newtown Square	PA	19073	610-353-9300		6
Web: www.emcoutdoor.com						

Name / Address	City	State	Zip	Phone	Fax	Class
Emc2 3518 Riverside Dr Ste 202	Columbus	OH	43221	614-459-3200		256
Web: www.emc-sq.com						
EMCC (East Mississippi Community College)						
1512 Kemper St PO Box 158	Scooba	MS	39358	662-476-8442		162
EMCO Chemical Distributors Inc						
2100 Commonwealth Ave	North Chicago	IL	60064	847-689-2200		146
TF: 800-652-9297 ■ *Web:* www.emcochem.com						
EMCO Corp 1108 Dundas St	London	ON	N5W3A7	519-453-9600	645-2465	612
TF: 800-267-8508 ■ *Web:* www.emcoltd.com						
Emco Enterprises Inc 2121 E Walnut	Des Moines	IA	50317	515-265-6101		499
Web: www.emcodoors.com						
Emco Wheaton USA Inc						
9111 Jackrabbit Rd	Houston	TX	77095	281-856-1300	856-1325	429
Web: www.emcowheaton.com						
EMCOR Construction Services Inc						
1420 Spring Hill Rd Ste 500	McLean	VA	22102	703-556-8000	556-0890	189-4
Web: www.emcorgroup.com						
Emcor Enclosures 1600 Fourth Ave NW	Rochester	MN	55901	507-289-3371	287-3405*	254
**Fax:* Sales ■ *Web:* www.crenlo.com						
EMCOR Group Inc 301 Merritt 7 6th Fl	Norwalk	CT	06851	203-849-7800	849-7900	189-4
NYSE: EME ■ *TF:* 866-890-7794 ■ *Web:* www.emcorgroup.com						
EMCOR Hyre Electric Co						
2655 Garfield Ave	Highland	IN	46322	219-923-6100	838-3631	189-4
Web: www.emcorhyre.com						
EMCOR Services Betlem						
704 Clinton Ave S	Rochester	NY	14620	585-271-5500		261
TF: 800-423-8536 ■ *Web:* www.emcorbetlem.com						
EMCORE Corp 10420 Research Rd SE	Albuquerque	NM	87123	505-332-5000		696
NASDAQ: EMKR ■ *Web:* www.emcore.com						
EMC-Paradigm Publishing Co						
875 Montreal Way	Saint Paul	MN	55102	651-290-2800	328-4564*	637-2
**Fax Area Code:* 800 ■ *TF:* 800-328-1452 ■ *Web:* newmountainlearning.com						
EMC-Tempest Technical Support Services						
2190 E Winston Rd	Anaheim	CA	92806	714-778-1726		261
Web: www.emctempest.com						
Emcure Pharmaceuticals USA INC						
21/B Cotters Ln	East Brunswick	NJ	08816	732-238-7880		231
Web: www.emcureusa.com						
EMD Serono Inc 1 Technology Pl	Rockland	MA	02370	781-982-9000		85
TF: 800-283-8088 ■ *Web:* www.emdserono.com						
Emdeon Business Services LLC						
3055 Lebanon Pk	Nashville	TN	37214	615-932-3000		39
TF: 800-735-8254 ■ *Web:* www.emdeon.com						
Emeco 805 W Elm Ave	Hanover	PA	17331	717-637-5951	633-6018	319-1
TF: 800-366-5951 ■ *Web:* www.emeco.net						
eMedia Music Corp						
664 NE Northlake Way	Seattle	WA	98105	206-329-5657		180
TF: 888-363-3424 ■ *Web:* www.emediamusic.com						
Emek Hebrew Academy						
15365 Magnolia Blvd	Sherman Oaks	CA	91403	818-783-3663		685
Web: emek.nationbuilder.com						
Emelin Theater 153 Library Ln	Mamaroneck	NY	10543	914-698-0098	698-1404	572
Web: www.emelin.org						
EMEPA (East Mississippi Electric Power Assn)						
2128 Hwy 39 N PO Box 5517	Meridian	MS	39302	601-581-8600	482-0701	245
TF: 800-532-1502 ■ *Web:* www.emepa.com						
Emera Energy Inc						
1223 Lower Water St PO Box 910	Halifax	NS	B3J2W5	902-474-7800	428-6118	538
TF: 866-474-7800 ■ *Web:* www.emeraenergy.com						
Emerald Asset Advisors LLC						
2843 Executive Park Dr	Weston	FL	33331	954-385-9624		401
Web: www.emerald-eas.com						
Emerald Bay Energy Inc						
4015 - First St SE Ste 3A	Calgary	AB	T2G4X7	403-262-6000		536
Web: www.emeraldbayenergy.com						
Emerald Bay State Park						
138 Emerald Bay Rd	South Lake Tahoe	CA	96150	530-525-7232		565
Web: www.parks.ca.gov/default.asp?page_id=506						
Emerald Chinese Seafood Restaurant						
3709 Convoy St	San Diego	CA	92111	858-565-6888		671
Web: www.emeraldrestaurant.com						
Emerald City Graphics 23328 66th Ave S	Kent	WA	98032	253-520-2600	520-2607	627
TF General: 877-631-5178 ■ *Web:* www.emeraldcg.com						
Emerald Coast Utilities Authority (ECUA)						
9255 Sturdevant St	Pensacola	FL	32514	850-476-0480		787
Web: www.ecua.fl.gov						
Emerald Correctional Management LLC						
3800 N Central Ave Ste 460	Phoenix	AZ	85012	337-264-9777		652
Web: emeraldcm.com/ecm						
Emerald Creek Garnet Ltd						
59652 Hwy 3 Rt 4	Fernwood	ID	83830	208-245-2096		1
Emerald Downs						
2300 Emerald Downs Dr PO Box 617	Auburn	WA	98001	253-288-7000		133
TF: 888-931-8400 ■ *Web:* www.emeralddowns.com						
Emerald Hospitality Associates Inc						
2001 Crocker Rd Ste 300	Westlake	OH	44145	440-239-9848		195
Web: www.emeraldhospitality.com						
Emerald International Corp						
6895 Burlington Pk	Florence	KY	41042	859-525-2522	525-4052	501
Web: www.emeraldcoal.com						
Emerald Kalama Chemical LLC						
1296 Third St NW	Kalama	WA	98625	360-673-2550	673-3564	296-15
TF: 877-300-9545 ■ *Web:* www.emeraldmaterials.com						
Emerald Lake State Park						
65 Emerald Lake Ln	East Dorset	VT	05253	802-362-1655		565
Web: www.vtstateparks.com						
Emerald Packing						
2823 N Orange Blossom Trl	Orlando	FL	32804	407-423-0531		11-1
Emerald Queen Casino (EQC) 2024 E 29th St	Tacoma	WA	98404	253-594-7777		133
TF: 888-831-7655 ■ *Web:* www.emeraldqueen.com						
Emerald Queen Hotel & Casino						
5700 Pacific Hwy E	Fife	WA	98424	253-922-2000		379
TF: 888-820-3555 ■ *Web:* emeraldqueen.com						
Emerald Square Mall						
999 S Washington St	North Attleboro	MA	02760	508-699-7979		460
TF: 800-315-4000 ■ *Web:* www.simon.com/mall/?id=335						
e-Merchant Processing Inc						
3125 Sterling Cir	Boulder	CO	80301	303-577-0330		253
Emerge Energy Services LP						
1400 Civic Pl Ste 250	Southlake	TX	76092	817-488-7775		539
Web: www.emergelp.com						
Emergency Ambulance Service International Inc						
3200 E Birch St Ste A	Brea	CA	92821	714-990-1331		30
TF: 800-400-0689 ■ *Web:* www.emergencyambulance.com						
Emergency Communications for SW British Columbia Inc						
3301 E Pender St	Vancouver	BC	V5K5J3	604-215-5000		224
Web: www.ecomm911.ca						
Emergency Nurses Assn (ENA)						
915 Lee St	Des Plaines	IL	60016	847-460-4000	460-4001	49-8
TF: 800-900-9659 ■ *Web:* www.ena.org						
Emergency Physicians Medical Group Pc Inc						
2000 Green Rd Ste 300	Ann Arbor	MI	48105	734-995-3764	995-2913	374-3
Web: www.epmgpc.com						
EMERgency24 Inc 4179 W Irving Park Rd	Chicago	IL	60641	773-777-0707		693
Web: www.emergency24.com						
Emergent Biosolutions Inc						
2273 Research Blvd Ste 400	Rockville	MD	20850	301-795-1800	795-1899	85
TF: 800-419-7302 ■ *Web:* www.emergentbiosolutions.com						
Emergent Financial Group Inc						
3600 American Blvd W Ste 670	Bloomington	MN	55431	952-829-1212		690
Web: www.emergentfinancial.com						
Emerging Markets Traders Assn (EMTA)						
360 Madison Ave 18th Fl	New York	NY	10017	212-313-1100	313-1016	49-2
Web: www.emta.org						
Emerging Pictures 49 W 27th St	New York	NY	10001	212-245-6767		514
Web: www.emergingpictures.com						
Emerging Portfolio Fund Research Inc						
80 Sherman St	Cambridge	MA	02140	617-864-4999		637-9
Web: www.epfr.com						
Emerging Power Inc 200 Holt St	Hackensack	NJ	07601	201-441-3590		253
Web: www.emergingpower.com						
Emerging Vision Inc						
520 Eigth Ave Ste 2300	New York	NY	10018	646-737-1500		543
Web: www.emergingvision.com						
Emergo Group Inc						
816 Congress Ave Ste 1400	Austin	TX	78701	512-327-9997		193
Web: www.emergogroup.com						
Emergycare Inc 1701 Sassafras St	Erie	PA	16502	814-870-1010		30
TF: 800-814-1038 ■ *Web:* www.emergycare.org						
Emeril's 800 Tchoupitoulas St	New Orleans	LA	70130	504-528-9393	558-3925	671
Web: www.emerils.com						
Emeril's Delmonico						
1300 St Charles Ave	New Orleans	LA	70130	504-525-4937	595-2206	671
Web: www.emerils.com						
Emeril's Homebase						
829 St Charles Ave	New Orleans	LA	70130	504-524-4241		670
Web: www.emerils.com						
Emeril's New Orleans Fish House						
3799 Las Vegas Blvd S MGM Grand Hotel	Las Vegas	NV	89109	702-891-7374	891-7338	671
Web: emerilsrestaurants.com						
Emeril's Orlando						
6000 Universal Blvd Ste 702	Orlando	FL	32819	407-224-2424	224-2525	671
TF: 800-231-8395 ■ *Web:* www.emerils.com						
Emeril's Tchoup Chop						
6300 Hollywood Way	Orlando	FL	32819	407-503-2467		671
Web: www.emerils.com						
Emerson 835 Innovation Dr	Knoxville	TN	37932	865-675-2110	218-1764	472
TF: 800-675-4726 ■ *Web:* www2.emersonprocess.com						
emerson						
8100 W Florissant Ave Annex K	Saint Louis	MO	63136	314-553-1847	553-1982	201
Web: www.emersonprocess.com						
Emerson 7070 Winchester Cir	Boulder	CO	80301	303-530-8400		201
TF: 800-522-6277 ■						
Web: www2.emersonprocess.com/en-us/brands/micromotion						
Emerson Climate Technologies						
1675 Campbell Rd	Sidney	OH	45365	937-498-3011	498-3334	14
Web: www.emersonclimate.com						
Emerson Climate Technologies - Retail Solutions						
1065 Big Shanty Rd NW Ste 100	Kennesaw	GA	30144	770-425-2724	425-9319	202
TF: 800-829-2724 ■ *Web:* www.emersonclimate.com						
Emerson College 10 Boylston Pl	Boston	MA	02116	617-824-8500		166
TF: 888-627-7115 ■ *Web:* www.emerson.edu						
Emerson Equity LLC						
155 Bovet Rd Ste 725	San Mateo	CA	94402	650-312-0200		690
Web: www.emersonequity.com						
Emerson Hospital						
133 Old Rd To 9 Acre Corner	Concord	MA	01742	978-369-1400		374-3
Web: www.emersonhospital.org						
Emerson Industrial Automation						
8000 W Florissant Ave PO Box 4100	St Louis	MO	63136	952-995-8000		709
TF: 888-213-0970 ■ *Web:* www.emerson.com						
Emerson Network Power Connectivity Solutions						
1050 Dearborn Dr	Columbus	OH	43085	614-888-0246	841-6882	253
TF: 800-275-3500 ■ *Web:* www.emersonnetworkpower.com						
Emerson Resort & Spa 5340 Rt 28	Mount Tremper	NY	12457	845-688-2828		379
TF: 877-688-2828 ■ *Web:* www.emersonresort.com						
Emerson Thomson & Bennett LLC						
1914 Akron Peninsula Rd	Akron	OH	44313	330-434-9999		428
TF: 800-822-8113 ■ *Web:* www.etblaw.com						
Emerson-Swan Inc 300 Pond St	Randolph	MA	02368	781-986-2000	986-2028	612
TF: 800-346-9219 ■ *Web:* www.emersonswan.com						
Emery & Webb Inc 989 Main St	Fishkill	NY	12524	845-896-6727		390
TF: 800-942-5818 ■ *Web:* emerywebb.com						
Emery Air Charter Inc 1 Airport Cir	Rockford	IL	61109	815-968-8287		186
TF: 800-435-8090 ■ *Web:* www.emeryair.net						
Emery Corp PO Box 1104	Morganton	NC	28680	828-433-1536	433-6809	456
TF: 800-255-0537 ■ *Web:* www.emerycorp.com						
Emery County 75 E Main PO Box 907	Castle Dale	UT	84513	435-381-5106	381-5183	338
Web: www.emerycounty.com						
Emery Winslow Scale Co 73 Cogwheel Ln	Seymour	CT	06483	203-881-9333	881-9477	684
TF: 800-891-3952 ■ *Web:* www.emerywinslow.com						
Emery-Pratt Co 1966 W M 21	Owosso	MI	48867	989-723-5291		96
Web: www.emery-pratt.com						
EMF Corp 505 Pokagon Trl	Angola	IN	46703	260-665-9541		253
TF: 800-847-2818 ■ *Web:* www.emfusa.com						
Emf Inc 60 Foundry St	Keene	NH	03431	603-352-8400		175
TF: 800-992-3003 ■ *Web:* www.emfinc.com						

	Phone	Fax	Class
Emfluence 106 W 11th St Ste 2220 Kansas City MO 64105 *Web:* www.emfluence.com	816-472-5643		177
EMG Corp 10461 Mill Run Cir Ste 1100 Owings Mills MD 21117 **Fax Area Code:* 410 ■ *TF:* 800-733-0660 ■ *Web:* www.emgcorp.com	800-733-0660	785-6220*	656
Emgence Technologies Inc 11440 W Bernardo Ct San Diego CA 92127 *TF:* 800-228-8324 ■ *Web:* www.emgence.com	858-753-1985		196
Emhart Teknologies Inc 50 Shelton Technology Ctr PO Box 859 Shelton CT 06484 *Web:* www.stanleyengineeredfastening.com	203-924-9341		351
EMHS (Eastern Maine Healthcare Systems) 43 Whiting Hill Rd Brewer ME 04412 *TF:* 877-366-3662 ■ *Web:* www.emhs.org	207-973-7050	973-7139	353
EMHT (Evans Mechwart Hambleton & Tilton Inc) 5500 New Albany Rd Columbus OH 43054 *Web:* www.emht.com	614-775-4500		261
EMI Consulting 83 Columbia St Ste 400 Seattle WA 98104 *Web:* emiconsulting.com	206-621-1160		196
EMI Music Canada 109 Atlantic Ave Suite 301 Toronto ON M5E1W7 *Web:* www.emimusic.ca	416-583-5000	583-5497	657
EMI Network Inc 312 Elm St Ste 1150 Cincinnati OH 45202 *Web:* www.eminetwork.com	513-579-1950		317
EMI Services Inc 301 A St Idaho Falls ID 83402 *Web:* www.emiservices.com	208-522-1117		463
Emida Corp 27442 Portola Pkwy Ste 150 Foothill Ranch CA 92610 *Web:* www.emida.net	949-699-1401		69
Emil Anderson Construction (EAC) Inc 907 Ethel St Kelowna BC V1Y2W1 *Web:* www.eac.bc.ca	250-762-9999	762-6171	652
Emil's 2012 E Michigan Ave Lansing MI 48912	517-482-4430		671
Emile's 545 S Second St San Jose CA 95112 *Web:* www.emilesrestaurant.com	408-289-1960		671
Emiliano's Cafe 7 SE First Ave Gainesville FL 32601 *Web:* www.emilianoscafe.com	352-375-7381		671
Emily Fowler Central Library 502 Oakland St Denton TX 76201	940-349-8752		434-3
Emily Morgan Hotel 705 E Houston St San Antonio TX 78205 *TF:* 800-824-6674 ■ *Web:* www.emilymorganhotel.com	210-225-5100		379
EMILY's List 1800 M St NW Ste 375N Washington DC 20036 *TF:* 800-683-6459 ■ *Web:* www.emilyslist.org	202-326-1400	326-1415	48-7
Eminence Speaker LLC 838 Mulberry Pike PO Box 360 Eminence KY 40019 *TF:* 800-897-8373 ■ *Web:* www.eminence.com	502-845-5622	845-5622	52
Emisare Inc 532 S Elm St Ste 200 Greensboro NC 27406 *Web:* www.emisare.com	336-378-0510		7
Emisphere Technologies Inc 240 Cedar Knolls Rd Ste 200 Cedar Knolls NJ 07927 *Web:* www.emisphere.com	973-532-8000	532-8115	85
Emission Monitoring Service Inc 400 S Hwy 146 Baytown TX 77520 *Web:* www.emsi-air.com	281-428-1140		196
Emitations.com 6162 Mission Gorge Rd Ste G San Diego CA 92120 *Web:* www.emitations.com	619-528-9100		791
EMJ Corp 2034 Hamilton Pl Blvd Ste 400 Chattanooga TN 37421 *Web:* www.emjcorp.com	423-855-1550	855-6857	186
Emjay Engineering & Construction Company Inc 1706 Whitehead Rd Baltimore MD 21207 *Web:* emjaycons.com	410-298-2000		261
EMK Consultants of Florida Inc 7815 N Dale Mabry Hwy Tampa FL 33614 *TF:* 800-347-2607 ■ *Web:* www.emkfla.com	813-931-8900		261
Emka Inc 1961 Fulling Mill Rd Middletown PA 17057 *TF:* 800-426-2052 ■ *Web:* www.emkausa.com	717-986-1111		350
Emkay Inc 805 W Thorndale Ave Itasca IL 60143 *TF:* 800-621-2001 ■ *Web:* www.emkay.com	630-250-7400	250-7400	289
EMKF (Ewing Marion Kauffman Foundation) 4801 Rockhill Rd Kansas City MO 64110 *Web:* www.kauffman.org	816-932-1000	932-1100	305
EML LLC 318 Seaboard Ln Ste 106 Franklin TN 37067 *Web:* www.eml1.com	615-771-2560		393
EMM (Episcopal Migration Ministries) 815 Second Ave New York NY 10017 *TF:* 800-334-7626 ■ *Web:* episcopalchurch.org	212-716-6258		48-5
Emma Pendleton Bradley Hospital 1011 Veterans Memorial Pkwy East Providence RI 02915 *Web:* lifespan.org	401-432-1000		166
Emma Willard School 285 Pawling Ave Troy NY 12180 *Web:* www.emmawillard.org	518-833-1300	833-1805	622
Emmanuel Bible College 100 Fergus Ave Kitchener ON N2A2H2 *Web:* emmanuelbiblecollege.ca	519-894-8900	894-5331	785
Emmanuel Books 702 Delaware St PO Box 321 New Castle DE 19720 *Web:* www.emmanuelbooks.com	302-325-9515		95
Emmanuel College 400 Fenway Boston MA 02115 *Web:* www.emmanuel.edu	617-735-9715	735-9801	166
Emmanuel College 181 Spring St Franklin Springs GA 30639 *TF:* 800-860-8800 ■ *Web:* www.ec.edu	706-245-7226	245-2876	166
Emmanuel Gospel Center Inc 2 San Juan St Boston MA 02118 *Web:* egc.org	617-262-4567		48-20
Emmart & Son Inc W H 305 Brick Kiln Rd Winchester VA 22601	540-662-3848		539
Emmaus Bible College 2570 Asbury Rd Dubuque IA 52001 *TF:* 800-397-2425 ■ *Web:* www.emmaus.edu	563-588-8000	588-1216	161
Emmaus Medical Inc 20725 S Western Ave Ste 136 Torrance CA 90501 *Web:* emmausmedical.com	310-214-0065		231
Emme E2MS LLC PO Box 2251 Bristol CT 06011 *TF:* 800-396-0523 ■ *Web:* www.getemme.com	800-396-0523		407
Emmer Group 2801 SW Archer Rd Gainesville FL 32608 *TF:* 800-293-5867 ■ *Web:* www.emmergroup.com	352-376-2444	376-2260	653
Emmer Tom (Rep R - MN) 315 Cannon HOB Washington DC 20515 *Web:* emmer.house.gov	202-225-2331	225-6475	342-2
Emmet County 609 First Ave N Estherville IA 51334 *Web:* www.emmetcountyia.com	712-362-4261	362-7454	338
Emmet County 200 Div St Ste 130 Petoskey MI 49770 *TF:* 866-731-1204 ■ *Web:* www.emmetcounty.org	231-348-1702	348-0602	338
Emmis Communications Corp 40 Monument Cir 1 Emmis Plz Ste 700 Indianapolis IN 46204 *NASDAQ: EMMS* ■ *Web:* www.emmis.com	317-266-0100		643
Emmons County 100 NW Fourth St PO Box 272 Linton ND 58552 *Web:* emmonscounty.tripod.com	701-254-5410		338
EMMsphere 102 W Third St Ste 1200 Winston-salem NC 27101 *Web:* www.marketspheremarketing.com	336-608-3060		196
Emmy Magazine 5220 Lankershim Blvd North Hollywood CA 91601 *Web:* emmys.com	818-754-2800		457-9
Emory & Henry College PO Box 10 Emory VA 24327 **Fax:* Admissions ■ *TF Admissions:* 800-848-5493 ■ *Web:* www.ehc.edu	276-944-4121	944-6935*	166
Emory & Henry College Kelly Library 30450 Armbrister Dr Emory VA 24327 *Web:* www.ehc.edu	276-944-6208	944-4592	434-6
Emory Conference Ctr Hotel 1615 Clifton Rd Atlanta GA 30329 *TF:* 800-933-6679 ■ *Web:* www.emoryconferencecenter.com	404-712-6000	712-6025	377
Emory Crawford Long Hospital 550 Peachtree St NE Atlanta GA 30308 *Web:* www.emoryhealthcare.org	404-686-4411		374-3
Emory L Bennett Memorial Veterans' Nursing Home 1920 Mason Ave Daytona Beach FL 32117	386-274-3460		793
Emory University 201 Dowman Dr Atlanta GA 30322 *TF Admissions:* 800-727-6036 ■ *Web:* www.emory.edu	404-727-6036	727-4303	166
Emory University Hospital 1364 Clifton Rd Atlanta GA 30322 *Web:* www.emoryhealthcare.org	404-712-2000		374-3
Emory University School of Law 1301 Clifton Rd Atlanta GA 30322 **Fax:* Admissions ■ *Web:* www.law.emory.edu	404-727-6816	727-6802*	167-1
Emory University School of Medicine 1440 Clifton Rd NE Atlanta GA 30322 **Fax:* Admissions ■ *Web:* www.med.emory.edu	404-727-5660	727-5456*	167-2
Emory University Woodruff Library 540 Asbury Cir Atlanta GA 30322 *Web:* emory.edu/home/academics/libraries/index.html	404-727-6861	727-0805	434-6
Emoteq Corp 10002 E 43rd St S Tulsa OK 74146 *Web:* www.emoteq.com	918-627-1845		518
Emotion Studios 85 Liberty Ship Way Sausalito CA 94965 *Web:* www.emotionstudios.com	415-331-6975		180
Empathylogic.com 15732 Los Gatos Blvd #434 Los Gatos CA 95032 *Web:* www.empathylogic.com	408-940-3951		196
Emperor of China Restaurant 1010 E Brady St Milwaukee WI 53202 *Web:* www.emperorofchinarestaurant.com	414-271-8889		671
Emperor's Palace 400 Cooper Pt Rd SW Olympia WA 98502 *Web:* www.eprestaurant.com	360-352-0777		671
Empire Advisory Group Inc 38 Chimney View Ln Springfield IL 62707	217-528-0047		466
Empire Airlines Inc 11559 N Atlas Rd Hayden ID 83835 *Web:* www.empireairlines.com	208-292-3850	292-3851	12
Empire Architectural 409 N Main St Freeport NY 11520 *Web:* www.empirearchitecturalproducts.com	516-377-8545		820
Empire Arts Ctr 415 DeMers Ave Grand Forks ND 58201 *Web:* www.empireartscenter.com	701-746-5500	746-0500	572
Empire Bakery Equipment 171 Greenwich St Hempstead NY 11550 *TF:* 800-878-4070 ■ *Web:* empirebake.com	516-538-1210		454
Empire Bldg Materials Inc PO Box 220 Bozeman MT 59771 **Fax Area Code:* 406 ■ *TF:* 800-332-4577 ■ *Web:* www.empireinc.com	800-548-8201	587-3144*	191-2
Empire Blended Products Inc 250 Hickory Ln Bayville NJ 08721 *TF:* 800-526-9377 ■ *Web:* empireblended.com	732-269-4949		183
Empire Building Services 1570 E Edinger Ave Santa Ana CA 92705 *TF:* 888-296-2078 ■ *Web:* www.ebuildingservices.com	714-836-7700		138
Empire Cheese Inc 4520 County Rd 6 Cuba NY 14727 *TF:* 800-362-9196 ■ *Web:* greatlakescheese.com	585-968-1552	968-2660	296-5
Empire Chinese Restaurant 410 E Green St Champaign IL 61820 *Web:* cu-empire.com	217-328-0832		671
Empire Cleaning Supply 12821 S Figueroa St Los Angeles CA 90061 *Web:* www.empirecleaningsupply.com	310-527-0132		151
Empire Comfort Systems Inc 918 Freeburg Ave Belleville IL 62222 *Web:* www.empirecomfort.com	618-233-7420	233-7097	357
Empire Company Ltd 115 King St Stellarton NS B0K1S0 *TSE: EMP.A* ■ *TF:* 800-387-0825 ■ *Web:* www.empireco.ca	902-755-4440	755-6477	185
Empire Diamond Corp 350 Fifth Ave Ste 4000 New York NY 10118 *TF:* 800-728-3425 ■ *Web:* www.dialadiamond.com	212-564-4777	564-4960	411
Empire Die Casting Co Inc 635 Highland Rd E Macedonia OH 44056 *Web:* www.empiredie.com	330-467-0750	467-9118	308
Empire District Electric Co, The 602 Joplin St PO Box 127 Joplin MO 64802 *NYSE: EDE* ■ *TF:* 800-206-2300 ■ *Web:* www.empiredistrict.com	417-625-5100		787
Empire Electric Assn Inc 801 N Broadway Cortez CO 81321 *TF:* 800-709-3726 ■ *Web:* www.eea.coop	970-565-4444		245
Empire Energy Corporation International Level 3 65 Murray St Hobart Tasmania Leawood KS 66211 *Web:* www.empireenergy.com	913-663-2310		536
Empire Food Brokers of Ohio Inc 11243 Cornell Pk Dr Cincinnati OH 45242 *Web:* www.empirefoods.com	513-793-6241		297-8

Phone | Fax | Class

Empire Industries Inc
180 Olcott St. . . . . Manchester CT 06040 860-647-1431 647-1160 595
TF: 800-243-4844 ■ *Web:* www.empireindustries.com

Empire Iron Works Ltd
21104 - 107 Ave. . . . . Edmonton AB T5S1X2 780-447-4650 105
Web: www.empireiron.com

Empire Justice Center
1 W Main St Ste 200. . . . . Rochester NY 14614 585-454-4060 428
Web: www.empirejustice.org

Empire Kosher Poultry Inc
247 Empire Dr . . . . . Mifflintown PA 17059 717-436-7055 619
Web: www.empirekosher.com

Empire Landmark Hotel & Conference Ctr
1400 Robson St . . . . . Vancouver BC V6G1B9 604-687-0511 379
TF: 800-830-6144 ■ *Web:* www.empirelandmarkhotel.com

Empire Level Manufacturing Corp
929 Empire Dr PO Box 800. . . . . Mukwonago WI 53149 800-558-0722 368-2127* 758
**Fax Area Code: 262* ■ *TF:* 800-558-0722 ■ *Web:* www.empirelevel.com

Empire Little Bar & Bistro, The
257 Granby St. . . . . Norfolk VA 23510 757-626-3100 671

Empire Livestock Marketing LLC
5001 Brittonfield Pkwy . . . . . East Syracuse NY 13057 315-433-9129 433-0068 446
TF: 800-462-8802 ■ *Web:* www.empirelivestock.com

Empire Maintenance Co Inc
624 S Palm Ave . . . . . Alhambra CA 91803 626-289-8755 104
Web: www.empiremaintenance.com

Empire Mall, The 5000 Empire Mall. . . . . Sioux Falls SD 57106 605-361-0586 362-0283 460
Web: simon.com/default.aspx

Empire Media Services Inc
2050 E Continental Blvd. . . . . Southlake TX 76092 469-855-5959 5
Web: www.empiremedia.net

Empire Mine State Historic Park
10791 East Empire St. . . . . Grass Valley CA 95945 530-273-8522 565
Web: www.parks.ca.gov/default.asp?page_id=499

Empire Office Inc
105 Madison Ave Ste 15. . . . . New York NY 10016 212-607-5500 320
Web: www.empireoffice.com

Empire Optical Inc 3238 E 21st St . . . . . Tulsa OK 74114 918-744-8005 543
Web: empireoptical.com

Empire Plow Company Inc
3140 E 65th St . . . . . Cleveland OH 44127 216-641-2290 441-4709 273
Web: www.mckayempire.com

Empire Recycling Corp 64 N Genesee St. . . . . Utica NY 13502 315-724-7161 660
Web: www.empirerecycling.com

Empire Resorts Inc 204 Rt 17B . . . . . Monticello NY 12701 845-807-0001 132
NASDAQ: NYNY ■ *Web:* www.empireresorts.com

Empire Resources Inc
2115 Linwood Ave . . . . . Fort Lee NJ 07024 201-944-2200 944-2226 485
NYSE: ERS ■ *Web:* www.empireresources.com

Empire Safety & Supply Inc
10624 Industrial Ave. . . . . Roseville CA 95678 916-781-3003 882-9060* 679
**Fax Area Code: 888* ■ *TF:* 800-995-1341 ■ *Web:* www.empiresafety.com

Empire Screen Printing Inc
N5206 Marco Rd PO Box 218. . . . . Onalaska WI 54650 608-783-3301 783-3306 687
Web: www.empirescreen.com

Empire Southwest Co
1725 S Country Club Dr. . . . . Mesa AZ 85210 480-633-4000 633-4000 358
TF: 800-367-4731 ■ *Web:* www.empire-cat.com

Empire State Aerosciences Museum
250 Rudy Chase Dr . . . . . Glenville NY 12302 518-377-2191 377-1959 520
TF: 800-258-3582 ■ *Web:* www.esam.org

Empire State Bank 68 N Plank Rd . . . . . Newburgh NY 12550 845-561-0003 70
Web: esbna.com

Empire State Bldg
350 Fifth Ave Ste 100. . . . . New York NY 10118 212-736-3100 50-4
TF: 877-692-8439 ■ *Web:* www.esbnyc.com

Empire Telephone Corp
34 Main St PO Box 349 . . . . . Prattsburgh NY 14873 607-522-3712 736
TF: 800-338-3300 ■ *Web:* www.empiretelephone.com

Empire Travel Services
2080 Wern Ave. . . . . Guilderland NY 12084 518-869-0738 772
Web: www.empiretravel.com

Empire Turkish Grill
12448 Memorial Dr . . . . . Houston TX 77024 713-827-7475 671
Web: www.empireturkishgrill.com

Empire Vision Centers
2921 Erie Blvd E. . . . . Syracuse NY 13224 315-446-5120 543
Web: www.visionworks.com/loc/01020

Empire West Inc
9270 Graton Rd PO Box 511. . . . . Graton CA 95444 707-823-1190 823-8531 602
TF: 800-521-4261 ■ *Web:* www.empirewest.com

Empire-Fulton Ferry State Park
1 Water St. . . . . Brooklyn NY 11201 718-222-9939 565

EmpireWorks Inc 1940 Olivera Rd . . . . . Concord CA 94520 888-278-8200 260
TF: 888-278-8200 ■ *Web:* www.empireworks.com

Empirical Testing Corp
4628 Northpark Dr . . . . . Colorado Springs CO 80918 719-264-9937 743
TF: 800-366-3067 ■ *Web:* empiricaltech.com

Empirix Inc
600 Technology Park Dr Ste 100 . . . . . Billerica MA 01821 978-313-7000 313-7001 178-12
Web: www.empirix.com

EmplawyerNet 2331 Westwood Blvd. . . . . Los Angeles CA 90064 800-270-2688 260
TF: 800-270-2688 ■ *Web:* www.emplawyernet.com

Emplicity 9851 Irvine Ctr Dr. . . . . Irvine CA 92618 714-668-1388 260
TF: 800-447-3237 ■ *Web:* www.emplicity.com

Employco USA Inc 350 E Ogden Ave . . . . . Westmont IL 60559 630-920-0000 260
Web: www.employco.com

Employee & Family Resources Inc (EFR)
505 Fifth Ave Ste 600. . . . . Des Moines IA 50309 515-288-9020 631
Web: www.efr.org

Employee Assistance Professionals Assn Inc (EAPA)
4350 N Fairfax Dr Ste 740 . . . . . Arlington VA 22203 703-387-1000 522-4585 49-12
TF: 800-937-8461 ■ *Web:* www.eapassn.org

Employee Benefit Research Institute (EBRI)
1100 13th St NW Ste 878. . . . . Washington DC 20005 202-659-0670 775-6312 634
Web: www.ebri.org

Employee benefits News
1 State St Plaza Fl 27 . . . . . New York NY 10004 212-803-8200 390
Web: www.benefitnews.com

Employee Benefits Security Administration
200 Constitution Ave NW Rm S2524 . . . . . Washington DC 20210 202-693-8300 219-5526 340-15
Web: www.dol.gov/ebsa

Employee Development Systems Inc
7308 S Alton Way Ste 2J . . . . . Centennial CO 80112 303-221-0710 179
TF: 800-282-3374 ■ *Web:* www.employeedevelopmentsystems.com

Employee Involvement Assn
11 W Monument Ave . . . . . Dayton OH 45402 937-586-3724 49-12

Employee Leasing Solutions Inc
1401 Manatee Ave W Ste 600. . . . . Bradenton FL 34205 941-746-6567 390

Employee Management Services
435 Elm St . . . . . Cincinnati OH 45202 513-651-3244 381-2764 631
TF: 888-651-1536 ■ *Web:* www.emshro.com

Employee Owned Holdings Inc
5500 N Sam Houston Pkwy W Ste 100. . . . . Houston TX 77086 281-569-7000 791
Web: www.eoh-inc.com

Employee Resource Systems Inc
29 E Madison St Ste 1600 . . . . . Chicago IL 60602 312-269-0287 196
Web: ers-eap.com

Employees Only Inc
3256 University Dr Ste 25. . . . . Auburn Hills MI 48326 248-276-0950 194
Web: www.employeesonly.net

EmployeeScreenIQ Inc
24500 Chagrin Blvd . . . . . Cleveland OH 44122 800-899-2272 466
TF: 800-899-2272 ■ *Web:* www.employeescreen.com

Employer Benefits Inc 31 Keystone Ave . . . . . Reno NV 89503 775-786-6381 390
Web: ebi-nv.com

Employer Flexible
7850 N Sam Houston Parkway W Ste 100 . . . . . Houston TX 77064 866-501-4942 734
TF: 866-501-4942 ■ *Web:* www.employerflexible.com

Employer Plan Services Inc
2180 N Loop W Ste 400. . . . . Houston TX 77018 713-351-3500 193
TF: 800-447-6588 ■ *Web:* www.epsibenefitsinc.com

Employer Solutions Group Inc
4844 N 300 W Ste 100. . . . . Provo UT 84604 801-223-7007 734
Web: www.esgnr.com

Employer's Hum Res Inc (EHRI)
75899 State Hwy 16 . . . . . Wagoner OK 74467 918-485-9404 631

Employers Association, The
3020 W Arrowood Rd . . . . . Charlotte NC 28273 704-522-8011 317
Web: www.employersassoc.com

Employers Choice Solutions Inc
22476 Sacramento Ave. . . . . Port Charlotte FL 33954 941-627-0777 631
Web: www.employerchoice.com

Employers Council on Flexible Compensation (ECFC)
927 15th St NW Ste 700. . . . . Washington DC 20005 202-659-4300 216-9646 49-12
Web: www.ecfc.org

Employers Group
400 N Continental Blvd Ste 300 . . . . . El Segundo CA 90015 800-748-8484 533
TF: 800-748-8484 ■ *Web:* www.employersgroup.com

Employers Insurance Company of Nevada
9790 Gateway Dr Ste 100 . . . . . Reno NV 89521 888-682-6671 390
TF: 888-682-6671 ■ *Web:* www.employers.com

Employers Resource Management Co
1301 S Vista Ave Ste 200. . . . . Boise ID 83705 208-376-3000 570
TF: 800-574-4668 ■ *Web:* www.employersresource.com

Employment & Training Administration
200 Constitution Ave NW . . . . . Washington DC 20210 866-487-2365 340-15
TF: 866-487-2365 ■ *Web:* www.doleta.gov
Region I - Boston
25 New Sudbury St Rm E-350. . . . . Boston MA 02203 617-788-0170 788-0101 340-15
Web: www.doleta.gov/regions/reg01bos
Region II-Philadelphia
170 S Independence Mall W Ste 825 E . . . . . Philadelphia PA 19106 215-861-5200 861-5260 340-15
Web: www.doleta.gov

Employment & Training Administration Regional Offices
Region 3- Atlanta
Federal Ctr 61 Forsyth St SW Rm 6M12 . . . . . Atlanta GA 30303 404-302-5300 302-5382 340-15
Web: www.doleta.gov/regions/reg03
Region 4- Dallas 525 Griffin St Rm 317 . . . . . Dallas TX 75202 972-850-4600 850-4605 340-15
Web: www.doleta.gov/regions/reg04
Region 5 - Chicago
Federal Bldg 230 S Dearborn St 6th Fl . . . . . Chicago IL 60604 312-596-5400 596-5401 340-15
Web: www.doleta.gov/regions/reg05

Employment Discrimination Report
1801 S Bell St. . . . . Arlington VA 22202 800-372-1033 531-7
TF: 800-372-1033 ■ *Web:* www.bna.com

Employment Guide LLC, The
4460 Corporation Ln Ste 317. . . . . Virginia Beach VA 23462 877-876-4039 260
TF: 877-876-4039 ■ *Web:* www.employmentguide.com

Employment Policies Institute
1090 Vermont Ave NW Ste 800. . . . . Washington DC 20005 202-463-7650 463-7107 634
Web: www.epionline.org

Employment Screening Services Inc
627 E Sprague St Ste 100. . . . . Spokane WA 99202 509-624-3851 321-2905* 635
**Fax Area Code: 800* ■ *TF:* 800-473-7778 ■ *Web:* www.employscreen.com

Employment Standards Administration
200 Constitution Ave NW Rm S2321 . . . . . Washington DC 20210 202-693-0200 340-15
TF: 866-487-2365 ■ *Web:* www.dol.gov
Office of Labor-Management Standards (OLMS)
200 Constitution Ave NW Rm N-1519. . . . . Washington DC 20210 866-487-2365 340-15
TF: 866-487-2365 ■ *Web:* www.dol.gov/olms
Wage & Hour Div
200 Constitution Ave NW. . . . . Washington DC 20210 202-693-0051 340-15
Web: doleta.gov

EMPO Corp
3100 West Lake St Ste 100. . . . . Minneapolis MN 55416 612-285-8707 631
Web: www.empocorp.com

Emporia Area Chamber of Commerce
719 Commercial St. . . . . Emporia KS 66801 620-342-1600 342-3223 139
TF: 800-279-3730 ■ *Web:* www.emporiakschamber.org

Emporia (Independent City)
201 S Main St. . . . . Emporia VA 23847 434-634-3332 634-0003 338
Web: www.ci.emporia.va.us

Emporia State University
1200 Commercial St. . . . . Emporia KS 66801 620-341-1200 341-5599 166
TF: 877-468-6378 ■ *Web:* www.emporia.edu

Phone | Fax | Class

Empower Financials Inc
305 E Eisenhower Ste 318 . . . Ann Arbor MI 48108 734-747-9393 177
Web: empowerfin.com

EmPower Research LLC
404 E 79th St Ste 16E . . . New York NY 10075 646-472-7908 668
Web: www.empowerresearch.com

Empower Rf Systems Inc
316 W Florence Ave . . . Inglewood CA 90301 310-412-8100 412-9232 647
Web: www.empowerrf.com

Empowered Networks Inc
1315 Pickering Pkwy Ste 200 . . . Pickering ON L1V7G5 905-837-6585 463
Web: emporednetworks.com

Empresas Berrios Inc PO Box 674 . . . Cidra PR 00739 787-653-9393 321

Empress Hotel 7766 Fay Ave . . . La Jolla CA 92037 858-454-3001 379
Web: www.empress-hotel.com

Empress of China 2648 N Belt Line Rd . . . Irving TX 75062 972-252-7677 671
Web: www.eocrestaurant.com

Empress Software Inc
11785 Beltsville Dr . . . Beltsville MD 20705 301-220-1919 220-1997 178-2
TF: 866-626-8888 ■ *Web:* www.empress.com

Emprise Corp
3900 Kennesaw 75 Pkwy N W Ste 125 . . . Kennesaw GA 30144 770-425-1420 261
TF: 800-278-2119 ■ *Web:* www.emprise-usa.com

Emprise Financial Corp
257 N Broadway St PO Box 2970 . . . Wichita KS 67202 316-383-4301 69
TF Cust Svc: 800-201-7118 ■ *Web:* www.emprisebank.com

Emprise Publishing Inc
1104 Murrayhill Rd . . . Vestal NY 13850 607-772-0559 94

Empson Drug Co 212 N Main St . . . Ashland City TN 37015 615-792-4644 237

EmpXtrack 150 Motor Pkwy Ste 401 . . . Hauppauge NY 11788 888-840-2682 41
TF: 888-840-2682 ■ *Web:* www.empxtrack.com

EMR Inc 2110 Delaware St Ste B . . . Lawrence KS 66046 785-842-9013 667
Web: www.emr-inc.com

Emrise Corp
101 Wood Ave S 5th Floor . . . Woodbridge NJ 08830 732-395-4400 253
Web: www.emrise.com

EMS (IEEE Engineering Management Society)
IEEE Operations Ctr 445 and 501 Hoes Ln . . . Piscataway NJ 08854 732-981-0060 562-6380 49-19
TF: 800-678-4333 ■ *Web:* www.ewh.ieee.org/soc/ems

Ems Industrial Inc 802 Live Oak Dr . . . Chesapeake VA 23320 757-424-0134 698

Emsar Inc 125 Access Rd . . . Stratford CT 06615 203-377-9874 596
Web: www.emsargroup.com

EMSD (East Maine School District 63)
10150 Dee Rd . . . Des Plaines IL 60016 847-299-1900 299-9963 685
TF: 866-752-6850 ■ *Web:* www.emsd63.org

Ems-tech Inc 699 Dundas St W . . . Belleville ON K8N4Z2 613-966-6611 256
TF: 844-450-8324 ■ *Web:* ems-tech.net

EMT International Inc
780 Centerline Dr . . . Hobart WI 54155 920-468-5475 100
Web: www.emtinternational.com

EMTA (Emerging Markets Traders Assn)
360 Madison Ave 18th Fl . . . New York NY 10017 212-313-1100 313-1016 49-2
Web: www.emta.org

EMTA (Erie Metropolitan Transit Authority)
127 E 14th St . . . Erie PA 16503 814-452-3515 468
TF: 800-692-6314 ■ *Web:* www.ride-the-e.com

Emtec Consultants, Professional Engineers PLLC
3555 Veterans Memorial Hw . . . Ronkonkoma NY 11779 631-981-3990 261
TF: 800-834-4663 ■ *Web:* www.emtec-engineers.com

Emtek Products Inc
15250 Stafford St . . . City of Industry CA 91744 626-961-0413 350
TF: 800-356-2741 ■ *Web:* www.emtek.com

Emteq Inc 5349 S Emmer Dr . . . New Berlin WI 53151 262-679-6170 679-6175 24
TF: 888-679-6170 ■ *Web:* www.emteq.com

Emtex Inc 42 Cherry Hill Dr # B . . . Danvers MA 01923 978-907-4500 745-2
TF: 800-840-7035 ■ *Web:* www.emtexinc.com

Emulation Technology Inc
759 Flynn Rd . . . Camarillo CA 93012 805-383-8480 201
TF: 800-232-7837 ■ *Web:* www.emulation.com

Emulso Corp 2750 Kenmore Ave . . . Tonawanda NY 14150 716-854-2889 854-2809 151
TF: 800-535-5053 ■ *Web:* www.emulso.com

EMW Carpets & Furniture
2141 S Broadway . . . Denver CO 80210 303-744-2754 131
Web: emwcarpets.com

EN Bisso & Son Inc
3939 N Causeway Blvd Ste 401 . . . Metairie LA 70002 504-828-3296 539
Web: www.enbisso.com

EN Engineering LLC
28100 Torch Pkwy Ste 400 . . . Warrenville IL 60555 630-353-4000 353-7777 261
Web: www.enengineering.com

ENA (Emergency Nurses Assn)
915 Lee St . . . Des Plaines IL 60016 847-460-4000 460-4001 49-8
TF: 800-900-9659 ■ *Web:* www.ena.org

EnablePath LLC
3475 Piedmont Rd NE Ste 1225 . . . Atlanta GA 30305 704-373-9000 463
TF: 866-372-2897 ■ *Web:* enablepath.com

Enabling Technologies Corp
12226 Long Green Pk . . . Glen Arm MD 21057 443-625-5100 177
Web: www.enablingtechcorp.com

Enagic USA Inc 4115 Spencer St . . . Torrance CA 90503 310-542-7700 610
Web: www.enagic.com

Enanta Pharmaceuticals Inc
500 Arsenal St . . . Watertown MA 02472 617-607-0800 668
Web: www.enanta.com

Enaxis Consulting
9 Greenway Plaza Ste 3005 . . . Houston TX 77046 713-881-9494 463
Web: www.enaxisconsulting.com

ENBALA Power Networks Ltd
360 Bay St Ste 401 . . . Toronto ON M5H2V6 416-623-2626 387
Web: www.enbala.com

Enbase LLC 3303 Louisiana St Ste 210 . . . Houston TX 77006 888-400-2719 538
TF: 888-400-2719 ■ *Web:* www.enbasesolutions.com

Enbridge Energy Partners LP
1100 Louisiana Ste 3300 . . . Houston TX 77002 713-821-2000 597
NYSE: EEP ■ *TF:* 800-481-2804 ■ *Web:* www.enbridgepartners.com

EnCana Corp 500 Ctr St SE Po Box 2850 . . . Calgary AB T2G1A6 403-645-2000 645-3400 536
NYSE: ECA ■ *TF:* 888-568-6322 ■ *Web:* www.encana.com

Encari LLC 1616 E Millbrook Rd Ste 210 . . . Raleigh NC 27609 919-256-5900 196
Web: www.encari.com

Enchanted Mansion Doll Museum
190 Lee Dr . . . Baton Rouge LA 70808 225-769-0005 520
TF: 800-955-8510 ■ *Web:* www.enchantedmansion.org

Enchanted Rock State Natural Area
16710 Ranch Rd 965 . . . Fredericksburg TX 78624 830-685-3636 565
Web: tpwd.texas.gov/state-parks/enchanted-rock

Enchantment Resort
525 Boynton Canyon Rd . . . Sedona AZ 86336 800-826-4180 282-9249* 669
**Fax Area Code: 928* ■ *TF:* 800-826-4180 ■ *Web:* www.enchantmentresort.com

Encima Global LLC
645 Madison Ave 5th Fl . . . New York NY 10022 212-876-4400 401
Web: www.encimaglobal.com

Encinitas Chamber of Commerce
527 Encinitas Blvd . . . Encinitas CA 92024 760-753-6041 753-6270 139
TF: 800-953-6041 ■ *Web:* www.encinitaschamber.com

Encinitas Union School District
101 S Rancho Santa Fe Rd . . . Encinitas CA 92024 760-944-4300 685
Web: www.eusd.k12.ca.us

Encino Chamber of Commerce
4933 Balboa Blvd . . . Encino CA 91316 818-789-4711 789-2485 139
Web: encinochamber.org

EnCirca Inc
400 W Cummings Pk Ste 1725-307 . . . Woburn MA 01801 781-942-9975 823-8911 396
Web: www.encirca.com

Encision Inc 6797 Winchester Cir . . . Boulder CO 80301 303-444-2600 444-2693 476
OTC: ECIA ■ *TF:* 800-998-0986 ■ *Web:* www.encision.com

Enclave Suites of Orlando
6165 Carrier Dr . . . Orlando FL 32819 407-351-1155 379
TF: 800-457-0077 ■ *Web:* www.enclavesuites.com

Enclos Corp 2770 Blue Water Rd . . . Eagan MN 55121 651-796-6100 994-6360 189-6
TF: 888-234-2966 ■ *Web:* www.enclos.com

Enclude Ltd 1220 19th St NW Ste 200 . . . Washington DC 20036 202-822-9100 466
Web: www.encludesolutions.com

ENCO Laboratories Inc
10775 Central Port Dr . . . Orlando FL 32824 407-826-5314 743
Web: encolabs.com

Encoder Products Co
464276 Hwy 95 S PO Box 249 . . . Sagle ID 83860 208-263-8541 263-0541 201
TF: 800-366-5412 ■ *Web:* www.encoder.com

Encoll Corp. Inc 4576 Enterprise St . . . Fremont CA 94538 510-795-8581 317
Web: www.encoll.com

Encompass Financial Advisors Inc
6107 SW Murray Blvd . . . Beaverton OR 97008 503-643-8075 401
Web: fiadvisor.com

Encompass Group LLC 615 Macon Rd . . . McDonough GA 30253 770-957-1211 155-19
TF: 800-284-4540 ■ *Web:* www.encompassgroup.net

Encompass Iowa LLC
1420 First Ave NE . . . Cedar Rapids IA 52402 319-862-0221 180
Web: www.encompassiowa.com

Encompass Media Inc 11-11 44th Dr . . . Long Island NY 11101 212-993-9429 5
Web: emgmediainc.com

Encon Group Inc 500-1400 Blair Pl . . . Ottawa ON K1J9B8 613-786-2000 390
TF: 800-267-6684 ■ *Web:* www.encon.ca

Encon Inc 6161 Ventnor Ave . . . Dayton OH 45414 937-898-2603 596
Web: www.enconco.com

Encon International
7307 Remcon Cir 101 . . . El Paso TX 79912 915-833-3740 261
Web: www.enconinternational.com

Encon Safety Products Co
6825 W Sam Houston Pkwy N PO Box 3826 . . . Houston TX 77041 713-466-1449 466-1703 678
TF: 800-283-6266 ■ *Web:* www.enconsafety.com

Encore Bank
3003 Tamiami Trail N Ste 100 . . . Naples FL 34103 239-919-5888 70
TF: 800-472-3272 ■ *Web:* www.encorebank.com

Encore Capital Group Inc
3111 Camino Del Rio N Ste 300 . . . San Diego CA 92108 858-560-2600 160
NASDAQ: ECPG ■ *TF:* 877-445-4581 ■ *Web:* www.encorecapital.com

Encore Cbt Co 5900 US-23 . . . Worthington OH 43085 614-888-4179 463

Encore Consumer Capital
111 Pine St Ste 1825 . . . San Francisco CA 94111 415-296-9850 194
Web: www.encoreconsumercapital.com

Encore Creative Inc 410 S Madison Dr . . . Tempe AZ 85281 480-736-2800 149
Web: www.encorecreative.com

Encore Event Technologies
1 N Arlington 1500 W Shure Dr
Ste 175 . . . Arlington Heights IL 60004 800-836-8361 358-3106* 52
**Fax Area Code: 847* ■ *TF:* 800-836-8361 ■ *Web:* encore-us.com

Encore Hollywood
6344 Fountain Ave . . . Los Angeles CA 90028 323-466-7663 512
Web: www.encorepost.com

Encore Image Group Inc
1445 W Sepulveda Blvd . . . Torrance CA 90509 800-729-4853 5
TF: 800-729-4853 ■ *Web:* www.encoreimagegroup.com

Encore Manufacturing Company Inc
2415 Ashland Ave . . . Beatrice NE 68310 800-267-4255 429
TF: 800-267-4255 ■ *Web:* www.encoreequipment.com

Encore Medical Corp 9800 Metric Blvd . . . Austin TX 78758 512-832-9500 834-6300 85
TF: 800-456-8696 ■ *Web:* www.djoglobal.com

Encore Networks Inc
3800 Concorde Pkwy Ste 1500 . . . Chantilly VA 20151 703-318-7750 787-4625 173-3
TF: 800-770-0906 ■ *Web:* www.encorenetworks.com

Encore Wire Corp 1329 Millwood Rd . . . McKinney TX 75069 972-562-9473 562-3644 813
NASDAQ: WIRE ■ *TF:* 800-962-9473 ■ *Web:* www.encorewire.com

Encotech Engineering Cnsltnts
8500 Bluffstone Cv . . . Austin TX 78759 512-338-1101 261
Web: www.encotechengineering.com

Encur Inc 200 Division St . . . Keyport NJ 07735 732-264-2098 261
Web: encur.com

Encyclopaedia Britannica Inc
331 N La Salle St . . . Chicago IL 60654 312-347-7159 294-2104* 637-2
**Fax: PR* ■ *TF:* 800-323-1229 ■ *Web:* www.britannica.com

Encyclopedia.com
360 N Michigan Ave Ste 1900 . . . Chicago IL 60601 312-224-5000 224-5001 397
Web: www.encyclopedia.com

End Point Corp 304 Park Ave S Ste 214 . . . New York NY 10010 212-929-6923 180
TF: 800-818-2361 ■ *Web:* www.endpoint.com

Endacea Inc 2 Davis Dr . . . Research Triangle Park NC 27709 919-406-1888 668
Web: www.endacea.com

Phone | Fax | Class

Endeavor Agency
9601 Wilshire Blvd 3rd Fl Beverly Hills CA 90210 310-859-4000 285-9010 731
TF: 800-767-4984 ■ *Web:* www.wmeentertainment.com

Endeavor Commerce Inc
13140 Coit Ste 450 Dallas TX 75240 214-736-7178 177
Web: endeavorcpq.com

Endeavor Hall 6008 Center St Clayton CA 94517 925-673-7300 720
TF: 800-750-4096 ■ *Web:* cityofclayton.org

Endeavor IP Inc
46TH Fl, 140 BROADWAY New York NY 10005 212-858-7514 317
Web: www.enip.com

Endeavour Capital Inc
760 SW Ninth Ave Ste 2300 Portland OR 97205 503-223-2721 690
Web: www.endeavourcapital.com

Endeavour international corp
811 Main St Ste 2100 Houston TX 77002 713-307-8700 538
OTC: ENDRQ ■ *Web:* www.endeavourcorp.com

Endeavour Software Technologies Inc
8140 N Mopac Expy Westpark 1 Ste 220 Austin TX 78759 512-464-1218 631
Web: www.techendeavour.com

Enderes Tool Co
1521 E Hawthorne St Albert Lea MN 56007 507-373-2396 373-2398 758
TF: 800-874-7776 ■ *Web:* www.enderes.com

Enderle Group Inc 389 Photinia Ln San Jose CA 95127 408-272-8560 463
Web: www.enderlegroup.com

Enders Island PO Box 399 Mystic CT 06355 860-536-0565 572-7655 673
Web: www.endersisland.com

Enders Reservoir State Recreation Area
73122 338th Ave Enders NE 69027 308-394-5118 565
Web: outdoornebraska.gov/endersreservoir

Endevco Corp
30700 Rancho Viejo Rd San Juan Capistrano CA 92675 949-493-8181 661-7231 472
TF: 800-982-6732 ■ *Web:* www.endevco.com

Endicott Clay Products Co
57120 707 Rd Endicott NE 68350 402-729-3315 729-5804 150
TF: 800 393-6343 ■ *Web:* www.endicott.com

Endicott College 376 Hale St Beverly MA 01915 978-232-2021 232-2520* 166
**Fax:* Admissions ■ *TF Admissions:* 800-325-1114 ■ *Web:* www.endicott.edu

Endicott Precision Inc
1328 Campville Rd Endicott NY 13760 607-754-7076 697
TF: 800-666-6523 ■ *Web:* www.endicottprecision.com

Endicott Research Group Inc
2601 Wayne St, Po Box 269 Endicott NY 13760 607-754-9187 696
Web: www.ergpower.com

Endicott Rock State Historic Site
17 Endicott St Laconia NH 03246 603-271-3556 565

Endicott Tile LLC 57120 707 Rd Endicott NE 68350 402-729-3315 729-5804 751
TF: 800-393-6343 ■ *Web:* www.endicott.com

Endo Pharmaceuticals Holdings Inc
100 Endo Blvd Chadds Ford PA 19317 610-558-9800 582
TF Cust Svc: 800-462-3636 ■ *Web:* www.endo.com

Endocrine Society
8401 Connecticut Ave Ste 900 Chevy Chase MD 20015 301-941-0200 941-0259 49-8
TF: 888-363-6274 ■ *Web:* www.endocrine.org

Endologix Inc 11 Studebaker Irvine CA 92618 949-457-9546 843-1500* 476
NASDAQ: ELGX ■ **Fax Area Code: 877* ■ *TF:* 800-983-2284 ■ *Web:* www.endologix.com

Endomedix Inc 211 Warren St Newark NJ 07103 848-248-1883 475
Web: www.endomedix.com

Endometriosis Assn 8585 N 76th Pl Milwaukee WI 53223 414-355-2200 355-6065 48-17
TF: 800-992-3636 ■ *Web:* www.endometriosisassn.org

EndoShape Inc
5425 Airport Blvd Ste 101 Boulder CO 80301 844-870-5070 475
TF: 844-870-5070 ■ *Web:* www.endoshape.com

Endot Industries Inc
60 Green Pond Rd Rockaway NJ 07866 973-625-8500 625-4087 596
TF: 800-443-6368 ■ *Web:* www.endot.com

Endotec Inc 20 Valley St South Orange NJ 07079 973-762-6100 475
TF: 800-649-5215 ■ *Web:* www.endotec.com

Endotronix Inc 815 Ogden Ave Ste 104 Lisle IL 60532 630-473-3200 743
TF: 877-363-6879 ■ *Web:* www.endotronix.com

Endress+Hauser Inc 2350 Endress Pl Greenwood IN 46143 317-535-7138 535-8498 201
TF: 888-363-7377 ■ *Web:* www.us.endress.com

Endries International Inc
714 W Ryan St PO Box 69 Brillion WI 54110 920-756-5381 756-3772 385
TF: 800-852-5821 ■ *Web:* www.endries.com

Endsight 1440 Fourth St Ste B Berkeley CA 94710 510-280-2000 196
TF: 800-972-2175 ■ *Web:* www.endsight.net

Endstream Communications LLC
401 E 34Th St New York NY 10016 212-786-7289 387
Web: www.endstream.com

Endura Coatings LLC
42250 Yearego Dr Sterling Heights MI 48314 586-739-0101 481
Web: www.enduracoatings.com

Endura Products Inc 8817 W Market St Colfax NC 27235 336-668-2472 236
TF: 800-334-2006 ■ *Web:* www.enduraproducts.com

Endurance IT Services
4646 Princess Anne Rd Ste 104 Virginia Beach VA 23462 757-216-3671 196
TF: 800-368-6511 ■ *Web:* www.endurance-it.com

Endurance Resources Holdings LLC
15455 Dallas Pkwy Ste 600 Addison TX 75001 214-996-0900 536
Web: www.enduranceresourcesllc.com

Endurant Business Solutions
12100 Singletree Ln Ste 163 Eden Prairie MN 55344 952-746-1373 317
Web: www.endurant.com

Enduro Composites Inc
16602 Central Green Blvd Houston TX 77032 713-358-4000 358-4100 601
TF: 800-231-7271 ■ *Web:* www.endurocomposites.com

End-User Computing
4841 MONROE ST Ste 307 Toledo OH 43623 419-474-1762 393

Endview Plantation
362 Yorktown Rd Newport News VA 23603 757-887-1862 888-3369 520
Web: www.endview.org

ENE Systems Inc 480 Neponset St Ste 11D Canton MA 02021 781-828-6770 256
Web: enesystems.com

Eneflux Armtek Magnetics Inc
700 Hicksville Rd Ste 110 Bethpage NY 11714 516-576-3434 458
TF: 877-363-3589 ■ *Web:* www.eamagnetics.com

Enerac Inc 67 Bond St Westbury NY 11590 516-997-2100 201
TF: 800-695-3637 ■ *Web:* www.enerac.com

ENERActive Solutions LLC
700 Mattison Ave Ste A Asbury Park NJ 07712 732-988-8850 256
Web: www.eneractivesolutions.com

Enerbank USA Inc
1245 E Brickyard Rd Ste 600 Salt Lake City UT 84106 888-390-1220 217
TF: 888-390-1220 ■ *Web:* www.enerbank.com

Enerco 750 Third Ave 9th Fl New York NY 10017 212-572-0784 610
Web: www.ener.co

EnerCom Inc 800 18th St Ste 200 Denver CO 80202 303-296-8834 261
Web: www.enercominc.com

Enercon Engineering Inc
201 Altorfer Ln East Peoria IL 61611 309-694-1418 694-3703 203
TF: 800-218-8831 ■ *Web:* www.enercon-eng.com

Enercon Services Inc
5100 E Skelly Dr Ste 450 Tulsa OK 74135 918-665-7693 665-7232 261
Web: www.enercon.com

Enerfab Inc 4955 Spring Grove Ave Cincinnati OH 45232 513-641-0500 91
TF: 800-772-5066 ■ *Web:* www.enerfab.com

Enerflex Systems Ltd
1331 Macleod Trail SE Ste 904 Calgary AB T2G0K3 403-387-6377 386
TSE: EFX ■ *TF:* 800-242-3178 ■ *Web:* www.enerflex.com

Ener-G Foods Inc
5960 First Ave S PO Box 84487 Seattle WA 98124 206-767-3928 764-3398 296-36
TF: 800-331-5222 ■ *Web:* www.ener-g.com

ENER-G Rudox 180 E Union Ave East Rutherford NJ 07073 201-438-0111 438-3403 518
Web: energ-rudox.com

Energage Inc 3405 Bonaire Xing Marietta GA 30066 770-321-0537 463
Web: energage.com

Energen Corp
605 Richard Arrington Blvd N Birmingham AL 35203 205-326-2700 360-5
NYSE: EGN ■ *TF:* 800-654-3206 ■ *Web:* www.energen.com

Energent Inc
22 Frederick St Ste 1114 Kitchener ON N2H6M6 519-725-0906 177
TF: 800-857-5308 ■ *Web:* www.energent.com

Energetic Services Inc
PO Box 6639 Fort St. John BC V1J4J1 250-785-4761 478
Web: www.energeticservices.com

Energetiq Technology Inc
7 Constitution Way Woburn MA 01801 781-939-0763 454
Web: www.energetiq.com

EnergX LLC 1000 B Clearview Ct Oak Ridge TN 37830 866-932-1333 483-9811* 193
**Fax Area Code: 865* ■ *TF:* 866-932-1333 ■ *Web:* www.energxllc.com

Energy & Environmental Building Alliance, The
6520 Edenvale Blvd Ste 112 Eden Prairie MN 55346 952-881-1098 242
TF: 800-460-2575 ■ *Web:* www.eeba.org

Energy & Environmental Research Ctr (EERC)
University of N Dakota
15 N 23rd St S 9018 Grand Forks ND 58202 701-777-5000 777-5181 668
Web: www.eerc.und.nodak.edu

Energy & Resource Solutions Inc
120 Water St Ste 350 North Andover MA 01845 978-521-2550 194
Web: www.ers-inc.com

Energy 103.7 Fm 8033 Linda Vista Rd San Diego CA 92111 858-571-7600 571-0326 645-144
TF: 888-388-1037 ■ *Web:* energy1037.cbslocal.com

Energy 95.3 FM
3651 Pegasus Dr Ste 107 Bakersfield CA 93308 661-393-1900 645-15
Web: www.energy953.com

Energy Absorption Systems Inc
35 E Wacker Dr Ste 1100 Chicago IL 60601 312-467-6750 467-1356 678
Web: www.energyabsorption.com

Energy Ace Inc
160 Clairemont Ave Ste 600 Decatur GA 30030 404-378-7800 463
Web: www.energyace.com

Energy Air Inc 5401 Energy Air Ct Orlando FL 32810 407-886-3729 610
Web: www.energyair.com

Energy Alloys LLC
350 Glenborough Ste 300 Houston TX 77067 832-601-5800 601-5801 490
TF: 866-448-9831 ■ *Web:* www.ealloys.com

Energy and Commerce, The
Energy & Commerce Committee
2125 Rayburn Bldg Washington DC 20515 202-225-2927 342-1
Web: www.energycommerce.house.gov

Energy Answers Corp 79 N Pearl St Albany NY 12207 518-434-1227 436-6343 660
Web: www.energyanswers.com

Energy Authority Inc, The
301 W Bay St Ste 2600 Jacksonville FL 32202 904-356-3900 463
Web: www.teainc.org

Energy Automation Systems Inc
145 Anderson Ln Hendersonville TN 37075 615-822-7250 194
Web: www.energyautomation.com

Energy BBDO 225 N Michigan Ave Chicago IL 60601 312-337-7860 5
Web: www.energybbdo.com

Energy Capital Solutions LP
2651 N Harwood Ste 410 Dallas TX 75201 214-219-8200 70
Web: www.nrgcap.com

Energy Concepts Inc
404 Washington Blvd Mundelein IL 60060 847-837-8191 703
TF: 800-621-1247 ■ *Web:* www.eci-info.com

Energy Conversion Devices Inc
2956 Waterview Dr Rochester Hills MI 48309 248-293-0440 253
OTC: ENERQ

Energy Conversion Technologies Inc
1271 Denison St Unit 56-59 Unit 56-59 Markham ON L3R4B5 905-947-4300 203
Web: www.energyconversiontech.com

Energy Efficiency & Renewable Energy Information Ctr
1000 Independence Ave SW Washington DC 20585 202-586-4849 236-2023* 197
**Fax Area Code: 360* ■ *TF:* 877-337-3463 ■ *Web:* energy.gov

Energy Engineering Assoc Inc
6615 Vaught Ranch Rd Ste 200 Austin TX 78730 512-328-0082 261

Energy Exchanger Co 1844 N Garnett Rd Tulsa OK 74116 918-437-3000 437-7144 91
Web: www.energyexchanger.com

Energy Focus Inc 32000 Aurora Rd Solon OH 44139 440-715-1300 715-1314 439
OTC: EFOI ■ *TF:* 800-327-7877 ■ *Web:* www.energyfocusinc.com

Energy Foundation, The
Fifth Fl 301 Battery St San Francisco CA 94111 415-561-6700 305
Web: www.ef.org

Energy Information Administration
1000 Independence Ave SW Washington DC 20585 202-586-8800 586-0727 340-9
Web: www.eia.gov

Name / Address	City	State	ZIP	Phone	Fax	Class
Energy Initiatives Group LLC 176 Worcester-Providence TurnPk Ste 102 *Web:* www.eig-llc.com	Sutton	MA	01590	508-865-8021		261
Energy Inspectors 2570 S Miller Ln *Web:* www.energyinspectors.com	Las Vegas	NV	89117	702-365-8080		610
Energy Institute Pennsylvania State University C 211 CUL *Web:* www.energy.psu.edu	University Park	PA	16802	814-865-3093	863-7432	668
Energy Intelligence Group 5 E 37th St 5th Fl *Web:* www.energyintel.com	New York	NY	10016	212-532-1112	532-4479	637-9
Energy Laboratories Inc 2393 Old Salt Creek Rd *Web:* solarenergy.com	Casper	WY	82601	307-995-3200		743
Energy Labs Inc 9651 Airway Rd Ste E *Web:* www.energylabs.com	San Diego	CA	92154	619-671-0100		14
Energy Management Solutions Inc 7935 Stone Creek Dr Ste 140 *Web:* www.emsenergy.com	Chanhassen	MN	55317	952-767-7450		463
Energy Mfg Co Inc 204 Plastic Ln *Web:* www.energymfg.com	Monticello	IA	52310	319-465-3537	465-5279	223
Energy Northwest 76 N Power Plant Loop *TF:* 800-468-6883 ■ *Web:* www.energy-northwest.com	Richland	WA	99354	509-372-5000		245
Energy Operators L P 1431 Graham Dr Ste 203 *Web:* energyoperators.com	Tomball	TX	77375	281-351-1780		538
Energy Panel Structures Inc Industrial Pk *Web:* www.epsbuildings.com	Graettinger	IA	51342	712-859-3219		106
Energy Petroleum Co 2130 Kienlen Ave *TF:* 800-536-6828 ■ *Web:* www.energypetroleum.com	St. Louis	MO	63121	314-383-3700		316
Energy Project, The 1 Larkin Plaza 4th Fl *Web:* theenergyproject.com	Yonkers	NY	10701	914-207-8800		463
Energy Recovery Council (IWSA) 2200 Wilson Blvd Ste 310 *Web:* energyrecoverycouncil.org	Arlington	VA	22201	202-467-6240		48-12
Energy Recovery Inc 1717 Doolittle Dr *NASDAQ: ERII* ■ *TF:* 888-455-2263 ■ *Web:* www.energyrecovery.com	San Leandro	CA	94577	510-483-7370	483-7371	806
Energy Research & Generation Inc 900 Stanford Ave *Web:* www.ergaerospace.com	Oakland	CA	94608	510-658-9785	658-7428	143
Energy Sciences Inc 42 Industrial Way *TF:* 800-932-7299 ■ *Web:* www.ebeam.com	Wilmington	MA	01887	978-694-9000	694-9046	386
Energy Security Analysis Inc 401 Edgewater Pl Ste 640 *Web:* www.esai.com	Wakefield	MA	01880	781-245-2036		401
Energy Services Group International Inc (ESG) 3601 La Grange Pkwy *Web:* www.esgi.net	Toano	VA	23168	757-741-4040	741-4045	721
Energy Services of America Corp 75 W third Ave *OTC: ESOA*	Huntington	WV	25701	304-399-6300	399-1096	186
Energy Spectrum Advisors Inc 5956 Sherry Ln Ste 900 *Web:* www.energyspectrumcapital.com	Dallas	TX	75225	214-987-6100		690
Energy Steel & Supply Co 3123 John Conley Dr *Web:* www.energysteel.com	Lapeer	MI	48446	810-538-4990		480
Energy Transfer Equity LP 3738 Oak Lawn Ave *NYSE: ETE* ■ *Web:* www.energytransfer.com	Dallas	TX	75219	214-981-0700		316
Energy Transfer Partners LP 3738 Oak Lawn Ave *NYSE: ETP* ■ *Web:* www.energytransfer.com	Dallas	TX	75219	214-981-0700		316
Energy Transformation Systems Inc 43353 Osgood Rd *TF:* 800-752-8208 ■ *Web:* www.etslan.com	Fremont	CA	94539	510-656-2012		767
Energy Water Solutions LLC 9595 Six Pines Dr Ste 8210 *Web:* www.energywatersolutions.com	The Woodlands	TX	77380	713-722-0408		536
Energy West Inc 1 First Ave S *TF:* 800-570-5688 ■ *Web:* www.ewst.com	Great Falls	MT	59401	406-791-7500	791-7560	787
Energy Worldnet 1210 S Bus Hwy 81/287 Decatur *Web:* www.energyworldnet.com	Decatur	TX	76234	940-626-1941		192
Energy XXI 1021 Main Ste 2626 *NASDAQ: EXXI* ■ *Web:* www.energyxxi.com	Houston	TX	77002	713-351-3000		538
EnergyExplorium 13339 Hagers Ferry Rd *TF:* 800-777-9898 ■ *Web:* m.duke-energy.com	Huntersville	NC	28078	980-875-5600		520
ENERGYneering Solutions Inc 15820 Barclay Dr *Web:* energyneeringsolutions.com	Sisters	OR	97759	541-549-8766		261
Energynet.com Inc 7201 I-40 W Ste 319 *Web:* www.energynet.com	Amarillo	TX	79106	806-351-2953		690
EnergySolutions LLC 423 West Broadway Ste 200 *Web:* www.energysolutions.com	Salt Lake City	UT	84101	801-649-2000	321-0453	804
EnergyUnited Electric Membership Corp PO Box 1831 *TF:* 800-522-3793 ■ *Web:* www.energyunited.com	Statesville	NC	28687	704-873-5241		245
EnergyWorks Inc 71 Old Mill Bottom Rd N Ste 101 *Web:* www.energyworks.com	Annapolis	MD	21409	410-349-2001		463
EnerNex Corp 620 Mabry Hood Rd Ste 300 *Web:* www.enernex.com	Knoxville	TN	37932	865-218-4600		192
Enernoc Inc 101 Federal St Ste 1100 *NASDAQ: ENOC* ■ *Web:* www.enernoc.com	Boston	MA	02110	617-224-9900	224-9910	463
Enerpac PO Box 3241 **Fax:* Cust Svc ■ *TF Cust Svc:* 800-433-2766 ■ *Web:* www.enerpac.com	Milwaukee	WI	53201	262-293-1600	781-1049*	759
Enerplus Resources Fund 3000 Dome Tower 333 Seventh Ave SW Ste 3000 *TF:* 800-319-6462 ■ *Web:* www.enerplus.com	Calgary	AB	T2P2Z1	403-298-2200	298-2211	405
Enersul LP 7210 Blackfood Terr SE *Web:* www.enersul.com	Calgary	AB	T2H1M5	403-253-5969	259-2771	143
EnerSys 2366 Bernville Rd *NYSE: ENS* ■ *TF:* 800-538-3627 ■ *Web:* enersys.com	Reading	PA	19605	610-208-1991	372-8457	74
EnerSys Inc 617 N Ridgeview Dr *Web:* www.enersys.com/globallanding.aspx	Warrensburg	MO	64093	660-429-2165		74
EnerTech Capital 625 W Ridge Pk Ste 1225 W *Web:* www.enertechcapital.com	Conshohocken	PA	19428	484-539-1872	539-1870	792
Enertech Consultants Inc 494 Salmar Ave 200 *Web:* www.enertech.net	Campbell	CA	95008	408-866-7266		261
Enertechnix Inc PO Box 469 *Web:* www.enertechnix.com	Maple Valley	WA	98038	425-432-1589		358
Ener-Tel Services Inc 4512 Adobe Dr *Web:* www.ener-tel.com	San Angelo	TX	76903	325-658-8375		175
Enertopia Corp Suite 950, 1130 W Pender St *Web:* www.enertopia.com	Vancouver	BC	V6E4A4	604-602-1675		536
EnerVision Inc 4170 Ashford Dunwoody Rd Ste 550 *TF:* 888-999-8840 ■ *Web:* www.enervision-inc.com	Atlanta	GA	30319	678-510-2900		194
Enesco LLC 225 Windsor Dr *TF:* 800-436-3726 ■ *Web:* www.enesco.com	Itasca	IL	60143	630-875-5300	875-5350	334
E-Net Corp 300 Valley St *Web:* www.enet.com	Sausalito	CA	94965	415-332-6200	339-9592	178-12
Enetics Inc 830 Canning Pkwy *TF:* 800-341-2525 ■ *Web:* www.enetics.com	Victor	NY	14564	585-924-5010		246
eNeura Therapeutics LLC 715 N Pastoria Ave *Web:* www.eneura.com	Sunnyvale	CA	94085	408-245-6400		743
Enevate Corp 101 Theory Ste 200 *Web:* www.enevate.com	Irvine	CA	92617	949-243-0399		253
En-fab Inc 3905 Jensen Dr *Web:* www.en-fabinc.com	Houston	TX	77026	713-225-4913	224-7937	537
Enfield Correctional Institution 289 Shaker Rd PO Box 1500 *Web:* www.ct.gov	Enfield	CT	06082	860-814-4300		213
Enfield Public Library 104 Middle Rd *Web:* www.enfield-ct.gov	Enfield	CT	06082	860-763-7510	763-7514	434-3
Enfield Square 90 Elm St *Web:* shopenfieldmall.com	Enfield	CT	06082	860-745-7000	745-3007	460
Enflite Inc 105 Cooperative Way *Web:* www.enflite.com	Georgetown	TX	78626	512-868-3399		22
Enflo Corp 315 Lake Ave *TF:* 888-887-4093 ■ *Web:* www.enflo.com	Bristol	CT	06010	860-589-0014	589-7179	600
Enfold Systems Inc 4617 Montrose Blvd *TF:* 800-561-3357 ■ *Web:* www.enfoldsystems.com	Houston	TX	77006	713-942-2377		177
Enforcer Products Inc PO Box 1060 *TF:* 888-805-4357 ■ *Web:* www.enforcer.com	Cartersville	GA	30120	888-805-4357		280
Enform 1538 25 Ave NE *Web:* www.enform.ca	Calgary	AB	T2E8Y3	403-250-9606		196
E-n-g Mobile Systems Inc-broadcast & Mobilab Divs 2245 Via De Mercados *Web:* www.e-n-g.com	Concord	CA	94520	925-798-4060		514
Engage Communications Inc 9565 Soquel Dr *TF:* 800-467-3753 ■ *Web:* www.engagecom.com	Aptos	CA	95003	831-688-1021	688-1421	173-3
Engage Learning Systems 110 Spadina Ave *Web:* www.engagelearn.com	Toronto	ON	M5V2K4	416-368-0188		242
Engage Technologies Corp 7041 Boone Ave N *TF:* 800-877-5658 ■ *Web:* www.engagetechnologies.net	Brooklyn Park	MN	55428	800-877-5658		388
Engage3 Inc 213 E St 2nd FL *Web:* www.engage3.com	Davis	CA	95616	530-231-5485		393
EngagePoint Inc 3901 Calverton Blvd Ste 110 **Fax Area Code:* 954 ■ *Web:* www.engagepoint.com	Calverton	MD	20705	301-388-7900	315-0903*	177
Engel Eliot (Rep D - NY) 2462 Rayburn HOB *Web:* engel.house.gov	Washington	DC	20515	202-225-2464	225-5513	342-2
Engel Machinery Inc 3740 Board Rd Ste 5 *Web:* www.engelglobal.com/engel_web/ena/en	York	PA	17406	717-764-6818		98
Engel Realty Company Inc 951 Eighteenth St S Ste 200 *Web:* www.engelrealty.com	Birmingham	AL	35201	205-939-6800		652
Engelberth Construction Inc 463 Mtn View Dr Ste 200 Second Fl *TF:* 800-639-9011 ■ *Web:* www.engelberth.com	Colchester	VT	05446	802-655-0100		186
Engelman Berger PC 3636 N Central Ave Ste 700 *Web:* www.eblawyers.com	Phoenix	AZ	85012	602-271-9090		428
Engelson Assoc 3317 Mormon Coulee Rd *Web:* cpas-4biz.com	La Crosse	WI	54601	608-788-2181		2
EngenderHealth 440 Ninth Ave 13th Fl *TF:* 800-564-2872 ■ *Web:* www.engenderhealth.org	New York	NY	10001	212-561-8000	561-8067	48-17
Engenius Inc 31077 Schoolcraft Rd *Web:* www.engenius.com	Livonia	MI	48150	734-522-2597		180
EnGenius Technologies Inc 1580 Scenic Ave *Web:* www.engeniustech.com	Costa Mesa	CA	92626	714-432-8668		246
Engent Inc 3140 Northwoods Pkwy Ste 300A *Web:* www.engentaat.com	Norcross	GA	30071	678-990-3320	990-3324	695
Engeo Inc 2010 Crow Canyon Pl Ste 250 *Web:* engeo.com	San Ramon	CA	94583	925-866-9000		261
Enghouse Systems Ltd 80 Tiverton Ct Ste 800 *TSE: ESL* ■ *TF:* 866-233-4606 ■ *Web:* www.enghouse.com	Markham	ON	L3R0G4	905-946-3200	946-3201	178-10
Engine Co No 28 644 S Figueroa St *Web:* www.engineco.com	Los Angeles	CA	90017	213-624-6996		671

Name / Address	City	State	ZIP	Phone	Fax	Class
Engine Components Inc (ECI) 9503 Middlex *TF:* 800-324-2359 ■ *Web:* eci.aero	San Antonio	TX	78217	210-820-8101	820-8102	21
Engine Control & Monitoring PO Box 40 *Web:* www.ecm-co.com	Los Altos	CA	94023	408-734-3433		317
Engine Interactive 1415 Tenth Ave 4 *Web:* www.enginei.com	Seattle	WA	98122	206-709-1955		180
Engine Manufacturers Assn (EMA) 333 W Wacker Dr Ste 810 *Web:* www.truckandenginemanufacturers.org	Chicago	IL	60606	312-929-1970	929-1975	49-13
Engine Parts Warehouse Inc 7301 Global Dr *Web:* www.enginepartswarehouse.net/epwhome.html	Louisville	KY	40258	502-937-7258		247
Engine Power Components Inc 1333 Fulton St *Web:* www.engpwr.com	Grand Haven	MI	49417	616-846-0110		60
Engine Power Source Inc 348 Bryant Blvd *TF:* 800-374-7522 ■ *Web:* www.enginepowersource.com	Rock Hill	SC	29732	704-944-1999		518
Engineer Sales Co 2500 25th Ave N *Web:* www.engineersales.com	Saint Petersburg	FL	33713	727-323-2100		256
Engineered Building Products Inc 18 Southwood Dr *Web:* www.ebpfab.com	Bloomfield	CT	06002	860-243-1110		492
Engineered Controls International Inc (ECII) 100 Rego Dr PO Box 247 *TF:* 800-650-0061 ■ *Web:* www.regoproducts.com	Elon	NC	27244	336-449-7707	449-6594	789
Engineered Environments Inc 1620 Timocuan Way Ste 130 *Web:* www.eeigc.net	Longwood	FL	32750	407-831-6998		116
Engineered Materials Solutions Inc 39 Perry Ave *Web:* www.emsclad.com	Attleboro	MA	02703	508-342-2100		567
Engineered Medical Systems Inc 2055 Executive Dr *Web:* www.engmedsys.com	Indianapolis	IN	46241	317-246-5500		475
Engineered Plastic Components Inc 1408 Zimmerman Dr S *Web:* www.epcmfg.com	Grinnell	IA	50112	641-236-3100		596
Engineered Plastics Inc 211 Chase St *TF:* 800-711-1740 ■ *Web:* www.engplas.com	Gibsonville	NC	27249	336-449-4121	449-6352	602
Engineered Polymer Solutions Inc 1400 N State St **Fax Area Code: 815* ■ *TF:* 800-654-4242 ■ *Web:* www.epscca.com/en/index.html	Marengo	IL	60152	800-654-4242	568-4145*	605-2
Engineered Precision Casting Company Inc 952 Palmer Ave *Web:* www.epcast.com	Middletown	NJ	07748	732-671-2424	671-8615	306
Engineered Products Co (EPCO) 601 Kelso St PO Box 108 *TF:* 888-414-3726 ■ *Web:* www.epcohardware.com	Flint	MI	48506	810-767-2050	767-5084	350
Engineered Products Inc 500 Furman Hall Rd *TF:* 888-301-1421 ■ *Web:* www.engprod.com	Greenville	SC	29609	864-234-4868	234-4860	207
Engineered Products Inc (EPI) 200 Jones St *TF:* 800-422-0614 ■ *Web:* www.epimetal.com	Verona	PA	15147	412-423-4000	423-4002	234
Engineered Profiles 2141 Fairwood Ave *Web:* www.craneplasticsmfg.com	Columbus	OH	43207	614-754-3700		596
Engineered Protection Systems Inc 750 Front Ave NW *TF:* 800-966-9199 ■ *Web:* www.epssecurity.com	Grand Rapids	MI	49504	616-459-0281		189-4
Engineered Sintering & Plastic Inc 140 Commercial St *Web:* www.engsin.com	Watertown	CT	06795	860-274-8877		596
Engineered Software PO Box 408 *Web:* www.engsw.com	Grafton	MA	01519	336-299-4843		178-5
Engineered Steel Products Inc 4977 Plainfield Rd *Web:* www.engineeredsteel.org	Sophia	NC	27350	336-495-5266		480
Engineered Storage Products Co 345 Harvestore Dr *TF:* 800-880-3663 ■ *Web:* www.cstindustries.com	DeKalb	IL	60115	815-756-1551	756-7821	91
Engineered Systems & Products Inc 11438 Cronridge Dr Ste O *Web:* www.engineeredsystemsonline.com	Owings Mills	MD	21117	410-998-9456		729
Engineering & Environmental Consultants Inc 4625 E Ft Lowell Rd *TF:* 800-887-2103 ■ *Web:* www.eec-info.com	Tucson	AZ	85712	520-321-4625	321-0333	261
Engineering & Equipment Company Inc 910 N Washington St *TF:* 800-688-8816 ■ *Web:* www.engineeringandequipmentcoalbany.com	Albany	GA	31701	229-435-5601		612
Engineering & Refrigeration Inc 56 Baldwin Ave *Web:* dupont.com	Jersey City	NJ	07306	201-333-4200		189-10
Engineering & Utility Contractors Assn 17 Crow Canyon Ct Ste 100	San Ramon	CA	94583	925-855-7900		256
Engineering Contractors' Assn (ECA) 2190 S Towne Centre Pl *Web:* www.ecaonline.net	Anaheim	CA	92806	714-937-5000	937-5030	49-19
Engineering Data Design Corp 105 Daventry Ln Ste 100 *TF:* 888-678-0683 ■ *Web:* ed2c.com	Louisville	KY	40223	502-412-4000		256
Engineering Design Technologies (EDT) 1705 Entp Way SE Ste 200 *Web:* www.edtinc.net	Marietta	GA	30067	770-988-0400	988-0300	685
Engineering Dynamics Inc 3925 S Kalamath St *Web:* www.engdynamics.com	Englewood	CO	80110	303-761-4367		743
Engineering Economics Inc 8700 Monrovia St Ste 310 *TF:* 800-869-6902 ■ *Web:* www.eeiengineers.com	Lenexa	KS	66215	303-239-8700		186
Engineering Management Concepts Inc 5051 Verdugo Way Ste 200 *Web:* www.emc-inc.com	Camarillo	CA	93012	805-484-9082	484-4607	463
Engineering News-Record (ENR) 350 fifth Ave Ste 6000 *TF:* 877-876-8208 ■ *Web:* www.enr.com	New York	NY	10118	646-849-7100		457-21
Engineering Outlook 1308 W Green St 306 Engineering Hall *TF:* 800-325-5516 ■ *Web:* engineering.illinois.edu	Urbana	IL	61801	217-333-2151	244-7705	531-13
Engineering Planning & Management Inc 959 Concord St *Web:* www.epm-inc.com	Framingham	MA	01701	508-875-2121	879-3291	261
Engineering Research Ctr for Net Shape Mfg 1971 Neil Ave Rm 339 *Web:* ercnsm.osu.edu	Columbus	OH	43210	614-292-9267	292-7219	668
Engineering Services Network Inc 2450 Crystal Dr Ste 1015 *Web:* www.esncc.com	Arlington	VA	22202	703-412-3640		193
Engineering Specialists Inc 21360 Gateway Ct *Web:* www.engspec.com	Brookfield	WI	53045	262-783-8000		256
Engineering.com Inc 5285 Solar Dr Ste 101 *TF:* 800-439-5071 ■ *Web:* www.engineering.com	Mississauga	ON	L4W5B8	905-273-9991		387
Engineers Canada 180 Elgin St Ste 1100 *TF:* 877-408-9273 ■ *Web:* www.engineerscanada.ca	Ottawa	ON	K2P2K3	613-232-2474	230-5759	48-1
Engineery System Solutions 4943 N 29th E Ste A *Web:* www.es2eng.com	Idaho Falls	ID	83401	208-552-9874		256
Enginetech Inc 1205 W Crosby Rd *TF:* 800-869-8711 ■ *Web:* www.enginetech.com	Carrollton	TX	75006	972-245-0110	245-2093	61
Enginetics Corp 7700 New Carlise Rd *Web:* www.enginetics.com	Huber Heights	OH	45424	937-878-3800		21
Enginuiti Inc 8321 Old Cthouse Rd *Web:* www.enginuiti.com	Vienna	VA	22182	703-620-2266		180
Enginuity Works Corp 2195 Defoor Hills Rd NW *TF:* 800-645-1148 ■ *Web:* www.enginuityworks.com	Atlanta	GA	30318	678-739-0001		256
Engis Corp 105 W Hintz Rd *TF:* 800-993-6447 ■ *Web:* www.engis.com	Wheeling	IL	60090	847-808-9400	808-9430	386
England & Company LLC 888 17th St NW Ste 304 *Web:* www.englandco.com	Washington	DC	20006	202-386-6500		691
England Logistics Inc 1325 South 4700 West *TF:* 800-848-7810 ■ *Web:* www.englandlogistics.com	Salt Lake City	UT	84104	801-656-4500		194
Englander Northeast 12 Esquire Rd *TF:* 800-489-9994 ■ *Web:* www.englander.com	North Billerica	MA	01862	800-489-9994		471
Englefield Oil Co 447 James Pkwy *TF Cust Svc:* 800-837-4458 ■ *Web:* www.englefieldoil.com	Heath	OH	43056	740-928-8215	928-1531	324
Engler Meier & Justus Inc 1030 Vandustrial Dr *Web:* www.westmontint.com	Westmont	IL	60559	630-852-4600		191-1
Englert Inc 1200 Amboy Ave *Web:* www.englertinc.com	Perth Amboy	NJ	08861	732-826-8614		697
Englewood Cafe 10904 E Winner Rd	Independence	MO	64052	816-461-9588		671
Englewood Chamber of Commerce 2-10 N Van Brunt St *Web:* www.englewood-chamber.com	Englewood	NJ	07631	201-567-2381		139
Englewood Electrical Supply 716 Belvedere Dr *TF:* 800-417-7543 ■ *Web:* wesco.com	Kokomo	IN	46901	765-452-4087		246
Englewood Hospital & Medical Ctr 350 Engle St *Web:* www.englewoodhealth.org	Englewood	NJ	07631	201-894-3000	894-1473	374-3
Englewood Public Library 31 Engle St *TF:* 800-590-4064 ■ *Web:* www.englewoodlibrary.org	Englewood	NJ	07631	201-568-2215		434-3
Englewood Public Library 1000 Englewood Pkwy Englewood Civic Ctr 1st Fl *TF:* 866-922-9006 ■ *Web:* www.englewoodgov.org	Englewood	CO	80110	303-762-2560	783-6890	434-3
Englewood Tire Wholesale Inc 757 Page Ave *TF:* 800-678-8973 ■ *Web:* www.englewoodtire.com	Lyndhurst	NJ	07071	800-678-8973		755
Englewood-Cape Haze Area Chamber of Commerce 601 S Indiana Ave *TF:* 800-603-7198 ■ *Web:* www.englewoodchamber.com	Englewood	FL	34223	941-474-5511	475-9257	139
Englewood-Northmont Chamber of Commerce PO Box 62 *Web:* www.northmontchamber.com	Englewood	OH	45322	937-836-2550	836-2485	139
English American Tailoring Co 411 N Cranberry Rd *Web:* www.englishamericanco.com	Westminster	MD	21157	410-857-5774	386-0417	155-12
English Connection Inc 77 Railroad Pl *Web:* esldirectory.com	Saratoga Springs	NY	12866	518-581-1478		423
English Construction Co Inc 615 Church St *TF:* 800-304-0059 ■ *Web:* www.englishconst.com	Lynchburg	VA	24504	434-845-0301	845-0306	188-4
English Inn, The 677 S Michigan Rd *TF:* 800-858-0598 ■ *Web:* www.englishinn.com	Eaton Rapids	MI	48827	517-663-2500	663-2643	671
English Language Ctr Inc (ELC) 10850 Wilshire Blvd Ste 210 *Web:* www.elc.edu	Los Angeles	CA	90024	617-536-9788		423
English Oaks Nursing & Rehabilitation Ctr 2633 W Rumble Rd *Web:* lifegen.net	Modesto	CA	95350	209-577-1001	577-0366	450
English Village Manor Nursing Home 1515 Canterbury Blvd *TF:* 800-213-0154 ■ *Web:* englishvillagemanor.net	Altus	OK	73521	580-477-1133		371
English, Lucas, Priest & Owsley LLP 1101 College St *Web:* www.elpolaw.com	Bowling Green	KY	42102	270-781-6500		428
English-Speaking Union of the US 144 E 39th St *TF:* 800-566-2524 ■ *Web:* www.esuus.org	New York	NY	10016	212-818-1200	818-1200	48-15

Phone | Fax | Class

ENGlobal Corp
654 N Sam Houston Pkwy E Ste 400 .... Houston TX 77060 281-878-1000 878-1010 173-2
NASDAQ: ENG ■ *Web:* www.englobal.com

Englund Marine & Industrial Supply Co
95 Hamburg Ave PO Box 296.................. Astoria OR 97103 503-325-4341 325-6421 221
TF: 800-228-7051 ■ *Web:* www.englundmarine.com

Engman-Taylor Company Inc (ETCO)
W142 N9351 Fountain Blvd .... Menomonee Falls WI 53051 262-255-9300 255-6512 385
TF: 800-236-1975 ■ *Web:* www.engman-taylor.com

Engravers Metal Fabricators
124 Imperial St......................... Merritt Island FL 32952 321-453-3670 697
Web: www.emfinc.net

ENGStudios Inc
1931 Newport Blvd Ste B .... Costa Mesa CA 92627 949-642-2325 256

Enhance Energy Inc
333 5 Ave SW Ste 900 .... Calgary AB T2P3B6 403-984-0202 536
Web: www.enhanceenergy.com

Enhanced Retail Solutions Inc
214 W 39th St Rm 1202a .... New York NY 10018 212-938-1991 129
Web: www.enhancedretailsolutions.com

Enhanced Software Products Inc
1811 N Hutchinson Rd .... Spokane WA 99212 509-534-1514 225
TF: 800-456-5750 ■ *Web:* www.espsolution.net

Enhanced Telecommunication Inc
6065 Atlantic Blvd .... Norcross GA 30071 770-242-3620 180
Web: etisoftware.com

enherent Corp
6800 Jericho Tpke Ste 116E.................. Syosset NY 11791 732-321-1004 177
Web: www.enherent.com

Eni Petroleum Co
1200 Louisiana St Ste 1707 .... Houston TX 77002 713-393-6100 536
TF: 800-570-8024 ■ *Web:* eni.com

Enid A. Haupt Conservatory
2900 Southern Blvd .... Bronx NY 10458 212-263-6058 263-2091 97
Web: www.nybg.org/garden/conservatory

Enid News & Eagle
227 W Broadway PO Box 3451.................... Enid OK 73701 580-548-8186 233-7645 532-2
TF: 800-299-6397 ■ *Web:* www.enidnews.com

Enidine Inc 7 Centre Dr .... Orchard Park NY 14127 716-662-1900 662-1909 472
TF: 800-852-8508 ■ *Web:* www.enidine.com

Enigma Marketing Trvl Solutions
8463 castlewood dr .... Indianapolis IN 46250 317-585-0100 463
Web: www.enigma-marketing.com

Enilon Group 1045 Foch St .... Fort Worth TX 76107 817-632-3200 177
Web: www.enilon.com

Enite Management LLC 101 W 13th St .... Houston TX 77008 713-298-6149 463
Web: enitegroup.com

Enjet Inc 5373 W Alabama Ste 502 .... Houston TX 77056 713-552-1559 580
TF: 800-423-6538 ■ *Web:* www.enjet.com

Enkeboll Designs 16506 Avalon Blvd............ Carson CA 90746 310-532-1400 200
Web: www.enkeboll.com

Enkei America Inc 2900 W Inwood Dr .... Columbus IN 47201 812-373-7000 247

ENLASO Corp 9543 W Emerald St Ste 105.......... Boise ID 83704 208-672-8500 466
Web: www.enlaso.com

Enlighten 3027 Miller Rd................... Ann Arbor MI 48103 734-668-6678 668-1883 180

Enlightened Inc
1100 15th St N W Ste 300 .... Washington DC 20005 202-728-7190 177
Web: www.nlightened.com

Enlisted Assn of the National Guard of the US (EANGUS)
3133 Mt Vernon Ave...................... Alexandria VA 22305 703-519-3846 519-3849 48-19
TF: 800-234-3264 ■ *Web:* www.memberconnections.com

Enlivant 330 N Wabash Ave Ste 3700............ Chicago IL 60611 312-725-7000 371
TF: 800-881-0678 ■ *Web:* www.enlivant.com

Enloe Medical Ctr 1531 Esplanade .... Chico CA 95926 530-332-7300 374-3
TF: 800-822-8102 ■ *Web:* www.enloe.org

Enmark Tool & Gage Co Inc
18100 Cross Dr .... Fraser MI 48026 586-293-2797 293-1037 493
Web: www.enmarktool.com

ENMAX Corp 141 50 Ave SE.................... Calgary AB T2G4S7 403-245-7222 787
TF: 877-571-7111 ■ *Web:* www.enmax.com

Enmetric Systems Inc
617 Mtn View Ave Ste 5 .... Belmont CA 94002 650-762-5757 201
Web: www.enmetric.com

Ennead Architects 320 W 13 St............... New York NY 10014 212-807-7171 261
Web: www.ennead.com

Ennis Containers Inc
211 Sandra Jackson Rd .... Auburndale FL 33823 863-967-2419 125

Ennis Inc PO Box D .... Wolfe City TX 75496 972-775-9801 453-2674* 413
**Fax Area Code:* 800 ■ *TF:* 800-527-1008 ■ *Web:* www.ennis.com/our-products/labels

Ennis Inc 2441 Presidential Pkwy............. Midlothian TX 76065 972-775-9801 627
TF: 800-972-1069 ■ *Web:* www.ennis.com

Ennis Independent School District
303 W Knox PO Box 1420 .... Ennis TX 75119 972-872-7000 875-8667 685
Web: www.ennis.k12.tx.us

Ennis Pellum & Assoc Cpas
5150 Belfort Rd S Bldg 600 .... Jacksonville FL 32256 904-396-5965 399-4094 2
Web: www.jaxcpa.com

Ennis State Bank 815 W Ennis Ave .... Ennis TX 75119 972-875-9676 70
Web: ennisstatebank.com

Ennis Steel Industries Inc
204 Metro Park Blvd.......................... Ennis TX 75119 972-878-0400 878-9563 480
Web: www.ennissteel.com

Eno River State Park 6101 Cole Mill Rd .... Durham NC 27705 919-383-1686 565
Web: www.ncparks.gov

Eno Vino Wine Bar & Bistro
601 Junction Rd .... Madison WI 53717 608-664-9565 671
Web: www.eno-vino.com

Enoch Manufacturing Co
14242 SE 82nd Dr .... Clackamas OR 97015 503-659-2660 621
TF: 888-659-2660 ■ *Web:* enochmachining.com

Enoch Pratt Free Library
400 Cathedral St........................... Baltimore MD 21201 410-396-5283 396-8134 434-3
TF: 800-735-2258 ■ *Web:* www.prattlibrary.org

ENOCHS Examining Room Furniture
PO Box 50559 .... Indianapolis IN 46250 800-428-2305 580-2944* 319-3
**Fax Area Code:* 317 ■ **Fax:* Cust Svc ■ *TF Cust Svc:* 800-428-2305 ■ *Web:* www.enochsmed.com

eNom Inc
5808 Lake Washington Blvd Ste 300 .... Kirkland WA 98033 425-974-4689 396
Web: www.enom.com

Enor Corp 245 Livingston St................... Northvale NJ 07647 201-750-1680 608
Web: www.enor.com

Enotria Cafe & Wine Bar
1431 Del Paso Blvd .... Sacramento CA 95815 916-922-6792 671
Web: enotria.com

Enounce Inc 2666 E Bayshore Rd .... Palo Alto CA 94303 650-494-6200 177
TF: 800-872-4786 ■ *Web:* www.enounce.com

Enovity Inc 100 Montgomery St........... San Francisco CA 94104 415-974-0390 261
Web: enovity.com

Enphase Energy Inc
1420 N Mcdowell Blvd .... Petaluma CA 94954 707-763-4784 696
TF: 877-797-4743 ■ *Web:* investor.enphase.com

Enpower Corp
2420 Camino Ramon Ste 101.................. San Ramon CA 94583 925-244-1100 787
TF: 800-555-5211 ■ *Web:* www.enpowercorp.com

Enprecis Inc
60 Courtneypark Dr W Unit 3 .... Mississauga ON L5W0B3 206-274-0122 387
Web: www.enprecis.com

Enpria Inc
10260 SW Greenburg Rd Ste 850.............. Portland OR 97223 503-293-8444 652

Enpro 19 National Dr......................... Franklin MA 02038 800-966-1102 536
TF: 800-966-1102 ■ *Web:* enpro.com

Enpro Inc 121 S LombaRd Rd.................... Addison IL 60101 630-629-3504 629-3512 385
TF: 800-323-2416 ■ *Web:* www.enproinc.com

EnPro Industries Inc
5605 Carnegie Blvd Ste 500................. Charlotte NC 28209 704-731-1500 326
NYSE: NPO

EnPro Industries Inc Fairbanks Morse Engine
701 White Ave................................ Beloit WI 53511 800-356-6955 262
TF: 800-356-6955 ■ *Web:* www.fairbanksmorse.com

Enprotech Corp 4259 E 49th St................ Cleveland OH 44125 216-206-0081 697
Web: www.enprotech.com

Enprotech Mechanical Services Inc
2200 Olds Ave .... Lansing MI 48915 517-372-0950 697
Web: www.enpromech.com

ENR (Engineering News-Record)
350 fifth Ave Ste 6000 .... New York NY 10118 646-849-7100 457-21
TF: 877-876-8208 ■ *Web:* www.enr.com

ENrG Inc 155 Rano St Ste 300 .... Buffalo NY 14207 716-873-2939 253
Web: www.enrg.com

Enrich LLC
3655 Brookside Pkwy Ste 265 .... Alpharetta GA 30022 770-667-0510 180
Web: www.enrichit.com

Enriching Spaces
1360 Kemper Meadow Dr.................... Cincinnati OH 45240 513-851-0933 742-6415 320
Web: www.enrichingspaces.com

Enroute Computer Solutions Inc
2511 Fire Rd Ste A4 .... Egg Harbor Township NJ 08234 609-569-9255 261
Web: enroute-computer.com

ENSA North America Inc 400 SW Ave......... Waukesha WI 53189 262-408-2282 393
Web: www.ensa-northamerica.com

Ensave Energy Performance Inc
65 Millet St Ste 105 .... Richmond VT 05477 800-732-1399 463
TF: 800-732-1399 ■ *Web:* www.ensave.com

Enscicon Corp
2420 W 26 Ave Ste 500 Bldg D .... Denver CO 80211 303-980-8600 180
Web: enscicon.com

ENSCO Inc
3110 Fairview Pk Dr Ste 300 .... Falls Church VA 22042 703-321-9000 321-7863 261
TF: 800-367-2682 ■ *Web:* www.ensco.com

Ensearch Management Consultants
905 E Cotati Ave............................. Cotati CA 94931 888-667-5627 721
TF: 888-667-5627 ■ *Web:* www.ensearch.com

Ensemble Theatre 3535 Main St .... Houston TX 77002 713-520-0055 520-1269 572
TF: 800-688-3625 ■ *Web:* www.ensemblehouston.com

Ensemble Theatre of Cincinnati
1127 Vine St.............................. Cincinnati OH 45202 513-421-3555 573-4
Web: www.cincyetc.com

Ensemble Travel 256 W 38th St 11th Fl .... New York NY 10018 212-545-7460 772
TF: 800-576-2378 ■ *Web:* www.ensembletravel.com

Ensenada
2824 Virginia Beach Blvd .... Virginia Beach VA 23452 757-631-1090 671

Enseo Inc 1680 Prospect Dr Ste 100 .... Richardson TX 75081 972-234-2513 174
Web: www.enseo.com

Enser Corp 1902 Taylor's Ln............... Cinnaminson NJ 08077 856-829-5522 454
Web: www.enser.com

Ensign Corp 201 Ensign Rd .... Bellevue IA 52031 563-872-3900 872-4575 767
TF: 888-797-8658 ■ *Web:* www.ensigncorp.com

Ensign Energy Services Inc
400 Fifth Ave SW Ste 1000.................... Calgary AB T2P0L6 403-262-1361 262-8215 540
TSE: ESI ■ *Web:* www.ensignenergy.com

Ensign Engineering p C 1111 Calhoun Ave......... Bronx NY 10465 718-863-5590 256
Web: www.ensignengineering.com

Ensign Group Inc, The
27101 Puerta Real Ste 450............... Mission Viejo CA 92691 949-487-9500 450
NASDAQ: ENSG ■ *Web:* www.ensigngroup.net

Ensign-Bickford Aerospace & Defense Co
640 Hopmeadow St PO Box 429............... Simsbury CT 06070 860-843-2289 268
Web: www.ebaerospaceanddefense.com

Ensinger Putnam Precision Molding
11 Danco Rd.................................. Putnam CT 06260 860-928-7911 928-2229 604
TF: 800-752-7865 ■ *Web:* www.ensinger-pc.com

EnSolve Biosystems Inc
5805 Departure Dr Ste B...................... Raleigh NC 27616 919-954-6196 194
Web: www.ensolve.com

Ensource Inc
7970 Bayberry Rd Ste 5 .... Jacksonville FL 32256 800-748-3446 224
TF: 800-748-3446

ENSTAR Natural Gas Co
401 E International Airport Rd.............. Anchorage AK 99518 907-277-5551 787
TF: 800-907-9767 ■ *Web:* www.enstargas.com

Enstar USA Inc 7035 Halcyon Pk Dr .... Montgomery AL 36117 334-834-5483 405
NASDAQ: ESGR ■ *Web:* www.enstargroup.com

Enstoa 655 Third Ave .... New York NY 10017 212-913-0870 205
Web: www.enstoa.com

Enstrom Helicopter Corp USA
2209 22nd St .... Menominee MI 49858 906-863-1200 863-6244 20
Web: www.enstromhelicopter.com

Name / Address	City	State	Zip	Phone	Fax	Class
EnSys Energy & Systems Inc 1775 Massachussets Ave *Web:* www.ensysenergy.com	Lexington	MA	02420	781-274-8454		195
Ensyte Energy Software International 770 S Post Oak Ln Ste 330 *Web:* www.ensyte.com	Houston	TX	77056	713-622-2875		177
Ent Federal Credit Union 7250 Campus Dr *TF:* 800-525-9623 ■ *Web:* www.ent.com	Colorado Springs	CO	80920	719-574-1100	388-9065	219
Entact LLC 3129 Bass Pro Dr *Web:* www.entact.com	Grapevine	TX	76051	972-580-1323		192
Entagon Inc 9805 Vly View Rd *Web:* entagon.com	Eden Prairie	MN	55344	952-941-5305		350
Entap Inc 136 E Market St *Web:* www.entap.com	Indianapolis	IN	46204	317-634-9523		225
Entec Composite Machines Inc 300 West 2975 South *TF:* 800-354-1696 ■ *Web:* www.entec.com	Salt Lake City	UT	84115	801-486-8721	484-4363	744
Entec Services Inc 30 Monroe Dr *Web:* www.entecservicesinc.com	Pelham	AL	35124	205-358-1011		192
Entech Instruments Inc 2207 Agate Ct *Web:* www.entechinst.com	Simi Valley	CA	93065	805-527-5939		419
Entegee Inc 70 BlanchaRd Rd Ste 102 *TF:* 800-368-3433 ■ *Web:* www.entegee.com	Burlington	MA	01803	781-221-5800		721
Entegral Energy Marketing Inc 1228 Kensington Rd NW Ste 205 *Web:* www.entegralenergy.com	Calgary	AB	T2N3P3	403-283-1133		195
EnteGreat Inc 1500 Urban Ctr Dr Ste 415 *Web:* www.entegreat.com	Vestavia Hills	AL	35242	205-968-3050		449
Entegrity Networks Inc 6220 Avanti Dr *Web:* entegritynetworks.com	Arlington	TX	76001	214-432-5418		45
Entek International LLC 250 Hansard Ave *Web:* entek.com/lead-acid	Lebanon	OR	97355	541-259-3901	259-3932	620
Entelechy Enterprises Inc 889 E Shore Dr *TF:* 800-376-8368 ■ *Web:* www.unlockit.com	Silver Lake	NH	03875	603-424-1237		463
Enterasys Networks Inc 50 Minuteman Rd *Web:* extremenetworks.com	Andover	MA	01810	978-684-1000		176
Entercom Boston 20 Guest St 3rd Fl *Web:* www.entercom.com	Boston	MA	02135	617-779-5800		645
Entercom Communications Corp 401 City Ave Ste 809 *NYSE: ETM* ■ *TF:* 800-776-9437 ■ *Web:* www.entercom.com	Bala Cynwyd	PA	19004	610-660-5610	660-5620	643
Enterey Inc 9900 Irvine Ctr Dr Ste 100 *TF:* 800-691-2349 ■ *Web:* www.enterey.com	Irvine	CA	92618	800-691-2349		463
Enterforce Inc 626 W Moreland Blvd *Web:* www.enterforce.com	Waukesha	WI	53188	262-542-2218		196
Entergy Arkansas Inc 425 W Capitol Ave *TF:* 800-368-3749 ■ *Web:* www.entergy-arkansas.com	Little Rock	AR	72201	800-368-3749		787
Entergy Corp 639 Loyola Ave *NYSE: ETR* ■ *TF:* 800-368-3749 ■ *Web:* www.entergy.com	New Orleans	LA	70113	504-576-4000		360-5
Entergy Louisiana Inc 639 Loyola Ave *TF Cust Svc:* 800-368-3749 ■ *Web:* www.entergy.com	New Orleans	LA	70113	504-576-6116		787
Entergy Mississippi Inc PO Box 1640 *Web:* www.entergy-mississippi.com	Jackson	MS	39215	601-969-2440		787
Entergy New Orleans Inc 639 Loyola Ave *TF Cust Svc:* 800-368-3749 ■ *Web:* www.entergy-neworleans.com	New Orleans	LA	70113	800-368-3749		787
Entergy Texas Inc 350 Pine St *TF:* 800-368-3749 ■ *Web:* www.entergy-texas.com	Beaumont	TX	77701	409-981-3245		787
Entero Corp 1040 Seventh Ave SW Ste 500 *TF:* 877-261-1820 ■ *Web:* www.entero.com	Calgary	AB	T2P3G9	403-261-1820		177
Enterprise Bancorp Inc 222 Merrimack St *NASDAQ: EBTC* ■ *Web:* www.enterprisebanking.com	Lowell	MA	01852	978-459-9000		360-2
Enterprise Bank of SC 13497 Broxton Bridge Rd PO Box 8 *TF:* 800-554-8969 ■ *Web:* www.ebanksc.com	Ehrhardt	SC	29081	803-267-3191	267-2316	70
Enterprise Community Partners Inc 10227 Wincopin Cir *TF:* 800-624-4298 ■ *Web:* www.enterprisecommunity.com	Columbia	MD	21044	410-964-1230	964-1918	48-5
Enterprise Computing Solutions Inc 26024 Acero *TF:* 800-573-1874 ■ *Web:* www.thinkecs.com	Mission Viejo	CA	92691	949-609-1980		177
Enterprise Electric Co 4204 Shannon Dr *Web:* www.eecompany.com	Baltimore	MD	21213	410-488-8200	488-6639	189-4
Enterprise Financial Services Corp 150 N Meramec Ave *NASDAQ: EFSG* ■ *TF:* 800-396-8141 ■ *Web:* www.enterprisebank.com	Clayton	MO	63105	314-725-5500		360-2
Enterprise Information Services Inc 1945 Old Gallows Rd Ste 500 *Web:* www.goeis.com	Vienna	VA	22182	703-749-0007		177
Enterprise Magazine 825 N 300 W Ste NE220 *Web:* www.slenterprise.com	Salt Lake City	UT	84103	801-533-0556	533-0684	457-5
Enterprise Partners Venture Capital (EPVC) 2223 Avenida de la Playa Ste 300	La Jolla	CA	92037	858-731-0300		792
Enterprise Precast Concrete Inc 13800 Giles Rd *Web:* www.enterpriseprecast.com	Omaha	NE	68138	402-895-3848		183
Enterprise Products Partners LP 1100 Louisiana St 10th Fl *NYSE: EPD* ■ *TF:* 866-230-0745 ■ *Web:* www.enterpriseproducts.com	Houston	TX	77002	713-381-6500		325
Enterprise Rent-A-Car 600 Corporate Pk Dr *TF:* 800-307-6666 ■ *Web:* www.enterprise.com	Saint Louis	MO	63105	314-512-5000		126
Enterprise Roofing & Sheet Metal Co 1021 Irving St *Web:* www.enterpriserfg.com	Dayton	OH	45419	937-298-8664		189-12
Enterprise State Community College (ESCC) 600 Plaza Dr *Web:* www.escc.edu	Enterprise	AL	36330	334-347-2623		162
Enterprise Welding & Fabricating Inc 6257 Heisley Rd *Web:* www.enterprisewelding.com	Mentor	OH	44060	440-354-4128		697
Enterprise Wireless Alliance (EWA) 8484 Westpark Dr Ste 630 *TF:* 800-482-8282 ■ *Web:* www.enterprisewireless.org	McLean	VA	22102	703-528-5115	524-1074	49-20
Enterprise-Ozark Community College 1975 Ave C *Web:* escc.edu	Mobile	AL	36615	251-438-2816	438-2816	800
EnterpriseWorks/VITA 1100 H StNW Ste 1200 *Web:* www.enterpriseworks.org	Washington	DC	20005	202-639-8660	639-8664	48-5
Entertainment Fusion Group 6420 Wilshire Blvd Ste 620 *Web:* www.efgpr.com	Los Angeles	CA	90048	310-432-0020		636
Entertainment Lighting Services 11440 Sheldon St *Web:* www.elslights.com	Sun Valley	CA	91352	818-769-9800		544
Entertainment Merchants Assn 16530 Ventura Blvd Ste 400 *TF:* 800-665-5576 ■ *Web:* www.entmerch.org	Encino	CA	91436	818-385-1500	933-0910	49-18
Entertainment Properties Trust 909 Walnut Ste 200 *NYSE: EPR* ■ *TF:* 800-377-4273 ■ *Web:* www.eprkc.com	Kansas City	MO	64106	816-472-1700		655
Entertainment Software Assn (ESA) 575 Seventh St NW Ste 300 *TF:* 800-949-3660 ■ *Web:* www.theesa.com	Washington	DC	20004	202-223-2400	223-2401	48-9
Entertainment Studios Inc 1925 Century Park E 10th Fl *Web:* www.es.tv	Los Angeles	CA	90067	310-277-3500	277-7298	514
Entertainment Weekly Magazine 225 Liberty St *TF:* 800-828-6882 ■ *Web:* www.ew.com	New York	NY	10018	800-828-6882		457-9
Entest Inc 2015 Midway Rd Ste 114 *Web:* www.entest.net	Carrollton	TX	75006	972-980-9876		711
Enthalpy Analytical Inc 800-1 Capitola Dr *Web:* www.enthalpy.com	Durham	NC	27713	919-850-4392		743
Enthermics Inc W164 N9221 Water St *TF:* 800-862-9276 ■ *Web:* www.enthermics.com	Menomonee Falls	WI	53051	262-251-8356		475
Enthone Inc 350 Frontage Rd *TF:* 800-431-2200 ■ *Web:* www.enthone.com	West Haven	CT	06516	203-934-8611	799-1513	145
Enthought Inc 515 Congress Ave Ste 2100 *Web:* www.enthought.com	Austin	TX	78701	512-536-1057		177
Enting Water Conditioning Inc 3211 Dryden Rd *Web:* enting.com	Dayton	OH	45439	937-294-5100		189-10
Entitle Direct Group Inc 200 Marshall Dr *TF:* 877-936-8485 ■ *Web:* www.entitledirect.com	Pittsburgh	PA	15108	877-936-8485	810-8531	391-6
Entium Technology Partners Llc 1200 Valley Forge Rd Ste 50 *Web:* entium.com	Valley Forge	PA	19482	610-415-7200		193
Entomological Society of America 10001 Derekwood Ln Ste 100 *TF:* 800-523-8635 ■ *Web:* www.entsoc.org	Lanham	MD	20706	301-731-4535	731-4538	49-19
Entravision Communications Corp 2425 Olympic Blvd Ste 6000 W *NYSE: EVC* ■ *Web:* www.entravision.com	Santa Monica	CA	90404	310-447-3870	447-3899	643
Entre Computer Solutions 8900 N Second St *TF:* 800-523-3304 ■ *Web:* www.entrerock.com	Machesney Park	IL	61115	815-399-5664		175
Entre Solutions 51 W Fairmont Ave	Savannah	GA	31406	912-352-1600		180
Entre Technology Service 1501 14th St W Ste 201 *Web:* www.entremt.com	Billings	MT	59102	406-256-5700		196
Entrepia Ventures Inc 2975 Bowers Ave Ste 223 *Web:* www.entrepia.com	Santa Clara	CA	95051	408-492-9040		792
Entrepreneur Media Inc 18061 Fitch *TF:* 800-779-5295 ■ *Web:* www.entrepreneur.com	Irvine	CA	92614	949-261-2325	261-7729	637-9
Entreprises Jf Faucher Inc 1100 Chemin De Saint-jean *TF:* 800-817-5835 ■ *Web:* www.botanix.com	La Prairie	QC	J5R2L5	450-659-2222		183
Entrust Inc 5400 LBJ Fwy Ste 1340 *TF Sales:* 888-690-2424 ■ *Web:* www.entrust.com	Dallas	TX	75240	972-728-0447	728-0440	178-12
Entrust Mfg Technologies Inc N 58 W 14630 Shawn Cir *Web:* www.entrustmt.com	Menomonee Falls	WI	53051	262-252-3802		455
Entrx Corp 800 Nicollet Mall Ste 2690	Minneapolis	MN	55402	612-333-0614		189-9
Entry Cove State Marine Park PO Box 1247 *Web:* dnr.alaska.gov/parks/units/pwssmp/smpwhit1.htm	Soldotna	AK	99669	907-262-5581		565
EntryPoint Consulting LLC 4700 Rockside Rd Summit Office Park Bldg 1 Ste 625 *TF:* 800-233-0361 ■ *Web:* www.entrypointconsulting.com	Independence	OH	44131	216-674-9070		196
Entwistle Co Dietzco Div 6 Bigelow St *TF:* 800-445-8909 ■ *Web:* www.entwistleco.com	Hudson	MA	01749	508-481-4000	481-4004	556
Enumclaw Area Chamber of Commerce 1421 Cole St *TF:* 800-833-6384 ■ *Web:* www.enumclawchamber.com	Enumclaw	WA	98022	360-825-7666	825-8369	139
Envar Services Inc 505 Milltown Rd *TF:* 800-890-0003 ■ *Web:* www.envarservices.com	North Brunswick	NJ	08902	732-296-9601		261
Envelope Manufacturers Assn (EMA) 500 Montgomery St Ste 550 *Web:* www.envelope.org	Alexandria	VA	22314	703-739-2200	739-2209	49-4
Envelopes & Forms Inc 2505 Meadowbrook Pkwy *Web:* efsurebill.com/envelopes-forms	Duluth	GA	30096	770-623-5140		627
Envelopes Etcetera Inc 69-71 Townsend St *Web:* envetc.com	Port Chester	NY	10573	914-937-6162		627

Name / Address	City	State	Zip	Phone	Fax	Class
Envelopes Only Inc 2000 S Park Ave *Web:* envelopesonly.net	Streamwood	IL	60107	630-213-2500		535
Enventure Global Technology LLC 15995 N Barkers Landing Ste 350 *Web:* www.enventuregt.com	Houston	TX	77079	281-552-2200		190
Enventys Partners LLC 520 Elliot St Ste 200 *Web:* www.enventys.com	Charlotte	NC	28202	704-333-5335		5
envest private Equity 2101 Parks Ave Ste 401 *Web:* www.envestventures.com	Virginia Beach	VA	23451	757-437-3000		792
Envestnet Inc 35 E Wacker Dr Ste 2400 *Web:* www.envestnet.com	Chicago	IL	60601	312-827-2800		690
Envieta LLC 7175 Columbia Gateway Dr Ste T *Web:* envieta.com	Columbia	MD	21046	410-290-1136		261
Enviro Clean Services LLC 11717 N Morgan Rd *Web:* www.envirocleanps.com	Yukon	OK	73099	405-373-4545		192
Enviro Systems Inc 12037 N Hwy 99 *Web:* www.enviro-ok.com	Seminole	OK	74868	405-382-0731	382-0737	22
Enviroapplications Inc 2831 Camino Del Rio S Ste 214 *Web:* www.enviroapplications.com	San Diego	CA	92108	619-291-3636		196
EnviroCap LLC 3401 W Cypress St ste 200 *Web:* www.envirocap.com	Tampa	FL	33606	813-341-3650		401
Envirocon Inc 101 International Dr *Web:* www.envirocon.com	Missoula	MT	59808	406-523-1150		261
Envirodyne Systems Inc 75 Zimmerman Dr *Web:* www.envirodynesystems.com	Camp Hill	PA	17011	717-763-0500		194
Envirologic Technologies Inc 2960 Interstate Pkwy *TF:* 800-272-7802 ■ *Web:* envirologic.com	Kalamazoo	MI	49048	269-342-1100		463
EnviroLogix Inc 500 Riverside Industrial Pkwy *TF:* 866-408-4597 ■ *Web:* www.envirologix.com	Portland	ME	04103	207-797-0300		743
Environamics Inc 1401 Freedom Dr *TF:* 800-262-3613 ■ *Web:* www.environamics-inc.com	Charlotte	NC	28208	704-376-3613		186
Environics Analytics Group Ltd 33 Bloor St E Ste 400 *TF:* 888-339-3304 ■ *Web:* www.environicsanalytics.ca	Toronto	ON	M4W3H1	416-969-2733		195
Environics Inc 69 Industrial Park Rd E *Web:* www.environics.com	Tolland	CT	06084	860-872-1111		419
Environment Associates Inc 9604 Variel Ave *Web:* www.eatest.com	Chatsworth	CA	91311	818-709-0568		794
Environment Control 3430 N First Ave *TF:* 800-433-3243 ■ *Web:* www.environmentcontrol.com	Tucson	AZ	85719	520-292-3992		256
Environment of Care Leader 9737 Washintonian Blvd Ste 100 *TF Cust Svc:* 800-929-4824 ■ *Web:* www.ucg.com	Gaithersburg	MD	20878	301-287-2700	287-2039	531-8
Environment One Corp 2773 Balltown Rd *Web:* www.eone.com	Niskayuna	NY	12309	518-346-6161		641
Environment Reporter 1801 S Bell St *TF:* 800-372-1033 ■ *Web:* www.bna.com/environment-reporter-p4885	Arlington	VA	22202	800-372-1033		531-5
Environmental & Safety Designs Inc 5724 Summer Trees Dr *TF:* 800-588-7962 ■ *Web:* www.ensafe.com	Memphis	TN	38134	901-372-7962	372-2454	192
Environmental Air Systems Inc 521 Banner Ave *TF:* 800-274-9000 ■ *Web:* www.easinc.net	Greensboro	NC	27401	336-273-1975	273-1975	14
Environmental Assessment & Remediation Management Inc 4097 Trl Creek Rd *Web:* www.earmanagement.com	Riverside	CA	92505	951-735-5575		256
Environmental Compliance Management Services 2377 Gold Meadow Way Ste 100 *Web:* www.ecms.com	Gold River	CA	95670	916-988-0867	988-2139	192
Environmental Consultants Inc 295 Buck Rd Ste 203 *Web:* www.eci-consulting.com	SouthHampton	PA	18966	215-322-4040		302
Environmental Data Resources Inc 440 Wheelers Farms Rd **Fax Area Code:* 800 ■ *TF:* 800-352-0050 ■ *Web:* www.edrnet.com	Milford	CT	06460	203-783-0300	231-6802*	387
Environmental Defense 257 Pk Ave S *TF:* 800-505-0703 ■ *Web:* www.edf.org	New York	NY	10010	212-505-2100	505-2100	48-13
Environmental Earthscapes Inc 5075 S Swan Rd *TF:* 800-571-1575 ■ *Web:* www.groundskeeper.com	Tucson	AZ	85706	520-571-1575	750-7480	422
Environmental Enterprises Inc (EEI) 10163 Cincinnati Dayton Rd *TF:* 800-722-2818 ■ *Web:* www.eeienv.com	Cincinnati	OH	45241	513-772-2818		667
Environmental Express Ltd 2345A Charleston Regional Pkwy *Web:* www.envexp.com	Charleston	SC	29492	843-881-6560		419
Environmental Health & Engineering Inc 117 Fourth Ave *TF:* 800-825-5343 ■ *Web:* www.eheinc.com	Needham	MA	02494	781-247-4300		256
Environmental Information Assn (EIA) 6935 Wisconsin Ave Ste 306 *TF:* 888-343-4342 ■ *Web:* www.eia-usa.org	Chevy Chase	MD	20815	301-961-4999	961-3094	48-13
Environmental Inks & Coatings Corp 1 Quality Products Rd *Web:* www.envinks.com	Morganton	NC	28655	828-433-1922		388
Environmental Law Institute (ELI) 2000 L St NW Ste 620 *TF:* 800-433-5120 ■ *Web:* www.eli.org	Washington	DC	20036	202-939-3800	939-3868	49-10
Environmental Management Inc 5200 NE Hwy 33 *TF:* 800-510-8510 ■ *Web:* www.emiok.com	Guthrie	OK	73044	405-282-8510		668
Environmental Materials LLC 6300 E Stapleton Dr S *Web:* www.estoneworks.com	Denver	CO	80216	303-309-3040		724
Environmental Pneumatics Inc 215 Bowers Rd S *Web:* www.ep-corp.com	Oakland	TN	38060	901-465-0211		697
Environmental Protection Agency (EPA) 1200 Pennsylvania Ave NW *TF:* 888-372-8255 ■ *Web:* www.epa.gov	Washington	DC	20460	202-564-4700	501-1450	340-20
US National Response Team 1200 Pennsylvania Ave NW *TF:* 800-424-9346 ■ *Web:* www.nrt.org	Washington	DC	20593	202-267-2675		340-20
Environmental Protection Agency Regional Offices						
Region 1 1 Congress St Ste 1100 *TF:* 888-372-7341 ■ *Web:* www.epa.gov	Boston	MA	02114	617-918-1111	918-0101	340-20
Region 2 290 Broadway *TF:* 800-621-8431 ■ *Web:* www.epa.gov	New York	NY	10007	212-637-3000		340-20
Region 3 1650 Arch St *TF:* 800-438-2474 ■ *Web:* www.epa.gov	Philadelphia	PA	19103	215-814-5000		340-20
Region 4 Sam Nunn Atlanta Federal Ctr 61 Forsyth St SW *TF:* 800-241-1754 ■ *Web:* www.epa.gov	Atlanta	GA	30303	404-562-9900	562-8174	340-20
Region 5 77 W Jackson Blvd *TF:* 800-621-8431 ■ *Web:* www.epa.gov	Chicago	IL	60604	312-353-2000		340-20
Region 6 1445 Ross Ave Ste 1200 *TF:* 800-887-6063 ■ *Web:* www.epa.gov	Dallas	TX	75202	214-665-2200	665-2182	340-20
Region 7 901 N Fifth St *TF:* 800-223-0425 ■ *Web:* www.epa.gov	Kansas City	KS	66101	913-551-7003		340-20
Region 8 1595 Wynkoop St *TF:* 800-227-8917 ■ *Web:* www.epa.gov	Denver	CO	80202	303-312-6312		340-20
Region 9 75 Hawthorne St *TF:* 866-372-9378 ■ *Web:* www.epa.gov	San Francisco	CA	94105	415-947-8000	947-3598	340-20
Region 10 1200 Sixth Ave Ste 900 *TF:* 800-424-4372 ■ *Web:* www.epa.gov	Seattle	WA	98101	206-553-1200	553-0059	340-20
Environmental Protection Information Ctr (EPIC) 145 G St Ste A *Web:* www.wildcalifornia.org	Arcata	CA	95521	707-822-7711	822-7712	48-13
Environmental Science Assoc 225 Bush St Ste 1700 *Web:* www.esassoc.com	San Francisco	CA	94104	415-896-5900	896-0332	668
Environmental Standards Inc 1140 Vly Forge Rd *Web:* www.envstd.com	Valley Forge	PA	19482	610-935-5577		192
Environmental Systems Products Inc 7 Kripes Rd *TF:* 800-446-4708 ■ *Web:* www.esp-global.com	East Granby	CT	06026	860-392-2100		407
Environmental Systems Research Institute Inc 380 New York St *TF Sales:* 800-447-9778 ■ *Web:* www.esri.com	Redlands	CA	92373	909-793-2853	793-5953	178-10
Environmental Technology Council (ETC) 1112 16th St Ste 420 *Web:* www.etc.org	Washington	DC	20036	202-783-0870		48-12
Environmental Tectonics Corp 125 James Way *OTC:* ETCC ■ *Web:* www.etcusa.com	SouthHampton	PA	18966	215-355-9100	357-4000	703
Environmental Traveling Companions (ETC) 2 Marina Blvd Bldg C *Web:* www.etctrips.org	San Francisco	CA	94123	415-474-7662	474-3919	48-23
Enviro-Pro-Tech Inc 3210 Barrancas Ave	Pensacola	FL	32507	850-458-5447		141
Envirosafe Services of Ohio Inc 876 Otter Creek Rd *Web:* envirosafeservices.com	Oregon	OH	43616	419-698-3500		196
Enviro-Sciences Inc 781 Rte 15 S Ste 108 *Web:* www.enviro-sciences.com	Lake Hopatcong	NJ	07849	973-398-8183		261
Envirosearch Operations Inc 4166-15 Side Rd *Web:* www.envirosearchoperations.ca	Rockwood	ON	N0B2K0	905-854-4441		261
Envirosell Inc 907 Broadway	New York	NY	10010	212-673-9100		466
Envirosep Fluid & Heat Recovery Systems 31 Aviation Blvd *Web:* www.envirosep.com	Georgetown	SC	29440	843-546-7400		196
EnviroServe JV 5502 Schaaf Rd *Web:* www.enviroserve.com	Cleveland	OH	44131	216-642-1311		196
Enviro-Shred LLC 1045 Second Ave NW *Web:* www.enviroshrednc.com	Hickory	NC	28601	828-328-9333		317
Envirosure Solutions Llc 1979 E Broadway Rd Ste 2 *TF:* 800-383-8047 ■ *Web:* envirosure.com	Tempe	AZ	85282	480-784-4621		196
Envirotech Financial Inc 500 N State College Ste 1100 *TF:* 800-490-9194 ■ *Web:* etfinancial.com	Orange	CA	92868	714-532-2731		196
Enviro-Tote Inc 4 Cote Ln *TF:* 800-868-3224 ■ *Web:* www.enviro-tote.com	Bedford	NH	03110	603-647-7171	647-0116	66
EnviroTrac Ltd 5 Old Dock Rd *Web:* www.envirotrac.com	Yaphank	NY	11980	631-924-3001		192
Envirovantage Inc 629 Calef Hwy Ste 200 *TF:* 800-640-5323 ■ *Web:* www.envirovantage.com	Epping	NH	03042	603-679-9682		667
Envisa Inc 281 Pleasant St *Web:* www.envisa.com	Framingham	MA	01701	508-405-1220		463
Envision Capital Management Inc 2301 Rosecrans Ave Ste 4180 *TF:* 800-400-0989 ■ *Web:* www.envisioncap.com	El Segundo	CA	90245	310-445-3252	445-3258	401
Envision Creative Group 3400 Northland Dr *Web:* www.envision-creative.com	Austin	TX	78731	512-292-1049		6
Envision Group 990 W 190th St Ste 220 *Web:* www.envisiongroup.com	Torrance	CA	90502	310-523-2000		194
Envision Healthcare 6200 S Syracuse Way Ste 200 *Web:* www.evhc.net	Greenwood Village	CO	80111	303-495-1200		360-3
Envision Inc 610 N Main St *TF:* 888-425-7072 ■ *Web:* www.envisionus.com	Wichita	KS	67203	316-440-1500	440-1540	48-6
Envision Marketing Inc 26941 Cabot Rd Ste 121 *Web:* www.envisionmarketing.net	Laguna Hills	CA	92653	949-367-7818		195
Envision Media Inc 331 Soquel Ave Ste 100 *Web:* www.envisionmedia.com	Santa Cruz	CA	95062	831-429-5400		344
Envision Online Media Inc 1150 Morrison Dr Ste 201 *TF:* 800-544-8614 ■ *Web:* www.envisiononline.ca	Ottawa	ON	K2H8S9	613-594-2804		225

	City	State	Zip	Phone	Fax	Class
Envision Payment Solutions Inc 3039 Premiere Pkwy Ste 600 *TF:* 800-290-3957 ■ *Web:* envisionpayments.com	Duluth	GA	30097	770-709-3000		179
Envision Peripherals Inc (EPI) 47490 Seabridge Dr	Fremont	CA	94538	510-770-9988	770-1088	173-4
Envision Technology Advisors LLC 999 Main St *Web:* www.envisionsuccess.net	Pawtucket	RI	02860	401-272-6688		177
Envision Telephony Inc 901 Fifth Ave Ste 3300 *Web:* www.envisioninc.com	Seattle	WA	98164	206-225-0800		178-10
Envisioneering Inc 5904 Richmond Hwy Ste 300 *Web:* www.envisioneeringinc.com	Alexandria	VA	22303	571-483-4100		261
Envisionit Chicago LLC 130 E Randolph St Ste 1600 *Web:* envisionitagency.com	Chicago	IL	60601	312-236-2000		344
Enviva Lp 7200 Wisconsin Ave Ste 1100 *Web:* www.envivabiomass.com	Bethesda	MD	20814	301-657-5560		820
Envivio Inc 400 Oyster Pt Blvd Ste 325 *Web:* www.envivio.com	South San Francisco	CA	94080	650-243-2700		647
Envoy Advisors 268 Summer St *Web:* www.envoyadvisors.com	Boston	MA	02210	617-292-7676		70
Envoy Inc 3317 N 107th St *Web:* www.envoyinc.com	Omaha	NE	68134	402-558-0637		5
Envoy Plan Services Inc 901 Calle Amanecer Ste 200 *TF:* 800-248-8858 ■ *Web:* www.envoyplanservices.com	San Clemente	CA	92673	949-366-5070		535
Enwood Structures Inc 5724 McCrimmon Pkwy PO Box 2002 *TF:* 800-777-8648 ■ *Web:* www.enwood.com	Morrisville	NC	27560	919-518-0464	469-2536	817
Enzi Michael B (Sen R - WY) 379A Russell Bldg *Web:* www.enzi.senate.gov	Washington	DC	20510	202-224-3424	228-0359	342-2
Enzio's Italian Kitchen 126 W Mountain Ave *Web:* www.enzios.com	Fort Collins	CO	80524	970-484-8466		671
Enzo Biochem Inc 527 Madison Ave *NYSE: ENZ* ■ *TF:* 800-522-5052 ■ *Web:* www.enzo.com	New York	NY	10022	212-583-0100	583-0150	231
Enzo Life Sciences Inc 10 Executive Blvd *TF:* 800-942-0430 ■ *Web:* www.enzolifesciences.com	Farmingdale	NY	11735	631-694-7070		231
Enzon Pharmaceuticals Inc 20 Kingsbridge Rd *NASDAQ: ENZN* ■ *Web:* www.enzon.com	Piscataway	NJ	08854	732-980-4500		85
Enzymatic Therapy 825 Challenger Dr *TF:* 800-783-2286 ■ *Web:* www.enzymatictherapy.com	Green Bay	WI	54311	920-469-1313	469-4444	799
EO Media Group 211 SE Byers Ave *Web:* www.eastoregonian.com	Pendleton	OR	97801	541-276-2211		532-3
Eoa Inc 1410 Jackson St *Web:* eoainc.com	Oakland	CA	94612	510-832-2852		261
Eoff Electric Company Inc 3241 NW Industrial St *TF:* 800-285-3633 ■ *Web:* www.eoff.com	Portland	OR	97210	503-222-9411		253
EOG Resources Inc 1111 Bagby Sky Lobby 2 *NYSE: EOG* ■ *TF:* 877-363-3647 ■ *Web:* www.eogresources.com	Houston	TX	77002	713-651-7000	651-6995	538
EOI Service Company Inc Flex 1820 E First St Ste 400 *Web:* eoiservice.com	Santa Ana	CA	92705	714-935-0503		390
EOIR Technologies Inc 10300 Spotsylvania Ave Ste 420 *Web:* www.eoir.com	Fredericksburg	VA	22408	540-834-4888		95
Eola Hills Wine Cellars 501 S Pacific Hwy 99 W *TF:* 800-291-6730 ■ *Web:* www.eolahillswinery.com	Rickreall	OR	97371	503-623-2405	623-0350	50-7
EON Reality Inc 39 Parker St Ste 100 *TF:* 800-579-9607 ■ *Web:* www.eonreality.com	Irvine	CA	92618	949-460-2000		174
E-ONE Inc 1601 SW 37th Ave *Web:* www.e-one.com	Ocala	FL	34474	352-237-1122	237-1151	516
EOR Energy Services Inc 3950 Braxton Ste 100 *Web:* www.eorenergy.com	Houston	TX	77063	713-914-9300		536
Eoriginal Inc 351 W Camden St Ste 800 *Web:* www.eoriginal.com	Baltimore	MD	21201	410-659-9796		177
Eos Partners LP 320 Pk Ave 9th Fl *Web:* www.eospartners.com	New York	NY	10022	212-832-5800	832-5815	402
Eos Systems Inc 72 River Park St Ste 4 *TF:* 855-453-2600 ■ *Web:* www.eos-systems.com	Needham	MA	02494	855-453-2600		180
EOSPACE Inc 6222 185th AVE NE *Web:* www.eospace.com	Redmond	WA	98052	425-869-8673		116
EP "Tom" Sawyer State Park 3000 Freys Hill Rd *Web:* www.parks.ky.gov	Louisville	KY	40241	502-429-7270	429-7273	565
EP Canada Film Services Inc 130 Bloor St W Ste 500 *Web:* epcanada.com	Toronto	ON	M5S1N5	416-923-9255		734
EP Foster Library 651 E Main St *Web:* www.vencolibrary.org	Ventura	CA	93001	805-648-2716		434-3
EP Henry Corp 201 Pk Ave *TF:* 800-444-3679 ■ *Web:* www.ephenry.com	Woodbury	NJ	08096	856-845-6200	845-0023	183
EP Wealth Advisors Inc 21515 Hawthorne Blvd Ste 1200 *TF:* 800-272-2328 ■ *Web:* www.epwealth.com	Torrance	CA	90503	310-543-4559		194
EPA (Environmental Protection Agency) 1200 Pennsylvania Ave NW *TF:* 888-372-8255 ■ *Web:* www.epa.gov	Washington	DC	20460	202-564-4700	501-1450	340-20
Epac Software Technologies Inc 42 Ladd St *TF:* 888-336-3722 ■ *Web:* www.epacst.com	East Greenwich	RI	02818	888-336-3722		177
E-pak Machinery Inc 1535 S State Rd 39 *TF:* 800-328-0466 ■ *Web:* www.epakmachinery.com	La Porte	IN	46350	219-393-5541	324-2884	547
Epc Consultants Inc 655 Davis St *Web:* www.epcconsultants.com	San Francisco	CA	94111	415-675-7580		180
EPCO (Engineered Products Co) 601 Kelso St PO Box 108 *TF:* 888-414-3726 ■ *Web:* www.epcohardware.com	Flint	MI	48506	810-767-2050	767-5084	350
Epcon Communities Inc 500 Stonehenge Pkwy *Web:* epconcommunities.com	Dublin	OH	43017	614-761-1010		653
Epcon Industrial Systems Inc 17777 IH- 45 S	Conroe	TX	77385	936-273-1774		18
EPCOS Inc 485-B Rt 1 S Ste 200 *TF:* 800-689-3717 ■ *Web:* en.tdk.eu	Iselin	NJ	08830	732-906-4304		253
EPCOT 1200 Epcot Resort Blvd *TF:* 888-800-5447 ■ *Web:* disneyworld.disney.go.com	Lake Buena Vista	FL	32830	407-824-4321		32
Epec LLC 174 Duchaine Blvd *Web:* www.epectec.com	New Bedford	MA	02745	508-995-5171		625
ePerformax Centers Inc 100 Saddle Springs Blvd ste 100 *Web:* www.eperformax.com	Thompsons Station	TN	37179	901-751-4800		393
Epes Carriers Inc 3400 Edgefield Ct *TF:* 800-869-3737 ■ *Web:* www.epestransport.com	Greensboro	NC	27409	336-668-3358	668-7008	780
Ephibian Inc 3180 N Swan Rd *TF:* 800-438-7325 ■ *Web:* www.ephibian.com	Tucson	AZ	85712	520-917-4747		177
Ephor Group LLC 24 E Greenway Plaza Ste 440 *TF:* 800-379-9330 ■ *Web:* www.ephorgroup.com	Houston	TX	77046	800-379-9330		463
Ephox Corp 2100 Geng Rd *Web:* ephox.com	Palo Alto	CA	94303	650-292-9659		177
Ephraim McDowell Regional Medical Ctr 217 S Third St	Danville	KY	40422	859-239-1000		374-3
EPI (Envision Peripherals Inc) 47490 Seabridge Dr	Fremont	CA	94538	510-770-9988	770-1088	173-4
EPI (Engineered Products Inc) 200 Jones St *TF:* 800-422-0614 ■ *Web:* www.epimetal.com	Verona	PA	15147	412-423-4000	423-4002	234
EPI labelers 1145 E Wellspring Rd *Web:* www.epilabelers.com	New Freedom	PA	17349	717-235-8345		547
Epi Marketing Group 30262 Crown Vly Pkwy Ste B458 *Web:* www.epi-marketing.com	Laguna Niguel	CA	92677	949-542-7743		463
EPI Marketing Services 5404 Wayne Rd *TF:* 800-562-9733 ■ *Web:* www.epiinc.com	Battle Creek	MI	49037	800-562-9733		627
EPIC (Environmental Protection Information Ctr) 145 G St Ste A *Web:* www.wildcalifornia.org	Arcata	CA	95521	707-822-7711	822-7712	48-13
EPIC (Electronic Privacy Information Ctr) 1718 Connecticut Ave NW Ste 200 *TF:* 800-838-6554 ■ *Web:* www.epic.org	Washington	DC	20009	202-483-1140	483-1248	48-9
Epic AIR LLC 22590 Nelson Rd *TF:* 888-359-3742 ■ *Web:* www.epicaircraft.com	Bend	OR	97701	541-318-8849		20
Epic Cos 10656 Hwy 23 *Web:* epiccompanies.com	Belle Chasse	LA	70037	504-681-1200	656-7701	226
Epic Labs Inc 95 Third St NE *TF:* 800-666-4513 ■ *Web:* www.epiclabs.com	Waite Park	MN	56387	320-656-1473		543
Epic Life Insurance Co 1717 W Broadway **Fax Area Code:* 608 ■ *TF Sales:* 800-520-5750 ■ *Web:* www.epiclife.com	Madison	WI	53713	800-520-5750	223-2159*	391-2
Epic Lift Systems LLC 14185 Hwy 377 S *Web:* www.epiclift.com	Fort Worth	TX	76126	817-443-3500		539
Epic Metals Corp 11 Talbot Ave *TF:* 877-696-3742 ■ *Web:* www.epicmetals.com	Rankin	PA	15104	412-351-3913	351-3913	697
Epic Research LLC 1105 N Market St Ste 1600 *Web:* www.epicresearch.net	Wilmington	DE	19801	302-467-5445		195
Epic Systems Corp 1979 Milky Way *Web:* epic.com	Verona	WI	53593	608-271-9000		180
Epicenter Network Inc 3500 188th St SW Ste 500 **Fax Area Code:* 801	Lynnwood	WA	98037	425-744-1474	858-6059*	7
Epicom Corporation 2815 Manor Rd Ste 201 *Web:* www.epicom.com	Austin	TX	78722	512-481-9000	870-9508	196
Epicurean Cutting Surfaces Inc 1325 N 59th Ave W *Web:* www.epicureancs.com	Duluth	MN	55807	218-740-3500		279
Epicurious LLC 4 Times Sq 17th Fl *Web:* www.epicurious.com	New York	NY	10036	212-381-7057		387
EPIEN Medical Inc 4225 White Bear Pkwy Ste 600 *TF:* 888-884-4675 ■ *Web:* www.epien.com	St Paul	MN	55110	651-653-3380		668
Epilepsy Foundation 8301 Professional Pl E *TF:* 800-332-1000 ■ *Web:* epilepsy.com	Landover	MD	20785	301-459-3700	577-2684	48-17
Epilog Corp 16371 Table Mtn Pkwy *TF:* 888-437-4564 ■ *Web:* www.epiloglaser.com	Golden	CO	80403	303-277-1188		544
Epimed International Inc 141 Sal Landrio Dr *Web:* www.epimed.com	Johnstown	NY	12095	518-725-0209		476
Epiomed Therapeutics Inc 25 Mauchly Ste 316 *Web:* www.epiomed.com	Irvine	CA	92618	949-398-7357		231
Epiphany Biosciences Inc 1 California St Ste 2800	San Francisco	CA	94111	415-765-7193	765-7200	668
Epiphany Productions Inc 104 Hume Ave *Web:* www.epiphanyproductions.com	Alexandria	VA	22301	703-683-7500		261
EPIQ Systems Inc 501 Kansas Ave *NASDAQ: EPIQ* ■ *Web:* www.epiqsystems.com	Kansas City	KS	66105	913-621-9500		178-10
EPIQ Technologies Inc 4711 Viewridge Ave Ste 230 *Web:* www.epiqtech.com	San Diego	CA	92123	858-467-9961		225
EPIR Technologies Inc 590 Territorial Dr Unit B *Web:* epirtech.com	Bolingbrook	IL	60440	630-771-0203		246
Episcopal Church USA 815 Second Ave *TF:* 800-334-7626 ■ *Web:* www.episcopalchurch.org	New York	NY	10017	212-716-6000	867-0395	48-20

Phone | Fax | Class

Episcopal Diocese of West Texas
111 Torcido Dr San Antonio TX 78209 210-824-5387 48-20
TF: 888-824-5387 ■ *Web:* dwtx.org

Episcopal Divinity School
99 Brattle St Cambridge MA 02138 617-868-3450 864-5385 167-3
Web: www.eds.edu

Episcopal Health Services Inc
327 Beach 19th St Far Rockaway NY 11691 718-869-7000 363
Web: www.ehs.org

Episcopal High School
1200 N Quaker Ln. Alexandria VA 22302 703-933-4062 622
TF: 877-933-4347 ■ *Web:* www.episcopalhighschool.org

Episcopal Life Magazine
815 Second Ave Episcopal Church Ctr New York NY 10017 212-716-6000 716-6000 457-18
TF: 800-334-7626 ■ *Web:* www.episcopalchurch.org

Episcopal Migration Ministries (EMM)
815 Second Ave New York NY 10017 212-716-6258 48-5
TF: 800-334-7626 ■ *Web:* episcopalchurch.org

Episcopal Relief & Development
815 Second Ave New York NY 10017 855-312-4325 687-5302* 48-5
**Fax Area Code:* 212 ■ *TF:* 800-334-7626 ■ *Web:* www.episcopalrelief.org

Epitec Inc 24800 Denso Dr Ste 150 Southfield MI 48033 248-353-6800 177
Web: epitec.com

Epitome Networks LLC
1600 E Parham Rd Richmond VA 23228 804-419-8300 196
Web: www.epitomenetworks.com

Epitomics Inc 863 Mitten Rd Ste 103 Burlingame CA 94010 888-772-2226 774-8286* 668
**Fax Area Code:* 877 ■ *TF:* 888-772-2226 ■ *Web:* www.epitomics.com

Epitomione 4502 Chews Vineyard Ellicott City MD 21043 443-540-2230 180
Web: www.epitomione.com

Epixx 3915 Heritage Colony Dr Missouri City TX 77459 281-208-1989 41
Web: www.epixx.com

EPKO Industries Inc
1200 Arthur Ave Elk Grove Village IL 60007 847-437-4000 550
Web: www.epko.com

EPL (Edison Price Lighting Inc)
41-50 22nd St Long Island NY 11101 718-685-0700 786-8530 439
TF: 800-929-3669 ■ *Web:* www.epl.com

EPLAN Software & Services LLC
37000 Grand River Ave Ste 380 Farmington Hills MI 48335 248-945-9204 179
Web: www.eplan.de

ePlus Inc 13595 Dulles Technology Dr. Herndon VA 20171 703-984-8400 984-8600 39
NASDAQ: PLUS ■ *TF:* 888-482-1122 ■ *Web:* www.eplus.com

Epoch 5 Public Relations
755 New York Ave. Huntington NY 11743 631-427-1713 636
TF: 800-628-7070 ■ *Web:* www.epoch5.com

Epoch Adv Agency Inc
888 E Brighton Ave Syracuse NY 13205 315-492-3270 4
Web: www.epoch-adv.com

Epoch Design 17617 NE 65th St Ste 2 Redmond WA 98052 425-284-0880 321
TF: 800-589-7990 ■ *Web:* www.epochbydesign.com

Epoch Investment Partners Inc
640 Fifth Ave 18th Fl New York NY 10019 212-303-7200 202-4948 401
NASDAQ: EPHC ■ *Web:* www.eipny.com

Epoch Online
324 W Pershing Blvd N Little Rock AR 72114 501-907-7500 180
Web: www.epochonline.com

Epoch Senior Living
51 Sawyer Rd Ste 500 Waltham MA 02453 781-891-0777 891-0774 672
Web: www.epochsl.com

Epoch Times Atlanta PO Box 2041 Suwanee GA 30024 678-485-0136 532-3
Web: www.epochtimes.com

Epoch Universal Inc 39 Musick Irvine CA 92618 949-268-3499 681
Web: epochuniversal.com

Epoque Hotels
2500 NE 135th St Ste 502 North Miami FL 33181 305-538-9697 379
TF: 866-376-7831 ■ *Web:* www.epoquehotels.com

Eportation LLC
401 S Second St Ste 305 Philadelphia PA 19147 215-627-2651 177
TF: 800-800-1513 ■ *Web:* www.eportation.com

E-power Marketing Inc
111 N Main St Ste 405 Oshkosh WI 54901 920-303-1244 195
Web: www.epower.com

Eppendorf North America Inc
102 Motor Pkwy Hauppage NY 11788 800-645-3050 334-7506* 419
**Fax Area Code:* 516 ■ *TF:* 800-645-3050 ■ *Web:* www.eppendorf.com/us-en

Eppinger Manufacturing Co
6340 Schaefer Rd Dearborn MI 48126 313-582-3205 710
TF: 888-771-8277 ■ *Web:* www.eppinger.net

Eppley Airfield 4501 Abbott Dr Ste 2300 Omaha NE 68110 402-661-8000 661-8000 27
Web: flyoma.com

Epps Aviation Inc
1 Aviation Way DeKalb Peachtree Airport Atlanta GA 30341 770-458-9851 458-0320 63
TF: 800-241-6807 ■ *Web:* www.eppsaviation.com

EPRI 3420 Hillview Ave Palo Alto CA 94304 650-855-2000 668
Web: www.epri.com

EPRI Journal 3420 Hillview Ave. Palo Alto CA 94304 650-855-2121 855-2121 457-21
TF: 800-313-3774 ■ *Web:* www.epri.com/journal

Epro Tile Inc 10890 E CR 6 Bloomville OH 44818 866-818-3776 343-8453 751
TF: 866-818-3776 ■ *Web:* www.eprotile.com

ePromos Promotional Products Inc
120 Broadway Ste 1360 New York NY 10271 212-286-8008 96
TF: 877-377-6667 ■ *Web:* www.epromos.com

EPS (Educators Publishing Service Inc)
625 Mt Auburn St Third Fl PO Box 9031 Cambridge MA 02139 800-225-5750 637-2
TF: 800-225-5750 ■ *Web:* eps.schoolspecialty.com

Eps Group, Inc Engineers, Planners & Surveyors
2045 S Vineyard Ste 101 Mesa AZ 85210 480-503-2250 261
Web: www.epsgroupinc.com

EPSA (Electric Power Supply Assn)
1401 New York Ave NW 11th Fl Washington DC 20005 202-628-8200 628-8260 48-12
Web: www.epsa.org

EPSCO International & Companies Inc
717 Georgia Ave Deer Park TX 77536 281-476-8100 612
Web: www.epscointl.com

Epsilon Greek Restaurant
422 Tyler St Monterey CA 93940 831-655-8108 671
Web: epsilonrestaurant.com

Epsilon Management Systems Inc
151 Fairchild Ave Ste 2 Plainview NY 11803 516-349-1440 180
Web: www.emscirc.com

Epsilon Sigma Phi Inc
450 Falls Ave Ste 106 Twin Falls ID 83301 208-736-4495 736-6081 48-16
TF: 800-727-9540 ■ *Web:* www.espnational.org

Epsilon Systems Solutions Inc
605 Commerce St. Portsmouth VA 23707 619-702-1700 698
Web: www.epsilonsystems.com

Epsilonium Systems Inc
201 E Southern Ave 205 Tempe AZ 85282 480-219-2629 180
TF: 800-874-2458 ■ *Web:* www.epsilonium.com

Epson America Inc
3840 Kilroy Airport Way Long Beach CA 90806 562-981-3840 290-5220 173-6
TF: 800-463-7766 ■ *Web:* www.epson.com

Epson Electronics America Inc
214 Devcon Dr San Jose CA 95112 800-228-3964 696
TF: 800-228-3964 ■ *Web:* www.eea.epson.com

Epson Portland Inc
3950 NW Aloclek Pl Hillsboro OR 97124 503-645-1118 625
Web: www.epi.epson.com

Epstein Becker & Green PC 250 Pk Ave. New York NY 10177 212-351-4500 661-0989 428
Web: www.ebglaw.com

Epstein Cole LLP 393 University Ave Toronto ON M5G1E6 416-862-9888 428
Web: www.epsteincole.com

ePublicEye.com 1010 N Central Ave Glendale CA 91202 818-547-0222 114

EPVC (Enterprise Partners Venture Capital)
2223 Avenida de la Playa Ste 300 La Jolla CA 92037 858-731-0300 792

Epygi Technologies Ltd
6900 Dallas Pkwy Ste 850 Plano TX 75024 972-692-1166 111
Web: www.epygi.com

EQ Inc 1255 Bay St Ste 400 Toronto ON M5R2A9 416-597-8889 5
Web: www.eqworks.com

EQC (Emerald Queen Casino) 2024 E 29th St Tacoma WA 98404 253-594-7777 133
TF: 888-831-7655 ■ *Web:* www.emeraldqueen.com

EQMM (Ellery Queen Mystery Magazine)
267 Broadway 4th Fl New York NY 10007 800-220-7443 457-11
TF: 800-220-7443 ■ *Web:* www.themysteryplace.com/eqmm

EQT Corp 625 Liberty Ave Ste 1700 Pittsburgh PA 15222 412-553-5700 787
NYSE: EQT ■ *TF:* 800-242-1776 ■ *Web:* www.eqt.com

Equal Employment Opportunity Commission (EEOC)
1801 L St NW Washington DC 20507 202-663-4191 340-20
TF: 800-669-4000 ■ *Web:* www.eeoc.gov

Equal Employment Opportunity Commission Regional Office

Atlanta District
100 Alabama St SW Ste 4R30 Atlanta GA 30303 800-669-6820 562-6909* 340-20
**Fax Area Code:* 404 ■ *TF:* 800-669-6820 ■ *Web:* www.eeoc.gov

Birmingham District
1130 22nd St S Ste 2000 Birmingham AL 35205 205-212-2100 212-2105 340-20
TF: 800-669-4000 ■ *Web:* www.eeoc.gov

Charlotte District
129 W Trade St Ste 400 Charlotte NC 28202 704-344-6682 344-6734 340-20
TF: 800-669-4000 ■ *Web:* www.eeoc.gov

Chicago District
500 W Madison St Ste 2800 Chicago IL 60661 312-353-2713 353-4041 340-20
TF: 800-669-4000 ■ *Web:* www.eeoc.gov

Dallas District 207 S Houston St 3rd Fl. Dallas TX 75202 214-253-2700 253-2720 340-20
TF: 800-669-4000 ■ *Web:* www.eeoc.gov

Houston District
1201 Louisiana St 6th Fl Houston TX 77002 800-669-4000 651-4987* 340-20
**Fax Area Code:* 713 ■ *TF:* 800-669-4000 ■ *Web:* www.eeoc.gov

Indianapolis District
101 W Ohio St Ste 1900 Indianapolis IN 46204 317-226-7212 226-7953 340-20
Web: www.eeoc.gov

Los Angeles District
255 E Temple St 4th Fl. Los Angeles CA 90012 800-669-4000 894-1118* 340-20
**Fax Area Code:* 213 ■ *TF:* 800-669-4000 ■ *Web:* www.eeoc.gov

Miami District
2 S Biscayne Blvd Ste 2700 Miami FL 33131 305-808-1740 808-1834 340-20
Web: www.eeoc.gov

New York District
33 Whitehall St 5th Fl New York NY 10004 212-336-3620 336-3790 340-20
TF: 866-408-8075 ■ *Web:* www.eeoc.gov

Philadelphia District
801 Market St Ste 1300 Philadelphia PA 19107 800-669-4000 440-2606* 340-20
**Fax Area Code:* 215 ■ *TF:* 800-669-4000 ■ *Web:* www.eeoc.gov/field/philadelphia

Phoenix District
3300 N Central Ave Ste 690 Phoenix AZ 85012 602-640-5000 640-5071 340-20
Web: www.eeoc.gov

Saint Louis District
1222 Spruce St Rm 8.100 Saint Louis MO 63103 314-539-7800 539-7894 340-20
TF: 800-669-4000 ■ *Web:* www.eeoc.gov

San Francisco District
450 Golden Gate Ave 5 W PO Box 36025 San Francisco CA 94102 800-669-4000 522-3415* 340-20
**Fax Area Code:* 415 ■ *TF:* 800-669-4000 ■ *Web:* www.eeoc.gov

Equal Rights Advocates (ERA)
1170 Market St Ste 700 San Francisco CA 94102 415-621-0672 621-6744 48-24
TF: 800-839-4372 ■ *Web:* www.equalrights.org

Equal Vision Records 136 Fuller Rd Albany NY 12205 518-458-8250 226
Web: www.equalvision.com

Equals Three Communications
7910 Woodmont Ave Ste 200 Bethesda MD 20814 301-656-3100 636

Equator Technologies 520 Pike St. Seattle WA 98101 206-267-4500 696

Equi Tax Inc
17111 Rolling Creek Dr Ste 200 Houston TX 77090 281-444-4866 317
Web: www.equitaxinc.com

Equias Alliance LLC
8000 Ctrview Pkwy Ste 525 Cordova TN 38018 901-754-4712 463
Web: www.equiasalliance.com

Equifax Credit Marketing Services
1550 Peachtree St NW Atlanta GA 30309 404-885-8000 218
NYSE: EFX ■ *TF Sales:* 800-660-5125 ■ *Web:* www.equifax.com

Equifax Inc 1550 Peachtree St NW. Atlanta GA 30309 404-885-8000 218
NYSE: EFX ■ *TF Sales:* 888-202-4025 ■ *Web:* www.equifax.com

EquiLend Holdings LLC
17 State St 9th Fl New York NY 10004 212-901-2200 360-3
Web: www.equilend.com

Equilibar LLC 320 Rutledge Rd Fletcher NC 28732 828-650-6590 789
Web: www.equilibar.com

	Phone	Fax	Class
Equilibrium Inc 100 Tamal Plaza Ste 225..................Corte Madera CA 94925 *TF:* 855 378 4542 ■ *Web:* equilibrium.com	415-332-4343	331-8374	178-8
Equine Canada 2685 Queensview Dr.............Ottawa ON K2B8K2 *TF:* 866-282-8395 ■ *Web:* www.equinecanada.ca	613-248-3484		652
Equinox 818 Connecticut Ave NW.............Washington DC 20006 *Web:* www.equinoxrestaurant.com	202-331-8118		671
Equinox Engineering Ltd 940 Sixth Ave SW 4th FL.....................Calgary AB T2P3T1 *Web:* www.equinox-eng.com	403-205-3833		256
Equinox Fitness Holdings Inc 895 Broadway..............................New York NY 10003 *TF:* 866-332-6549 ■ *Web:* www.equinox.com	212-677-0180		354
Equinox Gallery 2321 Granville St ....Vancouver BC V6H3G4 *Web:* www.equinoxgallery.com	604-736-2405	736-0464	42
Equinox Ltd 1307 Park Ave ....Williamsport PA 17701 *Web:* www.equinoxltd.com	570-322-5900		711
Equinox, The 3567 Main St...........Manchester Village VT 05254 *TF:* 800-362-4747 ■ *Web:* www.equinoxresort.com	802-362-4700	362-4861	669
Equiom Inc 3181 156th Ave SE Ste 200...........Bellevue WA 98007 *Web:* www.equiom.com	425-818-3043	650-6804	809
Equipment & Tool Institute (ETI) 134 W University Dr Ste 205 ....Rochester MI 48307 **Fax Area Code:* 603 ■ *Web:* etools.org	248-656-5080	971-2375*	49-13
Equipment Corporation of America 1000 Sta St PO Box 306...................Coraopolis PA 15108 *Web:* www.ecanet.com	412-264-4480		23
Equipment Dealers Assn (NAEDA) 165 N Meramec Ave Ste 430 ....St. Louis MO 63105 *Web:* www.equipmentdealer.org	636-349-5000	349-5443	49-18
Equipment Depot Ltd 4100 S I-35................Waco TX 76706 *Web:* www.eqdepot.com	254-662-4322		358
Equipment Development Company Inc 100 Thomas Johnson Dr ....Frederick MD 21702 *Web:* www.edcoinc.com	301-663-1600		1
Equipment Fabricating Corp 729 45th Ave.................................Oakland CA 94601 *Web:* www.equipmentfabricating.com	510-261-0343	261-0715	73
Equipment Leasing & Finance Assn (ELFA) 1825 K St NW Ste 900 ....Washington DC 20006 *Web:* www.elfaonline.org	202-238-3400	238-3401	49-18
Equipment Manufacturing Corp (EMC) 14930 Marquardt Ave.................Santa Fe Springs CA 90670 *TF:* 888-833-9000 ■ *Web:* www.equipmentmanufacturing.com	562-623-9394		386
Equipment Technology LLC 341 NW 122nd St......................Oklahoma City OK 73114 **Fax Area Code:* 405 ■ *TF:* 888-748-3841 ■ *Web:* etiequipment.com	888-748-3841	755-6829*	264-3
Equipment Today Magazine 1233 Janesville Ave ....Fort Atkinson WI 53538	920-563-1677		457-21
EquipNet Inc 5 Dan Rd..........................Canton MA 02021 *Web:* www.equipnet.com	781-821-3482		358
Equipoise Dental Laboratory Inc 05 Portland Avc ....Bergenfield NJ 07621 *TF:* 800-999-4950 ■ *Web:* www.equipoisedental.com	201-385-4750	385-3280	418
Equiptec Mechanical Inc 523 Capitola Ave.............................Capitola CA 95010	831-462-9511		610
EQUIPTO 225 Main St..........................Tatamy PA 18085 **Fax Area Code:* 888 ■ *TF:* 800-323-0801 ■ *Web:* www.equipto.com	610-253-2775	859-2121*	286
Equipto Electronics Corp 351 Woodlawn Ave...........................Aurora IL 60506 *TF:* 800-204-7225 ■ *Web:* www.equiptoelec.com	630-897-4691	897-5314	254
EQUIS Hospitality Management LLC 1034 S Brentwood Blvd Ste 2020..............St. Louis MO 63144 *Web:* www.equishospitality.com	314-932-3200		194
Equis International 90 South 400 West Ste 620 ....Salt Lake City UT 84101 *TF Sales:* 800-882-3040 ■ *Web:* www.metastock.com	801-265-9996	265-3999	178-10
Equisport Agency Inc 1113 Holland St.........................Birmingham MI 48012 *TF:* 800-432-1215 ■ *Web:* www.equisportagency.com	248 644-1215	644-1404	391-1
Equitable Bank 113 N Locust St..............Grand Island NE 68802 *TF:* 800-641-5046 ■ *Web:* equitableonline.com	308-382-3136		70
Equitable Building 730 17th St Ste 200...........Denver CO 80202 *Web:* www.stcharlestown.com	303-626-7000		205
Equitable Life & Casualty Insurance Co 3 Triad Ctr..............................Salt Lake City UT 84180 **Fax Area Code:* 801 ■ *TF Cust Svc:* 877-358-4060 ■ *Web:* www.equilife.com	877-358-4060	579-3790*	391-2
Equitec Group LLC 111 W Jackson Blvd Fl 20 ....Chicago IL 60604 *Web:* www.eqtc.com	312-692-5000		690
Equitrust Financial Group Ltd 570 Lake Cook Rd Ste 101...................Deerfield IL 60015 *Web:* www.equitrustfinancial.com	847-317-0200		463
Equity Communications LLC 1512 Grand Ave Ste 200................Santa Barbara CA 93103 *Web:* www.equitycommunications.com	805-897-1880		194
Equity Co-op Livestock Sales Assn 401 Commerce Ave..........................Baraboo WI 53913 *TF:* 800-362-3989 ■ *Web:* www.equitycoop.com	608-356-8311	356-0117	446
Equity Exploration Consultants Ltd 2075 Brigantine Dr........................Coquitlam BC V3K7B8	604-522-9807		256
Equity Funding 12505 Bel-Red Rd Ste 200.....................Bellevue WA 98005 *TF:* 866-332-3863 ■ *Web:* www.equity-funding.com	425-283-1040	283-1054	216
Equity Investment Corp 3007 Piedmont Rd Ste 200.......................Atlanta GA 30305 *TF:* 877-342-0111 ■ *Web:* www.eicatlanta.com	404-239-0111		528
Equity Lifestyle Properties Inc 2 N Riverside Plaza Ste 800 ....Chicago IL 60606 *NYSE: ELS* ■ *TF:* 800-274-7314 ■ *Web:* mymhcommunity.com	312-279-1400	279-1710	655
Equity Methods LLC 15300 N 90th St Ste 400 ....Scottsdale AZ 85260 *Web:* www.equitymethods.com	480-428-3344		196
Equity Office Properties Trust 2 N Riverside Plaza Ste 2100 ....Chicago IL 60606 *Web:* www.equityoffice.com	312-466-3300		655
Equity Residential 2 N Riverside Plaza...........................Chicago IL 60606 *NYSE: EQR* ■ *TF:* 800-733-5001 ■ *Web:* www.equityapartments.com	312-474-1300		655

	Phone	Fax	Class
Equity Transportation Company Inc 3685 Dykstra Dr NW.....................Grand Rapids MI 49544 *Web:* equityinc.com	616-466-5647		780
Equus 122 Sears Ave.........................Louisville KY 40207 *Web:* www.equusrestaurant.com	502-897-9721		671
Equus Computer Systems Inc 5801 Clearwater Dr.......................Minnetonka MN 55343 *TF:* 866-378-8727 ■ *Web:* www.equuscs.com	612-617-6200		173-2
Equus Magazine 656 Quince OrchaRd Rd Ste 600 ....Gaithersburg MD 20878 *TF Cust Svc:* 800-829-5910 ■ *Web:* equusmagazine.com	301-977-3900	990-9015	457-14
EQUUS Total Return Inc 700 Louisiana St 48th Fl.........................Houston TX 77002 **Fax Area Code:* 212 ■ *TF:* 888-323-4533 ■ *Web:* www.equuscap.com	888-323-4533	671-1534*	792
ER Jahna Industries Inc 202 E Stuart Ave.........................Lake Wales FL 33853 *Web:* www.jahna.com	863-676-9431	676-5137	503-4
Er Marketing 512 Delaware St...............Kansas City MO 64105 *TF:* 800-749-0381 ■ *Web:* www.ermarketing.net	816-471-1400		193
ER Precision Optical Corp 805 W Central Blvd..........................Orlando FL 32805 *Web:* www.eroptics.com	407-292-5395		542
ER Wagner Mfg Company Inc 4611 N 32nd St ....Milwaukee WI 53209 *TF:* 800-558-5596 ■ *Web:* www.erwagner.com	414-871-5080	449-8228	350
ERA (Equal Rights Advocates) 1170 Market St Ste 700 ....San Francisco CA 94102 *TF:* 800-839-4372 ■ *Web:* www.equalrights.org	415-621-0672	621-6744	48-24
ERA (Electronics Representatives Assn) 1325 S Arlington Heights Rd Ste 204..............................Elk Grove Village IL 60007 *Web:* www.era.org	312-419-1432	419-1660	49-18
ERA Grizzard Real Estate 1300 W N Blvd ....Leesburg FL 34748 *Web:* www.eragrizzard.com	352-787-6966		652
Era Helicopters LLC 600 Airport Service Rd PO Box 6550........Lake Charles LA 70606 *TF:* 888-503-8172 ■ *Web:* www.erahelicopters.com	337-478-6131	474-3918	13
ERA Naper Realty Inc 865 N Columbia St.........................Naperville IL 60563 *Web:* www.eranaper.com	630-961-1776		652
ERA Wilder Realty 120A Columbia Ave PO Box 610 ....Chapin SC 29036 *TF:* 866-593-7653 ■ *Web:* www.era.com/era-wilder-realty-947c	803-345-6713		652
Erath County 100 W Washington............Stephenville TX 76401 *Web:* www.co.erath.tx.us	254-965-1452	965-5732	338
Erawan Thai Cuisine 42-31 Bell Blvd ....Bayside NY 11361 *Web:* www.erawanthaibayside.com	718-428-2112		671
Erb Company Inc 1400 Seneca St................Buffalo NY 14210 *TF:* 800-875-2389 ■ *Web:* erbco.com	716-825-1400		38
Erb Equipment Co Inc 200 Erb Industrial Dr ....Fenton MO 63026 *TF:* 800-634-9661 ■ *Web:* www.erbequipment.com	636-349-0200	349-4426	358
Erb's Business Machines Inc 4935 Bowling St SW....................Cedar Rapids IA 52404 *Web:* ctsconnect.com	319-364-5159		179
ERC (Elbow River Casino) 218 18th Ave SE ......Calgary AB T2G1L1 *Web:* elbowrivercasino.com	403-289-8880		379
ERC Properties Inc 813 Fort St ....Barling AR 72923 *Web:* www.erc.com	479-452-9950		106
ERCCC (Elkins-Randolph County Chamber of Commerce) 200 Executive Plaza ....Elkins WV 26241 *Web:* www.ercc.com	304-636-2717	636-8046	139
Erchonia Corp 2021 Commerce Dr ....Mckinney TX 75069 *Web:* www.erchonia.com	214-544-2227		475
ERDC (US Army Engineer Research & Development Ctr) 3909 Halls Ferry Rd ....Vicksburg MS 39180 *Web:* www.erdc.usace.army.mil	601-634-3188		668
ERDCO Engineering Corp 721 Custer Ave............................Evanston IL 60202 *Web:* www.erdco.com	847-328-0550		201
Erdle Perforating Company Inc 100 Pixley Industrial Pkwy ....Rochester NY 14624 *Web:* www.erdle.com	585-247-4700		488
Erdman Anthony 145 Culver Rd Ste 200.........Rochester NY 14620 *Web:* erdmananthony.com	585-427-8888		261
Erdman Automation Corp 1603 14th St S ....Princeton MN 55371 *Web:* www.erdmanautomation.com	763-389-9475		454
Erdman Co 1 Erdman Pl.......................Madison WI 53717 *Web:* www.erdman.com	608-410-8000		186
Erect-A-Tube Inc 701 W Pk St PO Box 100 ....Harvard IL 60033 *TF:* 800-624-9219 ■ *Web:* www.erect-a-tube.com	815-943-4091	943-4095	105
ERGO (Euthanasia Research & Guidance Organization) 24829 Norris Ln.......................Junction City OR 97448 *Web:* www.finalexit.org	541-998-1873		48-17
Ergo Resource Management Inc 801 N Huntington St 7 ....Syracuse IN 46567 *TF:* 800-604-1995 ■ *Web:* ergo-syracuse.com	574-457-8020		463
Ergodyne Corp 1021 Bandana Blvd E Ste 220...............Saint Paul MN 55108 *TF:* 800-225-8238 ■ *Web:* www.ergodyne.com	651-642-9889	642-1882	477
ErgoGenesis Workplace Solutions LLC 1 BodyBilt Pl...............................Navasota TX 77868 *TF:* 800-364-5299 ■ *Web:* www.ergogenesis.com	936-825-1700	825-1725	319-3
Ergon Properties Inc PO Box 1639 ....Jackson MS 39215 *Web:* www.ergonproperties.com	601-933-3174		653
Ergon Refining 2611 Haining Rd..............Vicksburg MS 39183 *Web:* www.ergon.com	601-933-3000		580
Ergonomic Group Inc 609-3 Cantiague Rock Rd....................Westbury NY 11590 *Web:* www.ergogroup.com	516-746-7777		174
Ergos Technology Partners Inc 3831 Golf Dr...............................Houston TX 77018 *Web:* www.ergos.com	713-621-9220		196
Ergotron Inc 1181 Trapp Rd.................Saint Paul MN 55121 *TF Sales:* 800-888-8458 ■ *Web:* www.ergotron.com	651-681-7600	681-7710	319-1

				Phone	Fax	Class
Erhard Bmw Of Bloomfield Hills 4065 W Maple Rd *TF:* 888-481-4058 ■ *Web:* erhardbmw.com	Bloomfield Hills	MI	48301	248-642-6565		57
ERHC Energy Inc Ste 1440 5444 Westheimer Rd *TF:* 800-732-0330 ■ *Web:* erhc.com	Houston	TX	77056	713-626-4700		536
ERIC (Education Resource Information Ctr) 655 15th St NW Ste 500 *TF:* 800-538-3742 ■ *Web:* www.usa.gov	Washington	DC	20005	800-538-3742		197
Eric A. King 301 Grant St Ste 4300 *TF:* 888-742-2454 ■ *Web:* www.the-modeling-agency.com	Pittsburgh	PA	15219	281-667-4200		177
Eric Buchanan & Associates Pllc 414 Mccallie Ave *TF:* 877-634-2506 ■ *Web:* www.buchanandisability.com	Chattanooga	TN	37402	877-634-2506		445
Eric Electronics 2220 Lundy Ave *TF General:* 800-495-3742 ■ *Web:* www.ericnet.com	San Jose	CA	95131	408-432-1111	433-0570	246
Eric Johnson Associates Inc 201 Alameda Del Prado Ste 204	Novato	CA	94949	415-482-0923	482-0927	393
Eric Mower & Assoc 211 W Jefferson St *Web:* www.mower.com	Syracuse	NY	13202	315-466-1000		4
Eric's San Jose 6118 Garners Ferry Rd *Web:* ericssanjose.com	Columbia	SC	29209	803-783-6650		671
Erica Lane Enterprises Inc 3226 Bob Wallace Ave SW Ste 114 *Web:* www.eleinc.com	Huntsville	AL	35805	256-536-7117	536-7133	261
Erick Nielsen Enterprises Inc 4453 County Rd Mm # O *TF:* 800-844-9409 ■ *Web:* www.eneinc.com	Orland	CA	95963	530-865-9409		196
Erickson Inc 5550 SW Macadam Ave Ste 200 *TF:* 877-725-7539 ■ *Web:* www.ericksoninc.com	Portland	OR	97239	503-505-5800		20
Erickson Metals Corp 25 Knotter Dr *Web:* www.ericksonmetals.com	Cheshire	CT	06410	203-272-2918		492
Erickson Metals of Minnesota Inc 501 93rd Ave NW *Web:* www.ericksonmetalsmn.com	Coon Rapids	MN	55433	763-785-2340		492
Erickson Oil Products Inc 1231 Industrial St *Web:* www.freedomvalu.com	Hudson	WI	54016	715-386-8241	386-2022	324
Erickson Transport Corp 2255 N Packer Rd	Springfield	MO	65803	417-862-6741		780
Erickson's Flooring & Supply Company Inc 1013 Orchard St *TF:* 866-541-9663 ■ *Web:* www.ericksonsfloors.com	Ferndale	MI	48220	866-541-9663		361
ERICO Products Inc 34600 Solon Rd *TF:* 800-248-2677 ■ *Web:* www.erico.com	Solon	OH	44139	440-248-0100	248-0723	815
Ericson Elementary School 2309 Tulare St *Web:* fresnounified.org	Fresno	CA	93721	559-253-6450		685
Ericsson 1 Ericsson Dr *TF:* 800-521-2673 ■ *Web:* www.ericsson.com	Piscataway	NJ	08854	732-699-2000		178-10
Ericsson Inc 6300 Legacy Dr *Web:* www.ericsson.com	Plano	TX	75024	972-583-0000		735
Erie & Niagara Insurance Assn 8800 Sheridan Dr *Web:* www.enia.com	Williamsville	NY	14221	716-632-5433		391-2
Erie 2-Chautauqua Cattaraugus Boces (ECCB) 8685 Erie Rd *TF:* 800-228-1184 ■ *Web:* www.e2ccb.org	Angola	NY	14006	716-549-4454		685
Erie Art Museum 411 State St *Web:* www.erieartmuseum.org	Erie	PA	16501	814-459-5477	452-1744	520
Erie Bearings Company Inc 1432 E 12th St *TF:* 800-777-6871 ■ *Web:* www.eriebearings.com	Erie	PA	16503	814-453-6871		385
Erie Business Ctr *Erie* 246 W Ninth St	Erie	PA	16501	814-456-7504	456-4882	800
Erie Canal Museum 318 Erie Blvd E *Web:* www.eriecanalmuseum.org	Syracuse	NY	13202	315-471-0593	471-7220	520
Erie City Hall 626 State St *Web:* www.erie.pa.us	Erie	PA	16501	814-870-1234	870-1296	337
Erie Community College 121 Ellicott St *Web:* www.ecc.edu	Buffalo	NY	14203	716-842-2770	851-1129	162
North 6205 Main St *Web:* www.ecc.edu	Williamsville	NY	14221	716-634-0800	851-1429	162
South 4041 Southwestern Blvd **Fax:* Admissions ■ *Web:* www.ecc.edu	Orchard Park	NY	14127	716-851-1003	851-1687*	162
Erie County 92 Franklin St *Web:* www.erie.gov	Buffalo	NY	14202	716-858-8785	858-6550	338
Erie County 140 W Sixth St *Web:* www.eriecountypa.gov	Erie	PA	16501	814-451-6344	451-6334	338
Erie County 323 Columbus Ave 4th FL *Web:* www.erie-county-ohio.net	Sandusky	OH	44870	419-627-7782	627-6600	338
Erie County Chamber of Commerce 225 W Washington Row *Web:* eriecountychamber.com	Sandusky	OH	44870	419-625-6421	625-7914	139
Erie County Library System 160 E Front St *TF:* 800-352-0026 ■ *Web:* www.erielibrary.org	Erie	PA	16507	814-451-6900		434-3
Erie County Medical Ctr 462 Grider St *Web:* www.ecmc.edu	Buffalo	NY	14215	716-898-3000	898-5178	374-3
Erie County Water Authority (ECWA) 295 Main St Rm 350 *TF:* 855-748-1076 ■ *Web:* www.ecwa.org	Buffalo	NY	14203	716-849-8484	849-8467	787
Erie Engineered Products Inc 3949 Walden Ave *Web:* www.containers-cases.com	Lancaster	NY	14086	716-206-0204		198
Erie Family Life Insurance Co 100 Erie Insurance Pl *TF:* 800-458-0811 ■ *Web:* www.erieinsurance.com	Erie	PA	16530	814-870-2000		391-2
Erie Foods International Inc 401 Seventh Ave *TF:* 800-447-1887 ■ *Web:* www.eriefoods.com	Erie	IL	61250	309-659-2233	659-2822	296-10
Erie Forge & Steel Inc 1341 W 16th St *Web:* www.whemco.com/erie_forge_and_steel.aspx	Erie	PA	16502	814-452-2300		483
Erie Indemnity Co *Erie Insurance Group* 100 Erie Insurance Pl *NASDAQ: ERIE* ■ **Fax:* Mail Rm ■ *TF:* 800-458-0811 ■ *Web:* www.erieinsurance.com	Erie	PA	16530	814-870-2000	870-3126*	391-4
Erie Insurance Exchange 100 Erie Insurance Pl *TF:* 800-458-0811 ■ *Web:* www.erieinsurance.com	Erie	PA	16530	814-870-2000	870-3126	391-4
Erie Insurance Property & Casualty Co 100 Erie Insurance Pl *TF:* 800-458-0811 ■ *Web:* www.erieinsurance.com	Erie	PA	16530	814-870-2000		391-4
Erie International Airport 4411 W 12th St *Web:* www.erieairport.org	Erie	PA	16505	814-833-4258	833-0393	27
Erie Metropolitan Transit Authority (EMTA) 127 E 14th St *TF:* 800-692-6314 ■ *Web:* www.ride-the-e.com	Erie	PA	16503	814-452-3515		468
Erie Philharmonic 609 Walnut St *TF:* 800-859-8959 ■ *Web:* www.eriephil.org	Erie	PA	16502	814-455-1375	455-1377	573-3
Erie Playhouse 13 W Tenth St *TF:* 800-305-0669 ■ *Web:* www.erieplayhouse.org	Erie	PA	16501	814-454-2852	454-0601	573-4
Erie Press Systems 1253 W 12th St PO Box 4061 *TF:* 800-222-3608 ■ *Web:* www.eriepress.com	Erie	PA	16512	814-455-3941	456-4819	456
Erie Regional Chamber & Growth Partnership 208 E Bayfront Pkwy Ste 100 *Web:* www.eriepa.com	Erie	PA	16507	814-454-7191	459-0241	139
Erie Steel Treating Inc 5540 Jackman Rd *TF:* 800-622-6624 ■ *Web:* www.erie.com	Toledo	OH	43613	419-478-3743		492
Erie Strayer Co 1851 Rudolph Ave *TF:* 800-356-4848 ■ *Web:* www.eriestrayer.com	Erie	PA	16502	814-456-7001	452-3422	190
Erie Times-News 205 W 12th St *TF:* 800-352-0043 ■ *Web:* www.goerie.com	Erie	PA	16534	814-870-1600	870-1808	532-2
Erie VA Medical Ctr 135 E 38th St *TF:* 800-274-8387 ■ *Web:* www.erie.va.gov	Erie	PA	16504	814-868-8661		374-8
Erie Vehicle Co 60 E 51st St *TF:* 888-550-3743 ■ *Web:* erievehicle.com	Chicago	IL	60615	773-536-6300	536-5779	516
Erie Zoo 423 W 38th St *Web:* www.eriezoo.org	Erie	PA	16508	814-864-4091	864-1140	823
Erie-Western Pennsylvania Port Authority 208 E Bayfront Pkwy Ste 201 *Web:* www.porterie.org	Erie	PA	16507	814-455-7557	455-8070	618
Eriez Manufacturing Company Inc 2200 Asbury Rd *Web:* www.eriez.com	Erie	PA	16506	814-835-6000		207
Erik's Deli Cafe 365 Coral St *Web:* www.eriksdelicafe.com	Santa Cruz	CA	95060	831-458-1818	458-9797	670
Eriks Seals & Plastics Inc 15600 Trinity Blvd Ste 100 *TF:* 800-394-4448 ■ *Web:* www.eriksusa.com	Fort Worth	TX	76155	682-292-5060		326
Eris Exchange LLC 311 S Wacker Dr Ste 950 *Web:* www.erisfutures.com	Chicago	IL	60606	212-561-5472		691
Eritrea 800 Second Ave 18th Fl *Web:* www.eritrea-unmission.org	New York	NY	10017	212-687-3390	687-3138	784
Erlander Home Museum 404 S Third St *TF:* 800-785-6541 ■ *Web:* www.swedishhistorical.org	Rockford	IL	61104	815-963-5559	963-5559	520
Erlang Technology Inc 2138 Woodson Rd Ste 7 *Web:* www.erlangtech.com	St. Louis	MO	63114	314-428-6500	428-6501	393
Erlanger Health System 975 E Third St *TF:* 877-849-8338 ■ *Web:* www.erlanger.org	Chattanooga	TN	37403	423-778-7000		374-3
Erler Industries Inc 418 Stockwell St PO Box 219 *Web:* www.erler.com	North Vernon	IN	47265	812-346-4421		481
Erling Jensen Restaurant 1044 S Yates Rd *Web:* www.ejensen.com	Memphis	TN	38119	901-763-3700	763-3800	671
ER&M (Ecological Restoration & Management Inc) 9475 Deereco Rd Ste 406 *Web:* www.er-m.com	Timonium	MD	21093	410-337-4899	583-5678	186
ERMC (Edinburg Regional Medical Ctr) 1102 W Trenton Rd *TF:* 800-465-5585 ■ *Web:* www.southtexashealthsystem.com	Edinburg	TX	78539	956-388-6000		374-3
Ermco Inc 1625 W Thompson Rd *TF:* 800-306-7172 ■ *Web:* www.ermco.com	Indianapolis	IN	46217	317-780-2923	780-2853	189-4
Erminia 250 E 83rd St *Web:* erminiarestaurant.com	New York	NY	10028	212-879-4284		671
Ernan Roman Direct Marketing Corp 3 Melrose Ln *Web:* erdm.com	Little Neck	NY	11363	718-225-4151		463
Ernest Bock Jewelers 226 W Portal Ave	San Francisco	CA	94127	415-681-5362		410
Ernest F Mariani Company Inc 573 West 2890 South **Fax Area Code:* 801 ■ *TF:* 800-453-2927 ■ *Web:* efmco.com	Salt Lake City	UT	84115	800-453-2927	531-9615*	665
Ernest Hemingway Home & Museum 907 Whitehead St *TF:* 800-507-9955 ■ *Web:* www.hemingwayhome.com	Key West	FL	33040	305-294-1136	294-2755	50-3
Ernest Hemingway Museum 200 N Oak Pk Ave *Web:* www.ehfop.org	Oak Park	IL	60302	708-524-5383		520
Ernest Maier Inc 4700 Annapolis Rd *TF:* 888-927-8303 ■ *Web:* www.emcoblock.com	Bladensburg	MD	20710	301-927-8300	779-8924	183
Ernest N Morial Convention Ctr 900 Convention Ctr Blvd *Web:* www.mccno.com	New Orleans	LA	70130	504-582-3023	582-3088	205
Ernest Paper Products 5777 Smithway St *TF:* 800-233-7788 ■ *Web:* www.ernestpackaging.com	Commerce	CA	90040	800-233-7788		559
Ernest's Orleans Restaurant & Cocktail Lounge 1601 Spring St S *TF:* 800-551-8682 ■ *Web:* www.ernestsorleans.com	Shreveport	LA	71101	318-226-1325	425-0900	671
Ernesto's 1202 NW Hwy	Garland	TX	75041	972-681-8112		671
Ernesto's Mexican Food 1901 16th St *Web:* www.ernestosmexicanfood.com	Sacramento	CA	95811	916-441-5850		671

Name / Address	City	State	ZIP	Phone	Fax	Class
Ernie Ball 151 Suburban Rd *TF:* 866-823-2255 ■ *Web:* www.ernieball.com	San Luis Obispo	CA	93401	805-544-7726		527
Ernie Von Schledorn Country Inc N88 W14167 Main St *Web:* evsauto.com	Menomonee Falls	WI	53051	262-255-6000		57
Ernie Williams Ltd 2613 Hwy 18 E *TF:* 888-535-4096 ■ *Web:* www.erniewilliamsltd.com	Algona	IA	50511	515-295-3561		274
Ernie's Cafe 1005 E Walnut St *Web:* erniescolumbia.com	Columbia	MO	65201	573-874-7804		671
Ernie's Texas Lunch 58 Chambersburg St	Gettysburg	PA	17325	717-334-1970		671
Ernst & Young EY Tower 100 Adelaide St W *TF:* 800-291-3380 ■ *Web:* www.ey.com	Toronto	ON	M5H1S3	416-864-1234	864-1174	2
Ernst & Young 5 Times Sq **Fax:* Mail Rm ■ *Web:* www.ey.com	New York	NY	10036	212-773-3000	773-6350*	2
Ernst Auto Ctr Inc 615 E 23rd St *Web:* www.ernstauto.com	Columbus	NE	68601	402-835-4221		57
Ernst Enterprises Inc 3361 Successful Way *TF:* 800-353-1555 ■ *Web:* ernstconcrete.com	Dayton	OH	45414	937-233-5555		182
Ernst Enterprises of Georgia 540 Seaboard Industrial Dr *Web:* www.ernstga.com	Lawrenceville	GA	30046	770-995-9098		182
Ernst Joni (Sen R - IA) 111 Russell Senate Office Bldg *Web:* www.ernst.senate.gov	Washington	DC	20510	202-224-3254	224-9369	342-2
Ernst Publishing Co LLC 1 Commerce Plaza 99 Washington Ave Ste 309 *TF:* 800-345-3822 ■ *Web:* marketing.ernstinfo.com	Albany	NY	12210	800-345-3822	252-0906	637-9
Ernst Swedean & Assoc PC 4125 Gordon Dr *Web:* esacpaonline.com	Sioux City	IA	51106	712-274-6617		2
Ernst-Van Praag Inc 433 Plaza Real Ste 275 *Web:* www.evpconsulting.com	Boca Raton	FL	33432	561-447-0557		4
eROI Inc 505 NW Couch Ste 300 *Web:* www.eroi.com	Portland	OR	97209	503-221-6200		177
ERP Group Inc 88 Farwell St	West Haven	CT	06516	203-931-0490		189-10
ERP International LLC 603 Seventh St Ste 203 *Web:* www.erpinternational.com	Laurel	MD	20707	301-490-0080		196
Errand Solutions LLC 118 S Clinton St Ste 760 *TF:* 800-280-9389 ■ *Web:* www.errandsolutions.com	Chicago	IL	60661	312-475-3800		113
ERRC (Eastern Regional Research Ctr) 600 E Mermaid Ln *Web:* www.ars.usda.gov	Wyndmoor	PA	19038	215-233-6400	233-6559	668
ERS (Economic Research Service) US Dept of Agriculture 1400 Independence Ave SW, Mail Stop 1800 *Web:* www.ers.usda.gov	Washington	DC	20250-0002	202-694-5050		340-1
ERS Industries Inc 1005 Indian Church Rd *TF:* 800-993-6446 ■ *Web:* www.ersindustries.com	West Seneca	NY	14224	716-675-2040		770
Ershigs Inc 742 Marine Dr *TF:* 800-524-5979 ■ *Web:* www.ershigs.com	Bellingham	WA	98225	360-733-2620	733-2628	606
Erskine Academy 309 Windsor Rd *Web:* erskineacademy.org	South China	ME	04358	207-445-2962		148
Erskine College 2 Washington St *TF Admissions:* 888-359-4358 ■ *Web:* www.erskine.edu	Due West	SC	29639	888-359-4358		166
Erskine Theological Seminary 2 Washington St PO Box 338 *TF:* 888-359-4358 ■ *Web:* www.erskine.edu	Due West	SC	29639	864-379-6571		167-3
ERT 1818 Market St Ste 1000 *NASDAQ: ERT* ■ *TF:* 800-704-9698 ■ *Web:* www.ert.com	Philadelphia	PA	19103	215-972-0420	972-0414	178-10
Erte Restaurant 323 13th Ave NE *Web:* www.ertedining.com	Minneapolis	MN	55413	612-623-4211		671
Ervin & Smith Advertising & Public Relations Inc 16934 Frances St *Web:* www.ervinandsmith.com	Omaha	NE	68130	402-334-6969		7
Ervin Cohen & Jessup 9401 Wilshire Blvd 9th Fl *Web:* www.ecjlaw.com	Beverly Hills	CA	90212	310-273-6333		428
Ervin Equipment Inc 608 N Ohio St *TF:* 800-388-7950 ■ *Web:* www.ervinusa.com	Toledo	IL	62468	217-849-3125		449
Ervin Industries Inc 3893 Research Pk Dr *TF:* 800-748-0055 ■ *Web:* www.ervinindustries.com	Ann Arbor	MI	48108	734-769-4600	663-0136	1
Erving Paper Mills 97 E Main St *Web:* www.ervingpaper.com	Erving	MA	01344	413-422-2700		558
Erving State Forest 200 E Main St Rt 2A *Web:* www.mass.gov	Erving	MA	01344	978-544-3939		565
Erwin & Co 6311 Ranch Dr *Web:* erwinco.com	Little Rock	AR	72223	501-868-7486		2
Erwine Home Health & Hospice 270 Pierce St Ste 101 *Web:* erwinehealthcare.com	Kingston	PA	18704	570-288-1013		371
Erwin-Keith Inc 1529 Hwy 193 *TF:* 888-535-7333 ■ *Web:* progenyag.com	Wynne	AR	72396	870-238-2079		10-5
Erwin-Penland Inc 125 E Broad St *Web:* www.epandcompany.com	Greenville	SC	29601	864-271-0500		636
E&S International Enterprises Inc 7801 Hayvenhurst Ave *TF:* 800-892-5234 ■ *Web:* www.esintl.com	Van Nuys	CA	91406	818-887-0700		38
ES Originals Inc 440 Ninth Ave 7th Fl *TF General:* 800-677-6577 ■ *Web:* www.esoriginals.com	New York	NY	10001	212-736-8124	736-8366	301
ES3 Inc 1625 Star Batt Dr	Rochester Hills	MI	48309	248-537-0110		636
ESA (Ecological Society of America) 1990 M St Ste 700 *Web:* www.esa.org	Washington	DC	20036	202-833-8773	833-8775	49-19
ESA (Evangelicals for Social Action) PO Box 367 *TF:* 800-650-6600 ■ *Web:* www.evangelicalsforsocialaction.org	Wayne	PA	19087	484-384-2988		48-7
ESA (Electronic Security Assn Inc) 2300 Vly View Ln Ste 230 *TF:* 888-447-1689 ■ *Web:* www.esaweb.org	Irving	TX	75062	214-260-5970	260-5979	49-3
ESA (Entertainment Software Assn) 575 Seventh St NW Ste 300 *TF:* 800-949-3660 ■ *Web:* www.theesa.com	Washington	DC	20004	202-223-2400	223-2401	48-9
ESA Biosciences Inc 22 Alpha Rd	Chelmsford	MA	01824	978-250-7000		418
ESA Construction Inc 645 El Molino Blvd *Web:* www.esaconstruction.com	Las Cruces	NM	88005	505-884-2171	888-3150	186
Esab Welding & Cutting Products 411 S Ebenezer Rd PO Box 100545 **Fax:* Hum Res ■ *TF:* 800-372-2123 ■ *Web:* www.esabna.com	Florence	SC	29501	843-669-4411	664-4258*	811
Esage Group LLC 605 First Ave Ste 510 *Web:* www.esagegroup.com	Seattle	WA	98104	206-342-9981		180
Esalen Institute 55000 Hwy 1 *Web:* www.esalen.org	Big Sur	CA	93920	831-667-3000	667-2724	673
Esan Thai 221 E Kirkwood Ave *Web:* esanthairest.com	Bloomington	IN	47408	812-333-8424		671
Esanu Katsky Korins & Siger 605 Third Ave *Web:* www.ekks.com	New York	NY	10158	212-953-6000		445
Esbenshade Farms 220 Eby Chiques Rd *Web:* esbenshadefarmmill.com	Mount Joy	PA	17552	717-653-8061	653-6922	10-8
Escalade Inc 817 Maxwell Ave *NASDAQ: ESCA* ■ *TF Cust Svc:* 800-426-1421 ■ *Web:* www.escaladesports.com	Evansville	IN	47711	812-467-1200		710
Escalante State Park 710 N Reservoir Rd *Web:* www.stateparks.utah.gov	Escalante	UT	84726	435-826-4466		565
Escalera Inc 708 S Industrial Dr PO Box 1359 *TF:* 800-622-1359 ■ *Web:* www.escalera.com	Yuba City	CA	95993	530-673-6318	673-6376	470
Escalon Medical Corp 435 Devon Pk Dr Bldg 100 *NASDAQ: ESMC* ■ *TF:* 800-433-8197 ■ *Web:* www.escalonmed.com	Wayne	PA	19087	610-688-6830		476
Escalon Premier Brands 1905 McHenry Ave *TF:* 800-255-5750 ■ *Web:* www.escalon.net	Escalon	CA	95320	209-838-7341		296-20
Escambia County PO Box 040 *Web:* www.co.escambia.al.us	Brewton	AL	36427	251-867-0300		338
Escambia County Area Transit (ECAT) 1515 W Fairfield Dr *Web:* www.goecat.com	Pensacola	FL	32501	850-595-3228	595-3222	468
Escambia River Electric Co-op Inc 3425 Florida 4 *TF:* 800-235-3848 ■ *Web:* www.erec.com	Jay	FL	32565	850-675-4521	675-8415	245
Escamilla & Sons Inc 23820 Potter Rd	Salinas	CA	93908	831-771-5400		260
Escamilla, Poneck & Cruz LLP 850 Riverwalk Pl 700 N St Mary's St *Web:* www.escamillaponeck.com	San Antonio	TX	78205	210-225-0001		428
Escanaba Public Library 400 Ludington St *TF:* 800 992 9012 ■ *Web:* www.uproc.lib.mi.us	Escanaba	MI	49829	906-786-4463	786-0942	434-3
Escape Enterprises Ltd 222 Neilston St *Web:* www.steakescape.com	Columbus	OH	43215	614-224-0300	224-6460	670
Escapees RV Club 100 Rainbow Dr *TF:* 800-231-9896 ■ *Web:* www.escapees.com	Livingston	TX	77399	936-327-8873	327-4388	48-23
ESCC (Enterprise State Community College) 600 Plaza Dr *Web:* www.escc.edu	Enterprise	AL	36330	334-347-2623		162
Eschenbach Optik of America Inc 904 Ethan Allen Hwy *Web:* www.eschenbach.com	Ridgefield	CT	06877	203-438-7471		544
eScholar LLC 222 Bloomingdale Rd Ste 107 *Web:* www.escholar.com	White Plains	NY	10605	914-989-2900		658
Esco Corp 2141 NW 25th Ave *TF:* 800-523-3795 ■ *Web:* www.escocorp.com	Portland	OR	97210	503-228-2141	226-8071	190
ESCO Technologies Inc 9900A Clayton Rd *NYSE: ESE* ■ *TF:* 800-368-5948 ■ *Web:* www.escotechnologies.com	Saint Louis	MO	63124	314-213-7200	213-7250	360-3
Escondido Chamber of Commerce 720 N Broadway *TF:* 800-736-7401 ■ *Web:* www.escondidochamber.org	Escondido	CA	92025	760-745-2125	745-1183	139
Escondido Public Library 239 S Kalmia St *Web:* www.library.escondido.org	Escondido	CA	92025	760-839-4684		434-3
Escopazzo 1311 Washington Ave	Miami Beach	FL	33139	305-674-9450		671
Escot Bus Lines Inc 6890 142nd Ave *TF:* 800-553-9000 ■ *Web:* www.escotbuslines.com	Largo	FL	33771	727-545-2088		107
eScreen Inc 7500 W 110th St Ste 500 *TF:* 800-881-0722 ■ *Web:* www.escreen.com	Overland Park	KS	66210	913-327-5915		387
EscrowTech International Inc 3290 W Mayflower Way *Web:* www.escrowtech.com	Lehi	UT	84043	801-852-8202		393
ESD (Etiwanda School District) 6061 E Ave *TF:* 800-300-1506 ■ *Web:* www.etiwanda.k12.ca.us	Etiwanda	CA	91739	909-899-2451	899-1235	685
ESE Inc 3600 DownWind Dr *TF:* 800-236-4778 ■ *Web:* eseautomation.com	Marshfield	WI	54449	715-387-4778		256
ESE Solutions LLC 2131 Homestead Blvd Ste *Web:* www.esesolutions.com	Westborough	MA	01581	857-540-2679		192
ESEA a California Corp 280 Second St Ste 270 *Web:* esea.com	Los Altos	CA	94022	650-941-4175		256
eSecurityToGo LLC 2280 University Dr Ste 104 *Web:* www.esecuritysolutions.com/security-products	Newport Beach	CA	92660	949-261-5556		180
Eseeola Lodge, The 175 Linville Ave PO Box 99 *TF:* 800-742-6717 ■ *Web:* www.eseeola.com	Linville	NC	28646	828-733-4311		669
eSentio Technologies 700 12Th St NW Ste 700 *Web:* www.esentio.com	Washington	DC	20005	202-628-6010		261
ESG (Energy Services Group International Inc) 3601 La Grange Pkwy *Web:* www.esgi.net	Toano	VA	23168	757-741-4040	741-4045	721

Phone | Fax | Class

ESGR (National Committee for Employer Support of the Guard & Reserve)
1555 Wilson Blvd Ste 319 .... Arlington VA 22209 703-696-1386 48-19
TF: 800-336-4590 ■ *Web:* www.esgr.mil

ESH (Eastern State Hospital)
4601 Ironbound Rd. .... Williamsburg VA 23188 757-253-5161 374-5
TF: 800-994-6610 ■ *Web:* esh.dbhds.virginia.gov

Eshoo Anna G (Rep D - CA)
241 Cannon Bldg .... Washington DC 20515 202-225-8104 225-8890 342-2
Web: eshoo.house.gov

ESI FME Engineers
1800 E 16th St Ste B. .... Santa Ana CA 92701 714-835-2800 256
Web: www.esifme.com

ESI Inc of Tennessee
1250 Roberts Blvd .... Kennesaw GA 30144 770-427-6200 261
Web: esitenn.com

ESI Information Technologies
1550 Metcalfe St Ste 1100 .... Montreal QC H3A1X6 514-745-3311 196
Web: www.esitechnologies.com

ESI Software Inc
1465 Kelly Johnson Blvd Ste 305 .... Colorado Springs CO 80920 719-638-7033 387
Web: www.esisoft.us

eSignal 3955 Pt Eden Way .... Hayward CA 94545 510-266-6000 266-6100 178-1
TF: 800-815-8256 ■ *Web:* www.esignal.com

eSilicon Corp 501 Macara Ave. .... Sunnyvale CA 94085 408-616-4600 991-9567 253
TF: 877-769-2447 ■ *Web:* www.esilicon.com

ESIS Inc 7920 Arjons Dr Ste H .... San Diego CA 92126 858-625-0060 387
Web: www.esisinc.com

Eskaton Inc 5105 Manzanita Ave. .... Carmichael CA 95608 916-334-0810 338-1248 672
TF: 800-729-2999 ■ *Web:* www.eskaton.org

Eskaton Village 3939 Walnut Ave. .... Carmichael CA 95608 916-974-2000 974-2022 672
TF: 800-300-3929 ■ *Web:* www.eskaton.org

Esker Inc 1212 Deming Way Ste 350 .... Madison WI 53717 608-828-6000 828-6001 178-12
TF: 800-368-5283 ■ *Web:* www.esker.com

Eskridge & Assocs
595 Round Rock W Dr Ste 406 .... Round Rock TX 78681 512-244-7023 194

Eskridge Inc 1900 Kansas City Rd. .... Olathe KS 66061 913-782-1238 620
Web: www.eskridgeinc.com

ESL ElectroScience Inc
416 E Church Rd .... King Of Prussia PA 19406 610-272-8000 246
Web: www.electroscience.com

Esmark Steel Group
2500 Euclid Ave .... Chicago Heights IL 60411 708-756-0400 360-3
TF: 800-323-0340 ■ *Web:* www.esmark.com

Esmeralda County PO Box 547. .... Goldfield NV 89013 775-485-6309 485-6376 338
TF: 800-884-4072 ■ *Web:* www.accessesmeralda.com

ESN Interactive
440 Seaton St Ste 301 .... Los Angeles CA 90013 323-337-0600 195
Web: www.edusearch.com

Esna Technologies Inc
30 W Beaver Creek Rd Ste 101 .... Richmond Hill ON L4B3K1 905-707-9700 45
Web: www.esna.com

eSnipe Inc 12819 SE 38th St .... Bellevue WA 98006 425-260-5292 387
Web: www.esnipe.com

eSoft Inc
295 Interlocken Blvd Ste 500 .... Broomfield CO 80021 303-444-1600 176
TF: 866-233-2296 ■ *Web:* untangle.com/esoft

eSoftware Professionals Inc
10450 SW Nimbus Ave Ste B .... Portland OR 97223 503-608-3601 631
Web: www.esopro.com

ESOP Assn 1726 M St NW Ste 501. .... Washington DC 20036 202-293-2971 293-7568 49-12
TF: 866-366-3832 ■ *Web:* www.esopassociation.org

ESP (Electronic Systems Packaging LLC)
1175 W Victoria St .... Rancho Dominguez CA 90220 310-639-2535 632-6666 815
Web: www.espbus.com

ESP Solutions Group Inc
8627 N Mopac Ste 400. .... Austin TX 78759 512-879-5300 387
Web: www.espsolutionsgroup.com

Espa Corp Inc 7120 Grand Blvd Ste 100 .... Houston TX 77054 713-680-0080 261
Web: kci.com

Espaillat Adriano (Rep D - NY)
1630 Longworth HOB .... Washington DC 20515 202-225-4365 226-9731 342-2
Web: espaillat.house.gov/contact/offices

Espanola Valley Chamber of Commerce
1 Calle de las Espanolas Ste F & G. .... Espanola NM 87532 505-753-2831 753-1252 139
TF: 800-446-8117 ■ *Web:* www.espanolanmchamber.com

ESPE Mfg Company Inc
9220 Ivanhoe St .... Schiller Park IL 60176 847-678-8950 678-0253 350
TF Cust Svc: 800-367-3773 ■ *Web:* www.electricalinsulationguys.com

Espey Mfg & Electronics Corp
233 Ballston Ave. .... Saratoga Springs NY 12866 518-245-4400 245-4421 253
NYSE: ESP ■ *Web:* www.espey.com

Esplanade Tours
160 Commonwealth Ave Ste U-1A .... Boston MA 02116 617-266-7465 262-9829 760
TF: 800-628-4893 ■ *Web:* esplanadetravel.com

Esplendor Resort at Rio Rico
1069 Camino Caralampi. .... Rio Rico AZ 85648 520-281-1901 669
TF: 800-288-4746 ■ *Web:* www.esplendor-resort.com

ESPN 1530
8044 Montgomery Rd Ste 650 .... Cincinnati OH 45236 513-686-8300 645-37
Web: www.espn1530.com

ESPN Classic Inc 1 ESPN Plaza .... Bristol CT 06010 877-710-3776 740
TF: 877-710-3776 ■ *Web:* www.espn.com

ESPN Deportes
2 Alhambra Plaza 9th Fl .... Coral Gables FL 33134 305-567-3797 740
TF: 800-337-6783 ■ *Web:* espndeportes.espn.com

ESPN Digital Center 1 545 Middle St. .... Bristol CT 06010 860-766-5333 740
TF: 877-710-3776 ■ *Web:* www.espn.com

ESPN KCBF 820 Sports
529 Fifth Ave Ste 200 .... Fairbanks AK 99701 907-451-5910 451-5999 645-57
Web: www.820sports.com

ESPN Radio 1320 5345 Madison Ave .... Sacramento CA 95841 916-334-7777 645-140
Web: espn1320.net

ESPN Radio 1410 10 Columbus Blvd .... Hartford CT 06106 860-723-6000 645-72
Web: newsradio1410.iheart.com

Espo Engineering 855 Midway Dr. .... Willowbrook IL 60527 630-789-2525 256
Web: www.espocorp.com

Esposito Jewelry Inc 225 DuPont Dr. .... Providence RI 02907 401-943-1900 409

Esprida Corp 5180 Orbitor Dr .... Mississauga ON L4W5L9 905-629-0455 177
Web: www.esprida.com

Esprit Miami 11475 NW 39th St .... Miami FL 33178 305-591-2244 591-2603 293
TF: 800-327-2320 ■ *Web:* www.espritmiami.com

Espy Investigate Services
1264 Sapphire Ct .... Ripon CA 95366 209-609-2676 400
TF: 800-720-8955 ■ *Web:* www.espyinvestigations.com

Esquire Deposition Solutions
2700 Centennial Tower 101 Marietta St
101 Marietta St. .... Atlanta GA 30303 404-495-0777 445
Web: www.esquiresolutions.com

Esquire Grill 1213 K St .... Sacramento CA 95814 916-448-8900 671
Web: www.paragarys.com

Esquire Inc
21241 Bentura Blvd Ste 293 .... Los Angeles CA 91364 818-712-9700 260
Web: www.esquireresearch.com

Esquire Magazine
300 W 57th St 21st Fl. .... New York NY 10019 212-649-4020 457-11
Web: www.esquire.com

Esrey Energy Ltd
1075 Georgia St W Ste 250 .... Vancouver BC V6E3C9 778-373-0103 538
Web: www.esreyenergy.com

ESRI Canada Ltd 12 Concorde Pl Ste 900. .... Toronto ON M3C3R8 416-441-6035 174
TF: 866-625-4577 ■ *Web:* www.esri.ca

Esrock Recruitment Advertising
14550 S 94th Ave .... Orland Park IL 60462 708-349-8400 7
TF: 800-874-2458 ■ *Web:* www.esrock.com

ESS Technology Inc 48401 Fremont Blvd. .... Fremont CA 94538 510-492-1088 696
Web: www.esstech.com

Essco Inc 1933 Highland Rd .... Twinsburg OH 44087 216-524-4141 605-2
TF: 800-321-2664 ■ *Web:* www.essco.net

Essdack 1500 E 11th Ave Ste 200 .... Hutchinson KS 67501 620-663-9566 196
Web: www.essdack.org

Esseks Hefter & Angel 108 E Main St. .... Riverhead NY 11901 631-369-1700 445
Web: www.ehalaw.com

Essen Haus 514 E Wilson St .... Madison WI 53703 608-255-4674 258-8632 671
Web: www.essen-haus.com

Essence Communications Inc
225 Liberty St 9th Fl. .... New York NY 10048 800-274-9398 637-9
TF Sales: 800-274-9398 ■ *Web:* www.essence.com

Essence Magazine
225 Liberty St 9th Fl. .... New York NY 10048 800-274-9398 274-9398 457-11
TF: 800-274-9398 ■ *Web:* www.essence.com

Essence Printing Inc
270 Oyster Point Blvd Ste. .... South San Francisco CA 94080 650-952-5072 627
Web: www.essenceprinting.com

Essentia Health 502 E Second St .... Duluth MN 55805 218-786-8376 374-3
TF: 855-469-6532 ■ *Web:* www.essentiahealth.org

Essential Baking Co, The
5601 First Ave S .... Seattle WA 98108 206-545-3804 345
Web: www.essentialbaking.com

Essential Dental Systems Inc
89 Leuning St Ste 8 .... South Hackensack NJ 07606 201-487-9090 228
Web: www.edsdental.com

Essential Management Solutions Llc
1 S Second St. .... Pottsville PA 17901 570-621-9000 463
Web: emsolutionsllc.net

Essential Personnel Inc
3415 W State St Ste B. .... Grand Island NE 68803 308-381-4400 193
TF: 800-906-7107 ■ *Web:* www.essentialpersonnelinc.com

Essential Technologies Inc
1107 Hazeltine Blvd Ste 477 .... Chaska MN 55318 952-368-9001 368-3334 175
TF: 844-375-7219 ■ *Web:* www.essentialtechinc.com

Essentialtalk Network
1289 Highfield Cres SE .... Calgary AB T2G5M2 403-537-9690 225
Web: www.essentialtalk.com

Essentra PLC 7400 W Industrial Dr .... Forest Park IL 60130 800-847-0486 561-6617* 154
**Fax Area Code:* 886 ■ *TF:* 800-847-0486 ■ *Web:* us.essentracomponents.com

Esser Hayes Insurance Group Inc
1811 High Grove .... Naperville IL 60540 630-355-2077 390
Web: esserhayes.com

Essex Boat Works Inc Ferry St PO Box 37. .... Essex CT 06426 860-767-8276 767-1729 698
TF: 800-870-1285 ■ *Web:* essexboatworks.com

Essex County 7559 Ct St .... Elizabethtown NY 12932 518-873-3600 338

Essex County
465 Dr Martin Luther King Jr Blvd Rm 558. .... Newark NJ 07102 973-621-4400 435-2537* 338
**Fax Area Code:* 703 ■ *Web:* essexcountynj.org

Essex County 32 Federal St .... Salem MA 01970 978-741-0200 338
Web: essexcountyma.net

Essex County 305 Prince St. .... Tappahannock VA 22560 804-443-4611 445-1216 338
TF: 800-552-9745 ■ *Web:* www.essex-virginia.org

Essex County College
303 University Ave .... Newark NJ 07102 973-877-3000 877-3446* 162
**Fax:* Admissions ■ *Web:* www.essex.edu
West Essex 730 Bloomfield Ave. .... West Caldwell NJ 07006 973-877-3175 162
TF: 800-433-3243 ■ *Web:* www.essex.edu

Essex County Hospital Ctr
204 Grove Ave .... Cedar Grove NJ 07009 973-571-2800 374-5
Web: essexcountynj.org

Essex County Public Schools
109 Cross St PO Box 756. .... Tappahannock VA 22560 804-443-4366 443-4498 780
Web: www.essex.k12.va.us

Essex Electro Engineering Inc
2015 Mitchell Blvd .... Schaumburg IL 60193 847-891-4444 111
Web: www.essexelectro.com

Essex Financial Services Inc
176 Westbrook Rd .... Essex CT 06426 860-767-4300 528
TF: 800-900-5972 ■ *Web:* www.essex.financial

Essex Food Ingredients 9 Lee Blvd. .... Frazer PA 19355 610-647-3800 647-4990 297-11
TF: 800-441-1017 ■ *Web:* www.essexgrain.com

Essex Futures Inc
8105 Irvine Ctr Dr Ste 840 .... Irvine CA 92618 949-450-8221 169
Web: www.essexfutures.com

Essex Industries Inc
7700 Gravois Rd. .... Saint Louis MO 63123 314-832-4500 832-1633 807
TF: 800-558-6270 ■ *Web:* essexindustries.com

Essex Investment Management Company LLC
125 High St 29th Fl .... Boston MA 02110 617-342-3200 342-3280 401
Web: www.essexinvest.com

Company	City	State	ZIP	Phone	Fax	Class
Essex Manufacturing Inc PO Box 92864 *TF:* 888-643-7739 ■ *Web:* www.essexmfg.com	Southlake	TX	76092	817-847-4555		155-5
Essex Meadows 30 Bokum Rd *TF:* 866-721-4838 ■ *Web:* www.essexmeadows.com	Essex	CT	06426	860-767-7201		672
Essex Oil Co 2174 Springfield Ave *Web:* essexoil.com	Vauxhall	NJ	07088	973-372-7700		316
Essex PB&R Corp 8007 Chivvis Dr	Saint Louis	MO	63123	314-351-6116		576
Essex Property Trust Inc 925 E Meadow Dr *NYSE: ESS* ■ *TF:* 800-690-6903 ■ *Web:* www.essexapartmenthomes.com	Palo Alto	CA	94303	650-494-3700	494-8743	655
Essex Radez LLC 440 S LaSalle St Ste 1111 *Web:* www.essexradez.com	Chicago	IL	60605	312-212-1815		194
Essex Savings Bank PO Box 950 *TF:* 877-377-3922 ■ *Web:* www.essexsavings.com	Essex	CT	06426	860-767-4414		70
Essex Shoppes & Cinema 21 Essex Way Ste 107 *Web:* www.essexoutlets.com	Essex	VT	05451	802-878-4200	879-5080	460
Essex-Middle River-White Marsh Chamber of Commerce 405 Williams Ct Ste 108 *Web:* www.chesapeakechamber.org	Middle River	MD	21220	443-317-8763	317-8772	139
Essick Air Products Inc 5800 Murray St *TF:* 800-643-8341 ■ *Web:* www.essickair.com	Little Rock	AR	72209	501-562-1094		91
Essig Research Inc 497 Cir Fwy *Web:* www.essig.com	Cincinnati	OH	45246	513-942-7100		256
Essilor of America Inc 13515 N Stemmons Fwy *TF:* 800-542-5668 ■ *Web:* www.essilorusa.com	Dallas	TX	75234	214-496-4000		542
Essis & Sons Inc 6220 Carlisle Pk *Web:* carpetmechanicsburg.com	Mechanicsburg	PA	17050	717-697-9423		290
Esskay Inc 8422 Bellona Ln Ste 200 *TF:* 800-769-7788 ■ *Web:* www.esskaymeat.com	Towson	MD	21204	410-823-2100		473
Essmueller Co 334 Ave A PO Box 1966 *TF:* 800-325-7175 ■ *Web:* www.essmueller.com	Laurel	MS	39440	601-649-2400	649-4320	207
Essner Manufacturing LP 6651 Will Rogers Blvd *Web:* www.essner.com	Fort Worth	TX	76140	817-551-5511		21
Est Group LLC 1907 Ascension Blvd Ste 100 *Web:* www.est-grp.com	Arlington	TX	76006	817-382-8000		180
Estabrook Capital Management LLC 875 Third Ave 15th Fl *Web:* www.estabrookcap.com	New York	NY	10022	212-605-5595		41
Estabrook Corp 700 W Bagley Rd *Web:* www.estabrookcorp.com	Berea	OH	44017	440-234-8566		641
Estancia Club 27998 N 99th Pl *Web:* www.estanciaclub.com	Scottsdale	AZ	85262	480-473-4400		354
Estates Pharmacy Inc 169-01 Hillside Ave	Jamaica	NY	11432	718-739-0311		237
Estech Systems Inc 3701 East Plano Pkwy *Web:* www.esi-estech.com	Plano	TX	75074	972-422-9700	422-9705	246
Estee Mold & Die Inc 1467 Stanley Ave *Web:* www.esteemold.com	Dayton	OH	45404	937-224-7853	228-0257	757
Estep-Doctor & Company PC 3737 W Bethel Ave *Web:* edcpa.com	Muncie	IN	47304	765-289-5366		2
Esterline & Sons Mfg 6508 Old Clifton Rd *Web:* esterlineandsons.com	Springfield	OH	45502	937-265-5278		757
Esterline Defense Group 85901 Ave 53 *Web:* www.armtecdefense.com	Coachella	CA	92236	760-398-0143		21
Esterline Interface Technologies 600 W Wilbur Ave *TF:* 800-444-5923 ■ *Web:* www.esterline.com	Coeur d'Alene	ID	83815	208-765-8000	292-2275	173-1
Esterline Mason 13955 Balboa Blvd **Fax:* Sales ■ *TF:* 800-232-7700 ■ *Web:* www.esterline.com	Sylmar	CA	91342	818-361-3366	365-6809*	504
Esterline Technologies Corp 500 108th Ave NE Ste 1500 *NYSE: ESL* ■ *TF:* 800-982-4372 ■ *Web:* www.esterline.com	Bellevue	WA	98004	425-453-9400	453-2916	529
Estes Design & Mfg 470 S Mitthoeffer Dr *Web:* www.estesdm.com	Indianapolis	IN	46229	317-899-2203		567
Estes Equipment Company Inc 2007 Polk St *Web:* www.estes-equipment.com	Chattanooga	TN	37407	423-756-0090		358
Estes Express Lines Inc 3901 W Broad St PO Box 25612 **Fax:* Sales ■ *TF:* 800-832-5660 ■ *Web:* www.estes-express.com	Richmond	VA	23230	804-353-1900	353-8001*	780
Estes Mcclure & Assoc Inc 3608 Wway St *Web:* estesmcclure.com	Tyler	TX	75703	903-581-2677		261
Estes Ron (Rep R - KS) 2452 Rayburn HOB *Web:* estes.house.gov	Washington	DC	20515	202-225-6216		342-2
Estes-Cox Corp 1295 H St *TF:* 800-525-7561 ■ *Web:* www.estesrockets.com	Penrose	CO	81240	719-372-6565		762
Estes-Winn Memorial Automobile Museum 111 Grovewood Rd *TF:* 877-622-7238 ■ *Web:* www.grovewood.com	Asheville	NC	28804	828-253-7651		520
Estex Mfg Co Inc 402 E Broad St PO Box 368 **Fax Area Code:* 770 ■ *TF:* 800-749-1224 ■ *Web:* www.estexmfg.com	Fairburn	GA	30213	800-749-1224	964-7534*	733
Esther Pharmacy Inc 71 S Broadway *TF:* 800-666-7667 ■ *Web:* estherpharmacy.com	Yonkers	NY	10701	914-965-2661		237
Esther Price Candies Inc 1709 Wayne Ave *TF:* 800-782-0326 ■ *Web:* www.estherprice.com	Dayton	OH	45410	937-253-2121		296-8
Esti Consulting Services 812 Spadina Cres E *Web:* www.esti.ca	Saskatoon	SK	S7K3H4	306-242-2436		180
Estiatorio Milos 125 W 55th St *Web:* www.milos.ca	New York	NY	10019	212-245-7400		671
Estill County 130 Main St *Web:* www.estillky.com	Irvine	KY	40336	606-723-5156	723-5108	338

Company	City	State	ZIP	Phone	Fax	Class
Estimating Edge, The 1301 N Congress Ave Ste 400 *Web:* www.edgeestimating.com	Boynton Beach	FL	33426-3363	561-276-9100		809
Estis Compression LLC 545 Huey Lenard Loop *Web:* www.estiscompression.com	West Monroe	LA	71292	318-397-5557		172
Estonia 305 E 47th St 6th Fl **Fax Area Code:* 646 ■ *Web:* www.un.estemb.org	New York	NY	10017	212-883-0640	514-0099*	784
Consulate General 305 E 47th St 3 Dag Hammarskjold Plz Ste 6B *Web:* www.nyc.estemb.org	New York	NY	10017	212-883-0636	883-0648	257
Embassy 2131 Massachusetts Ave NW *Web:* www.estemb.org	Washington	DC	20008	202-588-0101	588-0108	257
Estrada Hinojosa & Company Inc 1717 Main St LB47 *TF:* 800-676-5352 ■ *Web:* www.estradahinojosa.com	Dallas	TX	75201	214-658-1670	658-1671	401
Estrada Strategies Franchise Inc 3400 Inland Empire Blvd Ste 101	Ontario	CA	91764	909-917-1771		193
eStrategy Solutions Inc 6601 Vaught Ranch Rd Ste 100 *Web:* www.esslearning.com	Austin	TX	78730	512-451-0100		194
Estrella Mountain Community College 3000 N Dysart Rd *Web:* www.estrellamountain.edu	Avondale	AZ	85392	623-935-8000		162
Estwing Manufacturing Co 2647 Eigth St *TF:* 800-331-4495 ■ *Web:* www.estwing.com	Rockford	IL	61109	815-397-9558	397-8665	758
Esty Elizabeth (Rep D - CT) 221 Cannon HOB **Fax Area Code:* 860 ■ *Web:* esty.house.gov	Washington	DC	20515	202-225-4476	225-7289*	342-2
eSupply Systems LLC 7800 W IH-10 Ste 130 *Web:* www.esupplysystems.com	San Antonio	TX	78230	210-979-6670		393
Esys Corp 1670 N Opdyke Rd *Web:* esysautomation.com	Auburn Hills	MI	48326	248-754-1900		256
ET Horn Co 16050 Canary Ave *TF:* 800-442-4676 ■ *Web:* www.ethorn.com	La Mirada	CA	90638	714-523-8050	670-6851	146
Et International 100 White Clay Ctr Ste 103	Newark	DE	19711	302-738-1438		177
ET Lowe Publishing Co 220 Great Circle Rd Ste 122 *Web:* www.etlowe.com	Nashville	TN	37228	615-254-8866	254-8867	781
Et Search Inc 1712 Valdes Dr	La Jolla	CA	92037	858-459-3443		193
ET Water Systems LLC 384 Bel Marin Keys Blvd Ste 145 *Web:* www.etwater.com	Novato	CA	94949	415-945-9383		407
ET Wright & Company Inc 1251 First Ave	Chippewa Falls	WI	54729	715-720-4288		459
ETA (Evangelical Training Assn) PO Box 327 *TF General:* 800-369-8291 ■ *Web:* www.etaworld.org	Wheaton	IL	60187	800-369-8291		48-20
ETA (Electronics Technicians Assn International) 5 Depot St *TF:* 800-288-3824 ■ *Web:* www.eta-i.org	Greencastle	IN	46135	765-653-8262	653-4287	49-19
Eta Sigma Gamma 2000 University Ave *TF:* 800-715-2559 ■ *Web:* www.etasigmagamma.org	Muncie	IN	47306	765-285-2258	285-3210	48-16
ETABS (East Texas Arboretum) 1601 Patterson Rd *Web:* www.easttexasarboretum.org	Athens	TX	75751	903-675-5630		97
Etalex Inc 8501 Jarry St E *Web:* www.etalex.ca	Montreal	QC	H1J1H7	514-351-2000		261
ETC (Environmental Technology Council) 1112 16th St Ste 420 *Web:* www.etc.org	Washington	DC	20036	202-783-0870		40-12
ETC (Educational Travel Consultants) PO Box 1580 *TF:* 800-247-7969 ■ *Web:* www.educationaltravelconsultants.com	Hendersonville	NC	28793	828-693-0412	692-1591	760
ETC (Environmental Traveling Companions) 2 Marina Blvd Bldg C *Web:* www.etctrips.org	San Francisco	CA	94123	415-474-7662	474-3919	48-23
ETC ComputerLand 3206 Kochs Ln *Web:* www.etccomputerland.com	Quincy	IL	62305	217-228-6180		177
Etc Group Inc 1997 South 1100 East *Web:* www.etcgrp.com	Salt Lake City	UT	84106	801-278-1927		261
ETCO (Engman-Taylor Company Inc) W142 N9351 Fountain Blvd *TF:* 800-236-1975 ■ *Web:* www.engman-taylor.com	Menomonee Falls	WI	53051	262-255-9300	255-6512	385
ETCO Inc 25 Bellows St *TF:* 800-689-3826 ■ *Web:* www.etco.com	Warwick	RI	02888	401-467-2400	467-9230	815
ETCO Inc Automotive Products Div 3004 62nd Ave E *TF:* 800-689-3826 ■ *Web:* www.etco.com	Bradenton	FL	34203	941-756-8426	758-7195	247
e-TechServices.com Inc 5220 SW 91st Terr *Web:* www.e-techservices.com	Gainesville	FL	32608	352-332-3200		174
Etegent Technologies Ltd 1775 Mentor Ave *TF:* 800-860-4867 ■ *Web:* www.sdltd.com	Cincinnati	OH	45212	513-631-0579		261
Etek It Services Inc 830 E Higgins Rd Ste 102 *Web:* etekit.com	Schaumburg	IL	60173	847-969-0200		196
Etelint Consulting Inc 1683 Moongate Cres *Web:* www.etelintconsulting.com	Mississauga	ON	L5M4T2	905-826-3977	826-2934	196
Etera Consulting 1100 17th St NW Ste 605 *TF:* 800-674-3141 ■ *Web:* www.eteraconsulting.com	Washington	DC	20036	202-349-0177		196
Etera Solutions Llc 354 TurnPk St Ste 203 *TF:* 888-536-6515 ■ *Web:* eterasolutions.com	Canton	MA	02021	888-536-6515		396
Eternabond 75 E Div St *TF:* 888-336-2663 ■ *Web:* www.eternabond.com	Mundelein	IL	60060	847-837-9400	837-9449	732
Eternal Word Television Network (EWTN) 5817 Old Leeds Rd *Web:* www.ewtn.com	Irondale	AL	35210	205-271-2900		740

Entry	City	State	ZIP	Phone	Fax	Class
Eternity Healthcare Inc Ste 1 8755 Ash St TF: 855-324-1110 ■ Web: eternityhealthcare.com	Vancouver	BC	V6P6T3	855-324-1110		476
Etex Telephone Co-op Inc 1013 Hwy 155 N Web: www.etex.net	Gilmer	TX	75644	903-797-4357		736
Ethan Allen Homestead 1 Ethan Allen Homestead TF: 800-427-1396 ■ Web: www.ethanallenhomestead.org	Burlington	VT	05408	802-865-4556		50-3
Ethan Allen Hotel 21 Lake Ave Ext TF: 800-742-1776 ■ Web: www.ethanallenhotel.com	Danbury	CT	06811	203-744-1776		379
Ethan Allen Interiors Inc Ethan Allen Dr NYSE: ETH ■ TF: 888-324-3571 ■ Web: www.ethanallen.com	Danbury	CT	06811	888-324-3571		321
Ethan Allen Personnel Group Inc 59 Academy St TF: 800-420-4707 ■ Web: www.eaworkforce.com	Poughkeepsie	NY	12601	845-471-9700		260
Ethan Ellenberg Literary Agency 548 Broadway Web: ethanellenberg.com	New York	NY	10012	212-431-4554		637-2
Ethel Walker School 230 Bushy Hill Rd Web: www.ethelwalker.org	Simsbury	CT	06070	860-408-4200		622
EtherCom Corp 1409 Fulton Pl Web: www.ethercom.com	Fremont	CA	94539	510-440-0242		174
Etheridge Printing Co 4434 Mcewen Rd	Dallas	TX	75244	214-827-8151		393
Ethex Corp 1 Corporate Woods Dr	Bridgeton	MO	63044	314-646-3750		583
Ethical Markets Media LLC 10 Carrera St Web: www.ethicalmarkets.com	St. Augustine	FL	32084	904-829-3140		463
Ethicon Endo-Surgery Inc 4545 Creek Rd Web: www.ethicon.com	Cincinnati	OH	45242	513-337-7000		476
Ethics & Public Policy Ctr 1730 M St NW TF: 800-935-0699 ■ Web: www.eppc.org	Washington	DC	20036	202-682-1200	408-0632	634
Ethics Resource Ctr 2345 Crystal Dr Ste 201 Web: www.ethics.org	Arlington	VA	22202	703-647-2185	647-2180	48-8
Ethier Associates 736 6 Ave SW Web: www.ethier.ca	Calgary	AB	T2P3T7	403-234-8960		449
Ethiopia 866 Second Ave Ste 3 Web: ethiopianembassy.org	New York	NY	10017	212-421-1830		784
Ethiopia Embassy 3506 International Dr NW TF: 800-624-0686 ■ Web: www.ethiopianembassy.org	Washington	DC	20008	202-364-1200	587-0195	257
Ethiopian Community Development Council Inc (ECDC) 901 S Highland St Web: www.ecdcus.org	Arlington	VA	22204	703-685-0510	685-0529	48-5
Ethis Communications Inc 44 Church St Ste 200 Web: www.ethiscommunications.com	White Plains	NY	10601	212-791-1440		194
Ethnic Dance Theatre 3507 Clinton Ave S TF: 800-892-0022 ■ Web: www.ethnicdancetheatre.com	Minneapolis	MN	55408	763-545-1333		573-1
Ethnic Heritage Ctr 270 Fitch St Southern Connecticut State University Web: www.southernct.edu	New Haven	CT	06515	203-392-6126	392-5140	520
Ethnic Heritage Museum 1129 S Main St Web: ethnicheritagemuseum.org	Rockford	IL	61101	815-962-7402		520
Ethos 17 Ash St Web: ethos-marketing.com	Westbrook	ME	04092	207-856-2610		195
Ethos Risk Services Inc 300 First Ave S Ste 402 Web: ethosrisk.com	St. Petersburg	FL	33701	727-822-9800		463
ethosIQ LLC 17121 W Rd 201 Web: www.ethosiq.com	Houston	TX	77095	281-616-5711		177
EthoStream LLC 10200 Innovation Dr Ste 300 Web: www.ethostream.com	Milwaukee	WI	53226	414-223-0473		387
Ethyl Corp 1000 N South St Web: www.ethyl.com	Pasadena	TX	77503	713-740-8300		580
ETI (Equipment & Tool Institute) 134 W University Dr Ste 205 *Fax Area Code: 603 ■ Web: etools.org	Rochester	MI	48307	248-656-5080	971-2375*	49-13
ETI Converting 1490-H Nobel St Web: www.eticonverting.com	Boucherville	QC	J4B5H3	450-641-7900		628
ETI Technical College of Niles 2076 Youngstown-Warren Rd Web: www.eticollege.edu	Niles	OH	44446	330-652-9919	652-4399	800
Etic Engineering 2285 Morello Ave Web: www.eticeng.com	Pleasant Hill	CA	94523	925-602-4710		256
Eti-Net 505 Maisonneuve W Ste 400 Web: www.etinet.com	Montreal	QC	H3A3C2	514-395-1200		177
Etiwanda School District (ESD) 6061 E Ave TF: 800-300-1506 ■ Web: www.etiwanda.k12.ca.us	Etiwanda	CA	91739	909-899-2451	899-1235	685
Etkin Equities LLC 200 Franklin Ctr 29100 NW Hwy Web: etkinllc.com	Southfield	MI	48034	248-358-0800		652
Etm Electromatic Inc 35451 Dumbarton Ct Web: www.etm-inc.com	Newark	CA	94560	510-797-1100	797-4358	647
ETNA Supply Company Inc 529 32nd St Web: www.etnasupply.com	Grand Rapids	MI	49548	616-241-5414		612
Etobicoke Ironworks Ltd 141 Rivalda Rd TF: 866-274-6971 ■ Web: www.eiw.ca	Weston	ON	M9M2M6	416-742-7111		480
Etonien LLC 222 N Sepulveda Blvd Ste 1507 Web: www.etonien.com	El Segundo	CA	90245	310-321-5800		734
Etopolos Design PO Box 751603 Web: www.etopolos.com	Petaluma	CA	94975-1603	415-845-8897		393

Entry	City	State	ZIP	Phone	Fax	Class
Etouch Federal Systems Llc 6167 Jarvis Ave Ste 281 Web: etouchfederal.com	Newark	CA	94560	510-764-2303		809
Etowah County 800 Forrest Ave Web: www.etowahcounty.org	Gadsden	AL	35901	256-549-5300	549-5400	338
Etowah Indian Mounds State Historic Site 813 Indian Mounds Rd SW Web: www.gastateparks.org	Cartersville	GA	30120	770-387-3747		565
EtQ Management Consultants Inc 399 Conklin St Ste 208 TF: 800-354-4476 ■ Web: www.etq.com	Farmingdale	NY	11735	516-293-0949		195
Etrafficers 881 S Orem Blvd Ste 1 Web: www.etrafficers.com	Orem	UT	84058	801-221-9400		180
ETS (Praxis Series Online Educational Testing Service Teaching & Learning Div) PO Box 6051 TF: 800-772-9476 ■ Web: www.ets.org	Princeton	NJ	08541	609-771-7395	530-0581	244
ETS (Ecumenical Theological Seminary) 2930 Woodward Ave Web: www.etseminary.org	Detroit	MI	48201	313-831-5200		167-3
ETS-Lindgren LP 1301 Arrow Pt Dr Web: www.ets-lindgren.com	Cedar Park	TX	78613	512-531-6400	531-6500	420
Etta's Seafood 2020 Western Ave Web: www.tomdouglas.com	Seattle	WA	98121	206-443-6000		671
ettain group Inc 127 W Worthington Ave Ste 100 Web: www.ettaingroup.com	Charlotte	NC	28203	704-525-5499		260
Ettika LLC 714 S Hill St Ste 405 Web: ettika.com	Los Angeles	CA	90014	213-817-5510		411
Ettl Engineers & Consultants Inc 1717 E Erwin St TF: 800-767-5950 ■ Web: www.ettlinc.com	Tyler	TX	75702	903-595-4421		743
Ettline Foods Corp 525 N State St Web: www.ettline.com	York	PA	17403	717-848-1564		297-8
Ettore Products Co 2100 N Loop Rd TF: 800-438-8673 ■ Web: www.ettore.com	Alameda	CA	94502	510-748-4130	748-4146	508
ETV (South Carolina Educational Television Commission) 1101 George Rogers Blvd TF: 800-922-5437 ■ Web: www.scetv.org	Columbia	SC	29201	803-737-3200		632
EU Services 649 N Horners Ln TF: 800-241-1605 ■ Web: www.euservices.com	Rockville	MD	20850	301-424-3300	424-3696	627
EUB (Edinboro University of Pennsylvania Baron-Forness Library) 200 Tartan Rd TF: 888-845-2890 ■ Web: edinboro.edu/home/page_not_found.dot	Edinboro	PA	16444	814-732-2273	732-2883	434-6
Eubanks Engineering Co 3022 Inland Empire Blvd TF: 800-729-4208 ■ Web: www.eubanks.com	Ontario	CA	91764	909-483-2456	483-2498	813
Eubel Brady & Suttman Asset Management Inc 10100 Innovation Dr Ste 410 TF: 800-391-1223 ■ Web: www.ebs-asset.com	Dayton	OH	45342	937-291-1223		194
Euclid Chamber of Commerce 22639 Euclid Ave PO Box 32611 Web: www.euclidchamber.com	Euclid	OH	44117	216-731-9322		139
Euclid Chemical Co 19218 Redwood Rd TF: 800-321-7628 ■ Web: www.euclidchemical.com	Cleveland	OH	44110	216-531-9222	531-9596	3
Euclid Heat Treating Co 1340 E 222nd St TF: 800-962-2909 ■ Web: www.euclidheattreating.com	Euclid	OH	44117	216-481-8444		484
Euclid Hospital 18901 Lake Shore Blvd Web: my.clevelandclinic.org	Euclid	OH	44119	216-531-9000		374-3
Euclid Industries Inc 1655 Tech Dr TF: 800-780-4707 ■ Web: www.euclidindustries.com	Bay City	MI	48706	989-686-8920		757
Euclid Public Library 631 E 222nd St Web: www.euclidlibrary.org	Euclid	OH	44123	216-261-5300		434-3
Euclid Spiral Paper Tube Corp 339 Mill St	Apple Creek	OH	44606	330-698-4711	698-1254	124
Euclid SR Partners 45 Rockefeller Plaza Ste 1910	New York	NY	10111	212-218-6880		792
Eudora Welty Library, The 300 N State St Web: jhlibrary.org	Jackson	MS	39201	601-968-5811		434-3
Eudy's Cabinet Shop Inc 12303 Renee Ford Rd Web: www.eudyscabinets.com	Stanfield	NC	28163	704-888-4454		321
EUE/Screen Gems Studios 603 Greenwich St Web: euescreengems.com	New York	NY	10014	212-450-1600		514
Eufaula/Barbour County Chamber of Commerce 333 E Broad St TF: 800-524-7529 ■ Web: eufaulachamber.com	Eufaula	AL	36027	334-687-6664		139
Eufloria Flowers 885 Mesa Rd Web: www.eufloriaflowers.com	Nipomo	CA	93444	805-929-4683		292
Eugene Airport 28801 Douglas Dr TF: 800-741-5097 ■ Web: www.eugene-or.gov	Eugene	OR	97402	541-682-5430	682-6838	27
Eugene Burger Management Corp 6600 Hunter Dr TF: 800-788-0233 ■ Web: www.ebmc.com	Rohnert Park	CA	94928	707-584-5123	584-5124	655
Eugene Cascades Coast 754 Olive St TF: 800-547-5445 ■ Web: www.eugenecascadescoast.org	Eugene	OR	97440	541-484-5307	343-6335	206
Eugene Chamber of Commerce 1401 Willamette St Web: www.eugenechamber.com	Eugene	OR	97401	541-484-1314	484-4942	139
Eugene City Hall 125 E Eighth Ave 2nd Fl Web: www.eugene-or.gov	Eugene	OR	97401	541-682-5010	682-5414	337
Eugene Lang College 65 W 11th St *Fax: Admissions ■ Web: www.newschool.edu/lang	New York	NY	10011	212-229-5600	229-5355*	166
Eugene O'Neill National Historic Site 1000 Kuss Rd *Fax Area Code: 410 ■ TF: 866-945-7920 ■ Web: www.nps.gov	Danville	CA	94526	925-838-0249	396-3393*	564
Eugene Public Library 100 W Tenth Ave TF: 800-896-0410 ■ Web: www.eugene-or.gov	Eugene	OR	97401	541-682-5450	682-5898	434-3
Eugene Sand & Gravel Inc 3000 Delta Hwy N Web: www.eugenesand.com	Eugene	OR	97408	541-683-6400		182
Eugene School District 4J 200 N Monroe St Web: www.4j.lane.edu	Eugene	OR	97402	541-687-3123	687-3691	685
Eugene Symphony 115 W Eigth Ave Ste 115 Web: www.eugenesymphony.org	Eugene	OR	97401	541-687-9487	687-0527	573-3

Phone | Fax | Class

Eugene T Mahoney State Park
28500 W Pk Hwy .... Ashland NE 68003 402-944-2523 565
Web: nebraskastateparks.reserveamerica.com

Eugene Weekly 1251 Lincoln St .... Eugene OR 97401 541-484-0519 484-4044 532-5
Web: www.eugeneweekly.com

Euler Hermes ACI
800 Red Brook Blvd 4th Fl .... Owings Mills MD 21117 410-753-0753 391-5
TF: 877-883-3224 ■ *Web:* eulerhermes.us

Euless Public Library 201 N Ector Dr .... Euless TX 76039 817-685-1480 434-3
Web: eulesstx.gov

Eunice Kennedy Shriver Ctr
200 Trapelo Rd .... Waltham MA 02452 774-455-6562 668
Web: www.umassmed.edu/shriver

Euphemia Haye
5540 Gulf of Mexico Dr .... Longboat Key FL 34228 941-383-3633 671
Web: www.euphemiahaye.com

Euphrat Museum of Art
21250 Stevens Creek Blvd .... Cupertino CA 95014 408-864-5464 520
Web: www.deanza.edu

Eureka Casino Hotel 275 Mesa Blvd .... Mesquite NV 89027 702-346-4600 443
Web: www.eurekamesquite.com

Eureka College 300 E College Ave .... Eureka IL 61530 309-467-6350 467-6576* 166
**Fax:* Admissions ■ *TF Admissions:* 888-438-7352 ■ *Web:* www.eureka.edu

Eureka County 10 S Main St .... Eureka NV 89316 775-237-5262 237-6015 338
TF: 800-824-2218 ■ *Web:* www.co.eureka.nv.us

Eureka Electrical Products Inc
79 Clay St .... North East PA 16428 814-725-9638 815

Eureka Foundry Co
1601 Reggie White Blvd .... Chattanooga TN 37402 423-267-3328 756-2607 307
TF: 800-922-7220 ■ *Web:* www.eurekafoundryco.com

Eureka Growth Capital
1717 Arch St 3420 Bell Atlantic Twr .... Philadelphia PA 19103 267-238-4200 238-4201 405
Web: www.eurekagrowth.com

Eureka Homestead
1922 Veterans Memorial Blvd .... Metairie LA 70005 504-834-0242 69
TF: 855-858-5179 ■ *Web:* www.eurekahomestead.com

Eureka Lighting
225 De Li ge ouest Ste 200 .... Montreal QC H2P1H4 514-385-3515 393
TF: 800-383-7323 ■ *Web:* www.eurekalighting.com

Eureka Resources LLC
419 Second St .... Williamsport PA 17701 570-323-2535 192
Web: www.eureka-resources.com

Eureka Software Solutions Inc
3305 Northland Dr Ste 305 .... Austin TX 78731 512-459-9292 177
Web: www.eurekasoft.com

Eureka Technocrats Inc
1985 W Big Beaver Rd .... Troy MI 48084 248-816-1617 177
TF: 800-824-2962 ■ *Web:* www.eurekatek.com

Eureka Union School District
5455 Eureka Rd .... Granite Bay CA 95746 916-791-4939 791-5527 685
Web: www.eurekausd.org

Eureka Water Co 729 SW Third St .... Oklahoma City OK 73109 405-235-8474 366
Web: ozarkah2o.com

Eureka Welding Alloys Inc
2000 E Avis Dr .... Madison Heights MI 48071 248-588-0001 585-7711 811
TF: 800-962-8560 ■ *Web:* www.eurekaweldingalloys.com

Euro Lloyd Travel Inc
1640 Hempstead Tpke .... East Meadow NY 11554 516-228-4904 228-8258 771
Web: www.lcc-eurolloyd.com

Euro Pacific Capital Inc
88 Post Rd W 2nd Fl .... Westport CT 06880 203-662-9700 70
TF: 800-727-7922 ■ *Web:* www.europac.com

Euro-American Finance Network Inc
1212 S Main St Ste B .... Wildwood FL 34785 352-504-1641 379
Web: www.eafninc.com

Eurofase Inc
33 W Beaver Creek Rd .... Richmond Hill ON L4B1L8 905-695-2055 41
TF: 800-660-5391 ■ *Web:* www.eurofase.com

Eurofins Frontier Global Sciences
11720 N Creek Pkwy Ste 400 .... Bothell WA 98011 425-686-1996 743
Web: www.frontiergs.com

Eurofins Lancaster Laboratories Environmental LLC
2425 New Holland Pk PO Box 12425 .... Lancaster PA 17601 717-656-2300 656-2681 743

Eurofins Product Safety Labs Inc
2394 Hwy 130 Ste E .... Dayton NJ 08810 732-438-5100 743
Web: www.productsafetylabs.com

Eurofins Scientific Inc
2200 Rittenhouse St Ste 150 .... Des Moines IA 50321 515-265-1461 266-5453 417
Web: www.eurofinsus.com

Eurofins Spectrum Analytical Inc
830 Silver St .... Agawam MA 01001 413-789-9018 789-4076 743
TF: 800-789-9115 ■ *Web:* www.spectrum-analytical.com

Eurogentec North America
3347 Industrial Ct Ste A .... San Diego CA 92121 858-793-2661 196
Web: www.eurogentec.com

Eurokera North America Inc
140 Southchase Blvd .... Fountain Inn SC 29644 864-963-8082 362
Web: www.eurokera.com

Euromarket Designs Inc
1250 Techny Rd .... Northbrook IL 60062 847-272-2888 527-1448* 362
**Fax Area Code:* 630 ■ *Web:* www.crateandbarrel.com

Euromoney Institutional Investor PLC
225 Pk Ave S .... New York NY 10003 212-224-3300 637-9
TF: 800-715-9197 ■ *Web:* www.institutionalinvestor.com

Euronet Worldwide Inc
3500 College Blvd .... Leawood KS 66211 913-327-4200 327-1921 255
NASDAQ: EEFT ■ *Web:* www.euronetworldwide.com

Europ Assistance USA Services Inc
4330 East-West Hwy Ste 1000 .... Bethesda MD 20814 240-330-1000 775
Web: www.europassistance-usa.com

Europa Bistro 2515 N Proctor St .... Tacoma WA 98406 253-761-5660 671
Web: www.europabistro.net

Europa Market Company Inc, The
8100 Water St .... Saint Louis MO 63111 314-631-7288 297-8
Web: www.europa-market.com

Europa Restaurant
1620 S Indian Trl .... Palm Springs CA 92264 760-327-2314 671
TF: 800-245-2314 ■ *Web:* www.villaroyale.com

Europa! 323 E 55th St .... Kansas City MO 64113 816-523-1212 671
Web: cafeeuropakc.com

Europe by Car 40 Exchange Pl Ste 1720 .... New York NY 10005 212-581-3040 246-1458 126
TF: 800-223-1516 ■ *Web:* www.europebycarblog.com

Europea 1227 de la Montagne .... Montreal QC H3G1Z2 514-397-9161 398-9718 671
Web: www.europea.ca

European Touch Ltd II
8301 W Parkland Ct .... Milwaukee WI 53223 414-357-7016 76

European-American Business Council
919 18th St NW Ste 220 .... Washington DC 20006 202-828-9104 828-9106 138
Web: transatlanticbusiness.org

Euro-Pharm International Canada Inc
9400 Boul Langelier .... Montreal QC H1P3H8 514-323-8757 323-6325 231
TF: 888-929-0835 ■ *Web:* www.euro-pharm.com

EuroPharma Inc 955 Challenger Dr .... Green Bay WI 54311 920-406-6500 345
TF: 866-598-5487 ■ *Web:* www.europharmausa.com

Europlast Ltd 100 Industrial Ln .... Endeavor WI 53930 608-587-2335 596
Web: www.europlastltdusa.com

Europlay Capital Advisors LLC
15260 Ventura Blvd 20th Fl .... Sherman Oaks CA 91403 818-444-4400 401
Web: www.europlaycapital.com

Euro-Suites Hotel
University Centre 501 Chestnut Ridge Rd .... Morgantown WV 26505 800-678-4837 379
TF: 800-678-4837 ■ *Web:* www.euro-suites.com

Eurotainer Inc 5810 Wilson Rd Ste 200 .... Humble TX 77396 832-300-5001 300-5050 264-5
Web: www.eurotainer.com

Eurotherm USA
44621 Guilford Dr Ste 100 .... Ashburn VA 20147 703-724-7300 724-7301 202
Web: www.eurotherm.com

Eurotire Inc 200 S Biscayne Blvd 55th Fl .... Miami FL 33131 305-900-2850 755
Web: www.eurotire.net

Eutaw Construction Company Inc
109 1/2 W Commerce St PO Box 36 .... Aberdeen MS 39730 662-369-8868 186
Web: www.eutawconstruction.com

Eutectic Corp
N 94 W 14355 Garwin Mace Dr .... Menomonee Falls WI 53051 262-532-4677 255-5542 811
TF: 800-558-8524 ■ *Web:* www.eutectic-na.com

Euthanasia Research & Guidance Organization (ERGO)
24829 Norris Ln .... Junction City OR 97448 541-998-1873 48-17
Web: www.finalexit.org

Euthymics Bioscience
43 Thorndike St .... Cambridge MA 02141 617-758-0300 231
Web: www.euthymics.com

EV Connect Inc
714 W Olympic Blvd Ste 939 .... Los Angeles CA 90015 310-751-7997 393
Web: www.evconnect.com

ev3 Inc 3033 Campus Dr .... Plymouth MN 55441 763-398-7000 398-7200 476
TF: 800-716-6700 ■ *Web:* www.ev3.net

EVA Airways
200 N Sepulveda Blvd Ste 1600 .... El Segundo CA 90245 310-362-6600 362-6660 25
TF: 800-695-1188 ■ *Web:* www.evaair.com

Eva Restaurant 2227 N 56th St .... Seattle WA 98103 206-633-3538 671
Web: evarestaurant.com

Evaheart Inc 6655 Travis ST Ste 590 .... Houston TX 77030 713-520-7979 475
Web: www.evaheart-usa.com

Evan B Donaldson Adoption Institute
120 E 38th St .... New York NY 10016 212-925-4089 796-6592* 48-6
**Fax Area Code:* 775 ■ *Web:* www.adoptioninstitute.org

Evan K Thalenberg Law Offices
216 E Lexington St .... Baltimore MD 21202 410-625-9100 428
TF: 800-778-1181 ■ *Web:* ektlaw.com

Evana Automation
5825 Old Boonville Hwy .... Evansville IN 47715 812-479-8246 207
TF: 800-468-6774 ■ *Web:* www.evanaautomation.com

Evangel Cathedral
13901 Central Ave .... Upper Marlboro MD 20774 301-249-9400 95
Web: www.evangelcathedral.net

Evangel University
1111 N Glenstone Ave .... Springfield MO 65802 417-865-2815 865-9599 166
TF: 800-382-6435 ■ *Web:* evangel.edu

Evangelical Christian Publishers Assn (ECPA)
9633 S 48th St Ste 140 .... Phoenix AZ 85044 480-966-3998 966-1944 49-16
Web: www.ecpa.org

Evangelical Church Alliance (ECA)
205 W Broadway St PO Box 9 .... Bradley IL 60915 815-937-0720 937-0720 48-20
TF: 888-855-6060 ■ *Web:* www.ecainternational.org

Evangelical Community Hospital
1 Hospital Dr .... Lewisburg PA 17837 570-522-2000 374-3
Web: www.evanhospital.com

Evangelical Council for Financial Accountability (ECFA)
440 W Jubal Early Dr Ste 130 .... Winchester VA 22601 540-535-0103 535-0533 48-5
TF: 800-323-9473 ■ *Web:* www.ecfa.org

Evangelical Fellowship of Canada (EFC)
600 Alden Rd Markham Industrial Pk Ste 300 .... Markham ON L3R0E7 905-479-5885 479-4742 48-20
TF: 866-302-3362 ■ *Web:* www.evangelicalfellowship.ca

Evangelical Free Church of America, The
901 E 78th St .... Minneapolis MN 55420 952-854-1300 48-20
TF: 800-745-2202 ■ *Web:* www.efca.org

Evangelical Lutheran Church in America (ELCA)
8765 W Higgins Rd .... Chicago IL 60631 773-380-2700 380-1465 48-20
TF: 800-638-3522 ■ *Web:* www.elca.org

Evangelical Lutheran Good Samaritan Foundation, The
4800 W 57th St .... Sioux Falls SD 57108 605-362-3100 305
Web: www.good-sam.com

Evangelical Presbyterian Church of Plant City
1107 Charlie Griffin Rd .... Plant City FL 33566 813-759-9383 48-20
Web: www.gracepointpc.org

Evangelical School of Theology
121 S College St .... Myerstown PA 17067 717-866-5775 866-4667 167-3
TF: 800-532-5775 ■ *Web:* www.evangelical.edu

Evangelical Training Assn (ETA)
PO Box 327 .... Wheaton IL 60187 800-369-8291 48-20
TF General: 800-369-8291 ■ *Web:* www.etaworld.org

Evangelicals for Social Action (ESA)
PO Box 367 .... Wayne PA 19087 484-384-2988 48-7
TF: 800-650-6600 ■ *Web:* www.evangelicalsforsocialaction.org

Evangeline Bank & Trust Co, The
497 W Main St .... Ville Platte LA 70586 337-363-5541 363-0678 70
Web: www.therealbank.com

Phone | Fax | Class

Evangeline Parish
200 Ct St Ste 104 .... Ville Platte LA 70586 337-363-5671 363-5780 338
Web: evangelineparishclerkofcourt.com/contact.aspx

Evangeline Parish Library
242 W Main St .... Ville Platte LA 70586 337-363-1369 363-2353 434-3
Web: evangelinelibrary.org

Evangeline's 1653 McFarland Blvd .... Tuscaloosa AL 35406 205-752-0830 671
Web: www.evangelinesrestaurant.com

Evangola State Park
10191 Old Lake Shore Rd .... Irving NY 14081 716-549-1802 565
Web: parks.ny.gov/parks/91/maps.aspx

Evan-Moor Educational Publishers Inc
18 Lower Ragsdale Dr .... Monterey CA 93940 831-649-5901 649-6256 243
TF: 800-777-4362 ■ *Web:* www.evan-moor.com

Evanov Communications Inc
5312 Dundas St W .... Toronto ON M9B1B3 416-213-1035 360-2
Web: www.evanovradio.com

Evans & Assoc Construction Company Inc
3320 N 14th St .... Ponca City OK 74601 580-765-6693 188-4
TF: 800-324-6693 ■ *Web:* evans-assoc.com

Evans & Sutherland Computer Corp
770 Komas Dr .... Salt Lake City UT 84108 801-588-1000 703
OTC: ESCC ■ *TF Sales:* 800-327-5707 ■ *Web:* www.es.com

Evans Analytical Group 810 Kifer Rd .... Sunnyvale CA 94086 408-530-3500 530-3501 743
TF: 800-632-4357 ■ *Web:* www.eag.com

Evans Army Community Hospital
1650 Cochran Cir .... Fort Carson CO 80913 719-526-7000 374-4
Web: www.evans.amedd.army.mil

Evans Bancorp Inc 1 Grimsby Dr .... Hamburg NY 14075 716-926-2000 926-2005* 360-2
NYSE: EVBN ■ **Fax:* Hum Res ■ *TF:* 866-310-0763 ■ *Web:* www.evansbank.com

Evans Cabinet Corp 1321 N Franklin St .... Dublin GA 31021 478-272-2530 115
TF: 800-472-5889 ■ *Web:* www.evanscabinet.com

Evans Caseload Inc 1915 Danforth Ave .... Toronto ON M4C1J5 416-762-0236 177
TF: 800-461-4131 ■ *Web:* caseload.com

Evans Concrete LLC 518 E Smith St .... Claxton GA 30417 912-739-3733 183

Evans Correctional Institution
610 Hwy 9 W .... Bennettsville SC 29512 843-479-4181 213
Web: doc.sc.gov

Evans County 3 Freeman St .... Claxton GA 30417 912-739-1141 338
Web: www.claxtonevanschamber.com

Evans Data Corp 340 Soquel Ave .... Santa Cruz CA 95062 831-425-8451 668
TF: 800-831-3080 ■ *Web:* www.evansdata.com

Evans Dedicated Systems Inc PO Box 9 .... Maywood CA 90270 323-725-2928 726-0796 780
TF: 800-427-6387 ■ *Web:* www.evansdedicated.com

Evans Delivery Company Inc
PO Box 268 .... Pottsville PA 17901 570-385-9048 311
TF: 800-666-7885 ■ *Web:* www.evansdelivery.com

Evans Distribution Systems
18765 Seaway Dr .... Melvindale MI 48122 313-388-3200 388-0136 803-1
TF: 800-653-8267 ■ *Web:* www.evansdist.com

Evans Dwight (Rep D - PA)
1105 Longworth HOB .... Washington DC 20515 202-225-4001 225-5392 342-2
Web: evans.house.gov

Evans Enterprises Inc
1536 S Western Ave .... Oklahoma City OK 73109 405-631-1344 246
TF: 800-423-8267 ■ *Web:* www.goevans.com

Evans Ewan & Brady Insurance Agency Inc
2404 Williams Dr .... Georgetown TX 78628 512-869-1511 390
Web: eebins.com

Evans Food Group Ltd
4118 S Halsted St .... Chicago IL 60609 773-254-7400 254-7791 296-35
TF: 888-643-8267 ■ *Web:* www.evansfood.com

Evans Fruit Farm
200 Cowiche City Rd PO Box 70 .... Cowiche WA 98923 509-678-4127 678-5450 315-3
TF: 800-495-7222 ■ *Web:* www.evansfruitco.com

Evans Hardy & Young Inc
829 De La Vina St .... Santa Barbara CA 93101 805-963-5841 4
Web: www.ehy.com

Evans Investment Advisors LLC
6713 Perkins Rd .... Baton Rouge LA 70808 225-761-7870 690

Evans Latham & Campisi
1 Post St Ste 600 .... San Francisco CA 94104 415-421-0288 428
Web: www.elc-law.com

Evans Mechwart Hambleton & Tilton Inc (EMHT)
5500 New Albany Rd .... Columbus OH 43054 614-775-4500 261
Web: www.emht.com

Evans Oil Company LLC
8450 Millhaven Rd .... Monroe LA 71203 318-345-1502 579

Evans Tempcon Inc 701 Ann St NW .... Grand Rapids MI 49504 616-361-2681 361-9646 15
TF: 800-433-1740 ■ *Web:* www.evanstempcon.com

Evans Tire & Service Centers Inc
510 N Broadway .... Escondido CA 92025 877-338-2678 62-5
TF: 877-338-2678 ■ *Web:* www.evanstire.com

Evansburg State Park
851 May Hall Rd .... Collegeville PA 19426 610-409-1150 565
Web: www.dcnr.state.pa.us

Evans-Hamilton Inc
4608 Union Bay Pl N E .... Seattle WA 98105 206-526-5622 256
Web: www.evanshamilton.com

Evans-Hydro
18128 S Santa Fe Ave .... Rancho Dominguez CA 90221 310-608-5801 641
TF: 800-429-7867 ■ *Web:* evanshydro.com

Evans-Mason Inc
1021 S Grand Ave E .... Springfield IL 62703 217-522-3396 522-3190 189-7
TF: 800-536-2225 ■ *Web:* evans-mason.com

Evans-Sherratt Co 13050 Northend Ave .... Oak Park MI 48237 248-584-5500 475

Evanston Chamber of Commerce
1840 Oak Ave .... Evanston IL 60201 847-328-1500 328-1510 139
Web: evchamber.com

Evanston Hospital 2650 Ridge Ave .... Evanston IL 60201 847-570-2000 374-3
TF: 888-364-6400 ■ *Web:* www.northshore.org

Evanston Lumber Co 1001 Sherman Ave .... Evanston IL 60202 847-864-7700 364
TF: 800-862-4657 ■ *Web:* www.evanstonlumber.com

Evanston Public Library
1703 Orrington Ave .... Evanston IL 60201 847-448-8600 866-0313 434-3
TF: 888-253-7003 ■ *Web:* epl.org

Evanston Publishing Inc
4824 Brownsboro Ctr .... Louisville KY 40207 502-899-1919 94
Web: www.evanstonpublishing.com

Evanston/Skokie School District 65
1500 Mcdaniel Ave .... Evanston IL 60201 847-859-8000 859-8707 685
Web: www.district65.net

Evansville City Hall
1 NW ML King Jr Blvd .... Evansville IN 47708 812-436-4992 436-4999 337
Web: www.evansvillegov.org

Evansville Civic Theatre
717 N Fulton St .... Evansville IN 47710 812-425-2800 423-2636 572
Web: www.evansvillecivictheatre.org

Evansville Convention & Visitors Bureau
401 SE Riverside Dr .... Evansville IN 47713 812-421-2200 421-2207 206
TF: 800-433-3025 ■ *Web:* www.visitevansville.com

Evansville Courier & Press
300 E Walnut St .... Evansville IN 47713 812-424-7711 422-8196 532-2
TF: 800-288-3200 ■ *Web:* www.courierpress.com

Evansville Museum of Arts History & Science
411 SE Riverside Dr .... Evansville IN 47713 812-425-2406 421-7509 520
Web: evansvillemuseum.org

Evansville Philharmonic Orchestra
401 SE Sixth St .... Evansville IN 47708 812-425-5050 426-7008 573-3
TF: 800-745-3000 ■ *Web:* evansvillephilharmonic.org

Evansville Regional Airport
7801 Bussing Dr .... Evansville IN 47725 812-421-4401 421-4412 27
Web: flyevv.com

Evansville Sheet Metal Works Inc
1901 W Maryland St .... Evansville IN 47712 812-423-7871 697
Web: www.esmw.com

Evansville Teachers Federal Credit Union
PO Box 5129 .... Evansville IN 47716 812-477-9271 473-9704 219
TF: 800-800-9271 ■ *Web:* www.etfcu.org

Evansville Vanderburgh Public Library
200 SE ML King Jr Blvd .... Evansville IN 47713 812-428-8200 428-8397 434-3
Web: www.evpl.org

Evapco Inc 5151 Allendale Ln .... Taneytown MD 21787 410-756-2600 756-6450 14
Web: www.evapco.com

Evaporated Coatings Inc
2365 Maryland Rd .... Willow Grove PA 19090 215-659-3080 711
Web: www.evaporatedcoatings.com

EVC Group Inc
122 East 42nd St Ste 2105 .... New York NY 10168 646-445-4800 401
Web: www.evcgroup.com

Evco Plastics 100 W N St PO Box 497 .... DeForest WI 53532 800-507-6000 251-0822 604
TF: 800-507-6000 ■ *Web:* www.evcoplastics.com

Evelinecharles Salons-spas
100 Anderson Rd SE Ste 5 .... Calgary AB T2J3V1 403-571-5666 77
Web: www.evelinecharles.com

Evelyn & Walter Haas Jr Fund
114 Sansome St Ste 600 .... San Francisco CA 94104 415-856-1400 856-1500 305
Web: www.haasjr.org

Evelyn Hill Inc 1 Liberty Island .... New York NY 10004 212-363-3180 327
Web: www.thestatueofliberty.com

Evena Medical Inc
339 S San Antonio Rd Ste 1C .... Los Altos CA 94022 650-209-0398 743
Web: www.evenamed.com

Evenflo Company Inc 1801 Commerce Dr .... Piqua OH 45356 800-233-5921 64
TF: 800-233-5921 ■ *Web:* www.evenflo.com

Evenglow Lodge Inc
215 E Washington St .... Pontiac IL 61764 815-844-6131 450
Web: www.evenglowlodge.org

Evening Call Publishing Co, The
75 Main St .... Woonsocket RI 02895 401-762-3000 532-2
Web: www.woonsocketcall.com

Evening Observer
8-10 E Second St PO Box 391 .... Dunkirk NY 14048 716-366-3000 366-3005 532-2
TF: 800-836-0931 ■ *Web:* www.observertoday.com

Evening Star Cafe
2000 Mt Vernon Ave .... Alexandria VA 22301 703-549-5051 671
Web: www.eveningstarcafe.net

Evening Sun
135 Baltimore St PO Box 514 .... Hanover PA 17331 717-637-3736 637-7730 532-2
TF: 888-256-0125 ■ *Web:* www.eveningsun.com

Evensky & Katz LLC
4000 Ponce de Leon Blvd Ste 850 .... Coral Gables FL 33146 305-448-8882 194
TF: 800-448-5435 ■ *Web:* www.evensky.com

eVent Medical Inc
971 Calle Amanecer Ste 101 .... San Clemente CA 92673 949-492-8368 475
Web: www.event-medical.com

Event Planning International Corp
10900 Granite St .... Charlotte NC 28273 980-233-3777 233-3800 184
TF: 800-940-2164 ■ *Web:* www.epicreg.com

Event Producers Inc
5724 Salmen St .... New Orleans LA 70123 504-466-4066 514
TF: 866-903-6949 ■ *Web:* eventproducers.com

Event Solutions International Inc
1757 Larchwood Dr .... Troy MI 48083 248-307-9400 393
Web: www.eventsolutions.net

Eventech 1833 alford ave .... Los Altos CA 94024 650-961-7845 463
TF: 800-388-8255 ■ *Web:* www.eventech.com

E-ventexe
8775 Sierra College Blvd Ste 300 .... Roseville CA 95661 916-458-5820 260
Web: www.e-ventexe.com

Eventide Inc 1 Alsan Way .... Little Ferry NJ 07643 201-641-1200 647
Web: www.eventide.com

Eventive LLC 817 W Superior St Ste 1 .... Chicago IL 60642 312-997-2393 196
TF: 800-680-8558 ■ *Web:* www.eventivellc.com

Eventnet Usa
1129 SE Fourth Ave .... Fort Lauderdale FL 33316 954-467-9898 175
Web: www.eventnetusa.com

EventPro Strategies LLC
Scottsdale Rd Ste B120 .... Scottsdale AZ 85253 480-449-4100 283-1190 5
Web: www.eventprostrategies.com

EventRebels com Inc
10013 Fox Den Rd .... Ellicott City MD 21042 877-883-1786 5
TF: 877-883-1786 ■ *Web:* www.eventrebels.com

Events Forum Inc
2 Oxford Xing Ste 4 .... New Hartford NY 13413 315-792-7600 196
Web: www.eventsforum.net

Eventsful Inc 305 E 40th St Apt 6f .... New York NY 10016 212-682-8405 195
Web: www.eventsful.com

Phone | Fax | Class

Eventure Interactive Inc
3420 Bristol St Fl 6 Costa Mesa CA 92626 855-986-5669 395
TF: 855-986-5669 ■ *Web:* www.eventure.com

Eventus Group
15280 NW 79th Ct Ste 100 Miami Lakes FL 33016 305-557-4443 196

Eventus Solutions Group
98 Inverness Dr E Ste 100 Englewood CO 80112 303-376-6161 180
Web: www.eventusg.com

Ever Roll Specialties Co
3988 Lawrenceville Dr Springfield OH 45504 937-964-1302 595
TF: 800-292-9744 ■ *Web:* www.ever-roll.com

Ever Win International Corp
17579 Railroad St City Of Industry CA 91748 626-810-8218 735
Web: www.everwin.com

Everbloom Growers Inc
20450 SW 248th St Homestead FL 33031 305-248-1478 292

Ever-Bloom Inc 4701 Foothill Rd Carpinteria CA 93013 805-684-5566 369
TF: 800-388-8112 ■ *Web:* www.ever-bloom.com

Everbridge Inc
500 N Brand Blvd Ste 1000 Glendale CA 91203 818-230-9700 224
Web: www.everbridge.com

Everbrite Inc
4949 S 110th St PO Box 20020 Greenfield WI 53220 414-529-3500 529-7191 701
TF: 800-558-3888 ■ *Web:* www.everbrite.com

Evercoat 6600 Cornell Rd Cincinnati OH 45242 513-489-7600 489-9229 60
TF: 800-729-7600 ■ *Web:* www.evercoat.com

Evercore Partners Inc 55 E 52nd St New York NY 10055 212-857-3100 401
Web: www.evercore.com

Eveready Printing Inc
20700 Miles Pkwy Cleveland OH 44128 216-587-2379 587-2260 627
Web: www.evereadyprint.com

Everest 440 S LaSalle St 40th Fl Chicago IL 60605 312-663-8920 671
Web: www.everestrestaurant.com

Everest College
14555 Potomac Mills Rd Ste 200 Woodbridge VA 22192 571-408-2100 800
TF: 888-223-8556 ■ *Web:* www.everest.edu

Everest College
1010 W Sunshine St Springfield MO 65807 417-864-7220 864-5697 800
TF: 888-223-8556 ■ *Web:* www.everest.edu

Everest College Alhambra
2215 W Mission Rd Alhambra CA 91803 626-979-4940 979-4960 800
TF: 888-223-8556 ■ *Web:* www.everest.edu

Everest College Anaheim
511 N Brookhurst Ste 300 Anaheim CA 92801 714-953-6500 953-4163 800
TF: 888-224-6684 ■ *Web:* www.everest.edu

Everest College Aurora
14280 E Jewell Ave Ste 100 Aurora CO 80012 303-745-6244 800
TF: 888-223-8556 ■ *Web:* www.everest.edu

Everest College City of Industry
12801 Crossroads Pkwy S City of Industry CA 91746 562-908-2500 800
TF: 888-224-6684 ■ *Web:* www.everest.edu

Everest College San Jose
1245 S Winchester Blvd Ste 102 San Jose CA 95128 408-246-4171 800
TF: 888-223-8556 ■ *Web:* www.everest.edu

Everest College Thornton
9065 Grant St Thornton CO 80229 303-457-2757 457-4030 800
TF: 888-223-8556 ■ *Web:* www.everest.edu

Everest Consulting Group Inc
3840 Pk Ave Ste 203 Edison NJ 08820 732-548-2700 548-6200 177
Web: www.everestconsulting.net

Everest Group Inc, The
9912 Carver Rd Ste 100 Cincinnati OH 45242 513-769-2500 690
Web: www.everestrealestate.com

Everest Institute
100 Forbes Ave Ste 1200 Pittsburgh PA 15222 412-261-4520 261-4546 800
TF: 800-603-2870 ■ *Web:* www.everest.edu

Everest Institute
5514 Big Tyler Rd Cross Lanes WV 25313 304-776-6290 776-6262 800
Web: www.everest.edu

Everest Institute 21107 Lahser Rd Southfield MI 48033 248-799-9933 799-2912* 800
**Fax:* Admissions ■ *TF General:* 800-611-2101 ■ *Web:* www.everest.edu

Everest Institute Long Beach
2161 Technology Pl Long Beach CA 90810 562-624-9530 800
TF: 888-223-8556 ■ *Web:* www.everest.edu

Everest Institute San Antonio
6550 First Pk Ten Blvd San Antonio TX 78213 210-732-7800 731-9313 800
Web: www.everest.edu

Everest on Grand 1278 Grand Ave Saint Paul MN 55105 651-696-1666 671
Web: www.everestongrand.com

Everest Production Corp
300 Franklin Sq Dr Somerset NJ 08873 732-560-0800 116
Web: www.everestpro.com

Everest Re Group Ltd
477 Martinsville Rd PO Box 830 Liberty Corner NJ 07938 908-604-3000 604-3322 360-4
TF: 800-269-6660 ■ *Web:* www.everestre.com

Everest Reinsurance Co
477 Martinsville Rd Liberty Corner NJ 07938 908-604-3000 604-3322 391-5
TF: 800-269-6660 ■ *Web:* www.everestregroup.com

Everest University
Brandon 3924 Coconut Palm Dr Tampa FL 33619 813-621-0041 800
TF Cust Svc: 888-223-8556 ■ *Web:* www.everest.edu
Jacksonville 8226 Phillips Hwy Jacksonville FL 32256 904-731-4949 800
TF: 800-611-2101 ■ *Web:* www.everest.edu
Lakeland 995 E Memorial Blvd Ste 110 Lakeland FL 33801 863-686-1444 682-1077 800
TF: 888-223-8556 ■ *Web:* www.everest.edu
Largo 1199 E Bay Dr Largo FL 33770 727-725-2688 373-4412 800
TF: 888-223-8556 ■ *Web:* www.everest.edu
Orange Park 805 Wells Rd Orange Park FL 32073 904-264-9122 264-9952 800
TF: 888-223-8556 ■ *Web:* www.everest.edu
Pompano Beach 225 N Federal Hwy Pompano Beach FL 33062 954-783-7339 783-7964 800
TF: 888-223-8556 ■ *Web:* www.everest.edu
South Orlando 9200 Southpark Ctr Loop Orlando FL 32819 407-851-2525 851-1477 800
TF: 800-611-2101 ■ *Web:* www.everest.edu
Tampa 3319 W Hillsborough Ave Tampa FL 33614 813-879-6000 871-2483 800
TF: 888-223-8556 ■ *Web:* www.everest.edu

Everett & Jones Barbeque 126 Broadway Oakland CA 94607 510-663-2350 671
Web: www.eandjbbq.com

Everett Carpet Co 318 Ashman St Midland MI 48640 989-835-7191 290
Web: everettcarpet.com

Everett Cash Mutual Insurance Co
10591 Lincoln Hwy Everett PA 15537 814-652-6111 390
Web: www.everettcash.com

Everett Chamber of Commerce
467 Broadway Everett MA 02149 617-387-9100 389-6655 139
Web: www.everettmachamber.com

Everett Charles Technologies (ECT)
700 E Harrison Ave Pomona CA 91767 909-625-5551 248
Web: www.ectinfo.com

Everett Charles Technologies Inc Test Equipment Div
700 E Harrison Ave Pomona CA 91767 909-625-5551 248
Web: www.ectinfo.com

Everett Community College
2000 Tower St Everett WA 98201 425-388-9100 388-9129* 162
**Fax:* Admissions ■ *TF:* 866-575-9027 ■ *Web:* www.everettcc.edu

Everett J Prescott Inc
32 Prescott St Gardiner ME 04345 207-582-1851 582-5637 612
TF: 800-357-2447 ■ *Web:* www.ejprescott.com

Everett Public Library 2702 Hoyt Ave Everett WA 98201 425-257-8010 434-3
Web: www.epls.org

Everett Studios Inc 5 N Greenwich Rd Armonk NY 10504 914-997-2200 7
TF: 800-371-2555 ■ *Web:* www.goeverett.com

Everfast Inc 203 Gale Ln Kennett Square PA 19348 610-444-9700 270
TF Cust Svc: 800-213-6366 ■ *Web:* www.calicocorners.com

Everfresh Food Corp
501 Huron Blvd SE Minneapolis MN 55414 612-331-6393 296-31

eVerge Group Inc
4965 Preston Pk Blvd Ste 700 Plano TX 75093 972-608-1803 608-1893 180
TF: 888-548-1973 ■ *Web:* www.evergegroup.com

Everglades Alligator Farm
40351 SW 192nd Ave Homestead FL 33034 305-247-2628 248-9711 823
Web: www.everglades.com

Everglades Boats 544 Air Pk Rd Edgewater FL 32132 386-409-2202 409-7939 90
TF: 800-368-5647 ■ *Web:* www.evergladesboats.com

Everglades Holiday Park
21940 Griffin Rd Fort Lauderdale FL 33332 954-434-8111 50-5
TF: 800-220-2244 ■ *Web:* www.evergladesholidaypark.com

Everglades National Park
40001 SR-9336 Homestead FL 33034 305-242-7700 242-7728 564
TF: 800-788-0511 ■ *Web:* www.nps.gov/ever

Everglades Safari Park
26700 SW Eighth St Miami FL 33194 305-226-6923 554-5666 823
TF: 800-352-0050 ■ *Web:* www.evergladessafaripark.com

Everglades Steel Corp 5901 NW 74th Ave Miami FL 33166 305-591-9460 492
Web: www.evergladessteel.com

Everglades Technologies
1 Union Sq W 3rd Fl New York NY 10003 212-741-0000 196
Web: www.etny.net

EverGlow NA Inc 1122 Industrial Dr Matthews NC 28105 704-841-2580 45
Web: www.everglow.us

Evergreen Advisors LLC
9256 Bendix Rd Ste 300 Columbia MD 21045 410-997-6000 401
TF: 800-289-9999 ■ *Web:* www.evergreenadvisorsllc.com

Evergreen Capital Management LLC
10500 N East 8th Ste 950 Bellevue WA 98004 425-467-4600 401
Web: www.evergreengavekal.com

Evergreen Engineering Portland LLC
7431 NW Evergreen Pkwy Ste 210 Hillsboro OR 97124 503-439-8777 186
Web: www.evergreenengineering.com

Evergreen Enterprises Inc
5915 Midlothian Trnpk Richmond VA 23225 804-231-1800 320
TF: 800-774-3837 ■ *Web:* www.myevergreen.com

Evergreen FS Inc 402 N Hershey Rd Bloomington IL 61704 309-663-2392 663-0494 276
TF: 877-963-2392 ■ *Web:* www.evergreen-fs.com

Evergreen Hospice Services
12822 124th Ln NE Kirkland WA 98034 425-899-1070 899-1033 371
TF: 877-980-7500 ■ *Web:* www.evergreenhealth.com

Evergreen Hospital Medical Ctr
12040 NE 128th St Kirkland WA 98034 425-899-1000 374-3
Web: www.evergreenhealth.com

Evergreen Lodge 250 S Frontage Rd W Vail CO 81657 970-476-7810 476-4504 379
TF: 800-284-8245 ■ *Web:* www.evergreenvail.com

Evergreen Lumber & Truss Inc
84 Central Industrial Row Purvis MS 39475 601-794-8404 364
Web: www.evergreentruss.com

Evergreen Marriott Conference Resort
4021 Lakeview Dr Stone Mountain GA 30083 770-879-9900 465-3264 377
TF: 800-228-9290 ■ *Web:* marriott.com/vanityredirect/atleg

Evergreen Park Chamber of Commerce
9449 S Kedzie Ave Ste 196 Evergreen Park IL 60805 708-423-1118 139
Web: www.evergreenparkchamber.org

Evergreen Plastics Inc
202 Watertower Dr Clyde OH 43410 419-547-1400 601
Web: www.evergreenplastics.com

Evergreen Printing Company Inc
101 Haag Ave Bellmawr NJ 08031 856-933-0222 532-3
Web: www.egpp.com

Evergreen Public Schools
13501 NE 28th St PO Box 8910 Vancouver WA 98668 360-604-4000 892-5307 685
Web: evergreenps.org

Evergreen Regional Library
55 First Ave PO Box 1140 Gimli MB R0C1B0 204-642-7912 642-8319 436
Web: erlibrary.ca

Evergreen Rehabilitation & Care Ctr
2030 Evergreen Ave Modesto CA 95350 209-577-1055 450
TF: 800-465-3203 ■ *Web:* www.evergreencare.com

Evergreen Resort 7880 Mackinaw Trail Cadillac MI 49601 800-634-7302 775-9621* 669
**Fax Area Code:* 231 ■ *TF:* 800-634-7302 ■ *Web:* www.evergreenresortmi.com

Evergreen Shipping Agency (America) Corp
1 Evertrust Plaza Jersey City NJ 07302 201-761-3000 360-3
Web: www.evergreen-america.com

Evergreen Speedway 14405 179th Ave SE Monroe WA 98272 360-805-6100 805-6110 515
Web: www.evergreenspeedway.com

Evergreen State College
2700 Evergreen Pkwy Olympia WA 98505 360-867-6000 867-5114 166
TF: 888-492-9480 ■ *Web:* www.evergreen.edu

Evergreen State College Evans Library
2700 Evergreen Pkwy NW Olympia WA 98505 360-867-6250 434-6
TF: 800-443-1083 ■ *Web:* www.evergreen.edu/library

Name / Address	City	State	Zip	Phone	Fax	Class
Evergreen Valley College 3095 Yerba Buena Rd *Fax: Admissions ■ Web: www.evc.edu	San Jose	CA	95135	408-274-7900	223-9351*	162
Evergreen Woods 88 Notch Hill Rd TF General: 866-413-6378 ■ Web: evergreen-woods.com	North Branford	CT	06471	203-488-8000		672
Evergreens, The 309 Bridgeboro Rd TF: 877-673-8234 ■ Web: www.evergreens.org	Moorestown	NJ	08057	856-439-2000		672
Everhard Products Inc 1016 Ninth St SW TF: 800-225-0984 ■ Web: www.everhard.com	Canton	OH	44707	330-453-7786		758
Everhart Museum 1901 Mulberry St TF: 800-462-0442 ■ Web: everhart-museum.org	Scranton	PA	18510	570-346-7186	346-0652	520
EverHome Mortgage Co 301 W Bay St TF Cust Svc: 888-882-3837 ■ Web: www.everbank.com	Jacksonville	FL	32202	888-882-3837		509
Everi Holdings Inc (GCA) 7250 S Tenaya Way Ste 100 NYSE: EVRI ■ TF: 800-833-7110 ■ Web: www.everi.com	Las Vegas	NV	89113	702-855-3000		56
Everingham & Kerr Inc 1300 Route 73 Ste 103 Web: www.everkerr.com	Mount Laurel	NJ	08054	856-546-6655		708
Everist Genomics Inc 709 W Ellsworth Rd TF: 855-383-7478 ■ Web: www.everisthealth.com	Ann Arbor	MI	48108	855-383-7478		743
Everite Machine Products Co 6995 Airport Hwy Ln TF: 800-208-6075 ■ Web: www.everite.net	Pennsauken	NJ	08110	856-330-6700		455
Everkrisp Vegetables Inc 9202 W Harrison St Web: everkrispvegetables.com	Tolleson	AZ	85353	623-936-3321		10-11
Everlast Plastic Lumber 800 Market St Web: plasticlumber.org	Auburn	PA	17922	570-754-7440		661
Everlaw 2020 Milvia St Ste 220 TF: 844-383-7529 ■ Web: everlaw.com	Berkeley	CA	94704	844-383-7529		387
Ever-Lite Company Inc 1717 N Bayshore Dr Web: www.ever-lite.com	Miami	FL	33132	305-577-0819		9
Everlube Products 100 Cooper Cir TF: 800-428-7802 ■ Web: everlubeproducts.com	Peachtree City	GA	30269	770-261-4800		481
EverMark LLC 1050 Northbrook Pkwy Web: www.evermark-lnl.com	Suwanee	GA	30024	678-455-5188		236
Everprint International Inc 18021 Cortney Ct	City of Industry	CA	91748	626-839-2569		175
Everpure LLC Pentair 1040 Muirfield Dr TF: 800-323-7873	Hanover Park	IL	60133	630-307-3000	307-3030	806
Everson Cordage Works Inc 7180 Everson-Goshen Rd Web: www.eversoncordage.com	Everson	WA	98247	360-966-4613		208
Everson Museum of Art 401 Harrison St TF: 800-548-4386 ■ Web: www.everson.org	Syracuse	NY	13202	315-474-6064	474-6943	520
Everson Tesla Inc 615 Daniel's Rd Web: www.eversontesla.com	Nazareth	PA	18064	610-746-1520	746-1520	518
Eversource 1 Nstar Way NW200 TF Cust Svc: 800-592-2000 ■ Web: nstar.com	Westwood	MA	02090	800-592-2000		787
Eversource 56 Prospect St TF: 800-286-2000 ■ Web: www.eversource.com	Hartford	MA	06103	860-665-3495		787
EverStaff LLC 6500 Rockside Rd Ste 385 Ste TF: 800-334-1655 ■ Web: www.everstaff.com	Cleveland	OH	44131	216-369-2566		260
EverTrue LLC 330 Congress St 2nd Fl TF: 855-387-8783 ■ Web: www.evertrue.com	Boston	MA	02210	855-387-8783		387
Everwise Corp 1178 Broadway 4th Fl TF: 888-734-0011 ■ Web: www.geteverwise.com	New York	NY	10001	888-734-0011		387
Every Promotional Product 30401 Agoura Rd Ste 102 TF: 800-438-7325 ■ Web: www.everypromotionalproduct.com	Agoura Hills	CA	91301	818-597-9900		184
Everyday Technologies Inc 2005 Campbell Rd Web: www.everydaytech.com	Sidney	OH	45365	937-492-4171		358
Everyman Theatre 315 W Fayette St *Fax Area Code: 443 ■ Web: www.everymantheatre.org	Baltimore	MD	21201	410-752-2208	615-7053*	572
EveryScape Inc 65 Chapel St Web: www.everyscape.com	Newton	MA	02458	781-250-4800		387
Everything Parking Inc 1415 S Church St Ste T TF: 877-751-6683 ■ Web: www.parkinc.com	Charlotte	NC	28203	704-377-1755		108
Evesham Township Board of Education 25 S Maple Ave Web: www.evesham.k12.nj.us	Marlton	NJ	08053	856-983-1800		685
EVH Mfg Company LLC 4895 Red Bluff Rd TF: 888-990-2555 ■ Web: hardeebyevh.com	Loris	SC	29569	843-756-2555	756-4436	273
Evidence Based Research Inc 1595 Spring Hill Rd Web: www.ebrinc.com	Vienna	VA	22182	703-893-6800		463
Evident Point Software Corp 160-3751 Shell Rd Web: www.evidentpoint.com	Richmond	BC	V6X2W2	604-241-2711		179
Evidentio Inc 11501 Dublin Blvd Ste 200 Web: evident.io	Dublin	CA	94568	408-802-0724		387
Eview 360 Corp 39255 Country Club Dr Ste B-1 Web: www.eview360.com	Farmington Hills	MI	48331	248-306-5191		195
Evil Eye Pictures LLC 665 Third St Ste 503 Web: evileyepictures.com	San Francisco	CA	94107	415-777-0666		514
EVINE Live Inc 6740 Shady Oak Rd TF: 800-676-5523 ■ Web: www.evine.com	Eden Prairie	MN	55344	800-676-5523		740
Evins Communications Ltd 830 Third Ave Web: www.evins.com	New York	NY	10022	212-688-8200	935-6730	7
Evins Personnel Consultants Inc 2013 W Anderson Ln Web: www.evinspersonnelconsultants.com	Austin	TX	78757	512-454-9561		260
Evins Regional Juvenile Ctr 3801 E Monte Cristo Rd	Edinburg	TX	78542	956-289-5500		412
eVision LLC 179 E Main St Web: www.evisionsem.com	Branford	CT	06405	203-481-8005		5
Evision Systems I Inc 2852 Antoine Dr	Houston	TX	77092	713-807-9555		463
Evite LLC 600 Wilshire Blvd 4th Fl Web: www.evite.com	Los Angeles	CA	90017	213-699-5005		387
Evo Exhibits 399 Wegner Dr TF: 888-404-4224 ■ Web: www.evoexhibits.com	West Chicago	IL	60185	630-520-0710		7
EVOenergy LLC 10211 219th St SE Web: www.evonrg.com	Snohomish	WA	98296	415-533-0998		536
Evogen Inc 9393 W 110th St Ste 500 Web: www.evogen.com	Overland Park	KS	66210	913-948-5640		743
Evok Advertising Inc 1485 International Pkwy Ste 3001 Web: www.evokad.com	Heathrow	FL	32746	407-302-4416		7
evoke interaction One 13 S Broad St Web: www.evokehealth.com	Philadelphia	PA	19107	267-765-4992		5
Evoke Research & Consulting LLC 1000 Wilson Blvd Ste 2500 TF: 800-367-5690 ■ Web: www.evokeconsulting.com	Arlington	VA	22209	703-415-1007		196
Evoke Technologies 7106 Corporate Way Web: www.evoketechnologies.com	Dayton	OH	45459	937-660-4925		196
Evola Music Center Inc 12745 23 Mile Rd Web: www.evola.com	Shelby Township	MI	48315	586-726-6570		526
Evolution Computing 7000 N 16th St Ste 120 514 TF: 800-874-4028 ■ Web: www.fastcad.com	Phoenix	AZ	85020	800-874-4028		178-5
Evolve Digital Labs 7374 Elm St Web: evolvedigitallabs.com	Maplewood	MO	63143	314-260-7455		260
Evolve Discovery Inc 611 Mission St 4th Fl TF: 866-488-1032 ■ Web: www.evolvediscovery.com	San Francisco	CA	94105	415-398-8600		113
Evolve IP LLC 989 Old Eagle School Rd Ste 815 Web: www.evolveip.net	Wayne	PA	19087	610-964-8000		737
Evolve Media 39 Mesa St Ste 101 Web: www.evolvemedia.tv	San Francisco	CA	94129	415-324-5002		7
Evolve Payment Systems 2974 Rice St Web: evolve-systems.com	Saint Paul	MN	55113	651-628-4000		180
Evonik Corp 299 Jefferson Rd Web: corporate.evonik.us	Parsippany	NJ	07054	973-929-8000		146
EVS Ltd 3702 W Sample St TF: 800-364-3218 ■ Web: www.evsltd.com	South Bend	IN	46619	574-233-5707		320
EVS Metal Inc 1 Kenner Ct TF: 800-257-8174 ■ Web: www.evsmetal.com	Riverdale	NJ	07457	973-839-4432		697
EVS-US Inc 319 Garlington Rd Ste B4	Greenville	SC	29615	864-288-9777		365
Evviva Brands LLC 2403 Mira Vista Dr Web: evvivabrands.com	El Cerrito	CA	94530	510-215-2783		195
Evy of California Inc 810A S Flower St Web: www.evy.com	Los Angeles	CA	90017	213-746-4647	746-9788	277
EW Brandt & Sons Inc (EWB) 561 Ragan Rd TF: 800-348-9701 ■ Web: rembrandtfruit.com	Wapato	WA	98951	509-877-3193		315-3
EW James & Sons Inc 1308-14 Nailling Dr Web: www.ewjamesandsons.com	Union City	TN	38261	731-885-0601		345
EW Scripps Co 312 Walnut St Ste 2800 NYSE: SSP ■ *Fax: Hum Res ■ TF: 800-888-3000 ■ Web: www.scripps.com	Cincinnati	OH	45202	513-977-3000	977-3800*	637-8
EW Scripps Co, The 1866 E Chisholm Web: www.kivitv.com	Nampa	ID	83687	208-336-0500	381-6682	741
EW Tompkins Company Inc 126 Sheridan Ave TF: 800-486-5019 ■ Web: www.thetompkinsgroup.com	Albany	NY	12210	518-462-6577	462-6570	189-10
EW Wylie Corp 1520 Second Ave NW *Fax Area Code: 701 ■ TF Cust Svc: 800-437-4132 ■ Web: www.wylietrucking.com	West Fargo	ND	58078	800-437-4132	281-0415*	780
EWA (Enterprise Wireless Alliance) 8484 Westpark Dr Ste 630 TF: 800-482-8282 ■ Web: www.enterprisewireless.org	McLean	VA	22102	703-528-5115	524-1074	49-20
EWA Inc (Electronic Warfare Assoc Inc) 13873 Pk Ctr Rd Ste 500 TF General: 888-392-0002 ■ Web: www.ewa.com	Herndon	VA	20171	703-904-5700	904-5779	180
Ewald Consulting Group Inc 1000 Westgate Dr Ste 252 Web: www.ewald.com	Saint Paul	MN	55114	651-290-6260	290-2266	47
eWareness Inc 1900 S Harbor City Blvd Ste 122 TF: 800-517-4130 ■ Web: www.ewarenessinc.com	Melbourne	FL	32901	321-953-2435		809
Ewart-Ohlson Machine Company Inc, The 1435 Main St PO Box 359 Web: www.ewart-ohlson.com	Cuyahoga Falls	OH	44222	330-928-2171		757
EWB (EW Brandt & Sons Inc) 561 Ragan Rd TF: 800-348-9701 ■ Web: rembrandtfruit.com	Wapato	WA	98951	509-877-3193		315-3
EWI (EastWest Institute) 1 E 26th St 20th Fl Web: www.eastwest.ngo	New York	NY	10010	212-824-4100	824-4149	634
EWI (Edison Welding Institute) 1250 Arthur E Adams Dr Web: www.ewi.org	Columbus	OH	43221	614-688-5000	688-5001	49-13
EWI (Executive Women International) 3860 S 2300 E TF: 877-439-4669 ■ Web: ewiconnect.com	Salt Lake City	UT	84109	801-355-2800		49-12
EWI (Eagle Wings Industries Inc) 400 Shellhouse Dr Web: www.ewiusa.com	Rantoul	IL	61866	217-892-4322		60
EWI (Elliott Wave International) PO Box 1618 TF Cust Svc: 800-336-1618 ■ Web: www.elliottwave.com	Gainesville	GA	30503	770-536-0309	536-2514	637-9
EWI Worldwide Inc 13211 Merriman Rd TF: 800-875-5250 ■ Web: www.ewiworldwide.com	Livonia	MI	48150	734-525-9010		5
EWIE Company Inc 1099 Highland Dr Ste D Web: www.ewie.com	Ann Arbor	MI	48108	734-971-6265		393
eWinery Solutions 1700 Soscol Ave Ste 3 TF: 800-750-3947 ■ Web: www.vinsuite.com/home	Napa	CA	94559	707-253-7400		5

Company	City	State	ZIP	Phone	Fax	Class
Ewing Cole 100 N Sixth St *TF:* 800-383-6060 ■ *Web:* ewingcole.com	Philadelphia	PA	19106	215-923-2020	574-9163	261
Ewing Construction Company Inc PO Box 4235 *Web:* www.ewingcc.com	Corpus Christi	TX	78469	361-882-6525		186
Ewing Marion Kauffman Foundation (EMKF) 4801 Rockhill Rd *Web:* www.kauffman.org	Kansas City	MO	64110	816-932-1000	932-1100	305
Ewing Morris & Company Investment Partners 1407 Yonge St Ste 500 *Web:* www.ewingmorris.com	Toronto	ON	M4T1Y7	416-640-2791		528
Ewing-Foley Inc 10061 Bubb Rd Ste 1000 *TF:* 800-399-3319 ■ *Web:* www.ewingfoley.com	Cupertino	CA	95014	408-342-1200		246
eWomenNetwork Inc 14900 Landmark Blvd Ste 540 *Web:* www.ewomennetwork.com	Dallas	TX	75254	972-620-9995		225
eWorkplace Solutions Inc 24461 Ridge Rt Dr Ste 210 *Web:* www.batchmaster.com	Laguna Hills	CA	92653	949-583-1646	271-4620	178-8
EWR Weather Radar 336 Leffingwell Ave *Web:* www.ewradar.com	Saint Louis	MO	63122	314-821-1022		529
EWTN (Eternal Word Television Network) 5817 Old Leeds Rd *Web:* www.ewtn.com	Irondale	AL	35210	205-271-2900		740
Exact Eye Care 431 Pierce St *TF:* 800-369-2640 ■ *Web:* www.exacteyecare.com	Sioux City	IA	51101	712-252-4691		543
Exact Inc 5285 Ramona Blvd	Jacksonville	FL	32205	904-783-6640		697
Exact Metrology 11575 Goldcoast Dr *TF:* 866-722-2600 ■ *Web:* www.exactmetrology.com	Cincinnati	OH	45249	513-831-6620		358
EXACT Sciences Corp 441 Charmany Dr *NASDAQ: EXAS* ■ *Web:* www.exactsciences.com	Madison	WI	53719	608-284-5700	284-5701	231
Exacta Corp 16595 W Bluemound Rd *Web:* exactacorp.com	Brookfield	WI	53005	262-796-0000		180
Exactax Inc 2301 W Lincoln Ave Ste 100 *TF:* 844-327-6740 ■ *Web:* www.exactax.com	Anaheim	CA	92801	714-284-4802		734
Exactearth Ltd 60 Struck Ct *Web:* www.exactearth.com	Cambridge	ON	N1R8L2	519-622-4445		387
Exactech Inc 2320 NW 66th Ct *NASDAQ: EXAC* ■ *TF:* 800-392-2832 ■ *Web:* www.exac.com	Gainesville	FL	32653	352-377-1140	378-2617	477
Exacto Spring Corp 1201 Hickory St *Web:* www.exacto.com	Grafton	WI	53024	262-377-3970	377-3854	719
ExaDigm Inc 2871 Pullman St *TF:* 800-933-0064 ■ *Web:* www.exadigm.com	Santa Ana	CA	92705	949-486-0320		194
Exair Corp 11510 Goldcoast Dr *Web:* www.dutch.exair.com	Cincinnati	OH	45249	513-671-3322		567
Exal Corp 1 Performance Pl *Web:* www.exal.com	Youngstown	OH	44502	330-744-2267		124
Exalpha Biologicals Inc 2 Shaker Rd Unit B101 **Fax Area Code: 978* ■ *TF:* 800-395-1137 ■ *Web:* www.exalpha.com	Shirley	MA	01464	800-395-1137	461-0436*	231
Exalt Integrated Technologies 3000 Northwoods Pkwy Ste 350 *Web:* www.exaltit.com	Norcross	GA	30071	678-920-3019		196
Examination Management Services Inc 15333 N Pima Rd Ste 330 *Web:* www.emsinet.com	Scottsdale	AZ	85260	214-689-3600	689-3644	225
ExamWorks Inc 3280 Peachtree Rd Ste 2625 *Web:* www.examworks.com	Atlanta	GA	30305	404-952-2400		415
Exane Inc 640 Fifth Ave 15th Fl *Web:* www.exane.com	New York	NY	10019	212-634-4990		690
Exar Corp 48720 Kato Rd *NYSE: EXAR* ■ *TF:* 855-755-1330 ■ *Web:* www.exar.com	Fremont	CA	94538	510-668-7000	668-7011	696
exas Parks and Wildlife Departmenty 1331 McKelligon Canyon Rd *Web:* tpwd.texas.gov	El Paso	TX	79930	915-566-6441		665
Exatron Inc 2842 Aiello Dr *Web:* www.exatron.com	San Jose	CA	95111	408-629-7600		253
Excalibre Engineering 9201 Irvine Blvd *TF:* 877-922-5427 ■ *Web:* www.excaliburengineering.com	Irvine	CA	92618	949-454-6603		743
Excalibur Associates Inc 8687 W 108th Ave *Web:* www.excaliburassociates.com	Westminster	CO	80021	303-464-1574		463
Excalibur Data Systems 115 Sagamore Hill Rd *Web:* www.excaliburdata.com	Pittsburgh	PA	15239	724-387-1331		175
Excalibur Engineering Services Inc 962 East 2100 North *Web:* www.excalibur-engineering-services.com	North Logan	UT	84341	435-787-9599		256
Excalibur Equipment LLC *Gregory Industrial Trucks* 285 Eldridge Rd *Web:* www.exequipment.com	Fairfield	NJ	07004	973-808-8399	808-8398	470
Excalibur Extrusions Inc 110 E Crowther Ave *TF:* 800-648-6804 ■ *Web:* www.excaliburextrusions.com	Placentia	CA	92870	714-528-8834	524-7453	596
Excalibur Hotel & Casino 3850 Las Vegas Blvd S *TF:* 877-750-5464 ■ *Web:* www.excalibur.com	Las Vegas	NV	89109	702-597-7777	597-7009	133
Excalibur Technology Corp 700 Fox Glen Lowr Level *TF:* 800-800-0197 ■ *Web:* www.excaltech.com	Barrington	IL	60010	847-842-9570		196
Excedo Solutions Llc 44 Baldwin Dr	Fredericksburg	VA	22406	703-725-3156		180
Exceed Consulting 8259 Woodstone Dr SE *Web:* www.exceed-corp.com	Byron Center	MI	49315	616-698-1800		180
Exceed Resources Inc 294 New Rd *TF:* 800-517-8408 ■ *Web:* www.exceedresourcesinc.com	Monmouth Junction	NJ	08852	732-329-2742		193
Exceed Staffing LLC 363 N Sam Houston Pkwy E Ste 1100 *TF:* 866-609-2884	Houston	TX	77060	866-609-2884		193
Exceed Technologies Inc 2605 Cleda Dr *Web:* www.exceedtech.net	Columbus	MS	39701	662-328-8333		225
Excel Bridge Manufacturing Co 12001 Shoemaker Ave *TF:* 800-548-0054 ■ *Web:* www.excelbridge.com	Santa Fe Springs	CA	90670	562-944-0701		480
Excel Computer Corp 6 Frost Dr *Web:* www.excelme.com	Bangor	ME	04401	207-990-3305	990-3032	180
Excel Decorators Inc 3748 Kentucky Ave *Web:* www.exceldecorators.com	Indianapolis	IN	46221	317-856-1300		184
Excel Diagnostic Imaging Clinics 9701 Richmond Ave Ste 122 *Web:* exceldiagnostics.com	Houston	TX	77042	713-781-6200		383
Excel Funds Management Inc 2810 Matheson Blvd E Ste 800 *Web:* www.excelfunds.com	Mississauga	ON	L4W4X7	905-813-7111		796
Excel Homes Inc 10642 S Susquehanna Trail	Liverpool	PA	17045	717-444-3395	444-7577	187
Excel Machinery Ltd 12100 I-40 E *TF:* 800-858-4002 ■ *Web:* www.excelmach.com	Amarillo	TX	79120	806-335-1553		757
Excel Management Systems Inc 691 N High St 2nd Fl *TF:* 800-276-2957 ■ *Web:* www.emsi.com	Columbus	OH	43215	614-224-4007		196
Excel Manufacturing Inc 1705 E Fourth St *Web:* www.excelmanufacturinginc.com	Seymour	IN	47274	812-523-6764		454
Excel Partners Inc 1177 Summer St *TF:* 800-664-6392 ■ *Web:* www.excel-partners.com	Stamford	CT	06905	203-978-6200		260
Excel Personnel Inc 10111 Inverness Main St Ste 419 *Web:* www.excelpersonnel.com	Englewood	CO	80112	303-427-4600		260
Excel Printing and Mailing 924 E 162nd St *Web:* www.excelprintmail.com	South Holland	IL	60473	708-333-0773		627
Excel Railcar Corp 28367 Davis Pkwy Cantera Lakes Office Campus Ste 300 *TF:* 800-333-5450 ■ *Web:* excelrailcar.com	Warrenville	IL	60555	630-657-1100		23
Excel Screen Printing & Embroidery Inc 10507 Delta Pkwy *TF:* 800-622-1911 ■ *Web:* www.excelscreenprinting.com	Schiller Park	IL	60176	847-801-5200		687
EXCEL Services Corp 11921 Rockville Pk Ste 100 *Web:* www.excelservices.com	Rockville	MD	20852	301-984-4400		256
Ex-Cel Solutions Inc 14618 Grover St *Web:* www.excels.com	Omaha	NE	68144	402-333-6541		175
Excel Sports Boulder 2045 32nd St *Web:* www.excelsports.com	Boulder	CO	80301	303-444-6737		711
Excel Staffing Cos 1700 Louisiana Boulvard NE Ste 210 *TF:* 800-884-3764 ■ *Web:* www.excelstaff.com	Albuquerque	NM	87110	505-262-1871		193
Excel Technologies LLC 3701 Pender Dr *Web:* excel-technologies.com	Fairfax	VA	22030	703-246-9002		180
Excel Telecommunications 433 Las Colinas Blvd Ste 400 *TF:* 877-668-0808 ■ *Web:* www.excel.com	Irving	TX	75039	972-910-1900		736
Excel Tool Inc 2020 First Ave *Web:* www.exceleti.com	Seymour	IN	47274	812-522-6880	522-6524	757
Excel Transportation Inc 333 Ongman Rd *Web:* exceltransportation.ca	Prince George	BC	V2K4K9	250-563-7356		311
Excelda Manufacturing Co 12785 Emerson Dr *TF:* 877-486-3801 ■ *Web:* www.excelda.com	Brighton	MI	48116	248-486-3800	486-3810	145
Exceletech Coating & Applications LLC 221 N Hwy 27 Ste I *TF:* 800-932-3049 ■ *Web:* www.excelcoatings.com	Clermont	FL	34711	352-394-2155		261
Excell Communications Inc 6247 Amber Hills Rd *Web:* www.excellcommunications.com	Trussville	AL	35173	205-956-0198		116
Excell Marketing L C 5501 Park Ave *Web:* www.excellmktg.com	Des Moines	IA	50321	515-244-0300		195
Ex-Cell Metal Products Inc 11240 Melrose St *TF:* 800-392-3557 ■ *Web:* www.ex-cell.com	Franklin Park	IL	60131	847-451-0451	261-9448	286
Excella Consulting Inc 2300 Wilson Blvd Ste 630 *Web:* www.excella.com	Arlington	VA	22201	703-840-8600		180
Excellance Inc 453 Lanier Rd *Web:* www.excellance.com	Madison	AL	35758	256-772-9321		30
Excellent Coffee Company Inc 259 E Ave *Web:* excellentcoffee.com	Pawtucket	RI	02860	401-724-6393	724-0560	296-7
Excelleris Technologies Inc 4445 Lougheed Hwy Ste 201 *TF:* 866-728-4777 ■ *Web:* www.excelleris.com	Burnaby	BC	V5C0E4	866-728-4777		45
Excelligence Learning Corp 2 Lower Ragsdale Dr Ste 125 *TF:* 800-627-2829 ■ *Web:* excelligence.com	Monterey	CA	93940	831-333-5572		243
Excelline Food Products LLC 20232 Sunburst St *Web:* www.excellinefoods.com	Chatsworth	CA	91311	818-701-7710		123
Excello Circuits & Mfg Corp 1924 Nancita Cr *Web:* www.excello.com	Placentia	CA	92870	714-993-0560		625
Excellon Automation Inc 20001 S Rancho Way *TF:* 800-392-3556 ■ *Web:* www.excellon.com	Rancho Dominguez	CA	90220	310-668-7700	668-7800	470
Excellus BlueCross BlueShield PO Box 22999 *TF:* 800-278-1247 ■ *Web:* www.excellusbcbs.com	Rochester	NY	14692	585-454-1700		391-3
Excellus BlueCross BlueShield of Central New York 333 Butternut Dr **Fax: Cust Svc* ■ *TF:* 800-633-6066 ■ *Web:* www.excellusbcbs.com	Syracuse	NY	13214	315-671-6400	671-6752*	391-3
Excelsior College 7 Columbia Cir **Fax: Admissions* ■ *TF:* 888-647-2388 ■ *Web:* www.excelsior.edu	Albany	NY	12203	518-464-8500	464-8833*	166
Excelsior Defense Inc 2232 Central Ave *TF:* 877-955-4636 ■ *Web:* www.excelsiordefense.com	Saint Petersburg	FL	33712	727-527-9600		693

Company	City	State	ZIP	Phone	Fax	Class
Excelsior Electric Membership Corp 986 SE Broad St *Web:* www.excelsioremc.com	Metter	GA	30439	912-685-2115	685-5782	245
Excelsior Grand 2380 Hylan Blvd *TF:* 800-532-7245 ■ *Web:* www.excelsiorgrand.com	Staten Island	NY	10306	718-987-4800	987-4803	299
Excelsior Marking Products 888 W Waterloo Rd *TF:* 800-433-3615 ■ *Web:* www.excelsiormarking.com	Akron	OH	44314	330-745-2300	745-2333	467
Excelsior Medical Corp 1933 Heck Ave *Web:* www.excelsiormedical.com	Neptune	NJ	07753	732-776-7525		596
Excelsior Printing Company Inc 123 MASS MoCA Way *Web:* www.excelsiorprinting.com	North Adams	MA	01247	413-663-3771		627
Excelsior Springs Standard 417 S Thompson Ave *Web:* www.excelsiorspringsstandard.com	Excelsior Springs	MO	64024	816-637-6155	637-8411	532-2
Excelsys 3230 N Braeswood Blvd. *Web:* excelsys.org	Houston	TX	77025	713-662-0172		768
Excelta Corp 60 Easy St. *TF:* 800-899-3611 ■ *Web:* www.excelta.com	Buellton	CA	93427	805-686-4686		351
Exceptional Home Care LLP 1510 E Grande Blvd *Web:* ehctx.com	Tyler	TX	75703	903-533-0290		363
Excet 8001 Braddock Rd Ste 360 *Web:* www.excetinc.com	Springfield	VA	22151	703-635-7089		624
Exchange Conference Ctr 212 Northern Ave *Web:* www.exchangeconferencecenter.com	Boston	MA	02210	617-790-1900		205
Exchange State Bank 3992 Chandler St PO Box 68 *TF:* 888-488-9300 ■ *Web:* www.exchangestatebank.com	Carsonville	MI	48419	810-657-9333		70
Exchange, The 3911 S Walton Walker Blvd *TF:* 800-527-2345 ■ *Web:* www.shopmyexchange.com	Dallas	TX	75236	800-527-2345	446-0163	791
Excipio Consulting LLC 1216 E Kenosha St *Web:* www.excipio.net	Broken Arrow	OK	74012	918-357-5507		401
Exclaim Inc 220 N Smith St Ste 204 *Web:* www.exclaim-inc.com	Palatine	IL	60067	847-392-0008		4
Exclaimit Inc 3825 Misty Landing Dr *Web:* www.exclaimit.com	Valrico	FL	33594	813-731-8718		195
EXCO Resources Inc 12377 Merit Dr Ste 1700 *NYSE:* XCO ■ *TF:* 888-788-9449 ■ *Web:* www.excoresources.com	Dallas	TX	75251	214-368-2084	368-2087	538
Exec Air Montana Inc 2430 Airport Rd *TF:* 800-513-2190 ■ *Web:* www.execairmontana.com	Helena	MT	59601	406-442-2190	442-2199	13
Exec Inc 277 Carolina St *Web:* iamexec.com	San Francisco	CA	94103	415-275-8094		387
ExecSuite 702 3 Ave SW Ste 702 *TF:* 800-667-4980 ■ *Web:* www.execsuite.ca	Calgary	AB	T2P3B4	403-294-5800	294-5959	210
Execulink Telecom Inc 619 Main St N *TF:* 866-706-1994 ■ *Web:* www.execulink.com	Burgessville	ON	N0J1C0	866-706-1994		224
ExecUNet Inc 295 Westport Ave *TF:* 800-637-3126 ■ *Web:* www.execunet.com	Norwalk	CT	06851	203-750-1030		260
Execupharm Inc 500 N Gulph Rd Ste 120 *Web:* www.execupharm.com	King Of Prussia	PA	19406	610-272-8771	272-8056	721
Execushield Inc 4104 24th St *Web:* www.execushield.com	San Francisco	CA	94114	415-508-0825		693
Execusys Inc 6767 N Wickham Rd *TF:* 800-454-3081 ■ *Web:* execusys.com	Melbourne	FL	32940	321-253-0077		177
Executech 4000 Genesee Pl Ste 213 *Web:* www.esc-techsolutions.com	Woodbridge	VA	22192	571-285-3331		179
Executive Administration Inc 85 W Algonquin Rd Ste 550 *Web:* www.execadmin.com	Arlington Heights	IL	60005	847-427-9600		47
Executive Air 2131 Airport Dr Austin Straubel International Airport *TF:* 800-335-1731 ■ *Web:* www.executiveair.com	Green Bay	WI	54313	920-498-4880	498-4890	63
Executive Arrangements 2460 Fairmount Blvd Ste 205 *Web:* www.executivearrangements.com	Cleveland	OH	44106	216-231-9311		184
Executive Business Media Inc 825 Old Country Rd *Web:* www.ebmpubs.com	Westbury	NY	11590	516-334-3030	334-3059	463
Executive Cabinetry 2838 Grandview Dr *Web:* www.executivecabinetry.com	Simpsonville	SC	29680	864-963-7011		115
Executive Car Leasing Inc 7807 Santa Monica Blvd *TF:* 800-994-2277 ■ *Web:* www.executivecarleasing.com	Los Angeles	CA	90046	323-654-5000	848-9015	289
Executive Coach Builders Inc 4400 W Production St *Web:* www.ecblimo.com	Springfield	MO	65803	417-831-3535		59
Executive Director Inc 555 E Wells St Ste 1100 *Web:* www.execinc.com	Milwaukee	WI	53202	414-276-6445	276-3349	47
Executive Diversity Services Inc 675 S Ln St Ste 305 *Web:* www.executivediversity.com	Seattle	WA	98104	206-224-9293		463
Executive Hotel Vintage Court 650 Bush St *TF:* 888-388-3932 ■ *Web:* www.executivehotels.net	San Francisco	CA	94108	415-392-4666	433-4065	379
Executive Inn 978 Phillips Ln *TF:* 888-205-8144 ■ *Web:* hotelplanner.com	Louisville	KY	40209	502-367-6161		379
Executive Inn Group Corp *Executive Hotels & Resorts* 1080 Howe St 8th Fl *TF:* 866-642-6888 ■ *Web:* www.executivehotels.net	Vancouver	BC	V6Z2T1	604-642-5250	642-5255	379
Executive Jet 4556 Airport Rd. *TF:* 877-356-5387 ■ *Web:* www.executivejetmanagement.com	Cincinnati	OH	45226	513-979-6600	979-6600	13
Executive Management Assoc 210 N Glenoaks Blvd Ste C *Web:* www.emaoffice.com	Burbank	CA	91502	818-843-5660	843-7423	47
Executive Monetary Management LLC 220 E 42nd St 32nd Fl *Web:* www.michaelbolton.com	New York	NY	10017	212-476-5555		401
Executive Office Concepts Inc 1705 S Anderson Ave *TF:* 800-421-5927 ■ *Web:* www.eoccorp.com	Compton	CA	90220	310-537-1657		319-1
Executive Office for Immigration Review 5107 Leesburg Pike *Web:* www.justice.gov	Falls Church	VA	22041	703-305-0289	605-0365	340-14
Executive Office for US Trustees 950 Pennsylvania Ave NW *TF:* 800-877-8339 ■ *Web:* www.justice.gov	Washington	DC	20530-0001	202-353-1555	307-2397	340-14
Executive Pacific Plaza Hotel 400 Spring St *TF:* 888-388-3932 ■ *Web:* executivehotels.net/downtownseattlehotel	Seattle	WA	98104	206-623-3900	623-2059	379
Executive Protection Institute 16 Penn Plaza Ste 1570 *TF:* 800-947-5827 ■ *Web:* www.personalprotection.com	New York	NY	10001	212-268-4555		766
Executive Resources International LLC 63 Atlantic Ave *Web:* erisearch.net	Boston	MA	02110	617-742-8970		193
Executive Self Storage Assoc Inc 5353 W Dartmouth Ave Ste 401 *Web:* www.executiveselfstorage.com	Denver	CO	80227	303-703-1289	703-1289	803-3
Executive Sounding Board Associates Inc 3959 Welsh Rd Ste 354 *TF:* 800-870-7244 ■ *Web:* www.esba.com	Willow Grove	PA	19090	215-568-5788		463
Executive Speakers Bureau 8567 Cordes Cir *TF:* 800-754-9404 ■ *Web:* www.executivespeakers.com	Germantown	TN	38139	901-754-9404	756-4237	708
Executive Suite Hotel 4360 SpenaRd Rd	Anchorage	AK	99517	907-243-6366		379
Executive Surf Club 309 N Water St *Web:* www.waterstmarketcc.com/executive-surf-club	Corpus Christi	TX	78401	361-884-7873		671
Executive Technologies Corp 8731 Northpark Blvd Ste B *Web:* www.executivetechcorp.com	Charleston	SC	29406	843-824-5906		693
Executive Travel Consultants Ltd 345 118th Ave SE Ste 130 *Web:* www.etctravel.com	Bellevue	WA	98005	425-453-8200		772
Executive Travel Inc 1212 O St *Web:* www.executivetravel.com	Lincoln	NE	68508	402-435-8888		772
Executive Visions Inc 7000 Miller Ct E *Web:* www.executivevisions.com	Norcross	GA	30071	770-416-6100		181
Executive Women International (EWI) 3860 S 2300 E *TF:* 877-439-4669 ■ *Web:* ewiconnect.com	Salt Lake City	UT	84109	801-355-2800		49-12
Executrade 9917 112 St NW *Web:* www.executrade.com	Edmonton	AB	T5K1L6	780-944-1122		260
Exedy America Corp 2121 Holston Bend Dr *Web:* eac.exedy.com	Mascot	TN	37806	865-932-3700		247
Exel 570 Polaris Pkwy *Web:* www.exel.com	Westerville	OH	43082	614-865-8500		449
eXelate 7 W 22nd St 9th Fl. *TF:* 877-896-3282 ■ *Web:* exelate.com	New York	NY	10010	646-380-4400	448-4541	466
Exelixis Inc 210 E Grand Ave *NASDAQ:* EXEL ■ *TF:* 800-732-0330 ■ *Web:* www.exelixis.com	South San Francisco	CA	94080	650-837-7000	837-8300	85
Exergen Corp 400 Pleasant St *Web:* www.exergen.com	Watertown	MA	02472	617-923-9900	923-9911	419
Exergonix Inc 101 SE 30th St *Web:* www.exergonix.com	Lees Summit	MO	64082	816-875-4790		262
Exergy LLC 320 Endo Blvd *Web:* www.exergyllc.com	Garden City	NY	11530	516-832-9300		480
Exerplay Inc 12001 State Hwy 14 N. *TF:* 800-457-5444 ■ *Web:* www.exerplay.com	Cedar Crest	NM	87008	505-281-0151		711
Exerve Inc 2909 Langford Rd Ste 400B *TF:* 800-364-0637 ■ *Web:* www.exerve.com	Norcross	GA	30071	770-447-1566		734
Exeter Hospital 5 Alumni Dr *Web:* www.exeterhospital.com	Exeter	NH	03833	603-580-6668		374-3
Exeter Unified School District 1107 E Rocky Hill Dr	Exeter	CA	93221	559-592-4420		685
EXFO Inc 400 Godin Ave *NASDAQ:* EXFO ■ *TF:* 800-663-3936 ■ *Web:* www.exfo.com	Quebec	QC	G1M2K2	418-683-0211	683-2170	248
Exhibit Concepts Inc 700 Crossroads Ct *TF:* 800-324-5063 ■ *Web:* www.exhibitconcepts.com	Vandalia	OH	45377	800-324-5063		184
Exhibit Designers & Producers Assn (EDPA) 19 Compo Rd S *Web:* www.edpa.com	Westport	CT	06880	203-557-6321		49-18
Exhibit Museum of Natural History 1109 Geddes Ave *Web:* www.lsa.umich.edu	Ann Arbor	MI	48109	734-764-0478	647-2767	520
Exhibit Source Inc, The 145 Wells Ave. *TF:* 800-370-0736 ■ *Web:* www.theexhibitsource.com	Newton Center	MA	02459	781-449-1600		393
Exhibitors Carpet Service Inc 6112 W 73rd St	Bedford Park	IL	60638	773-247-0604		264-2
Exhibits & More 7843 Goguen Dr *Web:* www.exhibitsandmore.com	Liverpool	NY	13090	315-652-0383		232
Exhibits Development Group LLC Landmark Ctr 432 75 W Fifth St *Web:* www.exhibitsdevelopment.com	Saint Paul	MN	55102	651-222-1121		184
exidacom LLC 64 N Main St *Web:* www.exida.com	Sellersville	PA	18960	215-453-1720		256
Exide Technologies 13000 Deerfield Pkwy Bldg 200 *NASDAQ:* XIDE ■ *TF:* 888-563-6300 ■ *Web:* www.exide.com	Milton	GA	30004	678-566-9000	566-9188	74
Exiss Aluminum Trailers Inc 900 East Trailer Blvd *TF:* 877-553-9477 ■ *Web:* www.exiss.com	El Reno	OK	73036	877-553-9477		120
EXIT Theatre 156 Eddy St *Web:* www.theexit.org	San Francisco	CA	94102	415-931-1094	931-2699	572
ExitCertified 8950 Cal Center Dr Bldg 1 Ste 110 *TF:* 800-803-3948 ■ *Web:* www.exitcertified.com	Sacramento	CA	95826	916-669-3970	669-3977	179

	Phone	Fax	Class
Exl Media Corp			
803 Tahoe Blvd Ste 7 . . . . . Incline Village NV 89451	775-832-0202		7
Web: www.exlmedia.com			
Exobase Corp 3150 De La Cruz Blvd . . . . . Santa Clara CA 95054	408-235-8808		180
Exocor Inc 271 Ridley Rd . . . . . St. Catharines ON L2R6P7	905-704-0603		111
TF: 888-317-2209 ■ *Web:* exocor.com			
Exodus Film Group Inc			
1255 Electric Ave . . . . . Venice CA 90291	310-392-7778	392-7728	514
Web: www.exodusfilmgroup.com			
Exodyne Inc 8433 N Black Canyon Hwy . . . . . Phoenix AZ 85021	602-995-3700	995-4091	261
Web: www.exodyne.com			
ExOne Co 127 Industry Blvd . . . . . North Huntingdon PA 15642	724-863-9663		628
TF: 800-893-6315 ■ *Web:* www.exone.com			
Exopack Advanced Coatings			
700 Crestdale St . . . . . Matthews NC 28105	704-847-9171	845-4307	552-1
Web: coverisadvancedcoatings.com			
Exopack LLC			
23810 China Lake Ct PO Box 5687 . . . . . Katy TX 77494	864-596-7140	596-7150	548
TF: 877-447-3539			
Exopolis Inc 3000 E Cesar Chavez . . . . . Austin TX 78702	512-708-1113		5
Web: www.exopolis.com			
Exordium Group Inc, The			
25670 Chapin Rd . . . . . Los Altos Hills CA 94022	435-940-0600		344
Web: www.exordiumgroup.com			
Exothermics Inc 5040 Enterprise Blvd . . . . . Toledo OH 43612	419-729-9726		91
Web: www.eclipsenet.com			
Exotic Automation & Supply Inc			
34700 Grand River Ave . . . . . Farmington Hills MI 48335	248-477-2122	477-0427	608
Web: www.exoticautomation.com			
Exotic Metals Forming Company LLC			
5411 S 226th St . . . . . Kent WA 98032	253-395-3710		22
Web: www.exoticmetals.com			
Exoxemis Inc 6029 N 16th St . . . . . Omaha NE 68110	402-884-2316		231
Expanding Light			
14618 Tyler Foote Rd . . . . . Nevada City CA 95959	530-478-7518	478-7519	673
TF: 800-346-5350 ■ *Web:* www.expandinglight.org			
Expanko Inc 180 Gordon Dr Ste 113 . . . . . Exton PA 19341	800-345-6202	363-0735*	291
**Fax Area Code:* 610 ■ *TF:* 800-345-6202 ■ *Web:* www.expanko.com			
Expansion Management Magazine			
1300 E Ninth St . . . . . Cleveland OH 44114	216-696-7000		457-5
TF: 866-505-7173 ■ *Web:* www.industryweek.com			
Expansion Strategies Inc			
17 Rollingwood Dr . . . . . New Hartford NY 13413	315-793-3137		463
Expanxion			
860 Hampshire Rd Ste I . . . . . Westlake Village CA 91361	650-261-0211		260
Web: expanxion.com			
Expedient Communications			
810 Parish St . . . . . Pittsburgh PA 15220	412-316-7800		398
TF: 877-570-7827 ■ *Web:* www.expedient.com			
Expedition Trips.com			
6553 California Ave SW . . . . . Seattle WA 98136	206-547-0700		772
TF: 877-412-8527 ■ *Web:* www.expeditiontrips.com			
Expeditor Systems Inc			
4090 Nine McFarland Dr . . . . . Alpharetta GA 30004	800-226-8158		475
TF: 800-226-8158 ■ *Web:* www.expeditor.com			
Expeditors International of Washington Inc			
1015 Third Ave 12th Fl . . . . . Seattle WA 98104	206-674-3400	682-9777	449
NASDAQ: EXPD ■ *Web:* www.expeditors.com			
Expense Reduction Analysts Inc			
16479 N Dallas Pkwy Bent Tree Twr II Ste 240 . . . . . Addison TX 75001	469-310-2970		463
TF: 800-383-0804 ■ *Web:* www.expensereduction.com			
ExpenseVisor 910 Kenyon Ct Ste 110 . . . . . Charlotte NC 28211	704-644-0019		809
Web: www.payservice.com			
Experian Information Solutions Inc			
475 Anton Blvd . . . . . Costa Mesa CA 92626	714-830-7000		218
TF Cust Svc: 888-397-3742 ■ *Web:* www.experian.com			
Experience Bryan College Station (BCSCVB)			
715 University Dr E . . . . . College Station TX 77840	979-260-9898	260-9800	206
TF: 800-777-8292 ■ *Web:* www.visitaggieland.com			
ExpERIEnce Children's Museum			
420 French St . . . . . Erie PA 16507	814-453-3743		521
Web: www.eriechildrensmuseum.org			
Experience Corp, The 127A E 71st St . . . . . New York NY 10021	212-794-8801		195
Web: richardattiasassociates.com			
Experience Works Inc			
4401 Wilson Blvd Ste 1100 . . . . . Arlington VA 22203	703-522-7272	522-0141	48-6
TF: 866-397-9757 ■ *Web:* www.experienceworks.org			
Experient Inc			
2500 E Enterprise Pkwy . . . . . Twinsburg OH 44087	330-425-8333	425-3299	184
TF: 800-935-0333 ■ *Web:* www.experient-inc.com			
Experimental Aircraft Assn (EAA)			
3000 Poberezny Rd . . . . . Oshkosh WI 54902	920-426-4800	426-4828	48-18
TF: 800-236-4800 ■ *Web:* www.eaa.org			
Experi-Metal Inc			
6385 Wall St . . . . . Sterling Heights MI 48312	586-977-7800	977-6981	697
Web: www.experi-metal.com			
Experis Data Centers Inc			
7272 Wisconsin Ave Ste 330 . . . . . Bethesda MD 20814	240-223-0607		387
Web: www.experisdatacenters.com			
Expert Choice Inc			
1501 Lee Hwy Ste 302 . . . . . Arlington VA 22209	703-243-5595	243-5587	178-12
TF: 888-259-6400 ■ *Web:* www.expertchoice.com			
Expert Communications Inc			
394 Pacific Ave . . . . . San Francisco CA 94111	415-981-9900		7
Web: www.eciww.com			
ExPert E&P Consultants LLC			
101 Ashland Way . . . . . Madisonville LA 70447	985-801-4040		539
TF: 888-231-8639 ■ *Web:* www.expertep.com			
Expert Evidence Report			
1801 S Bell St . . . . . Arlington VA 22202	800-372-1033		531-7
TF: 800-372-1033 ■ *Web:* www.bna.com/expert-evidence-report-p5463			
Expert Global Solutions, Inc			
507 Prudential Rd . . . . . Horsham PA 19044	215-441-3000	269-8669*	160
**Fax Area Code:* 866 ■ *Web:* www.ncogroup.com			
Expert Industries Inc 848 E 43rd St . . . . . Brooklyn NY 11210	718-434-6060		770
TF: 800-424-2282 ■ *Web:* www.rubiconhx.com			
Expert Laser Service			
62 Pleasant St PO Box 744 . . . . . Southbridge MA 01550	800-622-3535		175
TF: 800-622-3535 ■ *Web:* www.expertlaserservices.com			

	Phone	Fax	Class
Expert Recruiters 883 Helmcken St . . . . . Vancouver BC V6Z1B1	604-689-3600		260
TF: 888-407-7799 ■ *Web:* www.expertrecruiters.com			
Expert System Applications Inc			
2681 Ashley Rd . . . . . Shaker Heights OH 44122	440-668-8184		180
Web: www.expert-system.com			
Experts Exchange LLC			
PO Box 1062 . . . . . San Luis Obispo CA 93406	805-787-0603		177
Web: www.experts-exchange.com			
Experts Inc, The			
2400 E Commercial Blvd Ste 614 . . . . . Fort Lauderdale FL 33308	954-493-8040		177
Experts-conseils Cep Inc			
1345 Boul Louis-xiv . . . . . Quebec QC G2L1M4	418-622-4480		261
Web: www.expcep.com			
Explora 1701 Mtn Rd NW . . . . . Albuquerque NM 87104	505-224-8300	224-8325	520
Web: explora.us			
Exploration Place 300 N McLean Blvd . . . . . Wichita KS 67203	316-660-0600	660-0670	521
TF: 877-904-1444 ■ *Web:* www.exploration.org			
Exploratorium, The Pier 15 . . . . . San Francisco CA 94111	415-528-4444	561-0370	520
Web: www.exploratorium.edu			
Explore & More Hands-On Children's Museum			
20 E High St . . . . . Gettysburg PA 17325	717-337-9151		521
Web: www.exploreandmore.com			
Explore & More-A Children's Museum			
300 Gleed Ave . . . . . East Aurora NY 14052	716-655-5131		521
Web: www.exploreandmore.org			
Explore Communications Inc			
3213 Zuni St . . . . . Denver CO 80211	303-393-0567		4
Web: www.explorehq.com			
Explore Information Services LLC			
2750 Blue Water Rd Ste 200 . . . . . Eagan MN 55121	800-531-9125	681-4476*	635
**Fax Area Code:* 651 ■ *TF:* 800-531-9125 ■ *Web:* www.exploredata.com			
Exploreco International LLC			
11930 S Sam Houston Pkwy E . . . . . Houston TX 77089	713-796-6000		492
Web: www.exploreco.com			
Explorer Competition Products			
2360 Boswell Rd . . . . . Chula Vista CA 91914	619-216-1444		451
Web: www.explorerprocomp.com			
Explorica Inc 145 Tremont St . . . . . Boston MA 02111	888-310-7120	310-7088	760
TF: 888-310-7120 ■ *Web:* www.explorica.com			
Exploris 401 Hillsborough St . . . . . Raleigh NC 27603	919-715-3690		685
Web: www.exploris.org			
Explorium of Lexington			
440 W Short St . . . . . Lexington KY 40507	859-258-3253	258-3255	521
Web: www.explorium.com			
Expo Chemical Company Inc			
6807 Theall Rd Ste A . . . . . Houston TX 77066	281-895-9200		146
Web: expochem.com			
Expo Group, The 5931 W Campus Cir Dr . . . . . Irving TX 75063	972-580-9000	550-7877	184
TF: 800-736-7775 ■ *Web:* www.theexpogroup.com			
Expo Square 4145 E 21st St . . . . . Tulsa OK 74114	918-744-1113	744-8725	205
TF: 877-781-2660 ■ *Web:* www.exposquare.com			
ExpoMarketing LLC 2741 Dow Ave . . . . . Tustin CA 92780	949-250-3976		184
TF: 800-867-3976 ■ *Web:* www.expomarketing.com			
Expon Exhibits 909 Fee Dr . . . . . Sacramento CA 95815	916-924-1600		232
TF: 800-783-9766 ■ *Web:* www.exponexhibits.com			
Exponent Inc 149 Commonwealth Dr . . . . . Menlo Park CA 94025	650-326-9400	326-8072	668
NASDAQ: EXPO ■ *TF:* 888-656-3976 ■ *Web:* www.exponent.com			
Exponent Telegram 324 Hewes Ave . . . . . Clarksburg WV 26301	800-982-6034	624-4188*	532-2
**Fax Area Code:* 304 ■ *TF:* 800-982-6034 ■ *Web:* theet.com			
Exponential Engineering Co			
2950 East Harmony Rd Ste 265 . . . . . Fort Collins CO 80528	970-207-9648		261
Web: www.exponentialengineering.com			
ExpoPlus			
1055 Research Ctr Atlanta Dr SW . . . . . Atlanta GA 30331	404-699-0650		7
Web: www.expoplus.com			
Export Corp 6060 Whitmore Lake Rd . . . . . Brighton MI 48116	810-227-6153		549
TF: 800-644-4032 ■ *Web:* www.exportcorporation.com			
Export-Import Bank of the US			
811 Vermont Ave NW . . . . . Washington DC 20571	202-565-3946		340-20
TF: 800-565-3946 ■ *Web:* www.exim.gov			
Exporting Commodities International Inc			
12000 Lincoln Dr W Ste 108 . . . . . Marlton NJ 08053	856-797-2004		791
Web: www.eci-coal.com			
Expoships LLLP			
27598 Riverview Ctr Blvd . . . . . Bonita Springs FL 34134	239-949-5411		387
Exposition Gardens 1601 W Northmoor Rd . . . . . Peoria IL 61614	309-691-6332	691-2372	205
Web: www.expogardensinc.com			
Expositor, The 195 Henry St Bldg 4 . . . . . Brantford ON N3S5C9	519-756-2020	756-3285	532-1
Web: www.brantfordexpositor.ca			
Expotel Hospitality Services LLC			
401 Veterans Memorial Blvd Ste 102 . . . . . Metairie LA 70005	504-212-1492		463
TF: 800-345-8082 ■ *Web:* www.expotelhospitality.com			
Express 1 Limited Pkwy . . . . . Columbus OH 43230	888-397-1980		157-6
NYSE: EXPR ■ *TF:* 888-397-1980 ■ *Web:* www.express.com			
Express Construction Company Inc			
355 118th Ave SE Ste 100 . . . . . Bellevue WA 98005	206-230-8500		186
Web: www.expressconstruction.net			
Express Contracting 420 Milam . . . . . San Antonio TX 78202	210-337-2260		492
Web: www.expressmetalwork.com			
Express Diagnostics Int'l Inc			
1550 Industrial Dr . . . . . Blue Earth MN 56013	507-526-3951		415
Web: www.drugcheck.com			
Express Employment Professionals			
9701 Boardwalk Blvd . . . . . Oklahoma City OK 73162	405-840-5000		721
TF: 800-222-4057 ■ *Web:* www.expresspros.com			
Express Envelopes Unlimited LLP			
1745 Suburban Dr . . . . . De Pere WI 54115	920-997-0182		627
Web: expressenvelopesunlimited.com			
Express Image Inc 2942 Rice St . . . . . Little Canada MN 55113	866-482-8602		687
TF: 866-482-8602 ■ *Web:* expressimage.com			
Express Immigration & Paralegal Services			
10143 Sepulveda Blvd . . . . . Mission Hills CA 91345	818-894-4611		226
Express Logic Inc			
11423 W Bernardo Ct . . . . . San Diego CA 92127	858-613-6640		179
Web: www.expresslogic.com			
Express Manufacturing Inc			
3519 W Warner Ave . . . . . Santa Ana CA 92704	714-979-2228	556-0575	454
Web: www.eminc.com			

	City	State	Zip	Phone	Fax	Class
Express Marine Inc PO Box 329	Pennsauken	NJ	08110	856-541-4600	541-0338	312
TF: 800-222-4591 ■ *Web:* www.expressmarine.com						
Express Oil Change 1880 S Pk Dr	Hoover	AL	35244	205-945-1771		62-5
TF: 888-945-1771 ■ *Web:* www.expressoil.com						
Express Packaging of Ohio Inc						
301 Enterprise Dr	Newcomerstown	OH	43832	740-498-4700		393
Web: www.expresspackaging.net						
Express Printing & Graphics Inc						
1205 Alderwood Ave.	Sunnyvale	CA	94089	408-400-0223		627
Web: expressprintingusa.com						
Express Technologies						
117 Vip Dr Ste 110	Wexford	PA	15090	724-940-5000		525
Web: www.xpresstech.com						
Express Tire 1148 Industrial Ave	Escondido	CA	92029	760-741-4044		62-5
Web: www.expresstire.com						
Expresscopy.com 6623 NE 59th Pl.	Portland	OR	97218	503-234-4880		627
TF: 800-260-5887 ■ *Web:* www.expresscopy.com						
Expression Home Gallery						
2273 S La Crosse Ave Ste 105	Colton	CA	92324	909-433-3990		321
Expression Pathology Inc						
9620 Medical Ctr Dr Ste100	Rockville	MD	20850	301-977-3654		668
Web: www.expressionpathology.com						
ExpressJet Airlines Inc						
990 Toffie Terr.	Atlanta	GA	30354	404-856-1000		25
Web: www.expressjet.com						
ExpressJet Holdings Inc						
990 Toffie Terrac	Atlanta	GA	30354	404-856-1000		360-1
Web: www.expressjet.com						
Express-News Corp PO Box 2171	San Antonio	TX	78297	210-250-3000		637-8
TF: 800-555-1551 ■ *Web:* www.mysanantonio.com						
Express-Times 30 N Fourth St.	Easton	PA	18042	610-258-7171	258-7130	532-2
Web: www.lehighvalleylive.com						
Expressway Hotels 4303 17th Ave S	Fargo	ND	58103	701-239-4303		379
TF: 877-239-4303 ■ *Web:* expresswaysuitesfargo.com						
Expressworks International Inc						
5619 Scotts Vly Dr	Scotts Valley	CA	95066	831-440-9300		256
Web: www.expressworks.com						
ExRx.net LLC 4236 Bell St	Kansas City	MO	64111	913-481-9335		690
Web: www.exrx.net						
EXSIF Worldwide Inc						
2700 Westchester Ave Ste 400	Purchase	NY	10577	914-848-4200	848-4201	264-5
Web: www.exsif.com						
EXSL/Ultra Labs Inc 30921 Wiegman Rd	Hayward	CA	94544	510-324-4567	324-8881	406
TF: 800-535-5053 ■ *Web:* exsl.net						
Ex-Students' Association, The						
2110 San Jacinto Blvd	Austin	TX	78712	512-471-8839		138
Web: www.texasexes.org						
Extant Aerospace 1615 W NASA Blvd	Melbourne	FL	32901	321-254-1500	259-4122	735
Web: www.symetrics.com						
Extech LLC						
455 Main St Bldg 1 Ste A-B	Deep River	CT	06417	860-526-2610		261
Extended Care Hospital Westminster						
206 Hospital Cir	Westminster	CA	92683	714-891-2769	895-9069	450
TF: 800-236-9747						
Extended Presence						
3570 E 12th Ave Ste 200	Denver	CO	80206	303-892-5881		317
TF: 800-398-8957 ■ *Web:* www.extendedpresence.com						
Extended Stay America						
11525 N Community House Rd Ste 100	Charlotte	NC	28277	980-345-1600		379
TF: 800-804-3724 ■ *Web:* www.extendedstayamerica.com						
Extended Stay Hotels						
Crossland Economy Studios						
11525 N Community House Rd Ste 100	Charlotte	NC	28277	980-345-1600		379
TF: 877-398-3633 ■ *Web:* www.crosslandstudios.com						
Extended StayAmerica						
11525 N Community House Rd Ste 100	Charlotte	NC	28277	980-345-1600		379
TF: 800-804-3724 ■ *Web:* www.extendedstayamerica.com						
Extendicare Inc 3000 Steeles Ave E	Markham	ON	L3R9W2	905-470-4000	470-5588	451
NYSE: EXE ■ *Web:* www.extendicare.com						
Extensis 1800 SW First Ave Ste 500	Portland	OR	97201	503-274-2020	274-0530	177
TF: 800-796-9798 ■ *Web:* www.extensis.com						
Exterior Wood Inc 2685 Index St	Washougal	WA	98671	360-835-8561		818
TF: 800-222-1222 ■ *Web:* www.exteriorwood.com						
Externetworks 10 Corporate Pl S	Piscataway	NJ	08854	732-465-0001		177
TF: 800-238-6360 ■ *Web:* www.externetworks.com						
Exterran 16666 Northchase Dr	Houston	TX	77060	281-836-7000		385
Web: www.exterran.com						
Exterran Water Solutions Ltd						
1721 27th Ave North E	Calgary	AB	T2E7E1	403-219-2210		539
Web: www.exterran.com						
EXTOL International Inc						
529 Terry Reiley Way	Pottsville	PA	17901	570-628-5500	628-6983	178-7
TF: 800-542-7284 ■ *Web:* www.extol.com						
Extole Inc						
350 Sansome St Ste 700	San Francisco	CA	94104	415-625-0411		195
Web: www.extole.com						
Exton Region Chamber of Commerce						
185 Exton Square Mall	Exton	PA	19341	610-363-7746		139
TF: 800-666-0191 ■ *Web:* www.ercc.net						
Extra Help Inc 3911 W Ernestine Dr	Marion	IL	62959	618-993-9675		141
Web: www.extrahelpinc.com						
Extra Mile Mktg Inc						
12600 SE 38th St Ste 205	Bellevue	WA	98006	425-746-1572		194
TF: 866-907-1753 ■ *Web:* www.extramilemarketing.com						
Extraco Technology PO Box 2299	Waco	TX	76710	866-428-9070		509
TF: 866-428-9070 ■ *Web:* www.extraco.tech						
Extraordinary Events						
13425 Ventura Blvd Ste 300	Sherman Oaks	CA	91423	818-783-6112		149
Web: www.extraordinaryevents.net						
ExtraView Corp						
269 Mt Hermon Rd Ste 207	Scotts Valley	CA	95066	831-461-7100		174
Web: www.extraview.com						
Extrel CMS LLC 575 Epsilon Dr	Pittsburgh	PA	15238	412-963-7530		246
Web: www.extrel.com						
Extreme Engineering Solutions Inc						
3225 Deming Way Ste 120	Middleton	WI	53562	608-833-1155		261
Web: xes-inc.com						
Extreme Networks Inc						
3585 Monroe St	Santa Clara	CA	95051	408-579-2800	579-3000	176
NASDAQ: EXTR ■ *TF:* 888-257-3000 ■ *Web:* www.extremenetworks.com						
Extreme Packing Solutions 5 Dodge St	Beverly	MA	01915	978-232-9190		7
TF: 800-335-9996 ■ *Web:* extremepackingsolutions.com						
Extreme Pita 2187 Dunwin Dr	Mississauga	ON	L5L1X2	905-820-7887		310
TF: 800-563-6688 ■ *Web:* www.extremepita.com						
Extreme Plastics Plus						
360 Epic Circle Dr	Fairmont	WV	26554	866-408-2837		536
TF: 866-408-2837 ■ *Web:* www.extremeplasticsplus.com						
Extreme Reach Inc						
75 Second Ave Ste 720	Needham	MA	02494	781-577-2016		511
NASDAQ: DGIT ■ *TF:* 877-769-9382 ■ *Web:* extremereach.com						
Extron Electronics 1230 S Lewis St	Anaheim	CA	92805	714-491-1500	491-1517	52
TF Tech Supp: 800-633-9876 ■ *Web:* www.extron.com						
Extron Logistics LLC						
496 S Abbott Ave	Milpitas	CA	95035	510-353-0177		449
Web: www.extroninc.com						
Extrude Hone Corp 235 Industry Blvd	Irwin	PA	15642	724-863-5900	863-8759	455
TF: 800-835-3668 ■ *Web:* www.kennametal.com						
Extruded Aluminum Corp						
7200 Industrial Dr	Belding	MI	48809	616-794-0300		492
Web: www.extrudedaluminum.com						
Extrudex Aluminum Ltd						
411 Chrislea Rd	Woodbridge	ON	L4L8N4	416-745-4444		492
TF: 800-668-7210 ■ *Web:* www.extrudex.com						
Extrutech Plastics Inc D/B/A Epi						
5902 W Custer St	Manitowoc	WI	54220	920-684-9650		596
Web: www.epiplastics.com						
Exvere Inc 1301 Fifth Ave Ste 3405	Seattle	WA	98101	206-728-1800		401
Web: www.exvere.com						
Exxact Corp 45445 Warm Springs Blvd	Fremont	CA	94539	510-226-7366		174
Web: www.exxactcorp.com						
EXXCEL Project Management Inc						
328 S Civic Ctr Dr	Columbus	OH	43215	614-621-4500		186
Web: www.exxcel.com						
Exxon Mobil Corp 5959 Las Colinas Blvd	Irving	TX	75039	972-444-1000		536
NYSE: XOM ■ *TF:* 800-252-1800 ■ *Web:* www.exxonmobil.com						
ExxonMobil Foundation Inc						
5959 Las Colinas Blvd	Irving	TX	75039	972-444-1000		304
Web: exxonmobil.com						
ExxonMobil Pipeline Co						
800 Bell St Rm 653A	Houston	TX	77002	713-656-3636	656-9586	597
Web: www.exxonmobilpipeline.com						
Eyak Corp, The						
360 W Benson Blvd Ste 210	Anchorage	AK	99503	907-334-6971		360-3
TF: 800-478-7161 ■ *Web:* eyakcorporation.com						
Eyak Technology LLC						
360 W Benson Blvd Ste 210	Anchorage	AK	99501	907-276-4472		196
Web: www.eyaktek.com						
Eyde Co 4660 S Hagadorn Ste 660	East Lansing	MI	48823	517-351-2480	351-3946	187
TF: 800-422-3933 ■ *Web:* www.eyde.com						
Eye Bank Assn of America (EBAA)						
1015 18th St NW Ste 1010	Washington	DC	20036	202-775-4999	429-6036	49-8
TF: 888-491-8833 ■ *Web:* www.restoresight.org						
Eye Bank for Sight Restoration Inc						
120 Wall St 3rd Fl	New York	NY	10005	212-742-9000	269-3139	269
TF: 866-287-3937 ■ *Web:* www.eyedonation.org						
Eye Bank of British Columbia						
855 W 12th Ave JPPN - B205	Vancouver	BC	V5Z1M9	604-875-4567	875-5316	269
TF: 800-667-2060 ■ *Web:* www.eyebankofbc.ca						
Eye Bank of Canada Ontario Div						
1929 Bayview Ave	Toronto	ON	M5T3A9	416-978-7355	978-1522	269
Web: www.eyebank.utoronto.ca						
Eye Care for Animals						
372 S Milwaukee Ave	Wheeling	IL	60090	847-215-3933		237
Web: www.eyecareforanimals.com						
Eye Center Surgeons & Associates Ll						
401 Meridian St N Ste 200	Huntsville	AL	35801	256-705-3937		237
TF: 800-233-9083 ■ *Web:* www.eyecentersurgeons.com						
Eye Centers of Florida (ECOF)						
4101 Evans Ave	Fort Myers	FL	33901	239-939-3456	936-8776	798
TF: 888-393-2455 ■ *Web:* www.ecof.com						
Eye Communication Systems Inc						
455 E Industrial Dr	Hartland	WI	53029	262-367-1360	367-1362	496
TF: 800-558-2153 ■ *Web:* www.eyecom.com						
Eye Foundation of Kansas City						
2300 Holmes St	Kansas City	MO	64108	816-404-1780		303
Eye Glass World Inc						
2435 Commerce Ave Bldg 2200	Duluth	GA	30096	800-637-3597		543
TF: 800-637-3597 ■ *Web:* www.eyeglassworld.com						
Eye Lighting International NA						
9150 Hendricks Rd	Mentor	OH	44060	440-350-7000	350-7001	437
TF Cust Svc: 888-665-2677 ■ *Web:* www.eyelighting.com						
Eye To Eye Vision Ctr						
2255 Sewell Mill Rd Ste 310	Marietta	GA	30062	770-578-1900		543
Web: www.eyetoeyevisioncenter.com						
Eyeball Digital Inc 187 Lafayette St	New York	NY	10013	212-431-5324		195
Web: www.eyeballnyc.com						
Eyebeam Atelier 540 W 21st St	New York	NY	10011	212-937-6580		720
Web: www.eyebeam.org						
Eyecon Marketing Group						
6738 Jamestown Dr	Alpharetta	GA	30005	770-752-0043		7
TF: 800-334-2835 ■ *Web:* www.eyeconmktg.com						
Eyedro Green Solutions Inc						
151 Charles St W Ste 100	Kitchener	ON	N2G1H6	226-499-0944		407
Web: eyedro.com						
Eyefinity Inc						
10875 International Dr Ste 200	Rancho Cordova	CA	95670	877-448-0707		177
TF: 877-448-0707 ■ *Web:* www.eyefinity.com						
Eyejot 315 Fifth Ave S Ste 800	Seattle	WA	98104	206-274-7374		387
Web: www.eyejot.com						
Eye-Kraft Optical Inc						
8 McLeland Rd	Saint Cloud	MN	56303	888-455-2022	950-7070*	542
**Fax Area Code:* 800 ■ *TF:* 888-455-2022 ■ *Web:* www.eyekraft.com						
Eyelematic Mfg Company Inc						
1 Seemar Rd	Watertown	CT	06795	860-274-6791		286
Eyelet Crafters Inc 2712 S Main St	Waterbury	CT	06706	203-757-9221		483
Web: www.eyeletcrafters.com						

Name / Address	City	State	Zip	Phone	Fax	Class
Eyeline Golf 2990 W 29th St Unit 7	Greeley	CO	80631	970-353-0393		711
Web: www.eyelinegolf.com						
Eyelit Inc 5685 Whittle Rd	Mississauga	ON	L4Z3P8	905-502-6184		179
TF: 800-429-8983 ■ *Web:* www.eyelit.com						
EyeMarker Systems Inc						
886 Chestnut Ridge Rd Sixth Fl	Morgantown	WV	26506	304-598-1101		743
Eye-Mart Express Inc						
13800 Senlac Dr Ste 200	Farmers Branch	TX	75234	972-488-2002		543
TF: 888-372-2763 ■ *Web:* www.eyemartexpress.com						
Eye-Mate Inc 77 N Centre Ave	Rockville Centre	NY	11570	516-678-9613		543
EyeMed Vision Care 4000 Luxottica Pl	Mason	OH	45040	513-765-4321	765-6388	391-3
TF: 866-939-3633 ■ *Web:* portal.eyemedvisioncare.com						
eyeReturn Marketing						
110 Eglinton Ave E Ste 705	Toronto	ON	M4P2Y1	416-929-4834		5
TF: 866-878-3335 ■ *Web:* www.eyereturnmarketing.com						
EyeSee360 Inc 300 Fleet St Ste 250	Pittsburgh	PA	15220	412-922-6002		179
Web: eyesee360.com						
Eyetique Corp 2242 Murray Ave	Pittsburgh	PA	15217	412-422-5300		543
Web: www.eyetique.com						
Eye-To-Eye Communications Inc						
2624 W Canyon Ave	San Diego	CA	92123	858-565-9800		41
TF: 800-859-1446 ■ *Web:* www.eyetoeyepr.com						
EYP Inc NanoFab E 257 Fuller Rd 1st Fl	Albany	NY	12203	518-795-3800	431-3330	261
Web: www.eypae.com						
Eyre Bus Service Inc						
13600 Triadelphia Rd PO Box 239	Glenelg	MD	21737	410-442-1330	442-0010	107
TF: 800-321-3973 ■ *Web:* www.eyre.com						
EZ Electric Inc 1250 Birchwood Dr	Sunnyvale	CA	94089	408-734-4282		439
Web: www.ez-electric.com						
E-Z Form Cable Corp 285 Welton St	Hamden	CT	06517	203-785-8215		116
Web: www.ezform.com						
EZ Loader Boat Trailers Inc						
717 N Hamilton St	Spokane	WA	99202	509-489-0181	489-5729	763
TF: 800-398-5623 ■ *Web:* www.ezloader.com						
E-Z Mart Stores						
602 W Falvey Ave PO Box 1426	Texarkana	TX	75501	903-832-6502		204
Web: www.ezmart.com						
EZ Micro Solutions Inc						
2670 Lehigh St	Whitehall	PA	18052	610-264-1232		180
Web: www.ezmicro.com						
E-Z Mix Inc 11450 Tuxford St	Sun Valley	CA	91352	818-768-0568		191-1
Web: www.ezmixinc.com						
EZ Systems.com						
3400 W MacArthur Blvd Ste E	Santa Ana	CA	92704	714-662-4959	662-6859	175
Web: www.ezsystems.com						
EZ Trail Inc						
1050 E Columbia St PO Box 168	Arthur	IL	61911	217-543-3471	543-3473	273
TF: 800-677-2802 ■ *Web:* www.e-ztrail.com						
E-Z Trench Manufacturing Inc						
2315 Hwy 701 S	Loris	SC	29569	843-756-6444		190
Web: www.eztrench.com						
EZ8 Motels Inc 2484 Hotel Cir Pl	San Diego	CA	92108	619-291-4824		707
TF: 855-413-1222 ■ *Web:* www.ez8motels.com						
ezCater Inc 101 Arch St Ste 1510	Boston	MA	02110	800-488-1803		387
TF: 800-488-1803 ■ *Web:* www.ezcater.com						
EZCORP Inc 1901 Capital Pkwy	Austin	TX	78746	512-314-3400		560
NASDAQ: EZPW ■ *TF:* 800-873-7296 ■ *Web:* www.ezcorp.com						
Eze Castle Integration Inc						
260 Franklin St 12th Fl	Boston	MA	02110	617-217-3000	217-3001	195
TF: 800-752-1382 ■ *Web:* www.eci.com						
Eze Lap Diamond Products						
3572 Arrowhead Dr	Carson City	NV	89706	775-888-9500		697
TF: 800-843-4815 ■ *Web:* www.eze-lap.com						
Ezenia! Inc 14 Celina Ave Ste 17	Nashua	NH	03063	781-505-2100		176
TF: 800-966-2301 ■ *Web:* www.ezenia.com						
Ez-flo International Inc						
2750 E Mission Blvd	Ontario	CA	91761	909-947-5256	827-3012*	610
**Fax Area Code: 800* ■ *Web:* www.ez-flo.net						
EZG Manufacturing Corp 405 Watertown Rd	Waterford	OH	45786	740-749-3512		135
TF: 888-344-7688 ■ *Web:* www.ezgrout.com						
E-Z-GO 1451 Marvin Griffin Rd	Augusta	GA	30906	800-241-5855		516
TF: 800-241-5855 ■ *Web:* www.ezgo.com						
E-Z-GO Division of Textron Inc						
1451 Marvin Griffin Rd	Augusta	GA	30906	706-798-4311	771-4609	770
TF: 800-241-5855 ■ *Web:* ezgo.com						
Ezra Sutton Law Offices						
900 US Hwy 9 N Ste 201	Woodbridge	NJ	07095	732-634-3520		428
TF: 800-900-4250 ■ *Web:* ezrasutton.com						
e-Zsigma (Canada) Inc						
200 Town Centre Blvd Ste 402	Markham	ON	L3R8G5	905-947-8562		196
Web: www.ezsigmagroup.com						
EZSolution Corp 111 Centerville Rdy	Lancaster	PA	17601	717-291-4689		809
Web: www.ezsolution.com						
Ezzi Net 85 Tenth Ave Fl 7	New York	NY	10011	646-375-3390		387
Web: www.ezzi.net						

F

Name / Address	City	State	Zip	Phone	Fax	Class
F & A Dairy Products Inc						
212 State Rd 35 S	Dresser	WI	54009	715-755-3485		296-5
Web: www.fadairy.com						
F & D Head Co 3040 E Peden Rd	Fort Worth	TX	76179	817-236-8773	236-1061	723
TF: 800-451-2684 ■ *Web:* www.fwfdhead.com						
F & F Productions LLC						
14333 Myerlake Cir	Clearwater	FL	33760	727-530-5000	535-6547	514
Web: fandfhd.tv						
F & G Mechanical Corp						
348 New County Rd	Secaucus	NJ	07094	201-864-3580		610
Web: www.fgmech.com						
F & H Ribbon Co Inc 3010 S Pipeline Rd	Euless	TX	76040	800-877-5775	344-3010	777
TF: 800-877-5775 ■ *Web:* www.fhribbon.com						
F & H Solutions Group						
1300 19th St NW Ste 300	Washington	DC	20036	202-719-2000	719-2088	195
Web: fhsolutionsgroup.com						
F & M Bank & Trust Co 505 Broadway	Hannibal	MO	63401	573-221-6424		360-2
Web: bankfm.com						
F & M Hat Co Inc						
103 Walnut St PO Box 40	Denver	PA	17517	717-336-5505	336-0501	155-9
TF: 800-953-4287 ■ *Web:* www.fmhat.com						
F & ME Consultants 3112 Devine St	Columbia	SC	29205	803-254-4540		261
Web: fandme.com						
F & P Georgia Mfg Inc						
88 Enterprise Dr SE	Rome	GA	30161	706-291-7550		247
Web: www.fandpgeorgia.com						
F & R Installers Corp						
63 Flushing Ave Ste 270	Brooklyn	NY	11205	718-855-1600		480
F & W Forestry Services Inc						
1310 W Oakridge Dr	Albany	GA	31707	229-883-0505		302
Web: www.fwforestry.com						
F C Kerbeck & Sons 100 Rt 73 N	Palmyra	NJ	08065	855-581-5700		57
TF General: 855-846-1500 ■ *Web:* www.fckerbeck.com						
F D Rich Co 222 Summer St	Stamford	CT	06901	203-359-2900	328-7980	187
Web: www.fdrich.com						
F D Thomas Inc 217 Bateman Dr	Central Point	OR	97502	541-664-3010	664-1105	189-8
Web: www.fdthomas.com						
F E Myers 1101 Myers Pkwy	Ashland	OH	44805	419-289-1144		641
TF: 855-274-8947 ■ *Web:* www.femyers.com						
F G Quality Supply Inc						
41 N Hillside Ave	Hillside	IL	60162	708-449-0300		366
F Gs Inc 815 W Van Buren St Ste 302	Chicago	IL	60607	312-421-3060		671
Web: fgs-inc.com						
F H Paschen S N Nielsen Inc						
5515 N East River Rd	Chicago	IL	60656	773-444-3474	693-0064	188-4
Web: www.fhpaschen.com						
F H Video Inc						
6137 Geary Blvd Fl 2	San Francisco	CA	94121	415-221-6128		647
Web: www.fhvideo.com						
F Korbel & Bros Inc						
13250 River Rd	Guerneville	CA	95446	707-824-7000		80-3
Web: www.korbel.com						
F M Brush Manufacturing Co						
7002 72nd Pl	Glendale	NY	11385	718-821-5939		362
TF: 800-645-4111 ■ *Web:* www.fmbrush.com						
F M C of Plymouth Ohio Inc						
500 Donnenwirth Dr	Plymouth	OH	44865	419-687-8237		492
Web: www.fetzermfg.com						
F Mcconnell & Sons Inc						
11102 Lincoln Hwy E	New Haven	IN	46774	260-493-6607	749-6116	297-8
TF: 800-552-0835 ■ *Web:* www.fmcconnell.com						
F p i s Inc 220 Story Rd	Ocoee	FL	34761	407-656-8818		7
TF: 800-346-5977 ■ *Web:* www.fpis.com						
F Rodgers Corp 7901 National Dr	Livermore	CA	94550	925-960-2300		389
F S Prestress LLC 190 Prestress Rd	Princeton	LA	71067	318-949-2444		183
TF: 800-231-2222 ■ *Web:* www.fsprestress.com						
F Visions Services						
500 Greenwich St Fl 3	New York	NY	10013	212-625-1616		121
TF: 888-245-8333 ■ *Web:* www.visionsvcb.org						
F Ziegler Enterprises Ltd						
528 Harrison Ct	North Fond Du Lac	WI	54937	920-921-4084		454
Web: www.fziegler.com						
F+W, A Content + eCommerce Co						
10151 Carver Rd Ste 200	Cincinnati	OH	45236	513-531-2690	531-2690	637-9
TF Sales: 800-289-0963 ■ *Web:* www.fwcommunity.com						
F Gilbert Hills State Forest						
45 Mill St	Foxboro	MA	02035	508-543-5850		565
Web: www.mass.gov						
F.B.P. Insurance Services LLC						
130 Theory Ste 200	Irvine	CA	92617	949-955-1430		390
Web: www.preceptgroup.com						
F-11 Photo the print refinery						
16 E Main St	Bozeman	MT	59715	406-586-3281		119
Web: www.f11photo.com						
F5 Networks Inc 401 Elliott Ave W	Seattle	WA	98119	206-272-5555	272-5556	176
NASDAQ: FFIV ■ *TF:* 888-882-4447 ■ *Web:* www.f5.com						
FA (Food Addicts In Recovery Anonymous)						
400 W Cummings Pk Ste 1700	Woburn	MA	01801	781-932-6300		48-21
Web: www.foodaddicts.org						
FA Bartlett Tree Expert Co						
1290 E Main St	Stamford	CT	06902	203-323-1131		776
TF: 877-227-8538 ■ *Web:* www.bartlett.com						
FA Davis Co 1915 Arch St	Philadelphia	PA	19103	215-568-2270	568-5065	637-2
TF: 800-323-3555 ■ *Web:* www.fadavis.com						
FA Wilhelm Construction Co Inc						
3914 Prospect St	Indianapolis	IN	46203	317-359-5411		186
Web: www.fawilhelm.com						
FAA (Federal Aviation Administration)						
800 Independence Ave SW	Washington	DC	20591	866-835-5322		340-17
TF: 866-835-5322 ■ *Web:* www.faa.gov						
FAA (Federal Aviation Administration Regional Offices)						
Alaskan Region						
222 W Seventh Ave Ste 14	Anchorage	AK	99513	907-271-5438	271-2851	340-17
Web: www.faa.gov						
Faa Federal Credit Union						
3920 Whitebrook Dr	Memphis	TN	38118	901-366-0066		219
TF: 800-346-0069 ■ *Web:* faafcu.org						
Faac Inc 1229 Oak Valley Dr	Ann Arbor	MI	48108	734-761-5836	761-5368	703
TF: 877-322-2387 ■ *Web:* www.faac.com						
FAAN (Food Allergy & Anaphylaxis Network)						
11781 Lee Jackson Hwy Ste 160	Fairfax	VA	22033	703-691-3179	691-2713	48-17
TF: 800-929-4040 ■ *Web:* www.foodallergy.org						
Fab Industries Corp						
98 Cutter Mill Rd Ste 412-N	Great Neck	NY	11021	516-498-3200		745-4
Web: fab-industries.com						
FabArc Steel Supply Inc 111 Meadow Ln	Oxford	AL	36203	256-831-8770		492
Web: www.fabarc.com						
Fabbri Sausage Manufacturing Co						
166 N Aberdeen St	Chicago	IL	60607	312-829-6363		296-26
Web: www.fabbrisausage.com						
Fabco Automotive Corp						
151 Lawrence Dr	Livermore	CA	94551	925-454-9500		454
Web: www.fabcoautomotive.com						
Fabco Inc 30G Summer St	Winthrop	ME	04364	207-377-6909		454
Web: www.fabcomaine.com						

Phone Fax Class

Fabco Steel Fabrication Inc
14688 San Bernardino Ave ... Fontana CA 92335 909-350-1535 480
TF: 800-851-2774 ■ Web: www.fabcosteel.com
Fabco-Air Inc 3716 NE 49th Ave ... Gainesville FL 32609 352-373-3578 375-8024 223
TF: 800-993-3786 ■ Web: www.fabco-air.com
Fabcon Inc 6111 Hwy 13 W ... Savage MN 55378 952-890-4444 890-6657 183
TF: 800-727-4444 ■ Web: www.fabcon-usa.com
Fabcon LLC 3400 Jackson Pike ... Grove City OH 43123 614-875-8601 183
FabCorp Inc 6951 W Little York ... Houston TX 77040 713-466-3962 466-3470 595
Web: www.fabcorp.com
Faber Enterprises Inc
6606 Variel Ave ... Canoga Park CA 91303 818-999-1300 790
TF: 800-400-1717 ■ Web: www.faberent.com
Fabgroups Technologies Inc
1100 Saint Amour ... Saint-laurent QC H4S1J2 514-331-3712 111
TF: 800-561-8910 ■ Web: www.fabgroups.com
Fabian Oil Inc 20 Oak St PO Box 99 ... Oakland ME 04963 207-465-2000 324
Web: www.fabianoil.com
Fabick Inc 4118 Robertson Rd ... Madison WI 53714 608-242-1100 605-2
Web: www.fabick.com
Fablok Mills Inc 140 Spring St ... Murray Hill NJ 07974 908-464-1950 464-6520 745-3
Web: www.fablokmills.com
Fabral Inc 3449 Hempland Rd ... Lancaster PA 17601 717-397-2741 397-1040 480
TF: 800-477-2741 ■ Web: www.fabral.com
Fabre Engineering Inc
119 Gregory Sq ... Pensacola FL 32502 850-433-6438 261
TF: 800-882-5043 ■ Web: www.fabreinc.com
Fabreeka International Inc
1023 Tpke St ... Stoughton MA 02072 781-341-3655 341-3983 677
TF Cust Svc: 800-322-7352 ■ Web: www.fabreeka.com
Fabre-Kramer Pharmaceuticals Inc
5847 San Felipe Ste 2000 ... Houston TX 77057 713-975-6900 238
Web: www.fabrekramer.com
Fabric Images Inc 325 Corporate Dr ... Elgin IL 60123 847-488-9877 791
TF: 800-336-5019 ■ Web: www.fabricimages.com
Fabric Workshop & Museum
1214 Arch St ... Philadelphia PA 19107 215-561-8888 561-8887 520
Web: www.fabricworkshopandmuseum.org
Fabrica International Inc
3201 S Susan St ... Santa Ana CA 92704 949-261-7181 364
Web: www.fabrica.com
Fabricated Components Inc
PO Box 431 ... Stroudsburg PA 18360 570-421-4110 421-2553 482
TF: 800-233-8163 ■ Web: www.fabricatedcomponents.com
Fabricated Extrusion Company LLC
2331 Hoover Ave ... Modesto CA 95354 209-529-9200 608
Web: www.fabexco.com
Fabricated Metals LLC
6300 Kenjoy Dr ... Louisville KY 40214 502-363-2625 198
Web: www.fabricatedmetals.com
Fabrication Concepts Corp
1800 E St Andrew Pl ... Santa Ana CA 92705 714-881-2000 881-2001 697
Web: www.fabcon.com
Fabrication Designs Inc
7463 New Ridge Rd Ste A ... Hanover MD 21076 410-850-0042 234
Web: www.fabricationdesigns.com
Fabrication JR Tardif Inc
62 Blvd Cartier ... Rivi Re-Du-Loup QC G5R6B2 418-862-7273 273
TF: 877-962-7273 ■ Web: www.jrtardif.com
Fabrication Products Inc
4201 NE Minnehaha St ... Vancouver WA 98661 360-696-1324 480
Web: www.fabproducts.com
Fabrication Technologies Industries Inc
2200 Haffley Ave ... National City CA 91950 619-477-4141 54
Web: www.ftisd.com
Fabricators & Manufacturers Assn International (FMA)
833 Featherstone Rd ... Rockford IL 61107 815-399-8700 484-7700 49-13
TF: 888-394-4362 ■ Web: www.fmanet.org
Fabricon Products
1721 W Pleasant Ave ... River Rouge MI 48218 313-841-8200 841-4819 554
Web: www.fabriconproducts.com
Fabricut Inc 9303 E 46th St ... Tulsa OK 74145 918-622-7700 664-8919 361
TF: 800-999-8200 ■ Web: www.fabricut.com
Fabri-Form Co 200 S Friendship Dr ... New Concord OH 43762 740-826-5000 826-5001 602
TF: 800-837-2574 ■ Web: portal.pendaform.com
Fabrik Molded Plastics
5213 Prime Pkwy ... Mchenry IL 60050 815-385-9480 596
Web: www.fabrikind.com
Fabri-Kal Corp 600 Plastics Pl ... Kalamazoo MI 49001 269-385-5050 385-0197 602
TF: 800-888-5054 ■ Web: www.fabri-kal.com
Fabri-Quilt Inc
901 E 14th Ave ... North Kansas City MO 64116 816-421-2000 471-2853 258
TF: 800-279-0622 ■ Web: www.fabri-quilt.com
Fabritech Inc 5740 Salmen St ... New Orleans LA 70123 504-733-5009 745-8
TF: 888-733-5009 ■ Web: www.fabritechonline.com
Fabrizio, McLaughlin & Associates
2624 NE 15th St ... Ft Lauderdale FL 33304 703-684-4510 463
Web: www.fabriziolee.com
Fabtrol Systems Inc
1025 Willamette St Ste 300 ... Eugene OR 97401 541-345-1494 177
Web: www.fabtrol.com
Fabulous Fox, The
527 N Grand Blvd ... Saint Louis MO 63103 314-534-1678 534-1678 572
TF: 800-293-5949 ■ Web: www.fabulousfox.com
Fabulous Specialties Inc
600 Livingston Ave ... Livingston NJ 07039 973-535-6300 366
FAC (Fargo Assembly Co)
3300 Seventh Ave N PO Box 2340 ... Fargo ND 58102 701-298-3803 298-3806 814
Web: www.facnd.com
FACC (French-American Chamber of Commerce of Chicago)
35 E Wacker Dr Ste 670 ... Chicago IL 60601 312-578-0444 578-0445 138
Web: www.facc-chicago.com
FACC (French-American Chamber of Commerce of Philadelphia)
1617 John F Kennedy Blvd Ste 555 ... Philadelphia PA 19103 215-716-1996 138
Web: www.faccphila.org
FACC (Fostoria Area Chamber of Commerce)
121 N Main St ... Fostoria OH 44830 419-435-7789 435-0936 139
Web: www.fostoriaohio.org
FACC (Franklin Area Chamber of Commerce)
1327 Liberty St ... Franklin PA 16323 814-432-5823 437-2453 139
Web: www.franklinareachamber.org
Facchina Construction Co Inc
102 Centennial St Ste 201 ... La Plata MD 20646 240-776-7000 776-7001 188-4
FACCPNW (French-American Chamber of Commerce of the Pacific Northwest)
2200 Alaskan Way Ste 490 ... Seattle WA 98121 206-443-4703 448-4218 138
Web: www.faccpnw.org
Face Stockholm Ltd 324 Joslen Blvd ... Hudson NY 12534 518-828-6600 231
TF: 888-334-3223 ■ Web: www.facestockholm.com
Facekey Corp
900 NE Loop 410 Ste D401 ... San Antonio TX 78209 210-826-8811 569
TF: 800-826-7493 ■ Web: www.facekey.com
Facet Computers 2103 Court St ... Pekin IL 61554 309-353-4727 175
Web: www.facettech.com
Facets Multimedia Inc
1517 W Fullerton Ave ... Chicago IL 60614 773-281-9075 929-5437 511
TF Cust Svc: 800-331-6197 ■ Web: www.facets.org
Facey Medical Group & Foundation
11211 Sepulveda Blvd ... Mission Hills CA 91345 818-365-9531 305
Web: www.facey.com
Facilite Informatique Canada Inc
5 Pl Ville-Marie Bureau 1045 ... Montreal QC H3B2G2 514-284-5636 284-9529 180
Web: www.facilite.com
Facilitech Inc 1111 Vly View Ln ... Irving TX 75061 817-858-2000 320
Web: www.businessinteriors.com
Facility Construction Services Inc
8200 Lovett Ave ... Dallas TX 75227 214-381-0101 186
Web: www.fcsdallas.com
Facility Dynamics Engineering
6760 Alexander Bell Dr ... Columbia MD 21046 410-290-0900 261
Web: facilitydynamics.com
Facility Gateway Corp
4920 Triangle St ... Mcfarland WI 09363 608-838-6060 180
Web: www.facilitygateway.com
Facility Group Inc 2233 Lake Pk Dr ... Smyrna GA 30080 770-437-2700 186
Web: fdgatlanta.com
Facility Masters Inc 1604 Kerley Dr ... San Jose CA 95112 408-436-9090 256
Web: www.facilitymasters.com
Facility Merchandising Inc
5959 Topanga Canyon Blvd Ste 125 ... Woodland Hills CA 91367 818-703-6690 710
Facility Programming & Consulting Inc
100 W Houston St Ste 1100 ... San Antonio TX 78205 210-228-9600 196
Web: www.facilityprogramming.com
Facility Solutions Group (FSG)
4401 Westgate Blvd Ste 310 ... Austin TX 78745 512-440-7985 440-0399 246
TF: 800-854-6465 ■ Web: www1.fsgi.com
Facing History & Ourselves
16 HuRd Rd ... Brookline MA 02445 617-232-1595 232-0281 48-11
TF: 800-856-9039 ■ Web: www.facinghistory.org
FACS (Foundation for American Communications)
85 S Grand Ave ... Pasadena CA 91105 626-584-0010 49-14
Faction Media LLP 1401 17th St Ste 800 ... Denver CO 80202 303-339-0206 7
TF: 866-788-5306 ■ Web: www.factionmedia.com
Factor Gas Liquids Inc 240 Vidal St N ... Sarnia ON N7T5Y3 519-332-8978 316
TF: 800-265-7051 ■ Web: www.factorgas.com
Factor Sales Inc 676 N Archibald St ... San Luis AZ 85349 928-627-8033 345
Factory at Franklin 230 Franklin Rd ... Franklin TN 37064 615-791-1777 591-2511 460
Web: www.factoryatfranklin.com
Factory Design Labs 1037 Broadway Ste B ... Denver CO 80203 303-573-9100 7
Factory Direct Appliance Inc
14105 Marshall Dr ... Lenexa KS 66215 913-888-8028 38
Web: www.kcfda.com
Factory Direct Furniture & Mattress
2330 Freedom Dr ... Charlotte NC 28208 704-393-2750 321
Factory Steel & Metal Supply Co
14020 Oakland ... Detroit MI 48203 313-883-6300 492
Web: www.factorysteel.com
Factory Stores at North Bend
North Bend Premium Outlets
461 S Fork Ave SW Ste E-1 ... North Bend WA 98045 425-888-4505 460
Web: www.premiumoutlets.com
FactSet Research Systems Inc
601 Merritt 7 3rd Fl ... Norwalk CT 06851 203-810-1000 810-1000 404
NYSE: FDS ■ TF: 877-322-8738 ■ Web: www.factset.com
Factual Data Inc 5200 Hahns Peak Dr ... Loveland CO 80538 970-663-5700 929-3297* 218
*Fax Area Code: 800 ■ TF: 800-929-3400 ■ Web: www.krollfactualdata.com
Faculty of Education University of British Columbia
2125 Main Mall ... Vancouver BC V6T1Z4 604-822-5242 162
Web: educ.ubc.ca
FACVB (Fayetteville Area Convention & Visitors Bureau)
245 Person St ... Fayetteville NC 28301 910-483-5311 484-6632 206
TF: 800-255-8217 ■ Web: www.visitfayettevillenc.com
Faddis Concrete Products
2206 Horseshoe Pk ... Honey Brook PA 19344 610-269-4685 135
Web: www.faddis.com
Fader Agencies 83 Shore Rd ... Dartmouth NS B3A1A5 902-466-2333 518
FADER Inc, The 71 W 23 St Fl 13 ... New York NY 10010 212-741-7100 530
Web: www.thefader.com
Fadi's Mediterranean Cuisine
8383 Westheimer Rd ... Houston TX 77063 713-532-0666 671
Web: www.fadiscuisine.com
Fadi's Mediterranean Grill
3001 Knox St ... Dallas TX 75205 214-528-1800 671
Web: www.fadiscuisine.com
Fado Irish Pub 1735 19th St Ste 150 ... Denver CO 80202 303-297-0066 671
Web: www.fadoirishpub.com
Fado's Irish Pub 214 W Fourth St ... Austin TX 78701 512-457-0172 671
TF: 800-928-2086 ■ Web: www.fadoirishpub.com
FAE (Foundation for Acctg Education)
14 Wall St 19th Fl ... New York NY 10005 212-719-8300 719-3365 49-1
TF General: 800-537-3635 ■ Web: www.nysscpa.org
Faegre & Benson LLP
90 S Seventh St 2200 Wells Fargo Bldg ... Minneapolis MN 55402 612-766-7000 766-1600 428
TF: 800-328-4393 ■ Web: www.faegrebd.com
FAES (Foundation for Advanced Education in the Sciences)
1 Cloister Ct ... Bethesda MD 20814 301-496-7976 402-0174 49-19
Web: www.faes.org

	Phone	Fax	Class
FAF (Financial Acctg Foundation) 401 Merritt 7 PO Box 5116....................Norwalk CT 06856 *Web:* fasb.org	203-847-0700	849-9714	49-1
FAF (Form-A-Feed Inc) 740 Bowman St..........Stewart MN 55385 *TF:* 800-422-3649 ■ *Web:* www.formafeed.com	320-562-2413		447
FAF Inc 26 Lark Industrial Pkwy .... Greenville RI 02828 *TF:* 800-949-3311 ■ *Web:* www.faf.com	800-949-3311		411
Fafco Inc 435 Otterson Dr ....Chico CA 95928 *TF:* 800-994-7652 ■ *Web:* www.fafco.com	530-332-2100	332-2109	91
Fafinski Mark & Johnson PA 775 Prairie Center Dr Ste 400...............Eden Prairie MN 55344 *TF:* 855-806-1525 ■ *Web:* www.fmjlaw.com	952-995-9500		428
Fagan Co 3125 Brinkerhoff Rd PO Box 15238 ....Kansas City KS 66115 *Web:* www.faganco.com	913-621-4444	621-1735	189-10
Fagen Inc 501 W Hwy 212 PO Box 159 ....Granite Falls MN 56241 *Web:* www.fageninc.com	320-564-3324		194
Fagen Pharmacy 915 S Halleck St PO Box 662..................Demotte IN 46310 *TF:* 800-978-0531 ■ *Web:* www.fagenpharmacy.com	219-987-6468	987-7226	237
Fager's Island Restaurant 201 60th St..............................Ocean City MD 21842 *TF:* 855-432-4377 ■ *Web:* www.fagers.com	410-524-5500		671
Fagor Automation Corp 2250 Estes Ave.....................Elk Grove Village IL 60007 *Web:* www.fagorautomation.com	847-981-1500		188
Fagundes Agribusiness 8700 Fargo Ave.........Hanford CA 93230 *Web:* fagundes.net	559-582-2000	582-0683	315-3
FAHC (University of Vermont Medical Center, The) 111 Colchester Ave........................Burlington VT 05401 *TF:* 800-358-1144 ■ *Web:* www.uvmhealth.org/medcenter/pages/default.aspx	802-847-0000		374-3
Fahlgren Mortine 4030 Easton Stn Ste 300 ....Columbus OH 43219 *TF:* 800-731-8927 ■ *Web:* www.fahlgrenmortine.com	614-383-1500	383-1501	4
Fahr Beverage 1369 Martin Rd...............Waterloo IA 50701 *Web:* www.fahrbeverage.com	319-234-2605	234-5644	81-1
Fahrenheit 2417 Professor Ave ....Cleveland OH 44113 *Web:* chefroccowhalen.com/fahrenheit-cleveland	216-781-8858		671
Fahrenheit Group LLC, The 1700 Bayberry Court Ste 201 ....Richmond VA 23226 *Web:* thefahrenheitgroup.com	804-955-4440		260
FAIA (Pekin Insurance) 2505 Ct St...............Pekin IL 61558 *TF:* 800-322-0160 ■ *Web:* pekininsurance.com	309-346-1161		391-4
Faidley's Seafood 203 N Paca St...............Baltimore MD 21201 *Web:* www.faidleyscrabcakes.com	410-727-4898		671
Failsafe Controls LLC 2712 SW Dr ....New Iberia LA 70560 *TF:* 800-264-1170 ■ *Web:* failsafecontrols.com	337-365-2493		539
FAIR (Federation for American Immigration Reform) 25 Massachusetts Ave NW Ste 330 ....Washington DC 20009 *TF:* 877-627-3247 ■ *Web:* www.fairus.org	202-328-7004	387-3447	48-7
Fair Anderson & Langeman 3065 S Jones Blvd Ste 100.................Las Vegas NV 89146 *Web:* www.falcpa.com	702-870-7999		2
Fair Choice Systems Inc 505 Ct St............Brooklyn NY 11231	646-485-0890		463
Fair Grounds Race Course 1751 Gentilly Blvd ....New Orleans LA 70119 *TF:* 800-262-7983 ■ *Web:* www.fairgroundsracecourse.com	504-944-5515	948-1160	642
Fair Haven Beach State Park 14985 State Park Rd.......................Fair Haven NY 13156 *TF General:* 800-456-2267 ■ *Web:* parks.ny.gov/parks/12/hunting.aspx	315-947-5205		565
Fair Hill Natural Resources Management Area 300 Tawes Dr ....Elkton MD 21921 *Web:* dnr2.maryland.gov	410-398-1246		565
Fair Hills Resort 24270 County Hwy 20 ....Detroit Lakes MN 56501 *TF Resv:* 800-323-2849 ■ *Web:* www.fairhillsresort.com	218-847-7638		660
Fair Isaac Corp 2665 Long Lake Rd Bldg C...................Roseville MN 55113 *NYSE: FICO* ■ *TF Cust Svc:* 888-342-6336 ■ *Web:* www.fico.com	612-758-5200	758-5201	225
Fair Labor Assn (FLA) 1111 19th St NW Ste 401.................Washington DC 20036 *Web:* www.fairlabor.org	202-898-1000	898-9050	48-5
Fair Lawn Chamber of Commerce 12-45 River Rd..............................Fair Lawn NJ 07410 *TF:* 800-474-1299 ■ *Web:* www.fairlawnchamber.org	201-796-7050	475-0619	139
Fair Meadows at Tulsa 4609 E 21st St ....Tulsa OK 74114 *TF:* 877-781-2660 ■ *Web:* exposquare.com	918-743-7223		642
Fair Oaks Farms Inc 7600 95th St.........................Pleasant Prairie WI 53158 *Web:* www.fairoaksfarms.com	262-947-0320	947-0348	473
Fair Oaks Ford Inc 2055 Wodgen Ave ....Naperville IL 60540 *Web:* fairoaksford.com	630-355-8140		57
Fair Oaks Hospital 5352 Linton Blvd ....Delray Beach FL 33484 *TF:* 866-904-6871 ■ *Web:* www.delraymedicalctr.com	561-498-4440	495-3103	374-5
Fair Oaks Mall 11750 Lee Jackson Hwy ....Fairfax VA 22033 *Web:* www.shopfairoaksmall.com	703-359-8300		460
Fair View Nursing Home 1714 W 16th St ....Sedalia MO 65301 *Web:* fairviewnursinghomesedalia.com	660-827-1594		371
Fair Winds Air Charter 2525 SE Witham Field Hngr 7 ....Stuart FL 34996 **Fax Area Code:* 772 ■ *TF:* 800-989-9665 ■ *Web:* www.fwjets.com	800-989-9665	288-4230*	13
Fairbanks Chamber of Commerce 100 Cushman St Ste 102 ....Fairbanks AK 99701 *Web:* www.fairbankschamber.org	907-452-1105	456-6968	139
Fairbanks City Hall 800 Cushman St...........Fairbanks AK 99701 *Web:* www.fairbanksalaska.us	907-459-6771	452-5913	337
Fairbanks Convention & Visitors Bureau 101 Dunkel St Ste 111 ....Fairbanks AK 99701 *TF:* 800-327-5774 ■ *Web:* www.explorefairbanks.com	907-456-5774	459-3757	206
Fairbanks Correctional Ctr 1931 Eagan Ave ....Fairbanks AK 99701 *TF:* 844-934-2381 ■ *Web:* www.correct.state.ak.us/institutions/fairbanks	907-458-6700	458-6751	213
Fairbanks Daily News Miner 200 N Cushman St...........................Fairbanks AK 99707 *TF:* 800-656-3265 ■ *Web:* www.newsminer.com	907-456-6661	452-7917	532-2
Fairbanks Golden Nugget Hotel, The 900 Noble St..................................Fairbanks AK 99701 *Web:* www.golden-nuggethotel.com	907-452-5141		379
Fairbanks Hospital 8102 Clearvista Pkwy ....Indianapolis IN 46256 *TF:* 800-225-4673 ■ *Web:* fairbankscd.org	317-849-8222	849-8222	726
Fairbanks International Airport 6450 Airport Way ....Fairbanks AK 99709 *Web:* www.dot.state.ak.us/faiiap	907-474-2500		27
Fairbanks Memorial Hospital 1650 Cowles St ....Fairbanks AK 99701 *Web:* bannerhealth.com	907-452-8181		374-3
Fairbanks Museum & Planetarium 1302 Main St ....Saint Johnsbury VT 05819 *TF:* 800-521-2233 ■ *Web:* www.fairbanksmuseum.org	802-748-2372	748-1893	520
Fairbanks North Star Borough 809 Pioneer Rd................................Fairbanks AK 99701 *TF:* 800-331-6158 ■ *Web:* www.co.fairbanks.ak.us	907-459-1000	459-1224	338
Fairbanks North Star Borough Public Library 1215 Cowles St ....Fairbanks AK 99701 **Fax:* Admin ■ *Web:* fnsblibrary.org	907-459-1022	459-1024*	434-3
Fairbanks Princess Riverside Lodge 4477 Pikes Landing Rd........................Fairbanks AK 99709 *TF:* 800-426-0500 ■ *Web:* princesslodges.com	907-455-4477	455-4476	379
Fairbanks Scales Inc 821 Locust St ....Kansas City MO 64106 *TF:* 800-451-4107 ■ *Web:* www.fairbanks.com	816-471-0231	471-0241	684
Fairbanks Shakespeare Theatre PO Box 73447 ....Fairbanks AK 99707 *Web:* www.fairbankschamber.org	907-457-7638	457-4511	573-4
Fairbanks Symphony Orchestra 312 Tanana Dr................................Fairbanks AK 99775 *TF:* 800-441-2962 ■ *Web:* www.fairbankssymphony.org	907-474-5733		573-3
Fairbanks Youth Facility 1502 Wilbur St...............................Fairbanks AK 99701	907-451-2150		412
Fairborn Area Chamber of Commerce 12 N Central Ave.............................Fairborn OH 45324 *Web:* www.fairborn.com	937-878-3191	878-3197	139
Fairborne Energy Ltd 450 1 St SW ....Calgary AB T2P5H1	403-290-7750		536
Fairbridge Capital Markets Inc 48 Carr 165 Ste 801 ....Guaynabo PR 00968 *Web:* www.fairbridgecap.com	787-622-3473	763-5397	690
FairBridge Inns LLC 421 W Riverside Ave Ste 407 ....Spokane WA 99201 **Fax Area Code:* 925 ■ *TF:* 877-866-8090 ■ *Web:* www.fairbridgeinns.com	877-866-8090	905-4174*	378
Fairchild Air Force Base 100 W Ent St Ste 155 ....Fairchild AFB WA 99011 *Web:* www.fairchild.af.mil	509-247-1212		497-1
Fairchild Auto-mated Parts Inc 10 White St...................................Winsted CT 06098 *TF:* 800-927-2545 ■ *Web:* www.fairchildparts.com	860-379-2725	379-5340	621
Fairchild Imaging Inc 1801 McCarthy Blvd.........................Milpitas CA 95035 *TF:* 800-325-6975 ■ *Web:* www.fairchildimaging.com	408-433-2500	435-7352	696
Fairchild Industrial Products Co 3920 Westpoint Blvd...................Winston-Salem NC 27103 **Fax:* Sales ■ *TF:* 800-334-8422 ■ *Web:* www.fairchildproducts.com	336-659-3400	659-9323*	201
Fairchild Lobel & Rice PC 5123 W St Joseph ....Lansing MI 48917	517-321-5990		2
Fairchild Semiconductor Corp 82 Running Hill Rd.....................South Portland ME 04106 *NASDAQ: FCS* ■ *TF:* 800-341-0392 ■ *Web:* www.fairchildsemi.com	207-775-8100		696
Fairchild Tropical Botanic Garden 10901 Old Cutler Rd.....................Coral Gables FL 33156 *Web:* www.fairchildgarden.org	305-667-1651	661-8953	97
Fairfax County 12000 Government Ctr Pkwy ....Fairfax VA 22035 *Web:* fairfaxcounty.gov	703-324-2531	324-3056	338
Fairfax County Chamber of Commerce (FCCC) 8230 Old Courthouse Rd Ste 350...............Vienna VA 22182 *Web:* www.novachamber.org	703-749-0400	749-9075	139
Fairfax County Convention & Visitors Bureau (FXVA) 3702 Pender Dr Ste 420 ....Fairfax VA 22030 *TF:* 800-732-4732 ■ *Web:* www.fxva.com	703-790-0643		206
Fairfax County Public Library 12000 Government Ctr Pkwy Ste 324.............Fairfax VA 22035 *Web:* www.fairfaxcounty.gov/library	703-324-3100	222-3193	434-3
Fairfax County Times 1920 Association Dr Ste 500 ....Reston VA 20191 *TF:* 800-946-7773 ■ *Web:* www.fairfaxtimes.com	703-437-5400		532-4
Fairfax Financial Holdings Ltd 95 Wellington St W Ste 800 ....Toronto ON M5J2N7 *Web:* www.fairfax.ca	416-367-4941	367-4946	360-4
Fairfax Hospital 10200 NE 132nd St ....Kirkland WA 98034 *TF:* 800-435-7221 ■ *Web:* www.fairfaxhospital.com	425-821-2000		374-5
Fairfax (Independent City) 10455 Armstrong St...........................Fairfax VA 22030 *Web:* fairfaxcounty.gov	703-324-7329	385-7811	338
Fairfax Inn 8660 S Fairfax Rd..............Bloomington IN 47401 *Web:* www.thefairfaxinn.com	812-824-8552		671
Fairfax PET Imaging Ctr 8503 Arlington Blvd Ste 120 Lowr Level...........Fairfax VA 22031 *TF:* 800-358-8831 ■ *Web:* www.inova.org	703-698-4441		769
Fairfax Symphony Orchestra 2667 Prosperity Ave ....Fairfax VA 22031 *Web:* www.fairfaxsymphony.org	703-563-1990		573-3
Fairfax, The 9140 Belvoir Woods Pkwy ....Fort Belvoir VA 22060 *Web:* sunriseseniorliving.com	703-799-1200		672
Fairfield Chair Co PO Box 1710...............Lenoir NC 28645 *TF:* 800-841-6279 ■ *Web:* www.fairfieldchair.com	828-758-5571	758-0211	319-2
Fairfield Chamber of Commerce 1597 Post Rd ....Fairfield CT 06824 *TF:* 800-953-4467 ■ *Web:* www.fairfieldctchamber.com	203-255-1011	256-9990	139
Fairfield Chamber of Commerce 670 Wessel Dr ....Fairfield OH 45014 *Web:* www.fairfieldchamber.com	513-881-5500	881-5503	139
Fairfield Commons 4869 Nine Mile Rd.........Richmond VA 23223	804-222-4167		460

Name / Address	City	State	Zip	Phone	Fax	Class
Fairfield County 210 E Main St *TF:* 800-450-8845 ■ *Web:* www.co.fairfield.oh.us	Lancaster	OH	43130	740-652-7075	687-6048	338
Fairfield County 150 Danbury Rd *Web:* www.fairfieldsc.com	Ridgefield	CT	06877	803-712-6526	712-1506	338
Fairfield County 1061 Main St *Web:* www.jud.state.ct.us	Bridgeport	CT	06604	203-579-6527		338
Fairfield County District Library 219 N Broad St *Web:* www.fcdlibrary.org	Lancaster	OH	43130	740-653-2745		434-3
Fairfield Industries Inc 1111 Gillingham Ln *TF:* 800-231-9809 ■ *Web:* www.fairfieldnodal.com	Sugar Land	TX	77478	281-275-7500	275-7500	472
Fairfield Lake State Park 123 State Pk Rd 64 *Web:* tpwd.texas.gov/state-parks/fairfield-lake	Fairfield	TX	75840	903-389-4514		565
Fairfield Machine Company Inc 1143 Lower Elkton Rd PO Box 27 *TF:* 800-704-1078 ■ *Web:* www.fairfieldmachine.com	Columbiana	OH	44408	330-482-3388	482-5052	674
Fairfield Medical Ctr (FMC) 401 N Ewing St *TF:* 800-548-2627 ■ *Web:* www.fmchealth.org	Lancaster	OH	43130	740-687-8000		374-3
Fairfield Mfg Company Inc 2309 Concord Rd *Web:* www.oerlikon.com	Lafayette	IN	47909	765-772-4000	772-4001	709
Fairfield Museum & History Ctr 370 Beach Rd *Web:* www.fairfieldhistoricalsociety.org	Fairfield	CT	06824	203-259-1598		520
Fairfield Nursing & Rehabilitation 420 Moody St *TF:* 800-213-0154 ■ *Web:* fairfieldnursingandrehab.com	Fairfield	TX	75840	903-389-1236		450
Fairfield Processing Corp 88 Rose Hill Ave *TF:* 800-980-8000 ■ *Web:* www.fairfieldworld.com	Danbury	CT	06810	203-744-2090		605-1
Fairfield Public Library 1080 Old Post Rd *TF:* 800-200-2882 ■ *Web:* www.fairfieldpubliclibrary.org	Fairfield	CT	06824	203-256-3155		434-3
Fairfield Research Corp 65 Locust Ave Ste 200 *Web:* www.fairfieldbush.com	New Canaan	CT	06840	203-972-0404		401
Fairfield Theater 70 Sanford St *Web:* fairfieldtheatre.org	Fairfield	CT	06824	203-319-1404		748
Fairfield University 1073 N Benson Rd **Fax:* Admissions ■ *TF:* 800-822-8428 ■ *Web:* www.fairfield.edu	Fairfield	CT	06824	203-254-4000	254-4199*	166
Fairfield-Suisun Chamber of Commerce 1111 Webster St *Web:* fairfieldsuisunchamber.com	Fairfield	CA	94533	707-425-4625	425-0826	139
Fairhaven 7200 Third Ave *Web:* www.fairhavenccrc.org	Sykesville	MD	21784	410-795-8801		672
Fairhaven 435 W Starin Rd *TF:* 877-624-2298 ■ *Web:* www.fairhaven.org	Whitewater	WI	53190	262-473-2140	473-5468	672
Fairhill School & Diagnostic 16150 Preston Rd *Web:* fairhill.org	Dallas	TX	75248	972-233-1026		685
FairHope Hospice & Palliative Care Inc 282 Sells Rd *TF:* 800-994-7077 ■ *Web:* www.fairhopehospice.org	Lancaster	OH	43130	740-654-7077	654-6321	371
Fairlane Town Ctr 18900 Michigan Ave *TF:* 800-992-9500 ■ *Web:* www.shopfairlane.com	Dearborn	MI	48126	800-992-9500		460
Fairlawn Rehabilitation Hospital 189 May St *Web:* www.fairlawnrehab.org	Worcester	MA	01602	508-791-6351		374-6
Fairleigh Dickinson University 285 Madison Ave **Fax:* Admissions ■ *TF:* 800-338-8803 ■ *Web:* www.fdu.edu	Madison	NJ	07940	973-443-8500	443-8088*	166
Metropolitan 1000 River Rd *TF:* 800-338-8803 ■ *Web:* www.fdu.edu	Teaneck	NJ	07666	201-692-2000	692-2560	166
Fairly Painless Advertising Inc 44 E Eighth St *TF:* 800-506-1299 ■ *Web:* fairlypainless.com	Holland	MI	49423	616-394-5900		7
FairMarket Life Settlements Corp 435 Ford Rd Ste 120 *TF:* 866-326-3757 ■ *Web:* www.fairmarketlife.com	St Louis Park	MN	55426	866-326-3757		390
Fairmont Banff Springs PO Box 960 *TF:* 800-441-1414 ■ *Web:* www.fairmont.com	Banff	AB	T1L1J4	403-762-2211	762-5755	669
Fairmont Capital Inc 3350 E Birch St Ste 206 *TF:* 800-653-2465 ■ *Web:* www.fairmontcapital.com	Brea	CA	92821	714-524-4770	524-4775	405
Fairmont Chateau Lake Louise 111 Lake Louise Dr *TF:* 800-441-1414 ■ *Web:* www.fairmont.com	Lake Louise	AB	T0L1E0	403-522-3511	522-3834	669
Fairmont Chateau Whistler 4599 Chateau Blvd *TF:* 800-441-1414 ■ *Web:* www.fairmont.com	Whistler	BC	V0N1B4	604-938-8000	938-2291	669
Fairmont Convention & Visitors Bureau 323 E Blue Earth Ave *TF:* 800-657-3280 ■ *Web:* visitfairmontmn.com	Fairmont	MN	56031	507-235-8585		206
Fairmont Foods of Minnesota 905 E Fourth St *Web:* www.fairmontfoods.com	Fairmont	MN	56031	507-238-9001		296-36
Fairmont General Hospital (FGH) 1325 Locust Ave	Fairmont	WV	26554	304-367-7100	367-7246	374-3
Fairmont Homes Inc 502 S Oakland Ave *Web:* www.fairmonthomes.com	Nappanee	IN	46550	574-773-7941		505
Fairmont Hot Springs Resort 1500 Fairmont Rd *TF:* 800-332-3272 ■ *Web:* www.fairmontmontana.com	Fairmont	MT	59711	406-797-3241	797-3337	669
Fairmont Hotel Management Lp 950 Mason St *Web:* www.tongaroom.com	San Francisco	CA	94108	415-982-6500		378
Fairmont Hotels & Resorts Inc 100 Wellington St W PO Box 40 *TF General:* 800-441-3313 ■ *Web:* www.frhi.com	Toronto	ON	M5K1B7	416-874-2600	874-2601	379
Fairmont Kea Lani 4100 Wailea Alanui Dr *TF:* 800-659-4100 ■ *Web:* www.fairmont.com	Maui	HI	96753	808-875-4100	875-1200	669
Fairmont Le Chateau Montebello 392 Notre Dame St *TF:* 800-441-1414 ■ *Web:* www.fairmont.com	Montebello	QC	J0V1L0	819-423-6341	423-1133	669
Fairmont Olympic Hotel Seattle, The 411 University St *Web:* www.seattleskal.org	Seattle	WA	98101	206-621-1700		378
Fairmont Orchid Hawaii 1 N Kaniku Dr *TF:* 800-845-9905 ■ *Web:* www.fairmont.com/orchid	Kohala Coast	HI	96743	808-885-2000	885-5778	669
Fairmont San Francisco Hotel, The 950 Mason St *TF:* 800-257-7544 ■ *Web:* fairmont.com	San Francisco	CA	94108	415-772-5000		378
Fairmont Scottsdale Princess 7575 E Princess Dr *TF:* 800-257-7544 ■ *Web:* www.fairmont.com	Scottsdale	AZ	85255	480-585-4848	585-0086	669
Fairmont Sign Company Inc 3750 E Outer Dr *Web:* www.fairmontsign.com	Detroit	MI	48234	313-368-4000		701
Fairmont Sonoma Mission Inn & Spa, The PO Box 1447 *TF:* 866-540-4499 ■ *Web:* www.fairmont.com/sonoma	Sonoma	CA	95476	707-938-9000	938-4250	669
Fairmont State University 1201 Locust Ave **Fax:* Admissions ■ *TF Admissions:* 800-641-5678 ■ *Web:* www.fairmontstate.edu	Fairmont	WV	26554	304-367-4892	367-4789*	166
Fairmont Supply Co 437 Jefferson Ave **Fax Area Code:* 724 ■ *TF:* 800-245-9900 ■ *Web:* www.fairmontsupply.com	Washington	PA	15301	800-245-9900	261-5326*	385
Fairmount Behavioral Health System 561 Fairthorne Ave *TF:* 800-235-0200 ■ *Web:* www.fairmountbhs.com	Philadelphia	PA	19128	215-487-4000		374-5
Fairmount Foundry Inc 25 Second Ave *Web:* fairmountfdry.com	Woonsocket	RI	02895	401-769-1585		492
Fairmount Hotel, The 401 S Alamo St *TF:* 877-229-8808 ■ *Web:* www.thefairmounthotel-sanantonio.com	San Antonio	TX	78205	210-224-8800	475-0082	379
Fairmount Park 9301 Collinsville Rd **Fax Area Code:* 314 ■ *TF:* 800-228-7297 ■ *Web:* www.fairmountpark.com	Collinsville	IL	62234	618-345-4300	436-1516*	642
Fairmount Partners LP 100 Four Falls Corporate Ctr Ste 660 *Web:* fairmountpartners.com	West Conshohocken	PA	19428	610-260-6200		690
Fairmount Theatre 33 Main St Annex	New Haven	CT	06512	203-467-3832	467-3832	572
Fairplay Inc 4640 S Halsted St *Web:* www.fairplayfoods.com	Chicago	IL	60609	773-247-3077		345
FairPoint Communications Inc 521 E Morehead St Ste 250 *NASDAQ: FRP* ■ *TF:* 866-984-2001 ■ *Web:* www.fairpoint.com	Charlotte	NC	28202	704-344-8150		736
Fair-Rite Products Corp 1 Commerical Row PO Box J *TF:* 888-324-7748 ■ *Web:* www.fair-rite.com	Wallkill	NY	12589	845-895-2055	895-2629	249
Fairview Advisors LLC 3838 Tamiami Trl N Ste 416 *Web:* www.fairviewadvisors.com	Naples	FL	34103	239-213-1107		194
Fairview Capital Partners Inc 75 Isham Rd Ste 200 *Web:* www.fairviewcapital.com	West Hartford	CT	06107	860-674-8066	678-5108	405
Fairview Commons Nursing & Rehabilitation Ctr 151 Christian Hill Rd *Web:* www.fairviewcommons.org	Great Barrington	MA	01230	413-528-4560		450
Fairview Elementary School 300 Salem Dr *Web:* www.plymouth.k12.wi.us	Plymouth	WI	53073	920-892-2621		685
Fairview Farms 5911 Heuermann Rd *Web:* www.fairview-farm.com	Peoria	IL	61607	309-697-4111		671
Fairview Fellowship Home For Senior Citizens Inc 605 E State Rd *TF:* 800-579-7967 ■ *Web:* www.fellowshiphome.com	Fairview	OK	73737	580-227-3783		371
Fairview Health Services 2450 Riverside Ave *TF:* 800-824-1953 ■ *Web:* www.fairview.org	Minneapolis	MN	55454	612-672-6000		353
Fairview Hospice 2450 26th Ave S *TF:* 800-285-5647 ■ *Web:* www.fairview.org	Minneapolis	MN	55406	612-728-2455	728-2400	371
Fairview Hospital 18101 Lorain Ave *TF:* 800-801-2273 ■ *Web:* my.clevelandclinic.org	Cleveland	OH	44111	216-444-0261		374-3
Fairview Park Hospital 200 Industrial Blvd *Web:* www.fairviewparkhospital.com	Dublin	GA	31021	478-275-2000		374-3
Fairview Ridges Hospital - Burnsville 2450 Riverside Ave *Web:* www.fairview.org	Minneapolis	MN	55454	952-892-2000		374-3
Fairview Southdale Hospital 6401 France Ave S *Web:* www.fairview.org/hospitals/southdale/index.htm	Edina	MN	55435	952-924-5000		374-3
Fairview University Medical Ctr Mesabi 750 E 34th St *TF:* 888-870-8626 ■ *Web:* www.range.fairview.org	Hibbing	MN	55746	218-262-4881		374-3
Fairview-Riverside State Park 119 Fairview Dr *TF:* 888-677-3247 ■ *Web:* www.crt.state.la.us	Madisonville	LA	70447	985-845-3318		565
Fairway Consulting Group 300 Merrick Rd Ste 404 *Web:* fcgsearch.com	Lynbrook	NY	11563	516-596-2800		194
Fairway Golf Inc 5040 Convoy St *Web:* www.fairwaygolfusa.com	San Diego	CA	92111	858-268-1702		711
Fairway Injection Molding Systems 20109 Paseo Del Prado *Web:* www.fairwaymolds.com	Walnut	CA	91789	909-595-2201		596
Fairway Lincoln-Mercury Inc 10101 Abercorn St *TF:* 855-304-4911 ■ *Web:* www.fairwaylincolnmercury.com	Savannah	GA	31419	855-304-4911		57
Fairway Outdoor Advertising Inc 814 Duncan-Reidville Rd *Web:* fairwayoutdoor.com	Duncan	SC	29334	864-439-6371		8
Fairway Technologies Inc 7825 Fay Ave Ste 100 *Web:* fairwaytech.com	La Jolla	CA	92037	858-454-4471		177
Fairweather LLC 301 Calista Ct *Web:* www.fairweather.com	Anchorage	AK	99518	907-346-3247	349-1920	539

	Phone	Fax	Class
Fairwinds Federal Credit Union 3087 N Alafaya Trl. . . . . Orlando FL 32826 *Fax: Acctg ■ TF: 800-443-6887 ■ Web: www.fairwinds.org	407-277-5045	658-7937*	219
Fairwinds International Inc 128 Northpark Blvd. . . . . Covington LA 70433 TF: 800-673-3863 ■ Web: www.fairwindsintl.com	985-809-3808		261
Fairy Stone State Park 967 Fairystone Lake Dr. . . . . Stuart VA 24171 Web: www.dcr.virginia.gov/state-parks/fairy-stone#general_information	276-930-2424		565
Faith & Reason Institute 1730 Rhode Island Ave NW Ste 212. . . . . Washington DC 20036 Web: www.frinstitute.org	202-289-8775		634
Faith Baptist Bible College 1900 NW Fourth St. . . . . Ankeny IA 50023 Web: www.faith.edu	515-964-0601	964-1638	161
Faith Enterprises Inc 129 S Corona St. . . . . Colorado Springs CO 80903 Web: www.faithenterprisesinc.com	719-578-8281		186
Faith Group Company Inc 195 Route 9 Ste 205. . . . . Manalapan NJ 07726 Web: www.faith-group.com	732-431-1326		603
Faith Mfg Company Inc 406 Atascocita Rd. . . . . Humble TX 77396 Web: www.faithmfg.com	281-441-9595		539
Faith Popcorn's BrainReserve 55 E 59th St Ste 1700. . . . . New York NY 10022 Web: www.faithpopcorn.com	212-772-7778		195
Faith Regional Health Services 2700 W Norfolk Ave . . . . . Norfolk NE 68701 Web: www.frhs.org	402-371-4880		374-3
Faith Tabernacle Pentecostal Church of Montgomery County Mo 121 W Fourth St. . . . . Montgomery City MO 63361	573-564-3700		48-20
Faithbridge United Methodist Church 18000 Stuebner Airline Rd . . . . . Spring TX 77379 Web: faithbridge.org	281-320-7588		48-20
FaithTrust Institute 2400 N 45th St Ste 101 . . . . . Seattle WA 98103 TF: 877-860-2255 ■ Web: www.faithtrustinstitute.org	206-634-1903	634-0115	48-17
Fakahatchee Strand Preserve State Park 137 Coastland Dr . . . . . Copeland FL 34137 Web: www.floridastateparks.org	239-695-4593		565
Fakhoury Law Group Pc 5440 Corporate Dr Ste 100. . . . . Troy MI 48098 Web: www.employmentimmigration.com	248-643-4900		225
Fakouri Electrical Engineering Inc 30001 Comercio. . . . . Rancho Santa Margarita CA 92688 TF: 800-669-8862 ■ Web: www.fee-ups.com	800-669-8862		261
Fala Technologies Inc 430 Old Neighborhood Rd . . . . . Kingston NY 12401 Web: www.falatech.com	845-336-4000		256
Falafel King Restaurant 5461 Wern Ave Unit B. . . . . Boulder CO 80301 Web: falafelkingfoods.com	303-449-9321		671
Falasca Mechanical Inc 3329 N Mill Rd . . . . . Vineland NJ 00360 Web: www.falascamechanical.com	856 704 2010		610
Falcon Crest Aviation Supply Inc 8318 Braniff . . . . . Houston TX 77061 TF: 000-033-0229 ■ Web: www.faloonoroctaviation.com	713-644-2290		250
Falcon Executive Aviation Inc 4766 E Falcon Dr . . . . . Mesa AZ 85215 TF: 800-237-2359 ■ Web: www.falconaviation.com	480-832-0704		358
Falcon Express Inc 2250 E Church St . . . . . Philadelphia PA 19124 TF: 800-544-6566 ■ Web: www.falconexp.com	215-992-3140	992-3150	780
Falcon Express Transportation Inc 6804 Virginia Manor Rd . . . . . Beltsville MD 20705 TF: 800-296-9696 ■ Web: www.fxtran.com	240-264-1215		314
Falcon Foundry Co 96 Sixth St. . . . . Lowellville OH 44436 TF: 800-253-8624 ■ Web: www.falconfoundry.com	330-536-6221		308
Falcon Fuels Inc 7300 Alondra Blvd Ste 204. . . . . Paramount CA 90723 Web: www.falconfuelsinc.com	562-272-4226		579
Falcon Genomics Inc 2661 Clearview Rd Ste 1. . . . . Allison Park PA 15101 Web: www.falcongenomics.com	412-486-1108		743
Falcon Industries Inc 371 Campus Dr. . . . . Somerset NJ 08873 Web: www.falcon-industries.com	732-563-9889		697
Falcon Natural Gas Corp 2500 City W Blvd Ste 300. . . . . Houston TX 77019	604-899-1533		538
Falcon Plastics Inc 1313 Western Ave. . . . . Brookings SD 57006 Web: falconplastics.com	605-696-2500	696-2585	604
Falcon Printing Inc 6360 Fulton St E. . . . . Ada MI 49301 Web: falconprintinginc.com	616-676-3737		627
Falcon Safety Products Inc 25 Imclone Dr. . . . . Branchburg NJ 08876 TF: 800-332-5266 ■ Web: www.falconsafety.com	908-707-4900	707-8855	151
Falcon Seaboard 109 N Post Oak Ln Ste 540. . . . . Houston TX 77024 Web: www.falconseaboard.com	713-622-0055	622-0045	540
Falcon State Park PO Box 2. . . . . Falcon Heights TX 78545 Web: tpwd.texas.gov/state-parks/falcon	956-848-5327		565
FalconStor Software Inc 2 Huntington Quad Ste 2S01 . . . . . Melville NY 11747 NASDAQ: FALC ■ Web: www.falconstor.com	631-777-5188	501-7633	178-12
Falconwood Inc 1011 Camino Del Rio S Ste 610. . . . . San Diego CA 92108 Web: www.falconwood.biz	619-297-9080		175
Falk Harrison Creative Inc 1300 Baur Blvd. . . . . St. Louis MO 63132 Web: falkharrison.com	314-531-1410		344
Falk Marques Group LLC 9 Meriam St Ste 21. . . . . Lexington MA 02420 Web: www.falkmarquesgroup.com	781-652-0900		463
Falkenberg Capital Corp 600 S Cherry St Cherry Creek Plaza I Ste 1108 . . . . . Denver CO 80246 Web: www.falkenbergcapital.com	303-320-4800		401
Fall Creek Falls State Park 2009 Village Camp Rd . . . . . Spencer TN 38585 Web: www.state.tn.us	423-881-5298		565
Fall Creek State Recreation Area 84610 Peninsula Rd . . . . . Fall Creek OR 97438 TF: 800-551-6949 ■ Web: oregonstateparks.org	541-937-1173		565
Fall River County 906 N River St . . . . . Hot Springs SD 57747 Web: ujs.sd.gov	605-745-5131		338
Fall River Feedyard LLC 27962 Angostura Rd. . . . . Hot Springs SD 57747	605-745-4109		10-1
Fall River Group 670 S Main. . . . . Fall River WI 53932 Web: www.fallrivergroup.com	920-484-3311		308
Fall River Heritage State Park Davol St . . . . . Fall River MA 02720 Web: www.mass.gov	508-675-5759		565
Fall River News Co 25 Westwood Ave . . . . . New London CT 06320	860-442-4394		96
Fall River Public Library 104 N Main St . . . . . Fall River MA 02720 TF: 800-331-3764 ■ Web: www.sailsinc.org	508-324-2700	324-2707	434-3
Fall River Rural Electric Co-op Inc 1150 N 3400 E . . . . . Ashton ID 83420 TF: 800-632-5726 ■ Web: www.fallriverelectric.com	208-652-7431	652-7825	245
Fallbrook Chamber of Commerce 111 S Main Ave . . . . . Fallbrook CA 92028 Web: www.fallbrookchamberofcommerce.org	760-728-5845	728-4031	139
Fallbrook Printing Corp 504 E Alvarado St. . . . . Fallbrook CA 92028 TF: 800-479-1033 ■ Web: www.fallbrookprinting.com	760-731-2020		627
Fallbrook Shopping Ctr 6633 Fallbrook Ave. . . . . West Hills CA 91307 TF: 888-888-7642 ■ Web: www.roicreit.net	858-922-6825		460
Faller Davis & Assoc Inc 4200 W Cypress St. . . . . Tampa FL 33607 Web: www.fallerdavis.com	813-261-5136		302
Fallin Mary (R) Capitol Bldg 2300 Lincoln Blvd Rm. 212 . . . . Oklahoma City OK 73105 Web: www.gov.ok.gov	405 521 2342	521-3353	343
Falling Waters State Park 1130 State Pk Rd . . . . . Chipley FL 32428 Web: www.floridastateparks.org	850-638-6130		565
Fallingwater 1491 Mill Run Rd. . . . . Mill Run PA 15464 Web: waterlandlife.org	724-329-8501	329-0553	50-3
Fallon 901 Marquette Ave Ste 2400 . . . . . Minneapolis MN 55402 Web: www.fallon.com	612-758-2345		4
Fallon Chamber of Commerce 85 N Taylor St. . . . . Fallon NV 89406 TF: 800-242-0478 ■ Web: www.fallonchamber.com	775-423-2544	423-0540	139
Fallon Community Health Plan Inc 10 Chestnut St Ste 7. . . . . Worcester MA 01608 TF: 800-333-2535 ■ Web: www.fchp.org	508-799-2100		391-3
Fallon County 10 W Fallon St PO Box 1061 . . . . . Baker MT 59313 Web: www.falloncounty.net	406-778-3152		338
Falls Church (Independent City) 300 Pk Ave . . . . . Falls Church VA 22046 TF: 800-543-8911 ■ Web: www.fallschurchva.gov	703-248-5001	248-5146	338
Falls County 520 Lawrence St . . . . . Corpus Christi TX 78401 Web: www.texasfile.com	254-883-1408		338
Falls Lake State Recreation Area 13304 Creedmoor Rd . . . . . Wake Forest NC 27587 Web: www.ncparks.gov	919-676-1027		565
Falls Landing 200 E Eigth St . . . . . Sioux Falls SD 57103 Web: falls-landing.com	605-336-2290		671
Falls of the Ohio State Park 201 W Riverside Dr. . . . . Clarksville IN 47129 Web: www.in.gov	812-280-9970	280-7110	565
Falls Park on the Reedy 601 S Main St. . . . . Greenville SC 29601 Web: www.fallspark.com	064 467 4350		50-5
Falls River Group LLC 305 Fifth Ave S Ste 206 . . . . . Naples FL 34102 Web: www.fallsrivergroup.com	239-649-4222		401
Falls Terrace 106 Deschutes Way SW. . . . . Tumwater WA 98501 TF: 800-863-2318 ■ Web: www.fallsterrace.com	360-943-7830		671
Fallsview Casino Resort 6380 Fallsview Blvd . . . . . Niagara Falls ON L2G7X5 *Fax Area Code: 905 ■ TF: 888-325-5788 ■ Web: www.fallsviewcasinoresort.com	888-325-5788	371-7952*	669
Falmouth Chamber of Commerce 20 Academy Ln. . . . . Falmouth MA 02540 TF: 800-526-8532 ■ Web: www.falmouthchamber.com	508-548-8500	548-8521	139
Falmouth Hospital 100 Terr Heun Dr . . . . . Falmouth MA 02540 Web: www.capecodhealth.org	508-548-5300		374-3
Falmouth Inn 824 Main St. . . . . Falmouth MA 02540 Web: www.falmouthinn.com	508-540-2500		379
Falmouth Lumber Inc 670 Teaticket Hwy. . . . . East Falmouth MA 02536 Web: www.falmouthlumber.com	508-548-6868		191-3
Falmouth Public Library 300 Main St. . . . . Falmouth MA 02540 Web: www.falmouthpubliclibrary.org	508-457-2555		434-3
Falmouth Scientific Inc 1400 Route 28A. . . . . Cataumet MA 02534 Web: www.falmouth.com	508-564-7640		757
False Cape State Park 4001 Sandpiper Rd. . . . . Virginia Beach VA 23456 TF General: 800-933-7275 ■ Web: www.dcr.virginia.gov/state-parks/false-cape#general_information	757-426-7128	426-0055	565
Falstrom Co 147 Falstrom Ct. . . . . Passaic NJ 07055 Web: www.falstromcompany.com	973-777-0013		697
FAM (Fresno Art Museum) 2233 N First St. . . . . Fresno CA 93703 Web: www.fresnoartmuseum.org	559-441-4221	441-4227	520
Fam Funds 384 N Grand St PO Box 310 . . . . . Cobleskill NY 12043 TF: 800-721-5391 ■ Web: www.famfunds.com	518-234-4393	234-4473	317
fama PR Inc Liberty Wharf 250 Northern Ave Ste 300. . . . . Boston MA 02210 Web: www.famapr.com	617-986-5002		636
Famcor Oil Inc 7887 San Felipe Ste 250. . . . . Houston TX 77063	713-974-0002		536
Finance Authority of Maine 5 Community Dr PO Box 949 . . . . . Augusta ME 04332 TF: 800-228-3734 ■ Web: www.famemaine.com	207-623-3263	623-0095	725

				Phone	Fax	Class
Fame Industries Inc 51100 Grand River Ave *Web:* www.fameind.com	Wixom	MI	48393	248-348-7760		207
Families Against Mandatory Minimums (FAMM) 1612 K St NW Ste 700 *TF:* 800-435-7352 ■ *Web:* www.famm.org	Washington	DC	20006	202-822-6700	822-6704	48-8
Families USA 1201 New York Ave NW Ste 1100 *Web:* www.familiesusa.org	Washington	DC	20005	202-628-3030	347-2417	48-7
Familiprix Inc 6000 Rue Armand-Viau *TF:* 800-463-5160 ■ *Web:* www.familiprix.com/en	Quebec	QC	G2C2C5	418-847-3311		238
Family Arena 2002 Arena Pkwy *Web:* www.familyarena.com	Saint Charles	MO	63303	636-896-4242	896-4205	720
Family Behavioral Resources 4900 Perry Hwy Bldg 2 Ste 200 *Web:* www.familybehavioralresources.com	Pittsburgh	PA	15229	724-850-8118		726
Family Brands International LLC 1001 Elm Hill Rd PO Box 429 *TF:* 800-356-4455	Lenoir City	TN	37771	865-986-8005	986-7171	296-26
Family Business Institute Inc, The 4050 Wake Forest Rd Ste 110 *Web:* www.familybusinessinstitute.com	Raleigh	NC	27609	919-783-1880		463
Family Campers & RVers (FCRV) 4804 Transit Rd Bldg 2 *TF:* 800-245-9755 ■ *Web:* www.fcrv.org	Depew	NY	14043	716-668-6242		48-23
Family Career & Community Leaders of America (FCCLA) 1910 Assn Dr *TF:* 800-234-4425 ■ *Web:* www.fcclainc.org	Reston	VA	20191	703-476-4900	439-2662	48-11
Family Caregiver Alliance (FCA) 180 Montgomery St Ste 900 *TF:* 800-445-8106 ■ *Web:* www.caregiver.org	San Francisco	CA	94104	415-434-3388	434-3508	48-17
Family Centre, The 9912-106 St Northwest Ste 20 *TF:* 800-268-7708 ■ *Web:* www.the-family-centre.com	Edmonton	AB	T5K1C5	780-423-2831		393
Family Cir Magazine 375 Lexington Ave 9th Fl *TF:* 800-627-4444 ■ *Web:* www.familycircle.com	New York	NY	10017	800-627-4444		457-11
Family Circle Tennis Ctr 161 Seven Farms Dr *TF:* 800-677-2293 ■ *Web:* www.familycircletenniscenter.com	Daniel Island	SC	29492	843-856-7900		463
Family Credit Management 111 N Wabash Ste 1408 *TF:* 800-994-3328 ■ *Web:* www.familycredit.org	Chicago	IL	60602	800-994-3328		41
Family Dollar Stores Inc PO Box 1017 *NYSE: FDO* ■ *TF:* 866-377-6420 ■ *Web:* www.familydollar.com	Charlotte	NC	28201	704-847-6961		791
Family Firm Institute (FFI) 200 Lincoln St Ste 201 *Web:* www.ffi.org	Boston	MA	02111	617-482-3045	482-3049	49-12
Family Friends Veterinary Hospital & Kennel 864 Massachusetts Ave *TF:* 800-920-4160 ■ *Web:* www.familyfriendsvetandkennel.com	Boxborough	MA	01719	978-263-3412		794
Family Guidance Center of Warren County Inc 492 Route 57 W *TF:* 800-326-3264 ■ *Web:* www.fgcwc.org	Washington	NJ	07882	908-689-1000		726
Family Handyman Magazine 2915 Commers Dr Ste 700 *TF:* 800-285-4961 ■ *Web:* www.familyhandyman.com	Eagan	MN	55121	800-285-4961		457-14
Family Health Care Services Inc *Home Health Care Service* 1701 W Charleston Blvd	Las Vegas	NV	89102	702-383-0887		371
Family Health Center 117 W Paterson *Web:* www.fhcsd.org	Kalamazoo	MI	49007	269-349-2641		418
Family Healthcare Network 305 E Ctr Ave *Web:* www.fhcn.org	Visalia	CA	93291	559-737-4700		374-3
Family Hospice & Palliative Care 50 Moffett St *TF:* 800-513-2148 ■ *Web:* familyhospicepa.org	Pittsburgh	PA	15243	412-572-8800	572-8827	371
Family Hospice of Belleville Area 5110 W Main St *Web:* www.familyhospice.org	Belleville	IL	62226	618-277-1800	277-1074	371
Family House Inc 1509 N Knoxville Ave *Web:* www.familyhousepeoria.org	Peoria	IL	61603	309-685-5300	685-8122	372
Family Kingdom Amusement Park & Oceanfront Water Park 300 S Ocean Blvd *TF:* 800-978-4988 ■ *Web:* www.familykingdomfun.com	Myrtle Beach	SC	29577	843-626-3447		32
Family Law Reporter 1801 S Bell St *TF:* 800-372-1033 ■ *Web:* www.bna.com/family-law-reporter-p6014	Arlington	VA	22202	800-372-1033		531-7
Family Life Communications Inc PO Box 35300 *TF:* 800-776-1070 ■ *Web:* www.myflr.org	Tucson	AZ	85740	800-776-1070		644
Family Life Worship Center Worldwide Ministries Inc 1517 Joyner Pond Rd	Aiken	SC	29803	803-641-0218		48-20
Family Motor Coach Assn (FMCA) 8291 Clough Pk *TF:* 800-543-3622 ■ *Web:* www.fmca.com	Cincinnati	OH	45244	513-474-3622	474-2332	48-23
Family Motor Coaching Magazine 8291 Clough Pk *TF:* 800-543-3622 ■ *Web:* www.fmca.com	Cincinnati	OH	45244	513-474-3622	474-2332	457-22
Family of the Americas Foundation 5929 Talbot Rd *TF:* 800-443-3395 ■ *Web:* www.familyplanning.net	Lothian	MD	20711	301-627-3346		48-17
Family Pet Animal Hospital 1401 W Webster Ave *Web:* familypetanimalhospital.com	Chicago	IL	60614	773-935-2311		794
Family Practice Management 11400 Tomahawk Creek Pkwy *TF:* 800-274-2237 ■ *Web:* aafp.org/journals/fpm.html	Leawood	KS	66211	913-906-6000	906-6075	457-16
Family Radio 290 Hegenberger Rd *TF:* 800-543-1495 ■ *Web:* familyradio.org	Oakland	CA	94621	800-543-1495		643
Family Research Council (FRC) 801 G St NW *TF:* 800-225-4008 ■ *Web:* www.frc.org	Washington	DC	20001	202-393-2100	393-2134	48-6
Family Service Foundation Inc 5301 76th Ave *TF:* 800-422-0009 ■ *Web:* www.fsfinc.org	Landover Hills	MD	20784	301-459-2121		303
Family Stations Inc 290 Hegenberger Rd *TF:* 800-543-1495 ■ *Web:* familyradio.org	Oakland	CA	94621	800-543-1495		645
Family Tree Magazine 4700 E Galbraith Rd *Web:* www.familytreemagazine.com	Cincinnati	OH	45236	513-531-2690		457-14
Family Video 2500 Lehigh Ave *TF:* 888-332-6843 ■ *Web:* www.familyvideo.com	Glenview	IL	60026	847-904-9000		797
Familymeds Inc 312 Farmington Ave *TF:* 888-787-2800 ■ *Web:* www.familymeds.com	Farmington	CT	06032	888-787-2800		238
FamilySearch 35 N W Temple St *TF:* 866-406-1830 ■ *Web:* www.familysearch.org	Salt Lake City	UT	84150	866-406-1830		387
FamilyTime LLC 101 Merrittt Blvd Ste 102 *Web:* www.familytime.com	Trumbull	CT	06611	203-610-8265		387
FAMM (Families Against Mandatory Minimums) 1612 K St NW Ste 700 *TF:* 800-435-7352 ■ *Web:* www.famm.org	Washington	DC	20006	202-822-6700	822-6704	48-8
Famous Bonanza Casino 107 Main St *Web:* www.famousbonanza.com	Central City	CO	80427	303-582-5914		133
Famous Dave's 401 E Bismarck Expy *Web:* www.famousdaves.com	Bismarck	ND	58504	701-530-9800		671
Famous Dave's Barbeque 181 Jennifer Rd *TF:* 877-833-9335 ■ *Web:* www.famousdaves.com	Annapolis	MD	21401	410-224-2207		671
Famous Dave's Bar-B-Que 900 S Pk St *Web:* www.famousdaves.com	Madison	WI	53715	608-286-9400		671
Famous Dave's Bar-B-Que 3001 Hennepin Ave *Web:* www.famousdaves.com	Minneapolis	MN	55408	612-822-9900		671
Famous Dave's of America Inc 12701 Whitewater Dr Ste 200 *NASDAQ: DAVE* ■ *TF:* 800-929-4040 ■ *Web:* www.famousdaves.com	Minnetonka	MN	55343	952-294-1300		670
Famous Enterprises Inc 109 N Union St *Web:* www.famous-supply.com	Akron	OH	44304	330-762-9621		246
Famous Footwear 247 Junction Rd *TF Cust Svc:* 800-888-7198 ■ *Web:* www.famousfootwear.com	Madison	WI	53717	608-833-3340		301
Famous Tate Electric Co 8317 N Armenia Ave *Web:* www.famoustate.com	Tampa	FL	33604	813-935-3151		321
Fancy Feet Inc 26650 Harding St	Oak Park	MI	48237	248-398-8460		301
Fancy Foods Inc Bldg B-12 Hunts Point Cooperative Market *TF:* 800-333-0949 ■ *Web:* www.fancyfoodsinc.com	Bronx	NY	10474	718-617-3000		345
Fandango Inc 12200 W Olympic Blvd Ste 400 *Web:* www.fandango.com	Los Angeles	CA	90064	310-954-0278		116
Fandango Productions LLC 4601 Hollins Ferry Rd *TF:* 866-232-6326	Baltimore	MD	21227	866-232-6326		226
Fandel Retail Group 650 Fifth St Ste 405 *Web:* www.fandelretail.com	San Francisco	CA	94107	415-538-8355		463
Fandor Homes 68 Romina Dr *TF:* 800-844-9936 ■ *Web:* fandorhomes.com	Vaughan	ON	L4K4Z7	905-669-5820		187
Fanello Industries Inc 50 E Main St *Web:* www.fanelloindustries.com	Lavonia	GA	30553	706-356-5359		488
Faneuil Hall Marketplace 4 S Market Bldg 5th Fl *Web:* www.faneuilhallmarketplace.com	Boston	MA	02109	617-523-1300	523-1779	50-6
Faneuil Inc 2 Eaton St Ste 1002 *Web:* www.faneuil.com	Hampton	VA	23669	757-722-3235		196
Fanfare Sports & Entertainment 4415 S Westnedge Ave *Web:* www.fanfare-se.com	Kalamazoo	MI	49008	269-349-8866		95
Fannie & John Hertz Foundation 2300 First St Ste 250 *Web:* www.hertzfoundation.org	Livermore	CA	94550	925-373-1642		305
Fannie Mae 3900 Wisconsin Ave NW *OTC: FNMA* ■ *TF:* 800-732-6643 ■ *Web:* www.fanniemae.com	Washington	DC	20016	202-752-7000		509
Fannin Battleground State Historic Site 734 FM 2506 *Web:* www.thc.texas.gov	Fannin	TX	77960	512-463-7948		565
Fannin County 400 W Main St Ste 100 *Web:* fannincountyga.org	Blue Ridge	GA	30513	706-632-2203	632-2507	338
Fannin County 101 Sam Rayburn Dr County Courthouse Ste 301 *Web:* www.co.fannin.tx.us	Bonham	TX	75418	903-583-7448	583-7682	338
Fannin County Board of Education 2290 E First St *TF:* 800-308-2145 ■ *Web:* www.fannin.k12.ga.us	Blue Ridge	GA	30513	706-632-3771	632-7583	685
Fannin County Electric Co-op Inc 1530 Silo Rd *Web:* www.fcec.coop	Bonham	TX	75418	903-583-2117		245
Fanning Group Inc 1280 Main St Second Fl PO Box 479 *Web:* www.fanningnet.com	Hanson	MA	02341	781-293-4100	294-0808	47
Fanning Springs State Park 18020 NW Hwy 19 *Web:* www.floridastateparks.org	Fanning Springs	FL	32693	352-463-3420	463-3420	565
Fanning/Howey Assoc Inc 540 E Market St *TF:* 800-452-3573 ■ *Web:* www.fhai.com	Celina	OH	45822	419-586-7771	586-2141	261
Fannon Petroleum Services Inc 7755 Progress Ct *Web:* www.fannonpetroleum.com	Gainesville	VA	20155	703-468-2060	754-2590	579
Fanshawe College 1001 Fanshawe College Blvd *TF:* 800-717-4412 ■ *Web:* www.fanshawec.on.ca	London	ON	N5Y5R6	519-452-4430		165
Fansteel Inc 1746 Commerce Rd *Web:* www.fansteel.com	Creston	IA	50801	641-782-8521		483
FANTA Equipment Co 6521 Storer Ave *Web:* www.fantaequip.com	Cleveland	OH	44102	216-281-1515	281-7755	494
Fantagraphics Books 7563 Lake City Way NE *TF:* 800-657-1100 ■ *Web:* www.fantagraphics.com	Seattle	WA	98115	206-524-1967	524-2104	637-5

	Phone	Fax	Class
Fantastic Indoor Swapmeet 1717 S Decatur Blvd, Las Vegas NV 89102 *Web:* www.fantasticindoorswapmeet.com	702-877-0087		460
Fantastic Sams Inc 500 Cummings Ctr Ste 1100, Beverly MA 01915 *Web:* www.fantasticsams.com	651-770-1449		77
Fantastic Tours & Travel 6143 Jericho Tpke, Commack NY 11725 *TF:* 800-552-6262 ■ *Web:* www.fantastictours.com	631-462-6262	462-2311	760
Fan-Tastic Vent Corp 2083 S Almont Ave, Imlay City MI 48444 *TF:* 800-521-0298 ■ *Web:* www.fantasticvent.com	810-724-3818		37
Fantasy Cookie Co 12800 Arroyo St, Sylmar CA 91342 *Web:* www.fantasycookie.com	818-361-6901		805
Fantasy Diamond Corp 1550 W Carrol Ave, Chicago IL 60607 *TF:* 800-621-4445 ■ *Web:* endlessdiamond.com	312-583-3200	583-3434	410
Fantasy Springs Resort Casino 84-245 Indio Springs Pkwy, Indio CA 92203 *TF Cust Svc:* 800-827-2946 ■ *Web:* www.fantasyspringsresort.com	760-342-5000		133
Fanthorp Inn State Historic Site 579 Main St, Anderson TX 77830 *Web:* tpwd.texas.gov/state-parks/fanthorp-inn	936-873-2633		565
Fantini Baking Company Inc 375 Washington St, Haverhill MA 01832 *TF:* 800-223-9037 ■ *Web:* www.fantinibakery.com	978-373-1273	373-6250	296-1
Fantus Paper Products P.S. Greetings Inc 5730 N Tripp Ave, Chicago IL 60646 *TF Sales:* 800-621-8823 ■ *Web:* www.psg-fpp.com	773-267-6069	267-6055	130
FANUC America Corp 3900 W Hamlin Rd, Rochester Hills MI 48309 *TF:* 800-477-6268 ■ *Web:* www.fanucamerica.com/corporate-home.aspx	248-377-7000	377-7832	386
Fanzz 2657 S 1030 W Ste 10, Salt Lake City UT 84119 *TF:* 888-326-9946 ■ *Web:* www.fanzz.com	801-325-2700		711
Fapco Inc 216 Post Rd, Buchanan MI 49107 *TF:* 800-782-0167 ■ *Web:* www.fapcoinc.com	800-782-0167		549
FAPD (Federal APD Inc) 28100 Cabot Dr Ste 200, Novi MI 48377 *TF:* 877-992-7749 ■ *Web:* 3m.com	248-374-9600		692
FAPRI (Food & Agricultural Policy Research Institute) Iowa State University 578 Heady Hall, Ames IA 50011 *Web:* www.fapri.iastate.edu	515-294-1183	294-6336	634
Far Bank Enterprises Inc 8500 NE Day Rd, Bainbridge Island WA 98110 *Web:* www.farbank.com	206-780-8767		787
Far Best Foods Inc 4689 S 400 W PO Box 480, Huntingburg IN 47542 *Web:* www.farbestfoods.com	812-683-4200	683-4226	619
Far East Broadcasting Co Inc 15700 Imperial Hwy PO Box 1, La Mirada CA 90638 *TF:* 800-523-3480 ■ *Web:* www.febc.org	800-523-3480		643
Far East Energy Corp 400 N Sam Houston Pkwy Ste 205, Houston TX 77060 *Web:* www.fareastenergy.com	832-598-0470		536
Far Hills Group LLC 747 Third Ave 30th Fl, New York NY 10017 *Web:* www.farhills.com	212-840-7779		194
Far Horizons Montessori 264 N Main St, Orange CA 92868 *TF:* 800-362-6010 ■ *Web:* www.farhorizonsmontessori.org	714-997-8333		685
Far Niente Ristorante 204 1/2 N Brand Blvd, Glendale CA 91203 *Web:* farnienteglendale.com	818-242-3835		671
Far Niente Winery Inc 1350 Acacia Dr, Oakville CA 94562 *Web:* www.farniente.com	707-944-2861		10-11
Far Research Inc 2210 Wilhelmina Ct N E, Palm Bay FL 32905 *Web:* far-chemical.com	321-723-6160		583
Far Ridgeline Engagements Inc 285 W New York Ave, Southern Pines NC 28387 *Web:* www.frleinc.com	910-725-0303		180
Far Western Graphics Inc 1105 Kern Ave, Sunnyvale CA 94085 *TF:* 800-959-6560 ■ *Web:* fwgprinting.com	408-481-9777		175
Faradyne Motors Inc 2077 Division St, Palmyra NY 14522 *Web:* www.faradynemotors.com	315-502-0125		518
Farah Afaf Vicky 201 E Liberty St Ste 7, Ann Arbor MI 48104 *TF:* 800-201-3187 ■ *Web:* vickyfarah.com	734-663-9813		428
Farallon 450 Post St, San Francisco CA 94102 *Web:* www.farallonrestaurant.com	415-956-6969	834-1234	671
Farallones Marine Sanctuary Assn PO Box 29386, San Francisco CA 94129 *Web:* www.farallones.org	415-561-6625		41
Farber Financial Group 150 York St Ste 1600, Toronto ON M5H3S5 *Web:* www.farberfinancial.com	416-497-0150		401
Farber Specialty Vehicle Inc 7052 Americana Pkwy, Reynoldsburg OH 43068 *Web:* www.farberspecialty.com	614-863-6470		59
FarCountries com 150 W 25th St, Ste 1203, New York NY 10001	212-255-6550	255-4543	393
Fard Engineers Inc 309 Lennon Ln Ste 200, Walnut Creek CA 94598 *Web:* www.fard.com	925-932-5505		256
Farenthold Blake (Rep R - TX) 2331 Rayburn HOB, Washington DC 20515 *Web:* farenthold.house.gov	202-225-7742	226-1134	342-2
Farewell Bend State Recreation Area 23751 Old Hwy 30, Huntington OR 97907 *Web:* www.oregonstateparks.org	541-869-2365		565
Farfalla Trattoria 1978 Hillhurst Ave, Los Angeles CA 90027 *Web:* trattoriafarfalla.com	323-661-7365	661-5956	671
Fargo Air Museum 1609 19th Ave N, Fargo ND 58102 *Web:* www.fargoairmuseum.org	701-293-8043	293-8103	520
Fargo Assembly Co (FAC) 3300 Seventh Ave N PO Box 2340, Fargo ND 58102 *Web:* www.facnd.com	701-298-3803	298-3806	814
Fargo Assembly of Pennsylvania Inc 800 W Washington St PO Box 550, Norristown PA 19404 *Web:* www.fargopa.com	610-272-6850	272-6858	247
Fargo Automation Inc 969 34th St N, Fargo ND 58102 *Web:* www.fargoautomation.com	701-232-1780		111
Fargo C'mon Inn Hotel 4338 20th Ave SW, Fargo ND 58103 *TF:* 800-334-1570 ■ *Web:* www.cmoninn.com	701-277-9944	277-9117	379
Fargo City Hall 200 N Third St, Fargo ND 58102 *Web:* fargond.gov	701-241-1310	476-4136	337
Fargo Civic Ctr 207 N Fourth St, Fargo ND 58102 *Web:* fargond.gov	701-241-1480	241-1483	205
Fargo Glass & Paint Company Inc 1801 Seventh Ave N, Fargo ND 58102 *Web:* fargoglass.com	701-235-4441		191-2
Fargo Jet Center Inc 3802 20th St N, Fargo ND 58102 *TF:* 800-770-0538 ■ *Web:* www.fargojet.com	701-235-3600		63
Fargo Packing & Sausage Co 307 E Main Ave, West Fargo ND 58078 *Web:* qualitymeats.com	701-282-3211		296-26
Fargo Theatre 314 Broadway N, Fargo ND 58102 *Web:* www.fargotheatre.org	701-239-8385		572
FARGODOME 1800 N University Dr, Fargo ND 58102 *TF:* 855-694-6367 ■ *Web:* www.fargodome.com	701-241-9100	237-0987	720
Fargo-Moorhead Community Theatre 333 Fourth St S, Fargo ND 58103 *TF:* 800-322-4810 ■ *Web:* www.fmct.org	701-235-1901		573-4
Fargo-Moorhead Convention & Visitors Bureau 2001 44th St S, Fargo ND 58103 *TF:* 800-235-7654 ■ *Web:* www.fargomoorhead.org	701-282-3653	282-4366	206
Fargo-Moorhead Opera Co 3100 25th St S Ste A, Fargo ND 58103 *Web:* www.fmopera.org	701-239-4558		573-2
Faria Beede Instruments 88 Village St, Penacook NH 03303 *Web:* www.beede.com	603-753-6362		248
Faribault County 415 N Main St, Blue Earth MN 56013 *Web:* faribaultcountyrecorder.com	507-526-6252		338
Faribault Foods Inc 222 S Ninth St Ste 3380, Minneapolis MN 55402 *Web:* www.faribaultfoods.com	612-333-6461		296-20
Faribault Woolen MillCo 1500 NW Second Ave, Faribault MN 55021 *Web:* faribaultmill.com	507-412-5510		745-1
Faribo Insurance Agency Inc 1404 Seventh St NW, Faribault MN 55021 *TF:* 888-923-0430 ■ *Web:* insuranceagencymn.com	507-334-3929		390
Faris Machinery Co 5770 E 77th Ave, Commerce CO 80022 *Web:* www.farismachinery.com/default.htm	303-289-5743		358
Farley Appliance 814 W Main St, League City TX 77573	281-332-8000		35
Farley Printing Co Inc 96 Vandever Ave, Wilmington DE 19802	302-656-4466		627
Farley's 3499 Foothills Rd, Las Cruces NM 88011 *Web:* www.farleyspub.com	575-522-0466		671
Farley's & Sathers Candy Company Inc 1 Sather Plaza, Round Lake MN 56167 *Web:* www.ferrarausa.com	507-945-8181		296-8
Farm & Home Oil Co 3115 State Rd, Telford PA 18969 *TF:* 800-776-7263 ■ *Web:* www.suburbanpropane.com	800-776-7263		316
Farm Boy Meats 2761 N Kentucky Ave, Evansville IN 47711 *TF:* 800-852-3976 ■ *Web:* www.farmboyfoodservice.com	812-425-5231	425-5231	473
Farm Bureau Bank 2165 Green Vista Dr Ste 204, Sparks NV 89431 **Fax Area Code:* 866 ■ *TF:* 800-492-3276 ■ *Web:* farmbureaubank.com	775-673-4566	913-5087*	70
Farm Bureau Life Insurance Co 5400 University Ave, West Des Moines IA 50266 *TF:* 800-247-4170 ■ *Web:* www.fbfs.com	515-225-5400		391-2
Farm Bureau Press 10720 Kanis Rd, Little Rock AR 72211 *Web:* www.arfb.com	501-228-1300		457-1
Farm Business Consultants Inc 150 3015 Fifth Ave NE, Calgary AB T2A6T8 *TF:* 800-265-1002 ■ *Web:* www.fbc.ca	403-735-6105		734
Farm Credit Administration 1501 Farm Credit Dr, McLean VA 22102 *Web:* www.fca.gov	703-883-4000	734-5784	340-20
Farm Credit Administration Regional Offices			
Bloomington (MN) Field Office 1501 Farm Credit Dr, McLean VA 22102 *Web:* www.fca.gov	952-854-7151		340-20
Dallas Field Office 511 E Carpenter Fwy Ste 650, Irving TX 75062 *Web:* fca.gov	972-869-0550		340-20
Denver Field Office 3131 S Vaughn Way Ste 250, Aurora CO 80014 *Web:* www.fca.gov	303-696-9737		340-20
McLean Field Office 1501 Farm Credit Dr, McLean VA 22102 *Web:* www.fca.gov	703-883-4056	883-4056	340-20
Sacramento Field Office 2180 Harvard St Ste 300, Sacramento CA 95815 *Web:* www.fca.gov	916-648-1118		340-20
Farm Credit Council 50 F St NW Ste 900, Washington DC 20001 *TF:* 866-632-9992 ■ *Web:* www.fccouncil.com	202-626-8710	626-8718	49-2
Farm Credit Leasing (FCL) 600 Hwy 169 S Ste 300, Minneapolis MN 55426 *TF:* 800-444-2929 ■ *Web:* www.farmcreditleasing.com	952-417-7800		216
Farm Credit Of Central Florida Aca 115 S Missouri Ave Ste 400, Lakeland FL 33815 *TF:* 800-533-2773 ■ *Web:* www.farmcreditcfl.com	863-682-4117	688-9364	216
Farm Credit Of Northwest Florida Aca 5052 Hwy 90, Marianna FL 32446 *TF:* 800-527-0647 ■ *Web:* www.farmcredit-fl.com	850-526-4910	482-6597	216
Farm Credit of The Virginias Aca 106 Sangers Ln, Staunton VA 24401 *TF:* 800-559-1016 ■ *Web:* www.farmcreditofvirginias.com	540-886-3435		217
Farm Credit West 3755 Atherton Rd, Rocklin CA 95765 *Web:* www.farmcreditwest.com	916-780-1166	780-1820	217

Phone | Fax | Class

Farm Equipment Manufacturers Assn (FEMA)
1000 Executive Pkwy Ste 100 .... Saint Louis MO 63141 314-878-2304 732-1480 48-2
TF: 800-647-3061 ■ *Web:* www.farmequip.org

Farm Family Casualty Insurance Co
PO Box 656 .... Albany NY 12201 518-431-5000 391-4
TF: 800-843-3276 ■ *Web:* www.farmfamily.com

Farm Family Life Insurance Co
PO Box 656 .... Albany NY 12201 518-431-5000 391-2
TF: 800-948-3276 ■ *Web:* www.farmfamily.com

Farm Financial Strategies 2029 400th St .... Osage IA 50461 641-732-3636 734
Web: farmestate.com

Farm First Dairy Co-op
4001 Nakoosa Trl Ste 100.................... Madison WI 53714 608-244-3373 393
TF: 800-525-7704 ■ *Web:* www.farmfirstdairycooperative.com

Farm Implement & Supply Company Inc
1200 S Washington Hwy 183................. Plainville KS 67663 785-434-4824 434-7390 274
TF: 888-589-6029 ■ *Web:* www.farmimp.com

Farm Industry News
7900 International Dr Ste 300...............Minneapolis MN 55425 800-441-1410 457-1
TF Cust Svc: 800-722-5334 ■ *Web:* www.farmindustrynews.com

Farm Island Recreation Area
1301 Farm Island Rd ....Pierre SD 57501 605-773-2885 565
Web: gfp.sd.gov

Farm Journal 261 E Broadway St.............. Monticello MN 55362 763-271-3363 457-1

Farm Journal 30 S 15th Ste 900 ....Philadelphia PA 19102 215-557-8900 457-1
TF: 800-331-9310 ■ *Web:* www.farmjournalmedia.com

Farm Service Agency
1400 Independence Ave SW................Washington DC 20250 202-720-3865 340-1
Web: www.fsa.usda.gov

Farm Service Co-op 2308 Pine St............... Harlan IA 51537 712-755-3185 755-7098 276
TF: 800-452-4372 ■ *Web:* www.fscoop.com

Farm Show Magazine
20088 Kenwood Trial .... Lakeville MN 55044 800-834-9665 469-5575* 457-1
**Fax Area Code:* 952 ■ *TF:* 800-834-9665 ■ *Web:* www.farmshow.com

Farm Stores Corp
16777 Old Cutler Rd.................... Palmetto Bay FL 33157 305-677-0645 297-8
Web: www.farmstores.com

Farm, The 5321 S Sheridan Ste 27 .... Tulsa OK 74145 918-622-3860 622-4675 460
Web: www.farmshoppingcenter.com

Farmdale Creamery Inc
1049 W Baseline St .... San Bernardino CA 92411 909-889-3002 888-2541 296-5
TF: 800-346-7306 ■ *Web:* farmdale.net

Farmer & Irwin Corp 3300 Ave K...........Riviera Beach FL 33404 561-842-5316 842-5999 189-10
Web: www.fandicorp.com

Farmer Boy Ag 50 W Stoever Ave ....Myerstown PA 17067 800-845-3374 866-6233* 274
**Fax Area Code:* 717 ■ *TF:* 800-845-3374 ■ *Web:* www.farmerboyag.com

Farmer Bros Co 20333 S Normandie Ave ....Torrance CA 90502 310-787-5200 296-7
NASDAQ: FARM ■ *TF:* 800-735-2878 ■ *Web:* www.farmerbros.com

Farmer State Bank of Sublette
303 S Pennsylvania Ave PO Box 20............. Sublette IL 61367 815-849-5242 360-2
TF: 866-269-1722 ■ *Web:* www.sublettebank.com

Farmer's Co-op Assn
110 S Keokuk Wash Rd......................... Keota IA 52248 641-636-3748 48-2
TF: 877-843-4893 ■ *Web:* www.keotafarmerscoop.com

Farmer's State Bank
555 S Commercial .... Harrisburg IL 62946 618-252-2600 186
Web: www.farmersstatebank.com

Farmer, Lumpe & Mcclelland Advertising Agency Ltd
500 W Wilson Bridge Rd Ste 316...........Worthington OH 43085 614-601-5195 5
Web: www.wideopenthinking.com

Farmers Alliance Mutual Insurance Co
1122 N Main PO Box 1401................. McPherson KS 67460 620-241-2200 241-5482 391-4
TF: 800-362-1075 ■ *Web:* www.fami.com

Farmers Bank & Savings Company Inc
211 W Second St .... Pomeroy OH 45769 740-992-2136 667-3162 70
Web: www.fbsc.com

Farmers Bank, The
9 E Clinton St PO Box 129................... Frankfort IN 46041 765-654-8731 654-8738 70
TF: 888-643-9090 ■ *Web:* www.thefarmersbank.com

Farmers Branch Chamber of Commerce
2815 Valley view Ln Ste 118............Farmers Branch TX 75234 972-243-8966 139
Web: farmersbranchchamber.org

Farmers Building & Savings Bank
290 W Park St............................Rochester PA 15074 724-774-4970 70

Farmers Capital Bank Corp
PO Box 309 .... Frankfort KY 40602 502-227-1668 227-1692 360-2
NASDAQ: FFKT ■ *TF:* 800-776-9437 ■ *Web:* www.farmerscapital.com

Farmers Co-op 208 W Depot.................Dorchester NE 68343 402-946-2211 275
Web: www.farmersco-operative.com

Farmers Co-op
2105 Industrial Park Rd .... Van Buren AR 72956 479-474-6622 474-4787 48-2
Web: www.farmercoop.com

Farmers Co-op Creamery Inc (FCC)
700 N Hwy 99 W......................... McMinnville OR 97128 503-472-2157 296-3

Farmers Co-op Elevator Co
177 W Main St...........................Cottonwood MN 56229 507-423-5412 423-5551 447
Web: www.farmerscoopelevator.com

Farmers Co-op Elevator Co
109 Isabella St PO Box 200 ....Radcliffe IA 50230 515-899-2101 899-2105 447
Web: www.radcliffecoop.com

Farmers Co-op Society
317 Third St NW........................... Sioux Center IA 51250 712-722-2671 48-2
Web: www.farmerscoopsociety.com

Farmers Co-op Union, The
225 S Broadway PO Box 159 .... Sterling KS 67579 620-278-2141 11-1
TF: 800-238-1843 ■ *Web:* cpcoop.us

Farmers Educational & Co-op Union of America
20 F St NW Ste 300 ....Washington DC 20001 202-554-1600 554-1654 48-2
TF: 800-442-8277 ■ *Web:* www.nfu.org

Farmers Electric Co-op Inc
1959 Yoder Ave SW ....Kalona IA 52247 319-683-2510 245

Farmers Electric Co-op Inc
2000 E I-30.............................. Greenville TX 75402 903-455-1715 455-8125 245
TF: 800-541-2662 ■ *Web:* www.fecelectric.com

Farmers Electric Co-op Inc
3701 Thornton PO Box 550 .... Clovis NM 88101 575-762-4466 245
TF: 800-445-8541 ■ *Web:* fecnm.org

Farmers Feed & Grain Company Inc
306 Birch St PO Box 291 ....Riceville IA 50466 641-985-2147 985-4000 276
Web: www.ffgcoinc.com

Farmers Fire Insurance Co
2875 Eastern Blvd..............................York PA 17402 717-751-4435 390
TF: 800-537-0928 ■ *Web:* www.farmersfire.com

Farmers Insurance Exchange
6301 Owensmouth Ave.................Woodland Hills CA 91367 800-493-4917 217-1389* 391-4
**Fax Area Code:* 877 ■ **Fax:* Hum Res ■ *TF:* 855-808-6599 ■ *Web:* www.farmers.com

Farmers Insurance Group
6060 W Manchester Ave Ste 302 ....Los Angeles CA 90045 888-327-6335 2
TF: 888-327-6335 ■ *Web:* farmers.com

Farmers Livestock Auction Inc
1581 E Emma Ave..........................Springdale AR 72764 479-751-5727 446

Farmers Market Garden Ctr Inc
4110 N Elston Ave ....Chicago IL 60618 773-539-1200 323
TF: 800-679-2300 ■ *Web:* www.gardenchicago.com

Farmers Merchants Bank & Trust Co
100 S Main St PO Box 910.............. Breaux Bridge LA 70517 337-332-4132 332-5089 70
Web: www.fmbanking.com

Farmers Mutual Hail Insurance Company of Iowa
6785 Westown Pkwy..................West Des Moines IA 50266 515-282-9104 282-1220 391-4
TF: 800-247-5248 ■ *Web:* www.fmh.com

Farmers Mutual Insurance Company of Nebraska
501 S 13th St PO Box 81529 .... Lincoln NE 68501 402-434-8300 434-8351 391-4
TF: 800-742-7433 ■ *Web:* www.fmne.com

Farmers National Bank of Buhl
914 Main St PO Box 392 ....Buhl ID 83316 208-543-4351 70
Web: www.farmersbankidaho.com

Farmers National Bank of Prophetstown, The
114 W Third St.........................Prophetstown IL 61277 815-772-3700 70
Web: www.farmersnationalbank.com

Farmers National Co
11516 Nicholas St Ste 100.....................Omaha NE 68154 402-496-3276 390
Web: www.farmers-national.com

Farmers New World Life Insurance
3003 77th Ave SE.......................Mercer Island WA 98040 206-232-8400 391-2
Web: farmers.com

Farmers Ranchers Coop 224 S Main St .... Ainsworth NE 69210 402-387-2811 579
TF: 800-233-6627 ■ *Web:* www.farmersrancherscoop.com

Farmers Rice Co-op PO Box 15223.......... Sacramento CA 95851 916-923-5100 920-3321 296-23
TF: 800-326-2799 ■ *Web:* www.farmersrice.com

Farmers Rice Milling Co
3211 Hwy 397 S........................ Lake Charles LA 70615 337-433-5205 433-1735 296-23
Web: www.frmco.com

Farmers Rural Electric Co-op Corp
504 S Broadway St..........................Glasgow KY 42141 270-651-2191 651-7332 245
TF: 800-253-2191 ■ *Web:* www.farmersrecc.com

Farmers Select LLC 7321 N Loop Rd............ El Paso TX 79915 915-772-2736 296-27

Farmers State Bancshares Inc
100 W Main St PO Box 9 .... Mountain City TN 37683 423-727-8121 727-5382 70
Web: www.fsbankmctn.com

Farmers State Bank & Trust Co, The
200 W State St ....Jacksonville IL 62650 217-479-4000 70
Web: www.fsbtco.com

Farmers Supply Sales Inc 1409 E Ave .... Kalona IA 52247 319-656-2291 274
TF: 800-493-4917 ■ *Web:* www.farmers.com

Farmers Telecommunications Co-op (FTC)
144 McCurdy Ave N PO Box 217 ....Rainsville AL 35986 256-638-2144 638-4830 736
TF: 866-638-2144 ■ *Web:* www.farmerstel.com

Farmers Telephone Co-op Inc
1101 E Main St.............................Kingstree SC 29556 843-382-2333 382-2333 736
TF: 888-218-5050 ■ *Web:* www.ftc-i.net

Farmers Union Co-op 1913 Co Rd B32 .... Ossian IA 52161 563-532-9381 447

Farmers Union Oil Co of Southern Valley (FUOSV)
204 S Front St .... Fairmount ND 58030 701-474-5440 316
Web: www.fuosv.com

Farmers West 5300 Foothill Rd.............. Carpinteria CA 93013 805-684-5531 684-1528 369
TF: 800-549-0085 ■ *Web:* www.farmerswest.com

Farmers Win Coop (FFC)
110 N Jefferson ....Fredericksburg IA 50630 563-237-5324 237-6123 10-4
TF: 800-562-8389 ■ *Web:* farmerswincoop.agricharts.com/Fredericksburg

Farmers' Electric Co-op
201 W Business 36 PO Box 680.............Chillicothe MO 64601 660-646-4281 646-3569 245
TF: 800-279-0496 ■ *Web:* www.fec-co.com

Farmhouse Restaurant 119 W Main St.......... Branson MO 65616 417-334-9701 671
Web: farmhouserestaurantbranson.com

Farmingdale State University of New York
2350 Broadhollow Rd....................Farmingdale NY 11735 631-420-2000 420-2633 166
TF: 800-557-7392 ■ *Web:* www.farmingdale.edu

Farmington Capital Partners
PO Box 1461 ....Hartford CT 06144 860-284-1096 691
Web: www.farmingtoncapital.com

Farmington Center Salem an Oregon LP
960 Boone Rd SE .... Salem OR 97306 503-715-0727 77
Web: www.farmingtonsquare-salem.com

Farmington Chamber of Commerce
100 W Broadway.......................... Farmington NM 87401 505-325-0279 327-7556 139
Web: www.gofarmington.com

Farmington Convention & Visitors Bureau
3041 E Main St.......................... Farmington NM 87402 505-326-7602 206
TF: 800-448-1240 ■ *Web:* www.farmingtonnm.org

Farmington Correctional Ctr
1012 W Columbia St .... Farmington MO 63640 573-218-7100 213
TF: 800-844-6591 ■ *Web:* mo.gov

Farmington Displays Inc 21 Hyde Rd .... Farmington CT 06032 860-677-2497 677-1418 286
Web: www.fdi-group.com

Farmington Foods Inc
7419 W Franklin St....................... Forest Park IL 60130 708-771-3600 296-26
Web: www.farmingtonfoods.com

Farmington HealthCare Ctr
34225 Grand River Ave.................... Farmington MI 48335 248-477-7373 450

Farmington Historic Plantation
3033 BaRdstown Rd.........................Louisville KY 40205 502-452-9920 520

Farmington Press
218 N Washington St .... Farmington MO 63640 573-756-8927 756-9160 532-4
TF: 800-455-0206 ■ *Web:* dailyjournalonline.com

Phone Fax Class

Farmington Public Library
2101 Farmington Ave ... Farmington NM 87401 505-599-1270 599-1257 434-3
Web: www.infoway.org

Farmington School District R-7
1022 St Genevieve Ave ... Farmington MO 63640 573-701-1300 701-1309 187
Web: www.farmington.k12.mo.us

Farmland Dairies LLC 520 Main Ave ... Wallington NJ 07057 973-777-2500 296-27
Web: www.skimplus.com

Farmland Management Services
301 E Main St ... Turlock CA 95380 209-669-0742 10-10

FarmLink Marketing Solutions Inc
Suite 110-93 Lombard Ave ... Winnipeg MB R3B3B1 877-376-5465 195
TF: 877-376-5465 ■ *Web:* www.farmlinksolutions.ca

FarmTek 1440 Field of Dreams Way ... Dyersville IA 52040 563-875-2288 10-4
TF: 800-327-6835 ■ *Web:* www.farmtek.com

Farmway Inc 204 E Ct St PO Box 568 ... Beloit KS 67420 785-738-2241 738-9659 276
Web: www.farmwaycoop.com

Farner, Barley & Associates Inc
4450 NE 83rd Rd ... Wildwood FL 34785 352-748-3126 261
Web: www.farnerbarley.com

Farner-Bocken Co
1751 US Hwy 30 E PO Box 368 ... Carroll IA 51401 712-792-3503 792-3503 297-8
TF: 800-274-8692 ■ *Web:* farner-bocken.com

Farnsworth Art Museum 16 Museum St ... Rockland ME 04841 207-596-6457 596-0509 520
Web: www.farnsworthmuseum.org

Farnsworth Group Inc
2709 McGraw Dr ... Bloomington IL 61704 309-663-8435 261
Web: www.f-w.com

Farnsworth House Inn
401 Baltimore St ... Gettysburg PA 17325 717-334-8838 671
TF: 800-575-3760 ■ *Web:* www.farnsworthhouseinn.com

Farny State Park
c/o Ringwood State Pk 1304 Sloatsburg Rd ... Ringwood NJ 07456 973-962-7031 565
TF: 800-852-7899 ■ *Web:* www.njparksandforests.org/parks/farny.html

Farouk Systems Inc 250 Pennbright Dr ... Houston TX 77090 281-876-2000 214
TF: 800-237-9175 ■ *Web:* www.farouk.com

Farr Associates Inc
4194 Mendenhall Oaks Pkwy Ste 101 ... High Point NC 27265 336-812-8050 812-8051 463
Web: www.farrleadership.com

Farr Regional Library 1939 61st Ave ... Greeley CO 80634 888-861-7323 434-3
TF: 888-861-7323 ■ *Web:* www.mylibrary.us

Farr, Farr, Emerich, Hackett & Carr PA
Earl D Farr Bldg 99 Nesbit St ... Punta Gorda FL 33950 941-639-1158 428
TF: 855-327-7529 ■ *Web:* www.farr.com

Farragut Folklife Museum
11408 Municipal Ctr Dr ... Farragut TN 37934 865-966-7057 675-2096 520
Web: www.townoffarragut.org

Farragut State Park 13550 E Hwy 54 ... Athol ID 83801 208-683-2425 565
Web: www.visitidaho.org

Farragutpress 11863 Kingston Pike ... Knoxville TN 37934 865-675-6397 675-1675 532-4
Web: www.farragutpress.com

Farrar Corp 142 W Burns St ... Norwich KS 67118 620-478-2212 478-2200 307
TF: 800-536-2215 ■ *Web:* www.farrarusa.com

Farrar Pump & Machinery Company Inc
1701 S Big Bend Blvd ... Saint Louis MO 63117 314-644-1050 366
Web: farrarpump.com

Farrar Scientific LLC
30765 State Rt 7 ... Marietta OH 45750 740-374-8300 194
Web: www.farrarscientific.com

Farrel Corp 25 Main St ... Ansonia CT 06401 203-736-5500 735-5580 380
TF: 800-800-7290 ■ *Web:* www.farrel-pomini.com

Farrell Distributing 19 Delaware Ave ... Endicott NY 13760 607-754-0707 290
Web: www.farrelldistributing.com

Farrell e d Company Inc
1225 E Second St ... Jamestown NY 14701 716-488-1759 770
TF: 800-574-4544 ■ *Web:* www.edfarrell.com

Farrell Fritz EAB Plaza 14th Fl ... Uniondale NY 11556 516-227-0700 428
Web: www.farrellfritz.com

Farrell-Calhoun Inc
221 E Carolina Ave ... Memphis TN 38126 901-526-2211 774-4213 550
TF: 888-832-7735 ■ *Web:* www.farrellcalhoun.com

Farrey's Wholesale Hardware Company Inc
1850 NE 146th St ... North Miami FL 33181 305-947-5451 361
TF: 888-854-5483 ■ *Web:* www.farreys.com

Farris Evans Insurance Agency Inc
1568 Union Ave ... Memphis TN 38104 901-274-5424 390
TF: 800-395-8207 ■ *Web:* www.farrisevans.com

Farris Vaughan Wills & Murphy
700 W Georgia St Pacific Centre S 25th Fl
PO Box 10026 ... Vancouver BC V7Y1B3 604-684-9151 41
TF: 877-684-9151 ■ *Web:* www.farris.com

Farris, Riley & Pitt LLP
505 20th St N Ste 400 ... Birmingham AL 35203 205-324-1212 428
TF: 888-580-5176 ■ *Web:* www.frplegal.com

Farroh Roof Truss Company Inc
5 27th St NE ... Minot ND 58703 701-852-1717 817
Web: www.trussmasters.com

Farrs Better Foods
2575 South 300 West ... South Salt lake City UT 84115 801-484-8724 484-8768 296-25
TF: 877-553-2777 ■ *Web:* www.farrsicecream.com

FarSounder Inc 43 Jefferson Blvd ... Warwick RI 02888 401-784-6700 459
Web: www.farsounder.com

Farstad Oil Inc 100 NE 27th St ... Minot ND 58703 701-852-1194 580
Web: www.farstadoil.com

Farstone Technology Inc
1758-B N Shoreline Blvd ... Mountain View CA 94043 562-373-5370 969-4567* 658
**Fax Area Code:* 650 ■ *Web:* www.farstone.com

Faruki Ireland & Cox PLL
500 Courthouse Plaza SW 10 N Ludlow St ... Dayton OH 45402 937-227-3700 428
Web: www.ficlaw.com

Farwest Corrosion Control Co
1480 W Artesia Blvd ... Gardena CA 90248 310-532-9524 532-3934 261
TF: 888-532-7937 ■ *Web:* www.farwestcorrosion.com

Farwest Freight Systems Inc
4504 E Vly Hwy E ... Sumner WA 98390 253-826-4565 685

Farwest Sports Inc 4602 20th St E ... Fife WA 98424 253-922-2581 711
Web: sportco.com

Farwest Steel Corp 2000 Henderson Ave ... Eugene OR 97403 541-686-2000 681-7250* 492
**Fax:* Hum Res ■ *Web:* www.farwests teel.com

FAS (Federation of American Scientists)
1725 DeSales St NW Ste 600 ... Washington DC 20036 202-546-3300 49-19
Web: www.fas.org

FASB (Financial Acctg Standards Board)
401 Merritt 7 PO Box 5116 ... Norwalk CT 06856 203-847-0700 849-9714 49-1
TF: 800-748-0659 ■ *Web:* www.fasb.org

Fascet LLC 224 W 30 St Ste 203 ... New York NY 10001 212-448-9830 528
Web: fascet.com

FASCore LLC
8515 E Orchard Rd ... Greenwood Village CO 80111 800-537-2033 535
TF: 800-232-0859 ■ *Web:* www.fascore.com

FASEB (Federation of American Societies for Experimental Biology)
9650 Rockville Pk ... Bethesda MD 20814 301-634-7000 634-7001 49-19
TF: 800-433-2732 ■ *Web:* www.faseb.org

Fashion Architectural Designs
4005 Carnegie Ave ... Cleveland OH 44103 216-432-1600 802
TF Orders: 800-362-9930 ■ *Web:* www.fashionwallcoverings.com

Fashion Cabinet Mfg Inc
5440 Axel Pk Rd ... West Jordan UT 84081 801-280-0646 280-8934 115
Web: www.fashioncabinet.com

Fashion Glass & Mirrors 585 S I-35 E ... Desoto TX 75115 972-223-8936 362
Web: www.fashionglass.com

Fashion Group International Inc (FGI)
8 W 40th St 7th Fl ... New York NY 10018 212-302-5511 302-5533 49-4
TF: 800-520-2262 ■ *Web:* www.fgi.org

Fashion Institute of Design & Merchandising
Los Angeles 919 S Grand Ave ... Los Angeles CA 90015 213-624-1200 624-4799 164
TF Admissions: 800-624-1200 ■ *Web:* fidm.edu
Orange County 17590 Gillette Ave ... Irvine CA 92614 949-851-6200 851-6808 164
TF: 888-974-3436 ■ *Web:* fidm.edu
San Diego 350 Tenth Ave ... San Diego CA 92101 619-235-2049 232-4322 164
TF: 800-243-3436 ■ *Web:* fidm.edu
San Francisco 55 Stockton St ... San Francisco CA 94108 415-675-5200 296-7299 164
TF: 800-422-3436 ■ *Web:* fidm.edu

Fashion Institute of Technology
227 W 27th St ... New York NY 10001 212-217-7000 164
Web: www.fitnyc.edu

Fashion Island Shopping Ctr
401 Newport Ctr Dr ... Newport Beach CA 92660 949-721-2000 720-3350 460
TF: 855-658-8527 ■ *Web:* www.shopfashionisland.com

Fashion Place 6191 S State St ... Murray UT 84107 801-262-9447 460
Web: www.fashionplace.com

Fashion Show Mall
3200 Las Vegas Blvd S Ste 600 ... Las Vegas NV 89109 702-369-8382 460
Web: www.thefashionshow.com

Fashion Snoops Inc 39W 38th St ... New York NY 10018 212-768-8804 466
Web: www.fashionsnoops.com

Fashion Time
2700 Potomac Mills Cir ... Woodbridge VA 22192 703-490-1556 410
Web: www.shopfashiontime.com

Fashion Valley Mall 7007 Friars Rd ... San Diego CA 92108 619-688-9113 294-8291 460
Web: www.simon.com

Fasig-Tipton Co Inc
2400 Newtown Pike ... Lexington KY 40511 859-255-1555 254-0794 51
TF: 877-945-2020 ■ *Web:* www.fasigtipton.com

Faske Lay & Co 3508 Far W Blvd 300 ... Austin TX 78731 512-346-9623 346-8109 2
Web: www.faskelay.com

Fasken Martineau DuMoulin LLP
333 Bay St Bay Adelaide Centre
Ste 2400 PO Box 20 ... Toronto ON M5H2T6 416-366-8381 41
TF: 800-268-8424 ■ *Web:* www.fasken.com

Fasny Museum of Firefighting
117 Harry Howard Ave ... Hudson NY 12534 518-822-1875 520
TF: 800-732-6845 ■ *Web:* www.fasnyfiremuseum.com

Faso John (Rep R - NY)
1616 Longworth HOB ... Washington DC 20515 202-225-5614 225-1168 342-2
Web: faso.house.gov

Fassberg Construction Co
17000 Ventura Blvd Ste 200 ... Encino CA 91316 818-386-1800 186
TF: 800-795-1747 ■ *Web:* www.fassbergconstruction.com

Fast Company Magazine
7 World Trade Ctr ... New York NY 10007 212-389-5300 457-5
TF: 800-542-6029 ■ *Web:* www.fastcompany.com

Fast Heat Inc 776 Oaklawn Ave ... Elmhurst IL 60126 630-833-5400 833-2040 318
TF: 877-747-8575 ■ *Web:* www.fastheat.com

Fast Horse 240 Ninth Ave N ... Minneapolis MN 55401 612-746-4610 195
Web: www.fasthorseinc.com

Fast Undercar Inc 4277 Transport St ... Ventura CA 93003 805-676-3410 61
Web: www.fastundercar.com

FastAsset Inc 170 W Rd Ste 15 ... Portsmouth NH 03801 603-559-9900 314
Web: www.fastasset.com

Fastbolt Corp 200 Louis St ... South Hackensack NJ 07606 201-440-9100 350
TF: 800-631-1980 ■ *Web:* www.fastboltcorp.com

Fastco Industries Inc
PO Box 141427 ... Grand Rapids MI 49514 616-453-5428 278
Web: fastcoindustries.com

Fastec Industrial
2219 Eddie Williams Rd ... Johnson City TN 37601 800-837-2505 351
TF: 800-837-2505 ■ *Web:* www.fastecindustrial.com

Fastek International Ltd
1425 60th St NE ... Cedar Rapids IA 52402 319-294-6664 261
Web: www.fastekintl.com

Fastenal Co 2001 Theurer Blvd ... Winona MN 55987 507-454-5374 453-8049 351
NASDAQ: FAST ■ *TF:* 877-507-7555 ■ *Web:* www.fastenal.com

Fastenal Company Caok 5130 N Hwy 167 ... Catoosa OK 74015 918-266-8954 350
Web: fastenal.com

Fastener Supply Co
13410 S Ridge Dr PO Box 7369 ... Charlotte NC 28241 704-596-7634 598-0116 690
TF: 800-888-9519 ■ *Web:* www.fastenersupply.com

Faster Solutions
10 E Superior St Ste 200 ... Duluth MN 55802 218-733-3936 396
TF: 800-942-3520 ■ *Web:* www.fastersolutions.com

Fast-Fix Jewelry & Watch Repairs
451 Altamonte Ave ... Altamonte Springs FL 32701 407-261-1595 310
TF: 800-359-0407 ■ *Web:* www.fastfix.com

Fastframe USA Inc
1200 Lawrence Dr Ste 300 ... Newbury Park CA 91320 800-631-4964 45
TF: 800-631-4964 ■ *Web:* www.fastframe.com

Name / Address	City	State	Zip	Phone	Fax	Class
Fastfurnishings.com 340 S Lemon Ave Ste 6043 *TF:* 866-720-0126 ■ *Web:* www.fastfurnishings.com	Walnut	CA	91789	443-371-3278		321
Fast-Impact Consulting Inc 5190 Neil Rd Ste 430 *Web:* www.fast-impact.com	Reno	NV	89502	775-284-3704		463
FasTracKids International Ltd 6900 E Belleview Ave Ste 100 *TF:* 888-576-6888 ■ *Web:* fastrackids.com	Greenwood Village	CO	80111	303-224-0200	224-0222	310
Fastron Company Inc, The 11800 Franklin Ave *Web:* www.fastron.com	Franklin Park	IL	60131	630-766-5000		815
FASTSIGNS International Inc 2542 Highlander Way *TF:* 800-327-8744 ■ *Web:* www.fastsigns.com	Carrollton	TX	75006	214-346-5600		701
FastWeb Inc 444 N Michigan Ave Ste 600 *Fax Area Code: 312 ■ *TF:* 800-829-1040 ■ *Web:* www.fastweb.com	Chicago	IL	60611	444-536-1212	467-0638*	725
Fat Bob's Smokehouse 41 Virginia Pl *Web:* www.fatbobs.com	Buffalo	NY	14202	716-887-2971	332-1201	671
Fat Brain Toys LLC 20516 Nicholas Cir Ste 120 *TF:* 800-590-5987 ■ *Web:* www.fatbraintoys.com	Elkhorn	NE	68022	402-779-3181	779-3253	761
Fat Canary 410 W Duke of Gloucester St *Web:* fatcanarywilliamsburg.com	Williamsburg	VA	23185	757-229-3333		671
Fat Cats 2061 W Tenth St *Web:* coolplacestoeat.com	Cleveland	OH	44113	216-579-0200		671
Fat Matt's Rib Shack 1811 Piedmont Ave *Web:* www.fatmattsribshack.com	Atlanta	GA	30324	404-607-1622		671
Fat Willy's 2416 W Schubert Ave *Web:* www.fatwillys.com	Chicago	IL	60647	773-782-1800		671
FATA Automation Inc 6050 Nineteen Mile Rd *Web:* www.fatainc.com	Sterling Heights	MI	48314	586-323-9400		207
FATA Hunter Inc 1040 Iowa Ave Ste 100 *Web:* www.danielifatahunter.com	Riverside	CA	92507	951-328-0200	328-9205	261
Fatair Inc 17033 Evergreen Pl	City of Industry	CA	91745	626-839-7513		770
Fatburger North America Inc 9606 Santa Monica Blvd PH Ste 200 *Web:* www.fatburger.com	Beverly Hills	CA	90210	310-319-1850	319-1863	670
Fate Therapeutics Inc 3535 General Atomics Ct Ste 200 *Web:* www.fatetherapeutics.com	San Diego	CA	92121	858-875-1800		85
Father Hennepin State Park 41294 Father Hennepin Pk Rd PO Box 397 *TF:* 888-646-6367 ■ *Web:* www.dnr.state.mn.us	Isle	MN	56342	320-676-8763	676-3748	565
Father's Table LLC, The 2100 Country Club Rd *Web:* www.thefatherstable.com	Sanford	FL	32771	407-324-1200		345
Fathom Five National Marine Park PO Box 189 *Web:* www.pc.gc.ca	Tobermory	ON	N0H2R0	519-596-2233	596-2298	563
FatTail Inc 20969 Ventura Blvd Ste 209 *Web:* adserver.fattail.com	Woodland Hills	CA	91364	818-615-0380		179
Fatz Cafe 4324 Wade Hampton Blvd *Web:* www.fatz.com	Taylors	SC	29687	864-322-1331	322-1332	670
FAU (Florida Atlantic University) 777 Glades Rd *Fax: Admissions ■ *TF Admissions:* 800-299-4328 ■ *Web:* www.fau.edu	Boca Raton	FL	33431	561-297-3000	297-2758*	166
Faubion Associates Inc 1000 Forest Ave *Web:* www.faubionassoc.com	Dallas	TX	75215	469-607-7086		499
Faucet Queens Inc 650 Forest Edge Dr *Web:* faucetqueen.com	Vernon Hills	IL	60061	847-478-2800	821-0277	351
Faulk & Winkler LLC 6811 Jefferson Hwy *TF:* 800-927-6811	Baton Rouge	LA	70806	225-927-6811		194
Faulkner County 801 Locust St *Web:* www.faulknercounty.org	Conway	AR	72034	501-450-4909	450-4938	338
Faulkner Hospital 1153 Centre St *Web:* www.brighamandwomensfaulkner.org	Jamaica Plain	MA	02130	617-983-7000		374-3
Faulkner Information Services 7905 Browning Rd *TF:* 800-843-0460 ■ *Web:* www.faulkner.com	Pennsauken	NJ	08109	856-662-2070	662-0905	637-11
Faulkner Pontiac Buick Gmc Truck Inc 705 Autopark Blvd *Web:* www.faulknerauto.com	West Chester	PA	19382	610-436-5600		390
Faulkner State Community College *Bay Minette* 1900 Hwy 31 S *TF:* 800-381-3722 ■ *Web:* www.faulknerstate.edu	Bay Minette	AL	36507	251-580-2111	580-2134	162
Fairhope 440 Fairhope Ave *Fax: Admissions ■ *TF:* 800-231-3752 ■ *Web:* www.faulknerstate.edu	Fairhope	AL	36532	251-990-0420	580-2285*	162
Gulf Shores 3301 Gulf Shores Pkwy *TF:* 800-231-3752 ■ *Web:* www.faulknerstate.edu	Gulf Shores	AL	36542	251-968-3104	968-3120	162
Faulkner University 5345 Atlanta Hwy *TF:* 800-879-9816 ■ *Web:* www.faulkner.edu	Montgomery	AL	36109	334-272-5820		166
Faultless Caster 3438 Briley Pk Blvd N *TF Cust Svc:* 800-322-7359 ■ *Web:* www.faultlesscaster.com	Nashville	TN	37207	800-322-7359	322-9329	350
Faultless Linen 330 W 19th Terr *TF:* 800-676-2373 ■ *Web:* www.faultlesslinen.com	Kansas City	MO	64108	816-421-2373		442
Fauquier Bank, The (TFB) 10 Courthouse Sq *TF:* 800-638-3798 ■ *Web:* www.tfb.bank	Warrenton	VA	20186	540-347-2700		70
Fauquier Bankshares Inc 10 Courthouse Sq *NASDAQ: FBSS* ■ *TF:* 800-638-3798 ■ *Web:* www.tfb.bank	Warrenton	VA	20186	540-347-2700		360-2
Fauquier County 10 Hotel St Ste 204 *Web:* www.fauquiercounty.gov	Warrenton	VA	20186	540-422-8001	422-8022	338
Fauquier County Chamber of Commerce 98 Alexandria Pike *Web:* www.fauquierchamber.org	Warrenton	VA	20186	540-347-4414	347-7510	139
Fauquier County Public Schools 320 Hospital Dr Ste 40 *Web:* www.fcps1.org	Warrenton	VA	20186	540-422-7000	422-7057	780
Fauquier Hospital 500 Hospital Dr *TF:* 800-994-6610 ■ *Web:* www.fauquierhealth.org	Warrenton	VA	20186	540-316-5000		374-3
Fauquier Times-Democrat 39 Culpeper St *TF:* 888-351-1660 ■ *Web:* www.fauquier.com	Warrenton	VA	20186	540-347-4222	349-8676	532-4
Faurecia Exhaust Systems Inc 543 Matzinger Rd *Web:* www.faurecia.com	Toledo	OH	43612	419-727-5000		60
Fauser Energy Resources 106 Center St *Web:* www.fauserenergy.com	Elgin	IA	52141	563-426-5811		579
Fauske & Assoc LLC 16w070 83rd St *TF:* 877-328-7531 ■ *Web:* www.fauske.com	Burr Ridge	IL	60527	630-323-8750		192
Faust & Assoc 200 Third St *Web:* faustcpa.com	Mccomb	MS	39648	601-684-6382		2
Faust Goetz Schenker & Blee 2 Rector St Fl 20 *Web:* www.fgsb.com	New York	NY	10006	212-363-6900		506
Faustel Inc W 194 N 11301 McCormick Dr *Web:* www.faustel.com	Germantown	WI	53022	262-253-3333	253-3334	556
Fausto's Bistro 530 Veterans Memorial Blvd *Web:* www.faustosbistro.com	Metairie	LA	70005	504-833-7121		671
Fausto's Fried Chicken Inc 905 E Fourth St	Dequincy	LA	70633	337-786-7264		670
Faux Pas Prints Inc 620 Papworth Ave *Web:* www.fauxpasprints.com	Metairie	LA	70005	504-834-8342		687
Favaloro's 545 Lighthouse Ave *Web:* favalorosbignightbistro.com	Pacific Grove	CA	93950	831-373-8523		671
Faver-Dykes State Park 1000 Faver Dykes Rd *Fax Area Code: 386 ■ *Web:* www.floridastateparks.org	Saint Augustine	FL	32086	904-794-0997	446-6781*	565
Favori 3502 W First St *Web:* www.favorirestaurant.com	Santa Ana	CA	92703	714-531-6838		671
Favorite Office Automation 2011 W State St Ste B *Web:* www.favorite1.com	New Castle	PA	16101	724-658-8300		116
Favorite Plastics 1465 Utica Ave *Web:* www.favoriteplastics.com	Brooklyn	NY	11234	718-253-7000		596
Fawcett Memorial Hospital 21298 Olean Blvd *Web:* www.fawcetthospital.com	Port Charlotte	FL	33952	941-629-1181		374-3
Fawn Industries Inc 1920 Greenspring Dr Ste 140 *Web:* fawnplastics.com	Timonium	MD	21093	410-308-9200	308-9202	604
Faxaway 417 Second Ave W *TF:* 800-906-4329 ■ *Web:* www.faxaway.com	Seattle	WA	98119	206-301-7000	301-7500	736
FaxBack Inc 7007 SW Cardinal Ln Ste 105 *TF:* 800-329-2225 ■ *Web:* www.faxback.com	Portland	OR	97224	503-597-5350	597-5399	736
Faxon Machining Inc 11101 Adwood Dr *Web:* www.faxon-machining.com	Cincinnati	OH	45240	513-851-4644		454
Faxton Saint Luke's Healthcare *Faxton Campus* 1676 Sunset Ave *Web:* www.faxtonstlukes.com	Utica	NY	13502	315-624-6000		374-3
Saint Luke's Campus 1656 Champlin Ave *Web:* www.faxtonstlukes.com	New Hartford	NY	13413	315-624-6000		374-3
Fay Bainbridge State Park 15446 Sunrise Dr NE *Web:* www.parks.wa.gov	Bainbridge Island	WA	98110	206-842-3931		565
Fay Industries Inc 17200 Foltz Pkwy *Web:* www.fayindustries.com	Strongsville	OH	44149	440-572-5030		492
Fay School 48 Main St *Web:* www.fayschool.org	Southborough	MA	01772	508-485-0100	481-7872	622
Fay Sharpe LLP 1228 Euclid Ave Ste 500 *Web:* www.faysharpe.com	Cleveland	OH	44115	216-861-5582		445
Fay Spofford & Thorndike LLC 5 Burlington Woods *TF:* 800-835-8666 ■ *Web:* www.fstinc.com	Burlington	MA	01803	781-221-1000		261
FAYBLOCK Materials Inc 130 Builders Blvd *TF:* 800-326-9198 ■ *Web:* www.fayblock.com	Fayetteville	NC	28302	910-323-9198		191-1
Fayette Chamber of Commerce 65 W Main St *TF:* 800-916-9365 ■ *Web:* www.fayettechamber.com	Uniontown	PA	15401	724-437-4571	438-3304	139
Fayette County 500 N Central Ave	Connersville	IN	47331	765-825-4211		338
Fayette County 103 First Ave NW Courthouse Annex Ste 2 *Web:* fayettecountyal.org	Fayette	AL	35555	205-932-4510	932-2902	338
Fayette County 140 Stonewall Ave W *TF:* 800-266-2278 ■ *Web:* www.fayettecountyga.gov	Fayetteville	GA	30214	770-460-5730		338
Fayette County 310 Oyler Ave *Web:* www.fayettecounty.com	Oak Hill	WV	25901	304-465-5617		338
Fayette County 246 W Colorado St *Web:* www.co.fayette.tx.us	La Grange	TX	78945	979-968-3251	968-8531	338
Fayette County 133 S Main St Ste 401 *Web:* www.fayette-co-oh.com	Washington Court House	OH	43160	740-335-0720	333-3530	338
Fayette County 114 N Vine St *Web:* fayettecountyiowa.org	West Union	IA	52175	563-422-5694	422-3137	338
Fayette County Board of Education 210 Stonewall Ave *Web:* www.fcboe.org	Fayetteville	GA	30214	770-460-3535	460-8191	685
Fayette County Chamber of Commerce 600 W Lanier Ave Ste 250 *Web:* www.fayettechamber.org	Fayetteville	GA	30214	770-461-9983	461-9622	139
Fayette County Chamber of Commerce 504 N Central Ave *Web:* connersvillechamber.com	Connersville	IN	47331	765-825-2561	825-4613	139

Name / Address	Phone	Fax	Class
Fayette County Chamber of Commerce 101 E East St ... Washington Court House OH 43160 *Web:* www.fayettecountyohio.com	740-335-0761		139
Fayette County Clerk 162 E Main St ... Lexington KY 40507 *Web:* local.dmv.org	859-253-3344	231-9619	338
Fayette County Library 216 W Market St ... Somerville TN 38068 *TF:* 866-465-3591 ■ *Web:* www.fayettetn.us	901-465-5248	465-5271	434-3
Fayette County Public Library 531 Summit St ... Oak Hill WV 25901 *TF:* 855-275-5737 ■ *Web:* fayette.lib.wv.us	304-465-0121	465-5306	434-3
Fayette County Public Library 828 N Grand Ave ... Connersville IN 47331 *TF:* 844-829-3746 ■ *Web:* www.fcplibrary.lib.in.us	765-827-0883		434-3
Fayette County Public Schools 701 E Main St ... Lexington KY 40502 **Fax:* Hum Res ■ *TF:* 877-597-2331 ■ *Web:* fcps.net	859-381-4100	381-4271*	685
Fayette Daily News 210 Jeff Davis Pl ... Fayetteville GA 30214 *Web:* www.fayettedailynews.com	770-461-6317		532-3
Fayette Electric Co-op Inc 357 N Washington St ... La Grange TX 78945 *TF:* 800-874-8290 ■ *Web:* www.fayette.coop	979-968-3181		245
Fayette Mall 3401 Nicholasville Rd ... Lexington KY 40503 *Web:* www.shopfayette-mall.com	859-272-3493		460
Fayette Regional Health System (FRHS) 1941 Virginia Ave ... Connersville IN 47331 *Web:* www.fayetteregional.org	765-825-5131		374-3
FayetteÿCountyÿ 221 S Seventh St Rm 106 ... Vandalia IL 62471 *Web:* www.fayettecountyillinois.org	618-283-5000	283-5004	338
Fayetteville Area Convention & Visitors Bureau (FACVB) 245 Person St ... Fayetteville NC 28301 *TF:* 800-255-8217 ■ *Web:* www.visitfayettevillenc.com	910-483-5311	484-6632	206
Fayetteville Athletic Club 2920 E Zion Rd ... Fayetteville AR 72703 *Web:* www.fayac.com	479-587-0500		354
Fayetteville Chamber of Commerce 21 W Mtn Ste 300 ... Fayetteville AR 72701 *Web:* www.fayettevillear.com	479-521-1710	521-1791	139
Fayetteville Free Library Inc 300 Orchard St ... Fayetteville NY 13066 *Web:* fflib.org	315-637-6374		434-3
Fayetteville National Cemetery 700 S Government Ave ... Fayetteville AR 72701 *Web:* www.cem.va.gov	479-444-5051		136
Fayetteville Observer 458 Whitfield St ... Fayetteville NC 28306 *TF:* 800-345-9895 ■ *Web:* fayobserver.com	910-323-4848	486-3545	532-2
Fayetteville Public Utilities 408 W College St ... Fayetteville TN 37334 *TF:* 800-379-2534 ■ *Web:* www.fayelectric.com	931-433-1522	433-0646	245
Fayetteville State University 1200 Murchison Rd ... Fayetteville NC 28301 **Fax:* Admissions ■ *TF Admissions:* 800-222-2594 ■ *Web:* www.uncfsu.edu	910-672-1371	672-1414*	166
Fayetteville Technical Community College 2201 Hull Rd ... Fayetteville NC 28303 *TF:* 877-245-5520 ■ *Web:* www.faytechcc.edu	910-678-8400	678-8407	162
Fayetteville-Lincoln County Chamber of Commerce 208 S Elk Ave ... Fayetteville TN 37334 *TF:* 888-433-1238 ■ *Web:* www.fayettevillelincolncountychamber.com	931-433-1234	433-9087	139
Fayez Sarofim & Co 909 Fannin St Ste 2907 ... Houston TX 77010 *TF:* 800-645-6561 ■ *Web:* www.sarofim.com	713-654-4484		401
Faygo Beverages Inc 3579 Gratiot Ave ... Detroit MI 48207 *TF:* 800-347-6591 ■ *Web:* www.faygo.com	313-925-1600		80-2
Faz Restaurants Inc 5121 HopyaRd Rd ... Pleasanton CA 94588 *Web:* www.fazrestaurants.com	925-460-0444	469-1604	670
Fazio's Trattoria 294 Main St ... Hyannis MA 02601 *Web:* www.fazio.net	508-775-9400		671
FB Johnston Graphics Inc 300 E Boundary Rd ... Chapin SC 29036	803-345-7993	345-7917	627
FB Washburn Candy Corp 137 Perkins Ave ... Brockton MA 02302 *Web:* www.fbwashburncandy.com	508-588-0820	588-2205	296-8
FB Wright Company Inc 9999 Mercier Ave PO Box 770 ... Dearborn MI 48121 *Web:* www.fbwright.com	313-843-8250		326
FBA (Fibre Box Assn) 25 NW Pt Blvd Ste 510 ... Elk Grove Village IL 60007 *Web:* www.fibrebox.org	847-364-9600	364-9639	49-13
FBC (Florida Brick & Clay Company Inc) 1708 Turkey Creek Rd ... Plant City FL 33567 *Web:* www.floridabrickandclay.com	813-754-1521	754-5469	291
FBC Industries Inc 110 E Ave H ... Rochelle IL 61068 *Web:* www.fbcindustries.com	815-562-8169		345
FBFC (First Bank Financial Centre) 155 W Wisconsin Ave PO Box 1004 ... Oconomowoc WI 53066 *TF:* 888-569-9909 ■ *Web:* www.fbfcwi.com	262-569-9900		70
FBG Service Corp 407 S 27th Ave ... Omaha NE 68131 *TF:* 800-777-8326 ■ *Web:* www.fbgservices.com	402-346-4422		104
FBI (Federal Bureau of Investigation) 935 Pennsylvania Ave NW ... Washington DC 20535 *Web:* www.fbi.gov	202-324-3000		340-14
FBI Buildings Inc 3823 W 1800 S ... Remington IN 47977 *Web:* www.fbibuildings.com	219-261-2157		186
FBIAA (Federal Bureau of Investigation Agents Assn) PO Box 12650 ... Arlington VA 22219	703-247-2173	247-2175	49-7
FBL Financial Group Inc 5400 University Ave ... West Des Moines IA 50266 *NYSE:* FFG ■ *TF:* 800-289-9999 ■ *Web:* www.fblfinancial.com	515-225-5400		360-4
FBLA-PBL (Future Business Leaders of America-Phi Beta Lambda Inc) 1912 Assn Dr ... Reston VA 20191 **Fax Area Code:* 866 ■ *TF:* 800-325-2946 ■ *Web:* www.fbla-pbl.org	800-325-2946	500-5610*	48-11
FBN Metal Products 5020 S Nathaniel Lyon St ... Battlefield MO 65619 *TF:* 800-538-2830 ■ *Web:* fbnmetal.com	417-882-2830		295
FBS (Fullerton Bldg Systems Inc) 34620 250th St PO Box 308 ... Worthington MN 56187 *TF:* 800-450-9782 ■ *Web:* www.fullertonbuildingsystems.com	507-376-3128	376-9530	817
FBS Inc 3340 W College Ave ... State College PA 16801 *TF:* 800-490-1072 ■ *Web:* www.fbsworldwide.com	814-234-3437		407
FC Dallas 9200 World Cup Way Ste 202 ... Frisco TX 75034 *Web:* www.fcdallas.com/stadium	214-705-6700	705-6799	717
FC Haab Company Inc 2314 Market St ... Philadelphia PA 19103 *TF:* 800-486-5663 ■ *Web:* www.fchaab.com	215-563-0800	563-9448	316
FC Phillips Inc 471 Washington St ... Stoughton MA 02072 *Web:* www.fcphillips.com	781-344-9400		621
Fc Tucker Company Inc 9201 N Meridian St Ste 100 ... Indianapolis IN 46260 *Web:* talktotucker.com	317-571-2200		652
FCA (Family Caregiver Alliance) 180 Montgomery St Ste 900 ... San Francisco CA 94104 *TF:* 800-445-8106 ■ *Web:* www.caregiver.org	415-434-3388	434-3508	48-17
FCA (Fellowship of Christian Athletes) 8701 Leeds Rd ... Kansas City MO 64129 *TF:* 800-289-0909 ■ *Web:* www.fca.org	816-921-0909	921-8755	48-22
FCA (First Co-op Assn) 960 Riverview Dr PO Box 60 ... Cherokee IA 51012 *TF:* 877-753-5400 ■ *Web:* www.firstcoop.com	712-225-5400	225-5493	447
FCA Canada Inc 1 Riverside Dr W ... Windsor ON N9A5K3 *Web:* www.fcacanada.ca/en	519-973-2000		59
FCA Corp 791 Town & Country Blvd Ste 250 ... Houston TX 77024 *Web:* www.fcacorp.com	713-781-2856		401
FCA LLC 7601 John Deere Pkwy PO Box 758 ... Moline IL 61266 *Web:* www.fcapackaging.com	309-792-3444		111
FCC (First Community Corp) 5455 Sunset Blvd ... Lexington SC 29072 *NASDAQ:* FCCO ■ *TF:* 800-829-6372 ■ *Web:* www.firstcommunitysc.com	803-951-0555		360-2
FCC (Farmers Co-op Creamery Inc) 700 N Hwy 99 W ... McMinnville OR 97128	503-472-2157		296-3
FCC (Federal Communications Commission) 445 12th St SW ... Washington DC 20554 **Fax Area Code:* 202 ■ *TF:* 888-225-5322 ■ *Web:* www.fcc.gov	888-225-5322	418-0232*	340-20
FCC (Fremont Contract Carriers Inc) 865 S Bud Blvd ... Fremont NE 68025 *TF:* 800-228-9842 ■ *Web:* www.fcc-inc.com	800-228-9842		449
FCC Commercial Furniture Inc 8452 Old Hwy 99 N ... Roseburg OR 97470 *TF:* 800-322-7328 ■ *Web:* fcc-create.com	800-322-7328		321
FCC Services 7951 E Maplewood Ave Ste 225 ... Greenwood Village CO 80111 *Web:* www.fccservices.com	303-721-3200		463
FCCC (Fairfax County Chamber of Commerce) 8230 Old Courthouse Rd Ste 350 ... Vienna VA 22182 *Web:* www.novachamber.org	703-749-0400	749-9075	139
FCCI Insurance Group 6300 University Pkwy ... Sarasota FL 34240 *TF:* 800-226-3224 ■ *Web:* www.fcci-group.com	941-907-3224		391-4
FCCLA (Family Career & Community Leaders of America) 1910 Assn Dr ... Reston VA 20191 *TF:* 800-234-4425 ■ *Web:* www.fcclainc.org	703-476-4900	439-2662	48-11
FCCU (First Community Credit Union) 17151 Chesterfield Airport Rd PO Box 1030 ... Chesterfield MO 63005 *TF:* 800-767-8880 ■ *Web:* www.firstcommunity.com	636-728-3333		219
FCF (Fremont Correctional Facility) E US Hwy 50 Evans Blvd PO Box 999 ... Canon City CO 81215 *TF:* 800-886-7683 ■ *Web:* www.colorado.gov	719-269-5002	269-5020	213
FCFC (First Community Financial Corp) 4000 N Central Ave Ste 100 ... Phoenix AZ 85012 *OTC:* FMFP ■ **Fax Area Code:* 312 ■ *TF:* 877-777-4778 ■ *Web:* capitalsource.com	602-265-7715	577-7907*	216
FCG (Florida City Gas) 955 E 25th St ... Hialeah FL 33013 *TF:* 800-993-7546 ■ *Web:* www.floridacitygas.com	800-993-7546		787
FCG Advisors LLC 1 Main St Ste 202 ... Chatham NJ 07928 *Web:* www.fcgadvisors.com	973-635-7374		194
FCI (Fluid Controls Institute) 1300 Sumner Ave ... Cleveland OH 44115 *Web:* www.fluidcontrolsinstitute.org	216-241-7333	241-0105	49-13
FCI (Federal Correctional Institution) *Bastrop* 1341 Hwy 95 N PO Box 730 ... Bastrop TX 78602 *TF:* 800-995-6429 ■ *Web:* www.bop.gov	512-321-3903	304-0117	212
FCI Constructors Inc 3070 I-70 Business Loop # A ... Grand Junction CO 81504 *TF:* 800-964-3444 ■ *Web:* www.fciol.com	970-434-9093	434-7583	188-4
FCI Enterprises LLC 14170 Newbrook Dr Ste 100 ... Chantilly VA 20151 *Web:* www.femmecomp.com	703-961-1818		177
FCi Federal Inc 20135 Lakeview Center Plaza Ste 300 ... Ashburn VA 20147 *TF:* 877-775-7595 ■ *Web:* www.fedconsulting.com	703-443-1888	443-1352	463
FCI Inc 4661 Giles Rd ... Cleveland OH 44135 *TF:* 800-321-1032 ■ *Web:* www.fci-usa.com	216-251-5200	251-5206	621
FCI Lender Services Inc 8180 E Kaiser Blvd ... Anaheim Hills CA 92808 *TF:* 800-931-2424 ■ *Web:* www.trustfci.com	714-282-2424		393
FCL (Farm Credit Leasing) 600 Hwy 169 S Ste 300 ... Minneapolis MN 55426 *TF:* 800-444-2929 ■ *Web:* www.farmcreditleasing.com	952-417-7800		216
FCL Builders Inc 1150 Spring Lake Dr ... Itasca IL 60143 *Web:* www.fclbuilders.com	630-773-0050	773-4030	186
FCL Graphics Inc 4600 N Olcott Ave ... Harwood Heights IL 60706 *TF:* 800-274-3380 ■ *Web:* www.fclgraphics.com	708-867-5500		627
FCM Investments 2200 Ross Ave Ste 4600 W ... Dallas TX 75201 *Web:* www.fcminvest.com	214-665-6900	665-6940	401
FCNL (Friends Committee on National Legislation) 245 Second St NE ... Washington DC 20002 *TF:* 800-630-1330 ■ *Web:* www.fcnl.org	202-547-6000	547-6019	615

	Phone	Fax	Class
FCPL (Flagler County Public Library)			
2500 Palm Coast Pkwy NW .... Palm Coast FL 32137	386-446-6763		434-3
TF: 877-863-5244 ■ *Web:* www.flaglercounty.org			
FCPL (Frankfort Community Public Library)			
208 W Clinton St .... Frankfort IN 46041	765-654-8746	654-8747	434-3
Web: myfcpl.org			
FCPL (Frederick County Public Libraries)			
110 E Patrick St .... Frederick MD 21701	301-600-1613		434-3
TF: 800-248-2296 ■ *Web:* www.fcpl.org			
FCRC (Forest City Ratner Cos)			
1 MetroTech Ctr N. .... Brooklyn NY 11201	718-923-8400		653
Web: www.forestcity.net			
FCRV (Family Campers & RVers)			
4804 Transit Rd Bldg 2 .... Depew NY 14043	716-668-6242		48-23
TF: 800-245-9755 ■ *Web:* www.fcrv.org			
FCT Assembly Inc 1309 N 17th Ave .... Greeley CO 80631	970-346-8002		407
Web: www.fctassembly.com			
FCWI (Federal Compress & Warehouse Company Inc)			
6060 Primacy Pkwy Ste 400 .... Memphis TN 38119	901-524-4000		803-1
Web: www.federalcompress.com			
FCx Performance 3000 E 14th Ave .... Columbus OH 43219	800-253-6223	253-2033*	385
**Fax Area Code:* 614 ■ *TF:* 800-253-6223 ■ *Web:* www.fcxperformance.com			
FCX Systems Inc 400 Fcx Ln .... Morgantown WV 26501	304-983-0400		256
Web: www.fcxinc.com			
FD Lawrence Electric Company Inc			
3450 Beekman St .... Cincinnati OH 45223	513-542-1100	542-2422	246
TF Cust Svc: 800-582-4490 ■ *Web:* www.fdlawrence.com			
FD Roosevelt State Park			
2970 GA Hwy 190 .... Pine Mountain GA 31822	706-663-4858	663-8906	565
TF: 800-864-7275 ■ *Web:* www.gastateparks.org			
FDA (First District Assn)			
101 S Swift Ave .... Litchfield MN 55355	320-693-3236		296-5
Web: www.firstdistrict.com			
FDA (Food & Drug Administration)			
5600 Fishers Ln .... Rockville MD 20857	301-827-2410	443-3100	340-10
TF: 888-463-6332 ■ *Web:* www.fda.gov			
FDA (Food & Drug Administration Regional Offices)			
Central Region			
200 Chestnut St Rm 900 .... Philadelphia PA 19106	215-597-4390	597-4660	340-10
Web: www.fda.gov			
FDB (First DataBank Inc)			
701 Gateway Blvd Ste 600 .... South San Francisco CA 94080	800-633-3453		178-10
TF General: 800-633-3453 ■ *Web:* www.fdbhealth.com			
FDC (Federal Detention Ctr)			
Honolulu 351 Elliot St .... Honolulu HI 96820	808-838-4200		212
Web: www.bop.gov			
FDC Graphics Films Inc			
3820 William Richardson Dr. .... South Bend IN 46628	574-273-4400		514
TF: 800-634-7523 ■ *Web:* www.fdcfilms.com			
FDH Inc 1033 Skokie Blvd Ste 320 .... Northbrook IL 60062	224-757-0001	265-4882	261
Web: www.fdhvelocitel.com			
FDI Group Inc			
39500 High Pointe Blvd Ste 400 .... Novi MI 48375	800-828-0759		390
TF: 800-828-0759 ■ *Web:* www.hcaweb.net			
FDLI (Food & Drug Law Institute)			
1155 15th St NW Ste 800 .... Washington DC 20005	202-371-1420	371-0649	49-10
TF: 800-956-6293 ■ *Web:* www.fdli.org			
FDM Software Ltd			
949 W Third St Ste 113 .... North Vancouver BC V7P3P7	604-986-9941		179
Web: www.fdmsoft.com			
Fdr and Cp Services Llc 2503 Tabor Rd .... Bryan TX 77803	979-778-0333		196
Web: www.fdrservices.com			
FDR Services Corp of New Jersey Inc			
44 Newmans Ct .... Hempstead NY 11550	516-483-6111		442
Web: fdrcorp.com			
FDRA (Footwear Distributors & Retailers of America)			
1319 F St NW Ste 700 .... Washington DC 20004	202-737-5660		49-4
TF: 800-252-6232 ■ *Web:* www.fdra.org			
FDSI Logistics Inc			
5703 Corsa Ave .... Westlake Village CA 91362	818-971-3300		314
Web: www.fdsi.com			
FE Moran 2265 Carlson Dr .... Northbrook IL 60062	847-498-4800	498-9091	189-10
Web: femoran.com			
FE Moran Security Solutions			
201 W University Ave .... Champaign IL 61820	217-403-6444		693
Web: www.femoransecurity.com			
F&E Sportswear Corp			
1230 Newell Pkwy .... Montgomery AL 36110	334-244-6477		687
TF: 800-523-7762 ■ *Web:* fandesportswear.us			
Fearing's 2121 McKinney Ave .... Dallas TX 75201	214-922-4848		671
Web: www.fearingsrestaurant.com			
Fearless Records			
11783 Cardinal Cir .... Garden Grove CA 92843	714-638-7090		317
TF: 800-222-6000 ■ *Web:* www.fearlessrecords.com			
Fearrington House			
2000 Fearrington Village Ctr. .... Pittsboro NC 27312	919-542-2121		379
TF: 800-277-0130 ■ *Web:* www.fearrington.com			
Feast 3719 E Speedway .... Tucson AZ 85712	520-326-9363	326-9245	671
Web: www.eatatfeast.com			
Feather Publishing Co Inc			
287 Lawrence St .... Quincy CA 95971	530-283-0800	283-3952	637-8
TF: 800-800-8000 ■ *Web:* www.plumasnews.com			
Feather River College			
570 Golden Eagle Ave. .... Quincy CA 95971	530-283-0202	283-9961*	162
**Fax:* Admissions ■ *TF:* 800-442-9799 ■ *Web:* www.frc.edu			
Feather River Hospital (FRH)			
5974 Pentz Rd .... Paradise CA 95969	530-877-9361		374-3
Web: www.adventisthealth.org			
Featherlite Bldg Products Corp			
508 McNeil St. .... Round Rock TX 78681	512-255-2573	255-2572	183
TF: 800-792-1234 ■ *Web:* www.featherlitetexas.com			
Featherlite Trailers			
Hwy 63 & 9 PO Box 320 .... Cresco IA 52136	563-547-6000	547-6100	779
TF: 800-800-1230 ■ *Web:* www.fthr.com			
Fechheimer Bros Company Inc			
4545 Malsbary Rd .... Cincinnati OH 45242	513-793-5400	793-7819	155-19
TF: 800-543-1939 ■ *Web:* www.fechheimer.com			

	Phone	Fax	Class
Fedchoice Federal Credit Union			
10001 Willowdale Rd .... Lanham MD 20706	301-699-6100		219
Web: fedchoice.org			
Fedco Manufacturing Inc			
11585 Route 993 .... Larimer PA 15647	724-863-2252		567
Web: www.fedcomfg.com			
Fedco Steel Corp 785 Harrison Ave .... Harrison NJ 07029	973-481-1424		492
Web: www.fedcosteel.com			
Federal Acctg Standards Advisory Board			
441 G St NW Ste 6814 .... Washington DC 20548	202-512-7350	512-7366	340-20
Web: www.fasab.gov			
Federal APD Inc (FAPD)			
28100 Cabot Dr Ste 200 .... Novi MI 48377	248-374-9600		692
TF: 877-992-7749 ■ *Web:* 3m.com			
Federal Assistance Monitor			
8204 Fenton St .... Silver Spring MD 20910	301-588-6380	588-6385	531-7
TF: 800-666-6380 ■ *Web:* www.cdpublications.com			
Federal Aviation Administration (FAA)			
800 Independence Ave SW .... Washington DC 20591	866-835-5322		340-17
TF: 866-835-5322 ■ *Web:* www.faa.gov			
Aircraft Certification Service			
800 Independence Ave SW Ste 800 E ...... Washington DC 20591	202-267-8235	267-5364	340-17
Web: www.faa.gov			
Aviation Research Div			
800 Independence Ave SW Rm 528A .... Washington DC 20591	202-267-9251	267-5320	668
TF: 866-835-5322 ■ *Web:* www.faa.gov			
Commercial Space Transportation Office			
800 Independence Ave SW .... Washington DC 20591	202-267-7793	267-5450	340-17
Web: www.faa.gov			
FAA Academy			
Mike Monroney Aeronautical Ctr			
6500 S MacArthur Blvd .... Oklahoma City OK 73169	405-954-6900	954-3018	340-17
Web: www.faa.gov			
Flight Standards Service			
800 Independence Ave SW Rm 821 .... Washington DC 20591	202-267-8237	267-5230	340-17
Web: www.faa.gov			
Great Lakes Region			
2300 E Devon Ave .... Des Plaines IL 60018	847-294-7272	294-7036	340-17
Web: www.faa.gov			
International Aviation Office			
800 Independence Ave SW .... Washington DC 20591	202-385-8900	267-7198	340-17
Web: www.faa.gov			
Mike Monroney Aeronautical Ctr			
6500 S MacArthur Blvd .... Oklahoma City OK 73125	405-954-4821		340-17
Web: www.faa.gov/about/office_org			
Office of Accident Investigation & Prevention			
800 Independence Ave SW Rm 840 .... Washington DC 20591	202-267-9612		340-17
Web: www.faa.gov			
Safety Hotline			
800 Independence Ave SW .... Washington DC 20591	800-255-1111		340-17
TF: 800-255-1111 ■ *Web:* www.faa.gov			
William J Hughes Technical Ctr			
Atlantic City International Airport			
Bldg 300 4th Fl G34 .... Atlantic City NJ 08405	609-485-6675	485-4667	340-17
Web: www.faa.gov			
Federal Aviation Administration Northwest Mountain Region			
1601 Lind Ave SW .... Renton WA 98057	425-227-2001		340-17
TF: 800-220-5715 ■ *Web:* www.faa.gov			
Federal Aviation Administration Regional Offices (FAA)			
Alaskan Region			
222 W Seventh Ave Ste 14 .... Anchorage AK 99513	907-271-5438	271-2851	340-17
Web: www.faa.gov			
Central Region			
Federal Bldg 901 Locust St .... Kansas City MO 64106	816-329-3050		340-17
Web: www.faa.gov			
Eastern Region 159-30 Rockaway Blvd .... Jamaica NY 11434	718-553-3001		340-17
Web: www.faa.gov			
New England Region			
12 New England Executive Pk .... Burlington MA 01803	781-238-7020	238-7608	340-17
Web: www.faa.gov/airports/new_england			
Western Pacific Region			
15000 Aviation Blvd. .... Lawndale CA 90261	310-725-7800	725-6811	340-17
Web: www.faa.gov/airports/western_pacific			
Federal Aviation Administration Southern Region			
1701 Columbia Ave .... College Park GA 30337	404-305-5000		340-17
Web: www.faa.gov			
Federal Bar Council			
123 Main St Ste L100 .... White Plains NY 10601	914-682-8800		138
Web: federalbarcouncil.org			
Federal Block Corp 247 Walsh Ave .... New Windsor NY 12553	845-561-4108	561-5344	183
TF: 800-724-1999 ■ *Web:* www.montfortgroup.com			
Federal Bureau of Investigation (FBI)			
935 Pennsylvania Ave NW .... Washington DC 20535	202-324-3000		340-14
Web: www.fbi.gov			
Criminal Justice Information Services			
1000 Custer Hollow Rd .... Clarksburg WV 26306	304-625-4995		340-14
Web: fbi.gov/about-us/cjis/cjis			
FBI Laboratory 1970 E Parham Rd. .... Richmond VA 23228	804-261-1044		340-14
Web: www.fbi.gov			
Federal Bureau of Investigation Agents Assn (FBIAA)			
PO Box 12650 .... Arlington VA 22219	703-247-2173	247-2175	49-7
Federal Bureau of Prisons			
320 First St NW .... Washington DC 20534	202-307-3198	514-6620	340-14
TF: 800-535-0283 ■ *Web:* www.bop.gov			
Federal Bureau of Prisons (FPC)			
Bryan 320 First St NW .... Washington DC 20534	202-307-3198	821-3316*	212
**Fax Area Code:* 979 ■ **Fax:* Warden ■ *Web:* www.bop.gov			
FDC Houston 1200 Texas Ave .... Houston TX 77002	713-221-5400		212
Management & Specialty Training Ctr			
791 Chambers Rd .... Aurora CO 80011	303-340-7800		340-14
Web: www.bop.gov/about/facilities/training_centers.jsp			
National Institute of Corrections			
320 First St NW .... Washington DC 20534	202-307-3106		340-14
TF: 800-995-6423 ■ *Web:* nicic.gov			
National Institute of Corrections Information Cent			
11900 E Cornell Ave Unit C .... Aurora CO 80014	800-877-1461		340-14
TF: 800-877-1461 ■ *Web:* nicic.gov			
Phoenix 37900 N 45th Ave .... Phoenix AZ 85086	623-465-9757	465-5199	212
Web: www.bop.gov			

				Phone	Fax	Class
Federal Bureau of Prisons Regional Offices						
Mid-Atlantic Region						
302 Sentinel Dr Ste 200	Annapolis Junction	MD	20701	301-317-3100		340-14
TF: 800-968-7229 ■ *Web:* www.bop.gov						
North Central Region						
400 State Ave Twr II Ste 800	Kansas City	KS	66101	913-551-1061		340-14
Web: www.bop.gov/about/ro/ncr						
Northeast Region						
200 Chestnut St 7th Fl	Philadelphia	PA	19106	215-521-7301		340-14
Web: www.bop.gov						
South Central Region						
4211 Cedar Springs Rd	Dallas	TX	75219	214-224-3389		340-14
Web: www.bop.gov						
Southeast Region						
3800 Camp Creek Pk SW Bldg 2000	Atlanta	GA	30331	678-686-1200		340-14
Web: www.bop.gov						
Federal Business Products Inc						
95 Main Ave	Clifton	NJ	07014	973-667-9800		110
TF: 800-927-5123 ■ *Web:* www.feddirect.com						
Federal Cartridge Co 900 Ehlen Dr	Anoka	MN	55303	800-379-1732	323-2506*	284
**Fax Area Code:* 763 ■ **Fax:* Hum Res ■ *TF:* 800-379-1732 ■ *Web:* www.federalpremium.com						
Federal Communications Commission (FCC)						
445 12th St SW	Washington	DC	20554	888-225-5322	418-0232*	340-20
**Fax Area Code:* 202 ■ *TF:* 888-225-5322 ■ *Web:* www.fcc.gov						
Federal Compress & Warehouse Company Inc (FCWI)						
6060 Primacy Pkwy Ste 400	Memphis	TN	38119	901-524-4000		803-1
Web: www.federalcompress.com						
Federal Computer Week Magazine						
3141 Fairview Pk Dr Ste 777	Falls Church	VA	22042	703-876-5100	876-5100	457-7
TF: 877-534-2208 ■ *Web:* www.fcw.com						
Federal Contracts Report						
1801 S Bell St	Arlington	VA	22202	800-372-1033		531-7
TF: 800-372-1033 ■ *Web:* www.bna.com/federal-contracts-report-p6016						
Federal Correctional Complex						
Beaumont 5830 Knauth Rd	Beaumont	TX	77705	409-727-0101	720-5000	212
Web: www.bop.gov						
Coleman 846 NE 54th Terr	Coleman	FL	33521	352-689-5000	689-5027	212
TF: 877-623-8426 ■ *Web:* www.bop.gov						
Federal Correctional Institution (FCI)						
Bastrop 1341 Hwy 95 N PO Box 730	Bastrop	TX	78602	512-321-3903	304-0117	212
TF: 800-995-6429 ■ *Web:* www.bop.gov						
Big Spring 1900 Simler Ave	Big Spring	TX	79720	432-466-2300	466-2576	212
Web: www.bop.gov/locations/institutions/big						
Butner Old NC Hwy 75 PO Box 1000	Butner	NC	27509	919-575-4541	575-5023	212
TF: 877-623-8426 ■ *Web:* www.bop.gov						
Cumberland 14601 Burbridge Rd SE	Cumberland	MD	21502	301-784-1000	784-1008*	212
**Fax:* Hum Res ■ *Web:* www.bop.gov						
Edgefield						
501 Gary Hill Rd PO Box 723	Edgefield	SC	29824	803-637-1500	637-9840	212
Web: www.bop.gov						
El Reno PO Box 1000	El Reno	OK	73036	405-262-4875		212
Web: fedcrimlaw.com						
Englewood 9595 W Quincy Ave	Littleton	CO	80123	303-985-1566	763-2553	212
TF: 877-623-8426 ■ *Web:* www.bop.gov						
Fairton						
655 Fairton-Millville Rd PO Box 280	Fairton	NJ	08320	856-453-1177	453-4015	212
TF: 877-623-8426 ■ *Web:* www.bop.gov						
FCI McKean 6975 Rt 59	Lewis Run	PA	16738	814-362-8900	363-6821	212
TF: 877-623-8426 ■ *Web:* www.bop.gov						
Florence 5880 State Hwy 67 S	Florence	CO	81226	719-784-9100		212
Web: usmarshals.gov						
Forrest City						
1400 Dale Bumpers Rd	Forrest City	AR	72335	870-630-6000	494-4496	212
TF: 877-623-8426 ■ *Web:* www.bop.gov						
Jesup 2600 Hwy 301 S	Jesup	GA	31599	912-427-0870	427-1125	212
Web: www.bop.gov/locations/institutions/jes						
Loretto 772 St Joseph St	Loretto	PA	15940	814-472-4140	472-6040	212
TF: 877-623-8426 ■ *Web:* www.bop.gov						
Manchester						
805 Fox Hollow Rd PO Box 4000	Manchester	KY	40962	606-598-1900	599-4115	212
TF: 877-623-8426 ■ *Web:* www.bop.gov						
Milan PO Box 9999	Milan	MI	48160	734-439-1511	439-0949	212
Web: www.bop.gov/locations/institutions/mil						
Morgantown 446 Greenbag Rd	Morgantown	WV	26501	304-296-4416	284-3613	212
TF: 800-613-4012 ■ *Web:* www.bop.gov						
Oxford PO Box 500	Oxford	WI	53952	608-584-5511	584-6371	212
TF: 800-995-6423 ■ *Web:* www.bop.gov						
Pekin 2600 S Second St	Pekin	IL	61554	309-346-8588	477-4685	212
Web: www.bop.gov/locations/institutions/pek/index.jsp						
Ray Brook						
128 Ray Brook Rd PO Box 300	Ray Brook	NY	12977	518-897-4000	897-4216	212
Web: www.bop.gov						
Safford 1529 W Highway 366	Safford	AZ	85546	928-428-6600	348-1331	212
Web: www.bop.gov						
Talladega 565 E Renfroe Rd	Talladega	AL	35160	256-315-4100	315-4495	212
Web: www.bop.gov/locations						
Tallahassee 501 Capital Cir NE	Tallahassee	FL	32301	850-878-2173		212
Web: federalprisoncalls.net						
Terminal Island 1299 Seaside Ave	San Pedro	CA	90731	310-831-8961	732-5335	212
Web: www.bop.gov						
Yazoo City						
2225 Haley Barbour Pkwy PO Box 5050	Yazoo City	MS	39194	662-751-4800	751-4958	212
TF: 877-623-8426 ■ *Web:* www.bop.gov						
Federal Deposit Insurance Corp						
550 17th St NW	Washington	DC	20429	202-898-7192		340-20
TF: 877-275-3342 ■ *Web:* www.fdic.gov						
Federal Deposit Insurance Corp Regional Offices						
Atlanta Regional Office						
10 Tenth St NW Ste 800	Atlanta	GA	30309	678-916-2200		340-20
TF: 800-765-3342 ■ *Web:* www.fdic.gov						
Boston Area Office						
15 Braintree Hill Office Pk Ste 300	Braintree	MA	02184	781-794-5500		340-20
TF: 866-728-9953 ■ *Web:* www.fdic.gov						
Chicago Area Office						
300 S Riverside Plaza Ste 1700	Chicago	IL	60606	312-382-6000		340-20
TF: 800-944-5343 ■ *Web:* www.fdic.gov						
Dallas Area Office 1601 Bryan St	Dallas	TX	75201	214-754-0098		340-20
TF: 800-568-9161 ■ *Web:* www.fdic.gov						
Kansas City Area Office						
2345 Grand Blvd Ste 1200	Kansas City	MO	64108	816-234-8000		340-20
TF: 800-209-7459 ■ *Web:* www.fdic.gov						
Memphis Area Office						
5100 Poplar Ave Ste 1900	Memphis	TN	38137	901-685-1603		340-20
TF: 800-210-6354 ■ *Web:* www.fdic.gov						
New York Area Office						
350 Fifth Ave Ste 1200	New York	NY	10118	917-320-2500		340-20
TF: 800-334-9593 ■ *Web:* fdic.gov						
San Francisco Area Office						
25 Jessie St at Ecker Sq Ste 2300	San Francisco	CA	94105	415-546-0160		340-20
TF: 800-756-3558 ■ *Web:* www.fdic.gov						
Federal Detention Ctr (FDC)						
Honolulu 351 Elliot St	Honolulu	HI	96820	808-838-4200		212
Web: www.bop.gov						
Oakdale PO Box 5060	Oakdale	LA	71463	318-335-4466	215-2046	212
Web: www.bop.gov						
Philadelphia PO Box 572	Philadelphia	PA	19106	215-521-4000	521-7220	212
Web: www.bop.gov						
SeaTac 2425 S 200th St	Seattle	WA	98198	206-870-5700	870-5717	212
TF: 877-623-8426 ■						
Web: www.bop.gov/locations/institutions/set/index.jsp						
Federal Education Assn						
1201 16th St NW Ste 117	Washington	DC	20036	202-822-7850		414
Web: www.feaonline.org						
Federal EEO Advisor						
360 Hiatt Dr	Palm Beach Gardens	FL	33418	561-622-6520	622-2423	531-2
TF: 800-341-7874 ■ *Web:* www.lrp.com						
Federal Election Commission						
999 E St NW	Washington	DC	20463	202-694-1100		265
TF: 800-424-9530 ■ *Web:* www.fec.gov						
Federal Electronics Inc						
75 Stamp Farm Rd	Cranston	RI	02921	401-944-6200		625
Web: www.federalelec.com						
Federal Emergency Management Agency (FEMA)						
500 C St SW	Washington	DC	20472	800-621-3362		340-11
TF: 800-621-3362 ■ *Web:* www.fema.gov						
FEMA for Kids 500 C St SW Ste 714	Washington	DC	20472	800-621-3362		340-11
TF: 800-621-3362 ■ *Web:* www.fema.gov						
National Flood Insurance Program						
500 C St SW	Washington	DC	20472	888-379-9531	646-2818*	340-11
**Fax Area Code:* 202 ■ *TF:* 888-379-9531 ■ *Web:* www.floodsmart.gov						
US Fire Administration						
16825 S Seton Ave	Emmitsburg	MD	21727	301-447-1000		340-11
TF: 888-382-3827 ■ *Web:* www.usfa.fema.gov						
Region 3						
1 Independence Mall						
615 Chestnut St 6th Fl	Philadelphia	PA	19106	215-931-5500	931-5621	340-11
TF: 800-621-3362 ■ *Web:* www.fema.gov						
Federal Emergency Management Agency Regional Office (FEMA)						
Region 1 99 High St	Boston	MA	02110	617-956-7551		340-11
TF: 877-336-2627 ■ *Web:* www.fema.gov/region-i						
Region 4 3003 Chamblee-Tucker Rd	Atlanta	GA	30341	770-220-5200	220-5230	340-11
Web: www.fema.gov						
Region 5 536 S Clark St 6th Fl	Chicago	IL	60605	312-408-5500	408-5234	340-11
TF: 877-336-2627 ■ *Web:* www.fema.gov						
Region 2 1 World Trade Ctr	New York	NY	10007	212-680-3600		340-11
Web: www.fema.gov						
Region 6 800 N Loop 288	Denton	TX	76209	940-898-5399	898-5325	340-11
TF: 800-426-5460 ■ *Web:* www.fema.gov						
Region 7 9221 Ward Pkwy	Kansas City	MO	64114	816-283-7061		340-11
Web: www.fema.gov						
Region 8						
Denver Federal Ctr Bldg 710 PO Box 25267	Denver	CO	80225	303-235-4800	235-4976	340-11
Web: www.fema.gov						
Region 9 1111 Broadway Ste 1200	Oakland	CA	94607	510-627-7100		340-11
TF: 877-336-2627 ■ *Web:* www.fema.gov						
Region 10						
Federal Regional Ctr 130 228th St SW	Bothell	WA	98021	425-487-4600		340-11
Web: www.fema.gov						
Federal Energy Regulatory Commission						
888 First St NE	Washington	DC	20426	202-502-8004	208-2106	340-9
TF: 866-208-3372 ■ *Web:* www.ferc.gov						
Chicago 230 S Dearborn St Rm 3130	Chicago	IL	60604	312-596-4437	596-4460	340-9
Web: www.ferc.gov						
New York 19 W 34th St Ste 400	New York	NY	10001	212-273-5911	631-8124	340-9
Web: www.ferc.gov						
Portland						
805 SW Broadway Fox Tower Ste 550	Portland	OR	97205	503-552-2715	552-2799	340-9
TF: 866-208-3372 ■ *Web:* www.ferc.gov/contact-us/tel-num/regional.asp						
San Francisco						
100 First St Ste 2300	San Francisco	CA	94105	415-369-3318	369-3322	340-9
Web: www.ferc.gov						
Federal Envelope Co						
608 Country Club Dr	Bensenville	IL	60106	630-595-2000		263
Web: www.federalenvelope.com						
Federal Equipment Co 5298 River Rd	Cincinnati	OH	45233	513-621-5260	621-0524	172
TF: 877-435-4723 ■ *Web:* www.federalequipment.com						
Federal Express Europe Inc						
3610 Hacks Cross Rd	Memphis	TN	38125	901-369-3600		546
TF: 800-463-3339 ■ *Web:* www.fedex.com						
Federal Farm Credit Banks Funding Corp						
10 Exchange Pl Ste 1401	Jersey City	NJ	07302	201-200-8131	200-8109	402
Web: www.farmcreditfunding.com						
Federal Financing Bank						
U S Department of the Treasury						
1500 Pennsylvania Ave NW	Washington	DC	20220	202-622-2470	622-0707	340-20
Web: www.treasury.gov						
Federal Flange 4014 Pinemont St	Houston	TX	77018	713-681-0606	681-3005	483
TF: 800-231-0150 ■ *Web:* www.federalflange.com						
Federal Foam Technologies Inc						
600 Wisconsin Dr	New Richmond	WI	54017	715-246-9500	246-9500	601
TF: 800-898-9559 ■ *Web:* www.federalfoam.com						
Federal Hall National Memorial						
26 Wall St	New York	NY	10005	212-825-6990	668-2899	564
Web: www.nps.gov/feha/index.htm						
Federal Hearings & Appeals Services Inc						
117 W Main St	Plymouth	PA	18651	570-779-5122		533
TF: 800-664-7177 ■ *Web:* fhas.com						

Name / Address	City	State	ZIP	Phone	Fax	Class
Federal Heath Sign Co 4602 N Ave	Oceanside	CA	92056	760-941-0715	941-0719	701
Web: www.federalheath.com						
Federal Heating & Engineering Company Inc						
160 Cross St	Winchester	MA	01890	781-721-2468		610
Federal Highway Administration (FHWA)						
400 Seventh St SW	Washington	DC	20590	202-366-0660		340-17
Web: www.fhwa.dot.gov						
National Highway Institute						
4600 Fairfax Dr Ste 800	Arlington	VA	22203	703-235-0500	235-0593	340-17
TF: 877-558-6873 ■ *Web:* www.nhi.fhwa.dot.gov						
Federal Home Loan Bank of Indianapolis						
8250 Woodfield Crossing Blvd	Indianapolis	IN	46240	317-465-0200		434-3
Web: www.fhlbi.com						
Federal House Bar & Grille						
22 Market Space	Annapolis	MD	21401	410-268-2576	280-0195	671
Web: federalhouserestaurant.com						
Federal Housing Finance Board						
400 Seventh St SW	Washington	DC	20024	202-649-3800	649-1071	340-20
Web: www.fhfa.gov						
Federal Industries Div Standex Corp						
215 Federal Ave	Belleville	WI	53508	800-356-4206	424-3234*	664
**Fax Area Code:* 608 ■ *TF:* 800-356-4206 ■ *Web:* www.federalind.com						
Federal International Inc						
7935 Clayton Rd	Saint Louis	MO	63117	314-721-3377		660
Web: www.federalinternational.com						
Federal Judicial Ctr						
1 Columbus Cir NE	Washington	DC	20544	202-502-4000		341
Web: www.fjc.gov						
Federal Labor Relations Authority						
1400 K St NW	Washington	DC	20424	202-357-6029	482-6724	340-20
TF: 800-331-3572 ■ *Web:* www.flra.gov						
Federal Labor Relations Authority Regional Offices						
Atlanta Region 225 Peachtree St NE	Atlanta	GA	30303	404-331-5300	331-5280	340-20
Web: www.flra.gov						
Boston Region						
Thomas PO Neill Jr Federal Bldg						
10 Causeway St Ste 472	Boston	MA	02222	617-565-5100	565-6262	340-20
Web: www.flra.gov						
Chicago Region 55 W Monroe St Ste 1150	Chicago	IL	60603	312-886-3465	886-5977	340-20
TF: 800-222-0364 ■ *Web:* www.flra.gov						
Dallas Region						
525 S Griffin St Ste 926 LB-107	Dallas	TX	75202	214-767-6266	767-0156	340-20
Web: www.flra.gov						
Denver Region 1391 Speer Blvd # 300	Denver	CO	80204	303-844-5224	844-2774	340-20
Web: flra.gov						
San Francisco Region						
901 Market St Ste 470	San Francisco	CA	94103	415-356-5000	356-5017	340-20
TF: 800-331-3572 ■ *Web:* www.flra.gov/ogc_ro_sf						
Washington (DC) Region						
1400 K St NW 2nd Fl	Washington	DC	20424	202-357-6029	482-6724	340-20
Web: www.flra.gov						
Federal Laboratory Consortium for Technology Transfer						
950 Kings Hwy N Ste 208	Cherry Hill	NJ	08034	856-667-7727	667-8009	340-20
Web: www.federallabs.org						
Federal Law Enforcement Officers Assn (FLEOA)						
1100 Connecticut Ave NW Ste 900	Washington	DC	20036	202-293-1550		49-7
Web: www.fleoa.org						
Federal Law Enforcement Training Ctr						
1131 Chapel Crossing Rd	Glynco	GA	31524	912-267-2100		340-11
TF: 800-743-5382 ■ *Web:* www.fletc.gov						
Federal Life Insurance Co Mutual						
3750 W Deerfield Rd	Riverwoods	IL	60015	847-520-1900		391-2
TF: 800-233-3750 ■ *Web:* www.federallife.com						
Federal Management Systems Inc						
462 K St NW	Washington	DC	20001	202-842-3003	829-4470	2
TF: 877-637-8277 ■ *Web:* www.fmshq.com						
Federal Managers Assn (FMA)						
1641 Prince St	Alexandria	VA	22314	703-683-8700	683-8707	49-7
Web: www.fedmanagers.org						
Federal Maritime Commission						
800 N Capitol St NW	Washington	DC	20573	202-523-5725	523-0014	340-20
Web: www.fmc.gov						
Federal Maritime Commission Regional Offices						
Los Angeles Area						
800 N Capital St NW	Washington	DC	20573	310-514-4905		340-20
Web: www.fmc.gov						
New Orleans Area 1515 Poydras St	New Orleans	LA	70112	504-589-6662		340-20
Web: www.fmc.gov						
South Florida Area PO Box 813609	Hollywood	FL	33081	954-963-5362		340-20
Web: www.fmc.gov						
Federal Materials Concrete						
2425 Wayne Sullivan Dr	Paducah	KY	42003	270-442-5496	443-6484	182
Web: www.fmc1.com						
Federal Mediation & Conciliation Service						
2100 K St NW	Washington	DC	20427	202-606-8100	606-4251	340-20
Web: www.fmcs.gov						
Federal Mediation & Conciliation Service Regional Offices						
Eastern Region						
6161 Oak Tree Blvd Ste 120	Independence	OH	44131	216-520-4800		340-20
Web: www.fmcs.gov/internet						
Federal Medical Ctr						
Butner Old N Carolina Hwy 75	Butner	NC	27509	919-575-3900	575-4801	212
Web: www.bop.gov						
Lexington 3301 Leestown Rd	Lexington	KY	40511	859-255-6812	253-8821	212
Web: www.bop.gov/locations/institutions/lex						
Federal Mine Safety & Health Review Commission						
601 New Jersey Ave NW	Washington	DC	20001	202-434-9900	434-9944	340-20
Web: www.fmshrc.gov						
Federal Motor Carrier Safety Administration (FMCSA)						
1200 New Jersey Ave SE	Washington	DC	20590	800-832-5660		340-17
TF: 800-832-5660 ■ *Web:* www.fmcsa.dot.gov						
Federal Network Inc (FedNet)						
122 C St NW Ste 520	Washington	DC	20001	202-393-7300		530
Web: www.fednet.net						
Federal News Services 77 K St	Washington	DC	20002	202-650-6500		530
Web: www.fednews.com						
Federal Pacific PO Box 8200	Bristol	VA	24203	276-669-4084	669-1869	767
Web: www.federalpacific.com						
Federal Plastics Manufacturing Ltd						
5100 Fisher St	St-laurent	QC	H4T1J5	514-342-5411	342-3744	601
Web: www.fedplast.com						
Duluth 6902 Airport Rd PO Box 1400	Duluth	MN	55814	218-722-8634	733-4701	212
TF: 877-623-8426 ■ *Web:* www.bop.gov						
Montgomery Maxwell AFB	Montgomery	AL	36112	334-293-2100	293-2326	212
TF: 877-623-8426 ■ *Web:* www.bop.gov/locations/institutions/mon						
Federal Prison Industries Inc						
320 First St NW	Washington	DC	20534	800-827-3168		630
TF: 800-827-3168 ■ *Web:* www.unicor.gov						
Federal Program Integrators LLC						
12 Wabanaki Way	Indian Island	ME	04468	207-817-7307		279
Federal Protection Inc						
2500 N Airport Commerce Ave	Springfield	MO	65803	800-299-5400		693
TF: 800-299-5400 ■						
Web: www.federalprotection.com/contact-federal-protection						
Federal Railroad Administration						
1200 New Jersey Ave SE	Washington	DC	20590	202-493-6014		340-17
Web: www.fra.dot.gov						
Federal Railroad Administration Regional Offices (FRA)						
Region 1 55 Broadway Room 1077	Cambridge	MA	02142	617-494-2302	494-2967	340-17
TF: 800-724-5991 ■ *Web:* www.fra.dot.gov						
Region 2						
Baldwin Tower Ste 660 1510 Chester Pike	Crum Lynne	PA	19022	610-521-8200	521-8225	340-17
TF: 800-724-5991 ■ *Web:* www.fra.dot.gov						
Region 3 61 Forsyth St SW Ste 16T20	Atlanta	GA	30303	404-562-3800	562-3830	340-17
TF: 800-724-5993 ■ *Web:* www.fra.dot.gov						
Region 4 200 W Adams St	Chicago	IL	60606	312-353-6203	886-9634	340-17
TF: 800-724-5040 ■ *Web:* www.fra.dot.gov						
Region 5						
4100 International Plaza Ste 450	Fort Worth	TX	76109	817-862-2200	862-2204	340-17
Web: www.fra.dot.gov						
Region 6 901 Locust St Ste 464	Kansas City	MO	64106	816-329-3840	329-3867	340-17
TF: 800-724-5996 ■ *Web:* www.fra.dot.gov						
Region 7 801 'I' St Ste 466	Sacramento	CA	95814	916-498-6540	498-6546	340-17
Web: www.fra.dot.gov						
Region 8 703 Broadway St Ste 650	Vancouver	WA	98660	360-696-7536	696-7548	340-17
TF: 800-724-5998 ■ *Web:* www.fra.dot.gov						
Federal Realty Investment Trust						
1626 E Jefferson St	Rockville	MD	20852	301-998-8100	998-3700	655
NYSE: FRT ■ *TF:* 800-658-8980 ■ *Web:* www.federalrealty.com						
Federal Reserve Bank of Atlanta						
1000 Peachtree St NE	Atlanta	GA	30309	404-498-8353		71
TF: 888-500-7390 ■ *Web:* www.frbatlanta.org						
Birmingham Branch 524 Liberty Pkwy	Birmingham	AL	35242	205-968-6700		71
TF: 800-257-7013 ■ *Web:* www.frbatlanta.org						
Jacksonville Branch 800 Water St	Jacksonville	FL	32204	904-632-1000		71
Web: federalreserve.gov						
Miami Branch 9100 NW 36th St	Miami	FL	33178	305-591-2065		71
TF: 800-827-3340 ■ *Web:* frbatlanta.org						
Nashville Branch 301 Rosa L Parks	Nashville	TN	37203	615-251-7100		71
Web: www.frbatlanta.org						
New Orleans Branch						
525 St Charles Ave	New Orleans	LA	70130	504-593-3200		71
TF: 877-638-7003 ■ *Web:* www.frbatlanta.org						
Federal Reserve Bank of Boston						
600 Atlantic Ave	Boston	MA	02210	617-973-3000		71
Web: www.bostonfed.org						
Federal Reserve Bank of Chicago						
230 S LaSalle St	Chicago	IL	60604	312-322-5322		71
Web: www.chicagofed.org						
Detroit Branch 1600 E Warren Ave	Detroit	MI	48207	313-961-6880		71
Web: chicagofed.org						
Federal Reserve Bank of Cleveland						
1455 E Sixth St PO Box 6387	Cleveland	OH	44101	216-579-2000		71
TF: 877-372-2457 ■ *Web:* www.clevelandfed.org						
Cincinnati Branch 150 E Fourth St	Cincinnati	OH	45202	513-721-4787		71
TF: 877-372-2457 ■ *Web:* www.clevelandfed.org						
Federal Reserve Bank of Dallas						
2200 N Pearl St	Dallas	TX	75201	214-922-6000	922-5268	71
TF: 800-333-4460 ■ *Web:* www.dallasfed.org						
El Paso Branch 301 E Main St	El Paso	TX	79901	915-521-5200		71
TF: 800-333-4460 ■ *Web:* www.dallasfed.org						
Houston Branch 1801 Allen Pkwy	Houston	TX	77019	713-483-3000		71
Web: www.dallasfed.org						
San Antonio Branch 402 Dwyer Ave	San Antonio	TX	78204	210-978-1200		71
TF: 800-333-4460 ■ *Web:* www.dallasfed.org						
Federal Reserve Bank of Kansas City						
1 Memorial Dr PO Box 1200	Kansas City	MO	64198	816-881-2000	881-2704	71
TF: 800-333-1010 ■ *Web:* www.kansascityfed.org						
Denver Branch 1 Memorial Dr	Kansas City	MO	64198	888-851-1920	881-2704*	71
**Fax Area Code:* 816 ■ *TF:* 888-851-1920 ■ *Web:* kansascityfed.org						
Oklahoma City Branch						
226 Dean A McGee Ave	Oklahoma City	OK	73102	405-270-8400	270-8676	71
TF: 800-333-1030 ■ *Web:* www.kansascityfed.org						
Omaha Branch 2201 Farnam St	Omaha	NE	68102	402-221-5500		71
TF: 800-333-1040 ■ *Web:* www.kansascityfed.org						
Federal Reserve Bank of Minneapolis						
90 Hennepin Ave	Minneapolis	MN	55401	612-204-5000	204-5905	71
TF: 800-553-9656 ■ *Web:* www.minneapolisfed.org						
Helena Branch 100 Neill Ave	Helena	MT	59601	406-447-3800		71
Web: federalreserve.gov						
Federal Reserve Bank of Philadelphia						
10 Independence Mall	Philadelphia	PA	19106	215-574-6000		71
TF: 866-574-3727 ■ *Web:* www.philadelphiafed.org						
Federal Reserve Bank of Richmond						
701 E Byrd St	Richmond	VA	23219	804-697-8000		71
Web: www.richmondfed.org						
Baltimore Branch 502 S Sharp St	Baltimore	MD	21201	410-576-3300		71
TF: 800-446-7045 ■ *Web:* www.richmondfed.org						
Federal Reserve Bank of Saint Louis						
701 Convention Plaza	Saint Louis	MO	63101	314-444-8444		71
TF: 800-333-0810 ■ *Web:* www.stlouisfed.org						
Little Rock Branch						
111 Ctr St Ste 1000 Stephens Bldg	Little Rock	AR	72201	501-324-8300		71
TF: 877-372-2457 ■ *Web:* frbservices.org						
Louisville Branch						
101 S Fifth St Ste 1920	Louisville	KY	40202	502-568-9200		71
Web: frbservices.org						

	Phone	Fax	Class
Federal Reserve Bank of San Francisco (FRBSF)			
101 Market St San Francisco CA 94105	415-974-2000		71
TF: 800-227-4133 ■ *Web:* www.frbsf.org			
Los Angeles Branch			
950 S Grand Ave Los Angeles CA 90015	213-683-2300		71
TF: 800-925-4618 ■ *Web:* www.frbsf.org			
Portland Branch			
1500 SW First Ave Ste 100 Portland OR 97201	503-276-3000		71
TF: 800-227-4133 ■ *Web:* www.frbsf.org			
Salt Lake City Branch			
101 Market St San Francisco CA 94105	415-974-2000	974-2168	71
TF: 800-227-4133 ■ *Web:* www.frbsf.org			
Federal Reserve Money Museum			
701 E Byrd St Richmond VA 23219	804-697-8000		520
Web: www.richmondfed.org			
Federal Retirement Thrift Investment Board			
1250 H St NW Washington DC 20005	202-942-1600		340-20
Web: www.frtib.gov			
Federal Screw Works 34846 Goddard Rd Romulus MI 48174	734-941-4211		621
OTC: FSCR ■ *Web:* www.federalscrew.com			
Federal Signal Corp			
1415 W 22nd St Ste 1100 Oak Brook IL 60523	630-954-2000	954-2030	185
NYSE: FSS ■ *TF:* 800-548-7229 ■ *Web:* www.federalsignal.com			
Federal Signal Corp Emergency Products Div			
2645 Federal Signal Dr University Park IL 60466	708-534-3400		700
TF: 800-264-3578 ■ *Web:* www.fedsig.com			
Federal Square Inn & Extended Stay			
8781 Madison Blvd Madison AL 35758	256-772-8470		379
Federal Staffing Resources LLC			
2200 Somerville Rd Ste 300 Annapolis MD 21401	410-990-0795		260
TF: 866-886-2300 ■ *Web:* fsrpeople.com			
Federal Steel Supply Inc			
747 Goddard Ave PO Box 840 Chesterfield MO 63005	636-537-2393		492
Web: www.fedsteel.com			
Federal Technology Solutions Inc			
1828 Railroad St Corona CA 92880	951-808-9660		180
Web: www.federalsales.com			
Federal Trade Commission (FTC)			
600 Pennsylvania Ave NW Washington DC 20580	202-326-2222		340-20
TF: 877-382-4357 ■ *Web:* www.ftc.gov			
National Do Not Call Registry			
600 Pennsylvania Ave NW Washington DC 20580	888-382-1222		340-20
TF: 888-382-1222 ■ *Web:* www.ftc.gov			
Federal Trade Commission Regional Offices			
East Central Region			
1111 Superior Ave Ste 200 Cleveland OH 44114	216-263-3455	263-3426	340-20
TF: 877-382-4357 ■ *Web:* www.ftc.gov			
Midwest Region 55 W Monroe St Ste 1825 Chicago IL 20580	877-382-4357		340-20
TF: 877-382-4357 ■ *Web:* www.ftc.gov			
NortheastRegion			
1 Bowling Green Ste 318 New York NY 10004	212-607-2829	607-2822	340-20
TF: 877-382-4357 ■ *Web:* www.ftc.gov			
Northwest Region			
915 Second Ave Rm 2896 Seattle WA 98174	877-382-4357		340-20
TF: 877-382-4357 ■ *Web:* www.ftc.gov			
Southeast Region 60 Forsyth St SW Atlanta GA 30303	404-656-1390	656-1379	340-20
TF: 877-282-4357 ■ *Web:* www.ftc.gov			
Southwest Region 1999 Bryan St Ste 2150 Dallas TX 75201	877-382-4357		340-20
TF: 877 382 4357 ■ *Web:* www.ftc.gov			
Western Region			
901 Market St Ste 570 San Francisco CA 94103	877-382-4357	824-4380*	340-20
**Fax Area Code:* 310 ■ *TF:* 877-382-4357 ■ *Web:* ftc.gov			
Federal Transit Administration			
1200 New Jersey Ave SE Washington DC 20590	202-366-4043	366-9854	340-17
Web: www.transit.dot.gov			
Federal Transit Administration Regional Offices			
Region 1 55 Broadway Ste 920 Cambridge MA 02142	617-494-2055	494-2865	340-17
Web: www.transit.dot.gov			
Region 2 1 Bowling Green Rm 429 New York NY 10004	212-668-2170	668-2136	340-17
Web: www.transit.dot.gov			
Region 3 1760 Market St Ste 500 Philadelphia PA 19103	215-656-7100	656-7260	340-17
Web: www.transit.dot.gov			
Region 4 230 Peachtree St NW Ste 800 Atlanta GA 30303	404-865-5600	865-5605	340-17
Web: www.transit.dot.gov			
Region 5 200 W Adams St Ste 320 Chicago IL 60606	312-353-2789	886-0351	340-17
Web: www.transit.dot.gov			
Region 6 819 Taylor St Rm 8A36 Fort Worth TX 76102	817-978-0550	978-0575	340-17
Web: www.transit.dot.gov			
Region 7 901 Locust St Ste 404 Kansas City MO 64106	816-329-3920	329-3921	340-17
Web: www.transit.dot.gov			
Region 8 1961 Stout St Ste 13 301 Denver CO 80202	303-362-2400	362-2424	340-17
Web: www.transit.dot.gov			
Region 9 201 Mission St Ste 1650 San Francisco CA 94105	415-744-3133	744-2726	340-17
Web: www.transit.dot.gov			
Region 10			
Federal Transit Administration			
915 2nd Ave Ste 3142 Seattle WA 98174	206-220-7954	220-7959	340-17
Web: www.transit.dot.gov			
Federal Wage & Labor Institute			
7001 W 43rd St Houston TX 77092	713-690-5676		752
TF: 800-767-9243 ■ *Web:* www.fwlli.com			
Federal White Cement Ltd			
PO Box 1609 Woodstock ON N4S0A8	519-485-5410	485-5892	135
TF Sales: 800-265-1806 ■ *Web:* www.federalwhitecement.com			
Federalist Society for Law & Public Policy Studies			
1015 18th St NW Ste 425 Washington DC 20036	202-822-8138	296-8061	49-10
Web: www.fed-soc.org			
Federally Employed Women (FEW)			
455 Massachusetts Ave NW Ste 306 Washington DC 20001	202-898-0994		49-7
Web: www.few.org			
Federal-Mogul Corp			
27300 W 11 Mile Rd Southfield MI 48034	248-354-7700	354-7700	60
NASDAQ: FDML ■ *TF Cust Svc:* 800-325-8886 ■ *Web:* www.federalmogul.com			
Federated Adjustment Company Inc			
7929 N Port Washington Rd Milwaukee WI 53217	414-228-0900		160
Web: facpaid.com			
Federated Co-operatives Ltd			
401 22nd St E PO Box 1050 Saskatoon SK S7K0H2	306-244-3311	244-3403	275
TF: 800-848-6347 ■ *Web:* www.coopconnection.ca			

	Phone	Fax	Class
Federated Co-ops Inc			
502 S Second St Princeton MN 55371	763-389-2582		579
TF: 800-638-8228 ■ *Web:* www.federatedcoops.com			
Federated Group Inc			
3025 W Salt Creek Ln Arlington Heights IL 60005	847-577-1200	632-8302	345
TF: 800-234-0011 ■ *Web:* www.fedgroup.com			
Federated Insurance Cos			
121 E Pk Sq PO Box 328 Owatonna MN 55060	507-455-5200		360-4
TF: 800-533-0472 ■ *Web:* federatedinsurance.com			
Federated Investors			
1001 Liberty Ave Federated Investors Twr Pittsburgh PA 15222	412-288-1900		401
NYSE: FII ■ *TF:* 800-245-0242 ■ *Web:* www.federatedinvestors.com			
Federated Life Insurance Co			
121 E Pk Sq PO Box 328 Owatonna MN 55060	507-455-5200	455-7840	391-2
TF: 800-533-0472 ■ *Web:* federatedinsurance.com			
Federated Media 421 S Second St Elkhart IN 46516	574-295-2500		645-10
Web: www.federatedmedia.com			
Federated Mutual Insurance Co			
121 E Pk Sq PO Box 328 Owatonna MN 55060	507-455-5200		391-2
TF: 800-533-0472 ■ *Web:* federatedinsurance.com			
Federated Rural Electric Assn			
77100 US Hwy 71 PO Box 69 Jackson MN 56143	507-847-3520	728-8366	245
TF: 800-321-3520 ■ *Web:* www.federatedrea.com			
Federation Co-op			
108 N Water St Black River Falls WI 54615	715-284-5354	284-9672	276
TF: 800-944-1784 ■ *Web:* www.fedcoop.com			
Federation for American Immigration Reform (FAIR)			
25 Massachusetts Ave NW Ste 330 Washington DC 20009	202-328-7004	387-3447	48-7
TF: 877-627-3247 ■ *Web:* www.fairus.org			
Federation Forest State Park			
49201 SE Enumclaw Chinook Pass Rd Enumclaw WA 98022	360-902-8844		565
Web: www.parks.wa.gov			
Federation of American Hospitals			
750 Ninth St NW Ste 600 Washington DC 20001	202-624-1500	624-1500	49-8
Web: www.fah.org			
Federation of American Scientists (FAS)			
1725 DeSales St NW Ste 600 Washington DC 20036	202-546-3300		49-19
Web: www.fas.org			
Federation of American Societies for Experimental Biology (FASEB)			
9650 Rockville Pk Bethesda MD 20814	301-634-7000	634-7001	49-19
TF: 800-433-2732 ■ *Web:* www.faseb.org			
Federation of Families for Children's Mental Health (FFCMH)			
9605 Medical Ctr Dr Ste 280 Rockville MD 20850	240-403-1901	403-1909	49-15
Web: www.ffcmh.org			
Federation of State Medical Boards of the US Inc (FSMB)			
400 Fuller Wiser Rd Ste 300 Euless TX 76039	817-868-4000	868-4098	49-8
TF: 800-793-7939 ■ *Web:* www.fsmb.org			
Federation of Tax Administrators (FTA)			
444 N Capitol St NW Ste 348 Washington DC 20001	202-624-5890	624-7888	49-7
TF: 800-829-9188 ■ *Web:* www.taxadmin.org			
Federico Consulting Inc 333 W Shaw Ave Fresno CA 93704	559-224-5922		225
Web: www.federico.net			
FedEx 450 W First Ave Roselle NJ 07203	406-252-6265		110
TF: 800-463-3339 ■ *Web:* www.fedex.com/us/office/commercialpress			
FedEx Corp 3610 Hacks Cross Rd Memphis TN 38125	901-369-3600		360-3
NYSE: FDX ■ *TF:* 800-463-3339 ■ *Web:* www.fedex.com			
FedEx Corp Government Affairs			
942 S Shady Grove Rd Memphis TN 38120	901-818-7500		615
Web: www.fedex.com			
FedEx Custom Critical Inc			
1475 Boettler Rd Uniontown OH 44685	234-310-4090		546
TF Cust Svc: 800-762-3787 ■ *Web:* www.customcritical.fedex.com			
FedEx Field 1600 FedEx Way Landover MD 20785	301-276-6000	276-6001	720
Web: www.redskins.com			
FedEx Forum 191 Beale St Memphis TN 38103	901-205-1234		720
TF: 866-648-4668 ■ *Web:* www.nba.com/grizzlies			
FedEx Freight East			
942 S Shady Grove Rd Memphis TN 38120	901-818-7500		780
Web: www.fedex.com			
FedEx Kinko's Office & Print Services Inc			
7900 Legacy Dr Plano TX 75024	214-550-7000	550-7001	113
Web: fedex.com			
FedEx Supply Chain Services Inc			
5455 Darrow Rd Hudson OH 44236	901-369-3600		449
TF: 800-463-3339 ■ *Web:* www.fedex.com			
FedEx Trade Networks Inc			
6075 Poplar Ave Ste 300 Third Fl Memphis TN 38119	901-684-4800	684-4843	449
NYSE: FDX ■ *Web:* www.ftn.fedex.com			
Fedmet Resources Corp PO Box 278 Montreal QC H3Z2T2	514-931-5711	931-8378	663
TF: 800-609-5711 ■ *Web:* www.fedmet.com			
Fednav Ltd			
1000 Rue de la GauchetiFre O Bureau 3500 Montreal QC H3B4W5	514-878-6500	878-6642	313
TF General: 800-678-4842 ■ *Web:* www.fednav.com			
FedNet (Federal Network Inc)			
122 C St NW Ste 520 Washington DC 20001	202-393-7300		530
Web: www.fednet.net			
Fedtech Inc 4763 Mustang Cir Mounds View MN 55112	763-784-4600		454
Web: www.fedtech.com			
FedTek Inc			
12700 Black Forest Ln Ste 202 Woodbridge VA 22192	703-551-4718		180
Web: www.fedtek.com			
Feduke Ford 2200 Vestal Pkwy E Vestal NY 13850	607-754-5533		57
Web: fedukeford.com			
FEDUSA 13256 66th St N Ste 35 Largo FL 33773	800-403-1077		391-2
TF: 800-403-1077 ■ *Web:* www.directgeneral.com/fed-us-insurance			
Fedway Assoc Inc			
505 Westgate Dr Basking Ridge NJ 07920	973-624-6444		81-3
Web: www.fedway.com			
FEE (Foundation for Economic Education)			
30 S Broadway Irvington-on-Hudson NY 10533	404-554-9980		634
TF: 800-960-4333 ■ *Web:* www.fee.org			
Fee Bros Inc 453 Portland Ave Rochester NY 14605	585-544-9530		296-40
Web: www.feebrothers.com			
Fee Smith Sharp & Vitullo L L P			
3 Galleria Tower 13155 Noel Rd Ste 1000 Dallas TX 75240	972-934-9100		445
Web: www.feesmith.com			
Feeco International Inc			
3913 Algoma Rd Green Bay WI 54311	920-468-1000	469-5110	207
TF: 800-373-9347 ■ *Web:* www.feeco.com			

Name / Address	City	State	Zip	Phone	Fax	Class
Feed Forward Inc 1834 W Oak Pkwy *Web:* feedforward.com	Marietta	GA	30062	770-426-4422		261
Feed the Children (FTC) PO Box 36 *TF:* 800-627-4556 ■ *Web:* www.feedthechildren.org	Oklahoma City	OK	73101	405-942-0228		48-5
Feeley Bonaventura & Hyzy CPAsPc 5695 Main St *Web:* fbhcpa.com	Williamsville	NY	14221	716-632-0606		2
Feenaughty Machinery Co 4800 NE Columbia Blvd *TF:* 800-875-2566 ■ *Web:* www.feenaughty.com	Portland	OR	97218	503-282-2566		358
Feesers Inc 5561 Grayson Rd *TF:* 800-326-2828 ■ *Web:* www.feesers.com	Harrisburg	PA	17111	717-564-4636		297-8
Feheley Fine Arts 65 George St **Fax Area Code:* 647 ■ *TF:* 877-904-9114 ■ *Web:* www.feheleyfinearts.com	Toronto	ON	M5A4L8	416-323-1373	361-7667*	42
Fehr Bros Industries Inc 895 Kings Hwy *Web:* endurancehardware.com	Saugerties	NY	12477	845-246-9525		492
Fehr-Graham & Assoc LLC 221 E Main St Ste 200 *Web:* fehr-graham.com	Freeport	IL	61032	815-235-7643		261
FEI (Financial Executives International) 1250 Headquarters Plaza W Twr 7th Fl *Web:* www.financialexecutives.org	Morristown	NJ	07960	973-765-1000	765-1018	49-2
FEI Behavioral Health 11700 West Lake Pk Dr *TF:* 800-782-1948 ■ *Web:* www.feinet.com	Milwaukee	WI	53224	414-359-1055	359-1973	462
FEI Co 5350 NE Dawson Creek Dr *NASDAQ: FEIC* ■ **Fax:* Sales ■ *TF Cust Svc:* 866-693-3426 ■ *Web:* www.fei.com	Hillsboro	OR	97124	503-726-7500	726-2570*	419
Feiltd 37 Arnold'S Valley Rd	Natural Bridge Station	VA	24579	540-291-3398		480
Feinblanking Ltd 9461 Lesaint Dr *Web:* www.feinblanking.com	Fairfield	OH	45014	513-860-2100		488
Feingold & Feingold Insurance Agency Inc 22 Elm St *Web:* feingoldco.com	Worcester	MA	01608	508-831-9500		390
Feingold & Kam LLC 5100 PGA Blvd Ste 2	Palm Beach	FL	33418	561-630-6727		445
Feingold Association of the US 11849 Suncatcher Dr *TF:* 800-321-3287 ■ *Web:* www.feingold.org	Fishers	IN	46037	631-369-9340	369-2988	48-17
Feinstein Dianne (Sen D - CA) 331 Hart Bldg *Web:* www.feinstein.senate.gov	Washington	DC	20510	202-224-3841	228-3954	342-2
Feinstein Kean Healthcare 245 First St Fl 10 *Web:* www.fkhealth.com	Cambridge	MA	02142	617-577-8110		636
Feith Systems & Software Inc 425 Maryland Dr *Web:* feith.com	Ft Washington	PA	19034	215-646-8000		180
Feizy Import & Export Co Ltd 1949 Stemmons Fwy *TF:* 800-779-0877 ■ *Web:* feizy.com	Dallas	TX	75207	214-747-6000	760-0521	290
Felbro Food Products Inc 5700 W Adams Blvd *Web:* felbro.com	Los Angeles	CA	90016	323-936-5266		297-8
Felbro Inc 3666 E Olympic Blvd *TF:* 800-733-5276 ■ *Web:* www.felbrodisplays.com	Los Angeles	CA	90023	323-263-8686	263-8874	233
Felchar Manufacturing Corp 196 Corporate Dr *Web:* www.felchar.com	Binghamton	NY	13904	607-723-4076		360-3
FelCor Lodging Trust Inc 545 E John Carpenter Fwy Ste 1300 *NYSE: FCH* ■ *Web:* www.felcor.com	Irving	TX	75062	972-444-4900	444-4949	655
Feld Entertainment Inc 8607 Westwood Ctr Dr *TF:* 800-844-3545 ■ *Web:* www.feldentertainment.com	Vienna	VA	22182	703-448-4000		149
Felder Communications Group 50 Louis NW Trade Ctr Ste 600 *TF:* 800-536-8628 ■ *Web:* www.felder.com	Grand Rapids	MI	49503	616-459-1200		195
Feldesman Tucker Leifer Fidell LLP 1129 20th St NW Ste 400 *Web:* www.feldesmantucker.com	Washington	DC	20036	202-466-8960		428
Feldman Bros Electrical Supply Co 26 Maryland Ave *Web:* www.feldmanbros.com	Paterson	NJ	07503	973-742-7329	742-2220	246
Feldman Financial Advisors Inc 1001 Connecticut Ave NW Ste 840 *Web:* www.feldmanfinancial.com	Washington	DC	20036	202-467-6862		734
Feldman, Kramer & Monaco PC 330 Vanderbilt Motor Pkwy *Web:* www.fkmlaw.com	Hauppauge	NY	11788	631-231-1450		428
Feldmeier Equipment Inc 6800 Townline Rd *TF:* 800-258-0118 ■ *Web:* www.feldmeier.com	Syracuse	NY	13211	315-454-8608	454-3701	298
Felicia Oil Company Inc R78 Commercial St	Gloucester	MA	01930	978-283-3808		316
Felician College 262 S Main St **Fax:* Admissions ■ *TF:* 888-442-4551 ■ *Web:* www.felician.edu	Lodi	NJ	07644	201-559-6000	559-6138*	166
Rutherford 223 Montross Ave *TF:* 888-442-4551 ■ *Web:* www.felician.edu	Rutherford	NJ	07070	201-559-6000	559-3578	166
Felician Sisters CSSF 1600 W Oklahoma Ave	Milwaukee	WI	53215	414-645-5329		48-20
Felicita Resort 2201 Fishing Creek Valley Rd *Web:* www.felicitaresort.com	Harrisburg	PA	17112	717-599-5301		669
Felidia 243 E 58th St *TF:* 800-631-8130 ■ *Web:* www.felidia-nyc.com	New York	NY	10022	212-758-1479		671
Felins USA Inc 8306 W Parkland Ct *Web:* www.felins.com	Milwaukee	WI	53223	414-355-7747		111
Felipe's 2241 N Woodlawn *Web:* www.felipeswichita.com	Wichita	KS	67220	316-652-0027		671
Felix Neck Wildlife Sanctuary 100 Felix Neck Dr *TF:* 866-627-2267 ■ *Web:* massaudubon.org	Edgartown	MA	02539	508-627-4850	627-6052	823
Felix Schoeller North America Inc 179 County Rt 2A Ste 2A *Web:* www.felix-schoeller.com	Pulaski	NY	13142	315-298-5133	298-3664	552-1
Felix Storch Inc 770 Garrison Ave *TF:* 800-932-4267 ■ *Web:* www.summitappliance.com	Bronx	NY	10474	718-893-3900		38
Felix Valle House State Historic Site 198 Merchant St *Web:* mostateparks.com	Sainte Genevieve	MO	63670	573-883-7102		565
Felker Bros Corp 22 N Chestnut Ave *TF:* 800-826-2304 ■ *Web:* www.felkerbrothers.com	Marshfield	WI	54449	715-384-3121	387-6837	490
Fellini's 3910 Colley Ave *TF:* 800-456-2444 ■ *Web:* fellinisva.com	Norfolk	VA	23508	757-625-3000		671
Fellowes Inc 1789 Norwood Ave **Fax:* Cust Svc ■ *TF:* 800-945-4545 ■ *Web:* www.fellowes.com	Itasca	IL	60143	630-893-1600	893-1600*	111
Fellowship Community 3000 Fellowship Dr *Web:* www.fellowshipcommunity.com	Whitehall	PA	18052	610-799-3000		48-20
Fellowship Hall Inc 5140 Dunstan Rd *TF:* 800-659-3381 ■ *Web:* www.fellowshiphall.com	Greensboro	NC	27405	336-621-3381		726
Fellowship of Christian Athletes (FCA) 8701 Leeds Rd *TF:* 800-289-0909 ■ *Web:* www.fca.org	Kansas City	MO	64129	816-921-0909	921-8755	48-22
Fellowship Village Dining Service Dept 8000 Fellowship Rd *Web:* fellowshipseniorliving.org	Basking Ridge	NJ	07920	908-580-3806		48-20
Felly's Flowers Inc PO Box 6620 *TF:* 800-993-7673 ■ *Web:* www.fellys.net	Madison	WI	53716	800-993-7673		292
Fels Institute for Cancer Research & Molecular Biology Temple Univ School of Medicine 3400 N Broad St *TF:* 800-988-4861 ■ *Web:* www.temple.edu	Philadelphia	PA	19140	215-707-6356	707-2783	668
Felsburg Holt & Ullevig Inc 6300 S Syracuse Way Ste 600 *Web:* www.fhueng.com	Centennial	CO	80111	303-721-1440		256
Feltl & Company Inc 2100 LaSalle Plaza 800 LaSalle Ave *Web:* www.feltl.com	Minneapolis	MN	55402	612-492-8800		401
Felton Brush Inc 7 Burton Dr *TF:* 800-258-9702 ■ *Web:* www.feltoninc.com	Londonderry	NH	03053	603-425-0200	425-0200	103
Felts Field Aviation Inc 6205 E Rutter Ave *TF:* 800-676-5538 ■ *Web:* www.feltsfield.com	Spokane	WA	99212	509-535-9011	535-9014	63
Felts Lock & Alarm Company Inc 4000 E Indiana St *TF:* 800-640-6560 ■ *Web:* www.feltsonline.com	Evansville	IN	47715	812-473-4000		692
FEM Electric Assn Inc PO Box 468 *TF:* 800-587-5880 ■ *Web:* www.femelectric.coop	Ipswich	SD	57451	605-426-6891	426-6791	245
FEMA (Flavor & Extract Manufacturers Assn of the US) 1101 17th St NW Ste 700 *Web:* www.femaflavor.org	Washington	DC	20036	202-293-5800	463-8998	49-6
FEMA (Federal Emergency Management Agency) 500 C St SW *TF:* 800-621-3362 ■ *Web:* www.fema.gov	Washington	DC	20472	800-621-3362		340-11
FEMA (Farm Equipment Manufacturers Assn) 1000 Executive Pkwy Ste 100 *TF:* 800-647-3061 ■ *Web:* www.farmequip.org	Saint Louis	MO	63141	314-878-2304	732-1480	48-2
FEMA (Federal Emergency Management Agency Regional Office) *Region 1* 99 High St *TF:* 877-336-2627 ■ *Web:* www.fema.gov/region-i	Boston	MA	02110	617-956-7551		340-11
Female Health Co 515 N State St Ste 2225 *Web:* fc2femalecondom.com	Chicago	IL	60654	312-595-9123		477
Femco Machine Co 754 S Main St Ext *TF:* 800-458-3445 ■ *Web:* www.femcomachine.com	Punxsutawney	PA	15767	814-938-9763	938-8332	454
Feminist Majority Foundation-East Coast (FMF) 1600 Wilson Blvd Ste 801 *Web:* www.feminist.org	Arlington	VA	22209	703-522-2214	522-2219	48-24
Feminist Press at the City University of New York 365 Fifth Ave Ste 5406 *Web:* www.feministpress.org	New York	NY	10016	212-817-7915	817-1593	637-2
FemmePharma 37 W Ave 2nd Fl *Web:* www.femmepharma.com	Wayne	PA	19087	610-995-0801		194
Fencecrete America Inc 15089 Tradesman Dr *Web:* www.fencecrete.com	San Antonio	TX	78249	210-492-7911		183
Fender Musical Instruments Corp 17600 N Perimeter Dr Ste 100 *TF Cust Svc:* 800-488-1818 ■ *Web:* www.fender.com	Scottsdale	AZ	85255	480-596-9690	596-1384	527
Fendt Builders Supply Inc 22005 Gill Rd *Web:* www.fendtproducts.com	Farmington Hills	MI	48335	248-474-3211		183
Fene-Tech Inc 264 St-Benoit E Blvd *Web:* www.fene-tech.com	Amqui	QC	G5L2C5	418-629-4675	629-3982	236
Fenetres Lapco Inc 12995 Rue Du Parc *Web:* www.lapcoinc.com	Mirabel	QC	J7J1P3	450-971-0432		499
Fengate Capital Management Ltd 77 King St W Ste 4230 *Web:* fengate.com	Toronto	ON	M5K1H1	416-488-4184		528
Fenix Construtors Inc 215 Drow St SW *Web:* www.fenixci.com	Ardmore	OK	73401	580-223-4313	223-4315	780
Fennebresque & Company LLC 550 S Caldwell St NASCAR Plaza Ste 755 *Web:* www.fennebresque.com	Charlotte	NC	28202	704-295-8900		41
Fennell Spring LLC 295 Hemlock St	Horseheads	NY	14845	607-739-3541		719
Fennemore Craig PC 3003 N Central Ave Ste 2600 *Web:* www.fclaw.com	Phoenix	AZ	85012	602-916-5000		428
Fenner Drives 311 W Stiegel St *TF Sales:* 800-243-3374 ■ *Web:* www.fennerdrives.com	Manheim	PA	17545	717-665-2421	664-8214	370
Fenster & Fenster 1514 S D St *Web:* fensterandfenster.com	San Bernardino	CA	92408	909-889-0288		2
Fenton Art Glass Co 700 Elizabeth St *TF Cust Svc:* 800-933-6766 ■ *Web:* www.fentonartglass.com	Williamstown	WV	26187	304-375-6122	375-6459	334
Fenton Communications Inc 1010 Vermont Ave NW Ste 1100 *Web:* www.fenton.com	Washington	DC	20005	202-822-5200		514
Fenton Lake State Park 455 Fenton Lake	Jemez Springs	NM	87025	575-829-3630		565
Fenton Rigging & Contracting Inc 2150 Langdon Farm Rd *Web:* fenton1898.com	Cincinnati	OH	45237	513-631-5500		189-14

Name / Address	City	State	ZIP	Phone	Fax	Class
Fentress Bradburn Architects Ltd						
421 Broadway	Denver	CO	80203	303-722-5000		261
Web: www.fentressarchitects.com						
Fentress County						
101 Main St S PO Box 823	Jamestown	TN	38556	931-879-9948		338
Web: www.jamestowntn.org						
Fentress Inc 945 Sunset Vly Dr	Sykesville	MD	21784	888-329-0040		196
TF: 888-329-0040 ■ *Web:* www.fentress.com						
Fenway Health 1340 Boylston St	Boston	MA	02215	617-267-0900		743
Web: www.fenwayhealth.org						
Fenway Park 4 Yawkey Way	Boston	MA	02215	617-226-6000		720
TF: 877-733-7699 ■ *Web:* boston.redsox.mlb.com						
Fenwick Inn 13801 Coastal Hwy	Ocean City	MD	21842	410-250-1100	250-0087	379
TF: 800-492-1873 ■ *Web:* www.fenwickinn.com						
Fenwick Island State Park						
39415 Inlet Rd	Rehoboth Beach	DE	19971	302-227-2800	227-7400	565
Web: www.destateparks.com						
Feralloy Corp						
8755 W Higgins Rd Ste 970	Chicago	IL	60631	773-380-1500	380-1535	492
TF: 800-754-8867 ■ *Web:* www.feralloy.com						
FERC						
Atlanta 888 First St NE	Washington	DC	30096	678-245-3075	245-3010	340-9
Web: www.ferc.gov						
Ferche Millwork Inc 400 Division St	Rice	MN	56367	320-393-5700		499
Web: www.ferche.com						
Ferco Tech Corp 291 Conover Dr	Franklin	OH	45005	937-746-6696		21
Web: www.fercotech.com						
Fergus County 712 W Main St	Lewistown	MT	59457	406-535-5026	535-6076	338
Web: www.co.fergus.mt.us						
Fergus Electric Co-op Inc						
84423 US Hwy 87	Lewistown	MT	59457	406-538-3465		245
Web: www.ferguselectric.coop						
Fergus Partnership Consulting Inc						
14 Wall St # 3C	New York	NY	10005	212-767-1775		266
Web: www.ferguslex.com						
Ferguson & Redelsperger PC						
1026 Main St	Duncan	OK	73533	580-255-2190		2
Ferguson Buick Gmc 1015 N I- Dr	Norman	OK	73069	405-253-0918	360-8854	57
Web: fergusonchallenge.com						
Ferguson Construction Co 400 Canal St	Sidney	OH	45365	937-498-2381		186
Web: www.ferguson-construction.com						
Ferguson Drew (Rep R - GA)						
1032 Longworth HOB	Washington	DC	20515	202-225-5901		342-2
Web: ferguson.house.gov						
Ferguson Enterprises Inc						
12500 Jefferson Ave	Newport News	VA	23602	757-874-7795	989-2501	612
TF: 800-721-2590 ■ *Web:* www.ferguson.com						
Ferguson Enterprises Inc 5722 49th St	Maspeth	NY	11378	718-937-9500	937-9500	610
TF: 800-721-2590 ■ *Web:* ferguson.com/davis-and-warshow						
Ferguson Library						
1 Public Library Plaza	Stamford	CT	06904	203-964-1000	357-9098	434-3
Web: www.fergusonlibrary.org						
Ferguson Perforating & Wire Co						
130 Ernest St	Providence	RI	02905	401-941-8876		483
TF: 800-341-9800 ■ *Web:* www.fergusonperf.com						
Ferguson Production Inc						
2130 Industrial Dr	Mcpherson	KS	67460	620-241-2400		596
Web: www.fergusonproduction.com						
Ferguson Supply & Box Manufacturing Co						
10820 Quality Dr	Charlotte	NC	28278	704-597-0310	597-5623	100
TF: 800-821-1023 ■ *Web:* www.fergusonbox.com						
Ferguson Wellman Capital Management Inc						
888 S W Fifth Ave	Portland	OR	97204	503-226-1444		528
TF: 800-327-5765 ■ *Web:* www.fergusonwellman.com						
Ferguson, Case, Orr, Paterson, & Cunningham LLP						
1050 S Kimball Rd	Ventura	CA	93004	805-659-6800		428
Web: www.fcopc.com						
Ferma Corp 1265 Montecito Ave	Mountain View	CA	94043	650-961-2742		189-16
TF: 877-337-6211 ■ *Web:* www.fermacorp.com						
Fermi National Accelerator Laboratory						
PO Box 500	Batavia	IL	60510	630-840-3000	840-4343	668
Web: www.fnal.gov						
Fern Forest Nature Ctr						
201 Lyons Rd S	Coconut Creek	FL	33063	954-970-0150		50-5
Web: www.broward.org/parks						
Fernandes Steak House 158 Fleming Ave	Newark	NJ	07105	973-589-4344		671
Web: www.fernandessteakhouse.com						
Fernbank Museum of Natural History						
767 Clifton Rd NE	Atlanta	GA	30307	404-929-6300		522
Web: www.fernbankmuseum.org						
Fernbank Science Ctr						
156 Heaton Pk Dr NE	Atlanta	GA	30307	678-874-7102	874-7110	520
Web: fernbank.edu						
Fernco Inc 300 S Dayton St	Davison	MI	48423	810-653-9626	653-8714	596
TF: 800-521-1283 ■ *Web:* www.fernco.com						
Ferndale Chamber of Commerce						
407 E 9-Mile Rd	Ferndale	MI	48220	248-542-2160	542-8979	139
TF: 800-495-5464 ■ *Web:* www.ferndaleareachamber.com						
Ferndale Electric Company Inc						
915 E Drayton Ave	Ferndale	MI	48220	248-545-4404	545-8140	189-4
Web: www.ferndale-electric.com						
Ferndale Public Library						
222 E Nine-Mile Rd	Ferndale	MI	48220	248-546-2504	545-5840	434-3
Web: www.ferndalepubliclibrary.org						
Ferndale School District 502						
6041 Vista Dr PO Box 698	Ferndale	WA	98248	360-383-9200	383-9201	685
Web: ferndalesd.org						
Ferne Clyffe State Park PO Box 10	Goreville	IL	62939	618-995-2411		565
Web: www.dnr.illinois.gov/parks/pages/ferneclyffe.aspx						
Fernley & Fernley Inc						
100 N 20th St 4th Fl	Philadelphia	PA	19103	215-564-3484	564-2175	47
Web: www.fernley.com						
Ferno-Washington Inc 70 Weil Way	Wilmington	OH	45177	937-382-1451	382-1191	477
TF: 800-733-3766 ■ *Web:* www.ferno.com						
Fernwood Botanical Gardens & Nature Preserve						
13988 Range Line Rd	Niles	MI	49120	269-695-6491		97
Web: www.fernwoodbotanical.org						
Fernwood Resort						
5785 Milford Rd	East Stroudsburg	PA	18302	888-337-6966	588-7112*	669
**Fax Area Code:* 570 ■ *TF:* 800-337-6966 ■ *Web:* fernwoodresortpoconos.com						
Feroleto Steel Company Inc						
300 Scofield Ave	Bridgeport	CT	06605	203-366-3263	366-8058	723
TF: 800-243-2839 ■ *Web:* www.feroletosteel.com						
Ferragon Corp 11103 Memphis Ave	Cleveland	OH	44144	216-671-6161		295
Web: www.ferragon.com						
Ferran Services & Contracting						
530 Grand St	Orlando	FL	32805	407-422-3551	648-0961	189-10
TF: 800-561-3357 ■ *Web:* www.ferran-services.com						
Ferrandino & Son Inc						
71 Carolyn Blvd	Farmingdale	NY	11735	516-735-0097		610
TF: 866-571-4609 ■ *Web:* www.ferrandinoandson.com						
Ferrante Manufacturing Co						
6626 Gratiot Ave	Detroit	MI	48207	313-571-1111		286
TF: 800-229-3672 ■ *Web:* ferrantemfg.com						
Ferrara Fiorenza Larrison Barrett & Reitz PC						
5010 Campuswood Dr	East Syracuse	NY	13057	315-437-7600		428
TF: 800-777-4742 ■ *Web:* www.ferrarafirm.com						
Ferrara Fire Apparatus Inc PO Box 249	Holden	LA	70744	225-567-7100	567-5260	59
TF: 800-443-9006 ■ *Web:* www.ferrarafire.com						
Ferrara International Logistics Inc						
1319 N Broad St	Hillside	NJ	07205	908-282-9440		360-3
Web: www.ferrarainternational.com						
Ferrara Pan Candy Co						
7301 Harrison St	Forest Park	IL	60130	708-366-0500		296-8
Web: www.ferrarausa.com						
Ferrarabuckworth LLC 60 Pompton Ave	Verona	NJ	07044	973-857-8800		2
Ferrari North America Inc						
250 Sylvan Ave	Englewood Cliffs	NJ	07632	201-816-2600		59
Web: www.ferrari.com						
Ferraro Foods Inc						
287 S Randolphville Rd	Piscataway	NJ	08854	732-424-3400		805
Web: www.ferrarofoods.com						
Ferraro's 4480 Paradise Rd	Las Vegas	NV	89169	702-364-5300		671
Web: www.ferraroslasvegas.com						
Ferreira Cafe 1446 Peel St	Montreal	QC	H3A1S8	514-848-0988		671
Web: www.ferreiracafe.com						
Ferrell Capital Management LLC						
4 Greenwich Office Pk	Greenwich	CT	06831	203-862-9500		194
Web: www.ferrellcapital.com						
Ferrell Wealth Management Inc						
1400 W Fairbanks Ave	Winter Park	FL	32789	407-629-7008		2
Web: ferrellwm.com						
Ferrellgas Partners LP						
1 Liberty Plaza	Liberty	MO	64068	816-792-1600		316
NYSE: FGP ■ *TF:* 888-337-7355 ■ *Web:* www.ferrellgas.com						
Ferrell-Ross Roll Manufacturing Inc						
102 FM 2856 (Holly Sugar Rd)	Hereford	TX	79045	806-364-9051		295
Web: www.ferrellross.com						
Ferrer Freeman & Company LLC						
10 Glenville St	Greenwich	CT	06831	203-532-8011	532-8016	792
TF: 800-443-0778 ■ *Web:* www.ffandco.com						
Ferrero USA Inc 600 Cottontail Ln	Somerset	NJ	08873	732-764-9300	764-9300	296-8
TF: 800-688-3552 ■ *Web:* www.ferrerousa.com						
Ferrilli 41 S Haddon Ave Ste 7	Haddonfield	NJ	08033	888-864-3282		463
TF: 888-864-3282 ■ *Web:* ferrilli.com						
Ferring Pharmaceuticals Inc						
100 Interpace Pkwy	Parsippany	NJ	07054	973-796-1600		238
TF: 888-337-7464 ■ *Web:* www.ferringusa.com						
Ferriot Inc 1000 Arlington Cir	Akron	OH	44306	330-786-3000	786-3001	757
Web: ferriot.com						
Ferris Manufacturing Corp						
16W300 83rd St	Burr Ridge	IL	60527	630-887-9797		558
Web: www.polymem.com						
Ferris School 959 Centre Rd	Wilmington	DE	19805	302-993-3800	993-3820	412
TF: 800-292-9582 ■ *Web:* kids.delaware.gov						
Ferris State University						
1201 S State St	Big Rapids	MI	49307	231-591-2000	591-3944*	166
**Fax:* Admissions ■ *TF:* 800-433-7747 ■ *Web:* www.ferris.edu						
FLITE Library 1010 Campus Dr	Big Rapids	MI	49307	231-591-3602	591-3724	434-6
TF: 800-433-7747 ■ *Web:* www.ferris.edu/library						
Traverse City						
2200 Dendrinos Dr Ste 200H	Traverse City	MI	49684	231-995-1734	995-1736*	166
**Fax:* Admissions ■ *TF:* 866-857-1954 ■ *Web:* www.ferris.edu						
Ferro Corp						
6060 Parkland Blvd Ste 250	Mayfield Heights	OH	44124	216-875-5600	875-5627	605-2
Web: www.ferro.com						
Ferro Corp Electronic Materials Div						
4150 E 56th St	Cleveland	OH	44105	216-641-8580		143
Web: ferro.com						
Ferro Solutions Inc 5 Constitution Way	Woburn	MA	01801	781-935-7878		639
Web: www.ferrosi.com						
Ferronics Inc 45 O'Connor Rd	Fairport	NY	14450	585-388-1020	388-0036	249
Web: www.ferronics.com						
Ferrotherm Corp 4758 Warner Rd	Cleveland	OH	44125	216-883-9350		57
Web: www.ferrotherm.com						
Ferrousouth 38 County Rd 370	Iuka	MS	38852	662-424-0115		295
Web: www.ferrousmetalprocessing.com						
Ferrum College 215 Ferrum Mtn Rd	Ferrum	VA	24088	540-365-2121	365-4266	166
TF: 800-868-9797 ■ *Web:* www.ferrum.edu						
Ferry Beach State Park 95 Bayview Rd	Saco	ME	04072	207-283-0067		565
Web: www.maine.gov						
Ferry County 290 E Tessie Ave	Republic	WA	99166	509-775-5229	775-5230	338
Web: www.ferry-county.com						
Ferry Industries Inc 4445 Allen Rd	Stow	OH	44224	330-920-9200		454
Web: www.ferryindustries.com						
Ferry Plaza Wine Merchant Administration Offices						
101 The Embarcadero	San Francisco	CA	94105	415-288-0470		443
TF: 866-991-9400 ■ *Web:* www.fpwm.com						
Ferry Transportation Inc 5 Thames Ave	Laurel	MS	39440	601-425-5542		685
Web: www.ferrytrans.com						
Fertilizer Company of Arizona Inc						
2850 S Peart Rd	Casa Grande	AZ	85293	520-836-7477		791
Web: www.comptonag.com						
Fertilizer Institute, The (TFI)						
425 Third St SW Ste 950	Washington	DC	20024	202-962-0490	962-0577	48-2
Web: www.tfi.org						

Name / Address	Phone	Fax	Class
FESCO Agencies NA Inc 1000 Second Ave Ste 1310 . . . Seattle WA 98104 *TF:* 800-275-3372 ■ *Web:* www.fesco-na.com	206-583-0860	583-0889	311
FESCO Ltd 1000 Fesco Ave. . . . Alice TX 78332 *Web:* www.fescoinc.com	361-661-7000	661-7004	539
Fesnak & Associates LLP 1777 Sentry Pkwy W Ste 300 . . . Blue Bell PA 19422 *TF:* 800-274-3978 ■ *Web:* rsmus.com/who-we-are/welcome-fesnak-llp.html	267-419-2200		734
Fess Parker's Doubletree Resort (FPDTR) 633 E Cabrillo Blvd. . . . Santa Barbara CA 93103 *TF:* 800-879-2929 ■ *Web:* www.fessparkersantabarbarahotel.com	805-564-4333		669
Fessenden School 250 Waltham St . . . West Newton MA 02465 *Web:* www.fessenden.org	617-630-2300		622
Festiva Resorts 1 Vance Gap Rd. . . . Asheville NC 28805 *TF Resv:* 866-933-7848 ■ *Web:* festiva.com	828-254-3378		753
Festival Co 9841 Airport Blvd Ste 700 . . . Los Angeles CA 90045 *TF:* 800-800-1816 ■ *Web:* www.festivalcos.com	310-665-9600	665-9009	655
Festival Concert Hall *North Dakota State University* PO Box 5691 . . . Fargo ND 58105 *TF:* 800-726-1724 ■ *Web:* www.ndsu.edu	701-231-7932	231-2085	572
Festival Flea Market Mall 2900 W Sample Rd. . . . Pompano Beach FL 33073 *TF:* 800-353-2627 ■ *Web:* www.festival.com	954-979-4555		460
Festival Inn, The 1144 Ontario St. . . . Stratford ON N5A6Z3 *TF:* 800-463-3581 ■ *Web:* www.festivalinnstratford.com	519-273-1150		707
Festival Plaza 101 Crockett St . . . Shreveport LA 71101 *Web:* www.shreveportla.gov	318-673-5100	673-5105	205
Festive Holidays Inc 5501 New Jersey Ave . . . Wildwood Crest NJ 08260 *TF:* 800-257-8920 ■ *Web:* www.festiveholidays.com	609-522-6316	729-8606	760
Festo Corp 395 Moreland Dr . . . Hauppauge NY 11788 *TF:* 800-993-3786 ■ *Web:* www.festo.com/us	800-993-3786		454
Fet Engineering Inc 903 Nutter Dr. . . . Bardstown KY 40004 *Web:* www.fetusa.com	502-348-2130		596
Feta Med Inc 530 S Henderson Rd Ste D. . . . King Of Prussia PA 19406 *Web:* www.fetamed.com	610-205-0010		475
Fetch Logistics Inc 25 Northpointe Pkwy Ste 200. . . . Amherst NY 14228 *TF:* 800-964-4940 ■ *Web:* www.fetchlogistics.com	716-689-4556	689-9676	311
Fetch Recruiting Inc 21143 Hawthorne Blvd Ste 322 . . . Torrance CA 90503 *Web:* fetchrecruiting.com	310-375-4384		260
FetchBack Inc 100 W University Ste 101 . . . Tempe AZ 85281	480-289-5555		5
Fetco 600 Rose Rd . . . Lake Zurich IL 60047 *Web:* www.fetco.com	847-821-1177		296
Fetco Home Decor Inc 84 Teed Dr. . . . Randolph MA 02368 *Web:* www.fetcohomedecor.com	781-963-3636		361
Feussner'S Ford Inc 470 S St . . . Freeland PA 18224 *Web:* feussnersford.com	570-636-3920		57
Feutz Contractors Inc 1120 N Main St PO Box 130. . . . Paris IL 61944 *Web:* www.feutzcontractors.com	217-465-8402	463-2256	189-5
FEV Inc 4554 Glenmeade Ln. . . . Auburn Hills MI 48326 *Web:* fev.com	248-373-6000		261
FEW (Federally Employed Women) 455 Massachusetts Ave NW Ste 306 . . . Washington DC 20001 *Web:* www.few.org	202-898-0994		49-7
Fey Industries Inc 200 Fourth Ave N . . . Edgerton MN 56128 *TF:* 800-533-5340 ■ *Web:* fey-line.com	507-442-4311	442-3686	86
FEY Printing Co 910 29th Ave N. . . . Wisconsin Rapids WI 54495 *Web:* feyprinting.com	715-423-2400		627
FF Soucy Inc 191 Delage. . . . Riviere-du-Loup QC G5R3Z1 *Web:* www.ffsoucy.com	418-862-6941		557
FF Thompson Hospital 350 Parrish St. . . . Canandaigua NY 14424 *Web:* www.thompsonhealth.com	585-396-6000		374-3
FFB (First Financial Bancorp) 255 E Fifth St Ste 700. . . . Cincinnati OH 45202 *NASDAQ:* FFBC ■ *TF:* 877-322-9530 ■ *Web:* www.bankatfirst.com	877-322-9530		360-2
FFC (Farmers Win Coop) 110 N Jefferson . . . Fredericksburg IA 50630 *TF:* 800-562-8389 ■ *Web:* farmerswincoop.agricharts.com/Fredericksburg	563-237-5324	237-6123	10-4
FFC Inc 4010 Pilot Dr Ste 103 . . . Memphis TN 38118 *Web:* www.ffcfuelcells.com	901-842-7110		22
FFCMH (Federation of Families for Children's Mental Health) 9605 Medical Ctr Dr Ste 280 . . . Rockville MD 20850 *Web:* www.ffcmh.org	240-403-1901	403-1909	49-15
FFE Transportation Inc 1145 Empire Central Pl. . . . Dallas TX 75247 *TF:* 800-569-9200 ■ *Web:* www.ffeinc.com	214-630-8090	819-5625	780
FFF (Freedom From Fear) 308 Seaview Ave. . . . Staten Island NY 10305 *TF:* 800-550-3560 ■ *Web:* www.freedomfromfear.org	718-351-1717		48-17
FFF Enterprises Inc 41093 County Ctr Dr . . . Temecula CA 92591 *TF:* 800-843-7477 ■ *Web:* www.fffenterprises.com	951-296-2500		5
FFHSJ (Fried Frank Harris Shriver & Jacobson LLP) 1 New York Plaza . . . New York NY 10004 *Web:* www.friedfrank.com	212-859-8000	859-4000	428
FFI (Family Firm Institute) 200 Lincoln St Ste 201. . . . Boston MA 02111 *Web:* www.ffi.org	617-482-3045	482-3049	49-12
FFP (Food for the Poor Inc) 6401 Lyons Rd . . . Coconut Creek FL 33073 *TF:* 800-427-9104 ■ *Web:* www.foodforthepoor.org	954-427-2222		48-5
FFW Corp 1205 N Cass St . . . Wabash IN 46992 *OTC:* FFWC ■ *Web:* www.crossroadsbanking.com	260-563-3185	563-4841	360-2
FG Wilson Inc 10431 N Commerce Pkwy . . . Miramar FL 33025 *Web:* www.fgwilsonmiami.com	954-433-2212		191-1
FGH (Fairmont General Hospital) 1325 Locust Ave. . . . Fairmont WV 26554	304-367-7100	367-7246	374-3
FGI (Fashion Group International Inc) 8 W 40th St 7th Fl. . . . New York NY 10018 *TF:* 800-520-2262 ■ *Web:* www.fgi.org	212-302-5511	302-5533	49-4
FGI (FOIA Group Inc) 1250 Connecticut Ave NW Ste 200. . . . Washington DC 20036 **Fax Area Code:* 202 ■ *TF:* 888-461-7951 ■ *Web:* www.foia.com	888-461-7951	347-8419*	387
Fgmk LLC 2801 Lakeside Dr 3rd Fl. . . . Bannockburn IL 60015 *Web:* www.fgmk.com	847-374-0400		734
FGS (Freedom Graphic Systems Inc) 1101 S Janesville St . . . Milton WI 53563 *TF:* 800-334-3540 ■ *Web:* fgs.com	800-334-3540		110
FGX International Inc 500 George Washington Hwy . . . Smithfield RI 02917 *TF:* 800-283-3090 ■ *Web:* fgxi.com	401-231-3800		408
FH Bonn Co 4300 Gateway Blvd . . . Springfield OH 45502 *TF:* 800-323-0143 ■ *Web:* www.fhbonn.com	937-323-7024	323-0388	745-3
F&H Construction 1115 E Lockeford St . . . Lodi CA 95240 *Web:* www.f-hconst.com	209-931-3738		186
F&H Food Equipment Co 1526 S Enterprise Ave. . . . Springfield MO 65804 *Web:* www.fhfoodequipment.com	417-881-6114		358
FH Martin Constructors 28740 Mound Rd . . . Warren MI 48092 *TF:* 800-732-5569 ■ *Web:* www.fhmartin.com	586-558-2100	558-2921	187
FH Peterson Machine Corp 143 S St . . . Stoughton MA 02072 *Web:* www.fhpetersonmachine.com	781-341-4930	341-6022	456
FHG Inc 6809 Orchard Ridge Dr . . . Charlotte NC 28227 *Web:* www.fhg-inc.com	704-567-9548		536
FHL Capital Corp 2 N Twentieth St Ste 860. . . . Birmingham AL 35203 *Web:* www.fhlcapital.com	205-328-3098	323-0001	401
Fhm Insurance Co 4601 Touchton Rd E Bldg 300 Ste 3150 . . . Jacksonville FL 32246 **Fax Area Code:* 407 ■ *TF:* 800-393-0001 ■ *Web:* www.fhmic.com	904-724-9890	926-9419*	391-4
FHN Memorial Hospital 1045 W Stephenson St . . . Freeport IL 61032 *TF:* 800-747-4131 ■ *Web:* www.fhn.org	815-599-6000		374-3
FHWA (Federal Highway Administration) 400 Seventh St SW. . . . Washington DC 20590 *Web:* www.fhwa.dot.gov	202-366-0660		340-17
FIA (Futures Industry Assn) 2001 Pennsylvania Ave NW Ste 600. . . . Washington DC 20006 *Web:* fia.org	202-466-5460	296-3184	49-2
FIA (Forging Industry Assn) 1111 Superior Ave Ste 615. . . . Cleveland OH 44114 *Web:* www.forging.org	216-781-6260	781-0102	49-13
FIAF (French Institute Alliance Francaise) 22 E 60th St . . . New York NY 10022 *Web:* www.fiaf.org	212-355-6100	935-4119	48-14
Fiamma Trattoria 3799 Las Vegas Blvd S. . . . Las Vegas NV 89109 *Web:* mgmgrand.com	702-891-7600		671
Fiba Technologies Inc 1535 Grafton Rd PO Box 360 . . . Millbury MA 01527 *Web:* www.fibatech.com	508-887-7100	754-2254	198
Fibar Group LLC, The 80 Business Park Dr Suit 300. . . . Armonk NY 10504 *TF:* 800-342-2721 ■ *Web:* www.fibar.com	914-273-8770		711
Fiber Art Inc 124 Industrial Dr. . . . Cibolo TX 78108	210-658-8866		22
Fiber Bond Corp 110 Menke Rd . . . Michigan City IN 46360 *Web:* www.fiberbond.net	219-879-4541	874-7502	745-6
Fiber Conversion Inc 15 E Elm St . . . Broadalbin NY 12025 *Web:* fiberconversion.net	518-883-3431		745-8
Fiber Instruments Sales Inc 161 Clear Rd. . . . Oriskany NY 13424 *TF Sales:* 800-500-0347 ■ *Web:* www.fiberinstrumentsales.com	315-736-2206	736-2285	472
Fiber Materials Inc 5 Morin St . . . Biddeford ME 04005 *Web:* www.fibermaterialsinc.com	207-282-5911	282-7529	127
Fiber Optic Center New Trust 23 Centre St . . . New Bedford MA 02740 *TF:* 800-473-4237 ■ *Web:* www.focenter.com	508-992-6464		246
Fiber Pad Inc 17260 E Young St . . . Tulsa OK 74116 *Web:* www.fiberpad.com	918-438-7430		608
Fiber SenSys LLC 2925 NW Aloclek Dr Ste 120 . . . Hillsboro OR 97124 *TF:* 800-641-8150 ■ *Web:* www.fibersensys.com	503-692-4430		692
Fibercel Packaging LLC 46 Brooklyn St PO Box 610 . . . Portville NY 14770 *Web:* www.fibercel.com	716-933-8703		548
Fibercomm Lc 1605 Ninth St. . . . Sioux City IA 51101 *TF:* 800-836-2472 ■ *Web:* www.fibercomm.net	712-224-2020		116
Fibercorp Mills Inc 670 17th St NW . . . Massillon OH 44646 *Web:* fibercorr.com	330-837-5151		125
Fiberesin Industries Inc 37031 E Wisconsin Ave PO Box 88 . . . Oconomowoc WI 53066 *TF:* 800-450-0051 ■ *Web:* www.fiberesin.com	262-567-4427	567-4814	599
Fiberglass Specialties Inc PO Box 1340 . . . Henderson TX 75653 *TF:* 800-527-1459 ■ *Web:* www.fsiweb.com	903-657-6522	657-2318	608
Fibergrate Composite Structures Inc 5151 Beltline Rd Ste 700 . . . Dallas TX 75254 *TF:* 800-527-4043 ■ *Web:* www.fibergrate.com	972-250-1633	250-1530	606
FiberMark Inc 161 Wellington Rd . . . Brattleboro VT 05301 *TF:* 800-732-0330 ■ *Web:* www.fibermark.com	802-257-0365		561
FiberMark North America, Inc. 161 Wellington Rd . . . Brattleboro VT 05302 *TF Cust Svc:* 800-784-8558 ■ *Web:* www.fibermark.com	802-257-0365		561
Fibernetics Corp 605 Boxwood Dr . . . Cambridge ON N3E1A5 *TF:* 866-973-4237 ■ *Web:* www.fibernetics.ca	519-489-6700		224
Fiberoptics Technology Inc 1 Quassett Rd . . . Pomfret CT 06258 *TF Cust Svc:* 800-433-5248 ■ *Web:* www.fiberopticstech.com	860-928-0443	928-7664	330
FiberPlus Inc 8240 Preston Court Ste C . . . Jessup MD 20794 *TF:* 800-394-3301 ■ *Web:* www.fiberplusinc.com	301-317-3300		180
Fiber-Tech Industries Inc 2000 Kenskill Ave. . . . Washington Court House OH 43160 *TF:* 800-879-4377 ■ *Web:* fiber-tech.net	740-335-9400	335-4843	613
Fibertek Inc 13605 Dulles Technology Dr. . . . Herndon VA 20171 *Web:* www.fibertek.com	703-471-7671		256
FiberTower Corp 185 Berry St Ste 4800. . . . San Francisco CA 94107 *OTC:* FTWRQ ■ *TF:* 800-732-0330 ■ *Web:* www.fibertower.com	415-659-3500		736

Name / Address	City	State	Zip	Phone	Fax	Class
Fiberutilities Group 222 Third Ave SE Ste 500 *Web:* fiberutilities.com	Cedar Rapids	IA	52401	319-364-3200	364-8100	256
Fiberwave Corp 140 58th St Bldg B Unit 6E *TF:* 800-280-9011 ■ *Web:* www.fiberwave.com	Brooklyn	NY	11220	718-802-9011	802-0116	813
Fibre Box Assn (FBA) 25 NW Pt Blvd Ste 510 *Web:* www.fibrebox.org	Elk Grove Village	IL	60007	847-364-9600	364-9639	49-13
Fibre Converters Inc PO Box 130 *Web:* www.fibreconverters.com	Constantine	MI	49042	269-279-1700		548
Fibre Craft Materials Corp 7603 New Gross Point Rd *TF:* 800-323-4316 ■ *Web:* www.fibrecraft.com	Skokie	IL	60077	800-323-4316		761
Fibre Noire Internet Inc 550 Ave Beaumont Ste 320 *TF:* 877-907-3002 ■ *Web:* www.fibrenoire.ca	Montreal	QC	H3N1V1	877-907-3002		224
Fibrebond Corp 1300 Davenport Dr *TF:* 800-824-2614 ■ *Web:* www.fibrebond.com	Minden	LA	71055	318-377-1030		183
Fibreflex Packing & Manufacturing Company Inc 5101 Umbria St *Web:* www.fibreflex.com	Philadelphia	PA	19128	215-482-1490		326
Fibre-Metal 2000 Plainfield Pk *TF:* 800-430-4110 ■ *Web:* www.honeywellsafety.com	Cranston	RI	02921	800-430-4110	572-6346	576
Fibrenetics Inc 2 Cutters Dock Rd *Web:* www.fibglass.com	Woodbridge	NJ	07095	732-636-5670	636-6624	199
Fibrex Corp 401 Sharon Ave *Web:* www.fibrex.com	Burlington	WA	98233	360-755-1766		596
FibroGen Inc 409 Illinois St *Web:* www.fibrogen.com	San Francisco	CA	94158	415-978-1200		231
FIC Capital Inc 260 Madison Ave Ste 8035 *Web:* www.ficcapital.com	New York	NY	10016	212-679-2100		401
FIC Corp 12216 Parklawn Dr *Web:* www.ficcorp.com	Rockville	MD	20852	301-881-8124		729
Ficara's 577 Franklin Ave *Web:* www.ficarasrestaurant.com	Hartford	CT	06114	860-290-3230	290-3238	671
Ficomp Inc 3015 Advance Ln	Colmar	PA	18915	215-997-2600		174
Fiddler Gonzalez & Rodriguez PSC 254 Munoz Rivera Ave 6th Fl *Web:* www.fgrlaw.com	Hato Rey	PR	00918	787-753-3113		428
Fidelco Guide Dog Foundation Inc 103 Vision Way *TF:* 800-225-7566 ■ *Web:* fidelco.org	Bloomfield	CT	06002	860-243-5200		693
Fidelifacts 42 Broadway Ste 1548 *TF:* 800-678-0007 ■ *Web:* www.fidelifacts.com	New York	NY	10004	212-425-1520	248-5619	635
Fidelitone Inc 1260 Karl Ct *TF:* 800-475-0917 ■ *Web:* www.fidelitone.com	Wauconda	IL	60084	800-475-0917		246
Fidelity ActionsXchange Inc 200 Seaport Blvd *TF:* 800-370-6325 ■ *Web:* www.actionsxchange.com	Boston	MA	02210	617-392-2900		387
Fidelity Advisor Funds PO Box 770002 *TF:* 800-522-7297 ■ *Web:* www.advisor.fidelity.com	Cincinnati	OH	45277	800-522-7297		528
Fidelity Bancshares Nc Inc PO Box 8 *TF:* 800-816-9608 ■ *Web:* www.fidelitybanknc.com	Fuquay Varina	NC	27526	919-552-2242		70
Fidelity Bank 100 E English St *Fax Area Code: 316 ■ *TF:* 800-658-1637 ■ *Web:* www.fidelitybank.com	Wichita	KS	67201	800-658-1637	268-7383*	70
Fidelity Bank & Trust PO Box 277 *TF:* 800-403-8333 ■ *Web:* www.bankfidelity.com	Dyersville	IA	52040	800-403-8333		70
Fidelity Communications Company Inc 64 N Clark St *Web:* www.fidelitycommunications.com	Sullivan	MO	63080	573-468-8081		116
Fidelity Creditor Service Inc 216 S Louise St *TF:* 800-440-1981 ■ *Web:* fcscollect.com	Glendale	CA	91205	818-502-1981		160
Fidelity Engineering Corp 25 Loveton Cir PO Box 2500 *TF:* 800-787-6000 ■ *Web:* www.fidelityengineering.com	Sparks	MD	21152	410-771-9400		14
Fidelity Federal Bancorp 18 NW Fourth St *OTC:* FDLB ■ *TF:* 800-280-8280 ■ *Web:* www.unitedfidelity.com	Evansville	IN	47708	812-424-0921		360-2
Fidelity Investment Funds PO Box 770001 *TF:* 800-343-3548 ■ *Web:* www.fidelity.com	Cincinnati	OH	45277	800-343-3548		528
Fidelity Investments 483 Bay St Ste 200 *TF:* 800-263-4077 ■ *Web:* www.fidelity.ca	Toronto	ON	M5G2N7	416-307-5200		528
Fidelity Investments Charitable Gift Fund PO Box 770001 *Fax Area Code: 877 ■ *TF:* 800-262-6039 ■ *Web:* www.fidelitycharitable.org	Cincinnati	OH	45277	800-262-6039	665-4274*	405
Fidelity Investments Institutional Operations Co Inc PO Box 770002 *TF:* 877-208-0098 ■ *Web:* www.fidelity.com	Cincinnati	OH	45277	877-208-0098		528
Fidelity Investments Institutional Services Co Inc 82 Devonshire St *TF:* 800-343-3548 ■ *Web:* www.fidelity.com	Boston	MA	02109	617-563-9840		401
Fidelity National Title Group Inc 601 Riverside Ave *TF:* 888-866-3684 ■ *Web:* www.fntg.com	Jacksonville	FL	32204	904-854-8100		391-6
Fidelity National Title Insurance Co 601 Riverside Ave *Fax Area Code: 904 ■ *TF:* 888-866-3684 ■ *Web:* www.fntic.com	Jacksonville	FL	92705-5542	888-866-3684	357-1261*	391-6
Fidelity National Title Insurance Co of Oregon 900 SW Fifth Ave Mezzanine Level *TF:* 888-934-3354 ■ *Web:* www.fntic.com	Portland	OR	97204	503-223-8338	796-6611	391-6
Fidelity State Bank & Trust Co 600 S Kansas Ave *Web:* www.fidelitytopeka.com	Topeka	KS	66603	785-295-2100	233-7571	70
Fidelity Technologies Corp 2501 Kutztown Rd *Web:* www.fidelitytech.com	Reading	PA	19605	610-929-3330	929-1969	647
Fidessa Financial Corp 17 State St 42nd Fl *TF:* 800-525-7082 ■ *Web:* fidessa.com	New York	NY	10004	212-269-9000	943-0353	178-1

Name / Address	City	State	Zip	Phone	Fax	Class
Fido Solutions Inc 800 De La Gauchetiere St W Ste 4000 *Web:* www.fido.ca	Montreal	QC	H5A1K3	514-933-3436		736
Fiducial 10100 Old Columbia Rd *TF:* 800-323-9000 ■ *Web:* www.fiducial.com	Columbia	MD	21046	410-290-8296	910-5903	734
Fiduciary Capital Management Inc PO Box 80 *Web:* www.fcmstablevalue.com	Wallingford	CT	06492	203-269-0440	269-6440	401
Fiduciary Management Inc of Milwaukee 100 E Wisconsin Ave Ste 2200 *TF:* 800-264-7684 ■ *Web:* www.fiduciarymgt.com	Milwaukee	WI	53202	414-226-4545	226-4522	401
Fidus Partners LLC 227 W Trade St Ste 1910 *Web:* www.fiduspartners.com	Charlotte	NC	28202	704-334-2222	334-2202	690
Fiedor Van Epps & Associates 964 Fifth Ave *Web:* fiedorvanepps.com	San Diego	CA	92101	619-544-1422		463
Fieger Fieger Kenney & Giroux PC 19390 W 10-Mile Rd *Web:* www.fiegerlaw.com	Southfield	MI	48075	248-355-5555		428
Field & Stream Licenses Company LLC 18 Kings Hwy N	Westport	CT	06880	203-221-0050		360-3
Field Aviation Company Inc 2450 Derry Rd E Hngr 2 *Web:* www.fieldav.com	Mississauga	ON	L5S1B2	905-676-1540		21
Field Controls LLC 2630 Airport Rd *Web:* www.fieldcontrols.com	Kinston	NC	28504	252-522-3031	522-0214	17
Field Fresh Foods Inc 14805 S San Pedro St *Web:* www.fieldfresh.com	Gardena	CA	90248	310-719-8422		345
Field House Museum 634 S Broadway *Web:* www.eugenefieldhouse.org	Saint Louis	MO	63102	314-421-4689		520
Field Law 10235 101 St NW Ste 2000 *TF:* 800-222-6479 ■ *Web:* www.fieldlaw.com	Edmonton	AB	T5J3G1	780-423-3003		428
Field Museum, The 1400 S Lake Shore Dr *TF:* 800-438-9644 ■ *Web:* www.fieldmuseum.org	Chicago	IL	60605	312-922-9410		520
Field Nation LLC 901 Marquette Ave Ste 2300 *TF:* 877-573-4353 ■ *Web:* www.fieldnation.com	Minneapolis	MN	55402	877-573-4353		317
Field Paper Co 3950 D St *TF:* 800-969-3435 ■ *Web:* www.fieldpaper.com	Omaha	NE	68107	402-733-3600	731-7113	553
Field Service Express Inc 3336 E 32nd St Ste 208 *Web:* fsx.com	Tulsa	OK	74135	918-744-9679		365
Field System Machining Inc 720 Schneider Dr	South Elgin	IL	60177	847-468-1313		492
Field Trip Factory 2211 N Elston Ave Ste 304 *TF:* 800-987-6409 ■ *Web:* www.fieldtripfactory.com	Chicago	IL	60614	800-987-6409		297-8
Field, The 544 Fifth Ave *Web:* www.thefield.com	San Diego	CA	92101	619-232-9840	232-9842	671
Fieldale Farms Corp PO Box 558 *TF:* 800-241-5400 ■ *Web:* www.fieldale.com	Baldwin	GA	30511	800-241-5400		619
Fielder House Museum 1616 W Abram St *Web:* historicalarlington.org	Arlington	TX	76013	817-460-4001		520
Fielding Lake State Recreation Site 3700 Airport Way *Web:* www.dnr.alaska.gov	Fairbanks	AK	99709	907-451-2705	451-2706	565
Fieldman Rolapp & Assoc 19900 Macarthur Blvd *Web:* www.fieldman.com	Irvine	CA	92612	949-660-7300	474-8773	463
FieldPoint Petroleum Corp 609 Castle Ridge Rd Ste 335 *NYSE:* FPP ■ *Web:* www.fppcorp.com	Cedar Park	TX	78746	512-250-8692		536
Fieldpoint Private Bank & Trust 100 Field Pt Rd *TF:* 877-438-4338 ■ *Web:* www.fieldpointprivate.com	Greenwich	CT	06830	203-413-9300		690
Fields Company LLC 2240 Taylor Way *Fax Area Code: 253 ■ *TF:* 800-627-4098 ■ *Web:* www.fieldscorp.com	Tacoma	WA	98421	800-627-4098	383-2181*	46
Fields Group Inc 1919 South Blvd Ste 1010	Charlotte	IN	28203	704-372-7855		384
Fields Spring State Park 992 Pk Rd *Web:* www.parks.wa.gov	Anatone	WA	99401	509-256-3332		565
Fieldstone Homes 12896 S Pony Express Rd Ste 400 *Web:* www.fieldstone-homes.com	Draper	UT	84020	801-233-8300		653
Fieldstone Partners 1800 Bering Dr Ste 430 *Web:* fieldstone.com	Houston	TX	77057	713-850-0080		690
Fieldtech Avionics & Instruments Inc 4151 N Main St *Web:* www.ftav.com	Fort Worth	TX	76106	817-625-2719		770
FieldWorker Products Ltd 88 Queens Quay W *Web:* www.fieldworker.com	Toronto	ON	M5J0B8	416-483-3485		177
Fiera Foods Co 50 Marmora St *Web:* www.fierafoods.com	Toronto	ON	M9M2X5	416-746-1010		68
Fiesta Cafe 216 S First St *Web:* www.fiestacafe.com	Champaign	IL	61820	217-352-5902		671
Fiesta Cafe Bar 1645 N Broadway *Web:* fiestacafeandbar.com	Rochester	MN	55906	507-288-1116		671
Fiesta Canning Co Inc 1480 E Bethany Home Ste 110 *Web:* www.fiestacan.com	Phoenix	AZ	85014	602-212-2424	274-7233	296-36
Fiesta Fresh Mexican Grill 51 New Orleans Rd Ste 4 *Web:* fiestafreshmexicangrill.com	Hilton Head Island	SC	29928	843-785-4788		671
Fiesta Henderson 777 West Lake Mead Pkwy *TF:* 888-899-7770 ■ *Web:* www.fiestahenderson.sclv.com	Henderson	NV	89015	702-558-7000		379
Fiesta Mall 1445 W Southern Ave	Mesa	AZ	85202	480-969-6725		460
Fiesta Mart Inc 5235 Katy Fwy *Web:* www.fiestamart.com	Houston	TX	77007	713-869-5060		345
Fiesta Rancho Casino Hotel 2400 N Rancho Dr *TF Resv:* 800-731-7333 ■ *Web:* fiestarancho.sclv.com	Las Vegas	NV	89130	702-631-7000		133

Name / Address	City	State	ZIP	Phone	Fax	Class
Fiesta San Antonio Commission 2611 Broadway *Web:* www.fiesta-sa.org	San Antonio	TX	78215	210-227-5191		720
Fifield Land Co 4307 Fifield Rd *TF:* 800-536-6395 ■ *Web:* www.kfseeds.com	Brawley	CA	92227	760-344-6391	344-6394	276
Fifteen Beacon Hotel 15 Beacon St *Web:* www.xvbeacon.com	Boston	MA	02108	617-670-1500	670-6925	379
Fifth Avenue Grill 821 SE Fifth Ave Federal Hwy	Delray Beach	FL	33483	561-265-0122		671
Fifth Baptist Church of The City of st Louis Mo 3736 Natural Bridge Ave	Saint Louis	MO	63107	314-531-2602		48-20
Fifth Business Inc 24 Greenway Plaza Ste 1200 *Web:* www.fifthbusiness.com	Houston	TX	77046	713-622-5423		180
Fifth inc, The 221 Richmond St W *Web:* www.thefifth.com	Toronto	ON	M5V1W2	416-979-3000	979-3005	671
Fifth Quarter 201 Clendenin St *Web:* fifthquarterofcharleston.com	Charleston	WV	25301	304-345-3933		671
Fifth Street Public Market 296 E Fifth Ave *Web:* www.5stmarket.com	Eugene	OR	97401	541-484-0383	686-1220	50-6
Fifth Sun Inc 495 Ryan Ave *Web:* www.5sun.com	Chico	CA	95973	530-343-8725		393
Fifth Third Bank Central Ohio 21 E State St *TF:* 866-671-5353 ■ *Web:* www.53.com	Columbus	OH	43215	800-972-3030		70
Fig Garden Swim & Racquet Club 4722 N Maroa Ave *Web:* www.fig-garden.com	Fresno	CA	93704	559-222-4816		354
Fig Garden Village 790 W Shaw Ave *Web:* www.shopfiggardenvillage.com	Fresno	CA	93704	559-412-5296		460
FIG restaurant 232 Meeting St *Web:* www.eatatfig.com	Charleston	SC	29401	843-805-5900		671
Fig Tree 515 Villita St *Web:* www.figtreerestaurant.com	San Antonio	TX	78205	210-224-1976	271-9180	671
Figaretti's 1035 Mt de Chantel Rd *Web:* www.figarettis.net	Wheeling	WV	26003	304-243-5625		671
Figaro's Italian Pizza Inc 1500 Liberty St SE Ste 160 *TF:* 888-344-2767 ■ *Web:* www.figaros.com	Salem	OR	97302	503-371-9318	363-5364	670
Figg Engineering Group 424 N Calhoun St *Web:* www.figgbridge.com	Tallahassee	FL	32301	850-224-7400		256
Figge Art Museum 225 W Second St *Web:* www.figgeartmuseum.org	Davenport	IA	52801	563-326-7804	326-7876	520
FIGHTER Interactive Inc 388 Beale St Ste 1014 *Web:* www.wearefighter.com	San Francisco	CA	94105	917-434-6102		636
Figment LLC 118 E 64th St *Web:* www.figment.com	New York	NY	10065	212-893-8790		387
Figo Pasta/Osteria del Figo 1170 Collier Rd NW # B Ste B *Web:* www.figopasta.com	Atlanta	GA	30318	404-351-9667		671
Figtree Consulting Inc 101 Gibraltar Dr Ste 3D *Web:* www.figtree.com	Morris Plains	NJ	07950	973-539-9311		180
Figueroa Hotel 939 S Figueroa St *Web:* www.hotelfigueroa.com	Los Angeles	CA	90015	213-627-8971		379
Fiji Embassy 1707 L St NW Ste 200 *TF:* 800-932-3454 ■ *Web:* www.fijiembassydc.com	Washington	DC	20036	202-337-8320	466-8325	257
Fiji Visitors Bureau 5777 W Century Blvd Ste 220 *TF:* 800-932-3454 ■ *Web:* www.fiji.travel	Los Angeles	CA	90045	310-568-1616	670-2318	775
Fiji Water 11444 W Olympic Blvd 2nd Fl *TF:* 888-426-3454 ■ *Web:* www.fijiwater.com	Los Angeles	CA	90064	310-312-2850	312-2828	80-2
Fike Corp 704 SW Tenth St *TF:* 877-342-3453 ■ *Web:* www.fike.com	Blue Springs	MO	64015	816-229-3405		283
File Keepers LLC 6277 E Slauson Ave *TF:* 800-332-3453 ■ *Web:* www.filekeepers.com	Los Angeles	CA	90040	323-728-3133	728-0867	463
FileCatalyst Inc 1725 St Laurent Blvd Ste 205 *TF:* 877-327-9387 ■ *Web:* www.utechsoft.com	Ottawa	ON	K1G3V4	613-667-2439		177
FileMaker Inc 5201 Patrick Henry Dr *TF Cust Svc:* 800-325-2747 ■ *Web:* www.filemaker.com	Santa Clara	CA	95054	408-987-7000		178-1
Filer Mutual Telephone Co PO Box 89 *Web:* www.filertel.com	Filer	ID	83328	208-326-4331	326-3190	736
FileStream Inc 240 Glen Head Rd Ste 93 *Web:* www.filestream.com	Glen Head	NY	11545	516-759-4100	759-3011	178-12
FileTrail Inc 111 N Market St Ste 715 *Web:* www.filetrail.com	San Jose	CA	95113	408-289-1300		177
Filippo's 6915 W Lincoln Ave	Milwaukee	WI	53219	414-321-4040		671
Fill in Foods 10554 Scott Hwy	Helenwood	TN	37755	423-663-2749		297-8
Fillauer Inc PO Box 5189 *TF:* 800-251-6398 ■ *Web:* www.fillauer.com	Chattanooga	TN	37406	423-624-0946	629-7936	477
Fillip Metal Cabinet Co 4500 W 47th St *TF:* 800-535-0733 ■ *Web:* www.fillipmetal.com	Chicago	IL	60632	773-733-7527		319-1
Fillmore County 900 G St *Web:* www.fillmorecounty.org	Geneva	NE	68361	402-759-4931	759-4307	338
Fillmore County 101 Fillmore St *Web:* www.co.fillmore.mn.us	Preston	MN	55965	507-765-3356		338
Fillmore Detroit, The 2115 Woodward Ave *Web:* thefillmoredetroit.com	Detroit	MI	48201	313-961-5451		572
Fillmore Glen State Park 1686 St Rt 38 *TF:* 800-456-2267 ■ *Web:* parks.ny.gov/parks/157/hunting.aspx	Moravia	NY	13118	315-497-0130		565
Fillmore Group Inc, The 8501 La Salle Rd Ste 318 *Web:* www.thefillmoregroup.com	Towson	MD	21286	410-465-6335		177
Fillmore-Piru Citrus Assn (FPCA) 357 N Main St PO Box 350 *Web:* www.fillmorepirucitrus.com	Piru	CA	93040	805-521-1781	521-0990	11-1
Film Roman Inc 21600 Oxnard St Ste 1700 *Web:* www.filmroman.com	Los Angeles	CA	91367	818-748-4000		33
Film Society of Lincoln Center 70 Lincoln Center Plaza *TF:* 888-313-6085	New York	NY	10023	212-875-5610		457-9
Film Workers Club 1006 17th Ave S *Web:* www.filmworkers.com	Nashville	TN	37212	615-322-9337		514
Film-Pak Inc 201 S Magnolia *Web:* www.film-pak.com	Crowley	TX	76036	817-297-2231		596
Filmtech Corp 2121 31st St SW *Web:* www.filmtech-corp.com	Allentown	PA	18103	610-709-9999		601
Filmworks/Astro Lab 61 W Erie St *Web:* www.filmworkersastro.com	Chicago	IL	60654	312-280-5500		512
Filnor Inc 227 N Freedom Ave PO Box 2328 *Web:* www.filnor.com	Alliance	OH	44601	330-821-7667	829-3175	253
Filogix Limited Partnership 276 King St W Ste 400	Toronto	ON	M5V1J2	416-360-1777		627
Filoli 86 Canada Rd *Web:* www.filoli.org	Woodside	CA	94062	650-364-8300	366-7836	97
Filomena Ristorante 1063 Wisconsin Ave NW	Washington	DC	20007	202-338-8800		671
Filomeno & Company PC 80 S Main St *Web:* www.filomeno.com	Hartford	CT	06107	860-561-0020		2
Filson Historical Society Museum 1310 S Third St *TF:* 800-928-7000 ■ *Web:* www.filsonhistorical.org	Louisville	KY	40208	502-635-5083	635-5086	520
Filter Recycling 180 W Monte Ave *Web:* www.filterrecycling.com	Bloomington	CA	92316	909-873-4141		454
Filter Talent 1425 Fourth Ave Ste 1000 *TF:* 800-336-0809 ■ *Web:* www.filtertalent.com	Seattle	WA	98101	800-336-0809		260
FilterBoxx Water & Environmental Corp 200 Rivercrest Dr SE Ste 160 *TF:* 877-868-4747 ■ *Web:* filterboxx.com	Calgary	AB	T2C2X5	403-203-4747		317
Filterspun 624 N Fairfield St *TF:* 800-323-5431 ■ *Web:* www.serfilco.com	Amarillo	TX	79107	806-383-3840		806
Filtertech Inc 113 Fairgrounds Dr PO Box 527 *Web:* www.filtertech.com	Manlius	NY	13104	315-682-8815	682-8825	18
Filtertek Inc 11411 Price Rd *TF:* 800-248-2461 ■ *Web:* www.filtertek.com	Hebron	IL	60034	815-648-1001	648-2929	604
Filtra-Systems Co 23900 Haggerty Rd *Web:* www.filtrasystems.com	Farmington Hills	MI	48335	248-427-9090	427-9895	806
Filtration Engineering Co 12255 Ensign Av *Web:* www.filtrationeng.com	Champlin	MN	55316	763-421-2721		298
Filtration Group Inc 912 E Washington St **Fax Area Code:* 800 ■ *TF:* 877-603-1003 ■ *Web:* www.filtrationgroup.com	Joliet	IL	60433	815-726-4600	518-1162*	18
Filtration Lab Inc 193 Rang De L Eglise *TF:* 800-738-0168 ■ *Web:* www.filtrationlab.com	Saint Ligouri	QC	J0K2X0	450-754-4222		791
Filtrine Manufacturing Co 15 Kit St *Web:* www.filtrine.com	Keene	NH	03431	603-352-5500		14
FIMAC Solutions LLC Denver Technological Ctr 5299 DTC Blvd Ste 950 *TF:* 877-789-5905 ■ *Web:* www.fimacsolutions.com	Greenwood Village	CO	80111	303-320-1900		690
Fimbel Architectural Door Specialties LLC PO Box 96 *TF:* 800-888-4574 ■ *Web:* www.fimbelads.com	Whitehouse	NJ	08888	908-534-1732		234
Fimc Commercial Realty 1619 S Tyler St *TF:* 800-658-2616 ■ *Web:* fimcrealty.com	Amarillo	TX	79102	806-358-7151		652
Fin & Feather Resort Inc 445889 Hwy 10-A *Web:* finandfeather.publishpath.com	Gore	OK	74435	918-487-5148		669
Fin Pan Inc 3255 Symmes Rd *TF:* 800-833-6444 ■ *Web:* www.finpan.com	Hamilton	OH	45015	513-870-9200		183
Finagle-a-Bagel Inc 77 Rowe St *Web:* www.finagleabagel.com	Auburndale	MA	02466	617-213-8400		345
FinAid Page LLC PO Box 2056 *TF:* 800-433-3243 ■ *Web:* www.finaid.org	Cranberry Township	PA	16066	724-538-4500	538-4502	725
Final Draft Inc 26707 W Agoura Rd Ste 205 *TF:* 800-231-4055 ■ *Web:* www.finaldraft.com	Calabasas	CA	91302	818-995-8995	995-4422	178-10
Finance & Commerce 730 Second Ave S US Trust Bldg Ste 100 *TF:* 800-451-9998 ■ *Web:* www.finance-commerce.com	Minneapolis	MN	55402	612-333-4244	333-3243	457-5
Finance Ctr Federal Credit Union PO Box 26501 *TF:* 800-473-2328 ■ *Web:* www.fcfcu.com	Indianapolis	IN	46226	317-916-7700		219
Finance Factors Ltd 1164 Bishop St *TF:* 800-640-7136 ■ *Web:* www.financefactors.com	Honolulu	HI	96813	808-548-4940	548-5148	217
Finance of America Mortgage 300 Welsh Rd Bldg 5 *Web:* www.financeofamerica.com	Horsham	PA	19044	215-591-0222		217
Financial & Realty Services LLC 1110 Bonifant St Ste 301 *TF:* 800-650-9714 ■ *Web:* frsllc.com	Silver Spring	MD	20910	301-650-9112		271
Financial Acctg Foundation (FAF) 401 Merritt 7 PO Box 5116 *Web:* fasb.org	Norwalk	CT	06856	203-847-0700	849-9714	49-1
Financial Acctg Standards Board (FASB) 401 Merritt 7 PO Box 5116 *TF:* 800-748-0659 ■ *Web:* www.fasb.org	Norwalk	CT	06856	203-847-0700	849-9714	49-1
Financial Advisory Service Inc 4747 W 135th St *TF:* 888-700-9230 ■ *Web:* www.faskc.com	Leawood	KS	66224	913-239-2300		194
Financial America Securities Inc 1325 Carnegie Ave *Web:* www.fasinv.com	Cleveland	OH	44115	216-781-5060		690
Financial Courier Service Inc 6099 Mt Moriah Ext Ste 13	Memphis	TN	38115	901-761-4555		546
Financial Crimes Enforcement Network 2070 Chain Bridge Rd **Fax Area Code:* 202 ■ *Web:* www.fincen.gov	Vienna	VA	22182	703-905-3591	354-6411*	340-18

Name / Address	Phone	Fax	Class
Financial Designs Ltd 1775 Sherman St Ste 1800....................Denver CO 80203 *Web:* www.fdltd.com	303-832-6100		390
Financial Dimensions Group 3900 Northwoods Dr .... Saint Paul MN 55112 *TF:* 800-490-3717 ■ *Web:* www.fdg-advisors.com	651-481-6280		401
Financial Engines Inc 1804 Embarcadero Rd .... Palo Alto CA 94303 *NASDAQ: FNGN* ■ **Fax Area Code:* 650 ■ *TF:* 888-443-8577 ■ *Web:* www.corp.financialengines.com	408-498-6000	565-4905*	178-10
Financial Executives International (FEI) 1250 Headquarters Plaza W Twr 7th Fl........ Morristown NJ 07960 *Web:* www.financialexecutives.org	973-765-1000	765-1018	49-2
Financial Fedcorp Inc 6305 Humphreys Blvd ....Memphis TN 38120 *Web:* www.finfedmem.com	901-756-2848		509
Financial Guaranty Insurance Co 125 Pk Ave 6th Fl..........................New York NY 10017 *TF:* 800-352-0001 ■ *Web:* www.fgic.com	212-312-3000		391-5
Financial Industry Regulatory Authority (FINRA) 9509 Key W Ave ....Rockville MD 20850 *TF:* 800-321-6273 ■ *Web:* www.finra.org	301-590-6500		49-2
Financial Institutions Inc 220 Liberty St...........................Warsaw NY 14569 *NASDAQ: FISI* ■ *TF:* 866-296-3743 ■ *Web:* www.snl.com	585-786-1100		360-2
Financial Intelligence LLC 1451 Grant Rd Ste 200.................Mountain View CA 94040 *Web:* www.financial-intelligence.com	650-264-2252		734
Financial Management Assn International (FMA) 4202 E Fowler Ave .... Tampa FL 33620 *Web:* www.fma.org	813-974-2084		49-2
Financial Management Professionals Inc 6034 W Courtyard Dr Ste 380.................. Austin TX 78730 *Web:* www.fmprofessionals.com	512-329-5174		194
Financial Management Service 401 14th St SW ....Washington DC 20227 *Web:* www.fms.treas.gov	202-874-6950		340-18
Financial Managers Society (FMS) 100 W Monroe St Ste 810 ....Chicago IL 60603 *TF Cust Svc:* 800-275-4367 ■ *Web:* www.fmsinc.org	312-578-1300	578-1308	49-2
Financial Navigator Inc 883 N Shoreline Blvd Ste D-100..........Mountain View CA 94043 *Web:* www.finnav.com	650-962-0300		177
Financial Pacific Co 3455 S 344th Way Ste 300................Federal Way WA 98001 *TF:* 800-447-7107 ■ *Web:* www.finpac.com	800-447-7107	447-7106	216
Financial Partners Credit Union PO Box 7005 ....Downey CA 90241 *TF:* 800-950-7328 ■ *Web:* www.fpcu.org	562-923-0311		219
Financial Planning Assn (FPA) 7535 E Hampden Ave Ste 600 ....Denver CO 80231 *TF:* 800-322-4237 ■ *Web:* www.plannersearch.org	303-759-4900		49-2
Financial Publishing Co PO Box 570 .... South Bend IN 46624 *TF Cust Svc:* 800-433-0090 ■ *Web:* www.financial-publishing.com	574-243-6040	243-6060	637-2
Financial Resource Group LLC 12900 Preston Rd Ste 100, LB-104 .... Dallas TX 75230 *TF:* 800-290-0629 ■ *Web:* financialresourcegroup.co/index.html	972-960-7790		401
Financial Service Centers of America Inc (FiSCA) 21 Main St 1st Fl .... Hackensack NJ 07602 *Web:* www.fisca.org	201-487-0412	487-3954	49-2
Financial Service Corp 2300 Windy Ridge Pkwy Ste 1100 .... Atlanta GA 30339 *TF:* 800-547-2382 ■ *Web:* www.joinfsc.com	800-547-2382		690
Financial Services Inc 21 Harristown Rd .... Glen Rock NJ 07452	201-652-6000		225
Financial Services Roundtable 600 13th St NW Ste 400..................Washington DC 20005 **Fax Area Code:* 855 ■ *Web:* fsroundtable.org/bits	202-289-4322	802-9355*	49-2
Financial Software Systems Inc 100 Tournament Dr Ste 300 .... Horsham PA 19044 *TF:* 800-656-7356 ■ *Web:* www.finsoftware.com	215-784-1100		177
Financial Technology Partners LP 601 California St 22nd Fl .... San Francisco CA 94108 *Web:* www.ftpartners.com	415-512-8700		401
Financial Times 1330 Ave of the Americas......................New York NY 10019 *TF:* 800-628-8088 ■ *Web:* www.ft.com	207-873-3000		532-2
Financial Transmission Network Inc 13220 Birch Dr Ste 120..........................Omaha NE 68164 *TF:* 800-316-7342 ■ *Web:* www.ftni.com	402-502-8777		251
Financial West Investment Group Inc 4510 E Thousand Oaks Blvd........... Westlake Village CA 91362 *Web:* www.fwg.com	805-497-9222		690
FinancialCAD Corp 13450 102nd Ave Ste 1750 .... Surrey BC V3T5X3 *TF:* 800-304-0702 ■ *Web:* www.fincad.com	604-957-1200	957-1201	39
FINCA (Foundation for International Community Assistance) 1201 15th St NW 8th fl...................Washington DC 20005 *TF:* 855-903-4622 ■ *Web:* www.finca.org	202-682-1510	682-1535	48-5
Fincantieri Marine Systems North America Inc 800-C Principal Ct......................Chesapeake VA 23320 *TF:* 877-436-7643 ■ *Web:* www.fincantierimarinesystems.com	757-548-6000		690
Finch Paper LLC 1 Glen St ....Glens Falls NY 12801 *TF:* 800-833-9983 ■ *Web:* www.finchpaper.com	518-793-2541		557
Finchey Corp of California Dba Pacific Bmw 800 S Brand Blvd .... Glendale CA 91204	818-246-5600		57
Finck Cigar Co 414 Vera Cruz St..............San Antonio TX 78207 *TF Orders:* 800-221-0638 ■ *Web:* www.finckcigarcompany.com	210-226-4191	226-2825	756
FinCo Management LLC 18 Doaks Ln........ Marblehead MA 01945	781-639-6000		195
Find & Convert 36181 E Lake Rd Ste 188 .... Palm Harbor FL 34685 *Web:* www.findandconvert.com	727-234-0952		195
Find the Children 2656 29th St Ste 203 ....Santa Monica CA 90405 *TF:* 888-477-6721 ■ *Web:* www.findthechildren.com	310-314-3213		48-6
Find Your Dreams Inc 636 Plank Rd Ste 205.......................Clifton Park NY 12065 *Web:* www.internetmarketingninjas.com	518-631-6227		631
Findings Inc 160 Water St ....Keene NH 03431 *TF:* 800-225-2706 ■ *Web:* leachgarner.com	603-352-3717		407
FinditQuick.com Inc 1817 Saunders Settlement Rd............. Niagara Falls NY 14304 *Web:* www.finditquick.com	716-297-5292		225
FindLaw 610 Opperman Dr.........................Eagan MN 55123 **Fax Area Code:* 800 ■ *TF:* 800-392-6206 ■ *Web:* www.findlaw.com	651-687-6393	392-6206*	397
Findlay Automobile Club 1550 Tiffin Ave ....Findlay OH 45840 *TF:* 800-222-4357 ■ *Web:* www.aaa.com	419-422-4961	422-5620	53
Findlay Automotive Group 310 N Gibson Rd ....Henderson NV 89014 *Web:* www.findlayauto.com	702-558-8888		57
Findlay Country Club Pro. Shop 1500 Country Club Dr ....Findlay OH 45840 *Web:* www.findlaycc.com	419-422-9263		354
Findlay Hancock County District Public Library 206 Broadway..Findlay OH 45840 *TF:* 800-590-9755 ■ *Web:* www.findlaylibrary.org	419-422-1712	422-0638	434-3
Findlay Inn & Conference Ctr 200 E Main Cross St..............................Findlay OH 45840 *TF Cust Svc:* 800-825-1455 ■ *Web:* www.findlayinn.com	419-422-5682		379
Findlay Market PO Box 14727 .... Cincinnati OH 45250 *Web:* www.findlaymarket.org	513-665-4839		50-6
Findlay Publishing Co 701 W Sandusky St ....Findlay OH 45840 *Web:* www.thecourier.com	419-422-5151	422-2937	637-8
Findlay-Hancock County Chamber of Commerce 123 E Main Cross St..............................Findlay OH 45840 *Web:* findlayhancockchamber.com	419-422-3313	422-9508	139
Findley Davies 1 Seagate # 2050 .... Toledo OH 43604 *Web:* www.findleydavies.com	419-255-1360	259-5685	193
Findley State Park 25381 State Rt 58.........................Wellington OH 44090 *Web:* www.ohiodnr.com	440-647-4490		565
Findleys Pharmacy Inc 136 W Main St......... Somerset PA 15501 *Web:* findleyspharmacy.com	814-445-7939		237
Findorff JH & Son Inc 300 S Bedford St .... Madison WI 53703 *Web:* www.findorff.com	608-257-5321	257-5306	186
Findwell 920 Dexter Ave N .... Seattle WA 98109 *Web:* www.findwell.com	206-462-6200		652
Fine Arts Association, The 38660 Mentor Ave .... Willoughby OH 44094 *TF:* 800-314-2535 ■ *Web:* www.fineartsassociation.org	440-951-7500		138
Fine Arts Museums of San Francisco 50 Hagiwara Tea Garden Dr.............. San Francisco CA 94118 *TF:* 800-794-7576 ■ *Web:* deyoung.famsf.org	415-750-3600		397
Fine Book Club of Claifornia 312 Sutter St Ste 500 .... San Francisco CA 94108 *Web:* www.bccbooks.org	415-781-7532		533
FINE Design Group Inc 3450 Sansome St..................... San Francisco CA 94118 *Web:* www.wearefine.com	415-552-9300		506
Fine Furniture Inc 1107 N Main St........... High Point NC 27262 *Web:* www.ffdm.com	336-883-9918		194
Fine Homebuilding Magazine 63 S Main St PO Box 5506................... Newtown CT 06470 *TF:* 800-283-7252 ■ *Web:* www.finehomebuilding.com	203-426-8171	270-6753	457-21
Fine Hospitality Group LLC 545 W Lambert Rd Ste D ....Brea CA 92821 *Web:* www.finehospitality.com	714-990-8800		226
Fine Hotels Corp One Washington St ....Wellesley MA 02481 *Web:* finebergcompanies.com	781-431-1108		656
Fine Laboratories Inc 100 Ashley Park Dr.........................Piedmont MO 63957 *Web:* www.finelabs.com	573-223-2388		247
Fine Line Production 2221 Regal Pkwy........... Euless TX 76040 *TF:* 800-887-5625 ■ *Web:* www.finelineproduction.com	817-267-6750		483
FINE Mortuary College LLC 150 Kerry Pl .... Norwood MA 02062 *Web:* www.fine-ne.com	781-762-1211	762-7177	800
Fine Organics Corp 420 Kuller Rd PO Box 2277 .... Clifton NJ 07015 **Fax:* Sales ■ *TF:* 800-526-7480 ■ *Web:* www.fineorganicscorp.com	973-478-1000	478-6120*	151
Fine Technology Solutions 7936 Grado El Tupelo....................... Carlsbad CA 92009 *Web:* www.fineonline.com	760-274-2370		177
Fine Wine Brokers 4621 N Lincoln Ave ....Chicago IL 60625	773-989-8166		443
Fine Woodworking Magazine 63 S Main St PO Box 5506.................... Newtown CT 06470 *TF:* 800-283-7252 ■ *Web:* www.finewoodworking.com	203-426-8171	270-6753	457-14
Fineline Graphics & Design Inc 1820 Bellomy St......................... Santa Clara CA 95050 *Web:* finelinegd.com	408-261-7676		344
Fineline Printing Group 8081 Zionsville Rd.........................Indianapolis IN 46268 *TF:* 877-334-7687 ■ *Web:* finelineprintinggroup.com	317-872-4490		627
Fineline Technologies Inc 3145 Medlock Bridge Rd .... Norcross GA 30071 *Web:* www.finelinetech.com	678-969-0835		196
Finelite Inc 30500 Whipple Rd ....Union City CA 94587 *Web:* www.finelite.com	510-441-1100		4
Fin-feather-fur Outfitters 652 US Hwy 250 E ....Ashland OH 44805 *TF:* 800-362-1361 ■ *Web:* www.finfeatherfur.com	419-281-2557		711
Finfrock Industries Inc 2400 Apopka Blvd .... Apopka FL 32703 *Web:* finfrock.com	407-293-4000	297-0512	183
Finger Lake State Recreation Area 7278 E Bogard Rd...............................Wasilla AK 99654 *Web:* dnr.alaska.gov	907-745-3975		565
Finger Lakes Community College 4340 Lakeshore Dr......................Canandaigua NY 14424 *Web:* www.fingerlakes.edu	585-394-3500	394-5005	162
Finger Lakes Gaming & Race Track 5857 Rt 96 .... Farmington NY 14425 *TF:* 877-846-7369 ■ *Web:* www.fingerlakesgaming.com	585-924-3232	924-3967	642
Finger Lakes Library System 1300 Dryden Rd...................................Ithaca NY 14850 *TF:* 800-909-3557	607-273-4074	273-3618	434-3

				Phone	Fax	Class
Finger Lakes Livestock Exchange Inc 3865 Rts 5 & 20 Geneva Tpke *TF:* 800-352-3785 ■ *Web:* www.fingerlakeslivestockex.com	Canandaigua	NY	14424	585-394-1515	394-9151	446
Finger Lakes Racing Assn 5857 Rt 96 *TF:* 800-522-4700 ■ *Web:* www.fingerlakesgaming.com	Farmington	NY	14425	585-924-3232	924-3967	642
Finger Lakes State Park 1505 E Peabody Rd *Web:* www.mostateparks.com	Columbia	MO	65202	573-443-5315		565
Finger Lakes Stone Company Inc 33 Quarry Rd *Web:* www.fingerlakesstone.net	Ithaca	NY	14850	607-273-4646	273-4692	724
Finger Lakes Times 218 Genesse St PO Box 393 *TF:* 800-388-6652 ■ *Web:* www.fltimes.com	Geneva	NY	14456	315-789-3333	789-4077	637-8
Finger Lakes Visitors Connection 25 Gorham St *TF:* 877-386-4669 ■ *Web:* www.visitfingerlakes.com	Canandaigua	NY	14424	585-394-3915		206
Fingerhut 6250 Ridgewood Dr *TF:* 800-208-2500 ■ *Web:* www.fingerhut.com	St. Cloud	MN	56303	800-208-2500		459
Fingerpaint Mktg Inc 395 Broadway *Web:* fingerpaintmarketing.com	Saratoga Springs	NY	12866	518-693-6960		194
Finial Company Inc, The 4030 La Reunion Pkwy Ste 100 *TF:* 800-498-7932 ■ *Web:* www.thefinialcompany.com	Dallas	TX	75212	214-678-0805		361
Finisar Corp 1389 Moffett Pk Dr *NASDAQ: FNSR* ■ *Web:* www.finisar.com	Sunnyvale	CA	94089	408-548-1000	541-6129	176
Finish Line Ford Inc 2211 W Pioneer Pkwy *TF:* 888-484-1390 ■ *Web:* www.greenfordstore.com	Peoria	IL	61615	309-693-2525		57
Finish Line Inc, The 3308 N Mitthoeffer Rd *NASDAQ: FINL* ■ *TF:* 888-777-3949 ■ *Web:* www.finishline.com	Indianapolis	IN	46235	317-899-1022		301
Finishing Plus Inc 4546 W 47th St *Web:* finishingplus.com	Chicago	IL	60632	773-523-5510		92
FinishMaster Inc 115 W Washington St 700 S *TF:* 888-311-3678 ■ *Web:* www.finishmaster.com	Indianapolis	IN	46204	317-237-3678	237-2150	550
Finity Inc 1200 NW Natio Pkwy Ste 220 *TF:* 800-509-1346 ■ *Web:* www.finity.com	Portland	OR	97209	503-808-9240		195
Finkelstein & Partners LLP 1279 Route 300 *Web:* www.lawampm.com	Newburgh	NY	12551	845-562-0203		428
Finken Plumbing Heating & Cooling 628 19th Ave NE *TF:* 877-346-5367 ■ *Web:* www.finkens.com	Saint Joseph	MN	56374	320-258-2005	258-2006	610
Finkler & Company CPAs Inc 16600 Sprague Rd 285 *Web:* finklercpa.com	Middleburg Hts	OH	44130	440-826-1550		2
Finks Jewelry Inc 3545 Electric Rd *Web:* www.finks.com	Roanoke	VA	24018	540-342-2991	344-5385	410
Finland 866 UN Plaza Ste 222 *Web:* www.finlandun.org	New York	NY	10017	212-355-2100	759-6156	784
Consulate General 11900 W Olympic Blvd Ste 580 *Web:* www.finland.org	Los Angeles	CA	90064	310-203-9903	481-8981	257
Consulate General 866 UN Plaza Ste 250 *Web:* www.finland.org	New York	NY	10017	212-750-4400	750-4418	257
Embassy 3301 Massachusetts Ave NW *Web:* www.finland.org	Washington	DC	20008	202-298-5800	298-6030	257
Finlandia Sauna Products Inc 14010 SW 72nd Ave Ste B *TF:* 800-354-3342 ■ *Web:* www.finlandiasauna.com	Portland	OR	97224	503-684-8289		711
Finlandia University 601 Quincy St **Fax:* Admissions ■ *TF:* 800-682-7604 ■ *Web:* www.finlandia.edu	Hancock	MI	49930	906-482-5300	487-7383*	166
Finlay Printing LLC 44 Tobey Rd *Web:* www.finlay.com	Bloomfield	CT	06002	860-242-2800		627
Finley Engineering Company Inc 104 E 11th St *Web:* finleyusa.com	Lamar	MO	64759	417-682-5531		256
Finley Fire Equipment Company Inc 5255 N State Rt 60 NW *TF:* 800-697-8564 ■ *Web:* www.finleyfire.com	Mcconnelsville	OH	43756	740-962-4328		406
Finley Hospital 350 N Grandview Ave *TF:* 800-582-1891 ■ *Web:* www.unitypoint.org	Dubuque	IA	52001	563-582-1881		374-3
Finley Point State Park 490 N Meridian Rd *Web:* www.fwp.mt.gov	Kalispell	MT	59901	406-752-5501		565
Finley Resources Inc 1308 Lake St *TF:* 800-492-4403 ■ *Web:* www.finleyresources.com	Fort Worth	TX	76102	817-336-1924		581
Finley, Alt, Smith, Scharnberg, Craig, Hilmes 699 Walnut St Ste 1700 *Web:* www.finleylaw.com	Des Moines	IA	50309	515-288-0145		428
Finn & Porter 5000 Seminary Rd *Web:* www.finnandporter.com	Alexandria	VA	22311	703-379-2340	845-7662	671
Finn Corp 9281 Le St Dr *TF:* 800-543-7166 ■ *Web:* www.finncorp.com	Fairfield	OH	45014	513-874-2818	874-2914	273
Finn's Point National Cemetery 454 Ft Mott Rd *TF:* 800-827-1000 ■ *Web:* www.cem.va.gov/cems/nchp/finnspoint.asp	Pennsville	NJ	08070	215-504-5610	504-5611	136
Finney County 311 N Ninth St PO Box M *TF:* 800-344-7233 ■ *Web:* www.finneycounty.org	Garden City	KS	67846	620-272-3542	272-3599	338
Finney County Convention & Visitors Bureau 1511 E Fulton Terr *TF:* 866-267-4638 ■ *Web:* www.gardencity.net	Garden City	KS	67846	620-275-1900	276-3290	206
Finney County Public Library Garden City 605 E Walnut St *TF:* 800-244-5373 ■ *Web:* finneylibrary.org	Garden City	KS	67846	620-272-3680	272-3682	434-3
Finnish American Chamber of Commerce Inc 866 United Nations Plaza Ste 250 *Web:* www.facc-ny.com	New York	NY	10017	212-821-0225	750-4418	138
Finnleo Sauna 575 Cokato St E *TF:* 800-346-6536 ■ *Web:* www.finnleo.com	Cokato	MN	55321	800-346-6536		319-2
Fino Consulting LLC 20 W 37th St 12th Fl *TF:* 800-328-1422 ■ *Web:* www.finoconsulting.com	New York	NY	10018	212-532-0020		463
Finotex USA Corp 6942 NW 50th St *Web:* www.finotex.com	Miami	FL	33166	305-470-2400		693
FINRA (Financial Industry Regulatory Authority) 9509 Key W Ave *TF:* 800-321-6273 ■ *Web:* www.finra.org	Rockville	MD	20850	301-590-6500		49-2
FINRA 1735 K St NW *TF:* 800-289-9999 ■ *Web:* www.finra.org	Washington	DC	20006	202-728-8000		49-2
FinSer Corp 1 Alamo Ctr 106 S St Mary'S St Ste 600 *Web:* www.finser.com	San Antonio	TX	78205	210-224-5492	224-8787	194
Finsoft Consultants Inc 545 Eighth Ave Ste 4 *Web:* www.finsoftus.com	New York	NY	10018	212-239-9191		180
FinTrack Systems 194 Calyer St *Web:* www.fintrack.com	Brooklyn	NY	11222	212-742-1800		317
Fintronx LLC 5995 Chapel Hill Rd Ste 119 *TF:* 800-541-9082 ■ *Web:* www.fintronx.com	Raleigh	NC	27607	919-324-3960		77
Fin-West Group 1131 W Sixth St *OTC: FMOR*	Ontario	CA	91762	909-595-1996		509
Finzer Roller Co 129 Rawls Rd *TF:* 888-486-1900 ■ *Web:* www.finzerroller.com	Des Plaines	IL	60018	847-390-6200	390-6201	677
Fior D'Italia 2237 Mason St *Web:* www.fior.com	San Francisco	CA	94133	415-986-1886		671
Fiore Cantina Italiana 638 17th Ave SW *Web:* www.fiore.ca	Calgary	AB	T2S0B4	403-244-6603		671
Fiore Industries Inc 8601 Washington St NE Ste B *Web:* fiore-ind.com	Albuquerque	NM	87113	505-255-9797		261
Fiorella's Jack Stack Barbecue 13441 Holmes Rd *Web:* www.jackstackbbq.com	Kansas City	MO	64145	816-942-9141		671
Fiorella's Jack Stack Barbecue 9520 Metcalf Ave *Web:* www.jackstackbbq.com	Overland Park	KS	66212	913-385-7427		671
Fiorucci Foods Inc 1800 Ruffin Mill Rd *Web:* www.fioruccifoods.com	Colonial Heights	VA	23834	804-520-7775		297-8
FIP Construction Inc 1536 New Britain Ave *Web:* www.fipconstruction.com	Farmington	CT	06032	860-470-1800		186
Fire 13220 Shaker Sq *Web:* www.firefoodanddrink.com	Cleveland	OH	44120	216-921-3473		671
Fire & Life Safety America 3017 Vernon Rd *TF:* 800-252-5069 ■ *Web:* flsamerica.com	Richmond	VA	23228	804-222-1381	222-4393	283
Fire & Rain LLC 40 N First Ave *Web:* www.firerain.com	Evansville	IN	47710	812-464-5244		4
Fire Brick Engineers Co 2400 S 43rd St *Web:* www.firebrickengineers.com	Milwaukee	WI	53219	414-383-6000		191-4
Fire Creek Resources Ltd 206-11th Ave *Web:* www.fcrl.ca	Calgary	AB	T2G0X8	403-234-9309		539
Fire Engine Red 700 Locust St Apt A4 *Web:* fire-engine-red.com	Philadelphia	PA	19106	215-829-1850		177
Fire Fighter Sales & Service Co 791 Commonwealth Dr *TF:* 888-412-3473 ■ *Web:* www.firefighter-pgh.com	Warrendale	PA	15086	724-720-6000		610
Fire Fighters Equipment Co 3053 Rt 10 E *TF:* 800-523-7222 ■ *Web:* www.ffecnj.com	Denville	NJ	07834	973-366-4466		679
Fire Hall Theatre 412 Second Ave N *Web:* ggfct.com	Grand Forks	ND	58203	701-746-0847		572
Fire Island National Seashore 120 Laurel St *Web:* www.nps.gov/fiis	Patchogue	NY	11772	631-687-4750	289-4898	564
Fire Lite Alarms 1 Fire-Lite Pl *TF:* 800-627-3473 ■ *Web:* www.firelite.com	Northford	CT	06472	203-484-7161	484-7118	283
Fire Mountain Gems Inc 1 Fire Mountain Way *TF:* 800-355-2137 ■ *Web:* www.firemountaingems.com	Grants Pass	OR	97526	800-355-2137		411
Fire Museum of Maryland 1301 York Rd *Web:* www.firemuseummd.org	Lutherville	MD	21093	410-321-7500		520
Fire Museum of Memphis 118 Adams Ave *TF:* 800-780-5733 ■ *Web:* www.firemuseum.com	Memphis	TN	38103	901-320-5650	529-8422	520
Fire Protection Co 12828 S Ridgeway Ave	Alsip	IL	60803	708-371-4300		189-13
Fire Protection Service Inc 8050 Harrisburg Blvd *TF:* 800-453-2025 ■ *Web:* www.fps-usa.com	Houston	TX	77012	713-924-9600	923-6272	679
Fire Protection Systems Inc 22 Industrial Pk Dr *TF:* 800-499-0994 ■ *Web:* www.fireprotectionsys.com	Hendersonville	TN	37075	615-822-3600	822-3427	189-13
Fire Rock Products LLC 3620 Ave C *Web:* www.firerock.us	Birmingham	AL	35064	205-639-5000		364
Fire Systems West Inc 206 Frontage Rd N Ste C *Web:* www.firesystemswest.com	Pacific	WA	98047	253-833-1248	735-0113	283
Firecom Inc 39-27 59th St *TF:* 888-347-3269 ■ *Web:* firecominc.com	Woodside	NY	11377	718-899-6100	899-1932	283
Fire-End & Croker Corp 7 Westchester Plaza *TF:* 800-759-3473 ■ *Web:* www.fire-end.com	Elmsford	NY	10523	914-592-3640	592-3892	576
Firefighters Community Credit Union Inc 2300 St Clair Ave NE *TF:* 800-621-4644 ■ *Web:* www.ffcommunity.com	Cleveland	OH	44114	216-621-4644	694-3600	219
Firefighters' Museum 226 W Washington Blvd *TF:* 800-767-7752 ■ *Web:* fortwaynefiremuseum.com	Fort Wayne	IN	46802	260-426-0051		520
Firefly 4288 24th St *Web:* www.fireflyrestaurant.com	San Francisco	CA	94114	415-821-7652		671
FireFly Balloons 850 Meacham Rd *Web:* www.fireflyballoons.net	Statesville	NC	28677	704-878-9501	878-9505	28
Firefly Milward Brown 401 Merritt 7 3rd Fl *Web:* www.fireflymb.com	Norwalk	CT	06851	203-221-0411	221-0791	466

Name / Address	City	State	ZIP	Phone	Fax	Class
Firehouse Brewing Co 610 Main St *TF:* 800-487-3223 ■ *Web:* firehousebrewing.com	Rapid City	SD	57701	605-348-1915		671
Firehouse Image Ctr 2000 N Illinois St *TF:* 800-382-9179 ■ *Web:* onyx.fire-house.net	Indianapolis	IN	46202	317-236-1747		627
Firehouse Museum 1572 Columbia St *Web:* sandiegofirehousemuseum.com	San Diego	CA	92101	619-232-3473		520
Firehouse Restaurant 627 W Walnut St *TF:* 800-542-4546 ■ *Web:* www.thefirehouse.com	Johnson City	TN	37604	423-929-7377		671
Firehouse Restaurant Group Inc 3400 Kori Rd Ste 8 *Web:* www.firehousesubs.com	Jacksonville	FL	32257	904-886-8300		310
Firehouse, The 1112 Second St *Web:* www.firehouseoldsac.com	Sacramento	CA	95814	916-442-4772	442-6617	671
FireKing Security Group 101 Security Pkwy *TF:* 800-457-2424 ■ *Web:* www.fireking.com	New Albany	IN	47150	812-948-8400		692
Firelands Electric Co-op Inc 1 Energy Pl PO Box 32 *TF:* 800-533-8658 ■ *Web:* www.firelandsec.com	New London	OH	44851	419-929-1571	929-8550	245
Firelands Regional Medical Ctr 1111 Hayes Ave *TF:* 800-342-1177 ■ *Web:* www.firelands.com	Sandusky	OH	44870	419-557-7400	557-6977	374-3
Fireman's Fund Insurance Co 1465 N McDowell Blvd *TF:* 866-386-3932 ■ *Web:* www.firemansfund.com	Petaluma	CA	94954	866-386-3932		391-5
Fireplace 1634 Beacon St *Web:* www.fireplacerest.com	Brookline	MA	02446	617-975-1900		671
Fireplace & Bar-B-Q Center Inc 10470 Metcalf Ave *Web:* fireplacecenterkc.com	Overland Park	KS	66212	913-383-2286		362
Firepoint Technologies Inc 27-180 Wilkinson Rd *Web:* www.firepoint.ca	Brampton	ON	L6T4W8	905-874-9400		261
Fire-Safe Protection Services 1815 Sherwood Forest St *Web:* www.fire-safe.net	Houston	TX	77043	713-722-7800		428
Fireside Hearth & Home 7571 215th St W *Web:* www.fireside.com	Lakeville	MN	55044	651-452-3399		111
Fireside Inn & Suites 25 Airport Rd *TF:* 877-258-5900 ■ *Web:* www.firesideinnwestlebanon.com	West Lebanon	NH	03784	603-298-5900	298-0340	379
Fireside Restaurant 810 Woodward Ave	New Haven	CT	06512	203-466-1919		671
Firestone & Parson Inc 30 Newbury St	Boston	MA	02116	617-266-1858		410
Firestone Fibers & Textiles Co 100 Firestone Ln PO Box 1369 *TF:* 800-441-1336 ■ *Web:* www.firestonefibers.com	Kings Mountain	NC	28086	704-734-2132	734-2104	745-3
Firestone Industrial Products Co 250 W 96th St *TF:* 800-888-0650 ■ *Web:* www.firestoneip.com	Indianapolis	IN	46260	317-818-8600	818-8645	60
Firestone Tube Co 2700 E Main St *Web:* www.firestonetubes.com	Russellville	AR	72802	479-968-1443		754
Firetrol Protection Systems Inc 3696 West 900 South Ste A *Web:* www.firetrol.net	Salt Lake City	UT	84104	801-485-6900	485-6902	189-13
Fireworks 3307 Utah Ave S *TF:* 800-505-0002 ■ *Web:* www.fireworksgallery.net	Seattle	WA	98134	206-682-8707	467-6366	520
Fireye Inc 3 Manchester Rd *Web:* www.fireye.com	Derry	NH	03038	603-432-4100		407
Firezat 5173 Waring Rd Ste 158 *Web:* www.firezat.com	San Diego	CA	92120	619-955-6788		302
Firm Consulting Group 2107 W Cass St Ste B *TF:* 877-636-9525 ■ *Web:* www.firmconsultinggrp.com	Tampa	FL	33606	877-636-9525		463
Firm Realty Inc 1930 Harrison St Ste 505 *Web:* www.firmrealty.com	Hollywood	FL	33020	954-926-2510		652
FIRMA Foreign Exchange Corp 10205 101 St Edmonton City Ctr E Ste 400 *Web:* www.firmafx.com	Edmonton	AB	T5J4H5	780-426-4946		691
Firmenich Inc 250 Plainsvoro *Web:* www.firmenich.com	Plainsboro	NJ	08536	609-452-1000		296-15
Firmwater 20 Maud St Ste 405 *Web:* www.firmwater.com	Toronto	ON	M5V2M5	416-815-1496		180
FIRST 200 Bedford St *TF:* 800-871-8326 ■ *Web:* www.firstinspires.org	Manchester	NH	03101	603-666-3906	666-3907	48-11
First - Call Medical Inc 574 Boston Rd Unit 11 *Web:* www.fcminc.com	Billerica	MA	01821	978-670-5399		415
First & Last Tavern 939 Maple Ave *Web:* www.firstandlasttavern.com	Hartford	CT	06114	860-956-6000		671
First Act Inc 745 Boylston St *TF:* 888-551-1115 ■ *Web:* www.firstact.com	Boston	MA	02116	617-226-7888		526
First Action Security Security Team Inc 525 Northern Ave PO Box 2070 *TF Cust Svc:* 800-372-7447 ■ *Web:* www.firstactionteam.com	Hagerstown	MD	21742	301-797-2124		692
First Affirmative Financial Network LLC 5475 Mark Dabling Blvd Ste 108 *Web:* www.firstaffirmative.com	Colorado Springs	CO	80918	719-636-1045		401
First Alarm Security & Patrol Inc 1111 Estates Dr *TF:* 800-684-1111 ■ *Web:* www.firstalarm.com	Aptos	CA	95003	831-476-1111		693
First Alert Inc 3901 Liberty St Rd *TF:* 800-323-9005 ■ *Web:* www.firstalert.com	Aurora	IL	60504	630-851-7330		283
First Alliance Bank 51 Germantown Ct Ste 100 *Web:* fabtn.com	Cordova	TN	38018	901-753-8339		70
First American Bank 261 S Western Ave *Web:* www.firstambank.com	Carpentersville	IL	60110	847-426-6300	426-6300	70
First American Bank & Trust 2785 Hwy 20 W PO Box 550 *TF:* 800-738-2265 ■ *Web:* www.fabt.com	Vacherie	LA	70090	225-265-2265	265-7339	70
First American Bank Corp 1650 Louis Ave *TF:* 866-449-1150 ■ *Web:* www.firstambank.com	Elk Grove Village	IL	60009	847-952-3700		360-2
First American Corp 1 First American Way *NYSE: FAF* ■ *TF:* 800-854-3643 ■ *Web:* www.firstam.com	Santa Ana	CA	92707	714-250-3000		391-6
First American Funds PO Box 701 *TF:* 800-677-3863 ■ *Web:* www.firstamericanfunds.com	Milwaukee	WI	53201	800-677-3863		528
First American Home Buyers Protection 7833 Haskell Ave *Web:* homewarranty.firstam.com	Van Nuys	CA	91406	818-781-5050		390
First American Plastic Molding Enterprise 2 Choctaw Trl *Web:* www.firstamericanplastic.com	Ocean Springs	MS	39564	228-872-4635		608
First Analysis Corp 1 S Wacker Dr Ste 3900 *Web:* firstanalysis.com	Chicago	IL	60606	312-258-1400		792
First Annapolis Consulting Inc Three Park Pl Ste 200 *Web:* www.firstannapolis.com	Annapolis	MD	21401	410-855-8500	855-8599	463
First Arkansas Bank & Trust 600 W Main St *Web:* www.fabandt.com	Jacksonville	AR	72076	501-982-4511		70
First Assembly of God 1701 N E Ave *Web:* firstassemblypc.org	Panama City	FL	32405	850-769-3558		48-20
First Aviation Services Inc 15 Riverside Ave *Web:* www.firstaviation.com	Westport	CT	06880	203-291-3300	291-3330	770
First BanCorp PO Box 9146 *NYSE: FBP* ■ *TF:* 866-695-2511 ■ *Web:* www.1firstbank.com/pr/es	San Juan	PR	00908	787-725-2511		360-2
First Bancorp 341 N Main St *NASDAQ: FBNC* ■ *TF:* 800-548-9377 ■ *Web:* localfirstbank.com	Troy	NC	27371	910-576-6171	576-1070	360-2
First Bancorp of Indiana Inc 5001 Davis Lant Dr *OTC: FBPI*	Evansville	IN	47715	812-492-8100		360-2
First Bancshares Inc 142 E First St *NYSE: FBSI* ■ *Web:* www.firsthomesavingsbank.com	Mountain Grove	MO	65711	417-926-5151	926-4362	360-2
First Banctrust Corp 101 S Central Ave *OTC: FIRT* ■ *TF:* 800-228-6381 ■ *Web:* www.firstbanktrust.com	Paris	IL	61944	217-465-0381		360-2
First Bank Financial Centre (FBFC) 155 W Wisconsin Ave PO Box 1004 *TF:* 888-569-9909 ■ *Web:* www.fbfcwi.com	Oconomowoc	WI	53066	262-569-9900		70
First Bank Muleshoe 202 S 1st PO Box 565 *TF:* 888-653-9558 ■ *Web:* fbmuleshoe.com	Muleshoe	TX	79347	806-272-4515	272-4436	70
First Bank Of Highland Park 1835 First St *TF:* 877-651-7800 ■ *Web:* www.firstbankhp.com	Highland Park	IL	60035	847-432-7800	433-2156	685
First Bankers Trust Company NA 1201 Broadway PO Box 3566 *Web:* www.firstbankers.com	Quincy	IL	62305	217-228-8000	228-8091	70
First Banks Inc 135 N Meramec Ave *TF:* 800-760-2265 ■ *Web:* www.firstbanks.com	Clayton	MO	63105	314-854-4600		360-2
First Baptist Church Dallas 1707 San Jacinto St *Web:* www.firstdallas.org	Dallas	TX	75201	214-969-0111		48-20
First Baptist Church of Orlando Inc, The 3000 S John Young Pkwy *Web:* www.firstorlando.com	Orlando	FL	32805	407-425-2555	425-2954	48-20
First Bethany Bank & Trust 6500 NW 39th Expy *Web:* firstbethany.com	Bethany	OK	73008	405-789-1110		70
First Book 1319 F St NW Ste 1000 *Web:* www.firstbook.org	Washington	DC	20004	202-393-1222		48-5
First Busey Corp 100 W University Ave *NASDAQ: BUSE* ■ *TF:* 800-672-8739 ■ *Web:* www.busey.com	Champaign	IL	61820	217-365-4516		360-2
First Business Financial Services Inc 401 Charmany Dr *NASDAQ: FBIZ* ■ *TF:* 888-455-2263 ■ *Web:* www.firstbusiness.com	Madison	WI	53719	608-238-8008		70
First Calgary Savings 510 16th Ave NE **Fax Area Code:* 403 ■ *TF:* 866-923-4778 ■ *Web:* www.firstcalgary.com	Calgary	AB	T2E1K4	866-923-4778	276-5299*	70
First Call Computer Solutions Inc 500 N Higgins Ave Ste 201 *Web:* www.firstsolution.com	Missoula	MT	59802	406-721-6462		179
First Call International Inc 6329 Airport Fwy *Web:* www.firstcallintl.com	Fort Worth	TX	76117	817-831-2220		22
First Call Nursing Services Inc 1313 N Milpitas Blvd Ste 210 *Web:* www.firstcallnursingservices.com	Milpitas	CA	95035	408-262-1533		260
First Candle 49 Locust Ave Ste 210 *TF:* 800-221-7437 ■ *Web:* cjfirstcandle.org	New Canaan	CT	06840	410-653-8226		48-17
First Carolina Management Inc 300 N Winstead Ave *Web:* www.1stcarolina.net	Rocky Mount	NC	27804	252-937-8111		463
First Cash Financial Services Inc 690 E Lamar Blvd Ste 400 *NASDAQ: FCFS* ■ *TF:* 800-290-4598 ■ *Web:* ww2.firstcash.com	Arlington	TX	76011	817-460-3947	461-7019	569
First Chemical Corp 1001 Industrial Rd *TF:* 877-243-6178 ■ *Web:* dupont.com	Pascagoula	MS	39581	228-762-0870		144
First Choice Health Plan 600 University St Ste 1400 **Fax Area Code:* 206 ■ **Fax:* Cust Svc ■ *TF:* 800-467-5281 ■ *Web:* www.fchn.com	Seattle	WA	98101	800-467-5281	667-8062*	391-3
First Choice Packaging Solutions 1501 W State St *Web:* www.firstchoicepackaging.com	Fremont	OH	43420	419-333-4100		596
First Choice Software LLC PO Box 1657 *Web:* www.fcs-software.com	West Chester	PA	19380	610-436-6825		734
First Christian Church 531 Fifth St *Web:* www.fccoc.org	Columbus	IN	47201	812-379-4491		48-20
First Church of Christ in New Haven, The *Center Church on-the-Green* 311 Temple St *Web:* centerchurchonthegreen.org	New Haven	CT	06511	203-787-0121	787-2187	50-4
First Church of Christ Scientist 210 Massachusetts Ave P05-10 *TF:* 800-288-7155 ■ *Web:* www.christianscience.com	Boston	MA	02115	617-450-2000		48-20

	Phone	Fax	Class
First Citizens Bancorp Inc 1230 Main St .... Columbia SC 29201 *OTC:* FCBN ■ *TF:* 888-323-4732 ■ *Web:* www.firstcitizens.com	803-733-2025		360-2
First Citizens BancShares Inc 4300 Six Forks Rd .... Raleigh NC 27609 *NASDAQ:* FCNCA ■ *Web:* www.firstcitizens.com	919-716-7000		360-2
First Citizens Bank 350 S Beverly D Ste 150 .... Beverly Hills CA 90212 *TF:* 888-323-4732 ■ *Web:* www.firstcitizens.com	888-323-4732		360-2
First Citizens Bank & Trust Co Inc 1230 Main St .... Columbia SC 29201 *TF:* 888-323-4732 ■ *Web:* www.firstcitizens.com	919-716-4588		70
First Citizens National Bank Charitable Foundation PO Box 1708 .... Mason City IA 50402 *TF:* 800-423-1602 ■ *Web:* www.firstcitizensnb.com	641-423-1600	423-4600	360-2
First City Bank 1885 Northwest Blvd .... Columbus OH 43212 *Web:* www.myfirstcitybank.com	614-487-1010		70
First Class Air Repair 15380 County Rd 565A Ste G .... Groveland FL 34736 *Web:* firstclassairrepair.com	352-241-7684		529
First Class Foods Inc 12500 Inglewood Ave .... Hawthorne CA 90250 *Web:* www.firstclassfoods.com	310-676-2500		473
First Class Services Inc 9355 US Hwy 60 E .... Lewisport KY 42351 *TF General:* 800-467-8684 ■ *Web:* www.firstclassservices.com	270-295-3746		780
First Class Solutions Inc 11426 Dorsett Rd .... Maryland Heights MO 63043 *Web:* www.firstclasssolutions.com	314-209-7800		225
First Clinical Research LLC 2249 Sutter St .... San Francisco CA 94115 *Web:* www.firstclinical.com	650-465-0119		194
First Coast Energy LLP 7014 A C Skinner Pkwy Ste 290 .... Jacksonville FL 32256 *Web:* www.dailysstores.com	904-596-3200		345
First Coast Hearing Clinic Inc 1835 US Hwy 1 S Ste 121 .... Saint Augustine FL 32084 *Web:* www.firstcoasthearing.com	904-429-3823		475
First Coast Logistics Services Inc 11460 Boote Blvd Ste 1 .... Jacksonville FL 32256 *Web:* www.firstcoast.net	904-757-6008	751-6244	311
First Colony Mall 16535 SW Fwy Ste 1 .... Sugar Land TX 77479 *Web:* www.firstcolonymall.com	281-265-6123		460
First Command Financial Services Inc 1 FirstComm Plaza .... Fort Worth TX 76109 *TF:* 800-443-2104 ■ *Web:* www.firstcommand.com	817-731-8621		194
First Commonwealth Financial Corp 601 Philadelphia St .... Indiana PA 15701 *NYSE:* FCF ■ *TF:* 800-711-2265 ■ *Web:* www.fcbanking.com	724-349-7220		360-2
First Community Bank 420 Second Ave SW .... Cullman AL 35055 *Web:* www.fcbcullman.com	256-734-4863	737-8900	360-2
First Community Corp (FCC) 5455 Sunset Blvd .... Lexington SC 29072 *NASDAQ:* FCCO ■ *TF:* 800-829-6372 ■ *Web:* www.firstcommunitysc.com	803-951-0555		360-2
First Community Credit Union (FCCU) 17151 Chesterfield Airport Rd PO Box 1030 .... Chesterfield MO 63005 *TF:* 800-767-8880 ■ *Web:* www.firstcommunity.com	636-728-3333		219
First Community Financial Corp (FCFC) 4000 N Central Ave Ste 100 .... Phoenix AZ 85012 *OTC:* FMFP ■ **Fax Area Code:* 312 ■ *TF:* 877-777-4778 ■ *Web:* capitalsource.com	602-265-7715	577-7907*	216
First Community Village 1800 Riverside Dr .... Columbus OH 43212 *TF:* 877-364-2570 ■ *Web:* www.nationalchurchresidences.org	614-324-4455		672
First Congregational Church 62 Centre St .... Nantucket MA 02554 *Web:* nantucketfcc.org	508-228-0950		50-1
First Co-op Assn (FCA) 960 Riverview Dr PO Box 60 .... Cherokee IA 51012 *TF:* 877-753-5400 ■ *Web:* www.firstcoop.com	712-225-5400	225-5493	447
First Corporate Sedans Inc 60 E 42nd St Ste 2424 .... New York NY 10165 *TF:* 800-473-8876 ■ *Web:* www.fcsny.com	212-972-2282	286-9130	316
First County Bank Inc, The 117 Prospect St .... Stamford CT 06901 *Web:* www.firstcountybank.com	203-462-4407		70
First Dallas Securities 2905 Maple Ave .... Dallas TX 75201 *Web:* www.firstdallas.com	214-954-1177	954-1281	690
First DataBank Inc (FDB) 701 Gateway Blvd Ste 600 .... South San Francisco CA 94080 *TF General:* 800-633-3453 ■ *Web:* www.fdbhealth.com	800-633-3453		178-10
First Defiance Financial Corp 601 Clinton St .... Defiance OH 43512 *NASDAQ:* FDEF ■ *TF:* 800-472-6292 ■ *Web:* www.fdef.com	419-782-5015		360-2
First Dental Health 5771 Copley Dr Ste 101 .... San Diego CA 92111 *TF:* 800-334-7244 ■ *Web:* www.firstdentalhealth.com	800-334-7244		415
First District Assn (FDA) 101 S Swift Ave .... Litchfield MN 55355 *Web:* www.firstdistrict.com	320-693-3236		296-5
First Draft 316 N Michigan Ave Ste 400 .... Chicago IL 60601 **Fax Area Code:* 312 ■ *TF:* 800-878-5331 ■ *Web:* www.ragan.com/main/home.aspx	800-493-4867	960-4106*	531-11
First Eastern Mortgage Corp 100 Brickstone Sq .... Andover MA 01810 *TF:* 800-777-2240 ■ *Web:* www.firsteastern.com	978-749-3100		509
First Electric Co-op Corp 1000 S JP Wright Loop Rd .... Jacksonville AR 72076 *TF:* 800-489-7405 ■ *Web:* www.firstelectric.coop	501-982-4545		245
First Environment Inc 91 Fulton St .... Boonton NJ 07005 *Web:* www.firstenvironment.com	973-334-0003	334-0928	192
First Equipment Co PO Box 2129 .... Addison TX 75001 *TF:* 888-780-8631 ■ *Web:* www.firstequipment.com	972-380-2300	380-8350	264-1
First Equity Mortgage Bankers 9300 S Dadeland Blvd Ste 500 .... Miami FL 33156 *TF:* 800-973-3654 ■ *Web:* www.fembi.com	305-666-3333	666-3181	509
First Evangelical Free Church of st Louis County 1375 Carman Rd .... Manchester MO 63021 *Web:* efree.org	636-227-0125		48-20
First Farmers & Merchants National Bank 816 S Garden St PO Box 1148 .... Columbia TN 38401 *OTC:* FIME ■ *TF:* 800-882-8378 ■ *Web:* www.myfirstfarmers.com	931-388-3145		685
First Federal Bank Fsb 6900 N Executive Dr .... Kansas City MO 64120 *TF:* 888-651-4759 ■ *Web:* www.ffbkc.com	816-241-7800		70
First Federal Bank Of Ohio 1660 W Market St Ste A .... Tiffin OH 44883 *Web:* www.firstfederalbankofohio.com	419-468-1518		70
First Federal Lakewood 14806 Detroit Ave .... Lakewood OH 44107 *TF:* 800-966-7300 ■ *Web:* www.ffl.net	216-529-2700		70
First Federal of Northern Michigan 100 S Second Ave .... Alpena MI 49707 *NASDAQ:* FFNM ■ *TF:* 800-916-8800 ■ *Web:* www.first-federal.com	989-356-9041	354-8671	71
First Federal Savings Bank of Frankfort 216 W Main St PO Box 535 .... Frankfort KY 40602 *TF:* 888-818-3372 ■ *Web:* www.ffsbfrankfort.com	502-223-1638	223-7136	360-2
First Fidelity Capital Markets Inc 10463 Stonebridge Blvd Ste 400 .... Boca Raton FL 33498 *Web:* www.ffidelity.com	561-558-0730		401
First Fidelity Funding & Mortgage Corp 6000 Lake Forrest Dr Ste 290 .... Atlanta GA 30328 *TF:* 800-933-3810 ■ *Web:* firstfidelityfunding.com	404-943-1533		141
First Financial Bancorp (FFB) 255 E Fifth St Ste 700 .... Cincinnati OH 45202 *NASDAQ:* FFBC ■ *TF:* 877-322-9530 ■ *Web:* www.bankatfirst.com	877-322-9530		360-2
First Financial Bank 1 First Financial Plaza .... Terre Haute IN 47807 *TF:* 800-511-0045 ■ *Web:* www.first-online.com	812-238-6000	238-6000	70
First Financial Bank 300 High St .... Hamilton OH 45011 **Fax:* Cust Svc ■ *TF Cust Svc:* 877-322-9530 ■ *Web:* www.bankatfirst.com	513-867-4744	867-3111*	70
First Financial Bank PO Box 2122 .... Terre Haute IN 47802 *Web:* first-online.com	815-844-3171	842-2958	186
First Financial Bank 301 W Beauregard .... San Angelo TX 76903 *Web:* www.ffin.com	325-659-5900		70
First Financial Bankshares 400 Pine St PO Box 701 .... Abilene TX 79601 *NASDAQ:* FFIN ■ *Web:* www.ffin.com	806-363-8200		70
First Financial Bankshares Inc PO Box 701 .... Abilene TX 79604 *NASDAQ:* FFIN ■ *TF:* 888-588-2623 ■ *Web:* www.ffin.com	325-627-7155	627-7393	360-2
First Financial Corp 1 First Financial Plaza .... Terre Haute IN 47807 *NASDAQ:* THFF ■ *TF:* 800-511-0045 ■ *Web:* www.first-online.com	812-238-6000	232-5336	360-2
First Financial Equity Corp 7373 N Scottsdale Rd Ste D-120 .... Scottsdale AZ 85253 *Web:* www.ffec.com	480-951-0079		194
First Florida Credit Union 500 W First St .... Jacksonville FL 32202 *Web:* firstflorida.org	904-359-6800		219
First Foundation Bank 18101 Von Karman Ave Ste 750 .... Irvine CA 92612 *TF:* 800-224-7931 ■ *Web:* www.ff-inc.com	949-202-4100		70
First FSB 633 La Salle St .... Ottawa IL 61350 *TF:* 800-443-8780 ■ *Web:* www.ffsbweb.com	815-434-3500		71
First General Bank 1744 S Nogales St .... Rowland Heights CA 91748 *Web:* www.fgbusa.com	626-820-1234		70
First Generation Productions 410 Allentown Dr .... Allentown PA 18109 *Web:* www.firstgencom.com	610-437-4300		514
First Gold Hotel 270 Main St .... Deadwood SD 57732 *TF:* 800-274-1876 ■ *Web:* www.firstgold.com	605-578-9777	578-3979	379
First Green Partners 1550 Utica Ave S Ste 450 .... Minneapolis MN 55416	952-288-2760		528
First Growth Holdings Ltd 4388 Still Creek Dr Unit 235 .... Vancouver BC V5C6C6 *Web:* firstgrowthholdings.com	604-688-9588		224
First Hartford Corp 149 Colonial Rd .... Manchester CT 06042 *OTC:* FHRT ■ *Web:* www.firsthartford.com	860-646-6555	646-8572	653
First Hawaiian Bank 999 Bishop St .... Honolulu HI 96813 *TF:* 888-844-4444 ■ *Web:* www.fhb.com	808-525-6340		70
First Health Group Corp *Coventry* 3200 Highland Ave .... Downers Grove IL 60515 *TF:* 800-247-2898 ■ *Web:* www.firsthealth.com	630-737-7900		463
First Heartland Capital Inc 1839 Lake St Louis Blvd .... Lake Saint Louis MO 63367	636-625-0900		690
First Horizon National Corp 165 Madison .... Memphis TN 38103 *NYSE:* FHN ■ *TF:* 800-489-4040 ■ *Web:* www.firsthorizon.com	901-523-4444		360-2
First Industrial Realty Trust Inc 311 S Wacker Dr Ste 4000 .... Chicago IL 60606 *NYSE:* FR ■ *Web:* www.firstindustrial.com	312-344-4300	922-6320	655
First Infrastructure LLC 15 Wendover Rd .... Montclair NJ 07042 *Web:* www.1stinfrastructure.com	973-783-0088		463
First Insight Corp 22845 NW Bennett St Bldg B Ste 200 .... Hillsboro OR 97124 *TF:* 800-920-1940 ■ *Web:* www.first-insight.com	800-920-1940		177
First Insurance Company of Hawaii Ltd 1100 Ward Ave PO Box 2866 .... Honolulu HI 96803 *TF:* 800-272-5202 ■ *Web:* www.ficoh.com	808-527-7777		391-4
First Insurance Funding Corp 450 Skokie Blvd Ste 1000 .... Northbrook IL 60062 *TF:* 800-837-3707 ■ *Web:* www.firstinsurancefunding.com	800-837-3707	837-3709	217
First Intercontinental Bank, The 5593 Buford Hwy .... Doraville GA 30340 *Web:* firsticbank.com	770-451-7200		70
First International Health Foods Ltd 7 Hoover Ave .... Haverstraw NY 10927 *Web:* www.bradsorganic.com	845-429-9080		805

	Phone	Fax	Class
First Interstate Bancsystem Inc 401 N 31st St Billings MT 59101 *NASDAQ: FIBK* ■ *TF:* 888-752-3341 ■ *Web:* www.firstinterstatebank.com	406-255-5000		360-2
First Interstate Bank 401 N 31st St Billings MT 59101 *TF:* 888-752-3341 ■ *Web:* www.firstinterstatebank.com	406-255-5000		70
First Investors Financial Services Group Inc 380 Interstate N Pkwy 3rd Fl Atlanta GA 30339 *Web:* www.fifsg.com	713-977-2600		390
First Jackson Bank 43243 US Hwy 72 Stevenson AL 35772 *TF:* 888-950-2265 ■ *Web:* firstjacksonbank.com	256-437-2107		70
First Ladies National Historic Site 205 Market Ave S Canton OH 44702 *Web:* www.nps.gov	330-452-0876	456-3414	564
First Lease Inc 1 Walnut Grove Dr Ste 300 Horsham PA 19044 **Fax Area Code:* 215 ■ *TF:* 866-493-4778 ■ *Web:* www.firstleaseonline.com	866-493-4778	283-9870*	264-4
First London Securities Corp 2603 Fairmount St Dallas TX 75201 *Web:* www.firstlondon.com	214-220-0690		690
First Manhattan Co 399 Park Ave New York NY 10022 *TF:* 800-280-0780 ■ *Web:* www.firstmanhattan.com	212-756-3300		690
First Manhattan Consulting Group 90 Pk Ave 18th Fl New York NY 10016 *Web:* www.fmcgdirect.com	212-557-0500	338-9296	194
First Mercantile Trust Co 57 Germantown Ct 4th Fl Cordova TN 38018 *TF:* 800-753-3682 ■ *Web:* www.firstmerc.com	901-753-9080		70
First Merchants Corp 200 E Jackson St Muncie IN 47305 *NASDAQ: FRME* ■ *TF:* 800-205-3464 ■ *Web:* www.firstmerchants.com	765-747-1500		360-2
First Metro Bank 406 Avalon Ave Muscle Shoals AL 35661 *Web:* www.firstmetro.com	256-386-0600	386-0651	70
First Mid-Illinois Bank & Trust 1515 Charleston Ave Mattoon IL 61938 *OTC: FMBH* ■ *Web:* www.firstmid.com	217-234-7454	258-0426	70
First Midwest Bancorp Inc 1 Pierce Pl Ste 1500 Itasca IL 60143 *NASDAQ: FMBI* ■ *TF:* 800-322-3623 ■ *Web:* firstmidwest.com	630-875-7450		300-2
First National Bank PO Box 578 Fort Collins CO 80521 *TF:* 800-883-8773 ■ *Web:* www.1stnationalbank.com	970-495-9450		70
First National Bank 316 E Bremer Ave PO Box 837 Waverly IA 50677 *Web:* www.myfnbbank.com	319-352-1340	352-6323	70
First National Bank 4220 William Penn Hwy Monroeville PA 15146 *TF:* 800-555-5455 ■ *Web:* www.fnb-online.com	800-555-5455		360-2
First National Bank Alaska 101 W 36 Ave PO Box 100720 Anchorage AK 99510 *OTC: FBAK* ■ *TF:* 800-856-4362 ■ *Web:* www.fnbalaska.com	907-777-4362		70
First National Bank Creston PO Box 445 Creston IA 50801 *TF:* 877-782-2195 ■ *Web:* www.fnbcreston.com	641-782-2195		70
First National Bank In Alamogordo 414 Tenth St PO Box 9 Alamogordo NM 88311 *Web:* www.fnb4u.com	575-437-4880	437-1631	70
First National Bank In Tremont 134 S Sampson St PO Box 23 Tremont IL 61568 *Web:* www.tremontbank.com	309-925-2121	925-5448	70
First National Bank of Illinois Inc 3266 Ridge Rd Lansing IL 60438 *Web:* www.fnbiweb.com	708-474-1300		70
First National Bank Of Jasper 200 W 18th St Jasper AL 35501 *TF:* 800-334-9007 ■ *Web:* www.fnbjasper.com	706-649-4900		70
First National Bank of Muscatine 300 E Second St Muscatine IA 52761 *Web:* www.fnbmusc.com	563-263-4221		70
First National Bank of Omaha 1620 Dodge St Omaha NE 68197 *TF:* 800-462-5266 ■ *Web:* www.fnbomaha.com	402-341-0500		70
First National Bank of Oneida, The 18418 Alberta St PO Box 4699 Oneida TN 37041 *TF:* 866-546-8273 ■ *Web:* www.fnboneida.com	423-569-8586	569-9826	70
First National Bank of Paragould 200 W Ct St Paragould AR 72450 *Web:* www.fnbank.net	870-215-4000		70
First National Bank of Santa Fe PO Box 609 Santa Fe NM 87504 *TF:* 888-912-2265 ■ *Web:* www.firstnationalsantafe.com	505-992-2000		70
First National Bank of South Miami 5750 Sunset Dr Miami FL 33143 *Web:* fnbsm.com	305-667-5511		70
First National Bank of Tennessee 214 E Main St Livingston TN 38570 *Web:* www.fnbotn.com	931-823-1261		360-2
First National Bankers Bankshares Inc (FNBB) 7813 Office Pk Blvd Baton Rouge LA 70809 *TF:* 800-421-6182 ■ *Web:* www.bankers-bank.com	225-924-8015	952-0899	70
First National of Nebraska Inc PO Box 2490 Omaha NE 68197 *TF:* 800-688-7070 ■ *Web:* www.firstnational.com	402-341-0500	938-5302	360-2
First Nations Development Institute 2217 Princess Anne St Ste 111-1 Fredericksburg VA 22401 **Fax Area Code:* 888 ■ *TF:* 888-371-3686 ■ *Web:* www.firstnations.org	540-371-5615	371-3686*	48-14
First Nations University of Canada *Northern* 1301 Central Ave Prince Albert SK S6V4W1 *TF:* 800-267-6303	306-765-3333	765-3330	785
Saskatoon 229 Fourth Ave S Saskatoon SK S7K4K3 *TF:* 800-267-6303 ■ *Web:* fnuniv.ca	306-931-1800	931-1849	785
First NBC (CPB) 29092 Kretel Rd Lacombe LA 70445 *Web:* www.firstnbcbank.com	985-819-1200		70
First New York Securities LLC 90 Pk Ave Fl 5 New York NY 10016 *Web:* www.firstny.com	212-848-0600		690
First Niles Financial Inc 55 N Main St Niles OH 44446 *NYSE: FNFI*	330-652-2539		360-2
First of Long Island Corp 10 Glen Head Ave Glen Head NY 11545 *NASDAQ: FLIC* ■ *TF:* 800-554-8969 ■ *Web:* www.fnbli.com	516-671-4900	676-7900	360-2
First Office 1204 E Sixth St Huntingburg IN 47542 **Fax Area Code:* 812 ■ **Fax:* Cust Svc ■ *TF:* 800-983-4415 ■ *Web:* www.firstoffice.com	800-983-4415	683-7155*	319-1
First Operations LP 8273 Moberly Ln Dallas TX 75227 *Web:* www.firstco.com	214-388-5751	388-2255	14
First Options of Chicago Inc 70 W Madison St Ste 2100 Chicago IL 60602 *Web:* www.pftctrading.com	312-933-5884		690
First Pacific Advisors Inc 11400 W Olympic Blvd Ste 1200 Los Angeles CA 90064 *TF:* 800-982-4372 ■ *Web:* www.fpafunds.com	310-473-0225	996-5450	401
First Palmetto Savings Bank Fsb PO Box 430 Camden SC 29021 *TF:* 800-922-7411 ■ *Web:* www.firstpalmetto.com	803-432-2265		70
First Peoples Buffalo Jump State Park 342 Ulm Vaughn Rd Ulm MT 59485 *Web:* www.fwp.mt.gov	406-866-2217		565
First Personal Bank 14701 Ravinia Ave Orland Park IL 60462 *Web:* firstpersonalbank.net	708-226-2727		70
First Piedmont Corp 108 S Main St Chatham VA 24531 *Web:* www.relyonred.com	434-432-0211		525
First Potomac Realty Trust 7600 Wisconsin Ave 11th Fl Bethesda MD 20814 *NYSE: FPO* ■ *Web:* www.first-potomac.com	301-986-9200	986-5554	654
First Priority Health 19 N Main St Wilkes-Barre PA 18711 *TF:* 800-822-8753 ■ *Web:* www.bcnepa.com	800-822-8753		391-3
First Priority Inc 1590 Todd Farm Dr Elgin IL 60123 *TF:* 800-650-4899 ■ *Web:* www.prioritycare.com	847-289-1600		582
First Process Steel 2678 N Harvard Tulsa OK 74115 *Web:* www.firstprocesssteel.com	918-836-2929		567
First Pryority Bank 310 E Graham Pryor OK 74361 *Web:* www.firstpryoritybank.com	918-825-2121		70
First Quality Products Inc 121 N Rd Mcelhattan PA 17748 *TF:* 000 227 3551 ■ *Web:* www.firstquality.com	570-769-6900		476
First Quality Tissue 904 Woods Ave Lock Haven PA 17745 *Web:* www.firstquality.com/x122.php	570-748-1200		557
First Quantum Minerals Ltd 543 Granville St 8th Fl Vancouver BC V6C1X8 *TSE: FM* ■ *TF:* 888-688-6577 ■ *Web:* www.first-quantum.com	604-688-6577	688-3818	502
First Rate Staffing 2775 W Thomas Rd Ste 107 Phoenix AZ 85017 *Web:* www.first-ratestaffing.com	602-442-5277		260
First Real Estate Investment 505 Main St Hackensack NJ 07602 *Web:* freitnj.com	201-488-6400	487-1798	655
First Realty Management Corp 151 Tremont St PH 1 Boston MA 02111 *Web:* www.frmboston.com	617-423-7000		655
First Recruitin LLC 33 N LaSalle St Ste 2250 Chicago IL 60602 *Web:* www.firstassoc.com	312-253-4000		260
First Regional Library 370 W Commerce St Hernando MS 38632 *Web:* firstregional.org	662-429-4439	429-8853	434-3
First Reliance Bank 2170 W Palmetto St Florence SC 29501 *Web:* firstreliance.com	843-656-5000		70
First Reliance Holdings LLC 275 N Pointe Pkwy Ste 60 Amherst NY 14228 **Fax Area Code:* 888 ■ *TF:* 877-495-8938	877-495-8938	253-6254*	393
First Republic Bank 111 Pine St San Francisco CA 94111 *NYSE: FRC* ■ *TF:* 800-392-1400 ■ *Web:* www.firstrepublic.com	415-392-1400	392-1413	70
First Republic Corp of America 302 Fifth Ave Ste 6 New York NY 10001 *NYSE: FRPC*	212-279-6100	629-6848	655
First Resource Computer Inc 590 Reservoir Ave Cranston RI 02910 *Web:* www.frcomputers.com	401-941-2500		175
First Run Features 630 Ninth Ave Ste 1213 New York NY 10036 *TF:* 800-229-8575 ■ *Web:* www.firstrunfeatures.com	212-243-0600	989-7649	511
First Savings Bank 2804 N Telshor Blvd Las Cruces NM 88011 *TF:* 800-555-6895 ■ *Web:* www.firstsavingsbanks.com	575-521-7931		70
First Security Bank of Missoula 1704 Dearborn PO Box 4506 Missoula MT 59801 *TF:* 888-782-3115 ■ *Web:* www.fsbmsla.com	406-728-3115		70
First Security Bank of Sleepy Eye 100 Main St E PO Box 469 Sleepy MN 56085 *TF:* 800-535-8440 ■ *Web:* www.firstsecuritybanks.com	507-794-3911	794-5140	70
First Security Company Inc 212 Third Ave NW Hickory NC 28601 *Web:* firstsecuritycompany.com	828-322-4171	322-5094	390
First Sentinel Bank 315 Railroad Ave Richlands VA 24641 *Web:* firstsentinelbank.com	276-963-0836		70
First Shore Federal 106-108 S Div St PO Box 4248 Salisbury MD 21803 *TF:* 800-634-6309 ■ *Web:* www.firstshorefederal.com	410-546-1101	546-9590	71
First Signal LLC 1750 Enterprise Way SE Ste 107 Marietta GA 30067 *Web:* www.firstsignal.com	770-988-8744		647
First South Bancorp Inc 1311 Carolina Ave Washington NC 27889 *NASDAQ: FSBK* ■ *TF:* 888-993-7664 ■ *Web:* www.firstsouthnc.com	252-946-4178	946-3873	360-2
First Southern Bank 301 S Ct St Florence AL 35630 *TF General:* 800-625-7131 ■ *Web:* www.firstsouthern.com	256-718-4200	718-4296	360-2
First State Ballet Theatre 818 N Market St Wilmington DE 19801 *Web:* www.firststateballet.com	302-658-7897		573-1
First State Bank 730 Harry Sauner Rd Hillsboro OH 45133 *TF General:* 800-987-2566 ■ *Web:* www.fsb4me.com	937-393-9170		360-2
First State Bank 708 Azalea Dr PO Box 506 Waynesboro MS 39367 **Fax Area Code:* 601 ■ *TF:* 866-408-3582 ■ *Web:* www.firststatebnk.com	866-408-3582	735-0231*	70

Company	Phone	Fax	Class
First State Bank & Trust Co 1005 E 23rd St .... Fremont NE 68025 *TF:* 888-674-4344 ■ *Web:* www.firststatebankandtrust.com	402-721-2500		70
First State Bank of Kansas City 650 Kansas Ave .... Kansas City KS 66105 *TF:* 800-883-1242 ■ *Web:* www.cfbkc.com	913-371-1242	371-7516	70
First State Heritage Park 102 S State St .... Dover DE 19901 *Web:* www.destateparks.com/heritagepark	302-739-9194	739-6264	565
First Student Inc 600 Vine St .... Cincinnati OH 45202 *TF:* 800-367-5690 ■ *Web:* www.firststudentinc.com	513-241-2200		109
First Sun EAP 2700 Middleburg Dr Ste 312 .... Columbia SC 29204 *Web:* www.FirstSunEAP.com	803-376-2668		463
First Supply LLC 6800 Gisholt Dr .... Madison WI 53713 *TF:* 800-236-9795 ■ *Web:* www.1supply.com	608-222-7799	223-6621	612
First Surgical Partners Inc 411 First St .... Bellaire TX 77401 *Web:* www.firstsurgicalpartners.com/first-street-surgical-center.html	713-665-1111		787
First Tennessee Bank 165 Madison Ave .... Memphis TN 38103 *TF:* 800-382-5465 ■ *Web:* www.firsttennessee.com	901-523-4883		70
First Texas Bank 501 E Third St .... Lampasas TX 76550 *TF:* 866-220-1598 ■ *Web:* www.firstexbank.com	512-556-3691	556-6104	70
First Titan Energy LLC 495 Grand Blvd Ste 206 .... Miramar Beach FL 32550	850-269-7267		536
First to The Finish Inc 1325 N Broad St .... Carlinville IL 62626 *TF:* 800-747-9013 ■ *Web:* www.firsttothefinish.com	800-747-9013		711
First Tool Corp 612 Linden Ave .... Dayton OH 45403 *TF:* 800-771-1707 ■ *Web:* www.firsttoolcorp.com	937-254-6197	254-0625	757
First Trinity Financial Corp 7633 E 63rd Pl Ste 230 .... Tulsa OK 74133 *Web:* www.firsttrinityfinancial.com	918-249-2438		360-2
First Truck Centre Inc 11313 170 St .... Edmonton AB T5M3P5 *TF:* 888-882-8530 ■ *Web:* www.firsttruck.ca	780-413-8800		57
First Tryon Securities LLC 1355 Greenwood Cliff Ste 401 .... Charlotte NC 28204 *Web:* www.firsttryon.com	704-372-6118		690
First Unitarian Church of Philadelphia 2125 Chestnut St .... Philadelphia PA 19103 *Web:* www.philauu.org	215-563-3980	563-4209	50-1
First United Bank & Trust 19 S Second St .... Oakland MD 21550 *NASDAQ: FUNC* ■ **Fax Area Code:* 301 ■ **Fax:* Hum Res ■ *TF:* 888-692-2654 ■ *Web:* www.mybank4.com	888-692-2654	334-5784*	360-2
First UNUM Life Insurance Co 2211 Congress St .... Portland ME 04122 *TF:* 800-633-7491 ■ *Web:* www.unum.com	207-575-2211		391-2
First Utah BanCorp 3826 South 2300 East .... Salt Lake City UT 84109 *Web:* firstutahbank.com	801-272-9454		70
First Wave Aviation LLC 5440 S 101st E Ave .... Tulsa OK 74146	918-622-0007	280-0484	20
First West Virginia Bancorp Inc 1701 Warwood Ave .... Wheeling WV 26003 *NYSE: FWV* ■ *TF:* 800-732-0330 ■ *Web:* snl.com	304-277-1100		360-2
First Western Advisors 6440 Millrock Dr .... Salt Lake City UT 84121 *TF:* 800-937-3500 ■ *Web:* www.fwainvest.com	801-930-6500		463
First Western Bank & Trust PO Box 1090 .... Minot ND 58702 *TF:* 800-688-2584 ■ *Web:* bankfirstwestern.com	701-852-3711	857-7195	70
First Whitney Bank & Trust 223 Chestnut St .... Atlantic IA 50022 *Web:* firstwhitneybank.com	712-243-3195		70
Firstbase Services Ltd 34609 Delair Rd .... Abbotsford BC V2S2E1 *TF:* 800-758-2922 ■ *Web:* www.firstbase.ca	604-850-5334		344
FirstCare 1901 W Loop 289 Ste #9 .... Lubbock TX 79407 *TF:* 800-884-4901 ■ *Web:* www.firstcare.com	806-784-4300		391-2
FirstCom Music 1325 Capital Pkwy Ste 109 .... Carrollton TX 75006 *TF Cust Svc:* 800-858-8880 ■ *Web:* www.firstcom.com	972-446-8742	242-6526	525
FirstEnergy Corp 76 S Main St .... Akron OH 44308 *NYSE: FE* ■ *TF:* 800-633-4766 ■ *Web:* www.firstenergycorp.com	800-633-4766		360-5
Firstexpress Inc 1135 Freightliner Dr .... Nashville TN 37210 **Fax Area Code:* 615 ■ *TF:* 800-848-9203 ■ *Web:* firstexpress.com	800-848-9203	244-1448*	780
FirstFed Bancorp Inc 1630 Fourth Ave N PO Box 340 .... Bessemer AL 35020 *TF:* 800-436-5112 ■ *Web:* www.firstfedbessemer.com	205-428-8472	428-8652	360-2
FirstFuel Software Inc 420 Bedford St Ste 200 .... Lexington MA 02420 *TF:* 800-425-4081 ■ *Web:* www.firstfuel.com	781-862-6500		387
FirstGiving Inc 100 Cambridge Park Dr .... Cambridge MA 02210 *TF:* 800-687-8505 ■ *Web:* www.firstgiving.com	800-687-8505		387
Firsthand Capital Management Inc 150 Almaden Blvd Ste 1250 .... San Jose CA 95113 *Web:* www.firsthandcapital.com	408-886-7096		401
FirstHealth Hospice 5 Aviemore Dr .... Pinehurst NC 28374 *TF:* 800-496-1742 ■ *Web:* www.firsthealth.org	910-715-6000		371
FirsTier Bank (Kimball NE) 115 S Walnut .... Kimball NE 69145 *Web:* www.firstierbanks.com	308-235-4633		70
First-Knox National Bank 1 S Main St .... Mount Vernon OH 43050 *TF:* 800-837-5266 ■ *Web:* www.firstknox.com	740-399-5500		70
Firstline Business Systems Inc 211 E 11th St Ste 101 .... Vancouver WA 98660 *TF:* 800-318-9806 ■ *Web:* firstline-online.com	360-695-3138		535
FirstOption Staffing 8918 Tesoro Dr Ste 500 .... San Antonio TX 78217 *Web:* www.firstoptionstaffing.com	210-733-3700	733-3711	260
FirstPoint Inc 225 Commerce Pl .... Greensboro NC 27401 *Web:* www.firstpointresources.com	336-378-6300		393
Firstrust Savings Bank 15 E Ridge Pike 4th Fl .... Conshohocken PA 19428 *TF:* 800-220-2265 ■ *Web:* www.firstrust.com	610-941-9898	941-5544	70

Company	Phone	Fax	Class
FirstService Corp 1140 Bay St 1st Service Bldg Ste 4000 .... Toronto ON M5S2B4 *TSE: FSV* ■ *Web:* www.firstservice.com	416-960-9500	960-5333	185
Firstwave Technologies Inc 99 MedTech Dr .... Batavia NY 14020 *TF:* 800-540-6061 ■ *Web:* www.firstwavetechnologies.com	678-672-3112		178-11
Fisc Investment Services Corp 1849 Clairmont Rd .... Decatur GA 30033 *TF:* 800-241-3203 ■ *Web:* www.palmeragency.com	404-321-1212		690
FISCA (Financial Service Centers of America Inc) 21 Main St 1st Fl .... Hackensack NJ 07602 *Web:* www.fisca.org	201-487-0412	487-3954	49-2
Fischbach Gallery 210 11th Ave .... New York NY 10001 *Web:* www.fischbachgallery.com	212-759-2345		42
Fischbein Co 151 Walker Rd .... Statesville NC 28625 *Web:* www.fischbein.com	704-871-1159	872-3303	547
Fischer Cunnane & Assoc Ltd 11 Turner Ln .... West Chester PA 19380 *Web:* www.fischercunnane.com	610-431-1003		2
Fischer Deb (Sen R - NE) 454 Russell Senate Office Bldg .... Washington DC 20510 *Web:* www.fischer.senate.gov	202-224-6551	228-1325	342-2
Fischer Environmental Service Inc 1980 Surgi Dr .... Mandeville LA 70448 *TF:* 800-391-2565 ■ *Web:* www.fischerenv.com	800-391-2565		577
Fischer International Systems Corp 9045 Strada Stell Ct Ste 201 .... Naples FL 34109 *TF Tech Supp:* 800-776-7258 ■ *Web:* www.fisc.com	239-643-1500	643-3772	178-1
Fischer Special Manufacturing Co 1188 Industrial Rd .... Cold Spring KY 41076 *TF:* 800-990-6664 ■ *Web:* www.fischerspecial.com	859-781-1400	781-4702	621
Fischer Tool & Die Corp 7155 Industrial Dr .... Temperance MI 48182 *Web:* www.fischertool.com	734-847-4788	847-5027	757
Fiserv Credit Processing Services Ste 100 901 International Pkwy .... Lake Mary FL 32746	407-829-4200		463
Fiserv Inc 255 Fiserv Dr PO Box 979 .... Brookfield WI 53008 *NASDAQ: FISV* ■ *TF Sales:* 800-872-7882 ■ *Web:* www.fiserv.com	262-879-5000		69
Fiserv Lending Solutions 455 S Gulph Rd Ste 125 .... King of Prussia PA 19406 *Web:* www.fiserv.com	610-337-8686	337-7206	178-4
Fiserv Mortgage Products 3575 Moreau Ct Ste 2 .... South Bend IN 46628 *Web:* fiserv.com	574-282-3300		178-11
Fisgard Capital Corp 3378 Douglas St .... Victoria BC V8Z3L3 *TF:* 866-382-9255 ■ *Web:* www.fisgard.com	250-382-9255		690
Fish 442 King St .... Charleston SC 29403 *Web:* www.fishrestaurantcharleston.com	843-722-3474	937-0406	671
Fish & Richardson PC 1 Marina Park Dr .... Boston MA 02110 *TF:* 800-818-5070 ■ *Web:* www.fr.com	617-542-5070	542-8906	428
Fish City Grill 445 Coneflower Dr .... Garland TX 75040 *Web:* www.fishcitygrill.com	972-675-1600		671
Fish Enterprises 905 S Fair Oaks Ave .... Pasadena CA 91105 *Web:* www.fishenterprises.com	626-773-8800	773-8820	187
Fish House, The 600 S Barracks St .... Pensacola FL 32502 *Web:* greatsouthernrestaurants.com	850-470-0003	470-0694	671
Fish House, The 4919 N University St .... Peoria IL 61614 *Web:* fishhousepeoria.com	309-691-9358		671
Fish Market 105 King St .... Alexandria VA 22314 *Web:* www.fishmarketva.com	703-836-5676		671
Fish Oven & Equipment Corp 120 W Kent Ave .... Wauconda IL 60084 *TF:* 877-526-8720 ■ *Web:* www.fishoven.com	847-526-8686		298
Fish Window Cleaning Services Inc 200 Enchanted Pkwy .... Manchester MO 63021 *TF:* 877-707-3474 ■ *Web:* www.fishwindowcleaning.com	636-779-1500	530-7856	310
Fishbait Marketing Llc 1968 Long Creek Rd .... Wadmalaw Island SC 29487 *Web:* fishbaitmarketing.com	843-557-0535	557-0536	463
Fishbeck Thompson Carr & Huber Inc 1515 Arboretum Dr SE .... Grand Rapids MI 49546 *Web:* www.ftch.com	616-575-3824		261
Fishbio Environmental LLC 180 E Fourth St Ste 160 .... Chico CA 95928 *Web:* www.fishbio.com	530-892-9686		192
Fishbowl Brew Pub & Cafe 515 Jefferson St SE .... Olympia WA 98501 *Web:* www.fishbrewing.com/brewpub	360-943-3650		671
Fisher & Arnold Inc 9180 Crestwyn Hills Dr .... Memphis TN 38125 *TF:* 888-583-9724 ■ *Web:* www.fisherarnold.com	901-748-1811		194
Fisher & Ludlow Tru-Weld Grating 2000 Corporate Dr Ste 400 .... Wexford PA 15090 *TF:* 800-334-2047 ■ *Web:* www.nucorgrating.com	724-934-5320		491
Fisher & Paykel Appliances Inc 5900 Skylab Rd .... Huntington Beach CA 92647 **Fax Area Code:* 800 ■ *TF:* 888-936-7872 ■ *Web:* www.fisherpaykel.com	888-936-7872	547-1971*	36
Fisher & Paykel Healthcare Inc 173 Technology Dr Ste 100 .... Irvine CA 92618 *TF:* 800-446-3908 ■ *Web:* www.fphcare.co.nz	949-453-4000	453-4001	250
Fisher Air Heating & Air Conditioning Services 239 Viking Ave .... Brea CA 92821 *Web:* fisherair.com	714-529-9600		189-10
Fisher Athletic Equipment Inc 2060 Cauble Rd .... Salisbury NC 28144 *TF:* 800-438-6028 ■ *Web:* www.fisherathletic.com	704-636-5713		711
Fisher Auction Company Inc 2112 E Atlantic Blvd Ste 210 .... Pompano Beach FL 33060 *Web:* www.fisherauction.com	954-942-0917		655
Fisher Auto Parts 512 Greenville Ave PO Box 2248 .... Staunton VA 24401 *TF:* 800-622-6997 ■ *Web:* www.fisherautoparts.com	540-885-8901		61
Fisher Barton South Carolina Inc 100 Industrial Blvd .... Fountain Inn SC 29644 *Web:* www.fisherbarton.com	864-862-3138		488
Fisher Bio Svc Inc 14665 Rothgeb Dr .... Rockville MD 20850 *Web:* www.fisherbioservices.com	301-315-8460		587

	Phone	Fax	Class
Fisher Canvas Products Inc 415 St Mary St .... Burlington NJ 08016 *TF:* 800-892-6688 ■ *Web:* www.fishercanvas.com	800-892-6688		733
Fisher College 118 Beacon St. .... Boston MA 02116 **Fax:* Admissions ■ *TF:* 866-266-6007 ■ *Web:* www.fisher.edu	617-236-8800	236-5473*	162
Fisher Communications Inc 140 Fourth Ave N Ste 500. .... Seattle WA 98109 *NASDAQ: FSCI* ■ *Web:* www.sbgi.net	206-404-7000		738
Fisher Container Corp 1111 Busch Pkwy .... Buffalo Grove IL 60089 *TF:* 800-837-2247 ■ *Web:* www.fishercontainer.com	847-541-0000	541-0075	548
Fisher Controls International Inc 205 S Ctr St PO Box 190 .... Marshalltown IA 50158 *Web:* www.emerson.com	641-754-3011	754-2830	789
Fisher Corp 1625 W Maple Rd. .... Troy MI 48084 *Web:* www.fisherco.com	248-280-0808		489
Fisher County PO Box 368 .... Roby TX 79543 *TF:* 800-388-8075 ■ *Web:* www.co.fisher.tx.us	325-776-2401	776-3274	338
Fisher Dachs Assoc 22 W 19th St 6th Fl. .... New York NY 10011 *Web:* www.fda-online.com	212-691-3020		722
Fisher Development Inc 601 California St Ste 300 .... San Francisco CA 94108 *Web:* www.fisherinc.com	415-228-3060		186
Fisher Electric Technology 2801 72nd St N .... Saint Petersburg FL 33710 *Web:* www.fisherelectric.com	727-345-9122		247
Fisher Engineering 50 Gordon Dr .... Rockland ME 04841 *Web:* www.fisherplows.com	207-701-4200		516
Fisher Foods Mktg Inc 5215 Fulton Dr NW. .... Canton OH 44718 *Web:* www.fishersfoods.com	330-497-3000		297-8
Fisher Group Inc 4517 W 1730 S .... Salt Lake City UT 84115 *TF:* 800-365-8920 ■ *Web:* www.fishergroupinc.com	800-365-8920		393
Fisher Grove State Park 17290 Fishers Ln .... Frankfort SD 57440 *Web:* gfp.sd.gov	605-472-1336		565
Fisher Hawaii 450 Cooke St .... Honolulu HI 96813 *Web:* www.fisherhawaii.net	808-524-8770		535
Fisher Home Furnishings 2175 N Main St .... Logan UT 84341 *Web:* www.fisherhf.com	435-753-1018		321
Fisher Honey Co 1 Belle Ave Bldg 21 .... Lewistown PA 17044 *Web:* www.fisherhoney.com	717-242-4373		296-24
Fisher House Inc 7323 Hwy 90 W Ste 107. .... San Antonio TX 78227 *Web:* www.fisherhouseinc.org	210-673-7500		372
Fisher International Inc 50 Water St. .... Norwalk CT 06854 *Web:* www.fisheri.com	203-854-5390	854-5070	194
Fisher Investments 13100 Skyline Blvd. .... Woodside CA 94062 *TF:* 800-550-1071 ■ *Web:* www.fi.com	800-550-1071		401
Fisher Island Club & Resort 1 Fisher Island Dr. .... Miami FL 33109 *TF Resv:* 800-537-3708 ■ *Web:* www.fisherislandclub.com	305-535-6000	535-6003	669
Fisher Lynch Capital 2929 Campus Dr Ste 420 .... San Mateo CA 94403 *Web:* www.fisherlynch.com	650-287-2700	287-2701	792
Fisher Manufacturing Co PO Box 60 .... Tulare CA 93275 *TF:* 800-421-6162 ■ *Web:* www.fisher-mfg.com	800-421-6162	832-8238	609
Fisher Meats Inc 85 Front St N .... Issaquah WA 98027 *TF:* 800-561-3357 ■ *Web:* fischermeatsnw.com	425-392-3131	392-0168	296-26
Fisher Printing Inc 8640 S Oketo Ave .... Bridgeview IL 60455 *TF:* 800-366-0006 ■ *Web:* fisherprinting.com	708-598-1500		687
Fisher Products LLC 1320 W 22nd Pl .... Tulsa OK 74107 *TF:* 800-848-5759 ■ *Web:* www.fisherproductsllc.com	918-582-2204		757
Fisher Research Laboratory Inc 1465H Henry Brennan Ste H. .... El Paso TX 79936 *TF:* 800-685-5050 ■ *Web:* www.fisherlab.com	915 225 0333	225-0336	472
Fisher Sand & Gravel Co 3948 First ST SW .... Underwood ND 58576 *TF:* 800-932-8740 ■ *Web:* www.fisherind.com	701-442-5600		503-4
Fisher Science Education 4500 Turnberry Dr .... Hanover Park IL 60133 *TF:* 800-955-1177 ■ *Web:* www.fishersci.com	800-766-7000	955-0740	243
Fisher Scientific Company Inc 112 Colonnade Rd .... Ottawa ON K2E7L6 *TF:* 800-234-7437 ■ *Web:* www.fishersci.ca	613-226-8874	226-7658	419
Fisher Space Pen Co 711 Yucca St .... Boulder City NV 89005 *TF:* 800-102-7366 ■ *Web:* www.spacepen.com	702-293-3011	293-6616	571
Fisher Tank Co 3131 W Fourth St .... Chester PA 19013 *TF:* 800-220-3270 ■ *Web:* www.fishertank.com	610-494-7200	485-0157	91
Fisher Textiles Inc 139 Business Pk Dr .... Indian Trail NC 28079 *TF:* 800-554-8886 ■ *Web:* www.fishertextiles.com	704-821-8870	821-8880	745-6
Fisher Theatre 3011 W Grand Blvd. .... Detroit MI 48202 *TF:* 800-982-2787 ■ *Web:* www.broadwayindetroit.com	313-872-1000		572
Fisher Vista LLC 119 Marina Ave .... Aptos CA 95003 *Web:* www.fishervista.com	831-685-9700		5
Fisher-Barton Inc 1040 S 12th St. .... Watertown WI 53094 *Web:* www.fisherbarton.com	920-261-0131		484
Fisheries Museum of the Atlantic 68 Bluenose Dr PO Box 1363 .... Lunenburg NS B0J2C0 *TF:* 866-579-4909 ■ *Web:* museum.novascotia.ca	902-634-4794	634-8990	520
Fisheries Supply Co 1900 N Northlake Way .... Seattle WA 98103 *TF:* 800-426-6930 ■ *Web:* www.fisheriessupply.com	206-632-4462	634-4600	770
Fisherman's Island State Park Bells Bay Rd PO Box 456 .... Charlevoix MI 49720 *Web:* www.michigandnr.com	231-547-6641		565
Fisherman's Market 830 W Seventh Ave .... Eugene OR 97402 *Web:* eugenefishmarket.com	541-484-2722		671
Fisherman's Market & Grill 235 S Indian Canyon Dr .... Palm Springs CA 92262 *Web:* www.fishermans.com	760-327-1766		671
Fisherman's Wharf Inn 22 Commercial St. .... Boothbay Harbor ME 04538 *Web:* fishermanswharfinn.com	207-633-5090	633-5092	379
Fishermen's Memorial State Park 1011 Point Judith Rd .... Narragansett RI 02882 *Web:* www.riparks.com	401-789-8374		565
Fishermen's Pride Processors 4510 S Alameda St. .... Vernon CA 90058 *Web:* www.neptunefoods.com	323-232-8300	232-8833	296-14
Fisher-Price Inc 636 Girard Ave .... East Aurora NY 14052 *TF:* 800-432-5437 ■ *Web:* www.fisher-price.com	716-687-3000		762
Fisher-Titus Medical Ctr (FTMC) 272 Benedict Ave .... Norwalk OH 44857 *TF:* 800-589-3862 ■ *Web:* www.fishertitus.org	419-668-8101		374-3
FishHound LLC 15720 Ventura Blvd Ste 220. .... Encino CA 91436 *TF:* 800-469-0224 ■ *Web:* www.scout.com/outdoors/fishhound	800-469-0224		387
Fishing Holdings, LLC PO Box 179 .... Flippin AR 72634 *Web:* www.rangerboats.com	870-453-2222		90
Fishkind & Associates Inc 12051 Corporate Blvd. .... Orlando FL 32817 *TF:* 800-314-4035 ■ *Web:* www.fishkind.com	407-382-3256		463
Fishman & Tobin Inc 4000 Chemical Rd Ste 500 Metroplex Corp Ctr-1 .... Plymouth Meeting PA 19462 *Web:* www.fishmantobin.org	610-828-8400		155-12
Fishman's Fabrics Inc 1101 S Des Plaines St .... Chicago IL 60607 *TF:* 800-258-9816 ■ *Web:* www.fishmansfabrics.com	312-922-7250	922-7402	270
Fishmonger's 806 W Main St .... Durham NC 27701	919-682-0128		671
Fishmonger's Seafood 1901 N Central Expy. .... Plano TX 75075 *TF:* 800-442-1162 ■ *Web:* www.fishmongersplano.com	972-423-3699		671
Fishtech 5802 W Dempster St .... Morton Grove IL 60053 *TF:* 800-487-0199 ■ *Web:* www.fishtechmg.com	847-966-5900		711
Fishtrap Lake State Park 2204 Fishtrap Rd .... Shelbiana KY 41562 *Web:* www.stateparks.com	502-564-2172		565
Fick Electric Co 111 TC Jester Blvd .... Houston TX 77007 *Web:* www.fiskcorp.com	713-868-6111	880-2918	189-4
Fisk University 1000 17th Ave N. .... Nashville TN 37208 *TF:* 888-702-0022 ■ *Web:* www.fisk.edu	615-329-8500	329-8774	166
Fiskars Brands Inc 7800 Discovery Dr .... Middleton WI 53562 *TF:* 866-348-5661 ■ *Web:* www2.fiskars.com	866-348-5661		222
Fiske Bros Refining Co 129 Lockwood St .... Newark NJ 07105 *TF:* 800-733-4755 ■ *Web:* www.lubriplate.com	973-589-9150	589-4432	541
Fiske Planetarium 2414 Regent Dr .... Boulder CO 80309 *TF:* 800-254-3768 ■ *Web:* www.colorado.edu	303-492-5002	492-1725	598
FIT (Forest Industries Telecommunications) 1565 Oak St .... Eugene OR 97401 *Web:* www.landmobile.com	541-485-8441	485-7556	49-20
Fit America MD 4864 Arthur Kill Rd. .... Staten Island NY 10309 *TF:* 800-940-7546 ■ *Web:* fitamerica.com	718-227-4980		810
Fitch & Associates LLC 303 Marshall Rd Ste G .... Platte City MO 64079 *TF:* 800-363-9127 ■ *Web:* www.fitchassoc.com	816-431-2600		463
Fitch Co 2201 Russell St .... Baltimore MD 21230 *TF:* 800-933-4824 ■ *Web:* www.fitchco.com	410-539-1953	727-2244	406
Fitch Inc 585 S Front St Ste 300 .... Columbus OH 43215 *Web:* www.fitch.com	614 885-3453	885-4289	195
Fitch Ratings Inc 1 State St Plaza. .... New York NY 10004 *TF:* 800-753-4824 ■ *Web:* www.fitchratings.com	212-908-0500		218
Fitchburg Public Library 610 Main St .... Fitchburg MA 01420 *Web:* fitchburgpubliclibrary.org	978-829-1783		434-3
Fitcorp 800 Boylston St .... Boston MA 02199 *TF:* 800-301-1231 ■ *Web:* www.fitcorp.com	617-262-2050		354
Fite Building Company Inc 3116 Sexton Rd SE Ste A .... Decatur AL 35603 *Web:* www.fitebuilding.com	256-353-5759		186
Fitelson Lasky Aslan & Couture Atty 551 Fifth Ave Rm 605 .... New York NY 10176 *Web:* agnesdemilledances.com	212-586-4700		428
Fitger's Brewery Complex 600 E Superior St .... Duluth MN 55802 *TF:* 888-348-4377 ■ *Web:* www.fitgers.com	218-722-8826	722-8826	671
Fitger's Brewery Museum 600 E Superior St .... Duluth MN 55802 *TF:* 888-348-4377 ■ *Web:* www.fitgers.com	218-722-8826	722-8826	520
Fitger's Inn 600 E Superior St .... Duluth MN 55802 *TF:* 888-348-4377 ■ *Web:* www.fitgers.com	218-722-8826	722-8826	379
Fitness Club Warehouse Inc 2210 S Sepulveda Blvd. .... Los Angeles CA 90064 *TF:* 800-348-4537 ■ *Web:* www.fitnessblowout.com	310-235-2040		711
Fitness Ctr 1914 Round Barn Rd .... Champaign IL 61821 *Web:* www.fitcen.com	217-356-1616		354
Fitness Depot 1808 Lower Roswell Rd .... Marietta GA 30068 *TF:* 800-974-6828 ■ *Web:* www.thefitnessdepot.com	770-971-6828		354
Fitness Formula Ltd 619 W Jackson .... Chicago IL 60661 *Web:* ffc.com	312-648-4666		354
Fitness Marketing Systems LLC 427 N Theard St 239. .... Covington LA 70433 *Web:* www.netprofitexplosion.com	504-723-9649		711
Fitness Rx for Men Magazine 21 Bennetts Rd .... Setauket NY 11733 *TF:* 800-653-1151 ■ *Web:* www.fitnessrxformen.com	631-751-9696	751-9699	457-13
Fitness Rx for Women Magazine 21 Bennetts Rd Ste101 .... Setauket NY 11733 *Web:* www.fitnessrxwomen.com	631-751-9696		457-13
Fitness Zone 3439 Colonnade Pkwy Se 800 .... Birmingham AL 35243 *TF:* 800-875-9145 ■ *Web:* www.fitnesszone.com	800-875-9145		711
Fitocracy Inc 51 E 12th St 4th Fl. .... New York NY 10003 *Web:* www.fitocracy.com	646-450-3029		387
FitOrbit Inc 11611 San Vicente Blvd Ste 515. .... Los Angeles CA 90049 *Web:* www.fitorbit.com	424-652-9650	652-9659	387
Fitt Telecommunications Inc 1740 W Sam Houston Pkwy N .... Houston TX 77043 *Web:* fittcom.com	281-497-8181		196

Name	Address	City	State	ZIP	Phone	Fax	Class	Other
Fittje Bros Printing Co	804 Garden of the Gods Rd	Colorado Springs	CO	80907	719-392-4286		627	*TF:* 800-232-5411 ■ *Web:* www.fittje.com
Fitts Roberts & Co PC	5718 Westheimer Rd Ste 800	Houston	TX	77057	713-260-5230		2	*Web:* www.fittsroberts.com
Fitz Chem Corp	450 E Devon Ave Ste 175	Itasca	IL	60143	630-467-8383	467-1183	146	*Web:* www.fitzchem.com
Fitz Enterprises Inc	232 NE Middlefield Rd	Portland	OR	97211	503-286-9310		579	*Web:* www.staroilco.net
Fitzgerald & Co	3333 Piedmont Rd 11th Fl	Atlanta	GA	30305	404-504-6900		4	*Web:* www.fitzco.com
Fitzgerald & Halliday Inc	416 Asylum St	Hartford	CT	06103	860-247-7200	247-7206	256	*Web:* www.fhiplan.com
Fitzgerald Auto Mall	10915 Georgia Ave	Wheaton	MD	20902	855-776-0552		57	*TF:* 855-776-0552 ■ *Web:* www.fitzmall.com
Fitzgerald Auto Mall Inc	114 Baughmans Ln	Frederick	MD	21702	301-696-9200		57	*Web:* www.fitzmall.com
Fitzgerald Contractors Inc	7103 St Vincent Ave	Shreveport	LA	71106	318-869-3262	865-9640	189-10	*TF:* 800-259-3264 ■ *Web:* www.fitzgeraldcontractors.com
Fitzgerald Electro-mechanical Company Inc	6 S Linden Ave Ste 4	South San Francisco	CA	94080	650-589-9935		610	*Web:* www.fitzgeraldemco.com
Fitzgerald Formliners Inc	1500 E Chestnut Ave	Santa Ana	CA	92701	714-547-6710		183	*Web:* www.formliners.com
Fitzgerald Hotel	620 Post St	San Francisco	CA	94109	415-775-8100		379	*Web:* www.fitzgeraldhotel.com
Fitzgerald Industries International Inc	30 Sudbury Rd Ste 1A N	Acton	MA	01720	978-371-6446		231	*Web:* www.fitzgerald-fii.com
Fitzgerald Theater	10 E Exchange St	Saint Paul	MN	55101	651-290-1200		572	*Web:* fitzgeraldtheater.publicradio.org
Fitzgeralds Casino & Hotel Tunica	711 Lucky Ln	Robinsonville	MS	38664	662-363-5825		133	*TF:* 888-766-5825 ■ *Web:* www.fitzgeraldstunica.com
Fitzmartin Inc	2917 Central Ave Ste 211	Homewood	AL	35209	205-322-1010		4	*Web:* fitzmartin.com
Fitzpatrick & Weller Inc	12 Mill St PO Box 490	Ellicottville	NY	14731	716-699-2393	699-2893	683	*TF:* 800-349-9099 ■ *Web:* www.fitzweller.com
Fitzpatrick Cella Harper & Scinto	1290 Ave of the Americas	New York	NY	10104	212-218-2100	218-2200	428	*Web:* www.fitzpatrickcella.com
Fitzpatrick Co	832 Industrial Dr	Elmhurst	IL	60126	630-530-3333	530-0832	298	*Web:* www.fitzmill.com
Fitzpatrick Container Co	800 E Walnut St	North Wales	PA	19454	215-699-3515		100	*Web:* www.fitzbox.com
Fitzpatrick Engineering Group PLLC	19520 W Catawba Ave Ste 311	Cornelius	NC	28031	704-987-9114		261	*Web:* www.fegstructural.com
Fitzpatrick Manhattan Hotel	687 Lexington Ave	New York	NY	10022	212-355-0100	355-1371	379	*TF:* 800-367-7701 ■ *Web:* www.fitzpatrickhotels.com
Fitzpatrick Michael G (Rep R - PA)	514 Cannon HOB	Washington	DC	20515	202-225-4276	225-9511	342-2	*Web:* fitzpatrick.house.gov
Five Below Inc	1818 Market St	Philadelphia	PA	19103	215-546-7909	546-8099	762	*TF:* 844-452-3569 ■ *Web:* www.fivebelow.com
Five Civilized Tribes Museum	1101 Honor Heights Dr	Muskogee	OK	74401	918-683-1701	683-3070	520	*Web:* www.fivetribes.org
Five Fishermen Restaurant & Grill, The	1740 Argyle St	Halifax	NS	B3J2B6	902-422-4421		671	*Web:* www.fivefishermen.com
Five K Computers & Internet Services	104 S Sixth Ave	Yakima	WA	98902	509-575-3600		177	*TF:* 800-433-5778 ■ *Web:* www.fivek.com
Five Mile Pet Clinic Ps	6825 N Country Homes Blvd	Spokane	WA	99208	509-326-3465		794	*Web:* www.healthypets.com
Five Sails Restaurant	999 Canada Pl Ste 410	Vancouver	BC	V6C3E1	604-844-2855	682-6321	671	*Web:* www.fivesails.ca
Five Star Computing Inc	6316 Saint Andrews Rd Ste C	Columbia	SC	29212	803-561-0050		396	*Web:* ncsetoff.org
Five Star Distributing Inc	4055 E Parl 30 Dr	Columbia City	IN	46725	260-244-3775		81-1	*Web:* www.fivestardistributing.net
Five Star Dodge	3068 Riverside Dr	Macon	GA	31210	478-474-3700		57	*Web:* www.fivestarcdjr.com
Five Star Electric of Houston Inc	19424 Pk Row Dr Ste 100	Houston	TX	77084	281-492-7090		518	*TF:* 888-492-7090 ■ *Web:* vfd.com
Five Star Food Service Inc	6005 Century Oaks Dr Ste 100	Chattanooga	TN	37416	423-643-2600		299	*Web:* www.fivestar-food.com
Five Star Industries Inc	1308 Wells St Rd	Du Quoin	IL	62832	618-542-5421		186	*Web:* www.5starind.com
Five Star International LLC	6100 Wattsburg Rd	Erie	PA	16509	814-825-6150		57	*Web:* fivestarinternational.com
Five Star Productions	42 N Swinton Ave	Delray Beach	FL	33444	561-279-7827		742	*Web:* www.swoolleyentertainment.com
Five Star Professional Maids	8714 N 52nd Ave	Omaha	NE	68152	402-502-3100		256	
Five Star Quality Care Inc	400 Centre St	Newton	MA	02458	617-796-8387	796-8385	451	*NYSE: FVE* ■ *TF:* 866-230-1286 ■ *Web:* www.fivestarseniorliving.com
Five Star Trucking Inc	4380 Glenbrook Rd	Willoughby	OH	44094	440-953-9300		780	*TF:* 800-321-3658 ■ *Web:* www.fivestartrucking.com
Five Towns College	305 N Service Rd	Dix Hills	NY	11746	631-424-7000		166	*Web:* www.ftc.edu
FiveStars Loyalty Inc	321 11th St	San Francisco	CA	94103	860-578-2770		195	*Web:* www.fivestars.com
FIX Flyer LLC	225 Broadway Ste 1600	New York	NY	10007	888-349-3593		251	*TF:* 888-349-3593 ■ *Web:* www.fixflyer.com
Fixation Marketing Inc	4340 East-West Hwy Ste 200	Bethesda	MD	20814	240-207-2009		195	*Web:* www.fixation.com
Fixture Exchange Corp	3000 W Pafford St	Fort Worth	TX	76110	817-429-2496		115	*TF:* 800-848-0732 ■ *Web:* fixturex.com
Fixtureworks LLC	33792 Doreka	Fraser	MI	48026	586-294-1188		454	*TF:* 888-794-8687 ■ *Web:* www.fixtureworks.net
Fizzano Bros Concrete Products Inc	1776 Chester Pk	Crum Lynne	PA	19022	610-833-1100	833-5347	183	*Web:* www.fizzano.com
FJ McLain State Park	18350 Hwy M-203	Hancock	MI	49930	906-482-0278		565	*Web:* www.michigandnr.com
FJC	520 Eighth Ave 20th Fl	New York	NY	10018	212-714-0001		305	*TF:* 888-448-3352 ■ *Web:* www.fjc.org
FJC Security Services Inc	275 Jericho Tpke	Floral Park	NY	11001	516-328-6000		693	*TF:* 888-832-6352 ■ *Web:* www.fjcsecurity.com
FJH Music Company Inc, The	2525 Davie Rd Ste 360	Davie	FL	33317	954-382-6061		95	*TF:* 800-262-8744 ■ *Web:* www.fjhmusic.com
Fkg Oil Co	721 W Main	Belleville	IL	62220	618-233-6754		204	*TF:* 800-873-3546 ■ *Web:* www.mymotomart.com
FL Crane & Sons Inc	508 S Spring St PO Box 428	Fulton	MS	38843	662-862-2172	862-2649	189-9	*TF:* 800-748-9523 ■ *Web:* www.flcrane.com
FL Emmert Co Inc	2007 Dunlap St	Cincinnati	OH	45214	513-721-5808	721-6087	447	*TF:* 800-441-3343 ■ *Web:* www.emmert.com
FL Roberts & Company Inc	93 W Broad St	Springfield	MA	01105	413-781-7444	781-4328	324	*TF:* 800-837-4966 ■ *Web:* www.flroberts.com
FL Smidth Inc	2040 Ave C	Bethlehem	PA	18017	610-264-6011	264-6170	470	*TF:* 800-523-9482 ■ *Web:* www.flsmidth.com
FLA (Fair Labor Assn)	1111 19th St NW Ste 401	Washington	DC	20036	202-898-1000	898-9050	48-5	*Web:* www.fairlabor.org
FLA (Forest Landowners Assn)	900 Cir 75 Pkwy Ste 205	Atlanta	GA	30339	404-325-2954	325-2955	48-13	*TF:* 800-325-2954 ■ *Web:* www.forestlandowners.com
Flack Steel Ltd	425 West Lakeside Ave Ste 200	Cleveland	OH	44113	216-456-0700		492	*Web:* www.flacksteel.com
Flackman Goodman & Potter	106 Prospect St	Ridgewood	NJ	07450	201-445-0500		2	*Web:* www.fgpcpa.com
Flad & Assoc	644 Science Dr	Madison	WI	53711	608-238-2661	238-6727	261	*Web:* www.flad.com
Flagel Huber Flagel and Co	3400 S Dixie Dr	Dayton	OH	45439	937-299-3400		2	*Web:* fhf-cpa.com
Flagler College	74 King St	Saint Augustine	FL	32084	904-829-6481		166	*TF Admissions:* 800-304-4208 ■ *Web:* www.flagler.edu
Flagler County	1769 E Moody Blvd Bldg 2	Bunnell	FL	32110	386-313-4000		338	*TF:* 800-829-4933 ■ *Web:* www.flaglercounty.org
Flagler County Chamber of Commerce	20 Airport Rd Ste C	Palm Coast	FL	32164	386-437-0106	437-5700	139	*Web:* www.flaglerchamber.org
Flagler County Public Library (FCPL)	2500 Palm Coast Pkwy NW	Palm Coast	FL	32137	386-446-6763		434-3	*TF:* 877-863-5244 ■ *Web:* www.flaglercounty.org
Flagpole	PO Box 1027	Athens	GA	30603	706-549-9523	548-8981	532-5	*Web:* www.flagpole.com
Flagship All Suites Resort	60 N Maine Ave	Atlantic City	NJ	08401	609-343-7447		379	*TF:* 800-647-7890 ■ *Web:* www.fantasearesorts.com
Flagship Converters Inc	205 Shelter Rock Rd	Danbury	CT	06810	203-792-0034	797-0410	608	*Web:* www.flagshipconverters.com
Flagship Facility Services Inc	1050 N Fifth St	San Jose	CA	95112	408-977-0155		104	*Web:* www.flagshipinc.com
Flagship Fire Inc	1500 15th Ave dr e	Palmetto	FL	34221	941-723-7230		138	*TF:* 866-242-3307 ■ *Web:* www.flagshipfire.com
Flagship Investment Group Inc	3939 W Ridge Rd Ste A-103	Erie	PA	16506	814-835-1150		690	*Web:* raymondjames.com
Flagship Marinas Acquisitions LLC	950 E Paces Ferry Rd Ste 820	Atlanta	GA	30326	770-965-7605	965-7804	31	
Flagship Press Inc	150 Flagship Dr	North Andover	MA	01845	978-975-3100	975-0635	627	*TF:* 800-733-1520 ■ *Web:* www.flagshippress.com
Flagship Properties Corp	1 Greenway Plaza Ste 750	Houston	TX	77046	713-623-6000		653	*Web:* flagshipco.com
Flagship Ventures	1 Memorial Dr 7th Fl	Cambridge	MA	02142	617-868-1888	868-1115	792	*Web:* www.flagshipventures.com
Flagstaff Chamber of Commerce	101 W Rt 66	Flagstaff	AZ	86001	928-774-4505	779-1209	139	*TF:* 800-842-7293 ■ *Web:* www.flagstaffchamber.com
Flagstaff City Hall	211 W Aspen Ave	Flagstaff	AZ	86001	928-774-5281	779-7696	337	*Web:* www.flagstaff.az.gov
Flagstaff City-Coconino County Public Library System	300 W Aspen Ave	Flagstaff	AZ	86001	928-213-2330		434-3	*TF:* 800-379-0065 ■ *Web:* www.flagstaffpubliclibrary.org

Phone | Fax | Class

Flagstaff Convention & Visitors Bureau
323 W Aspen Ave ... Flagstaff AZ 86001 928-779-7611 556-1305 206
TF: 800-217-2367 ■ *Web:* www.flagstaffarizona.org
Flagstaff House 1138 Flagstaff Rd ... Boulder CO 80302 303-442-4640 442-8924 671
Web: www.flagstaffhouse.com
Flagstaff Medical Ctr
1200 N Beaver St ... Flagstaff AZ 86001 928-779-3366 374-3
Web: www.flagstaffmedicalcenter.com
Flagstaff Pulliam Airport
6200 S Pulliam Dr ... Flagstaff AZ 86001 928-556-1234 556-1288 27
TF: 800-463-1389 ■ *Web:* www.flagstaff.az.gov
Flagstaff Symphony Orchestra
113 E Aspen Ave # A ... Flagstaff AZ 86001 928-774-5107 774-5109 573-3
TF: 888-520-7214 ■ *Web:* www.flagstaffsymphony.org
Flagstar Bank FSB 5151 Corporate Dr ... Troy MI 48098 248-312-2000 70
TF: 800-945-7700 ■ *Web:* www.flagstar.com
Flagstop Corp 11031 Ironbridge Rd ... Chester VA 23831 804-768-0090 62-1
Web: www.flagstopcarwash.com
FlagZone LLC 105A Industrial Dr ... Gilbertsville PA 19525 800-976-4201 258
TF: 800-976-4201 ■ *Web:* www.theflagzone.com
Flaherty & Collins Properties Inc
8900 Keystone Crossing Ste 1200 ... Indianapolis IN 46240 317-816-9300 656
Web: flco.com
Flair Communications Agency Inc
214 W Erie St ... Chicago IL 60654 312-943-5959 9
Web: flairagency.com
FLAIR Flexible Packaging Corp
4100 72 Ave SE ... Calgary AB T2C2C1 403-207-3226 358
TF: 800-465-1914 ■ *Web:* www.flairpackaging.com
Flakeboard America Ltd
515 River Crossing Dr Ste 110 ... Fort Mill SC 29715 905-475-9686 820
Web: www.flakeboard.com
Flambeau Inc 15981 Valplast Rd ... Middlefield OH 44062 440-632-1631 632-1581 604
TF: 800-457-5252 ■ *Web:* www.flambeau.com
Flambeau River State Forest
W1613 County Rd ... Winter WI 54896 715-332-5271 565
Web: dnr.wi.gov
Flamboro Downs Ltd 967 Hwy 5 ... Hamilton ON L9H5E2 905-627-3561 642
Web: www.flamborodowns.com
Flamborough Chamber of Commerce
7 Innovation Dr Ste 227 ... Flamborough ON L9H7H9 905-689-7650 689-1313 137
Web: www.flamboroughchamber.ca
Flame Control Coatings LLC
4120 Hyde Park Blvd ... Niagara Falls NY 14305 716-282-1399 481
Web: www.flamecontrol.com
Flame Enterprises Inc
21500 Gledhill St ... Chatsworth CA 91311 818-700-2905 700-9168 246
TF: 800-854-2255 ■ *Web:* www.flamecorp.com
Flame Metals Processing Corp
12450 Ironwood Cir ... Rogers MN 55374 763-428-2596 428-3689 484
Web: flamemetals.com
Flame Retardancy News
49 Walnut Pk Bldg 2 ... Wellesley MA 02481 781-489-7301 253-3933 531-12
TF: 866-285-7215 ■ *Web:* www.bccresearch.com
Flame Spray Inc
4674 Alvarado Canyon Rd ... San Diego CA 92120 619-283-2007 567
Web: www.flamesprayinc.com
Flamenco Vivo Carlota Santana
4 W 43rd St Ste 608 ... New York NY 10036 212-736-4499 573-1
TF: 800-600-3168 ■ *Web:* flamenco-vivo.org
Flamers Charbroiled Hamburgers
1515 International Pkwy Ste 2013 ... Heathrow FL 32746 407-574-8363 670
TF: 866-749-4889 ■ *Web:* www.flamersgrill.com
Flamingo 2777 Fourth St ... Santa Rosa CA 95405 707-545-8530 378
Web: www.flamingoresort.com
Flamingo Gardens 3750 S Flamingo Rd ... Davie FL 33330 954-473-2955 473-1738 97
TF: 800-435-7352 ■ *Web:* www.flamingogardens.org
Flamingo Grille 7050 N Kings Hwy ... Myrtle Beach SC 29572 843-449-5388 671
TF: 800-930-0104 ■ *Web:* flamingogrill.com
Flamingo Las Vegas/O'Shea's Casino
3555 Las Vegas Blvd S ... Las Vegas NV 89109 702-733-3111 378
Web: www.flamingolasvegas.com
Flamingo Resort Hotel & Conference Ctr
2777 Fourth St ... Santa Rosa CA 95405 707-545-8530 669
TF: 800-848-8300 ■ *Web:* www.flamingoresort.com
Flamingo Seismic Solutions
4815 S Harvard Ste 401 ... Tulsa OK 74135 918-492-3773 538
Web: www.flamingoseismic.com
Flanagan Industries 25 Mill St ... Glastonbury CT 06033 860-633-9474 22
Web: www.flanaganindustries.com
Flanagan Instruments Inc
633 Village Ln N ... Mandeville LA 70471 985-626-3786 475
Web: www.flanagan.com
Flanagan's Restaurant & Pub
6525 Covington Rd ... Fort Wayne IN 46804 260-432-6666 671
Web: www.eatatflanagans.com
Flanary Group Inc, The
701 Decatur Ave North ... Golden Valley MN 55427 763-545-4564 390
Web: theflanarygroup.com
Flanders Corp
531 Flanders Filters Rd ... Washington NC 27889 252-946-8081 946-3425 18
OTC: FLDR ■ *TF:* 800-637-2803 ■ *Web:* www.flanderscorp.com
FLANDERS Inc
8101 Baumgart Rd PO Box 23130 ... Evansville IN 47724 812-867-7421 518
TF: 855-875-5888 ■ *Web:* www.flandersinc.com
Flanders Provision Company LLC
1104 Gilmore St ... Waycross GA 31501 912-283-5191 297-9
Web: www.flandersprovision.com
Flandrau Science Ctr & Planetarium
1601 E University Blvd ... Tucson AZ 85719 520-621-4516 621-8451 520
Web: www.flandrau.org
Flandrau State Park 1300 Summit Ave ... New Ulm MN 56073 507-233-9800 565
Web: www.dnr.state.mn.us
Flanigan's Enterprises Inc
5059 NE 18th Ave ... Fort Lauderdale FL 33334 954-377-1961 670
NYSE: BDL ■ *TF:* 800-833-5239 ■ *Web:* www.flanigans.net
Flans & Weiner Inc
16200 Ventura Blvd Ste 417 ... Encino CA 91436 818-501-4888 652
Web: flansweiner.com

Phone | Fax | Class

Flare Industries Inc
16310 Bratton Lnn Bldg 3 Ste 350 ... Austin TX 78728 512-836-9473 237
Web: www.flareindustries.com
Flash Foods Inc 215 Pendleton St ... Waycross GA 31501 912-285-4011 297-8
Web: www.flashfoods.com
Flash Market Inc
105 W Harrison St ... West Memphis AR 72301 870-732-2242 579
Web: flashmarketinc.com
Flash Technology Corp
332 Nichol Mill Ln ... Franklin TN 37067 615-503-2000 529
TF: 888-313-5274 ■ *Web:* www.spx.com
Flashbanc LLC
185 NW spanish river blvd ... Boca Raton FL 33431 561-278-8888 138
TF: 800-808-1622 ■ *Web:* www.flashbanc.com
Flashes Publishers Inc 595 Jenner Dr ... Allegan MI 49010 269-673-2141 673-4761 637-8
Web: www.flashespublishers.com
Flashman Studios LLC
4280 26Th St ... San Francisco CA 94131 415-826-7654 195
Web: www.flashmanstudios.com
Flaster Greenberg
1810 Chapel Ave W ... Cherry Hill NJ 08002 856-661-1900 428
Web: www.flastergreenberg.com
Flat Branch Pub & Brewing Co
115 S Fifth St ... Columbia MO 65201 573-499-0400 671
Web: www.flatbranch.com
Flat Rock Metal Inc (FRM)
26601 W Huron River Dr PO Box 1090 ... Flat Rock MI 48134 734-782-4454 782-5640 485
Web: www.frm.com
Flat Rock Playhouse
2661 Greenville Hwy ... Flat Rock NC 28731 828-693-0731 572
TF: 866-732-8008 ■ *Web:* www.flatrockplayhouse.org
Flat Top Grill 5201 W War Memorial Dr ... Peoria IL 61615 309-693-9966 671
Web: www.flattopgrill.com
Flathead Convention & Visitors Bureau
15 Depot Pk ... Kalispell MT 59901 406-756-9091 257-2500 206
TF: 800-543-3105 ■ *Web:* www.fcvb.org
Flathead County 800 S Main St ... Kalispell MT 59901 406-758-5503 758-5861 338
Web: flathead.mt.gov
Flathead Electric Co-op Inc
2510 Hwy 2 E ... Kalispell MT 59901 406-751-4483 245
TF: 800-735-8489 ■ *Web:* www.flatheadelectric.com
Flathead Lake Lodge & Ranch
150 Flathead Lodge Rd ... Bigfork MT 59911 406-837-4391 760
TF: 800-548-4487 ■ *Web:* flatheadlakelodge.com
Flathead Travel Service 500 Main St ... Kalispell MT 59901 406-752-8700 772
Web: www.flatheadtravel.com
Flathead Valley Community College
777 Grandview Dr ... Kalispell MT 59901 406-756-3822 756-3815 162
TF: 800-313-3822 ■ *Web:* www.fvcc.edu
Libby 225 Commerce Way ... Libby MT 59923 406-293-2721 293-5112* 162
**Fax:* Admissions ■ *TF:* 800-313-3822 ■ *Web:* www.fvcc.edu
Flatiron Constructors Corp
385 Interlocken Crescent Ste 900 ... Broomfield CO 80021 303-485-4050 485-3922 188-4
Web: www.flatironcorp.com
FlatIron Crossing
1 W Flatiron Crossing Dr ... Broomfield CO 80021 720-887-0888 50-6
Web: www.flatironcrossing.com
Flatiron Group, The
55 Fifth Ave Ste 2A ... New York NY 10003 212-966-8615 463
Web: www.theflatirongroup.com
Flatley Co, The
35 Braintree Hill Office Pk ... Braintree MA 02184 781-848-2000 655
Web: www.flatleyco.com
Flatness International Inc
104 Stony Mtn Rd ... Tunkhannock PA 18657 570-836-3527 836-1549 11-2
Web: www.flatnessintl.com
Flatout Inc 1422 Woodland Dr ... Saline MI 48176 734-944-4262 296
TF: 888-254-5480 ■ *Web:* www.flatoutbread.com
Flats Cat Boats 1565 Patton Rd ... Rosenberg TX 77471 281-342-3940 90
Web: www.flatscat.com
Flatter & Associates Inc
805 Princess Anne St Ste 201 ... Fredericksburg VA 22401 540-658-1922 261
Web: www.flatterassociates.com
Flavine North America Inc
10 Reuten Dr ... Closter NJ 07624 201-768-4190 768-2854 479
Web: www.flavine.com
Flavor & Extract Manufacturers Assn of the US (FEMA)
1101 17th St NW Ste 700 ... Washington DC 20036 202-293-5800 463-8998 49-6
Web: www.femaflavor.org
Flavor Dynamics Inc
640 Montrose Ave ... South Plainfield NJ 07080 908-822-8855 297-8
TF: 888-271-8424 ■ *Web:* www.flavordynamics.com
Flavorchem Corp 1525 Brook Dr ... Downers Grove IL 60515 630-932-8100 297-8
Web: www.flavorchem.com
Flavour Tech International LLC
66 Industrial Ave ... Little Ferry NJ 07643 201-440-3281 297-8
Flavurence Corp
1916 Tubeway Ave Commerce ... Commerce CA 90040 323-727-1957 296-37
Flax Art & Design
Fort Mason Ctr 2 Marina Blvd Bldg D ... San Francisco CA 94123 415-530-3510 45
TF: 844-352-9278 ■ *Web:* www.flaxart.com
Fleet Advantage LLC
401 E Las Olas Blvd 17th Fl ... Fort Lauderdale FL 33301 954-615-4400 177
Web: www.fleetadvantage.net
Fleet Brake Parts & Service Ltd
7707 54 St SE ... Calgary AB T2C4R7 403-279-8661 61
Web: www.fleetbrake.com
Fleet Engineers Inc
1800 E Keating Ave ... Muskegon MI 49442 231-777-2537 777-2720 516
TF Cust Svc: 800-333-7890 ■ *Web:* www.fleetengineers.com
Fleet Equipment Corp
567 Commerce St ... Franklin Lakes NJ 07417 201-337-3294 337-3294 516
TF: 800-631-0873 ■ *Web:* www.fcttrucks.com
Fleet Feet Inc 310 E Main St ... Carrboro NC 27510 919-942-3102 366
Web: fleetfeetsports.com
Fleet Landing Retirement Community
1 Fleet Landing Blvd ... Atlantic Beach FL 32233 904-246-9900 246-9900 672
TF General: 877-591-6547 ■ *Web:* www.fleetlanding.com

	Phone	Fax	Class
Fleet Management Solutions Inc 3426 Empresa Dr Ste 100 ... San Luis Obispo CA 93401 *Web:* www.fmsgps.com	805-787-0508		681
Fleet Products LLC 6510 Golden Groves Ln ... Tampa FL 33610 *Web:* www.fleetproductsfl.com	813-621-1734		61
Fleet Reserve Assn (FRA) 125 NW St ... Alexandria VA 22314 *TF:* 800-372-1924 ■ *Web:* www.fra.org	703-683-1400	549-6610	48-19
Fleet Safety Equipment Inc 1100 Hemlock St ... North Little Rock AR 72114 *Web:* www.fleetsafety.com	501-370-9500		647
FleetBoss Global Positioning Solutions Inc 241 O'Brien Rd ... Fern Park FL 32730 *TF:* 877-265-9559 ■ *Web:* www.fleetboss.com	407-265-9559	265-0365	735
Fleet-Fisher Engineering Inc 4250 E Camelback Rd Ste 410K ... Phoenix AZ 85018 *Web:* www.ffeng.com	602-264-3335		261
Fleetgistics Holdings Inc 2251 Lynx Ln Ste 7 ... Orlando FL 32804 *Web:* www.fleetgistics.com	407-843-6505		311
Fleetilla LLC 1745 Fritz Dr ... Trenton MI 48183 *Web:* www.fleetilla.com	734-676-5100		61
Fleetwash Inc 26 Law Dr ... Fairfield NJ 07004 **Fax Area Code:* 973 ■ *TF:* 800-847-3735 ■ *Web:* www.fleetwash.com	800-847-3735	882-0585*	62-1
Fleetway Inc 155 Chain Lake Dr Ste 200 ... Halifax NS B3S1B3 *TF:* 800-976-9819 ■ *Web:* www.fleetway.ca	902-494-5700		261
FleetWeather Group, The 2566 Route 52 ... Hopewell Junction NY 12533 *TF:* 800-704-2033 ■ *Web:* fleetweathergroup.com	845-226-8300		463
Fleetwing Corp 742 S Combee Rd ... Lakeland FL 33801 *TF:* 800-282-5678 ■ *Web:* www.fleetwingoil.com	863-665-7557		579
Fleetwood Group Inc 11832 James St ... Holland MI 49424 *TF:* 800-257-6390 ■ *Web:* www.fleetwoodgroup.com	616-396-1142		319-3
Fleetwood Homes of California Inc 7007 Jurupa Ave ... Riverside CA 92504 *TF:* 800-999-9265 ■ *Web:* www.fleetwoodhomes.com	951-351-2494		106
Fleetwood Homes of Idaho Inc 2611 E Comstock Ave ... Nampa ID 83687 *TF:* 800-334-8958 ■ *Web:* fleetwoodhomes.com	208-466-2438		505
Fleetwood Homes of Virginia Inc 90 Weaver St ... Rocky Mount VA 24151 *TF:* 866-890-6206 ■ *Web:* www.fleetwoodhomes.com	540-483-5171		505
Fleetwood Windows & Doors 395 Smitty Way ... Corona CA 92879 *Web:* www.fleetwoodusa.com	951-279-1070		362
Fleetwood-Fibre Packaging & Graphicsinc 15250 Don Julian Rd ... Industry CA 91745 *Web:* www.fleetwood-fibre.com	626-968-8503		548
Fleetwood-Signode 3624 West Lake Ave ... Glenview IL 60026 *TF:* 800-862-7997 ■ *Web:* www.fleetsig.com	847-657-5111	657-5116	559
Flegels Home Furnishings 870 Santa Cruz Ave ... Menlo Park CA 94025 *Web:* www.flegels.com	650-326-9661		321
Fleischmann Chuck (Rep R - TN) 2410 Rayburn HOB ... Washington DC 20515 *Web:* fleischmann.house.gov	202-225-3271	225-3494	342-2
Fleischmann Planetarium & Science Ctr University of Nevada ... Reno NV 89557 *Web:* planetarium.unr.nevada.edu	775-784-4811	784-4822	598
Fleishman-Hillard Inc 200 N Broadway ... Saint Louis MO 63102 *Web:* www.fleishmanhillard.com	314-982-1700		636
Fleming & Van Metre Advertising 600 W Germantown Pk ... Plymouth Meeting PA 19462 *Web:* thinkfvm.com	610-941-0395		4
Fleming College 200 Albert St S ... Lindsay ON K9V5E6 *TF:* 866-353-6464 ■ *Web:* flemingcollege.ca	705-324-9144		162
Fleming Door Products Ltd 101 Ashbridge Cir ... Woodbridge ON L4L3R5 *TF:* 800-263-7515 ■ *Web:* www.flemingdoor.com	800-263-7515		234
Fleming Mason Energy Co-op 1449 Elizaville Rd ... Flemingsburg KY 41041 *Web:* www.fmenergy.com	606-845-2661	845-1008	245
Fleming's Prime Steakhouse & Wine Bar 8970 University Ctr Ln ... San Diego CA 92122 *Web:* flemingssteakhouse.com	858-535-0078		671
Fleming's Prime Steakhouse & Wine Bar 2525 W End Ave ... Nashville TN 37203 *Web:* www.flemingssteakhouse.com	615-342-0131		671
Fleming's Prime Steakhouse & Wine Bar 4322 W Boy Scout Blvd ... Tampa FL 33607 *Web:* www.flemingssteakhouse.com	813-874-9463		671
Fleming's Prime Steakhouse & Wine Bar 217 Stuart St ... Boston MA 02116 *Web:* www.flemingssteakhouse.com	617-292-0808		671
Fleming's Prime Steakhouse & Wine Bar 20 South 400 West ... Salt Lake City UT 84101 *Web:* www.flemingssteakhouse.com	801-355-3704		671
Fleming's Prime Steakhouse & Wine Bar 6333 N Scottsdale Rd ... Scottsdale AZ 85250 *Web:* www.flemingssteakhouse.com	480-596-8265		671
Fleming's Prime Steakhouse & Wine Bar 103 Summit Blvd ... Birmingham AL 35243 *Web:* www.flemingssteakhouse.com	205-262-9463		671
Fleming's Prime Steakhouse & Wine Bar 140 Regency Pkwy ... Omaha NE 68114 *Web:* www.flemingssteakhouse.com	402-393-0811		671
Fleming's Prime Steakhouse & Wine Bar 8721 W Charleston Blvd ... Las Vegas NV 89117 *Web:* www.flemingssteakhouse.com	702-838-4774		671
Fleming's Prime Steakhouse & Wine Bar 2202 N West Shore Blvd Ste 500 ... Tampa FL 92660 *Web:* www.flemingssteakhouse.com	949-222-2223		671
Fleming-Lee Shue Inc 158 W 29th St 9th Fl ... New York NY 10001 *Web:* www.flemingleeshue.com	212-675-3225	675-3224	196
Flemington Fur Co 8 Spring St ... Flemington NJ 08822 *TF:* 800-990-8666 ■ *Web:* www.flemingtonfurs.com	908-782-2212		157-6

	Phone	Fax	Class
FLEOA (Federal Law Enforcement Officers Assn) 1100 Connecticut Ave NW Ste 900 ... Washington DC 20036 *Web:* www.fleoa.org	202-293-1550		49-7
Flesh Co 2118 59th St ... Saint Louis MO 63110 *TF:* 800-869-3330 ■ *Web:* www.fleshco.com	314-781-4400		110
Flesher & Associates Inc 445 S San Antonio Rd Ste 103 ... Los Altos CA 94022 *TF:* 800-704-9115 ■ *Web:* www.flesher.com	650-917-9900		260
Fletch's Inc 825 Charlevoix Ave PO Box 265 ... Petoskey MI 49770 *TF:* 888-764-0308 ■ *Web:* www.fletchs.com	231-347-9651		57
FletchAir Inc 103 Turkey Run Ln ... Comfort TX 78013 *TF:* 800-329-4647 ■ *Web:* www.fletchair.com	830-995-5900	995-5903	22
Fletcher & Assoc PC 424 E Jackson St ... Thomasville GA 31792 *Web:* fletchcpa.com	229-226-2241		2
Fletcher Csi LLC 237 Commerce St ... Williston VT 05495 *Web:* www.fletchercsi.com	802-660-9636		463
Fletcher Free Public Library 235 College St ... Burlington VT 05401 *TF:* 800-942-4288 ■ *Web:* www.fletcherfree.org	802-863-3403	865-7227	434-3
Fletcher Granite Company Inc 534 Groton Rd ... Westford MA 01886 *Web:* www.fletchergranite.com	978-320-4129	692-1325	503-6
Fletcher Jones Imports 7300 W Sahara Ave ... Las Vegas NV 89117 *TF:* 888-927-3675 ■ *Web:* www.fjimports.com	702-364-2700		57
Fletcher Music Centers Inc 3966 Airway Cir ... Clearwater FL 33762 *TF:* 800-258-1088 ■ *Web:* www.fletchermusic.com	727-571-1088		526
Fletcher Spaght Inc 500 Boylston St ... Boston MA 02116 *Web:* www.fletcherspaght.com	617-247-6700	247-7757	792
Fletcher'S Medical Supplies Inc 6851 S Distribution Ave ... Jacksonville FL 32256 *TF:* 855-541-7809 ■ *Web:* fletchermedical.com	904-387-4481		363
Fletcher, Heald & Hildreth PLC 1300 N 17th St 11th Fl ... Arlington VA 22209 *Web:* www.fhhlaw.com	703-812-0400		428
Fletcher-Terry Company Inc 65 Spring Ln ... Farmington CT 06032 *TF Cust Svc:* 800-843-3826 ■ *Web:* www.fletcherviscom.com	860-677-7331	676-8858	758
Fletcher-Thompson Inc 3 Corporate Dr Ste 500 ... Shelton CT 06484 *Web:* www.fletcherthompson.com	203-225-6500		261
Fleur De Lait Foods Inc 400 S Custer Ave ... New Holland PA 17557	717-355-8580		296-5
Flex Checks Inc PO Box 141215 ... Grand Rapids MI 49514 *Web:* www.flexchecks.com	616-791-7900		2
Flex Foam 617 N 21st Ave ... Phoenix AZ 85009 *TF:* 800-266-3626 ■ *Web:* www.flexfoam.net	602-252-5819		131
Flex Hr 10700 Medlock Bridge Rd Ste 206 ... Johns Creek GA 30097 *TF:* 877-735-3947 ■ *Web:* www.flexhr.com	770-814-4225	814-4123	354
Flex Magazine 21100 Erwin St ... Woodland Hills CA 91367 *TF:* 877-527-8342 ■ *Web:* www.flexonline.com	412-235-0203		457-13
Flex N Gate Forming Technologies LLC 26269 Groesbeck Hwy ... Warren MI 48089	586-773-0800		454
Flex Technologies 5479 Gundy Dr PO Box 400 ... Midvale OH 44653 *TF:* 800-326-6206 ■ *Web:* www.flextechnologies.com	740-922-5992	922-4416	625
Flexan Corp 6626 W Dakin St ... Chicago IL 60634 *Web:* www.flexan.com	773-685-6446		677
Flexaust Co 1510 Armstrong Rd ... Warsaw IN 46580 **Fax Area Code:* 800 ■ *TF:* 800-343-0428 ■ *Web:* www.flexaust.com	574-267-7909	382-8464*	370
Flexbar Machine Corp 250 Gibbs Rd ... Islandia NY 11749 *TF:* 800-879-7575 ■ *Web:* www.flexbar.com	631-582-8440		697
Flex-Cable Inc 5822 N Henkel Rd ... Howard City MI 49329 *TF:* 800-245-3539 ■ *Web:* www.flexcable.com	231-937-8000	937-8091	816
Flexcell International Corp 437 Dimmocks Mill Rd Ste 28 ... Hillsborough NC 27278 *Web:* www.flexcellint.com	919-732-1591		596
Flexco Products Inc 2415 Bryant St ... Elkhart IN 46516 *Web:* www.flexcoproducts.com	574-294-2502		697
FLEXcon Company Inc 1 Flexcon Industrial Pk ... Spencer MA 01562 *Web:* www.flexcon.com	508-885-8200	885-8400	600
FlexEnergy Inc 30 New Hampshire Ave ... Portsmouth NH 03801 *Web:* www.flexenergy.com	603-430-7000		194
Flexfab LLC 1699 W M-43 Hwy ... Hastings MI 49058 *TF:* 800-528-9230 ■ *Web:* www.flexfab.com	269-945-2433	945-4802	370
Flexfirm Products Inc 2300 N Chico Ave ... South El Monte CA 91733 *Web:* www.flexfirmproducts.com	626-448-7627	579-5116	745-2
FlexHead Industries Inc 56 Lowland St ... Holliston MA 01746 *TF:* 800-829-6975 ■ *Web:* www.flexhead.com	508-893-9596		52
Flexi Display Marketing Inc 24669 Halsted Rd Ste ... Farmington Hills MI 48335 *TF:* 800-875-1725 ■ *Web:* www.flexidisplay.com	248-987-6400		195
Flexial Corp 1483 Gould Dr ... Cookeville TN 38506 *Web:* www.flexial.com	931-432-1853		401
Flexible Business Systems 380 Oser Ave ... Hauppauge NY 11788 *TF:* 800-427-4120 ■ *Web:* www.flexiblesystems.com	631-756-0404		180
Flexible Concepts 1620 Middlebury St ... Elkhart IN 46516 *Web:* www.flexibleconcepts.com	574-296-0941		75
Flexible Lifeline Systems Inc 14325 W Hardy Rd ... Houston TX 77060 *Web:* www.fall-arrest.com	832-448-2900		477
Flexible Materials Inc 1202 Port Rd ... Jeffersonville IN 47130 *TF:* 800-244-6492 ■ *Web:* www.flexwood.com	812-280-7000	280-7001	613
Flexible Packaging Assn (FPA) 971 Corporate Blvd Ste 403 ... Linthicum MD 21090 *Web:* www.flexpack.org	410-694-0800	694-0900	49-13
Flexible Plan Investments Ltd 3883 Telegraph Rd Ste 100 ... Bloomfield Hills MI 48302 *TF:* 800-347-3539 ■ *Web:* www.flexibleplan.com	248-642-6640		401

Company	City	State	ZIP	Phone	Fax	Class
Flexible Products Co 2600 Auburn Ct *Web:* www.flexible-products.com	Auburn Hills	MI	48326	248-852-5500	852-8620	677
Flexible Resources Inc 304 Main Ave Ste 299 *Web:* www.flexibleresources.com	Norwalk	CT	06851	203-351-1180		260
Flexible Steel Lacing Co 2525 Wisconsin Ave *TF:* 800-323-3444 ■ *Web:* www.flexco.com	Downers Grove	IL	60515	630-971-0150		207
Flexible Technologies Inc 528 Carwellyn Rd *TF:* 800-459-7747 ■ *Web:* www.flexibletechnologies.com	Abbeville	SC	29620	800-459-7747		370
Flexible-Montisa 323 Acorn St *TF Cust Svc:* 800-875-6836 ■ *Web:* www.montisawork.com	Plainwell	MI	49080	269-924-0730	685-9195	319-1
Flexicell Inc 10463 Wilden Dr *Web:* flexicell.com	Ashland	VA	23005	804-550-7300		261
Flexicon Corp 2400 Emrick Blvd *TF:* 888-353-9426 ■ *Web:* www.flexicon.com	Bethlehem	PA	18020	610-814-2400		547
Flexicore of Texas 8634 McHard Rd *Web:* www.flexicoreoftexas.com	Houston	TX	77053	281-437-5700	437-8913	183
FlexiInternational Software Inc 2 Enterprise Dr *OTC: FLXI* ■ *TF:* 800-353-9492 ■ *Web:* www.flexi.com	Shelton	CT	06484	203-925-3040		178-1
Flexitallic Ltd 6915 Hwy 225 *Web:* www.flexitallic.com	Deer Park	TX	77536	281-604-2400		326
Flexi-Van Leasing Inc 251 Monroe Ave *TF:* 866-965-9288 ■ *Web:* www.flexi-van.com	Kenilworth	NJ	07033	908-276-8000	276-7666	264-5
Flexlink Systems Inc 6580 Snowdrift Rd Ste 200 *Web:* www.flexlink.com	Allentown	PA	18106	610-973-8200	973-8345	385
Flexmag Industries Inc 107 Industry Rd *TF:* 800-543-4426 ■ *Web:* www.arnoldmagnetics.com	Marietta	OH	45750	740-374-8024	374-5068	458
Flex-N-Gate Corp 5663 E Nine Mile Rd *TF:* 800-398-1496 ■ *Web:* www.flex-n-gate.com	Warren	MI	48091	800-398-1496		60
Flexo Impressions 8647 Eagle Creek Pkwy *TF:* 800-752-2357 ■ *Web:* www.flexoimpressions.com	Savage	MN	55378	952-884-9442		627
Flexo Transparent Inc 28 Wasson St *Web:* www.flexotransparent.com	Buffalo	NY	14210	716-825-7710		815
Flexographic Technical Assn (FTA) 3920 Veterans Memorial Hwy Ste 9 *TF:* 800-242-5216 ■ *Web:* www.flexography.org	Bohemia	NY	11716	631-737-6020	737-6813	49-16
Flexospan Steel Buildings Inc 253 Railroad St *TF:* 800-245-0396 ■ *Web:* www.flexospan.com	Sandy Lake	PA	16145	724-376-7221		106
Flexpak Corp 3720 W Washington St *Web:* www.nelipak.com	Phoenix	AZ	85009	602-269-7648		601
Flexpak Inc 1894 W 2425 S *Web:* www.flexpak.net	Woods Cross	UT	84087	801-956-0696		96
Flex-Pay Business Services Inc 723 Coliseum Dr Ste 200 *TF:* 800-457-2143 ■ *Web:* www.flex-pay.com	Winston-Salem	NC	27106	336-773-0128		194
FlexPlay Technologies Inc 3350 Peachtree Rd One Capital City Plaza Ste 1150 *Web:* www.flexplay.com	Atlanta	GA	30326	404-835-9900		173-8
FlexPrint Inc 2845 N Omaha St *TF:* 800-366-3888 ■ *Web:* www.flexprintinc.com	Mesa	AZ	85215	480-360-0011		589
FlexShopper Inc 2700 N Military Trl Ste 200 *TF:* 855-353-9289 ■ *Web:* www.flexshopper.com	Boca Raton	FL	33431	866-950-6669		23
FLEXSTAR Packaging Inc 13320 River Rd *TF:* 800-663-1177 ■ *Web:* www.flexstar.ca	Richmond	BC	V6V1W7	604-273-9277		601
Flexstar Technology Inc 1965 Concourse Dr *Web:* www.flexstar.com	San Jose	CA	95131	408-643-7000		407
Flexsteel Industries Inc 385 Bell St *NASDAQ: FLXS* ■ *TF:* 800-318-9806 ■ *Web:* www.flexsteel.com	Dubuque	IA	52001	563-556-7730		319-2
Flexsys America LP 260 Springside Dr *TF:* 800-455-5622 ■ *Web:* www.eastman.com	Akron	OH	44333	330-666-4111		676
Flexsystems USA Inc 727 W Main St *TF:* 800-656-7645 ■ *Web:* www.flexsystems.com	El Cajon	CA	92020	619-401-1858		599
Flextech Inc 7300 W 27th St *Web:* www.flextechfoam.com	St. Louis Park	MN	55426	952-345-0012		601
Flextron Industries Inc 720 Mt Rd *TF:* 800-633-2181 ■ *Web:* www.flextronindustries.com	Aston	PA	19014	610-459-4600	459-5379	548
Flexy Foam 12315 Colony Ave	Chino	CA	91710	909-465-5555		344
Flex-Y-Plan Industries Inc 6960 W Ridge Rd *TF Cust Svc:* 800-458-0552 ■ *Web:* www.fyp.com	Fairview	PA	16415	814-474-1565	474-2129	319-1
Flicker, Kerin, Kruger & Bissada LLP 120 B Santa Margarita Ave *Web:* www.fkkblaw.com	Menlo Park	CA	94025	650-289-1400		428
Flickinger Ctr for Performing Arts 1110 New York Ave *Web:* www.flickingercenter.com	Alamogordo	NM	88310	575-437-2202		572
Flight 93 National Memorial *National Park Service* PO Box 911 *Web:* www.nps.gov/flni/index.htm	Shanksville	PA	15560	814-893-6322	443-2180	564
Flight Deck Restaurant & Lounge 2680 Aerial Way *Web:* www.flightdeckrestaurant.com	Salem	OR	97302	503-581-5721		671
Flight Deck Specialists Inc 1288 Belmont Dr *Web:* www.flightdeckspecialists.com	Mcminnville	TN	37110	931-668-6761		22
Flight Dimensions International Inc 4835 Cordell Ave Ste 150 *TF:* 866-235-6870 ■ *Web:* www.flightexplorer.com	Bethesda	MD	20814	301-634-8201		21
Flight Director Inc 100 Michael Angelo Way *Web:* flightdirector.com	Austin	TX	78728	512-834-2000		770
Flight Landata Inc 250 Clark St	North Andover	MA	01845	978-682-7767		225
Flight Light Inc 2708 47th Ave *TF:* 800-806-3548 ■ *Web:* www.flightlight.com	Sacramento	CA	95822	916-394-2800		63
Flight Safety Foundation 801 N Fairfax St Ste 400 *Web:* www.flightsafety.org	Alexandria	VA	22314	703-739-6700	739-6708	49-21
Flight Systems Inc 505 Fishing Creek Rd *TF:* 800-403-3728 ■ *Web:* www.flightsystems.com	Lewisberry	PA	17339	717-932-9900		247
Flight Trak Inc 1872 Dover St *Web:* www.flighttrak.com	Broomfield	CO	80020	303-438-8640		196
FlightAware 8 Greenway Plaza Ste 1300 *TF:* 800-713-8570 ■ *Web:* www.flightaware.com	Houston	TX	77046	713-877-9010		19
Flightline Data Services Inc 138 Peachtree Ct *TF:* 800-659-9859 ■ *Web:* www.flightline.com	Fayetteville	GA	30215	770-487-3482		225
Flightline Group Inc 3256 Capital Cir SW *TF:* 800-226-4000 ■ *Web:* www.flightlinegroup.com	Tallahassee	FL	32310	850-574-4444	576-4210	63
Flightpath Inc 36 W 25Th St 8th Fl *Web:* www.flightpath.com	New York	NY	10010	212-674-5600		225
Flightsafety Services Corp 10770 E Briarwood Ave Ste 100 *Web:* www.flightsafety.com	Centennial	CO	80112	303-783-1023		21
Flightstar Corp 7 Airport Rd Willard Airport *TF:* 800-747-4777 ■ *Web:* www.flightstar.com	Savoy	IL	61874	217-351-7700	351-9843	13
FLIK Hotels & Conference Centers 3 International Dr 2nd Fl *Web:* www.flikccm.compass-usa.com	Rye Brook	NY	10573	914-935-5394		271
Flinchbaugh Engineering Inc 4387 Run Way *TF:* 866-967-5334 ■ *Web:* www.flinchbaughengineering.com	York	PA	17406	717-755-1900	840-3217	487
Flinn Broadcasting 6080 Mt Moriah Rd Ext *Web:* www.flinn.com	Memphis	TN	38115	901-375-9324		643
Flinn Foundation, The 1802 N Central Ave *Web:* www.flinn.org	Phoenix	AZ	85004	602-744-6800		305
Flint & Walling Inc 95 N Oak St *TF Sales:* 800-345-9422 ■ *Web:* www.flintandwalling.com	Kendallville	IN	46755	260-347-1600		641
Flint Children's Museum 1602 W University Ave *Web:* thefcm.org	Flint	MI	48504	810-767-5437	767-4936	521
Flint Cliffs Manufacturing Co 1600 Bluff Rd	Burlington	IA	52601	319-752-2781		273
Flint Community Schools 923 E Kearsley St *TF:* 800-227-6382 ■ *Web:* www.flintschools.org	Flint	MI	48503	810-760-1000		685
Flint Cultural Ctr Corp 1310 E Kearsley St *TF:* 800-214-7275 ■ *Web:* www.flintculturalcenter.com	Flint	MI	48503	810-237-7333		50-2
Flint Energies 3 S Macon St *TF:* 800-342-3616 ■ *Web:* www.flintenergies.com	Reynolds	GA	31076	478-847-3415		245
Flint Equipment Company - West Columbia 3464 Sunset Blvd *Web:* www.flintequipco.com	West Columbia	SC	29169	803-794-9340		190
Flint Group 33 S Third St Ste C *Web:* www.simmonsflint.com	Grand Forks	ND	58201	701-746-4573		7
Flint Hills Resources LP 4111 E 37th St N *Web:* www.fhr.com	Wichita	KS	67220	316-828-3477		579
Flint Hills Rural Electric Co-op Assn Inc 1564 S 1000 Rd *Web:* www.flinthillsrec.com	Council Grove	KS	66846	620-767-5144		245
Flint Institute of Arts 1120 E Kearsley St *TF:* 800-222-7270 ■ *Web:* www.flintarts.org	Flint	MI	48503	810-234-1695	234-1692	520
Flint Journal 200 E First St *TF Circ:* 800-875-6200 ■ *Web:* www.mlive.com	Flint	MI	48502	810-766-6100		532-2
Flint Machine Tools Inc 3710 Hewatt Ct *TF:* 800-984-2620 ■ *Web:* www.flintmachine.com	Snellville	GA	30039	770-985-2626		358
Flint Public Library 1026 E Kearsley St *Web:* fpl.info	Flint	MI	48502	810-232-7111		434-3
Flint River Mills Inc 1100 Dothan Rd *TF Cust Svc:* 800-841-8502 ■ *Web:* frmfeeds.com	Bainbridge	GA	39817	229-246-2232		447
Flint River Regional Library 800 Memorial Dr *Web:* frrls.net	Griffin	GA	30223	770-412-4770		434-3
Flint Surveying & Engineering Company Inc 5370 Miller Rd *TF:* 800-624-6089 ■ *Web:* fse.us	Swartz Creek	MI	48473	810-230-1333		261
Flintco LLC 1624 W 21st St *TF:* 800-947-2828 ■ *Web:* www.flintco.com	Tulsa	OK	74107	918-587-8451	582-7506	186
Flintridge Operating Foundation 236 W Mountain St Ste 106 *Web:* www.flintridge.org	Pasadena	CA	91103	626-449-0839		305
Flintridge Sacred Heart Academy 440 St Katherine Dr *Web:* www.fsha.org	La Canada	CA	91011	626-685-8333		622
Flip Publicity and Promotions 500 Bloor St W *Web:* www.flip-publicity.com	Toronto	ON	M5S1Y3	416-533-7710		6
Flippen Group, The 1199 Haywood Dr *TF:* 800-316-4311 ■ *Web:* www.flippengroup.com	College Station	TX	77845	979-693-7660		463
Flippo Lumber Corp 16415 Washington Hwy	Doswell	VA	23047	804-798-6616		683
FLIR Systems Inc 27700-A SW Pkwy Ave *NASDAQ: FLIR* ■ **Fax:* Sales ■ *TF:* 877-773-3547 ■ *Web:* www.flir.com	Wilsonville	OR	97070	503-498-3547	498-3904*	529
Flite Hockey Inc 3400 Ridgeway Dr Unit 2 *TF:* 800-275-5338 ■ *Web:* www.flitehockey.com	Mississauga	ON	L5L0A2	905-828-6030		711
Flixster Inc 208 Utah St 4th Fl *Web:* www.flixster.com	San Francisco	CA	94103	415-255-7215		174
FLM Graphics 123 Lehigh Dr *Web:* www.flmgraphics.com	Fairfield	NJ	07004	973-575-9450		588
Floataway Cafe 1123 Zonolite Rd Ste 15 *Web:* www.starprovisions.com	Atlanta	GA	30306	404-892-1414		671

				Phone	Fax	Class
Floating Island International Inc 10052 Floating Island Way *Web:* www.floatingislandinternational.com	Shepherd	MT	59079	406-373-5200		188
FlockTAG LLC 401 E Stadium Ste 106 *Web:* deals.flocktag.com	Ann Arbor	MI	48104	734-707-1250		5
Flodraulic Group Inc 3539 N 700 W *Web:* www.flodraulic.com	Greenfield	IN	46140	317-890-3700		358
Floe International Inc 48473 State Hwy 65 *Web:* www.floeintl.com	Mcgregor	MN	55760	218-426-3563		779
Flo-Form Industries Ltd 125 Hamelin St *Web:* www.floform.com	Winnipeg	MB	R3T3Z1	204-474-2334		115
Flood & Peterson Insurance Inc 4687 W 18th St *Web:* floodpeterson.com	Greeley	CO	80634	970-356-0123		390
Floodgate Entertainment LLC 55 Moody St Ste 31	Waltham	MA	02453	781-893-3500		174
Flook & Graham Pc 11 E Kansas St Ste 100 *Web:* flookandgraham.com	Liberty	MO	64068	816-792-0500		428
Floor Coverings International 5250 Triangle Pwy Ste 100 *TF Sales:* 800-955-4324 ■ *Web:* www.floorcoveringsinternational.com	Norcross	GA	30092	770-874-7600		290
Floor King Inc 10961 Research Blvd *Web:* floorking.net	Austin	TX	78759	512-346-7034		290
Floor Seal Technology Inc 1005 Ames Ave *Web:* www.floorseal.com	Milpitas	CA	95035	408-436-8181		291
FLOORgraphics Inc 200 American Metro Blvd	Hamilton Township	NJ	08619	609-528-9200		701
Flooring Sales Group 1251 First Ave S *TF:* 877-478-3577 ■ *Web:* www.greatfloors.com	Seattle	WA	98134	206-624-7800	622-8407	290
Floors Are Us Inc 2275 Seminole Ln	Charlottesville	VA	22901	434-978-4454		131
Floors by Foutch 5555 Woodland Hills Dr	Denton	TX	76208	940-383-4499		131
Flora Family Foundation, The 2121 Sand Hill Rd Ste 123 *Web:* www.florafamily.org	Menlo Park	CA	94025	650-233-1335		305
Flora Mfg & Distributing Ltd 7400 Fraser Park Dr *TF:* 888-436-6697 ■ *Web:* www.florahealth.com	Burnaby	BC	V5J5B9	604-436-6000		479
Floral Plant Growers LLC North 781 Curran Rd *Web:* www.naturalbeautygrowers.com	Denmark	WI	54208	920-863-2107		77
Floralawn Inc 734 S Combee Rd *Web:* www.floralawn.com	Lakeland	FL	33801	863-668-0494		776
Florance & Associates Consulting 1011 Hampshire Ln Ste 200 *Web:* floranceandassociates.com	Richardson	TX	75080	972-690-1909		196
Florence Area Chamber of Commerce 290 Hwy 101 *Web:* www.florencechamber.com	Florence	OR	97439	541-997-3128	997-4101	139
Florence Concrete Products Inc PO Box 5506 *Web:* www.florenceconcreteproducts.com	Florence	SC	29502	843-662-2549	667-0729	183
Florence Convention & Visitors Bureau 3290 W Radio Dr *TF General:* 800-325-9005 ■ *Web:* www.visitflo.com	Florence	SC	29501	843-664-0330	665-9480	206
Florence County 180 N Irby St *TF:* 800-523-3577 ■ *Web:* www.florenceco.org	Florence	SC	29501	843-665-3035	665-3070	338
Florence County 501 Lake Ave *Web:* www.florencecountywi.com	Florence	WI	54121	715-528-3201	528-4762	338
Florence County Library 509 S Dargan St *Web:* www.florencelibrary.org	Florence	SC	29506	843-662-8424	661-7544	434-3
Florence Eiseman company LLC 1966 S Fourth St *TF:* 800-558-9013 ■ *Web:* www.florenceeiseman.com	Milwaukee	WI	53204	800-558-9013		155-4
Florence Events Center 715 Quince St *TF:* 888-968-4086 ■ *Web:* www.ci.florence.or.us	Florence	OR	97439	541-997-1994	902-0991	205
Florence Motor Speedway 836 E Smith St *Web:* www.florencemotorspeedway.com	Timmonsville	SC	29161	843-346-7711		515
Florence National Cemetery 803 E National Cemetery Rd *TF:* 877-907-8585 ■ *Web:* www.cem.va.gov	Florence	SC	29506	843-669-8783	662-8318	136
Florence Savings Bank 85 Main St PO Box 60700 *Web:* www.florencebank.com	Florence	MA	01062	413-586-1300		70
Florence-Darlington Technical College 2715 W Lucas St *TF:* 800-228-5745 ■ *Web:* www.fdtc.edu	Florence	SC	29502	843-661-8324		800
Florence-Lauderdale Public Library (FLPL) 350 N Wood Ave *Web:* www.flpl.org	Florence	AL	35630	256-764-6564		434-3
Florens Container Services (USA) Ltd 275 Battery St Ste 800 *Web:* www.florens.com	San Francisco	CA	94111	415-348-2800		360-3
Florentine Opera Co 700 N Water St Ste 950 *TF:* 800-326-7372 ■ *Web:* www.florentineopera.org	Milwaukee	WI	53202	414-291-5700	291-5706	573-2
Flores Bill (Rep R - TX) 2440 Rayburn HOB *Web:* flores.house.gov	Washington	DC	20515	202-225-6105	225-0350	342-2
Flores Financial Services 314 Sage St Ste 100 *TF:* 800-782-7097 ■ *Web:* rflores.com	Lake Geneva	WI	53147	262-248-2771		251
Florestone Products Company Inc 2851 Falcon Dr *TF:* 800-446-8827 ■ *Web:* www.florestone.com	Madera	CA	93637	559-661-4171	661-2070	610
Floresville Independent School District 908 Tenth St *Web:* floresvilleathletics.us	Floresville	TX	78114	830-393-5300		685
Florexpo LLC 1960 Kellogg Ave *TF:* 800-830-3567 ■ *Web:* www.florexpo.com	Carlsbad	CA	92008	800-830-3567		708

Florida

				Phone	Fax	Class
Agriculture & Consumer Services Dept State Capitol PL-10 *Web:* www.freshfromflorida.com	Tallahassee	FL	32399	850-488-3022		339-10
Attorney General State Capitol PL-01 *TF:* 866-966-7226 ■ *Web:* myfloridalegal.com	Tallahassee	FL	32399	850-245-0140		339-10
Bill Status 111 W Madison St *Web:* www.flsenate.gov	Tallahassee	FL	32399	850-488-4371		433
Business & Professional Regulation Dept 2601 Blair Stone Rd *TF:* 866-532-1440 ■ *Web:* www.myfloridalicense.com/dbpr	Tallahassee	FL	32399	850-487-1395		339-10
Chief Financial Officer 200 E Gaines St *TF:* 877-693-5236 ■ *Web:* www.myfloridacfo.com	Tallahassee	FL	32399	850-413-3089		339-10
Citrus Dept 605 E Main St PO Box 9010 *Web:* www.floridacitrus.org	Bartow	FL	33830	863-272-8180		339-10
Colleges & Universities Div 325 W Gaines St Ste 1414 *TF:* 888-224-6684 ■ *Web:* www.fldoe.org	Tallahassee	FL	32399	850-245-3200	245-3233	339-10
Consumer Services Div 2005 Apalachee Pkwy **Fax Area Code:* 850 ■ *TF:* 800-435-7352 ■ *Web:* www.freshfromflorida.com	Tallahassee	FL	32399	800-435-7352	245-1330*	339-10
Corrections Dept 501 S Calhoun St *Web:* www.dc.state.fl.us	Tallahassee	FL	32399	850-488-5021		339-10
Cultural Affairs Div 329 N Meridian St *Web:* dos.myflorida.com/cultural	Tallahassee	FL	32301	850-254-6470	245-6454	339-10
Education Dept 325 W Gaines St Ste 1514 *TF:* 800-445-6739 ■ *Web:* www.fldoe.org	Tallahassee	FL	32399	850-245-0505	245-9667	339-10
Elder Affairs Dept 4040 Esplanade Way *Web:* www.elderaffairs.state.fl.us	Tallahassee	FL	32399	850-414-2000	414-2004	339-10
Emergency Management Div 605 Suwannee St *Web:* www.fdot.gov	Tallahassee	FL	32399	850-414-5336	488-7841	339-10
Environmental Protection Dept 3900 Commonwealth Blvd MS 49 *Web:* www.dep.state.fl.us	Tallahassee	FL	32399	850-245-2118	245-2128	339-10
Ethics Commission 3600 Maclay Blvd S Bldg E, Ste 200 *Web:* www.ethics.state.fl.us	Tallahassee	FL	32303	850-488-7864	488-3077	265
Financial Services Dept 200 E Gaines St *TF:* 800-342-2762 ■ *Web:* www.myfloridacfo.com	Tallahassee	FL	32399	850-413-3149		339-10
Fish & Wildlife Conservation Commission 620 S Meridian St *Web:* myfwc.com	Tallahassee	FL	32399	850-488-4676		339-10
Historical Resources Div 500 S Bronough St Ste 305 *Web:* www.flheritage.com	Tallahassee	FL	32399	850-245-6300	245-6435	339-10
Housing Finance Corp 227 N Bronough St Ste 5000 *Web:* www.floridahousing.org	Tallahassee	FL	32301	850-488-4197	488-9809	339-10
Information Technology Services 644 W Call St *Web:* www.its.fsu.edu	Tallahassee	FL	32306	850-644-4357		339-10
Insurance Regulation Office 200 E Gaines St *TF:* 800-342-2762 ■ *Web:* floir.com	Tallahassee	FL	32399	850-413-3140		339-10
Legislature 111 W Madison St *Web:* www.leg.state.fl.us	Tallahassee	FL	32399	850-488-4371		339-10
Lieutenant Governor State Capitol 400 S Monroe St *Web:* www.flgov.com	Tallahassee	FL	32399	850-488-7146	921-6114	339-10
Lottery Dept 250 Marriott Dr *Web:* www.flalottery.com	Tallahassee	FL	32301	850-487-7787	488-8049	452
Medical Quality Assurance Div 4052 Bald Cypress Way *Web:* www.floridahealth.gov	Tallahassee	FL	32399	850-488-0595	245-4791	339-10
Military Affairs Dept 82 Marine St *Web:* dma.myflorida.com	St. Augustine	FL	32084	904-823-0364		339-10
Office of the Governor 400 S Monroe St *Web:* www.flgov.com	Tallahassee	FL	32399	850-488-7146	922-9002	339-10
Parole Commission 4070 Esplanade Way *Web:* www.fcor.state.fl.us	Tallahassee	FL	32399	850-488-3417		339-10
Prepaid College Board PO Box 6567 **Fax Area Code:* 850 ■ **Fax:* Cust Svc ■ *TF:* 800-552-4723 ■ *Web:* www.myfloridaprepaid.com	Tallahassee	FL	32314	800-552-4723	309-1766*	725
Public Service Commission 2540 Shumard Oak Blvd *TF:* 800-342-3552 ■ *Web:* www.floridapsc.com	Tallahassee	FL	32399	850-413-6042		339-10
Recreation & Parks Div 3900 Commonwealth Blvd *TF Campground Resv:* 800-326-3521 ■ *Web:* www.floridastateparks.org	Tallahassee	FL	32399	850-245-2157		339-10
Secretary of State RA Gray Bldg 500 S Bronough St *TF:* 800-955-8771 ■ *Web:* dos.myflorida.com	Tallahassee	FL	32399	850-245-6500	245-6125	339-10
State Cts Administrator Office 500 S Duval St *Web:* www.flcourts.org	Tallahassee	FL	32399	850-922-5081		339-10
Student Financial Assistance Office 1940 N Monroe St Ste 70 *Web:* www.floridastudentfinancialaid.org	Tallahassee	FL	32303	850-410-5200	488-3612	725
Supreme Court 500 S Duval St *Web:* www.flcourts.org	Tallahassee	FL	32399	850-922-5081		339-10
Transportation Dept 605 Suwannee St *Web:* www.dot.state.fl.us	Tallahassee	FL	32399	850-414-5200		339-10
Veterans' Affairs Dept 11351 Ulmerton Rd Ste 311-K *Web:* www.floridavets.org	Largo	FL	33778	727-518-3202		339-10
Vital Records Bureau 1217 N Pearl St *Web:* www.floridahealth.gov	Jacksonville	FL	32202	904-359-6900		339-10

Phone | Fax | Class

Vocational Rehabilitation Services Div
4070 Esplanade Wayy — Tallahassee FL 32399 — 850-245-3399 — 339-10
TF: 800-451-4327 ■ *Web:* www.rehabworks.org

Workers' Compensation Div
200 E Gaines St — Tallahassee FL 32399 — 850-413-1609 — 339-10
Web: www.myfloridacfo.com

Florida A & M University
1700 Lee Hall Dr Rm G-7
Foote-Hilyer Administration Ctr — Tallahassee FL 32307 — 850-599-3000 — 599-3069 — 166
TF: 866-642-1198 ■ *Web:* www.famu.edu

Florida Agricultural Museum
7900 Old Kings Rd — Palm Coast FL 32137 — 386-446-7630 — 520
Web: www.myagmuseum.com

Florida Aquarium 701 Channelside Dr — Tampa FL 33602 — 813-273-4000 — 40
TF: 800-353-4741 ■ *Web:* www.flaquarium.org

Florida Aquastore & Utility Construction Inc
4722 NW Boca Raton Blvd Ste C-102 — Boca Raton FL 33431 — 561-994-2400 — 358
Web: www.florida-aquastore.com

Florida Assn of Realtors
7025 Augusta National Dr — Orlando FL 32822 — 407-438-1400 — 438-1411 — 656
TF: 800-669-4327 ■ *Web:* www.floridarealtors.org

Florida Association of Counties
100 S Monroe St — Tallahassee FL 32301 — 850-922-4300 — 138
TF: 800-375-3642 ■ *Web:* www.fl-counties.com

Florida Atlantic University (FAU)
777 Glades Rd — Boca Raton FL 33431 — 561-297-3000 — 297-2758* — 166
**Fax:* Admissions ■ *TF Admissions:* 800-299-4328 ■ *Web:* www.fau.edu

Davie 3200 College Ave — Davie FL 33314 — 954-236-1000 — 166
TF: 800-764-2222 ■ *Web:* www.fau.edu/broward/davie

Fort Lauderdale
111 E Las Olas Blvd — Fort Lauderdale FL 33301 — 954-236-1000 — 166

MacArthur 777 Glades Rd — Boca Raton FL 33431 — 561-799-8500 — 799-8721* — 166
**Fax:* Admissions ■ *Web:* www.fau.edu/jupiter

Treasure Coast 777 Glades Rd — Boca Raton FL 33431 — 772-873-3300 — 873-3304* — 166
**Fax:* Admissions ■ *TF:* 800-552-4723 ■ *Web:* www.fau.edu

Florida Bar 651 E Jefferson St — Tallahassee FL 32399 — 850-561-5600 — 561-1141 — 72
TF: 800-342-8060 ■ *Web:* www.floridabar.org

Florida Bar Journal
651 E Jefferson St — Tallahassee FL 32399 — 850-561-5600 — 681-3859 — 457-15
TF: 800-342-8060 ■ *Web:* www.floridabar.org

Florida Botanical Gardens
12520 Ulmerton Rd — Largo FL 33774 — 727-582-2100 — 97
Web: www.flbg.org

Florida Brick & Clay Company Inc (FBC)
1708 Turkey Creek Rd — Plant City FL 33567 — 813-754-1521 — 754-5469 — 291
Web: www.floridabrickandclay.com

Florida Business Interiors
767 Stirling Ctr Pl — Lake Mary FL 32746 — 407-805-9911 — 321
Web: www.4fbi.com

Florida Caverns State Park
3345 Caverns Rd — Marianna FL 32446 — 850-482-9598 — 565
Web: www.floridastateparks.org

Florida Chamber of Commerce
136 S Bronough St PO Box 11309 — Tallahassee FL 32302 — 850-521-1200 — 140
TF: 877-521-1230 ■ *Web:* www.flchamber.com

Florida Christian College
1011 Bill Beck Blvd — Kissimmee FL 34744 — 407-847-8966 — 206-2007* — 161
**Fax Area Code:* 321 ■ *TF:* 888-468-6322 ■ *Web:* johnsonu.edu/florida

Florida City Gas (FCG) 955 E 25th St — Hialeah FL 33013 — 800-993-7546 — 787
TF: 800-993-7546 ■ *Web:* www.floridacitygas.com

Florida Coast Equipment
9775 Boynton Beach Blvd — Boynton Beach FL 34104 — 561-369-0414 — 317
Web: www.floridacoasteq.com

Florida Coastal School of Law
8787 Bay Pine Rd — Jacksonville FL 32256 — 904-680-7700 — 680-7692* — 167-1
**Fax:* Admissions ■ *TF:* 877-210-2591 ■ *Web:* www.fcsl.edu

Florida College
119 N Glen Arven Ave — Temple Terrace FL 33617 — 813-988-5131 — 899-6772* — 166
**Fax:* Admissions ■ *TF:* 800-326-7655 ■ *Web:* www.floridacollege.edu

Florida College of Integrative Medicine
7100 Lake Ellenor Dr — Orlando FL 32809 — 407-888-8689 — 166
Web: www.fcim.edu

Florida Community College at Jacksonville
Downtown 101 State St W — Jacksonville FL 32202 — 904-633-8100 — 162
TF: 877-633-5950 ■ *Web:* www.fscj.edu

Kent 3939 Roosevelt Blvd — Jacksonville FL 32205 — 904-381-3400 — 162
TF: 800-700-2795 ■ *Web:* www.fccj.org

South 11901 Beach Blvd — Jacksonville FL 32246 — 904-646-2111 — 162
TF: 800-700-2795 ■ *Web:* www.fccj.org

Florida Cooling Supply Inc
1954 Carroll St — Clearwater FL 33765 — 727-449-1230 — 610
Web: www.flcoolingsupply.com

Florida Council Against Sexual Violence Inc
1820 E Park Ave Ste 100 — Tallahassee FL 32301 — 850-297-2000 — 41
TF: 888-956-7273 ■ *Web:* www.fcasv.org

Florida Crystals Corp
1 N Clematis St Ste 200 — West Palm Beach FL 33401 — 561-366-5100 — 366-5158 — 296-38
Web: www.floridacrystals.com

Florida Ctr for Addictions & Dual Disorders
100 W College Dr — Avon Park FL 33825 — 863-452-3858 — 452-3863 — 726
Web: tchsonline.org

Florida Custom Mold Inc 1806 Gunn Hwy — Odessa FL 33556 — 813-343-5080 — 711
Web: www.fla-mold.com

Florida Democratic Party
214 S Bronough St — Tallahassee FL 32301 — 850-222-3411 — 222-0916 — 616-1
TF: 855-352-7233 ■ *Web:* www.floridadems.org

Florida Dental Assn
1111 E Tennessee St — Tallahassee FL 32308 — 850-681-3629 — 561-0504 — 227
TF: 800-877-9922 ■ *Web:* www.floridadental.org

Florida Department of Corrections
8784 W US 27 — Mayo FL 32066 — 386-294-4500 — 829-4534* — 213
**Fax Area Code:* 904

Florida Detroit Diesel-Allison Inc
5040 University Blvd W — Jacksonville FL 32216 — 904-737-7330 — 385
TF: 888-812-4440 ■ *Web:* www.fdda.com

Florida Family Insurance Services LLC
27599 Riverview Ctr Blvd Ste 100
PO Box 136001 — Bonita Springs FL 34136 — 239-495-4700 — 391-4
TF: 888-850-4663 ■ *Web:* www.floridafamily.com

Florida Farm Bureau Casualty Insurance Co
5700 SW 34th St — Gainesville FL 32608 — 352-378-1321 — 374-1577 — 391-4
Web: floridafarmbureau.com

Florida Farm Bureau Insurance Cos
5700 SW 34th St — Gainesville FL 32608 — 352-378-1321 — 374-1577 — 391-4
TF: 866-275-7322 ■ *Web:* floridafarmbureau.com

Florida Fertilizer Company Inc
PO Box 1087 — Wauchula FL 33873 — 863-773-4159 — 276
Web: www.floridafertilizer.com

Florida Gateway College
149 SE College Pl — Lake City FL 32025 — 386-752-1822 — 754-4594* — 162
**Fax:* Admissions ■ *TF:* 800-261-2576 ■ *Web:* www.fgc.edu

Florida Grand Opera 8390 NW 25th St — Miami FL 33122 — 305-854-1643 — 856-1042 — 573-2
TF: 800-741-1010 ■ *Web:* www.fgo.org

Florida Handling Systems Inc
2651 State Rd 60 W — Bartow FL 33830 — 863-534-1212 — 358
TF: 800-664-3380 ■ *Web:* www.fhsinc.com

Florida Heritage Museum
167 San Marco Ave — Saint Augustine FL 32084 — 904-829-9729 — 520
TF: 800-268-7252 ■ *Web:* www.amtrakvacations.com

Florida Holocaust Museum
55 Fifth St S — Saint Petersburg FL 33701 — 727-820-0100 — 821-8435 — 520
TF: 800-388-4069 ■ *Web:* www.flholocaustmuseum.org

Florida Hospital Heartland Medical Ctr
4200 Sun 'n Lake Blvd — Sebring FL 33871 — 863-314-4466 — 402-3415 — 374-3
TF: 800-756-4447 ■ *Web:* floridahospital.com

Florida Hospital North Pinellas
1395 S Pinellas Ave — Tarpon Springs FL 34689 — 727-942-5000 — 374-3
TF: 800-558-6365 ■ *Web:* www.floridahospital.com

Florida Hospital Oceanside
264 S Atlantic Ave — Ormond Beach FL 32176 — 386-672-4161 — 374-3
TF: 800-558-6365 ■ *Web:* www.floridahospital.com

Florida Hospital Orlando
601 E Rollins St — Orlando FL 32803 — 407-303-2800 — 374-3
TF: 800-227-2345 ■ *Web:* www.floridahospital.com

Florida Hospital Zephyrhills
7050 Gall Blvd — Zephyrhills FL 33541 — 813-788-0411 — 374-3
TF: 800-558-6365 ■ *Web:* www.floridahospital.com

Florida Industrial Products Inc
1602 N 39th St — Tampa FL 33605 — 813-247-5356 — 610
Web: www.fiponline.com

Florida Institute of Technology
150 W University Blvd — Melbourne FL 32901 — 321-674-8000 — 674-8004* — 166
**Fax:* Admissions ■ *TF:* 800-888-4348 ■ *Web:* www.fit.edu

Florida Instructional Materials Ctr
5002 N Lois Ave — Tampa FL 33614 — 813-872-5281 — 95
Web: www.fimcvi.org

Florida International Museum
244 Second Ave N
St Petersburg College Downtown Ctr — Saint Petersburg FL 33701 — 727-341-7900 — 341-7908 — 520
Web: www.floridamuseum.org

Florida International University
11200 SW Eigth St — Miami FL 33199 — 305-348-2000 — 348-3648 — 166
TF: 800-677-6337 ■ *Web:* www.fiu.edu

Florida Keys Community College
5901 College Rd — Key West FL 33040 — 305-296-9081 — 292-5155* — 162
**Fax:* Admissions ■ *TF:* 866-567-2665 ■ *Web:* www.fkcc.edu

Florida Keys Electric Co-op Assn
91630 Overseas Hwy — Tavernier FL 33070 — 305-852-2431 — 853-5381 — 245
TF: 800-858-8845 ■ *Web:* www.fkec.com

Florida Mall
8001 S Orange Blossom Trl — Orlando FL 32809 — 407-851-6255 — 855-1827 — 460
Web: www.simon.com

Florida Mechanical LLC
3615 Fiscal Ct — Riviera Beach FL 33404 — 561-863-3606 — 610
Web: www.flamech.com

Florida Memorial University
15800 NW 42nd Ave — Miami Gardens FL 33054 — 305-626-3600 — 166
TF: 800-822-1362 ■ *Web:* www.fmuniv.edu

Florida Museum of Natural History
3215 Hull Rd — Gainesville FL 32611 — 352-392-1721 — 392-8783 — 520
TF: 800-595-7760 ■ *Web:* www.flmnh.ufl.edu

Florida National Cemetery
6502 SW 102nd Ave — Bushnell FL 33513 — 352-793-7740 — 793-9560 — 136
TF: 877-907-8585 ■ *Web:* www.cem.va.gov

Florida Newsclips LLC PO Box 2190 — Palm Harbor FL 34682 — 800-442-0332 — 736-5005* — 624
**Fax Area Code:* 727 ■ *TF:* 800-442-0332 ■ *Web:* www.newsclipsonweb.com

Florida Nurses Assn (FNA)
1235 E Concord St PO Box 536985 — Orlando FL 32853 — 407-896-3261 — 896-9042 — 533
Web: www.floridanurse.org

Florida Osteopathic Medical Association District 3 Inc
7855 Argyle Forest Blvd Ste 601 — Jacksonville FL 32244 — 904-406-3026 — 619-1080 — 533
Web: www.fomadistrict2.com

Florida Pest Control & Chemical Company Inc
116 NW 16th Ave — Gainesville FL 32601 — 352-376-2661 — 376-2791 — 577
Web: www.flapest.com

Florida Pharmacy Assn
610 N Adams St — Tallahassee FL 32301 — 850-222-2400 — 561-6758 — 585
Web: www.pharmview.com

Florida Pneumatic Manufacturing Corp
851 Jupiter Pk Ln — Jupiter FL 33458 — 561-744-9500 — 575-9134 — 759
TF: 800-327-9403 ■ *Web:* www.florida-pneumatic.com

Florida Power & Light Co (FPL)
700 Universe Blvd — Juno Beach FL 33408 — 561-697-8000 — 787
TF: 800-226-3545 ■ *Web:* www.fpl.com

Florida Presbyterian Homes
16 Lake Hunter Dr — Lakeland FL 33803 — 863-688-5521 — 672
TF: 866-294-3352 ■ *Web:* www.fphi.org

Florida Public Interest Research Group
926 E Pk Ave — Tallahassee FL 32301 — 850-224-3321 — 633
Web: www.floridapirg.org

Florida Public Utilities Co (FPUC)
401 S Dixie Hwy — West Palm Beach FL 33401 — 800-427-7712 — 787
TF: 800-427-7712 ■ *Web:* www.fpuc.com

Florida Repertory Theatre Inc
2267 Bay St — Fort Myers FL 33901 — 239-332-4665 — 720
TF: 877-787-8053 ■ *Web:* www.floridarep.org

Name / Address	City	State	Zip	Phone	Fax	Class
Florida Resources & Environmental Analysis Ctr *Florida State University* UCC 2200 FSU	Tallahassee	FL	32306	850-644-2007	644-7360	668
Web: www.freac.fsu.edu						
Florida Retail Federation Services Inc 227 S Adams St	Tallahassee	FL	32301	850-222-4082		138
Web: www.frf.org						
Florida School of the Arts 5001 St Johns Ave	Palatka	FL	32177	386-312-4300	312-4306	164
Web: floarts.org						
Florida Solar Energy Ctr 1679 Clearlake Rd	Cocoa	FL	32922	321-638-1000	638-1010	668
TF: 877-777-4778 ■ *Web:* www.fsec.ucf.edu						
Florida Southern College 111 Lake Hollingsworth Dr	Lakeland	FL	33801	863-680-4131	680-4120*	166
*Fax: Admissions ■ *TF Admissions:* 800-274-4131 ■ *Web:* www.flsouthern.edu						
Florida Sportsman Magazine 2700 S Kanner Hwy	Stuart	FL	34994	772-219-7400		457-20
Web: www.flsportsman.com						
Florida State College at Jacksonville *North* 4501 Capper Rd	Jacksonville	FL	32218	904-766-6500		162
Web: www.fccj.org						
Florida State Conference Center 555 W Pensacola St	Tallahassee	FL	32306	850-644-3801	644-2589	205
Web: alwayslearning.fsu.edu						
Florida State Prison 23916 NW 83rd Ave PO Box 800	Raiford	FL	32083	904-368-2500	368-2732	213
Web: dc.state.fl.us						
Florida State University College of Law 425 W Jefferson St	Tallahassee	FL	32306	850-644-3400	644-5487	167-1
Web: www.law.fsu.edu						
Florida State University College of Medicine 1115 W Call St	Tallahassee	FL	32306	850-644-1855	645-2846*	167-2
*Fax: Admissions ■ *Web:* www.med.fsu.edu						
Florida State University Museum of Fine Arts 530 W Call St Fine Arts Bldg	Tallahassee	FL	32306	850-644-6836	644-7229	520
TF: 800-953-2473 ■ *Web:* www.mofa.fsu.edu						
Florida State University Strozier Library Rm 314	Tallahassee	FL	32306	850-644-5211	644-5016*	434-6
*Fax: Admin ■ *Web:* www.lib.fsu.edu						
Florida State University, The 600 W College Ave	Tallahassee	FL	32306	850-644-4357		166
Web: www.fsu.edu						
Florida Surplus Lines Service Office 1441 Maclay Commerce Dr	Tallahassee	FL	32312	850-224-7676		41
TF: 800-562-4496 ■ *Web:* www.fslso.com						
Florida Technical College 12900 Challenger Pkwy	Orlando	FL	32826	407-447-7300	447-7301	800
TF General: 888-678-2929 ■ *Web:* www.ftccollege.edu						
Florida Theatre 128 E Forsyth St Ste 300	Jacksonville	FL	32202	904-355-5661	358-1874	572
TF: 800-734-4667 ■ *Web:* www.floridatheatre.com						
Florida Tile Industries Inc 998 Governors Ln Ste 300	Lexington	KY	40513	859-219-5200		751
TF Cust Svc: 800-352-8453 ■ *Web:* www.floridatile.com						
Florida Times-Union 1 Riverside Ave	Jacksonville	FL	32202	904-359-4111	359-4478	532-2
TF: 800-472-6397 ■ *Web:* jacksonville.com						
Florida Turbine Technologies Inc 1701 Military Trl Ste 110	Jupiter	FL	33458	561-427-6400		261
Web: www.fttinc.com						
Florida Venture Forum Inc, The 707 W Azeele St	Tampa	FL	33606	813-335-8116		138
TF: 888-375-7136 ■ *Web:* www.flventure.org						
Floridagriculture Magazine PO Box 147030	Gainesville	FL	32614	352-374-1535	374-1530	457-1
Web: www.floridagriculture.org						
Florig R & J Industrial Company Inc 910 Brook Rd	Conshohocken	PA	19428	610-825-6655	825-7424	480
Web: www.rjflorig.com						
Florim USA Inc 300 International Blvd	Clarksville	TN	37040	931-645-5100	647-5974	751
Web: www.florimusa.com						
Florissant Fossil Beds National Monument PO Box 185	Florissant	CO	80816	719-748-3253	748-3164	564
Web: www.nps.gov						
Florist Distributing Inc 2403 Bell Ave	Des Moines	IA	50321	515-243-5228	282-9241	293
TF: 800-373-3741 ■ *Web:* www.fdionline.net						
Florsheim Inc 333 W Estabrook Blvd	Glendale	WI	53212	866-454-0449	908-1601*	301
*Fax Area Code: 414 ■ *TF:* 866-454-0449 ■ *Web:* www.florsheim.com						
Flotation Technologies Inc 20 Morin St	Biddeford	ME	04005	207-282-7749		601
Web: www.flotec.com						
Flotech Inc 3330 Evergreen Ave	Jacksonville	FL	32206	904-358-1849		595
Web: www.flotechinc.com						
Floturn Inc 4236 Thunderbird Ln	Fairfield	OH	45014	513-860-8040	860-8044	697
Web: www.floturn.com						
Flourish Inc 1001 Huron Rd E Ste 102	Cleveland	OH	44115	216-696-9116		7
Web: www.freddiegeorges.com						
Flournoy Development Co 900 Brookstone Ctr Pkwy	Columbus	GA	31904	706-324-4000	324-4150	653
TF: 888-801-3404 ■ *Web:* flournoycompanies.com						
Flow Construction Company Inc 3628 Trousdale Dr Ste E	Nashville	TN	37204	615-832-0707		186
Web: flowconstruction.com						
Flow Consulting Inc 10340 SE 138th Pl Rd	Summerfield	FL	34491	386-208-6146		449
Web: www.flowconsulting.com						
Flow Dry Technology Inc 379 Albert Rd PO Box 190	Brookville	OH	45309	937-833-2161	833-3208	326
TF: 800-533-0077 ■ *Web:* flowdry.com						
Flow Dynamics & Automation Inc 1024 11th Ct W	Birmingham	AL	35204	205-581-1200		358
TF: 800-435-2526 ■ *Web:* www.flowdynamics.net						
Flow International Corp 23500 64th Ave S	Kent	WA	98032	253-850-3500	813-9377	455
NASDAQ: FLOW ■ *TF:* 800-446-3569 ■ *Web:* www.flowwaterjet.com						
Flow Petroleum Services Inc 209 Marcon Dr	Lafayette	LA	70507	337-593-9987		539
Web: www.flowps.com						
Flow Solutions Inc 4401 S Pinemont Ste 208	Houston	TX	77041	713-939-7000		358
Web: www.flowsolutionsinc.com						
Flow Sports Inc 1011 Calle Sombra Ste 220	San Clemente	CA	92673	949-361-5260		711
Web: www.sicmaui.com						
Flowell Electric Assn Inc 495 N 3200 W	Fillmore	UT	84631	435-743-6214		245
Flower City Communications LLC 1848 Lyell Ave	Rochester	NY	14606	585-458-5350		292
Web: flowercitycommunications.com						
Flower City Tissue Mills Inc 700 Driving Pk Ave	Rochester	NY	14613	585-458-9200		548
TF: 800-595-2030 ■ *Web:* www.flowercitytissue.com						
Flower Hospital 5200 Harroun Rd	Sylvania	OH	43560	419-824-1444		374-3
Web: www.promedica.org						
Flower Memorial Library 229 Washington St	Watertown	NY	13601	315-785-7705		434-3
Flower Mound Chamber of Commerce 700 Parker Sq Ste 100	Flower Mound	TX	75028	972-539-0500	539-4307	139
Web: www.flowermoundchamber.com						
Flower Patch Inc 4370 S 300 W	Murray	UT	84107	801-747-2824	263-7896	292
TF General: 888-865-6858 ■ *Web:* www.flowerpatch.com						
Flower Pot Florists 2314 N Broadway St	Knoxville	TN	37917	865-523-5121		292
TF: 800-824-7792 ■ *Web:* www.knoxvilleflowerpot.com						
Flowerbud.com PO Box 761	Lake Oswego	OR	97034	503-697-1790		292
Web: www.flowerbud.com						
Flowers & Fancies-greenlea 11404 Cronridge Dr	Owings Mills	MD	21117	410-653-0600		292
Web: www.flowersandfancies.com						
Flowers Auto Parts Co 935 Hwy 70 SE	Hickory	NC	28602	828-322-5414		61
TF Cust Svc: 800-538-6272 ■ *Web:* www.napaonline.com						
Flowers by Anthony Inc 3300 SW Ninth St Ste 1	Des Moines	IA	50315	515-288-6789		292
Web: flowersbyanthony.com						
Flowers By Burton Inc 426 Old Walt Whitman Rd	Melville	NY	11747	631-424-3377		292
Web: flowersbyburton.com						
Flowers by Sleeman for All Seasons & Reasons Ltd 1201 Memorial Rd	Houghton	MI	49931	906-482-4023		292
TF: 800-400-4023 ■ *Web:* flowersbysleeman.com						
Flowers Chemical Laboratories Inc 481 Newburyport Ave	Altamonte Springs	FL	32701	407-339-5984		292
Web: www.flowerslabs.com						
Flowers Foods Inc 1919 Flowers Cir	Thomasville	GA	31757	229-226-9110		296-1
NYSE: FLO ■ *Web:* www.flowersfoods.com						
Flowers Hospital 4370 W Main St	Dothan	AL	36305	334-793-5000	836-1888	374-3
TF: 877-456-9617 ■ *Web:* www.flowershospital.com						
Flowerwood Garden Ctr 7625 US Hwy 14	Crystal Lake	IL	60012	815-459-6200		323
TF: 800-643-5443 ■ *Web:* www.flowerwoodgardencenter.net						
Flow-Eze Co 3209 Auburn St	Rockford	IL	61101	815-965-1062	965-1329	687
TF: 800-435-4873 ■ *Web:* www.flow-eze.com						
Flowing Tide Pub 10580 N McCarran Blvd	Reno	NV	89503	775-747-7707		671
Web: www.flowingtidepub.com						
Flowline Inc 10500 Humbolt St	Los Alamitos	CA	90720	562-598-3015	431-8507	472
Web: www.flowline.com						
Flowmetrics Inc 9201 Independence Ave	Chatsworth	CA	91311	818-407-3420		250
Web: flowmetrics.com						
Flowroute LLC 1218 Third Ave 6th Fl	Seattle	WA	98101	206-641-8000		387
Web: www.flowroute.com						
Flowserve Corp 5215 N O'Connor Blvd Ste 2300	Irving	TX	75039	972-443-6500	443-6800	641
NYSE: FLS ■ *TF:* 800-543-3927 ■ *Web:* www.flowserve.com						
Floyd Bell Inc 720 Dearborn Park Ln	Columbus	OH	43085	614-294-4000		246
TF: 888-356-9323 ■ *Web:* www.floydbell.com						
Floyd Blinsky Trucking Inc 210 Keys Rd	Yakima	WA	98901	509-457-3484	457-0832	685
TF: 800-537-9599 ■ *Web:* www.blinsky.com						
Floyd Browne Group 3875 Embassy Pkwy	Akron	OH	44333	330-375-0800	665-0620	193
TF General: 800-362-2764 ■ *Web:* ctconsultants.com						
Floyd County 101 S Main St	Charles City	IA	50616	641-228-7777	228-7772	338
Web: www.floydcoia.org						
Floyd County PO Box 218	Floyd	VA	24091	540-745-9300	745-9305	338
TF: 800-367-7623 ■ *Web:* www.floydcova.org						
Floyd County 311 Hauss Sq	New Albany	IN	47150	812-948-4119	981-0352	338
Web: www.floydcounty.in.gov						
Floyd County 313 Westminster St Ste 210	Prestonsburg	KY	41653	606-886-0364		338
Web: www.floydcountykentucky.com						
Floyd County 12 E Fourth Ave Ste 209	Rome	GA	30162	706-291-5110	291-5248	338
TF: 800-436-7442 ■ *Web:* www.romefloyd.com						
Floyd County Board of Education 600 Riverside Pkwy NE	Rome	GA	30161	706-234-1031	236-1824	685
Web: www.floydboe.net						
Floyd E Tut Fann State Veterans Home 2701 Meridian St	Huntsville	AL	35811	256-851-2807	851-2967	793
TF: 855-212-8028 ■ *Web:* www.va.state.al.us						
Floyd Medical Ctr 304 Turner McCall Blvd	Rome	GA	30165	706-509-5000		374-3
TF: 866-874-2772 ■ *Web:* www.floyd.org						
Floyd Memorial Hospital 1850 State St	New Albany	IN	47150	812-944-7701		374-3
TF: 800-423-1513 ■ *Web:* floydmemorial.com						
FLPL (Florence-Lauderdale Public Library) 350 N Wood Ave	Florence	AL	35630	256-764-6564		434-3
Web: www.flpl.org						
Fluent 7319 104 St NW	Edmonton	AB	T6E4B9	855-238-4826		693
TF: 855-238-4826 ■ *Web:* myfluenthome.com						
Fluent Language Solutions Inc 8801 JM Keynes Dr Ste 400	Charlotte	NC	28262	704-532-7446		768
TF: 888-225-6056 ■ *Web:* www.fluentls.com						
Fluent Media Group LLC 5230 Alton Rd	Miami Beach	FL	33140	305-424-1030		116
Web: www.fluentmediagroup.com						

Name / Address	Phone	Fax	Class
Fluid Components International 1755 La Costa Meadows Dr................San Marcos CA 92078 *TF:* 800-863-8703 ■ *Web:* www.fluidcomponents.com	760-744-6950	736-6250	201
Fluid Conditioning Products Inc Kleine & Warwick Sts...........................Lititz PA 17543 *Web:* www.fcp-filters.com	717-627-1550		610
Fluid Controls Institute (FCI) 1300 Sumner Ave.........................Cleveland OH 44115 *Web:* www.fluidcontrolsinstitute.org	216-241-7333	241-0105	49-13
Fluid Delivery Solutions LLC 6795 Corporation Pkwy Ste 200.............Fort Worth TX 76126 *Web:* www.fdsllc.com	817-730-9761		539
Fluid Engineering Div 1432 Walnut St..............Erie PA 16502 *Web:* www.fluideng.com	814-453-5014		256
Fluid Equipment Development Company LLC 800 Ternes Dr..............................Monroe MI 48162 *Web:* www.fedco-usa.com	734-241-3935		641
Fluid Flow Products Inc 2108 Crown View Dr.......................Charlotte NC 28227 *Web:* www.fluidflow.com	704-847-4464		789
Fluid Imaging Technologies Inc 65 Forest Falls Dr..........................Yarmouth ME 04096 *Web:* www.fluidimaging.com	207-846-6100		419
Fluid Innovation Inc 911 N RR 620 Ste 205........................Austin TX 78734 *TF:* 866-934-7779	866-934-7779		809
Fluid Line Products Inc 38273 Western Pkwy.....................Willoughby OH 44094 *Web:* www.fluidline.com	440-946-9470		790
Fluid Management Inc 1023 S Wheeling Rd.......................Wheeling IL 60090 *TF:* 800-462-2466 ■ *Web:* www.fluidman.com	847-537-0880	537-3221	386
Fluid Metering Inc 5 Aerial Way Ste 500........................Syosset NY 11791 *TF:* 800-223-3388 ■ *Web:* fluidmetering.com	516-922-6050	624-8261	640
Fluid Power Distributors Assn (FPDA) PO Box 1420...........................Cherry Hill NJ 08034 *TF:* 800-843-2763 ■ *Web:* www.fpda.org	856-424-8998	424-9248	49-13
Fluid Power Equipment Inc 6305 Cunningham Rd.......................Houston TX 77041 *Web:* www.fluidpowerequipment.com	713-466-8088		641
Fluid Systems Inc 16619 Aldine Westfield Rd...................Houston TX 77032 *Web:* www.fluidsystems.com	832-467-9898	467-9897	539
Fluidic Inc 8455 N 90th St...................Scottsdale AZ 85258 *Web:* fluidicenergy.com	480-966-0242		74
Fluidmaster Inc 30800 Rancho Viejo Rd............San Juan Capistrano CA 92675 *TF:* 800-631-2011 ■ *Web:* www.fluidmaster.com	949-728-2000	728-2205	609
Fluidware 12 York St 2nd Fl..........................Ottawa ON K1N5S6 *TF:* 866-218-5127 ■ *Web:* www.fluidware.com	866-218-5127		387
Fluke Biomedical 6920 Seaway Blvd.............Everett WA 98203 *TF:* 800-443-5853 ■ *Web:* www.flukebiomedical.com	425-446-6945	446-5629	248
Fluke Corp 6920 Seaway Blvd..................Everett WA 98203 *TF:* 877-355-3225 ■ *Web:* www.fluke.com	425-446-6100	446-5116	248
Fluke Electronics Canada LP 400 Britannia Rd E Unit 1................Mississauga ON L4Z1X9 *Web:* www.fluke.com/fluke/caen/home/default.htm	905-890-7600		54
Fluke Inc 3550 Annapolis Ln N...........................Everett WA 98203 *Web:* en-us.fluke.com	425-446-6945		693
Fluke Networks Inc 6920 Seaway Blvd..........Everett WA 98203 *TF:* 800-283-5853 ■ *Web:* www.flukenetworks.com	425-446-4519	446-5043	248
Fluor Constructors International Inc 352 Halton Rd.............................Greenville SC 29607	864-234-7335		186
Fluor Corp 6700 Las Colinas Blvd.................Irving TX 75039 *TF:* 800-405-6637 ■ *Web:* www.fluor.com	469-398-7000	398-7255	194
Fluor Daniel Inc 6700 Las Colinas Blvd..........Irving TX 75039 *Web:* www.fluor.com	949-349-2000	349-2585	261
Fluoresco Lighting & Sign Corp 5505 S Nogales Hwy.........................Tucson AZ 85706 *Web:* www.fluoresco.com	520-623-7953	884-0161	261
Flushing Financial Corp 1979 Marcus Ave......................New Hyde Park NY 11042 *NASDAQ: FFIC* ■ *TF:* 800-581-2889 ■ *Web:* www.flushingbank.com	718-961-5400		360-2
Flushing Hospital Medical Ctr 4500 Parsons Blvd........................Flushing NY 11355 *Web:* www.flushinghospital.org	718-670-5000		374-3
Flushing Savings Bank FSB 144-51 Northern Blvd.......................Flushing NY 11354 *TF:* 800-435-4000 ■ *Web:* www.flushingbank.com	718-512-2929		70
Flutes Inc 8252 Zionsville Rd...............Indianapolis IN 46268 *Web:* www.flutesinc.com	317-870-6010		100
Fluvanna County 132 Main St..................Palmyra VA 22963 *TF:* 800-814-5339 ■ *Web:* www.fluvannacounty.org	434-591-1910	591-1911	338
Flw International 1147 W Ohio St.............Chicago IL 60642 *Web:* www.flwint.net	312-239-2174		225
Fly Fishing Shop E 67296 Hwy 26..............Welches OR 97067 *TF:* 800-266-3971 ■ *Web:* www.flyfishusa.com	503-622-4607		711
FlyData Inc 1043 N Shoreline Blvd Ste 200.............Mountain View CA 94043 *TF:* 855-427-9787 ■ *Web:* www.flydata.com	855-427-9787		624
Flyer.Com 201 Kelsey Ln.............................Tampa FL 33619 *TF:* 800-995-4433 ■ *Web:* theflyer.com	813-626-9430		637-10
Flying Aces Technology LLC 305 N Westgate Rd Ste 100............Mount Prospect IL 60056 *Web:* www.flying-aces.com	847-299-7815		39
Flying Biscuit Cafe 1655 McLendon Ave..........Atlanta GA 30307 *Web:* www.flyingbiscuit.com	404-687-8888		671
Flying Bridge Technologies 2709 Water Ridge Pkwy Ste 480..............Charlotte NC 28217 *Web:* www.flyingbridge.net	704-357-8011		4
Flying Dog Brewery LLC 4607 Wedgewood Blvd.......................Frederick MD 21703 *Web:* www.flyingdogales.com	301-694-7899		102
Flying E Ranch 2801 W Wickenburg Way.....................Wickenburg AZ 85390 *TF:* 888-684-2650 ■ *Web:* www.flyingeranch.com	928-684-2690	684-5304	239
Flying Fig 2523 Market St....................Cleveland OH 44113 *Web:* www.theflyingfig.com	216-241-4243		671
Flying Fish 300 Westlake Ave N..................Seattle WA 98109 *Web:* www.flyingfishseattle.com	206-728-8595	728-1551	671
Flying Fish Grill Mission St....................Carmel CA 93921 *Web:* flyingfishgrill.com	831-625-1962		671
Flying Food Group 5370 S Cicero Ave...........Chicago IL 60638 *Web:* www.flyingfood.com	312-243-2122		299
Flying Hippo Investments L L C 130 E Third St...........................Des Moines IA 50309 *Web:* www.flyinghippo.com	515-288-5316		525
Flying Leatherneck Aviation Museum Anderson Ave MCAS Miramar...............San Diego CA 92145 *TF:* 877-359-8762 ■ *Web:* www.flyingleathernecks.org	858-693-1723		520
Flying Magazine 460 N Orlando Ave Ste 200................Winter Park FL 32789 *TF Cust Svc:* 800-678-0797 ■ *Web:* www.flyingmag.com	407-628-4802		457-14
Flying Rhino Cafe 278 Shrewsbury St..........Worcester MA 01604 *Web:* flyingrhinocafe.com	508-757-1450	754-8102	671
Flying W Ranch Inc 3330 Chuckwagon Rd................Colorado Springs CO 80919 *TF:* 800-232-3599 ■ *Web:* www.flyingw.com	719-598-4000	598-4600	671
Flynn Burner Corp 425 Fifth Ave............New Rochelle NY 10801 *Web:* www.flynnburner.com	914-636-1320		612
Flynn Ctr for the Performing Arts 153 Main St...............................Burlington VT 05401 *Web:* www.flynncenter.org	802-863-5966	863-8788	572
Flynn Enterprises Inc 2203 Walnut St..........................Hopkinsville KY 42240	270-886-0223		155-11
Flynn Systems Corp 74 Northeastern Blvd........................Nashua NH 03062 *TF:* 800-730-6567 ■ *Web:* www.flynn.com	603-598-4444		225
Flynn Walker Diggin CPA PC 50 Seward St......................Saratoga Springs NY 12866 *Web:* flynnwalkerdiggin.com	518-583-1234		2
Flywheel Communications Inc 2501 Harrison St.....................San Francisco CA 94110 *Web:* www.flywheel.com	415-401-7290		387
FM 106.1 12100 W Howard Ave..............Greenfield WI 53220 *Web:* www.fm106.com	414-546-8000	327-3200	645
F&M Bank PO Box 1130....................Clarksville TN 37041 *TF:* 800-645-4199 ■ *Web:* www.myfmbank.com	931-645-2400		70
FM Brown's Sons Inc 205 Woodrow Ave PO Box 2116...........Sinking Spring PA 19608 **Fax Area Code:* 610 ■ *TF:* 800-334-8816 ■ *Web:* www.fmbrown.com	800-334-8816	678-7023*	447
FM Communications Inc 1914 Colvin Blvd........................Tonawanda NY 14150 *TF:* 800-895-5122 ■ *Web:* www.fmcommunications.com	716-832-2026		179
FM Corp 3535 Hudson Rd.......................Rogers AR 72756 *Web:* www.fmcorp.com	479-636-3540		601
F&M Expressions Inc 211 Island Rd...........Mahwah NJ 07430 *Web:* www.fmexpressions.com	201-512-3338		627
FM Global 270 Central Ave PO Box 7500.........Johnston RI 02919 *TF:* 800-343-7722 ■ *Web:* www.fmglobal.com	401-275-3000	275-3029	391-4
FM Industries Inc 221 Warren Ave.............Fremont CA 94539 *Web:* www.fmindustries.com	510-668-1900	668-1920	454
F&M Mafco Inc PO Box 11013...............Cincinnati OH 45211 *TF:* 800-333-2151 ■ *Web:* www.fmmafco.com	513-367-2151	367-0363	190
FM NEWS 101 KXL 1211 SW Fifth Ave Ste 6........................Portland OR 97204 *Web:* www.kxl.com	503-517-6000		645-128
Fm3 Systems Inc 20118 N 67th Ave Ste 300 609...........Glendale AZ 85305 *Web:* fm3systems.com	602-288-1410		177
FMA (Federal Managers Assn) 1641 Prince St..........................Alexandria VA 22314 *Web:* www.fedmanagers.org	703-683-8700	683-8707	49-7
FMA (Financial Management Assn International) 4202 E Fowler Ave.........................Tampa FL 33620 *Web:* www.fma.org	813-974-2084		49-2
FMA (Fabricators & Manufacturers Assn International) 833 Featherstone Rd......................Rockford IL 61107 *TF:* 888-394-4362 ■ *Web:* www.fmanet.org	815-399-8700	484-7700	49-13
FMA Advisory Inc 1631 N Front St...........Harrisburg PA 17102 *Web:* fma-advisory.com	717-232-8850		691
FMA Alliance Ltd 80 Garden Ctr Ste 3.....................Broomfield CO 80020 *TF:* 800-955-5598 ■ *Web:* www.fmaalliance.com	281-931-5050		160
FMC (Foothills Medical Centre) 1403 29th St NW...........................Calgary AB T2N2T9 **Fax Area Code:* 403 ■ *TF:* 888-342-2471 ■ *Web:* www.albertahealthservices.ca	780-342-2000	944-1663*	374-2
FMC (Fairfield Medical Ctr) 401 N Ewing St...........................Lancaster OH 43130 *TF:* 800-548-2627 ■ *Web:* www.fmchealth.org	740-687-8000		374-3
FMC Corp 2929 Walnut St.................Philadelphia PA 19104 *NYSE: FMC* ■ *TF:* 888-548-4486 ■ *Web:* www.fmc.com	215-299-6000	299-5998	143
FMC Ice Sports 100 Schoosett St Bldg 3..................Pembroke MA 02359 *TF:* 888-747-5283 ■ *Web:* www.fmcicesports.com	781-826-3085		717
FMC Technologies Inc 1803 Gears Rd..........Houston TX 77067 *NYSE: FTI* ■ *TF:* 800-356-4898 ■ *Web:* www.fmctechnologies.com	281-591-4000	591-4102	537
FMCA (Family Motor Coach Assn) 8291 Clough Pk..........................Cincinnati OH 45244 *TF:* 800-543-3622 ■ *Web:* www.fmca.com	513-474-3622	474-2332	48-23
FMCI (Grassley Group, The) 600 State St Ste A.......................Cedar Falls IA 50613 **Fax Area Code:* 703 ■ *TF:* 866-619-5580 ■ *Web:* www.grassleygroup.com	866-619-5580	342-0411*	47
FMCSA (Federal Motor Carrier Safety Administration) 1200 New Jersey Ave SE..................Washington DC 20590 *TF:* 800-832-5660 ■ *Web:* www.fmcsa.dot.gov	800-832-5660		340-17
FMF (Feminist Majority Foundation-East Coast) 1600 Wilson Blvd Ste 801..................Arlington VA 22209 *Web:* www.feminist.org	703-522-2214	522-2219	48-24
FMG Enterprises Inc 1125 Memorex Dr.........................Santa Clara CA 95050 *TF:* 800-327-6177 ■ *Web:* www.fmgvacpump.com	408-982-0110		641
FMI (Food Marketing Institute) 2345 Crystal Dr Ste 800...................Arlington VA 22202 *TF:* 800-732-2639 ■ *Web:* www.fmi.org	202-220-0600	429-4519	49-18
FMI Corp 5171 Glenwood Ave Ste 200............Raleigh NC 27612 *TF General:* 800-669-1364 ■ *Web:* www.fminet.com	919-787-8400	785-9320	194

	Phone	Fax	Class
Fmi Direct Mail 2100 Kubach Rd Rear .... Philadelphia PA 19116 *Web:* fmidm.com	215-464-0111		5
FMI Inc 2382 United Ln .... Elk Grove Village IL 60007 *Web:* www.fmimed.com	847-350-1535		475
FMOLHS (Franciscan Missionaries of Our Lady Health System) 4200 Essen Ln .... Baton Rouge LA 70809 *Web:* www.fmolhs.org	225-923-2701	926-4846	353
FMR Corp 82 Devonshire St .... Boston MA 02109 *TF:* 800-343-3548 ■ *Web:* www.fidelity.com	800-343-3548		401
FMS (Financial Managers Society) 100 W Monroe St Ste 810 .... Chicago IL 60603 *TF Cust Svc:* 800-275-4367 ■ *Web:* www.fmsinc.org	312-578-1300	578-1308	49-2
FMS Inc 8150 Leesburg Pk Ste 600 .... Vienna VA 22182 *TF:* 866-367-7801 ■ *Web:* www.fmsinc.com	703-356-4700	448-3861	178-2
FMS InfoServ Inc 6053 W Century Blvd 9th Fl .... Los Angeles CA 90045 *Web:* www.fmsinfoserv.com	310-981-9510		387
FN America LLC 797 Old Clemson Rd .... Columbia SC 29229 *Web:* www.fnamerica.com	803-736-0522		807
FNA (Florida Nurses Assn) 1235 E Concord St PO Box 536985 .... Orlando FL 32853 *Web:* www.floridanurse.org	407-896-3261	896-9042	533
FNBB (First National Bankers Bankshares Inc) 7813 Office Pk Blvd .... Baton Rouge LA 70809 *TF:* 800-421-6182 ■ *Web:* www.bankers-bank.com	225-924-8015	952-0899	70
FNF Construction Inc 115 S 48th St .... Tempe AZ 85281 *TF:* 800-767-3263 ■ *Web:* www.fnfinc.com	480-784-2910	829-8607	188-4
FNNB 100 N Second Ave W .... Newton IA 50208 *Web:* firstnnb.com	641-792-3010		70
FNS (Food & Nutrition Service Regional Offices) *Mid-Atlantic Regional Office* 300 Corporate Blvd .... Robbinsville NJ 08691 *Web:* fns.usda.gov	609-259-5025	259-5185	340-1
FOA (Friends of Animals Inc) 777 Post Rd Ste 205 .... Darien CT 06820 *TF:* 800-321-7387 ■ *Web:* www.friendsofanimals.org	203-656-1522	656-0267	48-3
Foam Fabricators Inc 950 Progress Blvd .... New Albany IN 47150 *TF:* 800-626-1197 ■ *Web:* www.foamfabricatorsinc.com	812-948-1696	948-2450	601
Foam Molders & Specialty Corp 20004 State Rd .... Cerritos CA 90703 *TF:* 800-378-8987 ■ *Web:* www.foammolders.com	800-378-8987		601
Foam Products Corp 350 Beamer Rd .... Calhoun GA 30701 *Web:* www.foamproducts.com	706-629-1256		601
Foam Rubber Products Inc 2000 Troy Ave .... New Castle IN 47362 *TF:* 800-827-5211 ■ *Web:* www.foamrubberllc.com	765-521-2000	521-2759	601
Foamcraft Inc 900 Industrial Pkwy .... Elkhart IN 46516 *Web:* www.foamcraftinc.com	574-293-8569		601
Foard County 101 S Main St .... Crowell TX 79227	940-684-1919		338
Focal Point Energy Inc 1650 Las Plumas Ave .... San Jose CA 95133 *Web:* www.focalpointenergy.com	408-923-1541		14
Focal Point LLC, The 501 14th St Ste 200 .... Oakland CA 94612 *TF:* 800-559-4534 ■ *Web:* www.thefocalpoint.com	510-208-1760		344
Focus 603 Park Point Dr Ste 200 .... Genesee CO 80401 *Web:* www.focus.org	303-962-5750		48-20
Focus 360 Inc 27721 La Paz Rd .... Laguna Niguel CA 92677 *TF:* 800-490-1621 ■ *Web:* www.focus360.com	949-234-0008		177
Focus Camera Inc 905 McDonald Ave .... Brooklyn NY 11218 *TF:* 800-221-0828 ■ *Web:* www.focuscamera.com	800-221-0828		119
Focus Center of Pittsburgh 651 Holiday Dr Plaza 5 Ste 300 .... Pittsburgh PA 15220 *TF:* 800-336-7674 ■ *Web:* www.fcpresearch.com	412-279-5900		463
Focus Daily News 1337 Marilyn Ave .... De Soto TX 75115 *Web:* www.focus-news.com	972-223-9175		532-2
Focus Diagnostics Inc 11331 Vly View St .... Cypress CA 90630 **Fax Area Code:* 714 ■ *TF:* 800-838-4548 ■ *Web:* www.focusdx.com	562-240-6500	243-4703*	418
Focus Direct LLC 9707 Broadway .... San Antonio TX 78217 *TF:* 800-555-1551 ■ *Web:* mysanantonio.com	210-805-9185		5
Focus Features 100 Universal City Plaza .... Universal City CA 91608 *Web:* www.focusfeatures.com	818-777-8738	866-4579	514
Focus Forward LLC 950 W Valley Rd Ste 2700 .... Wayne PA 19087 *Web:* www.focusfwd.com	215-367-4000		668
Focus Healthcare Management Inc 720 Cool Springs Blvd .... Franklin TN 37067	615-778-4000	778-0801	463
Focus Industrial Workforces 8651 Hauser Ct .... Lenexa KS 66215 *Web:* www.workatfocus.com	913-268-1222		260
Focus Logistics Inc 1311 Howard Dr .... West Chicago IL 60185 *TF:* 877-924-3600 ■ *Web:* focuslogisticsinc.com	630-231-8200		314
Focus Management Group USA Inc 5001 W Lemon St .... Tampa FL 33609 *TF:* 800-225-1025 ■ *Web:* www.focusmg.com	813-281-0062		463
Focus Media Inc 10 Matthews St .... Goshen NY 10924 *Web:* www.focusmediausa.com	845-294-3342		636
Focus Mfg 38127 Willoughby Pkwy .... Willoughby OH 44094 *Web:* www.focusmanufacturing.com	440-946-8766		567
Focus on the Family 8605 Explorer Dr .... Colorado Springs CO 80920 *TF Sales:* 800-232-6459 ■ *Web:* www.focusonthefamily.com	719-531-3400	531-3424	48-6
Focus Pointe 100 E Penn Sq Ste 1200 .... Philadelphia PA 19107 *Web:* www.phonelab.com	215-561-5500		668
Focus Receivables Management LLC 1130 Northchase Pkwy Ste 150 .... Marietta GA 30067 *TF:* 877-362-8766 ■ *Web:* www.focusrm.com	678-228-0000	228-0019	160
Focus Strategic Communications Inc 2474 Waterford St .... Oakville ON L6L5E6 *TF:* 866-263-6287 ■ *Web:* www.focussc.com	905-825-8757		94
Focus Technology Solutions Inc 93 Ledge Rd .... Seabrook NH 03874 *Web:* www.focustsi.com	603-766-0000		180

	Phone	Fax	Class
Focus Ventures 525 University Ave Ste 225 .... Palo Alto CA 94301 *Web:* www.focusventures.com	650-325-7400		792
Focus Vision 7 River Park Pl E Ste 110 .... Fresno CA 93720 *Web:* www.decipherinc.com	559-436-6940		668
FocusCFO LLC 1010 Jackson Hole Dr Ste 202 .... Columbus OH 43004 *TF:* 800-722-2289 ■ *Web:* focuscfo.com	614-944-5760		463
Focused Management Inc 6354 Walker Ln Ste 101 .... Franconia VA 22310 *TF:* 800-353-6561 ■ *Web:* www.focusedmgmtinc.com	703-922-9600		180
FocusVision Worldwide Inc 1266 E Main St .... Stamford CT 06902 *TF:* 800-433-8128 ■ *Web:* www.focusvision.com	203-961-1715		387
Fodera Guitars Inc 68 34th St Ste 3 .... Brooklyn NY 11232 *Web:* www.fodera.com	718-832-3455		526
Foellinger-Freimann Botanical Conservatory 1100 S Calhoun St .... Fort Wayne IN 46802 *TF:* 866-220-8842 ■ *Web:* www.botanicalconservatory.org	260-427-6440	427-6450	97
Foerster Instruments Inc 140 Industry Dr .... Pittsburgh PA 15275 *Web:* www.foerstergroup.com	412-788-8976	788-8984	813
Fogarty Creek State Recreation Area 725 Summer St NE Ste C .... Salem OR 97341 *TF:* 800-551-6949 ■ *Web:* www.oregonstateparks.org	800-551-6949		565
Fogel Capital Management Inc 453 Riverside Dr .... Stuart FL 34994 *Web:* fogelcapital.com	772-223-9686		401
Fogel International Inc 5110 N 32nd St Ste 206 .... Phoenix AZ 85018 *Web:* www.fogelinternational.com	602-508-0728		690
Fogelman Executive Conference Center & Hotel 330 Innovation Dr Ste 206 .... Memphis TN 38152 *Web:* bf.memphis.edu	901-678-2021	678-5329	377
Fogg Art Museum 32 Quincy St Harvard University .... Cambridge MA 02138 *TF:* 800-872-0500 ■ *Web:* www.harvardartmuseums.org	617-495-9400		520
Fogg Filler Co 3455 John F Donnelly Dr .... Holland MI 49424 *TF:* 800-813-6644 ■ *Web:* www.foggfiller.com	616-786-3644		111
Fogo de Chao 8250 Westheimer Rd .... Houston TX 77063 *Web:* www.fogodechao.com	713-978-6500		671
Fogo de Chao 3101 Piedmont Rd .... Atlanta GA 30305 *Web:* www.fogodechao.com	404-266-9988		671
Fogo de Chao 14881 Quorum Dr Ste 750 .... Dallas TX 75254 *Web:* www.fogodechao.com	972-960-9533		670
FOI Services Inc 704 Quince OrchaRd Rd Ste 275 .... Gaithersburg MD 20878 *TF:* 800-654-1147 ■ *Web:* www.foiservices.com	301-975-9400	975-0702	387
FOIA Group Inc (FGI) 1250 Connecticut Ave NW Ste 200 .... Washington DC 20036 **Fax Area Code:* 202 ■ *TF:* 888-461-7951 ■ *Web:* www.foia.com	888-461-7951	347-8419*	387
Foit-Albert Assoc 763 Main St .... Buffalo NY 14203 *Web:* www.foit-albert.com	716-856-3933		261
Fokker Services Inc 5169 Southridge Pkwy Ste 100 .... Atlanta GA 30349	770-991-4373	991-4360	770
Folbot Inc 4209 Pace St .... Charleston SC 29405 *TF:* 800-533-5099 ■ *Web:* www.folbot.com	843-744-3483	744-7783	710
Folderwave 238 Littleton Rd Ste 204 .... Westford MA 01886 *Web:* www.folderwave.com	978-392-2055		177
Folding Shutter Corp 7089 Hemstreet Pl .... West Palm Beach FL 33413 *TF:* 800-643-6371 ■ *Web:* www.foldingshutters.com	800-643-6371		234
FoldRx Pharmaceuticals Inc 100 Acorn Park Dr 5th Fl .... Cambridge MA 02140 *Web:* www.foldrx.com	617-252-5500		238
Foley & Lardner LLP 777 E Wisconsin Ave .... Milwaukee WI 53202 *Web:* www.foley.com	414-271-2400	297-4900	428
Foley Carrier Services LLC 140 Huyshope Ave .... Hartford CT 06106 *TF:* 800-253-5506 ■ *Web:* www.foleyservices.com	800-253-5506		463
Foley Equipment Co 1550 SW St .... Wichita KS 67213 **Fax:* Sales ■ *TF:* 800-475-4114 ■ *Web:* www.foleyeq.com	316-943-4211	943-0896*	358
Foley Group, The 1661 Front St Ste 3 .... Yorktown Heights NY 10598 *Web:* foleygraphics.com	914-245-3625	245-8587	627
Foley High School 1 Pride Pl .... Foley MN 36535 *TF:* 800-352-7550 ■ *Web:* www.foley.k12.mn.us	320-968-7246		685
Foley House Inn 14 W Hull St Chippewa Sq .... Savannah GA 31401 *TF:* 800-647-3708 ■ *Web:* www.foleyinn.com	912-232-6622		379
Foley Inc 855 Centennial Ave .... Piscataway NJ 08854 *TF:* 888-417-6464 ■ *Web:* www.foleyinc.com	732-885-5555		62-7
Foley Pattern Company Inc 500 W 11th St .... Auburn IN 46706	260-925-4113		567
Folger Adam Security Inc 4634 S Presa St .... San Antonio TX 78223 *TF:* 888-745-0530 ■ *Web:* www.southernfolger.com	210-533-1231	533-2211	350
Folger Levin LLP 199 Fremont St 20th Fl .... San Francisco CA 94105 *Web:* www.folgerlevin.com	415-625-1050		41
Folger Shakespeare Library 201 E Capitol St SE .... Washington DC 20003 *Web:* www.folger.edu	202-544-4600	544-4623	434-4
Folgergraphics Inc 2339 Davis Ave .... Hayward CA 94545 *Web:* www.folgergraphics.com	510-887-5656		174
Foliage 122 N Main Ave .... Scranton PA 18504	570-347-1071		671
Foliage Inc 20 N Ave .... Burlington MA 01803 *Web:* www.foliage.com	781-993-5500		525
Folio Weekly 45 W Bay St Ste 103 .... Jacksonville FL 32202 *Web:* www.folioweekly.com	904-260-9770	260-9773	532-5
Folk Alliance International 509 Delaware St Ste 101 .... Kansas City MO 64105 *Web:* www.folk.org	816-221-3655		48-4
Folk Art Ctr PO Box 9545 .... Asheville NC 28815 *TF:* 888-672-7717 ■ *Web:* www.southernhighlandguild.org	828-298-7928	298-7962	520

Phone | Fax | Class

Folk's Folly Prime Steak House
551 S Mendenhall Rd........................Memphis TN 38117 901-762-8200 671
Web: www.folksfolly.com

Folks Southern Kitchen
1384 Buford Business Blvd Ste 500..............Buford GA 30518 770-904-6595 904-6805 670
Web: www.folkskitchen.com

Follett Corp 1340 Ridgeview Dr................McHenry IL 60050 815-759-1700 759-9831 96
TF: 877-899-8550 ■ *Web:* www.follettlearning.com

Follett Corp
3 Westbrook Corporate Ctr Ste 200..........Westchester IL 60154 708-884-0000 96
TF: 800-365-5388 ■ *Web:* www.follett.com

Follett Corp 801 Church Ln................Easton PA 18040 610-252-7301 250-0169 664
TF Cust Svc: 800-523-9361 ■ *Web:* www.follettice.com

Follett Higher Education Group
3 Westbrook Corporate Ctr Ste 200..........Westchester IL 60154 800-323-4506 95
TF: 800-323-4506 ■ *Web:* www.follett.com/higher-ed

Follow Up Sales Systems
400 S Summit St......................Arkansas City KS 67005 620-442-2460 449
Web: fussinc.com

Folly Theater
300 W 12th St PO Box 26505...............Kansas City MO 64105 816-474-4444 842-8709 572
TF: 800-525-4514 ■ *Web:* follytheater.org

Folsom Buick Gmc 12640 Auto Mall Cir.........Folsom CA 95630 916-358-8963 57
Web: folsombuickgmc.com

Folsom Chamber of Commerce 200 Wool St.....Folsom CA 95630 916-985-2698 985-4117 139
TF: 800-585-4483 ■ *Web:* www.folsomchamber.com

Folsom Lake Ford 12755 Folsom Blvd...........Folsom CA 95630 916-353-2000 57
TF: 800-730-0457 ■ *Web:* www.folsomlakeford.com

Folsom Powerhouse State Historic Park
9980 Greenback Ln..........................Folsom CA 95630 916-985-4843 565
Web: www.parks.ca.gov

Folsom Ready Mix Inc
3401 Fitzgerald Rd...................Rancho Cordova CA 95742 916-851-8300 135
TF: 800-635-1486 ■ *Web:* www.folsomreadymix.com

Folsom State Prison 300 Prison Rd............Represa CA 95671 916-985-2561 213
Web: cdcr.ca.gov

Folsom Technology Group Inc
440 Trowbridge Ln..........................Folsom CA 95763 916-851-7330 180
Web: www.ftgroup.com

Foltz Concrete Pipe Co LLC
11875 N NC Hwy 150..................Winston-Salem NC 27127 800-229-8525 183
TF: 800-229-8525 ■ *Web:* www.foltzconcretepipe.com

Fomo Products Inc 2775 Barber Rd.............Norton OH 44203 330-753-4585 753-9566* 601
*Fax: Cust Svc ■ *TF:* 800-321-5585 ■ *Web:* www.fomo.com

Fona International Inc 1900 Averill Rd...........Geneva IL 60134 630-578-8600 123
Web: www.fona.com

Fonar Corp 110 Marcus Dr.....................Melville NY 11747 631-694-2929 390-7766 382
NASDAQ: FONR ■ *Web:* www.fonar.com

Fond du Lac Area Assn of Commerce
207 N Main St..........................Fond du Lac WI 54935 920-921-9500 921-9559 139
TF: 800-279-8811 ■ *Web:* www.fdlac.com

Fond du Lac Band of Lake Superior Chippewa
1720 Big Lake Rd..........................Cloquet MN 55720 218-879-4593 878-7169 132
TF: 888-888-6007 ■ *Web:* fdlrez.com

Fond du Lac Convention & Visitors Bureau
171 S Pioneer Rd.......................Fond du Lac WI 54935 920-923-3010 929-6846 206
TF: 800-937-9123 ■ *Web:* www.fdl.com

Fond du Lac County 160 S Macy St.........Fond du Lac WI 54935 920-929-3000 929-3293 338
Web: www.fdlco.wi.gov

Fond Du Lac Lutheran Home Inc
244 N Macy St..........................Fond Du Lac WI 54935 920-921-9520 371
Web: www.lutheranhomesfonddulac.org

Fond du Lac Public Library
32 Sheboygan St.......................Fond du Lac WI 54935 920-929-7080 929-7082 434-3
TF: 800-686-1346 ■ *Web:* fdlpl.org

Fond du Lac Tribal & Community College
2101 14th St..............................Cloquet MN 55720 218-879-0800 879-0814 165
TF: 800-657-3712 ■ *Web:* www.fdltcc.edu

Fonda & Fraser LLP
Watt Plaza 1925 Century Park E Ste 1380......Los Angeles CA 90067 310-553-3320 445
Web: www.fondafraserlaw.com

Fonda San Miguel 2330 W N Loop Blvd...........Austin TX 78756 512-459-4121 671
TF: 800-375-4685 ■ *Web:* www.fondasanmiguel.com

Fondaction
Bureau 103 2175 Blvd de Maisonneuve Est......Montreal QC H2K4S3 514-525-5505 528
TF: 800-253-6665 ■ *Web:* www.fondaction.com

Fonds de solidarite FTQ
545 Cremazie Blvd E Ofc 200................Montreal QC H2M2W4 514-383-8383 528
Web: www.fondsftq.com

FONEX Data Systems Inc
5400 Ch St-Francois......................St-Laurent QC H4S1P6 514-333-6639 224
Web: www.fonex.com

Fonkoze USA Inc
1718 Connecticut Ave NW Ste 201..........Washington DC 20009 202-628-9033 463
TF: 800-293-0308 ■ *Web:* www.fonkoze.org

Fonner Park 700 E Stolley Pk Rd............Grand Island NE 68801 308-382-4515 384-2753 642
TF: 800-456-3412 ■ *Web:* www.fonnerpark.com

Fontaine Fifth Wheel
7574 Commerce Cir........................Trussville AL 35173 205-661-4900 655-9982 60
TF: 800-874-9780 ■ *Web:* www.fifthwheel.com

Fontaine Modification Co
9827 Mt Holly Rd..........................Charlotte NC 28214 800-366-8246 516
TF: 800-366-8246 ■ *Web:* fontainemodification.com

Fontaine Trailer Co
430 Letson Rd PO Box 619..................Haleyville AL 35565 205-486-5251 779
TF: 800-821-6535 ■ *Web:* www.fontainetrailer.com

Fontaine Truck Equipment Co
7574 Commerce Cir........................Trussville AL 35173 205-661-4900 655-9982 516
TF: 800-874-9780 ■ *Web:* www.fontaine.com

Fontainebleau Miami Beach
4441 Collins Ave.......................Miami Beach FL 33140 305-538-2000 669
TF: 800-548-8886 ■ *Web:* fontainebleau.com

Fontainebleau State Park
67825 US Hwy 190.........................Mandeville LA 70448 985-624-4443 565
TF: 888-677-3668 ■ *Web:* www.crt.state.la.us

Fontana Chamber of Commerce
8491 Sierra Ave...........................Fontana CA 92335 909-822-4433 822-6238 139
Web: www.fontanachamber.org

Fontana CPAs Pa
2519 N Mcmullen Booth Rd Ste 5............Clearwater FL 33761 727-799-9533 2
Web: fontanacpas.com

Fontana Paper Mills Inc
13733 Valley Blvd...........................Fontana CA 92335 909-823-4100 557
Web: www.fontanaroof.com

Fontana Regional Library
33 Fryemont Rd.........................Bryson City NC 28713 828-488-2382 434-3
Web: www.fontanalib.org

Fontana Village Resort
300 Woods Rd PO Box 68................Fontana Dam NC 28733 828-498-2211 669
TF: 800-849-2258 ■ *Web:* fontanavillage.com

Food & Agricultural Policy Research Institute (FAPRI)
Iowa State University 578 Heady Hall.............Ames IA 50011 515-294-1183 294-6336 634
Web: www.fapri.iastate.edu

Food & Drug Administration (FDA)
5600 Fishers Ln..........................Rockville MD 20857 301-827-2410 443-3100 340-10
TF: 888-463-6332 ■ *Web:* www.fda.gov
Center for Devices & Radiological Health (CDRH)
10903 New Hampshire Ave WO66-5429...Silver Spring MD 20993 301-796-7100 847-8149 340-10
TF: 800-638-2041 ■ *Web:* www.fda.gov
Center for Veterinary Medicine
7519 Standish Pl........................Rockville MD 20855 240-276-9000 276-9115 340-10
Web: www.fda.gov/cvm
CFSAN 5100 Paint Branch Pkwy..........College Park MD 20740 888-723-3366 340-10
TF: 888-723-3366 ■ *Web:* www.fda.gov
National Center for Toxicological Research
3900 N Ctr Rd..........................Jefferson AR 72079 870-543-7000 543-7576 340-10
TF: 800-638-3321 ■ *Web:* www.fda.gov/nctr
Vaccines, Blood & Biologics
1401 Rockville Pike Ste 200N MS HFM-4.....Rockville MD 20852 301-827-0372 340-10
Web: www.fda.gov/cber

Food & Drug Administration Regional Offices (FDA)
Central Region
200 Chestnut St Rm 900................Philadelphia PA 19106 215-597-4390 597-4660 340-10
Web: www.fda.gov
Northeast Region 158-15 Liberty Ave...........Jamaica NY 11433 718-662-5416 662-5434 340-10
Web: www.fda.gov
Pacific Region 1301 Clay St Ste 1180N..........Oakland CA 94612 877-696-6775 340-10
TF: 877-696-6775 ■ *Web:* www.hhs.gov

Food & Drug Law Institute (FDLI)
1155 15th St NW Ste 800..................Washington DC 20005 202-371-1420 371-0649 49-10
TF: 800-956-6293 ■ *Web:* www.fdli.org

Food & Nutrition Service
3101 Pk Ctr Dr..........................Alexandria VA 22302 703-305-2062 340-1
Web: www.fns.usda.gov
Food Stamp Program
3101 Pk Ctr Dr Ste 808..................Alexandria VA 22302 703-305-2022 305-1117 340-1
TF: 800-221-5689 ■ *Web:* www.fns.usda.gov
Western Regional Office
90 Seventh St Ste 10-100.............San Francisco CA 94103 415-705-1310 705-1364 340-1
Web: www.fns.usda.gov

Food & Nutrition Service Regional Offices (FNS)
Mid-Atlantic Regional Office
300 Corporate Blvd....................Robbinsville NJ 08691 609-259-5025 259-5185 340-1
Web: fns.usda.gov
Midwest Region
77 W Jackson Blvd 20th Fl.................Chicago IL 60604 312-353-6664 340-1
Web: www.fns.usda.gov
Mountain Plains Region
1244 Speer Blvd Ste 903...................Denver CO 80204 303-844-0300 844-2160 340-1
Web: www.fns.usda.gov
Northeast Region 10 Cswy St Rm 501............Boston MA 02222 617-565-6370 565-6473 340-1
Web: www.fns.usda.gov
Southeast Region 61 Forsyth St SW.............Atlanta GA 30303 404-562-1801 562-1807 340-1
Web: www.fns.usda.gov/fns-regional-offices
Southwest Region
1100 Commerce St Rm 555.................Dallas TX 75242 214-290-9800 340-1
Web: www.fns.usda.gov

Food & Water Watch
1616 P St NW Ste 300.....................Washington DC 20036 202-683-2500 305
TF: 855-340-8083 ■ *Web:* www.foodandwaterwatch.org

Food & Wine Magazine
1120 Ave of the Americas Ste 9...............New York NY 10036 813-979-6625 457-11
TF: 800-333-6569 ■ *Web:* www.foodandwine.com

Food 4 Less 678 N Wilson Way..............Stockton CA 95205 209-466-2751 297-8
Web: myfood4less.com

Food Addicts In Recovery Anonymous (FA)
400 W Cummings Pk Ste 1700................Woburn MA 01801 781-932-6300 48-21
Web: www.foodaddicts.org

Food Allergy & Anaphylaxis Network (FAAN)
11781 Lee Jackson Hwy Ste 160...............Fairfax VA 22033 703-691-3179 691-2713 48-17
TF: 800-929-4040 ■ *Web:* www.foodallergy.org

Food Bank For New York City
39 Broadway 10th Fl......................New York NY 10006 212-566-7855 566-1463 299
TF: 866-692-3663 ■ *Web:* www.foodbanknyc.org

Food City 1005 N Arizona Ave.................Chandler AZ 85224 480-857-2198 345
TF: 800-755-7292 ■ *Web:* www.myfoodcity.com

Food Concepts Inc 2551 Parmenter St.........Middleton WI 53562 608-831-5006 463
TF: 800-280-2347 ■ *Web:* foodconcepts.com

Food Concepts International LP
2575 S Loop 289...........................Lubbock TX 79423 806-785-8686 785-8866 670
Web: www.abuelos.com

Food Consulting Co, The
13724 Recuerdo Dr.........................Del Mar CA 92014 858-793-4658 473
TF: 800-793-2844 ■ *Web:* www.foodlabels.com

Food Corps 281 Park Ave S....................New York NY 10010 212-596-7045 305
TF: 800-321-3054 ■ *Web:* foodcorps.org

Food Country USA 566 E Main St..............Abingdon VA 24210 276-628-3332 345
Web: foodcountryusainc.com

Food Fight Restaurant 5111 Monona Dr.........Monona WI 53716 608-467-3130 671
Web: www.foodfightinc.com

Food for the Poor Inc (FFP)
6401 Lyons Rd.......................Coconut Creek FL 33073 954-427-2222 48-5
TF: 800-427-9104 ■ *Web:* www.foodforthepoor.org

Food for Thought Inc 10704 Oviatt Rd............Honor MI 49640 231-326-5444 345
Web: www.foodforthought.net

Name / Address	City	State	Zip	Phone	Fax	Class
Food Giant Supermarkets 120 Industrial Dr. *Web:* foodgiant.com	Sikeston	MO	63801	573-471-3500		345
Food Ingredient News 49 Walnut Pk Bldg 2 *TF:* 866-285-7215 ■ *Web:* www.bccresearch.com	Wellesley	MA	02481	781-489-7301	253-3933	531-12
Food Management Associates Inc 22349 La Palma Ave Ste 115 *Web:* www.foodmgt.com	Yorba Linda	CA	92887	714-694-2828		194
Food Management Magazine 1300 E Ninth St *Web:* www.penton.com	Cleveland	OH	44114	216-696-7000		457-21
Food Marketing Institute (FMI) 2345 Crystal Dr Ste 800 *TF:* 800-732-2639 ■ *Web:* www.fmi.org	Arlington	VA	22202	202-220-0600	429-4519	49-18
Food Perspectives Inc 13755 First Ave N Ste 500 *Web:* foodperspectives.com	Plymouth	MN	55441	763-553-7787		261
Food Processing Magazine 555 W Pierce Rd Ste 301 *Web:* www.foodprocessing.com	Itasca	IL	60143	630-467-1300	467-1179	457-21
Food Research & Action Ctr (FRAC) 1875 Connecticut Ave NW Ste 540 *Web:* www.frac.org	Washington	DC	20009	202-986-2200	986-2525	48-6
Food Research Institute University of Wisconsin Madison 1550 Linden Dr. *Web:* fri.wisc.edu	Madison	WI	53706	608-263-7777	263-1114	668
Food Safety & Inspection Service 1400 Independence Ave SW *Web:* www.fsis.usda.gov	Washington	DC	20250	202-720-7025	205-0158	340-1
Food Service Technologies Inc 5256 Eisenhower Ave *Web:* www.mytech24.com	Alexandria	VA	22304	703-354-3835		610
Food Services of America Inc 16100 N 71st St Ste 400 *TF:* 800-528-9346 ■ *Web:* www.fsafood.com	Scottsdale	AZ	85254	480-927-4000	927-4299	297-8
Food Warming Equipment Company Inc 7900 S Rt 31 *TF Sales:* 800-222-4393 ■ *Web:* www.fwe.com	Crystal Lake	IL	60014	815-459-7500	459-7989	298
Foodbank of Southeastern Virginia 800 Tidewater Dr. *Web:* www.foodbankonline.org	Norfolk	VA	23517	757-627-6599		474
Foodbuy LLC 1105 Lakewood Pkwy *Web:* www.foodbuy.com	Alpharetta	GA	30009	678-256-8000		194
FoodChek Systems Inc 1414 8 St SW Ste 450 *TF:* 877-298-0208 ■ *Web:* www.foodcheksystems.com	Calgary	AB	T2R1J6	403-269-9424		407
Foodland Super Market Ltd 3536 Harding Ave *Web:* www.foodland.com	Honolulu	HI	96816	808-732-0791	737-6952	345
FoodLink Online LLC 475 Alberto Way Ste 100 *Web:* www.itradenetwork.com/login	Los Gatos	CA	95032	925-660-1100		387
Foods of All Nations 2121 Ivy Rd *Web:* www.foodsofallnations.com	Charlottesville	VA	22903	434-296-6131		345
Foodscience Corp 20 New England Dr Ste 10 *TF:* 800-451-5190 ■ *Web:* www.foodsciencecorp.com	Essex Junction	VT	05452	802-878-5508	878-0549	799
Foodservice & Packaging Institute (FPI) 7700 Leesburg Pk. *Web:* www.fpi.org	Falls Church	VA	22046	703-538-3551	241-5603	49-13
Fool Hollow Lake Recreation Area 1500 N Fool Hollow Lake Rd	Show Low	AZ	85901	928-537-3680		565
Foot Locker Inc 112 W 34th St *NYSE:* FL ■ *TF:* 800-952-5210 ■ *Web:* www.footlocker-inc.com	New York	NY	10120	212-720-3700		301
Foot of the Mountain Motel 200 W Arapahoe Ave. *TF:* 866-773-5489 ■ *Web:* www.footofthemountainmotel.com	Boulder	CO	80302	303-442-5688	442-5719	379
Foot Solutions Inc 4101 Roswell Rd Ste 800 *Web:* footsolutions.com	Marietta	GA	30062	770-984-0844		310
Foote Steel Corp 6635 Edgewater Dr *Web:* www.footesteel.com	Orlando	FL	32810	407-293-0120		480
Foothill College 12345 El Monte Rd. *Fax: Admissions ■ *TF:* 800-234-1597 ■ *Web:* www.foothill.edu	Los Altos Hills	CA	94022	650-949-7777	949-7048*	162
Foothill Presbyterian Hospital 250 S Grand Ave. *Web:* www.cvhp.org	Glendora	CA	91741	626-963-8411		374-3
Foothill Ready Mix Inc 11415 State Hwy 99W *Web:* foothillreadymix.com	Red Bluff	CA	96080	530-527-2565		191-1
Foothill Village 1400 S Foothill Dr *Web:* www.foothillvillage.com	Salt Lake City	UT	84108	801-487-6670		460
Foothills Asset Management Ltd 8767 E Via de Ventura Ste 175 *TF:* 800-663-9870 ■ *Web:* www.faml.net	Scottsdale	AZ	85258	480-777-9870		401
Foothills Correctional Institution 5150 Western Ave. *Web:* ncdps.gov	Morganton	NC	28655	828-438-5585	438-5598	412
Foothills Inn 1625 N La Crosse St. *TF:* 877-428-5666 ■ *Web:* www.thefoothillsinn.com	Rapid City	SD	57701	605-348-5640	348-0073	379
Foothills Mall 7401 N La Cholla Blvd *Web:* www.shopfoothillsmall.com	Tucson	AZ	85741	520-742-7191		460
Foothills Medical Centre (FMC) 1403 29th St NW *Fax Area Code: 403 ■ *TF:* 888-342-2471 ■ *Web:* www.albertahealthservices.ca	Calgary	AB	T2N2T9	780-342-2000	944-1663*	374-2
Footlocker.com Inc 112 W 34th St *TF:* 800-863-8932 ■ *Web:* www.footaction.com	New York	NY	10120	715-261-9719		301
Foot-So-Port Shoe Corp 405 E Forest St. *Web:* www.footsoport.com	Oconomowoc	WI	53066	262-567-4416		301
Footstar Inc 933 MacArthur Blvd. *TF:* 800-322-2885 ■ *Web:* www.footstar.com	Mahwah	NJ	07430	201-934-2000		301
Footwear Distributors & Retailers of America (FDRA) 1319 F St NW Ste 700 *TF:* 800-252-6232 ■ *Web:* www.fdra.org	Washington	DC	20004	202-737-5660		49-4
FOP (Fraternal Order of Police) 701 Marriott Dr. *TF:* 800-451-2711 ■ *Web:* www.fop.net	Nashville	TN	37214	615-399-0900	399-0400	48-15
Foppiano Wine Co 12707 Old Redwood Hwy *TF:* 800-678-4763 ■ *Web:* www.foppiano.com	Healdsburg	CA	95448	707-433-7272		443
For Eyes 285 W 74th Pl *TF:* 877-688-9891 ■ *Web:* www.foreyes.com	Hialeah	FL	33014	800-367-3937		543
For the Bride Magazine 222 W 37th St. *Web:* www.demetriosbride.com	New York	NY	10018	212-967-5222		457-11
Foraker Design LLC 5277 Manhattan Cir Ste 210 *Web:* www.foraker.com	Boulder	CO	80303	303-449-0202		809
Forbes Capretto 470 Cayuga Rd. *Web:* www.forbeshomes.com	Cheektowaga	NY	14225	716-688-5597	688-6674	187
Forbes Energy Services LLC 3000 S Business Hwy 28 *Web:* www.forbesenergyservices.com	Alice	TX	78333	361-664-0549		536
Forbes Hospice 4800 Friendship Ave *TF:* 800-381-8080 ■ *Web:* ahn.org	Pittsburgh	PA	15224	412-578-5000		371
Forbes Inc 60 Fifth Ave *TF:* 800-295-0893 ■ *Web:* www.forbes.com	New York	NY	10011	212-620-2200		637-9
Forbes Library 20 W St *TF:* 800-969-9778 ■ *Web:* www.forbeslibrary.org	NorthHampton	MA	01060	413-587-1012	587-1015	434-3
Forbes Magazine 60 Fifth Ave *TF:* 800-295-0893 ■ *Web:* www.forbes.com	New York	NY	10011	800-295-0893		457-5
Forbes Regional Hospital 2570 Haymaker Rd *TF:* 800-436-2461 ■ *Web:* ahn.org	Monroeville	PA	15146	412-858-2000		374-3
Forbes Snyder Tristate Cash 54 Northampton St *TF:* 800-222-4064 ■ *Web:* www.forbes-snyder.com	Easthampton	MA	01027	413-529-2950		253
Forbo Flooring North America 8 Maplewood Dr Humboldt Industrial Pk *Fax Area Code: 570 ■ *TF:* 800-842-7839 ■ *Web:* www.forbo.com/flooring/en-us	Hazleton	PA	18202	800-842-7839	450-0258*	131
Forbo Flooring Systems 8 Maplewood Dr Humboldt Industrial Pk *Fax Area Code: 570 ■ *Fax: Cust Svc ■ *TF Cust Svc:* 800-842-7839 ■ *Web:* www.forbo.com/flooring/en-us	Hazleton	PA	18202	800-842-7839	450-0258*	291
Forbo Siegling LLC 12201 Vanstory *Web:* www.forbo-siegling.com/us	Huntersville	NC	28078	704-948-0800		207
Force 3 Inc 2151 Priest Bridge Dr *Fax Area Code: 410 ■ *TF:* 800-391-0204 ■ *Web:* www.force3.com	Crofton	MD	21114	301-261-0204	721-5624*	180
FORCE America Inc 501 E Cliff Rd *TF:* 800-328-2732 ■ *Web:* www.forceamerica.com	Burnsville	MN	55337	952-707-1300		358
Force Capital Management LLC 767 Fifth Ave 12th Fl *Web:* www.forcecapital.com	New York	NY	10153	212-451-9150		690
Force Construction Company Inc 990 N National Rd *Web:* www.forceco.com	Columbus	IN	47201	812-372-8441	372-5424	264-3
Force Control Industries Inc 3660 Dixie Hwy *TF:* 800-829-3244 ■ *Web:* www.forcecontrol.com	Fairfield	OH	45014	513-868-0900	868-2105	620
Force Flow Inc 2430 Stanwell Dr *TF:* 800-893-6723 ■ *Web:* www.forceflow.com	Concord	CA	94520	800-893-6723		362
Force Management LLC 10815 Sikes Pl Ste 200 *Web:* www.forcemanagement.com	Charlotte	NC	28277	704-246-2400		463
Force Mass Acceleration 20 W 22nd St Ste 601 *Web:* www.fmaonline.com	New York	NY	10010	212-691-5000	691-5066	637-10
Force10 Networks Inc 1415 N McDowell Blvd. *TF:* 866-600-5100 ■ *Web:* www.force10networks.com	Petaluma	CA	94954	707-665-4400		681
Forcex Inc 2208 Charlotte Ave. *Web:* www.forcexinc.com	Nashville	TN	37203	931-368-0111		177
Forcum Lannom Contractors LLC 350 US Hwy 51 Bypass S *TF:* 800-903-5827 ■ *Web:* www.forcumlannom.com	Dyersburg	TN	38024	731-287-4700	287-4701	188-7
Ford & Harrison LLP 271 17th St NW Ste 1900 *Web:* www.fordharrison.com/Atlanta	Atlanta	GA	30363	404-888-3800		428
Ford Audio-Video Systems Inc 4800 W I- 40 *TF:* 800-654-6744 ■ *Web:* www.fordav.com	Oklahoma City	OK	73128	405-946-9966	946-9991	52
Ford Bacon & Davis 12021 Lakeland Pk Blvd *Web:* www.fbd.com	Baton Rouge	LA	70809	225-292-0050		261
Ford County 100 Gunsmoke St *Web:* www.fordcounty.net	Dodge City	KS	67801	620-227-4670	227-4699	338
Ford County Feed Yard Inc 12466 US Hwy 400	Ford	KS	67842	620-369-2252		10-1
Ford Development Corp 11148 Woodward Ln. *Web:* www.forddevelopment.com	Cincinnati	OH	45241	513-772-1521		186
Ford Equity Research Inc 11722 Sorrento Valley Rd Ste I *TF:* 800-842-0207 ■ *Web:* www.fordequity.com	San Diego	CA	92121	858-755-1327		401
Ford Family Foundation 1600 NW Stewart Pkwy *Web:* www.tfff.org	Roseburg	OR	97471	541-957-5574		305
Ford Fasteners Inc 110 S Newman St *TF:* 800-272-3673 ■ *Web:* www.fordfasteners.com	Hackensack	NJ	07601	201-487-3151	487-1919	278
Ford Field 2000 Brush St Ste 200 *TF:* 800-456-1701 ■ *Web:* www.detroitlions.com	Detroit	MI	48226	313-262-2000	262-2808	720
Ford Foundation 320 E 43rd St. *Web:* www.fordfoundation.org	New York	NY	10017	212-573-5000	351-3677	305
Ford Gum & Machine Company Inc 18 Newton Ave *TF:* 800-662-6776 ■ *Web:* www.fordgum.com	Akron	NY	14001	716-542-4561	542-4610	296-6
Ford Hotel Supply Company Inc 2204 N Broadway *TF:* 800-472-3673 ■ *Web:* www.fordstl.com	Saint Louis	MO	63102	314-231-8400		707

	Phone	Fax	Class

Ford Meter Box Company Inc, The
775 Manchester Ave PO Box 443 Wabash IN 46992 260-563-3171 610
Web: www.fordmeterbox.com

Ford Models Inc
11 East 26th St 14th Fl New York NY 10010 212-219-6500 966-5028 506
Web: www.fordmodels.com

Ford Motor Co PO Box 6248 Dearborn MI 48126 313-845-8540 59
NYSE: F ■ *TF:* 800-392-3673 ■ *Web:* www.ford.com

Ford Motor Credit Co One American Rd Dearborn MI 48126 313-322-3000 217
TF: 800-392-3673 ■ *Web:* credit.ford.com

Ford Nassen & Baldwin PC
8080 N Central Expy Ste 1600 LB 65 Dallas TX 75206 214-523-5100 428
TF: 800-373-0156 ■ *Web:* www.fordnassen.com

Ford of Montebello Inc
2747 Via Campo Montebello CA 90640 323-838-6920 57
TF: 888-313-2305 ■ *Web:* www.fordofmontebello.com

Ford of Ocala Inc 2816 NW Pine Ave Ocala FL 34475 352-732-4800 516
TF: 888-255-1788 ■ *Web:* www.fordofocala.com

Ford Theaters 2580 Cahuenga Blvd E Hollywood CA 90068 323-461-3673 871-5904 572
Web: www.fordamphitheatre.org

Ford's Theatre National Historic Site
511 Tenth St NW Washington DC 20004 202-233-0701 233-0706 564
Web: www.nps.gov/foth

FordDirect 1740 US Hwy 60 PO Box 700 Republic MO 65738 417-732-2626 57
TF: 888-578-8478 ■ *Web:* www.republicford.com

Fordham Auto Sales Inc 236 W Fordham Rd Bronx NY 10468 800-407-1153 57
TF: 800-407-1153 ■ *Web:* www.fordhamtoyota.com

Fordham Financial Management Inc
14 Wall St New York NY 10005 212-732-8500 690
Web: www.fordhamfinancial.com

Fordham Plastics
1204 Village Market Pl Ste 262 Morrisville NC 27560 919-467-0708 319-3
TF: 866-467-0708 ■ *Web:* www.fordhamplastics.com

Fordham University 441 E Fordham Rd Bronx NY 10458 718-817-3240 367-9404* 166
**Fax:* Admissions ■ *TF:* 800-367-3426 ■ *Web:* www.fordham.edu
College at Lincoln Ctr 113 W 60th St New York NY 10023 212-636-6000 636-7368 166
TF: 800-367-3426 ■ *Web:* www.fordham.edu
Westchester 400 Westchester Ave West Harrison NY 10604 914-332-8295 817-3921* 166
**Fax Area Code:* 718 ■ *TF:* 800-606-6090 ■ *Web:* www.fordham.edu

Fordham University School of Law
150 W 62nd St New York NY 10023 212-636-6000 636-7984* 167-1
**Fax:* Admissions ■ *Web:* www.law.fordham.edu

Fordia Inc
2745 de Miniac Ville Saint Laurent Saint Laurent QC H4S1E5 514-336-9211 358
TF: 800-768-7274 ■ *Web:* www.fordia.com

Fore Street 288 Fore St Portland ME 04101 207-775-2717 671
Web: forestreet.biz

Forecast International 22 Commerce Rd Newtown CT 06470 203-426-0800 426-1964 637-10
TF: 800-451-4975 ■ *Web:* www.forecastinternational.com

Forecaster Newsletter
19623 Ventura Blvd Tarzana CA 91356 818-345-4421 531-1

Forecaster, The 5 Fundy Rd Falmouth ME 04105 207-781-3661 781-2060 532-4
Web: www.theforecaster.net

Forefront Analytics LLC
1 Tower Bridge 100 Front St
Ste 1111 West Conshohocken PA 19428 610-341-3900 401
Web: www.forefrontanalytics.com

Foreign Affairs 58 E 68th St New York NY 10065 212-434-9527 457-17
TF Cust Svc: 800-829-5539 ■ *Web:* foreignaffairs.com

Foreign Agricultural Service
1400 Independence Ave SW Washington DC 20250 202-720-3935 340-1
Web: www.fas.usda.gov

Foreign Candy Company Inc
1 Foreign Candy Dr Hull IA 51239 712-439-1496 439-3207 297-3
TF: 800 831 8541 ■ *Web:* www.foreigncandy.com

Foreign Cinema 2534 Mission St San Francisco CA 94110 415-648-7600 671
Web: www.foreigncinema.com

Foreign Claims Settlement Commission of the US
600 E St NW Washington DC 20579 202-616-6975 616-6993 340-14
Web: www.justice.gov

Foreign Policy Assn (FPA) 470 Pk Ave S New York NY 10016 212-481-8100 481-9275 48-7
TF: 800-628-5754 ■ *Web:* www.fpa.org

Foreign Policy Institute
1740 Massachusetts Ave NW Nitze Bldg Washington DC 20036 202-663-5600 663-5769 634
Web: www.sais-jhu.edu

Foreign Policy Research Institute (FPRI)
1528 Walnut St Ste 610 Philadelphia PA 19102 215-732-3774 732-4401 634
Web: www.fpri.org

Foreign Service Institute
4000 Arlington Blvd Rt 50 Arlington VA 22204 703-302-6703 340-16
Web: www.state.gov/m/fsi

Foreign Trade Export Packing Co
1350 Lathrop St Houston TX 77020 713-672-8211 311
Web: www.ftep.com

Forell-Elsesser Engineers Inc
160 Pine St Ste 600 San Francisco CA 94111 415-837-0700 261
Web: www.forell.com

Foreman Tool & Mold Corp
3850 Swenson Ave Saint Charles IL 60174 630-377-6389 711
Web: www.foremantool.com

Foremost Farms USA E10889A Penny Ln Baraboo WI 53913 608-355-8700 355-8699 296-10
TF: 800-362-9196 ■ *Web:* www.foremostfarms.com

Foremost Industries Inc
2375 Buchanan Trail W Greencastle PA 17225 717-597-7166 106
Web: www.foremost-fit.com

Foremost Insurance Co
5600 Beech Tree Ln Caledonia MI 49316 800-532-4221 391-4
TF: 800-532-4221 ■ *Web:* www.foremost.com

Foremost Machine Builders Inc
23 Spielman Rd Fairfield NJ 07004 973-227-0700 111
TF: 800-328-5088 ■ *Web:* foremostmachine.com

Foremost Media 1337 Excalibur Dr Janesville WI 53546 608-758-4841 177
Web: foremostmedia.com

Foremost Mfg Company Inc 941 Ball Ave Union NJ 07083 908-687-4646 483
Web: www.foremost-mfg.com

Foremostco Inc 8457 NW 66th St Miami FL 33166 305-592-8986 426-1362* 694
**Fax Area Code:* 800 ■ *TF:* 800-421-8986 ■ *Web:* www.foremostco.com

Forensic Fluids Laboratories Inc
225 Parsons St Kalamazoo MI 49007 269-492-7700 743
TF: 866-492-2517 ■ *Web:* www.forensicfluids.com

Forensic It 57 E Southcrest Cir Edwardsville IL 62025 314-677-3950 743
TF: 877-483-3284 ■ *Web:* www.forensicit.us

Forent Energy Ltd 12th Ave SW Calgary AB T2R1L5 403-262-9444 539
Web: www.forentenergy.com

Forenta LP
2300 W Andrew Johnson Hwy Ste A Morristown TN 37814 423-586-5370 586-3470 427
Web: www.forentausa.com

Forepaugh's 276 S Exchange St Saint Paul MN 55102 651-224-5606 671
Web: www.forepaughs.com

Foresight Financial Group Inc
3106 N Rockton Ave Rockford IL 61103 815-847-7500 70
Web: foresightfg.com

Foresight Group Inc
2822 N Martin Luther King Jr Blvd Lansing MI 48906 517-485-5700 485-0202 687
Web: www.foresightgr.com

Foresite Group Inc
5185 Peachtree Pkwy Ste 240 Norcross GA 30092 770-368-1399 261
Web: fg-inc.net

Foresite Software LLC S2756A County T Baraboo WI 53913 608-393-1019 525
Web: www.foresitesoftware.com

Forest Agency Inc
7310 W Madison St Forest Park IL 60130 708-383-9000 390
Web: forestagency.com

Forest at Duke 2701 Pickett Rd Durham NC 27705 919-490-8000 490-0887 672
TF: 800-474-0258 ■ *Web:* www.forestduke.org

Forest Capital Museum State Park
204 Forest Pk Dr Perry FL 32348 850-584-3227 565
Web: www.floridastateparks.org

Forest City Equity Services Inc
50 Public Sq Ste 1170 Cleveland OH 44113 216-416-3500 653

Forest City Ratner Cos (FCRC)
1 MetroTech Ctr N Brooklyn NY 11201 718-923-8400 653
Web: www.forestcity.net

Forest City Residential Group
50 Public Sq Ste 1515 Cleveland OH 44113 216-416-3906 655
Web: www.forestcity.net

Forest City Technologies Inc
299 Clay St Wellington OH 44090 440-647-2115 647-2644 326
TF: 800-657-4413 ■ *Web:* www.forestcitytech.com

Forest City Trading Group LLC
10250 SW Greenburg Rd Ste 300 Portland OR 97223 503-246-8500 246-1116 191-3
TF: 800-767-3284 ■ *Web:* www.fctg.com

Forest County 200 E Madison St Crandon WI 54520 715-478-3475 478-3815 338
Web: www.forestcountywi.com

Forest County 526 Elm St Ste 3 Tionesta PA 16353 814-755-3537 755-8837 338
TF: 800-323-9997 ■ *Web:* www.co.forest.pa.us

Forest Electric Corp 1375 BRdway New York NY 10018 212-318-1500 318-1518 189-4
TF: 800-801-6984 ■ *Web:* www.forestelectric.net

Forest Guild
80 E San Francisco PO Box 519 Santa Fe NM 87504 505-983-8992 986-0798 48-13
Web: forestguild.org

Forest Haven Nursing & Rehabilitation Center LLC
171 Thrasher Dr Jonesboro LA 71251 318-259-2729 371
Web: www.foresthavennursingandrehab.com

Forest Hills Journal
394 Wards Corner Rd Ste 170 Loveland OH 45140 513-248-8600 688-7444* 532-4
**Fax Area Code:* 212 ■ *TF:* 888-894-2113

Forest Hills Local School
7550 Forest Rd Cincinnati OH 45255 513-231-3600 685
Web: www.foresthills.edu

Forest Hills Public Schools
6590 Cascade Rd SE Grand Rapids MI 49546 616-669-2700 493-8519 532-4

Forest History Society
701 William Vickers Ave Durham NC 27701 919-682-9319 682-2349 48-13
Web: www.foresthistory.org

Forest Industries Telecommunications (FIT)
1565 Oak St Eugene OR 97401 541-485-8441 485-7556 49-20
Web: www.landmobile.com

Forest Investment Assoc
15 Piedmont Ctr Ste 1250 Atlanta GA 30305 404-261-9575 261-9574 401
Web: www.forestinvest.com

Forest Laboratories Inc
909 Third Ave New York NY 10022 212-421-7850 583
Web: www.frx.com

Forest Lake Area Chamber of Commerce
20 Lake St N Forest Lake MN 55025 651-464-3200 464-3201 139
Web: forestlakechamber.org

Forest Lake Area School District
6100 210th St N Forest Lake MN 55025 651-982-8100 982-8137 685
TF: 866-632-9992 ■ *Web:* www.forestlake.k12.mn.us

Forest Lake State Park
397 Forest Lake Rd Dalton NH 03598 603-466-3860 565
Web: www.nhstateparks.org

Forest Landowners Assn (FLA)
900 Cir 75 Pkwy Ste 205 Atlanta GA 30339 404-325-2954 325-2955 48-13
TF: 800-325-2954 ■ *Web:* www.forestlandowners.com

Forest Lawn Memorial-Parks & Mortuaries
1712 S Glendale Ave Glendale CA 91205 323-254-3131 510
TF: 800-204-3131 ■ *Web:* www.forestlawn.com

Forest of Nisene Marks State Park
Aptos Creek Rd Aptos CA 95003 831-763-7063 565
Web: www.parks.ca.gov/?page_id=666

Forest Park Nature Ctr
5809 Forest Pk Dr Peoria Heights IL 61616 309-686-3360 50-5
Web: peoriaparks.org

Forest Preserve Dist of Dupage County
1717 31st St Oak Brook IL 60523 630-616-8424 226
TF: 800-526-0857 ■ *Web:* www.dupageforest.com

Forest Products Group Inc, The
1033 Dublin Rd Columbus OH 43215 614-488-9743 191-3
Web: www.forestproductsgroup.com

Forest Products Manufacturing Co
51 E 30th St Jasper IN 47547 812-482-5625 482-9148 683
TF: 800-838-2151 ■ *Web:* forestp.com

Phone · Fax · Class

Forest Products Society
2801 Marshall Ct ... Madison WI 53705 608-231-1361 231-2152 48-2
Web: www.forestprod.org

Forest Resources Assn Inc
600 Jefferson Plaza Ste 350 ... Rockville MD 20852 301-838-9385 49-3
Web: www.forestresources.org

Forest River Inc 58277 SR 19 S ... Elkhart IN 46517 574-296-7700 120
Web: www.forestriverinc.com

Forest Service (USFS)
1400 Independence Ave SW ... Washington DC 20050 202-205-8333 340-1
TF: 800-832-1355 ■ *Web:* www.fs.fed.us

Forest Service Employees for Environmental Ethics (FSEEE)
PO Box 11615 ... Eugene OR 97440 541-484-2692 484-3004 49-7
Web: www.fseee.org

Forest Service Regional Offices
Northern Region-Regional Office
26 Fort Missoula Rd ... Missoula MT 59804 406-329-3511 329-3347 340-1
Web: www.fs.fed.us
US Forest ServiceRocky Mountain Region
740 Simms St ... Golden CO 80401 303-275-5350 275-5366 340-1
Web: www.fs.fed.us
Region 3 (Southwestern Region)
333 Broadway Blvd SE ... Albuquerque NM 87102 505-842-3292 340-1
Web: www.fs.fed.us
Region 5 (Pacific Southwest Region)
1323 Club Dr ... Vallejo CA 94592 707-562-8737 562-9130 340-1
Web: www.fs.usda.gov/r5
Region 6 (Pacific Northwest Region)
333 SW First Ave PO Box 3623 ... Portland OR 97208 503-808-2468 808-2469 340-1
Web: www.fs.fed.us
Region 8 (Southern Region)
1720 Peachtree St Ste 760S ... Atlanta GA 30309 404-347-4177 347-4821 340-1
TF: 877-372-7248 ■ *Web:* www.fs.fed.us
Region 9 (Eastern Region)
626 E Wisconsin Ave ... Milwaukee WI 53202 414-297-3600 297-3808 340-1
Web: www.fs.fed.us

Forest Travel Agency
2440 NE Miami Gardens Dr Ste 107 ... Miami FL 33180 305-932-5560 772
Web: www.foresttravel.com

Forest Valley Veterinary Clinic
2555 Mosby Creek Rd ... Cottage Grove OR 97424 541-942-9132 794
Web: fvvet.com

Forestiere Underground Gardens
5021 W Shaw Ave ... Fresno CA 93722 559-271-0734 97
Web: www.undergroundgardens.com

Foreston Trends Inc
1483 W Via Plata St ... Long Beach CA 90810 310-952-8500 362
Web: www.forestontrends.com

Forestry Suppliers Inc
205 W Rankin St ... Jackson MS 39201 601-354-3565 292-0165 459
TF Cust Svc: 800-752-8460 ■ *Web:* www.forestry-suppliers.com

Forestville/Mystery Cave State Park
21071 County 118 ... Preston MN 55965 507-352-5111 352-5113 565
TF: 888-646-6367 ■ *Web:* www.dnr.state.mn.us

Foretravel Motorcoach Inc
1221 NW Stallings Dr ... Nacogdoches TX 75964 936-564-8367 120
TF: 800-955-6226 ■ *Web:* www.foretravel.com

Forever 21 Inc 2001 S Alameda St ... Los Angeles CA 90058 213-741-5100 157-6
TF Cust Svc: 800-966-1355 ■ *Web:* www.forever21.com

Forever Broadcasting
1 Forever Dr ... Hollidaysburg PA 16648 814-941-9800 643
Web: www.forevermediainc.com

Forever Living Products International Inc
7501 E McCormick Pkwy ... Scottsdale AZ 85258 480-998-8888 905-8451 214
TF: 888-440-2563 ■ *Web:* www.foreverliving.com

Forever Spring 2629 E Craig Rd Ste E ... Las Vegas NV 89030 702-633-4283 238
TF: 800-523-4334 ■ *Web:* www.foreverspring.com

Forex Newscom 55 Water St 50th Fl ... New York NY 10041 212-201-7300 387
TF: 888-503-6739 ■ *Web:* www.forexnews.com

Forge Energy LLC 10999 W I-10 ... San Antonio TX 78230 210-478-5950 536
TF: 800-270-7007 ■ *Web:* www.forgenergy.com

Forge Industries Inc
4450 Market St ... Youngstown OH 44512 330-782-8301 360-3

Forge, The 432 41st St ... Miami Beach FL 33140 305-538-8533 538-7733 671
Web: www.theforge.com

Forged Components Inc 14527 Smith Rd ... Humble TX 77396 281-441-4088 441-8899 483
Web: forgedcomponents.com

Forged Metals Inc 10685 Beech Ave ... Fontana CA 92337 909-350-9260 21

Forged Products Inc (FPI)
6505 N Houston Rosslyn Rd ... Houston TX 77091 713-462-3416 460-9404 483
TF: 800-876-3416 ■ *Web:* www.fpitx.com

Forgentum Inc 9312 W St ... Manassas VA 20110 703-906-8996 180
Web: www.forgentum.com

Forging Industry Assn (FIA)
1111 Superior Ave Ste 615 ... Cleveland OH 44114 216-781-6260 781-0102 49-13
Web: www.forging.org

Foria International Inc
18689 Arenth Ave ... City of Industry CA 91748 626-912-6100 156
Web: www.foria.com

Forino Company LP
555 Mtn Home Rd ... Sinking Spring PA 19608 610-670-2200 186
TF: 800-425-4450 ■ *Web:* www.forino.com

Fork 306 Market St ... Philadelphia PA 19106 215-625-9425 671
Web: www.forkrestaurant.com

Forkardt 2155 Traverse Field Dr ... Traverse City MI 49686 231-995-8300 995-8361 493
TF: 800-544-3823 ■ *Web:* www.forkardt.com

Forked Deer Electric Co-op PO Box 67 ... Halls TN 38040 731-836-7508 245
TF: 844-333-2729 ■ *Web:* www.forkeddeer.com

Forked Run State Park
63300 SR- 124 PO Box 127 ... Reedsville OH 45772 740-378-6206 565
TF: 866-644-6727 ■ *Web:* parks.ohiodnr.gov/forkedrun

Forklifts of Minnesota Inc
2201 W 94th St ... Bloomington MN 55431 952-887-5400 881-3030 385
TF: 800-752-4300 ■ *Web:* www.forkliftsofmn.com

Forks of Cheat Winery
2811 Stewart Town Rd ... Morgantown WV 26508 304-598-2019 50-7
TF: 877-989-4637 ■ *Web:* www.wvwines.com

Phone · Fax · Class

Form Cut Industries Inc
197 Mt Pleasant Ave ... Newark NJ 07104 973-483-5154 483-4512 621
TF: 800-480-9198 ■ *Web:* www.formcut.com

Form Grind Corp
30062 Aventura ... Rancho Santa Margarita CA 92688 949-858-7000 481
Web: www.kellysearch.com

Form House, The 4640 S Kolmar ... Chicago IL 60632 773-577-8500 523-9155 92
Web: theformhouse.com

Form Plastics Co 3825 Stern Ave ... Saint Charles IL 60174 630-443-1400 608
Web: www.formplastics.com

Form-A-Feed Inc (FAF) 740 Bowman St ... Stewart MN 55385 320-562-2413 447
TF: 800-422-3649 ■ *Web:* www.formafeed.com

Formaggio Kitchen on Line LLC
244 Huron Ave ... Cambridge MA 02138 617-354-4750 292
TF: 888-212-3224 ■ *Web:* www.formaggiokitchen.com

Formall Inc 3908 Fountain Vly Dr ... Knoxville TN 37918 865-259-6298 922-3941 602
TF: 800-643-3676 ■ *Web:* www.formall.com

Formaloy Corp 1080 W Jefferson St ... Morton IL 61550 309-266-5381 386

Forman Holt Eliades & Ravin LLC
66 Rte 17 N ... Paramus NJ 07652 201-845-1000 445
Web: www.formanlaw.com

Forman Mills
1070 Thomas Busch Memorial Hwy ... Pennsauken NJ 08110 856-486-1447 157-2
Web: formanmills.com

Forman School
12 Norfolk Rd PO Box 80 ... Litchfield CT 06759 860-567-1802 567-3501 622
Web: www.formanschool.org

For-Mar Nature Preserve & Arboretum
2142 N Genesee Rd ... Burton MI 48509 810-789-8567 823
Web: www.geneseecountyparks.org

Format International Inc
10715 Kahlmeyer Dr ... Saint Louis MO 63132 314-428-2671 317
TF: 800-208-6963 ■ *Web:* www.format-international.com

Formatech It Services
3263 Claremont Way # B ... Napa CA 94558 707-258-1492 196
TF: 800-573-1874 ■ *Web:* www.formatech-it.com

Formax Manufacturing Corp
168 Wealthy St SW ... Grand Rapids MI 49503 616-456-5458 456-7507 1
TF: 800-242-2833 ■ *Web:* formaxmfg.com

Formco Metal Products Inc
556 Clayton Ct ... Wood Dale IL 60191 630-766-4441 295
Web: www.formcometal.com

Formed Fiber Technologies Inc
125 Allied Rd PO Box 1300 ... Auburn ME 04211 207-784-1118 784-1137 606
Web: www.formedfiber.com

Former Governors' Mansion State Historic Site
612 E Blvd Ave ... Bismarck ND 58505 701-328-2666 328-3710 565
TF: 866-243-5352 ■ *Web:* www.nd.gov

Formers by Ernie Inc
7905 Almeda Genoa Rd Ste B ... Houston TX 77075 713-991-3455 358
TF: 866-991-3455 ■ *Web:* www.formersbyernie.net

Formetco Inc 2963 Pleasant Hill Rd ... Duluth GA 30096 770-476-7000 701
TF: 800-367-6382 ■ *Web:* www.formetco.com

Formex Manufacturing Inc
601 Hurricane Shoals Rd NW ... Lawrenceville GA 30046 770-962-9816 596
Web: www.formex.com

Formex Metal Industries Inc
N2b-221 Riverbend Dr ... Kitchener ON N2B2E8 519-745-2260 757
TF: 800-668-6810 ■ *Web:* www.formexmetal.com

FormFactor Inc 7005 SouthFront Rd ... Livermore CA 94551 925-290-4000 290-4010 695
NASDAQ: FORM ■ *TF:* 800-732-0330 ■ *Web:* www.formfactor.com

Formflex Inc PO Box 218 ... Bloomingdale IN 47832 800-255-7659 86
TF: 800-255-7659 ■ *Web:* www.formflexproducts.com

Formica Corp 10155 Reading Rd ... Cincinnati OH 45241 513-786-3400 599
TF: 800-367-6422 ■ *Web:* www.formica.com

Formosa Garden 1011 NE Loop 410 ... San Antonio TX 78209 210-828-9988 826-2566 671
Web: www.formosasa.com

Formosa Plastics Corp USA
9 Peach Tree Hill Rd ... Livingston NJ 07039 973-992-2090 605-2
TF: 888-664-4040 ■ *Web:* www.fpcusa.com

Formosa Restaurant 913 E Broadway ... Columbia MO 65201 573-449-3339 671
Web: www.formosatogo.com

Formosa's 3830 Washington Rd ... Augusta GA 30907 706-855-8998 671

Formost Construction Co PO Box 559 ... Temecula CA 92593 951-698-7270 698-6170 188-3
Web: www.formostconstruction.com

Formotus Inc
9725 SE 36th St Ste 400 ... Mercer Island WA 98040 206-973-5060 177
Web: www.formotus.com

Forms & Surfaces Inc 30 Pine St ... Pittsburgh PA 15223 412-781-9003 701
Web: www.forms-surfaces.com

Forms Manufacturers Inc
312 E Forest Ave ... Girard KS 66743 620-724-8225 724-8188 110
TF: 800-835-0614 ■ *Web:* www.ennis.com/our-network/forms-manufacturers

Formsprag Clutch Inc 23601 Hoover Rd ... Warren MI 40009 586-758-5000 770
Web: www.formsprag.com

Formtek Metal Forming Inc
4899 Commerce Pkwy ... Cleveland OH 44128 216-292-4460 674
TF: 800-631-0520 ■ *Web:* formtekgroup.com

Formula Consultants Inc
100 S Anaheim Blvd ... Anaheim CA 92805 714-778-0123 180
Web: www.formula.com

Formula Ford Inc 265 River St ... Montpelier VT 05602 802-223-5201 57
TF: 888-872-9439 ■ *Web:* formulatruckland.com

Formula Growth Ltd
1010 Sherbrooke St W Ste 2300 ... Montreal QC H3A2R7 514-288-5136 401
Web: www.formulagrowth.ca

Forney Corp
16479 N Dallas Pkwy Ste 600 ... Addison TX 75001 972-458-6100 201
TF Cust Svc: 800-356-7740 ■ *Web:* www.forneycorp.com

Forney Independent School District (Inc)
600 S Bois D ARC St ... Forney TX 75126 972-564-4055 685
Web: www.forneyisd.net

Forney Industries Inc
1830 LaPorte Ave ... Fort Collins CO 80521 800-521-6038 811
TF: 800-521-6038 ■ *Web:* www.forneyind.com

FORNEY LLC
310 Seven Fields Blvd One Adams Pl ... Seven Fields PA 16046 724-346-7400 419
Web: www.forneyonline.com

Name / Address	City	State	Zip	Phone	Fax	Class
Forney Museum of Transportation 4303 Brighton Blvd. *Web:* www.forneymuseum.org	Denver	CO	80216	303-297-1113		520
Fornos of Spain 47 Ferry St *Web:* www.fornosrestaurant.com	Newark	NJ	07105	973-589-4767		671
Forque Kitchen and Bar 330 Tijeras Ave NW Hyatt Regency Albuquerque	Albuquerque	NM	87102	505-843-2700		671
Forquer Group Inc 100 State St Ste 310 *Web:* www.forquer.com	Erie	PA	16507	814-453-3366		174
Forrest County 641 Main St *Web:* www.co.forrest.ms.us	Hattiesburg	MS	39401	601-545-6000		338
Forrest General Hospital 6051 US Hwy 49 *TF:* 800-503-5980 ■ *Web:* www.forresthealth.org	Hattiesburg	MS	39402	601-288-7000	288-4180	374-3
Forrest Hills Mountain Resort & Conference Ctr 135 Forrest Hills Rd *TF:* 800-654-6313 ■ *Web:* forresthillsresort.com	Dahlonega	GA	30533	706-864-6456		669
Forrest Machining Inc 27756 Ave Mentry *Web:* www.forrestmachining.com	Valencia	CA	91355	661-257-0231		529
ForSaleByOwnercom Corp 435 N Michigan Ave Fl 5 *Web:* www.forsalebyowner.com	Chicago	IL	60611	312-222-4653		387
Forsberg Real Estate Co 2422 Jolly Rd Ste 200 *Web:* www.lansingrealestate.com	Okemos	MI	48864	517-349-9330	349-7131	653
Forsbergs Inc 1210 Pennington Ave PO Box 510 *TF Cust Svc:* 800-654-1927 ■ *Web:* www.forsbergs.com	Thief River Falls	MN	56701	218-681-1927	681-2037	273
Forshaw Industries Inc 650 State St *Web:* www.forshaw.com	Charlotte	NC	28208	704-372-6790		690
Forster Electrical Engineering Inc 550 N Burr Oak Ave *Web:* www.forstereng.com	Oregon	WI	53575	608-835-9009		256
Forstmann Little & Co 767 Fifth Ave	New York	NY	10153	212-355-5656		405
Forsyth County 110 E Main St Ste 010 *TF:* 800-252-5119 ■ *Web:* forsythco.com	Cumming	GA	30040	770-781-2120		338
Forsyth County Board of Education 1120 Dahlonega Hwy *Web:* www.forsyth.k12.ga.us	Cumming	GA	30040	770-887-2461	781-6632	685
Forsyth County Public Library 201 N Chestnut St *TF:* 866-345-1884 ■ *Web:* www.forsyth.cc	Winston-Salem	NC	27101	336-703-2665	727-2549	434-3
Forsyth Medical Ctr 3333 Silas Creek Pkwy *Web:* novanthealth.org/forsythmedicalcenter.aspx	Winston-Salem	NC	27103	336-718-5000		374-3
Forsyth Technical Community College 2100 Silas Creek Pkwy *Web:* www.forsythtech.edu	Winston-Salem	NC	27103	336-723-0371	761-2399	800
Forsythe & Long Engineering 4560 Helton Dr	Florence	AL	35630	256-760-0000		261
Fort Abercrombie State Historic Site PO Box 140 *Web:* www.nd.gov	Abercrombie	ND	58001	701-553-8513		565
Fort Abraham Lincoln State Park 4480 Ft Lincoln Rd *Web:* www.parkrec.nd.gov/parks/falsp/falsp.html	Mandan	ND	58554	701-667-6340		565
Fort Adams State Park Harrison Ave *Web:* www.riparks.com	Newport	RI	02840	401-847-2400		565
Fort AP Hill 18436 Fourth St *Web:* www.army.mil	Fort AP Hill	VA	22427	804-633-8120	633-8105	497-2
Fort Atkinson Memorial Hospital 611 Sherman Ave E *TF:* 800-844-5575 ■ *Web:* www.forthealthcare.com	Fort Atkinson	WI	53538	920-568-5000		374-3
Fort Atkinson State Historical Park 201 S Seventh St *Web:* www.fortatkinsononline.org	Fort Calhoun	NE	68023	402-468-5611		565
Fort Atkinson State Preserve c/o Volga River State Recreation Area 10225 Ivy Rd *Web:* www.iowadnr.gov	Fayette	IA	52142	563-425-4161		565
Fort Bayard National Cemetery 200 Camino De Paz PO Box 44 *Web:* www.cem.va.gov/cems/nchp/ftbayard.asp	Fort Bayard	NM	88036	915-564-0201	564-3746	136
Fort Belknap Electric Co-op Inc 1302 W Main PO Box 486 *Web:* www.fortbelknapec.com	Olney	TX	76374	940-564-2343	564-3247	245
Fort Bend Chamber of Commerce 445 Commerce Green Blvd. *Web:* www.fortbendchamber.com	Sugar Land	TX	77478	281-491-0800	491-0112	139
Fort Bend County 301 Jackson St Ste 101 *TF:* 800-388-8075 ■ *Web:* www.fortbendcountytx.gov	Richmond	TX	77469	281-342-3411	341-8669	338
Fort Bend Herald 1902 S Fourth St *Web:* www.fbherald.com	Rosenberg	TX	77471	281-342-4474	342-3219	532-2
Fort Bend Museum 500 Houston St *Web:* www.fortbendmuseum.org	Richmond	TX	77469	281-342-6478		520
Fort Benning 1 Karker St McGinnis-Wickam Hall Ste W-141 *Web:* www.benning.army.mil	Fort Benning	GA	31905	706-545-2218	545-1604	497-2
Fort Bliss National Cemetery 5200 Fred Wilson Rd PO Box 6342 *TF:* 800-273-8255 ■ *Web:* www.cem.va.gov	El Paso	TX	79906	915-564-0201	564-3746	136
Fort Boonesborough State Park 4375 Boonesborough Rd *Web:* www.parks.ky.gov	Richmond	KY	40475	859-527-3131		565
Fort Bowie National Historic Site 3203 S Old Ft Bowie Rd *Web:* www.nps.gov/fobo	Bowie	AZ	85605	520-847-2500	847-2221	564
Fort Bragg Unified School District 312 S Lincoln St *TF:* 800-734-7793 ■ *Web:* www.fbusd.us	Fort Bragg	CA	95437	707-961-2850		685
Fort Bridger State Historic Site PO Box 35 *Web:* www.travelwyoming.com	Fort Bridger	WY	82933	307-782-3842		565
Fort Buford State Historic Site 15349 39th Ln NW *Web:* www.nd.gov	Williston	ND	58801	701-572-9034		565
Fort Caroline National Memorial 12713 Ft Caroline Rd *Web:* www.nps.gov/foca	Jacksonville	FL	32225	904-641-7155	641-3798	564
Fort Casey State Park 1280 S Engle Rd *Web:* www.parks.wa.gov	Coupeville	WA	98239	360-678-4519		565
Fort Caspar Museum 4001 Fort Caspar Rd *TF:* 800-877-7353 ■ *Web:* www.casperwy.gov	Casper	WY	82604	307-235-8462		520
Fort Churchill State Historic Park 10000 Hwy 95A *Web:* www.parks.nv.gov	Silver Springs	NV	89429	775-577-2345		565
Fort Clinch State Park 2601 Atlantic Ave *Web:* www.floridastateparks.org	Fernandina Beach	FL	32034	904-277-7274	277-7225	565
Fort Cobb Lake State Park 27022 Copperhead Rd *TF:* 800-622-6317 ■ *Web:* www.travelok.com	Fort Cobb	OK	73038	405-643-2249	643-5167	565
Fort Collins Area Chamber of Commerce 225 S Meldrum St *TF:* 877-652-8607 ■ *Web:* www.fortcollinschamber.com	Fort Collins	CO	80521	970-482-3746	482-3774	139
Fort Collins City Hall 300 Laporte Ave *Web:* www.fcgov.com	Fort Collins	CO	80521	970-221-6505	224-6107	337
Fort Collins Convention & Visitors Bureau 19 Old Town Sq Ste 137 *TF:* 800-274-3678 ■ *Web:* www.visitftcollins.com	Fort Collins	CO	80524	970-232-3840	232-3841	206
Fort Collins Museum 200 Matthews St *Web:* www.fcgov.com	Fort Collins	CO	80524	970-221-6738	416-2236	520
Fort Collins Museum of Contemporary Art 201 S College Ave *Web:* ftcma.org	Fort Collins	CO	80524	970-482-2787		520
Fort Collins Museum of Discovery 408 Mason Ct *Web:* www.fcmdsc.org	Fort Collins	CO	80524	970-221-6738		520
Fort Collins Symphony 214 S College Ave *TF:* 800-274-3678 ■ *Web:* www.fcsymphony.org	Fort Collins	CO	80524	970-482-4823	482-4858	573-3
Fort Columbia State Park Highway 101 *Web:* www.parks.wa.gov	Chinook	WA	98614	360-777-8221		565
Fort Cooper State Park 3100 S Old Floral City Rd *Web:* www.floridastateparks.org	Inverness	FL	34450	352-726-0315		565
Fort Custer National Cemetery 15501 Dickman Rd *TF:* 800-273-8255 ■ *Web:* www.cem.va.gov	Augusta	MI	49012	269-731-4164	731-2428	136
Fort Custer Recreation Area 5163 Ft Custer Dr *Web:* www.michigandnr.com	Augusta	MI	49012	269-731-4200		565
Fort Davidson State Historic Site 118 E Maple *Web:* www.mostateparks.com/ftdavidson.htm	Pilot Knob	MO	63663	573-546-3454		565
Fort Davis National Historic Site PO Box 1379 *TF:* 800-524-3015 ■ *Web:* www.nps.gov/foda	Fort Davis	TX	79734	432-426-3224	426-3122	564
Fort Dearborn Co 6035 W Gross Pt Rd *Web:* www.fortdearborn.com	Niles	IL	60714	773-774-4321	774-9105	627
Fort Defiance State Park 175th St 1500 Harpen St *Web:* www.iowadnr.gov	Milford	IA	51351	712-337-3211		565
Fort Delaware State Park PO Box 170 *Web:* www.destateparks.com	Delaware City	DE	19706	302-834-7941	836-2539	565
Fort Detrick 810 Schreider St *TF:* 800-256-7621 ■ *Web:* www.detrick.army.mil	Frederick	MD	21702	301-619-7613		497-2
Fort Docs 533 Pacific Ave *Web:* www.rmscd.com	Santa Rosa	CA	95407	707-571-8313		317
Fort Dodge Chamber of Commerce 24 N Ninth St Ste A *Web:* www.greaterfortdodge.com	Fort Dodge	IA	50501	515-955-5500	955-3245	139
Fort Dodge Correctional Facility 1550 L St *Web:* doc.iowa.gov	Fort Dodge	IA	50501	515-574-4700		213
Fort Dodge Public Library 424 Central Ave *Web:* www.fortdodgeiowa.org	Fort Dodge	IA	50501	515-573-8167	573-5422	434-3
Fort Donelson National Battlefield PO Box 434 *TF:* 800-426-8366 ■ *Web:* www.nps.gov	Dover	TN	37058	931-232-5706	232-4085	564
Fort Douglas Military Museum 32 Potter St Ft Douglas *TF:* 800-746-9882 ■ *Web:* www.fortdouglas.org	Salt Lake City	UT	84113	801-581-1251		520
Fort Dummer State Park 517 Old Guilford Rd *Web:* www.vtstateparks.com	Brattleboro	VT	05301	802-254-2610		565
Fort Duncan Regional Medical Ctr 3333 N Foster Maldonado Blvd **Fax:* Admissions ■ *TF:* 800-994-6610 ■ *Web:* www.fortduncanmedicalcenter.com	Eagle Pass	TX	78852	830-773-5321	872-2549*	374-3
Fort DuPont State Park 45 Clinton St *Web:* www.destateparks.com	Delaware City	DE	19706	302-834-7941		565
Fort East Martello Museum 3501 S Roosevelt Blvd *Web:* kwahs.com	Key West	FL	33040	305-296-3913		520
Fort Ebey State Park 400 Hill Vly Dr *Web:* www.parks.wa.gov	Coupeville	WA	98239	360-678-4636		565
Fort Edgecomb State Historic Site 66 Ft Rd *Web:* www.maine.gov	Edgecomb	ME	04556	207-882-7777		565
Fort Edward Express Company Inc 1402 Rt 9 *TF:* 800-342-1233 ■ *Web:* bulktransporter.com	Fort Edward	NY	12828	518-792-6571		780
Fort Erie Race Track 230 Catherine St PO Box 1130 *TF:* 800-295-3770 ■ *Web:* www.fortorieracing.com	Fort Erie	ON	L2A5N9	905-871-3200		642

Name / Address	City	State	Zip	Phone	Fax	Class
Fort Fetterman State Historic Site 752 Hwy 93 *Web:* www.wyoparks.state.wy.us	Douglas	WY	82633	307-358-2864		565
Fort Fisher State Recreation Area 1000 Loggerhead Rd *Web:* www.ncparks.gov	Kure Beach	NC	28449	910-458-5798		565
Fort Flagler State Park 10541 Flagler Rd *Web:* www.parks.wa.gov	Nordland	WA	98358	360-385-1259		565
Fort Fred Steele State Historic Site I-80 Exit 228 *Web:* wyoparks.state.wy.us	Sinclair	WY	82334	307-320-3013		565
Fort Frederica National Monument 6515 Frederica Rd *Web:* www.nps.gov	Saint Simons Island	GA	31522	912-638-3639	634-5357	564
Fort Frederick State Park 11100 Ft Frederick Rd *Web:* dnr2.maryland.gov	Big Pool	MD	21711	301-842-2155		565
Fort Gaines Historic Site 51 Bienville Blvd. *Web:* www.dauphinisland.org/fort.htm	Dauphin Island	AL	36528	251-861-6992		50-3
Fort Garry, The 222 Broadway *TF:* 800-665-8088 ■ *Web:* www.fortgarryhotel.com	Winnipeg	MB	R3C0R3	204-942-8251	956-2351	379
Fort George Island Cultural State Park 12157 Heckscher Dr *Web:* www.floridastateparks.org/fortgeorgeisland	Jacksonville	FL	32226	904-251-2320		565
Fort Gibson National Cemetery 1423 Cemetery Rd *Web:* www.cem.va.gov	Fort Gibson	OK	74434	918-478-2334	478-2661	136
Fort Gordon 201 Third Ave. *Web:* www.gordon.army.mil	Fort Gordon	GA	30905	706-791-0110	791-2061	497-2
Fort Griffin State Park & Historic Site 1701 N US Hwy 283 *Web:* www.thc.texas.gov	Albany	TX	76430	325-762-3592		565
Fort Griswold Battlefield State Park c/o Ft Trumbull State Pk 90 Walbach St *Web:* www.ct.gov	New London	CT	06320	860-444-7591		565
Fort Group Inc 100 Challenger Rd 8th Fl *Web:* www.fortgroupinc.com	Ridgefield Park	NJ	07660	201-445-0202		738
Fort Halifax State on the Kennebec c/o Bureau of Parks & Lands Ste 7 *Web:* maine.gov/dacf/parks/index.shtml	Bangor	ME	04401	207-941-4014		565
Fort Hamilton 230 Sheridan Loop Bldg 113 *Web:* www.hamilton.army.mil	Brooklyn	NY	11252	718-630-4101	630-4717	497-2
Fort Hamilton Hospital 630 Eaton Ave *TF:* 800-388-4483 ■ *Web:* www.ketteringhealth.org	Hamilton	OH	45013	513-867-2000		374-3
Fort Harrison State Park 5753 Glenn Rd *Web:* www.in.gov	Indianapolis	IN	46216	317-591-0904		565
Fort Hartsuff State Historical Park 82034 Fort Ave *Web:* outdoornebraska.gov/forthartsuff	Burwell	NE	68823	308-346-4715		565
Fort Hays State University 600 Pk St *TF Admissions:* 800-628-3478 ■ *Web:* www.fhsu.edu	Hays	KS	67601	785-628-4000		166
Fort Henry National Historic Site PO Box 213 *TF Cust Svc:* 800-437-2233 ■ *Web:* www.forthenry.com	Kingston	ON	K7L4V8	613-542-7388	542-3054	520
Fort Hill Construction Inc 8118 Hollywood Blvd *Web:* www.forthill.com	Los Angeles	CA	90069	323-656-7425		186
Fort Hill The John C Calhoun House Clemson University Ft Hill St *TF:* 800-777-1004 ■ *Web:* clemson.edu	Clemson	SC	29634	864-656-2475		50-3
Fort Hood 1001 761st Tank Battalion Ave Ste W105 *Web:* www.hood.army.mil	Fort Hood	TX	76544	254-286-5139	288-2750	497-2
Fort Huachuca Smith St Bldg 50010 *Web:* huachuca-www.army.mil	Fort Huachuca	AZ	85613	520-533-2330	533-3778	497-2
Fort Humboldt State Historic Park c/o N Coast Redwoods District Office PO Box 2006 *Web:* www.parks.ca.gov/default.asp?page_id=665	Eureka	CA	95502	707-445-6567		565
Fort Hunter Mansion & Park 5300 N Front St *TF:* 800-222-3373 ■ *Web:* www.forthunter.org	Harrisburg	PA	17110	717-599-5751	599-5838	50-3
Fort Jackson 5450 Strom Thurmond Blvd Rm 216 *Web:* jackson.armylive.dodlive.mil	Fort Jackson	SC	29207	803-751-7511		497-2
Fort Jesup State Historic Site 32 Geoghagan Rd *TF:* 888-677-5378 ■ *Web:* www.crt.state.la.us	Many	LA	71449	318-256-4117		565
Fort Kearny State Recreation Area 1020 V Rd 1020 'V' Rd *Web:* www.nps.gov/index.htm	Kearney	NE	68845	308-865-5305		565
Fort Kent State Historic Site 106 Hogan Rd. *TF:* 800-332-1501 ■ *Web:* www.maine.gov	Bangor	ME	04401	207-941-4014		565
Fort King George State Historic Site 1600 Wayne St *Web:* www.gastateparks.org	Darien	GA	31305	912-437-4770		565
Fort Knox PO Box 995 *Web:* www.knox.army.mil	Fort Knox	KY	40121	502-624-4985		497-2
Fort Knox Federal Credit Union PO Box 900 *TF:* 800-756-3678 ■ *Web:* www.fortknoxfcu.org	Radcliff	KY	40159	502-942-0254		219
Fort Knox State Historic Site 711 Ft Knox Rd. *Web:* maine.gov/dacf/parks/index.shtml	Prospect	ME	04981	207-469-7719		565
Fort Lancaster State Historic Site 629 Fort Lancaster Rd. *Web:* www.thc.texas.gov	Sheffield	TX	79781	432-836-4391		565
Fort Langley National Historic Site 23433 Mavis Ave *Web:* www.pc.gc.ca/eng/lhn-nhs/bc/langley/index.aspx	Fort Langley	BC	V1M2R5	604-513-4777	513-4798	563
Fort Laramie National Historic Site 965 Grey Rocks Rd *TF:* 800-444-7275 ■ *Web:* www.nps.gov/fola	Fort Laramie	WY	82212	307-837-2221	837-2120	564
Fort Larned National Historic Site 1767 Kansas Hwy 156 *Web:* www.nps.gov	Larned	KS	67550	620-285-6911	285-3571	564
Fort Lauderdale Antique Car Museum 1527 SW First Ave *Web:* www.antiquecarmuseum.org	Fort Lauderdale	FL	33315	954-779-7300		520
Fort Lauderdale City Hall 100 N Andrews Ave. *Web:* www.fortlauderdale.gov	Fort Lauderdale	FL	33301	954-828-5000	828-5017	337
Fort Lauderdale Executive Airport 5101 NW 21st Ave *TF:* 800-955-8770 ■ *Web:* fortlauderdale.gov	Fort Lauderdale	FL	33309	954-828-4955	938-4974	27
Fort Lauderdale Historical Society 219 SW Second Ave *Web:* www.fortlauderdalehistoricalsociety.org	Fort Lauderdale	FL	33301	954-463-4431		520
Fort Lauderdale Hospital 1601 E Las Olas Blvd *TF:* 800-585-7527 ■ *Web:* www.fortlauderdalehospital.org	Fort Lauderdale	FL	33301	954-463-4321	453-5497	374-5
Fort Lauderdale Museum of Art 1 E Las Olas Blvd *Web:* nsuartmuseum.org	Fort Lauderdale	FL	33301	954-525-5500		520
Fort Lauderdale/Hollywood International Airport 100 Aviation Blvd *TF:* 866-682-2258 ■ *Web:* www.broward.org	Fort Lauderdale	FL	33315	954-359-1200	359-0027	27
Fort Leaton State Historic Site PO Box 2349 *Web:* tpwd.texas.gov/state-parks/fort-leaton	Presidio	TX	79845	432-229-3613		565
Fort Leavenworth 881 Mcclellan Ave *Web:* usacac.army.mil	Fort Leavenworth	KS	66027	913-684-4021		497-2
Fort Leavenworth National Cemetery 395 Biddle Blvd *Web:* www.cem.va.gov	Fort Leavenworth	KS	66027	913-758-4105	758-4136	136
Fort Lee 500 Lee Ave *Web:* www.lee.army.mil	Fort Lee	VA	23801	804-765-3000		497-2
Fort Lee Free Public Library 320 Main St *TF:* 800-275-4278 ■ *Web:* www.bccls.org	Fort Lee	NJ	07024	201-592-3614	585-0375	434-3
Fort Lee Regional Chamber of Commerce (GFLCOC) 210 Whiteman St *Web:* www.fortleechamber.com	Fort Lee	NJ	07024	201-944-7575	944-5168	139
Fort Lewis College 1000 Rim Dr **Fax:* Admissions ■ *TF:* 877-352-2656 ■ *Web:* www.fortlewis.edu	Durango	CO	81301	970-247-7010	247-7179*	166
Fort Logan National Cemetery 4400 W Kenyon Ave *Web:* www.cem.va.gov	Denver	CO	80236	303-761-0117	781-9378	136
Fort Loudoun State Historic Park 338 Ft Loudoun Rd. *Web:* www.state.tn.us	Vonore	TN	37885	423-884-6217		565
Fort Lowell Museum 2900 N Craycroft Rd *TF:* 800-965-2030 ■ *Web:* arizonahistoricalsociety.org	Tucson	AZ	85712	520-885-3832		520
Fort Lyon National Cemetery 15700 County Rd HH *Web:* www.cem.va.gov	Las Animas	CO	81054	303-761-0117	781-9378	136
Fort MacArthur Museum 3601 S Gaffey St *Web:* www.ftmac.org	San Pedro	CA	90731	310-548-2631	241-0847	520
Fort Madison 614 Ninth St *Web:* fortmadison.com	Fort Madison	IA	52627	319-372-5471	372-6404	206
Fort Malden National Historic Site 100 Laird Ave *Web:* www.pc.gc.ca/eng/lhn-nhs/on/malden/index.aspx	Amherstburg	ON	N9V2Z2	519-736-5416	736-6603	563
Fort Marcy Hotel Suites 321 Kearney Ave *TF:* 888-667-2775 ■ *Web:* www.allseasonsresortlodging.com	Santa Fe	NM	87501	505-988-2800		379
Fort Massac State Park 1308 E Fifth St *Web:* www.dnr.illinois.gov/parks/pages/fortmassac.aspx	Metropolis	IL	62960	618-524-4712		565
Fort Matanzas National Monument 8635 A1A S *Web:* www.nps.gov/foma	Saint Augustine	FL	32080	904-471-0116	471-7605	564
Fort McAllister State Historic Park 3894 Ft McAllister Rd *TF:* 800-864-7275 ■ *Web:* www.gastateparks.org	Richmond Hill	GA	31324	912-727-2339	727-3614	565
Fort McClary State Historic Site Rt 103 *Web:* maine.gov/dacf/parks/index.shtml	Kittery point	ME	03905	207-384-5160		565
Fort McDowell Casino 10424 N Ft McDowell Rd *TF:* 800-843-3678 ■ *Web:* www.fortmcdowellcasino.com	Fort Mcdowell	AZ	85264	800-843-3678		133
Fort McHenry National Monument & Historic Shrine 2400 E Fort Ave *TF:* 866-945-7920 ■ *Web:* www.nps.gov	Baltimore	MD	21230	410-962-4290	962-2500	520
Fort McKavett State Historic Site 7066 FM 864 Rd. *Web:* www.thc.texas.gov/historic-sites/fort-mckavett-state-historic-site	Fort McKavett	TX	76841	325-396-2358		565
Fort McMurray Chamber of Commerce 9612 Franklin Ave Ste 304 *Web:* www.fortmcmurraychamber.ca	Fort McMurray	AB	T9H2J9	780-743-3100	790-9757	137
Fort McNab National Historic Site C/O Halifax Citadel National Historic Site *Web:* www.pc.gc.ca/eng/lhn-nhs/ns/mcnab/contact.aspx	Halifax	NS	B3K5M7	902-426-5080	426-4228	563
Fort Meade Museum PO Box 164 PO Box 164 *TF:* 800-346-4383 ■ *Web:* www.fortmeademuseum.org	Fort Meade	SD	57741	605-347-9822		520
Fort Meigs State Memorial 29100 W River Rd. *TF:* 800-283-8916 ■ *Web:* www.fortmeigs.org	Perrysburg	OH	43551	419-874-4121	874-9446	50-3
Fort Mill School District 4 120 E Elliott St *Web:* www.fortmillschools.org	Fort Mill	SC	29715	803-548-2527		685
Fort Miller Company Inc, The 688 Wilbur Ave. *Web:* www.fortmiller.com	Greenwich	NY	12834	518-695-5000		183
Fort Mitchell National Cemetery 553 Hwy 165 *Web:* www.cem.va.gov	Fort Mitchell	AL	36856	334-855-4731	855-4740	136

Phone | Fax | Class

Fort Mojave Tribal Council
500 Merriman Ave — Needles CA 92363 — 760-629-4591 — 132
Web: mojaveindiantribe.com

Fort Montgomery State Historic Site
690 Route 9W PO Box 213 — Fort Montgomery NY 10922 — 845-446-2134 — 565
Web: parks.ny.gov/historic-sites/28/details.aspx

Fort Morgan Area Chamber of Commerce
300 Main St — Fort Morgan CO 80701 — 970-867-6702 — 139
TF: 800-354-8660 ■ *Web:* www.fortmorganchamber.org

Fort Morris State Historic Site
2559 Ft Morris Rd — Midway GA 31320 — 912-884-5999 — 565
Web: www.gastateparks.org

Fort Mose Historic State Park
15 Ft Mose Trl — Saint Augustine FL 32084 — 904-823-2232 — 565
Web: www.floridastateparks.org/fortmose

Fort Mott State Park
454 Ft Mott Rd — Pennsville NJ 08070 — 856-935-3218 — 565
Web: www.njparksandforests.org

Fort Mountain State Park
181 Ft Mtn Pk Rd — Chatsworth GA 30705 — 706-695-2621 — 565
Web: www.gastateparks.org

Fort Myer Construction Corp
Washington National Airport Gravely Pt — Washington DC 20018 — 202-636-9535 — 186
Web: www.fortmyer.com

Fort Myers Beach Chamber of Commerce
17200 San Carlos Blvd — Fort Myers Beach FL 33931 — 239-454-7500 — 454-7910 — 139
TF: 866-998-9250 ■ *Web:* www.fortmyersbeach.org

Fort Necessity National Battlefield
1 Washington Pkwy — Farmington PA 15437 — 724-329-5512 — 329-8682 — 564
Web: www.nps.gov

Fort Niagara State Park
1 Scott Ave — Youngstown NY 14174 — 716-745-7273 — 565
Web: parks.ny.gov/parks/175/details.aspx

Fort O'Brien State Historic Site
106 Hogan Rd — Bangor ME 04401 — 207-941-4014 — 565
TF: 800-332-1501 ■ *Web:* www.maine.gov

Fort Ontario State Historic Site
1 E Fourth St — Oswego NY 13126 — 315-343-4711 — 565
Web: parks.ny.gov/historic-sites/20/details.aspx

Fort Orange Press Inc 11 Sand Creek Rd — Albany NY 12205 — 518-489-3233 — 627
TF: 800-777-3233 ■ *Web:* www.fortorangepress.com

Fort Owen State Park PO Box 995 — Lolo MT 59847 — 406-273-4253 — 565
Web: stateparks.mt.gov

Fort Parker State Park 194 Pk Rd 28 — Mexia TX 76667 — 254-562-5751 — 565
Web: tpwd.texas.gov/state-parks/fort-parker

Fort Peck Community College PO Box 398 — Poplar MT 59255 — 406-768-6300 — 768-6301 — 165
TF: 800-313-3822 ■ *Web:* www.fpcc.edu

Fort Phil Kearny State Historic Site
528 Wagon Box Rd — Banner WY 82832 — 307-684-7629 — 565
Web: www.fortphilkearny.com

Fort Phoenix State Reservation
Green St — Fairhaven MA 02719 — 508-992-4524 — 565

Fort Pierce Inlet State Park
905 Shorewinds Dr — Fort Pierce FL 34949 — 772-468-3985 — 565
Web: www.floridastateparks.org

Fort Pillow State Historic Park
3122 Pk Rd — Henning TN 38041 — 731-738-5581 — 565
TF: 800-250-8015 ■ *Web:* www.state.tn.us

Fort Pitt Capital Group Inc
680 Andersen Dr Foster Plaza Ten — Pittsburgh PA 15220 — 412-921-1822 — 528
TF: 800-471-5827 ■ *Web:* www.fortpittcapital.com

Fort Pitt Museum
601 Commonwealth Pl,Bldg C — Pittsburgh PA 15222 — 412-471-1764 — 520
TF: 800-732-0999 ■ *Web:* fortpittblockhouse.com

Fort Point Capital Partners LLC
275 Sacramento St 8th Fl — San Francisco CA 94111 — 415-625-0909 — 401
Web: www.fortpointcap.com

Fort Point National Historic Site
Fort Mason Bldg 201 — San Francisco CA 94123 — 415-556-1693 — 561-4390 — 564
Web: www.nps.gov/fopo

Fort Point State Park
Bureau of Parks & Lands
106 Hogan Rd 4th Fl Ste 7 — Bangor ME 04401 — 207-941-4014 — 941-4222 — 565
Web: maine.gov/dacf/parks/index.shtml

Fort Polk 2030 14th St — Fort Polk LA 71459 — 337-531-2911 — 497-2
TF: 800-752-4658 ■ *Web:* www.jrtc-polk.army.mil

Fort Popham State Historic Site
10 Perkins Farm Ln — Phippsburg ME 04562 — 207-389-1335 — 565
Web: www.maine.gov

Fort Pulaski National Monument
PO Box 30757 — Savannah GA 31410 — 912-786-8182 — 786-6023 — 564
TF: 800-228-5150 ■ *Web:* www.nps.gov/fopu/index.htm

Fort Raleigh National Historic Site
1401 National Pk Dr — Manteo NC 27954 — 252-473-5772 — 473-2595 — 564
Web: www.nps.gov

Fort Ransom State Park
5981 Walt Hjelle Pkwy — Fort Ransom ND 58033 — 701-973-4331 — 565
Web: www.parkrec.nd.gov/parks/frsp/frsp.html

Fort Recovery Industries Inc
2440 Ohio 49 — Fort Recovery OH 45846 — 419-375-4121 — 375-4194 — 199
Web: www.fortrecoveryindustries.com

Fort Richardson National Cemetery
Bldg 58-512 Davis Hwy Bldg 58 — Fort Richardson AK 99505 — 907-384-7075 — 384-7111 — 136
Web: www.cem.va.gov/cems/nchp/ftrichardson.asp

Fort Richardson State Park Historic Site & Lost Creek Reservoir State Trailway
228 State Pk Rd 61 — Jacksboro TX 76458 — 940-567-3506 — 565
Web: tpwd.texas.gov

Fort Ridgely State Park
72158 County Rd 30 — Fairfax MN 55332 — 507-426-7840 — 426-7112 — 565
TF: 888-646-6367 ■ *Web:* www.dnr.state.mn.us

Fort Riley 405 Pershing Ct — Fort Riley KS 66442 — 785-239-2022 — 239-2592 — 497-2
TF: 800-273-8255 ■ *Web:* www.riley.army.mil

Fort Robinson State Park PO Box 392 — Crawford NE 69339 — 308-665-2900 — 565
Web: www.stateparks.com

Fort Rock State Natural Area
725 Summer St NE Ste C — Salem OR 97739 — 800-551-6949 — 565
TF: 800-551-6949 ■ *Web:* www.oregonstateparks.org

Fort Rodd Hill National Historic Site
603 Ft Rodd Hill Rd — Victoria BC V9C2W8 — 250-478-5849 — 478-2816 — 563
Web: www.pc.gc.ca

Fort Roofing & Sheet Metal Works Inc
14 W Oakland Ave — Sumter SC 29150 — 803-773-9391 — 773-7711 — 189-12
Web: www.fortroofing.com

Fort Rosecrans National Cemetery
Cabrillo Memorial Dr — San Diego CA 92106 — 619-553-2084 — 553-6593 — 136
Web: www.cem.va.gov/cems/nchp/ftrosecrans.asp

Fort Ross State Historic Park
19005 Coast Hwy 1 — Jenner CA 95450 — 707-847-3286 — 565
Web: www.parks.ca.gov/default.asp?page_id=449

Fort Saint Jean Baptiste State Historic Site
155 Jefferson St — Natchitoches LA 71457 — 318-357-3101 — 565
TF: 888-677-7853 ■ *Web:* www.crt.state.la.us

Fort Saint John & District Chamber of Commerce
9325 100th St — Fort Saint John BC V1J4N4 — 250-785-6037 — 785-6050 — 137
Web: www.fsjchamber.com

Fort Sam Houston
3630 Stanley Rd — Fort Sam Houston TX 78234 — 210-221-8580 — 497-2
Web: www.cs.amedd.army.mil

Fort Sam Houston National Cemetery
1520 Harry Wurzbach Rd — San Antonio TX 78209 — 210-820-3891 — 820-3445 — 136
Web: www.cem.va.gov/cems/nchp/ftsamhouston.asp

Fort Sanders Regional Medical Ctr
1901 W Clinch Ave — Knoxville TN 37916 — 865-541-1111 — 374-3
Web: www.fsregional.com

Fort Scott Community College
2108 S Horton St — Fort Scott KS 66701 — 620-223-2700 — 223-6530* — 162
*Fax: Admissions ■ *TF:* 800-874-3722 ■ *Web:* www.fortscott.edu

Fort Scott National Cemetery
900 E National Ave — Fort Scott KS 66701 — 620-223-2840 — 223-2505 — 136
TF: 800-827-1000 ■ *Web:* www.cem.va.gov/cems

Fort Scott National Historic Site
PO Box 918 — Fort Scott KS 66701 — 620-223-0310 — 223-0188 — 564
Web: www.nps.gov

Fort Simcoe State Park
5150 Ft Simcoe Rd — White Swan WA 98952 — 509-874-2372 — 565
Web: www.parks.wa.gov

Fort Sisseton State Historical Park
11907 434th Ave — Lake City SD 57247 — 605-448-5474 — 565
Web: gfp.sd.gov/state-parks/directory/fort-sisseton

Fort Smith Convention & Visitors Bureau
2 N 'B' — Fort Smith AR 72901 — 479-783-8888 — 784-2421 — 206
TF: 800-637-1477 ■ *Web:* www.fortsmith.org

Fort Smith Convention Ctr
55 S Seventh St — Fort Smith AR 72901 — 479-788-8932 — 205
Web: www.fortsmith.org

Fort Smith Little Theatre
401 N Sixth St — Fort Smith AR 72913 — 479-783-2966 — 573-4
Web: www.fslt.org

Fort Smith Museum of History
320 Rogers Ave — Fort Smith AR 72901 — 479-783-7841 — 520
TF: 800-745-3000 ■ *Web:* www.fortsmithmuseum.org

Fort Smith National Cemetery
522 Garland Ave — Fort Smith AR 72901 — 479-783-5345 — 785-4189 — 136
TF: 800-535-1117 ■ *Web:* www.cem.va.gov

Fort Smith National Historic Site
301 Parker Ave — Fort Smith AR 72901 — 479-783-3961 — 783-5307 — 564
Web: www.nps.gov

Fort Smith Public Library
3201 Rogers Ave — Fort Smith AR 72903 — 479-783-0229 — 434-3
TF: 866-660-0885 ■ *Web:* fortsmithlibrary.org

Fort Smith Regional Airport
6700 McKennon Blvd Ste 200 — Fort Smith AR 72903 — 479-452-7000 — 452-7008 — 27
TF: 800-992-7433 ■ *Web:* www.fortsmithairport.com

Fort Smith Regional Chamber of Commerce
612 Garrison Ave — Fort Smith AR 72901 — 479-783-3111 — 783-6110 — 139
Web: www.fortsmithchamber.org

Fort Smith Trolley Museum
100 S Fourth St — Fort Smith AR 72901 — 479-783-0205 — 520
Web: www.fstm.org

Fort Snelling National Cemetery
7601 34th Ave — Minneapolis MN 55450 — 612-726-1127 — 136
Web: www.cem.va.gov

Fort Snelling State Park
101 Snelling Lake Rd — Saint Paul MN 55111 — 612-725-2389 — 725-2391 — 565
TF: 888-646-6367 ■ *Web:* www.dnr.state.mn.us

Fort Stark Historic Site
Wildrose Ln — New Castle NH 03854 — 603-436-1552 — 565
Web: www.nhstateparks.org

Fort Stevens State Park
100 Peter Iredale Rd — Hammond OR 97121 — 503-861-1671 — 565
Web: www.oregonstateparks.org

Fort Stevenson State Park
1252A 41st St NW — Garrison ND 58540 — 701-337-5576 — 565
Web: www.parkrec.nd.gov/parks/fssp/fssp.html

Fort Story 2600 Tarawa Ct — Norfolk VA 23521 — 757-462-8425 — 497-2
Web: www.cnic.navy.mil

Fort Sumter National Monument
1214 Middle St — Sullivans Island SC 29482 — 843-883-3123 — 883-3910 — 564
Web: www.nps.gov/fosu

Fort Tejon State Historic Park
c/o Central Valley District Office
22708 Broadway St — Columbia CA 95310 — 209-536-5930 — 248-8373* — 565
*Fax Area Code: 661 ■ *Web:* www.parks.ca.gov/default.asp?page_id=585

Fort Totten State Historic Site
PO Box 224 — Fort Totten ND 58335 — 701-766-4441 — 565
Web: www.nd.gov

Fort Trumbull State Park
90 Walbach St — New London CT 06320 — 860-444-7591 — 565
Web: www.ct.gov/dep/cwp/view.asp?a=2716&q=325200

Fort Union National Monument
PO Box 127 — Watrous NM 87753 — 505-425-8025 — 454-1155 — 564
Web: www.nps.gov

Fort Union Trading Post National Historic Site
15550 Hwy 1804 — Williston ND 58801 — 701-572-9083 — 572-7321 — 564
TF: 800-486-8173 ■ *Web:* www.nps.gov

Name / Address	City	State	ZIP	Phone	Fax	Class
Fort Valley State University 1005 State University Dr TF: 877-462-3878 ■ Web: www.fvsu.edu	Fort Valley	GA	31030	478-825-6211		166
Fort Vancouver National Historic Site 612 E Reserve St Web: www.nps.gov	Vancouver	WA	98661	360-816-6230		564
Fort Vancouver Regional Library 1007 E Mill Plain Blvd Web: www.fvrl.org	Vancouver	WA	98663	360-329-9906		434-3
Fort Walton Beach Medical Ctr (FWBMC) 1000 Mar-Walt Dr Web: www.fwbmc.com	Fort Walton Beach	FL	32547	850-862-1111		374-3
Fort Ward Museum & Historic Site 4301 W Braddock Rd Web: www.alexandriava.gov/FortWard	Alexandria	VA	22304	703-838-4848	671-7350	520
Fort Washington Investment Advisors Inc 303 Broadway Ste 1200 TF: 888-244-8167 ■ Web: www.fortwashington.com	Cincinnati	OH	45202	513-361-7600		401
Fort Washington Park 13551 Ft Washington Rd TF: 800-514-3849 ■ Web: www.nps.gov	Fort Washington	MD	20744	301-763-4600	763-1389	564
Fort Washington State Park 500 Bethlehem Pk Web: www.dcnr.state.pa.us	Fort Washington	PA	19034	215-591-5250		565
Fort Wayne Ballet Inc 300 E Main St Web: www.fortwayneballet.org	Fort Wayne	IN	46802	260-484-9646	484-9647	573-1
Fort Wayne Children's Zoo 3411 Sherman Blvd Web: kidszoo.org	Fort Wayne	IN	46808	260-427-6800	427-6820	823
Fort Wayne City Hall 1 Main St Web: www.cityoffortwayne.org	Fort Wayne	IN	46802	260-427-1221	427-1371	337
Fort Wayne Civic Theater 303 E Main St Web: www.fwcivic.org	Fort Wayne	IN	46802	260-422-8641		573-4
Fort Wayne Community Schools (FWCS) 1200 S Clinton St Web: www.fwcs.k12.in.us	Fort Wayne	IN	46802	260-467-2009		685
Fort Wayne Dance Collective 437 E Berry St Web: www.fwdc.org	Fort Wayne	IN	46802	260-424-6574		573-1
Fort Wayne International Airport 3801 W Ferguson Rd Ste 209 Web: www.fwairport.com	Fort Wayne	IN	46809	260-747-4146	747-1762	27
Fort Wayne Metals Inc 9609 Ardmore Ave Web: www.fwmetals.com	Fort Wayne	IN	46809	260-747-4154		295
Fort Wayne Museum of Art 311 E Main St Web: www.fwmoa.org	Fort Wayne	IN	46802	260-422-6467	422-1374	520
Fort Wayne Newspapers Inc 600 W Main St TF: 800-444-3303 ■ Web: www.fortwayne.com	Fort Wayne	IN	46802	260-461-8444		637-8
Fort Wayne Plastics Inc 510 Sumpter St Web: www.fortwayneplastics.com	Fort Wayne	IN	46804	260-432-2520		596
Fort Wayne Public Transportation Corp 801 Leesburg Rd TF: 800-743-3333 ■ Web: www.fwcitilink.com	Fort Wayne	IN	46808	260-432-4546	436-7729	468
Fort Wayne Wire Die Inc 2424 American Way Web: www.fwwd.com	Fort Wayne	IN	46809	260-747-1681	747-4269	757
Fort Wayne/Allen County Convention & Visitors Bureau 927 S Harrison St TF: 800-767-7752 ■ Web: www.visitfortwayne.com	Fort Wayne	IN	46802	260-424-3700	424-3914	206
Fort Wellington National Historic Site 370 Vankoughnet St Web: www.pc.gc.ca/eng/lhn-nhs/on/wellington/index.aspx	Prescott	ON	K0E1T0	613-925-2896	925-1536	563
Fort Wilkins State Park 15223 US Hwy 41 Web: www.michigandnr.com	Copper Harbor	MI	49918	906-289-4215		565
Fort William Henry Corp, The 48 Canada St TF: 800-234-0267 ■ Web: www.fortwilliamhenry.com	Lake George	NY	12845	518-668-3081		378
Fort Worden State Park 200 Battery Way Web: www.parks.wa.gov/fortworden	Port Townsend	WA	98368	360-344-4400		565
Fort Worth Botanic Garden 3220 Botanic Garden Blvd TF: 800-326-2289 ■ Web: www.fwbg.org	Fort Worth	TX	76107	817-392-5510		97
Fort Worth Chamber of Commerce 777 Taylor St Ste 900 TF: 800-433-5747 ■ Web: www.fortworthchamber.com	Fort Worth	TX	76102	817-336-2491	877-4034	139
Fort Worth Chop House 301 Main St Web: www.fortworthchophouse.com	Fort Worth	TX	76102	817-336-4129		671
Fort Worth City Credit Union PO Box 100099 TF: 888-732-3085 ■ Web: www.fwccu.org	Fort Worth	TX	76185	817-732-2803	377-7966	219
Fort Worth City Hall 1000 Throckmorton St TF: 800-211-4450 ■ Web: fortworthtexas.gov	Fort Worth	TX	76102	817-392-2255	392-6187	337
Fort Worth Community Credit Union 1905 Forest Ridge Dr PO Box 210848 TF: 800-817-8234 ■ Web: www.ftwccu.org	Bedford	TX	76021	817-835-5000	835-5235	219
Fort Worth Convention & Visitors Bureau 111 W Fourth St Ste 200 TF: 800-433-5747 ■ Web: www.fortworth.com	Fort Worth	TX	76102	817-336-8791	698-7823	206
Fort Worth Convention Ctr 1201 Houston St TF: 866-630-2588 ■ Web: fortworthtexas.gov	Fort Worth	TX	76102	817-392-6338	392-2756	205
Fort Worth Independent School District 100 N University Dr Web: fwisd.org	Fort Worth	TX	76107	817-871-2000		685
Fort Worth Museum of Science & History 1600 Gendy St TF: 888-255-9300 ■ Web: www.fortworthmuseum.org	Fort Worth	TX	76107	817-255-9300	732-7635	520
Fort Worth Opera 1300 Gendy St TF: 877-396-7372 ■ Web: www.fwopera.org	Fort Worth	TX	76107	817-731-0833	731-0835	573-2
Fort Worth Public Library 500 W Third St Web: fortworthtexas.gov	Fort Worth	TX	76102	817-392-7323		434-3
Fort Worth Star-Telegram 808 Throckmorton St Web: www.star-telegram.com/entertainment	Fort Worth	TX	76102	817-390-7400		532-2
Fort Worth Stockyards National Historic District PO Box 64203 Web: www.fortworthstockyards.org	Fort Worth	TX	76164	817-626-7921	740-8635	50-6
Fort Worth Symphony Orchestra Assn 330 E Fourth St Ste 200 Web: www.fwsymphony.org	Fort Worth	TX	76102	817-665-6500	665-6600	573-3
Fort Worth Weekly 3311 Hamilton Ave Web: www.fwweekly.com	Fort Worth	TX	76107	817-321-9700	335-9575	532-5
Fort Yargo State Park 210 S Broad St Web: www.gastateparks.org	Winder	GA	30680	770-867-3489		565
Fortbrand Services Inc 50 Fairchild Ct Web: www.fortbrand.com	Plainview	NY	11803	516-576-3200		641
Forte & Tablada Inc 9107 Interline Ave Web: forteandtablada.com	Baton Rouge	LA	70809	225-927-9321		261
Forte Data Systems Inc 3330 Paddock Pkwy TF: 800-571-8702 ■ Web: www.fortedata.com	Suwanee	GA	30024	678-208-0206		225
Forte Information Resources LLC 2000 S Colorado Blvd Twr II, Ste 400 Web: www.forteinformation.com	Denver	CO	80222	303-321-3888		463
Forte Research Systems Inc 1200 John Q Hammons Dr Ste 300	Madison	WI	53717	608-826-6000		238
Fortemedia Inc 810 E Arques Ave Web: www.fortemedia.com	Sunnyvale	CA	94085	408-861-8088		256
Fortenberry Jeff (Rep R - NE) 1514 Longworth Bldg Web: fortenberry.house.gov	Washington	DC	20515	202-225-4806	225-5686	342-2
Forth Inc 5959 W Century Blvd Ste 700 TF: 800-553-6784 ■ Web: www.forth.com	Los Angeles	CA	90045	310-999-6784	943-3806	178-2
Forthea Interactive Marketing 2727 Allen Pkwy Ste 1200 *Fax Area Code: 800 ■ TF: 800-882-5905 ■ Web: www.forthea.com	Houston	TX	77019	713-568-2763	580-8936*	5
Forti's Mexican Elder 321 Chelsea St Web: fortisrestaurant.com	El Paso	TX	79905	915-772-0066		671
Fortifiber Building Systems Group 300 Industrial Dr TF: 800-773-4777 ■ Web: www.fortifiber.com	Fernley	NV	89408	775-333-6400	333-6411	552-1
Fortifire Inc 46560 Fremont Blvd Ste 119 Web: www.fortifire.com	Fremont	CA	94538	510-651-7770		177
Fortin Consulting Inc 215 Hamel Rd TF: 844-273-3117 ■ Web: www.fortinconsulting.com	Hamel	MN	55340	763-478-3606		196
Fortis Construction Inc 1705 SW Taylor St Ste 200 TF: 800-364-2059 ■ Web: fortisconstruction.com	Portland	OR	97205	503-459-4477		261
Fortis Films 8581 Santa Monica Blvd Ste 1	West Hollywood	CA	90069	310-659-4533		514
Fortistar LLC 1 N Lexington Ave Web: www.fortistar.com	White Plains	NY	10601	914-421-4900		196
Fortitech Inc 2105 Technology Dr Web: www.fortitech.com	Schenectady	NY	12308	518-372-5155		583
Fortitude Business Solutions LLC PO Box 2095 TF: 877-577-2644	Daphne	AL	36526	877-577-2644		393
Fortney & Weygandt Inc 31269 Bradley Rd Web: www.fortneyweygandt.com	North Olmsted	OH	44070	440-716-4000		186
Fortney Scott LLC 1750 K St NW Ste 325 Web: fortneyscott.com	Washington	DC	20006	202-689-1200		428
Fortrend Corp 687 N Pastoria Ave TF: 888-937-3637 ■ Web: www.fortrend.com	Sunnyvale	CA	94085	408-734-9311	734-4299	695
Fortress Computer Pros 11305 Rancho Bernardo Rd Ste 116 TF: 800-405-4069 ■ Web: www.fortresscomputerpros.com	San Diego	CA	92127	858-451-7020		175
Fortress Integrated Technologies 5805 State Bridge Rd Ste G332	Johns Creek	GA	30097	404-394-9495		808
Fortress Technology Inc 51 Grand Marshall Dr TF: 888-220-8737 ■ Web: www.fortresstechnology.com	Toronto	ON	M1B5N6	416-754-2898		692
Fortrust LLC 4300 Brighton Blvd Web: www.fortrustdatacenter.com	Denver	CO	80216	720-264-2000		196
Fortun Insurance Agency Inc 365 Palermo Ave TF: 877-643-2055 ■ Web: www.fortuninsurance.com	Coral Gables	FL	33134	305-445-3535		390
Fortuna Technologies Inc 1270 A Lawrence Station Rd Web: www.fortuna.com	Sunnyvale	CA	94089	408-541-0200		809
Fortune Bay Resort & Casino 1430 Bois Forte Rd TF: 800-992-7529 ■ Web: fortunebay.com	Tower	MN	55790	218-753-6400		452
Fortune Brands Home & Hardware Inc 520 Lake Cook Rd Web: www.fbhs.com	Deerfield	IL	60015	847-484-4400		609
Fortune Brands Inc 520 Lake Cook Rd NYSE: FBHS ■ TF: 800-225-2719 ■ Web: www.fbhs.com	Deerfield	IL	60015	847-484-4400		185
Fortune Builders International 25082 Paseo Arboleda	Lake Forest	CA	92630	949-380-3080		652
Fortune Contract Inc 272 Kraft Dr Web: www.fortunecontract.com	Dalton	GA	30721	706-279-3669		131
Fortune Cookie 7006 University Ave Web: www.fortunecookietx.com	Lubbock	TX	79413	806-745-2205		671
Fortune Fabrics Inc *Wyoming Weavers* 315 Simpson St Web: www.wyomingweavers.com	Swoyersville	PA	18704	570-288-3666		745-1
Fortune House All Suites Hotel 185 SE 14th Terr Web: fortunehousehotel.com	Miami	FL	33131	305-349-5200		132

Name / Address	City	State	ZIP	Phone	Fax	Class
Fortune Industries Inc 6402 Corporate Dr *Web:* www.ffi.net	Indianapolis	IN	46278	317-532-1374		734
Fortune Metals Inc 330 Hwy 7 E Ste 201 *Web:* www.fortunemetals.com	Richmond Hill	ON	L4B3P8	905-707-0786		791
Fortune Practice Management 1265 El Camino Real Ste 205 *TF:* 800-628-1052 ■ *Web:* fortunemgmt.com	Santa Clara	CA	95050	800-628-1052		463
Fortune Small Business Magazine (FSB) 1271 Ave of the Americas *Web:* www.money.cnn.com/magazines/fsb	New York	NY	10020	212-522-1212		457-5
FortuNet Inc 3901 Graphic Dr *Web:* www.fortunet.com	Las Vegas	NV	89118	702-796-9090		322
Forum at Brookside 200 Brookside Dr *Web:* www.fivestarseniorliving.com	Louisville	KY	40243	502-245-3048		672
Forum at Desert Harbor, The 13840 N Desert Harbor Dr **Fax Area Code:* 617 ■ *Web:* www.fivestarseniorliving.com	Peoria	AZ	85381	623-972-0995	796-8385*	672
Forum at Lincoln Heights 311 W Nottingham Pl *Web:* www.fivestarseniorliving.com	San Antonio	TX	78209	210-824-2314	824-6556	672
Forum at Park Lane 7831 Pk Ln *Web:* www.fivestarseniorliving.com	Dallas	TX	75225	214-369-9902		672
Forum at Tucson 2500 N Rosemont Blvd *Web:* www.fivestarseniorliving.com	Tucson	AZ	85712	520-325-4800	319-4076	672
Forum Communications Co 101 Fifth St N *Web:* www.forumcomm.com	Fargo	ND	58102	701-235-7311		637-8
Forum Credit Union PO Box 50738 *TF:* 800-382-5414 ■ *Web:* www.forumcu.com	Indianapolis	IN	46250	317-558-6000		219
Forum Gallery 730 Fifth Ave *Web:* www.forumgallery.com	New York	NY	10019	212-355-4545	355-4547	42
Forum Manufacturing Inc 77 Brown St *Web:* www.forummfg.com	Milford Center	OH	43045	937-349-8685		321
Forum Motor Inn 800-814 Atlantic Ave PO Box 448 *Web:* www.theforuminoc.homestead.com	Ocean City	NJ	08226	609-399-8700		379
Forum One Communications Corp 2200 Mt Vernon Ave *Web:* www.forumone.com	Alexandria	VA	22301	703-548-1855		809
Forum Publishing Co 383 E Main St *TF:* 800-635-7654 ■ *Web:* www.forum123.com	Centerport	NY	11721	631-754-5000		637-9
Forum South 155-19 Lahn St *Web:* www.theforumnewsgroup.com	Howard Beach	NY	11414	718-845-3221		532-4
Forum, The 101 N Fifth St *TF:* 800-274-5445 ■ *Web:* www.inforum.com	Fargo	ND	58102	701-235-7311	241-5487	532-2
Forward Air Corp 1915 Snapps Ferry Rd Building N *NASDAQ: FWRD* ■ *TF:* 800-726-6654 ■ *Web:* www.forwardair.com	Greeneville	TN	37745	423-636-3380	783-9019	700
Forward Branding & Identity 34 May St *Web:* www.forwardbranding.com	Webster	NY	14500	585-872-9222		195
Forward Corp 219 N Front St *TF:* 800-664-4501 ■ *Web:* www.forwardcorp.com	Standish	MI	48658	989-846-4501		324
Forward Edge LLC 3428 Hauck Rd Ste K *Web:* www.forward-edge.net	Cincinnati	OH	45241	513-761-3343		260
Forward Industries Inc 477 S Rosemary Ave Ste 219 *Web:* www.forwardindustries.com	West Palm Beach	FL	33401	561-465-0030		453
Forward Publishing 125 Maiden Ln *Web:* www.forward.com	New York	NY	10038	212-889-8200	447-6406	637-8
Forward Technology Inc 260 Jenks Ave *TF Cust Svc:* 800-307-6040 ■ *Web:* www.forwardtech.com	Cokato	MN	55321	320-286-2578	286-2467	380
Forward Thinking Systems 105 Route 101A Ste 21 *Web:* forwardthinkingsys.com	Amherst	NH	03031	603-882-8465		180
Forward Ventures 4747 Executive Dr Ste 700 *Web:* www.forwardventures.com	San Diego	CA	92121	858-677-6077		792
Forza Silicon Corp 2947 Bradley St Ste 130 *Web:* www.forzasilicon.com	Pasadena	CA	91107	626-796-1182		256
Forzani Group Ltd 824 41st Ave NE *Web:* www.fglsports.com	Calgary	AB	T2E3R3	403-717-1400		711
Fosdick & Hilmer Inc 525 Vine St *Web:* www.fosdickandhilmer.com	Cincinnati	OH	45202	513-241-5640		261
Fosdick Fulfillment Corp 26 Barnes Industrial Park Rd *Web:* www.fosdickfulfillment.com	North Wallingford	CT	06492	203-269-0211		366
Foseco Metallurgical Inc 20200 Sheldon Rd *Web:* www.vesuvius.com/en/our-solutions/international/foundry.html	Cleveland	OH	44142	440-826-4548	243-7658	145
Foshay Electric 555 Laurel Bay Ln *Web:* www.foshayelectric.com	San Diego	CA	92154	858-277-7676	277-2629	189-4
Foss Maritime Co 1151 Fairview Ave N *TF:* 800-426-2885 ■ *Web:* www.foss.com	Seattle	WA	98109	206-281-3800		465
Foss National Leasing 7200 Yonge St *TF:* 800-461-3677 ■ *Web:* www.fossnational.com	Thornhill	ON	L4J1V8	905-886-4244		126
Foss Performance Materials 11 Merrill Industrial Dr *Web:* www.fossmfg.com	Hampton	NH	03842	603-929-6000	929-6010	745-6
Foss State Park 10252 Hwy 44 *TF:* 800-622-6317 ■ *Web:* www.travelok.com	Foss	OK	73647	580-592-4433	592-4701	565
Foss Waterway Seaport 705 Dock St *Web:* www.fosswaterwayseaport.org	Tacoma	WA	98402	253-272-2750		520
Fossil Butte National Monument 864 Chicken Creek Rd *Web:* www.nps.gov	Kemmerer	WY	83101	307-877-4455	877-4457	564
Fossil Creek Nursery Inc 7029 S College Ave *Web:* www.fossilcreeknursery.com	Fort Collins	CO	80525	970-226-4924		292
Fossil Creek Resources LLC 1521 N Cooper St Ste 650	Arlington	TX	76011	817-701-4970	701-4984	539
Fossil Energy Research Corp 23342 S Pointe Dr Ste C *TF:* 800-227-4224 ■ *Web:* www.ferco.com	Laguna Hills	CA	92653	949-859-4466		41
Fossil Power Systems Inc 10 Mosher Dr Burnside Industrial Pk *Web:* www.fossil.ca	Dartmouth	AB	B3B1N5	902-468-2743		407
Fossil Rim Wildlife Ctr 2299 County Rd 2008 *Web:* www.fossilrim.com	Glen Rose	TX	76043	254-897-2960		823
Fosta-Tek Optics Inc 320 Hamilton St *TF:* 866-221-9157 ■ *Web:* www.fosta-tek.com	Leominster	MA	01453	978-534-6511	537-2168	544
Foster & Motley Inc 7755 Montgomery Rd Ste 100 *Web:* www.fosterandmotley.com	Cincinnati	OH	45236	513-561-6640		401
Foster Bill (Rep D - IL) 1224 Longworth Bldg *Web:* foster.house.gov	Washington	DC	20515	202-225-3515	225-9420	342-2
Foster Blue Water Oil LLC 36065 Water St *Web:* www.fosteroil.com	Richmond	MI	48062	586-727-3996		579
Foster Botanical Garden 50 N Vineyard Blvd *Web:* www.honolulu.gov/parks/hbg/fbg.htm	Honolulu	HI	96817	808-522-7066	522-7050	97
Foster City Chamber of Commerce 1031 E Hillsdale Blvd Ste F *Web:* www.fostercitychamber.com	Foster City	CA	94404	650-573-7600	573-5201	139
Foster City Flowers & Gifts 1160 Chess Dr Ste 1 *TF:* 800-970-7673 ■ *Web:* www.fostercity-flowers.com	Foster City	CA	94404	650-573-6607		292
Foster Construction Products Inc 1105 S Frontenac St *TF:* 800-231-9541 ■ *Web:* www.fosterproducts.com	Aurora	IL	60504	800-231-9541	942-6856	3
Foster County PO Box 257 *TF:* 800-435-5663 ■ *Web:* www.fostercounty.com	Carrington	ND	58421	701-652-1001	652-2173	338
Foster Electric America 1000 E State Pkwy Ste G *Web:* www.fosterelectric.com	Schaumburg	IL	60173	847-310-8200		52
Foster Family Music Center LLC 2967 State St	Bettendorf	IA	52722	563-355-0647		520
Foster Farms Inc PO Box 306 *TF:* 800-255-7227 ■ *Web:* www.fosterfarms.com	Livingston	CA	95334	800-255-7227		10-8
Foster Fuels Inc 16720 Brookneal Hwy *TF:* 800-344-6457 ■ *Web:* www.fosterfuels.com	Brookneal	VA	24528	434-376-2322		579
Foster Grandparent Program c/o Senior Corps 1201 New York Ave NW *TF:* 800-942-2677 ■ *Web:* www.nationalservice.gov	Washington	DC	20525	202-606-5000		197
Foster Lake & Pond Management Inc 9020 White Oak Rd PO Box 1294 *Web:* www.fosterlake.com	Garner	NC	27529	919-772-8548		463
Foster Marketing LLC 3909-F Ambassador Caffery *Web:* www.fostermarketing.com	Lafayette	LA	70503	337-235-1848		7
Foster Pepper Pllc 1111 Third Ave Ste 3400 *TF:* 800-995-5902 ■ *Web:* www.foster.com	Seattle	WA	98101	206-447-4400	447-9700	428
Foster Printing Service Inc 4295 Ohio St *Web:* www.fosterprinting.com	Michigan City	IN	46360	219-879-8366		627
Foster Swift Collins & Smith 313 S Washington Sq *TF:* 800-222-0424 ■ *Web:* www.fosterswift.com	Lansing	MI	48933	517-371-8100		428
Foster Thomas Inc 1788 Forest Dr *TF:* 800-372-3626 ■ *Web:* www.fosterthomas.com	Annapolis	MD	21401	800-372-3626		391-3
Foster's Daily Democrat 150 Venture Dr *Web:* www.fosters.com	Dover	NH	03820	603-742-4455	749-7079	532-2
Foster-Miller Inc 350 Second Ave *Web:* www.qinetiq-na.com	Waltham	MA	02451	781-684-4000		256
fosters 150 Venture Dr *Web:* www.fosters.com	Dover	NH	03820	603-742-4455	749-7079	637-8
Fosters Freeze International LLC 400 E 18th St *Web:* www.fostersfreeze.com	Antioch	CA	94509	510-757-6441		670
Fostoria Area Chamber of Commerce (FACC) 121 N Main St *Web:* www.fostoriaohio.org	Fostoria	OH	44830	419-435-7789	435-0936	139
Foth & Van Dyke & Assoc Inc 2121 Innovation Ct PO Box 5095 *TF:* 800-362-4505 ■ *Web:* www.foth.com	Green Bay	WI	54115	920-497-2500	497-8516	261
Foto News 807 E First St *Web:* www.merrillfotonews.com	Merrill	WI	54452	715-536-7121		532-4
Foto Source Canada Inc 2333 Wyecroft Rd *Web:* www.fotosource.com	Oakville	ON	L6L6L4	905-465-2759	465-0470	119
Fotofabrication Corp 3758 W Belmont Ave *Web:* www.fotofab.com	Chicago	IL	60618	773-463-6211		492
Fotofest Inc 1113 Vine St Ste 101 *Web:* www.fotofest.org	Houston	TX	77002	713-223-5522		184
FotoKem Industries Inc 2801 W Alameda Ave *Web:* www.fotokem.com	Burbank	CA	91505	818-846-3101		225
Fotomedia Technologies LLC 155 Fleet St *Web:* www.fotomedialabs.com	Portsmouth	NH	03801	603-570-4843		387
Fotoprint 975 Pandora Ave *TF:* 888-382-8211 ■ *Web:* www.fotoprint.ca	Victoria	BC	V8V3P4	250-382-8218		627
Fotorecord Print Ctr 45 E Pittsburgh St *Web:* www.fotorecord.com	Greensburg	PA	15601	724-837-0530		627
Fought & Company Inc 14255 SW 72nd Ave *Web:* www.fought.org	Tigard	OR	97224	503-639-3141		189-14
Foulds Inc 520 E Church St *TF:* 800-253-0590 ■ *Web:* fouldspasta.com	Libertyville	IL	60048	847-362-3062		296-31
Foulk Bros Plumbing & Heating Co 322 W Seventh St *Web:* www.foulkbrothers.com	Sioux City	IA	51103	712-258-3388		189-10
Foulkeways at Gwynedd 1120 Meetinghouse Rd *TF:* 800-211-2713 ■ *Web:* www.foulkeways.org	Gwynedd	PA	19436	215-643-2200	646-2917	672

Name / Address	Phone	Fax	Class
Foulston & Siefkin LLP 1551 N Waterfront Pkwy Ste 100 .... Wichita KS 67206 *TF:* 800-526-6529 ■ *Web:* www.foulston.com	316-267-6371		428
Foundation Capital 250 Middlefield Rd .... Menlo Park CA 94025 *Web:* www.foundationcapital.com	650-614-0500		792
Foundation Constructors Inc 81 Big Break Rd .... Oakley CA 94561 *TF:* 800-841-8740 ■ *Web:* www.foundationpiledriving.com	925-754-6633	625-5783	189-5
Foundation Ctr 32 Old Slip 24th Fl............ New York NY 10005 *TF:* 800-424-9836 ■ *Web:* www.foundationcenter.org	212-620-4230	807-3691	48-11
Foundation Fighting Blindness 11435 Cron Hill Dr.................... Owings Mills MD 21117 *TF:* 800-683-5555 ■ *Web:* www.blindness.org	410-568-0150		48-17
Foundation for Acctg Education (FAE) 14 Wall St 19th Fl........................ New York NY 10005 *TF General:* 800-537-3635 ■ *Web:* www.nysscpa.org	212-719-8300	719-3365	49-1
Foundation for Advanced Education in the Sciences (FAES) 1 Cloister Ct............................ Bethesda MD 20814 *Web:* www.faes.org	301-496-7976	402-0174	49-19
Foundation for American Communications (FACS) 85 S Grand Ave.......................... Pasadena CA 91105	626-584-0010		49-14
Foundation for Economic Education (FEE) 30 S Broadway .... Irvington-on-Hudson NY 10533 *TF:* 800-960-4333 ■ *Web:* www.fee.org	404-554-9980		634
Foundation for International Community Assistance (FINCA) 1201 15th St NW 8th fl.................. Washington DC 20005 *TF:* 855-903-4622 ■ *Web:* www.finca.org	202-682-1510	682-1535	48-5
Foundation for Jewish Culture 330 Seventh Ave.......................... New York NY 10001	212-629-0500		48-14
Foundation for Montessori Education 291B Jane St .... Toronto ON M6S3Z3 *Web:* www.montessori-ami.ca	416-769-7457		166
Foundation for Moral Law PO Box 4086 .... Montgomery AL 36103 *Web:* www.morallaw.org	334-262-1245	262-1708	48-7
Foundation for the Carolinas 217 S Tryon St .... Charlotte NC 28202 *TF:* 800-973-7244 ■ *Web:* www.fftc.org	704-973-4500	973-4599	303
Foundation Laboratory 1716 W Holt Ave .... Pomona CA 91768 *TF:* 800-843-7190 ■ *Web:* www.foundationlaboratory.com	909-623-9301		415
Foundation on Economic Trends 4520 E W Hwy Ste 600.................... Bethesda MD 20814 *Web:* www.foet.org	301-656-6272	654-0208	49-12
Foundation Technologies Inc 1400 Progress Industrial Blvd .... Lawrenceville GA 30043 *TF:* 800-773-2368 ■ *Web:* www.foundationtechnologies.com	678-407-4640		191-1
Founders Federal Credit Union 607 N Main St .... Lancaster SC 29720 *TF Tech Supp:* 888-918-7403 ■ *Web:* www.foundersfcu.com	803-289-5927		219
Founders Financial Inc 1020 Cromwell Bridge Rd..................... Towson MD 21286 *TF:* 800-288-3035 ■ *Web:* www.foundersfinancial.com	410-308-9988		796
Founders Garden 2450 Milledge Ave .... Athens GA 30602 *Web:* gardenclub.uga.edu	706-227-5369	227-5370	97
Founders Inn 5641 Indian River Rd .... Virginia Beach VA 23464 *TF:* 800-926-4466 ■ *Web:* www.foundersinn.com	757-424-5511		377
Foundry 9 LLC 44 W 28th St 6th Fl .... New York NY 10001 *Web:* www.foundry9.com	212-989-7999		7
Fountain Circle Care & Rehabilitation Ctr 200 Glenway Rd .... Winchester KY 40391 *Web:* www.fountaincirclecare.com	859-744-1800		450
Fountain Construction Co 5655 Hwy 18 W .... Jackson MS 39209 *Web:* www.fountainconstruction.com	601-373-4162	373-4300	189-10
Fountain County 301 Fourth St County Courthouse .... Covington IN 47932 *TF:* 800-800-5556 ■ *Web:* www.in.gov/judiciary/2948.htm	765-793-2411		338
Fountain Grove Inn, The 101 Fountaingrove Pkwy .... Santa Rosa CA 95403 *TF:* 800-222-6101 ■ *Web:* www.fountaingroveinn.com	707-578-6101		378
Fountain House Inc 425 W 47th St .... New York NY 10036 *Web:* www.fountainhouse.org	212-582-0340		726
Fountain Industries Co 922 E 14th St .... Albert Lea MN 56007 *TF:* 800-328-3594 ■ *Web:* www.fountainindustries.com	507-373-2351		111
Fountain People Inc 4600 Hwy 123.......... San Marcos TX 78666 *Web:* fountainpeople.com	512-392-1155		183
Fountain Valley Chamber of Commerce 10055 Slater Ave Ste 250.............. Fountain Valley CA 92708 *Web:* www.fvchamber.com	714-962-3822		139
Fountain Valley Regional Hospital & Medical Ctr 17100 Euclid St .... Fountain Valley CA 92708 *TF:* 866-904-6871 ■ *Web:* www.fountainvalleyhospital.com	714-966-7200		374-3
Fountain Valley School of Colorado 6155 Fountain Vly School Rd.......... Colorado Springs CO 80911 *Web:* www.fvs.edu	719-390-7035		622
Fountain, The 1100 State Rt 17................. Ramsey NJ 07446 *Web:* www.thefountainspa.com	201-327-5155		77
Fountaindale Public Library 300 W Briarcliff Rd...................... Bolingbrook IL 60440 *TF:* 800-982-2787 ■ *Web:* www.fountaindale.org	630-759-2102		434-3
Fountainhead College of Technology 3203 Tazewell Pk .... Knoxville TN 37918 *TF:* 888-218-7335 ■ *Web:* www.fountainheadcollege.edu	865-688-9422	688-2419	800
Fountainhead Group Inc 23 Garden St.......................... New York Mills NY 13417 *TF:* 800-311-9903 ■ *Web:* www.thefountainheadgroup.com	315-736-0037	768-4220	172
Fountains America Inc 175 Barnstead Rd Ste 4 .... Pittsfield NH 03263 *Web:* www.fountainsamerica.com	603-435-8234		302
Fountains at Millbrook, The 79 Flint Rd .... Millbrook NY 12545 *Web:* www.watermarkcommunities.com	845-605-4457		672
Fountains Forestry Inc 175 Barnstead Rd.......................... Pittsfield NH 03263 *Web:* www.fountainforestry.com	603-435-8234	435-7274	302

Name / Address	Phone	Fax	Class
Four C's Holdings Ltd 330 Mackenzie Blvd .... Fort Mcmurray AB T9H4C4 *Web:* www.casman.ca	780-791-9283		499
Four Colour Print Group 2410 Frankfort Ave .... Louisville KY 40206 *Web:* www.fourcolour.com	502-896-9644		627
Four County Electric Membership Corp 1822 NC Hwy 53 W PO Box 667 .... Burgaw NC 28425 *TF:* 888-368-7289 ■ *Web:* www.fourcty.org	910-259-2171	259-1860	245
Four County Library System 304 Clubhouse Rd .... Vestal NY 13850 *Web:* www.4cls.org	607-723-8236	723-1722	434-3
Four Flags Area Chamber of Commerce 321 E Main St............................... Niles MI 49120 *TF:* 800-719-2188 ■ *Web:* www.nilesmi.com	269-683-3720	683-3722	139
Four Mile Creek State Park 1055 Lake Rd .... Youngstown NY 14174 *Web:* parks.ny.gov/parks/6/details.aspx	716-745-3802		565
Four Oaks Bank & Trust Co PO Box 309 .... Four Oaks NC 27524 *TF:* 877-963-6257 ■ *Web:* www.fouroaksbank.com	919-963-2177	963-2768	70
Four Points by Sheraton Charlotte 315 E Woodlawn Rd........................ Charlotte NC 28217 *TF:* 800-368-7764 ■ *Web:* www.starwoodhotels.com	704-522-0852		379
Four Points by Sheraton French Quarter 541 Bourbon St .... New Orleans LA 70130 *TF:* 866-716-8133 ■ *Web:* www.fourpointsfrenchquarter.com	504-524-7611	524-8273	379
Four Points By Sheraton Hotel & Suites Sfo 264 S Airport Blvd .... South San Francisco CA 94080 *Web:* fort-walton-beach-fl-us.hotels-x.net/Four-points-by-sheraton-destin-fort-walton-beach.html	650-624-3700		378
Four Points by Sheraton Norwood Hotel & Conference Ctr 1125 Boston-Providence Tpke (Rt 1) .... Norwood MA 02062 *Web:* www.fourpointsnorwood.com	781-769-7900	551-3552	377
Four Queens Hotel & Casino 202 Fremont St............................ Las Vegas NV 89101 *TF:* 800-634-6045 ■ *Web:* www.fourqueens.com	702-385-4011	387-5158	379
Four Roses Distillery LLC 1224 Bonds Mill Rd.................. Lawrenceburg KY 40342 *Web:* www.fourrosesbourbon.com	502-839-3436	839-8338	80-1
Four Sails Resort Hotel 3301 Atlantic Ave .... Virginia Beach VA 23451 *TF:* 800-227-4213 ■ *Web:* www.foursails.com	757-491-8100	491-0573	379
Four Seasons 280 Park Ave..................... New York NY 10017 *Web:* www.fourseasonsrestaurant.com	212-754-9494		671
Four Seasons Hospice & Palliative Care 571 S Allen Rd .... Flat Rock NC 28731 *TF:* 866-466-9734 ■ *Web:* www.fourseasonscfl.org	828-692-6178	233-0351	371
Four Seasons Hotel Austin 98 San Jacinto Blvd .... Austin TX 78701 *Web:* fourseasons.com	512-478-4500	478-3117	671
Four Seasons Hotels & Resorts 1165 Leslie St............................... Toronto ON M3C2K8 *TF:* 800-332-3442 ■ *Web:* www.fourseasons.com	416-449-1750	441-4374	753
Four Seasons Hotels Inc 1165 Leslie St............................... Toronto ON M3C2K8 *TF:* 800-332-3442 ■ *Web:* www.fourseasons.com	416-449-1750	441-4374	379
Four Seasons Hotels Ltd 2800 Pennsylvania Ave NW .... Washington DC 20007 *TF:* 800-819-5053 ■ *Web:* www.fourseasons.com/washington	202-944-2022		707
Four Seasons Inc 1801 Waters Ridge Dr....................... Lewisville TX 75057 *TF:* 888-505-4567 ■ *Web:* www.4s.com	972-316-8100		612
Four Seasons Resort & Club Dallas at Las Colinas 4150 N MacArthur Blvd .... Irving TX 75038 *TF:* 800-332-3442 ■ *Web:* www.fourseasons.com/dallas	972-717-0700	717-2550	669
Four Seasons Resort Hualalai 100 Ka'upulehu Dr .... Kailua-Kona HI 96740 *TF:* 888-340-5662 ■ *Web:* www.fourseasons.com/hualalai	808-325-8000	325-8200	669
Four Seasons Resort Jackson Hole 7680 Granite Loop Rd PO Box 544.......... Teton Village WY 83025 *TF:* 800-914-5110 ■ *Web:* www.fourseasons.com/jacksonhole	307-732-5000	732-5001	669
Four Seasons Resort Maui at Wailea 3900 Wailea Alanui Dr .... Wailea HI 96753 *TF:* 800-334-6284 ■ *Web:* www.fourseasons.com	808-874-8000	874-2244	669
Four Seasons Resort Palm Beach 2800 S Ocean Blvd....................... Palm Beach FL 33480 *TF:* 800-432-2335 ■ *Web:* www.fourseasons.com/palmbeach	561-582-2800	547-1374	669
Four Seasons Resort Santa Barbara 1260 Ch Dr.......................... Santa Barbara CA 93108 *TF:* 800-819-5053 ■ *Web:* www.fourseasons.com	805-969-2261	565-8323	669
Four Seasons Resort Scottsdale at Troon North 10600 E Crescent Moon Dr .... Scottsdale AZ 85262 *TF:* 800-332-3442 ■ *Web:* www.fourseasons.com	480-515-5700	515-5599	669
Four Seasons Resort Whistler 4591 Blackcomb Way........................ Whistler BC V0N1B4 *Web:* www.fourseasons.com/whistler	604-935-3400	935-3455	669
Four Seasons Retirement Ctr 1901 Taylor Rd .... Columbus IN 47203 *Web:* www.fourseasonsretirement.com	812-372-8481	378-6184	672
Four Seasons Solar Products LLC 5005 Veterans Memorial Hwy................. Holbrook NY 11741 *TF:* 800-368-7732 ■ *Web:* www.fourseasonssunrooms.com	631-563-4000	563-4010	105
Four Seasons Spa at the Four Seasons Hotel Las Vegas 3960 Las Vegas Blvd S...................... Las Vegas NV 89119 *TF:* 800-332-3442 ■ *Web:* www.fourseasons.com/lasvegas	702-632-5302		707
Four Seasons Spa at the Four Seasons Hotel Los Angeles at Beverly Hills 300 S Doheny Dr .... Los Angeles CA 90048 *TF:* 800-819-5053 ■ *Web:* www.fourseasons.com/losangeles	310-786-2229		707
Four Seasons Spa at the Four Seasons Resort Jackson Hole 7680 Granite Loop Rd PO Box 544.......... Teton Village WY 83025 *TF:* 800-819-5053 ■ *Web:* www.fourseasons.com/jacksonhole	307-732-5120		707
Four Seasons Spa at the Four Seasons Resort Maui 3900 Wailea Alanui Dr .... Wailea HI 96753 *TF:* 800-334-6284 ■ *Web:* www.fourseasons.com/maui	808-874-2925		707
Four Seasons Spa at the Four Seasons Resort Santa Barbara 1260 Ch Dr.......................... Santa Barbara CA 93108 *TF General:* 800-819-5053 ■ *Web:* www.fourseasons.com/santabarbara	805-565-8250		707

				Phone	Fax	Class
Four Seasons Town Centre 410 Four Seasons Town Centre *Web:* www.shopfourseasons.com	Greensboro	NC	27407	336-292-0171		460
Four States Livestock Sales 501 E First St *Web:* fourstateslivestocksales.com	Hagerstown	MD	21740	301-733-8120	733-7318	446
Four Wheel Campers 1460 Churchill Downs Ave *TF:* 800-242-1442 ■ *Web:* www.fourwh.com	Woodland	CA	95776	530-666-1442		120
Four Winds Casino Resort 11111 Wilson Rd *TF:* 866-494-6371 ■ *Web:* www.fourwindscasino.com	New Buffalo	MI	49117	866-494-6371		132
Four Winds Hospital 800 Cross River Rd. *TF:* 800-528-6624 ■ *Web:* www.fourwindshospital.com	Katonah	NY	10536	914-763-8151		374-5
Four Winds Manufacturing LLC 251 Mayfield Dr *Web:* www.fourwindsspas.com	Smyrna	TN	37167	615-220-8879		596
Four Winns Inc 925 Frisbie St. *Web:* www.fourwinns.com	Cadillac	MI	49601	231-775-1343	779-2345	90
Fourandhalf Inc 22320 Foothill Blvd Ste 620 *Web:* fourandhalf.com	Hayward	CA	94541	510-889-9921		195
FourCubed LLC 509 First Ave NE *Web:* fourcubed.com	Minneapolis	MN	55413	612-454-1509		195
FourFront Design Inc. 517 Seventh St *Web:* www.4front.biz	Rapid City	SD	57701	605-342-9470		256
Fournitures De Bureau Denis Inc 2990 boul Le Corbusier *Web:* www.denis.ca	Laval	QC	H7L3M2	450-687-3110		320
Foursome Inc 3570 Vicksveurg Ln N Ste 100 *TF:* 888-368-7766 ■ *Web:* www.thefoursome.com	Plymouth	MN	55447	763-473-4667	504-5555	157-2
Fourteen Company Ltd 18271 W McDurmott St Ste F *Web:* www.fourteengolf.com	Irvine	CA	92614	949-852-8811		711
Fourth Avenue 434 E Ninth St *TF:* 800-933-2477 ■ *Web:* www.fourthavenue.org	Tucson	AZ	85705	520-624-5004		50-6
Fourth Presbyterian Church 3016 Preston Hwy *Web:* fourthpc.org	Louisville	KY	40217	502-634-8021		48-20
Fourth Street Bowl 1441 N Fourth St *Web:* www.4thstreetbowl.com	San Jose	CA	95112	408-453-5555		99
Fourwinds Resort & Marina 9301 Fairfax Rd *TF:* 800-824-2628 ■ *Web:* www.bestinboating.com	Bloomington	IN	47401	812-824-2628		669
Foushee & Assoc Inc 3260 118th Ave SE *Web:* www.foushee.com	Bellevue	WA	98005	425-746-1000	746-3737	186
Fowler Foods Inc 139 SW Dr	Jonesboro	AR	72401	870-935-6032		345
Fowler Holding Company Inc 2721 NW 36th Ave *Web:* fowlerholding.com	Norman	OK	73072	405-573-9909		57
Fowler Museum at UCLA University of California 308 Charles E Young Dr *Web:* www.fowler.ucla.edu	Los Angeles	CA	90024	310-825-4361	206-7007	520
Fowler Packing Company Inc 8570 S Cedar Ave *Web:* fowlerpacking.com	Fresno	CA	93725	559-834-5911	834-5272	315-3
Fowler State Bank 300 E Fifth St PO Box 511 *TF:* 800-439-3951 ■ *Web:* www.fowlerstatebank.com	Fowler	IN	47944	765-884-1200		70
Fowler's Chocolate Co 100 River Rock Dr Ste 102 *TF:* 800-824-2263 ■ *Web:* www.fowlerschocolates.com	Buffalo	NY	14207	716-877-9983		296-8
Fowlers Furniture 410 N Peters Rd *Web:* www.fowlersfurnitureinc.com	Knoxville	TN	37922	865-539-0036		321
Fowlers Hollow State Park c/o Colonel Denning 1599 Doubling Gap Rd *Web:* www.dcnr.state.pa.us	Newville	PA	17241	717-776-5272		565
Fownes Bros & Company Inc 16 E 34th St *TF All:* 800-345-6837 ■ *Web:* urpowered.com	New York	NY	10016	212-683-0150		155-8
FOX - WRSR The G-4511 Miller Rd *Web:* www.classicfox.com	Flint	MI	48507	810-720-9510	720-9513	645-60
Fox 102.3 1900 Pineview Rd *Web:* fox1023.com	Columbia	SC	29209	803-695-8600		645-40
FOX 11 1999 S Bundy Dr. *Web:* www.foxla.com	Los Angeles	CA	90025	310-584-2000		741-76
FOX 29 WFLX.COM 4119 W Blue Heron Blvd *Web:* www.wflx.com	West Palm Beach	FL	33404	561-845-2929	863-1238	741-140
FOX 7 Austin 119 E Tenth St *Web:* www.fox7austin.com	Austin	TX	78701	512-476-7777	495-7060	741-9
Fox Broadcasting Co 10201 W Pico Blvd. *TF:* 800-367-8788 ■ *Web:* www.fox.com	Los Angeles	CA	90035	310-369-1350		739
Fox Chapel Area School District 611 Field Club Rd. *Web:* www.fcasd.edu	Pittsburgh	PA	15238	412-967-2453	967-0697	685
Fox Chase Cancer Ctr 333 Cottman Ave *TF:* 888-369-2427 ■ *Web:* www.foxchase.org	Philadelphia	PA	19111	215-728-6900		374-7
Fox Chase Rehabilitation & Nursing Ctr 2015 E W Hwy	Silver Spring	MD	20910	301-587-2400		450
Fox Cities Chamber of Commerce & Industry 125 N Superior St. *Web:* www.foxcitieschamber.com	Appleton	WI	54911	920-734-7101	734-7161	139
Fox Cities Convention & Visitors Bureau 3433 W College Ave *TF:* 800-236-6673 ■ *Web:* www.foxcities.org	Appleton	WI	54914	920-734-3358	734-1080	206
Fox Cities Performing Arts Ctr 400 W College Ave *TF:* 800-982-2787 ■ *Web:* foxcitiespac.com	Appleton	WI	54911	920-730-3782		522
Fox Communities Credit Union 3401 E Calumet St *Web:* foxcu.org	Appleton	WI	54915	920-993-9000		219
Fox Contractors Corp 5430 W Ferguson Rd Ste B. *Web:* www.foxcontractors.com	Fort Wayne	IN	46809	260-747-7461		188-4
Fox Converting Inc 1250 Cornell Rd *Web:* www.foxconverting.com	Green Bay	WI	54313	920-434-5272		638
Fox CPA Group Ltd 204 E Cherry St	Watseka	IL	60970	815-432-3126		2
Fox Creek Leather Inc 2029 Elk Creek Pkwy *TF:* 800-766-4165 ■ *Web:* www.foxcreekleather.com	Independence	VA	24348	276-773-3131		711
Fox Edward Photography 6133 N Northwest Hwy Ste A *Web:* www.edwardfox.com	Chicago	IL	60631	773-736-0200		590
Fox Electric Ltd 1104 Colorado Ln. *TF:* 800-925-6085 ■ *Web:* www.foxelectric.com	Arlington	TX	76015	817-461-2571	261-7311	189-4
FOX Engineering Associates Inc 414 S 17th St Ste 107 *TF:* 800-433-3469 ■ *Web:* www.foxeng.com	Ames	IA	50010	515-233-0000		261
Fox Galvin LLC 1 S Memorial Dr 12th Fl. *Web:* www.foxgalvin.com	St. Louis	MO	63102	314-588-7000		428
Fox Harb'r Resort & Spa 1337 Fox Harbour Rd *TF:* 866-257-1801 ■ *Web:* www.foxharbr.com	Wallace	NS	B0K1Y0	902-257-1801		707
Fox Hill Village 10 Longwood Dr *Web:* foxhillvillage.com	Westwood	MA	02090	781-329-4433	461-2464	672
Fox Hills Resort & Convention Ctr 250 W Church St *TF:* 800-950-7615 ■ *Web:* www.foxhillsresort.com	Mishicot	WI	54228	920-755-2376		669
Fox Industries Inc 3100 Falls Cliff Rd *TF:* 888-760-0369 ■ *Web:* strongtie.com	Baltimore	MD	21211	410-243-8856		3
Fox IV Technologies 6011 Enterprise Dr *TF:* 800-328-0466 ■ *Web:* www.foxiv.com	Export	PA	15632	724-387-3500		547
Fox Lake Correctional Institution PO Box 147 *Web:* doc.wi.gov	Fox Lake	WI	53933	920-928-3151	928-6929	213
Fox Lite Inc 8300 Dayton Rd *Web:* www.foxlite.com	Fairborn	OH	45324	937-864-1966	864-7010	608
Fox Lumber Sales Inc PO Box 1000. *Web:* www.foxlumber.com	Hamilton	MT	59840	406-363-5140		820
FOX News Ch 1211 Ave of the Americas **Fax:* News Rm ■ *TF:* 800-282-2882 ■ *Web:* www.foxnews.com	New York	NY	10036	212-301-3000	301-8274*	740
Fox Packaging Co 2200 Fox Dr *Web:* www.foxbag.com	McAllen	TX	78504	956-682-6176	682-5768	67
Fox Point State Park c/o Bellevue State Pk 800 Carr Rd *Web:* www.destateparks.com/foxpt/foxpt.htm	Wilmington	DE	19809	302-761-6963		565
Fox Pool Corp 3490 BoaRd Rd *TF:* 800-723-1011 ■ *Web:* www.foxpool.com	York	PA	17406	800-723-1011		728
Fox Richmond 1925 Westmoreland St. *Web:* www.foxrichmond.com	Richmond	VA	23230	804-358-3535	358-1495	741-100
Fox Ridge State Park 18175 State Pk Rd *Web:* www.dnr.illinois.gov/Parks/Pages/FoxRidge.aspx	Charleston	IL	61920	217-345-6416		565
Fox River Mall 4301 W Wisconsin Ave *TF:* 800-236-6673 ■ *Web:* www.foxrivermall.com	Appleton	WI	54913	920-739-4100		460
Fox River Mills Inc 227 Poplar Stq PO Box 298 *TF:* 800-247-1815 ■ *Web:* www.foxsox.com	Osage	IA	50461	641-732-3798		155-10
Fox Rothschild LLP 2000 Market St 10th Fl. *TF:* 800-580-9136 ■ *Web:* www.foxrothschild.com	Philadelphia	PA	19103	215-299-2000	299-2150	428
Fox Run Vineyards 670 SR- 14 *TF:* 800-636-9786 ■ *Web:* www.foxrunvineyards.com	Penn Yan	NY	14527	315-536-4616		443
Fox Searchlight Pictures 10201 W Pico Blvd Bldg 38 *Web:* www.foxsearchlight.com	Los Angeles	CA	90035	310-369-1530	369-1491	514
Fox Service Co PO Box 19047 *TF:* 866-668-4749 ■ *Web:* www.foxservice.com	Austin	TX	78760	512-442-6782		189-10
FOX Sports Net 10201 W Pico Blvd. *Web:* www.foxsports.com	Los Angeles	CA	90035	310-369-7069		740
FOX Studios 10201 W Pico Blvd *Web:* www.foxstudios.com	Los Angeles	CA	90035	310-369-1000		512
Fox Television Stations Inc 1999 S Bundy Dr *Web:* www.foxla.com	Los Angeles	CA	90025	310-584-2000	584-2012	738
Fox Theatre 660 Peachtree St NE. *TF:* 855-285-8499 ■ *Web:* www.foxtheatre.org	Atlanta	GA	30308	404-881-2100	872-2972	572
Fox Theatre 2211 Woodward Ave *TF:* 800-745-3000 ■ *Web:* www.olympiaentertainment.com	Detroit	MI	48201	313-471-3200		572
Fox Valley Fire & Safety Company Inc 2730 Pinnacle Dr *Web:* www.foxvalleyfire.com	Elgin	IL	60124	847-695-5990	695-3699	189-4
Fox Valley Spring Company Inc N915 Craftsmen Dr. *TF:* 800-776-2645 ■ *Web:* www.foxvalleyspring.com	Greenville	WI	54942	920-757-7777		492
Fox Valley Technical College 1825 N Bluemound Dr PO Box 2277 *TF:* 800-735-3882 ■ *Web:* www.fvtc.edu	Appleton	WI	54912	920-735-5600	735-2484	800
Fox's 80 Main St *Web:* www.foxs.com	Mineola	NY	11501	516-294-8321		157-6
Fox's Pizza Den Inc 4425 Willaim Penn Hwy *TF:* 800-899-3697 ■ *Web:* www.foxspizza.com	Murrysville	PA	15668	724-733-7888		670
FOX31 & Channel 2 100 E Speer Blvd *Web:* kwgn.com	Denver	CO	80203	303-595-3131		741-39
Foxcom Inc 136 Main St Ste 300b *Web:* www.foxcom.com	Princeton	NJ	08540	609-228-8104		246
Foxcroft School 22407 Foxhound Ln PO Box 5555 *Web:* www.foxcroft.org	Middleburg	VA	20118	540-687-5555	687-3675	622
Foxdale Village 500 E Marylyn Ave *TF:* 800-253-4951 ■ *Web:* www.foxdalevillage.org	State College	PA	16801	814-272-2117	238-2920	672
Foxes Music Co 416 S Washington St *TF:* 800-446-4414 ■ *Web:* www.foxesmusic.com	Falls Church	VA	22046	703-533-7393	536-2171	526

				Phone	Fax	Class
Foxfire Printing & Packaging Inc						
750 Dawson Dr	Newark	DE	19713	302-368-9466		627
Foxlink International Inc						
925 W Lambert Rd Ste C	Brea	CA	92821	714-256-1777		253
Web: www.foxlink.com						
FoxNet Solutions Inc 92 Erb St E	Waterloo	ON	N2J1L6	519-886-8895		180
Web: www.foxnetsolutions.com						
Foxworth-Galbraith Lumber Co						
4965 Preston Pk Blvd Ste 400	Plano	TX	75093	972-665-2400		191-3
TF: 800-688-8082 ■ *Web:* www.foxgal.com						
Foxx Equipment Co 421 SW Blvd	Kansas City	MO	64108	816-421-3600		358
TF: 800-821-2254 ■ *Web:* foxxequipment.com						
Foxx Virginia (Rep R - NC)						
2262 Rayburn HOB	Washington	DC	20515	202-225-2071	225-2995	342-2
Web: foxx.house.gov						
Foxy 104.3 Fm 8001-101 Creedmoor Rd	Raleigh	NC	27613	919-848-9736	848-4724	645-131
Web: foxync.com						
Foxy 107.1 8001-101 Creedmoor Rd	Raleigh	NC	27613	919-848-9736	848-4724	645-131
TF: 800-467-3699 ■ *Web:* foxync.com						
Foyer, The 3655 Perkins Rd	Baton Rouge	LA	70808	225-343-3655		460
F&P America Mfg Inc 2101 Corporate Dr	Troy	OH	45373	937-339-0212		59
Web: www.fandp.com						
FP Horak Co 401 Saginaw St	Bay City	MI	48708	989-892-6505		627
Web: www.fphorak.com						
FP Mailing Solutions						
140 N Mitchell Ct	Addison	IL	60101	630-827-5500		112
TF: 800-341-6052 ■ *Web:* www.fp-usa.com						
FPA (Foreign Policy Assn) 470 Pk Ave S	New York	NY	10016	212-481-8100	481-9275	48-7
TF: 800-628-5754 ■ *Web:* www.fpa.org						
FPA (Flexible Packaging Assn)						
971 Corporate Blvd Ste 403	Linthicum	MD	21090	410-694-0800	694-0900	49-13
Web: www.flexpack.org						
FPA (Financial Planning Assn)						
7535 E Hampden Ave Ste 600	Denver	CO	80231	303-759-4900		49-2
TF: 800-322-4237 ■ *Web:* www.plannersearch.org						
FPA Customs Brokers Inc						
152-31 134th Ave	Jamaica	NY	11434	718-527-2280	276-3345	311
FPC (Frank Phillips College) PO Box 5118	Borger	TX	79008	806-457-4200		162
TF: 800-394-5445 ■ *Web:* www.fpctx.edu						
FPC (Federal Bureau of Prisons)						
Bryan 320 First St NW	Washington	DC	20534	202-307-3198	821-3316*	212
**Fax Area Code:* 979 ■ **Fax:* Warden ■ *Web:* www.bop.gov						
FPC Flexible Packaging Corp						
1891 Eglinton Ave E	Toronto	ON	M1L2L7	416-288-3060	288-0808	548
TF: 888-288-7386 ■ *Web:* www.fpcflexible.com						
FPCA (Fillmore-Piru Citrus Assn)						
357 N Main St PO Box 350	Piru	CA	93040	805-521-1781	521-0990	11-1
Web: www.fillmorepirucitrus.com						
FPDA (Fluid Power Distributors Assn)						
PO Box 1420	Cherry Hill	NJ	08034	856-424-8998	424-9248	49-13
TF: 800-843-2763 ■ *Web:* www.fpda.org						
FPDTR (Fess Parker's Doubletree Resort)						
633 E Cabrillo Blvd	Santa Barbara	CA	93103	805-564-4333		669
TF: 800-879-2929 ■ *Web:* www.fessparkersantabarbarahotel.com						
FPI (Forged Products Inc)						
6505 N Houston Rosslyn Rd	Houston	TX	77091	713-462-3416	460-9404	483
TF: 800-876-3416 ■ *Web:* www.fpitx.com						
FPI (Franklin Precision Industry Inc)						
3220 Bowling Green Rd	Franklin	KY	42134	270-598-4300		60
Web: www.fpik.com						
FPI (Foodservice & Packaging Institute)						
7700 Leesburg Pk	Falls Church	VA	22046	703-538-3551	241-5603	49-13
Web: www.fpi.org						
FPI Management Inc 800 Iron Pt Rd	Folsom	CA	95630	916-357-5300		652
Web: www.fpimgt.com						
FPI Thermoplastic Technologies						
520 Speedwell Ave Ste 116	Morris Plains	NJ	07950	973-998-9801		604
Web: www.njmep.org						
FPL (Florida Power & Light Co)						
700 Universe Blvd	Juno Beach	FL	33408	561-697-8000		787
TF: 800-226-3545 ■ *Web:* www.fpl.com						
Fpl Food LLC 1301 New Savannah Rd	Augusta	GA	30901	706-722-2694		473
Web: fplfood.net						
FPL Group Inc						
NextEra Energy Inc						
700 Universe Blvd	Juno Beach	FL	33408	561-694-4000	694-4620	360-5
NYSE: NEE ■ *TF:* 888-218-4392 ■ *Web:* www.nexteraenergy.com						
Fpm Group Ltd 909 Marconi Ave	Ronkonkoma	NY	11779	631-737-6200		261
Web: www.fpm-group.com						
FPM LLC 1501 S Lively Blvd	Elk Grove Village	IL	60007	847-228-2525	228-5912	484
TF: 877-437-6432 ■ *Web:* www.fpmht.com						
FPMI Solutions Inc						
1033 N Fairfax St Ste 200	Alexandria	VA	22314	888-644-3764		193
TF: 888-644-3764 ■ *Web:* www.fpmi.com						
FPRI (Foreign Policy Research Institute)						
1520 Walnut St Ste 610	Philadelphia	PA	19102	215-732-3774	732-4401	634
Web: www.fpri.org						
FPSA (FPSA)						
1451 Dolley Madison Blvd Ste 101	McLean	VA	22101	703-761-2600	761-4334	49-13
Web: www.fpsa.org						
FPT Pontiac Div 500 Collier Rd	Pontiac	MI	48340	248-335-8141		686
Web: www.fptscrap.com						
FPT USA Corp 155 Bovet Rd Ste 303	San Mateo	CA	94402	650-349-5000		196
Web: fpt-software.com						
FPUC (Florida Public Utilities Co)						
401 S Dixie Hwy	West Palm Beach	FL	33401	800-427-7712		787
TF: 800-427-7712 ■ *Web:* www.fpuc.com						
Fpweb.net LC 1714 Gilsinn Ln	Fenton	MO	63026	636-600-8960		225
Web: www.fpweb.net						
FRA (Fleet Reserve Assn) 125 NW St	Alexandria	VA	22314	703-683-1400	549-6610	48-19
TF: 800-372-1924 ■ *Web:* www.fra.org						
FRA (Federal Railroad Administration Regional Offices)						
Region 1 55 Broadway Room 1077	Cambridge	MA	02142	617-494-2302	494-2967	340-17
TF: 800-724-5991 ■ *Web:* www.fra.dot.gov						
FRA Today 125 NW St	Alexandria	VA	22314	703-683-1400	549-6610	457-12
TF: 800-372-1924 ■ *Web:* www.fra.org						
FRAC (Food Research & Action Ctr)						
1875 Connecticut Ave NW Ste 540	Washington	DC	20009	202-986-2200	986-2525	48-6
Web: www.frac.org						
Frac Tech Services LLC 301 E 18th St	Cisco	TX	76437	817-850-1008		145
TF: 866-877-1008 ■ *Web:* www.ftsi.com						
Fractal Analytics Ltd						
951 Mariners Island Ste 307	San Mateo	CA	94404	650-378-1284		225
Web: www.fractalanalytics.com						
Fracture LLC 112 SW Sixth St	Gainesville	FL	32601	888-675-8044		627
TF: 888-675-8044 ■ *Web:* www.fractureme.com						
Fraen Corp 80 Newcrossing Rd	Reading	MA	01867	781-205-5300	942-2426	488
TF: 800-610-6053 ■ *Web:* www.fraen.com						
Fraen Machining Corp 324 New Boston St	Woburn	MA	01801	781-205-5400	205-5472	621
TF: 800-876-7833 ■ *Web:* www.fraen.com						
Fraenkel Gallery 49 Geary St	San Francisco	CA	94108	415-981-2661	981-4014	42
Web: www.artnet.com						
Fragrance Foundation						
621 Second Ave 2nd Fl	New York	NY	10016	212-725-2755		49-4
Web: fragrance.org						
Fraim & Fiorella PC						
150 Boush St Ste 601	Norfolk	VA	23510	757-227-5900		428
Web: fraimandfiorella.com						
Frain Group Inc, The						
9377 W Grand Ave	Franklin Park	IL	60131	630-629-9900		23
Web: www.fraingroup.com						
Frakes Engineering Inc						
7950 Castleway Dr Ste 160	Indianapolis	IN	46250	317-577-3000		256
Web: www.frakesengineering.com						
Fraley & Company Inc 6723 S Hwy 160	Cortez	CO	81328	970-565-8538	565-8743	579
Fralinger Engineering PA						
629 Shiloh Pk	Bridgeton	NJ	08302	856-451-2990		261
Web: fralinger.com						
Fram Trak Industries Inc						
205 Hallock Ave	Middlesex	NJ	08846	732-424-8400		711
Web: www.framtrak.com						
Framed on Madison Inc						
976 Lexington Ave Frnt 2	New York	NY	10021	212-734-4680		362
TF: 800-458-9214 ■ *Web:* framedonmadison.com						
Framingham Heart Study						
73 Mt Wayte Ave Ste 2	Framingham	MA	01702	508-935-3418	626-1262	668
TF: 800-854-7582 ■ *Web:* www.framinghamheartstudy.org						
Framingham State College						
100 State St PO Box 9101	Framingham	MA	01701	508-620-1220	626-4017*	166
**Fax:* Admissions ■ *TF:* 866-361-8970 ■ *Web:* www.framingham.edu						
Framingham Welding & Engineering Corp						
120 Leland St PO Box 112	Framingham	MA	01702	508-875-3563	626-4234	454
TF: 800-419-4923 ■ *Web:* www.framinghamwelding.com						
Framme Law Firm PC						
6800 Paragon Pl #233	Richmond	VA	23230	804-649-1334		428
Web: www.frammelaw.com						
Frampton Mailing Systems						
450 Horton St E	London	ON	N6B1M3	519-680-6245		5
Web: fms.ca						
France 1 Dag Hammarskjold Plaza # 36	New York	NY	10017	212-371-0480	421-6889	784
Web: www.un.int						
Consulate General						
1340 Poydras St Ste 1710	New Orleans	LA	70112	504-569-2870	569-2871	257
Web: www.consulfrance-nouvelleorleans.org						
Consulate General						
1395 Brickell Ave Ste 1050	Miami	FL	33131	305-403-4185	403-4187	257
TF: 877-624-8737 ■ *Web:* www.consulfrance-miami.org						
Consulate General						
205 N Michigan Ave Ste 3700	Chicago	IL	60601	312-327-5200	327-5201	257
TF: 866-858-4430 ■ *Web:* www.consulfrance-chicago.org						
Consulate General						
777 Post Oak Blvd Ste 600	Houston	TX	77056	713-572-2799	572-2911	257
TF: 888-902-5322 ■ *Web:* www.consulfrance-houston.org						
Consulate General						
10390 Santa Monica Blvd Ste 410	Los Angeles	CA	90025	310-235-3200	479-4813	257
Web: www.consulfrance-losangeles.org						
Consulate General 934 Fifth Ave	New York	NY	10021	212-606-3600	606-3614	257
TF: 800-772-1213 ■ *Web:* www.consulfrance-newyork.org						
Consulate General 540 Bush St	San Francisco	CA	94108	415-397-4330	433-8357	257
TF: 800-553-4133 ■ *Web:* www.consulfrance-sanfrancisco.org						
Consulate General						
3475 Piedmont Rd NE Ste 1840	Atlanta	GA	30305	404-495-1660	495-1661	257
TF: 888-937-2623 ■ *Web:* www.consulfrance-atlanta.org						
Consulate General						
31 St James Ave Ste 750	Boston	MA	02116	617-832-4400		257
Web: www.consulfrance-boston.org						
Embassy 4101 Reservoir Rd NW	Washington	DC	20007	202-944-6000	944-6175	257
TF: 800-622-6232 ■ *Web:* franceintheus.org						
Frances Collin Literary Agent PO Box 33	Wayne	PA	19087	610-254-0555	254-5029	444
Web: www.francescollin.com						
Frances Slocum State Park						
565 Mt Olivet Rd	Wyoming	PA	18644	570-696-3525		565
Web: www.dcnr.state.pa.us						
Francesca's on Taylor						
1400 W Taylor St	Chicago	IL	60607	312-829-2828	829-2831	671
Web: www.miafrancesca.com						
Francesco 325 Alcazar Ave	Coral Gables	FL	33134	305-446-1600		671
Web: www.francesco.com.pe						
Franchise Brands LLC 325 Bic Dr	Milford	CT	06461	800-797-2308		463
TF: 800-797-2308 ■ *Web:* www.franchisebrandsllc.com						
Franchise Capital Advisors Inc						
9903 E Bell Rd Ste 130	Scottsdale	AZ	85260	480-355-4390		70
Web: www.franchisecapitaladvisors.com						
Franchise Co, The (TFC)						
5399 Eglinton Ave W Ste 110	Etobicoke	ON	M9C5K9	416-620-3960	620-3961	463
TF: 800-294-5591 ■ *Web:* www.thefranchisecompany.com						
Franchise Handbook						
5555 N Port Washington Rd Ste 305	Milwaukee	WI	53217	414-882-2878		457-11
TF: 800-272-0246 ■ *Web:* franchisehandbook.com						
Franchise Information Services Inc						
4075 Wilson Blvd Ste 410	Arlington	VA	22203	703-740-4700		387
TF: 800-485-9570 ■ *Web:* www.frandata.com						
Franchising Business & Law Alert						
120 Broadway 5th Fl	New York	NY	10271	212-457-9400		531-7
TF: 877-256-2472 ■ *Web:* www.lawjournalnewsletters.com						
Franchising World Magazine						
1501 K St NW Ste 350	Washington	DC	20005	202-628-8000	628-0812	457-5
TF: 800-543-1038 ■ *Web:* www.franchise.org						

	Phone	Fax	Class
Franchoice Inc 7500 Flying Cloud Dr ..... Eden Prairie MN 55344 *TF:* 877-396-4238 ■ *Web:* www.franchoice.com	952-345-8400		194
Francis A Countway Library of Medicine, The 10 Shattuck St ..... Boston MA 02115 *Web:* www.countway.harvard.edu	617-432-2136	432-4739	434-1
Francis Bitter Magnet Laboratory Bldg NW14 166 Albany Street ..... Cambridge MA 02139 *Web:* web.mit.edu/fbml	617-253-5478	253-5405	668
Francis Cheney Family Place 2650 Siskiyou Blvd ..... Medford OR 97504 *Web:* www.asante.org	541-789-5876		372
Francis Coppola Winery LLC 300 Via Archimedes ..... Geyserville CA 95441 *Web:* www.francisfordcoppolawinery.com	707-857-1471		57
Francis Drilling Fluids Ltd 240 Jasmine Rd ..... Crowley LA 70526 *TF:* 800-252-3104 ■ *Web:* www.fdfltd.com	337-783-8685		146
Francis Investment Counsel LLC 21180 W Capitol Dr ..... Pewaukee WI 53072 *TF:* 866-232-6457 ■ *Web:* www.francisinvco.com	866-232-6457		796
Francis Land House 3131 Virginia Beach Blvd ..... Virginia Beach VA 23452 *Web:* museumsvb.org	757-385-5100		50-3
Francis Manufacturing Co 500 E Main St PO Box 400 ..... Russia OH 45363 *TF:* 800-745-1682 ■ *Web:* www.francismanufacturing.com	937-526-4551		492
Francis Marion Hotel, The 387 King St ..... Charleston SC 29403 *TF:* 877-756-2121 ■ *Web:* www.francismarionhotel.com	843-722-0600	853-2186	379
Francis Marion University PO Box 100547 ..... Florence SC 29501 **Fax:* Admissions ■ *TF:* 800-368-7551 ■ *Web:* www.fmarion.edu	843-661-1231	661-4635*	166
Francis Marion University Rogers Library PO Box 100547 ..... Florence SC 29502 *TF:* 800-368-7551 ■ *Web:* www.fmarion.edu/rogerslibrary/directory	800-368-7551		434-6
Francis O Day Construction Company Inc 850 E Gude Dr ..... Rockville MD 20850 *TF:* 800-984-3775 ■ *Web:* www.foday.com	301-652-2400	340-6592	188-4
Francis Scott Key Family Resort 12806 Ocean Gateway ..... Ocean City MD 21842 *TF:* 800-213-0088 ■ *Web:* www.fskmotel.com	410-213-0088	213-2854	669
Francis Tuttle Technology Ctr School District 21 12777 N Rockwell Ave ..... Oklahoma City OK 73142 *Web:* www.francistuttle.edu	405-717-7799		186
Franciscan Estates 1178 Galleron Rd ..... Saint Helena CA 94574 **Fax Area Code:* 585 ■ *TF:* 800-529-9463 ■ *Web:* www.franciscan.com	707-967-3830	396-7831*	80-3
Franciscan Health 20201 S Crawford Ave ..... Olympia Fields IL 60461 *Web:* www.franciscanalliance.org	708-747-4000	503-3270	374-3
Franciscan Health Hammond 5454 Hohman Ave ..... Hammond IN 46320 *Web:* www.franciscanalliance.org	219-932-2300	933-2585	374-3
Franciscan Health, Inc 1501 Hartford St ..... Lafayette IN 47904 *TF:* 800-371-6011 ■ *Web:* www.franciscanalliance.org/pages/default.aspx	765-423-6011		374-3
Franciscan Hospital for Children 30 Warren St ..... Boston MA 02135 *Web:* franciscanchildrens.org	617-254-3800		374-1
Franciscan Missionaries of Our Lady Health System (FMOLHS) 4200 Essen Ln ..... Baton Rouge LA 70809 *Web:* www.fmolhs.org	225-923-2701	926-4846	353
Franciscan Monastery of the Holly Land 1400 Quincy St NE ..... Washington DC 20017 *Web:* www.myfranciscan.org	202-526-6800		50-1
Franciscan School of Theology 1712 Euclid Ave ..... Berkeley CA 94709 *TF:* 855-355-1550 ■ *Web:* www.fst.edu	760-547-1800		167-3
Franciscan Sisters of Chicago Inc 11500 Theresa Dr ..... Lemont IL 60439 *TF:* 800-524-6126 ■ *Web:* www.franciscanministries.org	800-524-6126		48-20
Franciscan Skemp Health Care 700 W Ave S ..... La Crosse WI 54601 *TF:* 800-362-5454 ■ *Web:* mayoclinichealthsystem.org	608-785-0940		374-3
Franciscan Spirituality Ctr 920 Market St ..... La Crosse WI 54601 *TF:* 800-821-6819 ■ *Web:* www.franciscanspiritualitycenter.org	608-791-5295		673
Franciscan Villa 3601 S Chicago Ave ..... South Milwaukee WI 53172 *Web:* www.franciscanvilla.org	414-764-4100		450
Francisco Grande Hotel & Golf Resort 26000 Gila Bend Hwy ..... Casa Grande AZ 85222 *TF General:* 800-237-4238 ■ *Web:* www.franciscogrande.com	520-836-6444		669
Franck's Pharmacy Inc 7518 Soquel Dr ..... Aptos CA 95003	831-685-1100		238
Franco Mfg Company Inc 555 Prospect St ..... Metuchen NJ 08840 *Web:* franco-mfg.com	732-494-0500	494-8270	746
Franco's 6200 N Military Hwy ..... Norfolk VA 23518	757-853-0177		671
Franco's Ristorante Italiano 824 E Fifth St ..... Dayton OH 45402 *Web:* www.francos-italiano.com	937-222-0204	222-1380	671
Franconia Notch State Park 9 Franconia Notch Pkwy ..... Franconia NH 03580 *Web:* www.nhstateparks.org	603-745-8391		565
Francorp Inc 20200 Governors Dr ..... Olympia Fields IL 60461 *Web:* www.francorp.com	708-481-2900		463
Franczek Sullivan Pc 300 S Wacker Dr Ste 3400 ..... Chicago IL 60606 *Web:* www.franczek.com	312-786-6119		428
Frandsen Bank & Trust 501 Chestnut St W ..... Virginia MN 55792 *Web:* www.frandsenbank.com	507-744-2361		71
Frank B Fuhrer Wholesale Co 3100 E Carson St ..... Pittsburgh PA 15203 *TF:* 800-837-2212 ■ *Web:* www.fuhrerwholesale.com	412-488-8844	488-0195	81-1
Frank B Ross Co 970-H New Brunswick Ave ..... Rahway NJ 07065 *TF:* 800-541-6752 ■ *Web:* www.frankbross.com	732-669-0810	669-0814	151
Frank Bryan Inc 1263 Chartiers Ave ..... Mckees Rocks PA 15136	412-331-1630		182
Frank C. Alegre Trucking Inc PO Box 1508 ..... Lodi CA 95241 *TF:* 800-769-2440 ■ *Web:* www.alegretrucking.com	209-334-2112	367-0572	780
Frank Capurro & Son LLC 2250 Hwy 1 ..... Moss Landing CA 95039	831-786-0731		10-11
Frank Edmunds & Co 6111 S Sayre ..... Chicago IL 60638 *TF:* 800-447-3516 ■ *Web:* www.frankedmunds.com	773-586-2772	586-2783	820
Frank Edwards Co 3626 Pkwy Blvd ..... West Valley City UT 84120 *Web:* feco.net	801-736-8000		61
Frank Erwin Ctr 1701 Red River PO Box 2929 ..... Austin TX 78701 *Web:* www.uterwincenter.com	512-471-7744	471-9652	720
Frank Family Vineyards LLC 1091 Larkmead Ln ..... Calistoga CA 94515 *Web:* www.frankfamilyvineyards.com	707-942-0859		443
Frank Grisanti's 1022 S Shady Grove Rd ..... Memphis TN 38120 *Web:* frankgrisanti.com	901-761-9462		671
Frank H McClung Museum 1327 Cir Pk Dr University of Tennessee ..... Knoxville TN 37996 *Web:* mcclungmuseum.utk.edu	865-974-2144	974-3827	520
Frank Holten State Recreation Area 4500 Pocket Rd ..... East Saint Louis IL 62205 *Web:* www.dnr.illinois.gov/Parks/Pages/FrankHolten.aspx	618-874-7920		565
Frank J Larusso CPA PC 550 Mamaroneck Ave Ste 402 ..... Harrison NY 10528	914-698-8303		2
Frank J Zamboni & Company Inc 15714 Colorado Ave ..... Paramount CA 90723 *Web:* www.zamboni.com	562-633-0751	633-9365	516
Frank Jackson State Park 100 Jerry Adams Dr ..... Opp AL 36467 *TF:* 800-760-4089 ■ *Web:* www.alapark.com	334-493-6988	493-2478	565
Frank Kent Cadillac Inc 3800 W Loop 820 S ..... Fort Worth TX 76116 *TF:* 877-558-5468 ■ *Web:* www.frankkentcadillac.com	877-558-5468		57
Frank L. Blum Construction Co 830 E 25th St ..... Winston-Salem NC 27105 *Web:* www.flblum.com	336-724-5528		186
Frank Lill & Son Inc 785 Old Dutch Rd ..... Victor NY 14564 *Web:* www.franklillandson.com	585-265-0490	265-1842	189-10
Frank Lloyd Wright Home & Studio 951 Chicago Ave ..... Oak Park IL 60302 *Web:* flwright.org	708-848-1976	848-1248	520
Frank Lloyd Wright House in Ebbsworth Park 120 N Ballas Rd ..... Kirkwood MO 63122 *Web:* www.ebsworthpark.org	314-822-8359		50-3
Frank Lloyd Wright Preservation Trust *Special Collections* 931 Chicago Ave ..... Oak Park IL 60302 **Fax Area Code:* 708 ■ *Web:* flwright.org	312-994-4000	848-1248*	434-4
Frank Lloyd Wright's Martin House Complex 125 Jewett Pkwy ..... Buffalo NY 14214 *TF:* 877-377-3858 ■ *Web:* www.darwinmartinhouse.org	716-856-3858	856-4009	50-3
Frank Lloyd Wright's Pope-Leighey House 9000 Richmond Hwy ..... Alexandria VA 22309 *Web:* www.woodlawnpopeleighey.org	703-780-4000		50-3
Frank Lumber Company Inc PO Box 79 ..... Mill City OR 97360 *Web:* franklumberco.com	503-897-2371		683
Frank Lynn & Associates Inc 500 Park Blvd Ste 1300 ..... Itasca IL 60143 *TF:* 800-245-5966 ■ *Web:* www.franklynn.com	312-263-7888		196
Frank M Booth Inc 222 Third St ..... Marysville CA 95901 *TF:* 800-540-9369 ■ *Web:* www.frankbooth.com	530-742-7134	742-8109	189-10
Frank Mayer & Assoc Inc 1975 Wisconsin Ave ..... Grafton WI 53024 **Fax Area Code:* 262 ■ *TF:* 855-294-2875 ■ *Web:* www.frankmayer.com	855-294-2875	377-3449*	233
Frank Miller Lumber Company Inc 1690 Frank Miller Rd ..... Union City IN 47390 *TF:* 800-345-2643 ■ *Web:* www.frankmiller.com	765-964-3196		191-3
Frank Millman Distributors Inc 8 Progress St ..... Edison NJ 08820 *Web:* www.millmans.com	908-561-7300		54
Frank Novak & Sons Inc 23940 Miles Rd ..... Cleveland OH 44128	216-475-5440		189-2
Frank Paxton Lumber Co 7455 Dawson Rd ..... Cincinnati OH 45243 **Fax:* Sales ■ *TF:* 800-325-9800 ■ *Web:* www.paxtonwood.com	513-984-8200	984-9060*	191-3
Frank Phillips College (FPC) PO Box 5118 ..... Borger TX 79008 *TF:* 800-394-5445 ■ *Web:* www.fpctx.edu	806-457-4200		162
Frank Rewold & Son Inc 333 E Second St ..... Rochester MI 48307 *Web:* frankrewold.com	248-651-7242		186
Frank Rimerman & Company LLP 1801 Page Mill Rd ..... Palo Alto CA 94304 *TF:* 800-900-4250 ■ *Web:* www.frankrimerman.com	650-845-8100	494-1975	2
Frank Roberts & Sons Inc 1130 Robertsville Rd ..... Punxsutawney PA 15767 *TF:* 800-262-8955 ■ *Web:* frankrobertsandsons.com	814-938-5000		191-4
Frank Roth Company Inc 1795 Stratford Ave ..... Stratford CT 06615 *Web:* www.frankroth.com	203-377-2155		454
Frank Seringer & Chaney Inc 197 N Leavitt Rd ..... Amherst OH 44001 *Web:* fsc-cpa.com	440-984-2441		2
Frank Sterles Slovenian Restaurant 1401 E 55th St ..... Cleveland OH 44103 *Web:* www.sterlescountryhouse.com	216-881-4181		671
Frank Strategic Marketing Inc 8775 Centre Park Dr Ste 211 ..... Columbia MD 21043 *Web:* www.frankbiz.com	410-203-1228		232
Frank Thompson Transport Inc 1010 Paxton Rd ..... El Dorado AR 71731	870-862-5426		191-1
Frank W Diver Inc 2101 Pennsylvania Ave ..... Wilmington DE 19806 *Web:* www.diverchev.com	302-575-0161		57

Name / Address	City	State	Zip	Phone	Fax	Class
Frank W Mayborn Civic & Convention Ctr 3303 N Third St *Web:* ci.temple.tx.us	Temple	TX	76501	254-298-5720	298-5388	205
Frank Wardynski & Sons Inc 336 Peckham St *TF:* 800-255-8401 ■ *Web:* www.wardynski.com	Buffalo	NY	14206	716-854-6083		296-26
Frank's Great Outdoors 1212 N Huron Rd *TF:* 800-922-1219 ■ *Web:* www.franksgreatoutdoors.com	Linwood	MI	48634	989-697-5341		711
Franke Kindred Canada Ltd 1000 Kindred Rd **Fax Area Code:* 866 ■ *Web:* www.franke.com	Midland	ON	L4R4K9	705-526-5427	227-3035*	480
Frankel Lois (Rep D - FL) 1037 Longworth Bldg *Web:* frankel.house.gov	Washington	DC	20515	202-225-9890		342-2
Franken Al (Sen D - MN) 309 Hart Bldg *Web:* www.franken.senate.gov	Washington	DC	20510	202-224-5641		342-2
Frankenmuth Convention & Visitors Bureau 635 S Main St *TF:* 800-386-8696 ■ *Web:* www.frankenmuth.org	Frankenmuth	MI	48734	989-652-6106	652-3841	206
Frankenmuth Insurance 1 Mutual Ave *TF:* 800-234-4433 ■ *Web:* www.fmins.com	Frankenmuth	MI	48787	989-652-6121		391-4
Frankford Candy & Chocolate Co Inc 9300 Ashton Rd *Web:* www.frankfordcandy.com	Philadelphia	PA	19114	215-735-5200		296-8
Frankfort Area Chamber of Commerce 100 Capitol Ave *Web:* www.frankfortky.info	Frankfort	KY	40601	502-223-8261	223-5942	139
Frankfort City Hall 315 W Second St PO Box 697 *Web:* frankfort.ky.gov	Frankfort	KY	40601	502-875-8500		337
Frankfort Community Public Library (FCPL) 208 W Clinton St *Web:* myfcpl.org	Frankfort	IN	46041	765-654-8746	654-8747	434-3
Frankfort Convention Ctr 405 Mero St *Web:* www.frankfortconventioncenter.com	Frankfort	KY	40601	502-564-5335	564-3310	205
Frankfort Regional Medical Ctr 299 King's Daughters Dr *TF:* 888-696-4505 ■ *Web:* www.frankfortregional.com	Frankfort	KY	40601	502-875-5240	226-7936	374-3
Frankfort/Franklin County Tourist & Convention Commission 100 Capitol Ave *TF:* 800-960-7200 ■ *Web:* www.visitfrankfort.com	Frankfort	KY	40601	502-875-8687		206
Frankfurt Kurnit Klein & Selz Pc 488 Madison Ave 10th Fl *Web:* www.fkks.com	New York	NY	10022	212-980-0120	593-9175	428
Frankie Friend & Assoc Inc 2305 E Arapahoe Rd Ste 132 *Web:* www.frankiefriend.com	Centennial	CO	80122	303-768-8577		2
Frankie Rowland's Steakhouse 104 Jefferson St *Web:* frankierowlandssteakhouse.com	Roanoke	VA	24011	540-527-2333		671
Frankie's Barbecue 1583-1691 W Washington St	South Bend	IN	46628	574-287-8993		671
Frankies 457 Court Street Spuntino 457 Ct St *Web:* frankiesspuntino.com	Brooklyn	NY	11231	718-403-0033		671
Franklin & Marshall College PO Box 3003 **Fax:* Admissions ■ *TF:* 877-678-9111 ■ *Web:* www.fandm.edu	Lancaster	PA	17604	717-291-3951	291-4389*	166
Franklin & Marshall College Shadek-Fackenthal Library 450 College Ave *TF:* 866-366-7655 ■ *Web:* www.fandm.edu	Lancaster	PA	17604	717-358-3911		434-6
Franklin & Prokopik A Professional Corp The B & O Bldg 2 N Charles St Ste 600 *Web:* www.fandpnet.com	Baltimore	MD	21201	410-752-8700		428
Franklin American Mortgage Company Inc 501 Corporate Centre Dr Ste 400 *Web:* www.franklinamerican.com	Franklin	TN	37067	615-778-1000		217
Franklin Area Chamber of Commerce (FACC) 1327 Liberty St *Web:* www.franklinareachamber.org	Franklin	PA	16323	814-432-5823	437-2453	139
Franklin Cafe 278 Shawmut Ave *Web:* www.franklincafe.com	Boston	MA	02118	617-350-0010		671
Franklin Clothing Company Inc 208 Lurgan Ave	Shippensburg	PA	17257	717-532-4146		155-12
Franklin College 101 Branigin Blvd **Fax:* Admissions ■ *TF:* 800-852-0232 ■ *Web:* www.franklincollege.edu	Franklin	IN	46131	317-738-8000	738-8274*	166
Franklin Community Health Network 111 Franklin Health Commons *TF:* 800-398-6031 ■ *Web:* mainehealth.org/franklin-community-health-network	Farmington	ME	04938	207-778-6031	778-2548	374-3
Franklin Corp 600 Franklin Dr *Web:* franklincorp.com	Houston	MS	38851	662-456-4286		319-2
Franklin Correctional Ctr 5918 NC 39 Hwy S PO Box 155 *Web:* www.ncdps.gov	Bunn	NC	27508	919-496-6119	496-6032	213
Franklin Correctional Facility 62 Bare Hill Rd	Malone	NY	12953	518-483-6040		213
Franklin County 33 Market St Ste 203 *TF:* 800-352-3671 ■ *Web:* www.franklincountyflorida.com	Apalachicola	FL	32320	850-653-8861		338
Franklin County PO Box 607 *TF:* 800-833-2611 ■ *Web:* franklincountyil.gov	Benton	IL	62812	618-438-3221	435-3405	338
Franklin County 459 Main St *TF:* 800-622-4941 ■ *Web:* franklincounty.in.gov	Brookville	IN	47012	765-647-5111	647-3224	338
Franklin County 211 Athens St PO Box 313 *TF:* 800-520-7493 ■ *Web:* franklincountyga.gov	Carnesville	GA	30521	706-384-4390	384-3506	338
Franklin County 14 N MAIN ST *Web:* www.franklincountypa.gov	Chambersburg	PA	17201	717-264-4125	267-3438	338
Franklin County 369 S High St 3rd Fl *Web:* www.franklincountyohio.gov	Columbus	OH	43215	614-525-3800		338
Franklin County 615 Wilton Rd *Web:* www.franklincountymaine.org	Farmington	ME	04938	207-778-4215	778-2438	338
Franklin County 321 W Main St *Web:* franklincounty.ky.gov	Frankfort	KY	40601	502-875-8702	875-8755	338
Franklin County 405 15th Ave *Web:* co.franklin.ne.us	Franklin	NE	68939	308-425-6202	425-6093	338
Franklin County 12 First Ave NW Ste 203 *Web:* www.co.franklin.ia.us/pages/clerk	Hampton	IA	50441	641-456-5626	456-5628	338
Franklin County 113 Market St *Web:* www.franklincountync.us	Louisburg	NC	27549	919-496-5994	496-2683	338
Franklin County 355 W Main St *TF:* 800-397-8686 ■ *Web:* franklincony.org	Malone	NY	12953	518-481-1681	483-0141	338
Franklin County PO Box 267 *Web:* franklin.msghn.org	Meadville	MS	39653	601-384-2320		338
Franklin County 200 N Kaufman St *Web:* www.co.franklin.tx.us	Mount Vernon	TX	75457	903-537-2342		338
Franklin County 315 S Main St *TF:* 800-368-8683 ■ *Web:* www.franklincoks.org	Ottawa	KS	66067	785-229-3410	229-3419	338
Franklin County 211 W Commercial St	Ozark	AR	72949	479-667-3818		338
Franklin County 1016 N Fourth Ave *TF:* 800-647-7706 ■ *Web:* www.co.franklin.wa.us	Pasco	WA	99301	509-545-3535	545-3573	338
Franklin County 39 W Oneida St *Web:* www.franklincountyidaho.org	Preston	ID	83263	208-852-1090	852-1094	338
Franklin County 1255 Franklin St *Web:* www.franklincountyva.org	Rocky Mount	VA	24151	540-483-3030		338
Franklin County 405 N Jackson Ave PO Box 1028 *Web:* www.franklincountyal.org	Russellville	AL	35653	256-332-8850		338
Franklin County 17 Church St *Web:* www.visitfranklincountyvt.com	Saint Albans	VT	05478	802-524-2444		338
Franklin County 400 E Locust *Web:* www.franklinmo.org	Union	MO	63084	636-583-6355	583-7320	338
Franklin County 855 Dinah Shore Blvd Ste 3 *Web:* www.franklincotn.us	Winchester	TN	37398	931-967-2905		338
Franklin County Chamber of Commerce 395 Main St *Web:* franklincc.org	Greenfield	MA	01301	413-773-5463	773-7008	139
Franklin County Chamber of Commerce 103 N Jackson Ave *Web:* www.franklincountychamber.org	Russellville	AL	35653	256-332-1760	332-1740	139
Franklin County Chamber of Commerce 44 Chamber Way PO Box 280 *Web:* www.franklincountychamber.com	Winchester	TN	37398	931-967-6788		139
Franklin County Library 105 S Porter St *Web:* franklincountylibrary.org	Winchester	TN	37398	931-967-3706	962-1477	434-3
Franklin County Library 355 Franklin St *Web:* library.franklincountyva.org	Rocky Mount	VA	24151	540-483-3098	483-6652	434-3
Franklin County Library 906 N Main St *Web:* www.franklincountync.us	Louisburg	NC	27549	919-496-2111	496-1339	434-3
Franklin County Regional Chamber of Commerce 2 N Main St Ste 101 *Web:* www.visitfranklincountyvt.com	Saint Albans	VT	05478	802-524-2444		139
Franklin County Veterans Memorial 300 W Broad St	Columbus	OH	43215	614-221-4341		205
Franklin Covey Co 2200 West PkwyBlvd *NYSE:* FC ■ *TF:* 800-827-1776 ■ *Web:* www.franklincovey.com	Salt Lake City	UT	84119	801-817-1776		765
Franklin Crates Inc 311 NE Bay sixth Ave	Micanopy	FL	32667	352-466-3141		200
Franklin Credit Management Corp 101 Hudson St *TF:* 800-255-5897 ■ *Web:* www.franklincredit.com	Jersey City	NJ	07302	201-604-1800	839-4512	217
Franklin Creek State Natural Area 1872 Twist Rd *Web:* www.dnr.illinois.gov/INPC/Pages/Area1LeeFranklinCreek.aspx	Franklin Grove	IL	61031	815-456-2878		565
Franklin D Roosevelt Presidential Library & Museum 4079 Albany Post Rd *TF:* 800-337-8474 ■ *Web:* www.fdrlibrary.marist.edu	Hyde Park	NY	12538	845-486-7770	486-1147	434-2
Franklin D. Roosevelt State Park 2957 Crompond Rd *Web:* parks.ny.gov/parks/148/details.aspx	Yorktown Heights	NY	10598	914-245-4434		565
Franklin Delano Roosevelt Memorial 900 Ohio Dr SW *Web:* www.nps.gov/fdrm	Washington	DC	20024	202-426-6841		50-4
Franklin Development Co 21260 Gathering Oak Ste 101 *Web:* franklincompanies.com	San Antonio	TX	78260	210-694-2223		187
Franklin Electric Co Inc 9255 Coverdale Rd *NASDAQ:* FELE ■ *TF:* 800-962-3787 ■ *Web:* www.franklin-electric.com	Fort Wayne	IN	46809	260-824-2900	824-2909	518
Franklin Electric Co-op Inc 225 Franklin St NW *TF:* 800-410-2732 ■ *Web:* areapower.coop	Russellville	AL	35653	256-332-2730		245
Franklin Electric LP 916 Fulton St *Web:* www.franklinelectric.net	Pittsburgh	PA	15233	412-322-4477		186
Franklin Empire Inc 8421 Darnley Rd *TF:* 800-361-5044 ■ *Web:* www.feinc.com	Montreal	QC	H4T2B2	514-341-9720		253
Franklin Feed & Supply Co 1977 Philadelphia Ave *Web:* franklinhardwareandpetcenter.com	Chambersburg	PA	17201	717-264-6148	264-7865	447
Franklin Fibre-Lamitex Corp 903 E 13th St *TF:* 800-233-9739 ■ *Web:* www.franklinfibre.com	Wilmington	DE	19802	302-652-3621	571-9754	599
Franklin G Burroughs-Simeon B Chapin Art Museum 3100 S Ocean Blvd *Web:* www.myrtlebeachartmuseum.org	Myrtle Beach	SC	29577	843-238-2510		520
Franklin Homes Inc 10655 Hwy 43 **Fax Area Code:* 256 ■ *TF:* 800-332-4511 ■ *Web:* www.franklinhomesusa.com	Russellville	AL	35653	800-332-4511	331-2203*	505
Franklin Imaging LLC 500 Schrock Rd *TF:* 877-885-6894 ■ *Web:* www.franklinimaging.com	Columbus	OH	43229	614-885-6894		627
Franklin (Independent City) 1020 Pretlow St *Web:* www.courts.state.va.us	Franklin	VA	23851	757-562-8550	562-1156	338
Franklin Institute, The 222 N 20th St *Web:* www.fi.edu	Philadelphia	PA	19103	215-448-1200	448-1235	520

Phone | Fax | Class

Franklin Interiors Inc
2740 Smallman St Ste 600 ... Pittsburgh PA 15222 412-261-2525 321
Web: frankllninteriors.com

Franklin International 2020 Bruck St ... Columbus OH 43207 614-443-0241 3
TF: 800-877-4583 ■ *Web:* www.franklininternational.com

Franklin Iron & Metal Corp
1939 E First St ... Dayton OH 45403 937-253-8184 686
Web: frankliniron andmetal.liveonatt.com

Franklin Local School District
4000 Millers Ln ... Duncan Falls OH 43734 740-674-5203 685
TF: 800-846-4976 ■ *Web:* www.franklinlocalschools.org

Franklin Mills
1455 Franklin Mills Cir ... Philadelphia PA 19154 215-632-1500 632-7888 460
TF General: 877-746-6642 ■ *Web:* simon.com/mall/franklin-mills

Franklin Mutual Insurance Co
5 Broad St ... Branchville NJ 07826 973-948-3120 948-7190 391-4
TF: 800-842-0551 ■ *Web:* www.fmiweb.com

Franklin Parish 6550 Main St ... Winnsboro LA 71295 318-435-5133 338
Web: laclerksofcourt.org

Franklin Park Associates LLC
Franklin Park 251 St Asaphs Rd Three Bala Plaza
Ste 500 W ... Bala Cynwyd PA 19004 610-822-0500 401
Web: www.franklinparkllc.com

Franklin Park Conservatory & Botanical Gardens
1777 E Broad St ... Columbus OH 43203 614-715-8000 715-8199 97
Web: www.fpconservatory.org

Franklin Park Zoo 1 Franklin Pk Rd ... Boston MA 02121 617-541-5466 989-2025 823
Web: www.zoonewengland.org

Franklin Pierce University
Keene 17 Bradco St ... Keene NH 03431 603-899-4000 166
TF: 800-325-1090 ■ *Web:* www.franklinpierce.edu
Lebanon 24 Airport Rd Ste 19 ... West Lebanon NH 03784 603-298-5549 899-1065* 166
**Fax:* Admissions ■ *TF:* 800-325-1090 ■ *Web:* www.franklinpierce.edu
Manchester 670 N Commercial St ... Manchester NH 03101 603-626-4972 626-4815 166
TF Admissions: 800-437-0048 ■ *Web:* www.franklinpierce.edu
Portsmouth 73 Corporate Dr ... Portsmouth NH 03801 603-433-2000 899-1067* 166
**Fax:* Admissions ■ *TF:* 800-325-1090 ■ *Web:* www.franklinpierce.edu
Rindge 40 University Dr ... Rindge NH 03461 603-899-4000 899-4394* 166
**Fax:* Admissions ■ *TF Admissions:* 800-437-0048 ■ *Web:* www.franklinpierce.edu

Franklin Precision Industry Inc (FPI)
3220 Bowling Green Rd ... Franklin KY 42134 270-598-4300 60
Web: www.fpik.com

Franklin Press Inc
1391 Highland Rd ... Baton Rouge LA 70802 225-387-0504 5
Web: gofranklingo.com

Franklin Resources Inc
1 Franklin Pkwy Bdge 970 1st Fl ... San Mateo CA 94403 650-312-2000 525-7141* 401
NYSE: BEN ■ **Fax:* Hum Res ■ *TF:* 800-632-2301 ■ *Web:* www.franklintempleton.com

Franklin Rural Electric Co-op
1560 Hwy 65 PO Box 437 ... Hampton IA 50441 641-456-2557 456-5183 245
TF: 800-750-3557 ■ *Web:* www.franklinrec.coop

Franklin Special School District
507 New Hwy 96 W ... Franklin TN 37064 615-794-6624 790-4716 685
Web: www.fssd.org

Franklin Sports Inc
17 Campanelli Pkwy ... Stoughton MA 02072 781-344-1111 341-0333 710
TF: 800-225-8649 ■ *Web:* www.franklinsports.com

Franklin Square Hospital Ctr
9000 Franklin Sq Dr ... Baltimore MD 21237 443-777-7000 374-3
TF: 888-404-3549 ■ *Web:* www.medstarhealth.org

Franklin Square Public Library, The
19 Lincoln Rd ... Franklin Square NY 11010 516-488-3444 434-3
Web: franklinsquarepl.org

Franklin Street Properties Corp
401 Edgewater Pl Ste 200 ... Wakefield MA 01880 781-557-1300 654
NYSE: FSP ■ *TF:* 877-686-9496 ■ *Web:* www.franklinstreetproperties.com

Franklin Supply Inc 75 Lee St ... Franklin LA 70538 337-828-3208 297-8
Web: franklinsupplyinc.com

Franklin Templeton Investments
3344 Quality Dr ... Rancho Cordova CA 95670 650-312-2000 690
TF: 800-632-2350 ■ *Web:* www.franklintempleton.com

Franklin Township Chamber of Commerce
675 Franklin Blvd ... Somerset NJ 08873 732-545-7044 139
Web: www.franklinchamber.com

Franklin Township Public Library
485 DeMott Ln ... Somerset NJ 08873 732-873-8700 873-0746 434-3
TF: 800-944-6847 ■ *Web:* www.franklintwp.org

Franklin Truck Parts Inc
6925 Bandini Blvd ... Commerce CA 90040 323-726-1034 57
Web: www.franklintruckparts.com

Franklin University 201 S Grant Ave ... Columbus OH 43215 614-797-4700 166
TF: 877-341-6300 ■ *Web:* www.franklin.edu

Franklin W Olin College of Engineering
1000 Olin Way ... Needham MA 02492 781-292-2300 292-2210* 166
**Fax:* Admissions ■ *Web:* www.olin.edu

Franklin, The 164 E 87th St ... New York NY 10128 212-369-1000 369-8000 379
TF: 800-607-4009 ■ *Web:* www.franklinhotel.com

Franklin-Pierce Schools 315 129th St S ... Tacoma WA 98444 253-298-3000 685
Web: fpschools.org

Franklin-Southampton Area Chamber of Commerce
108 W Third Ave PO Box 531 ... Franklin VA 23851 757-562-4900 562-6138 139
Web: fsachamber.com

Franks International Services Inc
10260 Westheimer Rd Ste 700 ... Houston TX 77042 281-966-7300 45
Web: franksinternational.com

Franks Supply Company Inc
3311 Stanford Dr NE ... Albuquerque NM 87107 505-884-0000 884-1787 358
TF: 800-432-5254 ■ *Web:* www.franks-supply.com

Franks Trent (Rep R - AZ)
2435 Rayburn Bldg ... Washington DC 20515 202-225-4576 342-2
Web: franks.house.gov

Frankston Packaging
699 N Frankston Hwy ... Frankston TX 75763 903-876-2550 557
TF: 800-881-1495 ■ *Web:* frankstonpackaging.com

FranNet LLC
10302 Brookridge Village Blvd Ste 201 ... Louisville KY 40291 502-753-2380 196
Web: www.frannet.com

FRAN-PAC 1501 K St Ste 350 ... Washington DC 20005 202-628-8000 628-0812 615
TF: 800-543-1038 ■ *Web:* www.franchise.org

Phone | Fax | Class

Fransmart Inc
105 Oronoco St Ste 200 ... Alexandria VA 22314 703-537-5396 543-0750 195
Web: www.fransmart.com

Frantic Films Corp
70 Arthur St Ste 300 ... Winnipeg MB R3B1G7 204-949-0070 514
Web: www.franticfilms.com

Frantz Group Inc, The
1245 Cheyenne Ave ... Grafton WI 53024 262-204-6000 195
TF: 800-707-0064 ■ *Web:* www.thefrantzgroup.com

Frantz McConnell & Seymour LLP
550 Main Ave Ste 500 ... Knoxville TN 37902 865-546-9321 445
Web: www.fmsllp.com

Frantz Wholesale Nursery LLC
12161 Delaware Rd ... Hickman CA 95323 209-874-1459 292
Web: frantznursery.com

Franz Family Bakeries
2901 Sixth Ave S ... Seattle WA 98134 206-726-7535 296-1
Web: franzbakery.com

Franz Family Bakeries 340 NE 11th St ... Portland OR 97232 541-772-5816 296-1
Web: franzbakery.com

Franz Jevne State Park State Hwy 11 ... Birchdale MN 56629 218-783-6252 565
Web: www.dnr.state.mn.us/state_parks/franz_jevne

Franzen & Franzen LLP
125 E De La Guerra St Ste 201 ... Santa Barbara CA 93101 805-563-0821 2
Web: franzencpa.com

Franzen Graphics Inc
5300 State Hwy 42 ... Sheboygan WI 53083 920-565-4656 627
Web: www.franzenlitho.com

Frasca International Inc
906 E Airport Rd ... Urbana IL 61802 217-344-9200 344-9207 703
Web: www.frasca.com

Frascati 1901 Hyde St ... San Francisco CA 94109 415-928-1406 671
Web: www.frascatisf.com

Frasco Investigative Services
444 Washington St Ste 306 ... Woburn MA 01801 781-935-3888 400
Web: frasco.com

Fraser Direct Distribution Services Ltd
8300 Lawson Rd ... Milton ON L9T0A4 905-877-4411 314
Web: www.fraserdirect.ca

Fraser Forbes Co LLC
6862 Elm St Ste 620 ... Mclean VA 22101 703-790-9400 652
Web: www.fraserforbes.com

Fraser Hearing & Optical Ctr
32925 Groesbeck Hwy ... Fraser MI 48026 586-293-8888 237
Web: www.fraseroptical.com

Fraser Manufacturing Corp
7235 Boyington St ... Lexington MI 48450 810-359-5338 454

Fraser Shipyards Inc 1 Clough Ave ... Superior WI 54880 715-394-7787 394-2807 698
Web: www.frasershipyards.com

Fraser Stryker PC LLO
500 Energy Plaza 409 S 17th St ... Omaha NE 68102 402-341-6000 428
TF: 800-544-6041 ■ *Web:* www.fraserstryker.com

Fraser Trebilcock Davis & Dunlap PC
124 W Allegan St Ste 1000 ... Lansing MI 48933 517-482-5800 428
Web: www.fraserlawfirm.com

Fraser Yachts Florida Inc
1800 Southeast Tenth Ave Ste 400 ... Fort Lauderdale FL 33316 954-463-0600 41
Web: www.fraseryachts.com

Frasier Dean & Howard PLLC
3310 W End Ave Ste 550 ... Nashville TN 37203 615-383-6592 2
Web: www.fdhcpa.com

Fratelli 499 Terry Fox Dr ... Ottawa ON K2T1H7 613-592-0225 671
Web: www.fratelli.ca

Fratelli 124 N Nevada Ave ... Colorado Springs CO 80903 719-575-9571 671
Web: www.fratelliristorante.com

Fratello's Ristorante Italiano
155 Dow St ... Manchester NH 03101 603-624-2022 671
Web: www.fratellos.com

Fraternal Order of Alaska State Troopers Museum
245 W Fifth Ave ... Anchorage AK 99501 907-279-5050 279-5054 520
TF: 800-770-5050 ■ *Web:* www.alaskatroopermuseum.com

Fraternal Order of Police (FOP)
701 Marriott Dr ... Nashville TN 37214 615-399-0900 399-0400 48-15
TF: 800-451-2711 ■ *Web:* www.fop.net

Fraternity of Alpha Kappa Lambda
354 Gradle Dr ... Carmel IN 46032 317-564-8003 48-16
Web: www.akl.org

Frayman Group Inc, The
128 Brighton Beach Ave Ste 400 P.O. Box 299 ... Brooklyn NY 11235 718-648-7700 196

Fraze Pavilion 695 Lincoln Pk Blvd ... Dayton OH 45429 937-296-3300 296-3302 572
TF: 800-514-3849 ■ *Web:* www.fraze.com

Frazier & Deeter LLC
1230 Peachtree St NE Ste 1500 ... Atlanta GA 30309 404-253-7500 194
Web: www.frazierdeeter.com

Frazier & Frazier Industries Inc
817 S First St PO Box 279 ... Coolidge TX 76635 254-786-2293 786-2284 307
Web: www.ffcastings.com

Frazier Healthcare
601 Union St 2 Union Sq Ste 3200 ... Seattle WA 98101 206-621-7200 792
Web: www.frazierhealthcare.com

Frazier History Museum
829 W Main St ... Louisville KY 40202 502-753-5663 520
Web: fraziermuseum.org

Frazier Industrial Co
91 Fairview Ave ... Long Valley NJ 07853 908-876-3001 876-3615 286
TF: 800-859-1342 ■ *Web:* www.frazier.com

Frazier Rehabilitation Institute
220 Abraham Flexner Way ... Louisville KY 40202 502-582-7400 582-7477 374-6
TF: 800-333-2230 ■ *Web:* kentuckyonehealth.org

FRBSF (Federal Reserve Bank of San Francisco)
101 Market St ... San Francisco CA 94105 415-974-2000 71
TF: 800-227-4133 ■ *Web:* www.frbsf.org

FRC (Family Research Council)
801 G St NW ... Washington DC 20001 202-393-2100 393-2134 48-6
TF: 800-225-4008 ■ *Web:* www.frc.org

FRC Component Products Inc
1511 S Benjamin Ave ... Mason City IA 50401 641-424-0370 253
Web: frccorp.com

	City	State	ZIP	Phone	Fax	Class
FRCC (Front Range Community College) *Boulder County* 2190 Miller Dr **Fax:* Admissions ■ *TF:* 888-800-9198 ■ *Web:* www.frontrange.edu	Longmont	CO	80501	303-678-3722	678-3699*	162
Frecom 435 W Baltimore Pk *TF:* 800-261-0490 ■ *Web:* frecominc.com	West Grove	PA	19390	610-869-3307		196
Fred C Churchlnc 41 Wellman St *TF:* 800-225-1865 ■ *Web:* fredcchurch.com	Lowell	MA	01851	978-458-1865		390
Fred Christen & Sons Co 714 George St *Web:* toledochamber.com	Toledo	OH	43608	419-243-4161	243-1292	697
Fred D Pfening Co 1075 W Fifth Ave *Web:* www.pfening.com	Columbus	OH	43212	614-294-5361		207
Fred Flare Inc 300f Kingsland Ave	Brooklyn	NY	11222	718-599-9221		225
Fred Gannon Rocky Bayou State Park 4281 E Hwy 20 *Web:* www.floridastateparks.org	Niceville	FL	32578	850-833-9144		565
Fred Garrison Oil Co 1107 Walter Griffin St PO Box 100 *TF:* 800-721-4147 ■ *Web:* www.allstarfuel.com	Plainview	TX	79073	806-296-6353		579
Fred Heroman's Florist 6868 Florida Blvd *Web:* www.flowerlandflowers.com	Baton Rouge	LA	70806	225-927-6070		292
Fred Hutchinson Cancer Research Ctr 1100 Fairview Ave N PO Box 19024 *Web:* www.fredhutch.org/en.html	Seattle	WA	98109	206-667-5000	667-4051	668
Fred Jones Jr Museum of Art 555 Elm Ave University of Oklahoma *Web:* www.ou.edu	Norman	OK	73019	405-325-3272	325-7696	520
Fred Knapp Engraving Company Inc 5102 Douglas Ave *Web:* www.air-logic.com	Racine	WI	53402	262-639-9035		201
Fred Loya Insurance 1800 Lee Trevino Ste 201 *TF:* 800-554-0595 ■ *Web:* www.fredloya.com	El Paso	TX	79936	915-590-5692		390
Fred M Schildwachter & Sons Inc 1400 Ferris Pl *TF:* 800-642-3646 ■ *Web:* www.schildwachteroil.com	Bronx	NY	10461	718-828-2500	828-3661	316
Fred Olivieri Construction Company Inc 6315 Promway Ave NW *TF:* 800-847-5085 ■ *Web:* www.fredolivieri.com	North Canton	OH	44720	330-494-1007		186
Fred Porter & Assoc Inc Dba Porter & Assoc Inc 1200 21st St	Bakersfield	CA	93301	661-327-0362		261
Fred Pryor Seminars 9757 Metcalf Ave **Fax Area Code:* 913 ■ *TF:* 800-780-8476 ■ *Web:* www.pryor.com	Overland Park	KS	66212	800-780-8476	967-8842*	765
Fred Rau Dairy 10255 W Manning Ave	Fresno	CA	93706	559-237-3393		10-3
Fred Usinger Inc 1030 N Old World Third St *TF:* 800-558-9998 ■ *Web:* www.usinger.com	Milwaukee	WI	53203	414-276-9100	291-5277	296-26
Fred Weber Inc 2320 Creve Coeur Mill Rd *TF:* 866-739-8855 ■ *Web:* www.fredweberinc.com	Maryland Heights	MO	63043	314-344-0070	344-0970	188-4
Fred Wilson & Associates Inc 3970 Hendricks Ave *Web:* www.fredwilson.com	Jacksonville	FL	32207	904-398-8636		261
Fred's Inc 4300 New Getwell Rd *NASDAQ:* FRED ■ *TF:* 800-374-7417 ■ *Web:* www.fredsinc.com	Memphis	TN	38118	901-365-8880		229
Freddie Georges Production Group 15362 Graham St *Web:* www.freddiegeorges.com	La Palma	CA	92649	714-367-9260		184
Freddie Mac 8200 Jones Branch Dr *TF:* 800-424-5401 ■ *Web:* www.freddiemac.com	McLean	VA	22102	703-903-2000	903-2759	509
North Central Region 333 W Wacker Dr Ste 2500 *TF:* 800-373-3343 ■ *Web:* www.freddiemac.com	Chicago	IL	60606	312-407-7400		509
Northeast Region 8200 Jones Branch Dr *TF:* 800-373-3343 ■ *Web:* www.freddiemac.com	McLean	VA	22102	703-903-2000	903-2759	509
Southeast/Southwest Region 2300 Windy Ridge Pkwy Ste 200N *TF:* 800-373-3343 ■ *Web:* www.freddiemac.com	Atlanta	GA	30339	770-857-8800		509
Freddie's Beach Bar & Restaurant 555 23rd St S *Web:* freddiesbeachbar.com	Arlington	VA	22202	703-685-0555		671
Frederic Dorwart Lawyers Old City Hall 124 E Fourth St *Web:* www.fdlaw.com	Tulsa	OK	74103	918-583-9922		428
Frederic Printing Co 14701 E 38th Ave *Web:* www.fredericprinting.com	Aurora	CO	80011	303-371-7990		627
Frederic W Cook & Co Inc 685 Third Ave 28th Fl *Web:* www.fwcook.com	New York	NY	10017	212-986-6330		193
Frederick Community College 7932 Opossumtown Pk *Web:* www.frederick.edu	Frederick	MD	21702	301-846-2400		162
Frederick County 107 N Kent St *Web:* www.co.frederick.va.us	Winchester	VA	22601	540-665-5600	667-0370	338
Frederick County Chamber of Commerce 8420 Gas House Pk Ste B *Web:* www.frederickchamber.org	Frederick	MD	21701	301-662-4164	846-4427	139
Frederick County Public Libraries (FCPL) 110 E Patrick St *TF:* 800-248-2296 ■ *Web:* www.fcpl.org	Frederick	MD	21701	301-600-1613		434-3
Frederick Douglass Museum & Hall of Fame for Caring Americans 320 A St NE *Web:* www.caringinstitute.org	Washington	DC	20002	202-547-4273		520
Frederick Douglass National Historic Site 1900 Anacostia Dr SE *Web:* www.nps.gov/frdo	Washington	DC	20020	202-426-5961	426-0880	564
Frederick Goldman Inc 154 W 14th St *TF:* 800-221-3232 ■ *Web:* www.fgoldman.com	New York	NY	10011	800-221-3232		411
Frederick L Ehrman Medical Library *New York University Medical Ctr School of Medicine* 550 First Ave Medical Science Bldg ground fl *Web:* hsl.med.nyu.edu	New York	NY	10016	212-263-5395	263-6534	434-1
Frederick Law Olmsted National Historic Site 99 Warren St *Web:* www.nps.gov/frla	Brookline	MA	02445	617-566-1689	232-4073	564
Frederick Memorial Hospital 400 W Seventh St *Web:* www.fmh.org	Frederick	MD	21701	240-566-3300		374-3
Frederick Motor Co, The 1 Waverley Dr *TF:* 800-734-9118	Frederick	MD	21702	800-734-9118		57
Frederick News Post 200 E Patrick St *TF:* 800-486-1177 ■ *Web:* www.fredericknewspost.com	Frederick	MD	21701	301-662-1177		532-2
Frederick Quinn Corp 103 S Church St *TF:* 800-568-2433 ■ *Web:* www.fquinncorp.com	Addison	IL	60101	630-628-8500	628-8595	186
Frederick Taylor University 346 Rheem Blvd Ste 203 *TF:* 888-370-7589 ■ *Web:* www.ftu.edu	Moraga	CA	94556	800-988-4622		507
Frederick Wildman & Sons Ltd 307 E 53rd St *TF General:* 800-733-9463 ■ *Web:* www.frederickwildman.com	New York	NY	10022	212-355-0700	355-4719	81-3
Frederick's of Hollywood Inc 6255 Sunset Blvd 6th FL *TF:* 855-655-2514 ■ *Web:* www.fredericks.com	Los Angeles	CA	90028	323-466-5151		157-6
Fredericks Co, The 2400 Philmont Ave *TF:* 800-367-2919 ■ *Web:* www.frederickscompany.com	Huntingdon Valley	PA	19006	215-947-2500	947-7464	332
Fredericks Michael & Co 430 Park Ave *Web:* www.fm-co.com	New York	NY	10022	212-732-1600		401
Fredericksburg & Spotsylvania National Military Park 120 Chatham Ln *Web:* www.nps.gov/frsp	Fredericksburg	VA	22405	540-371-0802	371-1907	564
Fredericksburg Chamber of Commerce 302 E Austin St *TF:* 888-997-3600 ■ *Web:* www.fredericksburg-texas.com	Fredericksburg	TX	78624	830-997-6523	997-8588	206
Fredericksburg City Public Schools 817 Princess Anne St *Web:* www.cityschools.com	Fredericksburg	VA	22401	540-372-1130	372-1111	685
Fredericksburg (Independent City) 715 Princess Ann St *TF:* 800-649-8481 ■ *Web:* www.fredericksburgva.gov	Fredericksburg	VA	22401	540-372-1010	372-1201	338
Fredericksburg Regional Chamber of Commerce 2300 Fall Hill Ave Ste 240 *TF:* 888-338-0252 ■ *Web:* www.fredericksburgchamber.org	Fredericksburg	VA	22401	540-373-9400	373-9570	139
Fredericton Chamber of Commerce 364 York St Ste 200 *Web:* www.frederictonchamber.ca	Fredericton	NB	E3B3P7	506-458-8006	451-1119	137
Fredericton Tourism 11 Carleton St *Web:* www.fredericton.ca	Fredericton	NB	E3B4Y7	506-460-2041		772
Frederik Meijer Gardens & Sculpture Park 1000 E Beltline Ave NE *TF:* 877-975-3171 ■ *Web:* www.meijergardens.org	Grand Rapids	MI	49525	616-957-1580	957-5792	97
Fredonia State University of New York *Fredonia* 280 Central Ave *TF:* 800-642-4272 ■ *Web:* www.fredonia.edu	Fredonia	NY	14063	716-673-3111		166
Fredrick, Fredrick & Heller Engineers Inc 672 E Royalton Rd *TF:* 800-551-2658 ■ *Web:* www.ffhengineers.com	Broadview Heights	OH	44147	440-546-9696		261
Fredrickson, Mazeika & Grant LLP 5720 Oberlin Dr *TF:* 800-231-8440 ■ *Web:* fmglegal.com	San Diego	CA	92121	858-642-2002		428
Fredson Travel Inc 11077 Biscayne Blvd Ste 401 *TF:* 800-626-8422	Miami	FL	33161	800-626-8422		772
Free Flite Inc 2949 Canton Rd Ste 1000 *Web:* www.freeflite.com	Marietta	GA	30066	770-422-5237		711
Free Flow Packaging International Inc 1090 Mills Way *TF:* 800-866-9946 ■ *Web:* www.fpintl.com	Redwood City	CA	94063	650-261-5300	361-1713	601
Free Lance Star 616 Amelia St **Fax:* News Rm ■ *TF:* 800-877-0500 ■ *Web:* www.fredericksburg.com	Fredericksburg	VA	22401	540-374-5000	373-8455*	532-2
Free Library of Philadelphia 1901 Vine St *TF:* 800-732-0999 ■ *Web:* www.freelibrary.org	Philadelphia	PA	19103	215-686-5322		434-3
Free Methodist Foundation, The 8050 Spring Arbor Rd *TF:* 800-325-8975 ■ *Web:* fmfoundation.org	Spring Arbor	MI	49283	517-750-2727		305
Free Press 418 S Second St *TF:* 800-657-4662 ■ *Web:* www.mankatofreepress.com	Mankato	MN	56001	507-625-4451	388-4355	532-2
Free Press Standard, The 43 E Main St *Web:* www.freepressstandard.com	Carrollton	OH	44615	330-627-5591		532-3
Free Service Tire Co Inc PO Box 6187 *TF:* 855-646-1423 ■ *Web:* www.freeservicetire.com	Johnson City	TN	37602	423-979-2250	979-2262	755
Free Speech TV (FSTV) PO Box 44099 *Web:* www.freespeech.org	Denver	CO	80201	303-542-4813		740
Free Spirit Publishing Inc 217 Fifth Ave N Ste 200 *TF:* 800-735-7323 ■ *Web:* freespirit.com	Minneapolis	MN	55401	612-338-2068		637-2
Free State Growers Inc 12819 198th St *Web:* www.armasson.com	Linwood	KS	66052	913-301-3281	301-3288	369
Freebord Manufacturing Inc 455 Irwin St Unit 104 *Web:* www.freebord.com	San Francisco	CA	94107	415-285-2673		711
Freeborn & Peters 311 S Wacker Dr Ste 3000 *Web:* www.freeborn.com	Chicago	IL	60606	312-360-6000	360-6520	428
Freeborn County 411 S Broadway *Web:* www.co.freeborn.mn.us	Albert Lea	MN	56007	507-377-5116	377-5109	338
Freeborn-Mower Co-op Services 2501 E Main St *TF:* 800-734-6421 ■ *Web:* www.fmcs.coop	Albert Lea	MN	56007	507-373-6421	369-0259	245
Freed & Associates 412 Yale Ave *Web:* www.freedassociates.com	Berkeley	CA	94708	510-525-1853		196
Freed Advertising LP 1650 Hwy 6 Ste 400 *TF:* 800-438-7325 ■ *Web:* www.freedad.com	Sugar Land	TX	77478	281-240-4949		7
Freed Maxick & Battaglia CPAs 800 Liberty Bldg *Web:* www.freedmaxick.com	Buffalo	NY	14202	716-847-2651		2

Name / Address	City	State	ZIP	Phone	Fax	Class
Freed Photography Inc 4931 Cordell Ave Ste 101 *Web:* www.freedphoto.com	Bethesda	MD	20814	301-652-5452		590
Freed's Bakery LLC 299 Pepsi Rd	Manchester	NH	03109	603-627-7746		68
Freed's Fine Furnishings Inc 3645 Sturgis Rd *Web:* freedsfurniture.com	Rapid City	SD	57702	605-343-2538	343-3662	321
Freed'S Super Markets Inc 2024 Swamp Pk *Web:* freedsmarket.com	Gilbertsville	PA	19525	610-326-4189		345
Freeda Wigs 779 E Newyork Ave *TF:* 800-371-0550 ■ *Web:* www.freeda.com	Brooklyn	NY	11203	718-771-2000		348
Freed-Hardeman University 158 E Main St *TF:* 800-348-3481 ■ *Web:* www.fhu.edu	Henderson	TN	38340	731-989-6651	989-6047	166
Freedman & Goldberg CPA'S PC 31150 Northwestern Hwy Ste 200 *Web:* freedmangoldberg.com	Farmington Hills	MI	48334	248-626-2400		2
Freedman Financial Associates Inc 8 Essex Ctr Dr 3rd Fl *TF:* 800-588-8108 ■ *Web:* www.freedmanfinancial.com	Peabody	MA	01960	978-531-8108		251
Freedman Seating Co 4545 W Augusta Blvd *TF:* 800-443-4540 ■ *Web:* www.freedmanseating.com	Chicago	IL	60651	773-524-2440	252-7450	689
Freedom 95 Radio 645 Industrial Dr *TF:* 800-278-9200 ■ *Web:* www.freedom95.us	Franklin	IN	46131	317-736-4040	736-4781	645
Freedom Alliance 22570 Markey Ct Ste 240 *TF:* 800-475-6620 ■ *Web:* freedomalliance.org	Sterling	VA	20166	703-444-7940		615
Freedom Arms Inc 314 Wyoming 239 *Web:* www.freedomarms.com	Freedom	WY	83120	307-883-2468	883-2005	284
Freedom Cad Services Inc 20 Cotton Rd Ste 201 *TF:* 800-829-1226 ■ *Web:* www.freedomcad.com	Nashua	NH	03063	603-864-1300		41
Freedom Consulting Group Inc 9881 Broken Land Pkwy Ste 300 *Web:* freedomconsultinggroup.com	Columbia	MD	21046	410-290-9035		225
Freedom Designs Inc 2241 N Madera Rd *Web:* www.freedomdesigns.com	Simi Valley	CA	93065	805-582-0077		475
Freedom Fire Pro LLC 811 Lester Ln *Web:* www.freefirepro.com	Rogers	AR	72756	479-631-6363		610
Freedom Forum 555 Pennsylvania Ave NW *Web:* www.newseuminstitute.org	Washington	DC	20001	202-639-0537		48-7
Freedom From Fear (FFF) 308 Seaview Ave *TF:* 800-550-3560 ■ *Web:* www.freedomfromfear.org	Staten Island	NY	10305	718-351-1717		48-17
Freedom from Hunger 1460 Drew Ave Ste 300 *TF:* 800-708-2555 ■ *Web:* www.freedomfromhunger.org	Davis	CA	95618	530-758-6200	758-6241	48-5
Freedom Graphic Systems Inc (FGS) 1101 S Janesville St *TF:* 800-334-3540 ■ *Web:* fgs.com	Milton	WI	53563	800-334-3540		110
Freedom Greeting Card Company Inc 774 American Dr *TF Sales:* 800-359-3301	Bensalem	PA	19020	215-604-0300	604-0436	130
Freedom Investments Inc 375 Raritan Ctr Pkwy *TF:* 800-944-4033 ■ *Web:* www.freedominvestments.com	Edison	NJ	08837	800-944-4033	830-1855	690
Freedom Lights Our World (FLOW) Inc 1510 Falcon Ledge Dr *Web:* www.flowidealism.org	Austin	TX	78746	512-327-8860		393
Freedom Medical Inc 219 Welsh Pool Rd *TF:* 800-784-8849 ■ *Web:* www.freedommedical.com	Exton	PA	19341	610-903-0200	903-0180	264-4
Freedom Meditech Inc 5090 Shoreham Pl Ste 109	San Diego	CA	92122	858-638-1433		743
Freedom Middle School 3016 Ridgeland Ave *Web:* www.bsd100.org	Berwyn	IL	60402	708-795-5800		685
Freedom Oil Co 814 W Chestnut St *TF:* 800-397-6147 ■ *Web:* www.freedomoil.com	Bloomington	IL	61701	309-828-7750		324
Freedom Sausage Inc 4155 E 1650th Rd	Earlville	IL	60518	815-792-8276		296-26
Freedom Scientific Inc 11800 31st Ct N *TF:* 800-444-4443 ■ *Web:* www.freedomscientific.com	St. Petersburg	FL	33716	727-803-8000		177
Freedom Station Family Fun Ctr 2992 N Park Ave Ste A *Web:* www.freedomstationfun.com	Prescott Valley	AZ	86314	928-775-4040		31
Freedom Technologies Inc 1100 Wilson Blvd Ste 1200 *Web:* freedomtechnologiesinc.com	Arlington	DC	22209	202-371-2220		463
Freedom Trail 99 Chauncy St Ste 401 *Web:* www.thefreedomtrail.org	Boston	MA	02111	617-357-8300	357-8303	50-3
Freedom Village 23442 El Toro Rd *TF:* 800-584-8084 ■ *Web:* www.freedomvillage.org	Lake Forest	CA	92630	949-472-4700		672
Freedom Village 5275 Rt 14 PO Box 24 *TF:* 800-842-8679 ■ *Web:* freedomvillageusa.com/1.4.html	Lakemont	NY	14857	607-243-8126		672
FreedomWorks 400 N Capitol St NW Ste 765 *TF:* 888-564-6273 ■ *Web:* www.freedomworks.org	Washington	DC	20001	202-783-3870	942-7649	48-7
Freedonia Group Inc, The 767 Beta Dr *Web:* www.freedoniagroup.com	Cleveland	OH	44143	440-684-9600		466
FreeFlight Systems Inc 8150 Springwood Dr Ste 100 *Web:* www.freeflightsystems.com	Irving	TX	75063	254-662-0000		57
Freehold Raceway 130 Pk Ave *Web:* www.freeholdraceway.com	Freehold	NJ	07728	732-462-3800	462-2920	642
Freelancers Union 408 Jay St Ste 700 *Web:* www.freelancersunion.org	Brooklyn	NY	11201	718-532-1515		414
Freeland Contracting 11350 OH-335 *Web:* freelandcontracting.com	Lucasville	OH	45648	740-981-2819		610
Freeland Cooper & Foreman LLP 150 Spear St Ste 1800 *Web:* www.freelandlaw.com	San Francisco	CA	94105	415-541-0200		428
Freeline Sports Inc 10 Hughes Ste A-107 *TF:* 800-552-5595 ■ *Web:* freelinedistribution.com	Irvine	CA	92618	949-770-3478		711
Freelin-Wade Co 1730 NE Miller St *TF:* 888-373-9233 ■ *Web:* www.freelin-wade.com	McMinnville	OR	97128	503-434-5561	472-1989	370
Freeman & Mills Inc 350 S Figueroa St Ste 900 *TF:* 800-645-0895 ■ *Web:* www.freemanmills.com	Los Angeles	CA	90071	213-620-9535		463
Freeman Av 4545 W Davis St *Web:* www.freeman.com	Dallas	TX	75211	214-623-1300		179
Freeman Coliseum 3201 E Houston St *TF:* 800-745-3000 ■ *Web:* www.freemancoliseum.com	San Antonio	TX	78219	210-226-1177	226-5081	720
Freeman Corp, The 415 Magnolia St PO Box 96 *TF:* 800-682-9663 ■ *Web:* www.freemancorp.com	Winchester	KY	40392	859-744-4311	744-4363	613
Freeman Cos 1600 Viceroy Ste 100 *Web:* www.freemanco.com	Dallas	TX	75235	214-445-1000		184
Freeman Enterprises Inc 20 E 46th St Ste 800	New York	NY	10017	212-490-6565	490-6566	317
Freeman Freeman & Smiley LLP 1888 Century Pk E Ste 1900 *Web:* www.ffslaw.com	Los Angeles	CA	90067	310-255-6100	391-4042	428
Freeman Gas Inc 113 Peake Rd *TF:* 800-277-5730 ■ *Web:* www.freemangas.com	Roebuck	SC	29376	864-582-5475	582-0937	357
Freeman Health System 1102 W 32nd St *TF:* 800-297-3337 ■ *Web:* www.freemanhealth.com	Joplin	MO	64804	417-347-1111		374-3
Freeman Jewelers Inc 76 Merchants Row *TF:* 800-451-4167 ■ *Web:* rutlanddowntown.com	Rutland	VT	05701	802-773-2792		410
Freeman Manufacturing Co 900 W Chicago Rd *TF:* 800-253-2091 ■ *Web:* www.freemanmfg.com	Sturgis	MI	49091	269-651-2371	651-8248	477
Freeman Metal Products Inc 2124 US Hwy 13 S *Web:* www.freemanmetal.com	Ahoskie	NC	27910	252-332-5390		295
Freeman Mfg & Supply Co 1101 Moore Rd *TF:* 800-321-8511 ■ *Web:* www.freemansupply.com	Avon	OH	44011	440-934-1902	934-7200	567
Freeman Public Relations 16 Furler St	Totowa	NJ	07512	973-470-0400		636
FREEMAN WEBB CO 3810 Bedford Ave Ste 300 *Web:* www.freemanwebb.com	Nashville	TN	37215	615-271-2700		652
Freeman's Flowers & Event Consultants 2934 Duniven Cir *TF:* 800-846-3104 ■ *Web:* www.freemansflowers.com	Amarillo	TX	79109	806-355-4451		292
Freeman, The 30 S Broadway *TF Sales:* 800-960-4333 ■ *Web:* www.fee.org	Irvington-on-Hudson	NY	10533	914-591-7230		457-17
Freeman/Fine Arts of Philadelphia 1808 Chestnut St *TF:* 800-501-0277 ■ *Web:* www.freemansauction.com	Philadelphia	PA	19103	215-563-9275	563-8236	51
Freemason Abbey 209 W Freemason St *Web:* www.freemasonabbey.com	Norfolk	VA	23510	757-622-3966	622-3592	671
FreeMind Group LLC 423 Brookline Ave *Web:* www.freemindconsultants.com	Boston	MA	02215	617-648-0340		466
Freenters LLC 5555 S Ellis Ave **Fax Area Code:* 703 ■ *Web:* www.freenters.com	Chicago	IL	60637	773-834-1414	480-0488*	5
Freeport Area Chamber of Commerce 27 W Stephenson St *TF:* 800-942-2555 ■ *Web:* www.freeportilchamber.com	Freeport	IL	61032	815-233-1350	235-4038	139
Freeport Ctr Assoc PO Box 160466 *Web:* www.freeportcenter.com	Clearfield	UT	84016	801-825-9741	825-3587	655
Freeport Press Inc 121 Main St *Web:* www.freeportpress.com	Freeport	OH	43973	740-658-4000		627
Freeport Public Library 100 E Douglas St *Web:* www.freeportpubliclibrary.org	Freeport	IL	61032	815-233-3000	297-8236	434-3
Freer Gallery of Art / Arthur M. Sackler Gallery 1050 Independence Ave SW PO Box 37012 MRC 707 *Web:* www.asia.si.edu	Washington	DC	20013	202-633-1000	357-4911	520
Freer Gallery of Art (Smithsonian Institution) 1050 Independence Ave SW PO Box 37012 *Web:* www.asia.si.edu	Washington	DC	20013-7012	202-633-1000	357-4911	520
FreeRealTime com LLC 22365 El Toro Rd Ste 224 *Web:* www2.freerealtime.com	Lake Forest	CA	92630	949-458-6935		226
Freese & Nichols Inc 4055 International Plaza Ste 200 *Web:* www.freese.com	Fort Worth	TX	76109	817-735-7300	735-7491	261
Freeservers.com 1253 N Research Way Ste Q-2500 *TF:* 800-396-1999 ■ *Web:* www.freeservers.com	Orem	UT	04097	000-396-1999		808
Freestone County 103 E Main PO Box 1010 *Web:* www.co.freestone.tx.us	Fairfield	TX	75840	903-389-2635		338
Freestone Inn at Wilson Ranch 31 Early Winters Dr *TF:* 800-639-3809 ■ *Web:* www.freestoneinn.com	Mazama	WA	98833	509-996-3906		669
Freestone Resources Inc 101 W Ave D Ste 1350 *Web:* www.freestoneresources.com	Ennis	TX	75119	214-880-4870		539
Freestyle Photo Biz 5124 Sunset Blvd *TF:* 800-292-6137 ■ *Web:* www.freestylephoto.biz	Hollywood	CA	90027	800-292-6137		590
Freetech Plastics Inc 2211 Warm Springs Ct *Web:* freetechplastics.com	Fremont	CA	94539	510-651-9996		608
Freetown Village Living History Museum PO Box 1041 *TF:* 800-283-8904 ■ *Web:* www.freetown.org	Indianapolis	IN	46206	317-631-1870	631-0224	520
Freetown-Fall River State Forest 110 Slab Bridge Rd *Web:* www.mass.gov	Assonet	MA	02702	508-644-5522		565
FreeWave Technologies Inc 5395 Pearl Pkwy *TF Cust Svc:* 866-923-6168 ■ *Web:* www.freewave.com	Boulder	CO	80301	303-381-9200	786-9948	173-3
Freeway Corp 9301 Allen Dr **Fax:* Sales ■ *Web:* www.freewaycorp.com	Cleveland	OH	44125	216-524-9700	524-7396*	75
Freeze Frame LLC 4205 Vineland Rd *Web:* www.freezeframe.com	Orlando	FL	32811	407-648-2111		590

Name / Address	City	State	Zip	Phone	Fax	Class
Freezetone Products Inc 7986 NW 14th St TF: 800-356-7223 ■ Web: www.freezetone-usa.com	Doral	FL	33126	305-640-0414		145
Freight Handlers Inc 310 N Judd Pkwy NE Web: fhiworks.com	Fuquay Varina	NC	27526	919-552-3157		314
Freight Logistics Inc PO Box 1712 TF: 800-866-7882 ■ Web: www.shipfli.com	Medford	OR	97501	541-734-5617		311
FreightCar America Inc 17 Johns St NASDAQ: RAIL ■ *Fax Area Code: 814 ■ TF: 800-458-2235 ■ Web: www.freightcaramerica.com	Johnstown	PA	15901	800-458-2235	533-5010*	650
Freightliner Custom Chassis Corp 552 Hyatt St Web: www.freightlinerchassis.com	Gaffney	SC	29341	864-487-1700		247
Freightliner Northwest 277 Stewart Rd SW *Fax Area Code: 253 ■ TF: 800-523-8014 ■ Web: www.valleyfreightliner.com	Pacific	WA	98047	800-523-8014	863-6473*	57
Freightliner of Hartford Inc 222 Roberts St TF: 800-453-6967 ■ Web: freightlinerofhartford.com	East Hartford	CT	06108	860-289-0201	610-6242	57
Freightliner Specialty Vehicles Inc 2300 S 13th St TF: 800-358-7624 ■ Web: www.sportchassis.com	Clinton	OK	73601	580-323-4100	323-4111	59
FreightPros 3307 Northland Dr Ste 360 TF: 888-297-6968 ■ Web: www.freightpros.com	Austin	TX	78731	888-297-6968		478
Freightquote.com Inc 16025 W 113th St TF: 800-323-5441 ■ Web: www.freightquote.com	Lenexa	KS	66219	800-323-5441		312
Freitag Weinhardt Inc 5900 N 13th St Web: www.freitaginc.com	Terre Haute	IN	47805	812-466-9861		610
Freixenet USA 967 Broadway Web: www.freixenetusa.com	Sonoma	CA	95476	707-996-4981		80-3
Frelinghuysen Rodney (Rep R - NJ) 2306 Rayburn HOB Web: frelinghuysen.house.gov	Washington	DC	20515	202-225-5034		342-2
Fremada Gold Inc 2 W 45th St Ste 1605 Web: www.fremadaspecials.com	New York	NY	10036	212-921-8829		411
Fremont Area Community Foundation 4424 W 48th St Web: facommunityfoundation.org	Fremont	MI	49412	231-924-5350		305
Fremont Bank PO Box 5101 TF: 800-359-2265 ■ Web: www.fremontbank.com	Fremont	CA	94538	510-792-2300		70
Fremont Beef Co 960 S Schneider St Web: www.fremontbeef.com	Fremont	NE	68025	402-727-7200		296-26
Fremont Chamber of Commerce 39488 Stevenson Pl Ste 100 Web: www.fremontbusiness.com	Fremont	CA	94539	510-795-2244	795-2240	139
Fremont City Hall PO Box 5006 TF: 800-462-3271 ■ Web: www.fremont.gov	Fremont	CA	94537	510-284-4000	284-4001	337
Fremont Company, The 802 N Front St	Fremont	OH	43420	419-334-8995	334-8120	296-20
Fremont Contract Carriers Inc (FCC) 865 S Bud Blvd TF: 800-228-9842 ■ Web: www.fcc-inc.com	Fremont	NE	68025	800-228-9842		449
Fremont Correctional Facility (FCF) E US Hwy 50 Evans Blvd PO Box 999 TF: 800-886-7683 ■ Web: www.colorado.gov	Canon City	CO	81215	719-269-5002	269-5020	213
Fremont County 615 Macon Ave Rm 102 Web: www.fremontco.com	Canon City	CO	81212	719-276-7330	276-7338	338
Fremont County 450 N Second St TF: 800-967-2297 ■ Web: fremontcountywy.org	Lander	WY	82520	307-332-2405	857-3682	338
Fremont County 151 W First N St Web: www.co.fremont.id.us	Saint Anthony	ID	83445	208-624-7332	624-7335	338
Fremont County 506 Filmore St PO Box 299 Web: www.co.fremont.ia.us	Sidney	IA	51652	712-374-2122	374-6202	338
Fremont County Library System 451 N Second St Web: fclsonline.org	Lander	WY	82520	307-332-5194	332-3909	434-3
Fremont Group Inc 199 Fremont St Web: www.fremontgroup.com	San Francisco	CA	94105	415-284-8500		405
Fremont Health 450 E 23rd St Web: www.famc.org	Fremont	NE	68025	402-721-1610	727-3656	374-3
Fremont Hotel & Casino 200 Fremont St TF: 800-634-6460 ■ Web: www.fremontcasino.com	Las Vegas	NV	89101	702-385-3232		133
Fremont Indian State Park & Museum 3820 W Clear Creek Canyon Rd Web: www.stateparks.utah.gov	Sevier	UT	84766	435-527-4631		565
Fremont Industries Inc 4400 Vly Industrial Blvd N PO Box 67 TF: 800-436-1238 ■ Web: www.fremontind.com	Shakopee	MN	55379	952-445-4121	496-3027	145
Fremont Lakes State Recreation Area 9677 County Rd 3 Web: www.visitfremontne.org	Nickerson	NE	68025	402-478-4296		565
Fremont Main Library 2400 Stevenson Blvd TF: 800-434-0222 ■ Web: www.aclibrary.org	Fremont	CA	94538	510-745-1400	797-6557	434-3
Fremont Market Broiler 43406 Christy St Web: www.marketbroiler.com	Fremont	CA	94538	510-791-8675		671
Fremont Medical Ctr 970 Plumas St Web: www.frhg.org	Yuba City	CA	95991	530-751-4000		374-3
Fremont Public Schools 220 W Pine St TF: 800-822-9433 ■ Web: www.fremont.net	Fremont	MI	49412	231-924-2350	924-5264	685
Fremont Realty Capital 199 Fremont St Ste 2200 Web: www.fremontgroup.com/fremont-realty-capital	San Francisco	CA	94105	415-284-8665		690
Fremont Unified School District 4210 Technology Dr TF: 800-544-5248 ■ Web: www.fremont.k12.ca.us	Fremont	CA	94538	510-657-2350	770-9851	685
Fremont/Sandusky County Convention & Visitors Bureau 712 N St Ste 102 TF: 800-255-8070 ■ Web: www.sanduskycounty.org	Fremont	OH	43420	419-332-4470	332-4359	206
French Broad Electric Membership Corp 3043 Nc 213 Hwy TF: 800-222-6190 ■ Web: www.frenchbroademc.com	Marshall	NC	28753	828-649-2051	649-2989	245
French Country Waterways Ltd 24 Bay Rd TF: 800-222-1236 ■ Web: www.fcwl.com	Duxbury	MA	02332	781-934-2454		221
French Creek Outfitters Inc 270 Schuylkill Rd Web: www.frenchcreekoutfitters.com	Phoenixville	PA	19460	610-933-7200		711
French Creek State Park 843 Pk Rd Web: www.dcnr.state.pa.us	Elverson	PA	19520	610-582-9680		565
French Culinary Institute 462 Broadway TF: 888-324-2433 ■ Web: www.internationalculinarycenter.com	New York	NY	10013	888-324-2433		163
French Government Tourist Office 9454 Wilshire Blvd Ste 210 Web: us.france.fr	Beverly Hills	CA	90212	310-271-6665		775
French Hen 7143 S Yale Ave Web: frenchhentulsa.net	Tulsa	OK	74136	918-492-2596		671
French Institute Alliance Francaise (FIAF) 22 E 60th St Web: www.fiaf.org	New York	NY	10022	212-355-6100	935-4119	48-14
French Legation Museum 802 San Marcos St Web: www.frenchlegationmuseum.org	Austin	TX	78702	512-472-8180		520
French Lick Resort 8670 W State Rd 56 TF: 888-936-9360 ■ Web: www.frenchlick.com	French Lick	IN	47432	812-936-9300	936-2100	669
French Market Grille 15717 Bernardo Heights Pkwy Web: frenchmarketgrille.com	San Diego	CA	92128	858-485-8055		671
French Market Grille 425 Highland Ave TF: 800-638-3101 ■ Web: www.thefrenchmarketgrille.com	Augusta	GA	30909	706-737-4865		671
French Oil Mill Machinery Co 1035 W Greene St Web: www.frenchoil.com	Piqua	OH	45356	937-773-3420	773-3424	386
French Paper Co 100 French St Web: www.frenchpaper.com	Niles	MI	49120	269-683-1100		552-1
French Park Care Ctr 600 E Washington Ave Web: frenchparkcarecenter.com	Santa Ana	CA	92701	714-973-1656	836-4349	450
French Quarter Suites Hotel 1119 N Rampart St TF: 800-457-2253 ■ Web: www.frenchquartersuites.com	New Orleans	LA	70116	504-524-7725	522-9716	379
French Room 1321 Commerce St Web: www.adolphus.com	Dallas	TX	75202	214-742-8200	651-3588	671
French West Vaughan 112 E Hargett St Web: fwv-us.com	Raleigh	NC	27601	919-832-6300		636
French-American Chamber of Commerce in New York 1350 Broadway Ste 2101 TF: 800-821-2241 ■ Web: www.faccnyc.org	New York	NY	10018	212-867-0123	867-9050	138
French-American Chamber of Commerce of Atlanta 3399 Peachtree Rd NE Ste 500 Web: www.facc-atlanta.com	Atlanta	GA	30326	404-997-6800	997-6810	138
French-American Chamber of Commerce of Chicago (FACC) 35 E Wacker Dr Ste 670 Web: www.facc-chicago.com	Chicago	IL	60601	312-578-0444	578-0445	138
French-American Chamber of Commerce of Florida 100 N Biscayne Blvd Ste 1105 Web: www.faccmiami.com	Miami	FL	33131	305-374-5000	358-8203	138
French-American Chamber of Commerce of Houston 777 Post Oak Blvd Ste 600	Houston	TX	77056	713-985-3280		138
French-American Chamber of Commerce of Philadelphia (FACC) 1617 John F Kennedy Blvd Ste 555 Web: www.faccphila.org	Philadelphia	PA	19103	215-716-1996		138
French-American Chamber of Commerce of San Francisco 26 O'Farrell St Ste 500 Web: www.faccsf.com	San Francisco	CA	94108	415-442-4717	442-4621	138
French-American Chamber of Commerce of the Pacific Northwest (FACCPNW) 2200 Alaskan Way Ste 490 Web: www.faccpnw.org	Seattle	WA	98121	206-443-4703	448-4218	138
Frenchie's 1041 NASA Pkwy Web: frenchiesvillacapri.com	Houston	TX	77058	281-486-7144	486-3952	671
Frenchman Valley Farmers Co-op Exchange 202 Broadway TF: 800-538-2667 ■ Web: www.fvcoop.com	Imperial	NE	69033	308-882-3200	882-3242	276
French-Reneker Assoc Inc 1501 S Main St PO Box 135	Fairfield	IA	52556	641-472-5145		261
Frenchtown Pond State Park 3201 Spurgin Rd FWP Reg 2 Ofc Web: stateparks.mt.gov	Missoula	MT	59804	406-542-5500		565
Frequency Electronics Inc 55 Charles Lindbergh Blvd NASDAQ: FEIM ■ Web: www.freqelec.com	Uniondale	NY	11553	516-794-4500	794-4340	248
Freres Lumber Company Inc PO Box 276 Web: www.frereslumber.com	Lyons	OR	97358	503-859-2121		613
Fresca Mexican Foods Inc 11193 W Emerald St Web: www.frescamex.com	Boise	ID	83713	208-376-6922		123
Fresco Italian Cafe 1513 S 1500 E	Salt Lake City	UT	84105	801-486-1300		671
Fresco Ristorante 514 S Brand Blvd TF: 800-442-1162 ■ Web: www.frescoristorante.com	Glendale	CA	91204	818-247-5541	247-1964	671
Fresenius Medical Care 2637 Shadeland Dr TF: 800-227-2572 ■ Web: www.freseniusmedicalcare.us	Walnut Creek	CA	94598	800-227-2572		475
Fresenius Medical Care North America 920 Winter St TF: 800-662-1237 ■ Web: fmcna.com	Waltham	MA	02451	781-699-9000		352
Fresh Air Educators Inc 203-1568 Carling Ave TF: 866-495-4868 ■ Web: www.freshaireducators.com	Ottawa	ON	K1Z7M4	866-495-4868		244
Fresh Air Fund 633 Third Ave 14th Fl TF: 800-367-0003 ■ Web: www.freshair.org	New York	NY	10017	800-367-0003		239
Fresh Air Media PO Box 6078 Web: freshairmedia.com	Auburn	CA	95604	530-888-7676		514
Fresh Ale Pubs LLC 1317 W Northern Lights Blvd	Anchorage	AK	99503	907-222-1560		102
Fresh Consulting LLC 14725 SE 36th St Ste 300 Web: www.freshconsulting.com	Bellevue	WA	98006	425-516-7597		195
Fresh Encounter Inc 317 W Main Cross St Web: www.freshencounter.com	Findlay	OH	45840	419-422-8090		345

				Phone	Fax	Class
Fresh Express Inc 4757 The Grove Rd Ste 1212 *TF Cust Svc:* 800-242-5472 ■ *Web:* www.freshexpress.com	Windermere	NC	34786	800-242-5472		11-1
Fresh Foods Corp of America 1528 S Hayford Rd *Web:* www.cyruspies.com	Airway Heights	WA	99001	509-624-5000		297-8
Fresh Grocer at Chester Avenue, The 5406 Chester Ave *Web:* thefreshgrocer.com	Philadelphia	PA	19143	215-730-0881		297-8
Fresh Ideas Group 3350 Brighton Blvd Ste 201 *Web:* www.freshideasgroup.com	Denver	CO	80216	303-449-2108		636
Fresh Mark Inc 1888 Southway St SE *TF:* 800-860-6777 ■ *Web:* www.freshmark.com	Massillon	OH	44646	330-832-7491	830-3174	473
Fresh Meadow Mechanical Corp 65-01 Fresh Meadow Ln. *Web:* www.fmmcorp.com	Fresh Meadows	NY	11365	718-961-6634		610
Fresh Start Bakeries 145 S State College Blvd Ste 200 *Web:* www.freshstartbakeries.com	Brea	CA	92821	714-256-8900		296-1
Fresh Start Janitorial & Property Services Inc 806 E Ninth St *Web:* www.freshstartjanitorial.com	South Sioux City	NE	68776	402-494-9980		104
FreshAddress Inc 36 Crafts St *TF:* 800-321-3009 ■ *Web:* www.freshaddress.com	Newton	MA	02458	617-965-4500		196
FreshDirect Inc 23-30 Borden Ave *TF:* 866-511-1240 ■ *Web:* www.freshdirect.com	Long Island	NY	11101	718-928-1000		345
Freshens Quality Brands 1750 The Exchange *TF:* 800-633-4519 ■ *Web:* www.freshens.com	Atlanta	GA	30339	678-627-5400	627-5454	381
FreshGrade Inc 301-1447 Ellis St. *TF:* 877-957-7757 ■ *Web:* www.freshgrade.com	Kelowna	BC	V1Y2A3	877-957-7757		224
FreshPoint Inc 1390 Enclave Pkwy *Web:* www.freshpoint.com	Houston	TX	77077	281-899-4242		297-7
Freshwater Farm Products LLC 4554 State Hwy 12 E PO Box 850	Bolzoni	MS	30038	662-247-4205	247-4442	296-14
Freshwater Fish Mktg Corp 1199 Plessis Rd *Web:* www.freshwaterfish.com	Winnipeg	MB	R2C3L4	204-983-6601		297-9
Freshwater Society 2500 Shadywood Rd. *TF:* 888-471-9773 ■ *Web:* www.freshwater.org	Excelsior	MN	55331	952-471-9773	471-7685	48-13
Freshway Foods 601 Stolle Ave *Web:* www.freshwayfoods.com	Sidney	OH	45365	937-498-4664	498-4124	297-7
Freskeeto Frozen Foods Inc 8019 Rt 209 *TF:* 800-356-3663 ■ *Web:* www.freskeeto.com	Ellenville	NY	12428	845-647-5111		296-18
Fresno & Clovis Convention & Visitors Bureau 1550 E Shaw Ave Ste 101 *TF:* 800-788-0836 ■ *Web:* www.playfresno.org	Fresno	CA	93710	559-981-5500	445-0122	206
Fresno Area Express 2223 G St *Web:* www.fresno.gov	Fresno	CA	93706	559-621-7433	488-1065	468
Fresno Art Museum (FAM) 2233 N First St *Web:* www.fresnoartmuseum.org	Fresno	CA	93703	559-441-4221	441-4227	520
Fresno Bee 1626 E St. *TF:* 800-877-3400 ■ *Web:* www.fresnobee.com	Fresno	CA	93786	559-441-6111	441-6436	532-2
Fresno Chaffee Zoo 894 W Belmont Ave *Web:* www.fresnochaffeezoo.org	Fresno	CA	93728	559-498-5910		823
Fresno Chamber of Commerce 2331 Fresno St *Web:* www.fresnochamber.com	Fresno	CA	93721	559-495-4000	495-4011	139
Fresno City College 1101 E University Ave. *TF:* 866-245-3276 ■ *Web:* www.fresnocitycollege.edu	Fresno	CA	93741	559-442-4600		162
Fresno City Hall 2600 Fresno St. *Web:* www.fresno.gov	Fresno	CA	93721	559-621-7770	621-7776	337
Fresno Convention Ctr 848 M St. *TF:* 800-745-3000 ■ *Web:* www.fresnoconventioncenter.com	Fresno	CA	93721	559-445-8100	445-8110	205
Fresno County 1100 Van Ness Ave *Web:* www.co.fresno.ca.us	Fresno	CA	93721	559-488-1710	488-1830	338
Fresno County Public Library 2420 Mariposa St. *TF:* 800-798-4809 ■ *Web:* www.fresnolibrary.org	Fresno	CA	93721	559-600-7323		434-3
Fresno Distributing Company Inc 2055 E McKinley Ave *TF:* 800-655-2542 ■ *Web:* www.fresnod.com	Fresno	CA	93703	559-442-8800	264-3809	612
Fresno District Fair 1121 S Chance Ave *TF:* 866-275-3772 ■ *Web:* www.fresnofair.com	Fresno	CA	93702	559-650-3247	650-3226	642
Fresno Grand Opera 2405 Capitol St Ste 103 *Web:* www.fresnograndopera.org	Fresno	CA	93721	559-442-5699		573-2
Fresno Philharmonic 7170 N Financial Dr Ste 135. *Web:* www.fresnophil.org	Fresno	CA	93720	559-261-0600	261-0700	573-3
Fresno Unified School District 2309 Tulare St. *Web:* www.fresno.k12.ca.us	Fresno	CA	93721	559-457-3000		685
Fresno Valves & Castings Inc 7736 E Springfield Ave PO Box 40 *TF:* 800-333-1658 ■ *Web:* www.fresnovalves.com	Selma	CA	93662	559-834-2511	834-2017	790
Fresno Yosemite International Airport 5175 E Clinton Way *TF:* 866-275-7772 ■ *Web:* www.fresno.gov	Fresno	CA	93727	559-621-4500	251-4825	27
FRETTE Inc 850 Third Ave 10th Fl **Fax Area Code:* 347 ■ *Web:* www.frette.com	New York	NY	10022	212-299-0400	862-9309*	442
Freud America Inc 218 Feld Ave *TF:* 800-334-4107 ■ *Web:* www.freudtools.com	High Point	NC	27263	336-434-3171		350
Freudenberg-NOK General Partnership 47690 E Anchor Ct *Web:* www.fst.com	Plymouth	MI	48170	734-451-0020	451-0043	326
Freund, Freeze & Arnold, A Legal Professional Assn 1 S Main St Fifth Third Ctr Ste 1800. *TF:* 800-455-5600 ■ *Web:* ffalaw.com	Dayton	OH	45402	937-222-2424		428
Freundlich Supply Co Inc 2200 Arthur Kill Rd. *TF:* 800-221-0260 ■ *Web:* www.fresupco.com	Staten Island	NY	10309	718-356-1500	356-3661	770
Frey Vineyards Winery 14000 Tomki Rd *Web:* freywine.com	Redwood Valley	CA	95470	707-485-5177		443
Freyberg Hinkle Ashland Powers & Stowell Sc CPA 15420 W Capitol Dr *TF:* 000-413-0799 ■ *Web:* www.freyberg hinkle.com	Brookfield	WI	53005	262-784-6210		2
Freyer & Laureta Inc 144 N San Mateo Dr. *Web:* www.freyerlaureta.com	San Mateo	CA	94401	650-344-9901	344-9920	261
Freyssinet Inc 44880 Falcon Pl Ste 100 *TF:* 800-423-6587 ■ *Web:* www.freyssinetusa.com	Sterling	VA	20166	703-378-2500		261
FRH (Feather River Hospital) 5974 Pentz Rd *Web:* www.adventisthealth.org	Paradise	CA	95969	530-877-9361		374-3
FRHS (Fayette Regional Health System) 1941 Virginia Ave. *Web:* www.fayetteregional.org	Connersville	IN	47331	765-825-5131		374-3
Friars Club 57 E 55th St. *Web:* www.friarsclub.com	New York	NY	10022	212-751-7272		48-15
Friary of Lakeview Ctr, The 4400 Hickory Shores Blvd *TF:* 800-332-2271 ■ *Web:* www.thefriary.org	Gulf Breeze	FL	32563	850-932-9375	934-1281	726
Frick Art & Historical Ctr 7227 Reynolds St *Web:* thefrickpittsburgh.org	Pittsburgh	PA	15208	412-371-0600		520
Frick Collection 1 E 70th St. *Web:* www.frick.org	New York	NY	10021	212-288-0700	628-4417	520
Frick Hospital 508 S Church St. *TF:* 877-771-1234 ■ *Web:* www.excelahealth.org	Mount Pleasant	PA	15666	724-547-1500		374-3
Frick Services Inc 570 E Boundary Rd. *Web:* www.frickservices.com	Portage	IN	46368	219-787-8548	787-8101	275
Fricke-Parks Press Inc 33250 Transit Ave. *Web:* www.fricke-parks.com	Union City	CA	94587	510-489-6543		627
Friction Zone Magazine 60166 Hop Patch Spring Rd *Web:* www.friction-zone.com	Mountain Center	CA	92561	951-659-9500		457-3
Friday, Eldredge & Clark LLP 400 W Capitol Ave Ste 2000. *TF:* 800-655-1336 ■ *Web:* www.fridayfirm.com	Little Rock	AR	72201	501-376-2011		428
Fridgedoor.com 65 School St. *TF:* 800-955-3741 ■ *Web:* www.fridgedoor.com	Quincy	MA	02169	617-770-7913	801-8026	328
Fried Frank Harris Shriver & Jacobson LLP (FFHSJ) 1 New York Plaza *Web:* www.friedfrank.com	New York	NY	10004	212-859-8000	859-4000	428
Frieda's Inc 4465 Corporate Ctr Dr **Fax:* Sales ■ *Web:* www.friedas.com	Los Alamitos	CA	90720	714-826-6100	816-0273*	297-7
Friedemann Goldberg LLP 420 Aviation Blvd Ste 201 *Web:* www.frigolaw.com	Santa Rosa	CA	95403	707-543-4900		428
Friedman & Feiger LLP 5301 Spring Valley Rd Ste 200. *Web:* www.fflawoffice.com	Dallas	TX	75254	972-788-1400		428
Friedman & Huey Assoc LLP 1313 W 175th St. *Web:* www.fhassoc.com	Homewood	IL	60430	708-799-6800		2
Friedman Bros Decorative Arts 9015 NW 105th Way. *TF:* 800-327-1065 ■ *Web:* www.friedmanmirrors.com	Medley	FL	33178	305-887-3170	885-5331	334
Friedman Deborah s Dvm 1612 Washington Blvd *Web:* www.animaleyecare.com	Fremont	CA	94539	510-623-0444		794
Friedman Electric 1321 Wyoming Ave. *TF:* 800-545-5517 ■ *Web:* www.friedmanelectric.com	Exeter	PA	18643	570-654-3371	655-6194	246
Friedman Group, The 5759 Uplander Way *Web:* www.thefriedmangroup.com	Culver City	CA	90230	310-590-1248		190
Friedman LLP 1700 Broadway *TF:* 800-372-1033 ■ *Web:* www.friedmanllp.com	New York	NY	10019	212-842-7000	842-7001	2
Friedman Michael G. Atty. 77 N Bridge St *Web:* www.maurosavolaw.com	Somerville	NJ	08876	908-526-0707		428
Friedman Recycling Co 3640 W Lincoln St *Web:* www.friedmanrecycling.com	Phoenix	AZ	85009	602-269-9324		660
Friedrich 10001 Reunion Pl Ste 500 *TF:* 800-541-6645 ■ *Web:* www.friedrich.com	San Antonio	TX	78216	210-546-0500	357-4480	14
Friend Tire Co 11 Industrial Dr **Fax Area Code:* 417 ■ *TF:* 800-950-8473 ■ *Web:* www.friendtire.com	Monett	MO	65708	800-950-8473	235-3062*	755
Friend's of Pruyn House 207 Old Niskayuna Rd PO Box 1254 *Web:* www.pruynhouse.org	Latham	NY	12110	518-783-1435		50-3
Friend's Professional Stationery Inc 1535 Lewis Ave. *TF:* 800-323-4394 ■ *Web:* www.friendsstationery.com	Zion	IL	60099	800-323-4394	323-1535	535
Friendemic Inc 375 200 S Ste 5200 *Web:* friendemic.com	Salt Lake City	UT	84101	801-415-9314		5
Friendfinder Network Inc 6800 Broken Sound Pkwy Ste 200 *TSE:* FFN ■ *TF:* 888-575-8383 ■ *Web:* ffn.com	Boca Raton	FL	33487	561-912-7000		226
Friendly Cruises 3081 S Sycamore Village Dr. *TF:* 800-842-1786 ■ *Web:* www.friendlycruises.com	Superstition Mountain	AZ	85118	480-358-1496		771
Friendly Excursions Inc PO Box 69. *TF:* 800-775-5018 ■ *Web:* www.friendlyexcursions.net	Sunland	CA	91041	818-353-7726	353-3903	760
Friendly Express # 14 507 City Blvd *Web:* friendlyexpress.com	Waycross	GA	31503	912-285-7703		345
Friendly Gift Shop Inc 1812 Marsh Rd. *TF:* 800-442-1162 ■ *Web:* facebook.com	Wilmington	DE	19810	302-475-6560		327
Friendly Ice Cream Corp 1855 Boston Rd *TF:* 800-966-9970 ■ *Web:* www.friendlys.com	Wilbraham	MA	01095	413-543-1624		670
Friendly Solutions Corp 3837 N Panama Ave. *Web:* friendlysol.com	Chicago	IL	60634	773-957-7800		180
Friends Committee on National Legislation (FCNL) 245 Second St NE. *TF:* 800-630-1330 ■ *Web:* www.fcnl.org	Washington	DC	20002	202-547-6000	547-6019	615

Phone | Fax | Class

Friends General Conference
1216 Arch St Ste 2B Philadelphia PA 19107 215-561-1700 48-20
TF: 800-966-4556 ■ *Web:* www.fgcquaker.org
Friends Hospital
4641 Roosevelt Blvd Philadelphia PA 19124 215-831-4600 374-5
TF: 800-889-0548 ■ *Web:* www.friendshospital.com
Friends of Animals Inc (FOA)
777 Post Rd Ste 205 Darien CT 06820 203-656-1522 656-0267 48-3
TF: 800-321-7387 ■ *Web:* www.friendsofanimals.org
Friends of the Earth
1717 Massachusetts Ave NW Ste 600 Washington DC 20036 202-783-7400 783-0444 48-13
TF: 877-843-8687 ■ *Web:* www.foe.org
Friends of the Earth Magazine
1100 15th St NW Washington DC 20005 202-783-7400 783-0444 457-19
TF: 877-843-8687 ■ *Web:* www.foe.org
Friends of the Everglades
11767 S Dixie Hwy Ste 232 Miami FL 33156 305-669-0858 48-13
Web: www.everglades.org
Friends of the River
1418 20th St Ste 100 Sacramento CA 95811 916-442-3155 442-3396 48-13
TF: 888-464-2477 ■ *Web:* www.friendsoftheriver.org
Friends of the Topiary Park
480 E Town St Columbus OH 43215 614-645-0197 97
Web: www.topiarygarden.org
Friends Research Institute Inc
1040 Pk Ave Ste 103 Baltimore MD 21201 410-823-5116 823-5131 668
TF: 800-822-3677 ■ *Web:* www.friendsresearch.org
Social Research Ctr
1040 Pk Ave Ste 103 Baltimore MD 21201 410-837-3977 752-4218 668
TF: 800-705-7757 ■ *Web:* www.friendsresearch.org
Friends School of Wilmington Inc
350 Peiffer Ave Wilmington NC 28409 910-792-1811 685
Web: www.fsow.org
Friends University 2100 University St Wichita KS 67213 316-295-5000 166
TF: 800-794-6945 ■ *Web:* www.friends.edu
Friendship Automotive Inc
1855 Volunteer Pkwy Bristol TN 37620 423-652-6200 57
Web: friendshipford.com
Friendship Hill National Historic Site
223 New Geneva Rd Point Marion PA 15474 724-725-9190 725-1999 564
Web: www.nps.gov/frhi
Friendship Hospital for Animals
4105 Brandywine St NW Washington DC 20016 202-363-7300 794
TF: 800-548-2423 ■ *Web:* www.friendshiphospital.com
Friendship House PO Box 3778 Scranton PA 18505 570-342-8305 685
Web: www.friendshiphousepa.org
Friendship Manor 1209 21st Ave Rock Island IL 61201 309-786-9667 794-9141 672
Web: www.friendshipmanor.org
Friendship Village 600 Pk Ln Waterloo IA 50702 319-291-8100 672
TF: 800-248-4504 ■ *Web:* www.friendshipvillageiowa.com
Friendship Village
8100 Highwood Dr Bloomington MN 55438 952-831-7500 672
Web: lifespacecommunities.com
Friendship Village Kalamazoo
1400 N Drake Rd Kalamazoo MI 49006 269-381-0560 672
TF: 800-613-3984 ■ *Web:* www.friendshipvillagemi.com
Friendship Village of columbus
5800 Forest Hills Blvd Columbus OH 43231 614-890-8282 672
Web: www.fvcolumbus.org
Friendship Village of South County
12503 Village Cir Dr Saint Louis MO 63127 314-842-6840 672
Web: www.friendshipvillagestl.com
Friendship Village of South Hills
1290 Boyce Rd Upper Saint Clair PA 15241 724-941-3100 672
Web: lifespacecommunities.com/senior-living-pittsburgh
Friendship Village of Tempe
2645 E Southern Ave Tempe AZ 85282 480-831-5000 672
Web: www.friendshipvillageaz.com
Friendsview Retirement Community
1301 E Fulton St Newberg OR 97132 503-538-3144 672
TF: 866-307-4371 ■ *Web:* friendsview.org
Friendswood Chamber of Commerce
1100 S Friendswood Dr Friendswood TX 77546 281-482-3329 139
Web: www.friendswood-chamber.com
Friendswood Development Co
11506 Island Manor St Pearland TX 77584 713-436-6951 653
Friendswood Public Library
416 S Friendswood Dr Friendswood TX 77546 281-482-7135 434-3
Web: www.friendswood.lib.tx.us
Friesens Corp 1 Printers Way Altona MB R0G0B0 204-324-6401 324-1333 626
Web: www.friesens.com
Frigel North America Inc
150 Prairie Lake Rd East Dundee IL 60118 847-540-0160 610
Web: www.frigel.com
Fringale 570 Fourth St San Francisco CA 94107 415-543-0573 671
Web: www.fringalesf.com
Fringe Benefits Management Co
3101 Sessions Rd Tallahassee FL 32303 850-425-6200 425-6220 390
TF: 800-872-0345 ■ *Web:* www.fbmc.com
Fringe Theatre Adventures Society
10330 84 Ave NW Edmonton AB T6E2G9 780-448-9000 749
Web: www.fringetheatre.ca
Frio County
500 E San Antonio St PO Box 8 Pearsall TX 78061 830-334-8073 334-0047 338
Web: www.co.frio.tx.us
Friona Feedyard 2370 FM 3140 Friona TX 79035 806-265-3574 10-1
Web: www.frionaindustries.com
Friona Industries
500 S Taylor St Ste 601 Ste 601 Amarillo TX 79101 806-374-1811 374-3003 10-1
TF: 800-658-6014 ■ *Web:* www.frionaindustries.com
Frisbie Memorial Hospital
11 Whitehall Rd Rochester NH 03867 603-332-5211 374-3
Web: www.frisbiehospital.com
Frisch's Restaurants Inc
2800 Gilbert Ave Cincinnati OH 45206 513-961-2660 559-5160 670
NYSE: FRS ■ *TF:* 800-873-3633 ■ *Web:* www.frischs.com
Fristam Pumps USA LP
2410 Parview Rd Middleton WI 53562 608-831-5001 641
TF: 800-841-5001 ■ *Web:* www.fristam.com

Frit Car Inc 1965 South Blvd Brewton AL 36426 251-867-7752 650
Web: www.fritcar.com
Frit Industries Inc
1792 Jodie Parker Rd Ozark AL 36360 334-774-2515 774-9306 280
TF: 800-633-7685 ■ *Web:* www.fritind.com
Frite Alors! 1562 Laurier St E Montreal QC H2J1H9 514-524-6336 671
Web: www.fritealors.com
Frito-Lay North America 7701 Legacy Dr Plano TX 75024 800-352-4477 296-35
TF: 800-352-4477 ■ *Web:* www.fritolay.com
Fritti 309 N Highland Ave Atlanta GA 30307 404-880-9559 671
Web: www.frittirestaurant.com
Fritz & Alfredo's 1007 S McCord Rd Toledo OH 43611 419-729-9775 671
Web: toledostripletreat.com
Fritz Enterprises Inc
1650 W Jefferson Ave Trenton MI 48183 734-362-3200 660
Web: www.fritzinc.com
Fritz Industries Inc
180 Gordon Dr Ste 113 Exton PA 19341 800-345-6202 363-0735* 183
**Fax Area Code:* 610 ■ *TF:* 800-345-6202 ■ *Web:* www.fritztile.com
Fritz's Wagon Wheel Restaurant
2709 S MacArthur Blvd Springfield IL 62704 217-546-9888 671
Frize Corp 16605 Gale Ave City Of Industry CA 91745 626-369-6088 186
TF: 800-834-2127 ■ *Web:* www.frizecorp.com
Frizzelle & Parsons Die Sinking Co
6602 John Deere Rd Moline IL 61265 309-796-1030 757
Web: www.frizzelle-parsons.com
FRL Furniture 460 Grand Blvd Westbury NY 11590 516-333-4400 333-4759 664
TF: 800-529-4375 ■ *Web:* www.frlalternatives.com
FRM (Flat Rock Metal Inc)
26601 W Huron River Dr PO Box 1090 Flat Rock MI 48134 734-782-4454 782-5640 485
Web: www.frm.com
FRM Weekly 54 Adams St Garden City NY 11530 516-746-6700 531-6
FRMC (Frye Regional Medical Ctr)
420 N Ctr St Hickory NC 28601 828-315-5000 374-3
Web: www.fryemedctr.com
Froedtert Hospital
9200 W Wisconsin Ave Milwaukee WI 53226 414-805-4311 805-7790 374-3
Web: www.froedtert.com
Froedtert Hospital Bone Marrow Transplant Program
9200 W Wisconsin Ave Milwaukee WI 53226 414-805-3666 769
TF: 800-272-3666 ■ *Web:* www.froedtert.com
Froehling & Robertson Inc
3015 Dumbarton Rd Richmond VA 23228 804-264-2701 264-1202 743
Web: www.fandr.com
Frog Street Press Inc
800 Industrial Blvd Ste 100 Grapevine TX 76051 800-884-3764 759-3828 243
TF: 800-884-3764 ■ *Web:* www.frogstreet.com
Frog Switch & Mfg Co 600 E High St Carlisle PA 17013 717-243-2454 307
TF: 800-233-7194 ■ *Web:* www.frogswitch.com
Frogco Amphibious Equipment Inc
2280 Coteau Rd Houma LA 70364 985-853-2200 567
Web: www.frogco-amphibious.com
Frogdesign Inc
660 Third St 4th Fl San Francisco CA 94107 415-442-4804 442-4803 4
Web: www.frogdesign.com
FROGGY 107.7 1560 Fairfield Rd Gettysburg PA 17325 717-334-3101 334-5822 645
TF: 800-366-9489 ■ *Web:* www.foreveryork.com
Frohm Kelley Butler & Ryan PC
333 Ft St Port Huron MI 48060 810-987-2727 2
Fromm Electric Supply
2101 Centre Ave PO Box 15147 Reading PA 19605 610-374-4441 374-8756 246
TF: 800-360-4441 ■ *Web:* www.frommelectric.com
Fronk Oil Co Inc PO Box F Booker TX 79005 806-658-4565 579
Web: www.fronkoil.com
Front End Audio
130 Hunter Village Dr Ste D Irmo SC 29063 803-748-0914 526
TF: 888-228-4530 ■ *Web:* www.frontendaudio.com
Front Porch Barbecue & Seafood
205 Thornhill Dr Hattiesburg MS 39401 601-264-3536 671
Front Porch Communities & Services
303 N Glenoaks Blvd Burbank CA 91502 800-233-3709 450
TF: 800-233-3709 ■ *Web:* www.frontporch.net
Front Range Community College (FRCC)
Boulder County 2190 Miller Dr Longmont CO 80501 303-678-3722 678-3699* 162
**Fax:* Admissions ■ *TF:* 888-800-9198 ■ *Web:* www.frontrange.edu
Larimer 4616 S Shields St Fort Collins CO 80526 970-226-2500 204-8484 162
TF: 888-800-9198 ■ *Web:* www.frontrange.edu
Westminster 3645 W 112th Ave Westminster CO 80031 303-404-5000 466-1623* 162
**Fax:* Admissions ■ *Web:* www.frontrange.edu
Front Range Energy LLC
31375 Great Western Dr Windsor CO 80550 970-674-2910 143
Web: www.frontrangeenergy.com
Front Row Motorsports
2670 Peachtree Rd Statesville NC 28625 704-873-6445 717
Web: teamfrm.com
Front Row USA Entertainment
900 N Federal Hwy Ste 200 Hallandale FL 33009 305-940-8499 750
TF: 800-277-8499 ■ *Web:* www.frontrowusa.com
Front Royal-Warren County Chamber of Commerce
106 Chester St Front Royal VA 22630 540-635-3185 635-9758 139
Web: www.frontroyalchamber.com
Front Runner Consulting LLC
6850 O'Bannon Bluff Loveland OH 45140 513-697-6850 194
TF: 877-328-3360 ■ *Web:* www.frontrunnerconsulting.com
Front Street 230 Commercial St Provincetown MA 02657 508-487-9715 671
Web: www.frontstreetrestaurant.com
Front Street Capital
33 Yonge St Ste 600 Toronto ON M5E1G4 416-364-1990 401
TF: 800-513-2832 ■ *Web:* www.frontstreetcapital.com
Frontage Laboratories LLC
700 Pennsylvania Dr Exton PA 19341 610-232-0100 743
Web: www.frontagelab.com
Frontenac Bank 8021 Olive Blvd Saint Louis MO 63130 314-212-1500 70
Web: www.frontenacbank.com
Frontenac Co 1 S Wacker Ste 2980 Chicago IL 60606 312-368-0044 368-9520 792
Web: www.frontenac.com
Frontenac State Park
29223 County 28 Blvd Frontenac MN 55026 651-345-3401 345-3694 565
TF: 888-646-6367 ■ *Web:* www.dnr.state.mn.us

Company	City	State	Zip	Phone	Fax	Class
Frontend Graphics Inc 1951 Old Cuthbert Rd Ste 404 *Web:* www.frontendgraphics.com	Cherry Hill	NJ	08034	856-547-1600		627
Frontera Foods Inc 449 N Clark St Ste 205 *TF:* 800-509-4441 ■ *Web:* www.fronterafiesta.com	Chicago	IL	60654	312-595-1624		345
Frontera Grill 445 N Clark St *TF:* 800-321-1499 ■ *Web:* www.rickbayless.com	Chicago	IL	60654	312-661-1434	661-1830	671
Frontier Adjusters of America Inc 4745 N Seventh St Ste 320 *TF:* 800-426-7228 ■ *Web:* www.frontieradjusters.com	Phoenix	AZ	85014	800-426-7228	553-4799	390
Frontier Airlines Ctr 400 W Wisconsin Ave *TF:* 800-745-3000 ■ *Web:* wisconsincenter.org	Milwaukee	WI	53203	414-908-6000	908-6010	205
Frontier Airlines Inc 7001 Tower Rd *TF:* 800-265-5505 ■ *Web:* www.flyfrontier.com	Denver	CO	80249	720-374-4200		360-1
Frontier Aluminum Corp 2480 Railroad St *Web:* www.frontier-aluminum.com	Corona	CA	92880	951-735-1770		492
Frontier Asset Management LLC 201 N Connor St Ste 250 *Web:* www.frontierasset.com	Sheridan	WY	82801	307-673-5675		401
Frontier Central School District 5120 Orchard Ave *Web:* www.frontier.wnyric.org	Hamburg	NY	14075	716-926-1711		685
Frontier City Theme Park 11501 NE Expy *TF:* 800-364-7111 ■ *Web:* www.frontiercity.com	Oklahoma City	OK	73131	405-478-2140	478-2118	32
Frontier Communications Corp 3 High Ridge Pk *NASDAQ: FTR* ■ *TF:* 800-877-4390 ■ *Web:* www.frontier.com	Stamford	CT	06905	203-614-5600	614-4602	736
Frontier Computer Corp 1275 Business Pk Dr *TF:* 866-226-6344 ■ *Web:* www.frontiercomputercorp.com	Traverse City	MI	49686	231-929-1386		180
Frontier Consulting Inc 10101 SW Fwy Ste 202 *TF:* 877-324-8729 ■ *Web:* www.frontier-consulting.com	Houston	TX	77074	713-778-0799		180
Frontier Co-op 211 S Lincoln PO Box 37 *TF:* 800-869-0379 ■ *Web:* www.frontiercooperative.com	Brainard	NE	68626	402-545-2811	545-2821	275
Frontier Cooperative Herbs 3021 78th St *TF:* 800-669-3275 ■ *Web:* www.frontiercooperative.com	Norway	IA	52318	800-669-3275		805
Frontier County PO Box 40 *Web:* www.co.frontier.ne.us	Stockville	NE	69042	308-367-8641	367-8730	338
Frontier Electronic Systems Corp 4500 W Sixth Ave *TF:* 800-677-1769 ■ *Web:* www.fescorp.com	Stillwater	OK	74074	405-624-1769		529
Frontier Ford 3701 Stevens Creek Blvd *TF:* 844-501-7699 ■ *Web:* frontierford.com	Santa Clara	CA	95051	844-501-7699		57
Frontier Health 1167 Spratlin Pk Dr PO Box 9054 *Web:* www.frontierhealth.org	Gray	TN	37615	423-467-3600		462
Frontier Homes Inc 1225 Willow Creek Rd *Web:* www.frontierhomes.com	Corvallis	MT	59828	406-961-3115		106
Frontier Industries Inc 1911 Commercial Ave *Web:* www.fbs.us	Anacortes	WA	98221	300-293-4500		603
Frontier Investment Management Co 8401 N Central Expy Ste 300 *TF:* 800-553-8034 ■ *Web:* www.frontierinvest.com	Dallas	TX	75225	972-934-2590		401
Frontier Logistic Services 1700 N Alameda St *Web:* www.frontier-logistics.com	Compton	CA	90222	310-604-8208		449
Frontier Logistics LP 1806 S 16th St **Fax Area Code:* 281 ■ *TF:* 800-610-6808 ■ *Web:* www.frontierlogistics.com	La Porte	TX	77571	800-610-6808	307-2399*	311
Frontier Mechanical Inc 2771 W Mansfield Ave *Web:* www.frontiermech.net	Englewood	CO	80110	303-806-5400		610
Frontier Metal Stamping Inc 3764 Puritan Way *TF:* 888-316-1266 ■ *Web:* www.frontiermetal.com	Erie	CO	80516	303-458-5129		483
Frontier Natural Products Co-op 3021 78th St PO Box 299 *TF:* 800-669-3275 ■ *Web:* www.frontiercoop.com	Norway	IA	52318	319-227-7996		296-37
Frontier Networks Inc 530 Kipling Ave *TF:* 866-833-2323 ■ *Web:* frontiernetworks.ca	Toronto	ON	M8Z5E3	416-847-5240		387
Frontier Power Co 770 S Second St PO Box 280 *TF:* 800-624-8050 ■ *Web:* www.frontier-power.com	Coshocton	OH	43812	740-622-6755	622-0711	245
Frontier Steel Company Inc 4990 Grand Ave *Web:* www.frontiersteel.com	Pittsburgh	PA	15225	412-865-4444	865-0030	492
Frontier Supply Inc 981 Van Horn Rd *Web:* www.frontierplumbing.com	Fairbanks	AK	99701	907-374-3500	374-3570	612
Frontier-Kemper Constructors Inc 1695 Allen Rd *TF:* 877-554-8600 ■ *Web:* www.frontierkemper.com	Evansville	IN	47710	812-426-2741	428-0337	188-10
Frontiers International Travel PO Box 959 *TF:* 800-245-1950 ■ *Web:* www.frontierstravel.com	Wexford	PA	15090	724-935-1577	935-5388	760
Frontiers of Flight Museum 6911 Lemon Ave *TF:* 800-568-8924 ■ *Web:* www.flightmuseum.com	Dallas	TX	75209	214-350-1651		520
Frontline Communications PO Box 98 **Fax Area Code:* 845 ■ **Fax:* Sales ■ *TF:* 888-376-6854 ■ *Web:* www.frontline.net	Orangeburg	NY	10962	888-376-6854	680-6541*	398
Frontline Group of Texas LLC 15021 Katy Fwy Ste 575 *TF:* 800-285-5512 ■ *Web:* www.frontline-group.com	Houston	TX	77094	281-453-6000		765
Frontline Logistics Inc 10315 Grand River Ste 300 *TF:* 800-245-6632 ■ *Web:* www.frontlinelogistics.com	Brighton	MI	48116	734-449-9474		314
Frontline Systems Inc PO Box 4288 *TF:* 888-831-0333 ■ *Web:* www.solver.com	Incline Village	NV	89450	775-831-0300	831-0314	809
FrontPage Local 1660 Hotel Cir N Ste 600 *TF:* 800-219-1755 ■ *Web:* www.frontpagelocal.com	San Diego	CA	92108	800-219-1755		631
Frontpoint 1310 W 233 N Ste 101 *Web:* www.frontpoint-it.com	Centerville	UT	84014	801-312-9400		393
Frosch International Travel Inc 1 Greenway Plaza Ste 800 *TF:* 800-866-1623 ■ *Web:* www.froschtravel.com	Houston	TX	77046	800-866-1623		772
Frost & Sullivan 7550 IH 10 W Ste 400 **Fax Area Code:* 888 ■ *TF:* 877-463-7678 ■ *Web:* www.frost.com	San Antonio	TX	78229	210-348-1000	690-3329*	531-12
Frost Art Museum at Florida International University 10975 SW 17th St *Web:* frost.fiu.edu	Miami	FL	33199	305-348-2890	348-2762	520
Frost Brown Todd 2200 PNC Ctr 201 E Fifth St *Web:* www.frostbrowntodd.com	Cincinnati	OH	45202	513-651-6800	651-6981	428
Frost Cutlery Company LLC 6861 Mtn View Rd *Web:* www.frostcutlery.com	Ooltewah	TN	37363	423-894-6079		351
Frost PLLC 425 W Capitol Ave Ste 3300 *Web:* www.frostpllc.com	Little Rock	AR	72201	501-376-9241		2
Frost Roofing Inc 2 Broadway St *Web:* www.frost-roofing.com	Wapakoneta	OH	45895	419-739-2701		697
Frost Ruttenberg & Rothblatt PC 111 S Pfingsten Rd Ste 300 *Web:* www.marcumllp.com	Deerfield	IL	60015	847-282-6300		2
Frost Securities Inc 2727 N Harwood St Ste 1000 *Web:* www.frostbank.com	Dallas	TX	75201	214-515-4435		690
Frost Valley Ymca 2000 Frost Valley Rd *Web:* www.frostvalley.org	Claryville	NY	12725	845-985-2291		379
Frostburg State University 101 Braddock Rd **Fax:* Admissions ■ *Web:* www.frostburg.edu	Frostburg	MD	21532	301-687-4000	687-7074*	166
Frozen Fire Films Inc 325 N St Paul St *Web:* frozenfire.com	Dallas	TX	75201	214-745-3456		5
Frozen Head State Natural Area 964 Flat Fork Rd *TF:* 800-250-8615 ■ *Web:* www.state.tn.us	Wartburg	TN	37887	423-346-3318		565
Frozen Specialties Inc 8600 S Wilkinson Wy Ste G *TF:* 800-510-3811 ■ *Web:* www.frozenspecialties.com	Perrysburg	OH	43551	419-867-2005		296-36
Fruit & Spice Park 24801 SW 187th Ave *Web:* www.floridaplants.com/fruit&spice	Homestead	FL	33031	305-247-5727	245-3369	97
Fruit Basket Flowerland 765 28th St SW *Web:* www.myflowerland.com	Wyoming	MI	49509	616-532-7404	531-7858	323
Fruit Co, The 2900 Van Horn Dr *TF:* 800-387-3100 ■ *Web:* www.thefruitcompany.com	Hood River	OR	97031	541-387-3100		292
Fruit Growers Laboratory Inc 853 Corporation St *TF:* 800-440-7821 ■ *Web:* www.fglinc.com	Santa Paula	CA	93060	805-392-2000		743
Fruit Growers Supply Company Inc 27770 N Entertainment Dr *Web:* www.fruitgrowers.com	Valencia	CA	91355	818-986-6480	783-1941	274
Fruit of The Earth Inc 3101 High Rver Rd Ste 175 *Web:* www.fote.com	Fort Worth	TX	76155	972-790-0808	790-1322	214
Fruit of the Loom Inc 1 Fruit of the Loom Dr PO Box 90015 *TF:* 888-378-4029 ■ *Web:* www.fruitactivewear.com	Bowling Green	KY	42102	270-781-6400	781-1754	155-3
Fruit Yard, The 7948 Yosemite Blvd *TF:* 800-561-3357 ■ *Web:* www.thefruityard.com	Modesto	CA	95357	209-577-3093	577-0600	671
Fruitful Yield Inc 229 W Roosevelt Rd *Web:* www.fruitfulyield.com	Lombard	IL	60148	630-545-9098		799
Fruitridge Printing & Lithograph Inc 3258 Stockton Blvd *TF:* 800-835-4846 ■ *Web:* www.fruitridgeprinting.com	Sacramento	CA	95820	916-452-9213		627
Frullati Cafe & Bakery 9311 E Via de Ventura *TF:* 866-452-4252 ■ *Web:* www.frullati.com	Scottsdale	AZ	85258	480-362-4800	362-4812	670
Frutarom Corp 9500 Railroad Ave **Fax:* Cust Svc ■ *TF:* 866-229-7198 ■ *Web:* www.frutarom.com	North Bergen	NJ	07047	201-861-9500	861-9267*	296-15
Fruth Pharmacy Inc 4016 Ohio River Rd *TF:* 800-438-5390 ■ *Web:* www.fruthpharmacy.com	Point Pleasant	WV	25550	304-675-1612		237
FRWD 120 First Ave N Ste 300 *Web:* frwdco.com	Minneapolis	MN	55401	612-235-5030		5
FRX Polymers Inc 200 Turnpike Rd *TF:* 800-865-2478 ■ *Web:* www.frxpolymers.com	Chelmsford	MA	01824	978-244-9500		601
Fry Communications Inc 800 W Church Rd *TF:* 800-334-1429 ■ *Web:* www.frycomm.com	Mechanicsburg	PA	17055	800-334-1429		627
Fry Fastening Systems 2150 Waycross Rd *Web:* www.frysys.com	Cincinnati	OH	45240	513-851-2233		351
Fry Steel Company Inc 13325 Molette St *Web:* www.frysteel.com	Santa Fe Springs	CA	90670	562-802-2721		492
Fry's Electronics 600 E Brokaw Rd **Fax:* PR ■ *Web:* www.frys.com	San Jose	CA	95112	408-350-1484	487-4700*	35
Fry's Food Stores of Arizona Inc 500 S 99th Ave *TF:* 866-221-4141 ■ *Web:* www.frysfood.com	Tolleson	AZ	85353	866-221-4141		345
Frye Art Museum 704 Terry Ave *Web:* smoking.vapingguide.org	Seattle	WA	98104	206-622-9250		520
Frye Properties 300 W Freemason St *Web:* www.fryeproperties.com	Norfolk	VA	23510	757-627-1980		652
Frye Regional Medical Ctr (FRMC) 420 N Ctr St *Web:* www.fryemedctr.com	Hickory	NC	28601	828-315-5000		374-3
Fryeburg Academy 745 Main St *Web:* www.fryeburgacademy.org	Fryeburg	ME	04037	207-935-2013	935-5013	622
Fryer-Knowles Inc 205 S Dawson St *TF:* 800-544-6052 ■ *Web:* www.fryerk.com	Seattle	WA	98108	206-767-7710		291

Company	Phone	Fax	Class
Frymaster LLC 8700 Line Ave .... Shreveport LA 71106 *TF Cust Svc:* 800-221-4583 ■ *Web:* www.frymaster.com	318-865-1711		298
Frymire Engineering Company Inc 2818 Satsuma Dr .... Dallas TX 75229 *TF:* 877-379-6473 ■ *Web:* www.frymire.com	877-379-6473		261
Fry-Wagner Moving & Storage Co 3700 Rider Trl S .... Earth City MO 63045 *TF:* 800-899-4035 ■ *Web:* www.fry-wagner.com	314-291-4100		780
FS Precision Tech Co LLC 3025 E Victoria St.................. Rancho Dominguez CA 90221 *Web:* www.fs-precision.com	310-638-0595		306
FS Tool Corp 71 Hobbs Gate .... Markham ON L3R9T9 *TF:* 800-387-9723 ■ *Web:* www.fstoolcorp.com	905-475-1999		697
FSB (Fortune Small Business Magazine) 1271 Ave of the Americas.................... New York NY 10020 *Web:* www.money.cnn.com/magazines/fsb	212-522-1212		457-5
FSB Warner Financial 1001 Peoples Sq .... Waterloo IA 50702 *TF:* 800-747-9999 ■ *Web:* fsbfs.com	319-235-6561		690
FSEEE (Forest Service Employees for Environmental Ethics) PO Box 11615 .... Eugene OR 97440 *Web:* www.fseee.org	541-484-2692	484-3004	49-7
FS-Elliott Company LLC 5710 Mellon Rd .... Export PA 15632 *Web:* www.fs-elliott.com	724-387-3200		172
FSG (Facility Solutions Group) 4401 Westgate Blvd Ste 310.................. Austin TX 78745 *TF:* 800-854-6465 ■ *Web:* www1.fsgi.com	512-440-7985	440-0399	246
FSG Lighting 4401 Westgate Blvd Ste 310.......... Austin TX 78745 *TF:* 800-854-6465 ■ *Web:* www.fsgi.com	512-440-7985		246
FSI International Inc 3455 Lyman Blvd........... Chaska MN 55318 *NASDAQ: FSII* ■ *Web:* www.tel.com	952-448-5440	448-2825	695
FSI Technologies Inc 668 E Western Ave .... Lombard IL 60148 *TF:* 800-468-6009 ■ *Web:* www.fsinet.com	630-932-9380	932-0016	203
FSMB (Federation of State Medical Boards of the US Inc) 400 Fuller Wiser Rd Ste 300.................... Euless TX 76039 *TF:* 800-793-7939 ■ *Web:* www.fsmb.org	817-868-4000	868-4098	49-8
FSNA 1052 St Laurent Blvd .... Ottawa ON K1K3B4 *TF:* 855-304-4700 ■ *Web:* www.fsna.com	613-745-2559		138
FSO Knowledge Xchange LLC 208 Shepard Way .... Manalapan NJ 07726 *TF:* 800-713-7278 ■ *Web:* www.fsokx.com	732-462-3763		396
FSO Onsite Outsourcing 19 W 44th St 9th Fl.......................... New York NY 10036 *Web:* fso-outsourcing.com	212-204-1193		260
Fsr Inc 244 Bergen Blvd .... Woodland Park NJ 07424 *Web:* www.fsrinc.com	973-998-2300		127
FST Logistics Inc 2040 Atlas St .... Columbus OH 43228 *Web:* www.fstlogistics.com	614-529-7900		194
FSTV (Free Speech TV) PO Box 44099 .... Denver CO 80201 *Web:* www.freespeech.org	303-542-4813		740
FTA (Federation of Tax Administrators) 444 N Capitol St NW Ste 348................. Washington DC 20001 *TF:* 800-829-9188 ■ *Web:* www.taxadmin.org	202-624-5890	624-7888	49-7
FTA (Flexographic Technical Assn) 3920 Veterans Memorial Hwy Ste 9............ Bohemia NY 11716 *TF:* 800-242-5216 ■ *Web:* www.flexography.org	631-737-6020	737-6813	49-16
FTC (Federal Trade Commission) 600 Pennsylvania Ave NW .... Washington DC 20580 *TF:* 877-382-4357 ■ *Web:* www.ftc.gov	202-326-2222		340-20
FTC (Farmers Telecommunications Co-op) 144 McCurdy Ave N PO Box 217 .... Rainsville AL 35986 *TF:* 866-638-2144 ■ *Web:* www.farmerstel.com	256-638-2144	638-4830	736
FTC (Feed the Children) PO Box 36 .... Oklahoma City OK 73101 *TF:* 800-627-4556 ■ *Web:* www.feedthechildren.org	405-942-0228		48-5
FTD Inc 3113 Woodcreek Dr.............. Downers Grove IL 60515 *TF Cust Svc:* 800-736-3383 ■ *Web:* www.ftd.com	800-736-3383		292
FTF Engineering Inc 1916 Mcallister St .... San Francisco CA 94115 *Web:* ftfengineering.com	415-931-8460		261
FTG Inc 725 Marshall Phelps Rd................ Windsor CT 06095 *TF:* 888-610-6020	860-610-6000	610-6001	246
FTI Consulting 909 Commerce Rd Ste 1400................. Annapolis MD 21401 *NYSE: FCN* ■ *TF:* 800-334-5701 ■ *Web:* www.fticonsulting.com	410-224-8770	224-9740	445
FTI Flow Technology Inc 8930 S Beck Ave Ste 107 .... Tempe AZ 85284 *Web:* www.ftimeters.com	480-240-3400		201
FTJ FundChoice LLC 2300 Litton Ln Ste 102......................... Hebron KY 41048 *TF:* 800-379-2513 ■ *Web:* www.ftjfundchoice.com	800-379-2513		387
FTMC (Fisher-Titus Medical Ctr) 272 Benedict Ave .... Norwalk OH 44857 *TF:* 800-589-3862 ■ *Web:* www.fishertitus.org	419-668-8101		374-3
FTR Associates Inc 2881 Grandma Barnes Rd.................. Nashville IN 47448 *Web:* ftrintel.com	812-988-1699		463
FTS International Express Inc 400 Country Club Dr .... Bensenville IL 60106 *Web:* www.fts.com	630-694-0644	694-0778	311
FTZ Industries Inc 515 Palmetto Dr .... Simpsonville SC 29681 *Web:* www.ftzind.com	864-963-5000	963-5352	815
Fu Lin Chinese Restaurant 200 N Bowman Rd .... Little Rock AR 72211	501-225-8989		671
Fuchs Lubricants Canada Ltd Eastern Canada Div 405 Dobbie Dr PO Box 909 .... Cambridge ON N1R5X9 *Web:* www.fuchs.com	519-622-2040		541
Fuchs Lubricants Co 17050 Lathrop Ave.......... Harvey IL 60426 *Web:* www.fuchs.com	708-333-8900		541
Fuchs North America 9740 Reisterstown Rd.................... Owings Mills MD 21117 *TF:* 800-365-3229 ■ *Web:* www.fuchsna.com	410-363-1700	363-6619	296-37
Fudge Marcia L (Rep D - OH) 2344 Rayburn HOB.......................... Washington DC 20515 *Web:* fudge.house.gov	202-225-7032	225-1339	342-2
Fuego 330 E Palace Ave .... Santa Fe NM 87501 *Web:* www.laposadadesantafe.com	505-986-0000		671
FUEL Digital Marketing & Branding 25 E Court St Ste 100..................... Greenville SC 29601 *TF:* 800-438-7325 ■ *Web:* www.fuelingbrands.com	864-627-1676		5
Fuel Education LLC 2300 Corporate Park Dr .... Herndon VA 20171 *TF:* 866-912-8588 ■ *Web:* www.fueleducation.com	866-912-8588		178-3
Fuel Masters LLC 133 Caddo Dr................ Abilene TX 79602 *TF:* 866-455-3835 ■ *Web:* www.fuelmasters.com	325-676-3835	676-3841	579
Fuel South Inc 3020 Harris Rd .... Waycross GA 31503	912-284-0264		345
Fuel Tech Inc 27601 Bella Vista Pkwy .... Warrenville IL 60555 *NASDAQ: FTEK* ■ *TF General:* 800-666-9688 ■ *Web:* www.ftek.com	630-845-4500	845-4502	18
FuelCell Energy Inc 3 Great Pasture Rd .... Danbury CT 06810 *NASDAQ: FCEL* ■ *TF:* 800-278-7980 ■ *Web:* www.fuelcellenergy.com	203-825-6000		253
FuelFX LLC 1811 Bering Dr .... Houston TX 77057 *TF:* 855-472-7316 ■ *Web:* www.fuelfx.com	855-472-7316		195
Fuga 3853 N Southport Ave...................... Chicago IL 60613 *Web:* www.salonfuga.com	773-880-1280		77
Fugro Consultants LP 6100 Hillcroft Ave........................... Houston TX 77081 *Web:* www.fugro.com	713-369-5400		261
Fugro Pelagos Inc 3574 Ruffin Rd .... San Diego CA 92123 *TF:* 800-439-8205 ■ *Web:* www.fugro-pelagos.com	858-292-8922	292-5308	727
Fugro-Roadware Inc 2505 Meadowvale Blvd................. Mississauga ON L5N5S2 *TF:* 800-828-2726 ■ *Web:* www.roadware.com	905-567-2870		407
Fuji 8226 E 71st St .... Tulsa OK 74133 *Web:* www.fujisushibar.com	918-250-1821		671
Fuji Do Restaurant 1701 Paxton St .... Harrisburg PA 17104	717-232-1437		671
Fuji Health Science Inc 3 Terri Ln Ste 12......................... Burlington NJ 08016 *TF:* 877-385-4777 ■ *Web:* www.fujihealthscience.com	609-386-3030		297-8
Fuji Steakhouse & Sushi Bar 12817 Preston Rd............................. Dallas TX 75230 *Web:* www.fujisteakhouse-sd.com	972-661-5662		671
Fuji Vegetable Oil Inc 1 Barker Ave .... White Plains NY 10601 *Web:* www.fujioilusa.com	914-761-7900		296-30
FUJIFILM Graphic System USA Inc 45 Crosby Dr .... Bedford MA 01730 *TF:* 800-755-3854 ■ *Web:* www.fujifilmusa.com	781-271-4400		385
Fujifilm Mfg USA Inc 211 Pucketts Ferry Rd...................... Greenwood SC 29649 *Web:* fujifilmusa.com/about	864-223-2888		658
Fujii Farms Inc 2511 S Troutdale Rd PO Box 188 .... Troutdale OR 97060 *Web:* fujiifarms.com	503-665-6659	661-2799	315-1
Fujikin of America Inc 4677 Old Ironsides Dr .... Santa Clara CA 95054 *Web:* www.fujikin.com	408-980-8269	980-0572	612
Fujimi Corp 11200 SW Leveton Dr.............. Tualatin OR 97062 *Web:* www.fujimiam.com	503-682-7822		1
Fujisankei Communications International Inc 150 E 52nd St 34th Fl....................... New York NY 10022 *Web:* www.fujisankei.com	212-753-8100		514
Fujitec America Inc 7258 Innovation Way......... Mason OH 45040 *Web:* www.fujitecamerica.com	513-932-8000		256
Fujitsu America Inc 1250 E Arques Ave........................ Sunnyvale CA 94085 *TF:* 800-538-8460 ■ *Web:* www.fujitsu.com	408-746-6200	746-6260	735
Fujitsu Components America Inc 250 E Caribbean Dr .... Sunnyvale CA 94089 *Web:* www.fujitsu.com	408-745-4900	745-4970	253
Fujitsu Computer Products of America Inc 1255 E Arques Ave........................ Sunnyvale CA 94085 *TF:* 800-626-4686 ■ *Web:* www.fujitsu.com	408-746-7000	746-6910	173-8
Fujitsu Computer Systems Corp 1250 E Arques Ave........................ Sunnyvale CA 94085 *TF:* 800-538-8460 ■ *Web:* solutions.us.fujitsu.com	408-746-6000		176
Fujitsu Consulting 1250 E Arques Ave........................ Sunnyvale CA 94085 *TF:* 800-831-3183 ■ *Web:* fujitsu.com	800-831-3183		180
Fujitsu General America Inc 353 Rt 46 W .... Fairfield NJ 07004 *TF:* 888-888-3424 ■ *Web:* www.fujitsugeneral.com	973-575-0380		610
Fujitsu Ten Corp of America 19600 S Vermont Ave........................ Torrance CA 90502 *TF:* 800-233-2216 ■ *Web:* www.eclipse-web.com	310-327-2151		52
Fuji-Ya 600 West Lake St .... Minneapolis MN 55408 *Web:* www.fujiyasushi.com	612-871-4055		671
Fujiyama 283 N Milwaukee St .... Boise ID 83704 *Web:* www.fujiyamaboise.com	208-672-8227	672-8247	671
Fujiyama Japanese Steakhouse 5149 Victory Dr .... Indianapolis IN 46203 *Web:* www.fujiyama-indy.com	317-787-7900		671
Fukuvi USA Inc 7631 Progress Ct.......... Huber Heights OH 45424 *Web:* www.fukuvi-usa.com	937-236-7288		596
Fulbright & Fulbright CPA PA 5302 NC Hwy 55 Ste 104 PO Box 13156 .... Durham NC 27713 *Web:* www.moneyful.com	919-544-0398	544-8719	2
Fulbright & Jaworski LLP 1301 McKinney St Ste 5100.................. Houston TX 77010 *TF:* 866-385-2744 ■ *Web:* www.nortonrosefulbright.com	713-651-5151	651-5246	428
Fulco Fulfillment Inc 26 Richboynton Rd .... Dover NJ 07801 *Web:* www.fulcofulfillment.com	973-361-1700		317
Fulcrum Analytics Inc 70 W 40th St 10th Fl....................... New York NY 10018 *Web:* www.fulcrumanalytics.com	212-651-7000		195
Fulcrum Financial Inquiry LLP 888 S Figueroa St Ste 2000 .... Los Angeles CA 90017 *Web:* www.fulcrum.com	213-787-4100		463
Fulcrum Group Inc, The 5751 Kroger Dr Ste 279 .... Fort Worth TX 76244 *Web:* www.fulcrum.pro	817-337-0300		180
Fulcrum International Ltd 280 Railroad Ave......................... Greenwich CT 06830 *Web:* www.fulcrum-intl.com	203-869-8181		194

				Phone	Fax	Class
Fulcrum Technologies Inc 712 Aurora Ave N *Web:* www.fulcrum.net	Seattle	WA	98109	206-336-5656		177
Fuld & Company Inc 131 Oliver St 3rd Fl *Web:* www.fuld.com	Boston	MA	02110	617-492-5900		463
Fulenwider Enterprises Inc 104 Mull St. *Web:* www.fulenwider.net	Morganton	NC	28655	828-437-8000		194
Fulfillment Concepts Inc 2200 Ampere Dr *Web:* www.fulfillmentconcepts.com	Jeffersontown	KY	40299	502-266-5555		5
Fulflex Inc 32 Justin Holden Dr **Fax:* Cust Svc ■ *TF:* 800-283-2500 ■ *Web:* www.fulflex.com	Brattleboro	VT	05301	802-257-5256	257-5602*	745-5
Fulghum Industries 317 S Main St. *Web:* www.fulghum.com	Wadley	GA	30477	478-252-5223		683
Fulghum Macindoe & Associates Inc 10330 Hardin Valley Rd Ste 201 *Web:* www.fulghummacindoe.com	Knoxville	TN	37932	865-690-6419		261
Fulham & Company Inc 593 Washington St *Web:* www.fulhamco.com	Wellesley	MA	02482	781-235-2266		528
Fulkerson Services Inc 111 Parce Rd *Web:* fulkersonservices.com	Fairport	NY	14450	585-223-2541		321
Full Access Brokerage 1240 Charnelton St. *TF:* 866-890-5743 ■ *Web:* fullaccess.org	Eugene	OR	97401	541-284-5070		690
Full Cir Bookstore 1900 NW Expy *Web:* www.fullcirclebooks.com	Oklahoma City	OK	73118	405-842-2900	842-2894	95
Full E-media Marketing Inc 2122 S El Camino Real Ste F	San Clemente	CA	92672	949-940-0198		5
Full Employment Council Inc 1740 Paseo Blvd. *Web:* www.feckc.org	Kansas City	MO	64108	816-471-2330		260
Full Frame Documentary Film Festival 320 Blackwell St Ste 101 *Web:* www.fullframefest.org	Durham	NC	27701	919-687-4100		282
Full House Resorts Inc 4670 S Fort Apache Rd Ste 190 *NASDAQ: FLL* ■ *Web:* www.fullhouseresorts.com	Las Vegas	NV	89147	702-221-7800		132
Full Life Financial LLC 604 Georgetown Dr. *Web:* www.FullLifeFinancial.com	Nashville	TN	37205	615-356-4164		463
Full Sail University 3300 University Blvd Ste 160 *TF:* 800-226-7625 ■ *Web:* www.fullsail.edu	Winter Park	FL	32792	407-679-6333		800
Full Spectrum Software 225 Tpke Rd *Web:* www.fullspectrumsoftware.com	Southborough	MA	01772	508-620-6400		177
Full Swing Golf Inc 10890 Thornmint Rd. *TF:* 800-798-9094 ■ *Web:* www.fullswinggolf.com	San Diego	CA	92127	858-675-1100		253
Fullen Dock & Warehouse Inc 382 Klinke Rd *TF:* 800-467-7104 ■ *Web:* www.fullendock.com	Memphis	TN	38127	901-358-9544	357-2879	191-1
Fuller Box Co 150 Chestnut St. *TF:* 800-243-1816 ■ *Web:* www.fullerbox.com	North Attleboro	MA	02760	508-695-2525	695-2187	488
Fuller Brush Co, The PO Box 729 1 Fuller Way *TF Cust Svc:* 800-522-0499 ■ *Web:* www.fuller.com	Great Bend	KS	67530	620-792-1711		103
Fuller Craft Museum 455 Oak St *TF:* 800-639-4808 ■ *Web:* fullercraft.org	Brockton	MA	02301	508-588-6000	587-6191	520
Fuller Engineering Co 4135 W 99th St *Web:* fullerengr.com	Carmel	IN	46032	317-228-5800		186
Fuller Industrial 65 Nelson Rd *TF:* 888-524-3777 ■ *Web:* www.fullerindustrial.com	Lively	ON	P3Y1P4	705-682-2777	682-4777	595
Fuller Landau SENCRL 1010 De La Gauchetiere St W Pl du Canada Ste 200 *Web:* www.fullerlandau.com	Montreal	QC	H3B2S1	514-875-2865		2
Fuller Theological Seminary 135 N Oakland Ave *TF:* 800-235-2222 ■ *Web:* www.fuller.edu	Pasadena	CA	91182	626-584-5200	795-8767	167-3
Fullerton & Knowles PC 12644 Chapel Rd Ste 206 *Web:* www.fullertonlaw.com	Clifton	VA	20124	703-818-2600		428
Fullerton Arboretum 1900 Associated Rd *Web:* www.fullertonarboretum.org	Fullerton	CA	92831	657-278-3407	278-7066	97
Fullerton Bldg Systems Inc (FBS) 34620 250th St PO Box 308 *TF:* 800-450-9782 ■ *Web:* www.fullertonbuildingsystems.com	Worthington	MN	56187	507-376-3128	376-9530	817
Fullerton Chamber of Commerce 444 N Harbor Blvd Ste 200 *Web:* www.nocchamber.com	Fullerton	CA	92832	714-871-3100	871-2871	139
Fullerton College 321 E Chapman Ave. *Web:* www.fullcoll.edu	Fullerton	CA	92832	714-992-7000		162
Fullerton Public Library 353 W Commonwealth Ave. *Web:* www.ci.fullerton.ca.us	Fullerton	CA	92832	714-738-6333	447-3280	434-3
Fullerton Tool Company Inc 121 Perry St *TF:* 855-722-7243 ■ *Web:* www.fullertontool.com	Saginaw	MI	48602	989-799-4550	792-3335	493
Fulmer Co 122 Gayoso Ave *Web:* www.fulmerlogistics.com	Memphis	TN	38103	901-248-7189		517
Fultech Solutions Inc 7837 Bayberry Rd *TF:* 800-759-8888 ■ *Web:* www.fultechsolutions.com	Jacksonville	FL	32256	904-992-6624		180
Fulton Concrete Company Inc 11470 N Fulton Industrial	Alpharetta	GA	30009	770-475-6504		182
Fulton Corp 303 Eigth Ave **Fax Area Code:* 815 ■ *TF:* 800-252-0002 ■ *Web:* www.fultoncorp.com	Fulton	IL	61252	800-252-0002	589-4433*	350
Fulton Correctional Facility 1511 Fulton Ave	Bronx	NY	10457	718-583-8000		213
Fulton Cos 972 Centerville Rd *Web:* www.fulton.com	Pulaski	NY	13142	315-298-5121	298-6390	357
Fulton County 141 Pryor St *Web:* www.co.fulton.ga.us	Atlanta	GA	30303	404-612-4000		338
Fulton County 2216 Myron Cory Dr Ste 1 *Web:* fultoncounty.ky.gov	Hickman	KY	42050	270-236-2594	236-7904	338
Fulton County 2 N Main St *Web:* fultonmontgomeryny.org	Gloversville	NY	12078	518-725-0641	725-0643	338
Fulton County 100 N Main St *Web:* www.fultonco.org	Lewistown	IL	61542	309-547-3041	547-3326	338
Fulton County 116 W Market St Ste 203 *TF:* 800-328-0058 ■ *Web:* www.co.fulton.pa.us	McConnellsburg	PA	17233	717-485-3691	485-9411	338
Fulton County 815 Main St *TF:* 800-382-9467 ■ *Web:* www.co.fulton.in.us	Rochester	IN	46975	574-223-4824	223-8304	338
Fulton County 123 S Main St Courthouse Sq *TF:* 800-637-9314 ■ *Web:* www.argenweb.net/fulton	Salem	AR	72576	870-895-3310		338
Fulton County 152 S Fulton St Ste 270 *Web:* www.fultoncountyoh.com	Wauseon	OH	43567	419-337-9255	337-9285	338
Fulton County Rural Electric Membership Corp 1448 W State Rd 14 PO Box 230 *Web:* faqs.org	Rochester	IN	46975	574-223-3156		245
Fulton Five 5 Fulton St.	Charleston	SC	29401	843-853-5555		671
Fulton Homes Corp 9140 S Kyrene Rd Ste 202 *TF:* 800-570-2289 ■ *Web:* www.fultonhomes.com	Tempe	AZ	85284	480-753-6789	753-5554	187
Fulton Industries Inc 135 E Linfoot St PO Box 377 *TF:* 800-537-5012 ■ *Web:* www.fultonindoh.com	Wauseon	OH	43567	419-335-3015	335-3215	439
Fulton Iron & Mfg LLC 3844 Walsh St *Web:* www.fultoniron.net	Saint Louis	MO	63116	314-752-2400		298
Fulton Opera House Foundation 12 N Prince St PO Box 1865 *TF:* 888-480-1265 ■ *Web:* www.thefulton.org	Lancaster	PA	17603	717-397-7425	397-3780	572
Fulton Precision Industries 300 Success Dr *Web:* www.fultonprecision.com	McConnellsburg	PA	17233	717-485-5158		14
Fulton School District 58 2 Hornet Dr *TF:* 800-456-2634 ■ *Web:* www.fulton58.org	Fulton	MO	65251	573-590-8000		685
Fulton State Hospital 600 E Fifth St *Web:* dmh.mo.gov	Fulton	MO	65251	573-592-4100	592-3000	374-5
Fulton-Denver Co 3500 Wynkoop St. *TF:* 800-521-1414 ■ *Web:* fultonpacific.com	Denver	CO	80216	303-294-9292		67
Fulton-Montgomery Community College 2805 New York 67 *Web:* www.fmcc.edu	Johnstown	NY	12095	518-762-4651	762-4334	162
Fults Hill Prairie & Kidd Lake State Natural Areas c/o Randolph County State Recreation Area 4301 S Lk Dr	Chester	IL	62233	618-826-2706		565
Fultz Maddox Hovious & Dickens PLC 2700 National City Tower 101 S Fifth St *Web:* www.fmhd.com	Louisville	KY	40202	502-588-2000		428
Fun 101.3 FM 1996 Auction Rd *TF:* 800-655-4101 ■ *Web:* www.fun1013.com	Manheim	PA	17545	717-653-0800	653-0122	645
Fun Town Splash Town USA Inc US Rt 1 774 Portland Rd. *Web:* www.funtownsplashtownusa.com	Saco	ME	04072	207-284-5139	283-4716	32
Funagain Games of Ashland 1060 Ashland St *Web:* funagain.com	Ashland St	OR	97520	541-482-1939		761
Funai Corp 201 Rt 17 N Ste 903 *Web:* www.funai.us	Rutherford	NJ	07070	201-727-4560		52
Function Engineering Inc 163 Everett Ave *Web:* function.com	Palo Alto	CA	94301	650-326-8834		261
Function Point Productivity Software Inc 2034 11th Ave W Ste 140 *Web:* www.functionpoint.com	Vancouver	BC	V6J2C9	604-731-2522		809
Functional Genetics Inc 708 Quince Orchard Rd	Gaithersburg	MD	20878	240-631-6790		668
Fund for American Studies, The 1706 New Hampshire Ave NW *Web:* www.tfas.org	Washington	DC	20009	202-986-0384		242
Fund for Animals, The 200 W 57th St *Web:* www.fundforanimals.org	New York	NY	10019	212-757-3425		48-3
Fund for Peace, The 1101 14th St Ste 1020 *Web:* global.fundforpeace.org	Washington	DC	20005	202-223-7940		48-5
Fundcraft Publishing Inc 410 Hwy 72 W *TF:* 800-964-5715 ■ *Web:* www.fundcraft.com/fundraising-cookbooks/index.asp	Collierville	TN	38027	901-853-7070	853-6196	627
Funder America Inc 200 Funder Dr *Web:* www.funderamerica.com	Mocksville	NC	27028	336-751-3501		819
Fundquest 1 Winthrop Sq *Web:* www.fundquestadvisor.com	Boston	MA	02110	617-526-0766		401
FundThrough Inc 260 Spadina Ave Ste 400 *TF:* 800-766-0460 ■ *Web:* www.fundthrough.com	Toronto	ON	M5T2E4	800-766-0460		224
Funeral Consumers Alliance 33 Patchen Rd *TF:* 800-765-0107 ■ *Web:* www.funerals.org	South Burlington	VT	05403	802-865-8300	865-2626	48-10
Funeral Service Insider 3349 Hwy 138 Bldg D Ste D *TF:* 800-500-4585 ■ *Web:* www.kates-boylston.com	Wall	NJ	07719	800-500-4585		531-13
Fung's Kitchen 7320 SW Fwy Ste 115 *Web:* eatatfungs.com	Houston	TX	77074	713-779-2288	271-2288	671
FUNimation Entertainment Ltd 1200 Lakeside Pkwy Bldg 1 *Web:* www.funimation.com	Flower Mound	TX	75028	972-355-7300		514
Funix Inc 184 Westward Dr. *Web:* www.funix.com	Miami	FL	33166	305-884-8800		463
Funnel Science Internet Marketing LLC 1802 N Carson St *TF:* 877-301-0001 ■ *Web:* www.funnelscience.com	Carson City	NV	89701	877-301-0001		5
Fun-Tees 4735 Corporate Dr Ste 100 *Web:* www.funtees.com	Concord	NC	28027	704-788-3003		155-3
Funter Bay State Marine Park 400 Willoughby Ave PO Box 111071	Juneau	AK	99811	907-465-3400	586-2954	565

				Phone	Fax	Class
Funville Mobile Carnival 415 Plainview Heights Cir *Web:* funvilleisfun.com	Greeneville	TN	37745	423-638-9818		366
FUOSV (Farmers Union Oil Co of Southern Valley) 204 S Front St *Web:* www.fuosv.com	Fairmount	ND	58030	701-474-5440		316
Fuqua Homes Inc 7100 S Cooper St	Arlington	TX	76001	817-465-3211		505
Fuquay-Varina Area Chamber of Commerce 121 N Main St *TF:* 800-334-9880 ■ *Web:* www.fuquay-varina.com	Fuquay Varina	NC	27526	919-552-4947	552-1029	139
Furgo 6100 Hillcroft St *Web:* www.fugrochance.com	Houston	TX	77081	713-346-3700		727
Furino & Son Inc 66 Columbia Rd *Web:* www.furinoandsons.com	Branchburg	NJ	08876	908-756-7736		186
Furiwa Seafood 13826 Brookhurst St *Web:* furiwa.com	Garden Grove	CA	92843	714-534-3996		671
FURMAN 1690 Corporate Cir *TF:* 877-486-4738 ■ *Web:* www.furmansound.com	Petaluma	CA	94954	707-763-1010	763-1310	52
Furman Roth Advertising 801 Second Ave Rm 1400 *TF:* 800-908-5395 ■ *Web:* www.furmanroth.com	New York	NY	10017	212-687-2300		7
Furman University 3300 Poinsett Hwy **Fax:* Admissions ■ *Web:* www.furman.edu	Greenville	SC	29613	864-294-2000	294-2018*	166
Furmanite America 101 Old Underwood Rd *TF:* 800-444-5572 ■ *Web:* www.furmanite.com	La Porte	TX	77571	281-842-5100	842-5111	454
Furmano Foods Inc 770 Cannery Rd PO Box 500 *TF:* 877-877-6032 ■ *Web:* www.furmanos.com	Northumberland	PA	17857	570-473-3516	473-7367	296-20
Furnas County PO Box 387 *Web:* furnascounty.ne.gov	Beaver City	NE	68926	308-268-4145	268-3205	338
Furniture Buy Consignment Inc 1348 W Main St *Web:* furniturebuyconsignment.com	Lewisville	TX	75067	972-436-4389		321
Furniture by Thurston 12250 Charles Dr *TF:* 800-994-0165 ■ *Web:* thurstonmfg.net	Grass Valley	CA	95945	530-272-4331	272-4962	319-3
Furniture Consultants Inc 1 Penn Plaza 55th Fl *TF:* 800-541-5545 ■ *Web:* www.fcifurnitureconsultants.com	New York	NY	10119	212-229-4500	807-0036	320
Furniture Factory Outlet LLC 901 Industrial Park Rd	Muldrow	OK	74948	918-427-0241		321
Furniture Fair 7200 Dixie Hwy *TF:* 800-966-3040 ■ *Web:* www.furniturefair.com	Fairfield	OH	45014	513-874-5553		321
Furniture Mall of Kansas 1901 SW Wanamaker Rd *Web:* www.furnituremallofkansas.com	Topeka	KS	66604	785-271-0684		321
Furniture Medic 3839 S Forest Hill Irene Rd *TF:* 800-877-9933 ■ *Web:* www.furnituremedic.com	Memphis	TN	38125	800-877-9933		310
Furniture Outlets USA Inc 140 E Hinks Ln *TF:* 877-395-8998 ■ *Web:* www.thefurnituremart.com	Sioux Falls	SD	57104	605-336-5000	336-5010	290
Furniture Values International LLC 601 N 75th Ave *Web:* www.aspenhome.net	Phoenix	AZ	85043	602-442-5600		319-2
Furniture/Today Magazine 7025 Albert Pick Rd Ste 200 *TF:* 800-395-2329 ■ *Web:* www.furnituretoday.com	Greensboro	NC	27409	336-605-0121	605-1143	457-21
FurnitureDealer.net Inc 507 E Travelers Trail *TF:* 866-387-6357 ■ *Web:* www.furnituredealer.net	Burnsville	MN	55337	952-345-7171		530
Furnitureland South Inc 5635 Riverdale Rd *Web:* www.furniturelandsouth.com	Jamestown	NC	27282	336-822-3000		321
Furst & Jinks PA 170 Changebridge Rd *Web:* furstandjinks.com	Montville	NJ	07045	973-575-9191		2
Furst-McNess Co 120 E Clark St *TF:* 800-435-5100 ■ *Web:* www.mcness.com	Freeport	IL	61032	815-235-6151		447
Furuno USA Inc 4400 NW Pacific Rim Blvd *Web:* www.furuno.com	Camas	WA	98607	360-834-9300		770
Furusato 10012 82nd Ave *Web:* furusatojapaneserestaurant.com	Edmonton	AB	T6E1Y9	780-439-1335		671
Fusco Corp 555 Long Wharf Dr Long Wharf Maritime Ctr Ste 14 *Web:* www.fusco.com	New Haven	CT	06511	203-777-7451		186
Fuscoe Engineering Inc 16795 Von Karman Ave Ste 100 *Web:* www.fuscoe.com	Irvine	CA	92606	949-474-1960		256
Fuse Inc 802 N First St *TF:* 800-677-1997 ■ *Web:* www.fuseadvertising.com	St. Louis	MO	63102	314-421-4040		7
Fusebox Inc 36 W 20th St *Web:* www.fusebox.com	New York	NY	10011	212-929-7644		809
fuseproject LLC 1401 16th St *Web:* www.fuseproject.com	San Francisco	CA	94103	415-908-1492	908-1491	196
Fusibond Piping Systems Inc 2615 Curtiss St *Web:* www.fusibond.com	Downers Grove	IL	60515	630-969-4488	969-2355	596
Fusicology LLC 2658 Griffith Park Blvd #128 *Web:* fusicology.com	Los Angeles	CA	90039	323-988-2424		393
FUSION b2b Inc 1548 Bond St Ste 114 *Web:* www.fusionb2b.com	Naperville	IL	60563	630-579-8300		7
Fusion Design 440 N Central Ave *Web:* www.fusionnet.com	Campbell	CA	95008	408-378-9980		256
Fusion Geophysical LLC 103 W Boyd St	Norman	OK	73069	405-364-8663	321-7571	536
Fusion Grill 550 Academy Rd *Web:* fusiongrill.mb.ca	Winnipeg	MB	R3N0E3	204-489-6963		671
Fusion Hardware Group 5730 Oakbrook Pkwy Ste 105 *Web:* www.fusionhardware.com	Norcross	GA	30093	678-990-1676		361
Fusion Imaging inc 601 Boro St *Web:* www.fusionimaging.com	Kaysville	UT	84037	801-546-4567		5
Fusion Inc 4658 E 355th St *TF:* 800-626-9501 ■ *Web:* www.fusion-inc.com	Willoughby	OH	44094	440-946-3300	942-9083	386
Fusion Optix Inc 19 Wheeling Ave *Web:* www.fusionoptix.com	Woburn	MA	01801	781-995-0805		608
Fusion Packaging Solutions Inc 3333 Welborn St - Ste 400 *Web:* fusionpkg.com	Dallas	TX	75219	214-747-2004		393
Fusion Recruitment Group Ltd 900 Howa St Ste 330	Vancouver	BC	V6Z2M4	604-678-5627		260
Fusion Risk Management Inc 3601 W Algonquin Rd Ste 510 *Web:* www.fusionrm.com	Rolling Meadows	IL	60008	847-632-1002		195
Fusion Solutions Inc 16901 N Dallas Pkwy Ste 114 *TF:* 888-817-1951 ■ *Web:* www.fusionsolutionsinc.com	Dallas	TX	75001	972-764-1708		194
Fusion Tech 218 20th Ave *Web:* www.ftiinc.org	Roseville	IL	61473	309-774-4275		791
Fusion Telecommunications International Inc 420 Lexington Ave Ste 1718 *OTC: FSNN* ■ *TF:* 888-301-1721 ■ *Web:* fusionconnect.com	New York	NY	10170	212-201-2400	972-7884	736
Fusionary Media 220 Grandville SW *TF:* 800-438-7325 ■ *Web:* www.fusionary.com	Grand Rapids	MI	49503	616-454-2357		7
Fusionbox Inc 2031 Curtis St *Web:* www.fusionbox.com	Denver	CO	80205	303-952-7490		7
Fusionist LLC 438 Amapola Ave Ste 225 *Web:* www.fusionist.com	Torrance	CA	90501	310-787-7877		225
FusionOne Inc 11 N Roselle Rd *TF:* 877-387-6300	Roselle	IL	60172	877-387-6300		177
FusionStorm 2 Bryant St Ste 150 *TF:* 800-228-8324 ■ *Web:* www.fusionstorm.com	San Francisco	CA	94105	415-623-2626		177
Fusionworks Inc 120 Condado Ave Pico Ctr Ste 102 *TF:* 800-634-2718 ■ *Web:* www.fwpr.com	San Juan	PR	00907	787-721-1039		180
Fuss & O'Neill Consulting Engineers Inc 146 Hartford Rd *TF:* 800-286-2469 ■ *Web:* www.fando.com	Manchester	CT	06040	860-646-2469	533-5143	261
Fust Charles Chambers LLP 5786 Widewaters Pkwy *Web:* www.fcc-cpa.com	Syracuse	NY	13214	315-446-3600		2
Futaba Corp of America 711 E State Pkwy *Web:* www.futaba.com	Schaumburg	IL	60173	847-884-1444	884-1635	173-4
FUTEK Advanced Sensor Technology Inc 10 Thomas *TF:* 800-233-8835 ■ *Web:* www.futek.com	Irvine	CA	92618	949-465-0900		256
Futrend Technology Inc 8605 Westwood Ctr Dr Ste 502 *TF:* 866-388-7363 ■ *Web:* www.futrend.com	Vienna	VA	22182	703-556-0016	556-0199	177
Futrex Inc 130 Western Maryland Pkwy *Web:* www.futrex.com	Hagerstown	MD	21740	301-733-9368		250
Futura Industries 11 Freeport Ctr Bldg H *TF:* 800-824-2049 ■ *Web:* www.futuraind.com	Clearfield	UT	84016	800-824-2049		234
Futuramic Tool & Engineering Co 24680 Gibson Dr *Web:* www.futuramic.com	Warren	MI	48089	586-758-2200	758-0641	757
Future Acquisition Company LLC 9990 Richmond Ave Ste 202s *Web:* www.futureacq.com	Houston	TX	77042	832-831-3700	831-3719	536
Future Business Leaders of America-Phi Beta Lambda Inc (FBLA-PBL) 1912 Assn Dr **Fax Area Code:* 866 ■ *TF:* 800-325-2946 ■ *Web:* www.fbla-pbl.org	Reston	VA	20191	800-325-2946	500-5610*	48-11
Future Com Ltd 3600 William D Tate Ave Ste 300 *TF:* 888-710-5250 ■ *Web:* www.myfuturecom.com	Grapevine	TX	76051	817-510-1100	510-1159	180
Future Computing Solutions Inc 23800 Via Del Rio *Web:* www.fcsinet.com	Yorba Linda	CA	92887	714-692-9120		177
Future Electronics 237 Hymus Blvd *TF Cust Svc:* 800-675-1619 ■ *Web:* www.futureelectronics.com	Pointe-Claire	QC	H9R5C7	514-694-7710	695-3707	246
Future Financial Planners Inc 847 Broadway *TF:* 866-968-4848 ■ *Web:* ffpinc.com	Bayonne	NJ	07002	201-823-1030		463
Future Foam Inc 1610 Ave N Council Bluffs *TF:* 800-733-8061 ■ *Web:* www.futurefoam.com	Council Bluffs	IA	51501	712-323-9122		601
Future Force Inc 15800 NW 57th Ave *TF:* 800-683-0681 ■ *Web:* www.futureforcepersonnel.com	Miami Lakes	FL	33014	305-557-4900		260
Future Harvest Development Ltd 725 Evans Crt *Web:* futureharvest.com	Kelowna	BC	V1X6G4	250-491-0255		429
Future Home Technology Inc 33 Ralph St *TF:* 800-342-8650	Port Jervis	NY	12771	800-342-8650		364
Future Inns 30 Fairfax Dr *Web:* www.futureinns.co.uk	Halifax	NS	B3S1P1	902-443-4333		379
Future Media Concepts Inc 299 Broadway Ste 1510 *Web:* www.fmctraining.com	New York	NY	10007	212-233-3500		772
Future of Flight Foundation 8415 Paine Field Blvd *TF:* 888-467-4777 ■ *Web:* www.futureofflight.org	Mukilteo	WA	98275	425-438-8100		129
Future Path Medical Holding Company LLC 7757 Auburn Rd Ste 21 *Web:* www.future-path.net	Concord	OH	44077	440-354-4044		743
Future Pipe Industries Inc 11811-11812 Proctor Rd *Web:* www.futurepipe.com	Houston	TX	77038	281-847-2987		595
Future Products Tool Corp 885 Rochester Rd S *TF:* 800-237-5754 ■ *Web:* www.future-products.com	Troy	MI	48083	248-588-1060	588-7303	757
Future Research Corp 675 Discovery Dr Bldg 2 Ste 102 *Web:* www.future-research.com	Huntsville	AL	35806	256-430-4304		261
Future Tech Enterprise Inc 101-8 Colin Dr *Web:* www.ftei.com	Holbrook	NY	11741	631-472-5500	472-6599	177

Phone | Fax | Class

Future Technologies Inc
3877 Fairfax Ridge Rd .... Fairfax VA 22030 703-278-0199 385-0886 261
Web: www.ftechi.com
Future Test Inc 24430 N 20th Dr .... Phoenix AZ 85085 623-580-0162 516-4934 256
Web: www.futuretest.com
Future Visions Inc
3424 Stony Spring Cir .... Louisville KY 40220 502-499-6337 177
Web: futurevisions.com
Futurebiotics LLC 70 Commerce Dr .... Hauppauge NY 11788 631-273-6300 799
TF: 800-367-5433 ■ Web: www.futurebiotics.com
FutureCare Canton Harbor
1300 S Ellwood Ave .... Baltimore MD 21224 410-342-6644 450
TF: 800-553-8082 ■ Web: futurecare.com
Futurecom Systems Group Inc
3277 Langstaff Rd .... Concord ON L4K5P8 905-660-5548 246
TF: 800-701-9180 ■ Web: www.futurecom.com
Futuredontics Inc
6060 Center Dr 7th Fl .... Los Angeles CA 90045 310-215-6400 195
Web: www.futuredontics.com
FutureFuel Corp
8235 Forsyth Blvd 4th Fl .... Clayton MO 63105 805-565-9800 146
NYSE: FF ■ Web: www.futurefuelcorporation.com
Futureguard Building Products Inc
101 Merrow Rd .... Auburn ME 04211 207-795-6536 256
Web: www.futureguard.net
FutureMark Paper Co 13101 S Pulaski Rd .... Alsip IL 60803 708-272-8700 557
FutureNet Group Inc 12801 Auburn St .... Detroit MI 48223 313-544-7117 186
Web: www.futurenetgroup.com
Futureproof LLC
2374 St Claude Ave .... New Orleans LA 70119 504-822-8995 196
Web: www.futureproofnola.com
Futures Co, The
11 Madison Ave 12th flr .... New York NY 10010 212-896-8112 466
Web: thefuturescompany.com
Futures Industry Assn (FIA)
2001 Pennsylvania Ave NW Ste 600 .... Washington DC 20006 202-466-5460 296-3184 49-2
Web: fia.org
Futures Magazine
222 S Riverside Plaza Ste 620 .... Chicago IL 60606 312-846-4600 457-5
Web: www.futuresmag.com
FutureSoft Inc 1660 Townhurst Dr Ste E .... Houston TX 77043 281-496-9400 496-1090 178-7
TF: 800-989-8908 ■ Web: www.futuresoft.com
Futurewise 816 Second Ave Ste 200 .... Seattle WA 98104 206-343-0681 415
Web: futurewise.org
Futurex Inc 864 Old Boerne Rd .... Bulverde TX 78163 830-980-9782 438-8782 176
TF: 800-251-5112 ■ Web: www.futurex.com
Futurist Magazine
7910 Woodmont Ave Ste 450 .... Bethesda MD 20814 800-989-8274 457-11
TF: 800-989-8274 ■ Web: www.wfs.org
Fuze Fit for a Kid
15405 Los Gatos Blvd Ste 103 .... Los Gatos CA 95032 408-358-7529 810
Web: www.fuzefit.com
Fuzio Universal Pasta
1020 Tenth St Ste 100 .... Modesto CA 95354 209-557-9711 671
Web: www.fuzio.com
FVB Energy Inc 3901 Hwy 7 Ste 300 .... Vaughan ON L4L8L5 905-265-9777 256
Web: www.fvbenergy.com
FW Gartner Thermal Spraying Ltd
25 Southbelt Industrial Dr .... Houston TX 77047 713-225-0010 481
TF: 888-439-4872 ■ Web: www.fwgts.com
FW Spencer & Son Inc 99 S Hill Dr .... Brisbane CA 94005 415-468-5000 468-4579 189-10
TF: 800-897-4100 ■ Web: www.fwspencersoninc.com
FW Webb Co 160 Middlesex Tpke .... Bedford MA 01730 781-272-6600 275-3354 385
TF: 800-343-7555 ■ Web: www.fwwebb.com
FWBMC (Fort Walton Beach Medical Ctr)
1000 Mar-Walt Dr .... Fort Walton Beach FL 32547 850-862-1111 374-3
Web: www.fwbmc.com
FWCS (Fort Wayne Community Schools)
1200 S Clinton St .... Fort Wayne IN 46802 260-467-2009 685
Web: www.fwcs.k12.in.us
FWT LLC 5750 E I-20 .... Fort Worth TX 76119 817-255-3060 480
TF: 800-433-1816 ■ Web: fwtllc.com
FXC Corp 3410 S Susan St .... Santa Ana CA 92704 714-556-7400 641-5093 203
TF: 800-845-8753 ■ Web: www.pia.com
FXCM Inc 32 Old Slip .... New York NY 10005 212-897-7660 229-0004* 178-10
NYSE: FXCM ■ *Fax Area Code: 877 ■ TF: 888-503-6739 ■ Web: www.fxcm.com
FXI 1400 N Providence Rd .... Media PA 19063 610-744-2300 601
TF: 800-355-3626 ■ Web: fxi.com
FXVA (Fairfax County Convention & Visitors Bureau)
3702 Pender Dr Ste 420 .... Fairfax VA 22030 703-790-0643 206
TF: 800-732-4732 ■ Web: www.fxva.com
Fyda Freightliner Youngstown Inc
5260 76th Dr .... Youngstown OH 44515 330-797-0224 797-0230 62-5
TF: 800-837-3932 ■ Web: www.fydafreightliner.com
Fyfe Co LLC 3940 Ruffin Rd Ste C .... San Diego CA 92123 858-642-0694 444-2982 191-1
Web: www.fyfeco.com
FYI Systems Inc 35 Waterview Blvd .... Parsippany NJ 07054 973-331-9050 331-9055 180
Web: www.fyisolutions.com
Fys Group Corp 131 S Brent Cir .... Walnut CA 91789 909-468-0072 787
Web: fysonline.com

G

Phone | Fax | Class

G & a Label Inc 1601 Wyoming Ave .... El Paso TX 79902 915-544-1766 627
Web: www.ganda-printandlabel.com
G & C Equipment Corp
1875 W Redondo Beach Blvd Ste 102 .... Gardena CA 90247 310-515-6715 515-5046 264-3
TF: 800-559-5529 ■ Web: www.gandccorp.com
G & F Industries Inc
709 Main St, Rte 20 .... Sturbridge MA 01566 508-347-9132 596
Web: www.gandf.us
G & G Fitness Equipment Inc
7350 Transit Rd .... Williamsville NY 14221 716-633-2527 354
TF: 800-537-0516 ■ Web: www.livefit.com
G & G Instrument Corp
466 Saw Mill River Rd .... Ardsley NY 10502 914-693-6000 693-6738 476
Web: www.datacut.com
G & G Mfg 4432 Mckinley .... Omaha NE 68112 402-453-9595 620
Web: www.ggmfg.com
G & G Oil Company of Indiana Inc
220 E Centennial Ave .... Muncie IN 47303 765-288-7795 579
Web: www.ggoil.com
G & H Art Co 4300 Hamilton Rd .... Columbus GA 31904 706-576-5551 45
G & H Decoys Inc PO Box 1208 .... Henryetta OK 74437 918-652-3314 710
TF Orders: 800-443-3269 ■ Web: www.ghdecoys.com
G & H Towing Company Inc
200 Pennzoil Rd .... Galveston TX 77554 409-744-6311 465
Web: www.gandhtowing.com
G & H Wire Company Inc
2165 Earlywood Dr .... Franklin IN 46131 317-346-6655 228
TF: 800-526-1026 ■ Web: www.ghorthodontics.com
G & J Land & Marine Food Distributors
506 Front St .... Morgan City LA 70380 985-385-2620 345
TF: 800-256-9187 ■ Web: www.gjfood.com
G & K Services Inc
5995 Opus Pkwy Ste 500 .... Minnetonka MN 55343 952-912-5500 912-5999 442
TF: 800-452-2737 ■ Web: www.gkservices.com
G & L Manufacturing Inc
1975 Fisk Rd .... Cookeville TN 38506 931-528-1732 492
Web: www.glmanufacturing.com
G & L Motion Control Inc
672 S Military Rd .... Fond Du Lac WI 54935 920-921-7100 203
Web: kdn.kollmorgen.com
G & m Compliance Inc 154 S Cypress St .... Orange CA 92866 714-628-1020 261
Web: www.gmcompliance.com
G & M Electrical Contractors Co
1746 N Richmond St .... Chicago IL 60647 773-278-8200 278-8038 189-4
TF: 800-359-0077 ■ Web: www.gm-electric.com
G & O Thermal Supply Co
5435 N Northwest Hwy .... Chicago IL 60630 773-763-1300 111
TF: 800-621-4997 ■ Web: www.gothermal.com
G & R Foods Inc PO Box 610 .... Reedsburg WI 53959 608-524-3776 524-1752 10-3
Web: www.grfoodsinc.com
G & R Labs 2996 scott blvd .... Santa Clara CA 95054 408-986-0377 743
Web: www.grlabs.com
G & S Metal Products Company Inc
3330 E 79th St .... Cleveland OH 44127 216-441-0700 441-0736 486
Web: www.gsmetal.com
G & S Packing 16600 Florida 25 .... Weirsdale FL 32195 352-821-2251 315-2
G & T Industries Inc
1001 76th St SW .... Byron Center MI 49315 800-968-6035 583-1524* 601
*Fax Area Code: 616 ■ TF: 800-968-6035 ■ Web: www.gtindustries.com
G & W Commercial Flooring Inc
6407 S 211th St .... Kent WA 98032 253-479-1760 290
TF: 800-240-0806 ■ Web: gwcfloor.com
G & W Engineering Corp
138 Weldon Pkwy .... Maryland Heights MO 63043 314-469-3737 261
Web: gandwengineering.com
G & W Foods Inc
2041 Railroad Dr .... Willow Springs MO 65793 417-469-4000 345
Web: gwfoodsinc.com
G & W Laboratories Inc
111 Coolidge St .... South Plainfield NJ 07080 908-753-2000 582
TF: 800-922-1038 ■ Web: www.gwlabs.com
G Bar M Ranch PO Box 29 .... Clyde Park MT 59018 406-686-4423 239
TF: 800-476-6045 ■ Web: www.gbarm.com
G D C Inc 815 Logan St .... Goshen IN 46528 574-533-3128 601
Web: www.gdc-corp.com
G D G Environment Group Ltd
430, rue St-Laurent .... Trois-RiviŠres QC G8T6H3 888-567-8567 192
TF: 888-567-8567 ■ Web: www.gdg.ca
G Dc Home 695 Coleman Blvd .... Mount Pleasant SC 29464 843-849-0711 393
Web: www.gdchome.com
G E Tignall & Company Inc
14 Mccann Ave .... Cockeysville MD 21030 410-666-3000 189-10
Web: getignall.com
G f Studio Inc 540 Ravine Ct .... Wyckoff NJ 07481 201-445-1002 592
Web: www.gfstudio.net
G F Vaughan Tobacco Company Inc
1247 Versailles Rd .... Lexington KY 40508 859-254-4705 275
G G Schmitt & Sons Inc
2821 Old Tree Dr .... Lancaster PA 17603 717-394-3701 291-9739 350
TF: 866-724-6488 ■ Web: www.ggschmitt.com
G Greene Construction Company Inc
300 Longwood Ave .... Boston MA 02115 617-782-1100 186
Web: www.ggreene.com
G K Partners 401 E 74th St Apt 18h .... New York NY 10021 212-535-5617 193
Web: gk-partners.com
G L Wilson Bldg Co
190 Wilson Pk Rd .... Statesville NC 28625 704-872-2411 872-8281 186
Web: www.glwilson.com
G Michael's Bistro 595 S Third St .... Columbus OH 43215 614-464-0575 671
Web: gmichaelsbistroandbar.com
G P Aviation Services 95 Round Hill Rd .... Armonk NY 10504 914-273-0123 23
Web: gpaviation.com
G r Manufacturing Inc
4800 Commerce Dr .... Trussville AL 35173 205-655-8001 297-8
TF: 800-841-8001 ■ Web: www.grtractors.com
G Robert Cotton Correctional Facility
3500 N Elm Rd .... Jackson MI 49201 517-780-5000 780-5100 213
TF: 855-444-3911 ■ Web: www.michigan.gov/corrections
G S Design 6665 N Sidney Pl .... Milwaukee WI 53209 414-228-9666 4
Web: www.gsdesign.com
G Schirmer Inc 257 Pk Ave S 20th Fl .... New York NY 10010 212-254-2100 254-2013 637-7
Web: www.musicsalesclassical.com
G Sp Group Inc 1343 Boswall Dr .... Worthington OH 43085 614-888-7502 195
Web: gspgroup.com
G Stephens Inc 133 N Summit St .... Akron OH 44304 330-762-1386 196
Web: www.gstephensinc.com
G Systems LP
1240 Campbell Rd Ste 100 .... Richardson TX 75081 972-234-6000 261
Web: www.gsystems.com

Phone Fax Class

G Tj Consulting 20100 Cornillie Dr — Roseville MI 48066 586-293-9600 196
TF: 800-385-0563 ■ *Web:* gtjonline.com

G. & M. Die Consulting Company Inc
284 Richert Rd — Wood Dale IL 60191 630-595-2340 358
Web: www.gmdiecasting.com

G. A. Bove & Sons Inc
76 Railroad St — Mechanicville NY 12118 518-664-5111 316
Web: www.bovefuels.com

G. R. Rush & Co
5720 Skurlock Rd 6500 Bldg Osborne Office Pk
— Chattanooga TN 37411 423-899-5162 2
Web: www.rushcpa.com

G.M. Crisalli Associates Inc
843 Hiawatha Blvd W — Syracuse NY 13204 315-454-0000 186
Web: gmca.com

G.N. Plastics Company Ltd
345 Old Trunk 3 — Chester NS B0J1J0 902-275-3571 358
Web: www.gnplastics.com

G.S. Proctor & Associates Inc
14408 Old Mill Rd Ste 201 — Upper Marlboro MD 20772 301-952-8885 463
Web: www.gsproctor.com

G.V. (Sonny) Montgomery VA Medical Ctr
1500 E Woodrow Wilson Dr — Jackson MS 39216 601-362-4471 368-3811* 374-8
**Fax:* Hum Res ■ *Web:* www.jackson.va.gov

G2 Investment Group LLC
142 W 57th St 12th Fl — New York NY 10019 212-887-1150 691
Web: www.g2investmentgroup.com

G2 Secure Staff LLC
400 E Las Colians Blvd Ste 750 — Irving TX 75039 972-915-6979 393
Web: www.g2securestaff.com

G2 Software Systems Inc
4025 Hancock St Ste 105 — San Diego CA 92110 619-222-8025 177
Web: g2ss.com

G2 Solutions LLC 11410 NE 124th St — Kirkland WA 98034 425-789-0200 21
Web: g2globalsolutions.com

G2 USA 200 Fifth Ave — New York NY 10010 212-537-3700 5
Web: www.geometry.com

G2 Web Services LLC
1750 112th Ave NE Ste C101 — Bellevue WA 98004 425-749-4040 180
TF: 888-788-5353 ■ *Web:* www.g2webservices.com

G3 Communications
411 State Rt 17 S Ste 410 — Hasbrouck Heights NJ 07604 888-603-3626 195
TF: 888-603-3626 ■ *Web:* gthreecom.com

G3 Enterprises Inc 502 E Whitmore Ave — Modesto CA 95358 800-321-8747 124
TF: 800-321-8747 ■ *Web:* www.g3enterprises.com

G3 Technologies Inc
10280 Old Columbia Rd Ste 260 — Columbia MD 21046 410-290-8110 261
Web: www.g3ti.net

G3 Telecom Inc 1039 McNicoll Ave — Toronto ON M1W3W6 416-499-2121 387
Web: www.g3telecom.com

G4S PLC 1395 University Blvd — Jupiter FL 33458 561-691-6669 631
Web: www.g4s.com

G-51 Capital Management
900 S Capital of Texas Hwy Ste 151 — Austin TX 78746 512-929-5151 732-0886 792
Web: www.g51-amplify.com

G6 Hospitality LLC
Motel 6 4001 International Pkwy — Carrollton TX 75007 972-360-9000 379
TF: 800-466-8356 ■ *Web:* www.motel6.com

GA (Gamblers Anonymous) PO Box 17173 — Los Angeles CA 90017 626-960-3500 960-3501 48-21
Web: www.gamblersanonymous.org

GA Braun Inc 79 General Irwin Blvd — Syracuse NY 13212 315-475-3123 475-4130 427
TF: 800-432-7286 ■ *Web:* www.gabraun.com

GA Industries Inc
9025 Marshall Rd — Cranberry Township PA 16066 724-776-1020 776-1254 789
Web: www.gaindustries.com

GA Repple & Co 101 Normandy Rd — Casselberry FL 32707 407-339-9090 194
TF: 800-289-9999 ■ *Web:* www.garepple.com

GA Telesis LLC
1850 NW 49th St — Fort Lauderdale FL 33309 954-676-3111 676-9998 21
Web: www.gatelesis.com

GA Wintzer & Son Co
204 W Auglaize St — Wapakoneta OH 45895 419-739-4900 738-9058 296-12
TF: 800-331-1801 ■ *Web:* www.gawintzer.com

Gabbard Tulsi (Rep D - HI)
1433 Longworth HOB — Washington DC 20515 202-225-4906 225-4987 342-2
Web: gabbard.house.gov

Gabberts Inc 3501 Galleria — Minneapolis MN 55435 952-927-1500 321
Web: www.gabberts.com

Gable- Peritz- Miskin & Co
323 NORRISTOWN Rd — Spring House PA 19477 215-628-0500 2
Web: gpmllp.net

Gabler Trucking Inc
5195 Technology Ave — Chambersburg PA 17201 717-261-1492 780
Web: www.hcgabler.com

Gables Engineering Inc
247 Greco Ave — Coral Gables FL 33146 305-774-4400 774-4465 529
Web: www.gableseng.com

Gables Residential Trust
3399 Peachtree Rd NE Ste 600 — Atlanta GA 30326 561-997-9700 654
Web: www.gables.com

Gables Search Group Inc
37721 Vine St Ste 1 — Willoughby OH 44094 440-951-9990 261

GableSigns Inc 7440 Ft Smallwood Rd — Baltimore MD 21226 410-255-6400 437-5336 701
TF: 800-854-0568 ■ *Web:* www.gablesigns.com

GableStage
1200 Anastasia Ave Biltmore Hotel — Coral Gables FL 33134 305-446-1116 445-8645 573-4
Web: www.gablestage.org

Gabriel Container Co
8844 S Millergrove Dr — Santa Fe Springs CA 90670 562-699-1051 557
Web: www.gabrielcontainer.com

Gabriel deGrood Bendt
515 Washington Ave N Ste 200 — Minneapolis MN 55401 612-547-5000 7
Web: www.gdbagency.com

Gabriel E Senor PC 90 N Central Ave — Hartsdale NY 10530 914-422-0070 727

Gabriel Roeder Smith & Co
1 Towne Sq Ste 800 — Southfield MI 48076 248-799-9000 799-9020 193
TF: 800-521-0498 ■ *Web:* www.grsconsulting.com

Gabriel Venture Partners
999 Baker Way Ste 400 — San Mateo CA 94404 650-551-5000 551-5001 792
Web: www.gabrielvp.com

Gabriella 3907 Jonestown Rd — Harrisburg PA 17109 717-540-0040 671
Web: gabriellaristorante.com

Gabrielli Truck Sales Ltd
153-20 S Conduit Ave — Jamaica NY 11434 718-977-7348 57
Web: www.gabriellitruck.com

Gabriels Technology Solutions Inc
250 Hudson St Rm 1002 — New York NY 10013 212-741-0700 224
Web: www.gabriels.net

Gachina Landscape Management Inc
1130 O'Brien Dr — Menlo Park CA 94025 650-853-0400 776
TF: 800-891-7710 ■ *Web:* www.gachina.com

Gachman Metals & Recycling Company Inc
2600 Shamrock Ave — Fort Worth TX 76107 817-334-0211 877-1528 686
TF: 800-749-0423 ■ *Web:* www.gachman.com

Gaco Western Inc
200 W Mercer St Ste 202 — Seattle WA 98119 206-575-0450 575-0587 601
TF: 800-456-4226 ■ *Web:* www.gaco.com

Gadabout Inc
6393 E Grant Near Grant and Tanque Verde Near Cost
— Tucson AZ 85715 520-885-0000 77
TF: 800-600-3662 ■ *Web:* www.gadabout.com

Gadabout Vacations
1801 E Tahquitz Canyon Way Ste 100 — Palm Springs CA 92262 760-325-5556 325-5127 760
TF: 800-952-5068 ■ *Web:* www.gadaboutvacations.com

GadellNet Consulting Services LLC
1520 S Vandeventer — St. Louis MO 63110 314-431-0358 180
Web: www.gadellnet.com

Gadsby's Tavern Museum Society
134 N Royal St — Alexandria VA 22314 703-746-4242 520
Web: www.gadsbystavernmuseum.us

Gadsden & Etowah County Chamber
1 Commerce Sq — Gadsden AL 35901 256-543-3472 543-9887 139
TF: 800-659-2955 ■ *Web:* www.etowahchamber.org

Gadsden County 10 E Jefferson St — Quincy FL 32351 850-875-8601 875-8612 338
TF: 800-517-0035 ■ *Web:* www.gadsdengov.net

Gadsden County Chamber of Commerce
208 N Adams St — Quincy FL 32351 850-627-9231 875-3299 139
TF: 800-627-9231 ■ *Web:* www.gadsdencc.com

Gadsden County Public Library
732 Pat Thomas Pkwy — Quincy FL 32351 850-627-7106 434-3
Web: www.gcpls.org

Gadsden Public Library 254 College St — Gadsden AL 35901 256-549-4699 434-3
Web: www.gadsdenlibrary.org

Gadsden Regional Medical Ctr
1007 Goodyear Ave — Gadsden AL 35903 256-494-4000 494-4474 374-3
TF: 800-548-2546 ■ *Web:* www.gadsdenregional.com

Gadsden State Community College
1001 George Wallace Dr PO Box 227 — Gadsden AL 35902 256-549-8200 549-8205* 162
**Fax:* Admissions ■ *TF:* 800-226-5563 ■ *Web:* www.gadsdenstate.edu

Gadsden Times 401 Locust St — Gadsden AL 35901 256-549-2000 549-2105 532-2
Web: www.gadsdentimes.com

Gaebler Ventures
12301 Whitewater Dr — Minnetonka MN 55343 952-936-9333 936-9755 457-20
Web: www.gaebler.com

Gaetz Matt (Rep R - FL)
507 Cannon HOB — Washington DC 20515 202-225-4136 342-2
Web: gaetz.house.gov

GAF Materials Corp 1361 Alps Rd — Wayne NJ 07470 973-628-3000 46
TF: 800-365-7353 ■ *Web:* www.gaf.com

Gaffney-Kroese Supply Corp
60 Kingsbridge Rd — Piscataway NJ 08854 732-885-9000 385
Web: www.gaffney-kroese.com

Gaffoglio Family Metalcrafters Inc
11161 Slater Ave — Fountain Valley CA 92708 714-444-2000 489
Web: www.metalcrafters.com

Gage 10000 Hwy 55 — Minneapolis MN 55441 763-595-3800 737
Web: www.gage.com

Gage Brothers Concrete Products Inc
4301 W 12th St — Sioux Falls SD 57106 605-336-1180 183
Web: www.gagebrothers.com

Gage County 612 Grant St Rm 21 — Beatrice NE 68310 402-223-1344 223-1380 338
Web: www.gagecountynebraska.us

Gage E Services LLC
601 S Phillips Ave Ste 100 — Sioux Falls SD 57104 605-332-1242 225
Web: www.geshosting.com

Gage Industries Inc
6710 McEwan Rd — Lake Oswego OR 97035 503-639-2177 602

Gage Pattern & Model Inc
32070 Townley — Madison Heights MI 48071 248-585-2476 547
Web: www.gpminc.com

Gagemaker LP 712 Southmore Ave — Pasadena TX 77502 713-472-7360 639
Web: gagemaker.com

Gagen, McCoy, McMahon, Koss, Markowitz & Raines A Professional Corp
279 Front St — Danville CA 94526 925-837-0585 428
Web: www.gagenmccoy.com

Gaggle Net 1319 n veterans pkwy — Bloomington IL 61704 309-665-0572 225
Web: www.gaggle.net

Gahanna Area Chamber of Commerce
181 Granville St Ste 200 — Gahanna OH 43230 614-471-0451 471-5122 139
Web: www.gahannaareachamber.com

GAI Consultants Inc
385 E Waterfront Dr — Homestead PA 15120 412-476-2000 261
Web: www.gaiconsultants.com

Gaiam Inc 833 W S Boulder Rd Ste C — Louisville CO 80027 303-222-3600 459
NASDAQ: GAIA ■ *TF:* 877-989-6321 ■ *Web:* www.gaiam.com

Gail & Rice Productions Inc
30700 Northwestern Hwy — Farmington Hills MI 48334 248-799-5000 513
Web: www.gail-rice.com

Gail Rosen CPA PC
2032 Washington Valley Rd — Martinsville NJ 08836 732-469-4202 2
Web: gailrosencpa.com

Gaillard Municipal Auditorium
77 Calhoun St — Charleston SC 29401 843-577-7400 572

Gainans Flowers 1211 24th St W Ste 3 — Billings MT 59102 406-652-1650 292
Web: www.gainans.com

Name / Address	City	State	Zip	Phone	Fax	Class
Gaines County 101 S Main St PO Box 847 *Web:* co.gaines.tx.us	Seminole	TX	79360	432-758-5411		338
Gaines Motor Lines Inc 2349 13th Ave SW PO Box 1549 *TF:* 800-438-7311 ■ *Web:* www.gainesml.com	Hickory	NC	28603	828-322-2000		186
Gainesville Area Chamber of Commerce 300 E University Ave Ste 100 *TF:* 888-795-2707 ■ *Web:* www.gainesvillechamber.com	Gainesville	FL	32601	352-334-7100	334-7141	139
Gainesville City Schools 508 Oak St *TF:* 800-533-0682 ■ *Web:* www.gcssk12.net	Gainesville	GA	30501	770-536-5275	287-2019	685
Gainesville Correctional Institution 2845 NE 39th Ave	Gainesville	FL	32609	352-955-2001	334-1675	213
Gainesville Raceway 11211 N County Rd 225 *Web:* gainesvilleraceway.com	Gainesville	FL	32609	352-377-0046	371-4212	515
Gainesville State College University of N Georgia Gainesville Campus 3820 Mundy Mill Rd *Web:* ung.edu/visitors/campuses/gainesville	Oakwood	GA	30566	678-717-3639		162
Gainesville State School 1379 FM 678	Gainesville	TX	76240	940-665-0701	665-0469	412
Gainesville Sun Publishing Co 2700 SW 13th St *Web:* www.gvillesun.com	Gainesville	FL	32608	352-378-1411		532-3
Gainesville Times 345 Green St NW *TF:* 800-395-5005 ■ *Web:* www.gainesvilletimes.com	Gainesville	GA	30501	770-532-1234	532-0457	532-2
Gainesway Farm 3750 Paris Pk *Web:* www.gainesway.com	Lexington	KY	40511	859-293-2676	299-9371	368
Gainey Suites Hotel 7300 E Gainey *TF:* 800-970-4666 ■ *Web:* www.gaineysuiteshotel.com	Scottsdale	AZ	85258	480-922-6969		378
Gainshare Inc 3110 N Central Ave Ste 160 *TF:* 800-264-9029 ■ *Web:* www.interfacett.com	Phoenix	AZ	85012	602-266-8500		764
GainSpan Corp 3590 N First St Ste 300 *Web:* www.gainspan.com	San Jose	CA	95134	408-627-6500		201
Gaiser Tool Co 4544 McGrath St *Web:* www.gaisertool.com	Ventura	CA	93003	805-644-5583		493
Gaithersburg-Germantown Chamber of Commerce 910 Clopper Rd Ste 205N *Web:* www.ggchamber.org	Gaithersburg	MD	20878	301-840-1400	963-3918	139
GAI-Tronics Corp 400 E Wyomissing Ave *TF:* 800-492-1212 ■ *Web:* www.gai-tronics.com	Mohnton	PA	19540	610-777-1374	775-6540	735
Galanga 1129 Broadway *Web:* www.galangathai.com	Tacoma	WA	98402	253-272-3393		671
Galapagos Partners LP 55 Waugh Dr Ste 1130 *Web:* www.gplp.com	Houston	TX	77007	713-803-4326		610
Galasso's Inc 10820 San Sevaine Way *TF:* 800-339-7494 ■ *Web:* www.galassos.com	Mira Loma	CA	91752	951-360-1211		68
Galatea Associates LLC 20 Holland St Ste 405 *Web:* www.galatea-associates.com	Somerville	MA	02144	617-623-5466		225
Galatoire's 209 Bourbon St *TF:* 800 476 1651 ■ *Web:* www.galatoires.com	New Orleans	LA	70130	504 525 2021	525-5900	671
Galax (Independent City) 111 E Grayson St *Web:* www.galaxva.com	Galax	VA	24333	276-236-5773	236-2889	338
Galax-Carroll-Grayson Chamber of Commerce 405 N Main St *Web:* twincountychamber.com	Galax	VA	24333	276-236-2184	236-1338	139
Galaxie Coffee Services 110 Sea Ln *TF:* 800-564-9104 ■ *Web:* galaxiecoffee.com	Farmingdale	NY	11735	631-694-2688		113
Galaxie Defense Marketing Services 5330 Napa St *TF:* 888-711-3427 ■ *Web:* www.galaxiemgmt.com	San Diego	CA	92110	619-299-9950		186
Galaxy Aquatics Inc 1075 W Sam Houston Pkwy N Ste 210 *Web:* www.galaxy-aquatics.com	Houston	TX	77043	713-464-0303		375
Galaxy Builders Ltd 4729 College Pk *Web:* thegalaxycompanies.com	San Antonio	TX	78249	210-493-0550	493-1238	187
Galaxy Communications LP 235 Walton St *Web:* www.galaxycommunications.com	Syracuse	NY	13202	315-472-9111	472-1888	643
Galaxy Glass 208 N W Blvd	Newfield	NJ	08344	856-697-3934		292
Galaxy Hotel Systems LLC 15621 Red Hill Ave Ste 100 *TF:* 800-624-2953 ■ *Web:* www.galaxylightspeed.com/home.jsf	Tustin	CA	92780	714-258-5800	258-5880	178-11
Galaxy Integrated Technologies 100 Leo M Birmingham Pkwy *Web:* www.galaxyintegrated.com	Brighton	MA	02135	617-202-6388		693
Galaxy Nutritional Foods Inc 66 Whitecap Dr *TF:* 800-441-9419 ■ *Web:* goveggiefoods.com	North Kingstown	RI	02852	401-667-5000		296-5
Galaxy Software Solutions Inc 5820 N Lilley Rd Ste 8 *TF:* 877-269-4774 ■ *Web:* www.galaxy-soft.com	Canton	MI	48187	734-983-9030		260
Galbraith Laboratories Inc 2323 Sycamore Dr *TF:* 800-323-0749 ■ *Web:* www.galbraith.com	Knoxville	TN	37921	865-546-1335		743
Galco Industrial Electronics Inc 26010 Pinehurst Dr *TF:* 888-783-4611 ■ *Web:* www.galco.com	Madison Heights	MI	48071	248-542-9090	542-8031	246
Galderma Laboratories Inc 14501 N Fwy *TF:* 866-735-4137 ■ *Web:* www.galderma.com	Fort Worth	TX	76177	817-961-5000		582
Gale Cengage Learning 27500 Drake Rd **Fax Area Code: 877* ■ *TF Cust Svc:* 800-877-4253 ■ *Web:* www.gale.com	Farmington Hills	MI	48331	248-699-4253	363-4253*	637-2
Gale Force Petroleum Inc 100 King St W Ste 5700 *TF:* 888-440-3411	Toronto	ON	M5X1C7	888-440-3411		317
Galecki Financial Management Inc 7743 W Jefferson Blvd *TF:* 800-838-6441 ■ *Web:* www.galecki.com	Fort Wayne	IN	46804	260-436-8525		528
Galectin Therapeutics 4960 Peachtree Industrial Blvd Ste 240 *TF:* 000-206-0010 ■ *Web:* www.galectintherapeutics.com	Norcross	GA	02459	617-559-0033	928-3450	85
Galen e Wilson Petroleum Co 3057 Davenport Ave *Web:* gewilsonpetroleum.com	Saginaw	MI	48602	989-793-2181		579
Galena Gazette 716 S Bench St *TF:* 800-373-6397 ■ *Web:* www.galenagazette.com	Galena	IL	61036	815-777-0019	777-3809	532-4
Galena/Jo Daviess County Convention & Visitors Bureau (GJDCCVB) 720 Park Ave *TF General:* 800-747-9377 ■ *Web:* www.galena.org	Galena	IL	61036	815-777-3557	777-3566	206
Galera Therapeutics Inc 2 W Liberty Blvd Ste 405 *Web:* www.galeratx.com	Malvern	PA	19355	610-725-1500		231
Galerie Lelong 528 W 26th St *Web:* www.galerie-lelong.com	New York	NY	10001	212-315-0470		42
Galerie Saint Etienne 24 W 57th St *Web:* www.gseart.com	New York	NY	10019	212-245-6734	765-8493	42
Galerie Valentin 1490 Sherbrooke Quest Ste 200 *Web:* www.galerievalentin.com	Montreal	QC	H3G1L3	514-939-0500	939-0413	42
Galesburg Area Chamber of Commerce 185 S Kellogg St *Web:* www.galesburg.org	Galesburg	IL	61401	309-343-1194		139
Galesburg Area Convention & Visitors Bureau 2163 E Main St *TF:* 800-916-3330 ■ *Web:* www.visitgalesburg.com	Galesburg	IL	61401	309-343-2485		206
Galesburg Castings Inc 940 Ave C St *Web:* www.galesburgcastings.com	Galesburg	IL	61401	309-343-6178		492
Galesburg Cottage Hospital (GCH) 695 N Kellogg St *Web:* www.cottagehospital.com	Galesburg	IL	61401	309-343-8131		374-3
Galesburg Printing & Publishing Co 140 S Prairie St *TF:* 800-733-2767 ■ *Web:* www.galesburg.com	Galesburg	IL	61401	309-343-7181	343-2382	637-8
Galesburg Public Library 40 E Simmons St *Web:* www.galesburglibrary.org	Galesburg	IL	61401	309-343-6118	343-4877	434-3
Galileo Global Advisors LLC 10 Rockefeller Plaza Ste 1001 *Web:* galileoglobaladvisors.com	New York	NY	10020	212-332-6055		690
Galison Publishing LLC 28 W 44th St Ste 1411 *TF:* 800-670-7441 ■ *Web:* www.galison.com	New York	NY	10036	212-354-8840		130
Gallade Chemical Inc 1230 E St Gertrude Pl *TF:* 888-830-9092 ■ *Web:* www.galladechem.com	Santa Ana	CA	92707	714-546-9901	546-2501	146
Gallagher & Burk Inc 344 High St *Web:* www.gallagherandburk.com	Oakland	CA	94601	925-361-1645		188-4
Gallagher Asphalt Corp 18100 S Indiana Ave *TF:* 800-536-7160 ■ *Web:* www.gallagherasphalt.com	Thornton	IL	60476	708-877-7160	877-5222	188-4
Gallagher Corp 3908 Morrison Dr *TF:* 800-524-8597 ■ *Web:* www.gallaghercorp.com	Gurnee	IL	60031	847-249-3440		605-2
Gallagher Flynn & Company LLP 55 Community Dr *Web:* www.gfc.com	South Burlington	VT	05403	802 863 1331	651-7305	2
Gallagher Mike (Rep R - WI) 1007 Longworth HOB *Web:* gallagher.house.gov	Washington	DC	20515	202-225-5665	225-5665	342-2
Gallagher Systems Group Inc 2502 N Clark St	Chicago	IL	60614	773-348-5400		177
Gallagher, Gams, Pryor, Tallan & Littrell LLP 471 E Broad St 19th Fl *TF:* 866-378-1624 ■ *Web:* www.ggptl.com	Columbus	OH	43215	614-228-5151		428
Gallagher-Kaiser Corp 13710 Mt Elliott St *Web:* www.gkcorp.com	Detroit	MI	48212	313-368-3100	368-3109	550
Galland Henning Nopak Inc 1025 S 40th St *Web:* www.nopak.com	West Milwaukee	WI	53215	414-645-6000	645-6048	223
Gallant & Wein Corp 11-20 43Rd Rd *Web:* www.galwein.com	Long Island	NY	11101	718-784-5210		814
Gallant Greetings Corp 4300 United Pkwy *TF:* 800-621-4279 ■ *Web:* www.gallantgreetings.com	Schiller Park	IL	60176	847-671-6500		130
Gallatin County 311 W Main St *Web:* gallatincomt.virtualtownhall.net	Bozeman	MT	59715	406-582-3050	582-3068	338
Gallatin County 200 Washington St PO Box 144 *Web:* gallatincounty.ky.gov	Warsaw	KY	41095	859-567-5691	567-4764	338
Gallaudet University 800 Florida Ave NE *TF:* 800-995-0550 ■ *Web:* www.gallaudet.edu	Washington	DC	20002	202-651-5000	651-5744	166
Gallaudet University Library 800 Florida Ave NE *TF:* 800-995-0550 ■ *Web:* www.gallaudet.edu/library.html	Washington	DC	20002	202-651-5217	651-5213	434-6
Gallaudet University Press 800 Florida Ave NE *TF:* 800-621-2736 ■ *Web:* gupress.gallaudet.edu	Washington	DC	20002	202-651-5488	651-5489	637-4
Gallego Ruben (Rep D - AZ) 1218 Longworth House Office Bldg *Web:* rubengallego.house.gov	Washington	DC	20515	202-225-4065		342-2
Gallegos Corp PO Box 821 *TF:* 800-425-5346 ■ *Web:* www.gallegoscorp.com	Vail	CO	81658	970-926-3737	926-3727	189-7
Galleher Corp 9303 Greenleaf Ave *Web:* www.galleher.com	Santa Fe Springs	CA	90670	562-944-8885		361
Galleon Pharmaceuticals Inc 213 Witmer Rd *Web:* www.galleonpharma.com	Horsham	PA	19044	267-803-1970		668
Galleon Resort & Marina 617 Front St *TF:* 800-544-3030 ■ *Web:* www.galleonresort.com	Key West	FL	33040	305-296-7711	296-0821	669
Galleria at Fort Lauderdale 2414 E Sunrise Blvd *Web:* www.galleriamall-fl.com	Fort Lauderdale	FL	33304	954-564-1015	566-9976	460
Galleria at Pittsburgh Mills 590 Pittsburgh Mills Cir *Web:* www.pittsburghmills.com	Tarentum	PA	15084	724-904-9010		460

Phone | Fax | Class

Galleria at Sunset
1300 W Sunset Rd Ste 1400 ..... Henderson NV 89014 702-434-2409 434-0259 460
Web: www.galleriaatsunset.com

Galleria at Tyler
1299 Galleria at Tyler St ..... Riverside CA 92503 951-351-3112 460
Web: www.galleriatyler.com

Galleria at White Plains
100 Main St ..... White Plains NY 10601 914-682-0111 460
Web: simon.com/default.aspx

Galleria Park Hotel
191 Sutter St ..... San Francisco CA 94104 415-781-3060 379
TF: 800-325-3589 ■ *Web:* www.jdvhotels.com

Galleria Woods
3850 Galleria Woods Dr ..... Birmingham AL 35244 205-918-7972 672
Web: brookdale.com

Galleria, The
5085 Westheimer Rd Ste 4850 ..... Houston TX 77056 713-966-3500 966-3596 460
TF: 800-333-5032 ■ *Web:* www.simon.com

Gallerie 454
15105 Kercheval Ave ..... Grosse Pointe Park MI 48230 313-822-4454 822-3768 520
TF: 800-914-3538 ■ *Web:* www.gallerie454.com

Galleries of Syracuse, The
441 S Salina St ..... Syracuse NY 13202 315-475-5351 460

Gallery 78 Inc 796 Queen St ..... Fredericton NB E3B1C6 506-454-5192 42
TF: 888-883-8322 ■ *Web:* www.gallery78.com

Gallery Model Homes Inc 6006 N Fwy ..... Houston TX 77076 713-694-5570 321
Web: www.galleryfurniture.com

Gallery Moos Ltd 622 Richmond St W ..... Toronto ON M5V1Y9 416-504-5445 42
TF: 800-551-2465 ■ *Web:* www.gallerymoos.com

Gallery of History Inc
3601 W Sahara Ave ..... Las Vegas NV 89102 702-364-1000 364-1285 51
TF: 800-425-5379 ■ *Web:* www.galleryofhistory.com

Gallery One 121 Scollard St ..... Toronto ON M5R1G4 416-929-3103 42
Web: www.artgalleryone.com

Gallery Paule Anglim
14 Geary St ..... San Francisco CA 94108 415-433-2710 42
Web: www.gallerypauleanglim.com

Galletto Ristorante 1101 J St ..... Modesto CA 95354 209-523-4500 671
Web: www.galletto.biz

Gallia County Chamber of Commerce
16 State St PO Box 465 ..... Gallipolis OH 45631 740-446-0596 338
Web: galliacountychamber.org

Galliard Capital Management Inc
800 La Salle Ave Ste 1100 ..... Minneapolis MN 55402 612-667-3220 402
TF: 800-717-1617 ■ *Web:* www.galliard.com

Gallier House Museum
1132 Royal St PO Box 56836 ..... New Orleans LA 70156 504-525-5661 568-9735 520
Web: www.hgghh.org

Galliker Dairy Company Inc
143 Donald Ln ..... Johnstown PA 15907 814-266-8702 296-27
TF: 800-477-6455 ■ *Web:* www.gallikers.com

Gallina LLP
925 Highland Pointe Dr Ste 450 ..... Roseville CA 95678 916-638-1188 638-1782 2
TF: 877-638-1188 ■ *Web:* www.gallina.com

Gallo Equipment Company Inc
11835 S Ave O ..... Chicago IL 60617 773-374-5515 54
TF: 800-322-5438 ■ *Web:* www.galloequipment.com

Gallo Salame 2411 Baumann Ave ..... San Lorenzo CA 94580 800-988-6464 296-26
TF: 800-988-6464 ■ *Web:* gallosalame.com

Gallon Takacs Boissoneault & Schaffer Company LPA
Jack Gallon Bldg 3516 Granite Cir ..... Toledo OH 43617 419-843-2001 428
TF: 800-352-1976 ■ *Web:* www.gallonlaw.com

Galloon e s & Associates
40 W Fourth St Ste 2200 ..... Dayton OH 45402 937-586-3100 428
TF: 800-998-4374 ■ *Web:* esgallon.com

Galloup 3838 Clay Ave SW ..... Wyoming MI 49548 269-965-4005 965-3263 191-2
TF: 888-755-3110 ■ *Web:* www.galloup.com

Galloway Company Inc
601 S Commercial St ..... Neenah WI 54956 920-722-7741 296-10
Web: www.gallowaycompany.com

Galloway Field Service Inc Dba Galloway Research Service
4751 Hamilton-Wolfe ..... San Antonio TX 78229 210-734-4346 466
Web: gallowayresearch.com

Galloway, Lucchese, Everson & Picchi A Professional
2300 Contra Costa Blvd Ste 500 ..... Pleasant Hill CA 94523 925-930-9090 428
Web: www.glattys.com

Galls Inc 2680 Palumbo Dr ..... Lexington KY 40509 859-266-7227 576
TF: 800-477-7766 ■ *Web:* www.galls.com

Gallun Snow 1920 Market St Ste 201 ..... Denver CO 80202 303-433-9500 393
TF: 866-846-7514 ■ *Web:* www.gallunsnow.com

Gallup Inc 1001 Gallup Dr ..... Omaha NE 68102 402-951-2003 466
TF: 888-500-8282 ■ *Web:* gallup.com

Gallup Independent 500 N Ninth St ..... Gallup NM 87301 505-863-6811 532-2
Web: www.gallupindependent.com

Gallup Indian Medical Ctr
516 E Nizhoni Blvd ..... Gallup NM 87301 505-722-1000 374-3

Gallup Organization 901 F St NW ..... Washington DC 20004 202-715-3030 715-3045 466
TF: 877-242-5587 ■ *Web:* www.gallup.com

Gallus Inc 2800 Black Lake Pl ..... Philadelphia PA 19154 215-677-9600 627
TF: 800-248-7649 ■ *Web:* www.gallus.org

Gally Public Affairs Inc
111 Cathedral St Ste 203 ..... Annapolis MD 21401 410-990-0069 636
Web: www.gallypublicaffairs.com

Galman Group, The
261 Old York Rd Ofc ..... Jenkintown PA 19046 215-886-2000 652

Galpin Motors Inc
15505 Roscoe Blvd ..... North Hills CA 91343 818-787-3800 57
TF: 800-256-7137 ■ *Web:* www.galpin.com

Galson Laboratories Inc
6601 Kirkville Rd ..... East Syracuse NY 13057 315-432-5227 743
TF: 800-458-1158 ■ *Web:* www.galsonlabs.com

Galt House Hotel 140 N Fourth St ..... Louisville KY 40202 502-589-5200 379
TF: 800-843-4258 ■ *Web:* www.galthouse.com

Galt Toys 900 N Michigan Ave ..... Chicago IL 60611 312-440-9550 761
Web: www.galtbaby.com

Galtere Ltd 515 Madison Ave 35th Fl ..... New York NY 10022 212-598-1837 194
Web: www.galtere.com

Galvan Industries Inc
7320 Millbrook Rd ..... Harrisburg NC 28075 704-455-5102 455-5215 481
TF General: 800-277-5678 ■ *Web:* www.galvan-ize.com

Galvanic Applied Sciences USA Inc
41 Wellman St ..... Lowell MA 01851 978-848-2701 201
TF: 866-252-8470 ■ *Web:* www.galvanic.com

Galveston Central Appraisal District
9850 Emmett F Lowry Expy Ste A ..... Texas City TX 77591 409-935-1980 317
TF: 866-277-4725 ■ *Web:* www.galvestoncad.org

Galveston College 4015 Ave Q ..... Galveston TX 77550 409-944-4242 944-1501* 162
*Fax: Admissions ■ *TF:* 866-483-4242 ■ *Web:* www.gc.edu

Galveston Computer Solutions LLC
523 24th St Ste 5 ..... Galveston TX 77550 409-762-4326 379
Web: galvestoncs.com

Galveston County
600 59th St Second Fl Ste 2001
PO Box 17253 ..... Galveston TX 77550 409-766-2200 338
Web: www.galvestoncountytx.gov

Galveston County Daily News
8522 Teichman Rd PO Box 628 ..... Galveston TX 77553 409-683-5200 740-3421 532-2
TF: 800-561-3611 ■ *Web:* www.galvnews.com

Galveston Independent School District (GISD)
3904 Ave T PO Box 660 ..... Galveston TX 77550 409-766-5100 762-8391 685
Web: www.gisd.org

Galveston Island State Park
14901 Termini San Luis Pass Rd ..... Galveston TX 77554 409-737-1222 565
Web: tpwd.texas.gov/state-parks/galveston-island

Galvestonian Condominium Association
1401 E Beach Dr ..... Galveston TX 77550 409-765-6161 707
TF: 888-526-6161 ■ *Web:* www.galvestonian.com

Galvin Flying Services
7001 Perimeter Rd ..... Seattle WA 98108 206-763-9706 63
Web: www.galvinflying.com

Galway Bay Irish Pub
63 Maryland Ave ..... Annapolis MD 21401 410-263-8333 671
Web: www.galwaybayannapolis.com

Galway Group LP
3009 Post Oak Blvd Ste 950 ..... Houston TX 77056 713-952-0186 70
Web: www.galwaylp.com

GAMA (General Aviation Manufacturers Assn)
1400 K St NW Ste 801 ..... Washington DC 20005 202-393-1500 842-4063 49-21
TF: 866-427-3287 ■ *Web:* www.gama.aero

Gama Aviation Inc
2 Corporate Dr Ste 1050 ..... Shelton CT 06484 203-337-4600 21
TF: 800-468-1110 ■ *Web:* www.gamaaviationllc.com

GAMA International
2901 Telestar Ct ..... Falls Church VA 22042 800-345-2687 49-9
TF Cust Svc: 800-345-2687 ■ *Web:* gamaweb.com

Gamajet Cleaning Systems Inc
604 Jeffers Cir ..... Exton PA 19341 610-408-9940 408-9945 386
TF Sales: 877-426-2538 ■ *Web:* www.gamajet.com

Gam-Anon International Service Office Inc
PO Box 157 ..... Whitestone NY 11357 718-352-1671 746-2571 48-21
TF: 800-477-6291 ■ *Web:* www.gam-anon.org

Gambardella's Pasta Bella
706 Second Ave ..... Fairbanks AK 99701 907-457-4992 456-3425 671
TF: 800-314-0858 ■ *Web:* www.gambardellas.com

Gamber-Johnson Inc
3001 Borham Ave ..... Stevens Point WI 54481 715-344-3482 295
Web: www.gamberjohnson.com

Gambia 800 Second Ave Ste 400F ..... New York NY 10017 212-949-6640 856-9820 784

Gambit Weekly 3923 Bienville St ..... New Orleans LA 70119 504-486-5900 483-3116 532-5
Web: www.bestofneworleans.com

Gamble Plantation Historic State Park
3708 Patten Ave ..... Ellenton FL 34222 941-723-4536 565
Web: www.floridastateparks.org

Gamblers Anonymous (GA) PO Box 17173 ..... Los Angeles CA 90017 626-960-3500 960-3501 48-21
Web: www.gamblersanonymous.org

Gambone Bros Development Co
1030 W Germantown Pk ..... East Norriton PA 19403 610-539-4700 539-4701 653
Web: www.gambone.com

Gambone Steel Company Inc
545 Foundry Rd ..... Norristown PA 19403 610-539-6505 480
Web: www.gambonesteelcompany.com

Gambrill State Park
8602 Gambrill Pk Rd ..... Frederick MD 21702 301-271-7574 565
TF: 800-830-3974 ■ *Web:* dnr.maryland.gov/Pages/default.aspx

Gambrinus Co, The
14800 San Pedro 3rd Fl ..... San Antonio TX 78232 210-490-9128 490-9984 81-1
TF: 800-596-6486 ■ *Web:* www.gambrinusco.com

Gambro BCT 10811 W Collins Ave ..... Lakewood CO 80215 303-231-4357 231-4357 419
TF: 877-339-4228 ■ *Web:* www.terumobct.com

GAMCO Investors Inc 1 Corporate Ctr ..... Rye NY 10580 914-921-5100 921-5118 528
NYSE: GBL ■ *TF:* 800-422-3554 ■ *Web:* www.gabelli.com

Game & Parks Commission
301 E State Farm Rd ..... North Platte NE 69101 308-535-8025 565

Game Country USA 2403 Commerce Ln ..... Albany GA 31707 229-883-4706 883-4766 710
Web: www.gamecountry.biz

Game Creek Video LLC 23 Executive Dr ..... Hudson NH 03051 603-882-5222 514
Web: www.gamecreekvideo.com

Game Informer 724 N First St Fl 3 ..... Minneapolis MN 55401 612-486-6100 761
Web: www.gameinformer.com

GameChanger Products LLC
2207 Harbor Bay Pkwy ..... Alameda CA 94502 510-521-7985 196
Web: gamechanger.net

GameFly Inc 3000 Ocean Pk Blvd ..... Santa Monica CA 90405 310-664-6400 93
Web: www.gamefly.com

GamePlan Financial Marketing LLC
300 ParkBrooke Pl Ste 200 ..... Woodstock GA 30189 678-238-0601 402
TF Cust Svc: 800-886-4757 ■ *Web:* www.gameplanfinancial.com

Gamesa Wind US LLC
2050 Cabot Blvd W ..... Langhorne PA 19047 215-710-3100 518
Web: www.gamesacorp.com

GameStop Corp 625 Westport Pkwy ..... Grapevine TX 76051 817-424-2000 424-2002 179
NYSE: GME ■ *TF:* 800-883-8895 ■ *Web:* www.gamestop.com

Gamesville Inc 100 Fifth Ave ..... Waltham MA 02451 781-370-2700 452
TF: 800-223-2064 ■ *Web:* www.gamesville.com

Gamewell FCI 12 Clintonville Rd ..... Northford CT 06472 203-484-7161 484-7118 283
TF: 800-606-1983 ■ *Web:* www.gamewell-fci.com

Phone | Fax | Class

Gaming Laboratories International Inc
600 Airport Rd, Lakewood NJ 08701 — 732-942-3999 — 942-0043 — 193
Web: www.gaminglabs.com

Gaming Partners International Corp
3945 W Cheyenne Ave Ste 208, Las Vegas NV 89032 — 702-384-2425 — 384-1965 — 322
NASDAQ: GPIC ■ *TF:* 800-728-5766 ■ *Web:* gpigaming.com

Gamma Beta Phi Society
5204 Kingston Pk Ste 31-33, Knoxville TN 37919 — 865-483-6212 — 48-16
TF: 800-628-9920 ■ *Web:* www.gammabetaphi.org

Gamma Construction Co 2808 Joanel St, Houston TX 77027 — 713-963-0086 — 963-0961 — 186
Web: www.gammaconst.com

Gamma Dynacare Medical Laboratories Inc
115 Midair Ct, Brampton ON L6T5M3 — 800-668-2714 — 415
TF: 800-668-2714 ■ *Web:* www.dynacare.ca

Gamma Engineering Inc
601 Airport Dr, Mansfield TX 76063 — 817-477-2193 — 256
Web: www.gammaeng.com

Gamma Medica Inc 12 Manor Pkwy Unit 3, Salem NH 03079 — 603-952-4441 — 743
TF: 888-720-3152 ■ *Web:* www.gammamedica.com

Gamma Phi Beta International Sorority (GPB)
12737 E Euclid Dr, Centennial CO 80111 — 303-799-1874 — 799-1876 — 48-16
TF: 800-526-1870 ■ *Web:* www.gammaphibeta.org

Gamma Sports 200 Waterfront Dr, Pittsburgh PA 15222 — 412-323-0335 — 323-0317 — 710
TF: 800-333-0337 ■ *Web:* www.gammasports.com

Gamma Vacuum LLC 2915 133rd St W, Shakopee MN 55379 — 952-445-4841 — 419
Web: www.gammavacuum.com

Gammon Technical Products Inc
2300 Hwy 34, Manasquan NJ 08736 — 732-223-4600 — 358
Web: www.gammontech.com

Gams Communications LLC
308 W Erie St Ste 4, Chicago IL 60654 — 312-280-2740 — 195
Web: www.gamscom.com

Gamse Lithographing Company Inc
7413 Pulaski Hwy, Baltimore MD 21237 — 410-866-4700 — 174
Web: www.gamse.com

GaN Corp 11247 S Memorial Pkwy, Huntsville AL 35803 — 256-489-2471 — 261
Web: www.geeksandnerds.com

GANA (Glass Assn of North America)
800 SW Jackson St Ste 1500, Topeka KS 66612 — 785-271-0208 — 271-0166 — 49-13
Web: www.glasswebsite.com

Ganahl Lumber Co 1220 E Ball Rd, Anaheim CA 92805 — 714-772-5444 — 772-0639 — 364
Web: www.ganahl.com

Ganaraska Region Conservation
2216 28 Hwy, Port Hope ON L1A3V8 — 905-885-8173 — 192
Web: www.grca.on.ca

GANCOM Inc 209 Senate Ave, Camp Hill PA 17011 — 717-763-7387 — 344
Web: www.gancom.com

Gander & Area Chamber of Commerce
109 Trans Canada Hwy, Gander NL A1V1P6 — 709-256-7110 — 256-4080 — 137
Web: www.ganderchamber.nf.ca

Gander Mountain Co
180 Fifth St E Ste 1300, Saint Paul MN 55101 — 651-325-4300 — 711
Web: gandermountain.com

Gandhi 150 W Ft Lowell Rd, Tucson AZ 85705 — 520-292-1738 — 671
Web: gandhicuisineofindia.com

Gandhi 1 Central Ave, Albany NY 12210 — 518-449-5577 — 449-8941 — 671
Web: www.albanygandhi.com

Gandhi 554 Queen St W, Toronto ON M5V2B7 — 416-504-8155 — 671

Gandhi India's Cuisine
4080 Paradise Rd, Las Vegas NV 89169 — 702-734-0094 — 671
Web: www.gandhicuisine.com

Gandy Co 528 Gandrud Rd, Owatonna MN 55060 — 507-451-5430 — 451-2857 — 273
TF: 800-443-2476 ■ *Web:* www.gandy.net

Gandy Dancer 401 Depot St, Ann Arbor MI 48104 — 734-769-0592 — 769-0415 — 671
Web: www.muer.com

Gandy's Dairies Inc
201 University Blvd, Lubbock TX 79415 — 806-762-8844 — 296-25
TF: 877-382-4357 ■ *Web:* search.lubbockonline.com

Ganesh Machinery 20869 Plummer St, Chatsworth CA 91311 — 818-349-9166 — 385
TF: 888-542-6374 ■ *Web:* www.ganeshmachinery.com

Ganna Walska Lotusland
695 Ashley Rd, Santa Barbara CA 93108 — 805-969-3767 — 969-4423 — 97
Web: www.lotusland.org

Ganneston Construction Corp
3025 N Belfast Ave, Augusta ME 04332 — 207-621-8505 — 186
Web: gannestonconstruction.com

Gannett Company Inc
7950 Jones Branch Dr, McLean VA 22107 — 703-854-6000 — 738
NYSE: GCI ■ *TF:* 800-778-3299 ■ *Web:* www.gannett.com

Gannett Direct Marketing Services Inc
3400 Robards Ct, Louisville KY 40218 — 502-454-6660 — 5

Gannett Fleming Inc 207 Senate Ave, Camp Hill PA 17011 — 717-763-7211 — 763-8150 — 261
TF: 800-233-1055 ■ *Web:* www.gannettfleming.com

Gannett Offset 7950 Jones Branch Dr, McLean VA 22107 — 703-854-6000 — 627
Web: www.gannett.com

Gannett Welsh & Kotler LLC
222 Berkeley St, Boston MA 02116 — 617-236-8900 — 236-1815 — 401
TF: 800-225-4236 ■ *Web:* www.gwkinvest.com

Gannon University 109 University Sq, Erie PA 16541 — 814-871-7000 — 871-5803 — 166
TF Admissions: 800-426-6668 ■ *Web:* www.gannon.edu

Ganondagan State Historic Site
SR 444 Victor-Bloomfield Rd, Victor NY 14564 — 585-924-5848 — 565
Web: parks.ny.gov/historic-sites/26/hunting.aspx

Ganong Bros Ltd 1 Chocolate Dr, Saint Stephen NB E3L2X5 — 506-465-5600 — 465-5610 — 296-8
Web: www.ganong.com

Gans Ink & Supply Company Inc
1441 Boyd St, Los Angeles CA 90033 — 323-264-2200 — 264-2916 — 388
TF: 800-421-6167 ■ *Web:* www.gansink.com

Ganser German Translations
602 Fairway Rd, Belton MO 64012 — 816-561-3777 — 768

Gant Travel Management
400 W Seventh St Ste 233, Bloomington IN 47404 — 800-742-4198 — 771
TF Cust Svc: 800-742-4198 ■ *Web:* www.ganttravel.com

Gantec Corp 1111 Plaza Dr Ste 310, Schaumburg IL 60173 — 847-885-7655 — 196
Web: www.gantecusa.com

Gantec Publishing Solutions LLC
1111 N Plaza Dr Ste 652, Schaumburg IL 60173 — 847-598-1144 — 530
Web: www.gantecpublishing.com

Ganther Construction & Architecture Inc
4825 County Rd A, Oshkosh WI 54901 — 920-426-4774 — 186
TF: 800-847-2404 ■ *Web:* www.ganther.com

Gantry Plaza State Park
4-09 47th Rd, Long Island NY 11101 — 718-786-6385 — 565
Web: parks.ny.gov/parks/149/details.aspx

GAO (Government Accountability Office)
441 G St NW, Washington DC 20548 — 202-512-4800 — 342
Web: www.gao.gov

Gap Engineering Inc 802 Dominion Dr, Katy TX 77450 — 281-578-0500 — 261
Web: www.gap-eng.com

Gap Inc 2 Folsom St, San Francisco CA 94105 — 650-952-4400 — 157-4
NYSE: GPS ■ *TF:* 800-333-7899 ■ *Web:* www.gapinc.com

Gap International Inc
700 Old Marple Rd, Springfield PA 19064 — 610-328-0308 — 463
Web: www.gapinternational.com

GAP Solutions Inc
205 Van Buren St Ste 205, Herndon VA 20170 — 703-707-2090 — 317
Web: www.gapsi.com

Gapco Inc 2151 Centennial Dr, Gainesville GA 30504 — 770-534-7928 — 811
Web: www.gapco.com

Gar Enterprises 418 E Live Oak Ave, Arcadia CA 91006 — 626-574-1175 — 174
Web: www.kgselectronics.com

GAR Foundation
Andrew Jackson House 277 E Mill St, Akron OH 44308 — 330-576-2926 — 305
Web: garfoundation.org

Gar Wood Securities LLC
440 S LaSalle St Ste 2201, Chicago IL 60605 — 312-566-0740 — 690
Web: www.garwoodsecurities.net

Garaga Inc 8500 25th Ave, St Georges QC G6A1K5 — 418-227-2828 — 227-6282 — 480
TF: 800-464-2724 ■ *Web:* www.garaga.com

Garamendi John (Rep D - CA)
2438 Rayburn Bldg, Washington DC 20515 — 202-225-1880 — 225-5914 — 342-2
Web: garamendi.house.gov

Garan Lucow Miller PC
1000 Woodbridge St, Detroit MI 48207 — 313-446-1530 — 428
TF: 800-875-1530 ■ *Web:* www.garanlucow.com

Garavi Gujarat Publications
2020 Beaver Ruin Rd, Norcross GA 30071 — 770-263-7728 — 532-3
TF: 800-980-6559 ■ *Web:* www.amg.biz

Garban Capital Markets LLC
1100 Plaza Five, Jersey City NJ 07311 — 212-732-6900 — 690
Web: www.icap.com

GARBC (General Assn of Regular Baptist Churches)
1300 N Meacham Rd, Schaumburg IL 60173 — 847-585-0816 — 48-20
TF: 888-588-1600 ■ *Web:* www.garbcinternational.org

Garbe Iron Works Inc Manufacturing Div
500 N Broadway, Aurora IL 60505 — 630-897-5100 — 480
Web: www.giwinc.com

Garber C s & Sons Inc
7928 Boyertown Pk, Boyertown PA 19512 — 610-689-9500 — 711
TF: 800-947-8631 ■ *Web:* www.csgarber.com

Garb-ko Inc 3925 Fortune Blvd, Saginaw MI 48603 — 989-799-6937 — 299
Web: 7-eleven.com

Garcia & Assoc Inc 1 Saunders Ave, San Anselmo CA 94960 — 415-458-5803 — 194
Web: www.garciaandassociates.com

Garcia Express LLC 639 S 54th Ave, Phoenix AZ 85043 — 602-352-0150 — 311
Web: www.garciaexpress.com

Garcia Foods Inc PO Box 13280, San Antonio TX 78213 — 210-349-6262 — 296-26
Web: www.garciafoods.com

Garcia Galuska & De Sousa Inc
370 Faunce Corner Rd, North Dartmouth MA 02747 — 508-998-5700 — 261
TF: 800-909-7763 ■ *Web:* www.g-g-d.com

Garcia Hamilton & Associates LP
5 Houston Ctr 1401 McKinney Ste 1600, Houston TX 77010 — 713-853-2322 — 401
Web: www.dhja.com

Garcia Research Associates Inc
300 E Magnolia Blvd, Burbank CA 91502 — 818-566-7722 — 466
TF: 800-627-8334 ■ *Web:* www.garciaresearch.com

Garcia's 398 NW N River Dr, Miami FL 33128 — 305-375-0765 — 671
Web: garciasmiami.com

Garco Bldg Systems
2714 S Garfield Rd, Airway Heights WA 99001 — 509-244-5611 — 244-2850 — 105
TF: 800-941-2291 ■ *Web:* www.garcobuildings.com

Garco Construction Inc
4114 E Broadway, Spokane WA 99202 — 509-535-4688 — 186
TF: 800-572-3706 ■ *Web:* www.garco.com

Garcon Restaurant
1101 Valencia St, San Francisco CA 94110 — 415-401-8959 — 671
Web: www.garconsf.com

Gard Communications
1140 SW 11th Ave Fl 3, Portland OR 97205 — 503-221-0100 — 636
Web: gardcommunications.com

Garda World Security Corp
1390 Barre St, Montreal QC H3C1N4 — 514-281-2811 — 281-2811 — 693
TSE: GW ■ *TF:* 800-859-1599 ■ *Web:* www.garda.com

Garde Arts Ctr 325 State St, New London CT 06320 — 860-444-7373 — 701-0189 — 572
Web: www.gardearts.org

Garden City Area Chamber of Commerce
1511 E Fulton Terr, Garden City KS 67846 — 620-275-1900 — 139
TF: 800-219-8941 ■ *Web:* www.gardencity.net

Garden City Community College
801 N Campus Dr, Garden City KS 67846 — 620-276-7611 — 276-9573 — 162
TF: 800-658-1696 ■ *Web:* www.gcccks.edu

Garden City Ctr 100 Midway Rd Ste 14, Cranston RI 02920 — 401-942-2800 — 460
Web: www.gardencitycenter.com

Garden City Feed Yard
1805 W Annie Scheer Rd, Garden City KS 67846 — 620-275-4191 — 10-1
TF: 800-272-4191 ■ *Web:* www.aztx.com

Garden City Group LLC 105 Maxess Rd, Melville NY 11747 — 631-470-5000 — 428
TF: 888-404-8013 ■ *Web:* www.gardencitygroup.com

Garden City Hospital (GCH)
6245 Inkster Rd, Garden City MI 48135 — 734-458-3300 — 374-3
Web: www.gch.org

Garden City Hotel 45 Seventh St, Garden City NY 11530 — 516-747-3000 — 747-1414 — 379
TF: 877-549-0400 ■ *Web:* www.gardencityhotel.com

Garden City Plumbing & Heating Inc
4025 Flynn Ln, Missoula MT 59808 — 406-728-5550 — 610
Web: www.gardencityplumbing.com

	Phone	Fax	Class
Garden City Public Library 31735 Maplewood St, Garden City MI 48135 *Web:* www.gardencitylib.org	734-793-1830	793-1831	434-3
Garden Compass 1660 Union St, San Diego CA 92101 *Web:* gardencompass.com	619-239-2202		457-19
Garden County 611 Main St, Oshkosh NE 69154 *TF:* 800-563-0012 ■ *Web:* www.co.garden.ne.us	308-772-3924	772-0124	338
Garden Court Hotel 520 Cowper St, Palo Alto CA 94301 *TF:* 800-824-9028 ■ *Web:* www.gardencourt.com	650-322-9000	324-3609	379
Garden District Animal Hospital, The 1302 Perkins Rd, Baton Rouge LA 70806 *Web:* www.gardendistrictanimalhospital.com	225-381-9661		794
Garden Fresh Restaurant Corp 15822 Bernardo Ctr Dr Ste A, San Diego CA 92127 *TF:* 800-874-1600 ■ *Web:* www.souplantation.com	858-675-1600	675-1032	670
Garden Grove Chamber of Commerce 12866 Main St Ste 102, Garden Grove CA 92840 *TF:* 800-959-5560 ■ *Web:* gardengrovechamber.com	714-638-7950	636-6672	139
Garden Grove City Hall 11222 Acacia Pkwy, Garden Grove CA 92840 *Web:* www.ci.garden-grove.ca.us	714-741-5000	741-5044	337
Garden Grove Hospital & Medical Ctr 12601 Garden Grove Blvd, Garden Grove CA 92843 *Web:* www.gardengrovehospital.com	714-537-5160		374-3
Garden Grove Regional Library 11200 Stanford Ave, Garden Grove CA 92840 *Web:* www.ocsd.org	714-530-0711		434-3
Garden Grove Unified School District 10331 Stanford Ave, Garden Grove CA 92840 *Web:* www.ggusd.us	714-663-6000	663-6100	685
Garden Island State Recreation Area c/o Zippel Bay State Pk 3684 54th Ave NW, Williams MN 56686 *Web:* www.dnr.state.mn.us/state_parks/garden_island	218-783-6252		565
Garden of Life Inc 4200 NorthCrop Pkwy Ste 200, Palm Beach Gardens FL 33410 *TF:* 866-465-0051 ■ *Web:* www.gardenoflife.com	561-748-2477	472-9298	799
Garden Spa at MacArthur Place 29 E MacArthur St, Sonoma CA 95476 *TF:* 800-722-1866 ■ *Web:* www.macarthurplace.com	707-933-3193	933-9833	707
Garden Spot Distributors Inc 191 Commerce Dr, New Holland PA 17557 *Web:* www.gardenspotdist.com	717-354-4936		297-11
Garden State Community Bank (GSCB) 36 Ferry St, Newark NJ 07105 *NYSE:* NYB ■ *TF:* 877-786-6560	973-589-8616	589-1202	70
Garden State Engine & Equipment Co 3509 US Hwy 22, Somerville NJ 08876 *TF:* 800-479-3857 ■ *Web:* gseecrane.com	908-534-5444	534-5623	358
Garden State Exhibit Ctr 50 Atrium Dr, Somerset NJ 08873 *TF:* 800-246-2287 ■ *Web:* www.gsec.com	732-469-4000		205
Garden State Growers 99 Locust Grove Rd, Pittstown NJ 08867 *TF:* 800-288-8484 ■ *Web:* www.gardenstategrowers.com	908-730-8888	730-6676	369
Garden State Lumber Products 18 Muller Rd, Oakland NJ 07436 *Web:* www.gardenstatelumber.com	201-651-1600		186
Garden State Mltple Lsting Services 1719 SR- 10 Ste 223, Parsippany NJ 07054 *Web:* www.gsmls.com	973-898-1900		652
Garden State Orthopaedic Center Inc 9 Post Rd, Oakland NJ 07436 *Web:* gsortho.com/Garden_State_Orthopaedic/Main.html	201-337-5566		238
Garden State Plaza 1 Garden State Plaza, Paramus NJ 07652 *TF:* 800-436-7734 ■ *Web:* www.westfield.com	201-843-2121		460
Garden State Precast Inc 1630 Wyckoff Rd, Wall NJ 07727 *Web:* www.gardenstateprecast.com	732-938-4436		183
Garden State Tile Distributors Inc 5001 Industrial Rd, Farmingdale NJ 07727 *Web:* www.gstile.com	732-938-6675		191-1
Gardena Valley Chamber of Commerce 1204 W Gardena Blvd Ste E, Gardena CA 90247 *Web:* www.gardenachamber.com	310-532-9905	329-7307	139
Gardena Valley News 15005 S Vermont Ave, Gardena CA 90247 *TF:* 800-329-6351 ■ *Web:* gvnoffset.com	310-329-6351	329-7501	532-4
Gardener's Supply Co 128 Intervale Rd, Burlington VT 05401 *TF:* 800-863-1700 ■ *Web:* www.gardeners.com	802-660-3500		323
Gardeners' Guild Inc 2780 Goodrick Ave, Richmond CA 94801 *Web:* www.gardenersguild.com	510-439-3700		776
Gardens Alive Inc 5100 Schenley Pl, Lawrenceburg IN 47025 *TF:* 800-222-1222 ■ *Web:* www.gardensalive.com	513 354 1482	354 1484	459
Gardens Hotel 526 Angela St, Key West FL 33040 *TF:* 800-526-2664 ■ *Web:* www.gardenshotel.com	305-294-2661		379
Gardens Mall, The 3101 PGA Blvd, Palm Beach Gardens FL 33410 *Web:* www.thegardensmall.com	561-622-2115	694-9380	460
Gardens of Salonica 19 NE Fifth St, Minneapolis MN 55413 *Web:* gardensofsalonica.com	612-378-0611		671
Gardens of the American Rose Ctr 8877 Jefferson-Paige Rd, Shreveport LA 71119 *TF:* 800-637-6534 ■ *Web:* rose.org/arc/gardens.htm	318-938-5402	938-5402	97
Gardens on Spring Creek 2145 Centre Ave, Fort Collins CO 80526 *Web:* www.fcgov.com	970-416-2486	416-2280	97
Gardenside Ltd 808 Anthony St Ste 140, Berkeley CA 94710 *TF:* 888-999-8325 ■ *Web:* www.gardenside.com	415-455-4500	455-4505	319-4
Gardenswartz & Dodds PC 600 17th St Ste 1800 N, Denver CO 80202 *Web:* gndpc.com	303-534-6770		2
Gardien Services USA Inc 3700 24th Ave Bldg A, Forest Grove OR 97116 *Web:* www.gardien.com	503-430-8980		393

	Phone	Fax	Class
Gardiner Museum 111 Queen's Pk, Toronto ON M5S2C7 *TF:* 800-222-7270 ■ *Web:* www.gardinermuseum.on.ca	416-586-8080	586-8085	520
Gardner Cory (Sen R - CO) 354 Russell Senate Office Bldg, Washington DC 20510 *Web:* www.gardner.senate.gov	202-224-5941	224-6524	342-2
Gardner Cryogenics 2136 City Line Rd, Bethlehem PA 18017 *Web:* www.gardnercryo.com	610-264-4523		763
Gardner Denver Inc 1800 Gardner Expy, Quincy IL 62305 *NYSE:* GDI ■ *Web:* www.gardnerdenver.com	217-222-5400		172
Gardner Denver Nash 1800 Gardner Expy, Quincy IL 62305 *Web:* www.gardnerdenver.com	217-222-5400		172
Gardner Denver Nash LLC Alta Vista Business Park 200 Simko Blvd, Charleroi PA 15022 *Web:* www.gdnash.com	724-239-1500		172
Gardner Denver Thomas - Products Div 1419 Illinois Ave, Sheboygan WI 53081 *Web:* www.gd-thomas.com	920-457-4891		641
Gardner Denver Water Jetting Systems Inc 12300 N Houston Rosslyn, Houston TX 77086 *Web:* www.gardnerdenver.com	281-448-5800		172
Gardner Glass Products Inc 301 Elkin Hwy PO Box 1570, North Wilkesboro NC 28659 *TF:* 800-334-7267 ■ *Web:* www.gardnerglass.com	800-334-7267		334
Gardner Hotel 311 E Franklin Ave, El Paso TX 79901 *TF:* 800-891-7022 ■ *Web:* www.gardnerhotel.com	915-532-3661		379
Gardner Inc 3641 Interchange Rd, Columbus OH 43204 *TF:* 800-848-8946 ■ *Web:* www.gardnerinc.com	614-456-4000	456-4001	274
Gardner James Nakken Hugo & Nolan 429 First St, Woodland CA 95695 *Web:* yololaw.com	530-662-7367		428
Gardner Linn Burkhart & Flory Llp 2851 Charlevoix Dr SE Ste 207, Grand Rapids MI 49546 *TF:* 800-208-6315 ■ *Web:* vglb.com	616-975-5500		445
Gardner Manufacturing Inc 1201 West Lake St, Horicon WI 53032 *Web:* www.gardnermfg.com	920-485-4303		198
Gardner Mattress Corp 254 Canal St, Salem MA 01970 *Web:* www.gardnermattress.com	978-341-4780		321
Gardner Publications Inc 6915 Valley Ave, Cincinnati OH 45244 *TF:* 800-950-8020 ■ *Web:* www.gardnerweb.com	513-527-8800	527-8801	637-9
Gardner Rich & Co 401 S Financial Pl, Chicago IL 60605	312-922-3333		690
Gardner Village 1100 W 7800 S, West Jordan UT 84088 *TF:* 800-662-4335 ■ *Web:* www.gardnervillage.com	801-566-8903		460
Gardner White Furniture Company Inc 21001 Groesbeck Hwy, Warren MI 48089 *Web:* www.gardner-white.com	586-774-8853		321
Gardner's Seafood & Pasta 111 Thurston Ave NW, Olympia WA 98501 *Web:* gardnersrestaurant.com	360-786-8466		671
Gardner-Gibson PO Box 5449, Tampa FL 33675 *TF:* 800-237-1155 ■ *Web:* www.gardner-gibson.com	813-248-2101	248-6768	46
Gardners Candies Inc 2600 Adams Ave PO Box E, Tyrone PA 16686 *TF:* 800-242-2639 ■ *Web:* www.gardnerscandies.com	814-684-3925	684-3928	123
Gardner-Webb University PO Box 817, Boiling Springs NC 28017 **Fax:* Admissions ■ *TF:* 800-253-6472 ■ *Web:* www.gardner-webb.edu	704-406-4498	406-4488*	166
Gardner-Webb University M Christopher White School of Divinity 110 S Main St PO Box 997, Boiling Springs NC 28017 *Web:* gardner-webb.edu	704-406-4000		167-3
Gardner-Zemke Company Inc 6821 Academy Parkway NE, Albuquerque NM 87109 *Web:* gardnerzemke.com	505-881-0555	884-2191	189-4
Garduno's 10031 Coors Blvd NW, Albuquerque NM 87114 *Web:* www.gardunosrestaurants.com	505-890-7000		670
Gare Inc 165 Rosemont St, Haverhill MA 01832 **Fax Area Code:* 800 ■ *TF:* 888-289-4273 ■ *Web:* www.gare.com	978-373-9131	292-0885*	43
Gared Sports Inc 707 N Second St Ste 202, Saint Louis MO 63102 *TF:* 800-325-2682 ■ *Web:* www.garedsports.com	314-421-0044	421-6014	710
Garelick Manufacturing Co 644 Second St, Saint Paul Park MN 55071 *Web:* www.garelick.com	651-459-9795		350
Garfield County 250 S 8th PO Box 218, Burwell NE 68823 *Web:* www.garfieldcounty.ne.gov	308-346-4161		338
Garfield County 114 W Broadway Rm 106, Enid OK 73701 *Web:* www.qpublic.net	580-237-0220	249-5989	338
Garfield County 108 Eigth St, Glenwood Springs CO 81601 *TF:* 800-423-1108 ■ *Web:* www.garfield-county.com	970-945-2377	947-1078	338
Garfield County PO Box 370, Jordan MT 59337 *Web:* www.garfieldcounty.com	406-557-6178		338
Garfield County 375 N 700 W, Panguitch UT 84759 *TF:* 800-844-6591 ■ *Web:* gcutsheriff.com	435-676-2678		338
Garfield County 789 Main St PO Box 915, Pomeroy WA 99347 *Web:* www.co.garfield.wa.us	509-843-3731		338
Garfield Elementary School 1514 S Ninth Ave, Maywood IL 60153 *Web:* www.maywood89.org	708-450-2009		685
Garfield Free Public Library 500 Midland Ave, Garfield NJ 07026 *Web:* www.bccls.org	973-478-3800	478-7162	434-3
Garfield Heights Chamber of Commerce 5522 Turney Rd, Garfield Heights OH 44125 *Web:* www.garfieldchamber.com	216-475-7775		139
Garfield Industries 62 Clinton Rd, Fairfield NJ 07004 *Web:* garfieldbuff.com	973-575-8800	575-6840	1
Garfield Medical Ctr 525 N Garfield Ave, Monterey Park CA 91754 *TF:* 800-742-7343 ■ *Web:* www.garfieldmedicalcenter.com	626-573-2222	571-8972	374-3
Garfield Park Conservatory 300 N Central Pk Ave, Chicago IL 60624 *Web:* www.garfield-conservatory.org	312-746-5100		97
Garfield Park Library 705 Woodrow Ave, Santa Cruz CA 95060 *Web:* www.santacruzpl.org	831-427-7713		434-3

Phone | Fax | Class

Garfield Refining Co
810 East Cayuga St ... Philadelphia PA 19124 800-523-0968 410
TF: 800-523-0968 ■ *Web:* www.garfieldrefining.com

Garfield Suites Hotel
2 Garfield Pl ... Cincinnati OH 45202 513-421-3355 379

Garfunkel Wild & Travis PC
111 Great Neck Rd Ste 503 ... Great Neck NY 11021 516-393-2200 428
TF: 800-973-0424 ■ *Web:* www.garfunkelwild.com

Garganigo, Goldsmith & Weiss
14 Penn Plaza Ste 1020 ... New York NY 10122 212-643-6400 428
Web: www.ggw.com

Gargiulo Inc 15000 Old 41 N ... Naples FL 34110 239-597-3131 194
Web: www.gargiulo.com

Gargoyles Inc
500 George Washington Hwy ... Smithfield RI 02917 401-231-3800 542
TF: 866-807-0195 ■ *Web:* gargoyleseyewear.com

Gari Melchers Home and Studio
224 Washington St ... Fredericksburg VA 22405 540-654-1015 654-1785 97
Web: garimelchers.umw.edu

Garibaldi Cafe 315 W Congress St ... Savannah GA 31401 912-232-7118 671
Web: garibaldisavannah.com

Garibaldi's 307 N Carson St ... Carson City NV 89701 775-884-4574 671
Web: garibaldisristoranteitaliano.com

Garibaldis 347 Presidio Ave ... San Francisco CA 94115 415-563-8841 671
Web: www.hurleyhafen.com

Garick Corp 13600 Broadway Ave ... Cleveland OH 44125 216-581-0100 820
Web: www.garick.com

Garing Taylor & Assoc Inc
141 S Elm St ... Arroyo Grande CA 93420 805-489-1321 261

Garkane Energy Co-op Inc
120 W 300 S PO Box 465 ... Loa UT 84747 435-836-2795 836-2497 245
TF: 800-747-5403 ■ *Web:* www.garkaneenergy.com

Gar-Kenyon Technologies
106 Evansville Ave PO Box 559 ... Meriden CT 06451 203-729-4900 729-4950 790
Web: www.garkenyon.com

Garland & Mason LLC
Manalapan Corporate Plaza 195 Rt 9 S ... Manalapan NJ 07726 732-358-2028 358-2029 428
TF: 800-922-1233 ■ *Web:* www.kmrslaw.com

Garland C Norris Co 1101 Terry Rd ... Apex NC 27502 919-387-1059 387-1325 559
TF: 800-331-8920 ■ *Web:* www.gcnorris.com

Garland Chamber of Commerce
520 N Glenbrook Dr ... Garland TX 75040 972-272-7551 276-9261 139
Web: www.garlandchamber.com

Garland City Hall 200 N Fifth St ... Garland TX 75040 972-205-2000 205-2504 337
Web: www.ci.garland.tx.us

Garland Civic Theatre
2703 National Pl ... Garland TX 75040 972-485-8884 573-4
Web: www.garlandcivictheatre.org

Garland Commercial Industries
185 S St ... Freeland PA 18224 570-636-1000 624-0218* 298
**Fax Area Code:* 800 ■ *TF:* 800-424-2411 ■ *Web:* www.garland-group.com

Garland Company Inc 3800 E 91st St ... Cleveland OH 44105 216-641-7500 641-0633 46
TF: 800-321-9336 ■ *Web:* www.garlandco.com

Garland County 501 Ouachita Ave ... Hot Springs AR 71901 501-622-3610 624-0665 338
TF: 800-482-5964 ■ *Web:* www.garlandcounty.org

Garland Independent School District (GISD)
501 S Jupiter PO Box 469026 ... Garland TX 75046 972-494-8201 485-4936 685
TF: 800-252-5555 ■ *Web:* www.garlandisd.net

Garland Landmark Museum
200 Museum Plaza Dr ... Garland TX 75040 972-205-2749 520
Web: garlandhistorical.org

Garland Light & Power Co 755 Hwy 14A ... Powell WY 82435 307-754-2881 245
Web: garlandpower.org

Garland Power & Light PO Box 469002 ... Garland TX 75046 972-205-2650 41
Web: www.gpltexas.org

Garland Resort 4700 N Red Oak Rd ... Lewiston MI 49756 989-786-2211 669
TF: 877-442-7526 ■ *Web:* www.garlandusa.com

Garland Sales Inc PO Box 1870 ... Dalton GA 30720 706-278-7880 131
TF: 800-524-0361 ■ *Web:* www.garlandrug.com

Garland, The
4222 Vineland Ave ... North Hollywood CA 91602 818-980-8000 766-0112 379
TF: 800-238-3759 ■ *Web:* www.thegarland.com

Garlic Bros 6629 Embarcadero Dr ... Stockton CA 95219 209-474-6585 671
Web: garlicbrothersonline.com

Garlich Printing Co 525 Rudder Rd ... Fenton MO 63026 636-349-8000 626
TF: 800-276-2622 ■ *Web:* www.garlich.com

Garling Construction Inc
1120 11th St ... Belle Plaine IA 52208 319-444-3409 444-2437 186
Web: www.garlingconstruction.com

Garlington Landeweer Marine Inc
3370 SE Slater St ... Stuart FL 34997 772-283-7124 90
Web: www.garlingtonyachts.com

Garlington Lohn Robinson PLLP
350 Ryman St ... Missoula MT 59802 406-523-2500 445
TF: 800-683-4281 ■ *Web:* www.garlington.com

Garlin-Neumann Leathers Company Inc
66-D River Rd ... Hudson NH 03051 603-595-6319 881-9431 431
Web: leatherusa.com

Garlock Bearings Inc
700 Mid Atlantic Pkwy ... West Deptford NJ 08066 856-848-3201 75

Garlock Equipment Co
2601 Niagara Ln N ... Plymouth MN 55447 763-694-2624 190
Web: www.garlockequip.com

Garlock Printing & Converting Corp
164 Fredette St ... Gardner MA 01440 978-630-1028 627
TF: 800-473-1328 ■ *Web:* garlockprinting.com

Garment Graphics LLC
220 W Ft Lowell Rd ... Tucson AZ 85705 520-544-0529 687
Web: www.garmentgraphics.net

Garmin Ltd 1200 E 151st St ... Olathe KS 66062 913-397-8200 397-8282 529
NASDAQ: GRMN ■ *TF:* 888-442-7646 ■ *Web:* www.garmin.com

Garms Group, The 553 N Ave Ste 250 ... Barrington IL 60010 847-382-7200 260
TF: 800-446-3037 ■ *Web:* garms.com

Garner 825 E Cooley Ave ... San Bernardino CA 92408 909-799-3030 385
TF: 800-282-9120 ■ *Web:* www.garnerholt.com

Garner Correctional Institution
50 Nunnawauk Rd ... Newtown CT 06470 203-270-2800 213
Web: ct.gov

Garner Environmental Services Inc
1717 W 13th St ... Deer Park TX 77536 281-930-1200 667
Web: www.garner-es.com

Garner Industries Inc
7201 N 98th St PO Box 29709 ... Lincoln NE 68507 402-434-9100 434-9133 608
TF: 800-228-0275 ■ *Web:* www.garnerindustries.com

Garner Printing Co
1697 NE 53rd Ave ... Des Moines IA 50313 515-266-2171 627
TF: 800-747-2171 ■ *Web:* www.garnerprint.com

Garnet A Wilson Public Library of Pike County
207 N Market St ... Waverly OH 45690 740-947-4921 947-2918 434-3
Web: www.pike.lib.oh.us

Garnet Hill Inc 231 Main St ... Franconia NH 03580 603-823-5545 842-9696* 745-1
**Fax Area Code:* 888 ■ *TF:* 800-870-3513 ■ *Web:* www.garnethill.com

Garnett & Helfrich Capital
1200 Park Pl Ste 330 ... San Mateo CA 94403 650-234-4200 194
Web: www.garnetthelfrich.com

Garnett State Savings Bank
106 E Fifth St PO Box 329 ... Garnett KS 66032 785-448-3111 70
Web: www.gssb.us.com

Garney Cos Inc 1333 NW Vivion Rd ... Kansas City MO 64118 816-741-4600 741-4488 188-10
TF: 800-832-1517 ■ *Web:* www.garney.com

Garozzo's 526 Harrison St ... Kansas City MO 64106 816-221-2455 671
Web: www.garozzos.com

Garozzo's 9950 College Blvd ... Overland Park KS 66210 913-491-8300 671
Web: www.garozzos.com

GARP Research 406 Main St ... Reisterstown MD 21136 410-764-1300 401
Web: www.garpresearch.com

Garr Tool Co 7800 N Alger Rd ... Alma MI 48801 989-463-6171 463-3609 493
TF: 800-248-9003 ■ *Web:* www.garrtool.com

Garrard County 15 Public Sq ... Lancaster KY 40444 859-792-3531 792-2010 338
Web: garrardcounty.us

Garrett & Tully A Professional Corp
225 S Lake Ave Ste 1400 ... Pasadena CA 91101 626-577-9500 428
Web: www.garrett-tully.com

Garrett College 687 Mosser Rd ... McHenry MD 21541 301-387-3000 387-3038* 162
**Fax:* Admissions ■ *TF:* 866-554-2773 ■ *Web:* www.garrettcollege.edu

Garrett County 203 S Fourth St Rm 207 ... Oakland MD 21550 301-334-8970 334-5000 338
Web: www.garrettcounty.org

Garrett County Chamber of Commerce
15 Visitors Ctr Dr ... McHenry MD 21541 301-387-4386 387-2080 139
TF: 888-387-5237 ■ *Web:* www.visitdeepcreek.com

Garrett Metal Detectors
1881 W State St ... Garland TX 75042 972-494-6151 494-1881 472
TF: 800-234-6151 ■ *Web:* www.garrett.com

Garrett Nagle & Company Inc
300 Unicorn Park Dr 3rd Fl ... Woburn MA 01801 617-737-9090 528
Web: www.garrettnagle.com

Garrett Printing & Graphics Inc
331 Riverside Ave ... Bristol CT 06010 860-589-6710 627
Web: www.garrettprinting.us

Garrett State Forest
1431 Potomac Camp Rd ... Oakland MD 21550 301-334-2038 565
Web: dnr.maryland.gov/Pages/default.aspx

Garrett Thomas (Rep R - VA)
415 Cannon HOB ... Washington DC 20515 202-225-4711 225-5681 342-2
Web: tomgarrett.house.gov

Garrett's Cafe 1631 N Bell School Rd ... Rockford IL 61107 815-484-9473 671
Web: www.garrettsrestaurantbar.com

Garrett's Desert Inn
311 Old Santa Fe Trl ... Santa Fe NM 87501 505-982-1851 989-1647 379
TF: 800-888-2145 ■ *Web:* www.garrettsdesertinn.com

Garrigan Lyman Group Inc, The
1524 Fifth Ave Ste 400 ... Seattle WA 98101 206-223-5548 7
TF: 800-332-1736 ■ *Web:* www.glg.com

Garrison Forest School
300 Garrison Forest Rd ... Owings Mills MD 21117 410-363-1500 622
Web: www.gfs.org

Garrison Investment Group LP
1290 Ave of the Americas Ste 914 ... New York NY 10104 212-372-9500 401
Web: www.garrisoninv.com

Garrison-Ross Agency Inc
602 W Flint PO Box 18 ... Davison MI 48423 810-653-2101 390
Web: www.garrisonross.com

Garrity Print Solutions
109 Research Dr ... Harahan LA 70123 504-733-9654 627
TF: 877-568-1555 ■ *Web:* www.garritysolutions.com

Garrott Bros Continous Mix Inc
PO Box 419 ... Gallatin TN 37066 615-452-2385 182
Web: www.garrottbros.com

Garry Packing Inc 11272 E Central Ave ... Del Rey CA 93616 559-888-2126 296-18
TF: 800-248-2126 ■ *Web:* www.garryscs.com

Garsite LLC 539 S Tenth St ... Kansas City KS 66105 913-342-5600 342-0638 21
TF: 888-427-7483 ■ *Web:* www.garsite.com

Garston Sign & Screen Printing
570 Tolland St ... East Hartford CT 06108 860-289-3040 492
Web: www.garston.com

Gart Cos Inc, The
299 Milwaukee St Ste 500 ... Denver CO 80206 303-333-1933 652
Web: www.gartcompanies.com

Gartech Enterprises Inc
3037 W State Rd 256 ... Austin IN 47102 812-794-4796 256
Web: gartechenterprises.com

Gartenhaus Furs 7101 Wisconsin Ave ... Bethesda MD 20814 301-656-2800 157-6
Web: www.fursbygartenhaus.com

Garth Fagan Dance 50 Chestnut St ... Rochester NY 14604 585-454-3260 573-1
Web: www.garthfagandance.org

Gartland & Mellina Group Corp
1385 Broadway Ste 912 ... New York NY 10018 212-418-4780 463
Web: www.gartlandandmellina.com

Gartland Foundry Company Inc
330 Grant St ... Terre Haute IN 47802 812-232-0226 232-7569 307
Web: www.gartlandfoundry.com

Gartner Inc 56 Top Gallant Rd ... Stamford CT 06902 203-964-0096 316-6300 466
NYSE: IT ■ *TF:* 866-471-2526 ■ *Web:* www.gartner.com

Gartner Studios Inc
220 Myrtle St E ... Stillwater MN 55082 651-351-7700 590
Web: www.gartnerstudios.com

Phone | Fax | Class

Garton Tractor Inc
2400 N Golden State Blvd. Turlock CA 95382 209-632-3931 632-8006 274
TF: 877-872-2767 ■ *Web:* gartontractor.com

Garvan Woodland Gardens
550 Arkridge Rd PO Box 22240 Hot Springs AR 71903 501-262-9300 262-9301 97
TF: 800-366-4664 ■ *Web:* www.garvangardens.org

Garver Engineers
4701 Northshore Dr North Little Rock AR 72118 501-376-3633 261
Web: www.garverusa.com

Garvey Corp 208 S Rt 73 Blue Anchor NJ 08037 609-561-2450 561-2328 207
TF: 800-257-8581 ■ *Web:* www.garvey.com

Garvey Group LLC, The 7400 N Lehigh Ave Niles IL 60714 847-647-1900 787
Web: www.thegarveygroup.com

Garvey Wholesale Beverage Inc
2542 San Gabriel Blvd Rosemead CA 91770 626-280-5244 80-3
TF: 800-287-2075 ■ *Web:* garveywholesalebeverage.com

Garvin & Hickey LLC
181 E Livingston Ave Columbus OH 43215 614-225-9000 428
TF: 800-543-5589 ■ *Web:* garvin-hickey.com

Garvin County 201 W Grant St Pauls Valley OK 73075 405-238-2772 338
TF: 800-231-8668 ■ *Web:* okcountyrecords.com

Garvin Industries Inc
3700 Sandra St Franklin Park IL 60131 847-455-0188 488
Web: www.garvinindustries.com

Garvin-Allen Solutions Ltd
Unit 12 155 Chain Lake Dr Halifax NS B3S1B3 902-453-3554 180
TF: 877-325-9062 ■ *Web:* www.garvin-allen.com

Gary & Leos Inc 730 First St Havre MT 59501 406-265-1404 345
Web: garyandleos.com

Gary A Halpert CPA
20335 Ventura Blvd Ste 400 Woodland Hills CA 91364 818-715-9081 2

Gary Chamber of Commerce
839 Broadway Ste S103 Gary IN 46402 219-885-7407 139
Web: www.garychamber.com

Gary d Mccallister & Associates LLC
120 N La Salle St Ste 2800 Chicago IL 60602 312-345-0611 428
Web: www.mccallisterlawgroup.com

Gary Doupnik Manufacturing Inc
3237 Rippey Rd Loomis CA 95650 916-652-9291 106

Gary Draper & Associates of Atlanta Inc
5665 New Northside Dr NW Ste 100 Atlanta GA 30328 404-256-3601 361
Web: www.draperandassociates.com

Gary Jet Center Inc 5401 Industrial Hwy Gary IN 46406 219-944-1210 316
Web: www.garyjetcenter.com

Gary K Walch
23801 Calabasas Rd Ste 1019 Calabasas CA 91302 818-222-3400 428
Web: www.walchlaw.com

Gary L Schutz PC 900 NW Joy Ave Portland OR 97229 503-520-1120 2

Gary Mathews Motors Inc
1100 Ashland City Rd Clarksville TN 37040 931-552-7100 516
Web: www.garymathewsmotors.com

Gary Merlino Construction Co
9125 Tenth Ave S Seattle WA 98108 206-762-9125 763-4178 183

Gary Plastic Packaging Corp
1340 Viele Ave Bronx NY 10474 718-893-2200 378-2141 600
TF: 800-221-8150 ■ *Web:* www.plasticboxes.com

Gary Pools Inc 438 Sandau Rd San Antonio TX 78216 210-341-5153 341-5154 728
Web: www.garypools.com

Gary Public Library 220 W Fifth Ave Gary IN 46402 219-886-2484 886-6829 434-3
Web: www.garypubliclibrary.org

Gary Public Transportation Corp
2101 W 35th Ave Gary IN 46408 219-884-6100 108
Web: www.gptcbus.com

Gary Raub Assoc
4345 Murphy Canyon Rd San Diego CA 92123 858-565-2775 393

Gary Soren Smith Ctr for the Fine & Performing Arts
Ohlone College 43600 Mission Blvd Fremont CA 94539 510-659-6031 659-6188 572
TF: 800-309-2131 ■ *Web:* www.ohlone.edu/org/smithcenter

Gary Stock Co 7 Sutton Pl Brewster NY 10509 914-276-2700 7
Web: www.gstockco.com

Gary's House 97 State St Portland ME 04101 207-535-1320 372

Gary's Wine & Marketplace 121 Main St Madison NJ 07940 973-822-0200 443
Web: www.garyswine.com

Garza County PO Box 366 Post TX 79356 806-495-4430 495-4431 338
Web: www.garzacounty.net

Garza Creative Group PO Box 190595 Dallas TX 75219 214-720-3888 4
Web: www.garzacommunications.com

Garza Enterprises Inc
840 W Rhapsody Dr San Antonio TX 78216 210-377-3500 179
Web: www.costx.com

GAS (Glass Art Society)
6512 23rd Ave NW Ste 329 Seattle WA 98117 206-382-1305 382-2630 48-4
TF: 800-636-2377 ■ *Web:* www.glassart.org

Gas 'n' Shop Inc 701 Marina Bay Pl Lincoln NE 68528 402-475-1101 475-0976 324
Web: gitnsplit.com

Gas Co, The 515 Kamake'e St Honolulu HI 96814 808-535-5933 535-5934 787
TF: 866-499-3941 ■ *Web:* www.hawaiigas.com

Gas Daily 1200 G St NW Ste 1000 Washington DC 20005 202-383-2000 383-2024 531-5
TF: 800-752-8878 ■ *Web:* www.platts.com/products/gasdaily

Gas Depot Oil Company Inc
8700 N Waukegan Rd Ste 200 Morton Grove IL 60053 847-581-0303 324
Web: www.gasdepot.com

Gas Equipment Company Inc
11616 Harry Hines Blvd Dallas TX 75229 972-241-2333 620-1403 385
TF: 800-821-1829 ■ *Web:* www.gasequipment.com

Gas Field Specialists Inc
2107 SR- 44 S Shinglehouse PA 16748 814-698-2122 698-2124 539
Web: www.gfsinc.net

Gas Inc 77 Jefferson Pkwy Newnan GA 30263 770-502-8800 316
Web: www.gasinc.net

Gas Liquids Engineering Ltd
2749-39th Ave NE Ste 300 Calgary AB T1Y4T8 403-250-2950 539
Web: www.gasliquids.com

Gas Processors Assn (GPA) 6526 E 60th St Tulsa OK 74145 918-493-3872 493-3875 48-12
Web: www.gpaglobal.org

Gas Processors Suppliers Assn (GPSA)
6526 E 60th St Tulsa OK 74145 918-493-3872 48-12
Web: www.gpaglobal.org

Gas Technology Energy Concepts LLC
401 William L Gaiter Pkwy Ste 4 Buffalo NY 14215 800-451-8294 172
TF: 800-451-8294 ■ *Web:* www.gas-tec.com

Gas Technology Institute (GTI)
1700 S Mt Prospect Rd Des Plaines IL 60018 847-768-0500 768-0501 668
Web: www.gastechnology.org

Gas Transmission-Northwest
1400 SW Fifth Ave Ste 900 Portland OR 97201 888-750-6275 325
TF: 888-750-6275 ■ *Web:* www.gastransmissionnw.com

Gas Turbine Controls Corp
6 Skyline Dr Hawthorne NY 10532 914-693-0830 693-3824 362
Web: www.gasturbinecontrols.com

Gas Unlimited
15999 City Walk Ste 200 Sugar Land TX 77479 281-295-5600 256
Web: www.gasunlim.com

GasAmerica Services Inc
2700 W Main St Greenfield IN 46140 317-468-2515 864-3091* 324
**Fax Area Code:* 937 ■ *TF:* 800-643-1948 ■ *Web:* www.speedway.com

Gasbarre Products Inc 590 Division St Dubois PA 15801 814-371-3015 697
Web: www.gasbarre.com

Gasboy International Inc
7300 W Friendly Ave Greensboro NC 27420 336-547-5000 444-5569* 639
**Fax Area Code:* 800 ■ **Fax:* Cust Svc ■ *TF Sales:* 800-444-5579 ■ *Web:* www.gasboy.com

Gasch Printing LLC 1780 Crossroads Dr Odenton MD 21113 301-362-0700 627
TF: 800-634-3475 ■ *Web:* www.gaschprinting.com

Gasconade County 119 E First St Rm 23 Hermann MO 65041 573-486-3100 486-3693 338
TF: 800-392-1261 ■ *Web:* www.gasconadecountyassessor.com

Gascosage Electric Co-op
803 S Hwy 28 PO Box G Dixon MO 65459 573-759-7146 759-6020 245
TF: 866-568-8243 ■ *Web:* www.gascosage.com

Gas-Fired Products Inc
305 Doggett St Charlotte NC 28203 704-372-3485 332-5843 318
TF: 800-830-3983 ■ *Web:* www.gasfiredproducts.com

Gaska-Tape Inc 1810 W Lusher Ave Elkhart IN 46517 574-294-5431 293-4504 732
TF: 800-423-1571 ■ *Web:* www.gaska.com

Gasket & Seal Fabricators Inc
1640 Sauget Industrial Pkwy Sauget IL 62206 618-332-0425 326
Web: www.gasketandseal.com

Gasket Engineering Company Inc
4500 E 75th Terr Kansas City MO 64132 816-363-8333 363-3558 326
Web: www.gasketeng.com

Gasket Manufacturing Co 18001 Main St Gardena CA 90248 310-217-5600 217-5608 326
TF: 800-442-7538 ■ *Web:* www.gasketmfg.com

Gaskets Inc 301 W Hwy 16 Rio WI 53960 920-992-3137 992-3124 326
TF: 800-558-1833 ■ *Web:* www.gasketsinc.com

Gaskins Surveying Company Inc
1266 Powder Springs Rd Marietta GA 30064 770-424-7168 261
Web: www.gscsurvey.com

Gaslamp Plaza Suites 520 E St San Diego CA 92101 619-232-9500 238-9945 379
Web: www.gaslampplaza.com

Gaslamp Quarter Assn
614 Fifth Ave Ste E San Diego CA 92101 619-233-5227 233-4693 50-6
Web: www.gaslamp.org

Gaslight Media 120 E Lake St Petoskey MI 49770 231-487-0692 180
Web: gaslightmedia.com

Gasoline Alley
870 N Cleveland Massillon Rd Akron OH 44333 330-666-2670 671
Web: gasolinealleyinbath.com

Gaspard Inc 200 N Janacek Rd Brookfield WI 53045 262-784-6800 784-7567 155-14
TF: 800-784-6868 ■ *Web:* www.gaspardinc.com

Gasparilla Island State Park
880 Belche Rd Boca Grande FL 33921 941-964-0375 565
Web: www.floridastateparks.org/gasparillaisland

GasPedal LLC 333 W N Ave Ste 500 Chicago IL 60610 312-932-9000 195
TF: 800-716-4408 ■ *Web:* www.gaspedal.com

Gassaway Mansion 106 Dupont Dr Greenville SC 29607 864-271-0188 242-9935 50-3
TF: 888-912-7469 ■ *Web:* www.gassawaymansion.com

Gassco 7515 Lindsay Rd Bakersfield CA 93313 661-832-7406 832-9795 579
TF: 800-390-7837 ■ *Web:* gasscoinc.com

Gasser & Sons Inc 440 Moreland Rd Commack NY 11725 631-543-6600 543-6649 488
Web: www.gasser.com

Gast Mfg Inc
2300 M-139 Hwy PO Box 97 Benton Harbor MI 49023 269-926-6171 925-8288 172
Web: www.gastmfg.com

Gastar Exploration Ltd
1331 Lamar St Ste 1080 Houston TX 77010 713-739-1800 739-0458 536
NYSE: GST ■ *Web:* www.gastar.com

Gasthaus Gutenberger
2583 Portage Ave Winnipeg MB R3J0P5 204-888-3133 671
Web: www.gasthausgutenberger.com

Gaston Chamber of Commerce
601 W Franklin Blvd Gastonia NC 28052 704-864-2621 854-8723 139
TF: 800-933-3909 ■ *Web:* www.gastonchamber.com

Gaston College 201 Hwy 321-S Dallas NC 28034 704-922-6200 922-2344* 162
**Fax:* Admissions ■ *TF:* 800-634-7854 ■ *Web:* gaston.edu

Gaston Correctional Ctr 520 Justice Ct Dallas NC 28034 704-922-3861 213
Web: www.doc.state.nc.us

Gaston County
128 W Main Ave PO Box 1578 Gastonia NC 28053 704-866-3111 866-3147 338
Web: www.gastongov.com

Gaston County Dyeing Machine Co
PO Box 308 Stanley NC 28164 704-822-5000 822-0753 744
Web: www.gaston-county.com

Gaston County Family Ymca
3210 Union Rd Gastonia NC 28056 704-865-2193 354
Web: www.gastonymca.org

Gaston County Public Library
1555 E Garrison Blvd Gastonia NC 28054 704-868-2164 853-0609 434-3
Web: gastonlibrary.org

Gaston County School
943 Osceola St PO Box 1397 Gastonia NC 28053 704-866-6117 685
Web: www.gaston.k12.nc.us

Gaston County Travel & Tourism
620 N Main St Belmont NC 28012 704-825-4044 206
TF: 800-849-9994 ■ *Web:* www.gastongov.com

Gaston Gazette 1893 Remount Rd Gastonia NC 28054 704-869-1700 867-5751 532-2
TF: 800-273-3315 ■ *Web:* www.gastongazette.com

	Phone	Fax	Class
Gaston's White River Resort 1777 River Rd. Lakeview AR 72642 *Web:* www.gastons.com	870-431-5202		669
Gastonian, The 220 E Gaston St. Savannah GA 31401 *TF:* 800-322-6603 ■ *Web:* www.gastonian.com	912-232-2869	232-0710	379
Gastronomy Inc 48 W Market St Ste 250. Salt Lake City UT 84101 *Web:* marketstreetgrill.com	801-322-2020	363-5275	670
Gatan Inc 5794 W Las Positas Blvd. Pleasanton CA 94588 *TF:* 888-887-3377 ■ *Web:* www.gatan.com	925-463-0200		419
Gatco Inc 1550 Factor Ave. San Leandro CA 94577 *TF:* 800-227-5640 ■ *Web:* www.gatco-inc.com	510-352-8770		787
Gate Petroleum Co 9540 San Jose Blvd PO Box 23627. Jacksonville FL 32241 *TF:* 866-571-1982 ■ *Web:* www.gatepetro.com	904-737-7220	732-7660	324
Gate6 Inc 16624 N 90th Ste 111. Phoenix AZ 85260 *Web:* www.gate6.com	623-572-7725		5
Gatehouse Group Inc, The 120 Forbes Blvd Ste 180. Mansfield MA 02048 *Web:* www.gatehousemgt.com	508-337-2500		653
GateHouse Media Inc 350 Willowbrook Office Pk. Fairport NY 14450 *NYSE: GHSE* ■ *TF:* 800-544-9218 ■ *Web:* www.gatehousemedia.com	585-598-0030	248-2631	637-8
Gatekeeper Systems Inc 8 Studebaker. Irvine CA 92618 *TF:* 888-808-9433 ■ *Web:* www.gatekeepersystems.com	949-453-1940	453-8148	199
Gates Albert Inc 3434 Union St. North Chili NY 14514 *TF:* 800-937-9311 ■ *Web:* www.gatesalbert.com	585-594-9401	594-4305	621
Gates Bar-B-Q 10440 E US Hwy 40. Independence MO 64055 *Web:* www.gatesbbq.com	816-353-5880		671
Gates Bar-B-Q 4621 Paseo Blvd. Kansas City MO 64110 *TF:* 800-662-7427 ■ *Web:* www.gatesbbq.com	816-923-0900		670
Gates Bar-B-Que 1026 State Ave. Kansas City KS 66102 *Web:* www.gatesbbq.com	913-621-1134		671
Gates Business Solutions LLC 2418 Crossroads Dr Ste 3000. Madison WI 53718	608-661-0810		177
Gates Capital Management Inc 1177 Ave of the Americas between 45th and 46th Sts 46th Fl. New York NY 10036 *Web:* www.gatescap.com	212-626-1421		401
Gates Corp 1551 Wewatta St. Denver CO 80202 *TF:* 800-709-6001 ■ *Web:* www.gates.com	303-744-1911	744-4000	370
Gates County 200 Court St. Gatesville NC 27938 **Fax:* Financial ■ *TF:* 800-272-9829 ■ *Web:* www.gatescounty.govoffice2.com	252-357-2411	357-0073*	338
Gates Family Foundation 1390 Lawrence St. Denver CO 80204 *TF:* 866-590-4377 ■ *Web:* www.gatesfamilyfoundation.org	303-722-1881	316-3038	305
Gates of the Arctic National Park & Preserve 4175 Geist Rd. Fairbanks AK 99709 *TF:* 866-869-6887 ■ *Web:* www.nps.gov/gaar	907-457-5752	455-0601	564
Gates Public Library 1605 Buffalo Rd. Rochester NY 14624 *Web:* www.gateslibrary.org	585-247-6446	426-5733	434-3
Gates, O'Doherty, Gonter & Guy LLP 15373 Innovation Dr Ste 170. San Diego CA 92128 *Web:* gogglaw.com	949-769-2481		428
Gatesworth at One Mcknight Place, The 1 Mcknight Pl. Saint Louis MO 63124 *Web:* thegatesworth.com	314-993-0111		371
Gateway Arch 50 S Leonor K Sullivan Blvd. Saint Louis MO 63102 *TF:* 877-982-1410 ■ *Web:* www.gatewayarch.com	877-982-1410		50-4
Gateway Clipper Fleet 350 W Stn Sq Dr. Pittsburgh PA 15219 *Web:* www.gatewayclipper.com	412-355-7980	355-7987	221
Gateway Communications Services 220 Log Canoe Cir. Stevensville MD 21666 *Web:* www.gatewaycsi.com	410-670-4399		194
Gateway Community & Technical College (GCTC) 1025 Amsterdam Rd. Covington KY 41011 *TF:* 855-346-4282 ■ *Web:* www.gateway.kctcs.edu	859-441-4500		800
GateWay Community College 108 N 40th St. Phoenix AZ 85034 *TF:* 888-994-4433 ■ *Web:* www.gatewaycc.edu	602-286-8000	286-8072	162
Gateway Community College 60 Sargent Dr. New Haven CT 06510 **Fax:* Admissions ■ *TF:* 800-390-7723 ■ *Web:* www.gatewayct.edu	203-285-2000	285-2260*	162
Gateway Ctr 1 Gateway Dr. Collinsville IL 62234 *TF:* 800-289-2388 ■ *Web:* gatewaycenter.com	618-345-8998	345-9024	205
Gateway Design Inc 4299 San Felipe St Ste 100. Houston TX 77027	713-572-9600	572-0777	7
Gateway Energy Services Corp 400 Rella Blvd Ste 300. Montebello NY 10901 *TF:* 800-805-8586 ■ *Web:* www.gesc.com	800-805-8586		316
Gateway Foundation Inc 1080 E Pk St. Carbondale IL 62901 *TF:* 877-505-4673 ■ *Web:* www.recovergateway.org	877-505-4673		726
Gateway Group One Inc 604-608 Market St. Newark NJ 07105 *Web:* www.gatewaygroupone.com	973-465-8006		692
Gateway Hospitality LLC 111 Stonemark Ln Ste 202. Columbia SC 29210 *Web:* gatewayhospitality.com	803-798-7979		379
Gateway Inc 7565 Irvine Ctr Dr. Irvine CA 92618 *TF:* 800-846-2000 ■ *Web:* www.gateway.com	949-471-7040		173-2
Gateway Limousines 1550 Gilbreth Rd. Burlingame CA 94010 *TF:* 800-486-7077 ■ *Web:* gatewayglobalsf.com	650-697-5548		441
Gateway Logistics Group Inc, The 18201 Viscount Rd. Houston TX 77032 *TF:* 800-338-8017 ■ *Web:* www.gateway-group.com	281-443-7447		311
Gateway Mortgage Group LLC 244 S Gateway Pl PO Box 974. Jenks OK 74037 *TF:* 877-764-9319 ■ *Web:* www.gatewayloan.com	877-406-8109		217
Gateway National Recreation Area 210 New York Ave. Staten Island NY 10305 *Web:* www.nps.gov/gate	718-354-4606	354-4605	564
Gateway News 1050 W Main St. Kent OH 44240 *TF:* 800-560-9657 ■ *Web:* www.recordpub.com	330-541-9400	296-2698	532-4
Gateway Newspapers 610 Beatty Rd. Monroeville PA 15146 *Web:* triblive.com	412-856-7400		637-8
Gateway Newstands 240 Chrlslea Rd. Woodbridge ON L4L0V1 *TF:* 800-942-5351 ■ *Web:* www.gatewaynewstands.com	905 851 9652		530
Gateway Pacific Contractors Inc 8055 Freeport Blvd. Sacramento CA 95832	916-665-4100		610
Gateway Packaging Co 100 S Fourth St Ste 600. St Louis MO 63102 *Web:* www.gatewaypackaging.com	618-451-0010		548
Gateway Plastics Inc 5650 W County Line Rd. Mequon WI 53092 *Web:* www.gatewayplastics.com	262-242-2020		596
Gateway Products Recycling Inc 4223 E 49th St. Cleveland OH 44125 *Web:* www.gatewayrecycle.com	216-341-8777		638
Gateway Regional Chamber of Commerce 135 Jefferson Ave PO Box 300. Elizabeth NJ 07207 *TF:* 800-424-5430 ■ *Web:* www.gatewaychamber.com	908-352-0900	352-0865	139
Gateway Regional Medical Ctr (GRMC) 2100 Madison Ave. Granite City IL 62040 *TF General:* 800-422-6237 ■ *Web:* www.gatewayregional.net	618-798-3000		374-3
Gateway Shoe Co 910 Kehro Mill Rd Ste 112. Ballwin MO 63011 *TF:* 800-539-6063 ■ *Web:* www.gatewayshoes.com	636-256-7050	527-3797	301
Gateway Supply Company Inc 1312 Hamrick St. Columbia SC 29202 *TF:* 800-922-5312 ■ *Web:* www.gatewaysupply.net	803-771-7160		612
Gateway Technical College 3520 30th Ave. Kenosha WI 53144 *TF:* 800-247-7122 ■ *Web:* www.gtc.edu	262-564-2200	564-2201	800
Gateway to Care 3611 Ennis St. Houston TX 77004 *TF:* 800-272-3900 ■ *Web:* gatewaytocare.org	713-783-4616		363
Gateway Travel Service Inc 28470 W 13 Mile Rd Ste 200. Farmington Hills MI 48334 *TF:* 800-423-4898 ■ *Web:* www.gatewaytrvl.com	248-432-8600		772
Gateway Truck & Refrigeration 921 Fournie Ln. Collinsville IL 62234 *TF:* 800-449-2131 ■ *Web:* www.gipower.com	618-345-0123	242-8420	57
Gateway Unified School Disrict 4411 Mtn Lakes Blvd. Redding CA 96003 *Web:* www.gateway-schools.org	530-245-7900		685
Gateway, The 18 N Rio Grande St. Salt Lake City UT 84101 *Web:* www.shopthegateway.com	801-456-0000	456-0005	50-6
Gateways Inn 51 Walker St. Lenox MA 01240 *TF:* 888-492-9466 ■ *Web:* www.gatewaysinn.com	413-637-2532	637-1432	379
Gatewood Hughey & Company CPA 2000 W First St. Winston-Salem NC 27104	336-724-4446		2
Gator Media Group LLC 40 Fairfield Pl. West Caldwell NJ 07006 *Web:* www.gatormediagroup.com	973-244-5900		627
Gator of Florida Inc 5002 N Howard Ave. Tampa FL 33603 *Web:* gatorofflorida.com	813-877-8267		155-21
Gator Park 24050 SW Eigth St. Miami FL 33194 *TF:* 800-559-2205 ■ *Web:* www.gatorpark.com	305-559-2255		823
Gatorade Sports Science Institute 617 W Main St. Barrington IL 60010 *TF:* 800-616-4774 ■ *Web:* www.gssiweb.org	800-616-4774		668
Gatorland 14501 S Orange Blossom Trl. Orlando FL 32837 *TF:* 800-393-5297 ■ *Web:* www.gatorland.com	407-855-5496		823
Gatorland Toyota-scion 2985 N Main St. Gainesville FL 32609 *Web:* gatorlandtoyota.com	352-376-3262		57
GATRA 2 Oak St. Taunton MA 02780 *TF:* 800-483-2500 ■ *Web:* www.gatra.org	508-823-8828		108
Gatterdam Industrial Services 114 N 30th St. Louisville KY 40212 *Web:* www.gatterdam.com	502-776-3937		454
Gatto's Tires & Auto Service 15 W Hibiscus Blvd. Melbourne FL 32901 *Web:* www.gattos.com	321-727-3322		54
GATX Rail Canada 1801 Magill College Ave. Montreal QC H3A2N4 *Web:* www.cgtx.com	514-931-7343		264-5
Gaucho's Churrascaria 62 Lowell St. Manchester NH 03101 *TF:* 866-669-9460 ■ *Web:* www.gauchosbraziliansteakhouse.com	603-669-9460		671
Gaudenzia 106 W Main St. Norristown PA 19401 *TF:* 800-255-2335 ■ *Web:* www.gaudenzia.org	610-239-9600	239-9195	726
Gauger & Associates 360 Post St Ste 901. San Francisco CA 94108 *Web:* www.gauger-associates.com	415-434-0303		7
Gauley River National Recreation Area 104 Main St PO Box 246. Glen Jean WV 25846 *Web:* www.nps.gov/gari	304-465-0508	465-0591	564
Gauntlett & Associates 18400 Von Karman Ave Ste 300. Irvine CA 92612 *TF:* 800-638-8437 ■ *Web:* www.gauntlettlaw.com	949-553-1010		428
Gausman & Moore Assoc 1700 Hwy 36 W. Roseville MN 55113 *Web:* www.gausman.com	651-639-9606	639-9618	256
Gaussian Inc 340 Quinnipiac St Bldg 40. Wallingford CT 06492 *TF:* 800-536-7386 ■ *Web:* www.gaussian.com	203-284-2501		261
Gauthier Biomedical Inc 2221 Washington St. Grafton WI 53024 *TF:* 800-210-2677 ■ *Web:* www.gauthierbiomedical.com	262-546-0010		476
Gauthier Industries Inc 3105 22nd St NW. Rochester MN 55901 *TF:* 800-568-6601 ■ *Web:* www.gauthind.com	507-289-0731		697
Gavco Plastics 9840 S 219th E Ave. Broken Arrow OK 74014 *Web:* www.gavcoplastics.com	918-455-7888		608
Gavel International Corp 935 Lakeview Pkwy Ste 190. Vernon Hills IL 60061 *TF:* 800-544-2835 ■ *Web:* www.gavelintl.com	800-544-2835		184
Gaver Technologies Inc 340 W Patrick St. Frederick MD 21701 *TF:* 800-903-1360 ■ *Web:* www.gtifederal.com	301-698-5795		463
Gavilan College 5055 Santa Teresa Blvd. Gilroy CA 95020 **Fax:* Admissions ■ *Web:* www.gavilan.edu	408-847-1400	846-4940*	162

Name / Address	City	State	Zip	Phone	Fax	Class
Gavin de Becker & Assoc						
11684 Ventura Blvd Ste 440	Studio City	CA	91604	818-760-4213	506-0426	194
Web: www.gavindebecker.com						
Gavis Pharmaceuticals LLC						
400 Campus Dr	Somerset	NJ	08873	908-603-6080		238
Web: www.gavispharma.com						
Gawfco Enterprises Inc						
587 Ygnacio Valley Rd	Walnut Creek	CA	94596	925-979-0560		324
Web: www.gawfco.com						
Gawthrop Greenwood PC						
17 E Gay St Ste 100	West Chester	PA	19381	610-696-8225		428
Web: www.gawthrop.com						
Gay & Robinson Inc PO Box 156	Kaumakani	HI	96747	808-335-3133		10-9
Gay Ad Network 1628 NE 17th Way	Ft Lauderdale	FL	33305	954-485-9910		7
Web: gayadnetwork.com						
Gay City State Park 435 North St	Hebron	CT	06248	860-295-9523		565
Web: www.ct.gov						
Gay Men's Health Crisis (GMHC)						
119 W 24th St	New York	NY	10011	212-367-1000		48-17
TF: 800-243-7692 ■ *Web:* www.gmhc.org						
Gay WW Mechanical Contractor Inc						
524 Stockton St	Jacksonville	FL	32204	904-388-2696		189-10
Web: wwgmc.com						
Gayesco International LP						
2859 Wside Dr	Pasadena	TX	77502	713-941-8540		256
Web: www.gayesco.com						
Gayla Industries Inc PO Box 920800	Houston	TX	77292	800-231-7508	682-1357*	762
**Fax Area Code: 713 ■ TF:* 800-231-7508 ■ *Web:* www.gaylainc.com						
Gayle Mfg Company Inc						
1455 E Kentucky Ave	Woodland	CA	95776	530-662-0284		480
Web: gaylemfg.com						
Gayle's Chocolates						
417 S Washington Ave	Royal Oak	MI	48067	248-398-0001		296-8
TF: 800-682-2760 ■ *Web:* www.gayleschocolates.com						
Gaylor Electric						
5750 Castle Creek Pkwy N Dr Ste 400	Indianapolis	IN	46250	317-843-0577	848-0364	189-4
TF: 800-878-0577 ■ *Web:* www.gaylor.com						
Gaylord Bros 7282 William Barry Blvd	Syracuse	NY	13212	800-448-6160	272-3412	319-3
TF: 800-345-5330 ■ *Web:* www.gaylord.com						
Gaylord Hospital						
Gaylord Farms Rd PO Box 400	Wallingford	CT	06492	203-284-2800	294-8705	374-6
TF: 866-429-5673 ■ *Web:* www.gaylord.org						
Gaylord Industries Inc						
10900 SW Avery St	Tualatin	OR	97062	503-691-2010	692-6048	18
TF: 800-547-9696 ■ *Web:* gaylordventilation.com						
Gaylord Manufacturing Co						
1088 Montclaire Dr	Ceres	CA	95307	209-538-3313		816
TF: 800-375-0091 ■ *Web:* www.gaylordmfg.com						
Gaylord Nelson Insurance Agency Inc						
8516 S Pulaski Rd	Chicago	IL	60652	773-581-0844		390
Web: gaylordnelson.net						
Gaylord Opryland Hotel & Convention Ctr						
2800 Opryland Dr	Nashville	TN	37214	615-889-1000	885-3054	379
TF: 888-236-2427 ■ *Web:* www.marriott.com						
Gaylord Palms Resort & Convention Ctr						
6000 W Osceola Pkwy	Kissimmee	FL	34746	407-586-0000		669
Web: www.marriott.com						
Gaylord Texan Resort & Convention Ctr						
1501 Gaylord Trl	Grapevine	TX	76051	817-778-2000		707
Web: www.marriott.com						
Gaymar Industries Inc						
10 Centre Dr	Orchard Park	NY	14127	716-662-2551		476
TF: 800-828-7341 ■ *Web:* stryker.com						
Gaytan Foods						
15430 Proctor Ave	City Of Industry	CA	91745	626-330-4553		296-26
TF: 800-242-9826 ■ *Web:* www.gaytanfoods.com						
Gazebo Works Too Inc						
5235 Rainbow Dr	Central Point	OR	97502	541-664-2000		106
Web: www.gazeboworkstoo.com						
Gazelle Sports 3930 28th St SE	Grand Rapids	MI	49512	616-940-9888		711
Web: www.gazellesports.com						
Gazelle Transportation Inc						
34915 Gazelle Ct	Bakersfield	CA	93308	661-322-8868		311
Web: www.gazelletrans.com						
Gazelles Publishing Inc						
21246 Dubois Ct	Ashburn	VA	20147	703-858-2400		449
TF: 800-266-9432 ■ *Web:* www.gazelles.com						
Gazette Newspapers Inc						
9030 Comprint Ct	Gaithersburg	MD	20877	301-948-3120		637-8
TF: 888-670-7100 ■ *Web:* www.gazette.net						
Gazette Publishing Inc 1114 Broadway	Wheaton	MN	56296	320-563-8146	563-8147	627
TF: 000-567-8303 ■ *Web:* www.mnnews.com						
Gazette, The 885 W Liberty St	Medina	OH	44256	330-725-4299		532-2
TF: 800-633-4623 ■ *Web:* medinagazette.northcoastnow.com						
Gazette, The 501 Second Ave SE	Cedar Rapids	IA	52401	319-398-8333		532-2
TF: 800-397-8333 ■ *Web:* www.thegazette.com						
GazetteXtra						
Janesville Gazette						
1 S Parker Dr PO Box 5001	Janesville	WI	53547	608-755-8250	755-8349*	532-2
**Fax:* Edit ■ *TF:* 800-362-6712 ■ *Web:* www.gazettextra.com						
GB Collects LLC 145 Bradford Dr	West Berlin	NJ	08091	856-768-9995		160
TF: 800-462-2070 ■ *Web:* www.gbcollects.com						
GB Manufacturing Co 1120 E Main St	Delta	OH	43515	419-822-5323		483
Web: www.gbmfg.com						
G&B Oil Company Inc 667 N Bridge St	Elkin	NC	28621	336-835-3607		581
TF: 800-784-3839 ■ *Web:* www.gbenergy.com						
G&B Solutions Inc						
1861 Wiehle Ave Ste 200	Reston	VA	20190	703-883-1140	883-1143	180
G&B Specialties Inc 535 W Third St	Berwick	PA	18603	570-752-5901		480
Web: www.gandbspecialties.com						
GB Tubulars Inc						
950 Threadneedle St Ste 130	Houston	TX	77079	713-465-3585		492
TF: 888-245-3848 ■ *Web:* www.gbtubulars.com						
GBCVB (Greater Boston Convention & Visitors Bureau)						
2 Copley Pl Ste 105	Boston	MA	02116	617-536-4100	424-7664	206
TF: 888-733-2678 ■ *Web:* www.bostonusa.com						
GBF Enterpnrises Inc						
2709 Halladay St	Santa Ana	CA	92705	714-979-7131		454
Web: www.gbfenterprises.com						
GBF Inc 2427 Penny Rd	High Point	NC	27265	336-665-0205		627
Web: www.gbf-inc.com						
GBH Communications Inc						
1309 S Myrtle Ave	Monrovia	CA	91016	800-222-5424		246
TF: 800-222-5424 ■ *Web:* www.gbh.com						
GBI (Grand Beach Inn)						
198 E Grand Ave	Old Orchard Beach	ME	04064	207-934-4621		379
Web: grandbeachinnmaine.com						
GBI Tile & Stone Inc						
5900 Skylab Rd Ste 150	Huntington Beach	CA	92647	949-567-1880		361
Web: www.gbitile.com						
GBMC (Greater Baltimore Medical Ctr)						
6701 N Charles St	Baltimore	MD	21204	443-849-2000		374-3
Web: www.gbmc.org						
GBPD (Guardian Building Products)						
979 Batesville Rd	Greer	SC	29651	864-297-6101	281-3558	191-3
TF: 800-569-4262 ■ *Web:* guardianbp.com						
GBQ Partners LLC 230 W St Ste 700	Columbus	OH	43215	614-221-1120		2
Web: www.gbq.com						
GBRA (Guadalupe-Blanco River Authority)						
933 E Ct St	Seguin	TX	78155	830-379-5822	379-9718	245
Web: www.gbra.org						
GBS (Greater Bridgeport Symphony)						
446 University Ave	Bridgeport	CT	06604	203-576-0263		573-3
Web: www.bptsym.org						
GBS Corp 7233 Freedom Ave NW	North Canton	OH	44720	330-494-5330		534
TF: 800-552-2427 ■ *Web:* www.gbscorp.com						
GBS Filing Solutions 224 Morges Rd	Malvern	OH	44644	330-494-5330		560
TF: 800-873-4427 ■ *Web:* www.gbscorp.com						
GBS Financial Corp 558 B St	Santa Rosa	CA	95401	707-568-2400		690
Web: www.gbsfinancial.com						
GBTA (Global Business Travel Assn, The)						
123 N Pitt St	Alexandria	VA	22314	703-684-0836	684-0263	48-23
TF: 888-574-6447 ■ *Web:* www.gbta.org						
GC America Inc 3737 W 127th St	Alsip	IL	60803	708-597-0900	371-5103*	228
**Fax:* Cust Svc ■ *TF Cust Svc:* 800-323-7063 ■ *Web:* www.gcamerica.com						
GC Broach Co 7667 E 46th Pl	Tulsa	OK	74145	918-664-7420	627-4083	318
Web: www.broach.com						
GC Engineering Inc						
10010 Indian School Rd NE	Albuquerque	NM	87112	505-275-0022		256
Web: www.occamconsultinggroup.com						
Gc Marketing Services						
10 E 23rd St Ste 300	New York	NY	10010	212-780-5200		195
TF: 800-927-6306 ■ *Web:* www.gcmarketingservices.com						
GC Packaging 877 N Larch Ave	Elmhurst	IL	60126	630-758-4100	833-1058	554
Web: www.graphicconverting.com						
GC Partners Inc						
3816 Forrestgate Dr	Winston-Salem	NC	27103	336-767-1600		299
Web: www.gcpartners.com						
GC Services LP 6330 Gulfton St	Houston	TX	77081	713-777-4441		160
TF: 800-756-6524 ■ *Web:* www.gcserv.com						
GCA (Greeting Card Assn)						
1444 I St NW Ste 700	Washington	DC	20005	202-216-9627	216-9646	49-16
Web: www.greetingcard.org						
GCA (Everi Holdings Inc)						
7250 S Tenaya Way Ste 100	Las Vegas	NV	89113	702-855-3000		56
NYSE: EVRI ■ *TF:* 800-833-7110 ■ *Web:* www.everi.com						
GCA Law Partners LLP						
2570 W El Camino Real Ste 400	Mountain View	CA	94040	650-428-3900	428-3901	428
Web: www.gcalaw.com						
GCA Services Group						
1350 Euclid Ave Ste 1500	Cleveland	OH	44115	800-422-8760		152
TF: 800-422-8760 ■ *Web:* www.gcaservices.com						
Gcas Inc 1531 Grand Ave Ste A	San Marcos	CA	92078	760-591-4227		180
Web: www.gcas.net						
GCC Printers USA 209 Burlington Rd	Bedford	MA	01730	781-275-1115		173-6
Web: www.gccprinters.de/en						
GCCA						
Cherry Creek Plaza 1						
600 S Cherry St 10th Fl	Glendale	CO	80246	303-739-5900	739-5938	135
Web: www.gccusa.com						
GCCO (Geneva Construction Co)						
1350 Aurora Ave	Aurora	IL	60507	630-892-4357	892-7738	186
Web: www.genevaconstruction.net						
GCE Industries Inc						
1891 Nirvana Ave	Chula Vista	CA	91911	619-421-1151		529
Web: www.gceindustries.com						
GCEC (Grayson-Collin Electric Co-op)						
PO Box 548	Van Alstyne	TX	75495	903-482-7100		245
TF: 800-967-5235 ■ *Web:* www.gcec.net						
GCF (General Credit Forms Inc)						
3595 Rider Trl S	Earth City	MO	63045	314-216-8600	216-8570	110
TF: 888-423-6397 ■ *Web:* www.gcfinc.com						
GCFB (Granite City Food & Brewery Ltd)						
1636 42nd St SW	Fargo	ND	58103	701-293-3000		671
Web: www.gcfb.com						
GCG Marketing						
2421 W Seventh St Ste 400	Fort Worth	TX	76107	817-332-4600		466
Web: www.gcgmarketing.com						
GCH (Garden City Hospital)						
6245 Inkster Rd	Garden City	MI	48135	734-458-3300		374-3
Web: www.gch.org						
GCH (Galesburg Cottage Hospital)						
695 N Kellogg St	Galesburg	IL	61401	309-343-8131		374-3
Web: www.cottagehospital.com						
GCH International Inc						
330 Boxley Ave	Louisville	KY	40209	502-636-1374		454
Web: www.gchintl.com						
GCI Affiliated Cos						
20875 Crossroads Cir Ste 100	Waukesha	WI	53186	262-798-5080		360-3
Web: gcionline.com						
GCI Outdoor Inc 66 Killingworth Rd	Higganum	CT	06441	860-345-9595		321
TF: 800-956-7328 ■ *Web:* www.gcioutdoor.com						
GCI Technologies Inc 1301 Precision Dr	Plano	TX	75074	972-423-8411		256
Web: gcitechnologies.com						
GCM (Aging Life Care Association)						
3275 W Ina Rd Ste 130	Tucson	AZ	85741	520-881-8008	325-7925	49-8
TF: 800-677-1116 ■ *Web:* www.aginglifecare.org						

Name	Address	City	State	ZIP	Phone	Fax	Class	TF / Web
GCM North American Aerospace LLC	21719 84th Ave S	Kent	WA	98032	253-872-7488		529	
GCMC (Grove City Medical Ctr)	631 N Broad St Ext	Grove City	PA	16127	724-450-7000	450-7179	374-3	Web: www.gcmcpa.org
GCMC (Gulf Coast Medical Ctr)	10141 US 59 Rd	Wharton	TX	77488	979-532-2500	282-6190	374-3	TF: 800-345-8082 ■ Web: www.gulfcoastmedical.com
Gcom Software Inc	24 Madison Ave Ext	Albany	NY	12203	518-869-1671		177	TF: 800-467-4448 ■ Web: www.gcomsoft.com
GCR Inc	2021 Lakeshore Dr Ste 500	New Orleans	LA	70122	504-304-2500		463	TF: 800-456-2009 ■ Web: www.gcrincorporated.com
GCS (Georgia Cancer Specialists Pc)	1872 Montreal Rd	Tucker	GA	30084	770-496-9443	496-9490	374-7	TF: 800-491-5991 ■ Web: www.gacancer.com
GCS Inc	7640 Omnitech Pl	Victor	NY	14564	585-742-9100		647	Web: www.globalcoms.com
GCS Service Inc	370 Wabasha St N	St. Paul	MN	55102	800-822-2303		393	TF: 800-822-2303 ■ Web: www.equipmentcare.com
GCSAA (Golf Course Superintendents Assn of America)	1421 Research Pk Dr	Lawrence	KS	66049	785-841-2240		48-2	TF: 800-472-7878 ■ Web: www.gcsaa.org
GCT (Gold Coast Transit)	301 E Third St	Oxnard	CA	93030	805-487-4222	487-0925	468	Web: www.goldcoasttransit.org
GCT Semiconductor Inc	2121 Ringwood Ave	San Jose	CA	95131	408-434-6040	434-6050	696	Web: www.gctsemi.com
GCTC (Gateway Community & Technical College)	1025 Amsterdam Rd	Covington	KY	41011	859-441-4500		800	TF: 855-346-4282 ■ Web: www.gateway.kctcs.edu
GCube Insurance Services Inc	3101 Wcoast Hwy Ste 100	Newport Beach	CA	92663	949-515-9981		390	TF: 877-903-4777 ■ Web: www.gcube-insurance.com
G&D Integrated	50 Commerce Dr	Morton	IL	61550	800-451-6680		186	TF: 800-451-6680 ■ Web: www.gdintegrated.com
GDA (Global Design Alliance Inc)	26 Grammercy Pk S 4B	New York	NY	10003	917-887-3860		261	Web: www.globalda.com
GDB International Inc	1 Home News Row	New Brunswick	NJ	08901	732-246-3001	246-3004	313	Web: www.gdbinternational.com
GDBA Investments LLLP	1440 Blake St Ste 310	Denver	CO	80202	720-932-9395		401	
GDC (Ginsburg Development Cos LLC)	100 Summit Lake Dr	Valhalla	NY	10595	914-747-3600		653	Web: www.gdc-homes.com
GDEB (General Dynamics Electric Boat Corp)	75 Eastern Pt Rd	Groton	CT	06340	860-433-3000	433-1400*	698	*Fax: Hum Res ■ TF: 800-742-9692 ■ Web: gdeb.com
GDI Infotech Inc	3775 Varsity Dr	Ann Arbor	MI	48108	734-477-6900		177	Web: www.gdii.com
GDKN Corp	1779 N University Dr Ste 102	Pembroke Pines	FL	33024	954-905-6650		387	Web: www.gdkn.com
GDP Technologies	1180 Eisenhower Pkwy	Macon	GA	31206	478-781-8991	788-5459	317	Web: www.gadup.com
GDS Associates Inc	1850 Pkwy Pl Ste 800	Marietta	GA	30067	770-425-8100		261	Web: www.gdsassociates.com
GDS Publishing Ltd	40 Wall St Trump Bldg Ste 5	New York	NY	10005	212-796-2000	796-7010	387	Web: gdsgroup.com
GE Aircraft Engines	1 Neumann Way	Cincinnati	OH	45215	513-243-2000		21	Web: www.geaviation.com
GE Analytical Instruments Inc	6060 Spine Rd	Boulder	CO	80301	303-444-2009		692	TF: 800-255-6964 ■ Web: www.geinstruments.com
GE Aviation	1 Neumann Way	Cincinnati	OH	45215	513-243-2000		21	Web: www.geaviation.com
GE Aviation Services	901 Main Ave	Norwalk	CT	06851	203-842-5200		23	Web: www.gecas.com
GE Aviation Systems Div	3290 Patterson Ave SE	Grand Rapids	MI	49512	616-241-8274		22	Web: www.geaviation.com
GE Betz	4636 Somerton Rd	Trevose	PA	19053	215-355-3300		145	TF Cust Svc: 866-439-2837 ■ Web: www.gewater.com
GE Capital Solutions Franchise Finance	8377 E Hartford Dr Ste 200	Scottsdale	AZ	85255	866-438-4333		654	TF: 866-438-4333 ■ Web: www.gefranchisefinance.com
GE Equipment Services	120 Long Ridge Rd	Stamford	CT	06902	203-357-4000		289	
GE Fanuc Embedded Systems Inc	7401 Snaproll NE	Albuquerque	NM	87109	505-875-0600		625	TF: 888-790-1820 ■ Web: www.geautomation.com
GE Foodland Inc	1105 E Beltline Rd	Carrollton	TX	75006	972-245-0470		345	Web: elrodscostplus.com
GE Foundation	3135 Easton Tpke	Fairfield	CT	06828	203-373-2211		304	Web: www.ge.com
GE Healthcare	8200 W Tower Ave	Milwaukee	WI	53223	414-355-5000		250	TF: 800-558-5102 ■ Web: gehealthcare.com
GE Healthcare Bio-Sciences Corp	800 Centennial Ave	Piscataway	NJ	08855	732-457-8000		743	TF: 800-810-9118 ■ Web: www.gelifesciences.com
GE Healthcare Financail Services	500 W Monroe	Chicago	IL	60661	312-697-3999		216	Web: www.gehcfinance.com
GE Infrastructure Sensing	1100 Technology Pk Dr	Billerica	MA	01821	978-437-1000		201	TF: 800-833-9438 ■ Web: www.gemeasurement.com
GE Johnson Construction Co	25 N Cascade Ave Ste 400	Colorado Springs	CO	80903	719-473-5321		186	Web: www.gejohnson.com
GE Lighting Systems Inc	3010 Spartanburg Hwy	East Flat Rock	NC	28726	828-693-2000		439	TF: 888-694-3533 ■ Web: gelighting.com/lightingweb/na
Ge Mathis Co	6100 S Oak Park Ave	Chicago	IL	60638	773-586-3800		697	Web: www.gemathis.com
GE Richards Graphic Supplies Company Inc	928 Links Ave	Landisville	PA	17538	717-898-3151		690	TF: 800 233-0410 ■ Web: www.gerichards.com
GE Transportation Rail	2901 E Lake Rd	Erie	PA	16531	814-875-2234		650	TF Prod Info: 800-285-6545 ■ Web: www.getransportation.com
GE Vendor Financial Services	1719 Rt 10 E Ste 306	Parsippany	NJ	07054	973-292-0025	292-0019	216	TF: 800-626-2000
GE Walker Inc	4420 E Adamo Dr Ste 206	Tampa	FL	33605	800-749-2483	621-4291*	475	*Fax Area Code: 813 ■ TF: 800-749-2483 ■ Web: www.gewalker.com
GE Water & Process Technologies	4636 Somerton Rd	Trevose	PA	19053	215-355-3300		806	TF: 866-439-2837 ■ Web: www.gewater.com
Geaghan's Restaurant & Pub	570 Main St	Bangor	ME	04401	207-945-3730	941-6758	671	TF: 800-765-7238 ■ Web: www.geaghans.com
Gear Energy Ltd	2600 500 - Fourth Ave SW	Calgary	AB	T2P2V6	403-538-8435		536	TF: 877-494-3430 ■ Web: www.gearenergy.com
Gear for Sports Inc	9700 Commerce Pkwy	Lenexa	KS	66219	913-693-3200		155-1	TF: 800-255-1065 ■ Web: www.gearforsports.com
Gear Motions Inc	1750 Milton Ave	Syracuse	NY	13209	315-488-0100	488-0196	709	TF: 800-491-1073 ■ Web: www.gearmotions.com
Gearbox Software LLC	101 E Park Blvd Ste 1200	Plano	TX	75074	972-312-8202		174	Web: www.gearboxsoftware.com
Gearench Inc	4450 S Hwy 6 PO Box 192	Clifton	TX	76634	254-675-8651	675-6100	537	Web: www.gearench.com
Gearhart By the Sea	1157 N Marion Ave	Gearhart	OR	97138	503-738-8331	738-0881	669	TF: 800-547-0115 ■ Web: www.gearhartresort.com
Geartronics Industries Inc	100 Chelmsford Rd	North Billerica	MA	01862	978-663-6566	667-3130	709	TF: 800-221-5452 ■ Web: www.geartronics.com
Geary County	200 E 8th	Junction City	KS	66441	785-238-3912	238-5419	338	Web: ks-geary.manatron.com
Geary Pacific Corp	1908 N Enterprise St	Orange	CA	92865	714-279-2950		690	TF: 800-444-3279 ■ Web: www.gearypacific.com
GEARYS Beverly Hills	351 N Beverly Dr	Beverly Hills	CA	90210	310-273-4741		362	TF: 800-793-6670 ■ Web: www.gearys.com
Geauga County	470 Ctr St Bldg 8 Ste D	Chardon	OH	44024	440-285-2222		338	Web: www.co.geauga.oh.us
Geauga County Public Library	12701 Ravenwood Dr	Chardon	OH	44024	440-286-6811		434-3	Web: www.geauga.lib.oh.us
Geauga County Transit	12555 Merritt Rd	Chardon	OH	44024	440-279-2150	285-9476	108	TF Cust Svc: 888-287-7190 ■ Web: www.geaugatransit.org
GeBBS Healthcare Solutions Inc	560 Sylvan Ave 2nd Fl	Englewood Cliffs	NJ	07632	888-539-4282		177	TF: 888-539-4282 ■ Web: www.gebbs.com
Gebco Insurance Assoc	8600 LaSalle Rd Ste 338	Towson	MD	21286	410-668-3100	882-2872	390	TF: 800-464-3226 ■ Web: www.gogebco.com
Gebhard Woods State Park	401 Ottawa St PO Box 272	Morris	IL	60450	815-942-0796		565	Web: www.dnr.illinois.gov/parks/pages/gebhardwoods.aspx
Gebsco Inc	245 S Eau Claire St	Mondovi	WI	54755	715-926-4234		70	
GEC Inc	8282 Goodwood Blvd	Baton Rouge	LA	70806	225-612-3000		256	Web: www.gecinc.com
Gecko Grill	855 N 13th St	San Jose	CA	95112	408-971-1826		671	
Geddy's Pub	19 Main St PO Box 955	Bar Harbor	ME	04609	207-288-5077	288-9927	671	TF: 800-345-4617 ■ Web: www.geddys.com
Gedeon Grc Consulting	6901 Jericho Tpke Ste 216	Syosset	NY	11791	516-873-7010		256	Web: gedeongrc.com
Geehan Group	40 N Main St Ste 1570	Dayton	OH	45423	937-226-1622		463	TF: 800-434-7300 ■ Web: www.geehangroup.com
Geeks.com	43195 Business Park Dr	Temecula	CA	92590	951-694-4335		179	Web: www.geeksstore.com/About_The_Geeks
GEEP Ecosys Inc	220 John St	Barrie	ON	L4N2L2	705-725-1919	725-1920	192	Web: www.geepecosys.com
Geep International	2501 N Great SW Pkwy	Grand Prairie	TX	75050	972-602-2900		660	TF: 888-832-4929 ■ Web: www.geepglobal.com
Geer Tank Trucks Inc	1136 S Main St	Jacksboro	TX	76458	940-567-2677		579	
GEFCO (GEFCO Inc)	2215 S Van Buren	Enid	OK	73703	580-234-4141		537	TF: 800-759-7441 ■ Web: www.gefco.com
GEFCO Inc (GEFCO)	2215 S Van Buren	Enid	OK	73703	580-234-4141		537	TF: 800-759-7441 ■ Web: www.gefco.com
Geffen Mesher & Co	888 SW Fifth Ave Ste 800	Portland	OR	97204	503-221-0141		466	Web: www.gmco.com
Geffen Playhouse	10886 Le Conte Ave	Los Angeles	CA	90024	310-208-5454	208-8383	749	Web: www.geffenplayhouse.org
Geffen Records	2220 Colorado Ave	Santa Monica	CA	90404	310-865-1000		657	Web: www.interscope.com
Gefran ISI Inc	8 Lowell Ave	Winchester	MA	01890	781-729-5249		201	TF: 888-888-4474 ■ Web: www.gefran.com
Gehan Homes	15725 N Dallas Pkwy Ste 300	Addison	TX	75001	972-383-4300	383-4399	653	Web: www.gehanhomes.com
Gehl Foods	N116 W15970 Main St	Germantown	WI	53022	262-251-8572	250-6847	296-10	TF: 800-521-2873 ■ Web: www.gehls.com
Gehr Industries	7400 E Slauson Ave	Los Angeles	CA	90040	323-728-5558	728-1983	813	Web: gehr.com
Gehring LP	24800 Drake Rd	Farmington Hills	MI	48335	248-478-8060		393	Web: www.gehring.de/en-us
Gehring Textiles Inc	1225 Franklin Ave Ste 300	Garden City	NY	11530	516-747-4555	747-8885	745-4	TF: 800-570-3010 ■ Web: www.gehring-tricot.com
GEI Consultants Inc	400 Unicorn Pk Dr	Woburn	MA	01801	781-721-4000	721-4073	261	TF: 888-434-9679 ■ Web: www.geiconsultants.com
Geiger	70 Mt Hope Ave	Lewiston	ME	04240	207-755-2000	755-2422	9	TF: 800-203-9917 ■ Web: www.geiger.com

Name / Address	City	State	Zip	Phone	Fax	Class
Geiger & Peters Inc 761 S Sherman Dr PO Box 33807 *Web:* www.gpsteel.com	Indianapolis	IN	46203	317-359-9521	359-9525	91
Geiger Inc 660 W Sunset Dr *Web:* www.geigerawards.com	Waukesha	WI	53189	262-542-4856		222
Geiger International Inc 6095 Fulton Industrial Blvd SW *TF:* 800-456-6452 ■ *Web:* www.geigerfurniture.com	Atlanta	GA	30336	404-344-1100	836-7519	319-1
Geiger Ready Mix Company Inc PO Box 50 *Web:* www.geigerreadymix.com	Leavenworth	KS	66048	913-772-4010		182
Geis Cos, The 10020 Aurora Hudson Rd *Web:* www.buildgeis.com	Streetsboro	OH	44241	330-528-3500		186
Geisinger Columbia Montour Hospice 410 Glenn Ave *Web:* www.geisinger.org	Bloomsburg	PA	17815	570-784-1723		371
Geisinger Health Plan 100 N Academy Ave *TF:* 800-447-4000 ■ *Web:* www.thehealthplan.com	Danville	PA	17822	570-271-8760	271-7218	391-3
Geisinger Health System (CMC) 1800 Mulberry St *TF:* 800-230-4565 ■ *Web:* www.geisinger.org	Scranton	PA	18510	570-703-8000		374-3
Geisinger South Wilkes-Barre (GSWB) 25 Church St *TF:* 800-230-4565 ■ *Web:* www.geisinger.org	Wilkes-Barre	PA	18765	570-808-3100		374-3
Geisinger Wyoming Valley Medical Ctr 1000 E Mountain Dr *TF:* 800-230-4565 ■ *Web:* www.geisinger.org	Danville	PA	17822	570-271-8600		374-3
Geja's Cafe 340 W Armitage Ave *Web:* www.gejascafe.com	Chicago	IL	60614	773-281-9101		671
Gekakis & Co 901 Mariners Island Blvd Ste 610	San Mateo	CA	94404	650-349-5700		2
Gekkeikan Sake USA Inc 1136 Sibley St *Web:* www.gekkeikan-sake.com	Folsom	CA	95630	916-985-3111	985-2221	80-1
Gekko Engineering Inc 1210 E 223rd St *Web:* gekkoeng.com	Carson	CA	90745	310-513-0000		261
GEL Group Inc, The 2040 Savage Rd *Web:* www.gel.com	Charleston	SC	29407	843-556-8171		256
Gelfand Rennert & Feldman LLP 1880 Century Park E Ste 1600 *Web:* www.grfllp.com	Los Angeles	CA	90067	310-553-1707		2
Gelia, Wells & Mohr Inc 390 S Youngs Rd *TF:* 800-438-7325 ■ *Web:* www.gelia.com	Williamsville	NY	14221	716-629-3200		636
Gelita USA Inc PO Box 927 *TF:* 800-223-9244 ■ *Web:* www.gelita.com	Sioux City	IA	51102	712-943-5516	943-3372	296-22
Gellman Research Associates Inc 115 W Ave Ste 201 *Web:* gra-inc.com	Jenkintown	PA	19046	215-884-7500		449
Gelmart International Industries 48 W 38th St 10th Fl *TF General:* 800-746-0014 ■ *Web:* www.gelmart.com	New York	NY	10018	212-743-6900	725-7248	155-18
GELPAKÿ 31398 Huntwood Ave *TF:* 888-621-4147 ■ *Web:* www.gelpak.com	Hayward	CA	94544	510-576-2220	576-2282	696
Gelson's Markets 16400 Ventura Blvd Ste 240 **Fax Area Code:* 818 ■ *Web:* www.gelsons.com	Encino	CA	91436	310-638-2842	788-4018*	345
Gem City College 700 State St *Web:* www.gemcitycollege.com	Quincy	IL	62301	217-222-0391	222-1557	800
Gem City Engineering & Mfg Co, The 401 Leo St *Web:* www.gemcity.com	Dayton	OH	45404	937-223-5544	226-1908	695
Gem County 415 E Main St *Web:* www.co.gem.id.us	Emmett	ID	83617	208-365-4561	365-7795	338
Gem Dandy Inc 200 W Academy St *TF:* 800-334-5101 ■ *Web:* www.gem-dandy.com	Madison	NC	27025	336-548-9624		155-2
Gem East Corp 8639 Pacific Ave Tacoma *Web:* www.gemeast.com	Tacoma	WA	98444	253-537-5572	531-8237	409
GEM Edwards Inc 5640 Hudson Industrial Pkwy PO Box 429 *TF:* 800-733-7976 ■ *Web:* www.gemcomedical.com	Hudson	OH	44236	800-733-7976		476
Gem Engineering Inc 1762 Watterson Trl *Web:* www.gemeng.com	Louisville	KY	40299	502-493-7100		261
Gem Equipment of Oregon Inc PO Box 359 *Web:* www.gemequipment.com	Woodburn	OR	97071	503-982-9902	981-6316	298
GEM Group 9 International Way *TF:* 800-800-3200 ■ *Web:* gemline.com	Lawrence	MA	01843	978-691-2000	691-2085	67
Gem Health Care Services Inc-services De Sant Gem Inc 304-383 Parkdale Ave *TF:* 800-445-0626 ■ *Web:* www.gemhealthcare.com	Ottawa	ON	K1Y4R4	613-761-7474		363
Gem Manufacturing Company Inc 78 Brookside Rd *TF:* 800-678-7931 ■ *Web:* www.gemmfg.com	Waterbury	CT	06708	203-574-1466		711
Gem Mobile Treatment Services Inc 2525 Cherry Ave Ste 105 *Web:* gem.evergreenes.com	Signal Hill	CA	90755	562-595-7075		668
Gem of India 211 W Battlefield St *Web:* gemofindia.net	Springfield	MO	65807	417-881-9558		671
Gem Services USA Inc 2880 Lakeside Dr *Web:* www.gemservices.com	Santa Clara	CA	95054	408-566-8866		695
Gem State Paper & Supply Co 1801 Highland Ave E *TF:* 800-727-2737 ■ *Web:* www.gemstatepaper.com	Twin Falls	ID	83303	208-733-6081		559
GEM Systems Inc 135 Spy Ct *Web:* www.gemsys.ca	Markham	ON	L3R5H6	905-752-2202		639
GEM Technologies Inc 2033 Castaic Ln *Web:* www.gemtechnologiesinc.com	Knoxville	TN	37932	865-560-9434		610
GEM Technology International Corp 2665 S Bayshore Dr Ste M103-5 *Web:* www.gemtechnology.com	Miami	FL	33133	305-447-1344	447-3830	652
Gem Theater Cultural & Performing Arts Ctr 1615 E 18th St *TF:* 800-745-3000 ■ *Web:* americanjazzmuseum.com	Kansas City	MO	64108	816-474-6262		572
Gem Theatre & Century Grille 333 Madison Ave *Web:* gemcolonyevents.com	Detroit	MI	48226	313-963-9800	963-0873	572
GEMCH (Greater El Monte Community Hospital) 1701 Santa Anita Ave *TF:* 800-954-8000 ■ *Web:* www.greaterelmonte.com	South El Monte	CA	91733	626-579-7777	350-0368	374-3
GEMCOR Corp 100 Gemcor Dr *TF:* 800-325-1596 ■ *Web:* www.gemcor.com	West Seneca	NY	14224	716-674-9300	674-3171	456
Gem-Craft Inc 1420 Elmwood Ave	Cranston	RI	02910	401-854-1200		408
Gemeinhardt Company LLC 57882 State Rd 19 S *Web:* www.gemeinhardt.com	Elkhart	IN	46517	574-295-5280		527
Gemex Systems Inc 6040 W Executive Dr Ste A *TF:* 866-694-3639 ■ *Web:* www.gemex.com	Mequon	WI	53092	262-242-1111		411
GEMGroup LP 1200 Three Gateway Ctr *Web:* www.gemgrouplp.com	Pittsburgh	PA	15222	412-471-2885		535
Gemini Coatings Inc 421 SE 27th St *TF:* 800-262-5710 ■ *Web:* www.gemini-coatings.com	El Reno	OK	73036	405-262-5710		550
Gemini Computer Systems 4855 E State St Ste 15 *Web:* geminicomputersystems.com	Rockford	IL	61108	815-227-5800	227-5606	180
Gemini Duplication Inc 9645 W Grove Ave *Web:* geminiduplication.com	Visalia	CA	93291	559-739-7481		396
Gemini Engineering Inc 5940 Macleod Trail SW Ste 700	Calgary	AB	T2H2G4	403-255-2006		261
Gemini Fund Services LLC 450 Wireless Blvd *Web:* www.geminifund.com	Hauppauge	NY	11788	631-470-2600		401
Gemini Inc 103 Mensing Way *TF:* 800-538-8377 ■ *Web:* www.geminisignproducts.com	Cannon Falls	MN	55009	507-263-3957	263-4887	701
Gemini Industries Inc 200 Wheeler Rd N Tower *Web:* www.gemini-ind.com	Burlington	MA	01803	781-203-0100		610
Gemini Investors LLC 20 William St Ste 250 *Web:* www.gemini-investors.com	Wellesley	MA	02481	781-237-7001	237-7233	402
Gemini Pharmaceuticals Inc 87 Modular Ave *Web:* www.geminipharm.com	Commack	NY	11725	631-543-3334		479
Gemini Valve 2 Otter Ct *TF:* 800-370-0936 ■ *Web:* www.geminivalve.com	Raymond	NH	03077	603-895-4761	895-6785	789
Gemma Power Systems LLC 769 Hebron Ave *Web:* www.gemmapower.com	Glastonbury	CT	06033	860-659-0509		256
Gemmar Systems International Inc 11450 Cote de Liesse *Web:* www.gsi.ca	Dorval	QC	H9P1A9	514-631-3336		178-1
Gemmel Pharmacy Group Inc 143 N Euclid Ave *TF:* 888-302-0229 ■ *Web:* www.gemmelrx.com	Ontario	CA	91762	909-988-0591		237
Gemmus Pharma Inc 409 Illinois St *Web:* www.gemmuspharma.com	San Francisco	CA	94158	415-978-2151		668
Gemmy Industries Corp 117 Wrangler Dr *Web:* gemmy.com	Coppell	TX	75019	972-538-4200		364
Gemological Institute of America (GIA) 5345 Armada Dr *TF:* 800-421-7250 ■ *Web:* www.gia.edu	Carlsbad	CA	92008	760-603-4000	603-4003	49-4
Gems Sensors Inc 1 Cowles Rd *TF:* 800-378-1600 ■ *Web:* www.gemssensors.com	Plainville	CT	06062	860-747-3000	747-4244	201
Gemstone Systems Inc 1260 NW Waterhouse Ave Ste 200 *TF:* 800-243-4772 ■ *Web:* www.gemstone.com	Beaverton	OR	97006	503-533-3000	629-8556	178-1
Gemtex Abrasives 234 Belfield Rd *TF:* 800-387-5100 ■ *Web:* www.gemtexabrasives.com	Toronto	ON	M9W1H3	416-245-5605	245-3723	1
Gemtor Inc One Johnson Ave *TF:* 800-405-9048 ■ *Web:* www.gemtor.com	Matawan	NJ	07747	732-583-6200	290-9391	678
Gemu Valves Inc 3800 Camp Creek Pkwy SW **Fax Area Code:* 404 ■ *Web:* www.gemu-group.com/en_us	Atlanta	GA	30331	678-553-3400	344-9350*	789
Gemveto Co Inc 18 E 48th St Ste 502 *Web:* www.gemveto.com	New York	NY	10017	212-755-2522	755-2027	409
Genability 221 Main St Ste 400 *Web:* www.genability.com	San Francisco	CA	94105	415-371-0136		387
Genaera Corp 5110 Campus Dr	Plymouth Meeting	PA	19462	610-941-4020	941-5399	85
Genal Strap Inc 31-00 47th Ave *Web:* voguestrap.com	Long Island	NY	11101	718-706-8700		411
GenArts Inc 955 Massachusetts Ave *Web:* www.genarts.com	Cambridge	MA	02139	617-492-2888		225
Genatt Associates Inc 3333 New Hyde Park Rd Ste 400 *Web:* www.genatt.com	New Hyde Park	NY	11042	516-869-8666		390
GenBio 15222 Ave of Science Ste A *TF Tech Supp:* 800-288-4368 ■ *Web:* www.genbio.com	San Diego	CA	92128	858-592-9300		231
Genco Energy Services Inc 1701 W Hwy 107 *Web:* www.genco.us	Mcallen	TX	78504	956-380-3710		539
Genco Shipping & Trading Ltd 299 Pk Ave 12th Fl *NYSE:* GNK ■ *Web:* www.gencoshipping.com	New York	NY	10171	646-443-8550		313
Genco Stamping & Manufacturing Co 2001 Genco Dr *TF:* 800-223-4583 ■ *Web:* gencostamping.com	Cookeville	TN	38506	931-528-5574	528-8379	489
Gencor Industries Inc 5201 N Orange Blossom Trail *NASDAQ:* GENC ■ **Fax:* Sales ■ *TF General:* 888-887-1266 ■ *Web:* www.gencor.com	Orlando	FL	32810	407-290-6000	578-0577*	190
Gene & Georgetti 500 N Franklin St *Web:* www.geneandgeorgetti.com	Chicago	IL	60654	312-527-3718	527-2039	671
Gene B Glick Company Inc 8801 River Crossing Blvd Ste 200 *Web:* www.genebglick.com	Indianapolis	IN	46240	317-469-0400		655
Gene By Gene LTD 1445 N Loop W 820 *Web:* www.genebygene.com	Houston	TX	77008	832-381-5410		415
Gene Codes Corp 775 Technology Dr *TF:* 800-497-4939 ■ *Web:* www.genecodes.com	Ann Arbor	MI	48108	734-769-7249		177

Phone | Fax | Class

Gene Langley Ford Inc 3500 E End Dr..........Humboldt TN 38343 731-784-9311 57
Web: genelangleyford.com
Gene's Place 3730 Rocky River Dr ....Cleveland OH 44111 216-252-1741 671
Gene's Steak House
3674 W International Speedway Blvd ....Daytona Beach FL 32124 386-255-2059 671
Genealogy.com 360 W 4800 N.....................Provo UT 84604 801-705-7000 705-7001 397
TF: 800-262-3787 ■ *Web:* www.genealogy.com
GeneChem 1 Westmount Sq Ste 800 .... Montreal QC H3Z2P9 514-849-7696 528
Web: www.genechem.com
Genemed Biotechnologies Inc
458 Carlton Ct S San Francisco .... San Francisco CA 94080 650-952-0110 668
TF: 877-436-3633 ■ *Web:* www.genemed.com
Geneos Wealth Management Inc
9055 E Mineral Cir Ste 200 ....Centennial CO 80112 303-785-8470 690
TF: 888-812-5043 ■ *Web:* www.geneoswealth.com
GenePharm Inc 1237 Midas Way .... Sunnyvale CA 94085 408-773-0106 668
Web: www.genepharminc.com
GenePOC Inc
360 Rue Franquet Porte 3 Technology Pk......... Quebec QC G1P4N3 418-650-3535 743
TF: 844-616-1544 ■ *Web:* www.genepoc-diagnostics.com
Gener8 Inc 500 Mercury Dr .... Sunnyvale CA 94085 650-940-9898 506
Web: www.gener8.net
Generac Power Systems Inc PO Box 8........ Waukesha WI 53187 262-544-4811 544-4851 518
TF: 888-436-3722 ■ *Web:* www.generac.com
General Air Service & Supply Company Inc
1105 Zuni St.................................Denver CO 80204 303-892-7003 146
TF: 877-782-8434 ■ *Web:* www.generalair.com
General Asphalt Co Inc 4850 NW 72nd Ave .... Miami FL 33166 305-592-3480 46
General Assn of Regular Baptist Churches (GARBC)
1300 N Meacham Rd .... Schaumburg IL 60173 847-585-0816 48-20
TF: 888-588-1600 ■ *Web:* www.garbcinternational.org
General Atlantic LLC
600 Steamboat Rd Ste 105..................Greenwich CT 06830 203-629-8600 622-8818 792
Web: www.generalatlantic.com
General Atomics
3550 General Atomics Ct PO Box 85608 .... San Diego CA 92121 858-455-3000 455-3621 668
TF: 800-669-6820 ■ *Web:* www.ga.com
General Atomics Aeronautical Systems
16761 Via Del Campo Ct .... San Diego CA 92127 858-385-7850 21
Web: www.ga-asi.com
General Automatic Transfer Co
100 Larkin Williams Industrial Ct................ Fenton MO 63026 636-343-6370 207
Web: www.gat-systems.com
General Automotive Mfg LLC
5215 W Airways Ave.........................Franklin WI 53132 414-423-6400 621
Web: www.gamfg.com
General Aviation Industries Inc
415 Jones Rd ....Weatherford TX 76088 817-598-4848 22
Web: www.gaiinc.net
General Aviation Manufacturers Assn (GAMA)
1400 K St NW Ste 801 ....Washington DC 20005 202-393-1500 842-4063 49-21
TF: 866-427-3287 ■ *Web:* www.gama.aero
General Aviation Services LLC
1155 E Ensell Rd .... Lake Zurich IL 60047 847-726-5000 726-7668 770
Web: www.genav.com
General Baptist Nursing Home
US Hwy 62 W............................Campbell MO 63933 573-246-2155 672
Web: generalbaptisthealthcare.com
General Bearing Corp 44 High St .... West Nyack NY 10994 845-358-6000 358-6277 75
TF Sales: 800-431-1766 ■ *Web:* www.generalbearing.com
General Beer Distributors
6169 McKee Rd ....Fitchburg WI 53719 608-271-1234 81-3
Web: visitmadison.com
General Biodiesel Inc
6333 First Ave S............................. Seattle WA 98108 206-932-1600 580
Web: www.gbdnw.com
General Broach Co 307 Salisbury St .... Morenci MI 49256 517-458-7555 493
TF: 800-889-7555 ■ *Web:* www.generalbroach.com
General Burnside Island State Park
8801 S Hwy 27........................... Burnside KY 42519 606-561-4104 565
Web: www.parks.ky.gov
General Butler State Resort Park
1608 US Hwy 227..................... Carrollton KY 41008 502-732-4384 669
TF: 866-462-8853 ■ *Web:* www.parks.ky.gov
General Cable Corp
4 Tesseneer Dr ....Highland Heights KY 41076 859-572-8000 814
NYSE: BGC ■ *TF:* 800-572-8000 ■ *Web:* www.generalcable.com
General Carbide Corp
1151 Garden St........................ Greensburg PA 15601 724-836-3000 836-6274 757
TF: 800-245-2465 ■ *Web:* www.generalcarbide.com
General Code Publishers Corp
72 Hinchey Rd ....Rochester NY 14624 585-328-1810 428
TF: 800-836-8834 ■ *Web:* www.generalcode.com
General Coffee State Park
46 John Coffee Rd ....Nicholls GA 31554 912-384-7082 565
Web: www.gastateparks.org
General Collection Inc
310 N Walnut PO Box 1423 .... Grand Island NE 68802 308-381-1423 160
TF: 800-475-7526 ■ *Web:* www.generalcollection.com
General Communication Inc
2550 Denali St Ste 1000.................... Anchorage AK 99503 907-265-5600 868-5676 736
NASDAQ: GNCMA ■ *TF:* 800-770-7886 ■ *Web:* www.gci.com
General Credit Forms Inc (GCF)
3595 Rider Trl S..........................Earth City MO 63045 314-216-8600 216-8570 110
TF: 888-423-6397 ■ *Web:* www.gcfinc.com
General Crook House Museum
5730 N 30th St Ste 11B ....Omaha NE 68111 402-455-9990 50-3
General Cutting Tools
6440 N Ridgeway Ave.................... Lincolnwood IL 60712 847-677-8770 493
Web: www.generalcuttingtools.com
General Daniel Bissell House
10225 Bellefontaine Rd.................... Saint Louis MO 63137 314-544-5714 50-3
Web: stlouisco.com
General Data Co Inc
4354 Ferguson Dr........................ Cincinnati OH 45245 513-752-7978 752-6947* 174
**Fax:* Sales ■ *TF:* 800-733-5252 ■ *Web:* www.general-data.com
General DataComm Inc 6 Rubber Ave.......... Naugatuck CT 06770 203-729-0271 723-2883 176
Web: www.gdc.com

Phone | Fax | Class

General Devices Company Inc
1410 S Post Rd.........................Indianapolis IN 46239 317-897-7000 201
TF: 000-021-3520 ■ *Web:* www.generaldevices.com
General Die Casters Inc
2150 Highland Rd......................... Twinsburg OH 44087 330-657-2300 657-2192 308
TF: 800-332-2278 ■ *Web:* www.generaldie.com
General Digital Corp
8 Nutmeg Rd S ....South Windsor CT 06074 860-282-2900 282-2244 173-4
TF: 800-952-2535 ■ *Web:* www.generaldigital.com
General Distributing Co
5350 Amelia Earhart Dr..................Salt Lake City UT 84116 801-531-7895 363-4924 81-1
Web: generaldistributing.weebly.com
General Doors Corp
1 Monroe St PO Box 205 .... Bristol PA 19007 215-788-9277 788-9450 236
Web: www.general-doors.com
General Dynamics Advanced Information Systems
12450 Fair Lakes Cir .... Fairfax VA 22033 877-449-0600 529
TF: 877-449-0600 ■ *Web:* gdmissionsystems.com
General Dynamics Armament & Technical Products Inc
2118 Water Ridge Pkwy .... Charlotte NC 28217 704-714-8000 21
Web: www.gdatp.com
General Dynamics C4 Systems
400 John Quincy Adams Rd Bldg 80 .... Taunton MA 02780 877-449-0600 178-10
TF: 877-449-0600 ■ *Web:* www.gdc4s.com
General Dynamics Corp
2941 Fairview Pk Dr Ste 100 .... Falls Church VA 22042 703-876-3000 876-3125 807
NYSE: GD ■ *Web:* www.generaldynamics.com
General Dynamics Electric Boat Corp (GDEB)
75 Eastern Pt Rd............................Groton CT 06340 860-433-3000 433-1400* 698
**Fax:* Hum Res ■ *TF:* 800-742-9692 ■ *Web:* gdeb.com
General Dynamics Information Technology
3211 Jermantown Rd .... Fairfax VA 22030 703-246-0200 180
TF: 800-242-0230 ■ *Web:* www.gdit.com
General Dynamics NASSCO
2798 E Harbor Dr .... San Diego CA 92113 619-544-3400 544-3541 698
TF: 800-810-4853 ■ *Web:* www.nassco.com
General Dynamics Ordnance & Tactical Systems Inc
11399 16th Ct N Ste 200 .... Saint Petersburg FL 33716 727-578-8100 268
Web: www.gd-ots.com
General Dynamics SATCOM Technologies
3111 Fujita St................................Torrance CA 90505 828-464-4141 464-4147 647
TF: 888-874-7646 ■ *Web:* www.gdsatcom.com/prodelin.php
General Dynamics SATCOM Technologies
1500 Prodelin Dr .... Newton NC 28658 828-464-4141 464-5725 647
TF: 888-874-7646 ■ *Web:* www.gdsatcom.com
General Ecology Inc 151 Sheree Blvd ....Exton PA 19341 610-363-7900 427
Web: www.generalecology.com
General Educational Development Testing Service
American Council on Education
1 Dupont Cir NW......................Washington DC 20036 202-939-9300 244
TF: 866-205-6267 ■ *Web:* www.acenet.edu
General Electric Company PAC
1299 Pennsylvania Ave NW Ste 900........... Washington DC 20004 202-637-4000 637-4006 615
General Electrodynamics Corporation Inc
8000 Calendar Rd.........................Arlington TX 76001 817-572-0366 22
TF: 800-551-6038 ■ *Web:* www.gecscales.com
General Employment Enterprises Inc
184 Shuman Blvd Ste 420 .... Naperville IL 60563 630-954-0400 954-0447 721
NYSE: JOB ■ *Web:* www.generalemployment.com
General Engineering Co
26485 Hillman Hwy ....Abingdon VA 24212 276-628-6068 628-4311 223
Web: generalengr.com
General Engineering Works
1515 W Wrightwood Ct ....Addison IL 60101 630-543-8000 543-8005 621
Web: www.gewinc.com
General Equipment & Supplies Inc
4300 Main Ave ....Fargo ND 58103 701-282-2662 364-2190 358
TF: 800-437-2924 ■ *Web:* www.genequip.com
General Equipment Co
620 Alexander Dr SW PO Box 334 ....Owatonna MN 55060 507-451-5510 451-5511 386
TF Cust Svc: 800-533-0524 ■ *Web:* www.generalequip.com
General Extrusions Inc
4040 Lake Pk Rd.........................Youngstown OH 44512 330-783-0270 788-1250 485
Web: www.genext.com
General Fasteners Co
37584 Amrhein Rd Ste 150......................Livonia MI 48150 734-452-2400 452-2257 351
TF: 800-945-2658 ■ *Web:* www.genfast.com
General Federation of Women's Clubs (GFWC)
1734 N St NW...........................Washington DC 20036 202-347-3168 835-0246 48-24
TF: 800-443-4392 ■ *Web:* www.gfwc.org
General Films Inc 645 S High St .... Covington OH 45318 937-473-2051 600
Web: www.generalfilms.com
General Filters Inc
43800 Grand River Ave..........................Novi MI 48375 866-476-5101 349-2366* 18
**Fax Area Code:* 248 ■ *TF:* 866-476-5101 ■ *Web:* www.generalfilters.com
General Financial Supply Inc
1235 N Ave...................................Nevada IA 50201 515-382-3549 627
TF: 800-759-4374 ■ *Web:* www.generalfinancialsupply.com
General Floor Industries Inc
190 Benigno Blvd.......................... Bellmawr NJ 08031 856-931-0012 361
Web: www.generalfloor.com
General Foam Plastics Corp
3321 E Princess Anne Rd ....Norfolk VA 23502 757-857-0153 857-0033 601
Web: www.genfoam.com
General Formulations Inc
309 S Union St.............................. Sparta MI 49345 616-887-7387 887-0537 600
TF: 800-253-3664 ■ *Web:* www.generalformulations.com
General Genetics Corp
MSC3ARP, Box 30001 3655 Research Dr.......Las Cruces NM 88003 575-646-7850 646-6060 743
Web: www.ggcdna.com
General Grand Chapter Order of the Eastern Star
1618 New Hampshire Ave NW ....Washington DC 20009 202-667-4737 462-5162 48-15
Web: www.easternstar.org
General Grant National Memorial
Riverside Dr & W 122nd St.................New York NY 10027 212-666-1640 932-9631 564
TF: 800-246-8872 ■ *Web:* www.nps.gov/gegr
General Growth Properties Inc
110 N Wacker Dr.............................Chicago IL 60606 312-960-5000 960-5475 655
NYSE: GGP ■ *TF:* 888-395-8037 ■ *Web:* www.ggp.com

Phone | Fax | Class

General Health System (GHS)
3600 Florida Blvd ... Baton Rouge LA 70806 | 225-387-7000 | | 353
Web: www.brgeneral.org

General Healthcare Resources Inc
2250 Hickory Rd Ste 240 ... Plymouth Meeting PA 19462 | 610-834-1122 | 834-7525 | 363
TF: 800-879-4471 ■ *Web:* www.ghresources.com

General Hearing Corp
175 Brookhollow Esplanade ... Harahan LA 70123 | 504-733-3767 | | 237
TF: 800-824-3021 ■ *Web:* www.generalhearing.com

General Hotels Corp
2501 S High School Rd ... Indianapolis IN 46241 | 317-243-1000 | | 707
Web: genhotels.com

General Hydronics Inc 1001 Zuni Dr ... Alamogordo NM 88310 | 575-437-6512 | | 189-10

General Insulation Company Inc
278 Mystic Ave Ste 209 ... Medford MA 02155 | 781-391-2070 | 391-3094 | 191-4
TF: 800-229-9148 ■ *Web:* www.generalinsulation.com

General John J. Pershing Boyhood Home State Historic Site
1100 Pershing Dr ... Laclede MO 64651 | 660-963-2525 | | 565
Web: www.mostateparks.com

General Kinematics Corp
5050 Rickert Rd ... Crystal Lake IL 60014 | 815-455-3222 | 455-2285 | 207
TF: 800-345-4946 ■ *Web:* generalkinematics.com

General Kinetics Engineering Corp
110 E Dr ... Brampton ON L6T1C1 | 905-458-0888 | | 21
Web: www.generalkinetics.com

General Loose Leaf Bindery Co
3811 Hawthorn Ct ... Waukegan IL 60087 | 847-244-9700 | 244-9741 | 86
TF: 800-621-0493 ■ *Web:* www.looseleaf.com

General Machine Products Company Inc
3111 Old Lincoln Hwy ... Trevose PA 19053 | 215-357-5500 | 357-6216 | 758
TF Tech Supp: 800-345-6009 ■ *Web:* www.gmptools.com

General Magnaplate Corp 1331 Us Rt 1 ... Linden NJ 07036 | 908-862-6200 | | 487
TF: 800-441-6173 ■ *Web:* www.magnaplate.com

General Maritime Corp
299 Pk Ave Ste 2 ... New York NY 10171 | 212-763-5600 | | 313
Web: www.gener8maritime.com

General Metal Finishing Company Inc (GMF)
42 Frank Mossberg Dr ... Attleboro MA 02703 | 508-226-5606 | | 481
Web: www.pepgenmetal.com

General Microcircuits Inc
1133 N Main St PO Box 748 ... Mooresville NC 28115 | 704-663-5975 | 663-6569 | 253
Web: www.gmimfg.com

General Mills Foundation
PO Box 9452 ... Minneapolis MN 55440 | 800-248-7310 | 764-8330* | 304
**Fax Area Code:* 763 ■ *TF:* 800-248-7310 ■ *Web:* www.generalmills.com

General Mills Inc
1 General Mills Blvd ... Minneapolis MN 55426 | 800-248-7310 | 764-8330* | 299
NYSE: GIS ■ **Fax Area Code:* 763 ■ **Fax:* PR ■ *TF:* 800-248-7310 ■ *Web:* www.generalmills.com

General Mitchell International Airport
5300 S Howell Ave ... Milwaukee WI 53207 | 414-747-5300 | 747-4525 | 27
Web: www.mitchellairport.com

General Moly Inc
1726 Cole Blvd Ste 115 ... Lakewood CO 80401 | 303-928-8599 | | 502
Web: www.generalmoly.com

General Morgan Inn 111 N Main St ... Greeneville TN 37743 | 423-787-1000 | | 379
Web: generalmorganinn.com

General Motors Acceptance Corp (GMAC)
200 Renaissance Ctr ... Detroit MI 48265 | 877-320-2559 | 428-4622* | 217
**Fax Area Code:* 800 ■ *TF:* 800-200-4622 ■ *Web:* www.ally.com

General Motors Corp (GMC)
100 Renaissance Ctr ... Detroit MI 48265 | 313-556-5000 | | 59
NYSE: GM ■ *TF:* 800-462-8782 ■ *Web:* www.gm.com

General Motors Corp Buick Motor Div
300 Renaissance Ctr PO Box 33136 ... Detroit MI 48265 | 800-521-7300 | | 59
TF Cust Svc: 800-521-7300 ■ *Web:* www.buick.com

General Motors Foundation Inc
PO Box 33170 ... Detroit MI 48232 | 800-222-1020 | | 304
TF: 800-222-1020 ■ *Web:* www.gm.com

General Music Corp
605 Country Club Dr ... Bensenville IL 60106 | 630-766-8230 | | 527

General Networks Corp
3524 Ocean View Blvd ... Glendale CA 91208 | 818-249-1962 | | 174
Web: www.gennet.com

General Nuclear Corp
3519 Wheeler St ... New Stanton PA 15672 | 724-925-3565 | | 454
Web: www.generalnuclearcorp.com

General Office Products Co
4521 Hwy 7 ... Minneapolis MN 55416 | 952-925-7500 | 925-7531 | 320
Web: www.gopco.com

General Oil Equipment Company Inc
60 John Glenn Dr ... Amherst NY 14228 | 716-691-7012 | | 358
Web: www.goe-amhfab.com

General Partitions Manufacturing Corp
1702 Peninsula Dr PO Box 8370 ... Erie PA 16505 | 814-833-1154 | 838-3473 | 286
TF: 800-393-6343 ■ *Web:* generalpartitions.com

General Parts LLC
11311 Hampshire Ave S ... Bloomington MN 55438 | 952-944-5800 | | 690
Web: generalparts.com

General Pattern Company Inc
3075 84th Ln NE ... Blaine MN 55449 | 763-780-3518 | | 567
TF: 800-587-1541 ■ *Web:* www.generalpattern.com

General Pencil Co Inc
3160 Bay Rd ... Redwood City CA 94063 | 650-369-4889 | 369-7169 | 571
TF: 800-537-0734 ■ *Web:* www.generalpencil.com

General Pet Supply Inc
7711 N 81st St ... Milwaukee WI 53223 | 414-365-3400 | | 96
TF: 800-433-9786 ■ *Web:* www.generalpet.com

General Petroleum Inc
7404 Disalle Blvd ... Fort Wayne IN 46825 | 260-489-8504 | | 579
Web: www.genpet.com

General Pickett's Buffet
571 Steinwehr Ave ... Gettysburg PA 17325 | 717-334-7580 | | 671
TF: 800-367-1797 ■ *Web:* generalpickettsbuffets.com

General Plastic Extrusions Inc
1238 Kasson Dr ... Prescott WI 54021 | 715-262-3806 | 262-3836 | 548
TF: 800-532-3888 ■ *Web:* www.generalplastic.com

General Plastics & Composites Lp
5727 Ledbetter ... Houston TX 77087 | 713-644-1449 | | 599
Web: www.genplastics.com

General Plastics Mfg Co
4910 S Burlington Way ... Tacoma WA 98409 | 253-473-5000 | 473-5104 | 601
TF: 800-806-6051 ■ *Web:* www.generalplastics.com

General Plug & Mfg Co Inc 455 Main St ... Grafton OH 44044 | 440-926-2411 | 926-3305 | 595
TF: 800-289-7584 ■ *Web:* www.generalplug.com

General Plumbing Supply Company Inc
1530 San Luis Rd PO Box 4666 ... Walnut Creek CA 94597 | 925-939-4622 | 939-1548 | 612
Web: www.generalplumbingsupply.com

General Polymeric Corp
1136 Morgantown Rd ... Reading PA 19607 | 610-374-5171 | | 596

General Press Corp
110 Allegheny Dr ... Natrona Heights PA 15065 | 724-224-3500 | | 627
Web: www.generalpress.com

General Produce Co 1330 N 'B' St ... Sacramento CA 95814 | 916-441-6431 | 441-2483 | 297-7
TF: 800-366-4991 ■ *Web:* www.generalproduce.com

General Products 4045 N Rockwell St ... Chicago IL 60618 | 773-463-2424 | | 86

General Resonance LLC
1 Resonance Way ... Havre De Grace MD 21078 | 410-939-2343 | | 668

General Revenue Corp
4660 Duke Dr Ste 300 ... Mason OH 45040 | 800-234-6258 | | 160
TF: 800-234-6258 ■ *Web:* www.generalrevenue.com

General Scientific Corp
1201 M St SE Ste 120 ... Washington DC 20003 | 202-547-4299 | 547-7550 | 544
Web: www.genscicorp.com

General Security Services Corp
9110 Meadowview Rd ... Minneapolis MN 55425 | 952-858-5000 | | 693
Web: www.gssc.net

General Service Bureau Inc
8429 Blondo St ... Omaha NE 68134 | 402-255-5025 | | 160
Web: www.gsbcollect.com

General Services Administration (GSA)
1275 F St NE ... Washington DC 20417 | 202-501-0800 | | 340-20
Web: www.gsa.gov
Federal Citizen Information Center
PO Box 100 ... Pueblo CO 81009 | 888-878-3256 | | 340-20
TF: 888-878-3256 ■ *Web:* publications.usa.gov
Regulatory Information Service Ctr
1800 F St NW Rm 3039 ... Washington DC 20405 | 202-482-7340 | | 340-20
Web: www.gsa.gov

General Services Administration Regional Offices
Region 1 - New England
10 Cswy St Rm 1010
Thomas P O'Neill Federal Bldg ... Boston MA 02222 | 617-565-5860 | | 340-20
TF: 866-734-1727 ■ *Web:* www.gsa.gov
Region 2 - Northeast & Caribbean
26 Federal Plaza ... New York NY 10278 | 212-264-2600 | | 340-20
Web: www.gsa.gov
Region 3 - Mid-Atlantic
Strawbridge Bldg 20 N 8th St ... Philadelphia PA 19107 | 215-446-5100 | | 340-20
TF: 800-333-4636 ■ *Web:* www.gsa.gov
Region 4 - Southeast Sunbelt
1800 F St NW Ste 600 ... Washington DC 20405 | 800-333-4636 | 331-0931* | 340-20
**Fax Area Code:* 404 ■ *TF:* 800-333-4636 ■ *Web:* www.gsa.gov
Region 6 - Heartland 1800 F St NW ... Washington DC 20405 | 816-823-5320 | 926-7513 | 340-20
Web: www.gsa.gov
Region 7 - Greater Southwest
819 Taylor St ... Fort Worth TX 76102 | 817-978-2321 | | 340-20
Web: www.gsa.gov
Region 8 - Rocky Mountain
Denver Federal Ctr Bldg 41 ... Denver CO 80225 | 303-236-7329 | | 340-20
TF: 888-999-4777 ■ *Web:* www.gsa.gov
Region 9 - Pacific Rim
450 Golden Gate Ave ... San Francisco CA 94102 | 530-756-3082 | | 340-20
Web: www.gsa.gov
Region 10 - Northwest/Arctic
400 15th St SW ... Auburn WA 98001 | 253-931-7000 | | 340-20
Web: www.gsa.gov
Region 11 - National Capital Region
301 Seventh St SW ... Washington DC 20407 | 202-708-9100 | | 340-20

General Shale Products LLC
3015 Bristol Hwy ... Johnson City TN 37601 | 423-282-4661 | 952-4104 | 150
TF: 800-414-4661 ■ *Web:* www.generalshale.com

General Shelters of Texas Ltd
1639 State Hwy 87 N ... Center TX 75935 | 936-598-3389 | 598-1432 | 106
Web: www.generalshelters.com

General Ship Repair Corp, The
1449 Key Hwy ... Baltimore MD 21230 | 410-752-7620 | | 698
TF: 800-222-1980 ■ *Web:* www.generalshiprepair.com

General Star National Insurance Co
695 E Main St Financial Ctr ... Stamford CT 06901 | 203-328-5000 | | 391-4
TF: 800-624-5237 ■ *Web:* www.generalstar.com

General Steamship Agencies Inc
575 Redwood Hwy Ste 200 ... Mill Valley CA 94941 | 415-389-5200 | 389-9020 | 465
Web: www.gensteam.com

General Steel Drum LLC 4500 S Blvd ... Charlotte NC 28209 | 704-525-7160 | | 198
Web: www.generalsteeldrum.com

General Steel Inc PO Box 1503 ... Macon GA 31202 | 478-746-2794 | | 492
TF: 800-476-2794 ■ *Web:* www.steeldeal.com

General Theming Contractors LLC
3750 Courtright Ct ... Columbus OH 43227 | 614-252-6342 | | 344

General Theological Seminary
440 W 21st St ... New York NY 10011 | 212-243-5150 | 727-3907 | 167-3
TF: 888-487-5649 ■ *Web:* gts.edu

General Thermodynamics Inc
4700 Ironwood Dr ... Franklin WI 53132 | 414-761-4500 | | 247
Web: www.thermasys.com/general_thermo

General Tool & Supply Co Inc
2705 NW Nicolai St ... Portland OR 97210 | 503-226-3411 | | 385
TF: 800-526-9328 ■ *Web:* www.motionindustries.com

General Tool Co 101 Landy Ln ... Cincinnati OH 45215 | 513-733-5500 | 733-5604 | 757
TF: 800-314-9817 ■ *Web:* www.gentool.com

General Tool Inc 2025 Alton Pkwy ... Irvine CA 92606 | 949-261-2322 | | 190
Web: www.gtdiamond.com

General Tools Mfg Company LLC
80 White St ... New York NY 10013 | 212-431-6100 | 431-6499 | 758
TF: 800-697-8665 ■ *Web:* www.generaltools.com

General Tours 53 Summer St ... Keene NH 03431 | 800-221-2216 | 357-4548* | 760
**Fax Area Code:* 603 ■ *TF:* 800-221-2216 ■ *Web:* alexanderroberts.com

	Phone	Fax	Class
General Truck Body 7110 Jensen Dr, Houston TX 77093 *TF:* 000-395-8585 ■ *Web:* www.generalbody.com	713-692-5177	692-0700	516
General Truck Parts & Equipment Co 4040 W 40th St, Chicago IL 60632 *TF:* 800-621-3914 ■ *Web:* www.generaltruckparts.com	773-247-6900	247-2632	61
General Utilities Inc 100 Fairchild Ave, Plainview NY 11803 *Web:* www.generalutilities.com	516-349-8989		580
General Vision Services LLC 520 Eigth Ave 9th Fl, New York NY 10018 *TF:* 855-653-0586 ■ *Web:* www.generalvision.com	212-729-5300	967-4781	543
General Wax & Candle Co 6863 Beck Ave PO Box 9398, North Hollywood CA 91605 *TF:* 800-929-7867 ■ *Web:* www.generalwax.com	818-765-5800	765-0555	122
General Welding Supply Company and Propane Co 15 Lombard St, Martins Ferry OH 43935 *Web:* www.generalwelding.net	740-635-1324		45
General Welding Works Inc 2060 N Loop W Ste 200 PO Box 925749, Houston TX 77018 *Web:* www.generalwelding.com	713-869-6401	869-5405	91
General Wire Spring Co 1101 Thompson Ave, McKees Rocks PA 15136 *TF:* 800-245-6200 ■ *Web:* www.generalwirespring.com	412-771-6300	771-6317	718
Generate Content LLC 1545 26th St Ste 200, Santa Monica CA 90404 *Web:* www.defymedia.com	310-255-0460		260
Generations Restaurant & Pub 338 National Rd, Wheeling WV 26003 *Web:* www.generationswhg.com	304-232-7917		671
Generations United (GU) 1333 H St NW Ste 500-W, Washington DC 20005 *TF:* 800-677-1116 ■ *Web:* www.gu.org	202-289-3979	289-3952	48-6
Generex Biotechnology Corp 4145 N Service Rd Ste 200, Burlington ON L7L6A3 *OTC: GNBT* ■ **Fax Area Code:* 647 ■ *TF:* 800-391-6755 ■ *Web:* www.generex.com	416-364-2551	547-7104*	85
Generic Theater 215 St Paul's Blvd, Norfolk VA 23510 *TF:* 800-745-3000 ■ *Web:* www.generictheater.org	757-441-2160		573-4
Genesco Inc 1415 Murfreesboro Rd, Nashville TN 37217 *NYSE: GCO* ■ *TF:* 800-732-0330 ■ *Web:* www.genesco.com	615-367-7000		301
Genesee & Wyoming Inc 66 Field Pt Rd, Greenwich CT 06830 *NYSE: GWR* ■ *TF:* 800-230-1059 ■ *Web:* www.gwrr.com	203-629-3722		648
Genesee Community College 1 College Rd, Batavia NY 14020 *TF:* 866-225-5422 ■ *Web:* www.genesee.edu	585-343-0055	345-6810	162
Genesee Country Village & Museum 1410 Flint Hill Rd, Mumford NY 14511 *Web:* www.gcv.org	585-538-6822	538-6927	520
Genesee County 15 Main St Ste 1, Batavia NY 14020 *Web:* www.co.genesee.ny.us	585-344-2550	344-8582	338
Genesee County 900 S Saginaw St, Flint MI 48502 *Web:* www.co.genesee.mi.us	810-424-4355	257-3464	338
Genesee County Chamber of Commerce 210 E Main St, Batavia NY 14020 *TF:* 877-788-6846 ■ *Web:* www.geneseeny.com	585-343-7440	343-7487	139
Genesee County Parks & Recreation 5045 Stanley Rd, Flint MI 48506 *TF:* 800-648-7275 ■ *Web:* 'www.geneseecountyparks.org	810-736-7100	736-7220	50-5
Genesee District Library *Flint Township-McCarty Library* 2071 Graham Rd, Flint MI 48532 *TF:* 866-732-1120 ■ *Web:* www.thegdl.org	810-732-9150	732-0878	434-3
Genesee Grande Hotel 1060 E Genesee St, Syracuse NY 13210 *Web:* www.geneseegrande.com	315-476-4212	471-4663	379
Genesee Group Inc 1470 Ave T, Grand Prairie TX 75050 *Web:* www.geneseegroup.com	972-623-2004	623-0404	488
Genesee Intermediate School District 2413 W Maple Ave, Flint MI 48507 *Web:* www.geneseeisd.org	810-591-4400		685
Genesee Packaging Inc 2010 Dort Hwy, Flint MI 48506 *TF:* 800-743-3323 ■ *Web:* www.genpackaging.com	810-235-6120		88
Genesee Regional Chamber of Commerce 519 S Saginaw St Ste 200, Flint MI 48502 *Web:* www.flintandgenesee.org	810-600-1404	600-1461	139
Genesee Reserve Supply Inc 200 Jefferson Rd, Rochester NY 14623 *Web:* www.geneseereserve.com	585-292-7040		191-3
Genesee Theatre 203 N Genesee St, Waukegan IL 60085 *Web:* www.geneseetheatre.com	847-782-2366	782-2355	749
Genesee Valley Ctr 3341 S Linden Rd, Flint MI 48507 *TF:* 866-236-1128 ■ *Web:* www.geneseemall.com	810-732-4000	732-4343	460
Genesee Valley Penny Saver Inc 1471 W Henrietta Rd, Avon NY 14414 *Web:* www.gvpennysaver.com	585-226-8111		532-3
Geneseo Community Unit School District 228 209 S College Ave, Geneseo IL 61254 *Web:* www.dist228.org	309-945-0450		685
Genesic Semiconductor Inc 43670 Trade Center Pl, Sterling VA 20166 *Web:* www.genesicsemi.com	703-996-8200		696
Genesis Attachments LLC 1000 Genesis Dr, Main St, Superior WI 54880 *Web:* www.genesisattachments.com	715-395-5252		190
Genesis Automation Inc 3480 Swenson Ave, St. Charles IL 60174 *Web:* www.genesisautomation.com	630-587-0444		358
Genesis Bicycles 126 Bushkill St, Easton PA 18042 *TF:* 800-561-3357 ■ *Web:* genesisbicycles.com	610-253-1140		711
Genesis Biosystems Inc 1500 Eagle Ct # 75057, Lewisville TX 75057 *TF:* 888-577-7335 ■ *Web:* www.genesisbiosystems.com	972-315-7888		77
Genesis Capital LLC 3414 Peachtree Rd NE Ste 700, Atlanta GA 30326 *TF:* 800-998-8479 ■ *Web:* www.genesis-capital.com	404-816-7540		70
Genesis Communications Inc 900 Technology Pkwy Ste 300, Cedar Falls IA 50613 *Web:* www.phantomefx.com	319-266-3656		514
Genesis Concepts & Consultants LLC 1777 NE Loop 410 Ste 1009, San Antonio TX 78217 *Web:* www.genconcepts.com	210-451-5100		177
Genesis Corp 950 Third Ave Fl 26, New York NY 10022 *TF:* 800-261-1776 ■ *Web:* www.genesis10.com	212-688-5522	421-6292	180
Genesis Diamonds Cool Springs LLC 3742 Hillsboro Pk, Nashville TN 37215 *Web:* genesisdiamonds.net	615-269-6996		411
Genesis Direct 8514 Sunstate St, Tampa FL 33634 *Web:* www.genesisdirect.com	813-855-4274		5
Genesis Energy LP 919 Milam Ste 2100, Houston TX 77002 *NYSE: GEL* ■ *TF:* 800-284-3365 ■ *Web:* www.genesisenergy.com	713-860-2500	860-2640	597
Genesis Engineers Inc 1850 Gravers Rd, Plymouth Meeting PA 19462 *Web:* www.geieng.com	610-592-0280		261
Genesis Global Group Inc 28 Highland Rd, Westport CT 06880 *Web:* www.g3global.com	203-222-1795		193
Genesis HealthCare Corp 101 E State St, Kennett Square PA 19348 *TF:* 800-944-7776 ■ *Web:* www.genesishcc.com	610-444-6350	925-4000	451
Genesis Home Care Inc 116 E Heritage Dr, Tyler TX 75703 *TF:* 800-947-0273 ■ *Web:* genesishomecare.net	903-509-3374		363
Genesis Industries Inc 601 Pro Ject Dr, Elmwood WI 54740 *Web:* www.genesisindustriesinc.com	715-639-2435		596
Genesis International Inc 1040 Fox Chase Industrial Dr, Arnold MO 63010 *Web:* www.genesis-international.com	636-282-0011		203
Genesis Medical Ctr 1227 E Rusholme St, Davenport IA 52803 *Web:* www.genesishealth.com	563-421-1000		374-3
Genesis Medical Ctr Illini Campus 801 Illini Dr, Silvis IL 61282 *TF:* 800-250-6020 ■ *Web:* www.genesishealth.com	309-792-9363	792-4274	374-3
Genesis Plastics Welding Inc 720 E Broadway, Fortville IN 46040 *Web:* www.genesisplasticswelding.com	317-485-7887		393
Genesis Press Inc 7112 Augusta Rd, Piedmont SC 29673	864-552-2000		637-10
Genesis Products Inc 2608 Almac Ct, Elkhart IN 46514 *Web:* www.genesisproductsinc.com	574-266-8292		492
Genesis Publisher Services 3310 Eagle Pk Dr NE Ste 200, Grand Rapids MI 49525 *TF:* 800-828-1022 ■ *Web:* www.genesispubservices.com	616-831-2800	831-0831	637-6
Genesis Spiritual Life Ctr 53 Mill St, Westfield MA 01085 *Web:* genesisspiritualcenter.org	413-562-3627		673
Genesisfour Corp 7747 Ten Acre Rd, Andrews SC 29510 **Fax Area Code:* 978	843-461-4117	443-1303*	177
Genesys Creative Inc 500 Queens Quay W Ste 103e, Toronto ON M5V3K8 *Web:* www.genesisxd.com	416-595-9823		344
Genesys Engineering PC 629 Fifth Ave Bldg 3, Pelham NY 10803 *Web:* www.genesysengineering.net	914-251-0540		196
Genesys Telecommunications Laboratories Inc 2001 Junipero Serra Blvd, Daly City CA 94014 *TF:* 888-436-3797 ■ *Web:* genesys.com	650-466-1100	466-1260	735
Genesys Venture Inc 4-1250 Waverley St, Winnipeg MB R3T6C6 *Web:* www.genesysventure.com	204-478-5007		191
Genetec Inc 2280 Alfred-Nobel Blvd Ste 400, Montreal QC H4S2A4 *TF:* 866-684-8006 ■ *Web:* www.genetec.com	514-332-4000		225
GeneThera Inc 7577 W 103rd Ave Ste 212, Westminster CO 80021 *Web:* www.genethera.net	303-439-2085		85
Genetic Alliance Inc 4301 Connecticut Ave NW Ste 404, Washington DC 20008 *TF:* 800-860-8747 ■ *Web:* www.geneticalliance.org	202-966-5557	966-8553	48-17
Genetic Assays Inc 4711 Trousdale Dr Ste 209, Nashville TN 37220 *Web:* www.geneticassays.com	615-781-0709		415
Genetic Engineering News 140 Huguenot St 3rd Fl, New Rochelle NY 10801 *TF:* 888-211-4235 ■ *Web:* www.genengnews.com	914-740-2100	740-2101	531-12
Genetic Los Angeles 2344 E 38th St, Los Angeles CA 90058 *Web:* geneticlosangeles.com	323-364-8600		157-2
Genetic Profiles Corp 10675 Treena St Ste 103, San Diego CA 92131 *TF:* 800-551-7763 ■ *Web:* www.geneticprofiles.com	800-551-7763		417
Genetica DNA Laboratories Inc 1737 Tennessee Ave, Cincinnati OH 45229 *TF:* 800-433-6848 ■ *Web:* www.genetica.com	513-985-9777		417
Genetics & IVF Institute Inc 3015 Williams Dr, Fairfax VA 22031 *Web:* www.givf.com	703-698-7355		415
Genetics Associates Inc 1916 Patterson St Ste 400, Nashville TN 37203 *TF:* 800-331-4363 ■ *Web:* www.geneticsassociates.com	615-327-4532		415
Genetics Society of America (GSA) 9650 Rockville Pk, Bethesda MD 20814 *TF:* 866-486-4363 ■ *Web:* www.genetics-gsa.org	301-634-7300	634-7079	49-19
Genetrack Biolabs Inc 401-1508 Broadway W, Vancouver BC V6J1W8 *TF:* 888-828-1899 ■ *Web:* www.genetrack.com	604-325-7282		418
Genetti Lycoming Hotel 200 W Fourth St, Williamsport PA 17701 *Web:* genetti.com	570-326-6600		377
Geneva Area Chamber of Commerce 866 E Main St PO Box 84, Geneva OH 44041 *Web:* www.genevachamber.org	440-466-8694		139
Geneva Capital LLC 522 Broadway St Ste 4, Alexandria MN 56308 *TF:* 800-408-9352 ■ *Web:* www.gogc.com	800-408-9352		194
Geneva College 3200 College Ave, Beaver Falls PA 15010 **Fax:* Admissions ■ *TF:* 800-847-8255 ■ *Web:* www.geneva.edu	724-847-6500	847-6776*	166

Company	City	State	ZIP	Phone	Fax	Class
Geneva Construction Co (GCCO) 1350 Aurora Ave *Web:* www.genevaconstruction.net	Aurora	IL	60507	630-892-4357	892-7738	186
Geneva Consulting Group Inc 14 Vanderventer Ave Ste 250 *Web:* www.genevaconsulting.com	Port Washington	NY	11050	212-244-9595		180
Geneva County 200 N Commerce St *Web:* www.genevacounty.us	Geneva	AL	36340	334-684-5660		338
Geneva County Board of Education PO Box 250 *Web:* www.genevacountyschools.com	Geneva	AL	36340	334-684-5690		685
Geneva General Hospital 196 N St *TF:* 800-227-2345 ■ *Web:* www.flhealth.org	Geneva	NY	14456	315-787-4000		374-3
Geneva Laboratories Inc 1001 Proctor Dr *Web:* www.genevalabs.com	Elkhorn	WI	53121	262-723-5669		743
Geneva on the Lake 1001 Lochland Rd *Web:* www.genevaonthelake.com	Geneva	NY	14456	315-789-7190	789-0332	379
Geneva Pipe Inc 1465 W 400 N *Web:* www.genevapipe.com	Orem	UT	84057	801-225-2416		183
Geneva Rock Products Inc 302 W 5400 S Ste 200 *TF:* 855-614-6497 ■ *Web:* www.genevarock.com	Murray	UT	84107	801-281-7900		182
Geneva Scientific Inc 11 N Batavia Ave *TF:* 800-338-2697 ■ *Web:* www.barcoproducts.com	Batavia	IL	60510	800-338-2697		385
Geneva State Park 4499 Pandanarum Rd *TF:* 866-644-6727 ■ *Web:* parks.ohiodnr.gov/geneva	Geneva	OH	44041	440-466-8400		565
Geneva Trading USA LLC 190 S Lasalle St Ste 1800 *Web:* www.geneva-trading.com	Chicago	IL	60603	312-587-7000		691
Geneva Woods Pharmacy Inc 501 W International Airport Rd Ste 1A *TF:* 800-478-0005 ■ *Web:* www.genevawoods.com	Anchorage	AK	99518	907-565-6100		237
Genex Co-op Inc/CRI 117 E Green Bay St *TF:* 888-333-1783 ■ *Web:* genex.crinet.com	Shawano	WI	54166	715-526-2141		11-2
Genex Interactive 800 Corporate Pointe *Web:* meredithxceleratedmarketing.com	Culver City	CA	90230	424-672-9500		809
Genex Services Inc 440 E Swedesford Rd Ste 1000 *TF:* 888-464-3639 ■ *Web:* www.genexservices.com	Wayne	PA	19087	610-964-5100	964-1919	194
Genghis Cohen 740 N Fairfax Ave *Web:* www.genghiscohen.com	Los Angeles	CA	90046	323-653-0640		671
Genghis Grill 18900 Dallas Pkwy Ste 125 *TF:* 888-436-4447 ■ *Web:* www.genghisgrill.com	Dallas	TX	75287	888-436-4447		671
Genie Co 1 Door Dr PO Box 67 *TF:* 800-354-3643 ■ *Web:* www.geniecompany.com	Mount Hope	OH	44660	800-354-3643		350
Genie Industries Inc 18340 NE 76th St *TF:* 800-536-1800 ■ *Web:* www.genielift.com	Redmond	WA	98052	425-881-1800	883-3475	470
Genie Manufacturing Corp 999 Rush Henrietta Townli *TF:* 800-640-8680 ■ *Web:* www.geniemfg.com	Rush	NY	14543	585-359-4100		88
Genie Repros Inc 2211 Hamilton Ave *TF:* 877-496-6611 ■ *Web:* www.genierepros.com	Cleveland	OH	44114	216-696-6677		627
Genieco Inc 200 N Laflin St *TF:* 800-223-8217 ■ *Web:* gonesh.com	Chicago	IL	60607	312-421-2383	421-3042	145
Genius Jones Inc 49 NE 39th St *TF:* 866-436-4875 ■ *Web:* www.geniusjones.com	Miami	FL	33137	866-436-4875		174
Genius SIS Inc 150 S Pine Island Rd Ste 420 *Web:* www.geniussis.com	Plantation	FL	33324	954-667-7747		387
Genki Sushi Hawaii 677 Ala Moana Blvd Ste 612 *Web:* www.genkisushiusa.com	Honolulu	HI	96813	808-523-3315	523-3316	671
Genmab Inc 902 Carnegie Ctr Ste 301 *Web:* www.genmab.com	Princeton	NJ	08540	609-430-2481		743
Genmark Automation Inc 46723 Lakeview Blvd *Web:* www.genmarkautomation.info	Fremont	CA	94538	510-897-3400		386
Gennaro Inc 1725 Pontiac Ave *Web:* www.gennaroinc.com	Cranston	RI	02920	401-632-4100		411
Gennaro's Ristorante 1109 N Brand Blvd *TF:* 800-204-3131 ■ *Web:* www.gennarosristorante.com	Glendale	CA	91202	818-243-6231		671
Gennesaret Media LLC 1990 Main St Ste 750	Sarasota	FL	34236	941-621-2504		5
Genoa Business Forms Inc 445 Pk Ave *Fax Area Code: 815 ■ *TF:* 800-383-2801 ■ *Web:* www.genoabusforms.com	Sycamore	IL	60178	800-383-2801	895-8206*	110
Genocea Biosciences Inc 100 Acorn Park Dr *Web:* www.genocea.com	Cambridge	MA	02140	617-876-8191		668
GenomeDx 1038 Homer St *TF:* 888-975-4540 ■ *Web:* genomedx.com	Vancouver	BC	V6B2W9	888-975-4540		743
Genomic Health Inc 101 Galveston Dr *NASDAQ: GHDX* ■ *TF:* 866-662-6897 ■ *Web:* www.genomichealth.com	Redwood City	CA	94063	650-556-9300	556-1132	85
Genova Diagnostics 63 Zillicoa St *Fax: Cust Svc ■ *TF:* 800-522-4762 ■ *Web:* www.gdx.net	Asheville	NC	28801	828-253-0621	252-9303*	418
Genova Products Inc 7034 E Court St *TF:* 800-521-7488 ■ *Web:* www.genovaproducts.com	Davison	MI	48423	810-744-4500		608
Genova Technologies Inc 4250 River Center Ct NE Ste A *Web:* www.genovatech.com	Cedar Rapids	IA	52402	319-378-8455		177
Genpak Carthage 505 E Cotton St *TF:* 800-626-6695 ■ *Web:* www.genpak.com	Carthage	TX	75633	903-693-7151		300
Genpak Corp 68 Warren St *TF:* 800-626-6695 ■ *Web:* www.genpak.com	Glens Falls	NY	12801	518-798-9511		548
GenPore 1136 Morgantown Rd PO Box 380 *TF:* 800-654-4391 ■ *Web:* www.genpore.com	Reading	PA	19607	610-374-5171	374-4990	608
Gen-Probe Inc 10210 Genetic Center Dr *Fax Area Code: 800 ■ *TF:* 800-523-5001 ■ *Web:* www.hologic.com	San Diego	CA	92121	858-410-8000	288-3141*	231
GenQuest DNA Analysis Laboratory 133 Coney Island Dr *TF:* 877-362-5227 ■ *Web:* www.genquestdnalab.com	Sparks	NV	89431	775-358-0652		417
Genscape Inc 1140 Garvin Pl *Web:* www.genscape.com	Louisville	KY	40203	502-583-3435	583-3464	463
Gensco Equipment (1990) Inc 53 Carlaw Ave *TF:* 800-268-6797 ■ *Web:* www.genscoequip.com	Toronto	ON	M4M2R6	416-465-7521		258
Gensco Inc 4402 20th St E *TF:* 877-620-8203 ■ *Web:* www.gensco.com	Tacoma	WA	98424	253-620-8203	926-2073	612
GenServe Inc 80 Sweeneydale Ave *TF:* 800-247-7215 ■ *Web:* www.genserveinc.com	Bay Shore	NY	11706	631-435-0437		111
Gensler 2 Harrison St Ste 400 *Web:* gensler.com	San Francisco	CA	94105	415-433-3700	836-4599	261
Gentec Inc 2625 Dalton *TF:* 800-463-4480 ■ *Web:* gentec.ca	Quebec	QC	G1P3S9	418-651-8000		203
Gentech Systems Management LLC PO Box 3426 *Web:* www.gentech.com	Trenton	NJ	08619	609-890-2522		196
Gentek Bldg Products Inc 11 Craigwood Rd *TF:* 800-489-1144 ■ *Web:* www.gentekinc.com	Avenel	NJ	07001	732-381-0900		697
Gentell 3600 Boundbrook Ave *Web:* www.gentell.com	Feasterville Trevose	PA	19053	215-788-2700		238
Gentex Corp 600 N Centennial St *NASDAQ: GNTX* ■ *Web:* www.gentex.com	Zeeland	MI	49464	616-772-1800	772-7348	329
GENTEX Corp 324 Main St *TF:* 888-894-1755 ■ *Web:* www.gentexcorp.com	Simpson	PA	18407	570-282-3550	282-8555	542
Gentile Pismeny & Brengel LLP 159 Northern Blvd *Web:* www.gpb.net	Great Neck	NY	11021	516-487-4110		2
Gentiva Health Services Inc 680 S Fourth St Ste 1400 *NASDAQ: GTIV* ■ *TF:* 855-865-5894 ■ *Web:* www.gentiva.com	Louisville	KY	40202	855-865-5894	865-5894	363
Gentle Dental 22 Alpine Ln *TF:* 800-456-8715 ■ *Web:* www.gentledental.com	Chelmsford	MA	01824	978-256-7581		390
Gentry County 200 W Clay St *TF:* 800-392-8222 ■ *Web:* www.gentrycounty.net	Albany	MO	64402	660-726-3618	726-4102	338
Gentry Homes Ltd 560 N Nimitz Hwy *Fax: Sales ■ *Web:* www.gentryhawaii.com	Honolulu	HI	96809	808-599-5558	599-8347*	653
Gentry Locke Rakes & Moore LLP 10 Franklin Rd S E Ste 900 *TF:* 866-983-0866 ■ *Web:* www.gentrylocke.com	Roanoke	VA	24011	540-983-9300		428
Genuine Parts Co 2999 Cir 75 Pkwy *NYSE: GPC* ■ *TF:* 800-388-9993 ■ *Web:* www.genpt.com	Atlanta	GA	30339	770-953-1700		61
Genuitec LLC 2221 Justin Rd Ste 119-340 *Web:* www.genuitec.com	Flower Mound	TX	75028	214-224-0461		180
Genuity Concepts Inc 507 N Church St *TF:* 800-348-6616 ■ *Web:* www.genuityconcepts.com	Greensboro	NC	27401	336-379-1850		184
Genus Capital Management Inc 900 W Hastings St 6th Fl *Web:* www.genuscap.com	Vancouver	BC	V6C1E5	604-683-4554		401
Genus Oncology LLC 650 Albany St *Web:* genusoncology.com	Boston	MA	02118	847-549-6500		231
Genus Technologies LLC 6600 France Ave S Ste 425 *Web:* www.genusllc.com/en	Minneapolis	MN	55435	952-844-2644	844-2670	387
GenVec Inc 65 W Watkins Mill Rd *NASDAQ: GNVC* ■ *Web:* www.genvec.com	Gaithersburg	MD	20878	240-632-0740	632-0735	85
Genwest Systems Inc PO Box 397 *TF:* 800-235-6488 ■ *Web:* www.genwest.com	Edmonds	WA	98020	425-771-2700		180
Genzyme Corp 500 Kendall St *TF:* 800-745-4447 ■ *Web:* www.sanofigenzyme.com	Cambridge	MA	02142	617-252-7500		85
Genzyme Genetics 3400 Computer Dr *TF:* 800-255-7357 ■ *Web:* www.labcorp.com	Westborough	MA	01581	508-898-9001		417
GEO Care South Florida State Hospital 800 E Cypress Dr	Pembroke Pines	FL	33025	954-392-3000		374-5
GEO Drilling Fluids Inc 1431 Union Ave *TF:* 800-438-7436 ■ *Web:* www.geodf.com	Bakersfield	CA	93305	661-325-5919	325-5648	540
Geo Group 6 Odana Ct Ste 205 *TF:* 800-886-4709 ■ *Web:* www.thegeogroup.com	Madison	WI	53719	608-230-1000		768
Geo Heiser Body Company Inc 11210 Tukwila International Blvd *Web:* www.heiserbody.com	Seattle	WA	98168	206-622-7985	622-7135	516
Geo M Robinson & Co 1461 Atteberry Ln	San Jose	CA	95131	408-432-6264		189-13
Geo Products LLC 8615 Golden Spike Ln *TF:* 800-434-4743 ■ *Web:* www.geoproducts.org	Houston	TX	77086	281-820-5493		819
GEO Specialty Chemicals Inc 401 S Earl Ave *Web:* www.geosc.com	Lafayette	IN	47904	765-448-9412		145
Geo Strata Environmental Consultants Inc 4710 College Pk	San Antonio	TX	78249	210-492-7282		256
Geocal Inc 7290 S Fraser St *Web:* www.geocal.us	Centennial	CO	80112	303-337-0338		256
Geocapital Partners 1 Executive Dr Ste 160	Fort Lee	NJ	07024	201-461-9292	461-7793	792
Geocel Corp 2504 Marina Dr *TF:* 800-348-7615 ■ *Web:* www.geocelusa.com	Elkhart	IN	46514	800-348-7615	348-7009	3
Geo-Cleanse International Inc 400 State Rt 34 Ste B *Web:* www.geocleanse.com	Matawan	NJ	07747	908-206-1250		463
Geocom Inc 366 Madison Ave 10th Fl *Web:* www.geocom-inc.com	New York	NY	10017	212-949-0712		194
Geo-Comm Inc 601 W St Germain St *Web:* www.geo-comm.com	St. Cloud	MN	56301	320-240-0040		196
Geocomp Corp 1145 Massachusetts Ave *TF Cust Svc:* 800-822-2669 ■ *Web:* www.geocomp.com	Boxborough	MA	01719	978-635-0012	635-0266	178-5
Geo-Con Inc 1250 Fifth Ave *TF:* 800-544-6235 ■ *Web:* www.geocon.net	New Kensington	PA	15235	412-856-7700	373-3357	189-5
Geoconcepts Engineering 19955 Highland Vista Dr *Web:* geoconcepts-eng.com	Ashburn	VA	20147	703-726-8030		261
Geode Partners Inc 15851 N Dallas Pkwy Ste 600	Dallas	TX	75001	214-352-1002		463

	Phone	Fax	Class
Geode State Park 3333 Racine Ave, Danville IA 52623	319-392-4601		565
Web: www.iowadnr.gov			
Geodetic Designs			
2300 N Grand River Ave, Lansing MI 48906	517-908-0008		727
Web: geodeticdesigns.com			
GeoDigital International Inc			
175 Longwood Rd S McMaster Innovation Pk			
Ste 400A, Hamilton ON L8P0A1	905-667-7204		407
Web: www.geodigital.com			
Geodis Wilson Canada Ltd			
3061 Orlando Dr, Mississauga ON L4V1R4	905-677-5266		311
Web: www.geodis.com			
GeoEngineers Inc 8410 154th Ave NE, Redmond WA 98052	425-861-6000		261
TF: 888-624-8373 ■ *Web:* www.geoengineers.com			
Geofields Inc			
1201 W Peachtree St Ste 2450, Atlanta GA 30309	404-253-1000	875-2442	178-10
Web: www.geofields.com			
Geoforce Inc 750 Canyon Dr Ste 140, Coppell TX 75019	972-546-3878		536
TF: 888-574-3878 ■ *Web:* www.geoforce.com			
GeoGlobal Resources Inc (GGR)			
625 Fourth Ave SW, Calgary AB T2P0K2	403-777-9250		538
OTC: GGLR ■ *Web:* www.geoglobal.com			
Geographics 108 Main St 3rd Fl, Norwalk CT 06851	800-436-4919	520-1955*	552-2
**Fax Area Code:* 866 ■ *TF:* 800-436-4919 ■ *Web:* www.geographics.com			
Geo-instruments Inc			
24 Celestial Dr, Narragansett RI 02882	800-477-2506		463
TF: 800-477-2506 ■ *Web:* www.geo-instruments.com			
Geokinetics Management Inc			
1500 Citywest Blvd Ste 800, Houston TX 77042	713-850-7600		727
Web: www.geokinetics.com			
Geokon Inc 48 Spencer St, Lebanon NH 03766	603-448-1562	448-3216	472
Web: www.geokon.com			
Geolo Capital			
Pier 5 The Embarcadero Ste 102, San Francisco CA 94111	415-694-5802		528
Web: www.geolo.com			
Geologic Data Systems Inc			
2145 S Clermont St, Denver CO 80222	303-837-1699		536
Web: www.geologicdata.com			
Geological Museum			
1000 E University Ave, Laramie WY 82071	307-766-2646	766-6679	520
TF: 800-842-2776 ■ *Web:* www.uwyo.edu/geomuseum			
Geological Society of America, The (GSA)			
3300 Penrose Pl PO Box 9140, Boulder CO 80301	303-357-1000	357-1070	49-19
TF: 800-472-1988 ■ *Web:* www.geosociety.org			
GeoLogics Corp			
5285 Shawnee Rd Ste 300, Alexandria VA 22312	703-750-4000	750-4010	180
TF: 800-684-3455 ■ *Web:* geologics.com			
GeoMark Research Ltd 218 Higgins St, Humble TX 77338	832-644-1184		536
Web: www.geomarkresearch.com			
Geomedia Inc			
4242 Medical Dr Ste 4200, San Antonio TX 78229	210-614-5900		514
Web: www.geomedia.com			
Geomet Technologies LLC			
20251 Century Blvd, Germantown MD 20874	301-428-9898		193
TF: 877-407-8033 ■ *Web:* www.geomet.com			
Geometric Americas Inc			
50 Kirts Blvd Ste A, Troy MI 48084	248-404-3500		261
Web: geometricglobal.com			
Geometrica Inc 12300 Dundee Ct Ste 200, Cypress TX 77429	832-220-1200		198
Web: www.geometrica.com			
Geometrics Inc 2190 Fortune Dr, San Jose CA 95131	408-954-0522	954-0902	472
Web: www.geometrics.com			
GeoMicro Inc			
3200 El Camino Real Ste 140, Irvine CA 92602	714-505-0000		35
TF: 800-787-2337 ■ *Web:* www.geomicro.com			
Geonautics Manufacturing Inc			
506 Merrimac St, Newburyport MA 01950	978-462-7161		608
Web: www.geonauticsmfg.com			
Geopentech 5251 California Ave Ste 210, Irvine CA 92617	714-796-9100		261
Web: geopentech.com			
Geophysical Fluid Dynamics Laboratory			
NOAA/OAR/GFDL 201 Forrestal Rd, Princeton NJ 08540	609-452-6500	987-5063	668
Web: www.gfdl.noaa.gov			
Geophysical Pursuit Inc			
3501 Allen Pkwy, Houston TX 77019	713-529-3000		539
TF: 800-762-2123 ■ *Web:* www.geopursuit.com			
Geophysical Research Letter			
2000 Florida Ave NW, Washington DC 20009	202-462-6900	328-0566	531-12
TF: 800-966-2481 ■ *Web:* onlinelibrary.wiley.com			
Geophysics GPR International Inc			
100 - 2545 Delorimier Stree, Longueuil QC J4K3P7	450-679-2400		727
TF: 800-672-4774 ■ *Web:* www.geophysicsgpr.com			
Geoprofessional Business Assn			
1300 Piccard Dr LL14, Rockville MD 20850	301-565-2733	589-2017	49-19
Web: www.geoprofessional.org			
GeoResources Inc			
110 Cypress Stn Dr Ste 220, Williston ND 58802	281-537-9920	537-8324	536
NASDAQ: GEOI ■ *TF:* 855-538-0599 ■ *Web:* www.halconresources.com			
Georesults Inc 309 Pirkle Ferry Rd, Cumming GA 30040	770-205-8111		463
Web: www.georesults.com			
George 111 Queen St E, Toronto ON M5C1S2	416-863-6006	368-6093	671
Web: www.georgeonqueen.com			
George & Lynch Inc 150 Lafferty Ln, Dover DE 19901	302-736-3031		188-4
Web: www.geolyn.com			
George & Sons 11291 E Via Linda, Scottsdale AZ 85259	480-661-6336		671
Web: www.georgeandsonsasiancuisine.com			
George Adams Gallery 525 W 26th St, New York NY 10001	212-564-8480	564-8485	42
Web: www.artnet.com			
George Bagley & Company LLC			
1315 W 22nd St Ste 305, Oak Brook IL 60523	630-990-0355		2
Web: bagleycpa.com			
George Borchardt Inc 136 E 57th St, New York NY 10022	212-753-5785		444
Web: gbagency.com			
George Bush Library & Museum			
1000 George Bush Dr W, College Station TX 77845	979-691-4000		434-2
George Butler Assoc Inc			
9801 Renner Blvd, Lenexa KS 66219	913-492-0400		261
Web: www.gbateam.com			
George C Marshall Foundation			
VMI Parade, Lexington VA 24450	540-463-7103		520
Web: www.marshallfoundation.org			
George C Page Museum at La Brea Tar Pits			
5801 Wilshire Blvd, Los Angeles CA 90036	323-857-6300		520
Web: www.tarpits.org			
George County Hospital PO Box 607, Lucedale MS 39452	601-947-3161		374-3
Web: www.georgeregional.com			
George Darling Consulting Group Inc			
Towle Office Bldg 260 Merrimac St, Newburyport MA 01950	978-463-0400		463
Web: www.darlingconsulting.com			
George E DeLallo Co Inc 6390 Rt 30, Jeannette PA 15644	724-523-6577		297-8
TF: 877-335-2556 ■ *Web:* www.delallo.com			
George E Masker Inc 887 71st Ave, Oakland CA 94621	510-568-1206	638-2530	189-8
TF: 800-664-2656 ■ *Web:* www.maskerpainting.com			
George E Warren Corp			
3001 Ocean Dr Ste 203, Vero Beach FL 32963	772-778-7100	778-7171	579
Web: www.gewarren.com			
George Eastman House			
Menschel Library 900 E Ave, Rochester NY 14607	585-271-3361		434-4
Web: www.eastman.org			
George Eastman House & Gardens			
900 E Ave, Rochester NY 14607	585-271-3361		50-3
Web: www.eastman.org			
George Fox Evangelical Seminary			
12753 SW 68th Ave, Portland OR 97223	503-554-6150	554-6111	167-3
TF: 800-493-4937 ■ *Web:* www.georgefox.edu			
George Fox University			
414 N Meridian St, Newberg OR 97132	503-538-8383	554-3110*	166
**Fax:* Admissions ■ *TF:* 800-765-4369 ■ *Web:* www.georgefox.edu			
George G Sharp Inc			
22 Cortlandt St Ste 10, New York NY 10007	212-732-2800	732-2809	261
Web: www.georgesharp.com			
George H Swatek Inc			
1095 Edgewater Ave, Ridgefield NJ 07657	201-941-2400	941-8681	559
George H Wilson Inc			
250 Harvey W Blvd, Santa Cruz CA 95060	831-423-9522	423-9903	189-10
Web: www.geohwilson.com			
George H. Crosby Manitou State Park			
c/o Tettegouche State Pk 5702 Hwy 61, Silver Bay MN 55614	218-353-8800	226-6366	565
TF: 888-646-6367 ■ *Web:* www.dnr.state.mn.us			
George Harms Construction Co Inc			
PO Box 817, Farmingdale NJ 07727	732-938-4004	938-2782	188-4
Web: www.ghcci.com			
George Heinl & Co 201 Church St, Toronto ON M5B1Y7	416-363-0093		527
TF: 800-387-7858 ■ *Web:* www.georgeheinl.com			
George Industries Inc 1 S Page St, Endicott NY 13760	607-748-3371		492
Web: www.georgeindustries.com			
George J Igel & Company Inc			
2040 Alum Creek Dr, Columbus OH 43207	614-445-8421	445-8205	189-5
Web: www.igelco.com			
George J. Shaw Construction Co			
1601 Bellefontaine Ave, Kansas City MO 64127	816-231-8200		186
Web: georgeshawconstruction.com			
George K Baum & Co			
4801 Main St Ste 500 Ste 500, Kansas City MO 64112	816-474-1100	283-5180	690
TF: 800-821-7195 ■ *Web:* www.gkbaum.com			
George K's Catering & Banquet Hall			
2108 Cedar Fork Dr, Greensboro NC 27407	336-854-0008		671
George Kaiser Family Foundation			
7030 S Yale Ave Ste 600, Tulsa OK 74136	918-392-1612		305
Web: www.gkff.org			
George Kelk Corp 48 Lesmill Rd, Toronto ON M3B2T5	416-445-5850		407
TF: 888-275-5355 ■ *Web:* www.kelk.com			
George Koch Sons LLC 10 S 11th Ave, Evansville IN 47712	812-465-9600	465-9814*	386
**Fax:* Sales ■ *TF:* 888-873-5624 ■ *Web:* www.kochllc.com			
George L Luthy Memorial Botanical Gardens			
2520 N Prospect, Peoria IL 61603	309-686-3362		97
Web: www.peoriaparks.org			
George L Throop Co			
444 N Fair Oaks Ave, Pasadena CA 91103	626-796-0285		183
TF: 800-796-0285 ■ *Web:* www.throop.com			
George L. Smith State Park			
371 Geo L Smith St Pk Rd, Twin City GA 30471	478-763-2759		565
Web: www.gastateparks.org			
George Mason Mortgage Corp			
4100 Monu Crnr Dr Ste 100, Fairfax VA 22030	703-273-2600	934-9122	509
TF: 800-867-6859 ■ *Web:* www.gmmllc.com			
George Mason University			
4400 University Dr, Fairfax VA 22030	703-993-1000		166
TF: 888-627-6612 ■ *Web:* www.gmu.edu			
Fenwick Library 4400 University Dr, Fairfax VA 22030	703-993-2240		434-6
Web: library.gmu.edu			
George Mason University School of Law			
3301 N Fairfax Dr, Arlington VA 22201	703-993-8000	993-8088	167-1
Web: www.law.gmu.edu			
George Mason University's Ctr for the Arts			
George Mason University			
4400 University Dr MS 2F5, Fairfax VA 22030	703-993-8888	993-8650	572
Web: cfa.gmu.edu			
George Mcelroy & Associates Inc			
1349 Empire Central Ste 600, Dallas TX 75247	214-905-3700		463
TF: 800-935-4775 ■ *Web:* www.gmainc.com			
George Memorial Library			
1001 Golfview Dr, Richmond TX 77469	281-342-4455	341-2689	434-3
TF: 800-332-7143 ■ *Web:* www.fortbend.lib.tx.us			
George P. Johnson Co			
3600 Giddings Rd, Auburn Hills MI 48326	248-475-2500		195
Web: www.gpj.com			
George Pappas' Liberty Lanes			
2501 S York Rd, Gastonia NC 28052	704-868-2695		99
Web: www.georgepappaslibertylanes.com			
George Patton Assoc Inc			
55 Broadcommon Rd, Bristol RI 02809	401-247-0333		701
TF: 800-572-2194 ■ *Web:* www.displays2go.com			
George R Brown Convention Ctr			
1001 Avenida de Las Americas, Houston TX 77010	713-853-8000	853-8090	205
TF: 800-427-4697 ■ *Web:* www.grbhouston.com			

	Phone	Fax	Class
George R Peters Assoc Inc PO Box 850 ... Troy MI 48099 TF: 800-929-5972 ■ Web: www.grpeters.com	248-524-2211	524-1758	246
George Ranch Historical Park 10215 FM 762 ... Richmond TX 77469 Web: www.georgeranch.org	281-343-0218	343-9316	520
George Reed Inc 140 Empire Ave ... Modesto CA 95354 TF: 800-431-2584 ■ Web: www.georgereed.com	209-523-0734		261
George Risk Industries Inc 802 S Elm St ... Kimball NE 69145 OTC: RSKIA ■ TF Sales: 800-523-1227 ■ Web: www.grisk.com	308-235-4645	235-2609	692
George Rogers Clark National Historical Park 401 S Second St ... Vincennes IN 47591 Web: www.nps.gov	812-882-1776	882-7270	564
George S & Dolores Dore Eccles Foundation 79 S Main St 14th Fl ... Salt Lake City UT 84111 Web: www.gsecclesfoundation.org	801-246-5340	350-3510	305
George S Coyne Chemical Co 3015 State Rd ... Croydon PA 19021 TF: 800-523-1230 ■ Web: www.coynechemical.com	215-785-3000	785-1585	146
George S. Mickelson Trail 11361 Nevada Gulch Rd ... Lead SD 57754 TF: 800-888-1798 ■ Web: gfp.sd.gov/state-parks/directory/mickelson-trail	605-584-3896		565
George Schmitt & Company Inc 251 Boston Post Rd ... Guilford CT 06437 Web: www.georgeschmitt.com	203-453-4334		627
George School 1690 Newtown-Langhorne Rd ... Newtown PA 18940 TF: 888-804-1300 ■ Web: www.georgeschool.org	215-579-6547	579-6549	622
George Sollitt Construction 790 N Central Ave ... Wood Dale IL 60191 Web: www.sollitt.com	630-860-7333		186
George STREET Photo & Video LLC 230 W Huron St Ste 3W ... Chicago IL 60654 TF: 866-831-4103 ■ Web: www.georgestreetphoto.com	866-831-4103		590
George Street Playhouse 9 Livingston Ave ... New Brunswick NJ 08901 Web: www.georgestreetplayhouse.org	732-246-7717	247-9151	749
George T. Bagby State Park & Lodge 330 Bagby Pkwy ... Fort Gaines GA 39851 TF: 877-591-5575 ■ Web: www.gastateparks.org	229-768-2571		565
George Uhe Company Inc 219 River Dr ... Garfield NJ 07026 TF: 800-850-4075 ■ Web: www.uhe.com	201-843-4000	843-7517	479
George W Auch Co 735 S Paddock St ... Pontiac MI 48341 Web: www.auchconstruction.com	248-334-2000	334-3404	189-1
George Warshaw & Associates PC 77 Newbury St Fl 4 ... Boston MA 02116 Web: www.warshawdicarlo.com	617-262-7800		428
George Washington Birthplace National Monument 1732 Popes Creek Rd ... Washington's Birthplace VA 22443 Web: www.nps.gov/gewa	804-224-1732	224-2142	564
George Washington Carver Museum & Cultural Ctr 1165 Angelina St ... Austin TX 78702 Web: austintexas.gov/search404	512-974-4926	974-3699	520
George Washington Carver National Monument 5646 Carver Rd ... Diamond MO 64840 Web: www.nps.gov	417-325-4151	325-4231	564
George Washington Masonic National Memorial 101 Callahan Dr ... Alexandria VA 22301 TF: 800-435-7352 ■ Web: www.gwmemorial.org	703-683-2007	519-9270	50-4
George Washington Memorial Parkway Turkey Run Pk ... McLean VA 22101 Web: www.nps.gov/gwmp	703-289-2500	289-2598	564
George Washington University 2121 'I' St NW ... Washington DC 20052 TF: 866-498-3382 ■ Web: www.gwu.edu	202-994-1000	994-9619	166
Gelman Library 2130 H St NW ... Washington DC 20052 Web: library.gwu.edu	202-994-6558		434-6
Mount Vernon College 2100 Foxhall Rd NW ... Washington DC 20007 *Fax: Admissions ■ TF: 800-447-3765 ■ Web: www.gwu.edu	202-994-1000	994-0325*	166
George Washington University Hospital 900 23rd St NW ... Washington DC 20037 TF: 888-449-3627 ■ Web: www.gwhospital.com	202-715-4000		374-3
George Washington University Inn 824 New Hampshire Ave NW ... Washington DC 20037 Web: www.universityinndc.com	202-337-6620		379
George Washington University Law School 2000 H St NW ... Washington DC 20052 *Fax: Admissions ■ Web: www.law.gwu.edu	202-994-6261	994-7230*	167-1
George Washington University School of Medicine & Health Sciences 2300 Eye St NW Ross Hall ... Washington DC 20037 TF: 866-846-1107 ■ Web: smhs.gwu.edu	202-994-3506	994-1753	167-2
George Washington's Grist Mill 5513 Mt Vernon Memorial Hwy ... Mount Vernon VA 22309 Web: mountvernon.org	703-780-3383		565
George Washington's Mount Vernon 3200 Mt Vernon Memorial Hwy PO Box 110 ... Mt Vernon VA 22121 Web: www.mountvernon.org	703-780-2000		50-3
George Weston Ltd 22 St Clair Ave E ... Toronto ON M4T2S7 TSE: WN ■ TF: 800-564-6253 ■ Web: www.weston.ca	416-922-2500	922-4395	360-3
George Wood Farms Inc 113 N Carolina 343 ... Camden NC 27921	252-335-4357		10-11
George Wyth State Park 3659 Wyth Rd ... Waterloo IA 50703 Web: www.iowadnr.gov	319-232-5505		565
George's Greek Cafe 5316 E Second St ... Long Beach CA 90803 Web: georgesgreekcafe.com	562-433-1755		671
George, Miles & Buhr LLC 206 W Main St ... Salisbury MD 21801 TF: 800-789-4462 ■ Web: www.gmbnet.com	410-742-3115		261
Georges Inc 402 W Robinson Ave ... Springdale AR 72764 TF: 800-800-2449 ■ Web: georgesinc.com	479-927-7000		619
Georges Music Inc 912 Third St S ... Jacksonville Beach FL 32250 Web: www.georgesmusic.com	904-270-2220		526
Georgeson Securities Corp 480 Washington Blvd 27th Fl ... Jersey City NJ 07310 TF: 800-428-0717 ■ Web: www.georgesonsecurities.com	800-428-0717		690
Georgetown Chamber of Commerce 1 Chamber Wy ... Georgetown TX 78626 Web: www.georgetownchamber.org	512-930-3535	930-3587	139
Georgetown College 400 E College St ... Georgetown KY 40324 TF Admissions: 800-788-9985 ■ Web: www.georgetowncollege.edu	502-863-8000		166
Georgetown Convention & Visitors Bureau 1101 N College St ... Georgetown TX 78626 TF: 800-436-8696 ■ Web: www.visit.georgetown.org	512-930-3545		206
Georgetown County 129 Screven St PO Box 421270 ... Georgetown SC 29442 TF: 800-868-2284 ■ Web: www.georgetowncountysc.org	843-545-3063	545-3292	338
Georgetown County Chamber of Commerce 531 Front St ... Georgetown SC 29440 TF: 800-777-7705 ■ Web: www.visitgeorge.com	843-546-8436	520-4876	139
Georgetown Inn 1310 Wisconsin Ave ... Washington DC 20007 TF: 866-971-6618 ■ Web: www.georgetowninn.com	202-333-8900	333-8308	379
Georgetown Lombardi Comprehensive Cancer Center 3800 Reservoir Rd NW ... Washington DC 20057 Web: lombardi.georgetown.edu	202-444-0275		769
Georgetown Preparatory School 10900 Rockville Pk ... North Bethesda MD 20852 Web: www.gprep.org	301-493-5000		622
Georgetown Rail Equipment Co 111 Cooperative Way Ste 100 ... Georgetown TX 78626 Web: www.georgetownrail.com	512-869-1542		770
Georgetown Times 615 Front St ... Georgetown SC 29440 TF: 800-772-1213 ■ Web: www.southstrandnews.com	843-546-4148	264-5511	532-4
Georgetown Township Library 1525 Baldwin St ... Jenison MI 49428 Web: www.georgetown-mi.gov	616-457-9620		434-3
Georgetown University 37th & 'O' Sts NW ... Washington DC 20057 Web: www.georgetown.edu	202-687-3600	687-5084	166
Georgetown University Hotel & Conference Ctr 3800 Reservoir Rd NW ... Washington DC 20057 TF: 888-902-1606 ■ Web: www.acc-guhotelandconferencecenter.com	202-687-3200	687-3297	377
Georgetown University Law Ctr 600 New Jersey Ave NW ... Washington DC 20001 *Fax: Admissions ■ Web: www.law.georgetown.edu	202-662-9000	662-9439*	167-1
Georgetown University Library 37th 'O' St NW ... Washington DC 20057 Web: www.library.georgetown.edu	202-687-7452	687-1215	434-6
Georgetown University School of Medicine 3900 Reservoir Rd NW ... Washington DC 20057 Web: som.georgetown.edu	202-687-1154	687-3079	167-2
Georgetown-Scott County Chamber of Commerce 160 E Main St ... Georgetown KY 40324 Web: www.gtown.org	502-863-5424	863-5756	139
Georgia 1 Un Plaza 26th Fl ... New York NY 10017	212-759-1949		784
Administrative Office of the Cts 244 Washington St SW Ste 300 ... Atlanta GA 30334 Web: www.georgiacourts.org	404-656-5171		339-11
Aging Services Div 2 Peachtree St NW Fl 33 ... Atlanta GA 30303 Web: aging.dhs.georgia.gov	404-657-5258	657-5285	339-11
Agriculture Dept 19 ML King Jr Dr SW ... Atlanta GA 30334 Web: www.agr.state.ga.us	404-656-3627		339-11
Arts Council 260 14th St NW Ste 401 ... Atlanta GA 30318 TF: 800-222-6006 ■ Web: www.gpb.org/education	404-685-2400		339-11
Attorney General 40 Capitol Sq SW ... Atlanta GA 30334 Web: georgia.gov	404-656-3300	657-8733	339-11
Banking & Finance Dept 2990 Brandywine Rd Ste 200 ... Atlanta GA 30341 TF: 888-986-1633 ■ Web: www.ganet.org	770-986-1633	986-1654	339-11
Bill Status-House 309 State Capitol ... Atlanta GA 30334 Web: www.house.ga.gov	404-656-5015		433
Community Affairs Dept 60 Executive Pk S NE ... Atlanta GA 30329 TF: 800-359-4663 ■ Web: www.dca.state.ga.us	404-679-4940		339-11
Composite Medical Board 2 Peachtree St NW 36th Fl ... Atlanta GA 30303 TF: 800-436-7442 ■ Web: medicalboard.georgia.gov	404-656-3913	656-9723	339-11
Corrections Dept 300 Patrol Rd Forsyth ... Atlanta GA 31029 TF: 888-343-5627 ■ Web: www.dcor.state.ga.us	404-656-4661		339-11
Department of Behavioral Health & Developmental Di 2 Peachtree St NW Fl 24 ... Atlanta GA 30303 TF: 800-436-7442 ■ Web: dbhdd.georgia.gov	404-657-2252		339-11
Departmentyof Driver Services 2206 E View Pkwy ... Conyers GA 30013 Web: www.dds.ga.gov	678-413-8400		339-11
Division of Child Support Services 2 Peachtree St NW ... Atlanta GA 30303 *Fax Area Code: 800 ■ Web: childsupport.georgia.gov	404-657-3865	436-7442*	339-11
Economic Development Dept 75 Fifth St NW Ste 845 ... Atlanta GA 30308 TF: 800-255-0056 ■ Web: www.georgia.org	404-962-4005		339-11
Education Dept 205 Jesse Hill Jr Dr SE ... Atlanta GA 30334 Web: www.gadoe.org	404-656-2800	651-8737	339-11
Emergency Management Agency (GEMA) 935 E Confederate Ave SE PO Box 18055 ... Atlanta GA 30316 TF: 800-879-4362 ■ Web: www.gema.ga.gov	404-635-7000		339-11
Employment Services Div 148 Andrew Young International Blvd NE ... Atlanta GA 30303 Web: www.dol.state.ga.us	404-232-3515		259
Environmental Protection Div 2 Martin Luther King Jr Dr Ste 1152 E Tower ... Atlanta GA 30334 TF: 888-373-5947 ■ Web: www.georgiaepd.org	404-657-5947		339-11
Family & Children Services Div 2 Peachtree St NW ... Atlanta GA 30303 Web: dfcs.dhs.georgia.gov	404-651-9361	657-5105	339-11
General Assembly State Capitol ... Atlanta GA 30334 Web: www.legis.ga.gov	404-656-5020		339-11
Governor 203 State Capitol 206 Washington St ... Atlanta GA 30334 Web: www.gov.georgia.gov	404-656-1776	657-7332	339-11

	Phone	Fax	Class
Governor's Office of Consumer Protection 2 ML King Jr Dr Ste 356 .... Atlanta GA 30334 *Fax Area Code: 404 ■ *TF:* 800-869-1123 ■ *Web:* consumer.georgia.gov	800-869-1123	651-9018*	339-11
Historic Preservation Div 2610 GA Hwy 155 SW .... Atlanta GA 30281 *Web:* www.georgiashpo.org	404-656-2840		339-11
Housing Finance Div 60 Executive Pk S NE .... Atlanta GA 30329 *Web:* www.dca.state.ga.us	404-679-0607	679-4837	339-11
Human Resources Dept 2 Peachtree St NW Ste 29-250 .... Atlanta GA 30303 *Web:* dhs.georgia.gov	404-656-6750	651-8669	339-11
Information Technology Office 258 Fourth St NW Rich Bldg .... Atlanta GA 30332 *Web:* www.oit.gatech.edu	404-894-7173		339-11
Insurance Commissioner 2 Martin Luther King, Jr Dr W Tower, Ste 704 .... Atlanta GA 30334 *TF:* 800-656-2298 ■ *Web:* www.oci.ga.gov	404-656-2070	656-4030	339-11
Labor Dept 148 Andrew Young International Blvd NE .... Atlanta GA 30303 *Web:* www.dol.state.ga.us	404-232-7300		339-11
Lieutenant Governor 240 State Capitol .... Atlanta GA 30334 *Web:* ltgov.georgia.gov	404-656-5030	656-6739	339-11
Natural Resources Dept 2 ML King Jr Dr SE Ste 1252E .... Atlanta GA 30334 *TF:* 800-366-2661 ■ *Web:* www.gadnr.org	404-656-3500	656-0770	339-11
Ports Authority 2 Main St .... Savannah GA 31402 *TF:* 800-342-8012 ■ *Web:* www.gaports.com	912-964-3811		618
Professional Licensing Boards Div 237 Coliseum Dr .... Macon GA 31217 *Web:* connect.georgia.gov	478-207-1640	207-1660	339-11
Public Health Div 2 Peachtree St NW Ste 15-470 .... Atlanta GA 30303 *Web:* dph.georgia.gov	404-657-2700		339-11
Public Service Commission 244 Washington St SW .... Atlanta GA 30334 *TF:* 800-282-5813 ■ *Web:* www.psc.state.ga.us	404-656-4501	656-2341	339-11
Rehabilitation Services Div 1718 Peachtree St NW Ste 376 S .... Atlanta GA 30309 *Web:* gvs.georgia.gov	404-232-7300		339-11
Revenue Dept 1800 Century Ctr Blvd NE .... Atlanta GA 30345 *TF:* 877-423-6711 ■ *Web:* www.etax.dor.ga.gov	404-417-6760		339-11
Secretary of State 214 State Capitol .... Atlanta GA 30334 *Web:* georgia.gov	404-656-2881		339-11
Securities & Business Regulation Div 2 Martin Luther King Jr Dr W Tower Ste 313 ..... Atlanta GA 30334 *TF:* 844-753-7825 ■ *Web:* sos.ga.gov/index.php/?section=securities	404-654-6023		339-11
State Government Information 7 Martin Luther King JrDr Ste 643 .... Atlanta GA 30334 *Web:* www.georgia.gov	404-656-6996		339-11
State Patrol PO Box 1456 .... Atlanta GA 30371 *Web:* www.dps.georgia.gov	404-624-7000		339-11
Student Finance Commission 2082 E Exchange Pl .... Tucker GA 30084 *TF:* 800-505-4732 ■ *Web:* gsfc.georgia.gov	770-724-9000		725
Supreme Court 244 Washington St SW Rm 572 State Office Annex Bldg .... Atlanta GA 30334 *Web:* www.gasupreme.us	404-656-3470		339-11
Tourism Div 75 Fifth St NW Ste 1200 .... Atlanta GA 30308 *TF Resv:* 800-255-0056 ■ *Web:* georgia.org/georgia_slide/tourism	404-962-4000		339-11
Transparency & Campaign Finance Commission 200 Piedmont Ave SE Ste 1416 W Tower .... Atlanta GA 30334 *TF:* 866-589-7327 ■ *Web:* ethics.ga.gov	404-463-1980	463-1988	265
University System Board of Regents 270 Washington St South W .... Atlanta GA 30334 *Web:* www.usg.edu	404-962-3049	651-9301	339-11
Veterans Service Dept Floyd Veterans Memorial Bldg Ste 970E .... Atlanta GA 30334 *TF:* 800-436-7442 ■ *Web:* veterans.georgia.gov	404-656-2300	657-9738	339-11
Vital Records Office 2600 Skyland Dr NE .... Atlanta GA 30319 *TF:* 800-436-7442 ■ *Web:* dph.georgia.gov	404-679-4701		339-11
Wildlife Resources Div 2070 US Hwy 278 SE .... Social Circle GA 30025 *Web:* georgiawildlife.org	770-918-6400		339-11
Workers' Compensation Board 270 Peachtree St NW .... Atlanta GA 30303 *Web:* www.sbwc.georgia.gov	404-656-2048	651-9467	339-11
Georgia Aquarium 225 Baker St .... Atlanta GA 30313 *Web:* www.georgiaaquarium.org	404-581-4000		40
Georgia Assn of Realtors 3200 Presidential Dr .... Atlanta GA 30340 *TF:* 866-280-0576 ■ *Web:* www.garealtor.com	770-451-1831	458-6992	656
Georgia Avenue Rock Creek East Family Support Collaborative 1104 Allison St NW .... Washington DC 20011 *TF:* 800-552-3431 ■ *Web:* gafsc-dc.org	202-722-1815		533
Georgia Ballet 1255 Field Pkwy .... Marietta GA 30066 *Web:* www.georgiaballet.org	770-528-0881		573-1
Georgia Bar Journal 104 Marietta St NW Ste 100 .... Atlanta GA 30303 *TF:* 866-773-2782 ■ *Web:* gabar.org	404-527-8700	527-8717	457-15
Georgia Boot Inc 39 E Canal St .... Nelsonville OH 45764 *TF:* 877-795-2410 ■ *Web:* www.georgiaboot.com	740-753-1951		301
Georgia Cancer Specialists Pc (GCS) 1872 Montreal Rd .... Tucker GA 30084 *TF:* 800-491-5991 ■ *Web:* www.gacancer.com	770-496-9443	496-9490	374-7
Georgia Chamber of Commerce 270 Peachtree St NW Ste 2000 .... Atlanta GA 30303 *TF:* 800-241-2286 ■ *Web:* www.gachamber.com	404-223-2264	223-2290	140
Georgia College & State University 231 W Hancock St CB 23 .... Milledgeville GA 31061 *Fax: Admissions ■ *TF:* 800-342-0471 ■ *Web:* www.gcsu.edu	478-445-5004	445-3653*	166
Macon 433 Cherry St .... Macon GA 31206 *TF:* 800-342-0471 ■ *Web:* www.gcsu.edu/future-students/graduate	478-752-4278		166
Georgia Correctional Industries 2984 Clifton Springs Rd .... Decatur GA 30034 *TF:* 800-282-7130 ■ *Web:* www.gci-ga.com	404-244-5100	244-5141	630

	Phone	Fax	Class
Georgia Crown Distributing Co 100 Georgia Crown Dr .... McDonough GA 30253 *TF:* 800-342-2350 ■ *Web:* www.georgiacrown.com	770-302-3000		81-3
Georgia Cu Affiliates 6705 Sugarloaf Pkwy Ste 200 .... Duluth GA 30097 *TF:* 800-768-4282 ■ *Web:* gcua.org	770-476-9625		219
Georgia Dental Assn 7000 Peachtree Dnwdy Rd NE Ste 200 Bldg 17 ..... Atlanta GA 30328 *TF:* 800-432-4357 ■ *Web:* www.gadental.org	404-636-7553	633-3943	227
Georgia Dome 1 Georgia Dome Dr NW .... Atlanta GA 30313 *TF:* 888-333-4406 ■ *Web:* www.gadome.com	404-223-9200	223-8011	720
Georgia Farm Bureau News 1620 Bass Rd .... Macon GA 31210 *TF:* 800-342-1192 ■ *Web:* www.gfb.org	478-474-8411		457-1
Georgia Flooring Outlet 1660 Hwy 155 S .... Mcdonough GA 30253 *Web:* www.georgiaflooringoutlet.com	770-474-9270		361
Georgia Grille 2290 Peachtree Rd .... Atlanta GA 30309	404-352-3517		671
Georgia Hardy Tours 20 Eglinton Ave E .... Toronto ON M4R1K8 *TF:* 800-813-4509 ■ *Web:* www.ghardytours.com	416-483-7533		772
Georgia Highlands College *Cartersville* 5441 Hwy 20 NE .... Cartersville GA 30121 *TF:* 800-332-2406 ■ *Web:* www.highlands.edu	678-872-8000	872-8013	162
Floyd 3175 Cedartown Hwy .... Rome GA 30161 *TF:* 800-332-2406 ■ *Web:* www.highlands.edu	706-802-5000	295-6341	162
Georgia Institute of Technology 225 N Ave NW .... Atlanta GA 30332 *Fax: Admissions ■ *Web:* www.gatech.edu	404-894-2000	894-9511*	166
Georgia Institute of Technology Library 266 Fourth St NW .... Atlanta GA 30332 *TF:* 888-225-7804 ■ *Web:* www.library.gatech.edu	404-894-4500	894-0399	434-6
Georgia International Convention Ctr 2000 Convention Ctr Concourse .... College Park GA 30337 *Web:* www.gicc.com	770-997-3566	994-8559	205
Georgia Lottery Corp 250 Williams St NW Ste 3000 .... Atlanta GA 30303 *TF:* 800-425-8259 ■ *Web:* www.galottery.com	404-215-5000		452
Georgia Military College 201 E Green St .... Milledgeville GA 31061 *Fax: Admissions ■ *TF:* 800-342-0413 ■ *Web:* www.gmc.edu	478-387-4900	445-6520*	162
Georgia Mountains Ctr 301 Main St SW PO Box 2496 .... Gainesville GA 30501 *Web:* www.gainesville.org	770-534-8420		205
Georgia Municipal Association 201 Pryor St SW .... Atlanta GA 30303 *TF:* 888-488-4462 ■ *Web:* www.gmanet.com	404-688-0472		533
Georgia Museum of Art 90 Carlton St University of Georgia .... Athens GA 30602 *TF:* 800-709-7406 ■ *Web:* www.uga.edu	706-542-4662		520
Georgia Northwestern Technical College Foundation Inc 1 Maurice Culberson Dr SW .... Rome GA 30161 *TF:* 866-983-4682 ■ *Web:* www.gntc.edu/community/foundation	706-295-6842		305
Georgia Nurses Assn (GNA) 3032 Briarcliff Rd NE .... Atlanta GA 30329 *TF:* 800-324-0462 ■ *Web:* www.georgianurses.org	404-325-5536	325-0407	533
Georgia O'Keeffe Museum 217 Johnson St .... Santa Fe NM 87501 *TF:* 800-898-6639 ■ *Web:* www.okeeffemuseum.org	505-946-1000		520
Georgia Perimeter College *Clarkston Campus* 555 N Indian Creek Dr .... Clarkston GA 30021 *Web:* perimeter.gsu.edu	678-891-3200		162
Decatur Campus 3251 Panthersville Rd .... Decatur GA 30034 *Web:* perimeter.gsu.edu	678-891-2300		162
Dunwoody Campus 2101 Womack Rd .... Dunwoody GA 30338 *Web:* perimeter.gsu.edu	770-274-5000		162
Georgia Pharmacy Assn (GPhA) 50 Lenox Pointe NE .... Atlanta GA 30324 *TF:* 888-871-5590 ■ *Web:* www.gpha.org	404-231-5074	237-0435	585
Georgia Poultry Improvement Assn 3235 Abit Massey Way .... Ganesville GA 30501	770-766-6810		138
Georgia Power Foundation Inc 96 Annex .... Atlanta GA 30396 *Web:* www.southerncompany.com	404-506-5000		304
Georgia Printco 90 S Oak St .... Lakeland GA 31635 *TF:* 866-572-0146 ■ *Web:* www.georgiaprintco.com	866-572-0146		627
Georgia Public Broadcasting (GPB) 260 14th St NW .... Atlanta GA 30318 *TF:* 800-222-6006 ■ *Web:* www.gpb.org	800-222-6006		632
Georgia Public Interest Research Group (PIRG) 817 W Peachtree St NW Ste 204 .... Atlanta GA 30308 *Web:* www.georgiapirg.org	404-892-3405		633
Georgia Public Library 1800 Century Pl NE Ste 150 .... Atlanta GA 30345 *TF:* 800-248-6701 ■ *Web:* www.georgialibraries.org	404-235-7200		31
Georgia Regional Hospital at Atlanta 3073 Panthersville Rd .... Atlanta GA 30034 *TF:* 800-436-7442 ■ *Web:* dbhdd.georgia.gov	404-243-2100		374-5
Georgia Regional Hospital at Savannah 1915 Eisenhower Dr .... Savannah GA 31406 *TF:* 800-436-7442	912-356-2011	356-2691	374-5
Georgia Republican Party 3110 Maple Dr Ste 200-E .... Atlanta GA 30305 *Web:* www.gagop.org	404-257-5559	257-0779	616-2
Georgia Society of Cpa's 6 Concourse Pkwy Ste 800 .... Atlanta GA 30328 *TF:* 800-330-8889 ■ *Web:* www.gscpa.org	404-231-8676		138
Georgia Southern University PO Box 8024 .... Statesboro GA 30460 *Web:* www.georgiasouthern.edu	912-478-5391		166
Georgia Southwestern State University 800 Gsw State University Dr .... Americus GA 31709 *TF Admissions:* 800-338-0082 ■ *Web:* www.gsw.edu	229-928-1273	931-2983	166
Georgia Sports Hall of Fame 301 Cherry St PO Box 4644 .... Macon GA 31201 *Web:* georgiasportshalloffame.com/site	478-752-1585	752-1587	522
Georgia State Prison 1978 Georgia Hwy 147 .... Reidsville GA 30453 *Web:* www.dcor.state.ga.us	912-557-7771	557-7163	213

Name / Address	City	State	Zip	Phone	Fax	Class
Georgia State University 33 Gilmer St SE *Web:* www.gsu.edu	Atlanta	GA	30303	404-413-2000	413-2002	166
Georgia State University College of Law 140 Decatur St *Web:* www.law.gsu.edu	Atlanta	GA	30303	404-651-2048		167-1
Georgia Straight 1701 W Broadway *Web:* www.straight.com	Vancouver	BC	V6J1Y3	604-730-7000	730-7010	532-5
Georgia Tech Fusion Research Ctr Boggs Bldg Rm 3-29 *Web:* www.frc.gatech.edu	Atlanta	GA	30332	404-894-3714	894-3733	668
Georgia Tech Research Institute (GTRI) *Georgia Institute of Technology* 250 14th St NW *Web:* www.gtri.gatech.edu	Atlanta	GA	30318	404-407-7400	894-9875	668
Georgia Timberlands Inc 3250 Waterville Rd *Web:* gatimberlands.com	Macon	GA	31206	478-788-4660		302
Georgia Trust, The 1516 Peachtree St NW *Web:* www.georgiatrust.org	Atlanta	GA	30309	404-881-9980	875-2205	50-3
Georgia Veterans State Park 2459 US 280 W *Web:* www.gastateparks.org	Cordele	GA	31015	229-276-2371		565
Georgia Veterinary Medical Assn 2200 Century Pkwy Ste 725 *TF:* 800-853-1625 ■ *Web:* www.gvma.net	Atlanta	GA	30345	678-309-9800	309-3361	795
Georgia War Veterans Nursing Home 1101 15th St	Augusta	GA	30901	706-721-2824		793
Georgia Winery, The 6469 Battlefield Pkwy *Web:* www.georgiawines.com	Ringgold	GA	30736	706-937-9463	937-9860	50-7
Georgia World Congress Ctr 285 Andrew Young International Blvd NW *Web:* www.gwcc.com	Atlanta	GA	30313	404-223-4200	223-4211	205
Georgia's Greek Cuisine 3550 Rosecrans St *Web:* www.georgiasgreekcuisine.com	San Diego	CA	92110	619-523-1007	523-2455	671
Georgia's Own Credit Union 1155 Peachtree St NE Ste 400 *TF:* 800-533-2062 ■ *Web:* www.georgiasown.org	Atlanta	GA	30309	404-874-1166	881-2950	219
Georgia-Carolina Radiocasting Cos LLC 233 Big A Rd *Web:* www.gacaradio.com	Toccoa	GA	30577	706-297-7264		643
Georgian College 1 Georgian Dr *Web:* www.georgianc.on.ca	Barrie	ON	L4M3X9	705-728-1968		179
Georgian Court Hotel 773 Beatty St *TF:* 800-663-1155 ■ *Web:* www.georgiancourthotelvancouver.com	Vancouver	BC	V6B2M4	604-682-5555	682-8830	379
Georgian Court University 900 Lakewood Ave **Fax Area Code: 732* ■ **Fax:* Admissions ■ *TF:* 800-458-8422 ■ *Web:* www.georgian.edu	Lakewood	NJ	08701	800-458-8422	987-2000*	166
Georgian Hotel 1415 Ocean Ave *TF:* 800-538-8147 ■ *Web:* www.georgianhotel.com	Santa Monica	CA	90401	310-395-9945		379
Georgian Partners 2 St Clair Ave W Ste 1400 *TF:* 800-567-0006 ■ *Web:* www.georgianpartners.com	Toronto	ON	M4V1L5	416-868-9696		401
Georgian Plantation Shutter Co 455 Wilbanks Dr *TF:* 888-684-0382 ■ *Web:* www.georgianshutters.com	Ball Ground	GA	30107	678-454-1100		361
Georgian Resort 384 Canada St *TF:* 800-525-3436 ■ *Web:* www.georgianresort.com	Lake George	NY	12845	518-668-5401	668-5870	379
Georgian Terrace Hotel 659 Peachtree St NE *TF:* 800-651-2316 ■ *Web:* www.thegeorgianterrace.com	Atlanta	GA	30308	404-897-1991		379
Georgian, The 411 University St *TF:* 888-363-5022 ■ *Web:* fairmont.com	Seattle	WA	98101	206-621-7889		671
Georgia-Pacific Corp 133 Peachtree St NE *Web:* www.gp.com	Atlanta	GA	30303	404-652-4000		558
Georgie's Ceramic & Clay Company Inc 756 NE Lombard St *TF:* 800-999-2529 ■ *Web:* www.georgies.com	Portland	OR	97211	503-283-1353	283-1387	43
Georgio's Cafe International 426 N Superior St *TF:* 800-243-4667 ■ *Web:* www.georgiostoledo.com	Toledo	OH	43604	419-242-2424		671
Georgio's Fine Food and Spirits 2971 Apalachee Pkwy *Web:* georgiostallahassee.com	Tallahassee	FL	32309	850-877-3211		671
Geoscape International Inc 2100 W Flagler St *TF:* 888-211-9353 ■ *Web:* www.geoscape.com	Miami	FL	33135	888-211-9353		180
Geo-slope International Ltd 633 6 Ave SW Ste 1400 *TF:* 800-965-4665 ■ *Web:* www.geo-slope.com	Calgary	AB	T2P2Y5	403-269-2002		261
Geosol Inc 5795 NW 151st St	Hialeah	FL	33014	305-828-4367		261
Geo-Solutions Inc 1250 Fifth Ave *Web:* www.geo-solutions.com	New Kensington	PA	15068	724-335-7273		188
GEOSPAN Corp 6901 E Fish Lake Rd Ste 156 *TF:* 800-436-7726 ■ *Web:* www.geospan.com	Minneapolis	MN	55369	763-493-9320	424-6633	225
Geospatial Information & Technology Assn (GITA) 14456 E Evans Ave *Web:* www.gita.org	Aurora	CO	80014	303-337-0513		49-19
Geospatial Systems Inc 150 Lucius Gordon Dr	West Henrietta	NY	14586	585-427-8310		21
GeoStrata Resources Inc 9727 Horton Rd SW *Web:* www.geostrata.ca	Calgary	AB	T2V2X5	403-319-0922		727
GeoStrut 1374 W 200 S	Lindon	UT	84042	801-356-1311		387
GeoSyntec Consultants Inc 5901 Broken Sound Pkwy NW Ste 300 *TF:* 866-676-1101 ■ *Web:* www.geosyntec.com	Boca Raton	FL	33487	561-995-0900	995-0925	261
GEOSYS Inc 3030 Harbor Ln *TF:* 866-782-4661 ■ *Web:* www.geosys.com	Plymouth	MN	55447	866-782-4661		194
Geosystems Inc 210 S Washington Ave *Web:* zippermast.com	Titusville	FL	32796	321-383-9585	747-0601	591
Geotab Inc 1081 S Service Rd W *TF:* 877-436-8221 ■ *Web:* www.geotab.com	Oakville	ON	L6L6K3	416-434-4309		387
Geotech Environmental Equipment Inc 2650 E 40th Ave *TF:* 800-833-7958 ■ *Web:* www.geotechenv.com	Denver	CO	80205	303-320-4764	322-7242	201
Geotech Ltd 245 Industrial Pkwy N *Web:* www.geotech.ca	Aurora	ON	L4G4C4	905-841-5004		727
Geotechnical Services Inc 9312 G Ct *Web:* gsinetwork.com	Omaha	NE	68127	402-339-6104		261
Geotechnologies Inc 3200 Wellington Court Ste G *Web:* www.geotechpa.com	Raleigh	NC	27615	919-954-1514		261
Geotek Engineering & Testing Services Inc 909 E 50th St N *TF:* 800-354-5512 ■ *Web:* www.geotekeng.com	Sioux Falls	SD	57104	605-335-5512		256
Geotest - Marvin Test Systems Inc 1770 Kettering *Web:* marvintest.com	Irvine	CA	92614	949-263-2222		201
Geotest Engineering Inc 5600 Bintliff Dr *Web:* geotesteng.com	Houston	TX	77036	713-266-0588	266-2977	261
Geotrace Technologies Inc 12141 Wickchester Ln	Houston	TX	77079	281-497-8440		225
GeoTrust Inc 350 Ellis St Bldg J *TF:* 866-511-4141 ■ *Web:* www.geotrust.com	Mountain View	CA	94043	650-426-5010	237-8871	178-7
GeoVera Holdings Inc 1455 Oliver Rd *Web:* www.geoveraholdingsinc.com	Fairfield	CA	94534	707-863-3700		391-6
Gerace Construction Company Inc 4055 S Saginaw Rd *Web:* www.geraceconstruction.com	Midland	MI	48640	989-496-2440	496-2465	186
Geragos & Geragos PC 644 S Figueroa St *Web:* www.geragos.com	Los Angeles	CA	90017	213-625-3900	625-1600	428
Gerald A Teel Co 974 Campbell Rd Ste 204 *Web:* www.valbridge.com/appraiser/43/houston-tx	Houston	TX	77024	713-467-5858	467-0704	652
Gerald H Phipps 5995 Greenwood Florida Plaza Blvd Ste 100 *TF:* 877-574-4777 ■ *Web:* www.ghphipps.com	Greenwood Village	CO	80111	303-571-5377	629-7467	186
Gerald J Sullivan & Assoc Inc 800 W Sixth St Ste 1800 *Web:* gjs.com	Los Angeles	CA	90017	213-626-1000		390
Gerald Printing Service Inc 105 Hunter Ct *TF:* 800-444-6787 ■ *Web:* www.geraldprinting.com	Bowling Green	KY	42103	270-781-4770		627
Gerald R Ford Conservation Ctr 1326 S 32nd St *TF:* 800-634-6932 ■ *Web:* www.nebraskahistory.org	Omaha	NE	68105	402-595-1180	595-1178	50-2
Gerald R Ford International Airport 5500 44th St SE *TF:* 866-289-9673 ■ *Web:* www.grr.org	Grand Rapids	MI	49512	616-233-6000	233-6025	27
Gerald R Ford Library 1000 Beal Ave *TF:* 800-410-8354 ■ *Web:* www.fordlibrarymuseum.gov	Ann Arbor	MI	48109	734-205-0555	205-0571	434-2
Gerald R Ford Museum 303 Pearl St NW *TF:* 800-888-9487 ■ *Web:* fordlibrarymuseum.gov	Grand Rapids	MI	49504	616-254-0400	254-0386	520
Geraldine R Dodge Foundation 14 Maple Ave *Web:* www.grdodge.org	Morristown	NJ	07962	973-540-8442	540-1211	305
Geraldo's 701 College Rd	Fairbanks	AK	99701	907-452-2299		671
Geralds of Northville Inc 41012 Five Mile Rd *Web:* www.geraldssalon.com	Plymouth	MI	48170	734-420-0111		77
Geranio Ristorante 722 King St *Web:* www.geranio.net	Alexandria	VA	22314	703-548-0088	548-0091	671
Gerard Daniel Worldwide 34 Barnhart Dr *TF:* 800-232-3332 ■ *Web:* www.gerarddaniel.com	Hanover	PA	17331	717-637-5901	633-7095	688
Gerard Design 28371 Davis Pkwy Ste 100 *Web:* www.gerardagency.com	Warrenville	IL	60555	630-355-0775		344
Gerardi Construction Inc 1604 N 19th St *Web:* www.gerardiconstruction.com	Tampa	FL	33605	813-248-4341		186
Gerbel & Company PC 830 Pleasant St PO Box 44 *Web:* gerbel.com	St Joseph	MI	49085	269-983-0534		2
Gerber Auto Collision & Glass Centers Inc 8250 Skokie Blvd *TF:* 877-743-7237 ■ *Web:* www.gerbercollision.com	Skokie	IL	60077	847-679-0510		62-4
Gerber Childrenswear Inc 7005 Pelham Rd Ste D *TF:* 800-642-4452 ■ *Web:* www.gerberchildrenswear.com	Greenville	SC	29615	864-987-5200	987-5264	155-4
Gerber Collision & Glass 44700 Enterprise Dr *TF General:* 877-743-7237 ■ *Web:* www.gerbercollision.com	Clinton Township	MI	48038	586-954-3850	954-0912	62-4
Gerber Legendary Blades Inc 14200 SW 72nd Ave *Web:* gerbergear.com	Portland	OR	97224	503-639-6161		222
Gerber Life Insurance Co 1311 Mamaroneck Ave *TF:* 800-704-2180 ■ *Web:* www.gerberlife.com	White Plains	NY	10605	914-272-4000		391-2
Gerber Metal Supply Co 2 Boundary Rd *Web:* www.gerbermetal.com	Somerville	NJ	08876	908-823-9150		492
Gerber Plumbing Fixtures LLC 2500 International Pkwy *TF:* 888-648-6466 ■ *Web:* www.gerberonline.com	Woodridge	IL	60517	888-648-6466		611
Gerber Products Co 445 State St *TF:* 800-284-9488 ■ *Web:* www.gerber.com	Fremont	MI	49413	800-284-9488		296-36
Gerber Scientific Inc 24 Industrial Pk Rd W *Web:* www.gerbertechnology.com	Tolland	CT	06084	860-870-2890		386
Gerber Technology Inc 24 Industrial Pk Rd W *TF:* 800-826-3243 ■ *Web:* www.gerbertechnology.com	Tolland	CT	06084	860-871-8082		744
Gerber Tours Inc 100 Crossways Park Dr W Ste 400 *TF:* 800-645-9145 ■ *Web:* www.gerbertours.com	Woodbury	NY	11797	516-826-5000		760

Phone | Fax | Class

Gerber/Hart Library & Archives
6500 N Clark St ... Chicago IL 60626 773-381-8030 381-8030 434-3
Web: www.gerberhart.org

Gerdau Ameristeel
2300 Oklahoma 97 ... Sand Springs OK 74063 918-245-1335 723

Gerdau AmeriSteel Corp
4221 W Boy Scout Blvd Ste 600 ... Tampa FL 33607 813-286-8383 723
TF Sales: 800-876-7833 ■ *Web:* www.gerdau.com

Gerhard's Appliances
290 N Keswick Ave ... Glenside PA 19038 215-884-8650 884-0349 38
Web: www.gerhardsappliance.com

Gerhart Systems & Controls Corp
754 Roble Rd Ste 140 ... Allentown PA 18109 610-264-2800 639
TF: 888-437-4278 ■ *Web:* gerhart.com

Gerken Capital Associates
110 Tiburon Blvd Ste 5 ... Mill Valley CA 94941 415-383-1464 194
Web: gerkencapital.com

Gerland Corp 3131 Pawnee St ... Houston TX 77054 713-746-3600 345
Web: www.gerlands.com

Gerling & Associates Inc
138 Stelzer Ct ... Sunbury OH 43074 740-965-2888 779
Web: www.gerlinggroup.com

Gerlinger Foundry & Machine Works Inc
1527 Sacramento St ... Redding CA 96001 530-243-1053 480
TF: 800-342-7673 ■ *Web:* www.gerlinger.com

Gerloff Company Inc
14955 Bulverde Rd ... San Antonio TX 78247 210-490-2777 494-0610 186
TF: 800-486-3621 ■ *Web:* www.gerloffinc.com

Germain Motor Co
Mercedes-Benz of Easton
4300 Morse Crossing ... Columbus OH 43219 855-217-5986 57
TF: 855-217-5986 ■ *Web:* www.germain.com

German Academic Exchange Service (DAAD)
871 United Nations Plaza ... New York NY 10017 212-758-3223 755-5780 48-11
Web: www.daad.org

German American Bancorp 711 Main St ... Jasper IN 47546 812-482-1314 482-0758 360-2
NASDAQ: GABC ■ *TF:* 800-482-1314 ■ *Web:* www.germanamerican.com

German Marshall Fund of the United States
1744 R St NW ... Washington DC 20009 202-745-3950 784
TF: 800-276-5680 ■ *Web:* www.gmfus.org

German National Tourist Office
122 E 42nd St Ste 2000 ... New York NY 10168 212-661-7176 775
Web: www.germany.travel/en

German Press Agency
529 14th St NW Ste 1112 ... Washington DC 20045 202-662-1220 530
Web: www.dpa.com

German Village 588 S Third St ... Columbus OH 43215 614-221-8888 222-4747 50-3
Web: germanvillage.com

German-American Chamber of Commerce Inc
75 Broad St 21st Fl ... New York NY 10004 212-974-8830 974-8867 138
Web: www.gaccny.com

German-American Chamber of Commerce Inc - Philadelphia
200 S Broad St Ste 910 ... Philadelphia PA 19103 215-501-7102 665-0375 138
Web: www.gaccphiladelphia.com

German-American Chamber of Commerce of the Midwest Inc
321 N Clark St Ste 1425 ... Chicago IL 60654 312-644-2662 644-0738 138
Web: www.gaccmidwest.org

German-American Chamber of Commerce of the Southern US Inc
1170 Howell Mill Rd Ste 300 ... Atlanta GA 30318 404-586-6800 586-6820 138
Web: www.gaccsouth.com

German-American National Congress (DANK)
4740 N Western Ave Ste 206 ... Chicago IL 60625 773-275-1100 275-4010 48-14
TF: 888-872-3265 ■ *Web:* www.dank.org

GermanDeli.com
601 Westport Pkwy, Ste 100 ... Grapevine TX 76051 817-410-9955 345
TF: 877-437-6269 ■ *Web:* www.germandeli.com

Germania Farm Mutual Insurance Assn
507 Hwy 290 E ... Brenham TX 77833 979-836-5224 836-1977 391-4
TF: 800-392-2202 ■ *Web:* www.germaniainsurance.com

Germanna Community College
Fredericksburg
10000 Germanna Pt Dr ... Fredericksburg VA 22408 540-891-3000 710-2092* 162
**Fax: Admissions* ■ *Web:* www.germanna.edu
Locust Grove 2130 Germanna Hwy ... Locust Grove VA 22508 540-423-9030 727-3207 162
Web: www.germanna.edu

Germantown Area Chamber of Commerce
2195 S Germantown Rd ... Germantown TN 38138 901-755-1200 755-9168 139
Web: www.germantownchamber.com

Germantown Community Library
N112 W16957 Mequon Rd ... Germantown WI 53022 262-253-7760 253-7763 434-3
Web: germantownlibrarywi.org

Germantown Performing Arts Centre (GPAC)
1801 Exeter Rd ... Germantown TN 38138 901-751-7500 572
Web: www.gpacweb.com

Germany 871 UN Plaza ... New York NY 10017 212-940-0400 784
Web: www.new-york-un.diplo.de
Consulate General
1330 Post Oak Blvd Ste 1850 ... Houston TX 77056 713-627-7770 627-0506 257
Web: germany.info
Consulate General
1960 Jackson St ... San Francisco CA 94109 415-775-1061 775-0187 257
Web: www.germany.info
Consulate General
676 N Michigan Ave Ste 3200 ... Chicago IL 60611 312-202-0480 202-0466 257
Web: germany.info
Consulate General
285 Peachtree Ctr Ave NE Ste 901 ... Atlanta GA 30303 404-659-4760 659-1280 257
TF: 866-687-8561 ■ *Web:* germany.info
Consulate General
6222 Wilshire Blvd Ste 500 ... Los Angeles CA 90048 323-930-2703 930-2805 257
TF: 800-780-5733 ■ *Web:* germany.info
Consulate General
100 Biscayne Blvd Ste 2200 ... Miami FL 33132 305-358-0290 358-0307 257
Web: germany.info
Consulate General 871 UN Plaza ... New York NY 10017 212-610-9700 610-9702 257
TF: 800-232-4636 ■ *Web:* germany.info
Embassy 4645 Reservoir Rd NW ... Washington DC 20007 202-298-4000 257
TF: 800-826-2181 ■ *Web:* www.germany.info

Phone | Fax | Class

Germer Gertz LLP 550 Fannin Ste 400 ... Beaumont TX 77701 409-654-6700 428
TF: 800-973-1177 ■ *Web:* www.germer.com

Germiphene Corp 1379 Colborne St E ... Brantford ON N3T5M1 800-265-9931 759-1625* 582
**Fax Area Code: 519* ■ *TF:* 800-265-9931 ■ *Web:* www.germiphene.com

Gerner & Kearns Co L P A
335 E Third St ... Newport KY 41071 513-241-7722 445
Web: www.gernerlaw.com

Gerome Mfg Co Inc
80 Laurel View Dr ... Smithfield PA 15478 724-438-8544 437-5608 697
Web: www.geromemfg.com

Geron Corp 149 Commonwealth Dr ... Menlo Park CA 94025 650-473-7700 473-7750 85
NASDAQ: GERN ■ *Web:* www.geron.com

Geronimo 724 Canyon Rd ... Santa Fe NM 87501 505-982-1500 671
TF: 800-280-4654 ■ *Web:* www.geronimorestaurant.com

Gerontological Society of America, The
1220 L St NW Ste 901 ... Washington DC 20005 202-842-1275 842-1150 49-8
TF: 800-677-1116 ■ *Web:* www.geron.org

Gerotech Inc 29220 Commerce Dr ... Flat Rock MI 48134 734-379-7788 379-2244 385
Web: www.gerotechinc.com

Gerref Industries 206 N York St ... Belding MI 48809 616-794-3110 697
Web: www.gerref.com

Gerresheimer Glass Inc
537 Crystal Ave ... Vineland NJ 08360 856-692-3600 333
Web: www.gerresheimer.com

Gerretsen Bldg Supply Co
1900 NE Airport Rd ... Roseburg OR 97470 541-672-2636 191-3
Web: www.gerretsen.com

Gerrish McCreary Smith PC
700 Colonial Rd Ste 200 ... Memphis TN 38117 901-767-0900 428
Web: www.gerrish.com

Gerrity Baker Williams Inc
3 Goldmine Rd ... Flanders NJ 07836 973-426-1500 390
TF: 800-548-2329 ■ *Web:* gbwinsurance.com

Gerrity Stone Inc 225 Merrimac St ... Woburn MA 01801 781-938-1820 191-1
Web: www.gerritystone.com

Gerrity's Supermarket Inc 950 N S Rd ... Scranton PA 18504 570-342-4144 345
Web: www.gerritys.com

Gerrus Maintenance Inc
95 Northfield Ave ... Edison NJ 08837 732-225-0662 104
Web: www.gerrus.com

Gerry Cosby & Company Inc
11 Pennsylvania Plaza ... New York NY 10001 212-563-6464 967-0876 711
TF: 877-563-6464 ■ *Web:* www.cosbysports.com

Gersh Agency 9465 Wilshire Blvd ... Beverly Hills CA 90212 310-274-6611 731
Web: www.gershcomedy.com

Gersh Agency, The (TGA)
41 Madison Ave 33rd Fl ... New York NY 10010 212-997-1818 731
TF: 800-908-1302 ■ *Web:* www.gershcomedy.com

Gershman, Brickner & Bratton Inc
8550 Arlington Blvd Ste 304 ... Fairfax VA 22031 703-573-5800 192
TF: 800-573-5801 ■ *Web:* www.gbbinc.com

Gershow Recycling Corp
71 Peconic Ave PO Box 526 ... Medford NY 11763 631-289-6188 289-6368 686
Web: www.gershow.com

Gerson Co 1450 S Lone Elm Rd ... Olathe KS 66061 913-262-7400 535-7592 411
TF: 800-444-8172 ■ *Web:* www.gersoncompany.com

Gerstein Science Information Centre
University of Toronto
9 King's College Cir
Sigmund Samuel Library Bldg ... Toronto ON M5S1A5 416-978-2280 434-1
Web: gerstein.library.utoronto.ca

Gertrude Hawk Chocolates Inc
9 Keystone Pk ... Dunmore PA 18512 800-822-2032 338-0947* 296-8
**Fax Area Code: 570* ■ *TF:* 866-932-4295 ■ *Web:* www.gertrudehawkchocolates.com

Gertrude Herbert Institute of Art
506 Telfair St ... Augusta GA 30901 706-722-5495 722-3670 520
Web: www.ghia.org

Gertrude's 10 Art Museum Dr ... Baltimore MD 21218 410-889-3399 671
Web: gertrudesbaltimore.com

Gertsch-Baker Engineering & Design Inc
104 S Fourth St Ste 100 ... Laramie WY 82070 307-742-6116 256
Web: www.gertschbaker.com

Gervais & Vine 620-A Gervais St ... Columbia SC 29201 803-799-8463 671
Web: www.gervine.com

GES 7000 Lindell Rd ... Las Vegas NV 89118 702-515-5500 515-5765 184
TF: 800-443-9767 ■ *Web:* www.ges.com

GES (Grangeville Environmental Services)
GES Property Pros LLC
352 Pine Run Rd ... New Oxford PA 17331 717-637-6152 630-2713 83
Web: www.gespropertypros.com

GES Global Energy Services Inc
3220 Cypress Creek Pkwy ... Houston TX 77068 888-523-6797 190
TF: 888-523-6797 ■ *Web:* www.global-energy.ca

Ges USA Inc 101 W Elm St Ste 550 ... Conshohocken PA 19428 610-940-6088 787
Web: services-ges.com

Gesa Credit Union
51 Gage Blvd PO Box 500 ... Richland WA 99352 509-946-1611 219
TF: 888-946-4372 ■ *Web:* www.gesa.com

GESD Capital Partners
50 Francisco St Ste 235 ... San Francisco CA 94133 415-477-8200 194
Web: www.gesd.net

Gessner Products Company Inc
241 N Main St ... Ambler PA 19002 215-646-7667 608
TF: 800-874-7808 ■ *Web:* gessnerproducts.com

Gestion Fonds Capital Culture Quebec Inc
485 McGill St Ste 900 ... Montreal QC H2Y2H4 514-940-6820 528
Web: capitalculture.ca

Gestion P R Maintenance Inc
639 King St W Ste 203 ... Kitchener ON N2G1C7 905-304-8300 192
TF: 800-719-2828 ■ *Web:* www.prmaintenance.com

Get & Go Market 10950 Beech Daly Rd ... Taylor MI 48180 313-295-3434 297-8

Get a Clue Design 1026 14th Ave Dr NW ... Hickory NC 28601 828-324-4262 4

GET Engineering Corp 9350 Bond Ave ... El Cajon CA 92021 619-443-8295 443-8613 203
TF: 877-494-1820 ■ *Web:* www.getntds.com

Get Found First LLC 160 W Second S ... Rexburg ID 83440 208-991-3463 5
TF: 800-261-1537 ■ *Web:* www.getfoundfirst.com

Get In Shape For Women
75 Second Ave Ste 220 ... Needham MA 02494 781-444-1913 354
Web: www.getinshapeforwomen.com

	Phone	Fax	Class
Get It LLC 128 N Pitt St Ste 2 .... Alexandria VA 22314 TF: 877-285-7861 ■ Web: get.it	877-285-7861		387
Get Noticed Promotions Inc 152 Sonwil Dr. .... Buffalo NY 14225 Web: getnoticedpromotions.com	716-688-8152		129
Get Smart Content Inc 3000 E Cesar Chavez St .... Austin TX 78702 Web: www.getsmartcontent.com	512-583-1853		387
Getabl Inc 11 Elkins St. .... Boston MA 02127 Web: pingup.com	617-752-1691		387
Getboards.com 40905 Big Bear Blvd. .... Big Bear Lake CA 92315 Web: www.getboards.com	909-878-3155		711
Getconnect 14114 Dallas Pkwy Ste 430 .... Dallas TX 75254 TF: 888-200-1831 ■ Web: www.getconnect.com	888-200-1831		366
Getinge USA Inc 1777 E Henrietta Rd .... Rochester NY 14623 TF: 800-424-9300 ■ Web: www.getinge.com/us-ca	585-475-1400		477
Getintegrated Inc 616 Water St Ste 329 .... Baltimore MD 21202 Web: www.getintegrated.com	410-685-6100	685-1701	260
GetMeFriends 7801 Broadway St .... San Antonio TX 78209 TF: 888-663-9143 ■ Web: www.getmefriends.com	888-663-9143		631
Gettel Automotive Group 3500 Bee Ridge Rd .... Sarasota FL 34239 Web: www.gettel.com	941-921-2655		57
Gettig Technologies Inc 1 Streamside Pl E .... Spring Mills PA 16875 Web: springmillsmfg.com	814-422-8892	422-8011	476
Getty Realty Corp 2 Jericho Plaza Ste 110 .... Jericho NY 11753 NYSE: GTY ■ TF: 800-946-0706 ■ Web: www.gettyrealty.com	516-478-5400		324
Gettysburg Battle Theatre 571 Steinwehr Ave .... Gettysburg PA 17325 TF: 800-830-5775 ■ Web: www.gettysburgbattlefieldtours.com	717-334-6100		520
Gettysburg Borough Hall 59 E High St .... Gettysburg PA 17325 TF: 800-433-7317 ■ Web: www.gettysburg-pa.gov	717-334-1160	334-7258	337
Gettysburg College 300 N Washington St .... Gettysburg PA 17325 *Fax: Admissions ■ TF: 800-431-0803 ■ Web: www.gettysburg.edu	717-337-6000	337-6145*	166
Gettysburg Convention & Visitors Bureau 571 W Middle St. .... Gettysburg PA 17325 TF: 800-337-5015 ■ Web: destinationgettysburg.com/index.asp	717-334-6274	334-1166	206
Gettysburg Heritage Center 297 Steinwehr Ave .... Gettysburg PA 17325 Web: www.gettysburgmuseum.com	717-334-6245		520
Gettysburg Hospital 147 Gettys St PO Box 3786 .... Gettysburg PA 17325 Web: wellspan.org/offices-locations/hospitals	717-334-2121	334-1302	374-3
Gettysburg Hotel 1 Lincoln Sq .... Gettysburg PA 17325 TF: 866-378-1797 ■ Web: www.hotelgettysburg.com	717-337-2000	337-2075	671
Gettysburg National Military Park 97 Taneytown Rd. .... Gettysburg PA 17325 Web: www.nps.gov/gett	717-334-1124	334-1891	564
Gettysburg National Military Park Library & Research Ctr 97 Taneytown Rd. .... Gettysburg PA 17325 Web: nps.gov/nps/404.htm	717-334-1124	334-1997	434-4
Gettysburg Times, The 1570 Fairfield Rd .... Gettysburg PA 17325 Web: www.gettysburgtimes.com	717-334-1131	334-4243	532-2
Gettysburg-Adams County Area Chamber of Commerce 18 Carlisle St Ste 203 .... Gettysburg PA 17325 TF: 800-699-1176 ■ Web: www.gettysburg-chamber.org	717-334-8151	334-3368	139
GetWireless LLC 10901 Red Cir Dr. .... Minnetonka MN 55343 Web: www.getwirelessllc.com	952-890-6669		736
Getzen Company Inc 530 S Cty Hwy H PO Box 440. .... Elkhorn WI 53121 TF: 800-366-5584 ■ Web: www.getzen.com	262-723-4221	723-4245	527
Getzschman Heating LLC 1700 E 23rd St .... Fremont NE 68025 Web: getzschman.com	402-721-6301		189-10
Geutebruck Security Inc 750 Miller Dr Ste A-5 .... Leesburg VA 20175 Web: geutebrueck.com	703-378-4856		693
Geva Theatre Ctr 75 Woodbury Blvd .... Rochester NY 14607 Web: www.gevatheatre.org	585-232-1366	232-4031	573-4
Gevity Consulting Inc 375 Water St Ste 350 .... Vancouver BC V6B5C6 TF: 800-785-3303 ■ Web: www.global-village.net	604-608-1779		177
Gexco 3460 Vine St. .... Norco CA 92860 Web: gexcoenterprises.com	951-735-4951		710
Geyer Printing Company Inc 55 38th St. .... Pittsburgh PA 15201 Web: www.geyerprinting.com	412-682-3633		626
Geygan & Geygan Ltd 8050 Hosbrook Rd Ste 107 .... Cincinnati OH 45236 Web: geygan.net	513-791-1673		428
GF Health Products Inc 2935 NE Pkwy .... Atlanta GA 30360 *Fax Area Code: 800 ■ TF: 800-347-5678 ■ Web: www.grahamfield.com	770-447-1609	726-0601*	477
GF Machining Solutions 560 Bond St .... Lincolnshire IL 60069 TF: 800-282-1336 ■ Web: www.gfms.com/content/gfac/country_us/en.html	847-913-5300	913-5340	455
GF Management Inc 1628 John F Kennedy Blvd 8 Penn Ctr 23rd Fl .... Philadelphia PA 19103 Web: www.gfhotels.com	215-972-2222		378
GF Piping Systems 3401 Aero Jet Ave .... El Monte CA 91731 Web: www.gfps.com	626-571-2770	573-2057	201
GF Piping Systems 300 Kuebler Rd .... Easton PA 18040 Web: gfps.com	610-252-7355	253-4436	350
GfG Instrumentation Inc 1194 Oak Vly Dr Ste 20 .... Ann Arbor MI 48108 TF: 800-959-0329 ■ Web: www.gfg-inc.com	734-769-0573		201
GFI Energy Ventures LLC 333 S Grand Ave 28 Fl .... Los Angeles CA 90071 Web: www.oaktreecapital.com	213-830-6300	830-6293	792
GFI Genfare 751 Pratt Blvd. .... Elk Grove Village IL 60007 TF: 877-247-3797 ■ Web: www.spx.com	847-593-8855	593-1824	472
GFI Group Inc 55 Water St .... New York NY 10041 NYSE: GFIG ■ TF: 888-750-5884 ■ Web: www.gfigroup.com	212-968-4100	968-2386	169

	Phone	Fax	Class
GFK Custom Research Inc 8401 Golden Valley Rd .... Minneapolis MN 55427 Web: gfk.com/us/pages/default.aspx	763-542-0800		466
GFLCOC (Fort Lee Regional Chamber of Commerce) 210 Whiteman St .... Fort Lee NJ 07024 Web: www.fortleechamber.com	201-944-7575	944-5168	139
GFMCO (Goldens' Foundry & Machine Co) 600 12th St. .... Columbus GA 31902 Web: www.gfmco.com	706-323-0471		307
GFOA (Government Finance Officers Assn) 203 N LaSalle St Ste 2700 .... Chicago IL 60601 Web: www.gfoa.org	312-977-9700	977-4806	49-7
G-Force Protective Services & Training Academy Inc 14331 SW 120 St Ste 103 .... Miami FL 33186 Web: www.gforcemiami.com	305-380-1212		260
GFRC Cladding Systems LLC 118 N Shiloh Rd .... Garland TX 75042 Web: www.gfrccladding.com	972-494-9000	494-1900	183
GFS Building Maintenance Inc 20 Blaine St .... Manchester NH 03102 Web: www.gfsservices.com	603-668-6612		104
GFWC (General Federation of Women's Clubs) 1734 N St NW. .... Washington DC 20036 TF: 800-443-4392 ■ Web: www.gfwc.org	202-347-3168	835-0246	48-24
GFX International Inc 333 Barron Blvd .... Grayslake IL 60030 TF: 800-274-3225 ■ Web: www.gfxi.com	847-543-4600		687
G&G Outfitters Inc 4901 Forbes Blvd .... Lanham MD 20706 TF: 800-233-9787 ■ Web: www.ggoutfitters.com	301-731-2099		258
G&G Steel Inc PO Box 179 .... Russellville AL 35653 Web: www.ggsteel.com	256-332-6652	332-0143	697
G&G Technologies Inc 1517 Old Apex Rd Ste 100 .... Cary NC 27513 Web: www.gandgtech.com	919-461-9848		809
GGB North America 700 Mid Atlantic Pkwy PO Box 189 .... Thorofare NJ 08086 *Fax: Sales ■ Web: www.ggbearings.com	856-848-3200	848-5115*	620
GGC Engineers Inc 148 N High St .... Gahanna OH 43230	614-471-7310		261
Ggi Worldwide Inc 552 Forest Crest Lk .... St. Louis MO 63367 Web: ggiww.com	636-561-4900		711
GGLO LLC 1301 First Ave Ste 301 .... Seattle WA 98101 Web: www.gglo.com	206-467-5828		393
GGMC Parking LLC 1651 Third Ave .... New York NY 10128 Web: www.ggmcparking.com	212-996-6363		562
GGP Publishing Inc 105 Calvert St Ste 201 .... Harrison NY 10528 Web: ggppublishing.com	914-834-8896	834-7566	94
GGR (GeoGlobal Resources Inc) 625 Fourth Ave SW .... Calgary AB T2P0K2 OTC: GGLR ■ Web: www.geoglobal.com	403-777-9250		538
GGS Technical Publications Services 3265 Farmtrail Rd .... York PA 17406 TF: 800-927-4474 ■ Web: ggsinc.com	717-764-2222		781
GH International Inc 2540 Rena Rd .... Mississauga ON L4T3C9 Web: www.ghinternational.ca	905-677-5522		481
GH Metal Solutions Inc 2890 Airport Rd NW .... Fort Payne AL 35968 Web: www.ghmetalsolutions.com	256-845-5411		295
Gh Package Product & Testing Consulting Inc 4090 Thunderbird Ln .... Fairfield OH 45014 TF: 800-922-2054 ■ Web: www.ghtesting.com	513-870-0080		196
GHA design studios 1100 Ave des Canadiens-de-Montr,al Ste 130 .... Montreal QC H3B2S2 Web: www.ghadesign.com	514-843-5812		393
Ghafari Assoc Inc 17101 Michigan Ave .... Dearborn MI 48126 TF: 800-289-7822 ■ Web: www.ghafari.com	313-441-3000		261
Ghana 19 E 47th St .... New York NY 10017 Web: www.un.int/ghana	212-832-1300	751-6743	784
Consulate General 19 E 47th St. .... New York NY 10017 Web: ghanaconsulatenewyork.org	212-832-1300	751-6743	257
Embassy 3512 International Dr NW .... Washington DC 20008 TF: 800-424-8580 ■ Web: www.ghanaembassy.org	202-686-4520	686-4527	257
GHBLP (Grand Haven Board of Lightand & Power) 1700 Eaton Dr. .... Grand Haven MI 49417 Web: www.ghblp.org	616-846-6250	846-3114	245
GHC Mechanical Inc 990 Pauly Dr. .... Elk Grove Village IL 60007 TF: 800-579-7368 ■ Web: www.ghcmech.com	847-593-0123		14
GHD Inc 2235 Mercury Way Ste 150 .... Santa Rosa CA 95407 TF: 800-800-0490 ■ Web: www.ghd.com	707-523-1010		261
Gheens Science Hall & Rauch Planetarium Rauch Planetarium University of Louisville .... Louisville KY 40292 TF: 800-996-7566 ■ Web: louisville.edu/planetarium	502-852-6664	852-0831	598
Ghent Manufacturing Inc 2999 Henkle Dr. .... Lebanon OH 45036 TF: 800-543-0550 ■ Web: www.ghent.com	513-932-3445	932-9252	243
GHG Corp 960 Clear Lake City Blvd. .... Webster TX 77598 TF: 866-380-4146 ■ Web: www.ghg.com	281-488-8806	488-1838	178-10
Ghiotto & Assoc Inc 2426 Phillips Hwy .... Jacksonville FL 32207 TF: 844-304-7262 ■ Web: www.ghiotto.com	844-304-7262		727
Ghirardelli Chocolate Co 1111 139th Ave. .... San Leandro CA 94578 TF: 800-877-9338 ■ Web: www.ghirardelli.com	800-877-9338		296-8
Ghirardelli Square 900 N Pt St Ste E-100. .... San Francisco CA 94109 TF: 800-836-3470 ■ Web: www.ghirardellisq.com	415-775-5500	775-0912	50-6
Ghirardo CPA 7200 Redwood Blvd Ste 403 .... Novato CA 94945 Web: www.ghirardocpa.com	415-897-5678		2
GHJ&M (Goldner Hawn Johnson & Morrison Inc) 90 S Seventh St 3700 Wells Fargo Ctr .... Minneapolis MN 55402 Web: www.ghjm.com	612-338-5912		403
GHO Ventures LLC 92 Nassau St 2nd Fl .... Princeton NJ 08542 Web: www.ghoventures.com	609-497-6333		696
Ghost Armor LLC 1470 N Horne St .... Gilbert AZ 85233 TF: 888-960-2766 ■ Web: www.ghost-armor.com	480-921-3161		791

Phone | Fax | Class

Ghost Town Museum
400 S 21st St .... Colorado Springs CO 80904 719-634-0696 520
Web: www.ghosttownmuseum.com
Ghost Town Partners LLC 16 Fie Top Rd .... Maggie NC 28751 828-926-1130 32
Web: www.ghosttowninthesky.com
Ghostnet Inc 38 Wall St Ste 109 .... Jasper GA 30143 706-253-1013 175
Web: www.ghostnetinc.com
GHR Engineers & Assoc Inc
1615 S Neil St .... Champaign IL 61820 217-356-0536 261
Web: ghrinc.com
GHS (General Health System)
3600 Florida Blvd .... Baton Rouge LA 70806 225-387-7000 353
Web: www.brgeneral.org
GHS (Greenville Hospital System)
701 Grove Rd .... Greenville SC 29605 864-455-8976 353
TF: 877-447-4636 ■ *Web:* www.ghs.org
GHS Corp 2813 Wilber Ave .... Battle Creek MI 49037 800-388-4447 860-6913 527
TF: 800-388-4447 ■ *Web:* www.ghsstrings.com
GHS Interactive Security Inc
21031 Warner Center Ln Ste D .... Woodland Hills CA 91367 855-447-4961 693
TF: 855-447-4961 ■ *Web:* ghssecurity.com
GHSP Co 1250 S Beechtree St .... Grand Haven MI 49417 616-842-5500 842-7230 489
Web: www.ghsp.com
GHX (Global Health Care Exchange LLC)
1315 W Century Dr .... Louisville CO 80027 720-887-7000 887-7200 225
TF: 800-968-7449 ■ *Web:* www.ghx.com
GIA (Gemological Institute of America)
5345 Armada Dr .... Carlsbad CA 92008 760-603-4000 603-4003 49-4
TF: 800-421-7250 ■ *Web:* www.gia.edu
Giact Systems Inc 700 Central Expy S .... Allen TX 75013 866-918-2409 225
TF: 866-918-2409 ■ *Web:* www.motio.com
Gianforte Greg (Rep R - MT)
1419 Longworth HOB .... Washington DC 20515 202-225-3211 342-2
Web: gianforte.house.gov
Giannelli Cabinets
19443 Londelius St .... Northridge CA 91324 818-882-9787 286
Giannini Garden Ornaments Inc
225 Shaw Rd .... South San Francisco CA 94080 650-873-4493 183
TF: 800-431-1993 ■ *Web:* www.gianninigarden.com
Giant Bicycle USA
3587 Old Conejo Rd .... Newbury Park CA 91320 805-267-4600 82
Web: www.giant-bicycles.com
Giant City State Park
235 Giant City Rd .... Makanda IL 62958 618-457-4836 565
Web: www.dnr.illinois.gov/parks/pages/giantcity.aspx
Giant Communications Inc
418 W Fifth St Ste C .... Holton KS 66436 785-362-9331 116
TF: 800-346-9084 ■ *Web:* www.giantcomm.net
Giant Crab 9597 N Kings Hwy .... Myrtle Beach SC 29572 843-449-1097 671
Web: www.giantcrab.com
Giant Eagle Inc 101 Kappa Dr .... Pittsburgh PA 15238 412-963-6200 345
TF Cust Svc: 800-553-2324 ■ *Web:* www.gianteagle.com
Giant Food Inc
8301 Professional Pl Ste 115 .... Landover MD 20785 888-469-4426 618-4998* 345
*Fax Area Code: 301 ■ *Fax: Cust Svc ■ *TF:* 888-469-4420 ■ *Web:* www.giantfood.com
Giant Food Stores 1200 W Market St .... West York PA 17404 717-845-5214 345
Web: www.ahold.com/Media/Giant-Carlisle.htm
Giant Food Stores Inc
1149 Harrisburg Pike .... Carlisle PA 17013 717-240-4000 960-1356* 345
*Fax: Mail Rm ■ *TF:* 888-814-4268 ■ *Web:* www.giantfoodstores.com
Giant Oil Inc 1806 N Franklin St .... Tampa FL 33602 813-740-0422 579
Web: www.giantoil.com
Giant Realm Inc 254 W 31St St 8th Fl .... New York NY 10001 212-488-1740 747-7757* 387
*Fax Area Code: 646
Giant Resource Recovery Company Inc
654 Judge St PO Box 352 .... Harleyville SC 29488 803-496-2200 192
TF: 800-637-4023 ■ *Web:* www.grr-giant.com
Giant Springs State Park
4600 Giant Springs Rd .... Great Falls MT 59405 406-454-5840 761-8477 565
TF: 855-922-6768 ■ *Web:* www.fwp.mt.gov
Giantbank.com
6300 NE First Ave .... Fort Lauderdale FL 33334 877-446-4200 493-8969* 70
*Fax Area Code: 954 ■ *TF:* 877-446-4200 ■ *Web:* www.giantbank.com
Giardoni Foods Inc
44 W Jefryn Blvd Ste R .... Deer Park NY 11729 631-586-2331 297-8
Web: giardonifoods.com
Gibbes Museum of Art
135 Meeting St .... Charleston SC 29401 843-722-2706 720-1682 520
Web: www.gibbesmuseum.org
Gibbon Conservation Ctr
19100 Esguerra Rd .... Santa Clarita CA 91390 661-296-2737 823
Web: www.gibboncenter.org
Gibbons & Conley
3480 Buskirk Ave Ste 200 .... Pleasant Hill CA 94523 925-932-3600 932-1623 445
Web: gibbons-conley.com
Gibbons & Kawash
707 Virginia St Bank One Ctr Ste 500 .... Charleston WV 25301 304-345-8400 2
Web: gandkcpas.com
Gibbons PC 1 Gateway Ctr .... Newark NJ 07102 973-596-4500 428
Web: www.gibbonslaw.com
Gibbs & Assoc 323 Science Dr .... Moorpark CA 93021 805-523-0004 523-0006 178-5
TF Cust Svc: 800-654-9399 ■ *Web:* gibbscam.com
Gibbs & Soell, Inc.
60 E 42nd St Fl 44 .... New York NY 10165 212-697-2600 697-2646 636
TF: 800-359-7600 ■ *Web:* www.gscommunications.com
Gibbs Bob (Rep R - OH)
2446 Rayburn HOB .... Washington DC 20515 202-225-6265 225-3394 342-2
Web: gibbs.house.gov
Gibbs Construction LLC
5736 Citrus Blvd Ste 200 .... New Orleans LA 70123 504-733-4336 186
Web: www.gibbsconstruction.net
Gibbs Die Casting Corp
369 Community Dr .... Henderson KY 42420 270-827-1801 827-7840 308
TF: 800-872-2657 ■ *Web:* www.gibbsdc.com
Gibbs Flying Service Inc
3717 John J Montgomery Dr .... San Diego CA 92123 858-277-0310 277-0678 63
Web: gibbsflyingservice.com

Gibbs Museum of Pioneer & Dakotah Life
2097 W Larpenteur Ave .... Saint Paul MN 55113 651-646-8629 520
Web: www.rchs.com
Gibbs Wire & Steel Company Inc
Metals Dr PO Box 520 .... Southington CT 06489 860-621-0121 628-7780 492
TF: 800-800-4422 ■ *Web:* www.gibbswire.com
Gibgot Willenbacher & Co
310 E Shore Rd .... Great Neck NY 11023 516-482-3660 2
Web: gw-cpa.com
Gibraltar 488 Royer Dr .... Lancaster PA 17601 717-397-2790 671
Web: gibraltargrille.com
Gibraltar Industries Inc
3556 Lakeshore Rd .... Buffalo NY 14219 716-826-6500 826-1589* 723
NASDAQ: ROCK ■ *Fax: Sales ■ *TF:* 800-247-8368 ■ *Web:* www.gibraltar1.com
Gibraltar Savings Bank
1039 S Orange Ave .... Newark NJ 07106 973-372-1221 70
Web: gibraltarbanknj.com
Gibraltar Steel Furniture Inc
9976 Westwanda Dr .... Beverly Hills CA 90210 310-276-8889 321
TF: 800-416-3635 ■ *Web:* www.gibraltarfurniture.com
Gibraltar Trade Ctr Inc
237 N River Rd .... Mt Clemens MI 48043 586-465-6440 366
Web: www.gibraltartrade.com
Gibson 309 Plus Pk Blvd .... Nashville TN 37217 615-871-4500 889-5509 527
TF: 800-444-2766 ■ *Web:* www.gibson.com
Gibson & Barnes
1900 Weld Blvd Ste 140 .... El Cajon CA 92020 619-440-6977 748-6694* 155-19
*Fax Area Code: 800 ■ *TF Sales:* 800-748-6693 ■ *Web:* www.gibson-barnes.com
Gibson Arnold & Assoc
5433 Westheimer Rd Ste 1016 .... Houston TX 77056 713 572-3000 721
TF: 800-879-2007 ■ *Web:* www.gibsonarnold.com
Gibson Corrugated 1920 E Main St .... Tupelo MS 38804 662-842-1862 100
Web: www.gibsoncorrugated.com
Gibson County 101 N Main .... Princeton IN 47670 812-385-4885 385-3089 338
Web: gibsoncounty-in.gov
Gibson Dunn & Crutcher LLP
333 S Grand Ave Ste 4600 .... Los Angeles CA 90071 213-229-7000 229-7520 428
TF: 888-203-1112 ■ *Web:* www.gibsondunn.com
Gibson Electric Company Inc
3100 Woodcreek Dr .... Downers Grove IL 60515 630-288-3800 743-2100 189-4
Web: www.gibsonelec.com
Gibson Electric Membership Corp
1207 S College St PO Box 47 .... Trenton TN 38382 731-855-4740 245
TF: 800-977-4076 ■ *Web:* www.gibsonemc.com
Gibson Energy Inc
440 - Second Ave SW Ste 1700 .... Calgary AB T2P5E9 403-206-4000 536
Web: www.gibsons.com
Gibson Engineering Company Inc
90 Broadway .... Norwood MA 02062 781-769-3600 256
Web: www.gibsonengineering.com
Gibson Guitar Corp 309 Plus Pk Blvd .... Nashville TN 37217 615-871-4500 527
TF: 800-444-2766 ■ *Web:* www2.gibson.com
Gibson House Museum 137 Deacon St .... Boston MA 02116 617-267-6338 267-6338 520
Web: www.thegibsonhouse.org
Gibson Insurance Agency Inc
130 S Main St Ste 400 .... South Bend IN 46601 574-245-3500 390
Web: www.gibsonins.com
Gibson Laboratories Inc
1040 Manchester St .... Lexington KY 40508 859-254-9500 253-1476 231
TF: 800 477 4763 ■ *Web:* gibsonbioscience.com
Gibson Performance Exhaust
1270 Webb Cir .... Corona CA 92879 951-372-1220 247
Web: www.gibsonperformance.com
Gibsons Steakhouse 1028 N Rush St .... Chicago IL 60611 312-266-8999 266-3327 671
Web: www.gibsonssteakhouse.com
Gibson-Thomas Engineering Company Inc
1004 Ligonier St .... Latrobe PA 15650 724-539-8562 261
Web: www.gibson-thomas.com
GIC Group Inc, The 1434 Duke St .... Alexandria VA 22314 703-684-1366 463
Web: www.gicgroup.com
Gichner Systems Group Inc
490 E Locust St .... Dallastown PA 17313 717-244-7611 246-5496 105
TF: 800-786-2929 ■ *Web:* www.gichner.us
Giddings Independent Schl Dst
2337 N Main St .... Giddings TX 78942 979-542-2854 542-9264 685
Web: giddingsisd.net
Giddings Manufacturing Company Inc
1426 Us Route 7 .... Pittsford VT 05763 802-483-2292 817
TF: 800-303-4312 ■ *Web:* giddingsvt.com
Giddings State School
2261 James Turman Rd PO Box 600 .... Giddings TX 78942 979-542-4500 542-0177 412
Web: www.tjjd.texas.gov/aboutus/facilities.aspx
GIDEON Informatics Inc
8721 Santa Monica Blvd Ste 234 .... Los Angeles CA 90069 323-934-0000 177
Web: www.gideononline.com
Gideon Putnam Resort & Spa
24 Gideon Putnam Rd .... Saratoga Springs NY 12866 518-584-3000 379
TF: 800-452-7275 ■ *Web:* www.gideonputnam.com
Gieger Laborde & Laperouse L L C
701 Poydras St Ste 4800 .... New Orleans LA 70139 504-561-0400 561-1011 445
Web: glllaw.com
Giering Metal Finishing Inc
2655 State St .... Hamden CT 06517 203-248-5583 481
Web: www.gieringmetalfinishing.com
Giesecke & Devrient America Inc
45925 Horseshoe Dr .... Sterling VA 20166 703-480-2000 596
Web: www.gi-de.com
Giesecke Devrient Cardtech Inc
2020 Enterprise Pkwy .... Twinsburg OH 44087 330-425-1515 596
Gif Services Inc
2525 Brunswick Ave Ste 204 .... Linden NJ 07036 908-474-1270 311
TF: 800-772-9550 ■ *Web:* www.gifservices.com
Giffels-Webster Engineers Inc
28 W Adams Ste 1200 .... Detroit MI 48226 313-962-4442 261
Web: giffelswebster.com
Giffin Interior & Fixture Inc
500 Scotti Dr .... Bridgeville PA 15017 412-221-1166 221-3745 499
Web: giffininterior.com

Phone | Fax | Class

Gifford Arboretum
1301 Memorial Dr University of Miami....... Coral Gables FL 33146 305-284-5364 284-3039 97
Web: www.bio.miami.edu/arboretum

Gifford Fong Associates Inc
3658 Mt Diablo Blvd Ste 200.............. Lafayette CA 94549 925-299-7800 463
TF: 800-653-2465 ■ *Web:* www.gfong.com

Gifford Pinchot State Park
2200 Rosstown Rd.......................Lewisberry PA 17339 717-432-5011 565
Web: www.dcnr.state.pa.us

Gifford Woods State Park
34 Gifford Woods.........................Killington VT 05751 802-775-5354 565
Web: www.vtstateparks.com

Gift Box Corp America
305 Veterans Blvd............................ Carlstadt NJ 07072 201-933-9777 561
Web: www.800giftbox.com

Gift Card Partners Inc
47 pine plain rd.............................Wellesley MA 02482 800-413-9101 7
TF: 800-413-9101 ■ *Web:* www.giftcardpartners.com

Gift of Hope Organ & Tissue Donor Network
425 Spring Lake Dr.............................Itasca IL 60143 630-758-2600 545
TF: 877-577-3747 ■ *Web:* www.giftofhope.org

Gift of Life Bone Marrow Foundation
800 Yamato Rd Ste 101.................... Boca Raton FL 33431 561-982-2900 48-17
TF: 800-962-7769 ■ *Web:* www.giftoflife.org

Gift of Life Donor Program
401 N Third St..........................Philadelphia PA 19123 215-557-8090 545
TF: 800-543-6391 ■ *Web:* www.donors1.org

Gift of Life Foundation
3861 Research Park Dr..................... Ann Arbor MI 48108 734-973-1577 292
TF: 866-500-5801 ■ *Web:* giftoflifemichigan.org

Gift of Life Transplant House
705 Second St SW........................Rochester MN 55902 507-288-7470 372
TF: 800-479-7824 ■ *Web:* www.gift-of-life.org

Gift Planning Assoc
4417 11th St NW....................... Albuquerque NM 87107 415-970-2380 317
Web: www.giftplanner1.com

Gift Wrap Co 338 Industrial Blvd................ Midway GA 31320 800-443-4429 548
TF General: 800-443-4429 ■ *Web:* www.giftwrapcompany.com

GiftCertificates.com 11510 Blondo St..........Omaha NE 68164 800-773-7368 327
TF: 800-773-7368 ■ *Web:* www.giftcertificates.com

Gifting Services LLC
7494-B Santa Monica Blvd..............West Hollywood CA 90046 323-874-4156 195
Web: www.giftingservices.com

Gifts for You LLC
2425 Curtiss St...................... Downers Grove IL 60515 630-771-0095 292
TF: 866-443-8748 ■ *Web:* www.giftsforyounow.com

Gifts On Time LLC 80 Front St Ste 21........... Scituate MA 02066 781-545-0799 690

Giftwares Co 436 First Ave...................Royersford PA 19468 610-792-8177 292
Web: www.giftwaresco.com

GIG (Gluten Intolerance Group)
31214 124th Ave SE..........................Auburn WA 98092 253-833-6655 833-6675 48-17
Web: www.gluten.org

Gig Harbor/Peninsula Area Chamber of Commerce
3125 Judson St Ste 101......................Gig Harbor WA 98332 253-851-6865 851-6881 139
Web: www.gigharborchamber.net

Gigabyte Technology Inc
17358 Railroad St..................... City of Industry CA 91748 626-854-9338 625
Web: gigabyte.com

GigaCrete Inc
6775 Speedway Blvd Ste M105 .... Las Vegas NV 89115 702-643-6363 225
Web: www.gigacrete.com

Gigante Vaz Partners Inc
915 Bwy Ste 1408.........................New York NY 10010 212-343-0004 4
Web: www.gigantevaz.com

Gigasonic 260 E Gish Rd................... San Jose CA 95112 408-573-1400 526
TF: 888-246-4442 ■ *Web:* www.gigasonic.com

Giga-Tronics Inc
4650 Norris Canyon Rd................. San Ramon CA 94583 925-328-4650 328-4700 248
NASDAQ: GIGA ■ *TF:* 800-726-4442 ■ *Web:* www.gigatronics.com

Gigi's Restaurant 257 E Ferry St............... Buffalo NY 14208 716-883-1438 671

GigMasters.com Inc 33 S Main St............. Norwalk CT 06854 866-342-9794 387
TF: 866-342-9794 ■ *Web:* www.gigmasters.com

GIH (Grantmakers in Health)
1100 Connecticut Ave NW Ste 1200..........Washington DC 20036 202-452-8331 452-8340 48-5
Web: www.gih.org

G-III Apparel Group Ltd
512 Seventh Ave..........................New York NY 10018 212-403-0500 403-0551 155-5
NASDAQ: GIII ■ *Web:* www.giii.com

Gil Haugan Construction Inc
200 E 60th St N..........................Sioux Falls SD 57104 605-336-6082 186
Web: www.gilhaugan.com

Gil Tours Travel Inc
1511 Walnut St 2nd Fl...................Philadelphia PA 19102 215-568-6655 568-0696 771
TF: 800-223-3855 ■ *Web:* www.giltravel.com

Gila Cliff Dwellings National Monument
HC 68 PO Box 100..................... Silver City NM 88061 575-536-9461 536-9344 564
Web: www.nps.gov/gicl

Gila County 1400 E Ash St......................Globe AZ 85501 928-425-3231 338
TF: 800-304-4452 ■ *Web:* co.gila.az.us

Gila Regional Medical Ctr
1313 E 32nd St........................ Silver City NM 88061 575-538-4000 374-3
Web: www.grmc.org

Gila River Arena 9400 W Maryland Ave......... Glendale AZ 85305 623-772-3800 720
Web: gilariverarena.com

Gila River Telecommunications Inc
7065 W Allison Dr........................ Chandler AZ 85226 520-796-3333 196
TF: 800-421-5711 ■ *Web:* www.gilanet.net

Gilardi's 820 E Walnut St....................Springfield MO 65806 417-862-6400 671
Web: www.gilardis.com

Gilbane Bldg Co 7 Jackson Walkway...........Providence RI 02903 401-456-5800 188-7
TF: 800-445-2263 ■ *Web:* www.gilbaneco.com

Gilbane Bldg Co New England Regional Office
7 Jackson Walkway.......................Providence RI 02903 401-456-5800 456-5936 186
TF: 800-445-2263 ■ *Web:* www.gilbaneco.com

Gilbane Bldg Company Southwest Regional Office
1331 Lamar St Ste 1170.......................Houston TX 77010 713-209-1873 186
TF: 800-445-2263 ■ *Web:* www.gilbaneco.com

Gilbane Inc 7 Jackson Walkway...............Providence RI 02903 401-456-5890 456-5996 653
TF: 800-445-2263 ■ *Web:* www.gilbaneco.com

Phone | Fax | Class

Gilbane Report, The
763 Massachusetts Ave......................Cambridge MA 02139 617-497-9443 395
Web: gilbane.com

Gilbarco Inc 7300 W Friendly Ave............ Greensboro NC 27420 336-547-5000 547-5890* 639
**Fax:* Mktg ■ *Web:* www.gilbarco.com

Gilbert & Barnhill pa
503 Belle Hall Pkwy Unit 101............ Mount Pleasant SC 29464 843-856-9227 445
Web: gilbertbarnhill.publishpath.com

Gilbert & Calabrese LLC 181 Rt 206............Flanders NJ 07863 973-448-1099 2
Web: gcllc-cpa.com

Gilbert Associates Inc
2880 Gateway Oaks Dr Ste 100.............. Sacramento CA 95833 916-646-6464 2
TF: 800-889-4410 ■ *Web:* www.gilbertcpa.com

Gilbert Chamber of Commerce
119 N Gilbert Rd Ste 101 PO Box 527............Gilbert AZ 85299 480-892-0056 139
Web: www.gilbertaz.com

Gilbert Displays Inc 110 Spagnoli Rd.......... Melville NY 11747 631-577-1100 232
TF: 855-577-1100 ■ *Web:* www.gilbertdisplays.com

Gilbert Industries Inc
5611 Krueger Dr......................... Jonesboro AR 72401 870-932-6070 577
TF: 800-643-0400 ■ *Web:* www.gilbertinc.com

Gilbert Kelly Crowley & Jennett LLP
550 S Hope St Ste 2200...................Los Angeles CA 90071 213-615-7000 428
Web: www.gilbertkelly.com

Gilbert Lake State Park 18 CCC Rd............ Laurens NY 13796 607-432-2114 565
Web: parks.ny.gov/parks/19/details.aspx

Gilbert Mechanical Contractors Inc
4451 W 76th St.................................Edina MN 55435 952-835-3810 835-4765 697
TF: 800-325-8476 ■ *Web:* www.gilbertmech.com

Gilbert Metzger & Madigan LLP
6029 Park Dr PO Box 677....................Charleston IL 61920 217-345-2128 2
Web: gmmcpa.com

Gilbert Plumbing Co PO Box 8........... West Simsbury CT 06092 860-658-4653 610
TF: 800-567-7537 ■ *Web:* gilbertplumbingllc.com

Gilbert Southern Corp 3555 Farnam St............Omaha NE 68131 402-342-2052 271-2829* 188-4
**Fax:* Hum Res ■ *TF:* 800-901-1087 ■ *Web:* www.kiewit.com

Gilbert's Chowder House
92 Commercial St...........................Portland ME 04101 207-871-5636 671
Web: gilbertschowderhouse.com

Gilberti Stinziano Heintz & Smith PC
555 E Genesee St.......................... Syracuse NY 13202 315-442-0100 428
Web: www.gilbertilaw.com

Gilbreth Packaging Systems
3001 State Rd..............................Croydon PA 19021 800-630-2413 785-4077* 413
**Fax Area Code:* 215 ■ *TF:* 800-630-2413 ■ *Web:* www.gilbrethusa.com

Gilbride, Tusa, Last & Spillane
31 Brookside Dr PO Box 658................. Greenwich CT 06836 203-622-9360 428
Web: www.gtlslaw.com

Gilchrist County 112 S Main St.................Trenton FL 32693 352-463-3170 463-3166 338
Web: gilchrist.fl.us

Gilchrist Hospice Care
11311 McCormick Rd..................... Hunt Valley MD 21031 443-849-8200 371
TF: 800-735-2258 ■ *Web:* www.gilchristhospice.org

Gilchrist Metal Fabricating Company Inc
18 Park Ave................................. Hudson NH 03051 603-889-2600 492
TF: 800-541-4424 ■ *Web:* www.gmfco.com

Gilcrease Museum
1400 N Gilcrease Museum Rd................... Tulsa OK 74127 918-596-2700 596-2770 520
TF: 888-655-2278 ■ *Web:* gilcrease.org

Gilead 333 Lakeside Dr.......................Foster City CA 94404 650-574-3000 578-9264 85
TSE: GILD ■ *Web:* www.gilead.com

Gilead Group LLC
12444 Powerscourt Dr Ste 375.................St Louis MO 63131 314-821-2500 10-11
Web: www.gileadgroup.net

Gilead Sciences Inc
333 Lakeside Dr.......................Foster City CA 94404 650-574-3000 578-9264 85
NASDAQ: GILD ■ *TF:* 800-445-3235 ■ *Web:* www.gilead.com

Giles & Kendall Inc
3470 Maysville Rd NE PO Box 188........... Huntsville AL 35804 256-776-2978 817
TF: 800-225-6738 ■ *Web:* cedarsafe.com

Giles & Lambert PC 1 E Main St............ Martinsville VA 24112 276-632-7000 428
Web: www.gileslambert.com

Giles & Ransome Inc Ransome Engine Power Div
2975 Galloway Rd..........................Bensalem PA 19020 215-639-4300 245-2830 274
TF: 877-726-7663 ■ *Web:* www.ransome.com

Giles Chemical Corp
102 Commerce St........................Waynesville NC 28786 828-452-4784 452-4786 143
Web: www.gileschemical.com

Giles Communications LLC
2975 Westchester Ave Ste 402................ Purchase NY 10577 914-644-3500 636
Web: giles.com

Giles County 315 N Main St..................Pearisburg VA 24134 540-921-1722 921-3825 338
Web: virginiasmtnplayground.com

Giles County 1 Public Sq..........................Pulaski TN 38478 931-363-1509 424-4795 338
Web: www.gilescounty-tn.us

Giles County Chamber of Commerce
110 N Second St..............................Pulaski TN 38478 931-363-3789 363-7279 139
Web: www.gilescountychamber.com

Giles County Public Library
122 S Second St.............................Pulaski TN 38478 931-363-2720 434-3
TF: 800-346-8460 ■ *Web:* www.gilescountylibrary.org

Giles Craig Communications Inc
504 Snidow St........................... Pembroke VA 24136 540-544-2288 224
Web: www.pemtel.com

Giles Engineering Assoc Inc
N8 W22350 Johnson Dr..................... Waukesha WI 53186 262-544-0118 256
TF: 800-782-0610 ■ *Web:* www.gilesengr.com

Giles Enterprises Inc
2750 Gunter Park Dr W.................... Montgomery AL 36109 334-272-1457 123
Web: www.gilesent.com

Giles Industries Inc
405 S Broad St.........................New Tazewell TN 37825 423-626-7243 626-7243 505
Web: www.gilesindustries.com

Gilford Corp
4600 Powder Mill Rd Ste 350................ Beltsville MD 20705 301-931-3900 186
Web: www.gilfordcorp.com

Gilford Securities Inc 777 Third Ave...........New York NY 10017 212-888-6400 690

Phone | Fax | Class

Gilkey Window Company Inc
3625 Hauck Rd .... Cincinnati OH 45241 513-769-4527 596
Web: www.gilkey.com
Gill Athletics Inc 2808 Gemini Ct. .... Champaign IL 61822 217-367-8438 367-8440 710
TF Cust Svc: 800-637-3090 ■ *Web:* www.gillathletics.com
Gill Elrod Ragon Owen & Sherman PA
425 W Capitol Ave Ste 3800 .... Little Rock AR 72201 501-376-3800 428
Web: gill-law.com
Gill Foundation Inc 2215 market st .... Denver CO 80205 303-292-4455 303
Web: gillfoundation.org
Gill Industries Inc
5271 Plainfield Ave NE .... Grand Rapids MI 49525 616-559-2700 689
Web: www.gill-industries.com
Gill Manufacturing Ltd
9 Kenview Blvd .... Brampton ON L6T5G5 905-792-0999 454
TF: 800-800-4018 ■ *Web:* www.gillmanufacturing.com
Gill Mike Pluming & Heating 46 Temi Rd .... Hudson MA 01749 978-568-8086 610
Web: mikegillplumbing.com
Gill Services Inc
650 Aldine Bender Rd .... Houston TX 77060 281-820-5400 358
TF: 800-375-7881 ■ *Web:* www.gillservicesinc.com
Gill Studios Inc 10800 Lackman Rd .... Lenexa KS 66219 913-888-4422 687
Web: www.gill-line.com
Gillespie County
101 W Main St Unit 13 .... Fredericksburg TX 78624 830-997-6515 997-9958 338
TF: 800-272-9829 ■ *Web:* www.gillespiecounty.org
Gillespie County Fairgrounds
530 Fair Dr PO Box 526 .... Fredericksburg TX 78624 830-997-2359 997-4923 642
Web: gillespiefair.net
Gillespie Graphics
27676 SW Pkwy Ave .... Wilsonville OR 97070 503-682-1122 687
TF: 800-547-6841 ■ *Web:* www.gillespie-graphics.com
Gillespie Museum of Minerals
421 N Woodland Blvd Unit 8403 .... DeLand FL 32723 386-822-7330 520
TF: 800-688-0101 ■ *Web:* www.stetson.edu
Gillespie, Prudhon & Associates Inc
16111 SE 106th Ave Ste 100 .... Clackamas OR 97015 503-657-0424 261
TF: 800-595-2145 ■ *Web:* www.gpatelecom.com
Gillette Air Conditioning Company Inc
1215 San Francisco .... San Antonio TX 78201 210-735-9235 736-1932 189-10
Gillette Castle State Park
67 River Rd .... East Haddam CT 06423 860-526-2336 565
Web: www.ct.gov
Gillette Children's Specialty Healthcare
200 E University Ave .... Saint Paul MN 55101 651-291-2848 374-1
TF: 800-719-4040 ■ *Web:* www.gillettechildrens.org
Gillette Generators Inc 1340 Wade Dr .... Elkhart IN 46514 574-264-9639 518
TF: 800-777-9639 ■ *Web:* www.gillettegenerators.com
Gillette Stadium 1 Patriots Pl .... Foxboro MA 02035 508-543-8200 720
Web: www.gillettestadium.com
Gilliam and Sons Inc
9831 Rosedale Hwy .... Bakersfield CA 93312 661-589-0913 539
Web: www.gilliamandsons.com
Gilliam Youth Services Ctr
2844 Downing St .... Denver CO 80205 303-291-8951 412
Gillibrand Kirsten E (Sen D - NY)
478 Russell Bldg .... Washington DC 20510 202-224-4451 228-0282 342-2
Web: www.gillibrand.senate.gov
Gillies & Prittie Inc
151 Pleasant Hill Rd .... Scarborough ME 04074 207-883-7815 752
TF: 800-298-6565 ■ *Web:* www.gilliesandprittie.com
Gillig Corp 25800 Clawiter Rd .... Hayward CA 94545 510-785-1500 785-6819 516
TF: 800-735-1500 ■ *Web:* www.gillig.com
Gilligan & Ferneman LLC
1754 Business Ctr Ln .... Kissimmee FL 34758 800-720-4152 317
TF: 800-720-4152
Gillis Gilkerson
150 W Market St Ste 200 Riverview Commons ... Salisbury MD 21801 410-749-4821 186
Web: www.gillisgilkerson.com
Gillispie & Ogilbee Pc
4400 N Meridian Ave .... Oklahoma City OK 73112 405-947-3030 942-0017 2
Web: www.gocpas.com
Gillmore Security Systems Inc
26165 Broadway Ave .... Cleveland OH 44146 440-232-1000 693
TF: 800-899-8995 ■ *Web:* www.gillmoresecurity.com
Gill-Simpson Inc 2834 Loch Raven Rd .... Baltimore MD 21218 410-467-3335 366-4557 189-4
Gilltek Systems Intl Inc
2409 S Rural Rd Ste C .... Tempe AZ 85282 480-831-5565 177
Gilman & Pastor LLP
63 Atlantic Ave 3rd Fl .... Boston MA 02110 617-742-9700 192
TF: 877-428-7374 ■ *Web:* www.gilmanlawllp.com
Gilman Brothers Co, The Gilman Rd .... Gilman CT 06336 860-889-8444 596
Web: gilmanbrothers.com
Gilman USA 1230 Cheyenne Ave PO Box 5 .... Grafton WI 53024 262-377-2434 377-9438 493
TF: 800-445-6267 ■ *Web:* gilmanprecision.com
Gil-Mar Manufacturing Company Inc
7925 Ronda Dr .... Canton MI 48187 734-459-4803 358
Web: www.gil-mar.com
Gilmer Area Chamber of Commerce
106 Buffalo St .... Gilmer TX 75644 903-843-2413 843-3759 139
Web: gilmerareachamber.wix.com/chamber
Gilmer Chamber
696 First Ave PO Box 505 .... East Ellijay GA 30540 706-635-7400 635-7410 338
Web: www.gilmerchamber.com
Gilmer County 10 Howard St .... Glenville WV 26351 304-462-7641 462-5134 338
Web: courtswv.gov
Gilmer Junior High 111 Bruce St .... Gilmer TX 75645 903-841-7600 685
Web: www.gilmerisd.org
Gilmer Mirror Co 214 E Marshall St .... Gilmer TX 75644 903-843-2503 843-5123 637-8
Web: www.gilmermirror.com
Gilmore Entertainment Group
8901-A Business 17 N .... Myrtle Beach SC 29572 843-913-4000 181
TF: 800-843-6779 ■ *Web:* thecarolinaopry.com
Gilmore Jasion & Mahler Ltd
1715 Indianwood Cir Ste 100 .... Maumee OH 43537 419-794-2000 2
Web: www.gjmltd.com
Gilmore Services Inc
31 E Fairfield Dr .... Pensacola FL 32501 850-434-1054 358
TF: 800-537-3287 ■ *Web:* www.gilmoreservices.com

Phone | Fax | Class

Gilmour 7800 Discovery Dr .... Middleton WI 53562 866-348-5661 429
TF Cust Svc: 866-348-5661 ■ *Web:* www.gilmour.com
Gilmour Academy 34001 Cedar Rd .... Gates Mills OH 44040 440-442-1104 473-8010 622
TF: 800-533-5140 ■ *Web:* www.gilmour.org
Gilmour Craves
455 Irwin St Ste 201 .... San Francisco CA 94107 415-431-9955 4
Web: gilmourcraves.com
Gilpin County 203 Eureka St .... Central City CO 80427 303-582-5321 582-3086 338
Web: www.co.gilpin.co.us
Gilpin Hotel Casino 111 Main St .... Black Hawk CO 80422 303-582-1133 133
Web: thegilpincasino.com
Gilroy Chamber of Commerce
7471 Monterey St .... Gilroy CA 95020 408-842-6437 842-6010 139
Web: www.gilroy.org
Gilroy Chevrolet Cadillac Inc
6720 Bear Cat Ct .... Gilroy CA 95020 408-842-9301 57
TF: 800-201-7241 ■ *Web:* gilroychevy.com
Gilroy Gardens Family Theme Park
3050 Hecker Pass Hwy .... Gilroy CA 95020 408-840-7100 97
Web: www.gilroygardens.org
Gilroy Unified School District
7810 Arroyo Cir .... Gilroy CA 95020 408-847-2700 842-1158 685
Web: www.gusd.k12.ca.us
Gilsanz, Murray, Steficek LLP
129 W 27th St Fl 5 .... New York NY 10001 212-254-0030 261
Web: www.gmsllp.com
Gilsbar Inc PO Box 998 .... Covington LA 70434 844-413-1989 871-1855* 462
**Fax Area Code:* 985 ■ *TF:* 844-413-1989 ■ *Web:* www.gilsbar.com
Gilster-Mary Lee Corp
1037 State St PO Box 227 .... Chester IL 62233 618-826-2361 826-2973 296-16
TF: 800-851-5371 ■ *Web:* gilstermarylee.com
Gilton Solid Waste Management
755 S Yosemite Ave .... Oakdale CA 95361 209-527-3781 804
Web: www.gilton.com
Gina B & Company Inc
23811 Aliso Creek Rd Ste 130 .... Laguna Niguel CA 92677 949-643-1430 361
Web: www.ginab.com
Gina B Designs Inc
12700 Industrial Pk Blvd Ste 40 .... Plymouth MN 55441 763-559-7595 559-3899 130
TF: 800-228-4856 ■ *Web:* www.ginabdesigns.com
Ginac Group Inc, The
8834 N Capital of Texas Hwy Ste 200 .... Austin TX 78730 512-943-6801 943-6801 194
Giner Inc 89 Rumford Ave .... Newton MA 02466 781-529-0500 668
Web: www.ginerinc.com
Ginger Bay Salon Group Ltd
437 S kirkwood Rd .... Kirkwood MO 63122 314-966-0655 77
Web: www.gingerbay.com
Ginger Cove 4000 River Crescent Dr .... Annapolis MD 21401 410-266-7300 672
TF: 800-299-2683 ■ *Web:* www.gingercove.com
Ginger G 3616 Noakes St .... Los angeles CA 90023 323-266-0202 366
Ginkgo International
8102 Lemont Rd Ste 1100 .... Woodridge IL 60517 630-910-5244 362
Web: www.ginkgoint.com
Ginkgo Petrified Forest State Park
4511 Huntzinger Rd .... Vantage WA 98950 509-856-2700 565
Web: www.parks.wa.gov
Ginkgo Residential LLC
301 S College St Ste 3850 .... Charlotte NC 28202 704-944-0100 655
Web: ginkgores.com
Ginn Group Inc, The
200 Westpark Dr Ste 100 .... Peachtree City GA 30269 404-669-9214 256
Web: www.theginngroup.com
Ginny's Printing 8410-B Tuscany Way .... Austin TX 78754 512-454-6874 453-2178 627
Web: www.ginnysprinting.com
Gino Morena Enterprises LLC
111 Starlite St .... South San Francisco CA 94080 800-227-6905 77
TF: 800-227-6905 ■ *Web:* www.ginomorena.com
Gino's 4542 Bennington Ave .... Baton Rouge LA 70808 225-927-7156 671
Web: www.ginosrestaurant.com
Gino's Restaurant & Lounge
2809 Sixth Ave .... Des Moines IA 50313 515-282-4029 671
Ginsberg's Foods Inc
29 Ginsberg Ln PO Box 17 .... Hudson NY 12534 518-828-4004 355
TF: 800-999-6006 ■ *Web:* www.ginsbergs.com
Ginsburg & Misk Attys
21548 Jamaica Ave .... Queens Village NY 11428 718-468-0500 428
TF: 800-337-6968 ■ *Web:* www.gmlawyers.net
Ginsburg Bakery Inc
300 N Tennessee Ave .... Atlantic City NJ 08401 609-345-2265 345-2268 297-11
Web: www.ginsburgbakery.com
Ginsburg Development Cos LLC (GDC)
100 Summit Lake Dr .... Valhalla NY 10595 914-747-3600 653
Web: www.gdc-homes.com
Ginsburg Ruth Bader
US Supreme Ct Bldg 1 1st St NE .... Washington DC 20543 202-479-3000 341-4
Web: www.supremecourt.gov
Ginza 16 Hudson St .... Boston MA 02111 617-338-2261 671
Ginza Sushi House 1105 Carnegie Ave .... Cleveland OH 44115 216-589-8503 671
Gioffre Cos Inc 6262 Eiterman Rd .... Dublin OH 43016 614-764-0032 764-1620 187
Web: www.gioffreconstruction.com
Giordano Construction Company Inc
1155 Main St .... Branford CT 06405 203-488-7264 186
Web: www.giordano-construction.com
Giordano s Solid Waste Removal
110 N Mill Rd .... Vineland NJ 08360 856-696-2068 660
TF: 800-636-8625 ■ *Web:* www.giordanosrecycling.com
Giordano, Halleran & Ciesla PC
125 Half Mile Rd .... Middletown NJ 07748 732-741-3900 428
Web: www.ghclaw.com
Giorgio Foods Inc PO Box 96 .... Temple PA 19560 610-926-2139 926-7012 296-20
TF: 800-220-2139 ■ *Web:* www.giorgiofoods.com
Giorgio Restaurants
222 boul Saint Laurent .... Montreal QC H2Y2Y3 514-845-4221 844-0071 670
Web: www.giorgio.ca
Giorgio's 1131 NW Hoyt St .... Portland OR 97209 503-221-1888 671
Web: www.giorgiospdx.com
Giovanni's 362 Preston St .... Ottawa ON K1S4M7 613-234-3156 671
Web: www.giovannis-restaurant.com

	Phone	Fax	Class
Giovanni's 5201 Shaw Ave ... Saint Louis MO 63110 *TF:* 800-916-0404 ■ *Web:* www.giovannisonthehill.com	314-772-5958		671
Giovanni's Restaurant & Convention Ctr 610 N Bell School Rd ... Rockford IL 61107 *TF:* 877-926-8300 ■ *Web:* www.giodine.com	815-398-6411		671
Giovanni's Ristorante 330 S Oakwood Blvd ... Detroit MI 48217 *Web:* www.giovannisristorante.com	313-841-0122		671
Giovatto Advertising & Consulting Inc 95 New Jersey 17 ... Paramus NJ 07652 *Web:* www.giovatto.com	201-226-9700		7
Gipe Assoc Inc 8719 Brooks Dr ... Easton MD 21601 *Web:* gipe.net	410-822-8688		261
Gipson Hoffman & Pancione 1901 Ave of The Stars 11th Fl ... Los Angeles CA 90067 *Web:* www.ghplaw.com	310-556-4660		428
Girard College 2101 S College Ave ... Philadelphia PA 19121 *Web:* www.girardcollege.com	215-787-2600		622
Girard Equipment Inc 531 Hwy 146 N ... La Porte TX 77571 *Web:* www.girardequip.com	281-842-7500		789
Girard Machine Company Inc 700 Dot St ... Girard OH 44420 *Web:* www.girardmachine.com	330-545-9731		492
Girardi Distributors LLC 5 Railroad Pl ... Athol MA 01331 *Web:* businessfinder.masslive.com	978-249-3581		81-1
Girardin Minibus Inc 3000 rue Girardin ... Drummondville QC J2E0A1 *TF:* 800-951-7867 ■ *Web:* www.girardin.com	819-477-2012		108
Girasole Ristorante & Lounge 3108 Pacific Ave ... Atlantic City NJ 08401 *Web:* www.girasoleac.com	609-345-5554		671
Girl Scouts of the USA 420 Fifth Ave ... New York NY 10018 *TF:* 800-478-7248 ■ *Web:* www.girlscouts.org	212-852-8000	852-6517	48-15
Girl Skateboard Company Inc, The 22500 S Vermont Ave ... Torrance CA 90502 *Web:* www.girlskateboards.com	310-783-1900		711
Girls Inc 120 Wall St ... New York NY 10005 *TF:* 800-374-4475 ■ *Web:* www.girlsinc.org	212-509-2000	509-8708	48-24
Girls Inc of Alameda County 510 16th St ... Oakland CA 94612 *Web:* www.girlsinc-alameda.org	510-357-5515		533
Girls Nation *American Legion Auxiliary* 8945 N Meridian St ... Indianapolis IN 46260 *TF:* 800-504-4098 ■ *Web:* www.alaforveterans.org	317-569-4500	569-4502	48-7
Girls' Life Acqusition Co 4529 Hartford Rd ... Baltimore MD 21214 *TF:* 800-931-2237 ■ *Web:* www.girlslife.com	410-426-9600		457-6
Giroux Glass Inc 850 W Washington Blvd ... Los Angeles CA 90015 *Web:* www.girouxglass.com	213-747-7406	747-8778	189-6
Girtz Industries Inc 5262 N E Shafer Dr ... Monticello IN 47960 *Web:* www.girtz.com	574-278-7510		697
Girvin Inc 121 Stewart St Ste 212 ... Seattle WA 98101 *Web:* www.girvin.com	206-674-7808	674-7909	344
Gis Assocs Inc 806a NW 16th Ave ... Gainesville FL 32601 *Web:* gis-associates.com	352-384-1465		317
Gisbiz Inc 25 Century Blvd Ste 602 ... Nashville TN 37214 *TF:* 800-642-2325 ■ *Web:* www.gisbiz.com	615-465-8287		177
GISD (Garland Independent School District) 501 S Jupiter PO Box 469026 ... Garland TX 75046 *TF:* 800-252-5555 ■ *Web:* www.garlandisd.net	972-494-8201	485-4936	685
GISD (Galveston Independent School District) 3904 Ave T PO Box 660 ... Galveston TX 77550 *Web:* www.gisd.org	409-766-5100	762-8391	685
Giselle's Travel Inc 1300 Ethan Way Ste 100 ... Sacramento CA 95825 *TF:* 800-782-5545 ■ *Web:* www.globaltrav.com	916-922-5500	679-3090	771
Gislason & Hunter LLP 2700 S Broadway ... New Ulm MN 56073 *TF:* 800-469-0234 ■ *Web:* www.gislason.com	507-354-3111		428
Gistics Inc 92 Templar Pl ... Oakland CA 94618 *Web:* gistics.com	510-450-9999		224
GITA (Geospatial Information & Technology Assn) 14456 E Evans Ave ... Aurora CO 80014 *Web:* www.gita.org	303-337-0513		49-19
Gita Sporting Goods Ltd 12500 Steele Creek Rd ... Charlotte NC 28273 *Web:* www.gitabike.com	704-588-7555		711
GitHub Inc 88 Colin P Kelly Junior St ... San Francisco CA 94107 *Web:* github.com	415 735-4488	520-5597	387
Gitlin & Assoc LLP 55 S Main St ... Liberty NY 12754	845-292-7780		2
Gitman & Co 2309 Chestnut St ... Ashland PA 17921 *TF:* 800-526-3929 ■ *Web:* www.gitman.com	570-875-3100		155-12
Gitman Bros 544 Hamilton St ... Allentown PA 18101 *Web:* www.gitman.com	610-433-7625		155-12
Gitomer & Berenholz PC 445 Shady Ln ... Huntingdon Valley PA 19006 *Web:* gbm-cpa.com	215-379-3500		2
Gits Manufacturing Co 1739 Commerce Dr ... Creston IA 50801 *Web:* www.gitsmfg.com	641-782-2105		247
Giuffre Bros Cranes Inc 6635 S 13th St ... Milwaukee WI 53221 *Web:* giuffre.com	414-764-9200		358
Giuffrida Assoc Inc 204 E St NE ... Washington DC 20002 *Web:* www.giuffrida.org	202-547-6340		47
Giunta's Meat Farms 1067 Route 112 ... Port Jefferson NY 11776 *Web:* www.giuntasmeatfarms.com	631-474-3910		345
Giuseppe's 4141 S Grand Blvd ... Saint Louis MO 63118 *Web:* www.giuseppesongrand.com	314-832-3779	832-7598	671
Giuseppe's 17937 SE Stark St ... Portland OR 97233 *Web:* giuseppespdx.com	503-669-8767		671
Giuseppe's Italian Kitchen 2824 E Indian School Rd ... Phoenix AZ 85016 *Web:* giuseppeson28th.com	602-381-1237	381-3669	671
Giusto Enterprises Inc 7525 Mission St ... Daly City CA 94014 *Web:* elcaminoinn.com	650-992-7090		379
Givaudan Flavors Corp 1199 Edison Dr ... Cincinnati OH 45216 *Web:* www.givaudan.com	513-948-8000		296-15
Giveanything.com LLC 307 Fifth Ave 4th Fl ... New York NY 10016 *Web:* www.giveanything.com	212-689-1200		387
Giveaway, The 183 E McClain St ... Scottsburg IN 47170 *Web:* www.gbpnews.com	812-752-3171		532-4
Givenhansco Inc 2400 Corporate Exchange Dr Ste 103 ... Columbus OH 43231 *TF:* 800-321-3231 ■ *Web:* www.givenhansco.com	614-310-0060		177
Givhans Ferry State Park 746 Givhans Ferry Rd ... Ridgeville SC 29472 *Web:* www.southcarolinaparks.com	843-873-0692		565
Giving Institute 303 W Madison St Ste 2650 ... Chicago IL 60606 *Web:* givinginstitute.org	312-981-6794		48-5
GIVINGTRAX 7921 S Hosmer Ste A ... Tacoma WA 98408 *Web:* www.givingtrax.com	206-486-0185		387
GIW Industries Inc 5000 Wrightsboro Rd ... Grovetown GA 30813 *TF:* 888-832-4449 ■ *Web:* www.ksb.com	706-863-1011	860-5897	641
Gizmo Art Production Inc 1315 Egbert Ave ... San Francisco CA 94124 *Web:* www.gizmosf.com	415-222-6181		279
GJ Chemical Co 370-376 Adams St ... Newark NJ 07105 *Web:* www.gjchemical.com	973-589-1450	589-5786	146
GJ Grewe Inc 9109 Watson Rd ... Saint Louis MO 63126 *Web:* www.gjgrewe.com	314-962-6300		653
GJ Littlewood & Son Inc 4045 Main St ... Philadelphia PA 19127 *TF:* 800-843-1728 ■ *Web:* www.littlewooddyers.com	215-483-3970	483-6129	745-7
GJ Nikolas & Company Inc 2800 Washington Blvd ... Bellwood IL 60104 *Web:* www.finish1.com	708-544-0320		549
G&J Seiberlich & Company LLP 3264 Villa Ln ... Napa CA 94558 *Web:* www.gjscollp.com	707-224-7948		734
GJDCCVB (Galena/Jo Daviess County Convention & Visitors Bureau) 720 Park Ave ... Galena IL 61036 *TF General:* 800-747-9377 ■ *Web:* www.galena.org	815-777-3557	777-3566	206
GK (Grand-Kahn Electric) 2455 W Grand Ave ... Chicago IL 60612 *Web:* www.grandkahn.com	312-298-1500	298-1501	189-4
GK Industries Ltd 50 Precidio Ct ... Brampton ON L6S6E3 *TF:* 800-463-8889 ■ *Web:* www.gkindustries.com	905-799-1972	799-0852	61
GKCCF (Greater Kansas City Community Foundation & Affiliated Trusts) 1055 Broadway Ste 130 ... Kansas City MO 64105 *Web:* www.growyourgiving.org	816-842-0944	842-8079	303
GKG (Global Knowledge Group Inc) 302 N Bryan Ave ... Bryan TX 77803 *TF:* 866-776-7584 ■ *Web:* www.gkg.net	866-776-7584		808
gkkworks Construction Services Inc 2355 Main St Ste 220 ... Irvine CA 92614 *Web:* gkkworks.com	949-250-1500		256
GKN Aerospace Bandy Machining Inc 3420 N San Fernando Blvd ... Burbank CA 91504 *Web:* www.gkn.com	818-846-9020		22
GKN Aerospace Chem-tronics Inc 1150 W Bradley Ave ... El Cajon CA 92020 *TF:* 800-377-8808 ■ *Web:* www.gkn.com	619-448-2320	258-5270	22
GKN Armstrong Wheels Inc 801 E Skinner St ... Wichita KS 67211	316-943-3571		57
GKN Rockford Inc 1200 Windsor Rd ... Loves Park IL 61111 *TF:* 800-394-5051 ■ *Web:* www.gkn.com	815-633-7460	633-1311	620
GKV 1500 Whetstone Way 4th Fl ... Baltimore MD 21230 *Web:* www.gkv.com	410-539-5400		4
GL Communications Inc 818 W Diamond Ave 3rd Fl ... Gaithersburg MD 20878 *Web:* www.gl.com	301-670-4784		177
GL Homes of Florida Corp 1600 Sawgrass Corporate Pkwy Ste 400 ... Sunrise FL 33323 *Web:* www.glhomes.com	954-753-1730		653
G&L Realty Corp 439 N Bedford Dr ... Beverly Hills CA 90210 *Web:* www.glrealty.com	310-273-9930		655
GL Seaman & Co 4201 International Pkwy ... Carrollton TX 75007 *Web:* glsc.com	214-764-6400	764-6420	320
G-L Veneer Co Inc 2224 E Slauson Ave ... Huntington Park CA 90255 *TF:* 800-588-5003 ■ *Web:* www.glveneer.com	323-582-5203	582-9681	613
Glacial Energy 2701 N Dallas Pkwy Ste 120 ... Plano TX 75093 *Web:* www.glacialenergy.com	469-467-8332		192
Glacial Lakes Energy LLC 301 20th Ave SE PO Box 933 ... Watertown SD 57201 *TF:* 866-934-2676 ■ *Web:* www.glaciallakesenergy.com	605-882-8480		579
Glacial Lakes State Park 25022 County Rd 41 ... Starbuck MN 56381 *TF:* 888-646-6367 ■ *Web:* www.dnr.state.mn.us	320-239-2860	239-4605	565
Glacial Ridge Hospital Foundation Inc 10 Fourth Ave SE ... Glenwood MN 56334 *TF:* 866-667-4747 ■ *Web:* www.glacialridge.org	320-634-4521		374-3
Glacial Waters Spa at Grand View Lodge 23521 Nokomis Ave ... Nisswa MN 56468 *TF:* 866-801-2951 ■ *Web:* www.grandviewlodge.com	218-963-2234		707
Glacier Bancorp Inc PO Box 27 ... Kalispell MT 59903 *NASDAQ: GBCI* ■ *TF:* 800-735-4371 ■ *Web:* www.glacierbank.com	406-756-4200		360-2
Glacier Bay Country Inn 35 Tong Rd ... Gustavus AK 99826 *Web:* www.glacierbayalaska.com	907-697-2288		379
Glacier Brew House 737 W Fifth Ave ... Anchorage AK 99501 *Web:* www.glacierbrewhouse.com	907-274-2739		671
Glacier Clear Enterprises Inc 3291 Thomas St ... Innisfil ON L9S3W3 *TF Cust Svc:* 800-668-5118 ■ *Web:* www.glacierclear.com	705-436-6363	436-4949	805

Name / Address	City	State	Zip	Phone	Fax	Class
Glacier County 512 E Main St.	Cut Bank	MT	59427	406-873-2711		338
Web: www.glaciercountygov.com						
Glacier Electric Co-op Inc 410 E Main St.	Cut Bank	MT	59427	406-873-5566		245
TF: 844-834-4457 ■ *Web:* www.glacierelectric.com						
Glacier Gardens Rainforest Adventure 7600 Old Glacier Hwy.	Juneau	AK	99801	907-790-3377	790-3907	97
Web: www.glaciergardens.com						
Glacier Hills 1200 Earhart Rd.	Ann Arbor	MI	48105	734-769-6410		672
Web: www.glacierhills.org						
Glacier National Park PO Box 350	Revelstoke	BC	V0E2S0	250-837-7500	837-7536	563
TF: 866-787-6221 ■ *Web:* www.pc.gc.ca						
Glacier National Park PO Box 128	West Glacier	MT	59936	406-888-7800	888-7808	564
Web: www.nps.gov/glac						
Glacier Park Inc PO Box 2025	Columbia Falls	MT	59912	406-892-2525	892-1375	669
TF: 844-868-7474 ■ *Web:* www.glacierparkinc.com						
Glacier Real Estate Finance Inc 2800 156th Ave Ste 210	Bellevue	WA	98007	425-746-6446		652
Web: www.glacier.com						
Glacier Restaurant Lounge 1873 Shell Simmons Dr Ste 220	Juneau	AK	99801	907-789-9538		671
Glacier Technologies LLC 1200 Golden Key Cir Ste 400	El Paso	TX	79925	915-751-6014		261
TF: 800-438-7325 ■ *Web:* www.glacier-tech.com						
Glacier Water Services Inc 1385 Pk Ctr Dr	Vista	CA	92081	760-560-1111		55
OTC: GWSV ■ *TF:* 800-452-2437 ■ *Web:* www.glacierwater.com						
Glad Tidings Assembly of God Church 1110 Snyder Rd	Reading	PA	19609	610-678-0266		48-20
Web: www.gladtidingsonline.com						
Glad Works 545 Pawtucket Ave	Pawtucket	RI	02860	401-724-4523		344
TF: 800-610-3458 ■ *Web:* www.gladworks.com						
Gladding Braided Products LLC 110 Country Rd	South Otselic	NY	13155	315-653-7211	653-4492	208
Web: gladdingbraid.com						
Gladding-Hearn Shipbuilding 1 Riverside Ave PO Box 300	Somerset	MA	02726	508-676-8596	672-1873	698
Web: www.gladding-hearn.com						
Glade & Grove Supply Inc 305 CR 17A W	Avon Park	FL	33825	561-996-3095	996-2048	274
TF: 800-433-4451 ■ *Web:* www.gladeandgroveused.com						
Glade Springs Resort 255 Resort Dr	Daniels	WV	25832	866-562-8054		669
TF: 866-562-8054 ■ *Web:* www.gladesprings.com						
Glades County 500 Ave K PO Box 1527	Moore Haven	FL	33471	863-946-6000	946-2860	338
Web: www.myglades.com						
Gladstein Neandross & Associates LLC 3015 Main St Ste 300	Santa Monica	CA	90405	310-314-1934		196
TF: 800-993-0302 ■ *Web:* www.gladstein.org						
Gladstone Area Chamber of Commerce 7001 N Oak Trfwy	Gladstone	MO	64118	816-436-4523	436-4352	139
Web: gladstonechamber.com						
Gladstone Care & Rehabilitation Ctr 435 E Gladstone St	Glendora	CA	91740	626-963-5955	963-8683	450
Web: www.gladstonecare.com						
Gladstone Dodge 5610 N Oak Trafficway	Gladstone	MO	64118	866-695-2043		57
TF: 866-695-2043 ■ *Web:* www.gladstonedodgekansascity.com						
Gladstone School District 115 17789 Webster Rd	Gladstone	OR	97027	503-655-2777	655-5201	685
TF: 800-328-0272 ■ *Web:* www.gladstone.k12.or.us						
Gladwin County 401 W Cedar Ave.	Gladwin	MI	48624	989-426-7351	426-6917	338
Web: gladwincounty-mi.gov						
Gladys Porter Zoo 500 Ringgold St	Brownsville	TX	78520	956-546-7187		823
Web: www.gpz.org						
Glamorise Foundations Inc 135 Madison Ave	New York	NY	10016	212-684-5025		155-18
TF: 800-928-1963 ■ *Web:* glamorise.com						
Glamos Wire Products Company Inc 5561 N 152nd St	Hugo	MN	55038	651-429-5386	429-7733	73
TF: 800-328-5062 ■ *Web:* www.glamoswire.com						
Glance Networks Inc 1167 Massachusetts Ave	Arlington	MA	02476	781-646-8505		225
TF: 877-452-6236 ■ *Web:* www.glance.net						
Glancy Prongay & Murray LLP 1801 Ave Of The Stars	Los Angeles	CA	90067	310-201-9150		428
TF: 888-773-9224 ■ *Web:* www.glancylaw.com						
Glascock County PO Box 66	Gibson	GA	30810	706-598-2671	598-0124	338
TF: 800-436-7442 ■ *Web:* www.glascockcountyga.com						
Glas-Col LLC 711 Hulman St.	Terre Haute	IN	47802	812-235-6167		14
Web: www.glascol.com						
Glaser Technology Inc 123 W Madison St 1100	Chicago	IL	60602	312-578-0377		177
Glaser Weil Fink Jacobs Howard Avchen & Shapiro LLP 10250 Constellation Blvd 19th Fl	Los Angeles	CA	90067	310-553-3000	556-2920	428
Web: glaserweil.com						
Glasfloss Industries Inc PO Box 150469	Dallas	TX	75315	214-741-7056	435-8377*	18
**Fax Area Code:* 800 ■ *Web:* www.glasfloss.com						
Glasgow Inc 104 Willow Grove Ave	Glenside	PA	19038	215-884-8800	884-1465	188-4
TF: 877-222-5514 ■ *Web:* www.glasgowinc.com						
Glasgow-Barren County Chamber of Commerce 118 E Public Sq	Glasgow	KY	42141	270-651-3161	651-3122	139
TF: 800-264-3161 ■ *Web:* www.glasgowbarrenchamber.com						
Glass & Company CPAs PC 515 Congress Ave Ste 1900	Austin	TX	78701	512-480-8182		2
Web: glasscpa.com						
Glass Art Society (GAS) 6512 23rd Ave NW Ste 329	Seattle	WA	98117	206-382-1305	382-2630	48-4
TF: 800-636-2377 ■ *Web:* www.glassart.org						
Glass Assn of North America (GANA) 800 SW Jackson St Ste 1500	Topeka	KS	66612	785-271-0208	271-0166	49-13
Web: www.glasswebsite.com						
Glass House Inn 3202 W 26th St.	Erie	PA	16506	814-833-7751	833-4222	379
TF: 800-956-7222 ■ *Web:* www.glasshouseinn.com						
Glass Magazine 8200 Greensboro Dr Ste 302	McLean	VA	22102	703-442-4890		457-21
Web: www.glassmagazine.com						
Glass McClure Inc 2700 J St	Sacramento	CA	95816	916-448-6956		5
Web: glassagency.com						

Name / Address	City	State	Zip	Phone	Fax	Class
Glass Packaging Institute (GPI) 700 N Fairfax St Ste 510	Alexandria	VA	22314	703-684-6359	299-1543	49-13
TF: 800-949-8305 ■ *Web:* www.gpi.org						
Glass, Jacobson and Medallion Financial Services LLC 10711 Red Run Blvd Ste 101	Owings Mills	MD	21117	410-356-1000		2
TF: 800-356-7666 ■ *Web:* www.glassjacobson.com						
Glasscock County 117 E Currie St	Garden City	TX	79739	432-354-2371		338
TF: 800-433-0567 ■ *Web:* www.co.glasscock.tx.us						
GlassCraft Door Co 2002 Brittmoore Rd.	Houston	TX	77043	713-690-8282		234
TF: 800-766-2196 ■ *Web:* www.gcdoor.com						
Glasses Ltd 50 E Oak St Apt Bsmt	Chicago	IL	60611	312-944-6876		543
Web: www.glasses.com						
Glassfab Tempering Services Inc 1448 Mariani Ct	Tracy	CA	95376	209-229-1060		261
TF: 800-535-2133 ■ *Web:* www.glassfabtempering.com						
Glasshouse Grille 709 Beechurst Ave	Morgantown	WV	26505	304-296-8460		671
Web: www.theglasshousegrille.com						
Glassline Corp PO Box 147	Perrysburg	OH	43552	419-666-5942	666-1549	493
Web: www.glassline.com						
Glassmere Fuel Service Inc 1967 Saxonburg Blvd	Tarentum	PA	15084	724-265-4646		316
TF: 800-235-9054 ■ *Web:* www.glassmerefuel.com						
GlassPoint Solar Inc 46485 Landing Pkwy	Fremont	CA	94538	415-778-2800		14
Web: www.glasspoint.com						
GlassRatner 3445 Peachtree Rd Ste 1225	Atlanta	GA	30326	678-904-1990		796
Web: www.glassratner.com						
Glassybaby LLC 3406 E Union St	Seattle	WA	98122	206-518-9071		362
Web: www.glassybaby.com						
Glast Phillips & Murray 14801 Quorum Dr Ste 500	Dallas	TX	75254	972-419-8300		445
Web: www.glastphillips.com						
Glasteel-stabilit America Inc 285 Industrial Dr.	Moscow	TN	38057	901-877-3010		608
TF: 800-238-5546 ■ *Web:* www.glasteel.com						
Glastender Inc 5400 N Michigan Rd.	Saginaw	MI	48604	989-752-4275	752-4444	386
TF: 800-748-0423 ■ *Web:* www.glastender.com						
Glastonbury Chamber of Commerce 2400 Main St Ste 2	Glastonbury	CT	06033	860-659-3587	659-0102	139
TF: 800-452-0949 ■ *Web:* www.glastonburychamber.net						
Glastonbury Citizen Inc PO Box 373	Glastonbury	CT	06033	860-633-4691	657-3258	637-8
Web: www.glcitizen.com						
Glastonbury Southern Gage 46 Industrial Pk Rd.	Erin	TN	37061	931-289-4242	242-7142*	493
**Fax Area Code:* 800 ■ *TF:* 800-251-4243 ■ *Web:* www.gsgage.com						
Glastron 925 Frisbie St.	Cadillac	MI	49601	800-354-3141		90
TF: 800-354-3141 ■ *Web:* www.glastron.com						
Glatfelter 96 S George St Ste 500	York	PA	17401	717-225-4711	846-7208	557
Web: www.glatfelter.com						
Glatt Air Techniques Inc 20 Spear Rd.	Ramsey	NJ	07446	201-825-8700	825-0389	385
Web: www.glatt.com						
Glauber Equipment Corp 1600 Commerce Pkwy	Lancaster	NY	14086	716-681-1234		358
TF: 888-452-8237 ■ *Web:* www.glauber.com						
Glaucoma Foundation (TGF) 80 Maiden Ln Ste 700	New York	NY	10038	212-285-0080	651-1888	48-17
Web: www.glaucomafoundation.org						
Glaucoma Research Foundation 251 Post St Ste 600	San Francisco	CA	94108	415-986-3162	986-3763	48-17
TF: 800-826-6693 ■ *Web:* www.glaucoma.org						
Glaval Bus 914 County Rd 1	Elkhart	IN	46514	574-262-2212		59
TF: 800-445-2825 ■ *Web:* www.glavalbus.com						
GlaxoSmithKline Inc 7333 Mississauga Rd N	Mississauga	ON	L5N6L4	905-819-3000	819-3099	582
TF: 800 387-7374 ■ *Web:* ca.gsk.com						
Glazer's Wholesale Drug Company Inc 14911 Quorum Dr Ste 150	Dallas	TX	75254	972-392-8200	702-8508	81-3
Web: www.southernglazers.com						
Glaz-Tech Industries Inc 2207 E Elvira Rd.	Tucson	AZ	85756	520-629-0268	629-8811	329
TF: 800-755-8062 ■ *Web:* www.glaztech.com						
Glb Insurance Group of Nevada 4455 S Pecos Rd	Las Vegas	NV	89121	702-735-9333		390
Web: glbins.com						
GLC (God's Learning Ch) PO Box 61000	Midland	TX	79711	432-563-0420	563-1736	740
TF: 800-707-0420 ■ *Web:* www.glc.us.com						
GLE Associates Inc 5405 Cypress Center Dr Ste 110	Tampa	FL	33609	813-241-8350		192
TF: 888-453-4531 ■ *Web:* www.gleassociates.com						
Gleacher & Co Inc 1290 Ave of the Americas	New York	NY	10104	212-273-7100		690
Web: www.gleacher.com						
Gleaner's Food Bank of Indianapolis 3737 Waldemere Ave	Indianapolis	IN	46241	317-925-0191		305
TF: 800-944-9166 ■ *Web:* www.gleaners.org						
Gleason Corp 1000 University Ave.	Rochester	NY	14607	585-473-1000	461-4348	455
TF: 800-727-6333 ■ *Web:* www.gleason.com						
Gleason Corp 1351 Windsor Rd.	Loves Park	IL	61111	815-877-8900	877-0264	493
TF: 800-438-5021 ■ *Web:* www.gleason.com						
Gleason Industrial Products Inc 8575 Forest Home Ave Ste 100	Greenfield	WI	53228	414-529-8357		554
Web: www.milwaukeehandtrucks.com						
Gleason Law Offices PC 163 Merrimack St.	Haverhill	MA	01830	978-521-4044		428
Web: www.gleasonlawoffices.com						
Gleason M & M Precision Systems Corp 300 Progress Rd.	Dayton	OH	45449	937-859-8273	859-4452	248
TF: 800-727-6333 ■ *Web:* www.gleason.com						
Gleason Reel Corp 600 S Clark St	Mayville	WI	53050	920-387-4120	387-4189	117
TF: 888-504-5151 ■ *Web:* www.hubbell-gleason.com						
Gleason Research Associates Inc 5030 Bradford Dr NW Bldg One Ste 220	Huntsville	AL	35805	256-883-7000		261
Web: www.grainc.net						
Gleim Publications Inc 4201 NW 95th Blvd	Gainesville	FL	32606	352-375-0772		532-3
Web: www.gleim.com						

	Phone	Fax	Class
Gleim The Jeweler Inc 322 University Ave .... Palo Alto CA 94301 *Web:* www.gleimjewelers.com	650-323-1331		410
Glen Canyon National Recreation Area 691 Scenic View Dr PO Box 1507................ Page AZ 86040 *Web:* www.nps.gov/glca	928-608-6200	608-6259	564
Glen Cove Hospital 101 St Andrews Ln......................... Glen Cove NY 11542	516-674-7300		374-3
Glen Cove Mansion Hotel & Conference Ctr 200 Dosoris Ln.......................... Glen Cove NY 11542 *TF:* 877-782-9426 ■ *Web:* www.glencovemansion.com	516-671-6400		377
Glen Eagles 3700 N Carson St.............. Carson City NV 89706 *Web:* www.gleneaglesrestaurant.com	775-884-4414		671
Glen Eden Corp 25999 Glen Eden Rd ....Corona CA 92883 *TF:* 800-843-6833 ■ *Web:* www.gleneden.com	951-277-4650		121
Glen Elder State Park 2131 180 Rd.............. Glen Elder KS 67446 *Web:* ksoutdoors.com/state-parks/locations/glen-elder	785-545-3345		565
Glen Ellyn Chamber of Commerce 800 Roosevelt Rd Bldg D Ste 108.............. Glen Ellyn IL 60137 *TF:* 800-622-9000 ■ *Web:* www.glenellynchamber.com	630-469-0907	469-0426	139
Glen Ellyn Public Library 400 Duane St .... Glen Ellyn IL 60137 *Web:* www.gepl.org	630-469-0879		435
Glen Ellyn School District 41 793 N Main St .... Glen Ellyn IL 60137 *Web:* www.d41.org	630-790-6400	790-1867	685
Glen Foerd on the Delaware 5001 Grant Ave...........................Philadelphia PA 19114 *Web:* www.glenfoerd.org	215-632-5330		50-3
Glen Grove Elementary School 3900 Glenview Rd......................... Glenview IL 60025 *TF:* 800-222-1222 ■ *Web:* www.glenview34.org	847-998-5030		685
Glen Grove Suites 2837 Yonge St.............. Toronto ON M4N2J6 *TF:* 800-565-3024 ■ *Web:* www.glengrove.com	416-489-8441	440-3065	379
Glen Meadows 11630 Glen Arm Rd............Glen Arm MD 21057 *TF:* 800-630-4689 ■ *Web:* www.presbyterianseniorliving.org	800-630-4689		672
Glen Mills Schools PO Box 5001 .... Concordville PA 19331 *TF:* 800-441-2064 ■ *Web:* www.glenmillsschool.org	610-459-8100	558-1493	623
Glen Oak Park 2218 N Prospect Rd.............. Peoria IL 61603 *Web:* www.peoriazoo.org	309-686-3365	685-6240	823
Glen Oaks Community College 62249 Shimmel Rd.........................Centreville MI 49032 *Fax: Admissions ■ *TF:* 888-994-7818 ■ *Web:* www.glenoaks.edu	269-467-9945	467-9068*	162
Glen Raven Inc 232 Glen Raven Rd.......... Glen Raven NC 27217 *Web:* www.glenraven.com	336-227-6211	226-8133	745-1
Glen Research Corp 22825 Davis Dr .... Sterling VA 20164 *TF:* 800-327-4536 ■ *Web:* www.glenres.com	703-437-6191		668
Glenair Inc 1211 Air Way........................ Glendale CA 91201 *TF:* 888-465-4094 ■ *Web:* www.glenair.com	818-247-6000	500-9912	815
Glenbeigh 2863 SR 45.................... Rock Creek OH 44084 *TF:* 800-234-1001 ■ *Web:* www.glenbeigh.com	440-563-3400	563-9619	726
Glenbow Museum 130-9 Ave SE.................. Calgary AB T2G0P3 *Web:* www.glenbow.org	403-268-4100	265-9769	520
Glenbriar Technologies Inc 736-1100 8 Ave SW.......................... Calgary AB T2P1H4 *Web:* www.glenbriar.com	403-233-7300		177
Glenbrook Square 4201 Coldwater Rd ....Fort Wayne IN 46805 *Web:* www.glenbrooksquare.com	260-483-2119		460
Glenco Steel Corp 8657 Live Oak Ave .... Fontana CA 92335	909-854-9000		480
Glencoe/McGraw-Hill 8787 Orion Pl.......... Columbus OH 43240 *TF:* 800-848-1567 ■ *Web:* www.glencoe.com	800-848-1567		637-2
Glencom Systems Inc 25 E Price St.............Linden NJ 07036 *Web:* www.glen.com	908-486-0420		180
Glencrest Farm 1576 Moores Mill Rd PO Box 4468 .... Midway KY 40347 *TF:* 800-903-0136 ■ *Web:* www.glencrest.com	859-233-7032	233-9404	368
Glencroft 8611 N 67th Ave.................... Glendale AZ 85302 *Web:* www.glencroft.com	623-939-9475		672
Glendale Adventist Medical Ctr 1509 Wilson Terr .... Glendale CA 91206 *Web:* www.adventisthealth.org	818-409-8000		374-3
Glendale (AZ) City Hall 5850 W Glendale Ave .... Glendale AZ 85301 *TF:* 800-367-8939 ■ *Web:* www.glendaleaz.com	623-930-2000	930-2690	337
Glendale (CA) City Hall 613 E Broadway Rm 110.................... Glendale CA 91206 *Web:* glendaleca.gov	818-548-2090	241-5386	337
Glendale Centre Theatre 324 N Orange St.......................... Glendale CA 91203 *Web:* www.glendalecentretheatre.com	818-244-8481	244-5042	572
Glendale Chamber of Commerce 200 S Louise St .... Glendale CA 91205 *Web:* www.glendalechamber.com	818-240-7870	240-2872	139
Glendale Civic Ctr 5750 W Glenn Dr .... Glendale AZ 85301 *Web:* www.glendaleciviccenter.com	623-930-4300	930-4319	205
Glendale Community College 6000 W Olive Ave........................ Glendale AZ 85302 *Web:* www2.gccaz.edu	623-845-3000		162
North Campus 5727 W Happy Valley Rd......... Phoenix AZ 85310 *Web:* www.gc.maricopa.edu/gccnorth	623-888-7000		162
Glendale Galleria 100 W Broadway .... Glendale CA 91210 *TF:* 800-786-1000 ■ *Web:* www.glendalegalleria.com	818-246-6737		460
Glendale Infiniti 812 S Brand Blvd.............. Glendale CA 91204	818-543-5000		57
Glendale Memorial Hospital & Health Ctr 1420 S Central Ave........................ Glendale CA 91204 *Web:* www.glendalememorialhospital.org	818-502-1900		374-3
Glendale News Press 202 W First St 2nd Fl.....................Los Angeles CA 90012 *Web:* www.latimes.com/socal/glendale-news-press	818-637-3200	241-1975	637-8
Glendale Public Library 5959 W Brown St.......................... Glendale AZ 85302 *Web:* www.glendaleaz.com	623-930-3530		434-3
Glendale Public Library 222 E Harvard St.......................... Glendale CA 91205 *TF:* 800-427-2200 ■ *Web:* www.glendaleca.gov	818-548-2030	548-7225	434-3
Glendale Securities Inc 15233 Ventura Blvd Ste 712.............Sherman Oaks CA 91403 *Web:* www.glendalesecurities.com	818-907-1505		690

	Phone	Fax	Class
Glendale Star 7122 N 59th Ave................ Glendale AZ 85301 *Web:* www.glendalestar.com	623-842-6000		532-3
Glendalough State Park 25287 Whitetail Ln........................Battle Lake MN 56515 *Web:* www.dnr.state.mn.us	218-864-0110	864-0587	565
Glendinning Marine Products 740 Century Cir .... Conway SC 29526 *TF:* 800-500-2380 ■ *Web:* www.glendinningprods.com	843-399-6146	399-5005	203
Glendo Corp PO Box 1153.....................Emporia KS 66801 *TF:* 800-835-3519 ■ *Web:* www.glendo.com	620-343-1084		295
Glendo State Park 397 Glendo Pk Rd............Glendo WY 82213 *Web:* wyoparks.state.wy.us	307-735-4433		565
Glendora Chamber of Commerce 131 E Foothill Blvd......................... Glendora CA 91741 *Web:* www.glendora-chamber.org	626-963-4128	914-4822	139
Glendora Highlander Press 1210 N Azusa Canyon Rd................ West Covina CA 91790 *TF:* 800-788-1200 ■ *Web:* sgvtribune.com/highlanders	626-962-8811		532-4
Glendora Public Library & Cultural Ctr 140 S Glendora Ave .... Glendora CA 91741 *TF:* 866-275-3772 ■ *Web:* www.ci.glendora.ca.us	626-852-4891	852-4899	434-3
Glendorn 1000 Glendorn Dr..................Bradford PA 16701 *TF:* 800-843-8568 ■ *Web:* www.glendorn.com	814-362-6511		379
Gleneden Beach State Recreation Site 198 NE 123rd St.........................Newport OR 97365 *TF:* 800-551-6949 ■ *Web:* www.oregonstateparks.org	800-551-6949		565
Glenerin Inn, The 1695 The Collegeway.................. Mississauga ON L5L3S7 *TF:* 877-991-9971 ■ *Web:* www.glenerininn.com	905-828-6103		379
Glen-Gery Corp 1166 Spring St PO Box 7001 ....Wyomissing PA 19610 *Web:* www.glengery.com	610-374-4011	374-1622	150
Glenmede Funds 1650 Market St Ste 1200 ....Philadelphia PA 19103 *TF:* 800-966-3200 ■ *Web:* www.glenmede.com	215-419-6000		528
Glenmoor Country Club 4191 Glenmoor Rd ....Canton OH 44718 *TF:* 800-462-9964 ■ *Web:* www.glenmoorcc.com	330-966-3600	966-3611	669
Glenmore Inn 2720 Glenmore Trl SE .... Calgary AB T2C2E6 *TF:* 800-661-3163 ■ *Web:* www.glenmoreinn.com	403-279-8611	236-8035	379
Glenmount Global Solutions 5960 Southport Rd.......................... Portage IN 46368 *Web:* www.glenmountglobal.com	219-762-0700		261
Glenn County 526 W Sycamore St Ste B1 .... Willows CA 95988 *TF:* 800-795-3272 ■ *Web:* www.countyofglenn.net	530-934-6400	934-6419	338
Glenn H. Johnson Construction 1776 Winthrop Dr...................... Des Plaines IL 60018 *Web:* www.ghjohnson.com	847-297-4700		186
Glenn m Gelman & Assoc Certified Public Accountants 1940 E 17th St .... Santa Ana CA 92705 *Web:* www.gelmanllp.com	714-667-2600		2
Glenn Miller Insurance Agency Inc 404 E N Ave ....Northlake IL 60164 *Web:* glennmilleragency.com	708-562-3404		390
Glenn O Hawbaker Inc 1952 Waddle Rd Ste 203 ....State College PA 16803 *TF:* 800-221-1355 ■ *Web:* www.goh-inc.com	814-237-1444		46
Glenn Research Ctr 21000 Brookpark Rd.......................Cleveland OH 44135 *Web:* www.nasa.gov/centers/glenn/home	216-433-4000	433-8000	668
Glennville Sentinel Inc, The 105 W Barnard St......................... Glennville GA 30427 *Web:* www.glennvillesentinel.net	912-654-2515		532-3
GlenOaks Hospital 701 Winthrop Ave.....................Glendale Heights IL 60139 *TF:* 866-751-7127 ■ *Web:* www.keepingyouwell.com	630-545-8000	545-3920	374-3
Glenro Inc 39 McBride Ave..................... Paterson NJ 07501 *TF:* 888-453-6761 ■ *Web:* www.glenro.com	973-279-5900	279-9103	318
Glenrock International Inc 985 E Linden Ave ....Linden NJ 07036 *TF:* 800-453-6762 ■ *Web:* glenrock.com	908-862-3433	862-0430	724
Glens Falls City School District 15 Quade St..............................Glens Falls NY 12801 *Web:* www.gfsd.org	518-792-1212		685
Glens Falls Hospital 100 Pk St ....Glens Falls NY 12801 *TF:* 800-994-6610 ■ *Web:* www.glensfallshospital.org	518-926-1000		374-3
Glensheen Mansion 3300 London Rd .... Duluth MN 55804 *TF:* 888-454-4536 ■ *Web:* www.d.umn.edu	218-726-8910	726-8911	50-3
Glentek Inc 208 Standard St .... El Segundo CA 90245 *TF:* 877-470-6742 ■ *Web:* www.glentek.com	310-322-3026	322-7709	518
Glenview Chamber of Commerce 2320 Glenview Rd......................... Glenview IL 60025 *TF:* 800-459-4250 ■ *Web:* www.glenviewchamber.com	847-724-0900	724-0202	139
Glenview Mansion 511 Warburton Ave Hudson River Museum .... Yonkers NY 10701 *Web:* www.hrm.org	914 963-4550		50-3
Glenview Public Library 1930 Glenview Rd.......................... Glenview IL 60025 *Web:* www.glenviewpl.org	847-729-7500	729-7558	434-3
Glenview State Bank 800 Waukegan Rd .... Glenview IL 60025 *Web:* gsb.com	847-729-1900		70
Glenville State College 200 High St........... Glenville WV 26351 *Fax: Admissions ■ *TF Admissions:* 800-924-2010 ■ *Web:* www.glenville.edu	304-462-7361	462-8619*	166
Glenwood Foods LLC 20850 Jackson Ln .... Jetersville VA 23083	804-561-3447		10-8
Glenwood LLC 111 Cedar Ln.................Englewood NJ 07631 *TF:* 800-542-0772 ■ *Web:* www.glenwood-llc.com	201-569-0050	569-0250	583
Glenwood Park Retirement Village 1924 Glenwood Pk Rd ....Princeton WV 24739 *Web:* www.gwpinc.org	304-425-8128		450
Glenwood Regional Medical Ctr 503 McMillan Rd ....West Monroe LA 71291 *Web:* www.grmc.com	318-329-4200	329-4710	374-3
Glenwood Resource Ctr 711 S Vine St .... Glenwood IA 51534 *Web:* dhs.iowa.gov	712-527-4811		230
Glenwood State Bank 5 E Minnesota Ave PO Box 197 .... Glenwood MN 56334 *TF:* 800-207-7333 ■ *Web:* www.glenwoodstate.com	320-634-5111	634-5114	70

	Phone	Fax	Class
GLERL (Great Lakes Environmental Research Laboratory) 4840 S State St ... Ann Arbor MI 48108 *TF:* 800-222-1222 ■ *Web:* www.glerl.noaa.gov	734-741-2235	741-2055	668
Glessner House Museum 1800 S Prairie Ave ... Chicago IL 60616 *TF:* 800-657-0687 ■ *Web:* www.glessnerhouse.org	312-326-1480		520
Glex Inc 12900 Fm 529 Rd ... Houston TX 77041 *TF:* 800-900-4805 ■ *Web:* www.glexinc.com	713-849-4985		261
Glhn Architects & Engineers Inc 2939 E Broadway Blvd ... Tucson AZ 85716 *Web:* glhn.com	520-881-4546		261
Glickenhaus & Co 546 Fifth Ave 7th Fl ... New York NY 10036 *Web:* www.glickenhaus.com	212-953-7800	867-9779	690
Glidden House 1901 Ford Dr ... Cleveland OH 44106 *TF:* 866-812-4537 ■ *Web:* www.gliddenhouse.com	216-231-8900	231-2130	379
GlideSlope LLC 133 W 19th St Sixth Fl ... New York NY 10011 *Web:* www.theglideslope.com	212-776-1817		463
Glidewell Laboratories Inc 4141 MacArthur Blvd ... Newport Beach CA 92660 *TF:* 800-854-7256 ■ *Web:* www.glidewelldental.com	800-854-7256		743
Glidewell Specialties Foundry Company Inc 600 Foundry Rd ... Calera AL 35040 *Web:* www.glidewell-foundry.com	205-668-1881		492
Glik Co 3248 Nameoki Rd ... Granite City IL 62040 *TF:* 800-622-1911 ■ *Web:* www.gliks.com	618-876-1065	876-7819	229
Glimmerglass Festival 7300 State Hwy 80 PO Box 191 ... Cooperstown NY 13326 *TF:* 866-568-2388 ■ *Web:* www.glimmerglass.org	607-547-0700		573-2
Glimmerglass Networks Inc 26142 Eden Landing Rd ... Hayward CA 94545 *TF:* 877-723-1900 ■ *Web:* www.glimmerglass.com	510-723-1900	780-9851	178-10
Glimmerglass State Park 1527 County Hwy 31 ... Cooperstown NY 13326 *Web:* parks.ny.gov/parks/28/details.aspx	607-547-8662		565
Glines & Rhodes Inc 189 E St ... Attleboro MA 02703 *TF:* 800-343-1196 ■ *Web:* www.glinesandrhodes.com	508-226-2000	226-7136	485
Glinsmann & Glinsmann, Chartered 12 Russell Ave ... Gaithersburg MD 20877 *Web:* mygreencardlawyer.com	301-987-0030		428
Glint Inc 808 Winslow St ... Redwood City CA 94063 *Web:* www.glintinc.com	650-817-7240		224
Glissen Chemical Company Inc 1321 58th St ... Brooklyn NY 11219	718-436-4200		151
Glitterex Corp 7 Commerce Dr ... Cranford NJ 07016 *Web:* glitterex.com	908-272-9121		761
GLK Foods LLC 11 Clark St ... Shortsville NY 14548 *TF:* 855-572-8800 ■ *Web:* www.glkfoods.com	855-572-8800		296-19
GLM Industries LP 1508 - Eighth St ... Nisku AB T9E7S6 *TF:* 800-661-9828 ■ *Web:* www.glmindustries.com	780-955-2233		480
GLMC (UMMC Grenada) 960 Avent Dr ... Grenada MS 38901 *Web:* www.glmc.net	662-227-7000		374-3
GLMV Chamber of Commerce 1123 S Milwaukee Ave ... Libertyville IL 60048 *Web:* www.glmvchamber.org	847-680-0750	680-0760	139
GLNX Corp 10077 Grogan's Mill Rd Ste 450 ... The Woodlands TX 77380 *Web:* www.glnx.com	281-363-7053	363-7060	264-5
Globa li 7948 E 23rd Ave ... Denver CO 80238 *Web:* www.globa.li	303-895-9583		393
GlobaFone Inc 1950 Lafayette Rd Ste 207 ... Portsmouth NH 03801 *TF:* 800-826-6152 ■ *Web:* globafone.com	603-433-7232		387
Global Air Response 5919 Approach Rd ... Sarasota FL 34238 **Fax Area Code:* 941 ■ *TF:* 800-631-6565 ■ *Web:* www.airresponse.net	800-631-6565	926-7690*	30
Global Aquaculture Alliance 2 International Dr Ste 105 ... Portsmouth NH 03801 *Web:* www.aquaculturealliance.org	603-317-5000		474
Global Arena Capital Corp 708 Third Ave 11th Fl ... New York NY 10017	212-508-4700		690
Global Bakeries Inc 13336 Paxton St ... Pacoima CA 91331 *Web:* www.globalbakeriesinc.com	818-896-0525		805
Global Banks Premium Income Trust 1375 Kerns Rd ... Burlington ON L7P4V7 *Web:* www.portlandic.com	905-331-4242		403
Global Benefits Group Inc 26000 Towne Centre Dr Ste 100 ... Foothill Ranch CA 92610 *Web:* www.gbg.com	949-470-2100		391-2
Global Body & Equipment Co 2061 Sylvan Rd ... Wooster OH 44691 *Web:* www.cncmetalproducts.com	330-264-6640		454
Global Brass & Copper Inc 475 N Martingale Rd Ste 1050 ... Schaumburg IL 60173 *Web:* gbcholdings.com	847-240-4700		492
Global Building Services Inc 25129 The Old Rd Ste 102 ... Stevenson Ranch CA 91381 *TF:* 800-675-6643 ■ *Web:* www.globalbuildingservices.com	800-675-6643	914-2485	393
Global Business Travel Assn, The (GBTA) 123 N Pitt St ... Alexandria VA 22314 *TF:* 888-574-6447 ■ *Web:* www.gbta.org	703-684-0836	684-0263	48-23
Global Cash Card 7 Corporate Pk Ste 130 ... Irvine CA 92606 *TF:* 888-220-4477 ■ *Web:* www.globalcashcard.com	949-751-0360		401
Global Center for Economic Enabling Environments 273 24th Ave ... San Francisco CA 94121 *Web:* www.gceee.com	206-877-2460		463
Global Change Assoc Inc 2576 Broadway ... New York NY 10025 *Web:* www.global-change.com	212-316-0223		194
Global Children's Organization 3580 Wilshire Blvd # 1800 ... Los Angeles CA 90010	213-368-8385		48-5
Global Citizen Year Inc 1625 Clay St Ste 400 ... Oakland CA 94612 *Web:* globalcitizenyear.org	415-963-9293		305
Global Cloud Ltd 901 Adams Xing Unit 2 ... Cincinnati OH 45202 *Web:* www.globalcloud.net	513-333-0450		196
Global Communication Semiconductors Inc 23155 Kashiwa Ct ... Torrance CA 90505 *Web:* www.gcsincorp.com	310-530-7274	517-8200	695
Global Computer Supplies Inc 11 Harbor Pk Dr ... Port Washington NY 11050 *TF:* 888-978-7759 ■ *Web:* www.globalindustrial.com	800-446-9662		174
Global Concepts Enterprise Inc 785 Waverly Ct ... Holland MI 49423 *Web:* www.globalconcepts.com	616-355-7657	355-7662	757
Global Consultants Inc 25 Airport Rd ... Morristown NJ 07960 *TF:* 877-264-6424 ■ *Web:* www.collabera.com	973-889-5200	292-1643	180
Global Contact Services LLC 101 Martin Dr ... Mount Hope WV 25880 *TF:* 800-379-2381 ■ *Web:* www.gcsagents.com	304-877-0427		393
Global Corporate College 6001 Cochran Rd Ste 305 ... Solon OH 44139 *Web:* globalcorporatecollege.com	440-793-0202		317
Global Credit Advisers LLC 101 Park Ave 26th Fl ... New York NY 10178 *Web:* www.globalcreditadvisers.com	212-949-1860		401
Global Data Consultants LLC 1144 Kennebec Dr ... Chambersburg PA 17201 *Web:* gdcitsolutions.com	717-262-2080		225
Global Design Alliance Inc (GDA) 26 Grammercy Pk S 4B ... New York NY 10003 *Web:* www.globalda.com	917-887-3860		261
Global Digital Media Xchange Inc 5432 W 102nd St ... Los Angeles CA 90045	818-972-0200		514
Global Domains International Inc 701 Palomar Airport Rd Ste 300 ... Carlsbad CA 92011 *Web:* www.worldsite.ws	760-602-3000	602-3099	736
Global Educational Tours 7216 Madison Ave Ste U ... Indianapolis IN 46227	317-787-2787	787-2765	760
Global Electronic Music PO Box 2186 ... La Jolla CA 92038	610-320-9927		525
Global Elite Group 825 E Gate Blvd Ste 301 ... Garden City NY 11530 *TF:* 877-425-0999 ■ *Web:* www.globaleliteinc.com	516-414-0487		693
Global Endowment Management LP 550 S Tryon St Ste 3500 ... Charlotte NC 28202 *Web:* www.globalendowment.com	704-333-8282		303
Global Energy Services USA Inc Unit A3, 3220 FM 1960W ... Houston TX 77068 *Web:* www.global-energy.ca	281-866-8544	770-0149	538
Global Enterprises Inc 7951 Shoal Creek Ste 200 ... Austin TX 78757	512-451-8280		772
Global Entertainment Corp 6751 N Sunset Blvd Ste 200 ... Glendale AZ 85305 *OTC:* GNTP	480-994-0772	994-0759	360-3
Global Environment & Technology Foundation 2900 S Quincy St Ste 375 ... Arlington VA 22206 *TF:* 800-407-0261 ■ *Web:* www.getf.org	703-379-2713		196
Global Equipment Marketing Inc PO Box 810483 ... Boca Raton FL 33481 *TF:* 866-750-8662 ■ *Web:* www.globalmagnetics.com	561-750-8662	750-9507	358
Global Equipment Services Corp 5215 Hellyer Ave Ste 130 ... San Jose CA 95138 *Web:* www.geservs.com	669-234-1110		696
Global Equity Capital LLC 6260 Lookout Rd ... Boulder CO 80301 *Web:* www.globalequitycap.com	303-531-1000		194
Global Exchange 2017 Mission St Ste 303 ... San Francisco CA 94110 *TF:* 800-497-1994 ■ *Web:* www.globalexchange.org	415-255-7296	255-7498	48-7
Global Experiences Inc 14 Annapolis St ... Annapolis MD 21401 *Web:* www.globalexperiences.com	410-267-7306		194
Global Fabrication Inc 235 Beaver Dr ... Dubois PA 15801 *Web:* www.globalfabricationinc.com	814-372-1500		480
Global Filtration Inc 9207 Emmott St ... Houston TX 77040 *TF:* 888-717-0888 ■ *Web:* www.globalfiltration.com	713-856-9800		57
Global Finance Magazine E 20th St ... New York NY 10003 *Web:* www.gfmag.com	212-447-7900		457-5
Global Fitness Center Inc 215 Hamilton St ... Leominster MA 01453 *Web:* www.globalfitnesscenter.com	978-537-2100		354
Global Flow Inc 5796 - 40th St SE ... Calgary AB T2C2A1 *Web:* globalflowinc.com	403-219-7373		538
Global Fulfillment 4 S Idaho St ... Seattle WA 98134 *Web:* www.globalful.com	206-405-3350		781
Global Gaming Solutions LLC 210 N Broadway ... Ada OK 74820 *Web:* www.globalgamingsol.com	580-559-0886		642
Global Gear & Machining LLC 2500 Curtiss St ... Downers Grove IL 60515 *Web:* www.globalgearllc.com	630-969-9400		295
Global Geophysical Services Inc 13927 S Gessner Rd ... Missouri City TX 77489 *NYSE:* GGS ■ *Web:* www.globalgeophysical.com	713-972-9200	972-1008	225
Global Graphics Software Inc 31 Nagog Pk Ste 315 ... Acton MA 01720 *Web:* www.globalgraphics.com	978-849-0011		225
Global Ground Support LLC 540 Old Hwy 56 ... Olathe KS 66061 *TF:* 888-780-0303 ■ *Web:* www.globalgroundsupport.com	913-780-0300	780-0829	22
Global Health Care Exchange LLC (GHX) 1315 W Century Dr ... Louisville CO 80027 *TF:* 800-968-7449 ■ *Web:* www.ghx.com	720-887-7000	887-7200	225
Global Help Desk Services Inc 2080 Silas Deane Hwy ... Rocky Hill CT 06067 *TF:* 800-770-1075 ■ *Web:* www.ghdsi.com	800-770-1075		180
Global Hope Network 934 N Magnolia Ave Ste 310 ... Orlando FL 32803 *Web:* www.ghni.org	407-207-3256		138
Global HR Research LLC 24201 Walden Ctr Dr Ste 206 ... Bonita Springs FL 34134 *TF:* 800-790-1205 ■ *Web:* www.ghrr.com	239-274-0048		260
Global ID Group 504 N Fourth St ... Fairfield IA 52556 *Web:* www.global-id-group.com	641-472-9979		743
Global Imaging Inc 2011 Cherry St Ste 116 ... Louisville CO 80027 *TF:* 800-787-9801 ■ *Web:* www.globalimaginginc.com	303-673-9773		41

	City	State	ZIP	Phone	Fax	Class
Global Imaging Systems 3903 Northdale Blvd Ste 200W *TF:* 888-628-7834 ■ *Web:* www.gisx.com	Tampa	FL	33624	813-960-5508	264-7877	112
Global Industries Inc 17 W Stow Rd *TF:* 800-220-1900 ■ *Web:* www.globalfurnituregroup.com/us	Marlton	NJ	08053	856-596-3390	596-5684	319-1
Global Industries Ltd 8000 Global Dr PO Box 442	Sulphur	LA	70665	337-583-5000	583-5100	539
Global Inflight Products 8918 152nd Ave NE *Web:* www.gipusa.com	Redmond	WA	98052	425-558-2778		196
Global Infotek Inc 1920 Association Dr Ste 200 *Web:* globalinfotek.com	Reston	VA	20191	703-652-1600		180
Global Inventures Inc 2400 Camino Ramon Bishop Ranch 6 Ste 375 *Web:* www.inventures.com	San Ramon	CA	94583	925-275-6690		194
Global IT Communications Inc 6720 Bright Ave *Web:* globalit.com	Whittier	CA	90601	562-698-2500		196
Global Knowledge Group Inc (GKG) 302 N Bryan Ave *TF:* 866-776-7584 ■ *Web:* www.gkg.net	Bryan	TX	77803	866-776-7584		808
Global Knowledge Training LLC 9000 Regency Pkwy Ste 500 *TF:* 800-268-7737 ■ *Web:* www.globalknowledge.com	Cary	NC	27518	919-461-8600	461-8646	764
Global Learning Resources Inc 46330 Sentinel Dr *Web:* www.glresources.com	Fremont	CA	94539	510-659-0179		428
Global Linguist Solutions LLC 3190 Fairview Park Dr Ste 1000 *Web:* www.gls-corp.com	Falls Church	VA	22042	817-224-7807		393
Global Logistics 99 W Hawthorne Ave L-12 Valley Stream *Web:* www.globallog.com	New York	NY	11580	516-825-2922	825-1143	449
Global LT Inc 1871 Woodslee Dr *Web:* www.global-lt.com	Troy	MI	48083	248-786-0999		260
Global Management Systems Inc (GMSI) 2201 Wisconsin Ave NW Ste 300 *Web:* www.gmsi.com	Washington	DC	20007	202-471-4674		180
Global Market Development Ctr (GMDC) 1275 Lake Plaza Dr *Web:* www.gmdc.org	Colorado Springs	CO	80906	719-576-4260	576-2661	49-18
Global Market Perspective PO Box 1618 *TF:* 800-336-1618 ■ *Web:* www.elliottwave.com/products/gmp	Gainesville	GA	30503	770-536-0309	536-2514	531-9
Global Material Technologies 1540 E Dundee Rd Ste 210 *Web:* www.gmt-inc.com	Palatine	IL	60074	847-202-7000	215-4838	1
Global Maxfin Investments Inc 100 Mural St Ste 201 *TF:* 866-666-5266 ■ *Web:* www.globalmaxfin.ca	Richmond Hill	ON	L4B1J3	416-741-1544		690
Global Medical Imaging LLC 222 Rampart St *TF:* 800-958-9986 ■ *Web:* www.gmi3.com	Charlotte	NC	28203	800-958-9986		475
Global Medical LLC 8332 Bristol Ct *TF:* 800-528-1001	Jessup	MD	20794	800-528-1001		475
Global Medical Solutions Ltd 14140 Ventura Blvd *Web:* globalmedicalsolutions.com	Sherman Oaks	CA	91423	818-783-2915		363
Global MetalForm LP 733 Davis St *Web:* www.markreuther.com/global401web	Scranton	PA	18505	570-346-3871	346-1612	254
Global Micro Solutions Inc 21250 Hawthorne Blvd Ste 540 *Web:* www.gmsnet.com	Torrance	CA	90503	310-218-5678		177
Global Mktg Group Worldwide LLC 704 Executive Blvd Ste I *Web:* www.gmgww.com	Valley Cottage	NY	10989	201-475-7755		194
Global Nest LLC 281 State Rt 79 N Ste 208 *TF:* 866-850-5872 ■ *Web:* www.globalnest.com	Morganville	NJ	07751	732-333-5848		177
Global Neuro-Diagnostics LP 2670 Firewheel Dr Ste B *TF:* 866-848-2522 ■ *Web:* www.globalneuro.net	Flower Mound	TX	75028	866-848-2522		418
Global New Beginnings Inc 4042 W 82nd Ct *Web:* www.gnbiusa.com	Merrillville	IN	46410	219-738-3600		463
Global Offset & Countertrade Assn (GOCA) 818 Connecticut Ave NW 12th Fl *Web:* www.globaloffset.org	Washington	DC	20006	202-887-9011		49-18
Global Oil Tools Inc 5343 Hwy 311 *Web:* globaloiltools.com	Houma	LA	70360	985-868-3404		358
Global Organization and Planning Services Llc 1 Mapes Ave Apt 2f *Web:* globalorganizationplanning.com	Newark	NJ	07112	973-374-6637		193
Global Outsourcing Services Inc 40 Fleetwood Ct Ste 2 *Web:* www.gostechnicalservices.com	Ronkonkoma	NY	11779	631-471-6798		180
Global Pacific Financial Services Ltd 10430 144 St *TF:* 800-561-1177 ■ *Web:* www.globalpacific.com	Surrey	BC	V3T4V5	800-561-1177		317
Global Partitions 2171 Liberty Hill Rd *TF:* 800-393-6343 ■ *Web:* www.globalpartitions.com	Eastanollee	GA	30538	706-827-2700	827-2710	609
Global Partners LP 800 South St Ste 200 *NYSE: GLP* ■ *TF:* 800-685-7222 ■ *Web:* www.globalp.com	Waltham	MA	02454	781-894-8800		579
Global Parts Distributors LLC 3279 Avondale Mill Rd *Web:* www.globalpartsdist.com	Macon	GA	31216	478-781-9854		61
Global Parts Support Inc 2799 SW 32nd Ave *Web:* www.globalpartssupport.com	Hollywood	FL	33023	954-989-5988		770
Global Payment Technologies Inc 170 Wilbur Pl *OTC: GPTX*	Bohemia	NY	11716	631-563-2500		111
Global Payments Inc 10 Glenlake Pkwy N Twr *NYSE: GPN* ■ *TF:* 800-560-2960 ■ *Web:* www.globalpaymentsinc.com	Atlanta	GA	30328	770-829-8000		255
Global Power Equipment Group Inc 400 E Las Colinas Blvd Ste 400 *NASDAQ: GLPW* ■ *Web:* www.globalpower.com	Irving	TX	75039	214-574-2700	853-4744	697
Global Precast Inc 2101 Teston Rd *TF:* 800-424-3996 ■ *Web:* www.globalprecast.com	Maple	ON	L6A1R3	905-832-4307	832-4388	106
Global Productivity Solutions LLC 19176 Hall Rd Ste 250 *Web:* globalproductivitysolutions.com	Clinton Township	MI	48038	586-412-9609		196
Global Public Affairs Inc 50 O'Connor St Ste 901 *Web:* globalpublicaffairs.ca	Ottawa	ON	K1P6L2	613-782-2336		194
Global Pump Company LLC 10162 E Coldwater Rd *Web:* www.globalpump.com	Davison	MI	48423	810-653-4828		641
Global Quality Assurance Inc 2822 S Alafaya Trl Ste 150 *TF:* 888-322-3330 ■ *Web:* www.globalqualityassurance.com	Orlando	FL	32828	888-322-3330		463
Global Reach Internet Productions LLC 2321 N Loop Dr Ste 101 *TF:* 877-254-9828 ■ *Web:* www.globalreach.com	Ames	IA	50010	515-996-0996		177
Global Relay Communications Inc 220 cambie St *TF:* 866-484-6630 ■ *Web:* www.globalrelay.com	Vancouver	BC	V6B2M9	604-484-6630		224
Global Resources International Inc 4142 Industry Way *Web:* www.gri-usa.com	Flowery Branch	GA	30542	678-866-0550		475
Global Results Communications 201 E Sandpointe Ave Ste 650 *Web:* www.globalresultspr.com	Santa Ana	CA	92707	949-608-0276		636
Global Safety & Security Inc 4713 Trenton St	Metairie	LA	70006	504-454-6933		418
Global SATCOM Technology Inc 9141 Arbuckle Dr *Web:* www.globalsatcom.com	Gaithersburg	MD	20877	301-963-0088		194
Global Science & Technology Inc 7855 Walker Dr Ste 200 *Web:* www.gst.com	Greenbelt	MD	20770	301-474-9696		387
Global Search Network Inc 118 S Fremont Ave *TF:* 800-254-3398 ■ *Web:* www.globalsearchnetwork.com	Tampa	FL	33606	813-832-8300		193
Global Security Glazing 616 Selfield Rd *Web:* www.security-glazing.com	Selma	AL	36703	334-875-1900		329
Global Security Management Agency Inc 1781 Vineyard Dr *Web:* gsmasecurity.com	Antioch	CA	94509	925-262-4181		690
Global Shop Solutions Inc 975 Evergreen Cir *TF Sales:* 800-364-5958 ■ *Web:* www.globalshopsolutions.com	The Woodlands	TX	77380	281-681-1959	681-2663	178-1
Global Software Inc 3201 Beechleaf Ct Ste 170 *TF:* 800-326-3444 ■ *Web:* globalsoftwareinc.com	Raleigh	NC	27604	919-872-7800	876-8205	178-1
Global Solar Energy Inc 8500 S Rita Rd *Web:* www.globalsolar.com	Tucson	AZ	85747	520-546-6313	546-6318	696
Global Solutions Network Inc 121 Congressional Ln Ste 302 *Web:* www.gsnhome.com	Rockville	MD	20852	301-881-7012		177
Global Sports & Entertainment Inc 300 N Continental Blvd Ste 140 *Web:* www.globalsports-ent.com	El Segundo	CA	90245	310-414-2690		717
Global Steering Systems LLC 156 Park Rd *Web:* www.globalsteering.com	Watertown	CT	06795	860-945-5400		247
Global Stock Trends Corp 1 Park Place 621 NW 53rd St Ste 240 *Web:* www.globalstocktrends.com	Boca Raton	FL	33487	401-885-4606		194
Global Strategic Investments LLC 701 Brickell Ave Ste 1420 *Web:* www.gscorporation.com	Miami	FL	33131	305-373-3326		690
Global Strategy Group LLC 895 Broadway 5th Fl *Web:* www.globalstrategygroup.com	New York	NY	10003	212-260-8813		194
Global Systems Technologies Inc 109 Floral Vale Blvd *Web:* www.gstpa.com	Yardley	PA	19067	215-579-8200		256
Global Tax Network US LLC 7950 Main St N Ste 200 *TF:* 888-486-2695 ■ *Web:* www.gtn.com	Minneapolis	MN	55369	763-746-4556	252-0304	734
Global Technology Resources Inc 990 S Broadway Ste 300 *TF:* 877-603-1984 ■ *Web:* www.gtri.com	Denver	CO	80209	303-455-8800		180
Global Tissue Group 870 Express Dr S *Web:* www.gtgtissue.com	Medford	NY	11763	631-419-1300		548
Global Trading & Sourcing Corp 1587 College Park Business Ctr Rd *Web:* www.gtsco.com	Orlando	FL	32804	407-532-7600		360-3
Global Travel 900 W Jefferson St *TF:* 800-584-8888 ■ *Web:* www.globaltrav.com	Boise	ID	83702	208-387-1000		771
Global Travel International 2600 Lake Lucien Dr Ste 201 *TF:* 800-715-4440 ■ *Web:* www.globaltravel.com	Maitland	FL	32751	407-660-7800	875-0711	772
Global Trim Sales Inc 22835 Savi Ranch Pkwy Ste A *TF:* 800-622-1911 ■ *Web:* www.globaltrim.com	Yorba Linda	CA	92887	714-998-4400		627
Global Turnkey Systems Inc 2001 US 46 *TF:* 800-221-1746 ■ *Web:* www.gtsystems.com	Parsippany	NJ	07054	973-331-1010		178-10
Global TV Concepts Ltd 676 S Military Trl *TF:* 800-873-0894 ■ *Web:* www.globaltvconcepts.com	Deerfield Beach	FL	33442	954-570-9999		7
Global University 1211 S Glenstone Ave *TF:* 800-443-1083 ■ *Web:* www.globaluniversity.edu	Springfield	MO	65804	417-862-9533	865-7167	766
Global Ventures Inc 12835 Bel-Red Rd Ste 305 *Web:* www.globalventuresinc.com	Bellevue	WA	98005	206-292-1428	292-1426	194
Global Village English Centres 888 Cambie St *Web:* www.gvenglish.com	Vancouver	BC	V6B2P6	604-684-1118		423

Phone | Fax | Class

Global Village Marketing & Data Services Inc
2710 Thomes Ave.......Cheyenne WY 82001 307-222-4135 7
Web: www.globalvillagemktg.com

Global Voyages Group LLC
320 120th Ave NE Ste 100.......Bellevue WA 98005 425-637-8558 463
Web: www.globalvoyagesgroup.com

Global Warranty Group LLC
500 Middle Country Rd.......St. James NY 11780 631-750-0300 390

Global Wildlife Ctr 26389 Hwy 40.......Folsom LA 70437 985-796-3585 796-9487 823
TF: 800-542-7520 ■ *Web:* www.globalwildlife.com

Global Window Solutions
128 Industrial Park Rd.......Richibucto NB E4W4A4 506-523-4900 499
Web: www.globalwindows.ca

Global X-Ray & Testing Corp
PO Box 1536.......Morgan City LA 70381 985-631-2426 743
Web: www.globalxray.com

GlobalDie 1130 Minot Ave PO Box 1120.......Auburn ME 04211 207-514-7252 514-7202 757
TF: 800-910-3747 ■ *Web:* www.globaldie.com

Globalfoundries Inc
2600 Great America Way.......Santa Clara CA 95054 408-462-3900 308
Web: www.globalfoundries.com

GlobalGiving Foundation Inc
1110 Vermont Ave NW Ste 550.......Washington DC 20005 202-232-5784 305
Web: www.globalgiving.org

GlobalMedia Group LLC
15020 N 74th St.......Scottsdale AZ 85260 480-922-0044 922-1090 52
Web: www.globalmed.com

GlobalPartsaero 901 Industrial Rd.......Augusta KS 67010 316-733-9240 57
Web: www.globalparts.aero

GlobalPhone Corp
137 N Washington St.......Falls Church VA 22046 703-533-2122 194
Web: www.gphone.com

Globalscale Technologies Inc
1200 N Van Buren St Ste D.......Anaheim CA 92807 714-632-9239 787
Web: globalscaletechnologies.com

Globalspec Inc 350 Jordan Rd.......Troy NY 12180 510-000-0200 880-0260 180
TF: 800-261-2052 ■ *Web:* www.globalspec.com

Globalstar 300 Holiday Square Blvd.......Covington LA 70433 408-933-4000 933-4100 681
TF: 877-728-7466 ■ *Web:* www.globalstar.com

Globalstor Data Corp
9960 Congoga Ave Unit D9.......Chatsworth CA 91311 818-701-7771 761
Web: www.globalstor.com

GlobalWorks Group LLC 220 Fifth Ave.......New York NY 10001 212-252-8800 4

Global-Z International Inc
395 Shields Dr.......Bennington VT 05201 802-445-1011 196
TF: 800-447-3978 ■ *Web:* www.globalz.com

Globat LLC
11684 Ventrura Blvd Ste 825.......Studio City CA 91604 323-874-9000 225
Web: www.globat.com

Globe & Mail Inc, The 444 Front St W.......Toronto ON M5V2S9 416-585-5000 585-5085 532-1
Web: www.theglobeandmail.com

Globe Dar-Restaurant
3455 St Laurent Blvd.......Montreal QC H2X2T6 514-284-3823 284-3531 671

Globe Business Interiors
6454 Centre Park Dr.......West Chester OH 45069 513-771-5550 321
Web: www.g b i.com

Globe Consultants Inc
3112 Porter St Ste D.......Soquel CA 95073 800-208-0663 193
TF: 800-208-0663 ■ *Web:* www.globeconsultants.com

Globe Die-Cutting Products Inc
76 Liberty St.......Metuchen NJ 08840 732-494-7744 561
Web: www.globediecutting.com

Globe Electronic Hardware Inc
34-24 56th St.......Woodside NY 11377 718-457-0303 457-7493 203
TF: 800-221-1505 ■ *Web:* www.globelectronics.com

Globe Energy Services LLC
3204 W Hwy 180.......Snyder TX 79549 325-573-1310 539
Web: globeenergyservices.com

Globe Engineering Company Inc
1539 S St Paul St PO Box 12407.......Wichita KS 67213 316-943-1266 943-3089 22
Web: www.globeeng.com

Globe Food Equipment Co 2153 Dryden Rd.......Dayton OH 45439 937-299-5493 299-8623 298
TF: 800-347-5423 ■ *Web:* www.globefoodequip.com

Globe Iron Foundry Inc
5649 E Randolph St.......Commerce CA 90040 323-723-8983 492
Web: www.globeiron.com

Globe Life 133 NW 122nd St.......Oklahoma City OK 73114 405-755-8282 194
Web: globeontheweb.com

Globe Life Park In Arlington
1000 Ballpark Way.......Arlington TX 76011 817-273-5222 720
Web: www.mlb.com/rangers

Globe Machine Manufacturing Company Inc
701 E D St.......Tacoma WA 98421 253-383-2584 190
Web: www.globemachine.com

Globe Metallurgical Inc
County Rd 32 PO Box 157.......Beverly OH 45715 740-984-2361 984-8691 485
TF: 800-845-6238 ■ *Web:* www.glbsm.com/globemetallurgical

Globe Mfg Co 37 Loudon Rd.......Pittsfield NH 03263 603-435-8323 435-6388 576
TF: 800-232-8323 ■ *Web:* www.globeturnoutgear.com

Globe Motors Inc 2275 Stanley Ave.......Dayton OH 45404 937-228-3171 57
TF: 800-433-5700 ■ *Web:* www.globe-motors.com

Globe Products Inc 5051 Kitridge Rd.......Dayton OH 45424 937-233-0233 233-5290 386
Web: www.globe-usa.com

Globe Tax Services Inc
90 Broad St 16th Fl.......New York NY 10004 212-747-9100 194
Web: www.globetax.com

Globe Ticket & Label Co
350 Randy Rd Ste 1.......Carol Stream IL 60188 800-523-5968 627
TF: 800-523-5968

Globe Turbocharger Specialties Inc
201 Edison Way.......Reno NV 89502 775-856-7337 262
Web: www.globeturbocharger.com

Globe University
5101 S Broadband Ln.......Sioux Falls SD 57108 605-977-0705 166
Web: globeuniversity.edu

Globe Vacation Inc
13527 Roosevelt Ave Ste 2.......Flushing NY 11354 718-539-3385 772
Web: wkka.com

Globecomm Systems Inc 45 Oser Ave.......Hauppauge NY 11788 631-231-9800 231-1557 647
NASDAQ: GCOM ■ *TF:* 866-499-0223 ■ *Web:* www.globecomm.com

Globe-Gazette
300 N Washington St PO Box 271.......Mason City IA 50402 641-421-0500 421-7108 532-2
TF: 800-421-0546 ■ *Web:* www.globegazette.com

Globespan Capital Partners
1 Boston Pl Ste 2810.......Boston MA 02108 617-305-2300 792
Web: www.globespancapital.com

Globetrotters Engineering Corp
300 S Wacker Dr Ste 400.......Chicago IL 60606 312-922-6400 261
Web: www.gec-group.com

Globex Corp 3620 Stutz Dr.......Canfield OH 44406 330-533-0030 256
TF: 800-533-8610 ■ *Web:* www.globexcorp.com

Globex International Inc
570 Lexington Ave 15th Fl.......New York NY 10022 212-308-2300 308-0202 196
Web: www.globexusa.com

Globitech Inc 200 Fm 1417 W.......Sherman TX 75092 903-957-1999 186
Web: www.globitech.com

Globus 5301 S Federal Cir.......Littleton CO 80123 866-755-8581 760
TF: 866-755-8581 ■ *Web:* www.globusjourneys.com

Glock Inc 6000 Highlands Pkwy.......Smyrna GA 30082 770-432-1202 433-8719 284
Web: www.glock.com

Glo-Quartz Electric Heater Company Inc
7084 Maple St.......Mentor OH 44060 440-255-9701 255-7852 318
TF Sales: 800-321-3574 ■ *Web:* www.gloquartz.com

Glori Energy Inc 4315 S Dr.......Houston TX 77053 713-237-8880 48-20
Web: www.glorienergy.com

Gloria Ferrer Caves & Vineyards
23555 Arnold Dr.......Sonoma CA 95476 707-996-7256 226
Web: www.gloriaferrer.com

Glorietta Bay Inn
1630 Glorietta Blvd.......Coronado CA 92118 619-435-3101 435-6182 379
TF: 800-283-9383 ■ *Web:* www.gloriettabayinn.com

Glory Foods Inc 901 Oak St.......Columbus OH 43205 614-252-2042 297-8
Web: www.gloryfoods.com

Glorybee Foods Inc 120 N Seneca Rd.......Eugene OR 97402 541-689-0913 689-9692 296-24
TF: 800-456-7923 ■ *Web:* www.glorybee.com

Gloss Mountain State Park Hwy 412.......Fairview OK 73737 580-227-2512 227-2513 565
Web: www.travelok.com/listings/view.profile/id.3030

Glotech 2551 Eltham Ave Ste A.......Norfolk VA 23513 757-499-3650 180
Web: glotech.net

Gloto Corp 8171 Maple Lawn Blvd Ste 250.......Fulton MD 20759 301-317-9800 177
Web: gloto.com

Gloucester County 6467 Main St.......Gloucester VA 23061 804-693-4042 693-6004 338
Web: gloucesterva.info

Gloucester County
2 S Broad St PO Box 337.......Woodbury NJ 08096 856-853-3237 853-3327 338
Web: gloucestercountynj.gov

Gloucester County Library
6920 Main St.......Gloucester VA 23061 804-693-2998 693-1477 434-3
Web: gloucesterva.info

Gloucester County Library System
389 Wolfert Stn Rd.......Mullica Hill NJ 08062 856-223-6000 223-6039 434-3
Web: www.gcls.org

Gloucester County Times
309 S Broad St.......Woodbury NJ 08096 856-845-3300 845-5480 532-2
TF: 800-300-9321 ■ *Web:* www.nj.com

Glover Foods Inc
119 Old Anderson Ville Rd.......Americus GA 31719 229-924-2974 297-8

Glover Sales Group LLC
221 Cockeysville Rd.......Cockeysville MD 21030 410-771-8000 771-8010 320

Gloves Inc 1950 Collins Blvd.......Austell MA 30106 770-944-9186 944-0012 155-8
TF: 800-476-4568 ■ *Web:* www.glovesinc.com/contacts

Glovia International Inc
2250 E Imperial Hwy Ste 200.......El Segundo CA 90245 310-563-7000 563-7300 178-1
TF: 888-245-6842 ■ *Web:* www.glovia.com

Glowbal Grill & Satay Bar
302 Water St.......Vancouver BC V6B1B6 604-602-0835 671
Web: www.glowbalgroup.com

Gloyer'S Pharmacy Inc 1010 W Main St.......Tomball TX 77375 281-351-5454 237
Web: www.gloyers.com

GLP Inc 360 W Superior St.......Chicago IL 60654 312-640-8300 393
Web: www.garyleepartners.com

GLS (Government Liaison Services Inc)
200 N Glebe Rd Ste 321.......Arlington VA 22203 703-524-8200 525-8451 635
TF: 800-642-6564 ■ *Web:* www.trademarkinfo.com

GLS Companies Inc
6845 Winnetka Cir.......Brooklyn Park MN 55428 763-535-7277 195
TF: 800-882-1844 ■ *Web:* glsprecisionmarketing.com

Gls Group Inc 27850 Detroit Rd.......Westlake OH 44145 440-899-7770 184
TF: 800-955-9435 ■ *Web:* glsgroup.com

Glu Mobile Inc
500 Howard St Ste 300.......San Francisco CA 94105 415-800-6100 177
Web: www.glu.com

Glumac Inc 150 California St.......San Francisco CA 94111 415-398-7667 256
Web: www.glumac.com

Glunt Industries Inc 319 N River Rd NW.......Warren OH 44483 330-399-7585 393-0387 386
Web: www.glunt.com

Glunz & Jensen K&F Inc
12633 Industrial Dr.......Granger IN 46530 574-272-9950 628
Web: www.glunz-jensen.com

Gluten Intolerance Group (GIG)
31214 124th Ave SE.......Auburn WA 98092 253-833-6655 833-6675 48-17
Web: www.gluten.org

Glynn & Finley LLP
100 Pringle Ave Ste 500.......Walnut Creek CA 94596 925-210-2800 428
Web: www.glynnfinley.com

Glynn County 701 G St.......Brunswick GA 31520 912-554-7400 554-7596 338
Web: www.glynncounty.org

Glynndevins Adv & Mktg
11230 College Blvd.......Overland Park KS 66210 913-491-0600 4
Web: www.glynndevins.com

Glyph Language Services Inc
126 NW Canal St Ste 110.......Seattle WA 98107 206-315-0994 768
Web: glyphservices.com

Glyphic Technologies Inc
1001 Ave Of The Amrcas.......New York NY 10018 212-625-9170 708
Web: www.glytec.com

Phone | Fax | Class

Glytec LLC 770 Pelham Rd Ste 210 Greenville SC 29615 864-370-3297 743
Web: www.glytecsystems.com

Gly-Tech Services Inc 2054 Paxton St Harvey LA 70058 504-348-8566 539
Web: www.glytech.com

GM Cable Contractors Inc
9232 Joor Rd Baton Rouge LA 70818 225-261-9800 116
Web: gmcable.com

Gm Financial Consultants Corp
191 Presidental Blvd Ste W-1 Bala Cynwyd PA 19004 610-664-4088 390
Web: jackgrossman.metlife.com

GM Nameplate Inc 2040 15th Ave W Seattle WA 98119 206-284-2200 284-3705 481
TF: 800-366-7668 ■ *Web:* www.gmnameplate.com

GMA (Gospel Music Assn)
741 Cool Springs Blvd Franklin TN 37067 615-242-0303 254-9755 48-4
TF: 800-846-8499 ■ *Web:* www.gospelmusic.org

GMAC (General Motors Acceptance Corp)
200 Renaissance Ctr Detroit MI 48265 877-320-2559 428-4622* 217
**Fax Area Code:* 800 ■ *TF:* 800-200-4622 ■ *Web:* www.ally.com

GMAC (Graduate Management Admission Council)
11921 Freedom Dr Ste 300 Reston VA 20190 703-668-9600 668-9601 48-11
TF: 866-505-6559 ■ *Web:* www.gmac.com

GMarie Group Inc, The
5621 W Beverly Ln Glendale AZ 85306 602-864-1385 196
Web: www.gmariegroup.com

GMBHA (Greater Miami & The Beaches Hotel Assn)
1674 Meridian Ave Ste 420 Miami Beach FL 33139 305-531-3553 531-8954 376
Web: gmbha.com

GMC (General Motors Corp)
100 Renaissance Ctr Detroit MI 48265 313-556-5000 59
NYSE: GM ■ *TF:* 800-462-8782 ■ *Web:* www.gm.com

GMD Studios 7057 University Blvd Winter Park FL 32792 407-657-8990 180

GMDC (Global Market Development Ctr)
1275 Lake Plaza Dr Colorado Springs CO 80906 719-576-4260 576-2661 49-18
Web: www.gmdc.org

GMF (General Metal Finishing Company Inc)
42 Frank Mossberg Dr Attleboro MA 02703 508-226-5606 481
Web: www.pepgenmetal.com

GMHC (Gay Men's Health Crisis)
119 W 24th St New York NY 10011 212-367-1000 48-17
TF: 800-243-7692 ■ *Web:* www.gmhc.org

GMI Building Services Inc
8001 Vickers St San Diego CA 92111 866-803-4464 256
TF: 866-803-4464 ■ *Web:* www.gmiweb.com

GMI Composites Inc
1355 W Sherman Blvd Muskegon MI 49441 231-755-1611 755-1613 606
TF: 800-330-4045 ■ *Web:* www.gmicomposites.com

Gmi Inc 4822 E 355th St Willoughby OH 44094 440-953-8811 326
Web: www.gmiincusa.com

GMO (Grantham Mayo Van Otterloo & Company LLC)
40 Rowes Wharf Boston MA 02110 617-330-7500 401
Web: www.gmo.com

GMO Trust Funds 40 Rowes Wharf Boston MA 02110 617-330-7500 528
Web: www.gmo.com

GMP Laboratories of America Inc
2931 E La Jolla St Anaheim CA 92806 714-630-2467 237-1374 582
Web: www.gmplabs.com

GMP Metal Products Inc
3883 Delor St Saint Louis MO 63116 314-481-0300 481-1379 273
TF: 800-325-9808 ■ *Web:* www.gmpmetal.com

Gmp Networks Llc
4729 E Sunrise Dr Ste 121 Tucson AZ 85718 520-577-3891 180
TF: 800-553-2447 ■ *Web:* www.gmpnet.net

GMP Securities LLC
530 Fifth Ave 15th Fl New York NY 10036 212-692-5100 690
Web: www.gmpsecuritiesllc.com

GMPIU 608 E Baltimore Pike Media PA 19063 610-565-5051 565-0983 414
Web: www.gmpiu.org

GMR Marketing LLC 5000 S Towne Dr New Berlin WI 53151 262-786-5600 636
TF: 800-477-8560 ■ *Web:* www.gmrmarketing.com

GMRMC (Merit Health Gilmore Memorial)
1105 Earl Frye Blvd Amory MS 38821 662-256-7111 374-3
TF: 800-636-7622 ■ *Web:* www.merithealthgilmore.com

GMS Group LLC, The
5 N Regent St Ste 513 Livingston NJ 07039 973-535-5000 690
Web: www.gmsgroup.com

GMSI (Global Management Systems Inc)
2201 Wisconsin Ave NW Ste 300 Washington DC 20007 202-471-4674 180
Web: www.gmsi.com

GMW Associates Inc
955 Industrial Rd San Carlos CA 94070 650-802-8292 358
Web: www.gmw.com

GMX Resources Inc
9400 Broadway Extension Hwy Oklahoma City OK 73114 405-600-0711 536
NYSE: GMXRQ ■ *Web:* www.gmxresources.com

GN Diamond LLC 800 Chestnut St Philadelphia PA 19107 215-925-0217 410
TF: 800-724-8810 ■ *Web:* www.gndiamond.com

GN ReSound North America
8001 E Bloomington Fwy Bloomington MN 55420 888-735-4327 250
TF: 888-735-4327 ■ *Web:* www.gnresound.com

GN US Inc 77 NE Blvd Nashua NH 03062 603-598-1100 598-1122 735
TF: 800-327-2230 ■ *Web:* www.jabra.com

GNA (Georgia Nurses Assn)
3032 Briarcliff Rd NE Atlanta GA 30329 404-325-5536 325-0407 533
TF: 800-324-0462 ■ *Web:* www.georgianurses.org

Gnaden Huetten Memorial Hospital
211 N 12th St Lehighton PA 18235 610-377-1300 374-3
Web: www.ghmh.org

Gnarus Advisors LLC
4350 N Fairfax Dr Ste 830 Arlington VA 22203 571-384-2444 463
TF: 800-767-3263 ■ *Web:* www.gnarusllc.com

GNC Consulting Inc
21195 S LaGrange Rd Frankfort IL 60423 815-469-7255 196
TF: 800-677-1997 ■ *Web:* www.gnc-consulting.com

GNC Inc 300 Sixth Ave 14th Fl Pittsburgh PA 15222 877-462-4700 355
NYSE: GNC ■ *TF:* 877-462-4700 ■ *Web:* www.gnc.com

GNFCC (Greater North Fulton Chamber of Commerce)
11605 Haynes Bridge Rd Ste 100 Alpharetta GA 30009 770-993-8806 594-1059 139
TF: 866-840-5770 ■ *Web:* www.gnfcc.com

Phone | Fax | Class

GNP Audio Video Inc
122-A Foothill Blvd Ste 326 Arcadia CA 91006 626-577-7767 35
Web: www.gnpaudiovideo.com

GNP Computers Inc
555 E Huntington Dr Monrovia CA 91016 626-305-8484 809
Web: www.gnp.com

Go 2 Group 138 N Hickory Ave Bel Air MD 21014 410-879-8102 177
TF: 877-442-4669 ■ *Web:* www.go2group.com

Go 96.3 420 N Fifth St Ste 150 Minneapolis MN 55401 612-659-4848 645
Web: www.gomn.com/radio

Go Apply Inc
27081 Aliso Creek Rd Ste 200 Aliso Viejo CA 92656 888-435-3239 569
TF: 888-435-3239 ■ *Web:* www.eleadz.com

GO Carlson Inc
350 Marshallton Thorndale Rd Downingtown PA 19335 610-384-2800 383-3429 723
TF: 800-338-5622 ■ *Web:* www.electralloy.com

Go Edit Inc 5542 Satsuma Ave North Hollywood CA 91601 818-284-6260 985-6260 512
Web: www.goedit.tv

Go Fish! Ocean Emporium
1505 W First Ave Vancouver BC V6J1E8 604-730-5040 671

Go Industries Inc 420 N Grove Rd Richardson TX 75081 972-783-7444 54
Web: goindustries.com

Go Medico 1515 S 75th St Omaha NE 68124 402-391-6900 391-2
TF: 800-228-6080 ■ *Web:* gomedico.com

Go Native Yacht Charters
1900 Purdy Ave Miami Beach FL 33139 954-791-4692 148
TF: 800-359-9808 ■ *Web:* www.gnyc.com

Go Next 8000 W 78th St Ste 345 Minneapolis MN 55439 952-918-8950 918-8975 760
TF: 800-842-9023 ■ *Web:* www.gonext.com

Go Pro Management Inc 22 Cynthia Rd Needham MA 02494 781-444-5753 196
Web: www.gopromanagement.com

GO Transit 20 Bay St Ste 600 Toronto ON M5J2W3 416-869-3200 869-3525 468
TF: 888-438-6646 ■ *Web:* www.gotransit.com

Go Travel 205 Parnell St Merritt Island FL 32953 321-453-1702 775
TF: 800-528-1358 ■ *Web:* gotravel.com

Go West Adventures Inc
PO Box 882319 Los Angeles CA 90009 310-216-2522 760
Web: www.gowestadventures.com

Go West Tours Inc
790 Eddy St at Van Ness San Francisco CA 94109 415-837-0154 775
Web: www.gowesttours.com

Go! Retail Group 6411 Burleson Rd Austin TX 78744 512-386-7220 369-6192 626
Web: calendarholdings.com/index.asp

Go...With Jo! Tours & Travel Inc
910 Dixieland Rd Harlingen TX 78552 956-423-1446 760
TF: 800-999-1446 ■ *Web:* www.gowithjo.com

Go2 Communications Inc
8 Cedar St Ste 57 Woburn MA 01801 781-376-2100 371-0369* 5
**Fax Area Code:* 815 ■ *Web:* www.go2communications.com

GO2 Media Design Inc
40 Oakridge Pkwy Peekskill NY 10566 914-734-1430 631
TF: 800-747-1453 ■ *Web:* www.go2mediadesign.com

Goal Sporting Goods Inc
37 Industrial Pk Rd PO Box 236 Essex CT 06426 800-334-4625 767-9121* 710
**Fax Area Code:* 860 ■ *TF:* 800-334-4625 ■ *Web:* www.goalsports.com

GoalLine Solutions
3115 Harvester Rd Ste 200 Burlington ON L7N3H8 866-788-4625 195
TF: 866-788-4625 ■ *Web:* www.goallinesolutions.com

Goals & Poles 7575 Jefferson Hwy Baton Rouge LA 70806 225-923-0622 710
TF: 800-275-0317 ■ *Web:* www.goalsandpoles.com

Goalsetter Systems Inc
1041 Cordova Ave Lynnville IA 50153 800-362-4625 594-3343* 710
**Fax Area Code:* 641 ■ *TF:* 800-362-4625 ■ *Web:* www.goalsetter.com

Gobbell Hays Partners Inc
10500 E 54th Ave J Denver CO 80239 303-574-0082 463
Web: www.ghp1.com

Gobin's Inc 615 N Santa Fe Ave Pueblo CO 81003 719-544-2324 544-2378 535
TF: 800-425-2324 ■ *Web:* www.gobins.com

Goblin Valley State Park
PO Box 637 Green River UT 84525 435-275-4584 565
Web: www.utah.com

GOCA (Global Offset & Countertrade Assn)
818 Connecticut Ave NW 12th Fl Washington DC 20006 202-887-9011 49-18
Web: www.globaloffset.org

God Owns This Company Inc
777 Hill Ave Muskegon MI 49442 231-727-3333 48-20
Web: godownsthiscompany.com

God's Bible School & College
1810 Young St Cincinnati OH 45202 513-721-7944 161
Web: www.gbs.edu

God's Learning Ch (GLC) PO Box 61000 Midland TX 79711 432-563-0420 563-1736 740
TF: 800-707-0420 ■ *Web:* www.glc.us.com

GoDaddy Inc 14455 N Hayden Rd Scottsdale AZ 85260 480-505-8800 387
Web: www.godaddy.com

Godbersen-Smith Construction Company Inc
5784 Iowa 175 Ida Grove IA 51445 712-364-3388 188-4

Goddard College 123 Pitkin Rd Plainfield VT 05667 802-454-8311 454-1029* 166
**Fax:* Admissions ■ *TF:* 800-468-4888 ■ *Web:* goddard.edu

Goddard Institute for Space Studies
2880 Broadway New York NY 10025 212-678-5510 678-5552 668
TF: 888-661-1620 ■ *Web:* www.giss.nasa.gov

Goddard Memorial State Park
1095 Ives Rd Warwick RI 02818 401-884-2010 885-7720 565
Web: riparks.com

Goddard Space Flight Ctr
8800 Greenbelt Rd Greenbelt MD 20771 301-286-2000 286-1707* 668
**Fax:* PR ■ *Web:* www.nasa.gov/centers/goddard

Goddard Systems Inc
1016 W Ninth Ave King of Prussia PA 19406 610-265-8510 310
TF: 800-463-3273 ■ *Web:* www.goddardschool.com

Godfathers Pizza Inc 2808 N 108th St Omaha NE 68164 402-391-1452 670
Web: godfathers.quikorder.net

Godfrey & Kahn SC
833 E Michigan St Ste 1800 Milwaukee WI 53202 414-273-3500 428
TF: 800-344-7040 ■ *Web:* www.gklaw.com

Godfrey & Wing Inc 220 Campus Dr Aurora OH 44202 330-562-1440 308
Web: www.godfreywing.com

Godfrey Adv Inc 40 N Christian St Lancaster PA 17602 717-393-3831 4
Web: www.godfrey.com

Company	Phone	Fax	Class
Godfrey Chevrolet-Buick Inc 1701 N Mitchell St ... Cadillac MI 49601 *Web:* www.godfreychevroletbuick.com	231-775-4661		57
Godfrey Trucking Inc 6173 W 2100 S ... West Valley City UT 84128 *TF:* 800-444-7669 ■ *Web:* www.godfreytrucking.com	801-972-0660	972-0709	780
Godshall & Godshall Personnel Po Box 1984 ... Greenville SC 29602 *TF:* 800-523-6802 ■ *Web:* www.sccareersearch.com	864-242-3491		721
Godwin Plumbing Inc 3703 Division Ave ... Grand Rapids MI 49548 *Web:* godwinplumbing.com	616-243-3131		189-10
Goebel Fixture Co 528 Dale St ... Hutchinson MN 55350 *Web:* www.gf.com	320-587-2112		286
Goehring, Rutter & Boehm 437 Grant St Ste 1424 ... Pittsburgh PA 15219 *Web:* www.grblaw.com	412-281-0587		428
Goelzer Investment Management Inc 111 Monument Cir Ste 500 ... Indianapolis IN 46204 *TF:* 800-428-1618 ■ *Web:* www.goelzerinc.com	317-264-2600		401
Goethe Institut Atlanta/German Cultural Ctr 1197 Peachtree St NE ... Atlanta GA 30361 *Web:* www.goethe.de	404-892-2388	892-3832	520
Goetting Rowe Engineering 12042 Blanco Rd Ste 301 ... San Antonio TX 78216 *Web:* www.goettingrowe.com	210-530-7800		256
Goettsch Partners Inc *Goettsch Partners* 224 S Michigan Ave 17th Fl ... Chicago IL 60604 *Web:* www.gpchicago.com	312-356-0600	356-0601	261
Goetz Energy Corp 1319 Military Rd ... Tonawanda NY 14217 *Web:* www.goetzenergy.com	716-876-4324		579
Goetz Insurors Inc 227 Main St ... Fort Morgan CO 80701 *Web:* goetzinsurors.com	970-867-8246		390
Goetz Printing Co, The 7939 Angus Ct ... Springfield VA 22153 *TF:* 866-245-0977 ■ *Web:* www.goetzprinting.com	703-569-0232		627
Goetze Dental 3939 NE 33 Terr ... Kansas City MO 64117 *TF:* 800-692-0804 ■ *Web:* www.goetzedental.com	816-413-1200		475
Goetze's Candy Company Inc 3900 E Monument St ... Baltimore MD 21205 *TF Orders:* 800-295-8058 ■ *Web:* www.goetzecandy.com	410-342-2010	522-7681	296-8
GOFCC (Greater Oswego-Fulton Chamber of Commerce) 44 E Bridge St ... Oswego NY 13126 *Web:* www.oswegofultonchamber.com	315-343-7681	342-0831	139
Goff Backa Alfera & Company LLC 3325 Saw Mill Run Blvd ... Pittsburgh PA 15227 *Web:* www.gbaco.com	412-885-5045		734
Goffa International 200 Murray Hill Pkwy Ste 1 ... East Rutherford NJ 07073 *Web:* www.goffausa.com	201-528-8999	528-8133	762
GOG (Gynooologic Oncology Group) 1600 JFK Blvd Ste 1020 ... Philadelphia PA 19103 *TF:* 800-225-3053 ■ *Web:* www.gog.org	215-854-0770	854-0716	49-8
Gogebic Community College E 4946 Jackson Rd ... Ironwood MI 49938 **Fax:* Admissions ■ *TF:* 800-682-5910 ■ *Web:* www.gogebic.cc.mi.us	906-932-4231	932-0868*	162
Gogebic County 200 N Moore St ... Bessemer MI 49911 *TF:* 800-258-1152 ■ *Web:* www.gogebic.org	906-663-4518	663-4660	338
Gogebic Medical Care Facility 402 N St ... Wakefield MI 49968 *Web:* www.gogebicmedicalcare.com	906-224-9811		371
Gogo Inc 1250 N Arlington Heights Rd Ste 500 ... Itasca IL 60143 *Web:* www.gogoair.com	630-647-1400		387
GOGO WorldWide Vacations 5 Paragon Dr Ste 200 ... Montvale NJ 07446 **Fax Area Code:* 201 ■ *TF:* 800-254-3477 ■ *Web:* www.gogowwv.com	800-254-3477	934-3764*	771
Gohmann Asphalt & Construction Inc 1630 Broadway St ... Clarksville IN 47129	812-282-1349	288-2168	188-4
Gohmert Louie (Rep R - TX) 2243 Rayburn HOB ... Washington DC 20515 *Web:* gohmert.house.gov	202-225-3035	226-1230	342-2
Going Bonkers Inc 229 N 48th St ... Quincy IL 62305 *Web:* www.goingbonkers.com	217-223-6331		31
Goizueta Foundation 4401 Northside Pkwy Ste 520 ... Atlanta GA 30327 *Web:* www.goizuetafoundation.org	404-239-0390	239-0018	305
GOJO Industries Inc 1 GOJO Plaza Ste 500 ... Akron OH 44311 **Fax Area Code:* 800 ■ *TF:* 800-321-9647 ■ *Web:* www.gojo.com	330-255-6000	329-4656*	214
Gokeyless 3646 Cargo Rd ... Vandalia OH 45377 *TF:* 877-439-5377 ■ *Web:* www.gokeyless.com	937-890-2333		41
Golan Christie Taglia LLP 70 W Madison St Ste 1500 ... Chicago IL 60602 *Web:* www.golanchristie.com	312-263-2300	263-0939	445
Golberg Companies Inc 4179 County Rd 40 NW ... Garfield MN 56332 *Web:* www.gcilift.com	320-834-2211		295
Gold Bond Inc 5485 Hixson Pike ... Hixson TN 37343 *Web:* www.goldbondinc.com	423-842-5844		9
Gold Canyon Golf Resort 6100 S Kings Ranch Rd ... Gold Canyon AZ 85118 *TF:* 800-827-5281 ■ *Web:* www.gcgr.com	480-982-9090	830-5211	669
Gold Capital LLC 3566 Olivet Church Rd ... Paducah KY 42001 *Web:* www.goldcapitalky.com	270-408-4653		106
Gold Coast Animal Hospital 225 W Division St ... Chicago IL 60610 *Web:* www.goldcoastah.com	312-337-7387		794
Gold Coast Freightways Inc 12250 NW 28th Ave ... Miami FL 33167 *TF:* 877-465-3585 ■ *Web:* www.gcfreight.com	305-687-3560		311
Gold Coast Hotel & Casino 4000 W Flamingo Rd ... Las Vegas NV 89103 *TF:* 800-331-5334 ■ *Web:* www.goldcoastcasino.com	702-367-7111		133
Gold Coast Ingredients Inc 2429 Yates Ave ... Commerce CA 90040 *TF:* 800-352-8673 ■ *Web:* www.goldcoastinc.com	323-724-8935		297-8
Gold Coast Jazz Society 1350 E Sunrise Blvd ... Fort Lauderdale FL 33304 *Web:* www.goldcoastjazz.org	954-524-0805	525-7880	48-4
Gold Coast Limousines 3463 State St Ste 408 ... Santa Barbara CA 93105 *Web:* www.goldcoastlimos.com	805-966-5466		441
Gold Coast Tours 105 Gemini Ave ... Brea CA 92821 *TF:* 800-638-6427 ■ *Web:* www.goldcoasttours.com	714-449-6888		107
Gold Coast Transit (GCT) 301 E Third St ... Oxnard CA 93030 *Web:* www.goldcoasttransit.org	805-487-4222	487-0925	468
Gold Dust West Carson City 2171 E William St ... Carson City NV 89701 *TF:* 877-519-5567 ■ *Web:* www.gdwcasino.com	775-885-9000	888-8018	133
Gold Eagle Co 4400 S Kildare Ave ... Chicago IL 60632 **Fax Area Code:* 773 ■ *TF:* 800-367-3245 ■ *Web:* www.goldeagle.com	800-367-3245	376-5749*	145
Gold Harbor Commodities Inc 9750 Third Ave NE ... Seattle WA 98115 *Web:* www.goldharbor.com	206-527-3494		297-7
Gold Hill Corp 2233 W Lindsey Ste 117 ... Norman OK 73069	405-321-8371		536
Gold Key Resorts Phr Career Center 313 Laskin Rd Ste 103 ... Virginia Beach VA 23451 *Web:* goldkeyphr.com	757-213-4344		707
Gold Key Solutions Inc 18757 Burbank Blvd Ste 212 ... Los Angeles CA 91356 *Web:* www.goldkeysolutions.com	818-865-0006		179
Gold Key Technology Solutions Inc 220 S Second St ... Temple TX 76501 *TF:* 800-433-5778 ■ *Web:* goldkeytechnology.com	254-774-9035		180
Gold Line Connector Inc PO Box 500 ... West Redding CT 06896 *Web:* www.gold-line.com	203-938-2588	938-8740	248
Gold Mechanical Inc 4735 W Division St ... Springfield MO 65802 *TF:* 877-873-9770 ■ *Web:* goldmechanical.com	417-873-9770		189-10
Gold Medal PO Box 9452 ... Minneapolis MN 55440 **Fax Area Code:* 763 ■ *TF:* 800-248-7310 ■ *Web:* www.generalmills.com	800-248-7310	764-8330*	296-23
Gold Medal Bakery Inc 1397 Bay St ... Fall River MA 02724 *TF:* 800-642-7568 ■ *Web:* www.goldmedalbakery.com	508-674-5766	674-6090	68
Gold Medal Products Co 10700 Medallion Dr ... Cincinnati OH 45241 *Web:* www.gmpopcorn.com	513-769-7676		298
Gold Meltzer Plasky & Wise PA 505 Pleasant Vly Ave ... Moorestown NJ 08057 *Web:* www.gmpw.com	856-727-0100		2
Gold Metal Recyclers 4305 S Lamar ... Dallas TX 75215 *Web:* www.goldmetal.com	214-421-0247		492
Gold Newsletter PO Box 84900 ... Phoenix AZ 85071 *TF:* 800-877-8847 ■ *Web:* jeffersoncompanies.com	800-877-8847		531-9
Gold Point Lodging & Realty Inc 75 Snowflake Dr ... Breckenridge CO 80424 *Web:* www.grandtimber.com	970-453-4440		653
Gold Pure Food Products Inc 1 Brooklyn Rd ... Hempstead NY 11550 *Web:* www.goldshorseradish.com	516-483-5600		296-19
Gold Ranch Casino & RV Resort 350 Gold Ranch Rd ... Verdi NV 89439 *Web:* www.goldranchrvcasino.com	775-345-6789		133
Gold Reserve Inc 926 W Sprague Ave Ste 200 ... Spokane WA 99201 *TSE:* GRZ ■ *TF:* 800-625-9550 ■ *Web:* www.goldreserveinc.com	509-623-1500	623-1634	502
Gold Room 127 N Franklin St ... Juneau AK 99801 *TF:* 800-544-0970 ■ *Web:* www.westmarkhotels.com/juneau-food.php	907-586-2660	586-8315	671
Gold Room 245 E Ina Rd ... Tucson AZ 85704 *Web:* westwardlook.com	520-297-1151		671
Gold Shield Fiberglass of Ind 2004 Patterson St ... Decatur IN 46733 *Web:* www.goldshield.com	260-728-2476		596
Gold Spike 217 Las Vegas Blvd N ... Las Vegas NV 89101 *Web:* goldspike.com	702-476-1082		133
Gold Standard Baking Inc 3700 S Kedzie Ave Ste A ... Chicago IL 60632 *Web:* www.gsbaking.com	773-523-2333		345
Gold Standard Enterprises Inc 5100 W Dempster St ... Skokie IL 60077 *TF:* 888-942-9463 ■ *Web:* www.binnys.com	847-674-4200	568-9905	443
Gold Star Chili 650 Lunken Pk Dr ... Cincinnati OH 45226 *TF:* 800-643-0465 ■ *Web:* www.goldstarchili.com	513-231-4541	624-4415	670
Gold Star FS Inc 101 NE St ... Cambridge IL 61238 *TF:* 800-443-8497 ■ *Web:* www.goldstarfs.com	309-937-3369	937-5465	276
Gold Star Sausage Co 2800 Walnut St ... Denver CO 80205 *Web:* www.goldstarsausage.com	303-295-6400		296-26
Gold Stars Speakers Bureau 7478 N La Cholla Blvd ... Tucson AZ 85741 *Web:* www.goldstars.com	520-742-4384		195
Gold Street Caffe 218 Gold Ave SW ... Albuquerque NM 87102 *Web:* goldstreetcaffe.com	505-765-1633		671
Gold Strike Casino Resort 1010 Casino Ctr Dr ... Tunica Resorts MS 38664 *TF Resv:* 888-245-7829 ■ *Web:* www.goldstrike.com/en.html	662-357-1111		133
Gold Strike Hotel & Gambling Hall 1 Main St ... Jean NV 89019 *TF:* 800-634-1359 ■ *Web:* goldstrikejean.com	702-477-5000		133
Gold Tip LLC 584 E 1100 S Ste 5 ... American Fork UT 84003 *TF:* 800-551-0541 ■ *Web:* www.goldtip.com	800-551-0541		711
Goldbelt Hotel Juneau 3025 Clinton Dr ... Juneau AK 99801 *TF:* 800-770-5866 ■ *Web:* www.goldbelt.com/subsidiaries/gbhj.html	907-586-6900	463-3567	379
Goldbelt Raven LLC 14117 Robert Paris Ct ... Chantilly VA 20151	703-871-2091	871-0026	180
Goldberg & Connolly G&C Bldg 66 N Village Ave ... Rockville Centre NY 11570 *Web:* www.goldbergconnolly.com	516-764-2800		428
Goldberg & Osborne 4423 E Thomas Rd Ste 3 ... Phoenix AZ 85018 *TF:* 800-843-3245 ■ *Web:* 1800theeagle.com	602-808-6200		445
Goldberg Bros Inc 8000 E 40th Ave ... Denver CO 80207 *Web:* www.goldbergbrothers.com	303-321-1099	388-0749	697

Phone | Fax | Class

Goldberg Harder Adelstein & Co
132 Lincoln St ... Boston MA 02111 | 617-426-3350 | | 2

Goldberg Testa & Company Inc
6201 Ft Hamilton Pkwy ... Brooklyn NY 11219 | 718-748-4851 | | 180

Goldberg Weisman Cairo
1 E Wacker Dr Ste 3800 ... Chicago IL 60601 | 312-464-1234 | | 428
TF: 800-464-4772 ■ *Web:* www.gwclaw.com

Goldberg, Persky & White PC
1030 Fifth Ave ... Pittsburgh PA 15219 | 412-471-3980 | | 428
TF: 800-266-7539 ■ *Web:* www.gpwlaw.com

Goldbug Inc 18245 E 40th Ave ... Aurora CO 80011 | 303-371-2535 | | 157-1
TF: 800-942-9442 ■ *Web:* goldbuginc.com

Goldcorp Inc 666 Burrard St Ste 3400 ... Vancouver BC V6C2X8 | 604-696-3000 | 696-3001 | 502
NYSE: G ■ *TF:* 800-567-6223 ■ *Web:* www.goldcorp.com

Goldcrest Investments
2525 McKinnon St Ste 550 ... Dallas TX 75201 | 214-303-1112 | | 401

Goldcrest Wallcoverings
PO Box 245 ... Slingerlands NY 12159 | 518-478-7214 | 478-7216 | 802
TF: 800-535-9513 ■ *Web:* www.wallcovering.com

Gold-Eagle Co-op
PO Box 280 PO Box 280 ... Goldfield IA 50542 | 800-825-3331 | | 10-4
TF: 800-825-3331 ■ *Web:* www.goldeaglecoop.com

Goldec Hamm's Manufacturing Ltd
6760 65 Ave ... Red Deer AB T4P1A5 | 403-343-6607 | | 393
TF: 800-661-1665 ■ *Web:* www.goldec.com

Golden & Silver Falls State Natural Area
89814 Cape Arago Hwy ... Coos Bay OR 97420 | 541-888-3778 | | 565
Web: www.oregonstateparks.org

Golden Acres 2525 Centerville Rd ... Dallas TX 75228 | 214-327-4503 | | 371
Web: www.goldenacresliving.com

Golden Aluminum Inc
1405 E 14th St ... Fort Lupton CO 80621 | 800-838-1004 | | 492
TF: 800-838-1004 ■ *Web:* goldenaluminum.com

Golden Anchor Travel
1909 Southwood St ... Sarasota FL 34231 | 941-922-4070 | | 775
TF: 800-299-1125 ■ *Web:* www.goldenanchortravel.com

Golden Artists Colors Inc
188 Bell Rd ... New Berlin NY 13411 | 607-847-6154 | 847-6767 | 43
TF: 800-959-6543 ■ *Web:* www.goldenpaints.com

Golden Bear International Inc
11780 US Hwy 1 ... North Palm Beach FL 33408 | 561-626-3900 | | 422
Web: www.nicklaus.com

Golden Bridge International Inc
9700 Harbour Pl Ste 129 ... Mukilteo WA 98275 | 425-493-1801 | | 231
Web: www.gbi-inc.com

Golden Capital Management LLC
10715 David Taylor Dr Ste 400 ... Charlotte NC 28262 | 704-593-1144 | | 401
Web: www.gcm1.com

Golden Chair Inc 958 Washington Rd ... Houlka MS 38850 | 662-568-7830 | | 321
Web: www.goldenchair.com

Golden Cheese Company of California
1138 W Rincon St ... Corona CA 92880 | 951-493-4700 | | 296-5
Web: waterboards.ca.gov

Golden Chick 1131 Rockingham Dr ... Richardson TX 75080 | 972-831-0911 | 831-0401 | 310
Web: www.goldenchick.com

Golden Chopsticks 329 N York St ... Wheeling WV 26003 | 304-232-2888 | | 671

Golden Corral Corp 5151 Glenwood Ave ... Raleigh NC 27612 | 919-781-9310 | | 670
Web: goldencorral.com

Golden Dawn 1245 Logan Ave ... Youngstown OH 44505 | 330-746-0393 | | 671

Golden Door 777 Deer Springs Rd ... San Marcos CA 92069 | 760-744-5777 | 471-2393 | 706
TF: 866-420-6414 ■ *Web:* www.goldendoor.com

Golden Dynasty 3433 Washington Blvd ... Ogden UT 84401 | 801-621-6789 | | 671

Golden Eagle Distributors Inc
705 E Ajo Way ... Tucson AZ 85713 | 520-884-5999 | | 81-1
Web: www.gedaz.com

Golden Eagle Extrusions Inc
1762 State Rt 131 ... Milford OH 45150 | 513-248-8292 | | 603
Web: www.goldeneagleextrusions.com

Golden Eagle Insurance Corp
525 B St ... San Diego CA 92101 | 610-832-8240 | | 391-4
TF: 888-398-8924 ■ *Web:* libertymutualgroup.com/business

Golden Eagle of Arkansas Inc
1900 E 15th St ... Little Rock AR 72202 | 501-372-2800 | | 81-1

Golden Eagle Resort 511 Mountain Rd ... Stowe VT 05672 | 802-253-4811 | 253-2561 | 379
TF: 866-970-0786 ■ *Web:* www.goldeneagleresort.com

Golden Eagle Syrup Company Inc
205 First Ave SE ... Fayette AL 35555 | 205-932-5294 | | 296-39
Web: www.goldeneaglesyrup.com

Golden Empire Transit District
1830 Golden State Ave ... Bakersfield CA 93301 | 661-324-9874 | 869-6394 | 468
Web: www.getbus.org

Golden Equipment Co
721 Candelaria NE ... Albuquerque NM 87107 | 505-345-7811 | 345-0401 | 358
Web: www.goldenequipment.com

Golden Flake Snack Foods Inc
1 Golden Flake Dr ... Birmingham AL 35205 | 205-323-6161 | | 296-35
TF: 800-239-2447 ■ *Web:* www.goldenflake.com

Golden Flower 205 W Fifth St ... Reno NV 89503 | 775-323-1628 | | 671
Web: goldenflowerreno.com

Golden Flowers 2600 NW 79th Ave ... Doral FL 33122 | 305-599-0193 | | 292
Web: terrafloristvancouver.com

Golden Foods/Golden Brands LLC
2520 Seventh St Rd ... Louisville KY 40208 | 502-636-3712 | 636-3904 | 296-30

Golden Franchising Corp
1131 Rockingham Ste 250 ... Richardson TX 75080 | 972-831-0911 | 831-0401 | 670
Web: www.goldenchick.com

Golden Gate 2640 W Baseline Rd ... Mesa AZ 85202 | 480-897-1335 | | 671

Golden Gate Baptist Theological Seminary
201 Seminary Dr ... Mill Valley CA 94941 | 415-380-1300 | | 167-3

Golden Gate Bridge
Golden Gate Bridge Toll Plaza Presidio Stn
PO Box 9000 ... San Francisco CA 94129 | 415-921-5858 | 956-1663 | 50-4
TF: 877-229-8655 ■ *Web:* www.goldengate.org

Golden Gate Canyon State Park
92 Crawford Gulch Rd ... Golden CO 80403 | 303-582-3707 | 582-3712 | 565
TF: 866-265-6447 ■ *Web:* cpw.state.co.us

Golden Gate Capital
1 Embarcadero Ctr Fl 39 ... San Francisco CA 94111 | 415-983-2700 | 983-2701 | 405
Web: goldengatecap.com

Golden Gate Fields
1100 Eastshore Hwy ... Berkeley CA 94710 | 510-559-7300 | | 642
Web: www.goldengatefields.com

Golden Gate National Cemetery
1300 Sneath Ln ... San Bruno CA 94066 | 650-589-7737 | 873-6578 | 136
Web: www.cem.va.gov/cems/nchp/goldengate.asp

Golden Gate National Recreation Area
Fort Mason Bldg 201 ... San Francisco CA 94123 | 415-561-4700 | 561-4750* | 564
*Fax: Hum Res ■ *Web:* www.nps.gov/goga

Golden Gate Park 970 47th Ave ... San Francisco CA 94121 | 415-751-8987 | | 50-5
Web: goldengateparkgolf.com

Golden Gate Rehabilitation & Health Care Ctr
191 Bradley Ave ... Staten Island NY 10314 | 718-698-8800 | | 450
Web: goldengaterehab.com

Golden Gate University
Roseville
7 Sierra Gate Plaza Ste 101 ... Roseville CA 95678 | 916-648-1446 | | 800
TF: 800-448-4968 ■ *Web:* www.ggu.edu
San Francisco 536 Mission St ... San Francisco CA 94105 | 415-442-7000 | 442-7807* | 800
*Fax: Admissions ■ *TF:* 800-448-4968 ■ *Web:* www.ggu.edu

Golden Gate University School of Law
536 Mission St ... San Francisco CA 94105 | 415-442-6600 | 442-6609 | 167-1
TF: 800-448-4968 ■ *Web:* law.ggu.edu

Golden Gates Casino 300 Main St ... Black Hawk CO 80422 | 303-582-5600 | | 133
Web: thegoldengatescasino.com

Golden Glow Investigative & Protective Services
147 Belmont Blvd ... Elmont NY 11003 | 516-437-7486 | | 693
Web: goldenglowsecurity.com

Golden Grain Energy LLC
1822 43rd St SW ... Mason City IA 50401 | 641-423-8525 | | 10-5
TF: 888-443-2676 ■ *Web:* www.ggecorn.com

Golden Griddle Corp, The
20 Woodlawn Rd E ... Guelph ON N1H1G7 | 519-836-4590 | | 670
Web: www.goldengriddleinc.com

Golden Hill Nursing Home Inc
520 Friendship St ... New Castle PA 16101 | 724-654-7791 | | 371
TF: 800-660-4464 ■ *Web:* goldenhill.com

Golden Hill State Park
9691 Lower Lake Rd ... Barker NY 14012 | 716-795-3885 | | 565
Web: parks.ny.gov/parks/143/details.aspx

Golden Hotel, The 800 11th St ... Golden CO 80401 | 303-279-0100 | 279-9353 | 379
TF: 800-233-7214 ■ *Web:* www.thegoldenhotel.com

Golden Hunan Restaurant
3309 Belmont Ave ... Youngstown OH 44505 | 330-759-7197 | | 671

Golden India 2097 Madison Ave ... Memphis TN 38104 | 901-728-5111 | | 671

Golden Ink Litho & Design
7602 Vickers St ... San Diego CA 92111 | 858-541-2259 | | 627
TF: 800-590-0150 ■ *Web:* www.goldeninklitho.com

Golden Krust Carribean Bakery & Grill
3958 Pk Ave ... Bronx NY 10457 | 718-655-7878 | 583-1883 | 310
Web: www.goldenkrustbakery.com

Golden Light Cafe 2908 W Sixth Ave ... Amarillo TX 79106 | 806-374-9237 | | 671
Web: www.goldenlightcafe.com

Golden Living Ctr
350 Old Gilkeson Rd ... Pittsburgh PA 15228 | 412-564-3988 | 257-8226 | 450
Web: www.goldenlivingcenters.com/mt-lebanon

Golden LivingCenter - Western Reserve
5220 Tennyson Pkwy ... Plano TX 75024 | 972-372-6300 | | 450
Web: www.goldenliving.com/home.aspx?showpage=true

Golden Mardi Gras 300 Main St ... Black Hawk CO 80422 | 303-582-5600 | | 133
Web: thegoldengatescasino.com

Golden Memorial State Park
2104 Damascus Rd ... Walnut Grove MS 39189 | 601-253-2237 | | 565
Web: www.mdwfp.com/parkview/parks.asp?id=4843

Golden Mfg Company Inc 125 Hwy 366 ... Golden MS 38847 | 662-454-3428 | | 155-19

Golden Moon 4527 Miller Rd ... Flint MI 48507 | 810-733-7030 | | 671
Web: goldenmoonflint.com

Golden Neo-Life Diamite International
3500 Gateway Blvd ... Fremont CA 94538 | 800-432-5842 | 657-7563* | 366
*Fax Area Code: 510 ■ *TF:* 800-432-5842 ■ *Web:* us.gnld.com

Golden Nugget Hotel
129 E Fremont St ... Las Vegas NV 89101 | 702-385-7111 | 385-7111 | 669
TF: 800-634-3454 ■ *Web:* www.goldennugget.com

Golden Nugget Hotels & Casinos
151 Beach Blvd ... Biloxi MS 39530 | 228-435-5400 | | 133
TF: 800-777-7568 ■ *Web:* www.goldennugget.com

Golden Nugget Laughlin
2300 S Casino Dr ... Laughlin NV 89029 | 702-298-7111 | | 133
TF: 800-950-7700 ■ *Web:* www.goldennugget.com

Golden Oaks Village 5801 N Oakwood Rd ... Enid OK 73703 | 580-249-2600 | | 672
TF: 800-259-0914 ■ *Web:* www.goldenoaks.com

Golden Palace 2195 Carling Ave ... Ottawa ON K2B7E8 | 613-820-8444 | | 671
Web: goldenpalacerestaurant.ca

Golden Peanut Company LLC
100 N Pt Ctr E Ste 400 ... Alpharetta GA 30022 | 770-752-8160 | | 11-1
Web: www.goldenpeanut.com

Golden Pheasant Foods 6931 S 234th St ... Kent WA 98032 | 253-520-9299 | | 123
Web: www.goldenpheasantfoods.com

Golden Phoenix 2421 W Main St ... Rapid City SD 57702 | 605-348-4195 | | 671

Golden Platter Foods Inc
37 Tompkins Point Rd ... Newark NJ 07114 | 973-242-0290 | | 297-8
Web: goldenplatter.com

Golden Rod Broilers Inc
2352 County Rd 719 ... Cullman AL 35055 | 256-734-0941 | | 619

Golden Sands General Contractors Inc
2500 NW 39 St ... Miami FL 33142 | 305-633-3336 | | 186
TF: 888-994-4742 ■ *Web:* www.goldensandsgc.com

Golden Specialty Foods LLC
14605 Best Ave ... Norwalk CA 90650 | 562-802-2537 | | 296-37
Web: www.goldenspecialtyfoods.com

Golden Spike Event Ctr 1000 N 1200 W ... Ogden UT 84404 | 801-399-8798 | | 205
Web: www.goldenspikeeventcenter.com

Golden Spike National Historic Site
PO Box 897 ... Brigham City UT 84302 | 435-471-2209 | 471-2341 | 564
Web: www.nps.gov/gosp

Name / Address	City	State	ZIP	Phone	Fax	Class
Golden Sports Tours 301 W Parker Rd Ste 206 *TF:* 800-966-8258 ■ *Web:* www.goldensports.com	Plano	TX	75023	800-966-8258		771
Golden Star Inc 4770 N Belleview Ave Ste 209 *TF:* 800-821-2792 ■ *Web:* www.goldenstar.com	Kansas City	MO	64116	816-842-0233	842-1129	508
Golden Star Resources Ltd 150 King St W Ste 1200 *NYSE: GSS* ■ *TF:* 800-553-8436 ■ *Web:* www.gsr.com	Toronto	ON	M5H1J9	416-583-3800		502
Golden State Engineering Inc 15338 Garfield Ave *Web:* www.goldenstateeng.com	Paramount	CA	90723	562-634-3125		454
Golden State Foods 18301 Von Karman Ave Ste 1100 *Web:* www.goldenstatefoods.com	Irvine	CA	92612	949-252-2000		473
Golden State Health Centers Inc 13347 Ventura Blvd *Web:* www.goldenstatehealth.com	Sherman Oaks	CA	91423	818-385-3200		371
Golden State Medical Supply Inc 5187 Camino Ruiz *TF:* 800-284-8633 ■ *Web:* www.gsms.us	Camarillo	CA	93012	805-477-9866		231
Golden State Warriors 1011 Broadway **Fax Area Code:* 404 ■ *TF:* 866-648-4668 ■ *Web:* www.nba.com	Oakland	CA	94607	510-986-2200	827-3880*	714-1
Golden Technologies Inc 401 Bridge St *TF:* 800-624-6374 ■ *Web:* www.goldentech.com	Old Forge	PA	18518	800-624-6374		475
Golden Thai 105 Church St *Web:* www.goldenthai.ca	Toronto	ON	M5C2G3	416-868-6668		671
Golden Valley Bank 190 Cohasset Rd Ste 170 *TF:* 800-472-3272 ■ *Web:* www.goldenvalley.bank	Chico	CA	95926	530-894-1000	894-4938	70
Golden Valley County 150 First Ave SE *Web:* www.beachnd.com	Beach	ND	58621	701-872-3713		338
Golden Valley County 107 Kemp St PO Box 10 *Web:* www.co.golden-valley.mt.us	Ryegate	MT	59074	406-568-2231	568-2428	338
Golden Valley Electrical Assn Inc 758 Illinois St *TF:* 800-770-4832 ■ *Web:* www.gvea.com	Fairbanks	AK	99701	907-452-1151	458-6365	245
Golden Valley Memorial Hospital 1600 N Second St *Web:* www.gvmh.org	Clinton	MO	64735	660-885-5511		374-3
Golden West Casino 1001 S Union Ave *TF:* 800-426-2537 ■ *Web:* www.goldenwestcasino.net	Bakersfield	CA	93307	661-324-6936		133
Golden West College 15744 Golden West St PO Box 2748 **Fax:* Admissions ■ *Web:* www.goldenwestcollege.edu	Huntington Beach	CA	92647	714-892-7711	895-8960*	162
Golden West Telecommunications 415 Crown St PO Box 411 *TF:* 866-279-2161 ■ *Web:* www.goldenwest.com	Wall	SD	57790	605-279-2161	279-2727	736
Golden Wok 8822 Wurzbach Rd *Web:* www.goldenwoksa.com	San Antonio	TX	78240	210-615-8282		671
Golden Wok Buffet 1311 Plaza Dr	Garland	TX	75041	972-686-8691		671
Goldenberg Group Inc, The 630 Sentry Pkwy Ste 300 *Web:* www.goldenberggroup.com	Blue Bell	PA	19422	610-260-9600		653
Goldendale Observatory State Park 1602 Observatory Dr *Web:* www.parks.wa.gov	Goldendale	WA	98620	509-773-3141		565
Goldener Hirsch Inn 7570 Royal St E *TF Cust Svc:* 800-252-3373 ■ *Web:* www.goldenerhirschinn.com	Park City	UT	84060	435-649-7770		379
GoldenRAM Computer Products 13 Whatney *TF:* 800-222-8861 ■ *Web:* www.goldenram.com	Irvine	CA	92618	949-460-9000		625
Goldenrod Area Chamber of Commerce 4755 Palmetto Ave PO Box 61	Winter Park	FL	32792	407-677-5980		139
Goldens' Foundry & Machine Co (GFMCO) 600 12th St *Web:* www.gfmco.com	Columbus	GA	31902	706-323-0471		307
Goldense Group Inc 1346 South St *Web:* www.goldensegroupinc.com	Needham	MA	02492	781-444-5400		195
GoldenSource Corp 22 Cortlandt St *Web:* www.thegoldensource.com	New York	NY	10007	212-798-7100	798-7238	178-10
Golden-Tech International Inc 2461 152nd Ave NE *TF:* 800-311-8090 ■ *Web:* www.gtiinc.com	Redmond	WA	98052	425-869-1461	867-1368	297-5
Goldenwest Electric Co-op Inc 119 1 Ave SW	Wibaux	MT	59353	406-796-2423		245
Golder Assoc Inc 3730 Chamblee Tucker Rd *Web:* www.golder.com	Atlanta	GA	30341	770-496-1893	934-9476	261
Goldey Beacom College 4701 Limestone Rd **Fax:* Admissions ■ *TF:* 800-833-4877 ■ *Web:* www.gbc.edu	Wilmington	DE	19808	302-998-8814	996-5408*	166
Goldfarb & Lipman LLP 1300 Clay St 11th Fl *Web:* www.goldfarblipman.com	Oakland	CA	94612	510-836-6336	836-1035	428
Goldfield Corp 1684 W Hibiscus Blvd *NYSE: GV* ■ *Web:* www.goldfieldcorp.com	Melbourne	FL	32901	321-724-1700		189-4
Goldfield Ghost Town & Mine 4650 N Mammouth Rd *Web:* www.goldfieldghosttown.com	Goldfield	AZ	85119	480-983-0333		50-3
Goldin & Company Ltd 263 Stanley St	Winnipeg	MB	R3A0W8	204-982-1188		292
Goldin Associates LLC 350 Fifth Ave The Empire State Bldg *Web:* www.goldinassociates.com	New York	NY	10118	212-593-2255		194
Golding Holden & Pope Llp 6701 Carmel Rd Ste 105 *TF:* 800-554-6728 ■ *Web:* ghplaw.net	Charlotte	NC	28226	704-374-1600		445
Goldline International 110 N Shaver St *Web:* www.goldlineinternationalinc.com	Pasadena	TX	77506	713-475-1201		480
Goldline International Inc 1601 Cloverfield Blvd 100 S Tower *TF:* 877-376-2646 ■ *Web:* goldline.com	Santa Monica	CA	90404	310-587-1423	319-0265	491
Goldman Antonetti & Cordova 250 Munoz Rivera Ave Ste 1400 *Web:* www.gaclaw.com	San Juan	PR	00918	787-759-8000		428
Goldman Sachs 200 W St *NYSE: GS* ■ *TF:* 800-526-7384 ■ *Web:* www.goldmansachs.com	New York	NY	10282	212-902-1000		528
Goldman Sachs Asset Management (GSAM) 200 W St *TF:* 800-526-7384 ■ *Web:* www.goldmansachs.com	New York	NY	10282	212-902-1000		401
Goldman Sloan Nash & Haber LLP 480 University Ave Ste 1600 *Web:* www.gsnh.com	Toronto	ON	M5G1V2	416-597-9922		41
Goldmark Group Inc, The 1155 Bloomfield Ave *TF:* 800-632-9632 ■ *Web:* www.goldmarkgroup.com	Clifton	NJ	07012	973-777-5720		344
Goldner Hawn Johnson & Morrison Inc (GHJ&M) 90 S Seventh St 3700 Wells Fargo Ctr *Web:* www.ghjm.com	Minneapolis	MN	55402	612-338-5912		403
Goldrich & Kest Industries 5150 Overland Ave *Web:* www.goldrichkest.com	Culver City	CA	90230	310-204-2050	204-1900	653
Goldring Gulf Distributing Co 8245 Opportunity Dr *Web:* www.goldringgulf.com	Milton	FL	32583	850-432-9883	432-5509	81-3
Goldsboro Milling Co 938 Millers Chapel Rd *Web:* cals.ncsu.edu	Goldsboro	NC	27534	919-778-3130		447
Goldsboro News-Argus 310 N Berkeley Blvd *TF:* 800-752-7504 ■ *Web:* www.newsargus.com	Goldsboro	NC	27534	919-778-2211	778-5408	637-8
Goldshield Elite 1501 Northpoint Pkwy	West Palm Beach	FL	33407	561-615-4701		366
Goldsmith & Eggleton Inc 300 First St *TF:* 800-321-0954 ■ *Web:* www.goldsmith-eggleton.com	Wadsworth	OH	44281	330-336-6616	334-4709	605-2
Goldsmith New York at Studio 350 601 W 26th St Ste 350 *Web:* www.goldsmith-inc.com	New York	NY	10001	212-366-9040		464
Goldston Oil Corp 1819 Saint James Pl *Web:* goldstonoil.com	Houston	TX	77056	713-355-3408		539
Goldwater Dube 3500 Boul De Maisonneuve O *Web:* www.goldwaterdube.com	Montreal	QC	H3Z3C1	514-861-4367		428
Goldwater Institute 500 E Coronado Rd *Web:* www.goldwaterinstitute.org	Phoenix	AZ	85004	602-462-5000	256-7045	634
Goleta Union School District 401 N Fairview Ave *Web:* www.goleta.k12.ca.us	Goleta	CA	93117	805-681-1200		685
Goleta Valley Chamber of Commerce 5662 Calle Real Ste 204 *Web:* goletachamber.com	Goleta	CA	93117	805-967-2500		139
Goleta Water District 4699 Hollister Ave *Web:* www.goletawater.com	Goleta	CA	93110	805-964-6761		787
Golf & Ski Warehouse Inc 290 Plainfield Rd *TF:* 800-219-1113 ■ *Web:* www.golfskiwarehouse.com	West Lebanon	NH	03784	603-298-8282		711
Golf Course Superintendents Assn of America (GCSAA) 1421 Research Pk Dr *TF:* 800-472-7878 ■ *Web:* www.gcsaa.org	Lawrence	KS	66049	785-841-2240		48-2
Golf Creations 18250 Beck Rd *TF:* 800-553-3384 ■ *Web:* lohmann.com	Marengo	IL	60152	815-923-1868		188
Golf Development Construction Inc PO Box 197249 *Web:* www.golfdev.com	Louisville	KY	40259	502-894-8916		188-3
Golf Etc Granburyÿ 2461 E Hwy 377 *Web:* www.golfetcgranbury.com	Granbury	TX	76048	817-579-5400		711
Golf Instruments Co 3210 Production Ave Unit A *Web:* www.golfinstruments.com	Oceanside	CA	92058	760-712-2345	967-7268	710
Golf Mill Shopping Ctr 239 Golf Mill Ctr *Web:* www.golfmill.com	Niles	IL	60714	847-699-1070		460
Golf Shack Inc 1631 N Bell School Rd *Web:* www.golfshack.com	Rockford	IL	61107	815-397-3709		711
Golf Shoe Centers of America 9899 N Kings Hwy *Web:* www.golfshoesonly.com	Myrtle Beach	SC	29572	843-497-0507		711
Golf Visions LLC 344 E Lyndale Ave *Web:* golfvisions.net	Northlake	IL	60164	708-562-5247		188-3
Golf Works Inc 3660 Stone Ridge Rd	Austin	TX	78746	512-327-8089		188-3
Golfballs.com Inc 126 Arnould Blvd *Web:* www.golfballs.com	Lafayette	LA	70506	337-210-4653		711
GolfBC Holdings Inc 1800-1030 W Georgia St *TF:* 800-446-5322 ■ *Web:* www.golfbc.com	Vancouver	BC	V6E2Y3	800-446-5322		787
Golfland Entertainment Centers Inc 155 W Hampton Ave *Web:* www.golfland.com	Mesa	AZ	85210	480-834-8319		31
Golflogix Inc 15685 N Greenway-Hayden Loop Ste 100A *TF:* 877-977-0162 ■ *Web:* www.golflogix.com	Scottsdale	AZ	85260	877-977-0162		148
Golfsmith International Inc 11000 N IH-35 *TF Sales:* 800-396-0099 ■ *Web:* www.golfgalaxy.com	Austin	TX	78753	512-821-4050	837-1245	711
GolfWorks, The 4820 Jacksontown Rd PO Box 3008 *TF:* 800-848-8358 ■ *Web:* www.golfworks.com	Newark	OH	43055	740-328-4193	323-0311	710
Goliad County 127 N Courthouse Sq PO Box 50 *Web:* www.co.goliad.tx.us	Goliad	TX	77963	361-645-3294		338
Goliad Independent School District PO Box 830 *Web:* www.goliadisd.org	Goliad	TX	77963	361-645-3259		685
Goliad State Park 108 Pk Rd 6 *Web:* tpwd.texas.gov/state-parks/goliad	Goliad	TX	77963	361-645-3405		565
Gollob Morgan Peddy & Company CPA 1001 Ese Loop 323 Ste 300 *Web:* www.gmpcpa.com	Tyler	TX	75701	903-534-0088		401
Goltens New York Corp 160 Van Brunt St *TF:* 800-524-5979 ■ *Web:* www.goltens.com	Brooklyn	NY	11231	718-855-7200	802-1147	698

Name / Address	City	State	ZIP	Phone	Fax	Class
Golub Corp 461 Nott St *TF:* 800-666-7667 ■ *Web:* pricechopper.com	Schenectady	NY	12308	800-666-7667		345
Go-Mart Inc 915 Riverside Dr *Web:* gomart.com	Gassaway	WV	26624	304-364-8000		204
gomembers Inc 1155 Perimeter Ctr W *TF:* 855-411-2783 ■ *Web:* www.aptean.com	Atlanta	GA	30338	855-411-2783		178-10
Gomez & Associates Company LLC 3216 Industry Dr Ste C *Web:* www.cryogenics.net	North Charleston	SC	29418	843-552-4552		697
Gomez & Sullivan PC 288 Genesee St *Web:* gomezandsullivan.com	Utica	NY	13502	315-724-4860		261
Gomez Construction Co 7100 SW 44th St *Web:* www.gomezconstruction.com	Miami	FL	33155	305-661-7660	661-0504	186
GoMotion Inc 10 Kendrick Rd Unit 3 *Web:* www.gomotiongear.com	Wareham	MA	02571	508-322-7695		253
Gompers 6601 N 27th Ave *Web:* www.gomperscenter.org	Phoenix	AZ	85017	602-336-0061		256
Gompers & Assoc PLLC 117 Edgington Ln *TF:* 844-805-9844 ■ *Web:* gomperscpa.com	Wheeling	WV	26003	304-242-9300		2
Gongos Research Inc 2365 Pontiac Rd *Web:* www.gongos.com	Auburn Hills	MI	48326	248-239-2300		668
Gonnella Baking Co 1117 E Wiley Rd **Fax Area Code:* 312 ■ *TF:* 800-322-8829 ■ *Web:* www.gonnella.com	Schaumburg	IL	60173	800-322-8829	733-7056*	68
Gonser Gerber 1776 Legacy Cir Ste 100 *Web:* www.gonsergerber.com	Naperville	IL	60563	630-505-1433		317
Gonzaga University 502 E Boone Ave **Fax:* Admissions ■ *TF:* 800-986-9585 ■ *Web:* www.gonzaga.edu	Spokane	WA	99258	509-323-6572	323-5780*	166
Gonzaga University Foley Library 502 E Boone Ave *TF:* 800-498-5941 ■ *Web:* gonzaga.edu/campus%2dresources	Spokane	WA	99258	509-323-5931	323-5904	434-6
Gonzaga University School of Law 721 N Cincinnati St PO Box 3528 *TF Admissions:* 800-793-1710 ■ *Web:* www.law.gonzaga.edu	Spokane	WA	99220	509-313-3700		167-1
Gonzales County 427 St George Ste 200 *Web:* www.co.gonzales.tx.us/default.aspx?Gonzales_County/County.Clerk	Gonzales	TX	78629	830-672-2801	672-2636	338
Gonzales Hoblit Ferguson LLP 802 N Carancahua St Ste 2000	Corpus Christi	TX	78470	361-888-9392		428
Gonzales Inquirer, The 1000 Civic Ctr Loop *TF:* 800-210-5909 ■ *Web:* gonzalesinquirer.com	San Marcos	TX	78666	830-672-2861	672-7029	789
Gonzalez 29401 Stephenson Hwy *Web:* www.gonzalez-group.com	Madison Heights	MI	48071	248-548-6010	548-3160	487
Gonzalez Defino 7 E 14th St Ste 20s *Web:* www.gonzalezdefino.com	New York	NY	10003	212-414-1058		94
Gonzalez Design Group 29401 Stevenson Hwy *TF:* 800-799-9625 ■ *Web:* www.gonzalez-group.com	Madison Heights	MI	48071	248-548-6010	548-3160	261
Gonzalez Strength & Assoc 2176 Pkwy Lake Dr *TF:* 800-262-2219 ■ *Web:* www.gonzalez-strength.com	Hoover	AL	35244	205-942-2486		261
Gonzalez Vicente (Rep D - TX) 113 Cannon HOB *Web:* gonzalez.house.gov	Washington	DC	20515	202-225-2531		342-2
Gonzalez-Colon Jenniffer (Rep D - PR) 1529 Longworth HOB *Web:* gonzalez-colon.house.gov	Washington	DC	20515	202-225-2615	225-2154	342-2
Gooch & Housego (Ohio) LLC 676 Alpha Dr *Web:* www.goochandhousego.com	Cleveland	OH	44143	216-486-6100		544
Goochland County 1800 Sandy Hook Rd *Web:* www.goochlandva.us	Goochland	VA	23063	804-556-5800	556-4617	338
Good Company Players 928 E Olive Ave *TF:* 800-371-4747 ■ *Web:* gcplayers.com	Fresno	CA	93728	559-266-0660	266-1342	572
Good Day Pharmacy 2033 Boise Ave *Web:* www.gooddaypharmacy.com	Loveland	CO	80538	970-669-7500		237
Good Design LLC 450 Industrial Park Rd *TF:* 800-497-4861 ■ *Web:* gooddesignusa.com	Deep River	CT	06417	860-526-1600		177
Good Dog Design 21 Corte Madera Ave Ste 2 *Web:* gooddogdesign.com	Mill Valley	CA	94941	415-383-0110		180
Good Earth Inc PO Box 290 *TF:* 800-877-0848 ■ *Web:* www.goodearth.org	Lancaster	NY	14086	716-684-8111	684-3722	280
Good Earth Lighting Inc 5260 Capitol Dr *Web:* www.goodearthlighting.com	Wheeling	IL	60090	847-808-1133	808-0838	439
Good Earth Teasinc 831 Almar Ave *TF:* 888-625-8227 ■ *Web:* www.goodearthteas.com	Santa Cruz	CA	95060	888-625-8227		123
Good Eats Inc 12200 Stemmons Fwy Ste 100 *TF:* 800-275-1337 ■ *Web:* www.goodeatsgrill.com	Dallas	TX	75234	972-241-5500		670
Good Food Inc 4960 Horseshoe Pike *Web:* www.goodfoodinc.org	Honey Brook	PA	19344	610-273-3776		805
Good Friends 507 E Lincolnway	Cheyenne	WY	82001	307-778-7088		671
Good Hope Lutheran Church 3359 New Zoarville Rd NE *Web:* www.nclutheran.org	Zoarville	OH	44656	330-859-2480		48-20
Good Hospitality Services Inc 1051 Southpoint Dr Ste A *Web:* goodhsi.com	Valparaiso	IN	46385	219-462-6265		379
Good Hotel *Good Hotel* 112 Seventh St *TF:* 800-444-5819 ■ *Web:* www.haiyi-hotels.com/thegoodhotel	San Francisco	CA	94103	415-621-7001	626-3974	379
Good Jobs Inc, The 2120 E Jarvis St *Web:* www.thegoodjobs.com	Milwaukee	WI	53211	414-949-5627		260
Good Lad Apparel 431 E Tioga St *Web:* goodlad.com	Philadelphia	PA	19134	215-739-0200		155-4
Good Leads 224 Main St Unit 2B *TF:* 866-894-5323 ■ *Web:* www.goodleads.com	Salem	NH	03079	603-894-5323		393
Good Old Boat Magazine 1501 Eigth Ave NW *Web:* www.goodoldboat.com	Jamestown	ND	58401	701-952-9433	952-9434	457-4
Good Printers Inc 213 Dry River Rd *TF:* 800-296-3731 ■ *Web:* www.goodprinters.com	Bridgewater	VA	22812	540-828-4663		174
Good Roads Inc 537 State Rd 28 E *Web:* www.goodroadsinc.com	Williamsport	IN	47993	765-762-1111		59
Good Sam Club PO Box 6888 *TF:* 800-234-3450 ■ *Web:* www.goodsamclub.com	Englewood	CO	80155	800-234-3450		48-23
Good Samaritan Hospice 2408 Electric Rd *TF:* 888-466-7809 ■ *Web:* www.goodsamhospice.com	Roanoke	VA	24018	540-776-0198	776-0841	371
Good Samaritan Hospital 10 E 31st St *TF:* 800-277-4306 ■ *Web:* chihealthgoodsamaritan.org	Kearney	NE	68847	308-865-7100		374-3
Good Samaritan Hospital 375 Dixmyth Ave *Web:* www.trihealth.com	Cincinnati	OH	45220	513-569-5400		374-3
Good Samaritan Hospital 255 Lafayette Ave *Web:* www.goodsamhosp.org	Suffern	NY	10901	845-368-5000		374-3
Good Samaritan Hospital 520 S Seventh St *Web:* www.gshvin.org	Vincennes	IN	47591	812-882-5220		374-3
Good Samaritan Hospital 2222 Philadelphia Dr *Web:* www.goodsamdayton.org	Dayton	OH	45406	937-278-2612	734-8214	374-3
Good Samaritan Hospital 2425 Samaritan Dr **Fax:* Admitting ■ *TF:* 800-307-7631 ■ *Web:* www.goodsamsanjose.com	San Jose	CA	95124	408-559-2011	559-2675*	374-3
Good Samaritan Hospital 1225 Wilshire Blvd *Web:* www.goodsam.org	Los Angeles	CA	90017	213-977-2121		374-3
Good Samaritan Hospital (GSH) 407 14th Ave SE *TF:* 800-776-4048 ■ *Web:* www.multicare.org/goodsam	Puyallup	WA	98372	253-697-4000		374-3
Good Samaritan Hospital of Maryland 5601 Loch Raven Blvd *TF:* 855-633-5655 ■ *Web:* www.medstarhealth.org	Baltimore	MD	21239	410-532-8000		374-3
Good Samaritan Medical Ctr 235 N Pearl St *TF:* 800-488-5959 ■ *Web:* steward.org	Brockton	MA	02301	508-427-3000		374-3
Good Samaritan Regional Medical Ctr 3600 NW Samaritan Dr *TF:* 888-872-0760 ■ *Web:* www.samhealth.org	Corvallis	OR	97330	541-768-5111		374-3
GOOD SEARCH LLC, The 4 Valley Rd *Web:* tgsus.com	Westport	CT	06880	203-539-0847		260
Good Shepherd Hospice 4350 Will Rogers Pkwy Ste 400 *TF:* 800-687-9008 ■ *Web:* www.goodshepherdhospice.com	Oklahoma City	OK	73108	405-943-0903		371
Good Shepherd Hospice 200 Belle Terre Rd *Web:* goodshepherdhospice.chsli.org	Port Jefferson	NY	11777	631-642-4200		371
Good Shepherd Medical Ctr 700 E Marshall Ave *Web:* www.gsmc.org	Longview	TX	75601	903-315-2000		374-3
Good Shepherd Rehabilitation & Nursing Ctr 20 Plantation Dr *Web:* www.cc-nh.org	Jaffrey	NH	03452	603-532-8762		450
Good Shepherd Rehabilitation Hospital 850 S Fifth St *Web:* www.goodshepherdrehab.org	Allentown	PA	18103	610-776-3585		374-6
Good Sports Outdoor Outfitters 12730 W I-10 Ste 300 *Web:* www.goodsports.com	San Antonio	TX	78230	210-694-0881		711
Good Time Tours 455 Corday St *TF:* 800-446-0886 ■ *Web:* www.goodtimetours.com	Pensacola	FL	32503	850-476-0046	476-7637	760
Good Times Restaurants Inc 141 Union Blvd Ste 400 *NASDAQ: GTIM* ■ *Web:* www.goodtimesburgers.com	Lakewood	CO	80228	303-384-1400		670
Good Times Travel Inc 17132 Magnolia St *TF:* 888-488-2287 ■ *Web:* www.goodtimestravel.com	Fountain Valley	CA	92708	714-848-1255	848-2855	760
Good Wildman Hegness & Walley 5000 Campus Dr *Web:* www.goodwildman.com	Newport Beach	CA	92660	949-955-1100		445
Good Will Publishers Inc PO Box 269 *TF:* 800-219-4663 ■ *Web:* www.goodwillpublishers.com	Gastonia	NC	28052	704-865-1256		637-2
Good Zoo & Benedum Planetarium 465 Lodge Dr *TF:* 800-624-6988 ■ *Web:* www.oglebay-resort.com/goodzoo	Wheeling	WV	26003	304-243-4030	243-4110	823
Good's Store 1338 Main St *TF:* 800-828-8218 ■ *Web:* www.goodsstores.com	East Earl	PA	17519	717-354-4026		229
Good4Utah.com 2175 W 1700 S *Web:* www.4utah.com	Salt Lake City	UT	84104	801-975-4444	924-8099	741-115
Goodale & Barbieri Co 818 W Riverside Ave Ste 300 *Web:* www.g-b.com	Spokane	WA	99201	509-459-6109	344-4939	655
Goodale State Park 650 Pk Rd *Web:* www.southcarolinaparks.com	Camden	SC	29020	803-432-2772		565
Goodall Manufacturing Co 7558 Washington Ave S *TF:* 800-328-7730 ■ *Web:* www.goodallmfg.com	Eden Prairie	MN	55344	952-941-6666		247
Goodby Silverstein & Partners 720 California St *Web:* www.goodbysilverstein.com	San Francisco	CA	94108	415-392-0669		4
Goodcity 5049 W Harrison St *TF:* 800-278-1239 ■ *Web:* www.goodcitychicago.org	Chicago	IL	60644	773-473-4790		305
Goode Casseb Jones Riklin Choate & Watson A Professional 2122 N Main Ave *TF:* 800-677-5584 ■ *Web:* www.goodelaw.com	San Antonio	TX	78212	210-733-6030		428
Goode Co Texas Barbecue 5109 Kirby Dr *TF:* 800-627-3502 ■ *Web:* www.goodecompany.com	Houston	TX	77098	713-522-2530		671
Goode Company Seafood 2621 Westpark Dr *Web:* goodecompany.com	Houston	TX	77098	713-523-7154		671
Goodell Devries Leech & Dann LLP 1 S St 20th Fl *TF:* 888-229-4354 ■ *Web:* www.gdldlaw.com	Baltimore	MD	21202	410-783-4000	783-4040	428
Goodfellow Air Force Base 351 Kearney Blvd *Web:* www.goodfellow.af.mil	Goodfellow AFB	TX	76908	325-654-3877		497-1
Goodfellow Inc 225 Goodfellow St *TF:* 800-361-6503 ■ *Web:* www.goodfellowinc.com	Delson	QC	J5B1V5	450-635-6511	635-3729	817

	City	State	ZIP	Phone	Fax	Class
Goodgame Company Inc 2311 Third Ave S	Pell City	AL	35128	205-338-2551		261
TF: 800-239-8017 ■ *Web:* www.goodgamecompany.com						
GoodGuide Inc 98 Battery St Ste 400	San Francisco	CA	94111	415-732-7722		387
Web: www.goodguide.com						
Goodhart Sons Inc 2515 Horseshoe Rd	Lancaster	PA	17605	717-656-2404	656-3301	91
Web: www.goodhartsons.com						
Goodheart-Willcox Publisher 18604 W Creek Dr	Tinley Park	IL	60477	708-687-5000	409-3900*	637-2
**Fax Area Code:* 888 ■ *TF:* 800-323-0440 ■ *Web:* www.g-w.com						
Goodhue County 454 W Sixth St	Red Wing	MN	55066	651-267-4800		338
Web: www.co.goodhue.mn.us						
Goodhue County Co-op Electric Assn 1410 Northstar Dr	Zumbrota	MN	55992	507-732-5117	732-5110	245
TF: 800-927-6864 ■ *Web:* www.gccea.com						
Goodin Co 2700 N Second St	Minneapolis	MN	55411	612-588-7811	588-7820	612
TF: 800-328-8433 ■ *Web:* www.goodinco.com						
Gooding Co Inc 5568 Davison Rd	Lockport	NY	14094	716-266-6252	434-9778	627
Web: www.microfolders.com						
Gooding County 624 Main St	Gooding	ID	83330	208-934-4841	934-5085	338
Web: www.goodingcounty.org						
Goodland Star-News 1205 Main St	Goodland	KS	67735	785-899-2338	899-6186	532-2
TF: 800-886-2423 ■ *Web:* www.nwkansas.com						
Goodlatte Bob (Rep R - VA) 2309 Rayburn HOB	Washington	DC	20515	202-225-5431	225-9681	342-2
Web: goodlatte.house.gov						
GoodLife Fitness *London King & Wellington Gym* 355 Wellington St	London	ON	N6A3N7	519-433-0601		354
Web: www.goodlifefitness.com						
Goodman Allen & Filetti PLLC 4501 Highwoods Pkwy Ste 210	Glen Allen	VA	23060	804-346-0600		428
Web: www.goodmanallen.com						
Goodman Correctional Institution 4556 Broad River Rd	Columbia	SC	29210	803-896-8505	896-1671	213
TF: 866-230-7761 ■ *Web:* doc.sc.gov						
Goodman Couture 224 W 30th St	New York	NY	10001	212-244-7422		155-7
Goodman Decorating Co 3400 Atlanta Industrial Pkwy NW	Atlanta	GA	30331	404-965-3626	965-2558	189-8
Web: www.goodman-decorating.com						
Goodman Factors 3010 LBJ Fwy Ste 140	Dallas	TX	75234	972-241-3297	243-6285	272
TF: 877-446-6362 ■ *Web:* www.goodmanfactors.com						
Goodman Mfg Company LP 5151 San Felipe St Ste 500	Houston	TX	77056	713-861-2500		15
Web: www.goodmanmfg.com						
Goodman Networks Inc 6400 International Ste 1000	Plano	TX	75093	972-406-9692		194
Web: www.goodmannetworks.com						
Goodman Real Estate Inc 2801 Alaskan Way Ste 310	Seattle	WA	98121	206-448-0259		656
Web: www.goodmanre.com						
Goodman Theatre 170 N Dearborn St	Chicago	IL	60601	312-443-3811	443-3821	572
Web: www.goodmantheatre.org						
Goodmanagement 603 Pilot House Dr Ste 225	Newport News	VA	23606	757-596-5215		379
Web: www.goodmanagement.com						
Goodmans LLP 333 Bay St Ste 3400	Toronto	ON	M5H2S7	416-979-2211		41
Web: www.goodmans.ca						
Goodmind LLC 41 E 11Th St 11Th Fl	New York	NY	10003	212-660-0110		41
Web: www.goodmind.com						
Good-Nite Inn Fremont 4135 Cushing Pkwy	Fremont	CA	94538	510-656-9307	656-9110	379
TF: 800-648-3466 ■ *Web:* www.goodnite.com						
Goodrich Corp 2730 W Tyvola Rd 4 Coliseum Ctr	Charlotte	NC	28217	704-423-7000	423-7002	529
NYSE: GR ■ *TF:* 800-735-7899 ■ *Web:* utcaerospacesystems.com						
Goodrich Landing Gear Div 1400 S Service Rd W	Oakville	ON	L6L5Y7	905-827-7777	825-1583	22
Web: customers.goodrich.com						
Goodrich Petroleum Corp 801 Louisiana Ste 700	Houston	TX	77002	713-780-9494	780-9254	539
NYSE: GDP ■ *TF:* 800-937-5449 ■ *Web:* www.goodrichpetroleum.com						
GoodShip International Inc 699 Lively Blvd	Elk Grove Village	IL	60007	847-621-1444		311
Web: www.goodship.com						
Goodsill Anderson Quinn & Stifel 1099 Alakea St Ste 1800	Honolulu	HI	96813	808-547-5600		428
Web: www.goodsill.com						
Goodsons' Supermarkets Inc US Rt 52	Welch	WV	24801	304-436-8481		345
Goodspeed Musicals PO Box A	East Haddam	CT	06423	860-873-8664	873-2329	749
Web: www.goodspeed.org						
Goodstay Gardens 26002800 Pennsylvania Ave	Wilmington	DE	19806	302-573-4450		97
Web: www.udel.edu						
Goodway Print & Copy Inc 15121 Ventura Blvd	Sherman Oaks	CA	91403	818-783-5172		627
Web: www.goodwayprintcopy.com						
Goodwill Easter Seals of Gulf Coast 2448 Gordon Smith Dr	Mobile	AL	36617	251-471-1581		242
Web: gesgc.org						
Goodwill Ind of Fort Worth PO Box 15520	Fort Worth	TX	76119	817-332-7866		104
Web: www.goodwillfortworth.org						
Goodwill Industries International Inc 15810 Indianola Dr	Rockville	MD	20855	301-530-6500		48-5
TF: 800-741-0197 ■ *Web:* www.goodwill.org						
Goodwill Industries of Akron Ohio Inc, The 570 E Waterloo Rd	Akron	OH	44319	330-724-6995		193
TF: 800-989-8428 ■ *Web:* www.goodwillakron.org						
Goodwill Industries of Central Texas 1015 Norwood Park Blvd	Austin	TX	78753	512-637-7106	637-7400	48-15
TF: 800-735-2989 ■ *Web:* www.goodwillcentraltexas.org						
Goodwill Keystone Area Inc 1150 Goodwill Dr	Harrisburg	PA	17101	717-232-1831		260
TF: 800-432-4483 ■ *Web:* www.yourgoodwill.org						
Goodwill of the East Bay 1301 30th Ave	Oakland	CA	94601	510-698-7200		256
TF: 800-388-2227 ■ *Web:* www.eastbaygoodwill.org						
Goodwin & Associates Hospitality Services LLC 11 S Main St Ste 200	Concord	NH	03301	603-223-0303		393
Web: goodwinhospitality.com						
Goodwin - Lasiter Inc 1609 S Chestnut St Ste 202	Lufkin	TX	75901	936-637-4900		256
Web: glstexas.com						
Goodwin Biotechnology Inc 1850 NW 69th Ave	Plantation	FL	33313	954-327-9656		231
Web: www.goodwinbio.com						
Goodwin Company Inc, The 12102 Industry St	Garden Grove	CA	92841	714-894-0531	894-6293	151
Web: www.goodwininc.com						
Goodwin House 4800 Fillmore Ave	Alexandria	VA	22311	703-578-1000		672
Web: www.goodwinhouse.org						
Goodwin House Bailey's Crossroads 3440 S Jefferson St	Falls Church	VA	22041	703-820-1488		672
TF: 800-451-5121 ■ *Web:* www.goodwinhouse.org						
Goodwin Procter LLP 53 State St	Boston	MA	02210	617-570-1000	523-1231	428
Web: www.goodwinlaw.com						
Goodwood Museum & Gardens 1600 Miccosukee Rd	Tallahassee	FL	32308	850-877-4202	877-3090	520
Web: www.goodwoodmuseum.org						
Goodyear Canada Inc 450 Kipling	Toronto	ON	M8Z5E1	416-201-4300		755
TF: 800-387-3288 ■ *Web:* www.goodyear.ca						
Goodyear Tire & Rubber Co 200 Innovation Way	Akron	OH	44316	330-796-2121	796-2222*	754
NASDAQ: GT ■ **Fax:* Cust Svc ■ *TF Cust Svc:* 800-321-2136 ■ *Web:* www.goodyear.com						
Goody-Goody Liquors Inc 10301 Harry Hines Blvd	Dallas	TX	75220	214-459-9962		443
Web: www.goodygoody.com						
Google Inc 1600 Amphitheatre Pkwy	Mountain View	CA	94043	650-253-0000	253-0001	397
NASDAQ: GOOG ■ *TF:* 800-123-1234 ■ *Web:* www.google.co.in						
Goomzee Corp 4852 Kendrick Pl Ste 1	Missoula	MT	59808	406-542-9955		387
Web: www.goomzee.com						
Goose Creek State Park 2190 Camp Leach Rd	Washington	NC	27889	252-923-2191		565
TF: 877-722-6762 ■ *Web:* www.ncparks.gov						
Goose Egg Inn 10580 Goose Egg Rd	Casper	WY	82604	307-473-8838		671
Goose Island State Park 202 S Palmetto St	Rockport	TX	78382	361-729-2858		565
Web: tpwd.texas.gov/state-parks/goose-island						
Goose Lake Prairie State Natural Area 5010 N Jugtown Rd	Morris	IL	60450	815-942-2899		565
Web: www.dnr.illinois.gov						
Gooseberry Falls State Park 3206 Hwy 61	Two Harbors	MN	55616	218-834-3855	834-3787	565
TF: 888-646-6367 ■ *Web:* www.dnr.state.mn.us/state_parks/gooseberry_falls						
Gooseneck Trailer Mfg Co 4400 E Hwy 21 PO Box 832	Bryan	TX	77808	979-778-0034	778-0615	763
TF Cust Svc: 800-688-5490 ■ *Web:* www.gooseneck.net						
Goosenecks State Park c/o Edge of the Cedars State Park Museum 660 W 400 N	Blanding	UT	84511	435-678-2238		565
Web: stateparks.utah.gov						
Goosepond Mountain State Park 1198 New York 17M Administration Bldg Rt 9 W	Chester	NY	10918	845-786-2701		565
Web: parks.ny.gov/parks/55/details.aspx						
Gootee Construction Inc 2400 N Arnoult Rd	Metairie	LA	70001	504-831-1909		186
TF: 800-321-2424 ■ *Web:* www.gootee.com						
Gopa It Consultants Inc 247 N San Mateo Dr	San Mateo	CA	94401	650-249-3200		196
Web: www.novigo.com						
GOPAC 2300 Clarendon Blvd Ste 1305	Arlington	VA	22201	703-566-0376		615
Web: www.gopac.org						
Gopher Electronics Company Inc 222 Little Canada Rd	Saint Paul	MN	55117	651-490-4900		179
TF: 800-592-9519 ■ *Web:* www.gopherelectronics.com						
Gopher Pattern Works Inc 422 Roosevelt St NE	Minneapolis	MN	55413	612-331-5512		567
Gopher Sign Co 1310 Randolph Ave	Saint Paul	MN	55105	651-698-5095	699-3727	701
TF: 800-383-3156 ■ *Web:* www.gophersign.com						
Gorant Candies 8301 Market St	Youngstown	OH	44512	330-726-8821	726-0325	123
TF: 800-572-4139 ■ *Web:* gorant.com						
Gorat's Steakhouse 4917 Ctr St	Omaha	NE	68106	402-551-3733		671
Web: www.goratsomaha.com						
Gordley Group 2540 N Tucson Blvd	Tucson	AZ	85716	520-327-6077	327-4687	344
Web: www.gordleygroup.com						
Gordman 12100 W Ctr Rd	Omaha	NE	68144	402-691-4000	691-4269	229
TF: 800-743-8730 ■ *Web:* www.gordmans.com						
Gordon & Betty Moore Foundation PO Box 29910	San Francisco	CA	94129	415-561-7700		305
TF: 800-776-0188 ■ *Web:* www.moore.org						
Gordon & Rees LLP 275 Battery St Ste 2000	San Francisco	CA	94111	415-986-5900		41
Web: www.gordonrees.com						
Gordon & Silver Ltd 3960 Howard Hughes Pkwy 9th Fl	Las Vegas	NV	89169	702-796-5555		445
Web: www.gordonsilver.com						
Gordon Aluminum Industries Inc 1000 Mason St	Schofield	WI	54476	715-359-6101		492
Web: www.gordonaluminum.com						
Gordon Brush Mfg Company Inc 3737 Capitol Ave	City of Industry	CA	90601	323-724-7777	724-1111	103
TF: 800-950-7950 ■ *Web:* www.gordonbrush.com						
Gordon C James Public Relations Inc 4715 N 32nd St Ste 104	Phoenix	AZ	85018	602-274-1988		636
Web: www.gcjpr.com						
Gordon College 255 Grapevine Rd	Wenham	MA	01984	978-927-2300	867-4682*	166
**Fax:* Admissions ■ *TF:* 800-343-1379 ■ *Web:* www.gordon.edu						
Gordon Companies Inc 384 Broadway	Albany	NY	12207	518-462-7411		377
Web: www.gordoncompanies.net						
Gordon Composites Inc 2350 Air Park Way	Montrose	CO	81401	970-240-4460		599
Web: www.gordoncomposites.com						
Gordon County 201 N Wall St	Calhoun	GA	30701	706-629-3795	629-9516	338
Web: www.gordoncounty.org						

Phone Fax Class

Gordon County Board of Education
205 Warrior Path PO Box 12001................Calhoun GA 30703 706-629-7366 685
Web: www.gcbe.org
Gordon County Chamber of Commerce
300 S Wall St..............................Calhoun GA 30701 706-625-3200 625-5062 139
Web: www.gordoncountychamber.com
Gordon Ctr for Performing Arts
3506 Gwynnbrook Ave...................Owings Mills MD 21117 410-356-7469 356-7605 572
Web: www.jcc.org
Gordon Energy Solutions LLC
11286 Hadley St........................Overland Park KS 66210 913-451-9539 463
Web: www.gordonenergysolutions.com
Gordon Feinblatt Rothman Hoffberger & Hollander LLC
233 E Redwood St..........................Baltimore MD 21202 410-576-4156 576-4246 428
Web: www.gfrlaw.com
Gordon Flesch Company Inc
2675 Research Pk Dr........................Madison WI 53711 800-677-7877 264-2
TF: 800-333-5905 ■ *Web:* gfcleasing.com
Gordon Glass Co
5116 Warrensville Center Rd............Maple Heights OH 44137 216-663-9830 330
TF: 888-663-9830 ■ *Web:* www.technologylk.com
Gordon L Seaman Inc 29 Old Dock Rd...........Yaphank NY 11980 631-567-8000 194
TF: 800-866-9473 ■ *Web:* www.gordonlseaman.com
Gordon Paper Company Inc PO Box 1806........Norfolk VA 23501 757-464-3581 363-9355 552-2
TF: 800-457-7366 ■ *Web:* www.gordonpaper.com
Gordon Petroleum Inc 950 Holmdel Rd.........Holmdel NJ 07733 732-946-6000 539
Web: www.gordonpetroleum.com
Gordon Ramsay at the London
151 W 54th St...............................New York NY 10019 866-690-2029 671
TF: 866-690-2029 ■ *Web:* www.thelondonnyc.com
Gordon Schanzlin New Vision Institute
8910 University Ctr Ln Ste 800..............San Diego CA 92122 858-455-6800 798
Web: www.gwsvision.com
Gordon Sevig Trucking Co (GSTC)
400 Hwy 151 E.................................Walford IA 52351 319-846-5500 846-5541 685
Web: www.gstcinc.com
Gordon Sign 2930 W Ninth Ave.................Denver CO 80204 303-629-6121 701
Web: www.gordonsign.com
Gordon Stockman & Waugh PC
8726 Industrial Rd...........................Peoria IL 61615 309-692-4030 692-4159 2
Web: gswcpa.com
Gordon Terminal Service Co
1000 Ella St.........................Mckees Rocks PA 15136 412-331-9410 541
Web: www.gtscofpa.com
Gordon Thomas Honeywell LLP
1201 Pacific Ave Ste 2100.....................Tacoma WA 98402 253-620-6500 620-6565 428
Web: www.gth-law.com
Gordon, Fournaris & Mammarella PA
1925 Lovering Ave.......................Wilmington DE 19806 302-652-2900 428
Web: gfmlaw.com
Gordon-Conwell Theological Seminary
130 Essex St........................South Hamilton MA 01982 978-468-7111 468-6691 167-3
TF: 800-428-7329 ■ *Web:* www.gordonconwell.edu
Gordon-Darby Inc 2410 Ampere Dr.............Louisville KY 40299 502-266-5797 407
Web: www.gordon-darby.com
Gordonderr Llp 2025 First Ave Ste 500...........Seattle WA 98121 206-382-9540 445
Web: www.gordonderr.com
Gordon-Lee Mansion 217 Cove Rd.........Chickamauga GA 30707 706-375-4728 50-3
Web: leeandgordonsmills.com
Gordons Specialties Inc
720 W Wintergreen Rd........................Hutchins TX 75141 972-225-1660 697
TF: 800-626-4653 ■ *Web:* www.gsihighway.com
Gordys County Market Downtown
212 Bay St..........................Chippewa Falls WI 54729 715-726-2500 345
Web: www.gordysinc.com
Gore Design Completions Ltd
2060 Eagle Pkwy............................Fort Worth TX 76177 210-496-5614 57
Web: www.gdctechnics.com
Gores Technology Group
9800 Wilshire Blvd......................Beverly Hills CA 90212 310-209-3010 209-3310 405
Web: www.gores.com
Gorfaine/Schwartz Agency
4111 W Alameda Ave Ste 509.................Burbank CA 91505 818-260-8500 731
Web: www.gsamusic.com
Gorfine Schiller & Gardyn PA
10045 Red Run Blvd Ste 250..............Owings Mills MD 21117 410-356-5900 2
Gorges Motor Company Inc
2660 S Oliver St.............................Wichita KS 67210 316-265-6400 57
Gorges State Park
976 Grassy Ridge Rd........................Sapphire NC 28774 828-966-9099 565
TF: 800-277-9611 ■ *Web:* www.ncparks.gov
Gorham Savings Bank 64 Main St..............Gorham ME 04038 207-839-4450 839-4790 70
Web: www.gorhamsavingsbank.com
Gorilla Capital Inc 1342 High St...............Eugene OR 97401 541-344-7867 652
Web: www.gorillacapital.com
Gorilla Marketing
4100 Flat Rock Dr Ste A....................Riverside CA 92505 951-353-8133 195
Web: www.gorillamarketing.net
Gorman & Assoc PC Certifi
1825 Franklin St Ste B..................Northampton PA 18067 610-262-1280 2
Web: www.gaapc.com
Gorman's 29145 Telegraph Rd................Southfield MI 48034 248-353-9880 321
Web: www.gormans.com
Gorman-Rupp Co
PO Box 1217 PO Box 1217..................Mansfield OH 44901 419-755-1011 641
NYSE: GRC ■ *Web:* www.gormanrupp.com
Gorman-Rupp Industries
180 Hines Ave...............................Bellville OH 44813 419-886-3001 886-2338 641
TF: 800-833-4882 ■ *Web:* www.gripumps.com
Gorrie Marketing Services
2770 Matheson Blvd E..................Mississauga ON L4W4M5 416-760-9100 7
Web: www.gorrie.com
Gorton Studios
4640 Nicols Rd Ste 205....................Saint Paul MN 55122 651-365-7891 177
TF: 800-845-0787 ■ *Web:* gortonstudios.com
Gorton's Inc 128 Rogers St................Gloucester MA 01930 978-283-3000 296-14
TF: 800-222-6846 ■ *Web:* www.gortons.com

Gosar Paul A (Rep R - AZ)
2057 Rayburn HOB.......................Washington DC 20515 202-225-2315 342-2
Web: gosar.house.gov
Gosar Paul A (Rep R - AZ)
1626 Longworth HOB.....................Washington DC 20515 202-225-2635 342-2
Web: biggs.house.gov
Goschie Farms Inc
7365 Meridian Rd NE......................Silverton OR 97381 503-873-5638 10-6
Web: goschiefarms.com
Goshen Chamber of Commerce
232 S Main St...............................Goshen IN 46526 574-533-2102 533-2103 139
TF: 800-307-4204 ■ *Web:* www.goshen.org
Goshen College 1700 S Main St................Goshen IN 46526 574-535-7000 535-7609* 166
*Fax: Admissions ■ *TF:* 800-348-7422 ■ *Web:* www.goshen.edu
Goshen County
2125 E A St Ste 37 PO Box 160.............Torrington WY 82240 307-532-4051 532-7375 338
Web: www.goshencounty.org
Goshen County School District 1
626 W 25th Ave...........................Torrington WY 82240 307-532-2171 532-7085 685
Web: www.goshen.k12.wy.us
Goshen Historic Track Inc 44 Pk Pl............Goshen NY 10924 845-294-5333 294-3998 642
Web: www.goshenhistorictrack.com
Goshen News 114 S Main St PO Box 569.........Goshen IN 46527 574-533-2151 534-8830 532-2
TF: 800-487-2151 ■ *Web:* www.goshennews.com
Gosiger Inc 108 McDonough St.................Dayton OH 45402 937-228-5174 228-5189 385
TF: 877-288-1538 ■ *Web:* www.gosiger.com
GoSolo Technologies Inc
5410 Mariner St Ste 175.......................Tampa FL 33609 866-246-7656 617
TF: 866-246-7656 ■ *Web:* www.teamgosolo.com
GOSPEL 1590 AM 11131 Colorado Ave........Kansas City MO 64137 816-763-2040 645-83
Web: www.kprt.com
Gospel Light Publications
1957 Eastman Ave..........................Ventura CA 93003 805-644-9721 637-3
TF: 800-446-7735 ■ *Web:* www.gospellight.com
Gospel Music Assn (GMA)
741 Cool Springs Blvd......................Franklin TN 37067 615-242-0303 254-9755 48-4
TF: 800-846-8499 ■ *Web:* www.gospelmusic.org
Gospel Publishing House
1445 N Boonville Ave.....................Springfield MO 65802 417-862-2781 626
TF Orders: 800-641-4310 ■ *Web:* www.gospelpublishing.com
Gosper County 507 Smith Ave PO Box 136.........Elwood NE 68937 308-785-2611 785-2300 338
Goss & DeLeeuw Machine Co
100 Harding St...........................Kensington CT 06037 860-828-4121 493
Web: goss-deleeuw.com
Goss Inc 1511 William Flynn Hwy.............Glenshaw PA 15116 412-486-6100 486-6844 811
TF: 800-367-4677 ■ *Web:* www.gossonline.com
Goss International 121 Technology Dr...........Durham NH 03824 603-750-6600 750-6860 629
Web: www.gossinternational.com
Gossen /Corp 2030 W Bender Rd.............Milwaukee WI 53209 414-228-9800 228-9077 191-2
TF: 800-558-8984 ■ *Web:* www.gossencorp.com
Gossner Foods Inc 1051 N 1000 W..............Logan UT 84321 435-227-2500 227-2550 296-5
TF: 800-944-0454 ■ *Web:* www.gossner.com
Gotco International
11410 Spring Cypress Rd.....................Tomball TX 77377 281-376-3784 537
Web: www.gotco-usa.com
GotData.com Inc
25431 Cabot Rd Ste 202..................Laguna Hills CA 92653 949-716-7500 269-9161 809
Gotech Inc 8383 Bluebonnet Blvd...........Baton Rouge LA 70810 225-766-5358 256
Web: www.gotech-inc.com
Goten Japanese Steak & Sushi Bar
1719 W End Ave Ste 101W...................Nashville TN 37203 615-321-4537 671
Gotham Bar & Grill 12 E 12th St..............New York NY 10003 212-620-4020 671
TF: 800-592-3295 ■ *Web:* www.gothambarandgrill.com
Gotham Distributing Corp
60 Portland Rd........................Conshohocken PA 19428 610-649-7650 649-0315 523
TF: 800-446-8426 ■ *Web:* oldies.com
Gotham Growth Group 301 Tory Turn.............Wayne PA 19087 484-433-9806 42
Web: www.gothamgrowth.com
Gotham Sales Co 302 Main St.................Millburn NJ 07041 973-912-8412 38
Web: www.gothamsales.com
Gotham Steakhouse & Cocktail Bar
615 Seymour St..........................Vancouver BC V6B3K3 604-605-8282 671
Web: www.gothamsteakhouse.com
Gotham Technology Group LLC
1 Paragon Dr Ste 200......................Montvale NJ 07645 201-474-4200 174
Web: www.gothamtg.com
Gothic Cabinet Craft Inc 5877 57th St..........Maspeth NY 11378 347-881-1458 321
Web: www.gothiccabinetcraft.com
GotPrint 7651 N San Fernando Rd...............Burbank CA 91505 818-252-3000 781
TF: 877-922-7374 ■ *Web:* gotprint.com
Gottheimer Josh (Rep D - NJ)
213 Cannon HOB..........................Washington DC 20515 202-225-4465 225-9048 342-2
Web: gottheimer.house.gov
Gottlieb Bros Inc 55 E Washington.............Chicago IL 60602 312-609-2222 411
Gottlieb Flekier & Company PA
12721 Metcalf Ave Ste 201..............Overland Park KS 66213 913-491-6655 2
Web: gfccpa.com
Gottlieb Martin & Associates Inc
4932 Sunbeam Rd........................Jacksonville FL 32257 904-346-3088 463
TF: 800-833-9986 ■ *Web:* www.gottlieb.com
Gottlieb Memorial Hospital
701 W N Ave...........................Melrose Park IL 60160 708-681-3200 374-3
TF: 800-424-4840 ■ *Web:* www.gottliebhospital.org
Gottsch Feeding Corp
20507 Nicholas Cir Ste 100..................Elkhorn NE 68022 402-463-6215 10-1
Web: gottschcattlecompany.com
Gottscho Printing Systems Inc
740 Veterans Cir.........................Warminster PA 18974 267-387-3005 387-3015 547
Web: www.gottscho.com
Goucher College 1021 Dulaney Valley Rd.........Towson MD 21204 410-337-6000 337-6354* 166
*Fax: Admissions ■ *TF:* 800-468-2437 ■ *Web:* www.goucher.edu
Gough Financial Group Inc
9415 E Harry St Ste 602.....................Wichita KS 67207 316-683-8400 251
Web: www.gfgks.com
Gougler Industries 705 Lake St..................Kent OH 44240 330-673-5821 454
Web: www.gougler.com
Gougler Industries Inc 711 Lake St...............Kent OH 44240 330-673-5826 677-1616 386
TF: 800-527-2282 ■ *Web:* www.frdusa.com

Phone | Fax | Class

Gould & Goodrich Leather Inc
709 E McNeil St Lillington NC 27546 910-893-2071 893-4742 431
TF: 800-277-0732 ■ *Web:* www.gouldusa.com

Gould & Ratner 222 N LaSalle Ste 800 Chicago IL 60601 312-236-3003 41
Web: www.gouldratner.com

Gould Academy PO Box 860 Bethel ME 04217 207-824-7777 622
Web: www.gouldacademy.org

Gould Asset Management LLC
341 W First St Ste 200 Claremont CA 91711 909-445-1291 401
Web: www.gouldasset.com

Gould Electronics Inc
2929 W Chandler Blvd Chandler AZ 85224 480-899-0343 295

Gould Evans International
4041 Mill St Kansas City MO 64111 816-931-6655 261
Web: www.gouldevans.com

Gould Investors LP
60 Cutter Mill Rd Ste 303 Great Neck NY 11021 516-466-3100 405
Web: gouldlp.com

Gould Technology LLC
1121 Benfield Blvd Stes J-P Millersville MD 21108 410-987-5600 544
TF: 800-544-6853 ■ *Web:* www.gouldfo.com

Gould's Styling Salons
2760 N Germantown Pkwy Ste 197 Memphis TN 38133 901-386-5101 77
Web: gouldsalonspa.com

Goulds Pumps Inc Goulds Water Technologies Group
240 Fall St Seneca Falls NY 13148 315-568-2811 568-2418 789
TF: 800-327-7700 ■ *Web:* www.gouldspumps.com

Gouldsboro State Park
c/o Tobyhanna State Pk 114 Campground Rd Tobyhanna PA 18466 570-894-8336 565
Web: www.dcnr.state.pa.us

Goulston & Storrs 400 Atlantic Ave Boston MA 02110 617-482-1776 428
Web: www.goulstonstorrs.com

Goulston Technologies Inc
700 N Johnson St Monroe NC 28110 704-289-6464 296-6400 145
Web: www.goulston.com

Gourmet Settings Inc
245 W Beaver Creek Rd Ste 10 Richmond Hill ON L4B1L1 905-707-0336 361
Web: www.gourmetsettings.com

GourmetSpot
StartSport Mediaworks Inc 1840 Oak Ave Evanston IL 60201 847-866-1830 866-1880 397
Web: gourmetspot.com

Gouverneur Correctional Facility
112 Scotch Settlement Rd Gouverneur NY 13642 315-287-7351 213

Gouverneur Hotel Montreal (Place-Dupuis)
1000 Sherbrooke St W Ste 2300 Montreal QC H3A3R3 888-910-1111 379
TF: 888-910-1111 ■ *Web:* www.gouverneur.com

Govconnection Inc 7503 Standish Pl Rockville MD 20855 800-998-0009 423-6192* 179
**Fax Area Code:* 603 ■ *TF:* 800-998-0009 ■ *Web:* www.govconnection.com

Gove County
520 Washington St Ste 105 PO Box 128 Gove KS 67736 785-938-2300 938-4486 338
Web: www.govecountyks.com/county-clerk

Gove Group Real Estate LLC
70 Portsmouth Ave Stratham NH 03885 603-778-6400 652
TF: 866-778-6400 ■ *Web:* www.thegovegroup.com

Governair Corp
4841 N Sewell Ave Oklahoma City OK 73118 405-525-6546 14
Web: governair.com

Governing Magazine
1100 Connecticut Ave NW Ste 1300 Washington DC 20036 202-862-8802 457-12
TF: 800-940-6039 ■ *Web:* www.governing.com

Government Accountability Office (GAO)
441 G St NW Washington DC 20548 202-512-4800 342
Web: www.gao.gov
Atlanta Office
2635 Century Pkwy Ste 700 Atlanta GA 30345 404-679-1900 679-1819 342
Web: www.gao.gov
Boston Office 10 Cswy St Rm 575 Boston MA 02222 617-788-0500 788-0505 342
Web: www.gao.gov
Dallas Office 1999 Bryan St Ste 2200 Dallas TX 75201 214-777-5600 777-5758 342
Web: www.gao.gov
Dayton Office
2196 D St Area B Bldg 39 Wright-Patterson AFB OH 45433 937-258-7900 258-7118 342
Web: www.gao.gov
Denver Office 1244 Speer Blvd Ste 800 Denver CO 80204 303-572-7306 572-7433 342
Web: www.gao.gov
Huntsville Office
6767 Old Madison Pike Bldg 5 Ste 520 Huntsville AL 35806 256-922-7500 971-9240 342
Web: www.gao.gov
Los Angeles Office
350 S Figueroa St Ste 1010 Los Angeles CA 90071 213-830-1000 830-1180 342
TF: 800-772-1213 ■ *Web:* www.gao.gov
Norfolk Office
5029 Corporate Woods Dr Ste 300 Virginia Beach VA 23462 757-552-8100 552-8197 342
Web: www.gao.gov
San Francisco Office
301 Howard St Ste 1200 San Francisco CA 94105 415-904-2000 904-2111 342
Web: www.gao.gov
Seattle Office 701 Fifth Ave Ste 2700 Seattle WA 98104 206-287-4800 287-4872 342
Web: www.gao.gov

Government Canyon State Natural Area
12861 Galm Rd San Antonio TX 78254 210-688-9055 565
Web: tpwd.texas.gov

Government Contracting Resources Inc
315 Page Rd PO Box 7 Pinehurst NC 28374 910-215-1900 549
Web: www.gcrinc.net

Government Employee Relations Report
1801 S Bell St Arlington VA 22202 800-372-1033 531-2
TF: 800-372-1033 ■
Web: www.bna.com/government-employee-relations-p5468

Government Finance Officers Assn (GFOA)
203 N LaSalle St Ste 2700 Chicago IL 60601 312-977-9700 977-4806 49-7
Web: www.gfoa.org

Government Island State Recreation Area
7005 NE Marine Dr Portland OR 97218 503-281-0944 565
TF: 800-551-6949 ■ *Web:* www.oregonstateparks.org/park_250.php

Government Liaison Services Inc (GLS)
200 N Glebe Rd Ste 321 Arlington VA 22203 703-524-8200 525-8451 635
TF: 800-642-6564 ■ *Web:* www.trademarkinfo.com

Government National Mortgage Assn
451 Seventh St SW Rm B-133 Washington DC 20410 202-708-1535 509
TF: 800-234-4662 ■ *Web:* www.ginniemae.gov

Government Research Service
1516 SW Boswell Ave Topeka KS 66604 785-232-7720 232-1615 637-2
TF: 800-346-6898 ■ *Web:* statelegislativesourcebook.com

Government Systems Technologies Inc
3159 Schrader Rd Dover NJ 07801 973-361-2627 177
TF: 800-573-1874 ■ *Web:* www.gstiusa.com

Governor Calvert House 58 State Cir Annapolis MD 21401 410-263-2641 268-3613 379
TF: 800-847-8882 ■ *Web:* www.historicinnsofannapolis.com

Governor Control Systems Inc
3101 SW Third Ave Fort Lauderdale FL 33315 954-462-7404 407
Web: www.govconsys.com

Governor Daniel Dunklin's Grave State Historic Site
104 Dunklin Dr Herculaneum MO 63048 800-334-6946 565
TF: 800-334-6946 ■ *Web:* www.mostateparks.com

Governor Dodge State Park
4175 State Hwy 23 N Dodgeville WI 53533 608-935-2315 565
Web: dnr.wi.gov

Governor Dummer Academy 1 Elm St Byfield MA 01922 978-499-3120 462-1278 622
Web: www.thegovernorsacademy.org

Governor Henry Lippitt House Museum
199 Hope St Providence RI 02906 401-453-0688 520
Web: preserveri.org

Governor Knowles State Forest
325 SR 70 Grantsburg WI 54840 715-463-2898 565
Web: dnr.wi.gov/newurl.html

Governor Nelson State Park
5140 County Hwy M Waunakee WI 53597 608-831-3005 565
Web: www.dnr.wi.gov

Governor Patterson Memorial State Recreation Site
5580 S Coast Hwy 5580 S Coast Hwy Waldport OR 97394 800-551-6949 565
TF: 800-551-6949 ■ *Web:* www.oregonstateparks.org

Governor Thompson State Park
N10008 Paust Ln Crivitz WI 54114 715-757-3979 565
TF: 800-986-2267 ■ *Web:* www.dnr.wi.gov

Governor Wentworth Historic Site
Rt 109 Wolfeboro NH 03894 603-823-7722 565
Web: www.nhstateparks.org

Governor's Inn 700 W Sioux Ave Pierre SD 57501 605-224-4200 379
TF General: 877-523-0080 ■ *Web:* www.govinn.com

Governor's Inn 210 Richards Blvd Sacramento CA 95811 916-448-7224 448-7382 379
TF: 800-999-6689 ■ *Web:* www.governorsinnhotel.com

Governor's Mansion State Historic Park
1526 H St Sacramento CA 95814 916-323-3047 565
Web: www.parks.ca.gov

Governor's Square
1500 Apalachee Pkwy Tallahassee FL 32301 850-877-8106 460
Web: www.governorssquare.com

Governors America Corp 720 Silver St Agawam MA 01001 413-786-5600 203
Web: www.governors-america.com

Governors Inn 209 S Adams St Tallahassee FL 32301 850-681-6855 222-3105 379
Web: thegovinn.org

Governors State University
1 University Pkwy University Park IL 60484 708-534-5000 534-1640* 166
**Fax:* Admissions ■ *TF:* 800-478-8478 ■ *Web:* www.govst.edu

Govind Development LLC
9359 IH 37 Ste A Corpus Christi TX 78409 361-241-2777 256
TF: 800-456-2009 ■ *Web:* www.govinddevelopment.com

Gow School 2491 Emery Rd PO Box 85 South Wales NY 14139 716-652-3450 652-3457 622
Web: www.gow.org

Gowan Company LLC PO Box 5569 Yuma AZ 85366 928-783-8844 276
TF: 800-883-1844 ■ *Web:* www.gowanco.com

Gowan Construction Inc PO Box 228 Oslo MN 56744 701-699-5171 699-3400 188-4
Web: www.gowanconstruction.com

Gowan Inc 5550 Airline Dr Houston TX 77076 713-696-5400 695-1726 189-10
TF: 800-800-5615 ■ *Web:* www.gowaninc.com

Gowanda Correctional Facility
S Rd PO Box 350 Gowanda NY 14070 716-532-0177 213
Web: www.doccs.ny.gov

Gowans-Knight Co Inc 49 Knight St Watertown CT 06795 860-274-8801 274-7937 516
TF: 800-352-4871 ■ *Web:* www.gowansknight.com

Goway Travel Ltd 3284 Yonge St Ste 300 Toronto ON M4N3M7 416-322-1034 772
TF: 800-665-4432 ■ *Web:* www.goway.com

Gowdy Trey (Rep R - SC)
2418 Rayburn HOB Washington DC 20515 202-225-6030 226-1177 342-2
Web: gowdy.house.gov

Gower Corp 355 Woodruff Rd Greenville SC 29607 864-234-4829 360-3
Web: www.gower.co.uk

Gowling WLG
100 King St W 1 First Canadian Pl Ste 1600 Toronto ON M5X1G5 416-862-7525 862-7661 41
Web: www.gowlings.com

Goyette & Associates Inc
2366 Gold Meadow Way Ste 200 Gold River CA 95670 916-851-1900 428
TF: 888-993-1600 ■ *Web:* goyetteassociates.com

Goyette Mechanical Co 3842 Gorey Ave Flint MI 48501 810-743-6883 743-9090 189-10
TF: 877-469-3883 ■ *Web:* www.goyettemechanical.com

GP Harmon Recycling LLC
2 Jericho Plaza Ste 110 Jericho NY 11753 516-997-3400 661
Web: www.eharmongp.com

GP Solutions Inc
201 N Charles St Ste 2406 Baltimore MD 21201 410-244-8548 177
Web: www.gpsonline.com

GP Strategies Corp
11000 Broken Land Pkwy Ste 200 Columbia MD 21044 443-367-9600 180
TF: 888-843-4784 ■ *Web:* www.gpstrategies.com

GPA (Gas Processors Assn) 6526 E 60th St Tulsa OK 74145 918-493-3872 493-3875 48-12
Web: www.gpaglobal.org

Gpa Specialty Printable Sbstrt
8740 W 50th St McCook IL 60525 773-650-2020 395-3581* 553
**Fax Area Code:* 800 ■ *TF:* 800-395-9000 ■ *Web:* www.askgpa.com

GPA Technologies Inc
2368 Eastman Ave Ste 8 Ventura CA 93003 805-643-7878 643-7474 256
Web: www.gpatech.com

GPAC (Germantown Performing Arts Centre)
1801 Exeter Rd Germantown TN 38138 901-751-7500 572
Web: www.gpacweb.com

Phone | Fax | Class

GPB (Georgia Public Broadcasting)
260 14th St NW Atlanta GA 30318 800-222-6006 632
TF: 800-222-6006 ■ *Web:* www.gpb.org

GPB (Gamma Phi Beta International Sorority)
12737 E Euclid Dr Centennial CO 80111 303-799-1874 799-1876 48-16
TF: 800-526-1870 ■ *Web:* www.gammaphibeta.org

GPB Education 260 14th St NW Atlanta GA 30318 404-685-2550 685-2556 632
TF: 888-501-8960 ■ *Web:* www.gpb.org

GPC Systems Inc 2108B Gallows Rd Vienna VA 22182 703-760-9700 177

GPCCVB (Greenville-Pitt County Convention & Visitors Bureau)
417 Cotanche St Ste 100 Greenville NC 27858 252-329-4200 329-4205 206
TF: 800-537-5564 ■ *Web:* www.visitgreenvillenc.com

GPD Group 520 S Main St Ste 2531 Akron OH 44311 330-572-2100 261
Web: www.gpdgroup.com

GPhA (Georgia Pharmacy Assn)
50 Lenox Pointe NE Atlanta GA 30324 404-231-5074 237-8435 585
TF: 888-871-5590 ■ *Web:* www.gpha.org

GPI (Glass Packaging Institute)
700 N Fairfax St Ste 510 Alexandria VA 22314 703-684-6359 299-1543 49-13
TF: 800-949-8305 ■ *Web:* www.gpi.org

GPK Products Inc 1601 43rd St NW Fargo ND 58102 701-277-3225 277-9286 608
TF: 800-437-4670 ■ *Web:* www.gpk-fargo.com

GPM Inc 4432 Venture Ave Duluth MN 55811 218-722-9904 358
Web: virginiachamber.com

GPM Investments LLC
8565 Magellan Pkwy Ste 400 Richmond VA 23227 804-730-1568 345
Web: gpminvestments.com

GPO (US Government Printing Office Bookstore)
732 N Capitol St NW Washington DC 20401 202-512-1800 512-2104 342
TF: 866-512-1800 ■ *Web:* bookstore.gpo.gov

GPS Insight LLC
21803 N Scottsdale Rd Ste 220 Scottsdale AZ 85255 480-663-9454 177
Web: www.gpsinsight.com

GPSA (Gas Processors Suppliers Assn)
6526 E 60th St Tulsa OK 74145 918-493-3872 48-12
Web: www.gpaglobal.org

GPShopper LLC 584 Broadway Ste 904 New York NY 10012 212-488-2222 736
TF: 800-696-6474 ■ *Web:* www.gpshopper.com

GPSi LLC 25307 Dequindre Rd Madison Heights MI 48071 248-399-4731 647
Web: www.guidepointsystems.com

GR Sponaugle & Sons Inc
4391 Chambers Hill Rd Harrisburg PA 17111 717-564-1515 564-3675 189-10
TF: 800-868-9353 ■ *Web:* www.grsponaugle.com

GRA Inc 2317 Falling Creek Rd Silver Spring MD 20904 301-989-9659 260-1444* 193
**Fax Area Code:* 240

GRAA (Greater Rockford Auto Auction Inc)
5937 Sandy Hollow Rd Rockford IL 61109 815-874-7800 874-1325 51
TF: 800-830-4722 ■ *Web:* www.graa.net

Grabar Voice and Data Inc
101 Slate Dr Ste 4 Bismarck ND 58503 701-258-3528 250-8850 525
TF: 888-239-1311 ■ *Web:* www.grabarvoice.com

Grabber Construction Products Inc
20 W Main St Ct Ste 200 Alpine UT 84004 925-680-0777 350
Web: www.grabberman.com

Graber Olive House Inc
315 E Fourth St Ontario CA 91764 800-996-5483 984-2180* 336
**Fax Area Code:* 909 ■ *TF:* 800-996-5483 ■ *Web:* www.graberolives.com

Grabill Cabinet Company Inc
13844 Sawmill Dr Grabill IN 46741 877-472-2782 115
TF: 877-472-2782 ■ *Web:* www.grabillcabinets.com

Grace & Wild Inc
23689 Industrial Park Dr Farmington Hills MI 48335 248-471-6010 33
TF: 800-381-7542 ■ *Web:* www.ringsidecreative.com

Grace A Dow Memorial Library
1710 W St Andrews Rd Midland MI 48640 989-837-3430 837-3468 434-3
TF: 800-422-5245 ■ *Web:* cityofmidlandmi.gov

Grace Bible College
1011 Aldon St SW PO Box 910 Grand Rapids MI 49509 616-538-2330 538-0599 161
TF: 800-968-1887 ■ *Web:* www.gbcol.edu

Grace Church 802 Broadway New York NY 10003 212-254-2000 48-20
Web: www.gracechurchnyc.org

Grace College 200 Seminary Dr Winona Lake IN 46590 574-372-5100 372-5120* 166
**Fax:* Admissions ■ *TF:* 800-544-7223 ■ *Web:* www.grace.edu

Grace College & Theological Seminary
200 Seminary Dr Winona Lake IN 46590 574-372-5100 167-3
TF: 800-544-7223 ■ *Web:* gts.grace.edu

Grace Communion International
PO Box 5005 Glendora CA 91740 626-650-2300 637-9
TF: 800-423-4444 ■ *Web:* www.gci.org

Grace Creek Media Inc
100 Cathedral St Ste 9 Annapolis MD 21401 410-280-8528 514
Web: www.gracecreek.com

Grace Davison 7500 Grace Dr Columbia MD 21044 410-531-4000 531-4197 145
TF: 800-638-6014 ■ *Web:* www.grace.com

Grace Episcopal Church
33 Church St White Plains NY 10601 914-949-2874 48-20
Web: www.gracecommunitycenter.org

Grace Financial Group LLC
83 Jobs Ln Southampton NY 11968 631-287-4633 690
Web: www.gracefg.com

Grace General Hospital 300 Booth Dr Winnipeg MB R3J3M7 204-837-0111 831-0029 374-2
Web: www.gracehospital.ca

Grace Hospice 6400 S Lewis Ave Ste 1000 Tulsa OK 74136 918-744-7223 371
TF: 800-659-0307 ■ *Web:* www.gracehospice.com

Grace Hospital 2201 S Sterling St Morganton NC 28655 828-580-5000 374-3
TF: 800-624-3004 ■ *Web:* www.blueridgehealth.org/grace-hospital.html

Grace Manufacturing Inc
614 SR 247 Russellville AR 72802 479-968-5455 295
Web: www.gracemfg.com

Grace Marketing Co
Mount Vernon Sq Bldg 6700 Beta Dr
3rd Fl Mayfield Village OH 44143 440-442-7000 442-7005 195
Web: www.gracemarketingco.com

Grace Museum 102 Cypress St Abilene TX 79601 325-673-4587 675-5993 520
TF: 800-283-8904 ■ *Web:* www.thegracemuseum.org

Grace Place Wellness Ministries
10733 Sunset Office Dr Ste 263 Saint Louis MO 63127 314-842-3077 842-3099 48-20
Web: graceplacewellness.org

Grace Plaza of Great Neck Inc
15 St Paul's Pl Great Neck NY 11021 516-466-3001 450
Web: www.graceplaza.com

Grace Presbyterian Village
550 E Ann Arbor Ave Dallas TX 75216 214-376-1701 672
Web: www.gracepresvillage.org

Grace To You 28001 Harrison Pkwy Valencia CA 91355 661-295-5777 116
Web: gty.org

Grace University 1311 S Ninth St Omaha NE 68108 402-449-2800 341-9587 161
TF: 800-383-1422 ■ *Web:* www.graceuniversity.edu

Graceland (Elvis Presley Mansion)
3734 Elvis Presley Blvd Memphis TN 38116 901-332-3322 520
TF: 800-238-2000 ■ *Web:* www.graceland.com

Graceland Fruit Inc 1123 Main St Frankfort MI 49635 231-352-7181 352-4711 296-18
TF: 800-352-7181 ■ *Web:* www.gracelandfruit.com

Graceland University 1 University Pl Lamoni IA 50140 641-784-5000 784-5480* 166
**Fax:* Admissions ■ *TF:* 800-859-1215 ■ *Web:* www.graceland.edu

Graceland University Independence
1401 W Truman Rd Independence MO 64050 816-833-0524 833-2990* 166
**Fax:* Admissions ■ *TF:* 800-833-0524 ■ *Web:* www.graceland.edu

Graceway Pharmaceuticals LLC
340 Martin Luther King Junior Blvd Ste 500 Bristol TN 37620 423-274-2100 274-2199 231

Graceworks Church Inc
16131 Hwy 44 Prairieville LA 70769 225-622-7805 48-20

Graceworks Lutheran Services
6430 Inner Mission Way Dayton OH 45459 937-433-2140 371
Web: www.graceworks.org

Gracie Films
10201 W Pico Blvd Bldg 41/42 Los Angeles CA 90064 310-369-7222 514
Web: www.graciefilms.com

Gracie Mansion 88th St & E End Ave New York NY 10128 212-570-4751 50-3
Web: www.nyc.gov/html/om/html/gracie.html

Gracies Contemporary Bistro
151 S Putnam St Williamston MI 48895 517-655-1100 671
Web: www.graciesplacewilliamston.com

Gracious Home 1220 Third Ave New York NY 10021 212-517-6300 362
TF: 800-338-7809 ■ *Web:* www.gracioushome.com

Gracious Living Corp
7200 Martin Grove Rd Woodbridge ON L4L9J3 905-264-5660 321
TF: 800-465-5660 ■ *Web:* www.graciousliving.com

Gracious Living Innovations Inc
151 Courtney Park Dr W Mississauga ON L5W1Y5 905-795-5505 795-5523 601
TF: 800-251-9566 ■ *Web:* www.glinnov.com

Graco Inc
88 11th Ave NE PO Box 1441 Minneapolis MN 55413 612-623-6000 623-6777* 641
NYSE: GGG ■ **Fax:* Hum Res ■ *TF Cust Svc:* 800-328-0211 ■ *Web:* www.graco.com

Graco Supply Co 1001 Miller Ave Fort Worth TX 76105 817-535-3200 21
Web: www.gracosupply.com

Gradall Industries Inc
406 Mill Ave SW New Philadelphia OH 44663 330-339-2211 339-8468 190
TF: 800-382-8302 ■ *Web:* www.gradall.com

Gradco USA Inc
871 Coronado Ctr Dr Ste 200 Henderson NV 89052 702-940-2266 111
Web: www.gradco.com

Grade A 9 Slack Rd Ste 200 Ottawa ON K2G0B7 613-721-3331 196
Web: www.gradea.ca

Grade A Markets Inc 563 Newfield Ave Stamford CT 06905 203-356-1662 961-8135 345
Web: shoprite.com

Grade Finders Inc PO Box 944 Exton PA 19341 610-524-7070 269-7077 637-2
TF: 800-777-8074 ■ *Web:* www.gradefinders.com

Gradient Corp 20 University Rd Cambridge MA 02138 617-395-5000 395-5001 194
Web: www.gradientcorp.com

Graduate Institute of Applied Linguistics Inc
7500 W Camp Wisdom Rd Dallas TX 75236 972-708-7340 166
Web: www.gial.edu

Graduate Management Admission Council (GMAC)
11921 Freedom Dr Ste 300 Reston VA 20190 703-668-9600 668-9601 48-11
TF: 866-505-6559 ■ *Web:* www.gmac.com

Graduate Theological Union
2400 Ridge Rd Berkeley CA 94709 510-649-2400 649-1730 167-3
TF: 800-826-4488 ■ *Web:* www.gtu.edu

Grady County 250 N Broad St Cairo GA 39828 229-377-1512 377-1039 338
Web: www.gradycountyga.gov

Grady County 326 Choctaw St Chickasha OK 73018 405-224-7388 222-4506 338
Web: www.gradycountyok.com

Grady Electric Membership Corp (EMC)
1499 US Hwy 84 W Cairo GA 39828 229-377-4182 245
TF: 877-757-6060 ■ *Web:* www.gradyemc.com

Grady Gammage Memorial Auditorium
1200 S Forest Ave Tempe AZ 85281 480-965-3434 965-3583 572
TF: 800-283-6734 ■ *Web:* www.asugammage.com

Grady Health System
80 Jesse Hill Jr Dr SE Atlanta GA 30303 404-616-1000 374-3
Web: www.gradyhealth.org

Grady Management Inc
8630 Fenton St Ste 625 Silver Spring MD 20910 301-587-3330 655
Web: www.gradymgt.com

Grady Memorial Hospital
2220 Iowa Ave Chickasha OK 73018 405-224-2300 779-2413 374-3
TF: 800-299-9665 ■ *Web:* www.gradymem.org

Grady-White Boats Inc
5121 Martin Luther King Jr Hwy Greenville NC 27834 252-752-2111 90
Web: www.gradywhite.com

Graebel Van Lines Inc
16346 Airport Cir Aurora CO 80011 303-214-6683 519
TF: 800-723-6683 ■ *Web:* www.graebel.com

Grae-Con Construction Inc
PO Box 1778 Steubenville OH 43952 740-282-6830 186
Web: www.graecon.com

GRAEF-USA Inc 125 S 84th St Ste 401 Milwaukee WI 53214 414-259-1500 259-0037 261
Web: graef-usa.com

Graeter's Inc 2145 Reading Rd Cincinnati OH 45202 513-721-3323 296-25
TF: 800-721-3323 ■ *Web:* www.graeters.com

Graf & Sons 4050 S Clark St Mexico MO 65265 573-581-2266 711
TF: 800-531-2666 ■ *Web:* www.grafs.com

Graff Californiawear
1515 E 15th St Los Angeles CA 90021 213-749-0171 155-21

Name / Address	City	State	Zip	Phone	Fax	Class
Graff Truck Centers Inc 1401 S Saginaw St *TF:* 888-870-4203 ■ *Web:* www.grafftruckcenter.com	Flint	MI	48503	810-239-8300	239-8561	57
Graffiti's Italian Restaurant 7811 Cantrell Rd *Web:* littlerockgraffitis.net	Little Rock	AR	72227	501-224-9079		671
Grafico Inc 15320 Cornet Ave *Web:* www.grafico.com	Santa Fe Springs	CA	90670	562-921-6731		627
Grafik Marketing Communications Ltd 625 N Washington St Ste 302 *TF:* 800-750-9772 ■ *Web:* www.grafik.com	Alexandria	VA	22314	703-299-4500		7
Grafika Commercial Printing Inc 710 Johnston St *Web:* www.grafikaprint.com	Sinking Spring	PA	19608	610-678-8630		627
GrafTech International Holdings Inc 12900 Snow Rd *NYSE: GTI* ■ *TF:* 800-424-9300 ■ *Web:* www.graftech.com	Parma	OH	44130	216-676-2000		127
Grafton City Hospital Inc 500 Market St *Web:* www.graftonhospital.com	Grafton	WV	26354	304-265-0400		374-3
Grafton Correctional Institution 2500 S Avon Beldon Rd *TF:* 800-828-4508 ■ *Web:* drc.ohio.gov	Grafton	OH	44044	440-748-1161	748-2521	213
Grafton County 3855 Dartmouth College Hwy PO Box 4 *Web:* www.nhdeeds.com/grafton/GrHome.html	North Haverhill	NH	03774	603-787-6921		338
Grafton National Cemetery 431 Walnut St *TF:* 800-535-1117 ■ *Web:* www.cem.va.gov	Grafton	WV	26354	304-265-2044	265-4336	136
Grafton Notch State Park 1941 Bear River Rd *Web:* www.maine.gov	Newry	ME	04261	207-824-2912		565
Grafton on Sunset 8462 W Sunset Blvd *TF:* 800-821-3660 ■ *Web:* www.graftononsunset.com	West Hollywood	CA	90069	323-654-4600	654-5918	379
Gragg Advertising Inc 450 E Fourth St Ste 100 *TF:* 800-860-9560 ■ *Web:* www.graggadv.com	Kansas City	MO	64106	816-931-0050		7
Grahall LLC 50 Fairlee Rd *Web:* www.grahall.com	Waban	MA	02468	917-453-4341		260
Graham & Assoc 3000 Riverchase Galleria Ste 310 *Web:* www.grahammktres.com	Birmingham	AL	35244	205-443-5399	443-5389	466
Graham Advertising 525 Communication Cir *Web:* www.grahamoleson.com	Colorado Springs	CO	80905	719-635-7335		5
Graham Architectural Products Corp 1551 Mt Rose Ave *TF:* 800-755-6274 ■ *Web:* www.grahamwindows.com	York	PA	17403	717-849-8100		234
Graham C- Stores Co 33978 N US Hwy 45 *Web:* www.grahamcstores.com	Grayslake	IL	60030	847-726-8188		579
Graham Cadillac 1515 W Fourth St *Web:* www.grahamchevycadillac.com	Mansfield	OH	44906	419-989-4012		516
Graham Co, The 1 Penn Sq W 25th Fl *TF:* 888-472-4262 ■ *Web:* www.grahamco.com	Philadelphia	PA	19102	215-567-6300		390
Graham Communications 40 Oval Rd *Web:* www.grahamcomm.com	Quincy	MA	02170	617-328-0069		7
Graham Corp 20 Florence Ave *NYSE: GHM* ■ *TF Orders:* 800-828-8150 ■ *Web:* www.graham-mfg.com	Batavia	NY	14020	585-343-2216	343-1097	386
Graham Correctional Ctr 12078 Illinois Rt 185 PO Box 499 *Web:* www.illinois.gov/idoc/facilities/Pages/grahamcorrectionalcenter.aspx	Hillsboro	IL	62049	217-532-6961	532-6799	213
Graham Cos 6843 Main St *Web:* www.miamilakes.com	Miami Lakes	FL	33014	305-821-1130	557-0313	655
Graham County 34 Wall St Ste 407 *TF:* 866-962-6246 ■ *Web:* www.main.nc.us	Asheville	NC	28801	828-255-0182	254-2286	338
Graham County 921 W Thatcher Blvd *Web:* www.graham.az.gov	Safford	AZ	85546	928-428-3250	428-5951	338
Graham County Chamber of Commerce 1111 Thatcher Blvd *TF:* 888-837-1841 ■ *Web:* www.graham-chamber.com	Safford	AZ	85546	928-428-2511	428-0744	139
Graham County Electric Inc 9 W Center St *TF:* 800-577-9266 ■ *Web:* www.gce.coop	Pima	AZ	85543	928-485-2451	485-9491	245
Graham Curtin & Sheridan PA 4 Headquarters Plaza PO Box 1991 *TF:* 800-255-0408 ■ *Web:* www.grahamcurtin.com	Morristown	NJ	07962	973-292-1700		428
Graham Engineering Corp 1203 Eden Rd *Web:* www.grahamengineering.com	York	PA	17402	717-848-3755		480
Graham Enterprise Inc 628 N Lake St *Web:* www.grahamei.com	Mundelein	IL	60060	847-837-0777	837-0778	324
Graham Group Inc, The 2014 W Pinhook Rd Ste 210 *Web:* www.graham-group.com	Lafayette	LA	70508	337-232-8214		4
Graham Hospital 210 W Walnut St *Web:* www.grahamhealthsystem.org	Canton	IL	61520	309-647-5240		374-3
Graham Lindsey (Sen R - SC) 290 Russell Bldg *Web:* www.lgraham.senate.gov	Washington	DC	20510	202-224-5972	224-3808	342-2
Graham Lundberg & Peschel 2153 Bethel Rd SE *Web:* www.glpattorneys.com	Port Orchard	WA	98366	360-876-5005		428
Graham Medical Products 2273 Larsen Rd *TF Cust Svc:* 800-558-6765 ■ *Web:* www.grahammedical.com	Green Bay	WI	54303	920-494-8701		576
Graham Packaging Company Inc 2401 Pleasant Valley Rd *TF:* 800-777-0065 ■ *Web:* www.grahampackaging.com	York	PA	17402	717-849-8500	854-4269	98
Graham Personnel Services 2100 w cornwallis dr *Web:* www.grahamjobs.com	Greensboro	NC	27408	336-288-9330		260
Graham, The 1075 Thomas Jefferson St NW *TF:* 855-341-1292 ■ *Web:* thegrahamgeorgetown.com	Washington	DC	20007	202-337-0900	333-6526	379
Graham-Pelton Consulting Inc 39 Beechwood Rd *Web:* grahampelton.com	Summit	NJ	07901	908-608-1388		463
Graham-White Manufacturing Co 1242 Colorado St PO Box 1099 *Web:* www.grahamwhite.com	Salem	VA	24153	540-387-5600	387-5697	650
Grain Belt Supply Company Inc PO Box 615 *TF:* 800-447-0522 ■ *Web:* www.grainbeltsupply.com	Salina	KS	67402	785-827-4491	827-4494	480
Grain Dealers Mutual Insurance Co 6201 Corporate Dr *TF:* 800-428-7081 ■ *Web:* www.graindealers.com	Indianapolis	IN	46278	317-388-4500	295-9434	391-4
Grain Inspection Packers & Stockyards Administration 1400 Independence Ave SW Rm 2055-S Bldg *Web:* www.gipsa.usda.gov	Washington	DC	20250	202-720-0219		340-1
Grain Processing Corp 1600 Oregon St *TF:* 800-851-9618 ■ *Web:* www.grainprocessing.com	Muscatine	IA	52761	563-264-4265	264-4289	296-23
Grainger County 7810 Rutledge Pk P. O. Box 639 *Web:* www.graingertn.com	Rutledge	TN	37861	865-828-4222	828-8972	338
Gram Lumber Co 985 NW Second St *Web:* rsgfp.com	Kalama	WA	98625	360-673-5231	673-5558	683
Grambling State University 403 Main St *TF:* 800-569-4714 ■ *Web:* www.gram.edu	Grambling	LA	71245	318-247-3811		166
Grambling State University Lewis Memorial Library (GSU) 403 Main St PO Box 4256 *Web:* www.gram.edu/research/library	Grambling	LA	71245	318-274-3354	274-3268	434-6
Gramercy Advisors LLC 20 Dayton Ave *Web:* www.gramercyadvisors.com	Greenwich	CT	06830	203-552-1900		401
Gramercy Brokerage Inc 97-77 Queens Blvd *Web:* www.gramercy1.com	Rego Park	NY	11374	718-896-2300		390
Gramercy Capital Corp 420 Lexington Ave *NYSE: GKK* ■ *Web:* www.gptreit.com	New York	NY	10170	212-297-1000	297-1090	654
Gramercy Park Hotel 2 Lexington Ave *TF:* 866-784-1300 ■ *Web:* www.gramercyparkhotel.com	New York	NY	10010	212-920-3300	673-5890	379
Gramercy Park Nursing Center Inc 17475 S Dixie Hwy *Web:* seniorsmanagement.com	Miami	FL	33157	305-255-1045		371
Gramercy Tavern 42 E 20th St *Web:* www.gramercytavern.com	New York	NY	10003	212-477-0777		671
Grammer Industries Inc 6320 E State St *TF:* 800-333-7410 ■ *Web:* www.grammerindustries.com	Columbus	IN	47201	812-579-5655	579-5643	780
Grammy Magazine 3030 Olympic Blvd *TF:* 800-423-2017 ■ *Web:* www.grammy.com	Santa Monica	CA	90404	310-392-3777		457-9
Grammy Museum Foundation Inc 800 W Olympic Blvd Ste 305 *Web:* www.grammymuseum.org	Los Angeles	CA	90015	213-765-6800		522
Gran Tierra Energy Inc 200 150 13th Ave SW *TF:* 800-732-0330 ■ *Web:* www.grantierra.com	Calgary	AB	T2R0V2	403-265-3221		536
Granada Hills Chamber of Commerce 17723 Chatsworth St *TF:* 800-843-5678 ■ *Web:* www.granadachamber.com	Granada Hills	CA	91344	818-368-3235		139
Granahan Investment Management Inc 404 Wyman St Ste 460 *Web:* www.granahan.com	Waltham	MA	02451	781-890-4412		401
Grand 1894 Opera House 2020 Postoffice St *TF:* 800-821-1894 ■ *Web:* www.thegrand.com	Galveston	TX	77550	409-765-1894	763-1068	572
Grand Aerie Fraternal Order of Eagles 1623 Gateway Cir S *Web:* www.foe.com	Grove City	OH	43123	614-883-2200	883-2201	48-15
Grand Aire Express Inc 11777 W Airport Service Rd **Fax Area Code:* 419 ■ *TF:* 800-704-7263 ■ *Web:* www.grandaire.com	Swanton	OH	43558	800-704-7263	865-2965*	63
Grand America Hotel 555 S Main St *TF:* 800-304-8696 ■ *Web:* www.grandamerica.com	Salt Lake City	UT	84111	801-258-6000	258-6911	379
Grand Avenue 649 Grand Ave *Web:* www.grandave.com	Saint Paul	MN	55105	651-699-0029	699-7775	460
Grand Avenue Worldwide 186 N First St *TF:* 866-455-2823 ■ *Web:* www.grandavenuelimo.com	Nashville	TN	37213	615-714-5466		441
Grand Banks Yachts Ltd 2288 W Commodore Way Ste 200 *Web:* www.grandbanks.com	Seattle	WA	98199	206-352-0116	352-1711	90
Grand Beach Inn (GBI) 198 E Grand Ave *Web:* grandbeachinnmaine.com	Old Orchard Beach	ME	04064	207-934-4621		379
Grand Blanc Cement Products 10709 Ctr Rd *TF:* 800-875-7500 ■ *Web:* GRANDBLANCCEMENTproducts.COM	Grand Blanc	MI	48439	810-694-7500	694-2995	183
Grand Blanc Chamber of Commerce 512 E Grand Blanc Rd *Web:* www.grandblancchamber.com	Grand Blanc	MI	48439	810-695-4222		139
Grand Cafe Key West 314 Duval St *Web:* www.grandcafekeywest.com	Key West	FL	33040	305-292-4740		671
Grand Canyon National Park PO Box 129 **Fax:* Mail Rm ■ *Web:* www.nps.gov	Grand Canyon	AZ	86023	928-638-7888	638-7797*	564
Grand Canyon National Park Museum Collection Grand Canyon National Pk 2C Albright Ave *Web:* www.nps.gov	Grand Canyon	AZ	86023	928-638-7769		520
Grand Canyon Railway Inc 1201 W Rt 66 Ste 200 *Web:* www.thetrain.com	Flagstaff	AZ	86001	928-773-1976		649
Grand Canyon Trust 2601 N Fort Valley Rd *TF:* 800-827-5722 ■ *Web:* www.grandcanyontrust.org	Flagstaff	AZ	86001	928-774-7488	774-7570	48-13
Grand Canyon University 3300 W Camelback Rd *TF:* 800-800-9776 ■ *Web:* www.gcu.edu	Phoenix	AZ	85017	602-639-7500		166
Grand Casino Hinckley 777 Lady Luck Dr *TF:* 800-472-6321 ■ *Web:* www.grandcasinomn.com	Hinckley	MN	55037	800-472-6321		133

Phone | Fax | Class

Grand Casino Mille Lacs
777 Grand Ave PO Box 343 Onamia MN 56359 800-626-5825 133
TF: 800-626-5825 ■ *Web:* www.grandcasinomn.com

Grand Central Graphics Inc
272 N 12th St Milwaukee WI 53233 414-273-7446 627
Web: grandcentralgraphics.com

Grand China 658 Kirkwood Mall Bismarck ND 58504 701-222-1518 671
Web: www.grandchinabismarck.com

Grand China Restaurant
2905 Peachtree Rd NE Atlanta GA 30305 404-231-8690 671
Web: www.grandchinaatl.com

Grand Concourse 100 W Stn Sq Dr Pittsburgh PA 15219 412-261-1717 261-6041 671
TF: 800-859-8589 ■ *Web:* www.muer.com

Grand Country Inn
Grand Country Sq 1945 W Hwy 76 Branson MO 65616 417-335-3535 379
TF: 888-505-4096 ■ *Web:* www.grandcountry.com/lodging

Grand County
308 W Byers Ave Hot Sulphur Springs CO 80451 970-725-3347 725-0100 338
Web: www.co.grand.co.us

Grand County 125 E Ctr St Moab UT 84532 435-259-1321 259-2959 338
TF: 800-635-6622 ■ *Web:* www.grandcountyutah.net

Grand Del Mar 5300 Grand Del Mar Ct San Diego CA 92130 858-314-2000 314-2001 379
TF: 855-314-2030 ■ *Web:* www.fairmont.com/san-diego

Grand Electric Co-op Inc
801 Coleman Ave PO Box 39 Bison SD 57620 605-244-5211 245
TF: 800-592-1803 ■ *Web:* www.grandelectric.coop

Grand European Tours
6000 Meadows Rd Ste 520 Lake Oswego OR 97035 503-718-2262 718-5198 760
TF: 877-622-9109 ■ *Web:* www.getours.com

Grand Forks Air Force Base
344 Tuskegee Airmen Blvd Grand Forks AFB Grand Forks ND 58205 701-747-3316 497-1
Web: www.grandforks.af.mil

Grand Forks Chamber of Commerce
202 N Third St Grand Forks ND 58203 701-772-7271 772-9238 139
TF: 855-233-6362 ■ *Web:* www.gochamber.org

Grand Forks City Hall
255 N Fourth St Grand Forks ND 58203 701-746-2626 787-3740 337
Web: www.grandforksgov.com

Grand Forks County
124 S Fourth St Grand Forks ND 58206 701-787-2730 338
Web: www.gfcounty.nd.gov

Grand Forks Herald
375 Second Ave N Grand Forks ND 58203 701-780-1100 780-1123 532-2
Web: www.grandforksherald.com

Grand Forks Human Nutrition Research Ctr
USDA/ARS 2420 Second Ave N Grand Forks ND 58203 701-795-8353 795-8395 668
Web: www.ars.usda.gov/Main/docs.htm?docid=3898

Grand Furniture Discount Store
836 E Little Creek Rd Norfolk VA 23518 757-588-1331 321
Web: www.grandfurniture.com

Grand Gateway Hotel
1721 N LaCrosse St Rapid City SD 57701 605-342-8853 342-0663 379
TF: 866-742-1300 ■ *Web:* www.grandgatewayhotel.com

Grand Geneva Resort & Spa
7036 Grand Geneva Way Lake Geneva WI 53147 262-248-8811 249-4763 669
TF: 800-558-3417 ■ *Web:* www.grandgeneva.com

Grand Harbor Resort & Waterpark
350 Bell St Dubuque IA 52001 563-690-4000 669
TF: 866-690-4006 ■ *Web:* www.grandharborresort.com

Grand Haven Board of Lightand & Power (GHBLP)
1700 Eaton Dr Grand Haven MI 49417 616-846-6250 846-3114 245
Web: www.ghblp.org

Grand Haven Plastics Inc
1425 Aerial View Dr Grand Haven MI 49417 616-846-4950 596
Web: www.ghplastics.com

Grand Haven State Park
1001 S Harbor Ave Grand Haven MI 49417 616-847-1309 565
Web: www.michigandnr.com

Grand Home Furnishings
4235 Electric Rd SW Roanoke VA 24018 540-776-7000 321
Web: www.grandhomefurnishings.com

Grand Homes Inc 5150 Keller Springs Rd Dallas TX 75001 214-750-6528 750-6849 653
Web: www.grandhomes.com

Grand Hotel & Conference Center Peoria
4400 N Brandywine Dr Peoria IL 61614 309-686-8000 707
TF: 800-345-8082 ■ *Web:* travelodgepeoria.com

Grand Hotel & Suites Toronto
225 Jarvis St Toronto ON M5B2C1 416-863-9000 379
Web: www.grandhoteltoronto.com

Grand Hotel Edmonton 10266 103rd St Edmonton AB T5J0Y8 780-422-6365 379
Web: www.thegrandedmonton.ca

Grand Hotel Marriott Resort Golf Club & Spa
1 Grand Blvd PO Box 639 Point Clear AL 36564 251-928-9201 928-1149 707
TF: 800-544-9933 ■ *Web:* www.marriott.com

Grand Hotel Minneapolis, The
615 Second Ave S Minneapolis MN 55402 612-288-8888 373-0407 379
TF: 866-843-4726 ■ *Web:* www.grandhotelminneapolis.com

Grand Hotel of Cape May Beach Ave Cape May NJ 08204 609-884-5611 379
TF: 800-257-8550 ■ *Web:* www.grandhotelcapemay.com

Grand Hotel, The 149 State Rt 64 Tusayan AZ 86023 928-638-3333 379
Web: www.grandcanyongrandhotel.com

Grand Hyatt Denver 1750 Welton St Denver CO 80202 303-295-1234 378
Web: denver.grand.hyatt.com/en/hotel/home.html

Grand Hyatt Kauai Resort & Spa
1571 Poipu Rd Koloa HI 96756 808-742-1234 742-1557 669
TF: 800-233-1234 ■ *Web:* kauai.grand.hyatt.com/en/hotel/home.html

Grand Hyatt Tampa Bay 2900 Bayport Dr Tampa FL 33607 813-874-1234 378
Web: tampabay.grand.hyatt.com/en/hotel/home.html

Grand Hyatt Washington
1000 H St NW Washington DC 20001 202-582-1234 379
Web: washingtondc.grand.hyatt.com/en/hotel/home.html

Grand Image Inc 560 Main St Ste 3 Hudson MA 01749 978-567-9408 8
TF: 800-444-2742 ■ *Web:* www.grandimageinc.com

Grand Island Area Chamber of Commerce
309 W Second St Grand Island NE 68802 308-382-9210 382-1154 139
TF: 800-809-8802 ■ *Web:* gichamber.com

Grand Island Independent
422 W First St Grand Island NE 68801 308-382-1000 382-8129 532-2
TF: 800-658-3160 ■ *Web:* www.theindependent.com

Grand Island Veterans' Home
2300 W Capital Ave Grand Island NE 68803 308-385-6252 793
TF: 800-358-8802 ■ *Web:* dhhs.ne.gov

Grand Isle County
9 Hyde Rd PO Box 49 Grand Isle VT 05458 802-372-8830 372-8815 338
Web: www.grandislevt.org

Grand Isle State Park
Admiral Craik Dr Grand Isle LA 70358 985-787-2559 565
TF: 888-787-2559 ■ *Web:* www.crt.state.la.us

Grand Isle State Park 36 E Shore S Grand Isle VT 05458 802-372-4300 565
Web: www.vtstateparks.com

Grand Junction Area Chamber of Commerce
360 Grand Ave Grand Junction CO 81501 970-242-3214 242-3694 139
TF: 800-352-5286 ■ *Web:* www.gjchamber.org

Grand Junction Concrete Pipe Co
2868 I-70 Business Loop Grand Junction CO 81501 970-243-4604 135
Web: www.gjpipe.com

Grand Junction VA Medical Ctr
2121 N Ave Grand Junction CO 81501 970-242-0731 244-1323 374-8
Web: www.grandjunction.va.gov

Grand Junction Visitors & Convention Bureau
740 Horizon Dr Grand Junction CO 81506 970-244-1480 243-7393 206
TF: 800-962-2547 ■ *Web:* www.visitgrandjunction.com

Grand Lake Casino 24701 S 655 Rd Grove OK 74344 918-786-8528 452
TF: 800-426-4640 ■ *Web:* grandlakecasino.com

Grand Lake Gardens
401 Santa Clara Ave Oakland CA 94610 800-416-6091 672
TF: 800-416-6091 ■ *Web:* www.grandlakegardens.com

Grand Lake Mental Health Center Inc
114 W Delaware Nowata OK 74048 918-273-1841 726
TF: 800-722-3611 ■ *Web:* www.glmhc.net

Grand Lodge Crested Butte
6 Emmons Rd Crested Butte CO 81225 970-349-8000 349-4265 669
TF: 877-547-5143

Grand Mesa Youth Sevices Ctr
360 28th Rd Grand Junction CO 81501 970-242-1521 242-8127 412
TF: 800-507-8662 ■ *Web:* www.colorado.gov

Grand Oaks Hotel
2315 Green Mountain Dr Branson MO 65616 800-553-6423 379
TF: 800-553-6423 ■ *Web:* www.grandoakshotel.net

Grand Ole Opry 2804 Opryland Dr Nashville TN 37214 615-871-6779 572
TF: 800-733-6779 ■ *Web:* www.opry.com

Grand Opera House 651 Mulberry St Macon GA 31201 478-301-5470 572
Web: www.thegrandmacon.com

Grand Pacific Palisades Resort & Hotel
5805 Armada Dr Carlsbad CA 92008 760-827-3200 669
TF: 800-725-4723 ■ *Web:* www.grandpacificpalisades.com

Grand Pacific Resorts Inc
Grand Pacific Plaza 5900 Pasteur Ct Ste 200 Carlsbad CA 92008 760-431-8500 378
Web: www.grandpacificresorts.com

Grand Palms Hotel & Golf Resort
110 Grand Palms Dr Pembroke Pines FL 33027 954-431-8800 435-5988 669
TF: 800-327-9246 ■ *Web:* www.grandpalmsresort.com

Grand Peaks Properties Inc
4582 S Ulster St Pkwy Ste 1200 Denver CO 80237 720-889-9200 656
Web: www.grandpeaks.com

Grand Portage Lodge & Casino
PO Box 233 Grand Portage MN 55605 218-475-2401 475-2309 669
TF: 800-543-1384 ■ *Web:* www.grandportage.com

Grand Portage National Monument
PO Box 426 Grand Portage MN 55605 218-475-0123 564
Web: www.nps.gov

Grand Portage State Park
9393 E Hwy 61 Grand Portage MN 55605 218-475-2360 475-2365 565
TF: 888-646-6367 ■ *Web:* www.dnr.state.mn.us

Grand Power Logistics Group Inc
Ste 2806 505 - Sixth St SW Ste 2806 Calgary AB T2P1X5 403-237-8211 313
Web: www.grandpowerlogistics.com

Grand Prix of Long Beach
3000 Pacific Ave Long Beach CA 90806 562-981-2600 642
TF: 888-827-7333 ■ *Web:* www.gplb.com

Grand Rapids Area Chamber of Commerce
1 NW Third St Grand Rapids MN 55744 218-326-6619 326-4825 139
TF: 800-472-6366 ■ *Web:* www.grandmn.com

Grand Rapids Area Chamber of Commerce
111 Pearl St NW Grand Rapids MI 49503 616-771-0300 771-0318 139
Web: www.grandrapids.org

Grand Rapids Art Museum
101 Monroe Ctr Grand Rapids MI 49503 616-831-1000 831-1001 520
TF: 800-272-8258 ■ *Web:* www.artmuseumgr.org

Grand Rapids Ballet Co
341 Ellsworth Ave SW Grand Rapids MI 49503 616-454-4771 454-0672 573-1
TF: 800-982-2787 ■ *Web:* www.grballet.com

Grand Rapids Business Journal (GRBJ)
549 Ottawa Ave NW Ste 201 Grand Rapids MI 49503 616-459-4545 457-5
Web: grbj.com

Grand Rapids Children's Museum
11 Sheldon Ave NE Grand Rapids MI 49503 616-235-4726 235-4728 521
Web: www.grcm.org

Grand Rapids City Hall
300 Monroe Ave NW Grand Rapids MI 49503 616-456-3010 456-4607 337
TF: 800-860-8610 ■ *Web:* grcity.us

Grand Rapids Civic Theatre
30 N Div Ave Grand Rapids MI 49503 616-222-6650 572
Web: www.grct.org

Grand Rapids Community College
143 Bostwick Ave NE Grand Rapids MI 49503 616-234-4000 234-4107* 162
*Fax: Admissions ■ *Web:* www.grcc.edu

Grand Rapids Controls
825 Northland Dr NE Rockford MI 49341 616-884-7100 247
Web: www.grcontrols.com

Grand Rapids Label Co
2351 Oak Industrial Dr NE Grand Rapids MI 49505 616-459-8134 459-4543 413
TF: 800-552-5215 ■ *Web:* www.grlabel.com

Grand Rapids Public Library
111 Library St NE Grand Rapids MI 49503 616-988-5400 434-3
Web: grpl.org

Phone | Fax | Class

Grand Rapids Public Schools (GRPS)
1331 Franklin St SE PO Box 117 Grand Rapids MI 49506 616-819-2000 819-2104 685
Web: www.grps.org

Grand Rapids Scale Company Inc
4215 Stafford Ave SW Grand Rapids MI 49548 616-538-7080 362
TF: 800-348-5701 ■ *Web:* www.grmetrology.com

Grand Rapids Symphony
300 Ottawa Ave NW Ste 100 Grand Rapids MI 49503 616-454-9451 454-7477 573-3
TF: 800-982-2787 ■ *Web:* www.grsymphony.org

Grand Rapids/Kent County Convention & Visitors Bureau
171 Monroe Ave NW Ste 700 Grand Rapids MI 49503 616-459-8287 206
TF: 800-678-9859 ■ *Web:* www.experiencegr.com

Grand River Academy
3042 College St Austinburg OH 44010 440-275-2811 275-1825 622
Web: www.grandriver.org

Grand River Agricultural Society
7445 Wellington Rd Ste 21 Elora ON N0B1S0 519-846-5455 642
TF: 800-898-7792 ■ *Web:* www.grandriverraceway.com

Grand River Hospital Kitchener-Waterloo Health Centre
835 King St W PO Box 9056 Kitchener ON N2G1G3 519-749-4300 374-2
Web: www.grhosp.on.ca

Grand River Rubber & Plastics Co
2029 Aetna Rd Ashtabula OH 44004 440-998-2900 677
Web: www.grrp.com

Grand Seas Resort Partners
2424 N Atlantic Ave Daytona Beach FL 32118 386-677-7880 378

Grand Sierra Resort & Casino
2500 E Second St Reno NV 89595 775-789-2000 669
TF: 800-501-2651 ■ *Web:* www.grandsierraresort.com

Grand Strand Airport
2800 Terminal St North Myrtle Beach SC 29582 843-848-7400 63

Grand Strand Regional Medical Ctr
809 82nd Pkwy Myrtle Beach SC 29572 843-692-1000 692-1109 374-3
TF: 800-342-2383 ■ *Web:* www.grandstrandmed.com

Grand Street Cafe 4740 Grand Ave Kansas City MO 64112 816-561-8000 671
Web: grandstreetkc.com

Grand Street Theater 325 N Pk Ave Helena MT 59601 406-442-4270 447-1573 572
Web: www.grandstreettheatre.com

Grand Summit Hotel 570 Springfield Ave Summit NJ 07901 908-273-3000 273-4228 379
TF: 800-346-0773 ■ *Web:* grandsummit.com

Grand Targhee Resort 3300 E Ski Hill Rd Alta WY 83414 307-353-2300 353-8148 669
TF: 800-827-4433 ■ *Web:* www.grandtarghee.com

Grand Terrace Healthcare Ctr
12000 Mt Vernon Ave Grand Terrace CA 92313 909-825-5221 783-4811 450
Web: grandterracecare.com

Grand Teton Lodge Company & Jackson Lake Lodge
5 Miles N Hwy 89 Ste 250 Moran WY 83013 307-543-2811 543-3143* 669
**Fax:* Resv ■ *TF Resv:* 800-628-9988 ■ *Web:* www.gtlc.com

Grand Teton National Park
Teton Pk Rd PO Box 170 Moose WY 83012 307-739-3300 739-3438 564
Web: www.nps.gov/grte

Grand Transformers Inc
1500 Marion Ave Grand Haven MI 49417 616-842-5430 767
Web: www.gtipower.com

Grand Traverse County
400 Boardman Ave Traverse City MI 49684 231-922-4760 922-4658 338
TF: 800-882-5941 ■ *Web:* www.co.grand-traverse.mi.us

Grand Traverse Machine (GTM)
1247 Boon St Traverse City MI 49686 231-946-8006 621
Web: www.gtmachine.com

Grand Traverse Resort & Spa
100 Grand Traverse Blvd PO Box 404 Acme MI 49610 231-534-6000 669
TF: 800-236-1577 ■ *Web:* www.grandtraverseresort.com

Grand Union Motel & Crystal Spa
120 S Broadway Saratoga Springs NY 12866 518-584-9000 378
Web: www.grandunionmotel.com

Grand Valley Advance PO Box 9 Jenison MI 49428 616-669-2700 532-4
Web: www.mlivemediagroup.com/advance-weeklies

Grand Valley Mfg Co (GVM)
701 E Spring St Bldg 52 Titusville PA 16354 814-827-2707 827-4349 454
TF: 800-704-1078 ■ *Web:* www.grandvalleymfg.com

Grand Valley Rural Power Lines Inc
845 22 Rd PO Box 190 Grand Junction CO 81505 970-242-0040 245
TF: 877-760-7435 ■ *Web:* www.gvp.org

Grand Valley State University
1 Campus Dr Allendale MI 49401 616-331-5000 331-2000 166
TF: 800-748-0246 ■ *Web:* www.gvsu.edu

Grand Valley State University Zumberge Library
1 Campus Dr Allendale MI 49401 616-331-3252 434-6
TF: 800-879-0581 ■ *Web:* www.gvsu.edu/library

Grand View College
1200 Grandview Ave Des Moines IA 50316 515-263-2800 263-2974* 166
**Fax:* Admissions ■ *TF:* 800-444-6083 ■ *Web:* www.gvc.edu

Grand View Glass & Metal Inc
2134 S Green Privado Ontario CA 91761 909-923-9544 362
TF: 800-454-1207 ■ *Web:* www.grandviewglass.com

Grand View Hospital 700 Lawn Ave Sellersville PA 18960 215-453-4000 374-3
Web: www.gvh.org

Grand View Lodge 23521 Nokomis Ave Nisswa MN 56468 218-963-2234 669
TF: 866-801-2951 ■ *Web:* www.grandviewlodge.com

Grand View Media Group Inc (GVMG)
200 Croft St Ste 1 Birmingham AL 35242 205-408-3700 637-9
TF: 888-431-2877 ■ *Web:* grandviewmedia.com

Grand Wailea Resort & Spa
3850 Wailea Alanui Dr Wailea HI 96753 808-875-1234 879-4077 669
TF: 800-888-6100 ■ *Web:* www.grandwailea.com

Grand Wayne Convention Ctr
120 W Jefferson Blvd Fort Wayne IN 46802 260-426-4100 420-9080 205
Web: www.grandwayne.com

Grand, The 818 N Market St Wilmington DE 19801 302-658-7897 572
TF: 800-374-7263 ■ *Web:* www.thegrandwilmington.org

GrandBanks Capital
65 William St Ste 330 Wellesley MA 02481 781-997-4300 997-4301 792
Web: www.grandbankscapital.com

Grandbridge Real Estate Capital LLC
271 17th St NW Ste 750 Atlanta GA 30363 704-332-4454 216
Web: www.gbrecap.com

Grande Cheese Co 301 E Main St Lomira WI 53048 800-772-3210 269-1445* 296-5
**Fax Area Code:* 920 ■ *TF:* 800-772-3210 ■ *Web:* www.grandecig.com

Grande Colonial 910 Prospect St La Jolla CA 92037 888-828-5498 454-5679* 379
**Fax Area Code:* 858 ■ *TF:* 888-828-5498 ■ *Web:* www.thegrandecolonial.com

Grande Communications Networks LLC
401 Carlson Cir San Marcos TX 78666 512-878-4000 194
Web: mygrande.com

Grande Plateau Casino 131 Main St Black Hawk CO 80422 303-777-1111 582-0311 133
Web: www.blackhawkcolorado.com

Grande Prairie & District Chamber of Commerce
11330 106th St Ste 127 Grande Prairie AB T8V6T7 780-532-5340 532-2926 137
Web: www.grandeprairiechamber.com

Grande Prairie Public Library
3479 W 183rd St Hazel Crest IL 60429 708-798-5563 798-5874 434-3
TF: 800-321-9511 ■ *Web:* www.grandeprairie.org

Grande Prairie Regional College
10726 106 Ave Grande Prairie AB T8V4C4 780-539-2911 165
TF: 888-539-4772 ■ *Web:* www.gprc.ab.ca

Grandite Inc PO Box 47133 Quebec QC G1S4X1 581-318-2018 703-0924 178-1
TF: 866-808-3932 ■ *Web:* www.grandite.com

Grand-Kahn Electric (GK)
2455 W Grand Ave Chicago IL 60612 312-298-1500 298-1501 189-4
Web: www.grandkahn.com

GrandLife Hotels Inc 310 W Broadway New York NY 10013 212-965-3000 378
TF: 800-965-3000 ■ *Web:* www.grandlifehotels.com

Grandma Brown's Beans Inc
5837 Scenic Ave Mexico NY 13114 315-963-7221 296-36

Grandma Hattie's 2811 S Carson St Carson City NV 89701 775-882-4900 671

Grandma's Bakery Inc
1765 Buerkle Rd White Bear Lake MN 55110 651-779-0707 345
Web: www.grandmasbakery.com

Grandma's Saloon & Grill
522 Lake Ave S Duluth MN 55802 218-727-4192 671
TF: 800-706-7672 ■ *Web:* www.grandmasrestaurants.com/gmas_cp.htm

Grandma's Sports Garden 425 Lake Ave S Duluth MN 55802 218-722-4724 720-3804 671
Web: www.grandmasrestaurants.com

Grandmark Lodging 3300 28th St SW Grandville MI 49418 616-534-7641 379

Grandmother's Buttons Museum
9814 Royal St Saint Francisville LA 70775 225-635-4107 635-6067 520
TF: 800-580-6941 ■ *Web:* www.grandmothersbuttons.com

Grandover Resort & Conference Ctr
1000 Club Rd Greensboro NC 27407 336-294-1800 856-9991 377
TF: 800-472-6301 ■ *Web:* www.grandover.com

Grandparents Rights Organization (GRO)
1760 S Telegraph Rd Ste 250 Bloomfield Hills MI 48304 248-646-7177 48-6
Web: www.grandparentsrights.org

Grandstand Publishing LLC
990 Grove St Ste 400 Evanston IL 60201 847-491-6440 491-0459 637-9
Web: baseballdigest.com

Grandview Heights City School District
1587 W Third Ave Columbus OH 43212 614-481-3600 685
Web: www.ghcsd.org

Grandview Medical Ctr 405 W Grand Ave Dayton OH 45405 937-395-3963 395-8327 374-3
Web: www.ketteringhealth.org

Grandview Pharmacy
474 Southpoint Cir Brownsburg IN 46112 866-827-7575 237
TF: 866-827-7575 ■ *Web:* www.grandviewpharmacy.com

Grandview Products Co
1601 Superior Dr Parsons KS 67357 620-421-6950 421-4211 115
TF: 800-247-9105 ■ *Web:* www.grandviewcabinets.com

Grandview Speedway
43 Passmore Rd Bechtelsville PA 19505 610-754-7688 515
Web: www.grandviewspeedway.com

Grandville Printing Company Inc
4719 Ivanrest Ave SW Grandville MI 49418 800-748-0248 627
TF: 800-748-0248 ■ *Web:* www.gpco.com

Grandvue Medical Care Facility
1728 S Peninsula Rd East Jordan MI 49727 231-536-2286 371
Web: grandvue.org

Grandwell Industries Inc
6109 S NC Hwy 55 Fuquay Varina NC 27526 919-557-1221 552-9830 701
TF Cust Svc: 800-338-6554 ■ *Web:* www.grandwell.com

Grange Hall 1067 State Rd Vineyard Haven MA 02568 508-627-4440 627-8088 50-3
Web: www.mvpreservation.org

Grange Insurance 671 S High St Columbus OH 43206 800-422-0550 391-2
TF: 800-422-0550 ■ *Web:* grangeinsurance.com

Grange Mutual Casualty Co
671 S High St Columbus OH 43206 800-422-0550 391-4
TF: 800-422-0550 ■ *Web:* grangeinsurance.com

Granger Construction Co
6267 Aurelius Rd Lansing MI 48911 517-393-1670 393-1382 186
TF: 800-303-8629 ■ *Web:* www.grangerconstruction.com

Granger House Museum 970 Tenth St Marion IA 52302 319-377-6672 520
TF: 800-824-1424 ■ *Web:* grangerhousemuseum.org

Granger Kay (Rep R - TX)
1026 Longworth HOB Washington DC 20515 202-225-5071 225-5683 342-2
Web: kaygranger.house.gov

Granger Plastics Co, The
1600 MADE Industrial Dr Middletown OH 45044 513-424-1955 596
Web: www.grangerplastics.com

Grangetto's Farm & Garden Supply Co
1105 W Mission Ave Escondido CA 92025 760-745-4671 276
TF: 800-536-4671 ■ *Web:* www.grangettos.com

Grangeville Environmental Services (GES)
GES Property Pros LLC
352 Pine Run Rd New Oxford PA 17331 717-637-6152 630-2713 83
Web: www.gespropertypros.com

Granicor Inc
300 Rue De Rotterdam Saint-augustin-de-desmaures QC G3A1T4 418-878-3530 878-3208 191-1
Web: www.granicor.com

Granite Bay State Marine Park
PO Box 1247 Soldotna AK 99669 907-262-5581 565
Web: dnr.alaska.gov/parks/units/pwssmp/smpwhit2.htm

Granite Broadcasting Corp
767 Third Ave 34th Fl New York NY 10017 212-826-2530 826-2858 738

Granite Business Solutions Inc
233 Technology Way Ste 4 Rocklin CA 95765 916-577-2181 174

Granite City Electric Supply Co
19 Quincy Ave Quincy MA 02169 617-472-6500 472-8661 362
TF: 800-850-9400 ■ *Web:* www.granitecityelectric.com

Name / Address	City	State	ZIP	Phone	Fax	Class
Granite City Food & Brewery Ltd (GCFB)						
1636 42nd St SW	Fargo	ND	58103	701-293-3000		671
Web: www.gcfb.com						
Granite Construction Inc						
585 W Beach St	Watsonville	CA	95076	831-724-1011	722-9657	188-4
NYSE: GVA ■ *TF:* 800-642-1687 ■ *Web:* www.graniteconstruction.com						
Granite County						
220 N Sansome St PO Box 925	Philipsburg	MT	59858	406-859-3771	859-3817	338
Web: www.co.granite.mt.us						
Granite Falls Energy LLC						
15045 Hwy 23 SE	Granite Falls	MN	56241	320-564-3100		297-8
TF: 877-485-8595 ■ *Web:* www.granitefallsenergy.com						
Granite Falls School District						
307 N Alder Ave	Granite Falls	WA	98252	360-691-7717	691-4459	685
TF: 888-651-8931 ■ *Web:* www.gfalls.wednet.edu						
Granite Farms Estates						
1343 W Baltimore Pike	Media	PA	19063	610-358-3440		672
TF: 888-499-2287 ■ *Web:* www.actsretirement.org						
Granite Gaming Group 115 N First St	Las Vegas	NV	89101	702-385-4250		132
Granite Ghost Town State Park						
3201 Spurgin Rd	Missoula	MT	59804	406-542-5500		565
Web: stateparks.mt.gov						
Granite Group Wholesalers LLC						
6 Storrs St	Concord	NH	03301	603-224-1901	224-4125	612
TF: 800-258-3690 ■ *Web:* www.thegranitegroup.com						
Granite Industries Inc						
595 E Lugbill Rd	Archbold	OH	43502	419-445-4733		492
Web: www.graniteind.com						
Granite Information Systems						
1490 Union Lake Rd	White Lake	MI	48386	248-360-8400		180
TF: 800-278-6575 ■ *Web:* graniteinfosys.com						
Granite Knitwear Inc						
805 S Salberry Ave Hwy 52S	Granite Quarry	NC	28072	704-279-5526	279-8205	155-12
TF Cust Svc: 800-476-9944 ■ *Web:* www.calcru.com						
Granite Links Golf Club						
100 Quarry Hills Dr	Quincy	MA	02169	617-689-1900		42
Web: www.granitelinksgolfclub.com						
Granite Microsystems Inc						
10202 N Enterprise Dr	Mequon	WI	53092	262-242-8800		173-2
Web: www.granitemicrosystems.com						
Granite Point Capital Management LP						
109 State St 5th Fl	Boston	MA	02109	617-587-7500		401
Web: www.granitepoint.com						
Granite Security Products Inc						
4801 Esco Dr	Fort Worth	TX	76140	469-735-4901		350
TF: 877-948-6723 ■ *Web:* www.winchestersafes.com						
Granite State College						
8 Old Suncook Rd	Concord	NH	03301	603-228-3000	513-1389	166
TF: 888-228-3000 ■ *Web:* www.granite.edu						
Berlin 25 Hall St Rm 144	Concord	NH	03301	603-447-3970		166
TF: 855-472-4255 ■ *Web:* www.granite.edu						
Portsmouth 51 International Dr	Portsmouth	NH	03801	603-332-8335		166
Web: www.granite.edu						
Granite State Independent Living Foundation						
21 Chenell Dr	Concord	NH	03301	603-228-9680		305
TF: 800-826-3700 ■ *Web:* www.gsil.org						
Granite State Manufacturing Co						
124 Joliette St	Manchester	NH	03102	800-464-7646		454
TF: 800-464-7646 ■ *Web:* gogsmgo.com						
Granite Telecommunications LLC						
100 Newport Ave Ext	Quincy	MA	02171	617-933-5500	328-0312	736
TF: 866-847-1500 ■ *Web:* www.granitenet.com						
Granite Tower Capital						
324 Traders Blvd E	Mississauga	ON	L4Z1W7	905-366-2551		691
Web: www.granitetowercapital.com						
Graniterock Co						
350 Technology Dr PO Box 50001	Watsonville	CA	95077	831-768-2000	768-2201	191-1
TF: 888-762-5100 ■ *Web:* www.graniterock.com						
Granite-Tops Inc 1480 Prairie Dr	Cold Spring	MN	56320	320-685-3005		115
Web: www.granite-tops.com						
Granitize Products Inc						
11022 Vulcan St	South Gate	CA	90280	562-923-5438	861-3475	151
TF: 800-424-9300 ■ *Web:* www.granitize.com						
Grant & Weber Inc						
26610 Agoura Rd Ste 209	Calabasas	CA	91302	818-871-7700	878-7777	393
TF: 800-333-1656 ■ *Web:* www.grantweber.com						
Grant Assembly Technologies						
90 Silliman Ave	Bridgeport	CT	06605	203-366-4557	366-0370	456
TF: 800-227-2150 ■ *Web:* www.grantriveters.com						
Grant Bennett Accountants						
1375 Exposition Blvd Ste 230	Sacramento	CA	95815	916-922-5109		2
TF: 888-763-7323 ■ *Web:* www.gbacpa.com						
Grant Career Center 718 W Plane St	Bethel	OH	45106	513-734-6222		685
Web: www.grantcareer.com						
Grant Cottage State Historic Site						
1000 Mt McGregor Rd	Wilton	NY	12831	518-587-8277		565
Web: parks.ny.gov/historic-sites/9/details.aspx						
Grant County 301 W Main St	John Day	OR	97845	541-575-0547		338
TF: 800-769-5664 ■ *Web:* www.gcoregonlive.com						
Grant County 106 Second Ave PO Box 164	Carson	ND	58529	701-622-3615	622-3717	338
Web: grantcountynd.com						
Grant County 10 Second St NE	Elbow Lake	MN	56531	218-685-4825	685-5349	338
Web: www.co.grant.mn.us						
Grant County 35 C St NW PO Box 37	Ephrata	WA	98823	509-754-2011	765-2160	338
TF: 800-572-0119 ■ *Web:* www.grantcountywa.gov						
Grant County 105 E Harrison St	Hyannis	NE	69350	308-458-2422	471-4020*	338
**Fax Area Code:* 402 ■ *Web:* local.dmv.org						
Grant County 111 S Jefferson St	Lancaster	WI	53813	608-723-2675	723-4048	338
TF: 800-514-0066 ■ *Web:* www.grantcounty.org						
Grant County 101 E Fourth St	Marion	IN	46952	765-668-8121	668-6541	338
Web: www.grantcounty.net						
Grant County 112 E Guthrie St Rm 105	Medford	OK	73759	580-395-2284		338
Web: grantcountyok.com						
Grant County 210 E Fifth Ave	Milbank	SD	57252	605-432-6711	432-9004*	338
**Fax:* Acctg ■ *Web:* grantcounty.sd.gov						
Grant County PO Box 114	Petersburg	WV	26847	304-257-2168	257-5454	338
TF: 800-252-5627 ■ *Web:* www.grantcounty-wv.com						
Grant County 101 W Ctr St	Sheridan	AR	72150	870-942-2631	942-3564	338
Web: grantcountyar.com						
Grant County 1400 Hwy 180	Silver City	NM	88061	575-574-0000	574-0073	338
Web: www.grantcountynm.com						
Grant County 108 S Glenn St	Ulysses	KS	67880	620-356-1335	356-3081	338
TF: 800-368-8683 ■ *Web:* www.grantcoks.org						
Grant County 105 Baton Rouge Rd	Williamstown	KY	41097	859-824-3321	824-3391	338
Web: grantcounty.ky.gov						
Grant County Herald						
35 Central Ave N	Elbow Lake	MN	56531	218-685-5326		532-3
TF: 877-852-2796 ■ *Web:* www.grantherald.com						
Grant County Journal 29 A St SW	Ephrata	WA	98823	509-754-4636		637-8
Grant Family Farms 12155 NCR 15	Wellington	CO	80549	970-568-7654		10-11
Web: www.grantfarms.com						
Grant Industries Inc						
33415 Groesbeck Hwy	Fraser	MI	48026	586-293-9200		489
Web: www.grantgrp.com						
Grant J Milleret CPA						
10777 W Twain Ave	Las Vegas	NV	89135	702-367-0341		2
Grant Medical Ctr 111 S Grant Ave	Columbus	OH	43215	614-566-9000		374-3
TF: 800-780-5733 ■ *Web:* www.ohiohealth.com						
Grant Parish 512 Main St PO Box 208	Colfax	LA	71417	318-627-3274	627-5931	338
TF: 800-776-4663 ■ *Web:* www.gpsb.org						
Grant Park Orchestra						
205 E Randolph St	Chicago	IL	60601	312-742-7638	742-7662	573-3
TF: 800-928-2086 ■ *Web:* www.grantparkmusicfestival.com						
Grant Piston Rings 1360 Jefferson St	Anaheim	CA	92807	714-996-0050		128
TF: 800-854-3540 ■ *Web:* www.grantpistonrings.com						
Grant Plaza Hotel 465 Grant Ave	San Francisco	CA	94108	415-434-3883	434-3886	379
TF: 800-472-6899 ■ *Web:* www.grantplaza.com						
Grant Street Group Inc						
339 Sixth Ave Ste 1400	Pittsburgh	PA	15222	412-391-5555		225
TF: 800-410-3445 ■ *Web:* www.grantstreet.com						
Grant Supply Company Inc						
901 Joyce Kilmer Ave	North Brunswick	NJ	08902	732-545-1018		189-10
Web: grantsupply.com						
Grant Thornton (CCRLLP)						
1400 Computer Dr	Westborough	MA	01581	508-926-2200		2
Web: www.grantthornton.com						
Grant Thornton International Ltd						
175 W Jackson Blvd 20th Fl	Chicago	IL	60604	312-856-0200		2
Web: www.grantthornton.com						
Grant Thornton LLP						
175 W Jackson Blvd 20th Fl	Chicago	IL	60604	312-856-0200	602-8099	2
Web: www.grantthornton.com						
Grant's 977 Farmington Ave	West Hartford	CT	06107	860-236-1930		671
Web: billygrant.com						
Grant's Farm 10501 Gravois Rd	Saint Louis	MO	63123	314-843-1700		368
Web: anheuser-busch.com						
Grant, Herrmann, Schwartz & Klinger						
675 Third Ave	New York	NY	10017	212-682-1800		428
Web: www.ghsklaw.com						
Grant, Konvalinka & Harrison PC						
Republic Ctr 633 Chestnut St Ninth Fl						
Ste 900	Chattanooga	TN	37450	423-756-8400		428
Web: www.gkhpc.com						
Grantek Systems Integration Inc						
4480 Harvester Rd	Burlington	ON	L7L4X2	905-634-0844		180
Web: grantek.com						
Grantham Distributing Co Inc						
2685 Hansrob Rd	Orlando	FL	32804	407-299-6446		81-3
Grantham Mayo Van Otterloo & Company LLC (GMO)						
40 Rowes Wharf	Boston	MA	02110	617-330-7500		401
Web: www.gmo.com						
Grantham Poole CPAs						
1062 Highland Colony Pkwy Ste 201	Ridgeland	MS	39157	601-499-2400		2
Web: www.granthampoole.com						
Grantham University Inc						
7200 NW 86th St	Kansas City	MO	64153	816-595-5759		166
Web: www.grantham.edu						
Grant-Kohrs Ranch National Historic Site						
266 Warren Ln	Deer Lodge	MT	59722	406-846-2070	846-3962	564
Web: www.nps.gov						
Grantmakers in Health (GIH)						
1100 Connecticut Ave NW Ste 1200	Washington	DC	20036	202-452-8331	452-8340	48-5
Web: www.gih.org						
Grants Pass Chamber of Commerce						
1995 NW Vine St PO Box 970	Grants Pass	OR	97526	541-476-7717	476-9574	139
TF: 800-547-5927 ■ *Web:* www.grantspasschamber.org						
Grants Pass Visitors & Convention Bureau						
1995 NW Vine St	Grants Pass	OR	97526	541-476-7574	476-9574	206
TF: 800-547-5927 ■ *Web:* travelgrantspass.com						
Grants State Bank						
824 W Santa Fe Ave PO Box 1088	Grants	NM	87020	505-285-6611		70
TF: 877-285-6611 ■ *Web:* www.grantsbank.com						
Grants.gov						
Dept of Health & Human Services						
200 Independence Ave SW HHH Bldg	Washington	DC	20201	800-518-4726		197
TF: 800-518-4726 ■ *Web:* www.grants.gov						
Grants/Cibola County Chamber of Commerce						
100 N Iron Ave	Grants	NM	87020	505-287-4802	287-8224	139
TF: 866-270-5110 ■ *Web:* www.grants.org						
Granutech-Saturn Systems Corp						
201 E Shady Grove	Grand Prairie	TX	75050	972-790-7800		494
Web: www.granutech.com						
Granville Arts Center 200 N Fifth St	Garland	TX	75040	972-205-2000		572
Web: www.garlandarts.com						
Granville Central School District						
58 Quaker St	Granville	NY	12832	518-642-1051	642-4544	685
Web: www.granvillecsd.org						
Granville County						
141 Williamsboro St PO Box 1286	Oxford	NC	27565	919-693-4761		338
TF: 800-685-8916 ■ *Web:* www.granvillecounty.org						
Granville County Chamber of Commerce						
124 Hillsboro St	Oxford	NC	27565	919-693-6125	693-6126	139
Web: www.granville-chamber.com						
Granville Island Hotel						
1253 Johnston St	Vancouver	BC	V6H3R9	604-683-7373	683-3061*	379
**Fax:* Admin ■ *TF Resv:* 800-663-1840 ■ *Web:* www.granvilleislandhotel.com						

Name / Address	City	State	ZIP	Phone	Fax	Class
Granville State Forest						
323 W Hartland Rd	Granville	MA	01034	413-357-6611		565
Web: www.mass.gov						
Grape Wine Company of San Antonio Inc, The						
1747 Citadel Plaza Ste 112	San Antonio	TX	78209	210-828-2222		443
Grape, The 2808 Greenville Ave	Dallas	TX	75206	214-828-1981		671
Web: www.thegraperestaurant.com						
Grapeland Elementary School						
PO Box 249	Grapeland	TX	75844	936-687-2317		685
Web: www.grapelandisd.net						
Grapevine Chamber of Commerce						
200 Vine St	Grapevine	TX	76051	817-481-1522	424-5208	139
TF: 866-322-8667 ■ *Web:* www.grapevinechamber.org						
Grapevine Communications International Inc						
5201 Paylor Ln	Sarasota	FL	34240	941-351-0024		7
TF: 800-266-6866 ■ *Web:* www.grapeinc.com						
Grapevine Convention Ctr, The						
1209 S Main St	Grapevine	TX	76051	817-410-3459		205
TF: 866-782-7897 ■ *Web:* www.grapevinetexasusa.com						
Grapevine Executive Recruiters Inc						
269 Richmond St W	Toronto	ON	M5V1X1	416-581-1445		260
Web: www.grapevinerecruiters.com						
Grapevine Media & Marketing						
1055 E Colorado Blvd Fl 5	Pasadena	CA	91101	626-240-4667		7
Web: www.grapevinemediaandmarketing.com						
Grapevine Mills						
3000 Grapevine Mills Pkwy	Grapevine	TX	76051	972-724-4900	724-4920	460
Web: www.simon.com/mall/grapevine-mills						
Grapevine Public Library						
1201 Municipal Way	Grapevine	TX	76051	817-410-3400		434-3
TF: 800-621-0508 ■ *Web:* grapevinetexas.gov						
Graphcom Inc 1219 Chambersburg Rd	Gettysburg	PA	17325	717-334-3107		627
TF: 800-871-9244 ■ *Web:* www.graphcom.com						
Graphel Corp 6115 Centre Pk Dr	West Chester	OH	45069	513-779-6166	777-8959	500
TF: 800-255-1104 ■ *Web:* www.graphel.com						
Graphic Artists Guild Inc						
32 Broadway Ste 1114	New York	NY	10004	212-791-3400	791-0333	414
TF: 800-878-2753 ■ *Web:* www.graphicartistsguild.org						
Graphic Arts Association						
1210 Northbrook Dr Ste 200	Trevose	PA	19053	215-396-2300		138
TF: 800-475-6708 ■ *Web:* www.graphicartsassociation.org						
Graphic Arts Finishers Inc						
32 Cambridge St	Charlestown	MA	02129	617-241-9292		555
Web: graphicartsfinishers.com						
Graphic Communications International Union						
25 Louisiana Ave NW	Washington	DC	20036	202-624-6800		414
Web: www.teamster.org						
Graphic Connections Group LLC						
174 Chesterfield Industrial Blvd	Chesterfield	MO	63005	636-519-8320		174
Web: www.gcfrog.com						
Graphic Controls LLC 400 Exchange St	Buffalo	NY	14204	800-669-1535	347-2420	628
TF: 800-669-1535 ■ *Web:* www.graphiccontrols.com						
Graphic Creations Inc						
213 E Fourth Ave	Knoxville	TN	37916	865-522-6221		184
Web: www.graphiccreations.com						
Graphic Design Inc						
315 Second St E PO Box 307	Hastings	MN	55033	651 437 6459		627
Web: www.gd-Inc.com						
Graphic Equipment Corp 55 Wester Ave	Metuchen	NJ	08840	732-494-5350		454
Web: www.gecorp.com						
Graphic Innovators Inc						
855 Morse Ave	Elk Grove Village	IL	60007	847-718-1516	718-1517	629
Web: www.graphicinnovators.com						
Graphic Management Specialty Products Inc						
139 Evergreen Rd PO Box 408	Oconto	WI	54153	920-835-3299		174
Web: www.gmsp.com						
Graphic Packaging International						
1500 Riveredge Parkway NW Ste 100	Atlanta	GA	30328	770-240-7200		101
NYSE: GPK ■ *TF:* 888-548-8395 ■ *Web:* www.graphicpkg.com						
Graphic Partners Inc 4300 II Rt 173	Zion	IL	60099	847-872-9445		174
Web: www.graphicpartners.com						
Graphic Products Inc PO Box 4030	Beaverton	OR	97076	503-644-5572	646-0183	174
TF: 888-326-9244 ■ *Web:* www.graphicproducts.com						
Graphic Reproduction						
1381 Franquette Ave Bldg B1	Concord	CA	94520	925-674-0900		344
TF: 800-498-9939 ■ *Web:* www.graphic4u.com						
Graphic Solutions Group Inc						
8575 Cobb Intl Blvd NW	Kennesaw	GA	30152	770-424-2300		781
Web: www.gsghome.com						
Graphic Specialties Inc						
3110 Washington Ave N	Minneapolis	MN	55411	612-522-5287		701
TF: 800-486-4605 ■ *Web:* www.signsbygsi.com						
Graphic Systems Inc						
2632 26th Ave S	Minneapolis	MN	55406	612-721-6100		588
Web: www.graphicsystems.com						
Graphic Technology of Maryland Inc						
8620 Old Dorsey Run Rd	Jessup	MD	20794	301-317-0100		627
TF: 800-896-8023 ■ *Web:* www.graphtec.com						
Graphic Trends Inc 7301 Adams St	Paramount	CA	90723	562-531-2339		687
Web: www.graphictrends.net						
Graphic World Inc 11687 Adie Rd	Hazelwood	MO	63043	314-567-9854		781
Web: www.gwinc.com						
Graphica 4501 Lyons Rd	Miamisburg	OH	45342	937-866-4013		4
Web: www.graphicadesign.com						
Graphicast Inc 36 Knight St	Jaffrey	NH	03452	603-532-4481		492
Web: www.graphicast.com						
Graphics & Mailing Service Inc						
2026 Locust St	Montgomery	AL	36107	334-263-3419		5
Web: www.graphicsandmailing.com						
Graphics Group 2800 Taylor St	Dallas	TX	75226	214-749-2222		781
Web: www.graphicsgroup.com						
Graphics Plus Inc 1808 Ogden Ave	Lisle	IL	60532	630-968-9073		627
Web: www.gpdelivers.com						
Graphics Service Bureau						
370 Park Ave S	New York	NY	10010	212-684-3600		344
Web: www.gsbinc.net						
Graphics Type & Color Enterprises Inc						
2300 NW Seventh Ave	Miami	FL	33127	305-591-7600		627
TF: 800-433-9298 ■ *Web:* www.clubflyers.com						
Graphicworks 5611 Silverado Way # D	Anchorage	AK	99518	907-272-7400		627
Web: www.graphicworks.net						
Graphik Dimensions Ltd						
2103 Brentwood St	High Point	NC	27263	336-887-3500		200
Web: www.pictureframes.com						
Graphique De France 9 State St	Woburn	MA	01801	781-935-3405		130
TF Sales: 800-444-1464 ■ *Web:* www.graphiquedefrance.com						
Graphiques m & H 87 Rue Prince	Montreal	QC	H3C2M7	514-866-6736		627
Web: mh.ca						
Graphite Machining Inc 240 N Main St	Topton	PA	19562	610-682-0080		127
Web: www.graphitemachininginc.com						
Graphite Metallizing Corp						
1050 Nepperhan Ave	Yonkers	NY	10703	914-968-8400	968-8468	500
Web: www.graphalloy.com						
Graphite Sales Inc						
16710 W Pk Cir Dr	Chagrin Falls	OH	44023	440-543-8221	543-5183	500
TF: 800-321-4147 ■ *Web:* www.graphitesales.com						
Graphite Systems Inc						
1613 Danciger Dr	Fort Worth	TX	76112	817-457-1851		127
Graphnet 40 Fultron St 28th Fl	New York	NY	10038	212-994-1100		736
TF: 800-327-1800 ■ *Web:* www.graphnet.com						
Graph-Pak Corp						
11250 Addison Ave	Franklin Park	IL	60131	847-451-7400		100
Web: www.graphpakcustompackaging.com						
Graphtech 1310 Crooked Hill Rd	Harrisburg	PA	17110	717-238-5751		627
Web: www.thinkgraphtech.com						
Grapnel Tech Services LLC						
6905 Vista Dr	West Des Moines	IA	50266	515-953-5767		177
Web: www.grapneltech.com						
Grappa 690 The Queensway	Etobicoke	ON	M8Y1K8	416-535-3337		671
Web: www.grapparestaurant.ca						
Grasan Equipment Co						
440 S Illinois Ave	Mansfield	OH	44907	419-526-4440		207
Web: www.grasan.com						
Grasing's 6th & Mission Sts	Carmel	CA	93923	831-624-6562	624-7431	671
Web: www.grasings.com						
Grask Peterbilt 9201 Sixth St SW	Cedar Rapids	IA	52404	888-434-2511	848-4302*	780
**Fax Area Code:* 319 ■ *TF:* 888-434-2511 ■ *Web:* www.cedarrapidstruckcenter.com						
Grass America Inc 1202 Hwy 66 S	Kernersville	NC	27284	800-334-3512		350
TF: 800-334-3512 ■ *Web:* www.grassusa.com						
Grass Point State Park						
42247 Grassy Pt Rd	Alexandria Bay	NY	13607	315-686-4472		565
Web: parks.ny.gov/parks/139/details.aspx						
Grass Valley Inc						
3499 Douglas-B-Floreani	Montreal	QC	H4S2C6	514-333-1772	333-9828	52
Web: www.grassvalley.com						
Grasshopper Co, The						
105 Old US Hwy 81 PO Box 637	Moundridge	KS	67107	620-345-8621	345-2301	429
Web: www.grasshoppermower.com						
Grassi & Co 488 Madison Ave	New York	NY	10022	212-661-6166		2
Web: www.grassicpas.com						
Grassi Investment Management LLC						
2350 Mission College Blvd Ste 190	Santa Clara	CA	95054	650-934-0770		401
Web: www.grassiinvest.com						
Grassland Dairy Products Company Inc						
N 8790 Fairgrounds Ave	Greenwood	WI	54437	800-428-8837	267-6044*	296-3
**Fax Area Code:* 715 ■ *TF:* 800-428-8837 ■ *Web:* www.grassland.com						
Grassland Equipment & Irrigation Corp						
892-898 Troy Schenectady Rd	Latham	NY	12110	518-785-5841	785-5740	429
TF: 800-564-5587 ■ *Web:* www.grasslandcorp.com						
Grassley Chuck (Sen R - IA)						
135 Hart Bldg	Washington	DC	20510	202-224-3744	224-6020	342-2
Web: www.grassley.senate.gov						
Grassley Group, The (FMCI)						
600 State St Ste A	Cedar Falls	IA	50613	866-619-5580	342-0411*	47
**Fax Area Code:* 703 ■ *TF:* 866-619-5580 ■ *Web:* www.grassleygroup.com						
Grassroots Motorsports Magazine						
915 Ridgewood Ave	Holly Hill	FL	32117	386-239-0523	239-0573	457-3
TF: 800-520-8292 ■ *Web:* www.grassrootsmotorsports.com						
Gratiot Area Chamber of Commerce						
110 W Superior St PO Box 516	Alma	MI	48801	989-463-5525	463-6588	139
TF: 800-952-0178 ■ *Web:* www.gratiot.org						
Gratiot County						
County Courthouse 214 E Ctr St PO Box 437	Ithaca	MI	48847	989-875-5215	875-5254	338
Web: www.gratiotmi.com						
Gratiot-Isabella Regional Education Service District						
1131 E Ctr St PO Box 310	Ithaca	MI	48847	989-875-5101	875-2858	685
Web: giresd.net						
Gratry & Company LLC						
3201 Enterprise Pkwy Ste 495	Beachwood	OH	44122	216-283-8423		401
Web: www.gratry.com						
Gratz College 7605 Old York Rd	Melrose Park	PA	19027	215-635-7300		166
TF: 800-475-4635 ■ *Web:* www.gratz.edu						
Gratz Park Inn 120 W Second St	Lexington	KY	40507	859-231-1777		671
TF: 800-752-4166 ■ *Web:* www.gratzparkinn.com						
Graulich International Inc						
6411 NW 35th Ave	Miami	FL	33147	305-836-1700		311
Gravel & Shea						
76 St Paul St PO Box 369	Burlington	VT	05402	802-658-0220		428
Web: www.gravelshea.com						
Gravely & Pearson LLP						
425 Soledad St Ste 600	San Antonio	TX	78205	210-472-1111		428
Web: www.gplawfirm.com						
Graver Technologies LLC 200 Lake Dr	Newark	DE	19702	302-731-1700	731-1707	806
TF: 800-249-1990 ■ *Web:* www.gravertech.com						
Graver Water Systems						
675 Central Ave Ste 3	New Providence	NJ	07974	908-516-1400	516-1401	806
TF: 877-472-8379 ■ *Web:* www.graver.com						
Graves & Company PC						
20550 Vernier Rd	Harper Woods	MI	48225	313-886-8892		2
Web: gravescpa.com						
Graves Bros Co						
2770 Indian River Blvd Ste 201	Vero Beach	FL	32960	772-562-3886	562-3565	315-2
Web: www.gravesbrotherscompany.com						
Graves County 101 E S St	Mayfield	KY	42066	270-247-3626	247-1274	338
Web: gravescounty.ky.gov						
Graves Garret (Rep R - LA)						
430 Cannon HOB	Washington	DC	20515	202-225-3901	225-7313	342-2
Web: garretgraves.house.gov						

Name	Address	City	State	ZIP	Phone	Fax	Class	Details
Graves Lumber Co	1315 S Cleveland-Massillon Rd	Copley	OH	44321	330-666-1115	666-1377	499	*TF:* 877-500-5515 ■ *Web:* www.graveslumber.com
Graves Menu Maker Foods Inc	913 Big Horn Dr	Jefferson City	MO	65109	573-893-3000	893-2172	297-7	*Web:* www.menumakerfoods.com
Graves Metal Products Inc	220 Commerce St	Jackson	TN	38301	731-422-1925		492	*Web:* www.gravesmetal.com
Graves Piano & Organ Company Inc	5798 Karl Rd	Columbus	OH	43229	614-847-4322		526	*TF:* 800-686-4322 ■ *Web:* gravespianos.com
Graves Sam (Rep R - MO)	1135 Longworth HOB	Washington	DC	20515	202-225-7041	225-8221	342-2	*Web:* graves.house.gov
Graves Tom (Rep R - GA)	2078 Rayburn HOB	Washington	DC	20515	202-225-5211	225-8272	342-2	*Web:* tomgraves.house.gov
Gravett & Associates	4054 Sandstone Ct	Cincinnati	OH	45245	513-753-8870		193	*Web:* www.gravett.com
Gravina Smith & Matte Inc	12474 Brantley Commons Ct	Fort Myers	FL	33907	239-275-5758		636	*Web:* gsma.pro
Gravitec Systems Inc	9453 Coppertop Loop NE	Bainbridge Island	WA	98110	206-780-2898		261	*TF:* 800-755-8455 ■ *Web:* www.gravitec.com
Gravity Group	107 E Water St	Harrisonburg	VA	22801	540-433-3071		195	*Web:* www.gravitygroup.com
Gravity Switch Inc	89 Market St	Northampton	MA	01060	413-586-9596		344	*Web:* www.gravityswitch.com
Gravity Tank Inc	114 W Illinois St Fl 3	Chicago	IL	60654	312-988-3000		466	*TF:* 800-438-7325 ■ *Web:* www.gravitytank.com
Gravograph-New Hermes Inc	2200 Northmont Pkwy	Duluth	GA	30096	770-623-0331	533-7637*	629	**Fax Area Code:* 800 ■ *TF:* 800-843-7637 ■ *Web:* www.gravograph.com
Gravy Train Express LLC	65 Gravy Train Ln	Lewistown	PA	17044	717-242-8515		311	*Web:* gravytrainllc.com
Gray & Associates Diversity Advertising & Public Relations	2677 Tritt Springs Trce NE	Marietta	GA	30062	678-560-9272		7	*Web:* www.grayassoc.net
Gray & Co	3325 W Polk Rd	Hart	MI	49420	503-248-4729	248-4729	296-20	*Web:* www.cherryman.com
Gray & Osborne Inc	701 Dexter Ave N Ste 200	Seattle	WA	98109	206-284-0860		256	*Web:* www.g-o.com
Gray & Sons Inc	430 W Padonia Rd	Timonium	MD	21093	410-771-4311	771-8125	188-4	*Web:* www.graynson.com
Gray Blodgett & Company Pllc	629 24th Ave SW	Norman	OK	73069	405-360-5533		2	*Web:* cpagray.com
Gray Callison & Company PA	3813 Forrestgate Dr	Winston-Salem	NC	27103	336-760-3210		2	*Web:* graycallison.com
Gray Chevrolet Cadillac	1245 N Ninth St	Stroudsburg	PA	18360	570-517-5500		57	*Web:* graychevrolet.com
Gray Construction	10 Quality St	Lexington	KY	40507	859-281-5000	252-5300	186	*TF:* 800-814-8468 ■ *Web:* www.gray.com
Gray County	PO Box 487	Cimarron	KS	67835	620-855-3618	855-3107	338	*Web:* www.grayco.org
Gray County	PO Box 1902	Pampa	TX	79066	806-669-8004		338	*Web:* www.co.gray.tx.us
Gray County Feed Yard Inc	23405 SR 23	Cimarron	KS	67835	620-855-3486		10-1	
Gray Glass Co	217-44 98th Ave	Queens Village	NY	11429	718-217-2943	217-0280	329	*TF:* 800-523-3320 ■ *Web:* www.grayglass.net
Gray Hunter Stenn LLP	500 Maine St	Quincy	IL	62301	217-222-0304		2	*Web:* www.gray-hunter-stenn.com
Gray Line Worldwide	1835 Gaylord St	Denver	CO	80206	303-394-6920		760	*TF:* 800-472-9546 ■ *Web:* www.grayline.com
Gray Metal Products Inc	495 Rochester St	Avon	NY	14414	585-226-8660		295	*Web:* www.graymetal.com
Gray Mfg Industries LLC	6258 Icehouse Rd	Hornell	NY	14843	607-281-1325		650	*Web:* gmihornell.com
Gray Plant Mooty Inc	500 IDS Ctr 80 S Eighth St	Minneapolis	MN	55402	612-632-3000		428	*Web:* www.gpmlaw.com
Gray Rust St Amand Moffett & Brieske LLP	950 E Paces Ferry Rd NE	Atlanta	GA	30326	404-870-7373		41	*Web:* www.grsmb.com
Gray Television Inc	4370 Peachtree Rd NE	Atlanta	GA	30319	404-504-9828		738	*NYSE: GTN* ■ *Web:* www.gray.tv
Gray Tools Canada Inc	299 Orenda Rd	Brampton	ON	L6T1E8	905-457-3014	457-1050	350	*Web:* www.graytools.com
Gray Transportation Inc	2459 GT Dr	Waterloo	IA	50703	319-234-3930	234-8841	685	*TF:* 800-234-3930 ■ *Web:* www.graytran.com
Gray, Layton, Kersh, Solomon, Sigmon, Furr & Smith, PA	516 S New Hope Rd	Gastonia	NC	28054	704-865-4400		428	*TF:* 800-447-5375 ■ *Web:* www.gastonlegal.com
Graybar Electric Co Inc	34 N Meramec Ave	Saint Louis	MO	63105	314-573-9200		246	*TF:* 800-472-9227 ■ *Web:* www.graybar.com
Graybill Bartz & Thompson	135 S Cottage Hill	Elmhurst	IL	60126	630-941-9460	832-3491	401	*Web:* www.graybillbartz.com
Graybill Machines Inc	221 W Lexington Rd	Lititz	PA	17543	717-626-5221		296	*Web:* www.graybillmachines.com
Graycon Group Ltd	325 Tenth Ave SW	Calgary	AB	T2R0A5	844-745-8122		177	*TF:* 844-745-8122 ■ *Web:* www.graycon.com
Grayd-A Metal Fabricators	13233 Florence Ave	Santa Fe Springs	CA	90670	562-944-8951	944-2326	697	*Web:* www.grayd-a.com
Grayhill Inc	561 W Hillgrove Ave	La Grange	IL	60525	708-354-1040	354-2820	729	*TF:* 800-683-0366 ■ *Web:* www.grayhill.com
Grayling Industries	1008 Branch Dr	Alpharetta	GA	30004	770-751-9095	751-3710	548	*TF:* 800-635-1551 ■ *Web:* www.graylingindustries.com
Graylyn International Conference Center Inc	1900 Reynolda Rd	Winston-Salem	NC	27106	336-758-2600		184	*TF:* 800-472-9596 ■ *Web:* graylyn.com
Graymills Corp	3705 N Lincoln Ave	Chicago	IL	60613	773-477-4100	477-4133	641	*TF:* 877-465-7867 ■ *Web:* www.graymills.com
Graymont Inc	10991 Shellbridge Way Ste 200	Richmond	BC	V6X3C6	604-276-9331	276-9337	440	*TF:* 866-207-4292 ■ *Web:* www.graymont.com
Grayrose Marketing Group	9631 NE Colfax St	Portland	OR	97220	503-281-1922		195	*TF:* 800-875-1922 ■ *Web:* www.grayrose.com
Grays Harbor Chamber of Commerce	506 Duffy St	Aberdeen	WA	98520	360-532-1924	533-7945	139	*TF:* 800-321-1924 ■ *Web:* www.graysharbor.org
Grays Harbor College	1620 Edward P Smith Dr	Aberdeen	WA	98520	360-532-9020	538-4293*	162	**Fax:* Admissions ■ *TF:* 800-562-4830 ■ *Web:* www.ghc.edu
Grays Harbor Community Hospital	920 Anderson Dr	Aberdeen	WA	98520	360-532-5122		374-3	*Web:* www.ghcares.org
Grays Harbor County	100 W Broadway	Montesano	WA	98563	360-249-3842		338	*Web:* www.co.grays-harbor.wa.us
Grays Harbor Paper LP	801 23rd St	Hoquiam	WA	98550	360-532-9600		557	*TF:* 800-869-3557 ■ *Web:* www.ghpaper.com
Grays Harbor Raceway	32 Elma McCleary Rd PO Box 911	Elma	WA	98541	360-482-4374	892-6582	642	*TF:* 800-667-7711 ■ *Web:* www.graysharborraceway.com
Grays Harbor Tourism	PO Box 1229	Elma	WA	98541	360-482-2651		206	*TF:* 800-621-9625 ■ *Web:* visitgraysharbor.com
Grayson County	100 W Houston St	Sherman	TX	75090	903-813-4207		338	*Web:* www.co.grayson.tx.us
Grayson County Chamber of Commerce	425 S Main St	Leitchfield	KY	42754	270-259-5587		338	*Web:* www.graysoncountychamber.com
Grayson County College	6101 Grayson Dr	Denison	TX	75020	903-465-6030	463-5284*	162	**Fax:* Admissions ■ *TF:* 800-424-2246 ■ *Web:* www.grayson.edu
Grayson Lake State Park	314 Grayson Lake Pk Rd	Olive Hill	KY	41164	606-474-9727		565	*Web:* www.parks.ky.gov
Grayson Rural Electric Co-op Corp	109 Bagby Pk	Grayson	KY	41143	606-474-5136	474-5862	245	*TF:* 800-562-3532 ■ *Web:* www.graysonrecc.com
Grayson-Collin Electric Co-op (GCEC)	PO Box 548	Van Alstyne	TX	75495	903-482-7100		245	*TF:* 800-967-5235 ■ *Web:* www.gcec.net
Graystone Group Advertising	2710 N ave	Bridgeport	CT	06604	203-549-0060		7	*TF:* 800-544-0005 ■ *Web:* www.graystoneadv.com
Grayton Beach State Park	357 Main Pk Rd	Santa Rosa Beach	FL	32459	850-267-8300		565	*Web:* www.floridastateparks.org/graytonbeach
Graytor Printing Company Inc	149 Park Ave	Lyndhurst	NJ	07071	201-933-0100		627	*TF:* 800-553-0931 ■ *Web:* www.graytor.com
GrayWolf Sensing Solutions LLC	6 Research Dr	Shelton	CT	06484	203-402-0477		419	*TF:* 800-218-7997 ■ *Web:* www.wolfsense.com
Graziano's	9227 SW 40th St	Miami	FL	33165	305-225-0008		671	*Web:* grazianosgroup.com
Grazie Italian Eatery	106 W Sixth St	Bloomington	IN	47401	812-323-0303		671	*Web:* www.grazieitaliano.com
Grazies Italian Grill	2851 S Oneida St	Green Bay	WI	54304	920-499-6365		671	*Web:* www.graziesitaliangrill.com
Grb Entertainment Inc	13400 Riverside Dr Ste 300	Sherman Oaks	CA	91423	818-728-7600		514	*Web:* grbtv.com
GRBJ (Grand Rapids Business Journal)	549 Ottawa Ave NW Ste 201	Grand Rapids	MI	49503	616-459-4545		457-5	*Web:* grbj.com
GRE America Inc	425 Harbor Blvd	Belmont	CA	94002	650-591-1400		173-3	*TF:* 800-233-5973 ■ *Web:* www.greamerica.com
Grease Monkey International	7450 E Progress Pl	Greenwood Village	CO	80111	303-308-1660	308-5908	62-5	*TF:* 800-822-7706 ■ *Web:* www.greasemonkeyintl.com
Great American Bancorp Inc	1311 S Neil St	Champaign	IL	61820	217-356-2265	356-2502	360-2	*OTC: GTPS* ■ *TF:* 800-962-4284 ■ *Web:* www.greatamericanbancorp.com
Great American Casino	10117 S Tacoma Way	Lakewood	WA	98499	253-396-0500		133	*Web:* www.greatamericancasino.com
Great American Cookie Company Inc	3300 Chambers Rd Ste 170	Horseheads	NY	14845	877-639-2361		68	*TF:* 877-639-2361 ■ *Web:* www.greatamericancookies.com
Great American Custom Insurance Services Inc	725 S Figueroa St	Los Angeles	CA	90017	213-430-4300		390	*Web:* www.gamcustom.com
Great American Farms Inc	1255 W Atlantic Blvd Ste 218	Pompano Beach	FL	33069	954-785-9400		10-4	
Great American Group Inc	21860 Burbank Blvd Ste 300	Woodland Hills	CA	91367	818-884-3737	884-2976	655	*OTC: GAMR* ■ *Web:* www.greatamerican.com
Great American Home Store	5295 Pepper Chase Dr	Southaven	MS	38671	662-996-1000		321	*Web:* www.greatamericanhomestore.com
Great American Insurance Co	580 Walnut St	Cincinnati	OH	45202	513-369-5000		391-4	*Web:* www.greatamericaninsurancegroup.com
Great American Products Inc	1661 S Seguin Ave	New Braunfels	TX	78130	830-620-4400	620-8430	702	*TF:* 800-341-4436 ■ *Web:* www.gap1.com

Name / Address	Phone	Fax	Class
Great American Supplemental Benefits PO Box 26580 ....Austin TX 78755 *TF:* 866-459-4272 ■ *Web:* www.cigna.com	866-459-4272		391-3
Great Arrow Graphics 2495 Main St Ste 457.........................Buffalo NY 14214 *TF:* 800-835-0490 ■ *Web:* www.greatarrow.com	716-836-0408	836-0702	130
Great Basin College 1500 College Pkwy ....Elko NV 89801 **Fax:* Admissions ■ *TF:* 888-590-6726 ■ *Web:* www.gbcnv.edu	775-738-8493	753-2311*	166
Great Basin National Park 100 Great Basin National Pk.....................Baker NV 89311 *Web:* www.nps.gov/grba	775-234-7331	234-7269	564
Great Basin Scientific Inc 420 E S Temple Ste A...................Salt Lake City UT 84111 *TF:* 888-360-4022 ■ *Web:* www.gbscience.com	801-990-1055		476
Great Bay Distributors Inc 2750 Eagle Ave N......................St. Petersburg FL 33716 *Web:* www.greatbaybud.com	727-584-8626	585-9425	81-1
Great Bend Feeding Inc 2006 Broadway Ave ....Great Bend KS 67530 *Web:* www.ilsbeef.com	620-793-9200		10-1
Great Bend Industries Inc 8701 Sixth St ....Great Bend KS 67530 *TF:* 800-333-4266 ■ *Web:* www.greatbendindustries.com	620-792-4368	792-3935	223
Great Books Foundation 35 E Wacker Dr Ste 400 ....Chicago IL 60601 *TF:* 800-222-5870 ■ *Web:* www.greatbooks.org	312-332-5870		48-11
Great Brook Farm State Park 165 N Rd......... Carlisle MA 01741 *Web:* www.mass.gov	978-369-6312		565
Great Clips Inc 4400 W 78th St Ste 700....................Minneapolis MN 55435 *TF:* 800-999-5959 ■ *Web:* www.greatclips.com	952-893-9088	844-3444	77
Great Dane Trailers Inc 602 E Lathrop Ave.........................Savannah GA 31415 *Web:* greatdanetrailers.com	912-644-2100		779
Great Day Improvements LLC 700 E Highland Rd ....Macedonia OH 44056 *TF:* 800-230-8301 ■ *Web:* www.greatdayimprovements.com	330-468-0700		236
Great Divide Lodge 550 Village Rd PO Box 8059 ....Breckenridge CO 80424 *TF:* 888-400-9590 ■ *Web:* www.breckresorts.com	970-547-5550		379
Great Eastern Energy LLC 1515 Sheephead Bay Rd.....................Brooklyn NY 11235 *Web:* www.greateasternenergy.com	718-648-0900		316
Great Eastern Sun Trading Company Inc 92 Mcintosh Rd ....Asheville NC 28806 *Web:* www.great-eastern-sun.com	828-665-7790		805
Great Ecology 315 W 36th St 10th fl............New York NY 10018 *Web:* www.greatecology.com	212-579-6800		192
Great Escape & Splashwater Kingdom Po Box 511.............................Lake George NY 12845 *TF:* 800 836 2582 ■ *Web:* www.sixflags.com	518-792-3500	792-3404	32
Great Events & Teams Inc 2170 S Parker Rd Ste 290.......................Denver CO 80231 *Web.* www.geteams.com	303-394-2022	394-3450	184
Great Expectations 14180 Dallas Pkwy Ste 100 ....Dallas TX 75254	972-448-7900	448-7969	226
Great Explorations Children's Museum 1925 Fourth St N .... Saint Petersburg FL 33704 *Web:* greatex.org	727-821-8992	823-7287	521
Great Falls Area Chamber of Commerce 100 First Ave N.........................Great Falls MT 59401	406-761-4434	761-6129	139
Great Falls Historic District Cultural Ctr 65 McBride Ave Ext..........................Paterson NJ 07501 *Web:* www.patersonnj.gov	973-279-9587	279-0587	50-2
Great Falls International Airport 2800 Terminal Dr ....Great Falls MT 59404 *Web:* flygtf.com	406-727-3404	727-6929	27
Great Falls Marketing LLC 121 Mill St.............Auburn ME 04210 *TF:* 800-221-8895 ■ *Web:* www.greatfallsmarketing.com	800-221-8895		195
Great Falls Public Library 301 Second Ave N ....Great Falls MT 59401 *Web:* www.greatfallslibrary.org	406-453-0349	453-0181	434-3
Great Falls Region Chamber of Commerce 5 Westminster St.........................Bellows Falls VT 05101 *Web:* www.gfrcc.org	802-463-4280		139
Great Falls Tribune 205 River Dr S ....Great Falls MT 59405 **Fax:* News Rm ■ *TF:* 800-438-6600 ■ *Web:* www.greatfallstribune.com	406-791-1444	791-1431*	532-2
Great Floors LLC 524 E Sherman Ave..................... Coeur d'Alene ID 83814 *Web:* greatfloors.com	208-664-5405		290
Great GetAways Inc 313 Cambridge St ....Boston MA 02114 *Web:* www.ggatravel.com	617-720-6100		772
Great Harvest Bread Co 28 S Montana St..........Dillon MT 59725 *TF:* 800-442-0424 ■ *Web:* www.greatharvest.com	406-683-6842	683-5537	68
Great Hill Partners LLC 1 Liberty Sq ....Boston MA 02109 *Web:* www.greathillpartners.com	617-790-9400	790-9401	792
Great Lake Woods Inc 3303 John F Donnelly Dr..................... Holland MI 49424 *Web:* www.greatlakewoods.com	616-399-3300		550
Great Lakes Aquarium 353 Harbor Dr............ Duluth MN 55802 *Web:* www.glaquarium.org	218-740-3474	740-2020	40
Great Lakes Aviation Ltd 1022 Airport Pkwy ....Cheyenne WY 82001 *OTC: GLUX* ■ *TF:* 800-554-5111 ■ *Web:* www.greatlakesav.com	307-432-7000		25
Great Lakes Case & Cabinet Company Inc 4193 Route 6N ....Edinboro PA 16412 *Web:* www.werackyourworld.com	814-734-7303		567
Great Lakes Castings LLC 800 N Washington Ave..................... Ludington MI 49431 *Web:* www.greatlakescastings.com	231-843-2501	845-1534	307
Great Lakes Cheese Company Inc 17825 Great Lakes Pkwy.........................Hiram OH 44234 *Web:* www.greatlakescheese.com	440-834-2500	834-1002	296-5
Great Lakes Christian College 6211 W Willow Hwy ....Lansing MI 48917 *TF Admissions:* 800-937-4522 ■ *Web:* www.glcc.edu	517-321-0242	321-5902	161
Great Lakes Construction Co 2608 Great Lakes Way ....Hinckley OH 44233 *TF:* 800-893-3665 ■ *Web:* greatlakesway.com	330-220-3900	220-7670	188-4
Great Lakes Crossing Outlets 4000 Baldwin Rd .... Auburn Hills MI 48326 *TF:* 877-746-7452 ■ *Web:* www.greatlakescrossingoutlets.com	248-454-5000		50-6
Great Lakes Cruise Co 3270 Washtenaw Ave .... Ann Arbor MI 48104 **Fax Area Code:* 734 ■ *TF:* 888-891-0203 ■ *Web:* www.greatlakescruising.com	888-891-0203	677-1428*	220
Great Lakes Dart Manufacturing Inc S84 W19093 Enterprise Dr................... Muskego WI 53150 *TF:* 800-225-7593 ■ *Web:* www.gldproducts.com	262-679-8730		761
Great Lakes Dredge & Dock Co 2122 York Rd .... Oak Brook IL 60523 *NASDAQ: GLDD* ■ *Web:* www.gldd.com	630-574-3000	574-2909	188-5
Great Lakes Energy Co-op 1323 Boyne Ave.............................Boyne City MI 49712 **Fax Area Code:* 231 ■ **Fax:* Cust Svc ■ *TF:* 888-485-2537 ■ *Web:* www.gtlakes.com	888-485-2537	582-6213*	245
Great Lakes Environmental Research Laboratory (GLERL) 4840 S State St........................... Ann Arbor MI 48108 *TF:* 800-222-1222 ■ *Web:* www.glerl.noaa.gov	734-741-2235	741-2055	668
Great Lakes Filters 301 Arch Ave .... Hillsdale MI 49242 *TF:* 800-521-8565 ■ *Web:* www.greatlakesfilters.com	800-521-8565		18
Great Lakes Foods 1230 48th Ave .... Menominee MI 49858 *Web:* www.greatlakesfoods.com	906-863-5503		186
Great Lakes Gypsum & Supply 33900 Concord Rd ....Livonia MI 48150	734-421-1170		191-3
Great Lakes Institute of Technology Toni & Guy Hair 5100 Peach St .... Erie PA 16509 *TF:* 800-394-4548 ■ *Web:* www.glit.edu	814-864-6666		166
Great Lakes International Inc 1905 Kearney Ave............................ Racine WI 53403 *Web:* www.greatlakesintl.com	262-634-2386		427
Great Lakes Mall 7850 Mentor Ave ....Mentor OH 44060 *TF:* 877-746-6642 ■ *Web:* www.simon.com	440-255-8932		460
Great Lakes Mdf LLC 300 Commerce Dr ....Lackawanna NY 14218 *Web:* www.greatlakesmdf.com	716-827-3008		819
Great Lakes Orthodontic Laboratories Div 200 Cooper Ave ....Tonawanda NY 14150 *TF:* 800-828-7626 ■ *Web:* www.greatlakesortho.com	800-828-7626		228
Great Lakes Packaging Corp W 190 N 11393 Carnegie Dr.............. Germantown WI 53022 *TF:* 800-261-4572 ■ *Web:* www.glpc.com	262-255-2100	255-7290	100
Great Lakes Packers Inc 400 Great Lakes Pkwy..........................Bellevue OH 44811	419-483-2956		11-1
Great Lakes Packing Co 1535 W 43rd St ....Chicago IL 60609 *Web:* glpacking.com	773-927-6660	927-8587	296-26
Great Lakes Plumbing & Heating Company Inc 4521 W Diversey Ave ....Chicago IL 60639 *Web:* www.glph.com	773-489-0400	489-1402	14
Great Lakes Power Products Inc 7455 Tyler Blvd.............................Mentor OH 44060 *Web:* www.glpower.com	440-951-5111		350
Great Lakes Rubber Company Inc 30573 Beck Rd ....Wixom MI 48442 *Web:* www.greatlakesrubberco.com	248-624-5710		789
Great Lakes Science Ctr 601 Erieside Ave...........................Cleveland OH 44114 *Web:* www.greatscience.com	216-694-2000		520
Great Lakes Theater Festival 1501 Euclid Ave Ste 300.....................Cleveland OH 44115 *Web:* www.greatlakestheater.org	216-241-5490	241-6315	749
Great Lakes Towing Co 4500 Div Ave ....Cleveland OH 44102 *TF:* 800-321-3663 ■ *Web:* www.thegreatlakesgroup.com	216-621-4854	621-7616	465
Great Lakes Veneer Inc 222 S Parkview Ave PO Box 476 ....Marion WI 54950 *Web:* www.greatlakesveneer.com	715-754-2501	754-2582	191-3
Great Lakes Window Inc 30499 Tracy Rd.......................... Walbridge OH 43465 *TF:* 844-247-6226 ■ *Web:* www.greatlakeswindow.com	844-247-6226		234
Great Lakes Woodworking Co 11345 Mound Rd .... Detroit MI 48212 *Web:* www.g-l-w.com	313-892-8500		499
Great Mall 447 Great Mall Dr.................. Milpitas CA 95035 *Web:* www.simon.com	408-945-4022		460
Great Meadow Correctional Facility 11739 SR 22 PO Box 51.................... Comstock NY 12821 *Web:* www.doccs.ny.gov/faclist.html	518-639-5516		213
Great Neck Saw Manufacturing Inc 165 E Second St............................Mineola NY 11501 *TF Cust Svc:* 800-457-0600 ■ *Web:* www.greatnecksaw.com	516-746-5352		682
Great North Artists Management 350 Dupont St .... Toronto ON M5R1V9 *Web:* tamac.ca	416-925-2051	925-3904	731
Great Northern Corp 395 Stroebe Rd .... Appleton WI 54914 *TF:* 800-236-3671 ■ *Web:* www.greatnortherncorp.com	920-739-3671		100
Great Northern Insurance Co 15 Mtn View Rd ....Warren NJ 07059 *TF Cust Svc:* 800-252-4670 ■ *Web:* www.chubb.com	908-903-2000		391-4
Great Northern Iron Ore Properties 332 Minnesota St Rm W1290............... Saint Paul MN 55101 *NYSE: GNI* ■ *TF:* 800-468-9716 ■ *Web:* www.gniop.com	651-224-2385	224-2387	675
Great Northern Products Ltd 2700 Plainfield Pk .... Cranston RI 02921 *Web:* northernproducts.com	401-490-4590	490-5595	296-14
Great Pacific Fixed Income Securities Inc 151 Kalmus Dr Ste H-8.................... Costa Mesa CA 92626 *TF:* 800-284-4804 ■ *Web:* www.greatpac.com	714-619-3000	619-3018	690
Great Plains Art Museum 1155 Q St PO Box 880214 .... Lincoln NE 68588 *Web.* www.unl.edu	402-472-6220	472-0463	520
Great Plains Coca-Cola Bottling Company Inc 600 N May Ave.........................Oklahoma City OK 73107 *TF:* 800-753-2653 ■ *Web:* www.greatplainscocacola.com	405-280-2000		80-2
Great Plains Correctional Facility 700 Sugar Creek Dr .... Hinton OK 73047 *Web:* www.geogroup.com	405-542-3711		213

Name / Address	City	State	ZIP	Phone	Fax	Class
Great Plains Energy Inc						
1200 Main St PO Box 418679	Kansas City	MO	64106	816-556-2200		360-5
NYSE: GXP ■ *Web:* www.greatplainsenergy.com						
Great Plains Ethanol LLC						
27716-462nd Ave	Chancellor	SD	57015	605-647-0040		579
Web: www.poetenergy.com						
Great Plains Health Alliance Inc						
625 Third St	Phillipsburg	KS	67661	785-543-2111		353
TF: 800-432-2779 ■ *Web:* www.gpha.com						
Great Plains Industries Inc						
5252 E 36th St N	Wichita	KS	67220	316-686-7361	686-6746	641
TF Sales: 800-835-0113 ■ *Web:* www.gpi.net						
Great Plains Laboratory Inc						
11813 W 77th St	Lenexa	KS	66214	913-341-8949		418
TF: 800-288-0383 ■ *Web:* www.greatplainslaboratory.com						
Great Plains Lions Eye Bank						
Texas Tech University Health Sciences Ctr						
3601 Fourth St Ste BAB104-HSC	Lubbock	TX	79430	806-743-2242		269
Web: www.ttuhsc.edu/eye						
Great Plains Nature Ctr						
6232 E 29th St N	Wichita	KS	67220	316-683-5499	688-9555	50-5
TF: 800-222-1222 ■ *Web:* www.gpnc.org						
Great Plains State Park						
22487 E 1566 Rd	Mountain Park	OK	73559	580-569-2032	569-2375	565
TF: 800-622-6317 ■ *Web:* www.travelok.com						
Great Plains Transportation Museum						
700 E Douglas St	Wichita	KS	67202	316-263-0944		520
Web: www.gptm.us						
Great Plains Tribal Chairmen's Health Board						
1770 Rand Rd	Rapid City	SD	57702	605-721-1922		194
TF: 800-745-3466 ■ *Web:* www.aatchb.org						
Great Plains Zoo						
805 S Kiwanis Ave	Sioux Falls	SD	57104	605-367-7003		823
Web: www.greatzoo.org						
Great Planes Model Distributors						
PO Box 9021	Champaign	IL	61826	217-398-3630	398-1104	762
TF: 800-637-7660 ■ *Web:* www.gpmd.com						
Great Point Investors LLC						
2 Center Plaza Ste 410	Boston	MA	02108	617-526-8800		401
Web: www.gpinvestors.com						
Great Point Partners LLC						
165 Mason St 3rd Fl	Greenwich	CT	06830	203-971-3300		194
Web: www.greatpointpartnersllc.com						
Great River Bluffs State Park						
43605 Kipp Dr	Winona	MN	55987	507-643-6849	643-6849	565
TF: 888-646-6367 ■ *Web:* www.dnr.state.mn.us						
Great River Energy						
12300 Elm Creek Blvd	Maple Grove	MN	55369	763-445-5000	445-5050	245
TF: 888-521-0130 ■ *Web:* www.greatriverenergy.com						
Great River Medical Ctr						
1221 S Gear Ave	West Burlington	IA	52655	319-768-1000		374-3
Web: www.greatrivermedical.org						
Great River Regional Library						
1300 W St Germain St	Saint Cloud	MN	56301	320-650-2500	650-2501	434-3
TF: 800-581-0081 ■ *Web:* www.griver.org						
Great Salt Lake Book Festival						
Utah Humanities Council 202 W 300 N	Salt Lake City	UT	84103	801-359-9670	531-7869	281
TF: 877-786-7598 ■ *Web:* www.utahhumanities.org						
Great Salt Plains State Park						
23280 S Spillway Dr	Jet	OK	73749	580-626-4731	626-4730	565
Web: www.travelok.com						
Great Sand Dunes National Park & Preserve						
11500 Hwy 150	Mosca	CO	81146	719-378-6300	378-6310	564
Web: www.nps.gov/grsa						
Great Seal State Park						
4908 Marietta Rd	Chillicothe	OH	45601	740-663-2125		565
Web: www.ohiodnr.com						
Great Seats Inc						
7338 Baltimore Ave Ste 108A	College Park	MD	20740	301-985-6250	985-6254	750
TF: 800-664-5056 ■ *Web:* www.greatseats.com						
Great Skate Hockey Supl Co						
3395 Sheridan Dr	Buffalo	NY	14226	716-838-5100		711
TF: 800-828-7496 ■ *Web:* www.greatskate.com						
Great Smoky Mountains National Park						
107 Park Headquarters Rd	Gatlinburg	TN	37738	865-436-1200	436-1204	564
Web: www.nps.gov						
Great Source Education Group						
181 Ballardvale St	Wilmington	MA	01887	800-289-4490	289-3994	243
TF: 800-289-4490 ■ *Web:* www.hmhco.com						
Great South Texas Corp						
814 Arion Pkwy	San Antonio	TX	70216	210-369-0300		177
TF: 800-531-3858 ■ *Web:* www.comsoltx.com						
Great Southern Coaches						
900 Burke Ave	Jonesboro	AR	72401	870-935-5569		107
Web: yellowpagesgoesgreen.org						
Great Southern Wood Preserving						
1050 N Main St	Rocky Mount	VA	24151	540-483-5264		818
Web: www.greatsouthernwood.com						
Great Southern Wood Preserving Inc						
1100 US Hwy 431 N	Abbeville	AL	36310	334-585-2291	585-4353	818
Web: www.yellawood.com						
Great Southwest Paper Co						
5707 Harvey Wilson Dr	Houston	TX	77020	713-223-5050	223-3030	554
TF: 800-544-1512 ■ *Web:* www.gswpaper.com						
Great Steak & Potato Co						
9311 E Via de Ventura	Scottsdale	AZ	85258	480-362-4800	362-4812	670
TF: 866-452-4252 ■ *Web:* www.thegreatsteak.com						
Great Wall 410 N Hillside Ave	Wichita	KS	67214	316-688-0881		671
Web: greatwallwichita.com						
Great Wall 1649 Bedford Row	Halifax	NS	B3J3J4	902-422-6153		671
Web: www.thegreatwall.ca						
Great West Casualty Co						
1100 W 29th St PO Box 277	South Sioux City	NE	68776	402-494-2411		391-4
TF: 800-228-8602 ■ *Web:* info.gwccnet.com						
Great Western Bank 6015 NW Radial Hwy	Omaha	NE	68104	402-952-6000	223-6057*	70
**Fax Area Code:* 515 ■ *TF:* 800-952-2043 ■ *Web:* www.greatwesternbank.com						
Great Western Drilling Co Inc						
700 W Louisiana St	Midland	TX	79701	432-682-5241		536
Web: www.gwdc.com						
Great Western Ink Inc						
2100 NW 22nd Ave	Portland	OR	97210	503-226-3595		388
Web: www.gw-inks.com						
Great Western Malting Co						
1701 NW Harborside Dr	Vancouver	WA	98660	360-693-3661		461
Web: www.greatwesternmalting.com						
Great Western Mfg Co Inc						
2017 S Fourth St PO Box 149	Leavenworth	KS	66048	913-682-2291	682-1431	298
TF: 800-682-3121 ■ *Web:* www.gwmfg.com						
Great Western Recycling Industries Inc						
521 Barge Channel Rd	St Paul	MN	55107	651-224-4877		492
Great Western Supply Inc						
2626 Industrial Dr	Ogden	UT	84401	801-621-5412		612
Web: www.gwsupply.com						
Great White Energy Services LLC						
14201 Caliber Dr Ste 300	Oklahoma City	OK	73134	405-285-5812		538
Great White Pressure Control LLC						
4500 SE 59th St	Oklahoma City	OK	73135	405-605-2700		540
Web: www.greatwhitepressurecontrol.com						
Great Wolf Lodge of Sandusky LLC						
4600 Milan Rd US 250	Sandusky	OH	44870	800-641-9653		378
TF: 800-641-9653 ■ *Web:* www.greatbearlodge.com						
Great Wolf Lodge Williamsburg						
549 E Rochambeau Dr	Williamsburg	VA	23188	757-229-9700	229-9780	669
TF: 800-551-9653 ■ *Web:* www.greatwolf.com						
Great Wolf Resorts Inc						
525 Junction Rd Ste 6000 S	Madison	WI	53717	608-253-2222		669
NASDAQ: WOLF ■ *Web:* www.greatwolf.com						
Great Wraps! Inc						
4 Executive Pk E Ste 315	Atlanta	GA	30329	404-248-9900		670
Web: www.greatwraps.com						
Greater Aiken Chamber of Commerce						
121 Richland Ave E PO Box 892	Aiken	SC	29802	803-641-1111	641-4174	139
TF: 800-251-7234 ■ *Web:* www.aikenchamber.net						
Greater Akron Chamber						
1 Cascade Plaza 17th Fl	Akron	OH	44308	330-376-5550	379-3164	139
TF: 800-733-5627 ■ *Web:* www.greaterakronchamber.org						
Greater Albuquerque Chamber of Commerce						
115 Gold Ave SW # 201	Albuquerque	NM	87102	505-764-3700	764-3714	139
Web: www.abqchamber.com						
Greater Atlanta Christian						
1575 Indian Trl Lilburn Rd	Norcross	GA	30093	770-243-2000		48-20
TF: 800-450-1327 ■ *Web:* www.greateratlantachristian.org						
Greater Atlantic City Chamber						
12 S Virginia Ave	Atlantic City	NJ	08401	609-345-4524	345-1666	139
TF: 800-123-4567 ■ *Web:* acchamber.com						
Greater Augusta Regional Chamber of Commerce						
30 Ladd Rd PO Box 1107	Fishersville	VA	22939	540-324-1133	324-1136	139
TF: 866-922-2514 ■ *Web:* augustava.com						
Greater Austin Performing Arts Center Inc						
701 W Riverside Dr	Austin	TX	78704	512-457-5100		720
TF: 800-735-2989 ■ *Web:* thelongcenter.org						
Greater Bakersfield Chamber of Commerce						
1725 Eye St	Bakersfield	CA	93301	661-327-4421	327-8751	139
Web: www.bakersfieldchamber.org						
Greater Bakersfield Convention & Visitors Bureau						
515 Truxtun Ave	Bakersfield	CA	93301	661-852-7282	325-7074	206
TF: 866-425-7353 ■ *Web:* www.visitbakersfield.com						
Greater Baltimore Medical Ctr (GBMC)						
6701 N Charles St	Baltimore	MD	21204	443-849-2000		374-3
Web: www.gbmc.org						
Greater Bangor Convention & Visitors Bureau						
40 Harlow St	Bangor	ME	04401	207-947-5205		206
TF: 800-916-6673 ■ *Web:* www.visitbangormaine.com						
Greater Barrie Chamber of Commerce						
97 Toronto St	Barrie	ON	L4N1V1	705-721-5000	726-0973	137
Web: www.barriechamber.com						
Greater Baton Rouge Chamber of Commerce						
564 Laurel St	Baton Rouge	LA	70801	225-381-7125		139
Web: www.brac.org						
Greater Beauregard Chamber of Commerce						
111 N Washington St	DeRidder	LA	70634	337-463-5533	463-2244	139
Web: www.beauchamber.org						
Greater Beloit Chamber of Commerce						
500 Public Ave	Beloit	WI	53511	608-365-8835	365-6850	139
TF: 866-981-5969 ■ *Web:* greaterbeloitchamber.org						
Greater Bentonville Area Chamber of Commerce (BBVCC)						
200 E Central St PO Box 330	Bentonville	AR	72712	479-273-2841	273-2180	139
Web: www.bbvchamber.com						
Greater Bethesda Chamber of Commerce, The						
7910 Woodmont Ave Ste 1204	Bethesda	MD	20814	301-652-4900	657-1973	139
Web: www.bccchamber.org						
Greater Big Rapids Convention & Visitors Bureau						
246 N State St	Big Rapids	MI	49307	231-796-7640		206
Web: www.bigrapids.org						
Greater Binghamton Chamber of Commerce						
49 Ct St	Binghamton	NY	13901	607-772-8860	722-4513	139
Web: www.greaterbinghamtonchamber.com						
Greater Binghamton Convention						
49 Ct St Second Fl PO Box 995	Binghamton	NY	13902	607-772-8860	722-4513	206
Web: greaterbinghamtonchamber.com						
Greater Binghamton Health Ctr						
425 Robinson St	Binghamton	NY	13904	607-724-1391	773-4387	374-5
Web: www.omh.ny.gov						
Greater Birmingham Convention & Visitors Bureau						
2200 Ninth Ave N	Birmingham	AL	35203	205-458-8000	458-8086	206
TF: 800-458-8085 ■ *Web:* birminghamal.org						
Greater Bloomington Chamber of Commerce						
400 W Seventh St Ste 102	Bloomington	IN	47404	812-336-6381	336-0651	139
Web: www.chamberbloomington.org						
Greater Boca Raton Chamber of Commerce						
1800 N Dixie Hwy	Boca Raton	FL	33432	561-395-4433	392-3780	139
TF: 800-435-7352 ■ *Web:* www.bocaratonchamber.com						
Greater Boston Chamber of Commerce						
265 Franklin St	Boston	MA	02110	617-227-4500	227-7505	139
TF: 800-476-3094 ■ *Web:* www.bostonchamber.com						
Greater Boston Convention & Visitors Bureau (GBCVB)						
2 Copley Pl Ste 105	Boston	MA	02116	617-536-4100	424-7664	206
TF: 888-733-2678 ■ *Web:* www.bostonusa.com						

Phone Fax Class

Greater Bowie Chamber of Commerce
1525 Pointer Ridge Pl Ste 117 .... Bowie MD 20715 301-262-0920 262-0921 139
Web: www.bowiechamber.org

Greater Boynton Beach Chamber of Commerce
1880 N Congress Ave Ste 106 .... Boynton Beach FL 33426 561-732-9501 734-4304 139
Web: www.boyntonbeach.org

Greater Brandon Chamber of Commerce
330 Pauls Dr Ste 100 .... Brandon FL 33511 813-689-1221 689-9440 139
TF: 800-594-9620 ■ *Web:* www.brandonchamber.com

Greater Bridgeport Conference & Vistors Ctr
164 W Main St .... Bridgeport WV 26330 304-842-7272 206
TF: 800-368-4324 ■ *Web:* www.greater-bridgeport.com

Greater Bridgeport Symphony (GBS)
446 University Ave .... Bridgeport CT 06604 203-576-0263 573-3
Web: www.bptsym.org

Greater Brighton Area Chamber of Commerce
218 E Grand Riv .... Brighton MI 48116 810-227-5086 227-5940 139
Web: www.brightoncoc.org

Greater Bristol Chamber of Commerce
200 Main St .... Bristol CT 06010 860-584-4718 584-4722 139
TF: 855-344-1874 ■ *Web:* www.centralctchambers.org

Greater Brookfield Chamber of Commerce
17100 W Bluemound Rd Ste 202 .... Brookfield WI 53005 262-786-1886 786-1959 139
TF: 800-600-0134 ■ *Web:* www.brookfieldchamber.com

Greater Capital Area Assn of Realtors
15201 Diamondback Dr Ste 100.............. Rockville MD 20850 301-590-2000 656
Web: www.gcaar.com

Greater Cedar Falls Chamber of Commerce
312 W First St.......................... Cedar Falls IA 50613 319-266-3593 277-4325 139
Web: cedarvalleyalliance.com

Greater Cedar Valley Chamber of Commerce
10 W Fourth St Ste 310 .... Waterloo IA 50703 319-232-1156 233-4580 139
TF: 800-288-1047 ■ *Web:* cedarvalleyalliance.com

Greater Chambersburg Chamber of Commerce
100 Lincoln Way E Ste A ....Chambersburg PA 17201 717-264-7101 267-0399 139
TF: 800-840-9081 ■ *Web:* www.chambersburg.org

Greater Charlottetown Area Chamber of Commerce
PO Box 67 .... Charlottetown PE C1A7K2 902-628-2000 368-3570 137
Web: www.charlottetownchamber.com

Greater Cheyenne Chamber of Commerce
121 W 15th St Ste 204 ....Cheyenne WY 82001 307-638-3388 778-1407 139
TF: 800-227-5122 ■ *Web:* www.cheyennechamber.org

Greater Cincinnati Convention & Visitors Bureau
525 Vine St Ste 1500 .... Cincinnati OH 45202 513-621-2142 621-5020 206
TF: 800-543-2613 ■ *Web:* www.cincyusa.com

Greater Cincinnati Foundation
200 W Fourth St .... Cincinnati OH 45202 513-241-2880 852-6886 303
TF: 800-742-6253 ■ *Web:* www.gcfdn.org

Greater Cleveland Partnership
1240 Huron Rd E Ste 300....................Cleveland OH 44115 216-621-3300 621-6013 139
TF: 888-304-4769 ■ *Web:* www.gcpartnership.com

Greater Cleveland Regional Transit Authority (RTA)
1240 W Sixth St ....Cleveland OH 44113 216-621-9500 468
Web: www.riderta.com

Greater Columbia Chamber of Commerce
930 Richland St ....Columbia SC 29201 803-733-1110 733-1149 139
Web: www.columbiachamber.com

Greater Columbus Chamber of Commerce
1200 Sixth Ave PO Box 1200 .... Columbus GA 31902 706-327-1566 327-7512 139
TF: 800-360-8552 ■ *Web:* www.columbusgachamber.com

Greater Columbus Convention & Visitors Bureau
277 W Nationwide Blvd Ste 125............. Columbus OH 43215 614-221-6623 221-5618 206
TF: 866-397-2657 ■ *Web:* www.experiencecolumbus.com

Greater Columbus Convention Ctr
400 N High St.............................. Columbus OH 43215 614-827-2500 221-7239 205
TF: 800-626-0241 ■ *Web:* www.columbusconventions.com

Greater Concord Chamber of Commerce
2280 Diamond Blvd Ste 200..................Concord CA 94520 925-685-1181 685-5623 139
TF: 800-427-8686 ■ *Web:* www.concordchamber.com

Greater Concord Chamber of Commerce
49 S Main St...............................Concord NH 03301 603-224-2508 224-8128 139
TF: 800-360-4839 ■ *Web:* www.concordnhchamber.com

Greater Conroe/Lake Conroe Area Chamber of Commerce
PO Box 2347 ....Conroe TX 77305 936-756-6644 756-6462 139
TF: 800-825-8829 ■ *Web:* www.conroe.org

Greater Conroe-Lake Conroe Area Chamber of Commerce
505 W Davis St.............................Conroe TX 77301 936-756-6644 756-6462 139
Web: www.conroe.org

Greater Corner Brook Board of Trade
11 Confederation Dr PO Box 475 ....Corner Brook NL A2H6E6 709-634-5831 639-9710 137
Web: www.gcbbt.com

Greater Crofton Chamber of Commerce
2138 Priest Bridge Ct Ste 1 PO Box 4146......... Crofton MD 21114 410-721-9131 274-6060* 139
**Fax Area Code:* 443 ■ *Web:* www.greatercroftonchamberofcommerce.wildapricot.or

Greater Danbury Chamber of Commerce
39 West St ....Danbury CT 06810 203-743-5565 794-1439 139
TF: 800-722-2936 ■ *Web:* www.danburychamber.com

Greater Data & Mailing Inc
551 Acorn St...............................Deer Park NY 11729 631-667-1450 5
Web: greaterdata.com

Greater Decatur Chamber of Commerce
101 S Main St Ste 102 .... Decatur IL 62523 217-422-2200 422-4576 139
Web: www.decaturchamber.com

Greater Deerfield Beach Chamber of Commerce
1601 E Hillsboro Blvd.................. Deerfield Beach FL 33441 954-427-1050 427-1056 139
TF: 866-551-9805 ■ *Web:* www.deerfieldchamber.com

Greater Delray Beach Chamber of Commerce
140 NE First St......................... Delray Beach FL 33444 561-278-0424 278-6012 139
Web: www.delraybeach.com

Greater Derry Chamber of Commerce
29 W Broadway.............................. Derry NH 03038 603-432-8205 139
Web: www.gdlchamber.org

Greater Des Moines Convention & Visitors Bureau
400 Locust St Ste 265 .... Des Moines IA 50309 515-286-4960 244-9757 206
TF: 800-451-2625 ■ *Web:* www.catchdesmoines.com

Greater Des Moines Partnership
700 Locust St Ste 100 .... Des Moines IA 50309 515-286-4950 286-4902 139
Web: www.dsmpartnership.com

Greater Dover Chamber of Commerce
550 Central Ave ....Dover NH 03820 603-742-2218 749-6317 139
TF: 800-277-2130 ■ *Web:* www.dovernh.org

Greater Durham Chamber of Commerce
300 W Morgan St Ste 1400 PO Box 3829......... Durham NC 27702 919-328-8700 688-8351 139
Web: www.durhamchamber.org

Greater Easley Chamber of Commerce
2001 E Main St PO Box 241.................... Easley SC 29641 864-859-2693 859-1941 139
Web: www.easleychamber.net

Greater East Aurora Chamber of Commerce
652 Main St .... East Aurora NY 14052 716-652-8444 652-8384 139
TF: 800-441-2881 ■ *Web:* www.eanycc.com

Greater Edmonds Chamber of Commerce
121 Fifth Ave N............................. Edmonds WA 98020 425-670-1496 712-1808 139
TF: 800-592-9995 ■ *Web:* www.edmondswa.com

Greater El Monte Community Hospital (GEMCH)
1701 Santa Anita Ave .... South El Monte CA 91733 626-579-7777 350-0368 374-3
TF: 800-954-8000 ■ *Web:* www.greaterelmonte.com

Greater El Paso Chamber of Commerce
10 Civic Ctr Plaza........................... El Paso TX 79901 915-534-0500 534-0510 139
Web: www.elpaso.org

Greater Elkhart Chamber of Commerce
418 S Main St...............................Elkhart IN 46516 574-293-1531 294-1859 139
Web: www.elkhart.org

Greater Enid Chamber of Commerce
PO Box 907 ....Enid OK 73702 580-237-2494 237-2497 139
TF: 877-334-2665 ■ *Web:* www.enidchamber.com

Greater Eureka Chamber of Commerce, The
2112 Broadway............................... Eureka CA 95501 707-442-3738 442-0079 139
TF: 866-267-4255 ■ *Web:* www.eurekachamber.com

Greater Fayetteville Chamber
159 Maxwell St...........................Fayetteville NC 28301 910-483-8133 483-0263 139
Web: www.faybiz.com

Greater Federal Way Chamber of Commerce
31919 First Ave S Ste 202 ....Federal Way WA 98003 253-838-2605 661-9050 139
TF: 800-390-8370 ■ *Web:* www.federalwaychamber.com

Greater Fort Lauderdale Chamber of Commerce
512 NE Third Ave .... Fort Lauderdale FL 33301 954-462-6000 527-8766 139
Web: www.ftlchamber.com

Greater Fort Lauderdale Convention & Visitors Bureau
100 E Broward Blvd Ste 200............ Fort Lauderdale FL 33301 954-765-4466 765-4467 206
TF: 877-272-5465 ■ *Web:* www.sunny.org

Greater Fort Lauderdale-Broward County Convention Ctr
1950 Eisenhower Blvd .... Fort Lauderdale FL 33316 954-765-5900 205
TF: 800-327-1390 ■ *Web:* www.ftlauderdalecc.com

Greater Fort Myers Chamber of Commerce
2310 Edwards Dr .... Fort Myers FL 33901 239-332-3624 332-7276 139
TF: 800-366-3622 ■ *Web:* www.fortmyers.org

Greater Fort Walton Beach Chamber of Commerce
34 Miracle Strip Pkwy SE .... Fort Walton Beach FL 32548 850-244-8191 244-1935 139
TF: 800-225-5797 ■ *Web:* www.fwbchamber.org

Greater Fort Wayne Chamber of Commerce
826 Ewing St .... Fort Wayne IN 46802 260-424-1435 139
Web: greaterfortwayneinc.com

Greater Fort Worth Assn of Realtors Inc
2650 Parkview Dr......................... Fort Worth TX 76102 817-336-5165 652
Web: www.gfwar.org

Greater Franklin County Chamber of Commerce, The
11 E Nash St PO Box 62.................... Louisburg NC 27549 919-496-3056 496-0422 139
Web: www.franklin-chamber.org

Greater Gardner Chamber of Commerce
29 Parker St PO Box 1381 .... Gardner MA 01440 978-632-1780 630-1767 139
TF: 800-523-6373 ■ *Web:* www.gardnerma.com

Greater Gibson County Area Chamber of Commerce
200 E Eaton St .... Trenton TN 38382 731-855-0973 855-0979 139
Web: www.gibsoncountytn.com

Greater Giving Inc
1920 N W Amberglen Pkwy Ste 140...........Beaverton OR 97006 800-276-5992 317
TF: 800-276-5992 ■ *Web:* greatergiving.com

Greater Golden Chamber of Commerce
1010 Washington Ave.........................Golden CO 80401 303-279-3113 139
Web: goldenchamber.org

Greater Grand Forks Convention & Visitors Bureau
4251 Gateway Dr ....Grand Forks ND 58203 701-746-0444 746-0775 206
TF: 800-866-4566 ■ *Web:* www.visitgrandforks.com

Greater Green Bay Chamber
PO Box 1660 .... Green Bay WI 54305 920-437-8704 139
Web: www.titletown.org

Greater Green Bay Convention & Visitors Bureau
1901 S Oneida St .... Green Bay WI 54304 920-494-9507 405-1271 206
TF: 888-867-3342 ■ *Web:* www.greenbay.com

Greater Greenbrier Chamber of Commerce
200 W Washington St Ste C .... Lewisburg WV 24901 304-645-2818 139
Web: www.greenbrierwvchamber.org

Greater Greenville Chamber of Commerce
24 Cleveland St .... Greenville SC 29601 864-242-1050 282-8509* 139
**Fax:* PR ■ *TF:* 866-485-5262 ■ *Web:* www.greenvillechamber.org

Greater Greenville Convention & Visitors Bureau
148 River St Ste 222...................... Greenville SC 29601 864-421-0000 421-0005 206
TF: 800-351-7180 ■ *Web:* www.visitgreenvillesc.com

Greater Greenwood Chamber of Commerce
65 Airport Pkwy .... Greenwood IN 46143 317-888-4856 865-2609 139
TF: 800-462-7585 ■ *Web:* www.greenwoodchamber.com

Greater Hackensack Chamber of Commerce
5 University Plaza Dr .... Hackensack NJ 07601 201-489-3700 489-1741 139
Web: www.hackensackchamber.org

Greater Hall Chamber of Commerce
230 EE Butler Pkwy.......................Gainesville GA 30501 770-532-6206 535-8419 139
Web: www.ghcc.com

Greater Hamilton Chamber of Commerce
201 Dayton St............................. Hamilton OH 45011 513-844-1500 844-1999 139
Web: www.hamilton-ohio.com

Greater Hammonton Chamber of Commerce, The
10 S Egg Harbor Rd ....Hammonton NJ 08037 609-561-9080 139
Web: www.hammontonnj.us

Greater Hartsville Chamber of Commerce
214 N Fifth St .... Hartsville SC 29551 843-332-6401 332-8017 139
TF: 866-747-0060 ■ *Web:* www.hartsvillechamber.org

Name	Address	City	State	Zip	Phone	Fax	Class	TF / Web
Greater Haverhill Chamber of Commerce	80 Merrimack St	Haverhill	MA	01830	978-373-5663	373-8060	139	*Web:* www.haverhillchamber.com
Greater Heights Area Chamber of Commerce	545 W 19th St 2nd Fl	Houston	TX	77008	713-861-6735	861-9310	139	*Web:* www.heightschamber.com
Greater Hernando County Chamber of Commerce	15588 Aviation Loop Dr	Brooksville	FL	34604	352-796-0697	796-3704	139	*Web:* www.hernandochamber.com
Greater Hollywood Chamber of Commerce	330 N Federal Hwy	Hollywood	FL	33020	954-923-4000		139	*Web:* www.hollywoodchamber.org
Greater Holy Temple Christian Academy	5575 N 76th St	Milwaukee	WI	53218	414-265-4131		148	*Web:* greaterholy.org
Greater Holyoke Chamber of Commerce	177 High St	Holyoke	MA	01040	413-534-3376		139	*TF:* 800-462-2301 ■ *Web:* www.holycham.com
Greater Hot Springs Chamber of Commerce	659 Ouachita Ave	Hot Springs	AR	71901	501-321-1700	321-3551	139	*TF:* 800-992-7552 ■ *Web:* www.hotspringschamber.com
Greater Houston Convention & Visitors Bureau	901 Bagby St Ste 100	Houston	TX	77002	713-437-5200		206	*TF:* 800-446-8786 ■ *Web:* www.visithoustontexas.com
Greater Houston Partnership	1200 Smith St Ste 700	Houston	TX	77002	713-844-3600	844-0200	139	*TF:* 800-829-1040 ■ *Web:* www.houston.org
Greater Huntington Park Area Chamber of Commerce	6330 Pacific Blvd Ste 208	Huntington Park	CA	90255	323-585-1155	585-2176	139	*TF:* 800-866-1752 ■ *Web:* www.hpchamber.org
Greater Hutchinson Convention & Visitors Bureau	117 N Walnut St PO Box 519	Hutchinson	KS	67504	620-662-3391	662-2168	206	*TF:* 800-691-4262 ■ *Web:* www.hutchchamber.com
Greater Iberia Chamber of Commerce	111 W Main St	New Iberia	LA	70560	337-364-1836	367-7405	139	*TF:* 800-346-1958 ■ *Web:* iberiachamber.org
Greater Illinois Title Co	120 N La Salle St Ste 900	Chicago	IL	60602	312-236-7300	236-0284	391-6	*Web:* www.gitc.com
Greater Indianapolis Chamber of Commerce	111 Monument Cir Ste 1950	Indianapolis	IN	46204	317-464-2200	464-2217	139	*Web:* www.indychamber.com
Greater Irvine Chamber	2485 McCabe Way Ste 150	Irvine	CA	92614	949-660-9112	660-0829	139	*Web:* www.irvinechamber.com
Greater Issaquah Chamber of Commerce	155 NW Gilman Blvd	Issaquah	WA	98027	425-392-7024	392-8101	139	*Web:* www.issaquahchamber.com
Greater Jackson Chamber of Commerce	141 S Jackson St	Jackson	MI	49201	517-782-8221	780-3688	139	*TF:* 800-366-3699 ■ *Web:* www.jacksonchamber.org
Greater Jackson Chamber Partnership	PO Box 22548	Jackson	MS	39225	601-948-7575	352-5539	139	*TF:* 800-339-7781 ■ *Web:* www.greaterjacksonpartnership.com
Greater Jackson County Chamber of Commerce, The	407 E Willow St	Scottsboro	AL	35768	256-259-5500	259-4447	139	*TF:* 800-259-5508 ■ *Web:* www.jacksoncountychamber.com
Greater Johnstown/Cambria County Chamber of Commerce	245 Market St Ste 100	Johnstown	PA	15901	814-536-5107	539-5800	139	*TF:* 800-790-4522 ■ *Web:* www.johnstownchamber.com
Greater Johnstown/Cambria County Convention & Visitors Bureau	111 Roosevelt Blvd Ste A	Johnstown	PA	15906	814-536-7993	539-3370	206	*TF:* 800-237-8590 ■ *Web:* www.visitjohnstownpa.com
Greater Kansas City Chamber of Commerce	911 Main St Ste 2600	Kansas City	MO	64105	816-221-2424	221-7440	139	*Web:* www.kcchamber.com
Greater Kansas City Community Foundation & Affiliated Trusts (GKCCF)	1055 Broadway Ste 130	Kansas City	MO	64105	816-842-0944	842-8079	303	*Web:* www.growyourgiving.org
Greater Keene Chamber of Commerce	48 Central Sq	Keene	NH	03431	603-352-1303	358-5341	139	*Web:* www.keenechamber.com
Greater Killeen Chamber of Commerce	1 Santa Fe Plaza	Killeen	TX	76540	254-526-9551	526-6090	139	*TF:* 866-790-4769 ■ *Web:* www.killeenchamber.com
Greater Kingston Chamber of Commerce	67 Brock St	Kingston	ON	K7L1R8	613-548-4453	548-4743	137	*Web:* kingstonchamber.ca
Greater Kirkland Chamber of Commerce	440 Central Way Ste 102	Kirkland	WA	98033	425-822-7066	827-4878	139	*TF:* 800-501-7772 ■ *Web:* www.kirklandchamber.org
Greater Lafourche Port Commission	PO Box 490	Galliano	LA	70354	985-632-6701	632-6703	618	*Web:* www.portfourchon.com
Greater Lake Placid Chamber of Commerce	18 N Oak Ave	Lake Placid	FL	33852	863-465-4331	465-2588	139	*Web:* www.lpfla.com
Greater Lake Worth Chamber of Commerce	501 Lake Ave	Lake Worth	FL	33460	561-582-4401		139	*TF:* 800-955-8770 ■ *Web:* www.cpbchamber.com
Greater Lansing Ballet Co	2225 E Grand River Ave	Lansing	MI	48912	517-372-9887		573-1	*Web:* greaterlansingballet.com
Greater Lansing Convention & Visitors Bureau	500 E Michigan Ave Ste 180	Lansing	MI	48912	517-487-0077	487-5151	206	*TF:* 888-252-6746 ■ *Web:* www.lansing.org
Greater Las Cruces Chamber of Commerce	760 W Picacho Ave	Las Cruces	NM	88005	575-524-1968	527-5546	139	*TF:* 800-786-9199 ■ *Web:* www.lascruces.org
Greater Lawrence County Area Chamber of Commerce	216 Collins Ave	South Point	OH	45680	740-377-4550	377-2091	139	*TF:* 800-408-1334 ■ *Web:* www.lawrencecountyohio.org
Greater Lawrence Township Chamber of Commerce	9120 Otis Ave Ste 100	Indianapolis	IN	46216	317-541-9876	541-9875	139	*Web:* www.lawrencechamberofcommerce.org
Greater Lehigh Valley Chamber of Commerce	840 Hamilton St Ste 205	Allentown	PA	18101	610-841-5800	437-4907	139	*TF:* 800-845-7941 ■ *Web:* www.lehighvalleychamber.org
Greater Lehigh Valley Chamber of Commerce	1 E Broad St Ste 560	Bethlehem	PA	18018	610-841-5862	758-9533	139	*Web:* www.lehighvalleychamber.org
Greater Lexington Chamber of Commerce Inc	330 E Main St Ste 100	Lexington	KY	40507	859-254-4447	233-3304	139	*TF:* 800-848-1224 ■ *Web:* www.commercelexington.com
Greater Limestone County Chamber of Commerce	101 S Beaty St	Athens	AL	35611	256-232-2600	232-2609	139	*TF:* 866-953-6565 ■ *Web:* www.tourathens.com
Greater Lincoln Lakes Region Chamber of Commerce	256 W Broadway	Lincoln	ME	04457	207-794-8065		139	*Web:* www.lincolnmechamber.org
Greater Liverpool Chamber of Commerce	314 Second St	Liverpool	NY	13088	315-457-3895	234-3226	139	*TF:* 800-388-2000 ■ *Web:* www.liverpoolchamber.com
Greater Long Branch Chamber of Commerce	228 Broadway PO Box 628	Long Branch	NJ	07740	732-222-0400		139	*Web:* www.longbranchchamber.org
Greater Louisville Inc	614 W Main St	Louisville	KY	40202	502-625-0000	625-0010	139	*Web:* www.greaterlouisville.com
Greater Lowell Chamber of Commerce	131 Merrimack St	Lowell	MA	01852	978-459-8154	452-4145	139	*TF:* 800-338-0221 ■ *Web:* greaterlowellcc.org
Greater Macon Chamber of Commerce	305 Coliseum Dr	Macon	GA	31217	478-621-2000	621-2021	139	*Web:* www.maconchamber.com
Greater Madison Chamber of Commerce	PO Box 71	Madison	WI	53701	608-256-8348	256-0333	139	*TF:* 800-750-5437 ■ *Web:* www.greatermadisonchamber.com
Greater Madison Convention & Visitors Bureau	615 E Washington Ave	Madison	WI	53703	608-255-2537	258-4950	206	*TF:* 800-373-6376 ■ *Web:* www.visitmadison.com
Greater Mahopacs-Carmel Chamber of Commerce	953 S Lake Blvd PO Box 160	Mahopac	NY	10541	845-628-5553	628-5962	139	*Web:* www.mahopaccarmelonline.com
Greater Manchester Chamber of Commerce	20 Hartford Rd	Manchester	CT	06040	860-646-2223	646-5871	139	*TF:* 800-369-6153 ■ *Web:* www.manchesterchamber.com
Greater Mankato Growth	1961 Premier Dr	Mankato	MN	56001	507-385-6640	345-4451	206	*TF:* 800-697-0652 ■ *Web:* www.greatermankato.com
Greater Maple Valley-Black Diamond Chamber of Commerce	23745 225th Way SE Ste 205	Maple Valley	WA	98038	425-432-0222		139	*Web:* www.maplevalleychamber.org
Greater Marathon Chamber of Commerce	12222 Overseas Hwy	Marathon	FL	33050	305-743-5417	289-0183	139	*TF:* 800-262-7284 ■ *Web:* www.floridakeysmarathon.com
Greater Marion Area Chamber of Commerce	2305 W Main St	Marion	IL	62959	618-997-6311	233-8765	139	*Web:* www.marionillinois.com
Greater Marshall Chamber of Commerce	213 W Austin St	Marshall	TX	75670	903-935-7868		139	*Web:* www.marshall-chamber.com
Greater Media Detroit Wcsx Wmg	3033 Rivieria Dr	Naples	FL	48220	248-591-6800		116	*Web:* www.greatermedia.biz/greatermediadetroit
Greater Media Inc	35 Braintree Hill Pk Ste 300	Braintree	MA	02184	781-348-8600		637-8	
Greater Memphis Chamber	22 N Front St Ste 200	Memphis	TN	38103	901-543-3500	543-3510	139	*TF:* 800-829-1040 ■ *Web:* www.memphischamber.com
Greater Menomonie Area Chamber of Commerce	342 E Main St	Menomonie	WI	54751	715-235-9087	235-2824	139	*TF:* 800-283-1862 ■ *Web:* www.menomoniechamber.org
Greater Merced Chamber of Commerce	1640 N St Ste 120	Merced	CA	95340	209-384-7092	384-8472	139	*Web:* www.merced-chamber.com
Greater Meriden Chamber of Commerce	3 Colony St Ste 301	Meriden	CT	06451	203-235-7901	686-0172	139	*TF:* 877-283-8158 ■ *Web:* www.midstatechamber.com/default.asp
Greater Merrimack Valley Convention & Visitors Bureau	40 French St 2nd Fl	Lowell	MA	01852	978-459-6150	459-4595	206	*TF:* 800-443-3332 ■ *Web:* www.merrimackvalley.org
Greater Miami & The Beaches Hotel Assn (GMBHA)	1674 Meridian Ave Ste 420	Miami Beach	FL	33139	305-531-3553	531-8954	376	*Web:* gmbha.com
Greater Miami Chamber of Commerce	1601 Biscayne Blvd	Miami	FL	33132	305-350-7700	374-6902	139	*TF:* 888-660-5955 ■ *Web:* www.miamichamber.com
Greater Miami Convention & Visitors Bureau	701 Brickell Ave Ste 2700	Miami	FL	33131	305-539-3000	530-5859	206	*TF:* 800-933-8448 ■ *Web:* www.miamiandbeaches.com
Greater Milwaukee Convention & Visitors Bureau	648 N Plankinton Ave Ste 425	Milwaukee	WI	53203	414-273-7222	273-5596	206	*TF:* 800-554-1448 ■ *Web:* www.visitmilwaukee.org
Greater Milwaukee Foundation	101 W Pleasant St Ste 210	Milwaukee	WI	53212	414-272-5805	272-6235	303	*Web:* www.greatermilwaukeefoundation.org
Greater Moncton Chamber of Commerce	1273 Main St Ste 200	Moncton	NB	E1C0P4	506-857-2883	857-9209	137	*Web:* www.gmcc.nb.ca
Greater Monmouth Chamber of Commerce	10 E Main St Ste 1A	Freehold	NJ	07728	732-462-3030	462-2123	139	*Web:* www.monmouthregionalchamber.com
Greater Monticello Chamber of Commerce	116 N Main St	Monticello	IN	47960	574-583-7220	583-3399	139	*TF:* 800-541-7906 ■ *Web:* www.monticelloin.com
Greater Morgantown Convention & Visitors Bureau	68 Donley St	Morgantown	WV	26501	304-292-5081	291-1354	206	*TF:* 800-458-7373 ■ *Web:* www.tourmorgantown.com
Greater Mount Airy Chamber of Commerce	200 N Main St	Mount Airy	NC	27030	336-786-6116	786-1488	139	*TF:* 800-948-0949 ■ *Web:* www.mtairyncchamber.org
Greater Muskogee Area Chamber of Commerce	PO Box 797	Muskogee	OK	74402	918-682-2401	682-2403	139	*TF:* 866-381-6543 ■ *Web:* www.visitmuskogee.com

Phone | Fax | Class

Greater Nanaimo Chamber of Commerce
2133 Bowen Rd ... Nanaimo BC V9S1H8 250-756-1191 756-1584 137
Web: www.nanaimochamber.bc.ca

Greater Naples Chamber of Commerce, The
2390 Tamiami Trl N Ste 210 ... Naples FL 34103 239-262-6376 262-8374 139
Web: www.napleschamber.org

Greater Naples Marco Island Everglades Convention & Visitors Bureau
2800 Horseshoe Dr ... Naples FL 34104 239-252-2384 252-2404 206
TF: 800-688-3600 ■ *Web:* www.paradisecoast.com

Greater Nashua Chamber of Commerce
142 Main St ... Nashua NH 03060 603-881-8333 881-7323 139
Web: www.nashuachamber.com

Greater New Braunfels Chamber of Commerce Inc, The
390 S Seguin Ave PO Box 311417 ... New Braunfels TX 78130 830-625-2385 625-7918 206
TF: 800-572-2626 ■ *Web:* innewbraunfels.com

Greater New Britain Chamber of Commerce
1 Ct St 4th Fl ... New Britain CT 06051 860-229-1665 223-8341 139
Web: greaternewbritainchamber.com

Greater New Haven Chamber of Commerce
900 Chapel St 10th Fl ... New Haven CT 06510 203-787-6735 782-4329 139
TF: 800-953-4467 ■ *Web:* www.gnhcc.com

Greater New Milford Chamber of Commerce
11 Railroad St ... New Milford CT 06776 860-354-6080 354-8526 139
TF: 800-998-2984 ■ *Web:* www.newmilford-chamber.com

Greater New Orleans Hotel & Lodging Assn
2020 St Charles Ave 5th Fl ... New Orleans LA 70130 504-525-2264 210-0356 376
TF: 866-366-1121 ■ *Web:* www.gnohla.com

Greater New York Dental Meeting
801 Fourth St ... Sioux City IA 51101 712-279-4800 279-4900 206
TF: 800-593-2228 ■ *Web:* www.visitsiouxcity.org

Greater New York Dental Meeting
200 W 41st St Ste 800 ... New York NY 10036 212-398-6922 398-6934 194
TF: 844-797-7469 ■ *Web:* www.gnydm.com

Greater New York Chamber of Commerce
20 W 44th St 4th Fl ... New York NY 10036 212-686-7220 686-7232 139
TF: 800-344-6088 ■ *Web:* www.chamber.nyc/default.asp

Greater Newport Chamber of Commerce
555 SW Coast Hwy ... Newport OR 97365 541-265-8801 265-5589 139
TF: 800-262-7844 ■ *Web:* www.newportchamber.org

Greater Niagara General Hospital
5546 Portage Rd ... Niagara Falls ON L2E6X2 905-378-4647 374-2
Web: www.niagarahealth.on.ca

Greater North County Chamber of Commerce
420 W Washington St ... Florissant MO 63031 314-831-3500 831-9682 139
Web: greaternorthcountychamber.com

Greater North Fulton Chamber of Commerce (GNFCC)
11605 Haynes Bridge Rd Ste 100 ... Alpharetta GA 30009 770-993-8806 594-1059 139
TF: 866-840-5770 ■ *Web:* www.gnfcc.com

Greater North Miami Chamber of Commerce
13100 W Dixie Hwy ... North Miami FL 33161 305-891-7811 893-8522 139
TF: 800-939-3848 ■ *Web:* www.northmiamichamber.com

Greater Northampton Chamber of Commerce
99 Pleasant St ... NorthHampton MA 01060 413-584-1900 584-1934 139
TF: 800-392-6090 ■ *Web:* www.explorenorthampton.com

Greater Northeast Philadelphia Chamber of Commerce
8025 Roosevelt Blvd Ste 200 ... Philadelphia PA 19152 215-332-3400 332-6050 139
Web: www.nephilachamber.com

Greater Norwalk Chamber of Commerce
101 E Ave ... Norwalk CT 06851 203-866-2521 852-0583 139
TF: 800-473-4868 ■ *Web:* www.norwalkchamberofcommerce.com

Greater O'Hare Assn of Industry & Commerce
PO Box 1516 ... Elk Grove Village IL 60009 630-773-2944 139
TF: 877-355-4768 ■ *Web:* thegoa.com

Greater Ocean City Chamber of Commerce
12320 Ocean Gateway ... Ocean City MD 21842 410-213-0144 213-7521 139
TF: 888-626-3386 ■ *Web:* www.oceancity.org

Greater Oklahoma City Chamber of Commerce
123 Pk Ave ... Oklahoma City OK 73102 405-297-8900 297-8916 139
TF: 800-225-5652 ■ *Web:* www.okcchamber.com

Greater Olean Area Chamber of Commerce
120 N Union St ... Olean NY 14760 716-372-4433 372-7912 139
Web: www.oleanny.com

Greater Omaha Chamber of Commerce
1301 Harney St ... Omaha NE 68102 402-346-5000 346-7050 139
TF: 800-852-2622 ■ *Web:* www.omahachamber.org

Greater Omaha Convention & Visitors Bureau
1001 Farnam St Ste 200 ... Omaha NE 68102 402-444-4660 444-4511 206
TF: 866-937-6624 ■ *Web:* www.visitomaha.com

Greater Omaha Packing Company Inc
3001 L St ... Omaha NE 68107 402-731-1700 473
TF: 800-747-5400 ■ *Web:* www.greateromaha.com

Greater Orange Area Chamber of Commerce
1012 Green Ave ... Orange TX 77630 409-883-3536 139
Web: www.orangetexaschamber.org

Greater Oshawa Chamber of Commerce
44 Richmond St W Ste 100 ... Oshawa ON L1G1C7 905-728-1683 432-1259 137
Web: www.oshawachamber.com

Greater Oswego-Fulton Chamber of Commerce (GOFCC)
44 E Bridge St ... Oswego NY 13126 315-343-7681 342-0831 139
Web: www.oswegofultonchamber.com

Greater Owensboro Chamber of Commerce
200 E Third St PO Box 825 ... Owensboro KY 42302 270-926-1860 926-3364 139
Web: www.owensboro.com

Greater Palm Harbor Area Chamber of Commerce
1151 Nebraska Ave ... Palm Harbor FL 34683 727-784-4287 786-2336 139
Web: www.palmharborcc.org

Greater Paramus Chamber of Commerce
58 E Midland Ave ... Paramus NJ 07652 201-261-3344 261-3346 139
Web: paramuschamber.org

Greater Parkersburg Convention & Visitors Bureau
350 Seventh St ... Parkersburg WV 26101 304-428-1130 428-8117 206
TF: 800-752-4982 ■ *Web:* www.greaterparkersburg.com

Greater Paterson Chamber of Commerce
100 Hamilton Plaza Ste 1201 ... Paterson NJ 07505 973-881-7300 881-8233 139
TF: 800-220-2892 ■ *Web:* www.greaterpatersoncc.org

Greater Peoria Mass Transit District
407 SW Adams St ... Peoria IL 61602 309-676-4040 468

Greater Peterborough Chamber of Commerce
175 George St N ... Peterborough ON K9J3G6 705-748-9771 743-2331 137
TF: 877-640-4037 ■ *Web:* www.peterboroughchamber.ca

Greater Pflugerville Chamber of Commerce
101 S Third St PO Box 483 ... Pflugerville TX 78691 512-251-7799 251-7802 139
Web: www.pfchamber.com

Greater Philadelphia Chamber of Commerce
200 S Broad St Ste 700 ... Philadelphia PA 19102 215-545-1234 790-3600 139
Web: chamberphl.com

Greater Phoenix Chamber of Commerce
201 N Central Ave Ste 2700 ... Phoenix AZ 85004 602-495-2195 495-8913 139
TF: 800-283-6372 ■ *Web:* www.phoenixchamber.com

Greater Phoenix Convention & Visitors Bureau
400 E Van Buren St Ste 600 ... Phoenix AZ 85004 602-254-6500 253-4415 206
TF: 877-225-5749 ■ *Web:* www.visitphoenix.com

Greater Pittsburgh Chamber of Commerce
425 Sixth Ave Ste 1100 ... Pittsburgh PA 15219 412-281-1890 392-1040 139
TF: 877-392-1300 ■ *Web:* www.alleghenyconference.org

Greater Pittsburgh Convention & Visitors Bureau
120 Fifth Ave 5th Ave Pl Ste 2800 ... Pittsburgh PA 15222 412-281-7711 644-5512 206
TF: 800-359-0758 ■ *Web:* www.visitpittsburgh.com

Greater Plant City Chamber of Commerce
106 N Evers St ... Plant City FL 33563 813-754-3707 752-8793 139
Web: www.plantcity.org

Greater Plantation Chamber of Commerce
7401 NW Fourth St ... Plantation FL 33317 954-587-1410 587-1886 139
Web: www.plantationchamber.org

Greater Pocatello Chamber of Commerce
324 S Main St ... Pocatello ID 83204 208-233-1525 233-1527 139
TF: 800-632-0905 ■ *Web:* www.pocatelloidaho.com

Greater Pompano Beach Chamber of Commerce
2200 E Atlantic Blvd ... Pompano Beach FL 33062 954-941-2940 785-8358 139
TF: 888-939-5711 ■ *Web:* www.pompanobeachchamber.com

Greater Port Arthur Chamber of Commerce
4749 Twin City Hwy Ste 300 ... Port Arthur TX 77642 409-963-1107 962-1997 139
Web: www.portarthurtexas.com

Greater Portage Chamber of Commerce
2642 Eleanor St ... Portage IN 46368 219-762-3300 763-2450 139
Web: www.portageinchamber.com

Greater Portland Convention & Visitors Bureau
94 Commercial St Ste 300 ... Portland ME 04101 207-772-4994 874-9043 206
Web: www.visitportland.com

Greater Portland Transit District
114 Valley St ... Portland ME 04102 207-774-0351 468
Web: gpmetrobus.net

Greater Portsmouth Chamber of Commerce
500 Market St PO Box 239 ... Portsmouth NH 03802 603-610-5510 436-5118 139
Web: www.portsmouthchamber.org

Greater Providence Chamber of Commerce
30 Exchange Terr ... Providence RI 02903 401-521-5000 621-6109 139
Web: www.providencechamber.com

Greater Pueblo Chamber of Commerce
302 N Santa Fe Ave ... Pueblo CO 81003 719-542-1704 542-1624 139
TF: 800-233-3446 ■ *Web:* www.pueblochamber.org

Greater Raleigh Chamber of Commerce
PO Box 2978 ... Raleigh NC 27602 919-664-7000 664-7097 139
TF: 888-456-8535 ■ *Web:* www.raleighchamber.org

Greater Raleigh Convention & Visitors Bureau
421 Fayetteville St Mall Ste 1505 ... Raleigh NC 27602 919-834-5900 831-2887 206
TF: 800-849-8499 ■ *Web:* www.visitraleigh.com

Greater Reading Chamber of Commerce & Industry
201 Penn St ... Reading PA 19601 610-376-6766 376-4135 139
TF: 800-227-2345 ■ *Web:* www.greaterreadingchamber.org

Greater Redding Chamber of Commerce
747 Auditorium Dr ... Redding CA 96001 530-225-4433 225-4398 139
Web: www.reddingchamber.com

Greater Renton Chamber of Commerce
625 S Fourth St ... Renton WA 98057 425-226-4560 226-4287 139
TF: 877-467-3686 ■ *Web:* www.gorenton.com

Greater Reston Chamber of Commerce
1886 Metro Center Dr ... Reston VA 20190 703-707-9045 139
Web: www.restonchamber.org

Greater Richmond Chamber of Commerce
600 E Main St 7th Fl ... Richmond VA 23219 804-648-1234 783-9366 139
Web: www.grcc.com

Greater Richmond Convention Ctr
403 N Third St ... Richmond VA 23219 804-783-7300 205
Web: www.richmondcenter.com

Greater Riverside Chambers of Commerce
3985 University Ave ... Riverside CA 92501 951-683-7100 683-2670 139
TF: 800-951-2411 ■ *Web:* www.riverside-chamber.com

Greater Riverview Chamber of Commerce
10011 Water Works Ln ... Riverview FL 33578 813-234-5944 234-5945 139
Web: www.riverviewchamber.com

Greater Rochester Chamber of Commerce
18 S Main St ... Rochester NH 03867 603-332-5080 332-5216 139
Web: www.rochesternh.org

Greater Rochester International Airport
1200 Brooks Ave ... Rochester NY 14624 585-753-7020 753-7008 27
Web: www.monroecounty.gov

Greater Rockford Airport
60 Airport Dr ... Rockford IL 61109 815-969-4000 969-4001 27
TF: 800-517-2000 ■ *Web:* www.flyrfd.com

Greater Rockford Auto Auction Inc (GRAA)
5937 Sandy Hollow Rd ... Rockford IL 61109 815-874-7800 874-1325 51
TF: 800-830-4722 ■ *Web:* www.graa.net

Greater Rome Chamber of Commerce
1 Riverside Pkwy ... Rome GA 30161 706-291-7663 232-5755 139
Web: www.romega.com

Greater Rome Convention & Visitors Bureau
402 Civics Ctr Dr ... Rome GA 30161 706-295-5576 206
TF: 800-444-1834 ■ *Web:* www.romegeorgia.org

Greater Saint Charles Convention & Visitors Bureau
230 S Main St ... Saint Charles MO 63301 636-946-7776 949-3217 206
TF: 800-366-2427 ■ *Web:* www.historicstcharles.com

Greater Salem Chamber of Commerce
81 Main St ... Salem NH 03079 603-893-3177 894-5158 139
TF: 800-367-3364 ■ *Web:* www.gschamber.com

Phone · Fax · Class

Greater San Antonio Chamber of Commerce
602 E Commerce St ..... San Antonio TX 78205 210-229-2100 229-1600 139
TF: 888-828-8680 ■ *Web:* www.sachamber.org

Greater Sarasota Chamber of Commerce
1945 Fruitville Rd ..... Sarasota FL 34236 941-955-8187 366-5621 139
Web: www.sarasotachamber.com

Greater Saskatoon Chamber of Commerce
104-202 Fourth Ave N ..... Saskatoon SK S7K0K1 306-244-2151 244-8366 137
Web: www.saskatoonchamber.com

Greater Scranton Chamber of Commerce
222 Mulberry St ..... Scranton PA 18503 570-342-7711 347-6262 139
Web: www.scrantonchamber.com

Greater Seattle Chamber of Commerce
1301 Fifth Ave Ste 1500 ..... Seattle WA 98101 206-389-7200 139
TF: 866-978-2997 ■ *Web:* www.seattlechamber.com

Greater Sebring Chamber of Commerce
227 US 27 N ..... Sebring FL 33870 863-385-8448 385-8810 139
Web: sebring.org

Greater Seminole Area Chamber of Commerce
7777 131st St N ..... Seminole FL 33772 727-392-3245 397-7753 139
Web: www.seminolechamber.net

Greater Severna Park Chamber of Commerce
1 Holly Ave ..... Severna Park MD 21146 410-647-3900 647-3999 139
TF: 800-626-2326 ■ *Web:* www.severnaparkchamber.com

Greater Shawnee Area Chamber of Commerce
231 N Bell ..... Shawnee OK 74801 405-273-6092 275-9851 139
Web: www.shawneechamber.com

Greater Shelby County Chamber of Commerce
1301 County Services Dr ..... Pelham AL 35124 205-663-4542 663-4524 139
Web: www.shelbychamber.org

Greater Sherman Oaks Chamber of Commerce
14827 Ventura Blvd Ste 207 ..... Sherman Oaks CA 91403 818-906-1951 139
Web: www.shermanoakschamber.org

Greater Shreveport Chamber of Commerce
400 Edwards St ..... Shreveport LA 71101 318-677-2500 677-2541 139
Web: www.shreveportchamber.org

Greater Sierra Vista Area Chamber of Commerce
21 E Wilcox Dr ..... Sierra Vista AZ 85635 520-458-6940 452-0878 139
Web: www.sierravistachamber.org

Greater Silver Spring Chamber of Commerce
8601 Georgia Ave Ste 203 ..... Silver Spring MD 20910 301-565-3777 565-3377 139
Web: www.gsscc.org

Greater Smithfield-Selma Area Chamber of Commerce
1115 Industrial Pk Dr ..... Smithfield NC 27577 919-934-9166 934-1337 139
Web: www.smithfieldselma.com

Greater Southington Chamber of Commerce
31 Liberty St Ste 210 ..... Southington CT 06489 860-628-8036 139
Web: www.southingtonchamber.com

Greater Spokane Inc
801 W Riverside Ave Ste 100 ..... Spokane WA 99201 509-624-1393 747-0077 139
TF: 800-776-5263 ■ *Web:* www.greaterspokane.org

Greater Springfield Chamber of Commerce
6434 Brandon Ave Ste 208 ..... Springfield VA 22150 703-866-3500 866-3501 139
Web: www.springfieldchamber.org

Greater Springfield Chamber of Commerce, The
1011 S Second St ..... Springfield IL 62701 217-525-1173 525-8768 139
Web: www.gscc.org

Greater Springfield Convention & Visitors Bureau
1441 Main St ..... Springfield MA 01103 413-787-1548 781-4607 206
TF: 800-723-1548 ■ *Web:* www.valleyvisitor.com

Greater Springfield Convention & Visitors Bureau
20 S Limestone St Ste 100 ..... Springfield OH 45502 937-325-7621 325-8765 206
TF: 800-803-1553 ■ *Web:* www.greaterspringfield.com

Greater Starkville Development Partnership
200 E Main St ..... Starkville MS 39759 662-323-3322 323-5815 139
TF: 800-649-8687 ■ *Web:* www.starkville.org

Greater Stillwater Chamber of Commerce
200 Chestnut St E Ste 204 ..... Stillwater MN 55082 651-439-4001 139
Web: www.ilovestillwater.com

Greater Stockton Chamber of Commerce
445 W Weber Ave Ste 220 ..... Stockton CA 95203 209-547-2770 139
TF: 800-766-4463 ■ *Web:* www.stocktonchamber.org

Greater Sudbury Chamber of Commerce
40 Elm St Ste 1 ..... Sudbury ON P3C1S8 705-673-7133 673-1951 137
Web: sudburychamber.ca

Greater Summerville-Dorchester County Chamber of Commerce
402 N Main St ..... Summerville SC 29483 843-873-2931 875-4464 139
TF: 800-966-6631 ■ *Web:* greatersummerville.org

Greater Sumter Chamber of Commerce
32 E Calhoun St ..... Sumter SC 29150 803-775-1231 775-0915 139
Web: www.sumterchamber.com

Greater Susquehanna Valley Chamber of Commerce
2859 N Susquehanna Trl PO Box 10 ..... Shamokin Dam PA 17876 570-743-4100 743-1221 139
TF: 800-410-2880 ■ *Web:* www.gsvcc.org

Greater Tacoma Convention & Trade Ctr
1500 Broadway ..... Tacoma WA 98402 253-830-6601 573-2363 205
TF: 800-745-3000 ■ *Web:* www.tacomaconventioncenter.com

Greater Talent Network Inc
437 Fifth Ave ..... New York NY 10016 212-645-4200 627-1471 708
TF: 800-326-4211 ■ *Web:* www.greatertalent.com

Greater Talladega Area Chamber of Commerce
210 E St S ..... Talladega AL 35160 256-362-9075 362-9093 139
Web: talladegachamber.chambermaster.com

Greater Tallahassee Chamber of Commerce
115 N Calhoun St ..... Tallahassee FL 32301 850-224-8116 561-3860 139
Web: www.talchamber.com

Greater Tampa Chamber of Commerce
201 N Franklin St Ste 201 ..... Tampa FL 33602 813-228-7777 223-7899 139
TF: 800-707-8846 ■ *Web:* www.tampachamber.com

Greater Tehachapi Chamber of Commerce
209 E Tehachapi Blvd PO Box 401 ..... Tehachapi CA 93581 661-822-4180 822-9036 139
Web: www.tehachapi.com

Greater Texas Federal Credit Union
6411 N Lamar Blvd ..... Austin TX 78752 512-458-2558 219
Web: gtfcu.org

Greater Texas Foundation
6100 Foundation Pl Dr ..... Bryan TX 77807 979-779-6100 305
Web: greatertexasfoundation.org

Greater Toledo Convention & Visitors Bureau
401 Jefferson Ave ..... Toledo OH 43604 419-321-6404 206
TF: 800-243-4667 ■ *Web:* www.dotoledo.org

Greater Topeka Chamber of Commerce
120 SE Sixth St Ste 110 ..... Topeka KS 66603 785-234-2644 234-8656 139
Web: www.topekachamber.org

Greater Toronto Airports Authority
Toronto Pearson International Airport 3111 Convair
PO Box 6031 ..... Toronto ON L5P1B2 416-776-3000 63
Web: www.torontopearson.com

Greater Trenton Symphony Orchestra
28 W State St Ste 202 ..... Trenton NJ 08608 609-394-1338 573-3
TF: 800-351-1440 ■ *Web:* www.trentonsymphony.org

Greater Tulare Chamber of Commerce
220 E Tulare Ave ..... Tulare CA 93274 559-686-1547 686-4915 139
TF: 800-427-2200 ■ *Web:* www.tularechamber.org

Greater University Chamber of Commerce
4710 University Way NE Ste 114 ..... Seattle WA 98105 206-547-4417 139
Web: udistrictpartnership.org

Greater Valley Area Chamber of Commerce
2102 S Broad Ave PO Box 205 ..... Lanett AL 36863 334-642-1411 642-1410 139
TF: 800-245-2244 ■ *Web:* www.greatervalleyarea.com

Greater Valley Chamber of Commerce
900 Bridgeport Ave 2nd Fl ..... Shelton CT 06484 203-925-4981 925-4984 139
TF: 800-290-5619 ■ *Web:* www.greatervalleychamber.com

Greater Vancouver Chamber of Commerce
1101 Broadway Ste 100 ..... Vancouver WA 98660 360-694-2588 693-8279 139
Web: www.vancouverusa.com

Greater Vancouver Convention & Visitors Bureau
200 Burrard St ..... Vancouver BC V6C3L6 604-682-2222 682-1717 206
TF: 800-561-0123 ■ *Web:* www.tourismvancouver.com

Greater Vernon Chamber of Commerce
PO Box 1228 ..... Leesville LA 71496 337-238-0349 238-0340 139
Web: www.chambervernonparish.com

Greater Vernon Chamber of Commerce
2901 32nd St Ste 102 ..... Vernon BC V1T5M2 250-545-0771 545-3114 137
Web: vernonchamber.ca

Greater Victoria Chamber of Commerce
852 Ft St Ste 100 ..... Victoria BC V8W1H8 250-383-7191 385-3552 137
Web: www.victoriachamber.ca

Greater Vineland Chamber of Commerce
2115 S Delsea Dr ..... Vineland NJ 08360 856-691-7400 691-2113 139
TF: 800-922-1766 ■ *Web:* www.vinelandchamber.org

Greater Waco Chamber of Commerce
101 S Third St ..... Waco TX 76701 254-757-5600 752-6618 139
Web: www.wacochamber.com

Greater Washington Publishing Inc
1800 Alexander Bell Dr Ste 120 ..... Reston VA 20191 703-992-1100 893-8356 637-9
Web: www.gwpi.net

Greater Waterbury Chamber of Commerce
83 Bank St ..... Waterbury CT 06702 203-757-0701 139
Web: www.waterburychamber.com

Greater Watertown-North Country Chamber of Commerce
1241 Coffeen St ..... Watertown NY 13601 315-788-4400 788-3369 139
TF: 800-924-5145 ■ *Web:* www.watertownny.com

Greater Waynesboro Chamber of Commerce
118 Walnut St Ste 111 ..... Waynesboro PA 17268 717-762-7123 762-7124 139
Web: www.waynesboro.org

Greater West Chester Chamber of Commerce
119 N High St ..... West Chester PA 19380 610-696-4046 696-9110 139
TF: 800-210-8008 ■ *Web:* www.greaterwestchester.com

Greater Westfield Chamber of Commerce
16 N Elm St ..... Westfield MA 01085 413-568-1618 139
TF: 800-316-8559 ■ *Web:* www.westfieldbiz.org/contact-us.html

Greater Wilkes-Barre Chamber of Business & Industry
2 Public Sq PO Box 5340 ..... Wilkes-Barre PA 18710 570-823-2101 822-5951 139
TF: 800-701-8449 ■ *Web:* www.wilkes-barre.org

Greater Williamsburg Chamber & Tourism Alliance
421 N Boundary St ..... Williamsburg VA 23185 757-229-6511 229-2047 139
TF: 800-368-6511 ■ *Web:* www.williamsburgcc.com

Greater Wilmington Chamber of Commerce
1 Estell Lee Pl ..... Wilmington NC 28401 910-762-2611 762-9765 139
TF: 800-829-4477 ■ *Web:* www.wilmingtonchamber.org

Greater Wilmington Convention & Visitors Bureau
100 W Tenth St Ste 20 ..... Wilmington DE 19801 800-489-6664 652-4726* 206
**Fax Area Code:* 302 ■ *TF:* 800-489-6664 ■ *Web:* www.visitwilmingtonde.com

Greater Winston-Salem Chamber of Commerce
411 W Fourth St Ste 211 ..... Winston-Salem NC 27101 336-728-9200 721-2209 139
Web: www.winstonsalem.com

Greater Winter Haven Area Chamber of Commerce
401 Ave 'B' NW ..... Winter Haven FL 33881 863-293-2138 297-5818 139
TF: 800-260-9220 ■ *Web:* winterhavenchamber.com

Greater Woodfield Convention & Visitors Bureau
1375 E Woodfield Rd Ste 120 ..... Schaumburg IL 60173 847-490-1010 490-1212 206
TF: 800-847-4849 ■ *Web:* www.chicagonorthwest.com

Greater Yakima Chamber of Commerce
10 N Ninth St PO Box 1490 ..... Yakima WA 98901 509-248-2021 248-0601 139
TF: 800-375-5283 ■ *Web:* www.yakima.org

Greater Yellowstone Coalition (GYC)
215 S Wallace Ave Ste 2 ..... Bozeman MT 59715 406-586-1593 556-2839 48-13
TF: 800-775-1834 ■ *Web:* www.greateryellowstone.org

Greatlookz 4635 N Black Canyon Hwy ..... Phoenix AZ 85015 602-218-5976 791
Web: www.greatlookz.com

Great-West Life & Annuity Insurance Co
8515 E OrchaRd Rd ..... Greenwood Village CO 80111 303-737-3000 391-2
TF: 800-537-2033 ■ *Web:* www.greatwest.com

Great-West Life Assurance Co
100 Osborne St ..... Winnipeg MB R3C3A5 204-946-1190 391-2
TF: 800-990-6654 ■ *Web:* www.greatwestlife.com

Greatwide Logistics Services LLC
12404 Pk Central Dr Ste 300S ..... Dallas TX 75251 972-228-7300 780
Web: www.greatwide.com

Greddy Performance Products Inc Mnmt
9 Vanderbilt ..... Irvine CA 92618 949-588-8300 588-6318 61
Web: www.greddy.com

Greece 866 Second Ave 13th Fl ..... New York NY 10017 212-888-6900 888-4440 784
Web: www.mfa.gr

	Phone	Fax	Class
Consulate General 12424 Wilshire Blvd Ste 800 .... Los Angeles CA 90025 *Web:* www.mfa.gr	310-826-5555	826-8670	257
Consulate General 650 N St Clair St .... Chicago IL 60611 *Web:* www.mfa.gr	312-335-3915	335-3958	257
Consulate General 86 Beacon St .... Boston MA 02108 *Web:* www.mfa.gr	617-523-0100	523-0511	257
Consulate General 69 E 79th St .... New York NY 10075 *Web:* www.mfa.gr	212-988-5500	734-8492	257
Consulate General 2441 Gough St .... San Francisco CA 94123 *Web:* www.mfa.gr	415-775-2102	776-6815	257
Embassy 2217 Massachusetts Ave .... Washington DC 20008 *Web:* www.mfa.gr/usa/en/the-embassy	202-939-1300	939-1324	257
Greece Public Library 2 Vince Tofany Blvd .... Greece NY 14612 *TF:* 800-767-7539 ■ *Web:* greecepubliclibrary.org	585-225-8951		434-3
Greek Catholic Union of the USA 5400 Tuscarawas Rd .... Beaver PA 15009 *TF:* 800-722-4428 ■ *Web:* www.gcuusa.com	724-495-3400		391-2
Greek Islands 3821 Ctr St .... Omaha NE 68105 *TF:* 800-228-9100 ■ *Web:* greekislandsomaha.com	402-346-1528	345-7428	671
Greek Islands Restaurant 906 S Meridian St .... Indianapolis IN 46225 *TF:* 800-793-7469 ■ *Web:* www.greekislandsrestaurant.com	317-636-0700		671
Greek Islands Taverna 3300 N Ocean Blvd .... Fort Lauderdale FL 33308 *Web:* www.greekislandstaverna.com	954-565-5505		671
Greek Isles Grille & Taverna 3309 N Central Expy Ste 370 .... Plano TX 75023 *Web:* greekislesgrille.com	972-423-7778		671
Greek National Tourism Organization 800 Third Ave 23rd FL .... New York NY 10022 *Web:* www.visitgreece.gr	212-421-5777		775
Greek Palace 8878 Clairmont Mesa Blvd .... San Diego CA 92123 *Web:* www.greekpalace.com	858-573-0155	573-9645	671
Greek Peak Mountain Resort 2000 NYS Rt 392 .... Cortland NY 13045 *TF:* 800-541-2501 ■ *Web:* www.greekpeak.net	607-835-6300		194
Greek Peak Mountain Resort 2000 State Rt 392 .... Cortland NY 13045 *Web:* greekpeakmtnresort.com	607-835-6300		707
Greek, Theatre, The 2700 N Vermont Ave .... Los Angeles CA 90027 *Web:* www.greektheatrela.com	323-665-5857	666-8202	572
Greektown Superholdings Inc 555 E Lafayette .... Detroit MI 48226 *Web:* www.greektowncasino.com	313-223-2999		133
Greeley & Hansen 100 S Wacker Dr Ste 1400 .... Chicago IL 60606 *TF:* 800-837-9779 ■ *Web:* www.greeley-hansen.com	312-558-9000	558-1006	261
Greeley Convention & Visitors Bureau 902 Seventh Ave .... Greeley CO 80631 *TF:* 800-449-3866 ■ *Web:* www.greeleychamber.com	970-352-3567	352-3572	206
Greeley County PO Box 287 .... Greeley NE 68842 *Web:* greeleycounty.ne.gov	308-428-3625	428-3022	338
Greeley County 510 Broadway PO Box 656 .... Tribune KS 67879 *TF:* 888-204-1781 ■ *Web:* www.greeleycounty.org	620-376-2540	376-2549	338
Greeley Tribune 501 Eigth Ave .... Greeley CO 80631 *TF:* 800-275-0321 ■ *Web:* www.greeleytribune.com	970-352-0211	356-5780	532-2
Greeley-Weld Chamber of Commerce 902 Seventh Ave .... Greeley CO 80631 *TF:* 800-449-3866 ■ *Web:* www.greeleychamber.com	970-352-3566	352-3572	139
Green Acres Baptist Church 16163 N Peninsula Rd .... Whitehouse TX 75791 *Web:* www.gabc.org	903-566-2515		48-20
Green Acres Contracting Company Inc 703 Pennsylvania Ave .... Scottdale PA 15683 *Web:* www.greenacrescontracting.com	724-887-8096		186
Green Acres Mall 2034 Green Acres Mall .... Valley Stream NY 11581 *Web:* www.greenacresmallonline.com	516-561-1157		460
Green Al (Rep D - TX) 2347 Rayburn HOB .... Washington DC 20515 *Web:* algreen.house.gov	202-225-7508	225-2947	342-2
Green Bay Botanical Garden 2600 Larsen Rd .... Green Bay WI 54303 *TF:* 877-355-4224 ■ *Web:* www.gbbg.org	920-490-9457	490-9461	97
Green Bay City Hall 100 N Jefferson St .... Green Bay WI 54301	920-448-3000	448-3016	337
Green Bay Correctional Institution 2833 Riverside Dr .... Green Bay WI 54307 *Web:* doc.wi.gov	920-432-4877	448-6545	213
Green Bay Drop Forge 1341 State St .... Green Bay WI 54304 *TF:* 800-824-4896 ■ *Web:* www.greenbaydropforge.com	920-432-6401	432-0859	483
Green Bay Packaging Inc 1700 Webster Ct .... Green Bay WI 54302 *TF:* 800-236-8400 ■ *Web:* www.gbp.com	920-433-5111		548
Green Bay Packers 1265 Lombardi Ave PO Box 10628 .... Green Bay WI 54304 *TF:* 800-895-0071 ■ *Web:* www.packers.com	920-569-7500	569-7301	715-3
Green Bay Press-Gazette Media PO Box 3249 .... Milwaukee WI 53201 *TF:* 800-422-7128 ■ *Web:* www.greenbaypressgazette.com	920-431-8400	431-8379	532-2
Green Brick Partners Inc 2805 Dallas Pkwy Ste 400 .... Plano TX 75093 *TF:* 800-374-0137 ■ *Web:* greenbrickpartners.com	469-573-6755		787
Green Canary Sustainability Consulting LLC 1717 W Sixth St Ste 400 .... Austin TX 78703 *Web:* www.greencanary.net	512-476-4368		5
Green Circle Growers Inc 51051 US Hwy 20 .... Oberlin OH 44074 *TF:* 800-368-4759 ■ *Web:* www.greencirclegrowers.com	440-775-1411	774-1465	369
Green County 203 W Ct St .... Greensburg KY 42743 *Web:* www.greencounty.ky.gov	270-932-4024	932-3635	338
Green County 1016 16th Ave .... Monroe WI 53566 *TF:* 800-947-3529 ■ *Web:* www.co.green.wi.gov	608-328-9430	328-2835	338

	Phone	Fax	Class
Green Crow Corp 727 E Eigth St PO Box 2469 .... Port Angeles WA 98362 *Web:* www.greencrow.com	360-452-3325		448
Green Dental Laboratories Inc 1099 Wilburn Rd .... Heber Springs AR 72543 *Web:* greendentallab.com	501-362-3132		418
Green Depot Inc 1 Ivy Hill Rd .... Brooklyn NY 11211 *TF:* 800-238-5008 ■ *Web:* greendepot.com	718-782-2991		429
Green Diamond Resource Co 1301 Fifth Ave Ste 2700 .... Seattle WA 98101 *Web:* www.greendiamond.com	206-224-5800		302
Green Door 198 Main St .... Ottawa ON K1S1C6 *Web:* www.greendoor.ca	613-234-9597		671
Green Dot Corp 3465 E Foothill Blvd .... Pasadena CA 91107 *TF:* 800-473-3636 ■ *Web:* www.greendot.com	626-765-2000		215
Green Earth Cleaning 51 W 135th St .... Kansas City MO 64145 *TF:* 877-926-0895 ■ *Web:* www.greenearthcleaning.com	816-926-0895		116
Green Field Churrascaria 5305 E Pacific Coast Hwy .... Long Beach CA 90804 *Web:* greenfieldlongbeach.com	562-597-0906		671
Green Field Paper Co 7196 Clairemont Mesa Blvd .... San Diego CA 92111 *TF:* 888-402-9979 ■ *Web:* www.greenfieldpaper.com	858-565-2585		557
Green Foods Corp 2220 Camino Del Sol .... Oxnard CA 93030 *TF:* 800-777-4430 ■ *Web:* www.greenfoods.com	805-983-7470		296-25
Green Gateau 330 S Tenth St .... Lincoln NE 68508 *Web:* www.greengateau.com	402-477-0330		671
Green Gene (Rep D - TX) 2470 Rayburn HOB .... Washington DC 20515 *Web:* green.house.gov	202-225-1688	225-9903	342-2
Green Grass Golf Corp 282 Newbridge Rd .... Hicksville NY 11801 *Web:* www.greengrassgolf.com	516-935-6722	935-7064	710
Green Harbor Resort 182 Baxter Ave .... West Yarmouth MA 02673 *Web:* www.greenharborresort.com	508-771-1126		379
Green Haven Correctional Facility 594 Rt 216 .... Stormville NY 12582 *Web:* www.doccs.ny.gov	845-221-2711		213
Green Hills Antique Mall 4108 Hillsboro Pk .... Nashville TN 37215 *TF:* 888-316-6255	615-383-9851	383-4886	460
Green Hills Software Inc 30 W Sola St .... Santa Barbara CA 93101 *TF:* 800-765-4733 ■ *Web:* www.ghs.com	805-965-6044	965-6343	178-2
Green Idea 950 page st .... San Francisco CA 94117 *Web:* www.greenidea.com	415-863-2157		225
Green Job Interview 3050 Pullman Ave Ste D .... Costa Mesa CA 92626 *Web:* greenjobinterview.com	714-444-5500		387
Green Lake Conference Center W2511 State Rd 23 .... Green Lake WI 54941 *Web:* www.glcc.org	920-294-3323		205
Green Lake County 492 Hill St .... Green Lake WI 54941 *TF:* 800-664-3588 ■ *Web:* www.co.green-lake.wi.us	920-294-4005	294-4009	338
Green Lake Jewelry Works 550 NE Northgate Way .... Seattle WA 98125 *Web:* www.seattlejewelry.com	206-527-1108		410
Green Lakes State Park 7900 Green Lakes Rd .... Fayetteville NY 13066 *Web:* parks.ny.gov/parks/172	315-637-6111		565
Green Lawn Fertilizing Inc 1004 Saunders Ln .... West Chester PA 19380 *TF:* 888-581-5296 ■ *Web:* www.greenlawnfertilizing.com	880-581-5296		577
Green Leads Holdings LLC 183 Rockingham Rd .... Windham NH 03087 *Web:* www.greenleads.com	978-633-3233		195
Green Line Hose & Fittings (B.C.) Ltd 1477 Derwent Way .... Delta BC V3M6N3 *TF:* 800-665-5444 ■ *Web:* www.greenlinehose.com	604-525-6700		358
Green Mechanical Construction Inc 322 W Main St .... Glasgow KY 42141 *Web:* gmci.com	270-651-8978		189-10
Green Mill Restaurant & Bar 1342 Grand Ave .... Saint Paul MN 55105 *Web:* www.greenmill.com	651-203-3100		671
Green Mountain at Fox Run 262 Fox Ln PO Box 358 .... Ludlow VT 05149 *TF:* 800-448-8106 ■ *Web:* www.fitwoman.com	802-228-8885	228-8887	706
Green Mountain College 1 Brennan Cir .... Poultney VT 05764 *TF Admissions:* 800-776-6675 ■ *Web:* www.greenmtn.edu	802-287-8000	287-8099	166
Green Mountain Energy Co PO Box 25211 .... Lehigh Valley PA 18002 *Web:* www.greenmountainenergy.com	512-691-6100		787
Green Mountain Inn 18 Main St PO Box 60 .... Stowe VT 05672 *TF:* 800-253-7302 ■ *Web:* www.greenmountaininn.com	802-253-7301	253-5096	379
Green Mountain Power Corp 163 Acorn Ln .... Colchester VT 05446 *TF:* 888-835-4672 ■ *Web:* www.greenmountainpower.com	802-864-5731		787
Green Mountain Rifle Barrel Co 153 W Main St PO Box 2670 .... Conway NH 03818 *Web:* www.gmriflebarrel.com	603-447-1095	447-1099	284
Green Oak Tire Inc 7480 Kensington Rd .... Brighton MI 48116 *Web:* www.greenoaktire.com	248-437-1753		54
Green Oaks Hospital 7808 Clodus Fields Dr .... Dallas TX 75251 *TF:* 800-866-6554 ■ *Web:* medicalcitygreenoaks.com	972-991-9504		374-5
Green Papaya 256 Preston St .... Ottawa ON K1R7R5 *Web:* www.greenpapaya.ca	613-231-8424		671
Green Papaya 3211 Oak Lawn Ave Ste B .... Dallas TX 75219 *Web:* www.greenpapayadallas.com	214-521-4811		671
Green Park Inn 9239 Valley Blvd .... Blowing Rock NC 28605 *Web:* www.greenparkinn.com	828-414-9230		379
Green Pastures 811 W Live Oak St .... Austin TX 78704	512-444-1888		671
Green Peak Partners PO Box 6064 .... Denver CO 80206 *Web:* www.greenpeakpartners.com	303-841-7098		463

Phone Fax Class

Green Pharmaceuticals Inc
591 Constitution Ave Ste A .... Camarillo CA 93012 805-388-0600 231
Web: snorestop.com

Green Plains Renewable Energy Inc
450 Regency Pkwy Ste 400 .... Omaha NE 68114 402-884-8700 884-8776 143
NASDAQ: GPRE ■ *TF:* 877-886-2288 ■ *Web:* www.gpreinc.com

Green Ridge State Forest
28700 Headquarters Dr NE .... Flintstone MD 21530 301-478-3124 565
Web: dnr2.maryland.gov

Green River Community College
12401 SE 320th St .... Auburn WA 98092 253-833-9111 288-3454* 162
**Fax:* Admissions ■ *TF:* 800-291-7593 ■ *Web:* www.greenriver.edu

Green River Correctional Complex
1200 River Rd .... Central City KY 42330 270-754-5415 213
Web: corrections.ky.gov

Green River Lake State Park
179 Pk Office Rd .... Campbellsville KY 42718 270-465-8255 565
Web: www.parks.ky.gov

Green River Reservoir State Park
1393 Green River Dam Rd .... Hyde Park VT 05655 802-888-1349 565
Web: www.vtstateparks.com

Green River State Park PO Box 637 .... Green River UT 84525 435-564-3633 565
Web: www.utah.com

Green River State Wildlife Area
375 Game Rd .... Harmon IL 61042 815-379-2324 565
Web: dnr.illinois.gov/Lands/Landmgt/PARKS/R1/green.htm

Green Room at the Hotel duPont
42 W 11th St .... Wilmington DE 19801 302-594-3100 594-3108 671
TF: 800-441-9019 ■ *Web:* www.hoteldupont.com

Green Seal
1001 Connecticut Ave NW Ste 827 .... Washington DC 20036 202-872-6400 872-4324 48-10
Web: www.greenseal.org

Green Seal Environmental Inc
114 State Rd Bldg B .... Sagamore Beach MA 02562 508-888-6034 192
Web: www.gseenv.com

Green Spring Gardens Park
4603 Green Spring Rd .... Alexandria VA 22312 703-642-5173 642-8095 97
Web: www.fairfaxcounty.gov/parks/gsgp

Green Tangerine Spa & Salon
238 Patriot Pl .... Foxborough MA 02035 508-203-9414 77
Web: www.greentangerinespa.com

Green Tape Llc
5300 Dtc Pkwy Ste 450 .... Greenwood Village CO 80111 303-221-1306 463
Web: www.greentapellc.com

Green Technology Group, Llc, The
10619 Canterberry Rd .... Fairfax Station VA 22039 202-285-4748 180
Web: tgtgconsulting.com

Green Tokai Company Ltd
55 Robert Wright Dr .... Brookville OH 45309 937-833-5444 604

Green Top Sporting Goods Corp
PO Box 1015 .... Glen Allen VA 23060 804-550-2188 711
Web: www.greentophuntfish.com

Green Tortoise Adventure Travel & Hostels
494 Broadway .... San Francisco CA 94133 415-834-1000 956-4900 760
TF: 800-867-8647 ■ *Web:* www.greentortoise.com

Green Transfer & Storage Co
10099 N Portland Rd .... Portland OR 97203 503-286-0673 780
Web: greentransfer.com

Green Tree Event Consultants
35 Storer St .... Saco ME 04072 207-781-2982 149
Web: www.nemadeshows.com

Green Tree Packing Co 65 Central Ave .... Passaic NJ 07055 973-473-1305 296-26
Web: www.greentreepacking.com

Green Turtle Bay Inc
239 Jetty Dr .... Grand Rivers KY 42045 270-362-8364 378
Web: www.greenturtlebay.com

Green Valley Consulting Engineers
335 Tesconi Cir .... Santa Rosa CA 95401 707-579-0388 256
Web: www.gvalley.com

Green Valley Corp
777 N First St 5th Fl .... San Jose CA 95112 408-287-0246 998-1737 187
Web: www.barryswensonbuilder.com

Green Valley Floral Co
24999 Potter Rd .... Salinas CA 93908 831-424-7691 424-4473 369
TF: 800-228-1255 ■ *Web:* www.greenvalleyfloral.com

Green Valley Grill
622 Green Valley Rd .... Greensboro NC 27408 336-854-2015 671
Web: www.greenvalleygrill.com

Green Valley Pecan Co
1625 E Sahuarita Rd .... Sahuarita AZ 85629 520-791-2852 791-2853 10-10
TF: 800-533-5269 ■ *Web:* greenvalleypecan.com

Green Valley Ranch Resort Casino & Spa
2300 Paseo Verde Pkwy .... Henderson NV 89052 702-617-7777 379
TF Resv: 866-782-9487 ■ *Web:* greenvalleyranch.sclv.com

Green Valley Recreation Inc
921 W Via Rio Fuerte .... Green Valley AZ 85614 520-393-0360 354
Web: www.gvrec.org

Green Valley Spa & Resort
1871 W Canyon View Dr .... Saint George UT 84770 800-237-1068 706
TF: 800-237-1068 ■ *Web:* www.greenvalleyspa.com

Green Valley State Park 1480 130th St .... Creston IA 50801 641-782-5131 565
Web: www.iowadnr.gov

Green Zebra 1460 W Chicago Ave .... Chicago IL 60642 312-243-7100 671
Web: www.greenzebrachicago.com

Greenan, Peffer, Sallander & Lally LLP
6111 Bollinger Canyon Rd Ste 500 .... San Ramon CA 94583 925-866-1000 428
Web: www.gpsllp.com

GREENandSAVE LLC
Greater Philadelphia 204 Old Lancaster Rd Ste ...... Devon PA 19333 610-628-1300 192
Web: www.greenandsave.com

Greenbank Mill 500 Greenbank Rd .... Wilmington DE 19808 302-999-9001 50-3
Web: www.greenbankmill.org

Greenbaum, Rowe, Smith, Ravin, Davis & Himmel LLP
Metro Corporate Campus 99 Wood Ave S ..... Woodbridge NJ 07095 732-549-5600 428
Web: www.greenbaumlaw.com

Greenbelt Electric Co-op Inc
PO Box 948 .... Wellington TX 79095 806-447-2536 245
TF: 800-527-3082 ■ *Web:* www.greenbeltelectric.coop

Phone Fax Class

Greenbelt Park 6565 Greenbelt Rd .... Greenbelt MD 20770 301-344-3948 564
TF: 800-562-5771 ■ *Web:* www.nps.gov/gree

Greenberg & Lieberman
314 Philadelphia Ave .... Takoma Park MD 20912 202-625-7000 445
Web: www.aplegal.com

Greenberg Ettlin & Assoc PA
109 Bridge St .... Elkton MD 21921 410-398-1961 2
Web: ge-cpa.com

Greenberg Farrow 44 W 28th St .... New York NY 10001 212-725-9530 261
Web: www.greenbergfarrow.com

Greenberg Glusker Fields Claman & Machtinger LLP
1900 Ave of the Stars 21st Fl .... Los Angeles CA 90067 310-553-3610 553-0687 428
Web: www.greenbergglusker.com

Greenberg Rosenblatt Kull & Bitsoli PC
The Day Bldg 306 Main St Ste 400 .... Worcester MA 01615 508-791-0901 2
Web: www.grkb.com

Greenberry Industrial
2273 NW Professional Dr .... Corvallis OR 97330 541-757-8458 610
Web: www.greenberry.com

Greenblatt & Laube Pc
200 N Eighth St .... Vineland NJ 08360 856-691-0424 445
Web: greenblattlaube.com

Greenbriar Animal Hospital LLC
4307 N Green River Rd .... Evansville IN 47715 812-479-0867 794
Web: www.greenbrieranimalhospital.com

Greenbriar Inn, The
8735 N Foothills Hwy .... Boulder CO 80302 303-440-7979 449-2054 671
TF: 800-253-1474 ■ *Web:* www.greenbriarinn.com

Greenbriar Mall
2841 Greenbriar Pkwy SW .... Atlanta GA 30331 404-344-6611 460
Web: www.shopgreenbriar.com

Greenbrier Co
1 Centerpointe Dr Ste 200 .... Lake Oswego OR 97035 503-684-7000 684-7553 650
NYSE: GBX ■ *TF:* 800-343-7188 ■ *Web:* www.gbrx.com

Greenbrier County
200 W Washington St .... Lewisburg WV 24901 304-647-6602 338
TF: 800-833-2068 ■ *Web:* www.greenbrierwv.com

Greenbrier County Convention & Visitors Bureau
200 W Washington St .... Lewisburg WV 24901 304-645-1000 647-3001 206
TF: 800-833-2068 ■ *Web:* www.greenbrierwv.com

Greenbrier Farms Inc
225 Sign Pine Rd .... Chesapeake VA 23322 757-421-2141 323
TF: 800-829-2141 ■ *Web:* www.historicgreenbrierfarms.com

Greenbrier State Park
21843 National Pk .... Boonsboro MD 21713 301-791-4767 565
Web: dnr2.maryland.gov

Greenbrier Valley Medical Ctr
202 Maplewood Ave .... Ronceverte WV 24970 304-647-4411 647-6010 374-3
Web: www.gvmc.com

Greenbrier, The
300 W Main St .... White Sulphur Springs WV 24986 304-536-1110 536-7854 669
TF: 800-453-4858 ■ *Web:* www.greenbrier.com

Greenbusch Group Inc
1900 W Nickerson St Ste 201 .... Seattle WA 98119 206-378-0569 196
TF: 855-476-2874 ■ *Web:* www.greenbusch.com

Greencastle Associates Consulting LLC
627 Swedesford Rd .... Malvern PA 19355 610-640-9958 463
TF: 800-241-7246 ■ *Web:* www.greencastleconsulting.com

Greencastle Chamber of Commerce
16 S Jackson St .... Greencastle IN 46135 765-653-4517 139
Web: www.gogreencastle.com

GreenChem Industries LLC
222 Clematis St Ste 207 .... West Palm Beach FL 33401 561-659-2236 690
Web: www.greenchemindustries.com

GREENCREST Marketing Inc
120 Northwoods Blvd .... Columbus OH 43235 614-885-7921 4
Web: www.greencrest.com

Greencroft Retirement Communities Inc
1721 Greencroft Blvd .... Goshen IN 46527 574-537-4000 672
TF: 800-733-4111 ■ *Web:* www.greencroft.org

Greene & Bradford Inc
3501 Constitution Dr .... Springfield IL 62711 217-793-8844 727
Web: greeneandbradford.com

Greene & Schermer
601 12th St W Ste 505 .... Bradenton FL 34205 941-747-1871 745-2866 445
Web: www.manateelegal.com

Greene Consulting Associates LLC
Waterstone Bldg 4751 Best Rd Ste 450 .... Atlanta GA 30337 404-324-4600 196
Web: www.greeneconsults.com

Greene Correctional Facility
165 Plank Rd PO Box 8 .... Coxsackie NY 12051 518-731-2741 213
Web: www.doccs.ny.gov

Greene Correctional Institution
2699 Hwy 903 N PO Box 39 .... Maury NC 28554 252-747-3676 747-4432 213
Web: www.ncdps.gov

Greene County 411 Main St .... Catskill NY 12414 518-719-3270 719-3793 338
TF: 800-355-2287 ■ *Web:* www.greenegovernment.com

Greene County 400 Morrow Ave .... Eutaw AL 35462 205-372-3598 338
Web: www.greenecountyalabama.com

Greene County 204 N Cutler St .... Greeneville TN 37745 423-798-1708 338
TF: 800-732-6847 ■ *Web:* www.greenecountytngov.com

Greene County 1034 Silver Dr .... Greensboro GA 30642 706-453-7716 453-9555 338
TF: 800-248-7689 ■ *Web:* www.greenecountyga.gov

Greene County 114 N Chestnut St .... Jefferson IA 50129 515-386-2516 386-2321 338
Web: www.co.greene.ia.us

Greene County 450 High St .... Jackson MS 39201 601-359-3694 359-2407 338

Greene County 301 N Greene St .... Snow Hill NC 28580 252-747-4700 338
TF: 800-822-9388 ■ *Web:* www.co.greene.nc.us

Greene County 940 N Boonville Ave .... Springfield MO 65802 417-868-4055 868-4170 338
TF: 800-735-2966 ■ *Web:* www.greenecountymo.org

Greene County 22 Ct St .... Stanardsville VA 22973 434-985-5208 985-6723 338
Web: www.greenecountyva.gov

Greene County 35 Green St .... Xenia OH 45385 937-562-5006 562-5331 338
TF: 800-426-4791 ■ *Web:* www.co.greene.oh.us

Greene County Bancorp Inc
302 Main St .... Catskill NY 12414 518-943-2600 943-3756 360-2
NASDAQ: GCBC ■ *TF:* 888-439-4272 ■ *Web:* thebankofgreenecounty.com

				Phone	Fax	Class
Greene County Chamber of Commerce 327 Main St PO Box 248	Catskill	NY	12414	518-943-4222	943-1700	139
TF: 800-888-3586 ■ *Web:* greenecountychamber.com						
Greene County Convention & Visitors Bureau 1221 Meadowbridge Dr	Beavercreek	OH	45434	937-429-9100	429-7726	206
TF: 800-733-9109 ■ *Web:* www.greenecountyohio.org						
Greene County Partnership & Chamber of Commerce 115 Academy St	Greeneville	TN	37743	423-638-4111	638-5345	139
TF: 800-562-5907 ■ *Web:* www.greenecountypartnership.com						
Greene County Public Library 76 E Market St PO Box 520	Xenia	OH	45385	937-352-4000	372-4673	434-3
TF: 800-829-1040 ■ *Web:* greenelibrary.info						
Greene Espel PLLP 222 S Ninth St Campbell Mithun Tower Ste 2200	Minneapolis	MN	55402	612-373-0830	373-0929	445
Greene Lyon Group Inc 100 Cummings Ctr Ste 207P	Beverly	MA	01915	978-496-3455	496-3454	192
Web: www.greenelyon.com						
Greene Memorial Hospital 1141 N Monroe Dr	Xenia	OH	45385	937-352-2000		374-3
Web: ketteringhealth.org						
Greene Memorial Museum 3209 N Maryland Ave Lapham Hall UWM Campus	Milwaukee	WI	53211	414-229-4561	229-5452	520
Web: www.uwm.edu						
Greene Metal Products Inc 24500 Capital Blvd	Clinton Township	MI	48036	586-465-6800		697
Greene Resources 6601 Six Forks Rd	Raleigh	NC	27615	919-862-8602		260
TF: 800-784-9619 ■ *Web:* www.greeneresources.com						
Greene Rubber Company Inc 20 Cross St	Woburn	MA	01801	781-937-9909		385
TF: 800-558-3206 ■ *Web:* www.greenerubber.com						
Greene Tweed & Co 2075 Detwiler Rd	Kulpsville	PA	19443	215-256-9521	256-0189	326
Web: www.gtweed.com						
Greene Wealth Management LLC 1301 Fifth Ave Ste 3410	Seattle	WA	98101	206-623-2200		390
Web: www.greenewealthmgmt.com						
Greene-Niesen Insurance Agency Inc 6810 University Ave	Middleton	WI	53562	608-831-3168		390
Web: greeneniesen.com						
Greenerd Press & Machine Company Inc 41 Crown St PO Box 886	Nashua	NH	03061	603-889-4101	889-7601	456
TF: 800-877-9110 ■ *Web:* www.greenerd.com						
GreenerU Inc 480 Pleasant St Ste C300	Watertown	MA	02472	781-891-3750		192
Web: greeneru.com						
Greenery Speciality Care 2200 Hill Church-Houston Rd	Canonsburg	PA	15317	724-745-8000	746-8780	450
Web: greenerycenter.com						
Greeneville Light & Power System PO Box 1690	Greeneville	TN	37744	423-636-6200		245
TF: 866-466-1438 ■ *Web:* www.glps.net						
Greeneville Sun 121 W Summer St	Greeneville	TN	37743	423-638-4181	638-7348	532-2
Web: www.greenevillesun.com						
Greenfield Chamber of Commerce 4818 S 76th St Ste 129	Greenfield	WI	53220	414-327-8500		139
Web: www.thegreenfieldchamber.com						
Greenfield Community College 1 College Dr	Greenfield	MA	01301	413-775-1837	775-1827*	162
**Fax:* Admissions ■ *Web:* gcc.mass.edu						
Greenfield Public Library 5310 W Layton Ave	Greenfield	WI	53220	414-321-9595	321-8595	434-3
Web: www.greenfieldlibrary.org						
Greenfield Savings Bank 400 Main St PO Box 1537	Greenfield	MA	01302	413-774-3191		70
TF: 888-324-3191 ■ *Web:* www.greenfieldsavings.com						
Greenfield Union School District 1624 Fairview Rd	Bakersfield	CA	93307	661-837-6000	832-2873	685
Web: www.gfusd.k12.ca.us						
Greenfield Village 20900 Oakwood Blvd	Dearborn	MI	48124	313-271-1620	982-6225*	520
**Fax:* Cust Svc ■ *TF:* 800-835-5237 ■ *Web:* thehenryford.org/village						
Greengate Power Corp 407 - Second St SW	Calgary	AB	T2P2Y3	403-514-0556		612
Web: www.greengatepower.com						
GreenGeeks LLC 5739 Kanan Rd Ste 300	Agoura Hills	CA	91301	310-496-8946		225
TF: 877-326-7483 ■ *Web:* www.greengeeks.com						
Greenhaus Inc 2660 First Ave	San Diego	CA	92103	619-744-4024		7
TF: 800-561-3357 ■ *Web:* greenhaus.com						
Greenheart Farms Inc 902 Zenon Way	Arroyo Grande	CA	93420	805-481-2234	481-7374	10-11
TF: 800-549-5531 ■ *Web:* www.greenheartfarms.com						
Greenheck Fan Corp 1100 Greenheck Dr PO Box 410	Schofield	WI	54476	715-359-6171	355-2399	18
TF: 800-355-5354 ■ *Web:* www.greenheck.com						
Greenhill & Company Inc 300 Pk Ave 23rd Fl	New York	NY	10022	212-389-1500	389-1700	401
NYSE: GHL ■ *Web:* www.greenhill.com						
Greenhorn Creek Guest Ranch 2116 Greenhorn Ranch Rd	Quincy	CA	95971	530-283-0930		239
TF: 800-334-6939 ■ *Web:* www.greenhornranch.com						
Greenhorn Creek Resort 711 McCauley Ranch Rd	Angels Camp	CA	95222	209-729-8111		669
TF: 888-736-5900 ■ *Web:* www.greenhorncreek.com						
GreenHouse Holdings Inc 5171 Santa Fe St Ste I	San Diego	CA	92109	858-273-2626		360-2
Greenhurst Nursing Center 226 Skyler Dr	Charleston	AR	72933	479-965-7373		371
TF: 800-877-8339 ■ *Web:* greenhurst.net						
Greening of Detroit 1418 Michigan Ave	Detroit	MI	48216	313-237-8733		196
Web: greeningofdetroit.com						
Greenlancer Energy Inc 1150 Griswold St	Detroit	MI	48226	313-312-5101		256
Web: www.greenlancer.com						
Greenland (America) Inc 1905 Woodstock Rd Ste 2200	Roswell	GA	30075	770-435-1100		690
Web: www.greenlandamerica.com						
Greenland International Consulting Ltd 120 Hume St	Collingwood	ON	L9Y1V5	705-444-8805		192
TF: 800-461-0219 ■ *Web:* www.grnland.com						
Greenleaf Ctr 2209 Pineview Dr	Valdosta	GA	31602	229-671-6700		726
TF: 800-247-2747 ■ *Web:* www.greenleafhospital.com						
Greenleaf Inc 1955 Jerrold Ave	San Francisco	CA	94124	415-647-2991		345
Web: www.greenleafsf.com						
Greenleaf Media 1917 Winnebago St Ste 100	Madison	WI	53704	608-240-9611		177
TF: 800-561-3357 ■ *Web:* greenleafmedia.com						
Greenleaf Nursery Co 28406 Hwy 82	Park Hill	OK	74451	918-457-5172	407-5550*	369
**Fax Area Code:* 800 ■ *TF:* 800-331-2982 ■ *Web:* www.greenleafnursery.com						
Greenleaf State Park Hwy 10 S	Braggs	OK	74423	918-487-5196	487-5406	565
Web: www.travelok.com						
Greenlee County 223 Fifth St	Clifton	AZ	85533	928-865-2072	865-4417	338
TF: 800-793-6181 ■ *Web:* www.co.greenlee.az.us						
Greenlee Textron 1390 Aspen Way	Vista	CA	92081	760-598-8900		253
TF: 800-642-2155 ■ *Web:* greenlee.com						
Greenlee Textron Inc 4455 Boeing Dr	Rockford	IL	61109	800-435-0786	451-2632	759
TF: 800-435-0786 ■ *Web:* www.greenlee.com						
Greenline Emeritus Consulting 29 S Lasalle St Ste 333	Chicago	IL	60603	312-436-1883		463
Web: www.greenlineemeritus.com						
Greenline Equipment 14750 S Pony Express Rd	Bluffdale	UT	84065	801-966-4231	966-4313	274
TF: 888-201-5500 ■ *Web:* stotzequipment.com						
GreenLine Foods Inc 4575 W Main St PO Box 727	Guadalupe	CA	93434	419-353-2326		345
Web: www.greenlinefoods.com						
Greenline Industries Inc 2425 Larkspur Landing Cir	Larkspur	CA	94939	415-472-6890		580
GreenLine Paper Company Inc 631 S Pine St	York	PA	17403	717-845-8697	846-3806	553
TF: 800-641-1117 ■ *Web:* www.greenlinepaper.com						
Greenlining Institute, The 360 14th St 2nd FL	Oakland	CA	94612	510-926-4001	926-4010	765
Web: greenlining.org						
Greenlite Ventures Inc 810 Peace Portal Dr Ste 201	Blaine	WA	98230	360-220-5218		538
Web: www.greenlitecarboncredits.com						
GreenMan Technologies Inc 7 Kimball Ln Bldg A	Lynnfield	MA	01940	781-224-2411		660
TF: 866-994-7697 ■ *Web:* www.americanpowergroupinc.com						
Greenman-Pedersen Inc 325 W Main St	Babylon	NY	11702	631-587-5060	587-5029	261
Web: www.gpinet.com						
Greenpages Inc 33 Badgers Island W	Kittery	ME	03904	207-439-7310	439-7334	180
TF: 888-687-4876 ■ *Web:* www.greenpages.com						
Greenpath Inc 36500 Corporate Dr	Farmington Hills	MI	48331	248-553-5400		810
TF: 800-550-1961 ■ *Web:* www.greenpath.com						
Greenpeace Canada 33 Cecil St	Toronto	ON	M5T1N1	416-597-8408		48-13
TF: 800-320-7183 ■ *Web:* www.greenpeace.org						
Greenpeace USA 702 H St NW Ste 300	Washington	DC	20001	202-462-1177	462-4507	48-13
TF: 800-326-0959 ■ *Web:* www.greenpeace.org						
Greenpoint Metals Inc 301 Shotwell Dr	Franklin	OH	45005	937-743-4075		492
Web: www.greenpointmetals.com						
GreenPointe Holdings LLC 7807 Baymeadows Rd E Ste 205	Jacksonville	FL	32256	904-996-2485		360-3
Web: www.greenpointellc.com						
Greenridge Business Systems Corp 2701 - 83 Garry St	Winnipeg	MB	R3C4J9	204-775-3500		260
Web: www.greenridge.ca						
Greens Fort Mason Ctr Bldg A	San Francisco	CA	94123	415-771-6222		671
Web: www.greensrestaurant.com						
Greensboro Area Convention & Visitors Bureau 2200 Pinecroft Rd Ste 200	Greensboro	NC	27407	336-274-2282	230-1183	206
TF: 800-344-2282 ■ *Web:* visitgreensboronc.com						
Greensboro Children's Museum 220 N Church St	Greensboro	NC	27401	336-574-2898	574-3810	521
TF: 800-745-3000 ■ *Web:* www.gcmuseum.com						
Greensboro City Hall 300 W Washington St PO Box 3136	Greensboro	NC	27401	336-373-2489	373-2117	337
Web: www.greensboro-nc.gov						
Greensboro Coliseum Complex 1921 W Lee St	Greensboro	NC	27403	336-373-7400	373-2170	572
TF: 800-745-3000 ■ *Web:* www.greensborocoliseum.com						
Greensboro College 815 W Market St	Greensboro	NC	27401	336-272-7102	378-0154*	166
**Fax:* Admissions ■ *TF:* 800-346-8226 ■ *Web:* greensboro.edu						
Greensboro Pathology LLC 706 Green Valley Rd Ste 104	Greensboro	NC	27408	336-271-4930		418
Web: www.greensboropathology.com						
Greensboro Public Library 219 N Church St	Greensboro	NC	27401	336-373-2471		434-3
Web: www.greensboro-nc.gov						
Greensboro Science Center 4301 Lawndale Dr	Greensboro	NC	27455	336-288-3769	288-2531	520
TF: 800-344-2282 ■ *Web:* www.greensboroscience.org						
Greensboro Symphony Orchestra 200 N Davie St Ste 301	Greensboro	NC	27401	336-335-5456	335-5580	573-3
Web: www.greensborosymphony.org						
Greensburg State Bank 240 S Main St	Greensburg	KS	67054	620-723-2131		70
Web: bestbank.us						
Greenscape Pump Services Inc 1425 Whitlock Ln Ste 108	Carrollton	TX	75006	972-446-0037		612
TF: 877-401-4774 ■ *Web:* www.greenscapepump.com						
Greenscapes Home & Garden Products Inc 200 Union Grove Rd SE	Calhoun	GA	30701	706-629-6652		429
Web: www.greenscapesinc.net						
GreenSeed Contract Packaging 1025 Paramount Pkwy	Batavia	IL	60510	630-761-8544		393
TF: 800-238-0001 ■ *Web:* greenseedcp.com						
GreenSky Trade Credit LLC 1797 Northeast Expy Ste 100	Atlanta	GA	30329	866-936-0602		224
TF: 866-936-0602 ■ *Web:* www.greenskycredit.com						
GreensLedge Group LLC, The 399 Park Ave 37th Fl	New York	NY	10022	212-792-5270		70
Web: www.greensledge.com						

Name / Address	City	State	ZIP	Phone	Fax	Class
Greenspan Humphrey Lavine Barristers 15 Bedford Rd. *TF:* 800-387-5164 ■ *Web:* www.15bedford.com	Toronto	ON	M5R2J7	416-868-1755		445
Greenspoint Mall 12300 IH-45 N Fwy *Web:* www.greenspointmall.com	Houston	TX	77060	281-875-4201		460
Greenspring Assoc Inc 100 Painters Mill Rd Ste 700 *Web:* greenspringassociates.com	Owings Mills	MD	21117	410-363-2725		792
Greenspun Corp Inc, The 2275 Corporate Cir Ste 300	Henderson	NV	89074	702-259-4098	952-4010	690
Greenspun Media Group LLC, The 2360 Corporate Cir 3rd Fl. *TF:* 800-522-4700 ■ *Web:* www.gmgvegas.com	Henderson	NV	89074	702-990-2550		532-3
Greenstar Environmental Solutions LLC 6 Gellatly Dr *TF:* 800-428-2508 ■ *Web:* www.greenstarsolutions.com	Wappingers Falls	NY	12590	845-223-9944		196
Greenstein Rogoff Olsen & Company LLP 39159 Paseo Padre Pkwy Ste 315 *Web:* www.groco.com	Fremont	CA	94538	510-797-8661		2
Greenstone Farm Credit Services Aca 3515 West Rd *TF:* 800-444-3276 ■ *Web:* www.greenstonefcs.com	East Lansing	MI	48823	800-968-0061		216
Greensville Correctional Ctr 901 Corrections Way *Web:* vadoc.virginia.gov	Jarratt	VA	23870	434-535-7000		213
Greensville County 337 S Main St *Web:* www.greensvillecountyva.gov	Emporia	VA	23847	434-348-4215	348-4020	338
Greentec International Inc 95 Struck Ct *TF:* 888-858-1515 ■ *Web:* www.greentec.com	Cambridge	ON	N1R8L2	519-624-3300		660
Green-Tek Inc 3708 Enterprise Dr *TF:* 800-747-6440 ■ *Web:* www.green-tek.com	Janesville	WI	53546	608-754-7336		601
GreenTree Financial Group Inc 7951 SW Sixth St Ste 216 *Web:* www.gtfinancial.com	Plantation	FL	33324	954-424-2345		463
Greentree Group Inc, The 1360 Technology Court Ste 100 *Web:* www.greentreegroup.com	Dayton	OH	45430	937-490-5500		463
Greenup County 301 Main St *Web:* greenupcountyclerk.com	Greenup	KY	41144	606-473-7394	473-5354	338
Greenview Data Inc 8178 Jackson Rd *TF:* 800-458-3348 ■ *Web:* www.greenviewdata.com	Ann Arbor	MI	48103	734-426-7500		196
Greenview Regional Hospital 1801 Ashley Cir *TF:* 800-605-1466 ■ *Web:* tristargreenviewregional.com	Bowling Green	KY	42104	270-793-1000		374-3
Greenville Advocate, The PO Box 507 *Web:* www.greenvilleadvocate.com	Greenville	AL	36037	334-382-3111	382-7104	532-4
Greenville Area Chamber of Commerce 1 Depot Sq *Web:* www.greenvillealchamber.com	Greenville	AL	36037	334-382-3251		139
Greenville Business Magazine 303 Haywood Rd *Web:* www.greenvillebusinessmag.com	Greenville	SC	29607	864-271-1105	271-1165	457-5
Greenville City Hall 206 S Main St *TF:* 800-829-4477 ■ *Web:* www.greenvillesc.gov	Greenville	SC	29601	864-232-2273		337
Greenville College 315 E College Ave. **Fax:* Admissions ■ *TF:* 800-345-4440 ■ *Web:* www.greenville.edu	Greenville	IL	62246	618-664-7100	664-9841*	166
Greenville County 305 E N St. *Web:* www.greenvillecounty.org	Greenville	SC	29601	864-467-8551	467-8540	338
Greenville County Library System 25 Heritage Green Pl. *Web:* www.greenvillelibrary.org	Greenville	SC	29601	864-242-5000	235-8375	434-3
Greenville County Museum of Art 420 College St *Web:* www.gcma.org	Greenville	SC	29601	864-271-7570		520
Greenville First Bank 100 Verdae Blvd Ste 100 *TF:* 877-679-9646 ■ *Web:* www.southernfirst.com	Greenville	SC	29072	864-679-9000	679-9099	70
Greenville Hospital System (GHS) 701 Grove Rd *TF:* 877-447-4636 ■ *Web:* www.ghs.org	Greenville	SC	29605	864-455-8976		353
Greenville Library 1 Lou Finney Ln *TF:* 800-227-2345 ■ *Web:* www.ci.greenville.tx.us	Greenville	TX	75401	903-457-2992	457-2961	434-3
Greenville Little Theatre 444 College St *Web:* www.greenvillelittletheatre.org	Greenville	SC	29601	864-233-6238		572
Greenville Memorial Hospital 701 Grove Rd *TF:* 800-994-6610 ■ *Web:* www.ghs.org	Greenville	SC	29605	864-455-7000		374-3
Greenville Museum of Art 802 S Evans St *Web:* www.gmoa.org	Greenville	NC	27834	252-758-1946	758-7989	520
Greenville News 305 S Main St *TF:* 800-800-5116 ■ *Web:* www.greenvilleonline.com	Greenville	SC	29601	864-298-4100	298-4395	532-2
Greenville Symphony Orchestra 200 S Main St. *Web:* www.greenvillesymphony.org	Greenville	SC	29601	864-232-0344	467-3113	573-3
Greenville Technical College						
Barton 506 S Pleasantburg Dr *TF All:* 800-723-0673 ■ *Web:* www.gvltec.edu	Greenville	SC	29607	864-250-8000		162
Brashier 1830 W Georgia Rd *Web:* www.gvltec.edu/brashier	Simpsonville	SC	29680	864-250-7950		162
Greer 2522 Locust Hill Rd *TF:* 800-723-0673 ■ *Web:* www.gvltec.edu/greer	Taylors	SC	29687	800-723-0673		162
Greenville Tool & Die Co 1215 S Lafayette St. *Web:* www.gtd.com	Greenville	MI	48838	616-754-5693	754-5500	757
Greenville Zoo 150 Cleveland Pk Dr *TF:* 800-877-8339 ■ *Web:* www.greenvillezoo.com	Greenville	SC	29601	864-467-4300	467-4314	823
Greenville-Muhlenberg Chamber of Commerce 100 E Main Cross *Web:* www.greatermuhlenberg.com	Greenville	KY	42345	270-338-5422		139
Greenville-Pitt County Chamber of Commerce 302 S Greene St *Web:* www.greenvillenc.org	Greenville	NC	27834	252-752-4101	752-5934	139
Greenville-Pitt County Convention & Visitors Bureau (GPCCVB) 417 Cotanche St Ste 100 *TF:* 800-537-5564 ■ *Web:* www.visitgreenvillenc.com	Greenville	NC	27858	252-329-4200	329-4205	206
Greenville-Spartanburg Airport (GSP) 2000 GSP Dr Ste 1 *TF:* 800-331-1212 ■ *Web:* www.gspairport.com	Greer	SC	29651	864-877-7426	848-6225	27
Greenvity Communications Inc 673 S Milpitas Blvd Ste 204 *Web:* www.greenvity.com	Milpitas	CA	95035	408-935-9434		201
Greenwald Industries 212 Middlesex Ave *TF:* 800-221-0982 ■ *Web:* www.greenwaldindustries.com	Chester	CT	06412	860-526-0800	526-4205	495
Greenway Enterprises Inc PO Box 5553 *Web:* www.greenwayent.com	Helena	MT	59604	406-458-9411	458-6516	186
Greenway Print Solutions 5425 E Bell Rd #120 *TF:* 800-367-5793 ■ *Web:* www.greenwayprintsolutions.com	Scottsdale	AZ	85254	602-482-1100		627
Greenway Station 1650 Deming Way *Web:* www.greenwayshopping.com	Middleton	WI	53562	608-824-9111		460
Greenwell Chisholm Printing Co 420 E Parrish Ave *TF:* 800-844-1876 ■ *Web:* www.gc1919.com	Owensboro	KY	42303	270-684-3267		627
Greenwell State Park 25450 Rosedale Manor Ln PO Box 198 *Web:* www.greenwellfoundation.org	Hollywood	MD	20636	301-373-9775		565
Greenwich Assoc LLC 6 High Ridge Pk *TF:* 800-704-1027 ■ *Web:* www.greenwich.com	Stamford	CT	06905	203-629-1200	629-1229	194
Greenwich Chamber of Commerce 45 E Putnam Ave Ste 121 *Web:* www.greenwichchamber.com	Greenwich	CT	06830	203-869-3500	869-3502	139
Greenwich Hospital 5 Perryridge Rd *TF:* 800-657-8355 ■ *Web:* www.greenwichhospital.org	Greenwich	CT	06830	203-863-3000	863-3845	374-3
Greenwich Hospitality Group LLC 500 Steamboat Rd *Web:* www.thedelamar.com	Greenwich	CT	06830	203-661-9800		378
Greenwich Hotel, The 377 Greenwich St *Web:* www.thegreenwichhotel.com	New York	NY	10013	212-941-8900		378
Greenwich Symphony Orchestra PO Box 35 *TF:* 800-200-2882 ■ *Web:* www.greenwichsymphony.org	Greenwich	CT	06836	203-869-2664		573-3
Greenwood Athletic Club 5801 S Quebec St. *Web:* www.greenwoodathleticclub.com	Greenwood Village	CO	80111	303-770-2582	850-9219	354
Greenwood Chamber of Commerce 110 Phoenix St *Web:* www.greenwoodscchamber.org	Greenwood	SC	29646	864-223-8431	229-9785	139
Greenwood Communities & Resorts Inc 104 Maxwell Ave. *Web:* www.greenwoodcr.com	Greenwood	SC	29646	864-941-4044		653
Greenwood Convention & Visitors Bureau 2600 Sugarloaf Pkwy *TF:* 800-748-9064 ■ *Web:* www.gcvb.com	Dullath	GA	30097	662-453-9197	453-5526	206
Greenwood County 311 N Main St *Web:* www.greenwoodcounty.org	Eureka	KS	67045	620-583-8121	583-8124	338
Greenwood County 600 Monument St Park Plaza Ste 102 PO Box P-103 *Web:* www.greenwoodsc.gov	Greenwood	SC	29646	864-942-8596	942-8566	338
Greenwood Cultural Ctr 322 N Greenwood Ave *Web:* www.greenwoodculturalcenter.com	Tulsa	OK	74120	918-596-1020		50-2
Greenwood Furnace State Park 15795 Greenwood Rd *Web:* www.dcnr.state.pa.us	Huntingdon	PA	16652	814-667-1800		565
Greenwood House 53 Walter St *TF:* 800-367-6543 ■ *Web:* www.greenwoodhouse.org	Ewing	NJ	08628	609-883-5391		371
GreenWood Inc 160 Milestone Way Ste A *Web:* www.gwood.com	Greenville	SC	29615	864-244-9669		186
Greenwood King Properties 2 Inc 1616 S Voss Rd Ste 900 *TF:* 800-403-0888 ■ *Web:* www.greenwoodking.com	Houston	TX	77057	713-784-0888		196
Greenwood Leflore Hospital 1401 River Rd *Web:* www.glh.org	Greenwood	MS	38930	662-459-7000		374-3
Greenwood Mills Inc 300 Morgan Ave. *Web:* www.greenwoodmills.com	Greenwood	SC	29646	864-227-2121		745-1
Greenwood Mop & Broom Inc 312 Palmer St *TF:* 800-635-6849 ■ *Web:* www.greenwoodmopandbroom.com	Greenwood	SC	29646	864-227-8411	227-3200	103
Greenwood Park Mall 1251 US Hwy 31 N *TF:* 877-746-6642 ■ *Web:* simon.com/mall?id=165	Greenwood	IN	46142	317-881-6758	887-8606	460
Greenwood Plantation 6838 Highland Rd. *TF:* 800-259-4475 ■ *Web:* www.greenwoodplantation.com	Saint Francisville	LA	70775	225-655-4475	655-3292	50-3
Greenwood Racing Inc 3001 St Rd *TF:* 888-238-2946 ■ *Web:* www.parxracing.com	Bensalem	PA	19020	215-639-9000		360-2
Greenwood School 14 Greenwood Ln. *Web:* greenwood.org	Putney	VT	05346	802-387-4545		622
Greenwood School District 50 1855 Calhoun Rd PO Box 248 *TF:* 888-260-9430 ■ *Web:* www.gwd50.org	Greenwood	SC	29648	864-941-5400	941-5427	685
Greenwood Village South 295 Village Ln *TF:* 800-435-5601 ■ *Web:* www.greenwoodvillagesouth.com	Greenwood	IN	46143	317-881-2591	881-1299	672
Greenwood-Leflore County Chamber of Commerce 402 Hwy 82 *Web:* www.greenwoodms.com	Greenwood	MS	38930	662-453-4152	453-8003	139
Greenwood-Leflore Public Library 405 W Washington St. *Web:* glpls.com	Greenwood	MS	38930	662-453-3634	453-0683	434-3
Greer Capital Advisors LLC 2200 Woodcrest Pl Ste 309 *Web:* www.greercap.com	Birmingham	AL	35209	205-445-0800	445-1013	792
Greer County PO Box 207	Mangum	OK	73554	580-782-3664	782-3803	338

Phone | Fax | Class

Greer Galloway Group Inc, The
973 Crawford Dr . . . Peterborough ON K9J3X1 705-743-5780 743-9592 256
TF: 800-461-0219 ■ *Web:* www.greergalloway.com

Greer Garson Theatre Ctr
1600 St Michael's Dr. . . . Santa Fe NM 87505 505-473-6011 572
TF: 800-456-2673 ■ *Web:* www.santafeuniversity.edu

Greer Herz & Adams LLP
2525 S Shore Blvd Ste 203. . . . League City TX 77573 281-480-5278 428
TF: 800-201-3187 ■ *Web:* www.greerherz.com

Greer Laboratories Inc
639 Nuway Cir NE PO Box 800. . . . Lenoir NC 28645 828-754-5327 754-5320 479
TF Cust Svc: 800-378-3906 ■ *Web:* www.greerlabs.com

Greer Management Group Inc
3109 Charles B Root Wynd. . . . Raleigh NC 27612 919-571-0051 260
TF: 800-888-5894 ■ *Web:* www.thegreergroup.com

Greer Steel Co 624 Blvd . . . Dover OH 44622 330-343-8811 343-1700 723
TF Sales: 800-388-2868 ■ *Web:* www.greersteel.com

Greer Tank Inc
2921 International Airport Rd . . . Anchorage AK 99502 907-243-2455 480
Web: www.greertank.com

Greeters of Hawaii Ltd
300 Rodgers Blvd Ste 266 . . . Honolulu HI 96819 808-836-0161 292
TF: 800-366-8559 ■ *Web:* www.greetersofhawaii.com

Greeting Card Assn (GCA)
1444 I St NW Ste 700. . . . Washington DC 20005 202-216-9627 216-9646 49-16
Web: www.greetingcard.org

Grefe & Sidney P L C
500 W Ct Ave Ste 200. . . . Des Moines IA 50309 515-245-4300 445
Web: www.grefesidney.com

Greg Malik Real Estate Group Inc
7450 Morro Rd. . . . Atascadero CA 93422 805-466-2540 652
Web: gregmalik.com

Greg Norman Collection
134 W 37th St Ste 4 . . . New York NY 10018 646-840-5200 155-12
Web: gregnormancollection.com

Greg'S Heating & Air Cond Inc
2115 Pacific Blvd SE . . . Albany OR 97321 541-926-8950 189-10
Web: gregsheating.com

Gregg Appliances Inc
4151 E 96th St . . . Indianapolis IN 46240 317-848-8710 848-8723 35
NYSE: HGG ■ *TF:* 800-284-7344 ■ *Web:* www.hhgregg.com

Gregg County 101 E Methvin Ste 200 . . . Longview TX 75601 903-236-8430 237-2574 338
Web: www.co.gregg.tx.us

Gregg Distributors Ltd 16215-118 Ave . . . Edmonton AB T5V1C7 780-447-3447 652
Web: www.greggdistributors.ca

Gregg Engineering Inc
403 Julie Rivers Dr. . . . Sugar Land TX 77478 281-494-8100 177
Web: www.greggeng.com

Gregg Investigations Inc
500 E Milwaukee St . . . Janesville WI 53545 800-866-1976 400
TF: 800-866-1976 ■ *Web:* www.gregginvestigations.com

Gregg Ruth & Co
22809 Pacific Coast Hwy . . . Malibu CA 90265 310-456-1888 410
Web: greggruth.com

Gregg's Greenlake Cycle
7007 Woodlawn Ave NE . . . Seattle WA 98115 206-523-1822 711
TF: 800-786-9796 ■ *Web:* www.greggscycles.com

Gregor Technologies LLC
529 Technology Park Dr . . . Torrington CT 06790 860-482-2569 454
Web: www.gregortech.com

Gregory & Assoc Pllc 14 E Tabb St . . . Petersburg VA 23803 804-733-4511 2
Web: gregory-cpas.com

Gregory Electric Company Inc
2124 College St . . . Columbia SC 29205 803-748-1122 189-4
Web: www.gregoryelectric.com

Gregory Logistics Inc
2844 Fair St . . . Poplar Bluff MO 63901 573-785-1088 57
Web: www.gregorylogistics.com

Gregory Poole Equipment Co
4807 Beryl Rd PO Box 469. . . . Raleigh NC 27606 919-828-0641 386
TF: 800-451-7278 ■ *Web:* www.gregorypoole.com

Gregory Welteroth Advertising Inc
356 Laurens Rd . . . Montoursville PA 17754 570-433-3366 5
TF: 866-294-5765 ■ *Web:* www.gwa-inc.com

Gregory Wood Products Inc
2800 Woodtech Dr . . . Newton NC 28658 704-462-0001 683

Gregory's Foods Inc 1301 Trapp Rd. . . . Eagan MN 55121 651-454-0277 454-2254 297-11
Web: www.gregorysfoods.com

Gregory, Sharer & Stuart PA
100 Second Ave S Ste 600 . . . Saint Petersburg FL 33701 727-821-6161 2
Web: www.gsscpa.com

Gregs Japanese Auto Parts & Service
1506 S 348th St . . . Federal Way WA 98003 253-815-1500 57
Web: www.gregs.com

Gregstrom Corp 64 Holton St . . . Woburn MA 01801 781-935-6600 935-4905 602
Web: www.gregstrom.com

Greibok Designs LLC 3 E Read St. . . . Baltimore MD 21202 410-244-8861 514
TF: 800-704-3655 ■ *Web:* www.greibo.com

Greif Inc 425 Winter Rd . . . Delaware OH 43015 740-549-6000 657-6592 198
NYSE: GEF ■ *TF:* 877-781-9797 ■ *Web:* www.greif.com

Greiner Construction Inc
625 Marquette Ave . . . Minneapolis MN 55402 612-338-1696 186
Web: www.greinermn.com

Greitens Eric (R)
Capitol Bldg Rm 218, PO Box 720 . . . Jefferson City MO 65102 573-751-3222 526-3291 343
Web: governor.mo.gov

Gremada Industries Inc
825 28th St SW Unit E . . . Fargo ND 58103 701-356-0814 757
Web: www.gremada.com

Grenada 800 Second Ave Ste 400-K. . . . New York NY 10017 212-599-0301 599-1540 784
Web: www.un.int/grenada
Embassy 1701 New Hampshire Ave NW . . . Washington DC 20009 202-265-2561 265-2468 257
TF: 800-333-4636 ■ *Web:* www.grenadaembassyusa.org

Grenada County 59 Green St Ste 8 . . . Grenada MS 38902 662-226-1941 227-2865 338
TF: 800-368-3749 ■ *Web:* www.grenadamississippi.com

Grenelefe Golf & Tennis Resort
3271 Camelot Dr . . . Haines City FL 33844 863-422-7511 669
Web: www.thelefe.com

Greno Industries Inc 2820 Amsterdam Rd . . . Scotia NY 12302 518-393-4195 454
Web: www.greno.com

Grenzebach Corp 10 Herring Rd . . . Newnan GA 30265 770-253-4980 253-5189 386
Web: www.grenzebach.com

Grenzebach Glier & Assoc Inc
401 N Michigan Ave Ste 2800 . . . Chicago IL 60611 312-372-4040 589-6358 317
TF: 800-222-9233 ■ *Web:* www.grenzebachglier.com

Gresham Area Chamber of Commerce
701 NE Hood Ave . . . Gresham OR 97030 503-665-1131 666-1041 139
Web: www.greshamchamber.org

Gresham Petroleum Co
415 Pershing Ave P O Box 690. . . . Indianola MS 38751 662-884-5000 581
TF: 800-748-8934 ■ *Web:* www.greshampetroleum.com

Gresham Smith & Partners
511 Union St 1100 Nashville City Ctr. . . . Nashville TN 37219 615-770-8100 261
Web: www.greshamsmith.com

Gressco Ltd 328 Moravian Valley Rd . . . Waunakee WI 53597 608-849-6300 321
TF: 800-345-3480 ■ *Web:* gresscoltd.com

Gretz Beer Company
2801 E Township Line Rd . . . Hatfield PA 19440 610-275-0285 81-1
TF General: 800-310-5099 ■ *Web:* gretzbeer.com

Grey Bruce Health Services
1800 Eigth St E PO Box 1800. . . . Owen Sound ON N4K6M9 519-376-2121 374-2
Web: www.gbhs.on.ca

Grey Group 200 Fifth Ave . . . New York NY 10010 212-546-2000 546-1495 4
Web: www.grey.com

Grey Healthcare Group Inc
200 Fifth Ave. . . . New York NY 10010 212-886-3000 4
Web: www.ghgroup.com

Grey House Publishing
4919 Rt 22 PO Box 56 . . . Amenia NY 12501 518-789-8700 789-0556 637-2
TF: 800-562-2139 ■ *Web:* www.greyhouse.com

Grey Law of Ventura County Inc
3585 Maple St Ste 126. . . . Ventura CA 93003 805-658-2266 428
Web: www.greylaw.us

Grey Matter Group Inc
131 Division Ave S Ste 300 . . . Grand Rapids MI 49503 616-458-8750 7
Web: groymattergroup.com

Grey Moss Inn 19010 Scenic Loop Rd. . . . Helotes TX 78023 210-695-8301 695-3237 671
Web: www.grey-moss-inn.com

Greybrook Capital Inc
890 Yonge St 7th Fl . . . Toronto ON M4W3P4 416-322-9700 528
Web: www.greybrook.com

GreyCastle Security LLC
500 Federal St Ste 540 . . . Troy NY 12180 518-274-7233 196
TF: 800-403-8350 ■ *Web:* www.greycastlesecurity.com

Greycliff Prairie Dog Town State Park
2300 Lake Elmo Dr. . . . Billings MT 59105 406-247-2940 565
Web: stateparks.mt.gov

Greycroft Partners LLC
292 Madison Ave . . . New York NY 10017 212-756-3508 832-0117 401
Web: greycroft.com

Greyfield Inn
4 N Second St Ste 300 . . . Fernandina Beach FL 32034 904-261-6408 379
TF: 866-401-8581 ■ *Web:* www.greyfieldinn.com

GREYHAWK North America LLC
260 Crossways Park Dr . . . Woodbury NY 11797 516-921-1900 194
Web: www.greyhawk.com

Greyhound Canada Transportation Corp
1111 International Blvd Ste 700 . . . Burlington ON L7L6W1 800-661-0747 107
TF: 800-661-8747 ■ *Web:* www.greyhound.ca

Greyhound Friends Inc
167 Saddle Hill Rd . . . Hopkinton MA 01748 508-435-5969 48-3
Web: www.greyhoundfds.org

Greyhound Hall of Fame
407 S Buckeye Ave . . . Abilene KS 67410 785-263-3000 522
TF: 800-932-7881 ■ *Web:* www.greyhoundhalloffame.com

Greylock Federal Credit Union
150 W St. . . . Pittsfield MA 01201 413-236-4000 443-0292 219
TF: 800-207-5555 ■ *Web:* greylock.org

Greystar Development & Construction LP
750 Bering Dr Ste 400 . . . Houston TX 77057 713-966-5000 225
Web: www.greystar.com

Greyston Bakery Inc 104 Alexander St. . . . Yonkers NY 10701 914-375-1510 375-1514 296-1
TF: 800-289-2253 ■ *Web:* greyston.com

Greystone Construction Co
500 S Marschall Rd Ste 300. . . . Shakopee MN 55379 952-496-2227 186
TF: 888-742-6837 ■ *Web:* www.greystoneconstruction.com

Greystone Healthcare Management Corp
4042 Park Oaks Blvd Ste 300. . . . Tampa FL 33610 813-635-9500 196
Web: www.greystonehealth.com

Greystone Investment Management LLC
3805 Edwards Rd Ste 180. . . . Cincinnati OH 45209 513-731-8444 528
TF: 877-293-0908 ■ *Web:* www.greystoneinvestment.com

Greystone Managed Investments Inc
300 Park Centre 1230 Blackfoot Dr. . . . Regina SK S4S7G4 306-779-6400 401
TF: 800-213-4286 ■ *Web:* www.greystone.ca

Greystone of Lincoln Inc
7 Wellington Rd . . . Lincoln RI 02865 401-333-0444 334-5745 621
TF: 800-446-1761 ■ *Web:* greyst.com

Greystone Oil & Gas LLP
1616 S Voss Rd Ste 400. . . . Houston TX 77057 832-333-4000 324

Greystone Park Psychiatric Hospital
59 Koch Ave . . . Morris Plains NJ 07950 973-538-1800 374-5
Web: www.nj.gov/humanservices/dmhs/oshm/gpph

Greystone Power Corp
4040 Bankhead Hwy. . . . Douglasville GA 30134 770-942-6576 489-0940 245
Web: www.greystonepower.com

Greystone the Steakhouse
658 Fifth Ave. . . . San Diego CA 92101 619-232-0225 671
Web: www.greystonesteakhouse.com

GRFI Ltd 400 E Randolph St Ste 700. . . . Chicago IL 60601 888-856-5161 466
TF: 888-856-5161 ■ *Web:* grfiltd.com

Grid Dynamics Consulting Services Inc
4600 Bohannon Dr Ste 220 . . . Menlo Park CA 94025 650-523-5000 225
Web: www.griddynamics.com

Grid Net Inc
126 S Park St Ste 501. . . . San Francisco CA 94107 415-872-5097 177
Web: www.grid-net.com

Name / Address	City	State	Zip	Phone	Fax	Class
Grid One Solutions Inc 700 Turner Way Ste 205 *TF:* 800-606-7981 ■ *Web:* www.gridonesolutions.com	Aston	PA	19014	800-606-7981		393
Grid4 Communications Inc 2107 Crooks Rd *Web:* www.grid4.com	Troy	MI	48084	248-244-8100		387
Gridley & Company LLC 10 E 53rd St 24th Fl *Web:* www.gridleyco.com	New York	NY	10022	212-400-9720	400-9717	690
Gridley Country Ford-mercury 1709 State Hwy 99 *Web:* www.gridleycountryford.com	Gridley	CA	95948	530-846-4724		57
GridPoint Inc 2801 Clarendon Blvd Ste 100 *Web:* www.gridpoint.com	Arlington	VA	22201	703-667-7000	667-7001	787
GridSpeak Corp 555 12th St Ste 2040 *Web:* www.gridspeak.com	Oakland	CA	94607	510-463-8800		387
Grier School 2522 Grier Rd PO Box 308 *Web:* www.grier.org	Tyrone	PA	16686	814-684-3000		622
Grier-Musser Museum 403 S Bonnie Brae St *Web:* griermussermuseum.org	Los Angeles	CA	90057	213-413-1814		520
Gries Financial LLC 1801 E Ninth St Ste 1600 *TF:* 800-541-7774 ■ *Web:* www.gries.com	Cleveland	OH	44114	216-861-1148		194
Gries Seed Farms Inc 2348 N Fifth St *TF:* 800-472-4797 ■ *Web:* seedtoday.com	Fremont	OH	43420	419-332-5571		694
Grieve Corp, The 500 Hart Rd *Web:* www.grievecorp.com	Round Lake	IL	60073	847-546-8225		591
Griff's of America Inc 1202 Richardson Dr Ste 312 *TF:* 800-442-1162 ■ *Web:* griffshamburgers.com	Richardson	TX	75080	972-238-9561		670
Griffel, Dorshow & Johnson, Chartered 1809 Plymouth Rd Ste 222 *TF:* 800-447-5375 ■ *Web:* www.612law3333.com	Hopkins	MN	55305	612-529-3333		428
Griffin & Assoc 119 Dartmouth Dr SE *TF:* 800-758-5262 ■ *Web:* www.griffinassoc.com	Albuquerque	NM	87106	505-764-4444		636
Griffin Communitcations Group 3101 Nasa Pkwy Ste L *Web:* www.griffincommgroup.com	Seabrook	TX	77586	281-335-0200		463
Griffin Filters 106 Metropolitan Park Dr *Web:* www.griffinfilters.com	Liverpool	NY	13088	315-451-5300	451-2338	18
Griffin Gate Marriott Resort 1800 Newtown Pk *TF:* 800-228-9290 ■ *Web:* www.marriott.com	Lexington	KY	40511	859-231-5100	255-9944	669
Griffin Gear Inc 131 Railroad St *Web:* www.griffingear.com	Roebuck	SC	29376	864-576-6495		744
Griffin Home Health Care Inc 4231 Monroe Rd *TF:* 800-955-8510 ■ *Web:* www.griffinhomehealthcare.com	Charlotte	NC	28205	704-347-1993		475
Griffin Hospital 130 Div St *Web:* www.griffinhealth.org	Derby	CT	06418	203-735-7421	732-7569	374-3
Griffin Industries Inc 4413 Tanner Church Rd *TF:* 800-536-3935 ■ *Web:* griffinind.com	Ellenwood	GA	30294	404-363-1320		296-12
Griffin Lumber Co 1284 Charity Hwy *Web:* www.griffithlumber.net	Woolwine	VA	24185	276-930-2727		683
Griffin Memorial Hospital 900 E Main St *TF General:* 800-955-3468 ■ *Web:* ok.gov	Norman	OK	73071	405-321-4880		374-5
Griffin Pipe Products Co 1011 Warrenville Rd Ste 200 *Web:* uspipe.com	Lisle	IL	60532	630-719-6500		595
Griffin Publishing Group 18022 Cowan	Irvine	CA	92614	949-263-3733		626
Griffin Ranches Inc 9490 W County 19th St	Somerton	AZ	85350	928-627-8809		10-11
Griffin Thermal Products 100 Hurricane Creek Rd *TF:* 800-722-3723 ■ *Web:* www.griffinrad.com	Piedmont	SC	29673	864-845-5000	845-5001	60
Griffin Transport Services 5360 Capital Ct *TF:* 800-361-5028 ■ *Web:* legacyscs.com	Reno	NV	89502	775-331-8010		449
Griffin-Spalding Chamber of Commerce 143 N Hill St *TF:* 800-356-3094 ■ *Web:* www.griffinchamber.com	Griffin	GA	30223	770-228-8200	228-8031	139
Griffith ID Inc 735 S Market St *Web:* www.idgriffith.com	Wilmington	DE	19801	302-656-8253	656-8268	189-10
Griffith Morgan (Rep R - VA) 2202 Rayburn HOB *Web:* morgangriffith.house.gov	Washington	DC	20515	202-225-3861	225-0076	342-2
Griffith Rubber Mills 2625 NW Industrial St *TF:* 800-321-9677 ■ *Web:* griffithrubber.com	Portland	OR	97210	503-226-6971	226-6976	677
Griffiths Corp 2717 Niagara Ln N *TF:* 800-322-7663 ■ *Web:* www.griffithscorp.com	Minneapolis	MN	55447	763-557-8935		488
Griffon Aerospace 106 Commerce Cir *Web:* www.griffon-aerospace.com	Madison	AL	35758	256-258-0035		256
Griffon Corp 712 Fifth Ave 18th Fl *NYSE:* GFF ■ *TF:* 800-378-1475 ■ *Web:* www.griffon.com	New York	NY	10019	212-957-5000	957-5040	185
Grifols USA LLC 2410 Lillyvale Ave *TF:* 888-474-3657 ■ *Web:* www.grifolsusa.com	Los Angeles	CA	90032	888-474-3657		85
Grigg Graphic Services Inc 20982 Bridge St *Web:* www.grigg.com	Southfield	MI	48033	248-356-5005		627
Griggs County 808 Rollin Ave SW *Web:* www.cooperstownnd.com	Cooperstown	ND	58425	701-797-3613		338
Griggs Steel Company Inc 1200 Souter Dr *Web:* www.griggssteel.com	Troy	MI	48083	248-298-0540		492
Grignard Company LLC 505 Capobianco Plaza *TF:* 800-424-9300 ■ *Web:* www.grignard.com	Rahway	NJ	07065	732-340-1111		146
Grijalva Raul (Rep D - AZ) 1511 Longworth Bldg *Web:* grijalva.house.gov	Washington	DC	20515	202-225-2435	225-1541	342-2
Grill 225 225 E Bay St *TF:* 877-440-2250 ■ *Web:* www.marketpavilion.com/grill225.cfm	Charleston	SC	29401	843-266-4222	723-4320	671
Grill 23 & Bar 161 Berkeley St *Web:* www.grill23.com	Boston	MA	02116	617-542-2255	542-5114	671
Grill at Hacienda del Sol 5501 N Hacienda del Sol Rd *TF:* 800-728-6514 ■ *Web:* www.haciendadelsol.com	Tucson	AZ	85718	520-529-3500		671
Grill Concepts Inc 6300 Canoga Ave Ste 600 *OTC:* GLLC ■ *Web:* www.dailygrill.com	Woodland Hills	CA	91367	818-251-7000	999-4745	670
Grill of India 354 Ludlow Ave *Web:* amolindiacincinnati.com	Cincinnati	OH	45220	513-961-3600		671
Grill on, The Alley, The 172 S Market St *Web:* www.thegrill.com	San Jose	CA	95113	408-294-2244	294-2255	671
Grill83 83 Madison Ave *Web:* www.eighty3memphis.com	Memphis	TN	38103	901-333-1224		671
Grillfish 1444 Collins Ave *Web:* www.grillfish.com	Miami Beach	FL	33139	305-538-9908		671
Grimaud Farms of California Inc 1320-A S Aurora St *Web:* www.grimaudfarms.com	Stockton	CA	95206	209-466-3200		619
Grimbleby Coleman CPA's Inc 200 W Roseburg Ave *Web:* www.grimbleby-coleman.com	Modesto	CA	95350	209-527-4220		2
Grimco Inc 1585 Fencorp Dr *TF:* 800-542-9941 ■ *Web:* www.grimco.com	Fenton	MO	63026	800-542-9941		350
Grimes Legal 8264 Louisville Rd *TF:* 800-875-3820 ■ *Web:* www.grimeslegal.com	Bowling Green	KY	42101	270-782-3820		260
Grimmway Farms Inc PO Box 81498 *TF:* 800-301-3101 ■ *Web:* www.grimmway.com	Bakersfield	CA	93380	800-301-3101		10-11
Grimstad S84w18887 Enterprise Dr *TF:* 877-474-6782 ■ *Web:* www.grimstad.com	Muskego	WI	53150	414-422-2300		358
Grindall Island State Marine Park 400 Willoughby Ave PO Box 111071 *Web:* www.dnr.alaska.gov	Juneau	AK	99811	907-465-4563		565
Grinders 417 E 18th St *Web:* grinderspizza.com	Kansas City	MO	64108	816-472-5454		671
Grinding & Dicing Services Inc 925 Berryessa Rd *Web:* www.wafergrind.com	San Jose	CA	95133	408-451-2000		696
Grinding Products Company Inc 11084 E 9 Mile Rd *TF:* 800-521-3661 ■ *Web:* grindingproducts.net	Warren	MI	48089	586-757-2118		757
Grindmaster-Cecilware Inc 4003 Collins Ln *TF:* 800-695-4500 ■ *Web:* www.grindmaster.com	Louisville	KY	40245	502-425-4776	425-4664	298
Griner Engineering Inc 2500 N Curry Pk *Web:* www.griner.com	Bloomington	IN	47404	812-332-2220	332-2229	621
Grinnell College 1115 Eighth Ave *TF:* 800-247-0113 ■ *Web:* www.grinnell.edu	Grinnell	IA	50112	641-269-3600	269-4800	166
Grinnell College Burling Library 6th Ave High St *TF:* 800-247-0113 ■ *Web:* www.grinnell.edu	Grinnell	IA	50112	641-269-3371	269-4283	434-6
Grinnell Mutual Reinsurance Co 4215 Hwy 146 PO Box 790 *TF:* 800-362-2041 ■ *Web:* grinnellmutual.com	Grinnell	IA	50112	641-269-8000	236-2840	391-4
Grinner's Food Systems Ltd 105 Walker *Web:* www.greco.ca	Truro	NS	B2N4B1	902-893-4141		670
Grinstead Group Inc 13289 O'Bannon Stn Way	Louisville	KY	40223	502-966-9020		61
Grip Ltd 179 John St 6th Fl *Web:* www.griplimited.com	Toronto	ON	M5T1X4	416-340-7111		7
Grisham Consulting Services 3514 E Tropicana Ave *Web:* grishamconsultingservices.com	Las Vegas	NV	89121	702-450-6523		196
Grismer Tire Co PO Box 337 *Web:* www.grismertire.com	Dayton	OH	45401	937-643-2526		755
Griswold Home Care 717 Bethlehem Pike Ste 300 **Fax Area Code:* 469 ■ *TF:* 855-303-9470 ■ *Web:* www.griswoldhomecare.com	Erdenheim	PA	19038	215-402-0200	277-3820*	310
Griswold Industries 1701 Placentia Ave *Web:* www.cla-val.com	Costa Mesa	CA	92627	949-722-4805		789
Griswold LLC 1 River St PO Box 638 *TF:* 800-472-8788 ■ *Web:* www.griswoldcorp.com	Moosup	CT	06354	860-564-3321	564-9103	676
Griswold Machine & Engineering Inc 8530 M 60 *TF:* 800-248-2054 ■ *Web:* www.gme-shields.com	Union City	MI	49094	517-741-4300		475
Grit Commercial Printing Inc 80 Choate Cir *TF:* 800-872-0409 ■ *Web:* www.gritprinting.com	Montoursville	PA	17754	570-368-8021		627
Grizzly & Wolf Discovery Ctr 201 S Canyon St *TF:* 800-257-2570 ■ *Web:* www.grizzlydiscoveryctr.org	West Yellowstone	MT	59758	406-646-7001	646-7004	823
Grizzly Oil Sands ULC 605 - 5 Ave SW Ste 2600 *Web:* www.grizzlyoilsands.com	Calgary	AB	T2P3H5	403-930-6450		536
Grizzly Peak Brewing Co 120 W Washington St *Web:* www.grizzlypeak.net	Ann Arbor	MI	48104	734-741-7325		671
GRMC (Gateway Regional Medical Ctr) 2100 Madison Ave *TF General:* 800-422-6237 ■ *Web:* www.gatewayregional.net	Granite City	IL	62040	618-798-3000		374-3
GRO (Grandparents Rights Organization) 1760 S Telegraph Rd Ste 250 *Web:* www.grandparentsrights.org	Bloomfield Hills	MI	48304	248-646-7177		48-6
Grob Inc 1731 Tenth Ave *TF:* 800-225-6481 ■ *Web:* www.grobinc.com	Grafton	WI	53024	262-377-1400	377-2106	455
Grobet File Company of America Inc 750 Washington Ave *TF:* 800-847-4188 ■ *Web:* www.grobetusa.com	Carlstadt	NJ	07072	201-939-6700	939-5067	758
Grocers Supply 3131 E Holcombe Blvd *Web:* www.grocerssupply.com	Houston	TX	77021	713-747-5000		297-8
Grocery People Ltd, The 14505 Yellowhead Trl *TF:* 800-461-9401 ■ *Web:* www.tgp.ca	Edmonton	AB	T5L3C4	780-447-5700		297-8
Grocery Supply Co 130 Hillcrest Dr *TF:* 800-231-1938 ■ *Web:* www.grocerysupply.com	Sulphur Springs	TX	75482	903-885-7621	439-3249	297-8

				Phone	Fax	Class
Grocery, The 288 Smith St *Web:* www.thegroceryrestaurant.com	Brooklyn	NY	11231	718-596-3335		671
Groendyke Transport Inc 2510 Rock Island Blvd *TF:* 800-843-2103 ■ *Web:* www.groendyke.com	Enid	OK	73701	580-234-4663		780
Groezinger Provisions Inc 1200 Seventh Ave *Web:* alexianpate.com	Neptune	NJ	07753	732-775-3220		473
Groff NetWorks LLC 11 State St *Web:* www.groffnetworks.com	Troy	NY	12180	518-320-8906		196
Grogans Health Care Supply Inc 1016 S Broadway St *TF:* 800-365-1020 ■ *Web:* www.grogans.com	Lexington	KY	40504	859-254-6661	254-6666	475
Grohe America Inc 241 Covington Dr *TF:* 800-444-7643 ■ *Web:* www.grohe.com	Bloomingdale	IL	60108	630-582-7711	582-7722	609
Gromwell LLC 15 W 39th St 11th Fl *Web:* www.gromwell.com	New York	NY	10018	212-972-9300		260
Groom Energy Solutions LLC 96 Swampscott Rd *Web:* www.groomenergy.com	Salem	MA	01970	978-306-6052		256
Groople Inc 1732 Wazee St Ste 202 *Web:* www.groople.com	Denver	CO	80202	817-987-9004		393
Groove 99.3 FM 3651 Pegasus Dr Ste 107 *Web:* www.groove993.com	Bakersfield	CA	93308	661-393-1900		645-15
Groovfold Inc 1050 W State St *TF:* 800-367-1133 ■ *Web:* www.groovfold.com	Newcomerstown	OH	43832	740-498-8363	498-8782	309
Gros Ventre River Ranch PO Box 151 *Web:* grosventreriverranch.com	Moose	WY	83012	307-733-4138	733-4272	239
Grosh Scenic Rentals 4114 Sunset Blvd **Fax Area Code:* 323 ■ *TF:* 877-363-7998 ■ *Web:* www.grosh.com	Los Angeles	CA	90029	877-363-7998	664-7526*	722
Gros-Ite Industries 1790 New Britain Ave *TF:* 877-777-4778 ■ *Web:* www.edactechnologies.com	Farmington	CT	06032	860-677-2603		21
Gross Electric Inc 2807 N Reynolds Rd *Web:* www.grosselectric.com	Toledo	OH	43615	419-537-1818		246
Gross Mendelsohn & Associates PA 36 S Charles St 18th fl *TF:* 800-899-4623 ■ *Web:* www.gma-cpa.com	Baltimore	MD	21201	410-685-5512		2
Grosse Ile Township Schools 23276 E River Rd *Web:* www.gischools.org	Grosse Ile	MI	48138	734-362-2555		685
Grosse Pointe News 96 Kercheval Ave *Web:* www.grossepointenews.com	Grosse Pointe Farms	MI	48236	313-882-6900	882-1585	532-4
Grossel Tool Co 34190 Doreka *Web:* www.grosseltool.com	Fraser	MI	48026	586-294-3660	294-7134	811
Grossenburg Implement Inc 31341 US Hwy 18 *TF:* 800-658-3440 ■ *Web:* www.grossenburg.com	Winner	SD	57580	605-842-2040	842-3485	274
Grossinger Motorcorp Inc 6900 N McCormick Blvd *Web:* grossinger.com	Lincolnwood	IL	60712	847-674-9000		57
Grossinger Motors 1430 Fort Jesse Rd *TF:* 888-719-0095 ■ *Web:* www.sudsmotorcars.com	Normal	IL	61761	880-719-0095		57
Grossman & Grossman LLP 4 Executive Park Dr	Albany	NY	12203	518-438-3509		2
Grossman & Keith Engineering Co 10408 Greenbriar Pl *Web:* grossman-keith.com	Oklahoma City	OK	73159	405-691-3213		261
Grossman Iron & Steel 5 N Market St *TF:* 800-969-9423 ■ *Web:* www.grossmaniron.com	Saint Louis	MO	63102	314-231-9423	231-6983	686
Grossman's Inc 90 Hawes Way *Web:* www.bargain-outlets.com	Stoughton	MA	02072	781-297-3300	297-0180	364
Grossman, Tucker, Perreault & Pfleger PLLC 55 S Commercial St *Web:* gtpp.com	Manchester	NH	03101	603-668-6560		428
Grossmont College 8800 Grossmont College Dr **Fax:* Admissions ■ *Web:* www.grossmont.edu	El Cajon	CA	92020	619-644-7000	644-7933*	162
Grossmont Ctr 5500 Grossmont Ctr Dr *Web:* www.grossmontcenter.com	La Mesa	CA	91942	619-465-2900		460
Grosvenor Funds 888 17th St NW Ste 214 *Web:* www.grosvenorfund.com	Washington	WA	20006	202-861-5650	861-5653	792
Grote & Weigel Inc 76 Granby St *Web:* www.groteandweigel.com	Bloomfield	CT	06002	860-242-8528		296-26
Grote Industries Inc 2600 Lanier Dr *TF:* 800-628-0809 ■ *Web:* www.grote.com	Madison	IN	47250	812-273-2121	265-8440	60
Groth Corp 13650 N Promenade Blvd *TF:* 800-354-7684 ■ *Web:* www.grothcorp.com	Stafford	TX	77477	281-295-6800	295-6999	789
Groth Gates Heating & Sheet Metal Inc 2614 SE Hwy 101 *Web:* www.grothgates.com	Lincoln City	OR	97367	541-994-2631		610
Grothman Glenn (Rep R - WI) 1217 Longworth HOB *Web:* grothman.house.gov	Washington	DC	20515	202-225-2476	225-2356	342-2
Groton Partners LLC 640 Fifth Ave Ste 1700 *Web:* www.grotonpartners.com	New York	NY	10019	212-430-1800		194
Groton Public Library 52 Newtown Rd *TF:* 800-989-0900 ■ *Web:* www.groton-ct.gov/library	Groton	CT	06340	860-441-6750	448-0363	434-3
Groton School 282 Farmers Row PO Box 991 *Web:* www.groton.org	Groton	MA	01450	978-448-3363		622
Groton-Dunstable Regional School District PO Box 729 *Web:* www.gdrsd.org	Groton	MA	01450	978-448-5505	448-9402	449
Grotto 37 Bowdoin St *Web:* www.grottorestaurant.com	Boston	MA	02114	617-227-3434		671
Grotto Pizza Inc 20376 Coastal Hwy *TF:* 800-464-5377 ■ *Web:* www.grottopizza.com	Rehoboth Beach	DE	19971	302-227-3567	227-4566	670
Grotto Ristorante 129 E Fremont St *TF:* 800-634-3454 ■ *Web:* www.goldennugget.com	Las Vegas	NV	89101	702-385-7111		671
Grotto, The 8840 NE Skidmore St *TF:* 800-342-6529 ■ *Web:* www.thegrotto.org	Portland	OR	97220	503-254-7371	254-7948	97
Ground Control Systems Inc 3100 El Camino Real *Web:* www.groundcontrol.com	Atascadero	CA	93422	805-783-4600		681
Ground Penetrating Radar Systems Inc 7540 New West Rd *Web:* www.gp-radar.com	Toledo	OH	43617	419-843-9804		727
Ground Round 15 Main St Ste 210 *Web:* www.groundround.com	Freeport	ME	04032	207-623-0022		671
Ground Water Protection Council (GWPC) 13308 N MacArthur Blvd *TF:* 800-364-2274 ■ *Web:* www.gwpc.org	Oklahoma City	OK	73142	405-516-4972	516-4973	48-13
GroundMetrics Inc 4217 Ponderosa Ave Ste A *Web:* www.groundmetrics.com	San Diego	CA	92123	619-786-8023		407
Grounds For Play Inc 1050 Columbia Dr **Fax Area Code:* 817 ■ *TF:* 800-552-7529 ■ *Web:* www.groundsforplay.com	Mansfield	TX	76063	800-552-7529	477-1140*	346
GroundSwell 1776 Park Ave Ste 4-175 *Web:* www.groundswellinc.com	Park City	UT	84060	435-214-2997		528
Groundwater & Environmental Services Inc 1599 Rte 34 Ste 1 **Fax Area Code:* 866 ■ *TF:* 800-220-3068 ■ *Web:* www.gesonline.com	Wall Township	NJ	07727	800-220-3068	902-2187*	192
Group 1 Automotive Inc 800 Gessner Ste 500 *NYSE:* GPI ■ *TF:* 888-707-4094 ■ *Web:* www.group1auto.com	Houston	TX	77024	713-647-5700		57
Group 22 Inc 1661 E Franklin Ave *Web:* www.group22.com	El Segundo	CA	90245	310-322-2210		344
Group 3 Marketing 1907 Wayzata Blvd Ste 200	Wayzata	MN	55391	952-475-3269		195
Group 55 Marketing Inc 3011 W Grand Blvd 329 Fisher Bldg *TF:* 800-438-7325 ■ *Web:* www.group55.com	Detroit	MI	48202	313-875-1155		5
Group Builders Inc 511 Mokauea St *Web:* www.groupbuilders.net	Honolulu	HI	96819	808-832-0888		189-9
Group Delta Consultants 370 Amapola Ave Ste 212 *Web:* www.groupdelta.com	Torrance	CA	90501	310-320-5100		256
Group for Organizational Effectiveness Inc, The 727 Waldens Pond Rd *Web:* groupoe.com	Albany	NY	12203	518-456-7738		195
Group Health Co-op 320 Westlake Ave N Ste 100 *TF:* 888-901-4636 ■ *Web:* www.ghc.org	Seattle	WA	98109	206-448-5600		391-3
Group Health Solutions Inc 148 Madison Ave Fl 15 *Web:* www.grouphealthsolutions.com	New York	NY	10016	212-779-4158		226
Group Ist 545 Eighth Ave Ste 720 *Web:* www.groupist.com	New York	NY	10018	212-594-8787		636
Group Management Services Inc 3296 Columbia Rd Ste 101 *TF:* 888-823-2084 ■ *Web:* www.groupmgmt.com	Richfield	OH	44286	330-659-0100		463
Group Manufacturing Services Inc 1928 Hartog Dr *Web:* www.groupmanufacturing.com	San Jose	CA	95131	408-436-1040		697
Group O Inc 4905 77th Ave *TF Cust Svc:* 800-752-0730 ■ *Web:* www.groupo.com	Milan	IL	61264	309-736-8300		113
Group One Trading LP 440 S La Salle Ste 3232 *Web:* www.group1.com	Chicago	IL	60605	312-922-2620		600
Group Transportation Services Inc 5876 Darrow Rd	Hudson	OH	44236	330-342-8700		311
Group Voyagers Inc 5301 S Federal Cir *Web:* www.globusandcosmos.com	Littleton	CO	80123	303-703-7000		760
Group Wellesley 307 S Dithridge St *Web:* www.groupwellesley.com	Pittsburgh	PA	15213	412-363-3481		428
Group360 Inc 1227 Washington Ave *Web:* www.group360.com	Saint Louis	MO	63103	314-260-6360		232
Groupe Ameublement Focus Inc 1310 Rue Nobel *Web:* www.groupefocus.com	Boucherville	QC	J4B5H3	514-644-5551		321
Groupe BBA Inc 375 Sir-Wilfrid-Laurier Blvd *Web:* www.bba.ca	Mont-saint-hilaire	QC	J3H6C3	450-464-2111		463
Groupe Canimex 285 Saint-Georges St *TF:* 855-777-1335 ■ *Web:* www.canimex.com	Drummondville	QC	J2C4H3	819-477-1335		358
Groupe de Scieries GDS Inc 207 Rt 295 *Web:* www.groupgds.com	Degelis	QC	G5T1R1	418-853-2566		820
Groupe Deschenes Inc 3901 Jarry St E Ste 250 *Web:* www.groupedeschenes.com	Montreal	QC	H1Z2G1	514-253-3110		612
Groupe Desgagnes Inc 21 March-Champlain St *TF:* 800-463-0680 ■ *Web:* www.groupedesgagnes.com	Quebec	QC	G1K8Z8	418-692-1000		313
Groupe Germain Inc 1200 des-Soeurs-du-Bon-Pasteur Ste 500 *TF:* 800-484-6267 ■ *Web:* www.groupegermain.com	Quebec	QC	G1S0B1	418-687-1123		707
Groupe Gsc 10 905 Blvd Louis-H Lafontaine Bureau 200 *Web:* groupe-gsc.qc.ca	Montr,al	QC	H1J2E8	514-354-4222		180
Groupe Informatique TechSolCom Inc 1450 City Councillors Ste 340 *Web:* www.techsolcom.ca	Montreal	QC	H3A2E6	514-392-9997		180
Groupe Lacasse LLC 99 St-Pierre St **Fax Area Code:* 888 ■ **Fax:* Cust Svc ■ *TF:* 888-522-2773 ■ *Web:* www.groupelacasse.com	Sainte-Pie	QC	J0H1W0	450-772-2495	248-1865*	319-1
Groupe Lelys Inc 3275 Ave Francis Hughes *Web:* www.lelys.com	Laval	QC	H7L5A5	450-662-7161		627
Groupe Lou-Tec Inc 8500 Jules L,ger *TF:* 800-567-0422 ■ *Web:* www.loutec.com	Anjou	QC	H1J1A7	514-356-0047		23
Groupe Maskatel Inc 3455 Blvd Choquette *TF:* 800-567-6353 ■ *Web:* www.maskatel.ca	Saint-Hyacinthe	QC	J2S7Z8	450-250-5050		224
Groupe Meloche Inc 491 Boul Des Rables *Web:* www.melocheinc.com	Salaberry-de-valleyfield	QC	J6T6G3	450-371-4646	371-4957	454

	Phone	Fax	Class
Groupe PARIMA Inc 4450 Cousens Rue, Montreal QC H4S1X6 *Web:* groupeparima.com	514-338-3780		743
Groupe Plombaction Inc 575 boul Pierre-Roux est, Victoriaville QC G6T1S7 *Web:* www.groupeplombaction.com	819-752-6064		186
Groupe Sante Sedna Inc 1010 Sherbrooke W Ste 2405, Montreal QC H3A2R7 *Web:* www.groupesedna.ca	514-844-8760		194
Groupe Savoie Inc 251, Rt 180, St-Quentin NB E8A2K9 *Web:* www.groupesavoie.com	506-235-2228	235-3200	683
Groupe SYGIF Inc 120 Montee Industrielle-et-Commerciale, Rimouski QC G5M1B1 *Web:* groupesygif.ca	418-721-5353		180
GroupGifting.com Inc 445 Broad Hollow Rd Ste 25, Melville NY 11747 *Web:* www.egifter.com	516-882-1200		387
Groupon Inc 600 W Chicago Ave Ste 620, Chicago IL 60654 *Web:* www.groupon.com	312-676-5773		345
Grouse Mountain Resorts Ltd 6400 Nancy Greene Way, North Vancouver BC V7R4K9 *Web:* www.grousemountain.com	604-984-0661		707
Grove City College 100 Campus Dr, Grove City PA 16127 **Fax:* Admissions ■ *Web:* www.gcc.edu	724-458-2000	458-3395*	166
Grove City Medical Ctr (GCMC) 631 N Broad St Ext, Grove City PA 16127 *Web:* www.gcmcpa.org	724-450-7000	450-7179	374-3
Grove Consultants International, The 1000 Oreilly Ave, San Francisco CA 94129 *TF:* 800-494-7683 ■ *Web:* www.grove.com	415-561-2500		463
Grove Grill 4550 Poplar Ave, Memphis TN 38117 *Web:* www.thegrovegrill.com	901-818-9951		671
Grove Hotel, The 245 S Capitol Blvd, Boise ID 83702 *Web:* www.grovehotelboise.com	208-333-8000	333-8800	379
Grove Park Inn Resort & Spa 290 Macon Ave, Asheville NC 28804 *TF:* 800-438-5800 ■ *Web:* www.omnihotels.com/hotels/asheville-grove-park	828-252-2711		669
Grove Printing Corp 4225 Howard Ave, Kensington MD 20895 *TF:* 877-290-5793 ■ *Web:* www.groveprinting.com	301-571-1024		627
Grove Street Advisors 2221 Washington St Bldg 1 Ste 201, Newton MA 02462 *Web:* grovestreet.com	781-263-6100	263-6101	792
Grove, The 189 The Grove Dr, Los Angeles CA 90036 *TF:* 888-315-8883 ■ *Web:* www.thegrovela.com	323-900-8080		460
Grove/Atlantic Inc 841 Broadway 4th Fl, New York NY 10003 *Web:* www.groveatlantic.com	212-614-7850	614-7886	637-2
Grove-Madsen Industries 390 E Sixth St, Reno NV 89512 *Web:* www.g-m-i.net	775-322-3400	322-3495	246
Grover Cleveland Birthplace State Historic Site 207 Bloomfield Ave, Caldwell NJ 07006 *Web:* www.njparksandforests.org	973-226-0001		565
Grover Corp 2759 S 28th St, Milwaukee WI 53234 *TF:* 800-776-3602 ■ *Web:* www.grovercorp.com	414-384-9472	384-0201	128
Grover Landscape Services Inc 6224 Stoddard Rd, Modesto CA 95356 *Web:* www.groverlandscapeservices.com	209-545-4401		776
Groves Industrial Supply Inc 7301 Pinemont Dr, Houston TX 77040 *TF:* 800-343-8923 ■ *Web:* www.grovesindustrial.com	713-675-4747		111
GroveWare Technologies Ltd 90 Eglinton Ave E Ste 411, Toronto ON M4P2Y3 *TF:* 877-701-9378 ■ *Web:* www.groveware.com	877-701-9378		317
Grow Company Inc 55 Railroad Ave, Ridgefield NJ 07657 *Web:* www.growco.us	201-941-8777	941-1881	296-11
GROW Inc 2403 W Springfield Ave PO Box 3667, Champaign IL 61826 *Web:* www.growinamerica.org	217-352-6989		48-21
Grow (Norfolk, VA) 427 Granby St, Norfolk VA 23510 *Web:* www.thisisgrow.com	757-248-5274		5
Grower Direct Fresh Cut Flowers 6303 Wagner Rd, Edmonton AB T6E4N4 *TF:* 877-277-4787 ■ *Web:* www.growerdirect.com	780-436-7774	436-3336	292
Grower, Ketcham Advocates, Counselors & Litigators 901 N Lake Destiny Rd Ste 450, Maitland FL 32751 *Web:* www.growerketcham.com	407-423-9545		428
Growers Co-op Grape Juice Company Inc 112 N Portage St, Westfield NY 14787 *Web:* www.concordgrapejuice.com	716-326-3161	326-6566	296-20
Growers Express LLC 1219 Abbott St PO Box 948, Salinas CA 93901 **Fax:* Sales ■ *Web:* www.growersexpress.com	831-757-9700	422-4246*	315-4
Growing Leaders Inc 270 Scientific Dr NW Ste 10, Norcross GA 30092 *Web:* www.growingleaders.com	770-495-3332		393
GROWMARK Inc 1701 Towanda Ave, Bloomington IL 61701 *TF:* 800-728-7511 ■ *Web:* www.growmark.com	309-557-6000		276
Growth Assn of Southwestern Illinois 5800 Godfrey Rd Alden Hall, Godfrey IL 62035 *TF:* 855-852-9460 ■ *Web:* www.growthassociation.com	618-467-2280	466-8289	139
Growth Coach, The 10700 Montgomery Rd Ste 300, Cincinnati OH 45242 *TF:* 888-292-7992 ■ *Web:* www.thegrowthcoach.com	888-292-7992		310
Growth Design Corp 225 E St Paul Ave Ste 201, Milwaukee WI 53202 *Web:* www.growthdesign.com	414-224-0586		463
Growth Energy 777 N Capitol St NE Ste 805, Washington DC 20002 *Web:* www.growthenergy.org	202-545-4000		192
Growth Fund Guide 4020 Jackson Blvd, Rapid City SD 57702 *Web:* marketwatch.com	605-341-1971		531-9
Growth Industries Inc 12523 Third St PO Box 900, Grandview MO 64030 *Web:* www.growthind.com	816-763-7676	765-4925	22
Growth Products Ltd 80 Lafayette Ave, White Plains NY 10603 *TF:* 800-648-7626 ■ *Web:* www.growthproducts.com	914-428-1316		276
Growth Properties Investment Managers Inc 1329 Bristol Pike Ste 182, Bensalem PA 19020 *Web:* www.gpim.net	215-546-5980		656
GrowthForce LLC 800 Rockmead Ste 200, Kingwood TX 77339 *Web:* growthforce.com	281-358-2007		194
Growthpoint Inc 926 76th Ave S, Fargo ND 58104 *TF:* 800-366-5775 ■ *Web:* growthpoint-inc.com	701-235-1600		195
GRPS (Grand Rapids Public Schools) 1331 Franklin St SE PO Box 117, Grand Rapids MI 49506 *Web:* www.grps.org	616-819-2000	819-2104	685
GRSS (IEEE Geoscience & Remote Sensing Society) IEEE Operations Ctr 445 and 501 Hoes Ln, Piscataway NJ 08854 *TF:* 800-678-4333 ■ *Web:* www.ewh.ieee.org	732-562-5550		49-19
GRTC Transit System 301 E Belt Blvd, Richmond VA 23224 *TF:* 800-221-1212 ■ *Web:* www.ridegrtc.com	804-358-3871	342-1933	468
Grubb Company Inc, The 1960 Mountain Blvd, Oakland CA 94611 *Web:* www.grubbco.com	510-339-0400		652
Grubbs Infiniti Ltd 1661 Airport Fwy, Euless TX 76040 *TF:* 800-685-1111 ■ *Web:* infiniti.grubbs.com	817-318-1200	359-4100	57
Gruber Systems Inc 25636 Ave Stanford, Valencia CA 91355 *TF:* 800-257-4070 ■ *Web:* www.gruber-systems.com	661-257-4060	257-4791	604
Grudi Associates Inc PO Box 626, Palmyra PA 17078 *TF:* 800-638-7990 ■ *Web:* www.grudiassociates.com	717-838-5022		463
Gruet Winery 8400 Pan American Fwy NE, Albuquerque NM 87113 *Web:* www.gruetwinery.com	505-821-0055		50-7
Gruhn Guitars 2120 Eight Ave S, Nashville TN 37204 *TF:* 800-734-9199 ■ *Web:* guitars.com	615-256-2033	255-2021	526
Gruma Corp 1159 Cottonwood L Ste 200, Irving TX 75038 *TF:* 800-147-8629 ■ *Web:* www.gruma.com	972-232-5000	232-5176	11-1
Grunau Company Inc 1100 W Anderson Ct, Oak Creek WI 53154 *TF:* 800-365-1920 ■ *Web:* www.grunau.com	414-216-6900	768-7950	189-10
Grundfos Pumps Corp 17100 W 118th Terr, Olathe KS 66061 *Web:* grundfos.com	913-227-3400	227-3500	641
Grundmann's Athletic Co 3018 Galleria Dr, Metairie LA 70001 *Web:* www.grundmanns.com	504-833-6602	833-6899	710
Grundy County 68 Cumberland St PO Box 177, Altamont TN 37301 *Web:* www.grundycountytn.net	931-692-3721	692-3718	338
Grundy County 706 G Ave, Grundy Center IA 50638 *Web:* www.grundycounty.org	319-824-5229		338
Grundy County PO Box 675, Morris IL 60450 *TF:* 800-669-5556 ■ *Web:* www.grundyco.org	815-941-3222	942-2222	338
Grundy County 700 Main St, Trenton MO 64683 *Web:* www.grundycountymo.com	660-359-4040	359-6786	338
Grundy County Chamber of Commerce & Industry 909 Liberty St, Morris IL 60450 *Web:* www.grundychamber.com	815-942-0113	942-0117	139
Grundy County Rural Electric Co-op 102 E 'G' Ave, Grundy Center IA 50638 *TF:* 800-390-7605 ■ *Web:* www.grundycountyrecia.com	319-824-5251	824-3118	245
Grundy Electric Co-op Inc 4100 Oklahoma Ave, Trenton MO 64683 *TF:* 800-279-2249 ■ *Web:* www.grundyec.com	660-359-3941	359-6030	245
Grunley Construction Company Inc 15020 Shady Grove Rd Ste 500, Rockville MD 20850 *Web:* www.grunley.com	240-399-2000	399-2001	186
Grupe Co 3255 W March Ln Ste 400, Stockton CA 95219 *TF:* 877-984-7873 ■ *Web:* www.grupe.com	209-473-6000	473-6001	187
Grupo Antolin Kentucky Inc 208 Commerce Ct, Hopkinsville KY 42240 *Web:* www.grupoantolin.com	270-885-2703		61
Grupo Gallegos 401 E Ocean Blvd Sixth Fl, Long Beach CA 90802 *Web:* www.grupogallegos.com	562-256-3600		7
Grupo Golan Company Inc 18619 Long Lake Dr, Boca Raton FL 33496	561-483-9972		693
Grupo -sms 2525 Main St Ste 200, Irvine CA 92614 *Web:* www.grupo-sms.com	949-223-9240		177
Grupo Uno Intl 2199 Ponce De Leon Blvd Fl 5, Coral Gables FL 33134 *Web:* www.grupouno.com	305-448-6111		7
GRUS Inc 109 N Brush St Unit 160 Unit 160, Tampa FL 33602-4157 **Fax Area Code:* 888 ■ *Web:* www.gruspersonnel.com	727-791-6205	230-9909*	260
Gruzen Samton LLC 320 W 13th St 9th Fl, New York NY 10014 *Web:* www.gruzensamton.com	212-477-0900		261
GRW Engineers Inc 801 Corporate Dr, Lexington KY 40503 *Web:* www.grwinc.com	859-223-3999		261
Gryphon International Engineering Services Inc 80 King St Ste 404, Saint Catharines ON L2R7G1 *TF:* 800-268-9242 ■ *Web:* www.gryphoneng.com	905-984-8383		256
Gryphon Investment Counsel Inc 20 Bay St Ste 1905, Toronto ON M5J2N8 *Web:* www.gryphon.ca	416-364-2299		528
Gryphon Mobile Electronics LLC 489 Yorbita Rd, La Puente CA 91744 *Web:* gryphonmobile.com	626-810-7770		57
Gryphtech Inc 2595 Skymark Ave Ste 206, Mississauga ON L4W4L5 *Web:* gryphtech.com	416-362-0543		180
GS Blodgett Corp 44 Lakeside Ave, Burlington VT 05401 *TF:* 800-331-5842 ■ *Web:* www.blodgett.com	802-658-6600	864-0183	298
G-S Company Inc, The 7920 Stansbury Rd, Baltimore MD 21222 *Web:* www.g-sco.com	410-284-9549		693
GS Engineering Consultants Inc 2080 N Talbot Rd RR 1, Windsor ON N9A6J3 *Web:* www.gsengineering.ca	519-737-9162		256
GS Engineering Inc 47500 US Hwy 41, Houghton MI 49931	906-482-1235		261
Gs Foods Inc 5925 S Alcoa Ave, Vernon CA 90058 *Web:* www.gsfoods.com	323-581-6161	589-2106	345

Company	Phone	Fax	Class
GS Precision Inc 101 John Seitz Dr Exit One Industrial Pk Brattleboro VT 05301 *Web:* www.gsprecision.com	802-257-5200	257-7937	112
G-S Supplies 1150 University Ave Ste 5 Rochester NY 14607 *TF:* 800-295-3050 ■ *Web:* www.gssupplies.com	585-295-0250	241-2375	544
GSA (US General Services Administration) 1275 First St NW Washington DC 20405 *TF:* 800-424-5210 ■ *Web:* www.gsa.gov/portal/category/100000	202-208-7642		340-20
GSA (General Services Administration) 1275 F St NE Washington DC 20417 *Web:* www.gsa.gov	202-501-0800		340-20
GSA (Geological Society of America, The) 3300 Penrose Pl PO Box 9140 Boulder CO 80301 *TF:* 800-472-1988 ■ *Web:* www.geosociety.org	303-357-1000	357-1070	49-19
GSA (Genetics Society of America) 9650 Rockville Pk Bethesda MD 20814 *TF:* 866-486-4363 ■ *Web:* www.genetics-gsa.org	301-634-7300	634-7079	49-19
GSAM (Goldman Sachs Asset Management) 200 W St New York NY 10282 *TF:* 800-526-7384 ■ *Web:* www.goldmansachs.com	212-902-1000		401
Gsat Inc 100 W Oak St Ste 200 Denton TX 76201 *TF:* 866-977-4728 ■ *Web:* www.gsati.com	469-287-6771		180
GSB (Guilford Savings Bank) PO Box 369 Guilford CT 06437 *TF:* 866-878-1480 ■ *Web:* www.gsb-yourbank.com	203-453-2015		70
GSC W189 N11161 Kleinmann Dr Germantown WI 53022 *Web:* www.gxsc.com	262-790-1080		180
GSC Enterprises Inc 130 Hillcrest Dr PO Box 638 Sulphur Springs TX 75483 *Web:* www.grocerysupply.com	903-885-7621		360-3
GSC Logistics Inc 530 Water St 5th Fl Oakland CA 94607 *Web:* www.gschq.com	510-844-3700		803-1
GSC Packaging Inc 575 Wharton Dr Atlanta GA 30336 *TF:* 800-467-9967 ■ *Web:* www.gscpackaging.com	404-505-9925		88
GSCB (Garden State Community Bank) 36 Ferry St Newark NJ 07105 *NYSE: NYB* ■ *TF:* 877-786-6500	973-589-8616	589-1202	70
GSD & M Idea City 828 W Sixth St Austin TX 78703 *Web:* www.gsdm.com	512-242-4736		4
GSE Construction Company Inc 6950 Preston Ave Livermore CA 94551 *TF:* 800-456-2009 ■ *Web:* www.gseconstruction.com	925-447-0292	447-0962	188-10
GSE Dynamics Inc 25 Corporate Dr Hauppauge NY 11788 *Web:* www.gsedynamics.com	631-231-1044		22
GSE Lining Technology Inc 19103 Gundle Rd Houston TX 77073 *TF:* 800-435-2008 ■ *Web:* www.gseworld.com	281-443-8564	875-6010	600
GSE Systems Inc 1332 Londontown Blvd Ste 200 Sykesville MD 21784 *NYSE: GVP* ■ *TF Cust Svc:* 800-638-7912 ■ *Web:* www.gses.com	410-970-7800	970-7997	178-1
GS&F 209 Tenth Ave S Ste 222 Nashville TN 37203 *Web:* www.gsandf.com	615-385-1100		4
Gsg Associates Inc 1010 E Union St Ste 203 Pasadena CA 91106 *TF:* 866-808-4742 ■ *Web:* www.gsga.net	866-808-4742		463
GSH (Good Samaritan Hospital) 407 14th Ave SE Puyallup WA 98372 *TF:* 800-776-4048 ■ *Web:* www.multicare.org/goodsam	253-697-4000		374-3
GSI Group Inc 1004 E Illinois St Assumption IL 62510 *Web:* www.grainsystems.com	217-226-4421		273
GSI Interactive Inc 1075 First Ave King Of Prussia PA 19406	610-491-7100	265-3528	195
GSI Technology Inc 2360 Owen St Santa Clara CA 95054 *NASDAQ: GSIT* ■ *Web:* www.gsitechnology.com	408-980-8388	980-8377	696
GSL Electric 8540 S Sandy Pkwy Sandy UT 84070 *Web:* www.gslelectric.com	801-565-0088	565-0099	189-4
GSL Fine Lithographers 8386 Rovana Cir Sacramento CA 95828 *TF:* 800-877-3678 ■ *Web:* www.gslitho.com	916-231-1410		627
GSL Solutions Inc 1411 N Westshore Blvd Ste 204 Tampa FL 33607 *Web:* www.gslsolutions.com	813-637-8535		177
Gsolutionz Inc 625 E Santa Clara St Ste 100 Ventura CA 93001 *Web:* www.gsolutionz.com	805-662-1500		246
GSP (Greenville-Spartanburg Airport) 2000 GSP Dr Ste 1 Greer SC 29651 *TF:* 800-331-1212 ■ *Web:* www.gspairport.com	864-877-7426	848-6225	27
Gsp International Inc 90 Woodbridge Ctr Dr Ste 110 Woodbridge NJ 07095 *Web:* gspintl.com	732-602-0100		260
GSP Marketing Technologies Inc 14055 46th St N Ste 1112 Clearwater FL 33760 *Web:* www.gspretail.com	727-532-0647		344
GSPANN Technologies Inc 362 Fairview Way Milpitas CA 95035 *Web:* www.gspann.com	408-263-3435		196
GSS Infotech Inc 1699 Wall St Ste 201 Mt. Prospect IL 60056 *Web:* www.gssinfotech.com	847-640-3700		196
GST AutoLeather Inc 20 Oak Hollow Dr Ste 300 Southfield MI 48033 *Web:* www.gstautoleather.com	248-436-2300	436-2390	432
GST Inc 13043 166th St Cerritos CA 90703 *TF:* 800-833-0128 ■ *Web:* www.gstes.com	562-345-8700	345-8701	177
GSTC (Gordon Sevig Trucking Co) 400 Hwy 151 E Walford IA 52351 *Web:* www.gstcinc.com	319-846-5500	846-5541	685
Gstek 911 Cedar Rd Chesapeake VA 23322 *Web:* www.gstekinc.com	757-548-1597		261
GSU (Grambling State University Lewis Memorial Library) 403 Main St PO Box 4256 Grambling LA 71245 *Web:* www.gram.edu/research/library	318-274-3354	274-3268	434-6
GSVlabs Inc 425 Broadway St Redwood City CA 94063 *Web:* gsvlabs.com	650-421-2000		463
GSW Worldwide 500 Old Worthington Rd Westerville OH 43082 *Web:* www.gsw-w.com	614-848-4848		4
GSWB (Geisinger South Wilkes-Barre) 25 Church St Wilkes-Barre PA 18765 *TF:* 800-230-4565 ■ *Web:* www.geisinger.org	570-808-3100		374-3
GT Advanced Technologies Inc 243 DANIEL WEBSTER Hwy Merrimack NH 03054 *TF:* 800-763-0885 ■ *Web:* www.gtat.com	603-883-5200		696
GT Consultants Inc 3050 Eagle Watch Dr Woodstock GA 30189	770-591-1343		184
GT Distributors Inc 100 McFarland Ave Rossville GA 30741 *Web:* www.gtdist.com	706-866-2764		237
GT Grandstands Inc 2810 Sydney Rd Plant City FL 33566 *TF:* 800-458-5872 ■ *Web:* www.gtgrandstands.com	813-305-1415		320
GT Technologies Inc 5859 Executive Dr Westland MI 48185 *Web:* www.gttechnologies.com	734-467-8371		256
GT Urological LLC 960 E Hennepin Ave Minneapolis MN 55414	612-379-3578		476
GT Water Products Inc 5239 N Commerce Ave Moorpark CA 93021 *TF:* 800-862-5647 ■ *Web:* www.gtwaterproducts.com	805-529-2900	529-4558	607
GTC Biotherapeutics Inc 175 Crossing Blvd Framingham MA 01702 *Web:* revobiologics.com	508-620-9700	370-3797	85
GTC Systems Inc 504 W Mission Ave Ste 203 Escondido CA 92025	858-560-5800		174
GTC Technology Inc 1001 S Dairy Ashford Ste 500 Houston TX 77077 *Web:* gtctech.com	281-597-4800		146
Gtcbio 635 W Foothill Blvd Monrovia CA 91016 *TF:* 800-422-8386 ■ *Web:* gtcbio.com	626-256-6405		184
GTC-GTC LLC 14574 Weld County Rd 64 Greeley CO 80631	970-351-6000		11-1
GTCO CalComp Inc 7125 Riverwood Dr Columbia MD 21046 *TF:* 800-344-4723 ■ *Web:* gtcocalcomp.com	410-381-6688		173-1
GTCR Golder Rauner LLC 300 N Lasalle Ste 5000 Chicago IL 60654 *Web:* www.gtcr.com	312-382-2200		792
GTE Federal Credit Union PO Box 172599 Tampa FL 33672 *TF:* 888-871-2690 ■ *Web:* www.gtefinancial.org	813-871-2690		219
Gtek Computers LLC 4111 FM 2986 Portland TX 78374 *Web:* gtek.biz	361-777-1400		175
GTFSD (Parker Gas Turbine Fuel Systems Div) 8940 Tyler Blvd Mentor OH 44060 *Web:* parker.com	440-266-2300	266-2311	21
GTI (Gas Technology Institute) 1700 S Mt Prospect Rd Des Plaines IL 60018 *Web:* www.gastechnology.org	847-768-0500	768-0501	668
GTI Corporate Travel 111 Township Line Rd Jenkintown PA 19046 *TF:* 800-223-3863 ■ *Web:* gtitravel.com	215-379-6800		772
GTM (Grand Traverse Machine) 1247 Boon St Traverse City MI 49686 *Web:* www.gtmachine.com	231-946-8006		621
Gtm Wholesale Liquidators Inc 1462 Corporate Center Dr Ste 130 A San Diego CA 92154 *Web:* www.gtmstores.com	619-596-7486		175
GTMIT Means A Lot 239 Walker St SW Atlanta GA 30313 *Web:* www.gtmcentral.com	404-522-0486		463
GTO 2000 Inc PO Box 2819 Gainesville GA 30503 *Web:* www.gto2000.com	770-287-9233		311
GTP Inc 1801 Rutherford Rd Greenville SC 29609 *Web:* www.globaltextilepartner.com	864-288-5475		744
Gtr Manufacturing Inc 1 Jonathan Dr Brockton MA 02301 *Web:* www.gtrmfg.com	508-588-3240		697
GTRI (Georgia Tech Research Institute) *Georgia Institute of Technology* 250 14th St NW Atlanta GA 30318 *Web:* www.gtri.gatech.edu	404-407-7400	894-9875	668
Gts Communications & Cabling Co 11953 Prospect Rd Strongsville OH 44149 *TF:* 877-487-8866 ■ *Web:* www.gtscommunications.com	440-878-8866		179
GTS Consultants 2 Monmouth Ave Freehold NJ 07728 *TF:* 800-742-0407 ■ *Web:* gtsconsultants.com	732-409-0900		317
Gts Technologies Inc 441 Friendship Rd Harrisburg PA 17111 *Web:* gtstech.com	717-236-3006		261
GTSI Corp 2553 Dulles View Dr Ste 100 Herndon VA 20171 *NASDAQ: GTSI* ■ *TF:* 800-999-4874 ■ *Web:* unicomgov.com	703-502-2000		174
GTT Communications Inc 7900 Tysons One Pl Ste 1450 McLean VA 22102 *NYSE: GTT* ■ *Web:* www.gtt.net	703-442-5500		736
GTT Global 600 Data Dr Ste 101 Plano TX 75075 *TF:* 800-485-6828 ■ *Web:* www.gttglobal.com	800-983-5388		16
GTX Corp 117 W Ninth St Ste 1214 Los Angeles CA 90015 *TF:* 877-489-3019 ■ *Web:* www.gtxcorp.com	213-489-3019		736
GTx Inc 175 Toyota Plaza 7th Fl Memphis TN 38103 *NASDAQ: GTXI* ■ *Web:* www.gtxinc.com	901-523-9700	844-8075	85
GU (Generations United) 1333 H St NW Ste 500-W Washington DC 20005 *TF:* 800-677-1116 ■ *Web:* www.gu.org	202-289-3979	289-3952	48-6
Guadalajara 314 W Sioux Ave Pierre SD 57501 *Web:* www.eatguads.com	605-224-2771		671
Guadalajara 1745 Dell Range Blvd Cheyenne WY 82009	307-432-6803		671
Guadalajara Family Mexican 17 N 29th St Billings MT 59101	406-259-8930		671
Guadalupe County 211 W Ct St Seguin TX 78155 *TF:* 800-388-8075 ■ *Web:* www.co.guadalupe.tx.us	830-303-4188	401-0300	338
Guadalupe County Correctional Facility S Hwy 54 PO Box 520 Santa Rosa NM 88435 *TF:* 800-315-7043 ■ *Web:* geogroup.com	575-472-1001		213
Guadalupe Credit Union 3601 Mimbres Ln Santa Fe NM 87507 *TF:* 800-540-5382 ■ *Web:* www.guadalupecu.org	505-982-8942		219
Guadalupe Cultural Arts Ctr 1300 Guadalupe St San Antonio TX 78207 *Web:* www.guadalupeculturalarts.org	210-271-3151		50-2

				Phone	Fax	Class
Guadalupe Mountains National Park						
400 Pine Canyon Rd	Salt Flat	TX	79847	915-828-3251	828-3269	564
Web: www.nps.gov						
Guadalupe River Park & Gardens						
438 Coleman Ave	San Jose	CA	95110	408-298-7657	288-9048	97
Web: www.grpg.org						
Guadalupe River State Park						
3350 Pk Rd 31	Spring Branch	TX	78070	830-438-2656		565
Web: tpwd.texas.gov/state-parks/guadalupe-river						
Guadalupe Valley Electric Co-op Inc						
825 E Sarah Dewitt Dr	Gonzales	TX	78629	830-857-1200		245
TF: 800-223-4832 ■ *Web:* www.gvec.org						
Guadalupe Valley Telephone Co-op (GVTC)						
36101 FM 3159	New Braunfels	TX	78132	830-885-4411	885-2400	736
TF: 800-367-4882 ■ *Web:* www.gvtc.com						
Guadalupe-Blanco River Authority (GBRA)						
933 E Ct St	Seguin	TX	78155	830-379-5822	379-9718	245
Web: www.gbra.org						
Guajillo 1727 Wilson Blvd	Arlington	VA	22201	703-807-0840		671
Web: guajillomexican.com						
Guarantee Electrical Co						
3405 Bent Ave	Saint Louis	MO	63116	314-772-5400		189-4
Web: www.geco.com						
Guarantee Real Estate Corp						
5380 N Fresno Ave Ste 103	Fresno	CA	93710	559-650-6088		652
Web: www.guarantee.com						
Guarantee Specialties Inc						
9401 Carr Ave	Cleveland	OH	44108	216-451-9744		488
Guarantee Trust Life Insurance Co						
1275 Milwaukee Ave	Glenview	IL	60025	847-699-0600	699-2355	391-2
TF: 800-338-7452 ■ *Web:* www.gtlic.com						
Guaranteed Industries Ltd						
5420 Rue Pare	Montreal	QC	H4P1R3	514-342-3400		610
Web: www.guaranteedindustries.com						
Guaranteed Rate Inc 3940 N Ravenswood	Chicago	IL	60613	773-290-0505		217
TF: 866-934-7283 ■ *Web:* www.guaranteedrate.com						
Guaranteed Supply Company of South Carolina Inc						
1211 Rotherwood Rd	Greensboro	NC	27406	336-273-6140		191-1
Web: www.guaranteedsupply.com						
Guaranty Bancshares Inc						
100 W Arkansas St PO Box 1158	Mount Pleasant	TX	75455	903-572-9881	572-9658	360-2
TF: 888-572-9881 ■ *Web:* www.gnty.com						
Guaranty Bank 4000 W Brown Deer Rd	Brown Deer	WI	53209	800-235-4636	332-0491*	70
**Fax Area Code:* 855 ■ *TF:* 800-235-4636 ■ *Web:* www.guarantybank.com						
Guaranty Bank & Trust Co						
PO Box 1807	Cedar Rapids	IA	52406	319-286-6200	362-7894	70
TF: 800-362-2119 ■ *Web:* www.guaranty-bank.com						
Guaranty State Bank & Trust Co Beloit Kansas, The						
201 S Mill St	Beloit	KS	67420	785-738-3501		70
TF: 888-738-8000 ■ *Web:* guarantystate.com						
Guard Publishing Co PO Box 10188	Eugene	OR	97440	541-485-1234		637-8
TF: 800-377-7428 ■ *Web:* www.registerguard.com						
Guard Systems Inc						
1190 Monterey Pass Rd	Monterey Park	CA	91754	323-881-6711	261-7841	693
TF: 800-606-6711 ■ *Web:* www.guardsystemsinc.com						
Guardair Corp 47 Veterans Dr	Chicopee	MA	01022	413-594-4400	594-4884	172
TF: 800-482-7324 ■ *Web:* www.guardair.com						
Guardian Alarm 20800 Southfield Rd	Southfield	MI	48075	248-423-1000	423-3009	692
TF: 800-782-9688 ■ *Web:* www.guardianalarm.com						
Guardian Building Products (GBPD)						
979 Batesville Rd	Greer	SC	29651	864-297-6101	281-3558	191-3
TF: 800-569-4262 ■ *Web:* guardianbp.com						
Guardian Credit Union						
4501 W Greenfield Ave	West Milwaukee	WI	53214	414-546-7450		219
Web: guardiancu.org						
Guardian Electric Mfg Company Inc						
1425 Lake Ave	Woodstock	IL	60098	815-334-3600	337-0377	203
TF: 800-762-0369 ■ *Web:* www.guardian-electric.com						
Guardian Energy LLC 4745 380th Ave	Janesville	MN	56048	507-234-5000		580
Web: www.guardiannrg.com						
Guardian Industries Corp						
2300 Harmon Rd	Auburn Hills	MI	48326	248-340-1800	340-9988	329
TF: 800-822-5599 ■ *Web:* www.guardian.com						
Guardian Interlock Systems of Northeast Georgia Inc						
228 Church St	Marietta	GA	30060	770-499-0499		407
Web: www.guardianinterlock.com						
Guardian Jet LLC 102 BRd St	Guilford	CT	06437	203-453-0800		57
Web: www.guardianjet.com						
Guardian Life Insurance Company of America						
7 Hanover Sq	New York	NY	10004	888-482-7342		391-2
TF: 888-600-4667 ■ *Web:* www.guardianlife.com						
Guardian Lima LLC 2485 Houx Pkwy	Lima	OH	45804	567-940-9500		580
Web: www.guardianlima.com						
Guardian Mobility Corp 43 Auriga Dr	Ottawa	ON	K2E7Y8	613-225-8885		647
TF: 888-817-8159 ■ *Web:* www.guardianmobility.com						
Guardian Packaging Inc						
3615 Security St	Garland	TX	75042	214-349-1500		601
TF: 800-259-1502 ■ *Web:* www.guardianpackaging.com						
Guardian Protection Services Inc						
174 Thorn Hill Rd	Warrendale	PA	15086	855-779-2001		693
TF Cust Svc: 877-314-7092 ■ *Web:* www.guardianprotection.com						
Guardian Technologies LLC						
7700 Saint Clair Ave	Mentor	OH	44060	866-603-5900		35
TF: 866-603-5900 ■ *Web:* www.guardiantechnologies.com						
Guardian, The 165 Prince St	Charlottetown	PE	C1A4R7	902-629-6000	566-3808	532-1
Web: www.theguardian.pe.ca						
Guard-Line Inc						
215 S Louise St PO Box 1030	Atlanta	TX	75551	903-796-4111	796-7262*	155-8
**Fax:* Orders ■ *TF:* 800-527-8822 ■ *Web:* www.guardline.com						
guardNOW Inc						
16209 Victory Blvd Ste 302	Van Nuys	CA	91406	877-482-7366		693
TF: 877-482-7366 ■ *Web:* www.guardnow.com						
Guatemala 57 Pk Ave	New York	NY	10016	212-679-4760	685-8741	784
Web: www.un.int						
Consulate General						
3013 Fountain View Dr Ste 210	Houston	TX	77057	713-953-9531		257
Embassy 2220 R St NW	Washington	DC	20008	202-745-4953		257
Web: www.consulateofguatemalaindenver.org						
Guelph Chamber of Commerce						
111 Farquhar St	Guelph	ON	N1H3N4	519-822-8081	822-8451	137
Web: www.guelphchamber.com						
Guelph General Hospital 115 Delhi St	Guelph	ON	N1E4J4	519-822-5350	837-6773	374-2
Web: www.gghorg.ca						
Guenther House 205 E Guenther St	San Antonio	TX	78204	210-227-1061		50-3
TF: 800-235-8186 ■ *Web:* www.guentherhouse.com						
Guerbet LLC						
120 W Seventh St Ste 108	Bloomington	IN	47404	812-333-0059		231
TF: 877-729-6679 ■ *Web:* www.guerbet-us.com						
Guerin & Vreeland Engineering Inc						
272 Rt 206	Flanders	NJ	07836	973-252-9340		261
Guernsey County						
627 Wheeling Ave Ste 300	Cambridge	OH	43725	740-432-9200	432-9359	338
Web: www.guernseycounty.org						
Guernsey County District Public Library						
800 Steubenville Ave	Cambridge	OH	43725	740-432-5946	432-7142	434-3
Web: www.gcdpl.lib.oh.us						
Guernsey Industries						
60772 Southgate Rd	Byesville	OH	43723	740-439-5017		88
Web: guernseycountydd.org						
Guernsey Office Products						
45070 Old Ox Rd	Dulles	VA	20166	703-968-8200		535
Web: www.buyguernsey.com/thm103home.aspx						
Guernsey State Park 2301 Central Ave	Cheyenne	WY	82002	307-836-2334		565
Web: wyoparks.state.wy.us/site/siteinfo.aspx?siteid=7						
Guernsey-Muskingum Electric Co-op						
17 S Liberty St	New Concord	OH	43762	740-826-7661	826-7171	245
TF: 800-521-9879 ■ *Web:* www.gmenergy.com						
Guess CPA PC						
4000 Eagle Point Corporate Dr	Birmingham	AL	35242	205-259-1905		2
Guest Communications Corp						
15009 W 101st Terr	Shawnee Mission	KS	66215	913-888-1217		5
TF: 800-637-8525 ■ *Web:* www.gcckc.com						
Guest Informant Magazine 725 Broad St	Augusta	GA	30901	706-724-0851		457-22
TF: 800-622-6358 ■ *Web:* morris.com						
Guest Inn 2533 N Piccoli Rd	Stockton	CA	95215	209-931-6675		379
Guest Services Inc						
3055 Prosperity Ave	Fairfax	VA	22031	703-849-9300		299
TF: 800-345-7534 ■ *Web:* www.guestservices.com						
Guest Supply Inc						
4301 US Hwy 1 PO Box 902	Monmouth Junction	NJ	08852	609-514-9696	514-2692	214
TF Cust Svc: 800-446-7819 ■ *Web:* www.guestsupply.com						
Guestlogix Inc 111 Peter St Ste 302	Toronto	ON	M5V2H1	416-642-0349		253
TF: 800-375-8181 ■ *Web:* www.guestlogix.com						
Guest-tek Ltd 777 8 Ave SW Ste 600	Calgary	AB	T2P3R5	403-509-1010		177
TF: 866-509-1010 ■ *Web:* www.guesttek.com						
Guggenheim Hermitage Museum						
3355 Las Vegas Blvd S						
Venetian Resort Hotel & Casino	Las Vegas	NV	89109	212-423-3575		520
TF: 800-329-6109 ■ *Web:* guggenheim.org						
Guggisberg Cheese Inc						
5060 SR- 557	Millersburg	OH	44654	330-893-2500		292
Web: www.babyswiss.com						
Guhring Inc 1445 Commerce Ave	Brookfield	WI	53045	262-784-6730	784-9096	493
TF: 800-776-6170 ■ *Web:* www.guhring.com						
Guida, Slavich & Flores PC						
750 N Saint Paul St Ste 200	Dallas	TX	75201	214-692-0009	692-6610	428
Web: www.guidaslavichflores.com						
Guidance Charter School, The						
1125 E Palmdale Blvd # B	Palmdale	CA	93550	661-272-1701		685
Web: www.thegcs.org						
Guidance Software Inc						
1055 E Colorado Blvd	Pasadena	CA	91106	626-229-9191	229-9199	178-10
TF: 866-229-9199 ■ *Web:* guidancesoftware.com						
Guidance Solutions Inc						
4134 Del Rey Ave	Marina del Rey	CA	90292	310-754-4000	754-4010	736
Web: www.guidance.com						
Guidant Group Inc						
3414 Peachtree Rd NE Ste 375	Atlanta	GA	30326	404-920-6100		463
Web: www.guidantgroup.com						
Guidant Partners						
1410 Donelson Pike Ste B5	Nashville	TN	37217	615-327-9111		196
TF: 800-526-9002 ■ *Web:* www.guidantpartners.com						
Guida-Seibert Dairy Co 433 Pk St	New Britain	CT	06051	800-832-8929		296-27
TF: 800-832-8929 ■ *Web:* www.supercow.com						
Guide Dog Foundation for the Blind Inc						
371 E Jericho Tkpe	Smithtown	NY	11787	800-548-4337		48-17
TF: 800-548-4337 ■ *Web:* www.guidedog.org						
Guide Dogs for the Blind						
350 Los Ranchitos Rd	San Rafael	CA	94903	415-499-4000	499-4035	48-17
TF: 800-295-4050 ■ *Web:* www.guidedogs.com						
Guide Dogs of America						
13445 Glenoaks Blvd	Sylmar	CA	91342	818-362-5834	362-6870	48-17
TF: 800-459-4843 ■ *Web:* www.guidedogsofamerica.org						
Guide Productions LLC						
30589 Monarch Ct	Evergreen	CO	80439	604-669-0500	688-6566	196
Web: www.guideproductions.com						
Guide, The 24904 Sussex Hwy	Seaford	DE	19973	302-629-5060		627
TF: 800-984-8433 ■ *Web:* www.theguide.com						
Guidecraft USA 55508 Hwy 19 W	Winthrop	MN	55396	507-647-5030	647-3254	762
TF: 800-524-3555 ■ *Web:* www.guidecraft.com						
Guided Delivery Systems						
2355 Calle de Luna	Santa Clara	CA	95054	408-727-1105	727-6615	723
Guided Discoveries Inc						
27282 Calle Arroyo	San Juan Capistrano	CA	91711	909-625-6194		239
Web: guideddiscoveries.org						
Guided Therapeutics Inc						
5835 Peachtree Corners E Ste D	Norcross	GA	30092	770-242-8723	242-8639	477
OTC: GTHP ■ *Web:* www.guidedinc.com						
Guided Wave Inc						
3033 Gold Canal Dr	Rancho Cordova	CA	95670	916-638-4944		201
Web: www.guidedwave.com						
Guidemark Health Inc 6 Campus Dr	Parsippany	NJ	07054	201-740-6160		5
Web: www.guidemarkhealth.com						
GuideOne Mutual Insurance Co						
1111 Ashworth Rd	West Des Moines	IA	50265	515-267-5000		391-4
TF: 877-448-4331 ■ *Web:* www.guideone.com						

Company / Address	City	State	ZIP	Phone	Fax	Class
Guidepoint Global LLC 730 Third Ave 11th Fl *Web:* www.guidepoint.com	New York	NY	10017	212-375-2980		466
Guidesoft Inc 5875 Castle Creek Pkwy Ste 400 *TF:* 877-256-6948 ■ *Web:* www.knowledgeservices.com	Indianapolis	IN	46250	317-578-1700		41
Guido Perla & Associates Inc 701 Fifth Ave Ste 1200 *TF:* 800-252-5232 ■ *Web:* www.gpai.com	Seattle	WA	98104	206-768-1515		261
Guiffre Distributing Co 6839 Industrial Rd *Web:* guiffredistributing.com	Springfield	VA	22151	703-642-1700		81-1
Guild Assoc Inc, The 389 Main St Ste 202 *Web:* www.guildassoc.com	Malden	MA	02148	781-397-8870		47
Guild Investment Management Inc 12400 Wilshire Blvd Ste 1080 *TF:* 800-645-4100 ■ *Web:* www.guildinvestment.com	Los Angeles	CA	90025	310-826-8600		528
Guild Mortgage Co 5898 Copley Dr 4th & 5th Fl *TF:* 800-365-4441 ■ *Web:* www.guildmortgage.com	San Diego	CA	92111	800-365-4441		509
Guild of American Luthiers 8222 S Pk Ave *TF:* 800-836-0901 ■ *Web:* www.luth.org	Tacoma	WA	98408	253-472-7853		48-4
Guild Shop of The Church of st John The Divine, The 2009 Dunlavy St *Web:* theguildshop.org	Houston	TX	77006	713-528-5095		48-20
Guildcraft Inc 100 Fire Tower Dr *TF:* 800-345-5563 ■ *Web:* www.guildcraftinc.com	Tonawanda	NY	14150	800-345-5563		711
Guilderland Chamber of Commerce 2050 Western Ave Ste 109 *TF:* 800-803-8508 ■ *Web:* www.guilderlandchamber.com	Guilderland	NY	12084	518-456-6611	456-6690	139
Guilford College 5800 W Friendly Ave *Fax: Admissions ■ *TF Admissions:* 800-992-7759 ■ *Web:* www.guilford.edu	Greensboro	NC	27410	336-316-2000	316-2954*	166
Guilford County PO Box 3427 *Web:* www.co.guilford.nc.us	Greensboro	NC	27402	336-641-3383		338
Guilford County Schools 617 W Market St *TF:* 866-286-7337 ■ *Web:* www.gcsnc.com	Greensboro	NC	27401	336-370-8100	370-8398	685
Guilford Courthouse National Military Park 2332 New Garden Rd *Web:* www.nps.gov/guco	Greensboro	NC	27410	336-288-1776	282-2296	564
Guilford Lake State Park 6835 E Lake Rd *Web:* www.ohiodnr.com	Lisbon	OH	44432	330-222-1712		565
Guilford Savings Bank (GSB) PO Box 369 *TF:* 866-878-1480 ■ *Web:* www.gsb-yourbank.com	Guilford	CT	06437	203-453-2015		70
Guilford Technical Community College 601 Highpoint Rd PO Box 309 *Web:* www.gtcc.edu	Jamestown	NC	27282	336-334-4822		162
Guill Tool & Engineering Company Inc 10 Pike St *Web:* guill.com	West Warwick	RI	02893	401-828-7600	823-5310	757
Guinea 140 E 39th St *Web:* www.un.int	New York	NY	10016	212-687-8115	687-8248	704
Guinea Embassy 2112 Leroy Pl NW *Web:* www.guineaembassyusa.com	Washington	DC	20008	202-986-4300		257
Guinness World Records Museum 4943 Clifton Hill *TF:* 866-656-0310 ■ *Web:* falls.com	Niagara Falls	ON	L2G3N5	905-357-4330		520
Guitar Center Inc 5795 Lindero Canyon Rd *Web:* www.guitarcenter.com	Westlake Village	CA	91362	818-735-8800		526
Guitar Player Magazine 28 E 28th St 12th Fl *TF Cust Svc:* 800-289-9839 ■ *Web:* www.guitarplayer.com	New York	NY	10016	212-378-0400		457-9
Guittard Chocolate Co 10 GuittaRd Rd *TF:* 800-468-2462 ■ *Web:* www.guittard.com	Burlingame	CA	94010	650-697-4427	692-2761	296-8
Gulf & Ohio Railways Inc 422 W Cumberland Ave PO Box 2408 *Web:* www.gulfandohio.com	Knoxville	TN	37901	865-525-9400		360-3
Gulf & Pacific Equities Corp 1300 Bay St Ste 300 *Web:* www.gpequities.com	Toronto	ON	M5R3K8	416-968-3337		186
Gulf Asphalt Corp 4116 US Hwy 231 *Web:* www.gaccontractors.com	Panama City	FL	32404	850-785-4675	769-3456	188-4
Gulf Bay Hotels Inc 8156 Fiddler's Creek Pkwy *Web:* www.gulfbay.com	Naples	FL	34114	239-732-9402		378
Gulf Beaches Historical Museum 115 Tenth Ave *TF:* 800-344-5999 ■ *Web:* gulfbeachesmuseum.com	Saint Pete Beach	FL	33706	727-552-1610		520
Gulf Branch Nature Ctr & Park Grounds 3608 N Military Rd *Web:* arlingtonva.us	Arlington	VA	22207	703-228-3403		50-5
Gulf Breeze News Inc 913 Gulf Breeze Pkwy Ste 35 *Web:* www.gulfbreezenews.com	Gulf Breeze	FL	32561	850-932-8986		610
Gulf Business Forms Inc 2460 IH-35 S *TF:* 800-433-4853 ■ *Web:* www.gulfforms.com	San Marcos	TX	78666	512-353-8313	353-8866	110
Gulf Coast Autoplex Inc 414 W Fred&Ruth Zingler Dr *TF:* 888-526-2391 ■ *Web:* gulfcoastautoplex.net	Jennings	LA	70546	888-526-2391		57
Gulf Coast Bank 4310 Johnston St *TF:* 800-722-5363 ■ *Web:* www.gcbank.com	Lafayette	LA	70503	337-989-1133		70
Gulf Coast Bank & Trust Co 200 St Charles Ave *TF:* 800-223-2060 ■ *Web:* www.gulfbank.com	New Orleans	LA	70130	504-561-6100		685
Gulf Coast Collection Bureau Inc 5630 Marquesas Cir *TF:* 866-991-7358 ■ *Web:* www.gulfcoastcollection.com	Sarasota	FL	34233	941-927-6999		160
Gulf Coast Community College 5230 W Hwy 98 *Fax: Admissions ■ *TF:* 800-311-3685 ■ *Web:* www.gulfcoast.edu	Panama City	FL	32401	850-769-1551	913-3308*	162
Gulf Coast Electric Co-op Inc 722 W Hwy 22 PO Box 220 *TF:* 800-333-9392 ■ *Web:* www.gcec.com	Wewahitchka	FL	32465	850-639-2216	639-5061	245
Gulf Coast Exploreum Science Ctr 65 Government St *Web:* www.exploreum.com	Mobile	AL	36602	251-208-6893	208-6889	521
Gulf Coast Machine & Supply Company Inc 6817 Industrial Rd *TF:* 800-231-3032 ■ *Web:* www.gulfco.com	Beaumont	TX	77705	409-842-1311	842-4621	723
Gulf Coast Manufacturing LLC 3622 W Main St *Web:* gulfcoastmfg.com	Gray	LA	70359	985-872-0187		537
Gulf Coast Medical Ctr 449 W 23rd St *TF:* 800-296-2611 ■ *Web:* www.gcmc-pc.com	Panama City	FL	32405	850-769-8341		374-3
Gulf Coast Medical Ctr (GCMC) 10141 US 59 Rd *TF:* 800-345-8082 ■ *Web:* www.gulfcoastmedical.com	Wharton	TX	77488	979-532-2500	282-6190	374-3
Gulf Coast Mental Health Center 1600 Broad Ave *TF:* 800-681-0798 ■ *Web:* www.gcmhc.com	Gulfport	MS	39501	228-863-1132		726
Gulf Coast Paper Company Inc 3705 Houston Hwy *Web:* www.gulfcoastpaper.com	Victoria	TX	77901	361-576-1237		612
Gulf Coast Pre-stress Inc 494 Market St	Pass Christian	MS	39571	228-452-9486		183
Gulf Coast Regional Blood Ctr 1400 La Concha Ln *TF:* 888-482-5663 ■ *Web:* www.giveblood.org	Houston	TX	77054	713-790-1200		89
Gulf Coast Research Laboratory 703 E Beach Dr	Ocean Springs	MS	39564	228-872-4200		40
Gulf Coast Signs of Sarasota Inc 1713 Northgate Blvd *Web:* www.gulfcoastsigns.com	Sarasota	FL	34234	941-355-8841		701
Gulf Coast Tmc 7670 Hwy 10 *TF:* 888-683-6638 ■ *Web:* www.gulfcoasttmc.com	Ethel	LA	70730	225-683-6636		636
Gulf Coast Treatment Ctr 1015 Mar-Walt Dr *TF:* 800-537-5433 ■ *Web:* www.gulfcoastyouthservices.com	Fort Walton Beach	FL	32547	850-863-4160	863-8576	374-1
Gulf Coast Veterinary Avian 1111 W Loop S *TF:* 800-345-4767 ■ *Web:* www.gcvs.com	Houston	TX	77027	713-693-1133		794
Gulf Coast Village 1333 Santa Barbara Blvd *TF:* 800-573-8490 ■ *Web:* www.gulfcoastvillage.com	Cape Coral	FL	33991	239-772-1333		672
Gulf Compress 201 N 19th St *Web:* www.gulfcompress.com	Corpus Christi	TX	78408	361-882-5489		803-1
Gulf Copper & Mfg Corp 7200 Hwy 87 *Web:* www.gulfcopper.com	Port Arthur	TX	77642	409-989-0300		698
Gulf Correctional Institution 500 Ike Steele Rd *Web:* dc.state.fl.us	Wewahitchka	FL	32465	850-639-1100	639-1182	213
Gulf County 1000 Cecil Costin Sr Blvd Rm 148 *Web:* www.gulfcounty-fl.gov	Port Saint Joe	FL	32456	850-229-6112	229-6174	338
Gulf County School District 150 Middle School Rd *Web:* www.thereddoor.com	Port Saint Joe	FL	32456	850-229-8256	229-6089	685
Gulf Craft LLC 320 Boro Ln *Web:* www.gulfcraft.com	Franklin	LA	70538	337-828-2580	828-2586	698
Gulf Crane Services Inc 73413 Bollfield Dr *Web:* www.gulfcraneservices.com	Covington	LA	70435	985-892-0056		190
Gulf Electric Company Inc of Mobile PO Box 2385 *Web:* www.gulfelec.com	Mobile	AL	36652	251-666-0654	666-6323	189-4
Gulf Engineering LLC 611 Hill St *TF:* 800-347-4749 ■ *Web:* www.gulfengineering.com	Jefferson	LA	70121	504-733-4868		188
Gulf Hills Hotel 13701 Paso Rd *TF:* 866-875-4211 ■ *Web:* www.gulfhillshotel.com	Ocean Springs	MS	39564	228-875-4211	875-4213	669
Gulf Interstate Engineering Co 16010 Barkers Pt Ln Ste 600 *TF:* 800-521-8879 ■ *Web:* www.gie.com	Houston	TX	77079	713-850-3400	850-3579	261
Gulf Island Fabrication Inc 567 Thompson Rd PO Box 310 *NASDAQ: GIFI* ■ *Web:* www.gulfisland.com	Houma	LA	70361	985-872-2100		537
Gulf Islands National Seashore (Florida) 1801 Gulf Breeze Pkwy *Web:* www.nps.gov	Gulf Breeze	FL	32563	850-934-2600	932-9654	564
Gulf Islands National Seashore (Mississippi) 3500 Pk Rd *Web:* www.nps.gov/guis	Ocean Springs	MS	39564	850-934-2600		564
Gulf Manufacturing Inc 1221 Indiana *Web:* www.gmigroup.com	Humble	TX	77396	281-446-0093		567
Gulf Marine & Industrial Supplies Inc 5501 Jefferson Hwy *Web:* www.gulfmarine.net	New Orleans	LA	70123	504-525-6252	525-4761	770
Gulf Marine Repair Corp 1800 Grant St *Web:* www.gulfmarinerepair.com	Tampa	FL	33605	813-247-3153		698
Gulf of Maine Research Institute, The 350 Commercial St *TF:* 866-447-2111 ■ *Web:* www.gmri.org	Portland	ME	04101	207-772-2321		466
Gulf Offshore Logistics LLC 120 White Rose Dr *TF:* 866-532-1060 ■ *Web:* www.gulf-log.com	Raceland	LA	70394	866-532-1060		539
Gulf Oil LP 80 William St Ste 400	Wellesley Hills	MA	01702	339-933-7200		579
Gulf Publishing Company Inc 2 Greenway Plaza Ste 1020 *Web:* www.gulfpub.com	Houston	TX	77046	713-529-4301		637-9
Gulf Regional Planning Commission 1635-G Popps Ferry Rd *Web:* grpc.com	Biloxi	MS	39531	228-864-1167		261
Gulf Seaboard General Contractors Inc 629 N Washington Hwy *TF:* 800-203-2678 ■ *Web:* www.gulfseaboard.com	Ashland	VA	23005	804-752-7600		186

Phone Fax Class

Gulf South Research Corp
8081 G S R I Rd .... Baton Rouge LA 70820 225-757-8088 463
TF: 800-206-8704 ■ *Web:* www.gsrcorp.com
Gulf State Park 20115 Alabama 135 .... Gulf Shores AL 36542 251-948-7275 948-7726 565
Web: www.alapark.com
Gulf States Distributors Inc
6000 E Shirley Ln .... Montgomery AL 36117 334-271-2010 711
Web: www.gulfstatesdist.com
Gulf States Engineering Inc
4110 Moffett Rd .... Mobile AL 36618 251-460-4646 791
Web: www.gseeng.com
Gulf Stream Coach Inc
503 S Oakland Ave PO Box 1005 .... Nappanee IN 46550 574-773-7761 773-5761 120
TF: 800-289-8787 ■ *Web:* www.gulfstreamcoach.com
Gulf Winds International Inc
411 Brisbane St .... Houston TX 77061 713-747-4909 747-5330 803-1
TF: 866-238-4909 ■ *Web:* www.gwii.com
Gulfland Office Supplies Inc
801 Brashear Ave .... Morgan City LA 70380 985-384-3250 535
Web: gulflandoffice.com
GulfMark Energy Inc
17 S Briar Hollow Ln Ste 100 .... Houston TX 77027 713-881-3603 538
Web: gulfmarkenergy.com
Gulfmark Offshore Inc
842 W Sam Houston Pkwy N Ste 400 .... Houston TX 77024 713-963-9522 539
NYSE: GLF ■ *Web:* www.gulfmark.com
Gulfport Chamber of Commerce
11975-E Seaway Rd .... Gulfport MS 39503 228-604-0014 604-0105 139
TF: 800-748-7626 ■ *Web:* mscoastchamber.com
Gulfport City Hall 2309 15th St .... Gulfport MS 39501 228-868-5700 868-5800 337
TF: 800-901-7072 ■ *Web:* gulfport-ms.gov
Gulfport Energy Corp
14313 N May Ave Ste 100 .... Oklahoma City OK 73134 405-848-8807 536
TF: 800-221-1037 ■ *Web:* www.gulfportenergy.com
Gulfport/Biloxi International Airport
14035 - L Airport Rd .... Gulfport MS 39503 228-863-5951 863-5953 27
Web: www.flygpt.com
Gulfside Hospice Inc
6224 Lafayette St .... New Port Richey FL 34652 727-845-5707 371
TF: 800-561-4883 ■ *Web:* www.ghppc.org
GulfSlope Energy Inc
Ste 800 2500 City W Blvd .... Houston TX 77042 281-918-4100 536
Web: www.gulfslope.com
Gulfstream Aerospace Corp
500 Gulfstream Rd .... Savannah GA 31408 912-965-3000 395-8222 20
Web: www.gulfstream.com
Gulfstream Park 901 S Federal Hwy .... Hallandale FL 33009 954-454-7000 457-6510 133
Web: www.gulfstreampark.com
Gull Industries 3404 Fourth Ave S .... Seattle WA 98134 206-624-5900 579
Gull Point State Park 1500 Harpen St .... Milford IA 51351 712-337-3211 565
Web: www.iowadnr.gov
Gullett & Associates Inc
7135 Office City Dr .... Houston TX 77087 713-644-3219 536
Web: www.gulonline.com
Gullett, Sanford, Robinson & Martin PLLC
150 Third Ave S Ste 1700 .... Nashville TN 37201 615-244-4994 428
Web: www.gsrm.net
Gulliver's Travel Service Inc
2800 S Hulen Ste 110 .... Fort Worth TX 76109 817-924-7766 772
Web: www.gullivers.com
Gully Transportation Inc
3820 Wismann Ln .... Quincy IL 62305 217-224-0770 224-9885 780
Web: www.gullyicx.com
Gulo Solutions LLC
1467 N Elston Ave Ste 105 .... Chicago IL 60642 773-276-8066 177
TF: 800-841-1055 ■ *Web:* www.gulosolutions.com
Gulph Creek Hotels Inc
150 Strafford Ave Ste 215 .... Wayne PA 19087 610-687-9283 132
Web: gulphcreekhotels.com
Gumas Advertising LLC
99 Shotwell St .... San Francisco CA 94103 415-621-7575 393
TF: 800-801-5856 ■ *Web:* www.gumas.com
Gumbiner Savett Inc
1723 Cloverfield Blvd .... Santa Monica CA 90404 310-828-9798 2
TF: 800-989-9798 ■ *Web:* www.gscpa.com
Gumbo Limbo Nature Ctr
1801 N Ocean Blvd .... Boca Raton FL 33432 561-544-8605 50-5
Web: www.gumbolimbo.org
Gumbo Pot 6333 W Third St .... Los Angeles CA 90036 323-933-0358 671
Web: www.thegumbopotla.com
Gump's 135 Post St .... San Francisco CA 94108 415-982-1616 984-9374 362
TF: 800-766-7628 ■ *Web:* www.gumps.com
Gun Barrel Steak & Game House
862 W Broadway .... Jackson WY 83002 307-733-3287 733-6090 671
Web: www.gunbarrel.com
Gun Parts Corp 226 Williams Ln .... Kingston NY 12401 845-679-4867 486-7278* 284
**Fax Area Code:* 877 ■ *TF:* 866-686-7424 ■ *Web:* www.gunpartscorp.com
Gund Co 2121 Walton Rd .... Saint Louis MO 63114 314-423-5200 423-9009 816
Web: www.thegundcompany.com
Gund Inc 1 Runyons Ln .... Edison NJ 08817 732-248-1500 762
TF Cust Svc: 800-448-4863 ■ *Web:* www.gund.com
Gunda Corporation LLC
6161 Savoy Dr Ste 550 .... Houston TX 77036 713-541-3530 186
Web: www.gundacorp.com
Gundaker Commercial Group
2458 Old Dorsett Rd Ste 100 .... Maryland Heights MO 63043 314-298-5200 298-5096 655
Web: www.coldwellbankerhomes.com/st-louis
Gundersen Lutheran at Home HomeCare & Hospice
914 Green Bay St .... La Crosse WI 54601 608-775-8435 371
TF General: 800-362-9567 ■ *Web:* www.gundersenhealth.org
Gundersen Lutheran Medical Ctr
1836 S Ave .... La Crosse WI 54601 608-782-7300 372-3253 374-3
TF: 800-362-9567 ■ *Web:* www.gundersenhealth.org
Gunderson Dettmer Stough Villeneuve Franklin & Hachigian LLP
1200 Seaport Blvd .... Redwood City CA 94063 650-321-2400 41
Web: www.gunder.com
Gunderson Palmer Nelson & Ashmore LLP
506 Sixth St .... Rapid City SD 57701 605-342-1078 445
Web: gpna.com

Phone Fax Class

Gundlach Champion Inc
180 Traders Mine Rd .... Iron Mountain MI 49801 906-779-2303 186
Web: www.gcfirst.com
Gunlock State Park 4405 W 3600 S .... Hurricane UT 84737 435-680-0715 565
Web: www.stateparks.utah.gov
Gunlocke Company LLC 1 Gunlocke Dr .... Wayland NY 14572 585-728-5111 319-1
TF Cust Svc: 800-828-6300 ■ *Web:* www.gunlocke.com
Gunn Automotive Group
227 Broadway .... San Antonio TX 78205 888-452-2856 57
TF: 888-452-2856 ■ *Web:* www.gunnauto.com
Gunn Memorial Public Library
161 Main St E .... Yanceyville NC 27379 336-694-6241 694-9846 434-3
Web: caswellcountync.gov
Gunnebo-Johnson Corp 1240 N Harvard Ave .... Tulsa OK 74115 918-832-8933 834-0984* 470
**Fax:* Cust Svc ■ *TF Sales:* 800-331-5460 ■ *Web:* www.gunnebojohnson.com
Gunnery, The 99 Green Hill Rd .... Washington CT 06793 860-868-7334 622
Web: www.gunnery.org/page
Gunnison Country Times
218 N Wisconsin St .... Gunnison CO 81230 970-641-1414 532-2
Web: www.gunnisontimes.com
Gunnison County
221 N Wisconsin St Ste C .... Gunnison CO 81230 970-641-1516 641-7956 338
Web: gunnisoncounty.org
Gunnison County Electric Assn Inc
37250 W Hwy 50 PO Box 180 .... Gunnison CO 81230 970-641-3520 245
TF: 800-726-3523 ■ *Web:* www.gcea.coop
Gunnison Energy Corp
1801 Broadway Ste 1200 .... Denver CO 80202 303-296-4222 536
Web: www.oxbow.com
Gunpowder Falls State Park
2813 Jerusalem Rd .... Kingsville MD 21087 410-592-2897 565
Web: dnr2.maryland.gov
Gunsite Academy Inc 2900 W Gunsite Rd .... Paulden AZ 86334 928-636-4565 711
Web: www.gunsite.com
Gunster Yoakley & Stewart Pa
777 S Flagler Dr Ste 500 E .... West Palm Beach FL 33401 561-655-1980 655-5677 428
TF: 800-749-1980 ■ *Web:* www.gunster.com
Gunstock Recreation Area
719 Cherry Valley Rd .... Gilford NH 03249 603-293-4341 378
Web: www.gunstock.com
Guntersville City Schools Board of Education
4200 Alabama 79 S .... Guntersville AL 35976 256-582-3159 186
Guntersville Public Library
1240 O'Brig Ave .... Guntersville AL 35976 256-571-7595 434-3
Web: www.guntersvillelibrary.org
Guntert & Zimmerman Construction Div Inc
222 E Fourth St .... Ripon CA 95366 209-599-0066 190
TF: 800-733-2912 ■ *Web:* www.guntert.com
Gunther Douglas Inc 3400 Mariposa St .... Denver CO 80211 303-534-4441 260
TF: 800-979-0209 ■ *Web:* www.guntherdouglas.com
Gunther Mele Ltd 30 Craig St .... Brantford ON N3R7J1 519-756-4330 601
TF: 888-486-8437 ■ *Web:* www.gunthermele.com
Gunze USA
2113 Wells Branch Pkwy Ste 5400 .... Austin TX 78728 512-990-3400 173-4
Web: www.gunzeusa.com
Gupton Marrs International Inc
75 S Broadway Ste 400 .... White Plains NY 10601 212-372-8880 463
Web: www.guptonmarrs.com
Gupton-Jones College of Funeral Service
5141 Snapfinger Woods Dr .... Decatur GA 30035 770-593-2257 593-1891 800
TF: 800-848-5352 ■ *Web:* www.gupton-jones.edu
Gurley Leep Automotive Group
5302 Grape Rd .... Mishawaka IN 46545 574-272-0990 256-5427 57
Web: www.gurleyleep.com
Gurley Motor Co 701 W Coal .... Gallup NM 87301 505-722-6621 57
Web: gurleymotor.com
Gurley's Foods 1118 E Hwy 12 .... Willmar MN 56201 320-235-0600 296-9
Web: www.gurleysfoods.com
Gurnee Mills 6170 W Grand Ave .... Gurnee IL 60031 847-263-7500 460
TF: 800-558-5911 ■ *Web:* www.simon.com
Gurney Productions Inc
8929 S Sepulveda Blvd Ste 510 .... Los Angeles CA 90045 310-645-1499 514
Web: www.gurneyproductions.com
Gurney's Montauk Resort & Seawater Spa
290 Old Montauk Hwy .... Montauk NY 11954 631-668-2345 669
TF: 800-848-7639 ■ *Web:* www.gurneysmontauk.com
Gurstel Chargo LLP
6681 Country Club Dr .... Golden Valley MN 55427 877-344-4002 428
TF: 877-750-6335 ■ *Web:* www.gurstel.com
Guru Labs
1148 W Legacy Crossing Blvd Ste 200 .... Centerville UT 84014 801-298-5227 298-1149 94
TF: 800-833-3582 ■ *Web:* www.gurulabs.com
Guru Studio 500-110 Spadina Ave .... Toronto ON M5V2K4 416-599-4878 514
Web: www.gurustudio.com
Guru.com 5001 Baum Blvd Ste 760 .... Pittsburgh PA 15213 412-687-1316 687-4466 260
TF: 888-678-0136 ■ *Web:* www.guru.com
Gurus Information Technology Services LLC
517 Georges Rd .... North Brunswick NJ 08902 732-247-7747 196
Web: www.gurusit.com
Gurwin Jewish Nursing & Rehabilitation Ctr
68 Hauppauge Rd .... Commack NY 11725 631-715-2000 363
Web: www.gurwin.org
Gurwitch Products LLC
135 East 57th St Ste 7 .... New York NY 10022 281-275-7000 214
TF: 888-637-2437 ■ *Web:* www.lauramercier.com
Gus Harrison Correctional Facility
2727 E Beecher St .... Adrian MI 49221 517-265-3900 213
TF: 800-326-4537 ■ *Web:* www.michigan.gov
Gusher Pumps 115 Industrial Dr .... Williamstown KY 41097 859-824-3100 824-7248 641
Web: www.gusher.com
Gusmer Enterprises Inc
1165 Globe Ave .... Mountainside NJ 07092 908-301-1811 14
Web: www.gusmerenterprises.com
Gustave A Larson Co
W233 N2869 Roundy Circle W .... Pewaukee WI 53072 262-542-0200 542-1400 665
TF: 800-829-9609 ■ *Web:* www.galarson.com
Gustavson Assoc LLC
5757 Central Ave Ste D .... Boulder CO 80301 303-443-2209 668
Web: www.gustavson.com

Phone Fax Class

Gustavus Adolphus College
800 W College Ave........Saint Peter MN 56082 507-933-8000 933-7474 166
TF: 800 487 8288 ■ Web: www.gustavus.edu

Gustman Chevrolet Sales Inc
1450 Delanglade St........Kaukauna WI 54130 920-766-3581 57
Web: www.gustman.com

Gusto 12022 Mayfield Rd........Cleveland OH 44106 216-791-9900 671
Web: www.gustolittleitaly.com

Gusto Brands Inc 707 Douglas St........LaGrange GA 30240 706-882-2573 882-2412 81-1
Web: gustobrands.com

Gutenberg College 1883 University St........Eugene OR 97403 541-683-5141 166
Web: www.gutenberg.edu

Guthrie & Associates Meeting & Event Management Inc
10889 La Alberca Ave........San Diego CA 92127 858-487-7759 5
Web: www.guthrie-meetings-events.com

Guthrie County 200 N Fifth St........Guthrie Center IA 50115 641-747-3415 338
Web: guthriecounty.org

Guthrie Healthcare System 1 Guthrie Sq........Sayre PA 18840 570-887-4401 353
TF: 888-448-8474 ■ Web: www.guthrie.org

Guthrie S Brett (Rep R - KY)
2434 Rayburn HOB........Washington DC 20515 202-225-3501 226-2019 342-2
Web: guthrie.house.gov

Guthrie Theater 818 S Second St........Minneapolis MN 55415 612-377-2224 572
TF Resv: 877-447-8243 ■ Web: www.guthrietheater.org

Guthy-Renker
100 N Sepulveda Blvd Ste 100........El Segundo CA 90245 310-581-6250 581-3232 514
Web: www.guthy-renker.com

Gutierrez Luis (Rep D - IL)
2408 Rayburn Bldg........Washington DC 20515 202-225-8203 225-7810 342-2
Web: gutierrez.house.gov

Gutirrez Co, The 1 Wall St........Burlington MA 01803 781-272-7000 272-3130 186
Web: www.gutierrezco.com

Gutknecht Construction Co
2280 Citygate Dr........Columbus OH 43219 614-532-5410 186
Web: www.gutknecht.com

Gutman, Mintz, Baker & Sonnenfeldt
813 Jericho Tpke........New Hyde Park NY 11040 516-775-7007 428
TF: 800-299-9470 ■ Web: www.gmbspc.com

Gutsy Women Travel LLC
801 E Katella Ave........Anaheim CA 92806 866-464-8879 760
TF: 866-464-8879 ■ Web: www.gutsywomentravel.com

Guttenplans Frozen Dough
100 Hwy 36........Middletown NJ 07748 732-495-9480 296-2
TF General: 888-422-4357 ■ Web: www.guttenplan.com

Guttmacher Institute (AGI)
125 Maiden Ln 7th Fl........New York NY 10038 212-248-1111 248-1951 48-5
TF: 800-355-0244 ■ Web: www.guttmacher.org

Guttman Development Strategies Inc
400 Valley Rd Ste 103........Mt. Arlington NJ 07856 973-770-7177 194
Web: www.guttmandev.com

Guttman Group LLC, The
200 Speers St........Belle Vernon PA 15012 724-483-3533 539
Web: www.guttmangroup.com

Guttmann & Blaevoet
2351 Powell St........San Francisco CA 94133 415-655-4000 539
TF: 800-582-6178 ■ Web: www.gb-eng.com

Guy & O'Neill Inc 617 Tower Dr........Fredonia WI 53021 262-692-2469 231
Web: www.guyandoneill.com

Guy Chemical Company Inc
150 Dominion Dr........Somerset PA 15501 814-443-9455 88
Web: www.guychemical.com

Guy Engineering Services Inc
10759 E Admiral Pl........Tulsa OK 74116 918-437-0282 256
Web: guyengr.com

Guy Evans Inc 82-585 Showcase Pkwy........Indio CA 92203 760-262-6300 499

Guy Ezzell Agency Inc 209 E High St........Lexington KY 40507 859-264-1021 390

Guy Hurley Blaser & Heuer LLC
1080 Kirts Blvd Ste 500........Troy MI 48084 248-519-1400 390
Web: www.ghbh.com

Guy M Turner Inc
4514 S Holden Rd PO Box 7776........Greensboro NC 27406 336-294-4660 294-6668 780
TF: 800-432-4859 ■ Web: www.guymturner.com

Guy Shavender Trucking Inc PO Box 206........Pantego NC 27860 252-943-3379 943-6434 685
TF: 800-682-2447 ■ Web: www.shavender.com

Guyana 801 Second Ave 5th Fl........New York NY 10017 212-573-5828 573-6225 784
Web: www.un.int/guyana
Consulate General 308 W 38th St........New York NY 10001 212-947-5110 947-5163 257
Web: www.guyana.org
Embassy 2490 Tracy Pl NW........Washington DC 20008 202-265-6900 232-1297 257
TF: 800-333-4636 ■ Web: guyana.org

Guynes Printing Company of Texas Inc
927 Tony Lama........El Paso TX 79915 915-772-2211 627
Web: www.guynesprinting.com

Guzman & Co 101 Aragon Ave........Coral Gables FL 33134 305-374-3600 690
Web: guzman.com

Guzzler Manufacturing Inc
1621 S Illinois St........Streator IL 61364 815-672-3171 672-2779* 386
*Fax: Sales ■ TF: 800-627-3171 ■ Web: www.guzzler.com

GVC Capital LLC
5350 S Roslyn St Ste 400........Greenwood Village CO 80111 303-694-0862 694-6287 690
Web: www.gvccap.com

GVD Commercial Properties Inc
1915 E Katella Ave Ste A........Orange CA 92867 714-639-2131 652
Web: www.gvdcommercialproperties.com

Gvd Corp 45 Spinelli Pl........Cambridge MA 02138 617-661-0060 603
Web: www.gvdcorp.com

GVI Medical Devices Corp
1470 Enterprise Pkwy........Twinsburg OH 44087 330-963-4083 743
TF: 888-247-8840 ■ Web: www.gvimd.com

GVM (Grand Valley Mfg Co)
701 E Spring St Bldg 52........Titusville PA 16354 814-827-2707 827-4349 454
TF: 800-704-1078 ■ Web: www.grandvalleymfg.com

GVMG (Grand View Media Group Inc)
200 Croft St Ste 1........Birmingham AL 35242 205-408-3700 637-9
TF: 888-431-2877 ■ Web: grandviewmedia.com

Gvnw Consulting
2270 La Montana Way Ste 200........Colorado Springs CO 80918 719-594-5800 196
Web: gvnw.com

GVTC (Guadalupe Valley Telephone Co-op)
36101 FM 3159........New Braunfels TX 78132 830-885-4411 885-2400 736
TF: 800-367-4882 ■ Web: www.gvtc.com

GVW (GVW Group LLC)
625 Roger Williams Ave........Highland Park IL 60035 847-681-8417 360-3
Web: www.gvwgroup.com

GVW Group LLC (GVW)
625 Roger Williams Ave........Highland Park IL 60035 847-681-8417 360-3
Web: www.gvwgroup.com

GW & Wade LLC 93 Worcester St........Wellesley MA 02481 781-239-1188 194
TF: 800-801-9942 ■ Web: www.gwwade.com

GW Berkheimer Company Inc
6000 Southport Rd........Portage IN 46368 219-764-5200 764-5203 612
TF: 800-589-2368 ■ Web: www.gwberkheimer.com

GW Fins 808 Bienville St........New Orleans LA 70112 504-581-3467 671
Web: www.gwfins.com

GW Lisk Company Inc 2 S St........Clifton Springs NY 14432 315-462-2611 462-7661 253
TF: 800-776-9528 ■ Web: www.gwlisk.com

GW Plastics Inc 239 Pleasant St........Bethel VT 05032 802-234-9941 234-9940 604
Web: www.gwplastics.com

Gw Technologies
1245 S Garfield Ave........Traverse City MI 49686 231-941-2250 415
Web: www.goodwillnmi.org

Gwa Electrical Engineers Inc
168 Laurelhurst Ave........Columbia SC 29210 803-252-6919 261
Web: www.gwainc.net

Gwaii Haanas National Park Reserve &Haida Heritage Site
60 Second Beach Rd........Queen Charlotte BC V0T1S0 250-559-8818 559-8366 563
Web: www.pc.gc.ca

GWAVA Inc 100 Alexis Nihon Rd Ste 500........Montreal QC H4M2P1 514-639-4850 41
Web: www.gwava.com

Gweenie's Old Alaska Restaurant
4333 SpenaRd Rd........Anchorage AK 99517 907-243-2090 671
Web: gwenniesrestaurant.com

GWI Engineering Inc
1411 Michigan St NE........Grand Rapids MI 49503 616-459-8274 386
Web: www.gwiengineering.com

GWI Inc 8 Pomerleau St........Biddeford ME 04005 207-286-8686 608
TF: 866-494-2020 ■ Web: www.gwi.net

Gwin Dobson & Foreman Inc
3121 Fairway Dr........Altoona PA 16602 814-943-5214 261
TF: 800-525-6464 ■ Web: www.gdfengineers.com

Gwin's Commercial Printing & Engraving
957 Spring Hill Ave........Mobile AL 36604 251-438-2226 687
Web: gwins.cc

Gwin's Travel Planners Inc
212 N Kirkwood Rd........Saint Louis MO 63122 314-822-1957 771
TF: 800-433-9211 ■ Web: www.gwins.com

Gwinnett Chamber of Commerce
6500 Sugarloaf Pkwy........Duluth GA 30097 770-232-3000 232-8807 139
TF: 800-241-2286 ■ Web: www.gwinnettchamber.org

Gwinnett College of Business
4230 Lawrenceville Hwy NW Ste 11........Lilburn GA 30047 770 381 7200 166
Web: www.gwinnettcollege.edu

Gwinnett County
75 Langley Dr
Gwinnett Justice & Administration Ctr........Lawrenceville GA 30045 770-822-8000 822-7097 338
TF: 800-772-1213 ■ Web: www.gwinnettcounty.com

Gwinnett County Public Library
1001 Lawrenceville Hwy........Lawrenceville GA 30046 770-822-4522 434-3
Web: www.gwinnettpl.org

Gwinnett Daily Post
725 Old Norcross Rd........Lawrenceville GA 30045 770-963-9205 339-8081 532-2
Web: www.gwinnettdailypost.com

Gwinnett Medical Ctr Lawrenceville
1000 Medical Ctr Blvd........Lawrenceville GA 30046 678-312-1000 374-3
Web: www.gwinnettmedicalcenter.org

Gwinnett Place Mall
2100 Pleasant Hill Rd........Duluth GA 30096 770-813-6840 460
Web: www.simon.com

GWK Enterprises 123 S Ctr St........Geneseo IL 61254 309-944-4969 157-6
Web: www.fourseasonsdirect.com

GWN Consulting LLC
1498 Sheridan Run Ct........Herndon VA 20170 571-318-1909 463

GWN Securities Inc
11440 N Jog Rd........Palm Beach Gardens FL 33418 561-472-2700 690
Web: www.gwnsecurities.com

GWPC (Ground Water Protection Council)
13308 N MacArthur Blvd........Oklahoma City OK 73142 405-516-4972 516-4973 48-13
TF: 800-364-2274 ■ Web: www.gwpc.org

Gwynedd-Mercy College
1325 Sunneytown Pk PO Box 901........Gwynedd Valley PA 19437 215-646-7300 641-5556* 166
*Fax: Admissions ■ TF Admissions: 800-342-5462 ■ Web: gmercyu.edu

Gwynn Group
600 E Las Colinas Blvd Ste 150........Irving TX 75039 214-485-5990 177
Web: www.gwynngroup.com

GX Technology Corp
2105 City West Blvd Ste 900........Houston TX 77042 713-789-7250 727
Web: www.iongeo.com

GXS Inc 9711 Washingtonian Blvd........Gaithersburg MD 20878 301-340-4000 340-5299 178-4
TF: 800-560-4347 ■ Web: www.gxs.com

GYC (Greater Yellowstone Coalition)
215 S Wallace Ave Ste 2........Bozeman MT 59715 406-586-1593 556-2839 48-13
TF: 800-775-1834 ■ Web: www.greateryellowstone.org

Gyford Productions 891 Trademark Dr........Reno NV 89521 775-829-7272 393
Web: www.standoffsystems.com

GY&K Antler 181 S St........Boston MA 02111 617-423-0011 195
Web: gykantler.com

Gym Source 40 E 52nd St........New York NY 10022 212-688-4222 750-2886 711
TF: 888-994-4890 ■ Web: www.gymsource.com

GYMA Laboratories of America Inc
135 Cantiague Rock Rd........Westbury NY 11590 516-933-0900 933-1075 479
Web: www.gyma.com

Gymboree Corp 500 Howard St........San Francisco CA 94105 415-278-7000 278-7100 157-1
NASDAQ: GYMB ■ TF: 877-449-6932 ■ Web: www.gymboree.com

Gynecologic Oncology Group (GOG)
1600 JFK Blvd Ste 1020........Philadelphia PA 19103 215-854-0770 854-0716 49-8
TF: 800-225-3053 ■ Web: www.gog.org

Company / Address	City	State	Zip	Phone	Fax	Class
Gyotaku 1824 King St *Web:* www.gyotakuhawaii.com	Honolulu	HI	96826	808-949-4584		671
Gypsum Assn 6525 Belcrest Rd Ste 480 *TF:* 800-874-4968 ■ *Web:* www.gypsum.org	Hyattsville	MD	20782	301-277-8686	277-8747	49-13
Gypsum Express Ltd 8280 Sixty Rd PO Box 268 *TF:* 800-621-7901 ■ *Web:* www.gypsumexpress.com	Baldwinsville	NY	13027	315-638-2201		449
Gypsum Supply Company Inc 859 74th St *Web:* www.gypsum-supply.com	Byron Center	MI	49315	616-583-9300		191-1
Gypsy Den 125 N Broadway Ave *Web:* www.gypsyden.com	Santa Ana	CA	92701	714-835-8840		671
Gyration Inc 3601-B Calle Tecate *Fax Area Code: 805 ■ *TF:* 888-340-0033 ■ *Web:* www.gyration.com	Camarillo	CA	93012	888-340-0033	987-6665*	173-1
Gyro Creative Group 400 Grand River Ave *Web:* www.gyrocreative.com	Detroit	MI	48226	313-964-0100		5
Gyrodata Inc 23000 Northwest Lake Dr *TF:* 800-348-6063 ■ *Web:* www.gyrodata.com	Houston	TX	77095	281-213-6300		190
Gyrodyne Company of America Inc 1 Flowerfield Ste 24 *NASDAQ:* GYRO ■ *TF:* 800-322-2885 ■ *Web:* www.gyrodyne.com	Saint James	NY	11780	631-584-5400	584-7075	655
Gyrus ACMI 6655 Wedgwood Rd Ste 160 *TF:* 800-387-0437 ■ *Web:* medical.olympusamerica.com	Maple Grove	MN	55311	763-416-3000		476
Gyrus Medical Inc ENT Div 136 Turnpike Rd *TF:* 800-757-2942 ■ *Web:* www.medical.olympusamerica.com	Southborough	MA	01772	508-804-2600		477

H

Company / Address	City	State	Zip	Phone	Fax	Class
H & B Mechanical Inc 111 Cal Ave	Barstow	CA	92311	760-256-8401		350
H & C Tool Supply Corp 235 Mt Read Blvd *TF:* 800-323-4624 ■ *Web:* www.hctoolsupply.com	Rochester	NY	14611	585-235-5700		350
H & E Equipment Services Inc 7500 Pecue Ln *NASDAQ:* HEES ■ *TF:* 866-467-3682 ■ *Web:* www.he-equipment.com	Baton Rouge	LA	70809	225-298-5200		264-3
H & G Sales Inc 11635 Lackland Rd *Web:* www.h-gsales.com	St. Louis	MO	63146	314-432-8188		499
H & H Chevrolet LLC 4645 S 84 St *Web:* hhchevy.com	Omaha	NE	68127	402-339-2222		57
H & H Color Lab Inc 8906 E 67th St *TF:* 800-821-1305 ■ *Web:* www.hhcolorlab.com	Raytown	MO	64133	816-358-6677	313-1480	588
H & H General Excavating Inc 660 Old Hanover Rd *Web:* www.h-hgenexc.com	Spring Grove	PA	17362	717-225-4669		683
H & H Graphics Inc 854 N Prince St *TF:* 866-338-7569 ■ *Web:* www.hhgraphicsgroup.com	Lancaster	PA	17603	717-393-3941		344
H & H Group Inc 2801 Syene Rd *Web:* www.hhindustries.com	Madison	WI	53713	608-273-3434	273-9654	189-10
H & H Industrial Corp 7612 Rt 130 *TF:* 800-982-0341 ■ *Web:* www.hhindustrial.com	Pennsauken	NJ	08110	856-663-4444	663-4446	697
H & H Mfg Company Inc 2 Horne Dr	Folcroft	PA	19032	610-532-8100		262
H & H Publishing Company Inc 1231 Kapp Dr *TF:* 800-366-4079 ■ *Web:* www.hhpublishing.com	Clearwater	FL	33765	727-442-7760	442-2195	244
H & H Swiss Screw Machine Products Company Inc 1478 Chestnut Ave *Fax Area Code: 908 ■ *TF:* 800-826-9985 ■ *Web:* www.hhswiss.com	Hillside	NJ	07205	800-826-9985	688-3503*	621
H & H Tube & Manufacturing Co 579 Garfield Ave *Web:* www.h-htube.com	Vanderbilt	MI	49795	989-983-2800		595
H & L Advantage Inc 3500 Busch Dr SW *TF:* 800-581-2343 ■ *Web:* hladvantage.com	Grandville	MI	49418	616-532-1012		350
H & L Tool Company Inc 32701 Dequindre Rd *Web:* www.hltool.com	Madison Heights	MI	48071	248-585-7474	585-5774	621
H & L Tooth Company Inc 10055 E 56 St N *TF:* 800-458-6684 ■ *Web:* www.hltooth.com	Tulsa	OK	74117	918-272-0951	272-0163	483
H & M Construction Company Inc 50 Security Dr *Web:* hmcompany.com	Jackson	TN	38305	731-664-6300		188-7
H & M International Transportation Inc 485B Rt 1 S *TF:* 800-446-4685 ■ *Web:* www.hmit.net	Iselin	NJ	08830	732-510-4640		780
H & M Systems Software Inc 600 E Crescent Ave Ste 203 *Web:* www.hm-software.com	Upper Saddle River	NJ	07458	201-934-3414	934-9206	178-11
H & O Centerless Grinding Inc 45 Bathurst Dr *TF:* 800-352-9993 ■ *Web:* www.cylindricalprecision.com	Waterloo	ON	N2V1N2	519-884-0322		393
H & P Leasing Inc 550 Hwy 49 S *Web:* www.hptrailerleasing.com	Jackson	MS	39218	601-939-9000	939-9037	393
H & P Sales Inc 2022 Victory Dr *Web:* www.handpsalesinc.com	Vista	CA	92084	760-727-2614		292
H & R 1871 60 Industrial Rowe *Fax Area Code: 336 ■ *TF:* 866-776-9292 ■ *Web:* www.hr1871.com	Gardner	MA	01440	866-776-9292	548-7801*	284
H & R Block Tax Services Inc 4400 Main St *TF:* 800-472-5625 ■ *Web:* www.hrblock.com	Kansas City	MO	64111	800-472-5625		734
H & R Mechanical Contractors Inc 106 Demand Ct *Web:* hrmech.com	Georgetown	KY	40324	502-863-4955		189-10
H & R Retail Inc 2800 Quarry Lake Dr Ste 320 *Web:* www.hrretail.com	Baltimore	MD	21209	410-308-0800	486-2733	655
H & S Bakery Inc 601 S Caroline St *TF:* 800-959-7655 ■ *Web:* www.hsbakery.com	Baltimore	MD	21231	410-276-7254		296-1
H & s Environmental Inc 160 E Main St Ste 2F *Web:* www.hsenv.com	Westborough	MA	01581	508-366-7442		667
H & s Floors & Furnishings Inc 210 Russell St	Darlington	SC	29532	843-393-0456		131
H & S Heat Treating 133 S St N *Web:* www.hsheat.com	Port Robinson	ON	L0S1K0	905-384-9355		484
H & S Manufacturing Co 2913 Singleton St *TF:* 800-899-9036 ■ *Web:* www.hsmfg.com	Rowlett	TX	75088	972-475-4747		697
H & S Manufacturing Company Inc 2608 S Hume *Web:* www.hsmfgco.com	Marshfield	WI	54449	715-387-3414		125
H & s Sports Plus 8015 Summerfield Rd *Web:* hssportsplus.com	Lambertville	MI	48144	734-847-3881		711
H & S Swansons' Tool Co 9000 68th St N *TF:* 800-942-1690 ■ *Web:* www.hsswansons.com	Pinellas Park	FL	33782	727-541-3575		454
H & W Computer Systems Inc 6154 N Meeker Pl Ste 100 *TF:* 800-338-6692 ■ *Web:* www.hwcs.com	Boise	ID	83713	208-377-0336	377-0069	177
H & W Management Co 1021 Majestic Dr Ste 380 *Web:* www.hwhotels.com	Lexington	KY	40513	859-263-0106		463
H & W Trucking Company Inc 1772 N Andy Griffith Pkwy PO Box 1545 *TF:* 800-334-9181 ■ *Web:* www.hwtrucking.com	Mount Airy	NC	27030	336-789-2188	789-7973	780
H A M Media Group 1058 N TAMIAMI Tl Ste 108-302 *Web:* www.hammedia.com	Sarasota	FL	34236	917-407-6014		401
H B Fuller Construction Products Inc 1105 S Frontenac Rd *TF:* 800-832-9002 ■ *Web:* www.tecspecialty.com	Aurora	IL	60504	800-832-9002		3
H Barber & Sons Inc 15 Raytkwich Rd *TF:* 800-355-8318 ■ *Web:* hbarber.com	Naugatuck	CT	06770	203-729-9000		667
H C Olsen Construction Company Inc 710 Los Angeles Ave *TF:* 800-219-1899 ■ *Web:* www.hcolsen.com	Monrovia	CA	91016	626-359-8900		186
H Chambers Co 1800 Washington Blvd Ste 111 *Web:* www.chambersusa.com	Baltimore	MD	21230	410-727-4535	727-6982	393
H Douglas Singer Mental Health & Development Ctr 4402 N Main St	Rockford	IL	61103	317-494-2294		374-5
H E Anderson Company Inc 2100 Anderson Dr *TF:* 800-331-9620 ■ *Web:* www.heanderson.com	Muskogee	OK	74403	918-687-4426		711
H E Bergeron Engineers Inc 2605 White Mtn Hwy *Web:* hebengineers.com	North Conway	NH	03860	603-356-6936		261
H E Whitlock Inc 4808 Dillon Dr PO Box 8030 *TF:* 866-933-0709 ■ *Web:* www.hewhitlock.com	Pueblo	CO	81008	866-933-0709		449
H Enterprises International Inc 120 S Sixth St	Minneapolis	MN	55402	612-340-8849		360-3
H Freeman & Son Inc 411 N Cranberry Rd *TF:* 800-876-7700 ■ *Web:* www.hfreemanco.com	Westminster	MD	21157	410-857-5774	857-1560	155-12
H G Makelim Co 219 Shaw Rd *TF:* 800-471-0590 ■ *Web:* www.hgmakelim.com	South San Francisco	CA	94080	650-873-4757	872-5438	385
H Gr Industrial Surplus 20001 Euclid Ave *TF:* 866-447-7117 ■ *Web:* www.hgrinc.com	Euclid	OH	44117	216-486-4567		358
H Hotel, The 111 W Main St *Web:* www.thehhotel.com	Midland	MI	48640	989-839-0500	837-6000	377
H I M on Call Inc 1033 Hamilton St *Web:* www.himoncall.com	Allentown	PA	18101	610-435-5724		196
H Ka Staffing Services 800 Waukegan Rd Ste 200 *Web:* www.hkastaffing.com	Glenview	IL	60025	847-998-9300		260
H Kramer & Co 1345 W 21st St *TF:* 800-621-2305 ■ *Web:* hkramer.com	Chicago	IL	60608	312-226-6600	226-4713	485
H Krevit & Company Inc 73 Welton St *TF:* 800-435-6856 ■ *Web:* www.hkrevit.com	New Haven	CT	06511	203-772-3350		145
H Lee Moffitt Cancer Ctr & Research Institute Blood & Marrow Transplantation Program 12902 Magnolia Dr *TF:* 888-663-3488 ■ *Web:* www.moffitt.org	Tampa	FL	33612	888-663-3488		769
H Muehlstein & Company Inc 10 Westport Rd *TF:* 800-257-3746 ■ *Web:* www.muehlstein.com	Wilton	CT	06897	203-855-6000		603
H Myers John & Son Inc 2200 Monroe St *Web:* www.jhmson.com	York	PA	17404	717-792-2500	792-5115	191-2
H O Wolding Inc 9642 Western Way *TF:* 800-950-0054 ■ *Web:* www.howolding.com	Amherst	WI	54406	715-824-5513		780
H Pearce Real Estate Co 393 State St *TF:* 800-373-3411 ■ *Web:* www.joelgalvin.com	North Haven	CT	06473	203-281-3400		652
H r Office Inc, The 2437 Commercial Blvd Ste 5 *Web:* www.thehrofficeinc.com	State College	PA	16801	814-238-3750		193
H Rubin Vision Centers 7539 Garners Sperry Rd *Fax: Cust Svc ■ *Web:* www.hrubinvision.com	Columbia	SC	29209	803-779-9313	779-9551*	543
H S C Foundation Inc 2013 H St NW *Web:* www.hschealth.org/foundation	Washington	DC	20006	202-454-1220		463
H Sattler Plastics Co Inc 5410 W Roosevelt Rd	Chicago	IL	60644	773-287-3600		603
H Schultz & Sons Inc 777 Lehigh Ave *Web:* www.housewaresandthings.com	Union	NJ	07083	908-687-5400	687-1788	38
H Smith Packing Corp 99 Ft Fairfield Rd *TF:* 800-393-9898 ■ *Web:* www.smithsfarm.com	Presque Isle	ME	04769	207-764-4540	764-2816	297-7
H Stern Jewelers Inc 645 Fifth Ave *TF:* 800-747-8376 ■ *Web:* www.hstern.net	New York	NY	10022	212-688-0300		410
H Wilson Co 2245 Delany Rd *TF:* 800-245-7224 ■ *Web:* www.luxorfurn.com	Waukegan	IL	60087	800-245-7224	327-1698	319-1
H. B. Van Duzer Forest State Scenic Corridor 8300 Salmon River Hwy *TF:* 800-551-6949 ■ *Web:* www.oregonstateparks.org	Otis	OR	97368	800-551-6949		565
H. E. Murdock Co Inc 88 Main St *TF:* 888-974-1805 ■ *Web:* www.daysjewelers.com	Waterville	ME	04901	207-873-7036		410

	Phone	Fax	Class
H. T. Berry Co Inc PO Box B ... Canton MA 02021 *TF:* 800-736-2206 ■ *Web:* www.htberry.com	781-828-6000	828-9788	559
H. T. Lyons Inc 7165 Ambassador Dr ... Allentown PA 18106 *Web:* m.htlyons.com	610-530-2600		261
H. W. Culp Lumber Co PO Box 235 ... New London NC 28127 *Web:* www.culplumber.com	704-463-7311	463-4100	191-3
H.M. Dunn Co 3301 House Anderson Rd ... Euless TX 76040 *Web:* www.hmdunn.com	817-283-3722		454
H.N. Funkhouser & Company Inc 2150 S Loudoun St ... Winchester VA 22601 *TF:* 800-343-6556 ■ *Web:* www.hnfunkhouser.com	540-662-9000		579
H.O.T. Printing & Graphics Inc 2595 Tracy Ct ... Northwood OH 43619 *TF:* 800-848-8259 ■ *Web:* www.h-o-tgraphics.com	419-242-7000	242-3299	627
H.P. Cummings Construction Co 14 Prospect St PO Box 29 ... Ware MA 01082 *Web:* www.hpcummings.com	413-967-6251		186
H.P. White Laboratory Inc 3114 Scarboro Rd ... Street MD 21154 *TF:* 800-872-2253 ■ *Web:* www.hpwhite.com	410-838-6550		743
H.Q.C Inc 230 Kendall Pt Dr ... Oswego IL 60543 *Web:* www.hqcinc.com	630-820-5550	820-5549	608
H.R. Lewis Petroleum Co 1432 Cleveland St ... Jacksonville FL 32209 *TF:* 800-638-6551 ■ *Web:* www.lewispetroleum.com	904-356-0731		579
H2 Engineering Surveying LLC 8880 N Hess St ... Hayden ID 83835 *Web:* h2survey.com	208-772-6600		727
H2 Plains LLC 10500 E Berkeley Sq Ste 100 ... Wichita KS 67206 *Web:* www.hartmanoil.com	316-636-2090	636-1155	536
H2 Pre-Cast Inc 3835 N Clemons ... East Wenatchee WA 98802 *Web:* www.h2precast.com	509-884-6644		183
H2O Consulting Inc 5870 Hwy 6 N Ste 215 ... Houston TX 77084 *Web:* h2oconsulting.net	281-861-6215		196
H2f Comedy Productions 102 E Magnolia Blvd ... Burbank CA 91502 *TF:* 800-252-4499 ■ *Web:* www.flapperscomedy.com	818-845-9721		708
H2O Concepts International Inc 1518 W Knudsen Dr Ste 100 ... Phoenix AZ 85027 *Web:* www.h2oconcepts.com	623-582-5222		364
H2O Plus Inc 845 W Madison St ... Chicago IL 60607 *TF Cust Svc:* 800-242-2284 ■ *Web:* www.h2oplus.com	312-850-9283		214
H3 Ranch 105 E Exchange Ave Stockyards Hotel ... Fort Worth TX 76164 *TF:* 800-433-5747 ■ *Web:* www.h3ranch.com	817-624-1246	624-2571	671
H3 Solutions Inc 10432 Balls Ford Rd Ste 230 ... Manassas VA 20109 *TF:* 855-464-5914 ■ *Web:* www.h3s-inc.com	855-464-5914		196
H5 Colo 12712 Park Central Dr Ste 200 ... Dallas TX 75251 *Web:* www.h5colo.com	469-533-0270		492
HA Guden Company Inc 99 Raynor Ave ... Ronkonkoma NY 11779 *TF:* 800-344-6437 ■ *Web:* www.guden.com	631-737-2900	737-2933	350
Ha Ha Tonka State Park 1491 State Rd D ... Camdenton MO 65020 *Web:* www.mostateparks.com	573-346-2986		565
HA Logistics Inc 5175 Johnson Dr ... Pleasanton CA 94588 *TF:* 800-449-5778 ■ *Web:* www.halogistics.com	925-251-9300	251-9333	311
Haag Engineering Co 4949 W Royal Ln ... Irving TX 75063 *TF:* 800-527-0168 ■ *Web:* haagengineering.com	214-614-6500		261
Haakon County 140 Howard PO Box 70 ... Philip SD 57567 *Web:* ujs.sd.gov/County_Information/haakon.aspx	605-859-2627	859-2257	338
Haakon Industries (Canada) Ltd 11851 Dyke Rd ... Richmond BC V7A4X8 *Web:* www.haakon.com	604-273-0161		14
Haapanen Brothers Inc 1400 Saint Paul Ave ... Gurnee IL 60031 *Web:* hb-graphics.net	847-662-2233		687
Haartz Corp 87 HaywaRd Rd ... Acton MA 01720 *TF:* 800-263-7377 ■ *Web:* www.haartz.com	978-264-2600	264-2601	745-2
Haas & Haynie Corp 400 Oyster Pt Blvd Ste 123 ... South San Francisco CA 94080 *Web:* www.hh1898.com	650-588-5600		653
Haas & Wilkerson Inc 4300 Shawnee Mission Pkwy ... Fairway KS 66205 *TF:* 800-821-7703 ■ *Web:* www.hwins.com	913-432-4400	432-6159	390
Haas Automation Inc 2800 Sturgis Rd ... Oxnard CA 93030 *TF:* 800-331-6746 ■ *Web:* int.haascnc.com	805-278-1800	278-2255	454
Haas Cabinet Company Inc 625 W Utica St ... Sellersburg IN 47172 *TF:* 800-457-6458 ■ *Web:* www.haascabinet.com	812-246-4431		115
Haas Environmental Inc 7 Red Lion Rd PO Box 2082 ... Vincentown NJ 08088	609-859-3100		393
Habana 2728 S Congress Ave ... Austin TX 78704 *Web:* www.habanaaustin.com	512-443-4252		671
Habana Inn 2200 NW 40th St ... Oklahoma City OK 73112 *TF:* 800-988-2221 ■ *Web:* www.habanainn.com	405-525-0730		379
Habanero Consulting Group Inc 510-1111 Melville St ... Vancouver BC V6E3V6 *TF:* 866-841-6201 ■ *Web:* www.habaneroconsulting.com	604-709-6201		225
Habasit ABT Inc 150 Industrial Pk Rd ... Middletown CT 06457 *TF:* 800-522-2358 ■ *Web:* www.habasit.com	860-632-2211	632-1710	370
Habasit America 805 Satellite Blvd ... Suwanee GA 30024 **Fax Area Code:* 678 ■ *TF:* 800-458-6431 ■ *Web:* www.habasit.com	800-458-6431	288-3651*	608
Habasit Belting Inc 1400 Clinton St ... Buffalo NY 14206 *TF:* 800-325-1585 ■ *Web:* www.habasit.com	716-824-8484		370
Habbersett Scrapple Inc 103 S Railroad Ave ... Bridgeville DE 19933 *TF:* 800-338-4727 ■ *Web:* www.habbersettscrapple.com	800-338-4727		296-26
habco 501 Gordon Baker Rd ... Toronto ON M2H2S6 *TF:* 800-448-0244 ■ *Web:* www.habcotech.com	416-491-6008	491-6982	803-1
Habegger Corp 4995 Winton Rd ... Cincinnati OH 45232 **Fax Area Code:* 513 ■ *TF:* 800-459-4822 ■ *Web:* www.habeggercorp.com	309-793-4328	681-9892*	612
Habelman Bros Co Inc 10688 Estate Rd ... Tomah WI 54660 *Web:* www.habelmancranberries.com	608-372-2444		315-1

	Phone	Fax	Class
Habenicht Novak & Birckbichler 287 Pittsburgh Rd ... Butler PA 16002 *Web:* hnbcpa.net	724-283-8661		2
Haber Vision LLC 15710 W Colfax Ave Ste 204 ... Golden CO 80401 *TF:* 800-621-4381 ■ *Web:* www.habervision.com	303-459-2220		45
Haberfeld Associates Inc 206 S 13th St Ste 1500 ... Lincoln NE 68508 *Web:* www.haberfeld.com	402-475-1191		196
Habersham County 555 Monroe St Ste 20 ... Clarkesville GA 30523 *Web:* www.habershamga.com	706-839-0200	839-0219	338
Habersham County Board of Education 132 W Stanford Mill Rd PO Box 70 ... Clarkesville GA 30523 *Web:* www.habershamschools.com	706-754-2118	754-1549	685
Habersham County Chamber of Commerce 668 Clarkesville St ... Cornelia GA 30531 *TF:* 800-835-2559 ■ *Web:* www.habershamchamber.com	706-778-4654	776-1416	139
Habersham Electric Membership Corp 6135 Georgia 115 ... Clarkesville GA 30523 **Fax Area Code:* 800 ■ *TF:* 800-640-6812 ■ *Web:* www.habershamemc.com	706-754-2114	640-6813*	245
Habersham Funding LLC 3495 Piedmont Rd NE Ste 910 ... Atlanta GA 30305 *TF:* 888-874-2402 ■ *Web:* www.habershamfunding.com	404-233-8275	233-9394	796
Habersham Metal Products Co 264 Stapleton Rd ... Cornelia GA 30531 *TF:* 800-592-8066 ■ *Web:* www.habershammetal.com	706-778-2212	778-2769	234
Habib American Bank 99 Madison Ave ... New York NY 10016 *Web:* www.habbank.com	212-532-4444		70
Habitat Company LLC, The 350 W Hubbard St Ste 500 ... Chicago IL 60610 *Web:* www.habitat.com	312-527-5400	527-7440	652
Habitat for Humanity International Inc 121 Habitat St ... Americus GA 31709 *TF:* 800-422-4828 ■ *Web:* www.habitat.org	229-924-6935	924-6541	48-5
Habitat Housewares 3801 Old Seward Hwy Ste 7 ... Anchorage AK 99503 *TF:* 800-770-1856 ■ *Web:* www.habitathousewares.com	907-561-1856		362
Habitat Suites 500 E Highland Mall Blvd ... Austin TX 78752 *TF:* 800-535-4663 ■ *Web:* www.habitatsuites.com	512-467-6000	467-6000	379
Habitec Security Inc 2926 S Republic Blvd ... Toledo OH 43615 *TF:* 888-422-4832 ■ *Web:* www.habitecsecurity.com	419-537-6768		693
Habush Habush & Rottier S C US Bank Ctr 777 E Wisconsin Ave Ste 2300 ... Milwaukee WI 53202 *Web:* habush.com	414-271-0900		445
HAC (Housing Assistance Council) 1025 Vermont Ave NW Ste 606 ... Washington DC 20005 *TF:* 866-234-2689 ■ *Web:* www.ruralhome.org	202-842-8600	347-3441	48-5
HACC (Howell Area Chamber of Commerce) 123 E Washington St ... Howell MI 48843 *TF:* 800-292-9555 ■ *Web:* www.howell.org	517-546-3920	546-4115	139
HACC (Hellenic-American Chamber of Commerce) 370 Lexington Ave 27th Fl ... New York NY 10017 *Web:* www.hellenicamerican.cc	212-629-6380	564-9281	138
Hach Co PO Box 389 ... Loveland CO 80539 *TF:* 800-227-4224 ■ *Web:* www.hach.com	970-669-3050	669-2932	419
Hachette Book Group 237 Pk Ave ... New York NY 10017 *TF:* 800-759-0190 ■ *Web:* www.hachettebookgroup.com	800-759-0190	331-1664	637-2
HACI Mechanical Contractors Inc 2108 W Shangri La Rd ... Phoenix AZ 85029 *Web:* www.hacimechanical.com	602-944-1555	678-0266	189-10
Hacienda del Sol Guest Ranch Resort 5501 N Hacienda Del Sol Rd ... Tucson AZ 85718 *TF:* 800-728-6514 ■ *Web:* www.haciendadelsol.com	520-299-1501		669
Hacienda Hotel 525 N Sepulveda Blvd ... El Segundo CA 90245	310-615-0015		379
Hacienda Mexican Restaurant 711 N First Ave ... Evansville IN 47710 *Web:* www.haciendafiesta.com	812-423-6355		671
Hacienda Mexican Restaurants 1501 N Ironwood Dr ... South Bend IN 46635 *TF:* 800-541-3227 ■ *Web:* www.haciendafiesta.com	800-541-3227		670
Hacienda Restaurant 102 McLean Blvd ... Paterson NJ 07514 *Web:* haciendanj.com	973-345-1255		671
Hacienda The at Hotel Santa Fe 1501 Paseo del Peralta ... Santa Fe NM 87501 *TF:* 855 825-9876 ■ *Web:* www.hotelsantafe.com/the_hacienda	505-955-7805		379
Hacienda, The 1725 College Ave ... Santa Ana CA 92706 *Web:* tivoliterrace.com/wedding-packages	714-558-1304		671
Hack Piro 30 Columbia Tpke PO Box 168 ... Florham Park NJ 07932 *Web:* www.hpomlaw.com	973-301-6500		445
Hackbarth Delivery Service Inc 3504 Brookdale Dr N ... Mobile AL 36618 *TF:* 800-277-3322 ■ *Web:* www.hackbarthdelivery.com	251-478-1401		314
Hackensack University Medical Ctr 30 Prospect Ave ... Hackensack NJ 07601 *Web:* hackensackumc.org	201-996-2000		374-3
Hacker Group Inc 1215 Fourth Ave Ste 2100 ... Seattle WA 98161 *Web:* hal2l.com	206-805-1500	805-1599	7
Hacker Johnson & Smith PA 500 N Wshore Blvd Ste 1000 ... Tampa FL 33609 *TF:* 800-366-7126 ■ *Web:* www.hackerjohnson.com	813-286-2424		2
Hacklebarney State Park 119 Hacklebarney Rd 119 Hacklebarney Rd ... Long Valley NJ 07853 *TF:* 800-659-4044 ■ *Web:* www.njparksandforests.org	908-638-6969		565
Hackley School 293 Benedict Ave ... Tarrytown NY 10591 *Web:* www.hackleyschool.org	914-631-0128		622
Hackney 911 W Fifth St PO Box 880 ... Washington NC 27889 *TF:* 800-763-0700 ■ *Web:* www.hackneyandsons.com	252-946-6521	975-8340	516
Hackney Ladish Inc 400 E Willow ... Enid OK 73701 *Web:* www.hackney.com	580-237-4212		608
Hackworth Reprographics 1700 Liberty St ... Chesapeake VA 23324 *TF:* 800-676-2424 ■ *Web:* www.hackworth.co	757-545-7675		113

Name / Address	City	State	ZIP	Phone	Fax	Class
HACU (Hispanic Assn of Colleges & Universities) 8415 Datapoint Dr Ste 400	San Antonio	TX	78229	210-692-3805	692-0823	49-5
TF: 800-780-4228 ■ *Web:* www.hacu.net						
Hadady Corp 510 W 172nd St	South Holland	IL	60473	708-596-5168	596-7563	621
Web: www.hadadycorp.com						
Haddad Restaurant Group Inc 4717 Grand Ave Ste 200	Kansas City	MO	64112	816-931-2261	931-9044	670
Haddox Reid Burkes & Calhoun PLLC PO Box 22507	Jackson	MS	39225	601-948-2924		2
Web: www.haddoxreid.com						
Haddrell's Point Tackle & Supply 47 Windermere Blvd	Charleston	SC	29407	843-573-3474		711
TF: 800-881-5201 ■ *Web:* www.haddrellspoint.com						
HadenStanziale PA 2200 W Main St Ste 560	Durham	NC	27705	919-286-7440		727
Web: www.hadenstanziale.com						
Hader/Seitz Inc 15600 W Lincoln Ave	New Berlin	WI	53151	877-388-2101		223
TF: 877-388-2101 ■ *Web:* www.haderind.com/seitz.htm						
Hadley Capital 1200 Central Ave Ste 300 Chase Bank Bldg	Wilmette	IL	60091	847-906-5300	906-5301	528
Web: www.hadleycapital.com						
Hadley Exhibits Inc 1700 Elmwood Ave	Buffalo	NY	14207	716-874-3666	874-9994	232
TF: 800-962-8088 ■ *Web:* hadleyexhibitsinc.com						
Hadley House Company PO Box 245	Madison Lake	MN	56063	952-983-8208	243-3698*	637-10
**Fax Area Code:* 507 ■ *TF:* 800-423-5390 ■ *Web:* www.hadleyhouse.com						
Hadron Technologies Inc 4941 Allison St Ste 15	Arvada	CO	80002	303-431-7798	431-6168	249
Web: www.hadrontechnologies.com						
Hadronics Inc 4570 Steel Pl	Cincinnati	OH	45209	513-321-9350		481
TF: 800-829-0826 ■ *Web:* www.hadronics.com						
Hadwen House 96 Main St	Nantucket	MA	02554	508-228-1894		50-3
Web: www.nha.org						
HAECO Americas 10262 Norris Ave	Pacoima	CA	91331	818-896-2938		319-3
Web: www.haeco.aero						
Haefele Tv Inc 24 E Tioga St	Spencer	NY	14883	607-589-6235		116
Web: www.htva.net						
Haemonetics Corp 400 Wood Rd	Braintree	MA	02184	781-848-7100	860-1512*	476
NYSE: HAE ■ **Fax Area Code:* 800 ■ *TF:* 800-225-5242 ■ *Web:* www.haemonetics.com						
Haemotec Inc 383 Joseph Carrier	Vaudreuil-Dorion	QC	J7V5V5	450-424-3615		231
Haena State Park 3060 Eiwa St Ste 306	Lihue	HI	96766	808-274-3444	274-3448	565
Web: dlnr.hawaii.gov/dsp/parks/kauai/haena-state-park						
Hafele America Company Inc 3901 Cheyenne Dr	Archdale	NC	27263	336-889-2322	325-6197*	491
**Fax Area Code:* 800 ■ *TF Cust Svc:* 800-423-3531 ■ *Web:* www.hafele.com						
Hafetz & Assoc LLC 609 New Rd	Linwood	NJ	08221	609-872-0001		390
Web: hafetzandassociates.com						
Haffenreffer Museum of Anthropology 300 Tower St	Bristol	RI	02809	401-253-8388	253-1198	520
Web: www.brown.edu						
Hagadone Printing Company Inc 274 Puuhale Rd	Honolulu	HI	96819	808-847-5310		626
Web: www.hagadoneprinting.com						
Hagan Kennington Oil 9250 S Carolina 9	Nichols	SC	29581	843-392-1300		579
Hagedorn Inc 1924 Broadway St Ste B	Vancouver	WA	98663	360-696-4428		727
Hagemeyer North America Inc 1460 Tobias Gadson Blvd	Charleston	SC	29407	843-745-2400	745-6942	385
TF: 877-462-7070 ■ *Web:* www.hagemeyerna.com						
Hagen Streiff Newton Oshiro PC 15601 Dallas Pkwy Ste 1050	Addison	TX	75001	972-980-5060		2
Web: www.hsno.com						
Hagen Wilka & Archer LLP 600 S Main Ave Ste 102	Sioux Falls	SD	57104	605-334-0005		428
Web: hwalaw.com						
Hagens Berman Sobol Shapiro LLP 1918 Eighth Ave Ste 3300	Seattle	WA	98101	206-623-7292		428
Web: www.hbsslaw.com						
Hager Co 139 Victor St	Saint Louis	MO	63104	314-772-4400	782-0149*	350
**Fax Area Code:* 800 ■ **Fax:* Sales ■ *TF:* 800-325-9995 ■ *Web:* www.hagerco.com						
Hager Sharp Inc 1030 15th St NW Ste 600 E	Washington	DC	20005	202-842-3600		636
Web: www.hagersharp.com						
Hagerman & Company Inc 505 Sunset Ct	Mount Zion	IL	62549	217-864-2326		809
TF: 800-755-5000 ■ *Web:* www.hagerman.com						
Hagerman Fossil Beds National Monument 221 N State St PO Box 570	Hagerman	ID	83332	208-933-4100	837-4857	564
Web: www.nps.gov						
Hagerman Inc 510 W Washington Blvd	Fort Wayne	IN	46802	260-424-1470		177
Web: www.thehagermangroup.com						
Hagerstown Community College 11400 Robinwood Dr	Hagerstown	MD	21742	301-790-2800	791-9165*	162
**Fax:* Admissions ■ *Web:* www.hagerstowncc.edu						
Hagerstown/Washington County Convention & Visitors Bureau 16 Public Sq	Hagerstown	MD	21740	301-791-3246	791-2601	206
TF: 888-257-2600 ■ *Web:* www.visithagerstown.com						
Hagerstown-Washington County Chamber of Commerce 28 W Washington St	Hagerstown	MD	21740	301-739-2015	739-1278	139
TF: 800-520-6685 ■ *Web:* www.hagerstown.org						
Hagerty Insurance Agency LLC 141 River's Edge Dr Ste 200 PO Box 1303	Traverse City	MI	49684	800-922-4050	941-8227*	391-4
**Fax Area Code:* 231 ■ *TF:* 877-922-9701 ■ *Web:* www.hagerty.com						
Hagerty Peterson & Company LLC 421 N Northwest Hwy Ste 201	Barrington	IL	60010	847-277-9900		401
Web: www.hagertypeterson.com						
Hagerty Steel & Aluminum Co 601 N Main	East Peoria	IL	61611	309-699-7251		697
TF: 800-322-2600 ■ *Web:* www.hagertysteel.com						
Hagey Coach & Tours Nrt 210 Schoolhouse Rd	Souderton	PA	18964	215-723-4381		760
TF: 800-544-2439 ■ *Web:* hagey.com						
Haggar Clothing Co 11511 Luna Rd 2 Colinas Crossing	Dallas	TX	75234	214-352-8481	956-4561	155-12
TF: 877-841-2219 ■ *Web:* www.haggar.com						
Haggard & Stocking Assoc 5318 Victory Dr	Indianapolis	IN	46203	317-788-4661	788-1645	385
TF: 800-622-4824 ■ *Web:* www.haggard-stocking.com						
Haggen Inc 2900 Woburn St	Bellingham	WA	98226	360-676-5300		345
TF: 800-995-1902 ■ *Web:* www.haggen.com						
Haggerty Enterprises Inc 370 Kimberly Dr	Carol Stream	IL	60188	630-315-3300		334
TF: 800-336-5282 ■ *Web:* www.lavalamp.com						
Haggin Museum, The 1201 N Pershing Ave	Stockton	CA	95203	209-940-6300	462-1404	520
Web: www.hagginmuseum.org						
Hagie Manufacturing Co 721 Central Ave W	Clarion	IA	50525	515-532-2861	532-3553	273
TF: 800-247-4885 ■ *Web:* www.hagie.com						
Hagle Lumber Company Inc 3100 Somis Rd PO Box 120	Somis	CA	93066	805-987-3887	987-7564	191-3
Web: www.haglelumber.com						
Hagley Museum & Library 298 Buck Rd E	Greenville	DE	19807	302-658-2400	658-0568	520
Web: www.hagley.org						
Hagopian & Sons Inc 14000 W 8 Mile Rd	Oak Park	MI	48237	248-399-2323		290
TF: 800-424-6742 ■ *Web:* www.originalhagopian.com						
HAGR (Hamilton Grange National Memorial) 122 St Riverside Dr	New York	NY	10027	212-666-1640		564
TF: 800-246-8872 ■ *Web:* www.nps.gov/hagr						
Hague Sahady & Company PC 126 President Ave Ste 201	Fall River	MA	02720	508-675-7889		2
Web: hague-sahady.com						
Hagyard-Davidson-McGee Assoc PSC 4250 Iron Works Pike	Lexington	KY	40511	859-255-8741	253-0196	11-2
TF: 888-323-7798 ■ *Web:* www.hagyard.com						
Hahl Inc 126 Glassmaster Rd	Lexington	SC	29072	803-359-0706		596
Hahn & Bowersock Corp 151 Kalmus Dr Ste L1	Costa Mesa	CA	92626	800-660-3187		445
TF: 800-660-3187 ■ *Web:* www.hahnbowersock.com						
Hahn Automotive Warehouse Inc 415 W Main St	Rochester	NY	14608	585-235-1595		61
Web: www.hahnauto.com						
Hahn Capital Management LLC 601 Montgomery St Ste 840	San Francisco	CA	94111	415-394-6512		401
Web: www.hahncap.com						
Hahn Engineering Inc 3060 S Dale Mabry Hwy	Tampa	FL	33629	813-831-8599		261
Web: www.hahneng.com						
Hahn Loeser & Parks LLP 200 Public Sq Ste 2800	Cleveland	OH	44114	216-621-0150	241-2824	445
Web: www.hahnlaw.com						
Hahn Manufacturing Co 5332 Hamilton Ave	Cleveland	OH	44114	216-391-9300		757
Web: www.hahnmfg.com						
Hahn Supply Inc 2101 Main St	Lewiston	ID	83501	208-743-1577		612
TF: 800-444-4246 ■ *Web:* www.hahnsupply.com						
Hahn Systems LLC 8416 Zionsville Rd	Indianapolis	IN	46268	317-243-3796	244-9079	385
TF: 800-201-4246 ■ *Web:* www.hahnsystems.com						
Hahnel Bros Co (HBC) 46 Strawberry Ave PO Box 1160	Lewiston	ME	04243	207-784-6477		189-12
TF: 800-448-7663 ■ *Web:* www.hahnelbrosco.com						
Hahnemann University Hospital 230 N Broad St	Philadelphia	PA	19102	215-762-7000		374-3
TF: 800-290-0836 ■ *Web:* www.hahnemannhospital.com						
HAI (Hightech American Industrial Laboratories Inc) 320 Massachusetts Ave	Lexington	MA	02420	781-862-9884	860-7722	477
Web: www.hailabs.com						
HAI (Helicopter Assn International) 1635 Prince St	Alexandria	VA	22314	703-683-4646	683-4745	49-21
TF: 800-435-4976 ■ *Web:* www.rotor.org						
HAI (Hohman Assoc Inc) 6951 W Little York	Houston	TX	77040	713-896-0978	896-9419	48-2
TF: 800-324-0978 ■ *Web:* www.hohmanassociates.com						
Haida Corp PO Box 89	Hydaburg	AK	99922	907-285-3721		752
TF: 800-478-3721 ■ *Web:* haidacorporation.com						
Haidar Capital Management LLC Carnegie Hall Tower 152 W 57th St	New York	NY	10019	212-752-5077		401
Web: www.haidarcapital.com						
Haig's Quality Printing 6360 Sunset Corporate Dr	Las Vegas	NV	89120	702-966-1000		627
TF: 800-691-7164 ■ *Web:* www.haigsprinting.com						
Haight Brown & Bonesteel LLP 555 S Flower St	Los Angeles	CA	90071	213-542-8000	542-8100	428
Web: www.hbblaw.com						
Haiku Poetic Food & Art 800 N High St	Columbus	OH	43215	614-294-8168	294-3868	671
Web: haikucolumbus.com						
Hail & Cotton Inc 2500 S Main St	Springfield	TN	37172	615-384-9576		756
TF: 800-561-7710 ■ *Web:* www.hailcotton.com						
Hailey, McNamara, Hall, Larmann & Papale LLP 1 Galleria Blvd Ste 1400	Metairie	LA	70001	504-836-6500		428
Web: www.hmhlp.com						
Hain Celestial Group Inc 4600 Sleepytime Dr	Boulder	CO	80301	877-612-4246		297-11
NASDAQ: HAIN ■ *TF:* 877-612-4246 ■ *Web:* www.hain-celestial.com						
Hainen Ford Inc 800 Hwy 5 S	Tipton	MO	65081	660-433-5545		57
Web: hainenford.com						
Haines & Company Inc 8050 Freedom Ave	North Canton	OH	44720	800-843-8452		637-6
TF: 800-843-8452 ■ *Web:* www.haines.com						
Haines Borough 103 Third Ave S PO Box 1209	Haines	AK	99827	907-766-2231	766-2716	338
TF: 800-572-8006 ■ *Web:* www.hainesalaska.gov						
Haines Centre for Strategic Management 1420 Monitor Rd	San Diego	CA	92110	619-275-6528		463
Web: hainescentre.com						
Haines City Citrus Growers Assn (HCCGA) 8 Railroad Ave PO Box 337	Haines City	FL	33844	863-422-1174		11-1
TF Sales: 800-327-6676 ■ *Web:* www.hilltopcitrus.com						

Name / Address	City	State	Zip	Phone	Fax	Class
Hair Club for Men LTD Inc 1515 S Federal Hwy Ste 401 *Web:* www.hairclub.com	Boca Raton	FL	33432	561-361-7600		77
Hair It Is 977 Perry Hwy Ste 4	Pittsburgh	PA	15237	412-366-5511		77
Hairart International Inc 400 W 157th St *Web:* hairartinc.com	Gardena	CA	90248	818-905-7730		77
Haiti						
Consulate General 220 S State St Ste 2110 *TF:* 800-860-8610 ■ *Web:* www.haitianconsulate.org	Chicago	IL	60604	312-922-4004	922-7122	257
Consulate General 815 Second Ave 6th Fl *Web:* www.embassypages.com/missions/embassy21725	New York	NY	10017	212-697-9767		257
Consulate General 259 SW 13th St *Web:* haiti.org	Miami	FL	33130	305-859-2003	854-7441	257
Consulate General 545 Boylston St Rm 201	Boston	MA	02116	617-266-3660	778-6898	257
Embassy 2311 Massachusetts Ave NW *TF:* 800-265-6723 ■ *Web:* www.haiti.org	Washington	DC	20008	202-332-4090	745-7215	257
Haitian American Community Development 181 NE 82 St Ste 2 *Web:* www.haitianamericancdc.org	Miami	FL	33138	305-759-2542		194
Hajoca Corp 127 Coulter Ave **Fax Area Code:* 505 ■ *TF:* 888-328-2383 ■ *Web:* www.hajoca.com	Ardmore	PA	19003	610-649-1430	884-2455*	612
Hajoca Corp Keenan Supply Div 127 Coulter Ave *Web:* www.hajoca.com	Ardmore	PA	19003	610-649-1430	649-1798	612
Hakanson Anderson Assoc Inc 3601 Thurston Ave *Web:* www.haa-inc.com	Anoka	MN	55303	763-427-5860		261
Hakim Optical Laboratory Ltd 128 Hazelton Ave *Web:* www.hakimoptical.ca	Toronto	ON	M5R2E5	416-924-5600		543
HAKS Engineers PC 40 Wall St *Web:* www.haks.net	New York	NY	10005	212-747-1997		261
Hal & Mal's 200 S Commerce St *Web:* www.halandmals.com	Jackson	MS	39201	601-948-0888		671
HAL Communications Corp 1201 W Kenyon Rd PO Box 365 *Web:* www.halcomm.com	Urbana	IL	61803	217-367-7373	367-1701	647
Hal Hays Construction Inc 4181 Latham St *Web:* www.halhays.com	Riverside	CA	92501	951-788-0703	275-0752	302
HAL Inc 11109 Cutten Rd Ste 200 *Web:* www.hal-inc.com	Houston	TX	77066	281-260-8101		177
Hal Leonard Corp 960 E Mark St *TF:* 800-321-3408 ■ *Web:* www.halleonard.com	Winona	MN	55987	507-454-2920		637-7
Hal Lewis Group 1700 Market St 6th Fl *Web:* www.hlg.com	Philadelphia	PA	19103	215-563-4461		4
Hal Smith Restaurant Group Inc 3101 W Tecumseh Rd *TF:* 800-333-9566 ■ *Web:* www.ehsrg.com	Norman	OK	73072	405-321-2600		670
Hal's on Old Ivy 30 Old Ivy Rd *Web:* www.hals.net	Atlanta	GA	30342	404-261-0025		671
Halabi Inc 2100 Huntington Dr *TF:* 800-660-4167 ■ *Web:* www.duracite.com	Fairfield	CA	94533	707-402-1600		115
Halbert Construction Company Inc 330 S Magnolia Ave Ste 203 *TF:* 800-724-2969 ■ *Web:* www.halbertco.com	El Cajon	CA	92020	619-593-3527		188
Halbrecht Lieberman Assoc Inc 32 Surf Rd *Web:* www.hlassoc.com	Westport	CT	06880	203-222-4890	222-4895	266
Halbrook & Miller Inc 2307 Springlake Rd Ste 110 *Web:* tmtel.com	Carrollton	TX	75006	972-243-4772		246
HALCO Industries LLC 1015 Norcross Industrial Ct *Web:* www.halcolubricants.com	Norcross	GA	30071	770-840-3480		579
Halco Products 100 Gordon St *Web:* www.halco-products.com	Elk Grove Village	IL	60007	847-956-1600		186
Haldeman-Homme Inc 430 Industrial Blvd NE	Minneapolis	MN	55413	612-331-4880		320
Halden Group, The 5948 Harbour Park Dr *Web:* www.haldengroup.com	Midlothian	VA	23112	804-595-2295		177
Hale Centre Theater 3333 S Decker Lake Dr *Web:* www.hct.org	West Valley City	UT	84119	801-984-9000	984-9009	572
Hale County 1001 Main St Rm 18 PO Box 100 *Web:* www.halecoso.com	Greensboro	AL	36744	334-624-3081	624-0218	338
Hale County 500 Broadway Rm 140 *Web:* whc.net	Plainview	TX	79072	806-291-5261		338
Hale County Board of Education 1115 Powers St *Web:* www.halek12.org	Greensboro	AL	36744	334-624-8836		685
Hale Ctr Theater Orem 225 W 400 N *TF:* 800-746-9882 ■ *Web:* www.haletheater.org	Orem	UT	84057	801-226-8600	852-3189	572
Hale Farm & Village 2686 Oakhill Rd PO Box 296 *TF:* 877-425-3327 ■ *Web:* westernreservepublicmedia.org	Bath	OH	44210	330-666-3711		520
Hale Group Ltd, The 8 Cherry St *Web:* www.halegroup.com	Danvers	MA	01923	978-777-9077		463
Hale Products Inc 700 Spring Mill Ave **Fax:* Cust Svc ■ *TF:* 800-220-4253 ■ *Web:* www.haleproducts.com	Conshohocken	PA	19428	610-825-6300	825-6440*	641
Hale Trailer Brake & Wheel Inc Rt 73 & Cooper Rd *TF:* 800-232-6535 ■ *Web:* www.haletrailer.com	Voorhees	NJ	08043	856-768-1330		126
Haleakala National Park PO Box 369 *Web:* www.nps.gov	Makawao	HI	96768	808-572-4400	572-1304	564
Halekii-Pihana Heiau State Monument 54 S High St Rm 101 *Web:* dlnr.hawaii.gov/dsp	Wailuku	HI	96793	808-984-8109	984-8111	565
Halekulani Hotel 2199 Kalia Rd *TF:* 800-367-2343 ■ *Web:* www.halekulani.com	Honolulu	HI	96815	808-923-2311	926-8004	379
Hales Machine Tool Inc 2730 Niagara Ln N *Web:* halesmachinetool.com	Minneapolis	MN	55447	763-553-1711		358
Halex Co 23901 Aurora Rd **Fax Area Code:* 440 ■ *TF:* 800-749-3261 ■ *Web:* www.halexco.com	Bedford Heights	OH	44146	800-749-3261	439-1792*	308
Haley & Aldrich Inc 465 Medford St Ste 2200 *TF:* 800-899-2573 ■ *Web:* www.haleyaldrich.com	Boston	MA	02129	617-886-7400	886-7600	261
Haley Bros Inc 6291 Orangethorpe Ave *TF:* 800-854-5951 ■ *Web:* www.haleybros.com	Buena Park	CA	90620	714-670-2112	994-6971	236
Haley Construction Inc 9 Aviator Way *Web:* rescongroup.com	Ormond Beach	FL	32174	386-944-0470		186
Haley Farm State Park c/o Ft Trumbull State Pk 90 Walbach St *Web:* www.ct.gov	New London	CT	06320	860-444-7591		565
Haley Industries Ltd 634 Magnesium Rd	Haley	ON	K0J1Y0	613-432-8841		21
Haley Marketing Group 6028 Sheridan Dr *Web:* www.haleymarketing.com	Buffalo	NY	14221	716-631-8981		195
Haley Miranda Group 8654 Washington Blvd *Web:* www.haleymiranda.com	Culver City	CA	90232	310-842-7369		4
Haley-Greer Inc 2257 -C Lombardy Ln *Web:* www.haleygreer.com	Dallas	TX	75220	972-556-1177	556-1384	186
Haleyville Drapery Manufacturing Co 1050 Hill Ave	Haleyville	AL	35565	205-486-9257		746
Half Hitch Tackle Company Inc 2206 Thomas Dr *TF:* 888-668-9810 ■ *Web:* www.halfhitch.com	Panama City	FL	32408	850-234-2621		711
Half Hollow Hills Community Library 55 Vanderbilt Pkwy *Web:* hhhlibrary.org	Dix Hills	NY	11746	631-421-4530		434-3
Half Moon Bay Lodge & Conference Ctr 2400 S Cabrillo Hwy *TF:* 800-710-0778 ■ *Web:* pacificahotels.com/halfmoonbaylodge	Half Moon Bay	CA	94019	650-726-9000	726-7951	379
Half Moon Bay State Beach c/o San Mateo Coast Sector Office 95 Kelly Ave *TF:* 800-444-7275 ■ *Web:* www.parks.ca.gov	Half Moon Bay	CA	94019	650-726-8819	726-8816	565
Half Moon Outfitters 15 E Broughton St *Web:* www.recarts.com	Savannah	GA	31401	912-201-9393		711
Half Moon Pond State Park 1621 Black Pond Rd *Web:* www.vtstateparks.com/htm/halfmoon.cfm	Fair Haven	VT	05743	802-273-2848		565
Half Price Books Records & Magazines Inc 5803 E Northwest Hwy *Web:* www.hpb.com	Dallas	TX	75231	214-360-0833	379-8010	95
Half Yard Productions LLC 4922 Fairmont Ave Ste 300 *Web:* www.halfyardproductions.com	Bethesda	MD	20814	240-223-3400		514
Halfacre Construction Co 7015 Professional Pkwy E *TF:* 800-741-3114 ■ *Web:* www.halfacreconstruction.com	Sarasota	FL	34240	941-907-9099		186
Halfaker & Associates LLC 2900 S Quincy St Ste 410 *Web:* www.halfakerandassociates.com	Arlington	VA	22206	703-434-3900		225
Halff Assoc Inc 1201 N Bowser Rd *Web:* www.halff.com	Richardson	TX	75081	214-346-6200	739-0095	261
Halibut Point State Park Gott Ave *Web:* www.mass.gov	Rockport	MA	01966	978-546-2997		565
Halifax Community College 100 College Dr *TF:* 800-228-8443 ■ *Web:* www.halifaxcc.edu	Weldon	NC	27890	252-536-2551	536-4144	162
Halifax County 33 S Granville St *Web:* www.halifaxnc.com	Halifax	NC	27839	252-583-1131	583-9921	338
Halifax County 134 S Main St *Web:* www.halifaxcountyva.gov	Halifax	VA	24558	434-476-3300	476-3384	338
Halifax County Chamber of Commerce 820 Bruce St PO Box 399 *Web:* www.halifaxchamber.net	South Boston	VA	24592	434-572-3085		139
Halifax County Library System PO Box 537 *Web:* www.halifaxnc.libguides.com	Scotland Neck	NC	27839	252-583-3631	583-8661	434-3
Halifax County Public Schools 1030 Mary Bethune St PO Box 1849 *TF:* 800-422-2083 ■ *Web:* www.halifax.k12.va.us	Halifax	VA	24558	434-476-2171	476-1858	685
Halifax Electric Membership Corp 208 Whitfield St *TF:* 800-690-0522 ■ *Web:* www.halifaxemc.com	Enfield	NC	27823	252-445-5111		245
Halifax Historical Museum 252 S Beach St *TF:* 800-677-6884 ■ *Web:* www.halifaxhistorical.org	Daytona Beach	FL	32114	386-255-6976	255-7605	520
Halifax Marriott Harborfront Hotel 1919 Upper Water St *TF:* 800-450-4442 ■ *Web:* www.marriott.com	Halifax	NS	B3J3J5	902-421-1700	422-5805	379
Halifax Port Authority 1215 Marginal Rd PO Box 336 *Web:* www.portofhalifax.ca	Halifax	NS	B3J2P6	902-426-8222	426-7335	618
Halifax Regional Health System (HRHS) 2204 Wilborn Ave *Web:* www.sentara.com	South Boston	VA	24592	434-517-3100		374-3
Halifax Regional Medical Ctr 250 Smith Church Rd *Web:* halifaxregional.org	Roanoke Rapids	NC	27870	252-535-8011	535-8466	374-3
Halifax Stanfield International Airport (HIAA) 1 Bell Blvd *Web:* halifaxstanfield.ca	Enfield	NS	B2T1K2	902-873-4422	873-4750	27
Hall & Evans 1001 17th St Ste 300 *Web:* www.hallevans.com	Denver	CO	80202	303-628-3300		428
Hall & Foreman Inc 17782 E 17th St Ste 200 *Web:* www.hfinc.com	Tustin	CA	92780	714-665-4500		261
Hall Automotive LLC 441 Viking Dr *Web:* www.hallauto.com	Virginia Beach	VA	23452	757-431-9944		57

				Phone	Fax	Class
Hall Capital Partners LLC 1 Maritime Plaza 5th Fl *Web:* www.hallcapital.com	San Francisco	CA	94111	415-288-0544		401
Hall Communications Inc 404 W Lime St *Web:* www.hallradio.com	Lakeland	FL	33815	863-682-8184		643
Hall Contracting Corp 6415 Lakeview Rd *Web:* hallcontracting.com	Charlotte	NC	28269	704-598-0818		188-10
Hall County 225 Green St SE *TF:* 800-735-4271 ■ *Web:* www.hallcounty.org	Gainesville	GA	30501	770-531-7025	531-7070	338
County Courthouse 512 Main St Ste 1 *Web:* www.texasfile.com	Memphis	TX	79245	806-259-2627	259-5078	338
Hall County Schools 711 Green St NW Ste 100 *TF:* 866-632-9992 ■ *Web:* www.hallco.org	Gainesville	GA	30501	770-534-1080	535-7404	685
Hall Family Foundation PO Box 419580 MD 323 *Web:* www.hallfamilyfoundation.org	Kansas City	MO	64141	816-274-8516	274-8547	305
HALL Group 2323 Ross Ave Ste 100 *Web:* www.hallfinancial.com	Dallas	TX	75201	214-269-9500		655
Hall Hodges & Associates Inc 700 N Brand Blvd Ste 650 *TF:* 800-490-1447 ■ *Web:* hall-hodges.com	Glendale	CA	91203	818-244-8930		463
Hall Industries Inc 514 Mecklem Ln *Web:* hallindustries.com	Ellwood City	PA	16117	724-752-2000	758-1558	621
Hall Kistler & Company LLP 220 Market Ave S Ste 700 *Web:* www.hallkistler.com	Canton	OH	44702	330-453-7633		2
Hall Laughlin China Co 672 Fiesta Dr *Fax Area Code: 800 ■ *TF:* 800-452-4462 ■ *Web:* www.hlcdinnerware.com/hall_china	Newell	WV	26050	330-385-2900	533-8918*	730
Hall Letter Shop Inc 5200 Rosedale Hwy *Web:* www.hallprintmail.com	Bakersfield	CA	93308	661-327-3228		627
Hall Manufacturing Corp 297 Margaret King Ave *Web:* www.hallmanufacturing.com	Ringwood	NJ	07456	973-962-6022		596
Hall Mark Global Technologies Inc 262 Chapman Rd Ste 101 *Web:* www.hgtechinc.net	Newark	DE	19702	302-366-8960		177
Hall of Flame Museum of Firefighting 6101 E Van Buren St *Web:* www.hallofflame.org	Phoenix	AZ	85008	602-275-3473	275-0896	520
Hall Render Killian Heath & Lyman Pc 1 American Sq Ste 2000 Ste 2000 *Web:* www.hallrender.com	Indianapolis	IN	46282	317-633-4884	633-4878	428
Hall Signs Inc 4495 W Vernal Pk *Fax Area Code: 812 ■ *TF:* 800-284-7446 ■ *Web:* www.hallsigns.com	Bloomington	IN	47404	800-284-7446	332-9816*	701
Hall, Estill, Hardwick, Gable, Golden & Nelson PC 320 S Boston Ave Ste 200 *Web:* www.hallestill.com	Tulsa	OK	74103	918-594-0400		428
Hallamore Motor Transportation Inc 795 Plymouth St *Fax Area Code: 920 ■ *TF:* 800-242-1300 ■ *Web:* www.hallamore.com	Holbrook	MA	02343	781-767-2000	683-6277*	780
Hallandale Beach Chamber of Commerce 400 S Federal Hwy Ste 192 *Web:* www.hallandalebeachchamber.com	Hallandale Beach	FL	33009	954-454-0541	454-0930	139
Hallcon Corp 3280 Bloor St W Ste 250 *Web:* hallcon.com	Toronto	ON	M8X2X3	416-964-9191		393
Hallcrest Inc 1820 Pickwick Ln *Web:* www.hallcrest.com	Glenview	IL	60026	847-998-8580	998-6866	202
Haller Enterprises Inc 212 Bucky Dr *Web:* www.hallerent.com	Lititz	PA	17543	717-207-9813		610
Hallett & Perrin PC 1445 Ross Ave Ste 2400 *Web:* www.hallettperrin.com	Dallas	TX	75202	214-953-0053	922-4142	445
Halliburton Energy Services 10200 Bellaire Blvd *Web:* www.halliburton.com	Houston	TX	77072	281-871-4000		538
Halliburton House Inn 5184 Morris St *TF:* 888-512-3344 ■ *Web:* www.thehalliburton.com	Halifax	NS	B3J1B3	902-420-0658	423-2324	379
Halliburton Investor Relations 14651 Dallas Pkwy Ste 800 *TF:* 800-727-8643 ■ *Web:* halliburtonir.com	Dallas	TX	75254	972-458-8000		636
Halliburton Screen Co 3000 N Sam Houston Pkwy E *NYSE: HAL* ■ *Web:* www.halliburton.com	Houston	TX	77032	281-871-4000		688
Hallie Ford Museum of Art 700 State St *TF:* 844-232-7228 ■ *Web:* willamette.edu/arts/hfma	Salem	OR	97301	503-370-6855	375-5458	520
Hallman Lindsay Paints Inc 1717 N Bristol St *Web:* www.hallmanlindsay.com	Sun Prairie	WI	53590	608-834-8844	837-1064	550
Hallmark Cards Inc 2501 McGee St *TF:* 800-425-5627 ■ *Web:* www.hallmark.com	Kansas City	MO	64108	816-274-5111		130
Hallmark Ch 12700 Ventura Blvd Ste 200 *TF:* 888-390-7474 ■ *Web:* www.hallmarkchannel.com	Studio City	CA	91604	818-755-2400		740
Hallmark Corp Foundation 2501 McGee St *TF:* 800-425-5627 ■ *Web:* corporate.hallmark.com	Kansas City	MO	64108	800-425-5627		304
Hallmark Financial Services Inc 777 Main St Ste 1000 *NASDAQ: HALL* ■ *Web:* www.hallmarkgrp.com	Fort Worth	TX	76102	817-348-1600		360-4
Hallmark Inns & Resorts 15455 Hallmark Dr Ste 200 *TF:* 888-448-4449 ■ *Web:* www.hallmarkinns.com	Lake Oswego	OR	97035	503-635-4555		379
Hallmark International PO Box 419034 *TF:* 800-425-5627 ■ *Web:* www.hallmark.com	Kansas City	MO	64141	816-274-5111		130
Hallmark Nameplate Inc 1717 E Lincoln Ave *TF:* 800-874-9063 ■ *Web:* www.hallmarknameplate.com	Mount Dora	FL	32757	352-383-8142		701
Hallmark Pharmacy 1316 Sycamore School Rd Ste 130	Fort Worth	TX	76134	817-293-2441		237
Hallmark, The 2960 N Lake Shore Dr *TF:* 800-254-9442 ■ *Web:* brookdale.com	Chicago	IL	60657	773-880-2960		672
Halloran & Sage Llp 1 Goodwin Sq *TF:* 800-826-3579 ■ *Web:* halloransage.com	Hartford	CT	06103	860-522-6103		445
Hallwalls Contemporary Arts Ctr 341 Delaware Ave *Web:* www.hallwalls.org	Buffalo	NY	14202	716-854-1694	854-1696	50-2
Hallwood Group Inc 3710 Rawlins St Ste 1500 *NYSE: HWG* ■ *Web:* www.hallwood.com	Dallas	TX	75219	214-528-5588		185
Halma Holdings Inc 11500 Northlake Dr Ste 306 *Web:* www.halma.com	Cincinnati	OH	45249	513-772-5501		201
Halmar International LLC 421 E Route 59 Nanuet *Web:* www.halmarinternational.com	New York	NY	10954	845-735-3511		188
HALO Branded Solutions Inc 1980 Industrial Dr *Web:* www.halo.com	Sterling	IL	61081	815-625-0980	632-6900	86
Halo Group LLC 39475 13 Mile Rd Ste 201 *Web:* www.halogroup.us	Novi	MI	48377	248-489-9500		449
HALO Pharmaceutical Inc 30 N Jefferson Rd *Web:* www.halopharma.com	Whippany	NJ	07981	973-428-4000		231
Halocarbon Products Corp PO Box 661 *TF:* 800-338-5803 ■ *Web:* www.halocarbon.com	River Edge	NJ	07661	201-262-8899		582
Halogen Software 495 March Rd *TF:* 866-566-7778 ■ *Web:* www.halogensoftware.com	Kanata	ON	K2K3G1	613-270-1011	270-8311	178-1
HaloSource Inc 1631 220th St SE Ste 100 *Web:* www.halosource.com	Bothell	WA	98021	425-881-6464	882-2476	787
Halozyme Therapeutics Inc 11388 Sorrento Valley Rd *NASDAQ: HALO* ■ *Web:* www.halozyme.com	San Diego	CA	92121	858-794-8889	704-8311	582
Halpern Capital Inc 20900 NE 30th Ave Ste 200 *Web:* www.halperncapital.com	Aventura	FL	33180	786-528-1400		401
Halron Lubricants Inc 1618 State St *TF:* 800-236-5845 ■ *Web:* www.halron.com	Green Bay	WI	54304	920-436-4000		579
Halsey & Griffith Inc 1983 Tenth Ave N *TF:* 800-875-7426 ■ *Web:* www.halseygriffith.com	Lake Worth	FL	33461	561-820-8000		535
Halstead International Inc 15 Oakwood Ave *TF:* 866-843-8453 ■ *Web:* www.mydiygenius.com	Norwalk	CT	06850	866-843-8453		361
Halstead Property LLC 770 Lexington Ave *Web:* www.halstead.com	New York	NY	10065	212-317-7800		652
Halsted Communications Ltd 13 Commerce Dr	Ballston Spa	NY	12020	518-885-8590		177
Halsted Corp 51 Commerce Dr Ste 3 *TF:* 800-843-5184 ■ *Web:* www.halstedbag.com	Cranbury	NJ	08512	609-235-4444		67
Halston LLC 1201 W Fifth St 11th fl *TF:* 844-425-7866 ■ *Web:* www.halston.com	Los Angeles	CA	90017	844-425-7866		157-2
Haltom City Public Library 4809 Haltom Rd *Web:* www.haltomcitytx.com	Haltom City	TX	76117	817-222-7786	834-1446	434-3
Haltoms Jewelers 317 Main St *Web:* www.haltoms.com	Fort Worth	TX	76102	817-336-4051		410
Halton Group Americas Inc 103 Industrial Dr *Web:* www.halton.com	Scottsville	KY	42164	270-393-7214		14
Halton Hills Chamber of Commerce 328 Guelph St *Web:* www.haltonhillschamber.on.ca	Georgetown	ON	L7G4B5	905-877-5117	877-5117	137
Halverson Co 235 Paxton Ave *Web:* www.halversoncompany.com	Salt Lake City	UT	84101	801-467-9423		362
Halverson Construction Company Inc 620 N 19th St *Web:* www.halversonconstruction.com	Springfield	IL	62702	217-753-0027	753-1904	188-4
Halvorson Trane 2220 NW 108th St *TF:* 800-798-0004 ■ *Web:* www.halvorsontrane.com	Clive	IA	50325	515-270-0004		610
Halvorson's Upstreet Cafe 16 Church St *Web:* halvorsonsupstreetcafe.com	Burlington	VT	05401	802-658-0278		671
Halyard Health 1400 Holcomb Bridge Rd *Web:* www.halyardhealth.com	Roswell	GA	30076	770-587-8000		477
Halyard Health 20202 Windrow Dr *TF:* 800-448-3569 ■ *Web:* www.halyardhealth.com	Lake Forest	CA	92630	949-206-2700		477
Halyard Health Inc 5405 Windward Pkwy *Web:* www.halyardhealth.com	Alpharetta	GA	30004	678-425-9273		475
Ham, Langston & Brezina LLP 11550 Fuqua St Ste 475 *Web:* www.hlb-cpa.com	Houston	TX	77034	281-481-1040		2
Hamacher Resource Group Inc W 229 N 2510 Duplainville Rd *Fax Area Code: 414 ■ *TF:* 800-888-0889 ■ *Web:* hamacher.com	Waukesha	WI	53186	800-888-0889	355-1032*	363
Hamachi House 5190 Morris St *Web:* www.hamachirestaurants.com	Halifax	NS	B3J1B3	902-425-7711	444-4068	671
Hamamatsu Corp 360 Foothill Rd *Web:* www.hamamatsu.com	Bridgewater	NJ	08807	908-231-0960		246
Hamasaku 11043 Santa Monica Blvd *Web:* www.hamasakula.com	Los Angeles	CA	90025	310-479-7636		671
Hamblen County 2415 N Davy Crockett Pkwy *Web:* www.hamblencountytn.gov	Morristown	TN	37814	423-318-1536	318-2508	338
Hamblen County Board of Education 210 E Morris Blvd *Web:* www.hcboe.net	Morristown	TN	37813	423-586-7700	586-7747	685
Hambro Forest Products Inc 445 Elk Valley Rd	Crescent City	CA	95531	707-464-6131		291
Hamburg Area School District (HASD) 701 Windsor St *Web:* www.hasdhawks.org	Hamburg	PA	19526	610-562-2241	562-2634	685
Hamburg Public Library 102 Buffalo St *Web:* buffalolib.org	Hamburg	NY	14075	716-649-4415	649-4160	434-3
Hamburg State Park 6071 Hamburg State Pk Rd *Web:* www.gastateparks.org	Mitchell	GA	30820	478-552-2393		565

Phone | Fax | Class

Hamburg Sud North America Inc
465 S St ... Morristown NJ 07960 973-775-5300 916-5901* 313
Fax Area Code: 770 ■ *TF:* 888-228-8241 ■ *Web:* www.hamburgsud.com
Hamdard Center for Health & Human Services
228 E Lake St Ste 300 ... Addison IL 60101 630-835-1430 317
Web: www.hamdardcenter.org
Hamden Chamber of Commerce
2969 Whitney Ave ... Hamden CT 06518 203-288-6431 288-4499 139
Web: hamdenregionalchamber.com
Hamden Library 2901 Dixwell Ave ... Hamden CT 06518 203-287-2686 434-3
Web: www.hamdenlibrary.org
Hamer Enterprises
4200-A N Bicentennial Dr ... Mcallen TX 78504 956-682-3466 174
TF: 800-374-9271 ■ *Web:* hecorp.com
Hamer LLC 14650 28th Ave N ... Plymouth MN 55447 763-231-0100 547
Web: hamerinc.com
Hamersley's Bistro 553 Tremont St ... Boston MA 02116 617-423-2700 671
Hamill Manufacturing Co
500 Pleasant Valley Rd ... Trafford PA 15085 724-744-2131 454
Web: www.hamillmfg.com
Hamilton Advisors Inc
373 Stanwich Rd ... Greenwich CT 06830 203-629-1112 629-1469 401
Web: www.hamiltonadvisors.com
Hamilton Area YMCA Inc
1315 Whitehorse-Mercerville Rd ... Hamilton NJ 08619 609-581-9622 354
TF: 800-582-7692 ■ *Web:* www.hamiltonymca.org
Hamilton Associates Inc
11403 Cronridge Dr ... Owings Mills MD 21117 410-363-9696 544
Web: www.atitest.com
Hamilton Beach/Proctor-Silex Inc
4421 Waterfront Dr ... Glen Allen VA 23060 804-273-9777 37
TF Cust Svc: 800-851-8900 ■ *Web:* www.hamiltonbeach.com
Hamilton BioVentures
990 Highland Dr Ste 302 ... Solana Beach CA 92075 858-314-2350 792
Hamilton Branch State Recreation Area
111 Campground Rd ... Plum Branch SC 29845 864-333-2223 565
Web: www.southcarolinaparks.com
Hamilton Bulldogs Hockey Club
101 York Blvd ... Hamilton ON L8R3L4 905-529-8500 706
Web: www.hamiltonbulldogs.com
Hamilton Capital Management
5025 Arlington Centre Blvd ... Columbus OH 43220 614-273-1000 401
TF: 888-833-5951 ■ *Web:* www.hamiltoncapital.com
Hamilton Caster & Manufacturing Co
1637 Dixie Hwy ... Hamilton OH 45011 513-863-3300 863-5508 350
Web: www.hamiltoncaster.com
Hamilton Chamber of Commerce
120 King St W Plaza level ... Hamilton ON L8P4V2 905-522-1151 522-1154 137
Web: www.hamiltonchamber.ca
Hamilton Chevrolet 5800 E 14 Mile Rd ... Warren MI 48092 586-264-1400 667-4007* 57
Fax Area Code: 313 ■ *Web:* hamiltonchevy.com
Hamilton City School District (HCSD)
533 Dayton St PO Box 627 ... Hamilton OH 45012 513-887-5000 887-5014 685
Web: www.hamiltoncityschools.com
Hamilton Co 4970 Energy Way ... Reno NV 89502 775-858-3000 419
TF: 800-648-5950 ■ *Web:* www.hamiltoncompany.com
Hamilton Co, The 39 Brighton Ave ... Allston MA 02134 617-783-0039 783-0568 653
Web: www.thehamiltoncompany.com
Hamilton College 198 College Hill Rd ... Clinton NY 13323 315-859-4421 859-4457* 166
*Fax: Admissions ■ *TF Admissions:* 800-843-2655 ■ *Web:* www.hamilton.edu
Hamilton Communications Group
20 N Wacker Dr ... Chicago IL 60606 312-321-5000 4
Hamilton Correctional Institution
10650 SW 46th St ... Jasper FL 32052 386-792-5151 213
Hamilton County 1111 13th St Ste 1 ... Aurora NE 68818 402-694-3443 338
TF: 800-368-8683 ■ *Web:* www.co.hamilton.ne.us
Hamilton County
625 Georgia Ave Rm 201 ... Chattanooga TN 37402 423-209-6500 209-6501 338
TF: 800-342-1003 ■ *Web:* www.hamiltontn.gov
Hamilton County 138 E Ct St Rm 603 ... Cincinnati OH 45202 513-946-4400 946-4444 338
Web: www.hamilton-co.org
Hamilton County
County Courthouse 102 N Rice Ste 107 ... Hamilton TX 76531 254-386-3518 386-8727 338
Web: www.hamiltoncountytx.org
Hamilton County 207 NE First St Rm 106 ... Jasper FL 32052 386-792-1288 792-3524 338
TF: 800-368-4274 ■ *Web:* www.hamiltoncountyflorida.com
Hamilton County
102 County View Dr ... Lake Pleasant NY 12108 518-548-7111 548-9740 338
Web: www.hamiltoncounty.com
Hamilton County
1 Hamilton County Sq Ste 106 ... Noblesville IN 46060 317-776-9629 338
Web: hamiltoncounty.in.gov
Hamilton County PO Box 1167 ... Syracuse KS 67878 620-384-5629 384-5853 338
Web: www.syracuseks.gov
Hamilton County 2300 Superior St ... Webster City IA 50595 515-832-9535 832-9514 338
Web: www.hamiltoncounty.org
Hamilton County Convention & Visitors Bureau Inc
37 E Main St ... Carmel IN 46032 317-848-3181 848-3191 206
TF: 800-776-8687 ■ *Web:* www.visithamiltoncounty.com
Hamilton County Dept of Education
3074 Hickory Valley Rd ... Chattanooga TN 37421 423-209-8400 209-8539* 685
*Fax: Hum Res ■ *Web:* www.hcde.org
Hamilton County Educational Service Ctr (HCESC)
11083 Hamilton Ave ... Cincinnati OH 45231 513-674-4200 742-8339 685
TF: 800-964-8211 ■ *Web:* www.hcesc.org
Hamilton County Electric Co-op Assn
420 N Rice St PO Box 753 ... Hamilton TX 76531 254-386-3123 245
TF: 800-595-3401 ■ *Web:* www.hamiltonelectric.coop
Hamilton County Speedway
1200 Bluff St ... Webster City IA 50595 515-832-1443 832-6972 515
TF: 800-873-1507 ■ *Web:* www.hamiltoncospeedway.com
Hamilton County State Fish & Wildlife Area
RR 4 PO Box 242 ... McLeansboro IL 62859 618-773-4340 565
Web: dnr.illinois.gov/Lands/Landmgt/PARKS/R5/HAMILTON.HTM
Hamilton Ctr Inc PO Box 4323 ... Terre Haute IN 47804 812-231-8323 374-5
TF: 800-742-0787 ■ *Web:* www.hamiltoncenter.org
Hamilton Engineering & Surveyi
3409 W Lemon St ... Tampa FL 33609 813-250-3535 261
Web: www.hamiltonengineering.us

Hamilton Equipment Inc
567 S Reading Rd PO Box 478 ... Ephrata PA 17522 717-733-7951 274
Web: www.haminc.com
Hamilton Form Company Ltd
7009 Midway Rd ... Fort Worth TX 76118 817-590-2111 595-1110 697
TF: 800-332-7090 ■ *Web:* www.hamiltonform.com
Hamilton Grange National Memorial (HAGR)
122 St Riverside Dr ... New York NY 10027 212-666-1640 564
TF: 800-246-8872 ■ *Web:* www.nps.gov/hagr
Hamilton Group
100 Elwood Davis Rd ... North Syracuse NY 13212 315-413-0086 413-0087 272
TF: 800-351-3066 ■ *Web:* www.hamiltongroup.net
Hamilton Health Sciences
1200 Main St W ... Hamilton ON L8N3Z5 905-521-2100 374-2
TF: 800-680-9868 ■ *Web:* www.hamiltonhealthsciences.ca
Hamilton House Estate Bed & Breakfast
132 Van Lyell Terr ... Hot Springs AR 71913 501-520-4040 520-4023 671
Web: www.hamiltonhouseestate.com
Hamilton Mall
4403 Black Horse Pk ... Mays Landing NJ 08330 609-646-8326 460
Web: www.shophamilton.com
Hamilton Medical Ctr
1200 Memorial Dr PO Box 1168 ... Dalton GA 30720 706-272-6000 374-3
Web: www.hamiltonhealth.com
Hamilton Park Hotel & Conference Ctr
175 Pk Ave ... Florham Park NJ 07932 973-377-2424 377
TF: 877-999-3223 ■ *Web:* www.hamiltonparkhotel.com
Hamilton Partners Inc
300 Park Blvd Ste 500 ... Itasca IL 60143 630-250-9700 653
Web: www.hamiltonpartners.com
Hamilton Place
2100 Hamilton Pl Blvd ... Chattanooga TN 37421 423-894-7177 460
Web: www.hamiltonplace.com
Hamilton Port Authority
605 James St N 6th Fl ... Hamilton ON L8L1K1 905-525-4330 618
TF: 800-263-2131 ■ *Web:* www.hamiltonport.ca
Hamilton Printing Co Inc
22 Hamilton Way ... CastletononHudson NY 12033 518-732-4491 626
Hamilton Sorter Co Inc
3158 Production Dr ... Fairfield OH 45014 513-870-4400 503-9963* 286
Fax Area Code: 800 ■ *TF:* 800-503-9966 ■ *Web:* www.hamiltonsorter.com
Hamilton Sundstrand Corp
1 Hamilton Rd ... Windsor Locks CT 06096 860-654-6000 504
TF: 800-227-7437 ■ *Web:* utcaerospacesystems.com
Hamilton Telephone Co 1001 12th St ... Aurora NE 68818 402-694-5101 116
TF: 800-821-1831 ■ *Web:* www.hamiltontelephone.com
Hamilton Watch Company Inc
1200 Harbor Blvd ... Weehawken NJ 07086 201-271-4680 153
Web: www.hamiltonwatch.com
Hamler State Bank
210 Randolph St PO Box 350 ... Hamler OH 43524 419-274-3955 70
TF: 888-508-3955 ■ *Web:* www.hamlerstatebank.com
Hamlet Homes
308 East 4500 South Ste 200 ... Salt Lake City UT 84107 801-281-2223 281-2224 653
Web: www.hamlethomes.com
Hamlet Village
200 Hamlet Hills Dr Ofc ... Chagrin Falls OH 44022 440-247-4201 371
Web: www.hamletretirement.com
Hamlin Beach State Park
1 Hamlin Beach Blvd W ... Hamlin NY 14464 585-964-2121 565
Hamlin County 300 Fourth St PO Box 208 ... Hayti SD 57241 605-783-3232 783-1330 338
Web: hamlincountysheriff.com
Hamlin Newco LLC 2741 Wingate Ave ... Akron OH 44314 330-753-7791 753-5577 489
Web: www.hnmetalstamping.com
Hamline University 1536 Hewitt Ave ... Saint Paul MN 55104 651-523-2207 523-2458 166
TF: 800-753-9753 ■ *Web:* www.hamline.edu
Hamm Inc 609 Perry Pl ... Perry KS 66073 785-597-5111 503-5
Web: www.nrhamm.com
Hamm Memorial Psychiatric Clnc
408 Saint Peter St Ste 429 ... Saint Paul MN 55102 651-224-0614 726
Web: www.hammclinic.org
Hammacher Schlemmer & Co
9307 N Milwaukee Ave ... Niles IL 60714 800-321-1484 362
TF: 800-321-1484 ■ *Web:* www.hammacher.com
Hammel Green & Abrahamson Inc
701 Washington Ave N ... Minneapolis MN 55401 612-758-4000 758-4199 261
TF: 888-442-8255 ■ *Web:* www.hga.com
Hammelmann Corp 600 Progress Rd ... Dayton OH 45449 937-859-8777 641
TF: 800-783-4935 ■ *Web:* www.hammelmann.de
Hammer & Hand Inc
1020 SE Harrison St ... Portland OR 97214 503-232-2447 186
TF: 800-274-6198 ■ *Web:* hammerandhand.com
Hammer Company Inc
9450 Rosemont Dr ... Streetsboro OH 44241 330-422-1471 81-3
Hammer Creative Inc 1020 N Cole Ave ... Hollywood CA 90038 323-606-4700 4
Web: www.hammercreative.com
Hammer Data Systems LLC
8138 Main St ... Garrettsville OH 44231 330-527-4018 177
TF: 800-677-9299 ■ *Web:* www.hammerdata.com
Hammer Museum 10899 Wilshire Blvd ... Los Angeles CA 90024 310-443-7000 443-7099 520
Web: www.hammer.ucla.edu
Hammer Nutrition Ltd
4952 Whitefish Stage Rd ... Whitefish MT 59937 406-862-1877 862-4543 799
TF Cust Svc: 800-336-1977 ■ *Web:* www.hammernutrition.com
Hammer Packaging Corp
200 Lucius Gordon Dr ... Rochester NY 14692 585-424-3880 627
Web: www.hammerpackaging.com
Hammer's Store
1415 W Dinah Shore Blvd ... Winchester TN 37398 931-967-2886 157-2
Web: hammersstore.com
Hammerman & Hultgren PC
3101 N Central Ave Ste 500 ... Phoenix AZ 85012 602-264-2566 41
Web: www.hammerman-hultgren.com
Hammerman Bros Inc
50 W 57th St 12th Fl ... New York NY 10019 212-956-2800 956-2769 409
TF: 800-223-6436 ■ *Web:* www.hammermanbrothers.com
Hammersmith Mfg & Sales Inc
401 Central Ave ... Horton KS 66439 785-486-2121 91
TF: 800-375-8245 ■ *Web:* www.vailproducts.com

	Phone	Fax	Class
Hammock Beach Resort 200 Ocean Crest Dr .... Palm Coast FL 32137 *TF:* 866-841-0287 ■ *Web:* www.hammockbeach.com	386-246-5500		669
Hammocks Beach State Park 1572 Hammock Beach Rd........ Swansboro NC 28584 *Web:* www.ncparks.gov	910-326-4881	326-2060	565
Hammonasset Beach State Park 1288 Boston Post Rd PO Box 271 .... Madison CT 06443 *Web:* www.ct.gov	203-245-2785	245-9201	565
Hammond & Irving Inc 254 N St .... Auburn NY 13021 *Web:* www.hammond-irving.com	315-253-6265	253-3136	483
Hammond Communications Group Inc 173 Trade St .... Lexington KY 40511 *TF:* 888-424-1878 ■ *Web:* www.hammondcg.com	859-254-1878		513
Hammond Drives & Equipment Inc 8527 Midland Rd .... Freeland MI 48623 *TF:* 888-695-2239 ■ *Web:* www.hammondeqp.com	989-695-2239		358
Hammond Electronics Inc 1230 W Central Blvd........ Orlando FL 32805 *TF Sales:* 800-929-3672 ■ *Web:* www.hammondelec.com	407-849-6060	872-0826	246
Hammond Manufacturing Company Ltd 394 Edinburgh Rd N........ Guelph ON N1H1E5 *Web:* www.hammfg.com	519-822-2960		201
Hammond North Condominium Assn 5300 Hamilton Ave........ Cincinnati OH 45224	513-541-5252		803-3
Hammond Public Library 564 State St........ Hammond IN 46320 *Web:* www.hammond.lib.in.us	219-931-5100	931-3474	434-3
Hammond Roto-Finish 1600 Douglas Ave........ Kalamazoo MI 49007 *Web:* www.hammondmach.com	269-327-7071	345-1710	455
Hammond Steakhouse 1402 N Fifth St .... Superior WI 54880 *Web:* hammondliquor.com	715-392-3269		671
Hammond Suzuki USA Inc 743 Annoreno Dr .... Addison IL 60101 *TF:* 888-765-2900 ■ *Web:* www.hammondorganco.com	630-543-0277		527
Hammond-Harwood House 19 Maryland Ave........ Annapolis MD 21401 *TF:* 800-492-7122 ■ *Web:* www.hammondharwoodhouse.org	410-263-4683		520
Hammonds House 503 Peeples St SW .... Atlanta GA 30310 *Web:* www.hammondshouse.org	404-612-0500	752-8733	50-3
Hamner Institutes for Health Sciences, The 6 Davis Dr PO Box 12137........ Research Triangle Park NC 27709 *Web:* www.thehamner.org	919-558-1200	558-1400	668
Hamon corp 58 E Main St .... Somerville NJ 08876 *TF:* 800-445-6578 ■ *Web:* www.hamon-researchcottrell.com	908-333-2000	333-2179	386
Hampden County 50 State St........ Springfield MA 01102 *Web:* hcbar.org	413-748-8600		338
Hampden Papers Inc 100 Water St .... Holyoke MA 01040 *Web:* www.hampdenpapers.com	413-536-1000	532-9161	554
Hampden-Sydney College PO Box 667 .... Hampden Sydney VA 23943 **Fax:* Admissions ■ *TF Admissions:* 800-755-0733 ■ *Web:* www.hsc.edu	434-223-6120	223-6120*	166
Hampel Oil Distributors Inc 3727 S W St........ Wichita KS 67217 *Web:* www.hampeloil.com	316-529-1162		581
Hampshire College 893 W St........ Amherst MA 01002 **Fax:* Admissions ■ *Web:* www.hampshire.edu	413-549-4600	559-5631*	166
Hampshire Country School 28 Patey Cir........ Rindge NH 03461 *Web:* www.hampshirecountryschool.org	603-899-3325	899-6521	622
Hampshire County 99 Main St .... NorthHampton MA 01060 *Web:* www.hampshirecog.org	413-584-1300	584-1465	338
Hampshire County 66 N High St........ Romney WV 26757 *Web:* hampshirecountyclerk.weebly.com	304-822-5112	822-4039	338
Hampshire Fire Protection Company Inc 8 N Wentworth Ave........ Londonderry NH 03053 *Web:* www.hampshirefire.com	603-432-8221		189-10
Hampson Aerospace Inc 2700 112th St Ste 300........ Grand Prairie TX 75050	214-988-0630		529
Hampson Archeological Museum State Park PO Box 156 .... Wilson AR 72395 *TF:* 888-742-8701 ■ *Web:* www.arkansasstateparks.com	870-655-8622		565
Hampstead Hospital 218 E Rd........ Hampstead NH 03841 *Web:* www.hampsteadhospital.com	603-329-5311	329-4746	374-5
Hampton Area Chamber of Commerce 1 Layfayette Rd........ Hampton NH 03842 *Web:* www.hamptonchamber.com	603-926-8718	926-9977	139
Hampton Beach State Park Rt 1A........ Hampton NH 03842 *Web:* www.nhstateparks.org	603-926-3784		565
Hampton Behavioral Health Center 650 Rancocas Rd .... Westampton NJ 08060 *TF:* 800-603-6767 ■ *Web:* hamptonhospital.com	800-603-6767		726
Hampton Coliseum 1000 Coliseum Dr........ Hampton VA 23666 *Web:* www.hamptoncoliseum.org	757-838-4203	838-2595	720
Hampton Conventions & Visitors Bureau 1919 Commerce Dr Ste 290........ Hampton VA 23666 *TF:* 800-487-8778 ■ *Web:* visithampton.com	757-722-1222	896-4600	206
Hampton County 200 Jackson Ave E........ Hampton SC 29924 *Web:* www.hamptoncountysc.org	803-914-2100	914-2107	338
Hampton Golf Inc 10401 Deerwood Park Blvd Ste 2130........ Jacksonville FL 32256 *Web:* hampton.golf	904-564-9129		760
Hampton Hydraulics Inc 712 First St NW .... Hampton IA 50441 *Web:* local.hamptonhydraulics.com	641-456-4871		789
Hampton (Independent City) 22 Lincoln St .... Hampton VA 23669 *TF:* 800-555-3930 ■ *Web:* hampton.gov	757-727-8311		338
Hampton Inn 2300 Carlisle NE........ Albuquerque NM 87117 *Web:* www.hamptoninn3.hilton.com	770-493-1966		378
Hampton Inn & Suites Atlanta Downtown Hotel 161 Spring St NW........ Atlanta GA 30303 *Web:* hamptoninn3.hilton.com/en/index.html	404-589-1111		379
Hampton Inn Brookhaven 2000 N Ocean Ave .... Farmingville NY 11738 *Web:* hamptoninn3.hilton.com	631-732-7300		378
Hampton Inn Philadelphia Ctr City-Convention Ctr 1301 Race St .... Philadelphia PA 19107 *TF:* 800-426-7866 ■ *Web:* www3.hilton.com	215-665-9100	665-9200	205
Hampton Inn Phoenix-Biltmore 2310 E Highland Ave .... Phoenix AZ 85016	602-956-5221		379
Hampton Inn (Pittsburgh Pennsylvania) 3315 Hamlet St........ Pittsburgh PA 15213 *Web:* www.pittsburghhamptoninn.com	412-681-1000		378
Hampton Jitney Inc (HJ) 395 County Rd 39A Ste 6........ SouthHampton NY 11968 *Web:* www.hamptonjitney.com	631-283-4600		107
Hampton Lumber 9600 SW Barnes Rd Ste 200........ Portland OR 97225 *Web:* www.hamptonaffiliates.com	503-297-7691		683
Hampton Lumber Mills Inc 1000 Willamina Creek Rd........ Willamina OR 97396	503-876-2322		683
Hampton Machine Shop Inc 900 39th St........ Newport News VA 23607 *Web:* www.hampmach.com	757-380-8500		757
Hampton Marina Hotel 700 Settlers Landing Rd........ Hampton VA 23669 *Web:* www.hamptonmarinahotel.com	757-727-9700		378
Hampton National Cemetery Cemetery Rd at Marshall Ave .... Hampton VA 23669 *Web:* www.cem.va.gov	757-723-7104		136
Hampton National Historic Site 535 Hampton Ln........ Towson MD 21286 *Web:* www.nps.gov	410-823-1309	823-8394	564
Hampton Office Products Inc 248 Donohoe Rd........ Greensburg PA 15601 *TF:* 800-466-8694 ■ *Web:* www.hamptonoffice.com	724-836-6430		321
Hampton Paper & Transfer Printing Inc 2230 Eddie Williams Rd .... Johnson City TN 37601 *Web:* www.hamptonprints.com	423-928-7247		627
Hampton Plantation State Historic Site 1950 Rutledge Rd........ McClellanville SC 29458 *TF:* 866-345-7275 ■ *Web:* southcarolinaparks.com/hampton/introduction.aspx	843-546-9361	527-4995	565
Hampton Ponds State Park 1048 N Rd........ Westfield MA 01085 *Web:* www.mass.gov	413-532-3985	533-1837	565
Hampton Products International Corp 50 Icon .... Foothill Ranch CA 92610 *TF:* 800-562-5625 ■ *Web:* www.hamptonproducts.com	949-472-4256		350
Hampton Public Library 4207 Victoria Blvd .... Hampton VA 23669 *TF:* 800-552-7096 ■ *Web:* www.hampton.gov	757-727-1154	727-1152	434-3
Hampton Roads Chamber of Commerce 500 E Main St Ste 700 .... Norfolk VA 23510 *TF:* 800-592-5482 ■ *Web:* www.hamptonroadschamber.com	757-622-2312	622-5563	139
Hampton Roads Chamber of Commerce-Suffolk 500 E Main St Ste 700 .... Norfolk VA 23510 *Web:* www.hamptonroadschamber.com	757-622-2312	622-5563	139
Hampton Roads Naval Museum 1 Waterside Dr Ste 248........ Norfolk VA 23510 *Web:* www.history.navy.mil/museums/hrnm/index.html	757-322-2987	445-1867	520
Hampton Securities Ltd 141 Adelaide St W Ste 1800........ Toronto ON M5H3L5 *TF:* 877-225-0229 ■ *Web:* www.hamptonsecurities.com	416-862-7800		690
Hampton Street Vineyard 1201 Hampton St........ Columbia SC 29202 *Web:* www.hamptonstreetvineyard.com	803-252-0850	931-0193	671
Hampton Technologies LLC 19 Scouting Blvd .... Medford NY 11763 *TF:* 800-229-1019 ■ *Web:* www.hamptontech.net	631-924-1335		467
Hampton University 100 E Queen St .... Hampton VA 23668 *TF:* 800-624-3341 ■ *Web:* www.hamptonu.edu	757-727-5000		166
Hampton, Lenzini & Renwick Inc 380 Shepard Dr .... Elgin IL 60123 *Web:* www.hlrengineering.com	847-697-6700		261
Hampton-Preston Mansion & Garden 1615 Blanding St .... Columbia SC 29201 *Web:* www.historiccolumbia.org	803-252-1770	929-7695	50-3
Hamptons Magazine 67 Hampton Rd Ste 201 .... SouthHampton NY 11968 *TF:* 866-891-3144 ■ *Web:* www.hamptons-magazine.com	631-283-7125	283-7854	457-22
Hamrick Inc 742 Peachoid Rd........ Gaffney SC 29341 *Web:* www.hamricks.com	864-489-6095		155-3
Hamrick Mills Inc 515 W Buford St PO Box 48........ Gaffney SC 29341 *TF:* 800-600-4305 ■ *Web:* www.hamrickmills.com	864-489-4731		745-1
Hamrock Inc 12521 Los Nietos Rd .... Santa Fe Springs CA 90670 *Web:* www.hamrock.com	562-944-0255		488
Hana Hou 1144 Tenth Ave Ste 401 .... Honolulu HI 96816 *TF:* 888-733-3336 ■ *Web:* www.hanahou.com	808-733-3333	733-3340	457-22
Hana Sushi 1101 E March Ln........ Stockton CA 95210	209-477-1667		671
Hana Sushi 1807 Fourth St SW .... Calgary AB T2S1W2	403-229-1499		671
Hana Tokyo Seafood & Steak House 1275 Post Rd .... Fairfield CT 06824 *Web:* www.hanatokyo.com	203-256-0800		671
Hana Yori 3601 Grape Rd........ Mishawaka IN 46545 *Web:* www.hanayori.com	574-258-5817		671
Hanabusa Colleen (Rep D - HI) 422 Cannon HOB .... Washington DC 20515 *Web:* hanabusa.house.gov	202-225-2726		342-2
Hanalei Bay Resort & Suites 5380 Honoiki Rd........ Princeville HI 96722 *TF:* 877-344-0688 ■ *Web:* www.hanaleibayresort.com	808-826-6522		669
Hanapin Marketing LLC 501 N Morton St Ste 212 .... Bloomington IN 47404 *Web:* www.hanapinmarketing.com	812-330-3134		195
Hanasho Japanese Restaurant 2938 N Belt Line Rd .... Irving TX 75062 *Web:* www.hanashojapaneserestaurant.com	972-258-0250		671
Hanauma Bay Nature Preserve 100 Hanauma Bay Rd........ Honolulu HI 96825 *TF:* 800-690-6200 ■ *Web:* www.honolulu.gov	808-396-4229	395-0468	50-5
Hanauma Bay State Underwater Park 3949 Diamond Head Rd .... Honolulu HI 96816 *Web:* www.hawaii.gov	808-587-0300		565

	Phone	Fax	Class
Hanchett Entry Systems Inc (HES) 22630 N 17th Ave.......... Phoenix AZ 85027 *TF:* 800-626-7590 ■ *Web:* www.hesinnovations.com	623-582-4626	582-4641	692
Hanchett Manufacturing Inc 20000 19 Mile Rd.......... Big Rapids MI 49307 *Fax Area Code: 231 ■ *TF:* 800-454-7463 ■ *Web:* www.hanchett.com	800-454-7463	796-4851*	455
Hancock & Moore PO Box 3444.......... Hickory NC 28603 *TF:* 800-692-6889 ■ *Web:* www.hancockandmoore.com	828-495-8235	495-3021	319-2
Hancock Concrete Products Inc 17 Atlantic Ave.......... Hancock MN 56244 *Web:* www.hancockconcrete.com	320-392-5207	392-5155	183
Hancock County 854 Highway 90 Ste A.......... Bay Saint Louis MS 39520 *Web:* www.hancockcounty.ms.gov	228-467-2100		338
Hancock County PO Box 189.......... Carthage IL 62321 *Web:* www.hancockcounty-il.gov	217-357-2616		338
Hancock County 50 State St Ste 7.......... Ellsworth ME 04605 *Web:* www.co.hancock.me.us	207-667-9542	667-1412	338
Hancock County 300 S Main St.......... Findlay OH 45840 *TF:* 888-534-1432 ■ *Web:* www.co.hancock.oh.us	419-424-7037	424-7801	338
Hancock County PO Box 70.......... Garner IA 50438 *TF:* 800-479-9071 ■ *Web:* www.hancockcountyia.org	641-923-2532		338
Hancock County 9 E Main St.......... Greenfield IN 46140 *TF:* 800-267-9882 ■ *Web:* www.hancockcoingov.org	317-477-1135		338
Hancock County 225 Main Cross St.......... Hawesville KY 42348 *TF:* 800-815-2666 ■ *Web:* www.hancockky.us	270-927-6117		338
Hancock County PO Box 367.......... New Cumberland WV 26047 *TF:* 800-642-9066 ■ *Web:* www.hancockcountywv.org	304-564-3311	564-5941	338
Hancock County 418 Harrison St PO Box 575.......... Sneedville TN 37869 *TF:* 800-332-0900 ■ *Web:* www.hancockcountytn.com	423-733-2519	733-4509	338
Hancock County 12630 Broad St.......... Sparta GA 31087 *TF:* 800-255-0135 ■ *Web:* hancockcountyga.gov	706-444-5746	444-6221	338
Hancock County Co-op Oil Assn 245 State St.......... Garner IA 50438 *TF:* 800-924-2667 ■ *Web:* www.hancockcountycoop.com	641-923-2635		345
Hancock County Library 312 Hwy 90.......... Bay Saint Louis MS 39520 *Web:* hancocklibraries.info	228-467-5282	467-5503	434-3
Hancock County-Bar Harbor Airport 115 Caruso Dr.......... Trenton ME 04605 *Web:* www.bhbairport.com	207-667-7329	667-0218	27
Hancock Fabrics Inc 1 Fashion Way.......... Baldwyn MS 38824 *Web:* hancockfabrics.com	662-365-6000		270
Hancock Holding Co 2510 14th St.......... Gulfport MS 39501	228-868-4727		360-2
Hancock House State Historic Site 3 Front St PO Box 139.......... Hancock's Bridge NJ 08038 *Web:* www.njparksandforests.org	856-935-4373		565
Hancock International Corp 351 Main Pl.......... Carol Stream IL 60188 *Web:* hancock-international.com	630-510-7697		311
Hancock State Prison 701 Prison Blvd.......... Sparta GA 31087 *Web:* dcor.state.ga.us	706-444-1000	444-1137	213
Hancock-Wood Electric Co-op Inc (HWEC) 1399 Business Pk Dr S PO Box 190.......... North Baltimore OH 45872 *TF:* 800-445-4840 ■ *Web:* www.hwe.coop	419-257-3241	257-3024	245
Hancor Inc PO Box 1047.......... Findlay OH 45839 *TF:* 888-892-2694 ■ *Web:* www.hancor.com	419-422-6521		596
Hand County 415 W First Ave Ste 11.......... Miller SD 57362 *Web:* ujs.sd.gov	605-853-3337	853-3779	338
Hand Era 2859 104th St.......... Des Moines IA 50322 *TF:* 800-544-3571 ■ *Web:* www.handera.com	515-252-7522		393
Hand Industries/Dirilyte Line 315 S Hand Ave.......... Warsaw IN 46580 *TF:* 800-426-0921 ■ *Web:* www.handindustries.com	574-267-3525	267-7349	146
Handa Travel Services Ltd 2269 Riverside Dr Billings Bridge Plaza.......... Ottawa ON K1H8K2	613-731-1111		772
Handbill Printers Inc 820 E Parkridge Ave.......... Corona CA 92879 *Web:* www.handbillprinters.com	951-547-5910		627
Handel & Haydn Society 300 Massachusetts Ave.......... Boston MA 02115 *TF:* 800-531-7663 ■ *Web:* www.handelandhaydn.org	617-262-1815	266-4217	573-3
Handel Group Llc, The 247 Limestone Rd.......... Ridgefield CT 06877 *TF:* 800-617-7040 ■ *Web:* www.handelgroup.com	917-670-8782		463
Handel Karen C (Rep R - GA) 1211 Longworth HOB.......... Washington DC 20515 *Web:* handel.house.gov	202-225-4501		342-2
Handelan-pedersen 1453 N Ashland Ave.......... Chicago IL 60622 *Web:* www.hpdesign.net	312-664-1200		344
Handgards Inc 901 Hawkins Blvd.......... El Paso TX 79915 *TF:* 800-351-8161 ■ *Web:* www.handgards.com	800-351-8161		576
Handi-Foil Corp 135 E Hintz Rd.......... Wheeling IL 60090 *Web:* www.handi-foil.com	847-520-1000		295
Handi-Ramp 510 N Ave.......... Libertyville IL 60048 *TF:* 800-876-7267 ■ *Web:* www.handiramp.com	847-680-7700		358
Handke's Cuisine 520 S Front St.......... Columbus OH 43215 *Web:* www.chefhandke.com	614-621-2500		671
Handlery Hotel & Resort 950 Hotel Cir N.......... San Diego CA 92108 *TF:* 800-676-6567 ■ *Web:* www.handlery.com	619-298-0511		669
Handlery Union Square Hotel 351 Geary St.......... San Francisco CA 94102 *TF:* 800-995-4874 ■ *Web:* www.handlery.com	415-781-7800	781-0216	379
Handley Industries Inc 2101 Brooklyn Rd.......... Jackson MI 49203 *TF:* 800-870-5088 ■ *Web:* www.handleyind.com	517-787-8821	787-3946	199
Handling Systems Inc 2659 E Magnolia St.......... Phoenix AZ 85034 *Web:* www.handlingsystems.com	602-275-2228		770
Handpicked Inc 150 Harbison Blvd Ste C.......... Columbia SC 29212 *Web:* www.behandpicked.com	803-749-6024		410
Hands of Heartland 211 Galvin Rd N.......... Bellevue NE 68005 *Web:* handsofheartland.com	402-933-0680		371

	Phone	Fax	Class
Hands On Children's Museum 414 Jefferson St NE.......... Olympia WA 98501 *Web:* www.hocm.org	360-956-0818	754-8626	521
Hands on Mailing & Fulfillment Inc 6840 Orangethorpe Ave Ste E.......... Buena Park CA 90620 *Web:* handsonmailing.com	714-522-3979		5
Hands on Technology Transfer Inc 1 Village Sq Ste 8.......... Chelmsford MA 01824 *Web:* traininghott.com	978-250-4299		764
Hands On! Regional Museum 315 E Main St.......... Johnson City TN 37601 *Web:* www.handsonmuseum.org	423-434-4263	928-6915	521
Hands-On House Children's Museum of Lancaster 721 Landis Valley Rd.......... Lancaster PA 17601 *TF:* 800-329-7466 ■ *Web:* www.handsonhouse.org	717-569-5437		521
Handweavers Guild of America (HGA) 1255 Hwy 23 NW Ste 211.......... Suwanee GA 30024 *TF:* 800-665-9786 ■ *Web:* www.weavespindye.org	678-730-0010	730-0836	48-18
Handy & Harman 1133 Westchester Ave Ste N222.......... White Plains NY 10604 *Web:* www.handyharman.com	914-461-1300		485
Handy Hardware Wholesale Inc 8300 Tewantin Dr.......... Houston TX 77061 *TF:* 800-364-3835 ■ *Web:* www.handyhardware.com	713-644-1495		351
Handy Industries LLC 600 W Second Ave PO Box 223.......... Sully IA 50251 *Web:* www.handyindustries.com	641-752-5446		697
Handy Kenlin Group, The 29 E Hintz Rd.......... Wheeling IL 60090 *TF:* 800-214-3545 ■ *Web:* www.handykenlin.com	847-459-0900	459-0902	744
Handy Networks LLC 1801 Calif St Ste 240.......... Denver CO 80202 *Web:* www.handynetworks.com	303-414-6910		224
Handy Store Fixtures Inc 337 Sherman Ave.......... Newark NJ 07114 *TF:* 800-631-4280 ■ *Web:* www.handystorefixtures.com	973-242-1600		286
Handy Tv Inc 224 Oxmoor Cir.......... Birmingham AL 35209 *Web:* www.handytv.com	205-290-0300		429
Handyman Connection Inc 11115 Kenwood Rd.......... Blue Ash OH 45242 *TF:* 800-466-5530 ■ *Web:* www.handymanconnection.com	513-771-3003	771-6439	189-11
Handyman Matters Inc 12567 W Cedar Dr.......... Lakewood CO 80228 *TF:* 866-349-6946 ■ *Web:* www.handymanmatters.com	303-984-0177		310
HandyTrac Systems LLC 510 Staghorn Ct.......... Alpharetta GA 30004 *TF:* 800-665-9994 ■ *Web:* www.handytrac.com	678-990-2305		692
Hanes Cos Inc 500 N McLin Creek Rd.......... Conover NC 28613 *TF:* 877-252-3052 ■ *Web:* www.hanescompanies.com	828-464-4673		594
Hanes Dye & Finish Inc 600 NW Blvd.......... Winston-Salem NC 27101 *Web:* www.hanescompanies.com	336-725-1391		745-7
Hanes Erie Inc 7601 Klier Dr S.......... Fairview PA 16415 *Web:* www.haneserie.com	814-474-1999		627
Hanes Mall 3320 Silas Creek Pkwy Ste 264.......... Winston-Salem NC 27103 *Web:* www.shophanesmall.com	336-765-8321		460
Hanford Chamber of Commerce 113 Ct St.......... Hanford CA 93230 *Web:* www.hanfordchamber.com	559-582-0483		139
Hanford Hotels Inc 4 Corporate Plaza Ste 102.......... Newport Beach CA 92660	949-640-8888		377
Hanford Nursing & Rehabilitation Hospital 1007 W Lacey Blvd.......... Hanford CA 93230 *Web:* hfcis.cdph.ca.gov	559-582-2871		450
Hanford Pharmaceuticals LLC 304 Oneida St.......... Syracuse NY 13202 *Web:* www.hanford.com	315-476-7418		231
Hangar On The Wharf 2 Marine Way Ste 106.......... Juneau AK 99801 *Web:* hangaronthewharf.com	907-586-5018	586-8173	671
Hangawi 12 E 32nd St.......... New York NY 10016 *Web:* www.hangawirestaurant.com	212-213-0077	689-0780	671
Hanger Orthopedic Group Inc 10910 Domain Dr Ste 300.......... Austin TX 78758 *TF:* 877-442-6437 ■ *Web:* www.hanger.com	512-777-3800		352
Hanger Prosthetics & Orthopedics Inc 10910 Domain Dr Ste 300.......... Austin TX 78758 *TF:* 877-442-6437 ■ *Web:* www.hanger.com	877-442-6437		477
Hangley Aronchick Segal & Pudlin PC 1 Logan Sq 18th and Cherry Sts.......... Philadelphia PA 19103 *Web:* www.hangley.com	215-568-6200		428
Hangman Products Inc 6400 Variel Ave.......... Woodland Hills CA 91367 *Web:* www.hangmanproducts.com	818-610-0487		320
Hangout Industries Inc 110 Chauncy St.......... Boston MA 02111 *Web:* www.hangout.net	617-447-2160		5
Hangsterfer's Laboratories Inc 175 Ogden Rd.......... Mantua NJ 08051 *TF:* 800-433-5823 ■ *Web:* www.hangsterfers.com	856-468-0216	468-0200	541
HANK AM 1550 AND 97.7 FM 730 Rayovac Dr.......... Madison WI 53711 *TF:* 888-974-4265 ■ *Web:* hankonline.net	608-273-1000		645-96
Hank's Seafood Restaurant 10 Hayne St.......... Charleston SC 29401 *TF:* 800-551-0181 ■ *Web:* www.hanksseafoodrestaurant.com	843-723-3474		671
Hankison International 1000 Philadelphia St.......... Canonsburg PA 15317 *Web:* www.spx.com	724-745-1555	745-6040	14
Hankook Tire America Corp 1450 Valley Rd.......... Wayne NJ 07470 *Fax Area Code: 800 ■ *TF:* 800-426-5665 ■ *Web:* www.hankooktire.com/us	973-633-9000	847-3765*	754
Hankscraft Inc 300 Wengel Dr.......... Reedsburg WI 53959 *TF:* 800-722-3530 ■ *Web:* www.hankscraft.com	608-524-4341	524-4342	518
Hanley House 7600 Westmoreland St.......... Clayton MO 63105 *Web:* hanleyhouse.blogspot.com	314-467-0712	290-8517	50-3
Hanley Industries Inc 3640 Seminary Rd PO Box 1058.......... Alton IL 62002 *Web:* www.hanleyindustries.com	618-465-8892		268

	Phone	Fax	Class
Hanley-Wood LLC 1 Thomas Cir NW Ste 600 .... Washington DC 20005 *TF:* 800-227-8839 ■ *Web:* www.hanleywood.com	202-452-0800	785-1974	637-9
Hanlin-Rainaldi Construction Corp 6610 Singletree Dr .... Columbus OH 43229 *Web:* www.hanlinrainaldi.com	614-310-1466		186
Hanlo Gages & Engineering Co 34403 Glendale .... Livonia MI 48150 *Web:* www.hanlogages.com	734-422-4224	422-2244	493
Hanmi Bank 3660 Wilshire Blvd Ste PH-A .... Los Angeles CA 90010 *TF:* 877-808-4266 ■ *Web:* www.hanmi.com	213-382-2200		360-2
Hanna Andersson Corp 1010 NW Flanders St .... Portland OR 97209 *TF Cust Svc:* 800-222-0544 ■ *Web:* www.hannaandersson.com	800-222-0544		459
Hanna Instruments Inc 584 Park E Dr .... Woonsocket RI 02895 *Web:* www.hannainst.com	401-765-7500		696
Hanna Plumbing & Supply Co 643 S Santa Fe Ave. .... Vista CA 92083	760-726-2002		189-10
Hanna Steel Corp 3812 Commerce Ave PO Box 558 .... Fairfield AL 35064 *TF:* 800-633-8252 ■ *Web:* www.hannasteel.com	205-780-1111	783-8368	490
Hannaford Bros Co 145 Pleasant Hill Rd .... Scarborough ME 04074 *TF:* 800-213-9040 ■ *Web:* www.hannaford.com	800-213-9040		297-8
Hannah Duston Memorial Exit 17 Off I-93 .... Boscawen NH 03303 *Web:* www.nhstateparks.org	603-271-3556		565
Hannah Lindahl Children's Museum 1402 S Main St. .... Mishawaka IN 46544 *Web:* www.hlcm.org	574-254-4540	254-4585	521
Hannay Reels Inc 553 SR-143 .... Westerlo NY 12193 *TF:* 877-467-3357 ■ *Web:* www.hannay.com	518-797-3791	797-3259	117
Hannibal Carbide Tool Inc 5000 Paris Gravel Rd .... Hannibal MO 63401 *TF:* 800-451-9436 ■ *Web:* www.hannibalcarbide.com	573-221-2775	221-1140	493
Hannibal Convention & Visitors Bureau 505 N Third St .... Hannibal MO 63401 *TF:* 877-423-4140 ■ *Web:* www.visithannibal.com	573-221-2477	221-6999	206
Hannibal Industries Inc 3851 S Santa Fe Ave. .... Los Angeles CA 90058 *TF:* 888-246-7074 ■ *Web:* www.hannibalindustries.com	323-588-4261	589-5640	490
Hannibal Regional Hospital 6500 Hospital Dr .... Hannibal MO 63401 *TF:* 888-426-6425 ■ *Web:* hospital.hannibalregional.org	573-248-1300		374-3
Hannibal-LaGrange College 2800 Palmyra Rd .... Hannibal MO 63401 *TF Admissions:* 800-454-1119 ■ *Web:* www.hlg.edu	573-221-3675	221-6594	166
Hanning Construction Inc 815 Swan St .... Terre Haute IN 47807 *Web:* www.hannigconstruction.com	812-235-6218	235-1218	685
Hannon Co, The 1605 Waynesburg Dr SE .... Canton OH 44707 *Web:* www.hanco.com	330-456-4728	456-3323	518
Hannon Hydraulics LLC 625 N Loop 12 .... Irving TX 75061 *TF:* 800-333-4266 ■ *Web:* www.hannonhydraulics.com	972-438-2870		223
Hannover Life Reassurance Co of America 200 S Orange Ave Ste 1900 .... Orlando FL 32801 *Web:* www.hannover-re.com	407-649-8411		391-2
Hanor Co E 4614 Hwy 14-60 .... Spring Green WI 53588 *Web:* hanorcompany.com	608-588-9170		10-6
Hanover Area Chamber of Commerce 146 Carlisle St .... Hanover PA 17331 *Web:* www.hanoverchamber.com	717-637-6130	637-9127	139
Hanover Area Chamber of Commerce 53 S Main St .... Hanover NH 03755 *Web:* www.hanoverchamber.org	603-643-3115	643-5606	139
Hanover College 484 Ball Dr. .... Hanover IN 47243 *TF:* 800-213-2178 ■ *Web:* www.hanover.edu	812-866-7000	866-7098	166
Hanover County 7497 County Complex Rd .... Hanover VA 23069 *TF:* 800-367-7623 ■ *Web:* hanovercounty.gov	804-365-6000	365-6234	338
Hanover Design Services PA 1123 Floral Pkwy .... Wilmington NC 28403	910-343-8002		727
Hanover Direct Inc 1200 Harbor Blvd .... Weehawken NJ 07086 *Web:* www.hanoverdirect.com	201-863-7300	272-3465	459
Hanover Engineering Assoc Inc 252 Brodhead Rd Ste 100 .... Bethlehem PA 18017 *Web:* www.hanovereng.com	610-691-5644		256
Hanover Foods Corp 1550 York St PO Box 334 .... Hanover PA 17331 *OTC:* HNFSA ■ *TF:* 800-888-4646 ■ *Web:* www.hanoverfoods.com	717-632-6000		296-36
Hanover Hospital 300 Highland Ave. .... Hanover PA 17331 *TF:* 800-673-2426 ■ *Web:* www.hanoverhospital.org	717-637-3711		374-3
Hanover Inn 2 E Wheelock St .... Hanover NH 03755 *TF:* 800-443-7024 ■ *Web:* www.hanoverinn.com	603-643-4300	643-4433	379
Hanover Insurance Co 440 Lincoln St .... Worcester MA 01653 *TF:* 800-853-0456 ■ *Web:* www.hanover.com	508-855-1000		391-4
Hanover Juvenile Correctional Ctr 7093 Broadneck Rd .... Hanover VA 23069 *Web:* www.djj.virginia.gov/pages/admin/human-resources.htm	804-537-5316	537-5907	412
Hanover Mall 1775 Washington St .... Hanover MA 02339 *Web:* www.hanovermall.com	781-826-4392		460
Hanover Marriott 1401 Route 10 E. .... Whippany NJ 07981 *Web:* www.marriott.com/hotels/travel/ewrho-hanover-marriott	973-538-8811		378
Hanover Partners Inc 425 California St Ste 1700 .... San Francisco CA 94104 *Web:* www.hanoverpartners.com	415-788-8680		690
Hanover Research 1700 K St NW 8th Fl. .... Washington DC 20006 *Web:* www.hanoverresearch.com	202-559-0050		196
Hanover Wire Cloth 500 E Middle St .... Hanover PA 17331 *Web:* www.newyorkwireind.com	717-637-3795		688
Hanoverr Architectural Products 240 Bender Rd .... Hanover PA 17331 *Web:* www.hanoverpavers.com	717-637-0500		183
Hanovia Corp 6 Evans St .... Fairfield NJ 07004 *TF:* 800-827-3920 ■ *Web:* www.hanovia-uv.com	973-651-5510	651-5550	437

	Phone	Fax	Class
Hanrahan Carey & Company PLC 306 S Troy St PO Box 1049 .... Royal Oak MI 48068 *Web:* www.hccplc.com	248-544-1484		2
Hans Herr House & Museum 1849 Hans Herr Dr .... Willow Street PA 17584 *Web:* www.hansherr.org	717-464-4438		50-3
Hans Johnsen Co 8901 Chancellor Row .... Dallas TX 75247 *TF Sales:* 800-879-1515 ■ *Web:* www.hjc.com	214-879-1550	879-1520	351
Hans Kissle Co LLC 9 Creek Brook Dr. .... Haverhill MA 01832 *Web:* www.hanskissle.com	978-556-4500		123
Hans P Kraus Jr Inc 962 Pk Ave. .... New York NY 10028 *Web:* www.sunpictures.com	212-794-2064		42
Hans Rudolph Inc 8325 Cole Pkwy. .... Shawnee KS 66227 *TF:* 800-456-6695 ■ *Web:* www.rudolphkc.com	913-422-7788		477
Hansa GCR LLC 308 SW First Ave .... Portland OR 97204 *TF:* 800-755-7683 ■ *Web:* www.hansagcr.com	503-241-8036		195
Hansa Language Centre of Toronto Inc 51 Eglinton Ave E .... Toronto ON M4P1G7 *Web:* www.hansacanada.com	416-487-8643		148
Hanscom Air Force Base 55 Grenier St .... Hanscom AFB MA 01731 *Web:* www.hanscom.af.mil	781-225-1110		497-1
Hanscom Inc 331 Market St. .... Warren RI 02885 *TF:* 877-725-6788 ■ *Web:* www.hanscominc.com	401-247-1999	247-4575	608
Hanseatic Management Services Inc 5600 Wyoming N E Ste 220 .... Albuquerque NM 87109 *Web:* www.hanseaticgroup.com	505-828-2824		401
Hansel 'n Gretel Brand Inc 79-36 Cooper Ave. .... Glendale NY 11385 *Web:* www.healthydeli.com	718-326-0041	326-2069	473
Hansell Tierney Inc 2955 80th Ave SE Ste 102 .... Mercer Island WA 98040 *Web:* hanselltierney.com	206-232-3080		260
Hansen Architectural Systems 5500 SE Alexander St. .... Hillsboro OR 97123 *TF:* 800-599-2965 ■ *Web:* aluminumrailing.com	503-356-0959		492
Hansen Balk Steel Treating Co 1230 Monroe Ave NW. .... Grand Rapids MI 49505 *Web:* www.hansenbalk.com	616-458-1414		484
Hansen Beverage Co 1 Monster Way .... Corona CA 92879 *Web:* www.hansens.com	951-739-6200		297-8
Hansen Company Inc, The 5665 Greendale Rd Ste A .... Johnston IA 50131 *Web:* www.hansencompany.com	515-270-1117	270-3829	186
Hansen Corp 901 S First St .... Princeton IN 47670 *TF:* 800-328-8996 ■ *Web:* www.hansen-motor.com	812-385-3415	385-3013	518
Hansen Engineering Company Inc 24050 Frampton Ave. .... Harbor City CA 90710 *Web:* www.hansenengineering.com	310-534-3870		22
Hansen International Inc 130 Zenker Rd .... Lexington SC 29072 *Web:* www.hansen-online.com	803-695-1500		697
Hansen Manufacturing Corp 5100 W 12th St. .... Sioux Falls SD 57107 *TF:* 800-328-1785 ■ *Web:* www.hiroller.com	605-332-3200		207
Hansen Mechanical Contractors Inc 4580 W Post Rd .... Las Vegas NV 89118 *Web:* www.hansenmechanical.com	702-361-5111		610
Hansen Medical Inc 800 E Middlefield Rd .... Mountain View CA 94043 *Web:* hansenmedical.com	650-404-5800		250
Hansen Plastic Corp 2758 Alft Ln .... Elgin IL 60124 *Web:* www.hansenplastics.com	847-741-4510		608
Hansen Software Corp 1855 Kirschner Rd Ste 380 .... Kelowna BC V1Y4N7 *TF:* 877-795-2274 ■ *Web:* www.hansensoftware.com	877-795-2274		525
Hansen Surfboards 1105 S Coast Hwy 101 .... Encinitas CA 92024 *TF:* 800-480-4754 ■ *Web:* www.hansensurf.com	760-753-6595		711
Hansen Technologies Corp 6827 High Grove Blvd .... Burr Ridge IL 60527 *TF:* 800-426-7368 ■ *Web:* www.hantech.com	630-325-1565	325-1572	202
Hansen Thorp Pellinen Olson Inc 7510 Market Pl Dr .... Eden Prairie MN 55344 *Web:* www.htpo.com	952-829-0700		256
Hansen, Jacobson, Teller, Hoberman, Newman, Warren, Richman, Rush & Kaller, LLP 450 N Roxbury Dr 8th Fl. .... Beverly Hills CA 90210 *Web:* www.hjth.com	310-271-8777		428
Hansen-Mueller Co 12231 Emmet St Ste 1 .... Omaha NE 68164 *Web:* www.hansenmueller.com	402-491-3385		690
Hanser & Associates Public Relations 4401 Westown Pkwy Ste 212 .... West Des Moines IA 50266 *TF:* 800-229-4879 ■ *Web:* www.hanser.com	515-224-1086		7
Hansford County 15 Northwest Ct. .... Spearman TX 79081 *Web:* www.co.hansford.tx.us	806-659-4110	659-4168	338
Hansford County Feeders LP 13800 County Rd 19. .... Spearman TX 79081 *TF:* 800-951-2533 ■ *Web:* hcflp.com	806-477-1900	477-1910	10-1
Hansgrohe Inc 1490 Bluegrass Lakes Pkwy .... Alpharetta GA 30004 *TF:* 800-334-0455 ■ *Web:* www.hansgrohe-usa.com	770-360-9880	360-9887	609
Hansome Energy Systems Inc 365 Dalziel Rd .... Linden NJ 07036	908-862-9044		518
Hanson County 720 Fifth St PO Box 127 .... Alexandria SD 57311 *Web:* ujs.sd.gov	605-239-4446	239-9446	338
Hanson Directory Service Inc 1501 N 15th Ave E .... Newton IA 50208 *Web:* www.hansondirectory.com	641-792-2855		4
Hanson Distributing Company Inc 10802 Rush St .... South El Monte CA 91733	626-448-4683	579-4053	61
Hanson House 380 E Paseo El Mirador .... Palm Springs CA 92262 *Web:* www.hansonhouse.org	760-416-5070	416-5071	372
Hanson Information System 2433 W White Oaks Dr .... Springfield IL 62704 *TF:* 888-245-8468 ■ *Web:* hansoninfosys.com	217-726-2400		177
Hanson Logistics 2900 S State St. .... Saint Joseph MI 49085 *TF:* 888-772-1197 ■ *Web:* www.hansonlogisticsgroup.com	269-982-1390	982-1506	449

Phone | Fax | Class

Hanson Lulic & Krall LLC
700 Northstar E 608 Second Ave S .... Minneapolis MN 55402 612-333-2530 428
TF: 800-455-3476 ■ Web: hlk.com

Hanson Medical Systems Inc
1954 Howell Branch Rd Ste 203 .... Winter Park FL 32792 407-671-3883 475
TF: 877-671-3883 ■ Web: www.hansonmedicalsystems.com

Hanson Professional Services Inc
1525 S Sixth St .... Springfield IL 62703 217-788-2450 788-2503 261
Web: www.hanson-inc.com

Hanson Sign & Screen Process Corp
82 Carter St .... Falconer NY 14733 716-484-8564 687
Web: www.hansonsign.com

Hanson Silo Co
11587 County Rd 8 SE .... Lake Lillian MN 56253 320-664-4171 664-4140 273
Web: www.hansonsilo.com

Hanson Watson Assoc 1411 15th St .... Moline IL 61265 309-764-8315 4
Web: www.hansonwatson.com

Hantronix Inc 10080 Bubb Rd .... Cupertino CA 95014 408-252-1100 252-1123 173-4
TF: 800-525-0811 ■ Web: www.hantronix.com

Hantz Group Inc 26200 America Dr .... Southfield MI 48034 248-304-2855 390
Web: hantzgroup.com

Hantzmon Wiebel LLP
818 E Jefferson St .... Charlottesville VA 22902 434-296-2156 2
Web: www.hantzmonwiebel.com

Hanwha International LLC 2559 Rt 130 .... Cranbury NJ 08512 609-655-2500 791
TF: 800-522-0910 ■ Web: www.hanwha-usa.com

Hanwha L&C Canada Inc
2860 Innovation Dr .... London ON N6M065 519-433-0486 317
Web: www.hanwhasurfaces.com

Hapa Sushi Grill & Sake Bar
2780 E Second Ave .... Denver CO 80206 303-322-9554 671
Web: www.hapasushi.com

Hapag-Lloyd America Inc
401 E Jackson St .... Tampa FL 33602 813-276-4600 313
TF: 800-282-8077 ■ Web: www.hapag-lloyd.com/en

Hapco Inc 26252 Hillman Hwy .... Abingdon VA 24210 276-628-7171 491
TF: 800-368-7171 ■ Web: www.hapco.com

Hapman 6002 E N Ave .... Kalamazoo MI 49048 269-343-1675 349-2477 207
TF: 800-427-6260 ■ Web: www.hapman.com

Happy & Healthy Products Inc
1600 S Dixie Hwy Ste 200 .... Boca Raton FL 33432 561-367-0739 368-5267 297-6
Web: www.fruitfull.com

Happy Chef Systems Inc
51646 US Hwy 169 .... Mankato MN 56001 507-388-2953 345-4585 670

Happy Faces Personnel Group Inc
4333 Lynburn Dr .... Tucker GA 30084 770-414-9071 260
TF: 800-230-0043 ■ Web: www.happyfaces.net

Happy Hen Toys Ltd 7246 W Foster Ave .... Chicago IL 60656 847-831-3630 761
Web: www.happyhentoys.com

Happy Hollow Park & Zoo
1300 Senter Rd .... San Jose CA 95112 408-794-6400 823
TF: 800-786-1000 ■ Web: www.hhpz.org

Happy Joe's Inc 2705 Happy Joe Dr .... Bettendorf IA 52722 563-332-8811 332-5822 670
Web: www.happyjoes.com

Happy Kids Inc 100 W 33rd St .... New York NY 10001 212-239-4563 155-4
Web: happykidspersonalized.com

Happy Mexican Restaurant & Cantina
6080 Primacy Pkwy .... Memphis TN 38119 901-683-0000 671
Web: www.happymexican.com

Happy Sumo at the Riverwoods
4801 N University Ave .... Provo UT 84604 801-225-9100 671
Web: www.happysumosushi.com

Happy Time Tours & Travel
1475 Walsh St W .... Thunder Bay ON P7E4X6 807-473-5955 772
TF: 800-473-5955 ■ Web: www.httours.com

Happys Potato Chip Co
3900 Chandler Dr .... Minneapolis MN 55421 612-781-3121 123

Hapuna Beach Prince Hotel
62-100 Kauna'oa Dr .... Kamuela HI 96743 808-880-1111 880-3142 669
TF: 800-882-6060 ■ Web: www.princeresortshawaii.com

Hapuna Beach State Recreation Area
75 Aupuni St Rm 204 PO Box 936 .... Hilo HI 96721 808-882-6206 961-9599 565
Web: dlnr.hawaii.gov/dsp

Harada Industry of America Inc
22925 Venture Dr .... Novi MI 48375 248-374-9000 374-9100 61
Web: www.harada.com

Haralson County 70 Murphy Campus Blvd .... Waco GA 30182 770-537-5594 537-5873 338
TF: 800-955-7766 ■ Web: www.haralson.org

Haram-Christensen Corp 125 Asia Pl .... Carlstadt NJ 07072 201-507-8544 360-3
Web: www.haramchris.com

Harbar LLC 320 Turnpike St .... Canton MA 02021 781-828-0848 68
Web: www.harber.com

Harbec Inc 358 Timothy Ln .... Ontario NY 14519 585-265-0010 265-1306 608
TF: 888-521-4416 ■ Web: www.harbec.com

Harben Inc 2010 Ronald Regan Blvd .... Cumming GA 30041 770-889-9535 887-9411 641
TF: 800-327-5387 ■ Web: www.harben.com

Harbert Management Corp
2100 Third Ave N Ste 600 .... Birmingham AL 35203 205-987-5500 580
Web: www.harbert.net

Harbin Hot Springs
18424 Harbin Springs Rd PO Box 782 .... Middletown CA 95461 707-987-2477 987-0616 673
Web: www.harbin.org

Harbinger Group Inc
450 Pk Ave 29th Fl .... New York NY 10022 212-906-8555 296-12
NYSE: HRG ■ Web: www.harbingergroupinc.com

Harbison-Fischer 901 N Crowley Rd .... Crowley TX 76036 817-297-2211 297-4248 537
TF: 800-364-7867 ■ Web: doverals.com

HarbisonWalker International
ANH Refractories Co
1305 Cherrington Pkwy Ste 100 .... Moon Township PA 15108 412-375-6800 375-6731 662
Web: thinkhwi.com

Harbor Bay Club 200 Packet Landing Rd .... Alameda CA 94502 510-521-5414 354
Web: harborbayclub.com

Harbor Capital Management Inc
831 E Morehead St Ste 350 .... Charlotte NC 28202 704-377-6945 528
TF: 800-745-4195 ■ Web: harborcapitalmgmt.com

Harbor Court Hotel
165 Steuart St .... San Francisco CA 94105 415-882-1300 882-1313 379
TF: 866-792-6283 ■ Web: www.harborcourthotel.com

Harbor Court Hotel 550 Light St .... Baltimore MD 21202 410-234-0550 659-5925 379
TF: 800-766-3782 ■ Web: www.sonesta.com

Harbor Credit Union 800 Weise St .... Green Bay WI 54302 920-431-6688 219
TF: 800-827-4645 ■ Web: harborcu.com

Harbor Cruises LLC 1 Long Wharf .... Boston MA 02110 617-227-4321 760
TF: 800-826-9300 ■ Web: www.bostonharborcruises.com

Harbor Defense Museum
230 Sheridan Loop .... Brooklyn NY 11252 718-630-4349 520
TF: 800-987-6409 ■ Web: harbordefensemuseum.com

Harbor Express Inc 501 Quay Ave .... Wilmington CA 90744 310-513-6478 835-3794 780

Harbor Freight Tools
3491 Mission Oaks Blvd .... Camarillo CA 93011 805-445-4791 351
TF: 800-444-3353 ■ Web: www.harborfreight.com

Harbor Freight Transport Corp
301 Craneway St .... Newark NJ 07114 973-589-6700 589-6677 311
Web: www.harborusa.com

Harbor Health Systems LLC
1 Venture Ste 130 .... Irvine CA 92618 949-273-7020 239
TF: 855-521-7082 ■ Web: www.harborsys.com

Harbor Hospital Ctr
3001 S Hanover St .... Baltimore MD 21225 410-350-3200 354-4440 374-3
TF: 800-280-9006 ■ Web: www.medstarhealth.org

Harbor Hotel Provincetown
698 Commercial St Cape Cod .... Provincetown MA 02657 508-487-1711 378
Web: www.harborhotelptown.com

Harbor House 28 Pier 21 .... Galveston TX 77550 409-763-3321 765-6421 379
TF: 800-874-3721 ■ Web: www.harborhousepier21.com

Harbor House Seafood
2510 N Roan St .... Johnson City TN 37601 423-282-5122 671
Web: www.harborhousejc.com

Harbor Ind 14130 172nd Ave .... Grand Haven MI 49417 616-842-5330 842-1385 233
Web: www.harbor-ind.com

Harbor Light Hospice
800 Roosevelt Rd Bldg C Ste 206 .... Glen Ellyn IL 60137 630-300-3716 942-0118 371
TF: 800-419-0542 ■ Web: harborlighthospice.com

Harbor Manufacturing Inc
8300 W 185th St .... Tinley Park IL 60487 708-614-6400 295
Web: www.harbormfg.com

Harbor Playhouse
1802 N Chaparral Bldg Ste 2 .... Corpus Christi TX 78401 361-882-5500 572
Web: www.harborplayhouse.com

Harbor Rail Services of California Inc
1550 W Colorado Blvd .... Pasadena CA 91105 626-398-4065 188

Harbor Sales 1000 Harbor Ct .... Sudlersville MD 21668 800-345-1712 868-9257 613
TF: 800-345-1712 ■ Web: www.harborsales.net

Harbor Steel & Supply Corp
1115 E Broadway .... Muskegon MI 49444 231-739-7152 492
Web: www.harborsteel.com

Harbor Technologies LLC
681 Riverside Dr .... Augusta ME 04330 207-725-4878 106
Web: www.harbortech.us

Harbor View Hotel
131 N Water St Martha's Vineyard PO Box 7 .... Edgartown MA 02539 508-627-7000 379
TF: 800-225-6005 ■ Web: www.harbor-view.com

Harbor View Restaurant
301 Savannah Hwy .... Charleston SC 29407 843-556-7100 671
Web: www.harborviewdining.com

HarborLink Network Ltd
3131 S Dixie Dr Ste 500 .... Dayton OH 45439 937-294-2954 387
Web: www.harborlink.net

Harborlite 130 Castilian Dr .... Santa Barbara CA 93117 805-562-0200 503-3
TF: 800-893-4445 ■ Web: www.worldminerals.com

HarborOne Credit Union
770 Oak St PO Box 720 .... Brockton MA 02301 508-895-1000 219
TF: 800-244-7592 ■ Web: www.harborone.com

Harborplace & the Gallery
201 E Pratt St .... Baltimore MD 21202 410-332-4191 547-7317 50-6
TF: 800-722-8614 ■ Web: www.harborplace.com

Harbors Home Health & Hospice
201 Seventh St .... Hoquiam WA 98550 360-532-5454 371
TF: 800-772-1319 ■ Web: myhhhh.org

Harborside Event Ctr
1375 Monroe St .... Fort Myers FL 33901 239-321-8110 205
Web: www.fmharborside.com

Harborside Hotel & Marina 55 W St .... Bar Harbor ME 04609 207-288-5033 288-3661 379
TF: 800-328-5033 ■ Web: www.theharborsidehotel.com

Harborside Inn 1 Christie's Landing .... Newport RI 02840 401-846-6600 379
TF: 800-427-9444 ■ Web: www.newportharborsideinn.com

Harborside Inn of Boston 185 State St .... Boston MA 02109 617-723-7500 670-6015 379
Web: www.harborsideinnboston.com

Harborside Suites At Little Harbor
536 Bahia Beach Blvd .... Ruskin FL 33570 800-327-2773 922-6171* 669
*Fax Area Code: 813 ■ TF: 800-327-2773 ■ Web: www.staylittleharbor.com

Harbortown Industries Inc
28477 N Ballard Dr .... Lake Forest IL 60045 847-327-9900 820
Web: www.harbortown.net

Harbor-UCLA Medical Ctr
1000 W Carson St .... Torrance CA 90509 310-222-2345 374-3
Web: www.humc.edu

Harbour Contractors Inc
23830 W Main St .... Plainfield IL 60544 815-254-5500 254-5505 186
TF: 800-561-3357 ■ Web: www.harbour-cm.com

Harbour Homes LLC
400 N 34th St Ste 300 .... Seattle WA 98103 206-315-8130 653
Web: www.harbourhomes.com

Harbour Industries Inc
4744 Shelburne Rd PO Box 188 .... Shelburne VT 05482 802-985-3311 985-9534 814
TF: 800-659-4733 ■ Web: www.harbourind.com

Harbour Investments Inc
575 D'Onofrio Dr Ste 300 .... Madison WI 53719 608-662-6100 401
Web: www.harbourinv.com

Harbour Sixty Steakhouse
60 Harbour St .... Toronto ON M5J1B7 416-777-2111 671
Web: www.harboursixty.com

Harbour Towers Hotel & Suites
345 Quebec St .... Victoria BC V8V1W4 250-385-2405 378
TF: 800-663-5896 ■ Web: www.harbourtowers.com

Harbour's Edge 401 E Linton Blvd .... Delray Beach FL 33483 561-272-7979 672
TF: 888-417-9281 ■ Web: lifespacecommunities.com

Phone | Fax | Class

Harbour, Smith, Harris & Merritt, PC
222 N Fredonia St. Longview TX 75601 903-757-4001 428
Web: www.harbourlaw.com

Harbourtowne Golf Resort & Conference Ctr
9784 Martingham Dr Saint Michaels MD 21663 410-745-9066 669
Web: www.harbourtowne.com

HarbourVest Partners LLC
1 Financial Ctr Boston MA 02111 617-348-3707 350-0305 792
Web: www.harbourvest.com

HARC (Houston Advanced Research Ctr)
4800 Research Forest Dr The Woodlands TX 77381 281-364-6000 363-7914 668
Web: www.harcresearch.org

Harch Capital Management LLC
7400 N Federal Hwy Ste A5 Boca Raton FL 33487 561-226-6199 690
Web: www.harchcapital.com

Harco Company Ltd
5915 Coopers Ave Mississauga ON L4Z1R9 905-890-1220 35
TF: 800-387-9503 ■ *Web:* www.harcoco.com

Harco Laboratories Inc 186 Cedar St Branford CT 06405 203-483-3700 201
Web: www.harcolabs.com

Harcourt Equipment
313 Hwy 169 & 175 E Harcourt IA 50544 515-354-5332 274
TF: 800-445-5646 ■ *Web:* www.kcnielsen.com

Harcourt Outlines Inc
7765 S 175 W PO Box 128 Milroy IN 46156 800-428-6584 278-5165 55
TF: 800-428-6584 ■ *Web:* www.harcourtoutlinesstore.com

Harcourt Pencil Co 7765 S 175 W Milroy IN 46156 800-428-6584 571
TF: 800-428-6584 ■ *Web:* www.harcourtoutlinesstore.com

Harcros Chemicals Inc
5200 Speaker Rd Kansas City KS 66106 913-321-3131 621-7718 146
TF: 800-424-9300 ■ *Web:* harcros.com

Harcum College 750 Montgomery Ave Bryn Mawr PA 19010 610-525-4100 526-6147* 162
**Fax:* Admissions ■ *TF:* 800-537-3000 ■ *Web:* www.harcum.edu

Hard Labor Creek State Park
5 Hard Labor Creek Rd Rutledge GA 30663 706-557-3001 565
Web: www.gastateparks.org

Hard Mfg Company Inc 230 Grider St Buffalo NY 14215 800-873-4273 319-3
TF: 800-873-4273 ■ *Web:* www.hardmfg.com

Hard Rock Cafe 999 E St NW Washington DC 20004 202-737-7625 671
Web: www.hardrock.com

Hard Rock Cafe 6050 Universal Blvd Orlando FL 32819 407-351-7625 351-3983 671
Web: www.hardrock.com

Hard Rock Cafe
Boardwalk at Virginia Ave Atlantic City NJ 08401 609-441-0007 449-1836 671
Web: www.hardrock.com

Hard Rock Cafe 111 W Crocket St San Antonio TX 78205 210-224-7625 224-7693 671
TF: 888-519-6683 ■ *Web:* www.hardrock.com

Hard Rock Cafe 3 S Second St Ste 117 Phoenix AZ 85004 602-261-7625 671
Web: www.hardrock.com

Hard Rock Cafe 45 Monroe St Detroit MI 48226 313-964-7625 671
TF: 888-519-6683 ■ *Web:* www.hardrock.com

Hard Rock Cafe Indianapolis
49 S Meridian St Indianapolis IN 46204 317-636-2550 671
Web: www.hardrock.com

Hard Rock Cafe International Inc
1837 Kapiolani Blvd Honolulu HI 96826 808-955-7383 671
Web: www.hardrock.com

Hard Rock Cafe International Inc
6100 Old Pk Ln Orlando FL 32835 407-445-7625 670
TF: 888-519-6683 ■ *Web:* www.hardrock.com

Hard Rock Cafe Key West 313 Duval St Key West FL 33040 305-293-0230 671
TF: 800-869-4631 ■ *Web:* www.hardrock.com

Hard Rock Hotel & Casino
4455 Paradise Rd Las Vegas NV 89169 702-693-5000 669
TF: 800-473-7625 ■ *Web:* www.hardrockhotel.com

Hard Rock Hotel & Casino Biloxi
777 Beach Blvd Biloxi MS 39530 228-374-7625 133
TF: 877-877-6256 ■ *Web:* www.hrhcbiloxi.com

Hard Rock Hotel at Universal Orlando Resort
5800 Universal Blvd Orlando FL 32819 407-503-2000 503-2010 669
TF: 888-430-4999 ■ *Web:* www.loewshotels.com

Hard Rock Hotel Chicago
230 N Michigan Ave Chicago IL 60601 312-345-1000 379
Web: www.hardrockhotelchicago.com

Hard Rock Hotel Palm Springs
150 S Indian Canyon Dr Palm Springs CA 92262 760-325-9676 707
Web: www.hrhpalmsprings.com

Hard Rock Hotel San Diego
207 Fifth Ave San Diego CA 92101 619-702-3000 702-3007 379
TF: 866-751-7625 ■ *Web:* www.hardrockhotelsd.com

Hard Times Cafe 1404 King St Alexandria VA 22314 703-837-0050 837-0057 670
Web: www.hardtimes.com

Hardaway Concrete Co Inc
2001 Taylor St Columbia SC 29204 803-254-4350 182

Hardaway Group 615 Main St Nashville TN 37206 615-254-5461 187
Web: www.hardaway.net

Hardee County
412 W Orange St Rm A-203 Wauchula FL 33873 863-773-6952 773-0958 338
Web: www.hardeecounty.net

Hardee County School District
1009 N Sixth Ave PO Box 1678 Wauchula FL 33873 863-773-9058 773-0069 685
Web: www.hardee.k12.fl.us

Hardeman County 100 N Main St Bolivar TN 38008 731-658-3541 338
TF: 800-336-2036 ■ *Web:* hardemancountytn.com

Hardeman County PO Box 30 Quanah TX 79252 940-663-2911 663-6302 338
Web: hardemantx.com

Hardeman County Correctional Facility
2520 Union Springs Rd PO Box 549 Whiteville TN 38075 731-254-6000 254-6060 213
Web: www.tn.gov

Harden Furniture Inc
8550 Mill Pond Way McConnellsville NY 13401 315-245-1000 245-2884 319-2
Web: www.hardenfurniture.com

Harden House, The
626 Grand Central St Clearwater FL 33756 727-442-7546 321

Harder Corp 7029 Raywood Rd Monona WI 53713 608-271-5127 271-4677 559
TF: 800-261-3400 ■ *Web:* www.hardercorp.com

Harder Mechanical Contractors Inc
2148 NE M L King Blvd Portland OR 97212 503-281-1112 189-10
Web: www.harder.com

Phone | Fax | Class

Hardesty & Hanover LLP
1501 Broadway Ste 310 New York NY 10036 212-944-1150 391-0297 261
Web: www.hardesty-hanover.com

HARDI Hydronic Heating & Cooling Council
445 Hutchinson Ave Ste 550 Columbus OH 43235 614-345-4328 49-18
TF: 888-253-2128 ■ *Web:* www.hardinet.org

Hardi Inc 1500 W 76th St Davenport IA 52806 563-386-1730 386-1280 273
TF: 866-770-7063 ■ *Web:* www.hardi-us.com

Hardide Coatings Inc 440 Louisiana St Houston TX 77002 713-221-9020 146
Web: www.hardide.com

Hardie-Tynes Company Inc
800 28th St N Birmingham AL 35203 205-252-5191 18
Web: www.hardie-tynes.com

Hardin & Company Ltd
113 S 19th Ave Ste C Bozeman MT 59718 406-587-1211 652
Web: hardinre.com

Hardin County
1215 Edgington Ave County Courthouse Eldora IA 50627 641-858-2328 858-2320 338
Web: www.hardincountyia.gov

Hardin County PO Box 124 Elizabethtown IL 62931 618-287-4333 338
TF: 800-248-4373 ■ *Web:* www.hardincountyil.org

Hardin County 14 Public Sq Elizabethtown KY 42701 270-765-2171 765-6193 338
TF: 800-437-0092 ■ *Web:* www.hccoky.org

Hardin County 1 Courthouse Sq Ste 100 Kenton OH 43326 419-674-2205 338
Web: www.co.hardin.oh.us

Hardin County 495 Main St Savannah TN 38372 731-925-3921 925-6987 338
TF: 800-552-3866 ■ *Web:* www.tourhardincounty.org

Hardin County Bank, The (HCB)
235 Wayne Rd Savannah TN 38372 731-925-9001 925-8106 70
Web: www.hardincountybank.com

Hardin County Chamber & Business Alliance (HCCBA)
225 S Detroit St Kenton OH 43326 419-673-4131 674-4876 139
Web: www.hardincountyoh.org

Hardin County News PO Box 8240 Lumberton TX 77657 409-755-4912 755-7731 532-4
Web: www.beaumontenterprise.com

Hardin County Public Library
100 Jim Owen Dr Elizabethtown KY 42701 270-769-6337 434-3
Web: www.hcpl.info

Hardin Library for the Health Sciences
100 Main Library 125 West Washington St Iowa City IA 52242 319-335-9871 353-3752 434-1
Web: www.lib.uiowa.edu/hardin

Hardin Memorial Hospital
913 W Dixie Ave Elizabethtown KY 42701 270-737-1212 374-3
TF: 800-955-9455 ■ *Web:* www.hmh.net

Hardin's Florist Supply
329 W Bowman Ave Liberty NC 27298 336-622-3035 292
TF: 800-672-8226 ■ *Web:* www.hardins.com

Hardin, Kundla, McKeon & Poletto PA
673 Morris Ave Springfield NJ 07081 973-912-5222 428
TF: 800-253-3855 ■ *Web:* www.hkmpp.com

Harding & Carbone Inc
3903 Bellaire Blvd Houston TX 77025 713-664-1215 734
Web: www.hctax.com

Harding County
410 Ramsland St PO Box 534 Buffalo SD 57720 605-375-3351 375-3432 338
Web: ujs.sd.gov

Harding Instruments
7741 Wagner Rd NW Edmonton AB T6E5X7 780-462-7100 201
TF: 888-792-1171 ■ *Web:* www.harding.ca

Harding Lake State Recreation Area
c/o Northern Area Office 3700 Airport Way Fairbanks AK 99709 907-451-2695 565
Web: www.dnr.alaska.gov/parks/units/harding.htm

Harding Poorman 4923 W 78th St Indianapolis IN 46268 317-876-3355 174
Web: www.hardingpoorman.com

Harding Shymanski & Company PSC
21 SE Third St Ste 500 Evansville IN 47708 812-464-9161 2
Web: www.hsccpa.com

Harding University 915 E Market Ave Searcy AR 72149 501-279-4000 279-4129 166
TF: 800-477-4407 ■ *Web:* www.harding.edu

Harding University Graduate School of Religion
915 E Market Ave Searcy AR 72143 501-279-4407 167-3
TF: 800-477-4407 ■ *Web:* harding.edu/bible/faculty

Hardinge Inc 1 Hardinge Dr Elmira NY 14902 607-734-2281 455
NASDAQ: HDNG ■ *TF:* 800-843-8801 ■ *Web:* www.hardinge.com

Hardings Market-West Inc
211 Bannister Plainwell MI 49080 269-685-9807 297-8
Web: www.hardings.com

Hardin-Simmons University
2200 Hickory St Abilene TX 79698 325-670-1206 671-2115* 166
**Fax:* Admissions ■ *TF:* 877-464-7889 ■ *Web:* www.hsutx.edu

Hardline Installation Inc
1759 Green Cove Rd St B Brasstown NC 28902 828-835-8209 317
TF: 800-975-4406 ■ *Web:* www.hardlineinstallation.com

Hardrives of Delray Inc
2101 S Congress Ave Delray Beach FL 33445 561-278-0456 278-2147 188-4
TF: 800-736-4255 ■ *Web:* www.hardrivespaving.com

Hardware & Forging Co
3270 E 79th St Cleveland OH 44104 216-641-5200 483
Web: www.clevelandhardware.com

Hardware Distribution Warehouses Inc (HDW)
6900 Woolworth Rd Shreveport LA 71129 318-686-8527 351
TF Cust Svc: 800-256-8527 ■ *Web:* www.hdwinc.com

Hardware Grill 9698 Jasper Ave Edmonton AB T5H3V5 780-423-0969 671
Web: www.hardwaregrill.com

Hardware Group Ltd
7667 Cahill Rd Ste 400 Minneapolis MN 55439 866-408-9273 196
TF: 866-408-9273

Hardware Sales Inc 2034 James St Bellingham WA 98225 360-734-6140 350
Web: www.hardwaresales.net

Hardware Specialty Company Inc
48-75 36th St Long Island NY 11101 718-361-9393 706-0238 246
Web: www.hardwarespecialty.com

Hardware Suppliers of America Inc (HSI)
1400 E Fire Tower Rd Greenville NC 27858 800-334-5625 351
TF: 800-334-5625 ■ *Web:* www.hardwaresuppliers.com

Hardwick Clothes Inc
3800 Old Tasso Rd Cleveland TN 37312 800-251-6392 155-12
TF: 800-251-6392 ■ *Web:* hardwick.com

Phone | Fax | Class

Hardwire LLC 1947 Clarke Ave. . . . . Pocomoke City MD 21851 410-957-3669 492
Web: www.hardwirellc.com

Hardwood Plywood & Veneer Assn (HPVA)
1825 Michael Faraday Dr . . . . Reston VA 20190 703-435-2900 435-2537 49-3
Web: www.hpva.org

Hardwoods of Michigan Inc 430 Div St . . . . Clinton MI 49236 517-456-7431 456-4931 683
TF: 800-327-2812 ■ *Web:* www.hmilumber.com

Hardy Bros Inc 6406 Siloam Rd . . . . Siloam NC 27047 336-374-5050 186
Web: www.hardybros.com

Hardy Corp 350 Industrial Dr . . . . Birmingham AL 35211 205-252-7191 326-6268 189-10
TF: 800-289-4822 ■ *Web:* www.hardycorp.com

Hardy County
204 Washington St Rm 111 . . . . Moorefield WV 26836 304-530-0250 530-0251 338
TF: 800-222-1222 ■ *Web:* hardycounty.com

Hardy Diagnostics Inc
1430 W Mccoy Ln . . . . Santa Maria CA 93455 805-346-2766 475
Web: www.hardydiagnostics.com

Hardy Lake 4171 E Harrod Rd . . . . Scottsburg IN 47170 812-794-3800 565
Web: www.in.gov

Harford Community College
401 Thomas Run Rd . . . . Bel Air MD 21015 410-879-8920 162
Web: www.harford.edu

Harford County Chamber of Commerce
108 S Bond St . . . . Bel Air MD 21014 410-838-2020 893-4715 139
TF: 800-682-8536 ■ *Web:* www.harfordchamber.org

Harford County Public Library
1221-A Brass Mill Rd . . . . Belcamp MD 21017 410-575-6761 273-5606 434-3
TF: 800-944-7403 ■ *Web:* www.hcplonline.org

Harford Refrigeration Company Inc
7915 Philadelphia Rd . . . . Rosedale MD 21237 410-866-6200 189-10
Web: harfordrefrigeration.com

Harford Systems Inc
2225 Pulaski Hwy PO Box 700 . . . . Aberdeen MD 21001 410-272-3400 482
TF: 800-664-7620 ■ *Web:* harfordsystems.com

Harger Inc 301 Ziegler Dr . . . . Grayslake IL 60030 847-548-8700 815
Web: www.harger.com

Hargis Engineers Inc
1201 Third Ave Ste 600 . . . . Seattle WA 98101 206-448-3376 256
Web: www.hargis.biz

Hargrave Military Academy (HMA)
200 Military Dr . . . . Chatham VA 24531 434-432-2481 432-3129 622
TF: 800-432-2480 ■ *Web:* www.hargrave.edu

Hargray Communications
870-C William Hilton Pkwy . . . . Hilton Head Island SC 29938 843-341-1501 736
TF: 800-726-1266 ■ *Web:* www.hargray.com

Hargreaves & Taylor LLP
750 B St Ste 2300 . . . . San Diego CA 92101 619-238-5501 428
TF: 800-968-5313 ■ *Web:* www.htfamlaw.com

Hargrove & Assoc
100 N Sixth St Ste 720C . . . . Minneapolis MN 55403 612-436-5500 396
Web: web.hargrove-epc.com

Hargrove Electric Company Inc
1522 Market Ctr Blvd . . . . Dallas TX 75207 214-742-8665 744-0846 189-4
Web: www.hargroveelectric.com

Hargrove Inc 1 Hargrove Dr . . . . Lanham MD 20706 301-306-9000 232
Web: www.caw.ca

Hari World Travel Inc
3400 Peachtree Rd NE Ste 815 . . . . Atlanta GA 30326 404-233-5005 772

Harig Manufacturing Corp
5757 W Howard St . . . . Niles IL 60714 847-647-9500 647-8351 757
Web: www.harigmfg.com

Harkcon 1390 Chain Bridge Rd 570 . . . . Mclean VA 22101 800-499-6456 463
TF: 800-499-6456 ■ *Web:* www.harkcon.com

Harken Energy Corp
180 State St Ste 200 . . . . Southlake TX 76092 817-424-2424 536
OTC: HKNI ■ *Web:* www.hkninc.com

Harker's Distribution Inc
801 Sixth St SW . . . . Le Mars IA 51031 712-546-8171 297-10
Web: lemarssentinel.com

Harkess-Ord LLC 263 W 38th St Ste 306 . . . . New York NY 10018 212-704-9989 463
Web: www.harkess-ord.com

Harkins Builders Inc
2201 Warwick Way . . . . Marriottsville MD 21104 410-750-2600 480-4299 186
TF: 800-227-2345 ■ *Web:* www.harkinsbuilders.com

Harkins Theatres
7511 E Mcdonald Dr . . . . Scottsdale AZ 85250 480-627-7777 748
Web: www.harkinstheatres.com

Harlan ARH Hospital 81 Ballpark Rd . . . . Harlan KY 40831 606-573-8100 374-3
TF: 800-274-9375 ■ *Web:* www.arh.org

Harlan Bakeries-Avon LLC
7597 E US Hwy 36 . . . . Avon IN 46123 317-272-3600 297-11
Web: www.harlanbakeries.com

Harlan Cabinets Inc
12707 Spencerville Rd . . . . Harlan IN 46743 260-657-5154 115
Web: www.harlancabinets.com

Harlan Community Television Inc
124 S First St . . . . Harlan KY 40831 606-573-2945 116
Web: www.harlanonline.net

Harlan Consulting Services Inc
2515 Briarpark Dr . . . . Houston TX 77042 713-464-2484 463
Web: www.harlanconsulting.com

Harlan County 311 Main St . . . . Alma NE 68920 800-762-5498 338
TF: 800-762-5498 ■ *Web:* www.harlantourism.org

Harlan County 201 S Main St . . . . Harlan KY 40831 606-573-4495 573-9485 338
TF: 800-988-4660 ■ *Web:* www.harlancountytrails.com

Harlan County Chamber of Commerce
PO Box 268 . . . . Harlan KY 40831 606-573-4717 139
Web: www.harlancountychamber.com

Harlan Materials Handling Corp
27 Stanley Rd . . . . Kansas City KS 66115 913-342-5650 321-5802 470
TF: 800-255-4262 ■ *Web:* www.harlan-corp.com

Harlandale Isd 102 Genevieve Dr . . . . San Antonio TX 78214 210-989-4300 685
Web: www.harlandale.net

Harlee Manor Nursing & Rehabilitation Center
463 W Sproul Rd . . . . Springfield PA 19064 610-544-2200 371
TF: 800-917-3049 ■ *Web:* harleemanor.com

Harlem Children's Zone Inc
35 E 125th St . . . . New York NY 10035 212-360-3255 289-0661 685
Web: www.hcz.org

Phone | Fax | Class

Harlem Globetrotters International Inc
400 E Van Buren St Ste 300 . . . . Phoenix AZ 85004 602-258-0000 258-5925 181
TF: 800-641-4667 ■ *Web:* www.harlemglobetrotters.com

Harlem Hospital Ctr 506 Lenox Ave . . . . New York NY 10037 212-939-1000 374-3
Web: nyc.gov

Harlequin 233 Broadway Ste 1001 . . . . New York NY 10279 212-553-4200 227-8969 637-2
TF: 800-873-8635 ■ *Web:* www.harlequin.com

Harlequin Enterprises Ltd
225 Duncan Mill Rd . . . . Don Mills ON M3B3K9 416-445-5860 637-2
TF: 888-343-9777 ■ *Web:* www.harlequin.com

Harley Marine Services Inc
910 SW Spokane St . . . . Seattle WA 98134 206-628-0051 803-1
Web: www.harleymarine.com

Harley-Davidson Financial Services Inc
PO Box 21489 . . . . Carson City NV 89721 888-691-4337 217
TF: 888-691-4337 ■ *Web:* www.harley-davidson.com

Harley-Davidson Inc
3700 W Juneau Ave . . . . Milwaukee WI 53208 414-342-4680 343-4621* 517
NYSE: HOG ■ *Fax:* Hum Res ■ *TF:* 800-424-9393 ■ *Web:* harley-davidson.com

Harleysville Bank 271 Main St . . . . Harleysville PA 19438 215-256-8828 513-9393 360-2
NASDAQ: HARL ■ *TF:* 888-256-8828 ■ *Web:* www.harleysvillesavings.com

Harleysville Group Inc
355 Maple Ave . . . . Harleysville PA 19438 215-256-5000 360-4
NASDAQ: HGIC ■ *TF:* 800-523-6344 ■ *Web:* www.harleysvillegroup.com

Harleysville Insurance Co of New Jersey
112 W Park Dr . . . . Mount Laurel NJ 08054 856-642-9779 642-9412* 391-4
Fax: Claims ■ *TF:* 800-322-5521 ■ *Web:* www.harleysvillegroup.com

Harleysville Mutual Insurance Co
355 Maple Ave . . . . Harleysville PA 19438 215-256-5000 391-2
TF: 800-523-6344 ■ *Web:* www.harleysville.com

Harleysville Worcester Insurance Co
120 Front St Ste 400 . . . . Worcester MA 01608 508-754-6666 752-7903* 391-4
Fax: Hum Res ■ *TF:* 800-225-7387 ■ *Web:* www.harleysvillegroup.com

Harlick & Company Inc
893 American St . . . . San Carlos CA 94070 650-593-2093 593-9704 710
Web: www.harlick.com

Harlingen Area Chamber of Commerce
311 E Tyler St . . . . Harlingen TX 78550 956-423-5440 425-3870 139
TF: 800-225-5345 ■ *Web:* www.harlingen.com

Harlingen High School
1201 Marshall St . . . . Harlingen TX 78550 956-427-3600 685
Web: hcisd.org

Harlingen Public Library
410 76th Dr . . . . Harlingen TX 78550 956-216-5800 434-3

Harllee Packing Inc 2308 US 301 N . . . . Palmetto FL 34221 941-722-7747 11-1
Web: www.harlleepacking.com

Harlo Corp PO Box 129 . . . . Grandville MI 49468 616-538-0550 470
TF: 800-391-4151 ■ *Web:* www.harlo.com

Harlo Corp 4210 Ferry St SW . . . . Grandville MI 49468 616-538-0550 190
Web: www.harlocorporation.com

Harlow Aerostructures LLC
1501 McLean Blvd S . . . . Wichita KS 67213 316-265-5268 22
Web: www.harlowair.com

Harlow's Casino 4280 Harlow Blvd . . . . Greenville MS 38701 662-335-9797 42
TF: 800-303-3321 ■ *Web:* www.harlowscasino.com

Harmac Medical Products Inc
2201 Bailey Ave . . . . Buffalo NY 14211 716-897-4500 476
Web: www.harmac.com

Harman Construction Inc
1633 Rogers Rd . . . . Fort Worth TX 76107 817-336-5780 336-5797 186
Web: harmanconstructioninc.net

Harman International Industries Inc
400 Atlantic St 15th Fl . . . . Stamford CT 06901 203-328-3500 52
NYSE: HAR ■ *TF:* 800-473-0602 ■ *Web:* www.harman.com

Harman Kardon Inc
250 Crossways Pk Dr . . . . Woodbury NY 11797 516-496-3400 52
Web: www.harmankardon.com

Harman Management Corp
199 First St Ste 212 . . . . Los Altos CA 94022 650-941-5681 670

Harman Music Group 8760 S Sandy Pkwy . . . . Sandy UT 84070 801-566-8800 566-7005 52
Web: www.dbxpro.com

Harman Press Inc, The
6840 Vineland Ave . . . . North Hollywood CA 91605 818-432-0570 627
Web: www.harmanpress.com

Harman, Claytor, Corrigan & Wellman PC
PO Box 70280 . . . . Richmond VA 23255 804-747-5200 428
TF: 877-747-4229 ■ *Web:* www.hccw.com

Harman/Becker Automotive Systems
39001 W 12 Mile Rd . . . . Farmington Hills MI 48331 248-994-2100 994-2900 52
Web: www.harman.com

Harmelin Media
525 Righters Ferry Rd . . . . Bala Cynwyd PA 19004 610-668-7900 6
TF: 800-276-2722 ■ *Web:* www.harmelin.com

Harmer Assoc 100 S Wacker Dr Ste 1950 . . . . Chicago IL 60606 312-407-7180 390
Web: www.harmer.com

Harmon Brewing Co 1938 Pacific Ave . . . . Tacoma WA 98402 253-383-2739 671
TF: 800-272-2662 ■ *Web:* harmonbrewingco.com

Harmon Curran Spielberg & Eisenberg
1726 M St NW Ste 600 . . . . Washington DC 20036 202-328-3500 428
TF: 800-900-4250 ■ *Web:* www.harmoncurran.com

Harmon Electric Assn Inc (HEA)
114 N First St PO Box 393 . . . . Hollis OK 73550 580-688-3342 245
TF: 800-643-7769 ■ *Web:* www.harmonelectric.com

Harmon Medical & Rehabilitation Hospital
2170 E Harmon Ave . . . . Las Vegas NV 89119 702-794-0100 794-0041 374-6
Web: fundltc.com

Harmon Stores Inc 650 Liberty Ave . . . . Union NJ 07083 866-427-6661 237
TF: 866-427-6661 ■ *Web:* www.harmondiscount.com

Harmonia Inc 2020 Kraft Dr Ste 1000 . . . . Blacksburg VA 24060 540-951-5900 177
Web: www.harmonia.com

Harmonic Drive LLC 247 Lynnfield St . . . . Peabody MA 01960 978-532-1800 61
TF: 800-921-3332 ■ *Web:* www.harmonicdrive.net

Harmonic Inc 4300 N First St . . . . San Jose CA 95134 408-542-2500 542-2511 647
NASDAQ: HLIT ■ *TF:* 800-322-2885 ■ *Web:* www.harmonicinc.com

Harmonic International LLC
10 E Lee St Ste 2704 . . . . Baltimore MD 21202 410-727-3554 7
Web: www.harmonicinternational.com

Phone | Fax | Class

Harmonie State Park
3451 Harmonie State Pk Rd — New Harmony IN 47631 — 812-682-4821 — 565
TF: 866-622-6746 ■ Web: www.in.gov

Harmonix Music Systems Inc
625 Massachusetts Ave — Cambridge MA 02139 — 617-491-6144 — 177
Web: harmonixmusic.com

Harmonix Technologies Inc
4915 Paseo De Norte NE Ste A — Albuquerque NM 87113 — 505-205-1585 — 180
TF: 800-800-7004 ■ Web: www.harmonixtechnologies.com

Harmons Grocery
3540 S 4000 W — West Valley City UT 84120 — 801-969-8261 — 964-1299 — 345
Web: www.harmonsgrocery.com

Harmony Castings LLC 251 Perry Hwy — Harmony PA 16037 — 724-452-5811 — 452-0118 — 308
Web: www.harmonycastings.com

Harmony Dental Lab
758 W Duval St — Jacksonville FL 32202 — 904-354-4467 — 418
TF: 888-354-3594 ■ Web: www.harmonydental.com

Harmony Foundation Inc
1600 Fish Hatchery Rd — Estes Park CO 80517 — 970-586-4491 — 726
TF: 866-686-7867 ■ Web: www.harmonyfoundationinc.com

Harmony Gold Music Inc
7655 W Sunset Blvd — Los Angeles CA 90046 — 323-851-4900 — 514
Web: www.harmonygold.com

Harmony Nursing & Rehabilitation Center Inc
3919 W Foster Ave — Chicago IL 60625 — 773-588-9500 — 371
TF: 800-422-9300 ■ Web: www.harmonychicago.com

Harmony Park Safari
431 Clouds Cove Rd SE — Huntsville AL 35803 — 256-723-3880 — 823

Harmony Press 717 W Berwick St — Easton PA 18042 — 610-559-9800 — 627
Web: www.harmonypress.com

Harmony Vegetarian Chinese Restaurant
4897 Buford Hwy Ste 109 — Chamblee GA 30341 — 770-457-7288 — 671
Web: www.harmonyvegetarian.com

Harms Charters 532 S Vly View Rd — Sioux Falls SD 57106 — 605-336-3339 — 336-8731 — 107

Harms Oil Co 337 22nd Ave S — Brookings SD 57006 — 605-696-5000 — 580
TF: 800-376-8476 ■ Web: www.harmsoil.net

Harn Homestead & 1889er Museum
1721 N Lincoln Blvd — Oklahoma City OK 73105 — 405-235-4058 — 235-4041 — 520
Web: www.harnhomestead.com

Harnack Co 6016 Nordic Dr — Cedar Falls IA 50613 — 319-277-0660 — 772-2027* — 429
*Fax Area Code: 800 ■ TF Cust Svc: 800-772-2022 ■ Web: www.harnack.net

Harness Racing Museum & Hall of Fame
240 Main St — Goshen NY 10924 — 845-294-6330 — 294-3463 — 522
Web: www.harnessmuseum.com

Harnett Correctional Institution
1210 McNeil St — Lillington NC 27546 — 910-893-2751 — 893-6432 — 213
Web: www.ncdps.gov/index2.cfm?a=000003,002391,002934

Harnett County PO Box 759 — Lillington NC 27546 — 910-893-7555 — 814-2662 — 338
Web: www.harnett.org

Harnett County Board of Education
1008 S 11th St — Lillington NC 27546 — 910-893-8151 — 893-8839 — 685
TF: 800-342-9647 ■ Web: www.harnett.k12.nc.us

Harnett County Public Library
601 S Main St — Lillington NC 27546 — 910-893-3446 — 893-3001 — 434-3
Web: harnett.libguides.com/library

Harney County 450 N Buena Vista Ste 14 — Burns OR 97720 — 541-573-6641 — 573-8370 — 338
Web: www.co.harney.or.us

Harney Electric Co-op Inc
277 Lottery Ln PO Box 587 — Hines OR 97738 — 541-573-2061 — 245
Web: www.harneyelectric.org

Harney Rock & Paving Co 457 S Date Ave — Burns OR 97720 — 541-573-7855 — 573-3532 — 503-5
TF: 888-298-2681 ■ Web: www.harneyrock.com

Harnois Groupe Petrolier Inc
80 Rt 158 — Saint Thomas QC J0K3L0 — 450-759-7979 — 579
Web: www.harnoisgroupepetrolier.com

Haro Bicycles 1230 Avenida Chelsea — Vista CA 92081 — 760-599-0544 — 599-1237 — 82
Web: www.harobikes.com

Harodite Industries Inc 66 S St — Taunton MA 02780 — 508-824-6961 — 880-0696 — 745-7
TF: 800-864-0303 ■ Web: www.harodite.com

Harold & Belle's
2920 W Jefferson Blvd — Los Angeles CA 90018 — 323-735-9023 — 671
Web: haroldandbellesrestaurant.com

Harold A Davison 1723 Claredon Ave NW — Canton OH 44708 — 330-454-1244 — 652

Harold Beck & Sons Inc 11 Terry Dr — Newtown PA 18940 — 215-968-4600 — 203
Web: www.haroldbeck.com

Harold G Butzer Inc
730 Wicker Ln — Jefferson City MO 65109 — 573-636-4115 — 636-7053 — 189-10
TF: 800-769-1065 ■ Web: hgbutzer.com

Harold Import Company Inc
747 Vassar Ave — Lakewood NJ 08701 — 732-367-2800 — 360-3
Web: www.haroldskitchen.com

Harold L King & Company Inc
1420 Stafford St — Redwood City CA 94063 — 650-368-2233 — 297-8
Web: king-coffee.com

Harold Levinson Assoc (HLA)
21 Banfi Plaza — Farmingdale NY 11735 — 631-962-2400 — 962-9000 — 297-3
TF: 800-325-2512 ■ Web: www.hlacigars.com

Harold Ober Assoc Inc
425 Madison Ave Ste 1001 — New York NY 10017 — 212-759-8600 — 759-9428 — 444
TF: 800-627-7377 ■ Web: www.haroldober.com

Harold Parker State Forest
305 Middleton Rd — North Andover MA 01845 — 978-686-3391 — 565
Web: www.mass.gov

Harp, The 4408 Detroit Ave — Cleveland OH 44113 — 216-939-0200 — 671
Web: www.the-harp.com

Harpel Oil Company Inc
5480 Brighton Blvd — Commerce CO 80022 — 303-292-5005 — 581
Web: www.harpeloil.com

Harper & Pearson Company PC
1 Riverway Ste 1000 — Houston TX 77056 — 713-622-2310 — 2
Web: harperpearson.com

Harper Brush Works Inc
400 N Second St — Fairfield IA 52556 — 641-472-5186 — 472-3187 — 103
TF: 800-223-7894 ■ Web: www.harperbrush.com

Harper Co 1648 Petersburg Rd — Hebron KY 41048 — 859-586-8890 — 586-8891 — 188-4
TF: 800-880-3290 ■ Web: harperco.com

Harper College 1200 W Algonquin Rd — Palatine IL 60067 — 847-925-6000 — 162
Web: www.harpercollege.edu

Harper Construction Company Inc
2241 Kettner Blvd Ste 300 — San Diego CA 92101 — 619-233-7900 — 186
Web: www.harperconstruction.com

Harper Corp General Contractors
35 W Ct St Ste 400 — Greenville SC 29601 — 864-527-2500 — 527-2536 — 187
Web: www.harpercorp.com

Harper Corporation of America
11625 Steele Creek Rd — Charlotte NC 28273 — 704-588-3371 — 629
Web: www.harperimage.com

Harper County 201 N Jennings Ave — Anthony KS 67003 — 620-842-5555 — 842-3455 — 338
TF: 877-537-2110 ■ Web: www.harpercountyks.gov

Harper County 311 SE 1st — Buffalo OK 73834 — 580-735-6023 — 338

Harper Engraving & Printing Co
2626 Fisher Rd — Columbus OH 43204 — 614-276-0700 — 627
TF: 800-848-5196 ■ Web: www.harperengraving.com

Harper Gregg (Rep R - MS)
2227 Rayburn HOB — Washington DC 20515 — 202-225-5031 — 225-5797 — 342-2
Web: harper.house.gov

Harper Grey LLP
3200 Vancouver Centre 650 W Georgia St — Vancouver BC V6B4P7 — 604-687-0411 — 428
Web: www.harpergrey.com

Harper Houf Peterson Righ
205 SE Spokane St — Portland OR 97202 — 503-221-1131 — 256
Web: www.hhpr.com

Harper Industries Inc
616 Northview St — Paducah KY 42001 — 270-442-2753 — 443-9154 — 188-4
TF: 800-669-0077 ■ Web: www.harper1.com

Harper Industries Inc 52 Virginia St — Lucedale MS 39452 — 601-947-2746 — 155-3

Harper Love Adhesives Corp
11101 Westlake Dr — Charlotte NC 28273 — 704-588-1350 — 3
Web: www.harperlove.com

Harper Motors Inc 200 Hwy 531 — Minden LA 71055 — 318-377-0395 — 198
TF: 800-259-0395 ■ Web: www.harperminden.com

Harper Trucks Inc PO Box 12330 — Wichita KS 67277 — 316-942-1381 — 942-8508 — 470
TF: 800-835-4099 ■ Web: www.harpertrucks.com

Harper's Bazaar Magazine
300 W 57th St — New York NY 10019 — 212-903-5000 — 457-11
Web: www.harpersbazaar.com

Harper's Magazine
666 Broadway 11th Fl — New York NY 10012 — 212-420-5720 — 457-11
TF: 800-444-4653 ■ Web: www.harpers.org

Harpers Ferry National Historic Park
PO Box 65 — Harpers Ferry WV 25425 — 304-535-6029 — 535-6244 — 564
Web: www.nps.gov/hafe

Harpeth Capital LLC
3100 W End Ave Ste 710 — Nashville TN 37203 — 615-296-9840 — 690
Web: www.harpethcapital.com

Harpo Films Inc
345 N Maple Dr Ste 315 — Beverly Hills CA 90210 — 310-278-5559 — 514

Harpo Productions Inc 110 N Carpenter — Chicago IL 60607 — 312-633-1000 — 514
Web: www.oprah.com

Harpoon Brewery 306 Northern Ave — Boston MA 02210 — 617-574-9551 — 102
Web: www.harpoonbrewery.com

Harps Food Stores Inc
918 S Gutensohn Rd — Springdale AR 72762 — 479-751-7601 — 345
Web: www.harpsfood.com

Harrah's Ak-Chin Casino Resort
15406 Maricopa Rd — Maricopa AZ 85139 — 480-802-5000 — 669
TF General: 800-427-7247 ■ Web: www.totalrewards.com

Harrah's Cherokee Casino & Hotel
777 Casino Dr — Cherokee NC 28719 — 828-497-7777 — 133
TF General: 877-811-0777 ■ Web: www.caesars.com/harrahs-cherokee

Harrah's Council Bluffs
1 Harrahs Blvd — Council Bluffs IA 51501 — 712-329-6000 — 133
TF: 800-342-7724 ■ Web: www.caesars.com/harrahs-council-bluffs

Harrah's Joliet 151 N Joliet St — Joliet IL 60432 — 815-740-7800 — 133
TF: 800-522-4700 ■ Web: www.caesars.com/harrahs-joliet

Harrah's Las Vegas
3475 Las Vegas Blvd S — Las Vegas NV 89109 — 702-369-5000 — 378
Web: www.harrahslasvegas.com/casinos/harrahs-las-vegas/hotel-casino/property-home.shtml

Harrah's Laughlin 2900 S Casino Dr — Laughlin NV 89029 — 702-298-4600 — 133
TF: 800-427-7247 ■ Web: www.totalrewards.com

Harrah's New Orleans 8 Canal St — New Orleans LA 70130 — 504-533-6000 — 133
TF: 800-427-7247 ■ Web: www.caesars.com/harrahs-new-orleans

Harrah's Resort Atlantic City
777 Harrah's Blvd — Atlantic City NJ 08401 — 609-441-5000 — 133
TF: 800-342-7724 ■ Web: www.caesars.com/harrahsac

Harrah's Rincon Casino & Resort
777 Harrah's Rincon Way — Valley Center CA 92082 — 760-751-3100 — 669
TF: 800-522-4700 ■ Web: www.totalrewards.com

Harrang Long Gary Rudnick PC
360 E Tenth Ave Ste 300 — Eugene OR 97401 — 541-485-0220 — 428
TF: 800-315-4172 ■ Web: www.harrang.com

Harraseeket Inn 162 Main St — Freeport ME 04032 — 207-865-9377 — 379
TF: 800-342-6423 ■ Web: www.harraseeketinn.com

Harrell Bancshares Inc
1325 Hwy 278 Byp — Camden AR 71701 — 870-837-8300 — 360-2

Harri Plumbing & Heating Inc
809 W 12th St — Juneau AK 99801 — 907-586-3190 — 612
Web: www.harriplumbing.com

Harriet Beecher Stowe House
2950 Gilbert Ave — Cincinnati OH 45206 — 513-751-0651 — 520
Web: www.ohiohistory.org

Harrigan Lumber Company Inc
1033 Hornady Dr — Monroeville AL 36460 — 251-575-4821 — 683
Web: www.harriganlumber.com

Harriman State Park
3489 Green Canyon Rd — Island Park ID 83429 — 208-558-7368 — 565
TF: 866-634-3246 ■ Web: www.stateparks.com

Harriman State Park
Palisades Pkwy Exit 17 — Bear Mountain NY 10911 — 845-942-2560 — 565
Web: parks.ny.gov/parks/145

Harrington Beach State Park
531 County Rd D — Belgium WI 53004 — 262-285-3015 — 565
Web: dnr.wi.gov

Harrington Co 4248 Pk Glen Rd — Minneapolis MN 55416 — 952-928-7477 — 929-1318 — 47
Web: www.harringtoncompany.com

Harrington Corp, The 3721 Cohen Pl — Lynchburg VA 24501 — 434-845-7094 — 596
Web: www.harcofittings.com

Name / Address	City	State	ZIP	Phone	Fax	Class
Harrington Group, The 873 Inverness Cir	Spartanburg	SC	29306	864-585-5850		193
TF: 800-301-1763 ■ *Web:* harringtongroup.net						
Harrington Hoists Inc 401 W End Ave	Manheim	PA	17545	717-665-2000	665-2861	386
TF: 800-233-3010 ■ *Web:* www.harringtonhoists.com						
Harrington Hospital (HMH) 100 South St	Southbridge	MA	01550	508-765-9771	765-3147	374-3
TF: 800-416-6072 ■ *Web:* www.harringtonhospital.org						
Harrington Industrial Plastics LLC 14480 Yorba Ave	Chino	CA	91710	909-597-8641	597-9826	385
TF: 800-213-4528 ■ *Web:* www.harringtonplastics.com						
Harrington Investments Inc 1001 Second St Ste 325	Napa	CA	94559	707-252-6166		401
TF: 800-788-0154 ■ *Web:* harringtoninvestments.com						
Harrington Mold 1906 S Quaker Ridge Pl	Ontario	CA	91761	909-923-2627		697
Web: www.harringtonmold.com						
Harrington Museum 108 Fleming St	Harrington	DE	19952	302-398-3698		520
Web: harrington.delaware.gov/harrington-historical-society						
Harrington Raceway 15 W Rider Rd	Harrington	DE	19952	302-398-7223		642
TF: 888-887-5687 ■ *Web:* casino.harringtonraceway.com						
Harrington Signal Co 2519 Fourth Ave	Moline	IL	61265	309-762-0731		283
Web: www.harringtonsignal.com						
Harrington Tool Co 105 N Rath Ave	Ludington	MI	49431	231-843-3445		455
Web: harringtontool.net						
Harris & Assoc Inc 1401 Willow Pass Rd	Concord	CA	94520	925-827-4900	356-0998*	261
**Fax Area Code:* 866 ■ *Web:* www.weareharris.com						
Harris & Hart Inc 1759 W 1200 S	Ogden	UT	84404	801-731-0577		189-10
Harris & Sloan Consulting Group Inc 2295 Gateway Oaks Dr Ste 165	Sacramento	CA	95833	916-921-2800		256
Web: www.hscgi.com						
Harris Andy (Rep R - MD) 1533 Longworth Bldg	Washington	DC	20515	202-225-5311	225-0254	342-2
Web: harris.house.gov						
Harris Assoc LP 111 S Wacker Dr Ste 4600	Chicago	IL	60606	312-646-3600		401
Web: www.harrisassoc.com						
Harris Beach LLP 99 Garnsey Rd 130 E Main St	Pittsford	NY	14534	585-419-8800		445
Web: www.harrisbeach.com						
Harris Beach State Park 1655 Hwy 101 N	Brookings	OR	97415	541-469-2021		565
Web: oregonstateparks.org						
Harris CapRock 4400 S Sam Houston Pkwy E	Houston	TX	77048	832-668-2300		387
Web: www.caprock.com						
Harris Civil Engineers LLC 1200 Hillcrest St Ste 200	Orlando	FL	32803	407-629-4777		261
Web: www.harriscivilengineers.com						
Harris Computer Systems Inc 1 Antares Dr Ste 400	Ottawa	ON	K2E8C4	613-226-5511		180
TF: 800-239-6224 ■ *Web:* www.harriscomputer.com						
Harris Corp 1025 W NASA Blvd	Melbourne	FL	32919	321-727-9100		647
NYSE: HRS ■ *TF:* 800-442-7747 ■ *Web:* www.harris.com						
Harris Corp Government Communication Systems Div 1710 Main St NE	Palm Bay	FL	32905	321-727-9100		647
Web: www.govcomm.harris.com						
Harris Corp RF Communications Div 1680 University Ave	Rochester	NY	14610	585-244-5830	242-4755	647
TF: 866-264-8040 ■ *Web:* rf.harris.com						
Harris Cos Inc 909 Montreal Cir	Saint Paul	MN	55102	651-602-6500	602-6699	189-3
TF: 800-466-3993 ■ *Web:* www.hmcc.com						
Harris County 159 S College St PO Box 426	Hamilton	GA	31811	706-628-0010	628-4429	338
TF: 888-478-0010 ■ *Web:* www.harriscountychamber.org						
Harris County 201 Caroline St 4th Fl	Houston	TX	77002	713-755-5000		338
TF: 800-983-9933 ■ *Web:* harriscountytx.gov						
Harris County Public Library System 8080 El Rio St	Houston	TX	77054	713-749-9000	749-9090	434-3
Web: www.hcpl.net						
Harris Environmental Systems Inc 11 Connector Rd	Andover	MA	01810	978-470-8600	475-7903	664
Web: www.harrisenv.com						
Harris Farms Inc 27366 W Oakland Ave	Coalinga	CA	93210	559-884-2859	884-2855	10-11
TF: 800-311-6211 ■ *Web:* www.harrisfarms.com						
Harris Financial Services Inc 940 Spokane Ave	Whitefish	MT	59937	406-862-4400		690
TF: 800-735-7095 ■ *Web:* harrisfsi.com						
Harris Freeman & Company LP 3110 E Miraloma Ave	Anaheim	CA	92806	714-765-1190		296-37
Web: www.harrisfreeman.com						
Harris Goldman Productions Inc 8885 Rio San Diego Dr Ste 335	San Diego	CA	92108	619-299-7951		31
Web: www.harrisgoldman.com						
Harris Group Inc 300 Elliott Ave W	Seattle	WA	98119	206-494-9400	494-9500	261
Web: www.harrisgroup.com						
Harris Industrial Gases 8475 Auburn Blvd	Citrus Heights	CA	95610	916-725-2168		789
Web: www.harrisgas.com						
Harris Industries Inc 5181 Argosy Ave	Huntington Beach	CA	92649	714-898-8048	898-7108	732
TF: 800-222-6866 ■ *Web:* www.harrisind.com						
Harris Kamala D (Sen D - CA) 112 Hart Senate Office Bldg	Washington	DC	20510	202-224-3553	224-2200	342-2
Web: www.harris.senate.gov						
Harris Law Firm 1125 17th St Ste 450	Denver	CO	80202	303-622-5502		428
Web: www.harrisfamilylaw.com						
Harris Machine Co 8623 Highway 1	Oakes	ND	58474	701-742-2536		480
Web: www.harrismachineco.com						
Harris Manufacturing Inc 4775 E Vine Ave	Fresno	CA	93725	559-268-7422		482
Web: www.harrismfg.com						
Harris Methodist Fort Worth 1301 Pennsylvania Ave	Fort Worth	TX	76104	817-882-2000		374-3
TF: 800-222-1222 ■ *Web:* www.texashealth.org						
Harris Methodist-HEB 1600 Hospital Pkwy	Bedford	TX	76022	817-848-4000		374-3
Web: www.texashealth.org						
Harris Miller Miller & Hanson Inc 77 S Bedford St Ste 120	Burlington	MA	01803	781-229-0707		196
Web: www.hmmh.com						
Harris Miniature Golf 141 W Burk Ave	Wildwood	NJ	08260	609-522-4200	729-0100	188-3
TF: 888-294-6530 ■ *Web:* www.harrisminigolf.com						
Harris Moran Seed Co PO Box 4938	Modesto	CA	95352	800-320-4672	527-5312*	694
**Fax Area Code:* 209 ■ *TF:* 800-808-7333 ■ *Web:* www.harrismoran.com						
Harris myCFO Inc 2200 Geng Rd Ste 100	Palo Alto	CA	94303	650-210-5000		404
TF: 866-966-1130 ■ *Web:* ctcmycfo.com						
Harris Originals of NY Inc 800 Prime Pl	Hauppauge	NY	11788	631-348-0303		410
Web: www.harrisjewelry.com						
Harris Packaging Corp 1600 Carson St	Haltom City	TX	76117	817-429-6262		100
Web: www.harrispackaging.com						
Harris Products Group 4501 Quality Pl	Mason	OH	45040	513-754-2000	754-8778*	811
**Fax:* Sales ■ *TF:* 800-733-4043 ■ *Web:* www.harrisproductsgroup.com						
Harris Ranch Beef Co 16277 S McCall Ave PO Box 220	Selma	CA	93662	800-742-1955		473
TF: 800-742-1955 ■ *Web:* www.harrisranchbeef.com						
Harris Smariga & Assoc Inc 125 S Carroll St Ste 100	Frederick	MD	21701	301-662-4488		261
Harris Steel Co 1223 S 55th Ct	Cicero	IL	60804	708-656-5500	656-0151	723
Web: www.harrissteelco.com						
Harris Tea Co 344 New Albany Rd	Moorestown	NJ	08057	856-793-0290		123
Web: www.harristea.com						
Harris Technology Services Inc 1603 Golf Course Rd SE Ste B	Rio Rancho	NM	87124	505-892-7364		180
Web: htsusa.com						
Harris Teeter Inc PO Box 10100	Mathews	NC	28106	800-432-6111		185
NYSE: HTSI ■ *TF:* 800-432-6111 ■ *Web:* www.harristeeter.com						
Harris Teeter Inc 701 Crestdale Rd PO Box 10100	Matthews	NC	28105	704-844-3100		345
TF Cust Svc: 800-432-6111 ■ *Web:* www.harristeeter.com						
Harris Woolf California Almonds 26060 Colusa Rd	Coalinga	CA	93210	559-884-2147		11-1
Web: www.harriswoolfalmonds.com						
Harris Wyatt & Amala Attorneys at Law 5778 Commercial St SE	Salem	OR	97306	503-378-7744		428
TF: 800-853-2144 ■ *Web:* www.salemattorneys.com						
Harris' Restaurant 2100 Van Ness Ave	San Francisco	CA	94109	415-673-1888	673-8817	671
Web: www.harrisrestaurant.com						
Harris, Deville & Associates Inc 521 Laurel St	Baton Rouge	LA	70801	225-344-0381		636
Web: hdaissues.com						
Harris, Harris, Bauerle & Sharma PA 1201 E Robinson St	Orlando	FL	32801	407-843-0404		787
TF: 800-747-7569 ■ *Web:* www.hhbslaw.com						
Harrisburg Area Community College 1 HACC Dr	Harrisburg	PA	17110	717-780-2300	231-7674*	162
**Fax:* Admissions ■ *TF:* 800-222-4222 ■ *Web:* www.hacc.edu						
Gettysburg 731 Old Harrisburg Rd	Gettysburg	PA	17325	717-337-3855	337-3015*	162
**Fax:* Admissions ■ *TF:* 800-222-4222 ■ *Web:* www.hacc.edu						
Lebanon 735 Cumberland St	Lebanon	PA	17042	717-270-4222	270-6385	162
TF: 800-222-4222 ■ *Web:* www.hacc.edu						
Harrisburg City Hall 10 N Second St	Harrisburg	PA	17101	717-255-3060	255-3081	337
Web: www.harrisburgpa.gov						
Harrisburg Dairies Inc 2001 Herr St	Harrisburg	PA	17105	717-233-8701	231-4584	296-27
TF: 800-692-7429 ■ *Web:* www.harrisburgdairies.com						
Harrisburg Hospital 111 S Front St	Harrisburg	PA	17101	717-782-3131	782-5536	374-3
TF: 888-782-5678 ■ *Web:* www.pinnaclehealth.org						
Harrisburg International Airport 1 Terminal Dr Ste 300	Middletown	PA	17057	717-948-3900	948-4636	27
Web: www.flyhia.com						
Harrisburg Regional Chamber 3211 N Front St Ste 201	Harrisburg	PA	17110	717-232-4099	232-5184	139
TF: 877-883-8339 ■ *Web:* www.harrisburgregionalchamber.org						
Harrisburg School District Inc 1601 State St	Harrisburg	PA	17103	717-703-4000		685
Web: www.hbgsd.k12.pa.us						
Harrisburg Symphony Orchestra 800 Corporate Cir Ste 101	Harrisburg	PA	17110	717-545-5527	545-6501	573-3
Web: www.harrisburgsymphony.org						
Harrisburg University of Science & Technology 215 Market St	Harrisburg	PA	17101	717-901-5100		166
Web: harrisburgu.edu						
HarrisData 13555 Bishops Ct Ste 300	Brookfield	WI	53005	262-784-9099	784-5994	178-1
TF: 800-225-0585 ■ *Web:* www.harrisdata.com						
Harris-Kearney House 4000 Baltimore St	Kansas City	MO	64111	816-561-1821		50-3
TF: 800-519-4800 ■ *Web:* www.westporthistorical.com						
Harrison & Held LLP 333 W Wacker Dr Ste 1700	Chicago	IL	60606	312-753-6185		428
Web: www.harrisonheld.com						
Harrison & Lear Inc 2310 Tower Pl Ste 105	Hampton	VA	23666	757-825-9100	838-2574	655
Web: www.harrison-lear.com						
Harrison & Shriftman 158 W 29th St 6th Fl	New York	NY	10018	917-351-8600		7
Web: www.hs-pr.com						
Harrison & Star 75 Varick St	New York	NY	10013	212-727-1330		4
TF: 800-458-4779 ■ *Web:* www.harrisonandstar.com						
Harrison Accountancy Corp 2850 Mesa Verde Dr E Ste 101	Costa Mesa	CA	92626	714-966-0644		734
Harrison Bay State Park 8411 Harrison Bay Rd	Harrison	TN	37341	423-344-6214		565
Web: www.state.tn.us						
Harrison County 1501 Main St PO Box 169	Bethany	MO	64424	660-425-3199		338
Web: harrisoncountysheriffmo.org						
Harrison County 100 W Market St	Cadiz	OH	43907	740-942-8510		338
Web: www.harrisoncountyohio.org						
Harrison County 301 W Main St County Courthouse	Clarksburg	WV	26301	304-624-8500	624-8673	338
TF: 800-786-6480 ■ *Web:* www.harrisoncountywv.com						

Name / Address	City	State	ZIP	Phone	Fax	Class
Harrison County 300 N Capitol Ave Rm 203 *Web:* harrisoncounty.in.gov	Corydon	IN	47112	812-738-4289	738-3126	338
Harrison County 313 Oddville Ave *Web:* www.harrisoncountyfiscalcourt.com	Cynthiana	KY	41031	859-234-7130	234-8049	338
Harrison County 1801 23rd Ave *TF:* 800-222-8000 ■ *Web:* www.co.harrison.ms.us	Gulfport	MS	39501	228-865-4036	868-1480	338
Harrison County 111 N Second Ave *Web:* www.harrisoncountyia.org	Logan	IA	51546	712-644-3123	644-2643	338
Harrison County Chamber of Commerce 520 W Main St *Web:* www.harrisoncountychamber.com	Clarksburg	WV	26301	304-624-6331	624-5190	139
Harrison County Clerk 200 W Houston PO Box 1365 Ste 143 *Web:* harrisoncountytexas.org	Marshall	TX	75671	903-935-8403		338
Harrison County Public Library District 105 N Capital Ave *Web:* www.hcpl.lib.in.us	Corydon	IN	47112	812-738-4110		434-3
Harrison County Rural Electric Co-op 105 Enterprise Dr PO Box 2 *Web:* www.hcrec.coop	Woodbine	IA	51579	712-647-2727		245
Harrison Edwards Inc 80 Business Park Dr Ste 303 *Web:* harrison-edwardspr.com	Armonk	NY	10504	914-242-0010		466
Harrison Group A YouGov Co 21 W Main St One Exchange Pl Fl 5 *Web:* research.yougov.com	Waterbury	CT	06702	203-573-0400		195
Harrison Hot Springs Resort & Spa 100 Esplanade Ave *TF:* 800-663-2266 ■ *Web:* www.harrisonresort.com	Harrison Hot Springs	BC	V0M1K0	604-796-2244	796-3682	669
Harrison Lake State Park 26246 Harrison Lake Rd *Web:* www.ohiodnr.com	Fayette	OH	43521	419-237-2593		565
Harrison Orr Air Conditioning LLC 4100 N Walnut *Web:* www.harrisonorr.com	Oklahoma City	OK	73105	405-528-3333		610
Harrison Paint Co 1329 Harrison Ave SW *TF:* 800-321-0680 ■ *Web:* www.harrisonpaint.com	Canton	OH	44706	330-455-5125	454-1750	550
Harrison Plaza Suite Hotel 409 S Cole Rd	Boise	ID	83709	208-376-3608		379
Harrison Regional Library 50 Lester St *Web:* www.shelbycounty-al.org	Columbiana	AL	35051	205-669-3910	669-3940	434-3
Harrison Scott Publications Inc 5 Marine View Plaza Ste 301 *Web:* www.hspnews.com	Hoboken	NJ	07030	201-659-1700		194
Harrison Senior Living Inc 300 Strode Ave *Web:* harrisonseniorliving.com	East Fallowfield	PA	19320	610-384-6310	383-3945	271
Harrison Steel Castings Co Inc 900 S Mound St *TF:* 800-659-4722 ■ *Web:* www.hscast.com	Attica	IN	47918	765-762-2481	762-2487	307
Harrison's Harbor Watch Restaurant 806 S Boardwalk *TF:* 800-228-5590 ■ *Web:* www.harborwatchrestaurant.com	Ocean City	MD	21842	410-289-5121		671
Harrison, Eichenberg & Murphy LLP PO Box 640 *Web:* www.hem-law.com	Agoura Hills	CA	91376	805-495-7379		428
Harrisonburg City Public Schools (HCPS) 317 S Main St *Web:* www.harrisonburg.k12.va.us	Harrisonburg	VA	22801	540-434-9916	434-5196	780
Harrisonburg (Independent City) 345 S Main St *TF:* 800-272-9829 ■ *Web:* www.harrisonburgva.gov	Harrisonburg	VA	22801	540-432-7701	432-7778	338
Harrisonburg-Rockingham Chamber of Commerce 800 Country Club Rd *Web:* www.hrchamber.org	Harrisonburg	VA	22802	540-434-3862	434-4508	139
Harrisonville Telephone Co 213 S Main St PO Box 149 *Web:* htc.net	Waterloo	IL	62298	618-939-6112	939-4826	736
Harriss & Covington Hosiery Mills Inc 1250 Hickory Chapel Rd *Web:* www.harrissandcov.com	High Point	NC	27260	336-882-6811		155-10
Harris-Stowe State University 3026 Laclede Ave *Web:* go.hssu.edu?CFID=4097332&CFTOKEN=23364537	Saint Louis	MO	63103	314-340-3366	340-3555	166
Harristown Development Corp 11 N Third St *Web:* strawberrysquare.com	Harrisburg	PA	17101	717-236-5061		653
Harrisville State Park 248 State Pk Rd PO Box 326 *Web:* www.michigan.org	Harrisville	MI	48740	989-724-5126		565
Harrogate 400 Locust St *Web:* harrogatelifecare.org	Lakewood	NJ	08701	732-905-7070	905-4059	672
Harry & David Holdings Inc 2500 S Pacific Hwy *TF Cust Svc:* 877-322-1200 ■ *Web:* www.harryanddavid.com	Medford	OR	97501	877-322-1200	233-2300	336
Harry & Jeanette Weinberg Foundation Inc, The 7 Park Ctr Ct *Web:* hjweinbergfoundation.org	Owings Mills	MD	21117	410-654-8500		305
Harry & Sons 820 N Highland Ave *Web:* surinofthailand.com	Atlanta	GA	30306	404-873-2009		671
Harry "Babe" Woodyard State Natural Area 19284 E 670 N	Georgetown	IL	61846	217-442-4915		565
Harry Browne's 66 State Cir *TF:* 800-296-7304 ■ *Web:* www.harrybrownes.com	Annapolis	MD	21401	410-263-4332		671
Harry C. Crooker & Sons Inc PO Box 5001 *Web:* www.crooker.com	Topsham	ME	04086	207-729-5511		189-5
Harry Cooper Supply Company Inc 605 N Sherman Pkwy *TF:* 800-426-6737 ■ *Web:* www.harrycooper.com	Springfield	MO	65802	417-865-8392	873-9146	612
Harry Davis & Co 1725 Blvd of Allies *TF:* 800-775-2289 ■ *Web:* www.harrydavis.com	Pittsburgh	PA	15219	412-765-1170	765-1170	51
Harry G Barr Co 6500 S Zero St *TF:* 800-829-2277 ■ *Web:* www.weatherbarr.com	Fort Smith	AR	72903	479-646-7891	646-8591	235
Harry Grodsky & Company Inc 33 Shaws Ln *TF:* 800-992-7386 ■ *Web:* www.grodsky.com	Springfield	MA	01104	413-785-1947	737-9870	189-10
Harry Hynes Memorial Hospice 313 S Market St *TF:* 800-767-4965 ■ *Web:* www.hynesmemorial.org	Wichita	KS	67202	316-265-9441	265-6066	371
Harry J Whelchel Co 1332 Stuart St	Chattanooga	TN	37406	423-698-4415		274
Harry Jernigan CPA Attorney PC 5101 Cleveland St Ste 200 *Web:* www.hjlaw.com	Virginia Beach	VA	23462	757-490-2200		466
Harry K Dupree Stuttgart National Aquaculture Research Ctr 2955 Hwy 130 E PO Box 1050 *Web:* www.ars.usda.gov	Stuttgart	AR	72160	870-673-4483	673-7710	668
Harry Klitzner Co, The 530 Wellington Ave Ste 11 *TF:* 800-621-0161 ■ *Web:* www.klitzner.com	Cranston	RI	02910	800-621-0161	622-9802	409
Harry Krantz Co 50 Heartland Blvd *Web:* www.harrykrantz.com	Edgewood	NY	11717	516-620-0111		246
Harry L Murphy Inc 42 Bonaventura Dr *Web:* harrylmurphyinc.com	San Jose	CA	95134	408-955-1100		290
Harry London Candies Inc 5353 Lauby Rd *TF Cust Svc:* 800-333-3629 ■ *Web:* www.fanniemay.com	North Canton	OH	44720	330-494-0833		296-8
Harry Miller Co Inc 850 Albany St *TF:* 800-878-7777 ■ *Web:* www.harrymiller.com	Boston	MA	02119	617-427-2300	442-1152	733
Harry N Abrams Inc 115 W 18th St 6th Fl *Web:* www.abramsbooks.com	New York	NY	10011	212-206-7715	519-1210	637-2
Harry P Leu Gardens 1920 N Forest Ave *Web:* www.leugardens.org	Orlando	FL	32803	407-246-2620	246-2849	97
Harry Ritchie's Jewelers Inc 956 Willamette St *TF Cust Svc:* 800-935-2850 ■ *Web:* www.harryritchies.com	Eugene	OR	97401	541-686-1787	485-8841	410
Harry S Truman Birthplace State Historic Site 1009 Truman St *Web:* www.mostateparks.com	Lamar	MO	64759	417-682-2279		565
Harry S Truman College 1145 W Wilson Ave **Fax:* Admissions ■ *TF:* 877-863-6339 ■ *Web:* www.ccc.edu	Chicago	IL	60640	773-878-1700	907-4464*	162
Harry S Truman Memorial Veterans Hospital 800 Hospital Dr *TF:* 800-273-8255 ■ *Web:* www.columbiamo.va.gov	Columbia	MO	65201	573-814-6000	814-6600	374-8
Harry S Truman National Historic Site 223 N Main St *TF:* 877-642-4743 ■ *Web:* www.nps.gov	Independence	MO	64050	816-254-2720	254-4491	564
Harry S Truman Presidential Library & Museum 500 W Hwy 24 *TF:* 800-833-1225 ■ *Web:* www.trumanlibrary.org	Independence	MO	64050	816-268-8200	268-8295	434-2
Harry S Truman Scholarship Foundation 712 Jackson Pl NW *Web:* www.truman.gov	Washington	DC	20006	202-395-4831	395-6995	725
Harry S Truman State Park 28761 State Pk Rd *Web:* www.mostateparks.com	Warsaw	MO	65355	660-438-7711		565
Harry S Truman's Little White House Museum 111 Front St *TF:* 800-435-7352 ■ *Web:* www.trumanlittlewhitehouse.com	Key West	FL	33040	305-294-9911	294-9988	520
Harry Walker Agency Inc (HWA) 355 Lexington Ave 21st Fl *Web:* www.harrywalker.com	New York	NY	10017	646-227-4900		708
Harry Winston Inc 718 Fifth Ave *TF:* 800-988-4110 ■ *Web:* www.harrywinston.com	New York	NY	10019	212-399-1000		409
Harry's 17711 NE Riverside Pkwy *TF:* 800-307-7687 ■ *Web:* www.harrysfresh.com	Portland	OR	97230	503-257-7687		297-8
Harry's Continental Kitchens 525 St Judes Dr *TF:* 800-843-4458 ■ *Web:* www.harryskitchen.com	Longboat Key	FL	34228	941-383-0777	383-2029	671
Harry's Savoy Grill 2020 Naamans Rd *TF:* 800-711-5882 ■ *Web:* harryshospitalitygroup.com/harrys-savoy-grill	Wilmington	DE	19810	302-475-3000	475-9990	671
Harry's Seafood Grill 101 S Market St *Web:* harryshospitalitygroup.com/harrys-seafood-grill	Wilmington	DE	19801	302-777-1500	777-2406	671
Harsco Corp 350 Poplar Church Rd *NYSE:* HSC ■ *TF:* 866-470-3900 ■ *Web:* www.harsco.com	Camp Hill	PA	17011	717-763-7064	763-6424	185
Harsco Industrial Air-X-Changers 5215 Arkansas Rd *TF:* 800-404-3904 ■ *Web:* www.harscoaxc.com	Catoosa	OK	74015	918-619-8000	384-5000	91
Harsco Rail (HTT) 2401 Edmund Rd PO Box 20 *Web:* www.harscorail.com	West Columbia	SC	29171	803-822-9160	822-8107	650
Harsh International Inc 600 Oak Ave *Web:* www.harshenviro.com	Eaton	CO	80615	970-454-2291		273
Hart & Price Corp PO Box 36368 *TF:* 800-777-9129 ■ *Web:* www.hartprice.com	Dallas	TX	75235	214-521-9129	350-4143	665
Hart Associates Inc 1915 Indian Wood Cir *TF:* 800-537-8827 ■ *Web:* www.hartinc.com	Maumee	OH	43537	419-893-9600		4
Hart Corp 900 Jaymor Rd *TF:* 800-368-4278 ■ *Web:* www.hartcorp.com	SouthHampton	PA	18966	215-322-5100	322-5840	652
Hart County 800 Chandler St *Web:* www.hartcountyga.org	Hartwell	GA	30643	706-376-2024	376-9477	338
Hart County 200 Main St *TF:* 800-829-4933 ■ *Web:* www.hartcounty.ky.gov	Munfordville	KY	42765	270-524-2751	524-0458	338
Hart County Charter System 284 Campbell Dr PO Box 696 *Web:* www.hart.k12.ga.us	Hartwell	GA	30643	706-376-5141	376-7046	685
Hart Crowser Inc 1700 Westlake Ave N Ste 200 *Web:* www.hartcrowser.com	Seattle	WA	98109	206-324-9530	328-5581	261
Hart Davis Hart Wine Co 363 W Erie St Ste 500W *Web:* www.hdhwine.com	Chicago	IL	60654	312-482-9996		443
Hart Electric Membership Corp 1071 Elberton Hwy **Fax Area Code:* 800 ■ *TF:* 800-241-4109 ■ *Web:* www.hartemc.com	Hartwell	GA	30643	706-376-4714	486-3277*	245

Name / Address	City	State	ZIP	Phone	Fax	Class
Hart Engineering Corp 800 Sconic View Dr *Web:* www.hartcompanies.com	Cumberland	RI	02864	401-658-4600		256
Hart Hotels Inc 617 Dingens St. *Web:* www.harthotels.com	Buffalo	NY	14206	716-893-6551		194
Hart Industries Inc 11412 Cronridge Dr *TF:* 800-638-2700 ■ *Web:* hartind.com	Owings Mills	MD	21117	410-581-1900		627
Hart InterCivic 15500 Wells Port Dr *TF:* 800-223-4278 ■ *Web:* www.hartintercivic.com	Austin	TX	78728	512-252-6400	252-6466	801
Hart King & Coldren 4 Hutton Centre Dr Ste 400 *Web:* www.hartkinglaw.com	Santa Ana	CA	92707	714-432-8700		445
Hart Petroleum 323 Skidmores Rd *TF:* 800-796-3342 ■ *Web:* www.harthomecomfort.com	Deer Park	NY	11729	631-667-3200		580
Hart Precision Products Inc 12700 Marion *Web:* www.hart-precision.com	Redford	MI	48239	313-537-0490		22
Hart Publications Inc 1616 S Voss Rd Ste 1000 *TF:* 800-874-2544 ■ *Web:* www.hartenergy.com	Houston	TX	77057	713-260-6400	840-8585	637-9
Hart Ranch Camping Resort Club 23756 Arena Dr *TF:* 800-605-4278 ■ *Web:* www.hartranchresort.com	Rapid City	SD	57702	605-399-2582		121
Hart Realty Advisers Inc 1 Mill Pond Ln *Web:* www.hartadvisers.com	Simsbury	CT	06070	860-651-4000		652
Hart Schaffner Marx (HSM) 1680 E Touhy Ave *Web:* www.hartschaffnermarx.com	Des Plaines	IL	60018	847-257-4644		155-12
Hart Scientific Inc 799 E Utah Vly Dr *TF:* 800-438-4278 ■ *Web:* us.flukecal.com	American Fork	UT	84003	801-763-1600	763-1010	201
Hart Specialties Inc 5000 New Horizons Blvd *Web:* www.newyorkeye.net	Amityville	NY	11701	631-226-5600		543
Hart State Park 330 Hart Pk Rd *Web:* www.gastateparks.org	Hartwell	GA	30643	706-376-8756		565
Hart-Boillot LLC 134 Rumford Ave Ste 307 *TF:* 800-553-6477 ■ *Web:* www.hbagency.com	Newton	MA	02466	781-893-0053		7
Harte Nissan Inc 165 W Service Rd *TF:* 866-687-8971 ■ *Web:* www.hartenissan.com	Hartford	CT	06120	860-549-2800		57
Harte-Hanks Inc 9601 McAllister Fwy Ste 610 *NYSE: HHS* ■ *TF:* 800-456-9748 ■ *Web:* hartehanks.com	San Antonio	TX	78216	210-829-9000	829-9403	5
Harte-Hanks Response Management 2800 Wells Branch Pkwy *TF:* 800-456-9748 ■ *Web:* hartehanks.com	Austin	TX	78728	512-434-1100		737
Harter Industries Inc 401 W Gemini Dr *TF:* 800-727-3337 ■ *Web:* www.harter.aero	Tempe	AZ	85283	480-345-9595		22
Harter Secrest & Emery LLP (HSE) 1600 Bausch & Lomb Pl *Web:* www.hselaw.com	Rochester	NY	14604	585-232-6500	232-2152	428
Hartford Aircraft Products Inc 94 Old Poquonock Rd	Bloomfield	CT	06002	860-242-8228		350
Hartford Beach State Park 13672 Hartford Beach Rd *Web:* gfp.sd.gov/state-parks/directory/hartford-beach	Corona	SD	57227	605-432-6374		565
Hartford Casualty Insurance Co 1 Hartford Plaza *TF:* 800-243-5860 ■ *Web:* www.thehartford.com	Hartford	CT	06155	860-547-5000		391-4
Hartford City Hall 550 Main St *Web:* www.hartford.gov	Hartford	CT	06103	860-522-4888		337
Hartford Computer Group Inc 10440 Little Patuxent Pkwy 3rd Fl *TF:* 800-370-5849 ■ *Web:* www.hcgi.com	Columbia	MD	21044	410-740-3020	740-8732	180
Hartford Correctional Ctr 177 Weston St *Web:* ct.gov	Hartford	CT	06120	959-200-3000	200-3008	213
Hartford Courant 285 Broad St *TF:* 800-524-4242 ■ *Web:* www.courant.com	Hartford	CT	06115	860-241-6200	520-6941	532-2
Hartford Despatch Moving & Storage Inc 225 Prospect St	East Hartford	CT	06108	860-528-9551		519
Hartford Electric Supply Co (HESCO) 30 Inwood Rd Ste 1 *TF:* 800-969-5444 ■ *Web:* www.hesconet.com	Rocky Hill	CT	06067	860-236-6363	236-0233	246
Hartford Financial Services Group Inc 690 Asylum Ave *NYSE: HIG* ■ *TF:* 866-553-5663 ■ *Web:* www.thehartford.com	Hartford	CT	06115	860-547-5000		360-4
Hartford Financial Services Group Inc, The 690 Asylum Ave *Web:* www.thehartford.com	Hartford	CT	06115	860-547-5000		391-4
Hartford Foundation for Public Giving 10 Columbus Blvd 8th Fl *Web:* www.hfpg.org	Hartford	CT	06106	860-548-1888	524-8346	303
Hartford Funds 30 Dan Rd Ste 55022 *TF:* 888-843-7824 ■ *Web:* www.hartfordfunds.com	Canton	MA	02021	888-843-7824		528
Hartford Hospital 80 Seymour St *TF:* 800-545-7664 ■ *Web:* hartfordhospital.org	Hartford	CT	06102	860-545-5000	545-3622	374-3
Hartford Investment Management Co 1 Hartford Plaza *Web:* www.himco.com	Hartford	CT	06155	860-297-6700		401
Hartford Life & Accident Insurance Co 1 Hartford Plaza *TF:* 877-896-9320 ■ *Web:* www.thehartford.com	Hartford	CT	06155	860-547-5000		391-2
Hartford News 563 Franklin Ave	Hartford	CT	06114	860-296-6128		532-4
Hartford Public Library 500 Main St *Web:* www.hplct.org	Hartford	CT	06103	860-695-6300	722-6900	434-3
Hartford Public Schools 960 Main St **Fax:* Hum Res ■ *Web:* www.hartfordschools.org	Hartford	CT	06103	860-695-8000	722-8454*	685
Hartford Seminary 77 Sherman St **Fax:* Admissions ■ *TF:* 877-860-2255 ■ *Web:* www.hartsem.edu	Hartford	CT	06105	860-509-9500	509-9509*	166
Hartford Stage Co 50 Church St *Web:* www.hartfordstage.org	Hartford	CT	06103	860-527-5151	247-8243	749
Hartford Technologies 1022 Elm St *TF:* 800-839-9007 ■ *Web:* www.hartfordtechnologies.com	Rocky Hill	CT	06067	860-571-3602	571-3604	75
Hartford York 2615 Boeing Way	Stockton	CA	95206	209-982-5462		184
Hartgrove Hospital 5730 W Roosevelt Rd *Web:* hartgrovehospital.com	Chicago	IL	60644	773-413-1700		374-5
Hartig Drug Co 703 Main St *Web:* www.hartigdrug.com	Dubuque	IA	52001	563-588-8700	588-8750	237
Hartig Hilepo Agency Ltd 54 W 21st St Ste 610 *Web:* hartighilepo.com	New York	NY	10010	212-929-1772		731
Hartington Telemarketing Inc 318 318 S Robinson Ave Ave *TF:* 800-354-6369 ■ *Web:* www.hartel.net	Hartington	NE	68739	402-254-2255		737
Hartley County 900 Main St *Web:* www.co.hartley.tx.us	Channing	TX	79018	806-235-3582	235-2316	338
Hartley Data Service Inc (HDS) 1807 Glenview Rd Ste 201 *Web:* hartleydata.com	Glenview	IL	60025	847-724-9280	729-2199	225
Hartley, Rowe & Fowler PC 6622 Broad St *Web:* www.hrflegal.com	Douglasville	GA	30134	770-920-2000		428
Hartley-Racon 1987 Placentia Ave *Web:* www.hartleyraconusa.com	Costa Mesa	CA	92627	949-646-9643	548-1220	571
Hartline Dacus Barger Dreyer 8750 N Central Expy Ste 1600 *Web:* www.hdbdlaw.com	Dallas	TX	75231	214-369-2100		428
Hartman Blitch & Gartside 4929 Atlantic Blvd *Web:* www.hbgcpa.com	Jacksonville	FL	32207	904-396-9802	396-1528	2
Hartman Creek State Park N2480 Hartman Creek Rd *Web:* dnr.wi.gov	Waupaca	WI	54981	715-258-2372		565
Hartman, Simons, Spielman & Wood LLP 6400 Powers Ferry Rd NW Ste 400 *TF:* 800-787-5340 ■ *Web:* www.hartmansimons.com	Atlanta	GA	30339	770-955-3555		428
Hartmann Studios Inc 1150 Brickyard Cove Rd Ste 202 *Web:* www.hartmannstudiosproductions.com	Point Richmond	CA	94801	510-970-3297		226
Hartman-Walsh Painting Co 7144 N Market St *Web:* www.hartmanwalsh.com	Saint Louis	MO	63133	314-863-1800	863-6964	189-8
Hart-Miller Island State Park c/o Gunpowder Falls State Pk 2813 Jerusalem Rd *Web:* dnr2.maryland.gov	Kingsville	MD	21087	410-592-2897		565
Hartnell College 156 Homestead Ave **Fax:* Admissions ■ *TF:* 888-678-2871 ■ *Web:* www.hartnell.edu	Salinas	CA	93901	831-755-6700	759-6014*	162
Hartness House Inn 30 Orchard St *Web:* hartnesshouse.com	Springfield	VT	05156	802-885-2115		379
Hartness International Inc 1200 Garlington Rd PO Box 26509 *TF:* 800-845-8791 ■ *Web:* www.hartness.com	Greenville	SC	29616	864-297-1200	288-5390	547
Hartnett Law Firm, The 2920 N Pearl St *TF:* 800-900-9702 ■ *Web:* www.hartnettlawfirm.com	Dallas	TX	75201	214-742-4655		428
Harts Nursery of Jefferson Inc 4049 Jefferson-Scio Rd *TF:* 800-356-9335 ■ *Web:* www.hartsnursery.com	Jefferson	OR	97352	541-327-3366		369
Hartselle Enquirer PO Box 929 *TF:* 800-772-9143 ■ *Web:* www.hartselleenquirer.com	Hartselle	AL	35640	256-773-6566	773-1953	532-4
Hartsfield-Jackson Atlanta International Airport 6000 N Terminal Pkwy Ste 4000 *TF:* 800-897-1910 ■ *Web:* www.atl.com	Atlanta	GA	30320	404-530-6600	530-6803	27
Hartson-kennedy Cabinet Top Company Inc 522 W 22nd St PO Box 3095 *TF:* 800-388-8144 ■ *Web:* www.hartson-kennedy.com	Marion	IN	46953	765-668-8144	662-3452	599
Hartsville Oil Mill 311 Washington St	Darlington	SC	29532	843-393-2855		296-29
Hartung Agalite Glass Co 17830 W Valley Hwy *TF:* 800-552-2227 ■ *Web:* www.hartung-glass.com	Seattle	WA	98188	425-656-2626	656-2601	329
Hartung Bros Inc 708 Heartland Trl Ste 2000 *TF:* 800-362-2522 ■ *Web:* www.hartungbrothers.com	Madison	WI	53717	608-829-6000	829-6001	10-11
Hartung Glass Industries 10450 SW Ridder Rd *TF:* 800-552-2227 ■ *Web:* hartung-glass.com	Wilsonville	OR	97070	503-682-3846		329
Hartwell Corp 900 Richfield Rd *Web:* www.hartwellcorp.com	Placentia	CA	92870	714-993-4200	579-4419	350
Hartwell Medical Corp 6354 Corte Del Abeto Ste F *TF:* 800-633-5900 ■ *Web:* www.hartwellmedical.com	Carlsbad	CA	92011	760-438-5500		476
Hartwell Vineyards 5815 Silverado Trl *TF:* 800-400-1353 ■ *Web:* www.hartwellvineyards.com	Napa	CA	94558	707-255-4269		443
Hartwick College 1 Hartwick Dr **Fax:* Admissions ■ *TF:* 888-427-8942 ■ *Web:* www.hartwick.edu	Oneonta	NY	13820	607-431-4150	431-4154*	166
Hartwick Pines State Park 4216 Ranger Rd *Web:* www.michigandnr.com	Grayling	MI	49738	989-348-7068		565
Hartwig Inc 10617 Trenton Ave *Web:* www.hartwiginc.com	Saint Louis	MO	63132	314-426-5300		358
Hartwood Mansion 200 Hartwood Acres *Web:* alleghenycounty.us	Pittsburgh	PA	15238	412-767-9200		50-3
Harty Press Inc, The 25 James St *TF:* 800-654-0562 ■ *Web:* www.hartynet.com	New Haven	CT	06513	203-562-5112	782-9168	627
Hartz Construction Co Inc 9026 Heritage Pkwy *Web:* www.hartzhomes.com	Woodridge	IL	60517	630-228-3800		653
Hartz Group Inc, The 667 Madison Ave **Fax Area Code:* 212 ■ *TF:* 800-999-3000 ■ *Web:* www.hartzmountain.com	New York	NY	10065	201-348-1200	838-8845*	360-3
Hartz Mountain Corp, The 400 Plaza Dr *TF:* 800-275-1414 ■ *Web:* www.hartz.com	Secaucus	NJ	07094	800-275-1414		578
Hartzell Engine Technologies LLC 2900 Selma Hwy *TF:* 877-359-5355 ■ *Web:* hartzell.aero	Montgomery	AL	36108	334-386-5400		21
Hartzell Fan Inc 910 S Downing St *TF:* 800-336-3267 ■ *Web:* www.hartzellairmovement.com	Piqua	OH	45356	937-773-7411	773-8994	18
Hartzell Hardwoods 1025 S Roosevelt Ave *TF:* 800-336-3267 ■ *Web:* www.hartzellhardwoods.com	Piqua	OH	45356	937-773-7054		683

Phone | Fax | Class

Hartzell Propeller Inc 1 Propeller Pl .... Piqua OH 45356 937-778-4200 778-4321 22
TF: 800-942-7767 ■ *Web:* www.hartzellprop.com

Hartzler Vicky (Rep R - MO)
2235 Rayburn HOB .... Washington DC 20515 202-225-2876 342-2
Web: hartzler.house.gov

Haruki East 172 Wayland Ave .... Providence RI 02906 401-223-0332 671
Web: harukisushi.com

Harvard Bioscience Inc
84 October Hill Rd .... Holliston MA 01746 508-893-8999 429-5732 419
NASDAQ: HBIO ■ *TF:* 800-272-2775 ■ *Web:* www.harvardbioscience.com

Harvard Book Store Inc
1256 Massachusetts Ave .... Cambridge MA 02138 617-661-1515 95
TF: 800-542-7323 ■ *Web:* harvard.com

Harvard Business Review 60 Harvard Way .... Boston MA 02163 617-783-7500 783-7555* 457-5
**Fax:* Cust Svc ■ *TF:* 800-274-3214 ■ *Web:* www.hbr.org

Harvard Business School Publishing
60 Harvard Way .... Boston MA 02163 800-795-5200 637-4
TF: 800-795-5200 ■ *Web:* www.harvardbusiness.org

Harvard Collection Services Inc
4839 N Elston Ave .... Chicago IL 60630 773-283-7500 160
Web: www.harvardcollect.com

Harvard Crimson Inc, The
14 Plympton St .... Cambridge MA 02138 617-576-6600 557
Web: thecrimson.com

Harvard Educational Review
8 Story St 1st Fl .... Cambridge MA 02138 617-495-3432 496-3584 457-8
TF: 877-930-4473 ■ *Web:* www.gse.harvard.edu

Harvard Law Review
1511 Massachusetts Ave Gannett House .... Cambridge MA 02138 617-495-4650 457-15
TF: 800-828-7571 ■ *Web:* www.harvardlawreview.org

Harvard Management Company Inc
600 Atlantic Ave .... Boston MA 02210 617-523-4400 792
Web: www.hmc.harvard.edu

Harvard Medical School 25 Shattuck St .... Boston MA 02115 617-432-1550 167-2
TF: 866-606-0573 ■ *Web:* www.hms.harvard.edu

Harvard Men's Health Watch
10 Shattuck St Ste 612 .... Cambridge MA 02115 617-432-4717 531-8
Web: www.health.harvard.edu

Harvard Museum of Natural History
26 Oxford St Harvard University .... Cambridge MA 02138 617-495-5891 496-8308 520
Web: www.mcz.harvard.edu

Harvard Pilgrim Health Care Inc
93 Worcester St .... Wellesley MA 02481 617-509-1000 509-2515 391-3
TF: 888-888-4742 ■ *Web:* www.harvardpilgrim.org

Harvard Square Co-op Society
1400 Massachusetts Ave .... Cambridge MA 02238 617-499-2000 95
Web: www.harvardsquare.com

Harvard Square Hotel
110 Mt Auburn St Harvard Sq .... Cambridge MA 02138 617-864-5200 864-2409 379
TF: 800-458-5886 ■ *Web:* www.harvardsquarehotel.com

Harvard Student Agencies Inc
67 Mt Auburn St .... Cambridge MA 02138 617-495-3030 260
TF: 800-440-7494 ■ *Web:* www.hsa.net

Harvard University 12 Holyoke St .... Cambridge MA 02138 617-495-1000 495-8821 166
Web: www.harvard.edu

Harvard University Press
79 Garden St .... Cambridge MA 02138 617-495-2600 406-9145* 637-4
**Fax Area Code:* 800 ■ *TF:* 800-405-1619 ■ *Web:* www.hup.harvard.edu

Harvard University Widener Library
Hardvar Yard Rm 110 .... Cambridge MA 02138 617-495-3650 434-6
Web: harvard.edu

Harvard Women's Health Watch
PO Box 9308 .... Big Sandy TX 75755 877-649-9457 531-8
TF: 877-649-9457 ■ *Web:* www.health.harvard.edu

Harvard-Smithsonian Ctr for Astrophysics
60 Garden St .... Cambridge MA 02138 617-495-7100 495-7468 668
Web: www.cfa.harvard.edu

Harvest 44 Brattle St .... Cambridge MA 02138 617-868-2255 671
Web: www.harvestcambridge.com

Harvest Capital Management Inc
114 N Main St Ste 301 .... Concord NH 03301 603-224-6994 528
Web: www.harvestcap.com

Harvest Christian Fellowship
6115 Arlington Ave .... Riverside CA 92504 951-687-6902 48-20
Web: harvest.org

Harvest Energy Trust
700 Second St SW Ste 2100 .... Calgary AB T2P2W1 403-265-1178 675
TF: 866-666-1178 ■ *Web:* www.harvestenergy.ca

Harvest Health Foods
1944 Eastern Ave SE .... Grand Rapids MI 49507 616-245-6268 297-8
Web: www.harvesthealthfoods.com

Harvest Inn 1 Main St .... Saint Helena CA 94574 707-963-9463 379
TF: 800-950-8466 ■ *Web:* www.harvestinn.com

Harvest Kitchen & Bar 400 W Waterman .... Wichita KS 67202 316-613-6300 293-1200 671
Web: wichita.regency.hyatt.com/en/hotel/dining.html

Harvest Land Co-op
711 Front St PO Box 278 .... Morgan MN 56266 507-249-3196 447
TF: 800-245-5819 ■ *Web:* www.harvestland.com

Harvest Natural Resources Inc
1177 Enclave Pkwy Ste 300 .... Houston TX 77077 281-899-5700 899-5702 536
NYSE: HNR ■ *Web:* www.harvestnr.com

Harvest Partners 280 Pk Ave 25th Fl .... New York NY 10017 212-599-6300 812-0100 792
TF: 866-771-1000 ■ *Web:* harvestpartners.com

Harvest Technical Service Inc
1839 Ygnacio Valley Rd Ste 390 .... Walnut Creek CA 94598 925-937-4874 260
TF: 800-767-3263 ■ *Web:* www.harvtech.com

Harvest Vine 2701 E Madison St .... Seattle WA 98112 206-320-9771 671
Web: www.harvestvine.com

Harvest Word of Life Ministries International Inc
2260 Lake Ave .... Fort Wayne IN 46805 260-422-5750 48-20

Harvey & Company LLC
5000 Birch St Ste 9200 .... Newport Beach CA 92660 949-757-0400 4
Web: www.harveyllc.com

Harvey & Daughters Inc
952 Ridgebrook Rd .... Sparks Glencoe MD 21152 410-771-5566 7
TF: 800-832-3008 ■ *Web:* www.harveyagency.com

Harvey Alpert & Company Inc
2014 S Sepulveda Blvd Ste 200 .... Los Angeles CA 90025 310-689-6000 297-8

Harvey Cadillac Co
2600 28th St SE .... Grand Rapids MI 49512 616-949-1140 954-1201 57
TF Sales: 877-845-1557 ■ *Web:* harveycadillac.com

Harvey County 800 N Main PO Box 687 .... Newton KS 67114 316-284-6840 284-6856 338
Web: www.harveycounty.com

Harvey Cushing/John Hay Whitney Medical Library
333 Cedar St .... New Haven CT 06510 203-785-5352 785-5636 434-1
Web: medicine.yale.edu

Harvey Gap State Park
c/o Rifle Gap State Pk 5775 Hwy 325 .... Rifle CO 81650 970-625-1607 565
Web: cpw.state.co.us

Harvey Hohauser & Associates
5600 New King Dr Ste 355 .... Troy MI 48098 248-641-1400 196
TF: 800-446-3037 ■ *Web:* www.hohauser.com

Harvey Industries Inc 1400 Main St .... Waltham MA 02451 800-598-5400 191-4
TF: 800-598-5400 ■ *Web:* www.harveybp.com

Harvey Klinger Inc 300 W 55th St .... New York NY 10019 212-581-7068 444
TF: 800-874-8844 ■ *Web:* www.harveyklinger.com

Harvey Mudd College
301 Platt Blvd Kingston Hall .... Claremont CA 91711 909-621-8011 607-7046* 166
**Fax:* Admissions ■ *TF:* 877-827-5462 ■ *Web:* www.hmc.edu

Harvey School 260 Jay St .... Katonah NY 10536 914-232-3161 622
Web: www.harveyschool.org

Harvey Software Inc
7050 Winkler Rd Ste 104 .... Fort Myers FL 33919 800-231-0296 177
TF: 800-231-0296 ■ *Web:* www.harveysoft.com

Harvey Vogel Manufacturing Co
425 Weir Dr .... Woodbury MN 55125 651-739-7373 739-8666 488
Web: www.harveyvogel.com

Harvey Watt & Co 475 N Central Ave .... Atlanta GA 30354 404-767-7501 761-8326 391-2
TF: 800-241-6103 ■ *Web:* www.harveywatt.com

Harvey Wheeler Community Ctr
1276 Main St .... Concord MA 01742 978-318-3020 720
Web: www.concordnet.org

Harvey-Cleary Builders
207a Perry Pkwy Ste 1 .... Gaithersburg MD 20877 301-519-2288 186
Web: www.harveycleary.com

Harveys Lake Tahoe
Hwy 50 at Stateline Ave PO Box 128 .... Lake Tahoe NV 89449 775-588-6611 133
TF: 800-522-4700 ■ *Web:* www.caesars.com/harveys-tahoe

Harvin Clarendon County Library
215 N Brooks St .... Manning SC 29102 803-435-8633 434-3
Web: www.clarendoncountylibrary.com

Harwood Engineering Consultant
255 N 21st St .... Milwaukee WI 53233 414-475-5554 256
Web: www.hecl.com

Harwood International Corp
4713 Gann Store Rd 100 Northshore Office Pk
.... Chattanooga TN 37343 423-870-5500 174
Web: www.harwood-intl.com

Harwood Lloyd LLC 130 Main St .... Hackensack NJ 07601 201-487-1080 428
TF: 800-973-1177 ■ *Web:* www.harwoodlloyd.com

Hasbro Inc 1027 Newport Ave .... Pawtucket RI 02861 401-431-8697 431-8082* 762
NASDAQ: HAS ■ **Fax:* Cust Svc ■ *TF:* 800-242-7276 ■ *Web:* www.hasbro.com

Hasbrouck Heights Board of Education
379 Blvd .... Hasbrouck Heights NJ 07604 201-288-6150 187
Web: www.hhschools.org

Hascall Steel Co
4165 Spartan Industrial Dr .... Grandville MI 49418 616-531-8600 492
Web: www.hascallsteel.com

HASCO America Inc
270 Rutledge Rd Unit B .... Fletcher NC 28732 828-650-2600 697
Web: www.hasco.com

Hasco Oil Company Inc
2800 Temple Ave .... Long Beach CA 90806 562-595-8491 579
TF: 800-456-8491 ■ *Web:* www.hascooil.com

Hasco Relays & Electronics International Corp
906 Jericho Tpke .... New Hyde Park NY 11040 516-328-9292 203
Web: www.hascorelays.com

HASD (Hamburg Area School District)
701 Windsor St .... Hamburg PA 19526 610-562-2241 562-2634 685
Web: www.hasdhawks.org

Hasd&ic 5575 Ruffin Rd Ste 225 .... San Diego CA 92123 858-614-0200 466
Web: www.hasdic.org

Haselden Construction LLC
6950 S Potomac St .... Centennial CO 80112 303-751-1478 186
Web: www.haselden.com

Haskel International Inc
100 E Graham Pl .... Burbank CA 91502 818-843-4000 841-4291* 641
**Fax:* Sales ■ *TF:* 800-743-2720 ■ *Web:* www.haskel.com

Haskel Thompson & Associates LLC
12734 Kenwood Ln Ste 74 .... Fort Myers FL 33907 239-437-4600 260
TF: 800-470-4226 ■ *Web:* haskelthompson.com

Haskell & White LLP
300 Spectrum Center Dr Ste 300 .... Irvine CA 92618 949-450-6200 2
Web: www.hwcpa.com

Haskell Co 111 Riverside Ave .... Jacksonville FL 32202 904-791-4500 791-4699 188-7
TF: 800-622-4326 ■ *Web:* haskell.com

Haskell Corp
1001 Meador Ave PO Box 917 .... Bellingham WA 98229 360-734-1200 734-5538 186
Web: www.haskellcorp.com

Haskell County 1 Ave D .... Haskell TX 79521 940-864-3448 338
Web: www.co.haskell.tx.us

Haskell County 202 E Main St .... Stigler OK 74462 918-967-2611 967-4640 338
Web: haskell.oklahoma.usassessor.com

Haskell County PO Box 518 .... Sublette KS 67877 620-675-2263 675-2681 338
TF: 800-262-8683 ■ *Web:* www.haskellcounty.org

Haskell Indian Nations University
155 Indian Ave PO Box 5031 .... Lawrence KS 66046 785-749-8454 749-8429* 165
**Fax:* Admissions ■ *Web:* www.haskell.edu

Haskins Laboratories Library
300 George St Ste 900 .... New Haven CT 06511 203-865-6163 434-3
Web: www.haskins.yale.edu

Haskris Co 100 Kelly St .... Elk Grove Village IL 60007 847-956-6420 14
Web: www.haskris.com

Haslam Bill (R) State Capitol .... Nashville TN 37243 615-741-2001 343
Web: www.state.tn.us/governor

Name / Address	City	State	ZIP	Phone	Fax	Class
Haslett Heating & Cooling Inc						
920 King Ave	Columbus	OH	43212	614-299-2133		189-10
Web: haslettmechanical.com						
Haslett Public School						
5593 Franklin St	Haslett	MI	48840	517-339-8242		685
Web: www.haslett.k12.mi.us						
Hass Avocado Board 38 Discovery Ste 150	Irvine	CA	92618	949-341-3250		138
Web: www.hassavocadoboard.com						
Hassan Margaret Wood (Sen D - NH)						
330 Hart Senate Office Bldg	Washington	DC	20510	202-224-3324		342-2
Web: www.hassan.senate.gov						
Hassayampa Inn 122 E Gurley St	Prescott	AZ	86301	800-322-1927	445-8590*	379
**Fax Area Code:* 928 ■ *TF Cust Svc:* 800-322-1927 ■ *Web:* www.hassayampainn.com						
Hassett Air Express						
18W100 22nd St Ste 109	Oakbrook Terrace	IL	60181	630-530-6515		311
Web: hassettexpress.com						
Hastings & Sons Publishing						
38 Exchange St	Lynn	MA	01901	781-593-7700		637-8
TF: 800-243-4636 ■ *Web:* www.itemlive.com						
Hastings Alcee L (Rep D - FL)						
2353 Rayburn Bldg	Washington	DC	20515	202-225-1313	225-1171	342-2
Web: www.alceehastings.house.gov						
Hastings Area Chamber of Commerce & Tourism Bureau						
111 E Third St	Hastings	MN	55033	651-437-6775	437-2697	139
TF: 877-524-5340 ■ *Web:* www.hastingsmn.org						
Hastings Automotive Inc						
3625 Vermillion St	Hastings	MN	55033	651-437-4030		57
Web: hastingsautos.com						
Hastings Bus Co 425 31st St E	Hastings	MN	55033	651-437-1888		109
TF: 800-210-6362 ■ *Web:* www.minnesotacoaches.com						
Hastings City Bank 150 W Court St	Hastings	MI	49058	269-945-2401		70
Web: hastingscitybank.com						
Hastings College 710 N Turner Ave	Hastings	NE	68901	402-463-2402	461-7490*	166
**Fax:* Admissions ■ *TF:* 800-532-7642 ■ *Web:* www.hastings.edu						
Hastings Co-op Creamery Co						
1701 Vermillion St PO Box 217	Hastings	MN	55033	651-437-9414		345
Web: www.hastingscreamery.com						
Hastings Equity Grain Bin Mfg Co						
1900 Summit Ave	Hastings	NE	68901	402-462-2189	462-2900	273
TF: 888-883-2189 ■ *Web:* www.hastingstanks.com						
Hastings Fiber Glass Products Inc						
770 Cook Rd PO Box 218	Hastings	MI	49058	269-945-9541	945-4623	758
Web: www.hfgp.com						
Hastings House Country House Hotel						
160 Upper Ganges Rd	Salt Spring Island	BC	V8K2S2	250-537-2362		379
TF: 800-661-9255 ■ *Web:* www.hastingshouse.com						
Hastings HVAC Inc						
3606 Yost Ave PO Box 669	Hastings	NE	68902	402-463-9821	463-6273	14
TF Cust Svc: 800-228-4243 ■ *Web:* www.hastingshvac.com						
Hastings Manufacturing Co						
325 N Hanover St	Hastings	MI	49058	269-945-2491	945-4667	128
TF: 800 776 1088 ■ *Web:* www.hastingspistonrings.com						
Hastings Pavement Company LLC						
200 Henry St	Lindenhurst	NY	11757	631-669-0600	669-8052	183
Web: www.hastingsarchitectural.com						
Hastings Pork 301 S Burlington Ave	Hastings	NE	68901	402 461 8400		10-6
Web: www.hastingschamber.com						
Hastings Public Library						
517 W Fourth St	Hastings	NE	68901	402-461-2346	461-2359	434-3
Web: hastingslibrary.us						
Hastings Veterans Home						
1200 E 18th St	Hastings	MN	55033	651-438-8500		793
TF: 877-838-3803 ■ *Web:* mn.gov						
Hastings Water Works Inc						
10331 Brecksville Rd	Brecksville	OH	44141	440-832-7700		104
TF: 800-822-4342 ■ *Web:* hastingswaterworks.com						
Hasty Plywood Co 100 N Austin St	Maxton	NC	28364	910-844-5267		613
Web: www.hasply.com						
Hat World Corp 7555 Woodland Dr	Indianapolis	IN	46278	888-564-4287		157-5
TF: 888-564-4287 ■ *Web:* www.lids.com						
Hatboro Federal Savings 221 S York Rd	Hatboro	PA	19040	215-675-4000	672-6684	70
Web: www.hatborofed.com						
Hatboro-Horsham School District						
229 Meetinghouse Rd	Horsham	PA	19044	215-672-5660	420-5262	685
TF: 866-771-3170 ■ *Web:* www.hatboro-horsham.org						
Hatch & Bailey Company Inc						
1 Meadow St Ext	Norwalk	CT	06854	203-866-5515	854-1712	191-3
Web: www.hatchandbailey.com						
Hatch & Kirk Inc 5111 Leary Ave NW	Seattle	WA	98107	206-783-2766	782-6482	262
TF: 800-426-2818 ■ *Web:* www.hatchkirk.com						
Hatch Ltd 2800 Speakman Dr	Mississauga	ON	L5K2R7	905-855-7600	855-8270	194
Web: www.hatch.com						
Hatch Mott Macdonald Group						
27 Bleeker St	Millburn	NJ	07041	973-379-3400	376-1072	261
Web: www.hatchmott.com						
Hatch Orrin G (Sen R - UT)						
104 Hart Bldg	Washington	DC	20510	202-224-5251	224-6331	342-2
Web: www.hatch.senate.gov						
Hatch Stamping Co 635 E Industrial Dr	Chelsea	MI	48118	734-475-8628	475-6255	489
Web: www.hatchstamping.com						
HatchBeauty Agency LLC						
10951 W Pico Blvd Ste 300	Los Angeles	CA	90404	877-428-2424		195
TF: 877-428-2424 ■ *Web:* hatchbeauty.com						
Hatcher Consultants Inc						
2955 SW Wanamaker Dr Click Here For A Map To Our	Topeka	KS	66614	785-271-5557		463
Hatchet Publications Inc						
2140 G St NW	Washington	DC	20052	202-847-0400		532-3
Web: www.gwhatchet.com						
Hatfield & Dawson						
9500 Greenwood Ave N	Seattle	WA	98103	206-783-9151		261
Web: hatdaw.com						
Hatfield Marine Science Ctr						
2030 SE Marine Science Dr	Newport	OR	97365	541-867-0100	867-0138	668
TF: 800-273-8255 ■ *Web:* www.hmsc.oregonstate.edu						
Hatfield Quality Meats Inc						
2700 Clemens Rd	Hatfield	PA	19440	215-368-2500		473
TF: 800-743-1191 ■ *Web:* www.hatfieldqualitymeats.com						
Hathaway Dinwiddie Construction Co						
275 Battery St Ste 300	San Francisco	CA	94111	415-986-2718		186
Web: www.hdcco.com						
Hathaway Inc 347 S Oak Ln	Waynesboro	VA	22980	540-949-8285	943-7619	559
Web: www.hathawaypaper.com						
Hathaway-Sycamores Child & Family Services						
210 S DeLacey Ave Ste 110	Pasadena	CA	91105	626-395-7100		726
Web: www.hathaway-sycamores.org						
Hatsize Learning Corp						
555 11 Ave SW Ste 200	Calgary	AB	T2R1P6	403-538-3295		764
Web: hatsize.com						
Hatteras 56 Park Rd	Tinton Falls	NJ	07724	732-223-9888		627
Web: www.hatteraspress.com						
Hatteras Hammocks Inc						
305 Industrial Blvd	Greenville	NC	27834	252-758-0641	758-0375	319-4
TF: 800-643-3522 ■ *Web:* www.hatterashammocks.com						
Hatteras Yachts Inc						
110 N Glenburnie Rd	New Bern	NC	28560	252-633-3101		90
Web: www.hatterasyachts.com						
Hattiesburg American						
825 N Main St	Hattiesburg	MS	39401	601-582-4321	583-9914*	532-2
**Fax:* News Rm ■ *TF:* 800-844-2637 ■ *Web:* www.hattiesburgamerican.com						
Hattiesburg City Hall						
City of Hattiesburg PO Box 1898	Hattiesburg	MS	39403	601-545-4500		337
Web: www.dev.hattiesburgms.com						
Hattiesburg Zoo 107 S 17th Ave	Hattiesburg	MS	39401	601-545-4500		823
TF: 800-733-2767 ■ *Web:* www.hattiesburgms.com						
Hattiesburg-Laurel Regional Airport						
1002 Terminal Dr	Moselle	MS	39459	601-649-2444	545-3155	27
TF: 800-433-7300 ■ *Web:* www.flypib.com						
Hatton Brown Publishers Inc						
PO Box 2268	Montgomery	AL	36102	334-834-1170		637-9
TF: 800-669-5613 ■ *Web:* www.hattonbrown.net						
Hatzel & Buehler Inc						
3600 Silverside Rd	Wilmington	DE	19803	302-478-4200	478-2750	189-4
TF: 800-461-1381 ■ *Web:* www.hatzelandbuehler.com						
Hauck & Assoc Inc						
1025 Thomas Jefferson St Ste 500 E	Washington	DC	20007	202-452-8100	833-3636	47
TF: 800-767-7777 ■ *Web:* www.hauck.com						
Hauck Manufacturing Co 100 N Harris St	Cleona	PA	17042	717-272-3051	273-9882	318
Web: www.hauckburner.com						
Haug Communications Inc 622 Neptune Dr	Seneca	KS	66538	785-336-3579		225
TF: 800-325-8646 ■ *Web:* www.bbwi.net						
Haulsey Engineering Inc						
10755 Scripps Poway Pkwy Ste 466	San Diego	CA	92131	858-271-1780		256
Web: www.haulseyengr.com						
Haumiller Engineering 445 Renner Dr	Elgin	IL	60123	847-695-9111		256
Web: www.haumiller.com						
Hauppauge Computer Works Inc						
91 Cabot Ct	Hauppauge	NY	11788	631-434-1600	434-3198	625
TF: 800-443-6284 ■ *Web:* www.hauppauge.com						
Hauppauge Digital Inc 91 Cabot Ct	Hauppauge	NY	11788	631-434-1600	434-3198	625
OTC: HAUP ■ *TF:* 800-443-6284 ■ *Web:* www.hauppauge.com						
Hauppauge School District (HSP)						
495 Hoffman Ln PO Box 6006	Hauppauge	NY	11788	631-761-8208		685
Web: www.hauppauge.k12.ny.us						
Haury Plumbing & Heating Inc						
1816 N Market St	Sparta	IL	62286	618-443-2416		189-10
Haus Murphy's						
5739 W Glendale Ave	Downtown Glendale	AZ	85301	623-939-2480		671
Web: www.hausmurphys.com						
Hause Machines 809 S Pleasant St	Montpelier	OH	43543	419-485-3158	485-3146	455
TF: 800-932-8665 ■ *Web:* www.hausemachines.com						
Hauser Agency Inc						
16 S Church St	Mount Pleasant	PA	15666	724-547-3536		390
Hauser Ctr for Nonprofit Organizations						
15 Eliot St	Cambridge	MA	02138	617-496-8866	495-0996	634
Web: www.hks.harvard.edu/hauser						
Hausermann Abrading Process Co						
300 Laura Dr	Addison	IL	60101	630-543-6688	543-6689	455
TF: 800-446-7404 ■ *Web:* www.hausermann.net						
Hausmann Industries Inc						
130 Union St	Northvale	NJ	07647	201-767-0255	767-1369	319-1
TF: 888-428-7626 ■ *Web:* www.hausmann.com						
Hausted Patient Handling Systems LLC						
2511 Midpark Rd	Montgomery	AL	36109	334-215-5151		567
Web: www.hausted.com						
Hautly Cheese Company Inc						
251 Axminister Dr	Fenton	MO	63026	636-533-4400	533-4401	297-4
TF: 800-729-9339 ■ *Web:* www.hautly.com						
Havana 318 Main St	Bar Harbor	ME	04609	207-288-2822		671
Web: havanamaine.com						
Havana National Bank, The						
112 S Orange St	Havana	IL	62644	309-543-3361		70
Havana's 255 Granby St	Norfolk	VA	23510	757-627-5800		671
Havanet Communications PO Box 91124	Portland	OR	97291	503-531-9048		225
Web: www.hevanet.com						
Havasu Newspapers Inc						
2225 Acoma Blvd W	Lake Havasu City	AZ	86403	928-453-4237		387
Web: www.havasunews.com						
Havasu Pest Control Inc						
2716 Maricopa Ave	Lake Havasu City	AZ	86406	800-858-1859		577
TF: 800-858-1859						
Havasu Regional Medical Ctr						
101 Civic Ctr Ln	Lake Havasu City	AZ	86403	928-855-8185		374-3
Web: www.havasuregional.com						
Havco Wood Products LLC						
3200 E Outer Rd	Scott City	MO	63780	573-334-6024		499
Web: www.havco.com						
Haven 1441 Dresden Dr NE Ste 100	Atlanta	GA	30319	404-969-0700	969-0701	671
Web: www.havenrestaurant.com						
Haven Homes Inc						
554 Eagle Valley Rd	Beech Creek	PA	16822	570-962-2111		106
Web: lockhaven.com						
Haven Manor Health Care Ctr						
1441 Gateway Blvd	Far Rockaway	NY	11691	718-471-1500		450
Haven Restaurant 2208 W Morrison Ave	Tampa	FL	33606	813-258-2233		671
Web: www.sideberns.com						

Name / Address	City	State	Zip	Phone	Fax	Class
Haven Steel Products Inc						
13206 S Willison Rd	Haven	KS	67543	620-465-2573		492
TF: 800-891-2773 ■ *Web:* www.havensteel.com						
Havenwood-Heritage Heights Havenwood Campus						
33 Christian Ave	Concord	NH	03301	603-224-5363		672
TF: 800-457-6833 ■ *Web:* www.hhhinfo.com						
Havenwoods State Forest						
6141 N Hopkins St	Milwaukee	WI	53209	414-527-0232	527-0761	565
TF: 888-936-7463 ■ *Web:* dnr.wi.gov						
Havenwyck Hospital						
1525 University Dr	Auburn Hills	MI	48326	248-373-9200	377-8160*	374-5
**Fax:* Admitting ■ *TF:* 800-401-2727 ■ *Web:* havenwyckhospital.com						
Haverford College 370 Lancaster Ave	Haverford	PA	19041	610-896-1000	896-1338	166
Web: www.haverford.edu						
Haverford Trust Co						
3 Radnor Corp Ctr Ste 450	Radnor	PA	19087	610-995-8700	995-8796	405
TF: 888-995-1979 ■ *Web:* www.haverfordquality.com						
Havergal College 1451 Ave Rd	Toronto	ON	M5N2H9	416-483-3519	483-6796	622
Web: www.havergal.on.ca						
Haverhill Gazette 100 Turnpike St	N Andover	MA	01831	978-946-2000	556-3703	532-2
TF: 888-411-3245 ■ *Web:* www.hgazette.com						
Haverhill Public Library 99 Main St	Haverhill	MA	01830	978-373-1586	373-8466	434-3
TF: 800-772-1213 ■ *Web:* www.haverhillpl.org						
Haverstock & Owens LLP						
162 N Wolfe Rd	Sunnyvale	CA	94086	408-530-9700		428
Web: hollp.com						
Haverty Furniture Cos Inc						
780 Johnson Ferry Rd NE Ste 800	Atlanta	GA	30342	404-443-2900	443-4169	321
NYSE: HVT ■ *TF:* 888-428-3789 ■ *Web:* www.havertys.com						
Haviland Enterprises Inc						
421 Ann St NW	Grand Rapids	MI	49504	616-361-6691	361-9772	146
TF: 800-456-1134 ■ *Web:* www.havilandusa.com						
Havre Daily News 119 Second St	Havre	MT	59501	406-265-6795		532-3
TF: 800-993-2459 ■ *Web:* www.havredailynews.com						
Hawaii						
Aging Office (HCOA)						
250 S Hotel St Rm 406	Honolulu	HI	96813	808-586-0100		339-12
Web: www.hcoahawaii.org						
Agriculture Dept 1428 S King St	Honolulu	HI	96814	808-973-9560		339-12
Web: hdoa.hawaii.gov						
Attorney General 425 Queen St	Honolulu	HI	96813	808-586-1500	586-1239	339-12
Web: ag.hawaii.gov						
Bill Status 415 S Beretania St Rm 401	Honolulu	HI	96813	808-587-0478		433
Web: www.capitol.hawaii.gov						
Budget & Finance Dept PO Box 150	Honolulu	HI	96810	808-586-1518	586-1976	339-12
Web: portal.ehawaii.gov						
Business Economic Development & Tourism Dept						
PO Box 2359	Honolulu	HI	96804	808-586-2355		339-12
Web: www.hawaii.gov						
Child Support Enforcement Agency						
601 Kamokila Blvd Kakuhihewa Bldg Ste 251	Kapolei	HI	96707	808-692-8265	692-7060	339-12
TF: 888-317-9081 ■ *Web:* ag.hawaii.gov						
Civil Defense Div						
3949 Diamond Head Rd	Honolulu	HI	96816	808-733-4260	733-4238	339-12
Web: scd.hawaii.gov						
Commerce & Consumer Affairs Dept						
335 Merchant St	Honolulu	HI	96813	808-587-3222		339-12
Web: cca.hawaii.gov						
Consumer Protection Office						
235 S Beretania St 8th fl	Honolulu	HI	96813	808-586-2630		339-12
TF: 800-394-1902 ■ *Web:* cca.hawaii.gov						
Department of Accounting & General Services						
1151 Punchbowl St	Honolulu	HI	96813	808-586-0400	586-0775	339-12
Web: www.hawaii.gov						
Education Dept 1390 Miller St	Honolulu	HI	96813	808-586-3230	586-3234	339-12
Web: www.hawaiipublicschools.org						
Forestry & Wildlife Div						
1151 Punchbowl St Rm 325	Honolulu	HI	96813	808-587-0166	587-0160	339-12
Web: hawaii.gov						
Governor						
415 S Beretania St State Capitol	Honolulu	HI	96813	808-586-0034	586-0006	339-12
Web: governor.hawaii.gov						
Historic Preservation Div						
601 Kamokila Blvd Ste 555	Kapolei	HI	96707	808-692-8015	692-8020	339-12
Web: dlnr.hawaii.gov						
Human Resources Development Dept						
235 S Beretania St Rm 1400	Honolulu	HI	96813	808-587-1100		339-12
Web: dhrd.hawaii.gov						
Human Services Dept						
1390 Miller St Rm 209	Honolulu	HI	96809	808-586-4993	586-4890	339-12
Web: humanservices.hawaii.gov						
Information Consortium						
1136 Union Mall Rm 600	Honolulu	HI	96813	808-587-1143	587-1146	339-12
Web: www.hawaii.gov						
Insurance Div 335 Merchant St Rm 213	Honolulu	HI	96813	808-586-2790	586-2806	339-12
Web: www.hawaii.gov						
Labor & Industrial Relations Dept						
830 Punchbowl St	Honolulu	HI	96813	808-586-8600		339-12
Web: labor.hawaii.gov						
Land & Natural Resources Dept						
1151 Punchbowl St Kalanimoku Bldg	Honolulu	HI	96813	808-587-0400	587-0390	339-12
Web: dlnr.hawaii.gov						
Legislature 415 S Beretania St	Honolulu	HI	96813	808-587-0478	587-0681	339-12
Web: www.capitol.hawaii.gov						
Lieutenant Governor						
415 S Beretania St 5th Fl	Honolulu	HI	96813	808-586-0255	586-0231	339-12
Web: ltgov.hawaii.gov						
Measurement Standards Branch						
1851 Auiki St	Honolulu	HI	96819	808-832-0690	832-0683	339-12
Web: hdoa.hawaii.gov/qad/measurement-standards-branch						
Motor Vehicle Safety Office						
601 Kamokila Blvd Rm 511	Kapolei	HI	96707	808-692-7650	692-7665	339-12
Web: hidot.hawaii.gov						
Paroling Authority						
1177 Alakea St Ground Fl	Honolulu	HI	96813	808-587-1300		339-12
Web: www.hawaii.gov						
Professional & Vocational Licensing Div						
335 Merchant St King Kalakaua Bldg Rm 301	Honolulu	HI	96813	808-586-3000		339-12
Web: cca.hawaii.gov/pvl						
Public Safety Dept						
919 Ala Moana Blvd Fl 4	Honolulu	HI	96814	808-587-1288	587-1282	339-12
Web: dps.hawaii.gov						
Public Utilities Commission						
465 S King St Ste 103	Honolulu	HI	96813	808-586-2020	586-2066	339-12
Web: puc.hawaii.gov						
Securities Compliance Div						
335 Merchant St Rm 205	Honolulu	HI	96813	808-586-2744	586-3977	339-12
Web: cca.hawaii.gov						
Sheriffs Div 1177 Alakea St Rm 418	Honolulu	HI	96813	808-587-2652		339-12
Web: dps.hawaii.gov						
State Foundation for Culture & the Arts						
250 S Hotel St 2nd Fl	Honolulu	HI	96813	808-586-0300	586-0308	339-12
Web: sfca.hawaii.gov						
State Government Information						
201 Merchant St Ste 1805	Honolulu	HI	96813	808-695-4620		339-12
Web: portal.ehawaii.gov						
State Parks Div PO Box 621	Honolulu	HI	96809	808-587-0300	587-0311	339-12
Web: www.state.hi.us						
Supreme Court 417 S King St	Honolulu	HI	96813	808-539-4919	539-4928	339-12
Web: www.courts.state.hi.us						
Taxation Dept 830 Punchbowl St Rm 221	Honolulu	HI	96813	808-587-4242	587-1488	339-12
TF: 800-222-3229 ■ *Web:* tax.hawaii.gov						
Teacher Standards Board						
650 Iwilei Rd Ste 201	Honolulu	HI	96817	808-586-2600	586-2606	339-12
Web: www.htsb.org						
Tourism Authority						
1801 Kalakaua Ave 1st Fl	Honolulu	HI	96815	808-973-2255	973-2253	339-12
Web: www.hawaiitourismauthority.org						
Transportation Dept 869 Punchbowl St	Honolulu	HI	96813	808-587-2160	587-2313	339-12
Web: www.hawaii.gov						
Veterans Services Office						
459 Patterson Rd E-Wing Rm 1-A103	Honolulu	HI	96819	808-433-0420	433-0385	339-12
Web: dod.hawaii.gov						
Vocational Rehabilitation Div						
1901 Bachelot St	Honolulu	HI	96817	808-586-9744		339-12
TF: 800-316-8005 ■ *Web:* humanservices.hawaii.gov/vocationalrehab						
Workforce Development Div						
201 Merchant St Ste 1805	Honolulu	HI	96813	808-695-4620	695-4618	259
Web: www.hawaii.gov						
Hawaii Assn of Realtors						
1136 12th Ave Ste 220	Honolulu	HI	96816	808-733-7060	737-4977	656
TF: 866-693-6767 ■ *Web:* www.hawaiirealtors.com						
Hawaii Bar Journal						
1100 Alakea St Ste 1000	Honolulu	HI	96813	808-537-1868	521-7936	457-15
TF: 888-586-1056 ■ *Web:* hsba.org						
Hawaii Children's Discovery Ctr						
111 Ohe St	Honolulu	HI	96813	808-524-5437	524-5400	521
Web: www.discoverycenterhawaii.org						
Hawaii Coffee Company Inc						
1555 Kalani St	Honolulu	HI	96817	808-847-3600		159
TF: 800-338-8353 ■ *Web:* hawaiicoffeecompany.com						
Hawaii Community College 200 W Kawili St	Hilo	HI	96720	808-934-2500		162
Web: www.hawcc.hawaii.edu						
Hawaii Community Foundation						
65-1279 Kawaihae Rd	Kamuela	HI	96743	808-537-6333	521-6286	303
TF: 888-731-3863 ■ *Web:* www.hawaiicommunityfoundation.org						
Hawaii Convention Ctr						
1801 Kalakaua Ave	Honolulu	HI	96815	808-943-3500	943-3599	205
TF: 800-295-6603 ■ *Web:* www.meethawaii.com						
Hawaii County 1055 Kinoole St Ste 101	Hilo	HI	96720	808-961-8255	961-8603	338
Web: www.hawaiicounty.gov						
Hawaii Democratic Party						
627 S St Ste 105	Honolulu	HI	96813	808-596-2980		616-1
TF: 844-596-2980 ■ *Web:* www.hawaiidemocrats.org						
Hawaii Dental Assn						
1345 S Beretania St Ste 301	Honolulu	HI	96814	808-593-7956	593-7636	227
TF: 800-359-6725 ■ *Web:* www.hawaiidentalassociation.net						
Hawaii Dental Service						
700 Bishop St Ste 700	Honolulu	HI	96813	808-521-1431	529-9368	391-3
TF: 800-232-2533 ■ *Web:* www.hawaiidentalservice.com						
Hawaii Dept of Education Honolulu District Office						
4967 Kilauea Ave	Honolulu	HI	96816	808-733-4950	733-4953	685
TF: 800-437-8641 ■ *Web:* www.hawaiipublicschools.org						
Hawaii Dept of Transportation Harbors Div						
79 S Nimitz Hwy	Honolulu	HI	96813	808-587-1927	587-1928	618
Web: www.hawaii.gov						
Hawaii Federal Credit Union						
1244 Kaumualii St	Honolulu	HI	96817	808-847-1371		219
Web: www.hawaiifcu.org						
Hawaii Health Matters PO Box 88900	Steilacoom	WA	98388	253-512-6600		213
Web: www.hawaiihealthmatters.org						
Hawaii Information Consortium (HIC)						
201 Merchant St Ste 1805	Honolulu	HI	96813	808-695-4620		565
TF: 800-295-0089 ■ *Web:* www.hawaii.gov						
Hawaii Insitute of Geophysics & Planetology						
1680 E West Rd PO Box 602B						
Pacific Ocean Science & Technology (POST) Bldg Rm 602	Honolulu	HI	96822	808-956-8760	956-3188	668
Web: www.higp.hawaii.edu						
Hawaii Island Chamber of Commerce						
117 Keawe St	Hilo	HI	96720	808-935-7178	961-4435	139
TF: 877-482-4411 ■ *Web:* hicc.biz						
Hawaii Lions Eye Bank & Makana Foundation						
405 N Kuakini St Ste 801	Honolulu	HI	96817	808-536-7416		269
Web: www.hlebmf.org						
Hawaii Medical Assn						
1360 S Beretania St	Honolulu	HI	96816	808-536-7702	528-2376	474
TF: 888-536-2792 ■ *Web:* www.hawaiimedicalassociation.org						
Hawaii Medical Service Assn						
818 Keeaumoku St	Honolulu	HI	96814	808-948-6111	948-5567*	391-3
**Fax:* Cust Svc ■ *TF:* 800-776-4672 ■ *Web:* www.hmsa.com						
Hawaii Modular Space Inc						
91-282 Kalaeloa Blvd	Kapolei	HI	96707	808-682-5559	682-5199	187
Web: www.hawaiimodularspace.com						
Hawaii National Bank 45 N King St	Honolulu	HI	96817	808-528-7711		69
TF: 800-528-2273 ■ *Web:* www.hawaiinational.com						

	Phone	Fax	Class
Hawaii Nurses Assn (HNA) 949 Kapiolani Blvd Ste 107 .... Honolulu HI 96814 *TF:* 800-617-2677 ■ *Web:* www.hawaiinurses.org	808-531-1020		533
Hawaii Nut & Bolt Inc 905 Ahua St .... Honolulu HI 96819 *TF:* 800-764-6887 ■ *Web:* www.hawaiinutandbolt.com	808-834-1919		351
Hawaii Opera Theatre 848 S Beretania St Ste 301 .... Honolulu HI 96813 *TF:* 800-836-7372 ■ *Web:* www.hawaiiopera.org	808-596-7372	596-0379	573-2
Hawaii Pacific Teleport LP 91-340 Farrington Hwy. .... Kapolei HI 96707 *Web:* www.hawaiiteleport.com	808-674-9157		116
Hawaii Pacific University 1164 Bishop St Ste 200 .... Honolulu HI 96813 **Fax:* Admissions ■ *TF:* 866-225-5478 ■ *Web:* www.hpu.edu	808-544-0200	544-1136*	166
Meader Library 1060 Bishop St. .... Honolulu HI 96813 *TF:* 866-225-5478 ■ *Web:* www.hpu.edu	808-544-0210	521-7998	434-6
Windward Hawaii Loa 1164 Bishop St. .... Honolulu HI 96813 *TF Admissions:* 866-225-5478 ■ *Web:* www.hpu.edu	808-544-0200		166
Hawaii Petroleum Inc 16 Railroad Ave Ste 202 .... Hilo HI 96720 *Web:* www.hawaiipetroleum.com	808-969-1405		579
Hawaii Planing Mill Ltd (HPM) 16-166 Melekahiwa St .... Keaau HI 96749 *TF:* 877-841-7633 ■ *Web:* www.hpmhawaii.com	808-966-5693	966-7564	191-3
Hawaii Preparatory Academy 65-1692 Kohala Mountain Rd. .... Kamuela HI 96743 *TF:* 800-644-4481 ■ *Web:* www.hpa.edu	808-885-7321	881-4045	622
Hawaii Prince Hotel Waikiki, The 100 Holomoana St .... Honolulu HI 96815 **Fax Area Code:* 808 ■ *TF:* 888-977-4623 ■ *Web:* www.princeresortshawaii.com	888-977-4623	944-4491*	669
Hawaii Public Television 2350 Dole St. .... Honolulu HI 96822 *TF:* 800-238-4847 ■ *Web:* www.pbshawaii.org	808-973-1000	973-1090	632
Hawaii Republican Party 725 Kapiolani Blvd Ste C105 .... Honolulu HI 96813 *Web:* www.gophawaii.com	808-593-8180	593-7742	616-2
Hawaii Reserves Inc 55-510 Kamehameha Hwy .... Laie HI 96762 *Web:* www.hawaiireserves.com	808-293-9201	293-6456	655
Hawaii State Ballet 1418 Kapiolani Blvd .... Honolulu HI 96814 *TF:* 800-367-7060 ■ *Web:* www.hawaiistateballet.com	808-947-2755		573-1
Hawaii State Bar Assn (HSBA) 1100 Alakea St Ste 1000. .... Honolulu HI 96813 *TF:* 800-932-0311 ■ *Web:* www.hsba.org	808-537-1868	521-7936	72
Hawaii State Hospital 45-710 Keaahala Rd .... Kaneohe HI 96744	808-247-2191		374-5
Hawaii State Parks Kalanimoku Bldg 1151 Punchbowl St Rm 310 .... Honolulu HI 96813 *Web:* dlnr.hawaii.gov/dsp	808-587-0300	587-0311	565
Hawaii State Public Library System (HSPLS) 44 Merchant St .... Honolulu HI 96813 *Web:* hawaii.sdp.sirsi.net	808-586-3700		434-5
Hawaii Stevedores Inc 1601 Sand Island Pkwy .... Honolulu HI 96819 *TF:* 800-767-7093 ■ *Web:* www.hawaiistevedores.com	808-527-3400		465
Hawaii Tribune-Herald 355 Kinoole St .... Hilo HI 96720 *Web:* www.hawaiitribune-herald.com	808-935-6621		532-2
Hawaii Tropical Botanical Garden 27-717 Old Mamalahoa Hwy PO Box 80 .... Papaikou HI 96781 *Web:* www.hawaiigarden.com	808-964-5233	964-1338	97
Hawaii Visitors & Convention Bureau 2270 Kalakaua Ave Ste 801 .... Honolulu HI 96815 *TF:* 800-464-2924 ■ *Web:* www.gohawaii.com	800-464-2924		206
Hawaii Volcanoes National Park PO Box 52 .... Hawaii National Park HI 96718 *Web:* www.nps.gov	808-985-6000	985-6004	564
Hawaii's Best Bed & Breakfasts 571 Pauku St .... Kailua HI 96734 *TF:* 800-262-9912 ■ *Web:* www.bestbnb.com	808-263-3100	262-5030	376
Hawaii's Plantation Village (HPV) 94-695 Waipahu St. .... Waipahu HI 96797 *Web:* www.hawaiiplantationvillage.org	808-677-0110	676-6727	520
Hawaiian Airlines HawaiianMiles PO Box 30008 .... Honolulu HI 96820 **Fax Area Code:* 808 ■ *TF:* 877-426-4537 ■ *Web:* www.hawaiianairlines.com	877-426-4537	838-6777*	26
Hawaiian Airlines Inc 3375 Koapaka St Ste G350 .... Honolulu HI 96819 *TF:* 800-367-5320 ■ *Web:* www.hawaiianairlines.com	808-835-3700	835-3690	25
Hawaiian Cement 99-1300 Halawa Vly St .... Aiea HI 96701 *TF:* 800-317-4161 ■ *Web:* www.hawaiiancement.com	808-532-3400	532-3499	182
Hawaiian Commercial & Sugar Co 1 Hansen St .... Puunene HI 96784 *Web:* www.hcsugar.com	808-877-0081	871-7663	296-38
Hawaiian Dredging & Construction Co 201 Merchant St. .... Honolulu HI 96813 *Web:* www.hdcc.com	808-735-3211	735-7416	188-5
Hawaiian Electric Industries Inc 1001 Bishop St Ste 2900 .... Honolulu HI 96813 *TF:* 877-871-8461 ■ *Web:* www.hei.com	808-543-5662		787
Hawaiian Express Service Inc 3623 Munster Ave. .... Hayward CA 94545 *Web:* www.hawaiianexpressinc.com	510-783-6100	782-5794	311
Hawaiian Falls Waterparks 4550 N Garland Ave .... Garland TX 75040 *Web:* hfalls.com	972-675-8888		31
Hawaiian Gardens Casino 11871 Carson St. .... Hawaiian Gardens CA 90716 *Web:* www.thegardenscasino.com	562-860-5887		133
Hawaiian Housewares Ltd 96-1282 Waihona St. .... Pearl City HI 96782	808-456-3334		361
Hawaiian Inn 2301 S Atlantic Ave. .... Daytona Beach Shores FL 32118 *TF:* 800-922-3023 ■ *Web:* www.hawaiianinn.com	386-255-5411	253-1209	379
Hawaiian Island Creations Inc 348 Hahani St. .... Kailua HI 96734 *Web:* www.hicsurf.com	808-266-6730		711

	Phone	Fax	Class
Hawaiian Isles Kona Coffee Co 2839 Mokumoa St .... Honolulu HI 96819 *TF Orders:* 800-657-7716 ■ *Web:* www.hawaiianisles.com	808-839-3255		296-7
Hawaiian Sun Products Inc 259 Sand Island Access Rd .... Honolulu HI 96819 *TF:* 800-445-5787 ■ *Web:* www.hawaiiansunproducts.com	808-845-3211	842-0532	296-20
Hawaiian Telcom Holdco Inc 1177 Bishop St. .... Honolulu HI 96813 *Web:* www.hawaiiantel.com	808-546-4511		787
Hawaiian Tug & Barge 1331 N Nimitz Hwy PO Box 3288 .... Honolulu HI 96817 *Web:* www.htbyb.com	808-543-9311		465
Hawk Eye, The 800 S Main St PO Box 10. .... Burlington IA 52601 *TF:* 800-397-1708 ■ *Web:* www.thehawkeye.com	319-754-8461	754-6824	532-2
Hawk Inn & Mountain Resort 75 Billings Rd. .... Plymouth VT 05056 *TF:* 800-685-4295 ■ *Web:* www.hawkresort.com	802-672-3811	672-5585	669
Hawk Isolutions Group Inc 6439 Plymouth Ave Ste 112 .... Saint Louis MO 63133 *TF:* 800-621-2349 ■ *Web:* www.hawkisg.com	636-256-7534		180
Hawk Mountain Lab Inc 201 W Clay Ave .... Hazle Township PA 18202 *TF:* 800-220-3675 ■ *Web:* hawkmtnlabs.com	570-455-6011		743
Hawk Mountain Sanctuary (HMS) 1700 Hawk Mtn Rd .... Kempton PA 19529 *Web:* www.hawkmountain.org	610-756-6961	756-4468	48-3
Hawk Ridge Systems 4 Orinda Way Bldg B Ste 100 .... Orinda CA 94563 **Fax Area Code:* 650 ■ *TF:* 877-266-4469 ■ *Web:* hawkridgesys.com	877-266-4469	428-1868*	177
Hawk Rope Access Inc 124 Parker Ave. .... Rodeo CA 94572	510-245-8728		539
Hawk Springs State Recreation Area 2301 Central Ave Barrett Building, 4th Fl .... Cheyenne WY 82002 *Web:* wyoparks.state.wy.us/index.php/places-to-go/hawk-springs	307-777-6323		565
Hawk Steel Industries Inc 4010 S Eden Rd .... Kennedale TX 76060 *Web:* www.hawksteel.com	817-483-7511	516-0200	492
Hawk Technology Ltd 8080 Centennial Expy .... Rock Island IL 61201 *Web:* www.hawktechnology.com	309-787-6200		261
Hawk's Cay Resort & Marina 61 Hawk's Cay Blvd .... Duck Key FL 33050 *TF:* 888-395-5539 ■ *Web:* www.hawkscay.com	305-743-7000	743-5215	669
Hawken House, The 1155 S Rock Hill Rd .... Saint Louis MO 63119 *Web:* thehotelnexus.com	314-968-1857		50-3
Hawker Pacific Aerospace 11240 Sherman Way. .... Sun Valley CA 91352 *Web:* www.hawker.com	818-765-6201	765-8073	24
Hawker Powersource Inc 9404 Ooltewah Industrial Dr PO Box 808 .... Ooltewah TN 37363 *TF:* 800-238-8658 ■ *Web:* www.hawkerpowersource.com	423-238-5700		74
Hawkeye 2828 Routh St Ste 300 .... Dallas TX 75201 *Web:* www.hawkeyeww.com	214-749-0000		5
Hawkeye Community College 1501 E Orange Rd. .... Waterloo IA 50704 **Fax:* Admissions ■ *TF:* 800-670-4769 ■ *Web:* www.hawkeyecollege.edu	319-296-2320	296-2874*	162
Hawkeye Corrugated Box Co 725 Ida St. .... Cedar Falls IA 50613 *Web:* www.hawkeyebox.com	319-268-0407		100
Hawkeye Hotels Inc 1601 N Roosevelt Ave. .... Burlington IA 52601 *Web:* www.hawkeyehotels.com	319-752-7400		378
Hawkeye Industries Inc 1126 N Eason Blvd. .... Tupelo MS 38804 *Web:* hawkeye.ws	662-842-3333		697
Hawkeye International Ltd 5760 VT Rt 100. .... North Hyde Park VT 05665 *Web:* www.hawkeyeintl.com/home.htm	802-635-7500	635-7900	732
Hawkeye Leisure Trailers Ltd 1419 11th St N .... Humboldt IA 50548 *Web:* www.yachtclubtrailers.com	515-332-1802	332-1833	763
Hawkeye LLC 100 Marcus Blvd Ste 1 .... Hauppauge NY 11788	631-447-3100		539
Hawkeye REC 24049 Iowa 9 .... Cresco IA 52136 *TF:* 800-658-2243 ■ *Web:* www.hawkeyerec.com	563-547-3801	547-4033	245
Hawkeye Stages Inc 703 Dudley St. .... Decorah IA 52101 *TF:* 877-464-2954 ■ *Web:* www.hawkeyestages.com	563-382-3639		107
Hawking Technologies Inc 35 Hammond Ste 150. .... Irvine CA 92618 *Web:* www.hawkingtech.com	949-206-6900		246
Hawkins & Associates Engineering Inc 436 Mitchell Rd .... Modesto CA 95354 *Web:* www.hawkins-eng.com	209-575-4295		261
Hawkins Assoc Inc 909 NE Loop 410 Ste 104. .... San Antonio TX 78209 *Web:* www.hawkinspersonnel.com	210-349-9911	349-3393	721
Hawkins Construction Co 2516 Deer Pk Blvd .... Omaha NE 68105 *Web:* www.hawkins1.com	402-342-1607		186
Hawkins County 110 E Main St. .... Rogersville TN 37857 *TF:* 800-378-3778 ■ *Web:* www.hawkinscountytn.gov	423-272-7002		338
Hawkins County Library System 407 E Main St. .... Rogersville TN 37857 *Web:* www.hawkinslibraries.org	423-272-8710	272-9261	434-3
Hawkins Inc 3100 E Hennepin Ave .... Minneapolis MN 55413 *NASDAQ:* HWKN ■ *TF:* 800-328-5460 ■ *Web:* www.hawkinsinc.com	612-331-6910	331-5304	143
Hawkins Parnell Thackston & Young LLP 4000 SunTrust Plaza 303 Peachtree St NE .... Atlanta GA 30308 *Web:* www.hptylaw.com	404-614-7400		428
Hawks Giffels & Pullin (Hgp) Inc 1308 Altamont Rd. .... Greenville SC 29608 *Web:* hgp-inc.com	864-370-0213		463
Hawks Nest State Park PO Box 857 .... Ansted WV 25812 *Web:* www.hawksnestsp.com	304-658-5212		565
Hawley Mountain Guest Ranch 4188 Main Boulder Rd .... McLeod MT 59052 *TF:* 877-496-7848 ■ *Web:* www.hawleymountain.com	406-932-5791		239

	Phone	Fax	Class
Hawley Troxell Ennis & Hawley LLP 877 Main St Ste 1000 Boise ID 83702 *Web:* www.hawleytroxell.com	208-344-6000		428
Hawn State Park 12096 Pk Dr Sainte Genevieve MO 63670 *Web:* www.mostateparks.com	573-883-3603		565
Haworth Inc 1 Haworth Ctr. Holland MI 49423 *TF:* 800-344-2600 ■ *Web:* www.haworth.com	616-393-3000	393-1570	319-1
Haworth Marketing & Media Co 45 S Seventh St Plaza 7 Bldg Ste 2400 Minneapolis MN 55402 *Web:* www.haworthmedia.com	612-677-8900		6
Haworth, Bradshaw, Stallknecht & Barber Inc 4380 Auburn Blvd. Sacramento CA 95841 *Web:* www.haworthlaw.com	916-484-4354		428
Haws Corp 1455 Kleppe Ln Sparks NV 89431 *TF:* 888-640-4297 ■ *Web:* www.hawsco.com	775-359-4712	359-7424	664
Hawthorn Bancshares Inc 300 SW Longview Blvd. Lees Summit MO 64081 *NASDAQ: HWBK* ■ *Web:* www.exchangebancshares.com	816-347-8100		360-2
Hawthorn Ctr 18471 Haggerty Rd Northville MI 48167 *TF:* 855-444-3911 ■ *Web:* michigan.gov	248-349-3000	349-8259	374-1
Hawthorn Group LC 625 Slaters Ln # 100 Alexandria VA 22314 *TF:* 800-561-3357 ■ *Web:* www.hawthorngroup.com	703-299-4499	299-4488	636
Hawthorne Animal Hospital 1516 Alarth Dr Troy IL 62294 *Web:* glencarbonhawthorne.com	618-667-4900		794
Hawthorne Boulevard Cutters 1744 SE Hawthorne Blvd Portland OR 97214	503-239-0382		460
Hawthorne Chamber of Commerce 12519 Crenshaw Blvd. Hawthorne CA 90250 *Web:* www.hawthorne-chamber.com	310-676-1163		139
Hawthorne Executive Search 6303 Oleander Dr Ste 104b Wilmington NC 28403 *Web:* hawthornesearch.com	910-798-1800		260
Hawthorne Hotel 18 Washington Sq W. Salem MA 01970 *TF:* 800-729-7829 ■ *Web:* www.hawthornehotel.com	978-744-4080		379
Hawthorne Inn & Conference Ctr 420 High St Winston-Salem NC 27101 *TF:* 877-777-3099 ■ *Web:* www.wakehealth.edu	336-777-3000	777-3282	379
Hawthorne LLC 2280 W Tyler Ave Ste 200. Fairfield IA 52556 *Web:* www.hawthornedirect.com	641-472-3800		720
Hawthorne Machinery Co 16945 Camino San Bernardo San Diego CA 92127 *TF:* 800-437-4228 ■ *Web:* www.hawthornecat.com	858-674-7000		264-3
Hawthorne Race Course 3501 S Laramie Ave Cicero IL 60804 *Web:* www.hawthorneracecourse.com	708-780-3700		642
Hay Communications 72863 Blind Line PO Box 99 Zurich ON N0M2T0 *TF:* 800-665-3337 ■ *Web:* www.hay.net	519-236-4333		224
Hay Group Inc 1650 Arch St Ste 2300 Philadelphia PA 19107 *TF:* 800-716-4429 ■ *Web:* www.haygroup.com	215-861-2000	861-2111	194
Hay House Inc PO Box 5100 Carlsbad CA 92018 **Fax Area Code:* 800 ■ *TF:* 800-654-5126 ■ *Web:* www.hayhouse.com	760-431-7695	650-5115*	637-3
Hay-Adams Hotel 800 16th St NE Washington DC 20006 *TF:* 800-853-6807 ■ *Web:* www.hayadams.com	202-638-6600	638-2716	379
Haycock Petroleum Co 715 W Bonanza Rd Las Vegas NV 89106 *TF:* 800-876-1965 ■ *Web:* www.haycockpetroleum.com	702-382-1620		580
Hayden Automotive 1801 Waters Ridge Dr. Lewisville TX 75057 *TF:* 888-505-4567 ■ *Web:* www.haydenauto.com	888-505-4567		60
Hayden Consulting Engineers In 12480 SW 68th Ave Tigard OR 97223 *Web:* hayden-engineers.com	503-968-9994		261
Hayden Planetarium 81st St & Central Pk W. New York NY 10024 *Web:* www.amnh.org	212-769-5606	769-5427	598
Hayden Technologies Inc 333 Sandy Springs Cir Ste 127 Atlanta GA 30328 *Web:* www.haydentechnologies.com	404-303-9935		180
Hayden Twist Drill & Tool Company Inc 22822 Globe St. Warren MI 48089 *TF:* 800-521-1780 ■ *Web:* www.haydendrills.com	586-754-7700	754-3312	493
Haydon Building Corp 4640 E Cotton Gin Loop Phoenix AZ 85040 *TF:* 800-810-3761 ■ *Web:* www.haydonbc.com	602-296-1496		186
Hayes & Stolz Industrial Manufacturing Co 3521 Hemphill St PO Box 11217 Fort Worth TX 76110 *TF:* 800-725-7272 ■ *Web:* www.hayes-stolz.com	817-926-3391	926-4133	298
Hayes & Wiesel Independent Solutions Inc 78365 United States Hwy 111 Ste 316 La Quinta CA 92253 *Web:* www.hwisolutions.com	760-347-5505		193
Hayes Bolt & Supply Inc 2950 National Ave. San Diego CA 92113 *TF:* 800-222-9221 ■ *Web:* www.hayesbolt.com	619-231-5966		351
Hayes Convalescent Hospital 1250 Hayes St San Francisco CA 94117 *Web:* www.hayesconvalescent.com	415-931-8806		371
Hayes County 505 Troth St PO Box 370 Hayes Center NE 69032 *Web:* www.hayescounty.ne.gov	308-286-3413	286-3208	338
Hayes Group International Inc, The 4400 Silas Creek Pkwy Ste 301 Winston-salem NC 27104 *Web:* www.thehayesgroupintl.com	336-765-6764		463
Hayes Handpiece Franchises Inc 5375 Avenida Encinas Ste C. Carlsbad CA 92008 *TF:* 800-228-0521 ■ *Web:* www.hayeshandpiece.com	760-602-0521		310
Hayes James & Associates Inc 3005 Breckinridge Blvd Duluth GA 30096 *Web:* www.hayesjames.com	770-923-1600		261
Hayes Lake State Park 48990 County Rd 4. Roseau MN 56751 *Web:* www.dnr.state.mn.us/state_parks/hayes_lake	218-425-7504		565
Hayes Pump Inc 66 Old Powder Mill Rd I West Concord MA 01742 *Web:* www.hayespump.com	978-369-8800		358
Hayes School Publishing Co Inc 321 Pennwood Ave. Pittsburgh PA 15221 **Fax Area Code:* 513 ■ *TF:* 800-926-0704 ■ *Web:* www.hayespub.com	412-371-2373	527-4526*	243
Hayes Specialties Corp 1761 E Genesee. Saginaw MI 48601 *TF:* 800-248-3603 ■ *Web:* www.ehayes.com	989-755-6541	755-2341	328
Haylor Freyer & Coon 231 Salina Meadows N Syracuse NY 13212 *Web:* www.haylor.com	315-451-1500		390
Hayman Capital Management LP 2101 Cedar Springs Rd Ste 1400 Dallas TX 75201 *Web:* www.haymancapitalmanagement.com	214-347-8050		360-3
Haynes & Boone LLP 2323 Victory Ave #700 Dallas TX 75219 *Web:* www.haynesboone.com	214-651-5000	651-5940	428
Haynes Corp 3581 Mercantile Ave Naples FL 34104 *Web:* www.haynesco.com	239-643-3013		247
Haynes Furniture Company Inc 5324 Virginia Beach Blvd Virginia Beach VA 23462 *Web:* www.haynesfurniture.com	757-497-9681		321
Haynes International Inc 1020 W Pk Ave PO Box 9013 Kokomo IN 46904 *NASDAQ: HAYN* ■ *TF:* 800-354-0806 ■ *Web:* www.haynesintl.com	765-456-6000	456-6905	485
Haynesville Correctional Ctr 421 Barnfield Rd PO Box 129 Haynesville VA 22472 *Web:* www.vadoc.virginia.gov	804-333-3577		213
Hayneville Telephone Company Inc PO Box 175 Hayneville AL 36040 *Web:* www.htcnet.net	334-548-2101		736
Haynsworth Sinkler Boyd PA 134 Meeting St 3rd Fl Charleston SC 29402 *Web:* www.hsblawfirm.com	843-722-3366		428
Hays Consolidated I S D 21003 I- 35 Kyle TX 78640 *Web:* www.hayscisd.net	512-268-2141	268-2147	685
Hays Convention & Visitors Bureau 2700 Vine St PO Box 490 Hays KS 67601 *TF:* 800-569-4505 ■ *Web:* www.haysusa.com	785-628-8202	628-1471	206
Hays County 110 E Martin Luther King St San Marcos TX 78666 *Web:* www.co.hays.tx.us	512-393-7738	393-7735	338
Hays Feeders LLC 1174 Feedlot Rd Hays KS 67601 *TF:* 800-569-4505 ■ *Web:* www.prattfeeders.com	785-625-3415		10-1
Hays Financial Consulting LLC Atlanta Financial Ctr 3343 Peachtree Rd Ste 200 Atlanta GA 30326 *Web:* haysconsulting.net	404-926-0060		196
Hays Fluid Controls 114 Eason Rd. Dallas NC 28034 *TF:* 800-354-4297 ■ *Web:* www.haysfluidcontrols.com	704-922-9565	922-9595	790
Hays Medical Ctr (HMC) 2220 Canterbury Dr Hays KS 67601 *TF:* 800-248-0073 ■ *Web:* haysmed.com	785-650-2759		374-3
Haysite Reinforced Plastics 5599 Perry Hwy Erie PA 16509 *TF:* 800-259-9007 ■ *Web:* www.haysite.com	814-868-3691	864-7803	606
Haystack Mountain State Park c/o Burr Pond State Pk 385 Burr Mtn Rd Torrington CT 06790 *Web:* www.ct.gov	860-482-1817		565
Haystak Digital Marketing LLC 1514 Broadway Ste 201 Fort Myers FL 33901 *TF:* 866-292-0194 ■ *Web:* www.haystak.com	866-292-0194		5
Hayward Baker Inc 1130 Annapolis Rd Ste 202 Odenton MD 21113 *TF:* 800-456-6548 ■ *Web:* www.haywardbaker.com	410-551-8200		189-5
Hayward Chamber of Commerce 22561 Main St Hayward CA 94541 *TF:* 800-847-7037 ■ *Web:* www.hayward.org	510-537-2424		139
Hayward Lumber Co 429 Front St. Salinas CA 93901 *Web:* www.haywardlumber.com	831-755-8800	755-8821	364
Hayward Pool Products Inc 620 Div St. Elizabeth NJ 07207 *Web:* www.hayward-pool.com	908-351-5400	351-5675	357
Hayward Public Library 835 C St Hayward CA 94541 *Web:* www.hayward-ca.gov/public-library	510-293-8685		434-3
Hayward Quartz Technology Inc 1700 Corporate Way Fremont CA 94539 *Web:* www.haywardquartz.com	510-657-9605		454
Hayward Tyler Inc 480 Roosevelt Hwy Colchester VT 05446 *Web:* www.haywardtyler.com	802-655-4444	655-4682	641
Hayward Unified School District (HUSD) 24411 Amador St Hayward CA 94544 *Web:* www.husd.k12.ca.us	510-784-2600	784-2641	685
Haywood Community College 185 Freedlander Dr. Clyde NC 28721 **Fax:* Admissions ■ *TF:* 866-468-6422 ■ *Web:* www.haywood.edu	828-627-2821	627-4513*	162
Haywood County 1 N Washington St. Brownsville TN 38012 *TF:* 800-273-8712 ■ *Web:* www.haywoodcountybrownsville.com	731-772-1432	772-3864	338
Haywood County 1233 N Main St Annex II. Waynesville NC 28786 *Web:* www.haywoodnc.net	828-452-6633	452-6750	338
Haywood County Chamber of Commerce 28 Walnut St. Waynesville NC 28786 *Web:* haywoodchamber.com	828-456-3021	452-7265	139
Haywood County Public Library 678 S Haywood St Waynesville NC 28786 *Web:* haywoodlibrary.libguides.com	828-452-5169		434-3
Haywood County School District 900 E Main St. Brownsville TN 38012 *Web:* www.haywoodschools.com	731-772-9613		187
Haywood Electric Membership Corp 376 Grindstone Rd Waynesville NC 28785 *TF:* 800-951-6088 ■ *Web:* www.haywoodemc.com	828-452-2281		245
Haywood Hall House & Gardens 211 New Bern Pl. Raleigh NC 27601 *Web:* haywoodhall.org	919-832-8357		50-3
Haywood Mall 700 Haywood Rd Greenville SC 29607 *TF:* 800-331-5479 ■ *Web:* www.simon.com	864-288-0511	297-6018	460
Haywood Park Hotel 1 Battery Pk Ave Asheville NC 28801 *TF:* 800-741-5072 ■ *Web:* www.haywoodpark.com	828-252-2522	253-0481	379

Name / Address	City	State	ZIP	Phone	Fax	Class
Haywood Securities Inc						
Waterfront Centre 200 Burrard St Ste 700	Vancouver	BC	V6C3L6	604-697-7100		401
TF: 800-663-9499 ■ *Web:* www.haywood.com						
Hayzlett Companies Inc, The						
4912 S Technopolis Dr	Sioux Falls	SD	57106	605-275-4075		636
Web: hayzlett.com						
Hazard Communication Systems LLC						
190 Old Milford Rd	Milford	PA	18337	570-296-5686		627
Web: www.clarionsafety.com						
Hazard Community & Technical College						
1 Community College Dr	Hazard	KY	41701	606-436-5721	487-3614	162
TF: 800-246-7521 ■ *Web:* hazard.kctcs.edu						
Hazard Campus 101 Vo Tech Dr	Hazard	KY	41701	606-436-5721	487-8417	162
TF: 800-246-7521 ■ *Web:* hazard.kctcs.edu						
Lees College Campus Library						
601 Jefferson Ave	Jackson	KY	41339	606-666-7521		162
TF: 800-246-7521 ■ *Web:* www.hazard.kctcs.edu						
Hazel Park Raceway						
1650 E 10 Mile Rd	Hazel Park	MI	48030	248-398-1000	398-5236	642
TF: 800-794-8001 ■ *Web:* www.hazelparkraceway.com						
Hazelden Chicago 867 N Dearborn St	Chicago	IL	60610	312-943-3534		726
TF: 800-257-7810 ■ *Web:* www.hazelden.org						
Hazelden Ctr for Youth & Families (HCYF)						
11505 36th Ave N	Plymouth	MN	55441	763-509-3800		726
TF: 800-257-7810 ■ *Web:* www.hazelden.org						
Hazelden Foundation						
15251 Pleasant Valley Rd	Center City	MN	55012	651-213-4200		726
TF: 800-257-7810 ■ *Web:* www.hazelden.org						
Hazelden New York						
322 Eigth Ave 12th Fl	New York	NY	10001	212-420-9520	420-9664	726
TF: 800-257-7800 ■ *Web:* www.hazelden.org						
Hazelden Springbrook 1901 Esther St	Newberg	OR	97132	503-554-4300		726
TF: 866-866-4662 ■ *Web:* www.hazelden.org						
Hazelett Strip-Casting Corp						
135 West Lakeshore Dr PO Box 600	Colchester	VT	05446	802-863-6376		787
Web: www.hazelett.com						
Hazelnut Growers of Oregon						
401 N 26th Ave	Cornelius	OR	97113	800-382-5339		11-1
TF: 800-273-4676 ■ *Web:* www.westnut.com						
Hazelwood Enterprises Inc						
402 N 32nd St	Phoenix	AZ	85008	602-275-7709		327
Web: hazelwoods.com						
Hazelwood Historic Home Museum						
1008 S Monroe Ave	Green Bay	WI	54301	920-437-1840	455-4518	520
TF: 800-895-0071 ■ *Web:* www.browncohistoricalsoc.org						
Hazen & Sawyer PC						
498 Seventh Ave 11th Fl	New York	NY	10018	212-777-8400	614-9049	261
TF: 888-514-2936 ■ *Web:* www.hazenandsawyer.com						
Hazen Paper Co						
240 S Water St PO Box 189	Holyoke	MA	01041	413-538-8204	533-1420	554
Web: www.hazen.com						
Hazen Research Inc 4601 Indiana St	Golden	CO	80403	303-279-4501	278-1528	668
Web: www.hazenresearch.com						
Hazen Transport Inc 27050 Wick Rd	Taylor	MI	48180	313-292-2120	946-4452*	780
**Fax Area Code: 734* ■ *TF:* 800-251-2120 ■ *Web:* www.hazentransport.com						
Hazle Park Packing Co						
260 Washington Ave Hazle Pk	Hazletownship	PA	18202	570-455-7571	455-6030	296-26
TF: 800-238-4331 ■ *Web:* hazlepark.com						
Hazleton Standard Speaker						
21 N Wyoming St	Hazleton	PA	18201	570-455-3636	455-4244	532-2
TF Cust Svc: 800-843-6680 ■ *Web:* www.standardspeaker.com						
Hazlett Burt & Watson Inc						
1300 Chapline St	Wheeling	WV	26003	304-233-3312		690
Web: www.hazlettburt.com						
Hazmat Environmental Group Inc						
60 Commerce Dr	Buffalo	NY	14218	716-827-7200		194
Web: www.hazmatinc.com						
HazMat Systems Inc						
501 Slaters Ln Ste 1024	Alexandria	VA	22314	703-652-4512	734-0961	809
Web: www.hazmatsystems.com						
Hazmateam Inc 12 Kimball Hill Rd	Hudson	NH	03051	603-882-6247		196
Web: www.hazmateam.com						
Hazmed Inc 9410 Annapolis Rd Ste 200	Lanham	MD	20706	301-577-9339		463
Web: www.hazmed.com						
Haztek Inc 143 Medford - Mt Holly Rd	Medford	NJ	08055	609-714-1003		41
TF: 800-610-1771 ■ *Web:* www.haztekinc.com						
HB Communications Inc						
60 Dodge Ave	North Haven	CT	06473	203-234-9246	234-2013	38
TF: 800-243-4414 ■ *Web:* www.hbcommunications.com						
HB Frazer Co 514 Shoemaker Rd	King of Prussia	PA	19406	610-768-0400	992-5070	189-4
TF: 800-679-9567 ■ *Web:* hbfrazer.com						
HB Fuller Co						
1200 Willow Lake Blvd PO Box 64683	Saint Paul	MN	55164	651-236-5900		3
NYSE: FUL ■ *TF:* 888-423-8553 ■ *Web:* www.hbfuller.com						
HB Management Group Inc						
7100 Broadway Ste 6L	Denver	CO	80221	866-440-1100		104
TF: 866-440-1100 ■ *Web:* www.hbmgmt.com						
Hb Mcclure Co 600 S 17th St	Harrisburg	PA	17104	717-232-4328		697
Web: www.hbmcclure.com						
HB Mellot Estate Inc						
100 Mellott Dr	Warfordsburg	PA	17267	301-678-2050	678-2051	503-5
TF: 800-634-5634 ■ *Web:* www.mellottcompany.com						
HB Rentals LC 5813 Hwy 90 E	Broussard	LA	70518	337-839-1641	839-1628	264-3
TF: 800-262-6790 ■ *Web:* hbrentals.com						
HB Smith Company Inc						
47 Westfield Industrial Pk Rd	Westfield	MA	01085	413-568-3148		91
Web: hbsmith.com						
HB Stubbs Co 27027 Mound Rd	Warren	MI	48092	586-574-9700	574-9741	232
Hba Architecture Engineering And Interior Design						
1 Columbus Ctr Ste 1000	Virginia Beach	VA	23462	757-490-9048		393
Web: www.hbaonline.com						
HBC (Hahnel Bros Co)						
46 Strawberry Ave PO Box 1160	Lewiston	ME	04243	207-784-6477		189-12
TF: 800-448-7663 ■ *Web:* www.hahnelbrosco.com						
HBD Construction Inc						
5517 Manchester Ave	Saint Louis	MO	63110	314-781-8000		186
Web: www.hbdgc.com						
HBD Inc 3901 Riverdale Rd	Greensboro	NC	27406	336-275-4800		67
TF: 800-403-2247 ■ *Web:* www.hbdinc.com						

Name / Address	City	State	ZIP	Phone	Fax	Class
HBD Industries Inc						
5200 Upper Metro Pl Ste 110	Dublin	OH	43017	614-526-7000		610
TF: 800-314-4755 ■ *Web:* www.hbdindustries.com						
HBD/Thermoid Inc						
1301 W Sandusky Ave	Bellefontaine	OH	43311	937-593-5010	593-4354	370
TF: 800-543-8070 ■ *Web:* www.thermoid.com						
HBE Corp 11330 Olive Blvd	Saint Louis	MO	63141	314-567-9000		186
HB&G Inc PO Box 589	Troy	AL	36081	334-566-5000	566-4629	499
TF: 800-264-4424 ■ *Web:* www.hbgcolumns.com						
HBI (Hickory Brands Inc) 429 27th St NW	Hickory	NC	28601	800-438-5777	422-3279	745-5
TF: 800-438-5777 ■ *Web:* www.hickorybrands.com						
Hbm Integrated 600-1496 Bedford Hwy	Bedford	NS	B4A1E5	902-835-9611		177
TF: 800-337-5764 ■ *Web:* www.hbmintegrated.com						
HBP (Huttig Bldg Products Inc)						
555 Maryville University Dr Ste 400	Saint Louis	MO	63141	314-216-2600	216-2601	499
OTC: HBPI ■ *TF:* 800-325-4466 ■ *Web:* www.huttig.com						
HBP Inc 952 Frederick St	Hagerstown	MD	21740	301-733-2000		627
TF: 800-638-3508 ■ *Web:* www.hbp.com						
HBPH (Huntington Beach Playhouse)						
7111 Talbert Ave	Huntington Beach	CA	92648	714-375-0696		573-4
Web: www.hbplayhouse.com						
HBPL (Huntington Beach Public Library)						
7111 Talbert Ave	Huntington Beach	CA	92648	714-842-4481	375-5180	434-3
TF: 800-565-0148 ■ *Web:* www.huntingtonbeachca.gov						
HBS Consulting Inc						
53 Golden Aster Ste	Brisbane	CA	94005	415-508-1541		196
Web: www.hbsconsult.com						
HC Miller Press 3030 Lowell Dr	Green Bay	WI	54311	920-465-3030	465-3035	86
Web: hcmillerpress.com						
HC Nutting Co						
Terracon Co 611 Lunken Pk Dr	Cincinnati	OH	45226	513-321-5816	321-0294	261
Web: www.terracon.com						
HC Starck Inc 45 Industrial Pl	Newton	MA	02461	617-630-5800		485
Web: www.hcstarck.com						
HC Wainwright & Co Inc						
430 Park Ave 4th Fl	New York	NY	10022	212-356-0500		690
Web: www.hcwainwright.com						
HCA Gulf Coast 7400 Fannin Ste 650	Houston	TX	77054	713-852-1500		363
Web: hcagulfcoast.com						
HCA Holdings Inc 1 Pk Plaza	Nashville	TN	37203	615-344-9551		353
NYSE: HCA ■ *TF:* 800-732-0330 ■ *Web:* www.hcahealthcare.com						
HCA Midwest Health System						
903 E 104th St Ste 500	Kansas City	MO	64131	816-508-4000		353
TF: 800-386-9355 ■ *Web:* www.hcamidwest.com						
HCAA (National CPA Health Care Advisors Assn)						
1801 W End Ave Ste 800	Nashville	TN	37203	615-373-9880	377-7092	49-1
TF: 800-231-2524 ■ *Web:* www.hcaa.com						
HCB (Hardin County Bank, The)						
235 Wayne Rd	Savannah	TN	38372	731-925-9001	925-8106	70
Web: www.hardincountybank.com						
HCC (Highland Community College)						
606 W Main	Highland	KS	66035	785-442-6000	442-6106*	162
**Fax:* Admissions ■ *TF:* 800-985-9781 ■ *Web:* www.highlandcc.edu						
HCC (Hillsborough Community College)						
Brandon 10414 E Columbus Dr	Tampa	FL	33619	813-253-7801		162
Web: www.hccfl.edu/campus/br						
HC&C Communications Inc						
5427 Telegraph Ave Unit P	Oakland	CA	94609	510-655-1193	655-7299	175
Web: www.hcccom.net						
HCC Inc 1501 First Ave	Mendota	IL	61342	815-539-9371	539-3135	273
TF: 800-548-6633 ■ *Web:* www.hccincorporated.com						
HCC Industries Inc						
4232 Temple City Blvd	Rosemead	CA	91770	626-443-8931	575-2437	253
HCCBA (Hardin County Chamber & Business Alliance)						
225 S Detroit St	Kenton	OH	43326	419-673-4131	674-4876	139
Web: www.hardincountyoh.org						
HCCC (Elizabethtown-Hardin County Chamber of Commerce)						
111 W Dixie Ave	Elizabethtown	KY	42701	270-765-4334	737-0690	139
TF: 800-437-0092 ■ *Web:* hardinchamber.com						
HCCGA (Haines City Citrus Growers Assn)						
8 Railroad Ave PO Box 337	Haines City	FL	33844	863-422-1174		11-1
TF Sales: 800-327-6676 ■ *Web:* www.hilltopcitrus.com						
HCD Research Inc						
260 US Hwy 202/31 Ste 1000	Flemington	NJ	08822	908-788-9393		466
Web: www.hcdi.net						
HCDPL (Holmes County District Public Library)						
3102 Glen Dr	Millersburg	OH	44654	330-674-5972	674-1938	434-3
Web: www.holmeslibrary.org						
HCEA (Healthcare Convention & Exhibitors Assn)						
7918 Jones Branch Dr Ste 300	Atlanta	GA	30342	703-935-1961	506-3266	49-18
TF: 800-798-1822 ■ *Web:* www.hcea.org						
HCESC (Hamilton County Educational Service Ctr)						
11083 Hamilton Ave	Cincinnati	OH	45231	513-674-4200	742-8339	685
TF: 800-964-8211 ■ *Web:* www.hcesc.org						
HCF Inc 1100 Shawnee Rd	Lima	OH	45805	419-999-2010	999-6284	451
TF: 800-489-2648 ■ *Web:* www.hcfinc.com						
HCI (Health Communications Inc)						
3201 SW 15th St	Deerfield Beach	FL	33442	954-360-0909	360-0034	637-2
TF Cust Svc: 800-441-5569 ■ *Web:* www.hcibooks.com						
HCI Group, The						
6440 Southpoint Pkwy Ste 300	Jacksonville	FL	32216	904-337-6300		196
TF: 866-793-2484 ■ *Web:* thehcigroup.com						
HCL (Hennepin County Library)						
12601 Ridgedale Dr	Minnetonka	MN	55305	612-543-8800	847-8600*	434-3
**Fax Area Code: 952* ■ *Web:* www.hclib.org						
HCL America Inc 330 Potrero Ave	Sunnyvale	CA	94085	408-733-0480		196
Web: www.hcl.com						
Hcl Global Systems Inc						
24543 Indoplex Cir Ste 220	Farmington	MI	48335	248-473-0720		180
Web: www.hclglobal.com						
HCM (Henry Community Health)						
1000 N 16th St	New Castle	IN	47362	765-521-0890	521-1555	374-3
Web: www.hcmhcares.org						
HCMC (Hennepin County Medical Ctr)						
701 Pk Ave	Minneapolis	MN	55415	612-873-3000		374-3
Web: www.hcmc.org						
HCP Packaging USA Inc						
370 Monument Rd	Hinsdale	NH	03451	603-256-3141	256-6979	548
Web: www.hcpackaging.com						

Name / Address	City	State	Zip	Phone	Fax	Class
Hcpro Inc 75 Sylvan St Ste A-10 *TF:* 800-650-6787 ■ *Web:* www.hcpro.com	Danvers	MA	01923	800-650-6787		195
HCPS (Harrisonburg City Public Schools) 317 S Main St. *Web:* www.harrisonburg.k12.va.us	Harrisonburg	VA	22801	540-434-9916	434-5196	780
HCR Manor Care 333 N Summit St PO Box 10086 *Web:* www.hcr-manorcare.com	Toledo	OH	43699	419-252-5500		451
HCR ManorCare Inc 333 N Summit St *TF:* 800-366-1232 ■ *Web:* hcr-manorcare.com	Toledo	OH	43604	419-252-5500		450
HCREC (Humboldt County Rural Electric Co-op) 1210 13th St N *Web:* www.midlandpower.coop	Humboldt	IA	50548	515-332-1616		245
Hcs Group Inc 1030 E First St *Web:* hcsgroup.com	Humble	TX	77338	281-540-4838	540-6105	261
HCSD (Hamilton City School District) 533 Dayton St PO Box 627 *Web:* www.hamiltoncityschools.com	Hamilton	OH	45012	513-887-5000	887-5014	685
HCSG (Healthcare Services Group Inc) 3220 Tillman Dr Ste 300 *Web:* www.hcsgcorp.com	Bensalem	PA	19020	215-639-4274	639-2152	442
HCTec LLC 7105 S Springs Dr Ste 208 *Web:* www.hctec.com	Franklin	TN	37067	615-577-4030		260
HCYF (Hazelden Ctr for Youth & Families) 11505 36th Ave N *TF:* 800-257-7810 ■ *Web:* www.hazelden.org	Plymouth	MN	55441	763-509-3800		726
H-D Electric Co-op Inc 423 Third Ave S *TF:* 800-781-7474 ■ *Web:* h-delectric.coop	Clear Lake	SD	57226	605-874-2171	874-8173	245
HD Hudson Manufacturing Co 500 N Michigan Ave *TF:* 800-977-7293 ■ *Web:* www.hdhudson.com	Chicago	IL	60611	312-644-2830	644-7989	273
HD Supply Waterworks Ltd PO Box 1419 *TF:* 800-492-6909 ■ *Web:* www.hdswaterworks.com	Thomasville	GA	31799	800-950-7659		385
HD Vest Financial Services 6333 N State Hwy 161 4th Fl *TF:* 866-218-8206 ■ *Web:* hdvest.com	Irving	TX	75038	972-870-6000	870-6128	401
HDF (Hereditary Disease Foundation) 3960 Broadway 6th Fl. *Web:* www.hdfoundation.org	New York	NY	10032	212-928-2121	928-2172	48-17
HDF Group 1800 S Oak St Ste 203 *Web:* www.hdfgroup.org	Champaign	IL	61820	217-531-6100		177
Hdl Companies 1340 Vly Vista Dr Ste 200 *TF:* 800-325-9818 ■ *Web:* www.hdlcompanies.com	Diamond Bar	CA	91765	909-861-4335		463
HDM Hydraulics LLC 125 Fire Tower Dr *Web:* www.hdmhydraulics.com	Tonawanda	NY	14150	716-694-8004	694-4164	262
HDMA (Healthcare Distribution Management Assn) 901 N Glebe Rd Ste 1000 *Web:* www.healthcaredistribution.org	Arlington	VA	22203	703-787-0000	935-3200	49-18
HDMG Corp 555 First Ave NE *Web:* www.hdmg.com	Minneapolis	MN	55413	612-224-9500	224-9515	512
HDR Engineering Inc 8404 Indian Hills Dr **Fax:* Hum Res ■ *TF:* 800-366-4411 ■ *Web:* www.hdrinc.com	Omaha	NE	68114	402-399-1000	548-5015*	261
HDS (Hartley Data Service Inc) 1807 Glenview Rd Ste 201 *Web:* hartleydata.com	Glenview	IL	60025	847-724-9280	729-2199	225
HDSA (Huntington's Disease Society of America) 505 Eigth Ave Ste 902 *TF:* 800-345-4372 ■ *Web:* www.hdsa.org	New York	NY	10018	212-242-1968	239-3430	48-17
HDSB (Holmes District School Board) 701 E Pennsylvania Ave *Web:* www.hdsb.org	Bonifay	FL	32425	850-547-9341	547-3568	685
HDSP (High Desert State Prison) 475-750 Rice Canyon Rd PO Box 750 *Web:* www.cdcr.ca.gov	Susanville	CA	96127	530-251-5100		213
HDT Global 30500 Aurora Rd Ste 100 **Fax Area Code:* 440 ■ *TF:* 800-969-8527 ■ *Web:* www.hdtglobal.com	Solon	OH	44139	216-438-6111	248-1691*	15
HDW (Hardware Distribution Warehouses Inc) 6900 Woolworth Rd *TF Cust Svc:* 800-256-8527 ■ *Web:* www.hdwinc.com	Shreveport	LA	71129	318-686-8527		351
HE Neumann Inc 100 Middle Creek Rd *TF:* 800-627-5312 ■ *Web:* www.heneumann.com	Triadelphia	WV	26059	304-232-3040	232-7858	189-10
HE Williams Inc 831 W Fairview Ave. *TF:* 866-358-4065 ■ *Web:* www.hew.com	Carthage	MO	64836	417-358-4065	358-6015	439
HEA (Harmon Electric Assn Inc) 114 N First St PO Box 393 *TF:* 800-643-7769 ■ *Web:* www.harmonelectric.com	Hollis	OK	73550	580-688-3342		245
HEAB (Wisconsin Higher Educational Aids Board) 131 W Wilson S PO Box 7885 *Web:* www.heab.state.wi.us	Madison	WI	53707	608-267-2206	267-2808	725
Head in the Cloud Inc 220A Twin Dolphin Dr. *Web:* www.hitcloud.com	Redwood Shores	CA	94065	650-234-7100		196
Head Injury Hotline 212 Pioneer Bldg *Web:* www.headinjury.com	Seattle	WA	98104	206-621-8558		48-17
Head Johnson & Kachigian Pc 228 W 17th Pl. *Web:* www.hjklaw.com	Tulsa	OK	74119	918-587-2000		445
Head Start of Greater Dallas Inc 3954 Gannon Ln. *Web:* www.hsgd.org	Dallas	TX	75237	972-283-6400		148
HEAD USA Inc 1 Selleck St. *TF:* 800-874-3235 ■ *Web:* www.head.com	Norwalk	CT	06855	800-874-3235		710
Headcovers Unlimited 35 Tiffany Plaza *Web:* www.headcovers.com	Ardmore	OK	73401	580-226-5871		348
Headington Oil Co 2711 N Haskell Ave Ste 2800 *Web:* www.headington.com	Dallas	TX	75204	214-696-0606		536
Headlands Beach State Park Geneva State Pk 4499 Padanarum Rd. *Web:* www.dnr.state.oh.us	Geneva	OH	44041	440-466-8400		565
Headley-Whitney Museum 4435 Old Frankfort Pike *TF:* 800-755-6956 ■ *Web:* www.headley-whitney.org	Lexington	KY	40510	859-255-6653	255-8375	520
Headliner Talent Marketing 39398 Moonlight Bay Trl *Web:* headlinertalent.com	Pelican Rapids	MN	56572	218-863-1367		390
Headquarter Toyota 5895 NW 167th St *TF:* 800-549-0947 ■ *Web:* www.headquartertoyota.com	Miami	FL	33015	305-364-9800		57
Headquarters.Com Inc 625 Walnut Ridge Dr Ste 108	Hartland	WI	53029	262-369-0600		809
Headquist International Corp 230 Florence St *Web:* hedquistintl.com	Crystal Lake	IL	60014	815-479-1700		260
Headrick Companies Inc, The 1 Freedom Sq *TF:* 800-933-1365 ■ *Web:* www.headricks.com	Laurel	MS	39440	601-649-1977		5
Headsets Direct Inc 1454 W Gurley St Ste A *TF:* 800-914-7996 ■ *Web:* www.headsetsdirect.com	Prescott	AZ	86305	928-777-9100		246
Headstart Hair For Men Inc 3395 Cypress Gardens Rd *TF:* 800-645-6525 ■ *Web:* www.headstarthairformen.com	Winter Haven	FL	33884	863-324-5559	324-5673	348
Headwall Photonics Inc 601 River St *Web:* www.headwallphotonics.com	Fitchburg	MA	01420	978-353-4100		639
Headwaters Health Care Ctr 100 Rolling Hills Dr *Web:* www.headwatershealth.ca	Orangeville	ON	L9W4X9	519-941-2410	942-0483	374-2
Headwaters Inc 10701 S River Front Pkwy Ste 300 *NYSE:* HW ■ *Web:* www.headwaters.com	South Jordan	UT	84095	801-984-9400	984-9410	804
Headway Corporate Resources Inc 421 Fayetteville St Ste 1020 *Web:* www.headwaycorp.com	Raleigh	NC	27601	919-376-4929		721
Headway Technologies Inc 682 S Hillview Dr *Web:* headway.com	Milpitas	CA	95035	408-934-5300		173-8
Headwest Inc 15650 S Avalon Blvd. *Web:* www.headwestinc.com	Compton	CA	90220	310-532-5420	532-5920	332
Heald College *Salinas* 1450 N Main St.	Salinas	CA	93906	831-443-1700		800
Healing the Children (HTC) 2624 W Beacon Ave *Web:* www.healingthechildren.org	Spokane	WA	99208	509-327-4281	327-4284	48-5
Health & Environment Dept 130 S Market St Ste 6050 *TF:* 800-842-0078 ■ *Web:* www.kdheks.gov	Wichita	KS	67202	316-337-6020		804
Health & Human Services Administration *Region 1* 200 Independence Ave *Web:* www.hrsa.gov	Washington	DC	20201	301-443-3376		340-10
Health & Safety Institute Inc 1450 Westec Dr *TF:* 800-447-3177 ■ *Web:* www.hsi.com	Eugene	OR	97402	800-447-3177		764
Health Advocacy Strategies Llc 4126 E Madison St Ste 200 *Web:* www.hastrategies.com	Seattle	WA	98112	206-861-1000		636
Health After 50 750 Third Ave Fl 6 *TF:* 800-829-0422 ■ *Web:* www.healthafter50.com	New York	NY	10017	800-829-0422		531-8
Health Alliance of MidAmerica LLC, The 10401 Holmes Rd Ste 280	Kansas City	MO	64131	816-941-3800		474
Health Alliance Plan 2850 W Grand Blvd **Fax:* Hum Res ■ *TF:* 800-422-4641 ■ *Web:* www.hap.org	Detroit	MI	48202	313-872-8100	664-5866*	391-3
Health Care Daily Report 1801 S Bell St. *TF:* 800-372-1033 ■ *Web:* www.bna.com/health-care-daily-p6781	Arlington	VA	22202	800-372-1033		531-8
Health Care Property Investors Inc 1920 Main St Ste 1200. *TF:* 800-690-6903 ■ *Web:* www.hcpi.com	Irvine	CA	92614	949-407-0700		655
Health Care Software Inc PO Box 2430 **Fax Area Code:* 732 ■ *TF:* 800-524-1038 ■ *Web:* www.hcsinteractant.com	Farmingdale	NJ	07727	800-524-1038	938-5380*	177
Health Care Unlimited Inc 1100 E Laurel Ave. *Web:* www.hcuinc.com	Mcallen	TX	78501	956-994-9911		237
Health Coalition Inc 8320 NW 30th Terr *TF:* 800-456-7283 ■ *Web:* healthcoalition.com	Doral	FL	33122	305-662-2988		238
Health Communications Inc (HCI) 3201 SW 15th St *TF Cust Svc:* 800-441-5569 ■ *Web:* www.hcibooks.com	Deerfield Beach	FL	33442	954-360-0909	360-0034	637-2
Health Connect Partners Inc 65 Business Park Dr *Web:* www.hlthcp.com	Lebanon	TN	37090	615-449-6234		184
Health Decisions Inc 2510 Meridian Pkwy Ste 300 *TF:* 800-574-7374 ■ *Web:* www.healthdec.com	Durham	NC	27713	919-967-1111		463
Health Dimensions Group 4400 Baker Rd Ste 100 *Web:* www.healthdimensionsgroup.com	Minneapolis	MN	55343	763-537-5700		194
Health Facilities Management Magazine 155 N Wacker Dr Ste 400 *Web:* www.hfmmagazine.com	Chicago	IL	60606	312-893-6800	422-4500	457-5
Health First Cape Canaveral Hospital 701 W Cocoa Beach Cswy *Web:* www.health-first.org	Cocoa Beach	FL	32931	321-799-7111	434-6103	374-3
Health Forum 155 N Wacker Dr Ste 400 *TF:* 800-621-6902 ■ *Web:* healthforum.com	Chicago	IL	60606	312-893-6800		637-11
Health Hut 1512 First Ave NE. *Web:* healthhutcr.com	Cedar Rapids	IA	52402	319-362-7345		296-11
Health Industry Business Communications Council (HIBCC) 2525 E Arizona Biltmore Cir Ste 127 *TF:* 800-755-5505 ■ *Web:* www.hibcc.org	Phoenix	AZ	85016	602-381-1091	381-1093	49-8
Health Industry Distributors Assn (HIDA) 310 Montgomery St *TF:* 800-549-4432 ■ *Web:* www.hida.org	Alexandria	VA	22314	703-549-4432	549-6495	49-18
Health Information Designs Inc 391 Industry Dr.	Auburn	AL	36832	334-502-3262		177
Health Integrated Inc 10008 N Dale Mabry Hwy *Web:* www.healthintegrated.com	Tampa	FL	33618	813-388-4000		194
Health Law Reporter 1801 S Bell St *TF:* 800-372-1033 ■ *Web:* www.bna.com/health-law-reporter-p6785	Arlington	VA	22202	800-372-1033		531-7

				Phone	Fax	Class
Health Law Week 590 Dutch Valley Rd NE *TF:* 800-926-7926 ■ *Web:* www.straffordpub.com	Atlanta	GA	30324	404-881-1141	881-0074	531-8
Health Management Services Inc 9100 SW Fwy Ste 114 *Web:* www.hmssleep.com	Houston	TX	77074	713-541-2727		194
Health Management Systems Inc 401 Pk Ave S *TF:* 877-357-3268 ■ *Web:* www.hms.com	New York	NY	10016	212-857-5000	857-5004	225
Health Net Inc 21650 Oxnard St *NYSE: HNT* ■ *TF:* 800-848-4747 ■ *Web:* www.healthnet.com	Woodland Hills	CA	91367	818-676-6000		391-3
Health Net Of Arizona Inc 1230 W Washington St *TF:* 800-291-6911 ■ *Web:* www.healthnet.com	Tempe	AZ	85281	602-794-1400		353
Health Network America Inc 745 Hope Rd *Web:* www.healthnetworkamerica.com	Tinton Falls	NJ	07724	732-676-2630		390
Health Network Laboratory 2024 Lehigh St *TF:* 877-402-4221 ■ *Web:* www.healthnetworklabs.com	Allentown	PA	18103	610-402-8170		418
Health Partners 8170 33rd Ave S *TF:* 800-247-7015 ■ *Web:* healthpartners.com	Minneapolis	MN	55425	952-883-6877		371
Health Physics Society 1313 Dolley Madison Blvd Ste 402 *TF:* 888-624-8373 ■ *Web:* www.hps.org	McLean	VA	22101	703-790-1745	790-2672	48-17
Health Plan of Nevada Inc PO Box 15645 *Web:* www.myhpnonline.com/Member	Las Vegas	NV	89114	702-242-7300		391-3
Health Products Corp 1060 Nepperhan Ave *Web:* healthproductscorporation.com	Yonkers	NY	10703	914-423-2900		799
Health Resources & Services Administration (HRSA) 5600 Fishers Ln *TF:* 888-275-4772 ■ *Web:* hrsa.gov	Rockville	MD	20857	301-443-2216		340-10
Health Revenue Assurance Holdings Inc Ste 304 8551 W Sunrise Blvd	Plantation	FL	33322	954-472-2340		317
Health Sciences Centre 820 Sherbrook St *Web:* www.hsc.mb.ca	Winnipeg	MB	R3A1R9	204-787-3661		374-2
Health Services of Coshocton County 230 S Fourth St *Web:* healthservicescoshocton.com	Coshocton	OH	43812	740-622-7311		363
Health Smart Rx 1301 E Ninth St **Fax Area Code:* 216 ■ *TF:* 800-681-6912 ■ *Web:* www.healthsmart.com	Cleveland	OH	44114	800-681-6912	479-2015*	586
Health Systems 2000 1901 Oak Park Blvd *Web:* www.hhc2000.com	Lake Charles	LA	70601	337-562-1140		363
Health Technology Exchange, The 439 University Ave 5th Fl	Toronto	ON	M5G1Y8	437-836-3101		528
Health Tradition Health Plan 1808 E Main St *TF:* 800-545-8499 ■ *Web:* www.healthtradition.com	Onalaska	WI	54650	608-781-9692		391-3
Health Unit Brant County 194 Ter Hill St *TF:* 800-565-8603 ■ *Web:* www.bchu.org	Brantford	ON	N3R1G7	519-753-4937		138
HealthAlliance Leominster Hospital 60 Hospital Rd *TF:* 800-462-5540 ■ *Web:* umassmemorialhealthcare.org	Leominster	MA	01453	978-466-2000		374-3
HealthAmerica Pennsylvania Inc 3721 Tecport Dr PO Box 67103 *TF:* 800-788-6445 ■ *Web:* healthamerica.coventryhealthcare.com	Harrisburg	PA	17111	800-788-6445		391-3
HealthAxis Inc 7301 N State Hwy 161 *TF:* 888-974-2947 ■ *Web:* www.healthaxis.com	Irving	TX	75039	972-443-5000		463
Healthbridge 11300 Cornell Park Dr Ste 360 *Web:* www.healthbridge.org	Blue Ash	OH	45242	513-469-7222		225
HealthCap Partners LLC 5910 N Central Expy Ste 1000 *Web:* healthcap.com	Dallas	TX	75206	214-953-1722		528
Healthcare Administrative Partners LLC 112 Chesley Dr *Web:* www.hapusa.com	Media	PA	19063	610-892-8889		225
Healthcare Analytics 125-310 Village Blvd	Princeton	NJ	08540	609-452-2488	452-2668	194
Healthcare Automation Inc 41 Sharpe Dr *TF:* 800-738-8850 ■ *Web:* www.healthcare-automation.com	Cranston	RI	02920	401-572-3040	572-3350	177
Healthcare Consultancy Group 488 Madison Ave 5th Fl *Web:* www.hcgrp.com	New York	NY	10022	212-849-7900	627-4764	4
Healthcare Convention & Exhibitors Assn (HCEA) 7918 Jones Branch Dr Ste 300 *TF:* 800-790-1822 ■ *Web:* www.hcea.org	Atlanta	GA	30342	703-935-1961	506-3266	49-18
Healthcare Disparities Report 8204 Fenton St *TF:* 800-666-6380 ■ *Web:* www.cdpublications.com	Silver Spring	MD	20910	301-588-6385	588-6380	531-8
Healthcare Distribution Management Assn (HDMA) 901 N Glebe Rd Ste 1000 *Web:* www.healthcaredistribution.org	Arlington	VA	22203	703-787-0000	935-3200	49-18
Healthcare Financial Management Assn (HFMA) 2 Westbrook Corporate Ctr Ste 700 *TF:* 800-252-4362 ■ *Web:* www.hfma.org	Westchester	IL	60154	708-531-9600	531-0032	49-8
Healthcare Information & Management Systems Society (HIMSS) 230 E Ohio St Ste 500 *TF:* 800-982-2182 ■ *Web:* www.himss.org	Chicago	IL	60611	312-664-4467	664-6143	49-8
Healthcare Leadership Council (HLC) 750 Ninth St NW Ste 500 *Web:* hlc.org	Washington	DC	20001	202-452-8700	296-9561	48-17
Healthcare Management Systems Inc (HMS) 3102 W End Ave Ste 400	Nashville	TN	37203	615-383-7300	383-6093	387
Healthcare Realty Trust Inc 3310 W End Ave Ste 700 *NYSE: HR* ■ *Web:* www.healthcarerealty.com	Nashville	TN	37203	615-269-8175		655
Healthcare Services Group Inc (HCSG) 3220 Tillman Dr Ste 300 *Web:* www.hcsgcorp.com	Bensalem	PA	19020	215-639-4274	639-2152	442
HealthCare USA 10 S Broadway Ste 1200 *TF:* 800-213-7792 ■ *Web:* coventryhealthcare.com	Saint Louis	MO	63102	314-241-5300		391-3
HealthCareSource Inc 100 Sylvan Rd Ste 100 *TF:* 800-869-5200 ■ *Web:* www.healthcaresource.com	Woburn	MA	01801	800-869-5200	829-6600	260
Healthcasts Meded 55 E Ninth St Apt 7l	New York	NY	10003	212-533-1111		194
Health-Chem Diagnostics LLC 3341 SW 15th St *Web:* www.healthchemdiagnostics.com	Pompano Beach	FL	33069	954-979-3845	979-7997	743
Healthco Information Systems Inc 7657 SW Mohawk St *Web:* www.healthcosystems.com	Tualatin	OR	97062	503-612-1666		177
Healthcom 1600 W Jackson St *TF:* 800-525-6237 ■ *Web:* www.healthcominc.com	Sullivan	IL	61951	800-525-6237		475
HealthDrive Corp 888 Worcester St *TF:* 888-964-6681 ■ *Web:* www.healthdrive.com	Wellesley	MA	02482	888-964-6681	662-0859	352
Healtheast 559 Capitol Blvd *Web:* www.healtheast.org	Saint Paul	MN	55103	651-232-2000		353
HealthEdge Investment Partners 5550 W Executive Dr Ste 230 *Web:* www.healthedgepartners.com	Tampa	FL	33609	813-490-7100		401
HEALTHeLINK The Commons at Walden 2568 Walden Ave Ste 107 *Web:* www.wnyhealthelink.com	Buffalo	NY	14225	716-206-0993		415
HEALTHEON Inc 201 St Charles Ave Ste 4310 *Web:* www.healtheoninc.com	New Orleans	LA	70170	504-599-5982		415
HealthFocus International 449 Central Ave Ste 205 *Web:* www.healthfocus.com	St. Petersburg	FL	33701	727-821-7499		466
HealthForce Ontario Marketing & Recruitment Agency 163 Queen St E *TF:* 800-596-4046 ■ *Web:* www.healthforceontario.ca	Toronto	ON	M5A1S1	416-862-2200		260
Healthforce Partners Inc 18323 Bothell Everett Hwy *TF:* 877-437-2497 ■ *Web:* www.healthforcepartners.com	Bothell	WA	98012	425-806-5700		194
HealthInsight Inc 756 E Winchester St Ste 200 *Web:* www.healthinsight.org	Salt Lake City	UT	84107	801-892-0155		194
Healthlinx Transitional Leadership Inc 1404 Goodale Blvd Ste 400 *TF:* 800-980-4820 ■ *Web:* www.healthlinx.com	Columbus	OH	43212	614-444-5400		463
Healthmark Services 217 Lakewood Rd	Van Buren	AR	72956	479-471-9797		195
HealthMarkets Inc 9151 Blvd 26 *TF:* 800-827-9990 ■ *Web:* www.healthmarketsinc.com	North Richland Hills	TX	76180	800-827-9990		360-4
Healthnotes 215 NW Park Ave *Web:* aisle7.com	Portland	OR	97209	503-234-4092		177
Healthpac Computer Systems Inc 1010 E Victory Dr *TF:* 800-825-0224 ■ *Web:* www.healthpac.net	Savannah	GA	31405	912-341-7420		225
HealthPartners Inc PO Box 1309 *TF:* 800-883-2177 ■ *Web:* www.healthpartners.com	Minneapolis	MN	55440	952-883-5000		391-3
Healthplex Inc 333 Earl Ovington Blvd *TF Cust Svc:* 800-468-0608 ■ *Web:* www.healthplex.com	Uniondale	NY	11553	516-542-2200		391-3
HealthPlus of Michigan 2050 S Linden Rd *TF:* 800-332-9161 ■ *Web:* www.healthplus.org	Flint	MI	48532	810-230-2000		391-3
Healthpoint 3909 Hulen St *TF Cust Svc:* 800-441-8227 ■ *Web:* www.smith-nephew.com	Fort Worth	TX	76107	817-900-4000		583
HealthSCOPE Benefits Inc 27 Corporate Hill Dr *Web:* www.healthscopebenefits.com	Little Rock	AR	72205	501-225-1551		390
Healthsense Inc 1191 Northland Dr Ste 100 *TF:* 800-904-3775 ■ *Web:* www.healthsense.com	Mendota Heights	MN	55120	952-400-7300		743
Healthshare Inc 1108 Lavaca *Web:* www.healthshare-tha.com	Austin	TX	78701-2180	512-465-1028	465-1090	138
HealthSource Saginaw 3340 Hospital Rd *TF:* 800-662-6848 ■ *Web:* www.healthsourcesaginaw.org	Saginaw	MI	48603	989-790-7700		726
HealthSouth Bakersfield Rehabilitation Hospital 5001 Commerce Dr *Web:* healthsouthbakersfield.com	Bakersfield	CA	93309	661-323-5500		374-6
HealthSouth Braintree Rehabilitation Hospital 250 Pond St *TF:* 800-242-0030 ■ *Web:* www.healthsouthbraintree.com	Braintree	MA	02184	781-348-2500	356-2748	374-6
HealthSouth Chattanooga Rehabilitation Hospital 3660 Grandview Pkwy Ste 200 *TF:* 800-765-4772 ■ *Web:* www.healthsouth.com	Birmingham	AL	35243	205-967-7116		374-6
HealthSouth City View Rehabilitation Hospital 6701 Oakmont Blvd *TF:* 800-325-3591 ■ *Web:* healthsouthcityview.com	Fort Worth	TX	76132	817-370-4700		374-6
HealthSouth Corp 3660 Grandview Pkwy Ste 200 *NYSE: HLS* ■ *TF:* 800-765-4772 ■ *Web:* healthsouth.com	Birmingham	AL	35243	205-967-7116		352
HealthSouth Deaconess Rehabilitation Hospital 4100 Covert Ave *TF:* 800-677-3422 ■ *Web:* www.healthsouthdeaconess.com	Evansville	IN	47714	812-476-9983		374-6
HealthSouth Harmarville Rehabilitation Hospital 320 Guys Run Rd *TF:* 800-765-4772 ■ *Web:* www.healthsouthharmarville.com	Pittsburgh	PA	15238	412-828-1300		374-6
HealthSouth Hospital of Pittsburgh 320 Guys Run Rd *TF:* 800-765-4772 ■ *Web:* www.healthsouthharmarville.com	Pittsburgh	PA	15238	412-828-1300		374-6
HealthSouth Houston Rehabilitation Institute 13031 Wortham Ctr Dr *Web:* www.healthsouth.com	Houston	TX	77065	832-280-2500		374-6
HealthSouth Humble Rehabilitation Hospital 19002 McKay Dr *Web:* www.healthsouthhumble.com	Humble	TX	77338	281-446-6148		374-6
HealthSouth Lakeshore Rehabilitation Hospital 3660 Grandview Pkwy Ste 200 *TF:* 800-310-4919 ■ *Web:* www.healthsouth.com	Birmingham	AL	35243	205-967-7116		374-6
HealthSouth MountainView Regional Rehabilitation Hospital 1160 Van Voorhis Rd *TF:* 800-388-2451 ■ *Web:* www.healthsouthmountainview.com	Morgantown	WV	26505	304-598-1100	598-1103	374-6

	Phone	Fax	Class
HealthSouth Nittany Valley Rehabilitation Hospital 550 W College Ave .... Pleasant Gap PA 16823 *TF:* 800-842-6026 ■ *Web:* www.nittanyvalleyrehab.com	814-359-3421	359-5898	374-6
HealthSouth Plano Rehabilitation Hospital 2800 W 15th St. .... Plano TX 75075 *TF:* 800-765-4772 ■ *Web:* www.healthsouthplano.com	972-612-9000		374-6
HealthSouth Reading Rehabilitation Hospital 1623 Morgantown Rd .... Reading PA 19607 *Web:* www.healthsouthreading.com	610-796-6000		374-6
HealthSouth Rehabilitation Hospital of Albuquerque 7000 Jefferson St NE .... Albuquerque NM 87109 *Web:* www.healthsouthnewmexico.com	505-344-9478		374-6
HealthSouth Rehabilitation Hospital of Altoona 2005 Vly View Blvd. .... Altoona PA 16602 *TF:* 800-873-4220 ■ *Web:* www.healthsouthaltoona.com	814-944-3535		374-6
HealthSouth Rehabilitation Hospital of Arlington 3200 Matlock Rd .... Arlington TX 76015 *Web:* www.healthsoutharlington.com	817-468-4000		374-6
HealthSouth Rehabilitation Hospital of Austin 330 W Ben White Blvd .... Austin TX 78704 *TF:* 800-765-4772 ■ *Web:* www.healthsouthaustin.com	512-730-4800		374-6
HealthSouth Rehabilitation Hospital of Columbia 2935 Colonial Dr .... Columbia SC 29203 *Web:* www.healthsouthcolumbia.com	803-254-7777		374-6
HealthSouth Rehabilitation Hospital of Erie 143 E Second St .... Erie PA 16507 *TF:* 800-765-4772 ■ *Web:* healthsoutherie.com	814-878-1200		374-6
HealthSouth Rehabilitation Hospital of Fayetteville 153 E Monte Painter .... Fayetteville AR 72703 *TF:* 800-749-2257 ■ *Web:* www.healthsouth.com	479-444-2200		374-6
HealthSouth Rehabilitation Hospital of Florence 900 E Cheves St .... Florence SC 29506 *TF:* 800-951-4090 ■ *Web:* www.healthsouthflorence.com	843-679-9000		374-6
HealthSouth Rehabilitation Hospital of Fort Smith 1401 S J St .... Fort Smith AR 72901 *Web:* www.healthsouthfortsmith.com	479-785-3300		374-6
HealthSouth Rehabilitation Hospital of Fort Worth 1212 W Lancaster .... Fort Worth TX 76102 *TF:* 800-870-2336 ■ *Web:* www.healthsouthfortworth.com	817-870-2336		374-6
HealthSouth Rehabilitation Hospital of Jonesboro 1201 Fleming Ave .... Jonesboro AR 72401 *Web:* www.healthsouthjonesboro.com	870-932-0440		374-6
HealthSouth Rehabilitation Hospital of Kingsport 113 Cassel Dr .... Kingsport TN 37660 *TF:* 800-454-7422 ■ *Web:* www.healthsouthkingsport.com	423-246-7240		374-6
HealthSouth Rehabilitation Hospital of Largo 901 N Clearwater-Largo Rd .... Largo FL 33770 *TF:* 800-561-3357 ■ *Web:* healthsouthlargo.com	727-586-2999		374-6
HealthSouth Rehabilitation Hospital of Memphis 4100 Austin Peay Hwy .... Memphis TN 38128 *Web:* www.healthsouthnorthmemphis.com	901-213-5400		374-6
HealthSouth Rehabilitation Hospital of Montgomery 4465 Narrow Ln Rd .... Montgomery AL 36116 *Web:* www.healthsouthmontgomery.com	334-284-7700		374-6
HealthSouth Rehabilitation Hospital of New Jersey 14 Hospital Dr .... Toms River NJ 08755 *Web:* www.rehabnjtomsriver.com	732-244-3100		374-6
HealthSouth Rehabilitation Hospital of North Alabama 107 Governors Dr .... Huntsville AL 35801 *TF:* 800-467-3422 ■ *Web:* healthsouth.com	256-535-2300		374-6
HealthSouth Rehabilitation Hospital of Sarasota 6400 Edgelake Dr .... Sarasota FL 34240 *Web:* healthsouth.com	941-921-8600		374-6
HealthSouth Rehabilitation Hospital of Tallahassee 1675 Riggins Rd .... Tallahassee FL 32308 *Web:* www.healthsouthtallahassee.com	850-656-4800		374-6
HealthSouth Rehabilitation Hospital of Texarkana 515 W 12th St .... Texarkana TX 75501 *Web:* www.healthsouthtexarkana.com	903-735-5000		374-6
HealthSouth Rehabilitation Hospital of Utah 8074 S 1300 E .... Sandy UT 84094 *Web:* www.healthsouthutah.com	801-565-6666		374-6
HealthSouth Rehabilitation Institute of Tucson 2650 N Wyatt Dr .... Tucson AZ 85712 *TF:* 800-943-6667 ■ *Web:* www.rehabinstituteoftucson.com	520-325-1300		374-6
HealthSouth Riosa 9119 Cinnamon Hill .... San Antonio TX 78240 *Web:* www.hsriosa.com	210-691-0737		374-6
HealthSouth Sea Pines Rehabilitation Hospital 101 E Florida Ave .... Melbourne FL 32901 *Web:* www.healthsouthseapines.com	321-984-4662		374-6
HealthSouth Sunrise Rehabilitation Hospital 4399 Nob Hill Rd .... Sunrise FL 33351 *Web:* healthsouthsunrise.com	954-749-0300		374-6
HealthSouth Treasure Coast Rehabilitation Hospital 1600 37th St .... Vero Beach FL 32960 *TF:* 800-481-2910 ■ *Web:* healthsouthtreasurecoast.com	772-778-2100		374-6
HealthSouth Tustin Rehabilitation Hospital 14851 Yorba St .... Tustin CA 92780 *Web:* tustinrehab.com	714-832-9200		374-6
Healthspace USA Inc 4860 Cox Rd Ste 200 .... Glen Allen VA 23060 *TF:* 866-860-4224 ■ *Web:* www.healthspace.ca	804-935-8532		201
HealthSTAR Communications Inc 1000 Wyckoff Ave .... Mahwah NJ 07430 *Web:* www.healthstarcom.com	201-560-5370		4
HealthStream Inc 209 Tenth Ave S Ste 450 .... Nashville TN 37203 *NASDAQ: HSTM* ■ *TF:* 800-933-9293 ■ *Web:* www.healthstream.com	615-301-3100	301-3200	765
Healthtek Solutions Inc 109 E Main St .... Norfolk VA 23510 *Web:* ww12.healthtek.com	757-625-0800		463
Healthtrax Fitness & Wellness 2345 Main St .... Glastonbury CT 06033 *TF:* 800-998-0880 ■ *Web:* www.healthtrax.com	860-652-7066	652-7066	354
HealthTronics Inc 9825 Spectrum Dr Bldg 3 .... Austin TX 78717 *TF:* 888-252-6575 ■ *Web:* www.healthtronics.com	512-328-2892	439-8303	250
Healthways Inc 701 Cool Springs Blvd. .... Franklin TN 37067 *NASDAQ: HWAY* ■ **Fax Area Code:* 615 ■ *TF:* 800-327-3822 ■ *Web:* www.healthways.com	800-327-3822	665-7697*	352
HealthWorks! Kids' Museum 111 W Jefferson Blvd Ste 200 .... South Bend IN 46601 *Web:* www.healthworkskids.org	574-647-5437		521
Healthy Back Store LLC 10300 Southard Dr .... Beltsville MD 20705 *TF:* 800-469-2225 ■ *Web:* www.healthyback.com	800-469-2225		321
Healthy Companies International Inc 2101 Wilson Blvd Ste 1002 .... Arlington VA 22201 *Web:* healthycompanies.com	703-351-9901		194
Healthy Directions LLC 7811 Montrose Rd .... Potomac MD 20854 *TF:* 866-599-9491 ■ *Web:* www.healthydirections.com	866-599-9491		637-9
Healthy n Fit International 435 Yorktown Rd .... Croton On Hudson NY 10520 *Web:* behealthynfit.com	914-271-6040		231
Healthy Pet 6960 Salashan Pkwy. .... Ferndale WA 98248 *TF:* 800-242-2287 ■ *Web:* www.healthy-pet.com	360-734-7415	671-1588	578
Healthy Pets of Westgate Inc 3588 W Broad St .... Columbus OH 43228 *Web:* healthypetsofohio.com	614-279-8415		794
Healthy Teen Network 1501 St Paul St Ste 124 .... Baltimore MD 21202 *Web:* www.healthyteennetwork.org	410-685-0410	685-0481	48-6
Healy Group Inc, The 53800 Generations Dr. .... South Bend IN 46635 *TF:* 800-667-4613 ■ *Web:* www.healygroup.com	574-271-6000		390
Healy Long & Jevin Inc 2000 Rodman Rd .... Wilmington DE 19805 *Web:* www.healylongjevin.com	302-654-8039	654-8153	189-3
Healy Systems Inc 3760 Marsh Rd. .... Madison WI 53718 *Web:* www.franklinfueling.com	608-838-8786		610
Heapy Engineering Inc 1400 W Dorothy Ln .... Dayton OH 45409 *Web:* heapy.com	937-224-0861		261
Heard & Smith LLP 3737 Broadway Ste 310 .... San Antonio TX 78209 *TF:* 800-584-3700 ■ *Web:* www.heardandsmith.com	210-820-3737		428
Heard County PO Box 40 .... Franklin GA 30217 *TF:* 800-436-7442 ■ *Web:* www.heardcountyga.com	706-675-3821	675-2493	338
Heard Museum 2301 N Central Ave. .... Phoenix AZ 85004 *Web:* www.heard.org	602-252-8840	252-9757	520
Heard Natural Science Museum & Wildlife Sanctuary 1 Nature Pl .... McKinney TX 75069 *TF:* 800-645-3226 ■ *Web:* www.heardmuseum.org	972-562-5566	548-9119	520
Hearing Loss Assn of America 7910 Woodmont Ave Ste 1200 .... Bethesda MD 20814 *TF:* 800-221-6827 ■ *Web:* www.hearingloss.org	301-657-2248	913-9413	48-17
Hearn Co, The 875 N Michigan Ave Ste 4100 .... Chicago IL 60611 *Web:* www.hearncompany.com	312-408-3000	408-3010	653
Hearn Kirkwood 7251 Standard Dr .... Hanover MD 21076 *TF General:* 800-777-9489 ■ *Web:* www.hearnkirkwood.com	410-712-6000	712-0020	297-7
Hearn Paper Co 556 N Meridian Rd .... Youngstown OH 44509 *TF:* 800-225-2989 ■ *Web:* www.hearnpaper.com	330-792-6533	792-4762	553
Hearst Corp 300 W 57th St .... New York NY 10019 *Web:* www.hearst.com	212-649-2275		637-8
Hearst Entertainment & Syndication Group 300 W 57th St. .... New York NY 10019 *Web:* hearst.com/entertainment	212-969-7553		514
Hearst Foundation, The 300 W 57th St 26th Fl. .... New York NY 10019 *TF:* 800-841-7048 ■ *Web:* hearstfdn.org	212-649-3750	586-1917	305
Hearst Magazines Div 300 W 57th St .... New York NY 10019 *Web:* www.hearst.com	212-649-2275		637-9
Hearst Newspapers 300 W 57th St. .... New York NY 10019 *Web:* www.hearst.com/newspapers	212-649-2000		637-8
Hearst San Simeon State Historical Monument 750 Hearst Castle Rd .... San Simeon CA 93452 *TF:* 800-444-4445 ■ *Web:* www.parks.ca.gov/default.asp?page_id=591	805-927-2020		565
Heart & Crown 67 Clarence St. .... Ottawa ON K1N5P5 *Web:* www.heartandcrown.ca	613-562-0674		671
Heart & Soul Magazine 15480 Annapolis Rd Ste 202-225 .... Bowie MD 20715 *TF:* 800-834-8813 ■ *Web:* www.heartandsoul.com	800-834-8813		457-13
Heart O' Texas Speedway 784 N McLennan Dr .... Elm Mott TX 76640 *Web:* www.heartotexasspeedway.com	254-829-2294		515
Heart of the Valley Chamber of Commerce 101 E Wisconsin Ave .... Kaukauna WI 54130 *Web:* www.heartofthevalleychamber.com	920-766-1616	766-5504	139
Heart of Virginia Council Inc Boy Scouts of America 4015 Fitzhugh Ave .... Richmond VA 23230 *Web:* hovc.org	804-355-4306		138
Heart of Wisconsin Business & Economic Alliance 1120 Lincoln St .... Wisconsin Rapids WI 54494 *Web:* www.wisconsinrapidschamber.com	715-423-1830	423-1865	139
Heart Rhythm Society 1400 K St NW Ste 500 .... Washington DC 20005 *Web:* www.hrsonline.org	202-464-3400	464-3401	49-8
Heart Six Ranch 16985 Buffalo Valley Rd PO Box 70 .... Moran WY 83013 *TF:* 888-543-2477 ■ *Web:* heartsix.com	888-543-2477		239
Heart to Heart International 401 S Clairborne Rd Ste 302 .... Olathe KS 66062 *Web:* www.hearttoheart.org	913-764-5200		48-5
Heartbeat Ideas 1 Penn Plaza 5th Fl. .... New York NY 10119 *Web:* www.heartbeatdigital.com	212-812-2233		5
HEARTBEAT/Survivors After Suicide Inc 2015 Devon St .... Colorado Springs CO 80909 *Web:* www.heartbeatsurvivorsaftersuicide.org	719-596-2575		48-21
Hearth & Home Technologies Inc 7571 215th St W. .... Lakeville MN 55044 *TF:* 888-427-3973 ■ *Web:* www.hearthnhome.com	952-985-6000		357
Hearth Patio & Barbecue Assn (HPBA) 1901 N Moore St Ste 600 .... Arlington VA 22209 *TF:* 800-677-6278 ■ *Web:* www.hpba.org	703-522-0086	522-0548	49-4
Hearthstone at Green Lake, The 6720 E Green Lake Way N. .... Seattle WA 98103 *Web:* www.hearthstone.org	206-525-9666		672

	Phone	Fax	Class
Hearthstone of Round Rock 401 Oakwood Blvd ... Round Rock TX 78681 *Web:* www.seniorcarecentersltc.com	512-388-7494	388-2166	450
Heartland Behavioral Healthcare 3000 S Erie St ... Massillon OH 44646 *Web:* mha.ohio.gov	330-833-3135	833-6564	374-5
Heartland Bldg Company Inc 117 William St ... Middlesex NJ 08846	732-302-9277		186
Heartland Blood Centers 1200 N Highland Ave ... Aurora IL 60506 *TF:* 800-786-4483 ■ *Web:* www.heartlandbc.org	630-892-7055	892-4590	89
Heartland Community College 1500 W Raab Rd ... Normal IL 61761 *Web:* www.heartland.edu	309-268-8000	268-7992	162
Heartland Co-op 2829 Westown Pkwy Ste 350 ... West Des Moines IA 50266 *TF:* 800-513-3938 ■ *Web:* www.heartlandcoop.com	515-225-1334	225-8511	275
Heartland Engineered Products LLC 355 Industrial Dr ... Harrison OH 45030 *Web:* www.heartlandengineeredproducts.com	513-367-0080		480
Heartland Equipment Inc 2100 N Falls Blvd ... Wynne AR 72396 **Fax Area Code:* 870 ■ *TF:* 800-530-7617 ■ *Web:* www.tractorscraper.com	800-530-7617	238-8545*	273
Heartland Express Inc 901 N Kansas Ave ... North Liberty IA 52317 *NASDAQ: HTLD* ■ **Fax Area Code:* 319 ■ *TF:* 800-654-1175 ■ *Web:* www.heartlandexpress.com	800-654-1175	626-3311*	780
Heartland Film Festival 1043 Virginia Ave Ste 2 ... Indianapolis IN 46203 *Web:* heartlandfilm.org	317-464-9405	464-9409	282
Heartland Financial USA Inc 1398 Central Ave ... Dubuque IA 52001 *NASDAQ: HTLF* ■ *TF:* 888-739-2100 ■ *Web:* www.htlf.com	563-589-2100		360-2
Heartland Funds 789 N Water St Ste 500 ... Milwaukee WI 53202 *TF:* 800-432-7856 ■ *Web:* www.heartlandadvisors.com/heartland-advisors	414-347-7777		528
Heartland Hands-Hope Hospice 137 N Belt Hwy ... Saint Joseph MO 64506 *TF:* 800-443-1143 ■ *Web:* www.mymosaiclifecare.org	816-271-7190	271-7672	371
Heartland Health Care & Rehabilitation Ctr 5401 Sawyer Rd ... Sarasota FL 34233	941-925-3427		450
Heartland Health Care Ctr Bedford 2001 Forest Ridge Dr ... Bedford TX 76021 *Web:* www.heartland-manorcare.com	817-571-6804	267-4176	450
Heartland Health Care Ctr Bloomfield Hills 2975 N Adams Rd ... Bloomfield Hills MI 48304 *Web:* www.hcr-manorcare.com	248-645-2900		450
Heartland Health Care Ctr Boynton Beach 3600 Old Boynton Rd ... Boynton Beach FL 33436 *Web:* www.heartland-manorcare.com	561-736-9992	364-9527	450
Heartland Health Care Ctr Charleston 1800 Eagle Landing Blvd ... Hanahan SC 29410 *Web:* www.heartland-manorcare.com	843-553-0656	553-9773	450
Heartland Health Care Ctr University 28550 Five Mile Rd ... Livonia MI 48154 *Web:* heartland-manorcare.com	734-427-8270	427-2135	450
Heartland Health Care Ctr-South Jacksonville 3648 University Blvd S ... Jacksonville FL 32216 *Web:* www.heartland-manorcare.com	904-733-7440	448-9425	450
Heartland Hospice Services 333 N Summit St ... Toledo OH 43604 *TF:* 800-366-1232 ■ *Web:* www.hcr-manorcare.com	419-252-5500		371
Heartland Industrial Partners LP 177 Broad St 10th Fl ... Stamford CT 06901 *TF:* 800-338-5815 ■ *Web:* www.heartlandpartners.com	203-327-1202		360-3
Heartland Inns 87-2nd St ... Coralville IA 52241 *TF Resv:* 800-334-3277 ■ *Web:* www.heartlandinns.com	319-351-8132		379
Heartland Institute 3939 N Wilke Rd Ste 903 ... Arlington Heights IL 60004 *Web:* www.heartland.org	312-377-4000	377-5000	634
Heartland Investment Associates Inc 2202 Heritage Green Dr ... Hiawatha IA 52233	319-393-8913		690
Heartland Label Printers Inc 1700 Stephen St ... Little Chute WI 54140 **Fax Area Code:* 920 ■ *TF General:* 800-236-7914 ■ *Web:* www.hbs.net	800-236-7914	788-7739*	246
Heartland Library Co-op 319 W Ctr Ave ... Sebring FL 33870 *Web:* www.myhlc.org	863-402-6716		434-3
Heartland Lions Eye Bank 10100 N Ambassador Dr Ste 200 ... Kansas City MO 64153 *TF:* 800-753-2265 ■ *Web:* www.saving-sight.org	816-454-5454	454-5446	269
Heartland Lions Eye Bank 10801 Pear Tree Ln Ste 170 ... Saint Ann MO 63074	314-428-4373		269
Heartland Meat Company Inc 3461 Main St ... Chula Vista CA 91911 *TF:* 888-407-3668 ■ *Web:* www.heartlandmeat.com	619-407-3668	407-3678	297-9
Heartland Multiple Listing Service Inc 11150 Overbrook Rd Ste 100 ... Leawood KS 66211 *Web:* matrix.heartlandmls.com	913-661-1600	661-1618	652
Heartland of Beavercreek 1974 N Fairfield Rd ... Dayton OH 45432	937-429-1106		450
Heartland Paper Co 808 W Cherokee St ... Sioux Falls SD 57104 *TF Cust Svc:* 800-843-7922 ■ *Web:* www.heartland-paper.com	605-336-1190	332-8378	559
Heartland Park Topeka 7530 SW Topeka Blvd ... Topeka KS 66619 *TF:* 844-200-6472 ■ *Web:* heartlandpark.com	785-862-4781		515
Heartland Payment Systems Inc 90 Nassau St ... Princeton NJ 08542 *NYSE: HPY* ■ *TF:* 888-798-3131 ■ *Web:* www.heartlandpaymentsystems.com	609-683-3831		251
Heartland Petroleum LLC 4001 E Fifth Ave ... Columbus OH 43219 *TF:* 800-889-7831 ■ *Web:* www.heartland-petroleum.com	614-441-4001		579
Heartland Power Co-op 216 Jackson St PO Box 65 ... Thompson IA 50478 *TF:* 888-584-9732 ■ *Web:* www.heartlandpower.com	641-584-2251	584-2253	245
Heartland Precision Fasteners Inc 301 Prairie Village Dr ... New Century KS 66031 *Web:* www.heartlandfasteners.com	913-829-4447		22
Heartland Rural Electric Co-op 110 Enterprise St ... Girard KS 66743 *TF:* 888-835-9585 ■ *Web:* www.heartland-rec.com	620-724-8251	724-8253	245
Heartland Spa 1237 E 1600 N Rd ... Gilman IL 60938 *TF:* 800-545-4853 ■ *Web:* www.heartlandspa.com	800-545-4853		706
Heartland Video Systems Inc 1311 Pilgrim Rd ... Plymouth WI 53073 *Web:* hvs-inc.com	920-893-4204		116
Heartline Fitness Products Inc 8041 Cessna Ave Ste 200 ... Gaithersburg MD 20879 *TF:* 800-262-3348 ■ *Web:* www.heartlinefitness.com	301-921-0661		267
HeartSine Technologies Inc 121 Friends Ln Ste 400 ... Newtown PA 18940 *Web:* heartsine.com	215-860-8100		476
HeartWare Inc 4750 Wiley Post Way Ste 120 ... Salt Lake City UT 84116 *NASDAQ: WHRT* ■ *Web:* heartware.com	801-355-6255	355-7622	250
Heat & Control Inc 21121 Cabot Blvd ... Hayward CA 94545 *TF:* 800-227-5980 ■ *Web:* www.heatandcontrol.com	510-259-0500	259-0600	298
Heat Controller Inc 1900 Wellworth Ave ... Jackson MI 49203	517-787-2100	787-9341	14
Heat Pipe Technology Inc 4340 NE 49th Ave ... Gainesville FL 32609 *Web:* www.heatpipe.com	352-367-0999		14
Heat Seal LLC 4580 E 71st St ... Cleveland OH 44125 *TF:* 800-342-6329 ■ *Web:* www.heatsealco.com	216-341-2022	341-2163	547
Heat Transfer Products Group LLC 201 Thomas French Dr ... Scottsboro AL 35769 *TF:* 800-288-9488 ■ *Web:* www.htpgusa.com	256-259-7400		610
Heat Transfer Sales of the Carolinas Inc 4101 Beechwood Dr ... Greensboro NC 27410 *TF:* 800-842-3328 ■ *Web:* www.heattransfersales.com	336-294-3838		612
Heat USA Inc PO Box 50240 ... College Point NY 11356-0240 *Web:* www.heatusa.com	212-254-4328		538
Heatcraft Refrigeration Products 2175 W Pk Pl Blvd ... Stone Mountain GA 30087 *TF:* 800-321-1881 ■ *Web:* www.heatcraftrpd.com	770-465-5600	465-5990	664
Heateflex Corp 405 Santa Clara St ... Arcadia CA 91006 *Web:* www.heateflex.com	626-599-8566		14
Heath Ceramics Ltd 400 Gate Five Rd ... Sausalito CA 94965 *Web:* www.heathceramics.com	415-332-3732		361
Heath Consultants Inc 9030 Monroe Rd ... Houston TX 77061 *TF:* 800-432-8487 ■ *Web:* www.heathus.com	713-844-1300	844-1309	192
Heath Manufacturing Co 140 Mill St ... Coopersville MI 49404 *Web:* heathoutdoorproducts.com	616-997-8181		578
Heath Village 430 Schooley's Mtn Rd ... Hackettstown NJ 07840 *Web:* heathvillage.com	908-852-4801		371
Heath/Norton Assoc 301 Crocus Ct Ste L-7 ... Dayton NJ 08810	732-329-4663		266
Heathco'S Pizza & Variety 375 Court St ... Auburn ME 04210 *Web:* heathcos.com	207-689-9175		204
Heathcote Botanical Gardens 210 Savannah Rd ... Fort Pierce FL 34982 *Web:* www.heathcotebotanicalgardens.org	772-464-4672		97
Heathman Lodge 7801 NE Greenwood Dr ... Vancouver WA 98662 *TF:* 800-727-2478 ■ *Web:* www.heathmanlodge.com	360-254-3100		379
Heathman Restaurant 1001 SW Broadway ... Portland OR 97205 *Web:* www.heathmanrestaurantandbar.com	503-790-7752		671
Heathwood Hall Episcopal School 3000 S Beltline Blvd ... Columbia SC 29201 *Web:* www.heathwood.org	803-765-2309		48-20
Heating & Plumbing Engineers Inc 407 Fillmore Pl ... Colorado Springs CO 80907 *Web:* www.hpeinc.com	719-633-5414	633-4031	189-10
Heatrex Inc PO Box 515 ... Meadville PA 16335 *TF:* 800-394-6589 ■ *Web:* www.heatrex.com	814-724-1800	333-6580	318
Heatron Inc 3000 Wilson ... Leavenworth KS 66048 *Web:* www.heatron.com	913-651-4420		697
Heat-Timer Corp 20 New Dutch Ln ... Fairfield NJ 07004 *TF:* 800-424-3996 ■ *Web:* www.heat-timer.com	973-575-4004		407
Heatwave Labs Inc 195 Aviation Way Ste 100 ... Watsonville CA 95076 *Web:* www.cathode.com	831-722-9081		261
Heaven Group Inc 515 Broadway Ste 2AF ... New York NY 10012 *Web:* www.heavengroup.com	347-983-9339		5
Heaven's Best Carpet & Upholstery Cleaning PO Box 607 ... Rexburg ID 83440 *TF:* 800-359-2095 ■ *Web:* www.heavensbest.com	208-359-1106	359-1236	152
Heavener Runestone State Park 18365 Runestone Rd ... Heavener OK 74937 *Web:* travelok.com	918-653-2241		565
Heavenhill Distilleries Inc 1064 Loretto Rd ... Bardstown KY 40004 *Web:* heavenhill.com	502-348-3921		80-1
Heavner, Scott, Beyers & Mihlar LLC 111 E Main St Ste 200 ... Decatur IL 62523 *TF:* 800-578-1363 ■ *Web:* hsbattys.com	217-422-1719		428
Heavy Earth Resources Inc 625 Second St Ste 280 ... San Francisco CA 94107	415-813-5079		536
Heavy Machines Inc 3926 E Rains Rd ... Memphis TN 38118 *TF:* 888-366-9028 ■ *Web:* www.heavymachinesinc.com	901-260-2200		358
Hebco Products Inc 1232 Whetstone St ... Bucyrus OH 44820	419-562-7987	562-8577	61
Hebeler Corp 2000 Military Rd ... Tonawanda NY 14150 *TF:* 800-486-4709 ■ *Web:* www.hebeler.com	716-873-9300	873-7538	620
Heberly & Associates 615 First W ... Havre MT 59501 *Web:* www.heberlyeng.com	406-265-6741		261
Hebrew Academy of The Five Towns & Rockaway Inc 389 Central Ave ... Lawrence NY 11559 *Web:* www.haftr.org	516-569-3370		685
Hebrew Health Care Inc 1 Abrahms Blvd ... West Hartford CT 06117 *Web:* www.hebrewhealthcare.org	860-523-3800	523-3949	450
Hebrew Hospital Home Continuum of Care 61 Grasslands Rd ... Valhalla NY 10595 *Web:* www.hebrewhospitalhome.org	914-681-8400		374-7

Name / Address	City	State	ZIP	Phone	Fax	Class
Hebrew Immigrant Aid Society (HIAS) 333 Seventh Ave 16th Fl	New York	NY	10001	212-967-4100	967-4483	48-5
TF: 800-442-7714 ■ *Web:* www.hias.org						
Hebrew Theological College 7135 Carpenter Rd	Skokie	IL	60077	847-982-2500		165
TF: 800-798-8100 ■ *Web:* www.htc.edu						
Hebrew Union College Cincinnati 3101 Clifton Ave	Cincinnati	OH	45220	513-221-1875	221-0321*	166
*Fax: Admissions ■ *Web:* www.huc.edu						
Hebrew Union College Los Angeles 3077 University Ave	Los Angeles	CA	90007	213-749-3424	747-6128*	166
*Fax: Admissions ■ *TF:* 800-899-0925 ■ *Web:* www.huc.edu						
Hebron Academy 339 Rd PO Box 309	Hebron	ME	04238	207-966-2100		622
TF: 888-432-7664 ■ *Web:* www.hebronacademy.org						
Hebron Savings Bank (HSB) 101 N Main St PO Box 59	Hebron	MD	21830	410-749-1185	543-0703	70
Web: www.hebronsavingsbank.com						
Heceta Head Lighthouse State Scenic Viewpoint 93111 Hwy 101 N	Florence	OR	97439	800-551-6949		565
TF: 800-551-6949 ■ *Web:* www.oregonstateparks.org						
Hecht Solberg Robinson Goldberg & Bagley LLP 1 America Plaza 600 W Broadway Ste 800	San Diego	CA	92101	619-239-3444		445
Web: www.hechtsolberg.com						
Heck Denny (Rep D - WA) 425 Cannon HOB	Washington	DC	20515	202-225-9740	225-0129	342-2
Web: dennyheck.house.gov						
Heckaman Homes Inc 2676 E Market St	Nappanee	IN	46550	574-773-4167		106
Web: www.heckamanhomes.com						
Heckethorn Manfacturing Cos Inc 2005 Forrest St	Dyersburg	TN	38024	731-285-3310	286-2739	60
Web: www.hecomfg.com						
Heckler & Koch Inc 5675 Transport Blvd	Columbus	GA	31907	706-568-1906	568-9151	284
TF: 800-331-0852 ■ *Web:* www.hk-usa.com						
Hecks Direct Mail & Printing Service Inc 202 W Florence Ave	Toledo	OH	43605	419-661-6000	661-6036	5
TF: 800-997-4325 ■ *Web:* www.heckspringting.com						
Heckscher State Park 1 Heckscher State Pkwy	East Islip	NY	11730	631-581-2100		565
Web: parks.ny.gov/parks/136/maps.aspx						
Hecla Mining Co 800 W Pender St Ste 970	Vancouver	BC	V6C2V6	604-682-6201	682-6215	502
NYSE: HL ■ *TF:* 800-432-5291 ■ *Web:* hecla-mining.com						
Hecla Mining Co 6500 N Mineral Dr Ste 200	Coeur d'Alene	ID	83815	208-769-4100		502
NYSE: HL ■ *Web:* www.hecla-mining.com						
HECO Inc 2350 Del Monte St	West Sacramento	CA	95691	916-372-5411		709
Web: www.hecogear.com						
Hector International Airport 2801 32nd Ave NW	Fargo	ND	58102	701-241-1501	241-1538	27
TF: 800-451-5333 ■ *Web:* www.fargoairport.com						
Hed Cycling Products 1735 Terrace Dr	Roseville	MN	55113	651-653-0202		517
TF: 888-246-3639 ■ *Web:* www.hedcycling.com						
Hedahls Inc 100 East Broadway	Bismarck	ND	58502	701-223-8393	221-4251	61
TF: 800-433-2457 ■ *Web:* www.hedahls.com						
Hedberg Public Library (HPL) 316 S Main St	Janesville	WI	53545	608-758-6600	758-6583	434-3
Web: www.hedbergpubliclibrary.org						
Hedgehog Hosting 10387 Main St Ste 300	Fairfax	VA	22030	703-218-4170		396
Web: www.hedgehoghosting.com						
Hedges Engineering & Consulting Inc 913 Kincaid Ave	Sumner	WA	98390	253-891-9365		261
Hedgeye Risk Management LLC 1 High Ridge Pk	Stamford	CT	06905	203-562-6500		401
Web: www2.hedgeye.com						
Hedrick Associates Inc 2360 Oak Industrial Dr NE	Grand Rapids	MI	49505	616-454-1218		180
TF: 800-222-5877 ■ *Web:* hedrickassoc.com						
Hedrick Brothers Construction Company Inc 2200 Centrepark W Dr Ste 100	West Palm Beach	FL	33409	561-689-8880		186
Web: www.hedrickbrothers.com						
Hedstrom Lumber Company Inc 1504 Gunflint Trl	Grand Marais	MN	55604	218-387-2995	387-2204	683
Web: www.hedstromlumber.com						
Hedwin Corp 1600 Roland Heights Ave	Baltimore	MD	21211	410-467-8209	889-5189*	199
*Fax: Cust Svc ■ *TF:* 800-638-1012 ■ *Web:* www.hedwin.com						
Hedy Holmes Staffing Services 3031 W March Ln	Stockton	CA	95219	209-957-9630		260
Web: www.hedyholmesstaffing.com						
Hee Been 6231 Little River Tpke	Alexandria	VA	22312	703-941-3737		671
Web: www.heebeen.com						
Hee Hing 449 Kapahulu Ave	Honolulu	HI	96815	808-735-5544	732-6026	671
Web: www.heehinghawaii.com						
Heeia State Park 46-465 Kamehameha Hwy	Kaneohe	HI	96744	808-235-6509	235-6519	565
Web: www.heeiastatepark.org						
Heely-Brown Company Inc 1280 Chattahoochee Ave	Atlanta	GA	30318	404-352-0022	350-2693	46
TF: 800-241-4628 ■ *Web:* www.heelybrown.com						
Heerema Co 200 Sixth Ave	Hawthorne	NJ	07506	973-423-0505		711
TF: 800-346-4729 ■ *Web:* www.heeremacompany.com						
Heeren Bros Inc 1055 7 Mile Rd NW	Comstock Park	MI	49321	616-452-2101	243-7070	297-7
Web: www.heerenbros.com						
Heery International Inc 999 Peachtree St NE	Atlanta	GA	30309	404-881-9880	946-2398	261
TF: 800-524-3379 ■ *Web:* www.heery.com						
Hef Usa Corp 2015 Progress Rd	Springfield	OH	45505	937-323-2556		261
TF: 800-272-2525 ■ *Web:* www.hefusa.net						
Heffel Gallery Ltd 2247 Granville St	Vancouver	BC	V6H3G1	604-732-6505	732-4245	42
TF: 800-528-9608 ■ *Web:* www.heffel.com/gallery						
Hefren - Tillotson Inc 308 Seventh Ave	Pittsburgh	PA	15222	412-434-0990		194
Web: www.hefren.com						
Hegele Logistic LLC 1460 Brummel Ave	Elk Grove	IL	60007	847-690-0430		475
Web: www.hegelelogistic.com						
Hegemony Inc 520 W Roosevelt Rd	Wheaton	IL	60187	630-690-5200		261
TF: 800-692-4415 ■ *Web:* hegemony.com						
Hehr International Inc 3333 Casitas Ave	Los Angeles	CA	90039	323-663-1261	666-2372	234
TF: 800-642-9988 ■ *Web:* www.hehrintl.com						
HEI Hospitality LLC 101 Merritt 7 Corporate Pk 1st Fl	Norwalk	CT	06851	203-849-8844		378
Web: www.heihotels.com						
HEICO Corp 3000 Taft St	Hollywood	FL	33021	954-987-4000	987-8228	21
NYSE: HEI ■ *Web:* www.heico.com						
Heid Music Company Inc 308 East College Ave	Appleton	WI	54911	920-734-1969		526
Web: www.heidmusic.com						
Heide & Cook Ltd 1714 Kanakanui St	Honolulu	HI	96819	808-841-6161	841-4889	189-10
Web: www.heidecook.com						
Heidecke Lake State Fish & Wildlife Area 5010 N Jugtown Rd	Morris	IL	60450	815-942-6352		565
Web: dnr.illinois.gov/Lands/Landmgt/PARKS/R2/Heidecke.htm						
Heidel House Resort 643 Illinois Ave	Green Lake	WI	54941	920-294-3344	294-6128	669
TF: 800-444-2812 ■ *Web:* www.heidelhouse.com						
Heidelberg University 310 E Market St	Tiffin	OH	44883	419-448-2000	448-2334	166
TF: 800-434-3352 ■ *Web:* www.heidelberg.edu						
Heidelberg USA Inc 1000 Gutenberg Dr	Kennesaw	GA	30144	770-419-6500	419-6550	629
TF Cust Svc: 888-472-9655 ■ *Web:* www.heidelberg.com/us/en/index.jsp						
Heidell, Pittoni, Murphy & Bach LLP 99 Park Ave	New York	NY	10016	212-286-8585		428
TF: 800-286-8586 ■ *Web:* www.hpmb.com						
Heidenhain Corp 333 E State Pkwy	Schaumburg	IL	60173	847-490-1191	490-3931	493
Web: www.heidenhain.com						
Heidi's 1020 N Carson St	Carson City	NV	89701	530-544-8113		671
Web: heidislaketahoe.com						
Heidler Roofing Services Inc 2120 Alpha Dr	York	PA	17408	717-792-3549	792-4660	189-12
TF: 866-792-3549 ■ *Web:* www.heidlerroofing.com						
Heidman Law Firm Po Box 3086	Sioux City	IA	51101	712-255-8838		445
Web: www.heidmanlaw.com						
Heidrick & Struggles International Inc 233 S Wacker Dr Ste 4900	Chicago	IL	60606	312-496-1000	496-1048	266
NASDAQ: HSII ■ *TF:* 800-879-1193 ■ *Web:* www.heidrick.com						
Heidtman Steel Products Inc 2401 Front St	Toledo	OH	43605	419-691-4646	698-1150	723
Web: www.heidtman.com						
Heifer International 1 World Ave	Little Rock	AR	72202	501-907-2600	907-2902	48-5
TF: 800-422-0474 ■ *Web:* www.heifer.org						
Height Analytics LLC 1775 Pennsylvania Ave NW 5th Fl	Washington	DC	20006	202-629-0000		401
Web: www.heightllc.com						
Heights Insurance Group Inc 2048 S Hacienda Blvd	Hacienda Heights	CA	91745	626-855-8288		390
Web: www.kcal.net						
Heil Environmental Ltd 2030 Hamilton Pl Blvd Ste 200	Chattanooga	TN	37421	423-899-9100		516
TF: 866-367-4345 ■ *Web:* www.heil.com						
Heil Trailer International Co 1125 Congress Pkwy NE	Athens	TN	37303	423-745-5830		779
Web: www.heiltrailer.com						
HEILBrice Inc 9840 Irvine Ctr Dr	Irvine	CA	92618	949-336-8800		4
Web: www.heilbrice.com						
Heilind Electronics Inc 58 Jonspin Rd	Wilmington	MA	01887	978-657-4870	658-0278	246
TF: 800-400-7041 ■ *Web:* www.heilind.com						
Heim LP 6360 W 73rd St	Chicago	IL	60638	708-496-7450	496-7428	456
TF: 800-927-9393 ■ *Web:* www.theheimgroup.com						
Hein & Assoc LLP 1999 Broadway Ste 4000	Denver	CO	80202	303-298-9600	298-8118	2
TF: 800-234-5573 ■ *Web:* www.heincpa.com						
Heineken USA 360 Hamilton Ave Ste 1103	White Plains	NY	10601	914-681-4100		102
Web: www.heineken.com						
Heinemann 361 Hanover St	Portsmouth	NH	03801	603-431-7894	431-7840	637-2
TF: 800-541-2086 ■ *Web:* www.heinemann.com						
Heinemann's Bakeries LLC PO Box 558265	Chicago	IL	60655	616-885-9094	885-9031	296-1
Web: www.heinemanns.com						
Heinen's Inc 4540 Richmond Rd	Cleveland	OH	44128	855-475-2300	514-4788*	345
*Fax Area Code: 216 ■ *TF:* 855-475-2300 ■ *Web:* www.heinens.com						
Heiners Bakery Inc 1300 Adams Ave	Huntington	WV	25704	304-523-8411		296-1
TF: 800-776-8411 ■ *Web:* heinersbakery.com						
Heinfeld Meech & Company PC 10120 N Oracle Rd	Tucson	AZ	85704	520-742-2611		2
Web: heinfeldmeech.com						
Heinrich Envelope Corp 925 Zane Ave N	Minneapolis	MN	55422	763-544-3571	544-6287	263
TF: 800-346-7957 ■ *Web:* www.heinrichenvelope.com						
Heinrich Martin (Sen D - NM) 303 Hart Senate Office Bldg	Washington	DC	20510	202-224-5521	228-2841	342-2
Web: www.heinrich.senate.gov						
Heintz & Weber Co Inc 150 Reading Ave	Buffalo	NY	14220	716-852-7171	852-7173	296-41
TF: 800-438-6878 ■ *Web:* www.webersmustard.com						
Heinz Field 100 Art Rooney Ave	Pittsburgh	PA	15212	412-697-7181	697-7701	720
Web: www.steelers.com						
Heinz Hall for the Performing Arts 600 Penn Ave	Pittsburgh	PA	15222	412-392-4900	392-3328	572
TF: 800-743-8560 ■ *Web:* www.pittsburghsymphony.org						
Heinzeroth Marketing Group 415 Y Blvd Ste 3	Rockford	IL	61107	815-967-0929		195
Web: www.heinzeroth.com						
Heisler Industries Inc 224 Passaic Ave	Fairfield	NJ	07004	973-227-6300	227-7627	547
TF: 800-496-7621 ■ *Web:* www.heislerind.com						
Heisler's Cloverleaf Dairy 743 Catawissa Rd	Tamaqua	PA	18252	570-668-3399	668-3041	296-25
TF: 800-238-7245 ■ *Web:* www.heislersdairy.com						
Hei-Tek Automation 2102 W Quail Ave Ste 4	Phoenix	AZ	85027	602-269-7931		358
Web: www.heitek.com						
Heitkamp Heidi (Sen D - ND) SH-110 Hart Senate Office Bldg	Washington	DC	20510	202-224-2043	224-7776	342-2
Web: www.heitkamp.senate.gov						

Name / Address	City	State	Zip	Phone	Fax	Class
Heitman LLC 191 N Wacker Dr Ste 2500 *TF:* 800-289-9999 ■ *Web:* www.heitman.com	Chicago	IL	60606	312-855-5700		655
Heizer Aerospace Inc 8750 Pevely Industrial Dr *Web:* www.haiusa.com	Pevely	MO	63070	636-475-6300		22
Hekman 860 E Main Ave *TF:* 800-998-5018 ■ *Web:* www.hekman.com	Zeeland	MI	49464	616-748-2660	748-2645	319-2
Helac Corp 225 Battersby Ave *TF:* 800-327-2589 ■ *Web:* www.helac.com	Enumclaw	WA	98022	360-825-1601	825-1603	223
Helbling & Associates Inc 9000 Brooktree Rd Ste 150 *Web:* www.helblingsearch.com	Wexford	PA	15090	724-935-7500		721
Heldenfels Enterprises Inc 5700 IH-35 S (Exit 199) *Web:* heldenfels.com	San Marcos	TX	78666	512-396-2376	396-2381	183
Helen B Hoffman Plantation Library 501 N Fig Tree Ln *TF:* 800-774-5866 ■ *Web:* plantation.org	Plantation	FL	33317	954-797-2140	797-2767	434-3
Helen DeVos Children's Hospital 100 Michigan NE *TF:* 866-989-7999 ■ *Web:* www.helendevoschildrens.org	Grand Rapids	MI	49503	616-391-9000		769
Helen Hall Library (HHL) 100 W Walker St *TF:* 800-449-1600 ■ *Web:* www.leaguecity.com	League City	TX	77573	281-554-1111		434-3
Helen Hayes Theatre 240 W 44th St *TF:* 800-447-7400 ■ *Web:* telecharge.com/go.aspx?md=102&pid=8417	New York	NY	10036	212-239-6200		747
Helen Keller Hospital 1300 S Montgomery Ave *Web:* www.helenkeller.com	Sheffield	AL	35660	256-386-4196		374-3
Helen Keller International 352 Pk Ave S Ste 1200 *Web:* www.hki.org	New York	NY	10010	212-532-0544		48-5
Helen M Plum Memorial Library 110 W Maple St *Web:* helenplum.org	Lombard	IL	60148	630-627-0316	627-0336	434-3
Helen of Troy Ltd 1 Helen of Troy Plaza *NASDAQ:* HELE ■ *TF:* 800-487-8432 ■ *Web:* www.hotus.com	El Paso	TX	79912	915-225-8000	225-8004	38
Helen's 2527 W Main St *Web:* helensrva.com	Richmond	VA	23220	804-358-4370		671
Helena Area Chamber of Commerce 225 Cruse Ave *TF:* 800-743-5362 ■ *Web:* www.helenachamber.com	Helena	MT	59601	406-442-4120	447-1532	139
Helena Chemical Co 225 Schilling Blvd Ste 300 *TF:* 800-883-0234 ■ *Web:* www.helenachemical.com	Collierville	TN	38017	901-761-0050	821-5455	280
Helena City Hall 316 N Pk Ave *Web:* www.helenamt.gov	Helena	MT	59623	406-447-8000		337
Helena Civic Ctr 340 Neill Ave *Web:* www.helenaciviccenter.com	Helena	MT	59601	406-447-8481	447-8480	205
Helena Laboratories Inc 1530 Lindbergh Dr *TF:* 800-231-5663 ■ *Web:* www.helena.com	Beaumont	TX	77704	409-842-3714		231
Helena Regional Airport 2850 Skyway Dr *Web:* www.helenaairport.com	Helena	MT	59601	406-442-2821	449-2340	27
Helena Regional Medical Ctr 1801 ML King Dr *Web:* www.helenarmc.com	Helena	AR	72342	870-338-5800		374-3
Helene Fuld College of Nursing 24 E 120th St *TF:* 800-262-3257 ■ *Web:* www.helenefuld.edu	New York	NY	10035	212-616-7200	616-7299	800
Helfrich Bros Boiler Works Inc 39 Merrimack St *Web:* www.hbbwinc.com	Lawrence	MA	01843	978-683-7244		492
Helga's German Restaurant 14197 E Exposition Ave *Web:* www.helgasdeli.com	Aurora	CO	80012	303-344-5488		671
Helgesen Industries Inc 7261 Hwy 60 W *Web:* www.helgesen.com	Hartford	WI	53027	262-673-4444		386
Heliae Development LLC 614 E Germann Rd *Web:* www.heliae.com	Gilbert	AZ	85297	480-424-2875		466
Helical Products Co Inc 901 W McCoy Ln *TF:* 877-353-9873 ■ *Web:* www.heli-cal.com	Santa Maria	CA	93455	805-928-3851	928-2369	620
Helicomb International Inc 1402 S 69th E Ave *Web:* www.pccaero.com/companies/helicomb-int	Tulsa	OK	74112	918-835-3999	834-4451	24
Helicopter Assn International (HAI) 1635 Prince St *TF:* 800-435-4976 ■ *Web:* www.rotor.org	Alexandria	VA	22314	703-683-4646	683-4745	49-21
Helicopter Support Inc (HSI) 124 Quarry Rd	Trumbull	CT	06611	203-416-4000	416-4291	770
Helicopter Tech Inc 452 Swedeland Rd *Web:* www.helicoptertechinc.com	King Of Prussia	PA	19406	610-272-8090		25
Helicopter Transport Services Inc (HTS) 701 Wilson Pt Rd *Web:* www.htshelicopters.com	Baltimore	MD	21220	410-391-7722		359
Heliene Inc 520 Allen'S Side Rd *Web:* www.heliene.ca	Sault Sainte Marie	ON	P6A6K4	705-575-6556	575-4432	253
Heli-Mart Inc 3184 Airway Ave Unit E *TF:* 800-826-6899 ■ *Web:* www.helimart.com	Costa Mesa	CA	92626	714-755-2999	755-2995	770
Helinet Aviation Services LLC 16303 Waterman Dr *Web:* www.helinet.com	Van Nuys	CA	91406	818-902-0229		359
HELIO LLC 10960 Wilshire Blvd Ste 700 *Web:* www.helio.com	Los Angeles	CA	90024	310-445-7000		387
Helio Precision Products Inc 601 N Skokie Hwy *Web:* www.hnprecision.com	Lake Bluff	IL	60044	847-473-1300		128
Heliodyne Corp 4910 Seaport Ave *TF:* 888-878-8750 ■ *Web:* www.heliodyne.com	Richmond	CA	94804	510-237-9614		321
Heli-One 120 NE Frontage Rd *Web:* www.heli-one.ca	Fort Collins	CO	80524	970-492-1000		20
HelioPower Inc 25767 Jefferson Ave *Web:* www.heliopower.com	Murrieta	CA	92562	951-677-7755		610
Helios & Matheson North America Inc 350 Fifth Ave Ste 7520 *Web:* www.tact.com	New York	NY	10018	212-979-8228		180
HELIOS GROUP 2099 Fernand-Lafontaine blvd *Web:* www.helios-group.com	Longueuil	QC	J4G2J4	450-646-1903		393
Heliotrope 248 W Ponce De Leon Ave	Decatur	GA	30030	404-371-0100		321
Helitune Inc 190 Gordon St *Web:* www.helitune.com	Elk Grove Village	IL	60007	847-228-0985		407
Helix Biopharma Corp 305 Industrial Pkwy S Unit 3 *TSE:* HBP ■ *Web:* www.helixbiopharma.com	Aurora	ON	L4G6X7	905-841-2300	841-2244	85
Helix Commerce International Inc 117 Melrose Ave *Web:* www.helixcommerce.com	Toronto	ON	M5M1Y8	647-477-6254		196
Helix Computer Systems Inc 2401 Hydraulic Rd *TF:* 800-433-5778 ■ *Web:* www.helixsystems.com	Charlottesville	VA	22901	434-963-4900		177
Helix Design Inc 175 Lincoln St Unit 201 *Web:* www.helixdesign.net	Manchester	NH	03103	603-644-1408		463
Helix Energy Solutions Inc 400 N Sam Houston Pkwy E Ste 400 *NYSE:* HLX ■ *TF:* 888-345-2347 ■ *Web:* www.helixesg.com	Houston	TX	77060	281-618-0400	618-0500	539
Helix Enterprises Inc 4300 Forbes Blvd Ste 140 *Web:* helixenterprises.com	Lanham	MD	20706	301-429-0880		194
HELIX Environmental Planning Inc 7578 El Cajon Blvd Ste 200 *Web:* www.helixepi.com	La Mesa	CA	91942	619-462-1515		194
Helix Technologies Inc 8550 W Main St *Web:* helixtec.net	French Lick	IN	47432	812-936-2525		175
Helixis Inc 5421 Avenida Encinas Ste B *Web:* support.illumina.com	Carlsbad	CA	92008	760-688-0104		743
Helixstorm Inc 41619 Margarita Rd Ste 202 *TF:* 888-434-3549 ■ *Web:* www.helixstorm.com	Temecula	CA	92591	888-434-3549		387
Hell Creek State Park PO Box 1630 *Web:* fwp.mt.gov	Miles City	MT	59301	406-557-2362		565
Hella Corporate Center USA Inc 43811 Plymouth Oaks Blvd *Web:* www.hella.com	Plymouth	MI	48170	734-414-0900		48-20
Hellam Varon & Company Inc PS 1750 112th Ave NE *Web:* hellamvaron.com	Bellevue	WA	98004	425-453-9192		2
Hellas Construction Inc 12710 Research Blvd Ste 240 *Web:* www.hellasconstruction.com	Austin	TX	78759	512-250-2910		186
Hellenic College-Holy Cross School of Theology 50 Goddard Ave **Fax:* Admissions ■ *Web:* www.hchc.edu	Brookline	MA	02445	617-731-3500	850-1460*	166
Hellenic Heritage Museum 1650 Senter Rd *Web:* hhisj.org	San Jose	CA	95112	408-247-4685		520
Hellenic Museum & Cultural Ctr 333 S Halsted Ave *Web:* www.nationalhellenicmuseum.org	Chicago	IL	60661	312-655-1234	655-1221	520
Hellenic-American Chamber of Commerce (HACC) 370 Lexington Ave 27th Fl *Web:* www.hellenicamerican.cc	New York	NY	10017	212-629-6380	564-9281	138
Heller Consulting Inc 1736 Franklin St Ste 600 *Web:* www.teamheller.com	Oakland	CA	94612	510-841-4222		177
Heller Dean (Sen R - NV) 324 Hart Bldg *Web:* www.heller.senate.gov	Washington	DC	20510	202-224-6244	228-6753	342-2
Heller Real Estate Group Inc, The 171 Saxony Rd Ste 205 *Web:* www.hellerthehomeseller.com	Encinitas	CA	92024	760-632-8408		652
Hellman & Friedman LLC 1 Maritime Plaza 12th Fl *Web:* www.hf.com	San Francisco	CA	94111	415-788-5111	788-0176	405
Hellman Associates Inc 1225 W Fourth St PO Box 627 *TF:* 800-747-7055 ■ *Web:* www.hellman.com	Waterloo	IA	50704	319-234-7055		7
Hello Direct Inc 77 NE Blvd **Fax:* Sales ■ *TF:* 800-435-5634 ■ *Web:* www.hellodirect.com	Nashua	NH	03062	800-435-5634	456-2566*	459
Hello World Communications 118 W 22nd St Fl 2 *Web:* www.hwc.tv	New York	NY	10011	212-243-8800		514
HelloWorld 3000 Town Ctr ste 2100 *TF:* 877-837-7493 ■ *Web:* www.helloworld.com	South Field	MI	48075	877-837-7493		7
Hells Canyon Preservation Council 105 First St Ste 327 PO Box 2768 *Web:* www.hellscanyon.org	La Grande	OR	97850	541-963-3950		48-13
Hells Gate State Park 5100 Hells Gate Rd *Web:* www.idahoparks.org	Lewiston	ID	83501	208-799-5015		565
Helly Hansen US Inc 4104 C St NE Ste 200 *Web:* www.hellyhansen.com	Auburn	WA	98002	253-372-3000		155-5
Helm Inc 47911 Halyard Dr *TF:* 800-445-4831 ■ *Web:* www.helm.com	Plymouth	MI	48170	800-445-4831		88
Helm Surgical Systems LLC 5895 E Evans Ave Ste 100 *Web:* www.helmsurgical.com	Denver	CO	80222	720-524-1900		475
Helm US Chemical Corp 1110 Centennial Ave *TF:* 800-255-3924 ■ *Web:* www.helmus.com	Piscataway	NJ	08854	732-981-1116	981-0528	146
Helmand Restaurant 143 First St *Web:* www.helmandrestaurantcambridge.com	Cambridge	MA	02142	617-492-4646		671
Helmand, The 806 N Charles St *Web:* www.helmand.com	Baltimore	MD	21201	410-752-0311		671
Helmark Steel Inc 813 S Market St *Web:* www.helmarksteel.com	New Castle	DE	19720	302-652-3341		480

Phone | Fax | Class

Helmel Engineering Products Inc
6520 Lockport Rd .... Niagara Falls NY 14305 716-297-8644 174
TF: 800-237-8266 ■ *Web:* www.helmel.com

Helmerich & Payne Inc
1437 S Boulder Ave .... Tulsa OK 74119 918-742-5531 540
NYSE: HP ■ *TF:* 800-205-4913 ■ *Web:* www.hpinc.com

Helmet House Inc
26855 Malibu Hill Rd .... Calabasas Hills CA 91301 818-880-0000 576
Web: www.helmethouse.com

Helmut Guenschel Inc 10 Emala Ave........... Baltimore MD 21220 410-686-5900 115
TF: 800-852-2525 ■ *Web:* www.guenschel.com

Help At Home Inc 1 N State St Ste 800........... Chicago IL 60602 312-762-0900 704-0022 363
TF: 800-404-3191 ■ *Web:* www.helpathome.com

Help Button, The 3109 W Market St............... Akron OH 44333 330-867-4357 809
Web: thehelpbutton.net

Help Foundation Inc
3622 Prospect Ave E........................ Cleveland OH 44115 216-432-4810 305
TF: 800-233-8611 ■ *Web:* www.helpfoundationinc.org

Help Me Computers LLC
903 Austin Hwy .... San Antonio TX 78209 210-822-8817 175
Web: www.helpmecomputers.com

HELP USA 115 E 13th St .... New York NY 10004 212-400-7000 400-7005 48-5
TF: 800-311-7999 ■ *Web:* www.helpusa.org

Helping Hand Nursing Service Inc
8305 S Saginaw St .... Grand Blanc MI 48439 810-606-8400 260
Web: hhnsinc.com

Helpjuice Inc 211 E Seventh St Ste 620 .... Austin TX 78701 888-230-3420 387
TF: 855-256-0808 ■ *Web:* helpjuice.com

Help-U-Sell Real Estate
240 N Washington Blvd .... Sarasota FL 34236 941-951-7707 652
Web: www.helpusell.com

Helvoet Pharma Inc
9012 Pennsauken Hwy .... Pennsauken NJ 08110 856-663-2202 663-2636 477
Web: www.datwyler.com

Helwig Carbon Products Inc
8900 W Tower Ave .... Milwaukee WI 53224 414-354-2411 354-2421 127
TF: 800-365-3113 ■ *Web:* www.helwigcarbon.com

Helzberg Diamonds
1825 Swift Ave .... North Kansas City MO 64116 816-842-7780 627-1301* 410
**Fax:* Sales ■ *TF:* 800-435-9237 ■ *Web:* www.helzberg.com

Hemacare Corp
15350 Sherman Way Ste 350................. Van Nuys CA 91406 818-226-1968 251-5300 89
TF: 877-310-0717 ■ *Web:* www.hemacare.com

Hemagen Diagnostics Inc
9033 Red Branch Rd........................ Columbia MD 21045 443-367-5500 997-7812* 231
OTC: HMGN ■ **Fax Area Code:* 410 ■ *TF:* 800-436-2436 ■ *Web:* www.hemagen.com

HemaSource Inc 4158 Nike Dr Ste B .... West Jordan UT 84088 801-280-5151 475
Web: www.hemasource.com

Hemco Industries Inc 2408 Karbach St.......... Houston TX 77092 713-681-2426 480
Web: www.hemcoind.com

Hemenway's Seafood Grille
121 S Main St............................ Providence RI 02903 401-351-8570 351-8594 671
TF: 888-759-5557 ■ *Web:* www.hemenwaysrestaurant.com

Hemet Bancorp 3715 Sunnyside Dr .... Riverside CA 92506 951-784-5771 70

Hemet Jacinto Valley Chamber of Commerce
615 N San Jacinto St .... Hemet CA 92543 951-658-3211 766-5013 139
Web: hsjvc.com

Hemet Public Library 300 E Latham Ave .... Hemet CA 92543 951-765-2440 434-3
Web: hemetpubliclibrary.org

Hemet, California 445 E Florida Ave .... Hemet CA 92543 951-765-2330 192
TF: 800-510-3304 ■ *Web:* www.cityofhemet.org

Hemingway Apparel Manufacturing Inc
60 Apparel Dr............................ Hemingway SC 29554 843-558-2525 157-6
Web: www.hemingwayapparel.com

Hemingway's Blue Water Cafe
1935 S Campbell .... Springfield MO 65898 417-891-5100 887-5204 671
Web: restaurants.basspro.com

Hemisphere 9300 Airport Blvd.................. Orlando FL 32827 407-825-1234 671
Web: www.hyatt.com

Hemispheres Restaurant & Bistro
108 Chestnut St .... Toronto ON M5G1R3 416-599-8000 977-9513 671
TF: 800-668-6600 ■ *Web:* www.metropolitan.com

Hemispherx Biopharma Inc
1617 JFK Blvd Ste 500.................... Philadelphia PA 19103 215-988-0080 85
NYSE: HEB ■ *Web:* www.hemispherx.net

Hemlock Bluffs Nature Preserve
2616 Kildaire Farm Rd .... Cary NC 27518 919-387-5980 50-5
TF: 800-827-1000 ■ *Web:* townofcary.org

Hemlock Public Schools District
PO Box 260 .... Hemlock MI 48626 989-642-5282 685
Web: www.hemlock.k12.mi.us

Hemlock Semiconductor Corp
12334 Geddes Rd.......................... Hemlock MI 48626 989-301-5000 696
Web: www.hscpoly.com

Hemmelgarn & Sons Inc
3763 Philothea Rd .... Coldwater OH 45828 419-678-2351 297-10

Hemmings Motor News 222 Main St............ Bennington VT 05201 802-442-3101 447-9631 457-3
TF: 800-227-4373 ■ *Web:* www.hemmings.com

HemoShear LLC
501 Locust Ave Ste 301 .... Charlottesville VA 22902 434-872-0196 872-0199 668
Web: www.hemoshear.com

Hempel (USA) Inc 600 Conroe Park N Dr .... Conroe TX 77303 936-523-6000 550
Web: www.hempel.com

Hemphill County 400 Main St................. Canadian TX 79014 806-323-6521 323-5260 338
Web: co.hemphill.tx.us

Hempstead & Company Inc
807 Haddon Ave.......................... Haddonfield NJ 08033 856-795-6026 463
TF: 800-686-8476 ■ *Web:* www.hempsteadco.com

Hempstead County 400 S Washington Hope .... Hope AR 71801 870-777-6164 338
Web: www.hempsteadcountyar.com

Hempstead Lake State Park
Lakeside Dr......................... West Hempstead NY 11552 516-766-1029 565
Web: parks.ny.gov/parks/31

Hempstead Public Library
115 Nichols Ct .... Hempstead NY 11550 516-481-6990 481-6719 434-3
Web: www.hempsteadlibrary.info

Hempt Bros Inc 205 Creek Rd................. Camp Hill PA 17011 717-737-3411 761-5019 188-4
TF: 800-999-1018 ■ *Web:* hemptbros.com

Hemstreet Development Co
16100 NW Cornell Rd Ste 100 .... Beaverton OR 97006 503-531-4000 531-4001 655
TF: 800-995-4063 ■ *Web:* www.hemstreet.com

Hencorp Inc 777 Brickell Ave Ste 1010 .... Miami FL 33131 305-373-9000 690
Web: www.hencorp.com

Hendee Enterprises Inc
9350 S Point Dr .... Houston TX 77054 713-796-2322 796-0494 361
Web: www.hendee.com

Henderson Area Chamber of Commerce
201 N Main St .... Henderson TX 75652 903-657-5528 657-9454 139
Web: www.hendersontx.com

Henderson Auctions
13340 Florida Blvd PO Box 336.............. Livingston LA 70754 225-686-2252 686-0647 51
TF: 800-334-7443 ■ *Web:* www.hendersonauctions.com

Henderson Beach State Park
17000 Emerald Coast Pkwy .... Destin FL 32541 850-837-7550 565
Web: www.floridastateparks.org

Henderson Chamber of Commerce
590 S Boulder Hwy........................ Henderson NV 89015 702-565-8951 565-3115 139
Web: www.hendersonchamber.com

Henderson Community College
2660 S Green St .... Henderson KY 42420 270-827-1867 831-9612* 162
**Fax:* Admissions ■ *TF:* 800-696-9958 ■ *Web:* henderson.kctcs.edu

Henderson Convention Ctr
200 S Water St .... Henderson NV 89015 702-267-2171 205
TF: 877-775-5252 ■ *Web:* www.visithenderson.com

Henderson Corp 575New Jersey 28.............. Raritan NJ 08869 908-685-1300 186

Henderson County
125 N Prairieville St Rm 101 .... Athens TX 75751 903-675-6140 675-6105 338
Web: henderson-county.com

Henderson County 20 N Main St .... Henderson KY 42420 270-826-3971 338
Web: www.hendersoncounty.ky.gov

Henderson County
1 Historic Courthouse Sq................ Hendersonville NC 28792 828-697-4808 692-9855 338
Web: www.hendersoncountync.org

Henderson County 17 Monroe Ave Ste 2 .... Lexington TN 38351 731-968-2856 968-6644 338
TF: 800-342-1003 ■ *Web:* hendersoncountytn.gov

Henderson County PO Box 308 .... Oquawka IL 61469 309-867-2911 338
Web: www.cyberdriveillinois.com

Henderson County Conservation Area
PO Box 118 .... Keithsburg IL 61442 309-374-2496 565
Web: dnr.illinois.gov/Lands/Landmgt/PARKS/R1/HENDERSO.HTM

Henderson County CW Murchison Memorial Library
121 S Prairieville .... Athens TX 75751 903-677-7295 434-3
Web: www.koha.org

Henderson County Public Library
301 N Washington St .... Hendersonville NC 28739 828-697-4725 434-3
Web: www.henderson.lib.nc.us

Henderson County Tourist Commission
101 N Water St Ste B .... Henderson KY 42420 270-826-3128 826-0234 206
TF: 800-648-3128 ■ *Web:* www.hendersonky.org

Henderson Glass Inc
715 S Blvd E......................... Rochester Hills MI 48307 800-694-0672 332
TF: 800-694-0672 ■ *Web:* www.hendersonglass.com

Henderson Hills Baptist Church
1200 E I 35 Frontage Rd...................... Edmond OK 73034 405-341-4639 48-20
TF: 877-901-4639 ■ *Web:* www.hhbc.com

Henderson House Museum
602 Deschutes Way .... Tumwater WA 98501 360-754-4217 520
Web: www.ci.tumwater.wa.us

Henderson Isd PO Box 728 .... Henderson TX 75653 903-655-5000 657-9271 685
Web: www.hendersonisd.org

Henderson Manufacturing Inc
1085 S Third St .... Manchester IA 52057 563-927-2828 927-2521 273
TF: 800-359-4970 ■ *Web:* www.henderson-mfg.com

Henderson Paddon & Associates Ltd
945 Third Ave E Ste 212................. Owen Sound ON N4K2K8 519-376-7612 376-8008 261

Henderson Properties Inc
919 Norland Rd .... Charlotte NC 28205 704-535-1122 652
Web: www.hendersonproperties.com

Henderson Sewing Machine Company Inc
Waits Dr Industrial Pk...................... Andalusia AL 36420 334-222-2451 358
TF: 800-824-5113 ■ *Web:* www.hendersonsewing.com

Henderson State University
1100 Henderson St......................... Arkadelphia AR 71999 870-230-5000 230-5066* 166
**Fax:* Admissions ■ *TF:* 800-228-7333 ■ *Web:* www.hsu.edu

Henderson Wheel & Warehouse Supply
1825 South 300 West.................. Salt Lake City UT 84115 801-486-2073 486-0353 61
TF: 800-748-5111 ■ *Web:* www.hendersonwheel.com

Henderson, Caverly, Pum & Charney LLP
12750 High Bluff Dr Ste 300................. San Diego CA 92130 858-755-3000 428
Web: www.hcesq.com

Henderson-Johnson Co Inc
918 Canal St.............................. Syracuse NY 13210 315-479-5561 479-5585 189-9
TF: 800-492-3434 ■ *Web:* www.hjcoinc.com

Henderson-Vance County Chamber of Commerce
414 S Garnett St.......................... Henderson NC 27536 252-438-8414 139
Web: www.hendersonvance.org

Hendersonville Area Chamber of Commerce
100 Country Dr Ste 104 .... Hendersonville TN 37075 615-824-2818 250-3637 139
Web: www.hendersonvillechamber.com

Hendersonville County Chamber of Commerce
204 Kanuga Rd .... Hendersonville NC 28739 828-692-1413 693-8802 139
TF: 800-758-8130 ■ *Web:* www.hendersoncountychamber.org

Hendersonville Public Library
140 Saundersville Rd .... Hendersonville TN 37075 615-824-0656 434-3

Hendlin Visual Communications Inc
129 N Second St Ste 101................ Minneapolis MN 55401 612-338-1663 514

Hendrick Automotive Group
6000 Monroe Rd Ste 100 .... Charlotte NC 28212 704-568-5550 57
Web: www.hendrickauto.com

Hendrick Buick GMC Cadillac
1151 W 104th St.......................... Kansas City MO 64114 888-202-4773 57
TF: 888-255-9362 ■ *Web:* www.hendrickcadillackansascity.com

Hendrick Health System 1900 Pine St .... Abilene TX 79601 325-670-2000 374-3
Web: www.hendrickhealth.org

Hendrick Hospice Care 1682 Hickory St......... Abilene TX 79601 325-677-8516 371
TF: 800-622-8516 ■ *Web:* www.hendrickhospice.org

	Phone	Fax	Class

Hendrick Hudson Free Library
185 Kings Ferry Rd Montrose NY 10548 914-739-5654 434-3
Web: www.westchesterlibraries.org

Hendrick Manufacturing Co
1 Seventh Ave Carbondale PA 18407 800-225-7373 282-1506* 488
**Fax Area Code:* 570 ■ **Fax:* Sales ■ *TF Cust Svc:* 800-225-7373 ■ *Web:* www.hendrickcorp.com/perforated

Hendrick Motorsports Museum
4400 Papa Joe Hendrick Blvd Charlotte NC 28262 877-467-4890 455-0346* 522
**Fax Area Code:* 704 ■ *TF:* 877-467-4890 ■ *Web:* www.hendrickmotorsports.com

Hendricks & Assoc Inc
190 W Huffaker Ln Ste 403 Reno NV 89511 775-674-6000 390
Web: hendricks-inc.com

Hendricks County 355 S Washington St Danville IN 46122 317-745-9231 338
Web: www.co.hendricks.in.us

Hendricks County Flyer
8109 Kingston St Ste 500 Avon IN 46123 317-272-5800 272-5887 532-4
TF: 800-359-3747 ■ *Web:* www.flyergroup.com

Hendricks Holding Company Inc
690 Third St Beloit WI 53511 608-362-8000 360-3
Web: hendricksholding.com

Hendricks Park & Gardens
Summit Ave and Skyline Blvd Eugene OR 97403 541-682-4800 97
Web: www.eugene-or.gov

Hendricks Power Co-op
86 N County Rd 500 E Avon IN 46123 317-745-5473 245
TF: 800-876-5473 ■ *Web:* www.hendrickspower.com

Hendricks Regional Health Danville
1000 E Main St Danville IN 46122 317-745-4451 374-3
TF: 800-800-5556 ■ *Web:* www.hendricks.org

Hendrickson International
800 S Frontage Rd Woodridge IL 60517 630-910-2800 910-2899 60
TF: 855-743-3733 ■ *Web:* www.hendrickson-intl.com

Hendrix Batting Co 2310 Surrett Dr High Point NC 27263 336-431-1181 361
Web: hendrixbatting.com

Hendrix College 1600 Washington Ave Conway AR 72032 501-329-6811 450-3843* 166
**Fax:* Admissions ■ *TF:* 800-277-9017 ■ *Web:* www.hendrix.edu

Hendrix Wire & Cable Inc
53 Old Wilton Rd Milford NH 03055 603-673-2040 673-1497 813
Web: www.hendrix-wc.com

Hendry County PO Box 1760 LaBelle FL 33975 863-675-5217 338
Web: www.hendryfla.net

Hendy Woods State Park
18599 Philo-Greenwood Rd Philo CA 95466 707-895-3141 565
Web: www.parks.ca.gov/default.asp?page_id=438

Hengehold Capital Management LLC
6116 Harrison Ave Cincinnati OH 45247 513-598-5120 401
TF: 877-598-5120 ■ *Web:* www.hengeholdcapital.com

Henggeler Packing Company Inc
6730 Elmore Rd Fruitland ID 83619 208-452-4212 315-3
Web: www.henggelerpacking.com

Henig Inc 4135 Carmichael Rd Montgomery AL 36106 334-277-7610 157-6
TF: 800-521-2037 ■ *Web:* www.henigfurs.com

Henke Manufacturing Corp
3070 Wilson Ave Leavenworth KS 66048 913-682-9000 190
Web: www.henkemfg.com

Henkel Corp 1 Henkel Way Rocky Hill CT 06067 860-571-5100 571-5465 3
TF Cust Svc: 800-243-4874 ■ *Web:* www.henkel.com

Henkel Harris Company Inc
2983 S Pleasant Valley Rd Winchester VA 22601 540-667-4900 667-8261 319-2
TF: 800-582-3111 ■ *Web:* www.henkelharris.com

Henley & Company LLC 1290 RXR Plaza Uniondale NY 11556 516-794-5520 690
Web: www.henleyandcompany.com

Henley Park Hotel
926 Massachusetts Ave NW Washington DC 20001 202-638-5200 379
TF: 800-222-8474 ■ *Web:* www.henleypark.com

Henlopen Hotel 511 N Boardwalk Rehoboth Beach DE 19971 302-227-2551 227-8147 379
TF: 800-441-8450 ■ *Web:* www.henlopenhotel.com

Henna Chevrolet Inc 8805 N Ih 35 Austin TX 78753 512-832-1888 57
Web: www.hennachevyaustin.com

Hennegan Co 7455 Empire Dr Florence KY 41042 859-282-3600 627
Web: www.hennegan.com

Henneman Engineering
1605 S State St Champaign IL 61820 217-359-1531 261
Web: henneman.com

Hennepin Canal Parkway State Park
16006 875 E St Sheffield IL 61361 815-454-2328 565
Web: www.dnr.illinois.gov/Parks/Pages/HennepinCanal.aspx

Hennepin County 300 S Sixth St Minneapolis MN 55487 612-348-3081 348-8701 338
TF: 800-772-1213 ■ *Web:* hennepin.us

Hennepin County Library (HCL)
12601 Ridgedale Dr Minnetonka MN 55305 612-543-8800 847-8600* 434-3
**Fax Area Code:* 952 ■ *Web:* www.hclib.org

Hennepin County Medical Ctr (HCMC)
701 Pk Ave Minneapolis MN 55415 612-873-3000 374-3
Web: www.hcmc.org

Hennepin History Museum
2303 Third Ave S Minneapolis MN 55404 612-870-1329 520
Web: www.hennepinhistory.org

Hennepin Technical College
9000 Brooklyn Blvd Brooklyn Park MN 55445 952-995-1300 488-2944* 800
**Fax Area Code:* 763 ■ *TF:* 800-345-4655 ■ *Web:* www.hennepintech.edu

Hennepin Theatre Trust
615 Hennepin Ave Ste 140 Minneapolis MN 55403 612-455-9500 455-9502 572
Web: hennepintheatretrust.org

Hennessee Group LLC
500 Fifth Ave 47th Fl New York NY 10110 212-857-4400 401
Web: www.hennesseegroup.com

Hennessy Construction Services Corp
2300 22nd St N Saint Petersburg FL 33713 727-821-3223 186
Web: www.hcsfl.com

Hennessy Industries Inc
1601 JP Hennesey Dr La Vergne TN 37086 855-876-3864 60
TF: 800-688-6359 ■ *Web:* www.hennessyind.com

Hennessy River View Ford
2200 US Hwy 30 Oswego IL 60543 630-897-8900 57
Web: www.riverviewford.com

Henning Construction Company Inc
PO Box 394 Johnston IA 50131 515-253-0943 253-0942 186
Web: www.henningcompanies.com

Henning Industrial Software Inc
102 First St Ste 211 Hudson OH 44236 330-650-4212 177
Web: henningsoftware.com

Henninger Media Services Inc
1320 N Courthouse Rd Arlington VA 22201 703-243-3444 243-5697 512
Web: www.henninger.com

Henninger's Tavern 1812 Bank St Baltimore MD 21231 410-342-2172 671
Web: www.henningerstavern.com

Hennings Super Market Inc
290 Main St Harleysville PA 19438 215-256-9533 345
Web: henningsmarket.com

Henningsen Foods Inc
14334 Industrial Rd Omaha NE 68144 402-330-2500 330-0875 619
TF: 800-226-0561 ■ *Web:* www.henningsenfoods.com

Hennis Care Ctr 1720 Cross St Dover OH 44622 330-364-8849 364-2128 450
Web: www.henniscarecentre.com

Henny Penny Corp 1219 US 35 W PO Box 60 Eaton OH 45320 937-456-8400 417-8402* 298
**Fax Area Code:* 800 ■ *TF:* 800-417-8417 ■ *Web:* www.hennypenny.com

Henri Bendel Inc 712 Fifth Ave New York NY 10019 212-247-1100 157-6
TF: 866-875-7975 ■ *Web:* lb.com

Henri's Food Products Company Inc
8622 N 87th St Milwaukee WI 53224 414-365-5720 296-19

Henricksen & Co
1101 W River Pkwy Ste 100 Minneapolis MN 55415 612-455-2200 877-3300 320
Web: www.henricksen.com

Henrico County 4301 E Parham Rd Henrico VA 23228 804-501-4000 501-5214 338
Web: henrico.us

Henrico County Public Library
1001 N Laburnum Ave Henrico VA 23223 804-501-1900 270-2982 434-3
Web: www.henricolibrary.org

Henrico Doctor's Hospital
1602 Skipwith Rd Richmond VA 23229 804-289-4500 374-3
Web: hcavirginia.com

Henricus Historical Park
Henricus Pk Rd Chester VA 23836 804-748-1613 520
TF: 800-514-3849 ■ *Web:* www.henricus.org

Henrietta Public Library
455 Calkins Rd Rochester NY 14623 585-359-7092 334-6369 434-3
Web: www.hpl.org

Henry & Peters PC
3310 S Broadway Ste 100 Tyler TX 75701 903-597-6311 2
Web: www.henrypeters.com

Henry A Bromelkamp & Co
106 E 24th St Minneapolis MN 55404 612-870-9087 180
TF: 877-767-6703 ■ *Web:* www.bromelkamp.com

Henry A Fox Sales Co
4494 36th St SE Grand Rapids MI 49512 616-949-1210 81-1
TF: 800-551-0777 ■ *Web:* henryfoxsales.com

Henry Art Gallery
University of Washington
15th Ave NE & NE 41st St Seattle WA 98195 206-543-2281 520
TF: 800-497-7997 ■ *Web:* www.henryart.org

Henry B Ball Co 5254 Dressler Rd NW Canton OH 44718 330-499-3000 410
Web: henrybball.com

Henry B Gonzalez Convention Ctr
200 E Market St San Antonio TX 78205 210-207-8500 223-1495 205
TF: 877-504-8895 ■ *Web:* www.sahbgcc.com

Henry B Plant Museum 401 W Kennedy Blvd Tampa FL 33606 813-254-1891 258-7272 520
TF: 800-975-3177 ■ *Web:* www.plantmuseum.com

Henry Brick Co Inc 3409 Water Ave Selma AL 36703 334-875-2600 150
TF: 800-218-3906 ■ *Web:* www.henrybrick.com

Henry C Smither Roofing Company Inc
6050 E 32nd St Indianapolis IN 46226 317-545-1304 546-4764 189-12
Web: www.smitherroofing.com

Henry Carlson Co
1205 W Russell St Sioux Falls SD 57104 605-336-2410 332-1314 685
Web: henrycarlson.com

Henry Co
909 N Sepulveda Blvd Ste 650 El Segundo CA 90245 310-955-9200 223-1285* 46
**Fax Area Code:* 866 ■ **Fax:* Cust Svc ■ *TF:* 800-598-7663 ■ *Web:* www.henry.com

Henry Community Health (HCM)
1000 N 16th St New Castle IN 47362 765-521-0890 521-1555 374-3
Web: www.hcmhcares.org

Henry County 101 Ct Sq Ste B Abbeville AL 36310 334-585-2753 338
Web: www.henrycountyal.com

Henry County 307 W Ctr St Cambridge IL 61238 309-937-3578 338
Web: www.henrycty.com

Henry County 100 W Franklin St Clinton MO 64735 660-885-7204 338
Web: henrycomo.com

Henry County PO Box 7 Collinsville VA 24078 276-634-4601 634-4781 338
Web: www.henrycountyva.gov/Collinsville-District.html

Henry County 140 Henry Pkwy McDonough GA 30253 770-954-2400 288-7616 338
TF: 800-955-7766 ■ *Web:* www.co.henry.ga.us

Henry County
100 E Washington St Mount Pleasant IA 52641 319-385-2632 385-4144 338
Web: www.henrycountyiowa.us

Henry County 1853 Oakwood Ave Napoleon OH 43545 419-592-4876 338
Web: www.henrycountyohio.com

Henry County 1215 Race St PO Box B New Castle IN 47362 765-529-6401 521-7046 338
Web: www.henryco.net

Henry County PO Box 202 New Castle KY 40050 502-845-5707 338
Web: www.henryweb.com

Henry County 101 W Washington St Paris TN 38242 731-642-5212 642-6531 338
Web: henrycountytn.org

Henry County Chamber of Commerce
1709 Hwy 20 W McDonough GA 30253 770-957-5786 957-8030 139
Web: www.henrycounty.com

Henry County Medical Ctr 301 Tyson Ave Paris TN 38242 731-642-1220 374-3
Web: www.hcmc-tn.org

Henry Cowell Redwoods State Park
c/o Santa Cruz District Office
303 Big Trees Park Rd Felton CA 95018 831-335-4598 565
Web: www.parks.ca.gov/default.asp?page_id=546

Henry Doorly Zoo 3701 S Tenth St Omaha NE 68107 402-733-8401 733-7868 823
Web: www.omahazoo.com

Henry Equestrian Insurance Brokers
28 Victoria St Aurora ON L4G1P9 905-727-1144 727-4986 391-1
TF: 800-565-4321 ■ *Web:* www.hep.ca

Phone | Fax | Class

Henry F Teichmann Inc
3009 Washington Rd .... McMurray PA 15317 724-941-9550 941-3479 318
Web: www.hft.com

Henry Ford Bi-County Hospital
13355 E Ten-Mile Rd .... Warren MI 48089 586-759-7300 374-3
Web: hospital-data.com

Henry Ford Centennial Library
16301 Michigan Ave......................... Dearborn MI 48126 313-943-2330 434-3
TF: 800-266-2278 ■ *Web:* dearbornlibrary.org

Henry Ford Community College
5101 Evergreen Rd......................... Dearborn MI 48128 313-845-9600 845-9891* 162
**Fax:* Admissions ■ *TF:* 800-585-4322 ■ *Web:* www.hfcc.edu

Henry Ford Health System 1 Ford Pl .... Detroit MI 48202 800-436-7936 874-6380* 353
**Fax Area Code:* 313 ■ *TF:* 800-436-7936 ■ *Web:* www.henryford.com

Henry Ford Health System
Department of Food and Nutrition Services
2799 W Grand Blvd .... Detroit MI 48202 313-916-1071 371
TF: 800-436-7936 ■ *Web:* www.henryford.com

Henry Ford Hospital 2799 W Grand Blvd.......... Detroit MI 48202 313-916-2600 374-3
TF: 800-999-4340 ■ *Web:* www.henryford.com

Henry Ford Macomb Hospital
15855 19-Mile Rd .... Clinton Township MI 48038 586-263-2300 374-3
Web: henryford.com/homepage_macomb.cfm?id=48346

Henry Ford Museum 20900 Oakwood Blvd ...... Dearborn MI 48124 313-271-1620 982-6225 520
TF: 800-835-5237 ■ *Web:* thehenryford.org

Henry Ford OptimEyes
655 W 13-Mile Rd .... Madison Heights MI 48071 248-588-9300 543
TF: 800-393-2273 ■ *Web:* henryford.com/homepage_optimeyes.cfm?id=51936

Henry Ford Wyandotte Hospital
2333 Biddle Ave .... Wyandotte MI 48192 734-246-6000 374-3
Web: henryford.com

Henry Glass & Co 49 W 37th St .... New York NY 10018 917-229-1080 532-3525* 745-1
**Fax Area Code:* 212 ■ *TF:* 800-294-9495 ■ *Web:* www.henryglassfabrics.com

Henry H Armstrong Associates Inc
1 Gateway Ctr 420 Ft Duquesne Blvd
Ste 1825................................ Pittsburgh PA 15222 412-471-1551 690
Web: www.henryarmstrong.com

Henry Horton State Resort Park
4358 Nashville Hwy .... Chapel Hill TN 37034 931-364-2222 565
Web: tnstateparks.com/parks/about/henry-horton

Henry J Kaiser Family Foundation
2400 Sand Hill Rd .... Menlo Park CA 94025 650-854-9400 854-4800 305
Web: www.kff.org

Henry Luce Foundation Inc
51 Madison Ave 30th Fl .... New York NY 10010 212-489-7700 581-9541 305
Web: www.hluce.org

Henry M. Jackson Foundation For the Advancement of Military Medicine
6720-A Rockledge Dr Ste 100 .... Bethesda MD 20817 240-694-2000 305
Web: www.hjf.org

Henry Margu Inc 540 Commerce Dr.............. Yeadon PA 19050 610-622-0515 348
TF: 800-345-8284 ■ *Web:* www.henrymargu.com

Henry Mayo Newhall Memorial Hospital
23845 McBean Pkwy .... Valencia CA 91355 661-253-8000 374-3
Web: www.henrymayo.com

Henry Morrison Flagler Museum
1 Whitehall Way .... Palm Beach FL 33480 561-655-2833 655-2826 520
Web: www.flaglermuseum.us

Henry Pratt Co 401 S Highland Ave .... Aurora IL 60506 630-844-4000 844-4124 790
TF: 877-436-7977 ■ *Web:* www.henrypratt.com

Henry Products Inc 302 S 23rd Ave............. Phoenix AZ 85009 602-253-3191 254-2325 191-1
TF: 800-525-5533 ■ *Web:* www.henryproducts.com

Henry Quentzel Plumbing Supply Co
379 Throop Ave .... Brooklyn NY 11221 718-455-6600 612
TF: 800-889-2294 ■ *Web:* www.quentzel.com

Henry Schein Inc 135 Duryea Rd .... Melville NY 11747 631-843-5500 843-5652 475
NASDAQ: HSIC ■ *TF:* 800-582-2702 ■ *Web:* www.henryschein.com

Henry Schmieder Arboretum
Delaware Valley College
700 E Butler Ave .... Doylestown PA 18901 215-489-2283 489-2404 97
Web: www.delval.edu

Henry Street Settlement 265 Henry St......... New York NY 10002 212-766-9200 363
Web: www.henrystreet.org

Henry Technologies 701 S Main St .... Chatham IL 62629 217-483-2406 483-2408 14
TF: 800-964-3679 ■ *Web:* www.henrytech.com

Henry Troemner LLC 201 Wolf Dr.............. Thorofare NJ 08086 856-686-1600 476
TF: 800-352-7705 ■ *Web:* www.troemner.com

Henry V Events 6360 NE ML K Jr Blvd .... Portland OR 97211 503-232-6666 184
Web: www.henryvevents.com

Henry Vilas Park Zoo
702 S Randall Ave.......................... Madison WI 53715 608-266-4732 823
Web: www.vilaszoo.org

Henry W. Coe State Park
c/o Monterey District Office 2211 Garden Rd ..... Monterey CA 93940 408-779-2728 565
Web: www.parks.ca.gov/default.asp?page_id=561

Henry Waldinger Memorial Library
60 Verona Pl............................ Valley Stream NY 11582 516-825-6422 434-3
Web: www.nassaulibrary.org/valleyst

Henry Whitfield State Museum
248 Old Whitfield St........................ Guilford CT 06437 203-453-2457 453-7544 520
Web: www.cultureandtourism.org

Henry Wurst Inc
1331 Saline St .... North Kansas City MO 64116 816-842-3113 627
TF: 800-577-7045 ■ *Web:* www.henrywurst.com

Henry's Foods Inc 104 Mckay Ave N .... Alexandria MN 56308 320-763-3194 297-8
Web: www.henrysfoods.com

Henry's Hi-life 301 W St John St.............. San Jose CA 95110 408-295-5414 671
Web: henryshilife.com

Henry's Smokehouse
240 Wade Hampton Blvd .... Greenville SC 29607 864-232-7774 232-7237 671
Web: www.henryssmokehouse.com

Henrys Lake State Park
3917 E 5100 N .... Island Park ID 83429 208-558-7532 565
Web: idahostateparks.reserveamerica.com

Henryville Correctional Facility
PO Box 148 .... Henryville IN 47126 812-294-4372 294-1523 213
TF: 800-451-6028 ■ *Web:* www.in.gov/idoc/2398.htm

Hensarling Jeb (Rep R - TX)
2228 Rayburn HOB....................... Washington DC 20515 202-225-3484 226-4888 342-2
Web: hensarling.house.gov

Phone | Fax | Class

Hensarling Jeb (Rep R - TX)
2228 Rayburn HOB....................... Washington DC 20515 202-225-3484 226-4888 342-2
Web: hensarling.house.gov

Henschen & Associates Inc
432 W Gypsy Ln...................... Bowling Green OH 43402 419-352-5454 177
Web: henschen.com

Hensel Phelps 420 Sixth Ave.................. Greeley CO 80631 970-352-6565 346-7252 186
Web: www.henselphelps.com

Hensley & Co 4201 N 45th Ave .... Phoenix AZ 85031 602-264-1635 81-1
Web: www.abwholesaler.com

Hensley Industries Inc
2108 Joe Field Rd........................... Dallas TX 75229 972-241-2321 241-0915* 190
**Fax:* Cust Svc ■ *TF:* 888-406-6262 ■ *Web:* www.hensleyind.com

Hensley, Elam & Associates LLC
163 E Main St Ste 401 .... Lexington KY 40507 859-389-8182 177
Web: www.hea.biz

Henson & Efron PA
220 S Sixth St Ste 1800................... Minneapolis MN 55402 612-339-2500 428
Web: www.hensonefron.com

Henson Robinson Zoo
1100 E Lake Dr.......................... Springfield IL 62712 217-585-1821 529-8748 823
Web: www.springfieldparks.org

Hentzen Coatings Inc 6937 W Mill Rd......... Milwaukee WI 53218 414-353-4200 353-0286 550
TF: 800-236-6589 ■ *Web:* www.hentzen.com

HEPA Corp 3071 E Coronado St............... Anaheim CA 92806 714-630-5700 18
Web: www.hepa.com

Hepaco Inc
2711 Burch Dr PO Box 26308 .... Charlotte NC 28269 704-598-9782 598-7823 693
TF: 800-888-7689 ■ *Web:* www.hepaco.com

Hepatitis Foundation International (HFI)
504 Blick Dr .... Silver Spring MD 20904 301-622-4200 48-17
TF: 800-891-0707 ■ *Web:* www.hepfi.org

Hepburnia Coal Co PO Box I................. Grampian PA 16838 814-236-0473 501

HeplerBroom LLC
211 N Broadway Ste 2700 .... St Louis MO 63102 314-241-6160 241-6116 445
Web: www.heplerbroom.com

Heppner Gazette Times
188 Willow St PO Box 337................... Heppner OR 97836 541-676-9228 532-3
Web: www.heppner.net

Her Interactive Inc
1150 114th Ave SE Ste 200 .... Bellevue WA 98004 425-460-8787 460-8788 178-6
TF Orders: 800-461-8787 ■ *Web:* www.herinteractive.com

Heraeus Holding 1 Summit Sq Ste 1........... Langhorne PA 19047 215-944-9000 944-9000 201
Web: www.heraeus-electro-nite.com

Heraeus Medical Components LLC
5030 Centerville Rd .... St Paul MN 55127 651-792-8500 718

Heraeus Shin-Etsu America Inc
4600 NW Pacific Rim Blvd .... Camas WA 98607 360-834-4004 253
Web: sehamerica.com

Herald & Review 601 E Williams St .... Decatur IL 62523 217-429-5151 421-6913 532-2
TF: 800-437-2533 ■ *Web:* www.herald-review.com

Herald Bulletin 1133 Jackson St.............. Anderson IN 46016 765-622-1212 640-4815 532-2
TF: 800-750-5049 ■ *Web:* www.heraldbulletin.com

Herald Democrat 603 S Sam Rayburn Fwy....... Sherman TX 75090 903-893-8181 868-1930 532-2
TF: 800-827-7183 ■ *Web:* www.heralddemocrat.com

Herald Democrat 331 W Woodard .... Denison TX 75020 903-465-7171 532-2
Web: www.heralddemocrat.com

Herald Journal 75 W 300 N..................... Logan UT 84321 435-752-2121 753-6642 532-2
TF: 800-275-0423 ■ *Web:* www.hjnews.com

Herald News 207 Pocasset St Ste 8............ Fall River MA 02722 973-569-7000 569-7268* 532-2
**Fax:* Edit ■ *Web:* www.northjersey.com

Herald Publishing Co PO Box 153............. Houston TX 77001 713-630-0391 630-0404 637-8
TF: 888-421-1866 ■ *Web:* www.jhvonline.com

Herald Times Reporter
902 Franklin St.......................... Manitowoc WI 54221 920-684-4433 532-2
TF: 800-783-7323 ■ *Web:* www.htrnews.com

Herald, The 102 Manatee Ave W .... Bradenton FL 34205 941-748-0411 745-7097 532-2
Web: www.bradenton.com

Herald, The 52 S Dock St...................... Sharon PA 16146 724-981-6100 981-5116 532-2
TF: 800-981-1692 ■ *Web:* www.sharonherald.com

Herald/Country Market
500 Brown Blvd .... Bourbonnais IL 60914 815-933-1131 933-3785 532-4
TF: 800-323-0794 ■ *Web:* www.bbherald.com

Herald-Dispatch 946 Fifth Ave .... Huntington WV 25701 304-526-4000 526-2857 532-2
TF: 800-444-2446 ■ *Web:* www.herald-dispatch.com

Herald-Mail Co, The
100 Summit Ave PO Box 439 .... Hagerstown MD 21741 301-733-5131 714-0245 637-8
TF: 800-626-6397 ■ *Web:* www.heraldmailmedia.com

Herald-Palladium
3450 Hollywood Rd .... Saint Joseph MI 49085 269-429-2400 429-4398 532-2
TF: 800-356-4262 ■ *Web:* www.heraldpalladium.com

Herald-Republican 45 S Public Sq.............. Angola IN 46703 260-665-3117 532-2
Web: www.kpcnews.com

Herald-Standard 8 E Church St.............. Uniontown PA 15401 724-439-7500 439-7559 532-2
TF: 800-342-8254 ■ *Web:* www.heraldstandard.com

Herald-Star 401 Herald Sq.................. Steubenville OH 43952 740-283-4711 284-7355 637-8
TF: 800-526-7987 ■ *Web:* heraldstaronline.com

Herald-Sun, The 2828 Pickett Rd .... Durham NC 27705 919-419-6500 532-2
TF: 866-348-6479 ■ *Web:* www.heraldsun.com

Herald-Times Inc PO Box 909 .... Bloomington IN 47402 812-332-4401 331-4285 637-8
TF: 800-422-0070 ■ *Web:* www.heraldtimesonline.com

Herb Chambers 259 McGrath Hwy .... Somerville MA 02145 617-666-8333 57
Web: www.herbchambers.com

Herb Chambers I 95 Inc 107 Andover St......... Danvers MA 01923 877-907-1965 57
TF: 877-907-1965 ■ *Web:* www.herbchamberschevrolet.com

Herb Easley Motors Inc
1125 Central Fwy .... Wichita Falls TX 76306 940-723-6631 57
Web: www.herbeasley.com

Herb Gordon Nissan
3131 Automobile Blvd .... Silver Spring MD 20904 877-345-9869 57
TF: 877-345-9869 ■ *Web:* www.herbgordonnissan.com

Herb Growing & Marketing Network (HGMN)
PO Box 245 .... Silver Spring PA 17575 717-393-3295 393-9261 48-2
TF: 800-753-9199 ■ *Web:* www.herbworld.com

Herb Pharm LLC 20260 Williams Hwy.......... Williams OR 97544 541-846-6262 345
Web: www.herb-pharm.com

Phone Fax Class

Herb Redl Inc
80 Washington St Ste 100 ... Poughkeepsie NY 12601 845-471-3388 471-3851 655
TF: 800-678-5581 ■ *Web:* www.hredlproperties.com

Herb Research Foundation (HRF)
4140 15th St ... Boulder CO 80304 303-449-2265 449-7849 48-17
TF: 800-748-2617 ■ *Web:* www.herbs.org

Herbal Magic Inc 1867 Yonge St Ste 700 ... Toronto ON M4S1Y5 416-487-7009 194
Web: www.herbalmagic.ca

Herbalist, The 2106 NE 65th St ... Seattle WA 98115 206-523-2600 522-3253 799
TF: 800-694-3727 ■ *Web:* store.theherbalist.com

Herbein & Company Inc
2763 Century Blvd ... Reading PA 19610 610-378-1175 2
Web: herbein.com

Herber Aircraft Service Inc
1401 E Franklin Ave ... El Segundo CA 90245 310-322-9575 480
TF: 800-544-0050 ■ *Web:* www.herberaircraft.com

Herberger Theater Ctr 222 E Monroe St ... Phoenix AZ 85004 602-254-7399 258-9521 572
Web: www.herbergertheater.org

Herbert F Johnson Museum of Art
114 Central Ave ... Ithaca NY 14853 607-255-6464 520
Web: www.museum.cornell.edu

Herbert Gary Richard (R)
Utah State Capitoly Ste 200 ... Salt Lake City UT 84114 801-538-1000 538-1557 343
Web: www.utah.gov/governor

Herbert H & Grace A Dow Foundation
1018 W Main St ... Midland MI 48640 989-631-3699 631-0675 305
Web: www.hhdowfoundation.org

Herbert H. Landy Insurance Agency Inc
75 Second Ave Ste 410 ... Needham MA 02494 800-336-5422 449-7908* 390
**Fax Area Code:* 781 ■ *TF:* 800-336-5422 ■ *Web:* www.landy.com

Herbert Hoover National Historic Site
110 Parkside Dr PO Box 607 ... West Branch IA 52358 319-643-2541 643-7864 564
Web: www.nps.gov/hoho

Herbert Hoover Presidential Library & Museum
210 Parkside Dr ... West Branch IA 52358 319-643-5301 643-6045 434-2
TF: 800-234-8861 ■ *Web:* www.hoover.archives.gov

Herbert K Horita Realty Inc
98-150 Kaonohi St Ste B128 ... Aiea HI 96701 808-487-1561 652
Web: www.hicentral.com

Herbert Mines Assoc
600 Lexington Ave 2nd Fl ... New York NY 10022 212-355-0909 266
Web: www.herbertmines.com

Herbert Rowland & Grubic Inc (HRG)
369 E Pk Dr ... Harrisburg PA 17111 717-564-1121 564-1158 261
Web: www.hrg-inc.com

Herbert Yentis & Company Inc
7300 City Line Ave ... Philadelphia PA 19151 215-878-7300 652
Web: yentis.com

Herbfarm, The 14590 NE 145th St ... Woodinville WA 98072 425-485-5300 424-2925 671
Web: www.theherbfarm.com

Herbsaint Bar & Restaurant
701 St Charles Ave ... New Orleans LA 70130 504-524-4114 671
Web: herbsaint.com

Hercon Laboratories Corp
101 Sinking Springs Ln ... Emigsville PA 17318 717-764-1191 503
Web: www.herconlabs.com

Hercules Chemical Company Inc
111 S St ... Passaic NJ 07055 973-778-5000 3
TF: 800-221-9330 ■ *Web:* www.oatey.com

Hercules Engine Components Co
2770 S Erie St ... Massillon OH 44646 330-830-2498 262

Hercules Industries Inc
1310 W Evans Ave ... Denver CO 80223 303-937-1000 937-0903 612
TF: 800-356-5350 ■ *Web:* www.herculesindustries.com

Hercules Machine Tool & Die Co
13920 E Ten-Mile Rd ... Warren MI 48089 586-778-4120 778-0070 757
Web: www.hmtd.com

Hercules Manufacturing Co
800 Bob Posey St ... Henderson KY 42420 270-826-9501 826-0439 516
TF: 800-633-3031 ■ *Web:* www.herculesvanbodies.com

Hercules Offshore Inc
9 Greenway Plaza Ste 2200 ... Houston TX 77046 713-350-5100 350-5105 540
NASDAQ: HERO ■ *TF:* 888-647-1715 ■ *Web:* www.herculesoffshore.com

Hercules Technology Growth Capital Inc
400 Hamilton Ave Ste 310 ... Palo Alto CA 94301 650-289-3060 473-9194 792
NYSE: HTGC ■ *Web:* htgc.com

Hercules Tire & Rubber Co
16380 E US Rt 224 - 200 ... Findlay OH 45840 419-425-6400 425-6404 754
TF: 800-677-9535 ■ *Web:* www.herculestire.com

Hercules Tire Sales Inc 10130 E 51st St ... Tulsa OK 74146 918-627-7353 754
Web: www.herculestiresales.com

Herc-U-Lift Inc 5655 Hwy 12 W ... Maple Plain MN 55359 763-479-2501 479-2296 385
TF: 800-362-3500 ■ *Web:* www.herculift.com

Herculite Products Inc
105 E Sinking Springs Ln ... Emigsville PA 17318 717-764-1192 764-5211* 745-2
**Fax:* Acctg ■ *TF Cust Svc:* 800-772-0036 ■ *Web:* www.herculite.com

Herd Company Cattle Co
83973 489th Ave ... Bartlett NE 68622 402-482-5931 10-1

Herdrich Petroleum 210 E US 52 ... Rushville IN 46173 765-932-3224 932-4622 579
Web: herdrich.com

Hereditary Disease Foundation (HDF)
3960 Broadway 6th Fl ... New York NY 10032 212-928-2121 928-2172 48-17
Web: www.hdfoundation.org

Hereford Independent School District
601 N 25 Mile Ave ... Hereford TX 79045 806-363-7600 363-7699 685
Web: www.herefordisd.net

Heritage Auctions Inc
3500 Maple Ave 17th Fl ... Dallas TX 75219 214-528-3500 626
Web: www.ha.com

Heritage Bags 1648 Diplomat Dr ... Carrollton TX 75006 800-527-2247 66
TF: 800-527-2247 ■ *Web:* www.heritage-bag.com

Heritage Bank 101 N Main St ... Jonesboro GA 30236 770-478-8881 360-2
TF: 866-971-0106 ■ *Web:* www.heritagebank.com

Heritage Bank 201 Fifth Ave SW ... Olympia WA 98501 360-943-1500 360-2
TF: 800-455-6126 ■ *Web:* www.heritagebanknw.com/home/home

Heritage Bible College
1747 Bud Hawkins Rd PO Box 1628 ... Dunn NC 28334 910-892-3178 892-1809 166
TF: 800-297-6351 ■ *Web:* www.heritagebiblecollege.edu

Heritage Canada Foundation
5 Blackburn Ave ... Ottawa ON K1N8A2 613-237-1066 48-13
TF: 866-964-1066 ■ *Web:* www.nationaltrustcanada.ca

Heritage Christian University
3625 Helton Dr PO Box HCU ... Florence AL 35630 256-766-6610 161
TF: 800-367-3565 ■ *Web:* www.hcu.edu

Heritage Co, The
2402 Wildwood Ave Ste 500 ... North Little Rock AR 72120 501-835-5000 5
TF: 800-643-8822 ■ *Web:* www.theheritagecompany.com

Heritage College & Seminary
175 Holiday Inn Dr ... Cambridge ON N3C3T2 519-651-2869 651-2870 785
TF: 800-465-1961 ■ *Web:* heritagecambridge.com

Heritage Commerce Corp
150 Almaden Blvd ... San Jose CA 95113 408-947-6900 947-6910 360-2
NASDAQ: HTBK ■ *TF:* 800-468-9716 ■ *Web:* www.heritagecommercecorp.com

Heritage Corridor Convention & Visitors Bureau
339 W Jefferson St ... Joliet IL 60435 815-727-2323 727-2324 206
TF: 800-926-2262 ■ *Web:* www.heritagecorridorcvb.com

Heritage Ctr 1201 W Buena Vista Rd ... Evansville IN 47710 812-429-0700 429-1849 450
TF: 800-704-0700 ■ *Web:* www.holidayhealthcare.com

Heritage Dairy Stores Inc
376 Jessup Rd ... Thorofare NJ 08086 856-845-2855 845-8392 204
Web: www.heritages.com

Heritage Enterprises Inc
115 W Jefferson St ... Bloomington IL 61702 309-828-4361 450
Web: www.heritageofcare.com

Heritage Environmental Services Inc
7901 W Morris St ... Indianapolis IN 46231 317-243-0811 804
Web: www.heritage-enviro.com

Heritage Equipment Co
9000 Heritage Dr ... Plain City OH 43064 614-873-3941 358
TF: 800-282-7961 ■ *Web:* www.heritage-equipment.com

Heritage Farmstead Museum
1900 W 15th St ... Plano TX 75075 972-881-0140 422-6481 520
Web: heritagefarmstead.org

Heritage Financial Consultants LLC
307 International Cir Ste 390 ... Hunt Valley MD 21030 410-785-0033 194
Web: heritageconsultants.com

Heritage Financial Corp
201 Fifth Ave SW ... Olympia WA 98501 360-943-1500 360-2
NASDAQ: HFWA ■ *TF:* 800-962-4284 ■ *Web:* www.hf-wa.com

Heritage Foods LLC
4002 Westminster Ave ... Santa Ana CA 92703 714-775-5000 775-7677 296-27
TF Orders: 800-321-5960 ■ *Web:* stremicksheritagefoods.com

Heritage Ford Inc 2100 Sisk Rd ... Modesto CA 95350 209-529-5110 57
Web: www.heritagefordmodesto.com

Heritage Foundation
214 Massachusetts Ave NE ... Washington DC 20002 202-546-4400 634
TF: 800-546-2843 ■ *Web:* www.heritage.org

Heritage Gas Ltd
238 Brownlow Ave Ste 200 ... Dartmouth NS B3B1Y2 902-466-2003 580
Web: www.heritagegas.com

Heritage Global Solutions Inc
230 N Maryland Ave ... Glendale CA 91206 818-547-4474 196
TF: 800-915-4474 ■ *Web:* www.heritageglobalsolutions.com

Heritage Group Inc 1101 12th St ... Aurora NE 68818 402-694-3136 70
TF: 888-463-6611 ■ *Web:* www.bankonheritage.com

Heritage Hill Historic District
126 College Ave SE ... Grand Rapids MI 49503 616-459-8950 459-2409 50-3
TF: 800-968-5121 ■ *Web:* www.heritagehillweb.org

Heritage Hill State Historical Park
2640 S Webster Ave ... Green Bay WI 54301 920-448-5150 565
TF: 800-721-5150 ■ *Web:* heritagehillgb.org

Heritage Hills Golf Resort & Conference Ctr
2700 Mt Rose Ave ... York PA 17402 717-755-0123 669
TF: 877-782-9752 ■ *Web:* www.heritagehillsresort.com

Heritage Hospice
120 Enterprise Dr PO Box 1213 ... Danville KY 40423 859-236-2425 371
TF: 800-203-6633 ■ *Web:* www.heritagehospice.com

Heritage Hospital 111 Hospital Dr ... Tarboro NC 27886 252-641-7700 374-3
Web: www.vidanthealth.com

Heritage Hotel 522 Heritage Rd ... Southbury CT 06488 203-264-8200 377
Web: www.heritagesouthbury.com

Heritage Hotels & Resorts Inc
201 Third St NW Ste 1500 ... Albuquerque NM 87102 505-836-6700 379
Web: www.heritagehotelsandresorts.com

Heritage India
2400 Wisconsin Ave NW ... Washington DC 20007 202-333-3120 671
Web: heritageindiausa.com

Heritage Inn, The 34521 Postal Ln ... Lewes DE 19958 800-669-9399 379
TF: 800-669-9399 ■ *Web:* www.rehobothheritage.com

Heritage Insurance Managers Inc
922 Isom Rd ... San Antonio TX 78216 210-829-7467 391-5

Heritage Lace Inc 309 S St ... Pella IA 50219 641-628-4949 361
TF: 800-354-0668 ■ *Web:* www.heritagelace.com

Heritage Log Homes Inc
119 W Dumplin Valley Rd ... Kodak TN 37764 865-932-0202 106
Web: thegreatsmokeymountainsparkway.com

Heritage Mechanical Services Inc
305 Suburban Ave ... Deer Park NY 11729 516-558-2000 667-8613* 189-10
**Fax Area Code:* 631 ■ *TF:* 800-734-0384 ■ *Web:* www.heritagemech.com

Heritage Mfg Inc
16175 NW 49th Ave ... Miami Lakes FL 33014 305-685-5966 687-6721 284
Web: www.heritagemfg.com

Heritage Mint Ltd PO Box 13750 ... Scottsdale AZ 85267 480-860-1300 730
TF: 888-860-6245 ■ *Web:* www.heritagemint.com

Heritage Museum of Orange County, The
3101 W Harvard St ... Santa Ana CA 92704 714-540-0404 520
Web: heritagemuseumoc.org

Heritage Newspapers Inc
1 Heritage Pl Ste 100 ... Southgate MI 48195 734-246-0800 637-8
Web: www.heritagenews.com

Heritage of the Americas Museum
12110 Cuyamaca College Dr W ... El Cajon CA 92019 619-670-5194 520
Web: www.heritageoftheamericasmuseum.com

Heritage Office Furnishings
1588 Rand Ave ... Vancouver BC V6P3G2 604-688-2381 320
TF: 888-775-4555 ■ *Web:* www.heritageoffice.com

				Phone	Fax	Class
Heritage Optical Center Inc 19010 Livernois Ave *Web:* www.heritageoptical.com	Detroit	MI	48221	313-863-9581		543
Heritage Petroleum LLC 516 N Seventh Ave *Web:* www.heritageoil.com	Evansville	IN	47719	812-422-3251		579
Heritage Place Inc 2829 S MacArthur *TF:* 888-343-9831 ■ *Web:* www.heritageplace.com	Oklahoma City	OK	73128	405-682-4551	686-1267	51
Heritage Plastics Inc 1002 Hunt St *TF:* 800-245-4623 ■ *Web:* www.heritage-plastics.com	Picayune	MS	39466	601-798-8663		605-2
Heritage Products Inc 2000 Smith Ave *Web:* www.heritageproductsinc.com	Crawfordsville	IN	47933	765-364-9002		489
Heritage Rehabilitation Ctr 21414 S Vermont Ave *Web:* heritagerehabcenter.com	Torrance	CA	90502	310-320-8714	320-1809	450
Heritage Solar 5035 surfside dr	San diego	CA	92154	619-200-9073		138
Heritage Square Museum 3800 Homer St *TF:* 800-375-1771 ■ *Web:* www.heritagesquare.org	Los Angeles	CA	90031	323-225-2700	225-2725	520
Heritage Summit HealthCare of Florida Inc PO Box 2928 *TF:* 800-282-7644 ■ *Web:* www.summitholdings.com	Lakeland	FL	33806	863-665-6629	665-5177	391-3
Heritage University 3240 Ft Rd *Fax: Admissions ■ *TF:* 888-272-6190 ■ *Web:* www.heritage.edu	Toppenish	WA	98948	509-865-8500	865-8659*	166
Heritage Valley Health System 1000 Dutch Ridge Rd *TF:* 877-771-4847 ■ *Web:* www.heritagevalley.org	Beaver	PA	15009	724-728-7000		374-3
Heritage Village Museum 11450 Lebanon Pk *TF:* 800-944-4773 ■ *Web:* www.heritagevillagecincinnati.org	Cincinnati	OH	45241	513-563-9484	563-0914	520
Heritage-Crystal Clean Inc 2175 Pt Blvd Ste 375 *TF:* 877-938-7948 ■ *Web:* www.crystal-clean.com	Elgin	IL	60123	847-836-5670		151
Heritagenergy Inc 625 Sawkill Rd *TF:* 800-451-3835 ■ *Web:* www.heritagenergy.com	Kingston	NY	12401	845-336-2000		316
Herker Industries Inc N57 W13760 Carmen Ave *Web:* www.herker.com	Menomonee Falls	WI	53051	262-781-8270		621
Herkimer County 109 Mary St Ste 1111 *Web:* www.herkimercounty.org	Herkimer	NY	13350	315-867-1129	867-1349	338
Herkimer County Chamber of Commerce 28 W Main St *TF:* 877-984-4636 ■ *Web:* www.herkimercountychamber.com	Mohawk	NY	13407	315-866-7820	866-7833	139
Herkimer County Community College 100 Reservoir Rd *Fax: Admissions ■ *TF:* 844-464-4375 ■ *Web:* www.herkimer.edu	Herkimer	NY	13350	315-866-0300	866-0062*	162
Herkimer Home State Historic Site 200 SR- 169 *Web:* parks.ny.gov/historic-sites/14/details.aspx	Little Falls	NY	13365	315-823-0398		565
Herlache Enterprises 6417 W 87th St Ste 3 *TF:* 888-446-8854 ■ *Web:* telassist.com	Oak Lawn	IL	60453	888-446-8854		226
Herman & Kittle Properties Inc 500 E 96th St Ste 300 *Web:* hermankittle.com	Indianapolis	IN	46240	317-846-3111		652
Herman Davis State Park Corner of Ark 18 Baltimore St *TF:* 888-287-2757 ■ *Web:* www.arkansasstateparks.com/hermandavis	Manila	AR	72201	888-287-2757		565
Herman Goldner Co Inc 7777 Brewster Ave *TF:* 800-355-5997 ■ *Web:* www.goldner.com	Philadelphia	PA	19153	215-365-5400	492-6486	189-10
Herman H Sticht Company Inc 45 Main St Ste 701 *TF:* 800-221-3203 ■ *Web:* www.stichtco.com	Brooklyn	NY	11201	718-852-7602	852-7915	472
Herman Herman Katz & Cotlar LLP 820 Okeefe Ave *TF:* 844-943-7626 ■ *Web:* hhklawfirm.com	New Orleans	LA	70113	504-581-4892		428
Herman Miller Inc 855 E Main Ave *NASDAQ: MLHR* ■ *TF:* 888-443-4357 ■ *Web:* www.hermanmiller.com	Zeeland	MI	49464	616-654-3000		319-1
Herman Seekamp Inc 1120 W Fullerton Ave *TF:* 888-874-6814 ■ *Web:* www.clydesdonuts.com	Addison	IL	60101	888-874-6814		296-1
Herman Strauss Inc 35th & McColloch St *Web:* www.strauss-ind.com	Wheeling	WV	26003	304-748-0699		791
Herman Weissker Inc 1645 Brown Ave *Web:* www.hermanweissker.com	Riverside	CA	92509	951-826-8800		194
Herman's Inc 2820 Blackhawk Rd *TF:* 800-447-1295 ■ *Web:* hermansinc.com	Rock Island	IL	61201	309-788-9568	786 8296	156
Hermann Companies Inc 7701 Forsyth Blvd Ste 1000 *Web:* www.hermanncompanies.com	St. Louis	MO	63105	314-863-9200		601
Hermann Oak Leather Co 4050 N First St *TF:* 800-325-7950 ■ *Web:* www.hermannoakleather.com	Saint Louis	MO	63147	314-421-1173	421-6152	432
Hermann Sons Life 515 S Saint Marys St PO Box 1941 *TF:* 800-234-4124 ■ *Web:* www.hermannsonslife.org	San Antonio	TX	78205	210-226-9261	892-0299	707
Hermanos Cocina Mexicana 11 Hills Ave *TF:* 800-360-4839 ■ *Web:* www.hermanosmexican.com	Concord	NH	03301	603-224-5669		671
Hermary Opto Electronics Inc 104-1500 Hartley Ave *Web:* www.hermarymachinevision.com	Coquitlam	BC	V3K7A1	604-517-4625		256
Hermell Products Inc 9 Britton Dr *TF:* 800-233-2342 ■ *Web:* www.hermell.com	Bloomfield	CT	06002	860-242-6550		477
Hermes Abrasives Ltd 524 Viking Dr *TF:* 800-464-8314 ■ *Web:* www.hermesabrasives.com	Virginia Beach	VA	23452	757-486-6623	431-2370	1
Hermes Trading Company Inc 830 N Cage Blvd *TF:* 844-437-6371 ■ *Web:* www.hermes-music.com	Pharr	TX	78577	844-437-6371		526
Hermiston Chamber of Commerce 415 S Hwy 395 PO Box 185 *Web:* www.hermistonchamber.com	Hermiston	OR	97838	541-567-6151	564-9109	139
Hermitage Foundation Museum 7637 N Shore Rd *Web:* www.thehermitagemuseum.org	Norfolk	VA	23505	757-423-2052	423-2410	520
Hermitage Hotel 231 Sixth Ave N *TF:* 888-888-9414 ■ *Web:* www.thehermitagehotel.com	Nashville	TN	37219	615-244-3121	254-6909	379
Hermitage State Historic Site, The 335 N Franklin Tpke *Web:* www.thehermitage.org	Ho-Ho-Kus	NJ	07423	201-445-8311		565
Hermitage The (Home of Andrew Jackson) 4580 Rachel's Ln *Web:* www.thehermitage.com	Hermitage	TN	37076	615-889-2941	889-9289	520
Hermitage, The 1600 Westwood Ave *Web:* www.hermitage-vumh.com	Richmond	VA	23227	804-474-1800		672
Hermosa Inn 5532 N Palo Cristi Rd *TF:* 800-241-1210 ■ *Web:* www.hermosainn.com	Paradise Valley	AZ	85253	602-955-8614		379
Hernandez Consulting LLC 3221 Tulane Ave *Web:* www.hernandezconsulting.com	New Orleans	LA	70119	504-305-8571		196
Hernandez Cos Inc 3734 E Anne St *Web:* www.hernandezcompanies.com	Phoenix	AZ	85040	602-438-7825		187
Hernandez Office Solution 119 N 17th St *Web:* www.hernandezsupply.com	Nederland	TX	77627	409-724-0135		321
Hernando County 16110 Aviation Loop Dr *TF:* 800-601-4580 ■ *Web:* www.co.hernando.fl.us	Brooksville	FL	34604	352-754-4000	754-4477	338
Hernando County Public Library System 238 Howell Ave *Web:* hernandocountylibrary.us	Brooksville	FL	34601	352-754-4043	754-4044	434-3
Hernando Today 15299 Cortez Blvd *Web:* www.hernandotoday.com	Brooksville	FL	34613	352-544-5200	799-5246	532-4
Hernco Fabrication & Service 2131 Commerce Dr *Web:* herncoinc.com	Midland	TX	79703	432-522-1444		538
Herndon Plant Oakley Ltd 800 N Shoreline Blvd Ste 2200 South *TF:* 800-888-4894 ■ *Web:* www.hpo.com	Corpus Christi	TX	78401	361-888-7611	888-9342	401
HERO Entertainment Marketing Inc 4590 Ish Dr Ste 140 *TF:* 800-562-1231 ■ *Web:* www.heropp.com	Simi Valley	CA	93063	805-527-2000		5
Hero Systems Inc. 7327 SW Barnes Rd Ste 718 *Web:* www.bigtownhero.com	Portland	OR	97225	503-228-4376	228-8778	670
Heroix Corp 165 Bay State Dr *TF:* 800-229-6500 ■ *Web:* www.heroix.com	Braintree	MA	02184	781-848-1701	843-3472	178-12
Herold & Sager, Attorneys at Law 550 Second St Ste 200 *Web:* www.heroldsagerlaw.com	Encinitas	CA	92024	760-487-1047		428
Herold Precision Metals LLC 1370 Hammond Rd White Bear Township *Web:* www.heroldprecision.com	Saint Paul	MN	55110	651-490-5550		697
Herold's Salads Inc 17512 Miles Ave *TF:* 800-427-2523 ■ *Web:* www.heroldssalads.com	Cleveland	OH	44128	216-991-7500		296-33
Heron Point of Chestertown 501 E Campus Ave *TF:* 800-327-9138 ■ *Web:* www.actsretirement.org	Chestertown	MD	21620	410-778-7300		672
Heron Systems Inc 20945 Great Mills Rd Ste 201 *Web:* www.heronsystems.com	Lexington Park	MD	20653	301-866-0330		743
Heron Therapeutics Inc 123 Saginaw Dr *OTC: HRTX* ■ *Web:* www.herontx.com	Redwood City	CA	94063	650-366-2626		582
HEROweb Marketing and Design Inc 1976 Garden Ave *TF:* 888-257-2567 ■ *Web:* www.hero-web.com	Eugene	OR	97403	541-746-6418		5
Herpes Resource Center, The (HRC) PO Box 13827 *TF:* 877-478-5868	Research Triangle Park	NC	27709	919-361-8400	361-8425	48-17
Herr Foods Inc 20 Herr Dr PO Box 300 *TF:* 800-344-3777 ■ *Web:* www.herrs.com	Nottingham	PA	19362	610-932-9330	932-1190	296-35
Herr Industrial Inc 610 E Oregon Rd *Web:* www.herrindustrial.com	Lititz	PA	17543	717-569-6619		697
Herr Tavern & Public House 900 Chambersburg Rd *TF:* 800-362-9849 ■ *Web:* www.innatherrridge.com	Gettysburg	PA	17325	717-334-4332		671
Herrera Beutler Jaime (Rep R - WA) 1170 Longworth Bldg *Web:* herrerabeutler.house.gov	Washington	DC	20515	202-225-3536	225-3478	342-2
Herrero Brothers Inc 2100 Oakdale Ave *Web:* www.herrero.com	San Francisco	CA	94124	415-824-7675		186
Herrick & White Ltd 3 Flat St *Web:* herrick-white.com	Cumberland	RI	02864	401-658-0440		499
Herrick Corp 3003 E Hammer Ln *Web:* www.herricksteel.com	Stockton	CA	95212	209-956-4751		480
Herrick Feinstein LLP 2 Park Ave *TF:* 800-926-7926 ■ *Web:* www.herrick.com	New York	NY	10016	212-592-1400		428
Herring Impact Group LLC, The 12977 N Outer 40 Dr Ste 300 *TF:* 800-420-2420 ■ *Web:* www.impactgrouph.com	St. Louis	MO	63141	314-453-9002		260
Herrington Manor State Park 222 Herrington Ln *Web:* dnr2.maryland.gov	Oakland	MD	21550	301-334-9180		565
Herrling Clark Hartzheim & Siddall Ltd 800 N Lynndale Dr *Web:* www.herrlingclark.com	Appleton	WI	54914	920-739-7366		445
Herrman & Goetz Inc 225 S Lafayette Blvd	South Bend	IN	46601	574-282-2596		610
Herrman Lumber Co 1917 S State Hwy N *Web:* www.herrmanlumber.com	Springfield	MO	65802	417-862-3737		364
Herrod Technology Inc Po Box 152495 *Web:* herrodtech.com	Arlington	TX	76015	214-202-0999		180
Herrschners Inc 2800 Hoover Rd *TF:* 800-713-1239 ■ *Web:* www.herrschners.com	Stevens Point	WI	54481	715-341-8686	341-2250	258
Herr-Voss Corp 130 Main St *Web:* www.herr-voss.com	Callery	PA	16024	724-538-3180		295
HERS (Hysterectomy Educational Resources & Services Foundation) 422 Bryn Mawr Ave *TF:* 888-750-4377 ■ *Web:* www.hersfoundation.com	Bala Cynwyd	PA	19004	610-667-7757	667-8096	48-17

	Phone	Fax	Class
Hersam Acorn Newspapers 16 Bailey Ave .... Ridgefield CT 06877 *TF:* 800-372-2790 ■ *Web:* hersamacorn.com	203-438-6544		637-8
Herschel-Adams Inc 1301 N 14th St .... Indianola IA 50125 *TF:* 800-247-2167 ■ *Web:* www.alamo-group.com	800-247-2167		273
Herschend Family Entertainment Corp (HFE) 5445 Triangle Pkwy Ste 200........... Peachtree Corners GA 30092 *Web:* hfecorp.com	770-441-1940		31
Hersha Hospitality Trust 510 Walnut St 9th Fl...................... Philadelphia PA 19106 *NYSE: HT* ■ *TF:* 800-289-0572 ■ *Web:* www.hersha.com	215-238-1046	238-0157	655
Hershey Co 100 Crystal A Dr .... Hershey PA 17033 *NYSE: HSY* ■ *TF Cust Svc:* 800-468-1714 ■ *Web:* www.thehersheycompany.com	800-468-1714		296-8
Hershey Creamery Co 301 S Cameron St .... Harrisburg PA 17101 *TF:* 888-240-1905 ■ *Web:* www.hersheyicecream.com	717-238-8134	233-7195	296-25
Hershey Entertainment & Resorts Co 27 W Chocolate Ave .... Hershey PA 17033 *TF:* 800-437-7439 ■ *Web:* www.hersheypa.com	800-437-7439		669
Hershey Gardens 170 Hotel Rd................ Hershey PA 17033 *Web:* www.hersheygardens.org	717-534-3492		97
Hershey Harrisburg Region Visitors Bureau 3211 N Front St Ste 301-A................ Harrisburg PA 17110 *TF:* 877-727-8573 ■ *Web:* www.visithersheyharrisburg.org	717-231-7788		206
Hershey Lodge 325 University Dr .... Hershey PA 17033 *TF:* 844-330-1802 ■ *Web:* www.hersheylodge.com	717-533-3311	533-9642	379
Hershey Trust Co 100 Mansion Rd E .... Hershey PA 17033 *TF:* 800-322-3248 ■ *Web:* www.hersheytrust.com	717-520-1100		401
Hersheypark 100 Hershey Pk Dr................ Hershey PA 17033 *TF:* 844-330-1813 ■ *Web:* www.hersheypark.com	717-534-3900	534-3153	32
Hersheypark Arena & Stadium 550 W Hersheypark Dr..................... Hershey PA 17033 *TF:* 800-745-3000 ■ *Web:* www.hershyeentertainment.com/giant-center	717-534-3911	534-8996	720
Hershner Hunter LLP 180 E 11th Ave............. Eugene OR 97401 *TF:* 800-469-4663 ■ *Web:* www.hershnerhunter.com	541-686-8511		428
Herson's Inc 15525 Frederick Rd............... Rockville MD 20855 *TF:* 888-203-8318 ■ *Web:* www.hersonsauto.com	888-203-8318		57
Hertford County School District 701 N Martin St .... Winton NC 27986 *Web:* www.hertford.k12.nc.us	252-358-1761	358-4745	685
Hertrich Family of Automobile Dealerships 26905 Sussex Hwy.......................... Seaford DE 19973 *Web:* www.hertrichs.com	302-629-4553		57
Hertz Global Holdings Inc 225 Brae Blvd.......................... Park Ridge NJ 07656 *NYSE: HTZ* ■ *TF:* 800-654-3131 ■ *Web:* www.hertz.com	201-307-2000		126
Hertz Schram & Saretsky Pc 1760 S Telegraph Rd Ste 300........... Bloomfield Hills MI 48302 *TF:* 866-775-5987 ■ *Web:* www.hertzschram.com	248-335-5000		428
Herweck's Art & Drafting Supplies 300 Broadway St......................... San Antonio TX 78205 *TF:* 800-725-1349 ■ *Web:* www.herwecks.com	210-227-1349		45
Herzing College *Atlanta* 3393 Peachtree Rd Ste 1003 .... Atlanta GA 30326 *TF:* 800-573-4533 ■ *Web:* www.herzing.edu/atlanta	404-816-4533	816-5576	800
Herzing College Birmingham 280 W Valley Ave .... Birmingham AL 35209 **Fax:* Admissions ■ *TF:* 800-425-9432 ■ *Web:* www.herzing.edu/birmingham	205-916-2800	916-2807*	800
Herzing College Madison 5218 E Terr Dr............................ Madison WI 53718 *TF:* 800-582-1227 ■ *Web:* www.herzing.edu	608-249-6611	249-8593	800
Herzing College Toronto 220 Yonge St Eaton Centre Galleria Offices Ste 202.................................... Toronto ON M5B2H1 *TF:* 800-561-1818 ■ *Web:* www.herzing.ca	416-599-6996		162
Herzog & Co 4640 Lankershim Blvd Ste 400......... North Hollywood CA 91602 *Web:* www.herzogcompany.com	818-762-4640		41
Herzog Contracting Corp 600 S Riverside Rd...................... Saint Joseph MO 64507 *TF:* 800-541-7846 ■ *Web:* www.herzog.com	816-233-9001	233-9881	188-4
Herzum Inc 175 N Franklin St Ste 301........... Chicago IL 60606 *Web:* www.herzum.com	312-602-1001		180
HES (Hanchett Entry Systems Inc) 22630 N 17th Ave.......................... Phoenix AZ 85027 *TF:* 800-626-7590 ■ *Web:* www.hesinnovations.com	623-582-4626	582-4641	692
HESCO (Hartford Electric Supply Co) 30 Inwood Rd Ste 1 .... Rocky Hill CT 06067 *TF:* 800-969-5444 ■ *Web:* www.hesconet.com	860-236-6363	236-0233	246
Heska Corp 3760 Rocky Mtn Ave............... Loveland CO 80538 *NASDAQ: HSKA* ■ *TF:* 800-464-3752 ■ *Web:* www.heska.com	970-493-7272		584
Hesley Hunt & Assoc Ltd 2607 White Bear Ave N................... Maplewood MN 55109 *Web:* heshcpa.com	651-770-8505		2
Heslin, Rothenberg, Farley, & Mesiti PC 5 Columbia Cir............................. Albany NY 12203 *Web:* www.hrfmlaw.com	518-452-5600		428
Hesperia Chamber of Commerce 16816 Main St Ste D .... Hesperia CA 92345 *Web:* www.hesperiacc.com	760-244-2135	244-1333	139
Hesperia Resorter PO Box 400937............ Hesperia CA 92345 *TF:* 800-815-2666 ■ *Web:* www.valleywidenewspaper.com	760-244-0021	244-6609	532-4
Hess Co 420 Hook Rd........................ Bayonne NJ 07002 *Web:* hess.com	201-437-1017		597
HESS Construction + Engineering Services Inc 804 W Diamond Ave Ste 300 .... Gaithersburg MD 20878 *Web:* www.hessedu.com	301-670-9000		256
Hess Corp 1185 Ave of the Americas .... New York NY 10036 *Web:* www.hess.com	212-997-8500		304
Hess Sweitzer Inc 2805 S 160th St .... New Berlin WI 53151 *Web:* www.hessswеitzerpainting.com	262-641-9100		189-8
Hesse Inc 6700 St John Ave................. Kansas City MO 64123 *TF:* 800-821-5562 ■ *Web:* www.grouphesse.com	816-483-7808	241-9010	779
Hesser Toyota Scion 1811 Humes Rd .... Janesville WI 53545 *Web:* www.hessertoyota.com	608-754-7754		57
Hesston College 325 S College Dr PO Box 3000 .... Hesston KS 67062 *TF:* 800-995-2757 ■ *Web:* www.hesston.edu	620-327-4221	327-8300	162
HET (Historic Elsinore Theatre) 170 High St SE.............................. Salem OR 97301 *TF:* 800-992-8499 ■ *Web:* www.elsinoretheatre.com	503-375-3574	375-0284	572
Hethcoat & Davis Inc 278 Franklin Rd Ste 200.................... Brentwood TN 37027 *Web:* www.hdengr.com	615-577-4300		261
Hetran Inc 70 Pinedale Industrial Rd .... Orwigsburg PA 17961 *TF:* 800-313-4022 ■ *Web:* www.hetranb.com	570-366-1411	366-1829	455
Hettinger County 336 Pacific Ave................. Mott ND 58646 *Web:* www.hettingercounty.net	701-824-4227		338
Hettrick Cyr & Assoc Inc 287 Main St .... East Hartford CT 06118 *TF:* 800-226-0911 ■ *Web:* www.hettrickcyr.com	860-568-2999		400
Heubel Material Handling Inc 6311 NE Equitable Rd.................... Kansas City MO 64120 *TF:* 800-283-4177 ■ *Web:* www.heubelshaw.com	800-283-4177		770
Heuer Insurance Agency Inc 5050 Vista Blvd Ste 101 .... Sparks NV 89436 *Web:* heuerinsurance.com	775-358-5554		390
Heuristic Park Inc 1512 Emory Rd NE........... Atlanta GA 30306 *Web:* www.heuristicpark.com	404-373-7786		177
Heuristic Workshop Inc 203 W Jackson Ave........................ Knoxville TN 37902 *Web:* www.heuristicworkshop.com	865-523-9867		321
Heuss Printing Inc 903 N Second St .... Ames IA 50010 *TF:* 800-232-6710 ■ *Web:* www.heuss.com	515-232-6710		627
Hewitt Equipment Ltd 5001, Trans-Canada Hwy .... Pointe-Claire QC H9R1B8 *TF:* 800-265-1048 ■ *Web:* www.hewitt.ca	514-630-3100		112
Hewitt Material Handling Inc 425 Millway Ave........................... Concord ON L4K3V8 *TF:* 800-563-5438 ■ *Web:* www.hewittmaterialhandling.ca	905-669-6590		111
Hewlett-Packard (Canada) Ltd (HP) 5150 Spectrum Way .... Mississauga ON L4W5G1 *TF:* 888-447-4636 ■ *Web:* welcome.hp.com	905-206-4725		173-2
Hewlett-Packard Co 3000 Hanover St.......... Palo Alto CA 94304 *NYSE: HPQ* ■ *TF Sales:* 800-752-0900 ■ *Web:* www.hp.com	650-857-1501	857-5518	173-2
Hexacon Electric Co 161 W Clay Ave .... Roselle Park NJ 07204 *Web:* www.hexaconelectric.com	908-245-6200	245-6176	758
Hexagon Manufacturing Intelligence 250 Circuit Dr...................... North Kingstown RI 02852 *Web:* www.sheffieldmeasurement.com	401-886-2000	886-2727	472
Hexavest Inc 1250 Blvd Rene-Levesque O Ste 4200.......... Montreal QC H3B4W8 *TF:* 800-225-6265 ■ *Web:* www.hexavest.com	514-390-8484		463
Hexaware Technologies Inc 1095 Cranbury Rd .... Jamesburg NJ 08831 *Web:* www.hexaware.com	609-409-6950	409-6910	180
Hexcel Corp 281 Tresser Blvd 16th Fl .... Stamford CT 06901 *NYSE: HXL* ■ *TF:* 800-444-3923 ■ *Web:* www.hexcel.com	800-688-7734		605-1
Hexion Specialty Chemicals Inc 180 E Broad St .... Columbus OH 43215 *Web:* www.momentive.com	614-225-4000		3
Heyburn State Park 57 Chatcolet Rd .... Plummer ID 83851 *TF:* 866-634-3246 ■ *Web:* www.parksandrecreation.idaho.gov	208-686-1308		565
Heyco Metals Inc 1069 Stinson Dr............. Reading PA 19605 *Web:* heycometals.com	610-926-4131		481
Heyco Products 1800 Industrial Way N .... Toms River NJ 08755 *TF:* 800-526-4182 ■ *Web:* www.heyco.com	732-286-1800	244-8843	488
Heyl & Patterson Inc 2000 Cliff Mine Rd PO Box 36 .... Pittsburgh PA 15230 *TF:* 800-505-9665 ■ *Web:* www.heylpatterson.com	412-788-9810	788-9822	470
Heyl Royster Voelker & Allen Pc 124 SW Adams St Ste 600 .... Peoria IL 61602 *Web:* www.heylroyster.com	309-676-0400		428
Heyman HospiceCare 420 E Second Ave.......... Rome GA 30161 *TF:* 800-324-1078 ■ *Web:* www.floyd.org	706-509-3200		371
Heymann Performing Arts Ctr 1373 S College Rd .... Lafayette LA 70503 *TF:* 800-745-3000 ■ *Web:* heymanncenter.com	337-291-5540	291-5580	572
Heyrman Printing LLC 2083 Holmgren Way...................... Green Bay WI 54304 *TF:* 800-236-4815 ■ *Web:* heyrman.com	920-499-4815		627
Heyward-Washington House 87 Church St .... Charleston SC 29403 *Web:* charlestonmuseum.org	843-722-0354		50-3
Heywood Hospital 242 Green St................ Gardner MA 01440 *Web:* www.heywood.org	978-632-3420		374-3
Hezel Associates LLC 731 James St Ste 44........................ Syracuse NY 13203 *Web:* www.hezel.com	315-422-3512	422-3513	463
HF Group Inc 203 W Artesia Blvd............... Compton CA 90220 *TF:* 800-421-5000 ■ *Web:* www.hf76.com	310-605-0755		496
HF Group, The 8844 Mayfield Rd............ Chesterland OH 44026 *TF:* 800-444-7534 ■ *Web:* hfgroup.com/index.php	440-729-2445		92
HF Lenz Co 1407 Scalp Ave .... Johnstown PA 15904 *Web:* www.hflenz.com	814-269-9300		261
HF scientific Inc 3170 Metro Pkwy............ Fort Myers FL 33916 *Web:* www.hfscientific.com	239-337-2116		203
HFA (Humane Farming Assn) PO Box 3577 .... San Rafael CA 94912 *TF:* 800-295-4050 ■ *Web:* www.hfa.org	415-485-1495	485-0106	48-3
HFA (Hospice Foundation of America) 1710 Rhode Island Ave NW Ste 400.......... Washington DC 20036 *TF:* 800-854-3402 ■ *Web:* www.hospicefoundation.org	202-457-5811	457-5815	49-8
HFE (Herschend Family Entertainment Corp) 5445 Triangle Pkwy Ste 200.......... Peachtree Corners GA 30092 *Web:* hfecorp.com	770-441-1940		31
HFES (Human Factors & Ergonomics Society) 1124 Montana Ave Ste B PO Box 1369....... Santa Monica CA 90406 *TF:* 800-233-1234 ■ *Web:* www.hfes.org	310-394-1811	394-2410	48-17
Hff Inc 301 Grant St Ste 600............... Pittsburgh PA 15219 *NYSE: HF* ■ *Web:* www.hfflp.com	412-281-8714	281-2792	653
HFI (Hepatitis Foundation International) 504 Blick Dr .... Silver Spring MD 20904 *TF:* 800-891-0707 ■ *Web:* www.hepfi.org	301-622-4200		48-17

				Phone	Fax	Class
HFI LLC 2421 McGaw Rd *Web:* hfi-inc.com	Obetz	OH	43207	614-491-0700		745-3
HFI Wealth Management Inc 620 Newport Center Dr Ste 500 *Web:* www.unitedcp.com/wv1	Newport Beach	CA	92660	304-876-2619		401
HFIA (Home Furnishings Independents Assn) 2050 Stemmons World Fwy Ste 292 *TF:* 800-422-3778 ■ *Web:* myhfa.org	Dallas	TX	75207	800-422-3778		49-4
HFM FoodService Inc 716 Umi St *Web:* www.hfmfoodservice.com	Honolulu	HI	96819	808-843-3200		10-11
HFMA (Healthcare Financial Management Assn) 2 Westbrook Corporate Ctr Ste 700 *TF:* 800-252-4362 ■ *Web:* www.hfma.org	Westchester	IL	60154	708-531-9600	531-0032	49-8
HFPA (Hollywood Foreign Press Assn) 646 N Robertson Blvd *Web:* www.goldenglobes.com/hfpa	West Hollywood	CA	90069	310-657-1731		48-4
HFS Chicago Scholars 1074 W Taylor St Ste 201 *Web:* www.hfschicagoscholars.com	Chicago	IL	60607	312-421-4070		196
HFS Consultants 505 Fourteenth St 5th Fl *Web:* www.hfsconsultants.com	Oakland	CA	94612	510-768-0066		401
HFTP (Hospitality Financial & Technology Professionals) 11709 Boulder Ln Ste 110 *TF:* 800-646-4387 ■ *Web:* www.hftp.org	Austin	TX	78726	512-249-5333	249-1533	49-1
Hfw Industries Inc 196 Philadelphia St PO Box 8	Buffalo	NY	14207	716-875-3380	875-3385	386
HG Energy LLC 5260 Dupont Rd *TF:* 800-344-6601 ■ *Web:* hgenergyllc.com	Parkersburg	WV	26101	304-420-1100		536
HG Marketing Group LLC 150 E State St *TF:* 800-889-7676 ■ *Web:* www.hgmarketing.com	Doylestown	PA	18901	215-340-3606		636
HG Reynolds Co Inc 113 Contract Dr	Aiken	SC	29801	803-641-1402		186
Hg Solutions 3701 S Lawrence St *TF:* 866-988-2626 ■ *Web:* www.hughesgroup.biz	Tacoma	WA	98409	253-588-2626		463
HG Weber & Company Inc 725 Fremont St *Web:* www.holwegweber.com	Kiel	WI	53042	920-894-2221		556
HGA (Handweavers Guild of America) 1255 Hwy 23 NW Ste 211 *TF:* 800-665-9786 ■ *Web:* www.weavespindye.org	Suwanee	GA	30024	678-730-0010	730-0836	48-18
HGBD (Hussey Gay Bell) 329 Commercial Dr Ste 200 *Web:* www.husseygaybell.com	Savannah	GA	31406	912-354-4626		261
HGI Skydyne 100 River Rd *TF:* 800-428-2273 ■ *Web:* www.skydyne.com	Port Jervis	NY	12771	800-428-2273		199
HGK Asset Management Inc 525 Washington Blvd Newport Tower Ste 2000 *Web:* www.hgk.com	Jersey City	NJ	07310	201-659-3700		401
HGM Associates Inc 640 Fifth Ave *Web:* www.hgmonline.com	Council Bluffs	IA	51501	712-323-0530		261
HGMN (Herb Growing & Marketing Network) PO Box 245 *TF:* 800-753-9199 ■ *Web:* www.herbworld.com	Silver Spring	PA	17575	717-393-3295	393-9261	48-2
HGS Engineering Inc 1121 Noble St *Web:* hgsengineeringinc.com	Anniston	AL	36201	256-236-1848		261
Hgs Financial Services 680 Craig Rd *Web:* www.hgsfinancialservices.com	Saint Louis	MO	63141	314-432-5341		226
HH Angus & Assoc Ltd 1127 Leslie St *TF:* 866-955-8201 ■ *Web:* www.hhangus.com	Toronto	ON	M3C2J6	416-443-8200		256
HH Arnold Co Inc 529 Liberty St *TF:* 866-878-9603 ■ *Web:* www.hharnold.com	Rockland	MA	02370	781-878-0346	878-7944	744
HH Brown Shoe Company Inc 124 W Putnam Ave *Web:* www.hhbrown.com	Greenwich	CT	06830	203-661-2424	661-1818	301
HH Halferty & Sons Inc 1300 S US Hwy 169 *TF:* 800-303-4312 ■ *Web:* www.halfertyandsons.com	Smithville	MO	64089	816-532-0221		274
Hh Technologies Inc 1733 County Rd 68 *Web:* www.hired-hand.com	Bremen	AL	35033	256-287-7000		596
H&H Total Care Services Inc 8382 156 St *Web:* www.hhtotalcare.com	Surrey	BC	V3S3R7	604-597-7931		672
H&H X-Ray Services Inc 104 Enterprise St *TF:* 800-551-5093 ■ *Web:* www.hhxray.com	West Monroe	LA	71292	800-551-5093		743
HHI (Hoag Hospital Irvine) 16200 Sand Canyon Ave *TF:* 800-309-9729 ■ *Web:* www.hoag.org	Irvine	CA	92618	949-764-4624		374-3
HHI Corp 736 W Harrisville Rd *Web:* www.hhicorp.com	Ogden	UT	84404	385-333-4400		186
HHL (Helen Hall Library) 100 W Walker St *TF:* 800-449-1600 ■ *Web:* www.leaguecity.com	League City	TX	77573	281-554-1111		434-3
HHP (Horizon House Publications Inc) 685 Canton St *Web:* www.horizonhouse.com	Norwood	MA	02062	781-769-9750	762-9071	637-9
HHS (Department of Health & Human Services) 330 Independence Ave SW *TF:* 877-696-6775 ■ *Web:* www.hhs.gov	Washington	DC	20201	202-619-0150		340-10
Hi Caliber IT Soluitons 38 VALLEY WOOD DR *Web:* www.hicaliberit.com	Somerset	NJ	08873	732-828-7482		393
HI Development Corp 111 W Fortune St *Web:* www.hidevelopment.com	Tampa	FL	33602	813-229-6686		379
Hi Nabor Supermarket Inc 7201 Winbourne Ave *Web:* hinabor.com	Baton Rouge	LA	70805	225-357-1448		345
Hi Rel Connectors Inc 760 Wharton Dr *Web:* www.hirelco.net	Claremont	CA	91711	909-626-1820	399-0626	815
Hi Tech Data Floors Inc 1885 Swarthmore Ave *TF:* 800-544-8321 ■ *Web:* hitechdatafloors.com	Lakewood	NJ	08701	732-905-1799		290
Hi Tech Seals Inc 9211-41 Ave *TF:* 800-661-6055 ■ *Web:* www.hitechseals.com	Edmonton	AB	T6E6R5	780-438-6055	434-5866	350
HI TecMetal Group Inc 1101 E 55th St *TF:* 877-484-2867 ■ *Web:* www.htg.cc	Cleveland	OH	44103	216-881-8100	426-6690	484
HIAA (Halifax Stanfield International Airport) 1 Bell Blvd *Web:* halifaxstanfield.ca	Enfield	NS	B2T1K2	902-873-4422	873-4750	27
Hialeah Chamber of Commerce & Industries 240 E First Ave Ste 217	Hialeah	FL	33010	305-888-7780		139
Hialeah City Hall 501 Palm Ave *Web:* hialeahfl.gov	Hialeah	FL	33010	305-883-5820	883-5814	337
HIAS (Hebrew Immigrant Aid Society) 333 Seventh Ave 16th Fl *TF:* 800-442-7714 ■ *Web:* www.hias.org	New York	NY	10001	212-967-4100	967-4483	48-5
Hiasun Inc 5218 Atlantic Ave PO Box 785 *Web:* hiasun.com	Mays Landing	NJ	08330	609-625-0565		177
Hiatus Spa & Retreat 5560 W Lovers Ln Ste 250 *Web:* hiatusspa.com	Dallas	TX	75209	214-352-4111		354
Hiawatha Correctional Facility 4533 W Industrial Pk Dr *TF:* 800-642-4838 ■ *Web:* www.michigan.gov	Kincheloe	MI	49786	906-495-5661		213
Hiawatha Rubber Co 1700 67th Ave N *TF:* 800-782-7776 ■ *Web:* www.hiawatharubber.com	Minneapolis	MN	55430	763-566-0900	566-9537	677
Hiawatha World 607 Utah St *Web:* cityofhiawatha.org	Hiawatha	KS	66434	785-742-2111	742-2276	532-2
HI-AYH (Hostelling International USA - American Youth Hostels) 8401 Colesville Rd Ste 600 *TF:* 888-449-8727 ■ *Web:* www.hiusa.org	Silver Spring	MD	20910	240-650-2100	650-2094	48-23
Hibachi Japanese Steak House 3091 University Ave *Web:* www.mangoeskeywest.com	Morgantown	WV	26505	304-598-7140		671
Hibachi Japanese Steak House 3000 W 12th St *TF:* 800-442-1162 ■ *Web:* www.hibachijapan.com	Erie	PA	16505	814-838-2495		671
Hibachi Master 8160 Beechmont Ave *Web:* hibachimaster.com	Cincinnati	OH	45255	513-474-9888		671
Hibachi Steak House 108 S Fairmont Blvd	Anaheim	CA	92808	714-998-4110		671
Hibar Systems Ltd 35 Pollard St *TF:* 800-289-5986 ■ *Web:* www.hibar.com	Richmond Hill	ON	L4B1A8	905-731-2400	731-6035	547
Hibbert Company Inc, The 400 Pennington Ave *Web:* www.hibbertgroup.com	Trenton	NJ	08650	609-394-7500		5
Hibbett Sporting Goods Inc 451 Industrial Ln *Web:* www.hibbett.com	Birmingham	AL	35211	205-942-4292		711
Hibbing Community College 1515 E 25th St **Fax: Admissions* ■ *TF:* 800-224-4422 ■ *Web:* hibbing.edu	Hibbing	MN	55746	218-262-7200	262-6717*	162
Hibbing Taconite Co 4950 County Rd 5 N *TF:* 800-586-5336 ■ *Web:* cliffsnaturalresources.com	Hibbing	MN	55746	218-262-5950		502
Hibbs Hallmark & Co 501 Shelley Dr **Fax Area Code: 903* ■ *TF:* 800-765-6767 ■ *Web:* www.hibbshallmark.com	Tyler	TX	75701	800-765-6767	581-5988*	390
HIBCC (Health Industry Business Communications Council) 2525 E Arizona Biltmore Cir Ste 127 *TF:* 800-755-5505 ■ *Web:* www.hibcc.org	Phoenix	AZ	85016	602-381-1091	381-1093	49-8
Hibco Plastics Inc 1820 Us 601 Hwy *TF:* 800-849-8683 ■ *Web:* www.hibco.com	Yadkinville	NC	27055	336-463-2391	463-5591	601
HiBeam Internet & Voice 400 S Woods Mill Rd Ste 305	Chesterfield	MO	63017	636-203-9400		224
Hibernia Bancorp Inc 325 Carondelet St *Web:* hibbank.com	New Orleans	LA	70130	504-522-3203		70
Hibernia Management & Development Company Ltd 100 New Gower St Ste 1000 *Web:* www.hibernia.ca	St. John's	NL	A1C6K3	709-778-7000		536
Hibiscus Spa at the Myrtle Beach Marriott Resort at Grande Dunes 8400 Costa Verde Dr *Web:* www.csspagroup.com	Myrtle Beach	SC	29572	843-692-3730		707
Hibon Inc 12055 Cote de Liesse *Web:* www.hibon.com	Dorval	QC	H9P1B4	514-631-3501		358
HIC (Hawaii Information Consortium) 201 Merchant St Ste 1805 *TF:* 800-295-0089 ■ *Web:* www.hawaii.gov	Honolulu	HI	96813	808-695-4620		565
Hicaps Inc 600 N Regional Rd *Web:* www.hicaps.com	Greensboro	NC	27409	336-665-1234		194
Hice Jody (Rep R - GA) 324 Cannon HOB *Web:* hice.house.gov	Washington	DC	20515	202-225-4101	226-0776	342-2
Hickel Investment Co 930 W Fifth Ave *Web:* hickelinvestment.com	Anchorage	AK	99501	907-343-2400		655
Hicken, Scott, Howard & Anderson PA 2150 Third Ave Ste 300 *Web:* www.hshalaw.com	Anoka	MN	55303	763-421-4110		428
Hickenlooper John (D) 136 State Capitol *Web:* www.colorado.gov/governor	Denver	CO	80203	303-866-2471		343
Hickey Freeman 1155 N Clinton Ave *TF Cust Svc:* 844-755-7344 ■ *Web:* www.hickeyfreeman.com	Rochester	NY	14621	585-467-7021		155-12
Hickman County 114 N Central Ave # 202 *Web:* www.hickmancountytn.com	Centerville	TN	37033	931-729-2621	729-9951	338
Hickman County 110 E Clay St County Courthouse *TF:* 800-815-2666 ■ *Web:* hickmancountyclerkky.com	Clinton	KY	42031	270-653-2131		338
Hicko CPA Group PC, The 310 E 90th Dr	Merrillville	IN	46410	219-738-2863		2
Hickok Inc 10514 Dupont Ave *OTC:* HICKA ■ *TF:* 800-342-5080 ■ *Web:* www.hickok-inc.com	Cleveland	OH	44108	216-541-8060	761-9879	248
Hickory Brands Inc (HBI) 429 27th St NW *TF:* 800-438-5777 ■ *Web:* www.hickorybrands.com	Hickory	NC	28601	800-438-5777	422-3279	745-5
Hickory Bridge Farm 96 Hickory Bridge Rd *Web:* www.hickorybridgefarm.com	Orrtanna	PA	17353	717-642-5261		671

Phone | Fax | Class

Hickory County Library
100 New Hermitage Dr ... Hermitage MO 65668 417-745-6939 745-2132 338
Web: www.hickorylibrary.org

Hickory Daily Record 1100 Pk Pl. ... Hickory NC 28602 828-322-4510 532-2
TF: 800-849-8586 ■ *Web:* www.hickoryrecord.com

Hickory Farms Inc 811 Madison Ave ... Toledo OH 43604 800-753-8558 893-0164* 336
**Fax Area Code:* 419 ■ *TF:* 800-753-8558 ■ *Web:* www.hickoryfarms.com

Hickory House Ribs
Aspen 730 W Main St ... Aspen CO 81611 970-925-2313 671
Web: www.hickoryhouseribs.com

Hickory Knob State Resort Park
1591 Resort Dr ... McCormick SC 29835 864-391-2450 391-5390 565
TF: 800-491-1764 ■ *Web:* www.southcarolinaparks.com

Hickory Metro Convention & Visitors Bureau
1960 13th Ave Dr SE ... Hickory NC 28602 828-322-1335 206
TF: 800-509-2444 ■ *Web:* www.hickorymetro.com

Hickory Motor Speedway 3130 Hwy 70 SE ... Newton NC 28658 828-464-3655 465-5017 515
TF: 800-843-8725 ■ *Web:* www.hickorymotorspeedway.com

Hickory Point Bank & Trust FSB
PO Box 2548 ... Decatur IL 62525 217-875-3131 70
TF Cust Svc: 800-872-0081 ■ *Web:* www.hickorypointbank.com

Hickory Printing Group Inc
725 Reese Dr SW ... Conover NC 28613 828-465-3431 465-2517 627
TF: 800-442-5679 ■ *Web:* www.hickoryprinting.com

Hickory Ridge Mall 6075 Winchester Rd ... Memphis TN 38115 901-795-8844 460
Web: www.hickoryridge.com

Hickory Ridge Marriott Conference Hotel
10400 Fernwood Rd ... Bethesda IL 20817 301-380-3000 377
TF: 800-334-0344 ■ *Web:* www.marriott.com

Hickory Run State Park PO Box 81 ... White Haven PA 18661 570-443-0400 565
Web: www.dcnr.state.pa.us

Hickory Springs Mfg Co
235 Second Ave NW ... Hickory NC 28601 800-438-5341 719
TF: 800-438-5341 ■ *Web:* www.hsmsolutions.com

Hickory Veterinary Hospital
2303 Hickory Rd ... Plymouth Meeting PA 19462 610-828-3054 794
Web: hickoryvet.com

Hickory Yarns Inc 1025 Tenth St NE ... Hickory NC 28601 828-322-1550 322-1627 745-9
TF: 800-713-1484 ■ *Web:* www.hickoryyarns.com

Hicks & Company Inc 1504 W Fifth St ... Austin TX 78703 512-478-0858 196
Web: hicksenv.com

Hicks Oils & Hicksgas Inc
204 Hwy 54 E ... Roberts IL 60962 217-395-2281 581
TF: 800-747-7323 ■ *Web:* www.hicksoils.com

Hicks Partners LLC
10 W Broad St Ste 900 ... Columbus OH 43215 614-221-2800 636
Web: www.hickspartners.com

Hicks Plastics Company Inc
51300 Industrial Dr ... Macomb MI 48042 586-786-5640 608
Web: www.hicksplastics.com

Hicksville Chamber of Commerce
10 W Marie St ... Hicksville NY 11801 516-931-7170 931-8546 139
Web: www.hicksvillechamber.com

HICO America Sales & Technology Inc
3 Penn Ctr W Ste 300 ... Pittsburg PA 15276 412-787-1170 246
Web: www.hicoamerica.com

HID Global Corp 611 Center Ridge Dr ... Austin TX 78753 512-776-9000 776-9930 178-12
TF: 800-237-7769 ■ *Web:* www.hidglobal.com

Hid Inc 119 Starwood Cir Lot 16 ... Jacksonville NC 28540 910-455-8884 401

HIDA (Health Industry Distributors Assn)
310 Montgomery St ... Alexandria VA 22314 703-549-4432 549-6495 49-18
TF: 800-549-4432 ■ *Web:* www.hida.org

Hidalgo County 100 N Closner ... Edinburg TX 78539 956-318-2100 318-2105 338
TF: 888-318-2811 ■ *Web:* tx-hidalgocounty.civicplus.com

Hiday & Ricke pa
4100 E Southpoint Dr Ste 3 ... Jacksonville FL 32216 904-363-2769 428
TF: 800-713-0670 ■ *Web:* www.hidayricke.com

Hidden America PO Box 4202 ... River Edge NJ 07661 201-487-1190 773
Web: journeysinto.com

Hidden Lake Gardens 6214 Monroe Rd ... Tipton MI 49287 517-431-2060 431-9148 97
Web: www.hiddenlakegardens.msu.edu

Hidden Springs State Forest
RR 1 PO Box 200 ... Strasburg IL 62465 217-644-3091 565

Hidden Valley Resort & Conference Ctr
1 Craighead Dr PO Box 4420 ... Hidden Valley PA 15502 814-443-8000 377
TF: 800-452-2223 ■ *Web:* www.hiddenvalleyresort.com

Hidden Variable Studios LLC
1800 S Brand Blvd Ste 204 ... Glendale CA 91204 818-985-4263 225
Web: www.hiddenvariable.com

Hideout Lodge and Guest Ranch, The
PO Box 206 ... Shell WY 82441 307-765-2080 765-2681 239
TF: 800-354-8637 ■ *Web:* www.thehideout.com

Hi-Desert Publishing Co
56445 29 Palms Hwy ... Yucca Valley CA 92284 760-365-3315 637-8
Web: www.hidesertstar.com

Hidi Rae Consulting Engineers Inc
155 Gordon Baker Rd Ste 200 ... Toronto ON M2H3N5 416-364-2100 463
Web: www.hidi.com

Hiebing Group, The 315 Wisconsin Ave ... Madison WI 53703 608-256-6357 225
Web: www.hiebing.com

Hierl Insurance Inc 258 S Main St ... Fond Du Lac WI 54935 920-921-5921 390
Web: hierl.com

Higbee Inc 6741 Thompson Rd ... Syracuse NY 13211 315-432-8021 326
Web: higbee.sealanddesign.com

Higdon Florist 201 E 32nd St ... Joplin MO 64804 417-624-7171 292
TF: 800-641-4726 ■ *Web:* www.higdonflorist.com

Higgins Armory Museum
100 Barber Ave ... Worcester MA 01606 508-853-6015 520
Web: www.higgins.org

Higgins Brian (Rep D - NY)
2459 Rayburn Bldg ... Washington DC 20515 202-225-3306 226-0347 342-2
Web: higgins.house.gov

Higgins Clay (Rep R - LA)
1711 Longworth HOB ... Washington DC 20515 202-225-2031 342-2
Web: clayhiggins.house.gov

Higgins Electric Inc. of Dothan
1350 Columbia Hwy ... Dothan AL 36301 334-793-4859 246
Web: www.higginselectric.com

Higgins Restaurant & Bar
1239 SW Broadway ... Portland OR 97205 503-222-9070 671
Web: higginsportland.com

Higgins Supply Company Inc 18-23 S St ... Mcgraw NY 13101 607-836-6474 836-6913 250
Web: www.higginssupply.com

Higgins, Marcus & Lovett Inc
800 S Figueroa St Ste 710 ... Los Angeles CA 90017 213-617-7775 41
Web: www.hmlinc.com

High & Assoc Inc Dba Financial Services Group
105 Old Hewitt Rd Ste 400 ... Waco TX 76712 254-776-7283 390
Web: highandassociates.net

High Arctic Energy Services Inc
444 , Fifth Ave, SW Ste 2010 ... Calgary AB T2P2T8 403-340-9825 540
Web: www.haes.ca

High Choice Feeders LLC
553 W Rd 40 ... Scott City KS 67871 620-872-7271 10-1
Web: highchoicefeeders.com

High Cliff State Park
N7630 State Pk Rd ... Sherwood WI 54169 920-989-1106 565
Web: dnr.wi.gov/newurl.html

High Concrete Structures Inc
125 Denver Rd ... Denver PA 17517 717-336-9300 336-9301* 183
**Fax:* Sales ■ *TF:* 800-773-2278 ■ *Web:* www.highconcrete.com

High Country Bancorp Inc
7360 W Hwy 50 PO Box 309 ... Salida CO 81201 719-539-2516 530-8881 360-2
OTC: HCBC ■ *TF:* 800-201-0557 ■ *Web:* www.highcountrybank.net

High Country Beverage Corp
5706 Wright Dr ... Loveland CO 80538 970-622-8444 297-8
Web: www.highcountrybeverage.com

High Country News 119 Grand Ave ... Paonia CO 81428 970-527-4898 532-3
TF: 800-311-5852 ■ *Web:* www.hcn.org

High Country Performance 4x4 Inc
1695 W Hamilton Pl ... Englewood CO 80110 303-761-7379 57
Web: hcp4x4.com

High Country Tek Inc
208 Gold Flat Ct ... Nevada City CA 95959 530-265-3236 203
Web: www.highcountrytek.com

High Country Transportation Inc
400 N Saint Paul St Ste 400 ... Dallas TX 75201 800-635-7687 780
TF: 800-635-7687 ■ *Web:* www.highcountrytrans.com

High Desert Museum 59800 S Hwy 97 ... Bend OR 97702 541-382-4754 382-5256 520
TF: 866-632-9992 ■ *Web:* www.highdesertmuseum.org

High Desert State Prison (HDSP)
475-750 Rice Canyon Rd PO Box 750 ... Susanville CA 96127 530-251-5100 213
Web: www.cdcr.ca.gov

High End Systems Inc
2105 Gracy Farms Ln ... Austin TX 78758 512-836-2242 837-5290 439
TF: 800-890-8989 ■ *Web:* www.highend.com

High Falls Film Festival
45 E Ave Ste 400 ... Rochester NY 14604 585-279-8312 282
Web: www.highfallsfilmfestival.com

High Falls Museum 60 Browns Race ... Rochester NY 14614 585-325-2030 50-3
Web: www.cityofrochester.gov/highfallsmuseum

High Falls State Park
76 High Falls Pk Dr ... Jackson GA 30233 478-993-3053 565
Web: www.gastateparks.org

High Grade Beverage Inc
891 Georges Rd ... Monmouth Junction NJ 08852 732-821-7600 821-2898 81-1
Web: www.highgradebeverage.com

High Hampton Inn & Country Club
1525 Hwy 107 S ... Cashiers NC 28717 828-743-2450 743-5991 669
TF: 800-334-2551 ■ *Web:* www.highhamptoninn.com

High Industries Inc
1853 William Penn Way ... Lancaster PA 17601 717-293-4444 189-14
Web: www.high.net

High Level Components LLC
147 Locust Level Dr ... Locust NC 28097 704-781-2520 817

High Liner Foods Inc (HLF)
High Liner Foods Incorporated,100 Battery Point
P.O. Box 910 ... Lunenburg NS B0J2C0 902-634-8811 296-13
NYSE: HLF ■ *Web:* www.highlinerfoods.com

High Meadows Camp 1055 Willeo Rd ... Roswell GA 30075 770-993-7975 239
Web: highmeadows.org

High Mesa Consulting Group Inc
6010 Midway Park Blvd NE Ste B ... Albuquerque NM 87109 505-345-4250 261
Web: highmesacg.com

High Mowing School 222 Isaac Frye Hwy ... Wilton NH 03086 603-654-2391 654-6588 622
Web: www.highmowing.org

High Museum of Art
1280 Peachtree St NE ... Atlanta GA 30309 404-733-4400 733-4502 520
Web: www.high.org

High Peaks Resort
2384 Saranac Ave ... Lake Placid NY 12946 518-523-4411 523-1120 669
TF: 800-755-5598 ■ *Web:* highpeaksresort.com

High Performance Computing Collaboratory
2 Research Blvd ... Starkville MS 39759 662-325-8278 325-7692 668
TF: 800-521-4041 ■ *Web:* www.erc.msstate.edu

High Plains Livestock Exchange LLC
28601 US Hwy 34 ... Brush CO 80723 970-842-5115 842-5088 446
Web: www.hplivestock.com

High Plains Pizza Inc 7 W PkwyBlvd ... Liberal KS 67901 620-624-5638 670
Web: highplainspizza.com

High Plains Power Inc
1775 E Monroe PO Box 713 ... Riverton WY 82501 307-856-9426 856-4207 245
TF: 800-445-0613 ■ *Web:* www.highplainspower.org

High Plains Publishers Inc
1500 W Wyatt Earp Blvd ... Dodge City KS 67801 620-227-7171 227-7173 637-8
TF: 800-452-7171 ■ *Web:* hpj.com

High Point Chamber of Commerce
1634 N Main St ... High Point NC 27262 336-882-5000 889-9499 139
Web: www.highpointchamber.org

High Point Convention & Visitors Bureau
300 S Main St ... High Point NC 27260 336-884-5255 206
TF: 800-720-5255 ■ *Web:* www.highpoint.org

High Point Enterprise
210 Church Ave ... High Point NC 27262 336-888-3500 532-2
Web: www.hpenews.com

Phone | Fax | Class

High Point Furniture Industries Inc
1104 Bedford St PO Box 2063 .... High Point NC 27261 336-431-7101 434-1964 319-1
TF: 800-447-3462 ■ *Web:* www.hpfi.com

High Point Public Library (HPPL)
901 N Main St .... High Point NC 27262 336-883-3660 883-3636 434-3
Web: www.highpointnc.gov/749/library

High Point Regional Health System (HPRHS)
601 N Elm St PO Box HP-5 .... High Point NC 27262 336-878-6000 374-3
TF: 877-878-7644 ■ *Web:* www.highpointregional.com

High Point Solutions Inc 5 Gail Ct .... Sparta NJ 07871 973-940-0040 940-0041 176
Web: www.highpoint.com

High Point Sprinkler Inc
2 Regency Industrial Blvd .... Thomasville NC 27360 336-475-6181 189-13

High Point State Park 1480 Rt 23 .... Sussex NJ 07461 973-875-4800 565
Web: www.njparksandforests.org

High Point University
833 Montlieu Ave .... High Point NC 27262 336-841-9216 888-6382* 166
**Fax:* Admissions ■ *TF:* 800-345-6993 ■ *Web:* www.highpoint.edu

High Power Technical Services Inc (HPTS)
2230 Ampere Dr .... Louisville KY 40299 502-271-2469 116
TF: 866-398-3474 ■ *Web:* www.hpts.tv

High Precision Inc 375 Morse St .... Hamden CT 06517 203-777-5395 773-1976 621
TF: 800-517-9207 ■ *Web:* www.highprecisioninc.com

High Purity Systems Inc
8432 Quarry Rd .... Manassas VA 20110 703-330-5094 189-10
Web: www.highpurity.com

High Q Lighting Inc
11439 E Lakewood Blvd .... Holland MI 49424 616-396-3591 439
TF: 800-543-3765 ■ *Web:* www.hql.net

High Ridge Partners
140 S Dearborn Ste 420 .... Chicago IL 60603 312-456-5636 194
Web: www.high-ridge.com

High River Hospital
560 Ninth Ave W .... High River AB T1V1B3 403-652-2200 652-0199 374-2
TF: 800-332-1414 ■ *Web:* albertahealthservices.ca

High Road Craft Ice Cream Inc
1730 W Oak Commons Ct .... Marietta GA 30062 678-701-7623 296-25
Web: www.highroadcraft.com

High Speed Productions Inc
1303 Underwood Ave .... San Francisco CA 94124 415-822-3083 514
TF: 888-520-9099 ■ *Web:* www.juxtapoz.com

High Standards Technology
17000 El Camino Real .... Houston TX 77058 281-990-9422 225
Web: www.weredown.com

High Steel Service Center Inc
400 Steel Way .... Lancaster PA 17604 717-299-8989 492
Web: www.highsteelservicecenter.com

High Steel Structures Inc
1915 Old Philadelphia Pike PO Box 10008 .... Lancaster PA 17605 717-390-4270 399-4102 189-14
Web: www.highsteel.com

High Swartz Roberts & Seidel
40 E Airy St .... Norristown PA 19404 610-275-2823 445
Web: www.highswartz.com

High Tech Design Safety LLC
15304 Rainbow One St Ste 101 .... Austin TX 78734 512-266-0222 317
Web: hightechdesignsafety.com

High Tech Fire Protection Company Inc
84 Hackett Mills Rd .... Poland ME 04274 207-998-2551 610

High Tech Tool Inc 7803 S Loop E .... Houston TX 77012 713-641-2303 641-6664 493
Web: www.hightechtool.com

High Technology Inc 109 Production Rd .... Walpole MA 02081 508-660-2221 535
TF: 800-916-5600 ■ *Web:* www.htmed.com

High Tide Creative 208 Bridge St .... Bridgeton NC 28519 252-671-7087 195
Web: www.hightidecreative.com

High Tor State Park
417 S Mountain Rd .... New City NY 10956 845-634-8074 565

High Vacuum Apparatus LLC (HVA)
12880 Moya Blvd .... Reno NV 89506 775-359-4442 359-1369 789
TF: 800-551-4422 ■ *Web:* www.highvac.com

High Velocity Communications LLC
1720 Dolphin Dr Ste D .... Waukesha WI 53186 262-544-6600 4
Web: www.highvelocityllc.com

High West Energy Inc (HWE)
6270 County Rd 212 .... Pine Bluffs WY 82082 307-245-3261 245-9292 245
TF: 888-834-1657 ■ *Web:* www.highwestenergy.com

High Winds Casino 61475 E 100 Rd .... Miami OK 74354 918-541-9463 452
Web: highwindscasino.com

HighBeam Research Inc
65 E Wacker Pl Ste 400 .... Chicago IL 60601 312-782-3900 782-3901 397
Web: www.highbeam.com

Highcom Security Inc
2451 McMullen Booth Rd Ste 242 .... Clearwater FL 33759 727-592-9400 693
TF: 800-413-5155 ■ *Web:* highcomsecurity.com

Higher Dimension Research Inc
570 Hale Ave .... Oakdale MN 55128 651-730-6203 463
Web: www.superfabric.com

Higher Ed Growth LLC
5400 S Lakeshore Dr Ste 101 .... Tempe AZ 85283 866-433-8532 449
TF: 866-433-8532 ■ *Web:* www.higheredgrowth.com

Higher Education Assistance Group Inc, The
60 Walnut St 4th Fl .... Wellesley Hills MA 02481 617-928-1975 242
Web: www.heag.us

Higher Gear Group Inc, The
145 W Central Rd .... Schaumburg IL 60195 847-843-6800 179
Web: www.onecommand.com/what-we-do-auto/highergear-crm

Higher One Inc 115 Munson St .... New Haven CT 06511 203-776-7776 177
Web: higherone.com

Higher Technology Solutions Inc
1547 Old Forge Rd Ste 1111 .... Bartlett IL 60103 630-830-7638 809
Web: www.htsglobal.com

HigherMe inc 27 Parsons St .... Boston MA 02135 617-784-1052 260
Web: www.higherme.com

Highfield Manufacturing Co
380 Mtn Grove St .... Bridgeport CT 06605 203-384-2281 368-3906 595
TF: 800-423-1323 ■ *Web:* www.highfield-mfg.com

Highfleet Inc
3600 Odonnell St Ste 600 .... Baltimore MD 21224 410-675-1201 177
Web: highfleet.com

Highgate Hotels Inc
545 E John Carpenter Fwy Ste 1400 .... Irving TX 75062 972-444-9700 378
Web: www.highgateholdings.com

HighJump Software
5600 W 83rd St Ste 600 .... Minneapolis MN 55437 952-947-4088 178-1
TF: 800-328-3271 ■ *Web:* www.highjump.com

Highland Area Chamber of Commerce
27255 Messina St .... Highland CA 92346 909-864-4073 864-4583 139
TF: 800-504-6070 ■ *Web:* www.highlandchamber.org

Highland Associates Ltd
102 Highland Ave .... Clarks Summit PA 18411 570-586-4334 256
Web: www.highlandassociates.com

Highland Capital Management LP
300 Crescent Ct Ste 700 .... Dallas TX 75201 972-628-4100 405
Web: www.highlandcapital.com

Highland Capital Partners
92 Hayden Ave .... Lexington MA 02421 781-861-5500 792
Web: www.hcp.com

Highland Central School District
320 Pancake Hollow Rd .... Highland NY 12528 845-691-1000 685
Web: www.highland-k12.org

Highland Community Bank
307 Thacker Ave PO Box 1059 .... Covington VA 24426 540-962-2265 70
Web: www.highlandscommunitybank.com

Highland Community College
2998 W Pearl City Rd .... Freeport IL 61032 815-235-6121 235-6130* 162
**Fax:* Admissions ■ *Web:* www.highland.edu

Highland Community College (HCC)
606 W Main .... Highland KS 66035 785-442-6000 442-6106* 162
**Fax:* Admissions ■ *TF:* 800-985-9781 ■ *Web:* www.highlandcc.edu

Highland Computer Forms Inc
1025 W Main St .... Hillsboro OH 45133 937-393-4215 842-6485* 110
**Fax Area Code:* 800 ■ **Fax:* Sales ■ *TF:* 800-669-5213 ■ *Web:* www.hcf.com

Highland Containers 100 Ragsdale Rd .... Jamestown NC 27282 336-887-5400 701
Web: www.stronghaven.com

Highland County
119 Governor Foraker Pl .... Hillsboro OH 45133 937-393-1911 393-5850 338
TF: 800-774-1202 ■ *Web:* www.co.highland.oh.us

Highland County
County Offices Main St .... Monterey VA 24465 540-468-2347 468-3447 338
Web: www.highlandcova.org

Highland County Chamber of Commerce
PO Box 183 .... Hillsboro OH 45133 937-393-1111 139
Web: www.highlandcountychamber.com

Highland County District Library
10 Willettsville Pk .... Hillsboro OH 45133 937-393-3114 393-2985 434-3
Web: highlandco.org

Highland Engineering & Surveying Inc
1426 Memorial Dr .... Oakland MD 21550 301-334-6185 256
Web: highland-engineering.com

Highland Exchange Service Co-op
5916 Waverly Rd PO Box K .... Waverly FL 33877 863-439-3661 439-5383 315-2
Web: www.hesco-fl.com

Highland Falls-Ft Montgomery School District
PO Box 287 .... Highland Falls NY 10928 845-446-9575 685
Web: www.hffmcsd.org

Highland Fruit Growers Inc
8304 Wide Hollow Rd .... Yakima WA 98908 509-966-3990 315-3

Highland Helicopters Ltd
4240 Agar Dr .... Richmond BC V7B1A3 604-273-6161 273-6088 359
Web: www.highland.ca

Highland Homes
5601 Democracy Dr Ste 300 .... Dallas TX 75024 972-789-3500 653
TF: 800-570-2289 ■ *Web:* www.highlandhomes.com

Highland Hospital of Rochester
1000 S Ave .... Rochester NY 14620 585-473-2200 341-8350 374-3
TF: 800-499-9298 ■ *Web:* www.urmc.rochester.edu

Highland Lakes Newspapers Inc
304-A Highlander Cir .... Marble Falls TX 78654 830-693-4367 532-3
Web: www.highlandernews.com

Highland Lakes State Park
55-223 Tamms Rd .... Middletown NY 10911 845-786-2701 565
Web: parks.ny.gov/parks/5/details.aspx

Highland Machine 700 Fifth St .... Highland IL 62249 618-654-2103 654-8016 621
Web: www.highlandmachine.com

Highland Mills Inc 340 E 16th St .... Charlotte NC 28206 704-375-3333 342-0391 155-10
Web: www.highlandmills.com

Highland Nursing Home Inc
182 Highland Rd .... Massena NY 13662 315-769-9956 371
Web: www.highlandnursinghome.com

Highland Park Chamber of Commerce
508 Central Ave Ste 206 .... Highland Park IL 60035 847-432-0284 432-2802 139
Web: www.chamberhp.com

Highland Park Hospital
777 Pk Ave W .... Highland Park IL 60035 847-432-8000 374-3
Web: www.northshore.org

Highland Park Market of Farmington LLC
317 Highland St .... Manchester CT 06040 860-646-4277 345
Web: www.highlandparkmarket.com

Highland Park Public Library
494 Laurel Ave .... Highland Park IL 60035 847-432-0216 432-9139 434-3
TF: 800-566-5239 ■ *Web:* www.hplibrary.org

Highland Partnership Inc
285 Bay Blvd .... Chula Vista CA 91910 619-498-2900 186
Web: www.highlandpartnership.net

Highland Recreation Area
5200 E Highland Rd .... White Lake MI 48383 248-889-3750 565
Web: www.michigandnr.com

Highland Ridge Hospital 7309 S 180 W .... Midvale UT 84047 801-569-2153 726
TF: 800-821-4357 ■ *Web:* www.highlandridgehospital.com

Highland Rim Regional Library Ctr
2118 E Main St .... Murfreesboro TN 37130 615-893-3380 895-6727 434-3
Web: tennessee.gov

Highland Systems Inc
66 W Colorado Ave .... Memphis TN 38106 901-946-8677 115
Web: www.highlandsystems.net

Highland Tank & Manufacturing Co
1 Highland Rd .... Stoystown PA 15563 814-893-5701 893-6126 91
Web: www.highlandtank.com

Name / Address	City	State	Zip	Phone	Fax	Class
Highland Threads Inc 11700 Gloger St	Houston	TX	77039	281-986-5100	986-5151	350
Web: www.highlandthreads.com						
Highlander Charter School, The						
42 Lexington Ave	Providence	RI	02907	401-277-2600		237
Web: www.highlandercharter.org						
Highlands Bar & Grill						
2011 11th Ave S	Birmingham	AL	35205	205-939-1400	939-1405	671
TF: 800-292-4008 ■ *Web:* www.highlandsbarandgrill.com						
Highlands County 430 S Commerce Ave	Sebring	FL	33870	863-402-6500	402-6507	338
TF: 800-282-3655 ■ *Web:* www.hcbcc.net						
Highlands Diversified Services Inc						
250 Westinghouse Dr	London	KY	40741	606-878-1856		198
Web: www.hds-usa.com						
Highlands Fuel Delivery LLC						
190 Commerce Way	Portsmouth	NH	03801	888-310-1924		579
TF: 888-310-1924 ■ *Web:* www.irvingenergy.com						
Highlands Hammock State Park						
5931 Hammock Rd	Sebring	FL	33872	863-386-6094	386-6095	565
Web: www.floridastateparks.org/highlandshammock						
Highlands Medical Ctr						
380 Woods Cove Rd	Scottsboro	AL	35768	256-259-4444		374-3
Web: www.highlandsmedcenter.com						
Highlands Pathology Consultants Pc						
2175 Hwy 75 Ste 4	Blountville	TN	37617	423-323-5290		415
TF: 877-696-6775 ■ *Web:* www.highlandspath.com						
Highlands Regional Medical Ctr						
5000 KY Rt 321	Prestonsburg	KY	41653	606-886-8511		374-3
TF: 800-737-2723 ■ *Web:* www.hrmc.org						
Highlands Today 315 US Hwy 27 N	Sebring	FL	33870	863-386-5800		532-2
Web: www.highlandstoday.com						
Highlights for Children Inc						
1800 Watermark Dr	Columbus	OH	43216	614-486-0631	324-1630	637-9
TF Cust Svc: 800-255-9517 ■ *Web:* www.highlights.com						
Highline Community College						
2400 S 240th St	Des Moines	WA	98198	206-878-3710	870-4855	800
TF: 800-526-4629 ■ *Web:* www.highline.edu						
Highline Electric Assn						
1300 S Interocean Ave	Holyoke	CO	80734	970-854-2236	854-3652	245
TF: 800-816-2236 ■ *Web:* www.hea.coop						
Highline Lake State Park 1800 118 Rd	Loma	CO	81524	970-858-7208		565
Web: cpw.state.co.us						
Highline Medical Ctr						
16251 Sylvester Rd SW	Burien	WA	98166	206-244-9970		374-3
Web: www.chifranciscan.org/highline-medical-center						
Highline Portafab Inc						
20105 Broadway Ave SE	Snohomish	WA	98296	425-486-8031		480
Web: www.hpf.com						
Highline SeaTac Botanical Gardens						
13735 24th Ave S PO Box 69384	SeaTac	WA	98168	206-391-4003		97
Web: www.highlinegarden.org						
Highline United Methodist Church						
13015 First Ave S	Burien	WA	98168	206-241-5520		48-20
Web: highlineunitedmethodistchurch.org						
Highlines Construction Company Inc						
701 Bridge City Ave	Westwego	LA	70094	504-436-3961		189-4
Highmark Inc 120 Fifth Ave Pl	Pittsburgh	PA	15222	412-544-7000	302-7182*	391-3
**Fax Area Code:* 717 ■ **Fax:* Hum Res ■ *TF:* 800-992-0246 ■ *Web:* www.highmark.com						
HighPoint Technology Solutions Inc						
2332 Galiano St 2nd Fl	Coral Gables	FL	33134	800-767-0893		260
TF: 800-767-0893 ■ *Web:* www.mhighpoint.com						
HighPointe Hotel Corp						
311 Gulf Breeze Pkwy	Gulf Breeze	FL	32561	850-932-9314		378
Web: www.highpointe.com						
HighQuest Group						
300 Rosewood Dr Ste 260	Danvers	MA	01923	978-887-8800		463
Web: www.highquestgroup.com						
HighRes Biosolutions Inc						
299 Washington St	Woburn	MA	01801	781-932-1912		256
Web: www.highresbio.com						
Highroad Press LLC 220 Anderson Ave	Moonachie	NJ	07074	212-675-6500		627
Web: www.highroadpress.com						
Highstead Arboretum						
127 Lonetown Rd PO Box 1097	Redding	CT	06875	203-938-8809		97
Web: highstead.net						
Hightech American Industrial Laboratories Inc (HAI)						
320 Massachusetts Ave	Lexington	MA	02420	781-862-9884	860-7722	477
Web: www.hailabs.com						
Hightower Advertising Agency						
970 Ebenezer Blvd PO Box 622	Madison	MS	39110	601-853-1822		7
Web: www.hightoweragency.com						
Hightowers Petroleum Co						
3577 Commerce Dr	Middletown	OH	45005	513-423-4272		579
Web: hpc1952.businesscatalyst.com						
HighVista Strategies LLC						
200 Clarendon St John Hancock Tower 50th Fl	Boston	MA	02116	617-406-6500		194
Web: www.highvistastrategies.com						
Highway 11 Food Mart 322 Chesnee Hwy	Gaffney	SC	29341	864-489-4958		297-8
Highway Equipment Co						
1330 76th Ave SW	Cedar Rapids	IA	52404	319-363-8281	286-3350	190
Web: www.highwayequipment.com						
Highway Machine Company Inc (HMC)						
3010 S Old US Hwy 41	Princeton	IN	47670	812-385-3639	385-8186	454
TF: 866-990-9462 ■ *Web:* www.hmcgears.com						
Highway Safety Corp						
239 Commerce St	Glastonbury	CT	06033	860-633-9445		567
Web: www.highwaysafety.net						
Highway To Health Inc						
1 Radnor Corporate Ctr Ste 100	Radnor	PA	19087	888-243-2358	254-8797*	391-7
**Fax Area Code:* 610 ■ *TF:* 888-243-2358 ■ *Web:* www.hthtravelinsurance.com						
Highway Transport Logistics Inc (HTL)						
6420 Baum Dr	Knoxville	TN	37919	865-584-8631		780
Web: www.hytt.com						
Highwire Public Relations Inc						
727 sansome st	San Francisco	CA	94111	415-963-4174		636
Web: www.highwirepr.com						
Highwood USA LLC 87 Tide Rd	Tamaqua	PA	18252	570-668-6113		820
Web: www.highwood-usa.com						
Highwoods Properties Inc						
3100 Smoketree Ct Ste 600	Raleigh	NC	27604	919-872-4924		655
NYSE: HIW ■ *TF:* 866-449-6637 ■ *Web:* www.highwoods.com						
Higley Flow State Park						
442 Cold Brook Dr	Colton	NY	13625	315-262-2880		565
Web: parks.ny.gov/parks/58/details.aspx						
Higman Marine Services						
1980 Post Oak Blvd Ste 1101	Houston	TX	77056	713-552-1101	552-0732	465
TF: 800-375-5003 ■ *Web:* higman.com						
Hignell Book Printing 488 Burnell St	Winnipeg	MB	R3G2B4	204-784-1030		393
Web: www.hignell.mb.ca						
HII Technologies Inc						
8588 Katy Fwy Ste 430	Houston	TX	77024	713-821-3157		539
Web: www.hiitinc.com						
Hikaru 607 S Second St	Philadelphia	PA	19147	215-627-7110		671
Web: hikaruphilly.com						
Hikvision USA Inc						
908 Canada Ct	City Of Industry	CA	91748	909-895-0400		692
Web: hikvision.com						
Hiland Dairy Co PO Box 2270	Springfield	MO	65801	417-862-9311		296-27
TF: 800-641-4022 ■ *Web:* www.hilanddairy.com						
Hiland Toyota 5500 45th Ave Dr	Moline	IL	61265	309-764-2481		57
Web: www.hilandtoyota.com						
Hilbert College 5200 S Pk Ave	Hamburg	NY	14075	716-649-7900	649-1152	166
TF: 800-649-8003 ■ *Web:* www.hilbert.edu						
Hilburn & Lein CPA'S						
5520 S Ft Apache	Las Vegas	NV	89148	702-597-1945		2
Web: hilburn-lein.com						
Hilco Electric Co-op Inc						
115 E Main PO Box 127	Itasca	TX	76055	254-687-2331		245
TF: 800-338-6425 ■ *Web:* hilco.coop						
Hilco Federal Credit Union						
PO Box 291717	Kerrville	TX	78029-1717	830-257-8238	792-6865	219
Web: hilcocu.com						
Hilco Industrial LLC						
31555 W Fourteen Mile Rd Ste 207	Farmington Hills	MI	48334	248-254-9999		690
Web: www.hilcoind.com						
Hilco Merchant Resources LLC						
5 Revere Dr Ste 206	Northbrook	IL	60062	847-509-1100		690
Web: www.hilcomerchantresources.com						
Hilco Technologies Inc						
4172 Danvers Ct SE	Grand Rapids	MI	49512	616-957-1081		608
Web: www.hilcotech.com						
Hilco Transport Inc						
7700 Kenmont Rd	Greensboro	NC	27409	336-273-9441	273-9701	186
Web: www.hilcotransport.com						
Hile Group 1100 Beech St Bldg 15	Normal	IL	61761	309-888-4453		196
Web: www.hilegroup.com						
Hileman Enterprises LLC						
2217 E Ninth St Ste 200	Cleveland	OH	44115	216-923-1445		393
TF: 800-920-1023 ■ *Web:* www.hilemangroup.com						
Hi-Lex America Inc 5200 Wayne Rd	Battle Creek	MI	49037	269-968-0781		516
Web: www.hi-lex.com						
Hilford Moving & Storage						
1595 Arundell Ave	Ventura	CA	93003	805-642-0221		519
TF: 800-739-6683 ■ *Web:* www.hilford.com						
Hilgard House Hotel & Suites						
927 Hilgard Ave	Los Angeles	CA	90024	310-208-3945	208-1972	379
TF: 800-826-3934 ■ *Web:* www.hilgardhouse.com						
Hilgraeve Inc 115 E Elm Ave	Monroe	MI	48162	734-243-0576	243-0645	178-7
TF Sales: 800-826-2760 ■ *Web:* www.hilgraeve.com						
Hi-Life Cafe						
3000 N Federal Hwy	Fort Lauderdale	FL	33306	954-563-1395		671
Hi-Line Inc 2121 Vly View Ln	Dallas	TX	75234	972-247-6200		246
Web: www.hi-line.com						
Hilite International Inc						
250 Kay Industrial Dr	Orion	MI	48359	248-475-4580	475-4581	61
Web: www.hilite.com						
Hill & Company Real Estate Inc						
1880 Lombard St	San Francisco	CA	94123	415-921-6000		652
Web: www.marinadistrictrealestate.com						
Hill & Griffith Co 1085 Summer St	Cincinnati	OH	45204	513-921-1075	244-4199	500
TF: 800-543-0425 ■ *Web:* www.hillandgriffith.com						
Hill & Knowlton Inc 825 Third Ave	New York	NY	10022	212-885-0300		636
Web: www.hillandknowlton.com						
Hill & Ponton pa						
605 E Robinson St Ste 635	Orlando	FL	32801	386-257-2100		445
Web: www.hillandponton.com						
Hill & Stone Insurance Agency Inc						
900 N Shore Dr Ste 225	Lake Bluff	IL	60044	847-295-3030		390
Hill & Valley Premium Bakery						
320 44th St	Rock Island	IL	61201	309-793-0161	793-0183	68
TF: 800-480-0055 ■ *Web:* www.hillandvalley.net						
Hill Aerospace Museum						
7961 WaRdleigh Rd Bldg 1955	Hill AFB	UT	84056	801-777-6818	775-3034	520
Web: www.aerospaceutah.org						
Hill Aerosystems Inc						
911 Battersby Ave	Enumclaw	WA	98022	360-802-8300		22
Web: www.hillaerosystems.com						
Hill Air Force Base						
7981 Georgia St Bldg 1102	Hill Air Force Base	UT	84056	801-777-5201		497-1
Web: www.hill.af.mil						
Hill Barth & King LLC 6603 Summit Dr	Canfield	OH	44406	330-758-8613	758-0357	2
TF: 800-733-8613 ■ *Web:* www.hbkcpa.com						
Hill Bros Chemical Co 1675 N Main St	Orange	CA	92867	714-998-8800	998-6310	146
TF: 800-994-8801 ■ *Web:* www.hillbrothers.com						
Hill City Oil Company Inc 1409 Dunn St	Houma	LA	70360	985-851-4000		579
TF: 800-492-8377 ■ *Web:* www.hillcityoil.com						
Hill Co 8040 Germantown Ave	Philadelphia	PA	19118	215-247-7600	247-7603	319-4
Web: www.hill-company.com						
Hill College 112 Lamar Dr	Hillsboro	TX	76645	254-659-7500	582-7591*	162
**Fax:* Admissions ■ *Web:* www.hillcollege.edu						
Hill Correctional Ctr						
600 S Linwood Rd	Galesburg	IL	61401	309-343-4212		213
Hill Country Christian School of Austin						
12124 Ranch Rd 620 N	Austin	TX	78750	512-331-7036		148
Web: www.hillcountrychristianschool.org						

Name / Address	City	State	ZIP	Phone	Fax	Class
Hill Country Furniture Partners Ltd 1431 Fm 1101	New Braunfels	TX	78130	830-515-1400		321
Web: www.hillcountryholdings.com						
Hill Country State Natural Area 10600 Bandera Creek Rd	Bandera	TX	78003	830-796-4413		565
Web: tpwd.texas.gov/state-parks/hill-country						
Hill County 315 Fourth St	Havre	MT	59501	406-265-5481		338
Web: www.hillcounty.us						
Hill County PO Box 398	Hillsboro	TX	76645	254-582-4030	582-4003	338
Web: www.co.hill.tx.us						
Hill County Electric Co-op Inc PO Box 2330	Havre	MT	59501	877-394-7804		245
TF: 877-394-7804 ■ *Web:* www.hcelectric.com						
Hill Crest Behavioral Health Services 6869 Fifth Ave S	Birmingham	AL	35212	205-833-9000		374-5
TF: 800-292-8553 ■ *Web:* www.hillcrestbhs.com						
Hill Distributing Co 2555 Harrison Rd	Columbus	OH	43204	614-276-6533		81-1
Hill French (Rep R - AR) 1229 Longworth House Office Bldg	Washington	DC	20515	202-225-2506	225-5903	342-2
Web: hill.house.gov						
Hill Home Furnishings Inc 116 N Fifth St	Beatrice	NE	68310	402-228-4085		321
Web: hillhomefurnishings.com						
Hill International Inc 303 Lippincott Ctr	Marlton	NJ	08053	856-810-6200	810-1309	261
NYSE: HIL ■ *TF:* 800-732-0330 ■ *Web:* www.hillintl.com						
Hill Larson Walth & Benda Pa 326 N Main St	Austin	MN	55912	507-433-2264		2
Web: hlwb-cpa.com						
Hill Mechanical Group 11045 Gage Ave	Franklin Park	IL	60131	847-451-5000	451-5011	189-10
TF: 800-233-8990 ■ *Web:* www.hillgrp.com						
Hill Mfg Company Inc 1500 Jonesboro Rd SE	Atlanta	GA	30315	404-522-8364	522-9694	151
TF: 800-445-5123 ■ *Web:* www.hillmfg.com						
Hill Museum & Manuscript Library PO Box 7300	Collegeville	MN	56321	320-363-3514		434-3
TF: 800-654-0476 ■ *Web:* www.hmml.org						
Hill PHOENIX Inc 1003 Sigman Rd	Conyers	GA	30013	770-285-3264	285-3080	664
TF: 800-518-6630 ■ *Web:* www.hillphoenix.com						
Hill Physicians Medical Group Inc 2409 Camino Ramon PO Box 5080	San Ramon	CA	94583	925-820-8300		463
TF: 800-445-5747 ■ *Web:* www.hillphysicians.com						
Hill School 717 E High St	Pottstown	PA	19464	610-326-1000	705-1753	622
TF: 877-651-2800 ■ *Web:* www.thehill.org						
Hill Schroderus & Company LLP 923 Spring St	Petoskey	MI	49770	231-347-4136		2
Web: hs-co.com						
Hill Times 69 Sparks St	Ottawa	ON	K1P5A5	613-232-5952		532-3
TF: 800-858-9242 ■ *Web:* www.hilltimes.com						
Hill View Retirement Ctr 1610 Twenty-Eighth St	Portsmouth	OH	45662	740-354-3135		371
TF: 800-545-4121 ■ *Web:* www.hillviewretirement.org						
Hill Ward Henderson 101 E Kennedy Blvd Ste 3700	Tampa	FL	33602	813-221-3900		428
Web: www.hwhlaw.com						
Hill Wood Products Inc 9483 Ashawa Rd	Cook	MN	55723	218-666-5933	666-5726	551
TF: 800-788-9689 ■ *Web:* www.hillwoodproducts.com						
Hill's Lexington Barbecue 4005 Patterson Ave	Winston-Salem	NC	27105	336-767-2184		671
Web: ncbbqsociety.com						
Hill's Pet Nutrition Inc 400 SW Eigth St	Topeka	KS	66603	785-354-8523		578
Web: www.hillspet.com						
Hill, Farrer & Burrill LLP 300 S Grand Ave 37th Fl	Los Angeles	CA	90071	213-620-0460		428
Web: www.hillfarrer.com						
Hillcraft Ltd 2202 Advance Rd	Madison	WI	53718	608-221-3220		225
TF: 800-447-2257 ■ *Web:* hillcraft.com						
Hillcrest Baptist Medical Ctr 3000 Herring Ave	Waco	TX	76708	254-202-2000		374-3
TF: 800-793-6030 ■ *Web:* sw.org/location/waco-hillcrest-hospital						
Hillcrest Church of Christ 307 Oak St	Tunnel Hill	GA	30755	706-673-2234		48-20
Hillcrest Foods 2695 E 40th St	Cleveland	OH	44115	216-361-4625		297-4
Web: www.hillcrestfoods.com						
Hillcrest Garden 95 W Century Rd	Paramus	NJ	07652	201-599-3030		292
TF: 800-437-7000 ■ *Web:* hillcrestgarden.com						
Hillcrest Historic District Markham & Kavanaugh	Little Rock	AR	72216	501-371-0075	374-8142	50-6
TF: 877-637-0037 ■ *Web:* www.arkansas.com						
Hillcrest Homes 2705 Mtn View Dr	La Verne	CA	91750	909-392-4375		672
TF: 800-811-6617 ■ *Web:* www.livingathillcrest.org						
Hillcrest Hospital 6780 Mayfield Rd	Mayfield Heights	OH	44124	440-312-4500		374-3
TF: 800-707-8922 ■ *Web:* my.clevelandclinic.org						
Hillcrest Medical Ctr 1120 S Utica Ave	Tulsa	OK	74104	918-579-1000		374-3
Web: www.hillcrest.com						
Hillcrest Youth Correctional Facility 2450 Strong Rd SE	Salem	OR	97302	503-986-0400	986-0406	412
Web: oregon.gov						
Hilldale Church of Christ Inc 501 Hwy 76	Clarksville	TN	37043	931-647-5264		48-20
Web: hilldalecc.org						
Hillel: The Foundation for Jewish Campus Life 800 Eighth St NW	Washington	DC	20001	202-449-6500		48-20
Web: www.hillel.org						
Hillenbrand Industries Inc 1 Batesville Blvd	Batesville	IN	47006	812-934-7500	934-7613	250
NYSE: HI ■ *Web:* www.hillenbrand.com						
Hiller Aviation Museum 601 Skyway Rd	San Carlos	CA	94070	650-654-0200		520
TF: 888-500-1555 ■ *Web:* hiller.org						
Hiller Inc 630 N Washington	Wichita	KS	67214	316-264-8022		22
Web: www.hillerinc.com						
Hiller Inc 24359 Northwestern Hwy Ste 150	Southfield	MI	48075	248-355-2122		345
Hillerich & Bradsby Company Inc 800 W Main St	Louisville	KY	40202	502-585-5226		710
TF: 800-282-2287 ■ *Web:* www.slugger.com						
Hillfield Strathallan College 299 Fennell Ave W	Hamilton	ON	L9C1G3	905-389-1367		623
Web: www.hsc.on.ca						
Hilliard Corp 100 W Fourth St	Elmira	NY	14902	607-733-7121	733-3009	620
Web: www.hilliardcorp.com						
Hilliard Energy Inc 3001 W Loop 250 N Ste E103	Midland	TX	79705	432-683-9100		539
TF: 800-287-0014 ■ *Web:* www.hilliardenergy.com						
Hilliker Corp 1401 S Brentwood Blvd Ste 650	St Louis	MO	63144	314-781-0001		652
Web: www.hillikercorp.com						
Hillis, Clark, Martin & Peterson PS 1221 Second Ave Ste 500	Seattle	WA	98101	206-623-1745		428
Web: www.hcmp.com						
Hillman Group Inc 10590 Hamilton Ave	Cincinnati	OH	45231	513-851-4900	851-4997	351
TF: 800-800-4900 ■ *Web:* www.hillmangroup.com						
Hillman, Brown & Darrow PA 221 Duke Of Gloucester St	Annapolis	MD	21401	410-263-3131		428
Web: www.hbdlaw.com						
Hillmann & Carr Inc 2233 Wisconsin Ave NW Ste 425	Washington	DC	20007	202-342-0001		514
Web: www.hillmanncarr.com						
Hill-Rom Services Inc 1069 SR 46 E	Batesville	IN	47006	812-934-7777	934-8189	319-3
TF: 800-267-2337 ■ *Web:* www.hill-rom.com						
Hills Bank & Trust Co 131 Main St PO Box 70	Hills	IA	52235	319-679-2291	679-2180	70
TF: 800-445-5725 ■ *Web:* www.hillsbank.com						
Hills Communities Inc 4901 Hunt Rd	Cincinnati	OH	45242	513-984-0300		653
Web: www.hillsinc.com						
Hills Creek State Park 111 Spillway Rd	Wellsboro	PA	16901	570-724-4246		565
Web: www.dcnr.state.pa.us						
HILLS Inc 7785 Ellis Rd	West Melbourne	FL	32904	321-724-2370		111
TF: 800-209-8043 ■ *Web:* www.hillsinc.net						
Hills Materials Co 3975 Sturgis Rd	Rapid City	SD	57702	605-394-3300	341-3446	503-4
Web: www.hillsmaterials.com						
Hillsboro Argus 1500 SW First Ave	Portland	OR	97201	503-648-1131	648-9191	532-4
TF: 800-544-0505 ■ *Web:* www.oregonlive.com						
Hillsboro Chamber of Commerce 5193 NE Elam Young Pkwy Ste A	Hillsboro	OR	97124	503-648-1102		139
Web: hillsborochamberor.com						
Hillsboro City Schools 39 Willetsville Pk	Hillsboro	OH	45133	937-393-3475		685
Web: www.hillsboro.k12.oh.us						
Hillsboro Community Unit School District 3 1311 Vandalia Rd	Hillsboro	IL	62049	217-532-2942	532-3137	685
Web: www.hillsboroschools.net						
Hillsboro Equipment Inc E18898 Hwy 33	Hillsboro	WI	54634	608-489-2275	489-2717	274
TF: 800-521-5133 ■ *Web:* www.hillsboroequipment.com						
Hillsboro Public Library 2850 NE Brookwood Pkwy	Hillsboro	OR	97124	503-615-6500		434-3
Web: www.wccls.org/libraries/hillsboro						
Hillsboro School District 3083 NE 49th Pl	Hillsboro	OR	97124	503-844-1500	844-1540	685
Web: www.hsd.k12.or.us						
Hillsborough Community College (HCC)						
Brandon 10414 E Columbus Dr	Tampa	FL	33619	813-253-7801		162
Web: www.hccfl.edu/campus/br						
Dale Mabry 4001 Tampa Bay Blvd	Tampa	FL	33614	813-253-7000		162
TF: 866-253-7077 ■ *Web:* www.hccfl.edu						
Plant City 1206 N Pk Rd	Plant City	FL	33566	813-757-2102		162
Web: www.hccfl.edu						
Ybor City 2112 N 15th St PO Box 5096	Tampa	FL	33675	813-253-7602		162
Web: www.hccfl.edu						
Hillsborough County 329 Mast Rd	Goffstown	NH	03045	603-627-5600	627-5603	338
Web: www.hillsboroughcountynh.org						
Hillsborough County 800 E Twigg St	Tampa	FL	33602	813-276-8100		338
Web: www.hillsboroughcounty.org						
Hillsborough County Public Schools 901 E Kennedy Blvd	Tampa	FL	33602	813-272-4000	272-4073	685
TF: 800-962-2873 ■ *Web:* www.sdhc.k12.fl.us						
Hillsborough Regional Juvenile Detention Ctr West 3948 ML King Jr Blvd	Tampa	FL	33614	813-871-7650	871-4764	412
TF: 800-355-2280 ■ *Web:* www.djj.state.fl.us						
Hillsborough River State Park 15402 US 301 N	Thonotosassa	FL	33592	813-987-6771		565
Web: www.floridastateparks.org						
Hillsborough Township Board of Education 379 S Branch Rd	Hillsborough	NJ	08844	908-431-6600	369-8286	685
Web: www.htps.us						
Hillsdale College 33 E College St	Hillsdale	MI	49242	517-437-7341	437-3923*	166
**Fax:* Admissions ■ *TF:* 888-886-1174 ■ *Web:* www.hillsdale.edu						
Hillsdale County 29 N Howell St	Hillsdale	MI	49242	517-437-3391	437-3392	338
TF: 800-315-3593 ■ *Web:* www.co.hillsdale.mi.us						
Hillsdale Free Will Baptist College PO Box 7208	Moore	OK	73153	405-912-9000	912-9050*	166
**Fax:* Admissions ■ *TF:* 800-460-6328 ■ *Web:* www.hc.edu						
Hillsdale Investment Management Inc 100 Wellington St W Ste 2100 TD Centre	Toronto	ON	M5K1J3	416-913-3900	913-3901	401
Web: www.hillsdaleinv.com						
Hillsdale Shopping Ctr 60 31st Ave	San Mateo	CA	94403	650-345-8222		460
Web: www.hillsdale.com						
Hillsdale State Park 26001 W 255th St	Paola	KS	66071	913-783-4507		565
Web: ksoutdoors.com/state-parks/locations/hillsdale						
Hillshire Brands 2200 W Don Tyson Pkwy	Springdale	AR	72762	479-290-6397		214
Web: www.tysonfoods.com/hillshire-brands.aspx						
Hillside Candy Co 35 Hillside Ave	Hillside	NJ	07205	973-926-2300	926-4440	296-8
TF: 800-524-1304 ■ *Web:* www.hillsidecandy.com						
Hillside Cemetery Assn 1401 Woodland Ave	Scotch Plains	NJ	07076	908-756-1729		510
Web: hillsidecemetery.com						

Phone | Fax | Class

Hillside Plastics Inc
262 Millers Falls Rd .... Turners Falls MA 01376 413-863-2222 98
Web: www.hillsideplastics.com

Hillside Rehabilitation Hospital (HRH)
8747 Squires Ln NE .... Warren OH 44484 330-841-3893 374-6
Web: valleycareofohio.com

Hillside School 404 Robin Hill Rd. .... Marlborough MA 01752 508-485-2824 485-4420 622
TF: 800-344-8328 ■ *Web:* www.hillsideschool.net

Hill-Stead Museum 35 Mountain Rd .... Farmington CT 06032 860-677-4787 677-0174 520
Web: www.hillstead.org

Hillstone Restaurant Group
147 S Beverly Dr. .... Beverly Hills CA 90212 800-230-9787 670
TF: 800-230-9787 ■ *Web:* www.hillstone.com

Hilltop Arboretum
11855 Highland Rd. .... Baton Rouge LA 70810 225-767-6916 768-7740 97
Web: sites01.lsu.edu/wp/hilltop

Hilltop Basic Resources Inc
1 W Fourth St Ste 1100 .... Cincinnati OH 45202 513-651-5000 684-8222 182
Web: www.hilltopbasicresources.com

Hilltop Elementary School
2615 W Lincoln Rd. .... Mchenry IL 60051 815-385-4421 685
Web: www.d15.org

Hilltop Enterprises Inc
1157 Phoenixville Pk Ste 102. .... West Chester PA 19380 610-430-6920 192
Web: www.hilltopenterprises.com

Hilltop Garden & Nature Ctr
Indiana University Campus
2367 E Tenth St .... Bloomington IN 47408 812-855-8808 97

Hilltop Inn of Vermont
3472 Airport Rd .... Montpelier VT 05602 802-229-5766 229-5766 379
TF: 877-609-0003 ■ *Web:* www.hilltopinnvt.net

Hilltop Lodge Retirement Community
815 N Independence .... Beloit KS 67420 785-738-3516 371
Web: www.hilltoplodgeretirementcomm.org

Hilltop Mall 2200 Hilltop Mall Rd .... Richmond CA 94806 510-223-6900 460
Web: www.shophilltop.com

Hilltop Slate
3 County Rt 21 PO Box 201 .... Middle Granville NY 12849 518-642-2270 642-1220 724
Web: www.hilltopslate.com

Hilltop Village 25900 Euclid Ave. .... Euclid OH 44132 216-261-8383 261-6816 672
TF: 800-805-3621 ■ *Web:* www.hilltopvillage.com

Hilltown Pork Inc 12948 SR-22 .... Canaan NY 12029 518-781-4050 473
Web: www.hilltownpork.com

Hillview Capital Advisors LLC
777 THIRD AVE 28th Fl. .... New York PA 10017 484-708-4720 401
Web: www.hillviewcap.com

Hillwig-Goodrow Inc
31407 Outer Hwy 10. .... Redlands CA 92373 909-794-2673 727
Web: hillwig-goodrow.com

Hillwood Estate Museum & Gardens
4155 Linnean Ave NW .... Washington DC 20008 202-686-5807 966-7840 520
Web: www.hillwoodmuseum.org

Hillwood International Energy L P
3090 Olive St Ste 420. .... Dallas TX 75219 214-754-2316 506
Web: www.hillwood.com

Hillyard Chemical Company Inc
302 N Fourth St PO Box 909 .... Saint Joseph MO 64501 816-233-1321 861-0256* 151
**Fax Area Code:* 800 ■ *TF:* 800-365-1555 ■ *Web:* www.hillyard.com

Hilman Inc 12 Timber Ln .... Marlboro NJ 07746 732-462-6277 462-6355 470
TF Cust Svc: 888-276-5548 ■ *Web:* www.hilmanrollers.com

Hilmar Cheese Company Inc PO Box 910 .... Hilmar CA 95324 209-667-6076 634-1408 296-5
TF: 800-577-5772 ■ *Web:* www.hilmarcheese.com

Hilo Medical Ctr 1190 Waianuenue Ave .... Hilo HI 96720 808-932-3000 974-4746 374-3
Web: www.hilomedicalcenter.org

Hi-lo Motel Cafe & Rv Park
88 S Weed Blvd .... Weed CA 96094 530-938-2904 378
Web: www.sisdevco.com

Hilscher Clarke Electric Co
519 Fourth St NW. .... Canton OH 44703 330-452-9806 189-4
Web: www.hilscher-clarke.com

Hilti Inc 5400 S 122nd E Ave .... Tulsa OK 74146 918-252-6000 879-7000* 759
**Fax Area Code:* 800 ■ *TF Cust Svc:* 800-879-8000 ■ *Web:* www.us.hilti.com

Hilton Akron Fairlawn
3180 W Market St. .... Fairlawn OH 44333 330-867-5024 707
Web: www.akronhilton.com

Hilton Anaheim 777 W Convention Way .... Anaheim CA 92802 714-750-4321 379
Web: www3.hilton.com

Hilton Atlanta Northeast
5993 Peachtree Industrial Blvd. .... Norcross GA 30092 770-447-4747 379
Web: hilton.com

Hilton Charleston Harbor Resort & Marina
20 Patriots Pt Rd. .... Mount Pleasant SC 29464 843-856-0028 856-8333 669
Web: www.charlestonharborresort.com

Hilton Checkers Los Angeles
535 S Grand Ave. .... Los Angeles CA 90071 213-624-0000 671
Web: www3.hilton.com

Hilton Concord 1970 Diamond Bouleverd .... Concord CA 94520 925-827-2000 378
Web: www3.hilton.com/en/hotels/california/hilton-concord-CONCHHF/index.html

Hilton Galveston Island Resort
5400 Seawall Blvd .... Galveston TX 77551 409-744-5000 740-2209 669
TF: 800-475-3386 ■ *Web:* www3.hilton.com/en/index.html

Hilton Garden Inn Baton Rouge Airport
3330 Harding Blvd .... Baton Rouge LA 70807 225-357-6177 378
Web: www.pinkshell.com

Hilton Garden Inn (Burlington Canada)
985 Syscon Rd .... Burlington ON L7L5S3 905-631-7000 631-7000 379
Web: hiltongardeninn3.hilton.com

Hilton Garden Inn Greenville
108 Carolina Point Pkwy .... Greenville SC 29605 864-284-0111 379
Web: hiltongardeninn3.hilton.com

Hilton Grand Vacations Company LLC
6355 Metro W Blvd Ste 180 .... Orlando FL 32835 407-722-3100 753
TF: 800-230-7068 ■ *Web:* www.hiltongrandvacations.com

Hilton Hawaiian Village
2005 Kalia Rd. .... Honolulu HI 96815 808-949-4321 951-5458 669
TF: 800-445-8667 ■ *Web:* www.hilton.com

Hilton Head Health Institute
14 Valencia Rd .... Hilton Head Island SC 29928 843-785-3919 706
TF: 800-292-2440 ■ *Web:* www.hhhealth.com

Hilton Head Island Airport
120 Beach City Rd .... Hilton Head Island SC 29926 843-255-2950 689-5411 27
Web: bcgov.net

Hilton Head Island Beach & Tennis Resort
40 Folly Field Rd .... Hilton Head Island SC 29928 843-842-4402 669
TF Resv: 800-475-2631 ■ *Web:* www.hhibeachandtennis.com

Hilton Head Island Town Hall
1 Town Ctr Ct .... Hilton Head Island SC 29928 843-341-4600 842-7728 337
Web: www.hiltonheadislandsc.gov

Hilton Head Island Visitor & Convention Bureau, The
1 Chamber of Commerce Dr
PO Box 5647 .... Hilton Head Island SC 29938 843-785-3673 785-7110 139
TF: 800-523-3373 ■ *Web:* www.hiltonheadisland.org

Hilton Head Island Visitors & Convention Bureau
1 Chamber of Commerce Dr
PO Box 5647 .... Hilton Head Island SC 29938 843-785-3673 785-7110 206
TF: 800-523-3373 ■ *Web:* www.hiltonheadisland.org

Hilton Head Library
11 Beach City Rd .... Hilton Head Island SC 29926 843-255-6500 434-3
Web: beaufortcountylibrary.org

Hilton Head Regional Medical Ctr
25 Hospital Ctr Blvd .... Hilton Head Island SC 29926 843-681-6122 374-3
Web: www.hiltonheadregional.com

Hilton Hotel Waco
113 S University Parks Dr. .... Waco TX 76701 254-754-8484 378
Web: www.hiltonwaco.com

Hilton Jackson 1001 E County Line Rd. .... Jackson MS 39211 601-957-2800 379
Web: www.hiltonjackson.com

Hilton La Jolla Torrey Pines
10950 N Torrey Pines Rd .... La Jolla CA 92037 858-558-1500 379
Web: hilton.com

Hilton Long Beach Hotel & Executive Meeting Center
701 W Ocean Blvd .... Long Beach CA 90831 562-983-3400 379
Web: hiltonlb.com

Hilton Longboat Key Beach Resort
4711 Gulf of Mexico Dr .... Longboat Key FL 34228 941-383-2451 383-7979 669
Web: www3.hilton.com/en/index.html

Hilton Marco Island Beach Resort
560 S Collier Blvd .... Marco Island FL 34145 239-394-5000 394-8410 669
Web: www3.hilton.com/en/index.html

Hilton Miami Downtown
1601 Biscayne Blvd .... Miami FL 33132 305-374-0000 378
Web: www.hiltonmiamidowntown.com

Hilton Myrtle Beach Resort
10000 Beach Club Dr .... Myrtle Beach SC 29572 843-449-5000 497-0168 669
TF: 800-445-8667 ■ *Web:* www.hilton.com

Hilton Mystic 20 Coogan Blvd. .... Mystic CT 06355 860-572-0731 707
Web: www.hiltonmystic.com

Hilton New Orleans Riverside
2 Poydras St. .... New Orleans LA 70130 504-561-0500 653
Web: www3.hilton.com

Hilton Orlando Buena Vista Palace
1900 E Buena Vista Dr .... Lake Buena Vista FL 32830 407-827-2727 669
Web: www.buenavistapalace.com

Hilton Pasadena Hotel
168 S Los Robles Ave. .... Pasadena CA 91101 626-577-1000 707
Web: www.daytonahilton.com

Hilton Ponce Golf & Casino Resort
1150 Ave Caribe .... Ponce PR 00716 787-259-7676 132
Web: www3.hilton.com

Hilton Providence 21 Atwells Ave. .... Providence RI 02903 401-831-3900 379
Web: hilton.com

Hilton San Diego Resort
1775 E Mission Bay Dr. .... San Diego CA 92109 619-276-4010 275-8944 669
TF: 800-445-8667 ■ *Web:* www.hilton.com

Hilton Sandestin Beach Golf Resort & Spa
4000 Sandestin Blvd S .... Destin FL 32550 850-267-9500 267-3076 669
TF: 800-559-1805 ■ *Web:* hiltonsandestinbeach.com

Hilton Savannah Desoto
15 E Liberty St .... Savannah GA 31401 912-232-9000 378
TF: 800-874-9600 ■ *Web:* www.desotohilton.com

Hilton Scranton & Conference Ctr
100 Adams Ave. .... Scranton PA 18503 570-343-3000 343-8415 377
TF: 800-445-8667 ■ *Web:* www.hilton.com

Hilton Sedona Resort & Spa
90 Ridge Trl Dr .... Sedona AZ 86351 928-284-4040 669
TF General: 877 273-3762 ■ *Web:* www3.hilton.com/en/index.html

Hilton Short Hills 41 JFK Pkwy. .... Short Hills NJ 07078 973-379-0100 379-6870 707
TF: 800-445-8667 ■ *Web:* www3.hilton.com

Hilton St Louis Hotel at BaLLPark
1 S Broadway .... Saint Louis MO 63102 314-421-1776 379
Web: www3.hilton.com

Hilton Suites Atlanta Perimeter
6120 Peachtree Dunwoody Rd NE .... Atlanta GA 30328 770-668-0808 379
Web: hilton.com

Hilton Suites Toronto/Markham Conference Ctr
8500 Warden Ave .... Markham ON L6G1A5 905-470-8500 477-8611 707
TF: 800-445-8667 ■ *Web:* www3.hilton.com

Hilton Tampa Airport Westshore, The
2225 N Lois Ave .... Tampa FL 33607 813-877-6688 707
Web: www3.hilton.com

Hilton Valve 14520 NE 91st Ct .... Redmond WA 98052 425-883-7000 789
Web: www.dezurik.com

Hilton Waikoloa Village
425 Waikoloa Beach Dr. .... Waikoloa HI 96738 808-886-1234 886-2900 669
TF: 866-931-1679 ■ *Web:* www.hiltonwaikoloavillage.com

Hilton Whistler Resort & Spa
4050 Whistler Way .... Whistler BC V0N1B4 604-932-1982 966-5093 669
TF: 800-515-4050 ■ *Web:* www.hiltonwhistler.com

Hilton Winnipeg Airport Suites
1800 Wellington Ave. .... Winnipeg MB R3H1B2 204-783-1700 786-6588 378
Web: www3.hilton.com

Hilton Woodcliff Lake
200 Tice Blvd .... Woodcliff Lake NJ 07677 201-391-3600 378
Web: www.hiltonwoodclifflake.com

Hilton Worldwide 7930 Jones Branch Dr .... McLean VA 22102 703-883-1000 379
TF: 800-445-8667 ■ *Web:* www.hiltonworldwide.com

	Phone	Fax	Class
Himalayan Institute Ctr for Health & Healing 952 Bethany Tpke........................Honesdale PA 18431 TF: 800-822-4547 ■ Web: www.himalayaninstitute.org	570-253-5551		706
Himebaugh Consulting Inc 4940 Munson St NW Ste 2100..................Canton OH 44718 TF: 800-362-0622 ■ Web: www.hcd.net	330-493-9700		196
HiMEC Mechanical 1400 Seventh St NW........Rochester MN 55901 Web: www.himec.com	507-281-4000	281-5206	189-10
Himes Jim (Rep D - CT) 1227 Longworth HOB....................Washington DC 20515 Web: himes.house.gov	202-225-5541	225-9629	342-2
Himes Vending Inc 4654 Groves Rd..........Columbus OH 43232 Web: himesvending.com	614-868-6931		113
Himoinsa Power Systems Inc 16002 W 110th St............................Lenexa KS 66219 TF: 866-710-2988 ■ Web: www.hipowersystems.com	913-495-5557		518
HIMSS (Healthcare Information & Management Systems Society) 230 E Ohio St Ste 500......................Chicago IL 60611 TF: 800-982-2182 ■ Web: www.himss.org	312-664-4467	664-6143	49-8
Hinchcliff Products Co 13550 Falling Water Rd..................Strongsville OH 44136 TF: 800-752-1220 ■ Web: www.hinchcliffproducts.com	440-238-5200	238-5202	551
Hinckley Allen & Snyder LLP 28 State St..................................Boston MA 02109 Web: www.hinckleyallen.com	617-345-9000		428
Hinckley Co, The 1 Little Harbor Landing...................Portsmouth RI 02871 TF: 866-446-2553 ■ Web: www.hinckleyyachts.com	401-683-7005		90
Hinda Incentives Inc 2440 W 34th St..........Chicago IL 60608 Web: www.hinda.com	773-890-5900	890-4606	765
Hinderliter Construction Inc 3601 N Saint Joseph Ave..................Evansville IN 47720 Web: www.hinderliterconstruction.com	812-425-4137		186
Hindley Mfg Company Inc 9 Havens St...........................Cumberland RI 02864 TF: 800-323-9031 ■ Web: www.hindley.com	401-722-2550	722-3083	350
Hinds Community College 501 E Main St PO Box 1100..................Raymond MS 39154 *Fax: Admissions ■ TF: 800-446-3722 ■ Web: www.hindscc.edu	601-857-5261	857-3539*	162
Rankin 3805 Hwy 80 E.........................Pearl MS 39208 Web: www.hindscc.edu	601-932-5237		162
Hinds County 316 S President St...............Jackson MS 39201 Web: www.co.hinds.ms.us	601-968-6508	968-6794	338
Hinds County School District 13192 Hwy 18...........................Raymond MS 39154 Web: www.hinds.k12.ms.us	601-857-5222	857-8548	685
Hinds Hospice 1616 W Shaw Ste C-1............Fresno CA 93711 TF: 800-400-4677 ■ Web: www.hindshospice.org	559-248-8591	222-4782	371
Hindsdale Nurseries Inc 7200 S Madison Rd.....................Willowbrook IL 60527 Web: www.hinsdalenurseries.com	630-323-1411		422
Hinduja Global Solutions Inc 4355 Weaver Pkwy Ste 310...............Warrenville IL 60555 Web: www.teamhgs.com	309-229-2837		393
Hines Corp 1218 Pontaluna Rd Ste B..........Spring Lake MI 49456 Web: www.hinescorp.com	231-799-6240	799-6298	360-3
Hines Group Inc, The 5680 Old Hwy 54 E..........................Philpot KY 42366 TF: 800-345-8082 ■ Web: www.thehinesgroup.com	270-729-4242		489
Hines Interest LP 2800 Post Oak Blvd..........Houston TX 77056 Web: www.hines.com	713-621-8000		653
Hines Nut Co Inc 990 S St Paul St...............Dallas TX 75201 TF: 800-561-6374 ■ Web: www.hinesnut.com	214-939-0253		296-28
Hines Park Lincoln Inc 40601 Ann Arbor Rd.......................Plymouth MI 48170 Web: www.hinesparklincoln.com	734-619-6272	453-8333	57
Hingham Institution for Savings 55 Main St................................Hingham MA 02043 NASDAQ: HIFS ■ Web: www.hinghamsavings.com	781-749-2200	740-4889	70
Hingham Mutual Fire Insurance Co 230 Beal St..............................Hingham MA 02043 TF: 800-341-8200 ■ Web: www.hinghammutual.com	781-749-0841	749-4477	391-4
Hingham School District 220 Central St............................Hingham MA 02043 Web: www.hingham-ma.com	781-741-1500		685
Hiniker Co 58766 240th St...................Mankato MN 56002 *Fax: Sales ■ TF: 800-433-5620 ■ Web: www.hiniker.com	507-625-6621	625-5883*	273
Hinkle Contracting Corp 395 N Middletown Rd.........................Paris KY 40361 TF: 800-442-8878 ■ Web: www.hinklecontracting.com	859-987-3670	987-0727	188-4
Hinkle Elkouri Law Firm LLC 2000 Epic Ctr 301 N Main St.................Wichita KS 67202 Web: hinklaw.com	316-267-2000		428
Hinkle Insurance Agency Inc 600 Olde Hickory Rd Ste 200................Lancaster PA 17601 TF: 877-408-1418 ■ Web: hinkleinsurance.com	717-560-9733		390
Hinkle Metals & Supply Company Inc 3300 11th Ave N.........................Birmingham AL 35234 Web: hinklemetals.com	205-326-3300		612
Hinkley Lighting 12600 Berea Rd.............Cleveland OH 44111 TF: 800-446-5539 ■ Web: www.hinkleylighting.com	216-671-3300	671 4537	439
Hinman, Howard & Kattell LLP 700 Security Mutual 80 Exchange St.........Binghamton NY 13901 Web: www.hhk.com	607-723-5341		428
Hinsdale County 311 N Henson St.............Lake City CO 81235 TF: 877-944-7575 ■ Web: www.hinsdalecountycolorado.us	970-944-2225	944-2630	338
Hinshaw & Culbertson LLP 222 N LaSalle St Ste 300....................Chicago IL 60601 Web: www.hinshawlaw.com	312-704-3000		428
Hinshaws Acura/Honda 5955 20th St E..............Fife WA 98424 TF: 800-752-2872 ■ Web: hinshawsacura.com	253-922-8830		57
Hinterland Brewery & Restaurant 313 Dousman St..........................Green Bay WI 54303 Web: www.hinterlandbeer.com	920-438-8050		671
Hinton Lakeview Inns & Suites 500 Smith St...............................Hinton AB T7V2A1 TF: 877-355-3500 ■ Web: www.lakeviewhotels.com	780-865-2575		378
Hintzsche Fertilizer Inc 2 S 181 County Line Rd...................Maple Park IL 60151	630-557-2406		280
HiPerSoft (Center for High Performance Software Research) Rice University 6100 Main St MS-41............Houston TX 77005 Web: www.hipersoft.rice.edu	713-348-5186	348-3111	668
Hippocrates Health Institute Life-Change Ctr 1443 Palmdale Ct....................West Palm Beach FL 33411 TF: 800-842-2125 ■ Web: www.hippocratesinst.org	561-471-8876	471-9464	706
Hippodrome State Theatre 25 SE Second Pl..........................Gainesville FL 32601 Web: thehipp.org	352-373-5968		720
HipSwap Inc 2436 Second St..............Santa Monica CA 90405 Web: www.hipswap.com	310-396-5400		387
Hiram College PO Box 67.........................Hiram OH 44234 *Fax: Admissions ■ TF Admissions: 800-362-5280 ■ Web: www.hiram.edu	330-569-5169	569-5944*	166
Hire Demand 106 Pinehurst Dr.................Cranberry Township PA 16066 TF: 866-344-8014 ■ Web: hiredemand.com	724-538-3434		260
Hire Dynamics LLC 1845 Satellite Blvd Ste 800....................Duluth GA 30097 Web: www.hiredynamics.com	678-482-0200		193
Hire Image LLC 6 Alcazar Ave................Johnston RI 02919 TF: 888-433-0090 ■ Web: www.hireimage.com	401-490-2202		721
Hire Profile Inc 2225 Laurel Mill Way............Roswell GA 30076 Web: www.hire-profile.com	404-806-2285		193
Hire Quest LLC 4560 Great Oak Dr.................North Charleston SC 29418 TF: 800-835-6755 ■ Web: hirequestllc.com	843-723-7400		260
Hire Source Inc, The 24 Wooster Ave Ste 1.....................Waterbury CT 06708 Web: thehiresource.com	203-757-4000		260
HireAbility.com LLC 25 Nashua Rd Ste C6...................Londonderry NH 03053 Web: www.hireability.com	603-432-6653		387
Hired 1200 Plymouth Ave N.................Minneapolis MN 55411 TF: 800-582-5260 ■ Web: www.hired.org	612-529-3342		260
Hired Inc 1455 Market St Fl 19............San Francisco CA 94103 TF: 800-778-7879 ■ Web: hired.com	415-813-4987		260
Hiregenics 2400 Meadowbrook Pkwy.............Duluth GA 30096 TF: 866-315-5489 ■ Web: hiregenics.acsicorp.com	770-493-5588		570
Hireko Trading Company Inc 16185 Stephens St.....................City of Industry CA 91745 TF: 800-367-8912 ■ Web: www.hirekogolf.com	800-367-8912		710
Hireology Inc 640 N Lasalle St Ste 650...........Chicago IL 60654 Web: www.hireology.com	312-253-7870		387
HireRight Inc 5151 California Ave.................Irvine CA 92617 TF: 800-400-2761 ■ Web: www.hireright.com	949-428-5800		635
HIRO 88 Restaurants 3655 N 129th St............Omaha NE 68164 Web: www.hiro88.com	402-933-0091		671
Hirono Mazie K (Sen D - HI) 730 Hart Senate Office Bldg...............Washington DC 20510 Web: www.hirono.senate.gov	202-224-6361	224-2126	342-2
Hirose Electric (USA) Inc 2688 Westhills Ct.......................Simi Valley CA 93065 Web: www.hirose.com	805-522-7958		253
Hiroshi Eurasian Tapas 500 Ala Moana Blvd.........................Honolulu HI 96813	808-533-4476		671
Hirotec America Inc 4567 Glenmeade Ln.....................Auburn Hills MI 48326 Web: www.hirotecamerica.com	248-836-5100	836-5101	386
Hirschbach Motor Lines Inc 18355 US Hwy 20......................East Dubuque IL 61025 TF: 800-554-2969 ■ Web: www.hirschbach.com	402-494-5000		780
Hirschfeld Industries LP 112 W 29th St PO Box 3768..............San Angelo TX 76903 TF: 800-472-1113 ■ Web: www.carolinasteel.com	325-486-4201	486-4380	480
Hirschl & Adler Galleries Inc 730 Fifth Ave..............................New York NY 10019 TF: 800-642-4235 ■ Web: www.hirschlandadler.com	212-535-8810	772-7237	42
Hirschvogel Inc 2230 S Third St.............Columbus OH 43207 TF: 800-827-7455 ■ Web: hirschvogel.com	614-445-6060	445-7335	483
Hirsh Industries Inc 3636 Westown Pkwy Ste 100...........West Des Moines IA 50266 TF: 800-383-7414 ■ Web: www.hirshindustries.com	515-299-3200	299-3300	319-1
Hirshfield's Inc 725 Second Ave N...........Minneapolis MN 55405 Web: www.hirshfields.com	612-377-3910	436-3384	550
Hirshhorn Museum & Sculpture Garden (Smithsonian Institution) Independence Ave SW & Seventh St SW......Washington DC 20560 Web: www.hirshhorn.si.edu	202-633-1000	786-2682	520
Hirzel Canning Company & Farms 411 Lemoyne Rd........................Northwood OH 43619 TF: 800-837-1631 ■ Web: www.deifratelli.com	419-693-0531	693-4859	296-20
Hirzel Capital Management LLC 3963 Maple Ave Ste 170.......................Dallas TX 75129 Web: www.hirzelcapital.com	214-999-0014		690
His radio 89.3 2420 Wade Hampton Blvd..................Greenville SC 29615 TF: 800-447-7234 ■ Web: www.hisradio.com	864-292-6040	292-8428	645-68
His Tackle Box Inc 40 Chestnut Ave.................South San Francisco CA 94080 TF: 800-300-4916 ■ Web: www.histackleboxshop.com	650-588-1200		711
Hisada America Inc 1191 S Walnut St.........Edinburgh IN 46124	812-526-0756		247
Hispanic Assn of Colleges & Universities (HACU) 8415 Datapoint Dr Ste 400..................San Antonio TX 78229 TF: 800-780-4228 ■ Web: www.hacu.net	210-692-3805	692-0823	49-5
Hispanic Communications Network 50 F St NW 8th Floor......................Washington DC 20001 Web: www.hcnmedia.com	202-637-8800		644
Hispanic Information & Telecommunications Network Inc 63 Flushing Ave Unit 281.....................Brooklyn NY 11205 Web: www.hitn.org	212-966-5660		740
Hispanic Link Inc 1420 N St NW............Washington DC 20005	202-234-0280		530
Hispanic Society of America 613 W 155th St..........................New York NY 10032 Web: www.hispanicsociety.org	212-926-2234		48-14
Hispanics in Philanthropy 414 13th St Ste 200.........................Oakland CA 94612 Web: www.hiponline.org	415-837-0427		305
Hispano Unidos Multiservice Inc 6051 Arlington Blvd.....................Falls Church VA 22044 Web: www.tm.org	703-534-9800		772

				Phone	Fax	Class
Histopath Billing 3853 S Alameda St *Web:* www.histopath.com	Corpus Christi	TX	78411	361-992-4040		415
Historic Aircraft Restoration Museum 3127 Creve Coeur Mill Rd *Web:* www.historicaircraftrestorationmuseum.org	Saint Louis	MO	63146	314-434-3368	878-6453	520
Historic Annapolis Foundation 18 Pinkney St *Web:* www.annapolis.org	Annapolis	MD	21401	410-267-7619		50-3
Historic Annapolis Foundation Museum 77 Main St *Web:* www.annapolis.org	Annapolis	MD	21401	410-267-7619		520
Historic Arkansas Museum 200 E Third St *Web:* www.historicarkansas.org	Little Rock	AR	72201	501-324-9351		520
Historic Brownsville Museum 641 E Madison St *Web:* mitteculturaldistrict.org	Brownsville	TX	78520	956-548-1313		520
Historic Bullock Hotel 633 Main St *TF:* 800-336-1876 ■ *Web:* www.historicbullock.com	Deadwood	SD	57732	800-336-1876		379
Historic Camden Revolutionary War Site 222 Broad St *Web:* historiccamden.org	Camden	SC	29021	803-432-9841		564
Historic Deerfield PO Box 321 *TF:* 800-733-1830 ■ *Web:* www.historic-deerfield.org	Deerfield	MA	01342	413-774-5581	775-7220	520
Historic Elsinore Theatre (HET) 170 High St SE *TF:* 800-992-8499 ■ *Web:* www.elsinoretheatre.com	Salem	OR	97301	503-375-3574	375-0284	572
Historic Fort Snelling 200 Tower Ave Ft Snelling History Ctr *TF:* 800-657-3773 ■ *Web:* mnhs.org/visit	Saint Paul	MN	55111	612-726-1171		50-3
Historic Fort Worth Inc 1110 Penn St *Web:* www.historicfortworth.org	Fort Worth	TX	76102	817-332-5875		520
Historic French Market Inn 509 Decatur St *TF:* 800-366-2743 ■ *Web:* www.frenchmarketinn.com	New Orleans	LA	70130	504-561-5621	581-3802	379
Historic Governors' Mansion 300 E 21st St	Cheyenne	WY	82001	307-777-7878		565
Historic Hack House Museum 775 County St *Web:* www.michigan.org	Milan	MI	48160	734-439-7522		520
Historic Heritage Square 115 N Sixth St *Web:* www.phoenix.gov	Phoenix	AZ	85004	602-261-8063		50-3
Historic Inns of Annapolis 58 State Cir *TF:* 800-847-8002 ■ *Web:* www.historicinnsofannapolis.com	Annapolis	MD	21401	410-263-2641	268-3613	379
Historic Jonesborough Visitors Ctr & Museum 117 Boone St *TF:* 866-401-4223 ■ *Web:* jonesborough.com	Jonesborough	TN	37659	423-753-1010		520
Historic Latta Plantation 5225 Sample Rd *Web:* www.lattaplantation.org	Huntersville	NC	28078	704-875-2312	875-1724	50-3
Historic Mill Creek Discovery Park 9001 US-23 PO Box 370 **Fax Area Code:* 906 ■ *Web:* mackinacparks.com/parks-and-attractions	Mackinac Island	MI	49701	231-436-4100	847-3815*	565
Historic New England 141 Cambridge St *TF:* 800-722-2256 ■ *Web:* www.historicnewengland.org	Boston	MA	02114	617-227-3956	227-9204	48-13
Historic New Orleans Collection 533 Royal St *TF:* 800-535-9595 ■ *Web:* www.hnoc.org	New Orleans	LA	70130	504-523-4662	598-7108	520
Historic Old Town Fort Collins 19 Old Town Sq Ste 230 *TF:* 866-203-5939 ■ *Web:* www.downtownfortcollins.com	Fort Collins	CO	80524	970-484-6500		460
Historic Orpheum Theatre 910 Hennepin Ave *TF:* 800-295-5354 ■ *Web:* www.hennepintheatretrust.org	Minneapolis	MN	55403	612-339-7007		572
Historic Pantages Theatre 710 Hennepin Ave *Web:* www.hennepintheatretrust.org	Minneapolis	MN	55403	612-339-7007		572
Historic Pensacola Village 120 Church St PO Box 12866 *Web:* www.historicpensacola.org	Pensacola	FL	32502	850-595-5985	595-5989	50-3
Historic Rock Ford Plantation 881 Rockford Rd *TF:* 800-732-0999 ■ *Web:* www.rockfordplantation.org	Lancaster	PA	17602	717-392-7223		50-3
Historic Roswell District 617 Atlanta St *TF:* 800-776-7935 ■ *Web:* www.visitroswellga.com	Roswell	GA	30075	800-776-7935		50-3
Historic Samuel Cupples House 3673 W Pine Mall *Web:* www.slu.edu	Saint Louis	MO	63108	314-977-3575		50-3
Historic Tours of America Inc 201 Front St Ste 224 *TF General:* 800-844-7601 ■ *Web:* www.historictours.com	Key West	FL	33040	305-296-3609		760
Historic Trinity Lutheran Church 1345 Gratiot Ave *TF:* 800-268-3058 ■ *Web:* www.historictrinity.org	Detroit	MI	48207	313-567-3100	567-3209	50-1
Historic Union Pacific Rail Trail State Park PO Box 754 *Web:* www.stateparks.utah.gov	Park City	UT	84060	435-649-6839		565
Historic Valley Junction 137 Fifth St *Web:* www.valleyjunction.com	West Des Moines	IA	50265	515-222-3642	274-8407	460
Historic Washington State Park PO Box 129 *Web:* www.historicwashingtonstatepark.com	Washington	AR	71862	870-983-2684	983-2736	565
Historical Glass Museum 1157 Orange St *Web:* historicalglassmuseum.com	Redlands	CA	92374	909-798-0868		520
Historical Lawmen Museum 845 Motel Blvd *TF:* 877-827-7200 ■ *Web:* donaanacounty.org	Las Cruces	NM	88007	575-647-7200		520
Historical Museum of Southern Florida 101 W Flagler St *TF:* 800-966-1836 ■ *Web:* www.historical-museum.org	Miami	FL	33130	305-375-1492		520
Historical Research Ctr Inc 2107 Corporate Dr *TF:* 800-985-9956 ■ *Web:* www.names.com	Boynton Beach	FL	33426	800-985-9956		327
Historical Society of Erie County, The 356 W sixth St Erie County Historical Society *Web:* eriehistory.com	Erie	PA	16507	814-454-1813		520
Historical Society of Palm Beach County, The 300 N Dixie Hwy Ste 471 *Web:* www.historicalsocietypbc.org	West Palm Beach	FL	33401	561-832-4164		520
Historical Society of Washington DC 801 K St NW Historical Society of Washington DC *Web:* www.dchistory.org	Washington	DC	20001	202-249-3955		520
History Ch *A&E Television Networks LLC* 235 E 45th St 2nd Fl *TF:* 888-371-5848 ■ *Web:* www.history.com	New York	NY	10017	212-210-1400		740
History Colorado Ctr 1200 Broadway *Web:* www.historycolorado.org	Denver	CO	80203	303-447-8679		520
History Ctr 302 E Berry St *Web:* www.fwhistorycenter.com	Fort Wayne	IN	46802	260-426-2882	424-4419	520
History Ctr of Olmsted County 1195 W Cir Dr SW *Web:* olmstedhistory.com	Rochester	MN	55902	507-282-9447	289-5481	50-3
History Museum & Historical Society of Western Virginia 1 Market Sq *Web:* roanokehistory.org	Roanoke	VA	24011	540-342-5770		520
History Museum On The Square 155 Park Central Sq *Web:* historymuseumonthesquare.org	Springfield	MO	65806	417-864-1976		520
History Theatre 30 E Tenth St *Web:* www.historytheatre.com	Saint Paul	MN	55101	651-292-4323	292-4322	572
Hit Promotional Products Inc 7150 Bryan Dairy Rd *TF:* 800-237-6305 ■ *Web:* www.hitpromo.net	Largo	FL	33777	727-541-5561	541-5130	9
Hitachi America Ltd 50 Prospect Ave *TF:* 800-448-2244 ■ *Web:* www.hitachi.com	Tarrytown	NY	10591	914-332-5800	332-5555	185
Hitachi America Ltd Computer Div 2000 Sierra Pt Pkwy **Fax Area Code:* 650 ■ *TF:* 800-448-2244 ■ *Web:* www.hitachi-america.us	Brisbane	CA	94005	800-448-2244	244-7776*	173-8
Hitachi Automotive Systems Americas Inc 955 Warwick Rd *Web:* www.hap.com	Harrodsburg	KY	40330	859-734-9451	734-5309	247
Hitachi Canada Ltd 5450 Explore Dr Ste 501 *Web:* www.hitachi.ca	Mississauga	ON	L4W5N1	905-629-9300	290-0141	253
Hitachi Chemical Company America Ltd 10080 N Wolfe Rd Ste SW3-200 *Web:* www.hitachi-chemical.com	Cupertino	CA	95014	408-873-2200	873-2284	145
Hitachi Chemical Diagnostics 630 Clyde Ct *TF:* 800-233-6278 ■ *Web:* www.hcdiagnostics.com	Mountain View	CA	94043	650-961-5501	969-2745	231
Hitachi Consulting Corp 14643 Dallas Pkwy Ste 800 *Web:* www.hitachiconsulting.com	Dallas	TX	75254	214-665-7000	665-7010	178-1
Hitachi Credit America Ltd 800 Connecticut Ave *Web:* hitachicapitalamerica.com	Norwalk	CT	06854	203-275-5685		264-1
Hitachi Data Systems Corp 750 Central Expy *TF:* 877-437-3849 ■ *Web:* www.hds.com	Santa Clara	CA	95050	408-970-1000	727-8036	173-8
Hitachi High Technologies America Inc 10 N Martingale Rd Ste 500 *Web:* www.hitachi-hightech.com/us	Schaumburg	IL	60173	847-273-4141		419
Hitachi ID Systems Inc 500 1401 - First St SE Ste 500 *Web:* www.hitachi-id.com	Calgary	AB	T2G2J3	403-233-0740		177
Hitachi Kokusai Electric America Ltd 150 Crossways Pk Dr *TF:* 855-490-5124 ■ *Web:* www.hitachikokusai.us	Woodbury	NY	11797	516-921-7200	496-3718	847
Hitachi Medical Systems America Inc 1959 Summit Commerce Pk *TF:* 800-800-3106 ■ *Web:* www.hitachimed.com	Twinsburg	OH	44087	330-425-1313	425-1410	382
Hitachi Metals America Ltd 2 Manhattanville Rd Ste 301 *TF:* 800-777-5757 ■ *Web:* www.hitachimetals.com	Purchase	NY	10577	914-694-9200	694-9279	307
Hitch Enterprises Inc 309 Northridge Cir PO Box 1308 *TF:* 800-951-2533 ■ *Web:* hitchenterprises-public.sharepoint.com/contact-us	Guymon	OK	73942	580-338-8575		360-3
Hitchcock County 229 E D St *Web:* hitchcockcounty.ne.gov	Trenton	NE	69044	308-334-5646	334-5398	338
Hitchcock Fleming & Associates Inc 500 Wolf Ledges Pkwy *TF:* 800-477-6808 ■ *Web:* www.teamhfa.com	Akron	OH	44311	330-376-2111		7
Hitchiner Mfg Company Inc 594 Elm St *Web:* www.hitchiner.com	Milford	NH	03055	603-673-1100	673-7960	306
HITCO Carbon Composites Inc 1600 W 135th St *TF:* 800-421-5444 ■ *Web:* www.hitco.com	Gardena	CA	90249	310-527-0700	970-5468	504
Hite Co 3101 Beale Ave *TF:* 800-252-3598 ■ *Web:* www.hiteco.com	Altoona	PA	16601	814-944-6121	944-3052	246
HITEC Group Ltd 1743 Quincy Ave Unit 155 *TF:* 800-288-8303 ■ *Web:* www.hitec.com	Naperville	IL	60540	800-288-8303		246
Hi-Tec Industries Inc 1000 Sixth Ave NE *Web:* www.hitecindustries.ca	Portage La Prairie	MB	R1N3C5	204-239-4270		261
Hi-Tech Electric Inc 11116 W Little York Rd Bldg 8 *Web:* www.hitechelectric.com	Houston	TX	77041	832-243-0345	467-0132	189-4
Hi-Tech Fabrication Inc Leesville Industrial Park 8900 Midway W Rd *TF:* 800-359-7249 ■ *Web:* www.htfi.com	Raleigh	NC	27617	919-781-2552		697
Hi-Tech Healthcare Inc 1805 Shackleford Ct Ste 100	Norcross	GA	30093	770-449-6785		475
Hi-tech Machining & Engineering LLC 1075 E Wieding Rd *Web:* www.hi-techmachining.net	Tucson	AZ	85706	520-889-8325		261

Name / Address	City	State	Zip	Phone	Fax	Class
Hi-tech Optical Inc						
3139 Christy Way S	Saginaw	MI	48603	989-799-9390		543
Web: www.hi-techoptical.com						
Hi-Tech Systems Engineering Co						
2700 Old Centre Rd	Portage	MI	49024	269-488-7788		261
TF: 866-312-1893 ■ *Web:* www.htse.com						
Hi-Techniques Inc 2515 Frazier Ave	Madison	WI	53713	608-221-7500		246
Web: www.hi-techniques.com						
Hi-Tek Manufacturinginc 6050 Hi-Tek Ct	Mason	OH	45040	513-459-1094		454
Web: www.hitekmfg.com						
Hi-Temp Insulation Inc						
4700 Calle Alto	Camarillo	CA	93012	805-484-2774		389
Web: www.hi-tempinsulation.com						
Hi-Test Laboratories Inc						
1104 Arvon Rd	Arvonia	VA	23004	434-581-3204		261
Web: hitestlabs.com						
Hither Hills State Park						
164 Old Montauk Hwy	Montauk	NY	11954	631-668-2554		565
Web: parks.ny.gov/parks/122						
Hitran Corp 362 SR- 31	Flemington	NJ	08822	908-782-5525	782-9733	767
Web: www.hitrancorp.com						
HITS Inc 319 Main St	Saugerties	NY	12477	845-246-8833		31
TF: 800-342-5826 ■ *Web:* www.hitsshows.com						
Hitt Contracting Inc						
2900 Fairview Park Dr	Falls Church	VA	22042	703-846-9000	846-9110	186
TF: 800-777-7401 ■ *Web:* www.hitt-gc.com						
Hitt Marking Devices Inc						
3231 W MacArthur Blvd	Santa Ana	CA	92704	714-979-1405	979-1407	467
TF: 800-969-6699 ■ *Web:* www.hittmarking.com						
Hi-Vac Corp 117 Industry Rd	Marietta	OH	45750	740-374-2306		427
Web: www.hi-vac.com						
Hive Group Inc, The						
2201 N Central Expy Ste 180	Richardson	TX	75080	972-808-0400		177
Web: www.hivegroup.com						
Hive Modern Design 820 NW glisan st	Portland	OR	97209	503-242-1967		138
TF: 866-663-4483 ■ *Web:* hivemodern.com						
Hivelocity Ventures Corp						
8010 Woodland Ctr Blvd Ste 700	Tampa	FL	33614	813-471-0355		225
TF: 888-869-4678 ■ *Web:* www.hivelocity.net						
Hiwassee College						
225 Hiwassee College Dr	Madisonville	TN	37354	423-442-2001	442-8521*	162
**Fax:* Admissions ■ *TF:* 800-356-2187 ■ *Web:* www.hiwassee.edu						
Hi-Way Paving Inc 4343 Weaver Ct N	Hilliard	OH	43026	614-876-1700	876-1899	188-4
TF: 800-792-3822 ■ *Web:* www.hiwaypaving.com						
Hix Corp 1201 E 27th Terr	Pittsburg	KS	66762	620-231-8568	231-1598	744
TF: 800-835-0606 ■ *Web:* www.hixcorp.com						
Hixardt Technologies Inc						
119 W Intendencia St	Pensacola	FL	32502	850-439-3282		180
TF: 866-985-3282 ■ *Web:* www.hixardt.com						
HJ (Hampton Jitney Inc)						
395 County Rd 39A Ste 6	SoutHampton	NY	11968	631-283-4600		107
Web: www.hamptonjitney.com						
HJ Baker & Bros Inc						
2 Corporate Dr Ste 545	Shelton	CT	06484	203-682-9200	227-8351	280
Web: hjbaker.com						
H-J Enterprises Inc						
3010 High Ridge Blvd	High Ridge	MO	63049	636-677-3421		308
Web: www.h-j.com						
HJ Foundation Inc 8275 N W 80 St	Miami	FL	33166	305-592-8181		261
TF: 866-751-4545 ■ *Web:* www.hjfoundation.com						
HJ Heinz Company Foundation						
600 Grant St	Pittsburgh	PA	15219	651-450-4064		304
Web: www.kraftheinzcompany.com						
HJ Russell & Co						
171 17th St NW Ste 1600	Atlanta	GA	30363	404-330-1000	688-5179	186
Web: www.hjrussell.com						
HJM Precision Inc 9 New Tpke Rd	Troy	NY	12182	518-235-7407		385
Web: www.hjmprecision.com						
HK Enterprises Inc						
3190-B Coronado Dr	Santa Clara	CA	95054	408-988-5880		77
HK Payroll Services 2345 JFK Rd	Dubuque	IA	52004	563-556-0123		734
Web: www.hkpayroll.com						
HKA Enterprises Inc						
337 Spartangreen Blvd	Duncan	SC	29334	864-661-5100		192
TF: 800-825-5452 ■ *Web:* www.hkaa.com						
Hkm Direct Market Communications Inc						
5501 Cass Ave	Cleveland	OH	44102	216-651-9500	961-6330	5
TF General: 800-860-4456 ■ *Web:* www.hkmdirectmarket.com						
HKS Inc 1919 McKinney Ave	Dallas	TX	75201	214-969-5599	969-3397	261
Web: www.hksinc.com						
HL Dalis Inc 35-35 24th St	Long Island	NY	11106	718-361-1100	392-7654	246
TF: 800-453-2547 ■ *Web:* www.hldalis.com						
HL Turner Group Inc, The 27 Locke Rd	Concord	NH	03301	603-228-1122		261
TF: 800-305-2289 ■ *Web:* hlturner.com						
HLA (Harold Levinson Assoc)						
21 Banfi Plaza	Farmingdale	NY	11735	631-962-2400	962-9000	297-3
TF: 800-325-2512 ■ *Web:* www.hlacigars.com						
HL-A Company Inc 902 Ravenwood Dr	Selma	AL	36701	334-874-9010		350
Web: www.hla.com.my						
Hla Engineers Inc 7267 Envoy Ct	Dallas	TX	75247	214-267-0930	267-0970	261
Web: hlaengineers.com						
HLB Cinnamon Jang Willoughby						
Metro Tower II Ste 900-4720 Kingsway	Burnaby	BC	V5H4N2	604-435-4317		401
Web: www.cjw.com						
HLB Communications Inc						
875 N Michigan Ave	Chicago	IL	60611	312-649-0371		636
Hlb Systems Solutions 50 Malcolm Rd	Guelph	ON	N1K1A9	519-822-3450		180
Web: www.hlbsolutions.com						
HLC (Healthcare Leadership Council)						
750 Ninth St NW Ste 500	Washington	DC	20001	202-452-8700	296-9561	48-17
Web: hlc.org						
HLC Hotels Inc						
7080 Abercorn St PO Box 13069	Savannah	GA	31416	912-352-4493	352-0314	379
TF: 800-344-4378 ■ *Web:* www.hlchotels.com						
HLF (High Liner Foods Inc)						
High Liner Foods Incorporated,100 Battery Point						
P.O. Box 910	Lunenburg	NS	B0J2C0	902-634-8811		296-13
NYSE: HLF ■ *Web:* www.highlinerfoods.com						
HLI (Human Life International)						
4 Family Life Ln	Front Royal	VA	22630	540-635-7884	622-6247	48-6
TF Orders: 800-549-5433 ■ *Web:* www.hli.org						
HLI Energy Services Inc						
3600 W Hwy 67	Cleburne	TX	76033	817-558-1018		536
TF: 800-259-5544 ■ *Web:* www.hlienergy.com						
Hli Properties Inc						
1003 Central Ave	Fort Dodge	IA	50501	515-955-1600		637-9
TF: 800-247-2000 ■ *Web:* www.hlipublishing.com						
HLM Venture Partners						
222 Berkeley St 20th Fl	Boston	MA	02116	617-266-0030		792
Web: www.hlmvp.com						
Hln Consulting LLC						
7072 Santa Fe Canyon Pl	San Diego	CA	92129	858-538-2220		180
Web: www.hln.com						
HLW International						
115 Fifth Ave 5th Fl	New York	NY	10003	212-353-4600	353-4666	261
Web: www.hlw.com						
HM Richards Inc 414 Rd 2790	Guntown	MS	38849	662-365-9485		321
Web: www.hmrichards.com						
HM Royal Inc 689 Pennington Ave	Trenton	NJ	08618	609-396-9176	396-3185	146
TF: 800-257-9452 ■ *Web:* www.hmroyal.com						
H&M Shared Services Inc						
985 Jolly Rd	Blue Bell	PA	19422	215-283-7600	283-7659	188-10
TF: 888-436-5357 ■ *Web:* www.henkels.com						
HM Stauffer & Sons Inc						
33 Glenola Dr PO Box 567	Leola	PA	17540	717-656-2811	656-4392	817
TF: 800-662-2226 ■ *Web:* hmstauffer.com						
HM White Inc 12855 Burt Rd	Detroit	MI	48223	313-531-8477		697
Web: paintfinishingsystems.com						
HMA (Hargrave Military Academy)						
200 Military Dr	Chatham	VA	24531	434-432-2481	432-3129	622
TF: 800-432-2480 ■ *Web:* www.hargrave.edu						
HMA Public Relations						
3610 N 44th St Ste 110	Phoenix	AZ	85018	602-957-8881		636
Web: hmapr.com						
HMC (Highway Machine Company Inc)						
3010 S Old US Hwy 41	Princeton	IN	47670	812-385-3639	385-8186	454
TF: 866-990-9462 ■ *Web:* www.hmcgears.com						
HMC (Hays Medical Ctr) 2220 Canterbury Dr	Hays	KS	67601	785-650-2759		374-3
TF: 800-248-0073 ■ *Web:* haysmed.com						
HMC Archtiect 3546 Councours St	Ontario	CA	91764	909-989-9979	483-1400	261
TF: 800-350-9979 ■ *Web:* www.hmcarchitects.com						
HMC Corp 284 Maple St	Contoocook	NH	03229	603-746-4691	746-4819	821
TF: 800-992-3432 ■ *Web:* www.hmccorp.com						
HMC Holdings LLC						
1605 Old Rt 18 Ste 4-36	Wampum	PA	16157	724-535-1080		350
Hmc Products Inc 5196 27th Ave	Rockford	IL	61109	815-397-9145		88
TF: 800-275-8777 ■ *Web:* www.hmcproducts.com						
HMCS Haida National Historic Site						
57 Discovery Dr	Hamilton	ON	L8L8K4	905-526-6742	526-9734	563
Web: www.pc.gc.ca/eng/lhn-nhs/on/haida/index.aspx						
HME Inc 1950 Byron Ctr Ave	Wyoming	MI	49519	616-534-1463	534-1967	516
TF: 800-269-7335 ■ *Web:* www.firetrucks.com						
Hme Providers Inc 1410 White Dr	Titusville	FL	32780	321-267-7576		225
Web: www.hmeproviders.com						
HMG/Courtland Properties Inc						
1870 S Bayshore Dr	Coconut Grove	FL	33133	305-854-6803	856-7342	654
AMEX: HMG ■ *Web:* hmgcourtland.com						
HMH (Harrington Hospital)						
100 South St	Southbridge	MA	01550	508-765-9771	765-3147	374-3
TF: 800-416-6072 ■ *Web:* www.harringtonhospital.org						
HMHB (National Healthy Mothers Healthy Babies Coalition)						
4401 Ford Ave Ste 300	Alexandria	VA	22302	703-837-4792		48-17
Web: www.hmhb.org						
HMI (Hogan Manufacturing Inc) PO Box 398	Escalon	CA	95320	209-838-7323	838-7329	480
Web: www.hoganmfg.com						
HMJ Inc 212 W Colfax Ave	South Bend	IN	46601	574-232-3061		772
TF: 800-347-7986 ■ *Web:* www.travelmore.com						
HMN Financial Inc						
1016 Civic Ctr Dr NW	Rochester	MN	55901	507-535-1309		360-2
NASDAQ: HMNF ■ *TF:* 888-257-2000 ■ *Web:* www.hmnf.com						
HMS (Hawk Mountain Sanctuary)						
1700 Hawk Mtn Rd	Kempton	PA	19529	610-756-6961	756-4468	48-3
Web: www.hawkmountain.org						
HMS (Healthcare Management Systems Inc)						
3102 W End Ave Ste 400	Nashville	TN	37203	615-383-7300	383-6093	387
HMS Hawaii 841 Bishop St Stc 860	Honolulu	HI	96813	808-545-3755		792
Web: www.hmshawaii.com						
HMS Products Co 1200 E Big Beaver Rd	Troy	MI	48083	248-689-8120		454
Web: www.hmsproducts.com						
HMS Technologies Inc						
1 Discovery Pl	Martinsburg	WV	25403	304-596-5583		180
Web: www.hmstech.com						
HMSHost Corp 6905 Rockledge Dr # 1	Bethesda	MD	20817	240-694-4100		299
Web: www.hmshost.com						
Hn Burns Engineering Corp						
3275 Progress Dr Ste A	Orlando	FL	32826	407-273-3770		261
TF: 800-728-6506 ■ *Web:* www.hnbec.com						
H&N Printing & Graphics Inc						
1913 Greenspring Dr	Timonium	MD	21093	410-252-5300		627
TF: 800-882-1844 ■ *Web:* www.hnprinting.com						
HNA (Hawaii Nurses Assn)						
949 Kapiolani Blvd Ste 107	Honolulu	HI	96814	808-531-1628		533
TF: 800-617-2677 ■ *Web:* www.hawaiinurses.org						
HNA (Hockey North America)						
45570 Shepard Dr	Sterling	VA	20164	703-430-8100	421-9205	48-22
TF: 800-446-2539 ■ *Web:* www.hna.com						
HNH Mach Inc 110 Towerline Pl	London	ON	N6E2T1	519-680-3880		454
TF: 800-669-0988 ■ *Web:* www.hnhmachine.com						
HNP Pharmaceuticals						
381 Van Ness Ave Ste 1507	Torrance	CA	90501	310-783-7450		743
Web: www.hnppharmaceuticals.com						
HNTB Corp 715 Kirk Dr	Kansas City	MO	64105	816-472-1201	472-4060	261
Web: www.hntb.com						
HNW (Houston Northwest Chamber of Commerce)						
3920 Cypress Creek Pkwy	Houston	TX	77068	281-440-4160	440-5302	139
Web: www.houstonnwchamber.org						

Name / Address	City	State	Zip	Phone	Fax	Class
HO Bostrom Company Inc 818 Progress Ave *TF:* 800-332-5415 ■ *Web:* www.hobostrom.com	Waukesha	WI	53186	262-542-0222	542-3784	689
Ho Chow Restaurant 47966 Warm Springs Blvd *Web:* www.hochow.com	Fremont	CA	94539	510-657-0683		671
HO Penn Machinery Co Inc 122 Noxon Rd *Web:* www.hopenn.com	Poughkeepsie	NY	12603	845-452-1200		358
HO Trerice Co 12950 W Eight-Mile Rd *TF:* 888-873-7423 ■ *Web:* www.trerice.com	Oak Park	MI	48237	248-399-8000	399-7246	201
HO2 Partners 13455 Noel Rd 2 Galleria Tower Ste 1670 *Web:* www.ho2.com	Dallas	TX	75240	972-702-1107	702-8234	792
Hoag Hospital Irvine (HHI) 16200 Sand Canyon Ave *TF:* 800-309-9729 ■ *Web:* www.hoag.org	Irvine	CA	92618	949-764-4624		374-3
Hoag Memorial Hospital Presbyterian 1 Hoag Dr *Web:* www.hoag.org	Newport Beach	CA	92658	949-764-4624		374-3
Hoagland, Longo, Moran, Dunst & Doukas 40 Paterson St *Web:* www.hoaglandlongo.com	New Brunswick	NJ	08903	732-545-4717		428
Hoar Construction Inc 2 Metroplex Dr # 400 *Web:* www.hoar.com	Birmingham	AL	35209	205-803-2121	423-2323	186
Hoard's Dairyman Magazine 28 Milwaukee Ave W PO Box 801 *TF:* 800-245-8222 ■ *Web:* www.hoards.com	Fort Atkinson	WI	53538	920-563-5551	563-7298	457-1
Hoban & Assoc Dba Coast Real Estate Services 2829 Rucker Ave *TF:* 800-339-3634 ■ *Web:* www.coastmgt.com	Everett	WA	98201	425-339-3638		652
Hobart & William Smith Colleges 300 Pulteney St *TF Admissions:* 800-852-2256 ■ *Web:* www.hws.edu	Geneva	NY	14456	315-781-3000		166
Hobart Bros Co 101 Trade Sq E *TF:* 800-424-1543 ■ *Web:* www.hobartbrothers.com	Troy	OH	45373	937-332-4000	332-5178	811
Hobart Corp 701 S Ridge Ave *TF Cust Svc:* 800-333-7447 ■ *Web:* www.hobartcorp.com	Troy	OH	45374	937-332-3000	332-2852	298
Hobart Group Holdings LLC 240 Main St *TF:* 800-510-3401 ■ *Web:* thehobartgroup.com	Gladstone	NJ	07934	908-470-1780		5
Hobas Pipe USA LP 1413 E Richey Rd *TF:* 800-856-7473 ■ *Web:* www.hobaspipe.com	Houston	TX	77073	281-821-2200	821-7715	596
Hobbs & Towne Inc 1288 Vly Forge Rd PMB 269 PO Box 987 *Web:* hobbstowne.com	Valley Forge	PA	19482	610-783-4600		193
Hobbs Bonded Fibers Inc 200 Commerce Dr *TF:* 800-433-3357 ■ *Web:* www.hobbsbondedfibers.com	Waco	TX	76710	254-741-0040	772-7238	745-6
Hobbs Chamber of Commerce 400 N Marland Blvd *Web:* www.hobbschamber.org	Hobbs	NM	88240	575-397-3202	397-1689	139
Hobbs Herder 2240 University Dr *Web:* www.hobbsherder.com	Newport Beach	CA	92660	949-515-5000		7
Hobbs Public Library 509 N Shipp St *Web:* www.hobbspubliclibrary.org	Hobbs	NM	88240	575-397-9328		434-3
Hobbs State Park-Conservation Area 21392 E Hwy 12 *Web:* www.arkansasstateparks.com	Rogers	AR	72756	479-789-2380		565
Hobbs Straus Dean and Walker 117 Park Ave Ste 200 *Web:* hsdwlaw.com	Oklahoma City	OK	73102	405-602-9425		445
Hobby Ctr for the Performing Arts 800 Bagby St Ste 300 *Web:* www.thehobbycenter.org	Houston	TX	77002	713-315-2400	315-2402	572
Hobby Lobby 7717 SW 44th St *TF:* 800-888-0321 ■ *Web:* www.hobbylobby.com	Oklahoma City	OK	73179	405-745-1275		44
Hobby Lobby Creative Centers 7707 SW 44th St *TF:* 855-329-7060 ■ *Web:* www.hobbylobby.com	Oklahoma City	OK	73179	405-745-1100	745-1547	45
Hobby Lobby Stores Inc 7500 Jefferson Blvd *Web:* www.hobbylobby.com	Louisville	KY	40219	405-745-1721		761
Hobbytown USA 1233 Libra Dr *Web:* www.hobbytown.com	Lincoln	NE	68512	402-434-5050	434-5055	761
Hobe & Lucas 4807 Rockside Rd Ste 510 *Web:* www.hobe.com	Independence	OH	44131	216-524-8900		2
Hobe Sound Bible College PO Box 1065 *TF:* 800-881-5534 ■ *Web:* www.hsbc.edu	Hobe Sound	FL	33475	772-546-5534	545-1422	161
HOBI International Inc 1202 Nagel Blvd *Web:* www.hobi.com	Batavia	IL	60510	630-761-0500		174
Hobie Cat Co 4925 Oceanside Blvd *Web:* www.hobie.com	Oceanside	CA	92056	760-758-9100	758-1841	90
Hob-Nob Hill 2271 First Ave *Web:* hobnobhill.com	San Diego	CA	92101	619-239-8176		671
Hoboken Public Library (HPL) 500 Pk Ave *Web:* hobokenfol.org	Hoboken	NJ	07030	201-420-2346		434-3
Hoboken University Medical Ctr 308 Willow Ave *Web:* www.carepointhealth.org	Hoboken	NJ	07030	201-418-1000		374-3
Hobson & Motzer Inc 30 Air Line Dr *TF:* 800-476-5111 ■ *Web:* www.hobsonmotzer.com	Durham	CT	06422	860-349-1756	349-3602	488
Hobsons 50 E-Business Way Ste 300 *Web:* www.hobsons.com	Cincinnati	OH	45241	513-891-5444		177
Hobsons CollegeView 50 E Business Way Ste 300 *TF:* 800-927-8439 ■ *Web:* www.collegeview.com	Cincinnati	OH	45241	800-927-8439	891-8531	637-9
HOC Industries Inc 3511 N Ohio St *TF:* 800-633-8253 ■ *Web:* www.hocindustries.com	Wichita	KS	67219	316-838-4663		581
Hochberg d Peter Co Lpa Patent Attys 1301 E Ninth St Ste 3500 *Web:* www.dpeterhochberg.com	Cleveland	OH	44114	216-928-2903		445
Hochman, Salkin, Rettig, Toscher & Perez PC 9150 Wilshire Blvd Ste 300 *TF:* 800-926-7926 ■ *Web:* taxlitigator.com	Beverly Hills	CA	90212	310-281-3200		428
Ho-Chunk Casino S 3214 County Rd BD *TF:* 800-746-2486 ■ *Web:* www.ho-chunk.com	Baraboo	WI	53913	800-746-2486		133
Ho-chunk Golden Nickel Casino S3214 County Rd Bd *Web:* www.ho-chunkgaming.com	Baraboo	WI	53913	608-356-6210		452
Ho-Chunk Inc 1 Mission Dr *TF:* 800-439-7008 ■ *Web:* www.hochunkinc.com	Winnebago	NE	68071	402-878-2809		317
Hockaday School 11600 Welch Rd *Web:* www.hockaday100.org	Dallas	TX	75229	214-363-6311		622
Hockessin Library 1023 Valley Rd *TF:* 888-352-7722 ■ *Web:* www.nccde.org	Hockessin	DE	19707	302-239-5160	239-1519	434-3
Hockey Hall of Fame 30 Yonge St *TF:* 800-858-9242 ■ *Web:* www.hhof.com	Toronto	ON	M5E1X8	416-360-7735	360-1316	522
Hockey News Magazine 25 Sheppard Ave Ste 100 *TF:* 888-361-9768 ■ *Web:* www.thehockeynews.com	Toronto	ON	M2N6S7	514-848-7000		457-20
Hockey North America (HNA) 45570 Shepard Dr *TF:* 800-446-2539 ■ *Web:* www.hna.com	Sterling	VA	20164	703-430-8100	421-9205	48-22
Hockeytown Cafe 2301 Woodward Ave *TF:* 800-732-5569 ■ *Web:* hockeytowncafe.com	Detroit	MI	48201	313-471-3400		671
Hocking & Reid LLC 5757 S 34th St Ste 100	Lincoln	NE	68516	402-441-0140		2
Hocking College 3301 Hocking Pkwy *TF:* 877-462-5464 ■ *Web:* www.hocking.edu	Nelsonville	OH	45764	740-753-3591	753-7065	800
Hocking County 1 E Main St *TF:* 800-878-7828 ■ *Web:* www.co.hocking.oh.us	Logan	OH	43138	740-385-3000	385-7413	338
Hocking Hills Chamber of Commerce 96 W Hunter St *Web:* www.hockinghillschamber.com	Logan	OH	43138	740-385-6836	385-7259	139
Hocking Hills State Park 19852 State Rt 664 S *Web:* thehockinghills.org	Logan	OH	43138	740-385-6842		565
Hocking Valley Bank 7 W Stimson Ave *TF:* 888-482-5854 ■ *Web:* www.hvbonline.com	Athens	OH	45701	740-592-4441		70
Hockley County 802 Houston St Ste 213 *Web:* www.co.hockley.tx.us	Levelland	TX	79336	806-894-4404		338
Hocon Gas of Guilford LLC 736 Boston Post Rd *TF:* 800-992-2242 ■ *Web:* www.hocongas.com	Guilford	CT	06437	203-458-2790		579
Hodell-natco Industries Inc 7825 Hub Pkwy *TF:* 800-321-4862 ■ *Web:* www.hodell-natco.com	Cleveland	OH	44125	216-447-0165		351
Hodes Keating & Pilon 134 N La Salle St Ste 1300 *Web:* www.hkp-customs.com	Chicago	IL	60602	312-553-1440		428
Hodgdon Powder Company Inc 6231 Robinson St *Web:* www.hodgdon.com	Shawnee Mission	KS	66202	913-362-9455	362-1307	268
Hodgdon Yachts Inc 14 School St *TF:* 800-378-2181 ■ *Web:* www.hodgdonyachts.com	East Boothbay	ME	04544	207-633-4194		698
Hodge Engineering Inc 2615 Jahn Ave NW Ste E5 *Web:* hodgeengineering.squarespace.com	Gig Harbor	WA	98335	253-857-7055		261
Hodge Products Inc PO Box 1326 *TF:* 800 778 2217 ■ *Web:* www.hpionline.com	El Cajon	CA	92022	800-778-2217		295
Hodgeman County PO Box 247 *TF:* 800-262-8683 ■ *Web:* www.hodgemancountyks.com	Jetmore	KS	67854	620-357-6421	357-6313	338
Hodges & Associates PLLC 13642 Omega Ste 300 *Web:* www.hodgesarchitecture.biz	Dallas	TX	75244	972-387-1000		7
Hodges Harbin Newberry & Tribble 3920 Arkwright Rd *Web:* hhnt.com	Macon	GA	31210	478-743-7175		261
Hodges University 2655 Northbrooke Dr *TF:* 800-466-8017 ■ *Web:* www.hodges.edu	Naples	FL	34119	239-513-1122		166
Fort Myers 4501 Colonial Blvd *TF:* 800-466-0019 ■ *Web:* www.hodges.edu	Fort Myers	FL	33966	239-938-7701		166
Hodges-Mace Benefits Group Inc 5775-D Glenridge Dr Ste 350 *TF:* 800-643-2757 ■ *Web:* www.hodgesmace.com	Atlanta	GA	30328	404-574-6110		260
Hodgson Mill Inc 1100 Stevens Ave *TF:* 800-347-0105 ■ *Web:* www.hodgsonmill.com	Effingham	IL	62401	217-347-0105	347-0198	296-23
Hodgson Russ LLP 140 Pearl St The Guaranty Bldg Ste 100 *TF:* 800-973-1177 ■ *Web:* www.hodgsonruss.com	Buffalo	NY	14202	716-856-4000		428
Hodori 1116 S Dobson Rd *Web:* hodoriaz.com	Mesa	AZ	85202	480-668-7979		671
Hoeganaes Corp 1001 Taylors Ln *Web:* www.gkn.com	Cinnaminson	NJ	08077	856-829-2220		485
Hoegemeyer Hybrids Inc 1755 Hoegemeyer Rd *TF:* 800-245-4631 ■ *Web:* www.therightseed.com	Hooper	NE	68031	402-654-3399		10-5
Hoerbiger Corp of America Inc 3350 Gateway Dr *TF:* 800-888-8803 ■ *Web:* hoerbiger.com	Pompano Beach	FL	33069	954-974-5700	974-0964	789
Hoeven John (Sen R - ND) 338 Russell Bldg *Web:* www.hoeven.senate.gov	Washington	DC	20510	202-224-2551		342-2
HOF Construction Inc 3137 Jamieson Ave *Web:* www.hofconstruction.com	Saint Louis	MO	63139	314-645-2200		186
Hof's Hut Restaurants Inc 2601 E Willow St *Web:* www.hofshut.com	Signal Hill	CA	90755	562-596-0200		670
Hoff Cos Inc 1840 N Lakes Ave *Web:* www.hoffcompanies.com	Meridian	ID	83646	208-884-2002		499
Hoff Enterprises Inc 151 Freidhoff Ln *Web:* www.hoffent.com	Johnstown	PA	15902	814-535-8371		115
Hoffbrau Steaks 7203-G IH- I-40 W *Web:* www.hoffbrausteaks.com	Amarillo	TX	79106	806-358-6595		671
Hoffer Pest Solutions 12329 NW 35 St *Web:* www.hofferpest.com	Coral Springs	FL	33065	954-945-7979		577
Hoffer Plastics Corp 500 N Collins St *Web:* www.hofferplastics.com	South Elgin	IL	60177	847-741-5740	741-3086	604

Name / Address	City	State	Zip	Phone	Fax	Class
Hoffinger Industries Inc 315 Sebastian St.	West Helena	AR	72390	870-572-3466		728
Hoffland Environmental Inc 10391 Silver Springs Rd. *Web:* heienv.com	Conroe	TX	77303	936-856-4515		201
Hoffman Alvary & Company LLC 7 Wells Ave. *Web:* hoffmanalvary.com	Newton	MA	02459	617-758-0500		428
Hoffman California Fabrics Inc 25792 Obrero Dr. *Fax Area Code: 949 ■ *TF:* 800-547-0100 ■ *Web:* www.hoffmanfabrics.com	Mission Viejo	CA	92691	800-547-0100	770-4022*	594
Hoffman Car Wash 1757 Central Ave *Web:* www.hoffmancarwash.com	Albany	NY	12205	518-869-3218		62-1
Hoffman Construction Corp 805 SW Broadway Ste 2100 *Web:* www.hoffmancorp.com	Portland	OR	97205	503-221-8811		186
Hoffman Engineering Corp PO Box 4430 *Web:* www.hoffmanengineering.com	Stamford	CT	06907	203-425-8900	425-8910	743
Hoffman Equipment Inc 300 S Randolphville Rd *Web:* www.hoffmanequip.com	Piscataway	NJ	08854	732-752-3600		358
Hoffman Estates Chamber of Commerce 2200 W Higgins Rd Ste 201 *TF:* 800-422-8186 ■ *Web:* www.hechamber.com	Hoffman Estates	IL	60169	847-781-9100	781-9172	139
Hoffman G W Inc 757 Post Rd. *Web:* www.gwhoffman.com	Darien	CT	06820	203-655-8321		7
Hoffman Hills State Recreation Area 921 BrickyaRd Rd *Web:* www.dnr.wi.gov	Menomonie	WI	54751	715-232-1242		565
Hoffman Homes for Youth PO Box 4777 *Web:* www.hoffmanhomes.com	Gettysburg	PA	17325	717-359-7148	359-2600	653
Hoffman House 7550 E State St. *Web:* www.hoffmanhouserockford.com	Rockford	IL	61108	815-397-5800		671
Hoffman Memorial State Wayside Hoffman Memorial Myrtle Grove. *TF:* 800-551-6949 ■ *Web:* www.oregonstateparks.org	Mytrle Point	OR	97458	800-551-6949		565
Hoffman Planning, Design, & Construction Inc 122 E College Ave Ste 1G. *TF:* 800-236-2370 ■ *Web:* www.hoffman.net	Appleton	WI	54911	920-731-2322		186
Hoffman Products 9600 Vly View Rd *Fax Area Code: 866 ■ *TF:* 800-645-2014 ■ *Web:* www.tpcwire.com	Macedonia	OH	44056	216-525-4320	896-3017*	815
Hoffmann & Baron LLP 6900 Jericho Tpke *TF:* 800-387-4652 ■ *Web:* www.hbiplaw.com	Syosset	NY	11791	516-822-3550		428
Hoffmann & Feige Inc 3 Fallsview Ln *TF:* 800-258-7968 ■ *Web:* hoffmann-feige.com	Brewster	NY	10509	845-277-4401		261
Hoffmann Die Cast Corp 229 Kerth St *Web:* www.hoffmanndc.com	Saint Joseph	MI	49085	269-983-1102	983-2928	308
Hoffmann Hospice of the Valley 8501 Brimhall Rd Bldg 100 *TF:* 888-833-3900 ■ *Web:* www.hoffmannhospice.org	Bakersfield	CA	93312	661-410-1010	410-1110	371
Hoffmann-LaRoche Inc 340 Kingsland St *Web:* www.roche.com	Nutley	NJ	07110	973-235-5000		582
Hoffmaster 2920 N Main St. *TF:* 800-327-9774 ■ *Web:* www.hoffmaster.com	Oshkosh	WI	54901	920-235-9330	235-1642	558
Hoffmeier Inc 3210 N Lewis Ave. *Web:* www.hoffmeier.com	Tulsa	OK	74110	918-428-5823	430-0820	685
Hofmann Co, The 1380 Galaxy Way *Web:* www.hofmannhomes.com	Concord	CA	94520	925-682-4830	682-4771	653
Hofmann Industries Inc 3145 Shillington Rd *Web:* www.hofmann.com	Sinking Spring	PA	19608	610-678-8051	670-2221	490
Hofstra University 1000 Fulton Ave *Fax: Admissions ■ *TF:* 800-463-7872 ■ *Web:* www.hofstra.edu/home	Hempstead	NY	11549	516-463-6600	463-5100*	166
Hofstra University Axinn Library 123 Hofstra University *Web:* www.hofstra.edu	Hempstead	NY	11549	516-463-5940		434-6
Hofwyl-Broadfield Plantation State Historic Site 5556 US Hwy 17 N *Web:* www.gastateparks.org	Brunswick	GA	31525	912-264-7333		565
Hog Heaven 115 27th Ave N. *Web:* www.hogheavenbbq.com	Nashville	TN	37203	615-329-1234		671
Hog Heaven Bar-B-Q 2419 Guess Rd *Web:* www.hogheavenbarbecue.com	Durham	NC	27705	919-286-7447		671
Hog Island Oyster Co 1 Ferry Bldg # 11A *Web:* hogislandoysters.com	San Francisco	CA	94111	415-391-7117		671
Hog Slat Inc PO Box 300 *TF:* 800-949-4647 ■ *Web:* www.hogslat.com	Newton Grove	NC	28366	910-594-0219	594-1392	10-6
Hog's Breath Saloon Key West 400 Front St Ste C *TF:* 800-826-6969 ■ *Web:* www.hogsbreath.com	Key West	FL	33040	305-296-4222		671
Hogan Assessment Systems Inc 2622 E 21st St *Web:* www.hoganassessments.com	Tulsa	OK	74114	918-749-0632		463
Hogan Inc J Taylor 308 Libbie Ave. *Web:* www.jtaylorhogan.com	Richmond	VA	23226	804-282-4474		393
Hogan Larry (R) 100 State Cir *Web:* www.gov.state.md.us	Annapolis	MD	21401	410-974-3901	974-3275	343
Hogan Manufacturing Inc (HMI) PO Box 398 *Web:* www.hoganmfg.com	Escalon	CA	95320	209-838-7323	838-7329	480
Hogan Marren Ltd 321 N Clark St Ste 1301 *Web:* www.hmltd.com	Chicago	IL	60654	312-946-1800		428
Hogan's Hideaway 197 Pk Ave *Web:* www.hoganshideaway.com	Rochester	NY	14607	585-442-4293		671
Hogan-Knotts Financial Group, The 298 Broad St. *TF:* 800-801-3190 ■ *Web:* hkfg.biz	Red Bank	NJ	07701	732-842-7400		690
Hoge Lumber Co 701 S Main St *Web:* www.hoge.com	New Knoxville	OH	45871	419-753-2263	753-2963	683
Hoggan Health Industries Inc 8020 S 1300 W. *TF:* 800-678-7888 ■ *Web:* hogganhealth.net	West Jordan	UT	84088	801-572-6500		267
Hogle-Ireland Inc 2860 Michelle Dr Ste 100.	Irvine	CA	92606	949-553-1427		261
Hogue Cellars 2800 Lee Rd. *Fax Area Code: 509 ■ *TF:* 800-565-9779 ■ *Web:* www.hoguecellars.com	Prosser	WA	99350	800-565-9779	786-4580*	80-3
Hohl Industrial Services Inc 770 Riverview Blvd *Web:* www.hohlind.com	Buffalo	NY	14150	716-332-0466		186
Hohl Machine & Conveyor Company Inc 1580 Niagara St *Web:* www.hohlmachine.com	Buffalo	NY	14213	716-882-7210		207
Hohman Assoc Inc (HAI) 6951 W Little York *TF:* 800-324-0978 ■ *Web:* www.hohmanassociates.com	Houston	TX	77040	713-896-0978	896-9419	48-2
Hohmann & Barnard Inc 30 Rasons Ct *TF:* 800-645-0616 ■ *Web:* www.h-b.com	Hauppauge	NY	11788	631-234-0600	234-0683	278
Hohner Inc 12020 Volunteer Blvd. *TF:* 888-627-3987 ■ *Web:* www.hohnerusa.com	Mt. Juliet	TN	37122	888-627-3987		527
Hohokam Pima National Monument c/o Casa Grande Ruins National Monument 1100 W Ruins Dr *TF:* 866-705-5711 ■ *Web:* www.nps.gov/pima	Coolidge	AZ	85228	520-723-3172	723-7209	564
Hoigaards Inc 5425 Excelsior Blvd *TF:* 800-266-8157 ■ *Web:* www.hoigaards.com	Minneapolis	MN	55416	952-929-1351		711
Hoist Fitness Systems Inc 9990 Empire St Ste 130 *TF:* 800-548-5438 ■ *Web:* www.hoistfitness.com	San Diego	CA	92126	858-578-7676	578-9558	267
Hoke Correctional Institution 243 Old Hwy 211 *Web:* www.doc.state.nc.us	Raeford	NC	28376	910-944-7612		213
Hoke County 227 N Main St. *Web:* www.hoke-raeford.com	Raeford	NC	28376	910-875-8751		338
Hoke Inc 405 Centura Ct PO Box 4866 *Web:* www.hoke.com	Spartanburg	SC	29305	864-574-7966		790
Hoku's 5000 Kahala Ave *Web:* www.kahalaresort.com	Honolulu	HI	96816	808-739-8888		671
Holabird Sports LLC 9220 Pulaski Hwy. *TF:* 866-860-1416 ■ *Web:* www.holabirdsports.com	Middle River	MD	21220	410-687-6400		711
Holaday Circuits Inc 11126 Bren Rd W *TF:* 800-362-3303 ■ *Web:* www.holaday.com	Minnetonka	MN	55343	952-933-3303		625
Holaday-Parks Inc 4600 S 134 Pl *Web:* www.holadayparks.com	Seattle	WA	98168	206-248-9700	248-8700	189-10
HolaDoctor Inc 30 Mansell Court Ste 215 *Web:* www.holadoctor.net	Roswell	GA	30076	770-649-0298		177
Holbrook Island Sanctuary PO Box 35 *Web:* www.maine.gov	Brooksville	ME	04617	207-326-4012		565
Holbrook Manufacturing Inc 291 Province St *Web:* www.holbrookmfg.com	Franklin	IN	46131	317-736-9387		697
Holcomb & Hoke Mfg Company Inc 1545 Van Buren St *TF:* 800-869-9685 ■ *Web:* www.foldoor.com	Indianapolis	IN	46203	317-784-2448	781-9164	286
Holcomb Bridge at Grimes Bridge 690 Holcomb Bridge Rd *Web:* www.myfriendsplacedeli.com	Roswell	GA	30076	770-594-9117		670
Holcomb Enterprises 25108 Marguerite Pkwy B-206 *Web:* www.holcombenterprises.com	Mission Viejo	CA	92692	949-458-0292		180
Holcomb Eric (R) State Housey Rm 206 *Web:* www.in.gov/gov/index.htm	Indianapolis	IN	46204	317-232-4567	232-3443	343
Hold Bros On-Line Capital 10 W 46th St Ste 2450 *Web:* www.holdbrothers.com	New York	NY	10036	212-792-0900		405
Holden Advisors Corp 35 Forest Ridge Ste 160 *TF:* 800-272-0047 ■ *Web:* www.holdenadvisors.com	Concord	MA	01742	978-405-0020		195
Holden Arboretum 9500 Sperry Rd. *TF:* 800-858-1549 ■ *Web:* www.holdenarb.org	Kirtland	OH	44094	440-946-4400	602-3857	97
Holden Industries Inc 5624 S State Hwy 43 *TF:* 800-488-4487 ■ *Web:* www.holdentrailers.com	South West City	MO	64863	417-762-3218		779
Holden Marketing Support Services 5000 Lima St	Denver	CO	80239	720-374-3700		737
Holder Construction Co 3333 Riverwood Pkwy Ste 400 *Web:* www.holderconstruction.com	Atlanta	GA	30339	770-988-3000		186
Holderness School Chapel Ln PO Box 1879 *TF:* 877-262-1492 ■ *Web:* www.holderness.org	Plymouth	NH	03264	603-536-1747		622
Holding George (Rep R - NC) 1110 Longworth HOB *Web:* holding.house.gov	Washington	DC	20515	202-225-3032	225-0181	342-2
Holdrege & Kull Consulting Engineers & Geologists 792 Searls Ave *Web:* handk.net	Nevada City	CA	95959	530-478-1305		261
Holdrege Daily Citizen 418 Garfield St	Holdrege	NE	68949	308-995-4441		532-2
Holdren Brothers Inc 301 Runkle. *Web:* www.holdrenbrothers.com	West Liberty	OH	43357	937-465-7050		757
Holdsworth Financial Group 40 Eagle Vly ct *Web:* www.holdsworthfinancial.com	Broadview Heights	OH	44147	440-746-8100		463
Hole in One International 6195 Ridgeview Ct Ste A *TF:* 800-827-2249 ■ *Web:* www.holeinoneinternational.com	Reno	NV	89519	775-828-4653		760
Hole in the Wall Gang Camps Inc 265 Church St Ste 503 *Web:* www.seriousfunnetwork.org	New Haven	CT	06510	203-562-1203	562-1207	48-5
Ho-Lee-Chow 2204 Danforth Ave. *Web:* www.holeechow.com	Toronto	ON	M4C1K3	416-465-3333		670
Holiday Acres Resort 4060 S Shore Dr PO Box 460 *TF:* 800-261-1500 ■ *Web:* www.holidayacres.com	Rhinelander	WI	54501	715-369-1500		669
Holiday Automotive 321 N Rolling Meadows Dr. *Web:* www.holidayautomotive.com	Fond Du Lac	WI	54937	920-921-8898		516

Phone | Fax | Class

Holiday Builders Inc
2293 W Eau Gallie Blvd, Melbourne FL 32935 — 321-610-5172 — 653
TF: 866-431-2533 ■ *Web:* www.holidaybuilders.com

Holiday Cos
4567 American Blvd W PO Box 1224, Bloomington MN 55437 — 952-830-8700 — 185
TF: 800-745-7411 ■ *Web:* www.holidaystationstores.com

Holiday Diver Inc
180 Gulf Stream Way, Dania Beach FL 33004 — 954-925-7630 — 711
TF: 800-348-3872 ■ *Web:* www.diversdirect.com

Holiday Express Corp
721 S 28th St, Estherville IA 51334 — 712-362-5812 — 362-3019 — 685
TF: 800-831-5078 ■ *Web:* www.holidayxpress.net

Holiday Hair 7201 Metro Blvd, Minneapolis MN 55439 — 800-345-7811 — 77
TF: 800-345-7811 ■
Web: www.signaturestyle.com/brands/holiday-hair.html

Holiday Image Inc 760 First St, Harrison NJ 07029 — 718-369-3212 — 369-3262 — 344
Web: www.holidayimagellc.com

Holiday Inn 301 Government St, Mobile AL 36602 — 251-694-0100 — 379
TF: 888-465-4329 ■ *Web:* www.ihg.com

Holiday Inn Ann Arbor-Near the Univ of MI
3600 Plymouth Rd, Ann Arbor MI 48105 — 734-769-9800 — 378
Web: www.hiannarbor.com

Holiday Inn Baltimore Inner Harbor Hotel
301 W Lombard St, Baltimore MD 21201 — 410-685-3500 — 378
TF: 877-834-3613 ■ *Web:* www.innerharborhi.com

Holiday Inn By the Bay 88 Spring St, Portland ME 04101 — 207-775-2311 — 378
TF: 800-345-5050 ■ *Web:* www.innbythebay.com

Holiday Inn Express & Suites
5001 Brougham Dr, Drayton Valley AB T7A0A1 — 780-515-9888 — 514-2734 — 376
TF: 877-444-3110 ■ *Web:* www.ihg.com/h

Holiday Inn Express & Suites Oceanfront
3301 S Atlantic Ave, Daytona Beach Shores FL 32118 — 386-767-1711 — 669
TF: 800-633-8464 ■ *Web:* www.ihg.com

Holiday Inn Express DFW North
4550 W John Carpenter Fwy, Irving TX 75063 — 800-465-4329 — 379
TF: 800-465-4329 ■ *Web:* www.ihg.com

Holiday Inn Hotel
2501 S High School Rd, Indianapolis IN 46241 — 317-244-6861 — 378
Web: www.holidayinn.com/hotels/us/en/cincinnati/cvgem/hoteldetail

Holiday Inn Los Angeles International Airport
9901 La Cienega Blvd, Los Angeles CA 90045 — 310-649-5151 — 378
Web: www.hilax.com

Holiday Inn Oceanfront at Surfside Beach
1601 N Ocean Blvd, Surfside Beach SC 29575 — 843-238-5601 — 669
Web: www.ihg.com

Holiday Inn Resort Daytona Beach Oceanfront
1615 S Atlantic Ave, Daytona Beach FL 32118 — 386-255-0921 — 379
TF: 800-874-0975 ■ *Web:* www.hiresortdaytona.com

Holiday Inn Resort Lake Buena Vista
13351 SR 535, Orlando FL 32821 — 407-239-4500 — 669
TF Sales: 866-808-8833 ■ *Web:* www.hiresortlbv.com

Holiday Inn Select Hotel & Suites in Oakville
2525 Wyecroft Rd, Oakville ON L6L6P8 — 905-847-1000 — 378
TF: 000-263-0009 ■ *Web:* www.oakvillehotel.com

Holiday Inn Select in Windsor Canada
1855 Huron Church Rd, Windsor ON N9C2L6 — 519-966-1200 — 378
TF: 800-265-3633 ■ *Web:* www.hIs-windsor.com

Holiday Inn SunSpree Resort Whistler Village
4295 Blackcomb Way, Whistler BC V0N1B4 — 604-938-0878 — 669
Web: www.ihg.com

Holiday Inn SunSpree Resort Wrightsville Beach
1706 N Lumina Ave, Wrightsville Beach NC 28480 — 910-256-2231 — 669
TF: 888-211-9874 ■ *Web:* www.ihg.com

Holiday Isle Beach Resort & Marina
84001 Overseas Hwy, Islamorada FL 33036 — 305-664-2321 — 664-2523 — 669
TF: 855-314-2829 ■ *Web:* www.holidayisle.com

Holiday Lanes 3316 Old Minden Rd, Bossier City LA 71112 — 318-746-7331 — 99
Web: www.bowlholidaylanes.com

Holiday Models Convention Services
3651 Lindell Rd Ste D140, Las Vegas NV 89103 — 702-735-7353 — 796-5676 — 184
Web: www.holidaymodels.com

Holiday Oil Co 3115 W 2100 S, West Valley City UT 84119 — 801-973-7002 — 579
Web: www.holidayoil.com

Holiday Retirement Corp
5885 Meadows Rd Ste 500, Lake Oswego OR 97035 — 503-370-7070 — 655
TF: 800-322-0999 ■ *Web:* www.holidaytouch.com

Holiday River Expeditions
544 East 3900 South, Salt Lake City UT 84107 — 801-266-2087 — 266-1448 — 760
TF: 800-624-6323 ■ *Web:* www.bikeraft.com

Holiday Stationstores
4567 American Blvd W, Bloomington MN 55437 — 952-830-8700 — 204
TF: 800-745-7411 ■ *Web:* www.holidaystationstores.com

Holiday Tours Inc
10367 Randleman Rd, Randleman NC 27317 — 336-498-9000 — 498-2204 — 760
TF: 800-733-9011 ■ *Web:* www.holidaytoursinc.com

Holiday Trails Resorts (Western) Inc
53730 Bridal Falls Rd, Rosedale BC V0X1X1 — 604-794-7876 — 794-3756 — 121
TF: 800-663-2265 ■ *Web:* www.holidaytrailsresorts.com

Holiday Travel of America
6405 El Camino Real, Carlsbad CA 92009 — 760-431-8600 — 772
Web: www.htoa.com

Holiday Tree Farms Inc
800 NW Cornell Ave, Corvallis OR 97330 — 541-753-3236 — 757-8028 — 752
TF: 800-289-3684 ■ *Web:* www.holidaytreefarm.com

Holiday Valley Resort
6557 Holiday Valley Rd PO Box 370, Ellicottville NY 14731 — 716-699-2345 — 699-5204 — 669
TF: 800-323-0020 ■ *Web:* www.holidayvalley.com

Holiday World & Splashin' Safari
452 E Christmas Blvd, Santa Claus IN 47579 — 812-937-4401 — 32
TF: 877-463-2645 ■ *Web:* www.holidayworld.com

Holihan Law
1101 N Lake Destiny Rd Ste 275, Maitland FL 32751 — 407-660-8575 — 428
TF: 800-863-1462 ■ *Web:* www.holihanlaw.com

Holladay Corp
3400 Idaho Ave NW Ste 500, Washington DC 20016 — 202-362-2400 — 655
Web: holladaycorp.com

Holland & Knight LLP
2115 Harden Blvd, Lakeland FL 33803 — 863-682-1161 — 41
Web: www.hklaw.com

Holland America Line
300 Elliott Ave W, Seattle WA 98119 — 206-281-3535 — 281-7110 — 220
TF: 800-426-0327 ■ *Web:* www.hollandamerica.com

Holland Area Chamber of Commerce
272 E Eigth St, Holland MI 49423 — 616-392-2389 — 392-7379 — 139
TF: 800-764-2836 ■ *Web:* www.westcoastchamber.org

Holland Area Convention & Visitors Bureau
76 E Eigth St, Holland MI 49423 — 616-394-0000 — 394-0122 — 206
TF: 800-506-1299 ■ *Web:* www.holland.org

Holland Bowl Mill 120 James St, Holland MI 49424 — 616-396-6513 — 279
Web: www.hollandbowlmill.com

Holland Capital Management LP
303 W Madison St Ste 700, Chicago IL 60606 — 312-553-4830 — 553-4848 — 401
TF: 800-295-9779 ■ *Web:* www.hollandcap.com

Holland Co 1000 Holland Dr, Crete IL 60417 — 708-672-2300 — 672-0119 — 650
TF: 800-895-4389 ■ *Web:* www.hollandco.com

Holland College 140 Weymouth St, Charlottetown PE C1A4Z1 — 902-566-9510 — 629-4239 — 162
TF: 800-446-5265 ■ *Web:* www.hollandc.pe.ca

Holland Community Hospital
602 Michigan Ave, Holland MI 49423 — 616-392-5141 — 374-3
Web: www.hollandhospital.org

Holland Inc 109 W 17th St, Vancouver WA 98660 — 360-694-1521 — 670
Web: www.hollandinc.com

Holland Land Title & Abstract Company Inc
110 Pearl St, Buffalo NY 14202 — 716-853-6529 — 390
Web: hollandtitle.com

Holland Litho Printing Service Inc
10972 Chicago Dr, Zeeland MI 49464 — 616-392-4644 — 592
TF: 800-652-6567 ■ *Web:* www.hollandlitho.com

Holland Mfg Co Inc
15 Main St PO Box 404, Succasunna NJ 07876 — 973-584-8141 — 584-6845 — 732
TF: 800-345-0492 ■ *Web:* www.hollandmfg.com

Holland NASCAR Motorsports Complex
11586 Holland Glenwood Rd, Holland NY 14080 — 716-537-2272 — 537-9749 — 515
TF: 866-655-0257 ■ *Web:* www.hollandspeedway.com

Holland Patent Central School District
9001 Main St, Holland Patent NY 13354 — 315-865-7200 — 685
Web: www.hpschools.org

Holland Public Schools 156 W 11th St, Holland MI 49423 — 616-494-2000 — 685
Web: www.hollandpublicschools.org

Holland Sentinel 54 W Eigth St, Holland MI 49423 — 616-546-4200 — 392-3526 — 532-2
Web: www.hollandsentinel.com

Holland State Park
2215 Ottawa Beach Rd, Holland MI 49424 — 616-399-9390 — 565
Web: www.michigandnr.com

Holland Transportation Management Inc
305 N Center St, Statesville NC 28677 — 704-872-4269 — 311
TF: 800-832-5660 ■ *Web:* www.hollandtms.com

Holland's Rose 132 Griegos Rd NW, Albuquerque NM 87107 — 505-345-2020 — 372
Web: www.hollandsrose.com

Hollander Home Fashions Corp
6501 Congress Ave Ste 300, Boca Raton FL 33487 — 561-997-6900 — 746
TF: 800-233-7666 ■ *Web:* www.hollander.com

Hollandia Dairy Inc
622 E Mission Rd, San Marcos CA 92069 — 760-744-3222 — 10-3
Web: www.hollandiadairy.com

Hollar & Greene Produce Co Inc
230 Cabbage Rd PO Box 3500, Boone NC 28607 — 828-264-2177 — 264-4413 — 297-7
TF: 800-222-1077 ■ *Web:* www.hollarandgreene.com

Hollar Co 2012 Rainbow Dr, Gadsden AL 35901 — 256-547-1644 — 204
Web: shell.com

Holler Classic 139 N Oregon St, Sanford FL 32771 — 888-894-9542 — 57
TF: 888-894-9542 ■ *Web:* www.hollerclassic.com

Holley Credit Union
1107 Mineral Wells Ave, Paris TN 38242 — 731-644-9031 — 219
Web: holleycreditunion.org

Holley Performance Products Inc
1801 Russellville Rd, Bowling Green KY 42101 — 270-782-2900 — 781-9940* — 128
**Fax:* Cust Svc ■ *Web:* www.holley.com

Holliday Lake State Park
2759 State Pk Rd, Appomattox VA 24522 — 434-248-6308 — 565
TF: 800-933-7275 ■
Web: www.dcr.virginia.gov/state-parks/holliday-lake#general_information

Hollidaysburg Veterans Home
PO Box 319, Hollidaysburg PA 16648 — 814-696-5201 — 793
Web: www.dmva.pa.gov/stateveteranshomes/hollidaysburg-veterans-home

Hollingsworth & Vose Co
112 Washington St, East Walpole MA 02032 — 508-850-2000 — 557
Web: www.hollingsworth-vose.com

Hollingsworth Concrete Products Inc
920 Kingsbridge Rd, Carrollton GA 30117 — 770-832-2581 — 182

Hollingsworth Trey (Rep R - IN)
641 Longworth HOB, Washington DC 20515 — 202-225-5315 — 342-2
Web: hollingsworth.house.gov

Hollins University PO Box 9707, Roanoke VA 24020 — 540-362-6401 — 362-6218* — 166
**Fax:* Admissions ■ *TF Admissions:* 800-456-9595 ■ *Web:* www.hollins.edu

Hollis D Segur Inc 156 Knotter Dr, Cheshire CT 06410 — 203-699-4500 — 390

Hollis Industries Inc
1485 Washington St, Holliston MA 01746 — 508-429-4328 — 454

Hollis Marketing 2130 Brenner St, Saginaw MI 48602 — 989-797-3300 — 195
TF: 866-797-3301 ■ *Web:* hollismarketing.com

Hollis Social Library 2 Monument Sq, Hollis NH 03049 — 603-465-7721 — 465-3507 — 434-3
Web: hollislibrary.org

Hollister Construction Co
4071 E La Palma Ave Ste A, Anaheim CA 92807 — 714-701-1400 — 186
Web: www.hollico.net

Hollister Hills State Vehicular Recreation Area
7800 Cienega Rd, Hollister CA 95023 — 831-637-8186 — 565
Web: www.parks.ca.gov

Hollister Inc 2000 Hollister Dr, Libertyville IL 60048 — 847-680-1000 — 477
TF: 800-323-4060 ■ *Web:* www.hollister.com

Hollister Moving & Storage
1650 Lana Way, Hollister CA 95023 — 831-636-5000 — 519
Web: hollistermovers.com

Hollister-Whitney Elevator Corp
2603 N 24th St, Quincy IL 62305 — 217-222-0466 — 222-0493 — 256
Web: www.hollisterwhitney.com

Holliway Insurance Agency Inc
5765 Olde Wadsworth Blvd, Arvada CO 80002 — 303-421-3046 — 390

Company	Phone	Fax	Class
Holloman Corp 333 N Sam Houston Pkwy E Ste 600 .... Houston TX 77060 *TF:* 800-521-2461 ■ *Web:* www.hollomancorp.com	281-878-2600		186
Hollow Inn 278 S Main St. .... Barre VT 05641 *Web:* www.hollowinn.com	802-479-9313	476-5242	379
Holloway Credit Solutions LLC 1286 Carmichael Way.................... Montgomery AL 36106 *Web:* hollowaycredit.com	334-396-1200		218
Holloway Houston Inc 5833 Armour Dr.......... Houston TX 77020 *Web:* www.hhilifting.com	713-674-5631		770
Holloway Sportswear Inc 2633 Campbell Rd .... Sidney OH 45365 *TF:* 800-331-5156 ■ *Web:* www.hollowayusa.com	800-331-5156		155-5
Holly A Carlin CPA 1912 Sidewinder Dr 211A................... Park City UT 84060 *Web:* carlincpa.com	435-649-0909		2
Holly C Roundtree 5001 Spring Valley Rd Ste 250E................. Dallas TX 75244 *Web:* hcroundtreecpa.com	972-404-4434		2
Holly Energy Partners LP 100 Crescent Ct Ste 1600...................... Dallas TX 75201 *TF:* 800-642-1687 ■ *Web:* www.hollyenergy.com	214-871-3555		360-5
Holly Hill Hospital 3019 Falstaff Rd .... Raleigh NC 27610 *TF:* 800-447-1800 ■ *Web:* www.hollyhillhospital.com	919-250-7000		374-5
Holly Hill Nursing Home 203 Lafayette St .... Anna IL 62906	618-833-3322		371
Holly Poultry Inc 2221 Berlin St............. Baltimore MD 21230 *TF:* 800-342-9464 ■ *Web:* www.hollypoultry.com	410-727-6210		345
Holly Recreation Area 8100 Grange Hall Rd .... Holly MI 48442 *Web:* www.michigandnr.com	248-634-8811		565
Holly Refining & Marketing Co 1700 S Union Ave............................ Tulsa OK 74107 *Web:* www.hollyfrontier.com	918-594-6600		324
Holly River State Park 680 State Park Rd....................... Hacker Valley WV 26222 *Web:* www.hollyriver.com	304-493-6353		565
Holly Shores Best Holiday 491 Route 9 .... Cape May NJ 08204 *TF:* 877-494-6559 ■ *Web:* www.hollyshores.com	609-886-1234		707
Hollyhock PO Box 127............... Mansons Landing BC V0P1K0 *TF:* 800-933-6339 ■ *Web:* www.hollyhock.ca	250-935-6576	935-6424	673
Hollyhock Hill 8110 N College Ave .... Indianapolis IN 46240 *Web:* www.hollyhockhill.com	317-251-2294		671
Hollymatic Corp 600 E Plainfield Rd....................... Countryside IL 60525 *Web:* www.hollymatic.com	708-579-3700	579-1057	298
Hollywood & Highland 6801 Hollywood Blvd....................... Hollywood CA 90028 *Web:* www.hollywoodandhighland.com	323-817-0200	460-6003	50-6
Hollywood Bed & Spring Manufacturing Co 5959 Corvette St.......................... Commerce CA 90040 *Web:* www.hollywoodbed.com	323-887-9500		321
Hollywood Blvd a Cinema Bar & Eatery 1001 75th St Ste 153 .... Woodridge IL 60517 *Web:* www.atriptothemovies.com	630-427-1880		748
Hollywood Bowl 2301 N Highland Ave .... Hollywood CA 90068 *TF:* 800-745-3000 ■ *Web:* www.hollywoodbowl.com	323-850-2000	850-2155	572
Hollywood Casino at Charles Town Races 750 Hollywood Dr....................... Charles Town WV 25414 *TF:* 800-795-7001 ■ *Web:* www.hollywoodcasinocharlestown.com	304-725-7001		642
Hollywood Casino at Penn National Race Course 777 Hollywood Blvd .... Grantville PA 17028 *Web:* www.hollywoodpnrc.com	717-469-2211		642
Hollywood Casino Baton Rouge 1717 River Rd N .... Baton Rouge LA 70802 *TF:* 800-447-6843 ■ *Web:* www.hollywoodbr.com	225-709-7777		133
Hollywood Casino Bay Saint Louis 711 Hollywood Blvd.................. Bay Saint Louis MS 39520 *TF:* 866-758-2591 ■ *Web:* hollywoodgulfcoast.com	866-758-2591		133
Hollywood Casino Joliet 777 Hollywood Blvd........................... Joliet IL 60436 *TF:* 800-426-2537 ■ *Web:* www.hollywoodcasinojoliet.com	800-426-2537		133
Hollywood Chamber of Commerce 7018 Hollywood Blvd....................... Hollywood CA 90028 *TF:* 800-524-6783 ■ *Web:* walkoffame.com	323-469-8311		139
Hollywood Foreign Press Assn (HFPA) 646 N Robertson Blvd................. West Hollywood CA 90069 *Web:* www.goldenglobes.com/hfpa	310-657-1731		48-4
Hollywood Museum 1660 N Highland Ave .... Hollywood CA 90028 *Web:* www.thehollywoodmuseum.com	323-464-7776		520
Hollywood Park Land Company LLC 1050 S Prairie Ave .... Inglewood CA 90301 *Web:* www.hollywoodpark.com	310-330-3515		642
Hollywood Presbyterian Medical Ctr 1300 N Vermont Ave.................... Los Angeles CA 90027 *TF:* 800-465-3203 ■ *Web:* www.hollywoodpresbyterian.com	213-413-3000		374-3
Hollywood Records Inc 500 S Buena Vista St .... Burbank CA 91521 *Web:* www.hollywoodrecords.com	818-560-5670		657
Hollywood Reporter 5055 Wilshire Blvd Ste 600 .... Los Angeles CA 90036 **Fax: Edit* ■ *TF:* 866-525-2150 ■ *Web:* www.hollywoodreporter.com	323-525-2000	525-2377*	457-9
Hollywood Roosevelt Hotel 7000 Hollywood Blvd .... Los Angeles CA 90028 *Web:* www.thompsonhotels.com	323-466-7000		379
Hollywood Scriptwriter Magazine PO Box 3761 .... Cerritos CA 90703 **Fax Area Code:* 562 ■ *Web:* www.hollywoodscriptwriter.com	310-283-1630	926-2060*	457-9
Hollywood Standard Hotel 8300 Sunset Blvd.................... West Hollywood CA 90069 *Web:* www.standardhotels.com	323-650-9090		379
Hollywood Super Market Inc 2670 W Maple Rd.............................. Troy MI 48084 *Web:* hollywoodmarkets.com	248-643-6770	643-0309	345
Hollywood Tans 11 Enterprise Crt................ Sewell NJ 08080 *Web:* www.hollywoodtans.com	856-716-2150		310
Hollywood Theater Holdings Inc 919 SW Taylor St Ste 800..................... Portland OR 97205 *Web:* www.regmovies.com	503-221-7090		748
Hollywood Wax Museum 3030 W Hwy 76........ Branson MO 65616 *TF:* 800-214-3661 ■ *Web:* www.hollywoodwaxmuseum.com	417-337-8277	334-8202	520
Hollywood Woodwork Inc 2951 Pembroke Rd......................... Hollywood FL 33020 *Web:* www.hollywoodwoodwork.com	954-920-5009		499
Hollywood.com LLC 560 Broadway Ste 404 .... New York NY 10012 *Web:* www.hollywood.com	212-817-9105		387
Hol-Mac Corp 2730-A Hwy 15 PO Box 349................ Bay Springs MS 39422 *TF:* 800-844-3019 ■ *Web:* www.hol-mac.com	601-764-4121	764-3438	223
Holman Aviation Co 1940 Airport Ct........................... Great Falls MT 59404 *Web:* www.holmanaviation.com	406-453-7613		63
Holman Cadillac Co 1200 Rt 73 S .... Mount Laurel NJ 08054 *TF:* 866-865-6973 ■ *Web:* holmancadillac.com	856-778-1000		57
Holman Correctional Facility 866 Ross Rd................................... Atmore AL 36503 *Web:* www.doc.state.al.us	251-368-8173	368-1095	213
Holman Distribution Ctr of Oregon Inc 2300 SE Beta St .... Milwaukie OR 97222 *Web:* holmanusa.com	503-652-1912		803-1
Holman Group 9451 Corbin Ave .... Northridge CA 91324 *TF:* 800-321-2843 ■ *Web:* www.holmangroup.com	818-704-1444	704-9339	462
Holman Transportation Services Inc 1010 Holman Ct .... Caldwell ID 83605 *TF:* 800-375-2416 ■ *Web:* holmantransport.com	208-454-0779		780
Holman'S of Nevada Inc 4445 S Vly View Blvd .... Las Vegas NV 89103 *Web:* www.holmansnv.com	702-222-1818		180
Holmberg Farms Inc 13430 Hobson Simmons Rd..................... Lithia FL 33547	813-689-3601		293
Holmes Body Shop Inc 1095 E Colorado Blvd....................... Pasadena CA 91106	626-795-6447		62-4
Holmes Cheese Co 9444 SR-39............. Millersburg OH 44654	330-674-6451		296-5
Holmes Community College PO Box 399....... Goodman MS 39079 *TF:* 800-465-6374 ■ *Web:* holmescc.edu	662-472-2312		162
Holmes County 106 E Byrd Ave................. Bonifay FL 32425 *Web:* www.holmescountyonline.com	850-547-6153		338
Holmes County 6 W Jackson St.............. Millersburg OH 44654 *Web:* holmescountychamber.com	330-674-3975		338
Holmes County Chamber of Commerce 104 W China St .... Lexington MS 39095 *TF:* 800-748-7626 ■ *Web:* www.holmescountymississippi.com	662-834-3372	834-4544	338
Holmes County Chamber of Commerce 35 N Monroe St .... Millersburg OH 44654 *Web:* www.holmescountychamber.com	330-674-3975	674-3976	139
Holmes County District Public Library (HCDPL) 3102 Glen Dr .... Millersburg OH 44654 *Web:* www.holmeslibrary.org	330-674-5972	674-1938	434-3
Holmes County State Park 5369 State Pk Rd .... Durant MS 39063 *Web:* www.mdwfp.com/parkview/parks.asp?id=3824	662-653-3351		565
Holmes District School Board (HDSB) 701 E Pennsylvania Ave .... Bonifay FL 32425 *Web:* www.hdsb.org	850-547-9341	547-3568	685
Holmes Foods Inc 101 S Liberty Ave .... Nixon TX 78140 *Web:* holmesfoods.com	830-582-1551		619
Holmes Limestone Co 4255 SR 39 .... Millersburg OH 44654 *Web:* holmeslimestone.com	330-893-2721	893-2941	501
Holmes Murphy & Assoc Inc 3001 Westown Pkwy.................. West Des Moines IA 50266 *TF:* 800-247-7756 ■ *Web:* www.holmesmurphy.com	515-223-6800		390
Holmes Public Library 470 Plymouth St .... Halifax MA 02338 *Web:* holmespubliclibrary.org	781-293-2271	294-8518	434-3
Holmes Regional Medical Ctr 1350 Hickory St .... Melbourne FL 32901 *TF:* 800-716-7737 ■ *Web:* www.health-first.org	321-434-7000	727-1200	374-3
Holmes Tile & Marble Company Inc 1202 Falls St .... Jonesboro AR 72401 *Web:* holmestile.com	870-932-8011		290
Holmes-Wayne Electric Co-op Inc 6060 Ohio 83 .... Millersburg OH 44654 *TF:* 866-674-1055 ■ *Web:* www.hwecoop.com	330-674-1055	674-1869	245
Holmstad, The 700 W Fabyan Pkwy .... Batavia IL 60510 *Web:* www.covenantretirement.org	630-879-4100		672
Holocaust Memorial Ctr 28123 OrchaRd Lake Rd............... Farmington Hills MI 48334 *TF:* 800-875-5275 ■ *Web:* www.holocaustcenter.org	248-553-2400	553-2433	520
Holocaust Memorial of the Greater Miami Jewish Federation 1933-1945 Meridian Ave .... Miami Beach FL 33139 *TF:* 800-704-2663 ■ *Web:* www.holocaustmmb.org	305-538-1663		50-4
Holocaust Museum & Resource Ctr 601 Jefferson Ave.......................... Scranton PA 18510 *TF:* 800-605-7518 ■ *Web:* www.jewishnepa.org	570-961-2300	346-6147	520
Holocaust Museum Houston 5401 Caroline St............................ Houston TX 77004 *Web:* www.hmh.org	713-942-8000	942-7953	520
Hologic Inc 35 Crosby Dr...................... Bedford MA 01730 *NASDAQ:* HOLX ■ *TF:* 800-523-5001 ■ *Web:* www.hologic.com	781-999-7300	280-0669	382
Holophane 3825 Columbus Rd Granville Business Park Bldg A .... Granville OH 43023 *TF:* 866-759-1577 ■ *Web:* www.holophane.com	866-759-1577	637-7069	439
Holorad 2929 S Main St................... Salt Lake City UT 84115 *TF:* 800-424-3827 ■ *Web:* www.holorad.com	801-983-6075		382
Holsted Marketing Inc 112 W 34th St Ste 1405 .... New York NY 10120	212-686-8537		195
Holstein Assn USA Inc 1 Holstein Pl PO Box 808................... Brattleboro VT 05302 *TF Orders:* 800-952-5200 ■ *Web:* www.holsteinusa.com	802-254-4551	254-8251	48-2
Holston Electric Co-op Inc 1200 W Main St .... Rogersville TN 37857 *Web:* www.holstonelectric.com	423-272-8821		245

Phone | Fax | Class

Holston Valley Hospital & Medical Ctr
130 W Ravine Rd .... Kingsport TN 37660 423-224-4000 374-3
TF: 800-828-1120 ■ *Web:* www.wellmont.org

Holsum of Fort Wayne Inc
136 Murray St .... Fort Wayne IN 46803 260-456-2130 297-8
Web: www.holsum.com

Holt & Bugbee Co 1600 Shawsheen St .... Tewksbury MA 01876 978-851-7201 851-3941 191-3
TF: 800-325-6010 ■ *Web:* www.holtandbugbee.com

Holt County 204 N Fourth St PO Box 329 .... O'Neill NE 68763 402-336-1762 336-1762 338
Web: www.co.holt.ne.us

Holt County 102 W Nodaway St PO Box 437 .... Oregon MO 64473 660-446-3303 446-3353 338
Web: holtcounty.org

Holt Equipment Co LLC
PO Box 436317 .... Louisville KY 40223 502-797-5075 429
Web: www.holtgascompression.com

Holt Hosiery Mills Inc
733 Koury Dr .... Burlington NC 27215 336-227-1431 227-8614 155-10
Web: holthosiery.com

Holt Integrated Circuits Inc
23351 Madero .... Mission Viejo CA 92691 949-859-8800 859-9643 696
Web: www.holtic.com

Holt Marketing Services Inc
3075 Boardwalk Dr Unit 2 .... Saginaw MI 48603 989-791-2475 463
TF: 800-698-2449 ■ *Web:* marketingholt.com

Holt Sublimation Printing & Products
2208 Air Pk Dr .... Burlington NC 27215 336-222-3600 745-7

HOLT Texas Ltd 3302 S WW White Rd .... San Antonio TX 78222 210-648-1111 648-0079 274
TF: 800-275-4658 ■ *Web:* www.holtcat.com

Holter Museum of Art 12 E Lawrence St .... Helena MT 59601 406-442-6400 520
Web: www.holtermuseum.org

Holthouse Carlin & Van Trigt LLP
11444 W Olympic Blvd Ste 300-S .... Los Angeles CA 90064 310-566-1900 566-1901 2
Web: www.hcvt.com

Holts Cigar Co 1522 Walnut St .... Philadelphia PA 19102 215-732-8500 732-4988 756
TF: 800-523-1641 ■ *Web:* www.holts.com

Holts Landing State Park 89 Kings Hwy .... Dover DE 19901 302-227-2800 565
Web: www.destateparks.com

Holtzbrinck Publishers 175 Fifth Ave .... New York NY 10010 646-307-5151 637-2
TF: 800-221-7945 ■ *Web:* macmillan.com

Holtzman Enterprises Inc
8501 Turnpike Dr Ste 103 .... Westminster CO 80031 303-428-3364 77
Web: greatclips.com

Holum & Sons Company Inc
740 Burr Oak Dr .... Westmont IL 60559 630-654-8222 654-2929 86
TF: 800-447-4479 ■ *Web:* www.holumandsons.com

Holy Apostles College & Seminary
33 Prospect Hill Rd .... Cromwell CT 06416 860-632-3077 166
Web: www.holyapostles.edu

Holy Cross College 54515 SR 933 N .... Notre Dame IN 46556 574-239-8400 239-8323* 166
**Fax:* Admissions ■ *TF:* 800-742-0891 ■ *Web:* www.hcc-nd.edu

Holy Cross Energy
PO Box 2150 .... Glenwood Springs CO 81602 970-945-5491 945-4081 245
TF: 877-833-2555 ■ *Web:* www.holycross.com

Holy Cross Family Ministries
518 Washington St .... North Easton MA 02356 508-238-4095 48-20
TF: 800-299-7729 ■ *Web:* www.hcfm.org

Holy Cross Hospital 2701 W 68th St .... Chicago IL 60629 773-884-9000 374-3
Web: www.holycrosshospital.org

Holy Cross Hospital
4725 N Federal Hwy .... Fort Lauderdale FL 33308 954-771-8000 492-5741 374-3
TF: 888-419-3456 ■ *Web:* www.holy-cross.com

Holy Cross Hospital
1500 Forest Glen Rd .... Silver Spring MD 20910 301-754-7000 754-7012 374-3
Web: www.holycrosshealth.org

Holy Cross Monastery 1615 Rt 9W .... West Park NY 12493 845-384-6660 384-6031 673
TF: 800-313-5114 ■ *Web:* www.holycrossmonastery.com

Holy Cross Village At Notre Dame Inc
54515 State Rd 933 N PO Box 303 .... Notre Dame IN 46556 574-287-1838 371
TF: 800-622-4484 ■ *Web:* www.holycrossvillage.com

Holy Family Hospital 70 E St .... Methuen MA 01844 978-687-0151 374-3
Web: steward.org

Holy Family Institute
8235 Ohio River Blvd .... Pittsburgh PA 15202 412-766-4030 242
Web: www.hfi-pgh.org

Holy Family Memorial Medical Ctr
2300 Western Ave PO Box 1450 .... Manitowoc WI 54220 920-320-2011 374-3
TF: 800-994-3662 ■ *Web:* www.hfmhealth.org

Holy Family University
9801 Frankford Ave .... Philadelphia PA 19114 215-637-7700 166
TF: 800-422-0010 ■ *Web:* holyfamily.edu

Holy Land 677 Rand Ave .... Oakland CA 94610 510-272-0535 671

Holy Name Hospital 718 Teaneck Rd .... Teaneck NJ 07666 201-833-3000 374-3
Web: www.holyname.org

Holy Names University
3500 Mountain Blvd .... Oakland CA 94619 510-436-1000 436-1325* 166
**Fax:* Admissions ■ *TF:* 800-430-1321 ■ *Web:* www.hnu.edu

Holy Redeemer Home Care & Hospice
12265 Townsend Rd Ste 400 .... Philadelphia PA 19154 888-678-8678 371
TF: 888-678-8678 ■ *Web:* www.holyredeemer.com

Holy Redeemer Hospital & Medical Ctr
1648 Huntingdon Pk .... Meadowbrook PA 19046 215-947-3000 374-3
TF: 800-818-4747 ■ *Web:* www.holyredeemer.com

Holy Rosary Healthcare
2600 Wilson St .... Miles City MT 59301 406-233-2600 233-4214 374-3
TF: 800-843-3820 ■
Web: www.sclhealth.org/locations/holy-rosary-healthcare

Holy See 25 E 39th St .... New York NY 10016 212-370-7885 370-9622 784
Web: www.holyseemission.org
Apostolic Nunciature
3339 Massachusetts Ave NW .... Washington DC 20008 202-333-7121 337-4036 257
Web: www.holyseemission.org

Holy Spirit Catholic School
540 N Seventh Ave .... Pocatello ID 83201 208-232-5763 48-20
Web: www.hscssa.org

Holy Spirit Hospital 503 N 21st St .... Camp Hill PA 17011 717-763-2100 972-7676 374-3
Web: www.hsh.org

Holy Trinity Catholic Church
315 Marshall St .... Shreveport LA 71101 318-221-5990 50-1
Web: www.holytrinity-shreveport.com

Phone | Fax | Class

Holyoke Community College
303 Homestead Ave .... Holyoke MA 01040 413-538-7000 552-2192* 162
**Fax:* Admissions ■ *TF:* 800-325-3252 ■ *Web:* www.hcc.edu

Holyoke Heritage State Park
221 Appleton St .... Holyoke MA 01040 413-534-1723 565
Web: mass.gov

Holyoke Machine Co
514 Main St PO Box 988 .... Holyoke MA 01040 413-534-5612 532-9244 556
Web: www.holyokemachine.com

Holyoke Mall at Ingleside
50 Holyoke St .... Holyoke MA 01040 413-536-1441 460
Web: holyokemall.com

Holyoke Medical Ctr 575 Beech St .... Holyoke MA 01040 413-534-2500 374-3
Web: www.holyokehealth.com

Holyoke Public Library 335 Maple St .... Holyoke MA 01040 413-322-5640 434-3
Web: www.holyokelibrary.org

Holyoke Soldiers Home 110 Cherry St .... Holyoke MA 01040 413-532-9475 538-7968 793
TF: 800-315-6338 ■ *Web:* mass.gov

Holz Motors Inc 5961 S 108th Pl .... Hales Corners WI 53130 414-425-2400 57
Web: www.holzmotors.com

Holz Rubber Company Inc
1129 S Sacramento St .... Lodi CA 95240 209-368-7171 368-3246 677
TF: 800-285-1600 ■ *Web:* www.holzrubber.com

Holzer Health Systems
100 Jackson Pk .... Gallipolis OH 45631 740-446-5000 374-3
Web: www.holzer.org

Holzmueller Productions Corp
1000 25th St .... San Francisco CA 94107 415-826-8383 826-2608 722
TF: 800-284-2024 ■ *Web:* www.holzmueller.com

Homark Company Inc
100 Third St PO Box 309 .... Red Lake Falls MN 56750 218-253-2777 253-2116 505
TF: 800-382-1154 ■ *Web:* www.detroiter.com

Homasote Co
932 Lower Ferry Rd PO Box 7240 .... West Trenton NJ 08628 609-883-3300 883-3497 819
OTC: HMTC ■ *TF:* 800-257-9491 ■ *Web:* www.homasote.com

Homax Products Inc
1835 Barkley Blvd .... Bellingham WA 98226 360-733-9029 140
Web: www.homaxproducts.com

Homcare Inc 875 W Summit Ave .... Muskegon MI 49441 231-755-6951 363
Web: homcareinc.com

Home & Away Magazine 10703 J St Ste 100 .... Omaha NE 68127 402-592-5000 457-22
Web: www.homeandawaymagazine.com

Home & Garden Showplace
8600 W Bryn Mawr .... Chicago IL 60631 773-695-5000 323
TF: 877-502-4641 ■ *Web:* truevaluecompany.com/gardencenters

Home & Hearth 2090 E Main St .... Cortlandt Manor NY 10567 914-734-9773 321
Web: www.homeandhearth-mainst.com

Home Accents Mart
5521 McFarland Blvd .... Northport AL 35476 205-339-6550 362

Home Aides of Central New York Inc
723 James St .... Syracuse NY 13203 315-476-4295 363
Web: homeaidescny.org

Home Automated Living Inc
14401 Sweitzer Ln Ste 600 .... Laurel MD 20707 301-498-7000 174
TF: 800-935-5313

Home Bound Healthcare Inc
1615 Vollmer Rd .... Flossmoor IL 60422 708-798-0800 363
TF: 800-444-7028 ■ *Web:* www.homeboundhealth.com

Home Capital Group Inc
145 King St W Ste 2300 .... Toronto ON M5H1J8 416-360-4663 363-7611 360-3
TSE: HCG ■ *TF:* 800-990-7881 ■ *Web:* www.homecapital.com

Home Care & Elder Services
2141 NW Fillmore Ave .... Corvallis OR 97330 541-757-0214 363

Home Care Industries Inc ALFCO Div
1 Lisbon St .... Clifton NJ 07013 973-365-1600 365-1770 18
TF Cust Svc: 800-325-1908 ■ *Web:* www.homecareind.com

Home Care Network Inc
190A E Spring Valley Rd .... Centerville OH 45458 937-435-1142 363
TF: 800-417-0291 ■ *Web:* www.hcnmidwest.net

Home Care Partners
1234 Massachusetts Ave NW Ste C-1002 .... Washington DC 20005 202-638-2382 363
Web: www.homecarepartners.org

Home Care Specialists Inc
113 Neck Rd .... Haverhill MA 01835 978-373-7771 475
Web: www.hcshme.com

Home City Financial Corp
2454 N Limestone St .... Springfield OH 45503 937-390-0470 390-0876 360-2
OTC: HCFL ■ *TF:* 866-421-2331 ■ *Web:* www.homecityfederal.com

Home Comfort Furniture & Mattress Center Inc
7016 Glenwood Ave .... Raleigh NC 27612 919-781-3900 321
Web: www.homecomfortfurniture.com

Home Depot Inc 2455 Paces Ferry Rd NW .... Atlanta GA 30339 770-433-8211 364
NYSE: HD ■ *TF Cust Svc:* 800-553-3199 ■ *Web:* www.homedepot.com

Home Depot Supply
3100 Cumberland Blvd Ste 1480 .... Atlanta GA 30339 770-852-9000 351
TF: 855-615-8372 ■ *Web:* www.hdsupply.com

Home Design Outlet Ctr
400 County Ave .... Secaucus NJ 07094 800-701-0388 361
TF: 800-701-0388 ■ *Web:* www.homedesignoutletcenter.com

Home Dynamix LLC 1 Carol Pl .... Moonachie NJ 07074 800-726-9290 131
TF: 800-726-9290 ■ *Web:* www.homedynamix.com

Home Entertainment Distribution Inc
120 Shawmut Rd .... Canton MA 02021 781-821-0087 200-3764* 38
**Fax Area Code:* 866 ■ *Web:* www.enservio.com

Home Essentials & Beyond Inc
200 Theodore Conrad Dr .... Jersey City NJ 07305 732-590-3600 361
TF: 800-417-6218 ■ *Web:* www.homeessentials.com

Home Federal Bank
1602 Cumberland Ave .... Middlesboro KY 40965 606-248-1095 242-1010* 360-2
OTC: HFBA ■ **Fax:* Hum Res ■ *TF:* 800-354-0182 ■ *Web:* www.homefederalbank.com

Home Federal Bank
221 S Locust St .... Grand Island NE 68801 308-382-4000 71
Web: www.homefederalne.com

Home Furnishings Independents Assn (HFIA)
2050 Stemmons World Fwy Ste 292 .... Dallas TX 75207 800-422-3778 49-4
TF: 800-422-3778 ■ *Web:* myhfa.org

Home Furniture Mart 5301 Sheila St .... Commerce CA 90040 800-610-6605 791
TF: 888-936-6673 ■ *Web:* www.homefurnituremart.com

Name / Address	City	State	Zip	Phone	Fax	Class
Home Health & Hospice Care 7 Executive Park Dr. *TF:* 800-887-5973 ■ *Web:* www.hhhc.org	Merrimack	NH	03054	603-882-2941		371
Home Health Corp of America Inc *Healthcare Investment Corp of America* 620 Freedom Business Ctr Ste 105 *TF:* 800-332-2056 ■ *Web:* www.healthinvcorp.com	King of Prussia	PA	19406	484-690-1200	751-9100	363
Home Health Line 11300 Rockville Pk Ste 1100 *TF:* 800-929-4824 ■ *Web:* www.ucg.com	Rockville	MD	20852	301-287-2700	816-8945	531-8
Home Healthcare, Hospice & Community Services Inc 312 Marlboro St *TF:* 800-541-4145 ■ *Web:* www.hcsservices.org	Keene	NH	03431	603-352-2253		363
Home Hospice Care of Rhode Island 1085 N Main St *TF:* 800-338-6555 ■ *Web:* www.hopehospiceri.org	Providence	RI	02904	401-415-4200		371
Home Hospice of Grayson County 505 W Ctr St *TF:* 888-233-7455 ■ *Web:* www.homehospice.org	Sherman	TX	75090	903-868-9315	893-2772	371
Home Instead Inc 13323 California St *TF:* 888-484-5759 ■ *Web:* www.homeinstead.com	Omaha	NE	68154	402-498-4466		363
Home IV Care & Nutritional Service 30 Ebco Cir Ste 102 *TF:* 800-552-6576	Waynesboro	VA	22980	800-552-6576		363
Home Loan Financial Corp 413 Main St *OTC:* HLFN ■ *Web:* www.homeloansavingsbank.com	Coshocton	OH	43812	740-622-0444	623-6000	360-2
Home Made Brand Foods Inc 2 Opportunity Way	Newburyport	MA	01950	978-462-3663		296-33
Home Market Foods Inc 140 Morgan Dr. *TF:* 800-367-8325 ■ *Web:* www.homemarketfoods.com	Norwood	MA	02062	781-948-1500		296-36
Home Media Retailing 4590 MacArthur Ste 500 **Fax Area Code:* 540 ■ **Fax:* Sales ■ *Web:* www.homemediamagazine.com	Newport Beach	CA	92660	714-759-4661	248-4107*	457-21
Home Meridian International Inc 2485 Penny Rd Ste 310 *TF:* 800-659-7297 ■ *Web:* www.homemeridian.com	High Point	NC	27265	336-819-7200		787
Home News Enterprises 333 Second St *TF:* 800-876-7811 ■ *Web:* homenewsenterprises.com	Columbus	IN	47201	800-876-7811		637-8
Home News Tribune 92 E Main St Ste 202 *TF:* 800-627-4663 ■ *Web:* www.mycentraljersey.com	Somerville	NJ	08876	732-246-5500		532-2
Home of Franklin D Roosevelt National Historic Site 4097 Albany Post Rd *Web:* www.nps.gov/hofr	Hyde Park	NY	12538	845-229-9115	229-0739	564
Home Paramount Pest Control Cos Inc PO Box 850 *TF:* 888-888-4663 ■ *Web:* www.homeparamount.com	Forest Hill	MD	21050	410-510-0700		577
Home Products International Inc 4501 W 47th St *TF:* 800-457-9881 ■ *Web:* www.homzproducts.com	Chicago	IL	60632	773-890-1010	890-0523	607
Home Properties 11459 Cronhill Dr Ste P *NYSE:* HME ■ *Web:* www.homeproperties.com	Owings Mills	MD	21117	410-356-3320		655
Home Properties Inc 850 Clinton Sq *NYSE:* HME ■ *TF:* 800-421-3483 ■ *Web:* www.homeproperties.com	Rochester	NY	14604	585-546-4900		655
Home Ranch PO Box 822 *TF:* 800-688-2982 ■ *Web:* www.homeranch.com	Clark	CO	80428	970-879-1780	879-1795	239
Home Run Inn Frozen Foods Corp 1300 International Pkwy *Web:* www.homeruninnpizza.com	Woodridge	IL	60517	630-783-9696		296-36
Home Savings & Loan Company of Youngstown 275 W Federal St *TF:* 888-822-4751 ■ *Web:* www.homesavings.com	Youngstown	OH	44503	330-742-0500	742-0615	70
Home Security of America Inc 310 N Midvale Blvd **Fax Area Code:* 877 ■ *TF:* 800-367-1448 ■ *Web:* www.onlinehsa.com	Madison	WI	53705	800-367-1448	638-1741*	367
Home Staff Inc 5517 N Cumberland Ave Ste 915 *TF:* 800-806-6924 ■ *Web:* homestaffinc.com	Chicago	IL	60656	773-467-6002		363
Home Staff LLC 40 Millbrook St *Web:* www.homestaffma.com	Worcester	MA	01606	508-755-4600		363
Home Team Marketing LLC 812 Huron Rd E Ste 205 *Web:* www.hometeammarketing.com	Cleveland	OH	44115	216-566-8326		195
Home Tester, The 10555 SW Tigard St Apt 57 *Web:* www.thehometester.com	Tigard	OR	97223	503-515-1833		104
Home Town Cable TV LLC 10486 SW Village Ctr Dr	Port Saint Lucie	FL	34987	772-345-6000		116
Home2 Suites by Hilton 4035 Sycamore Dairy Rd *Web:* home2suites3.hilton.com/en/index.html	Fayetteville	NC	28303	910-223-1170		707
HomeAdvisor 14023 Denver W Pkwy Ste 200 *TF:* 800-474-1596 ■ *Web:* www.homeadvisor.com	Golden	CO	80401	303-963-7200	980-3003	397
HomeAway.com Inc 1011 W Fifth St Ste 300 *Web:* www.homeaway.com	Austin	TX	78703	512-782-0805		225
HomeCare & Hospice 1225 W State St *TF:* 800-339-7011 ■ *Web:* www.homecare-hospice.org	Olean	NY	14760	716-372-5735		371
Homecare Homebase LLC 6688 N Central Expy Ste 1200 *Web:* www.hchb.com	Dallas	TX	75206	214-239-6700		363
HomeCare of East Alabama Medical Ctr 665 Opelika Rd *TF:* 866-542-4768 ■ *Web:* www.lhcgroup.com	Auburn	AL	36830	334-826-3131		371
Homecare of Mid Missouri Inc 102 W Reed St *TF:* 800-246-6400 ■ *Web:* www.homecaremo.org	Moberly	MO	65270	660-263-1517		363
HomeCrest Cabinetry 1002 Eisenhower Dr N *TF:* 800-737-1500 ■ *Web:* www.homecrestcabinetry.com	Goshen	IN	46526	574-535-9300		115
HomeGain.com Inc 6001 Shellmound St Ste 550 *TF:* 888-542-0800 ■ *Web:* www.homegain.com	Emeryville	CA	94608	510-655-0800	655-0848	652
HomeGoods Inc 770 Cochituate Rd *Web:* www.homegoods.com	Framingham	MA	01701	508-390-1000		362
Homeland Security Funding Week 8204 Fenton St *TF:* 800-666-6380 ■ *Web:* www.cdpublications.com	Silver Spring	MD	20910	301-588-6380	588-6385	531-7
Homeland Security Information Ctr National Technical Information Service 5301 Shawnee Rd *Web:* www.ntis.gov	Alexandria	VA	22312	703-605-6000	487-4639	197
Homeland Vinyl Products Inc 3300 Pinson Valley Pkwy *Web:* www.homelandvinyl.com	Birmingham	AL	35217	205-854-4330		596
Homelegance Inc 495 S Grand Central Pkwy Ste 625A *Web:* www.homelegance.com	Las Vegas	NV	89106	510-783-8010	783-3089	321
Homeplace Ranch RR 1 Site 2 *Web:* www.homeplaceranch.com	Priddis	AB	T0L1W0	403-969-4444		239
HomePortfolio Inc 288 Walnut St Ste 300 *Web:* www.homeportfolio.com	Newton	MA	02460	617-965-0565		362
HomEquity Bank 1881 Yonge St Ste 300 *TF:* 866-522-2447 ■ *Web:* www.homequitybank.ca	Toronto	ON	M4S3C4	416-925-4757		69
Homer Central School District PO Box 500 *Web:* www.homercentral.org	Homer	NY	13077	607-749-7241		685
Homer Electric Assn Inc 3977 Lake St *TF:* 800-478-8551 ■ *Web:* www.homerelectric.com	Homer	AK	99603	907-235-8551	235-3313	245
Homer Group, The 2605 Egypt Rd *Web:* www.homergroup.com	Trooper	PA	19403	610-539-8400		344
Homer Laughlin China Co 672 Fiesta Dr *TF:* 800-452-4462 ■ *Web:* hlcdinnerware.com	Newell	WV	26050	304-387-1300	387-0593	730
Homer Optical Company Inc 2401 Linden Ln *TF:* 800-627-2710 ■ *Web:* www.homeroptical.com	Silver Spring	MD	20910	301-585-9060	585-5934	542
Homer Public Library 500 Hazel Ave *TF:* 800-478-4441 ■ *Web:* www.cityofhomer-ak.gov/library	Homer	AK	99603	907-235-3180	235-3136	434-3
Homereach Hospice 800 McConnell Dr *TF:* 800-837-2455 ■ *Web:* www.ohiohealth.com	Columbus	OH	43214	614-566-5377		371
HomeRunAutoSales 301 Green Ave N *Web:* homerunautogroup.com	Stevens Point	WI	54481	715-341-2440		57
Homes & Land Magazine Affiliates LLC 1830 E Pk Ave *TF:* 800-277-7800 ■ *Web:* www.homesandland.com	Tallahassee	FL	32301	850-575-0189		637-9
Homes by Keystone Inc 13338 Midvale Rd PO Box 69 *TF:* 800-890-7926 ■ *Web:* www.homesbykeystone.com	Waynesboro	PA	17268	800-890-7926		106
Homes.com Inc 150 Granby St *TF:* 866-675-1058 ■ *Web:* www.homes.com	Norfolk	VA	23510	866-675-1058		387
HomeServices of America Inc 333 S Seventh St 27th Fl *TF:* 888-485-0018 ■ *Web:* www.homeservices.com	Minneapolis	MN	55402	888-485-0018		652
HomeSmart International LLC 8388 E Hartford Dr Ste 100 *Web:* homesmart.com	Scottsdale	AZ	85255	602-230-7600		652
Homestead Hospital 975 Baptist Way *Web:* www.baptisthealth.net	Homestead	FL	33033	786-243-8000		374-3
Homestead Inn 420 Field Pt Rd *Web:* www.homesteadinn.com	Greenwich	CT	06830	203-869-7500	869-7502	379
Homestead Inn 800 Kuser Rd	Trenton	NJ	08619	609-890-9851		671
Homestead Mills 221 N River St PO Box 1115 *TF:* 800-652-5233 ■ *Web:* www.homesteadmills.com	Cook	MN	55723	218-666-5233	666-5236	296-4
Homestead National Monument of America 8523 W State Hwy 4 *TF:* 800-752-3965 ■ *Web:* www.nps.gov	Beatrice	NE	68310	402-223-3514	228-4231	564
Homestead Pasta Co 315 S Maple Ave Bldg 106 *Web:* www.homesteadpasta.com	South San Francisco	CA	94080	650-615-0750	615-0764	296-36
Homestead Resort 700 N Homestead Dr *TF:* 888-327-7220 ■ *Web:* www.homesteadresort.com	Midway	UT	84049	888-327-7220		669
Homestead Resort, The 1 Wood Ridge Rd *Web:* www.thehomesteadresort.com	Glen Arbor	MI	49636	231-334-5000	334-5246	669
Homestead Technologies Inc 180 Jefferson Dr *TF:* 800-797-2958 ■ *Web:* www.homestead.com	Menlo Park	CA	94025	650-944-3100		808
Homestead-Miami Speedway 1 Speedway Blvd *Web:* www.homesteadmiamispeedway.com	Homestead	FL	33035	305-230-5000	230-5140	515
HomeSteps 500 Plano Pkwy *TF:* 800-972-7555 ■ *Web:* www.homesteps.com	Carrollton	TX	75010	800-972-7555		509
HomeStreet Bank 601 Union St Ste 2000 *TF:* 800-654-1075 ■ *Web:* homestreet.com	Seattle	WA	98101	206-623-3050	389-4458	70
Homestyle Dining LLC 3701 W Plano Pkwy Ste 200 *Web:* www.ponderosasteakhouses.com	Plano	TX	75075	972-244-8900		670
HomeStyle Industries 1323 11th Ave N *Web:* www.home-style.com	Nampa	ID	83687	208-466-8481		471
HomeTeam Inspection Service Inc 575 Chamber Dr *TF:* 800-598-5297 ■ *Web:* www.hometeam.com	Milford	OH	45150	800-598-5297		365
Hometown America LLC 150 N Wacker Dr Ste 2800 *TF:* 888-735-4310 ■ *Web:* www.hometownamerica.com	Chicago	IL	60606	312-604-7500	604-7501	505
Hometown Bank 245 N Peters Ave *TF:* 877-261-2220 ■ *Web:* www.htbwi.com	Fond du Lac	WI	54935	920-907-2220		70
HomeTown Daily News 202 Courtney St *Web:* www.hometowndailynews.com	Branson	MO	65616	417-334-6003		645-10
Hometown Quotes LLC 304 Inverness Pkwy S Ste 395 *Web:* www.hometownquotes.com	Englewood	TN	80112	615-599-5506		390
Hometown Sportsweary 3692 Us Rt 60 E *Web:* hometownsportswear.com	Barboursville	WV	25504	304-736-4021		711
Hometrust Bank, The PO Box 10 *TF:* 800-627-1632 ■ *Web:* www.hometrustbanking.com	Asheville	NC	28802	828-259-3939		70
HomeVestors of America Inc 6500 Greenville Ave Ste 400 *TF:* 866-200-6475 ■ *Web:* www.homevestors.com	Dallas	TX	75206	972-761-0046	761-9022	310

Name / Address	City	State	Zip	Phone	Fax	Class
Homewatch International Inc						
7100 E Belleview Ave Ste 303	Greenwood Village	CO	80111	303-758-5111		363
TF: 800-777-9770 ■ Web: www.homewatchcaregivers.com						
Homewood at Williamsport						
16505 Virginia Ave	Williamsport	MD	21795	301-582-1750		672
TF: 877-849-9244 ■ Web: www.homewood.com						
Homewood Disposal Service Inc						
1501 W 175th St	Homewood	IL	60430	708-798-1004		804
Web: mydisposal.com						
Homewood FSB 3228-30 Eastern Ave	Baltimore	MD	21224	410-327-5220	558-1719	70
TF: 800-554-8969 ■ Web: www.homewoodfsb.com						
Homewood Museum						
3400 N Charles St Johns Hopkins University	Baltimore	MD	21218	410-516-5589	516-7859	520
Web: www.museums.jhu.edu						
Homewood Suites 1011 Pike St	Seattle	WA	98101	206-682-8282	682-5315	379
Web: homewoodsuites3.hilton.com						
Hominy Grill 207 Rutledge Ave	Charleston	SC	29403	843-937-0930		671
Web: www.hominygrill.com						
Homosassa Springs Wildlife State Park						
4150 S Suncoast Blvd	Homosassa	FL	34446	352-628-5343	628-4243	565
Web: www.floridastateparks.org						
Homrich & Berg Inc						
3060 Peachtree Rd Ste 830	Atlanta	GA	30305	404-264-1400		194
Web: www.homrichberg.com						
HON Co 200 Oak St	Muscatine	IA	52761	563-272-7100	328-7257*	319-1
*Fax Area Code: 800 ■ TF: 800-553-8230 ■ Web: www.hon.com						
Honda Aircraft Company Inc						
6430 Ballinger RdGreensboro	Greensboro	NC	27410	336-662-0246		20
Web: www.hondajet.com						
Honda Carland 11085 Alpharetta Hwy	Roswell	GA	30076	770-993-2805		57
Web: hondacarland.com						
Honda Ctr 2695 E Katella Ave	Anaheim	CA	92806	714-704-2400		720
Web: www.hondacenter.com						
Honda Mfg of Alabama LLC						
1800 Honda Dr	Lincoln	AL	35096	205-355-5000		59
Web: www.hondaalabama.com						
Honda of Santa Monica						
1726 Santa Monica Blvd	Santa Monica	CA	90404	310-264-4900		57
TF: 800-269-2031 ■ Web: www.hondaofsantamonica.com						
Honda of Tiffany Springs						
9200 NW Prairie View Rd	Kansas City	MO	64153	816-452-7000		516
Web: www.hondaoftiffanysprings.com						
Honda Precision Parts of Georgia LLC						
550 Honda Pkwy	Tallapoosa	GA	30176	770-574-3400		489
Web: www.cevalogistics.com						
Honda World 10645 Studebaker Rd	Downey	CA	90241	562-929-7000		57
TF: 888-458-9404 ■ Web: www.lahondaworld.com						
Hondros College						
4140 Executive Pkwy	Westerville	OH	43081	888-466-3767		166
TF: 888-466-3767 ■ Web: www.hondros.edu						
Honduras 866 UN Plaza Ste 417	New York	NY	10017	212-752-3370	223-0498	784
Web: www.un.int						
Consulate General						
4439 W Fullerton Ave	Chicago	IL	60639	773-342-8281		257
Web: hondurasemb.org						
Consulate General						
3550 Wilshire Blvd Ste 410	Los Angeles	CA	90010	213-383-9244	383-9306	257
Web: www.consulate-los-angeles.com/honduras.html						
Consulate General						
870 Market St Ste 875	San Francisco	CA	94102	415-392-0076	392-6726	257
Web: www.hondurasemb.org						
Embassy 3007 Tilden St NW	Washington	DC	20008	202-966-7702	966-9751	257
TF: 800-375-5283 ■ Web: www.hondurasemb.org						
Honegger Ringger & Company Inc						
1905 N Main St	Bluffton	IN	46714	260-824-4107		2
TF: 888-853-5906 ■ Web: www.hrc-cpa.com						
Honestly Now Inc 5 S Bedford Rd	Pound Ridge	NY	10576	917-453-5262		5
Web: www.honestlynow.com						
Honey Acres 1557 Hwy 67 N	Ashippun	WI	53003	800-558-7745		296-24
TF: 800-558-7745 ■ Web: www.honeyacres.com						
Honey Baked Ham Company of Ohio						
4967 Crooks Rd Ste 200	Troy	MI	48098	248-641-8300	641-0652	345
Web: www.honeybaked.com						
Honey Bee Manufacturing Ltd						
Friggstad Rd 4km S PO Box 120	Frontier	SK	S0N0W0	306-296-2297		274
Web: www.honeybee.ca						
Honey Creek State Natural Area						
c/o Guadalupe River State Pk						
3350 Park Rd 31	Spring Branch	TX	78070	830-438-2656		565
Web: tpwd.texas.gov/state-parks/honey-creek						
Honey Creek State Park						
12194 Honey Creek Pl	Moravia	IA	52571	641-724-3739	724-9846	565
Web: www.iowadnr.gov						
Honey Creek State Park 901 State Pk Rd	Grove	OK	74344	918-786-9447	787-5634	565
TF: 800-622-6317 ■ Web: www.travelok.com						
Honey Dew Assoc Inc 2 Taunton St	Plainville	MA	02762	508-699-3900	699-3949	68
TF: 800-946-6393 ■ Web: www.honeydewdonuts.com						
Honey Farms Inc 505 Pleasant St	Worcester	MA	01609	508-753-7678		297-8
Web: www.myhoneyfarms.com						
Honeycomb Co of America Inc						
1950 Limbus Ave	Sarasota	FL	34243	941-756-8781		22
Honeys Place Inc						
640 Glenoaks Blvd	San Fernando	CA	91340	800-910-3246		231
TF: 800-910-3246 ■ Web: www.honeysplace.com						
Honeytree Inc 8570 M 50	Onsted	MI	49265	517-467-2482		296-24
TF: 800-968-1889 ■ Web: honeytreehoney.com						
Honeyville Grain Inc						
11600 Dayton Dr	Rancho Cucamonga	CA	91730	909-980-9500	980-6503	296-4
TF: 888-810-3212 ■ Web: www.honeyville.com						
Honeyville Metal Inc 4200 S 900 W	Topeka	IN	46571	260-593-2266	593-2486	18
TF: 800-593-8377 ■ Web: www.honeyvillemetal.com						
Honeywell 101 Columbia Rd	Morristown	NJ	07960	973-455-2000	455-4807	145
TF: 800-822-7673 ■ Web: www.honeywell.com						
Honeywell Aerospace						
3520 Westmoor St	South Bend	IN	46628	574-231-2000		22
TF: 800-707-4555 ■ Web: honeywell.com						
Honeywell Aerospace						
1944 E Sky Harbor Cir	Phoenix	AZ	85034	800-601-3099	365-3343*	22
*Fax Area Code: 602 ■ TF: 800-601-3099 ■ Web: www.honeywell.com						
Honeywell Automation & Control Solutions						
115 Tabor Rd	Morris Plains	IL	61032	480-353-3020		201
Web: www.honeywell.com						
Honeywell Building Solutions Inc						
1985 Douglas Dr N	Golden Valley	MN	55422	763-954-5421		664
Web: buildingsolutions.honeywell.com/en-US/Pages/default.aspx						
Honeywell Electronic Materials						
1349 Moffett Pk Dr	Sunnyvale	CA	94089	877-841-2840		253
TF: 877-841-2840 ■ Web: www.honeywell.com						
Honeywell Fluorine Products						
101 Columbia Rd	Morristown	NJ	07962	973-455-2000		145
TF: 800-951-1527 ■						
Web: honeywell.com/pages/redirect.aspx?redirectid=179						
Honeywell HomMed LLC						
3400 Intertech Dr Ste 200	Brookfield	WI	53045	262-783-5440		250
Web: www.honeywelllifecare.com						
Honeywell International Inc						
101 Columbia Rd PO Box 2245	Morristown	NJ	07962	480-353-3020		735
NYSE: HON ■ TF: 877-841-2840 ■ Web: www.honeywell.com						
Honeywell Safety Products						
2000 Plainfield Pike	Cranston	RI	02921	401-943-4400	572-6346*	576
*Fax Area Code: 800 ■ TF Cust Svc: 800-430-4110 ■ Web: honeywellsafety.com						
Honeywell Security Group						
2 Corporate Ctr Dr Ste 100	Melville	NY	11747	516-577-2000		692
TF: 800-467-5875 ■ Web: www.security.honeywell.com						
Honeywell Sensing & Control						
11 W Spring St	Freeport	IL	61032	815-235-5500		203
TF Cust Svc: 800-537-6945 ■ Web: www.honeywell.com						
Honeywood Winery 1350 Hines St SE	Salem	OR	97302	503-362-4111		50-7
TF: 800-726-4101 ■ Web: www.honeywoodwinery.com						
Hong Kong Buffet 927 E N St	Rapid City	SD	57701	605-716-4664		671
Web: cocopalaces.com						
Hong Kong Chinese Restaurant						
1055 E Interstate Ave	Bismarck	ND	58503	701-223-2130		671
Hong Kong Tea House						
565 W 200 S	Salt Lake City	UT	84101	801-531-7010	531-7033	671
Web: hongkongteahouse.yolasite.com						
Hong Kong Tourism Board						
5670 Wilshire Blvd Ste 1230	Los Angeles	CA	90036	323-938-4582	938-4583	775
TF: 800-282-4582 ■ Web: www.discoverhongkong.com						
Hong Kong Tourism Board						
370 Lexington Ave 2nd Fl	New York	NY	10017	212-421-3382		775
Web: www.discoverhongkong.com						
Honigman Miller Schwartz & Cohn LLP						
660 Woodward Ave Ste 2290	Detroit	MI	48226	313-465-7000		41
Web: www.honigman.com						
Honiron Corp 400 Canal St	Jeanerette	LA	70544	337-276-6314		273
Web: www.honiron.com						
Honkamp Krueger & Company PC						
2345 JFK Rd PO Box 699	Dubuque	IA	52004	563-556-0123	556-8762	2
TF: 888-556-0123 ■ Web: www.honkamp.com						
Honolulu Academy of Arts						
900 S Beretania St	Honolulu	HI	96814	808-532-8700	532-8787	520
TF: 866-385-3849 ■ Web: honolulumuseum.org						
Honolulu Advertiser						
500 Ala Moana Blvd	Honolulu	HI	96813	808-529-4747		532-2
TF: 800-801-5999 ■ Web: www.staradvertiser.com						
Honolulu Botanical Gardens						
50 N Vineyard Blvd	Honolulu	HI	96817	808-768-3003	768-3053	97
Web: www.honolulu.gov/parks/hbg						
Honolulu City & County						
530 S King St Rm 100	Honolulu	HI	96813	808-768-3810	768-3835	338
Web: www.honolulu.gov						
Honolulu City Hall 530 S King St	Honolulu	HI	96813	808-768-4141	768-5552	337
Web: www.honolulu.gov						
Honolulu Ford Lincoln & Mercury						
1370 N King St	Honolulu	HI	96817	808-824-3970		57
Web: www.honoluluford.com						
Honolulu International Airport						
300 Rodgers Blvd	Honolulu	HI	96819	808-831-3600		27
Web: www.honoluluairport.com						
Honolulu Magazine						
1000 Bishop St Ste 405	Honolulu	HI	96813	808-534-7546		457-22
TF: 800-788-4230 ■ Web: www.honolulumagazine.com						
Honolulu Publishing Co Ltd						
707 Richards St Ste PH3	Honolulu	HI	96813	808-524-7400	531-2306	637-9
TF: 800-272-5245 ■ Web: www.honolulupublishing.com						
Honolulu Weekly 1111 Ford St Mall	Honolulu	HI	96813	808-528-1475		532-5
Web: www.honoluluweekly.com						
Honolulu Wood Treating Co Ltd						
91-291 Hanua St	Kapolei	HI	96707	808-682-5704		818
Web: 66.28.63.139/hwt						
Honolulu Zoo 151 Kapahulu Ave	Honolulu	HI	96815	808-971-7171		823
TF: 800-548-6262 ■ Web: www.honoluluzoo.org						
Honolulu-Japanese Chamber of Commerce						
2454 S Beretania St Ste 201	Honolulu	HI	96826	808-949-5531	949-3020	138
Web: hjcc.org						
Honor Conservation Camp						
40 Pippin Rd	Newcastle	WY	82701	307-746-4436		213
Honor Foods 1801 N Fifth St	Philadelphia	PA	19122	215-236-1700		297-8
TF: 800-462-2890 ■ Web: honorfoods.com						
Honor Guard Security Inc						
1965 Bernice Rd Ste 1 NW	Lansing	IL	60438	708-418-3059		693
Web: www.hgsecurity.biz						
HonorHealth John C. Lincoln Medical Center						
250 E Dunlap Ave	Phoenix	AZ	85020	602-943-2381		374-3
TF: 800-223-3131 ■ Web: www.honorhealth.com						
Honshy Electric Company Inc						
7345 SW 41st St	Miami	FL	33155	305-264-5500	266-3159	189-4
Web: www.honshyelectric.com						
Honstein Oil Co 11 Pasco Real	Santa Fe	NM	87507	505-471-1800		541
Web: www.honsteinoil.com						
Hontoon Island State Park						
2309 River Ridge Rd	DeLand	FL	32720	386-736-5309		565
Web: www.floridastateparks.org						
Hoober Inc						
3452 Old Philadelphia Pk PO Box 518	Intercourse	PA	17534	717-768-8231	768-3005	274
TF: 800-732-0017 ■ Web: www.hoober.com						

Phone | Fax | Class

Hood College 401 Rosemont Ave. .... Frederick MD 21701 301-696-3400 696-3819* 166
*Fax: Admissions ■ TF: 800-922-1599 ■ Web: www.hood.edu

Hood Construction Company Inc
1050 Shop Rd Ste A .... Columbia SC 29201 803-765-2940 186
Web: www.hoodconstruction.com

Hood Corp 3166 Horseless Carriage Rd .... Norco CA 92860 951-520-4282 188-10
Web: www.hoodcorp.com

Hood Cos Inc 623 N Main St Ste 300 .... Hattiesburg MS 39401 601-582-4486 613
Web: www.hoodcompanies.com

Hood County 100 E Pearl St Ste 5 .... Granbury TX 76048 817-579-3222 579-3227 338
TF: 800-829-4933 ■ Web: www.co.hood.tx.us

Hood County News 1501 S Morgan St .... Granbury TX 76048 817-573-7066 532-3
Web: www.hcnews.com

Hood County Public Library
222 N Travis St .... Granbury TX 76048 817-573-3569 573-3969 434-3
TF: 800-452-9292 ■ Web: www.co.hood.tx.us

Hood Industries Inc
15 Professional Pkwy # 8 .... Hattiesburg MS 39402 601-264-2559 296-4755 613
Web: www.hoodindustries.com

Hood Packaging Corp 25 Woodgreen Pl .... Madison MS 39110 601-853-7260 853-7299 65
TF: 800-321-8115 ■ Web: www.hoodpkg.com

Hood River County 601 State St .... Hood River OR 97031 541-386-3970 386-9392 338
Web: www.co.hood-river.or.us

Hood Theological Seminary
1810 Lutheran Synod Dr .... Salisbury NC 28144 704-636-7611 167-3
Web: www.hoodseminary.edu

Hooker County PO Box 184 .... Mullen NE 69152 308-546-2244 546-2490 338
TF: 800-368-8683 ■ Web: www.co.hooker.ne.us

Hooker Furniture Corp
440 E Commonwealth Blvd .... Martinsville VA 24112 276-632-0459 388-2289* 319-2
NASDAQ: HOFT ■ *Fax Area Code: 800 ■ *Fax: Cust Svc ■ TF Cust Svc: 800-422-1511 ■ Web: www.hookerfurniture.com

Hookflash Solutions Inc
6679 1A Ave Unit 1 .... Delta BC V4M3B3 604-628-9688 224
Web: www.hookflash.ca

Hoop Group, The 1930 Heck Ave Bldg 3 .... Neptune NJ 07753 732-502-2255 196
Web: www.hoopgroup.com

Hooper Corp 2030 Pennsylvania Ave .... Madison WI 53704 608-249-0451 249-7360 189-10
TF: 877-630-7554 ■ Web: www.hoopercorp.com

Hooper Handling Inc 5590 Camp Rd .... Hamburg NY 14075 716-649-5590 358
TF: 800-649-5590 ■ Web: www.hooperhandling.com

Hooper Holmes Inc
170 Mt Airy Rd .... Basking Ridge NJ 07920 908-766-5000 352
NYSE: HH ■ Web: www.hooperholmes.com

Hoosac School 14 Pine Valley Rd .... Hoosick NY 12089 518-686-7331 622
Web: www.hoosac.org

Hoosier Co
5421 W 86th St PO Box 681064 .... Indianapolis IN 46268 317-872-8125 872-7183 286
TF: 800-521-4184 ■ Web: www.hoosierco.com

Hoosier Gasket Corp
2400 Enterprise Pk Pl .... Indianapolis IN 46218 317-545-2000 545-5500 326
Web: www.hoosiergasket.com

Hoosier Hills Credit Union
630 Lincoln Ave .... Bedford IN 47421 812-279-6644 219
Web: hoosierhillscu.org

Hoosier Park Racing & Casino
4500 Dan Patch Cir .... Anderson IN 46013 765-642-7223 608-2754 642
TF: 800-526-7223 ■ Web: www.hoosierpark.com

Hoosier Tank & Manufacturing Inc
1710 N Sheridan St .... South Bend IN 46628 574-232-8368 480
Web: hoosiertank.com

Hoosier Village 5300 W 96th St .... Indianapolis IN 46268 317-873-3349 672
TF: 800-321-1245 ■ Web: www.hoosiervillage.com

Hooters Casino Hotel
115 E Tropicana Ave .... Las Vegas NV 89109 702-739-9000 133
TF: 866-584-6687 ■ Web: www.hooterscasinohotel.com

Hooven-Dayton Corp 511 Byers Rd .... Miamisburg OH 45342 937-233-4473 627
Web: www.hoovendayton.com

Hoover & Strong Inc
10700 Trade Rd .... North Chesterfield VA 23236 800-759-9997 616-9997 485
TF Cust Svc: 800-759-9997 ■ Web: www.hooverandstrong.com

Hoover Chamber of Commerce
PO Box 36005 .... Hoover AL 35236 205-988-5672 988-8383 139
TF: 800-231-2222 ■ Web: www.hooverchamber.org

Hoover Construction Co Inc
PO Box 1007 .... Virginia MN 55792 218-741-3280 741-6804 188-4
TF: 800-741-0970 ■ Web: www.hooverconstruction.biz

Hoover Dam Lodge
18000 Highway 93 .... Boulder City NV 89005 702-293-5000 378
Web: hooverdamlodge.com

Hoover Ferguson Group Inc
2135 Hwy Six S .... Houston TX 77077 281-870-8402 295
Web: www.hooversolutions.com

Hoover Inc 1205 Bridgestone Pkwy .... Lavergne TN 37086 615-793-2600 182
Web: hoover.com

Hoover Institution on War Revolution & Peace
Stanford University 434 Galvez Mall .... Stanford CA 94305 650-723-1754 723-1687 634
Web: www.hoover.org

Hoover Precision Products Inc
2200 Pendley Rd .... Cumming GA 30041 770-889-9223 889-0828 485
Web: www.hooverprecision.com

Hoover Public Library (HPL)
200 Municipal Dr .... Hoover AL 35216 205-444-7800 444-7878 434-3
TF: 800-231-2222 ■ Web: www.hooverlibrary.org

Hoover Toyota 2686 Hwy 150 .... Hoover AL 35244 205-978-2600 57
TF: 866-980-8082 ■ Web: www.hoovertoyota.com

Hoover Treated Wood Products Inc
154 Wire Rd .... Thomson GA 30824 706-595-1264 818
Web: www.frtw.com

Hoover's Inc 5800 Airport Blvd .... Austin TX 78752 512-374-4500 374-4501 637-6
TF: 800-486-8666 ■ Web: www.hoovers.com

Hop-A-Jet Inc
5525 NW 15th Ave Ste 150 .... Fort Lauderdale FL 33309 954-771-5779 772-6981 13
TF: 800-556-6633 ■ Web: www.hopajetworldwide.com

Hopatcong State Park PO Box 8519 .... Landing NJ 07850 973-398-7010 565
Web: www.njparksandforests.org

Hope Amundson 1301 Third Ave Ste 300 .... San Diego CA 92101 619-232-4673 256
Web: hope-amundson.com

Hope College 69 E Tenth St PO Box 9000 .... Holland MI 49422 616-395-7850 395-7130* 166
*Fax: Admissions ■ TF Admissions: 800-968-7850 ■ Web: www.hope.edu

Hope College Van Wylen Library
53 Graves Pl .... Holland MI 49423 616-395-7790 395-7965 434-6
TF: 800-968-7850 ■ Web: www.hope.edu

Hope Foundation Inc
1252 N Loesch Rd .... Bloomington IN 47404 812-355-6000 196
Web: alanblankstein.org/the-hope-foundation

Hope Global Engineered Textile Solutions
50 Martin St .... Cumberland RI 02864 401-333-8990 334-6442 745-5
Web: www.hopeglobal.com

Hope Group 70 Bearfoot Rd .... Northborough MA 01532 508-393-7660 393-8203 385
Web: www.thehopegroup.com

Hope Hospice 9470 HealthPark Cir .... Fort Myers FL 33908 239-482-4673 371
TF: 800-835-1673 ■ Web: www.hopehospice.org

Hope Hospice 611 N Walnut Ave .... New Braunfels TX 78130 830-625-7500 606-1388 371
TF: 800-499-7501 ■ Web: www.hopehospice.net

Hope Industries Inc
351 Industrial Park Rd .... Madisonville TN 37354 423-442-4471 596
Web: www.hopeindustries.com

Hope International University
2500 E Nutwood Ave .... Fullerton CA 92831 714-879-3901 526-0231* 166
*Fax: Admissions ■ TF: 866-722-4673 ■ Web: www.hiu.edu

Hope Lodge Hershey Pennsylvania
125 Lucy Ave .... Hummelstown PA 17036 717-533-5111 372
Web: www.cancer.org

Hope Network
3075 Orchard Vista Dr SE .... Grand Rapids MI 49546 616-301-8000 301-8010 450
TF: 800-695-7273 ■ Web: www.hopenetwork.org

Hope Pharmaceuticals Inc
16416 N 92nd St Ste 125 .... Scottsdale AZ 85260 800-755-9595 607-1971* 582
*Fax Area Code: 480 ■ TF: 800-755-9595 ■ Web: www.hopepharm.com

HOPE Worldwide
1285 Drummers Ln Ste 330 .... San Diego CA 92117 610-254-8800 254-8989 48-5
Web: www.hopeww.org

Hope's Windows Inc
84 Hopkins Ave PO Box 580 .... Jamestown NY 14702 716-665-5124 665-3365 234
Web: www.hopeswindows.com

HopeLink 115 Constitution Dr Ste 7 .... Menlo Park CA 94025 650-470-0123 396

Hopeville Pond State Park
193 Roode Rd .... Jewett City CT 06351 860-376-2920 565
Web: www.ct.gov

Hopewell Culture National Historical Park
16062 SR-104 .... Chillicothe OH 45601 740-774-1126 774-1140 564
Web: www.nps.gov/hocu

Hopewell Furnace National Historic Site
2 Mark Bird Ln .... Elverson PA 19520 610-582-8773 582-2768 564
TF: 866-705-5711 ■ Web: www.nps.gov

Hopewell (Independent City)
300 N Main St Rm 217 .... Hopewell VA 23860 804-541-2243 541-2248 338
TF: 800-552-7096 ■ Web: www.hopewellva.gov

Hopewell Veterinary Group Inc
230 Hopewell Pennington Rd .... Hopewell NJ 08525 609-466-0131 794
Web: saintsbury.com

Hopewell-Prince George Chamber of Commerce
210 N Second Ave .... Hopewell VA 23860 804-458-5536 139
Web: hpgchamber.org

HopFed Bancorp Inc
2700 Ft Campbell Blvd .... Hopkinsville KY 42240 270-885-1171 889-0313 360-2
NASDAQ: HFBC ■ TF: 800-872-2657 ■ Web: www.bankwithheritage.com

Hopital Brome Missisquoi-Perkins
950 Rue Principale .... Cowansville QC J2K1K3 450-266-4342 263-8669 374-2
Web: www.santemonteregie.qc.ca

Hopital de Papineau 500 Rue Belanger .... Gatineau QC J8L2M4 819-986-3341 986-4000 374-2
Web: www.cssspapineau.qc.ca

Hopital du Haut-Richelieu
920 Boul du Seminaire N .... Saint-Jean-sur-Richelieu QC J3A1B7 450-359-5000 374-2

Hopital Jean-Talon
1385 Jean-Talon St E .... Montreal QC H2E1S6 514-495-6767 374-2

Hopkes Logging Company Inc
2235 Hadley Rd N .... Tillamook OR 97141 503-842-2491 448

Hopkins & Carley A Law Corp
PO Box 1469 .... San Jose CA 95109 408-286-9800 998-4790 428
Web: www.hopkinscarley.com

Hopkins County 24 Union St .... Madisonville KY 42431 270-821-7361 338
Web: www.hopkinscountykentucky.org

Hopkins County 118 Church St .... Sulphur Springs TX 75482 903-438-4074 338
Web: www.hopkinscountytx.org

Hopkins County Chamber of Commerce
300 Connally St .... Sulphur Springs TX 75482 903-885-6515 885-6516 139
Web: www.sulphursprings-tx.com

Hopkins County Schools
320 S Seminary St .... Madisonville KY 42431 270-825-6000 825-6072 685
Web: hopkins.k12.ky.us

Hopkins Ctr for the Arts
6041 Wilson Hall .... Hanover NH 03755 603-646-2422 646-1375 572
TF: 800-451-4067 ■ Web: dartmouth.edu

Hopkins Financial Corp 100 E Havens .... Mitchell SD 57301 605-996-7775 70
Web: cortrustbank.com

Hopkins Manufacturing Corp
428 Peyton St .... Emporia KS 66801 620-342-7320 340-8590 60
TF: 800-524-1458 ■ Web: www.hopkinsmfg.com

Hopkins Planetarium
1 Market Square SE .... Roanoke VA 24011 540-342-5710 224-1240 598
TF: 800-533-1410 ■ Web: www.smwv.org

Hopkins Printing Inc
2246 CityGate Dr .... Columbus OH 43219 614-509-1080 627
TF: 800-319-3352 ■ Web: www.hopkinsprinting.com

Hopkins Sporting Goods Inc
5485 NW Beaver Dr .... Johnston IA 50131 515-270-0132 711
TF: 800-362-2937 ■ Web: www.hopkinssportinggoods.com

Hopkins-Carter Company Inc
3300 NW 21st St .... Miami FL 33142 305-635-7377 633-1310 465
TF: 800-595-9656 ■ Web: www.hopkins-carter.com

Hopkinsville Community College
720 N Dr .... Hopkinsville KY 42240 270-886-3921 886-0237* 162
*Fax: Admissions ■ TF: 866-534-2224 ■ Web: www.hopkinsville.kctcs.edu

	Phone	Fax	Class
Hopkinsville Milling Co PO Box 669 .... Hopkinsville KY 42241 *Web:* sunflourflour.com	270-886-1231	886-6407	296-23
Hopkinsville-Christian County Chamber of Commerce 2800 Port Campbell Blvd .... Hopkinsville KY 42240 *TF:* 800-842-9959 ■ *Web:* www.christiancountychamber.com	270-885-9096		139
Hopkinton State Park 71 Cedar St .... Hopkinton MA 01748 *Web:* www.mass.gov	508-435-4303		565
Hop-on Inc PO Box 940 Ste 222 .... Temecula CA 92593 *TF:* 800-579-9607 ■ *Web:* hop-on.com	949-756-9008		736
Hoppe North America Inc 205 E Blackhawk Dr .... Fort Atkinson WI 53538 *Web:* www.us.hoppe.com	920-563-2626		350
Hoppe Technologies Inc 107 First Ave .... Chicopee MA 01020 *Web:* www.hoppetech.com	413-592-9213	592-4688	493
Hopper Engineering Assoc Inc 300 Vista Del Mar .... Redondo Beach CA 90277 *Web:* www.hopperengineering.com	310-373-5573		256
Hopsports Inc 24715 Ave Rockefeller .... Valencia CA 91355 *TF:* 800-225-7749 ■ *Web:* www.hopsports.com	661-702-8946		514
Hoque & Assoc Inc 4325 S 34th St .... Phoenix AZ 85040 *Web:* www.hoqueandassociates.com	480-921-1368		256
Hoquiam Plywood Company Inc 1000 Woodlawn Rd .... Hoquiam WA 98550	360-533-3060		613
Horace Mann Educators Corp 1 Horace Mann Plaza .... Springfield IL 62715 *NYSE: HMN* ■ *TF:* 800-999-1030 ■ *Web:* www.horacemann.com	217-789-2500		360-4
Horace Mann Life Insurance Co 1 Horace Mann Plaza .... Springfield IL 62715 *TF:* 800-999-1030 ■ *Web:* www.horacemann.com	217-789-2500		391-2
Horace W Goldsmith Foundation 375 Pk Ave Rm 1602 .... New York NY 10152 *Web:* akfengyo.com.tr	212-319-8700		305
Horah Group, The 351 Manville Rd Ste 105 .... Pleasantville NY 10570 *Web:* www.horah.com	914-495-3200		652
Horan Associates Inc 4990 E Galbraith Rd .... Cincinnati OH 45236 *Web:* www.horanassoc.com	513-745-0707		690
Horan Capital Management LLC 20 Wight Ave Ste 115 .... Hunt Valley MD 21030 *TF:* 800-592-7534 ■ *Web:* www.horancm.com	410-494-4380		194
HORIBA ABX Diagnostics Inc 34 Bunsen Dr .... Irvine CA 92618	949-453-0500		743
Horiba Instruments Inc 17671 Armstrong Ave .... Irvine CA 92614 *TF:* 800-446-7422 ■ *Web:* www.horiba.com	949-250-4811	250-0924	419
Horix Manufacturing Co 1384 Island Ave .... McKees Rocks PA 15136	412-771-1111		298
Horizen 3103 E Strong St .... Pensacola FL 32503 *Web:* horizenpensacola.com	850-432-7899		671
Horizon Air Freight Inc 152-15 Rockaway Blvd .... Jamaica NY 11434 *TF:* 800-221-6028 ■ *Web:* www.haf.com	718-528-3800	949-0655	449
Horizon Bank 515 Franklin Sq .... Michigan City IN 46360 *Web:* www.horizonbank.com	219-874-9245		360-2
Horizon Books 243 E Front St .... Traverse City MI 49684 *TF:* 800-587-2147 ■ *Web:* www.horizonbooks.com	231-946-7290		95
Horizon Business Solutions Inc 1589 Brice Rd .... Reynoldsburg OH 43068 *Web:* horizonbiz.com	614-577-1700		2
Horizon Christian Fellowship PO Box 17480 .... San Diego CA 92177 *Web:* www.horizonchristianfellowship.org	858-277-4991		48-20
Horizon Consulting Inc 44135 Woodridge Pkwy Ste 100 .... Lansdowne VA 20176 *Web:* horizon-inc.com	703-726-6430		196
Horizon Convention Ctr 401 S High St .... Muncie IN 47305 *TF:* 888-288-8860 ■ *Web:* www.horizonconvention.com	765-288-8860	751-9190	205
Horizon Credit Union 13224 E Mansfield Ste 300 .... Spokane Valley WA 99216 *TF:* 800-808-6402 ■ *Web:* hzcu.org	800-808-6402		219
Horizon Dart Supply 2415 S 50th St .... Kansas City KS 66106 *Web:* www.horizondarts.com	913-236-9111		761
Horizon Distribution Inc PO Box 1021 .... Yakima WA 98907 *Web:* www.horizondistribution.com	509-453-3181	457-5769	351
Horizon Distributors Inc 5214 S 30th St .... Phoenix AZ 85040 *Web:* www.horizononline.com	480-337-6750	337-6701	422
Horizon Environmental Corp 4771 50th St SE .... Grand Rapids MI 49512 *Web:* horizonenv.com	616-554-3210		261
Horizon Equipment 402 Sixth St .... Manning IA 51455 *TF:* 800-626-6409 ■ *Web:* horizonequip.com	712-653-2574		274
Horizon Freight Lines Inc 6579 S US Hwy 31 .... Edinburgh IN 46124 *Web:* www.horizonfreightlines.com	812-526-3380		314
Horizon Freight System Inc 6600 Bessemer Ave .... Cleveland OH 44127 *TF:* 800-480-6829 ■ *Web:* www.horizonfreightsystem.com	216-341-7410	429-3523	468
Horizon Group Properties Inc 5000 Hakes Dr .... Muskegon MI 49441 *Web:* www.horizongroup.com	231-798-9100	798-5100	655
Horizon Holding Inc 6101 S 58th St Ste B .... Lincoln NE 68516 *Web:* www.horizonholding.com	402-421-6400		360-3
Horizon Home Care & Hospice 11400 West Lake Park Dr .... Milwaukee WI 53224 *Web:* www.horizonhch.com	414-365-8300	365-8330	371
Horizon Hotels Ltd 99 Corvett Way Ste 302 .... Eatontown NJ 07724 *Web:* www.horizonhotels.com	732-935-9553		707
Horizon House Publications Inc (HHP) 685 Canton St .... Norwood MA 02062 *Web:* www.horizonhouse.com	781-769-9750	762-9071	637-9
Horizon Juvenile Ctr 560 Brook Ave .... Bronx NY 10455 *Web:* www1.nyc.gov	718-292-0065		412
Horizon Medical Ctr 111 Hwy 70 E .... Dickson TN 37055 *Web:* beta.ehc.com	615-446-0446		374-3
Horizon Mfg Industries Inc 11417 Cyrus Way Ste 1 .... Mukilteo WA 98275 *Web:* www.horizonman.com	425-493-1220	493-0042	621
Horizon Mud Co 4417 N Lovington Hwy .... Hobbs NM 88240 *TF:* 800-570-8024 ■ *Web:* www.horizonmud.com	575-393-8641		538
Horizon Paper Co Inc 1010 Washington Blvd .... Stamford CT 06901 *TF:* 866-358-0855 ■ *Web:* www.horizonpaper.com	203-358-0855		552-1
Horizon Publications Inc 1120 N Carbon St Ste 100 .... Marion IL 62959	618-993-1711		532-3
Horizon Services Co 250 Governor St .... East Hartford CT 06108 *TF:* 800-949-5323 ■ *Web:* www.horizonsvcs.com	800-949-5323		104
Horizon Shipbuilding Inc 13980 Shell Belt Rd .... Bayou La Batre AL 36509 *TF:* 800-777-2014 ■ *Web:* www.horizonshipbuilding.com	251-824-1660		698
Horizon Snack Foods Inc 7066 Las Positas Rd Ste G .... Livermore CA 94551	925-373-7700		68
Horizon Software International LLC 2915 Premier Pkwy Ste 300 .... Duluth GA 30097 *Web:* www.horizonsoftware.com	770-554-6353		177
Horizon Solutions LLC 175 Josons Dr .... Rochester NY 14623 *Web:* hs-e.com	585-424-7376		180
Horizon Termite & Pest Control Corp 45 Cross Ave .... Midland Park NJ 07432 *TF:* 888-612-2847 ■ *Web:* www.horizonpestcontrol.com	201-447-2530		577
Horizon USA Data Supplies Inc 1595 Meadow Wood Ln Ste 1 .... Reno NV 89502 *TF:* 800-325-1199 ■ *Web:* www.horizonusa.com	775-858-2300		174
Horizon Wealth Management 8280 Ymca Plaza Dr Bldg 5 .... Baton Rouge LA 70810 *Web:* www.horizonfg.com	225-612-3820		401
Horizon Wellness Group 20 Jerusalem Ave 3rd Fl .... Hicksville NY 11801 *Web:* www.horizonhealthfairs.com	516-326-2020		507
Horizons Conference Ctr 6200 State St .... Saginaw MI 48603 *Web:* www.horizonscenter.com	989-799-4122	799-4188	205
Horizons Video & Film Inc 4000 Horizons Dr .... Columbus OH 43220 *Web:* www.horizonscompanies.com	614-481-7200		514
Horizons Window Fashions Inc 1705 Waukegan Rd .... Waukegan IL 60085 *TF:* 800-858-2352 ■ *Web:* horizonshades.com	800-858-2352		361
Hormel Foods Corp 1 Hormel Pl .... Austin MN 55912 *NYSE: HRL* ■ *TF:* 800-523-4635 ■ *Web:* www.hormel.com	507-437-5611		296-26
Horn 1600 Steeles Ave W Ste 412 .... Concord ON L4K4M2 *TF:* 800-897-1039 ■ *Web:* www.horn.com	905-761-8000		445
Hornady Manufacturing Co 3625 W Old Potash Hwy .... Grand Island NE 68803 *TF:* 800-338-3220 ■ *Web:* www.hornady.com	308-382-1390	382-5761	284
Hornbacher's 2510 N Broadway .... Fargo ND 58102 *Web:* www.hornbachers.com	701-293-5444		345
Hornbeck Offshore Services Inc 103 Northpark Blvd Ste 300 .... Covington LA 70433 *NYSE: HOS* ■ *TF:* 800-642-9816 ■ *Web:* www.hornbeckoffshore.com	985-727-2000	727-2006	465
Hornby Zeller Associates Inc 48 Fourth St Ste 300 .... Troy NY 12180 *Web:* www.hornbyzeller.com	518-273-1614		463
Horne LLP 26 Security Dr .... Jackson TN 38305 *Web:* hornellp.com	731-668-7070		2
Horner & Shifrin Inc 5200 Oakland Ave .... St Louis MO 63110 *Web:* www.hornershifrin.com	314-531-4321		256
Horner Millwork Corp 1255 Grand Army Hwy .... Somerset MA 02726 *TF:* 800-543-5403 ■ *Web:* www.hornermillwork.com	508-679-6479		499
Horner Rausch Optical Super Store 960 Main St .... Nashville TN 37206 *Web:* hornerrauschoptical.com	615-226-0251		543
Hornerxpress Inc 5755 Powerline Rd .... Fort Lauderdale FL 33309 *TF:* 800-432-6966 ■ *Web:* www.hornerxpress.com	954-772-6966	772-6970	728
Horning Bros 3333 14th St NW Ste 300 .... Washington DC 20010 *Web:* www.horningbrothers.com	202-659-0700		655
Hornor Townsend & Kent Inc (HTK) 600 Dresher Rd Ste C1C .... Horsham PA 19044 **Fax Area Code: 215* ■ *TF:* 800-289-9999 ■ *Web:* www.htk.com	800-289-9999	956-7750*	402
Hornung's Golf Products Inc 815 Morris St .... Fond du Lac WI 54935 *TF:* 800-323-3569 ■ *Web:* www.hornungs.com	920-922-2640		328
Hornwood Inc 766 Hailey's Ferry Rd .... Lilesville NC 28091 *Web:* www.hornwoodinc.com	704-848-4121	848-4555	745-4
Horowitt, Darryl J. - Coleman & Horowitt LLP 499 W Shaw Ave Ste 116 .... Fresno CA 93704 *TF:* 800-891-8362 ■ *Web:* www.ch-law.com	559-248-4820		428
Horrocks Engineers Inc 2162 Grove Pkwy Ste 400 .... Pleasant Grove UT 84062 *Web:* horrocksengineers.com	801-763-5100		256
Horry County 1301 Second Ave .... Conway SC 29526 *TF:* 800-433-0567 ■ *Web:* www.horrycounty.org	843-915-5080	915-6081	338
Horry County Solid Waste Authority Inc 1886 Hwy 90 .... Conway SC 29526 *TF:* 800-768-7348 ■ *Web:* www.solidwasteauthority.org	843-347-1651		660
Horry Electric Co-op Inc 2774 Cultra Rd .... Conway SC 29526 *TF:* 800-824-6779 ■ *Web:* www.horryelectric.com	843-369-2211		245
Horry Telephone Co-op Inc (HTC) 3480 Hwy 701 N PO Box 1820 .... Conway SC 29528 *TF:* 800-824-6779 ■ *Web:* www.htcinc.net	843-365-2151	365-0855	736
Horry-Georgetown Technical College 2050 E Hwy 501 .... Conway SC 29526 *TF:* 855-544-4482 ■ *Web:* www.hgtc.edu	843-347-3186	347-4207	800
Grand Strand Campus 743 Hemlock Ave .... Myrtle Beach SC 29577 *TF:* 855-544-4482 ■ *Web:* www.hgtc.edu	843-477-0808	477-0775	800

				Phone	Fax	Class
Horsburgh & Scott Co 5114 Hamilton Ave *Web:* www.horsburgh-scott.com	Cleveland	OH	44114	216-431-3900	432-5850	709
Horse Illustrated Magazine 3 Burroughs *TF:* 888-588-4677 ■ *Web:* www.horsechannel.com	Irvine	CA	92618	949-855-8822		457-14
Horse of Course Tack Shop 506 W Will Rogers Blvd *Web:* thehorseofcourse.com	Claremore	OK	74017	918-341-6293		711
Horse Prairie Cabin 420 Barrett St *TF:* 888-726-2454 ■ *Web:* www.ranchlife.com	Dillon	MT	59725	406-681-3166		239
Horsehead Corp 4955 Steubenville Pk Ste 405 *TF:* 800-648-8897 ■ *Web:* www.horsehead.net	Pittsburgh	PA	15205	724-774-1020		143
Horseheads Printing 2077 Grand Central Ave *TF:* 800-497-6530 ■ *Web:* horseheadsprinting.com	Horseheads	NY	14845	607-796-2681		627
HorseLoverZ com 254 N Cedar St *TF:* 877-804-7810 ■ *Web:* www.horseloverz.com	Hazleton	PA	18201	570-579-0054		157-5
Horseman's Guarantee Corp of America 25 W Palatine Rd *Web:* www.hgcaonline.com	Palatine	IL	60067	847-394-4210		39
Horsemen's Park 6303 Q St *Web:* www.horsemenspark.com	Omaha	NE	68117	402-731-2900	731-5122	133
Horseneck Beach State Reservation 5 John Reed Rd *Web:* www.mass.gov	Westport	MA	02791	508-636-8816		565
Horseradish Grill 4320 Powers Ferry Rd *Web:* www.horseradishgrill.com	Atlanta	GA	30342	404-255-7277		671
Horseshoe Bay State Marine Park PO Box 1247 *Web:* dnr.alaska.gov/parks/units/pwssmp/smpwhit2.htm	Soldotna	AK	99669	907-262-5581		565
Horseshoe Bend National Military Park 11288 Horseshoe Bend Rd *Web:* www.nps.gov	Daviston	AL	36256	256-234-7111	329-9905	564
Horseshoe Bend Regional Library 207 NW St *Web:* www.horseshoebendlibrary.org	Dadeville	AL	36853	256-825-9232		434-3
Horseshoe Casino 777 Casino Ctr Dr *TF:* 800-522-4700 ■ *Web:* www.totalrewards.com	Hammond	IN	46320	219-473-7000		133
Horseshoe Council Bluffs 2701 23rd Ave *TF:* 800-895-0711 ■ *Web:* www.totalrewards.com	Council Bluffs	IA	51501	712-323-2500		133
Horseshoe Lake State Fish & Wildlife Area (Alexander County) PO Box 81 *Web:* dnr.illinois.gov/Lands/Landmgt/PARKS/R5/HORSHU.HTM	Olive Branch	IL	62969	618-776-5689		565
Horseshoe Lake State Park (Madison County) 3321 Hwy 111 *Web:* www.dnr.illinois.gov/Parks/Pages/HorseshoeLakeMadison.aspx	Granite City	IL	62040	618-931-0270		565
Horseshoe Restaurant & Lounge 908 W Market St	Johnson City	TN	37604	423-928-8992		671
Horseshoe Valley Resort Ltd 1101 Horseshoe Valley Rd - Comp 10 RR 1 *TF:* 800-461-5627 ■ *Web:* www.horseshoeresort.com	Barrie	ON	L4M4Y8	705-835-2790		378
Horsham Clinic 722 E Butler Pk **Fax:* Admissions ■ *TF:* 800-237-4447 ■ *Web:* www.horshamclinic.com	Ambler	PA	19002	215-643-7800	654-1148*	374-5
Horsley Co, The 1630 South 4800 West Ste D *Web:* www.horsleyco.com	Salt Lake City	UT	84104	801-401-5500		207
Horsley Witten Group Inc 90 Route 6A Unit 1 *TF:* 800-675-2756 ■ *Web:* www.horsleywitten.com	Sandwich	MA	02563	508-833-6600		196
Horspool & Romine Manufacturing Inc 5850 Marshall St **Fax Area Code:* 510 ■ *TF:* 800-446-2263 ■ *Web:* www.horspool.com	Oakland	CA	94608	800-446-2263	652-3455*	621
Horst Engineering & Mfg Co 36 Cedar St *Web:* www.horstengineering.com	East Hartford	CT	06108	860-289-8209		22
Horst Group Inc 320 Granite Run Dr PO Box 3330 *Web:* www.horstgroup.com	Lancaster	PA	17604	717-581-9800	581-9816	186
Hortau Inc 3485 Sacramento Dr Ste B *Web:* www.hortau.com	San Luis Obispo	CA	93401	418-839-2852		407
Hortica Insurance 1 Horticultural Ln PO Box 428 *TF:* 800-851-7740 ■ *Web:* www.hortica.com	Edwardsville	IL	62025	618-656-4240	656-7581	391-4
Horton & Converse Pharmacy 120 Newport Ctr Dr Ste 250 *TF:* 800-213-0154 ■ *Web:* www.hortonandconverse.com	Newport Beach	CA	92660	949-640-1231		237
Horton & Horton Printing Co 12412 Sardis Rd *Web:* hortonandhorton.com	Mabelvale	AR	72103	501-455-3168		627
Horton Components 117 Milledgeville Rd *Web:* www.hortoncomponents.com	Eatonton	GA	31024	706-485-5480		820
Horton Emergency Vehicles 3800 McDowell Rd *TF:* 800-282-5113 ■ *Web:* www.hortonambulance.com	Grove City	OH	43123	614-539-8181	539-8165	59
Horton Grand Hotel 311 Island Ave *TF:* 800-542-1886 ■ *Web:* www.hortongrand.com	San Diego	CA	92101	619-544-1886		379
Horton Group 136 Rosa L Parks Blvd *TF:* 800-799-7233 ■ *Web:* www.hortongroup.com	Nashville	TN	37203	615-292-8642		177
Horton Group, The 10320 Orland Pkwy *TF:* 800-383-8283 ■ *Web:* www.thehortongroup.com	Orland Park	IL	60467	708-845-3000	845-3001	390
Horton Haven Christian Camp 3711 Reed Harris Rd *TF:* 800-882-0722 ■ *Web:* www.hortonhaven.org	Lewisburg	TN	37091	931-364-7656		239
Horton Homes Inc 101 Industrial Blvd	Eatonton	GA	31024	706-485-8506	485-4446	505
Horton Inc 2565 Walnut St *TF:* 800-621-1320 ■ *Web:* www.hortonww.com	Saint Paul	MN	55113	651-361-6400		620
Horton International LLC 29 S Main St *Web:* www.hortoninternational.com	West Hartford	CT	06107	860-521-0101		266
Horton, Oberrecht, Kirkpatrick & Martha, Attorneys At Law A Professional Corp NBC Bldg 225 Broadway Ste 2200 *Web:* www.hortonfirm.com	San Diego	CA	92101	619-232-1183		428
Horvath Communications Inc 312 W Colfax Ave *Web:* www.horvathcommunications.com	South Bend	IN	46601	574-237-0464		116
Horvitz & Levy LLP 15760 Ventura Blvd Ste 1800 *Web:* horvitzlevy.com	Encino	CA	91436	818-995-0800		428
Horwath Hotel Tourism & Leisure Consulting 1200 Ashwood Pkwy Ste 185 *Web:* www.horwathhtl.com	Atlanta	GA	30338	404-410-7800		463
Horween Leather Co 2015 N Elston Ave *TF:* 800-826-6379 ■ *Web:* www.horween.com	Chicago	IL	60614	773-772-2026	772-9235	432
Horwith Trucks Inc PO Box 7 *TF:* 800-220-8807 ■ *Web:* www.horwithfreightliner.com	NorthHampton	PA	18067	610-261-2220	261-2916	57
Horwitz/NSI 4401 Quebec Ave N *TF:* 800-236-2500 ■ *Web:* www.horwitzinc.com	New Hope	MN	55428	763-533-1900	235-9810	189-10
Hosanna 2421 Aztec Rd NE *TF:* 800-545-6552 ■ *Web:* www.faithcomesbyhearing.com	Albuquerque	NM	87107	505-881-3321		95
Hosanna Health Care 1001 N Conway Ave	Mission	TX	78572	956-519-1000		363
Hose Master LLC 1233 E 222nd St *Web:* www.hosemaster.com	Cleveland	OH	44117	216-481-2020		790
Hoselton Chevrolet Inc 909 Fairport Rd *Web:* hoselton.com	East Rochester	NY	14445	585-586-7373		57
Hoshino USA Inc 1726 Winchester Rd *Web:* www.ibanez.com	Bensalem	PA	19020	215-638-8670	245-8583	527
Hoshizaki America Inc 618 Highway 74 S *Web:* hoshizakiamerica.com	Peachtree City	GA	30269	770-487-2331		14
Hosley International Inc 20530 Stony Island Ave	Lynwood	IL	60411	708-758-1000		361
Hosmer-Dorrance Corp 561 Div St *Web:* www.hosmer.com	Campbell	CA	95008	408-379-5151	379-5263	477
Hosokawa Micron Powder Systems 10 Chatham Rd *Web:* www.hosokawamicron.co.jp/en/global.html	Summit	NJ	07901	908-273-6360		386
Hosokawa Polymer Systems 63 Fuller Way *TF:* 800-233-6112 ■ *Web:* www.polysys.com	Berlin	CT	06037	860-828-0541	829-1313	386
Hosparus Inc 502 Hausfeldt Ln *TF:* 800-895-5633 ■ *Web:* www.hosparushealth.org	New Albany	IN	47150	812-945-4596	945-4733	371
Hospi Tel Manufacturing Corp 545 N Arlington Ave Ste 7 *TF:* 800-631-0462 ■ *Web:* www.hospitel.com	East Orange	NJ	07017	973-678-7100		475
Hospicare of Tompkins County 172 E King Rd *Web:* www.hospicare.org	Ithaca	NY	14850	607-272-0212	272-0237	371
Hospice & Palliative Care of Buffalo 225 Como Pk Blvd *TF:* 800-342-9871 ■ *Web:* www.hospicebuffalo.com	Cheektowaga	NY	14227	716-686-1900	686-8181	371
Hospice & Palliative Care of Cabarrus County 5003 Hospice Ln *Web:* www.hpccc.org	Kannapolis	NC	28081	704-935-9434	935-9435	371
Hospice & Palliative Care of Cape Cod Inc 765 Attucks Ln *TF:* 800-642-2423 ■ *Web:* hopehealthco.org	Hyannis	MA	02601	508-957-0200		371
Hospice & Palliative Care of Northern Colorado 2726 W 11th St Rd *TF:* 800-564-5563 ■ *Web:* www.hospiceofnortherncolorado.org	Greeley	CO	80634	970-352-8487	475-0037	371
Hospice & Palliative Care of Western Colorado 2754 Compass Dr Ste 377 *TF:* 866-310-8900 ■ *Web:* www.hopewestco.org	Grand Junction	CO	81506	970-241-2212	257-2400	371
Hospice & Palliative CareCenter 101 Hospice Ln *TF:* 888-876-3663 ■ *Web:* www.hospicecarecenter.org	Winston-Salem	NC	27103	336-768-3972	659-0461	371
Hospice & VNA of the Florida Keys 1319 William St *TF:* 800-434-1399 ■ *Web:* www.hospicevna.com	Key West	FL	33040	305-294-8812		371
Hospice Alliance 10220 Prairie Ridge Blvd *TF:* 800-830-8344 ■ *Web:* www.hospicealliance.org	Pleasant Prairie	WI	53158	262-652-4400	652-4516	371
Hospice at Charlotte 1420 E Seventh St *TF:* 800-835-5306 ■ *Web:* www.hpccr.org	Charlotte	NC	28204	704-375-0100	375-8623	371
Hospice at Greensboro 2500 Summit Ave *Web:* www.hospicegso.org	Greensboro	NC	27405	336-621-2500	621-4516	371
Hospice at Home 4025 Health Pk Ln *TF:* 800-717-3811 ■ *Web:* www.lakelandhealth.org/hospice-at-home-cares	Saint Joseph	MI	49085	269-429-7100	428-3499	371
Hospice at the Texas Medical Ctr 1905 Holcombe Blvd *TF:* 800-630-7894 ■ *Web:* www.houstonhospice.org	Houston	TX	77030	713-467-7423		371
Hospice Atlanta-Visiting Nurse Health System 1244 Pk Vista Dr *Web:* www.vnhs.org	Atlanta	GA	30319	404-869-3000	215-6005	371
Hospice Austin 4107 Spicewood Springs Rd Ste 100 *TF:* 800-445-3261 ■ *Web:* www.hospiceaustin.org	Austin	TX	78759	512-342-4700	795-9053	371
Hospice Brazos Valley 502 W 26th St *TF:* 800-824-2326 ■ *Web:* www.hospicebrazosvalley.org	Bryan	TX	77803	979-821-2266	821-0041	371
Hospice by the Bay 1902 Van Ness Ave 2nd Fl *TF:* 800-919-8090 ■ *Web:* hospicebythebay.org	San Francisco	CA	94109	415-626-5900		371
Hospice By the Bay 17 E Sir Francis Drake Blvd *TF:* 800-511-2300 ■ *Web:* www.hospicebythebay.org	Larkspur	CA	94939	415-927-2273		371
Hospice Care in Westchester & Putnam Inc 540 White Plains Rd Ste 300 *Web:* www.vnahv.org	Tarrytown	NY	10591	914-666-4228	666-0378	371
Hospice Care Inc 4277 Middle Settlement Rd *TF:* 800-317-5661 ■ *Web:* www.hospicecareinc.org	New Hartford	NY	13413	315-735-6484	793-8852	371
Hospice Care Network 99 Sunnyside Blvd *TF:* 800-405-6731 ■ *Web:* hospicecarenetwork.org	Woodbury	NY	11797	516-832-7100	832-7160	371
Hospice Care of Southwest Michigan 222 N Kalamazoo Mall Ste 100 *Web:* www.hospiceswmi.org	Kalamazoo	MI	49007	269-345-0273		371

Phone | Fax | Class

Hospice Care Team
1708 N Amburn Rd Ste C ... Texas City TX 77591 409-938-0070 371
Web: www.hospicecareteam.org

Hospice Caring Project of Santa Cruz County
940 Disc Dr ... Scotts Valley CA 95066 831-430-3000 430-9272 371
TF: 800-369-7437 ■ *Web:* www.hospicesantacruz.org

Hospice Chautauqua County
20 W Fairmount Ave ... Lakewood NY 14750 716-753-5383 371
Web: www.hospicechautco.org

Hospice Community Care PO Box 993 ... Rock Hill SC 29731 803-329-1500 329-5935 371
TF: 800-895-2273 ■ *Web:* www.hospicecommunitycare.org

Hospice Family Care 550 E Main St ... Batavia NY 14020 585-343-7596 343-7629 371
TF: 800-719-7129 ■ *Web:* www.homecare-hospice.org

Hospice Family Care
1550 S Alma School Rd ... Mesa AZ 85210 480-461-3144 371
Web: www.hfc-az.com

Hospice Foundation of America (HFA)
1710 Rhode Island Ave NW Ste 400 ... Washington DC 20036 202-457-5811 457-5815 49-8
TF: 800-854-3402 ■ *Web:* www.hospicefoundation.org

Hospice Hawaii 860 Iwilei Rd ... Honolulu HI 96817 808-924-9255 922-9161 371
Web: www.hospicehawaii.org

Hospice Home Care 2200 S Bowman ... Little Rock AR 72211 501-296-9043 296-9978 371
TF: 800-479-1219 ■ *Web:* www.hospicehomecare.com

Hospice House Foundation Inc
903 n sam houston ave ... Odessa TX 79761 432-580-0067 371
TF: 877-428-3581 ■ *Web:* www.homehospicewtx.com

Hospice Life Care 575 Beech St ... Holyoke MA 01040 413-533-3923 371
TF: 800-606-4519 ■ *Web:* holyokevna.org

Hospice Ministries
450 Towne Center Blvd ... Ridgeland MS 39157 601-898-1053 371
TF: 800-273-7724 ■ *Web:* www.hospiceministries.org

Hospice of Acadiana
2600 Johnston St Ste 200 ... Lafayette LA 70503 337-232-1234 232-1297 371
TF: 800-738-2226 ■ *Web:* hospice0.wixsite.com/hospiceacadiana

Hospice of Alamance Caswell
914 Chapel Hill Rd ... Burlington NC 27215 336-532-0100 371
TF: 800-588-8879 ■ *Web:* www.hospiceac.org

Hospice of Anchorage
2612 E Northern Lights Blvd ... Anchorage AK 99508 907-561-5322 561-0334 371
TF: 800-662-4357 ■ *Web:* www.hospiceofanchorage.org

Hospice of Arizona
19620 N Seventh Ave Ste 130 ... Phoenix AZ 85027 602-678-1313 242-2178 371

Hospice of Baton Rouge
9063 Siegen Ln ... Baton Rouge LA 70810 225-767-4673 769-8113 371
TF: 888-447-0433 ■ *Web:* www.hospicebr.org

Hospice of Bend-La Pine 2075 NE Wyatt Ct ... Bend OR 97701 541-382-5882 371
TF: 800-555-2431 ■ *Web:* www.partnersbend.org

Hospice of Boulder County
2594 Trlridge Dr E ... Lafayette CO 80026 303-449-7740 371
TF: 877-986-4766 ■ *Web:* www.trucare.org

Hospice of Burke County 1721 Enon Rd ... Valdese NC 28690 828-879-1601 879-3500 371
TF: 800-282-4914 ■ *Web:* www.burkehospice.org

Hospice of Central Ohio
2269 Cherry Valley Rd ... Newark OH 43055 740-788-1400 371
TF: 800-804-2505 ■ *Web:* www.hospiceofcentralohio.org

Hospice of Central Pennsylvania
1320 Linglestown Rd ... Harrisburg PA 17110 717-732-1000 732-5348 371
TF: 866-779-7374 ■ *Web:* www.hospiceofcentralpa.org

Hospice of Chattanooga
4411 Oakwood Dr ... Chattanooga TN 37416 423-892-4289 371
TF: 800-267-6828 ■ *Web:* www.hospiceofchattanooga.org

Hospice of Cincinnati
4360 Cooper Rd ... Cincinnati OH 45242 513-891-7700 792-6980 371
TF: 800 691-7255 ■ *Web:* www.hospiceofcincinnati.org

Hospice of Cleveland County
951 Wendover Heights Dr ... Shelby NC 28150 704-487-4677 481-8050 371
Web: www.hospicecares.cc

Hospice of Cullman County
1912 Alabama Hwy 157 ... Cullman AL 35058 256-737-2502 737-2504 371
TF: 877-271-4176 ■ *Web:* cullmanregional.com

Hospice of Dayton 324 Wilmington Ave ... Dayton OH 45420 937-256-4490 256-9802 371
TF: 800-653-4490 ■ *Web:* www.hospiceofdayton.org

Hospice of East Texas
4111 University Blvd ... Tyler TX 75701 903-266-3400 371
TF: 800-777-9860 ■ *Web:* www.hospiceofeasttexas.org

Hospice of El Paso 1440 Miracle Way ... El Paso TX 79925 915-532-5699 532-7822 371
Web: www.hospiceelpaso.org

Hospice of Gaston County
258 E Garrison Blvd PO Box 3984 ... Gastonia NC 28054 704-861-8405 865-0590 371
Web: www.gastonhospice.org

Hospice of Hilo 1011 Waianuenue Ave ... Hilo HI 96720 808-969-1733 969-4863 371
TF: 800-474-2113 ■ *Web:* www.hospiceofhilo.org

Hospice of Holland Inc
270 Hoover Blvd ... Holland MI 49423 616-396-2972 396-2808 371
TF: 800-255-3522 ■ *Web:* www.hollandhospice.org

Hospice of Huntington
1101 Sixth Ave ... Huntington WV 25701 304-529-4217 523-6051 371
TF: 800-788-5480 ■ *Web:* www.hospiceofhuntington.org

Hospice of Jefferson County
425 Washington St ... Watertown NY 13601 315-788-7323 788-9653 371
Web: jeffersonhospice.org

Hospice of Kankakee Valley Inc
482 Main St NW ... Bourbonnais IL 60914 815-939-4141 371
TF: 855-871-4695 ■ *Web:* hkvcares.org

Hospice of Lake Cumberland
100 Pkwy Dr ... Somerset KY 42503 606-679-4389 371
TF: 800-937-9596 ■ *Web:* www.hospicelc.org

Hospice of Lancaster County
685 Good Dr PO Box 4125 ... Lancaster PA 17604 717-295-3900 391-9582 371
TF: 888-236-9563 ■ *Web:* www.hospiceandcommunitycare.org

Hospice of Lansing 3186 Pine Tree Rd ... Lansing MI 48911 517-882-4500 882-3010 371
Web: hospiceoflansing.org

Hospice of Lincolnland
1000 Health Ctr Dr ... Mattoon IL 61938 800-454-4055 347-7197* 371
**Fax Area Code:* 217 ■ *TF:* 800-454-4055 ■ *Web:* www.sarahbush.org/hospice

Hospice of Marion County
3231 SW 34th Ave ... Ocala FL 34474 352-873-7400 873-7435 371
TF: 888-482-5018 ■ *Web:* www.hospiceofmarion.com

Hospice of Marshall County
408 Martling Rd ... Albertville AL 35951 256-891-7724 891-7754 371
TF: 888-334-9336 ■ *Web:* www.hospicemc.org

Hospice of Medina County
5075 Windfall Rd ... Medina OH 44256 330-722-4771 722-5266 371
TF: 800-700-4771 ■ *Web:* www.hospiceofmedina.org

Hospice of Miami County
550 Summit Ave Ste 101 ... Troy OH 45373 937-335-5191 371
Web: www.hospiceofmiamicounty.org

Hospice of Michigan 400 Mack Ave ... Detroit MI 48201 313-578-5000 371
TF: 888-247-5701 ■ *Web:* www.hom.org

Hospice of Midland 911 W Texas Ave ... Midland TX 79701 432-682-2855 682-2989 371
Web: hospicemidland.org

Hospice of NE Georgia Medical Ctr
2150 Limestone Pkwy Ste 222 ... Gainesville GA 30501 770-533-8888 219-8887 371
TF: 888-572-3900 ■ *Web:* www.nghs.com

Hospice of New Jersey
400 Broadacres Dr 1St Fl ... Bloomfield NJ 07003 973-893-0818 893-0828 371
TF: 800-501-0451 ■
Web: www.nj.gov/cgi-bin/dhss/healthfacilities/hospitaldisplay.pl?id=22741

Hospice of North Central Ohio
1050 Dauch Dr ... Ashland OH 44805 419-281-7107 371
TF: 800-952-2207 ■ *Web:* www.hospiceofnorthcentralohio.org

Hospice of North Ottawa Community
1309 Sheldon Rd ... Grand Haven MI 49417 616-842-3600 371
TF: 800-742-5877 ■ *Web:* www.noch.org/main.aspx?id=115

Hospice of Northeast Florida
4266 Sunbeam Rd ... Jacksonville FL 32257 904-268-5200 371
TF: 866-253-6681 ■ *Web:* www.communityhospice.com

Hospice of Northwest Ohio
30000 E River Rd ... Perrysburg OH 43551 419-661-4001 661-4015 371
TF: 866-661-4001 ■ *Web:* www.hospicenwo.org

Hospice of Oklahoma County
4334 NW Expy Ste 106 ... Oklahoma City OK 73116 405-848-8884 841-4899 371
TF: 800-994-6610 ■ *Web:* integrisok.com

Hospice of Orange & Sullivan Counties
800 Stony Brook Ct ... Newburgh NY 12550 845-561-6111 561-2179 371
TF: 800-924-0157 ■ *Web:* www.hospiceoforange.com

Hospice of Palm Beach County
5300 East Ave ... West Palm Beach FL 33407 561-494-6888 494-6889 371
TF: 877-494-6890 ■ *Web:* www.hpbcf.org

Hospice of Randolph County
416 Vision Dr ... Asheboro NC 27203 336-672-9300 672-0868 371
TF: 800-772-1213 ■ *Web:* www.hospiceofrandolph.org

Hospice of Redlands Community Hospital
350 Terracina Blvd ... Redlands CA 92373 909-335-5643 371
TF: 888-397-4999 ■ *Web:* redlandshospital.org

Hospice of Reno County
1600 N Lorraine ... Hutchinson KS 67502 620-665-2473 669-5959 371
TF: 800-267-6891 ■ *Web:* hutchregional.com

Hospice of Rockingham County Inc
2150 NC Hwy 65 PO Box 281 ... Wentworth NC 27375 336-427-9022 427-9030 371
TF: 800-227-2345 ■ *Web:* www.hospiceofrockinghamcounty.com

Hospice of Rowan County Inc
720 Grove St ... Salisbury NC 28144 704-637-7645 371
Web: hospicecarecenter.org

Hospice of Rutherford County
374 Hudlow Rd PO Box 336 ... Forest City NC 28043 828-245 0095 248-1035 371
TF: 800-218-2273 ■ *Web:* www.hospiceofrutherford.org

Hospice of Saint Francis Inc
1250 Grumman Pl Ste B ... Titusville FL 32780 321-269-4240 371
TF: 866-269-4240 ■ *Web:* www.hospiceofstfrancis.com

Hospice of Saint Lawrence Valley
6805 State Hwy 11 ... Potsdam NY 13676 315-265-3105 371
TF: 888-827-1000 ■ *Web:* hospiceslv.org

Hospice of San Angelo
36 E Twohig St PO Box 471 ... San Angelo TX 76903 325-658-6524 658-8895 371
TF: 800-499-6524 ■ *Web:* www.hospiceofsanangelo.org

Hospice of San Joaquin
3888 Pacific Ave ... Stockton CA 95204 209-957-3888 957 3986 371
Web: www.hospicesj.org

Hospice of Siouxland
4300 Hamilton Blvd ... Sioux City IA 51104 712-233-4100 233-1123 371
TF: 800-383-4545 ■ *Web:* www.hospiceofsiouxland.com

Hospice of South Louisiana
6500 W Main St ... Houma LA 70360 985-868-3095 868-3910 371
Web: www.hospiceofsouthlouisiana.com

Hospice of South Texas
605 E Locust Ave ... Victoria TX 77901 361-572-4300 371
TF: 800-874-6908 ■ *Web:* www.hospiceofsouthtexas.org

Hospice of Southeastern Connecticut Inc
227 Dunham St ... Norwich CT 06360 860-848-5699 848-6898 371
TF: 877-654-4035 ■ *Web:* www.hospicesect.org

Hospice of Southern Illinois
305 S Illinois St ... Belleville IL 62220 618-235-1703 371
TF: 800-233-1708 ■ *Web:* hospice.org

Hospice of Southern Kentucky
5872 Scottsville Rd ... Bowling Green KY 42104 270-782-3402 371
Web: www.hospicesoky.org

Hospice of Southwest Georgia
114 A Mimosa Dr ... Thomasville GA 31792 229-584-5500 371
TF: 800-290-6567 ■ *Web:* www.archbold.org

Hospice of Spokane 121 S Arthur St ... Spokane WA 99202 509-456-0438 371
TF: 800-467-7423 ■ *Web:* www.hospiceofspokane.org

Hospice of Stanly County
960 N First St ... Albemarle NC 28001 704-983-4216 983-6662 371
TF: 800-230-4236 ■ *Web:* www.hospiceofstanly.org

Hospice of the Bluegrass
2312 Alexandria Dr ... Lexington KY 40504 859-276-5344 371
Web: www.hospicebg.com

Hospice of the Calumet Area
600 Superior Ave ... Munster IN 46321 219-922-2732 922-1947 371
TF: 888-303-0180 ■ *Web:* www.hospicecalumet.org

Hospice of the Chesapeake
445 Defense Hwy ... Annapolis MD 21401 410-987-2003 837-1505* 371
**Fax Area Code:* 443 ■ *TF General:* 877-462-1101 ■ *Web:* www.hospicechesapeake.org

Hospice of the Cleveland Clinic
6801 Brecksville Rd Ste 10 ... Independence OH 44131 216-444-9819 520-1973 371
TF: 800-263-0403 ■ *Web:* my.clevelandclinic.org

Name / Address	City	State	ZIP	Phone	Fax	Class
Hospice of the Comforter 480 W Central Pkwy *Fax: Admissions ■ TF: 877-696-6775 ■ Web: www.hospiceofthecomforter.org	Altamonte Springs	FL	32714	407-682-0808	303-0721*	371
Hospice of the Florida Suncoast 5771 Roosevelt Blvd Web: thehospice.org	Clearwater	FL	33760	727-586-4432		371
Hospice of the North Shore 75 Sylvan St Ste B102 TF: 888-283-1722 ■ Web: caredimensions.org	Danvers	MA	01923	978-774-7566	774-4389	371
Hospice of the Ozarks 701 Burnett Dr Web: www.baxterregional.org	Mountain Home	AR	72653	870-508-1000		371
Hospice of the Panhandle 330 Hospice Ln TF: 800-345-6538 ■ Web: www.hospiceotp.org	Kearneysville	WV	25430	304-264-0406	264-0409	371
Hospice of the Piedmont 675 Peter Jefferson Pkwy Ste 300 TF: 800-975-5501 ■ Web: www.hopva.org	Charlottesville	VA	22911	434-817-6900	245-0187	371
Hospice of the Piedmont 1801 Westchester Dr Web: hospiceofthepiedmont.org	High Point	NC	27262	336-889-8446		371
Hospice of the Rapidan 1200 Sunset Ln Ste 2320 TF: 800-272-3900 ■ Web: www.hotr.org	Culpeper	VA	22701	540-825-4840		371
Hospice of the Red River Valley 1701 38th St S Ste 101 TF: 800-237-4629 ■ Web: www.hrrv.org	Fargo	ND	58103	701-356-1500		371
Hospice of the Upstate 1835 Rogers Rd TF: 800-261-8636 ■ Web: www.hospicehouse.net	Anderson	SC	29621	864-224-3358	328-1132	371
Hospice of the Valley 5190 Market St TF: 800-640-5180 ■ Web: www.hospiceofthevalley.com	Youngstown	OH	44512	330-788-1992	788-1998	371
Hospice of the Valley 240 Johnston St SE TF: 877-260-3657 ■ Web: www.hospiceofthevalley.net	Decatur	AL	35601	256-350-5585	350-5567	371
Hospice of the Western Reserve 300 E 185th St TF: 800-707-8922 ■ Web: www.hospicewr.org	Cleveland	OH	44119	216-383-2222	383-3750	371
Hospice of Union County 700 W Roosevelt Blvd TF: 800-222-1222 ■ Web: www.carolinashealthcare.org	Monroe	NC	28110	704-292-2100	292-2190	371
Hospice of Visiting Nurse Service 3358 Ridgewood Rd TF: 800-335-1455 ■ Web: www.vnsa.com	Akron	OH	44333	330-665-1455	668-4680	371
Hospice of Volusia/Flagler 3800 Woodbriar Trl	Port Orange	FL	32129	386-322-4701		371
Hospice of Wake County Inc 250 Hospice Cir TF: 888-900-3959 ■ Web: transitionslifecare.org	Raleigh	NC	27607	919-828-0890		371
Hospice of Washington County Inc 747 Northern Ave Web: www.hwc-md.org	Hagerstown	MD	21742	301-791-6360		374-7
Hospice of West Alabama 3851 Loop Rd TF: 877-362-7522 ■ Web: hospiceofwestal.com	Tuscaloosa	AL	35404	205-523-0101	523-0102	371
Hospice of Westchester 1025 Westchester Ave Ste 200 TF: 800-860-9808 ■ Web: www.hospiceofwestchester.com	White Plains	NY	10604	914-682-1484	682-9425	371
Hospice of Wichita Falls 4909 Johnson Rd TF: 800-378-2822 ■ Web: www.hospiceofwf.org	Wichita Falls	TX	76310	940-691-0982	691-1608	371
Hospice Program of Hackensack University Medical Center 25 E Salem St	Hackensack	NJ	07601	201-342-7766	489-7275	371
Hospice Savannah Inc PO Box 13190 TF: 888-355-4911 ■ Web: www.hospicesavannah.org	Savannah	GA	31416	912-355-2289		371
HospiceCare 5395 E Cheryl Pkwy TF: 800-553-4289 ■ Web: www.agrace.org	Madison	WI	53711	608-276-4660	276-4672	371
HospiceCare of the Piedmont 408 W Alexander Ave TF: 800-465-4454 ■ Web: www.hospicepiedmont.org	Greenwood	SC	29646	864-227-9393	227-9377	371
Hospicomm Inc 41 N Third St Ste 200 Web: www.hospicomm.com	Philadelphia	PA	19106	215-925-5158		463
Hospira Boulder Inc 4876 Sterling Dr Web: hospira.com	Boulder	CO	80301	303-938-1250		231
Hospira Healthcare Corp 1111 Dr Frederik-Philips Blvd Ste 600 TF: 800-268-5860 ■ Web: www.hospira.ca	Saint-laurent	QC	H4M2X6	514-905-2600		475
Hospira Inc 275 N Field Dr NYSE: HSP ■ TF: 877-946-7747 ■ Web: www.hospira.com	Lake Forest	IL	60045	224-212-2000		477
Hospital Billing & Collection Service Ltd 118 Lukens Dr TF: 877-254-9580 ■ Web: www.hbcs.org	New Castle	DE	19720	302-552-8000		160
Hospital Complex Sagamie, The 305 Ave St Vallier CP 5006 Web: www.usherbrooke.ca	Chicoutimi	QC	G7H5H6	418-541-1000		374-2
Hospital Cooperative Laundry Inc 6225 E 38th Ave Web: hospitalcooperative.com	Denver	CO	80207	303-329-6662		363
Hospital De La Concepcion Carr #2 Km 1734 Bo Cain Alto Web: www.hospitalconcepcion.net	San German	PR	00683	787-892-1860		127
Hospital Employee Labor Pool 5400 Orange Ave Web: www.helpstaffs.com	Cypress	CA	90630	714-243-3510		260
Hospital for Special Care 2150 Corbin Ave Web: www.hfsc.org	New Britain	CT	06053	860-223-2761	612-6304	374-6
Hospital for Special Surgery 535 E 70th St Web: www.hss.edu	New York	NY	10021	212-606-1000		374-7
Hospital Forms & Systems Corp 8900 Ambassador Row TF: 800-527-5081 ■ Web: www.hforms.com	Dallas	TX	75247	214-634-8900		110
Hospital Hospitality House of Louisville 120 W Broadway Web: www.hhhlouisville.org	Louisville	KY	40202	502-625-1360	625-1363	372
Hospital Hospitality House of SW Michigan Inc 527 W S St Web: www.hhhkz.org	Kalamazoo	MI	49007	269-341-7811	341-7817	372
Hospital Marketing Services Company Inc 162 Great Hill Rd TF: 800-786-5094 ■ Web: www.hmsmedical.com	Naugatuck	CT	06770	203-723-1466		476
Hospital of Saint Raphael 1450 Chapel St TF: 888-700-6543 ■ Web: www.ynhh.org	New Haven	CT	06511	203-789-3000		374-3
Hospital of the University of Pennsylvania 3400 Spruce St TF: 800-789-7366 ■ Web: www.pennmedicine.org	Philadelphia	PA	19104	215-662-4000		374-3
Hospital Physician Magazine 125 Strafford Ave Ste 220 Web: turner-white.com	Wayne	PA	19087	610-975-4541	975-4564	457-16
Hospital Sisters Health System 4936 Laverna Rd Web: www.hshs.org	Springfield	IL	62707	217-523-4747		353
Hospitality Builders Inc 150 Knollwood Dr Web: www.hospitalitybuilders.com	Rapid City	SD	57701	605-791-3400		186
Hospitality Enterprises 4220 Howard Ave Web: www.bigeasy.com	New Orleans	LA	70125	504-529-4567		773
Hospitality Financial & Technology Professionals (HFTP) 11709 Boulder Ln Ste 110 TF: 800-646-4387 ■ Web: www.hftp.org	Austin	TX	78726	512-249-5333	249-1533	49-1
Hospitality House 121 Fifth Ave NE	Hickory	NC	28601	828-324-4544		372
Hospitality House of Charlotte 1400 Scott Ave Web: www.hospitalityhouseofcharlotte.org	Charlotte	NC	28203	704-376-0060	376-0059	372
Hospitality House of Methodist Hospital Foundation 990 Oak Ridge Tpke PO Box 2529 Web: www.mmcoakridge.com	Oak Ridge	TN	37830	865-835-5261		372
Hospitality House of Tulsa 1135 S Victor Ave Web: www.hhtulsa.org	Tulsa	OK	74014	918-794-0088		372
Hospitality Inn 3709 NW 39th St	Oklahoma City	OK	73112	405-942-7730		379
Hospitality International Inc 1726 Montreal Cir TF: 800-251-1962 ■ Web: www.bookroomsnow.com	Tucker	GA	30084	800-251-1962		379
Master Hosts Inns & Resorts 1726 Montreal Cir Ste 110 TF: 800-892-8405 ■ Web: www.bookroomsnow.com	Tucker	GA	30084	770-270-1180		379
Passport Inn 1726 Montreal Cir TF: 800-251-1962 ■ Web: www.bookroomsnow.com	Tucker	GA	30084	800-251-1962		379
Red Carpet Inn 1726 Montreal Cir TF: 800-247-4677 ■ Web: www.bookroomsnow.com	Tucker	GA	30084	800-247-4677		379
Scottish Inns 1726 Montreal Cir TF: 800-251-1962 ■ Web: www.bookroomsnow.com	Tucker	GA	30084	800-251-1962		379
Hospitality Investments LP 16114 E Indiana Ave Ste 200 Web: www.hospitalityassociates.com	Spokane Valley	WA	99216	509-928-3736		610
Hospitality Law 360 Hiatt Dr TF: 800-621-5463 ■ Web: www.lrp.com	Palm Beach Gardens	FL	33418	561-622-6520	622-2423	531-7
Hospitality Properties Trust 255 Washington St NYSE: HPT ■ TF: 800-475-6701 ■ Web: www.hptreit.com	Newton	MA	02458	617-964-8389	969-5730	655
Hospitality Real Estate Counselors 6400 S Fiddler'S Green Cir Ste 1730 Web: www.hrec.com	Greenwood Village	CO	80111	303-267-0057		652
Hospitality Sales & Marketing Assn International (HSMAI) 1760 Old Meadow Rd Ste 500 Web: www.hsmai.org	McLean	VA	22102	703-506-3280	610-9005	49-18
Hospitality Suites Resort 409 N Scottsdale Rd TF: 800-445-5115 ■ Web: www.hospitalitysuites.com	Scottsdale	AZ	85257	480-949-5115		379
Hospitality Ventures Management LLC 5 Concourse Pkwy Ste 2828 Web: www.hvmg.com	Atlanta	GA	30328	404-467-9299	467-1962	463
Hospitals & Health Networks Magazine 155 N Wacker Ste 400 TF: 800-621-6902 ■ Web: www.hhnmag.com	Chicago	IL	60606	312-893-6800	422-4500	457-5
Hoss's Steak & Sea House 170 Patchway Rd TF: 800-992-4677	Duncansville	PA	16635	814-695-7600	695-3865	670
Hoss's Steak & Sea House 3302 W 26th St	Erie	PA	16506	814-838-6718		671
Host America Corporate Dining Inc 1 Leonardo Dr	North Haven	CT	06473	203-239-4678		299
Host Department LLC 45277 Fremont Blvd Ste 11 TF: 866-887-4678 ■ Web: www.hostdepartment.com	Fremont	CA	94538	866-887-4678		387
Host Depot Inc 4613 N University Dr Ste 227 TF: 888-340-3527 ■ Web: www.hostdepot.com	Coral Springs	FL	33067	954-340-3527	340-3539	808
Host Engineering Inc 593 Aa Deakins Rd Web: hosteng.com	Jonesborough	TN	37659	423-913-2587		256
Host Hotels & Resorts Inc 6903 Rockledge Dr Ste 1500 NYSE: HST ■ Web: www.hosthotels.com	Bethesda	MD	20817	240-744-1000		654
Host t Parker of Maryland Inc 2200 Broening Hwy Ste 102 TF: 800-732-0204 ■ Web: www.tparkerhost.com	Baltimore	MD	21224	410-633-4666		23
Hostcentric Inc 70 BlanchaRd Rd 3rd Fl TF Tech Supp: 866-897-5418 ■ Web: www.hostcentric.com	Burlington	MA	01803	602-716-5396		808
Hostedware Corp 16 Technology Dr Ste 116 TF: 800-211-6967 ■ Web: www.hostedware.com	Irvine	CA	92618	949-585-1500		808
Hostelling International USA - American Youth Hostels (HI-AYH) 8401 Colesville Rd Ste 600 TF: 888-449-8727 ■ Web: www.hiusa.org	Silver Spring	MD	20910	240-650-2100	650-2094	48-23
Hosteria Romana 429 Espanola Way Web: www.hosteriaromana.com	Miami Beach	FL	33139	305-532-4299		671
Hostexcellence com 1774 Dividend Dr TF: 800-792-1197 ■ Web: www.hostexcellence.com	Columbus	OH	43228	614-534-1962		396

	Phone	Fax	Class
Hostmark Hospitality Group 1300 E Woodfield Rd Ste 400 .... Schaumburg IL 60173 *Web:* www.hostmark.com	847-517-9100	517-9797	379
HostMySite Inc 650 Pencader Dr ....Newark DE 19702 *Web:* www.hostmysite.com	302-731-4948		396
Hostnet Inc 1301 E Arapaho Rd Ste 104 .... Richardson TX 75081 *Web:* www.hostnet.com.br	214-800-5501		809
Hostos Community College 500 Grand Concourse.........................Bronx NY 10451 **Fax:* Admissions ■ *TF:* 888-993-7650 ■ *Web:* www.hostos.cuny.edu	718-518-4444	518-4256*	162
Hostvedt Pavoni Inc 30 S Pine St .... Doylestown PA 18901 *Web:* www.hpisales.com	215-489-7300		518
Hostway Corp 100 N Riverside Plaza 8th Fl..................Chicago IL 60606 *TF:* 866-467-8929 ■ *Web:* www.hostway.com	312-238-0125		808
Hosung NY Inc 300 Kingsland Ave .... Brooklyn NY 11222 *Web:* www.hosungny.com	718-389-8233		761
Hot & Hot Fish Club 2180 11th Ct S.........Birmingham AL 35205 *Web:* www.birminghammenus.com	205-933-5474		671
Hot 102.9 717 E David Rd ....Dayton OH 45429 *Web:* www.hot1029.com	937-294-5858		645-45
Hot 103.1 1355 California St PO Box 968..............Las Cruces NM 88001 *Web:* www.hot103.fm	575-525-9298	525-9419	645
HOT 106.3 1502 Wampanoag Trail.................East Providence RI 02914 *Web:* www.hot1063.com	401-433-4200		645
Hot Dog on a Stick 5942 Priestly Dr............ Carlsbad CA 92008 *TF:* 877-639-2361 ■ *Web:* www.hotdogonastick.com	877-639-2361		670
Hot Melt Technologies Inc 1723 W Hamlin Rd.................... Rochester Hills MI 48309 *Web:* www.hotmelt-tech.com	248-853-2011		711
Hot Rod Magazine 6420 Wilshire Blvd........................Los Angeles CA 90048 *TF Orders:* 800-800-4681 ■ *Web:* www.hotrod.com	323-782-2000	782-2223	457-3
Hot Rod Network 774 S Placentia Ave .... Placentia CA 92870 *Web:* www.hotrod.com/popular-hot-rodding-magazine	949-705-3100		457-3
Hot Rooms 875 N Michigan Ave Ste 3100 ....Chicago IL 60611 **Fax Area Code:* 312 ■ *TF:* 800-468-3500 ■ *Web:* www.hotrooms.com	773-468-7666	649-0559*	376
Hot Shot Delivery Inc 747 N Shepherd Dr Ste 100 PO Box 701189 ......Houston TX 77007 *TF:* 866-261-3184 ■ *Web:* www.hotshot-delivery.com	713-869-5525	862-6354	546
Hot Spring County 210 Locust St ....Malvern AR 72104	501-332-2291		338
Hot Springs City Hall 133 Convention Blvd ....Hot Springs AR 71901 *Web:* www.cityhs.net	501-321-6843	321-6809	337
Hot Springs Convention & Visitors Bureau 134 Convention Blvd ....Hot Springs AR 71901 *TF:* 800-543-2284 ■ *Web:* www.hotsprings.org	501-321-2277		206
Hot Springs Convention Ctr (HSCVB) 134 Convention Blvd PO Box 6000 ....Hot Springs AR 71902 *TF:* 800-625-7576 ■ *Web:* www.hotsprings.org	501-321-2277		205
Hot Springs County 415 Arapahoe St........................ Thermopolis WY 82443 *Web:* www.hscounty.com	307-864-3515	864-3333	338
Hot Springs Documentary Film Festival (HSDFF) 659 Ouachita Ave PO Box 6450 ....Hot Springs AR 71901 *Web:* www.hsdfi.org	501-538-0452		282
Hot Springs Lodge & Pool 415 E Sixth St....................Glenwood Springs CO 81601 *TF:* 800-537-7946 ■ *Web:* www.hotspringspool.com	970-945-6571	947-2950	669
Hot Springs Memorial Field 525 Airport Rd ....Hot Springs AR 71913 *TF:* 000-992-7433 ■ *Web:* cityhs.net/442/flight-information	501-321-6750	321-6754	27
Hot Springs National Park 101 Reserve St ....Hot Springs AR 71901 *TF:* 800-582-2244 ■ *Web:* www.nps.gov	501-620-6715	620-6778	564
Hot Stuff Pizza 2930 W Maple St ....Sioux Falls SD 57107 *TF:* 800-336-1320 ■ *Web:* www.hotstuffpizza.com	605-336-6961		68
Hot Tomato's 1 Union Pl ....Hartford CT 06103 *TF:* 800-222-5901 ■ *Web:* www.hottomatos.net	860-249-5100		671
Hot Topic Inc 18305 E San Jose Ave .... City of Industry CA 91748 *NASDAQ:* HOTT ■ *Web:* www.hottopic.com	626-839-4681		157-5
Hot Tuna Bar & Grill 2817 Shore Dr .... Virginia Beach VA 23451 *Web:* hottunavb.com	757-481-2888		671
Hot Water Products Inc 7254 N Teutonia Ave.........................Milwaukee WI 53209 *Web:* www.hotwaterproducts.com	414-434-1371		612
Hotaling Investment Management LLC 100 W Lancaster Ave Ste 105.................... Wayne PA 19087 *Web:* www.hotalingllc.com	610-688-0616		528
Hotan Corp 751 N Canyons Pkwy............. Livermore CA 94551 *TF:* 800-656-1888 ■ *Web:* www.hotan.com	925-290-1000		246
Hotcards Com Inc 2400 Superior Ave...........Cleveland OH 44114 *TF:* 800-787-4831 ■ *Web:* www.hotcards.com	216-241-4040		344
Hotchkis & Wiley Capital Management LLC 725 S Figueroa St Fl 39 ....Los Angeles CA 90017 *Web:* www.hwcm.com	213-430-1000	430-1001	463
Hotchkiss School 11 Interlaken Rd PO Box 800 .... Lakeville CT 06039 *Web:* www.hotchkiss.org	860-435-3102		622
Hotel & Restaurant Supply Inc 5020 Arundel Rd PO Box 6.................... Meridian MS 39302 *TF:* 800-782-6651 ■ *Web:* www.hnrsupply.com	601-482-7127	482-7170	300
Hotel & Suites Normandin 4700 Pierre-Bertrand Blvd .... Quebec QC G2J1A4 *TF:* 800-463-6721 ■ *Web:* www.hotelnormandin.com	418-622-1611	622-9277	379
Hotel 140 140 Clarendon St.......................Boston MA 02116 *Web:* www.hotel140.com	617-585-5600		379
Hotel 373 Fifth Avenue 373 Fifth Ave ....New York NY 10016 *TF:* 800-315-4642 ■ *Web:* www.373uhotels.com	212-213-3388		707
Hotel 43 981 Grove St..........................Boise ID 83702 *TF:* 800-243-4622 ■ *Web:* www.hotel43.com	208-342-4622	344-5751	379
Hotel 71 71 St Pierre St .... Quebec QC G1K4A4 *TF:* 888-692-1171 ■ *Web:* www.hotel71.ca	418-692-1171		379
Hotel Abri 127 Ellis St .... San Francisco CA 94102 *TF:* 866-778-6169 ■ *Web:* www.hotelabrisf.com	415-392-8800		379
Hotel Adagio 550 Geary St .... San Francisco CA 94102 *TF:* 855-687-7262 ■ *Web:* www.jdvhotels.com	415-775-5000	775-0388	379
Hotel Alex Johnson 523 Sixth St .... Rapid City SD 57701 *Web:* www.alexjohnson.com	605-342-1210		379
Hotel Allegro Chicago 171 W Randolph St............................Chicago IL 60601 *TF:* 800-643-1500 ■ *Web:* www.allegrochicago.com	312-236-0123		379
Hotel Ambassadeur 3401 Blvd Ste-Anne......... Quebec QC G1E3L4 *TF:* 800-363-4619 ■ *Web:* www.hotelambassadeur.ca	418-666-2828	666-2775	379
Hotel Andra 2000 Fourth Ave.......................... Seattle WA 98121 *TF:* 877-448-8600 ■ *Web:* www.hotelandra.com	206-448-8600	441-7140	379
Hotel Andrew Jackson 919 Royal St......... New Orleans LA 70116 *Web:* www.frenchquarterinns.com	504-561-5881		379
Hotel Angeleno 170 N Church Ln............Los Angeles CA 90049 *Web:* hotelangeleno.com	310-476-6411		379
Hotel Astor 956 Washington Ave .... Miami Beach FL 33139 *TF:* 800-933-3306 ■ *Web:* www.hotelastor.com	305-531-8081	531-3193	379
Hotel at Auburn University & Dixon Conference Ctr, The 241 S College St.............................Auburn AL 36830 *TF:* 800-228-2876 ■ *Web:* www.auhcc.com	334-821-8200	826-8746	377
Hotel at Old Town Wichita 830 E First St .... Wichita KS 67202 *TF:* 877-265-3869 ■ *Web:* www.hotelatoldtown.com	316-267-4800	267-4840	379
Hotel Avante 860 E El Camino Real..................Mountain View CA 94040 *TF:* 800-538-1600 ■ *Web:* jdvhotels.com	650-940-1000	968-7870	379
Hotel Beacon 2130 Broadway ....New York NY 10023 *TF:* 800-572-4969 ■ *Web:* www.beaconhotel.com	212-787-1100	724-0839	379
Hotel Bel-Air 701 Stone Canyon Rd..........Los Angeles CA 90077 *TF:* 800-648-4097 ■ *Web:* www.dorchestercollection.com	310-472-1211	276-2251	379
Hotel Bethlehem 437 Main St................. Bethlehem PA 18018 *Web:* www.hotelbethlehem.com	610-625-5000		379
Hotel Bijou 111 Mason St .... San Francisco CA 94102 *TF:* 877-568-2733 ■ *Web:* www.jdvhotels.com	415-771-1200		379
Hotel Blake 500 S Dearborn St ....Chicago IL 60605 *Web:* www.hotelblake.com	312-986-1234		379
Hotel Blue 717 Central Ave NW .... Albuquerque NM 87102 *TF:* 877-878-4868 ■ *Web:* www.thehotelblue.com	505-924-2400		378
Hotel Boulderado 2115 13th St .... Boulder CO 80302 *TF:* 800-433-4344 ■ *Web:* www.boulderado.com	303-442-4344	442-4378	379
Hotel Captain Cook 939 W Fifth Ave .... Anchorage AK 99501 *TF:* 800-843-1950 ■ *Web:* www.captaincook.com	907-276-6000		379
Hotel Carlton 1075 Sutter St.............. San Francisco CA 94109 *Web:* www.jdvhotels.com	415-673-0242		379
Hotel Casa del Mar 1910 Ocean Way........................Santa Monica CA 90405 *Web:* www.hotelcasadelmar.com	310-581-5533		379
Hotel Chateau Bellevue 16 Rue de la Porte .... Quebec QC G1R4M9 *TF:* 877-849-1877 ■ *Web:* www.hoteloldquebec.com/en	418-692-2573	692-4876	379
Hotel Chateau Laurier 1220 Pl George-V Ouest....................... Quebec QC G1R5B8 *TF:* 877-522-8108 ■ *Web:* hotelchateaulaurier.com	418-522-8108	524-8768	379
Hotel Cheribourg 2603 Ch du Parc............. Orford QC J1X8C8 *TF:* 877-845-5344 ■ *Web:* www.hotelsvillegia.com	819-843-3308	843-2639	669
Hotel Classique 2815 Laurier Blvd .... Quebec QC G1V4H3 *TF:* 800-463-1885 ■ *Web:* www.hotelclassique.com	418-658-2793	658-6816	379
Hotel Cleaning Services Inc 9609 N 22nd Ave ....Phoenix AZ 85021 *Web:* www.hotelcleaningservices.com	602-588-0864		192
Hotel Colorado 526 Pine St...........Glenwood Springs CO 81601 *TF:* 800-544-3998 ■ *Web:* www.hotelcolorado.com	970-945-6511	945-7030	379
Hotel Commonwealth 500 Commonwealth Ave.......................Boston MA 02215 *TF:* 866-784-4000 ■ *Web:* www.hotelcommonwealth.com	617-933-5000	266-6888	379
Hotel Congress 311 E Congress St...............Tucson AZ 85701 *TF:* 800-722-8848 ■ *Web:* www.hotelcongress.com	520-622-8848	792-6366	379
Hotel Contessa 306 W Market St ....San Antonio TX 78205 *TF:* 866-435-0900 ■ *Web:* www.thehotelcontessa.com	210-229-9222		379
Hotel Crescent Court 400 Crescent Ct............ Dallas TX 75201 *Web:* www.rosewoodhotels.com	214-871-3200	871-3272	379
Hotel de Anza 233 W Santa Clara St .... San Jose CA 95113 *TF:* 800-843-3700 ■ *Web:* www.destinationhotels.com/hotel-de-anza	408-286-1000	286-0500	379
Hotel De La Monnaie Owners Association Inc 405 Esplanade Ave .... New Orleans LA 70116 *Web:* hoteldelamonnaie.com	504-947-0009		379
Hotel Deca 4507 Brooklyn Ave NE................ Seattle WA 98105 *TF:* 800-899-0251 ■ *Web:* www.hoteldeca.com	206-634-2000		379
Hotel Del Coronado 1500 Orange Ave ....Coronado CA 92118 *TF:* 800-468-3533 ■ *Web:* www.hoteldel.com	619-435-6611		669
Hotel Del Sol 3100 Webster St.............. San Francisco CA 94123 *TF:* 877-433-5765 ■ *Web:* www.jdvhotels.com	415-921-5520		379
Hotel Deluxe 729 SW 15th Ave ....Portland OR 97205 *TF:* 866-895-2094 ■ *Web:* www.hoteldeluxeportland.com	503-219-2094	219-2095	379
Hotel Derek 2525 W Loop S ....Houston TX 77027 *TF:* 866-292-4100 ■ *Web:* www.destinationhotels.com/hotel-derek	713-961-3000	297-4392	379
Hotel Dieu Hospital 166 Brock St............. Kingston ON K7L5G2 *TF:* 855-544-3400 ■ *Web:* www.hoteldieu.com	613-544-3310		374-2
Hotel Drisco 2901 Pacific Ave .... San Francisco CA 94115 *TF:* 800-634-7277 ■ *Web:* hoteldrisco.com	415-346-2880		379
Hotel du Lac 121 Rue Cuttle ....Mont-Tremblant QC J8E1B9 *TF:* 800-567-8341 ■ *Web:* www.hoteldulac.ca/accueil	819-425-2731		669
Hotel du Pont 11th & Market Sts............. Wilmington DE 19801 *TF:* 800-441-9019 ■ *Web:* www.hoteldupont.com	302-594-3100	594-3108	379
Hotel Edison 228 W 47th St...................New York NY 10036 *TF:* 800-637-7070 ■ *Web:* www.edisonhotelnyc.com	212-840-5000		379
Hotel El Convento 100 Cristo St Old San Juan ....San Juan PR 00901 *Web:* www.elconvento.com	787-723-9020		379
Hotel Elegante Event & Conference Ctr 2886 South Cir Dr .... Colorado Springs CO 80906 *TF:* 800-981-4012 ■ *Web:* www.hotelelegante.com	719-576-5900		707
Hotel Elysee 60 E 54th St ....New York NY 10022 *Web:* www.elyseehotel.com	212-753-1066		379

	Phone	Fax	Class
Hotel Encanto de Las Cruces 705 S Telshor Blvd . . . . Las Cruces NM 88011 *TF:* 866-383-0443 ■ *Web:* www.hotelencanto.com	575-522-4300	522-4300	379
Hotel Equities Inc 41 Perimeter Ctr E Ste 510 . . . . Atlanta GA 30346 *Web:* www.hotelequities.com	678-578-4444		378
Hotel Financial Strategies 468 N Camden Dr Ste 200 . . . . Beverly Hills CA 90210 *Web:* www.hotelfinancial.com	310-247-2101		379
Hotel Fusion 140 Ellis St . . . . San Francisco CA 94102 *TF:* 866-753-4244 ■ *Web:* hotelfusionsf.com	415-568-2525		132
Hotel Galvez - A Wyndham Historic Hotel 2024 Seawall Blvd . . . . Galveston TX 77550 *TF:* 800-996-3426 ■ *Web:* www.wyndhamhotels.com/wyndham	409-765-7721		379
Hotel Gault 449 Rue St-Helene St . . . . Montreal QC H2Y2K9 *Web:* www.hotelgault.com	514-904-1616		379
Hotel George 15 E St NW . . . . Washington DC 20001 *TF General:* 800-546-7866 ■ *Web:* www.hotelgeorge.com	202-347-4200	347-4213	379
Hotel Giraffe 365 Pk Ave S at 26th St . . . . New York NY 10016 *Web:* www.hotelgiraffe.com	212-685-7700	685-7771	379
Hotel Grand Pacific 463 Belleville St . . . . Victoria BC V8V1X3 *TF:* 800-663-7550 ■ *Web:* www.hotelgrandpacific.com	250-386-0450	380-4475	379
Hotel Grand Victorian 2325 W Hwy 76 . . . . Branson MO 65616 *TF:* 800-324-8751 ■ *Web:* www.hotelgrandvictorian.com	417-336-2935		379
Hotel Granduca 1080 Uptown Pk Blvd . . . . Houston TX 77056 *TF:* 888-472-6382 ■ *Web:* www.granducahouston.com	713-418-1000		379
Hotel Griffon 155 Steuart St . . . . San Francisco CA 94105 *TF:* 800-321-2201 ■ *Web:* www.hotelgriffon.com	415-495-2100		379
Hotel Group, The (THG) 110 James St Ste 102 . . . . Edmonds WA 98020 *Web:* www.thehotelgroup.com	425-771-1788	672-8280	379
Hotel Hershey, The 100 Hotel Rd . . . . Hershey PA 17033 *TF:* 844-330-1711 ■ *Web:* www.thehotelhershey.com	717-533-2171	534-8887	669
Hotel Highland 1023 20th St S . . . . Birmingham AL 35205 *Web:* www.thehotelhighland.com	205-933-9555	933-6918	379
Hotel Huntington Beach 7667 Ctr Ave . . . . Huntington Beach CA 92647 *Web:* www.hotelhb.com	714-891-0123		379
Hotel Icon 220 Main St . . . . Houston TX 77002 *Web:* www.hotelicon.com	713-224-4266		379
Hotel Indigo San Diego 509 Ninth Ave . . . . San Diego CA 92101 *Web:* www.hotelinsd.com	619-727-4000		379
Hotel Jerome 330 E Main St . . . . Aspen CO 81611 **Fax Area Code:* 970 ■ *TF:* 855-331-7213 ■ *Web:* hoteljerome.aubergeresorts.com	855-331-7213	920-2050*	379
Hotel Kabuki San Francisco 1625 Post St . . . . San Francisco CA 94115 *TF:* 800-533-4567 ■ *Web:* jdvhotels.com	415-922-3200		379
Hotel La Rose 308 Wilson St . . . . Santa Rosa CA 95401 *TF:* 800-527-6738 ■ *Web:* www.hotellarose.com	707-579-3200	579-3247	379
Hotel Le Bleu 370 Fourth Ave . . . . Brooklyn NY 11215 *TF:* 866-427-6073 ■ *Web:* www.hotellebleu.com	718-625-1500		379
Hotel Le Cantlie Suites 1110 Sherbrooke St W . . . . Montreal QC H3A1G9 *TF:* 800-567-1110 ■ *Web:* www.hotelcantlie.com	514-842-2000	844-7808	379
Hotel Le Capitole 972 St Jean St . . . . Quebec QC G1R1R5 *TF:* 800-261-9903 ■ *Web:* www.lecapitole.com	418-694-4444		379
Hotel Le Clos Saint-Louis 69 St Louis St . . . . Quebec QC G1R3Z2 *TF:* 800-461-1311 ■ *Web:* www.clossaintlouis.com	418-694-1311	694-9411	379
Hotel Le Marais 717 Conti St . . . . New Orleans LA 70130 *TF:* 800-935-8740 ■ *Web:* www.hotellemarais.com	504-525-2300		379
Hotel le Priori 15 du Sault-au-Matelot St . . . . Quebec QC G1K3Y7 *TF:* 800-351-3992 ■ *Web:* www.hotellepriori.com	418-692-3992		379
Hotel Le Soleil 567 Hornby St . . . . Vancouver BC V6C2E8 *TF:* 877-632-3030 ■ *Web:* www.hotellesoleil.com	604-632-3000	632-3001	379
Hotel Le St-James 355 St Jacques St . . . . Montreal QC H2Y1N9 *TF:* 866-841-3111 ■ *Web:* www.hotellestjames.com	514-841-3111	841-1232	379
Hotel Lombardy 2019 Pennsylvania Ave NW . . . . Washington DC 20006 *TF:* 800-424-5486 ■ *Web:* www.hotellombardy.com	202-828-2600		379
Hotel Lord-Berri 1199 Berri St . . . . Montreal QC H2L4C6 *TF:* 888-363-0363 ■ *Web:* www.lordberri.com	514-845-9236	849-9855	379
Hotel Los Gatos 210 E Main St . . . . Los Gatos CA 95030 *Web:* www.jdvhotels.com	408-335-1700		379
Hotel Lucia 400 SW Broadway . . . . Portland OR 97205 *TF:* 877-225-1717 ■ *Web:* www.hotellucia.com	503-225-1717	225-1919	379
Hotel Lusso 10 S Post St . . . . Spokane WA 99201 *TF General:* 800-899-1482 ■ *Web:* www.davenporthotelcollection.com	509-455-8888		379
Hotel Madera 1310 New Hampshire Ave NW . . . . Washington DC 20036 *TF:* 800-546-7866 ■ *Web:* www.hotelmadera.com	202-296-7600	293-2476	379
Hotel Majestic 1500 Sutter St . . . . San Francisco CA 94109 *Web:* www.thehotelmajestic.com	415-441-1100	673-7331	379
Hotel Manoir Victoria 44 Cote du Palais . . . . Quebec QC G1R4H8 *TF:* 800-463-6283 ■ *Web:* www.manoir-victoria.com	418-692-1030	692-3822	379
Hotel Maritime Plaza 1155 Guy St . . . . Montreal QC H3H2K5	514-932-1411		379
Hotel Marlowe Cambridge 25 Edwind H Land Blvd . . . . Cambridge MA 02141 *TF:* 800-825-7140 ■ *Web:* www.hotelmarlowe.com	617-868-8000	868-8001	379
Hotel Max 620 Stewart St . . . . Seattle WA 98101 *TF:* 866-833-6299 ■ *Web:* www.hotelmaxseattle.com	206-728-6299	443-5754	379
Hotel Mead 451 E Grand Ave . . . . Wisconsin Rapids WI 54494 *TF:* 800-843-6323 ■ *Web:* www.hotelmead.com	715-423-1500		379
Hotel Mela 120 W 44th St . . . . New York NY 10036 *TF:* 877-452-6352 ■ *Web:* www.hotelmela.com	212-710-7000		379
Hotel Metro 411 E Mason St . . . . Milwaukee WI 53202 *TF:* 877-638-7620 ■ *Web:* www.hotelmetro.com	414-272-1937		379
Hotel Metro 45 W 35th St . . . . New York NY 10001 *Web:* www.hotelmetronyc.com	212-947-2500		379
Hotel ML, The 915 Rt 73 . . . . Mt. Laurel NJ 08054 *TF:* 800-238-0767 ■ *Web:* www.thehotelml.com	856-234-7300		378
Hotel Modera 515 SW Clay St . . . . Portland OR 97201 *Web:* hotelmodera.com	503-484-1084		378
Hotel Monaco Chicago 225 N Wabash Ave . . . . Chicago IL 60601 *TF:* 866-610-0081 ■ *Web:* www.monaco-chicago.com	312-960-8500	960-1883	379
Hotel Monaco Denver 1717 Champa St . . . . Denver CO 80202 *TF:* 800-990-1303 ■ *Web:* www.monaco-denver.com	303-296-1717	296-1818	379
Hotel Monaco Portland 506 SW Washington at Fifth Ave . . . . Portland OR 97204 *TF:* 866-861-9514 ■ *Web:* www.monaco-portland.com	503-222-0001	222-0004	379
Hotel Monaco Salt Lake City 15 West 200 South . . . . Salt Lake City UT 84101 *TF Resv:* 800-805-1801 ■ *Web:* www.monaco-saltlakecity.com	801-595-0000	532-8500	379
Hotel Monaco Seattle 1101 Fourth Ave . . . . Seattle WA 98101 *TF:* 800-715-6513 ■ *Web:* www.monaco-seattle.com	206-621-1770	621-7779	379
Hotel Monte Vista 100 N San Francisco St . . . . Flagstaff AZ 86001 *TF:* 800-545-3068 ■ *Web:* www.hotelmontevista.com	928-779-6971	779-2904	379
Hotel Monteleone 214 Royal St . . . . New Orleans LA 70130 *TF:* 866-338-4684 ■ *Web:* www.hotelmonteleone.com	504-523-3341		379
Hotel Mortagne 1228 Rue Nobel . . . . Boucherville QC J4B5H1 *TF:* 877-655-9966 ■ *Web:* www.hotelmortagne.com	450-655-9966		707
Hotel Murano 1320 Broadway Plaza . . . . Tacoma WA 98402 *TF:* 888-862-3255 ■ *Web:* www.hotelmuranotacoma.com	253-238-8000	591-4105	379
Hotel Nelligan 106 Rue Saint-paul Ouest . . . . Montreal QC H2Y1Z3 *TF:* 800-362-2779 ■ *Web:* hotelnelligan.com	514-788-2040		707
Hotel Nikko San Francisco 222 Mason St . . . . San Francisco CA 94102 *TF:* 866-636-4556 ■ *Web:* www.hotelnikkosf.com	415-394-1111		379
Hotel Northampton 36 King St . . . . NorthHampton MA 01060 *TF:* 800-547-3529 ■ *Web:* www.hotelnorthampton.com	413-584-3100		379
Hotel Ocean 1230 Ocean Dr . . . . Miami Beach FL 33139 *Web:* www.hotelocean.com	305-672-2579		379
Hotel Oceana			
Oceana Santa Monica 849 Ocean Ave . . . . Santa Monica CA 90403 *Web:* www.hoteloceanasantamonica.com	310-393-0486		379
Santa Barbara 202 W Cabrillo Blvd . . . . Santa Barbara CA 93101 *TF:* 800-965-9776 ■ *Web:* hotelmilosantabarbara.com	805-965-4577		379
Hotel of Rivington 107 Rivington St . . . . New York NY 10002 *TF:* 800-915-1537 ■ *Web:* www.hotelonrivington.com	212-475-2600		378
Hotel Omni Mont-Royal 1050 Sherbrooke St W . . . . Montreal QC H3A2R6 *TF:* 800-843-6664 ■ *Web:* www.omnihotels.com	514-284-1110	845-3025	379
Hotel Orrington 1710 Orrington Ave . . . . Evanston IL 60201 *TF:* 888-677-4648 ■ *Web:* www.hotelorrington.com	847-866-8700	866-8724	379
Hotel Pacific 300 Pacific St . . . . Monterey CA 93940 *Web:* www.hotelpacific.com	831-373-5700	373-6921	379
Hotel Palomar Washington DC 2121 P St NW . . . . Washington DC 20037 *Web:* www.hotelpalomar-dc.com	202-448-1800		378
Hotel Park 1125 Ninth St . . . . Sacramento CA 95814	916-441-5361		377
Hotel Park City (HPC) 2001 Pk Ave . . . . Park City UT 84060 *Web:* www.hotelparkcity.com	435-200-2000	940-5001	379
Hotel Phillips 106 W 12th St . . . . Kansas City MO 64105 *TF:* 877-704-5341 ■ *Web:* www.hotelphillips.com	816-221-7000	221-3477	379
Hotel Plaza Athenee 37 E 64th St . . . . New York NY 10065 *TF:* 800-447-8800 ■ *Web:* www.plaza-athenee.com	212-734-9100	772-0958	379
Hotel Plaza Quebec 3031 Laurier Blvd . . . . Sainte-Foy QC G1V2M2 *TF:* 800-567-5276 ■ *Web:* www.hotelsjaro.com/plazaquebec/index-en.aspx	418-658-2727	658-6587	379
Hotel Plaza Real 125 Washington Ave . . . . Santa Fe NM 87501 *TF:* 855-752-9273 ■ *Web:* hotelchimayo.com	505-988-4900	983-9322	379
Hotel Plaza Valleyfield 40 Av Du Centenaire . . . . Salaberry-de-valleyfield QC J6S3L6 *Web:* www.plazavalleyfield.com	450-373-1990		377
Hotel Preston 733 Briley Pkwy . . . . Nashville TN 37217 *TF:* 800-407-4324 ■ *Web:* www.hotelpreston.com	615-361-5900		379
Hotel Pro Staffing LLC 1950 N Park Pl Ste 330 . . . . Atlanta GA 30339 *TF:* 800-889-9770 ■ *Web:* www.gohotelpro.com	770-937-9007		260
Hotel Provincial 1024 Rue Chartres . . . . New Orleans LA 70116 *TF:* 800-535-7922 ■ *Web:* www.hotelprovincial.com	504-581-4995	581-1018	379
Hotel Rex 562 Sutter St . . . . San Francisco CA 94102 *TF Resv:* 800-433-4434 ■ *Web:* jdvhotels.com	415-433-4434		379
Hotel Roanoke & Conference Ctr 110 Shenandoah Ave . . . . Roanoke VA 24016 *TF:* 866-594-4722 ■ *Web:* www.hotelroanoke.com	540-985-5900	853-8264	377
Hotel Rodney 142 Second St . . . . Lewes DE 19958 *TF:* 800-824-8754 ■ *Web:* www.hotelrodneydelaware.com	302-645-6466		379
Hotel Roger Williams 131 Madison Ave . . . . New York NY 10016 *TF Resv:* 888-448-7788 ■ *Web:* www.therogernewyork.com	212-448-7000	448-7007	379
Hotel Rose 50 SW Morrison St . . . . Portland OR 97204 *Web:* www.HotelFifty.com	503-221-0711		377
Hotel Rouge 1315 16th St NW . . . . Washington DC 20036 *TF:* 800-738-1202 ■ *Web:* www.rougehotel.com	202-232-8000	667-9827	379
Hotel Ruby Foo's 7655 Decarie Blvd . . . . Montreal QC H4P2H2 *TF:* 800-361-5419 ■ *Web:* www.hotelrubyfoos.com	514-731-7701		379
Hotel Saint Francis 210 Don Gaspar Ave . . . . Santa Fe NM 87501 *TF:* 800-529-5700 ■ *Web:* www.hotelstfrancis.com	505-983-5700	989-7690	379
Hotel Saint Marie 827 Toulouse St . . . . New Orleans LA 70112 *TF:* 800-366-2743 ■ *Web:* www.hotelstmarie.com	504-561-8951		379
Hotel Saint Pierre 911 Burgundy St . . . . New Orleans LA 70116 *Web:* www.frenchquarterinns.com	504-524-4401		379
Hotel Saint Regis Detroit 3071 W Grand Blvd . . . . Detroit MI 48202 *TF:* 800-449-4167 ■ *Web:* www.hotelstregisdetroit.com	313-873-3000	481-8408	379
Hotel San Carlos 202 N Central Ave . . . . Phoenix AZ 85004 *TF:* 866-253-4121 ■ *Web:* hotelsancarlos.com	602-253-4121	253-6668	379
Hotel Santa Barbara 533 State St . . . . Santa Barbara CA 93101 *TF:* 800-549-9869 ■ *Web:* www.hotelsantabarbara.com	805-957-9300	962-2412	379
Hotel Santa Fe 1501 Paseo de Peralta . . . . Santa Fe NM 87501 *TF:* 855-825-9876 ■ *Web:* www.hotelsantafe.com	505-982-1200		379
Hotel Sepia 3135 Ch St-Louis . . . . Sainte-Foy QC G1W1R9 *TF:* 888-301-6837 ■ *Web:* www.hotelsepia.ca	418-653-4941	653-0774	379

Phone | Fax | Class

Hotel Shangri La 1301 Ocean Ave........... Santa Monica CA 90401 310-394-2791 378
TF: 877-999-1301 ■ *Web:* www.shangrila-hotel.com
Hotel Shelley 844 Collins Ave.............. Miami Beach FL 33139 305-531-3341 674-0811 379
TF: 877-762-3477 ■ *Web:* www.hotelshelley.com
Hotel Solamar 435 Sixth Ave................ San Diego CA 92101 619-819-9500 379
TF: 877-230-0300 ■ *Web:* www.hotelsolamar.com
Hotel Sorella 800 sorella ct.................... Houston TX 77024 713-973-1600 707
Web: www.hotelsorella-citycentre.com
Hotel St Germain 2516 Maple Ave .... Dallas TX 75201 214-871-2516 871-0740 379
Web: www.hotelstgermain.com
Hotel st James Inc 109 W 45th St .... New York NY 10036 212-730-9444 379
Web: hotel-st-james.hotelapp.me
Hotel Strasburg, The
213 S Holliday St.......................... Strasburg VA 22657 540-465-9191 465-4788 379
TF: 800-348-8327 ■ *Web:* www.hotelstrasburg.com
Hotel Teatro 1100 14th St...................... Denver CO 80202 303-228-1100 379
TF: 888-727-1200 ■ *Web:* www.hotelteatro.com
Hotel The Queen Mary
1126 Queens Hwy........................ Long Beach CA 90802 562-435-3511 379
TF: 877-342-0738 ■ *Web:* www.queenmary.com
Hotel Triton 342 Grant Ave................ San Francisco CA 94108 415-394-0500 394-0555 379
TF: 800-800-1299 ■ *Web:* www.hoteltriton.com
Hotel Tybee 1401 Strand Ave................ Tybee Island GA 31328 912-786-7777 379
Web: www.hoteltybee.com
Hotel Universel 2300 Ch St-Foy................ Quebec QC G1V1S5 418-653-5250 653-4486 379
TF: 800-463-4495 ■ *Web:* www.hoteluniversel.qc.ca
Hotel Utica 102 Lafayette St...................... Utica NY 13502 315-724-7829 379
TF: 877-906-1912 ■ *Web:* www.hotelutica.com
Hotel Valencia Riverwalk
150 E Houston St........................ San Antonio TX 78205 210-227-9700 707
TF: 855-596-3387 ■ *Web:* www.hotelvalencia-riverwalk.com
Hotel Valencia Santana Row
355 Santana Row .... San Jose CA 95128 408-551-0010 551-0550 379
TF: 866-842-0100 ■ *Web:* www.hotelvalencia-santanarow.com
Hotel Valley Ho 6850 E Main St .... Scottsdale AZ 85251 480-376-2600 421-7782 379
TF: 866-882-4484 ■ *Web:* www.hotelvalleyho.com
Hotel Victoria 56 Yonge St.................... Toronto ON M5E1G5 416-363-1666 363-7327 379
Web: www.hotelvictoria-toronto.com
Hotel Viking 1 Bellevue Ave................. Newport RI 02840 401-847-3300 379
TF: 800-556-7126 ■ *Web:* www.hotelviking.com
Hotel Vintage Park 1100 Fifth Ave............... Seattle WA 98101 206-624-8000 623-0568 379
TF: 800-853-3914 ■ *Web:* hotelvintage-seattle.com
Hotel Wales 1295 Madison Ave.............. New York NY 10128 212-876-6000 379
TF: 866-925-3746 ■ *Web:* www.hotelwalesnyc.com
Hotel Weatherford, The
23 N Leroux St.......................... Flagstaff AZ 86001 928-779-1919 773-8951 379
Web: www.weatherfordhotel.com
Hotel Wolcott 4 W 31st St.................... New York NY 10001 212-268-2900 563-0096 379
Web: www.wolcott.com
Hotel ZaZa Dallas 2332 Leonard St .... Dallas TX 75201 214-468-8399 468-8397 379
TF: 800-597-8399 ■ *Web:* www.hotelzaza.com
Hotel ZaZa Houston 5701 Main St............ Houston TX 77005 713-526-1991 526-0359 379
TF Resv: 888-880-3244 ■ *Web:* www.hotelzaza.com/houston
Hotel, The 801 Collins Ave .... Miami Beach FL 33139 305-531-2222 531-3222 379
Web: www.thehotelofsouthbeach.com
Hotel-Dieu d'Arthabaska
5 Rue des Hospitalieres .... Victoriaville QC G6P6N2 819-357-2030 758-7281 374-2
Web: www.csssae.qc.ca
Hotel-Dieu de Sorel
400 Ave Hotel-Dieu...................... Sorel-Tracy QC J3P1N5 450-746-6003 746-6082 374-2
Web: fondationhoteldieusorel.org
Hotel-Dieu Grace Hospital
1030 Ouellette Ave......................... Windsor ON N9A1E1 519-973-4411 374-2
Web: www.hdgh.org
Hotelrooms.com Inc
108-18 Queens Blvd.................... Forest Hills NY 11375 718-730-6000 261-4598 397
TF: 800-486-7000 ■ *Web:* www.hotelrooms.com
Hotels at Home Inc 208 Passaic Ave .... Fairfield NJ 07004 973-882-8437 707
Web: www.hotelsathome.com
Hotels Etc Inc
7712 Hampton Pl Bldg 11C .... Loganville GA 30052 877-967-7283 377
TF: 877-967-7283 ■ *Web:* www.hotelsetc.com
Hotels Unlimited Inc
399 Monmouth St...................... East Windsor NJ 08520 609-632-0006 379
HOT-FM 96.3 (CHR)
21 E St Joseph St......................... Indianapolis IN 46204 317-266-9600 328-3870 645-77
Web: hot963.com
HOT-FM 98.3 (Urban) 3202 N Oracle Rd........... Tucson AZ 85705 520-618-2100 645-167
Web: hot983.iheart.com
Hot-Line Freight System Inc
PO Box 205 .... West Salem WI 54669 608-486-1600 486-1601 780
TF: 800-468-4686 ■ *Web:* www.hotlinefreight.com
Hotline to HR Inc
110 Confederation Pkwy..................... Concord ON L4K4T8 416-619-7867 260
HotLink Inc
3130 De La Cruz Blvd Ste 211 .... Santa Clara CA 95054 408-463-6130 7
Web: www.hotlink.com
Hotpadscom PO Box 53104................ Washington DC 20009 202-232-1581 652
TF: 888-876-1992 ■ *Web:* hotpads.com
Hotronic USA Inc 25 Omega Dr............... Williston VT 05495 802-862-7403 863-6519 37
Web: www.hotronic.com
Hotspex Inc 40 Eglinton Ave E Ste 801 .... Toronto ON M4P3A2 416-487-5439 466
Web: www.hotspex.com
Hotwatt Inc 128 Maple St .... Danvers MA 01923 978-777-0070 774-2409* 318
**Fax:* Sales ■ *Web:* www.hotwatt.com
Hotwire Communications LLC
2100 W Cypress Creek Rd Ste 1100......... Bala Cynwyd PA 19004 800-355-5668 224
TF: 800-355-5668 ■ *Web:* hotwirecommunications.com
Hotwire.com
655 Montgomery St Ste 600............. San Francisco CA 94111 415-343-8400 343-8401 773
TF Cust Svc: 866-468-9473 ■ *Web:* www.hotwire.com
HOU (William P Hobby Airport)
7800 Airport Blvd.......................... Houston TX 77061 713-640-3000 641-7703 27
Web: fly2houston.com/hobbyhome
Houchen Bindery Ltd 340 First St .... Utica NE 68456 402-534-2261 626
TF: 800-869-0420 ■ *Web:* www.houchenbindery.com

Houchens Industries Inc
700 Church St .... Bowling Green KY 42101 270-843-3252 345
Web: houchensindustries.com
Houchin Community Blood Bank
5901 Truxtun Ave .... Bakersfield CA 93309 661-327-8541 89
Web: www.hcbb.com
Houdini Museum 1433 N Main Ave............. Scranton PA 18508 570-342-5555 520
Web: www.houdini.org
Houff Transfer Inc 46 Houff Rd .... Weyers Cave VA 24486 540-234-9233 234-9011 780
TF: 800-476-4683 ■ *Web:* www.houff.com
Hougen Manufacturing Inc
3001 Hougen Dr........................ Swartz Creek MI 48473 810-635-7111 635-8277 493
TF Orders: 800-426-7818 ■ *Web:* www.hougen.com
Hough Petroleum Corp 340 Fourth St............ Ewing NJ 08638 609-771-1022 580
TF: 800-400-7154 ■ *Web:* houghpetroleum.com
Houghton Academy 9790 Thayer St............ Houghton NY 14744 585-567-8115 567-8048 622
Web: www.houghtonacademy.org
Houghton Chemical Corp
52 Cambridge St............................. Allston MA 02134 617-254-1010 145
TF: 800-777-2466 ■ *Web:* www.houghton.com
Houghton College
1 Willard Ave PO Box 128 .... Houghton NY 14744 585-567-9200 567-9522* 166
**Fax:* Admissions ■ *TF:* 800-777-2556 ■ *Web:* www.houghton.edu
Houghton County 401 E Houghton Ave.......... Houghton MI 49931 906-482-1150 483-0364 338
TF: 800-315-3593 ■ *Web:* www.houghtoncounty.net
Houghton International Inc
945 Madison Ave PO Box 930 .... Valley Forge PA 19482 610-666-4000 666-0174 3
TF: 888-459-9844 ■ *Web:* www.houghtonintl.com
Houghton Mifflin Harcourt
222 Berkeley St.............................. Boston MA 02116 617-351-5000 637-2
Web: www.eduplace.com
Houle Chevrier Engineering Ltd
32 Steacie Dr Ste .... Kanata ON K2K2A9 613-836-1422 261
Web: hceng.ca
Houlihan Capital LLC
500 W Madison St Ste 2600.................... Chicago IL 60661 312-450-8600 090
Web: www.houlihancapital.com
Houlihan Valuation Advisors Inc
28662 W Northwest Hwy Ste 3........... Lake Barrington IL 60010 847-381-3616 70
Web: www.houlihan-hva.com
Houlihan's Restaurants Inc
8700 State Line Rd Ste 100 .... Leawood KS 66206 913-901-2500 670
Web: www.houlihans.com
Houma Area Convention & Visitors Bureau
114 Tourist Dr.................................. Gray LA 70359 985-868-2732 206
TF: 800-688-2732 ■ *Web:* www.houmatravel.com
Houmas House Plantation & Gardens
40136 Hwy 942 .... Darrow LA 70725 225-473-9380 50-3
Web: www.houmashouse.com
Houma-Terrebonne Chamber of Commerce
6133 Louisiana 311 .... Houma LA 70360 985-876-5600 876-5611 139
TF: 800-649-7346 ■ *Web:* www.houmachamber.com
Hound Ears Lodge & Club
328 Shulls Mill Rd .... Boone NC 28607 828-963-4321 669
TF: 800-243-8652 ■ *Web:* www.houndears.com
Hour, The 1 Selleck St .... Norwalk CT 06851 203-846-3281 532-2
Web: www.thehour.com
Housatonic Community College
900 Lafayette Blvd .... Bridgeport CT 06604 203-332-5000 332-5123* 162
**Fax:* Admissions ■ *TF:* 800-908-9946 ■ *Web:* www.hctc.commnet.edu
Housatonic Meadows State Park
90 Rte 7 N.................................. Sharon CT 06069 860-672-6772 565
Web: www.ct.gov
Housatonic Museum of Art
Housatonic Community College
900 Lafayette Blvd .... Bridgeport CT 06604 203-332-5052 520
Web: www2.housatonic.edu/artmuseum
Housatonic Partners
800 Boylston St Ste 2220...................... Boston MA 02199 617-399-9200 267-5565 792
Web: www.housatonicpartners.com
Hou-scape Inc 17725 Telge Rd .... Cypress TX 77429 281-579-6741 776
Web: www.hou-scape.com
House 1230 Grant Ave.................... San Francisco CA 94133 415-986-8612 671
Web: www.thehse.com
House Chevrolet Co 410 Main St S .... Stewartville MN 55976 507-533-4255 57
Web: housechevrolet.com
Veterans Affairs Committee
335 Cannon Bldg...................... Washington DC 20515 202-225-3527 342-1
Web: veterans.house.gov
House Foods America Corp
7351 Orangewood Ave .... Garden Grove CA 92841 714-901-4350 296-20
TF: 877-333-7077 ■ *Web:* www.house-foods.com
House of Blues
8430 W Sunset Blvd .... West Hollywood CA 90069 310-734-1007 671
Web: www.houseofblues.com
House of Blues Entertainment Inc
7060 Hollywood Blvd....................... Hollywood CA 90028 323-769-4600 181
Web: www.houseofblues.com
House of Blues Orlando
1490 E Lake Buena Vista Dr .... Lake Buena Vista FL 32830 407-934-2583 671
TF: 800-835-7377 ■ *Web:* www.houseofblues.com
House of Brick Technologies LLC
9300 Underwood Ave Ste 300 .... Omaha NE 68114 402-445-0764 180
TF: 877-780-7038 ■ *Web:* www.houseofbrick.com
House of Broel's Historic Mansion & Dollhouse Museum
2220 St Charles Ave..................... New Orleans LA 70130 504-522-2220 520
Web: www.houseofbroel.com
House of Chang
1589 W El Camino Ave.................... Sacramento CA 95833 916-925-2138 671
House of Dynasty 7550 Telegraph Rd.......... Alexandria VA 22315 703-922-5210 671
Web: www.houseofdynasty.com
House of Flavors Inc
110 N William St .... Ludington MI 49431 231-845-7369 845-7371 380
TF: 800-930-7740 ■ *Web:* www.houseofflavors.com
House of Hunan 18 Public Sq Ste 1 .... Medina OH 44256 330-722-1899 671
Web: thehouseofhunan.com
House of India 8501 Delmar Blvd .... Saint Louis MO 63124 314-567-6850 671
Web: www.hoistl.com

Name / Address	City	State	Zip	Phone	Fax	Class
House of Ing 4113 S Cedar St *Web:* www.houseofing.com	Lansing	MI	48910	517-393-4848	393-6868	671
House of Packaging Inc 2225 Via Cerro Ste B *Web:* www.hopbox.com	Riverside	CA	92509	626-369-3371		101
House of Prime Rib 1906 Van Ness Ave *Web:* houseofprimerib.net	San Francisco	CA	94109	415-885-4605		671
House of Raeford Farms Inc 520 E Central Ave *Web:* www.houseofraeford.com	Raeford	NC	28376	910-875-5161		619
House of Schwan Inc 3636 Comotara St *Web:* wichitabeer.com	Wichita	KS	67226	316-636-9100		81-1
House of Shaw 227 Dorris Pl	Stockton	CA	95204	209-948-4300		671
House of Siam 151 S Second St *Web:* houseofsiamsanjose.com	San Jose	CA	95113	408-295-3397		671
House of Tang 114 River St *TF:* 800-442-1162 ■ *Web:* houseoftang.com	Montpelier	VT	05602	802-223-6020		671
House of the Seven Gables 115 Derby St *Web:* www.7gables.org	Salem	MA	01970	978-744-0991	741-4350	50-3
House of Tricks 114 E Seventh St *TF:* 800-346-3049 ■ *Web:* www.houseoftricks.com	Tempe	AZ	85281	480-968-1114	968-0080	671
House of Webster Inc, The 1013 N Second St *Web:* www.houseofwebster.com	Rogers	AR	72756	479-636-4640		345
House of, The Good Shepherd, The 1550 Champlin Ave *Web:* www.hgs-utica.com	Utica	NY	13502	315-235-7600		48-15
House Park & Dobratz Pc 605 W 47th St Ste 301 *Web:* www.hpdco.com	Kansas City	MO	64112	816-931-3393	931-9636	2
House-Autry Mills Inc 7000 US Hwy 301 S *TF:* 800-849-0802 ■ *Web:* www.house-autry.com	Four Oaks	NC	27524	800-849-0802		296-23
House-Hasson Hardware Inc 3125 Water Plant Rd *TF:* 800-333-0520 ■ *Web:* www.househasson.com	Knoxville	TN	37914	865-525-0471		351
HouseLens Inc 650 Rundle Ave *TF:* 888-552-3851 ■ *Web:* houselens.com	Nashville	TN	37210	888-552-3851		5
HouseMaster 92 E Main St Ste 301 *TF:* 800-526-3939 ■ *Web:* www.housemaster.com	Somerville	NJ	08876	732-469-6565	469-7405	365
Houser & Allison APC 9970 Research Dr *Web:* www.houser-law.com	Irvine	CA	92618	949-679-1111		428
Housh-the Home Energy Experts 18 S Main St *TF:* 800-793-6374 ■ *Web:* www.houshhomeenergy.com	Monroe	OH	45050	513-793-6374		610
Housing Assistance Council (HAC) 1025 Vermont Ave NW Ste 606 *TF:* 866-234-2689 ■ *Web:* www.ruralhome.org	Washington	DC	20005	202-842-8600	347-3441	48-5
Housing Authority Risk Retention Group Inc PO Box 189 *TF:* 800-873-0242 ■ *Web:* www.housingcenter.com	Cheshire	CT	06410	203-272-8220		390
Housing Data Systems 750 W City Hwy 16 PO Box 883 *Web:* www.housingdatasystems.com	West Salem	WI	54669	608-786-2366		179
Housley Communications Inc 3550 S Bryant Blvd *Web:* housleygroup.com	San Angelo	TX	76903	325-944-9905		186
Houston Academy of Medicine - Texas Medical Ctr 1133 John Freeman Blvd *Web:* www.library.tmc.edu	Houston	TX	77030	713-795-4200	790-7052	434-1
Houston Advanced Research Ctr (HARC) 4800 Research Forest Dr *Web:* www.harcresearch.org	The Woodlands	TX	77381	281-364-6000	363-7914	668
Houston Apartment Association Inc 4810 Westway Park Blvd *Web:* www.haaonline.org	Houston	TX	77041	713-595-0300		138
Houston Arboretum & Nature Ctr 4501 Woodway Dr *TF:* 866-510-7219 ■ *Web:* www.houstonarboretum.org	Houston	TX	77024	713-681-8433		50-5
Houston Area Safety Council 1301 W 13th St *TF:* 888-955-7233 ■ *Web:* www.hasc.com	Deer Park	TX	77536	281-476-9900		138
Houston Arts Alliance 3201 Allen Pkwy Ste 250 *Web:* www.houstonartsalliance.com	Houston	TX	77019	713-527-9330		720
Houston Asset Management Inc 1800 W Loop S *Web:* www.houstonassetmgmt.com	Houston	TX	77027	713-629-1534		690
Houston Astros Minute Maid Pk 501 Crawford St *TF:* 800-771-2303 ■ *Web:* houston.astros.mlb.com	Houston	TX	77002	713-259-8000		713
Houston Ballet 601 Preston St *TF:* 800-828-2787 ■ *Web:* www.houstonballet.org	Houston	TX	77002	713-523-6300	523-4038	573-1
Houston Baptist University 7502 Fondren Rd **Fax:* Admissions ■ *TF Admissions:* 800-969-3210 ■ *Web:* www.hbu.edu	Houston	TX	77074	281-649-3000	649-3217*	166
Houston Business Journal 1233 W Loop S Ste 1300 **Fax:* Edit ■ *TF:* 800-729-1906 ■ *Web:* www.bizjournals.com	Houston	TX	77027	713-688-8811	963-0482*	457-5
Houston Chronicle 801 Texas Ave *TF:* 800-735-3800 ■ *Web:* www.chron.com	Houston	TX	77002	713-362-7171	362-6806	532-2
Houston City Hall 901 Bagby St *Web:* www.houstontx.gov	Houston	TX	77002	713-247-1000	247-2355	337
Houston Coast Guard Air Station 1178 Ellington Field *Web:* www.uscg.mil/d8/airstahouston	Houston	TX	77034	713-578-3000		158
Houston Comets 1730 Jefferson St **Fax:* Hum Res ■ *Web:* www.wnba.com	Houston	TX	77003	713-739-7442	739-7709*	714-2
Houston Community College						
Central College 3100 Main St *Web:* central.hccs.edu	Houston	TX	77002	713-718-6000	718-7617	162
NortheastCollege 4638 Airline Dr *Web:* www.hccs.edu	Houston	TX	77022	713-718-8100	718-7500	162
Southwest College 3100 Main St *Web:* southwest.hccs.edu	Houston	TX	77002	713-718-2000		162
Houston County PO Box 370 *TF:* 800-275-8777 ■ *Web:* www.co.houston.tx.us	Crockett	TX	75835	936-544-3255	544-8061	338
Houston County 4725 E Main St PO Box 603 *Web:* www.houstoncochamber.com	Erin	TN	37061	931-289-3141		338
Houston County 200 Carl Vinson Pkwy *Web:* www.houstoncountyga.com	Warner Robins	GA	31088	478-542-2115	923-5697	338
Houston Crating Inc 18941 Aldine Westfield *Web:* www.houstoncrating.com	Houston	TX	77073	281-443-3222	443-3234	549
Houston Dynamic Service Inc 8150 Lawndale *Web:* www.houstondynamic.com	Houston	TX	77012	713-928-6200		757
Houston Dynamo 1001 Avenida de las Americas Ste 200 *Web:* www.houstondynamo.com	Houston	TX	77010	713-276-7500		717
Houston Endowment Inc 600 Travis St Ste 6400 *TF:* 800-591-9663 ■ *Web:* www.houstonendowment.org	Houston	TX	77002	713-238-8100	238-8101	303
Houston Fire Museum 2403 Milam St *Web:* www.houstonfiremuseum.org	Houston	TX	77006	713-524-2526	520-7566	520
Houston Foam Plastics Inc 2019 Brooks St *Web:* www.houstonfoam.com	Houston	TX	77026	713-224-3484	224-5511	601
Houston Food Bank, The 535 Portwall St *TF:* 866-384-4277 ■ *Web:* www.houstonfoodbank.org	Houston	TX	77029	713-223-3700		324
Houston Forward Times 4411 ALMEDA *Web:* forwardtimes.com	Houston	TX	77004	713-526-4727	526-3170	532-4
Houston Fuel Oil Terminal Co 16642 Jacintoport Blvd *TF:* 800-324-3755 ■ *Web:* www.hfotco.com	Houston	TX	77015	281-452-3390	452-6306	581
Houston Graduate School of Theology 4300-C W Bellfort Blvd *Web:* www.hgst.edu	Houston	TX	77035	713-942-9505	942-9506	167-3
Houston Grand Opera 510 Preston St *TF:* 800-626-7372 ■ *Web:* www.houstongrandopera.org	Houston	TX	77002	713-546-0200		573-2
Houston Grinding & Manufacturing Inc 3544 W 12th St	Houston	TX	77008	713-869-3573		641
Houston Harris Div Patrol Inc 6420 Richmond Ave *TF:* 877-975-9922 ■ *Web:* www.hhdpi.com	Houston	TX	77057	713-975-9922		693
Houston Independent School District 228 McCarty St *TF:* 800-446-2821 ■ *Web:* www.houstonisd.org	Houston	TX	77029	713-556-6000	556-6006	685
Houston Intercontinental Chamber of Commerce 250 N Sam Houston Pkwy E Ste 200 *Web:* www.houstonicc.org	Houston	TX	77060	281-408-0866		139
Houston LifeStyle Magazine 10707 Corporate Dr Ste 170 *TF:* 866-505-4456 ■ *Web:* www.houstonlifestyles.com	Stafford	TX	77477	281-240-2445	240-5079	457-22
Houston Livestock Show & Rodeo Inc NRG Ctr Three NRG Pk *Web:* www.rodeohouston.com	Houston	TX	77054	832-667-1000		446
Houston Maritime Museum 2204 Dorrington St *Web:* houstonmaritime.org	Houston	TX	77030	713-666-1910		520
Houston Medical Ctr 1601 Watson Blvd *Web:* www.hhc.org	Warner Robins	GA	31093	478-922-4281		374-3
Houston Medical Records Inc 2211 Norfolk St Ste 950 *Web:* www.houmedicalbilling.com	Houston	TX	77098	713-850-1190		180
Houston Mfg Specialty Company Inc 9909 Wallisville Rd *TF:* 800-231-6030 ■ *Web:* www.houmfg.com	Houston	TX	77013	713-675-7400		326
Houston Motorsports Park 11620 N Lake Houston Pkwy *TF:* 800-668-6775 ■ *Web:* www.houstonmotorsportspark.com	Houston	TX	77044	281-458-1972	458-2836	515
Houston Museum of Decorative Arts 201 High St *Web:* thehoustonmuseum.com	Chattanooga	TN	37403	423-267-7176		520
Houston Museum of Natural Science 5555 Hermann Pk Dr *Web:* www.hmns.org	Houston	TX	77030	713-639-4629		520
Houston National Cemetery 10410 Veterans Memorial Dr *Web:* www.cem.va.gov	Houston	TX	77038	281-447-8686	447-0580	136
Houston Newspapers- Herald & The Messenger 113 N Grand Ave *TF:* 800-568-1927 ■ *Web:* www.houstonherald.com	Houston	MO	65483	417-967-2000		532-3
Houston Northwest Chamber of Commerce (HNW) 3920 Cypress Creek Pkwy *Web:* www.houstonnwchamber.org	Houston	TX	77068	281-440-4160	440-5302	139
Houston Northwest Medical Ctr 710 FM 1960 W *Web:* www.hnmc.com	Houston	TX	77090	281-440-1000		374-3
Houston Numismatic Exchange Inc 2486 Times Blvd *TF:* 800-561-3357 ■ *Web:* www.hnex.com	Houston	TX	77005	713-528-2135		459
Houston Pilots 203 Deerwood Glen Dr Ste 118 *Web:* www.houston-pilots.com	Deer Park	TX	77017	713-645-9620		465
Houston Pipe Benders 14500 E Hardy Rd *Web:* www.hpbenders.com	Houston	TX	77039	281-449-8241		595
Houston Press 1621 Milam St Ste 100 *TF:* 877-926-8300 ■ *Web:* www.houstonpress.com	Houston	TX	77002	713-280-2400	280-2444	532-5
Houston Production Guide Film 2054 W Main St *Web:* www.houstonproductionguide.com	Houston	TX	77098	713-523-5387		5
Houston Public Library 500 McKinney St *Web:* www.houstonlibrary.org	Houston	TX	77002	832-393-1313	393-1324	434-3
Houston Raceway Park 2525 FM 565 S *Web:* www.royalpurpleraceway.com	Baytown	TX	77523	281-383-7223		515
Houston Rockets 1510 Polk St **Fax:* Hum Res ■ *TF:* 866-648-4668 ■ *Web:* www.nba.com/rockets	Houston	TX	77002	713-758-7200	758-7396*	714-1
Houston Service Industries Inc 7901 Hansen Rd *TF:* 800-725-2291 ■ *Web:* www.hsiblowers.com	Houston	TX	77061	713-947-1623	947-6409	18

	Phone	Fax	Class
Houston Symphony Orchestra 615 Louisiana St Ste 102 .... Houston TX 77002 *Web:* www.houstonsymphony.org	713-224-4240		573-3
Houston Texans 2 NRG Pk .... Houston TX 77054 *TF:* 800-745-3000 ■ *Web:* www.houstontexans.com	832-667-2002		715-3
Houston Trust Co 1001 Fannin St Ste 700 .... Houston TX 77002 *Web:* www.houstontrust.com	713-651-9400		401
Houston West Chamber of Commerce 10370 Richmond Ave Ste 125 .... Houston TX 77042 *Web:* www.hwcoc.org	713-785-4922	785-4944	139
Houston Wiper & Mill Supply Co 1234 Kress St .... Houston TX 77020 *Web:* www.houstonwiperandmill.com	713-672-0571	673-7637	508
Houston Wire & Cable Co (HWC) 10201 N Loop E .... Houston TX 77029 *TF:* 800-468-9473 ■ *Web:* www.houwire.com	713-609-2100	609-2101	246
Houston World Trade Ctr *Greater Houston Partnership* 701 Avenida de las Americas Ste 900 .... Houston TX 77010 *Web:* www.houston.org	713-844-3600		822
Houston Zoo Inc 1513 Cambridge .... Houston TX 77030 *TF:* 800-828-2787 ■ *Web:* www.houstonzoo.org	713-533-6500		823
Houston's 147 S Beverly Dr .... Beverly Hills MO 90212 *TF:* 800-230-9787 ■ *Web:* hillstone.com	800-230-9787		671
Houston's 215 S Orlando Ave .... Winter Park FL 32789 *Web:* www.hillstone.com	407-740-4005		671
Houstonian Hotel Club & Spa 111 N Post Oak Ln .... Houston TX 77024 *TF Resv:* 800-231-2759 ■ *Web:* www.houstonian.com	713-680-2626	680-2992	669
Houston-Pasadena Apache Oil Company LP 5136 Spencer Hwy .... Pasadena TX 77505 *TF:* 800-248-6388 ■ *Web:* www.apacheoilcompany.com	800-248-6388		581
HoustonStreet Inc 1 New Hampshire Ave Ste 207 .... Portsmouth NH 03801 *Web:* www.houstonstreet.com	603-766-8716		600
HOV Services LLC 1305 Stephenson Hwy Ste .... Royal Oak MI 48073 *Web:* www.hovservices.com	248-837-7100		631
hovelstay.com LLC 121 W Lexington Dr .... Glendale CA 91203 *Web:* hovelstay.com	818-480-5770		393
Hovenweep National Monument McElmo Rt .... Cortez CO 81321 *Web:* www.nps.gov/hove	970-562-4282	562-4283	564
Hover Networks Inc 40 Gardenville Pkwy Ste 102 .... Buffalo NY 14224 *Web:* www.hovernetworks.com	716-650-5650		224
Hoveround Corp 2151 Whitfield Industrial Way .... Sarasota FL 34243 *TF:* 800-542-7236 ■ *Web:* www.hoveround.com	941-739-6200		477
Hovione LLC 40 Lake Dr .... East Windsor NJ 08520 *Web:* www.hovione.com	609-918-2600		231
Hovnanian Enterprises Inc 1806 S Highland Ave .... Lombard IL 60148 *Web:* khov.com	630-953-2222		187
HOW Design Magazine 4700 E Galbraith Rd .... Cincinnati OH 45236 *TF Cust Svc:* 800-333-1115 ■ *Web:* www.howdesign.com	513-531-2690		457-2
Howard & Howard Attorneys Pc 2950 S State St Ste 360 .... Ann Arbor MI 48104 *Web:* howardandhoward.com	248-645-1483		428
Howard Bros Florists 8700 S Pennsylvania Ave .... Oklahoma City OK 73159 *TF:* 800-648-0524 ■ *Web:* www.howardbrothersflorist.com	405-632-4747	632-1672	292
Howard College 1001 Birdwell Ln .... Big Spring TX 79720 *Fax: Admissions ■ *TF:* 877-090-3833 ■ *Web:* www.howardcollege.edu	432-264-5000	264-5082*	162
Southwest Collegiate Institute for the Deaf 3200 Ave C .... Big Spring TX 79720 *Fax: Admissions ■ *TF:* 800-421-3481 ■ *Web:* www.howardcollege.edu	432-264-3700	264-3707*	162
Howard Community College 10901 Little Patuxent Pkwy .... Columbia MD 21044 *Fax: Admissions ■ *Web:* www.howardcc.edu	410-772-4800	876-8855*	162
Howard County 300 Main St .... Big Spring TX 79720 *Web:* www.co.howard.tx.us	432-264-2213	264-2215	338
Howard County 3430 Courthouse Dr .... Ellicott City MD 21043	410-313-2001	313-3297	338
Howard County 1 Courthouse Sq .... Fayette MO 65248 *Web:* mocounties.com/howard-county.php	660-248-2284		338
Howard County 104 N Buckeye St Ste 114 .... Kokomo IN 46901 *TF:* 800-913-6050 ■ *Web:* www.howardcountyin.gov	765-456-2204	456-2267	338
Howard County 421 N Main St .... Nashville AR 71852 *Web:* howardcountytaxcollection.com	870-845-7508	845-7505	338
Howard County 830 Hardy Rd PO Box 25 .... Saint Paul NE 68873 *Web:* www.howardcounty.ne.gov	308-754-4343	754-4266	338
Howard County Central Library 10375 Little Patuxent Pkwy .... Columbia MD 21044 *Web:* www.hclibrary.org	410-313-7800	313-7864	434-3
Howard County Chamber of Commerce 5560 Sterrett Pl Ste 105 .... Columbia MD 21044 *Web:* www.howardchamber.com	410-730-4111	730-4584	139
Howard County General Hospital 5755 Cedar Ln .... Columbia MD 21044 *TF:* 866-323-4615 ■ *Web:* www.hopkinsmedicine.org	410-740-7890	740-7610	374-3
Howard County Library 500 S Main St .... Big Spring TX 79720	432-264-2260		434-3
Howard County Tourism Council 8267 Main St Side Entrance .... Ellicott City MD 21043 *TF:* 866-313-6300 ■ *Web:* www.howardcountymd.gov	410-313-1900		206
Howard Cunningham Houchin & Turner LLP 6901 Quaker Ave Ste 100 .... Lubbock TX 79413 *Web:* hchtcpa.com	806-799-6699		2
Howard Design Group 707 State Rd Ste 103 .... Princeton NJ 08540 *TF:* 800-622-3542 ■ *Web:* howarddesign.com	609-924-1106		344
Howard E. Nyhart Company Inc, The 8415 Allison Pointe Blvd Ste 300 .... Indianapolis IN 46250 *TF:* 800-428-7106 ■ *Web:* www.nyhart.com	317-845-3500		260
Howard Electric Co-op 205 Hwy 5 & 240 N PO Box 391 .... Fayette MO 65248 *TF:* 877-352-0122 ■ *Web:* www.howardelectric.com	660-248-3311		245
Howard Engineering Company Inc 687 Wooster St PO Box 1315 .... Naugatuck CT 06770 *Web:* www.howardengineering.com	203-729-5213	729-3843	454
Howard F Baer Inc 1301 Foster Ave .... Nashville TN 37210 *TF:* 800-447-7430 ■ *Web:* hbitransport.com	615-255-7351	726-1529	780
Howard Fischer Assoc International 1800 Kennedy Blvd Ste 700 .... Philadelphia PA 19103 *Web:* www.hfischer.com	215-568-8363	568-4815	266
Howard Greeley Rural Power 422 Howard Ave PO Box 105 .... Saint Paul NE 68873 *TF:* 800-280-4962 ■ *Web:* www.howardgreeleyrppd.com	308-754-4457	754-4230	245
Howard Hughes Medical Institute 4000 Jones Bridge Rd .... Chevy Chase MD 20815 *Web:* www.hhmi.org	301-215-8500	215-8863	668
Howard Immel Inc 1820 Radisson St .... Green Bay WI 54302 *Web:* www.immel-builds.com	920-468-8208		186
Howard Industries Inc 3225 Pendorff Rd .... Laurel MS 39440 *TF:* 800-663-5598 ■ *Web:* www.howard-ind.com	601-425-3151	649-8090	767
Howard Leight Industries 7828 Waterville Rd .... San Diego CA 92154 *Fax Area Code: 401 ■ *TF:* 800-430-5490 ■ *Web:* www.howardleight.com	800-430-5490	232-3110*	477
Howard Lumber Co 475 Columbia Industrial Blvd .... Evans GA 30809 *Web:* howardlumbercompany.com	706-868-8400		191-3
Howard McLeod Correctional Ctr 1970 E Whippoorwill Ln .... Atoka OK 74525 *Web:* www.ok.gov	580-889-6651	889-2264	213
Howard Miller Clock Co 860 E Main Ave .... Zeeland MI 49464 *Web:* www.howardmiller.com	616-772-7277	772-1670	153
Howard Payne University 1000 Fisk Ave .... Brownwood TX 76801 *TF:* 800-950-8465 ■ *Web:* www.hputx.edu	325-646-2502		166
Howard Precision Metals Inc PO Box 240127 .... Milwaukee WI 53224 *TF:* 800-444-0311 ■ *Web:* www.howardprecision.com	414-355-9611	355-2637	492
Howard Price Turf Equipment Inc 18155 Edison Ave .... Chesterfield MO 63005 *TF:* 800-770-2777 ■ *Web:* www.howardpriceturf.com	636-532-7000	532-0201	429
Howard R Green Co 8710 Earhart Ln SW .... Cedar Rapids IA 52404 *Web:* www.hrgreen.com	319-841-4000		261
Howard Regional Health System Main Campus (HRHS) 3500 S Lafountain St .... Kokomo IN 46902 *Web:* ecommunity.com/howard	765-453-0702		374-3
Howard Regional Health System West Campus Specialty Hospital 829 N Dixon Rd .... Kokomo IN 46901 *TF:* 800-344-4067 ■ *Web:* ecommunity.com/howard	765-452-6700		374-6
Howard Sheppard Inc PO Box 797 .... Sandersville GA 31082 *TF:* 800-846-1726 ■ *Web:* www.howardsheppard.com	478-552-5127		780
Howard Simon & Associates Inc 304 Saunders Rd .... Riverwoods IL 60015 *TF:* 800-424-7526 ■ *Web:* hsimon.com	847-945-0340		463
Howard Systems International 2777 Summer St .... Stamford CT 06905 *Fax Area Code: 203 ■ *TF:* 800-326-4860 ■ *Web:* www.howardsystems.com	800-326-4060	324-7722*	180
Howard Ternes Packaging Co 12285 Dixie .... Redford MI 48239 *Web:* www.ternespackaging.com	313-531-5867	531-5868	546
Howard Uniform Co 1915 Annapolis Rd .... Baltimore MD 21230 *TF:* 800-628-8299 ■ *Web:* www.howarduniform.com	410-727-3086	727-3142	155-19
Howard University 2400 Sixth St NW .... Washington DC 20059 *Fax: Admissions ■ *TF:* 800-822-6363 ■ *Web:* www.howard.edu	202-806-6100	806-4465*	166
Howard University College of Medicine 520 W St NW .... Washington DC 20059 *Web:* healthsciences.howard.edu	202-806-6270	806-7934	167-2
Howard University Hospital 2041 Georgia Ave .... Washington DC 20060 *Web:* huhealthcare.com	202-865-6100	865-1360	374-3
Howard University School of Divinity 1400 Shepherd St NE .... Washington DC 20017 *TF:* 800-822-6363 ■ *Web:* www.howard.edu	202-806-0500	806-0711	167-3
Howard University School of Law 2900 Van Ness St NW .... Washington DC 20008 *Fax: Admissions ■ *TF:* 800-829-9019 ■ *Web:* www.law.howard.edu	202-806-8000	806-8162*	167-1
Howard, Kohn, Sprague & FitzGerald LLP 237 Buckingham St .... Hartford CT 06126 *Web:* www.hksflaw.com	860-525-3101		428
HowardSoft 7852 Ivanhoe Ave .... La Jolla CA 92037 *Web:* www.howardsoft.com	858-454-0121		178-9
Howco Metals Management 9611 Telge Rd .... Houston TX 77095 *TF:* 800-392-7720 ■ *Web:* www.howcogroup.com	281-649-8800		307
Howden Buffalo Inc 7909 Parklane Rd Ste 300 .... Columbia SC 29223 *Fax Area Code: 866 ■ *TF:* 866-757-0908 ■ *Web:* www.howden.com	803-741-2700	757-0908*	18
Howe Barnes Hoefer & Arnett Inc 222 S Riverside Plaza 7th Fl .... Chicago IL 60606 *Web:* www.howebarnes.com	312-655-3000		690
Howe Caverns Inc 255 Discovery Dr .... Howes Cave NY 12092 *Web:* www.howecaverns.com	518-296-8900		129
Howe Corp 1650 N Elston Ave .... Chicago IL 60642 *Web:* www.howecorp.com	773-235-0200	235-1530	664
Howe Electric Inc 4682 E Olive Ave .... Fresno CA 93702 *Web:* www.howe-electric.com	559-255-8992	255-9745	189-4
Howe Library 13 S St .... Hanover NH 03755 *Web:* www.thehowe.org	603-643-4120		434-3
Howe Military School PO Box 240 .... Howe IN 46746 *TF:* 888-462-4693 ■ *Web:* howemilitary.org	260-562-2131	562-3678	622
Howell Area Chamber of Commerce (HACC) 123 E Washington St .... Howell MI 48843 *TF:* 800-292-9555 ■ *Web:* www.howell.org	517-546-3920	546-4115	139
Howell Care Center 3003 W Grand River Ave .... Howell MI 48843	517-546-4210	546-7661	450
Howell Chamber of Commerce 103 W Second St PO Box 196 .... Howell NJ 07731 *Web:* www.howellchamber.com	732-363-4114	363-8747	139

Name / Address	City	State	Zip	Phone	Fax	Class
Howell County 35 Court Sq Web: www.howellcounty.net	West Plains	MO	65775	417-256-2591	256-2512	338
Howell Furniture Galleries Inc 6095 Folsom Dr Web: howellfurniture.com	Beaumont	TX	77706	409-832-2544		321
Howell Instruments Inc 8945 S Fwy TF: 800-433-2873 ■ Web: www.howellinst.com	Fort Worth	TX	76140	817-336-7411	336-7874	472
Howell Tractor & Equipment LLC 480 Blaine St TF: 800-852-8816 ■ Web: www.howelltractor.com	Gary	IN	46406	800-852-8816		791
HOWELL'S FLORAL 6030 NE 112th Ave Web: www.howells-craftland.com	Portland	OR	97220	503-255-2001		44
Howell's Motor Freight Inc PO Box 12308 TF: 800-444-0585 ■ Web: www.howellsmotor.com	Roanoke	VA	24024	540-966-3200		780
Howell-Oregon Electric Co-op Inc 6327 N US Hwy 63 PO Box 649 TF: 855-385-9903 ■ Web: www.hoecoop.org	West Plains	MO	65775	417-256-2131		245
Hower House Museum - University of Akron 60 Fir Hill Web: www3.uakron.edu/howerhse	Akron	OH	44325	330-972-6909	384-2635	520
Howerton Engineering & Surveying 404 Main St Web: www.howertoneng.com	Greenup	KY	41144	606-473-5684		256
Howes & Jefferies Realtors 345 Fifth Ave S Web: howesandjefferies.com	Clinton	IA	52732	563-242-3265		652
HowGood Inc 93 Commercial St TF: 888-601-3015 ■ Web: howgood.com	Brooklyn	NY	11222	888-601-3015		463
Howick Associates 111 N Fairchild St TF: 800-292-4519 ■ Web: www.howickassociates.com	Madison	WI	53703	608-233-3377		463
Howland Capital Management Inc 75 Federal St Ste 1100 Web: www.howlandcapital.com	Boston	MA	02110	617-357-9110	357-5540	401
Howmet Castings 1 Misco Dr Web: www.alcoa.com	Whitehall	MI	49461	231-894-5686	894-7607	308
Howmet TMP Corp 3960 S Marginal Rd Web: www.arconic.com	Cleveland	OH	44114	216-391-3885	391-4842	757
Howred Corp 7887 San Felipe St Ste 122 TF: 800-535-5053 ■ Web: www.howred.com	Houston	TX	77063	713-781-3980	784-3985	191-4
Howrey LLP 1299 Pennsylvania Ave NW	Washington	DC	20004	202-383-6596		428
Howse Implement Company Inc 2013 Hwy 184 E Web: howseimplement.com	Laurel	MS	39443	601-428-0841	425-4900	273
Howson & Simon LLP 101 Ygnacio Valley Rd Ste 310	Walnut Creek	CA	94596	925-977-9060		2
Hoxie House 18 Water St	Sandwich	MA	02563	508-888-1173		50-3
Hoxie Implement Company Inc 933 Oak Ave PO Box 587 Web: www.hoxieimplement.com	Hoxie	KS	67740	785-675-3201	675-3438	274
Hoxworth Blood Ctr University of Cincinnati Medical Ctr 3130 Highland Ave ML0055 TF: 800-265-1515 ■ Web: www.hoxworth.org	Cincinnati	OH	45267	513-558-1200	558-1209	89
Hoya Holdings Inc 3285 Scott Blvd TF: 800-836-2788 ■ Web: www.hoya.co.jp	Santa Clara	CA	95054	408-654-2300		542
HOYA Optical Laboratories Inc 651 E Corporate Dr Web: www.hoyavision.com	Lewisville	TX	75057	972-221-4141		543
Hoyer Steny H (Rep D - MD) 1705 Longworth Bldg Web: hoyer.house.gov	Washington	DC	20515	202-225-4131	225-4300	342-2
Hoyle Holt Allied Services Co 710 W Broadway	Ardmore	OK	73401	580-223-5434		390
Hoyman Dobson & Company PA 215 Baytree Dr Web: www.hoyman.com	Melbourne	FL	32940	321-255-0088		2
Hoyt 543 N Neil Armstrong Rd TF: 800-474-8733 ■ Web: hoyt.com	Salt Lake City	UT	84116	801-363-2990	537-1470	710
Hoyt Arboretum 4000 SW Fairview Blvd Web: www.hoytarboretum.org	Portland	OR	97221	503-865-8733		97
Hoyt Group, The 760 US Hwy One The Hoyt Ctr Ste 300 Web: hoytgroup.org	North Palm Beach	FL	33408	561-694-7621		463
Hoyt Sherman Place 1501 Woodland Ave Web: www.hoytsherman.org	Des Moines	IA	50309	515-244-0507		520
Hoyt, Shepston & Sciaroni Inc 161a Starlite St # B TF: 800-321-8747 ■ Web: www.hoyt-shepston.com	South San Francisco	CA	94080	650-952-6930		449
Hoyt-Barnum House, The 713 Bedford St Web: www.stamfordhistory.org/hbh.htm	Stamford	CT	06903	203-329-1183	322-1607	50-3
HP (Hewlett-Packard (Canada) Ltd) 5150 Spectrum Way TF: 888-447-4636 ■ Web: welcome.hp.com	Mississauga	ON	L4W5G1	905-206-4725		173-2
HP Hotels Inc 1 Chase Corporate Dr Ste 210 Web: hp-hotels.com	Birmingham	AL	35244	205-879-7004		379
Hp Industries Inc 415 W Hickory St Web: hpind.com	Kirksville	MO	63501	660-627-2000		506
H-P Products Inc 512 W Gorgas St TF: 800-822-8356 ■ Web: www.h-pproducts.com	Louisville	OH	44641	330-875-5556		595
Hp2 Inc 1630 E Bethany Home Rd Web: hp2promo.com	Phoenix	AZ	85016	602-235-9099		366
HPA Development Group Inc 7800 Cooper Rd Ste 204 Web: www.hpadg.com	Cincinnati	OH	45242	513-793-2400		401
HPBA (Hearth Patio & Barbecue Assn) 1901 N Moore St Ste 600 TF: 800-677-6278 ■ Web: www.hpba.org	Arlington	VA	22209	703-522-0086	522-0548	49-4
HPC (Hotel Park City) 2001 Pk Ave Web: www.hotelparkcity.com	Park City	UT	84060	435-200-2000	940-5001	379
HPC Foods Ltd 288 Libby St TF: 877-370-0919 ■ Web: hpcfoods.com	Honolulu	HI	96819	808-848-2431		296-21
HPG International Inc 2121 N California Blvd Ste 625 Web: www.higginspurchasing.com	Walnut Creek	CA	94596	925-949-5700		393
HPH Corp 1529 SE 47th Terr TF: 800-654-9884 ■ Web: www.discounthairpiece.com	Cape Coral	FL	33904	239-540-0085		348
HPI LLC 15503 W Hardy Rd Web: www.hpi-llc.com	Houston	TX	77060	713-457-7500		610
HPL (Hoboken Public Library) 500 Pk Ave Web: hobokenlol.org	Hoboken	NJ	07030	201-420-2346		434-3
HPL (Hoover Public Library) 200 Municipal Dr TF: 800-231-2222 ■ Web: www.hooverlibrary.org	Hoover	AL	35216	205-444-7800	444-7878	434-3
HPL (Hyannis Public Library) 401 Main St TF: 800-827-1000 ■ Web: www.hyannislibrary.org	Hyannis	MA	02601	508-775-2280	790-0087	434-3
HPL (Hedberg Public Library) 316 S Main St Web: www.hedbergpubliclibrary.org	Janesville	WI	53545	608-758-6600	758-6583	434-3
HPL Stampings Inc 425 Enterprise Pkwy TF: 800-927-0397 ■ Web: www.hplstampings.com	Lake Zurich	IL	60047	847-540-1400	540-1422	488
HPM (Hawaii Planing Mill Ltd) 16-166 Melekahiwa St TF: 877-841-7633 ■ Web: www.hpmhawaii.com	Keaau	HI	96749	808-966-5693	966-7564	191-3
HPM Corp 4304 W 24th Ave Ste 100 Web: www.hpmcorporation.com	Kennewick	WA	99338	509-737-8939		463
HPM Inc 3231 Osgood Common TF: 800-957-5838 ■ Web: www.hpmnetworks.com	Fremont	CA	94539	510-353-0770		196
Hpn Worldwide Inc 119 W Vallette St Web: www.hpn.com	Elmhurst	IL	60126	630-941-9030		463
HPPL (High Point Public Library) 901 N Main St Web: www.highpointnc.gov/749/library	High Point	NC	27262	336-883-3660	883-3636	434-3
HPRHS (High Point Regional Health System) 601 N Elm St PO Box HP-5 TF: 877-878-7644 ■ Web: www.highpointregional.com	High Point	NC	27262	336-878-6000		374-3
HPTS (High Power Technical Services Inc) 2230 Ampere Dr TF: 866-398-3474 ■ Web: www.hpts.tv	Louisville	KY	40299	502-271-2469		116
HPV (Hawaii's Plantation Village) 94-695 Waipahu St Web: www.hawaiiplantationvillage.org	Waipahu	HI	96797	808-677-0110	676-6727	520
HPVA (Hardwood Plywood & Veneer Assn) 1825 Michael Faraday Dr Web: www.hpva.org	Reston	VA	20190	703-435-2900	435-2537	49-3
HR Advisors Inc 25411 Cabot Rd Ste 212 Web: www.hradvisors.com	Laguna Hills	CA	92653	949-497-7329		260
HR Affiliates 1930 Bishop Ln # 111 Web: www.hraffiliates.com	Louisville	KY	40218	502-485-9675		631
H&R Agri-Power Inc 4900 Eagle Way Web: www.hragripower.com	Hopkinsville	KY	42240	270-886-3918		190
Hr Alliance LLC 580 W Main St Web: hralliancewithyou.com	Wytheville	VA	24382	276-223-1718		195
Hr Answers Inc 7650 SW Beveland St Ste 130 Web: www.hranswers.com	Tigard	OR	97223	503-885-9815		195
H&R Construction Parts & Equipment Inc 20 Milburn St TF: 800-333-0650 ■ Web: www.hrparts.com	Buffalo	NY	14212	716-891-4311		57
Hr Consultants Inc 160 Jari Dr Ste 180 TF: 800-372-1033 ■ Web: www.hrconsults.com	Johnstown	PA	15904	814-266-3818		195
HR Focal Point LLC 5151 Headquarters Dr Ste 135 TF: 855-464-4737 ■ Web: www.hrfocalpoint.com	Plano	TX	75024	855-464-4737		196
HR People & Strategy (HRPS) 401 N Michigan Ave Ste 2200 TF: 800-337-9517 ■ Web: www.hrps.org	Chicago	IL	60611	312-321-6805	673-6944	49-12
Hr Resolutions 2033 Linglestown Rd Web: www.hrresolutions.com	Harrisburg	PA	17110	717-329-1107		226
Hr Strategies & Solutions 49663 Draper Cir Ste 200 Web: www.yourhrteam.net	Plymouth	MI	48170	734-455-1185		196
HR Wentzel Sons Inc 5521 Waggoners Gap Rd	Landisburg	PA	17040	717-789-3306		296-23
HR Works Inc 200 WillowBrook Ofc Pk TF: 877-219-9062 ■ Web: www.hrworks-inc.com	Fairport	NY	14450	585-381-8340		260
HR1 Services Inc 2030 Powers Ferry Rd NW #120 Web: www.hr1.com	Atlanta	GA	30339	770-541-7823		260
HRA - Healthcare Research & Analytics LLC 400 Lanidex Plaza TF: 800-929-5400 ■ Web: www.hraresearch.com	Parsippany	NJ	07054	973-240-1200		466
HR&A Advisors Inc 99 Hudson St 3rd Fl Web: www.hraadvisors.com	New York	NY	10013	212-977-5597		196
HRC (Herpes Resource Center, The) PO Box 13827 TF: 877-478-5868	Research Triangle Park	NC	27709	919-361-8400	361-8425	48-17
HRCG Inc 1202 E Dover Dr Web: hrcgtest.newsite.hrconsultinggroup.com	Provo	UT	84604	801-765-4417		260
Hrd Consulting Services 2310 Wineberry Terr Web: www.hrdconsultingservices.com	Baltimore	MD	21209	410-466-9023		196
Hrd Discount Book Society 2002 Renaissance Blvd TF: 800-633-4533 ■ Web: www.hrdqstore.com	King Of Prussia	PA	19406	610-279-2002		196
HRF (Herb Research Foundation) 4140 15th St TF: 800-748-2617 ■ Web: www.herbs.org	Boulder	CO	80304	303-449-2265	449-7849	48-17
HRG (Herbert Rowland & Grubic Inc) 369 E Pk Dr Web: www.hrg-inc.com	Harrisburg	PA	17111	717-564-1121	564-1158	261
HRG North America 16 E 34th St 3rd Fl TF: 800-225-4570 ■ Web: www.hrgworldwide.com	New York	NY	10016	212-404-8800		771
HRG Pllc 416 W Third St Web: hrgpllc.com	Owensboro	KY	42301	270-683-7558		727
HRH (Hillside Rehabilitation Hospital) 8747 Squires Ln NE Web: valleycareofohio.com	Warren	OH	44484	330-841-3893		374-6

Name / Address	City	State	ZIP	Phone	Fax	Class
HRHS (Howard Regional Health System Main Campus) 3500 S Lafountain St · *Web:* ecommunity.com/howard	Kokomo	IN	46902	765-453-0702		374-3
HRHS (Halifax Regional Health System) 2204 Wilborn Ave · *Web:* www.sentara.com	South Boston	VA	24592	434-517-3100		374-3
HRI Inc 1750 W College Ave · *TF:* 877-474-9999 ■ *Web:* www.hrico.com	State College	PA	16801	814-238-5071	238-0131	188-4
Hribar Trucking Inc 1521 Waukesha Rd · *TF:* 800-832-5660 ■ *Web:* hribarlogistics.com	Caledonia	WI	53108	262-835-4401		780
Hrizons 10749 108TH AVE N · *Web:* www.hrizons.com	Hanover	MN	55341	612-326-9677		393
Hrl Laboratories LLC 3011 Malibu Canyon Rd · *Web:* www.hrl.com	Malibu	CA	90265	310-317-5000	317-5483	261
HRM USA Inc 1044 Pulinski Rd · *Web:* www.heartratemonitorsusa.com	Warminster	PA	18974	215-259-2700		475
HRMagazine 1800 Duke St · *TF:* 800-283-7476 ■ *Web:* www.shrm.org/hrmagazine	Alexandria	VA	22314	703-548-3440	836-0367	457-5
HRMC (Huron Regional Medical Ctr) 172 Fourth St SE · *TF:* 800-529-0115 ■ *Web:* www.huronregional.org	Huron	SD	57350	605-353-6200	353-6300	374-3
HRO Partners LLC 1237 Yorkshire Cove · *Web:* www.hro-partners.com	Memphis	TN	38119	901-737-0123		260
Hrodey & Assoc 114 W Calhoun St · *Web:* www.hrodey.com	Woodstock	IL	60098	815-337-4636		400
HROplus com 65 Water St · *Web:* www.hroplus.com	Laconia	NH	03246	603-524-8762		393
HRP Associates Inc 197 Scott Swamp Rd · *TF:* 800-246-9021 ■ *Web:* www.hrpassociates.com	Farmington	CT	06032	800-246-9021		261
HR&P Solutions Inc 14550 Torrey Chase Ste 100 · *Web:* www.hrp.net	Houston	TX	77014	281-880-6525		2
HRPS (HR People & Strategy) 401 N Michigan Ave Ste 2200 · *TF:* 800-337-9517 ■ *Web:* www.hrps.org	Chicago	IL	60611	312-321-6805	673-6944	49-12
hrQ Inc 2859 Umatilla St · *Web:* www.hrqinc.com	Denver	CO	80211	303-455-1118		317
HRSA (Health Resources & Services Administration) 5600 Fishers Ln · *TF:* 888-275-4772 ■ *Web:* hrsa.gov	Rockville	MD	20857	301-443-2216		340-10
Hru Inc. Technical Resources 3451 Dunckel Rd · *TF:* 888-205-3446 ■ *Web:* www.hru-tech.com	Lansing	MI	48911	517-272-5888		463
Hrv Conformance Verification Associates Inc 420 Rouser Rd Ste 400 · *Web:* www.hrvinc.com	Moon Township	PA	15108	412-299-2000		41
HRValue LLC 1010 E 20th St · *Web:* www.4hrv.com	Tulsa	OK	74120	614-266-5926		463
H&S Constructors Inc 1616 Valero Way · *TF:* 800-727-8602 ■ *Web:* www.hsconstructors.com	Corpus Christi	TX	78469	361-289-5272		256
HS Die & Engineering Inc 0-215 Lake Michigan Dr NW · *Web:* www.hsdie.com	Grand Rapids	MI	49534	616-453-5451		697
HS International 9871 Irvine Ctr Dr · *Web:* www.hsi.net	Irvine	CA	92618	949-753-9153		731
HS Strygler & Company Inc 37 W 20th St Ste 1210	New York	NY	10011	212-727-7840		411
HSA Engineering Consulting Services Inc 5701 Euper Ln Ste A · *Web:* hsaconsultants.com	Fort Smith	AR	72903	479-452-8922		261
Hsa Lps 1520 S Beverly Glen Blvd Ste 305 · *Web:* www.hsa-lps.com	Los Angeles	CA	90024	310-286-2722		193
HSB (Hebron Savings Bank) 101 N Main St PO Box 59 · *Web:* www.hebronsavingsbank.com	Hebron	MD	21830	410-749-1185	543-0703	70
HSB Group Inc 1 State St	Hartford	CT	06103	860-722-1866	722-5106	391-4
HSBA (Hawaii State Bar Assn) 1100 Alakea St Ste 1000 · *TF:* 800-932-0311 ■ *Web:* www.hsba.org	Honolulu	HI	96813	808-537-1868	521-7936	72
HSBC Bank USA 2929 Walden Ave · **Fax Area Code:* 817 ■ *TF:* 800-338-4626 ■ *Web:* www.us.hsbc.com	Depew	NY	14043	800-338-4626	826-1874*	509
HSBC Bank USA 452 Fifth Ave · *TF:* 800-975-4722 ■ *Web:* www.banking.us.hsbc.com	New York	NY	10018	800-975-4722		401
HSBC North America Holdings Inc 2700 Sanders Rd · *TF:* 800-975-4722 ■ *Web:* www.hsbc.com	Prospect Heights	IL	60070	847-564-5000		360-2
HSC Pediatric Ctr 1731 Bunker Hill Rd NE · *TF:* 800-226-4444 ■ *Web:* www.hschealth.org/medical-programs-therapy	Washington	DC	20017	202-832-4400		374-1
HSCVB (Hot Springs Convention Ctr) 134 Convention Blvd PO Box 6000 · *TF:* 800-625-7576 ■ *Web:* www.hotsprings.org	Hot Springs	AR	71902	501-321-2277		205
HSDFF (Hot Springs Documentary Film Festival) 659 Ouachita Ave PO Box 6450 · *Web:* www.hsdfi.org	Hot Springs	AR	71901	501-538-0452		282
HSE (Harter Secrest & Emery LLP) 1600 Bausch & Lomb Pl · *Web:* www.hselaw.com	Rochester	NY	14604	585-232-6500	232-2152	428
HSE Integrated Ltd 630-6th Ave SW Ste 1000 · *Web:* www.hseintegrated.com	Calgary	AB	T2P0S8	403-266-1833		539
HSI (Helicopter Support Inc) 124 Quarry Rd	Trumbull	CT	06611	203-416-4000	416-4291	770
HSI (Hardware Suppliers of America Inc) 1400 E Fire Tower Rd · *TF:* 800-334-5625 ■ *Web:* www.hardwaresuppliers.com	Greenville	NC	27858	800-334-5625		351
HSM (Hart Schaffner Marx) 1680 E Touhy Ave · *Web:* www.hartschaffnermarx.com	Des Plaines	IL	60018	847-257-4644		155-12
HSMAI (Hospitality Sales & Marketing Assn International) 1760 Old Meadow Rd Ste 500 · *Web:* www.hsmai.org	McLean	VA	22102	703-506-3280	610-9005	49-18
HSMC Orizon LLC 16924 Frances St · *Web:* hsmcorizon.com/technology-consulting-services	Omaha	NE	68130	402-330-7008	330-6851	177
HSP (Hauppauge School District) 495 Hoffman Ln PO Box 6006 · *Web:* www.hauppauge.k12.ny.us	Hauppauge	NY	11788	631-761-8208		685
HSPLS (Hawaii State Public Library System) 44 Merchant St · *Web:* hawaii.sdp.sirsi.net	Honolulu	HI	96813	808-586-3700		434-5
HSQ Technology 26227 Research Rd · *TF:* 800-486-6684 ■ *Web:* www.hsq.com	Hayward	CA	94545	510-259-1334	259-1391	201
hss LLC 5446 Dixie Hwy · *Web:* www.valuepointsolutions.com	Saginaw	MI	48601	989-777-2983		393
Hsu's Gourmet Chinese Restaurant 192 Peachtree Ctr Ave · *Web:* www.hsus.com	Atlanta	GA	30303	404-659-2788		671
HSUS (Humane Society of the US) 2100 L St NW · *TF:* 866-720-2676 ■ *Web:* www.humanesociety.org	Washington	DC	20037	202-452-1100	778-6132	48-3
HT Hackney Co 502 S Gay St PO Box 238 · *TF:* 800-406-1291 ■ *Web:* www.hthackney.com	Knoxville	TN	37901	865-546-1291		185
HT Sweeney & Son Inc 308 Dutton Mill Rd · *TF:* 800-589-5704 ■ *Web:* htsweeney.com	Brookhaven	PA	19015	610-872-8896	874-6730	189-5
HTC (Healing the Children) 2624 W Beacon Ave · *Web:* www.healingthechildren.org	Spokane	WA	99208	509-327-4281	327-4284	48-5
HTC (Horry Telephone Co-op Inc) 3480 Hwy 701 N PO Box 1820 · *TF:* 800-824-6779 ■ *Web:* www.htcinc.net	Conway	SC	29528	843-365-2151	365-0855	736
HTC Global Services Inc 3270 W Big Beaver Rd · *Web:* htcinc.com	Troy	MI	48084	248-786-2500		177
HTC Purenergy Inc 002 2305 Victoria Ave · *Web:* www.htcenergy.com	Regina	SK	S4P0S7	306-352-6132		539
HTG Peer Groups 653 Oak Rd · *Web:* www.htgpeergroups.com	Harlan	IA	51537	712-794-7994		466
Hti Cybernetics 6701 Center Dr · *Web:* www.htitool.com	Sterling Heights	MI	48312	586-826-8346		454
HTK (Hornor Townsend & Kent Inc) 600 Dresher Rd Ste C1C · **Fax Area Code:* 215 ■ *TF:* 800-289-9999 ■ *Web:* www.htk.com	Horsham	PA	19044	800-289-9999	956-7750*	402
HTL (Highway Transport Logistics Inc) 6420 Baum Dr · *Web:* www.hytt.com	Knoxville	TN	37919	865-584-8631		780
HTS (Helicopter Transport Services Inc) 701 Wilson Pt Rd · *Web:* www.htshelicopters.com	Baltimore	MD	21220	410-391-7722		359
HTS 115 Norfinch Dr · *Web:* www.htseng.com	Toronto	ON	M3N1W8	416-661-3400		111
HTT (Harsco Rail) 2401 Edmund Rd PO Box 20 · *Web:* www.harscorail.com	West Columbia	SC	29171	803-822-9160	822-8107	650
HTT Inc. 1828 Oakland Ave · *TF:* 866-270-4710 ■ *Web:* www.htt-inc.com	Sheboygan	WI	53081	920-453-5300	453-5301	488
Hu's Szechwan Restaurant 10450 National Blvd · *Web:* www.husrestaurant.com	Los Angeles	CA	90034	310-837-0252		671
Hualalai Resort Corp PO Box 819 · *TF:* 800-983-3880 ■ *Web:* www.hualalairesort.com	Kailua-kona	HI	96745	808-325-8500	325-8501	707
Hualalai Sports Club & Spa at the Four Seasons Resort Hualalai 100 Kaupulehu Dr · *Web:* www.fourseasons.com/hualalai	Kaupulehu-Kona	HI	96740	808-325-8440		707
Hub City Inc 2914 Industrial Ave · *TF:* 800-482-2489 ■ *Web:* www.hubcityinc.com	Aberdeen	SD	57401	605-225-0360	225-0567	709
Hub Data Inc 70 Franklin St 7th Fl · *TF:* 800-327-2832 ■ *Web:* www.hubdata.com	Boston	MA	02110	617-530-1165		174
Hub Folding Box Co Inc 774 Norfolk St · *TF:* 800-334-1113 ■ *Web:* www.hubfoldingbox.com	Mansfield	MA	02048	508-339-0005		101
Hub Group Inc 2000 Clearwater Dr · *NASDAQ:* HUBG ■ *TF:* 800-377-5833 ■ *Web:* www.hubgroup.com	Oak Brook	IL	60523	630-271-3600	964-6475	449
HUB International Insurance Services 1091 N Shoreline Blvd Ste 200 · *Web:* hubinternational.com	Mountain View	CA	94043	650-964-8000		390
Hub International Ltd 1065 Ave of the Americas · *TF:* 800-456-5293 ■ *Web:* www.hubinternational.com	New York	NY	10018	212-338-2000	338-2100	390
Hub Pattern Corp 2113 Salem Ave · *TF:* 800-482-3505 ■ *Web:* www.hubcorp.net	Roanoke	VA	24016	540-342-3505	343-5337	567
Hub Strategy & Communication 39 Mesa St Ste 212 · *Web:* hubsanfrancisco.com	San Francisco	CA	94129	415-561-4345		7
Hubbard & Drake General Mechanical Contractors Inc PO Box 1867 · *TF:* 800-353-9245 ■ *Web:* www.hubbarddrake.com	Decatur	AL	35602	256-353-9244	350-5043	189-10
Hubbard Construction Co 1936 Lee Rd · *Web:* www.hubbard.com	Winter Park	FL	32789	407-645-5500		188-4
Hubbard County 301 Court Ave · **Fax:* Acctg ■ *Web:* www.co.hubbard.mn.us	Park Rapids	MN	56470	218-732-2300	732-3645*	338
Hubbard Feeds Inc 111 W Cherry St Ste 500 · *TF:* 800-869-7219 ■ *Web:* www.hubbardfeeds.com	Mankato	MN	56001	507-388-9400		447
Hubbard House, The 29 W Miller St · *TF:* 800-648-3818 ■ *Web:* www.orlandohealth.com	Orlando	FL	32806	407-649-6886	849-6447	372
Hubbard ISA 195 Main St · *Web:* www.hubbardbreeders.com	Walpole	NH	03608	603-756-3311	756-9034	10-8
Hubbard Museum of the American West 26301 Highway 70 PO Box 40	Ruidoso Downs	NM	88346	575-378-4142	378-4166	520
Hubbard Pipe & Supply Inc 463 Robeson St · *Web:* www.hubbardkitchenandbath.com	Fayetteville	NC	28301	910-484-9015		612
Hubbard Publishing Co 127 E Chillicothe Ave PO Box 40 · *TF:* 866-632-9992 ■ *Web:* www.examiner.org	Bellefontaine	OH	43311	937-592-3060	592-4463	637-8
Hubbard Street Dance Chicago 1147 W Jackson Blvd · *TF:* 800-982-2787 ■ *Web:* www.hubbardstreetdance.com	Chicago	IL	60607	312-850-9744	455-8240	573-1

	Phone	Fax	Class
Hubbard`s Impala Parts Inc			
1676 Anthony Rd .... Burlington NC 27215	336-227-1589		791
TF: 800-846-7252 ■ *Web:* www.impalaparts.com			
Hubbard-Hall Inc 563 S Leonard St .... Waterbury CT 06708	203-756-5521	756-9017	146
TF: 800-331-6871 ■ *Web:* www.hubbardhall.com			
Hubbell Group Inc, The			
859 Willard St Ste 201 .... Quincy MA 02169	781-878-8882		636
Web: www.hubbellgroup.com			
Hubbell Industrial Controls			
4301 Cheyenne Dr .... Archdale NC 27263	336-434-2800	434-2803	203
Web: www.hubbell-icd.com			
Hubbell Lighting Inc			
701 Millennium Blvd .... Greenville SC 29607	864-678-1000	678-1065	439
TF: 800-345-4928 ■ *Web:* www.hubbelllighting.com			
Hubbell Power Systems Inc			
210 N Allen St .... Centralia MO 65240	573-682-5521	682-8714	253
TF: 800-346-3062 ■ *Web:* www.hubbellpowersystems.com			
Hubbell Premise Wiring Inc 23 Clara Dr .... Mystic CT 06355	800-626-0005	535-8328*	815
**Fax Area Code:* 860 ■ *TF:* 800-626-0005 ■ *Web:* www.hubbell-premise.com			
Hubbell RACO 3902 W Sample St .... South Bend IN 46619	574-234-7151	722-6462*	816
**Fax Area Code:* 800 ■ *Web:* www.hubbell-rtb.com			
Hubbell Roth & Clark Inc			
555 Hulet Dr PO Box 824 .... Bloomfield Hills MI 48303	248-454-6300	338-2592	261
Web: hrcengr.com			
Hubbell Trading Post National Historic Site			
1/2 Mile W Hwy 191 on Hwy 264 PO Box 150 ..... Ganado AZ 86505	928-755-3475	755-3405	564
Web: www.nps.gov			
Hubbell Wiegmann 501 W Apple St .... Freeburg IL 62243	618-539-3193	539-5794	816
Web: www.hubbell-wiegmann.com			
Hubbell Wiring Device-Kellems			
40 Waterview Dr .... Shelton CT 06484	203-882-4800	882-4852*	815
**Fax:* Tech Supp ■ *TF Cust Svc:* 800-288-6000 ■ *Web:* www.hubbell-wiring.com			
Hubbuch & Co 324 W Main St................ Louisville KY 40202	502-583-2713	582-7375	393
Web: www.hubbuch.com			
Hubco Inc 215 S Poplar .... Hutchinson KS 67501	620-663-8301		67
Web: www.hubcoinc.com			
Huber & Associates Inc			
1400 Edgewood Dr .... Jefferson City MO 65109	573-634-5000		180
Web: www.teamhuber.com			
Huber Heights Chamber of Commerce			
4707 Brandt Pk PO Box 24006 .... Huber Heights OH 45424	937-233-5700		139
TF: 800-621-8001 ■ *Web:* huberheightschamber.com			
Huber's Orchard & Winery			
19816 Huber Rd .... Borden IN 47106	812-923-9463		50-7
TF: 800-345-9463 ■ *Web:* huberwinery.com			
Hubert Distributors Inc			
1200 Auburn Rd .... Pontiac MI 48342	248-858-2340		81-1
Web: www.abwholesaler.com			
Hubert H Humphrey Metrodome			
900 S Fifth St .... Minneapolis MN 55415	612-332-0386	332-8334	720
Web: msfa.com			
Hubris Communications Inc			
209 N Main............................. Garden City KS 67846	620-275-1900		387
Web: www.hubris.net			
HubTech 44 Norfolk Ave Ste 4 .... South Easton MA 02375	877-482-8324	238-1146*	180
**Fax Area Code:* 508 ■ *TF:* 877-482-8324 ■ *Web:* www.hubtechnical.com			
Hubtrucker Inc 315 Freeport St Ste B .... Houston TX 77015	713-547-5482		311
TF: 866-913-6553 ■ *Web:* hubtrucker.com			
Huck Group Inc, The			
510 W Sixth St Ste 1100.................. Los Angeles CA 90014	213-955-8080		344
Web: www.thehuckgroup.com			
Huckstep & Assoc LLC			
3734 S Ave Ste E .... Springfield MO 65807	417-889-8991		2
TF: 800-269-6466			
HUD (Department of Housing & Urban Development)			
451 Seventh St SW...................... Washington DC 20410	202-708-0685	619-8153	340-12
TF: 800-569-4287 ■ *Web:* www.hud.gov			
US Department of Housing and Urban Development			
451 Seventh St SW .... Washington DC 20410	202-708-1112		340-12
Web: portal.hud.gov			
HUD Office of Community Planning & Development			
451 Seventh St SW...................... Washington DC 20410	202-708-1112	708-1455	340-12
Web: www.hud.gov/offices/cpd			
HUD Office of Fair Housing & Equal Opportunity			
451 Seventh St SW...................... Washington DC 20410	202-708-1112	708-4483	340-12
TF: 800-669-9777 ■ *Web:* www.hud.gov/offices/fheo			
HUD Office of Public & Indian Housing			
Real Estate Assessment Ctr			
550 12th St SW Ste 100 .... Washington DC 20410	202-708-1112		340-12
TF: 888-245-4860 ■ *Web:* portal.hud.gov			
Hudapack Metal Treating Inc			
979 Koopman Ln .... Elkhorn WI 53121	262-723-3345		484
TF: 800-221-6827 ■ *Web:* www.hudapack.com			
Huddle House Inc			
5901 Peachtree Dunwoody Ste B450 .... Atlanta GA 30328	770-325-1300		670
Web: www.huddlehouse.com			
Hudson - Rpm Distributors LLC			
150 Blackstone River Rd Ste 4 .... Worcester MA 01607	617-328-9500		96
Web: www.hudsonrpm.com			
Hudson Advisors LLC			
2711 N Haskell Ave Ste 1800.................. Dallas TX 75204	214-754-8400		390
Web: www.hudson-advisors.com			
Hudson Bros Trailer Manufacturing Inc			
1508 Hwy 218 W .... Indian Trail NC 28079	704-753-4723		779
TF: 800-289-8787 ■ *Web:* www.hudsontrailers.com			
Hudson Color Concentrates Inc			
50 Francis St .... Leominster MA 01453	978-537-3538		550
TF: 888-858-9065 ■ *Web:* www.hudsoncolor.com			
Hudson Community Enterprises			
68-70 Tuers Ave .... Jersey City NJ 07306	201-434-3303		226
Web: www.hudsoncommunity.org			
Hudson Cook LLP 7037 Ridge Rd Ste 300........ Hanover MD 21076	410-684-3200		428
TF: 800-840-4956 ■ *Web:* www.hudsoncook.com			
Hudson County			
257 Cornelison Ave 4th Fl .... Jersey City NJ 07302	201-369-3470	369-3478	338
Web: www.hudsoncountyclerk.org			
Hudson County Chamber of Commerce			
857 Bergen Ave 3rd Fl .... Jersey City NJ 07306	201-386-0699	386-8480	139
Web: www.hudsonchamber.org			
Hudson County Community College			
162 Sip Ave .... Jersey City NJ 07306	201-714-7200	714-2136*	162
**Fax:* Admissions ■ *Web:* www.hccc.edu			
Hudson Fusion 30 State St................... Ossining NY 10562	914-762-0900		4
Web: www.hudsonfusion.com			
Hudson Gardens & Event Ctr			
6115 S Santa Fe Dr.......................... Littleton CO 80120	303-797-8565	797-8647	97
Web: www.hudsongardens.org			
Hudson Group			
1 Meadowlands Plaza Ste 902 .... East Rutherford NJ 07073	201-939-5050		530
Web: www.hudsongroup.com			
Hudson Highlands State Park Rt 9D .... Cold Spring NY 10516	845-225-7207		565
Web: www.nynjtc.org			
Hudson Institute			
1015 15th St NW Ste 600................. Washington DC 20005	202-974-2400	974-2410	634
TF: 888-554-1325 ■ *Web:* www.hudson.org			
Hudson Library & Historical Society			
96 Library St.............................. Hudson OH 44236	330-653-6658		434-3
Web: www.hudsonlibrary.org			
Hudson Liquid Asphalts Inc			
89 Ship St................................ Providence RI 02903	401-274-2200		191-1
Hudson Lock Inc 81 Apsley St .... Hudson MA 01749	800-434-8960	562-9859*	350
**Fax Area Code:* 978 ■ *TF:* 800-434-8960 ■ *Web:* www.hudsonlock.com			
Hudson Machinery Worldwide			
32 Stevens St .... Haverhill MA 01830	978-373-7295		456
Hudson Mann Inc			
710, Johnnie Dodds Blvd .... Mount Pleasant SC 29464	843-884-5557		463
Web: www.hudsonmann.com			
Hudson Marine Management Service			
4350 Haddonfield Rd # 302 .... Pennsauken NJ 08109	856-486-0800		463
Web: hudsonanalytix.com			
Hudson Museum			
5746 Collins Ctr for the Arts.................... Orono ME 04469	207-581-1901	581-1950	520
TF: 800-411-9671 ■ *Web:* www.umaine.edu/hudsonmuseum			
Hudson Printing & Graphic Design			
611 S Mobberly Ave .... Longview TX 75602	903-758-1773		344
TF: 800-530-4888 ■ *Web:* www.hudsonprint.com			
Hudson Richard (Rep R - NC)			
429 Cannon HOB .... Washington DC 20515	202-225-3715		342-2
Web: hudson.house.gov			
Hudson River Construction Co			
Port of Albany 101 Dunham Dr................. Albany NY 12202	518-434-6677	434-8638	188-4
Web: www.hudsonriverconstruction.com			
Hudson River Fruit Distributors			
65 Old Indian Rd........................... Milton NY 12547	800-640-2774		315-3
TF: 800-640-2774 ■ *Web:* hudsonriverfruit.com			
Hudson River Healthcare Inc			
1037 Main St .... Peekskill NY 10566	914-734-8800		352
Web: www.hrhcare.org			
Hudson River Islands State Park			
Schodack Island State Pk .... Schodack Landing NY 12156	518-732-0187		565
TF: 800-456-2267 ■ *Web:* parks.ny.gov/parks/98/details.aspx			
Hudson River Museum 511 Warburton Ave .... Yonkers NY 10701	914-963-4550	963-8558	520
Web: www.hrm.org			
Hudson RPO 10 S Wacker Dr Ste 2600........... Chicago IL 60606	312-795-4275		193
NASDAQ: HSON ■ *Web:* us.hudson.com			
Hudson Tool & Die Co			
Hudson Technologies 1327 N US 1........ Ormond Beach FL 32174	386-672-2000	676-6212*	757
**Fax:* Sales ■ *Web:* www.hudson-technologies.com			
Hudson Valley Community College			
80 Vandenburgh Ave............................ Troy NY 12180	518-629-4822	629-4576*	162
**Fax:* Admissions ■ *TF:* 877-325-4822 ■ *Web:* www.hvcc.edu			
Hudson Valley Federal Credit Union			
159 Barnegat Rd...................... Poughkeepsie NY 12601	845-463-3011	463-3613	219
TF: 800-468-3011 ■ *Web:* www.hvfcu.org			
Hudson Valley Gateway Chamber of Commerce			
1 S Div St .... Peekskill NY 10566	914-737-3600	737-0541	139
Web: www.hvgatewaychamber.com			
Hudson Valley Hospital Ctr			
1980 Crompond Rd .... Cortlandt Manor NY 10567	914-737-9000		374-3
Web: www.hvhc.org			
Hudson Valley Magazine			
2678 S Rd 2nd Fl .... Poughkeepsie NY 12601	845-463-0542	463-1544	457-22
Web: www.hvmag.com			
Hudson Valve Company Inc			
5301 Office Pk Dr Ste 330 .... Bakersfield CA 93309	661-869-1126	607-8731*	789
**Fax Area Code:* 800 ■ *TF:* 800-748-6218 ■ *Web:* www.hudsonvalve.com			
Hudson's Bar & Grill			
7805 NW Greenwood Dr.................... Vancouver WA 98662	360-816-6100		671
Web: www.hudsonsbarandgrill.com			
Hudson's Furniture Showroom Inc			
3290 W State Rd 46 .... Sanford FL 32771	407-708-5635		321
Web: www.hudsonsfurniture.com			
Hudson's Seafood House on the Docks			
1 Hudsons Rd..................... Hilton Head Island SC 29926	843-681-2772	681-2774	671
TF: 800-932-3652 ■ *Web:* www.hudsonsonthedocks.com			
Hudson-Webber Foundation			
333 W Ft St Ste 1310 .... Detroit MI 48226	313-963-7777		305
TF: 800-421-9512 ■ *Web:* www.hudson-webber.org			
Hudspeth County 109 Brown St .... Sierra Blanca TX 79851	915-369-2331	369-3005	338
TF: 888-368-4689 ■ *Web:* www.txdmv.gov			
Hue Restaurant 629 E Central Blvd............. Orlando FL 32801	407-849-1800		671
Web: socothorntonpark.com			
Hueco Tanks State Historic Site			
6900 Hueco Tanks Rd Ste 1 .... El Paso TX 79938	915-857-1135	845-1794*	565
**Fax Area Code:* 979 ■ *TF:* 800-792-1112 ■ *Web:* tpwd.texas.gov/state-parks/hueco-tanks			
Hueneme Elementary School Dist			
205 N Ventura Rd .... Port Hueneme CA 93041	805-488-3588	488-1779	685
TF: 866-431-2478 ■ *Web:* www.huensd.k12.ca.us			
Huerfano County 401 Main St Ste 201 .... Walsenburg CO 81089	719-738-2370	738-3996	338
TF: 800-466-4228 ■ *Web:* www.huerfano.us			
Hueston Woods Lodge & Conference Ctr			
5201 Lodge Rd................... College Corner OH 45003	513-664-3500	523-1522	669
TF: 800-282-7275 ■ *Web:* huestonwoodslodge.com			
Hueston Woods State Park			
6301 Pk Office Rd.................... College Corner OH 45003	513-523-6347		565
Web: www.ohiodnr.com			

Phone | Fax | Class

Huey P Long Medical Ctr
352 Hospital Blvd PO Box 5352 ... Pineville LA 71361 318-448-0811 374-3
Web: lsuhscshreveport.edu

Huey's 115 E River St ... Savannah GA 31401 912-234-7385 671
Web: hueysontheriver.net

Huey's 1927 Madison Ave ... Memphis TN 38104 901-726-4372 671
Web: www.hueyburger.com

Hueytown Public Library
1372 Hueytown Rd ... Hueytown AL 35023 205-491-1443 434-3
Web: www.hueytown.com

Hufcor Inc 2101 Kennedy Rd ... Janesville WI 53545 608-756-1241 756-1246 286
TF: 800-356-6968 ■ *Web:* www.hufcor.com

Huffman & Wright Logging Inc
801 SE Third St ... Canyonville OR 97417 541-839-4251 448

Huffman Corp 1050 Huffman Way ... Clover SC 29710 803-222-4561 222-7599 455
TF: 888-483-3626 ■ *Web:* huffman-llc.com

Huffman Finishing Co
4919 Hickory Blvd ... Granite Falls NC 28630 828-396-1741 745-7

Huffman Jared (Rep D - CA)
1406 Longworth HOB ... Washington DC 20515 202-225-5161 225-5163 342-2
Web: huffman.house.gov

Huffman Laboratories Inc
4630 Indiana St ... Golden CO 80403 303-278-4455 743
TF: 877-886-6225 ■ *Web:* www.huffmanlabs.com

Huffmaster Crisis Management
1300 Combermere Dr ... Troy MI 48083 248-588-1600 693
Web: huffmaster.com

Huffy Bicycle Co
6551 Centerville Business Pkwy ... Centerville OH 45459 937-865-2800 82
TF: 800-872-2453 ■ *Web:* www.huffybikes.com

Hu-Friedy Mfg Company Inc
3232 N Rockwell St ... Chicago IL 60618 773-975-6100 228
TF: 800-483-7433 ■ *Web:* www.hu-friedy.com

HUGE Inc 45 Main St 2nd Fl ... Brooklyn NY 11201 718-625-4843 225
Web: www.hugeinc.com

Huggins & Company CPA Pa
6148-D Brookshire Blvd ... Charlotte NC 28216 704-394-2364 2

Huggins Actuarial Services Inc
111 Veterans Sq 2nd Fl ... Media PA 19063 610-892-1824 390
Web: www.hugginsactuarial.com

Huggy Bear's Cupboards Inc
2731 N Hayden Island Dr ... Portland OR 97217 503-289-5541 321
Web: www.huggybear.com

Hugh Chatham Memorial Hospital
180 Parkwood Dr PO Box 560 ... Elkin NC 28621 336-527-7000 374-3
Web: www.hughchatham.org

Hugh M Cunningham Inc
13755 Benchmark Dr ... Dallas TX 75234 972-888-3800 612
Web: hughcunningham.com

Hugh Taylor Birch State Park
3109 E Sunrise Blvd ... Fort Lauderdale FL 33304 954-564-4521 565
Web: www.floridastateparks.org

Hughes & Sloan Inc
1360 Peachtree St NE ... Atlanta GA 30309 404-873-3421 266
Web: hughesandsloan.com

Hughes Agency, The
700 E 13th St ... North Little Rock AR 72114 501-791-3303 260
Web: www.hughesstaffingagency.com

Hughes Bros Inc
210 N 13th St PO Box 159 ... Seward NE 68434 402-643-2991 643-2149 816
TF: 800-869-0359 ■ *Web:* www.hughesbros.com

Hughes Capital Management Inc
916 Prince St ... Alexandria VA 22314 703-684-7222 684-7799 401

Hughes Commercial Properties Inc
110 E Court St Ste 501 PO Box 10440 ... Greenville SC 29603 864-233-0079 652
Web: www.hughescommercial.com

Hughes Corp Weschler Instruments Div
16900 Foltz Pkwy ... Cleveland OH 44149 440-238-2550 238-0660 248
TF: 800-557-0064 ■ *Web:* www.weschler.com

Hughes County
104 E Capitol Ave PO Box 1238 ... Pierre SD 57501 605-773-3713 773-3875 338
Web: ujs.sd.gov

Hughes Design Associates
7160 Beneva Rd ... Sarasota FL 34238 941-922-4767 41
Web: www.hughesdes.com

Hughes Federal Credit Union Inc
PO Box 11900 ... Tucson AZ 85734 520-794-8341 219
TF: 866-760-3156 ■ *Web:* www.hughesfcu.org

Hughes Furniture Industries Inc
952 S Stout Rd ... Randleman NC 27317 336-498-8700 319-2
Web: www.hughesfurniture.com

Hughes Group Inc 6200 E Hwy 62 ... Jeffersonville IN 47130 812-282-4393 283-0142 188-4
Web: hughesdevelopmentllc.com

Hughes Hardwood International Inc
500 Hwy 13 S ... Collinwood TN 38450 931-724-6258 724-6259 683
Web: www.hugheshardwood.com

Hughes Hubbard & Reed LLP
1 Battery Pk Plaza ... New York NY 10004 212-837-6000 422-4726 428
TF: 800-973-1177 ■ *Web:* www.hugheshubbard.com

Hughes Machinery Co 14400 College Blvd ... Lenexa KS 66215 913-492-0355 492-1420 385
Web: www.hughesmachinery.com

Hughes Marino Inc 1450 Front St ... San Diego CA 92101 619-238-2111 652
Web: www.hughesmarino.com

Hughes Network Systems LLC
11717 Exploration Ln ... Germantown MD 20876 301-428-5500 428-1868 735
Web: www.hughes.com

Hughes Parker Industries LLC
1604 Mahr Ave ... Lawrenceburg TN 38464 931-762-9403 483
Web: www.hughesparker.com

Hughes Production
1625 Berger Ln PO Box 3556 ... Jackson WY 83001 307-733-6505 733-0542 184
Web: www.hughesproduction.com

Hughes Spalding Children's Hospital
35 Jesse Hill Jr Dr SE ... Atlanta GA 30303 404-785-9500 374-3
Web: www.choa.org/hughesspalding

Hughes Supply Company of Thomasville Inc
175 Kanoy Rd PO Box 1003 ... Thomasville NC 27360 336-475-8146 454
TF: 800-747-8141 ■ *Web:* www.hughessupplyco.com

Phone | Fax | Class

Hughes Supply Inc 600 Ferguson Dr ... Orlando FL 32805 407-843-9100 612
Web: www.hughessupply.com

Hughes Western Sales Inc 4099 S 500 W ... Murray UT 84123 801-262-2900 361

Hughes-Anderson Heat Exchangers Inc
1001 N Fulton Ave ... Tulsa OK 74115 918-836-1681 836-5967 91
Web: www.hughesanderson.com

HughesNet 11717 Exploration Ln ... Germantown MD 20876 301-428-5500 428-1868 398
TF: 866-347-3292 ■ *Web:* www.hughesnet.com

Hughston Orthopedic Hospital
100 Frist Ct ... Columbus GA 31908 706-494-2100 374-7
TF: 855-795-3609 ■ *Web:* columbusregional.com

Hugo Boss Fashions Inc
601 W 26th St 8th fl ... New York NY 10001 212-940-0600 940-0619 155-12
Web: www.hugoboss.com/us

Hugo Neu Corp 120 Fifth Ave Ste 600 ... New York NY 10011 646-467-6700 492
Web: www.hugoneu.com

Hugo's 1600 Westheimer Rd ... Houston TX 77006 713-524-7744 671
Web: www.hugosrestaurant.net

Hugo's Cellar 202 Fremont St ... Las Vegas NV 89101 702-385-4011 671
TF: 800-634-6045 ■ *Web:* www.hugoscellar.com

Hugo's Restaurant 88 Middle St ... Portland ME 04101 207-774-8538 671
Web: www.hugos.net

Hugo's Restaurant 161 Stillwater Ave ... Stamford CT 06902 203-323-5577 671

Hugoton Royalty Trust
2911 Turtle Creek Blvd, Ste 850
Ste 850 PO Box 962020 ... Dallas TX 75219 855-588-7839 289-2431* 675
NYSE: HGT ■ **Fax Area Code:* 214 ■ *TF:* 855-588-7839 ■ *Web:* www.hgt-hugoton.com

Huguley Memorial Medical Ctr
11801 S Fwy ... Burleson TX 76028 817-293-9110 374-3
Web: www.texashealthhuguley.org

Huhtamaki Inc North America
9201 Packaging Dr ... DeSoto KS 66018 913-583-3025 583-8756* 548
**Fax:* Hum Res ■ *TF:* 800-255-4243 ■ *Web:* www2.huhtamaki.com

Huitt-Zollars Inc
1717 McKinney Ave Ste 1400 ... Dallas TX 75202 214-871-3311 871-0757 261
TF: 866-667-6572 ■ *Web:* www.huitt-zollars.com

Huizenga Bill (Rep R - MI)
2232 Rayburn HOB ... Washington DC 20515 202-225-4401 226-0779 342-2
Web: huizenga.house.gov

Huka Productions LLC
924 Valmont St Ste 103 ... New Orleans LA 70115 888-512-7469 684-5565* 195
**Fax Area Code:* 504 ■ *TF:* 888-512-7469 ■ *Web:* www.huka.com

Hula Hut 3825 Lake Austin Blvd ... Austin TX 78703 512-476-4852 671
Web: www.hulahut.com

Hulen Mall 4800 S Hulen St ... Fort Worth TX 76132 817-294-1200 460
Web: www.hulenmall.com

Hull & Assoc Inc
6397 Emerald Pkwy Ste 200 ... Dublin OH 43016 614-793-8777 261
Web: hullinc.com

Hull Lift Truck Inc 28747 Old US 33 W ... Elkhart IN 46516 574-293-8651 293-9709 385
TF: 888-284-0364 ■ *Web:* www.hullifttruck.com

Hull Street Blues 1222 Hull St ... Baltimore MD 21230 410-727-7476 576-2343 671
Web: www.hullstreetblues.com

Hulman & Co 900 Wabash Ave ... Terre Haute IN 47807 812-232-9446 360-2
Web: www.clabbergirl.com

Hulsey Harwood & Sheridan LLC
1900 Roselawn Ave ... Monroe LA 71201 318-325-6500 2
Web: hhcpa.net

Hulslander SUSAn d CPA PC
24 First Ave E Ste D ... Kalispell MT 59901 406-755-3092 2

Hult Ctr for the Performing Arts
1 Eugene Ctr ... Eugene OR 97401 541-682-5087 682-5426 572
TF: 800-735-2900 ■ *Web:* www.hultcenter.org

Hultgren Randy (Rep R - IL)
2455 Rayburn HOB ... Washington DC 20515 202-225-2976 225-0697 342-2
Web: hultgren.house.gov

Human Arc Corp 1457 East 40th St ... Cleveland OH 44103 216-431-5200 431-5201 390
Web: www.humanarc.com

Human Capital
2055 Crooks Rd Level B ... Rochester Hills MI 48309 888-736-9071 631
TF: 888-736-9071 ■ *Web:* www.human-capital.com

Human Development Foundation
1350 Remington Rd Ste W ... Schaumburg IL 60173 847-490-0100 305
Web: www.hdf.com

Human Dynamics Inc
11863 W 112th St Ste 110 ... Overland Park KS 66210 913-663-2088 663-2090 260
Web: www.hdynamics.com

Human Factors & Ergonomics Society (HFES)
1124 Montana Ave Ste B PO Box 1369 ... Santa Monica CA 90406 310-394-1811 394-2410 48-17
TF: 800-233-1234 ■ *Web:* www.hfes.org

Human Factors International Inc
410 W Lowe Ave ... Fairfield IA 52556 641-472-4480 472-5412 177
TF: 800-242-4480 ■ *Web:* www.humanfactors.com

Human Growth Foundation
997 Glen Cove Ave Ste 5 ... Glen Head NY 11545 516-671-4041 671-4055 48-17
TF: 800-451-6434 ■ *Web:* www.hgfound.org

Human Head Studios
1741 Commercial Ave Ste 200 ... Madison WI 53704 608-298-0643 177
Web: humanhead.com

Human International Academy
123 Camino de la Reina W-200 ... San Diego CA 92108 619-501-8091 423
Web: www.hiausa.com

Human Kinetics 1607 N Market St ... Champaign IL 61820 217-351-5076 351-2674 637-2
TF: 800-747-4457 ■ *Web:* www.humankinetics.com

Human Life International (HLI)
4 Family Life Ln ... Front Royal VA 22630 540-635-7884 622-6247 48-6
TF Orders: 800-549-5433 ■ *Web:* www.hli.org

Human Movement LLC 1501 Empire Rd ... Louisville CO 80027 720-255-5475 232
Web: www.humanmovement.me

Human Resource Development Press Inc
22 Amherst Rd ... Amherst MA 01002 413-253-3488 194
TF: 800-822-2801 ■ *Web:* www.hrdpressonline.com

Human Resource Executive Magazine
747 Dresher Rd Ste 500 ... Horsham PA 19044 215-784-0910 784-0275 457-5
Web: www.hreonline.com

Human Resources Inc
2127 Espey Ct Ste 306 ... Crofton MD 21114 410-451-4202 451-4206 631
Web: www.hri-online.com

Name / Address	Phone	Fax	Class
Human Resources Research Organization (HumRRO) 66 Canal Ctr Plaza Ste 400 .... Alexandria VA 22314 *Web:* www.humrro.org	703-549-3611	549-9025	668
Human Rights Campaign 1640 Rhode Island Ave NW .... Washington DC 20036 *TF:* 800-777-4723 ■ *Web:* www.hrc.org	202-628-4160	347-5323	48-8
Human Rights Watch 350 Fifth Ave 34th Fl .... New York NY 10118 *Web:* www.hrw.org	212-290-4700	736-1300	48-8
Human Touch 3030 Walnut Ave .... Long Beach CA 90807 *TF:* 800-742-5493 ■ *Web:* www.humantouch.com	562-426-8700	426-9690	319-2
Humana Foundation Inc 500 W Main St Ste 208 .... Louisville KY 40202 *Web:* www.humanafoundation.org	502-580-4140	580-1256	304
Humana Inc 500 W Main St .... Louisville KY 40202 *NYSE:* HUM ■ *TF:* 800-486-2620 ■ *Web:* www.humana.com	502-580-1000		391-3
Humana Military Healthcare Services 500 W Main St .... Louisville KY 40201 *TF General:* 800-444-5445 ■ *Web:* www.humana-military.com	800-444-5445		391-3
Humane Farming Assn (HFA) PO Box 3577 .... San Rafael CA 94912 *TF:* 800-295-4050 ■ *Web:* www.hfa.org	415-485-1495	485-0106	48-3
Humane Society of the US (HSUS) 2100 L St NW .... Washington DC 20037 *TF:* 866-720-2676 ■ *Web:* www.humanesociety.org	202-452-1100	778-6132	48-3
Humanetics II Ltd 1700 Columbian Club Dr .... Carrollton TX 75006 *Web:* www.humanetics.com	972-416-1304		697
Humantech Inc 1161 Oak Vly Dr .... Ann Arbor MI 48108 *Web:* www.humantech.com	734-663-6707		261
HumanZyme Inc 2201 W Campbell Park Dr Ste 24 .... Chicago IL 60612 *Web:* www.humanzyme.com	312-738-0127		231
Humber Arboretum 205 Humber College Blvd .... Toronto ON M9W5L7 *Web:* www.humberarboretum.on.ca	416-675-6622	675-2755	97
Humble Independent School District PO Box 2000 .... Humble TX 77347 *Web:* www.humbleisd.net	281-641-1000	641-1050	685
Humboldt Bay Harbor District 601 Startare Dr .... Eureka CA 95501 *Web:* humboldtbay.org	707-443-0801	443-0800	618
Humboldt Botanical Gardens 7707 Tompkins Hill Rd .... Eureka CA 95503 *Web:* www.hbgf.org	707-442-5139		97
Humboldt Brews 856 Tenth St .... Arcata CA 95521 *TF:* 800-346-3482 ■ *Web:* www.humbrews.com	707-826-2739		102
Humboldt County 203 Main St .... Dakota City IA 50529 *Web:* www.humboldtcountyia.org	515-332-1571		338
Humboldt County 825 Fifth St .... Eureka CA 95501 *Web:* www.humboldtgov.org	707-445-7256		338
Humboldt County 50 W Fifth St .... Winnemucca NV 89445 *Web:* www.hcnv.us	775-623-6300	623-6302	338
Humboldt County Convention & Visitors Bureau 1034 Second St .... Eureka CA 95501 *TF:* 800-346-3482 ■ *Web:* www.redwoods.info	707-443-5097	443-5115	206
Humboldt County Fair 1250 Fifth St .... Ferndale CA 95536 *Web:* www.humboldtcountyfair.org	707-786-9511	786-9450	642
Humboldt County Library 1313 Third St .... Eureka CA 95501 *Web:* www.humboldtgov.org/1346/public-library	707-269-1900		434-3
Humboldt County Rural Electric Co-op (HCREC) 1210 13th St N .... Humboldt IA 50548 *Web:* www.midlandpower.coop	515-332-1616		245
Humboldt Lagoons State Park c/o N Coast Redwoods District PO Box 2006 .... Eureka CA 95502 *Web:* www.parks.ca.gov/default.asp?page_id=416	707-677-3132		565
Humboldt Manufacturing Co 875 Tollgate Rd .... Elgin IL 60123 *TF:* 800-544-7220 ■ *Web:* www.humboldtmfg.com	708-456-6300		407
Humboldt Redwood Company LLC 108 Main St PO Box 565 .... Scotia CA 95565 *Web:* www.getredwood.com	707-764-4472		820
Humboldt Redwoods State Park PO Box 100 PO Box 2006 .... Weott CA 95571 *Web:* www.parks.ca.gov/default.asp?page_id=425	707-946-2409		565
Humboldt State University 1 Harpst St .... Arcata CA 95521 *Fax: Admissions ■ *TF:* 866-850-9556 ■ *Web:* www.humboldt.edu	707-826-3011	826-6190*	166
Humbug Mountain State Park PO Box 1345 .... Port Orford OR 97465 *Web:* www.oregonstateparks.org	541-332-6774		565
Humco Holding Group Inc 7400 Alumax Dr .... Texarkana TX 75501 *TF:* 800-662-3435 ■ *Web:* www.humco.com	903-334-6200	334-6300	582
Hume Lake Christian Camps Inc 5545 E Hedges Ave .... Fresno CA 93727 *Web:* hume.org/home2	559-305-7770		239
Hume Travel Corp 1130 W Pender St Ste 510 .... Vancouver BC V6E4A1 *TF:* 800-663-9787 ■ *Web:* www.hume-travel.com	604-682-7581	488-1138	772
Hummel Bros Inc 180 Sargent Dr .... New Haven CT 06511 *Web:* hummelbros.3dcartstores.com	203-787-4113		296-26
Hummel Gift Shop 1656 Garfield Rd .... New Springfield OH 44443	330-549-3728		327
Hummels Office Equipment Co 25 Canal St .... Mohawk NY 13407 *Web:* www.hummelsop.com	315-866-3860		320
Hummer Winblad Venture Partners Pier 33 S The Embarcadero Ste 300 .... San Francisco CA 94111 *Web:* hwvp.com	415-979-9600	979-9601	792
Hummer's Sports Cafe 2600 Paramount Blvd .... Amarillo TX 79109	806-353-0723		671
Hummert International Inc 4500 Earth City Expy .... Earth City MO 63045 *TF:* 800-325-3055 ■ *Web:* www.hummert.com	314-506-4500	506-4510	276
Humongo 155 Main St 4th Fl .... Danbury CT 06810 *Web:* www.humongoagency.com	203-730-6300		7
Humperdinks Restaurant and Brewpub 2208 W Northwest Hwy Ste 200 .... Dallas TX 75220	214-358-4159		670
Humphrey Company Ltd 6877 Wynnwood Ln .... Houston TX 77008	713-686-8606		189-10
Humphrey Products Co 5070 E N Ave PO Box 2008 .... Kalamazoo MI 49048 *TF:* 800-477-8707 ■ *Web:* www.humphrey-products.com	269-381-5500	381-4113	789
Humphrey's Half Moon Inn & Suites 2303 Shelter Island Dr .... San Diego CA 92106 *TF:* 800-542-7400 ■ *Web:* www.halfmooninn.com	619-224-3411	224-3478	379
Humphreys College 6650 Inglewood Ave .... Stockton CA 95207 *TF:* 800-433-3243 ■ *Web:* www.humphreys.edu	209-478-0800	478-8721	166
Humphreys County PO Box 547ÿ PO Box 547 .... Belzoni MS 39038 *Web:* humphreys.msghn.org	662-247-1740		338
Humphreys County 102 Thompson St .... Waverly TN 37185 *Web:* www.humphreystn.com	931-296-7795		338
Humphreys Restaurant 2241 Shelter Island Dr .... San Diego CA 92106 *Web:* humphreysrestaurant.com	619-224-3577	224-9438	671
Humpty's Restaurants International Inc 2505 Macleod Terr S .... Calgary AB T2G5J4 *Web:* www.humptys.com	403-269-4675	266-1973	670
HumRRO (Human Resources Research Organization) 66 Canal Ctr Plaza Ste 400 .... Alexandria VA 22314 *Web:* www.humrro.org	703-549-3611	549-9025	668
Hun School of Princeton 176 Edgerstoune Rd .... Princeton NJ 08540 *Web:* www.hunschool.org	609-921-7600		622
Hunan 1940 W William Cannon Dr .... Austin TX 78745 *Web:* www.hunanaustin.com	512-443-8848		671
Hunan 115 Southland Dr .... Lexington KY 40503 *Web:* hunanchineselexington.com	859-278-3811		671
Hunan Gate 4233 N Fairfax Dr .... Arlington VA 22203 *Web:* hunangate.com	703-243-5678		671
Hunan House 2350 E Dublin Granville Rd .... Columbus OH 43229 *Web:* www.hunancolumbus.com	614-895-3330		671
Hunan Restaurant 1416 Missouri Blvd .... Jefferson City MO 65109 *Web:* hunan-restaurant.com	573-634-5253		671
Hunan Springs 4939 Hamilton Blvd .... Wescosville PA 18106 *Web:* hunansprings.com	610-366-8338		671
Hunan Village 3311 S Shepherd Dr .... Houston TX 77098 *Web:* houstonhunanvillage.com	713-528-4651		671
Hunan Village Restaurant *Hunan Village Conroe* 1402 N Loop 336 W .... Conroe TX 77304 *Web:* www.hunanvillageconroe.com	936-539-6811		671
Hundley Farms Inc 28200 Florida 80 .... Belle Glade FL 33430	561-996-6855		10-11
Hunewill Cir H Ranch 1110 Hunewill Ranch Rd .... Bridgeport CA 93517 *Web:* www.hunewillranch.com	760-932-7710		239
Hungary 223 E 52nd St .... New York NY 10022 *Web:* www.un.int	212-752-0209		784
Hungary Consulate General 223 E 52nd St .... New York NY 10022	212-752-0669		257
Hunger Project, The 5 Union Sq W .... New York NY 10003 *TF:* 800-228-6691 ■ *Web:* www.thp.org	212-251-9100	532-9785	48-5
Hungerford & Terry Inc 226 N Atlantic Ave .... Clayton NJ 08312 *TF:* 800-817-3240 ■ *Web:* www.hungerfordterry.com	856-881-3200	881-6859	806
Hungry Howie's Pizza & Subs Inc 30300 Stephenson Hwy Ste 200 .... Madison Heights MI 48071 *TF:* 800-624-8122 ■ *Web:* www.hungryhowies.com	248-414-3300	414-3301	670
Hungry Mother State Park 2854 Pk Blvd .... Marion VA 24354 *Web:* www.dcr.virginia.gov/state-parks/hungry-mother#general_information	276-781-7400		565
Hungry Valley State Vehicular Recreation Area 46001 Orwin Way .... Gorman CA 93243 *Web:* www.parks.ca.gov	661-248-7007		565
Hunsaker & Assoc Irvine Inc 3 Hughes .... Irvine CA 92618 *Web:* www.hunsaker.com	949-583-1010	583-0759	261
Hunt & Behrens Inc 30 Lakeville St .... Petaluma CA 94952 *Web:* hbfeeds.com	707-762-4594	762-9164	447
Hunt & Faherty 40 Delaware Ave .... Lambertville NJ 08530 *Web:* hunt-faherty.hub.biz	609-397-0900		445
Hunt & Sons Inc 5750 S Watt Ave .... Sacramento CA 95829 *TF:* 800-734-2999 ■ *Web:* www.huntnsons.com	916-383-4868	383-1005	324
Hunt Adkins Inc 15 S Fifth St Ste 300 .... Minneapolis MN 55402 *Web:* www.huntadkins.com	612-339-8003		7
Hunt Bros 2404 Hunt Bros Rd SE .... Lake Wales FL 33898	863-676-9471		11-1
Hunt Conference Group Inc 611 S Main St Ste 410 .... Grapevine TX 76051 *Web:* www.huntconferencegroup.com	817-410-4660		196
Hunt Consolidated Inc 1900 N Akard St .... Dallas TX 75201 *TF:* 800-424-9300 ■ *Web:* www.huntoil.com	214-978-8000	978-8888	360-3
Hunt Construction Group 2450 S Tibbs Ave .... Indianapolis IN 46241 *Web:* www.huntconstructiongroup.com	317-227-7800		186
Hunt County PO Box 1316 .... Greenville TX 75403 *Web:* www.huntcounty.net	903-408-4130		338
Hunt Design Assoc Inc 25 N Mentor Ave .... Pasadena CA 91106 *TF:* 800-677-1997 ■ *Web:* www.huntdesign.com	626-793-7847		344
Hunt Electric Corp 7900 Chicago Ave S .... Bloomington MN 55420 *TF:* 800-257-5540 ■ *Web:* www.huntelec.com	651-646-2911	643-6575	189-4
Hunt Ford Inc 6825 Crain Hwy .... La Plata MD 20646 *Web:* huntfordinc.com	301-934-8186		57
Hunt Forest Products 401 E Reynolds Dr PO Box 1263 .... Ruston LA 71273 *TF:* 800-390-8589 ■ *Web:* www.huntforpro.com	318-255-2245		683
Hunt Guillot & Assoc LLC 603 Reynolds Dr .... Ruston LA 71270 *TF:* 866-255-6825 ■ *Web:* www.hga-llc.com	318-255-6825		256
Hunt Insurance Agency Inc 12000 S Harlem Ave .... Palos Heights IL 60463 *TF:* 800-772-6484 ■ *Web:* thehuntgroup.com	708-361-5300		390
Hunt Leibert Jacobson PC 50 Weston St .... Hartford CT 06120 *Web:* www.huntleibert.com	860-808-0606		428

				Phone	Fax	Class
Hunt Midwest Enterprises Inc 8300 NE Underground Dr *TF:* 800-551-6877 ■ *Web:* www.huntmidwest.com	Kansas City	MO	64161	816-455-2500		655
Hunt Midwest Mining Inc 8300 NE Underground Dr *TF:* 800-551-6877 ■ *Web:* www.huntmidwest.com	Kansas City	MO	64161	816-455-2500	455-4462	503-5
Hunt Midwest Residential Development 8300 NE Underground Dr *TF:* 800-551-6877 ■ *Web:* www.huntmidwest.com	Kansas City	MO	64161	816-455-2500		653
Hunt Oil Co 1900 N Akard St *Web:* www.huntoil.com	Dallas	TX	75201	214-978-8000	978-8888	580
Hunt Pan Am Aviation Inc 505 Amelia Earhart Dr *TF:* 800-888-7524 ■ *Web:* www.huntpanam.com	Brownsville	TX	78521	956-542-9111	542-9133	63
Hunt Refining Co 2200 Jack Warner Pkwy Ste 400 *Web:* www.huntrefining.com	Tuscaloosa	AL	35401	205-391-3300	758-8371	580
Hunt Regional Healthcare 4215 Joe Ramsey Blvd *TF:* 855-854-2283 ■ *Web:* www.huntregional.org	Greenville	TX	75401	903-408-5000		374-3
Hunt Valve Company Inc 1913 E State St *TF:* 800-321-2757 ■ *Web:* www.huntvalve.com	Salem	OH	44460	330-337-9535	337-3754	790
Hunter Banks Company Inc 29 Montford Ave *Web:* hunterbanks.com	Asheville	NC	28801	828-252-3005		711
Hunter Benefits Consulting Group Inc 119 E Palatine Rd Ste 104 *Web:* hunterbenefits.com	Palatine	IL	60067	847-776-2125		196
Hunter Business Group LLC 4650 N Port Washington Rd **Fax Area Code:* 414 ■ *TF:* 800-423-4010 ■ *Web:* www.hunterbusiness.com	Milwaukee	WI	53212	800-423-4010	203-8225*	195
Hunter College 695 Pk Ave Rm 1212W *Web:* www.hunter.cuny.edu	New York	NY	10065	212-772-4490	650-3472	166
Hunter Company Inc 3300 W 71st Ave *TF:* 800-676-4868 ■ *Web:* www.huntercompany.com	Westminster	CO	80030	303-427-4626		710
Hunter Contracting Co 701 N Cooper Rd *Web:* www.huntercontracting.com	Gilbert	AZ	85233	480-892-0521	892-4932	188-4
Hunter Display 14 Hewlett Ave *TF:* 800-767-2110 ■ *Web:* www.hunterdisplays.com	East Patchogue	NY	11772	631-475-5900	475-5950	233
Hunter Douglas Inc 1 Hunter Douglas Dr *TF:* 800-789-0331 ■ *Web:* my.hunterdouglas.com/dc	Cumberland	MD	21502	301-722-7700		87
Hunter Duncan D (Rep R - CA) 2429 Rayburn HOB *Web:* hunter.house.gov	Washington	DC	20515	202-225-5672	225-0235	342-2
Hunter Engineering Co 11250 Hunter Dr *TF:* 800-448-6848 ■ *Web:* www.hunter.com	Bridgeton	MO	63044	314-731-3020	731-1776	62-5
Hunter Events 1686 Union St Ste 305 *Web:* hunterproductionssf.com	San Francisco	CA	94123	415-563-8704		366
Hunter Fan Co 7130 Goodlett Farms Pkwy Ste 400 *TF:* 888-830-1326 ■ *Web:* www.hunterfan.com	Memphis	TN	38016	901-743-1360		37
Hunter Hamersmith 725 NE 125th St *Web:* www.hhadvertising.net	North Miami	FL	33161	305-895-8430		4
Hunter Heavy Equipment Inc 2829 Texas Ave *TF:* 800-562-7368 ■ *Web:* www.hunterheavyequipment.com	Texas City	TX	77590	409-945-2382	945-9145	190
Hunter House 54 Washington St *TF:* 800-326-6030 ■ *Web:* www.newportmansions.org	Newport	RI	02840	401-847-1000	847-1361	50-3
Hunter House Victorian Museum 240 W Freemason St *Web:* www.hunterhousemuseum.org	Norfolk	VA	23510	757-623-9814		520
Hunter Marine Transport Inc 6615 Robertson Ave *TF:* 800-876-2047 ■ *Web:* www.huntermarine.net	Nashville	TN	37209	615-352-6935		314
Hunter Memorial Presbyterian Church Inc 109 Rosemont Garden *Web:* hunterlex.org	Lexington	KY	40503	859-277-5126		48-20
Hunter Museum of American Art 10 Bluff View St *Web:* www.huntermuseum.org	Chattanooga	TN	37403	423-267-0968	267-9844	520
Hunter Public Relations 41 Madison Ave 5th Fl *TF:* 866-395-7710 ■ *Web:* www.hunterpr.com	New York	NY	10010	212-679-6600	679-6607	636
Hunter Woodworks Inc 21038 S Wilmington Ave PO Box 4937 *TF:* 800-966-4751 ■ *Web:* www.hunterpallets.com	Carson	CA	90749	323-775-2544	775-2540	551
Hunter World Travel 4683 Chabot Dr Ste 385 *TF:* 800-876-8785 ■ *Web:* www.hunterworldtravel.com	Pleasanton	CA	94588	925-463-0560		772
Hunter'S Friend LLC 340 Low Gap Frk *Web:* huntersfriend.com	Oil Springs	KY	41238	606-297-1011		711
Hunter's Specialties Inc 6000 Huntington Ct NE *Web:* www.hunterspec.com	Cedar Rapids	IA	52402	319-395-0321	395-0326	710
Hunter, Smith & Davis LLP 1212 N Eastman Rd *Web:* www.hsdlaw.com	Kingsport	TN	37664	423-378-8800		428
Hunter-Dawson State Historic Site PO Box 308 *Web:* www.mostateparks.com	New Madrid	MO	63869	573-748-5340		565
Hunterdon County 71 Main St *Web:* www.co.hunterdon.nj.us	Flemington	NJ	08822	908-788-1221	782-4068	338
Hunterdon County Chamber of Commerce 14 Mine St *Web:* www.hunterdon-chamber.org	Flemington	NJ	08822	908-782-7115	782-7283	139
Hunterdon County Democrat 8 Minneakoning Rd *TF:* 888-782-7533 ■ *Web:* www.nj.com	Flemington	NJ	08822	908-782-4747	782-6572	532-4
Hunterdon County Library 314 State Hwy 12 Bldg Ste 3 *TF:* 800-272-4630 ■ *Web:* www.hclibrary.us	Flemington	NJ	08822	908-788-1444	806-4862	434-3
Hunterdon Medical Ctr 2100 Westcott Dr *Web:* www.hunterdonhealthcare.org	Flemington	NJ	08822	908-788-6100		374-3
Hunterdon Transformer Co 75 Industrial Dr *TF:* 800-747-0845 ■ *Web:* www.hunterdontransformer.com	Alpha	NJ	08865	908-454-2400	454-6266	767
Hunters Ambulance Service Inc 47 N Plains Industrial Rd Ste A *Web:* www.huntersamb.com	Wallingford	CT	06492	203-269-6586		30
Hunting Energy Services Inc 2 Northpoint Dr Ste 400 *Web:* www.huntingplc.com	The Woodlands	TX	77060	281-442-7382	931-2450	190
Hunting Innova 8383 N Sam Houston Pkwy W *Web:* www.hunting-intl.com	Houston	TX	77064	281-653-5500	653-5501	253
Hunting Island State Park 2555 Sea Island Pkwy *Web:* www.southcarolinaparks.com	Hunting Island	SC	29920	843-838-2011	838-4263	565
Huntingdon College 1500 E Fairview Ave **Fax:* Admissions ■ *TF Admissions:* 800-763-0313 ■ *Web:* www.huntingdon.edu	Montgomery	AL	36106	334-833-4497	833-4497*	166
Huntingdon County 223 Penn St County Courthouse *TF:* 800-373-0209 ■ *Web:* www.huntingdoncounty.net	Huntingdon	PA	16652	814-643-3091	643-8152	338
Huntingdon County Business & Industry 9136 William Penn Hwy *Web:* www.hcbi.com	Huntingdon	PA	16652	814-506-8287		139
Huntingdon County Visitors Bureau 6993 Seven Pt Rd Ste 2 *TF:* 888-729-7869 ■ *Web:* www.raystown.org	Hesston	PA	16647	814-658-0060	658-0068	206
Huntington Bancshares Inc 7 Easton Oval *NASDAQ:* HBAN ■ *TF:* 800-480-2265 ■ *Web:* www.huntington.com	Columbus	OH	43219	800-480-2265		360-2
Huntington Beach Arts Ctr 538 Main St *TF:* 800-780-0347 ■ *Web:* huntingtonbeachartcenter.org	Huntington Beach	CA	92648	714-374-1650		50-2
Huntington Beach Chamber of Commerce 2134 Main St Ste 100 *Web:* hbchamber.com	Huntington Beach	CA	92648	714-536-8888	960-7654	139
Huntington Beach City Hall 2000 Main St *Web:* www.ci.huntington-beach.ca.us	Huntington Beach	CA	92648	714-536-5511	374-1557	337
Huntington Beach Independent 1375 Sunflower Ave *Web:* www.latimes.com/socal/hb-independent	Costa Mesa	CA	92626	714-966-4600		532-4
Huntington Beach Marketing & Visitors Bureau 301 Main St Ste 208 *TF:* 800-729-6232 ■ *Web:* www.surfcityusa.com	Huntington Beach	CA	92648	714-969-3492		206
Huntington Beach Playhouse (HBPH) 7111 Talbert Ave *Web:* www.hbplayhouse.com	Huntington Beach	CA	92648	714-375-0696		573-4
Huntington Beach Public Library (HBPL) 7111 Talbert Ave *TF:* 800-565-0148 ■ *Web:* www.huntingtonbeachca.gov	Huntington Beach	CA	92648	714-842-4481	375-5180	434-3
Huntington Beach State Park 16148 Ocean Hwy *TF:* 800-491-1764 ■ *Web:* www.southcarolinaparks.com	Murrells Inlet	SC	29576	843-237-4440		565
Huntington County 201 N Jefferson St *Web:* www.huntington.in.us	Huntington	IN	46750	260-358-4804	358-4823	338
Huntington County Visitors & Convention Bureau 407 N Jefferson St *TF:* 800-848-4282 ■ *Web:* www.visithuntington.org	Huntington	IN	46750	260-359-8687		206
Huntington Hospital Hospitality House 2801 S Staunton Rd	Huntington	WV	25702	304-522-1832		372
Huntington Hotel & Nob Hill Spa 1075 California St *TF:* 800-227-4683 ■ *Web:* thescarlethotels.com	San Francisco	CA	94108	415-474-5400	474-6227	379
Huntington Hotel Group LLC 105 Decker Ct Ste 500 *Web:* www.huntingtonhotelgroup.com	Irving	TX	75062	972-510-1200		194
Huntington Ingalls Industries 4101 Washington Ave *NYSE:* HII ■ *Web:* www.huntingtoningalls.com	Newport News	VA	23607	757-380-2000		698
Huntington Ingalls Industries Inc. 1000 Access Rd *TF:* 877-871-2058 ■ *Web:* ingalls.huntingtoningalls.com	Pascagoula	MS	39568	228-935-1122		698
Huntington Junior College 900 Fifth Ave *TF:* 800-344-4522 ■ *Web:* www.huntingtonjuniorcollege.com	Huntington	WV	25701	304-697-7550	697-7554	800
Huntington Learning Centers Inc 496 Kinderkamack Rd *TF:* 800-653-8400 ■ *Web:* huntingtonhelps.com	Oradell	NJ	07649	201-261-8400		148
Huntington Library Art Collections & Botanical Gardens, The 1151 Oxford Rd *Web:* www.huntington.org	San Marino	CA	91108	626-405-2100		97
Huntington Memorial Hospital 100 W California Blvd *Web:* www.huntingtonhospital.com	Pasadena	CA	91109	626-397-5000		374-3
Huntington Mortgage Co 7575 Huntington Pk Dr *TF:* 800-323-4695 ■ *Web:* huntington.com	Columbus	OH	43235	614-480-6505		509
Huntington Museum of Art Inc 2033 McCoy Rd *Web:* www.hmoa.org	Huntington	WV	25701	304-529-2701	529-7447	520
Huntington National Bank 41 S High St Huntington Ctr *TF:* 800-480-2265 ■ *Web:* www.huntington.com	Columbus	OH	43287	614-480-8300	480-4973	70
Huntington Park Rubber Stamp Co 2761 E Slauson Ave PO Box 519 *TF:* 800-882-0129 ■ *Web:* www.hprubberstamp.com	Huntington Park	CA	90255	323-582-6461	582-8046	467
Huntington Regional Chamber of Commerce 720 Fourth Ave *Web:* www.huntingtonchamber.org	Huntington	WV	25701	304-525-5131	525-5158	139
Huntington State Beach 21601 Pacific Coast Hwy *Web:* www.parks.ca.gov/?page_id=643	Huntington Beach	CA	92646	714-536-1454		565
Huntington State Park PO Box 1343 *TF:* 800-322-3770 ■ *Web:* stateparks.utah.gov	Huntington	UT	84528	435-687-2491		565
Huntington State Park 1343 Huntington *Web:* www.stateparks.utah.gov	Price	UT	84528	435-687-2491		565

Listing	City	State	Zip	Phone	Fax	Class
Huntington Steel & Supply Company Inc						
100 Third Ave	Huntington	WV	25714	304-522-8218		492
Web: www.huntingtonsteel.com						
Huntington Theatre Co						
264 Huntington Ave Boston University Theatre	Boston	MA	02115	617-266-7900	353-8300	749
Web: www.huntingtontheatre.org						
Huntington Township Chamber of Commerce						
164 Main St	Huntington	NY	11743	631-423-6100	351-8276	139
TF: 888-962-9932 ■ *Web:* www.huntingtonchamber.com						
Huntington Union Free School District 3						
PO Box 1500	Huntington	NY	11743	631-673-2185		685
Web: www.hufsd.edu						
Huntington University						
2303 College Ave	Huntington	IN	46750	260-356-6000	358-3699*	166
**Fax:* Admissions ■ *TF Admissions:* 800-642-6493 ■ *Web:* www.huntington.edu						
Huntington University						
935 Ramsey Lake Rd	Sudbury	ON	P3E2C6	705-673-4126	673-6917	785
TF: 800-461-6366 ■ *Web:* www.huntington.laurentian.ca						
Huntington Valley Health Care Ctr						
8382 Newman Ave	Huntington Beach	CA	92647	714-842-5551	848-5359	450
Web: hvhcc.com						
Huntington Veterans Affairs Medical Ctr						
1540 Spring Valley Dr	Huntington	WV	25704	304-429-6741	429-0270	374-8
TF: 800-827-8244 ■ *Web:* www.huntington.va.gov						
Huntington's Disease Society of America (HDSA)						
505 Eigth Ave Ste 902	New York	NY	10018	212-242-1968	239-3430	48-17
TF: 800-345-4372 ■ *Web:* www.hdsa.org						
Huntleigh Securities Corp						
7800 Forsyth Blvd 5th Fl	Saint Louis	MO	63105	314-236-2400	236-2401	690
TF: 800-727-5405 ■ *Web:* www.hntlgh.com						
Huntley-Sheehy Inc 520 Olive St	Marysville	CA	95901	530-743-9264		390
Web: huntley-sheehy.com						
Hunt-Morgan House (BGT) 201 N Mill St	Lexington	KY	40507	859-253-0362	259-9210	50-3
Web: www.bluegrasstrust.org/huntmorgantours.html						
Hunton & Williams LLP						
951 E Byrd St Riverfront Plz East Tower	Richmond	VA	23219	804-788-8200	788-8218	428
Web: www.hunton.com						
Hunton Group, The 10555 Westpark Dr	Houston	TX	77042	713-266-3900		14
Web: www.huntongroup.com						
Huntsinger & Jeffer Inc						
809 Brook Hill Cir	Richmond	VA	23227	804-266-2499		5
Web: www.huntsinger-jeffer.com						
Huntsman Corp 500 Huntsman Way	Salt Lake City	UT	84108	801-584-5700	584-5781	605-2
NYSE: HUN ■ *TF:* 888-490-8484 ■ *Web:* www.huntsman.com						
Huntsville Ballet 800 Regal Dr SW	Huntsville	AL	35801	256-539-0961		573-1
Web: www.communityballet.org						
Huntsville Board of Education						
200 White St	Huntsville	AL	35801	256-428-6800	428-6838*	685
**Fax:* Hum Res ■ *TF:* 877-517-0020 ■ *Web:* www.huntsvillecityschools.org						
Huntsville Botanical Garden						
4747 Bob Wallace Ave	Huntsville	AL	35805	256-830-4447	830-5314	97
TF: 877-930-4447 ■ *Web:* www.hsvbg.org						
Huntsville City Hall						
308 Fountain Cir	Huntsville	AL	35801	256-427-5240	427-5245	337
Web: www.huntsvilleal.gov/venue/city-hall						
Huntsville Hospital 101 Sivley Rd	Huntsville	AL	35801	256-265-1000		374-3
Web: www.huntsvillehospital.org						
Huntsville International Airport						
1000 Glenn Hearn Blvd Ste 20008	Huntsville	AL	35824	256-772-9395		27
Web: www.flyhuntsville.com						
Huntsville Memorial Hospital						
110 Memorial Hospital Dr	Huntsville	TX	77340	936-291-3411		374-3
TF: 800-833-5602 ■ *Web:* www.huntsvillememorial.com						
Huntsville Museum of Art						
300 Church St SW	Huntsville	AL	35801	256-535-4350	532-1743	520
TF: 800-786-9095 ■ *Web:* www.hsvmuseum.org						
Huntsville State Park PO Box 508	Huntsville	TX	77342	936-295-5644		565
Web: tpwd.texas.gov/state-parks/huntsville						
Huntsville Symphony Orchestra						
700 Monroe St PO Box 2400	Huntsville	AL	35801	256-539-4818	539-4819	573-3
Web: www.hso.org						
Huntsville/Madison County Convention & Visitor's Bureau						
500 Church St Ste 1	Huntsville	AL	35801	256-551-2230	551-2324	206
TF: 800-843-0468 ■ *Web:* www.huntsville.org						
Huntsville-Madison County Public Library						
915 Monroe St	Huntsville	AL	35801	256-532-5940		434-3
TF: 800-786-9095 ■ *Web:* hmcpl.org						
Huntsville-Walker County Chamber of Commerce						
1327 11th St	Huntsville	TX	77340	936-295-8113	295-0571	139
TF: 800-289-0389 ■ *Web:* www.chamber.huntsville.tx.us						
Huntwood Industries						
23800 E Apple Way	Liberty Lake	WA	99019	509-924-5858		115
TF: 800-873-7350 ■ *Web:* www.huntwood.com						
Huntzinger Management Group Inc, The						
72 Glenmaura National Blvd Ste 105	Moosic	PA	18507	570-824-4721		41
Web: huntzingergroup.com						
Hunzinger Construction Co						
21100 Enterprise Ave	Brookfield	WI	53045	262-797-0797		186
Web: www.hunzinger.com						
Huot Manufacturing Co						
550 Wheeler St N	Saint Paul	MN	55104	651-646-1869	646-0457	319-1
TF: 800-832-3838 ■ *Web:* www.huot.com						
Hupp & Assoc Inc 1690 Summit St	New Haven	IN	46774	260-748-8282		124
Web: www.huppaerospace.com						
Huppert Industries Inc						
16808 S Lathrop Ave	Harvey	IL	60426	708-339-2020	339-2225	318
Web: www.huppert.com						
Hurckman Mechanical Industries Inc						
PO Box 10977	Green Bay	WI	54307	920-499-8771		189-10
TF: 844-499-8771 ■ *Web:* www.hurckman.com						
Hurco Cos Inc 1 Technology Way	Indianapolis	IN	46268	317-293-5309	298-2621	455
NASDAQ: HURC ■ *TF Sales:* 800-634-2416 ■ *Web:* www.hurco.com						
Hurco Design & Mfg 200 W 33rd St	Ogden	UT	84401	905-567-2600		286
Hurco Technologies Inc						
409 Enterprise St	Harrisburg	SD	57032	800-888-1436		480
TF: 800-888-1436 ■ *Web:* hurcotech.com						
Hurd It Communications						
2106 Gallows Rd A	Vienna	VA	22182	703-442-3422		180
TF: 800-727-1624 ■ *Web:* www.hurdit.com						
Hurd State Park						
c/o Eastern District HQ 209 Hebron Rd	Marlborough	CT	06447	860-295-9523		565
Web: www.ct.gov						
Hurdman Communications						
1344 W 75 N	Centerville	UT	84014	801-292-7673		180
Web: hurdman.com						
Hurlen Corp						
9841 Bell Ranch Dr	Santa Fe Springs	CA	90670	562-941-5330		690
Web: kenigaero.com						
Hurley Communications Inc						
1113 Washington St	Norwood	MA	02062	781-762-3313		463
Web: hurleycommunications.com						
Hurley Medical Ctr 1 Hurley Plaza	Flint	MI	48503	810-262-9000		374-3
TF: 800-336-8999 ■ *Web:* www.hurleymc.com						
Hurley Rogner Miller Cox						
1560 Orange Ave Ste 500	Winter Park	FL	32789	407-571-7400		428
Web: www.hrmcw.com						
Hurley, Toevs, Styles, Hamblin & Panter PA						
4155 Montgomery Blvd NE	Albuquerque	NM	87109	505-888-1188		428
Web: hurleyfirm.com						
Huron Automatic Screw Co						
PO Box 610068	Port Huron	MI	48061	810-364-6636		621
Web: www.huronauto.com						
Huron Casting Inc						
7050 Hartley St PO Box 679	Pigeon	MI	48755	989-453-3933	453-3319	307
Web: www.huroncasting.com						
Huron Chamber & Visitors Bureau						
1725 Dakota Ave S	Huron	SD	57350	605-352-0000	352-8321	206
TF: 800-487-6673 ■ *Web:* www.huronsd.com						
Huron Community Bank 301 Newman St	East Tawas	MI	48730	989-362-6700		70
Web: bankhcb.com						
Huron Consulting Services LLC						
550 W Van Buren St	Chicago	IL	60607	312-583-8700		463
Web: www.huronconsultinggroup.com						
Huron County 250 E Huron Ave Rm 305	Bad Axe	MI	48413	989-269-6431	269-6152	338
TF: 800-358-4862 ■ *Web:* www.huroncounty.com						
Huron County						
County Courthouse 2 E Main St	Norwalk	OH	44857	419-668-5113		338
Web: www.hccommissioners.com						
Huron Daily Tribune						
211 N Heisterman St	Bad Axe	MI	48413	989-269-6461	269-9435	532-2
TF: 800-322-1184 ■ *Web:* www.michiganthumb.com						
Huron Inc 6554 Lakeshore Rd	Lexington	MI	48450	810-359-5344	359-7521	621
TF: 800-739-8188 ■ *Web:* huroninc.com						
Huron Machine Products Inc						
228 SW 21st Terr	Fort Lauderdale	FL	33312	800-327-8186	583-2154*	493
**Fax Area Code:* 954 ■ **Fax:* Sales ■ *TF:* 800-327-8186 ■ *Web:* www.huronmachine.com						
Huron Regional Medical Ctr (HRMC)						
172 Fourth St SE	Huron	SD	57350	605-353-6200	353-6300	374-3
TF: 800-529-0115 ■ *Web:* www.huronregional.org						
Huron Technologies International Inc						
550 Parkside Dr Unit B6	Waterloo	ON	N2L5V4	519-886-9013		743
TF: 800-601-9773 ■ *Web:* www.hurondigitalpathology.com						
Huron University College						
1349 Western Rd	London	ON	N6G1H3	519-438-7224	438-3938	785
Web: www.huronuc.on.ca						
Huron Valley Chamber of Commerce						
317 Union St	Milford	MI	48381	248-685-7129	685-9047	139
Web: www.huronvcc.com						
Huron Valley Correctional Facility						
3201 Bemis Rd	Ypsilanti	MI	48197	734-572-9900	572-9499	213
TF: 855-444-3911 ■ *Web:* www.michigan.gov						
Huron Valley Financial Inc						
2395 Oak Vly Dr Ste 200	Ann Arbor	MI	48103	734-669-8000		528
TF: 800-650-7441 ■ *Web:* www.huronvalleyfinancial.com						
Huron Valley Steel Corp						
1650 W Jefferson Ste 100	Trenton	MI	48183	734-479-3500	479-3413	723
TF: 800-666-4789 ■ *Web:* www.hvsc.net						
Hurricane Convention & Visitors Bureau						
3255 Teays Valley Rd PO Box 1086	Hurricane	WV	25526	304-562-5896	562-5858	206
Web: www.hurricanewv.com						
Hurricane Electric Internet Services						
760 Mission Ct	Fremont	CA	94539	510-580-4100	580-4151	808
Web: www.he.com						
Hurst Boiler & Welding Company Inc						
100 Boilermaker Ln	Coolidge	GA	31738	229-346-3545	346-3874	91
TF: 877-994-8778 ■ *Web:* www.hurstboiler.com						
Hurst Chemical Co						
2360 Eastman Ave Ste 108	Oxnard	CA	93030	800-723-2004		628
TF Cust Svc: 800-723-2004 ■ *Web:* www.hurstchemical.com						
Hurst Farm Supply Inc 105 Ave D	Abernathy	TX	79311	806-298-2541	298-2936	274
TF: 800-535-8903 ■ *Web:* www.hurstfs.com						
Hurst Group 500 Buck Pl	Lexington	KY	40511	859-255-4422	255-4421	535
TF: 800-926-4423 ■ *Web:* www.hurstgroup.net						
Hurst Place 209 Limeridge Rd E	Hamilton	ON	L9A2S6	289-426-5302	521-8166*	462
**Fax Area Code:* 905 ■ *TF:* 888-521-8300 ■ *Web:* www.mohawkssi.com						
Hurst Public Library						
901 Precinct Line Rd	Hurst	TX	76053	817-788-7300	590-9515	434-3
TF: 800-344-8377 ■ *Web:* hursttx.gov						
Hurst Rosche Engineers Inc						
601 N Bruns Ln Ste B	Springfield	IL	62702	217-787-1199		256
Web: hurst-rosche.com						
Hurst-Euless-Bedford Chamber of Commerce						
2109 Martin Dr	Bedford	TX	76021	817-283-1521	267-5111	139
Web: www.heb.org						
Hurth Yeager Sisk & Blakemore Llp						
4860 Riverbend Rd	Boulder	CO	80301	303-443-7900		445
Web: hurth.com						
Hurtigruten 405 Pk Ave	New York	NY	10022	212-319-1300		220
TF: 866-552-0371						
Hurwitz & Associates 13A Highland Cir	Needham	MA	02494	617-597-1724		463
Web: hurwitz.com						
Hurwitz-Mintz Furniture Co						
1751 Airline Dr	Metairie	LA	70001	504-378-1000		321
TF: 888-957-9555 ■ *Web:* www.hurwitzmintz.com						
Husar's House of Fine Diamonds						
131 N Main St	West Bend	WI	53095	262-334-3453		410
Web: www.husars.com						

Company	Phone	Fax	Class
Husch Blackwell LLP 4801 Main St Ste 1000 ... Kansas City MO 64108 *Web:* www.huschblackwell.com	816-983-8000		428
HUSCO International Inc 2239 Pewaukee Rd ... Waukesha WI 53188 *Web:* www.huscointl.com	262-513-4200	513-4514	790
HUSD (Hayward Unified School District) 24411 Amador St ... Hayward CA 94544 *Web:* www.husd.k12.ca.us	510-784-2600	784-2641	685
Huse Publishing Co 525 Norfolk Ave PO Box 977 ... Norfolk NE 68701 *TF:* 877-371-1020 ■ *Web:* www.norfolkdailynews.com	402-371-1020	371-5802	637-8
Hush Puppies Co 9341 Courtland Dr NE ... Rockford MI 49351 **Fax:* Acctg ■ *TF:* 866-699-7365 ■ *Web:* www.hushpuppies.com	616-866-5500	866-5625*	301
Husky Energy Inc 707 Eigth Ave SW PO Box 6525 ... Calgary AB T2P1H5 *TSE: HSE* ■ *TF:* 877-262-2111 ■ *Web:* www.huskyenergy.com	403-298-6111	298-7464	536
Husky Injection Molding Systems Ltd 500 Queen St S ... Bolton ON L7E5S5 *TF:* 800-465-4875 ■ *Web:* www.husky.co	905-951-5000	951-5384	386
Husnu's 547 State St ... Madison WI 53703 *Web:* www.husnus.com	608-256-0900		671
Husqvarna Construction Products 17400 W 119th St ... Olathe KS 66061 *TF:* 800-288-5040 ■ *Web:* www.husqvarna.com	800-288-5040	825-0028	493
Hussey Copper Ltd 100 Washington St ... Leetsdale PA 15056 *TF:* 800-733-8866 ■ *Web:* www.husseycopper.com	724-251-4200	251-4243	485
Hussey Gay Bell (HGBD) 329 Commercial Dr Ste 200 ... Savannah GA 31406 *Web:* www.husseygaybell.com	912-354-4626		261
Hussey Seating Co 38 Dyer St Ext ... North Berwick ME 03906 **Fax:* Sales ■ *TF:* 800-341-0401 ■ *Web:* www.husseyseating.com	207-676-2271	676-2222*	319-3
Hussian College 111 S Independence Mall E ... Philadelphia PA 19106 *Web:* www.hussianart.edu	215-574-9600	574-9800	164
Hussmann Corp 12999 St Charles Rock Rd ... Bridgeton MO 63044 *TF:* 800-592-2060 ■ *Web:* www.hussmann.com	314-291-2000	298-4756	664
Husson College 1 College Cir ... Bangor ME 04401 **Fax:* Admissions ■ *TF:* 800-448-7766 ■ *Web:* www.husson.edu	207-941-7000	941-7935*	166
Hussong Manufacturing Company Inc 204 Industrial Park Rd ... Lakefield MN 56150 *TF:* 800-253-4904 ■ *Web:* www.kozyheat.com	507-662-6641		362
Hussung Mechanical Contractors 6913 Enterprise Dr ... Louisville KY 40214 *TF:* 800-446-2738 ■ *Web:* www.hussung.com	502-375-3500		610
Hustler Conveyor Co 4101 Crusher Dr ... O'fallon MO 63368 *Web:* www.ampulverizer.com	636-441-8600		207
Huston-Patterson Corp 123 W N St Fl 4 ... Decatur IL 62522 *TF:* 800-866-5692 ■ *Web:* www.hustonpatterson.com	800-866-5692		112
Huston-Tillotson University 900 Chicon St ... Austin TX 78702 **Fax:* Admissions ■ *TF:* 800-343-3822 ■ *Web:* www.htu.edu	512-505-3000	505-3190*	166
Hutch's 1375 Delaware Ave ... Buffalo NY 14209 *Web:* www.hutchsrestaurant.com	716-885-0074		671
Hutch, The 6437 Avondale Dr Nichols Hills ... Plaza Oklahoma City OK 73116 *Web:* www.hutchokc.com	405-842-1000		671
Hutchens Construction Co 1007 Main St ... Cassville MO 65625 *TF:* 888-728-3482 ■ *Web:* www.hutchensconstruction.com	417-847-2489	847-5561	188-4
Hutchens Industries Inc 215 N Patterson Ave ... Springfield MO 65002 **Fax:* Cust Svc ■ *TF:* 800-654-8824 ■ *Web:* hutchensindustries.com	417-862-5012	862-2317*	60
Hutchens Petroleum Corp 22 Performance Dr ... Stuart VA 24171 *TF:* 800-537-7433 ■ *Web:* www.hutchenspetro.com	276-694-7000		580
Hutchings Museum 55 N Center St ... Lehi UT 84043 *Web:* www.lehi-ut.gov/recreation/museum	385-201-1020		520
Hutchins State Jail 1500 E Langdon Rd ... Dallas TX 75241 *Web:* tdcj.state.tx.us	972-225-1304		213
Hutchinson & Bloodgood LLP 579 Auto Center Dr ... Watsonville CA 95076 *Web:* www.hbllp.com	818-637-5000		2
Hutchinson Aerospace & Industry Inc 82 S St ... Hopkinton MA 01748 **Fax:* Sales ■ *TF:* 800-227-7962 ■ *Web:* www.hutchinsonai.com	508-417-7000	417-7224*	676
Hutchinson Asa (R) State Capitoly Rm 250 ... Little Rock AR 72201 *Web:* governor.arkansas.gov	501-682-2345	682-1382	343
Hutchinson Community College & Area Vocational School 1300 N Plum St ... Hutchinson KS 67501 **Fax:* Admissions ■ *TF:* 800-289-3501 ■ *Web:* www.hutchcc.edu	620-665-3500	728-8199*	162
Hutchinson Co-Op PO Box 158 ... Hutchinson MN 55350 *TF:* 800-795-1299 ■ *Web:* www.hutchcoop.com	320-587-4647		276
Hutchinson Correctional Facility PO Box 1568 ... Hutchinson KS 67504 *Web:* www.doc.ks.gov/facilities/hcf	620-662-2321	662-8662	213
Hutchinson County PO Box 1186 ... Stinnett TX 79083 *Web:* www.co.hutchinson.tx.us	806-878-4002		338
Hutchinson Leader Inc 36 Washington Ave W ... Hutchinson MN 55350 *Web:* www.crowrivermedia.com/hutchinsonleader	320-587-5000	587-6104	637-8
Hutchinson Manufacturing Inc 720 Hwy 7 W PO Box 487 ... Hutchinson MN 55350 *TF:* 800-795-1276 ■ *Web:* www.hutchmfg.com	320-587-4653		697
Hutchinson News 300 W Second St ... Hutchinson KS 67504 *TF:* 800-766-3311 ■ *Web:* www.hutchnews.com	620-694-5700	662-4186	532-2
Hutchinson Public Library 901 N Main St ... Hutchinson KS 67501 *Web:* www.hutchpl.org	620-663-5441		434-3
Hutchinson Regional Healthcare System 1701 E 23rd Ave ... Hutchinson KS 67502 *TF:* 800-267-6891 ■ *Web:* hutchregional.com	620-665-2000		374-3
Hutchinson Shockey Erley & Co 222 W Adams St Ste 1700 ... Chicago IL 60606 *Web:* www.hsemuni.com	312-443-1550		690
Hutchinson Technology Inc 40 W Highland Pk Dr ... Hutchinson MN 55350 *NASDAQ: HTCH* ■ *TF:* 800-419-1007 ■ *Web:* www.htch.com	320-587-3797		253
Hutchinson Zoo 6 Emerson Loop E ... Hutchinson KS 67501 *TF:* 800-362-3247 ■ *Web:* hutchgov.com	620-694-2693	694-1980	823
Hutchinson/Mayrath/TerraTrack Industries 514 W Crawford PO Box 629 ... Clay Center KS 67432 *TF:* 800-523-6993 ■ *Web:* www.hutchinson-mayrath.com	785-632-2161	632-5964	273
Hutchinson/Reno County Chamber of Commerce 117 N Walnut St ... Hutchinson KS 67501 *TF:* 800-691-4262 ■ *Web:* www.hutchchamber.com	620-662-3391	662-2168	139
Hutchison Engineering Inc 1801 W Lafayette Ave ... Jacksonville IL 62650 *Web:* hutchisoneng.com	217-245-7164		256
Hutchison Inc 7460 Hwy 85 PO Box 1158 ... Adams City CO 80022 *TF:* 800-525-0121 ■ *Web:* www.hutchison-inc.com	303-287-2826	289-3286	191-3
Huther Bros Inc 1290 University Ave ... Rochester NY 14607	585-473-9462		758
Hutson 306 Andrus Dr ... Murray KY 42071 *TF:* 866-488-7662 ■ *Web:* www.hutsoninc.com/h2	270-886-3994		429
Hutter Construction Corp 810 Turnpike Rd ... New Ipswich NH 03071 *Web:* hutterconstruction.com	603-878-2300		186
Huttig Bldg Products Inc (HBP) 555 Maryville University Dr Ste 400 ... Saint Louis MO 63141 *OTC: HBPI* ■ *TF:* 800-325-4466 ■ *Web:* www.huttig.com	314-216-2600	216-2601	499
Hutton Communications Inc 2520 Marsh Ln ... Carrollton TX 75006 *TF:* 800-725-5264 ■ *Web:* www.hol4g.com	972-417-0100	417-0180	246
Hutton Construction Corp 2229 S W St ... Wichita KS 67213 *Web:* www.huttonconstruction.com	316-942-8855		186
Hutton Hotel, The 1808 W End Ave ... Nashville TN 37203 *TF:* 800-325-2525 ■ *Web:* www.huttonhotel.com	615-340-9333		707
Huvepharma Inc 525 Westpark Dr Ste 230 ... Peachtree City GA 30269 *Web:* www.huvepharma.com	495-950-5000		231
Huxley Communications Co-op 102 N Main Ave ... Huxley IA 50124 *TF:* 800-231-4922 ■ *Web:* www.huxcomm.net	515-597-2212		224
Huy Fong Foods Inc 5001 Earle Ave ... Rosemead CA 91770 *Web:* www.huyfong.com	626-286-8328	286-8522	297-8
HV Food Products Co 1221 Broadway ... Oakland CA 94612 *Web:* www.hiddenvalley.com	510-271-7612	832-1463	296-19
HVA (High Vacuum Apparatus LLC) 12880 Moya Blvd ... Reno NV 89506 *TF:* 800-551-4422 ■ *Web:* www.highvac.com	775-359-4442	359-1369	789
Hvf West LLC 6581 E Drexel Rd ... Tucson AZ 85756 *Web:* www.hvfwest.com	520-750-9454		660
HVH Transportation Inc 181 E 56th Ave Ste 200 ... Denver CO 80216 *TF:* 800-525-4844 ■ *Web:* www.hvhtransportation.com	303-292-3656		780
HVS Executive Search 372 Willis Ave ... Mineola NY 11501 *Web:* www.hvs.com	516-248-8828		463
HW Metal Products Inc 19480 SW 118th Ave ... Tualatin OR 97062 *TF:* 800-498-1460 ■ *Web:* www.hwmetals.com	503-692-1690		295
H&W Printing Inc 1724 Sands Pl ... Marietta GA 30067 *Web:* www.hwprinting.com	770-951-9800		627
HW Wilson Co 10 Estes St ... Ipswich MA 01938 *TF:* 800-653-2726 ■ *Web:* www.ebscohost.com	978-356-6500		637-2
HWA (Harry Walker Agency Inc) 355 Lexington Ave 21st Fl ... New York NY 10017 *Web:* www.harrywalker.com	646-227-4900		708
Hwang-Kum 5908 Sherbrooke St W ... Montreal QC H4A1X7	514-487-1712		671
HWC (Houston Wire & Cable Co) 10201 N Loop E ... Houston TX 77029 *TF:* 800-468-9473 ■ *Web:* www.houwire.com	713-609-2100	609-2101	246
HWE (High West Energy Inc) 6270 County Rd 212 ... Pine Bluffs WY 82082 *TF:* 888-834-1657 ■ *Web:* www.highwestenergy.com	307-245-3261	245-9292	245
HWEC (Hancock-Wood Electric Co-op Inc) 1399 Business Pk Dr S PO Box 190 ... North Baltimore OH 45872 *TF:* 800-445-4840 ■ *Web:* www.hwe.coop	419-257-3241	257-3024	245
HWH Corp 2096 Moscow Rd ... Moscow IA 52760 *TF:* 800-321-3494 ■ *Web:* www.hwhcorp.com	563-724-3396	724-3408	60
Hx5 LLC 212 Eglin Pkwy SE ... Fort Walton Beach FL 32548 *TF:* 800-255-8607 ■ *Web:* www.hxfive.com	850-362-6551		177
Hy Cite Corp 333 Holtzman Rd ... Madison WI 53713 *Web:* www.hycite.com	608-273-3373		362
HY Connect 1000 N Water St Ste 1600 ... Milwaukee WI 53202 *Web:* www.hoffmanyork.com	414-289-9700	289-0417	7
Hy's Steak House 2440 Kuhio Ave ... Honolulu HI 96815 *Web:* hyswaikiki.com	808-922-5555	926-5089	671
Hy's Steakhouse & Cocktail Bar 1 Lombard Pl Main Fl Richardson Bldg ... Winnipeg MB R3B0X3 *Web:* www.hyssteakhouse.com	204-942-1000		671
Hyannis Area Chamber of Commerce 397 Main St ... Hyannis MA 02601 *Web:* www.hyannis.com	508-775-2201		139
Hyannis Holiday Motel 131 Ocean St ... Hyannis MA 02601 *TF:* 800-423-1551 ■ *Web:* hyannisholiday.com	508-775-1639	775-1672	379
Hyannis Public Library (HPL) 401 Main St ... Hyannis MA 02601 *TF:* 800-827-1000 ■ *Web:* www.hyannislibrary.org	508-775-2280	790-0087	434-3
Hyannis Travel Inn 18 N St ... Hyannis MA 02601 *TF:* 800-352-7190 ■ *Web:* www.hyannistravelinn.com	508-775-8200	775-8201	379
Hyatt & Weber P A 200 Westgate Cir Ste 500 ... Annapolis MD 21401 *Web:* www.hwlaw.com	410-266-0626		445
Hyatt at Fisherman's Wharf 555 N Point St ... San Francisco CA 94133 *Web:* fishermanswharf.centric.hyatt.com	415-563-1234		378
Hyatt Boston Harbor 101 Harborside Dr ... Boston MA 02128 *Web:* bostonharbor.regency.hyatt.com/en/hotel/home.html	617-568-1234		707
Hyatt Carmel Highlands 120 Highlands Dr ... Carmel CA 93923 *Web:* highlandsinn.hyatt.com/en/hotel/home.html	831-620-1234	626-1574	379

	Phone	Fax	Class

Hyatt Chicago Magnificent Mile
633 N Saint Clair St .... Chicago IL 60611 312-787-1234 378
Web: chicagomagnificentmile.centric.hyatt.com/en/hotel/home.html

Hyatt Corp 7331 Mazyck Rd............ North Charleston SC 29406 843-735-7100 378
Web: northcharleston.place.hyatt.com

Hyatt Deerfield 1750 Lake Cook Rd .... Deerfield IL 60015 847-945-3400 707
Web: deerfield.regency.hyatt.com

Hyatt Die Cast & Engineering Corp
4656 Lincoln Ave .... Cypress CA 90630 714-826-7550 256
Web: www.hyattdiecast.com

Hyatt Dulles 2300 Dulles Corner Blvd............ Herndon VA 20171 703-713-1234 378
Web: dulles.regency.hyatt.com/en/hotel/home.html

Hyatt Fair Lakes Hotel
12777 Fair Lakes Cir .... Fairfax VA 22033 703-818-1234 379
Web: fairpo.com

Hyatt Hotels Corp 71 S Wacker Dr .... Chicago IL 60606 312-750-1234 379
NYSE: H ■ *TF:* 888-591-1234 ■ *Web:* www.hyatt.com

Grand Hyatt Hotels 71 S Wacker Dr .... Chicago IL 60606 312-750-1234 379
TF Resv: 800-233-1234 ■ *Web:* www.hyatt.com

Hyatt Place Hotels 71 S Wacker Dr .... Chicago IL 60606 312-750-1234 379
TF: 888-492-8847 ■ *Web:* www.place.hyatt.com

Hyatt Regency Hotels 71 S Wacker Dr .... Chicago IL 60606 312-750-1234 379
TF Resv: 800-233-1234 ■ *Web:* www.hyatt.com

Park Hyatt Hotels 71 S Wacker Dr .... Chicago IL 60606 312-750-1234 379
TF Resv: 800-233-1234 ■ *Web:* www.hyatt.com

Hyatt Key West Resort & Spa
601 Front St .... Key West FL 33040 305-809-1234 378
Web: keywest.hyatt.com

Hyatt Place East End & Resort Marina
451 E Main St.................... Riverhead NY 11901 631-208-0002 378
Web: longislandeastend.place.hyatt.com

Hyatt Place New York Midtown South
52-54 W 36th.................... New York NY 10015 888-492-8847 377
TF: 888-492-8847 ■
Web: newyorkmidtown.place.hyatt.com/en/hotel/home.html

Hyatt Place San Jose Downtown
282 Almaden Blvd .... San Jose CA 95113 408-998-0400 378
Web: sanjose.place.hyatt.com/en/hotel/home.html

Hyatt Regency Albuquerque
330 Tijeras NW.................... Albuquerque NM 87102 505-842-1234 378
TF: 800-633-7313 ■
Web: albuquerque.regency.hyatt.com/en/hotel/home.html

Hyatt Regency Bethesda
1 Bethesda Metro Ctr 7400 Wisconsin Ave....... Bethesda MD 20814 301-657-1234 378
Web: bethesda.regency.hyatt.com/en/hotel/home.html

Hyatt Regency Boston
1 Ave de Lafayette.................... Boston MA 02111 617-912-1234 378
Web: boston.regency.hyatt.com/en/hotel/home.html

Hyatt Regency Century Plaza
2025 Ave of the Stars .... Los Angeles CA 90067 310-228-1234 378

Hyatt Regency Columbus 350 N High St ...... Columbus OH 43215 614-463-1234 378
Web: columbus.regency.hyatt.com/en/hotel/home.html

Hyatt Regency Huntington Beach Resort & Spa
21500 Pacific Coast Hwy .... Huntington Beach CA 92648 714-698-1234 845-4990 671
TF: 800-633-7313 ■ *Web:* huntingtonbeach.regency.hyatt.com

Hyatt Regency Jacksonville Riverfront
225 E Coastline Dr.................... Jacksonville FL 32202 904-588-1234 378
Web: jacksonville.regency.hyatt.com/en/hotel/home.html

Hyatt Regency La Jolla at Aventine
3777 La Jolla Village Dr.................... San Diego CA 92122 858-552-1234 378
Web: lajolla.regency.hyatt.com/en/hotel/home.html

Hyatt Regency Lake Tahoe Resort & Casino
111 Country Club Dr .... Incline Village NV 89451 775-832-1234 831-2171 133
TF: 800-233-1234 ■ *Web:* laketahoe.regency.hyatt.com/en/hotel/home.html

Hyatt Regency Lexington
401 W High St .... Lexington KY 40507 859-253-1234 378
Web: lexington.regency.hyatt.com/en/hotel/home.html

Hyatt Regency Maui Resort & Spa
200 Nohea Kai Dr.................... Lahaina HI 96761 808-661-1234 667-4497 669
Web: maui.regency.hyatt.com/en/hotel/home.html

Hyatt Regency Minneapolis
1300 Nicollet Mall .... Minneapolis MN 55403 612-370-1234 378
Web: minneapolis.regency.hyatt.com/en/hotel/home.html

Hyatt Regency Montreal
1255 Jeanne-Mance.................... Montreal QC H5B1E5 514-982-1234 378
Web: montreal.regency.hyatt.com/en/hotel/home.html

Hyatt Regency North Dallas
701 E Campbell Rd.................... Richardson TX 75081 972-231-9600 378
Web: northdallas.regency.hyatt.com/en/hotel/home.html

Hyatt Regency Phoenix 122 N Second St........ Phoenix AZ 85004 602-252-1234 378
Web: phoenix.regency.hyatt.com/en/hotel/home.html

Hyatt Regency Pittsburgh International Airport
1111 Airport Blvd PO Box 12420............ Pittsburgh PA 15231 724-899-1234 378
Web: pittsburghairport.regency.hyatt.com

Hyatt Regency Rochester
125 E Main St.................... Rochester NY 14604 585-546-1234 378
Web: rochester.regency.hyatt.com/en/hotel/home.html

Hyatt Regency San Francisco
5 Embarcadero Ctr .... San Francisco CA 94111 415-788-1234 378
Web: sanfrancisco.regency.hyatt.com/en/hotel/home.html

Hyatt Regency Santa Clara
5101 Great America Pkwy................ Santa Clara CA 95054 408-200-1234 378
Web: santaclara.regency.hyatt.com/en/hotel/home.html

Hyatt Regency Savannah 2 W Bay St.......... Savannah GA 31401 912-238-1234 378
Web: savannah.regency.hyatt.com/en/hotel/home.html

Hyatt Regency Scottsdale Resort at Gainey Ranch
7500 E Doubletree Ranch Rd .... Scottsdale AZ 85258 480-483-5558 707
TF: 800-233-1234 ■
Web: scottsdale.regency.hyatt.com/en/hotel/home.html

Hyatt Regency Suites Atlanta Northwest
2999 Windy Hill Rd .... Marietta GA 30067 770-956-1234 378
Web: atlantasuites.regency.hyatt.com

Hyatt Regency Tulsa 100 E Second St............ Tulsa OK 74103 918-582-9000 378
Web: tulsa.regency.hyatt.com/en/hotel/home.html

Hyatt Regency Valencia
24500 Town Ctr Dr.................... Valencia CA 91355 661-799-1234 378
Web: valencia.regency.hyatt.com/en/hotel/home.html

Hyatt Regency Washington DC on Capitol Hill
400 New Jersey Ave NW.................... Washington DC 20001 202-737-1234 378
Web: washingtondc.regency.hyatt.com/en/hotel/home.html

Hyatt regency Westlake
880 S Westlake Blvd.................. Westlake Village CA 91361 805-557-1234 379
Web: westlake.regency.hyatt.com/en/hotel/home.html

Hyatt Rosemont 6350 N River Rd .... Rosemont IL 60018 847-518-1234 707
Web: rosemont.hyatt.com

Hyatt Summerfield Suites Herndon
467 Herndon Pkwy .... Herndon VA 20170 703-437-5000 379
Web: herndonreston.house.hyatt.com/en/hotel/home.html

Hyatt Vacation Ownership Inc
140 Fountain Pkwy N Ste 570........... Saint Petersburg FL 33716 727-803-9400 753
TF: 800-926-4447 ■ *Web:* www.hyatt.com

Hyatts Market Inc 70 Mchann Rd .... Addison AL 35540 256-747-6005 345

Hybrid Design Associates Inc
230 S Siesta Ln .... Tempe AZ 85281 480-967-8989 729
Web: www.hda-smc.com

Hybrid Design Services 2479 Elliott Dr............ Troy MI 48083 248-298-3400 196
Web: hybriddesignservices.com

Hybrid Plastics
55 WL Runnels Industrial Dr................ Hattiesburg MS 39401 601-544-3466 545-3103 145
Web: www.hybridplastics.com

Hybrid Transit Systems Inc
818 Dows Rd SE.................... Cedar Rapids IA 52403 319-261-0749 478
Web: www.hybridtrans.com

Hy-capacity Engineering & Manufacturing Inc
1404 13th St S.................... Humboldt IA 50548 515-332-2125 256
Web: www.hy-capacity.com

Hyco Alabama LLC 218 Arad Thompson Rd.......... Arab AL 35016 256-586-8152 223
Web: www.hycoalabama.com

Hycomp Inc 17960 Englewood Dr .... Cleveland OH 44130 440-234-2002 608
Web: hycompinc.com

Hycor Biomedical Inc
7272 Chapman Ave.................... Garden Grove CA 92841 800-382-2527 933-3222* 231
**Fax Area Code:* 714 ■ *TF Cust Svc:* 800-382-2527 ■ *Web:* www.hycorbiomedical.com

Hydac Technology Corp
2260-2280 City Line Rd.................... Bethlehem PA 18017 610-266-0100 223
Web: www.hydac-na.com/sites/hydac-na

Hyde & Hyde Inc 300 El Sobrante Rd .... Corona CA 92879 951-817-2300 296-4
Web: www.hydeandhyde.com

Hyde Collection 161 Warren St.............. Glens Falls NY 12801 518-792-1761 792-9197 520
TF: 800-895-1648 ■ *Web:* www.hydecollection.org

Hyde Correctional Institution
620 Prison Rd.................... Fairfield NC 27826 252-926-1810 926-2306 213
Web: www.doc.state.nc.us

Hyde County 30 Oyster Creek Rd............ Swanquarter NC 27885 252-926-4178 926-3701 338
Web: hydecountync.gov

Hyde Hall State Historic Site
PO Box 721 .... Cooperstown NY 13326 518-486-1868 565
Web: parks.ny.gov/historic-sites/11/details.aspx

Hyde Memorial State Park
740 Hyde Pk Rd .... Santa Fe NM 87501 505-983-7175 565

Hyde Park Art Ctr 5020 S Cornell Ave .... Chicago IL 60615 773-324-5520 522
Web: hydeparkart.org

Hyde Park Bar & Grill 4206 Duval St............ Austin TX 78751 512-458-3168 671
Web: www.hpbng.com

Hyde Park Central School District (Inc)
PO Box 2033 .... Hyde Park NY 12538 845-229-4000 685
Web: www.hpcsd.org

Hyde Park Chamber of Commerce
5501 S Everett Ave .... Chicago IL 60637 773-288-0124 288-0464 139
Web: www.hydeparkchamberchicago.org

Hyde Park Chamber of Commerce
PO Box 17 .... Hyde Park NY 12538 845-229-8612 229-8638 139
TF: 800-356-3818 ■ *Web:* www.hydeparkchamber.org

Hyde Park Grille 4073 Medina Rd................ Akron OH 44333 330-670-6303 670-6174 671
Web: www.hydeparkrestaurants.com

Hyde Park Jewelers Inc
3000 E First Ave Ste 243 .... Denver CO 80206 303-333-4446 410
Web: www.hydeparkjewelers.com

Hyde Park Prime Steakhouse
569 N High St.................... Columbus OH 43215 614-224-2204 671
Web: hydeparkrestaurants.com

Hyde Park Restaurant Systems
26300 Chagrin Blvd Ste 1................ Beachwood OH 44122 216-464-0688 595-8267 670
Web: www.hydeparkrestaurants.com

Hyde Park Steakhouse
123 Prospect Ave W.................... Cleveland OH 44115 216-344-2444 344-2726 671
TF: 800-352-6343 ■ *Web:* www.hydeparkrestaurants.com

Hyde Park Village 744 S Village Cir............. Tampa FL 33606 813-251-3500 50-6
TF: 888-800-5447 ■ *Web:* www.hydeparkvillage.com

Hyde School 150 Rt 169 PO Box 237........... Woodstock CT 06281 860-963-4736 622
Web: www.hyde.edu

Hyde School 616 High St.................... Bath ME 04530 207-443-5584 622
Web: www.hyde.edu

Hyde Street Seafood House
1509 Hyde St .... San Francisco CA 94109 415-931-3474 671
Web: hydestseafoodhouse.com

Hyde Tools Co 54 Eastford Rd .... Southbridge MA 01550 508-764-4344 765-5250 758
TF: 800-872-4933 ■ *Web:* www.hydetools.com

Hyden Citizens Bank
22023 Main St PO Box 948 .... Hyden KY 41749 606-672-2344 672-3627 70
Web: www.hydencitizensbank.com

Hydra Baths 1632 W 139th St .... Gardena CA 90249 714-556-9133 375
Web: www.hydrabaths.com

Hydra-Fab Fluid Power Inc
3585 Laird Rd Unit 5 .... Mississauga ON L5L5Z8 905-569-1819 358
TF: 866-466-9866 ■ *Web:* www.hydrafab.com

Hydraflow Inc 1881 W Malvern Ave............ Fullerton CA 92833 714-773-2600 773-6351 350
Web: hydraflow.com

Hydraforce Inc 500 Barclay Blvd............ Lincolnshire IL 60069 847-793-2300 793-0087 790
TF: 877-237-9101 ■ *Web:* www.hydraforce.com

Hydratech Engineered Products LLC
10448 Chester Rd.................... Cincinnati OH 45215 513-827-9169 481
Web: hydratechllc.com

Hydraulic Controls Inc
4700 San Pablo Ave .... Emeryville CA 94608 510-658-8300 358
TF: 800-847-6900 ■ *Web:* www.hydraulic-controls.com

Company / Address	City	State	ZIP	Phone	Fax	Class
Hydraulic Press Brick Co						
5505 W 74th St	Indianapolis	IN	46268	317-290-1140	290-1071	500
Web: www.hpbhaydite.com						
Hydraulic Technology Inc						
3833 Cincinnati Ave	Rocklin	CA	95765	916-645-3317		697
TF: 800-727-4476 ■ *Web:* www.hydraulictechnology.com						
Hydraulics International Inc						
9201 Independence Ave	Chatsworth	CA	91311	818-998-1231	718-2459	385
Web: www.hiinet.com						
Hydreco Inc 200 Oakland Ave Ste D	Rock Hill	SC	29730	704-295-7575	210-9845*	128
**Fax Area Code:* 864 ■ *Web:* www.hydreco.com						
Hydrel 12881 Bradley Ave	Sylmar	CA	91342	866-533-9901	362-6548*	439
**Fax Area Code:* 818 ■ *TF:* 866-533-9901 ■ *Web:* hydrel.acuitybrands.com						
Hydril Company LP						
3300 N Sam Houston Pkwy	Houston	TX	77032	281-449-2000		538
TF: 800-375-7881 ■ *Web:* www.hydril.com						
Hydrite Chemical Co						
300 N Patrick Blvd	Brookfield	WI	53045	262-792-1450	792-8721	146
TF: 800-543-4560 ■ *Web:* www.hydrite.com						
Hydro Carbide 4439 SR-982	Latrobe	PA	15650	724-539-9701	539-8140	757
TF: 800-245-2476 ■ *Web:* www.hydrocarbide.com						
Hydro Geo Chem Inc						
6340 E Thomas Rd Ste 224	Scottsdale	AZ	85251	480-421-1501		196
TF: 800-727-5547 ■ *Web:* www.hgcinc.com						
Hydro One Inc 483 Bay St 15th Fl	Toronto	ON	M5G2P5	416-345-5000		787
TF: 888-664-9376 ■ *Web:* www.hydroone.com						
Hydro Systems 29132 Ave Paine	Valencia	CA	91355	661-775-0686	775-0668	375
TF: 800-747-9990 ■ *Web:* www.hydrosystem.com						
Hydro Tube Enterprises Inc						
137 Artino St	Oberlin	OH	44074	440-774-1022	774-1482	595
TF: 800-226-3553 ■ *Web:* www.hydrotube.com						
Hydro-Aire Inc 3000 Winona Ave	Burbank	CA	91504	818-526-2600	842-6117	22
TF: 800-493-7624 ■ *Web:* www.craneae.com						
HydroCAD Software Solutions LLC						
PO Box 477	Chocorua	NH	03817	603-323-8666	323-7467	178-8
TF: 800-927-7246 ■ *Web:* www.hydrocad.net						
Hydrocephalus Association						
870 Market St Ste 705	San Francisco	CA	94102	415-732-7040		533
Web: www.hydroassoc.org						
HYDRO-FIT Inc 160 Madison St	Eugene	OR	97402	541-484-4361	484-1443	267
TF Cust Svc: 800-346-7295 ■ *Web:* www.hydrofit.com						
Hydro-flo Products Inc						
3655 N 124th St	Brookfield	WI	53005	262-781-2810		612
TF: 800-843-3569 ■ *Web:* www.hydro-flo.com						
Hydroform USA Inc 2848 E 208th St	Long Beach	CA	90810	310-632-6353		483
Web: www.hydroforming.net						
Hydrolevel Co 83 Water St	New Haven	CT	06511	203-776-0473		203
TF: 800-654-0768 ■ *Web:* www.hydrolevel.com						
Hydromantis Environmental Software Solutions Inc						
407 King St W	Hamilton	ON	L8P1B5	905-522-0012		261
TF: 800-245-3006 ■ *Web:* www.hydromantis.com						
Hydromat Inc 11600 Adie Rd	Saint Louis	MO	63043	314-432-4644	432-7552*	455
**Fax:* Sales ■ *TF:* 800-683-1516 ■ *Web:* www.hydromat.com						
Hydromatic Pump Co 740 E Ninth St	Ashland	OH	44805	888-957-8677		641
TF: 888-957-8677 ■ *Web:* www.hydromatic.com						
Hydromotion Inc 85 E Bridge St	Spring City	PA	19475	610-948-4150		641
Web: www.hydromotion.com						
Hydro-Photon Inc 262 Ellsworth Rd	Blue Hill	ME	04614	207-374-5800		743
TF: 888-783-7473 ■ *Web:* www.steripen.com						
HydroPoint Data Systems Inc						
1720 Corporate Cir	Petaluma	CA	94954	800-362-8774		407
TF: 800-362-8774 ■ *Web:* www.hydropoint.com						
HydroPressure Cleaning Inc						
413 Dawson Dr	Camarillo	CA	93012	800-934-2399		641
TF: 800-934-2399 ■ *Web:* www.hydropressure.com						
Hydroscience Engineers Inc						
10569 Old Placerville Rd	Sacramento	CA	95827	916-364-1490		256
Web: hydroscience.com						
Hydro-stat Inc						
1111 SW First Way	Deerfield Beach	FL	33441	954-428-7677		743
TF: 800-233-5053 ■ *Web:* www.hydrostat.com						
Hydrotex Inc						
12920 Senlac D Ste 190	Farmers Branch	TX	75234	800-527-9439		541
TF: 800-527-9439 ■ *Web:* www.hydrotexlube.com						
Hydro-Thermal Corp 400 Pilot Ct	Waukesha	WI	53188	262-548-8900	548-8908	386
TF: 800-952-0121 ■ *Web:* www.hydro-thermal.com						
Hydrox Laboratories Inc 825 Tollgate Rd	Elgin	IL	60123	847-468-9400		743
Web: www.hydroxlabs.com						
Hydrozonix LLC						
333 N Rivershire Dr Ste 270	Conroe	TX	77304	936-441-0071		192
Web: www.hydrozonix.com						
Hygenic Corp 1245 Home Ave	Akron	OH	44310	330-633-8460	633-9359	228
TF: 800-321-2135 ■ *Web:* www.hygenic.com						
hygiena LLC 941 Avenida Acaso	Camarillo	CA	93012	805-388-8007		419
TF: 877-494-4364 ■ *Web:* www.hygiena.com						
Hygieneering Inc 7575 Plaza Ct	Willowbrook	IL	60527	630-654-2550		463
TF: 800-444-7154 ■ *Web:* hygieneering.com						
Hygolet Inc 349 SE Second Ave	Deerfield Beach	FL	33441	954-481-8601	481-8669	608
TF: 800-494-6538 ■ *Web:* www.hygolet.com						
Hygrade Metal Moulding Manufacturing Corp						
1990 Highland Ave	Bethlehem	PA	18020	610-866-2441	866-3761	234
TF: 800-645-9475 ■ *Web:* www.hygrademetal.com						
Hy-Grade Precast Concrete						
2411 First St	St Catharines	ON	L2R6P7	905-684-8568		183
TF: 800-229-8568 ■ *Web:* www.hygradeprecast.com						
Hygrade Precision Technologies Inc						
329 Cooke St	Plainville	CT	06062	860-747-5773	747-3179	757
TF: 800-457-1666 ■ *Web:* www.hygrade.com						
HyGreen Inc						
3630 SW 47th Ave Ste 100	Gainesville	FL	32608	877-574-9473		743
TF: 877-574-9473 ■ *Web:* hygreen.com						
Hygun Group Inc						
4180 Providence Rd Ste 109	Marietta	GA	30062	770-973-0838		261
Web: www.hygun.com						
Hy-Ko Products Co 60 Meadow Ln	Northfield	OH	44067	330-467-7446	467-7442	701
TF: 800-292-0550 ■ *Web:* www.hy-ko.com						
Hyland Levin LLP						
6000 Sagemore Dr Ste 6301	Marlton	NJ	08053	856-355-2900		428
TF: 800-973-1177 ■ *Web:* www.hylandlevin.com						
Hyland Screw Machine Products						
1900 Kuntz Rd	Dayton	OH	45404	937-233-8600	233-7067	621
Web: www.hylandmach.com						
Hyland Software Inc 28500 Clemens Rd	Westlake	OH	44145	440-788-5000	788-5100	178-7
TF: 888-495-2638 ■ *Web:* onbase.com						
Hylant Group 811 Madison Ave	Toledo	OH	43624	419-255-1020	255-7557	390
TF: 800-249-5268 ■ *Web:* www.hylant.com						
Hy-Line International						
1755 West Lakes Pkwy	West Des Moines	IA	50266	515-225-6030	225-6425	10-8
Web: www.hyline.com						
Hyman Phelps & Mcnamara Pc						
700 13th St NW Ste 1200	Washington	DC	20005	202-737-5600	737-9329	428
Web: www.hpm.com						
Hyner Run State Park						
86 Hyner Pk Rd	North Bend	PA	17760	570-923-6000		565
Web: www.dcnr.state.pa.us						
Hyner View State Park						
c/o Hyner Run State Pk 86 Hyner Pk Rd	Hyner	PA	17738	570-923-6000		565
Web: www.dcnr.state.pa.us						
Hynes Industries 3760 Oakwood	Youngstown	OH	44515	800-321-9257	799-9098*	492
**Fax Area Code:* 330 ■ *TF:* 800-321-9257 ■ *Web:* www.hynesindustries.com						
Hynix Semiconductor America Inc						
3101 N First St	San Jose	CA	95134	408-232-8000	232-8103	696
Web: www.hynix.com						
Hype Agency Llc, The 2 Dyer Ave	Salem	NH	03079	603-328-9019		195
Web: thehypeagency.com						
HyperBranch Medical Technology Inc						
800-12 Capitola Dr	Durham	NC	27713	919-433-3325		475
Web: www.hyperbranch.com						
HyperCube LLC						
3200 W Pleasant Run Rd Ste 300	Lancaster	TX	75146	469-727-1622		387
HyperDisk Marketing Inc						
18251 McDurmott W Ste A	Irvine	CA	92614	949-442-9850		177
TF: 800-241-1210 ■ *Web:* www.hyperdisk.com						
Hyperdynamics Corp						
12012 Wickchester Ln Ste 475	Houston	TX	77079	713-353-9400	353-9421	536
OTC: HDYN ■ *Web:* www.hyperdynamics.com						
Hyperion Biotechnology Inc						
13302 Langtry St	San Antonio	TX	78248	210-493-7452		668
Web: hyperionbiotechnology.com						
Hyperion Inc 1660 Intl Dr	Mclean	VA	22102	703-848-8850		225
Web: www.hyperioninc.com						
Hyperlogistics Group Inc						
9301 Intermodal Ct N	Columbus	OH	43217	614-497-0800		803-1
Web: www.hyperlog.com						
Hyperquake LLC						
205 W Fourth St Ste 1010	Cincinnati	OH	45202	513-563-6555		7
Web: www.hyperquake.com						
Hypertec BCDR Inc						
9300 Trans Canada Hwy	Saint-laurent	QC	H4S1K5	514-745-4540		393
Web: www.hypertecbcdr.com						
Hypertension Diagnostics Inc						
730 Bldg Ste 295	Minneapolis	MN	55402	612-361-5287		476
TF: 888-785-7392 ■ *Web:* www.hypertensiondiagnostics.com						
Hyper-Therm HTC						
18411 Gothard St Ste B	Huntington Beach	CA	92648	714-375-4085		127
Web: www.htcomposites.com						
Hypertherm Inc						
21 Great Hollow Rd PO Box 5010	Hanover	NH	03755	603-643-3441	643-5352	455
TF: 800-643-0030 ■ *Web:* www.hypertherm.com						
Hypex Inc 1000 Industrial Blvd	Southampton	PA	18966	215-322-0545		454
Web: www.hypex.com						
Hyphen 488 Madison Ave 5th Fl	New York	NY	10022	212-856-8700		4
Web: hyphendigital.com						
Hypneumat Inc 5900 W Franklin Dr	Franklin	WI	53132	414-423-7400	423-7414	455
TF: 800-228-9949 ■ *Web:* www.hypneumat.com						
Hypotenuse Enterprises Inc						
1545 East Ave	Rochester	NY	14610	585-473-7799		463
Web: www.hypot.com						
HyPro Inc						
600 S Jefferson St PO Box 370	Waterford	WI	53185	262-534-5141		295
Web: www.hypro.com						
Hyrum State Park 405 W 300 S	Hyrum	UT	84319	435-245-6866		565
Web: www.stateparks.utah.gov						
Hy-Safe Technology Inc						
960 Commerce Dr	Union Grove	WI	53182	262-752-2400		693
Web: www.hysafe.com						
Hysitron Inc 9625 W 76th St	Minneapolis	MN	55344	952-835-6366		696
Web: www.hysitron.com						
Hyson Products						
10367 Brecksville Rd	Brecksville	OH	44141	440-526-5900	838-7684	790
TF: 800-876-4976 ■ *Web:* www.hysonsolutions.com						
Hyspan Precision Products Inc						
1685 Brandywine Ave	Chula Vista	CA	91911	619-421-1355	421-1702	480
Web: www.hyspan.com						
Hysterectomy Educational Resources & Services Foundation (HERS)						
422 Bryn Mawr Ave	Bala Cynwyd	PA	19004	610-667-7757	667-8096	48-17
TF: 888-750-4377 ■ *Web:* www.hersfoundation.com						
Hy-Tape International Inc						
PO Box 540	Patterson	NY	12563	800-248-0101	878-4104*	477
**Fax Area Code:* 845 ■ *TF:* 800-248-0101 ■ *Web:* www.hytape.com						
Hytech Spring & Machine Corp						
950 Lincoln Pkwy	Plainwell	MI	49080	269-685-1768		492
TF: 800-879-2732 ■ *Web:* www.hytechspring.com						
Hytek Finishes Co 8127 S 216th St	Kent	WA	98032	253-872-7160		481
Web: www.hytekfinishes.com						
Hy-Tek Material Handling Inc						
2222 Rickenbacker Pkwy W	Columbus	OH	43217	614-497-2500		770
Web: www.hy-tek.net						
Hytel Group Inc 290 Industrial Dr	Hampshire	IL	60140	847-683-9800	683-7940	696
Web: www.hytel.com						
Hy-Test Packaging Corp 515 E 41st St	Paterson	NJ	07504	973-754-7000		88
Web: www.hy-testpackaging.com						
Hythane Company LLC						
12420 N Dumont Way	Littleton	CO	80125	303-486-1705		580
Web: www.hythane.com						
Hytrol Conveyor Company Inc						
2020 Hytrol St	Jonesboro	AR	72401	870-935-3700	852-3233*	207
**Fax Area Code:* 800 ■ *TF:* 800-852-3233 ■ *Web:* www.hytrol.com						

Phone | Fax | Class

Hyundai Ideal Electric Co
330 E First St .... Mansfield OH 44902 419-522-3611 518
Web: www.idealelectricco.com

Hyundai Motor America
10550 Talbert Ave .... Fountain Valley CA 92708 714-965-3000 59
TF Cust Svc: 800-633-5151 ■ Web: www.hyundaiusa.com

Hyundai Repair by Rally Sport Engineering Inc
2136 Newport Blvd .... Costa Mesa CA 92627 949-548-0978 256
Web: hyundairepair.net

I

Phone | Fax | Class

I & I Sling Inc PO Box 2423 .... Aston PA 19014 610-485-8500 208
TF: 800-874-3539 ■ Web: www.slingmax.com

I & M Heating & Appliance Service Inc
1628 S Michigan St .... South Bend IN 46613 574-288-3351 189-10
Web: www.imheatingandcooling.com

I Am Athlete LLC PO Box 667 .... Santa Monica CA 90406 877-462-7979 387
TF: 877-462-7979 ■ Web: www.imathlete.com

I B M Southeast Employees Federal Credit Union
PO Box 5090 .... Boca Raton FL 33431 561-982-4700 219
TF: 888-567-8688 ■ Web: www.ibmsecu.org

I C C Logistics Services Inc
960 S Broadway Ste 110 .... Hicksville NY 11801 516-822-1183 314
TF: 800-673-1044 ■ Web: www.icclogistics.com

I C Group 3985 Pinedale Ct .... Highlands Ranch CO 80126 303-972-2111 627
Web: www.ic-group.net

I C S Solutions Inc
11964 Oak Creek Pkwy .... Huntley IL 60142 847-515-8000 177
Web: www.icss.com

I D Booth Inc 620 William St PO Box 579 .... Elmira NY 14902 607-733-9121 733-9111 612
TF: 888-432-6684 ■ Web: www.idbooth.com

I E T Inc 3539 Glendale Ave .... Toledo OH 43614 419-385-1233 261
TF: 800-278-1031 ■ Web: www.ieteng.com

I Fratelli 7701 N MacArthur Blvd .... Irving TX 75063 972-501-9700 671
Web: www.ifratelli.net

I Have a Dream Foundation (IHAD)
330 Seventh Ave 20th Fl .... New York NY 10001 212-293-5480 48-5
Web: www.ihaveadreamfoundation.org

I Imagine Studio Inc
152 W Huron Ste 100 .... Chicago IL 60654 847-467-0308 5
TF: 855-792-7263 ■ Web: www.iimaginestudio.com

I J White Corp 20 Executive Blvd .... Farmingdale NY 11735 631-293-2211 207
Web: www.ijwhite.com

I Janvey & Sons Inc 218 Front St .... Hempstead NY 11550 516-489-9300 406
Web: www.janvey.com

I Love Mr Sushi 9443 Olive Blvd .... Saint Louis MO 63132 314-432-8898 671
Web: mrsushistl.com

I Macc 900 E Diehl Rd Ste 110 .... Naperville IL 60563 630-527-9052 196
TF: 800-804-3724 ■ Web: imacc.net

I Reservoir Com Corp
1490 W Canal Court Ste 2000 .... Littleton CO 80120 303-713-1112 539
Web: ireservoir.com

I Ricchi 1220 19th St NW .... Washington DC 20036 202-835-0459 671
Web: iricchidc.com

I Rice & Company Inc
11500 Roosevelt Blvd Bldg D .... Philadelphia PA 19116 215-673-7423 673-2616 296-15
TF: 800-232-6022 ■ Web: www.iriceco.com

I Sc International
9700 W Bluemound Rd .... Milwaukee WI 53226 414-476-7755 225
Web: www.iscinternational.com

I See Me! Inc 4305 Chimo E St .... Wayzata MN 55391 952-473-3939 95
TF: 800-962-2957 ■ Web: www.myveryownname.com

I Spiewak & Sons Inc 463 Seventh Ave .... New York NY 10018 212-695-1620 155-19
Web: www.spiewak.com

I T S Corp 300 E Esplanade Dr Ste 1450 .... Oxnard CA 93036 805-604-9191 604-9141 196
Web: www.itscorporation.com

I Wireless 4135 NW Urbandale Dr .... Urbandale IA 50322 515-258-7000 735
TF Cust Svc: 888-550-4497 ■ Web: www.iwireless.com

i Wireless Ctr 1201 River Dr .... Moline IL 61265 309-764-2001 764-2192 720
TF: 800-745-3000 ■ Web: www.iwirelesscenter.com

I. C. S. Customs Service Inc
1099 Morse Ave .... Elk Grove Village IL 60007 847-718-9998 311
Web: www.icscustoms.com

I. s Outsource Inc
19119 N Creek Pkwy Ste 200 .... Bothell WA 98011 206-374-0251 177
TF: 800-240-2821 ■ Web: www.isoutsource.com

I.B.I.S. Inc
30 Technology Pkwy S Ste 400 .... Norcross GA 30092 770-368-4000 695
TF: 866-714-8422 ■ Web: www.ibisinc.com

I.C. System Inc 444 Hwy 96 E .... St. Paul MN 55127 651-483-8201 160
Web: www.icsystem.com

i.d.e.a. 444 W Beech St .... San Diego CA 92101 619-295-8232 636
TF: 800-827-9990 ■ Web: www.theideabrand.com

I.M. Systems Group Inc
3206 Tower Oaks Blvd Ste 300 .... Rockville MD 20852 240-833-1889 180
TF: 866-368-9880 ■ Web: www.imsg.com

I.T. Blueprint Solutions Consulting Inc
170-422 Richards St .... Vancouver BC V6B2Z4 866-261-8981 196
TF: 866-261-8981 ■ Web: www.itblueprint.ca

I/O Magic Corp
20512 Crescent Bay Dr Ste 106 .... Lake Forest, CA 92630 949-707-4800 173-8
OTC: IOMG ■ Web: www.iomagic.com

i2a Technologies Inc
3399 W Warren Ave .... Fremont CA 94538 510-770-0322 696
Web: www.ipac.com

i2c Inc 1300 Island Dr Ste 105 .... Redwood City CA 94065 650-593-5400 80-3
Web: www.i2cinc.com

i2E Inc
840 Research Pkwy Research Pk Ste 250 .... Oklahoma City OK 73104 405-235-2305 466
Web: www.i2e.org

Phone | Fax | Class

i2M Inc
755 Oak Hill Rd Crestwood Industrial Pk
.... Mountain Top PA 18707 800-242-3909 600
TF: 800-242-3909 ■ Web: www.hpg-intl.com

i4DM 8227 Cloverleaf Dr Ste 312 .... Millersville MD 21108 410-729-7920 225
Web: www.i4dm.com

i4i Inc 116 Spadina Ave 5th Fl .... Toronto ON M5V2K6 416-504-0141 180
Web: www.i4i.com

I-95 95.7 Fm 49 Acme Rd .... Brewer ME 04412 207-989-5631 645
Web: i95rocks.com

IA (Irrigation Assn)
6540 Arlington Blvd .... Falls Church VA 22042 703-536-7080 536-7019 48-2
TF: 800-362-8774 ■ Web: www.irrigation.org

IAABO (International Assn of Approved Basketball Officials Inc)
PO Box 355 .... Carlisle PA 17013 717-713-8129 718-6164 48-22
Web: www.iaabo.org

IAAI (International Assn of Arson Investigators)
2111 Baldwin Ave # 203 .... Crofton MD 21114 410-451-3473 451-9049 49-7
TF: 800-468-4224 ■ Web: www.firearson.com

IAAO (International Assn of Assessing Officers)
314 W Tenth St .... Kansas City MO 64105 816-701-8100 701-8149 49-7
TF: 800-616-4226 ■ Web: www.iaao.org

IAAP (International Assn of Administrative Professionals)
10502 NW Ambassador Dr Ste 100 .... Kansas City MO 64153 816-891-6600 891-9118 49-12
Web: www.iaap-hq.org

IAAPA (International Assn of Amusement Parks & Attractions)
1448 Duke St .... Alexandria VA 22314 703-836-4800 836-6742 48-23
Web: www.iaapa.org

IAATI (International Assn of Auto Theft Investigators)
PO Box 223 .... Clinton NY 13323 315-853-1913 49-7
Web: www.iaati.org

IABC (International Assn of Business Communicators)
155 Montgomery St Ste 1210 .... San Francisco CA 94104 415-544-4700 544-4747 49-12
TF: 800-776-4222 ■ Web: www.iabc.com

IAC Industries 895 Beacon St .... Brea CA 92821 714-990-8997 990-0557 319-1
TF: 800-989-1422 ■ Web: www.iacindustries.com

IAC/InterActiveCorp 555 W 18th St .... New York NY 10011 212-314-7300 314-7309 185
NASDAQ: IACI ■ Web: www.iac.com

IACA (Indian Arts & Crafts Assn)
4010 Carlisle Blvd NE Ste C .... Albuquerque NM 87107 505-265-9149 265-8251 48-4
Web: www.iaca.com

IACC (International Assn of Conference Centers)
35 East Wacker Dr Ste 850 .... Chicago IL 60601 312-224-2580 644-8557 49-12
Web: www.iacconline.org

IACC (Italian American Chamber of Commerce of Chicago)
500 N Michigan Ave Ste 506 .... Chicago IL 60611 312-553-9137 553-9142 138
Web: www.iacc-chicago.com

IACC (International AntiCounterfeiting Coalition)
1730 M St NW .... Washington DC 20036 202-223-6667 49-13
Web: www.iacc.org

IACP (International Assn of Culinary Professionals)
45 Rockefeller Plaza Ste 2000 .... New York NY 10111 855-738-4227 358-2524* 49-6
*Fax Area Code: 866 ■ TF: 855-738-4227 ■ Web: www.iacp.com

IACP (International Academy of Compounding Pharmacists)
4638 Riverstone Blvd .... Missouri City TX 77459 281-933-8400 495-0602 49-8
TF: 800-927-4227 ■ Web: www.iacprx.org

IACP (International Assn of Chiefs of Police)
44 Canal Ctr Plaza Ste 200 .... Alexandria VA 22314 703-836-6767 836-4543 49-7
TF: 800-843-4227 ■ Web: www.theiacp.org

Iada Services Inc
1111 Office Park Rd .... West Des Moines IA 50265 515-440-7621 138
TF: 800-264-5384 ■ Web: www.iada.com

IADC (International Assn of Defense Counsel)
303 W Madison St Ste 925 .... Chicago IL 60606 312-368-1494 368-1854 49-10
TF: 800-575-1494 ■ Web: www.iadclaw.org

IADC (International Assn of Drilling Contractors)
10370 Richmond Ave Ste 760 .... Houston TX 77042 713-292-1945 292-1946 49-3
Web: www.iadc.org

IADR (International Assn for Dental Research)
1619 Duke St .... Alexandria VA 22314 703-548-0066 49-8
Web: www.iadr.org

iAdvantage Software Inc 404 E Chatham St .... Cary NC 27511 919-469-3888 177
Web: www.iadvantagesoftware.com

IAEA (International Atomic Energy Agency)
1 UN Plaza Rm DC1-1155 .... New York NY 10017 212-963-6010 367-4046* 783
*Fax Area Code: 917 ■ Web: www.iaea.org

IAEE (International Assn of Exhibitions & Events)
12700 Park Central Dr Ste 308 .... Dallas TX 75251 972-458-8002 458-8119 49-18
Web: www.iaee.com

IAEI (International Assn of Electrical Inspectors)
901 Waterfall Way Ste 602 .... Richardson TX 75080 972-235-1455 235-6858 49-3
TF: 800-786-4234 ■ Web: www.iaei.org

IAF (Institute for Alternative Futures)
100 N Pitt St Ste 307 .... Alexandria VA 22314 703-684-5880 49-12
Web: www.altfutures.com

IAF (Inter-American Foundation)
901 N Stuart St 10th Fl .... Arlington VA 22203 703-306-4301 306-4365 340-20
Web: www.iaf.gov

IAFC (International Assn of Fire Chiefs)
4025 Fair Ridge Dr Ste 300 .... Fairfax VA 22033 703-273-0911 273-9363 49-7
TF: 866-385-9110 ■ Web: www.iafc.org

IAFE (International Assn of Fairs & Expositions, The)
3043 E Cairo .... Springfield MO 65802 417-862-5771 48-23
TF: 800-516-0313 ■ Web: www.fairsandexpos.com

IAFF 1750 New York Ave NW Ste 300 .... Washington DC 20006 202-737-8484 737-8418 615
Web: client.prod.iaff.org

IAFF (International Assn of Fire Fighters)
1750 New York Ave NW 3rd Fl .... Washington DC 20006 202-737-8484 737-8418 414
Web: client.prod.iaff.org

IAFP (International Assn for Food Protection)
6200 Aurora Ave Ste 200W .... Des Moines IA 50322 515-276-3344 276-8655 49-6
TF General: 800-369-6337 ■ Web: www.foodprotection.org

IAFWA (International Assn of Fish & Wildlife Agencies)
444 N Capitol St NW Ste 725 .... Washington DC 20001 202-624-7890 624-7891 49-7
Web: www.fishwildlife.org

IAHB (Institute for the Advancement of Human Behavior)
PO Box 5527 .... Santa Rosa CA 95402 650-851-8411 755-3133* 49-8
*Fax Area Code: 707 ■ TF: 800-258-8411 ■ Web: www.iahb.org

Phone | Fax | Class

IAI (Integrity Applications Inc)
15020 Conference Ctr Dr Ste 100 — Chantilly VA 20151 — 703-378-8672 378-8978 261
Web: www.integrity-apps.com

IAIA (International Assn for Impact Assessment)
1330 23rd St S Ste C — Fargo ND 58103 — 701-297-7908 297-7917 49-12
TF: 800-873-7130 ■ *Web:* www.iaia.org

IAIA (Institute of American Indian Arts)
83 Avan Nu Po Rd — Santa Fe NM 87508 — 505-424-2300 424-0505 165
TF: 800-804-6422 ■ *Web:* www.iaia.edu

IAMAT (International Assn for Medical Assistance to Travellers)
67 Mowat Ave Ste 036 — Toronto ON M6K3E3 — 416-652-0137 652-1983 48-23
Web: www.iamat.org

IAMFC (International Assn of Marriage & Family Counselors)
5999 Stevenson Ave — Alexandria VA 22304 — 800-347-6647 473-2329 49-15
TF: 800-347-6647 ■ *Web:* www.counseling.org

IAMGOLD Corp
401 Bay St Ste 3200 PO Box 153 — Toronto ON M5H2Y4 — 416-360-4710 502
TSE: IMG ■ *TF:* 888-464-9999 ■ *Web:* www.iamgold.com

IAMS Co 3700 Ohio 65 — Leipsic OH 45856 — 419-943-4267 578
TF Cust Svc: 800-675-3849 ■ *Web:* www.iams.com

Ian Ryan & Assoc Inc
1400 E Touhy Ave Ste 220 — Des Plaines IL 60018 — 847-803-2050 514
Web: www.ianryan.com

IANA (Intermodal Assn of North America)
11785 Beltsville Dr Ste 1100 — Calverton MD 20705 — 301-982-3400 982-4815 49-21
TF: 877-438-8442 ■ *Web:* www.intermodal.org

Iao Valley State Monument
54 S High St Rm 101 — Wailuku HI 96793 — 808-984-8109 984-8111 565
Web: dlnr.hawaii.gov/dsp

IAP Worldwide Services Inc
7315 N Atlantic Ave — Cape Canaveral FL 32920 — 321-784-7100 271
TF: 877-296-8010 ■ *Web:* www.iapws.com

IAPA (Inter American Press Assn)
3511 NW 91st Ave — Doral FL 33172 — 305-634-2465 860-4264 49-14
Web: sipiapa.org/index.php

IAPA (International Airline Passengers Assn)
PO Box 700100 — Dallas TX 75370 — 972-404-9980 233-5348 48-23
TF: 800-821-4272 ■ *Web:* www.iapa.com

IAPD (International Assn of Plastics Distribution)
6734 W 121 St — Overland Park KS 66209 — 913-345-1005 345-1006 49-18
Web: www.iapd.org

IAPES (International Assn of Workforce Professionals)
1801 Louisville Rd — Frankfort KY 40601 — 502-223-4459 223-4127 49-12
Web: iawponline.org

IAPMO (International Assn of Plumbing & Mechanical Officials)
4755 E Philadelphia St — Ontario CA 91761 — 909-472-4100 472-4150 49-7
TF: 877-427-6601 ■ *Web:* www.iapmo.org

Iapp 170 Cider Hill Rd — York ME 03909 — 207-351-1500 533
Web: iapp.org

IAR Systems Software Inc
1065 E Hillsdale Blvd Century Plaza — Foster City CA 94404 — 650-287-4250 174
Web: iar.com

IARC (International Arctic Research Ctr)
930 N Koyukuk Dr PO Box 757340 — Fairbanks AK 99775 — 907-474-6016 474-5662 668
Web: www.iarc.uaf.edu

Iaria's Italian Restaurant
317 S College Ave — Indianapolis IN 46202 — 317-638-7706 671
Web: www.iariasrestaurant.com

Iars Systems Engineers
4121 Tytahun Cres Ste 200 — West Vancouver BC V0N3N1 — 778-772-9419 177
Web: www.iars-syseng.com

IASIS Healthcare Corp
117 Seaboard Ln Bldg E — Franklin TN 37067 — 615-844-2747 846-3006 353
TF: 877-898-6080 ■ *Web:* www.iasishealthcare.com

IASP (International Assn for the Study of Pain)
111 Queen Anne Ave N Ste 501 — Seattle WA 98109 — 206-283-0311 283-9403 48-17
TF: 866-574-2654 ■ *Web:* www.iasp-pain.org

IATSE (International Alliance of Theatrical Stage Employee)
1430 Broadway 20th Fl — New York NY 10018 — 212-730-1770 921-7699 414
TF: 800 456-3063 ■ *Web:* iatse.net

IATSE PAC 1430 Broadway 20th Fl — New York NY 10018 — 212-730-1770 730-7809 615
TF: 844-422-9273 ■ *Web:* iatse.net

IAVM (International Assn of Venue Managers Inc)
635 Fritz Dr Ste 100 — Coppell TX 75019 — 972-906-7441 906-7418 49-12
TF: 800-935-4226 ■ *Web:* www.iavm.org

IAWF (International Assn of Wildland Fire)
3416 Primm Ln — Birmingham AL 35216 — 205-824-7614 48-13
Web: www.iawfonline.org

Ibaset 27442 Portola Pkwy — Foothill Ranch CA 92610 — 949-598-5200 598-2600 180
TF: 877-422-7381 ■ *Web:* www.ibaset.com

iBasis Inc 20 Second Ave — Burlington MA 01803 — 781-505-7500 505-7300 736
Web: www.ibasis.com

Ibb Design Group 5798 Genesis Ct — Frisco TX 75034 — 214-618-6600 138
TF: 800-355-9195 ■ *Web:* www.ibbdesign.com

IBBA (International Brangus Breeders Assn)
5750 Epsilon Dr — San Antonio TX 78249 — 210-696-8231 696-8718 48-2
Web: www.gobrangus.com

IBC Advanced Alloys Corp
570 Granville St Ste 1200 — Vancouver BC V6C3P1 — 604-685-6263 502
TF: 800-373-3251 ■ *Web:* www.ibcadvancedalloys.com

IBC Coating Technologies
902 Hendricks Dr — Lebanon IN 46052 — 765-482-9802 481
Web: www.ibccoatings.com

IBCC Industries Inc 3200 S Third St — Milwaukee WI 53207 — 414-486-5460 194
Web: www.ibccind.com

Ibe Trade Corp 950 Third Ave 3rd Fl — New York NY 10022 — 212-593-3255 308-3642 280
Web: www.ibetrade.com

I-Behavior Inc
2051 Dogwood St Ste 220 — Louisville CO 80027 — 303-228-5000 194
Web: www.i-behavior.com

IBERDROLA Group 1125 NW Couch Ste 700 — Portland OR 97209 — 503-796-7000 796-6901 620
Web: www.iberdrolarenewables.us

Iberia Medical Ctr (IMC)
2315 E Main St — New Iberia LA 70560 — 337-364-0441 374-3
Web: www.iberiamedicalcenter.com

Iberia Parish 300 Iberia St Ste 400 — New Iberia LA 70560 — 337-365-8246 369-4470 338
Web: www.iberiaparishgovernment.com

Iberia Parish Library
445 E Main St — New Iberia LA 70560 — 337-364-7024 434-3
Web: iberialibrary.org

Iberia Peninsula Restaurant
67 Ferry St — Newark NJ 07105 — 973-344-5611 344-2067 671
TF: 800-442-1162 ■ *Web:* www.iberiarestaurants.com

Iberia Tiles Corp 2975 NW 77 Ave — Miami FL 33122 — 305-591-3880 191-1
Web: www.iberiatiles.com

IBERIABANK Corp 200 W Congress St — Lafayette LA 70501 — 800-968-0801 360-2
NASDAQ: IBKC ■ *TF:* 800-968-0801 ■ *Web:* www.iberiabank.com

Ibero American Investors Corp
817 E Main — Rochester NY 14605 — 585-256-8900 403
Web: www.iberoinvestors.com

Ibero-American Action League Inc
817 E Main St — Rochester NY 14605 — 585-256-8900 48-14
Web: www.iaal.org

IBEROSTAR Hotels & Resorts
70 Park Ave 38th St — New York NY 10016 — 212-973-2400 973-2401 379
Web: www.70parkave.com

Iberville Parish 58050 Meriam St — Plaquemine LA 70764 — 225-687-5190 338
Web: www.ibervilleparish.com

Iberville Parish Chamber of Commerce
23675 Church St — Plaquemine LA 70764 — 225-687-3560 687-3575 139
TF: 800-266-2692 ■ *Web:* www.ibervillechamber.com

Iberville Parish Library
24605 J Gerald Berret Blvd — Plaquemine LA 70764 — 225-687-2520 687-9719 434-3
Web: myipl.org

IBHS (Institute for Business & Home Safety)
4775 E Fowler Ave — Tampa FL 33617 — 813-286-3400 49-9
TF: 866-657-4247 ■ *Web:* www.disastersafety.org

IBI Armored Services Inc
37-06 61st St — Woodside NY 11377 — 718-458-4000 458-5371 693
Web: www.ibiarmored.com

IBIS Communications 1024 17th Ave S — Nashville TN 37212 — 615-777-1900 7
Web: www.ibiscommunications.com

Ibis Tek LLC 220 S Noah Dr — Saxonburg PA 16056 — 724-586-6005 330
Web: www.ibistek.com

IBISWorld Inc
11755 Wilshire blvd 11th fl — Los Angeles CA 90025 — 800-330-3772 387
TF: 800-330-3772 ■ *Web:* www.ibisworld.com

Ibiza Food & Wine Bar
2450 Louisiana St — Houston TX 77006 — 713-524-0004 671
Web: www.ibizafoodandwinebar.com

IBM (International Business Machines Corp)
1 New OrchaRd Rd — Armonk NY 10504 — 914-499-1900 173-2
NYSE: IBM ■ *TF:* 800-426-4968 ■ *Web:* www.ibm.com

IBM International Foundation
1 New OrchaRd Rd — Armonk NY 10504 — 914-499-1900 304
Web: www.ibm.com

IBM Research 650 Harry Rd — San Jose CA 95120 — 408-927-1080 466
Web: www.research.ibm.com/labs/almaden/index.shtml

IBM WebSphere Information Integration
26 Forest St — Marlborough MA 01752 — 508-366-3888 178-1
Web: www.ibm.com

iBox Network Inc
0600 Wash Blvd Apt 211 — Culver City CA 90232 — 323-855-0080 393
Web: www.lightboxnetwork.com

IBPA (Independent Book Publishers Assn, The)
1020 Manhattan Beach Blvd Ste 204 — Manhattan Beach CA 90266 — 310-546-1818 546-3939 49-10
TF: 800-327-5113 ■ *Web:* www.ibpa-online.org

IBPO (International Brotherhood of Police Officers)
159 Burgin Pkwy — Quincy MA 02169 — 617-376-0220 376-0285* 414
**Fax:* Legal Dept ■ *Web:* www.ibpo.org

IBS (International Biometric Society)
1444 'I' St NW Ste 700 — Washington DC 20005 — 202-712-9049 216-9646 49-19
Web: www.biometricsociety.org

IBS (International Bible Society)
Biblica 1820 Jet Stream Dr — Colorado Springs CO 80921 — 719-488-9200 48-20
TF Cust Svc: 800-524-1588 ■ *Web:* www.biblica.com

IBS Direct 431 Yerkes Rd — King of Prussia PA 19406 — 610-265-8210 265-7997 110
TF: 800-220-1255 ■ *Web:* www.ibsdm.com

IBS Electronics Inc
3506 West Lake Ctr Dr Ste D — Santa Ana CA 92704 — 714-751-6633 751-8159 246
TF: 800-527-2888 ■ *Web:* www.ibselectronics.com

IBT Enterprises LLC
1770 Indian Trail Rd Ste 300 — Norcross GA 30093 — 770-381-2023 194
TF: 877-242-8428 ■ *Web:* www.ibtenterprises.com

IBT Inc 9400 W 55th St — Merriam KS 66203 — 913-677-3151 677-3752 385
TF: 800-332-2114 ■ *Web:* www.ibtinc.com

IBTTA (International Bridge Tunnel & Turnpike Assn)
1146 19th St NW Ste 600 — Washington DC 20036 — 202-659-4620 659-0500 49-7
Web: www.ibtta.org

IBU (Inlandboatmen's Union of the Pacific)
1711 W Nickerson St Ste D — Seattle WA 98119 — 206-284-6001 414
TF: 800-562-6000 ■ *Web:* www.ibu.org

I-Bus Corp 3350 Scott Blvd Bldg 54 — Santa Clara CA 95054 — 408-450-7880 450-7881 625
Web: www.ibus.com

I-Business Network LLC
2617 Sandy Plains Rd Ste B — Marietta GA 30066 — 678-627-0646 627-0688 39
Web: www.i-bn.net

IBWA (International Bottled Water Assn)
1700 Diagonal Rd Ste 650 — Alexandria VA 22314 — 703-683-5213 683-4074 49-6
TF: 800-928-3711 ■ *Web:* www.bottledwater.org

IC Medical Inc 2340 W Shangri La Rd — Phoenix AZ 85029 — 623-780-0700 475
Web: www.icmedical.com

IC Thomasson Assoc Inc
2950 Kraft Dr Ste 500 — Nashville TN 37204 — 615-346-3400 261
Web: icthomasson.com

ICA (International Communication Assn)
1500 21st St NW — Washington DC 20036 — 202-955-1444 955-1448 49-14
TF: 800-590-1125 ■ *Web:* www.icahdq.org

ICA (International Chiropractors Assn)
6400 Arlington Blvd Ste 800 — Falls Church VA 22042 — 703-528-5000 528-5023 49-8
TF: 800-423-4690 ■ *Web:* www.chiropractic.org

ICAC (Institute of Clean Air Cos)
1730 M St NW Ste 206 — Washington DC 20036 — 202-457-0911 367-2114 48-12
TF: 800-631-9505 ■ *Web:* www.icac.com

iCAD Inc 98 Spit Brook Rd Ste 100 — Nashua NH 03062 — 603-882-5200 880-3843 382
NASDAQ: ICAD ■ *TF:* 866-280-2239 ■ *Web:* www.icadmed.com

Name / Address	City	State	Zip	Phone	Fax	Class
Icahn Enterprises LP						
767 Fifth Ave 47th Fl	New York	NY	10153	212-702-4300	750-5841	360-3
NASDAQ: IEP ■ *TF:* 800-255-2737 ■ *Web:* www.ielp.com						
Icahn School of Medicine at Mount Sinai						
1 Gustave L Levy Pl	New York	NY	10029	212-241-6500		48-17
TF: 800-862-1674 ■ *Web:* icahn.mssm.edu						
iCAIR (International Ctr for Advanced Internet Research)						
750 N Lake Shore Dr Ste 600	Chicago	IL	60611	312-503-0735		668
Web: www.icair.org						
ICAM Technologies Corp						
21500 Nassr St	Sainte-anne-de-bellevue	QC	H9X4C1	514-697-8033		179
TF: 800-827-4226 ■ *Web:* www.icam.com						
ICANN (Internet Corp for Assigned Names & Numbers)						
4676 Admiralty Way Ste 330	Marina del Rey	CA	90292	310-823-9358	823-8649	48-9
Web: www.icann.org						
Icare Industries Inc						
4399 35th St N	Saint Petersburg	FL	33714	727-526-0501		542
TF: 877-422-7352 ■ *Web:* www.icarelabs.com						
iCare Management LLC						
341 Bidwell St	Manchester	CT	06040	860-570-2140		371
TF: 800-244-6224 ■ *Web:* www.icaremanagement.com						
IcareLabs 4399 35th St N	Saint Petersburg	FL	33714	877-422-7352		542
TF: 877-422-7352 ■ *Web:* www.icarelabs.com						
ICAT Logistics Inc						
6805 Douglas Legum Dr	Elkridge	MD	21075	443-459-8070		311
Web: www.icatlogistics.com						
ICBA (Independent Community Bankers of America)						
1615 L St NW Ste 900	Washington	DC	20036	202-659-8111		49-2
TF: 800-422-8439 ■ *Web:* www.icba.org						
ICC (International Code Council)						
500 New Jersey Ave NW 6th Fl	Washington	DC	20001	202-370-1800	783-2348	49-3
TF: 888-422-7233 ■ *Web:* www.iccsafe.org						
Icc 6406 Odana Rd	Madison	WI	53719	608-277-8000		180
TF: 800-999-3355 ■ *Web:* www.iccnow.com						
ICC Capital 390 N Orange Ave Ste 2100	Orlando	FL	32801	407-839-8440		401
Web: www.icccapital.com						
ICC Chemical Corp 460 Pk Ave	New York	NY	10022	212-521-1700	521-1970	146
TF: 800-422-1720 ■ *Web:* www.iccchem.com						
ICC Chemicals						
4660 Spring Grove Ave	Cincinnati	OH	45232	513-541-7100	541-6880	145
Web: www.icc-chemicals.com						
ICC Industries Inc 460 Pk Ave	New York	NY	10022	212-521-1700	521-1970	144
TF: 800-422-1720 ■ *Web:* www.iccchem.com						
ICCFA (International Cemetery Cremation & Funeral Assn)						
107 Carpenter Dr Ste 100	Sterling	VA	20164	703-391-8400	391-8416	49-4
TF: 800-645-7700 ■ *Web:* www.iccfa.com						
Iccg Capital Inc 906 18th St Ste 122	Plano	TX	75074	972-424-5600		196
Web: www.iccgcapital.com						
ICCLOS (Indiana Convention Ctr & Lucas Oil Stadium)						
100 S Capitol Ave	Indianapolis	IN	46225	317-262-3400	262-3685	205
TF: 800-369-6220 ■ *Web:* www.icclos.com						
ICCP (Institute for Certification of Computing Professionals)						
2400 E Devon Ave Ste 281	Des Plaines	IL	60018	847-299-4227		48-9
TF: 800-843-8227 ■ *Web:* www.iccp.org						
ICD (International College of Dentists)						
51 Monroe St Ste 1400	Rockville	MD	20850	301-251-8861	738-9143	49-8
Web: www.icd.org						
ICD (International Ctr for the Disabled)						
340 E 24th St	New York	NY	10010	212-585-6020		48-17
TF: 800-246-4646 ■ *Web:* www.icdnyc.org						
ICD (Industrial Controls Distributors Inc)						
1776 Bloomsbury Ave	Ocean	NJ	07712	732-918-9000	922-4417	385
TF Sales: 800-281-4788 ■ *Web:* www.industrialcontrolsonline.com						
ICD Group International Inc						
600 Madison Ave Ste 1800	New York	NY	10022	212-644-1500		360-3
Web: www.icdgroup.com						
ICE (US Immigration & Customs Enforcement)						
425 'I' St NW	Washington	DC	20536	202-514-1900		340-11
TF: 866-347-2423 ■ *Web:* www.ice.gov						
Ice Air LLC 80 Hartford Ave	Mount Vernon	NY	10553	914-668-4700		664
Web: www.ice-air.com						
Ice Box Sports Ctr						
21902 Telegraph Rd	Brownstown Charter Twp	MI	48183	734-676-5500		711
Web: www.norianproperties.com						
Ice Cream Milk & Cheese PAC						
1250 H St NW Ste 900	Washington	DC	20005	202-737-4332	331-7820	615
Web: www.idfa.org						
Ice Cream Specialties						
8419 Hanley Industrial Ct	Saint Louis	MO	63144	314-962-2550		296-25
TF: 800-548-7777 ■ *Web:* www.northstarfrozentreats.com						
Ice Futures 1 N End Ave 13th Fl	New York	NY	10282	212-748-4000		691
TF: 800-821-5228 ■ *Web:* www.theice.com						
Ice House Cultural Ctr						
1925 Elm St Ste 500	Dallas	TX	75201	214-670-3687		50-2
TF: 800-255-5002 ■ *Web:* www.dallasculture.org						
Ice Industries Inc 3810 Herr Rd	Sylvania	OH	43560	419-842-3600		483
Web: www.iceindustries.com						
Ice Services Inc 2606 Ctr St	Anchorage	AK	99503	907-644-0385		393
Web: www.iceservices.net						
Ice Skating Institute (ISI)						
6000 Custer Rd Bldg 9	Plano	TX	75023	972-735-8800	735-8815	48-22
Web: www.skateisi.com						
Ice Specialty Entertainment Inc						
409 Santa Monica Blvd Ste E	Santa Monica	CA	90401	805-520-7465		354
Web: www.iceoplex.com						
Ice Technologies Inc 411 SE Ninth St	Pella	IA	50219	641-628-8724		180
TF: 877-754-8420 ■ *Web:* www.icetechnologies.com						
Icebox Cafe 1855 Purdy Ave	Miami Beach	FL	33139	305-538-8448		671
Web: www.iceboxcafe.com						
ICECORP Logistics Inc						
1600 Courtneypark Dr E	Mississauga	ON	L5T2W8	905-672-7400		314
Web: icecorp.ca						
Iceland 800 Third Ave 36th Fl	New York	NY	10022	212-593-2700	593-6269	784
Web: www.iceland.is						
Consulate General						
800 Third Ave 36th Fl	New York	NY	10022	646-282-9360	282-9369	257
Web: www.iceland.is/iceland-abroad						
Embassy						
House of Sweden 2900 K St NW Ste 509	Washington	DC	20007	202-265-6653	265-6656	257
Web: www.iceland.is/iceland-abroad/us						
Icelandair North America						
1900 Crown Colony Dr	Quincy	MA	02169	800-223-5500		26
TF: 800-223-5500 ■ *Web:* www.icelandair.com						
Icelandic State Park 13571 Hwy 5	Cavalier	ND	58220	701-265-4561		565
Web: www.parkrec.nd.gov/parks/isp/isp.html						
Icelandic-American Chamber of Commerce						
800 Third Ave 36th Fl	New York	NY	10022	212-593-2700	593-6269	138
Web: www.iceland.is						
Icemakers Inc 3711 Fifth Ct N	Birmingham	AL	35222	205-591-2791	591-2389	380
TF General: 800-467-2181 ■ *Web:* www.icemakers.net						
Ice-O-Matic 11100 E 45th Ave	Denver	CO	80239	303-371-3737	371-6296	664
TF: 800-423-3367 ■ *Web:* www.iceomatic.com						
Iceptstechnology Group Inc						
1301 Fulling Mill Rd	Middletown	PA	17057	717-704-1000	704-1010	174
TF: 888-477-7989 ■ *Web:* www.icepts.com						
ICF (International Contract Furnishings Inc)						
19 Ohio Ave	Norwich	CT	06360	860-886-1700	784-8209*	321
**Fax Area Code: 888* ■ *TF:* 800-237-1625 ■ *Web:* www.icfsource.com						
ICF International Inc 9300 Lee Hwy	Fairfax	VA	22031	703-934-3000	934-3740	261
NASDAQ: ICFI ■ *Web:* www.icf.com						
ICFG (International Church of the Foursquare Gospel)						
1910 W Sunset Blvd PO Box 26902	Los Angeles	CA	90026	213-989-4234	989-4590	48-20
TF: 888-635-4234 ■ *Web:* www.foursquare.org						
ICFL (Idaho Commission for Libraries)						
325 W State St	Boise	ID	83702	208-334-2150	334-4016	434-5
TF: 800-458-3271 ■ *Web:* www.libraries.idaho.gov						
ICG Castings Inc 9864 Church St	Bridgman	MI	49106	269-782-2108		308
ICG Consulting Inc						
8570 E Shea Blvd Ste 110	Scottsdale	AZ	85260	480-607-4040		463
Web: www.icgconsulting.com						
ICG Link Inc						
7003 Chadwick Dr Ste 111	Brentwood	TN	37027	615-370-1530		353
TF: 877-397-7605 ■ *Web:* www.icglink.net						
ICG/Holliston						
905 Holliston Mills Rd	Church Hill	TN	37642	423-357-6141	325-0351*	745-2
**Fax Area Code: 800* ■ *TF:* 800-251-0451 ■ *Web:* www.holliston.com						
iChange Networks Inc 801 N Harbor	Fullerton	CA	92832	714-447-4098		387
Web: www.ichange.com						
Ichetucknee Springs State Park						
12087 SW US Hwy 27	Fort White	FL	32038	850-245-2157		565
Web: www.floridastateparks.org						
Ichiban 338 Central Ave	Albany	NY	12206	518-432-0358		671
Web: ichibanjapanesechinese.com						
Ichiban 226 Union St	Bangor	ME	04401	207-262-9308		671
Web: bangorichiban.com						
Ichiban 19 S Orange Ave	Orlando	FL	32801	407-423-2688		671
Web: www.shakaiorlando.com						
Ichiban 1449 University Ave	San Diego	CA	92103	619-299-7203	299-7514	671
Web: www.ichibansushisandiego.com						
Ichiban 1914 Catasauqua Rd	Allentown	PA	18109	610-266-7781	266-7783	671
Web: ichibanpa.com						
Ichiban 189 Carlton St	Winnipeg	MB	R3C3H7	204-925-7400	957-1697	671
Web: www.ichiban.ca						
Ichp Building Company LLC						
4055 N Perryville Rd	Loves Park	IL	61111	815-227-9292		533
TF: 800-363-8012 ■ *Web:* ichpnet.org						
ICI (Investment Company Institute)						
1401 H St NW Ste 1200	Washington	DC	20005	202-326-5800	326-5841	49-2
Web: www.ici.org						
ICI (Investment Casting Institute)						
136 Summit Ave	Montvale	NJ	07645	201-573-9770	573-9771	49-13
Web: www.investmentcasting.org						
ICI (Industrial Contractors Inc)						
401 NW First St	Evansville	IN	47708	973-753-3500		186
Web: www.usa.skanska.com						
ICI Restaurant 246 DeKalb Ave	Brooklyn	NY	11205	718-789-2778		671
Web: www.icirestaurant.com						
ICI Services Corp						
500 Viking Dr Ste 400	Virginia Beach	VA	23452	757-340-6970		196
Web: www.icisrvcs.com						
ICIA (International Communications Industries Assn)						
11242 Waples Mill Rd Ste 200	Fairfax	VA	22030	703-273-7200	278-8082	49-20
TF: 800-659-7469 ■ *Web:* www.infocomm.org						
Icicle Seafoods Inc 4019 21st Ave W	Seattle	WA	98199	206-282-0988	282-7222	296-13
Web: www.icicleseafoods.com						
ICiDigital Inc						
4000 Westchase Blvd Ste 280	Raleigh	NC	27607	919-883-9467		195
Web: www.icidigital.com						
Icim Services Inc						
1401 H St NW Fl 10	Washington	DC	20005	202-682-4150		390
Web: www.icimutual.com						
iCIMS Inc						
90 Matawan Rd Pkwy 120 5th Fl	Matawan	NJ	07747	732-847-1941	876-0422	178-1
TF: 800-889-4422 ■ *Web:* www.icims.com						
Icio Inc 1373 Ridge Commons Blvd	Hanover	MD	21076	410-903-4166		225
TF: 800-595-0493 ■ *Web:* www.icioinc.com						
ICL Express 2307 Coney Island Ave	Brooklyn	NY	11223	718-376-1023	376-1073	12
TF: 800-229-2029 ■ *Web:* www.icl-express.com						
ICL Imaging Corp 51 Mellen St	Framingham	MA	01702	508-872-3280		174
Web: www.icl-imaging.com						
ICLA (International Collegiate Licensing Assn)						
24651 Detroit Rd	Westlake	OH	44145	440-892-4000	892-4007	48-22
TF: 877-887-2261 ■ *Web:* www.nacda.com/icla/nacda-icla.html						
ICM Asset Management Inc						
601 W Main Ave	Spokane	WA	99201	509-455-3588		401
TF: 800-488-4075 ■ *Web:* www.icmasset.com						
Icm Controls Corp						
7313 William Barry Blvd	North Syracuse	NY	13212	315-233-5266	233-5276	203
TF: 800-365-5525 ■ *Web:* www.icmcontrols.com						
ICM Inc 310 N First St	Colwich	KS	67030	316-796-0900		463
TF: 877-456-8588 ■ *Web:* www.icminc.com						
ICMA (International Card Manufacturers Assn)						
191 Clarksville Rd	Princeton Junction	NJ	08550	609-799-4900	799-7032	49-4
Web: www.icma.com						

	Phone	Fax	Class
ICMA (International Ctr of Medieval Art)			
The Cloisters Fort Tryon Pk New York NY 10040	212-928-1146	928-9946	48-4
Web: www.medievalart.org			
ICMA (International City/County Management Assn)			
777 N Capitol St NE Ste 500 Washington DC 20002	202-289-4262	962-3500	49-7
TF: 800-745-8780 ■ *Web:* www.icma.org			
ICMARC 777 N Capitol St NE Ste 600 Washington DC 20002	202-962-4600	962-4601	528
TF General: 800-669-7471 ■ *Web:* www.icmarc.org			
ICO (Inter City Oil Company Inc)			
1921 S St Duluth MN 55812	218-728-3641		579
TF: 800-642-5542 ■ *Web:* www.icofuel.com			
ICOI (International Congress of Oral Implantologists)			
248 Lorraine Ave 3rd Fl Upper Montclair NJ 07043	973-783-6300	295-8509*	49-8
**Fax Area Code:* 267 ■ *TF:* 800-442-0525 ■ *Web:* www.icoi.org			
iCollector Technologies Inc			
103-2071 Kingsway Ave Ste 114 Port Coquitlam BC V3C6N2	604-941-2221		51
TF: 866-313-0123 ■ *Web:* www.icollector.com			
ICOM America Inc 2380 116th Ave NE Bellevue WA 98004	425-454-8155	454-1509	647
TF: 800-872-4266 ■ *Web:* www.icomamerica.com			
iComp LLC 2524 Greenwich St San Francisco CA 94123	415-409-2070		463
TF: 866-432-2499			
ICON Advisers Inc			
5299 DTC Blvd Ste 1200 Greenwood Village CO 80111	303-790-1600		401
TF: 800-828-4881 ■ *Web:* www.iconadvisers.com			
ICON Creative Technologies Group			
202 E Huron St Ste 100 Ann Arbor MI 48104	734-239-3586		393
Icon Grill 1933 Fifth Ave Seattle WA 98101	206-441-6330		671
Web: www.icongrill.net			
ICON Health & Fitness Inc 1500 S 1000 W Logan UT 84321	435-750-5000		267
TF: 800-999-3756 ■ *Web:* www.iconfitness.com			
Icon International Inc			
4 Stamford 107 Elm St Plaza 15th Fl Stamford CT 06902	203-328-2300	328-2333	463
Web: www.icon-intl.com			
ICON Laboratories Inc			
123 Smith St Farmingdale NY 11735	631-777-8833		225
Web: iconplc.com			
Icon Media Direct Inc			
5910 Lemona Ave Sherman Oaks CA 91411	818-995-6400		5
Web: www.iconmediadirect.com			
Icon Productions			
808 Wilshire Blvd Santa Monica CA 90401	310-434-7300		514
Web: www.iconmovies.us			
Icon Ventures			
505 Hamilton Ave Ste 310 Palo Alto CA 94301	650-463-8800	463-8801	792
Web: www.jafco.com			
Icon West Inc			
520 S La Fayette Park Pl Ste 503 Los Angeles CA 90057	213-385-0027		187
TF: 800-400-7072 ■ *Web:* www.icon-west.com			
Icona Golden Inn 7849 Dune Dr Avalon NJ 08202	609-368-5155		378
Web: www.goldeninn.com			
Iconixx Software			
3420 Executive Ctr Dr Ste 250 Austin TX 78731	877-426-6499	651-3111*	180
**Fax Area Code:* 512 ■ *TF:* 877-426-6499 ■ *Web:* iconixx.com			
Iconma LLC 850 Stephenson Hwy Ste 612 Troy MI 48083	888-451-2519		631
TF: 888-451-2519 ■ *Web:* www.iconma.com			
IConnected Marketing Corp			
125 Tech Park Dr Rochester NY 14623	585-444-8500		5
Web: www.iconnectedmarketing.com			
Iconoculture Inc 244 First Ave N Minneapolis MN 55401	612-642-2222		668
Web: iconoculture.cebglobal.com			
Iconomics Inc 1 Dundas St W Ste 2108 Toronto ON M5G1Z3	416-703-6547		180
Web: www.iconomics-inc.com			
Icor Technology Inc 935 Ages Dr Ottawa ON K1G6L3	613-745-3600		690
TF: 877-483-7978 ■ *Web:* icortechnology.com			
ICO-RALLY Corp 2575 E Bayshore Rd Palo Alto CA 94303	650-856-9900	856-2006*	816
**Fax Area Code:* 800 ■ *Web:* www.icorally.com			
ICP (International Comfort Products Corp)			
650 Heil Quaker Ave Lewisburg TN 37091	931-359-3511		15
TF: 800-458-6650 ■ *Web:* www.icpusa.com			
ICPI (Interlocking Concrete Pavement Institute)			
14801 Murdock St Ste 230 Chantilly VA 20151	202-712-9036	408-0285	49-3
TF: 800-241-3652 ■ *Web:* www.icpi.org			
ICPM (Institute of Certified Professional Managers)			
James Madison University MSC 5504 Harrisonburg VA 22807	540-568-3247		49-12
TF: 800-460-8013 ■ *Web:* www.icpm.biz			
Icreon Tech 597 Fifth Ave 12th Fl New York NY 10017	212-706-6021		196
Web: www.icreon.us			
iCrossing Inc 300 W 57th St New York NY 10019	212-649-3900		466
TF: 800-908-5395 ■ *Web:* www.icrossing.com			
ICRW (International Ctr for Research on Women)			
1120 20th St NW Ste 500-N Washington DC 20036	202-797-0007	797-0020	48-24
Web: www.icrw.org			
ICS (International College of Surgeons)			
1516 N Lake Shore Dr Chicago IL 60610	312-642-3555		49-8
TF: 800-382-8270 ■ *Web:* www.icsglobal.org			
ICS (Integrated Computer Solutions Inc)			
54 Middlesex Tpke Ste B Bedford MA 01730	617-621-0060	621-9555	178-2
Web: www.ics.com			
ICS (Information & Computing Services Inc)			
1650 Prudential Dr Ste 300 Jacksonville FL 32207	904-399-8500		178-1
TF: 800-676-4427 ■ *Web:* www.icsfl.com			
ICS (Integrated Components Source)			
3977 Camino Ranchero Camarillo CA 93012	805-822-5100		246
Web: www.yourdrive.com			
ICS Blount Inc			
4909 SE International Way Portland OR 97222	800-321-1240	653-4201*	682
**Fax Area Code:* 503 ■ *TF:* 800-321-1240 ■ *Web:* www.icsdiamondtools.eu			
ICS Corp 100 Friars Blvd West Deptford PA 08086	888-223-2840		626
TF: 888-223-2840 ■ *Web:* ics-corporation.com			
ICS Marketing Services Inc			
4225 Legacy Pkwy Lansing MI 48911	517-394-1890		195
TF: 888-394-1890 ■ *Web:* www.icshq.com			
ICSA Labs			
1000 Bent Creek Blvd Ste 200 Mechanicsburg PA 17050	717-790-8100		387
Web: www.icsalabs.com			
ICSC (International Council of Shopping Centers)			
1221 Ave of the Americas 41st Fl New York NY 10020	646-728-3800	589-5555*	49-12
**Fax Area Code:* 212 ■ *Web:* www.icsc.org			

	Phone	Fax	Class
ICSNetwork LLC			
17450 Long Meadow Trl Chagrin Falls OH 44023	216-509-6000		41
Web: www.icsnetwork.com			
ICTA (International Ctr for Technology Assessment)			
660 Pennsylvania Ave SE Ste 302 Washington DC 20003	415-826-2770		49-19
Web: www.icta.org			
ICTA (Industry Council for Tangible Assets)			
1510 Circle Dr Annapolis MD 21409	410-626-7005		49-2
TF: 800-447-8848 ■ *Web:* www.ictaonline.org			
ICTC (Inter-Community Telephone Co)			
PO Box 8 Nome ND 58062	701-924-8815	924-8808	736
TF: 800-350-9137 ■ *Web:* www.ictc.com			
ICTV Brands Inc			
489 Devon Park Dr Ste 315 Wayne PA 19087	484-598-2300		225
TF: 800-839-4906 ■ *Web:* ictvbrands.com			
ICU Medical Inc			
951 Calle Amanecer San Clemente CA 92673	949-366-2183	366-8368	477
NASDAQ: ICUI ■ *TF:* 800-824-7890 ■ *Web:* www.icumed.com			
ICV Digital Media 3908 Valley Ave Pleasanton CA 94566	925-426-8230		514
Web: www.icvdm.com			
Icvm Group Inc 50 Love Ln Mattituck NY 11952	631-298-5505		225
Web: www.icvmgroup.com			
ICW Group 11455 El Camino Real San Diego CA 92130	858-350-2400		391-4
TF: 800-877-1111 ■ *Web:* www.icwgroup.com			
ICWM (Institute of Caster & Wheel Manufacturers)			
8720 Red Oak Blvd Ste 201 Charlotte NC 28217	704-676-1190	676-1199	49-13
TF: 877-522-5431 ■ *Web:* www.mhi.org			
IcwUSACom Inc 1487 Kingsley Dr Medford OR 97504	541-608-2824		321
TF: 800-558-4435 ■ *Web:* icwusa.com			
ICX Group Inc			
SunTrust Tower 76 S Laura St Ste 1300 Jacksonville FL 32202	904-208-2200		317
TF: 800-582-0828 ■ *Web:* www.icxgroup.com			
iCyt Visionary Bioscience Inc			
2100 S Oak St Champaign IL 61820	217-328-9396		261
Id Group LLC, The 2641 Irving Blvd Dallas TX 75207	214-638-6800		393
Web: www.idgroupdallas.com			
ID Systems Inc			
123 Tice Blvd Ste 101 Woodcliff Lake NJ 07677	201-996-9000	996-9144	647
NASDAQ: IDSY ■ *TF:* 866-410-0152 ■ *Web:* www.id-systems.com			
IDA (Institute for Defense Analyses)			
4850 Mark Ctr Dr Alexandria VA 22311	703-845-2000	845-2588	668
Web: www.ida.org			
IDA (In Defense of Animals)			
3010 Kerner Blvd San Rafael CA 94901	415-448-0048	454-1031	48-3
TF: 800-705-0425 ■ *Web:* www.idausa.org			
IDA (Industrial Diamond Assn of America)			
6081 Central Pk Dr Columbus OH 43231	614-797-2265		49-13
Web: www.superabrasives.org			
IDA (International Downtown Assn)			
1025 Thomas Jefferson St NW Ste 500 W Washington DC 20007	202-393-6801	393-6869	49-17
Web: www.ida-downtown.org/eweb			
IDA (International Dyslexia Assn, The)			
40 York Rd 4th Fl Towson MD 21204	410-296-0232	321-5069	48-17
Web: dyslexiaida.org			
Ida County 401 Moorehead St Ida Grove IA 51445	712-364-2626		338
TF: 800-368-8683 ■ *Web:* idacounty.org			
Ida Rupp Public Library			
310 Madison St Port Clinton OH 43452	419-732-3212		434-3
Web: www.idarupp.org			
IDACORP Inc 1221 W Idaho St Boise ID 83702	208-388-2200		360-5
NYSE: IDA ■ *TF:* 800-242-0681 ■ *Web:* www.idacorpinc.com			
Idaho			
Accountancy Board 3101 W Main St Ste 210 Boise ID 83702	208-334-2490	334-2615	339-13
Web: www.isba.idaho.gov			
Administrative Director of the Courts			
PO Box 83720 Boise ID 83720	208-334-2246	947-7590	339-13
Web: www.isc.idaho.gov			
Aging Commission (ICOA)			
341 W Washington Fl 3 PO Box 83720 Boise ID 83702	208-334-3833	334-3033	339-13
TF: 877-471-2777 ■ *Web:* www.idahoaging.com			
Agriculture Dept			
2270 Old Penitentiary Rd Boise ID 83712	208-332-8500	334-2170	339-13
Web: www.agri.state.id.us			
Arts Commission			
2410 Old Penitentiary Rd Boise ID 83712	208-334-2119		339-13
TF: 800-278-3863 ■ *Web:* www.arts.idaho.gov			
Attorney General			
PO Box 83720 PO Box 83720 Boise ID 83720	208-334-2400	854-8071	339-13
Web: www.ag.idaho.gov			
Bill Status PO Box 83720 Boise ID 83720	208-332-1000	334-2320	433
Web: www.legislature.idaho.gov			
Board of Medicine			
1755 N Westgate Dr Ste 140 PO Box 83720 Boise ID 83704	208-327-7000	327-7005	339-13
TF: 800-333-0073 ■ *Web:* www.bom.idaho.gov			
Child Support Services Bureau			
PO Box 83720 Boise ID 83720	208-334-2479	334-0666	339-13
Web: www.healthandwelfare.idaho.gov			
Consumer Protection Unit PO Box 83720 Boise ID 83720	208-332-0102		339-13
Web: www.state.id.us			
Correction Board			
1299 N Orchard St Ste 110 Boise ID 83706	208-658-2000	327-7404	339-13
Web: www.idoc.idaho.gov			
Crime Victims Compensation Program			
PO Box 83720 Boise ID 83720	208-334-6000	334-2321	339-13
TF: 800-950-2110 ■ *Web:* www.iic.idaho.gov			
Department of Commerce			
700 W State St PO Box 83720 Boise ID 83720	208-334-2470	334-2631	339-13
TF: 800-842-5858 ■ *Web:* commerce.idaho.gov			
Education Dept 650 W State St Boise ID 83702	208-332-6800	334-2228	339-13
Web: www.sde.idaho.gov			
Finance Dept			
800 Pk Blvd Ste 200 PO Box 83720 Boise ID 83712	208-332-8000		339-13
TF: 888-346-3378 ■ *Web:* www.finance.idaho.gov			
Fish & Game Dept 600 S Walnut St Boise ID 83712	208-334-3700	334-2114	339-13
Web: idfg.idaho.gov			
Health & Welfare Dept			
450 W State St Tenth Fl PO Box 83720 Boise ID 83720	877-456-1233	334-5926*	339-13
**Fax Area Code:* 208 ■ **Fax:* PR ■ *TF:* 877-456-1233 ■ *Web:* www.healthandwelfare.idaho.gov			

				Phone	Fax	Class
Historical Society 2205 Old Penitentiary Rd *Web:* history.idaho.gov	Boise	ID	83712	208-334-2682	334-2774	339-13
Homeland Security Bureau 4040 W Guard St Bldg 600 *Web:* www.bhs.idaho.gov	Boise	ID	83705	208-422-3040	422-3044	339-13
Housing & Finance Assn 565 W Myrtle Ave *TF:* 800-526-7145 ■ *Web:* www.idahohousing.com	Boise	ID	83702	208-331-4700		339-13
Insurance Dept 700 W State St Fl 3 *Web:* www.doi.idaho.gov	Boise	ID	83720	208-334-4250	334-4398	339-13
Lands Dept 300 N Sixth St Ste 103 PO Box 83720 *Web:* www.idl.idaho.gov	Boise	ID	83702	208-334-0200	334-5342	339-13
Legislature PO Box 83720 *Web:* www.legislature.idaho.gov	Boise	ID	83720	208-334-2475	334-2125	339-13
Lieutenant Governor State Capitol *Web:* www.lgo.idaho.gov	Boise	ID	83720	208-334-2200	334-3259	339-13
Lottery 1199 Shoreline Ln Ste 100 *TF:* 800-432-5688 ■ *Web:* www.idaholottery.com	Boise	ID	83702	208-334-2600		452
Motor Vehicles Div 3311 W State St PO Box 7129 *Web:* itd.idaho.gov	Boise	ID	83707	208-334-8000	334-8739	339-13
National Board For Professional Teaching Standards PO Box 83720 *Web:* www.sde.idaho.gov	Boise	ID	83720	208-332-6800	334-2228	339-13
Occupational Licenses Bureau 700 W State St *Web:* www.ibol.idaho.gov	Boise	ID	83702	208-334-3233		339-13
Office of the Governor 700 W Jefferson St, Ste 210 PO Box 83720 *Web:* www.ag.idaho.gov	Boise	ID	83720	208-334-2400	854-8071	339-13
Pardon & Parole Commission 3056 Elder St *Web:* www.parole.idaho.gov	Boise	ID	83705	208-334-2520		339-13
Parks & Recreation Dept 5657 Warm Springs Ave *TF:* 855-514-2429 ■ *Web:* www.parksandrecreation.idaho.gov	Boise	ID	83716	208-334-4199		339-13
Public Utilities Commission 472 W Washington Boise PO Box 83720 *TF:* 800-432-0369 ■ *Web:* www.puc.idaho.gov	Boise	ID	83720	208-334-0300	334-3762	339-13
Racing Commission 700 S Stratford Dr *Web:* isp.idaho.gov	Meridian	ID	83642	208-884-7080	884-7098	712
Real Estate Commission 575 E Parkcenter Blvd Ste 180 *Web:* www.irec.idaho.gov	Boise	ID	83706	208-334-3285	334-2050	339-13
Secretary of State 700 W Jefferson St Rm 205 *Web:* sos.idaho.gov	Boise	ID	83720	208-334-2300		339-13
Supreme Court PO Box 83720 *Web:* www.isc.idaho.gov	Boise	ID	83720	208-334-2210	947-7590	339-13
Tax Commission 800 E Pk Blvd Plz 4 *TF:* 800-972-7660 ■ *Web:* www.tax.idaho.gov	Boise	ID	83712	208-334-7660	334-7844	339-13
Tourism Development Div 700 W State St PO Box 83720 *TF General:* 800-847-4843 ■ *Web:* www.visitidaho.org	Boise	ID	83720	208-334-2470	334-2631	339-13
Transportation Dept PO Box 7129 *Web:* www.itd.idaho.gov	Boise	ID	83707	208-334-8000		339-13
Treasurer 700 W Jefferson St Ste 126 PO Box 83720 *Web:* sto.idaho.gov	Boise	ID	83720	208-334-3200	332-2960	339-13
Veterans Services Div 351 Collins Rd *Web:* www.veterans.idaho.gov	Boise	ID	83702	208-577-2310	780-1300	339-13
Vital Records & Health Statistics Bureau PO Box 83720 *Web:* www.healthandwelfare.idaho.gov	Boise	ID	83720	208-334-5988		339-13
Vocational Rehabilitation Div 650 W State St Rm 150 *Web:* www.vr.idaho.gov	Boise	ID	83720	208-334-3390	334-5305	339-13
Weights & Measures Bureau 2216 Kellogg Ln *Web:* www.agri.state.id.us	Boise	ID	83712	208-332-8690	334-2378	339-13
Idaho Assn of Commerce & Industry 816 W Bannock St Ste 5B PO Box 389 *TF:* 800-824-6883 ■ *Web:* www.iaci.org	Boise	ID	83701	208-343-1849		140
Idaho Assn of Realtors 10116 W Overland Rd *TF:* 800-621-7553 ■ *Web:* www.idahorealtors.com	Boise	ID	83702	208-342-3585	336-7958	656
Idaho Black History Museum 508 Julia Davis Dr *Web:* www.ibhm.org	Boise	ID	83702	208-789-2164		520
Idaho Botanical Garden 2355 N Penitentiary Rd *TF:* 877-527-8233 ■ *Web:* www.idahobotanicalgarden.org	Boise	ID	83712	208-343-8649	343-3601	97
Idaho Cedar Sales LLC 221 Main St *Web:* www.cedar.idahotimber.com	Troy	ID	83871	208-835-2161		820
Idaho Commission for Libraries (ICFL) 325 W State St *TF:* 800-458-3271 ■ *Web:* www.libraries.idaho.gov	Boise	ID	83702	208-334-2150	334-4016	434-5
Idaho Community Foundation Inc 210 W State St *TF:* 800-657-5357 ■ *Web:* www.idcomfdn.org	Boise	ID	83702	208-342-3535		305
Idaho Correctional Industries 1301 N Orchad Ste 110 *Web:* www.ci.idaho.gov	Boise	ID	83706	208-577-5555	577-5545	630
Idaho County 320 W Main St Rm 5 *Web:* www.idahocounty.org	Grangeville	ID	83530	208-983-2751		338
Idaho County Light & Power Co-op 1065 Hwy 13 *TF:* 877-212-0424 ■ *Web:* www.iclp.coop	Grangeville	ID	83530	208-983-1610		245
Idaho Democratic Party 943 W Overland Rd *TF:* 800-626-0471 ■ *Web:* idahodems.org	Meridian	ID	83642	208-336-1815		616-1
Idaho Falls Public Library 457 W Broadway *Web:* www.ifpl.org	Idaho Falls	ID	83402	208-612-8460		434-3
Idaho Falls School District 91 Education Foundation Inc 690 John Adams Pkwy *TF:* 888-993-7120 ■ *Web:* www.d91.k12.id.us	Idaho Falls	ID	83401	208-525-7500	525-7596	685
Idaho Historical Museum 610 N Julia Davis Dr *Web:* history.idaho.gov	Boise	ID	83702	208-334-2120	334-4059	520
Idaho Human Rights Education Ctr 777 S Eigth St *Web:* www.wassmuthcenter.org	Boise	ID	83702	208-345-0304		50-4
Idaho Innovation Center Inc 2300 N Yellowstone Hwy Ste 100 *Web:* innovateidaho.org	Idaho Falls	ID	83401	208-523-1026		194
Idaho Labor Dept 317 W Main St *TF:* 800-554-5627 ■ *Web:* labor.idaho.gov/dnn/idl	Boise	ID	83735	208-332-3570	334-6300	259
Idaho Lions Eye Bank 1090 N Cole Rd *TF:* 800-546-6889 ■ *Web:* www.idaholions.org	Boise	ID	83704	208-338-5466	338-6543	269
Idaho Maximum Security Institution (IMSI) PO Box 51 *Web:* www.idoc.idaho.gov	Boise	ID	83707	208-338-1635		213
Idaho Medical Assn 305 W Jefferson St *Web:* www.idmed.org	Boise	ID	83702	208-344-7888	344-7903	474
Idaho Military History Museum 4692 W Harvard St *Web:* museum.mil.idaho.gov	Boise	ID	83705	208-272-4841		520
Idaho Milk Transport Inc PO Box 1185 *Web:* www.idahomilktransport.com	Burley	ID	83318	208-878-5000		468
Idaho National Laboratory (INL) 2525 Fremont Ave *TF:* 866-495-7440 ■ *Web:* www.inl.gov	Idaho Falls	ID	83402	866-495-7440		668
Idaho Northern & Pacific Railroad 119 N Commercial Ave *Web:* www.rgpc.com	Emmett	ID	83617	208-365-6353		649
Idaho Nurses Assn (INA) 1850 E Southern Ave Ste 1 **Fax Area Code:* 404 ■ *TF:* 888-721-8904 ■ *Web:* www.idahonurses.org	Tempe	AZ	85282	888-721-8904	240-0998*	533
Idaho Pacific Lumber Company Inc (IdaPac) 1770 Spanish Sun Way *TF:* 800-231-2310 ■ *Web:* www.idapac.com	Meridian	ID	83642	208-375-8052	375-3054	191-3
Idaho Power Co 1221 W Idaho St *TF:* 800-488-6151 ■ *Web:* www.idahopower.com	Boise	ID	83702	208-388-2200		787
Idaho Press-Tribune 1618 N Midland Blvd *Web:* www.idahopress.com	Nampa	ID	83651	208-467-9251	467-9562	532-2
Idaho Primary Care Association Inc 1087 W River St Ste 160 *Web:* www.idahopca.org	Boise	ID	83702	208-345-2335		533
Idaho Public Television (IPTV) 1455 N Orchard St *TF:* 800-543-6868 ■ *Web:* idahoptv.org	Boise	ID	83706	208-373-7220	373-7245	632
Idaho Republican Party 101 S Capitol Blvd Ste 302 *Web:* www.idgop.org	Boise	ID	83702	208-343-6405	343-6414	616-2
Idaho Scholarship Office 650 W State St PO Box 83720 *Web:* www.boardofed.idaho.gov	Boise	ID	83720	208-334-2270	334-2632	725
Idaho State Bar 525 W Jefferson St *TF:* 800-221-3295 ■ *Web:* www.isb.idaho.gov	Boise	ID	83702	208-334-4500	334-4515	72
Idaho State Civic Symphony 921 S Eigth Ave S- 8099 *Web:* www.thesymphony.us	Pocatello	ID	83209	208-234-1587		573-3
Idaho State Correctional Institution PO Box 14 *Web:* idoc.idaho.gov	Boise	ID	83707	208-336-0740	334-2748	213
Idaho State Dental Assn 1220 W Hays St *Web:* theisda.org	Boise	ID	83702	208-343-7543		227
Idaho State Journal 305 S Arthur Ave *TF:* 800-669-9777 ■ *Web:* www.idahostatejournal.com	Pocatello	ID	83204	208-232-4161	233-8007	532-2
Idaho State Pharmacy Assn (ISPA) 816 W Bannock St Ste 105 *Web:* www.idahopharmacists.com	Boise	ID	83702	208-870-8312		585
Idaho State University 921 S Eigth Ave **Fax:* Admissions ■ *Web:* www.isu.edu	Pocatello	ID	83209	208-282-2475	282-4511*	166
Idaho State University Oboler Library 850 S Ninth Ave Bldg 50 Stop 8089 *Web:* www.isu.edu/library	Pocatello	ID	83209	208-282-2958	282-5847	434-6
Idaho State Veterans Home-Boise 320 Collins Rd *Web:* veterans.idaho.gov	Boise	ID	83702	208-780-1600	780-1601	793
Idaho State Veterans Home-Lewiston 821 21st Ave *Web:* veterans.idaho.gov	Lewiston	ID	83501	208-799-3422	799-3414	793
Idaho State Veterans Home-Pocatello 1957 Alvin Ricken Dr *TF:* 855-488-8440 ■ *Web:* veterans.idaho.gov	Pocatello	ID	83201	208-235-7800	235-7801	793
Idaho Statesman PO Box 40 *TF:* 800-635-8934 ■ *Web:* www.idahostatesman.com	Boise	ID	83707	208-377-6400	377-6449	532-2
Idaho Steel Products Co 255 E Anderson St *TF:* 800-835-5011 ■ *Web:* www.idahosteel.com	Idaho Falls	ID	83401	208-522-1275	522-6041	298
Idaho Supreme Potatoes Inc 614 E 800 N PO Box 246 *Web:* idahosupreme.com	Firth	ID	83236	208-346-6841	346-4104	296-18
Idaho Technology Council Inc 101 S Capitol Blvd Ste 208 *Web:* www.idahotechcouncil.org	Boise	ID	83702	208-917-5184		463
Idaho Veterinary Medical Assn (IVMA) 1841 W Secluded Ct *TF:* 800-552-7236 ■ *Web:* www.ivma.org	Kuna	ID	83634	208-922-9431	922-9435	795
Idaho-Pacific Corp 4723 E 100 N PO Box 478 *TF Sales:* 800-238-5503 ■ *Web:* www.idahopacific.com	Ririe	ID	83443	208-538-6971	538-5082	296-18
Idamerica 941 Corporate Ln *TF:* 800-876-1699 ■ *Web:* idamerica.com	Chesapeake	VA	23320	757-549-2300		344
IdaPac (Idaho Pacific Lumber Company Inc) 1770 Spanish Sun Way *TF:* 800-231-2310 ■ *Web:* www.idapac.com	Meridian	ID	83642	208-375-8052	375-3054	191-3
iData Research Inc 4211 Kingsway Ste 308 *Web:* idataresearch.com	Burnaby	BC	V5H1Z6	604-266-6933	266-6934	466

	Phone	Fax	Class

IDBB (Israel Discount Bank of New York)
511 Fifth Ave. New York NY 10017 — 212-551-8500 — 551-8540 — 70
Web: www.idbny.com

IDC (IDC) 5 Spoon St. Framingham MA 01701 — 508-872-8200 — 424-4829 — 466
TF: 800-343-4952 ■ *Web:* www.idcresearch.com

Idc Communications 1385 Niakwa Rd E Winnipeg MB R2J3T3 — 204-255-8389 — 736
Web: www.idccommunications.com

IDD Process & Packaging
5450 Tech Cir. Moorpark CA 93021 — 805-529-9890 — 261
TF: 800-621-4144 ■ *Web:* www.iddeas.com

IDDBA (International Dairy-Deli-Bakery Assn)
636 Science Dr. Madison WI 53711 — 608-310-5000 — 238-6330 — 49-6
TF: 877-399-4925 ■ *Web:* www.iddba.org

IDEA (International District Energy Assn)
24 Lyman St Ste 230. Westborough MA 01581 — 508-366-9339 — 366-0019 — 49-3
Web: www.districtenergy.org

Idea and Design Works LLC
5080 Santa Fe St Ste 106 San Diego CA 92109 — 858-270-1315 — 393
TF: 800-438-7325 ■ *Web:* www.idwpublishing.com

Idea Channel 2002 Filmore Ave Ste 1 Erie PA 16506 — 814-833-7107 — 740
Web: theideachannel.tv

Idea Engineering Inc
32 E Sola St Santa Barbara CA 93101 — 805-963-5399 — 256
Web: www.ideaengineering.com

Idea Foundry
4551 Forbes Ave Ste 200 Pittsburgh PA 15213 — 412-682-3067 — 260
Web: ideafoundry.org

IDEA Inc 10455 Pacific Ctr Ct San Diego CA 92121 — 858-535-8979 — 535-8234 — 48-22
TF: 800-999-4332 ■ *Web:* www.ideafit.com

Idea Lab Marketing
7 E Main St Ste 100 Moorestown NJ 08057 — 856-642-0007 — 7
Web: www.idealabmarketing.com

Idea Works Inc, The
100 W Briarwood Ln. Columbia MO 65203 — 573-445-4554 — 177
TF: 888-444-5772 ■ *Web:* www.ideaworks.com

IDEAL 4800 S Austin Ave. Chicago IL 60638 — 708-594-3100 — 594-3109 — 233
Web: www.idealpop.com

Ideal Adv & Printing
116 N Winnebago St. Rockford IL 61101 — 815-965-1713 — 4
TF: 800-208-0294 ■ *Web:* www.idealad.com

Ideal Builders Inc 1406 Emil St Madison WI 53713 — 608-271-8111 — 186
Web: www.idealbuildersinc.com

Ideal Chemical & Supply Co
4025 Air Pk St Memphis TN 38118 — 901-363-7720 — 366-0864 — 146
TF: 800-232-6776 ■ *Web:* www.idealchemical.com

Ideal Consulting Services Inco
521 American Legion Hwy Westport MA 02790 — 508-636-6615 — 196
TF: 866-254-6136 ■ *Web:* idealconsultingservices.com

Ideal Data Inc 420 River Rd North Arlington NJ 07031 — 201-998-9440 — 396

Ideal Fastener Corp 603 W Industry Dr. Oxford NC 27565 — 919-693-3115 — 693-3118 — 594
TF: 800-334-6653 ■ *Web:* www.idealfastener.com

Ideal Image Development Inc
1 N Dale Mabry Hwy Ste 100A Tampa FL 33609 — 813-286-8100 — 77
Web: www.idealimage.com

Ideal Industries Inc 1375 Pk Ave. Sycamore IL 60178 — 815-895-5181 — 816
TF: 800-435-0705 ■ *Web:* www.idealindustries.com

Ideal Innovations Inc
950 N Glebe Rd Ste 800 Arlington VA 22203 — 703-528-9101 — 528-1913 — 194
Web: www.idealinnovations.com

Ideal Integrations Inc
000 Regis Ave. Pittsburgh PA 15236 — 412-349-6680 — 180
Web: www.idealintegrations.net

Ideal Interiors Inc 450 Seventh Ave. New York NY 10123 — 212-262-7005 — 186
Web: www.ideal-interiors.com

Ideal Jacobs Corp 515 Valley St. Maplewood NJ 07040 — 973-275-5100 — 627
TF: 877-873-4332 ■ *Web:* idealjacobs.com

Ideal Manufacturing Inc
2011 Harnish Blvd Billings MT 59101 — 406-656-4360 — 492
TF: 800-523-3888 ■ *Web:* www.idealmfginc.com

Ideal Media US Inc
526 Seventh Ave Fl 7 New York NY 10018 — 646-681-3356 — 5
Web: idealmedia.com

Ideal Pet Products Inc
24735 Ave Rockefeller Valencia CA 91355 — 661-294-2266 — 608
TF: 800-378-4385 ■ *Web:* www.idealpetproducts.com

Ideal Pipe Ltd
Box 100 - 1100 Ideal Dr. Thorndale ON N0M2P0 — 519-473-2669 — 350
TF: 800-265-7098 ■ *Web:* www.idealpipe.ca

Ideal Power Inc
4120 Freidrich Ln Ste 100 Austin TX 78744 — 512-264-1542 — 767
TF: 800-732-0330 ■ *Web:* www.idealpower.com

Ideal Printers Inc 645 Olive St. Saint Paul MN 55130 — 651-855-1100 — 174
Web: www.idealprint.com

Ideal Ready Mix Company Inc
3902 W Mt Pleasant St West Burlington IA 52655 — 319-754-4747 — 182
Web: www.idealrm.com

Ideal Shield LLC 2525 Clark St. Detroit MI 48209 — 313-842-7290 — 295
TF: 866-825-8659 ■ *Web:* www.idealshield.com

Ideal Snacks Corp 89 Mill St. Liberty NY 12754 — 845-292-7000 — 292-7000 — 296-35
Web: www.idealsnacks.com

Ideal Software Systems Inc
4909 29th Ave. Meridian MS 39305 — 601-693-1673 — 177
TF: 800-964-3325 ■ *Web:* www.idealss.com

Ideal Supply Company Inc
2935 S Highland Dr Las Vegas NV 89109 — 702-731-3445 — 612
Web: www.idealsupplylv.com

Ideal Tape Co 1400 Middlesex St Lowell MA 01851 — 800-284-3325 — 458-0302* — 477
**Fax Area Code:* 978 ■ *TF:* 800-284-3325 ■ *Web:* www.idealtape.com

Ideal Welders Ltd 660 Caldew St Delta BC V3M5S2 — 604-525-5558 — 525-5313 — 595
Web: www.idealwelders.com

Ideal Window Manufacturing Inc
100 W Seventh St. Bayonne NJ 07002 — 800-631-3400 — 596
TF: 800-631-3400 ■ *Web:* www.idealwindow.com

Ideal Wire Works Inc 820 S Date Ave Alhambra CA 91803 — 626-282-0886 — 233

Idealab 130 W Union St Pasadena CA 91103 — 626-585-6900 — 535-2701 — 792
Web: www.idealab.com

Idealease Inc 430 N Rand Rd North Barrington IL 60010 — 847-304-6000 — 304-0076 — 778
TF: 800-435-3273 ■ *Web:* www.idealease.com

Idealliance 1600 Duke St Ste 420 Alexandria VA 22314 — 952-896-1908 — 49-16
TF: 800-255-8141 ■ *Web:* idealliance.org

Idealogical Systems Inc 2900 John St Markham ON L3R5G3 — 905-474-0772 — 180
TF: 855-554-4332 ■ *Web:* www.idealogical.com

Idealstor LLC
12400 St Hwy 71 W Ste 350-364 Austin TX 78738 — 512-279-4321 — 173-8
TF: 888-864-3257 ■ *Web:* www.idealstor.com

Ideaology Advertising Inc
4223 Glencoe Ave Ste A127 Marina Del Rey CA 90292 — 310-306-6501 — 7
Web: ideaologyinc.com

Ideas To Go Inc
1 Main St SE 5th Fl. Minneapolis MN 55414 — 612-331-1570 — 463
Web: www.ideastogo.com

Ideastream 1375 Euclid Ave Cleveland OH 44115 — 216-916-6100 — 741-31
Web: wviz.ideastream.org

IdeaTek 111 Old Mill Ln. Buhler KS 67522 — 620-543-2580 — 387
TF: 855-433-2835 ■ *Web:* www.ideatek.com

IdeaVillage Products Corp
155 Route 46 W 4th Fl Wayne NJ 07470 — 973-826-8418 — 76
Web: www.ideavillage.com

Ideaworks 1110 N Palafox St. Pensacola FL 32501 — 850-434-9095 — 7
TF: 800-874-1234 ■ *Web:* ideaworks.co

IDEC Corp 1175 Elko Dr Sunnyvale CA 94089 — 408-747-0550 — 744-9055 — 203
TF: 800-262-4332 ■ *Web:* www.idec.com

Idegy Inc 226 N Fifth St Ste 220. Columbus OH 43215 — 614-545-5000 — 545-4000 — 184
TF: 888-421-2288 ■ *Web:* idegy.com

Idem Translations Inc
550 California Ave Ste 310. Palo Alto CA 94306 — 650-858-4336 — 393
TF: 800-508-2484 ■ *Web:* www.idemtranslations.com

Iden Cosmetics Inc 15500 Texaco St. Paramount CA 90723 — 562-630-2580 — 238
Web: www.idencosmetics.com

Idenix Pharmaceuticals Inc
320 Bent St 4th fl Cambridge MA 02141 — 908-423-1000 — 631-5996* — 85
NYSE: MRK ■ **Fax Area Code:* 215 ■ *TF:* 800-770-4674 ■ *Web:* www.merck.com/contact/home.html

Ident-A-Kid Services of America
1780 102nd Ave N Ste 100. Saint Petersburg FL 33716 — 727-577-4646 — 576-8258 — 310
TF: 800-890-1000 ■ *Web:* www.identakid.com

Identatronics Inc
165 N Lively Blvd Elk Grove Village IL 60007 — 847-437-2654 — 591
TF Cust Svc: 800-323-5403 ■ *Web:* www.identatronics.com

IDenticard Systems Inc
25 Race Ave FL 1 Lancaster PA 17603 — 717-569-5797 — 569-2390 — 692
TF: 800-233-0298 ■ *Web:* www.identicard.com

Identification Plates Inc
1555 High Point Dr. Mesquite TX 75149 — 972-216-1616 — 934-8304* — 411
**Fax Area Code:* 800 ■ *TF:* 800-395-2570 ■ *Web:* www.idplates.com

Identifix Inc 2714 Patton Rd Saint Paul MN 55113 — 651-633-8007 — 624
TF: 800-745-9649 ■ *Web:* www.identifix.com

Identigene LLC
2495 South West Temple Salt Lake City UT 84115 — 801-462-1401 — 418
TF: 888-404-4363 ■ *Web:* www.dnatesting.com

Identity Automation LP
8833 N Sam Houston Pkwy W Houston TX 77064 — 877-221-8401 — 358
TF: 877-221-8401 ■ *Web:* www.identityautomation.com

Identity Genetics Inc 47927 213th St Aurora SD 57002 — 800-861-1054 — 417
TF: 800 861-1054 ■ *Web:* www.identitygenetics.com

Identity Group, The
505 N Tustin Ave Ste 234 Santa Ana CA 92705 — 714-573-0010 — 7
Web: www.identitygroup.com

Identity Theft Resource Center
3625 Ruffin Rd Ste 204. San Diego CA 92123 — 858-693-7935 — 631
TF: 888-400-5530 ■ *Web:* www.idtheftcenter.org

IdentityMine Inc
1201 Western Ave Ste 350 Seattle WA 98101 — 206-206-3500 — 180
Web: www.identitymine.com

IDEO 100 Forest Ave. Palo Alto CA 94301 — 650-289-3400 — 289-3707 — 261
Web: www.ideo.com

Idera Pharmaceuticals Inc
167 Sidney St. Cambridge MA 02139 — 617-679-5500 — 679-5592 — 85
NASDAQ: IDRA ■ *Web:* www.iderapharma.com

Idesco Corp 37 W 26th St New York NY 10010 — 212-889-2530 — 358
TF: 800-336-1383 ■ *Web:* www.idesco.com

Idesign Solutions Inc 51 Roysun Rd Woodbridge ON L4L8P9 — 416-213-8445 — 180
Web: www.idesignsol.com

IDEX Corp 1925 W Field Ct Ste 200 Lake Forest IL 60045 — 847-498-7070 — 641
NYSE: IEX ■ *Web:* www.idexcorp.com

IDEXX Laboratories Inc 1 IDEXX Dr Westbrook ME 04092 — 207-556-0300 — 556-4346 — 231
NASDAQ: IDXX ■ *TF:* 800-548-6733 ■ *Web:* www.idexx.com

IDF (Immune Deficiency Foundation)
40 W Chesapeake Ave Ste 308 Towson MD 21204 — 410-321-6647 — 321-9165 — 48-17
TF: 800-296-4433 ■ *Web:* www.primaryimmune.org

IDFA (International Dairy Foods Assn)
1250 H St NW Ste 900 Washington DC 20005 — 202-737-4332 — 331-7820 — 49-6
Web: www.idfa.org

IDFW (Institute for a Drug-Free Workplace)
10701 Parkridge Blvd Ste 300 Reston VA 20191 — 703-391-7222 — 391-7223 — 49-12
TF: 877-696-6775 ■ *Web:* www.drugfreeworkplace.org

IDG (International Data Group Inc)
1 Exeter Plaza 15th Fl. Boston MA 02116 — 617-534-1200 — 637-9
TF Orders: 800-343-4952 ■ *Web:* www.idg.com

IDG Ventures 1 Letterman Dr San Francisco CA 94129 — 415-439-4420 — 792
Web: www.idgvsf.com

IDG World Expo 3 Speen St Ste 320 Framingham MA 01701 — 508-879-6700 — 184
Web: www.idgworldexpo.com

IDI Distributors Inc
8303 Audubon Rd. Chanhassen MN 55317 — 952-279-6400 — 690
TF: 888-843-1318 ■ *Web:* idi-insulation.com

IDI Group Cos
1700 N Moore St Ste 2020. Arlington VA 22209 — 703-558-7300 — 558-7377 — 653
Web: www.idigroup.com

IDI Multimedia Inc
7250 Heritage Village Plaza Ste 201 Gainesville VA 20155 — 703-753-2141 — 637-10
Web: www.idimultimedia.com

Ididit Inc 610 S Maumee St Tecumseh MI 49286 — 517-424-0577 — 57
Web: www.ididitinc.com

Idilia Inc 1470 Peel St Twr B Ste 810. Montreal QC H3A1T1 — 514-843-6897 — 525

iDirect Marketing Inc
6789 Quail Hill Pkwy Ste 550 Irvine CA 92603 — 949-753-7300 — 269-0198 — 5
Web: www.idirectmarketing.com

Name / Address	Phone	Fax	Class
iDirect Technologies Inc 13865 Sunrise Valley Dr Ste 100 .... Herndon VA 20171 *TF:* 888-362-5475 ■ *Web:* www.idirect.net	703-648-8118		735
Idlewild & Soak Zone Rt 30 E PO Box C .... Ligonier PA 15658 *TF:* 800-487-4386 ■ *Web:* www.idlewild.com	724-238-3666	238-6544	32
Idm Computer Solutions Inc 5559 Eureka Dr............................ Hamilton OH 45011 *Web:* www.ultraedit.com	513-892-8600		225
Ido Bar & Grill 1537 S Main St .... Akron OH 44301 *Web:* www.idobar.com	330-773-1724		671
IDOM Inc 55 Madison Ave Ste 400........... Morristown NJ 07960 *Web:* www.idomusa.com	973-285-3328		463
IDP (Insurance Data Processing Inc) 8101 Washington Ln......................... Wyncote PA 19095 *TF:* 800-523-6745 ■ *Web:* www.idpnet.com	215-885-2150	887-4621	178-11
IDPR (Winchester Lake State Park) PO Box 186 .... Winchester ID 83555 *Web:* idahostateparks.reserveamerica.com	208-924-7563	924-5941	565
IDQ Holdings Inc 2901 W Kingsley Rd .... Garland TX 75041 *Web:* rechargeac.com	214-778-4600		3
IDRA (Intercultural Development Research Assn) 5815 Callaghan Rd Ste 101 .... San Antonio TX 78228 *Web:* www.idra.org	210-444-1710	444-1714	48-11
IDS Group Inc 1 Peters Canyon Rd................ Irvine CA 92606 *Web:* idsgi.com	949-387-8500		261
IDSA (IDSA) 1300 Wilson Blvd Ste 300........... Arlington VA 22209 *TF:* 888-463-6332 ■ *Web:* www.idsociety.org	703-299-0200	299-0204	49-8
IDSA (Industrial Designers Society of America) 45195 Business Ct Ste 250 .... Dulles VA 20166 *Web:* www.idsa.org	703-707-6000	787-8501	49-13
IDT Corp 520 Broad St .... Newark NJ 07102 *NYSE: IDT* ■ *Web:* www.idt.net	973-438-1000		736
IDT|RPM Consulting Services 1009 W Hawthorn Dr .... Itasca IL 60143 *TF:* 877-722-6438 ■ *Web:* www.idt-inc.com	630-875-1100		196
IDX Corp 1 Rider Trail Plaza Dr Ste 400................ Earth City MO 63045 *TF:* 800-395-7774 ■ *Web:* www.idxcorporation.com	314-739-4120	739-4129	286
Idyllwild Arts Academy 52500 Temecula Rd PO Box 38 .... Idyllwild CA 92549 *Web:* www.idyllwildarts.org	951-659-2171		622
IEA Inc 9625 55th St .... Kenosha WI 53144 *Web:* www.iearad.com	262-942-1414		61
IEAP (Interface EAP Inc) 10370 Richmond Ave Ste 1100 PO Box 421879.... Houston TX 77042 *TF:* 800-324-4327 ■ *Web:* www.ieap.com	713-781-3364	784-0425	462
IEC (International Environmental Corp) PO Box 2598 .... Oklahoma City OK 73101 *TF:* 800-264-5329 ■ *Web:* www.iec-okc.com	405-605-5000	605-5001	14
IEC Electronics Corp 105 Norton St............. Newark NY 14513 *NYSE: IEC* ■ *Web:* www.iec-electronics.com	315-331-7742	331-3547	625
Iec Group 3449 e copper point dr.............. Meridian ID 83642 *Web:* www.iecgroup.com	208-947-9522		463
IECA (Independent Educational Consultants Assn) 3251 Old Lee Hwy Ste 510.................... Fairfax VA 22030 *Web:* iecaonline.com	703-591-4850	591-4860	49-5
IEDC (International Economic Development Council) 734 15th St NW Ste 900.................. Washington DC 20005 *Web:* www.iedconline.org	202-223-7800	223-4745	49-12
IEEE Broadcast Technology Society (BTS) 445 Hoes Ln............................ Piscataway NJ 08854 *TF:* 800-678-4333 ■ *Web:* bts.ieee.org	732-562-5407	981-1769	49-19
IEEE Computational Intelligence Society (CIS) *IEEE CIS* 445 Hoes Ln.................... Piscataway NJ 08855 **Fax Area Code:* 858 ■ *Web:* cis.ieee.org	732-465-5892	455-1560*	49-19
IEEE Computer Graphics & Applications Magazine 10662 Los Vaqueros Cir PO Box 3014....... Los Alamitos CA 90720 *TF:* 800-272-6657 ■ *Web:* computer.org/portal/web/computingnow/cga	714-821-8380	821-4641	457-7
IEEE Computer Society 2001 L St NW Ste 700 .... Washington DC 20036 *TF:* 800-272-6657 ■ *Web:* www.computer.org	202-371-0101	728-9614	49-19
IEEE Computer Society Press 10662 Los Vaqueros Cir PO Box 3014....... Los Alamitos CA 90720 *TF:* 800-272-6657 ■ *Web:* computer.org/portal/web/cspress/home	714-821-8380	821-4010	637-9
IEEE Consumer Electronics Society (CES) 445 Hoes Ln............................ Piscataway NJ 08854 *Web:* cesoc.ieee.org	732-562-3844	981-9019	49-19
IEEE Electromagnetic Compatibility Society (EMC) IEEE Operations Ctr 445 and 501 Hoes Ln...... Piscataway NJ 08854 *TF:* 800-678-4333 ■ *Web:* www.ewh.ieee.org/soc/emcs	732-981-0060	562-6380	49-19
IEEE Electron Devices Society (EDS) IEEE Operations Ctr 445 Hoes Ln............ Piscataway NJ 08854 *TF:* 800-678-4333 ■ *Web:* eds.ieee.org	732-981-0060	562-6380	49-19
IEEE Engineering Management Society (EMS) IEEE Operations Ctr 445 and 501 Hoes Ln...... Piscataway NJ 08854 *TF:* 800-678-4333 ■ *Web:* www.ewh.ieee.org/soc/ems	732-981-0060	562-6380	49-19
IEEE Geoscience & Remote Sensing Society (GRSS) IEEE Operations Ctr 445 and 501 Hoes Ln...... Piscataway NJ 08854 *TF:* 800-678-4333 ■ *Web:* www.ewh.ieee.org	732-562-5550		49-19
IEEE Industrial Electronics Society (IES) IEEE Operations Ctr 445 Hoes Ln............ Piscataway NJ 08854 *TF:* 800-678-4333 ■ *Web:* www.ewh.ieee.org/soc/ies	732-981-0060	562-6380	49-19
IEEE Industry Applications Society 445 Hoes Ln............................ Piscataway NJ 08854 *Web:* ias.ieee.org	732-465-5804		49-19
IEEE Instrumentation & Measurement Society (IM) 445 Hoes Ln............................ Piscataway NJ 08854 *TF:* 800-327-6677 ■ *Web:* www.ieee-ims.org	732-562-3844	981-9019	49-19
IEEE Magnetics Society 445 Hoes Ln PO Box 459.................. Piscataway NJ 08855 *TF:* 800-678-4333 ■ *Web:* www.ieeemagnetics.org	908-981-0060		49-19
IEEE Micro Magazine 10662 Los Vaqueros Cir PO Box 3014....... Los Alamitos CA 90720 *TF:* 800-272-6657 ■ *Web:* computer.org/portal/web/computingnow/micro	714-821-8380	821-4641	457-7
IEEE Microwave Theory & Techniques Society (MTT-S) 5829 Bellanca Dr .... Elkridge MD 21075 *TF:* 800-678-4333 ■ *Web:* www.mtt.org	410-796-5866		49-19
IEEE Nuclear & Plasma Sciences Society (NPSS) 3 Park Ave.............................. New York NY 10016 *TF:* 800-678-4333 ■ *Web:* ieee-npss.org	732-981-0060		49-19
IEEE Power Engineering Society (PES) IEEE Operations Ctr 445 Hoes Ln............ Piscataway NJ 08854 *TF:* 800-678-4333 ■ *Web:* www.ieee-pes.org	732-562-3883	562-3881	49-19
IEEE Product Safety Engineering Society IEEE Operations Ctr 445 Hoes Ln............ Piscataway NJ 08854 *TF:* 800-678-4333 ■ *Web:* www.ieee.org	732-981-0060	562-6380	49-19
IEEE Reliability Society (RS) IEEE Operations Ctr 445 Hoes Ln............ Piscataway NJ 08854 *TF:* 800-678-4333 ■ *Web:* ieee.org	732-981-0060	562-6380	49-19
IEEE Signal Processing Society IEEE Operations Ctr 445 Hoes Ln............ Piscataway NJ 08854 *TF:* 800-678-4333 ■ *Web:* www.signalprocessingsociety.org	732-981-0060		49-19
IEEE Society on Social Implications of Technology (SSIT) IEEE Operations Ctr 445 and 501 Hoes Ln...... Piscataway NJ 08854 *TF:* 800-678-4333 ■ *Web:* standards.ieee.org	732-981-0060	562-6380	49-19
IEEE Solid State Circuits Society (SSCS) 445 Hoes Ln............................ Piscataway NJ 08854 *Web:* sscs.ieee.org	732-981-3400		49-19
IEEE Ultrasonics Ferroelectrics & Frequency Control Society IEEE Operations Ctr 445 Hoes Ln............ Piscataway NJ 08854 *TF:* 800-678-4333 ■ *Web:* www.ieee-uffc.org	732-981-0060		49-19
IEF (International Eye Foundation) 10801 Connecticut Ave................... Kensington MD 20895 *Web:* www.iefusa.org	240-290-0263	290-0269	48-5
Ieh Laboratories & Consulting Group 15300 Bothell Way NE .... Lake Forest Park WA 98155 *TF:* 800-491-7745 ■ *Web:* www.iehinc.com	800-491-7745		794
IEHA (International Executive Housekeepers Assn) 1001 Eastwind Dr Ste 301 .... Westerville OH 43081 *TF:* 800-200-6342 ■ *Web:* www.ieha.org	614-895-7166	895-1248	49-4
ieLinks Inc 2701 E Thomas Rd Ste B............ Phoenix AZ 85016 *Web:* ecampuslynx.com	602-852-0101		463
IEM (International Electronic Machines Corp) 850 River St .... Troy NY 12180 *Web:* www.iem.net	518-268-1636	268-1639	261
I-engineeringcom Inc 4 Armstrong Rd Ste 2....................... Shelton CT 06484 *Web:* www.i-engineering.com	203-402-0800		387
iEntertainment Network Inc 124 Quade Dr PO Box 3897 .... Cary NC 27519 *OTC: IENT* ■ *Web:* www.ient.com	919-238-4090		178-6
IEP Technologies LLC 400 Main St .... Ashland MA 01721 *TF:* 855-793-8407 ■ *Web:* www.ieptechnologies.com	855-793-8407		667
IER Fujikura Inc 8271 Bavaria Rd............ Macedonia OH 44056 *Web:* www.ierfujikura.com	330-425-7121	425-7596	677
IES (Institute of Ecosystem Studies) 2801 Sharon Tpke PO Box AB .... Millbrook NY 12545 *Web:* www.caryinstitute.org	845-677-5343	677-5976	668
IES (Integrated Electrical Services Inc) 5433 Westheimer Rd Ste 500................ Houston TX 77056 *NASDAQ: IESC* ■ *TF:* 800-732-0330 ■ *Web:* ies-corporate.com	713-860-1500		189-4
IES (Institute of Education Sciences) 550 12th St SW .... Washington DC 20024 *Web:* www.ies.ed.gov	202-245-6940	219-1466	668
IES (IEEE Industrial Electronics Society) IEEE Operations Ctr 445 Hoes Ln............ Piscataway NJ 08854 *TF:* 800-678-4333 ■ *Web:* www.ewh.ieee.org/soc/ies	732-981-0060	562-6380	49-19
IESCO (International Electrical Sales Corp) 7540 NW 66th St .... Miami FL 33166 *Web:* www.iescomia.com	305-591-8390		246
IeSmart Systems LLC 15200 E Hardy Rd .... Houston TX 77032 *TF:* 866-437-6278 ■ *Web:* www.iesmartsystems.com	281-447-6278		196
IESNA (Illuminating Engineering Society of North America) 120 Wall St 17th Fl....................... New York NY 10005 *Web:* www.ies.org	212-248-5000	248-5017	49-13
IEST (Institute of Environmental Sciences & Technology) 2340 S Arlington Heights Rd Ste 100............................ Arlington Heights IL 60005 *TF:* 800-699-9277 ■ *Web:* www.iest.org	847-981-0100	981-4130	49-19
IEWC (Industrial Electric Wire & Cable Inc) 5001 S Towne Dr .... New Berlin WI 53151 *TF:* 800-344-2323 ■ *Web:* www.iewc.com	262-782-2323		246
IEX Group Inc 4 World Trade Ctr 44th Fl .... New York NY 10007 *Web:* iextrading.com	646-568-2320		690
IFA (International Franchise Assn) 1501 K St NW Ste 350 .... Washington DC 20005 *TF:* 800-543-1038 ■ *Web:* www.franchise.org	202-628-8000	628-0812	49-18
IFAD (International Fund for Agricultural Development) 1775 K St NW Ste 410 .... Washington DC 20006 *Web:* www.ifad.org	202-331-9099	331-9366	783
IFAI (Industrial Fabrics Assn International) 1801 County Rd 'B' W...................... Roseville MN 55113 *TF:* 800-225-4324 ■ *Web:* www.ifai.com	651-222-2508	631-9334	49-13
IFAW (International Fund for Animal Welfare) 290 Summer St...................... Yarmouth Port MA 02675 *TF:* 800-932-4329 ■ *Web:* www.ifaw.org	508-744-2000		48-3
IFC Stone Crab 81532 Overseas Hwy PO Box 283 .... Islamorada FL 33036 **Fax Area Code:* 305 ■ *TF:* 800-258-2559 ■ *Web:* www.ifcstonecrab.com	800-258-2559	664-5071*	671
IFCA International 3520 Fairlane Ave SW.................... Grandville MI 49418 *TF:* 800-347-1840 ■ *Web:* www.ifca.org	616-531-1840	531-1814	48-20
IFCO (Interreligious Foundation for Community Organization) 418 W 145th St........................... New York NY 10031 *Web:* www.ifconews.org	212-926-5757	926-5842	48-7
Ifco Systems 3030 N Rocky Point Dr Ste 300 .... Tampa FL 33607 *TF:* 800-832-8480 ■ *Web:* www.ifco.com	813-463-4100	286-2070	551
IFDA (International Foodservice Distributors Assn) 1410 Spring Hill Rd Ste 210................. McLean VA 22102 *Web:* www.ifdaonline.org	703-532-9400	538-4673	49-18
IFEA (International Festivals & Events Assn) 2603 W Eastover Terr .... Boise ID 83706 *Web:* www.ifea.com	208-433-0950	433-9812	48-23

Name / Address	City	State	Zip	Phone	Fax	Class
IFEBP (International Foundation of Employee Benefit Plans) 18700 W Bluemound Rd. TF: 888-334-3327 ■ Web: www.ifebp.org	Brookfield	WI	53045	262-786-6700	786-8670	260
IFF (International Flavors & Fragrances Inc) 521 W 57th St. NYSE: IFF ■ Web: www.iff.com	New York	NY	10019	212-765-5500	708-7132	144
IFG Corp 1372 Broadway	New York	NY	10018	212-239-8615		155-4
IFIC (International Fidelity Insurance Co) 1 Newark Ctr 20th Fl. TF: 800-333-4167 ■ Web: www.ific.com	Newark	NJ	07102	973-624-7200	643-7116	391-5
IFIC (International Food Information Council Foundation) 1100 Connecticut Ave NW Ste 430. TF: 888-723-3366 ■ Web: www.foodinsight.org	Washington	DC	20036	202-296-6540	296-6547	49-6
iFly USA LLC 31310 Alvarado-Niles Rd TF: 800-759-3861 ■ Web: www.iflyworld.com/sfbay	Union City	CA	94587	510-489-4359		31
IFMA (International Facility Management Assn) 800 Gessner Rd Ste 900 Web: www.ifma.org	Houston	TX	77024	713-623-4362	623-6124	49-12
IFMA (International Foodservice Manufacturers Assn) 180 N Stetson Ave 2 Prudential Plz Ste 4400 Web: www.ifmaworld.com	Chicago	IL	60601	312-540-4400	540-4401	49-6
Ifocus Consulting Inc 100 39th St Ste 201 TF: 888-308-6192 ■ Web: www.ifocus.us	Astoria	OR	97103	503-338-7443		196
iFollo LLC 8461 Trails Dr	Park City	UT	84098	435-655-1511		366
Ifonoclast Inc 4620 Fortran Dr Ste 207 Web: www.phonevite.com	San Jose	CA	95134	408-946-9700		387
iforce LLC 1110 Morse Rd Ste 200 Web: www.iforceservices.com	Columbus	OH	43229	614-431-5100		260
iForem Inc 350 Marine Pkwy Ste 200	Redwood Shores	CA	94065	650-352-4750		387
IFOS Inc 2363 Calle Del Mundo Web: www.ifos.com	Santa Clara	CA	95054	408-565-9000		668
IFPRI (International Food Policy Research Institute) 2033 K St NW Web: www.ifpri.org	Washington	DC	20006	202-862-5600	467-4439	634
IFPW (International Federation of Pharmaceutical Wholesalers) 10569 Crestwood Dr. Web: www.ifpw.com	Manassas	VA	20109	703-331-3714	331-3715	49-18
IFRA (International Furniture Rental Assn) 950 F St NW 10th Fl. Web: www.ifra.org	Washington	DC	20004	202-239-3818	654-4818	49-4
Ifrah Financial Services Inc 17300 Chenal Pkwy Ste 150 TF: 800-954-3724 ■ Web: www.ifrahfinancial.com	Little Rock	AR	72223	501-821-7733		251
IFS Financial Services Inc 250 Brownlow Ave Ste 1 TF: 800-565-1153 ■ Web: www.ifs-finance.com	Dartmouth	NS	B3B1W9	902-481-6106		317
IFS North America Inc 300 Pk Blvd Ste 555 TF: 888-437-4968 ■ Web: www.ifsworld.com	Chicago	IL	60143	888-437-4968		178-1
IFSI (Illinois Foundation Seeds Inc) 1083 County Rd 900 N Web: www.ifsi.com	Tolono	IL	61880	217-485-6260	485-3687	10-5
IFT (Institute of Food Technologists) 525 W Van Buren St Ste 1000 TF: 800-438-3663 ■ Web: www.ift.org	Chicago	IL	60607	312-782-8424	782-8348	49-6
IFTA (Independent Film & Television Alliance) 10850 Wilshire Blvd 9th Fl. Web: www.ifta-online.org	Los Angeles	CA	90024	310-446-1047	446-1600	48-4
iFuturistics Inc 1007 Orange St Nemours Bldg Ste 1414 Web: www.ifuturistics.com	Wilmington	DE	19801	302-472-9271		796
IG Inc 720 S Sara Rd TF: 800-654-8433 ■ Web: www.igok.com	Mustang	OK	73064	405-376-9393	376-3933	326
IGA Inc 8745 W Higgins Rd Ste 350 TF: 800-321-5442 ■ Web: www.iga.com	Chicago	IL	60631	773-693-4520	693-4533	345
IGAF Worldwide 2250 Satellite Blvd Ste 115	Duluth	GA	30097	678-417-7730	417-6977	49-1
iGan Partners 60 Bloor St W 9th FL Web: www.iganpartners.com	Toronto	ON	M4W3B8	416-925-2433		528
Igarashi Motor Sales USA LLC 710 Colomba Ct Web: www.igusa.com	Saint Charles	IL	60174	630-587-1177		57
IGAS (International Graphoanalysis Society) 842 Fifth Ave. *Fax Area Code: 509 ■ Web: www.igas.com	New Kensington	PA	15068	724-472-9701	271-1149*	49-12
IGD Industries Inc 4150 C St SW Web: www.igdindustries.com	Cedar Rapids	IA	52404	319-396-2222		61
Ige David (D) Executive Chambers State Capitol. Web: governor.hawaii.gov	Honolulu	HI	96813	808-586-0034	586-0006	343
IGEL Technology Inc 5353 NW 35th Ave Web: www.igel.com	Fort Lauderdale	FL	33309	954-739-9990		177
Igenex 795 San Antonio Rd. TF: 800-832-3200 ■ Web: www.igenex.com	Palo Alto	CA	94303	650-424-1191		418
IGFA Fishing Hall of Fame & Museum 300 Gulf Stream Way TF: 800-227-7776 ■ Web: www.igfa.org	Dania Beach	FL	33004	954-922-4212	924-4220	522
IGI (Information Gatekeepers Inc) 1340 Soldiers Field Rd Ste 2 TF: 800-323-1088 ■ Web: www.igigroup.com	Brighton	MA	02135	617-782-5033	782-5735	637-11
IGI (Insight Global Inc) 4170 Ashford Dunwoody Rd Ste 250 TF: 888-336-7463 ■ Web: www.insightglobal.net	Atlanta	GA	30319	404-257-7900	257-1004	193
Iglesia Adventista Del Septimo Dia 9735 N Houston Rosslyn Rd.	Houston	TX	77088	713-937-1200		48-20
Iglesia Ni Cristo Church of Christ 505 E 36th St Web: incmedia.org	Long Beach	CA	90807	310-872-3487		48-20
Igloo Products Corp 777 Igloo Rd TF: 866-509-3503 ■ Web: www.igloocoolers.com	Katy	TX	77494	281-394-6800		607
IGLTA (International Gay & Lesbian Travel Assn) 1201 NE 26th St Ste 103 Web: www.iglta.org	Fort Lauderdale	FL	33305	954-630-1637	630-1652	48-23
Ignify Inc 200 Pine Ave 4th Fl TF: 888-599-4332 ■ Web: www.ignify.com	Long Beach	CA	90802	562-219-2000		177
IGNITE Group 255 Shoreline Dr	Redwood City	CA	94065	650-622-2005		792
Ignite Restaurant Group Inc 9900 Westpark Dr Ste 300 Web: igniterestaurants.com	Houston	TX	77063	713-366-7500		670
Ignite Technical Resources Ltd 1295 - 355 Burrard St. TF: 800-453-0214 ■ Web: www.ignitetechnical.com	Vancouver	BC	V6C2G8	604-687-6795		260
Ignite Venture Partners LLC 34522 N Scottsdale Rd Ste D7239 Web: www.ignite-vp.com	Scottsdale	AZ	85266	480-575-9717		463
Ignite! Learning Inc 4030 W Braker Ln Ste 175 Web: www.ignitelearning.com	Austin	TX	78759	512-697-7000		177
Ignited LLC 2221 Park Pl Web: ignitedusa.com	El Segundo	CA	90245	310-773-3100		7
Ignition Commerce 3820 Mansell Rd Ste 250 Web: www.ignitioncommerce.com	Alpharetta	GA	30022	770-640-6382		631
Ignition Systems & Controls LP 6300 W Hwy 80 TF: 800-777-5559 ■ Web: www.ignition-systems.com	Midland	TX	79706	432-697-6472	697-0563	247
Ignition Ventures Inc 1 Broadway Fl 14 Web: www.ignitionventures.com	Cambridge	MA	02142	617-398-0785		463
Ignitus Worldwide 1199 Haywood Dr Ste 417 Web: www.ignitusworldwide.org	College Station	TX	77845	979-574-6176		48-6
iGo Inc 17800 N Perimeter Dr Ste 200 NASDAQ: IGOI ■ TF: 888-205-0093 ■ Web: www.igo.com	Scottsdale	AZ	85255	480-596-0061	596-0349	176
I-Go Van & Storage 9820 S 142nd St. TF: 800-228-9276 ■ Web: www.igovanandstorage.com	Omaha	NE	68138	402-891-1222		519
iGov Technologies Inc 9211 Palm River Rd Ste 110 TF: 800-777-9375 ■ Web: www.igov.com	Tampa	FL	33619	813-612-9470		226
IGS (Institute of General Semantics) 72-11 Austin St *Fax Area Code: 718 ■ TF: 800-346-1359 ■ Web: www.generalsemantics.org	Forest Hills	NY	11375	212-729-7973	793-2527*	48-11
IGS (Industrial Gasket & Shim Company Inc) 200 Country Club Rd TF: 800-229-1447 ■ Web: www.igsind.com	Meadow Lands	PA	15347	724-222-5800		326
IGSHPA (International Ground Source Heat Pump Assn) Oklahoma State University 374 Cordell S. TF: 800-626-4747 ■ Web: igshpa.org	Stillwater	OK	74078	405-744-5175	744-5283	49-13
IGT (International Game Technology) 9295 Prototype Dr NYSE: IGT ■ TF: 800-522-4700 ■ Web: www.igt.com	Reno	NV	89521	775-448-7777		322
IGT Media Holdings Inc 21 SE First Ave Web: www.igtmh.com	Miami	FL	33131	305-573-2800		5
IGTI (ASME International Gas Turbine Institute) 6525 the Corners Pkwy. Web: www.asme.org	Norcross	GA	30092	404-847-0072	847-0151	49-19
Ih Services Inc PO Box 5033 Web: www.ihservices.com	Greenville	SC	29606	864-297-3740		152
IHA (International Housewares Assn) 6400 Shafer Ct Ste 650. TF: 800-752-1052 ■ Web: www.housewares.org	Rosemont	IL	60018	847-292-4200	292-4211	49-4
IHAD (I Have a Dream Foundation) 330 Seventh Ave 20th Fl. Web: www.ihaveadreamfoundation.org	New York	NY	10001	212-293-5480		48-5
IHC (International Homes of Cedar Inc) PO Box 886 TF: 800-767-7674 ■ Web: www.ihoc.com	Woodinville	WA	98072	360-668-8511	668-5562	106
iHealth Lab Inc 719 N Shoreline Blvd TF: 855-816-7705 ■ Web: www.ihealthlabs.com	Mountain View	CA	94043	855-816-7705		743
iHeartMedia San Diego 9660 Granite Ridge Dr Ste 100 *Fax Area Code: 210 ■ Web: star941fm.iheart.com	San Diego	CA	92123	858-292-2000	832-3149*	645-144
iHeartMedia, Inc 200 E Basse Rd. TF: 800-829-6551 ■ Web: www.iheartmedia.com	San Antonio	TX	78209	210-822-2828		185
IHFRA (International Home Furnishings Representatives Assn) 209 S Main St PO Box 670 TF: 800-873-4344 ■ Web: www.ihfra.org	High Point	NC	27261	336-889-3920		49-18
IHI (Institute for Healthcare Improvement) 20 University Rd 7th Fl TF: 866-787-0831 ■ Web: www.ihi.org	Cambridge	MA	02138	617-301-4800	301-4848	49-8
IHI Inc 150 E 52nd St Fl 24 Web: www.ihiincus.com	New York	NY	10022	212-599-8100	599-8111	770
IHI Southwest Technologies Inc 6766 Culebra Rd. Web: www.ihiswt.com	San Antonio	TX	78238	210-256-4100		261
i-Hire Inc 307 Sonora Dr Web: www.i-hire.com	San Mateo	CA	94402	650-678-2808		260
IHL Consulting Group 1064 Cedarview Ln. TF: 888-445-6777 ■ Web: www.ihlservices.com	Franklin	TN	37067	615-591-2955		463
IHLIC (Investors Heritage Life Insurance Co) 200 Capital Ave PO Box 717 TF: 800-422-2011 ■ Web: www.ihlic.com	Frankfort	KY	40602	502-223-2361	875-7084	391-2
IHMM (Institute of Hazardous Materials Management) 11900 Parklawn Dr Ste 450 Web: www.ihmm.org	Rockville	MD	20852	301-984-8969	984-1516	48-12
IHO (Institute of Human Origins) 951 South Cady Mall PO Box 874101 Web: iho.asu.edu	Tempe	AZ	85287	480-727-6580	727-6570	668
IHOP Corp 450 N Brand Blvd TF: 866-444-5144 ■ Web: www.ihop.com	Glendale	CA	91203	818-240-6055	637-4730	670
IHP Industrial Inc 1701 S Eigth St PO Box 578. Web: www.ihpindustrial.com	Saint Joseph	MO	64502	816-364-1581	232-4473	189-10
IHRIM (International Assn for Human Resource Information Management Inc) PO Box 1086 *Fax Area Code: 781 ■ TF: 800-804-3983 ■ Web: www.ihrim.org	Burlington	MA	01803	800-804-3983	998-8011*	49-12
IHRSA (International Health Racquet & Sportsclub Assn) 70 Fargo St. TF: 800-228-4772 ■ Web: www.ihrsa.org	Boston	MA	02210	617-951-0055	951-0056	48-22

Phone | Fax | Class

IHS (International Hearing Society)
16880 Middlebelt Rd Ste 4 .... Livonia MI 48154 734-522-7200 522-0200 48-17
TF: 800-521-5247 ■ Web: www.ihsinfo.org

IHS (Infirmary Health System Inc)
5 Mobile Infirmary Cir .... Mobile AL 36607 251-435-2400 660-8348 353
Web: www.infirmaryhealth.org

IHS (Indian Health Service)
801 Thompson Ave Ste 400 .... Rockville MD 20852 301-443-1083 340-10

IHS Energy Group 15 Inverness Way E .... Englewood CO 80112 303-736-3000 178-10
TF: 800-447-2273 ■ Web: www.ihs.com

IHS Inc 321 Inverness Dr S .... Englewood CO 80112 303-790-0600 178-11
NYSE: IHS ■ TF: 800-525-7052 ■ Web: www.ihs.com

Ihs Professional Services Inc
1632 Byron Nelson Pkwy .... Southlake TX 76092 817-296-1726 474
Web: www.ihsps.com

Ii Stanley Company Inc
1500 Hill Brady Rd .... Battle Creek MI 49037 269-660-7777 247
Web: www.iistanleybc.com

IIA (Institute of Internal Auditors)
247 Maitland Ave .... Altamonte Springs FL 32701 407-937-1100 937-1101 49-1
TF: 800-803-8367 ■ Web: na.theiia.org

IIABA (Independent Insurance Agents & Brokers of America Inc)
127 S Peyton St .... Alexandria VA 22314 703-683-4422 683-7556 49-9
TF: 800-221-7917 ■ Web: www.independentagent.com

IIB (Institute of International Bankers)
299 Pk Ave 17th Fl .... New York NY 10171 212-421-1611 421-1119 49-2
TF: 800-925-4618 ■ Web: www.iib.org

IIC (Indotronix International Corp)
331 Main St .... Poughkeepsie NY 12601 845-473-1137 473-1197 180
Web: www.iic.com

IICL (Institute of International Container Lessors)
1990 M St NW Ste 650 .... Washington DC 20036 202-223-9800 223-9810 49-21
Web: www.iicl.org

IICRC (Institute of Inspection Cleaning & Restoration Certification)
4043 S E Ave .... Las Vegas NV 89119 360-693-5675 49-4
Web: www.iicrc.org

IID (Imperial Irrigation District)
PO Box 937 .... Imperial CA 92251 760-482-9600 482-9611 203
TF: 800-303-7756 ■ Web: www.iid.com

IIDA (International Interior Design Assn)
222 Merchandise Mart Plaza Ste 567 .... Chicago IL 60654 312-467-1950 467-0779 48-4
TF: 888-799-4432 ■ Web: www.iida.org

IIE (Institute of Industrial & Systems Engineers)
3577 PkwyLn Ste 200 .... Norcross GA 30092 770-449-0461 441-3295 49-13
TF Cust Svc: 800-494-0460 ■ Web: www.iienet2.org

IIE (Institute of International Education)
809 United Nations Plaza # 1 .... New York NY 10017 212-883-8200 984-5358 48-11
Web: www.iie.org

IIF (Institute of International Finance)
1333 H St NW Ste 800-E .... Washington DC 20005 202-857-3600 775-1430 49-2
Web: www.iif.com

IIF Data Solutions Inc
7000 Gateway Ct Ste 120 .... Centreville VA 20120 703-531-1180 809
Web: www.iifdata.com

III (Insurance Information Institute Inc)
110 William St .... New York NY 10038 212-346-5500 732-1916 49-9
TF: 877-263-7995 ■ Web: www.iii.org

III Forks 111 Lavaca St .... Austin TX 78701 512-474-1776 671
Web: www.3forks.com

III Forks Steakhouse 17776 Dallas Pkwy .... Dallas TX 75287 972-267-1776 671
Web: 3forks.com

IIMC (International Institute of Municipal Clerks)
8331 Utica Ave Ste 200 .... Rancho Cucamonga CA 91730 909-944-4162 944-8545 49-7
TF: 800-251-1639 ■ Web: www.iimc.com

IIP Insurance Agency Inc
823 Clinton St .... Ottawa IL 61350 815-433-2680 390
Web: mylocalagent.com

IIRR (International Institute of Rural Reconstruction)
601 W 26th St Ste 325-1 .... New York NY 10001 917-410-7891 48-5
Web: www.iirr.org

IIS Group LLC
1015 Virginia Dr Ste 1 W .... Fort Washington PA 19034 855-443-5777 175
TF: 855-443-5777 ■ Web: www.iisgroupllc.com

IISRP (International Institute of Synthetic Rubber Producers Inc)
3535 Briarpark Dr Ste 250 .... Houston TX 77042 713-783-7511 783-7253 49-13
Web: www.iisrp.com

IIT Research Institute (IITRI)
10 W 35th St .... Chicago IL 60616 312-567-4000 668
TF: 800-878-8878 ■ Web: www.iitri.org

IITF (International Institute of Tropical Forestry)
Jardin Botanico Sur 1201 Calle Ceiba .... San Juan PR 00926 787-766-5335 766-6302 660
Web: www.fs.fed.us/global/iitf

IITRI (IIT Research Institute)
10 W 35th St .... Chicago IL 60616 312-567-4000 668
TF: 800-878-8878 ■ Web: www.iitri.org

II-VI Inc 375 Saxonburg Blvd .... Saxonburg PA 16056 724-352-4455 544
NASDAQ: IIVI ■ Web: www.ii-vi.com

IJ Research Inc 2919 Tech Ctr Dr .... Santa Ana CA 92705 714-546-8522 256
Web: www.ijresearch.com

Ijams Nature Ctr
2915 Island Home Ave .... Knoxville TN 37920 865-577-4717 577-1683 50-5
TF: 800-556-8974 ■ Web: www.ijams.org

IJO (Independent Jewelers Organization)
136 Old Post Rd .... Southport CT 06890 800-624-9252 254-7429* 49-4
*Fax Area Code: 203 ■ TF: 800-624-9252 ■ Web: www.ijo.com

Ikanos Communications
47669 Fremont Blvd .... Fremont CA 94538 510-979-0400 979-0500 696
NASDAQ: IKAN

Ikaros 4901 Eastern Ave .... Baltimore MD 21224 410-633-3750 633-7881 671
Web: www.ikarosrestaurant.com

ikaSystems Corp 134 Turnpike Rd .... Southborough MA 01772 508-229-0600 196
Web: www.ikasystems.com

Ika-Works Inc
2635 Northchase Pkwy SE .... Wilmington NC 28405 910-452-7059 452-7693 420
TF: 800-733-3037 ■ Web: www.ika.com

Ike Kinswa State Park 873 SR 122 .... Silver Creek WA 98585 360-983-3402 565
Web: www.parks.wa.gov

IKEA 420 Alan Wood Rd .... Conshohocken PA 19428 610-834-0180 321
TF: 800-434-4532 ■ Web: www.ikea.com

Ikegami Electronics USA Inc
37 Brook Ave .... Maywood NJ 07607 201-368-9171 569-1626 647
TF: 800-368-9171 ■ Web: www.ikegami.com

IKG Industries 1514 S Sheldon Rd .... Channelview TX 77530 281-452-6637 378-3987* 491
*Fax Area Code: 713 ■ Web: www.harscoikg.com

I-K-I Mfg Company Inc 116 Swift St .... Edgerton WI 53534 608-884-3411 884-4712 145
Web: www.ikimfg.com

Iknow LLC 100 Overlook Ctr 2nd Fl .... Princeton NJ 08540 609-419-0500 317
Web: www.iknow.us

IKO International Inc
91 Walsh Dr Fox Hill Industrial Pk .... Parsippany NJ 07054 973-402-0254 385
TF: 800-922-0337 ■ Web: www.ikont.com

IKON Global Markets Inc
88 Pine St Wall St Plaza 5th Fl .... New York NY 10005 212-482-8408 690
Web: www.ikongm.com

Ikonisys Inc 5 Science Pk .... New Haven CT 06511 203-776-0791 743
TF: 866-456-6832 ■ Web: www.ikonisys.com

Il Bistro 93-A Pike St .... Seattle WA 98101 206-682-3049 671
Web: www.ilbistro.net

Il Cantuccio 701 N Third St .... Philadelphia PA 19123 215-627-6573 671

Il Capriccio 888 Main St .... Waltham MA 02453 781-894-2234 671
Web: www.bostonchefs.com

Il Cortile Del Re 193 King St .... Charleston SC 29401 843-853-1888 671
Web: ilcortiledelre.com

Il Fornaio 400 Capitol Mall .... Sacramento CA 95814 916-446-4100 671
Web: www.ilfornaio.com

Il Fornaio America Corp
770 Tamalpais Dr Ste 400 .... Corte Madera CA 94925 415-945-0500 286-6632* 670
*Fax Area Code: 408 ■ TF: 888-454-6246 ■ Web: www.ilfornaio.com

Il Fornello Management Ltd
576 Danforth Ave .... Toronto ON M4K1R1 416-920-9410 707
Web: www.ilfornello.com

Il Gatto Nero 720 College St .... Toronto ON M6G1C2 416-536-3132 671

Il Giardino 910 Atlantic Ave .... Virginia Beach VA 23451 757-422-6464 671
Web: www.ilgiardino.com

IL Grano 11359 Santa Monica Blvd .... Los Angeles CA 90025 310-477-7775 671

IL MITO Trattoria e Enoteca
6913 W N Ave .... Wauwatosa WI 53213 414-443-1414 671
Web: www.ilmitotrattoriaeenoteca.com

IL Mulino 86 W Third St .... New York NY 10012 212-673-3783 671
Web: www.ilmulino.com

IL Mulino 1800 E Sunrise Blvd .... Fort Lauderdale FL 33304 954-524-1800 671
Web: www.ilmulinofl.com

Il Pasticcio Trattoria
11520 100th Ave .... Edmonton AB T5K1V4 780-488-9543 671
Web: www.ilpasticcio.ca

IL Porto Ristorante 121 King St .... Alexandria VA 22314 703-836-8833 671
Web: www.ilportoristorante.com

Il Terrazzo Carmine 411 First Ave S .... Seattle WA 98104 206-467-7797 671
Web: www.ilterrazzocarmine.com

IL Vicino 321 W San Francisco St .... Santa Fe NM 87501 505-986-8700 671

IL Vicino 11 S Tejon St .... Colorado Springs CO 80903 719-475-9224 671
Web: www.ilvicino.com

IL Vicino 4817 E Douglas .... Wichita KS 67218 316-612-7085 671
Web: www.ilvicino.com

ILA (Illinois Library Assn)
33 W Grand Ave Ste 401 .... Chicago IL 60654 312-644-1896 644-1899 435
TF: 877-565-1896 ■ Web: www.ila.org

ILAA (International Lawyers in Alcoholics Anonymous)
415-1080 Mainland St .... Vancouver BC V6B2T4 604-685-2171 48-21
TF: 888-685-2171 ■ Web: www.ilaa.org

Ilan Systems
1107 Fair Oaks Ave .... South Pasadena CA 91030 800-678-3526 180
TF: 800-678-3526 ■ Web: www.ilan.com

Ilani Shoes Ltd 1350 Broadway .... New York NY 10018 212-947-5830 301

ILC Dover Inc 1 Moonwalker Rd .... Frederica DE 19946 302-335-3911 335-0762 576
TF: 800-631-9567 ■ Web: www.ilcdover.com

ILC Resources 3301 106th Cir .... Urbandale IA 50322 515-243-8106 244-3200 503-3
TF: 800-247-2133 ■ Web: www.ilcresources.com

iLeads.com LLC
567 San Nicolas Dr Ste 180 .... Newport Beach CA 92660 877-245-3237 224
TF: 877-245-3237 ■ Web: www.ileads.com

iLearning Gateway Inc
2650 Vly View Ln Bldg 1 Ste 200 .... Dallas TX 75234 972-488-2298 387
Web: www.ilearninggateway.com

Ilene Industries Inc
301 Stanley Blvd .... Shelbyville TN 37160 931-684-8731 684-8735 326
TF: 800-251-1602 ■ Web: www.ileneindustries.com

Ilex Construction & Woodworking
3801 Northampton St NW Ste 3 .... Washington DC 20015 410-820-4393 820-4394 685
TF: 866-551-4539 ■ Web: www.ilexconstruction.com

ILF (Indiana Library Federation)
941 E 86th St Ste 260 .... Indianapolis IN 46240 317-257-2040 257-1389 435
TF: 800-326-0013 ■ Web: www.ilfonline.org

ILI (International Law Institute)
1055 Thomas Jefferson St NW Ste M-100 ..... Washington DC 20007 202-247-6006 247-6010 49-10
TF: 800-277-5508 ■ Web: www.ili.org

Iliff School of Theology
2201 S University Blvd .... Denver CO 80210 303-744-1287 777-0164 167-3
TF: 800-678-3360 ■ Web: www.iliff.edu

Ilikai Hotel & Suites
1777 Ala Moana Blvd .... Honolulu HI 96815 808-949-3811 947-0892 379
TF: 866-536-7973 ■ Web: www.ilikaihotel.com

iLinc Communications Inc
2999 N 44th St Ste 650 .... Phoenix AZ 85018 602-952-1200 952-0544 176
TF: 800-767-9054 ■ Web: www.ilinc.com

Iliniwek Village State Historic Site
c/o Battle of Athens State Historic Site Rt 1
PO Box 26 .... Revere MO 63465 660-877-3871 565
Web: www.mostateparks.com

Ilink Technology Inc
9840 Willows Rd Ste 202 .... Redmond CA 98052 425-869-8104 175
Web: ilinktechnology.com

Ilio DiPaolo's 3785 S Pk Ave .... Buffalo NY 14219 716-825-3675 825-1054 671
Web: www.iliodipaolos.com

Ilios Noche 11508 Providence Rd .... Charlotte NC 28277 704-814-9882 671
Web: www.xeniahospitality.com

Name / Address	City	State	Zip	Phone	Fax	Class
Illahee State Park						
3540 NE Bahia Vista Dr	Bremerton	WA	98310	360-478-6460		565
Web: www.parks.wa.gov						
ILLCO Inc 535 S River St	Aurora	IL	60506	630-892-7904	892-0318	612
Web: www.illco.com						
Illegal Pete's 1447 Pearl St	Boulder	CO	80302	303-440-3955		671
Web: illegalpetes.com						
Illingworth Engineering Co						
6855 Phillips Pkwy Dr S	Jacksonville	FL	32256	904-262-4700		610
Web: boiler.publishpath.com						
Illini State Park 2660 E 2350th Rd	Marseilles	IL	61341	815-795-2448		565
Web: www.dnr.illinois.gov/Parks/Pages/Illini.aspx						
Illinois						
Administrative Office of the Illinois Courts						
3101 Old Jacksonville Rd	Springfield	IL	62704	217-558-4490	785-3905	339-14
Web: www.state.il.us/court						
Aging Dept						
1 Natural Resources Way Ste 100	Springfield	IL	62701	217-785-3356	785-4477	339-14
TF: 800-252-8966 ■ *Web:* illinois.gov/aging						
Agriculture Dept PO Box 19281	Springfield	IL	62794	217-782-2172	785-4505	339-14
Web: www.agr.state.il.us						
Attorney General 500 S Second St	Springfield	IL	62701	217-782-1090		339-14
Web: www.illinoisattorneygeneral.gov						
Banks & Real Estate Div						
500 E Monroe St 3rd Fl	Springfield	IL	62701	217-782-3000	524-5941	339-14
TF: 877-793-3470 ■ *Web:* www.idfpr.com						
Bill Status 705 Stratton Bldg	Springfield	IL	62706	217-782-3944		433
Web: www.ilga.gov/legislation						
Child Support Enforcement Div						
509 S Sixth St	Springfield	IL	62701	217-524-6049		339-14
TF: 800-447-4278 ■ *Web:* www.childsupportillinois.com						
Children & Family Services Dept						
406 E Monroe St	Springfield	IL	62701	217-785-2509		339-14
Web: www.state.il.us/dcfs						
Commerce & Economic Opportunity Dept						
620 E Adams St	Springfield	IL	62701	217-782-7500		339-14
Web: illinois.gov/dceo						
Commerce Commission						
527 E Capitol Ave	Springfield	IL	62701	217-785-1407	785-1770	339-14
Web: www.state.il.us/icc						
Community College Board						
401 E Capitol Ave	Springfield	IL	62701	217-785-0123	524-4981	339-14
Web: www.iccb.org						
Crime Victims Services Div						
100 W Randolf Rd 13th Fl	Chicago	IL	60601	312-814-2581	814-7105	339-14
TF: 800-228-3368 ■ *Web:* www.illinoisattorneygeneral.gov						
Driver Services Office						
2701 S Dirksen Pkwy	Springfield	IL	62723	217-782-6212		339-14
Web: www.cyberdriveillinois.com/departments/drivers						
Emergency Management Agency						
2200 S Dirksen Pkwy	Springfield	IL	62703	217-782-2700		339-14
TF: 800-782-7860 ■ *Web:* www.state.il.us/iema						
Environmental Protection Agency						
1021 N Grand Ave E	Springfield	IL	62794	217-782-3397		339-14
TF: 800-782-7860 ■ *Web:* www.epa.state.il.us						
General Assembly						
705 Stratton Bldg	Springfield	IL	62706	217-782-2000		339-14
Web: www.ilga.gov						
Governor 207 State House	Springfield	IL	62706	217-558-3085	558-3094	339-14
Web: www.illinois.gov/gov						
Healthcare & Family Services Dept						
201 S Grand Ave E 3rd Fl	Springfield	IL	62763	217-782-1200	524-7979	339-14
Web: www.hfs.illinois.gov						
Higher Education Board						
1 N Old State Capitol Plaza Ste 333	Springfield	IL	62701	217-782-2551	782-8548	339-14
Web: www.ibhe.org						
Historic Preservation Agency						
1 Old State Capitol Plaza	Springfield	IL	62701	217-785-7930		339-14
TF: 888-440-9009 ■ *Web:* www.state.il.us						
Housing Development Authority						
401 N Michigan Ave Ste 900	Chicago	IL	60611	312-836-5200		339-14
Web: www.ihda.org						
Human Services Dept						
100 S Grand Ave E Harris Bldg 3rd Fl	Springfield	IL	62762	217-557-1601	557-1647	339-14
TF: 800-843-6154 ■ *Web:* www.dhs.state.il.us						
Insurance Div						
320 W Washington St 4th Fl	Springfield	IL	62767	217-782-4515	782-5020	339-14
Web: insurance.illinois.gov						
Labor Dept 160 N LaSalle St 13th Fl	Chicago	IL	60601	312-793-2800	793-5257	339-14
Web: www.illinois.gov						
Lottery 101 W Jefferson St	Springfield	IL	62702	217-524-6435		452
TF: 800-252-1775 ■ *Web:* www.illinoislottery.com						
Mental Health Div						
100 W Randolf St Ste 3-400	Chicago	IL	60601	312-814-2811		339-14
TF: 800-252-2923 ■ *Web:* illinois.gov/dceo						
Military Affairs Dept						
1301 N MacArthur Blvd	Springfield	IL	62702	217-761-3515	761-3527	339-14
Web: www2.illinois.gov/agencies/DMA						
Natural Resources Dept						
1 Natural Resources Way	Springfield	IL	62702	217-782-6302		339-14
Web: www.dnr.illinois.gov						
Professional Regulation Div						
320 W Washington St 3rd Fl	Springfield	IL	62786	888-473-4858		339-14
TF: 888-473-4858 ■ *Web:* www.ildpr.com						
Public Health Dept						
535 W Jefferson St	Springfield	IL	62761	217-782-4977		339-14
Web: www.idph.state.il.us						
Racing Board						
100 W Randolph St Ste 5-700	Chicago	IL	60601	312-814-2600	814-5062	712
Web: www.illinois.gov						
Revenue Dept 101 W Jefferson St	Springfield	IL	62702	217-782-3336		339-14
TF: 800-732-8866 ■ *Web:* www.revenue.state.il.us						
Secretary of State						
213 State Capitol	Springfield	IL	62756	217-782-2201		339-14
TF: 800-252-8980 ■ *Web:* www.cyberdriveillinois.com						
State Board of Education						
100 N First St	Springfield	IL	62777	217-782-4321		339-14
TF: 866-262-6663 ■ *Web:* www.isbe.state.il.us						
State Police 801 S Seventh St	Springfield	IL	62794	217-782-7263		339-14
Web: www.isp.state.il.us						
Student Assistance Commission						
1755 Lake Cook Rd	Deerfield	IL	60015	800-899-4722	519-4652*	725
**Fax:* Cust Svc ■ *TF:* 877-877-3724 ■ *Web:* collegeillinois.org						
Supreme Court 200 E Capitol Ave	Springfield	IL	62701	217-782-2035		339-14
Web: www.state.il.us/court						
Tourism Bureau						
100 W Randolph St Ste 3-400	Chicago	IL	60601	312-814-4732	814-6175	339-14
TF: 800-226-6632 ■ *Web:* www.enjoyillinois.com						
Treasurer						
Capitol Bldg 219 Statehouse	Springfield	IL	62706	866-458-7327	785-2777*	339-14
**Fax Area Code:* 217 ■ *TF:* 866-458-7327 ■ *Web:* www.treasurer.il.gov/contact-us.aspx						
Veterans Affairs Dept						
69 W Washington						
George Dunn County Bldg Ste 1620	Chicago	IL	60602	312-814-2460	814-2764	339-14
TF: 800-437-9824 ■ *Web:* www2.illinois.gov						
Vital Records Div						
605 W Jefferson St	Springfield	IL	62702	217-782-6553		339-14
Web: www.idph.state.il.us/vitalrecords						
Wildlife Resources Div						
1 Natural Resources Way	Springfield	IL	62702	217-785-5506		339-14
Web: www.dnr.state.il.us						
Workers' Compensation Commission						
100 W Randolph St Ste 8-200	Chicago	IL	60601	312-814-6611	814-6523	339-14
TF: 866-352-3033 ■ *Web:* www.iwcc.il.gov						
Illinois & Michigan Canal State Trail						
PO Box 272	Morris	IL	60450	815-942-0796		565
Web: www.dnr.illinois.gov/recreation/greenwaysandtrails/Pages/IMCanal.aspx						
Illinois & Midland Railroad Inc						
1500 N Grand Ave E	Springfield	IL	62702	217-788-8601		648
Web: www.gwrr.com						
Illinois Alcoholism & Drug Dependence Assn						
937 S Second St	Springfield	IL	62704	217-528-7335		533
Web: iadda.org						
Illinois Assn of Chamber of Commerce Executives						
215 E Adams St	Springfield	IL	62701	217-522-5512		139
Web: www.iacce.org						
Illinois Assn of Realtors						
522 S Fifth St	Springfield	IL	62701	217-529-2600	529-3904	656
Web: www.illinoisrealtor.org						
Illinois Auto Electric Co						
700 Enterprise St	Aurora	IL	60504	630-862-3300		385
TF: 800-683-8484 ■ *Web:* www.illinoisautoelectric.com						
Illinois Beach State Park Lake Front	Zion	IL	60099	847-662-4811	662-6433	565
Web: www.dnr.illinois.gov						
Illinois Blueprint Corp						
800 SW Jefferson Ave	Peoria	IL	61605	309-676-1300	676-1310	240
TF: 800-747-7070 ■ *Web:* www.illinoisblue.com						
Illinois Capacitor Inc						
3757 W Touhy Ave	Lincolnwood	IL	60712	847-675-1760	673-2850	253
Web: www.illinoiscapacitor.com						
Illinois Caverns State Natural Area						
4369 G Rd	Waterloo	IL	62298	618-458-6699		565
Web: dnr.illinois.gov/Lands/Landmgt/PARKS/R4/Ilc.htm						
Illinois Cement Co 1601 Rockwell Rd	La Salle	IL	61301	815-224-2112		135
Web: www.eaglematerials.com						
Illinois College						
1101 W College Ave	Jacksonville	IL	62650	217-245-3030	245-3034*	166
**Fax:* Admissions ■ *TF Admissions:* 866-464-5265 ■ *Web:* www.ic.edu						
Illinois Crane Inc 1621 W Chanute Rd	Peoria	IL	61615	309-692-0856		207
Web: www.illinoiscrane.com						
Illinois Fair Plan Assn						
130 East Randolph PO Box 81469	Chicago	IL	60601	312-861-0385	861-0485	690
TF: 800-972-4480 ■ *Web:* www.illinoisfairplan.com						
Illinois Foundation Seeds Inc (IFSI)						
1083 County Rd 900 N	Tolono	IL	61880	217-485-6260	485-3687	10-5
Web: www.ifsi.com						
Illinois Glove Co						
3701 Commercial Ave	Northbrook	IL	60062	847-291-1700	291-7722	155-8
TF: 800-342-5458 ■ *Web:* www.illinoisglove.com						
Illinois Health Care Association						
1029 S Fourth St	Springfield	IL	62703	217-528-6455		533
TF: 800-252-8988 ■ *Web:* www.ihca.com						
Illinois Institute of Art						
Chicago 350 N Orleans St Ste 136-L	Chicago	IL	60654	312-280-3500	280-8562	164
TF: 800-351-3450 ■ *Web:* www.artinstitutes.edu						
Schaumburg 1000 N Plaza Dr	Schaumburg	IL	60173	847-619-3450		164
TF: 800-314-3450 ■ *Web:* www.artinstitutes.edu						
Illinois Institute of Technology						
10 W 33rd St	Chicago	IL	60616	312-567-3025	567-6939*	166
**Fax:* Admissions ■ *TF:* 800-448-2329 ■ *Web:* www.iit.edu						
IIT Paul V. Galvin Library						
35 W 33rd St	Chicago	IL	60616	312-567-3616	567-5318	434-6
Web: library.iit.edu						
Rice 201 E Loop Rd	Wheaton	IL	60189	630-682-6000	682-6010*	166
**Fax:* Admissions ■ *Web:* www.iit.edu/rice						
Illinois International Port District						
3600 E 95th St	Chicago	IL	60617	773-646-4400	221-7678	618
Web: iipd.com						
Illinois Legal Aid Online						
17 N State St Ste 1590	Chicago	IL	60602	312-977-9047		428
Web: illinoislegalaid.org						
Illinois Library Assn (ILA)						
33 W Grand Ave Ste 401	Chicago	IL	60654	312-644-1896	644-1899	435
TF: 877-565-1896 ■ *Web:* www.ila.org						
Illinois Machine & Tool Works						
1961 Edgewater Dr	North Pekin	IL	61554	309-382-3045		454
Illinois Mutual Life Insurance Co						
300 SW Adams St	Peoria	IL	61634	309-674-8255		391-2
TF: 800-380-6688 ■ *Web:* www.illinoismutual.com						
Illinois National Bank						
322 E Capitol	Springfield	IL	62701	217-747-5500		70
TF: 877-771-2316 ■ *Web:* www.illinoisnationalbank.com						
Illinois Nurses Assn (INA)						
105 W Adams St Ste 2101	Chicago	IL	60603	312-419-2900	419-2920	533
TF: 800-262-2500 ■ *Web:* www.illinoisnurses.com						

				Phone	Fax	Class
Illinois Pharmacists Assn (IPhA) 204 W Cook St *Web:* www.ipha.org	Springfield	IL	62704	217-522-7300	522-7349	585
Illinois Principals Association 2940 Baker Dr *Web:* www.ilprincipals.org	Springfield	IL	62703	217-525-1383		533
Illinois Rural Electric Co-op 2 S Main St *TF:* 800-468-4732 ■ *Web:* e-co-op.com	Winchester	IL	62694	217-742-3128		245
Illinois Service Federal S & L 4619 S King Dr *Web:* www.isfbank.com	Chicago	IL	60653	773-624-2000	624-5340	70
Illinois South Tourism 4387 N Illinois St Ste 200 *TF:* 800-442-1488 ■ *Web:* www.illinoisouth.org	Swansea	IL	62226	618-257-1488	257-3403	206
Illinois Soybean Assoc 1605 Commerce Pkwy *Web:* www.ilsoy.org	Bloomington	IL	61704	309-662-3373		138
Illinois State Bar Assn 424 S Second St *TF:* 800-252-8908 ■ *Web:* www.isba.org	Springfield	IL	62701	217-525-1760	525-0712	72
Illinois State Chamber of Commerce 300 S Wacker Dr Ste 1600 *Web:* www.ilchamber.org	Chicago	IL	60606	312-983-7100	983-7101	140
Illinois State Dental Society 1010 S Second St *TF:* 888-286-2447 ■ *Web:* www.isds.org	Springfield	IL	62704	217-525-1406	525-8872	227
Illinois State Fairgrounds 801 E Sangamon Ave *TF:* 866-287-2999 ■ *Web:* www.agr.state.il.us	Springfield	IL	62702	217-782-4231	524-6194	642
Illinois State Library 300 S Second St *TF:* 800-665-5576 ■ *Web:* www.cyberdriveillinois.com	Springfield	IL	62701	217-782-2994	785-4326	434-5
Illinois State Medical Inter-Insurance Exchange (ISMIE) 20 N Michigan Ave Ste 700 *TF:* 800-782-4767 ■ *Web:* www.ismie.com	Chicago	IL	60602	312-782-2749	782-2023	391-5
Illinois State Medical Society 20 N Michigan Ave Ste 700 *TF:* 800-782-4767 ■ *Web:* www.isms.org	Chicago	IL	60602	312-782-1654	782-2023	474
Illinois State Military Museum 1301 N MacArthur Blvd *TF:* 800-732-8868	Springfield	IL	62702	217-761-3910	761-3709	520
Illinois State Museum 502 S Spring St *Web:* www.illinoisstatemuseum.org	Springfield	IL	62706	217-782-7386	782-1254	520
Illinois State University 100 N University St **Fax:* Admissions ■ *TF Admissions:* 800-366-2478 ■ *Web:* illinoisstate.edu	Normal	IL	61761	309-438-2111	438-3932*	166
Illinois State University Milner Library 201 N School St **Fax:* Admin ■ *TF:* 800-366-2478 ■ *Web:* www.illinoisstate.edu	Normal	IL	61790	309-438-3451	438-3676*	434-6
Illinois State Veterinary Medical Assn 1121 Chatham Rd *Web:* www.isvma.org	Springfield	IL	62704	217-546-8381	546-5633	795
Illinois Symphony Orchestra 524 E Capitol Ave *TF:* 800-401-7222 ■ *Web:* www.ilsymphony.org	Springfield	IL	62701	217-522-2838	522-7374	573-3
Illinois Tool Works Inc (ITW) 3600 West Lake Ave *NYSE: ITW* ■ *Web:* www.itw.com	Glenview	IL	60026	847-724-7500	657-4261	386
Illinois Valley Area Chamber of Commerce & Economic Development 1320 Peoria St *Web:* www.ivaced.org	Peru	IL	61354	815-223-0227	223-4827	139
Illinois Valley Community College 815 N Orlando Smith Ave **Fax:* Admissions ■ *Web:* www.ivcc.edu	Oglesby	IL	61348	815-224-2720	224-3033*	162
Illinois Valley Community Hospital 925 W St *Web:* www.ivch.org	Peru	IL	61354	815-223-3300		374-3
Illinois Veterans Home-Anna 792 N Main St *TF:* 800-437-9824 ■ *Web:* illinois.gov	Anna	IL	62906	618-833-6302		793
Illinois Veterans Home-La Salle 1015 O'Connor Ave *Web:* www.vfwil.org/lasalle.asp	La Salle	IL	61301	815-223-0303		793
Illinois Veterans Home-Manteno 1 Veterans Dr *TF:* 800-437-9824 ■ *Web:* vfwil.org	Manteno	IL	60950	815-468-6581		793
Illinois Veterans Home-Quincy 1707 N 12th St *Web:* quincyivh.org	Quincy	IL	62301	217-222-8641		793
Illinois Vietnam Veterans Memorial Oak Ridge Cemetery *TF:* 800-545-7300 ■ *Web:* www.illinois.gov	Springfield	IL	62702	217-782-2717		50-4
Illinois Wesleyan University 1312 Pk St **Fax:* Admissions ■ *TF Admissions:* 800-332-2498 ■ *Web:* www.iwu.edu	Bloomington	IL	61701	309-556-3031	556-3820*	166
Illinois Wholesale Cash Register Inc 2790 Pinnacle Dr *TF:* 800-544-5493 ■ *Web:* www.illinoiswholesale.com	Elgin	IL	60124	847-310-4200	310-8490	112
Illinois Youth Ctr Harrisburg 1201 W Poplar St **Fax Area Code:* 815 ■ *Web:* www.illinois.gov/idjj/Pages/Harrisburg_IYC.aspx	Harrisburg	IL	62946	618-252-8681	795-6869*	412
Illinois Youth Ctr Saint Charles 3825 Campton Hills Rd *Web:* www.illinois.gov/idjj/pages/st_charles_iyc.aspx	Saint Charles	IL	60175	630-584-0506	584-1014	412
Illumina Inc 9885 Towne Centre Dr *NASDAQ: ILMN* ■ *TF:* 800-809-4566 ■ *Web:* www.illumina.com	San Diego	CA	92121	858-202-4500	202-4545	419
Illumina Partners Inc 67 Yonge St Ste 600 *Web:* www.illuminapartners.com	Toronto	ON	M5E1J8	416-861-1717		528
Illuminate Education Inc 47 Discovery Ste 100 *Web:* www.illuminateed.com	Irvine	CA	92618	949-242-0343		387
Illuminating Engineering Society of North America (IESNA) 120 Wall St 17th Fl *Web:* www.ies.org	New York	NY	10005	212-248-5000	248-5017	49-13
Illuminet Inc 4501 Intelco Loop SE *Web:* www.illuminet.com	Olympia	WA	98507	360-493-6000	493-6253	177
Illuminous Enterprises Inc 3129 S Hacienda Blvd Ste 691 *Web:* www.illuminousinc.com	Hacienda Heights	CA	91745	626-600-2087		196
ILMA (Independent Lubricant Manufacturers Assn) 400 N Columbus St Ste 201 *TF:* 800-624-9663 ■ *Web:* www.ilma.org	Alexandria	VA	22314	703-684-5574	836-8503	49-13
ILMO Products Company Inc 7 Eastgate Dr *TF:* 888-243-9353 ■ *Web:* www.ilmoproducts.com	Jacksonville	IL	62650	217-245-2183		358
Ilmor Engineering Inc 43939 Plymouth Oaks Blvd *Web:* www.ilmor.com	Plymouth	MI	48170	734-456-3600		60
ILO (International Labour Organization) 220 E 42nd St Ste 3101 *Web:* www.ilo.org	New York	NY	10017	212-697-0150	697-5218	783
iLookabout Corp 383 Richmond St Ste 408 *TF:* 866-963-2015 ■ *Web:* www.ilookabout.com	London	ON	N6A3C4	519-963-2015		177
ILPEA Industries Inc 745 S Gardner St *Web:* www.ilpeaindustries.com	Scottsburg	IN	47170	812-752-2526		600
ILS (International Launch Services) 1875 Explorer St Ste 700 *TF:* 800-852-4980 ■ *Web:* www.ilslaunch.com	Reston	VA	20190	571-633-7400	633-7500	504
ILSC Education Group Inc, The 555 Richards St *TF:* 800-862-6307 ■ *Web:* www.ilsc.com	Vancouver	BC	V6B2Z5	604-689-9095		423
ILSCO 4730 Madison Rd *TF Sales:* 800-776-9775 ■ *Web:* www.ilsco.com	Cincinnati	OH	45227	513-533-6200		815
ILTA (Independent Liquid Terminals Assn) 1005 N Glebe Rd Ste 600 *Web:* www.ilta.org	Arlington	DC	22201	202-842-9200	326-8660	49-21
ILX Lightwave Corp 31950 E Frontage Rd *TF:* 800-459-9459 ■ *Web:* www.newport.com	Bozeman	MT	59715	406-586-1244	586-9405	248
IM (IEEE Instrumentation & Measurement Society) 445 Hoes Ln *TF:* 800-327-6677 ■ *Web:* www.ieee-ims.org	Piscataway	NJ	08854	732-562-3844	981-9019	49-19
IM Global 8201 Beverly Blvd 5th Fl **Fax Area Code:* 323 ■ *Web:* www.imglobalfilm.com	Los Angeles	CA	90048	310-777-3590	657-5354*	511
IM Group, The 1903 Post Rd Ste 201 *Web:* www.the-imgroup.com	Fairfield	CT	06824	203-307-2151		463
IMA (International Marketing Assn) 3509 Virginia Beach Blvd *Web:* www.imacorporate.com	Virginia Beach	VA	23452	757-490-9860	490-0716	301
IMA (Institute of Management Accountants Inc) 10 Paragon Dr Ste 1 *TF:* 800-638-4427 ■ *Web:* www.imanet.org	Montvale	NJ	07645	201-573-9000	474-1600	49-1
IMA (International Magnesium Assn) 1000 N Rand Rd Ste 214 *Web:* www.intlmag.org	Wauconda	IL	60084	847-526-2010	526-3993	49-13
IMA (Interchurch Medical Assistance Inc) 1730 M St Ste 1100 *TF:* 877-241-7952 ■ *Web:* www.imaworldhealth.org	Washington	DC	20036	410-635-8720	635-8726	48-5
IMA Financial Group Inc 8200 E 32nd St N PO Box 2992 *Web:* www.imacorp.com	Wichita	KS	67226	316-267-9221		390
IMA LIFE North America Inc 2175 Military Rd *Web:* www.ima.it	Tonawanda	NY	14150	716-695-6354		610
ImaCor Inc 839 Stewart Ave Ste 3 *Web:* www.imacor.com	Garden City	NY	11530	516-393-0970		476
Image API LLC 2002 Old St Augustine Rd Bldg D *TF:* 877-560-4274 ■ *Web:* www.imageapi.com	Tallahassee	FL	32301	850-222-1400		177
Image Architects Inc 784 Morris Tpke *Web:* www.imagearch.com	Short Hills	NJ	07078	973-912-9334		177
Image Craft LLC 3401 E Broadway Rd *TF:* 800-274-2422 ■ *Web:* www.imagecraft.com	Phoenix	AZ	85040	602-276-2082		592
Image Custom Engineering 5011 E Fifth St Ste 170A *Web:* www.image-ces.com	Katy	TX	77493	281-829-4000		261
Image Data Inc 18 Petra Ln *TF:* 800-225-5237 ■ *Web:* www.imgdata.com	Albany	NY	12205	518-862-2740		225
Image Diagnostics Inc 310 Authority Dr *TF:* 800-258-1946 ■ *Web:* www.imagediagnostics.com	Fitchburg	MA	01420	978-829-0009		723
Image Engineering Group Ltd 635 Westport Pkwy *Web:* www.iegltd.com	Grapevine	TX	76051	817-410-2858		261
Image Group 31 E Eighth St Ste 200 *Web:* www.imagegroup.com	Holland	MI	49423	616-393-9588		4
Image Inc 1100 S Lynndale Dr *Web:* www.imagestudios.com	Appleton	WI	54914	920-738-4080		592
Image Iv Systems Inc 512 S Varney St *TF:* 800-473-5424 ■ *Web:* imageiv.com	Burbank	CA	91502	818-841-0756		366
Image Labs International PO Box 1545 *TF:* 800-785-5995 ■ *Web:* www.imagelabs.com	Belgrade	MT	59714	406-585-7225		178-8
Image Matters LLC 201 Loudoun St SW *Web:* www.imagemattersllc.com	Leesburg	VA	20175	703-669-5510		195
Image National Inc 16265 Star Rd *Web:* www.imagenational.com	Nampa	ID	83687	208-345-4020	336-9886	701
Image One Corp 13201 Capital Ave *TF:* 800-799-5377 ■ *Web:* www.imageoneway.com	Oak Park	MI	48237	248-414-9955	414-9951	628
Image Process Design 36800 Woodward Ave Ste 300 *TF:* 800-426-9990 ■ *Web:* www.ipdsolution.com	Bloomfield Hills	MI	48304	248-723-9733	203-2566	178-1
Image Recordings 4736 Penn Ave Ste 200 *Web:* www.aspstation.net	Pittsburgh	PA	15224	412-362-4050		514
Image Resource Group 130 Pinnacle Point Ct Ste 101 *Web:* www.imageresourcegroup.com	Columbia	SC	29223	803-790-2121		463
Image Sensing Systems Inc 500 Spruce Tree Centre 1600 University Ave *TF:* 800-734-9293 ■ *Web:* www.imagesensing.com	St. Paul	MN	55104	651-603-7700		407
Image Sport Inc 1115 SE Westbrooke Dr *TF:* 800-919-0520 ■ *Web:* www.imagesport.com	Waukee	IA	50263	515-987-7699		687

Company	City	State	ZIP	Phone	Fax	Class
Image Works PO Box 443 *TF:* 800-475-8801 ■ *Web:* www.theimageworks.com	Woodstock	NY	12498	845-679-8500	679-0606	593
Imagecat Inc 400 Oceangate Ste 1050 *Web:* www.imagecatinc.com	Long Beach	CA	90802	562-628-1675		225
Imagemakers Inc 514 Lincoln Ave PO Box 368	Wamego	KS	66547	386-236-1200		4
ImageMark Business Services Inc 141 Robins St *Web:* www.imagemarkonline.com	Lowell	NC	28098	704-478-8988		627
imageMEDIA Inc 425 E Spruce *TF:* 866-885-4468 ■ *Web:* www.imagemedia.com	St Tarpon Springs	FL	34689	727-772-8889		627
Imagenation Systems 549 Pylon Dr *Web:* imagenationsystems.com	Raleigh	NC	27604	919-834-3440	834-3441	196
Imagenet Consulting 6411 S 216th St *Web:* www.imagenet.com	Kent	WA	98032	253-395-0110		225
Images USA 1320 Ellsworth Industrial Blvd *Web:* www.imagesusa.net	Atlanta	GA	30318	404-892-2931		7
Imageset 6611 Portwest Dr Ste 190 *Web:* www.imageset.com	Houston	TX	77024	713-869-7700		627
ImageShack Corp 236 N Santa Cruz Ave Ste 100 *Web:* www.imageshack.us	Los Gatos	CA	95030	408-354-5166		387
ImageSource Inc 612 Fifth Ave SW *Web:* www.imagesourceinc.com	Olympia	WA	98501	360-943-9273		225
ImageState New York 29 E 19th St	New York	NY	10003	212-982-1915		593
imageTech Marketing Inc 10388 S Randall St *TF:* 800-223-2500 ■ *Web:* www.imagetechmarketing.com	Orange	CA	92869	714-639-5411		179
ImageWare Systems Inc 10815 Rancho BernaRdo Rd Ste 310 *Web:* www.iwsinc.com	San Diego	CA	92127	858-673-8600	673-1770	178-10
Imagewerks Marketing 3758 Dunlap St N *Web:* www.iwmarketing.com	Arden Hills	MN	55112	651-770-1319		624
ImageWorks 250 Clearbrook Rd *TF:* 800 592 6666 ■ *Web:* www.imageworkscorporation.com	Elmsford	NY	10523	914-592-6100	592-6148	382
Imageworks Manufacturing Inc 49 S St *TF:* 800-275-8777 ■ *Web:* www.imageworksmfg.com	Park Forest	IL	60466	708-503-1122	503-1133	9
Imagina US 7291 NW 74th St *Web:* www.imaginaus.com	Miami	FL	33166	305-777-1900		514
Imaginarium of South Texas 5300 San Dario Ste 505 *Web:* www.imaginariumstx.org	Laredo	TX	78041	956-728-0404	725-7776	521
Imaginorium Science Discovery Ctr 625 C St *TF:* 800-770-3300 ■ *Web:* www.visit-ketchikan.com	Anchorage	AK	99501	907-225-6166		520
Imaginary Forces LLC 2254 S Sepulveda Blvd *Web:* www.imaginaryforces.com	Los Angeles	CA	90064	323-957-6868		514
Imaginasium Inc 110 S Washington St *Web:* www.imaginasium.biz	Green Bay	WI	54301	920-431-7872		4
Imagination Publishing 600 W Fulton St Ste 600 *Web:* www.imaginepub.com	Chicago	IL	60661	312-887-1000		637-10
Imagine Advertising & Publishing Inc 6141 Crooked Creek Rd *TF:* 866-832-3214 ■ *Web:* www.imagineadv.com	Norcross	GA	30092	770-734-0966		393
Imagine Air Jet Services LLC 460 Driscoe Blvd Ste 210 *Web:* www.imagineair.com	Lawrenceville	GA	30046	678-226-2329		21
Imagine Business Development 485 Ritchie Hwy Ste 201 *Web:* www.imaginellc.com	Severna Park	MD	21146	410-544-7878		463
Imagine Entertainment Inc 9465 Wilshire Blvd 7th Fl	Beverly Hills	CA	90212	310-858-2000	858-2020	514
Imagine Express 2633 Minnehaha Ave *Web:* imagine-express.com	Minneapolis	MN	55406	612-728-1500		658
Imagine GPS Inc 6847 S Ea Ste 104 *TF:* 866-477-2489 ■ *Web:* www.gpscity.com	Las Vegas	NV	89119	702-990-5600		647
Imagine IT 1043 Grand Ave Ste 206 *Web:* duralogic.com	Saint Paul	MN	55105	651-204-7222	204-7223	393
Imagine One Technology & Management Ltd 416 Colonial Ave *TF:* 800-517-8408 ■ *Web:* www.imagine-one.com	Colonial Beach	VA	22443	804-224-1555		261
Imagine Schools 1005 N Glebe Rd Ste 610 *Web:* www.imagineschools.org	Arlington	VA	22201	703-527-2600		242
Imagine! Print Solutions Inc 1000 Vly Park Dr *Web:* www.imagineps.com	Minneapolis	MN	55379	952-903-4400		627
Imaginet Resources Corp 233 Portage Ave *TF:* 800-989-6022 ■ *Web:* imaginet.com	Winnipeg	MB	R3B2A7	204-989-6022		177
Imaging & Microfilm Access Inc 150 Knickerbocker Ave Ste E *TF:* 800-221-5994 ■ *Web:* www.scanyourdocs.com	Bohemia	NY	11716	631-589-8100		396
Imaging Associates Inc 11110 Westlake Dr *Web:* www.imaginga.com	Charlotte	NC	28273	704-522-8094		590
Imaging Business Machines LLC 2750 Crestwood Blvd *TF:* 877-627-8325 ■ *Web:* www.ibml.com	Birmingham	AL	35210	205-439-7100	956-5309	111
Imaging Diagnostic Systems Inc 1291-B NW 65th Pl *OTC: IMDS* ■ *Web:* www.imds.com	Fort Lauderdale	FL	33309	954-581-9800	979-2420	382
Imaging Dynamics Company Ltd 3510 - 29 St NE *Web:* www.imagingdynamics.com	Calgary	AB	T1Y7E5	403-251-9939		476
Imaging Healthcare Specialists Medical Group Inc 6256 Greenwich Dr Ste 150 *TF:* 866-558-4320 ■ *Web:* www.imaginghealthcare.com	San Diego	CA	92122	866-558-4320		415
Imaging Locators Inc PO Box 3058 *Web:* www.imaginglocators.com	Pahrump	NV	89048	775-751-6931		693
Imaging Office Systems Inc 4505 E Park 30 Dr *TF:* 800-878-7731 ■ *Web:* www.imagingoffice.com	Columbia City	IN	46725	260-248-9696		45
Imaging Supplies Company Inc 804 Woodland Ave *TF:* 800-518-1152 ■ *Web:* www.imagingsuppliesco.com	Sanford	NC	27330	919-776-1152		589
Imaging Systems Technology Inc 4750 W Bancroft St *Web:* www.isttouch.com	Toledo	OH	43615	419-536-5741		180
Imagize LLC 2855 Telegraph Ave Ste 510 *Web:* www.imagizellc.com	Berkeley	CA	94705	510-540-0260		256
iMakeNews Inc 200 Fifth Ave *TF:* 866-964-6397 ■ *Web:* www.imninc.com	Waltham	MA	02451	781-890-4700	890-4701	180
Imalux Corp 11000 Cedar Ave Ste 250	Cleveland	OH	44106	216-502-0755		476
Iman Academy 10929 Almeda Genoa Rd *TF:* 800-214-5264 ■ *Web:* www.imanacademy.org	Houston	TX	77034	713-910-3626		685
IMANA (Islamic Medical Assn of North America) 101 W 22nd St Ste 106 *Web:* www.imana.org	Lombard	IL	60148	630-932-0000	932-0005	49-8
Imanami Corp 2301 Armstrong St Ste 211 *TF:* 800-684-8515 ■ *Web:* imanami.com	Livermore	CA	94551	925-371-3000		196
Imani Lee Translations Services; Ili International Services; Ili Business s 11297 Senda Luna Llena Bldg B *Web:* www.imanilee.com	San Diego	CA	92130	858-523-9733		768
IMAPS (International Microelectronics & Packaging Society) PO Box 110127 *Web:* www.imaps.org	Research Triangle Park	NC	27709	202-548-4001	548-6115	49-19
Imark Molding Inc 104 Park Ave *Web:* www.imarkmolding.com	Woodville	WI	54028	715-698-3144		608
Imata & Assoc Inc 171 Kapiolani St	Hilo	HI	96720	808-935-6827		261
iMatch LLC 1417 Fourth Ave Ste 810 *TF:* 800-264-1170 ■ *Web:* www.imatch.com	Seattle	WA	98101	206-262-1661		260
IMAX Corp 2525 Speakman Dr *NYSE: IMAX* ■ *TF:* 800-732-0330 ■ *Web:* www.imax.com	Mississauga	ON	L5K1B1	905-403-6500	403-6450	748
IMBA (International Mountain Bicycling Assn) 4888 Pearl E Cir Ste 200E *TF:* 888 442-4622 ■ *Web:* www.imba.com	Boulder	CO	80301	303-545-9011	545-9026	48-23
IMC (InterAmerican Motor Corp) 8901 Canoga Ave *TF:* 800-874-8925 ■ *Web:* www.imcparts.net	Canoga Park	CA	91304	818-678-1200		61
IMC (Iberia Medical Ctr) 2315 E Main St *Web:* www.iberiamedicalcenter.com	New Iberia	LA	70560	337-364-0441		374-3
IMC (International Medical Corps) 1919 Santa Monica Blvd Ste 400 *TF:* 800-481 4462 ■ *Web:* www.internationalmedicalcorps.org	Santa Monica	CA	90404	310-826-7800	442-6622	48-5
IMC Group of Cos 120 White Plains Rd Ste 405 *Web:* www.the-imc.com	Tarrytown	NY	10591	914-468-7050		266
IMC Inc 233 S Wacker Dr Ste 4300 *Web:* www.imc.com	Chicago	VA	22310	312-244-3300	244-3301	225
IMC Networks Corp 19772 Pauling *TF:* 800-624-1070 ■ *Web:* bb-elec.com	Foothill Ranch	CA	92610	949-465 3000	465-3020	170
Imc Resort Services LLC 2 Corpus Christie Pl Ste C104 *TF:* 800-955-4474 ■ *Web:* www.imcresortservices.com	Hilton Head Island	SC	29928	843 785-4775		707
IMC USA (Institute of Management Consultants USA Inc) 2025 M St NW Ste 800 *TF:* 800-221-2557 ■ *Web:* www.imcusa.org	Washington	DC	20036	202-367-1134	367-2134	49-12
IMCA (Investment Management Consultants Assn) 5619 DTC Pkwy Ste 500 *TF:* 800-250-9083 ■ *Web:* www.imca.org	Greenwood Village	CO	80111	303-770-3377	770-1812	49-2
IMCA (Insurance Marketing Communications Assn) 4248 Park Glen Rd *Web:* www.imcanet.com	Minneapolis	MN	55416	952-928-4644	929-1318	49-9
Imc-Metalsamerica LLC 135 Old Boiling Springs Rd *Web:* www.imc-ma.com	Shelby	NC	28152	704-482-8200		567
IMCO Carbide Tool Inc 28170 Cedar Park Blvd *Web:* www.imcousa.com	Perrysburg	OH	43551	419-661-6313		186
Imco General Construction Inc 2116 Buchanan Loop *TF:* 800-709-2187 ■ *Web:* imcoconstruction.com	Ferndale	WA	98248	360-671-3936		186
IMCO Inc 858 N Lenola Rd	Moorestown	NJ	08057	856-235-7254		697
IMCOR-Interstate Mechanical Corp 1841 E Washington St *TF:* 800-628-0211 ■ *Web:* www.imcor-az.com	Phoenix	AZ	85034	602-257-1319	271-0674	189-10
IMCU (Indiana Members Credit Union) 7110 W Tenth St *TF:* 800-556-9268 ■ *Web:* www.imcu.com	Indianapolis	IN	46214	317-248-8556		219
IME (Institute of Makers of Explosives) 1120 19th St NW Ste 310 *Web:* www.ime.org	Washington	DC	20036	202-429-9280	293-2420	49-13
IME (Intermountain Electric Inc) 5050 Osage St Ste 500 *Web:* imelect.com	Denver	CO	80221	303-733-7248	722-2410	189-4
Imec Technologies Inc 702 Bloomington Rd *TF:* 800-777-2922 ■ *Web:* www.imectechnologies.com	Champaign	IL	61820	217-643-7488		177
Imecom Group 8 Governor Wentworth Hwy *TF:* 800-329-9099 ■ *Web:* www.imecominc.com	Wolfeboro	NH	03894	603-569-0600	569-0609	178-7
I-MED Pharma Inc 1601 St Regis Blvd *Web:* www.imedpharma.com	Dollard-des-Ormeaux	QC	H9B3H7	514-685-8118	685-8998	543
Imedex Inc 4325 Alexander Dr *Web:* www.imedex.com	Alpharetta	GA	30022	770-751-7332	751-7334	800
iMemories 9181 E Bell Rd **Fax Area Code: 480* ■ *TF:* 800-845-7986 ■ *Web:* www.imemories.com	Scottsdale	AZ	85260	800-845-7986	767-2511*	588
Imerys USA Inc 100 Mansell Ct E Ste 300 *TF:* 800-843-3222 ■ *Web:* www.imerys-paper.com	Roswell	GA	30076	770-645-3300	645-3384	503-2
IMETCO (Innovative Metals Company Inc) 4648 S Old Peachtree Rd *TF:* 800-646-3826 ■ *Web:* www.imetco.com	Norcross	GA	30071	770-908-1030	908-2264	46
iMethods LLC 10748 Deerwood Park Blvd Ste 150 *TF:* 888-306-2261 ■ *Web:* www.imethods.com	Jacksonville	FL	32256	888-306-2261		196

Company	City	State	ZIP	Phone	Fax	Class
IMEX Research 1474 Camino Robles	San Jose	CA	95120	408-268-0800		463
Web: www.imexresearch.com						
Imex Veterinary Inc 1001 Mckesson Dr	Longview	TX	75604	903-295-2196		794
TF: 800-828-4639 ■ *Web:* www.imexvet.com						
IMF (International Monetary Fund)						
700 19th St NW	Washington	DC	20431	202-623-7000	623-4661	783
TF: 800-548-5384 ■ *Web:* www.imf.org						
IMG (International Motor Coach Group Inc)						
8695 College Blvd Ste 260	Overland Park	KS	66210	913-906-0111	906-0115	49-21
TF: 888-447-3466 ■ *Web:* www.imgcoach.com						
IMG Artists 7 W 54th St	New York	NY	10019	212-994-3500	994-3550	731
Web: www.imgartists.com						
IMG Inc 1360 E Ninth St	Cleveland	OH	44114	216-522-1200		731
Web: img.com						
IMG Models 304 Pk Ave S PH N	New York	NY	10010	212-253-8884	253-8883	506
Web: www.imgmodels.com						
Imh Financial Corp						
7001 N Scottsdale Rd Ste 2050	Scottsdale	AZ	85253	480-840-8400		216
TF: 800-510-6445 ■ *Web:* www.imhfc.com						
IMI (Irving Materials Inc)						
8032 N SR-9	Greenfield	IN	46140	317-536-6650	326-3105	182
Web: www.irvmat.com						
IMI (International Masonry Institute)						
17101 Science Dr	Bowie	MD	20715	800-803-0295	261-2855*	49-3
**Fax Area Code:* 301 ■ *TF:* 800-803-0295 ■ *Web:* www.imiweb.org						
IMI Assn Executives Inc						
110 Horizon Dr Ste 2100	Raleigh	NC	27615	919-459-2070	459-2075	47
Web: www.imiae.com						
IMI Cornelius Inc 101 Broadway St W	Osseo	MN	55369	763-488-8200		664
TF: 800-238-3600 ■ *Web:* www.cornelius.com						
IMI Data Search Inc						
275 E Hillcrest Dr Ste 102	Thousand Oaks	CA	91360	805-495-1149	495-0310	635
TF: 800-860-7779 ■ *Web:* www.imidatasearch.com						
Imic Hotels 1 Surrey Ct	Columbia	SC	29212	803-772-2629		377
TF: 800-345-8082 ■ *Web:* hamptoninn3.hilton.com						
I-Minerals Inc 880 - 580 Hornby St	Vancouver	BC	V6C3B6	604-303-6573		503-2
TF: 877-303-6573 ■ *Web:* www.imineralsinc.com						
iMirus 7715 E 111th St Ste 100	Tulsa	OK	74133	918-492-0660		393
Web: www.imirus.com						
Imko Enterprises Inc						
900 N Belt Hwy	Saint Joseph	MO	64506	816-233-4040		260
Web: www.imko.com						
IMLA (International Municipal Lawyers Assn)						
7910 Woodmont Ave Ste 1440	Bethesda	MD	20814	202-466-5424	785-0152	49-10
TF: 800-942-7732 ■ *Web:* www.imla.org						
Imlay City Ford Inc						
1788 S Cedar St	Imlay City	MI	48444	810-724-5900		57
Web: imlaycityford.com						
IMM Inc 758 Isenhauer Rd	Grayling	MI	49738	989-344-7619		697
Web: www.imm.net						
Immaculata University 1145 King Rd	Immaculata	PA	19345	610-647-4400	640-0836*	166
**Fax:* Admissions ■ *TF:* 877-428-6329 ■ *Web:* www.immaculata.edu						
Immanuel Lutheran Church						
2120 Lakewood Ave	Lima	OH	45805	419-222-2541		48-20
Web: www.wcoil.com						
Immanuel Lutheran College Inc						
501 Grover Rd	Eau Claire	WI	54701	715-836-6636		166
Web: ilc.edu						
Immanuel Lutheran Communities						
185 Crestline Ave	Kalispell	MT	59901	406-752-9622		48-20
Web: ilcorp.org						
Immanuel Medical Ctr 6901 N 72nd St	Omaha	NE	68122	402-572-2121		374-3
TF: 800-253-4368 ■ *Web:* chihealth.com/immanuel-medical-center						
IMMC (Iowa Methodist Medical Ctr)						
1200 Pleasant St	Des Moines	IA	50309	515-241-6212		374-3
Web: unitypoint.org						
Immecor 1650 Northpoint Pkwy	Santa Rosa	CA	95407	707-636-2550	636-2565	173-2
Web: www.immecor.com						
Immediatek Inc(NDA)						
3301 Airport Fwy Ste 200	Bedford	TX	76021	888-661-6565		224
TF: 888-661-6565 ■ *Web:* www.immediatek.com						
Immersion Corp 30 Rio Robles	San Jose	CA	95134	408-467-1900	467-1901	173-1
NASDAQ: IMMR ■ *Web:* www.immersion.com						
Immigrant and Employee Rights Section-U.S. Department of Justice Civil Rights Division						
950 Pennsylvania Ave NW IER, NYA 9000	Washington	DC	20530	202-616-5594	616-5509	340-14
TF: 800-255-7688 ■ *Web:* www.justice.gov						
Immtech Pharmaceuticals 1 N End Ave	New York	NY	10282	212-791-2911	791-2917	582
TF: 877-898-8038 ■ *Web:* www.immtechpharma.com						
ImmucorGamma Inc						
3130 Gateway Dr PO Box 5625	Norcross	GA	30091	770-441-2051	441-3807	231
NASDAQ: BLUD ■ *TF Cust Svc:* 800-829-2553 ■ *Web:* www.immucor.com						
Immunalysis Corp 829 Towne Ctr Dr	Pomona	CA	91767	909-482-0840		476
Web: immunalysis.com						
Immune Deficiency Foundation (IDF)						
40 W Chesapeake Ave Ste 308	Towson	MD	21204	410-321-6647	321-9165	48-17
TF: 800-296-4433 ■ *Web:* www.primaryimmune.org						
Immune Design Corp						
1616 Eastlake Ave E Ste 310	Seattle	WA	98102	206-682-0645		668
Web: www.immunedesign.com						
Immuno Concepts NA Ltd						
9825 Goethe Rd Ste 350	Sacramento	CA	95827	916-363-2649		743
TF: 800-251-5115 ■ *Web:* www.immunoconcepts.com						
ImmunoDiagnostics Inc						
1 Presidential Way Ste 104	Woburn	MA	01801	781-938-6300	938-7300	231
TF: 800-573-1700 ■ *Web:* www.immunodx.com						
ImmunoGen Inc 830 Winter St	Waltham	MA	02451	781-895-0600	895-0611	85
NASDAQ: IMGN ■ *Web:* www.immunogen.com						
Immunomedics Inc						
300 American Rd	Morris Plains	NJ	07950	973-605-8200	605-8282	85
NASDAQ: IMMU ■ *TF:* 800-327-7211 ■ *Web:* www.immunomedics.com						
ImmunoScience Inc 6670 Owens Dr	Pleasonton	CA	94588	925-828-1000		476
Web: www.immunoscience.com						
Immunotope Inc						
The Pennsylvania Biotechnology Ctr 3805 Old Easton	Doylestown	PA	18902	215-253-4180		668
Web: www.immunotope.com						
Immunovision Inc 1820 Ford Ave	Springdale	AR	72764	479-751-7005	751-7002	231
TF: 800-541-0960 ■ *Web:* www.immunovision.com						
IMMVAC Inc 6080 Bass Ln	Columbia	MO	65201	573-443-5363	874-7108	584
TF: 800-944-7563 ■ *Web:* www.immvac.com						
IMMY (IMMY) 2701 Corporate Centre Dr	Norman	OK	73069	405-360-4669		231
TF: 800-654-3639 ■ *Web:* www.immy.com						
Imo Pump 1710 Airport Rd	Monroe	NC	28110	704-289-6511	289-9273*	641
**Fax:* Sales ■ *TF:* 877-853-7867 ■ *Web:* www.imo-pump.com						
iModules Software Inc						
5101 College Blvd Ste 300	Leawood	KS	66211	913-888-0772		180
Web: www.imodules.com						
ImOn Communications LLC						
625 First St SE	Cedar Rapids	IA	52401	319-298-6484		116
Web: www.imon.net						
IMP Holdings LLC 409 Growth Pkwy	Angola	IN	46703	260-665-6112		253
Web: www.indianamarine.com						
Impac International 11445 Pacific Ave	Fontana	CA	92337	951-685-9660		8
TF: 800-227-9591 ■ *Web:* www.impac-international.com						
Impac Mortgage Holdings Inc						
19500 Jamboree Rd	Irvine	CA	92612	949-475-3600		654
NYSE: IMH ■ *TF:* 800-597-4101 ■ *Web:* www.impaccompanies.com						
Impact - Proven Solutions						
4600 Lyndale Ave N	Minneapolis	MN	55412	612-521-6245		4
Web: www.impactconnects.com						
Impact Benefit Management Services LLC						
10930 Crabapple Rd Ste 102	Roswell	GA	30075	770-709-6000		260
Impact Directories 1251 N Cole Rd	Boise	ID	83704	208-375-2220		5
Web: www.impactyp.com						
Impact Drug & Alcohol Treatment Ctr						
1680 N Fair Oaks Ave PO Box 93607	Pasadena	CA	91103	626-798-0884	798-6970	726
TF: 866-734-4200 ■ *Web:* www.impacthouse.com						
IMPACT Financial Services LLC						
381 Riverside Dr Ste 460	Franklin	TN	37064	615-771-9494		390
Web: www.impactfinancial.com						
Impact Guns 2710 S 1900 W	Ogden	UT	84401	801-393-2474		683
TF: 888-505-3086 ■ *Web:* www.impactguns.com						
Impact Incentives & Meetings Inc						
552 Valley Rd Ste 204	West Orange	NJ	07052	973-952-9052		384
Web: www.impactincentives.com						
Impact Industries Inc						
5120 Mills Industrial Pkwy	North Ridgeville	OH	44039	440-327-2360		488
Web: www.impactindustries.com						
Impact Instrumentation Inc						
27 Fairfield Pl	West Caldwell	NJ	07006	973-882-1212		250
Web: www.impactinstrumentation.com						
Impact Interactive						
5400 Laurel Springs Pkwy Ste 1003	Suwanee	GA	30024	678-679-6000		177
Web: impact.amwins.com						
Impact International Inc						
2600 Lockheed Way	Carson City	NV	89706	775-882-7834		596
Web: www.impactmenusystems.com						
Impact Label Corp 8875 Krum Ave	Galesburg	MI	49053	800-820-0362	381-1055*	413
**Fax Area Code:* 269 ■ *TF:* 800-820-0362 ■ *Web:* www.impactlabel.com						
Impact Mailing Services Inc						
100 Forsyth Hall Dr Ste A1	Charlotte	NC	28273	704-583-9490		5
Web: impactmailingservices.com						
Impact Makers Inc						
1707 Summit Ave Ste 201	Richmond	VA	23230	804-774-2600		180
TF: 800-438-7325 ■ *Web:* www.impactmakers.com						
Impact Management Services						
29792 Telegraph Rd Ste 150	Southfield	MI	48034	248-262-5200		193
TF: 800-395-9009 ■ *Web:* www.theimpactanswer.com						
Impact Marketing Inc						
7696 Golden Triangle Dr	Eden Prairie	MN	55344	952-562-6000		525
Web: www.impactmn.com						
Impact Planning Group						
11 Grumman Hill Rd	Wilton	CT	06897	203-854-1011		195
Web: www.impactplan.com						
Impact Products LLC 2840 Centennial Rd	Toledo	OH	43617	419-841-2891	841-7861	151
TF Cust Svc: 800-333-1541 ■ *Web:* www.impact-products.com						
Impact Resources Inc						
5910 Lone Oak Dr	Bethesda	MD	20814	301-581-9676		463
Web: www.ir-tech.com						
Impact Science & Technology Inc						
85 NW Blvd	Nashua	NH	03063	603-459-2255		193
Impact Seven Inc 147 Lake Almena Dr	Almena	WI	54805	715-357-3334	357-6233	402
TF: 800-685-9353 ■ *Web:* www.impactseven.org						
Impact Solutions Consulting Inc						
1300 Ridenour Blvd NW Ste 210	Kennesaw	GA	30152	770-795-9525		225
Impact Technologies Group Inc						
619 S Cedar St Ste J	Charlotte	NC	28202	704-549-1100		809
Web: www.impact-tech.com						
Impaq Corp 7785 W Sunset Blvd	Los Angeles	CA	90069	323-969-0088		195
Web: impaqcorp.com						
Impastato's 3400 16th St	Metairie	LA	70002	504-455-1545		671
Web: www.impastatos.com						
Impatica Inc 2430 Don Reid Dr Ste 200	Ottawa	ON	K1H1E1	613-736-9982		225
TF: 800-548-3475 ■ *Web:* www.impatica.com						
Impatto Custom Marketing Inc						
23235 Telegraph Rd	Southfield	MI	48033	248-415-5000		195
Web: impatto.com						
Impax Laboratories Inc						
30831 Hun2od Ave	Hayward	CA	94544	510-240-6450		583
NASDAQ: IPXL ■ *TF:* 877-994-6729 ■ *Web:* www.impaxlabs.com						
IMPCO Technologies Inc						
3030 S Susan St	Santa Ana	CA	92704	714-656-1200	656-1400*	128
**Fax:* Sales ■ *TF:* 800-325-4534 ■ *Web:* www.impcotechnologies.com						
Impelsys Inc 116 W 23rd St Ste 500	New York	NY	10011	212-239-4138	591-9536*	261
**Fax Area Code:* 917 ■ *Web:* www.impelsys.com						
Imperial Beach Chamber of Commerce & Visitors Bureau						
702 Seacoast Dr	Imperial Beach	CA	91932	619-424-3151	424-3008	139
TF: 800-829-1040 ■ *Web:* www.ib-chamber.com						
Imperial Bedding Co						
720 11th St PO Box 5347	Huntington	WV	25703	304-529-3321	525-5317	471
TF: 800-529-3321 ■ *Web:* www.imperialbedding.com						
Imperial Brands Inc						
11505 Fairchild Gardens Ave Ste 204	Palm Beach Gardens	FL	33410	561-624-5662		80-3
Web: www.ibrandsinc.com						

Phone | Fax | Class

Imperial Calcasieu Museum
204 W Sallier St Lake Charles LA 70601 337-439-3797 520
TF: 800-774-7394 ■ *Web:* www.imperialcalcasieumuseum.org

Imperial Capital LLC
10100 Santa Monica Blvd Ste 2400 Los Angeles CA 90067 310-246-3700 777-3000 401
TF: 800-929-2299 ■ *Web:* www.imperialcapital.com

Imperial Carbide Inc
10826 Mercer Pk Meadville PA 16335 814-724-3732 350
Web: www.imperialcarbide.com

Imperial Counters Inc
725 Spiral Blvd Hastings MN 55033 651-437-3903 438-3855 286
TF: 800-370-6545 ■ *Web:* www.imperialcounters.com

Imperial County 940 W Main St Rm 202 El Centro CA 92243 760-482-4427 482-4271 338
Web: www.co.imperial.ca.us

Imperial Dax Company Inc
120 New Dutch Ln Fairfield NJ 07004 973-227-6105 88
Web: www.daxhaircare.com

Imperial Die Casting Co
2249 Old Liberty Rd Liberty SC 29657 864-859-0202 855-1597 308
Web: www.rcmindustries.com

Imperial Distributors Inc 33 Sword St Auburn MA 01501 508-756-5156 756-0085 214
Web: www.imperialdist.com

Imperial Electric Co 1503 Exeter Rd Akron OH 44306 330-734-3600 734-3601 518
Web: www.imperialelectric.com

Imperial Electronic Assembly Inc
1000 Federal Rd Brookfield CT 06804 203-740-8425 740-8450 261
Web: www.impea.com

Imperial Graphics Inc
3100 Walkent Dr NW Grand Rapids MI 49544 800-777-2591 110
TF: 800-777-2591 ■ *Web:* www.imperialcrs.com

Imperial Hardware Company Inc
355 W Olive Ave El Centro CA 92243 760-353-5280 321
Web: www.imperialstores.com

Imperial High School
517 W Barioni Blvd Imperial CA 92251 760-355-3220 685
TF: 800-352-7550 ■ *Web:* imperialhighschool.org

Imperial Industries Inc
505 Industrial Pk Ave Rothschild WI 54474 715-359-0200 355-5349 105
TF: 800-558-2945 ■ *Web:* www.imperialind.com

Imperial Irrigation District (IID)
PO Box 937 Imperial CA 92251 760-482-9600 482-9611 203
TF: 800-303-7756 ■ *Web:* www.iid.com

Imperial Laundry Services LLC
1236 13th St Racine WI 53403 262-632-7997 426
Web: www.imperiallaundryservices.com

Imperial Manufacturing Group Inc
40 Industrial Park St Richibucto NB E4W4A4 506-523-9117 610
TF: 800-561-3100 ■ *Web:* www.imperialgroup.ca

Imperial Manufacturing Inc
2271 NE 194th Portland OR 97230 503-665-5539 106
Web: www.imperialmfg.com

Imperial Mechanical Inc
30685 Solon Industrial Pkwy Solon OH 44139 440-498-1788 610
Web: imperialhvac.com

Imperial Metals Corp
580 Hornby St Ste 200 Vancouver BC V6C3B6 604-669-8959 502
TSE: III ■ *Web:* www.imperialmetals.com

Imperial of Waikiki 205 Lewers St Honolulu HI 96815 808-923-1827 921-7586 379
TF: 800-347-2582 ■ *Web:* www.imperialofwaikiki.com

Imperial Oil Resources Ltd
237 Fourth Ave SW PO Box 2480 Stn M Calgary AB T2P3M9 800-567-3776 580
TF: 800-567-3776 ■ *Web:* www.imperialoil.ca

Imperial Palace 3415 E State St Rockford IL 61108 815-227-1442 316-0721 671
TF: 800-927-4738 ■ *Web:* imperialpalacerockford.com

Imperial Palace 701 N 27th St Lincoln NE 68503 402-474-2688 671
Web: imperialpalacene.net

Imperial Palace
4878 Princess Anne Rd Virginia Beach VA 23462 757-493-8838 671
Web: elegantchinesedining.com

Imperial Parking Corp
601 W Cordova St Ste 300 Vancouver BC V6B1G1 604-681-7311 562
Web: www.impark.com

Imperial PFS (UPAC) 8245 Nieman Rd Lenexa KS 66214 913-894-6150 216

Imperial Plastics Inc
21320 Hamburg Ave W Lakeville MN 55044 952-469-4951 596
Web: www.imperialplastics.com

Imperial Point Medical Ctr
6401 N Federal Hwy Fort Lauderdale FL 33308 954-776-8500 374-3
Web: www.browardhealth.org

Imperial Pools Inc 33 Wade Rd Latham NY 12110 518-786-1200 786-0954 728
TF: 800-444-9977 ■ *Web:* www.imperialpoolsb2b.com

Imperial Realty Company Inc
4747 W Peterson Ave Chicago IL 60646 773-736-4100 655
Web: imperialrealtyco.com

Imperial Salon & Spa Inc
3 Suntree Pl Melbourne FL 32940 321-254-4432 77
Web: www.imperialsalonandspa.com

Imperial Sprinkler Supply Inc
1485 N Manassero St Anaheim CA 92807 714-792-2925 429
Web: www.imperialsprinklersupply.com

Imperial Swan Hotel
4141 S Florida Ave Lakeland FL 33813 863-647-3000 379
TF: 800-327-3808 ■ *Web:* www.imperialswanlakeland.com

Imperial Theatre 249 W 45th St New York NY 10036 212-239-6200 747
TF: 800-447-7400 ■ *Web:* www.telecharge.com

Imperial Theatre 749 Broad St Augusta GA 30901 706-722-8293 312-1202 572
Web: www.imperialtheatre.com

Imperial Toy LLC 16641 Roscoe Pl North Hills CA 91343 818-536-6500 536-6501 762
TF: 800-497-9764 ■ *Web:* www.imperialtoy.com

Imperial Trading Co Inc
701 Edwards Ave Elmwood LA 70123 504-733-1400 297-8
TF Cust Svc: 800-775-4504 ■ *Web:* www.imperialtrading.com

Imperial Valley College
380 E Aten Rd PO Box 158 Imperial CA 92251 760-352-8320 355-2663* 162
*Fax: Admissions ■ *TF:* 800-336-1642 ■ *Web:* www.imperial.edu

Imperial Valley Press
205 N Eigth St El Centro CA 92243 760-337-3400 532-2
Web: www.ivpressonline.com

Imperial Valley Rop 687 W State St El Centro CA 92243 760-482-2600 685
Web: www.ivrop.org

Imperial Woodworking Co
310 N Woodwork Ln Palatine IL 60067 847-358-6920 358-0905 499
Web: www.imperialwoodworking.com

Imperial Woodworks Inc
PO Box 7835 PO Box 7835 Waco TX 76714 800-234-6624 741-0736* 319-3
*Fax Area Code: 254 ■ *TF:* 800-234-6624 ■ *Web:* www.pews.com

Imperium Inc 5901-F Ammendale Rd Beltsville MD 20705 301-431-2900 250
Web: www.imperiuminc.com

Imperium Renewables Inc
568 First Ave S Ste 600 Seattle WA 98104 206-254-0203 536
Web: www.imperiumrenewables.com

Impetus Capital LLC
145 W 57th St 16 Fl New York NY 10019 212-258-2782 691
Web: www.impetuscapital.com

Impinj Inc 400 Fairview Ave N Ste 1200 Seattle WA 98109 206-517-5300 517-5262 696

Implant Sciences Corp
500 Research Dr Wilmington MA 01887 978-752-1700 752-1711 476
OTC: IMSC ■ *Web:* www.implantsciences.com

Implantech Dental Laboratory
72415 Parkview Dr Palm Desert CA 92260 760-341-7388 415
Web: www.implantechlab.com

Implement Sales Company LLC
1574 Stone Ridge Dr Stone Mountain GA 30083 770-908-9439 908-8123 274
TF: 800-955-9592 ■ *Web:* implementsalesga.com

Implementation & Consulting Services Inc
500 Office Center Dr Ste 400 Washington PA 19073 844-432-8326 177
TF: 844-432-8326 ■ *Web:* www.ics-corporate.com

Impo International Inc PO Box 639 Santa Maria CA 93456 800-367-4676 301
TF: 800-367-4676 ■ *Web:* www.impo.com

Import Auto World 21571 Mission Blvd Hayward CA 94541 510-581-1200 581-1228 57
Web: importautoworldinc.com

IMPRES Technology Solutions Inc
10330 Pioneer Blvd Ste 280 Santa Fe Springs CA 90670 562-298-4030 196
Web: www.imprestechnology.com

Impression 5 Science Ctr
200 Museum Dr Lansing MI 48933 517-485-8116 520
Web: www.impression5.org

Imprex Inc 3260 S 108th St Milwaukee WI 53227 414-321-9300 480
Web: imprexusa.com

Imprimis Group Inc
4835 Lyndon B Johnson Fwy Dallas TX 75244 972-419-1700 419-1799 344
TF: 888-772-9682 ■ *Web:* www.imprimis.com

Improper Bostonian
142 Berkeley St 3rd Fl Boston MA 02116 617-859-1400 532-3
Web: www.improper.com

Improv Asylum 216 Hanover St Boston MA 02113 617-263-6887 522
TF: 888-396-6887 ■ *Web:* www.improvasylum.com

Improve Group Inc, The
1385 Mendota Heights Rd Ste 200b Mendota Heights MN 55120 877-467-7847 196
TF: 877-467-7847 ■ *Web:* www.theimprovegroup.com

Improved Construction Methods
1040 N Redmond Rd Jacksonville AR 72076 877-494-5793 358
TF: 877-494-5793 ■ *Web:* www.improvedconstructionmethods.com

Impulse Devices Inc
12731A Loma Rica Dr Grass Valley CA 95945 530-913-9753 273 5119 743

IMPulse NC Inc 100 IMPulse Way Mount Olive NC 28365 919-658-2200 658-2268 248
Web: www.impulsenc.com

Impulse Point LLC
5650 Breckenridge Park Dr Ste 201 Tampa FL 33610 813-607-2770 180
Web: www.impulse.com

Impulse Technologies Ltd
920 Gana Crt Mississauga ON L5S1Z4 905-564-9266 690
TF: 800-667-5475 ■ *Web:* impulsetechnologies.com

IMS Buhrke-Olson
511 W Algonquin Rd Arlington Heights IL 60005 847-981-7550 492
TF: 800-373-0464 ■ *Web:* www.metalstamper.com

IMS Health 535 Legget Dr Twr C 7th Fl Kanata ON K2K3B8 613-599-0711 178-12
NYSE: IMS ■ *Web:* www.imshealth.com

IMS Health Inc
485 Lexington Ave FL 26 New York NY 10017 917-542-5800 466
Web: www.imshealth.com

IMS inc 245 Commerce Blvd Liverpool NY 13088 800-466-4189 5
TF: 800-466-4189 ■ *Web:* imsdirect.com

IMS Productions 4555 W 16th St Indianapolis IN 46222 317-492-8770 513
Web: www.imsproductionstv.com

IMS Worldwide Inc 309 Henrietta Webster TX 77598 281-554-9099 463
TF: 800-741-9286 ■ *Web:* imsw.com

IMSA (International Municipal Signal Assn)
165 E Union St PO Box 539 Newark NY 14513 315-331-2182 331-8205 49-7
TF: 800-723-4672 ■ *Web:* www.imsasafety.org

IMshopping Inc
4699 Old Ironsides Dr Ste 450 Santa Clara CA 95054 408-228-4456 387
Web: www.imshopping.com

IMSI (Idaho Maximum Security Institution)
PO Box 51 Boise ID 83707 208-338-1635 213
Web: www.idoc.idaho.gov

IMSolutions LLC
3600 Pointe Ctr ct Ste 200 Dumfries VA 22026 703-221-2685 463
Web: www.imsolutionsllc.com

IMT (Iowa Mold Tooling Co Inc)
500 W US Hwy 18 Garner IA 50438 641-923-3711 923-6063 470
TF: 800-247-5958 ■ *Web:* www.imt.com

IMT Group, The PO Box 1336 Des Moines IA 50266 800-274-3531 391-4
TF: 800-274-3531 ■ *Web:* imtins.com

IMT Precision Inc 31902 Hayman St Hayward CA 94544 510-324-8926 454
Web: www.imtp.com

Imtec Acculine Inc 49036 Milmont Dr Fremont CA 94538 510-770-1800 770-1400 695
Web: www.imtecacculine.com

Imtech Graphics Inc 545 Dell Rd Carlstadt NJ 07072 800-468-3240 781
TF: 800-468-3240 ■ *Web:* imtechgraphics.com

Imtek Inc 175 Amherst St Nashua NH 03064 603-889-7610 7
Web: www.imtek.com

IMV (Institute for Molecular Virology)
413 RM Bock Laboratories 1525 Linden Dr Madison WI 53706 608-262-4540 262-4570 668
Web: virology.wisc.edu

IMVU Inc PO Box 390012 Mountain View CA 94039 650-321-8334 387
TF: 866-761-0975 ■ *Web:* www.imvu.com

Company / Address	City	State	ZIP	Phone	Fax	Class
In Business Magazine 200 River Pl Ste 250 *Web:* www.ibmadison.com	Madison	WI	53716	608-204-9655	204-9656	457-5
In Defense of Animals (IDA) 3010 Kerner Blvd *TF:* 800-705-0425 ■ *Web:* www.idausa.org	San Rafael	CA	94901	415-448-0048	454-1031	48-3
iN DEMAND 345 Hudson St 17th Fl *Web:* www.indemand.com	New York	NY	10014	646-638-8200		740
In Focus Adv Inc 29219 Canwood St Ste 101 *Web:* infocusadv.com	Agoura Hills	CA	91301	818-889-1342		4
In Focus Optical 202 Cherry St *Web:* www.infocussystems.com	Milford	CT	06460	203-882-7278		237
In The Line of Duty 10727 Indian Head Industrial Blvd *TF:* 800-462-5232 ■ *Web:* www.lineofduty.com	Saint Louis	MO	63132	314-890-8733		95
In the Raw Sushi 3321 S Peoria *Web:* www.intherawsushi.com	Tulsa	OK	74105	918-744-1300		671
In The Swim Inc 320 Industrial Dr **Fax Area Code:* 630 ■ *TF:* 800-288-7946 ■ *Web:* www.intheswim.com	West Chicago	IL	60185	800-288-7946	876-1091*	711
In Touch Business Consultants 11370 66th St 132 *TF:* 877-676-5492 ■ *Web:* www.affinityconsulting.com	Largo	FL	33773	877-676-5492		463
In Touch Marketing Inc 2793 Deerhaven Dr *Web:* intouchmarketinginc.net	Cincinnati	OH	45244	513-474-6317		195
In Touch Weekly Magazine 270 Sylvan Ave *Web:* www.intouchweekly.com	Englewood Cliffs	NJ	07632	201-569-6699		457-11
In Zone Brands 2859 Paces Ferry Rd SE Ste 2100 *Web:* www.good2grow.com	Atlanta	GA	30339	678-718-2000	718-2031	98
INA (Idaho Nurses Assn) 1850 E Southern Ave Ste 1 **Fax Area Code:* 404 ■ *TF:* 888-721-8904 ■ *Web:* www.idahonurses.org	Tempe	AZ	85282	888-721-8904	240-0998*	533
INA (Illinois Nurses Assn) 105 W Adams St Ste 2101 *TF:* 800-262-2500 ■ *Web:* www.illinoisnurses.com	Chicago	IL	60603	312-419-2900	419-2920	533
INA (Iowa Nurses Assn) 2400 86th St Ste 32 *Web:* www.iowanurses.org	Urbandale	IA	50322	515-225-0495		533
Inabata America Corp 1270 Ave of the Americas Ste 602 *Web:* us.inabata.com	New York	NY	10020	212-586-7764	245-2876	696
Inaho 157 Rt 6A *Web:* www.inahocapecod.com	Yarmouth Port	MA	02675	508-362-5522		671
Inair Aviation Services Co 8225 Country Club Pl *Web:* www.inairaviation.com	Indianapolis	IN	46214	317-271-0195		22
Inanovate Inc 2 Davis Dr Ste 13169 *Web:* www.inanovate.com	Research Triangle Park	NC	27709	919-354-1028		419
InBios International Inc 562 First Ave S Ste 600 *TF:* 866-462-4671 ■ *Web:* www.inbios.com	Seattle	WA	98104	206-344-5821		466
Inbound Call Experts LLC 700 Banyan Trl Ste 200 *Web:* www.inboundcallexperts.com	Boca Raton	FL	33431	561-705-0700		196
Inbox Group LLC 2100 W Northwest Hwy Ste 114-1135 *Web:* www.inboxgroup.com	Grapevine	TX	76051	214-530-5972		366
Inc Magazine 7 World Trade Ctr *TF:* 800-234-0999 ■ *Web:* www.inc.com	New York	NY	10007	212-389-5377		457-5
Inc ommand Technologies Inc 21 W William St *Web:* www.incommandtech.com	Corning	NY	14830	607-936-5066		180
Inc Solayre Inc 4568 N Hiatus Rd *Web:* www.solayre.com	Sunrise	FL	33351	954-389-4779		463
Inca Engineers Inc 400 112th Ave NE Ste 400	Bellevue	WA	98004	425-635-1000	635-1150	194
Incapital LLC 200 S Wacker Dr Ste 3700 *Web:* www.incapital.com	Chicago	IL	60606	312-379-3700		690
Incarnate Word High School 727 E Hildebrand Ave *Web:* www.incarnatewordhs.org	San Antonio	TX	78212	210-829-3100	829-3101	622
Incarnation Lutheran Church 4880 Hodgson Rd *Web:* www.incarnationmn.org	Saint Paul	MN	55126	651-766-0723		48-20
Incas 3312 S Holly Ave *Web:* incasiouxfalls.com	Sioux Falls	SD	57105	605-367-1992	367-1993	671
Incentive Group Inc, The 399 Knollwood Rd *Web:* www.incentivegroup.com	White Plains	NY	10603	914-948-0904		463
Incentive Publications Inc 2400 Crestmoor Dr *TF Mktg:* 800-967-5325 ■ *Web:* www.incentivepublications.com	Nashville	TN	37215	615-385-2934		243
Incentive Research Foundation 100 Chesterfield Business Pkwy Ste 200 *TF:* 800-262-1150 ■ *Web:* theirf.org	St. Louis	MO	63005	314-473-5601		305
Incentive Travel & Meetings (ITM) 970 Clementstone Dr Ste 100 *Web:* www.usaitm.com	Atlanta	GA	30342	404-252-2728	252-8328	384
Incepture Inc 8381 Dix Ellis Trl Ste 105 **Fax Area Code:* 904 ■ *TF:* 877-347-7151	Jacksonville	FL	32225	877-347-7151	363-4107*	260
INCERTEC LLC 160 83rd Ave NE *TF:* 800-638-2573 ■ *Web:* www.incertec.com	Fridley	MN	55432	763-717-7016		256
Incest Survivors Anonymous (ISA) PO Box 17245 *Web:* www.lafn.org/medical/isa	Long Beach	CA	90807	562-428-5599		48-21
Incharge Institute of America Inc 5750 Major Blvd *Web:* www.incharge.org	Orlando	FL	32819	407-291-7770		218
Inchcape Shipping Services Inc 11 N Water St Ste 9290 *Web:* www.iss-shipping.com	Mobile	AL	36602	251-461-2747		313
Inclinator Company of America 601 Gibson Blvd *Web:* www.inclinator.com	Harrisburg	PA	17104	717-939-8420		256
Inclind Inc Web Development Services 208 W Market St *Web:* www.inclind.com	Georgetown	DE	19947	302-856-2802		177
Incline Village/Crystal Bay Visitors Bureau 969 Tahoe Blvd *TF:* 800-468-2463 ■ *Web:* www.gotahoenorth.com	Incline Village	NV	89451	775-832-1606	832-1605	206
Incoe Corp 1740 E Maple Rd *Web:* www.incoe.com	Troy	MI	48083	248-616-0220	616-0225	757
Incom USA Inc 294 Southbridge Rd *Web:* www.incomusa.com	Charlton	MA	01507	508-765-9151	765-0041	330
Income Research & Management 100 Federal St 30th Fl *Web:* www.incomeresearch.com	Boston	MA	02110	617-330-9333		401
InComm Conferencing Inc 208 Harristown Rd Ste 101 *TF:* 877-804-2062 ■ *Web:* www.incommconferencing.com	Glen Rock	NJ	07452	877-804-2062		387
INCON Process Systems LLC PO Box 268 *Web:* www.incontech.com	St Charles	IL	60174	630-305-8556	477-0333	479
Incontact Inc 7730 S Union Pk Ave Ste 500 *NASDAQ: SAAS* ■ *TF:* 800-363-6177 ■ *Web:* www.incontact.com	Salt Lake City	UT	84047	801-320-3200		178-11
Incontrol Technology Inc 1651 e main st *Web:* incontroltechnology.com	El Cajon	CA	92021	619-270-1260		225
Incopro Corp 10827 Tower Oaks Blvd	Houston	TX	77070	281-894-9220		311
Incucomm Inc 5085 W Park Blvd Ste 100 *Web:* www.lone-star.com	Plano	TX	75093	972-690-9494		690
InCycle Software Inc 545 Promenade du Centropolis Ste 220 *TF:* 800-565-0510 ■ *Web:* www.incyclesoftware.com	Laval	QC	H7T0A3	450-682-4777		180
Incyte Corp 1801 Augustine Cut-Off *NASDAQ: INCY* ■ *TF:* 800-564-4220 ■ *Web:* www.incyte.com	Wilmington	DE	19803	302-498-6700		85
Incyte Diagnostics 13103 E Mansfield Ave *Web:* www.incytepathology.com	Spokane Valley	WA	99216	509-892-2700		415
IND Diagnostic Inc 1629 Fosters Way	Delta	BC	V3M6S7	604-522-1619		476
INDA: Assn of the Nonwoven Fabrics Industry 1100 Crescent Green Ste 115 *TF:* 800-628-2112 ■ *Web:* www.inda.org	Cary	NC	27518	919-233-1210	233-1282	49-13
Indaba Capital Management LP 1 Letterman Dr Bldg D Ste DM700 The Presidio of San Francisco *Web:* www.indabacapital.com	San Francisco	CA	94129	415-680-1180		401
Indaco Metal 3 American Way *TF:* 877-750-5614 ■ *Web:* www.indacometals.com	Shawnee	OK	74804	877-300-7334		106
Indak Manufacturing Corp 1915 Techny Rd *Web:* www.indak.com	Northbrook	IL	60062	847-272-0343		729
Indal Technologies Inc 3570 Hawkestone Rd *Web:* www.indaltech.cwfc.com	Mississauga	ON	L5C2V8	905-275-5300		21
Indalco Alloys Inc 939 Gana Ct *Web:* www.indalco.com	Mississauga	ON	L5S1N9	905-564-1151		811
Indco Inc 4040 Earnings Way *TF:* 800-942-4383 ■ *Web:* www.indco.com	New Albany	IN	47150	800-942-4383		190
Indeck Energy Services Inc 600 N Buffalo Grove Rd Ste 300 *Web:* indeckenergy.com	Buffalo Grove	IL	60089	847-520-3212		91
Indeck Keystone Energy LLC 5340 Fryling Rd Ste 200 *Web:* www.indeck-keystone.com	Erie	PA	16510	814-452-6421		612
Indeck Power Equipment Co 1111 Willis Ave *TF:* 800-446-3325 ■ *Web:* www.indeck.com	Wheeling	IL	60090	847-541-8300	541-9984	385
Indeco North America Inc 135 Research Dr *Web:* www.indeco-breakers.com	Milford	CT	06460	203-713-1030		532-3
Indelco Plastics Corp 6530 Cambridge St *TF:* 800-486-6456 ■ *Web:* www.indelco.com	Minneapolis	MN	55426	952-925-5075		605-2
Indel-Davis Inc 4401 S Jackson Ave *TF:* 800-331-6300 ■ *Web:* www.indel-davis.com	Tulsa	OK	74107	918-587-2151	446-1583	539
iNDELIBLE Media Corp 535 Eighth Ave 16th Fl	New York	NY	10018	212-629-0802		514
Indepak Inc 2136 NE 194th Ave *Web:* www.indepak.com	Portland	OR	97230	503-661-6774		596
Independant Insurance Services In 3956 N Pine St *TF:* 800-373-1562 ■ *Web:* qcfreequote.com	Davenport	IA	52806	563-383-5555		390
Independence Blue Cross 1901 Market St **Fax Area Code:* 215 ■ **Fax:* Hum Res ■ *TF:* 800-275-2583 ■ *Web:* www.ibx.com	Philadelphia	PA	19103	800-275-2583	241-0403*	391-3
Independence Bowl Foundation PO Box 1723	Shreveport	LA	71166	318-221-0712		720
Independence Chamber of Commerce 210 W Truman Rd *TF:* 800-222-6400 ■ *Web:* ichamber.biz	Independence	MO	64050	816-252-4745	252-4917	139
Independence City Hall 111 E Maple Ave *Web:* www.ci.independence.mo.us	Independence	MO	64050	816-325-7000	325-7012	337
Independence Community College 1057 W College Ave PO Box 708 **Fax:* Admissions ■ *TF:* 800-842-6063 ■ *Web:* indycc.squarespace.com	Independence	KS	67301	620-331-4100	331-0946*	162
Independence County 192 E Main St *Web:* www.independencecounty.com	Batesville	AR	72501	870-793-8800	793-8803	338
Independence Excavating 5720 Schaaf Rd *TF:* 800-524-3478 ■ *Web:* www.indexc.com	Independence	OH	44131	216-524-1700	524-1701	189-5
Independence FSB 1301 Ninth St NW *Web:* www.ifsb.com	Washington	DC	20001	202-628-5500		70
Independence Hall & Congress Hall Chestnut St-between Fifth & Sixth Sts *Web:* www.nps.gov/inde	Philadelphia	PA	19106	215-597-8787	861-4950	50-3

Phone | Fax | Class

Independence Lumber Inc
407 Lumber Ln. . . . . Independence VA 24348 276-773-3744 773-3723 683
Web: www.indlbr.com

Independence Mall 3500 Oleander Dr. . . . . Wilmington NC 28403 910-392-1776 460
TF: 800-245-4595 ■ *Web:* www.shopindependencemall.com

Independence National Historical Park
143 S Third St . . . . .Philadelphia PA 19106 215-597-8787 861-4950 564
TF: 800-537-7676 ■ *Web:* www.nps.gov/inde

Independence Rock State Historic Site
State Rt 220 . . . . Alcova WY 82620 307-577-5150 565

Independence Seaport Museum
211 S Columbus Blvd. .Philadelphia PA 19106 215-413-8655 925-6713 520
Web: www.phillyseaport.org

Independence Technology LLC
45 Technology Dr . . . . .Warren NJ 07059 908-412-2200 412-2205 477

Independence Tube Corp 6226 W 74th St . . . . . . .Chicago IL 60638 708-496-0380 492
Web: www.independencetube.com

Independent Agent Magazine
127 S Peyton St . . . . .Alexandria VA 22314 800-221-7917 457-5
TF: 800-221-7917 ■ *Web:* www.iamagazine.com

Independent Bank Corp 230 W Main St . . . . Ionia MI 48846 616-527-2400 527-4004 360-2
NASDAQ: IBCP ■ *TF:* 888-300-3193 ■ *Web:* www.independentbank.com

Independent Book Publishers Assn, The (IBPA)
1020 Manhattan Beach Blvd Ste 204 . . . . .Manhattan Beach CA 90266 310-546-1818 546-3939 49-16
TF: 800-327-5113 ■ *Web:* www.ibpa-online.org

Independent Can Co 1300 Brass Mill Rd. . . . . .Belcamp MD 21017 410-272-0090 273-7500 124
TF: 800-363-9822 ■ *Web:* www.independentcan.com

Independent Capital Management
4141 Inland Empire Blvd Ste 301 . . . . .Ontario CA 91764 909-948-1608 401
Web: www.icmfinancial.com

Independent Chemical Corp
79-51 Cooper Ave. . . . . Glendale NY 11385 718-894-0700 894-9224 146
TF: 800-892-2578 ■ *Web:* www.independentchemical.com

Independent Coach Corp 25 Wanser Ave . . . . .Inwood NY 11096 516-239-1100 109
TF: 800-640-4000 ■ *Web:* independentcoach.com

Independent Community Bankers of America (ICBA)
1615 L St NW Ste 900 .Washington DC 20036 202-659-8111 49-2
TF: 800-422-8439 ■ *Web:* www.icba.org

Independent Concrete Pipe Co
3756 Centennial Rd . . . . .Sylvania OH 43560 419-841-3361 183
Web: www.icpipe.com

Independent Educational Consultants Assn (IECA)
3251 Old Lee Hwy Ste 510. . . . . Fairfax VA 22030 703-591-4850 591-4860 49-5
Web: iecaonline.com

Independent Electric Supply Inc
1370 Bayport Ave . . . . .San Carlos CA 94070 650-594-9440 594-0484 246
Web: www.iesupply.com

Independent Equipment Co
2471 McMullen Booth Rd Ste 309 . . . . Clearwater FL 33759 727-796-7733 194
Web: www.iecvalue.com

Independent Film & Television Alliance (IFTA)
10850 Wilshire Blvd 9th Fl. . . . . .Los Angeles CA 90024 310-446-1047 446-1600 49-4
Web: www.ifta-online.org

Independent Financial Agents Inc
14 Walnut Ave. . . . . Clark NJ 07066 732-815-1202 390
TF: 800-388-0462 ■ *Web:* www.ifaauto.com

Independent Food Corp
2072 Orchard Dr E . . . . Twin Falls ID 83301 208-733-0980 473
Web: www.independentmeat.com

Independent Forge Co 692 N Batavia St . . . . .Orange CA 92868 714-997-7337 997-7546 483
Web: www.independentforge.com

Independent Health
511 Farber Lakes Dr . . . . .Buffalo NY 14221 716-631-3001 391-3
TF: 800-247-1466 ■ *Web:* www.independenthealth.com

Independent Ink Inc 13700 Gramercy Pl . . . . .Gardena CA 90249 310-523-4657 329-0943 388
TF: 800-446-5538 ■ *Web:* www.independentink.com

Independent Institute 100 Swan Way . . . . Oakland CA 94621 510-632-1366 568-6040 634
TF: 800-927-8733 ■ *Web:* www.independent.org

Independent Insurance Agents & Brokers of America Inc (IIABA)
127 S Peyton St . . . . Alexandria VA 22314 703-683-4422 683-7556 49-9
TF: 800-221-7917 ■ *Web:* www.independentagent.com

Independent Insurance Agents & Brokers of America PAC (INSURPAC)
412 First St SE Ste 300. . . . . .Washington DC 20003 202-863-7000 863-7015 615
Web: independentagent.com

Independent Jewelers Organization (IJO)
136 Old Post Rd . . . . .Southport CT 06890 800-624-9252 254-7429* 49-4
**Fax Area Code:* 203 ■ *TF:* 800-624-9252 ■ *Web:* www.ijo.com

Independent Liquid Terminals Assn (ILTA)
1005 N Glebe Rd Ste 600. Arlington DC 22201 202-842-9200 326-8660 49-21
Web: www.ilta.org

Independent Living Resource Center Inc, The
423 W Victoria St . . . . Santa Barbara CA 93101 805-963-1350 768
TF: 800-300-4326 ■ *Web:* www.ilrc-trico.org

Independent Lubricant Manufacturers Assn (ILMA)
400 N Columbus St Ste 201. . . . . .Alexandria VA 22314 703-684-5574 836-8503 49-13
TF: 800-624-9663 ■ *Web:* www.ilma.org

Independent Mechanical Industries Inc
4155 N Knox Ave . . . . .Chicago IL 60641 773-282-4500 282-2046 189-10
Web: www.independentmech.com

Independent Office Products & Furniture Dealers Assn (IOPFDA)
3601 E Joppa Rd . . . . .Baltimore MD 21234 410-931-8100 931-8111 49-4
TF: 800-252-6232 ■ *Web:* www.nopanet.org

Independent Order of Foresters (IOF)
789 Don Mills Rd . . . . Toronto ON M3C1T9 416-429-3000 271-6215* 48-5
**Fax Area Code:* 866 ■ *TF:* 800-828-1540 ■ *Web:* www.foresters.com

Independent Order of Odd Fellows
422 N Trade St . . . . Winston-Salem NC 27101 336-725-5955 722-7317 48-15
TF: 800-235-8358 ■ *Web:* www.ioof.org

Independent Packing Services Inc
7600-32nd Ave N . . . . .Crystal MN 55427 763-425-7155 549
Web: www.ipsipack.com

Independent Petroleum Assn of America (IPAA)
1201 15th St NW Ste 300. . . . . .Washington DC 20005 202-857-4722 857-4799 48-12
TF: 800-433-2851 ■ *Web:* www.ipaa.org

Independent Pipe & Supply Corp
Whitman Rd . . . . .Canton MA 02021 781-828-8500 612
Web: www.indpipe.com

Independent Protection Company Inc
1607 S Main St. . . . . Goshen IN 46526 574-533-4116 534-3719 815
TF: 800-860-8388 ■ *Web:* www.ipclp.com

Independent Publishers Group
814 N Franklin St . . . . .Chicago IL 60610 312-337-0747 337-5985 96
TF Orders: 800-888-4741 ■ *Web:* www.ipgbook.com

Independent Publishing Co
1000 Williamston Rd . . . . .Anderson SC 29621 864-224-4321 260-1276 637-8
TF: 800-859-6397 ■ *Web:* www.independentmail.com

Independent Record 317 Cruse Ave . . . . .Helena MT 59601 406-447-4000 447-4052 532-2
TF: 800-523-2272 ■ *Web:* www.helenair.com

Independent Rental Inc
2020 S Cushman St . . . . .Fairbanks AK 99701 888-456-6595 456-2927* 264-2
**Fax Area Code:* 907 ■ *TF:* 888-456-6595 ■ *Web:* www.independentrental.com

Independent Roofing Consultants
2901 Tullman St . . . . Santa Ana CA 92705 949-476-8626 476-9810 193
Web: www.irctech.com

Independent Sector
1602 L St NW Ste 900 .Washington DC 20036 202-467-6100 467-6101 48-5
Web: www.independentsector.org

Independent Stave Company Inc
1078 S Jefferson PO Box 104. . . . . .Lebanon MO 65536 417-588-4151 200
Web: independentstavecompany.com

Independent Television Service (ITVS)
651 Brannan St Ste 410 . . . . San Francisco CA 94107 415-356-8383 356-8391 742
TF: 888-572-8918 ■ *Web:* www.itvs.org

Independent Weekly PO Box 2690 . . . . Durham NC 27715 919-286-1972 286-4274 532-5
TF: 800-838-3006 ■ *Web:* www.indyweek.com

Independent, The 2250 First St . . . . Livermore CA 94550 925-447-8700 447-0212 532-4
TF: 877-952-3588 ■ *Web:* www.independentnews.com

Independents Service Co
2710 Market St. . . . . Hannibal MO 63401 573-221-4615 194
TF: 800-325-3694 ■ *Web:* www.isco.net

Indera Mills Co
350 W Maple St PO Box 309 . . . . Yadkinville NC 27055 336-679-4440 679-4475 155-18
TF: 800-334-8605 ■ *Web:* www.inderamills.com

Inderbitzin Distributors Inc
901 Valley Ave NW . . . . Puyallup WA 98371 253-922-2592 297-8
Web: www.inderbitzin.com

Index Engines Inc 960 Holmdel Rd . . . . .Holmdel NJ 07733 732-817-1060 54
Web: www.indexengines.com

Index Fresh Inc 18184 Slover Ave . . . . Bloomington CA 92316 909-877-0999 877-0495 11-1
TF: 800-352-6931 ■ *Web:* www.indexfresh.com

Index Funds Advisors Inc
19200 Von Karman Ave Ste 150. . . . . .Irvine CA 92612 949-502-0050 690
TF: 888-643-3133 ■ *Web:* ifa.com

Index Journal 610 Phoenix St. . . . . Greenwood SC 29648 864-223-1411 223-7331 532-2
Web: www.indexjournal.com

Index Packaging Inc
1055 White Mountain Hwy . . . . Milton NH 03851 603-652-4406 601
Web: www.indexpackaging.com

Indexing Technologies Inc
37 Orchard St . . . . Ramsey NJ 07446 201-934-6333 358
Web: www.ititooling.com

Indexx Inc 303 Haywood Rd. . . . . Greenville SC 29607 864-234-1024 627
TF: 800-252-8227 ■ *Web:* www.Indexx.com

India 235 E 43rd St . . . . .New York NY 10017 212-490-9660 490-9656 784
Web: www.un.int
Consulate General
540 Arguello Blvd . . . . San Francisco CA 94118 415-668-0662 668-9764 257
TF: 866-978-0055 ■ *Web:* www.cgisf.org
Consulate General
455 N Cityfront Plaza Dr Ste 850 . . . . .Chicago IL 60611 312-595-0405 595-0417 257
TF: 800-860-8610 ■ *Web:* www.indianconsulate.com
Embassy 2107 Massachusetts Ave NW . . . . . . .Washington DC 20008 202-939-7000 265-4351 257
TF: 800-333-4636 ■ *Web:* www.indianembassy.org
Embassy - Consular Wing
2536 Massachusetts Ave NW. . . . . .Washington DC 20008 202-939-9806 257
Web: www.indianembassy.org

India Bistro 2301 NW Market St . . . . Seattle WA 98107 206-783-5080 297-9069 671
Web: www.seattleindiabistro.com

India Community Center Inc
555 Los Coches St . . . . Milpitas CA 95035 408-934-1130 354
Web: www.indiacc.org

India Garden
830 Broad Ripple Ave . . . . .Indianapolis IN 46220 317-253-6060 253-2832 671
Web: www.indiagardenindy.com

India Garden 1107 N Broadway. . . . . .Rochester MN 55906 507-288-6280 671
Web: indiagardenrestaurantmn.com

India Garden 328 Atwood St . . . . Pittsburgh PA 15213 412-682-3000 671
Web: www.indiagarden.net

India Globalization Capital Inc
4336 Montgomery Ave . . . . Bethesda MD 20814 301-983-0998 465-0273* 188-4
NYSE: IGC ■ **Fax Area Code:* 240 ■ *Web:* www.indiaglobalcap.com

India House 1711 N University Dr . . . . Plantation FL 33322 954-565-5701 671
Web: www.indiahouserestaurant.com

India House Restaurant
207 Colchester Ave. . . . . Burlington VT 05401 802-862-7800 671

India K'Raja 9051 W Broad St. . . . . Richmond VA 23294 804-965-6345 671
Web: www.indiakraja.com

India Mahal 5970 Brainerd Rd. . . . . Chattanooga TN 37421 423-510-9651 671

India Oven 1031 Patricia . . . . .San Antonio TX 78213 210-366-1030 671
Web: www.indiaoven.biz

India Palace 413 Tate St . . . . Greensboro NC 27403 336-379-0744 671

India Palace 227 Don Gaspar Ave. . . . . .Santa Fe NM 87501 505-986-5859 671

India palace 3021 34th St. .Lubbock TX 79410 806-799-6772 671

India Palace 4213 Lafayette Rd . . . . .Indianapolis IN 46254 317-298-0773 671
Web: www.indiapalaceindy.com

India Palace 1720 Poplar Ave. . . . . Memphis TN 38104 901-278-1199 671

India Palace 377 Ct St. . . . . Salem OR 97301 503-371-4808 671

India Palace 2941 W Bell Rd. Phoenix AZ 85053 602-942-4224 671
Web: indiapalacephoenix.com

India Palace 319 W Superior St . . . . Duluth MN 55802 218-727-8767 671

India Palace Restaurant
12817 Preston Rd Ste 105 . . . . Dallas TX 75230 972-392-0190 671
TF: 800-290-0629 ■ *Web:* www.indiapalacedallas.com

				Phone	Fax	Class
India Palace Restaurant 6963 S Lewis Ave	Tulsa	OK	74136	918-492-8040		671
TF: 800-760-6700 ■ *Web:* theindiapalacetulsa.com						
India Palace Restaurant 8474 Fredericksburg Rd	San Antonio	TX	78229	210-692-5262		671
Web: www.indiapalacesa.com						
India Quality 484 Commonwealth Ave	Boston	MA	02215	617-267-4499	267-4477	671
Web: www.indiaquality.com						
India Tourist Office 3550 Wilshire Blvd Ste 204	Los Angeles	CA	90010	213-380-8855	380-6111	775
Web: www.incredibleindia.org						
India Tourist Office 1270 Ave of the Americas Ste 303	New York	NY	10020	212-586-4901	582-3274	775
Web: www.incredibleindia.org						
India's Restaurant 8921 East Hampden Ave	Denver	CO	80231	303-755-4284	752-9814	671
Web: www.indiasrestaurant.com						
India's Oven 11645 Wilshire Blvd	Los Angeles	CA	90025	310-207-5522		671
Web: www.laindiasoven.com						
India's Restaurant 5230 Essen Ln	Baton Rouge	LA	70809	225-769-0600		671
India's Tandoori 5468 Wilshire Blvd	Los Angeles	CA	90036	323-936-2050		671
Web: www.indiastandoori.net						
Indian Arts & Crafts Assn (IACA) 4010 Carlisle Blvd NE Ste C	Albuquerque	NM	87107	505-265-9149	265-8251	48-4
Web: www.iaca.com						
Indian Arts & Crafts Board Dept of the Interior 1849 C St NW MS 2528-MIB	Washington	DC	20240	202-208-3773	208-5196	340-20
TF: 888-278-3253 ■ *Web:* www.doi.gov/iacb						
Indian Bible College 2918 N Aris Ave	Flagstaff	AZ	86004	928-774-3890	774-2655	166
TF: 866-503-7789 ■ *Web:* www.indianbible.org						
Indian Biriyani House 1589 Bank St	Ottawa	ON	K1H7Z3	613-260-3893		671
Web: indianbiriyanihouse.ca						
Indian Capital Technology Ctr 2403 N 41st St E	Muskogee	OK	74403	918-687-6383		800
TF: 800-757-0877 ■ *Web:* www.ictctech.com						
Indian Cave State Park 65296 720 Rd	Shubert	NE	68437	402-883-2575		565
Web: gonebraskacity.com						
Indian Creek Fabricators 1350 Commerce Pk Dr	Tipp City	OH	45371	937-667-5818	667-4093	757
TF: 877-769-5880 ■ *Web:* www.indiancreekfab.com						
Indian Creek Foundation 420 Cowpath Rd	Souderton	PA	18964	267-203-1500		726
TF: 800-732-0999 ■ *Web:* www.indcreek.org						
Indian Creek Hotel 2727 Indian Creek Dr	Miami Beach	FL	33140	305-531-2727	531-5651	379
Web: www.thefreehand.com						
Indian Creek Nature Ctr 6665 Otis Rd SE	Cedar Rapids	IA	52403	319-362-0664		50-5
Web: www.indiancreeknaturecenter.org						
Indian Creek Recreation Area 12905 288th Ave	Mobridge	SD	57601	605-845-7112		565
Web: www.gfp.sd.gov/state-parks/directory/indian-creek						
Indian Ctr Museum 650 N Seneca St	Wichita	KS	67203	316-350-3340		520
Web: theindiancenter.org						
Indian Electric Co-op Inc 2506 E Hwy 64	Cleveland	OK	74020	918-358-2514		245
TF: 800-482-2750 ■ *Web:* www.iecok.com						
Indian Garden 247 E Ontario St 2nd Fl	Chicago	IL	60611	312-280-4910	280-4934	671
Web: www.indiangardenchicago.com						
Indian Grinding Rock State Historic Park 14881 Pine Grove-Volcano Rd	Pine Grove	CA	95665	209-296-7488		565
Web: www.parks.ca.gov/default.asp?page_id=553						
Indian Harvest Specialtifoods Inc 1012 Paul Bunyan Dr SE	Bemidji	MN	56601	800-346-7032	751-8519*	296-23
**Fax Area Code:* 218 ■ *TF Orders:* 800-346-7032 ■ *Web:* inharvest.com						
Indian Head Industries Inc 8530 Cliff Cameron Dr	Charlotte	NC	28269	704-547-7411	547-9367	60
TF: 800-527-1534 ■ *Web:* mgmbrakes.com						
Indian Health Service (IHS) 801 Thompson Ave Ste 400	Rockville	MD	20852	301-443-1083		340-10
Indian Hill Journal 394 Wards Corner Ste 170	Loveland	OH	45140	513-248-8600		637-8
Indian Hills Community College 525 Grandview Ave	Ottumwa	IA	52501	641-683-5111	683-5741	162
TF: 800-726-2585 ■ *Web:* www.indianhills.edu						
Indian Hills State Recreation Area & Resort 7302 14th St NW	Garrison	ND	58763	701-743-4122		565
Web: www.parkrec.nd.gov/recreationareas/ihra/ihra.html						
Indian Hot Springs 302 Soda Creek Rd PO Box 1990	Idaho Springs	CO	80452	303-989-6666		669
TF: 800-884-3201 ■ *Web:* www.indianhotsprings.com						
Indian Key Historic State Park 77200 Overseas Hwy	Islamorada	FL	33036	305-664-2540		565
Web: www.floridastateparks.org/indiankey						
Indian King Tavern State Historic Site 233 Kings Hwy	Haddonfield	NJ	08033	856-429-6792		565
Web: www.njparksandforests.org						
Indian Lake State Park 8970W County Rd 442	Manistique	MI	49854	906-341-2355		565
Web: www.michigandnr.com						
Indian Lake State Park 12774 State Rt 235 N	Lakeview	OH	43331	937-843-2717		565
Web: www.ohiodnr.com						
Indian Mountain School 211 Indian Mtn Rd	Lakeville	CT	06039	860-435-0871	435-0641	622
Web: www.indianmountain.org						
Indian Mountain State Park 143 State Pk Cir	Jellico	TN	37762	423-784-7958		565
Web: www.state.tn.us						
Indian Oven 1010 Howard St	Omaha	NE	68102	402-342-4856		671
Web: findmeglutenfree.com						
Indian Oven 233 Fillmore St	San Francisco	CA	94117	415-626-1628		671
Web: www.indianovensf.com						
Indian Oven 427 E Main St	Columbus	OH	43215	614-220-9390		671
Web: www.indianoven.com						
Indian Path Medical Ctr 2000 Brookside Dr	Kingsport	TN	37660	423-857-7000		374-3
Web: www.mountainstateshealth.com/ipmc						
Indian Pueblo Cultural Ctr 2401 12th St NW	Albuquerque	NM	87104	505-843-7270		520
TF: 866-855-7902 ■ *Web:* www.indianpueblo.org						
Indian River County 1801 27th St	Vero Beach	FL	32960	772-567-8000	978-1822	338
Web: www.ircgov.com						
Indian River County Chamber of Commerce 1216 21st St	Vero Beach	FL	32960	772-567-3491	778-3181	139
Web: www.indianriverchamber.com						
Indian River County Library (IRCL) 1600 21st St	Vero Beach	FL	32960	772-770-5060	770-5066	434-3
Web: www.irclibrary.org						
Indian River Estates 2250 Indian Creek Blvd W	Vero Beach	FL	32966	772-562-7400		672
TF Mktg: 800-544-0277 ■ *Web:* www.actsretirement.org						
Indian River Exchange Packers Inc 7355 Ninth St SW	Vero Beach	FL	32968	772-562-2252		11-1
Web: irexp.com						
Indian River Juvenile Correctional Facility 2775 Indian River Rd SW	Massillon	OH	44646	330-837-4211	837-4740	412
Web: www.dys.ohio.gov						
Indian River Lifesaving Station Museum 25039 Costal Hwy	Rehoboth Beach	DE	19971	302-227-6991	227-6438	520
TF: 877-987-2757 ■ *Web:* www.destateparks.com						
Indian River Medical Ctr 1000 36th St	Vero Beach	FL	32960	772-567-4311	562-5628	374-3
Web: www.indianrivermedicalcenter.com						
Indian River State College (IRSC) 3209 Virginia Ave	Fort Pierce	FL	34981	772-462-4772	462-4699	162
TF: 866-792-4772 ■ *Web:* www.irsc.edu						
Indian River Transport Co 2580 Executive Rd	Winter Haven	FL	33884	863-324-2430	326-9702	780
TF: 800-877-2430 ■ *Web:* www.indianrivertransport.com						
Indian Springs Mfg Company Inc 2095 W Genesse Rd	Baldwinsville	NY	13027	315-635-6101		326
Web: www.indiansprings.com						
Indian Springs Resort & Spa 1712 Lincoln Ave	Calistoga	CA	94515	707-942-4913	942-4919	669
TF: 800-877-3623 ■ *Web:* www.indianspringscalistoga.com						
Indian Springs School 190 Woodward Dr	Pelham	AL	35124	205-988-3350	988-3797	622
TF General: 888-843-9477 ■ *Web:* www.indiansprings.org						
Indian Springs State Park 678 Lake Clark Rd	Flovilla	GA	30216	770-504-2277		565
Web: www.gastateparks.org						
Indian Summer Carpet Mills Inc 601 Callahan Rd PO Box 3577	Dalton	GA	30719	706-277-6277	279-1884	131
TF: 800-824-4010 ■ *Web:* www.southwindcarpet.com						
Indian Summer Co-op 3958 W Chauvez Rd	Ludington	MI	49431	231-845-6248		296-20
Indian Temple Mound Museum 107 Miracle Strip Pkwy SW	Fort Walton Beach	FL	32548	850-833-9500	833-9640	520
TF: 866-847-1301 ■ *Web:* www.fwb.org						
Indian Trails Inc 109 E Comstock St	Owosso	MI	48867	989-725-5105		107
TF: 800-292-3831 ■ *Web:* www.indiantrails.com						
Indian Valley Chamber of Commerce 100 Penn Ave	Telford	PA	18969	215-723-9472	723-2490	139
Web: www.indianvalleychamber.com						
Indian Valley Industries Inc PO Box 810	Johnson City	NY	13790	607-729-5111	729-5158	67
TF: 800-659-5111 ■ *Web:* www.iviindustries.com						
Indian Well State Park c/o Osbornedale State Pk 555 Roosevelt Dr	Derby	CT	06418	203-735-4311		565
Web: www.ct.gov						
Indian Wells Resort Hotel 76-661 Hwy 111	Indian Wells	CA	92210	760-345-6466	772-5083	669
TF: 800-248-3220 ■ *Web:* www.indianwellsresort.com						
Indiana						
Agriculture Dept 101 W Ohio St Ste 1200	Indianapolis	IN	46204	317-234-7707		339-15
Web: www.in.gov/isda						
Arts Commission 150 W Market St Ste 618	Indianapolis	IN	46204	317-232-1268	232-5595	339-15
Web: www.in.gov/arts						
Attorney General 302 W Washington St 5th Fl	Indianapolis	IN	46204	317-232-6201	232-7979	339-15
Web: www.in.gov/attorneygeneral						
Bill Status State House 200 W Washington St	Indianapolis	IN	46204	317-232-9400		433
Web: www.in.gov/apps/lsa/session/billwatch						
Child Support Bureau 402 W Washington St	Indianapolis	IN	46204	317-233-5437		339-15
TF: 800-840-8757 ■ *Web:* www.in.gov/dcs/support						
Consumer Protection Div 402 W Washington St 5th Fl	Indianapolis	IN	46204	317-232-6330	233-4393	339-15
TF: 800-382-5516 ■ *Web:* www.in.gov						
Correction Dept 302 W Washington St Rm E334	Indianapolis	IN	46204	317-232-5711		339-15
Web: in.gov/idoc						
Disability Aging & Rehabilitative Services Div 402 W Washington St Ste W453	Indianapolis	IN	46207	317-232-1147	232-1240	339-15
TF: 800-545-7763 ■ *Web:* www.in.gov						
Economic Development Corp 1 N Capitol Ave Ste 700	Indianapolis	IN	46204	317-232-8800	232-4146	339-15
TF: 800-463-8081 ■ *Web:* www.iedc.in.gov						
Education Dept 115 W Washington St Ste 600	Indianapolis	IN	46204	317-232-6610		339-15
Environmental Management Dept 100 N Senate Ave	Indianapolis	IN	46204	317-232-8603		339-15
TF: 800-451-6027 ■ *Web:* www.in.gov/idem						
Family & Social Services Admin 402 W Washington St Rm W-392 PO Box 7083	Indianapolis	IN	46207	800-545-7763		339-15
TF: 800-403-0864 ■ *Web:* www.in.gov/fssa						
Finance Authority 1 N Capitol Ave Ste 900	Indianapolis	IN	46204	317-233-4332	232-6786	339-15
Web: www.in.gov						

Name / Address	City	State	ZIP	Phone	Fax	Class
Financial Institutions Dept 402 W Washington St PO Box 7083 *Web:* www.in.gov	Indianapolis	IN	46204	317-542-3449	232-6478	339-15
Fish & Wildlife Div 402 W Washington St Rm W273 *Web:* www.in.gov/dnr/fishwild	Indianapolis	IN	46204	317-232-4080	232-8150	339-15
General Assembly State House 200 W Washington St *TF:* 800-382-9842 ■ *Web:* www.in.gov/legislative	Indianapolis	IN	46204	317-232-9600	232-2554	339-15
Governor State House 200 W Washington St Rm 206 *Web:* www.in.gov	Indianapolis	IN	46204	317-232-6531	233-3283	339-15
Health Dept 2 N Meridian St *TF:* 800-382-9480 ■ *Web:* www.in.gov	Indianapolis	IN	46204	317-233-1325		339-15
Higher Education Commission 101 W Ohio St Ste 550 *Web:* www.in.gov	Indianapolis	IN	46204	317-464-4400	464-4410	339-15
Historical Bureau 140 N Senate Ave Rm 130 *Web:* www.in.gov/history	Indianapolis	IN	46204	317-232-2535	232-1659	339-15
Homeland Security Dept 302 W Washington St Rm E208 *TF:* 800-457-8283 ■ *Web:* www.in.gov/dhs	Indianapolis	IN	46204	317-232-3980		339-15
Horse Racing Commission 150 W Market St Ste 530 *Web:* www.in.gov	Indianapolis	IN	46204	317-233-3119	233-4470	712
Housing Finance Authority 30 S Meridian St Ste 1000 *TF:* 800-872-0371 ■ *Web:* www.in.gov	Indianapolis	IN	46204	317-232-7777		339-15
Insurance Dept 311 W Washington St Ste 300 *TF Cust Svc:* 800-622-4461 ■ *Web:* www.in.gov	Indianapolis	IN	46204	317-232-2385	232-5251	339-15
Labor Dept 402 W Washington St Rm W195 *Web:* www.in.gov/labor	Indianapolis	IN	46204	317-232-2655	233-3790	339-15
Lieutenant Governor 200 W Washington St Ste 230 *Web:* in.gov/lg	Indianapolis	IN	46204	317-232-9856		339-15
Motor Vehicles Bureau 100 N Senate Ave Rm 402 *Web:* www.in.gov	Indianapolis	IN	46204	317-233-6000	233-3135	339-15
Natural Resources Dept 402 W Washington St *TF:* 877-463-6367 ■ *Web:* www.in.gov/dnr	Indianapolis	IN	46204	317-232-4200	233-6811	339-15
Parole Services Div 302 W Washington St Rm E-334 *Web:* in.gov/ai/errors/idoc_404.html	Indianapolis	IN	46204	317-232-5757		339-15
Port Commission 150 W Market St Ste 100 *TF:* 800-232-7678 ■ *Web:* www.portsofindiana.com	Indianapolis	IN	46204	317-232-9200	232-0137	618
Professional Licensing Agency 302 W Washington St Rm E072 *Web:* www.in.gov/pla	Indianapolis	IN	46204	317-232-2980		339-15
Revenue Dept 100 N Senate Ave Rm N105 *Web:* www.in.gov/dor	Indianapolis	IN	46204	317-232-2240	232-1021	339-15
Secretary of State 200 W Washington St Rm 201 *Web:* www.in.gov	Indianapolis	IN	46204	317-232-6531	233-3283	339-15
Securities Div 302 W Washington St 5th Fl *TF:* 800-382-5516 ■ *Web:* www.in.gov	Indianapolis	IN	46204	317-232-6201	232-7979	339-15
State Court Administration Div 30 S Meridian St Ste 500 *Web:* www.in.gov	Indianapolis	IN	46204	317-232-2542	233-6586	339-15
State Ethics Commission 315 W Ohio St Rm 104 *TF:* 866-805-8498 ■ *Web:* www.in.gov/ig	Indianapolis	IN	46202	317-232-3850	232-0707	205
State Government Information 402 W Washington St Rm W160A *TF:* 800-457-8283 ■ *Web:* www.in.gov	Indianapolis	IN	46204	317-233-0800		339-15
State Parks & Reservoirs Div 402 W Washington St Rm W298 *TF:* 800-622-4931 ■ *Web:* www.in.gov	Indianapolis	IN	46204	317-232-4124	232-4132	339-15
State Police 100 N Senate Ave Ste N302 *Web:* www.in.gov/isp	Indianapolis	IN	46204	317-232-8262		339-15
Students Assistance Commission 150 W Market St Ste 500 *TF:* 888-528-4719 ■ *Web:* www.in.gov	Indianapolis	IN	46204	317-232-2350	232-3260	725
Supreme Court State House *Web:* www.in.gov/judiciary/supreme	Indianapolis	IN	46204	317-232-2540		339-15
Technology Office 100 N Senate Ave Room N-551 *TF:* 800-382-1095 ■ *Web:* www.in.gov	Indianapolis	IN	46204	317-234-4357	232-0748	339-15
Tourism Development Office 1 N Capitol Ave Ste 600 *TF:* 800-457-8283 ■ *Web:* www.in.gov	Indianapolis	IN	46204	317-232-8860	233-6887	339-15
Transportation Dept 100 N Senate Ave Rm N755 *Web:* www.in.gov	Indianapolis	IN	46204	317-232-5533	232-0238	339-15
Treasurer State House 200 W Washington St Rm 242 *Web:* www.in.gov/tos	Indianapolis	IN	46204	317-232-6386	233-1780	339-15
Utility Regulatory Commission 302 W Washington St Rm E306 *Web:* www.in.gov/iurc	Indianapolis	IN	46204	317-232-2701	232-6758	339-15
Veterans' Affairs Dept 302 W Washington St Rm E120 *Web:* www.in.gov	Indianapolis	IN	46204	317-232-3910	232-7721	339-15
Victims Services Div 101 W Washington St Ste 1170 East Tower *TF:* 800-353-1484 ■ *Web:* www.in.gov	Indianapolis	IN	46204	317-232-1233	233-3912	339-15
Vital Records Office PO Box 7125 *Web:* www.cdc.gov/nchs/w2w/indiana.htm	Indianapolis	IN	46206	317-233-2700		339-15
Weights & Measures Div 2525 Shadeland Ave Unit D3 *Web:* www.in.gov/isdh/23288.htm	Indianapolis	IN	46219	317-356-7078	351-2877	339-15
Worker's Compensation Board 402 W Washington St Rm W196 *Web:* in.gov/wcb	Indianapolis	IN	46204	317-232-3808		339-15
Workforce Development Dept 10 N Senate Ave Rm SE 203 *TF:* 800-891-6499 ■ *Web:* www.in.gov	Indianapolis	IN	46204	317-232-7670		259
Indiana Assn of Realtors 320 N Meridian St Ste 428 **Fax Area Code:* 303 ■ *TF:* 800-284-0084 ■ *Web:* www.indianarealtors.com	Indianapolis	IN	46204	800-284-0084	741-1070*	656
Indiana Association of School Principals Inc 11025 E 25th St *TF:* 800-285-2188 ■ *Web:* www.iasp.org	Indianapolis	IN	46229	317-891-9900		533
Indiana Automotive Fasteners Inc 1300 Anderson Blvd *Web:* www.iafi.com	Greenfield	IN	46140	317-467-0100		278
Indiana Bankers Assn 6925 Parkdale Pl *Web:* www.indianabankers.org	Indianapolis	IN	46254	317-387-9380		70
Indiana Basketball Hall of Fame 408 Trojan Ln *TF:* 800-677-9800 ■ *Web:* www.hoopshall.com	New Castle	IN	47362	765-529-1891	529-0273	522
Indiana Beach 5224 E Indiana Beach Rd *Web:* www.indianabeach.com	Monticello	IN	47960	574-583-4141		32
Indiana Black Expo Inc 3145 N Meridian St *Web:* www.indianablackexpo.com	Indianapolis	IN	46208	317-925-2702		138
Indiana Convention Ctr & Lucas Oil Stadium (ICCLOS) 100 S Capitol Ave *TF:* 800-369-6220 ■ *Web:* www.icclos.com	Indianapolis	IN	46225	317-262-3400	262-3685	205
Indiana County 350 N Fourth St *TF:* 888-559-6355 ■ *Web:* www.countyofindiana.org	Indiana	PA	15701	724-465-3805	465-3179	338
Indiana County Chamber of Commerce 1019 Philadelphia St *TF:* 800-522-2376 ■ *Web:* www.indianapa.com	Indiana	PA	15701	724-465-2511		139
Indiana County Tourist Bureau 2334 Oakland Ave Ste 68 *TF:* 877-746-3426 ■ *Web:* www.visitindianacountypa.org	Indiana	PA	15701	724-463-7505	465-3819	206
Indiana Credit Union League 5975 Castle Creek Pkwy N Ste 300 *TF:* 800-285-5300 ■ *Web:* icul.org	Indianapolis	IN	46250	317-594-5300		219
Indiana Democratic Party 115 W Washington St Ste 1165 *TF:* 800-223-3387 ■ *Web:* www.indems.org	Indianapolis	IN	46204	317-231-7100	231-7129	616-1
Indiana Dental Assn 1319 E Stop 10 Rd *TF:* 800-562-5646 ■ *Web:* www.indental.org	Indianapolis	IN	46227	317-634-2610	634-2612	227
Indiana Dimension Inc 1621 W Market St *TF:* 888-875-4434 ■ *Web:* indianadimension.com	Logansport	IN	46947	888-875-4434		683
Indiana Donor Network 3760 Guion Rd *TF:* 888-275-4676 ■ *Web:* indianadonornetwork.org	Indianapolis	IN	46222	317-685-0389		545
Indiana Dunes Environmental Learning Center Inc 700 Howe Rd *Web:* www.duneslearningcenter.org	Chesterton	IN	46304	219-395-9555		242
Indiana Dunes National Lakeshore 1100 N Mineral Springs Rd *TF:* 800-654-7309 ■ *Web:* www.nps.gov/indu	Porter	IN	46304	219-395-1772	926-7561	564
Indiana Dunes State Park 1600 N 25 E *Web:* www.in.gov	Chesterton	IN	46304	219-926-1952		565
Indiana Dunes the Casual Coast 1215 N State Rd 49 *TF:* 800-283-8687 ■ *Web:* www.indianadunes.com	Porter	IN	46304	219-926-2255	929-5395	206
Indiana Farm Bureau Insurance Co 225 SE St PO Box 1250 *TF:* 800-723-3276 ■ *Web:* www.infarmbureau.com	Indianapolis	IN	46206	317-692-7200		391-2
Indiana Farmers Mutual Insurance Co 10 W 106th St *TF:* 800-666-6460 ■ *Web:* www.indianafarmers.com	Indianapolis	IN	46290	317-846-4211		391-4
Indiana Football Hall of Fame 815 N A St PO Box 40 *TF:* 800-828-8414 ■ *Web:* www.indiana-football.org	Richmond	IN	47374	765-966-2235	966-5700	522
Indiana Furniture 1224 Mill St *TF:* 800-422-5727 ■ *Web:* www.indianafurniture.com	Jasper	IN	47546	812-482-5727	482-9035	319-1
Indiana Gazette 899 Water St *TF:* 800-321-0350 ■ *Web:* indianagazette.com	Indiana	PA	15701	724-465-5555	465-8267	532-2
Indiana Harbor Belt Railroad Co 2721 161st St *Web:* www.ihbrr.com	Hammond	IN	46323	219-989-4703	989-4707	651
Indiana Hardwood Specialists Inc 4341 N US Hwy 231 *Web:* indianahardwoodspec.com	Spencer	IN	47460	812-829-4866	829-4860	683
Indiana Health Information Exchange Inc 846 N Senate Ave Ste 300 *TF:* 800-275-8777 ■ *Web:* www.ihie.org	Indianapolis	IN	46202	317-644-1750		194
Indiana Heat Transfer Corp 500 W Harrison St *Web:* www.ihtc.net	Plymouth	IN	46563	574-936-3171		61
Indiana Knitwear Corp 230 E Osage St	Greenfield	IN	46140	317-462-4413		155-12
Indiana Library Federation (ILF) 941 E 86th St Ste 260 *TF:* 800-326-0013 ■ *Web:* www.ilfonline.org	Indianapolis	IN	46240	317-257-2040	257-1389	435
Indiana Medical History Museum 3045 W Vermont St *Web:* imhm.org	Indianapolis	IN	46222	317-635-7329	635-7349	520
Indiana Members Credit Union (IMCU) 7110 W Tenth St *TF:* 800-556-9268 ■ *Web:* www.imcu.com	Indianapolis	IN	46214	317-248-8556		219
Indiana Memorial Union Board 900 E Seventh St Rm 270 *TF:* 800-784-8669 ■ *Web:* www.imu.indiana.edu	Bloomington	IN	47405	812-855-4682		379
Indiana Mills & Manufacturing Inc 18881 US 31 N *Web:* www.imminet.com	Westfield	IN	46074	317-896-9531	896-2142	576

	City	State	Zip	Phone	Fax	Class
Indiana Newspapers Inc						
307 N Pennsylvania Pkwy	Indianapolis	IN	46206	317-444-4000		637-8
Web: indystar.com						
Indiana Pacers						
Conseco Fieldhouse						
125 S Pennsylvania St	Indianapolis	IN	46204	317-917-2500	917-2599	714-1
TF: 800-745-3000 ■ *Web:* www.nba.com/pacers						
Indiana Pharmacists Alliance						
729 N Pennsylvania St	Indianapolis	IN	46204	317-634-4968	632-1219	585
TF: 800-516-0313 ■ *Web:* netforum.avectra.com						
Indiana Precision Inc						
1201 E Elmore St	Crawfordsville	IN	47933	765-361-0247		596
Web: www.indianaprecision.com						
Indiana Printing & Publishing Co						
899 Water St PO Box 10	Indiana	PA	15701	724-465-5555	465-8267	637-8
TF: 800-262-3077 ■ *Web:* www.indianagazette.com						
Indiana Rail Road Co, The						
101 W Ohio St Ste 1600	Indianapolis	IN	46204	317-262-5140		649
TF: 888-596-2121 ■ *Web:* www.inrd.com						
Indiana Regional Medical Ctr						
835 Hospital Rd	Indiana	PA	15701	724-357-7000	357-7449	374-3
Web: www.indianarmc.org						
Indiana Repertory Theatre Inc						
140 W Washington St	Indianapolis	IN	46204	317-635-5277	236-0767	573-4
Web: www.irtlive.com						
Indiana Republican Party						
101 W Ohio St Ste 2200	Indianapolis	IN	46204	317-635-7561	632-8510	616-2
Web: indiana.gop						
Indiana Ribbon Inc 106 N Second St	Wolcott	IN	47995	219-279-2112		548
TF: 800-531-3100 ■ *Web:* www.giftwrapgifts.com						
Indiana State Bar Assn						
1 Indiana Sq Ste 530	Indianapolis	IN	46204	317-639-5465	266-2588	72
TF: 800-266-2581 ■ *Web:* www.inbar.org						
Indiana State Chamber of Commerce						
115 W Washington St Ste 850-S	Indianapolis	IN	46204	317-264-3110	264-6855	140
TF: 800-824-6885 ■ *Web:* www.indianachamber.com						
Indiana State Fairgrounds						
1202 E 38th St	Indianapolis	IN	46205	317-927-7500	927-7695	642
Web: www.in.gov						
Indiana State Library (ISL)						
140 N Senate Ave	Indianapolis	IN	46204	317-232-3694	232-3728	434-5
TF: 800-451-6028 ■ *Web:* www.in.gov/library						
Indiana State Medical Assn						
322 Canal Walk	Indianapolis	IN	46202	317-261-2060	261-2076	474
TF: 800-257-4762 ■ *Web:* www.ismanet.org						
Indiana State Museum						
650 W Washington St	Indianapolis	IN	46204	317-232-1637		520
TF: 800-382-9842 ■ *Web:* www.in.gov						
Indiana State Nurses Assn (ISNA)						
2915 N High School Rd	Indianapolis	IN	46224	317-299-4575	297-3525	533
Web: www.indiananurses.org						
Indiana State Prison 1 Pk Row	Michigan City	IN	46360	219-874-7258		213
Indiana State University						
200 N Seventh St	Terre Haute	IN	47809	800-468-6478	237-8023*	166
**Fax Area Code:* 812 ■ *TF:* 800-468-6478 ■ *Web:* www.indstate.edu						
Indiana Steel Fabricating Inc						
4545 W Bradbury Ave	Indianapolis	IN	46241	317-247-4545		480
Web: www.indianasteelfab.com						
Indiana Sugars Inc 911 Virginia St	Gary	IN	46402	219-886-9151	886-5124	297-11
Web: www.sugars.com						
Indiana Tech						
1600 E Washington Blvd	Fort Wayne	IN	46803	260-422-5561	422-7696	166
TF: 800-937-2448 ■ *Web:* www.indianatech.edu						
Indiana Trust & Investment Management Co						
4045 Edison Lakes Pkwy Ste 100	Mishawaka	IN	46545	574-271-0374		796
TF: 800-362-7905 ■ *Web:* www.indtrust.com						
Indiana Tube Corp						
2100 Lexington Ave	Evansville	IN	47720	812-424-9028		595
Web: www.indianatube.com						
Indiana University						
300 N Jordan Ave	Bloomington	IN	47405	812-855-0661	855-5102	166
Web: www.indiana.edu						
East 2325 Chester Blvd	Richmond	IN	47374	765-973-8208	973-8288*	166
**Fax:* Admissions ■ *TF:* 800-959-3278 ■ *Web:* www.iue.edu						
Kokomo 2300 S Washington St PO Box 9003	Kokomo	IN	46904	765-455-9217	455-9537*	166
**Fax:* Admissions ■ *TF:* 888-875-4485 ■ *Web:* www.iuk.edu						
Northwest 3400 Broadway	Gary	IN	46408	219-980-6500	981-4219*	166
**Fax:* Admissions ■ *TF:* 888-968-7486 ■ *Web:* www.iun.edu						
South Bend						
1700 Mishawaka Ave PO Box 7111	South Bend	IN	46634	574-520-4870		166
TF: 877-462-4872 ■ *Web:* www.iusb.edu						
Southeast 4201 Grant Line Rd	New Albany	IN	47150	812-941-2212	941-2595	166
TF: 800-852-8835 ■ *Web:* www.ius.edu						
Indiana University Art Museum						
1133 E Seventh St	Bloomington	IN	47405	812-855-5445	855-1023	520
Web: www.indiana.edu						
Indiana University Auditorium						
1211 E Seventh St	Bloomington	IN	47405	812-855-1103	855-4244	572
TF: 800-745-3000 ■ *Web:* www.iuauditorium.com						
Indiana University Bloomington						
Libraries 1320 E Tenth St	Bloomington	IN	47405	812-855-8028	855-2576	434-6
Web: libraries.indiana.edu						
Indiana University Hospital						
550 N University Blvd	Indianapolis	IN	46202	317-274-5000		374-3
TF: 800-248-1199 ■ *Web:* www.iuhealth.org						
Indiana University Melvin and Bren Simon Cancer Ctr						
535 Barnhill Dr	Indianapolis	IN	46202	317-278-0070		769
TF: 888-600-4822 ■ *Web:* cancer.iu.edu						
Indiana University of Pennsylvania						
1011 South Dr	Indiana	PA	15705	724-357-2100	357-6281*	166
**Fax:* Admissions ■ *TF:* 800-442-6830 ■ *Web:* www.iup.edu						
Indiana University of Pennsylvania Stapleton Library						
1011 S Dr	Indiana	PA	15705	724-357-2340	357-4891	434-6
TF: 888-342-2383 ■ *Web:* www.iup.edu/library						
Indiana University Press						
601 N Morton St	Bloomington	IN	47404	812-855-8817	855-8507	637-4
TF: 800-842-6796 ■ *Web:* www.iupress.indiana.edu						

	City	State	Zip	Phone	Fax	Class
Indiana University School of Law Bloomington						
211 S Indiana Ave	Bloomington	IN	47405	812-855-7995	855-0555	167-1
Web: www.law.indiana.edu						
Indiana University School of Law Indianapolis						
Lawrence W Inlow Hall 530 W New York St	Indianapolis	IN	46202	317-274-8523	274-3955	167-1
Web: mckinneylaw.iu.edu						
Indiana University School of Medicine						
340 W Tenth St Ste 6200	Indianapolis	IN	46202	317-274-8157		167-2
Web: www.medicine.iu.edu						
Indiana University South Bend						
Schurz Library						
1700 Mishawaka Ave PO Box 7111	South Bend	IN	46634	574-520-4440		434-6
TF: 800-350-6889 ■ *Web:* www.iusb.edu						
Indiana University-Purdue University						
Columbus 4601 Central Ave	Columbus	IN	47203	812-348-7271	348-7257	166
Web: iupuc.edu						
Fort Wayne 2101 E Coliseum Blvd	Fort Wayne	IN	46805	260-481-6100	481-6880*	166
**Fax:* Hum Res ■ *TF:* 800-324-4739 ■ *Web:* www.ipfw.edu						
Indianapolis 425 University Blvd	Indianapolis	IN	46202	317-274-5555	278-1862	166
Web: www.iupui.edu						
Indiana University-Purdue University Fort Wayne						
Helmke Library						
2101 E Coliseum Blvd	Fort Wayne	IN	46805	260-481-5404		434-6
Web: usdirectoryfinder.com						
Indiana University-Purdue University Indianapolis						
Library 755 W Michigan St	Indianapolis	IN	46202	317-274-0462	278-2300	434-6
TF: 888-422-0499 ■ *Web:* www.ulib.iupui.edu						
Indiana Veterans Home						
3851 N River Rd	West Lafayette	IN	47906	765-463-1502		793
TF: 800-400-4520 ■ *Web:* in.gov						
Indiana Veterinary Medical Assn						
201 S Capitol Ave Ste 405	Indianapolis	IN	46225	317-974-0888	974-0985	795
TF: 800-270-0747 ■ *Web:* www.invma.org						
Indiana Wesleyan University						
4201 S Washington St	Marion	IN	46953	765-677-2138	677-2333*	166
**Fax:* Admissions ■ *TF:* 800-332-6901 ■ *Web:* www.indwes.edu						
Indiana Women's Prison						
2596 N Girls School Rd	Indianapolis	IN	46214	317-244-3387	244-4670	213
TF: 800-451-6028 ■ *Web:* in.gov						
Indianapolis Art Ctr						
820 E 67th St	Indianapolis	IN	46220	317-255-2464		50-2
TF: 800-323-4639 ■ *Web:* indplsartcenter.org						
Indianapolis Artsgarden						
Above the Intersection of Washington						
Illinois St	Indianapolis	IN	46204	317-624-2563		572
Web: www.indyarts.org						
Indianapolis Business Journal						
41 E Washington St Ste 200	Indianapolis	IN	46204	317-634-6200	263-5406*	457-5
**Fax:* Edit ■ *TF:* 800-428-7081 ■ *Web:* www.ibj.com						
Indianapolis City Hall						
200 E Washington St Ste 2501	Indianapolis	IN	46204	317-327-3601	327-3980	337
Web: www.indy.gov						
Indianapolis Colts						
7001 W 56th St	Indianapolis	IN	46254	317-297-2658	297-8971	715-3
TF: 800-805-2658 ■ *Web:* www.colts.com						
Indianapolis Convention & Visitors Assn						
200 S Capitol Ave Ste 300	Indianapolis	IN	46225	317-262-3000		206
TF: 800-862-6912 ■ *Web:* www.visitindy.com						
Indianapolis Downtown Antique Mall						
1044 Virginia Ave	Indianapolis	IN	46203	317-635-5336		460
Indianapolis Fruit Company Inc						
4501 Massachusetts Ave	Indianapolis	IN	46218	317-546-2425	543-0521	297-7
TF: 800-377-2425 ■ *Web:* www.indyfruit.com						
Indianapolis Marriott Downtown						
350 W Maryland St	Indianapolis	IN	46225	317-822-3500		378
TF: 800-228-9290 ■ *Web:* www.indymarriott.com						
Indianapolis Monthly Magazine						
40 Monument Cir Ste 100	Indianapolis	IN	46204	317-237-9288	684-2080	457-22
TF Circ: 888-403-9005 ■ *Web:* www.indianapolismonthly.com						
Indianapolis Motor Speedway & Hall of Fame Museum						
4790 W 16th St	Indianapolis	IN	46222	317-492-6747		520
Web: www.indianapolismotorspeedway.com						
Indianapolis Motor Speedway Corp						
4790 W 16th St	Indianapolis	IN	46222	317-492-8500		642
Web: indianapolismotorspeedway.com						
Indianapolis Museum of Art						
4000 Michigan Rd	Indianapolis	IN	46208	317-923-1331	931-1978	520
Web: www.imamuseum.org						
Indianapolis Opera 250 E 38th St	Indianapolis	IN	46205	317-283-3531	923-5611	573-2
TF: 800-662-3311 ■ *Web:* www.indyopera.org						
Indianapolis Power & Light Co						
1 Monument Cir	Indianapolis	IN	46204	317-261-8261		787
Web: www.iplpower.com						
Indianapolis Public Schools						
120 E Walnut St	Indianapolis	IN	46204	317-226-4000		685
Web: www.myips.org						
Indianapolis Public Transportation Corp						
1501 W Washington St	Indianapolis	IN	46204	317-635-3344		108
Web: www.indygo.net						
Indianapolis Star						
307 N Pennsylvania St	Indianapolis	IN	46204	317-444-4000		532-2
TF: 800-669-7827 ■ *Web:* www.indystar.com						
Indianapolis Symphony Orchestra						
45 Monument Cir	Indianapolis	IN	46204	317-262-1100		573-3
TF: 800-366-8457 ■ *Web:* www.indianapolissymphony.org						
Indianapolis Zoo						
1200 W Washington St	Indianapolis	IN	46222	317-630-2001	630-5153	823
Web: www.indianapoliszoo.com						
Indianhead Federated Library System						
1538 Truax Blvd	Eau Claire	WI	54703	715-839-5082	839-5151	434-3
TF: 800-321-5427 ■ *Web:* iflsweb.org						
Indiantown Gap National Cemetery						
Indiantown Gap Rd RR 2 PO Box 484	Annville	PA	17003	717-865-5254	865-5256	136
Web: www.cem.va.gov/cems/nchp/indiantowngap.asp						
Indice Mode 5401 Boul Des Galeries	Quebec	QC	G2K1N4	418-624-9330		157-6
Web: lindicemode.com						
Indicon Corp 6125 Center Dr	Sterling Heights	MI	48312	586-274-0505		729
Indiemark LLC 120 Laurens St SW 2nd Fl	Aiken	SC	29801	214-716-0268		5
Web: www.indiemark.com						

Phone | Fax | Class

Indigen Armor Inc
793 Fort Mill Hwy ... Indian Land SC 29707 803-396-9600 59
Web: www.indigenarmor.com

Indigena Solutions LP
Ste 301 - 800 Carleton Ct ... Delta BC V3M6Y6 604-549-5800 463
Web: www.indigenasolutions.com

Indiggo Associates Inc
4600 E W Hwy Ste 875 ... Bethesda MD 20814 240-314-0533 193
Web: www.indiggoassociates.com

Indigo 3013 Lindbergh Blvd ... Springfield IL 62704 217-726-3487 671
Web: www.indigocuisine.com

Indigo BioSystems Inc
7820 Innovation Blvd Ste 250 ... Indianapolis IN 46278 317-493-2400 177
Web: www.indigobio.com

Indigo Books & Music Inc
468 King St W Ste 500 ... Toronto ON M5V1L8 416-364-4499 364-0355 95
NYSE: IDG ■ *TF Cust Svc:* 800-832-7569 ■ *Web:* www.chapters.indigo.ca

Indigo Dynamic Networks Llc
2413 W Algonquin Rd ... Algonquin IL 60102 888-464-6344 180
TF: 888-464-6344 ■ *Web:* www.indigodynamic.com

Indigo Grill 1536 India St ... San Diego CA 92101 619-234-6802 671
Web: www.cohnrestaurants.com

Indigo Inn 1 Maiden Ln ... Charleston SC 29401 843-577-5900 379
TF: 800-845-7639 ■ *Web:* www.indigoinn.com

Indigo Integrative Studio
1304 Eighth Ave ... Brooklyn NY 11215 718-832-3464 810
Web: www.indigo-pilates.com

Indigo Landing Restaurant
1 Marina Dr ... Alexandria VA 22314 703-548-0001 671
Web: indigolanding.com

Indigo ORB Inc 2454 Alton Pkwy ... Irvine CA 92606 949-784-0303 475
Web: www.indigo-orb.com

Indigo Rose Corp
123 Bannatyne Ave Ste 200 ... Winnipeg MB R3B0R3 204-946-0263 179
TF: 800-665-9668 ■ *Web:* www.indigorose.com

Indika 516 Westheimer Rd ... Houston TX 77006 713-524-2170 984-1755 671
Web: www.indikausa.com

Indio Chamber of Commerce
82921 Indio Blvd ... Indio CA 92201 760-347-0676 139
Web: www.indiochamber.org

Indique 3512 Connecticut Ave NW ... Washington DC 20008 202-244-6600 671
Web: www.indique.com

IndiSoft LLC 5550 Sterrett Pl Ste 311 ... Columbia MD 21044 410-730-0667 174
Web: www.indisoft.us

Indital USA Ltd 7947 Mesa Dr ... Houston TX 77028 713-694-6065 191-1
Web: www.indital.com

Individual Software Inc
4255 HopyaRd Rd Ste 2 ... Pleasanton CA 94588 925-734-6767 734-8337 178-3
TF: 800-822-3522 ■ *Web:* www.individualsoftware.com

Individualized Shirts Co
581 Cortland St ... Perth Amboy NJ 08861 732-826-8400 155-12
TF: 800-283-9490 ■ *Web:* individualizedshirts.com

Indmar Products Company Inc
5400 Old Millington Rd ... Millington TN 38053 901-353-9930 698
Web: www.indmar.com

Indochine Asian Dining Lounge
1924 Pacific Ave ... Tacoma WA 90402 253-272-8200 671
Web: www.indochinedowntown.com

Indoff Inc 11816 Lackland Rd ... Saint Louis MO 63146 314-997-1122 812-3932 385
TF: 800-486-7867 ■ *Web:* www.indoff.com

Indonesia 325 E 38th St ... New York NY 10016 212-972-0333 784
Web: www.indonesiamission-ny.org
Consulate General
211 W Wacker Dr 8th Fl ... Chicago IL 60606 312-920-1880 920-1881 257
Web: www.indonesiachicago.org
Consulate General 5 E 68th St ... New York NY 10065 212-879-0600 570-6206 257
Web: www.kemlu.go.id
Embassy 2020 Massachusetts Ave NW ... Washington DC 20036 202-775-5200 775-5365 257
Web: www.embassyofindonesia.org

Indoor Purification Systems Inc
Surround Air Div
334 N Marshall Way Ste C ... Layton UT 84041 801-547-1162 991-4838 17
TF: 888-812-1516 ■ *Web:* surroundair.com

InDorse Technologies Inc
424 W 33rd St ... New York NY 10001 646-495-0966 387

Indotronix International Corp (IIC)
331 Main St ... Poughkeepsie NY 12601 845-473-1137 473-1197 180
Web: www.iic.com

Indros Group 1 Meadow St Ste 202 ... Brooklyn NY 11206 718-417-1320 396
TF: 800-676-0134 ■ *Web:* www.indrosgroup.com

Indtai Inc 21525 Ridgetop Cir Ste 280 ... Sterling VA 20166 703-373-3188 180
Web: www.indtai.com

Inductoheat Inc
32251 N Avis Dr ... Madison Heights MI 48071 248-585-9393 589-1062 318
TF: 800-624-6297 ■ *Web:* www.inductoheat.com

Inductotherm Group
10 Indel Ave PO Box 157 ... Rancocas NJ 08073 609-267-9000 318
TF: 800-257-9527 ■ *Web:* www.inductotherm.com

Indufast Industrial Fasteners Ltd
111b-81 Golden Dr ... Coquitlam BC V3K6R2 604-464-6164 351
Web: indufast.com

INDUS Corp 1951 Kidwell Dr ... Vienna VA 22182 703-506-6700 177
Web: www.induscorp.com

Indus Instruments 721 Tristar Dr Ste C ... Webster TX 77598 281-286-1130 196
TF: 800-433-5778 ■ *Web:* www.indusinstruments.com

Indus International Inc
340 S Oak St PO Box 890 ... West Salem WI 54669 608-786-0300 786-0786 496
TF: 800-843-9377 ■ *Web:* www.indususa.com

Indus Technology Inc
2243 San Diego Ave ... San Diego CA 92110 619-299-2555 299-2444 261
Web: www.industechnology.com

Indusa Technical Corp
1 TransAm Plaza Dr Ste 350 ... Oakbrook Terrace IL 60181 630-424-1800 180
Web: www.indusa.com

Indusco Group 1200 W Hamburg St ... Baltimore MD 21230 410-727-0665 727-2538 470
TF: 800-727-0665 ■ *Web:* www.induscowirerope.com

Industrial Acoustics Company Inc
1160 Commerce Ave ... Bronx NY 10462 718-931-8000 863-1138 389
Web: www.iacacoustics.com

Industrial Air Centers Inc
731 E Market St ... Jeffersonville IN 47130 812-280-7070 280-7072 172
Web: www.iacserv.com

Industrial Air Inc
428 Edwardia Dr PO Box 8769 ... Greensboro NC 27409 336-292-1030 855-7763 697
Web: www.industrialairinc.com

Industrial Alliance Insurance & Financial Services Inc
1080 Grande Allee W PO Box 1907 Sta Therminus . Quebec QC G1K7M3 418-684-5405 688-0705 391-2
TF: 888-266-2224 ■ *Web:* ia.ca/individuals

Industrial Bank NA
4812 Georgia Ave NW ... Washington DC 20011 202-722-2000 461-5056* 70
**Fax Area Code:* 800 ■ *Web:* www.industrial-bank.com

Industrial Battery & Charger Inc
5831 Orr Rd ... Charlotte NC 28213 704-597-7330 74
TF: 800-833-8412 ■ *Web:* www.ibcipower.com

Industrial Brush Company Inc
105 Clinton Rd ... Fairfield NJ 07004 973-575-0455 575-6169 103
TF: 800-241-9860 ■ *Web:* www.indbrush.com

Industrial Chemicals Inc
2042 Montreat Dr ... Vestavia AL 35216 205-823-7330 978-0485 146
TF Cust Svc: 800-476-2042 ■ *Web:* www.industrialchem.com

Industrial Chrome Inc 834 NE Madison ... Topeka KS 66608 785-235-3463 247
Web: www.industrialchrome.com

Industrial Clutch 1701-3 Pearl St ... Waukesha WI 53186 262-547-3357 547-2949 620
TF: 800-964-3262 ■ *Web:* www.indclutch.com

Industrial Combustion Inc 351 21st St ... Monroe WI 53566 608-325-3141 325-4379 318
Web: www.ind-comb.com

Industrial Commodities Inc
PO Box 4380 ... Glen Allen VA 23060 800-523-7902 297-11
TF: 800-523-7902 ■ *Web:* www.industrialcommodities.com

Industrial Communications & Electronics Inc
40 Lone St ... Marshfield MA 02050 781-319-1100 647
TF: 800-822-9999 ■ *Web:* www.induscom.com

Industrial Components Inc
IC Assemblies Inc 2250 NW 102nd Ave ... Miami FL 33172 305-477-0387 594-7332 489
Web: www.icassemblies.com

Industrial Container & Supply Company Inc
1845 South 5200 West ... Salt Lake City UT 84104 801-972-1561 333
TF: 800-748-4250 ■ *Web:* www.industrialcontainer.com

Industrial Container Services
7152 First Ave S ... Seattle WA 98108 206-763-2345 198
TF: 800-273-3786 ■ *Web:* www.iconserv.com

Industrial Contractors Inc 701 Ch Dr ... Bismarck ND 58501 701-258-9908 258-9988 189-10
TF: 800-467-3089 ■ *Web:* www.icinorthdakota.com

Industrial Contractors Inc (ICI)
401 NW First St ... Evansville IN 47708 973-753-3500 186
Web: www.usa.skanska.com

Industrial Controls Distributors Inc (ICD)
1776 Bloomsbury Ave ... Ocean NJ 07712 732-918-9000 922-4417 385
TF Sales: 800-281-4788 ■ *Web:* www.industrialcontrolsonline.com

Industrial Custom Products Inc
2801 37th Ave NE ... Minneapolis MN 55421 612-781-2255 781-1144 326
TF: 800-654-0886 ■ *Web:* www.industrialcustom.com

Industrial Data Systems Inc
3822 E La Palma Ave ... Anaheim CA 92807 714-921-9212 399-0286 684
TF: 800-854-3311 ■ *Web:* www.industrialdata.com

Industrial Designers Society of America (IDSA)
45195 Business Ct Ste 250 ... Dulles VA 20166 703-707-6000 787-8501 49-13
Web: www.idsa.org

Industrial Diamond Assn of America (IDA)
6081 Central Pk Dr ... Columbus OH 43231 614-797-2265 49-13
Web: www.superabrasives.org

Industrial Dielectrics Inc
407 S Seventh St PO Box 357 ... Noblesville IN 46061 317-773-1766 773-3877 605-2
TF: 800-424-9300 ■ *Web:* www.idicomposites.com

Industrial Diesel Inc
8705 Harmon Rd ... Fort Worth TX 76177 817-232-1071 232-0354 385
TF: 800-323-3659 ■ *Web:* www.industrialdiesel.net

Industrial Door Company Inc
360 Coon Rapids Blvd ... Minneapolis MN 55433 763-786-4730 236
TF: 888-798-0199 ■ *Web:* www.idc-automatic.com

Industrial Door Contractors Inc
820 Mayberry Springs Rd ... Columbia TN 38401 931-380-0463 492
Web: www.hangardoor.com

Industrial Dynamics Company Ltd
3100 Fujita St ... Torrance CA 90505 310-325-5633 472
TF: 800-248-0888 ■ *Web:* www.filtec.com

Industrial Electric Wire & Cable Inc (IEWC)
5001 S Towne Dr ... New Berlin WI 53151 262-782-2323 246
TF: 800-344-2323 ■ *Web:* www.iewc.com

Industrial Equipment News
5 Penn Plaza ... New York NY 10001 212-695-0500 290-7362 457-21
Web: www.thomaspublishing.com

Industrial Fabricators Inc
403 N Cemetery St ... Thorp WI 54771 715-669-5512 669-5514 386
Web: industrialfabinc.com

Industrial Fabrics Assn International (IFAI)
1801 County Rd 'B' W ... Roseville MN 55113 651-222-2508 631-9334 49-13
TF: 800-225-4324 ■ *Web:* www.ifai.com

Industrial Gasket & Shim Company Inc (IGS)
200 Country Club Rd ... Meadow Lands PA 15347 724-222-5800 326
TF: 800-229-1447 ■ *Web:* www.igsind.com

Industrial Hardware & Specialties Inc
17B Kentucky Ave ... Paterson NJ 07503 973-684-4010 351
TF: 800-684-4010 ■ *Web:* www.industrialhardware.com

Industrial Health Council
3513 Seventh Ave S ... Birmingham AL 35222 205-326-4109 415
Web: www.i-h-c.org

Industrial Heater Corp 30 Knotter Dr ... Cheshire CT 06410 203-250-0500 250-0599 318
Web: www.industrialheater.com

Industrial Kinetics Inc
2535 Curtiss St ... Downers Grove IL 60515 630-655-0300 207
Web: www.iki.com

Industrial Laboratories Company Inc, The
4046 Youngfield St ... Wheat Ridge CO 80033 303-287-9691 287-0964 416
Web: www.industriallabs.net

Industrial Logic Inc
829 Bancroft Way ... Berkeley CA 94710 510-540-8336 177
Web: www.industriallogic.com

Company	City	State	Zip	Phone	Fax	Class
Industrial Louvers Inc 511 Seventh St S *TF:* 800-328-3421 ■ *Web:* www.industriallouvers.com	Delano	MN	55328	763-972-2981	972-2911	697
Industrial Manufacturing & Machining 5495 E 69th Ave *Web:* www.dualdraw.com	Commerce	CO	80022	303-287-2125		595
Industrial Marking Products 1415 Grovenburg Rd *TF:* 800-344-1161 ■ *Web:* www.industrialmarking.com	Holt	MI	48842	517-699-2160	699-1505	467
Industrial Material Corp 7701 Harborside Dr *TF:* 800-701-4462 ■ *Web:* www.industrialmaterial.com	Galveston	TX	77554	409-744-4538	744-1844	492
Industrial Molding Corp 616 E Slaton Rd *TF:* 800-869-3557 ■ *Web:* www.nninc.com	Lubbock	TX	79404	806-474-1000	474-1168	604
Industrial Motion Control LLC 1444 S Wolf Rd *Web:* www.destaco.com/camcoindex-redirect.html	Wheeling	IL	60090	847-459-5200	459-3064	709
Industrial Nut Corp 1425 Tiffin Ave *Web:* www.industrialnut.com	Sandusky	OH	44870	419-625-8543		350
Industrial Paper Tube Inc 1335 E Bay Ave **Fax Area Code:* 718 ■ *TF:* 800-345-0960 ■ *Web:* www.mailingtubes-ipt.com	Bronx	NY	10474	800-345-0960	378-0055*	125
Industrial Paramedic Services Ltd 630 Fourth Ave SW Ste 100 *Web:* ipsems.com	Calgary	AB	T2P0J9	403-264-6435		30
Industrial Partnership for Research in Interfacial & Materials Engineering (IPRIME) University of Minnesota 151 Amundson Hall 421 Washington Ave SE *Web:* www.iprime.umn.edu	Minneapolis	MN	55455	612-626-9509	626-7246	668
Industrial Parts Depot LLC 23231 Normandie Ave *Web:* www.ipdparts.com	Torrance	CA	90501	310-530-1900		262
Industrial Pipe & Supply Company Inc 1779 Martin Luther King Junior Blvd *TF:* 800-426-1458 ■ *Web:* www.industrialpipega.com	Gainesville	GA	30501	770-536-0517		612
Industrial Piping Inc 800 Culp Rd *TF:* 800-951-0988 ■ *Web:* www.goipi.com	Pineville	NC	28134	704-588-1100	588-5614	189-10
Industrial Power & Lighting Corp 60 Depost St Ste 500 *TF:* 800-639-3702 ■ *Web:* www.iplcorp.com	Buffalo	NY	14206	716-854-1811	854-1828	189-4
Industrial Realty Group LLC 11100 Santa Monica Blvd Ste 850 *Web:* www.industrialrealtygroup.com	Los Angeles	CA	90025	562-803-4761		652
Industrial Research Institute Inc (IRI) 2200 Clarendon Blvd Ste 1102 *Web:* www.iriweb.org	Arlington	VA	22201	703-647-2580	647-2581	49-19
Industrial Resources Inc PO Box 2648 *Web:* www.indres.com	Fairmont	WV	26554	304-363-4100		186
Industrial Revolution Inc 5835 Segale Park Dr Ste C **Fax Area Code:* 206 ■ *TF:* 888-297-6062 ■ *Web:* www.industrialrev.com	Tukwila	WA	98188	425-285-1111	812-2250*	697
Industrial Rubber Works 1700 Nicholas Blvd *TF:* 800-852-1855 ■ *Web:* www.abbottrubber.com	Elk Grove Village	IL	60007	847-952-1800		370
Industrial Scientific Corp 7848 Steubenville Pk *TF:* 800-338-3287 ■ *Web:* www.indsci.com	Oakdale	PA	15071	412-788-4353	788-8353	201
Industrial Shredders PO Box 38442 *Web:* www.industrialshredders.com	North Lima	OH	44452	330-549-9960	549-9961	111
Industrial Soap Co 722 S Vandeventer Ave *TF:* 800-405-7627 ■ *Web:* www.industrialsoap.com	Saint Louis	MO	63110	314-241-6363	533-5556	406
Industrial Source Inc 1574 W Sixth Ave *Web:* www.industrialsource.com	Eugene	OR	97402	541-344-1438		690
Industrial Specialty Contractors LLC 20480 Highland Rd *Web:* www.iscgrp.com	Baton Rouge	LA	70817	225-756-8001		189-4
Industrial Stainless Supply Inc 5265 Hanson Ct *Web:* www.issi-stainless.com	Minneapolis	MN	55429	763-535-5866		492
Industrial Steel Construction Inc 86 N Bridge St *Web:* www.iscbridge.com	Gary	IN	46404	219-885-5610		480
Industrial Steel Inc 3561 Industrial Rd *Web:* www.industrial-steel.com	Titusville	FL	32796	321-267-2341		480
Industrial Steel Treating Inc 613 Carroll St **Fax Area Code:* 866 ■ *TF:* 800-253-9534 ■ *Web:* www.indstl.com	Jackson	MI	49202	800-253-9534	550-7045*	484
Industrial Supply Solutions Inc 520 Elizabeth St *Web:* www.issimro.com	Charleston	WV	25311	304-346-5341		385
Industrial Tectonics Inc 7222 Huron River Dr *TF:* 866-816-8904 ■ *Web:* www.itiball.com	Dexter	MI	48130	734-426-4681	426-4701	485
Industrial Thermoform Inc 1211 Industrial Way *Web:* www.industrialthermoform.com	Cedar Hill	TX	75104	972-299-5391		596
Industrial Timber & Lumber Corp (ITL) 23925 Commerce Park Rd *TF:* 800-829-9663 ■ *Web:* www.itlcorp.com	Beachwood	OH	44122	216-831-3140	831-4734	683
Industrial Tool Inc 9210 52nd Ave N *TF Sales:* 800-776-4455 ■ *Web:* www.industrial-tool.com	New Hope	MN	55428	763-533-7244		454
Industrial Tools Inc (ITI) 1111 S Rose Ave *TF:* 800-266-5561 ■ *Web:* www.iti-abrasives.com	Oxnard	CA	93033	805-483-1111	483-6302	493
Industrial Tube & Steel Corp 4658 Crystal Pkwy *TF:* 800-662-9567 ■ *Web:* www.industrialtube.com	Kent	OH	44240	330-474-5530		690
Industrial Vehicles International Inc (IVI) 6737 E 12th St *Web:* www.indvehicles.com	Tulsa	OK	74112	918-836-6516	838-9529	470
Industrial Ventilation Inc W6395 Speciality Dr *Web:* www.ivinc.com	Greenville	WI	54942	920-757-6001		610
Industrial Welders & Machinists Inc 610 Opperman Dr *Web:* caselaw.findlaw.com	Eagan	MN	55123	218-628-1011	624-3319	811
Industries Bonneville Ltee 601 rue de l'Industrie *Web:* www.maisonsbonneville.com	Beloeil	QC	J3G4S5	450-464-1001		106
Industries for the Blind 445 S Curtis Rd *TF:* 800-642-8778 ■ *Web:* www.ibmilwaukee.com	West Allis	WI	53214	414-778-3040	778-3041	103
Industries of the Blind Inc 920 W Lee St *TF:* 800-909-7086 ■ *Web:* www.industriesoftheblind.com	Greensboro	NC	27403	336-274-1591		103
Industrios Software Inc 2150 Winston Park Dr Ste 214 *Web:* www.industrios.com	Oakville	ON	L6H5V1	905-829-2525		174
Industronics Service Co 489 Sullivan Ave *TF:* 800-878-1551 ■ *Web:* www.industronics.com	South Windsor	CT	06074	860-289-1551	289-3526	318
Industry Consulting Group Inc 2777 N Stemmons Fwy Ste 940 *Web:* www.icgtax.com	Dallas	TX	75207	972-991-0391		734
Industry Council for Tangible Assets (ICTA) 1510 Circle Dr *TF:* 800-447-8848 ■ *Web:* www.ictaonline.org	Annapolis	MD	21409	410-626-7005		49-2
Industry Products Co 500 E Statler Rd *Web:* www.industryproductsco.com	Piqua	OH	45356	937-778-0585		247
Industry Specific Solutions LLC 24901 Northwestern Hwy Ste 400 *TF:* 877-356-3450 ■ *Web:* industryspecificstaffing.com	Southfield	MI	48075	877-356-3450		260
Industry-Railway Suppliers Inc 811 Golf Ln *TF:* 800-728-0029 ■ *Web:* www.industryrailway.com	Bensenville	IL	60106	630-766-5708	766-0017	770
Indy Honda 8455 US 31 S *Web:* www.indyhonda.com	Indianapolis	IN	46227	317-887-0800		57
Indyne Inc 11800 Sunrise Vly Dr Ste 250 *Web:* www.indyneinc.com	Reston	VA	20191	703-903-6900	903-4997	743
InEdge 9800 Cavendish Blvd Ste 250 *Web:* www.inedge.com	Montreal	QC	H4M2V9	514-333-6600		463
Inek Technologies LLC 9200 Indian Creek Pkwy Ste 187 *Web:* www.inekinfo.com	Overland Park	KS	66210	913-469-1066		631
Ineo Technology LLC 3340-A Annapolis Ln	Plymouth	MN	55447	612-236-2100		179
Ineoquest Technologies Inc 170 Forbes Blvd *Web:* ineoquest.com	Mansfield	MA	02048	508-339-2497		180
INEOS Bio USA LLC 3030 Warrenville Rd Ste 650 *Web:* www.ineos.com	Lisle	IL	60532	630-857-7000		580
Inergy Automotive Systems USA LLC 2710 Bellingham Dr #400 *Web:* www.inergyautomotive.com	Troy	MI	48083	248-743-5700		247
Inertech Supply Inc 641 Monterey Pass Rd *Web:* inertech.com	Monterey Park	CA	91754	626-282-2000		326
Inertia Dynamics Inc 31 Industrial Park Rd *TF:* 800-800-6445 ■ *Web:* www.idicb.com	New Hartford	CT	06057	860-482-4444		203
Inertia Engineering 6665 Hardaway Rd *TF:* 800-791-9997 ■ *Web:* www.inertiaworks.com	Stockton	CA	95215	209-931-1670		729
INETCO Systems Ltd 4664 Lougheed Hwy Ste 258 *Web:* www.inetco.com	Burnaby	BC	V5C5T5	604-451-1567		174
Inetsolution 250 Monroe NW Ste 400 *TF:* 855-728-5839 ■ *Web:* www.inetsolution.com	Grand Rapids	MI	49503	586-726-9490		180
Infaith Community Foundation 625 Fourth Ave S Ste 1500 *TF:* 800-365-4172 ■ *Web:* infaithfound.org	Minneapolis	MN	55415	612-844-4110	844-4109	304
Infantino LLC 4920 Carroll Canyon Rd Ste 200 *TF:* 800-840-4916 ■ *Web:* www.infantino.com	San Diego	CA	92121	800-840-4916		64
Infection Control Today Magazine 3300 N Central Ave Ste 300 *TF:* 800-581-1811 ■ *Web:* www.infectioncontroltoday.com	Phoenix	AZ	85012	480-990-1101	990-0819	457-16
inferno LLC 505 Tennessee St Ste 108 *TF:* 800-713-7278 ■ *Web:* www.creativeinferno.com	Memphis	TN	38103	901-278-3773		7
Infi Net Solutions Inc 6430 S 84th St *TF:* 800-621-7440 ■ *Web:* www.omahait.com	Omaha	NE	68127	402-895-5777		225
INFICON Inc 2 Technology Pl *Web:* www.inficon.com	East Syracuse	NY	13057	315-434-1100	437-3803	201
Infilco Degremont Inc 8007 Discovery Dr PO Box 71390 *Web:* www.degremont-technologies.com	Richmond	VA	23255	804-756-7600	756-7643	806
Infinedi LLC 1437 S Boulder Ave Ste 1030 *Web:* www.infinedi.net	Tulsa	OK	74119	918-249-4450		708
Infinera Corp 140 Caspian Ct *NASDAQ: INFN* ■ *TF:* 877-742-3427 ■ *Web:* www.infinera.com	Sunnyvale	CA	94089	408-572-5200		735
Infinet Technologies 249 Oak St *TF:* 800-544-8614 ■ *Web:* www.infinet-technologies.com	Collingwood	ON	L9Y2Y2	705-445-2002		396
Infinia Group LLC 192 Lexington Ave 4th Fl *Web:* www.infiniagroup.com	New York	NY	10016	212-463-5100		195
Infiniedge Software Inc 14320 Infiniedge Way *Web:* www.infiniedge.com	Prairieville	LA	70769	225-677-8902	677-8513	177
Infinite Campus Inc 4321 109th Ave NE *TF:* 800-850-2335 ■ *Web:* www.infinitecampus.com	Blaine	MN	55449	651-631-0000		177
Infinite Dimensions Inc 1760 Reston Pkwy Ste 500 *Web:* www.infdim.com	Reston	VA	20191	703-435-9500		396
Infinite Graphics Inc 4611 E Lake St *OTC: INFG* ■ *TF:* 800-679-0676 ■ *Web:* www.igi.com	Minneapolis	MN	55406	612-721-6283	721-3802	178-5
Infinite Media Inc 491 Maple St Bldg 300 Ste 305 *Web:* www.infinitemediainc.com	Danvers	MA	01923	978-624-7106		627
Infinite Scale Design Group LLC 16 E Exchange Pl *TF:* 800-570-1443 ■ *Web:* www.infinitescale.com	Salt Lake City	UT	84111	801-363-1881		393

	Phone	Fax	Class
Infinite Wellness Solutions 3300 Reynolda Rd .... Winston-Salem NC 27106 *Web:* www.infinitewellnesssolutions.com	336-725-8624		466
Infiniti HR LLC 3905 National Dr Ste 400 .... Burtonsville MD 20866 *Web:* www.infinitihr.com	301-841-6380		734
INFINITT North America Inc 755 Memorial Pkwy Hillcrest Professional Plaza Ste 304 .... Phillipsburg NJ 08865 *TF:* 800-235-8690 ■ *Web:* www.infinittna.com	908-387-6960		624
Infinitude Creative Group LP 1820 Preston Park Blvd Ste 2100 .... Plano TX 75093 *Web:* www.nfinitude.com	972-867-6800		514
Infinity Capital Partners LLC 1075 Peachtree St NE Ste 2125 .... Atlanta GA 30309 *Web:* www.infinityfunds.com	404-458-4448		401
Infinity Contractors International Ltd 2563 E Loop 820 N .... Fort Worth TX 76118 *Web:* www.infinitycontractors.com	817-838-8700		610
Infinity Direct Inc 13220 County Rd 6 Ste 200 .... Plymouth MN 55441 *Web:* www.infinitydirect.com	763-559-1111		41
Infinity Engineering Consultants L L C 2626 Canal St Ste 202 .... New Orleans LA 70119 *Web:* www.infinityec.com	504-304-0548		256
Infinity Fasteners Inc 11028 Strang Line Rd .... Lenexa KS 66215 *Web:* www.infinityfasteners.com	913-438-2252		351
Infinity Hospice Care LLC 5110 N 40th St Ste 107 .... Phoenix AZ 85018 *Web:* www.infinityhospicecare.com	602-381-0375		371
Infinity Marketing Team Inc 6525 W Sunset Blvd Ste Gs2 .... Los Angeles CA 90028 *Web:* www.infinitymarketingteam.com	323-962-4784		195
Infinity Pharmaceuticals Inc 780 Memorial Dr .... Cambridge MA 02139 *NASDAQ: INFI* ■ *Web:* www.infi.com	617-453-1000	453-1001	582
Infinity Software Development Inc 1901 Commonwealth Ln .... Tallahassee FL 32303 *Web:* www.infinity-software.com	850-383-1011		180
Infinova Corp 51 Stouts Ln .... Monmouth Junction NJ 08852 *Web:* www.infinova.com	732-355-9100		692
Infirmary Health System Inc (IHS) 5 Mobile Infirmary Cir .... Mobile AL 36607 *Web:* www.infirmaryhealth.org	251-435-2400	660-8348	353
In-Fisherman Magazine 7819 Highland Scenic Rd .... Baxter MN 56425 *TF:* 800-235-1424 ■ *Web:* www.in-fisherman.com	218-829-1648		457-20
Infitec Inc 6500 Badgley Rd .... East Syracuse NY 13057 *TF:* 800-334-0837 ■ *Web:* www.infitec.com	315-433-1150		203
Inflection Point Ventures (IPV) 1 Innovation Way Ste 302 .... Newark DE 19711 *Web:* www.inflectpoint.com	302-452-1120	452-1122	792
Inflexxion Inc 320 Needham St Ste 100 .... Newton MA 02464 *TF:* 800-848-3895 ■ *Web:* www.inflexxion.com	617-332-6028		54
Influence Technologies Inc 3457 Ringsby Court Ste 111 .... Denver CO 80216	303-495-6980		393
Influxis 28110 Ave Stanford Unit D .... Valencia CA 91355 *Web:* www.influxis.com	661-775-3036		225
Info Cubic LLC 9250 E Costilla Ave Ste 525 .... Greenwood Village CO 80112 *TF:* 877-360-4636 ■ *Web:* www.infocubic.net	303-220-0170		317
Info Tech Inc 5700 SW 34th St Ste 1235 .... Gainesville FL 32608 *TF:* 888-352-2439 ■ *Web:* www.infotechfl.com	352-381-4400		178-10
Info X Distribution LLC 3 Aspen Dr Ste 1 .... Randolph NJ 07869 *Web:* www.info-x.com	973-386-1411		196
Info. Quality Healthcare 385b Highland Colony Pkwy Ste 504 .... Ridgeland MS 39157 *TF:* 800-844-0500 ■ *Web:* www.iqh.org	601-957-1575		138
InfoCision Management Corp 325 Springside Dr .... Akron OH 44333 *TF:* 800-210-6269 ■ *Web:* www.infocision.com	330-668-1400		737
InfoCommerce Group Inc 2 Bala Plaza Ste 300 .... Bala Cynwyd PA 19004 *Web:* www.infocommercegroup.com	610-649-1200	471-0515	637-10
InFocus Corp 13190 SW 68th Pkwy Ste 200 .... Portland OR 97223 *TF:* 877-388-8385 ■ *Web:* www.infocus.com	503-207-4700	207-1937	591
INFOCUS Marketing Inc 4245 Sigler Rd .... Warrenton VA 20187 *TF:* 800-708-5478 ■ *Web:* www.infocusmarketing.com	800-708-5478		463
Infodata Corp 181 Waukegan Rd Ste 300 .... Northfield IL 60093 *Web:* www.infodatacorp.com	847-486-0000	386-7166	194
InfoExpress Inc 170 S Whisman Rd Ste B .... Mountain View CA 94041 *Web:* www.infoexpress.com	650-623-0260		177
Infogain Corp 485 Alberto Way .... Los Gatos CA 95032 *Web:* www.infogain.com	408-355-6000		39
InfoGard Laboratories Inc 709 Fiero Ln Ste 25 .... San Luis Obispo CA 93401 *Web:* www.infogard.com	805-783-0810		180
Infoglide Software 6500 River Pl Blvd Bldg 2 .... Austin TX 78730 *Web:* www.infoglide.com	512-532-3500	532-3505	178-1
infoGroup Inc 1020 E First St .... Papillion NE 68046 *TF:* 866-414-7848 ■ *Web:* www.infousacity.com	402-836-5290		5
Infogrow Corp 2140 Front St .... Cuyahoga Falls OH 44221 *TF:* 800-897-9807 ■ *Web:* www.infogrowcorp.com	800-897-9807		196
Infolab Inc 17400 Hwy 61 N .... Clarksdale MS 38614	662-627-2283		419
Infolink 109 N Oregon St Ste 404c .... El Paso TX 79901 *Web:* infolinksa.com	915-577-9466		180
Info-Link Technologies Inc 601 Pittsburgh Ave .... Mount Vernon OH 43050 *Web:* www.infolinktechnologies.net	740-393-3100		180

	Phone	Fax	Class
Infomagnetics Technologies Corp 330 Saint Mary Ave .... Winnipeg MB R3C3Z5 *Web:* www.imt.ca	204-989-4630		261
InfoMart Inc 1582 Terrell Mill Rd .... Marietta GA 30067 *TF:* 800-800-3774 ■ *Web:* www.infomart-usa.com	770-984-2727		193
Infomax Office Systems Inc 1010 Illinois St .... Des Moines IA 50314 *Web:* infomaxoffice.com	515-244-5203		535
Infomax Shelf Management Inc 1000 Nevada Hwy Ste 204 .... Boulder City NV 89005 *TF:* 800-601-1125 ■ *Web:* infomaxshelfmgmt.com	702-293-3407		195
InfoMine Inc 580 Hornby St Ste 900 .... Vancouver BC V6C3B6 *TF:* 888-683-2037 ■ *Web:* www.infomine.com	604-683-2037		225
Infonaut Inc 255 Consumers Rd Ste 500 .... Toronto ON M2J1R4 *Web:* www.infonaut.ca	716-881-7578		2
Info-Power International Inc 3345 Silverstone Dr .... Plano TX 75023 *Web:* www.abw.com	972-424-4447		177
InfoPro Inc 8200 Greensboro Dr Ste 1450 .... Mclean VA 22102 *Web:* www.infopro.net	703-226-2520		360-3
Infopros 12325 Oracle Blvd Ste 100 .... Colorado Springs CO 80921 **Fax Area Code:* 719 ■ *TF:* 888-235-3231 ■ *Web:* infopros.com	888-235-3231	593-2996*	809
Infoquest Consulting Group Inc 68 Culver Rd Ste 106 .... Monmouth Junction NJ 08852 *Web:* www.infoquestgroup.com	609-409-5151		196
Infor Global Solutions 13560 Morris Rd Ste 4100 .... Alpharetta GA 30004 *TF:* 866-244-5479 ■ *Web:* www.infor.com	678-319-8000	319-8682	178-10
Inforeem Inc 1 Quality Pl .... Edison NJ 08820 *Web:* www.inforeem.com	732-494-4100		180
InForm Product Development Inc 1869 Haynes Dr .... Sun Prairie WI 53590 *Web:* www.in-form.com	608-825-4700		261
Informa 75 W St .... Walpole MA 02081 *Web:* informatp.com	508-668-0288		507
Informant Technologies Inc 19 Jenkins Ave Ste 200 .... Lansdale PA 19446 *TF:* 877-503-4636 ■ *Web:* www.informant-tech.com	215-412-9165		177
Informatica Corp 100 Cardinal Way .... Redwood City CA 94063 *NASDAQ: INFA* ■ *TF:* 800-653-3871 ■ *Web:* www.informatica.com	650-385-5000	385-5500	178-1
Information & Computing Services Inc (ICS) 1650 Prudential Dr Ste 300 .... Jacksonville FL 32207 *TF:* 800-676-4427 ■ *Web:* www.icsfl.com	904-399-8500		178-1
Information Analysis Inc 11240 Waples Mill Rd Ste 201 .... Fairfax VA 22030 *Web:* www.infoa.com	703-383-3000	293-7979	180
Information Builders Inc 2 Penn Plaza .... New York NY 10121 *TF:* 800-969-4636 ■ *Web:* www.informationbuilders.com	212-736-4433	967-6406	178-7
Information Gatekeepers Inc (IGI) 1340 Soldiers Field Rd Ste 2 .... Brighton MA 02135 *TF:* 800-323-1088 ■ *Web:* www.igigroup.com	617-782-5033	782-5735	637-11
Information Management Systems Inc 114 W Main St Ste 211 PO Box 2924 .... New Britain CT 06050 *TF:* 888-403-8347 ■ *Web:* www.imswebb.com	860-229-1119	225-5524	635
Information Network Assoc Inc 5235 N Front St .... Harrisburg PA 17110 *TF:* 800-443-0824 ■ *Web:* www.ina-inc.com	717-599-5505		693
Information Resources Inc 150 N Clinton St .... Chicago IL 60661 *TF:* 866-262-5973 ■ *Web:* www.iriworldwide.com	312-726-1221		466
Information Station Specialists Inc 3368 88th Ave .... Zeeland MI 49464 *Web:* www.theradiosource.com	616-772-2300		647
Information Systems & Networks Corp (ISN) 10411 Motor City Dr Ste700 .... Bethesda MD 20817 *Web:* www.isncorp.com	301-469-0400	469-0767	180
Information Systems Audit & Control Assn (ISACA) 3701 Algonquin Rd Ste 1010 .... Rolling Meadows IL 60008 *TF:* 888-491-8833 ■ *Web:* www.isaca.org	847-253-1545	253-1443	48-9
Information Systems Consulting 401 E East St .... Casper WY 82601 *Web:* www.isccorp.net	307-473-8933	473-8991	387
Information Systems Laboratories Inc 10070 Barnes Canyon Rd .... San Diego CA 92121 *Web:* www.islinc.com	858-535-9680	535-9848	28
Information Technology Industry Council (ITI) 1101 K St NW Ste 610 .... Washington DC 20005 *Web:* www.itic.org	202-737-8888	638-4922	48-9
Information Television Network 6650 Pk of Commerce Blvd .... Boca Raton FL 33487 *Web:* www.itvisus.com	561-997-7771	997-5208	742
Information Today Inc 143 Old Marlton Pike .... Medford NJ 08055 *TF:* 800-300-9868	609-654-6266	654-4309	637-9
Information Today Magazine 143 Old Marlton Pk .... Medford NJ 08055 *TF:* 800-300-9868 ■ *Web:* www.infotoday.com	609-654-6266	654-4309	457-7
Information Tycoon 1455 Old Alabama Rd Ste 140 .... Roswell GA 30076 *Web:* infotycoon.com	404-267-1506		387
InformationWEEK Labs 600 Community Dr .... Manhasset NY 11030 **Fax Area Code:* 516 ■ *Web:* www.informationweek.com	212-600-3157	562-5036*	743
InformationWeek Magazine 600 Community Dr .... Manhasset NY 11030 *TF:* 855-569-5945 ■ *Web:* www.informationweek.com	516-562-5000	562-5036	457-7
Informed Sources Inc 88 Sunnysd Blvd LI012 .... Plainview NY 11803 *Web:* www.informed-sources.com	516-576-0246		195
InforMedix Holdings Inc Georgetowne Park 5880 Hubbard Dr .... Rockville MD 20852	301-984-1566		743
Informity Network LTD 333 N Michigan Ave Ste 1650 .... Chicago IL 60601 *Web:* www.informitynetwork.com	312-361-6515	361-6520	246

	Phone	Fax	Class
INFORMS (Institute for Operations Research & the Management Sciences) 7240 Pkwy Dr Ste 300 ... Hanover MD 21076 *TF:* 800-446-3676 ■ *Web:* www.informs.org	443-757-3500	757-3515	49-19
Infortrend Corp 435 Lakeside Dr ... Sunnyvale CA 94085 *Web:* www.infortrend.com	408-988-5088		173-8
Infosat Communications Inc 3130-114 Ave SE ... Calgary AB T2Z3V6 *Web:* www.infosat.com	403-543-8188		246
InfoSearch Media Inc 6041 Bristol Pkwy 1st Fl ... Culver City CA 90230	310-437-7380		224
Infosec Inc 14001c Saint Germain Dr ... Centreville VA 20121 *Web:* www.infosecinc.com	703-825-1202		225
Infosemantics 2605 Sagebrush Dr Ste 207 ... Flower Mound TX 75028 *Web:* www.infosemantics.com	469-941-0266	941-0267	177
InfoSend Inc 4240 E La Palma Ave ... Anaheim CA 92807 *TF:* 800-955-9330 ■ *Web:* www.infosend.com	714-993-2690		393
Infoshred LLC 3 Craftsman Rd ... East Windsor CT 06088 *Web:* www.infoshred.com	860-627-5800		317
Infosight Corp PO Box 5000 ... Chillicothe OH 45601 *TF:* 800-401-0716 ■ *Web:* www.infosight.com	740-642-3600	642-5001	467
Infosilem Inc 99 Rue Emilien-marcoux ... Blainville QC J7C0B4 *TF:* 800-680-8925 ■ *Web:* www.infosilem.com	450-420-5565		177
Infosmart Systems Inc 5850 Town and Country Blvd Ste 1102 ... Frisco TX 75034 *Web:* www.infosmartsys.com	972-267-5900		196
Infosoft Group Inc 1123 N Water St Ste 400 ... Milwaukee WI 53202 *TF:* 800-984-3775 ■ *Web:* www.milwaukeejobs.com	414-278-0700		180
InfoSonics Corp 3636 Nobel Dr Ste 325 ... San Diego CA 92122 *NASDAQ: IFON* ■ *Web:* www.infosonics.com	858-373-1600	373-1503	246
Infosource Inc 1300 City View Ctr ... Oviedo FL 32765 *TF:* 800-393-4636 ■ *Web:* www.infosourcelearning.com	407-796-5200	796-5190	177
InfoSpace Inc 601 108th Ave NE Ste 1200 ... Bellevue WA 98004 *Web:* www.blucora.com	425-201-6100	201-6150	397
Infospan Inc 31878 Del Obispo St Ste 118 ... San Juan Capistrano CA 92675 *Web:* www.infospaninc.com	949-260-9990		393
Infostretch Corp 3200 Patrick Henry Dr Ste 250 ... Santa Clara CA 95054 *Web:* infostretch.com	408-727-1100		177
InfoSystems Inc 1317 Hickory Valley Rd ... Chattanooga TN 37421 *Web:* www.infosystems.biz	423-624-6551		180
Infosystems Technology Inc 4 Professional Dr Ste 118 ... Gaithersburg MD 20879 **Fax Area Code:* 301 ■ *Web:* www.rubix.com	202-412-0152	869-4667*	178-12
InfoTech Enterprises America Inc 330 Roberts St Ste 102 ... East Hartford CT 06108 *TF:* 866-746-2133 ■ *Web:* cyient.com	860-528-5430		256
Infotech Global Inc 371 Hoes Ln ... Piscataway NJ 08854 *TF:* 800-821-0887 ■ *Web:* www.igiusa.com	732-271-0600		225
Infotex Inc 2366 W Blvd ... Kokomo IN 46902 *Web:* www.infotex.com	765-236-2323		196
Infotier 7 Century Dr ... Parsippany NJ 07054 *Web:* infotier.com	973-538-2600		196
infoUSA Inc 5711 S 86th Cir ... Omaha NE 68127 **Fax Area Code:* 402 ■ **Fax:* Sales ■ *TF:* 800-321-0869 ■ *Web:* www.infousa.com	800-835-5856	331-1505*	387
Infovine Inc 1100 W 23rd St Ste 100 ... Houston TX 77008 *TF:* 800-460-8900 ■ *Web:* www.infovine.com	713-223-9994		627
InfoVista Corp 12950 Worldgate Dr Ste 250 ... Herndon VA 20170 *TF:* 866-921-9219 ■ *Web:* www.infovista.com	703-435-2435		178-1
InfoWorld Inc 501 Second St Fl 6 ... San Francisco CA 94107 *TF:* 800-227-8365 ■ *Web:* www.infoworld.com	415-243-4344	978-3120	457-7
InfoWorld Media Group Inc 501 Second St 6 Fl ... San Francisco CA 94107 *TF:* 800-227-8365 ■ *Web:* www.infoworld.com	415-243-0500	978-3120	637-9
InfoZen Inc 6700A Rockledge Dr Ste 300 ... Bethesda MD 20817 *Web:* www.infozen.com	301-605-8000		196
Infra Metals Co 4501 Curtis Ave ... Curtis Bay MD 21225 *Web:* www.infra-metals.com	410-355-2550		492
InfraBasic LLC The Trump Bldg 40 Wall St Ste 2800 ... New York NY 10005 *Web:* www.infrabasic.com	212-994-6333		693
Infradant Llc 15715 SE 89th Ct ... Summerfield FL 34491 *Web:* www.infradant.com	352-693-3581		463
Infralogix 1315 Jamestown Rd Ste 201 ... Williamsburg VA 23185 *Web:* www.infralogix.com	757-229-2965		365
InfraRed Imaging Systems Inc 22718 Holycross Epps Rd ... Marysville OH 43040 *TF:* 888-987-5768 ■ *Web:* www.irimagesys.com	888-987-5768		96
InfraReDx Inc 34 Third Ave ... Burlington MA 01803 *Web:* www.infraredx.com	781-221-0053		476
Infrastructure & Energy Alternatives LLC 2647 Waterfront Pkwy E Dr ste 100 ... Indianapolis IN 60154 *TF:* 800-688-3775 ■ *Web:* iea.net	800-688-3775		256
Infrastructure Alternatives 7888 Childsdale NE ... Rockford MI 49341 *Web:* infralt.com	616-866-1600		261
Infratech Corp 2036 Baker Ct ... Kennesaw GA 30144 *Web:* www.infratechcorp.com	770-792-8700		256
Infuse Medical 3369 W Mayflower Ave Ste 100 ... Lehi UT 84043 *Web:* www.infusemed.com	801-331-8610		415
Infusion Marketing Group LLC 18 Knights Bridge Rd ... Sherwood AR 72120 *Web:* infusionmarketinggroup.com	501-519-1969		393
Infusion Nurses Society (INS) 315 Norwood Pk S ... Norwood MA 02062 *TF:* 800-694-0298 ■ *Web:* www.ins1.org	781-440-9408	440-9409	49-8
Infusive Solutions Inc 411 Fifth Ave Rm 702 ... New York NY 10016 *Web:* www.infusivesolutions.com	212-566-1400		193
Infutor Data Solutions 1 Lincoln Ctr 18W140 Butterfield Rd Ste 1020 ... Oakbrook Terrace IL 60181 *Web:* www.infutor.com	312-348-7900		225
InfySource Ltd 8345 NW 66th St ... Miami FL 33166 *TF:* 800-275-7503 ■ *Web:* www.infy-source.com	800-275-7503		624
ING Financial Markets Llc 1325 Ave of the Americas ... New York NY 10019 *Web:* ing.com	646-424-6000		690
ING Funds 7337 E Doubletree Ranch Rd ... Scottsdale AZ 85258 **Fax Area Code:* 480 ■ *TF:* 800-992-0180 ■ *Web:* investments.voya.com	800-992-0180	477-2700*	528
INGAA (Interstate Natural Gas Assn of America) 10 G St NE Ste 700 ... Washington DC 20002 *Web:* www.ingaa.org	202-216-5900	216-0870	49-21
Ingalls Feed Yard 10505 US Hwy 50 ... Ingalls KS 67853 *Web:* www.irsikanddoll.com	620-335-5174		10-1
Ingalls Memorial Hospital 1 Ingalls Dr ... Harvey IL 60426 *Web:* www.ingalls.org	708-333-2300		374-3
Ingen Technologies Inc 3410 La Sierra Ave Ste F507 ... Riverside CA 92503 *Web:* www.ingen-tech.com	951-688-7840		476
Ingenicomm Inc 14120 Parke Long Court Ste 210 ... Chantilly VA 20151 *Web:* www.ingenicomm.net	703-665-4333		736
Ingenium Aerospace LLC 5389 International Dr ... Rockford IL 61109 *Web:* www.ingeniumaerospace.com	815-525-2000		350
Ingenium Corp 7474 Greenway Ctr Dr Maryland Trade Ctr II Ste 800 ... Greenbelt MD 20770 *Web:* www.ingenium.net	301-883-9800		180
Ingenium Technologies Corp 4216 Maray Dr ... Rockford IL 61107 *Web:* www.ingeniumtech.com	815-399-8803		256
Ingenuite Inc 7701 S Western Ave Ste 204 ... Oklahoma City OK 73139 *Web:* ingenuite.com	405-636-1802		177
Ingenuity Ieq 3600 Centennial Dr ... Midland MI 48642 *TF:* 800-669-9726 ■ *Web:* www.ingenuityieq.com	989-496-2233		610
Ingenuity Systems Inc 1700 Seaport Blvd 3rd Fl ... Redwood City CA 94063 *Web:* www.ingenuity.com	650-381-5100		177
Ingersoll Rand Air Solutions Group 800-D Beaty St ... Davidson NC 28036 *TF:* 800-866-5457 ■ *Web:* company.ingersollrand.com	704-655-4000		172
Ingersoll Watson & Mcmachen Inc 1133 E Milham Rd ... Portage MI 49002 *Web:* iwmeng.com	269-344-6165		727
Ingersoll-Rand Co 800-E Beaty St ... Davidson NC 28036 *Web:* www.ingersollrand.com	704-655-4000		641
Ingham County 315 S Jefferson St PO Box 179 ... Mason MI 48854 *Web:* www.ingham.org	517-676-7201	676-7254	338
Ingham Regional Medical Ctr 401 W Greenlawn Ave ... Lansing MI 48910 *TF:* 800-261-8018 ■ *Web:* www.mclaren.org	517-975-6000		374-3
Ingk Labs LLC 101 Fifth Ave ... New York NY 10003	646-350-3004		196
Ingle International 460 Richmond St W Ste 100 ... Toronto ON M5V1Y1 *TF:* 800-360-3234 ■ *Web:* ingleinternational.com	416-730-8488	730-1878	391-7
Ingles Markets Inc 2913 US Hwy 70 W ... Black Mountain NC 28711 *NASDAQ: IMKTA* ■ *TF:* 800-635-5066 ■ *Web:* www.ingles-markets.com	828-669-2941		345
Ingleside High School 2807 Mustang Dr ... Ingleside TX 78362 *TF:* 800-477-0177 ■ *Web:* www.inglesideisd.org	361-776-2712		685
Ingleside Inn 200 W Ramon Rd ... Palm Springs CA 92264 *TF:* 800-772-6655 ■ *Web:* www.inglesideinn.com	760-325-0046		379
Ingleside Plantation Nurseries 5870 Leedstown Rd ... Oak Grove VA 22443 *Web:* inglesidenurseries.com	804-224-7111		369
Ingleside Rock Creek 3050 Military Rd NW ... Washington DC 20015 *Web:* www.ircdc.org	202-363-8310		672
IngletBlair LLC 6207 Bee Cave Rd Ste 110 ... Austin TX 78746 *Web:* www.ingletblair.com	512-732-0498		225
Inglett & Stubbs LLC 5200 Riverview Rd ... Mableton GA 30126 *TF:* 800-561-3357 ■ *Web:* www.inglett-stubbs.com	404-881-1199	872-3101	189-4
Inglewood Associates LLC 9242 Headlands Rd ... Mentor OH 44060 *Web:* www.inglewoodassociates.com	216-672-5560		193
Inglewood Chamber of Commerce 330 E Queen St ... Inglewood CA 90301 *TF:* 800-682-8191 ■ *Web:* www.inglewoodchamber.com	310-677-1121	677-1001	139
Inglewood Park Cemetery Inc 720 E Florence Ave ... Inglewood CA 90301 *Web:* www.inglewoodparkcemetery.org	310-412-6500		510
Inglewood Public Library 101 W Manchester Blvd ... Inglewood CA 90301 *TF:* 800-984-4636 ■ *Web:* www.cityofinglewood.org/depts/library	310-412-5380		434-3
Ingomar Packing Co 9950 S Ingomar Grade PO Box 1448 ... Los Banos CA 93635 *TF:* 800-328-0026 ■ *Web:* www.ingomarpacking.com	209-826-9494	854-6292	296-20
Ingot Metal Company Ltd 111 Fenmar Dr ... Weston ON M9L1M3 *TF:* 800-567-7774 ■ *Web:* www.ingot.ca	416-749-1372		481
Ingram Barge Co 4400 HaRding Rd ... Nashville TN 37205 *Web:* www.ingrambarge.com	615-298-8200		314
Ingram Book Group 1 Ingram Blvd ... La Vergne TN 37086 *TF:* 800-937-7978 ■ *Web:* www.ingrambookgroup.com	615-793-5000	213-5710	96
Ingram Entertainment Inc 2 Ingram Blvd ... La Vergne TN 37089 *TF:* 800-621-1333 ■ *Web:* www.ingramentertainment.com	615-287-4000		511

Name / Address	City	State	ZIP	Phone	Fax	Class
Ingram Micro Inc 1600 E St Andrew Pl *NYSE:* IM ■ *Fax Area Code: 716 ■ *Fax:* Cust Svc ■ *TF Sales:* 800-456-8000 ■ *Web:* www.ingrammicro.com	Santa Ana	CA	92705	714-566-1000	565-8899*	174
Ingram Park Mall 6301 NW Loop 410 *TF:* 877-746-6642 ■ *Web:* www.simon.com	San Antonio	TX	78238	210-684-9570		460
Ingram Readymix Inc 3580 Fm 482 *Web:* www.ingramreadymixinc.com	New Braunfels	TX	78132	830-625-9156		182
Inhance Corp 609 Eighth St	Fort Madison	IA	52627	319-372-4920		379
Inhance Digital Corp 8057 Beverly Blvd Ste 200 *Web:* inhance.com	Los Angeles	CA	90048	323-297-7700		514
Inhand Electronics 30 W Gude Dr *Web:* inhand.com	Rockville	MD	20850	240-558-2014		261
Inhofe James M (Sen R - OK) 205 Russell Bldg *Web:* www.inhofe.senate.gov	Washington	DC	20510	202-224-4721	228-0380	342-2
inhouseIT 3193 Red Hill Ave *TF:* 800-431-2760 ■ *Web:* www.inhouseit.com	Costa Mesa	CA	92626	949-660-5655		177
INI Power Systems Inc 175 Southport Dr Ste 100 *Web:* inipowersystems.com	Morrisville	NC	27560	919-677-7112		262
Initial Outfitters Inc 209 Alabama St *Web:* www.initialoutfitters.com	Auburn	AL	36832	334-887-1856		195
Initiative Corp 5700 Wilshire Blvd Ste 400 *Web:* initiative.com	Los Angeles	CA	90036	323-370-8000		742
Initiative for a Competitive Inner City 200 High St Fl 3 *Web:* www.icic.org	Boston	MA	02110	617-292-2363		194
Initio Inc 2850 W Horizon Ridge Pkwy Ste 200 *Web:* initioinc.com	Henderson	NV	89052	201-621-0400		463
Initium 10300 old cutler rd *Web:* www.initium.com	Coral Gables	FL	33156	305-665-5212		463
Injen Technology Company Ltd 244 Pioneer Pl *Web:* www.injen.com	Pomona	CA	91768	909-839-0706		57
Injex Industries Inc 30559 San Antonio St *Web:* injexindustries.com	Hayward	CA	94544	510-487-4960		60
Injured Workers Insurance Fund 8722 Loch Raven Blvd *TF:* 800-264-4943 ■ *Web:* www.ceiwc.com	Towson	MD	21286	410-494-2000		391-4
InjuryFree Inc 20250 144Th Ave NE Ste 305 *Web:* www.ergostat.com	Woodinville	WA	98072	206-363-7676		260
Ink Custom Tees 400 Casey Dr *Web:* www.inkcustomtees.com	Maumelle	AR	72113	501-851-6916		687
Ink Inc 10561 Barkley St Ste 600 *Web:* www.inkincpr.com	Overland Park	KS	66212	816-753-6222		636
Ink Spot Inc, The 40 Oval Rd Ste 1 *TF:* 800-659-0069 ■ *Web:* theinkspot.com	Quincy	MA	02170	617-773-7605		627
Ink Technology Corp 18320 Lanken Ave *TF:* 800-633-2826 ■ *Web:* www.inktechnology.com	Cleveland	OH	44119	216-486-6720	486-6003	628
Inks Lake State Park 3630 Pk Rd 4 *Web:* tpwd.texas.gov/state-parks/inks-lake	Burnet	TX	78611	512-793-2223		565
Inkstone Printing Inc 129 Liberty St *Web:* www.inkstone.com	Brockton	MA	02301	508-587-5200		627
Inktel Direct Corp 13975 NW 58th Ct *TF:* 800-999-2100 ■ *Web:* www.inktel.com	Miami Lakes	FL	33014	305-523-1100		737
InkWell Management 521 Fifth Ave Ste 2600 *Web:* www.inkwellmanagement.com	New York	NY	10175	212-922-3500	922-0535	444
INL (Idaho National Laboratory) 2525 Fremont Ave *TF:* 866-495-7440 ■ *Web:* www.inl.gov	Idaho Falls	ID	83402	866-495-7440		668
Inland 2009 W Ave South *Web:* www.inlandpackaging.com	La Crosse	WI	54601	608-788-5800		627
Inland Aerial Surveys Inc 7117 Arlington Ave Ste A *Web:* inlandaerial.com	Riverside	CA	92503	951-687-4252		727
Inland Architect Magazine 3500 W Peterson Ave Ste 403 *Web:* www.inlandarchitectmag.com	Chicago	IL	60659	773-866-9900	866-9881	457-2
Inland Arts & Graphics Inc 14440 Edison Dr *TF:* 800-437-6003	New Lenox	IL	60451	800-437-6003		627
Inland Empire Magazine 3400 Central Ave Ste 160 *Web:* www.inlandempiremagazine.com	Riverside	CA	92506	951-682-3026	682-0246	457-22
Inland Empire Paper Co 3320 N Argonne Rd *TF:* 866-437-7711 ■ *Web:* www.iepco.com	Millwood	WA	99212	509-924-1911	927-8461	557
Inland Group Inc 2901 Butterfield Rd *TF:* 800-826-8228 ■ *Web:* www.inlandgroup.com	Oak Brook	IL	60523	630-218-8000		655
Inland Marine Industries Inc 3245 Depot Rd *Web:* www.inlandmetal.com	Hayward	CA	94545	510-785-8555		567
Inland Mortgage Corp 2901 Butterfield Rd *TF:* 800-826-8228 ■ *Web:* www.inlandgroup.com	Oak Brook	IL	60523	630-218-8000		509
Inland Northwest Blood Ctr 210 W Cataldo Ave *TF:* 800-423-0151 ■ *Web:* www.inbcsaves.org	Spokane	WA	99201	509-624-0151	232-4523	89
Inland Pacific Ballet 5050 Arrow Hwy *Web:* www.ipballet.org	Montclair	CA	91763	909-482-1590	482-1589	573-1
Inland Plastics Inc 201 Center St *Web:* www.inlandplastics.com	Rosedale	AB	T0J0Y0	403-823-6252		601
Inland Plywood Co 375 N Cass Ave *TF:* 800-521-4355 ■ *Web:* www.inlandplywood.com	Pontiac	MI	48342	248-334-4706	338-7407	613
Inland Power & Light Company Inc 10110 W Hallett Rd *TF:* 800-747-7151 ■ *Web:* www.inlandpower.com	Spokane	WA	99224	509-747-7151	747-7987	245
Inland Press Association 701 Lee St Ste 925 *Web:* inlandpress.org	Des Plaines	IL	60016	847-795-0380		138
Inland Productivity Solutions Inc 1153 W Ninth St *TF:* 800-314-6277 ■ *Web:* www.inland-prod.com	Upland	CA	91786	909-981-4500		177
Inland Real Estate Corp 2901 Butterfield Rd *NYSE:* IRC ■ *Fax:* Investor Rel ■ *Web:* www.inlandgroup.com	Oak Brook	IL	60523	630-218-8000	218-7357*	654
Inland Real Estate Development Corp 2901 Butterfield Rd *Web:* www.inlandgroup.com	Oak Brook	IL	60523	630-218-8000	990-5350	653
Inland Seafood Corp 1651 Montreal Cir *TF:* 800-883-3474 ■ *Web:* www.inlandseafood.com	Tucker	GA	30084	404-350-5850		297-5
Inland Technologies Inc 14 Queen St PO Box 253 *TF:* 877-633-5263 ■ *Web:* www.inlandgroup.ca	Truro	NS	B2N5C1	902-895-6346		192
Inland Valley Arbitration & Mediation Service (IVAMS) 8287 White Oak Ave *TF:* 800-244-8814 ■ *Web:* www.ivams.com	Rancho Cucamonga	CA	91730	909-466-1665	466-1796	41
Inland Valley Daily Bulletin 2041 E Fourth St *Web:* www.dailybulletin.com	Ontario	CA	91764	909-987-6397		532-2
Inlandboatmen's Union of the Pacific (IBU) 1711 W Nickerson St Ste D *TF:* 800-562-6000 ■ *Web:* www.ibu.org	Seattle	WA	98119	206-284-6001		414
Inlet Fish Producers Inc PO Box 114 *Web:* www.inletfish.com	Kenai	AK	99611	907-283-9275		296-13
Inlet Tower Hotel & Suites 1020 W 12th Ave *TF:* 800-544-0786 ■ *Web:* www.inlettower.com	Anchorage	AK	99501	907-276-0110	258-4914	379
InLine 600 Lakeshore Pkwy	Birmingham	AL	35209	205-278-8100		174
Inline Fibreglass Ltd 30 Constellation Ct *TF:* 866-566-5656 ■ *Web:* www.inlinefiberglass.com	Toronto	ON	M9W1K1	416-679-1171	679-1150	499
Inline Filling Systems Inc 216 Seaboard Ave *Web:* www.fillers.com	Venice	FL	34285	941-486-8800		547
Inline Packaging LLC 1205 18th Ave S *TF:* 800-419-6829 ■ *Web:* www.inlinepkg.com	Princeton	MN	55371	763-631-1555		317
Inline Plastics Corp 42 Canal St *TF:* 800-826-5567 ■ *Web:* www.inlineplastics.com	Shelton	CT	06484	203-924-5933	924-0370	602
Inline Services Inc 27731 Commercial Park Rd *Web:* www.inlineservices.com	Tomball	TX	77375	281-401-8142		358
inlingua International 551 Fifth Ave *Web:* www.inlinguametrony.com	New York	NY	10176	212-682-8585		423
Inman Mills 300 Pk Rd PO Box 207 *Web:* www.inmanmills.com	Inman	SC	29349	864-472-2121		745-1
Inman News 1100 Marina Village Pkwy Ste 102 *TF:* 800-775-4662 ■ *Web:* www.inman.com	Alameda	CA	94501	510-658-9252		530
Inman-EMJ Construction 88 Union Ave Ste 400	Memphis	TN	38103	901-682-4100		186
INMED Partnerships for Children 20110 Ashbrook Pl Ste 260 *TF:* 800-552-7096 ■ *Web:* www.inmed.org	Ashburn	VA	20147	703-729-4951	858-7253	48-5
Inmediata Health Group Corp 342 Calle San Luis Ste 203 *Web:* www.inmediata.com	San Juan	PR	00920	787-774-0606		225
Inmedius Inc 2247 Babcock Blvd *TF:* 800-697-7110 ■ *Web:* www.inmedius.com	Pittsburgh	PA	15237	800-697-7110		177
Inn & Spa at Loretto 211 Old Santa Fe Trl *TF:* 800-727-5531 ■ *Web:* www.destinationhotels.com/inn-at-loretto	Santa Fe	NM	87501	505-988-5531	984-7968	379
Inn Above Tide, The 30 El Portal *TF:* 800-893-8433 ■ *Web:* innabovetide.com	Sausalito	CA	94965	415-332-9535		379
Inn at Bay Harbor, The 3600 Village Harbor Dr *TF:* 800-462-6963 ■ *Web:* www.innatbayharbor.com	Bay Harbor	MI	49770	231-439-4000		669
Inn at Camachee Harbor 201 Yacht Club Dr *TF:* 800-688-5379 ■ *Web:* www.camacheeinn.com	Saint Augustine	FL	32084	904-825-0003	825-0048	379
Inn at Cherry Hill 500 17th Ave *Web:* www.swedish.org	Seattle	WA	98122	206-320-2164		372
Inn at Gig Harbor 3211 56th St NW *TF:* 800-795-9980 ■ *Web:* www.innatgigharbor.com	Gig Harbor	WA	98335	253-858-1111	851-5402	379
Inn at Harbour Town 7 Lighthouse Ln *TF Resv:* 800-732-7463	Hilton Head Island	SC	29928	843-363-8100		379
Inn at Henderson's Wharf 1000 Fell St *Web:* www.hendersonswharf.com	Baltimore	MD	21231	410-522-7777		379
Inn at Jackson Hole, The 3345 W Village Dr PO Box 328 *Web:* www.innatjacksonhole.com	Teton Village	WY	83025	307-733-2311		378
Inn at Lambertville Station 11 Bridge St *TF:* 800-524-1091 ■ *Web:* www.lambertvillestation.com	Lambertville	NJ	08530	609-397-4400		379
Inn at Langley 400 First St PO Box 835 *TF:* 800-843-3779 ■ *Web:* www.innatlangley.com	Langley	WA	98260	360-221-3033	221-3033	379
Inn at Little Washington Middle & Main St PO Box 300 *Web:* www.theinnatlittlewashington.com	Washington	VA	22747	540-675-3800	675-3100	379
Inn at Longshore 260 Compo Rd S *Web:* www.innatlongshore.com	Westport	CT	06880	203-226-3316		379
Inn at Mamas Fish House 799 Poho Pl *TF:* 800-860-4852 ■ *Web:* mamasfishhouse.com	Paia	HI	96779	808-579-8488		378
Inn at Montchanin Village 528 Montchanin Rd *TF:* 800-269-2473 ■ *Web:* www.montchanin.com	Montchanin	DE	19710	302-888-2133	691-0198	379
Inn at Montpelier, The 147 Main St *TF:* 800-666-8907 ■ *Web:* www.innatmontpelier.com	Montpelier	VT	05602	802-223-2727	223-0722	379
Inn at Morro Bay 60 State Pk Rd *TF:* 800-321-9566 ■ *Web:* www.innatmorrobay.com	Morro Bay	CA	93442	805-772-5651	772-4779	379
Inn at Mystic 3 Williams Ave PO Box 526 *TF:* 800-237-2415 ■ *Web:* www.innatmystic.com	Mystic	CT	06355	860-536-9604		379

	Phone	Fax	Class
Inn at National Hall 100 W Putnam Ave........................Greenwich CT 06830 *TF:* 800-628-4255 ■ *Web:* www.innatnationalhall.com	203-221-1351		379
Inn at Nichols Village 1101 Northern Blvd ....Clarks Summit PA 18411 *Web:* www.nicholsvillage.com	570-587-1135	586-7140	379
Inn at Otter Crest 301 Otter Crest Loop ....Otter Rock OR 97369 *TF:* 800-452-2101 ■ *Web:* www.innatottercrest.com	541-765-2111		379
Inn at Oyster Point 425 Marina Blvd.............................South San Francisco CA 94080 *Web:* www.innatoysterpoint.com	650-737-7633		379
Inn at Pelican Bay 800 Vanderbilt Beach Rd...........................Naples FL 34108 *TF:* 800-597-8770 ■ *Web:* www.innatpelicanbay.com	239-597-8777	597-8012	379
Inn at Perry Cabin 308 Watkins Ln.........................Saint Michaels MD 21663 *TF:* 800-722-2949 ■ *Web:* belmond.com/inn-at-perry-cabin-st-michaels	410-745-2200	745-3348	379
Inn at Queen Anne 505 First Ave N................Seattle WA 98109 *TF:* 800-952-5043 ■ *Web:* www.innatqueenanne.com	206-282-7357		379
Inn at Rancho Santa Fe 5951 Linea Del Cielo PO Box 869 ....Rancho Santa Fe CA 92067 *TF:* 800-843-4661 ■ *Web:* www.theinnatrsf.com	858-756-1131		669
Inn at Reading, The 1040 N Pk Rd..........Wyomissing PA 19610 *TF:* 800-383-9713 ■ *Web:* www.innatreading.com	610-372-7811		379
Inn at Saint John 939 Congress St..............Portland ME 04102 *TF:* 800-636-9127 ■ *Web:* www.innatstjohn.com	207-773-6481		379
Inn at Saint Mary's 53993 US Hwy 31-33 N ....South Bend IN 46637 *Web:* www.innatsaintmarys.com	574-232-4000		379
Inn at Sawmill Farm, The 7 Crosstown Rd ....West Dover VT 05356 *Web:* www.innatsawmillfarm.com	802-464-4300		379
Inn at Spanish Bay, The 2700 17-Mile Dr.........................Pebble Beach CA 93953 *TF:* 800-654-9300 ■ *Web:* www.pebblebeach.com	831-647-7500	622-3603	669
Inn at Spanish Head 4009 SW Hwy 101 ....Lincoln City OR 97367 *TF:* 800-452-8127 ■ *Web:* www.spanishhead.com	541-996-2161	996-4089	379
Inn at Stratton Mountain 5 Village Lodge Rd..................Stratton Mountain VT 05155 *TF:* 800-787-2886 ■ *Web:* www.stratton.com	802-297-2500		669
Inn at Tallgrass, The 2280 N Tara Cir ....Wichita KS 67226 *Web:* www.theinnattallgrass.com	316-684-3466		379
Inn at the Market 86 Pine St ....Seattle WA 98101 *TF:* 800-446-4484 ■ *Web:* www.innatthemarket.com	206-443-3600		379
Inn At The Quay 900 Quayside Dr....................New Westminster BC V3M6G1 *TF:* 800-663-2001 ■ *Web:* www.innatwestminsterquay.com	604-520-1776	520-5645	379
Inn at Union Square 440 Post St ....San Francisco CA 94102 *TF:* 800-288-4346 ■ *Web:* www.greystonehotels.com	415-397-3510	989-0529	379
Inn at USC Columbia South Caolina Hotel 1619 Pendleton St ....Columbia SC 29201 *Web:* www.innatusc.com	803-779-7779		378
Inn at Virginia Mason 1006 Spring St............Seattle WA 98104 *TF:* 800-283-6453 ■ *Web:* www.innatvirginiamason.com	206-583-6453		372
Inn at Virginia Tech & Skelton Conference Ctr 901 Prices Fork Rd.......................Blacksburg VA 24061 *TF:* 877-200-3360 ■ *Web:* www.innatvirginiatech.com	540-231-8000	231-0146	377
Inn at Wall Street Ltd, The 9 S William St.............................New York NY 10004 *Web:* www.thewallstreetinn.com	212-747-1500		772
Inn at, The Tides, The 800 Coast Hwy 1 ....Bodega Bay CA 94923 *TF:* 800-541-7788 ■ *Web:* www.innatthetides.com	707-875-2751	875-2669	379
Inn by the Sea 40 Bowery Beach Rd....................Cape Elizabeth ME 04107 *TF:* 800-888-4287 ■ *Web:* www.innbythesea.com	207-799-3134		669
Inn of Chicago Magnificent Mile 162 E Ohio St..............................Chicago IL 60611 *Web:* www.theinnofchicago.com	312-787-3100		379
Inn of Long Beach 185 Atlantic Ave ....Long Beach CA 90802 *TF:* 800-230-7500 ■ *Web:* www.innoflongbeach.com	562-435-3791	436-7510	379
Inn of the Anasazi 113 Washington Ave........................Santa Fe NM 87501 *TF:* 888-767-3966 ■ *Web:* www.rosewoodhotels.com	505-988-3030	988-3277	379
Inn of the Governors 101 W Alameda St ....Santa Fe NM 87501 *TF:* 800-234-4534 ■ *Web:* www.innofthegovernors.com	505-982-4333		379
Inn of the Hills River Resort 1001 Junction Hwy.........................Kerrville TX 78028 *TF:* 800-292-5690 ■ *Web:* www.innofthehills.com	830-895-5000		669
Inn of the Mountain Gods 287 Carrizo Canyon Rd....................Mescalero NM 88340 *TF:* 800-545-9011 ■ *Web:* www.innofthemountaingods.com	800-545-9011		669
Inn on Biltmore Estate 1 Antler Hill Rd.............................Asheville NC 28803 *TF:* 800-411-3812 ■ *Web:* www.biltmore.com	828-225-1600		379
Inn on Fifth 699 Fifth Ave S.....................Naples FL 34102 *TF:* 888-403-8778 ■ *Web:* innonfifth.com	239-403-8777	403-8778	379
Inn on Gitche Gumee 8517 Congdon Blvd.........Duluth MN 55804 *TF:* 800-317-4979 ■ *Web:* www.innongitchegumee.com	218-525-4979		379
Inn on Lake Superior 350 Canal Pk Dr............Duluth MN 55802 *TF:* 888-668-4352 ■ *Web:* www.theinnonlakesuperior.com	218-726-1111	727-3976	379
Inn on Long Wharf 5 Washington St............Newport RI 02840 *Web:* extraholidays.com	401-847-7800		669
Inn on the Alameda 303 E Alameda St...........Santa Fe NM 87501 *TF:* 888-984-2121 ■ *Web:* www.innonthealameda.com	505-984-2121		379
Inn on the Creek 295 N Millward Ave............Jackson WY 83001 *Web:* bedandbreakfast.com	307-739-1565		379
Inn on the Paseo 630 Paseo de Peralta ....Santa Fe NM 87501 *TF:* 855-984-8200 ■ *Web:* www.innonthepaseo.com	505-984-8200		379
Inner City Law Ctr 1309 E Seventh St ....Los Angeles CA 90021 *Web:* www.innercitylaw.org	213-891-2880		428
Inner Traditions International 1 Pk Row ....Rochester VT 05767 *TF:* 800-246-8648 ■ *Web:* www.innertraditions.com	802-767-3174	767-3726	637-2
Innergy Power Corp Inc 9051 Siempre Viva Rd Bldg 6 Ste AB..........San Diego CA 92154 *Web:* www.innergypower.com	619-710-0758		253
Innerspec Technologies Inc 2940 Perrowville Rd ....Forest VA 24551 *Web:* www.innerspec.com	434-948-1301		463
Innerstave LLC 21660 Eighth St E...............Sonoma CA 95476 *Web:* www.innerstave.com	707-996-8781		385
Innerworkings Inc 600 W Chicago Ave Ste 850...................Chicago IL 60654 *NASDAQ: INWK* ■ *Web:* www.inwk.com	312-642-3700		687
Innis Maggiore Group Inc 4715 Whipple Ave NW ....Canton OH 44718 *TF:* 800-460-4111 ■ *Web:* www.innismaggiore.com	330-492-5500	492-5568	4
Innisbrook Resort & Golf Club 36750 US Hwy 19 N .... Palm Harbor FL 34684 *TF:* 800-492-6899 ■ *Web:* www.innisbrookgolfresort.com	727-942-2000	942-5576	669
Inniswood Metro Gardens 940 S Hempstead Rd ....Westerville OH 43081 *Web:* www.inniswood.org	614-895-6216	895-6352	97
Innkeepers USA Trust 340 Royal Poinciana Way Ste 306 ....Palm Beach FL 33480	561-835-1800	835-0457	654
Innocean USA 180 Fifth St Ste 200 .... Huntington Beach CA 92648 *Web:* www.innocean.com	714-861-5200		5
Innocence Project of Florida Inc 1100 E Park Ave .... Tallahassee FL 32301 *TF:* 800-733-9529 ■ *Web:* www.floridainnocence.org	850-561-6767		428
Innodata-Isogen Inc 3 University Plaza Dr .... Hackensack NJ 07601 *NASDAQ: INOD* ■ *TF:* 877-454-8400 ■ *Web:* www.innodata.com	201-371-8000		178-12
Innography Inc 3900 N Capital Of Tx Hwy Ste 175 .... Austin TX 78746	512-306-8688		177
Innolect Inc 1004 Palmyra Dr .... Tega Cay SC 29708 *Web:* innolectinc.com	803-396-8500		193
InnoMedia Inc 1901 McCarthy Blvd ....Milpitas CA 95035 *Web:* www.innomedia.com	408-432-5400	941-8152	735
Innonet LLC 2 Huntley Rd.....................Old Lyme CT 06371 *Web:* www.innonetllc.com	860-395-0700		180
Innophos Holdings Inc 259 Prospect Plains Rd ....Cranbury NJ 08512 *NASDAQ: IPHS* ■ *Web:* www.innophos.com	609-495-2495		146
Innosight LLC 92 Hayden Ave ....Lexington MA 02421 *Web:* innosight.com	781-652-7200		463
InnoSource Inc 6085 Emerald Pkwy .... Dublin OH 43016 *Web:* innosource.com	614-775-1400		260
Innospec Inc 8375 S Willow St..................Littleton CO 80124 *NASDAQ: IOSP* ■ *Web:* www.innospecinc.com	303-792-5554		144
Innosphere Systems Development Group Ltd 147 Wyndham St N Ste 306....................Guelph ON N1H4E9 *Web:* innosphere.ca	519-766-9726		180
Innotap 200 N Warner Rd Ste 210............... King of Prussia PA 19406 *TF:* 855-438-4666 ■ *Web:* innotap.com	855-438-4666		225
Innotech-Execaire Aviation Group 10225 Ryan Ave Montreal International Airport ....Dorval QC H9P1A2 *Web:* www.innotech-execaire.com	514-636-8484		21
Innotek Corp 9140 Zachary Ln N............ Maple Grove MN 55369 *Web:* www.innotek-ep.com	763-493-2810		454
In-N-Out Burger Inc 4199 Campus Dr 9th Fl ....Irvine CA 92612 *TF Cust Svc:* 800-786-1000 ■ *Web:* www.in-n-out.com	949-509-6200		670
Innova Engineering Inc 2 Park Plaza Ste 510............................Irvine CA 92614 *Web:* www.innovaengineering.com	949-975-9965		256
INNOVA Medical Ophthalmics Inc 48 Carnforth Rd .... Toronto ON M4A2K7 *Web:* www.innovamed.com	416-615-0185		543
Innova Technologies Inc 1432 S Jones Blvd .... Las Vegas NV 89146 *Web:* www.innovanv.com	702-220-6640		261
InnoVactiv Inc 265 2E Rue E..................Rimouski QC G5L9H3 **Fax Area Code: 417* ■ *Web:* www.innovactiv.com	418-721-2308	721-2318*	146
Innovadex LLC 7930 Santa Fe 3rd Fl .... Overland Park KS 66204 *TF:* 877-292-7279 ■ *Web:* www.ulprospector.com	913-307-9010		393
Innovage LLC 19511 Pauling............Foothill Ranch CA 92610	949-587-9207		4
Innovairre Communications LLC 825 Hylton Rd...........................Pennsauken NJ 08110 *Web:* www.innovairre.com	856-663-2500		466
Innovara Inc 21 Pray St........................Amherst MA 01002 *Web:* www.innovara.com	413-549-5888		41
Innovasic Inc 5635 Jefferson St NE Ste A................ Albuquerque NM 87109 *Web:* www.innovasic.com	505-883-5263		180
Innovasium Inc 55 Albert St Ste 200............Markham ON L3P2T4 *Web:* www.innovasium.com	905-479-5555		225
Innovasys 36735 Metro Ct..............Sterling Heights MI 48312 *Web:* innovasys1.com	586-795-3000		358
Innovasystems International LLC 2385 Northside Dr Ste 300..................San Diego CA 92108 *Web:* www.innovasi.com	619-955-5800	955-5801	177
Innovate E-Commerce Inc 160 N Craig St .... Pittsburgh PA 15213 *TF:* 888-771-9606 ■ *Web:* innovateec.com	888-771-9606		631
InnovaTech Inc 1800 Diagonal Rd ....Alexandria VA 22314 *Web:* www.innovateteam.com	703-418-3919		177
Innovated Packaging Company Inc 38505 Cherry St..................................Newark CA 94560 *Web:* www.innovpak.com	510-745-8180		88
Innovatia Inc 1 Germain St...................Saint John NB E2L4V1 *TF:* 800-363-3358 ■ *Web:* www.innovatia.net	506-640-4000		463
Innovation Capital LLC 222 N Sepulveda Blvd Ste 1300............. El Segundo CA 90245 *Web:* www.innovation-capital.com	310-335-9333		194
Innovation Genesis LLC 75 Arlington St Ste 500 ....Boston MA 02116 *Web:* www.productgenesis.com	617-234-0070		261

Company / Address	City	State	Zip	Phone	Fax	Class
Innovation Works Inc 2000 Technology Dr Ste 250 — *Web:* www.innovationworks.org	Pittsburgh	PA	15219	412-681-1520	681-2625	792
Innovative Artists 1505 Tenth St — *Web:* www.innovativeartists.com	Santa Monica	CA	90401	310-656-0400		731
Innovative Components Inc 1050 National Pkwy — *Web:* www.inco-co.com	Schaumburg	IL	60173	847-885-9050		596
Innovative Configuration Inc 712 Via Palo Alto	Aptos	CA	95003	831-688-6917		529
Innovative Data Management Systems LLC 4006 W Azeele St — *TF:* 866-706-4588 ■ *Web:* idmsystems.com	Tampa	FL	33609	813-207-2025		177
Innovative Employee Solutions Inc 9665 Granite Ridge Dr Ste 420 — *Web:* www.innovativeemployeesolutions.com	San Diego	CA	92123	858-715-5100		734
Innovative Enterprises Inc 25 Town & Country Dr — *TF:* 800-280-0300 ■ *Web:* www.innovative-1.com	Washington	MO	63090	636-390-0300	390-4004	548
Innovative Fluid Handling Systems 3300 E Rock Falls Rd — *TF:* 800-435-7003 ■ *Web:* www.ifhgroup.com	Rock Falls	IL	61071	815-626-1018	626-1438	198
Innovative Hearth Products 1508 Elm Hill Pk Ste 108 — *Web:* ihp.us.com	Nashville	TN	37210	714-921-6100	921-6149	361
Innovative Industrial Solutions Inc 2830 Skyline Dr — *TF:* 888-684-8249 ■ *Web:* www.i-i-s.net	Russellville	AR	72802	479-968-4266		693
Innovative Information Solutions Inc 61 I- Ln. — *TF:* 800-343-8121 ■ *Web:* www.innovativeis.com	Waterbury	CT	06705	203-756-4243		179
Innovative Injection Technologies Inc 2360 Grand Ave — *Web:* www.i2-tech.com	West Des Moines	IA	50265	515-225-6707	225-9673	604
Innovative Integration Inc 2390-A Ward Ave — *Web:* www.innovative-dsp.com	Simi Valley	CA	93065	805-578-4260		637-10
Innovative Mattress Solutions LLC 1721 Jaggie Fox Way — *TF:* 800-766-4163 ■ *Web:* www.innovativemattresssolutions.com	Lexington	KY	40511	800-766-4163		321
Innovative Metals Company Inc (IMETCO) 4648 S Old Peachtree Rd — *TF:* 800-646-3826 ■ *Web:* www.imetco.com	Norcross	GA	30071	770-908-1030	908-2264	46
Innovative Optics Inc 6812 Hemlock Ln — *Web:* www.innovativeoptics.com	Maple Grove	MN	55369	763-425-7789		475
Innovative Packaging Corp 9400 W Heather Ave — *Web:* www.ipcsheets.com	Milwaukee	WI	53224	414-410-6000		100
Innovative Plastech Inc 1260 Kingsland Dr — *Web:* www.inplas.com	Batavia	IL	60510	630-232-1808		596
Innovative Plastics Corp 400 Rt 303 — *TF:* 800-290-1347 ■ *Web:* innovative-plastics.com	Orangeburg	NY	10962	845-359-7500	359-0237	601
Innovative Resources Consultant Group Inc 1 Pk Plaza Ste 600 — *Web:* www.ircginc.com	Irvine	CA	92614	949-252-0590	252-0592	194
Innovative Security Systems Inc 1809 Woodfield Dr — *Web:* gdc4s.com/pitbull	Savoy	IL	61874	217-355-6308		178-12
Innovative Solutions & Support Inc 720 Pennsylvania Dr. — *NASDAQ:* ISSC ■ *TF:* 866-359-7876 ■ *Web:* www.innovative-ss.com	Exton	PA	19341	610-646-9800	646-0149	529
Innovative Stamping Corp 2060 E Gladwick St. — *TF:* 800-400-0047 ■ *Web:* www.innovative-sys.com	Compton	CA	90220	310-537-6996	537-0312	488
Innovative Surfaces Inc 515 Spiral Blvd — *Web:* www.innovativesurfaces.com	Hastings	MN	55033	651-437-1004		115
Innovative Systems Group Inc 799 Roosevelt Rd — *TF:* 800-739-2400 ■ *Web:* www.innovativesys.com	Glen Ellyn	IL	60137	630-858-8500		177
Innovative Systems Inc 790 Holiday Dr Bldg 11 — *TF:* 800-622-6390 ■ *Web:* www.innovativesystems.com	Pittsburgh	PA	15220	412-937-9300		178-1
Innovative Technologies Corp (ITC) 1020 Woodman Dr Ste 100 — *TF:* 800-745-8050 ■ *Web:* www.itc-1.com	Dayton	OH	45432	937-252-2145	254-6853	178-10
Innovative Telecom Solutions Inc 9 Vela Way — *TF:* 800-510-3000 ■ *Web:* www.innovativetel.com	Edgewater	NJ	07020	800-510-3000		387
Innovative USA Inc 50 Washington St — *Web:* www.innovativekids.com	Norwalk	CT	06854	203-838-6400	855-5582	94
Innovent Air Handling Equipment 60 28th Ave N — *TF:* 877-218-4129 ■ *Web:* innoventair.com	Minneapolis	MN	55411	612-877-4800		358
Innovest Portfolio Solutions LLC 4643 S Ulster St Ste 1040 — *Web:* www.innovestinc.com	Denver	CO	80237	303-694-1900		401
Innovid Inc 30 Irving P Fl 12 — *Web:* www.innovid.com	New York	NY	10003	212-966-7555		5
Innovize Inc 500 Oak Grove Pkwy — *TF:* 877-605-6580 ■ *Web:* www.innovize.com	Saint Paul	MN	55127	877-605-6580		602
Innovus Pharmaceuticals, Inc. 1981 Murray Holladay R. — *Web:* innovuspharma.com	Salt Lake City	UT	84117	801-272-9294		85
InnoZen Inc 6429 Independence Ave	Woodland Hills	CA	91367	805-822-5091		231
InnQuest Software Corp 5300 W Cypress Ste 160 — *Web:* www.innquest.com	Tampa	FL	33607	813-288-4900		174
Inns at Mill Falls 312 Daniel Webster Hwy — *TF:* 800-622-6455 ■ *Web:* www.millfalls.com	Meredith	NH	03253	800-622-6455		379
Inns of America Suites 755 Raintree Dr Ste 200	Carlsbad	CA	92011	760-438-6661		379
InnSuites Hospitality Trust 1625 E Northern Ave Ste 105 — *NYSE:* IHT ■ *Web:* www.innsuitestrust.com	Phoenix	AZ	85020	602-944-1500		654
InnSuites Hospitality Trust InnSuites Hotels & Suites 475 N Granada Ave — *TF:* 800-842-4242 ■ *Web:* www.innsuites.com	Tucson	AZ	85701	520-622-0923		379
InnSuites Hotel Tempe/Phoenix Airport 1651 W Baseline Rd — *TF:* 800-842-4242 ■ *Web:* www.innsuites.com/tempe-hotel.html	Tempe	AZ	85283	480-897-7900	491-1008	379
InnSuites Hotel Tucson City Ctr 475 N Granada Ave — *Web:* www.innsuites.com/tucson_citycenter	Tucson	AZ	85701	520-622-3000		379
Ino.Com Inc 4800 Atwell Rd Discovery Village — *TF:* 800-538-7424 ■ *Web:* www.ino.com	Shady Side	MD	20764	410-867-2100		463
Inogen Inc 326 Bollay Dr — *Web:* www.inogen.com	Goleta	CA	93117	805-562-0500		476
Inolex Chemical Co 2101 S Swanson St — *Fax: Cust Svc ■ *TF Cust Svc:* 800-521-9891 ■ *Web:* www.inolex.com	Philadelphia	PA	19148	215-271-0800	271-6282*	144
Inotek Pharmaceuticals Corp 91 Hartwell Ave 2nd Fl — *Web:* inotekpharma.com	Lexington	MA	02421	781-676-2100		231
Inova Alexandria Hospital 4320 Seminary Rd — *TF:* 800-526-7101 ■ *Web:* www.inova.org	Alexandria	VA	22304	703-504-3000		374-3
Inova Diagnostics Inc 9900 Old Grove Rd — *TF:* 800-545-9495 ■ *Web:* www.inovadx.com	San Diego	CA	92131	858-586-9900	586-9911	231
Inova Fair Oaks Hospital 3600 Joseph Siewick Dr — *TF:* 800-208-8649 ■ *Web:* www.inova.org	Fairfax	VA	22033	703-391-3600	391-3273	374-3
Inova Fairfax Hospital 3300 Gallows Rd — *TF:* 800-838-8238 ■ *Web:* www.inova.org	Falls Church	VA	22042	703-776-4001	776-6128	374-3
Inova Federal Credit Union 358 S Elkhart Ave — *Web:* inovafcu.org	Elkhart	IN	46516	574-294-6553		70
INOVA Geophysical Equipment Ltd 12200 Parc Crest Dr — *Web:* www.inovageo.com	Stafford	TX	77477	281-568-2000		539
Inova Health System 8110 Gatehouse Rd — *Fax Area Code: 703 ■ *TF:* 855-694-6682 ■ *Web:* www.inova.org	Falls Church	VA	22042	855-694-6682	504-6607*	353
Inova Mount Vernon Hospital 2501 Parkers Ln — *Web:* www.inova.org	Alexandria	VA	22306	703-664-7000		374-3
Inova Payroll Inc 176 Thompson Ln Ste 204 — *TF:* 888-244-6106 ■ *Web:* www.inovapayroll.com	Nashville	TN	37211	615-921-0600		734
Inova Solutions Inc 110 Avon St — *TF:* 800-637-1077 ■ *Web:* www.inovasolutions.com	Charlottesville	VA	22902	434-817-8000	817-8002	178-1
Inovalon Inc 4321 Collington Rd — *Web:* www.inovalon.com	Bowie	MD	20716	301-809-4000		363
Inovar Inc 1073 W 1700 N — *TF:* 866-898-4949 ■ *Web:* www.inovar-inc.com	Logan	UT	84321	435-792-4949		393
Inovar Packaging Group LLC 602 Magic Mile — *Web:* www.inovarpkg.com	Arlington	TX	76011	817-277-6666		627
In-O-Vate Technologies Inc 810 Saturn St Ste 21 — *TF:* 888-443-7937 ■ *Web:* www.dryerbox.com	Jupiter	FL	33477	561-743-8696		191-1
Inovatia Laboratories LLC 120 E Davis St — *TF:* 800-280-1912 ■ *Web:* inovatia.com	Fayette	MO	65248	660-248-1911		743
Inovex Industries Inc 45681 Oakbrook Ct Ste 102 — *TF:* 888-374-3366 ■ *Web:* www.ride-on.com	Sterling	VA	20166	703-421-9778		3
Inovex Information Systems Inc 7240 Pkwy Dr Ste 140 — *TF:* 800-469-9705 ■ *Web:* www.inovexcorp.com	Hanover	MD	21076	443-782-1452		180
Inovio Pharmaceuticals Inc 660 W Germantown Pk Ste 110 — *NASDAQ:* INOVIO ■ *TF:* 877-446-6846 ■ *Web:* www.inovio.com	Plymouth	PA	19462	267-440-4200		250
Inovise Medical Inc 8770 SW Nimbus Ave Ste D — *TF:* 877-466-8473 ■ *Web:* www.inovise.com	Beaverton	OR	97008	503-431-3800		476
Inovo LLC 213 S Ashley St Ste 300 — *TF:* 888-464-6686 ■ *Web:* www.theinovogroup.com	Ann Arbor	MI	48104	888-464-6686		463
Inovonics Corp 397 S Taylor Ave. — *Web:* www.inovonics.com	Louisville	CO	80027	303-939-9336		693
Inpa System 22 Great Oaks Blvd — *Web:* www.inpasystems.com	San Jose	CA	95119	408-362-1541		226
InPath Devices 3610 Dodge St Ste 200 — *TF:* 800-988-1914 ■ *Web:* www.inpath.com	Omaha	NE	68131	402-345-9200		173-7
In-place Machining Company Inc 3811 N Holton St — *TF:* 800-833-3575 ■ *Web:* inplace.com	Milwaukee	WI	53212	414-562-2000		697
Inpower LLC 3555 Africa Rd — *TF:* 866-548-0965 ■ *Web:* www.inpowerdirect.com	Galena	OH	43021	740-548-0965		350
Inprov Ltd 2150 E Continental Blvd — *Web:* www.inprov.biz	Southlake	TX	76092	817-748-0300		463
Input 1 LLC 6200 Canoga Ave Ste 400 — *TF:* 888-882-2554 ■ *Web:* www.input1.com	Woodland Hills	CA	91367	818-713-2303		178-10
Input Solutions Inc 9250 Gaither Rd — *TF:* 800-914-2259 ■ *Web:* www.inputsolutions.com	Gaithersburg	MD	20877	301-948-6620		225
In-Q-Tel 2107 Wilson Blvd Ste 1100 — *Web:* www.iqt.org	Arlington	VA	22201	703-248-3000		792
InQuest Marketing Inc 9249 Ward Pkwy — *Web:* www.inquestmarketing.com	Kansas City	MO	64114	816-994-0994		636
Inquipco 2730 N Nellis Blvd — *TF:* 800-598-3465 ■ *Web:* www.inquipco.com	Las Vegas	NV	89115	702-644-1700		190
Inquiries Inc 129 N W St — *TF:* 866-987-3767 ■ *Web:* www.inquiriesinc.com	Easton	MD	21601	410-819-3711		400

Company / Address	City	State	Zip	Phone	Fax	Class
Inquiry Systems Inc 1195 Goodale Blvd TF: 800-508-1116 ■ Web: www.inquirysys.com	Columbus	OH	43212	614-464-3800		195
Inrad Inc 4375 Donker Ct SE TF: 800-558-4647 ■ Web: www.inrad-inc.com	Kentwood	MI	49512	616-301-7800		476
Inrad Optics Inc 181 Legrand Ave. Web: www.inradoptics.com	Northvale	NJ	07647	201-767-1910		253
In-Rel Properties Inc 2328 Tenth Ave N Ste 401 Web: in-rel.com	Lake Worth	FL	33461	561-533-0344		652
inRESONANCE Inc 32 Industrial Dr E Ste 100 Web: www.inresonance.com	Northampton	MA	01060	413-587-0236		177
INS (Infusion Nurses Society) 315 Norwood Pk S TF: 800-694-0298 ■ Web: www.ins1.org	Norwood	MA	02062	781-440-9408	440-9409	49-8
INS (International Neuropsychological Society) 700 Ackerman Rd Ste 625 TF: 800-999-6673 ■ Web: www.the-ins.org	Columbus	OH	43202	614-263-4200	263-4366	49-15
Insaco Inc 1365 Canary Rd Web: www.insaco.com	Quakertown	PA	18951	215-536-3500	536-7750	621
Inscape Publishing Inc 6465 Wayzata Blvd Ste 800 TF: 877-735-8383 ■ Web: everythingdisc.com	Minneapolis	MN	55426	763-765-2222	765-2277	178-3
Insco Distributing Inc 12501 Network Blvd TF: 855-282-4295 ■ Web: www.inscohvac.com	San Antonio	TX	78249	210-690-8400	690-1524	665
Insegment Inc 313 Washington St Ste 401 Web: www.insegment.com	Newton	MA	02458	617-965-0800		5
Insequence Inc 750 Jim Parker Dr Web: www.insequence.com	Smyrna	TN	37167	615-459-8943		177
Inserts East Inc 7045 Central Hwy Web: www.insertseast.com	Pennsauken	NJ	08109	856-663-8181		174
InService America Inc 129 Vista Centre Dr Web: www.inserviceamerica.com	Forest	VA	24551	434-316-7400		737
In-Shape Health Clubs 6 S El Dorado St Ste 600 TF: 877-446-7427 ■ Web: www.inshape.com	Stockton	CA	95210	209-472-2450	472-2235	354
Inside Edition Inc 1700 Broadway 33rd Fl. Web: www.insideedition.com	New York	NY	10019	212-817-5423		116
Inside Ideas Inc 49 Broadway St Ste 202 Web: www.thegossagency.com	Asheville	NC	28801	828-225-6888		7
Inside NRC 2 Penn Plaza 25th Fl TF: 800-752-8878 ■ Web: www.platts.com	New York	NY	10121	800-752-8878		531-5
Inside Publications 6221 N Clark St Web: www.insideonline.com	Chicago	IL	60660	773-465-9700	465-9800	532-4
Inside Self Storage Magazine 3300 N Central Ave Ste 300 TF: 800-528-1056 ■ Web: www.insideselfstorage.com	Phoenix	AZ	85012	480-990-1101	990-0819	457-21
Inside Source Inc 985 Industrial Rd Ste 101 Web: www.insidesource.com	San Carlos	CA	94070	650-508-9101		321
Inside Washington Publishers 1919 S Eads St Ste 201 TF: 800-424-9068 ■ Web: www.iwpnews.com	Arlington	VA	22202	703-416-8500	416-8543	637-9
InsideCounsel 120 Broadway 5th Fl *Fax Area Code: 312 ■ Web: www.insidecounsel.com	New York	NY	10271	212-457-9400	654-3525*	457-15
InsideFlyer Magazine 1930 Frequent Flyer Pt TF: 888-407-4747 ■ Web: www.insideflyer.com	Colorado Springs	CO	80915	719-597-8889		457-22
Insider Marketing 10801 E Northwest Hwy Web: www.insidermarketing.com	Dallas	TX	75238	214-348-4350		195
InsideUp Inc 9245 Activity Rd Ste 210 TF: 800-889-6178 ■ Web: www.insideup.com	San Diego	CA	92126	858-397-5735		393
Insight 444 Scott Dr TF: 800-467-4448 ■ Web: www.insight.com	Bloomingdale	IL	60108	800-467-4448		193
Insight Analytics Group 313 Gordon Dr	Exton	PA	19341	610-363-6353	363-6251	196
Insight Capital Investments 4101 Gateway Dr Web: www.onealinvestments.com	Colleyville	TX	76034	817-545-1959		690
Insight Computing LLC 448 Ignacio Blvd Ste 490 *Fax Area Code: 415 ■ TF: 800-380-8985 ■ Web: www.insight-computing.com	Novato	CA	94949	800-380-8985	532-2439*	175
Insight Designs Web Solutions 2006 Broadway St 300 Web: www.insightdesigns.com	Boulder	CO	80302	303-449-8567		180
Insight Enterprises Inc 6820 S Harl Ave NASDAQ: NSIT ■ TF: 800-467-4448 ■ Web: www.insight.com	Tempe	AZ	85283	480-333-3000		179
Insight Environmental Consultants Inc 5500 Ming Ave Ste 360 Web: www.insenv.com	Bakersfield	CA	93309	661-282-2200		194
Insight Global Inc (IGI) 4170 Ashford Dunwoody Rd Ste 250 TF: 888-336-7463 ■ Web: www.insightglobal.net	Atlanta	GA	30319	404-257-7900	257-1004	193
Insight Information 214 King St W Ste 300 *Fax Area Code: 866 ■ TF: 888-777-1707 ■ Web: www.insightinfo.com	Toronto	ON	M5H3S6	416-777-2020	777-1292*	765
Insight Instruments Inc 2580 SE Willoughby Blvd Web: www.insightinstruments.com	Stuart	FL	34994	772-219-9393		45
Insight Investments Corp 611 Anton Blvd Ste 700 TF: 888-442-1441 ■ Web: www.insightinvestments.com	Costa Mesa	CA	92626	714-939-2300		624
Insight Marketing Design Inc 401 E Eighth St Ste 304 Web: insightmarketingdesign.com	Sioux Falls	SD	57103	605-275-0011		195
Insight Media 2162 Broadway TF: 800-233-9910 ■ Web: www.insight-media.com	New York	NY	10024	212-721-6316	799-5309	511
Insight Medical Holdings Ltd 200 Meadowlark Health Ctr 156 St and 89 Ave TF: 866-771-9446 ■ Web: www.x-ray.ca	Edmonton	AB	T5R5W9	780-669-2222		415
Insight Performance Inc 990 Washington St Ste S109 Web: www.insightperformance.com	Dedham	MA	02026	781-326-8201		463
Insight Product Development 4660 N Ravenswood Ave Web: www.insightpd.com	Chicago	IL	60640	773-907-9500		256
Insight Public Sector Inc 444 Scott Dr Web: www.ips.insight.com	Bloomingdale	IL	60108	630-924-6801		366
Insight Resource Group 3 Altarinda Rd Ste 301 Web: www.insightresourcegroup.com	Orinda	CA	94563	925-254-4114		317
Insight Service 20338 Progress Dr TF: 800-465-4329 ■ Web: www.testoil.com	Strongsville	OH	44149	216-251-2510		743
Insight Technology Inc 9 Akira Way TF: 866-509-2040 ■ Web: www.insighttechnology.com	Londonderry	NH	03053	603-626-4800		21
Insight Technology Solutions Inc 17251 Melford Blvd Ste 100 Web: www.insighttsi.com	Bowie	MD	20715	301-860-1121		177
Insight USA Inc 23330 Cottonwood Pkwy Ste 333 Web: www.mds-inc.com	California	MD	20619	301-866-1990		60
Insights in Marketing LLC 444 Skokie Blvd Ste 200 Web: www.insightsinmarketing.com	Wilmette	IL	60091	847-853-0500		195
Insignia Systems Inc 8799 Brooklyn Blvd NASDAQ: ISIG ■ TF: 800-874-4648 ■ Web: www.insigniasystems.com	Minneapolis	MN	55445	763-392-6200	392-6222	701
Insigniam Performance 1205 N Coast Hwy Ste D Web: insigniam.com	Laguna Beach	CA	92651	949-494-4553		195
Insinger Machine Co 6245 State Rd TF: 800-344-4802 ■ Web: insingermachine.com	Philadelphia	PA	19135	215-624-4800	624-6966	298
In-Sink-Erator 4700 21st St. TF: 800-558-5712 ■ Web: www.insinkerator.com	Racine	WI	53406	262-554-5432		36
Insite Computer Group Inc 8920 Woodbine Ave Ste 104 Web: www.insite.ca	Markham	ON	L3R9W9	416-736-8386		180
Insite Managed Solutions LLC 1616 W Cape Coral Pkwy Ste 102 PMB 165 Web: insitemanagedsolutions.com	Cape Coral	FL	33914	239-313-1085		463
InSite Vision Inc 965 Atlantic Ave. OTC: INSV ■ TF: 800-642-1687 ■ Web: www.insitevision.com	Alameda	CA	94501	510-865-8800	865-5700	231
Insitu Inc 118 E Columbia River Way Web: insitu.com	Bingen	WA	98605	509-493-8600		261
InSitu Technologies Inc 539 Phalen Blvd Web: www.insitu-tech.com	St Paul	MN	55130	651-389-1017		476
Insituform Technologies Inc 17988 Edison Ave. TF Cust Svc: 800-234-2992 ■ Web: www.insituform.com	St. Louis	MO	63005	636-530-8000	519-8010	188-10
Inslee Jay (D) PO Box 40002 PO Box 40002 Web: www.governor.wa.gov	Olympia	WA	98504	360-902-4111	753-4110	343
Insl-X Products Corp 101 Paragon Dr TF Cust Svc: 800-225-5554 ■ Web: www.insl-x.com	Montvale	NJ	07645	800-225-5554		550
Insmed Inc 10 Finderne Ave Bldg 10 NASDAQ: INSM ■ Web: www.insmed.com	Bridgewater	NJ	08807	804-565-3000		85
Insparisk LLC 71-19 80th St Ste 8205 TF: 888-464-6772 ■ Web: www.insparisk.com	Glendale	NY	11385	888-464-6772		365
Inspec Group LLC 140 SW Arthur St Web: www.inspecgroup.com	Portland	OR	97201	503-595-6540		186
Inspectech Ltd 450 Midwest Rd Web: www.inspectech.ca	Toronto	ON	M1P3A9	416-757-1179		112
Inspection Depot Inc 7700 Sq Lake Blvd Unit 2 TF: 888-589-2112 ■ Web: www.inspectiondepot.com	Jacksonville	FL	32256	904-425-0001		365
Inspection Oilfield Services 2809 Youngsville Hwy 89 Web: www.iospci.com	Youngsville	LA	70592	337-856-9001		580
Insperity Inc 19001 Crescent Springs Dr TF: 800-237-3170 ■ Web: www.insperity.com/?redirect=true	Kingwood	TX	77339	866-715-3552		463
Inspirage Inc 600 108th Ave NE Ste 540 TF: 855-517-4250 ■ Web: www.inspirage.com	Bellevue	WA	98004	855-517-4250		631
Inspiration Software Inc 6443 SW Beaverton Hillsdale Hwy Ste 370 TF: 800-877-4292 ■ Web: www.inspiration.com	Portland	OR	97221	503-297-3004	297-4676	178-1
Inspirato with American Express 1625 Wazee St Ste 400 Web: www.inspirato.com	Denver	CO	80202	303-586-7771		652
Inspire Communications Inc 1414 Montauk Ct Web: inspiredcom.com	Bartlett	IL	60103	630-233-1331		224
Inspire Excellence 657 n W ave. TF: 800-863-4978 ■ Web: www.inspireexcellence.com	Elmhurst	IL	60126	630-279-7500		463
Inspired eLearning Inc 613 NW Loop 410 Ste 530 TF: 800-631-2078 ■ Web: www.inspiredelearning.com	San Antonio	TX	78216	210-579-0224		225
Inspired Studios 9920 Royal Cardigan Way Web: www.inspired-studios.com	West Palm Beach	FL	33411	561-333-9142		523
Inspirica Ltd 850 Seventh Ave Ste 403 Web: www.inspirica.com	New York	NY	10019	212-245-3888		765
Inspiring Wellness LLC 665 S Orange Ave Ste 7 Web: www.babybootcamp.com	Sarasota	FL	34236	941-953-5000		310
Inspironix Inc 3400 Cottage Way TF: 800-788-0233 ■ Web: www.inspironix.com	Sacramento	CA	95825	916-488-3222		179
INSTAAR (Institute of Arctic & Alpine Research) 4001 Discovery Dr Web: instaar.colorado.edu	Boulder	CO	80303	303-492-6387	492-6388	668
InstaGift LLC 117 W Glenwood Dr TF: 877-870-3463 ■ Web: instagift.com	Birmingham	AL	35209	877-870-3463		393

	City	State	Zip	Phone	Fax	Class
INSTALLS Inc 241 Main St 5th Fl *Web:* www.installs.com	Buffalo	NY	14203	716-854-1994		681
InstaMed Communications LLC 1880 John F Kennedy Blvd 12th Fl *TF:* 800-507-3800 ■ *Web:* www.instamed.com	Philadelphia	PA	19103	215-789-3680		300-3
Instanet Solutions 100 Wellington St Ste 201 *TF:* 800-668-8768 ■ *Web:* www.instanetsolutions.com	London	ON	N6B2K6	800-668-8768		179
Instant Imprints 5897 Oberlin Dr Ste 200 *TF:* 800-542-3437 ■ *Web:* www.instantimprints.com	San Diego	CA	92121	858-642-4848	453-6513	310
Instant Sign Ctr 1400 Providence Hwy Ste 2500 *Web:* www.instantsigncenter.com	Norwood	AL	02062	781-278-0150		627
Instantel Inc 309 Legget Dr *TF:* 800-267-9111 ■ *Web:* www.instantel.com	Ottawa	ON	K2K3A3	613-592-4642		253
Instantiations Inc Officers Row Ste 1325B *TF:* 855-476-2558 ■ *Web:* www.instantiations.com	Vancouver	WA	98661	503-649-3836	649-3836	178-2
Instantwhip Foods Inc 2200 Cardigan Ave **Fax:* Sales ■ *TF Cust Svc:* 800-544-9447 ■ *Web:* www.instantwhip.com	Columbus	OH	43215	614-488-2536	488-0307*	296-10
INSTEC (INSTEC) 1811 Centre Pt Cir Ste 115 *Web:* www.instec-corp.com	Naperville	IL	60563	630-955-9200		178-10
Insteel Industries Inc 1373 Boggs Dr *NASDAQ:* IIIN ■ *TF:* 800-334-9504 ■ *Web:* www.insteel.com	Mount Airy	NC	27030	336-786-2141	786-2144	813
Institute for a Drug-Free Workplace (IDFW) 10701 Parkridge Blvd Ste 300 *TF:* 877-696-6775 ■ *Web:* www.drugfreeworkplace.org	Reston	VA	20191	703-391-7222	391-7223	49-12
Institute for Alternative Futures (IAF) 100 N Pitt St Ste 307 *Web:* www.altfutures.com	Alexandria	VA	22314	703-684-5880		49-12
Institute for American Indian Studies, The 38 Curtis Rd PO Box 1260 *Web:* www.iaismuseum.org	Washington	CT	06793	860-868-0518	868-1649	520
Institute for Astronomy Institute for Astronomy 2680 Woodlawn Dr *TF:* 800-351-1330 ■ *Web:* www.ifa.hawaii.edu	Honolulu	HI	96822-1839	808-956-8312	988-2790	668
Institute for Basic Research in Developmental Disabilities 1050 Forest Hill Rd *Web:* opwdd.ny.gov	Staten Island	NY	10314	718-494-0600		668
Institute for Business & Home Safety (IBHS) 4775 E Fowler Ave *TF:* 866-657-4247 ■ *Web:* www.disastersafety.org	Tampa	FL	33617	813-286-3400		49-9
Institute for Certification of Computing Professionals (ICCP) 2400 E Devon Ave Ste 281 *TF:* 800-843-8227 ■ *Web:* www.iccp.org	Des Plaines	IL	60018	847-299-4227		48-9
Institute for Corporate Productivity Inc 411 First Ave S Ste 403 *TF:* 866-375-4427 ■ *Web:* www.i4cp.com	Seattle	WA	98104	206-624-6565		466
Institute for Defense Analyses (IDA) 4850 Mark Ctr Dr *Web:* www.ida.org	Alexandria	VA	22311	703-845-2000	845-2588	668
Institute for Diabetes Obesity & Metabolism 700 Clinical Research Bldg 415 Curie Blvd *Web:* www.med.upenn.edu/physiol/faculty.html	Philadelphia	PA	19104	215-898-4365	898-5408	668
Institute for Education & the Arts 1156 15th St NW Ste 600 *Web:* www.edartsinstitute.org	Washington	DC	20005	202-223-9721		48-11
Institute for Foreign Policy Analysis Inc 675 Massachusetts Ave 10th Fl *Web:* www.ifpa.org	Cambridge	MA	02139	617-492-2116	492-8242	634
Institute for Health Freedom 1825 I St NW *Web:* www.forhealthfreedom.org	Washington	DC	20006	202-429-6610	861-1973	48-8
Institute For Health Policy 3333 California St	San Francisco	CA	94118	415-476-4921		634
Institute for Healthcare Improvement (IHI) 20 University Rd 7th Fl *TF:* 866-787-0831 ■ *Web:* www.ihi.org	Cambridge	MA	02138	617-301-4800	301-4848	49-8
Institute for Humane Studies 3434 Washington Blvd MS 1C5 *TF:* 800-697-8799 ■ *Web:* www.theihs.org	Arlington	VA	22201	703-993-4880	993-4890	634
Institute for Justice 901 N Glebe Rd Ste 900 *TF:* 888-322-0397 ■ *Web:* www.ij.org	Arlington	VA	22203	703-682-9320	682-9321	634
Institute for Molecular Virology (IMV) 413 RM Bock Laboratories 1525 Linden Dr *Web:* virology.wisc.edu	Madison	WI	53706	608-262-4540	262-4570	668
Institute For Natural Resources PO Box 5757 *TF:* 877-246-6336 ■ *Web:* www.inrseminars.com	Concord	CA	94524	925-609-2820		21
Institute for Operations Research & the Management Sciences (INFORMS) 7240 Pkwy Dr Ste 300 *TF:* 800-446-3676 ■ *Web:* www.informs.org	Hanover	MD	21076	443-757-3500	757-3515	49-19
Institute for Philosophy & Public Policy Maryland School of Public Policy 3111 Van Munching Hall *Web:* www.msu.edu	College Park	MD	20742	301-405-4763		634
Institute for Policy Studies (IPS) 1112 16th St NW Ste 600 *Web:* www.ips-dc.org	Washington	DC	20036	202-234-9382		634
Institute for Professionals in Taxation (IPT) 600 Northpark Town Ctr 1200 Abernathy Rd Ste L-2 *Web:* www.ipt.org	Atlanta	GA	30328	404-240-2300	240-2315	49-10
Institute for Research on Poverty University of Wisconsin Madison 1180 Observatory D 3412 William H Sewell Social Sciences Bldg *TF:* 866-301-1753 ■ *Web:* www.irp.wisc.edu	Madison	WI	53706	608-262-6358	265-3119	668
Institute for Research on the Economics of Taxation (IRET) 529 14th St NW Ste 420 *Web:* www.iret.org	Washington	DC	20045	202-464-5113		634

	City	State	Zip	Phone	Fax	Class
Institute for Scientific Analysis 390 Fourth St Ste D *TF:* 800-251-8705 ■ *Web:* www.scientificanalysis.org	San Francisco	CA	94107	415-777-2352		668
Institute for Simulation & Training (IST) 3100 Technology Pkwy *Web:* www.ist.ucf.edu	Orlando	FL	32826	407-882-1300	658-5059	668
Institute for Social Behavioral & Economic Research University of California 2201 N Hall *Web:* www.isber.ucsb.edu	Santa Barbara	CA	93106	805-893-2548	893-7995	668
Institute for Social Research ISR-Thompson 426 Thompson St *Web:* home.isr.umich.edu	Ann Arbor	MI	48104	734-764-8354	647-4575	668
Institute for Supply Management (ISM) 2055 Centennial Cir *TF Cust Svc:* 800-888-6276 ■ *Web:* www.instituteforsupplymanagement.org	Tempe	AZ	85284	480-752-6276	752-7890	49-12
Institute for Systems Research University of Maryland 2173 AV Williams Bldg *TF:* 866-675-8967 ■ *Web:* www.isr.umd.edu	College Park	MD	20742	301-405-6615	314-9920	668
Institute for Telecommunications Sciences 325 Broadway *Web:* www.its.bldrdoc.gov	Boulder	CO	80305	303-497-5216		668
Institute for the Advancement of Human Behavior (IAHB) PO Box 5527 **Fax Area Code:* 707 ■ *TF:* 800-258-8411 ■ *Web:* www.iahb.org	Santa Rosa	CA	95402	650-851-8411	755-3133*	49-8
Institute for the North 1675 C St Ste 106 *Web:* www.institutenorth.org	Anchorage	AK	99501	907-786-6324		634
Institute of American Indian Arts (IAIA) 83 Avan Nu Po Rd *TF:* 800-804-6422 ■ *Web:* www.iaia.edu	Santa Fe	NM	87508	505-424-2300	424-0505	165
Institute of American Indian Arts Museum 108 Cathedral Pl *TF:* 800-965-2030 ■ *Web:* www.iaia.edu	Santa Fe	NM	87501	505-983-8900		520
Institute of Arctic & Alpine Research (INSTAAR) 4001 Discovery Dr *Web:* instaar.colorado.edu	Boulder	CO	80303	303-492-6387	492-0388	668
Institute of Behavioral Science University of Colorado 483 UCB *Web:* www.colorado.edu/IBS	Boulder	CO	80309	303-492-8147	492-6924	668
Institute of Caster & Wheel Manufacturers (ICWM) 8720 Red Oak Blvd Ste 201 *TF:* 877-522-5431 ■ *Web:* www.mhi.org	Charlotte	NC	28217	704-676-1190	676-1199	49-13
Institute of Certified Professional Managers (ICPM) James Madison University MSC 5504 *TF:* 800-460-8013 ■ *Web:* www.icpm.biz	Harrisonburg	VA	22807	540-568-3247		49-12
Institute of Clean Air Cos (ICAC) 1730 M St NW Ste 206 *TF:* 800-631-9505 ■ *Web:* www.icac.com	Washington	DC	20036	202-457-0911	367-2114	48-12
Institute of Consumer Financial Education PO Box 34070 *TF:* 800-685-1111 ■ *Web:* www.financial-education-icfe.org	San Diego	CA	92163	619-239-1401	923-3284	48-11
Institute of Contemporary Art 118 S 36th St University of Pennsylvania *Web:* www.icaphila.org	Philadelphia	PA	19104	215-898-7108	898-5050	520
Institute of Corporate Directors 602 - 40 University Ave *TF:* 877-593-7741 ■ *Web:* www.icd.ca	Toronto	ON	M5J1T1	416-593-7741		162
Institute of Culinary Education 50 W 23rd St *TF:* 800-522-4610 ■ *Web:* www.ice.edu	New York	NY	10010	212-847-0700	847-0723	163
Institute of Ecosystem Studies (IES) 2801 Sharon Tpke PO Box AB *Web:* www.caryinstitute.org	Millbrook	NY	12545	845-677-5343	677-5976	668
Institute of Education Sciences (IES) 550 12th St SW *Web:* www.ies.ed.gov	Washington	DC	20024	202-245-6940	219-1466	668
Institute of Environmental Sciences & Technology (IEST) 2340 S Arlington Heights Rd Ste 100 *TF:* 800-699-9277 ■ *Web:* www.iest.org	Arlington Heights	IL	60005	847-981-0100	981-4130	49-19
Institute of Food Technologists (IFT) 525 W Van Buren St Ste 1000 *TF:* 800-438-3663 ■ *Web:* www.ift.org	Chicago	IL	60607	312-782-8424	782-8348	49-6
Institute of General Semantics (IGS) 72-11 Austin St **Fax Area Code:* 718 ■ *TF:* 800-346-1359 ■ *Web:* www.generalsemantics.org	Forest Hills	NY	11375	212-729-7973	793-2527*	48-11
Institute of Gerontology University of Michigan 400 N Ingalls St *TF:* 877-865-2167 ■ *Web:* med.umich.edu	Ann Arbor	MI	48109	734-936-2107	936-2116	668
Institute of Government & Public Affairs Univ of Illinois 1007 W Nevada St *TF:* 866-794-3340 ■ *Web:* igpa.uillinois.edu	Urbana	IL	61001	217-333-3340	244-4817	634
Institute of Hazardous Materials Management (IHMM) 11900 Parklawn Dr Ste 450 *Web:* www.ihmm.org	Rockville	MD	20852	301-984-8969	984-1516	48-12
Institute of Human Origins (IHO) 951 South Cady Mall PO Box 874101 *Web:* iho.asu.edu	Tempe	AZ	85287	480-727-6580	727-6570	668
Institute of Industrial & Systems Engineers (IIE) 3577 PkwyLn Ste 200 *TF Cust Svc:* 800-494-0460 ■ *Web:* www.iienet2.org	Norcross	GA	30092	770-449-0461	441-3295	49-13
Institute of Inspection Cleaning & Restoration Certification (IICRC) 4043 S E Ave *Web:* www.iicrc.org	Las Vegas	NV	89119	360-693-5675		49-4
Institute of Internal Auditors (IIA) 247 Maitland Ave *TF:* 800-803-8367 ■ *Web:* na.theiia.org	Altamonte Springs	FL	32701	407-937-1100	937-1101	49-1
Institute of International Bankers (IIB) 299 Pk Ave 17th Fl *TF:* 800-925-4618 ■ *Web:* www.iib.org	New York	NY	10171	212-421-1611	421-1119	49-2
Institute of International Container Lessors (IICL) 1990 M St NW Ste 650 *Web:* www.iicl.org	Washington	DC	20036	202-223-9800	223-9810	49-21
Institute of International Education (IIE) 809 United Nations Plaza # 1 *Web:* www.iie.org	New York	NY	10017	212-883-8200	984-5358	48-11

Name / Address	City	State	Zip	Phone	Fax	Class
Institute of International Finance (IIF) 1333 H St NW Ste 800-E *Web:* www.iif.com	Washington	DC	20005	202-857-3600	775-1430	49-2
Institute of Makers of Explosives (IME) 1120 19th St NW Ste 310 *Web:* www.ime.org	Washington	DC	20036	202-429-9280	293-2420	49-13
Institute of Management Accountants Inc (IMA) 10 Paragon Dr Ste 1 *TF:* 800-638-4427 ■ *Web:* www.imanet.org	Montvale	NJ	07645	201-573-9000	474-1600	49-1
Institute of Management Consultants USA Inc (IMC USA) 2025 M St NW Ste 800 *TF:* 800-221-2557 ■ *Web:* www.imcusa.org	Washington	DC	20036	202-367-1134	367-2134	49-12
Institute of Materials Science University of Connecticut 97 N Eagleville Rd *TF:* 800-528-7411 ■ *Web:* www.ims.uconn.edu	Storrs	CT	06269-3136	860-486-4623	486-4745	668
Institute of Medicine 500 Fifth St NW *Web:* www.nationalacademies.org/hmd	Washington	DC	20001	202-334-2352	334-1412	49-8
Institute of Navigation Inc (ION) 8551 Rixlew Ln Ste 360 *TF:* 800-696-7353 ■ *Web:* www.ion.org	Manassas	VA	20109	703-366-2723	366-2724	49-21
Institute of Nuclear Power Operations 700 Galleria Pkwy SE Ste 100 *Web:* www.inpo.info	Atlanta	GA	30339	770-644-8000		48-12
Institute of Packaging Professionals (IoPP) 1833 Centre Point Cir Ste 123 *TF:* 800-432-4085 ■ *Web:* www.iopp.org	Naperville	IL	60563	630-544-5050	544-5055	49-13
Institute of Real Estate Management (IREM) 430 N Michigan Ave **Fax Area Code:* 800 ■ *TF:* 800-837-0706 ■ *Web:* www.irem.org	Chicago	IL	60611	312-329-6000	338-4736*	49-17
Institute of Scrap Recycling Industries Inc (ISRI) 1615 L St NW Ste 600 *TF:* 800-678-9595 ■ *Web:* www.isri.org	Washington	DC	20036	202-662-8500	626-0900	48-12
Institute of Scrap Recycling Industries Magazine 1615 L St NW Ste 6000 *TF:* 800-767-7236 ■ *Web:* www.isri.org	Washington	DC	20036	202-662-8500	626-0900	457-21
Institute of Texan Cultures 801 E Durango Blvd *Web:* www.texancultures.com	San Antonio	TX	78205	210-458-2300	458-2205	520
Institute of Transportation Engineers (ITE) 1099 14th St NW Ste 300W *TF:* 800-676-2775 ■ *Web:* www.ite.org	Washington	DC	20005	202-289-0222	289-7722	49-21
Institute of World Politics 1521 16th St NW *TF:* 888-566-9497 ■ *Web:* www.iwp.edu	Washington	DC	20036	202-462-2101	464-0335	634
Institute on Education & the Economy 525 W 120th St *Web:* www.tc.columbia.edu	New York	NY	10027	212-678-3091	678-3699	634
Institutional Advancement Programs Inc 65 Main St Ste 208	Tuckahoe	NY	10707	914-779-4092	961-3114	317
Institutional Investor Newsletters 225 Pk Ave S 8th Fl **Fax:* Cust Svc ■ *TF:* 800-437-9997 ■ *Web:* www.institutionalinvestor.com	New York	NY	10003	212-224-3300	224-3491*	637-9
Institutional Real Estate Inc 2274 Camino Ramon *Web:* www.irei.com	San Ramon	CA	94583	925-244-0500		652
Institutional Shareholder Services Inc 2099 Gaither Rd Ste 501 *Web:* www.issgovernance.com	Rockville	MD	20850	301-556-0500		401
Institutional Venture Partners 3000 Sand Hill Rd Bldg 2 Ste 250 *Web:* www.ivp.com	Menlo Park	CA	94025	650-854-0132	854-2009	792
Institutional Wholesale Co 535 Dry Valley Rd **Fax:* Cust Svc ■ *TF:* 800-239-9588 ■ *Web:* goiwc.com	Cookeville	TN	38506	931-537-4000	537-4017*	299
Instratek Inc 15200 Middlebrook Dr Ste G *TF:* 800-892-8020 ■ *Web:* www.instratek.com	Houston	TX	77058	281-890-8020		475
inStream Media Inc 260 Charles St Ste 300 *Web:* www.instreamglobal.com	Wellesley	MA	02453	781-419-6575		195
Instron Corp 825 University Ave *Web:* www.instron.us	Norwood	MA	02062	781-828-2500	575-5750	472
INSTRUMAR Ltd 39 Pippy Pl 3rd Fl *Web:* www.instrumar.com	St. John's	NL	A1B3X2	709-726-8460		261
Instrumed International Inc 626 Cooper Ct *Web:* www.instrumedinc.biz	Schaumburg	IL	60173	847-908-0292		475
Instrument 3529 N Williams Ave *Web:* www.instrument.com	Portland	OR	97227	503-928-3188		201
Instrument Development Corp Inc 820 Swan Dr *Web:* www.idcwi.com	Mukwonago	WI	53149	262-363-7307		653
Instrument Sales & Service Inc 16427 NE Airport Way *TF:* 800-333-7976 ■ *Web:* www.instrumentsales.com	Portland	OR	97230	503-239-0754		61
Instrument Technology Inc 33 Airport Rd *Web:* www.scopes.com	Westfield	MA	01085	413-562-3606		542
Instrumentation Laboratory Inc 180 Hartwell Rd *TF Sales:* 800-955-9525 ■ *Web:* www.instrumentationlaboratory.com	Bedford	MA	01730	781-861-0710	861-1908	419
Instruments Inc 7263 Engineer Rd Ste G *Web:* www.instrumentsinc.com	San Diego	CA	92111	858-571-1111	571-0188	729
Instyle Hair Designs Inc 175 Littleton Rd *Web:* www.instylehd.com	Westford	MA	01886	978-692-7851		77
Insulectro 20362 Windrow Dr *TF:* 800-279-7686 ■ *Web:* www.insulectro.com	Lake Forest	CA	92630	949-587-3200	454-0066	246
Insulet Corp 9 Oak Park Dr *TF:* 800-591-3455 ■ *Web:* investor.insulet.com	Bedford	MA	01730	781-457-5000		476
Insulfab Plastics Inc 834 Hayne St *TF:* 800-845-7599 ■ *Web:* www.insulfab.com	Spartanburg	SC	29301	864-582-7506	582-5215	599
Insultab Inc 45 Industrial Pkwy *TF Cust Svc:* 800-468-4822 ■ *Web:* www.insultab.com	Woburn	MA	01801	781-935-0800	935-0879	599
Insur IQ LLC 2 Corporate Dr Ste 636 *Web:* www.insuriq.com	Shelton	CT	06484	203-446-8070		387
Insurance Auto Auctions Inc 2 Westbrook Corporate Ctr Ste 500 *TF:* 800-872-1501 ■ *Web:* www.iaai.com	Westchester	IL	60154	708-492-7000		51
Insurance Company of the West 11455 El Camino Real *TF:* 800-877-1111 ■ *Web:* www.icwgroup.com	San Diego	CA	92130	858-350-2400	350-2616	391-4
Insurance Consultants International 1840 Deer Creek Rd Ste 200 **Fax Area Code:* 603 ■ *TF:* 800-576-2674 ■ *Web:* www.globalhealthinsurance.com	Monument	CO	80132	719-573-9080	843-6662*	391-7
Insurance Coverage Law Bulletin, The 120 Broadway 5th Fl *TF:* 877-256-2472 ■ *Web:* www.lawjournalnewsletters.com	New York	NY	10271	212-457-9400		531-7
Insurance Data Processing Inc (IDP) 8101 Washington Ln *TF:* 800-523-6745 ■ *Web:* www.idpnet.com	Wyncote	PA	19095	215-885-2150	887-4621	178-11
Insurance Information Institute Inc (III) 110 William St *TF:* 877-263-7995 ■ *Web:* www.iii.org	New York	NY	10038	212-346-5500	732-1916	49-9
Insurance Institute for Highway Safety 1005 N Glebe Rd Ste 800 *TF:* 888-327-4236 ■ *Web:* www.iihs.org	Arlington	VA	22201	703-247-1500	247-1588	49-9
Insurance Marketing Agencies Inc 306 Main St *TF:* 800-891-1226 ■ *Web:* www.imaagency.com	Worcester	MA	01608	508-753-7233		391-2
Insurance Marketing Center Inc 6101 Executive Blvd Ste 120 *Web:* www.imctr.com	Rockville	MD	20852	301-468-8888		390
Insurance Marketing Communications Assn (IMCA) 4248 Park Glen Rd *Web:* www.imcanet.com	Minneapolis	MN	55416	952-928-4644	929-1318	49-9
Insurance Research Council (IRC) 718 Providence Rd *TF:* 800-644-2101 ■ *Web:* www.insurance-research.org	Malvern	PA	19355	610-644-2212		49-9
Insurance Services Office Inc (ISO) 545 Washington Blvd **Fax:* Hum Res ■ *TF:* 800-888-4476 ■ *Web:* www.verisk.com/iso.html	Jersey City	NJ	07310	201-469-2000	748-1472*	390
Insurance Technology Consultants Inc (ITC) 2090 N Tustin Ave Ste 260 *Web:* www.itc-systems.com	Santa Ana	CA	92705	714-442-8702		177
Insurance Unlimited of La Inc 3111 Ryan St *Web:* insunlimited.com	Lake Charles	LA	70601	337-477-6922		390
InsurBanc 10 Executive Dr *TF:* 866-467-2262 ■ *Web:* www.insurbanc.com	Farmington	CT	06032	860-677-9701	677-9793	70
Insurity Inc 170 Huyshope Ave *TF:* 866-476-2606 ■ *Web:* insurity.com	Hartford	CT	06106	860-616-7721		177
INSURPAC (Independent Insurance Agents & Brokers of America PAC) 412 First St SE Ste 300 *Web:* independentagent.com	Washington	DC	20003	202-863-7000	863-7015	615
InsWeb Inc 11290 Pyrites Way	Gold River	CA	95670	916-853-3300		114
in-sync Consumer Insight Corp 90 Eglinton Ave E Ste 403 *Web:* www.insyncstrategy.com	Toronto	ON	M4P2Y3	416-932-0921		668
INSYS Group Inc 395 W Passaic St 4th Fl *Web:* www.insysus.com	Rochelle Park	NJ	07662	201-621-4797		196
In-Sys Solutions Inc 14048 W Petronella Dr *Web:* www.in-sys.com	Libertyville	IL	60048	847-996-0400		180
Insyst Inc 271 Rte 46 W Ste A201 *TF:* 800-317-5030 ■ *Web:* www.insystus.com	Fairfield	NJ	07004	973-227-6582		180
Insystech Inc 7064 Infantry Ridge Rd *Web:* www.insystechinc.com	Manassas	VA	20109	703-657-0472		396
INTA (International Trademark Assn) 655 Third Ave 10th Fl *TF:* 800-995-3579 ■ *Web:* www.inta.org	New York	NY	10017	212-768-9887	768-7796	49-12
Intacct Corp 300 Park Ave Ste 1400 *TF:* 877-437-7765 ■ *Web:* us.intacct.com	San Jose	CA	95110	408-878-0900		39
Intact Info Solutions LLC 3 Pointe Dr Ste 218 *TF:* 888-986-7736 ■ *Web:* www.intactinfo.com	Brea	CA	91765	888-986-7736		196
Intact Insurance 700 University Ave **Fax:* Claims ■ *TF:* 800-387-8823 ■ *Web:* www.intact.ca	Toronto	ON	M5G0A1	416-341-1464	344-8030*	391-4
Intag Inc 11469 Olive Bld Ste 400 *Web:* www.appliedws.com	Saint Louis	MO	63141	314-822-1102		175
Intaglio LLC 3 Mile Rd NW Ste 3106 *TF:* 800-632-9153 ■ *Web:* www.intaglioav.com	Grand Rapids	MI	49534	616-243-3300		513
Intalio Inc 644 Emerson St Ste 200 *Web:* www.intalio.com	Palo Alto	CA	94301	650-596-1800	249-0439	179
Intarcia Therapeutics Inc 24650 Industrial Blvd *Web:* www.intarcia.com	Hayward	CA	94545	510-782-7800	782-7801	85
Intat Precision Inc 2148 N State Rd 3 PO Box 488 *Web:* www.intat.com	Rushville	IN	46173	765-932-5323	932-3032	621
Intcomex Inc 3505 NW 107th Ave Ste 1 *Web:* www.intcomex.com	Miami	FL	33178	305-477-6230		174
Intec Group Inc 666 S Vermont St *Web:* www.intecgrp.com	Palatine	IL	60067	847-358-0088	358-4391	604
Intec Video Systems Inc 23301 Vista Grande Dr *TF:* 800-468-3254 ■ *Web:* www.intecvideo.com	Laguna Hills	CA	92653	949-859-3800		693
Intech Direct 105 E Marquardt Dr *TF:* 800-246-5538 ■ *Web:* intechdirect.com	Wheeling	IL	60090	847-850-5999		7
Intech Enterprises Inc 3825 Grant St *Web:* www.intechenterprises.net	Washougal	WA	98671	360-835-8785		463
Intech Inc 2802 Belle Arbor Ave *Web:* www.intech-intl.com	Chattanooga	TN	37406	423-622-3700		261
Intecon LLC 1325 AeroPlz Dr Ste 105 *Web:* www.inteconusa.com	Colorado Springs	CO	80906	303-771-5337		180
Intedge Mfg 1875 Chumley Rd *TF:* 866-969-9605 ■ *Web:* www.intedge.com	Woodruff	SC	29388	864-969-9601	969-9604	300

Company	City	State	ZIP	Phone	Fax	Class
INTEG Process Group Inc 2919 E Hardies Rd 1st Fl *Web:* www.integpg.com	Gibsonia	PA	15044	724-933-9350		225
Intega IT 210-1900 Merivale Rd *Web:* www.intega.ca	Ottawa	ON	K2G4N4	613-260-1114		196
Integra Capital Ltd 2020 Winston Park Dr Ste 200 *TF:* 800-363-2480 ■ *Web:* www.integra.com	Oakville	ON	L6H6X7	905-829-1131		401
Integra Graphix 160 Koser Rd *Web:* www.yourvisitorguide.com	Lititz	PA	17543	717-626-7895		627
Integra Group Inc 16 Triangle Park Dr Ste 1600 *TF:* 800-424-8384 ■ *Web:* www.integragrp.com	Cincinnati	OH	45246	513-326-5600		463
Integra Information Technologies Inc 101 South 27th St *TF:* 800-444-8688	Boise	ID	83702	208-336-2720		196
Integra LifeSciences Corp 311 Enterprise Dr *TF:* 800-654-2873 ■ *Web:* www.integralife.com	Plainsboro	NJ	08536	609-275-5363		475
Integra LifeSciences Holdings Corp 311 Enterprise Dr *NASDAQ: IART* ■ *TF:* 800-654-2873 ■ *Web:* www.integra-ls.com	Plainsboro	NJ	08536	609-275-0500	799-3297	85
Integra Marketing Group 206 Jackson St *Web:* www.integramarketinggroup.com	New Galilee	PA	16141	724-200-0005		7
Integra Services Technologies Inc 5000 Second E Unit E *Web:* www.integratechnologies.com	Benicia	CA	95410	707-751-0685	751-0678	385
Integra Technologies LLC 3450 N Rock Rd Bldg 100 Ste 111 *Web:* integra-tech.com	Wichita	KS	67226	316-630-6800		70
Integra Telecom Inc 1201 NE Lloyd Blvd Ste 500 *TF General:* 866-468-3472 ■ *Web:* www.integratelecom.com	Portland	OR	97232	503-453-8000	453-8221	736
IntegraColor 3210 Innovative Way *TF:* 800-933-9511 ■ *Web:* www.integracolor.com	Mesquite	TX	75149	972-289-0705	285-4881	627
IntegraCore LLC 6077 W Wells Park Rd *Web:* www.integracore.com	West Jordan	UT	84081	801-948-7100		311
Integral Automation Inc 16w171 Shore Ct *Web:* www.premiertool.com	Burr Ridge	IL	60527	630-654-4300	654-8519	189-1
Integral Group Inc 427 13th St *Web:* www.integralgroup.com	Oakland	CA	94612	510-663-2070		261
Integral Group LLC, The 191 Peachtree St NE Ste 4100 *Web:* www.integral-online.com	Atlanta	GA	30303	404-224-1860		401
Integral Hospitality Solutions LLC 3522 Vann Rd Ste 102 *Web:* www.integralhospitality.com	Birmingham	AL	35235	205-655-2097		463
Integral Networks Inc 4960 Rocklin Rd Ste 100 *Web:* www.integralnetworks.com	Rocklin	CA	95677	916-626-4000		174
Integral Products Inc 24030 Frampton Ave *Web:* www.integralproducts.com	Harbor City	CA	90710	310-326-8889		3
Integral Solutions LLC 450 Wofford St *Web:* www.integralsg.com	Spartanburg	SC	29301	864-574-8161		180
Integral Systems Inc 6721 Columbia Gateway Dr	Columbia	MD	21046	443-539-5008		647
Integral Transportation Networks Corp 6975 D Pacific Cir *Web:* www.itn-logistics.com	Mississauga	ON	L5T2H3	905-362-1111		314
Integranetics 325 Park Plaza Dr 2b *TF:* 800-291-9307 ■ *Web:* integranetics.net	Owensboro	KY	42301	270-685-6016		175
integraSoft Inc 2547 Tech Dr *TF:* 877-630-7960 ■ *Web:* integrasoft.com	Bettendorf	IA	52722	563-332-5030		196
Integrated Alliances LLC 1777 Larimer St Ste 1905 *Web:* www.integratedalliances.com	Denver	CO	80202	303-683-9600		177
Integrated Biometrics Inc 121 Broadcast Dr *TF:* 888-840-8034 ■ *Web:* www.integratedbiometrics.com	Spartanburg	SC	29303	864-990-3711		692
Integrated BioPharma Inc 225 Long Ave *OTC: INBP* ■ *TF:* 888-319-6962 ■ *Web:* www.chemintl.com	Hillside	NJ	07205	973-926-0816		799
Integrated BioTherapeutics Inc 4 Research Ct Ste 300 **Fax Area Code:* 301 ■ *TF:* 877-411-2041 ■ *Web:* www.integratedbiotherapeutics.com	Rockville	MD	20850	877-411-2041	515-0324*	743
Integrated Business Systems & Services Inc 1601 Shop Rd Ste E *TF:* 800-553-1038 ■ *Web:* www.ibss.net	Columbia	SC	29201	803-736-5595		178-1
Integrated Components Source (ICS) 3977 Camino Ranchero *Web:* www.yourdrive.com	Camarillo	CA	93012	805-822-5100		246
Integrated Computer Solutions Inc (ICS) 54 Middlesex Tpke Ste B *Web:* www.ics.com	Bedford	MA	01730	617-621-0060	621-9555	178-2
Integrated Data Services Inc 2141 Rosecrans Ave Ste 2050 *Web:* www.idserve.com	El Segundo	CA	90245	631-265-7162		177
Integrated Decisions & Systems Inc 8500 Normandale Lake Blvd Ste 1200 *Web:* www.ideas.com	Minneapolis	MN	55437	952-698-4200	698-4299	178-1
Integrated Design Tools Inc 1202 E Park Ave *Web:* www.idtvision.com	Tallahassee	FL	32301	850-222-5939	222-4591	591
Integrated Device Technology Inc 6024 Silver Creek Valley Rd *NASDAQ: IDTI* ■ *TF:* 800-345-7015 ■ *Web:* www.idt.com	San Jose	CA	95138	408-284-8200	284-2775	696
Integrated Digital Technologies Corp 1501 S Brand Blvd *TF:* 800-462-0730 ■ *Web:* www.idt.edu	Glendale	CA	91204	818-396-3511		177
Integrated Document Solutions Inc 3511 W Commercial Blvd *Web:* www.idssite.com	Fort Lauderdale	FL	33309	954-484-0969		177

Company	City	State	ZIP	Phone	Fax	Class
Integrated Electrical Services Inc (IES) 5433 Westheimer Rd Ste 500 *NASDAQ: IESC* ■ *TF:* 800-732-0330 ■ *Web:* ies-corporate.com	Houston	TX	77056	713-860-1500		189-4
Integrated Flow Solutions LLC 6461 Reynolds Rd *TF:* 800-859-7867 ■ *Web:* www.ifsolutions.com	Tyler	TX	75708	903-595-6511		641
Integrated Flow Systems LLC 43455 Osgood Rd	Fremont	CA	94539	510-659-4900		172
Integrated Health Management Services LLC 2632 E Thomas Rd Ste 103 *Web:* www.ihmsllc.com	Phoenix	AZ	85016	602-522-3240		194
Integrated Healthcare Holdings Inc 1301 N Tustin Ave *OTC: IHCH* ■ *Web:* www.ihhioc.com	Santa Ana	CA	92705	714-953-3652	953-3384	353
Integrated Industrial Technologies 221 Seventh St Ste 200 *Web:* www.isquaredt.com	Pittsburgh	PA	15238	412-828-1200		256
Integrated Magnetics Inc 11248 Playa Ct *TF:* 800-421-6692 ■ *Web:* www.intemag.com	Culver City	CA	90230	310-391-7213		253
Integrated Management Services PA 126 E Amite St *Web:* www.imsengineers.com	Jackson	MS	39201	601-968-9194		256
Integrated Microwave Corp 11353 Sorrento Valley Rd *Web:* www.imcsd.com	San Diego	CA	92121	858-259-2600		253
Integrated Mktg Services Inc 279 Wall St Research Pk *Web:* www.imsworld.com	Princeton	NJ	08540	609-683-9055		194
Integrated Print & Graphics (IPG) 645 Stevenson Rd *Web:* www.ipandginc.com	South Elgin	IL	60177	847-695-6777		110
Integrated Procurement Technologies Inc 320 Storke Rd Ste 100 *Web:* www.iptsb.com	Goleta	CA	93117	805-682-0842		770
Integrated Regional Laboratories Inc 5361 NW 33rd Ave *TF:* 800-522-0232 ■ *Web:* www.irlfl.com	Ft. Lauderdale	FL	33309	800-522-0232		415
Integrated Service Company LLC 1900 N 161st E Ave *TF:* 800-324-7035 ■ *Web:* www.inservusa.com	Tulsa	OK	74116	918-234-4150		539
Integrated Services Inc 15115 SW Sequoia Pkwy Ste 110 *TF:* 800-922-3099 ■ *Web:* www.lubenet.com	Portland	OR	97224	800-922-3099		174
Integrated Silicon Solution Inc (ISSI) 1940 Zanker Rd *NASDAQ: ISSI* ■ *TF:* 800-379-4774 ■ *Web:* www.issi.com	San Jose	CA	95112	408-969-6600	969-7800	696
Integrated Solution Group Inc, The 10 Cedar St *Web:* www.intsolgrp.com	Woburn	MA	01801	781-938-0712		225
Integrated Solutions Inc 16002 N 23rd Ave Ste 109 *Web:* www.isiaz.com	Phoenix	AZ	85023	602-437-5209		256
Integrated Support Command Miami Beach 100 MacArthur Cswy *TF:* 866-772-8724 ■ *Web:* www.uscg.mil/d7/sectmiami	Miami Beach	FL	33139	305-535-4300	535-4598	158
Integrated Surface Technologies Inc 1455 Adams St Ste 1125 *Web:* www.insurftech.com	Menlo Park	CA	94025	650-324-1824		481
Integrated Systems Analysts Inc 2001 N Beauregard St Ste 600 *TF:* 800-929-1024 ■ *Web:* www.isa.com	Alexandria	VA	22311	703-824-0700		180
Integrated Textile Solutions Inc 005 Cleveland Ave *Web:* www.intextile.com	Salem	VA	24153	540-389-8113	387-5855	155-19
Integrated Thermoforming Systems Inc 305 Hankes Ave *Web:* www.itspackaging.com	Aurora	IL	60505	630-906-6895		596
Integrated Title Insurance Services LLC 1092 E S Union Ave *Web:* www.itstitle.com	Midvale	UT	84047	801-307-0160		194
Integrated Tower Systems 2703 Dawson Rd *Web:* www.intelcotowers.com	Tulsa	OK	74110	918-749-8535		387
Integrated Wealth Counsel LLC 5375 Kietzke Ln Ste 210 *TF:* 866-898-1860 ■ *Web:* www.integratedwealth.com	Reno	NV	89511	866-898-1860		401
Integration Partners Inc 12 Hayden Ave *TF:* 800-377-4911 ■ *Web:* www.integrationpartners.com	Lexington	MA	02421	781-357-8100		180
Integration Technologies Group Inc 2745 Hartland Rd Ste 200 *TF:* 800-835-7823 ■ *Web:* www.itgonlinc.com	Falls Church	VA	22043	703-698-8282	698-0305	175
Integrative Logic Inc 2397 Huntcrest Way Ste 200 *Web:* www.integrativelogic.com	Lawrenceville	GA	30043	678-638-2600		4
Integretel Inc 5883 Rue Ferrari	San Jose	CA	95138	408-362-4000		737
Integri Net Solutions Inc 10020 W Fairview Ave 10 *TF:* 800-605-5530 ■ *Web:* www.insllc.net	Boise	ID	83704	208-376-0500		180
IntegriChain Inc 1628 JFK Blvd *Web:* www.integrichain.com	Philadelphia	PA	19103	609-806-5005		177
Integridata Inc 122 E 42nd St Ste 2900 *Web:* integri-data.com	New York	NY	10168	212-302-6200		180
INTEGRIS Baptist Medical Ctr 3300 NW Expy *TF:* 800-687-5170 ■ *Web:* www.integrisok.com	Oklahoma City	OK	73112	405-949-3011		374-3
INTEGRIS Baptist Regional Health Ctr 200 Second Ave SW *TF:* 888-951-2277 ■ *Web:* www.integrisok.com	Miami	OK	74355	918-542-6611	540-7605	374-3
INTEGRIS Bass Baptist Health Ctr 600 S Monroe *TF:* 888-951-2277 ■ *Web:* integrisok.com/bass-baptist-health-center-enid-ok	Enid	OK	73701	580-233-2300		374-3
INTEGRIS Health Inc 3300 NW Expy *TF:* 888-951-2277 ■ *Web:* www.integrisok.com	Oklahoma City	OK	73112	405-951-2277		353

Company / Address	City	State	Zip	Phone	Fax	Class
INTEGRIS Southwest Medical Ctr 4401 S Western St	Oklahoma City	OK	73109	405-636-7000		374-3
TF: 888-949-3816 ■ *Web:* www.integrisok.com/southwest						
Integritech LLC 5267 Gender Rd	Canal Winchester	OH	43110	614-920-3366		175
TF: 800-555-1234 ■ *Web:* www.integritech.us						
Integrity Applications Inc (IAI) 15020 Conference Ctr Dr Ste 100	Chantilly	VA	20151	703-378-8672	378-8978	261
Web: www.integrity-apps.com						
Integrity Building Systems Inc 2435 Housels Run Rd	Milton	PA	17847	570-522-3600		106
Web: www.integritybuild.com						
Integrity Business Solutions Inc 9470 Annapolis Rd	Lanham	MD	20706	301-306-3100		180
Web: www.integritybsi.com						
Integrity Group, The 20333 TX-249	Houston	TX	77070	281-955-0707		463
Web: www.go-integrity.com						
Integrity Interactive Corp 51 Sawyer Rd Ste 510	Waltham	MA	02453	781-891-9700		194
Integrity Marketing Solutions 100 E Park St Ste 2	Olathe	KS	66061	877-352-2021		195
TF: 877-352-2021 ■ *Web:* www.integritymarketingsolutions.com						
Integrity Music 1646 Westgate Cir Ste 106	Brentwood	TN	80918	888-888-4726		657
TF: 888-888-4726 ■ *Web:* www.integritymusic.com						
Integrity Parking Systems LLC 9828 E Washington St	Chagrin Falls	OH	44023	440-543-4123		562
Web: integrityparking.com						
Integrity Rotational Molding LLC 701 Carr Rd	Plainfield	IN	46168	317-837-1101		608
Web: www.integrityrotational.com						
Integrity Staffing Solutions Inc 700 Prides Crossing Ste 300	Newark	DE	19713	302-661-8776	661-8779	721
TF: 888-458-8367 ■ *Web:* www.integritystaffing.com						
Integrity Systems & Solutions LLC 1247 Highland Ave Ste 202	Cheshire	CT	06410	203-271-7971		177
TF: 866-446-8797 ■ *Web:* www.integrityss.com						
Integrity Tech Solutions 816 S Eldorado Rd Ste 4	Bloomington	IL	61704	309-662-7723		180
Web: integrityts.com						
Integro Earth Fuels Inc 6 Celtic Dr Ste A2	Arden	NC	28704	828-651-8988		580
Web: www.integrofuels.com						
Integron Corp 35 Bermar Pk	Rochester	NY	14624	585-426-6200		175
TF: 800-856-4605 ■ *Web:* www.integron.com						
Intek Plastic Inc 1000 Spiral Blvd	Hastings	MN	55033	888-468-3531	437-3805*	326
**Fax Area Code:* 651 ■ *TF:* 888-468-3531 ■ *Web:* www.intekplastics.com						
Intel Corp 2200 Mission College Blvd	Santa Clara	CA	95052	408-765-8080		696
NASDAQ: INTC ■ *TF Cust Svc:* 800-628-8686 ■ *Web:* www.intel.in						
Intel Museum 2200 Mission College Blvd	Santa Clara	CA	95052	408-765-5050		520
TF: 800-628-8686 ■ *Web:* www.intel.in						
Intela LLC 929 Pearl St Ste 200	Boulder	CO	80302	303-473-0000		195
Intelametrix 6246 Preston Ave	Livermore	CA	94551	925-606-7044		639
Web: www.intelametrix.com						
Intelect Corp 4000 Dillon St	Baltimore	MD	21224	410-327-0020		180
Web: intelectcorp.com						
Intelemark LLC 4545 E Shea Blvd Ste 280	Phoenix	AZ	85028	602-943-7111		737
Web: www.intelemark.com						
Intelestream Inc 27 N Wacker Dr Ste 370	Chicago	IL	60606	800-391-4055		196
TF: 800-391-4055 ■ *Web:* www.intelestream.net						
Intelesys Corp 6797 Dorsey Rd	Elkridge	MD	21075	410-540-9755		180
Web: www.intelesyscorp.com						
inTelesystems 17400 Dallas Pkwy	Dallas	TX	75287	972-852-8200		387
Web: www.intelesystems.com						
Intelex Technologies Inc 905 King St West Ste 600	Toronto	ON	M6K3G9	416-599-6009		179
Web: www.intelex.com						
Inteliport 103 N Church St	Hertford	NC	27944	252-426-4600		396
Web: www.inteliport.net						
Intelisearch Inc 60 Long Ride Rd Ste 304	Stamford	CT	06902	203-325-1389		193
Web: www.isimpact.com						
Intelitech Group Inc, The 12009 NE 99th St Ste 1480	Vancouver	WA	98682	360-260-9780		261
Web: www.intelitechgroup.com						
Intellect Resources Inc 3824 N Elm St Ste 102	Greensboro	NC	27455	877-554-8911		260
TF: 877-554-8911 ■ *Web:* www.intellectresources.com						
Intelletrace Inc 448 Ignacio Blvd	Novato	CA	94945	800-618-5877		387
TF: 800-618-5877 ■ *Web:* www.intelletrace.com						
Intellex Consulting Services Inc 4 Apple Row	Kennett Square	PA	19348	610-388-3939		194
Web: www.intellexinc.com						
IntelliChoice Energy LLC 2355 W Utopia Rd	Phoenix	AZ	85027	623-879-4664		664
TF: 800-769-2414 ■ *Web:* www.iccghp.com						
Intellicom Computer Consulting 1702 Second Ave	Kearney	NE	68847	308-237-0684		180
TF: 877-501-3375 ■ *Web:* www.intellicominc.com						
Intellicomm Inc 575 E Swedesford Rd	Wayne	PA	19406	610-687-8020		174
Web: www.intellicomm.com						
Intellicorp Inc 2460 N First St Ste 260	San Jose	CA	95131	408-454-3500	454-3529	178-1
TF: 800-343-6572 ■ *Web:* www.intellicorp.com						
Intelligencer Printing Co 330 Eden Rd	Lancaster	PA	17601	800-233-0107	834-1443*	627
**Fax Area Code:* 877 ■ *TF:* 800-233-0107 ■ *Web:* www.intellprinting.com						
Intelligencer, The 1500 Main St	Wheeling	WV	26003	304-233-0100	232-1399	532-2
Web: www.theintelligencer.net						
Intelligencer, The 333 N Broad St	Doylestown	PA	18901	215-345-3000		532-2
Web: www.phillyburbs.com						
Intelligent Automation Inc 15400 Calhoun Dr Ste 400	Rockville	MD	20855	301-294-5200	294-5201	261
Web: www.i-a-i.com						
Intelligent Capital Inc Market at Third St The Hearst Bldg Ste 810	San Francisco	CA	94103	415-974-1000		401
Web: www.intelligentcapital.com						
Intelligent Computer Solutions Inc 9350 Eton Ave	Chatsworth	CA	91311	818-998-5805		174
TF: 888-994-4678 ■ *Web:* www.ics-iq.com						
Intelligent Decisions Inc 21445 Beaumeade Cir	Ashburn	VA	20147	703-554-1600		180
TF: 800-929-8331 ■ *Web:* www.intelligent.net						
Intelligent Interiors Inc 16837 Addison Rd Ste 500	Addison	TX	75001	972-716-9979		321
Web: iispaces.com						
Intelligent Lighting Controls Inc 5229 Edina Industrial Blvd	Minneapolis	MN	55439	952-829-1900		203
Web: www.ilc-usa.com						
Intelligent Mechatronic Systems Inc 435 King St N	Waterloo	ON	N2J2Z5	519-745-8887		668
TF: 866-818-6637 ■ *Web:* www.intellimec.com						
Intelligent Software Solutions Inc 5450 Tech Ctr Dr	Colorado Springs	CO	80919	719-452-7000	452-7001	177
Web: www.issinc.com						
Intelligent Systems Corp 4355 Shackleford Rd	Norcross	GA	30093	770-381-2900	381-2808	792
NYSE: INS ■ *TF:* 800-937-5449 ■ *Web:* www.intelsys.com						
Intelligent Transportation Society of America (ITS) 1100 17th St NW Ste 1200	Washington	DC	20036	202-484-4847	484-3483	49-21
TF: 800-374-8472 ■ *Web:* www.itsa.org						
Intelligrated Products 475 E High St PO Box 899	London	OH	43140	513-701-7300		207
TF: 866-936-7300 ■ *Web:* www.intelligrated.com						
Intellimar Inc 7560 Main St	Sykesville	MD	21784	410-552-9940	552-9939	195
Web: www.intellimar.com						
Intellimed International Corp 1825 E Northern Ave Ste 175	Phoenix	AZ	85020	602-230-0333		194
Web: www.intellimed.com						
Intellimeter Canada Inc 1125 Squires Beach Rd	Pickering	ON	L1W3T9	905-839-9199		317
Web: intellimeter.on.ca						
Intelli-Mine Inc 1200 Quail St Ste 270	Newport Beach	CA	92660	949-486-2900		180
TF: 800-275-4885 ■ *Web:* www.intelli-mine.com						
IntelliNet Technologies Inc 1990 W New Haven Ave Ste 303	Melbourne	FL	32904	321-726-0686	726-0683	178-7
Web: diametriq.com/intellinet-tech						
Intellinetics 2190 Dividend Dr	Columbus	OH	43228	614-921-8170		177
Web: www.intellinetics.com						
IntelliQ Research and Strategy Inc 112 W Foster Ave Ste 202C	State College	PA	16801	814-234-2344		466
Web: www.intelliqresearch.com						
IntelliShop LLC 2025 Michael Owens Way	Perrysburg	OH	43551	419-872-5103		195
Web: www.intelli-shop.com						
IntelliSoft Group LLC 61 Spit Brook Rd	Nashua	NH	03060	888-634-4464		180
TF: 888-634-4464 ■ *Web:* www.intellisoftgroup.com						
IntelliStance LLC 213 Court St	Middletown	CT	06457	860-704-6381		225
Web: www.marketstance.com						
Intelliswift Software Inc 2201 Walnut Ave	Fremont	CA	94538	510-490-9240		180
Web: www.intelliswift.com						
Intellisys Technology LLC 1000 Jorie Blvd Ste 200	Oak Brook	IL	60523	630-928-1111		180
Web: www.intellisystechnology.com						
Intellithink LLC 1225 N 78 St Ste 200	Kansas City	KS	66112	913-766-0303		463
Web: www.intelli-think.com						
Intellys Corp 621 W College St	Grapevine	TX	76051	972-929-9000		180
Web: www.intellys.com						
Intelsat General Corp 6550 Rock Spring Dr Ste 450	Bethesda	MD	20817	301-571-1210		387
Web: www.intelsatgeneral.com						
Intelsat Ltd 3400 International Dr NW	Washington	DC	20008	703-559-6800		681
TF: 800-937-5449 ■ *Web:* www.intelsat.com						
Intematix Corp 46410 Fremont Blvd	Fremont	CA	94538	510-933-3300		668
Web: www.intematix.com						
Intensity Corp 12730 High Bluff Dr Ste 300	San Diego	CA	92130	858-876-9101		138
Web: intensity.com						
Intepros Consulting Inc 750 Marrett Rd	Lexington	MA	02421	781-761-1140		177
Web: www.intepros.com						
Inter American Press Assn (IAPA) 3511 NW 91st Ave	Doral	FL	33172	305-634-2465	860-4264	49-14
Web: sipiapa.org/index.php						
Inter City Oil Company Inc (ICO) 1921 S St	Duluth	MN	55812	218-728-3641		579
TF: 800-642-5542 ■ *Web:* www.icofuel.com						
Inter Mountain Cable Inc 20 Laynesville Rd PO Box 159	Harold	KY	41635	606-478-9406		116
TF: 800-635-7052 ■ *Web:* www.imctv.com						
Inter Parfums Inc 551 Fifth Ave Ste 1500	New York	NY	10176	212-983-2640	983-4197	574
NASDAQ: IPAR ■ *Web:* www.interparfumsinc.com						
Inter Technologies Corp 7716 Middle Valley Dr	Springfield	VA	22153	703-451-1083		113
Web: intertechav.com						
INTERA Inc 1812 Centre Creek Dr Ste 300	Austin	TX	78754	512-425-2000		261
Web: www.intera.com						
Interact Inc 1225 L St Ste 600	Lincoln	NE	68508	402-476-8786		178-7
Web: www.iivip.com						
Interact One Inc 4665 Cornell Rd Ste 255	Cincinnati	OH	45241	513-469-7042		196
TF: 800-869-9989 ■ *Web:* www.interactone.com						
Interact Performance Systems Inc 180 N Rverview Dr Ste 165	Anaheim	CA	92808	714-283-8288		463
TF: 800-944-7553 ■ *Web:* www.inter-ps.com						

	Phone	Fax	Class
InterAct PMTI 4567 Telephone Rd Ste 203 .... Ventura CA 93003 — *Web:* www.pacificmti.com	805-658-5600		539
Interaction Assoc 70 Fargo St Ste 908 .... Boston MA 02210 — *TF:* 800-347-8352 ■ *Web:* www.interactionassociates.com	617-234-2700	234-2727	194
Interactive Business Systems Inc 2625 Butterfield Rd .... Oak Brook IL 60523 — *TF:* 800-555-5427 ■ *Web:* www.ibs.com	630-571-9100	571-2490	180
Interactive Digital Solutions Inc 14701 Cumberland Rd Ste 400 .... Noblesville IN 46060 — *Fax Area Code:* 317 ■ *TF:* 877-880-0022 ■ *Web:* www.e-idsolutions.com	877-880-0022	770-3528*	52
Interactive Innovation Group Inc 413 W Channel Rd .... Santa Monica CA 90402 — *Web:* www.panjo.com	310-454-3023		387
Interactive Management Inc 12011 Tejon St Ste 700 .... Westminster CO 80234 — *Web:* www.imigroup.org	303-433-4446		47
Interactive Medical Connections Inc 700 Gemini St Ste 110 .... Houston TX 77058 — *TF:* 800-480-8040 ■ *Web:* www.edrugfree.com	281-486-4434		415
Interactive Motion Technologies Inc 80 Coolidge Hill Rd .... Watertown MA 02472 — *Web:* www.interactive-motion.com	617-926-4800		194
Interactive Tracking Systems Inc 820 51st St E Ste 150 .... Saskatoon SK S7K0X8 — *Web:* www.itracks.com	306-665-5026		225
Interagency Council on Homelessness 409 Third St SW Ste 310 .... Washington DC 20024 — *Web:* www.usich.gov	202-708-4663		340-20
Interamerican College of Physicians & Surgeons 233 Broadway .... New York NY 10279 — *TF:* 800-554-2245 ■ *Web:* icps.org	212-777-3642		49-8
Inter-American Commission of Women (CIM) 1889 F St NW .... Washington DC 20006 — *Web:* www.oas.org/cim	202-458-6084	458-6094	48-24
Inter-American Development Bank 1300 New York Ave NW .... Washington DC 20577 — *TF:* 877-782-7432 ■ *Web:* www.iadb.org	202-623-1000	623-3096	783
Inter-American Dialogue 1211 Connecticut Ave NW Ste 510 .... Washington DC 20036 — *Web:* www.thedialogue.org	202-822-9002	822-9553	634
Inter-American Foundation (IAF) 901 N Stuart St 10th Fl .... Arlington VA 22203 — *Web:* www.iaf.gov	703-306-4301	306-4365	340-20
InterAmerican Motor Corp (IMC) 8901 Canoga Ave .... Canoga Park CA 91304 — *TF:* 800-874-8925 ■ *Web:* www.imcparts.net	818-678-1200		61
Interamerican Trading & Products Corp 1800 Purdy Ave .... Miami Beach FL 33139	305-885-9666		297-5
Interbake Foods LLC 3951 Werre Pkwy .... Richmond VA 23233 — *Web:* www.interbake.com	804-755-7107		68
InterBank 4921 N May Ave .... Oklahoma City OK 73112 — *Web:* www.interbank.com	405-782-4200		70
InterBase Corp 22485 La Palma Ave Ste 200D .... Yorba Linda CA 92887 — *Web:* www.interbasecorp.com	714-701-3600		196
Interbond Corp of America 3200 SW 42nd St .... Fort Lauderdale FL 33312 — *TF:* 800-432-8579 ■ *Web:* www.brandsmartusa.com	000-432-8579		35
Interboro Systems Corp 206 San Jorge St .... San Juan PR 00912 — *Web:* www.interboropr.com	787-641-7777	641-7790	196
Interbrand Design Forum LLC 7575 Paragon Rd .... Dayton OH 45459 — *Web:* www.interbranddesignforum.com	937-439-4400		7
InterCall 8420 W Bryn Mawr Ste 1100 .... Chicago IL 60631 — *TF:* 800-374-2441 ■ *Web:* www.intercall.com	773-399-1600		736
Intercept Energy Services Inc 11464 149 St .... Edmonton AB T5M1W7 — *TF:* 877-975-0558 ■ *Web:* interceptenergy.ca	877-975-0558		538
Interceramic USA 2333 S Jupiter Rd .... Garland TX 75041-6007 — *Web:* www.interceramicusa.com	214-503-5500	503-5555	751
Interchem Corp 120 Rt 17 N .... Paramus NJ 07652 — *TF:* 800-261-7332 ■ *Web:* www.interchem.com	201-261-7333		479
InterChez Logistics Systems Inc 600 Alpha Pkwy .... Stow OH 44224 — *TF:* 800-780-4707 ■ *Web:* www.interchez.com	330-923-5080		449
Interchurch Medical Assistance Inc (IMA) 1730 M St Ste 1100 .... Washington DC 20036 — *TF:* 877-241-7952 ■ *Web:* www.imaworldhealth.org	410-635-8720	635-8726	48-5
Intercity Home Care 11 Dartmouth St .... Malden MA 02148 — *Web:* intercityhomecare.com	781-321-6300		363
Intercollegiate Studies Institute (ISI) 3901 Centerville Rd .... Wilmington DE 19807 — *TF:* 800-526-7022 ■ *Web:* home.isi.org	302-652-4600	652-1760	48-11
Inter-Community Telephone Co (ICTC) PO Box 8 .... Nome ND 58062 — *TF:* 800-350-9137 ■ *Web:* www.ictc.com	701-924-8815	924-8808	736
Intercomp Co 3839 County Rd 116 .... Medina MN 55340 — *TF:* 800-328-3336 ■ *Web:* www.intercompcompany.com	763-476-2531	476-2613	684
Interconnect Wiring Harnesses Inc 5024 W Vickery Blvd .... Fort Worth TX 76107 — *Web:* www.interconnect-wiring.com	817-377-9473	732-8667	247
Intercontinental Fuels 17617 Aldine Westfield Rd .... Houston TX 77073	281-821-2225		579
InterContinental Hotel Cleveland 9801 Carnegie Ave .... Cleveland OH 44106 — *Web:* www.ihg.com	216-707-4100		377
InterContinental Hotels Group 3315 Peachtree Rd NE .... Atlanta GA 30326 — *Web:* www.ihg.com	404-946-9000	946-9001	379
Crowne Plaza Hotels & Resorts 3 Ravinia Dr Ste 2900 .... Atlanta GA 30346 — *TF:* 800-621-0555 ■ *Web:* ihg.com	770-604-2000		379
Holiday Inn Hotels & Resorts 3 Ravinia Dr Ste 100 .... Atlanta GA 30346 — *Web:* www.ihgplc.com	770-604-2000		379
Hotel Indigo 3 Ravinia Dr Ste 100 .... Atlanta GA 30346 — *TF:* 800-990-1135 ■ *Web:* www.ihgplc.com	770-604-2000		379
Staybridge Suites 3 Ravinia Dr Ste 100 .... Atlanta GA 30346 — *TF:* 800-990-1135 ■ *Web:* www.ihgplc.com	770-604-2000		379
InterContinental Insurance Brokers LLC 175 Federal St Ste 725 .... Boston MA 02110 — *Web:* www.iibweb.com	617-648-5100		390
Intercontinental Marble Corp 8228 NW 56th St .... Miami FL 33166 — *TF:* 800-809-1465 ■ *Web:* www.intercontinentalmarble.com	305-591-2207		724
InterContinental Mark Hopkins San Francisco 999 California St .... San Francisco CA 94108 — *Web:* www.intercontinentalmarkhopkins.com	415-392-3434		378
InterContinental Montreal 360 St-Antoine St W .... Montreal QC H2Y3X4 — *Web:* www.montreal.intercontinental.com	514-987-9900		378
InterContinental New York Barclay, The 111 E 48th St .... New York NY 10017 — *Web:* www.ihg.com	212-755-5900		377
Intercontinental San Francisco 888 Howard St .... San Francisco CA 94103 — *TF:* 888-811-4273 ■ *Web:* www.intercontinentalsanfrancisco.com	888-811-4273		378
InterContinental Stephen F Austin Hotel 701 Congress Ave .... Austin TX 78701 — *Web:* www.austin.intercontinental.com	512-457-8800		378
InterCorr International Inc 14503 Bammel N Houston Ste 300 .... Houston TX 77014 — *Web:* www.intercorr.com	281-444-2282		743
Inter-County Bakers Inc 1095 Long Island Ave .... Deer Park NY 11729 — *TF:* 800-696-1350 ■ *Web:* www.icbakers.com	631-957-1350	957-1013	70
Intercounty Electric Co-op 102 Maple Ave .... Licking MO 65542 — *TF:* 888-771-7661 ■ *Web:* www.ieca.coop	573-674-2211		245
Inter-County Energy Co-op 1009 Hustonville Rd .... Danville KY 40422 — *TF:* 888-266-7322 ■ *Web:* www.intercountyenergy.net	859-236-4561	236-3627	245
Intercultural Communications College 810 Richards St Ste 200 .... Honolulu HI 96813 — *Web:* www.icchawaii.edu	808-946-2445	946-2231	423
Intercultural Development Research Assn (IDRA) 5815 Callaghan Rd Ste 101 .... San Antonio TX 78228 — *Web:* www.idra.org	210-444-1710	444-1714	48-11
Interdenominational Theological Ctr 700 Martin Luther King Jr Dr .... Atlanta GA 30314 — *TF:* 800-908-9946 ■ *Web:* www.itc.edu	404-527-7700	527-0901	168
InterDent Inc 9800 S La Cienega Blvd Ste 800 .... Inglewood CA 90301 — *Web:* www.interdent.com	310-765-2400	765-2456	463
InterDesign Group Inc 141 E Ohio St .... Indianapolis IN 46204 — *Web:* www.interdesign.com	317-263-9655		256
InterDev LLC 2650 Holcomb Bridge Rd Ste 310 .... Alpharetta GA 30022 — *TF:* 877-841-8069 ■ *Web:* www.interdev.com	770-643-4400		180
InterDigital Communications Corp 781 Third Ave .... King of Prussia PA 19406 — *Web:* www.interdigital.com	610-878-7800		690
Interdynamix 620-10180 101 St NW .... Edmonton AB T5J3S4 — *Web:* www.interdynamix.com	780-423-7005		177
Interool Corp 520 Third St Ste 555 .... San Francisco CA 94107	415-778-3900		652
Intereum 845 Berkshire Ln N .... Plymouth MN 55441 — *TF:* 800-447-2257 ■ *Web:* www.intereum.com	763-417-3300	417-3309	320
InterEx Exhibits 34 S Hunt Rd .... Amesbury MA 01913 — *Web:* www.interex.com	978-388-8755	388-8755	393
Interface Construction Corp 8401 Wabash Ave .... Saint Louis MO 63134 — *Web:* www.interfaceconstruction.com	314-522-1011	522-1022	186
Interface Displays & Controls Inc 4630 N Ave .... Oceanside CA 92056 — *Web:* www.interfacedisplays.com	760-945-0230		529
Interface EAP Inc (IEAP) 10370 Richmond Ave Ste 1100 PO Box 421879 .... Houston TX 77042 — *TF:* 800-324-4327 ■ *Web:* www.ieap.com	713-781-3364	784-0425	462
Interface Inc 7401 E Butherus Dr .... Scottsdale AZ 85260 — *TF:* 800-947-5598 ■ *Web:* www.interfaceforce.com	480-948-5555	948-1924	472
Interface Inc 2859 Paces Ferry Rd Ste 2000 .... Atlanta GA 30339 — *NASDAQ:* TILF ■ *Web:* www.interfaceglobal.com	770-437-6800		131
Interface Logic Systems Inc 3311 E Livingston Ave .... Columbus OH 43227 — *Web:* www.interfacelogic.com	614-236-8388		362
Interface Media Group Inc 1233 20th St NW .... Washington DC 20036 — *Web:* www.interfacemedia.com	202-861-0500		514
Interface Multimedia Inc 8505 Fenton St .... Silver Spring MD 20910 — *Web:* www.ifmm.com	301-585-0068		225
Interface Security Systems LLC 6340 International Pkwy Ste 100 .... Plano TX 75093 — *TF:* 866-593-3480	972-996-2800	996-2801	692
Interface Solutions Inc 216 Wohlsen Way .... Lancaster PA 17603 — *Fax Area Code:* 717 ■ *TF:* 800-942-7538 ■ *Web:* www.interfacematerials.com	800-942-7538	207-6080*	326
Interfaith Action of Greater Saint Paul 1671 Summit Ave .... Saint Paul MN 55105 — *Web:* interfaithaction.org	651-646-8805		48-20
Interfaith Alliance 2101 L St NW Ste 400 .... Washington DC 20037 — *TF:* 800-510-0969 ■ *Web:* www.interfaithalliance.org	202-466-0567	238-3301	48-7
Interfaith Medical Ctr 1545 Atlantic Ave .... Brooklyn NY 11213 — *Web:* www.interfaithmedical.com	718-613-4000	613-4101	374-3
Interfaith Ministries for Greater Houston 3303 Main St .... Houston TX 77002 — *TF:* 800-511-0999 ■ *Web:* www.imgh.org	713-533-4900		48-20
Interfoods of America Inc 9500 S Dadeland Blvd Ste 720 .... Miami FL 33156	305-670-0746	670-0767	670

Name / Address	City	State	ZIP	Phone	Fax	Class
Interfor Pacific Inc						
2211 Rimland Dr Ste 220	Bellingham	WA	98226	360-788-2299		683
Web: www.interfor.com						
Interfuel Llc 7102 Fullerton Rd	Springfield	VA	22150	703-455-1900		324
Web: www.interfuel.com						
Intergen 30 Corporate Dr	Burlington	MA	01803	781-993-3000		245
Web: www.intergen.com						
Intergraph Corp 19 Interpro Rd	Madison	AL	35758	256-730-2000	730-2048	178-5
TF: 800-345-4856 ■ *Web:* www.intergraph.com						
Interim HealthCare Inc						
1601 Sawgrass Corporate Pkwy	Sunrise	FL	33323	954-858-6000		721
TF: 800-338-7786 ■ *Web:* www.interimhealthcare.com						
Interior Architects Inc						
1726 Champa St Ste 100	Denver	CO	80202	303-292-4963	292-4971	466
Web: www.interiorarchitects.com						
Interior Construction Services Ltd						
2930 Market St	Saint Louis	MO	63103	314-534-6664	534-6663	189-9
Web: www.ics-stl.com						
Interior Crafts Inc						
2513 W Cullerton Ave	Chicago	IL	60608	773-376-8160	376-9578	319-2
Web: interiorcraftsinc.com						
Interior Design Services Inc						
209 Powell Pl	Brentwood	TN	37027	615-376-1200		321
TF: 800-433-7446 ■ *Web:* www.ids-tn.com						
Interior Move Consultants Inc						
5 W 19th St Rm 2c	New York	NY	10011	212-343-8624		463
Web: www.moveconsultants.com						
Interior Office Solutions Inc						
17800 Mitchell N	Irvine	CA	92614	949-724-9444		321
Web: www.interiorofficesolutions.com						
Interior Specialists Inc						
1630 Faraday Ave	Carlsbad	CA	92008	760-929-6700		291
TF: 800-959-8333 ■ *Web:* www.isidc.com						
Interiors by Steven G Inc						
2818 Centre Port Cir	Pompano Beach	FL	33064	954-735-8223		393
Web: www.interiorsbysteveng.com						
Interiors Inc 1325 N Dutton Ave	Santa Rosa	CA	95401	707-544-4770	544-0722	320
TF: 800-318-9806 ■ *Web:* interiorsincorporated.com						
Interis Consulting Inc						
275 Slater St 20th Fl	Ottawa	ON	K1P5H9	613-237-9331		796
Web: www.interis.ca						
Interkal Inc 5981 E Cork St	Kalamazoo	MI	49048	269-349-1521	349-6530	319-3
Web: www.interkal.com						
Interlake Steamship Co, The						
7300 Engle Rd	Middleburg Heights	OH	44130	440-260-6900		313
Web: www.interlake-steamship.com						
Interlaken Capital Inc						
475 Steamboat Rd 2nd Fl	Greenwich	CT	06830	203-629-8750		401
Web: www.interlakencapital.com						
Interlaken Inn						
74 Interlaken Rd Rt 12	Lakeville	CT	06039	860-435-9878	435-2980	669
TF: 800-222-2909 ■ *Web:* www.interlakeninn.com						
Interlectric Corp 1401 Lexington Ave	Warren	PA	16365	814-723-6061	723-1074	437
TF: 800-722-2184 ■ *Web:* www.interlectric.com						
Interleukin Genetics Inc						
135 Beaver St	Waltham	MA	02452	781-398-0700	398-0720	231
OTC: ILIU ■ *Web:* www.ilgenetics.com						
Interlex Communications						
4005 Broadway St	San Antonio	TX	78209	210-930-3339		7
Web: www.interlexusa.com						
Interlinc Direct Corp						
65 Superior Blvd	Mississauga	ON	L5T2X9	905-677-2620		224
Interline Brands Inc						
801 W Bay St	Jacksonville	FL	32204	904-421-1400		351
Web: www.interlinebrands.com						
Interline Creative Group						
553 North N Ct Ste 160	Palatine	IL	60067	847-358-4848		7
TF: 800-222-1208 ■ *Web:* www.interlinegroup.com						
Interlink Electronics Inc						
546 Flynn Rd	Camarillo	CA	93012	805-484-8855		173-1
OTC: LINK ■ *Web:* interlinkelectronics.com						
Interlink Network Systems Inc						
495 Cranbury Rd	East Brunswick	NJ	08816	732-846-2226		256
TF: 877-872-6947 ■ *Web:* www.ilinknet.com						
Interlochen Ctr for the Arts						
4000 Michigan 137	Interlochen	MI	49643	231-276-7200	276-7444	572
Web: www.interlochen.org						
Interlochen State Park M-137	Interlochen	MI	49643	231-276-9511		565
Web: www.michigandnr.com						
InterLock Industries Inc						
545 S Third St Ste 310	Louisville	KY	40202	502-569-2007		480
Web: www.interlockindustries.com						
Interlocking Concrete Pavement Institute (ICPI)						
14801 Murdock St Ste 2300	Chantilly	VA	20151	202-712-9036	408-0285	49-3
TF: 800-241-3652 ■ *Web:* www.icpi.org						
Interlog USA Inc						
2818A Anthony Ln S	Minneapolis	MN	55418	612-789-3456		313
TF: 800-603-6030 ■ *Web:* www.interlogusa.com						
Interlude Home Inc 25 Trefoil Dr	Trumbull	CT	06611	203-445-7617		361
Web: www.interludehome.com						
Intermap Technologies Inc						
8310 S Vly Hwy Ste 400	Englewood	CO	80112	303-708-0955		727
Web: www.intermap.com						
Intermarine LLC						
365 Canal St One Canal Pl Ste 2400	New Orleans	LA	70130	504-529-2100		312
Web: www.intelifuse.com						
Intermark Group Inc 101 25th St N	Birmingham	AL	35203	205-803-0000	870-3843	4
TF: 800-624-9239 ■ *Web:* www.intermarkgroup.com						
Intermatic Inc 7777 Winn Rd	Spring Grove	IL	60081	815-675-7000	675-7001	203
Web: www.intermatic.com						
Intermax Computer Associates Inc						
242 Big Run Rd	Lexington	KY	40503	859-277-5453		175
TF: 800-433-5778 ■ *Web:* intermaxcomputer.com						
Intermax Pharmaceuticals Inc						
228 Sherwood Ave	Farmingdale	NY	11735	631-777-3318		231
Web: synthopharmaceuticals.com						
Inter-Med Inc 2200 Northwestern Ave	Racine	WI	53404	262-636-9755		228
Web: www.vista-dental.com						

Name / Address	City	State	ZIP	Phone	Fax	Class
InterMetro Industries Corp						
651 N Washington St	Wilkes-Barre	PA	18705	570-825-2741		73
TF Cust Svc: 800-992-1776 ■ *Web:* www.metro.com						
Intermodal Assn of North America (IANA)						
11785 Beltsville Dr Ste 1100	Calverton	MD	20705	301-982-3400	982-4815	49-21
TF: 877-438-8442 ■ *Web:* www.intermodal.org						
Intermodal Cartage Co Inc						
5707 E Holmes Rd	Memphis	TN	38141	901-363-0050	432-6174	468
Web: www.imcg.com						
Intermolecular Inc 3011 N First St	San Jose	CA	95134	408-582-5700		696
TF: 877-251-1860 ■ *Web:* www.intermolecular.com						
Intermotive Inc 12840 Earhart Ave	Auburn	CA	95602	530-823-1048		350
Web: www.intermotive.net						
Intermountain Air LLC						
301 N 2370 W	Salt Lake City	UT	84116	801-322-1645		770
TF: 800-433-9617 ■ *Web:* keystoneaviation.com						
Intermountain Electric Inc (IME)						
5050 Osage St Ste 500	Denver	CO	80221	303-733-7248	722-2410	189-4
Web: imelect.com						
Intermountain Farmers Assn						
1147 West 2100 South	Salt Lake City	UT	84119	801-972-2122	972-2186	276
TF: 800-748-4432 ■ *Web:* www.ifa-coop.com						
Intermountain Gas Co Inc 555 S Cole Rd	Boise	ID	83709	208-377-6840	377-6081	787
TF Cust Svc: 800-548-3679 ■ *Web:* www.intgas.com						
Intermountain HealthCare						
36 S State St	Salt Lake City	UT	84111	801-442-2000		353
TF Hum Res: 800-843-7820 ■ *Web:* www.intermountainhealthcare.org						
Intermountain Healthcare Logan Regional Hospital						
500 E 1400 N	Logan	UT	84341	435-716-1000	716-5409	374-3
TF: 800-442-4845 ■ *Web:* www.intermountainhealthcare.org						
Intermountain Livestock Inc						
60654 Livestock Rd	La Grande	OR	97850	541-963-2158		446
Web: www.imlivestock.com						
InterMountain Management LLC						
2390 Tower Dr	Monroe	LA	71201	318-325-5561		379
Web: www.intermountainhotels.com						
Intermountain Rural Electric Assn						
5496 Hwy 85	Sedalia	CO	80135	303-688-3100	733-5872*	245
**Fax Area Code:* 720 ■ *TF:* 800-332-9540 ■ *Web:* www.irea.coop						
Intermountain Wood Products Inc						
1948 SW Temple	Salt Lake City	UT	84115	801-486-5414	466-0428	820
Web: www.intermountainwood.com						
Internal Audit Services by John Capizzi						
6231 Pga Blvd Ste 104	Palm Beach Gardens	FL	33418	561-626-7746		2
Web: internalauditservices.com						
Internal Auditor Magazine						
247 Maitland Ave	Altamonte Springs	FL	32701	407-937-1100	937-1101	457-5
Web: na.theiia.org						
Internal Intelligence Service Inc						
9-25 Alling St 1st Fl	Newark	NJ	07102	973-242-5400		693
Internal Medicine News						
5635 Fishers Ln Ste 6000	Rockville	MD	20852	240-221-2400	221-4400	457-16
TF: 877-524-9336 ■ *Web:* www.internalmedicinenews.com						
Internal Revenue Service (IRS)						
1111 Constitution Ave NW	Washington	DC	20224	202-622-9511		340-18
TF: 800-829-1040 ■ *Web:* www.irs.gov						
Appeals Office 77 K St NE	Washington	DC	20002	202-803-9000		340-18
Web: www.irs.gov						
Taxpayer Advocate Service						
77 K St NE Ste 1500	Washington	DC	20002	202-803-9000	810-2125*	340-18
**Fax Area Code:* 855 ■ *TF:* 877-777-4778 ■ *Web:* www.irs.gov/advocate						
Wage & Investment Div						
401 W Peachtree St NW	Atlanta	GA	30308	404-338-7060		340-18
Web: www.irs.gov						
Internap Network Services Corp						
250 Williams St Ste E-100	Atlanta	GA	30303	404-302-9700	475-0520	39
NASDAQ: INAP ■ *TF:* 877-843-7627 ■ *Web:* www.internap.com						
International Academy of Compounding Pharmacists (IACP)						
4638 Riverstone Blvd	Missouri City	TX	77459	281-933-8400	495-0602	49-8
TF: 800-927-4227 ■ *Web:* www.iacprx.org						
International Academy of Design & Technology						
Chicago 1 N State St Ste 500	Chicago	IL	60602	312-980-9200		164
TF: 877-222-3369 ■ *Web:* www.iadt.edu						
Las Vegas 2495 Village View Dr	Henderson	NV	89074	702-990-0150		164
TF: 866-400-4238 ■ *Web:* www.iadt.edu						
International Aid Inc						
17011 W Hickory St	Spring Lake	MI	49456	616-846-7490	846-3842	48-5
TF: 800-968-7490 ■ *Web:* www.internationalaid.org						
International Air Cargo Assn (TIACA)						
5600 NW 36th St Ste 620	Miami	FL	33266	786-265-7011	265-7012	49-21
TF: 800-262-9974 ■ *Web:* www.tiaca.org						
International Air Response Inc						
6250 S Taxiway Cir	Mesa	AZ	85212	480-840-9860	840-9866	302
Web: www.internationalairresponse.com						
International Air Transport Assn						
800 Pl Victoria PO Box 113	Montreal	QC	H4Z1M1	514-874-0202	874-9632	49-21
TF: 800-716-6326 ■ *Web:* www.iata.org						
International Airline Passengers Assn (IAPA)						
PO Box 700188	Dallas	TX	75370	972-404-9980	233-5348	48-23
TF: 800-821-4272 ■ *Web:* www.iapa.com						
International Alliance for Women (TIAW)						
1101 Pennsylvania Ave NW 3rd Fl	Washington	DC	20004	888-712-5200		48-24
TF: 888-712-5200 ■ *Web:* www.tiaw.org						
International Alliance of Theatrical Stage Employee (IATSE)						
1430 Broadway 20th Fl	New York	NY	10018	212-730-1770	921-7699	414
TF: 800-456-3863 ■ *Web:* iatse.net						
International AntiCounterfeiting Coalition (IACC)						
1730 M St NW	Washington	DC	20036	202-223-6667		49-13
Web: www.iacc.org						
International Arctic Research Ctr (IARC)						
930 N Koyukuk Dr PO Box 757340	Fairbanks	AK	99775	907-474-6016	474-5662	668
Web: www.iarc.uaf.edu						
International Armoring Corp						
80 N 1400 W	Centerville	UT	84014	801-393-1075	298-0858	59
Web: www.armormax.com						
International Assn for Dental Research (IADR)						
1619 Duke St	Alexandria	VA	22314	703-548-0066		49-8
Web: www.iadr.org						

	City	State	Zip	Phone	Fax	Class
International Assn for Food Protection (IAFP)						
6200 Aurora Ave Ste 200W	Des Moines	IA	50322	515-276-3344	276-8655	49-6
TF General: 800-369-6337 ■ *Web:* www.foodprotection.org						
International Assn for Human Resource Information Management Inc (IHRIM)						
PO Box 1000	Burlington	MA	01803	800-804-3983	998-8011*	49-12
**Fax Area Code:* 781 ■ *TF:* 800-804-3983 ■ *Web:* www.ihrim.org						
International Assn for Impact Assessment (IAIA)						
1330 23rd St S Ste C	Fargo	ND	58103	701-297-7908	297-7917	49-12
TF: 800-873-7130 ■ *Web:* www.iaia.org						
International Assn for Medical Assistance to Travellers (IAMAT)						
67 Mowat Ave Ste 036	Toronto	ON	M6K3E3	416-652-0137	652-1983	48-23
Web: www.iamat.org						
International Assn for the Study of Pain (IASP)						
111 Queen Anne Ave N Ste 501	Seattle	WA	98109	206-283-0311	283-9403	48-17
TF: 866-574-2654 ■ *Web:* www.iasp-pain.org						
International Assn of Administrative Professionals (IAAP)						
10502 NW Ambassador Dr Ste 100	Kansas City	MO	64153	816-891-6600	891-9118	49-12
Web: www.iaap-hq.org						
International Assn of Amusement Parks & Attractions (IAAPA)						
1448 Duke St	Alexandria	VA	22314	703-836-4800	836-6742	48-23
Web: www.iaapa.org						
International Assn of Approved Basketball Officials Inc (IAABO)						
PO Box 355	Carlisle	PA	17013	717-713-8129	718-6164	48-22
Web: www.iaabo.org						
International Assn of Arson Investigators (IAAI)						
2111 Baldwin Ave # 203	Crofton	MD	21114	410-451-3473	451-9049	49-7
TF: 800-468-4224 ■ *Web:* www.firearson.com						
International Assn of Assessing Officers (IAAO)						
314 W Tenth St	Kansas City	MO	64105	816-701-8100	701-8149	49-7
TF: 800-616-4226 ■ *Web:* www.iaao.org						
International Assn of Auto Theft Investigators (IAATI)						
PO Box 223	Clinton	NY	13323	315-853-1913		49-7
Web: www.iaati.org						
International Assn of Bridge Structural Ornamental & Reinforcing Iron Workers						
1750 New York Ave NW Ste 400	Washington	DC	20006	202-383-4800	638-4856	414
TF: 800-368-0105 ■ *Web:* www.ironworkers.org						
International Assn of Business Communicators (IABC)						
155 Montgomery St Ste 1210	San Francisco	CA	94104	415-544-4700	544-4747	49-12
TF: 800-776-4222 ■ *Web:* www.iabc.com						
International Assn of Chiefs of Police (IACP)						
44 Canal Ctr Plaza Ste 200	Alexandria	VA	22314	703-836-6767	836-4543	49-7
TF: 800-843-4227 ■ *Web:* www.theiacp.org						
International Assn of Conference Centers (IACC)						
35 East Wacker Dr Ste 850	Chicago	IL	60601	312-224-2580	644-8557	49-12
Web: www.iacconline.org						
International Assn of Culinary Professionals (IACP)						
45 Rockefeller Plaza Ste 2000	New York	NY	10111	855-738-4227	358-2524*	49-6
**Fax Area Code:* 866 ■ *TF:* 855-738-4227 ■ *Web:* www.iacp.com						
International Assn of Defense Counsel (IADC)						
303 W Madison St Ste 925	Chicago	IL	60606	312-368-1494	368-1854	49-10
TF: 800-575-1494 ■ *Web:* www.iadclaw.org						
International Assn of Drilling Contractors (IADC)						
10370 Richmond Ave Ste 760	Houston	TX	77042	713-292-1945	292-1946	49-3
Web: www.iadc.org						
International Assn of Electrical Inspectors (IAEI)						
901 Waterfall Way Ste 602	Richardson	TX	75080	972-235-1455	235-6858	49-3
TF: 800-786-4234 ■ *Web:* www.iaei.org						
International Assn of Exhibitions & Events (IAEE)						
12700 Park Central Dr Ste 308	Dallas	TX	75251	972-458-8002	458-8119	49-18
Web: www.iaee.com						
International Assn of Fairs & Expositions, The (IAFE)						
3043 E Cairo	Springfield	MO	65802	417-862-5771		48-23
TF: 800-516-0313 ■ *Web:* www.fairsandexpos.com						
International Assn of Fire Chiefs (IAFC)						
4025 Fair Ridge Dr Ste 300	Fairfax	VA	22033	703-273-0911	273-9363	49-7
TF: 866-385-9110 ■ *Web:* www.iafc.org						
International Assn of Fire Fighters (IAFF)						
1750 New York Ave NW 3rd Fl	Washington	DC	20006	202-737-8484	737 8418	414
Web: client.prod.iaff.org						
International Assn of Fish & Wildlife Agencies (IAFWA)						
444 N Capitol St NW Ste 725	Washington	DC	20001	202-624-7890	624-7891	49-7
Web: www.fishwildlife.org						
International Assn of Heat & Frost Insulators & Allied Workers						
9602 ML King Jr Hwy	Lanham	MD	20706	301-731-9101	731-5058	414
Web: www.insulators.org						
International Assn of Lions Clubs						
300 W 22nd St	Oak Brook	IL	60523	630-571-5466	571-8890	48-15
TF: 800-710-7822 ■ *Web:* www.lionsclubs.org						
International Assn of Machinists & Aerospace Workers						
9000 Machinists Pl	Upper Marlboro	MD	20772	301-967-4500		414
Web: www.goiam.org						
International Assn of Marriage & Family Counselors (IAMFC)						
5999 Stevenson Ave	Alexandria	VA	22304	800-347-6647	473-2329	49-15
TF: 800-347-6647 ■ *Web:* www.counseling.org						
International Assn of Plastics Distribution (IAPD)						
6734 W 121 St	Overland Park	KS	66209	913-345-1005	345-1006	49-18
Web: www.iapd.org						
International Assn of Plumbing & Mechanical Officials (IAPMO)						
4755 E Philadelphia St	Ontario	CA	91761	909-472-4100	472-4150	49-7
TF: 877-427-6601 ■ *Web:* www.iapmo.org						
International Assn of Venue Managers Inc (IAVM)						
635 Fritz Dr Ste 100	Coppell	TX	75019	972-906-7441	906-7418	49-12
TF: 800-935-4226 ■ *Web:* www.iavm.org						
International Assn of Wildland Fire (IAWF)						
3416 Primm Ln	Birmingham	AL	35216	205-824-7614		48-13
Web: www.iawfonline.org						
International Assn of Workforce Professionals (IAPES)						
1801 Louisville Rd	Frankfort	KY	40601	502-223-4459	223-4127	49-12
Web: iawponline.org						
International Atomic Energy Agency (IAEA)						
1 UN Plaza Rm DC1-1155	New York	NY	10017	212-963-6010	367-4046*	783
**Fax Area Code:* 917 ■ *Web:* www.iaea.org						
International Automotive Technicians' Network Inc						
PO Box 1599	Brea	CA	92822	714-257-1335		387
TF: 800-272-7467 ■ *Web:* www.iatn.net						
International Bakers Service Inc						
1902 N Sheridan St	South Bend	IN	46628	574-287-7111		345
Web: www.internationalbakers.com						
International Bancshares Corp						
1200 San Bernardo Ave	Laredo	TX	78040	956-722-7611	726-6637	360-2
NASDAQ: IBOC ■ *Web:* www.ibc.com						
International Baptist College						
2211 W Germann Rd	Chandler	AZ	85286	480-245-7900		166
TF General: 800-422-4858 ■ *Web:* www.tricityministries.org						
International Bible Society (IBS)						
Biblica 1820 Jet Stream Dr	Colorado Springs	CO	80921	719-488-9200		48-20
TF Cust Svc: 800-524-1588 ■ *Web:* www.biblica.com						
International Billiards Inc						
2311 Washington Ave	Houston	TX	77007	713-869-3237		710
TF: 800-255-6386 ■ *Web:* www.intlbilliards.com						
International Biometric Group LLC						
1 Battery Pk Plaza Ste 2901	New York	NY	10004	212-809-9491	809-6197	84
Web: www.ibgweb.com						
International Biometric Society (IBS)						
1444 'I' St NW Ste 700	Washington	DC	20005	202-712-9049	216-9646	49-19
Web: www.biometricsociety.org						
International Board of Jewish Missions Inc						
5106 Genesis Ln	Hixson	TN	37343	423-876-8150		520
Web: www.ibjm.org						
International Bottled Water Assn (IBWA)						
1700 Diagonal Rd Ste 650	Alexandria	VA	22314	703-683-5213	683-4074	49-6
TF: 800-928-3711 ■ *Web:* www.bottledwater.org						
International Boundary & Water Commission - US & Mexico						
2616 W Paisano Dr Ste C-100	El Paso	TX	79922	915-351-1030	832-4190	340-16
TF: 800-262-8857 ■ *Web:* www.ibwc.gov/home.html						
International Boundary Commission - US & Canada						
2000 L St NW Ste 615	Washington	DC	20036	202-736-9100	632-2008	340-16
Web: www.internationalboundarycommission.org						
International Bowling Museum & Hall of Fame						
621 Six Flags Dr	Arlington	TX	76011	817-385-8215	385-8210	522
TF: 800-514-2695 ■ *Web:* www.bowlingmuseum.com						
International Boxing Hall of Fame Museum						
1 Hall of Fame Dr	Canastota	NY	13032	315-697-7095	697 5356	522
Web: www.ibhof.com						
International Brangus Breeders Assn (IBBA)						
5750 Epsilon Dr	San Antonio	TX	78249	210-696-8231	696-8718	48-2
Web: www.gobrangus.com						
International Bridge Tunnel & Turnpike Assn (IBTTA)						
1146 19th St NW Ste 600	Washington	DC	20036	202-659-4620	659-0500	49-7
Web: www.ibtta.org						
International Broadcasting Bureau						
330 Independence Ave SW	Washington	DC	20237	202-203-4000	203-4585	643
Web: www.bbg.gov						
International Brotherhood of Boilermakers Iron Shipbuilders Blacksmiths Forgers & Helpers						
753 State Ave Ste 570	Kansas City	KS	66101	913-371-2640	281-8101	414
Web: www.boilermakers.org						
International Brotherhood of Electrical Workers						
900 Seventh St NW	Washington	DC	20001	202-833-7000		414
Web: www.ibew.org						
International Brotherhood of Police Officers (IBPO)						
159 Burgin Pkwy	Quincy	MA	02169	617-376-0220	376-0285*	414
**Fax:* Legal Dept ■ *Web:* www.ibpo.org						
International Brotherhood of Teamsters						
25 Louisiana Ave NW	Washington	DC	20001	202-624-6800	624-6918*	414
**Fax:* PR ■ *Web:* www.teamster.org						
International Business & Finance Daily						
1801 S Bell St	Arlington	VA	22202	703-341-5777		531-1
TF: 800-372-1033						
International Business College						
5699 Coventry Ln	Fort Wayne	IN	46804	260-459-4500		800
TF: 800-589-6363 ■ *Web:* www.ibcfortwayne.edu						
International Business Machines Corp (IBM)						
1 New OrchaRd Rd	Armonk	NY	10504	914-499-1900		173-2
NYSE: IBM ■ *TF:* 800-426-4968 ■ *Web:* www.ibm.com						
International Card Manufacturers Assn (ICMA)						
191 Clarksville Rd	Princeton Junction	NJ	08550	609-799-4900	799-7032	49-4
Web: www.icma.com						
International Carwash Assn						
230 E Ohio St	Chicago	IL	60611	888-422-8422	245-1085*	49-21
**Fax Area Code:* 312 ■ *TF:* 888-422-8422 ■ *Web:* www.carwash.org						
International Cemetery Cremation & Funeral Assn (ICCFA)						
107 Carpenter Dr Ste 100	Sterling	VA	20164	703-391-8400	391-8416	49-4
TF: 800-645-7700 ■ *Web:* www.iccfa.com						
International Ceramic Engineering						
235 Brooks St	Worcester	MA	01606	508-853-4700	852-4101	249
TF: 800-779-3321 ■ *Web:* www.intlceramics.com						
International Chauffeured Service Worldwide						
53 E 34th St	New York	NY	10016	212-213-0302	213-1373	441
TF: 800-266-5254 ■ *Web:* www.bookalimo.com						
International Checker Hall of Fame						
220 Lynn Ray Rd	Petal	MS	39465	601-582-7090		520
TF: 800-947-4666 ■ *Web:* ncheckers.org						
International Chemical Co						
2628-48 N Mascher St	Philadelphia	PA	19133	215-739-2313	423-7171	145
TF: 888-225-5422 ■ *Web:* www.e-icc.com						
International Chemical Workers Union Council						
1655 W Market St Fl 6	Akron	OH	44313	330-926-1444	926-0816	414
Web: www.icwuc.org						
International Chimney Corp						
55 S Long St	Williamsville	NY	14221	800-828-1446	634-3983*	189-7
**Fax Area Code:* 716 ■ *TF:* 800-828-1446 ■ *Web:* www.internationalchimney.com						
International Chiropractors Assn (ICA)						
6400 Arlington Blvd Ste 800	Falls Church	VA	22042	703-528-5000	528-5023	49-8
TF: 800-423-4690 ■ *Web:* www.chiropractic.org						
International Church of the Foursquare Gospel (ICFG)						
1910 W Sunset Blvd PO Box 26902	Los Angeles	CA	90026	213-989-4234	989-4590	48-20
TF: 888-635-4234 ■ *Web:* www.foursquare.org						
International City Theatre						
110 Pine Ave Ste 820 Ste 820	Long Beach	CA	90802	562-495-4595	436-7895	573-4
TF: 800-897-1952 ■ *Web:* www.ictlongbeach.org						
International City/County Management Assn (ICMA)						
777 N Capitol St NE Ste 500	Washington	DC	20002	202-289-4262	962-3500	49-7
TF: 800-745-8780 ■ *Web:* www.icma.org						
International Civil Rights Ctr & Museum						
134 S Elm St	Greensboro	NC	27401	336-274-9199	274-6244	520
TF: 800-748-7116 ■ *Web:* www.sitinmovement.org						

Organization	Phone	Fax	Class
International Coatings Co 13929 166th St Cerritos CA 90703 *TF:* 800-423-4103 ■ *Web:* www.iccink.com	562-926-1010	926-9486	388
International Code Council (ICC) 500 New Jersey Ave NW 6th Fl Washington DC 20001 *TF:* 888-422-7233 ■ *Web:* www.iccsafe.org	202-370-1800	783-2348	49-3
International Cold Storage Company Inc 215 E 13th St Andover KS 67002 *TF:* 800-835-0001 ■ *Web:* www.icsco.com	316-733-1385	733-2434	664
International College of Dentists (ICD) 51 Monroe St Ste 1400 Rockville MD 20850 *Web:* www.icd.org	301-251-8861	738-9143	49-8
International College of Surgeons (ICS) 1516 N Lake Shore Dr Chicago IL 60610 *TF:* 800-382-8270 ■ *Web:* www.icsglobal.org	312-642-3555		49-8
International Collegiate Licensing Assn (ICLA) 24651 Detroit Rd Westlake OH 44145 *TF:* 877-887-2261 ■ *Web:* www.nacda.com/icla/nacda-icla.html	440-892-4000	892-4007	48-22
International Comfort Products Corp (ICP) 650 Heil Quaker Ave Lewisburg TN 37091 *TF:* 800-458-6650 ■ *Web:* www.icpusa.com	931-359-3511		15
International Communication Assn (ICA) 1500 21st St NW Washington DC 20036 *TF:* 800-590-1125 ■ *Web:* www.icahdq.org	202-955-1444	955-1448	49-14
International Communications Industries Assn (ICIA) 11242 Waples Mill Rd Ste 200 Fairfax VA 22030 *TF:* 800-659-7469 ■ *Web:* www.infocomm.org	703-273-7200	278-8082	49-20
International Conference of Funeral Service Examining Boards Inc 1885 Shelby Ln Fayetteville AR 72704 *TF:* 800-709-0180 ■ *Web:* www.theconferenceonline.org	479-442-7076	442-7090	49-7
International Congress of Oral Implantologists (ICOI) 248 Lorraine Ave 3rd Fl Upper Montclair NJ 07043 **Fax Area Code:* 267 ■ *TF:* 800-442-0525 ■ *Web:* www.icoi.org	973-783-6300	295-8509*	49-8
International Contract Furnishings Inc (ICF) 19 Ohio Ave Norwich CT 06360 **Fax Area Code:* 888 ■ *TF:* 800-237-1625 ■ *Web:* www.icfsource.com	860-886-1700	784-8209*	321
International Contractors Inc 977 S Rt 83 Elmhurst IL 60126 *TF:* 800-847-5085 ■ *Web:* www.iciinc.com	630-834-8043		186
International Converter Inc 17153 Industrial Hwy Caldwell OH 43724 *TF:* 800-848-6623 ■ *Web:* www.i-convert.com	740-732-5665		554
International Copper Assn 260 Madison Ave 16th Fl New York NY 10016 *Web:* copperalliance.org	212-251-7240	251-7245	49-13
International Cornea Project 9246 Lightwave Ave Ste 120 San Diego CA 92123 *TF:* 800-393-2265 ■ *Web:* www.sdeb.org	858-694-0400	565-7368	269
International Council of Shopping Centers (ICSC) 1221 Ave of the Americas 41st Fl New York NY 10020 **Fax Area Code:* 212 ■ *Web:* www.icsc.org	646-728-3800	589-5555*	49-12
International Council on Hotel Restaurant & Institutional Education (CHRIE) 2810 N Parham Rd Ste 230 Richmond VA 23294 *Web:* www.chrie.org	804-346-4800	346-5009	49-5
International Ctr for Advanced Internet Research (iCAIR) 750 N Lake Shore Dr Ste 600 Chicago IL 60611 *Web:* www.icair.org	312-503-0735		668
International Ctr for Language Studies Inc 1133 15th St NW Ste 600 Washington DC 20005 *Web:* www.icls.edu	202-639-8800		423
International Ctr for Research on Women (ICRW) 1120 20th St NW Ste 500-N Washington DC 20036 *Web:* www.icrw.org	202-797-0007	797-0020	48-24
International Ctr for Technology Assessment (ICTA) 660 Pennsylvania Ave SE Ste 302 Washington DC 20003 *Web:* www.icta.org	415-826-2770		49-19
International Ctr for the Disabled (ICD) 340 E 24th St New York NY 10010 *TF:* 800-246-4646 ■ *Web:* www.icdnyc.org	212-585-6020		48-17
International Ctr of Medieval Art (ICMA) The Cloisters Fort Tryon Pk New York NY 10040 *Web:* www.medievalart.org	212-928-1146	928-9946	48-4
International Ctr of Photography 1133 Ave of the Americas New York NY 10036 *Web:* www.icp.org	212-857-0000		520
International Dairy Foods Assn (IDFA) 1250 H St NW Ste 900 Washington DC 20005 *Web:* www.idfa.org	202-737-4332	331-7820	49-6
International Dairy Queen Corp 7505 Metro Blvd Minneapolis MN 55439 *TF:* 866-793-7582 ■ *Web:* www.dairyqueen.com	952-830-0200		670
International Dairy-Deli-Bakery Assn (IDDBA) 636 Science Dr Madison WI 53711 *TF:* 877-399-4925 ■ *Web:* www.iddba.org	608-310-5000	238-6330	49-6
International Data Group Inc (IDG) 1 Exeter Plaza 15th Fl Boston MA 02116 *TF Orders:* 800-343-4952 ■ *Web:* www.idg.com	617-534-1200		637-9
International Delivery Solutions LLC 7340 S Howell Ave Milwaukee WI 53154 *TF:* 877-437-8722 ■ *Web:* www.idstrac.com	877-437-8722		5
International Digital Enterprise Alliance 1421 Prince St Ste 230 Alexandria VA 22314 *TF:* 800-942-7088 ■ *Web:* www.idealliance.org	703-837-1070	837-1072	49-16
International Display Systems Inc 5008 Veterans Memorial Hwy Holbrook NY 11741 *Web:* www.idsmenus.com	631-218-1802		701
International District Energy Assn (IDEA) 24 Lyman St Ste 230 Westborough MA 01581 *Web:* www.districtenergy.org	508-366-9339	366-0019	49-3
International Down & Feather Testing Laboratory 1455 S 1100 E Salt Lake City UT 84105 *Web:* www.idfl.com	801-467-7611		743
International Downtown Assn (IDA) 1025 Thomas Jefferson St NW Ste 500 W Washington DC 20007 *Web:* www.ida-downtown.org/eweb	202-393-6801	393-6869	49-17
International Dyslexia Assn, The (IDA) 40 York Rd 4th Fl Towson MD 21204 *Web:* dyslexiaida.org	410-296-0232	321-5069	48-17
International Economic Development Council (IEDC) 734 15th St NW Ste 900 Washington DC 20005 *Web:* www.iedconline.org	202-223-7800	223-4745	49-12
International Electrical Sales Corp (IESCO) 7540 NW 66th St Miami FL 33166 *Web:* www.iescomia.com	305-591-8390		246
International Electronic Machines Corp (IEM) 850 River St Troy NY 12180 *Web:* www.iem.net	518-268-1636	268-1639	261
International English Institute 640 Spence Ln Ste 121 Nashville TN 37217 *Web:* www.iei.edu	615-327-1715	399-9799	423
International Engraved Graphics Assn 305 Plus Pk Blvd Nashville TN 37217 *TF:* 800-821-3138 ■ *Web:* www.iega.org	800-821-3138		49-4
International Enterprises Inc 108 Allen St Talladega AL 35160 *TF:* 866-362-8562 ■ *Web:* www.ieionline.com	256-362-8562		21
International Environmental Corp (IEC) PO Box 2598 Oklahoma City OK 73101 *TF:* 800-264-5329 ■ *Web:* www.iec-okc.com	405-605-5000	605-5001	14
International Executive Housekeepers Assn (IEHA) 1001 Eastwind Dr Ste 301 Westerville OH 43081 *TF:* 800-200-6342 ■ *Web:* www.ieha.org	614-895-7166	895-1248	49-4
International Exotic Feline Sanctuary PO Box 637 Boyd TX 76023 *Web:* www.bigcat.org	940-433-5091	433-5092	823
International Extrusions Inc 5800 Venoy Rd Garden City MI 48135 *TF:* 800-242-8876 ■ *Web:* www.extrusion.net	734-427-8700	427-9319	482
International Eye Foundation (IEF) 10801 Connecticut Ave Kensington MD 20895 *Web:* www.iefusa.org	240-290-0263	290-0269	48-5
International Eyecare Center Inc 2445 Broadway Quincy IL 62301 *Web:* www.iec2020.com	217-222-8800		237
International Facility Management Assn (IFMA) 800 Gessner Rd Ste 900 Houston TX 77024 *Web:* www.ifma.org	713-623-4362	623-6124	49-12
International Federation of Accountants 545 Fifth Ave 14th Fl New York NY 10017 *TF:* 888-272-2001 ■ *Web:* www.ifac.org	212-286-9344	286-9570	49-1
International Federation of Pharmaceutical Wholesalers (IFPW) 10569 Crestwood Dr Manassas VA 20109 *Web:* www.ifpw.com	703-331-3714	331-3715	49-18
International Federation of Professional & Technical Engineers 8630 Fenton St Ste 400 Silver Spring MD 20910 *Web:* www.ifpte.org	301-565-9016	565-0018	414
International Festivals & Events Assn (IFEA) 2603 W Eastover Terr Boise ID 83706 *Web:* www.ifea.com	208-433-0950	433-9812	48-23
International Fiber Corp 50 Bridge St North Tonawanda NY 14120 *TF:* 888-698-1936 ■ *Web:* www.ifcfiber.com	716-693-4040	693-3528	605-1
International Fidelity Insurance Co (IFIC) 1 Newark Ctr 20th Fl Newark NJ 07102 *TF:* 800-333-4167 ■ *Web:* www.ific.com	973-624-7200	643-7116	391-5
International Financial Group 2530 Meridian Pkwy 2nd Fl Raleigh NC 27713 *Web:* www.ifgpr.com	919-806-4458	806-4829	260
International Fire Equipment Corp 500 Telser Rd Lake Zurich IL 60047 *TF:* 800-244-2343 ■ *Web:* www.intlfire.com	847-438-2343	438-1869	679
International Flavors & Fragrances Inc (IFF) 521 W 57th St New York NY 10019 *NYSE:* IFF ■ *Web:* www.iff.com	212-765-5500	708-7132	144
International Food Information Council Foundation (IFIC) 1100 Connecticut Ave NW Ste 430 Washington DC 20036 *TF:* 888-723-3366 ■ *Web:* www.foodinsight.org	202-296-6540	296-6547	49-6
International Food Policy Research Institute (IFPRI) 2033 K St NW Washington DC 20006 *Web:* www.ifpri.org	202-862-5600	467-4439	634
International Foodservice Distributors Assn (IFDA) 1410 Spring Hill Rd Ste 210 McLean VA 22102 *Web:* www.ifdaonline.org	703-532-9400	538-4673	49-18
International Foodservice Manufacturers Assn (IFMA) 180 N Stetson Ave 2 Prudential Plz Ste 4400 Chicago IL 60601 *Web:* www.ifmaworld.com	312-540-4400	540-4401	49-6
International Foundation of Employee Benefit Plans (IFEBP) 18700 W Bluemound Rd Brookfield WI 53045 *TF:* 888-334-3327 ■ *Web:* www.ifebp.org	262-786-6700	786-8670	260
International Franchise Assn (IFA) 1501 K St NW Ste 350 Washington DC 20005 *TF:* 800-543-1038 ■ *Web:* www.franchise.org	202-628-8000	628-0812	49-18
International Fraternity of Phi Gamma Delta 1201 Red Mile Rd PO Box 4599 Lexington KY 40544 *TF:* 888-668-4293 ■ *Web:* www.phigam.org	859-255-1848	253-0779	48-16
International Fund for Agricultural Development (IFAD) 1775 K St NW Ste 410 Washington DC 20006 *Web:* www.ifad.org	202-331-9099	331-9366	783
International Fund for Animal Welfare (IFAW) 290 Summer St Yarmouth Port MA 02675 *TF:* 800-932-4329 ■ *Web:* www.ifaw.org	508-744-2000		48-3
International Furniture Rental Assn (IFRA) 950 F St NW 10th Fl Washington DC 20004 *Web:* www.ifra.org	202-239-3818	654-4818	49-4
International Game Technology (IGT) 9295 Prototype Dr Reno NV 89521 *NYSE:* IGT ■ *TF:* 800-522-4700 ■ *Web:* www.igt.com	775-448-7777		322
International Gay & Lesbian Travel Assn (IGLTA) 1201 NE 26th St Ste 103 Fort Lauderdale FL 33305 *Web:* www.iglta.org	954-630-1637	630-1652	48-23
International Gourmet Foods Inc 7520 Fullerton Rd Springfield VA 22153 *TF:* 800-522-0377 ■ *Web:* www.igf-inc.com	703-569-4520		345
International Graphoanalysis Society (IGAS) 842 Fifth Ave New Kensington PA 15068 **Fax Area Code:* 509 ■ *Web:* www.igas.com	724-472-9701	271-1149*	49-12

Organization / Address	City	State	ZIP	Phone	Fax	Class
International Ground Source Heat Pump Assn (IGSHPA) Oklahoma State University 374 Cordell S *TF:* 800-626-4747 ■ *Web:* igshpa.org	Stillwater	OK	74078	405-744-5175	744-5283	49-13
International Group Inc 85 Old Eagle School Rd *TF:* 800-852-6537 ■ *Web:* www.igiwax.com	Wayne	PA	19087	610-687-9030		580
International Gymnastics Hall of Fame & Museum 2020 Remington Pl *Web:* www.ighof.com	Oklahoma City	OK	73111	405-602-6664		522
International Health Racquet & Sportsclub Assn (IHRSA) 70 Fargo St *TF:* 800-228-4772 ■ *Web:* www.ihrsa.org	Boston	MA	02210	617-951-0055	951-0056	48-22
International Hearing Society (IHS) 16880 Middlebelt Rd Ste 4 *TF:* 800-521-5247 ■ *Web:* www.ihsinfo.org	Livonia	MI	48154	734-522-7200	522-0200	48-17
International Herald Tribune 229 W 43rd St *TF:* 800-458-5522 ■ *Web:* international.nytimes.com	New York	NY	10036	212-556-7777		532-2
International Home Furnishings Ctr 210 E Commerce Ave	High Point	NC	27260	336-888-3700		205
International Home Furnishings Representatives Assn (IHFRA) 209 S Main St PO Box 670 *TF:* 800-873-4344 ■ *Web:* www.ihfra.org	High Point	NC	27261	336-889-3920		49-18
International Homes of Cedar Inc (IHC) PO Box 886 *TF:* 800-767-7674 ■ *Web:* www.ihoc.com	Woodinville	WA	98072	360-668-8511	668-5562	106
International Hotel 20 Second Ave SW **Fax Area Code:* 507 ■ *TF:* 800-940-6811 ■ *Web:* www.towersatkahlergrand.com	Rochester	MN	55902	800-940-6811	285-2767*	379
International Hotel of Calgary 220 Fourth Ave SW *TF:* 800-661-8627 ■ *Web:* internationalhotel.ca	Calgary	AB	T2P0H5	403-265-9600		379
International House Hotel 221 Camp St *Web:* www.ihhotel.com	New Orleans	LA	70130	504-553-9550	553-9560	379
International House Vancouver 200-1215 W BRdway Ste 2001 *Web:* www.ihvancouver.com	Vancouver	BC	V6H1G7	604-739-9030	739-9839	423
International Housewares Assn (IHA) 6400 Shafer Ct Ste 650 *TF:* 800-752-1052 ■ *Web:* www.housewares.org	Rosemont	IL	60018	847-292-4200	292-4211	49-4
International Ice Cream Assn 1250 H St NW Ste 900 *Web:* www.idfa.org	Washington	DC	20005	202-737-4332	331-7820	49-6
International Imaging Materials Inc 310 Commerce Dr *TF:* 888-464-4625 ■ *Web:* www.iimak.com	Amherst	NY	14228	716-691-6333		534
International Immunology Corp 25549 Adams Ave *TF:* 800-843-2853 ■ *Web:* www.nittobous.com	Murrieta	CA	92562	951-677-5629	677-6752	231
International Industrial Contracting Corp 35900 Mound Rd *Web:* www.iiccusa.com	Sterling Heights	MI	48310	586-264-7070		189-1
International Ingredient Corp 150 Larkin Williams Industrial Ct PO Box 26377 *Web:* www.iicag.com	Fenton	MO	63026	636-343-4111	349-4845	447
International Institute of Ammonia Refrigeration 1001 N Fairfax St Ste 503 *Web:* www.iiar.org	Alexandria	VA	22314	703-312-4200	312-0065	49-3
International Institute of Metropolitan Detroit 111 E Kirby St *Web:* www.iimd.org	Detroit	MI	48202	313-871-8600	871-1651	520
International Institute of Municipal Clerks (IIMC) 8331 Utica Ave Ste 200 *TF:* 800-251-1639 ■ *Web:* www.iimc.com	Rancho Cucamonga	CA	91730	909-944-4162	944-8545	49-7
International Institute of Rural Reconstruction (IIRR) 601 W 26th St Ste 325-1 *Web:* www.iirr.org	New York	NY	10001	917-410-7091		48-5
International Institute of Synthetic Rubber Producers Inc (IISRP) 3535 Briarpark Dr Ste 250 *Web:* www.iisrp.com	Houston	TX	77042	713-783-7511	783-7253	49-13
International Institute of Tropical Forestry (IITF) Jardin Botanico Sur 1201 Calle Ceiba *Web:* www.fs.fed.us/global/iitf	San Juan	PR	00926	787-766-5335	766-6302	668
International Interior Design Assn (IIDA) 222 Merchandise Mart Plaza Ste 567 *TF:* 888-799-4432 ■ *Web:* www.iida.org	Chicago	IL	60654	312-467-1950	467-0779	48-4
International Investigators Inc 3216 N Pennsylvania St *TF:* 800-403-8111 ■ *Web:* www.iiiweb.net	Indianapolis	IN	46205	317-925-1496	926-1177	400
International Isotopes Inc 4137 Commerce Cir *OTC:* INIS ■ *TF:* 800-699-3108 ■ *Web:* www.intisoid.com	Idaho Falls	ID	83401	208-524-5300	524-1411	231
International Jet Aviation Services 8511 Aviator Ln *TF:* 800-858-5891 ■ *Web:* www.internationaljet.com	Centennial	CO	80112	303-790-0414	790-4144	13
International Label & Printing Company Inc 2550 United Ln **Fax Area Code:* 630 ■ *TF:* 800-244-1442 ■ *Web:* www.internationallabel.com	Elk Grove Village	IL	60007	800-244-1442	595-1747*	413
International Labour Organization (ILO) 220 E 42nd St Ste 3101 *Web:* www.ilo.org	New York	NY	10017	212-697-0150	697-5218	783
International Labs Inc 2701 75th St N *Web:* www.internationallabs.com	St Petersburg	FL	33710	727-343-1548		583
International Language Institute 1717 Rhode Island Ave NW Ste 100 *Web:* ilidc.com	Washington	DC	20036	202-362-2505		423
International Launch Services (ILS) 1875 Explorer St Ste 700 *TF:* 800-852-4980 ■ *Web:* www.ilslaunch.com	Reston	VA	20190	571-633-7400	633-7500	504
International Law Institute (ILI) 1055 Thomas Jefferson St NW Ste M-100 *TF:* 800-277-5508 ■ *Web:* www.ili.org	Washington	DC	20007	202-247-6006	247-6010	49-10
International Lawyers in Alcoholics Anonymous (ILAA) 415-1080 Mainland St *TF:* 888-685-2171 ■ *Web:* www.ilaa.org	Vancouver	BC	V6B2T4	604-685-2171		48-21
International Longshore & Warehouse Union 1188 Franklin St 4th Fl *TF:* 866-266-0013 ■ *Web:* www.ilwu.org	San Francisco	CA	94109	415-775-0533	775-1302	414
International Magnesium Assn (IMA) 1000 N Rand Rd Ste 214 *Web:* www.intlmag.org	Wauconda	IL	60084	847-526-2010	526-3993	49-13
International Manufacturing Group Inc 879 F St Ste 120 *TF:* 800-775-6412	West Sacramento	CA	95605	800-775-6412		475
International Market Centers 209 S Main St *Web:* www.imchighpointmarket.com	High Point	NC	27260	336-888-3700		321
International Marketing Assn (IMA) 3509 Virginia Beach Blvd *Web:* www.imacorporate.com	Virginia Beach	VA	23452	757-490-9860	490-0716	301
International Masonry Institute (IMI) 17101 Science Dr **Fax Area Code:* 301 ■ *TF:* 800-803-0295 ■ *Web:* www.imiweb.org	Bowie	MD	20715	800-803-0295	261-2855*	49-3
International Medical Corps (IMC) 1919 Santa Monica Blvd Ste 400 *TF:* 800-481-4462 ■ *Web:* www.internationalmedicalcorps.org	Santa Monica	CA	90404	310-826-7800	442-6622	48-5
International Medical Device Regulatory Monitor 300 N Washington St Ste 200 *TF:* 888-838-5578 ■ *Web:* fdanews.com/publications/18	Falls Church	VA	22046	703-538-7600	538-7676	531-8
International Medical Laboratory Inc 6419 Parkland Dr *Web:* www.internationalmedicallab.com	Sarasota	FL	34243	941-756-0000		415
International Meeting Managers Inc 4550 Post Oak Pl Ste 342 *TF:* 800-423-7175 ■ *Web:* www.meetingmanagers.com	Houston	TX	77027	713-965-0566	960-0488	184
International Metal Hose Co 520 Goodrich Rd *TF:* 800-458-6855 ■ *Web:* www.metalhose.com	Bellevue	OH	44811	419-483-7690	483-8225	490
International Microelectronics & Packaging Society (IMAPS) PO Box 110127 *Web:* www.imaps.org	Research Triangle Park	NC	27709	202-548-4001	548-6115	49-19
International Mold Steel Inc 6796 Powerline Dr *TF:* 800-625-6653 ■ *Web:* www.imsteel.com	Florence	KY	41042	859-342-6000		492
International Monetary Fund (IMF) 700 19th St NW *TF:* 800-548-5384 ■ *Web:* www.imf.org	Washington	DC	20431	202-623-7000	623-4661	783
International Montessori Council & The Montessori Foundation 19600 SR 64 E *TF:* 800-655-5843 ■ *Web:* www.montessori.org	Bradenton	FL	34212	941-729-9565	729-9594	48-11
International Motor Coach Group Inc (IMG) 8695 College Blvd Ste 260 *TF:* 888-447-3466 ■ *Web:* www.imgcoach.com	Overland Park	KS	66210	913-906-0111	906-0115	49-21
International Motorsports Hall of Fame & Museum 3198 Speedway Blvd *Web:* www.motorsportshalloffame.com	Talladega	AL	35160	256-362-5002		522
International Mountain Bicycling Assn (IMBA) 4888 Pearl E Cir Ste 200E *TF:* 888-442-4622 ■ *Web:* www.imba.com	Boulder	CO	80301	303-545-9011	545-9026	48-23
International Municipal Lawyers Assn (IMLA) 7910 Woodmont Ave Ste 1440 *TF:* 800-942-7732 ■ *Web:* www.imla.org	Bethesda	MD	20814	202-466-5424	785-0152	49-10
International Municipal Signal Assn (IMSA) 165 E Union St PO Box 539 *TF:* 800-723-4672 ■ *Web:* www.imsasafety.org	Newark	NY	14513	315-331-2182	331-8205	49-7
International Museum of Cultures 411 US Hwy 67 Southbound Frontage Rd *Web:* www.internationalmuseumofcultures.org	Duncanville	TX	75137	972-572-0462		520
International Museum of Muslim Cultures 201 E Pascagoula St Ste 102 *Web:* www.muslimmuseum.org	Jackson	MS	39201	601-960-0440		520
International Museum of Photography & Film at George Eastman House 900 E Ave *Web:* www.eastman.org	Rochester	NY	14607	585-271-3361		520
International Museum of Surgical Science 1524 N Lake Shore Dr *Web:* www.imss.org	Chicago	IL	60610	312-642-6502		520
International Museum of the Horse 4089 Iron Works Pkwy *TF:* 800-678-8813 ■ *Web:* www.imh.org	Lexington	KY	40511	859-259-4232		520
International Musician 120 Walton St *TF:* 800-762-3444 ■ *Web:* www.internationalmusician.org	Syracuse	NY	13202	315-422-4488	422-3837	457-9
International Neuropsychological Society (INS) 700 Ackerman Rd Ste 625 *TF:* 800-999-6673 ■ *Web:* www.the-ins.org	Columbus	OH	43202	614-263-4200	263-4366	49-15
International OCD Foundation (OCF) PO Box 961029 *TF:* 800-331-3131 ■ *Web:* iocdf.org	Boston	MA	02196	617-973-5801	973-5803	48-17
International Order of the Golden Rule (OGR) 3520 Executive Ctr Dr Ste 300 *TF:* 800-637-8030 ■ *Web:* www.ogr.org	Austin	TX	78731	512-334-5504	334-5514	49-4
International Order-Hoo-Hoo 207 E Main St	Gurdon	AR	71743	870-353-4997		48-2
International Organization for Migration 1752 N St NW Ste 700 *Web:* www.iom.int	Washington	DC	20036	202-862-1826	862-1879	48-8
International Organization of Masters Mates & Pilots 700 Maritime Blvd *TF:* 877-667-5522 ■ *Web:* www.bridgedeck.org	Linthicum Heights	MD	21090	410-850-8700	850-0973	414
International Orthodox Christian Charities (IOCC) 110 W Rd Ste 360 *TF:* 877-803-4622 ■ *Web:* www.iocc.org	Towson	MD	21204	410-243-9820	243-9824	48-5
International Paper Co 6400 Poplar Ave *NYSE:* IP ■ *TF Prod Info:* 800-223-1268 ■ *Web:* www.internationalpaper.com	Memphis	TN	38197	901-419-9000		557
International Parking Institute (IPI) 1330 Braddock Pl Ste 350 *Web:* www.parking.org	Alexandria	VA	22314	571-699-3011		49-21
International Patterns Inc 50 Inez Dr	Bay Shore	NY	11706	631-952-2000		701
International Pentecostal Holiness Church (IPHC) PO Box 12609 *TF:* 888-474-2966 ■ *Web:* www.iphc.org	Oklahoma City	OK	73157	405-787-7110	789-3957	48-20

	Phone	Fax	Class
International Photography Hall of Fame & Museum 3415 Olive St ... St Louis MO 63103 *Web:* www.iphf.org	314-535-1999		520
International Planned Parenthood Federation - Western Hemisphere Region (IPPF/WHR) 125 Maiden Ln 9th Fl ... New York NY 10005 *TF:* 866-477-3947 ■ *Web:* www.ippfwhr.org	212-248-6400	248-4221	48-5
International Plant Nutrition Institute (IPNI) 3500 PkwyLn Ste 550 ... Norcross GA 30092 *Web:* www.ipni.net	770-447-0335	448-0439	48-2
International Plastics Inc 185 Commerce Ctr ... Greenville SC 29615 *TF:* 800-820-4722 ■ *Web:* interplas.com	864-297-8000		345
International Playthings Inc 75D Lackawanna Ave ... Parsippany NJ 07054 *TF:* 800-631-1272 ■ *Web:* www.intplay.com	973-316-2500	316-5883	762
International Plaza & Bay Street 2223 NW Shore Blvd ... Tampa FL 33607 *Web:* www.shopinternationalplaza.com	813-342-3790		50-6
International Poly Bag Inc 990 Pk Ctr Dr Ste F & G ... Vista CA 92081 *TF:* 800-976-5922 ■ *Web:* www.intlpolybag.com	760-598-2468	598-2469	66
International Port of Dutch Harbor 43 Raven Way ... Unalaska AK 99685 *TF:* 800-526-6731 ■ *Web:* ci.unalaska.ak.us	907-581-1251		618
International Precious Metals Institute (IPMI) 5101 N 12th Ave Ste C ... Pensacola FL 32504 *Web:* www.ipmi.org	850-476-1156	476-1548	49-4
International Precision Inc 9526 Vassar Ave ... Chatsworth CA 91313 *Web:* www.intlprecision.com	818-882-3933		22
International Primate Protection League (IPPL) 120 Primate Ln ... Summerville SC 29483 *Web:* www.ippl.org	843-871-2280	871-7988	48-3
International Procurement Agency Inc 4322 Avondale Ln NW ... Canton OH 44708 *Web:* www.usaipa.com	330-477-5020		225
International Production Specialists Inc 35006 Washington Ave ... Honey Creek WI 53138 *Web:* www.ipstanks.com	262-534-3130		480
International Professional Rodeo Assn (IPRA) 1412 S Agnew ... Oklahoma City OK 73108 *TF:* 800-639-9002 ■ *Web:* www.ipra-rodeo.com	405-235-6540		48-22
International Public Management Assn for Hum Res (IPMA-HR) 1617 Duke St ... Alexandria VA 22314 *TF:* 800-381-8378 ■ *Web:* www.ipma-hr.org	703-549-7100	684-0948	49-12
International Radio & Television Society Foundation Inc (IRTS) 1697 Broadway 10th Fl ... New York NY 10019 *Web:* www.irtsfoundation.org	212-867-6650		49-14
International Reprographic Assn (IRgA) 401 N Michigan Ave Ste 2200 ... Chicago IL 60611 *TF:* 800-833-4742 ■ *Web:* www.apdsp.org	312-245-1026	673-6724	49-16
International Rescue Committee (IRC) 122 E 42nd St ... New York NY 10168 *TF:* 800-435-7352 ■ *Web:* www.rescue.org	212-551-3000	551-3179	48-5
International Resistive Company Inc (IRC) 736 Greenway Rd ... Boone NC 28607 *Web:* www.irctt.com	828-264-8861	264-8865	253
International Restaurant Management Group Inc (IRMG) 4104 Aurora St ... Coral Gables FL 33146 *Web:* www.irmgusa.com	305-476-1611	476-9622	670
International Revolving Door Co 2138 N Sixth Ave ... Evansville IN 47710 *TF:* 800-745-4726 ■ *Web:* www.intlentrance.com	812-425-3311	426-2682	234
International Risk Management Institute Inc 12222 Merit Dr Ste 1600 ... Dallas TX 75251 *Web:* www.cvrdallas.com	972-960-7693		401
International Road Federation (IRF) 500 Mongomery St 5th Fl ... Alexandria VA 22314 *Web:* www.irfnet.ch	703-535-1001	535-1007	49-3
International Safe Transit Assn (ISTA) 1400 Abbott Rd Ste 160 ... East Lansing MI 48823 *TF:* 888-299-2208 ■ *Web:* www.ista.org	517-333-3437	333-3813	49-21
International Sanitary Supply Assn (ISSA) 3300 Dundee Rd ... Northbrook IL 60062 *TF:* 800-225-4772 ■ *Web:* global.issa.com	847-982-0800	982-1012	49-18
International Satellite Services Inc 1004 Collier Ctr Way Ste 205 ... Naples FL 34110 *Web:* www.internationalsatelliteservices.com	239-598-2241		681
International Sew-Right Co 6190 Don Murie St ... Niagara Falls ON L2G0B4 *Web:* www.safetyclothing.com	905-374-3600	374-6121	576
International Ship Repair & Marine Services Inc 1616 Penny St ... Tampa FL 33605 *Web:* www.internationalship.com	813-247-1118		698
International Shipholding Corp 11 N Water Ste 18290 ... Mobile AL 36602 *NYSE:* ISH ■ *TF:* 800-826-3513 ■ *Web:* www.intship.com	251-243-9100		313
International Sight Restoration Inc 3808 Gunn Hwy Ste B ... Tampa FL 33618 *TF:* 877-477-3210 ■ *Web:* www.internationalsight.com	813-264-6003	264-6007	269
International Sign Assn (ISA) 1001 N Fairfax St Ste 301 ... Alexandria VA 22314 *TF:* 866-949-7446 ■ *Web:* www.signs.org	703-836-4012	836-8353	49-4
International Sleep Products Assn (ISPA) 501 Wythe St ... Alexandria VA 22314 *Web:* www.sleepproducts.org	703-683-8371	683-4503	49-4
International Snowmobile Hall of Fame 1521 N Railroad St ... Eagle River WI 54521 *TF:* 800-746-8963 ■ *Web:* www.ishof.com	715-479-2186		522
International Society for Animal Rights (ISAR) PO Box F ... Clarks Summit PA 18411 *TF:* 888-589-6397 ■ *Web:* www.isaronline.org	570-586-2200	586-9580	48-3
International Society for Heart & Lung Transplantation (ISHLT) 14673 Midway Rd Ste 200 ... Addison TX 75001 *Web:* www.ishlt.org	972-490-9495	490-9499	49-8
International Society for Magnetic Resonance in Medicine (ISMRM) 2030 Addison St Ste 700 ... Berkeley CA 94704 *Web:* www.ismrm.org	510-841-1899	841-2340	49-8

	Phone	Fax	Class
International Society for Performance Improvement (ISPI) PO Box 13035 ... Silver Spring MD 20910 *TF:* 800-825-7550 ■ *Web:* www.ispi.org	301-587-8570	587-8573	49-12
International Society for Peritoneal Dialysis (ISPD) 66 Martin St ... Milton ON L9T2R2 *TF:* 888-834-1001 ■ *Web:* www.ispd.org	905-875-2456	875-2864	49-8
International Society for Pharmaceutical Engineering (ISPE) 3109 W Dr ML King Jr Blvd Ste 250 ... Tampa FL 33607 *TF:* 800-228-9290 ■ *Web:* www.ispe.org	813-960-2105	264-2816	49-19
International Society for Pharmacoepidemiology (ISPE) 5272 River Rd Ste 630 ... Bethesda MD 20816 *TF:* 888-887-7955 ■ *Web:* www.pharmacoepi.org	301-718-6500	656-0989	49-8
International Society for Technology in Education (ISTE) 1530 Wilson Blvd Ste 730 ... Arlington VA 22209 *TF General:* 800-336-5191 ■ *Web:* www.iste.org	202-861-7777		49-5
International Society for Traumatic Stress Studies (ISTSS) 111 Deer Lake Rd Ste 100 ... Deerfield IL 60015 *TF:* 877-469-7873 ■ *Web:* www.istss.org	847-480-9028	480-9282	49-15
International Society of Arboriculture (ISA) PO Box 3129 ... Champaign IL 61826 *TF:* 888-472-8733 ■ *Web:* www.isa-arbor.com	217-355-9411	355-9516	48-2
International Society of Automation, The 67 Alexander Dr PO Box 12277 ... Research Triangle Park NC 27709 *Web:* www.isa.org	919-549-8411	549-8288	49-19
International Society of Bassists (ISB) 14070 Proton Rd Ste 100 ... Dallas TX 75244 *Web:* www.isbworldoffice.com	972-233-9107	490-4219	48-4
International Society of Certified Electronics Technicians (ISCET) 3608 Pershing Ave ... Fort Worth TX 76107 *TF:* 800-946-0201 ■ *Web:* www.iscet.org	817-921-9101	921-3741	49-19
International Society of Certified Employee Benefits (ISCEBS) 18700 W Bluemond Rd PO Box 209 ... Brookfield WI 53008 *TF:* 888-334-3327 ■ *Web:* www.iscebs.org	262-786-8771	786-8650	49-12
International Society of Fire Service Instructors (ISFSI) 14001C St Germain Dr ... Centreville VA 20121 *TF:* 800-435-0005 ■ *Web:* www.isfsi.org	800-435-0005	435-0005	49-7
International Society of Political Psychology (ISPP) 126 Ward St Ste 1213 PO Box 1213 ... Columbus NC 28722 *TF:* 800-796-6094 ■ *Web:* www.ispp.org	828-894-5422	894-5422	48-7
International Society of Refractive Surgery (ISRS) 655 Beach St PO Box 7424 ... San Francisco CA 94109 *TF:* 866-561-8558 ■ *Web:* www.aao.org	415-561-8581	561-8575	49-8
International Society of Travel Medicine (ISTM) 315 W Ponce de Leon Ave Ste 245 ... Decatur GA 30030 *Web:* www.istm.org	404-373-8282	373-8283	49-8
International Society of Tropical Foresters (ISTF) 5400 Grosvenor Ln ... Bethesda MD 20814 **Fax Area Code:* 877 ■ *Web:* www.istf-bethesda.org	301-530-4514	665-6473*	48-13
International SOS 3600 Horizon Blvd Ste 300 ... Trevose PA 19053 *TF:* 800-523-6586 ■ *Web:* www.internationalsos.com	215-942-8000	942-8175	391-7
International Soundex Reunion Registry 901 E Second St ... Carson City NV 89701 *Web:* www.isrr.net	775-882-7755		48-6
International Speakers Bureau Inc 2128 Boll St ... Dallas TX 75204 *Web:* www.iasbweb.org	214-744-3885		708
International Specialty Products Inc (ISP) 1361 Alps Rd ... Wayne NJ 07470 *TF:* 800-622-4423 ■ *Web:* www.ashland.com	973-628-4000		144
International Spy Museum 800 F St NW ... Washington DC 20004 *Web:* www.spymuseum.org	202-393-7798	393-7797	520
International Studies Assn (ISA) 324 Social Sciences University of Arizona ... Tucson AZ 85721 *Web:* www.isanet.org	860-486-5850		48-11
International Submarine Engineering Ltd 1734 Broadway St ... Port Coquitlam BC V3C2M8 *Web:* www.ise.bc.ca	604-942-5223	942-7577	698
International Surfing Museum 411 Olive Ave ... Huntington Beach CA 92648 *Web:* www.surfingmuseum.org	714-960-3483		520
International Swaps & Derivatives Assn (ISDA) 360 Madison Ave 16th Fl ... New York NY 10017 *Web:* www2.isda.org	212-901-6000		49-2
International Swimming Hall of Fame 1 Hall of Fame Dr ... Fort Lauderdale FL 33316 *Web:* www.ishof.org	954-462-6536	525-4031	522
International Tax Monitor 1801 S Bell St ... Arlington VA 22202 *TF:* 800-372-1033	703-341-5777		531-1
International Technology Education Assn (ITEA) 1914 Assn Dr Ste 201 ... Reston VA 20191 *Web:* www.iteea.org	703-860-2100	860-0353	49-5
International Tennis Hall of Fame & Museum 194 Bellevue Ave ... Newport RI 02840 *TF:* 800-745-3000 ■ *Web:* www.tennisfame.com	401-849-3990		522
International Textile Group 804 Green Valley Rd Ste 300 ... Greensboro NC 27408 *Web:* www.itg-global.com	336-379-6220		360-3
International Thermal Systems LLC (ITS) 4697 W Greenfield Ave ... Milwaukee WI 53214 *TF:* 800-245-1869 ■ *Web:* internationalthermalsystems.com	414-672-7700	672-8800	318
International Ticketing Assn (INTIX) 5868 E 71st St Ste E367 ... Indianapolis IN 46220 *Web:* www.intix.org	212-629-4036	629-4036	48-4
International Titanium Assn (ITA) 2655 W Midway Blvd Ste 300 ... Broomfield CO 80020 *Web:* www.titanium.org	303-404-2221	404-9111	49-19
International Towing & Recovery Hall of Fame & Museum 3315 Broad St ... Chattanooga TN 37408 *Web:* www.internationaltowingmuseum.org	423-267-3132	267-0867	520
International Trade Administration 1401 Constitution Ave NW ... Washington DC 20230 *Web:* www.ita.doc.gov	202-482-3809	482-5819	340-2
International Trade Information Inc (ITI) 900 Las Vegas Blvd S Unit 908 ... Las Vegas NV 89101 *Web:* www.internationaltradeinformation.com	818-591-2255	591-2289	184

Name / Address	City	State	ZIP	Phone	Fax	Class
International Trademark Assn (INTA) 655 Third Ave 10th Fl	New York	NY	10017	212-768-9887	768-7796	49-12
TF: 800-995-3579 ■ *Web:* www.inta.org						
International Training Inc 1321 SE Decker Ave	Stuart	FL	34994	207-729-4201	436-7096*	31
**Fax Area Code:* 877 ■ *TF:* 888-778-9073 ■ *Web:* www.tdisdi.com						
International Transplant Nurses Society (ITNS) 8735 W Higgins Rd Ste 300	Chicago	IL	60631	847-375-6340	375-6341	49-8
TF: 800-776-8636 ■ *Web:* www.itns.org						
International Transportation Service Inc 1281 Pier J Way	Long Beach	CA	90802	562-435-7781	590-6761	465
Web: www.itslb.com						
International Travel Systems Inc 64 Madison Ave	Wood-Ridge	NJ	07075	201-727-0470		16
TF: 800-258-0135 ■ *Web:* international-travel-systems.com						
International Tsunami Information Ctr 1845 Wasp Blvd Bldg 176	Honolulu	HI	96818	808-532-6422	532-5576	783
Web: itic.ioc-unesco.org						
International Union of Bricklayers & Allied Craftworkers (BAC) 1776 eye St NW	Washington	DC	20006	202-783-3788	393-0219	414
TF: 888-880-8222 ■ *Web:* www.bacweb.org						
International Union of Elevator Constructors (IUEC) 7154 Columbia Gateway Dr	Columbia	MD	21046	410-953-6150		49-3
Web: www.iuec.org						
International Union of Operating Engineers 1125 17th St NW	Washington	DC	20036	202-429-9100		414
Web: www.iuoe.org						
International Union of Painters & Allied Trades (IUPAT) 7234 Pkwy Dr	Hanover	MD	21076	410-564-5900		414
TF: 800-554-2479 ■ *Web:* iupat.org						
International Union of Police Assn 1549 Ringling Blvd Ste 600	Sarasota	FL	34236	941-487-2560	487-2570	414
TF: 800-247-4872 ■ *Web:* iupa.org						
International Union Security Police & Fire Professionals of America (SPFPA) 25510 Kelly Rd	Roseville	MI	48066	586-772-7250	772-9644	414
TF: 800-228-7492 ■ *Web:* www.spfpa.org						
International Union United Automobile Aerospace & Agricultural Implement Workers of America 8000 E Jefferson Ave	Detroit	MI	48214	313-926-5000	823-6016	414
Web: www.uaw.org						
International Veterinary Acupuncture Society (IVAS) 1730 S College Ave Ste 301	Fort Collins	CO	80525	970-266-0666	266-0777	48-3
Web: www.ivas.org						
International Violin Co Ltd 1421 Clarkview Rd	Baltimore	MD	21209	410-832-2525	832-2528	526
TF: 800-542-3538 ■ *Web:* www.internationalviolin.com						
International Visual Corp (IVC) 11500 Blvd Armand Bombardier	Montreal	QC	H1E2W9	514-643-0570	643-4867	286
TF: 866-643-0570 ■ *Web:* www.ivcweb.com						
International Warehouse Logistics Assn (IWLA) 2800 S River Rd Ste 260	Des Plaines	IL	60018	847-813-4699	813-0115	49-21
Web: www.iwla.com						
International Webmasters Assn (IWA) 119 E Union St Ste A	Pasadena	CA	91103	626-449-3709		48-9
TF: 866-607-1773 ■ *Web:* www.iwanet.org						
International Wildlife Museum 4800 W Gates Pass Rd	Tucson	AZ	85745	520-629-0100		520
Web: www.thewildlifemuseum.org						
International Window Corp 5625 E Firestone Blvd	South Gate	CA	90280	562-928-6411	928-3492	234
TF: 800-477-4032 ■ *Web:* www.intlwindow.com						
International Women's Air & Space Museum 1501 N Marginal Rd Burke Lakefront Airport	Cleveland	OH	44114	216-623-1111	623-1113	520
TF: 877-287-4752 ■ *Web:* www.iwasm.org						
International Wood Products Assn (IWPA) 4214 King St	Alexandria	VA	22302	703-820-6696	820-8550	49-3
TF: 855-435-0005 ■ *Web:* www.iwpawood.org						
International Wrestling Institute & Museum 303 Jefferson St	Waterloo	IA	50701	319-233-0745	233-3477	522
Web: www.nwhof.org						
Internet Applications Group 999 Commercial St Ste 210	Palo Alto	CA	94303	650-424-0496		225
Web: inapp.com						
Internet Archive 300 Funston Ave	San Francisco	CA	94118	415-561-6767	840-0391	397
Web: www.archive.org						
Internet Broadcasting Systems Inc 355 Randolph Ave	Saint Paul	MN	55102	651-365-4000		171
Web: www.ibsys.com						
Internet Business Network 303 Ross Dr	Mill Valley	CA	94941	415-377-2255	380-8245	637-9
TF: 866-497-6747 ■ *Web:* www.interbiznet.com						
Internet Business Systems Inc 496 Millich Dr Ste 210	Campbell	CA	95008	408-850-9202	850-9200	4
Web: www.ibsystems.com						
Internet Corp for Assigned Names & Numbers (ICANN) 4676 Admiralty Way Ste 330	Marina del Rey	CA	90292	310-823-9358	823-8649	48-9
Web: www.icann.org						
Internet Creations Inc 2000 Waterview Dr Ste 100	Hamilton	NJ	08691	609-570-7200		225
Web: www.internetcreations.com						
Internet Crimes Group Inc PO Box 3599	Princeton	NJ	08543	609-806-5000	806-5001	400
Web: ithreat.com						
Internet Employment Linkage Inc 1010 Lake St Ste 611	Oak Park	IL	60301	708-848-4351		225
Web: www.ielinc.net						
Internet Exposure Inc 1101 Washington Ave S	Minneapolis	MN	55415	612-333-2606		344
Web: www.iexposure.com						
Internet Matrix Inc 10179 Huennekens St	San Diego	CA	92121	800-462-8749		7
TF: 800-462-8749 ■ *Web:* www.imatrix.com						
Internet Movie Database Inc 410 Terry Ave N	Seattle	WA	98109	206-266-4064		387
Web: www.imdb.com						
Internet Nebraska Inc 1719 N Cotner Blvd Ste B	Lincoln	NE	68505	402-434-8680		225
TF: 800-438-4638 ■ *Web:* www.inebraska.com						
Internet Society (ISOC) 1775 Wiehle Ave Ste 102	Reston	VA	20190	703-439-2120	326-9881	48-9
Web: www.internetsociety.org						
Internet Solver Inc 11308 Aurora Ave	Urbandale	IA	50322	515-224-9229		631
Internet2 1000 Oakbrook Dr Ste 300	Ann Arbor	MI	48108	734-913-4250	913-4255	48-9
Web: www.internet2.edu						
InternetSafety.com Inc 3979 S Main St Ste 230	Acworth	GA	30101	877-944-8080		178-7
TF: 877-944-8080 ■ *Web:* www.internetsafety.com						
InternetSpeech.com 6980 Santa Teresa Blvd Ste 201	San Jose	CA	95119	408-360-7730		617
Web: www.internetspeech.com						
Internexus 220 South 200 East Ste 200	Salt Lake City	UT	84111	801-487-2499		423
Web: www.internexus.to						
InterNiche Technologies Inc 1999 S Bascom Ave Ste 700	Campbell	CA	95008	408-540-1160		180
TF: 800-680-0529 ■ *Web:* www.iniche.com						
Internovo Inc PO Box 26258	Collegeville	PA	19426	610-409-9120		463
Web: www.internovo.com						
Interocean Systems 3738 Ruffin Rd	San Diego	CA	92123	858-565-8400		407
TF: 800-654-5382 ■ *Web:* www.interoceansystems.com						
Interop Technologies LLC 13500 Powers Ct	Fort Myers	FL	33912	239-425-3000		736
TF: 800-922-0204 ■ *Web:* www.interoptechnologies.com						
Inter-Pacific Corp 2257 Colby Ave	Los Angeles	CA	90064	310-473-7591	479-8701	301
TF: 877-605-8414 ■ *Web:* inter-pacific.com						
InterPark 200 N LaSalle St Ste 1400	Chicago	IL	60601	312-935-2800		562
Web: www.interparkholdings.com						
Interparts International Inc 190 Express St	Plainview	NY	11803	516-576-2000		60
Web: www.interparts.com						
Interphase Corp 4240 International Pkwy Ste 105	Carrollton	TX	75007	214-654-5000	654-5500	176
NASDAQ: INPH						
Interplastic Corp 1225 Wolters Blvd	Saint Paul	MN	55110	651-481-6860	481-9836	605-2
TF: 800-736-5497 ■ *Web:* www.interplastic.com						
Interplex Engineered Products 231 Ferris Ave	Rumford	RI	02916	401-434-6543	399-7655*	481
**Fax Area Code:* 508 ■ *Web:* www.interplex.com						
Interplex Medical LLC 25 Whitney Dr	Milford	OH	45150	513-248-5120		475
Web: www.interplexmedical.com						
Interpoint Corp PO Box 97005	Redmond	WA	98073	425-882-3100	882-1990	253
TF: 800-822-8782 ■ *Web:* www.interpoint.com						
INTERPOL (US National Central Bureau of INTERPOL) 600 E St NW Ste 600	Washington	DC	20530	202-616-9000	616-8400	340-14
Web: www.justice.gov						
Interpress Technologies Inc 1120 Del Paso Rd	Sacramento	CA	95834	916-929-9771		561
Web: www.iptec.com						
Interpreters Unlimited Inc 10050 Tierra St Ste 308	San Diego	CA	92131	800-726-9091		768
TF: 800-726-9091 ■ *Web:* www.interpretersunlimited.com						
Interprint Inc 12350 US Hwy 19 N	Clearwater	FL	33764	727-531-8957		627
TF: 800-749-5152 ■ *Web:* www.printerusa.com						
Interprint LLC 7111 Hayvenhurst Ave	Van Nuys	CA	91406	818-989-3600		627
TF: 800-926-9873 ■ *Web:* www.interprintusa.com						
Interprose Inc 2635 Steeplechase Dr	Reston	VA	20191	703-860-0577		636
Web: www.interprosepr.com						
Interpublic Group 1114 Ave of the Americas	New York	NY	10036	212-704-1200		4
NYSE: IPG ■ *TF:* 800-908-5395 ■ *Web:* www.interpublic.com						
Inter-quest Corp 304 S Spring St	Beaver Dam	WI	53916	920-885-0141		175
Web: www.wemaketechsimple.com						
Interra Credit Union 300 W Lincoln Ave	Goshen	IN	46526	574-534-2506		219
Web: interracu.com						
Interra Energy Inc 6456 Osler St	San Diego	CA	92111	858-522-0815		192
Web: interraenergy.us						
Interrad Medical Inc 181 Cheshire Ln Ste 100	Plymouth	MN	55441	763-225-6699		476
Web: www.interradmedical.com						
InterraTech Corp PO Box 4	Mount Ephraim	NJ	08059	856-854-5100	854-5102	178-1
TF: 888-589-4889 ■ *Web:* www.interratech.com						
InterRel Consulting Inc The Rangers Ballpark in Arlington 1000 Ballpark Wa Ste 304	Arlington	TX	76011	972-735-8716		180
TF: 800-366-9091 ■ *Web:* www.interrel.com						
Interreligious Foundation for Community Organization (IFCO) 418 W 145th St	New York	NY	10031	212-926-5757	926-5842	48-7
Web: www.ifconews.org						
Inter-Rock Minerals Inc 20 Toronto St 12th Fl	Toronto	ON	M5C2B8	416-367-3003		503-6
Interroll Corp 3000 Corporate Dr	Wilmington	NC	28405	910-799-1100		207
Web: www.interroll.es						
Interrupt Marketing 6622 Maplewood Ave	Sylvania	OH	43560	419-724-9900		5
TF: 800-847-0101 ■ *Web:* www.interruptdelivers.com						
Interschola 1004 Oreilly Ave	San Francisco	CA	94129	415-563-4100		387
Web: www.interschola.com						
Interscope Pathology Medical Group Inc 21114 Vanowen St	Canoga Park	CA	91303	818-992-7848		415
Web: www.interscopepath.com						
Interscope Records 2220 Colorado Ave	Santa Monica	CA	90404	310-865-1000		657
Web: www.interscope.com						
Intersect ENT Inc 1555 Adams Dr	Menlo Park	CA	94025	650-641-2100		476
Web: www.intersectent.com						
Intersect Media Solutions 610 Crescent Executive Ct Ste 112	Lake Mary	FL	32746	866-404-5913		195
TF: 866-404-5913 ■ *Web:* www.intersectmediasolutions.com						
Intersections Inc 3901 Stonecroft Blvd	Chantilly	VA	20151	703-488-6100		215
NASDAQ: INTX ■ *TF:* 800-695-7536 ■ *Web:* www.intersections.com						
Interserve USA PO Box 418	Upper Darby	PA	19082	610-352-0581		48-20
TF: 800-809-4440 ■ *Web:* www.interserveusa.org						
Intersil Corp 1001 Murphy Ranch Rd	Milpitas	CA	95035	408-432-8888	434-5351	696
NASDAQ: ISIL ■ *TF:* 888-468-3774 ■ *Web:* www.intersil.com						

Company	Phone	Fax	Class
Intersoft Corp 830 Stewart Dr Ste 220.......... Sunnyvale CA 94085 *Web:* www.intersoftusa.com	408-733-5300		809
InterSpec LLC 208 Fore St.......... Portland ME 04101 *Web:* www.e-specs.com	207-772-6135		463
InterStar Communications Inc 102 Sampson St.......... Clinton NC 28329 *TF:* 800-706-6538 ■ *Web:* www.starcom.net	910-564-4638		224
Inter-State Aviation 4800 Airport Complex N Airport Rd.......... Pullman WA 99163 *Web:* inter-stateaviation.com	509-332-6596	334-1751	63
Interstate Aviation 62 Johnson Ave.......... Plainville CT 06062 *TF:* 800-573-5519 ■ *Web:* www.interstateaviation.com	860-747-5519		63
Interstate Batteries 12770 Merit Dr Ste 400.......... Dallas TX 75251 *TF:* 800-541-8419 ■ *Web:* www.interstatebatteries.com	972-991-1444		61
Interstate Castings Co 3823 Massachusetts Ave.......... Indianapolis IN 46218 *TF:* 800-872-4246 ■ *Web:* www.interstatecastings.com	317-546-2427	546-4004	307
Interstate Chemical Co Inc 2797 Freedland Rd.......... Hermitage PA 16148 *TF:* 800-422-2436 ■ *Web:* www.interstatechemical.com	724-981-3771	981-8383	143
Interstate Connecting Components Inc 120 Mt Holly By Pass.......... Lumberton NJ 08048 **Fax Area Code: 856* ■ *TF:* 800-422-3911 ■ *Web:* www.connecticc.com	800-422-3911	722-9425*	246
Interstate Contract Cleaning Services Inc 509 Blairhill Rd.......... Charlotte NC 28217 *Web:* www.interstateccs.com	704-522-7773		104
Interstate Distributor Co 11707 21st Ave S.......... Tacoma WA 98444 *TF:* 800-426-8560 ■ *Web:* www.intd.com	800-426-8560		780
Interstate Electrical Supply Inc 2300 Second Ave.......... Columbus GA 31901 *TF:* 800-903-4409 ■ *Web:* ieselc.com	706-324-1000	576-5821	246
Interstate Foam & Supply Inc PO Box 338.......... Conover NC 28613 *Web:* interstatefoamandsupply.com	828-459-9700	459-0300	676
Interstate Glass Inc 1621 S Brightleaf Blvd.......... Smithfield NC 27577 *Web:* interstateglassinc.com	919-934-4121		329
Interstate Highway Sign Corp 7415 Lindsey Rd.......... Little Rock AR 72206 *Web:* www.interstatesigns.com	501-490-4242		701
Interstate Hotels & Resorts Inc 4501 N Fairfax Dr.......... Arlington VA 22203 *Web:* www.interstatehotels.com	703-387-3100		379
Interstate Meat Distributors Inc 9550 SE Last Rd.......... Clackamas OR 97015	503-656-0633		296-26
Interstate Mechanical Contractors Inc 3200 Henson Rd.......... Knoxville TN 37921 *Web:* interstatemechanical.com	865-588-0180	602-4124	189-10
Interstate NationaLease 2700 Palmyra Rd.......... Albany GA 31707 *Web:* inlleasing.com	229-883-7250		778
Interstate Natural Gas Assn of America (INGAA) 10 G St NE Ste 700.......... Washington DC 20002 *Web:* www.ingaa.org	202-216-5900	216-0870	49-21
Interstate Oil & Gas Compact Commission (IOGCC) 900 NE 23rd St PO Box 53127.......... Oklahoma City OK 73105 *Web:* iogcc.publishpath.com	405-522-8380	525-3592	48-12
Interstate Optical Co 680 Lindaire Ln.......... Mansfield OH 44901 *Web:* interstateoptical.com	419-529-6800		237
Interstate Paper LLC 2366 Interstate Rd.......... Riceboro GA 31323 *Web:* www.interstatepaper.com	912-884-3371		557
Interstate Paper Supply Co Inc (IPSCO) 103 Good St PO Box 670.......... Roscoe PA 15477 *TF:* 800-861-8584 ■ *Web:* www.ipscoinc.com	724-938-2218	938-3415	554
Interstate Resources Inc 1300 Wilson Blvd Ste 1075.......... Arlington VA 22209 *Web:* www.interstateresources.com	703-243-3355	243-4681	557
Interstate State Park 307 Milltown Rd PO Box 254.......... Taylors Falls MN 55084 *Web:* www.dnr.state.mn.us	651-465-5711		565
Interstate State Park PO Box 703.......... Saint Croix Falls WI 54024 *Web:* dnr.wi.gov	715-483-3747		565
Interstate Transport Inc 324 First Ave N.......... St Petersburg FL 33701 *TF:* 866-281-1281 ■ *Web:* www.interstate-transport.com	727-822-9999		650
Interstates Construction Services Inc 1520 N Main Ave.......... Sioux Center IA 51250 *TF:* 800-827-1662 ■ *Web:* www.interstates.com	712-722-1662	722-1667	189-4
Interstock Premium Cabinets LLC 6300 Bristol Pike.......... Levittown PA 19057 *TF:* 800-896-9842 ■ *Web:* www.interstockcabinets.com	267-288-1200	288-1206	745-9
Interstyle Ceramics & Glass Ltd 3625 Brighton Ave.......... Burnaby BC V5A3H5 *TF:* 800-667-1566 ■ *Web:* interstyleglass.com	604-421-7229	421-7544	751
Intersyn Technologies LP 2736 Albans.......... Houston TX 77005 *Web:* www.intersyn.com	713-866-4808		226
InterSystems Corp 1 Memorial Dr.......... Cambridge MA 02142 *TF:* 800-753-2571 ■ *Web:* intersystems.com	617-621-0600	494-1631	178-1
Intertape Polymer Group 3647 Cortez Rd W.......... Bradenton FL 34210 *Web:* www.itape.com	941-727-5788		124
InterTech Computer Products Inc 5225 S 39th St.......... Phoenix AZ 85040 *TF:* 800-456-6422 ■ *Web:* www.allcovered.com	602-437-0035		174
Intertech Corp 3240 N O'Henry Blvd Hwy 29 N.......... Greensboro NC 27405 *Web:* www.intertechcorp.com	336-621-1891		596
InterTech Group Inc 4838 Jenkins Ave.......... North Charleston SC 29405 *Web:* www.theintertechgroup.com	843-744-5174		605-1
Intertech Plastics Inc 12850 E 40th Ave.......... Denver CO 80239 *Web:* www.intertechplastics.com	303-371-4270		596
Intertech Training & Consulting Inc 25 Barcelona Ste 202.......... Irvine CA 92614 *Web:* www.intertechconsulting.net	949-852-1165		180
Inter-Technical Group Inc 175 Clearbrook Rd Ste 167.......... Elmsford NY 10523 *Web:* www.inter-technical.com	914-347-2474		246
Intertek AIM 601 W California Ave.......... Sunnyvale CA 94086 *TF:* 800-967-5352	800-967-5352		256
Intertek Automotive Research 5404 Bandera Rd.......... San Antonio TX 78238 *Web:* intertek.com/petroleum	210-684-2310	684-6074	743
Intertek Group PLC 801 Travis St Ste 1500.......... Houston TX 77002 *TF:* 800-967-5352 ■ *Web:* www.intertek.com	713-407-3500		261
Intertek Westport Technology Ctr 6700 Portwest Dr.......... Houston TX 77024 *Web:* www.intertek.com	713-479-8414		463
Intertractor America Corp 960 Proctor Dr.......... Elkhorn WI 53121 *Web:* www.intertractoramerica.com	262-723-6000		190
Intertrade Industries Ltd 14600 Commerce Ln.......... Huntington Beach CA 92649 *TF:* 800-944-9277 ■ *Web:* www.intertradeindustries.com	714-894-5566	894-3927	601
InterTrust Technologies Corp 920 Stewart Dr Ste 100.......... Sunnyvale CA 94085 *TF:* 800-393-2272 ■ *Web:* www.intertrust.com	408-616-1600	616-1626	178-12
Interuniversity Services Inc 1550 Bedford Hwy.......... Bedford NS B4A1E6 *Web:* www.interuniversity.ns.ca	902-453-2470		317
Interurban Railway Museum 901 E 15th St.......... Plano TX 75074 *Web:* www.plano.gov	972-941-2117		520
Inter-Urban Transit Partnership 300 Ellsworth St SW.......... Grand Rapids MI 49503 *TF:* 800-247-8726 ■ *Web:* www.ridetherapid.org	616-776-1100	456-1941	468
Interval International Inc 6262 Sunset Dr.......... Miami FL 33143 *TF:* 800-828-8200 ■ *Web:* www.intervalworld.com	305-666-1861	667-2072	753
Interval Management Inc 515 Nichols Blvd.......... Sparks NV 89431 *TF:* 800-788-4297 ■ *Web:* www.qmcorp.com	775-355-4040		463
Interval Servicing International Co 3363 W Commercial Blvd Ste 202.......... Ft Lauderdale FL 33309 *Web:* www.intervalservicing.com	954-485-5400		772
InterVarsity Christian Fellowship/USA 6400 Schroeder Rd.......... Madison WI 53711 *TF:* 866-734-4823 ■ *Web:* www.intervarsity.org	608-274-9001	274-7882	48-20
Interventional Spine Inc 13700 Alton Pkwy Ste 160.......... Irvine CA 92618 *TF:* 800-497-0484 ■ *Web:* www.i-spineinc.com	949-472-0006		476
Intervest Construction Inc 2379 Beville Rd.......... Daytona Beach FL 32119 *TF:* 855-215-2974 ■ *Web:* www.icihomes.com	844-349-6401		653
Intervest Mortgage Investment Co 180 Grand Ave Ste 1400.......... Oakland CA 94612 *Web:* www.intervestcref.com	510-622-8500		509
Interview Magazine 575 Broadway 5th Fl.......... New York NY 10012 *TF:* 800-925-9574 ■ *Web:* www.interviewmagazine.com	212-941-2900	941-2885	457-11
InterVision Systems Technologies Inc 2270 Martin Ave.......... Santa Clara CA 95050 *TF:* 800-787-6707 ■ *Web:* www.intervision.com	408-980-8550		180
Interwest Capital Corp 7724 Girard Ave Ste 300.......... La Jolla CA 92037 *TF:* 800-792-9639 ■ *Web:* www.interwestcapital.com	858-622-4900		690
InterWest Insurance Services Inc 3636 American River Dr 2nd Fl.......... Sacramento CA 95864 *TF:* 800-444-4134 ■ *Web:* www.iwins.com	916-488-3100	979-7992	390
InterWest Partners 2710 Sand Hill Rd Ste 200.......... Menlo Park CA 94025 *TF:* 866-803-9204 ■ *Web:* www.interwest.com	650-854-8585	854-4706	792
Inter-Wire Products (IWP) 355 Main St.......... Armonk NY 10504 *Web:* www.interwiregroup.com	914-273-6633		813
InterWorks Inc 1425 S Sangre Rd.......... Stillwater OK 74074 *TF:* 866-490-9643 ■ *Web:* www.interworks.com	405-624-3214		180
inTEST Corp 804 E Gate Dr Ste 200.......... Mount Laurel NJ 08054 *NYSE: INTT* ■ *Web:* www.intest.com	856-505-8800	505-8801	253
Intevac Inc 3560 Bassett St.......... Santa Clara CA 95054 *NASDAQ: IVAC* ■ *Web:* www.intevac.com	408-986-9888		544
Intex Recreation Corp 1665 Hughes Way.......... Long Beach CA 90810 *TF Cust Svc:* 800-234-6839 ■ *Web:* www.intexcorp.com	800-234-6839		710
Intex Solutions Inc 110 A St.......... Needham MA 02494 *Web:* www.intex.com	701-449-6222		177
INTIX (International Ticketing Assn) 5868 E 71st St Ste E367.......... Indianapolis IN 46220 *Web:* www.intix.org	212-629-4036	629-4036	48-4
Intland GmbH 968 Inverness Way.......... Sunnyvale CA 94087 *TF:* 866-468-5210 ■ *Web:* www.intland.com	866-468-5210		393
Intone Networks Inc 10 Austin Ave Ste A7.......... Iselin NJ 08830 *Web:* www.intonenetworks.com	732-721-3002		196
In-Touch Insight Systems Inc 400 March Rd.......... Ottawa ON K2K3H4 *TF:* 800-263-2980 ■ *Web:* www.intouchinsight.com	800-263-2980		177
Intoximeters Inc 2081 Craig Rd.......... Saint Louis MO 63146 *TF:* 800-451-8639 ■ *Web:* www.intox.com	314-429-4000		407
Intra Corp 885 Manufacturers Dr.......... Westland MI 48186 *Web:* www.intra-corp.net	734-326-7030	326-1410	472
Intracare North Hospital 1120 Cypress Stn.......... Houston TX 77090 *Web:* www.intracarehospital.com	713-790-0949		374-5
Intraco Corp 530 Stephenson Hwy.......... Troy MI 48083 *Web:* www.intracousa.com	248-585-6900		61
Intracorp Projects Ltd 900-666 Burrard St Ste 204.......... Vancouver BC V6C2X8 *Web:* intracorp.ca	905-940-6555		656
Intrada Technologies 31 Ashler Manor Dr.......... Muncy PA 17756 *Web:* intradatech.com	570-321-7370		396

	Phone	Fax	Class
Intradiem 3650 Mansell Rd Ste 500............ Alpharetta GA 30022 *TF:* 888-566-9457 ■ *Web:* www.intradiem.com	678-356-3500		178-10
Intrado Inc 1601 Dry Creek Dr............... Longmont CO 80503 *TF:* 877-262-3775 ■ *Web:* www.intrado.com	720-494-5800		736
IntraEdge Inc 80 N McClintock Dr Ste 2................... Chandler AZ 85226 *Web:* www.intraedge.com	480-240-5240		196
Intrafinity Inc 60 ADELAIDE St E............... Toronto ON M5C3E4 *TF:* 866-204-6147 ■ *Web:* www.intrafinity.com	416-848-9722		177
IntraLinks Inc 150 E 42nd St Ste 8............ New York NY 10017 *TF:* 888-546-5383 ■ *Web:* www.intralinks.com	212-543-7700	543-7978	39
Intralox LLC 8715 Bollman Pl ....Savage MD 20763 *Web:* www.intralox.com	301-575-2200		207
Intraprisetechknowlogies LLC 3615 Harding Ave Ste 209 .... Honolulu HI 96816 *TF:* 866-737-9991 ■ *Web:* www.intraprisetechknowlogies.com	866-737-9991		180
Intraspek Inc 8707 Timber Oak Ln .... Laurel MD 20723 *Web:* www.intraspek.com	301-617-0521		175
IntraSystems Inc 3 Allied Dr Ste 103 ....Dedham MA 02026 *TF:* 800-467-4448 ■ *Web:* www.intrasystems.com	781-986-1700		180
Intratek Computer Inc 5431 Industrial Dr................... Huntington Beach CA 92649 *TF:* 800-892-8282 ■ *Web:* www.intrapc.com	800-892-8282		175
Intrawest ULC 1621 18th St Ste 300 ....Denver CO 80202 *Web:* www.intrawest.com	303-749-8370		669
Intrax 600 California St Fl 10 .... San Francisco CA 94108 *Web:* www.staffordhouse.com/intrax.htm	415-434-1221	434-5404	423
InTren Inc 18202 W Union Rd ....Union IL 60180 *TF:* 800-832-5660 ■ *Web:* www.intren.com	815-923-2300		256
Intrepid Aviation Group Holdings LLC 263 Tresser Blvd One Stamford Plaza........... Stamford CT 06901 *Web:* www.intrepidaviation.com	203-905-4220		791
Intrepid Control Systems Inc 31601 Research Park Dr.............. Madison Heights MI 48071 *TF:* 800-859-6265 ■ *Web:* www.intrepidcs.com	586-731-7950		180
Intrepid Enterprises Inc 1848 Industrial Blvd ....Harvey LA 70058 *Web:* intrepidstone.com	504-348-2861	340-7018	191-1
Intrepid Potash Inc 700 17th St Ste 1700 ....Denver CO 80202 *NYSE: IPI* ■ *TF:* 800-451-2888 ■ *Web:* www.intrepidpotash.com	303-296-3006	298-7502	280
Intrepid Powerboats 11700 S Belcher Rd ....Largo FL 33773 *Web:* www.intrepidboats.com	727-548-1260	544-1796	90
Intrepid Sea-Air-Space Museum W 46th St & 12th Ave Pier 86................. New York NY 10036 *TF:* 877-957-7447 ■ *Web:* www.intrepidmuseum.org	212-245-0072		520
IntriCon Corp 1260 Red Fox Rd...............Arden Hills MN 55112 *NASDAQ: IIN* ■ *TF:* 800-732-0330 ■ *Web:* www.intricon.com	651-636-9770	636-9503	318
Intrigue Media Solutions Inc 55 Delhi St ....Guelph ON N1E4J3 *Web:* www.intrigueme.ca	519-265-4933		5
Intrinium Inc 609 N Argonne Rd .... Spokane Valley WA 99212 *TF:* 866-461-5099 ■ *Web:* www.intrinium.com	866-461-5099		196
Intrinsic Therapeutics Inc 30 Commerce Way ....Woburn MA 01801 *Web:* www.intrinsic-therapeutics.com	781-932-0222		475
IntrInsIx Corp 100 Campus Dr............. Marlborough MA 01752 *TF:* 800-783-0330 ■ *Web:* www.intrinsix.com	508-658-7600		261
Intrinzic Inc 1 Levee Way Ste 3121 ....Newport KY 41071 *TF:* 888-261-1537 ■ *Web:* intrinzicbrands.com	859-261-2200		195
introNetworks Inc 1482 E Valley Rd Ste 446................ Santa Barbara CA 93108 *Web:* www.intronetworks.com	805-722-1040		225
Intronix Technologies Inc 26 McEwan Dr W Unit 15......................... Bolton ON L7E1E6 *TF:* 800-819-9996 ■ *Web:* www.intronixtech.com	905-951-3361		317
Introtek International LP 150 Executive Dr.......................... Edgewood NY 11717 *Web:* www.introtek.com	631-242-5425		743
Introworks Inc 13911 Ridgedale Dr Ste 280............... Minnetonka MN 55305 *Web:* intro.works	952-593-1800		7
Intrusion Inc 1101 E Arapaho Rd............ Richardson TX 75081 *TF:* 888-637-7770 ■ *Web:* www.intrusion.com	972-234-6400		178-12
Intsel Steel Distributors LP 11310 W Little York ....Houston TX 77041 *TF:* 800-762-3316 ■ *Web:* www.intselsteel.com	713-937-9500	937-1091	723
Intuit Inc 2632 Marine Way ....Mountain View CA 94043 *NASDAQ: INTU* ■ *TF Cust Svc:* 800-446-8848 ■ *Web:* www.intuit.com	650-944-6000	944-5656	178-9
Intuit The Center for Intuitive & Outsider 756 N Milwaukee Ave........................Chicago IL 60642 *Web:* www.art.org	312-243-9088		520
Intuition Systems Inc 9428 Baymeadows Rd Ste 600 ....Jacksonville FL 32256 *Web:* www.intuitionsystems.com	904-421-7115		569
Intuitive Research & Technology Corp 5030 Bradford Dr NW # 205................. Huntsville AL 35805 *Web:* www.irtc-hq.com	256-922-9300	922-1122	178-1
Intuitive Surgical Inc 1266 Kifer Rd Bldg 101 .... Sunnyvale CA 94086 *NASDAQ: ISRG* ■ *TF:* 888-868-4647 ■ *Web:* www.intuitivesurgical.com	408-523-2100	523-1390	476
Inuit Gallery of Vancouver Ltd 206 Cambie St Gastown..................... Vancouver BC V6B2M9 *TF:* 888-615-8399 ■ *Web:* www.inuit.com	604-688-7323		42
Inuvialuit Regional Corp Bag Service #21..............................Inuvik NT X0E0T0 *TF:* 800-491-8885 ■ *Web:* www.irc.inuvialuit.com	867-777-2737		787
Invacare Canada LP 570 Matheson Blvd E Unit 8............... Mississauga ON L4Z4G4 *Web:* www.invacare.ca	905-890-8300		363
Invacare Corp 1 Invacare Way .... Elyria OH 44036 *NYSE: IVC* ■ **Fax Area Code:* 877 ■ *TF:* 800-333-6900 ■ *Web:* www.invacare.com	440-329-6000	619-7996*	477
Invaluable LLC 38 Everett St Ste 101.............Allston MA 02134 *Web:* www.invaluable.com	617-746-9800		809
Invena Corp 416 E Fifth St........................ Eureka KS 67045 *Web:* www.invena.com	620-583-8630		454
Invenio Marketing Solutions Inc 2201 Donley Dr Ste 200......................... Austin TX 78758 *TF:* 800-926-1754 ■ *Web:* www.inveniomarketing.com	800-926-1754		195
Invensense Inc 1197 Borregas Ave............ Sunnyvale CA 94089 *NYSE: INVN* ■ *Web:* www.invensense.com	408-988-7339	988-8104	696
Invenshure LLC 807 Broadway St NE Ste 148 ....Minneapolis MN 55405 *Web:* invenshure.com	612-520-7361		528
Invent Now, Inc 3701 Highland Park NW..................North Canton OH 44720 *TF:* 800-968-4332 ■ *Web:* www.invent.org	800-968-4332		520
Inventis Group Ltd 8400 Sugar Maple Dr Ste 305 .... Mason OH 45040 *Web:* www.inventisgroup.com	513-518-6691		466
Inventory Sales Co 9777 Reavis Rd.............St Louis MO 63123 *TF:* 866-417-3801 ■ *Web:* www.inventorysales.com	314-776-6200		350
Inver Hills Community College 2500 80th St E ....Inver Grove Heights MN 55076 *TF:* 866-576-0689 ■ *Web:* www.inverhills.edu	651-450-3000		162
Inverarden House National Historic Site 3350 Montreal Rd.......................... Cornwall ON K6H5R5 *Web:* www.pc.gc.ca/eng/lhn-nhs/on/inverarden/index.aspx	613-925-2896	925-1536	563
Inverness Management LLC 21 Locust Ave Ste 1D.....................New Canaan CT 06840 *Web:* www.invernessmanagement.com	203-966-4177		402
Inverrary Resort 3501 Inverrary Blvd .... Fort Lauderdale FL 33319 *TF:* 800-303-6009 ■ *Web:* inverrary.com	954-485-0500		669
Invesco 11 Greenway Plaza Ste 100.............Houston TX 77046 *TF:* 800-959-4246 ■ *Web:* invesco.com/us	713-626-1919		528
INVESCO Private Capital Inc 1166 Ave of the Americas 26th Fl.............New York NY 10036 *TF:* 800-959-4246 ■ *Web:* www.invesco.com	212-278-9000	278-9822	792
Invesco Trimark Ltd 5140 Yonge St Ste 800....................... Toronto ON M2N6X7 *TF:* 800-874-6275 ■ *Web:* www.invesco.ca	416-590-9855		528
InvestAmerica Investment Advisors Inc 101 Second St SE Ste 800 ....Cedar Rapids IA 52401 *Web:* www.investamericaventure.com	319-363-8249	363-9683	401
Investco Financial Corp 1302 Puyallup St .... Sumner WA 98390 *Web:* www.investco.com	253-863-6200		463
Investcorp International Inc 280 Park Ave Fl 37 ....New York NY 10017 *Web:* www.investcorp.com	212-599-4700		401
Investec Ernst & Co 1 Battery Park Plaza 2nd Fl...................New York NY 10004 *Web:* www.investec.com	212-898-6200		690
Investigative Services Inc 4381 S 153rd Cir ....Omaha NE 68137	402-894-5625		400
Investigator Support Services 1320 N Milwaukee Ave Fl 2 ....Chicago IL 60622 *TF:* 800-720-8955 ■ *Web:* www.researchsite.net	773-278-1567		196
Investing Daily 7600A Leesburg Pk W Bldg Ste 300......... Falls Church VA 22043 *TF:* 800-832-2330 ■ *Web:* www.investingdaily.com	703-394-4931	905-8100	531-9
Investment Casting Institute (ICI) 136 Summit Ave...........................Montvale NJ 07645 *Web:* www.investmentcasting.org	201-573-9770	573-9771	49-13
Investment Company Institute (ICI) 1401 H St NW Ste 1200 ....Washington DC 20005 *Web:* www.ici.org	202-326-5800	326-5841	49-2
Investment Counselors of Maryland LLC 803 Cathedral St...........................Baltimore MD 21201 *TF:* 800-421-9932 ■ *Web:* www.icomd.com	410-539-3838	625-9016	401
Investment Management & Consulting Group 97A Exchange St............................Portland ME 04101 *Web:* www.imcgrp.com	207-774-6552		194
Investment Management Consultants Assn (IMCA) 5619 DTC Pkwy Ste 500............Greenwood Village CO 80111 *TF:* 800-250-9083 ■ *Web:* www.imca.org	303-770-3377	770-1812	49-2
Investment Metrics LLC 3 Parklands Dr .... Darien CT 06820 *Web:* www.invmetrics.com	203-662-8400		466
Investment Performance Services LLC 7402 Hodgson Memorial Dr Ste 100 ....Savannah GA 31406 *Web:* www.ips-net.com	912-352-2862		401
Investment Planners Inc 226 W Eldorado St .... Decatur IL 62522 *Web:* www.investment-planners.com	217-425-6340		401
Investment Planning Counsel 2680 Skymark Ave Ste 700............... Mississauga ON L4W5L6 *TF:* 877-212-9799 ■ *Web:* www.ipcsecurities.com	905-212-9788		691
Investment Professionals Inc 16414 San Pedro Ave Ste 150 ....San Antonio TX 78232 *Web:* www.invpro.com	210-308-8800	308-8707	690
Investment Quality Trends (IQT) 2888 Loker Ave E Ste 116.................... Carlsbad CA 92010 **Fax Area Code:* 866 ■ *TF:* 800-763-8639 ■ *Web:* www.iqtrends.com	858-459-3818	927-5251*	531-9
Investment Scorecard Inc 601 Grassmere Park Dr Ste 1 ....Nashville TN 37211 *TF:* 800-555-6035 ■ *Web:* informais.com	615-301-1975		401
Investor Group Services LLC 855 Boylston St 6th Fl ....Boston MA 02116 *Web:* www.igsboston.com	617-371-4000		194
Investor Growth Capital Inc 1 Rockefeller Plaza Ste 2416..................New York NY 10020 *Web:* www.investorab.com	212-515-9000	515-9009	401
Investor Protection Trust 919 18th St NW Ste 300..................Washington DC 20006 *Web:* www.investorprotection.org	202-775-2111		49-2
Investor's Business Daily 12655 Beatrice St.......................Los Angeles CA 90066 **Fax:* Cust Svc ■ *TF:* 800-831-2525 ■ *Web:* www.investors.com	310-448-6000	577-7303*	532-2
InvestorIdeas.com 1385 Gulf Rd Ste 102.....................Point Roberts WA 98281 *TF:* 800-665-0411 ■ *Web:* www.investorideas.com	800-665-0411		466
InvestorPlace Media LLC 9201 Corporate Blvd Ste 200 .... Rockville MD 20850 *TF Cust Svc:* 800-219-8592 ■ *Web:* intelligencereport.investorplace.com	800-219-8592		531-9
InvestorPlace.com 2420A Gehman Ln 2420A Gehman Ln..........Lancaster PA 17602 *TF:* 800-219-8592 ■ *Web:* www.investorplace.com	800-219-8592		404

Name / Address	City	State	Zip	Phone	Fax	Class
Investors Bank 101 Wood Ave S	Iselin	NJ	08830	973-924-5100	765-0921	70
NASDAQ: ISBC ■ *TF:* 855-422-6548 ■ *Web:* www.myinvestorsbank.com						
Investors Group Inc 447 Portage Ave	Winnipeg	MB	R3B3H5	888-746-6344	202-1923*	401
NYSE: IGM ■ **Fax Area Code:* 866 ■ *TF:* 888-746-6344 ■ *Web:* www.investorsgroup.com						
Investors Heritage Life Insurance Co (IHLIC)						
200 Capital Ave PO Box 717	Frankfort	KY	40602	502-223-2361	875-7084	391-2
TF: 800-422-2011 ■ *Web:* www.ihlic.com						
Investors Management Corp						
801 N West St	Raleigh	NC	27603	919-653-7499	653-7498	360-3
Web: www.investorsmanagement.com						
Investors Title Co						
121 N Columbia St	Chapel Hill	NC	27514	919-968-2200		360-4
NASDAQ: ITIC ■ *TF:* 800-326-4842 ■ *Web:* invtitle.com						
Investrade Discount Securities						
950 N Milwaukee Ave Ste 102	Glenview	IL	60025	847-375-6080	367-8466*	690
**Fax Area Code:* 877 ■ **Fax:* Cust Svc ■ *TF Cust Svc:* 800-498-7120 ■ *Web:* www.investrade.com						
Invincible Office Furniture Co						
842 S 26th St PO Box 1117	Manitowoc	WI	54220	920-682-4601	683-2970	319-1
TF: 877-682-4601 ■ *Web:* www.invinciblefurniture.com						
Invisible Hand Networks Inc						
670 Broadway Ste 302	New York	NY	10012	212-400-7416		393
TF: 866-637-5286 ■ *Web:* www.invisiblehand.net						
Invisible Theatre 1400 N First Ave	Tucson	AZ	85719	520-882-9721	884-5410	573-4
Web: www.invisibletheatre.com						
InVision Communications Inc						
1280 Civic Dr 3rd Fl	Walnut Creek	CA	94596	925-944-1211		195
TF: 800-555-5211 ■ *Web:* www.iv.com						
InVision Software Inc						
110 Lake Ave S Ste 35	Nesconset	NY	11767	631-360-3400		177
TF: 800-722-1606 ■ *Web:* www.invisionsoft.com						
INVISTA 4123 E 37th St N	Wichita	KS	67220	316-828-1000		605-1
TF: 877-446-8478 ■ *Web:* www.invista.com						
InVite Health Inc						
1 Garden State Plaza	Paramus	NJ	07652	201-587-2222		345
TF: 800-349-0929 ■ *Web:* www.invitehealth.com						
Invitechange LLC						
110 Third Ave N Ste 102	Edmonds	WA	98020	425-778-3505		765
TF: 877-228-2622 ■ *Web:* www.invitechange.com						
Inviting Home.com						
4700 SW 51st St Unit 219	Davie	FL	33314	781-444-8001	616-8037*	321
**Fax Area Code:* 954 ■ *TF:* 866-751-6606 ■ *Web:* www.invitinghome.com						
InVitro International						
330 E Orangethorpe Ave Ste D	Placentia	CA	92870	949-851-8356	851-4985	231
TF: 800-246-8487 ■ *Web:* www.invitrointl.com						
Invivis Pharmaceuticals Inc						
547 Meadow Rd	Bridgewater	NJ	08807	908-818-9393		231
Web: www.invivis.com						
Invivo Therapeutics Holdings Corp						
1 Kendall Sq Ste B14402	Cambridge	MA	02139	617-863-5500		250
TF: 800-732-0330 ■ *Web:* www.invivotherapeutics.com						
Invivoscribe Technologies Inc						
6330 Nancy Ridge Dr Ste 106	San Diego	CA	92121	858-224-6600		231
TF: 866-623-8105 ■ *Web:* www.invivoscribe.com						
Invizeon Corp 113 W Front St Ste 101	Missoula	MT	59802	406-543-4059		180
Invodane Engineering Ltd						
30 Lesmill Rd Unit 2	Toronto	ON	M3B2T6	416-443-8049		261
TF: 800-387-2962 ■ *Web:* www.invodane.com						
Invoke Solutions Inc						
375 Totten Pond Rd	Waltham	MA	02451	781-810-2700		466
TF: 866-687-4367 ■ *Web:* www.invoke.com						
Involve LLC 16 E Poplar Ave	Columbus	OH	43215	614-545-3464		5
Web: www.getinvolve.com						
Invotec Engineering Inc						
10909 Industry Ln	Miamisburg	OH	45342	937-886-3232		256
Web: www.invotec.com						
InVue Security Products Inc						
10715 Sikes Pl Ste 200	Charlotte	NC	28277	704-206-7849		253
TF: 888-257-4272 ■ *Web:* www.alphaworld.com						
Invuity Inc 444 De Haro St	San Francisco	CA	94107	415-655-2100		475
Web: www.invuity.com						
INW Solutions						
4500 Holland Office Pk Ste #301	Virginia Beach	VA	23452	757-563-3572		196
Web: www.inwsolutions.com						
Inwood National Bank 7621 Inwood Rd	Dallas	TX	75209	214-358-5281		70
Web: www.inwoodbank.com						
inXile entertainment Inc						
2727 Newport Blvd	Newport Beach	CA	92663	949-675-3690		225
Web: www.inxile-entertainment.com						
Inyo County PO Box N	Independence	CA	93526	760-878-0292	878-2241	338
Web: www.inyocounty.us						
Inyxa LLC						
3501 W Algonguin Rd Ste 608	Rolling Meadows	IL	60008	224-325-4699		180
Web: inyxa.com						
I-O Corp						
14852 S Heritage Crest Way 1-A	Bluffdale	UT	84065	801-973-6767		696
Web: www.iocorp.com						
IO Environmental & Infrastructure Inc						
2840 Adams Ave Ste 301	San Diego	CA	92116	619-280-3278		610
Web: www.iosdv.com						
IO Industries Inc 1510 Woodcock St	London	ON	N6H5S1	519-663-9570		201
Web: www.ioindustries.com						
IO Integration Inc						
20480 Pacifica Dr Ste 1C	Cupertino	CA	95014	408-996-3420		180
Web: www.iointegration.com						
IO Semiconductor Inc						
4350 Executive Dr Ste 200	San Diego	CA	92121	858-373-0440		201
Web: www.iosemi.com						
IOA Re Inc						
190 W Germantown Pk Ste 200	East Norriton	PA	19401	610-940-9000		391-3
TF: 800-462-2300 ■ *Web:* www.ioare.com						
IOActive Inc 701 Fifth Ave Ste 6850	Seattle	WA	98104	206-784-4313		180
TF: 866-760-0222 ■ *Web:* www.ioactive.com						
IOCC (International Orthodox Christian Charities)						
110 W Rd Ste 360	Towson	MD	21204	410-243-9820	243-9824	48-5
TF: 877-803-4622 ■ *Web:* www.iocc.org						
IOF (Independent Order of Foresters)						
789 Don Mills Rd	Toronto	ON	M3C1T9	416-429-3000	271-6215*	48-5
**Fax Area Code:* 866 ■ *TF:* 800-828-1540 ■ *Web:* www.foresters.com						
IOGCC (Interstate Oil & Gas Compact Commission)						
900 NE 23rd St PO Box 53127	Oklahoma City	OK	73105	405-522-8380	525-3592	48-12
Web: iogcc.publishpath.com						
ioGenetics LLC						
3591 Anderson St Ste 218	Madison	WI	53704	608-310-9540		85
Web: www.iogenetics.com						
Iolani Palace State Monument						
364 S King St	Honolulu	HI	96813	808-522-0822		565
Web: www.iolanipalace.org						
Iolani School 563 Kamoku St	Honolulu	HI	96826	808-949-5355		623
TF: 888-879-8970 ■ *Web:* www.iolani.org						
Ioline Corp 14140 NE 200th St	Woodinville	WA	98072	425-398-8282	398-8383	744
TF: 800-598-0029 ■ *Web:* www.ioline.com						
I-ology Inc						
16767 N Perimeter Dr Ste 230	Scottsdale	AZ	85260	480-850-2800		180
Web: www.i-ology.com						
IOMEDIA Inc 640 W 28th St 9th Fl	New York	NY	10001	212-352-1115	352-1117	7
Web: www.io-media.com						
Iomer Internet Solutions						
10110 107 St NW Ste 202	Edmonton	AB	T5J1J4	780-424-3122		180
Web: www.iomer.com						
Iomosaic Corp 93 Stiles Rd	Salem	NH	03079	603-893-7009		196
TF: 844-466-6724 ■ *Web:* www.iomosaic.com						
ION (Institute of Navigation Inc)						
8551 Rixlew Ln Ste 360	Manassas	VA	20109	703-366-2723	366-2724	49-21
TF: 800-696-7353 ■ *Web:* www.ion.org						
Ion Art Inc 407 Radam Ln Ste A100	Austin	TX	78745	512-326-9333		8
Web: ionart.com						
ION Corp 7500 Equitable Dr	Eden Prairie	MN	55344	952-936-9490		21
Web: www.ioncorp.com						
Ion Design Inc 948 Seventh Ave W	Vancouver	BC	V5Z1C3	604-682-6787		7
Web: www.iondesign.ca						
ION Media Networks Inc						
7091 Grand National Dr Ste 100	Orlando	FL	32819	212-757-3100	659-4252*	741-95
**Fax Area Code:* 561 ■ *Web:* ionmedia.com						
ION Media Networks Inc						
2777 E Camelback Rd	West Palm Beach	FL	33401	561-659-4122	659-4252	741-140
Web: ionmedia.com						
Ion Networks Inc						
120 Corporate Blvd Ste A	South Plainfield	NJ	07080	908-546-3900	546-3901	178-7
TF: 800-722-8986 ■ *Web:* apitech.com						
Iona College 715 N Ave	New Rochelle	NY	10801	914-633-2502	633-2486	166
TF: 800-264-6350 ■ *Web:* www.iona.edu						
Iona Energy Inc						
333 Seventh Ave SW Ste 1600	Calgary	AB	T2P2Z1	587-889-8959		536
Web: www.ionaenergy.com						
IonBond LLC 200 Roundhill Dr	Rockaway	NJ	07866	973-586-4700	586-4729	481
Web: www.ionbond.com						
IonField Systems LLC						
1 Executive Dr Ste 8	Moorestown	NJ	08057	856-437-0330	823-1426	419
Web: ionfieldsystems.com						
Ionia County 100 W Main St	Ionia	MI	48846	616-527-5322	527-8201	338
TF: 800-649-3777 ■ *Web:* www.ioniacounty.org						
Ionia Maximum Correctional Facility						
1576 W Bluewater Hwy	Ionia	MI	48846	616-527-6331	527-6863	213
Web: www.michigan.gov/corrections						
Ionia Recreation Area 2880 W David Hwy	Ionia	MI	48846	616-527-3750		565
Web: www.michigandnr.com						
Ionian Technologies Inc						
4940 Carroll Canyon Rd Ste 100	San Diego	CA	92121	858-642-0998		668
Web: www.ionian-tech.com						
IonIdea Inc 3913 Old Lee Hwy Ste 33B	Fairfax	VA	22030	703-691-0400		180
Web: www.ionidea.com						
Ionit Technologies Inc						
601 Academy Dr	Northbrook	IL	60062	847-205-9651		693
Web: www.ionitusa.com						
IonSense Inc 999 Broadway Ste 404	Saugus	MA	01906	781-484-1043		419
TF: 800-229-8814 ■ *Web:* www.ionsense.com						
IOPFDA (Independent Office Products & Furniture Dealers Assn)						
3601 E Joppa Rd	Baltimore	MD	21234	410-931-8100	931-8111	49-4
TF: 800-252-6232 ■ *Web:* www.nopanet.org						
IoPP (Institute of Packaging Professionals)						
1833 Centre Point Cir Ste 123	Naperville	IL	60563	630-544-5050	544-5055	49-13
TF: 800-432-4085 ■ *Web:* www.iopp.org						
iORMYX Inc 1100-D Elden St Ste 304	Herndon	VA	20170	703-456-7010		195
Web: www.iormyx.com						
IOS Partners 311 Mendoza Ave	Coral Gables	FL	33134	305-648-2877		401
Web: www.iospartners.com						
IOS Technologies Inc						
3978 Sorrento Vly Blvd Ste 200	San Diego	CA	92121	858-202-3360		256
Web: www.ios3d.com						
Iosco County 422 West Lake St	Tawas City	MI	48763	989-362-3485		338
Web: www.iosco.net						
Iostudio LLC 565 Marriott Dr Ste 700	Nashville	TN	37214	615-256-6282		225
Web: www.iostudio.com						
iovation Inc						
111 SW Fifth Ave Ste 3200	Portland	OR	97204	503-224-6010		395
Web: www.iovation.com						
Iowa						
Adult Children & Family Services Div						
1305 E Walnut St	Des Moines	IA	50319	515-281-8977		339-16
TF: 800-735-2942 ■ *Web:* www.dhs.state.ia.us						
Agriculture & Land Stewardship Dept						
502 E Ninth St	Des Moines	IA	50319	515-281-5321		339-16
Web: www.iowaagriculture.gov						
Arts Council 600 E Locust st	Des Moines	IA	50319	515-281-5111	242-6498	339-16
Web: www.iowaartscouncil.org						
Attorney General						
1305 E Walnut St 2nd Fl	Des Moines	IA	50319	515-281-5164	281-4209	339-16
Web: www.state.ia.us/government/ag						
Banking Div 200 E Grand Ave Ste 300	Des Moines	IA	50309	515-281-4014	281-4862	339-16
Web: www.idob.state.ia.us						
Child Support Recovery Unit						
PO Box 9125	Des Moines	IA	50306	888-229-9223		339-16
TF: 888-229-9223 ■ *Web:* secureapp.dhs.state.ia.us/childsupport						
Community Development Div						
200 E Grand Ave	Des Moines	IA	50309	515-725-3000	725-3010	339-16
Web: www.iowaeconomicdevelopment.com/community						

				Phone	Fax	Class
Consumer Protection Div 1305 E Walnut St 2nd Fl TF: 888-777-4590 ■ Web: www.iowaalturneygeneral.org	Des Moines	IA	50319	515-281-5926	281-6771	339-16
Corrections Dept 420 Watson Powell Jr Way Web: www.doc.state.ia.us	Des Moines	IA	50319	515-242-5701		339-16
Economic Development Dept 200 E Grand Ave Web: ww.iowaeconomicdevelopment.com	Des Moines	IA	50309	515-725-3000		339-16
Education Dept 400 E 14th St Web: www.iowa.gov	Des Moines	IA	50319	515-281-3436	242-5988	339-16
Elder Affairs Dept 510 E 12th St Ste 2 TF: 800-532-3213 ■ Web: www.iowaaging.gov	Des Moines	IA	50319	515-242-3333		339-16
Emergency Management Div 7900 Hickman Rd Camp Dodge Bldg W-4 Web: homelandsecurity.iowa.gov	Des Moines	IA	50131	515-281-3231	725-3260	339-16
Environmental Services Div 11101 Aurora Ave Web: www.iesiowa.com	Urbandale	IA	50322	515-279-8042	279-1853	339-16
Ethics & Campaign Disclosure Board 510 E 12th St Ste 1-A Web: www.iowa.gov	Des Moines	IA	50319	515-281-4028	281-4073	265
General Assembly State Capitol 1007 E Grand Ave Web: www.legis.iowa.gov	Des Moines	IA	50319	515-281-5129		339-16
Governor 1007 East Grand Ave State Capitol Web: governor.iowa.gov	Des Moines	IA	50319	515-281-5211		339-16
Human Services Dept 1305 E Walnut St Fl 5 NE TF: 800-362-2178 ■ Web: dhs.iowa.gov	Des Moines	IA	50319	515-242-5880	242-6036	339-16
Information Technology Dept 1305 E Walnut St Level B Web: www.state.ia.us	Des Moines	IA	50319	515-281-5231		339-16
Insurance Div 601 Locust St 4th Fl TF: 877-955-1212 ■ Web: www.iid.state.ia.us	Des Moines	IA	50309	515-281-5705	281-3059	339-16
Lottery 13001 University Ave Web: www.ialottery.com	Clive	IA	50325	515-725-7900		452
Medical Examiners Board 400 SW Eigth St Ste C TF: 844-474-4321 ■ Web: medicalboard.iowa.gov	Des Moines	IA	50309	515-281-5171	242-5908	339-16
Motor Vehicle Div 100 Euclid Ave PO Box 9204 Web: www.dmvusa.com	Des Moines	IA	50306	515-244-9124		339-16
Natural Resource Dept 502 E Ninth St 4th Fl Web: www.iowadnr.gov	Des Moines	IA	50319	515-725-8200	725-8202	339-16
Natural Resources Dept 502 E Ninth St Web: www.iowadnr.gov	Des Moines	IA	50319	515-725-8200	725-8202	339-16
Office of Governor 1007 E Grand Ave Web: www.ltgovernor.iowa.gov	Des Moines	IA	50319	515-281-5211		339-16
Parks & Preserves Bureau 502 E Ninth St Web: iowadnr.gov	Des Moines	IA	50319	515 725 8200		339-16
Parole Board 510 E 12th St Ste 3 Web: www.bop.state.ia.us	Des Moines	IA	50319	515-725-5757		339-16
Professional Licensing & Regulation Div 200 E Grand Ave Ste 350 Web: plb.iowa.gov	Des Moines	IA	50309	515-725-9022	725-9032	339-16
Public Health Dept 321 E 12th St Web: www.idph.state.ia.us	Des Moines	IA	50319	515-281-5787		339-16
Regents Board 11260 Aurora Ave Web: regents.iowa.gov	Urbandale	IA	50322	515-281-3934	281-6420	339-16
Revenue & Finance Dept 1305 E Walnut FL 4 TF: 800-367-3388 ■ Web: www.iowa.gov	Des Moines	IA	50319	515-281-3114	242-6487	339-16
Secretary of State 321 E 12th St 1st Fl Web: sos.iowa.gov	Des Moines	IA	50319	515-281-5204		339-16
Securities Bureau 340 Maple St Web: www.iid.state.ia.us/securities_complaint	Des Moines	IA	50319	515-281-4441	281-3059	339-16
State Court Administration 1111 E Ct Ave Web: www.iowacourts.gov	Des Moines	IA	50319	515-281-5241		339-16
State Government Information 1305 E Walnut St Web: www.iowa.gov	Des Moines	IA	50319	515-281-5011		339-16
State Historical Society 600 E Locust St Web: www.iowahistory.org	Des Moines	IA	50319	515-281-5111		339-16
State Patrol Div 215 E Seventh St Web: www.dps.state.ia.us/isp	Des Moines	IA	50319	515-725-6090		339-16
Supreme Court 1111 E Ct Ave Iowa Judicial Branch Bldg Web: iowautility.org	Des Moines	IA	50319	515-281-5911		339-16
Transportation Dept 800 Lincoln Way Web: iowadot.gov	Ames	IA	50010	515-239-1101		339-16
Treasurer State Treasurer's Office Capitol Bldg Web: www.treasurer.state.ia.us	Des Moines	IA	50319	515-281-5368	281-7562	339-16
Utilities Board 1375 E Ct Ave Rm 69 TF: 877-565-4450 ■ Web: www.state.ia.us/government/com/util	Des Moines	IA	50319	515-725-7300	725-7399	339-16
Veterans Affairs Dept 7105 NW 70th Ave Camp Dodge Bldg A6A Web: va.iowa.gov	Johnston	IA	50131	515-252-4698	727-3713	339-16
Vital Records Bureau 321 E 12th St Lucas State Office Bldg TF: 866-834-9671 ■ Web: www.idph.state.ia.us	Des Moines	IA	50319	515-281-7689	281-0479	339-16
Vocational Rehabilitation Services Div 510 E 12th St Web: www.ivrs.iowa.gov	Des Moines	IA	50319	515-281-4311	281-7645	339-16
Weights & Measures Bureau 502 E Ninth St Web: www.iowaagriculture.gov/weightsandmeasures.asp	Des Moines	IA	50319	515-281-5321		339-16

				Phone	Fax	Class
Workforce Development 1000 E Grand Ave TF: 866 239 0843 ■ Web: www.iowaworkforcedevelopment.gov	Des Moines	IA	50319	515-281-5387		259
Iowa 80 Group Inc 515 Sterling Dr PO Box 639 TF: 800-553-8011 ■ Web: www.iowa80group.com	Walcott	IA	52773	563-284-6965		324
Iowa Arboretum 1875 Peach Ave Web: www.iowaarboretum.org	Madrid	IA	50156	515-795-3216		97
Iowa Assn of Business & Industry 400 E Ct Ave Ste 100 TF: 800-383-4224 ■ Web: www.iowaabi.org	Des Moines	IA	50309	515-280-8000		140
Iowa Assn of Realtors 1370 NW 114th St Ste 100 TF: 800-532-1515 ■ Web: www.iowarealtors.com	Clive	IA	50325	515-453-1064	453-1070	656
Iowa Beef Steakhouse 1201 E Euclid Ave Web: www.iowabeefsteakhouse.com	Des Moines	IA	50316	515-262-1138		671
Iowa Braille & Sight Saving School 1002 G Ave TF: 800-645-4579 ■ Web: www.iowa-braille.k12.ia.us	Vinton	IA	52349	319-472-5221		166
Iowa Central Community College 2031 Quail Ave TF: 800-362-2793 ■ Web: www.iccc.cc.ia.us	Fort Dodge	IA	50501	515-576-7201		162
Iowa City Area Chamber of Commerce 325 E Washington St Ste 100 Web: www.iowacityarea.com	Iowa City	IA	52240	319-337-9637	338-9958	139
Iowa City Public Library 123 S Linn St TF: 866-862-6877 ■ Web: www.icpl.org	Iowa City	IA	52240	319-356-5200	356-5494	434-3
Iowa City/Coralville Area Convention & Visitors Bureau 5353 E Margaret Dr TF: 800-366-3043 ■ Web: www.terrehaute.com	Terre Haute	IN	47803	800-366-3043		206
Iowa City/Coralville Area Convention & Visitors Bureau 900 First Ave Hayden Fry Way TF: 800-283-6592 ■ Web: www.iowacitycoralville.org	Coralville	IA	52241	319-337-6592	337-9953	206
Iowa College Student Aid Commission 430 East Grand Ave Fl 3 TF: 800-383-4222 ■ Web: www.iowacollegeaid.gov	Des Moines	IA	50309	515-725-3400	725-3401	725
Iowa Communications Network Inc Grimes State Office Bldg 400 E 14th St TF: 800-532-1290 ■ Web: icn.iowa.gov	Des Moines	IA	50319	515-725-4692		387
Iowa Correctional Institution for Women 420 Mill St SW Web: mitchellvilleprison.org	Mitchellville	IA	50169	515-725-5042	725-5015	213
Iowa County 222 N Iowa St Ste 102 Web: www.iowacounty.org	Dodgeville	WI	53533	608-935-0318	935-3024	338
Iowa County PO Box 266 Web: www.co.iowa.ia.us	Marengo	IA	52301	319-642-3914		338
Iowa Democratic Party 5661 Fleur Dr Web: www.iowademocrats.org	Des Moines	IA	50321	515-244-7292	244-5051	616-1
Iowa Dental Assn 8797 NW 54th Ave Ste 100 TF: 800-828-2181 ■ Web: www.iowadental.org	Johnston	IA	50131	515-331-2298	334-0007	227
Iowa Employment Solutions 430 E Grand Ave Web: www.iowaemploymentsolutions.com	Des Moines	IA	50309	515-281-9700		193
Iowa Farm Bureau Spokesman Magazine 5400 University Ave TF: 866-598-3693 ■ Web: iowafarmbureau.com	West Des Moines	IA	50266	515-225-5413	225-5419	457-1
Iowa Gold Star Military Museum 7105 NW 70th Ave TF: 800-294-6607 ■ Web: www.iowanationalguard.com	Johnston	IA	50131	515-252-4531		520
Iowa Health System 1200 Pleasant St Web: www.unitypoint.org	Des Moines	IA	50309	515-241-6161		353
Iowa Interstate Railroad 5900 Sixth St SW TF: 800-321-3891 ■ Web: www.iaisrr.com	Cedar Rapids	IA	52404	319-298-5400	298-5457	648
Iowa Juvenile Home 701 S Church St	Toledo	IA	52342	641-484-2560	484-2816	412
Iowa Lakes Community College 300 S 18th St *Fax: Admissions ■ TF: 800-242-5106 ■ Web: www.iowalakes.edu	Estherville	IA	51334	712-362-2604	362-8363*	162
Iowa Lakes Electric Co-op 702 S First St TF: 800-225-4532 ■ Web: www.ilec.coop	Estherville	IA	51334	712-362-7870		245
Iowa Laser Technology Inc 7100 Chancellor Dr Web: www.iowalaser.com	Cedar Falls	IA	50613	319-266-3561		567
Iowa Legal Aid 1111 Ninth St Ste 230 TF: 800-992-8161 ■ Web: www.iowalegalaid.org	Des Moines	IA	50314	515-243-1193		428
Iowa Masonic Library & Museum 813 First Ave SE TF: 800-358-3306 ■ Web: www.gl-iowa.org	Cedar Rapids	IA	52402	319-365-1438		520
Iowa Medical Society 515 E Locust St Ste 400 TF: 800-747-3070 ■ Web: www.iowamedical.org	Des Moines	IA	50309	515-223-1401	223-0590	474
Iowa Methodist Medical Ctr (IMMC) 1200 Pleasant St Web: unitypoint.org	Des Moines	IA	50309	515-241-6212		374-3
Iowa Mold Tooling Co Inc (IMT) 500 W US Hwy 18 TF: 800-247-5958 ■ Web: www.imt.com	Garner	IA	50438	641-923-3711	923-6063	470
Iowa Mortgage Association 8800 NW 62nd Ave TF: 800-800-2353 ■ Web: www.iowama.org	Johnston	IA	50131	515-286-4352		533
Iowa Northern Railway Co 305 Second St SE Paramount Theatre Bldg Ste 400 TF: 800-392-3342 ■ Web: www.iowanorthern.com	Cedar Rapids	IA	52401	319-297-6000		649
Iowa Nurses Assn (INA) 2400 86th St Ste 32 Web: www.iowanurses.org	Urbandale	IA	50322	515-225-0495		533
Iowa Pharmacy Assn 8515 Douglas Ave Ste 16 TF: 866-512-1800 ■ Web: www.iarx.org	Des Moines	IA	50322	515-270-0713	270-2979	585

Phone | Fax | Class

Iowa Precision Industries Inc
5480 Sixth St SW .... Cedar Rapids IA 52404 319-364-9181 493
Web: mestekmachinery.com

Iowa Prison Industries (IPI)
1445 E Grand Ave........ Des Moines IA 50316 515-242-5770 242-5779 630
TF: 800-670-4537 ■ *Web:* www.iaprisonind.com

Iowa Public Interest Research Group
3209 Ingersoll Ave........ Des Moines IA 50312 515-282-4193 633
Web: www.iowapirg.org

Iowa Public Television
6450 Corporate Dr PO Box 6450........ Johnston IA 50131 515-725-9700 725-9836 741
TF: 800-532-1290 ■ *Web:* www.iptv.org

Iowa Realty Company Inc
3501 Westown Pkwy........ West Des Moines IA 50266 515-453-6222 652
TF: 800-247-2430 ■ *Web:* www.iowarealty.com

Iowa Republican Party
621 E Ninth St........ Des Moines IA 50309 515-282-8105 616-2
Web: www.iowagop.org

Iowa Select Farms
811 S Oak St PO Box 400........ Iowa Falls IA 50126 641-648-4479 648-4251 10-6
Web: www.iowaselect.com

Iowa Soybean Association
4554 114th st........ Urbandale IA 50322 515-251-8640 138
TF: 800-383-1423 ■ *Web:* www.iasoybeans.com

Iowa Speedway LLC
3333 Rusty Wallace Dr........ Newton IA 50208 641-791-8000 642
Web: www.iowaspeedway.com

Iowa Spring Manufacturing & Sales Co
2112 Greene St........ Adel IA 50003 515-993-4791 492
TF: 800-622-2203 ■ *Web:* www.iowaspring.com

Iowa State Association of Counties
5500 Westown Pkwy 5500 Westown Pkwy West Des Moines IA 50266 515-244-7181 615
Web: www.iowacounties.org

Iowa State Bar Assn 625 E Ct Ave........ Des Moines IA 50309 515-243-3179 243-2511 72
TF: 800-457-3729 ■ *Web:* www.iowabar.org

Iowa State Fair (state House)
Po Box 57130........ Des Moines IA 50317 515-262-3111 720
Web: www.iowastatefair.org

Iowa State Library
1007 E Grand Ave Ste 214........ Des Moines IA 50319 515-281-4105 281-6191 434-5
TF: 800-248-4483 ■ *Web:* www.statelibraryofiowa.org

Iowa State Penitentiary
Ave E & First St PO Box 409........ Fort Madison IA 52627 319-372-1908 372-2856 213
TF: 800-382-0019 ■ *Web:* iaprisonind.com

Iowa State Savings Bank
401 W Adams St........ Creston IA 50801 641-782-1000 70
TF: 888-508-0142 ■ *Web:* issbbank.com

Iowa State University 100 Alumni Hall........ Ames IA 50011 515-294-4111 294-2592* 166
**Fax:* Admissions ■ *TF Admissions:* 800-262-3810 ■ *Web:* www.iastate.edu

Iowa State University Parks Library
Osborn Dr & Morrill Rd........ Ames IA 50011 515-294-3642 294-5525 434-6
Web: www.lib.iastate.edu

Iowa State University Research Park Corp
1805 Collaboration Pl Ste 1250........ Ames IA 50010-8648 515-296-7275 296-9924 166
Web: www.isupark.org

Iowa Veterans Home
7105 NW 70th Ave Camp Dodge Bldg 3465........ Johnston IA 50131 515-252-4698 727-3713 793
TF: 800-838-4692 ■ *Web:* va.iowa.gov

Iowa Veterinary Medical Assn
1605 N Ankeny Blvd Ste 110........ Ankeny IA 50023 515-965-9237 965-9239 795
TF: 800-369-9564 ■ *Web:* www.iowavma.org

Iowa Veterinary Supply Co (IVESCO)
124 Country Club Rd........ Iowa Falls IA 50126 641-648-2529 475

Iowa Wesleyan College
601 N Main St........ Mount Pleasant IA 52641 800-582-2383 385-6240* 166
**Fax Area Code:* 319 ■ **Fax:* Admissions ■ *TF:* 800-582-2383 ■ *Web:* www.iw.edu

Iowa Western Community College
Clarinda 923 E Washington St........ Clarinda IA 51632 712-542-5117 542-4608* 162
**Fax:* Admissions ■ *TF:* 800-521-2073 ■ *Web:* www.iwcc.cc.ia.us

IP Casino Resort & Spa 850 Bayview Ave........ Biloxi MS 39530 228-436-3000 133
TF Resv: 888-946-2847 ■ *Web:* www.ipbiloxi.com

Ip Convergence Inc 512 N Hwy 377 Ste 5........ Argyle TX 76226 940-464-2900 180
Web: www.ipcnv.com

IP Fabrics Inc
3720 SW 141st Ave Ste 201........ Beaverton OR 97005 503-444-2400 225
Web: www.ipfabrics.com

IP Network Solutions Inc 209 Elden St........ Herndon VA 20170 703-787-0095 180
Web: www.ipnsinc.com

IPAA (Independent Petroleum Assn of America)
1201 15th St NW Ste 300........ Washington DC 20005 202-857-4722 857-4799 48-12
TF: 800-433-2851 ■ *Web:* www.ipaa.org

IPAC Services Corp 8701 102 St........ Clairmont AB T0H0W0 780-532-7350 186
TF: 800-875-6180 ■ *Web:* www.ipacservices.com

iPacesetters LLC
135 Chestnut Ridge Rd........ Montvale NJ 07645 267-530-6001 396
Web: ipacesetters.com

iParty Corp 270 Bridge St Ste 301........ Dedham MA 02026 781-329-3952 566
NYSE: IPT ■ *Web:* partycity.com

iPass Inc 3800 Bridge Pkwy........ Redwood Shores CA 94065 650-232-4100 232-4111 394
NASDAQ: IPAS ■ *TF:* 877-236-3807 ■ *Web:* www3.ipass.com

iPayStation LLC 213 School St Ste 101........ Gardner MA 01440 978-632-6798 387
Web: www.paystation.com

IPC International Corp
2111 Waukegan Rd........ Bannockburn IL 60015 847-444-2000 693

IPC Systems Inc
Harborside Financial Plaza 10 15th Fl........ Jersey City NJ 07311 201-253-2000 253-2361 178-10
Web: www.ipc.com

IPC Technologies Inc
7200 Glen Forest Dr Ste 100........ Richmond VA 23226 877-947-2835 721
TF: 877-947-2835 ■ *Web:* www.ipctech.com

ipCapital Group Inc
426 Industrial Ave Ste 150........ Williston VT 05495 802-859-7800 463
Web: www.ipcapitalgroup.com

IPD Analytics LLC
1170 Kane Concourse Ste 300........ Bay Harbor Islands FL 33154 305-662-8515 463
TF: 800-861-7261 ■ *Web:* www.ipdanalytics.com

ipDataTel LLC 13110 SW Fwy........ Sugar Land TX 77478 713-452-2700 253
TF: 866-896-1818 ■ *Web:* www.ipdatatel.com

Phone | Fax | Class

IPextreme Inc
54 N Central Ave Ste 204........ Campbell CA 95008 408-540-0095 177
Web: www.ip-extreme.com

IPG (Integrated Print & Graphics)
645 Stevenson Rd........ South Elgin IL 60177 847-695-6777 110
Web: www.ipandginc.com

IPG Photonics Corp 50 Old Webster Rd........ Oxford MA 01540 508-373-1100 373-1103 425
NASDAQ: IPGP ■ *TF:* 877-980-1550 ■ *Web:* www.ipgphotonics.com

IPhA (Illinois Pharmacists Assn)
204 W Cook St........ Springfield IL 62704 217-522-7300 522-7349 585
Web: www.ipha.org

IPHC (International Pentecostal Holiness Church)
PO Box 12609........ Oklahoma City OK 73157 405-787-7110 789-3957 48-20
TF: 888-474-2966 ■ *Web:* www.iphc.org

Iphorgan Ltd
195 Arlington Heights Rd Ste 125........ Buffalo Grove IL 60089 847-808-5500 428
Web: iphorgan.com

IPI (Iowa Prison Industries)
1445 E Grand Ave........ Des Moines IA 50316 515-242-5770 242-5779 630
TF: 800-670-4537 ■ *Web:* www.iaprisonind.com

IPI (International Parking Institute)
1330 Braddock Pl Ste 350........ Alexandria VA 22314 571-699-3011 49-21
Web: www.parking.org

IPMA-HR (International Public Management Assn for Hum Res)
1617 Duke St........ Alexandria VA 22314 703-549-7100 684-0948 49-12
TF: 800-381-8378 ■ *Web:* www.ipma-hr.org

IPMI (International Precious Metals Institute)
5101 N 12th Ave Ste C........ Pensacola FL 32504 850-476-1156 476-1548 49-4
Web: www.ipmi.org

IPMobileNet LLC
1221 E Dyer Rd Ste 250........ Santa Ana CA 92705 714-434-6019 647
Web: www.ipmn.com

IPNI (International Plant Nutrition Institute)
3500 PkwyLn Ste 550........ Norcross GA 30092 770-447-0335 448-0439 48-2
Web: www.ipni.net

IPOfferings LLC 75 Montebello Rd........ Suffern NY 33487 845-337-6911 466
Web: www.ipofferings.com

IPOWER Inc 919 E Jefferson St........ Phoenix AZ 85034 888-511-4678 396
TF: 888-511-4678 ■ *Web:* www.ipower.com

IPPF/WHR (International Planned Parenthood Federation - Western Hemisphere Region)
125 Maiden Ln 9th Fl........ New York NY 10005 212-248-6400 248-4221 48-5
TF: 866-477-3947 ■ *Web:* www.ippfwhr.org

IPPL (International Primate Protection League)
120 Primate Ln........ Summerville SC 29483 843-871-2280 871-7988 48-3
Web: www.ippl.org

IPRA (International Professional Rodeo Assn)
1412 S Agnew........ Oklahoma City OK 73108 405-235-6540 48-22
TF: 800-639-9002 ■ *Web:* www.ipra-rodeo.com

IPREX Inc 2861 Kingsland Ct........ Atlanta GA 30339 770-433-9084 636
Web: www.iprex.com

IPRIME (Industrial Partnership for Research in Interfacial & Materials Engineering)
University of Minnesota
151 Amundson Hall 421 Washington Ave SE........ Minneapolis MN 55455 612-626-9509 626-7246 668
Web: www.iprime.umn.edu

IPRO (Island Peer Review Organization Inc)
1979 Marcus Ave........ New Hyde Park NY 11042 516-326-7767 328-2310 353
Web: www.ipro.org

IPRO Tech Inc 6811 E Mayo Blvd Ste 350........ Phoenix AZ 85054 602-324-4776 179
Web: www.iprotech.com

Iprocess Online Inc
1050 Hull St Ste 100........ Baltimore MD 21230 410-547-3270 2
Web: www.iprocessonline.com

IPS (Institute for Policy Studies)
1112 16th St NW Ste 600........ Washington DC 20036 202-234-9382 634
Web: www.ips-dc.org

IPS Corp 455 W Victoria St........ Compton CA 90220 310-898-3300 853-5008* 3
**Fax Area Code:* 901 ■ *TF:* 800-888-8312 ■ *Web:* www.ipscorp.com

IPS Group Inc 4343 Easton Rd........ Saint Joseph MO 64503 816-233-1800 207
Web: www.continentalscrew.com

IPS Worldwide LLC
265 Clyde Morris Blvd Ste 100........ Ormond Beach FL 32174 386-672-7727 225
Web: www.ipsww.com

IPSCO (Interstate Paper Supply Co Inc)
103 Good St PO Box 670........ Roscoe PA 15477 724-938-2218 938-3415 554
TF: 800-861-8584 ■ *Web:* www.ipscoinc.com

Ipsen Inc PO Box 6266........ Rockford IL 61125 815-332-4941 332-4995 318
TF: 800-727-7625 ■ *Web:* www.ipsenusa.com

Ipsenault Co, The 3791 River Rd N Ste F........ Keizer OR 97303 503-390-8968 195
TF: 866-240-7032 ■ *Web:* ipsenault.com

Ipsmarx Technology Inc
11710 Plaza America Dr Ste 2000........ Reston VA 20190 416-640-0375 180
Web: www.ipsmarx.com

Ipsos Reid Corp 160 Bloor St E Ste 300........ Toronto ON M4W1B9 416-324-2900 466
Web: www.ipsos.ca

Ipsos Understanding UnLtd
615 Elsinore Pl Third Fl 3rd Fl........ Cincinnati OH 45202 513-871-4644 193

Ipsos-ASI Inc
301 Merritt 7 Corporate Pk........ Norwalk CT 06851 203-840-3400 466
Web: www.ipsos.com

Ipss Inc 150 Isabella St........ Ottawa ON K1S1V7 613-232-2228 231-4888 693
TF: 866-532-2207 ■ *Web:* ipss.ca

Ipswich Shellfish Co Inc 8 Hayward St........ Ipswich MA 01938 978-356-4371 356-9235 297-5
TF: 866-477-3947 ■ *Web:* www.ipswichshellfish.com

Ipswitch Inc 83 Hartwell Ave........ Lexington MA 02421 781-676-5700 676-5710 178-12
TF: 800-793-4825 ■ *Web:* www.ipswitch.com

IPT (Institute for Professionals in Taxation)
600 Northpark Town Ctr
1200 Abernathy Rd Ste L-2........ Atlanta GA 30328 404-240-2300 240-2315 49-10
Web: www.ipt.org

IPTV (Idaho Public Television)
1455 N Orchard St........ Boise ID 83706 208-373-7220 373-7245 632
TF: 800-543-6868 ■ *Web:* idahoptv.org

IPV (Inflection Point Ventures)
1 Innovation Way Ste 302........ Newark DE 19711 302-452-1120 452-1122 792
Web: www.inflectpoint.com

IQ BackOffice LLC
2121 Rosecrans Ave Ste 3350........ El Segundo CA 90245 310-322-2311 194
Web: www.iqbackoffice.com

Name / Address	City	State	ZIP	Phone	Fax	Class
IQ Systems Inc 5595 Equity Ave Ste 300	Reno	NV	89502	775-352-2301		463
TF: 866-842-4748 ■ *Web:* www.iqisit.com						
IQE Inc 119 Technology Dr	Bethlehem	PA	18015	610-861-6930		696
Web: www.iqep.com						
IQMax Inc						
15720 Brixham Hill Ave Ste 300	Charlotte	NC	28277	704-377-2202		177
Web: iqmax.com						
IQMS Inc 2231 Wisteria Ln	Paso Robles	CA	93446	805-227-1122		177
TF: 800-713-1450 ■ *Web:* www.iqms.com						
Iqr Consulting Inc						
1915 gardenview cir	Santa Rosa	CA	95403	707-921-7071		225
TF: 800-848-9446 ■ *Web:* iqrconsulting.com						
IQT (Investment Quality Trends)						
2888 Loker Ave E Ste 116	Carlsbad	CA	92010	858-459-3818	927-5251*	531-9
**Fax Area Code:* 866 ■ *TF:* 800-763-8639 ■ *Web:* www.iqtrends.com						
IQware Inc						
5850 Coral Ridge Dr Ste 309	Coral Springs	FL	33076	954-698-5151		180
TF: 877-698-5151 ■ *Web:* www.iqwareinc.com						
Ira Davenport Memorial Hospital Inc						
7571 State Rt 54	Bath	NY	14810	607-776-8500		374-3
Web: www.arnothealth.org						
Ira G Steffy & Son Inc 460 Wenger Dr	Ephrata	PA	17522	717-733-2001	733-0971	363
Web: www.iragsteffyandson.com						
Ira Green Inc 177 Georgia Ave	Providence	RI	02905	401-467-4770		409
TF General: 800-663-7487 ■ *Web:* www.iragreen.com						
Ira Higdon 150 IGA WAY	Cairo	GA	39828	229-377-1272	377-8756	345
Web: irahigdongc.com						
IRA Services Trust Co						
1160 Industrial Rd Ste 1	San Carlos	CA	94070	650-593-2221		225
Web: www.iraservicestrust.com						
Irashiai Sushi Pub & Japanese Restaurant						
115 Pelham Rd	Greenville	SC	29615	864-271-0900		671
Web: www.irashiai.com						
IRC (International Rescue Committee)						
122 E 42nd St	New York	NY	10168	212-551-3000	551-3179	48-5
TF: 800-435-7352 ■ *Web:* www.rescue.org						
IRC (International Resistive Company Inc)						
736 Greenway Rd	Boone	NC	28607	828-264-8861	264-8865	253
Web: www.irctt.com						
IRC (Insurance Research Council)						
718 Providence Rd	Malvern	PA	19355	610-644-2212		49-9
TF: 800-644-2101 ■ *Web:* www.insurance-research.org						
Irc Building Sciences Group						
2121 Argentia Rd Ste 401	Mississauga	ON	L5N2X4	905-607-7244		463
TF: 888-607-5245 ■ *Web:* www.ircgroup.com						
IRCL (Indian River County Library)						
1600 21st St	Vero Beach	FL	32960	772-770-5060	770-5066	434-3
Web: www.irclibrary.org						
IRD LLC 4740 Allmond Ave	Louisville	KY	40209	502-366-0916		407
Web: www.irdbalancing.com						
Iredale Mineral Cosmetics Ltd						
28 Church St	Great Barrington	MA	01230	413-528-1078		238
TF: 877-869-9420 ■ *Web:* www.janeiredale.com						
Iredell County						
200 S Ctr St PO Box 788	Statesville	NC	28687	704-878-3000	878-5355	338
Web: www.co.iredell.nc.us						
Iredell County Library						
201 N Tradd St	Statesville	NC	28677	704-878-3090		434-3
Web: www.iredell.lib.nc.us						
Iredell Health Systemÿ						
557 Brookdale Dr	Statesville	NC	28677	704-873-5661	872-7924	374-3
TF: 800-508-5777 ■ *Web:* www.iredellhealth.org						
Ireland						
1 Dag Hammarskjold Plaza # 885	New York	NY	10017	212-421-6934	752-4726	784
Web: www.un.int						
Consulate General						
100 Pine St Ste 3350	San Francisco	CA	94111	415-392-4214	392-0885	257
TF: 800-777-0133 ■ *Web:* www.dfa.ie/irish-consulate/sanfrancisco						
Embassy 2234 Massachusetts Ave NW	Washington	DC	20008	202-462-3939	232-5993	257
TF: 866-560-1050 ■ *Web:* www.dfa.ie/irish-embassy/usa						
Ireland Army Community Hospital						
289 Ireland Ave	Fort Knox	KY	40121	502-624-9333		374-4
Web: www.iach.knox.amedd.army.mil						
Ireland Bank 33 Bannock St	Malad City	ID	83252	208-766-2254		70
Web: ireland-bank.com						
Ireland Chamber of Commerce in the US						
556 Central Ave	New Providence	NJ	07974	908-286-1300	286-1200	138
Web: www.iccusa.org						
Irell & Manella LLP						
1800 Ave of the Stars Ste 900	Los Angeles	CA	90067	310-277-1010	203-7199	428
TF: 800-973-1177 ■ *Web:* irell.com						
IREM (Institute of Real Estate Management)						
430 N Michigan Ave	Chicago	IL	60611	312-329-6000	338-4736*	49-17
**Fax Area Code:* 800 ■ *TF:* 800-837-0706 ■ *Web:* www.irem.org						
Irene's Cuisine 539 St Phillip St	New Orleans	LA	70116	504-529-8811		671
IRET 1400 31st Ave SW Ste 60 Ste 60	Minot	ND	58702	701-837-4738	838-7785	654
NYSE: IRET ■ *TF:* 888-478-4738 ■ *Web:* www.iretapartments.com						
IRET (Institute for Research on the Economics of Taxation)						
529 14th St NW Ste 420	Washington	DC	20045	202-464-5113		634
Web: www.iret.org						
Irex Contracting Group						
120 N Lime St	Lancaster	PA	17608	800-487-7255		189-9
TF: 800-487-7255 ■ *Web:* www.irexcontracting.com						
IRF (International Road Federation)						
500 Mongomery St 5th Fl	Alexandria	VA	22314	703-535-1001	535-1007	49-3
Web: www.irfnet.ch						
IRgA (International Reprographic Assn)						
401 N Michigan Ave Ste 2200	Chicago	IL	60611	312-245-1026	673-6724	49-16
TF: 800-833-4742 ■ *Web:* www.apdsp.org						
IRI (Industrial Research Institute Inc)						
2200 Clarendon Blvd Ste 1102	Arlington	VA	22201	703-647-2580	647-2581	49-19
Web: www.iriweb.org						
Iridescence 2901 Grand River Ave	Detroit	MI	48201	313-237-6732		671
Web: www.motorcitycasino.com						
Iridex Corp						
1212 Terra Bella Ave	Mountain View	CA	94043	650-940-4700	940-4710	424
NASDAQ: IRIX ■ *TF Cust Svc:* 800-388-4747 ■ *Web:* www.iridex.com						

Name / Address	City	State	ZIP	Phone	Fax	Class
Iridian Asset Management LLC						
276 Post Rd W	Westport	CT	06880	203-341-7800		194
Web: www.iridian.com						
Iridium Satellite LLC						
6701 Democracy Blvd	Bethesda	MD	20817	301-571-6200	571-6250	736
Web: www.iridium.com						
Irion County PO Box 736	Mertzon	TX	76941	325-835-2421		338
Web: www.co.irion.tx.us						
Iris Diagnostics Inc 9172 Eton Ave	Chatsworth	CA	91311	818-527-7000	700-9661	743
Iris Films 2600 Tenth St Ste 413	Berkeley	CA	94710	510-845-5415	841-3336	513
Web: www.irisfilms.org						
Iris Group Inc, The 1675 Faraday Ave	Carlsbad	CA	92008	760-431-1103		4
TF: 800-347-1103 ■ *Web:* www.irisgroup.com						
Iris Software Inc						
200 Metroplex Dr Ste 300	Edison	NJ	08817	732-393-0034		180
Web: www.irissoftware.com						
Iris USA Inc 11111 80th Ave	Pleasant Prairie	WI	53158	262-612-1000	612-1010	607
TF: 800-320-4747 ■ *Web:* www.irisusainc.com						
iRise 2301 Rosecrans Ave Ste 4100	El Segundo	CA	90245	800-556-0399		177
TF: 800-556-0399 ■ *Web:* www.irise.com						
Irish American Heritage Ctr						
4626 N Knox Ave	Chicago	IL	60630	773-282-7035		50-2
TF: 800-745-3000 ■ *Web:* www.irish-american.org						
Irish Classical Theatre 625 Main St	Buffalo	NY	14203	716-853-4282	853-0592	573-4
Web: www.irishclassicaltheatre.com						
Irish Construction Inc						
2641 River Ave	Rosemead	CA	91770	626-288-8530		188-10
Web: www.irishteam.com						
Irish Cultural & Heritage Ctr of Wisconsin						
2133 W Wisconsin Ave	Milwaukee	WI	53233	414-345-8800		50-2
Web: www.ichc.net						
Irish Democrat Pub						
3207 First Ave SE	Cedar Rapids	IA	52402	319-364-9896		671
Web: www.irishdemocrat.net						
Irish Lion 212 W Kirkwood Ave	Bloomington	IN	47404	812-336-9076		671
Web: www.irishlion.com						
IrishCentral LLC 875 Sixth Ave	New York	NY	10001	212-871-0111		387
Web: www.irishcentral.com						
IRMG (International Restaurant Management Group Inc)						
4104 Aurora St	Coral Gables	FL	33146	305-476-1611	476-9622	670
Web: www.irmgusa.com						
Irmscher Inc 1030 Osage St	Fort Wayne	IN	46808	260-422-5572		186
Iron & Metals Inc 5555 Franklin St	Denver	CO	80216	303-292-5555	292-0513	686
TF: 800-776-7910 ■ *Web:* www.ironandmetals.com						
Iron City Distributing Co						
2670 Commercial Ave	Mingo Junction	OH	43938	740-598-4171	598-4677	81-1
TF Cust Svc: 800-759-2671 ■ *Web:* www.ironcitydist.com						
Iron City Workplace Services						
6640 Frankstown Ave	Pittsburgh	PA	15206	412-661-2001	661-9356	442
TF: 800-532-2010 ■ *Web:* www.ironcityuniform.com						
Iron County 2 S Sixth St Ste 7	Crystal Falls	MI	49920	906-875-3221		338
Iron County 300 Taconite St Ste 101	Hurley	WI	54534	715-561-3375	561-2928	338
TF: 800-275-8777 ■ *Web:* www.co.iron.wi.gov						
Iron County 220 S Shepherd St	Ironton	MO	63650	573-546-7051		338
Web: icsomo.org						
Iron County 68 S 100 E	Parowan	UT	84761	435-477-8360	477-8847	338
Web: www.ironcounty.net						
Iron County Utah State Correctional Facility						
2136 N Main St	Cedar City	UT	84721	435-867-7555		213
Web: ironsheriff.net						
Iron Hill Brewery 2502 W Sixth St	Wilmington	DE	19805	302-472-2739		670
Web: www.ironhillbrewery.com						
Iron Horse 6034 SE Milwaukie Ave	Portland	OR	97202	503-232-1826		671
Web: www.portlandironhorse.com						
Iron Horse Energy Services Inc						
1901 Dirkson Dr NE	Redcliff	AB	T0J2P0	403 526 4600		540
TF: 877-526-4666 ■ *Web:* www.ihes.ca						
Iron Island Museum 998 E Lovejoy St	Buffalo	NY	14206	716-892-3084		520
TF: 800-745-3000 ■ *Web:* www.ironislandmuseum.com						
Iron Monkey 99 Greene St	Jersey City	NJ	07302	201-435-5756	433-0762	671
Web: ironmonkey.com						
Iron Mountain 745 Atlantic Ave	Boston	MA	02111	800-899-4766		803-1
NYSE: IRM ■ *TF:* 800-899-4766 ■ *Web:* www.ironmountain.com						
Iron Range Tourism Bureau						
403 N First St	Virginia	MN	55792	218-749-8161		206
TF: 800-777-8497 ■ *Web:* www.ironrange.org						
Iron Skillet Restaurant, The						
2489 W 30th St	Indianapolis	IN	46222	317-923-6353		671
Web: www.ironskillet.net						
Iron Tribe Franchise LLC						
300 27th St S	Birmingham	AL	35233	205-226-8669		354
Web: irontribefitness.com						
Iron Yard LLC, The						
101 N Main St Ste 400	Greenville	SC	29601	864-605-3976		528
Web: theironyard.com						
Iron-a-way Inc 220 W Jackson St	Morton	IL	61550	309-266-7232		362
Web: www.ironaway.com						
Ironbound Capital Management LP						
902 Carnegie Ctr Ste 300	Princeton	NJ	08540	609-951-5000		401
Web: www.ironboundcapital.com						
Ironco Enterprises LLC						
1025 E Broadway Rd	Phoenix	AZ	85040	602-243-5750		492
TF: 800-756-3333 ■ *Web:* www.ironco.net						
Irondequoit Public Library						
45 Cooper Rd	Rochester	NY	14617	585-336-6062		434-3
Web: www.libraryweb.org/irondequoit						
Ironman Magazine 1701 Ives Ave	Oxnard	CA	93033	805-385-3500		457-13
TF: 800-447-0008 ■ *Web:* www.ironmanmagazine.com						
Ironmark Inc 9040 Jct Dr	Annapolis Junction	MD	20701	888-775-3737		627
TF: 888-775-3737 ■ *Web:* www.ironmarkusa.com						
IronMaster LLC 14562 167th Ave SE	Monroe	WA	98272	360-217-7780	217-8415	267
TF: 800-533-3339 ■ *Web:* www.ironmaster.com						
Ironmind Enterprises Inc						
11992 Charles Dr	Grass Valley	CA	95945	530-272-3579		711
TF: 800-286-0567 ■ *Web:* www.ironmind.com						
Ironplanet Inc						
3825 Hopyard Rd Ste 250	Pleasanton	CA	94588	925-225-8600	225-8610*	51
**Fax:* Cust Svc ■ *TF Cust Svc:* 888-433-5426 ■ *Web:* www.ironplanet.com.au						

Name / Address	City	State	Zip	Phone	Fax	Class
Ironrock Capital Inc 1201 Millerton St SE *TF:* 800-325-3945 ■ *Web:* www.ironrock.com	Canton	OH	44707	800-325-3945		751
Ironside Capital 945 Concord St *Web:* www.ironsidecapital.com	Framingham	MA	01701	781-622-5800		792
Ironspeed 2870 Zanker Rd #210 *Web:* ironspeed.com	San Jose	CA	95134	408-228-3400		177
Irontouch Managed Services Inc 980 Mission Ct **Fax Area Code:* 408 ■ *Web:* www.irontouchms.com	Fremont	CA	94539	714-408-4700	943-8222*	631
Ironwood Capital Ltd 45 Nod Rd *Web:* www.ironwoodcap.com	Avon	CT	06001	860-409-2100		690
Ironwood Grille 400 Ave of the Champions *Web:* www.pgaresort.com	Palm Beach Gardens	FL	33418	561-627-4852		671
Ironwood Industries Inc 115 S Bradley Rd *Web:* www.ironind.com	Libertyville	IL	60048	847-362-8681	362-9190	604
Ironwood Lithographers Inc 455 S 52nd St *Web:* www.ironwoodlitho.com	Tempe	AZ	85281	480-829-7700		627
Ironwood Plastics Inc 1235 Wall St *Web:* www.ironwood.com	Ironwood	MI	49938	906-932-5025		608
Ironwood State Prison 19005 Wiley's Well Rd *Web:* www.cdcr.ca.gov/facilities_locator/isp.html	Blythe	CA	92225	760-921-3000		213
Ironworkers 1750 New York Ave NW Ste 400 *TF:* 800-368-0105 ■ *Web:* ironworkers.org	Washington	DC	20006	202-383-4800	638-4856	615
Iroquois County 1001 E Grant St Rm 106 *Web:* www.co.iroquois.il.us	Watseka	IL	60970	815-432-6978	432-6999	338
Iroquois County State Wildlife Area RR 1 2803 E 3300 N Rd *Web:* www.dnr.illinois.gov	Beaverville	IL	60912	815-435-2218		565
Iroquois Gas Transmission System LP 1 Corporate Dr Ste 600 *TF:* 800-888-3982 ■ *Web:* www.iroquois.com	Shelton	CT	06484	203-925-7200	929-9501	325
Iroquois Indian Museum 324 Caverns Rd *TF:* 800-724-0309 ■ *Web:* www.iroquoismuseum.org	Howes Cave	NY	12092	518-296-8949		520
Iroquois Industries Inc 25101 Groesbeck Hwy *Web:* www.iroquoisind.com	Warren	MI	48089	586-771-5734		489
Iroquois New York 49 W 44th St *TF:* 800-332-7220 ■ *Web:* www.iroquoisny.com	New York City	NY	10036	212-840-3080		379
Iroquois Products of Chicago 2220 W 56th St *TF:* 800-453-3355 ■ *Web:* www.iroquoisproducts.com	Chicago	IL	60636	800-453-3355		199
Irosoft 3100 Boul De La Cote-vertu *Web:* www.irosoft.com	Saint-laurent	QC	H4R2J8	514-920-0020		180
Irpinia Kitchens 278 Newkirk Rd *Web:* www.irpinia.com	Richmond Hill	ON	L4C3G7	905-780-7722		321
Irr Supply Centers Inc 908 Niagara Falls Blvd *Web:* www.irrsupply.com	North Tonawanda	NY	14120	716-692-1600	692-1611	612
Irregardless Cafe 901 W Morgan St *TF:* 800-365-5724 ■ *Web:* irregardless.com	Raleigh	NC	27603	919-833-8898		671
Irresistibles 7 Hawkes St *TF:* 800-555-9865 ■ *Web:* www.irresistibles.com	Marblehead	MA	01945	781-631-1248		157-6
Irridelco International Corp 440 Sylvan Ave	Englewood Cliffs	NJ	07632	201-569-3030		273
Irrigation Assn (IA) 6540 Arlington Blvd *TF:* 800-362-8774 ■ *Web:* www.irrigation.org	Falls Church	VA	22042	703-536-7080	536-7019	48-2
IRS (Internal Revenue Service) 1111 Constitution Ave NW *TF:* 800-829-1040 ■ *Web:* www.irs.gov	Washington	DC	20224	202-622-9511		340-18
IRS Practice Adviser 1801 S Bell St *TF:* 800-372-1033 ■ *Web:* www.bna.com/contact-us-form-p17179924216	Arlington	VA	22202	800-372-1033		531-7
IRSC (Indian River State College) 3209 Virginia Ave *TF:* 866-792-4772 ■ *Web:* www.irsc.edu	Fort Pierce	FL	34981	772-462-4772	462-4699	162
Irsfeld Pharmacy PC 33 Ninth St W *Web:* irsfeldpharmacy.com	Dickinson	ND	58601	701-483-4858		237
Irsik & Doll Co PO Box 847 *Web:* www.irsikanddoll.com	Cimarron	KS	67835	620-855-3111		10-1
IRTS (International Radio & Television Society Foundation Inc) 1697 Broadway 10th Fl *Web:* www.irtsfoundation.org	New York	NY	10019	212-867-6650		49-14
Irvin Automotive Products Inc 2600 Centerpoint Pkwy *Web:* www.irvinautomotive.com	Pontiac	MI	48341	248-451-4100	451-4101	60
Irvin Dick Inc 475 Wilson Ave	Shelby	MT	59474	406-434-5862		780
Irvin Simon Photographers Inc 146 Meacham Ave *TF:* 800-540-4700 ■ *Web:* www.irvinsimon.com	Elmont	NY	11003	516-437-4700		592
Irvine Access Floors Inc 9425 Washington Blvd *TF:* 800-969-8870 ■ *Web:* www.irvineaccessfloors.com	Laurel	MD	20723	301-617-9333	617-9907	491
Irvine Barclay Theatre 4242 Campus Dr *Web:* www.thebarclay.org	Irvine	CA	92612	949-854-4646		572
Irvine Co 550 Newport Ctr Dr *Web:* www.irvinecompany.com	Newport Beach	CA	92660	949-720-2000		653
Irvine Company Apartment Communities 550 Newport Center Dr Ste 300 *Web:* www.rental-living.com	Newport Beach	CA	92660	949-720-5500		655
Irvine Scientific 2511 Daimler St *TF:* 800-577-6097 ■ *Web:* www.irvinesci.com	Santa Ana	CA	92705	949-261-7800	261-6522	85
Irvine Sensors Corp 3001 Red Hill Ave B3-108vv *Web:* www.irvine-sensors.com	Costa Mesa	CA	92626	714-444-8700		696
Irvine Technology Corp 201 E Sandpointe Ave Ste 300 **Fax Area Code:* 714 ■ *TF:* 866-322-4482 ■ *Web:* www.irvinetechcorp.com	Santa Ana	CA	92707	866-322-4482	434-8869*	194
Irvine Valley College 5500 Irvine Ctr Dr *Web:* www.ivc.edu	Irvine	CA	92618	949-451-5100		162
Irving A Miller Inc 2550 W Chester Pk	Broomall	PA	19008	610-356-1130		652
Irving Arts Ctr 3333 N MacArthur Blvd *Web:* www.irvingartscenter.com	Irving	TX	75062	972-252-7558		572
Irving Burton Associates Inc 3150 Fairview Park Dr Ste 301 *Web:* www.ibacorp.us	Falls Church	VA	22042	703-575-8359		466
Irving City Hall 825 W Irving Blvd *Web:* www.ci.irving.tx.us	Irving	TX	75060	972-721-2600	721-2420	337
Irving Convention & Visitors Bureau 500 W Las Colinas Blvd *TF:* 800-247-8464 ■ *Web:* www.irvingtexas.com	Irving	TX	75039	972-252-7476		206
Irving Mall 3880 Irving Mall *TF:* 877-746-6642 ■ *Web:* www.simon.com	Irving	TX	75062	972-255-0571		460
Irving Materials Inc (IMI) 8032 N SR-9 *Web:* www.irvmat.com	Greenfield	IN	46140	317-536-6650	326-3105	182
Irving Public Library 801 W Irving Blvd *Web:* irving.net/irvingwiki/index.php?title=main_page	Irving	TX	75060	972-721-2606		434-3
Irving Ready-Mix Inc 13415 Coldwater Rd	Fort Wayne	IN	46845	260-443-9475		182
Irving Shipbuilding Inc 3099 Barrington St *TF:* 800-337-5764 ■ *Web:* www.irvingshipbuilding.com	Halifax	NS	B3K5M7	902-423-9271		698
Irving Tool & Mfg Company Inc 2249 Wall St *Web:* irvingtool.com	Garland	TX	75041	972-926-4000	926-4099	697
Irvington Public Library 5 Civic Sq *Web:* www.irvingtonpubliclibrary.org	Irvington	NJ	07111	973-372-6400	372-6860	434-3
Irwin Army Community Hospital 600 Caisson Hill Rd *Web:* iach.amedd.army.mil	Fort Riley	KS	66442	785-239-7000		374-4
Irwin Car and Equipment 9953 Broadway St *Web:* www.irwincar.com	Irwin	PA	15642	724-864-8900		480
Irwin County 620 S Irwin Ave *Web:* www.ocillachamber.net/irwin-county-commission	Ocilla	GA	31774	229-468-0050		338
Irwin Electric Membership Corp 915 W Fourth St *TF:* 800-237-3745 ■ *Web:* www.irwinemc.com	Ocilla	GA	31774	229-468-7415		245
Irwin Industries Inc 1580 W Carson St *Web:* www.irwinindustries.com	Long Beach	CA	90810	310-233-3000		186
Irwin Manufacturing Corp 398 Fitzgerald Hwy	Ocilla	GA	31774	229-468-9481		155-4
Irwin Naturals 5310 Beethoven St *TF:* 800-297-3273 ■ *Web:* www.appliednutrition.com	Los Angeles	CA	90066	310-306-3636		799
Irwin Seating Company Inc 3251 Fruit Ridge NW *TF:* 866-464-7946 ■ *Web:* www.irwinseating.com	Grand Rapids	MI	49544	616-574-7400		319-3
I&S Group Inc 115 E Hickory St Ste 300 *Web:* is-grp.com	Mankato	MN	56001	507-387-6651		261
ISA (International Sign Assn) 1001 N Fairfax St Ste 301 *TF:* 866-949-7446 ■ *Web:* www.signs.org	Alexandria	VA	22314	703-836-4012	836-8353	49-4
ISA (International Society of Arboriculture) PO Box 3129 *TF:* 888-472-8733 ■ *Web:* www.isa-arbor.com	Champaign	IL	61826	217-355-9411	355-9516	48-2
ISA (International Studies Assn) 324 Social Sciences University of Arizona *Web:* www.isanet.org	Tucson	AZ	85721	860-486-5850		48-11
ISA (Incest Survivors Anonymous) PO Box 17245 *Web:* www.lafn.org/medical/isa	Long Beach	CA	90807	562-428-5599		48-21
Isa 3324 Steiner St *Web:* www.isarestaurant.com	San Francisco	CA	94123	415-567-9588		671
Isaac Farrar Mansion 17 Second St *Web:* bangory.org	Bangor	ME	04401	207-941-2808	941-2812	50-3
Isaac's Deli Inc 354 N Prince St Ste 220 *Web:* www.isaacsrestaurants.com	Lancaster	PA	17603	717-394-0623	393-0955	670
Isaac's Restaurants 421 Friendship Rd *Web:* www.isaacsrestaurants.com	Harrisburg	PA	17111	717-920-5757	920-3955	671
Isaacson & Arfman PA 128 Monroe St NE *Web:* iacivil.com	Albuquerque	NM	87108	505-268-8828		256
Isaak Bond Investments Inc 3900 S Wadsworth Blvd Ste 590 *TF:* 800-279-4426 ■ *Web:* www.isaakbond.com	Lakewood	CO	80235	303-623-7500		690
Isabel Bloom LLC 736 Federal St Ste 2100 *TF:* 800-273-5436 ■ *Web:* www.ibloom.com	Davenport	IA	52803	800-273-5436		183
Isabella County 200 N Main St *Web:* www.isabellacounty.org	Mount Pleasant	MI	48858	989-772-0911	773-7431	338
Isabella Medical Care Facility 1222 North Dr *Web:* mcf.isabollacounty.org	Mount Pleasant	MI	48858	989-772-2957	772-3669	450
Isabella Stewart Gardner Museum 25 Evans Way *Web:* www.gardnermuseum.org	Boston	MA	02115	617-566-1401		520
ISACA (Information Systems Audit & Control Assn) 3701 Algonquin Rd Ste 1010 *TF:* 888-491-8833 ■ *Web:* www.isaca.org	Rolling Meadows	IL	60008	847-253-1545	253-1443	48-9
Isaco International Corp 5980 Miami Lakes Dr *Web:* www.isaco.com	Miami	FL	33014	305-594-4455	594-4496	155-15
I-Safe America Inc 5900 Pasteur Court Ste 100 *TF:* 800-423-8477 ■ *Web:* www.isafe.org	Carlsbad	CA	92008	760-603-7911		41
Isagenix International LLC 2225 S Price Rd *TF:* 877-877-8111 ■ *Web:* isagenix.com	Chandler	AZ	85286	480-889-5747	636-5386	296-11
Isakson Johnny (Sen R - GA) 131 Russell Bldg *Web:* www.isakson.senate.gov	Washington	DC	20510	202-224-3643	228-0724	342-2

Phone | Fax | Class

Isani Consultants
3143 Yellowstone Blvd ... Houston TX 77054 713-747-2399 261
Web: www.isaniconsultants.com
Isanti County 555 18th Ave SW ... Cambridge MN 55008 763-689-3859 689-8226 338
TF: 800-450-7463 ■ *Web:* www.co.isanti.mn.us
Isanti County News 234 S Main St ... Cambridge MN 55008 763-689-1981 689-4372 637-8
TF: 800-927-9233 ■ *Web:* www.isanticountynews.com
ISAR (International Society for Animal Rights)
PO Box F ... Clarks Summit PA 18411 570-586-2200 586-9580 48-3
TF: 888-589-6397 ■ *Web:* www.isaronline.org
ISB (International Society of Bassists)
14070 Proton Rd Ste 100 ... Dallas TX 75244 972-233-9107 490-4219 48-4
Web: www.isbworldoffice.com
ISBX Corp
3415 S Sepulveda Blvd Ste 1250 ... Los Angeles CA 90034 310-437-8010 177
TF: 800-962-4587 ■ *Web:* www.isbx.com
ISC Consultants Inc
345 Hoyt St Ste 1000 ... New York NY 11231 212-477-8800 477-9895 449
Web: www.isc.com
ISC Engineering 1730 Evergreen St ... Duarte CA 91010 909-596-3315 256
Web: www.iscengineering.com
ISC Group Inc 3500 Oak Lawn Ave Ste 400 ... Dallas TX 75219 214-520-1115 401
Web: www.iscgroup.com
Isc Kentucky
12305 Westport Rd Ste 1 ... Louisville KY 40245 502-292-5097 174
Web: iscky.com
Isc Sales Inc 4421 Tradition Trl ... Plano TX 75093 972-964-2700 177
TF: 800-836-7472 ■ *Web:* iscsales.com
ISCAR Metals 300 Wway Pl ... Arlington TX 76018 817-258-3200 360-2
Web: www.iscarmetals.com
ISCEBS (International Society of Certified Employee Benefits)
18700 W Bluemond Rd PO Box 209 ... Brookfield WI 53008 262-786-8771 786-8650 49-12
TF: 888-334-3327 ■ *Web:* www.iscebs.org
ISCET (International Society of Certified Electronics Technicians)
3608 Porching Ave ... Fort Worth TX 76107 817-921-9101 921-3741 49-19
TF: 800-946-0201 ■ *Web:* www.iscet.org
Isco Industries
926 Baxter Ave PO Box 4545 ... Louisville KY 40204 502-583-6591 596
TF: 800-345-4726 ■ *Web:* www.isco-pipe.com
ISCO International LLC
1450 Arthur Ave Ste A ... Elk Grove Village IL 60007 224-222-1666 222-1691 735
TF: 888-948-4726 ■ *Web:* www.iscointl.com
iScreen Vision Inc
110 Timber Creek Dr Ste 2 ... Cordova TN 38018 901-201-6132 743
Web: www.iscreenvision.com
ISD Inc
2500 W Higgins Rd Ste 250 ... Hoffman Estates IL 60169 847-519-1150 225
Web: www.isdinc.com
ISDA (International Swaps & Derivatives Assn)
360 Madison Ave 16th Fl ... New York NY 10017 212-901-6000 49-2
Web: www2.isda.org
ISE America Inc PO Box 267 ... Galena MD 21635 410-755-6300 755-6367 619
TF: 800-864-2220 ■ *Web:* www.iseamerica.com
ISEC Inc
6000 Greenwood Plaza Blvd Ste 200 ... Greenwood Village CO 80111 303-790-1444 248
Web: www.isecinc.com
isee systems Inc
Wheelock Office Park 31 Old Etna Rd Ste 7N ... Lebanon NH 03766 603-448-4990 177
Web: www.iseesystems.com
isekurity Inc 24663 Mound Rd ... Warren MI 48091 877-838-5734 693
TF: 877-838-5734 ■ *Web:* www.isekurity.com
iSelect Internet Inc
1420 W Kettleman Ln Ste E ... Lodi CA 95242 209-334-0496 837-1427* 398
**Fax Area Code:* 877 ■ *TF:* 877-837-1427 ■ *Web:* www.iselect.net
Iseli Co 402 N Main St ... Walworth WI 53184 262-275-2108 275-6094 621
TF: 800-403-8665 ■ *Web:* iseli.com
Iseman Cunningham Riester & Hyde LLP
9 Thurlow Terr ... Albany NY 12203 518-462-3000 428
Web: www.icrh.com
iSense Acquisition LLC
27700 SW 95th Ave ... Wilsonville OR 97070 503-783-5050 261
ISFSI (International Society of Fire Service Instructors)
14001C St Germain Dr ... Centreville VA 20121 800-435-0005 435-0005 49-7
TF: 800-435-0005 ■ *Web:* www.isfsi.org
ISG Novasoft (ISGN) 1333 Gateway Dr ... Melbourne FL 32901 860-656-7550 178-1
TF: 800-462-5545 ■ *Web:* www.isgn.com
ISG Prime LLC 12723 Mill Heights Ct ... Herndon VA 20171 703-624-9409 180
Web: www.isgprime.com
ISG Resources 11539 Park Woods Cir ... Alpharetta GA 30005 770-667-8830 256
TF: 800-225-5627 ■ *Web:* www.isg-resources.com
ISG Technologies 3333 St Rd Ste 330 ... Bensalem PA 19020 800-566-3310 824-9415* 175
**Fax Area Code:* 856 ■ *TF:* 800-566-3310 ■ *Web:* isgtechnologies.com
ISG Technology & Data Center
127 N Seventh St ... Salina KS 67401 785-823-1555 178-10
Web: www.isgtech.com
Isgett Distributors Inc
51 Highland Ctr Blvd ... Asheville NC 28806 828-667-9846 579
TF: 800-358-0080 ■ *Web:* www.isgettdistributors.com
ISGN (ISG Novasoft) 1333 Gateway Dr ... Melbourne FL 32901 860-656-7550 178-1
TF: 800-462-5545 ■ *Web:* www.isgn.com
Ish Entertainment LLC
34 W 27Th St 7TH FL ... New York NY 10001 212-377-3845 377-3845 260
Web: ish.tv
Isham-Terry House 211 High St ... Hartford CT 06103 860-247-8996 50-3
Web: www.ctlandmarks.org
iSherpa Capital LLC
6400 S Fiddlers Green Cir ... Greenwood Village CO 80111 303-645-0500 792
ISHLT (International Society for Heart & Lung Transplantation)
14673 Midway Rd Ste 200 ... Addison TX 75001 972-490-9495 490-9499 49-8
Web: www.ishlt.org
ISI (Intercollegiate Studies Institute)
3901 Centerville Rd ... Wilmington DE 19807 302-652-4600 652-1760 48-11
TF: 800-526-7022 ■ *Web:* home.isi.org
ISI (Ice Skating Institute)
6000 Custer Rd Bldg 9 ... Plano TX 75023 972-735-8800 735-8815 48-22
Web: www.skateisi.com
ISI Commercial Refrigeration LP
640 W Sixth St ... Houston TX 77007 214-631-7980 631-6813 665
TF: 800-777-5070 ■ *Web:* www.isi-texas.com

ISI Insulation Specialties Inc
2142 Rheem Dr Ste A ... Pleasanton CA 94588 925-846-7990 189-9
Isine Inc
4155 Veterans Memorial Hwy ... Ronkonkoma NY 11779 631-913-4400 261
Web: isine.com
Isis It Inc
88 Vilcom Ctr Dr Ste 180 ... Chapel Hill NC 27514 919-932-6150 180
TF: 877-970-4747 ■ *Web:* www.isisit.com
Isis Papyrus America Inc
301 Bank St ... Southlake TX 76092 817-416-2345 416-1223 177
Web: www.isis-papyrus.com
ISK Biosciences Corp
7474 Auburn Rd Ste 2 ... Painesville OH 44077 440-357-4640 317
Web: www.iskbc.com
Iskalo Development Corp
Harbinger Sq 5166 Main St ... Williamsville NY 14221 716-633-2096 653
Web: www.iskalo.com
ISKME 323 Harvard Ave ... Half Moon Bay CA 94019 650-728-3322 507
Web: iskme.org
iSky
1700 Pennsylvania Ave NW Ste 560 ... Washington DC 20006 240-456-4300 737
Web: www.isky.com
ISL (Indiana State Library)
140 N Senate Ave ... Indianapolis IN 46204 317-232-3694 232-3728 434-5
TF: 800-451-6028 ■ *Web:* www.in.gov/library
Islamic Center of Hawthorne
12227 Hawthorne Way ... Hawthorne CA 90250 310-973-8000 978-4036 685
Web: www.ichla.org
Islamic Medical Assn of North America (IMANA)
101 W 22nd St Ste 106 ... Lombard IL 60148 630-932-0000 932-0005 49-8
Web: www.imana.org
Islamorada Chamber of Commerce
PO Box 915 ... Islamorada FL 33036 305-664-4503 664-4289 139
TF: 800-322-5397 ■ *Web:* www.islamoradachamber.com
Island 98.5 650 Iwilei Rd Ste 400 ... Honolulu HI 96817 808-550-9200 645-73
Web: island985.iheart.com
Island Beach State Park
PO Box 37 ... Seaside Park NJ 08752 732-793-0506 565
Web: www.njparksandforests.org
Island Co
312 Clematis St Ste 401 ... West Palm Beach FL 33401 561-833-8110 514
Web: www.islandcompany.com
Island Computer Products Inc
20 Clifton Ave ... Staten Island NY 10305 718-556-6700 174
Web: www.icpcorp.com
Island Container Group
44 Island Container Plaza ... Wyandanch NY 11798 631-253-4400 100
Web: www.islandcontainer.com
Island County 1 NE Seventh St ... Coupeville WA 98239 360-679-7354 679-7381 338
Web: www.islandcountywa.gov/pages/home.aspx
Island Delight Caribbean Restaurant
323 Airbase Blvd ... Montgomery AL 36108 334-264-0041 671
Island Express Helicopter Service
1175 Queens Hwy S ... Long Beach CA 90802 310-510-2525 359
TF Cust Svc: 800-228-2566 ■ *Web:* www.islandexpress.com
Island Federal Credit Union
120 Motor Pkwy ... Hauppauge NY 11788 631-851-1100 219
TF: 800-475-5263 ■ *Web:* www.islandfcu.org
Island Global Yachting Ltd
717 Fifth Ave Ste 900 ... Fort Lauderdale FL 33301 212-705-5000 31
Web: www.igymarinas.com
Island Hotel, The
690 Newport Ctr Dr ... Newport Beach CA 92660 949-759-0808 759-0568 379
TF: 866-554-4620 ■ *Web:* www.islandhotel.com
Island Jerk 1800 Bank St ... Ottawa ON K1V0W3 613-737-5163 671
Island Key Computer Ltd 938 Howe St ... Vancouver BC V6Z1N9 604-669-8178 177
Web: www.islandkey.com
Island Lake Recreation Area
12950 E Grand River Rd ... Brighton MI 48116 810-229-7067 565
Web: www.michigandnr.com
Island Lincoln-Mercury Inc
1850 E Merritt Island Cswy ... Merritt Island FL 32952 321-452-9220 57
Island Micro Solutions Inc
3375 Koapaka St Ste B282 ... Honolulu HI 96819 808-833-6048 177
Web: solutionshawaii.com
Island Nature Trust PO Box 265 ... Charlottetown PE C1A7K4 902-566-9150 628-6331 48-13
Web: www.islandnaturetrust.ca
Island Oasis 141 Norfolk St PO Box 769 ... Walpole MA 02081 508-660-1176 299
TF: 800-777-4752 ■ *Web:* www.kerryfoodservice.com/brands/island-oasis
Island Pacific Inc
17310 Red Hill Ave Ste 320 ... Irvine CA 92614 800-994-3847 178-10
TF: 800-994-3847 ■ *Web:* www.islandpacific.com
Island Packet 10 Buck Island Rd ... Bluffton SC 29910 843-706-8100 706-3070 532-2
TF: 877-706-8100 ■ *Web:* www.islandpacket.com
Island Peer Review Organization Inc (IPRO)
1979 Marcus Ave ... New Hyde Park NY 11042 516-326-7767 328-2310 353
Web: www.ipro.org
Island Press 2000 M St NW Ste 650 ... Washington DC 20036 202-232-7933 234-1328 637-2
TF: 800-621-2736 ■ *Web:* www.islandpress.org
Island Pro Digital 35 Davids Dr ... Hauppauge NY 11788 631-293-4217 627
Web: www.islandprodigital.com
Island Staffing
4263 Oceanside Blvd Ste 106-160 ... Oceanside CA 92056 760-547-5018 260
TF: 800-559-1434 ■ *Web:* www.islandstaffing.us
Island Surf
1450 Miracle Strip Pkwy SE ... Fort Walton Beach FL 32548 800-272-2065 711
TF: 800-272-2065 ■ *Web:* www.islandsurf.com
Island Technologies
17408 Chatsworth St Ste 200 ... Granada Hills CA 91344 818-832-2310 177
Web: www.islandtechnologies.net
Island Terrace Nursing Home
57 Long Point Rd ... Lakeville MA 02347 508-947-0151 371
TF: 800-442-5581 ■ *Web:* islandterrace.com
Island Timberlands LP
65 Front St 4th Fl ... Nanaimo BC V9R5H9 250-755-3500 454
TF: 800-663-5555 ■ *Web:* www.islandtimberlands.com
Island View Casino Resort
3300 W Beach Blvd PO Box 1600 ... Gulfport MS 39502 228-314-2100 133
TF General: 888-777-9696 ■ *Web:* www.islandviewcasino.com

Phone | Fax | Class

Island Windjammers Inc 165 Shaw Dr ... Acworth GA 30102 877-772-4549 31
TF: 877-772-4549 ■ *Web:* www.islandwindjammers.com

Islander Resort, The
82100 Overseas Hwy PO Box 766 ... Islamorada FL 33036 305-664-2031 377
Web: guyharveyoutpostislamorada.com

Islands in the Sun Cruises & Tours Inc
348 Thompson Creek Mall Ste 107 ... Stevensville MD 21666 410-827-3812 782-2371* 771
**Fax Area Code:* 443 ■ *TF:* 800-278-7786 ■ *Web:* www.crus-sun.com

Islands Magazine
460 N Orlando Ave Ste 200 ... Winter Park FL 32789 515-237-3697 457-22
TF: 800-250-1523 ■ *Web:* www.islands.com

Islands Restaurants
5750 Fleet St Ste 120 ... Carlsbad CA 92008 760-268-1800 670
Web: www.islandsrestaurants.com

ISLC Inc 14 Savannah Hwy ... Beaufort SC 29906 843-770-1000 387
TF: 888-828-4752 ■ *Web:* www.islc.net

Isle of Capri Casino
1800 E Front St ... Kansas City MO 64120 816-855-7777 133
Web: www.kansas-city.isleofcapricasinos.com

Isle of Capri Casino Hotel Lake Charles
100 West Lake Ave ... Westlake LA 70669 610-241-1618 133
Web: www.lake-charles.isleofcapricasinos.com

Isle of Wight County
17090 Monument Cir # 123 ... Isle of Wight VA 23397 757-365-6204 338
Web: www.co.isle-of-wight.va.us

Isle Royale National Park
800 E Lakeshore Dr ... Houghton MI 49931 906-482-0984 482-8753 564
Web: www.nps.gov

Islip Public Library 71 Monell Ave ... Islip NY 11751 631-581-5933 434-3
Web: www.isliplibrary.org

ISM (Institute for Supply Management)
2055 Centennial Cir ... Tempe AZ 85284 480-752-6276 752-7890 49-12
TF Cust Svc: 800-888-6276 ■ *Web:* www.instituteforsupplymanagement.org

ISM Dickson Mounds Museum
10956 N Dickson Mounds Rd ... Lewistown IL 61542 309-547-3721 547-3189 520
Web: www.illinoisstatemuseum.org

ISMIE (Illinois State Medical Inter-Insurance Exchange)
20 N Michigan Ave Ste 700 ... Chicago IL 60602 312-782-2749 782-2023 391-5
TF: 800-782-4767 ■ *Web:* www.ismie.com

ISMRM (International Society for Magnetic Resonance in Medicine)
2030 Addison St Ste 700 ... Berkeley CA 94704 510-841-1899 841-2340 49-8
Web: www.ismrm.org

ISN (Information Systems & Networks Corp)
10411 Motor City Dr Ste700 ... Bethesda MD 20817 301-469-0400 469-0767 180
Web: www.isncorp.com

ISN Global Enterprises Inc
Po Box 1391 ... Claremont CA 91711 909-670-0601 192
TF: 877-376-4476 ■ *Web:* isnglobal.com

ISNA (Indiana State Nurses Assn)
2915 N High School Rd ... Indianapolis IN 46224 317-299-4575 297-3525 533
Web: www.indiananurses.org

iSnap 1715 I St Ste 14 ... Sacramento CA 95811 916-333-0330 387
Web: www.isnap.com

ISO (Insurance Services Office Inc)
545 Washington Blvd ... Jersey City NJ 07310 201-469-2000 748-1472* 390
**Fax:* Hum Res ■ *TF:* 800-888-4476 ■ *Web:* www.verisk.com/iso.html

Isobunkers LLC
5353 E Princess Anne Rd Ste F ... Norfolk VA 23502 757-855-0900 855-6200 579
Web: www.isoindustries.com

ISOC (Internet Society)
1775 Wiehle Ave Ste 102 ... Reston VA 20190 703-439-2120 326-9881 48-9
Web: www.internetsociety.org

ISOFlex Packaging 101 ISO Pkwy ... Gray Court SC 29645 864-876-4300 601
Web: www.isopoly.com

Isoflux Inc
10 Vantage Point Dr Ste 4 ... Rochester NY 14624 585-349-0640 350
Web: www.isofluxinc.com

Isolatek International Inc
41 Furnace St ... Stanhope NJ 07874 973-347-1200 389
TF: 800-631-9600 ■ *Web:* www.cafco.com

iSold It 1106 E Colorado Ave ... Pasadena CA 91106 626-584-0844 310
Web: www.i-soldit.com

Isolite Systems
6868A Cortona Dr ... Santa Barbara CA 93117 888-710-2268 966-6416* 228
**Fax Area Code:* 805 ■ *TF:* 888-710-2268 ■ *Web:* www.isolitesystems.com

Isomet Corp 5263 Port Royal Rd ... Springfield VA 22151 703-321-8301 321-8546 425
OTC: IOMT ■ *Web:* www.isomet.com

Isometric Tool & Design Inc
330 Wisconsin Dr ... New Richmond WI 54017 715-246-7005 711
Web: www.isotool.com

IsoRay Medical Inc
350 Hills St Ste 106 ... Richland WA 99354 509-375-5329 267-3670 360-3
Web: www.isoray.com

Isotech Laboratories Inc
1308 Parkland Ct ... Champaign IL 61821 217-398-3490 743
Web: www.isotechlabs.com

Isotech Pest Management Inc
12881 Ramona Blvd ... Baldwin Park CA 91706 909-594-8939 577
Web: www.isotechpest.com

Iso-Tex Diagnostics Inc
PO Box 909 ... Friendswood TX 77549 800-477-4839 482-1070* 231
**Fax Area Code:* 281 ■ *TF:* 800-477-4839 ■ *Web:* www.isotexdiagnostics.com

Isothermal Community College
286 ICC Loop Rd PO Box 804 ... Spindale NC 28160 828-286-3636 286-4014 162
Web: www.isothermal.edu

Isotron Corp
1443 N Northlake Way Ste 101 ... Seattle WA 98103 206-547-1196 547-1196 605-2

Isotropic Networks Inc
W2835 Krueger Rd ... Lake Geneva WI 53147 262-248-9600 116
Web: www.isosat.net

ISP (International Specialty Products Inc)
1361 Alps Rd ... Wayne NJ 07470 973-628-4000 144
TF: 800-622-4423 ■ *Web:* www.ashland.com

ISP Optics Corp 50 S Buckhout St ... Irvington NY 10533 914-591-3070 544
Web: www.ispoptics.com

ISPA (Idaho State Pharmacy Assn)
816 W Bannock St Ste 105 ... Boise ID 83702 208-870-8312 585
Web: www.idahopharmacists.com

ISPA (International Sleep Products Assn)
501 Wythe St ... Alexandria VA 22314 703-683-8371 683-4503 49-4
Web: www.sleepproducts.org

ISPA Inc 1100 Cir 75 Pkwy Ste 242 ... Atlanta GA 30339 770-690-2900 463
Web: www.ispainc.com

ISPD (International Society for Peritoneal Dialysis)
66 Martin St ... Milton ON L9T2R2 905-875-2456 875-2864 49-8
TF: 888-834-1001 ■ *Web:* www.ispd.org

ISPE (International Society for Pharmacoepidemiology)
5272 River Rd Ste 630 ... Bethesda MD 20816 301-718-6500 656-0989 49-8
TF: 888-887-7955 ■ *Web:* www.pharmacoepi.org

ISPE (International Society for Pharmaceutical Engineering)
3109 W Dr ML King Jr Blvd Ste 250 ... Tampa FL 33607 813-960-2105 264-2816 49-19
TF: 800-228-9290 ■ *Web:* www.ispe.org

ISPI (International Society for Performance Improvement)
PO Box 13035 ... Silver Spring MD 20910 301-587-8570 587-8573 49-12
TF: 800-825-7550 ■ *Web:* www.ispi.org

ISPN Inc 14303 W 95th St ... Lenexa KS 66215 913-859-9500 393
TF: 800-883-8839 ■ *Web:* www.ispn.net

ISPOR (ISPOR)
505 Lawrence Sq Blvd S ... Lawrenceville NJ 08648 609-586-4981 219-0774 49-8
TF: 800-992-0643 ■ *Web:* www.ispor.org

ISPP (International Society of Political Psychology)
126 Ward St Ste 1213 PO Box 1213 ... Columbus NC 28722 828-894-5422 894-5422 48-7
TF: 800-796-6094 ■ *Web:* www.ispp.org

Isr 264 Main St ... Sugar Grove IL 60554 630-466-7800 693
Web: www.isr-usa.com

ISR Info Way Inc
559 Donofrio Dr Ste 101 & 102 ... Madison WI 53719 608-827-7884 177
Web: www.isrinfo.com

Isra Surface Vision Inc
4470 Peachtree Lakes Dr ... Duluth GA 30096 770-449-7776 472
Web: www.lasorsystronics.com

Israel 800 Second Ave ... New York NY 10017 212-499-5000 499-5515 784
Web: embassies.gov.il
Consulate General
1100 Spring St NW Ste 440 ... Atlanta GA 30309 404-487-6500 257
Web: www.israelemb.org
Consulate General
456 Montgomery St Ste 2100 ... San Francisco CA 94104 415-844-7500 844-7555 257
Web: www.israelemb.org
Consulate General
100 Biscayne Blvd Ste 1800 ... Miami FL 33132 305-925-9400 257
Web: www.israelemb.org
Embassy of Israel to the United States, The
3514 International Dr NW ... Washington DC 20008 202-364-5500 257
Web: www.israelemb.org

Israel Discount Bank of New York (IDBB)
511 Fifth Ave ... New York NY 10017 212-551-8500 551-8540 70
Web: www.idbny.com

Israel Government Tourist Office
800 Second Ave 16th Fl ... New York NY 10017 646-779-6766 658-6543* 775
**Fax Area Code:* 323 ■ *TF:* 888-774-7723 ■ *Web:* www.goisrael.com

Isram World of Travel Inc
25 Broadway 9th Fl ... New York NY 10004 800-223-7460 370-1477* 760
**Fax Area Code:* 212 ■ *TF:* 800-223-7460 ■ *Web:* www.isram.com

ISRI (Institute of Scrap Recycling Industries Inc)
1615 L St NW Ste 600 ... Washington DC 20036 202-662-8500 626-0900 48-12
TF: 800-678-9595 ■ *Web:* www.isri.org

ISRS (International Society of Refractive Surgery)
655 Beach St PO Box 7424 ... San Francisco CA 94109 415-561-8581 561-8575 49-8
TF: 866-561-8558 ■ *Web:* www.aao.org

ISS Facilities Services Inc
1019 Central Pkwy N Ste 100 ... San Antonio TX 78232 210-495-6021 104
Web: www.us.issworld.com

ISS International Inc
Aspen Corporate Park 1480 US Hwy 9 N
Ste 202 ... Woodbridge NJ 07095 732-855-1111 692
Web: www.isscctv.com

ISS LLC 820 E 20th St ... Cookeville TN 38501 931-526-1106 273
Web: www.sproutnet.com

ISS Software Solutions Inc
5 Great Vly Pkwy Ste 110 ... Malvern PA 19355 610-560-4300 225
Web: www.intsoftinc.com

ISS Technologies 22 Business Park Cir ... Arden NC 28704 828-684-4248 463
Web: www.isstechnologies.com

ISSA (International Sanitary Supply Assn)
3300 Dundee Rd ... Northbrook IL 60062 847-982-0800 982-1012 49-18
TF: 800-225-4772 ■ *Web:* global.issa.com

Issa Darrell (Rep R - CA)
2269 Rayburn HOB ... Washington DC 20515 202-225-3906 225-3303 342-2
Web: issa.house.gov

Issaquah Dental Lab Inc
640 NW Gilman Blvd ... Issaquah WA 98027 425-392-5125 228
Web: www.issaquah-dl.com

Issaquah Press PO Box 1328 ... Issaquah WA 98027 425-392-6434 532-4
Web: www.theeastside.news/issaquah

Issaquah Swimming Pool
50 SE Clark St ... Issaquah WA 98027 425-837-3350 354
Web: ci.issaquah.wa.us

Issaquena County Regional Correctional Facility
PO Box 220 ... Mayersville MS 39113 662-873-2153 873-2956 213
Web: www.mdoc.ms.gov

ISSI (Integrated Silicon Solution Inc)
1940 Zanker Rd ... San Jose CA 95112 408-969-6600 969-7800 696
NASDAQ: ISSI ■ *TF:* 800-379-4774 ■ *Web:* www.issi.com

Isspro Inc 2515 NE Riverside Way ... Portland OR 97211 503-528-3400 495
Web: www.issproinc.com

Issuer Direct Corp
500 Perimeter Park Dr Ste D ... Morrisville NC 27560 877-481-4014 317
TF: 877-481-4014 ■ *Web:* www.issuerdirect.com

Issues & Answers Network Inc
5151 Bonney Rd Ste 100 ... Virginia Beach VA 23462 757-456-1100 668
Web: www.issans.net

IST (Institute for Simulation & Training)
3100 Technology Pkwy ... Orlando FL 32826 407-882-1300 658-5059 668
Web: www.ist.ucf.edu

Name / Address	City	State	ZIP	Phone	Fax	Class
IS&T (Society for Imaging Science & Technology) 7003 Kilworth Ln *TF:* 800-654-2240 ■ *Web:* www.imaging.org	Springfield	VA	22151	703-642-9090	642-9094	49-16
ISTA (International Safe Transit Assn) 1400 Abbott Rd Ste 160 *TF:* 888-299-2208 ■ *Web:* www.ista.org	East Lansing	MI	48823	517-333-3437	333-3813	49-21
ISTA Advocate Magazine 150 W Market St Ste 900 *TF:* 800-382-4037 ■ *Web:* ista-in.org	Indianapolis	IN	46204	317-263-3400	655-3700	457-8
Istaff Inc 1325 Satellite Blvd NW Ste 1305 *Web:* www.istaff.com	Suwanee	GA	30024	770-962-9604		260
iStar 1114 Ave of the Americas 39th Fl *NYSE:* STAR ■ *Web:* www.istarfinancial.com	New York	NY	10036	212-930-9400		216
ISTE (International Society for Technology in Education) 1530 Wilson Blvd Ste 730 *TF General:* 800-336-5191 ■ *Web:* www.iste.org	Arlington	VA	22209	202-861-7777		49-5
Istech Inc 4691 Raycom Rd *TF:* 800-555-4880 ■ *Web:* www.istech-inc.com	Dover	PA	17315	717-764-5565		180
ISTF (International Society of Tropical Foresters) 5400 Grosvenor Ln *Fax Area Code: 877 ■ *Web:* www.istf-bethesda.org	Bethesda	MD	20814	301-530-4514	665-6473*	48-13
Isthmus Publishing Company Inc 101 King St *Web:* isthmus.com	Madison	WI	53703	608-251-5627	251-2165	532-5
ISTM (International Society of Travel Medicine) 315 W Ponce de Leon Ave Ste 245 *Web:* www.istm.org	Decatur	GA	30030	404-373-8282	373-8283	49-8
iStores Inc 2311 Grant St	Vancouver	WA	98660	360-567-2520		393
iStreet Solutions LLC 1075 Triangle Ct Ste 130 *Web:* www.istreetsolutions.com	West Sacramento	CA	95605	916-792-3762		196
ISTSS (International Society for Traumatic Stress Studies) 111 Deer Lake Rd Ste 100 *TF:* 877-469-7873 ■ *Web:* www.istss.org	Deerfield	IL	60015	847-480-9028	480-9282	49-15
ISTT Inc 846 Broadway Ave *Web:* isttechnology.com	Bowling Green	KY	42101	270-781-5096		177
Isu Petasys Corp 12930 Bradley Ave *Web:* www.isupetasys.com	Sylmar	CA	91342	818-833-5800		625
iSyndica USA Inc 20A Northwest Blvd Ste 190 *Web:* www.isyndica.com	Nashua	NH	03063	603-452-7671	452-8762	366
ISYS Technologies Inc 801 W Mineral Ave Ste 105 *Web:* www.isystechnologies.com	Littleton	CO	80120	303-290-8922		681
IT America Inc 100 Metroplex Dr Ste 207 *Web:* www.itamerica.com	Edison	NJ	08817	732-985-5100		196
IT Company LLC, The 16 Emory Pl Ste 101 *Web:* www.theitco.net	Knoxville	TN	37917	865-862-6053		196
IT Direct LLC 67 Prospect Ave Ste 202 *TF:* 800-532-3722 ■ *Web:* www.gettingyouconnected.com	West Hartford	CT	06106	860-656-9110		624
It Doctors 2175 Northdale Blvd NW	Coon Rapids	MN	55433	763-267-6980		177
It Fitz Tools Inc 2064 Trlwood Dr W	Burleson	TX	76028	817-295-3093		366
It Healthtrack Inc 6500 Main St Ste 3 *Web:* ithealthtrack.com	Williamsville	NY	14221	716-630-0063		354
It Pitstop 10120 S Eastern Ave	Henderson	NV	89052	702-777-4445		396
It Pro Source 2600 Kitty Hawk Rd Ste 115 *TF:* 800-523-1950 ■ *Web:* www.itprosource.com	Livermore	CA	94551	925-455-7701		396
IT Prophets LLC 3030 Woodbridge Ln *TF:* 800-208-6137 ■ *Web:* www.itprophets.com	Canton	GA	30114	770-335-1410		180
IT Staffing Inc 5 Bliss Court Ste 200 *Web:* www.itstaffinc.com	Woodcliff Lake	NJ	07677	201-505-0493		631
IT Weapons 7965 Goreway Dr Unit 1 *TF:* 866-202-5298 ■ *Web:* www.itweapons.com	Brampton	ON	L6T5T5	905-494-1040		180
It's Just Lunch! Inc 121 W Wacker Dr Ste 663 *Web:* www.itsjustlunch.com	Chicago	IL	60611	312-644-9999		226
It4ce Inc 1200 Aerowood Dr *TF:* 877-470-0008 ■ *Web:* it4ce.com	Mississauga	ON	L4W2S7	905-206-9947		764
It4la Inc 8033 W Sunset Blvd 228 *Web:* www.it4la.com	West Hollywood	CA	90046	323-936-4900		396
ITA (International Titanium Assn) 2655 W Midway Blvd Ste 300 *Web:* www.titanium.org	Broomfield	CO	80020	303-404-2221	404-9111	49-19
Ita Inc 2162 Dana Ave *TF:* 800-899-8877 ■ *Web:* www.ita.com	Cincinnati	OH	45207	513-631-8877		525
Ita Software Inc 141 Portland St *Web:* www.itasoftware.com	Cambridge	MA	02139	617-714-2100	621-3913	178-10
ITAC Solutions LLC 700 Montgomery Hwy Ste 148 *Web:* www.itacsolutions.com	Birmingham	AL	35216	205-326-0004		193
ITAGroup 4600 Westown Pkwy *TF:* 800-257-1985 ■ *Web:* www.itagroup.com	West Des Moines	IA	50266	800-257-1985		384
Italgrani USA Inc 7900 Van Buren St *TF:* 800-274-1274 ■ *Web:* www.italgraniusa.com	Saint Louis	MO	63111	314-638-1447	752-7621	275
Italian American Chamber of Commerce of Chicago (IACC) 500 N Michigan Ave Ste 506 *Web:* www.iacc-chicago.com	Chicago	IL	60611	312-553-9137	553-9142	138
Italian Cafe 387 Las Colinas Blvd E *Web:* italianitaliancafe.com	Irving	TX	75039	972-401-0000	401-9193	671
Italian Government Tourist Board 500 N Michigan Ave Ste 1046 *Web:* www.italiantourism.com	Chicago	IL	60611	312-644-0996	644-3019	775
Italian Government Tourist Board 10850 Wilshire Blvd Ste 575 *TF:* 800-862-7822 ■ *Web:* www.italiantourism.com	Los Angeles	CA	90024	310-820-1898	470-7788	775
Italian Government Tourist Board 686 Park Ave Fl 3 *Web:* www.italiantourism.com	New York	NY	10065	212-245-5618		775
Italian Moon 810 S Washington St *Web:* www.italianmoon.com	Grand Forks	ND	58201	701-772-7277		671
Italian Village Pizza 711 Vandiver Dr Ste B *Web:* theitalianvillagepizza.com	Columbia	MO	65202	573-442-8821		671
iTalkBB CA 245 W Beaver Creek Rd Unit 9 *TF:* 877-482-5522 ■ *Web:* www.italkbb.com	Richmond Hill	ON	L4B1L1	877-482-5522		224
Italy 885 Second Ave 49th Fl *Web:* www.italyun.esteri.it	New York	NY	10017	212-486-9191	486-1036	784
Consulate General 2590 Webster St *Web:* www.conssanfrancisco.esteri.it	San Francisco	CA	94115	415-292-9200	931-7205	257
Consulate General 4000 Ponce de Leon Ste 590 *Web:* www.consmiami.esteri.it	Coral Gables	FL	33146	305-374-6322	374-7945	257
Consulate General 1300 Post Oak Blvd Ste 660 *TF:* 800-637-9314 ■ *Web:* www.conshouston.esteri.it	Houston	TX	77056	713-850-7520	850-9113	257
Consulate General 690 Park Ave *Web:* www.consnewyork.esteri.it	New York	NY	10065	212-737-9100	249-4945	257
Embassy 3000 Whitehaven St NW *TF:* 800-222-1222 ■ *Web:* www.ambwashingtondc.esteri.it	Washington	DC	20008	202-612-4400	518-2154	257
Italy-America Chamber of Commerce Inc 730 Fifth Ave Ste 600 *TF:* 800-862-2793 ■ *Web:* www.italchamber.org	New York	NY	10019	212-459-0044	459-0090	138
Italy-America Chamber of Commerce of Texas Inc 1800 W Loop S Ste 1120 *Web:* www.iacctexas.com	Houston	TX	77027	713-626-9303	626-9309	138
Italy-America Chamber of Commerce Southeast Inc 2 S Biscayne Blvd Ste 1880 *Web:* www.iacc-miami.com	Miami	FL	33131	305-577-9868	577-3956	138
Italy-America Chamber of Commerce West Inc 10537 Santa Monica Blvd Ste 210 *Web:* www.iaccw.net	Los Angeles	CA	90025	310-557-3017	557-1217	138
ITAMCO 6100 Michigan Rd *Web:* www.itamco.com	Plymouth	IN	46563	574-936-2112		454
Itasca Community College 1851 E US Hwy 169 *TF:* 800-996-6422 ■ *Web:* www.itascacc.edu	Grand Rapids	MN	55744	218-327-4460	327-4350	162
Itasca County 123 NE Fourth St *TF:* 800-657-3929 ■ *Web:* www.co.itasca.mn.us	Grand Rapids	MN	55744	218-327-2847	327-2848	338
Itasca State Park 36750 Main Pk Dr *Web:* www.dnr.state.mn.us	Park Rapids	MN	56470	218-266-2100		565
Itasca-Mantrap Co-op Electrical Assn 16930 County Rd 6 *TF:* 888-713-3377 ■ *Web:* www.itasca-mantrap.com	Park Rapids	MN	56470	218-732-3377	732-5890	245
Itawamba Community College *Fulton* 602 W Hill St *Fax: Admissions ■ *Web:* www.iccms.edu	Fulton	MS	38843	662-862-8000	862-8234*	162
Tupelo 2176 S Eason Blvd *Web:* www.iccms.edu	Tupelo	MS	38804	662-620-5000		162
Itawamba County 107 W Wiygul St *Web:* itawambams.com	Fulton	MS	38843	662-862-4571		338
ITB Group Ltd 39555 Orchard Hill Pl Ste 157 *Web:* itbgroup.com	Novi	MI	48375	248-380-6310		256
ITC (Innovative Technologies Corp) 1020 Woodman Dr Ste 100 *TF:* 800-745-8050 ■ *Web:* www.itc-1.com	Dayton	OH	45432	937-252-2145	254-6853	178-10
ITC (Insurance Technology Consultants Inc) 2090 N Tustin Ave Ste 260 *Web:* www.itc-systems.com	Santa Ana	CA	92705	714-442-8702		177
Itc Engineering Services Inc 9959 Calaveras Rd *Web:* www.itcemc.com	Sunol	CA	94586	925-862-2944		256
ITC Holding Company LLC 1791 O G Skinner Dr Ste A *Web:* www.itchold.com	West Point	GA	31833	706-645-9482		300-3
ITC Learning Corp 1616 Anderson Rd Ste 109 *TF:* 800-638-3757 ■ *Web:* www.itclearning.com	McLean	VA	22102	800-638-3757		765
Itco Solutions Inc 1003 Whitehall Ln *Web:* www.itcosolutions.com	Redwood City	CA	94061	650-367-0514		317
Itcon Services Llc 3701 S George Mason Dr Unit 2502n *Web:* www.itcon-inc.com	Falls Church	VA	22041	703-671-6437		180
ITE (Institute of Transportation Engineers) 1099 14th St NW Ste 300W *TF:* 800-676-2775 ■ *Web:* www.ite.org	Washington	DC	20005	202-289-0222	289-7722	49-21
ITEA (International Technology Education Assn) 1914 Assn Dr Ste 201 *Web:* www.iteea.org	Reston	VA	20191	703-860-2100	860-0353	49-5
Itech Consulting Partners LLC 30 Church Hill Rd Ste 7 *TF:* 800-501-5863 ■ *Web:* www.itechcp.com	Newtown	CT	06470	203-270-0051		196
Itech Digital LLC 4287 W 96th St *TF:* 866-733-6673 ■ *Web:* itechdigital.com	Indianapolis	IN	46268	317-704-0440		693
I-Tech Solutions Inc 10 New England Business Ctr Ste 302 *Web:* www.i-techsolutions.com	Andover	MA	01810	978-794-8333		260
ITechLaw Assn 401 Edgewater Pl Ste 600 *Fax Area Code: 781 ■ *Web:* www.itechlaw.org	Wakefield	MA	01880	703-506-2895	224-1239*	48-9
Iteck Solutions Llc 4909 Morning Glory Ct *Web:* www.itecksolutions.com	Rockville	MD	20853	301-929-1852		180
ITEL Laboratories Inc 6745 Philips Industrial Blvd *Web:* www.itelinc.com	Jacksonville	FL	32256	904-363-0196		743
itelligence Inc 10856 Reed Hartman Hwy *Web:* itelligencegroup.com	Cincinnati	OH	45242	513-956-2000		196
Item House Inc 2920 S Steele St *Web:* itemhouseinc.com	Tacoma	WA	98409	253-627-7168	627-1070	155-5
Item, The 20 N Magnolia St PO Box 1677 *TF:* 800-888-3566 ■ *Web:* www.theitem.com	Sumter	SC	29151	803-774-1200	774-1210	532-2
Iten Industries 4602 Benefit Ave *TF Orders:* 800-227-4836 ■ *Web:* www.itenindustries.com	Ashtabula	OH	44004	440-997-6134	992-4966	599

Company	Phone	Fax	Class
ITERA International Energy Corp 9995 Gate Pkwy N Ste 400 .... Jacksonville FL 32246	904-996-8800		196
Itergy 2075 University Ste 700 .... Montreal QC H3A2L1 *TF:* 866-522-5881 ■ *Web:* www.itergy.com	514-845-5881		180
Iteris Inc 1700 Carnegie Ave Ste 100 .... Santa Ana CA 92705 *NYSE: ITI* ■ *TF:* 888-254-5487 ■ *Web:* www.iteris.com	949-270-9400		647
Iterna 2600 Beverly Dr .... Aurora IL 60502 *Web:* iternacorp.com	630-585-7400		253
ITG Derivatives LLC 601 S LaSalle Ste 300 .... Chicago IL 60605	312-334-8000		690
ITG Inc 1 Liberty Plaza 165 Broadway .... New York NY 10006 *TF:* 800-215-4484 ■ *Web:* www.itg.com	212-588-4000		690
Itgroove Professional Services Ltd 1035 Nakini Pl .... Brentwood Bay BC V8M1A3 *Web:* itgroove.net	250-220-4575		317
Ithaca College 953 Danby Rd .... Ithaca NY 14850 **Fax:* Admissions ■ *TF Admissions:* 800-429-4274 ■ *Web:* www.ithaca.edu	607-274-3124	274-1900*	166
Ithaca College Library 953 Danby Rd .... Ithaca NY 14850 *Web:* library.ithaca.edu	607-274-3206		434-6
Ithaca Journal 123 W State St. .... Ithaca NY 14850 *TF:* 866-254-3068 ■ *Web:* www.ithacajournal.com	607-272-2321		532-2
Ithaca Times 109 N Cayuga St .... Ithaca NY 14850 *Web:* www.ithaca.com	607-277-7000		532-5
Ithaca/Tompkins County Convention & Visitors Bureau 904 E Shore Dr .... Ithaca NY 14850 *TF:* 800-284-8422 ■ *Web:* www.visitithaca.com	607-272-1313		206
itherX Pharmaceuticals Inc 10790 Roselle St .... San Diego CA 92121 *Web:* www.itxpharma.com	858-824-1100		668
ITI (Information Technology Industry Council) 1101 K St NW Ste 610 .... Washington DC 20005 *Web:* www.itic.org	202-737-8888	638-4922	48-9
ITI (Industrial Tools Inc) 1111 S Rose Ave. .... Oxnard CA 93033 *TF:* 800-266-5561 ■ *Web:* www.iti-abrasives.com	805-483-1111	483-6302	493
ITI (International Trade Information Inc) 900 Las Vegas Blvd S Unit 908 .... Las Vegas NV 89101 *Web:* www.internationaltradeinformation.com	818-591-2255	591-2289	184
ITI TranscenData 5303 DuPont Cir. .... Milford OH 45150 *Web:* www.iti-global.com	513-576-3900		387
ITL (Industrial Timber & Lumber Corp) 23925 Commerce Park Rd .... Beachwood OH 44122 *TF:* 800-829-9663 ■ *Web:* www.itlcorp.com	216-831-3140	831-4734	683
ITM (Incentive Travel & Meetings) 970 Clementstone Dr Ste 100. .... Atlanta GA 30342 *Web:* www.usaitm.com	404-252-2728	252-8328	384
Itm Marketing Inc 470 Downtowner Plaza .... Coshocton OH 43812 *TF:* 800-575-4283 ■ *Web:* www.itmmarketing.com	740-295-3575		624
ITN Energy Systems Inc 8130 Shaffer Pkwy .... Littleton CO 80127 *Web:* www.itnes.com	303-420-1141		668
ITNS (International Transplant Nurses Society) 8735 W Higgins Rd Ste 300 .... Chicago IL 60631 *TF:* 800-776-8636 ■ *Web:* www.itns.org	847-375-6340	375-6341	49-8
Ito Consulting Group Llc 90 Federal St .... Belchertown MA 01007 *Web:* www.itoconsultinggroup.com	413-323-8785		196
Itochu Logistics (USA) Corp 1830 W 205th St. .... Torrance CA 90501 *Web:* www.ilogi.co.jp	310-787-6500		314
Itochu Technology Inc 3945 Freedom Cir Ste 350 .... Santa Clara CA 95054 *Web:* www.ctc-america.com	408-727-8810	727-9391	174
Itp of Usa Inc 520 E Bainbridge St .... Elizabethtown PA 17022 *TF:* 800-561-3357 ■ *Web:* www.itpofusa.com	717-367-3670		627
ITP Worldwide Inc 20 N Main St Ste 300 .... Sherborn MA 01770 *Web:* www.itpww.com	508-650-1031	650-1503	260
ITR Economics 77 Sundial Ave Ste 510w .... Manchester NH 03103 *Web:* www.itreconomics.com	603-796-2500		466
ITR Group Inc 2520 Lexington Ave S Ste 500 .... Saint Paul MN 55120 *TF:* 866-290-3423 ■ *Web:* www.itrgroupinc.com	866-290-3423		193
ITR of Georgia Inc 3346 Montreal .... Tucker GA 30084 *Web:* itrps.com	770-496-0366		317
Itran Precision Rubber 375 Metuchen Rd .... South Plainfield NJ 07080 *Web:* www.itranrubber.com	908-754-8100	757-1820	676
ITRenew Inc 8356 Central Ave. .... Newark CA 94560 *Web:* www.itrenew.com	408-744-9600		225
Itron Inc 2111 N Molter Rd. .... Liberty Lake WA 99019 *NASDAQ: ITRI* ■ *TF:* 800-635-5461 ■ *Web:* www.itron.com	509-924-9900	891-3355	248
ITS (Intelligent Transportation Society of America) 1100 17th St NW Ste 1200 .... Washington DC 20036 *TF:* 800-374-8472 ■ *Web:* www.itsa.org	202-484-4847	484-3483	49-21
ITS (International Thermal Systems LLC) 4697 W Greenfield Ave .... Milwaukee WI 53214 *TF:* 800-245-1869 ■ *Web:* internationalthermalsystems.com	414-672-7700	672-8800	318
ITS Logistics LLC 555 Vista Blvd .... Sparks NV 89434 *TF:* 844-668-3487 ■ *Web:* www.its4logistics.com	775-358-5300		314
Its Technologies Inc 7060 Spring Meadows Dr W Ste D .... Holland OH 43528 *TF:* 800-432-6607 ■ *Web:* www.itstechnologies.com	419-842-2100		260
ITSource Technology Inc 1401 Los Gamos Dr Ste 102 .... San Rafael CA 94903 *TF:* 866-548-4911 ■ *Web:* www.itsourcetek.com	415-472-5700		180
ITSqc LLC 3945 Forbes Ave Ste 422 .... Pittsburgh PA 15213 *Web:* www.itsqc.org	412-436-5212		196
ITT Aerospace Controls 28150 Industry Dr. .... Valencia CA 91355 *TF:* 800-854-3028 ■ *Web:* www.ittaerospace.com	661-295-4000	294-1750	790
ITT Corp 1133 Westchester Ave .... White Plains NY 10604 **Fax:* Mktg ■ *Web:* www.bellgossett.com	914-641-2000	696-2950*	641
ITT Educational Services Inc 13000 N Meridian St .... Carmel IN 46032 *NYSE: ESI* ■ *TF:* 800-388-3368 ■ *Web:* www.ittesi.com	317-706-9200		242
ITT Goulds Pumps Industries/Goulds Industrial Pumps Group 240 Fall St .... Seneca Falls NY 13148 *TF:* 800-327-7700 ■ *Web:* www.gouldspumps.com	315-568-2811	568-2418	789
ITT Industries Inc 1133 Westchester Ave. .... White Plains NY 10604 *NYSE: ITT* ■ *TF:* 800-254-2823 ■ *Web:* www.itt.com	914-641-2000	696-2950	253
ITT Industries Inc Engineered Valves Div 33 Centerville Rd .... Lancaster PA 17603 *TF:* 800-366-1111 ■ *Web:* www.engvalves.com	717-509-2200	509-2336	789
ITT Standard 175 Standard Pkwy. .... Cheektowaga NY 14227 **Fax Area Code:* 716 ■ *TF:* 800-447-7700 ■ *Web:* www.ittstandard.com	800-281-4111	897-1777*	91
ITT Technical Institute *Torrance* 2555 W 190th St Ste 125 .... Torrance CA 90504 *Web:* www.itt-tech.edu	310-965-5900		800
ITT Technical Institute Arlington 551 Ryan Plaza Dr .... Arlington TX 76011 *TF:* 888-288-4950 ■ *Web:* www.itt-tech.edu	817-794-5100		800
ITT Technical Institute Austin 6330 Hwy 290 E Ste 150 .... Austin TX 78723 *TF:* 800-431-0677 ■ *Web:* www.itt-tech.edu	512-467-6800		800
ITT Technical Institute Boise 12302 W Explorer Dr .... Boise ID 83713 *TF:* 800-666-4888 ■ *Web:* www.itt-tech.edu	208-322-8844		800
ITT Technical Institute Dayton 3325 S- Eight Rd .... Dayton OH 45414 *TF:* 800-568-3241 ■ *Web:* www.itt-tech.edu	937-264-7700		800
ITT Technical Institute Grand Rapids 1980 Metro Ct SW .... Wyoming MI 49519 *TF:* 800-632-4676 ■ *Web:* www.itt-tech.edu	616-406-1200		800
ITT Technical Institute Greenfield 6300 W Layton Ave. .... Greenfield WI 53220 *TF:* 800-658-5744 ■ *Web:* www.itt-tech.edu	414-282-9494		800
ITT Technical Institute Harrisburg 449 Eisenhower Blvd Ste 100 .... Harrisburg PA 17111 *TF:* 800-847-4756 ■ *Web:* www.itt-tech.edu	717-565-1700		800
ITT Technical Institute Henderson 2300 Corporate Cir Ste 150 .... Henderson NV 89074 *Web:* www.itt-tech.edu	702-558-5404		800
ITT Technical Institute High Point 4050 Piedmont Pkwy .... High Point NC 27265 *TF:* 877-536-5231 ■ *Web:* www.itt-tech.edu	336-819-5900		800
ITT Technical Institute Houston 15651 N Fwy .... Houston TX 77090 *TF:* 800-879-6486 ■ *Web:* www.itt-tech.edu	281-873-0512		800
ITT Technical Institute Indianapolis 9511 Angola Ct. .... Indianapolis IN 46268 *TF:* 800-937-4488 ■ *Web:* www.itt-tech.edu	317-875-8640		800
ITT Technical Institute Jacksonville 7011 AC Skinner Pkwy Ste 140 .... Jacksonville FL 32256 *TF:* 800-318-1264 ■ *Web:* www.itt-tech.edu	904-573-9100		800
ITT Technical Institute Lexington 3020 Old Todds Rd. .... Lexington KY 40509 *Web:* www.itt-tech.edu	859-246-3300		800
ITT Technical Institute Mount Prospect 3800 N Wilke RD .... Arlington Heights IL 60004 *Web:* www.itt-tech.edu	847-454-1800		800
ITT Technical Institute Murray 920 Levoy Dr .... Murray UT 84123 *TF:* 800-365-2136 ■ *Web:* www.itt-tech.edu	801-263-3313		800
ITT Technical Institute Nashville 2845 Elm Hill Pk. .... Nashville TN 37214 *TF:* 800-331-8386 ■ *Web:* www.itt-tech.edu	615-889-8700		800
ITT Technical Institute Newburgh 10999 Stahl Rd. .... Newburgh IN 47630 *TF:* 800-832-4488 ■ *Web:* www.itt-tech.edu	812-858-1600		800
ITT Technical Institute Norfolk 5425 Robin Hood Rd Ste 100 .... Norfolk VA 23513 *TF:* 888-253-8324 ■ *Web:* www.itt-tech.edu	757-466-1260		800
ITT Technical Institute Omaha 1120 N 103rd Plaza Ste 200 .... Omaha NE 68114 *TF:* 800-677-9260 ■ *Web:* www.itt-tech.edu	402-331-2900		800
ITT Technical Institute Orland Park 11551 184th Pl. .... Orland Park IL 60467 *Web:* www.itt-tech.edu	708-326-3200		800
ITT Technical Institute Portland 9500 NE Cascades Pkwy .... Portland OR 97220 *TF:* 800-234-5488 ■ *Web:* www.itt-tech.edu	503-255-6500		800
ITT Technical Institute San Antonio 5700 NW Pkwy .... San Antonio TX 78249 *TF:* 800-880-0570 ■ *Web:* www.itt-tech.edu	210-694-4612		800
ITT Technical Institute Seattle 12720 Gateway Dr Ste 100 .... Seattle WA 98168 *TF:* 800-422-2029 ■ *Web:* www.itt-tech.edu	206-244-3300		800
ITT Technical Institute Springfield 7300 Boston Blvd .... Springfield VA 22153 *TF:* 888-253-8324 ■ *Web:* www.itt-tech.edu	703-440-9535		800
ITT Technical Institute Tempe 5005 S Wendler Dr .... Tempe AZ 85282 *TF:* 800-879-4881 ■ *Web:* www.itt-tech.edu	602-437-7500		800
ITT Technical Institute Troy 1522 E Big Beaver Rd .... Troy MI 40083 *TF:* 800-832-6817 ■ *Web:* www.itt-tech.edu	248-524-1000		800
ITT Technical Institute Tucson 1455 W River Rd. .... Tucson AZ 85704 *TF:* 800-870-9730 ■ *Web:* www.itt-tech.edu	520-408-7488		800
ITT Technical Institute Warrensville Heights 4700 Richmond Rd. .... Warrensville Heights OH 44128 *TF:* 800-741-3494 ■ *Web:* www.itt-tech.edu	216-896-6500		800
ITT Technical Institute Youngstown 1030 N Meridian Rd .... Youngstown OH 44509 *TF:* 800-832-5001 ■ *Web:* www.itt-tech.edu	330-270-1600		800
ITU AbsorbTech Inc 2700 S 160th St. .... New Berlin WI 53151 *TF:* 888-729-4884 ■ *Web:* www.ituabsorbtech.com	888-729-4884		442
Ituran USA Inc 1700 NW 64th St Ste 100 .... Fort Lauderdale FL 33309 *TF:* 800-667-6362 ■ *Web:* www.ituranusa.com	954-484-3806		224
ITUS Corp 12100 Wilshire Blvd Ste 1275 .... Los Angeles CA 90025 *OTC: COPY* ■ *Web:* ITUScorp.com	310-484-5200		735

Company	Phone	Fax	Class
ITV Studios America Inc 15303 Ventura Blvd Bldg C Ste 800, Los Angeles CA 91403 *Web:* www.itvstudios.com	818-455-4000		110
ITVS (Independent Television Service) 651 Brannan St Ste 410, San Francisco CA 94107 *TF:* 888-572-8918 ■ *Web:* www.itvs.org	415-356-8383	356-8391	742
ITW (Illinois Tool Works Inc) 3600 West Lake Ave, Glenview IL 60026 *NYSE:* ITW ■ *Web:* www.itw.com	847-724-7500	657-4261	386
ITW Brands 955 National Pkwy Ste 95500, Schaumburg IL 60173 *TF:* 877-489-2726 ■ *Web:* www.itwbrands.com	847-944-2260	619-8344	278
ITW Buildex 1349 W Bryn Mawr, Itasca IL 60143 *TF:* 800-848-5611 ■ *Web:* www.itwbuildex.com	630-595-3500	595-3549	278
ITW Coding Products 111 W Pk Dr, Kalkaska MI 49646 *Web:* www.codingproducts.com	231-258-5521	258-6120	628
ITW Drawform 500 Fairview Rd, Zeeland MI 49464 *TF:* 800-633-8078 ■ *Web:* www.drawform.com	616-772-1910	772-9572	489
ITW Dymon 805 E Old 56 Hwy, Olathe KS 66061 *TF:* 800-443-9536 ■ *Web:* itwprofessionalbrands.com	913-829-6296	397-8707	151
ITW Fluids North America 475 N Gary Ave, Carol Stream IL 60188 **Fax Area Code:* 913 ■ *TF:* 800-452-5823 ■ *Web:* itwfluidsna.com	800-452-5823	397-8704*	541
ITW Food Equipment Group 701 S Ridge Ave, Troy OH 45374 *Web:* www.hobartcorp.com	937-332-3000	332-2852	298
ITW Hi-Cone 1140 W Bryn Mawr Ave, Itasca IL 60143 *Web:* www.hicone.com	630-438-5300	438-5315	548
ITW Highland 1240 Wolcott St, Waterbury CT 06722 *Web:* www.itwhighland.com	203-574-3200	754-4019	489
ITW Industrial Finishing 195 International Blvd, Glendale Heights IL 60139	630-237-5000		172
ITW Insulation Systems 1370 E 40th St Ste 1 Bldg 7, Houston TX 77022 **Fax Area Code:* 713 ■ *TF:* 800-231-1024 ■ *Web:* www.itwinsulation.com	800-231-1024	691-7492*	389
ITW Minigrip Inc 8125 Cobb Ctr Dr, Kennesaw GA 30152 *Web:* www.minigrip.com	770-422-4187		601
ITW Polymers Sealants North America 111 S Nursery R, Irving TX 75060 *TF Hotline:* 800-878-7876 ■ *Web:* itwsealants.com	972-438-9111	554-3939	3
ITW Sexton Can Company Inc 3101 Sexton Rd, Decatur AL 35603 *TF:* 800-917-6171 ■ *Web:* www.sextoncan.com	256-355-5850		393
ITW Switches 195 E Algonquin Rd, Des Plaines IL 60016 *TF:* 800-544-3354 ■ *Web:* www.itwswitches.com	847-876-9400	876-9440	729
ITW United Silicone 4471 Walden Ave, Lancaster NY 14086 *TF:* 800-365-8222 ■ *Web:* www.unitedsilicone.com	716-681-8222	681-8789	386
ITW Vortec 10125 Carver Rd, Cincinnati OH 45242 *TF:* 800-441-7475 ■ *Web:* www.itw-air.com	513-891-7485	891-4092	14
ITworld.com Inc 492 Old Connecticut Path P.O. Box 9208, Framingham MA 01701 *Web:* www.itworld.com	508-820-8246		387
Itx Corp 1169 Pittsford Victor Rd Ste 100, Pittsford NY 14534 *TF:* 800-600-7785 ■ *Web:* www.itx.com	585-899-4888		224
IU Health Ball Memorial Hospital 2401 W University Ave, Muncie IN 47303 *Web:* www.iuhealth.org	765-747-3111	741-2848	374-3
IU School of Medicine - Office of Gift Development 1110 W Michigan St Lo 506, Indianapolis IN 46202 *TF:* 800-643-6975 ■ *Web:* medgifts.medicine.iu.edu	317-274-3270		305
IUEC (International Union of Elevator Constructors) 7154 Columbia Gateway Dr, Columbia MD 21046 *Web:* www.iuec.org	410-953-6150		49-3
iUniverse 1663 Liberty Dr, Bloomington IN 47403 *TF:* 800-288-4677 ■ *Web:* www.iuniverse.com	812-330-2909	355-4085	637-2
IUPAT (International Union of Painters & Allied Trades) 7234 Pkwy Dr, Hanover MD 21076 *TF:* 800-554-2479 ■ *Web:* iupat.org	410-564-5900		414
IV Most Consulting Inc 33 Park Dr, Mt Kisco NY 10549 *TF:* 800-448-6678 ■ *Web:* www.ivmost.com	914-864-2781		177
iv3 Solutions Corp 50 Minthorn Blvd Ste 301, Markham ON L3T7X8 *TF:* 877-995-2651 ■ *Web:* www.iv3solutions.com	877-995-2651		365
IVAMS (Inland Valley Arbitration & Mediation Service) 8287 White Oak Ave, Rancho Cucamonga CA 91730 *TF:* 800-244-8814 ■ *Web:* www.ivams.com	909-466-1665	466-1796	41
Ivan Allen Jr Braves Museum & Hall of Fame 755 Hank Aaron Dr SE, Atlanta GA 30315 *Web:* atlanta.braves.mlb.com	404-614-2310		522
Ivan C Dutterer Inc 115 Ann St, Hanover PA 17331 *Web:* www.ivancdutterer.com	717-637-8977		499
Ivan Franko Museum 200 McGregor St, Winnipeg MB R2W2K4 *TF:* 866-747-9323 ■ *Web:* www.museumsmanitoba.com	204-589-4397	942-3749	520
Ivanhoe Broadcast News 2745 W Fairbanks Ave, Winter Park FL 32789 *Web:* www.ivanhoe.com	407-740-0789	740-5320	742
Ivanhoe Cambridge Inc 1001 Sq Victoria bureau C-500, Montreal QC H2Z2B5 *Web:* www.ivanhoecambridge.com	514-841-7600		205
Ivanhoe Mines Ltd 654-999 Canada Pl, Vancouver BC V6C3E1 *Web:* www.ivanhoemines.com	604-688-6630		502
Ivanhoe Tool & Die Company Inc 590 Thompson Rd, Thompson CT 06277 *Web:* www.ivanhoetool.com	860-923-9541	923-2497	757
i-Vantage Inc 400 Talcott Ave, Watertown MA 02472 **Fax Area Code:* 253 ■ *Web:* www.i-vantage.com	617-393-2338	679-2959*	260
Ivar Jacobson Consulting Llc 211 N Union St Ste 100, Alexandria VA 22314 *Web:* www.ivarjacobson.com	703-434-3344		196
Ivar's Acres of Clams 1001 Alaskan Way Pier 54, Seattle WA 98104 *Web:* www.ivars.com	206-624-6852	624-4895	671
Ivarson Inc 3100 W Green Tree Rd, Milwaukee WI 53209 *TF:* 800-726-3331 ■ *Web:* ivarsoninc.com	414-351-0700		757
IVAS (International Veterinary Acupuncture Society) 1730 S College Ave Ste 301, Fort Collins CO 80525 *Web:* www.ivas.org	970-266-0666	266-0777	48-3
IVC (International Visual Corp) 11500 Blvd Armand Bombardier, Montreal QC H1E2W9 *TF:* 866-643-0570 ■ *Web:* www.ivcweb.com	514-643-0570	643-4867	286
IVCi LLC 601 Old Willets Path, Hauppauge NY 11788 *TF:* 800-224-7083 ■ *Web:* www.ivci.com	631-273-5800	273-7277	736
IVDiagnostics Inc 9800 Connecticut Dr, Crown Point IN 46307 *Web:* www.ivdiagnostics.com	219-840-0007		743
Ivenuecom 9925 Painter Ave Ste A, Whittier CA 90605 *TF:* 800-683-8314 ■ *Web:* www.ivenue.com	800-683-8314		177
Ivers-Lee Inc 31 Hansen S, Brampton ON L6W3H7 *TF:* 800-265-1009 ■ *Web:* jonespackaging.com	905-451-5535		85
Iverson Language Associates Inc 111 W Pleasant St Ste 102, Milwaukee WI 53212 *Web:* iversonlang.com	414-271-1144		768
Ives Group Inc 9 Main St Ste 2F, Sutton MA 01590 *Web:* www.ivesinc.com	508-476-7007		225
IVESCO (Iowa Veterinary Supply Co) 124 Country Club Rd, Iowa Falls IA 50126	641-648-2529		475
Ivey 5679 SE International Way, Portland OR 97222 *Web:* www.ivey.com	503-794-9800		184
Ivey Kay (R) State Capitol, 600 Dexter Ave, Montgomery AL 36130 *Web:* governor.alabama.gov	334-242-7100	242-7100	343
Ivey Spencer Leadership Ctr 551 Windermere Rd, London ON N5X2T1 *TF:* 800-407-9832 ■ *Web:* www.iveyspencerleadershipcentre.com	519-679-4546		377
Ivey, Barnum & O'mara LLC 170 Mason St, Greenwich CT 06830 *TF:* 800-479-2284 ■ *Web:* www.ibolaw.com	203-661-6000		428
IVG Energy Ltd 20 E Greenway Pl Ste 400, Houston TX 77046 *Web:* www.ivgenergy.com	713-554-3700		194
IVI (Industrial Vehicles International Inc) 6737 E 12th St, Tulsa OK 74112 *Web:* www.indvehicles.com	918-836-6516	838-9529	470
Ivie & Associates Inc 601 Silveron Blvd Ste 200, Flower Mound TX 75028 *TF:* 800-908-5395 ■ *Web:* www.ivieinc.com	972-899-5000		195
Ivision Inc 1430 W Peachtree St NW, Atlanta GA 30309 *TF:* 800-525-0130 ■ *Web:* ivision.com	678-999-3002		225
IVMA (Idaho Veterinary Medical Assn) 1841 W Secluded Ct, Kuna ID 83634 *TF:* 800-552-7236 ■ *Web:* www.ivma.org	208-922-9431	922-9435	795
Ivory Consulting Corp 325 Lennon Ln, Walnut Creek CA 94598 *TF:* 800-531-5086 ■ *Web:* www.ivorycc.com	925-926-1100		177
Ivory Homes 970 E Woodoak Ln, Salt Lake City UT 84117 **Fax Area Code:* 801 ■ *TF:* 888-455-5561 ■ *Web:* www.ivoryhomes.com	888-455-5561	747-7090*	653
Ivory Investment Management LP 11755 Wilshire Blvd Ste 1350, Los Angeles CA 90025 *Web:* ivorycapital.co	310-899-7300		401
Ivory Jack's 2581 Goldstream Rd, Fairbanks AK 99709 *Web:* www.ivoryjacks.alaskansavvy.com	907-455-6665		671
Ivy at the Shore 1535 Ocean Ave, Santa Monica CA 90401 *Web:* theivyrestaurant.com	310-393-3113		671
IVY Biomedical Systems Inc 11 Business Pk Dr, Branford CT 06405 *TF:* 800-247-4614 ■ *Web:* www.ivybiomedical.com	203-481-4183	481-8734	250
Ivy Planning Group 15204 Omega Dr Ste 110, Rockville MD 20850 *Web:* www.ivygroupllc.com	301-963-1669		463
Ivy Tech Columbus College *Columbus* 4475 Central Ave, Columbus IN 47203 *TF:* 800-922-4838 ■ *Web:* www.ivytech.edu/columbus	812-372-9925	372-0311	800
Ivy Tech Community College *Bloomington* 200 Daniels Way, Bloomington IN 47404 *TF:* 866-447-0700 ■ *Web:* www.ivytech.edu	812-330-6137	330-6140	800
Central Indiana 50 W Fall Creek Pkwy N Dr, Indianapolis IN 46208 *TF:* 888-489-5463 ■ *Web:* www.ivytech.edu/indianapolis	317-921-4800	921-4753	800
Kokomo 1815 E Morgan St, Kokomo IN 46901 *TF:* 800-459-0561 ■ *Web:* www.ivytech.edu/kokomo	765-459-0561	454-5111	800
Muncie 4301 S Cowan Rd, Muncie IN 47302 *TF:* 800-589-8324 ■ *Web:* www.ivytech.edu/eastcentral	765-289-2291	289-2292	800
North Central 220 Dean Johnson Blvd, South Bend IN 46601 *TF:* 888-489-3478 ■ *Web:* www.ivytech.edu	574-289-7001	236-7177	800
Northwest 1440 E 35th Ave, Gary IN 46409 *TF:* 888-489-5463 ■ *Web:* www.ivytech.edu	219-981-1111	981-4415	800
Richmond 2357 Chester Blvd, Richmond IN 47374 *TF:* 800-659-4562 ■ *Web:* www.ivytech.edu	765-966-2656	962-8741	800
Southeast 590 Ivy Tech Dr, Madison IN 47250 *TF:* 800-403-2190 ■ *Web:* www.ivytech.edu	812-265-2580	265-4028	800
Southern Indiana 8204 old Indiana 311, Sellersburg IN 47172 *TF:* 800-321-9021 ■ *Web:* www.ivytech.edu	812-246-3301	246-9905	800
Southwest Indiana 3501 N First Ave, Evansville IN 47710 *TF:* 800-621-7440 ■ *Web:* www.ivytech.edu	812-426-2865	429-9878	800
Wabash Valley 8000 S Education Dr, Terre Haute IN 47802 *TF:* 888-489-5463 ■ *Web:* www.ivytech.edu	812-298-2293	298-2294	800
Ivy, The 113 N Robertson Blvd, Los Angeles CA 90048 *Web:* theivyrestaurants.com	310-274-8303		671
IWA (International Webmasters Assn) 119 E Union St Ste A, Pasadena CA 91103 *TF:* 866-607-1773 ■ *Web:* www.iwanet.org	626-449-3709		48-9
Iwaki America Inc 5 Boynton Rd, Holliston MA 01746 *Web:* www.walchem.com	508-429-1110	429-7433	641
iWay Software 2 Penn Plaza, New York NY 10121 *TF:* 800-736-6130 ■ *Web:* www.informationbuilders.com	212-736-4433	967-6406	194

	City	State	ZIP	Phone	Fax	Class
IWCO Direct Holdings Inc						
7951 Powers Blvd	Chanhassen	MN	55317	952-470-6460		195
Web: www.iwco.com						
iWeb Group Inc 20 Place du Commerce	Montreal	QC	H3E1Z6	514-286-4242		225
Web: iweb.com						
IWITTS (National Institute for Women in Trades Technology & Science)						
1150 Ballena Blvd Ste 102	Alameda	CA	94501	510-749-0200	749-0500	49-19
Web: www.iwitts.org						
IWLA (International Warehouse Logistics Assn)						
2800 S River Rd Ste 260	Des Plaines	IL	60018	847-813-4699	813-0115	49-21
Web: www.iwla.com						
IWLA (Izaak Walton League of America)						
707 Conservation Ln	Gaithersburg	MD	20878	301-548-0150	548-0146	48-13
TF: 800-453-5463 ■ *Web:* www.iwla.org						
IWP (Inter-Wire Products) 355 Main St	Armonk	NY	10504	914-273-6633		813
Web: www.interwiregroup.com						
IWPA (International Wood Products Assn)						
4214 King St	Alexandria	VA	22302	703-820-6696	820-8550	49-3
TF: 855-435-0005 ■ *Web:* www.iwpawood.org						
Iwpc 610 Louis Dr	Warminster	PA	18974	215-293-9000		463
Web: www.iwpc.org						
IWSA (Energy Recovery Council)						
2200 Wilson Blvd Ste 310	Arlington	VA	22201	202-467-6240		48-12
Web: energyrecoverycouncil.org						
IWT (Anita Borg Institute for Women and Technology)						
1501 Page Mill Rd MS 1105	Palo Alto	CA	94304	650-352-7500	852-8172	48-9
Web: anitaborg.org						
Iwv Insurance 1310 N Norma St	Ridgecrest	CA	93555	760-446-3544		390
Web: www.ridgecrestcainsurancegroup.com						
IX Ctr 1-X Ctr Dr	Cleveland	OH	44135	216-676-6000		205
Web: www.ixcenter.com						
IXI Technology 23231 La Palma Ave	Yorba Linda	CA	92887	714-692-3800	692-3838	625
Web: ixitech.com						
Ixia 26601 W Agoura Rd	Calabasas	CA	91302	818-871-1800	871-1805	248
NASDAQ: XXIA ■ *TF:* 877-367-4942 ■ *Web:* www.ixiacom.com						
I-XL Building Products Ltd						
4900 102 Ave SE	Calgary	AB	T2X2X8	403-526-5901		150
Web: ixlmasonry.com						
iXP Corp						
Princeton Forrestal Village 103 Main St	Princeton	NJ	08540	609-759-5100		194
Web: www.ixpcorp.com						
Ixtapa 6132 Atlanta Hwy	Montgomery	AL	36117	334-272-5232		671
IXYS Corp 3540 Bassett St	Santa Clara	CA	95054	408-982-0700	748-9788	696
NASDAQ: IXYS ■ *Web:* www.ixys.com						
Iyka Enterprises 3890 E Main St	Saint Charles	IL	60174	630-372-3900		177
Web: www.iyka.com						
Izaak Walton League of America (IWLA)						
707 Conservation Ln	Gaithersburg	MD	20878	301-548-0150	548-0146	48-13
TF: 800-453-5463 ■ *Web:* www.iwla.org						
Izard County 80 E Main St PO Box 327	Melbourne	AR	72556	870-368-4316		338
Web: izardcountyar.org						
Izatys Golf Resort 40005 85th Ave	Onamia	MN	56359	320-532-4574		669
Web: www.izatys.com						
IZEA Inc 480 N Orlando Ave Ste 200	Winter Park	FL	32789	407-674-6911		7
Web: www.izea.com						
Izett & Assoc LLC 912 Killian Hill Rd	Lilburn	GA	30047	770-935-9575		390
I-Zu Japanese Restaurant & Grocery						
5252 N Dixie Dr	Dayton	OH	45414	937-277-9596		671
Izumi's 2150 N Prospect Ave	Milwaukee	WI	53202	414-271-5258		671
Web: www.izumis.com						
Izumo Sushi 4412 Ming Ave	Bakersfield	CA	93309	661-398-0608		671
Izzydesign 17237 Van Wagoner Rd	Spring Lake	MI	49456	616-916-9369		319-1
TF: 800-543-5449 ■ *Web:* www.izzyplus.com						

J

	City	State	ZIP	Phone	Fax	Class
J & A Freight Systems Inc						
4704 Irving Park Rd Ste 8	Chicago	IL	60641	877-668-3378	205-7725*	311
**Fax Area Code: 773* ■ *TF:* 877-668-3378 ■ *Web:* jandafreight.com						
J & A Printing Inc PO Box 457	Hiawatha	IA	52233	319-393-1781		627
TF: 800-793-1781 ■ *Web:* www.japrinting.com						
J & B Importers Inc 11925 SW 128th St	Miami	FL	33186	305-238-1866		710
Web: jbi.bike/web						
J & B Sausage Company Inc 100 Main St	Waelder	TX	78959	830-788-7511	788-7279	296-36
Web: www.jbfoods.com						
J & B Supply Inc 4915 S Zero St	Fort Smith	AR	72903	479-649-4915	649-4911	612
TF: 800-262-2028 ■ *Web:* www.jandbsupply.com						
J & D Interiors Inc						
8300 Briarwood St Ste A	Anchorage	AK	99518	907-349-9685		362
Web: ilovejd.com						
J & E Earl Manufacturing Co						
7925 215th St W	Lakeville	MN	55044	952-469-3933		483
Web: www.jecompanies.com						
J & E Earll Manufacturing						
4500 Vly Industrial Blvd S	Shakopee	MN	55379	952-445-4500		492
TF: 800-241-2718 ■ *Web:* www.nybo.com						
J & E Metal Fabricators 1 Coan Pl	Metuchen	NJ	08840	732-548-9650		697
Web: www.metalfab.com						
J & E Supply & Fastner Company Inc						
1903 SE 59th St	Oklahoma City	OK	73129	405-670-1234		351
TF: 800-677-7922 ■ *Web:* www.jandesupply.com						
J & G Sales Inc 440 Miller Valley Rd	Prescott	AZ	86301	928-445-9650		711
TF: 800-606-0370 ■ *Web:* jgsales.com						
J & G Steel Corp 2429 Industrial Rd	Sapulpa	OK	74066	918-227-3131		480
J & G's Steakhouse						
6000 E Camelback Rd	Scottsdale	AZ	85251	480-214-8000	214-8001	671
Web: www.jgsteakhousescottsdale.com						
J & H Oil Co 2696 Chicago Dr SW	Wyoming	MI	49519	616-534-2181		324
Web: www.jhoil.com						
J & J Industries Inc						
818 J & J Dr PO Box 1287	Dalton	GA	30721	706-529-2100	275-4433	131
TF: 800-241-4586 ■ *Web:* www.jjflooringgroup.com						
J & J Machine Inc						
12655 Industrial Blvd	Elk River	MN	55330	763-421-0114		757
Web: www.jandjmachine.com						
J & J Motor Service Inc						
2338 S Indiana Ave	Chicago	IL	60616	312-225-3323	225-9873	780
Web: jjexhibitors.com						
J & J Security Services Corp						
2922 Howland Blvd Ste 2	Deltona	FL	32725	386-789-5555		693
TF: 877-532-7233 ■ *Web:* www.jandjsecurity.com						
J & J Sheetmetal Works Inc						
414 Commerce Rd	Vestal	NY	13850	607-729-3566		567
Web: jjservicegroup.com						
J & J Snack Foods Corp						
6000 Central Hwy	Pennsauken	NJ	08109	856-665-9533	665-6718	296-25
NASDAQ: JJSF ■ *TF:* 800-486-9533 ■ *Web:* www.jjsnack.com						
J & K Contracting 8903 Pioneer Rd	Neenah	WI	54956	920-836-9539		697
J & L Mail Services Inc						
2100 Nelson Miller Pkwy	Louisville	KY	40223	800-346-9117		7
TF: 800-346-9117 ■ *Web:* www.jandlmarketing.com						
J & L Self Defense Products Inc						
70 Defense Dr	Berkeley Springs	WV	25411	304-258-2900		148
Web: www.selfdefenseproducts.com						
J & M Brown Company Inc						
267 Amory St	Jamaica Plain	MA	02130	617-522-6800	522-6422	189-4
Web: www.jmbco.com						
J & M Industries Inc						
300 Ponchatoula Pkwy	Ponchatoula	LA	70454	985-386-6000		67
TF: 800-989-1002 ■ *Web:* www.jm-ind.com						
J & M Machine Products Inc						
1821 Manor Dr	Muskegon	MI	49441	231-755-1622		757
Web: www.jmmachine.com						
J & M Plating Inc 4500 Kishwaukee St	Rockford	IL	61109	815-964-4975		481
TF: 877-344-3044 ■ *Web:* www.jmplating.com						
J & S Cafeteria Inc						
110 Westover Dr	High Point	NC	27265	336-884-0404		670
Web: www.jandscafeteria.com						
J & s Management						
702 Marshall St Ste 420	Redwood City	CA	94063	650-361-8350		652
J A Moss Construction PO Box 180460	Richland	MS	39218	601-939-4141		449
Web: www.jamossconstruction.com						
J A Piper Roofing Co						
209 Commerce Rd	Greenville	SC	29611	864-269-6645		697
Web: www.piperroofing.com						
J A Sauer Co 4559 Peoples Rd	Pittsburgh	PA	15237	412-931-7200		189-10
Web: jasauerco.com						
J A Sutherland Inc 228 MN St	Red Bluff	CA	96080	530-529-1470		670
Web: www.jasutherland.com						
J A T of Fort Wayne Inc						
5031 Industrial Rd	Fort Wayne	IN	46825	260-482-8447	482-9990	780
Web: www.jatoffortwayne.com						
J Alexander's Corp						
3401 W End Ave Ste 260	Nashville	TN	37203	615-269-1900	269-1999	670
NASDAQ: JAX ■ *TF:* 888-528-1991 ■ *Web:* www.jalexandersholdings.com						
J Alexanders 3320 Galleria Cir	Hoover	AL	35244	205-733-9995		671
NASDAQ: JAX ■ *Web:* www.jalexandersholdings.com						
J Allan Writing & Design Studios LLC						
115 12th Ave NE	Saint Petersburg	FL	33701	727-822-2526		344
Web: www.jallanstudios.com						
J B M Inc 2651 Scottish Pike	Knoxville	TN	37920	865-573-9800		480
Web: www.jbmincorporated.com						
J B Poindexter & Company Inc						
600 Travis St Ste 200	Houston	TX	77002	713-655-9800	951-9038	60
Web: www.jbpoindexter.com						
J Brand Holdings LLC						
1214 E 18th St	Los Angeles	CA	90021	213-749-3500		157-6
Web: www.jbrandjeans.com						
J Bulow Campbell Foundation						
3050 Peachtree Rd NW Ste 270	Atlanta	GA	30305	404-658-9066		305
Web: www.jbcf.org						
J Byrne Agency Inc						
5200 New Jersey Ave	Wildwood	NJ	08260	609-522-3406		390
Web: jbyrneagency.com						
J C Bamford Excavators Ltd						
2000 Bamford Blvd	Pooler	GA	31322	912-447-2000	447-2299	358
Web: www.jcb.com/en-us						
J C Foodservice Inc						
415 S Atlantic Blvd	Monterey Park	CA	91754	626-308-1988		111
TF: 800-443-4746 ■ *Web:* www.actionsales.com						
J C Hanlon Consulting Inc						
52611 Jessie Dr	Chesterfield	MI	48051	586-435-6231		196
Web: www.jchci.com						
J C Holliday Library 217 Graham St	Clinton	NC	28328	910-592-4153		434-3
J C Machine Works & Fabricating Inc						
1070 Neosho Ave	Baton Rouge	LA	70802	225-359-6117		454
J C Marketing Associates Inc						
467 Main St PO Box 289	Wakefield	MA	01880	781-245-7070		195
Web: jcmarketingassociates.com						
J C Millwork Inc						
501 Lakeside Pkwy Ste 150	Flower Mound	TX	75028	469-702-2570		499
TF: 800-254-3423 ■ *Web:* www.jcmillwork.com						
J C Snavely & Sons Inc						
150 Main St	Landisville	PA	17538	717-898-2241	898-5208	817
Web: www.jcsnavely.com						
J C Steele & Sons Inc						
710 S Mulberry St	Statesville	NC	28677	704-872-3681		454
TF: 800-278-3353 ■ *Web:* www.jcsteele.com						
J C Taylor Antique Automobile Agency Inc						
320 S 69th St	Upper Darby	PA	19082	800-345-8290		390
TF: 800-345-8290 ■ *Web:* www.jctaylor.com						
J C Wilkins Plumbing Company Inc						
840 Massengill Pond Rd	Angier	NC	27501	919-639-6201		610
J Carter Marketing Inc						
205 Smithtown Blvd	Nesconset	NY	11767	631-979-5620		195
Web: www.jcartermarketing.com						
J Crew Group Inc 770 Broadway	New York	NY	10003	212-209-2500	209-2666	459
TF: 800-562-0258 ■ *Web:* www.jcrew.com						
J D Beauty 5 Adams Ave	Hauppauge	NY	11788	631-273-2800		77
TF: 800-523-2889 ■ *Web:* www.jdbeauty.com						

Name / Address	City	St	ZIP	Phone	Fax	Class
J D H Contracting 8109 Network Dr *Web:* www.jdhcontracting.com	Plainfield	IN	46168	317-839-0520		186
J D Products Inc 405 Commerce Ct *Web:* www.jdproducts.com	Vadnais Heights	MN	55127	651-483-9166		596
J D Rush C Inc 5900 E Lerdo Hwy *Web:* www.jdrush.com	Shafter	CA	93263	661-392-1900	399-2728	490
J D'Addario & Company Inc 595 Smith St *TF:* 800-323-2746 ■ *Web:* www.daddario.com	Farmingdale	NY	11735	631-439-3300	439-3333	527
J e b Advertising Inc 616 E Market St Ste 618 *Web:* www.jebadvertising.com	Louisville	KY	40202	502-625-1800		7
J Edgar Eubanks & Assoc 1 Windsor Cove Ste 305 *TF:* 800-445-8629 ■ *Web:* www.jee.com	Columbia	SC	29223	803-252-5646	765-0860	47
J Erik Jonsson Central Library 1515 Young St *Web:* www.dallaslibrary2.org/central	Dallas	TX	75201	214-670-1400		434-3
J F C Construction Inc 4901 Pacheco Blvd *Web:* www.jfcconstruction.com	Martinez	CA	94553	925-228-0924		186
J F Jacobs Inc 31523 W 8 Mile Rd *Web:* jfjacobsinc.net	Livonia	MI	48152	248-476-7888		189-10
J f Sato & Assoc Inc 5878 S Rapp St *Web:* www.jfsato.com	Littleton	CO	80120	303-797-1200		256
J Fletcher Creamer & Son Inc 101 E Broadway *TF:* 800-835-9801 ■ *Web:* www.jfcson.com	Hackensack	NJ	07601	201-488-9800	488-2901	189-5
J Frank Schmidt & Son Company Inc 9500 SE 327th Ave *Web:* www.jfschmidt.com	Boring	OR	97009	503-663-4128		192
J Freirich Foods Inc 815 W Kerr St PO Box 1529 *TF:* 800-554-4788 ■ *Web:* freirich.com	Salisbury	NC	28144	704-636-2621		473
J Gilbert's Wood Fired Steaks 8700 State Line Rd Ste 100 *Web:* www.jgilberts.com	Leawood	KS	66206	913-642-8070		670
J H I Engineering 3420 SW Macadam Ave *Web:* www.jhiengineering.com	Portland	OR	97239	503-223-7799		256
J Hall & Associates Inc: Hall Johnathan W CPA 327 S Market St	Troy	OH	45373	937-339-8417		2
J Hl Mail Marketing 3100 Borham Ave *TF:* 800-236-0581 ■ *Web:* www.jhl.com	Stevens Point	WI	54481	715-341-0581		195
J J Curran Crane Co 865 S Ft St *Web:* www.jjcurran.com	Detroit	MI	48217	313-842-1700		190
J J Plumbing LLC 4210 B ST NW Ste K *Web:* jjplumbingllc.com	Auburn	WA	98001	253-939-1390		189-10
J Josephson Inc 35 Horizon Blvd **Fax:* Cust Svc ■ *Web:* www.jjosephson.com	South Hackensack	NJ	07606	201-440-7000	440-7109*	802
J K Consulting 990 E Ninth St *TF:* 866-634-9633 ■ *Web:* www.jkconsulting.net	Lockport	IL	60441	815-500-4530		196
J K Datta Consultants Inc 711 W 40th St Ste 355	Baltimore	MD	21211	410-243-2882		180
J Kokolakis Contracting Inc 1500 Ocean Ave *Web:* www.jkokolakis.com	Bohemia	NY	11716	631-744-6147	744-6156	186
J L A Consulting 1013 N Causeway Blvd *Web:* www.jlaconsulting.net	Metairie	LA	70001	504-835-9639		196
J L Business Interiors Inc 515 Schoenhaar Dr PO Box 303 *TF:* 866-338-5524 ■ *Web:* www.jlbusinessinteriors.com	West Bend	WI	53090	262-338-2221	338-2269	320
J L Manufacturing Inc 12310 WA-99	Everett	WA	98204	425-355-3330		295
J L Patterson & Associates 725 W Town And Country Rd Ste 300 *Web:* www.jlpatterson.com	Orange	CA	92868	714-835-6355		177
J L Wallace Inc 9111 W College Pointe Dr *Web:* www.jlwallaceinc.com	Fort Myers	FL	33919	239-437-1111		186
J Lawrence Hall Company Inc 17 Progress Ave *Web:* jlawrencehall.com	Nashua	NH	03062	603-882-2021		189-10
J Lohr Vineyards & Wines 1000 Lenzen Ave *Web:* www.jlohr.com	San Jose	CA	95126	408-288-5057	993-2276	50-7
J Lorber Company Inc 2659 Bristol Pk *Web:* www.jlorber.com	Bensalem	PA	19020	215-638-2300		610
J M Field Marketing Inc 3570 NW 53rd Ct *TF:* 844-523-1957 ■ *Web:* www.jmfieldmarketing.com	Fort Lauderdale	FL	33309	954-523-1957		317
J m Fox Associates Inc 616 Dekalb St *TF:* 800-701-8480 ■ *Web:* jmfox.com	Norristown	PA	19401	610-275-5957		7
J McLaughlin 236250 Greenpoint Ave 2nd Fl Bldg 6 *TF:* 844-532-5625 ■ *Web:* jmclaughlin.com	Brooklyn	NY	11222	212-879-9565		157-4
J Morgan's Steakhouse 100 State St *Web:* www.capitolplaza.com	Montpelier	VT	05602	802-223-5222		671
J P Diamond Co 25 E James St *Web:* www.jpdiamond.com	Falconer	NY	14733	716-665-4100		116
J P Kane's Town & Country Furniture 641 Missouri Ave N *Web:* jpkfurniture.com	Largo	FL	33770	727-584-2121		321
J p King Auction Company Texas Ltd 108 Fountain Ave *Web:* www.jpking.com	Gadsden	AL	35901	256-546-5217		41
J P Noonan Transportation Inc 415 W St *TF:* 800-922-8026 ■ *Web:* www.jpnoonan.com	West Bridgewater	MA	02379	508-583-2880		780
J P R Communications 20750 Ventura Blvd Ste 104 *Web:* www.jprcom.com	Woodland Hills	CA	91364	818-884-8282		636
J Paul Getty Museum 1200 Getty Ctr Dr **Fax:* Hum Res ■ *Web:* www.getty.edu	Los Angeles	CA	90049	310-440-7300	440-7720*	520
J Paul Leonard Library 1630 Holloway Ave *Web:* www.library.sfsu.edu	San Francisco	CA	94132	415-338-1854	338-1504	434-6
J Polep Distribution Services Inc 705 Meadow St *TF:* 800-447-6537 ■ *Web:* www.jpolep.com	Chicopee	MA	01013	413-592-4141	592-5870	756
J R C Transportation Inc 47 Maple Ave *Web:* www.jrctransportation.com	Thomaston	CT	06787	860-283-0207	742-9379	780
J r d Systems Inc 42450 Hayes Rd Ste 3 *Web:* www.jrdsi.com	Clinton Township	MI	48038	586-416-1500		261
J R Miller & Assoc 2700 Saturn St *Web:* www.jrma.com	Brea	CA	92821	714-524-1870		256
J R Roberts Corp 7745 Greenback Ln Ste 300 *TF:* 800-767-3263 ■ *Web:* www.jrroberts.com	Citrus Heights	CA	95610	916-729-5600		186
J Reese Construction Inc 10805 Thornmint Rd Ste 200 *Web:* www.debinc.com	San Diego	CA	92127	858-592-6500		188-4
J Reynolds & Company Inc 369 Sansom Blvd	Saginaw	TX	76179	817-381-2549		708
J Robert Scott Inc 500 N Oak St *TF:* 877-207-5130 ■ *Web:* www.jrobertscott.com	Inglewood	CA	90302	310-680-4300		319-4
J Rockcliff Realtors 15 Railroad Ave *Web:* www.rockcliff.com	Danville	CA	94526	925-855-4000		652
J Rubin & Company Inc 305 Peoples Ave *Web:* rockfordconsulting.com	Rockford	IL	61104	815-964-9471		492
J S Logistics 4550 Gustine Ave *TF:* 800-814-2634 ■ *Web:* www.jslogistics.com	Saint Louis	MO	63116	314-832-6008		314
J S Redpath Ltd 710 McKeown Ave *Web:* www.redpathmining.com	North Bay	ON	P1A7M2	705-474-2461		787
J Sargeant Reynolds Community College PO Box 85622 **Fax:* Admissions ■ *TF:* 800-922-3420 ■ *Web:* www.reynolds.edu	Richmond	VA	23285	804-371-3000	371-3650*	162
Downtown 700 E Jackson St *Web:* www.jsr.vccs.edu	Richmond	VA	23219	804-523-5455	371-3650	162
J Smith Lanier & Co 300 W Tenth St *TF:* 800-226-4522 ■ *Web:* www.jsmithlanier.com	West Point	GA	31833	706-645-2211	643-0606	390
J T M Technologies Inc 204 Industrial Ct *Web:* www.jtmtechnologies.com	Wylie	TX	75098	972-429-6575	635-6905	621
J T Turner Construction Co Inc 2250 E Victory Dr Ste 104 *Web:* www.jttconst.com	Savannah	GA	31404	912-356-5611		186
J T Walker Industries Inc 861 N Hercules Ave	Clearwater	FL	33765	727-461-0501		234
J V Northwest Inc 390 S Redwood St *TF:* 800-365-8555 ■ *Web:* www.jvnw.com	Canby	OR	97013	503-263-2058		480
J W Martin Library 709 Oklahoma Blvd *Web:* www.nwosu.edu	Alva	OK	73717	580-327-8574		434-3
J Walter Thompson 466 Lexington Ave *Web:* www.jwt.com	New York	NY	10017	212-210-7000		4
J Wda 2359 Fourth Ave Ste 300 *TF:* 800-424-3996 ■ *Web:* www.jwdainc.com	San Diego	CA	92101	619-233-6777		196
J. & M. Golf Inc 319 Industrial Dr *Web:* jandmgolf.com	Griffith	IN	46319	219-922-1787		711
J. C. Macelroy Company Inc PO Box 850 *TF:* 800-622-3576 ■ *Web:* www.macelroy.com	Piscataway	NJ	08855	732-572-7100	572-7112	480
J. Calnan & Assoc Inc 3 Batterymarch Pk 5th fl *Web:* www.jcalnan.com	Quincy	MA	02169	617-801-0200		403
J. D. Young Company Inc 116 W Third St *Web:* www.jdyoung.com	Tulsa	OK	74103	918-582-9955		45
J. Edward Roush Lake 517 N Warren Rd *Web:* www.in.gov	Huntington	IN	46750	260-468-2165		565
J. Ennis Fabrics Ltd 12122 - 68 St *TF:* 800-663-6647 ■ *Web:* www.jennisfabrics.com	Edmonton	AB	T5B1R1	800-663-6647		406
J. F. Brennan Co Inc 820 Bainbridge *Web:* www.jfbrennan.com	La Crosse	WI	54603	608-784-7173	785-2090	465
J. H. Bennett & Company Inc PO Box 8028 *TF General:* 800-837-5426 ■ *Web:* www.jhbennett.com	Novi	MI	48376	248-596-5100	596-0640	385
J. J. Collins' Sons Inc 7125 Janes Ave Ste 200 *Web:* www.jjcollins.com	Woodridge	IL	60517	630-960-2525		627
J. Joseph Consulting 21732 Hardy Oak Blvd *Web:* www.jjosephconsulting.com	San Antonio	TX	78258	210-587-2750		463
J. Knipper & Company Inc 1 Healthcare Way *TF:* 888-564-7737 ■ *Web:* www.knipper.com	Lakewood	NJ	08701	888-564-7737		195
J. Krug & Associates Inc 1350 W Northwest Hwy Ste 100 *Web:* www.jkrug.com	Mount Prospect	IL	60056	847-392-8585		393
J. Lieb Foods Inc PO Box 389 *Web:* www.jliebfoods.com	Forest Grove	OR	97116	503-359-9279		296-20
J. M. Martinac Shipbuilding Corp 401 E 15th St *Web:* www.martinacship.com	Tacoma	WA	98421	253-572-4005		698
J. P. Farley Corp 29055 Clemens Rd *TF:* 800-244-6224 ■ *Web:* www.jpfarley.com	Westlake	OH	44145	440-250-4300		463
J. Reckner Associates Inc 587 Bethlehem Pike Ste 800 *Web:* www.reckner.com	Montgomeryville	PA	18936	215-822-6220		466
J. s Firm LLC *Aviation Search Group* 11350 Cleveland Gibbs Rd *Web:* www.jsfirm.com	Roanoke	TX	76262	817-560-0300		260
J. Stokes & Associates Inc 1444 N Main St *TF:* 800-821-7019 ■ *Web:* jstokes.com	Walnut Creek	CA	94596	925-933-1624		195
J.a. Reinhardt & Co Inc Spruce Cabin Rd *Web:* jareinhardt.bethermalandpower.com	Mountainhome	PA	18342	570-595-7491		487

Company / Address	City	State	ZIP	Phone	Fax	Class
J.A. Riggs Tractor Company Inc 9125 I-30 *TF:* 800-759-3140 ■ *Web:* www.riggscat.com	Little Rock	AR	72209	501-570-3100		23
J.A. Street & Associates Inc 245 Birch St *Web:* www.jastreet.com	Blountville	TN	37617	423-323-8017		186
J.C. Watts Cos 600 13th St NW Ste 790 *TF:* 800-223-2571 ■ *Web:* www.wattsconsultinggroup.com	Washington	DC	20005	202-207-2854		636
J.F. Smith Group Inc 735 E Glenn Ave *Web:* www.jfsg.com	Auburn	AL	36831	334-502-5374		463
J.G. Edelen Company Inc 8901 Kelso Dr *Web:* www.jgedelen.com	Baltimore	MD	21221	410-918-1200		351
J.I. Garcia Construction Co 4717 East Hedges Ave *TF:* 800-768-5594 ■ *Web:* www.jigarcia.com	Fresno	CA	93703	559-276-7726		186
J.L. Souser & Associates Inc 3495 Industrial Dr *TF:* 800-757-0181 ■ *Web:* www.jlsautomation.com	York	PA	17402	717-505-3800		358
J.M. Bozeman Enterprises Inc 166 Seltzer Ln *TF General:* 800-472-1836 ■ *Web:* jmbozeman.com	Malvern	AR	72104	501-844-4060		685
J.M. Rodgers Company Inc 1975 Linden Blvd *TF:* 800-772-9550 ■ *Web:* www.jmrodgers.com	Elmont	NY	11003	516-872-5570		314
J.N. White Designs Digital Inc 129 N Ctr St PO Box 219 *Web:* www.jnwhitedesigns.com	Perry	NY	14530	585-237-5191		687
J.R. Automation Technologies LLC 13365 Tyler St *Web:* www.jrauto.com	Holland	MI	49424	616-399-2168		494
J.R. Henry Consulting Inc PO Box 9724 *Web:* www.psmarketing.org	Pittsburgh	PA	15229	412-931-2833		463
J.S. McCarthy Printers Inc 15 Darin Dr *Web:* www.jsmccarthy.com	Augusta	ME	04330	207-622-6241		627
J.V. Driver Installations Ltd 212- 3601 82 Ave *Web:* www.jvdriver.com	Leduc	AB	T9E0H7	780-980-5837		261
J.W. Design & Construction Inc 3563 Sueldo St Ste I *Web:* www.jwdci.com	San Luis Obispo	CA	93401	805-544-3130		186
J2 Engineering Inc 6921 Pistol Range Rd *Web:* www.j2-eng.com	Tampa	FL	33635	813-888-8861		256
J2 Global Communications Inc 6922 Hollywood Blvd *TF Sales:* 888-718-2000 ■ *Web:* www.j2global.com	Hollywood	CA	90028	323-860-9200		736
J2 Interactive LLC 2 13th St *Web:* www.j2interactive.com	Charlestown	MA	02129	617-241-7266		398
J2t Recruiting Consultants Inc 4101 S Quebec St *Web:* j2t-recruiting.com	Denver	CO	80237	303-741-6122		721
J4 Systems Inc 2521 Warren Dr Ste A *Web:* www.j4systems.com	Rocklin	CA	95677	916-303-7200		180
JA (Jenkins Arboretum) 631 Berwyn Baptist Rd *Web:* www.jenkinsarboretum.org	Devon	PA	19333	610-647-8870	647-6664	97
JA (Jewelers of America) 52 Vanderbilt Ave 19th Fl *TF:* 800-223-0673 ■ *Web:* www.jewelers.org	New York	NY	10017	646-658-0246	658-0256	49-4
JA & Kathryn Albertson Foundation 501 Baybrook Ct *Web:* www.jkaf.org	Boise	ID	83706	208-424-2600		305
JA Apparel Corp 650 Fifth Ave *Web:* www.josephabboud.com	New York	NY	10019	212-586-9140		157-3
JA Billipp Co 6925 Portwest Dr Ste 130 *TF:* 800-216-9013 ■ *Web:* www.jabillipp.com	Houston	TX	77024	713-426-5000		653
JA Mktg Inc 18160 Cottonwood Rd	Sun River	OR	97707	541-593-8113		345
JA Skinner State Park PO Box 91 *Web:* www.mass.gov	Hadley	MA	01035	413-586-0350		565
JA Tiberti Construction Co 1806 Industrial Rd *Web:* www.tiberti.com	Las Vegas	NV	89102	702-248-4000		186
JA Woollam Company Inc 645 M St Ste 102 *Web:* www.jawoollam.com	Lincoln	NE	68508	402-477-7501		256
Jaapharm Canada Inc 510 Rowntree Dairy Rd Bldg B *TF:* 800-465-9587 ■ *Web:* www.jaapharm.com	Woodbridge	ON	L4L8H2	905-851-7085	856-5838	582
Jaas Systems Ltd 555 Lancaster Ave *Web:* jaas.net	Reynoldsburg	OH	43068	614-759-4167		177
Jabil Circuit Inc 10560 ML King St N *NYSE: JBL* ■ *TF:* 877-217-6328 ■ *Web:* www.jabil.com	Saint Petersburg	FL	33716	727-577-9749		625
Jabo Supply Corp 5164 County Rd 64/66 *TF:* 800-334-5226 ■ *Web:* www.jabosupply.com	Huntington	WV	25705	304-736-8333	736-8551	385
J-A-C Electric Co-op Inc 1784 FM 172 *Web:* www.jacelectric.com	Bluegrove	TX	76352	940-895-3311		245
JACAN (Junior Achievement of Canada) 1 Eva Rd Ste 218 *TF:* 800-265-0699 ■ *Web:* jacanada.org	Toronto	ON	M9C4Z5	416-622-4602	622-6861	48-11
Jace Holdings Ltd 6649 Butler Crescent *TF:* 800-667-8280 ■ *Web:* www.thriftyfoods.com	Saanichton	BC	V8M1Z7	250-483-1715		297-8
Jacer Corp 10400 Eaton Pl Ste 501 *Web:* www.jacer.com	Fairfax	VA	22030	703-352-1964		180
Jaci Carroll Staffing Services Inc 751 Straits TurnPk Ste 3000 *Web:* www.jacicarroll.com	Middlebury	CT	06762	203-574-4838		260
JaCiva's Chocolate 4733 SE Hawthorne Ave *Web:* www.jacivas.com	Portland	OR	97215	503-234-8115		123
Jack & Giulio's 2391 San Diego Ave *Web:* jackandgiulios.com	San Diego	CA	92110	619-294-2074		671
Jack & Mary's Restaurant 655 N 114th St *Web:* www.jackandmarysrestaurant.com	Omaha	NE	68154	402-496-2090		671
Jack b Keenan Inc 1820 Georgetta Dr *Web:* www.jackbkeenan.com	San Jose	CA	95125	408-448-4686		507
Jack B Kelley Inc 801 S Fillmore St Ste 505 *TF:* 800-225-5525 ■ *Web:* www.jackbkelley.com	Amarillo	TX	79101	806-353-3553	353-7428	780
Jack B Parson Cos 2350 S 1900 W *TF:* 888-672-7766 ■ *Web:* www.stakerparson.com	Ogden	UT	84401	801-731-1111		188-4
Jack Becker Distributors Inc 6800 Suemac Pl *TF:* 800-488-8411 ■ *Web:* www.jackbecker.com	Jacksonville	FL	32254	800-488-8411		581
Jack Bros Co 551 W Main St	Brawley	CA	92227	760-344-3781		10-11
Jack Conway 137 Washington St *TF:* 800-283-1030 ■ *Web:* www.jackconway.com	Norwell	MA	02061	781-871-0080	878-2632	652
Jack Cooper Transport Co Inc 1100 Walnut St Ste 2400 *Web:* www.jackcooper.com	Kansas City	MO	64106	816-983-4000		780
Jack County 100 Main St *TF:* 800-368-8683 ■ *Web:* jackcounty.org	Jacksboro	TX	76458	940-567-2111		338
Jack Daniel Distillery 3310 W End Ave *TF:* 888-551-5225 ■ *Web:* www.jackdaniels.com	Lynchburg	TN	37352	931-759-6357		80-1
Jack Giambalvo Motor Co 1390 Eden Rd *Web:* jackgiambalvo.com	York	PA	17402	717-781-2154		57
Jack Gray Transport Inc 4600 E 15th Ave	Gary	IN	46403	219-938-7020		780
Jack Henry & Assoc Inc 663 W Hwy 60 PO Box 807 *NASDAQ: JKHY* ■ *TF:* 800-299-4222 ■ *Web:* www.jackhenry.com	Monett	MO	65708	417-235-6652	235-8406	178-11
Jack in the Box Inc 9330 Balboa Ave *NASDAQ: JACK* ■ *TF:* 800-955-5225 ■ *Web:* www.jackinthebox.com	San Diego	CA	92123	858-571-2121		670
Jack Jones Jefferson County Juvenile Detention Ctr 101 E Barraque St *Web:* www.jeffcoso.org	Pine Bluff	AR	71611	870-541-5351		412
Jack Kent Cooke Foundation 44325 woodridge pkwy *Web:* www.jkcf.org	Landsdowne	VA	20176	703-723-8000		303
Jack Kilgore & Company Inc 154 E 71st St 3rd Fl	New York	NY	10021	212-650-1149		42
Jack Laurence Corp 12831 W Golden Ln	San Antonio	TX	78249	210-696-0273		189-10
Jack Lawton Webb Convention Ctr 5300 S Range Line Rd	Joplin	MO	64804	417-781-4000		205
Jack London Inn 444 Embarcadero W *Web:* www.jacklondoninn.com	Oakland	CA	94607	510-444-2032		379
Jack London State Historic Park 2400 London Ranch Rd *Web:* www.parks.ca.gov/default.asp?page_id=478	Glen Ellen	CA	95442	707-938-5216		565
Jack Nadel International Inc 8701 Bellanca Ave *Web:* www.nadel.com	Los Angeles	CA	90045	310-815-2600		5
Jack Nicklaus Museum 2355 Olentangy River Rd *TF:* 800-686-6124 ■ *Web:* www.nicklausmuseum.org	Columbus	OH	43210	614-247-5959	247-5906	522
Jack O'Dwyer's PR Newsletter 271 Madison Ave Ste 600 *TF:* 866-395-7710 ■ *Web:* www.odwyerpr.com	New York	NY	10016	212-679-2471	683-2750	531-11
Jack O'Reilly Tuxedos LLC 2701 Fifth St Hwy *Web:* jackoreillytuxedos.com	Reading	PA	19605	610-929-9409		157-3
Jack of All Games Inc 9271 Meridian Way	West Chester	OH	45069	513-326-3020		174
Jack of All Trades Personnel Services 2701 Franklin Ave *Web:* www.joatwaco.com	Waco	TX	76710	254-754-7997		260
Jack Ogren & Company Inc 6929 Hohman Ave *TF:* 888-489-1371 ■ *Web:* ogreninsurance.com	Hammond	IN	46324	219-933-0076		390
Jack Powell Ford-Mercury Inc 1418 SE 1 St *Web:* jackpowellford.net	Mineral Wells	TX	76067	940-325-1331		57
Jack Richeson & Company Inc 557 Marcella Dr *TF:* 800-233-2404 ■ *Web:* www.richesonart.com	Kimberly	WI	54136	920-738-0744	738-9156	43
Jack Schwartz Shoes Inc 155 Ave of the Americas *Web:* www.lugz.com	New York	NY	10013	212-691-4700		301
Jack Tilton Gallery 8 E 76th St *Web:* www.jacktiltongallery.com	New York	NY	10021	212-737-2221	396-1725	42
Jack Williams Tire Co Inc PO Box 3655 *TF:* 800-833-5051 ■ *Web:* www.jackwilliams.com	Scranton	PA	18505	800-833-5051		62-5
Jack's Bar-B-Que 334 W Trinity Ln *Web:* www.jacksbarbque.com	Nashville	TN	37207	615-228-4600	228-4700	671
Jack's Family Restaurants Inc 2831 19th St S *TF:* 888-795-2707 ■ *Web:* www.eatatjacks.com	Homewood	AL	35209	205-879-9321	945-8167	670
Jack's Gourmet Restaurant 1903 Business Loop 70 E *Web:* www.jacksgourmetrestaurant.com	Columbia	MO	65201	573-449-3927	442-9881	671
Jack's Oyster House 42 State St *Web:* www.jacksoysterhouse.com	Albany	NY	12207	518-465-8854	434-2134	671
Jack's Tire & Oil Management Company Inc 1795 N Main St *TF:* 800-721-8253 ■ *Web:* www.jackstireandoil.com	North Logan	UT	84341	435-752-7811		54
Jackalope Pottery 2820 Cerrillos Rd *Web:* www.jackalope.com	Santa Fe	NM	87507	505-471-8539		362
Jackburn Manufacturing Inc 438 Church St *Web:* www.jackburn.com	Girard	PA	16417	814-774-3573	774-2854	491
Jackie Gleason Theater of the Performing Arts 1700 Washington Ave *Web:* fillmoremb.com	Miami Beach	FL	33139	305-673-7300		572
Jackie Matchett Personnel Inc 519 Heritage Rd Ste 2B *Web:* www.jackiematchett.com	Southbury	CT	06488	203-405-6111		260
Jacklin Steel Supply Co 2410 Aero Park Dr *Web:* www.jacklinsteel.com	Traverse City	MI	49686	231-946-8434		480

Phone | Fax | Class

Jacknob Corp
290 Oser Ave PO Box 18032 Hauppauge NY 11788 631-546-6560 231-0330 350
TF: 888-231-9333 ■ *Web:* www.jacknob.com

Jacko Law Group PC
5920 Friars Rd Ste 208 San Diego CA 92108 619-298-2880 428
TF: 866-497-2298 ■ *Web:* www.jackolg.com

Jackpot Junction Casino Hotel
39375 County Hwy 24 PO Box 420 Morton MN 56270 507-697-8000 133
TF: 800-946-2274 ■ *Web:* www.jackpotjunction.com

Jacksboro Public Library
585 Main St Ste 201 Jacksboro TN 37757 423-562-3675 562-9587 434-3
TF: 800-303-2220 ■ *Web:* www.jacksboropubliclibrary.org

Jackson & Blanc Inc 7929 Arjons Dr San Diego CA 92126 858-831-7900 527-1502 189-10
Web: www.jacksonandblanc.com

Jackson & Campbell 1120 20th St NW Washington DC 20036 202-457-1600 445
Web: www.jackscamp.com

Jackson & Hertogs
170 Columbus Ave Fl 4 San Francisco CA 94133 415-986-4559 428
TF: 800-780-2008 ■ *Web:* jackson-hertogs.com

Jackson & Perkins 2 Floral Ave Hodges SC 29653 800-292-4769 459
TF Cust Svc: 800-292-4769 ■ *Web:* www.jacksonandperkins.com

Jackson & Tull Chartered Engineers
12201 Distribution Way Beltsville MD 20705 301-937-8255 256
Web: www.jnt.com

Jackson Area Chamber of Commerce
197 Auditorium St Jackson TN 38301 731-423-2200 424-4860 139
Web: www.jacksontn.com

Jackson Area Chamber of Commerce
234 Broadway St Jackson OH 45640 740-286-2722 286-8443 139
TF: 800-796-4282 ■ *Web:* www.jacksonohio.org

Jackson Citizen Patriot
100 E Michigan Ave Ste 100 Jackson MI 49201 877-213-3754 532-2
TF: 877-213-3754 ■ *Web:* experiencejackson.com

Jackson Community College
2111 Emmons Rd Jackson MI 49201 517-787-0800 796-8631* 162
**Fax:* Admissions ■ *TF:* 888-522-7344 ■ *Web:* www.jccmi.edu
Hillsdale
3120 W Carleton Rd PO Box 712 Hillsdale MI 49242 517-437-3343 437-0232 162
Web: www.jccmi.edu

Jackson Correctional Institution
5563 Tenth St Malone FL 32445 850-569-5260 569-5996 213
TF: 800-299-4700 ■ *Web:* dc.state.fl.us

Jackson County 307 Main St Black River Falls WI 54615 715-284-0208 284-0270 338
Web: www.co.jackson.wi.us

Jackson County PO Box 318 Brownstown IN 47220 812-358-6116 358-6187 338
Web: www.jacksoncounty.in.gov

Jackson County 115 W Main St Rm 101 Edna TX 77957 361-782-3563 338
Web: www.co.jackson.tx.us

Jackson County 101 E Hull Ave Gainesboro TN 38562 931-268-9212 338
Web: www.jacksoncotn.com

Jackson County 400 New York Ave Ste 202 Holton KS 66436 785-364-2358 364-5257 338
Web: ks-jackson.manatron.com

Jackson County 405 Fourth St Ste 5 Jackson MN 56143 507-847 2763 847-4718 338
Web: www.co.jackson.mn.us

Jackson County 275 Portsmouth St Jackson OH 45640 740-286-3301 286 4754 338
Web: www.jacksoncountyohio.us

Jackson County 67 Athens St Jefferson GA 30549 706 367-6312 338
Web: www.jacksoncountygov.com

Jackson County 700 Main St PO Box 128 Kadoka SD 57543 605-837-2122 837-2120 338
Web: ujs.sd.gov/County_Information/jackson.aspx

Jackson County 415 E 12th St Kansas City MO 64106 816-881-3000 338
TF: 800-392-3738 ■ *Web:* 16thcircuit.org

Jackson County 201 W Platt St Maquoketa IA 52060 563-652-3144 652-4738 338
TF: 800-368-8683 ■ *Web:* www.co.jackson.ia.us

Jackson County PO Box 175 McKee KY 40447 606-287-8562 287-7190 338
Web: jacksoncounty.ky.gov

Jackson County 10 S Oakdale Ave Medford OR 97501 541-774-6029 338
Web: www.co.jackson.or.us

Jackson County
215 N 14th St County Courthouse Murphysboro IL 62966 618-687-7370 687-4046 338
Web: www.jacksoncounty-il.gov

Jackson County
3300 Theater Dr PO Box 647 Newport AR 72112 870-523-5842 523-7418 338
TF: 800-234-1040 ■ *Web:* www.jacksonsheriff.org

Jackson County
3104 Magnolia St PO Box 998 Pascagoula MS 39567 228 769-3040 769-3180 338
Web: www.co.jackson.ms.us

Jackson County PO Box 800 Ripley WV 25271 304-373-2220 373-0245 338
Web: jacksoncounty.wv.gov

Jackson County
102 E Laurel St Ste 307 Scottsboro AL 35768 256-574-9320 338
Web: jacksoncountyal.com

Jackson County 401 Grindstaff Cove Rd Sylva NC 28779 828-586-4055 338
TF: 800-962-1911 ■ *Web:* www.jacksonnc.org

Jackson County PO Box 1019 Walden CO 80480 970-723-4660 338
Web: www.jacksoncountyco.com

Jackson County Area Chamber of Commerce
270 Athens St PO Box 629 Jefferson GA 30549 706-387-0300 387-0304 139
Web: www.jacksoncountyga.com

Jackson County Chamber of Commerce
720 Krebs Ave Pascagoula MS 39567 228-762-3391 769-1726 139
TF: 800-748-7626 ■ *Web:* www.jcchamber.com

Jackson County Chamber of Commerce
773 W Main St Sylva NC 28779 828-586-2155 586-4887 139
TF: 800-962-1911 ■ *Web:* www.mountainlovers.com

Jackson County Chamber of Commerce
4318 Lafayette St Marianna FL 32446 850-482-8060 338
Web: www.jacksoncounty.com

Jackson County Convention & Visitors Bureau
141 S Jackson St Jackson MI 49201 517-764-4440 780-3688 206
TF: 800-245-5282 ■ *Web:* www.experiencejackson.com

Jackson County Courthouse, The
101 N Main St Altus OK 73521 580-482-2370 338
Web: jackson.okcounties.org

Jackson County Intermediate School District (JCISD)
6700 Browns Lake Rd Jackson MI 49201 517-768-5200 685
Web: www.jcisd.org/site/default.aspx

Jackson County Library System
205 S Central Ave Medford OR 97501 541-774-8679 434-3
Web: www.jcls.org

Jackson County Memorial Hospital
1200 E Pecan St Altus OK 73521 580-379-5000 374-3
TF: 800-595-0455 ■ *Web:* www.jcmh.com

Jackson County Public Library
208 Church St N Ripley WV 25271 304-372-5343 372-7935 434-3
Web: jackson.park.lib.wv.us

Jackson County Public Library (JCPL)
303 W Second St Seymour IN 47274 812-522-3412 522-5456 434-3
Web: www.myjclibrary.org

Jackson County Rural Electric Membership Corp
274 E Base Rd Brownstown IN 47220 812-358-4458 358-5719 245
TF: 800-288-4458 ■ *Web:* www.jacksonremc.com

Jackson County School District 6
300 Ash St Central Point OR 97502 541-494-6200 664-1637 685
TF: 800-978-3040 ■ *Web:* www.district6.org

Jackson County School District 9
11 N Royal PO Box 548 Eagle Point OR 97524 541-830-1200 685
Web: www.eaglepnt.k12.or.us

Jackson County School System
1660 Winder Hwy Jefferson GA 30549 706-367-5151 367-9457 685
TF: 800-760-3727 ■ *Web:* www.jackson.k12.ga.us

Jackson District Library
244 W Michigan Ave Jackson MI 49201 517-788-4087 434-3
Web: www.myjdl.com

Jackson Electric Co-op
N6868 County Rd F PO Box 546 Black River Falls WI 54615 715-284-5385 284-7143 245
TF: 800-370-4607 ■ *Web:* www.jackelec.com

Jackson Electric Membership Corp
850 Commerce Rd Jefferson GA 30549 706-367-5281 245
TF: 800-462-3691 ■ *Web:* www.jacksonemc.com

Jackson ElectricCo-op Inc
8925 State Hwy 111 S Ganado TX 77962 361-771-4400 771-4406 245
Web: www.jecec.com

Jackson Energy Authority
119 E College St Jackson TN 38301 731-422-7500 787
Web: www.jaxenergy.com

Jackson Energy Co-op
115 Jackson Energy Ln McKee KY 40447 606-364-1000 245
TF: 800-262-7480 ■ *Web:* www.jacksonenergy.com

Jackson George N Ltd
1139 Mcdermot Ave Winnipeg MB R3E0V2 204-786-3821 361
TF: 800-665-8978 ■ *Web:* www.jackson.ca

Jackson Grill 3736 W Mitchell St Milwaukee WI 53215 414-384-7384 671
Web: www.jacksongrill.com

Jackson Healthcare LLC
2655 Northwinds Pkwy Alpharetta GA 30009 770-643-5500 631
Web: www.jacksonhealthcare.com

Jackson Hewitt Inc
3 Sylvan Way Ste 301 Parsippany NJ 07054 800-234-1040 734
OTC: JHTXQ ■ *TF:* 800-234-1040 ■ *Web:* www.jacksonhewitt.com

Jackson Hole Airport
1250 E Airport Rd PO Box 159 Jackson WY 83001 307-733-7682 733-9270 27
Web: www.jacksonholeairport.com

Jackson Hole Central Reservations (JHCR)
140 E Broadway Ste 24 PO Box 2618 Jackson WY 83001 307-733-4005 733-1286 376
TF: 888-838-0000 ■ *Web:* www.jacksonholewy.com

Jackson Hole Chamber of Commerce
112 Center St Jackson WY 83001 307-733-3316 733-5585 139
Web: www.jacksonholechamber.com

Jackson Hole Historical Society & Museum
105 Mercill Jackson WY 83001 307-733-9605 739-9019 520
Web: www.jacksonholehistory.org

Jackson Hole Lodge
420 W Broadway PO Box 1805 Jackson WY 83001 307-733-2992 739 2144 379
TF: 800-604-9404 ■ *Web:* www.jacksonholelodge.com

Jackson Hole Mountain Resort
3395 Cody Ln PO Box 290 Teton Village WY 83025 307-733-2292 739-2737 669
TF: 800-450-0477 ■ *Web:* www.jacksonhole.com

Jackson Hole News & Guide
1225 Maple Way Jackson WY 83001 307-733-2047 733-2138 532-4
Web: jhnewsandguide.com

Jackson Hole Playhouse
145 W Deloney Ave Jackson WY 83001 307-733-6994 572
Web: jacksonholeplayhouse.com

Jackson HoleResort Lodging
3200 W McCollister Dr PO Box 510 Teton Village WY 83025 307-733-3990 669
TF: 800-443-8613 ■ *Web:* www.jhrl.com

Jackson Hospital 1725 Pine St Montgomery AL 36106 334-293-8000 374-3
TF: 800-815-8377 ■ *Web:* www.jackson.org

Jackson Hospital 4250 Hospital Dr Marianna FL 32446 850-526-2200 482-6374 374 3
Web: www.jacksonhosp.com

Jackson ImmunoResearch Laboratories Inc
872 W Baltimore Pk PO Box 9 West Grove PA 19390 610-869-4024 869-0171 231
TF: 800-367-5296 ■ *Web:* www.jacksonimmuno.com

Jackson International Airport
100 International Dr Ste 300 Jackson MS 39208 601-939-5631 939-3713 27
TF: 800-227-7368 ■ *Web:* www.jmaa.com

Jackson Kelly PLLC PO Box 553 Charleston WV 25322 304-340-1172 428
Web: www.jacksonkelly.com

Jackson Laboratory, The
600 Main St Bar Harbor ME 04609 207-288-6000 668
TF: 800-422-6423 ■ *Web:* www.jax.org

Jackson Lake Lodge PO Box 250 Moran WY 83013 307-543-2811 543-3143 669
TF: 800-628-9988 ■ *Web:* www.gtlc.com

Jackson Lake State Park
26363 County Rd 3 Orchard CO 80649 970-645-2551 565
Web: cpw.state.co.us

Jackson Lake State Park
35 Tommy Bcen Rd Oak Hill OH 45656 740-682-6197 565
Web: parks.ohiodnr.gov/jacksonlake

Jackson Lee Sheila (Rep D - TX)
2187 Rayburn HOB Washington DC 20515 202-225-3816 225-3317 342-2
Web: jacksonlee.house.gov

Jackson Local Schools District (JLSD)
7602 Fulton Dr Massillon OH 44646 330-830-8000 830-8008 186
Web: jackson.stark.k12.oh.us

Name / Address	City	State	ZIP	Phone	Fax	Class
Jackson Lumber & Millwork Company Inc PO Box 449 *Web:* www.jacksonlumber.com	Lawrence	MA	01842	978-686-4141		364
Jackson Marketing Group Inc 2 Task Industrial Ct *Web:* www.jacksonmg.com	Greenville	SC	29607	864-272-3000		7
Jackson Marking Products Co 9105 N Rainbow Ln *TF:* 800-782-6722 ■ *Web:* www.rubber-stamp.com	Mount Vernon	IL	62864	618-242-1334	242-7732	467
Jackson Mattress Company Inc 3154 Camden Rd *TF:* 800-763-7378 ■ *Web:* restonic.com	Fayetteville	NC	28306	910-425-0131	425-1602	471
Jackson Memorial Hospital 1611 NW 12th Ave *Web:* www.jacksonhealth.org	Miami	FL	33136	305-585-1111	326-9470	374-3
Jackson National Life Insurance Co 1 Corporate Way *TF:* 800-644-4565 ■ *Web:* www.jackson.com	Lansing	MI	48951	517-381-5500		391-2
Jackson Oil & Solvents Inc 1970 Kentucky Ave *TF:* 800-221-4603 ■ *Web:* www.jacksonoilsolvents.com	Indianapolis	IN	46221	317-636-4421	685-2403	541
Jackson Parish 500 E Ct St Ste 301 *Web:* www.jacksonparishpolicejury.org	Jonesboro	LA	71251	318-259-2361	259-5660	338
Jackson Public Schools 662 S President St *Web:* www.jackson.k12.ms.us	Jackson	MS	39201	601-960-8700	960-8713	685
Jackson Purchase Ag Credit Assn PO Box 309 *TF:* 877-422-4203 ■ *Web:* rivervalleyagcredit.com	Mayfield	KY	42066	270-247-5613		216
Jackson Purchase Energy Corp 2900 Irvin Cobb Dr *TF:* 800-633-4044 ■ *Web:* www.jpenergy.com	Paducah	KY	42002	270-442-7321	442-5337	245
Jackson Purchase Medical Ctr 1099 Medical Ctr Cir *TF:* 800-994-6610 ■ *Web:* www.jacksonpurchase.com	Mayfield	KY	42066	270-251-4100	251-4507	374-3
Jackson Ready Mix Concrete Inc 100 W Woodrow Wilson Dr *Web:* delta-ind.com	Jackson	MS	39213	601-354-3801		182
Jackson State Community College 2046 N Pkwy **Fax:* Admissions ■ *TF:* 800-250-1890 ■ *Web:* www.jscc.edu	Jackson	TN	38301	731-424-3520	425-9559*	162
Lexington-Henderson Ctr 932 E Church St *Web:* www.jscc.edu	Lexington	TN	38351	731-968-5722	968-1539	162
Jackson State University 1400 John R Lynch St **Fax:* Admissions ■ *TF:* 800-848-6817 ■ *Web:* www.jsums.edu	Jackson	MS	39217	601-979-2121	979-3445*	166
Jackson Sun 245 W LaFayette St *TF:* 800-372-3922 ■ *Web:* www.jacksonsun.com	Jackson	TN	38301	731-427-3333	425-9639	532-2
Jackson Technical LLC 427 S Boston Ave Ste 1010 *Web:* www.jacksontechnical.com	Tulsa	OK	74103	918-585-8324		180
Jackson Tidus A Law Corp 2030 Main St 12th Fl *Web:* www.jdtplaw.com	Irvine	CA	92614	949-752-8585		428
Jackson Tube Service Inc 8210 Industry Pk Dr *TF:* 800-543-8910 ■ *Web:* www.jackson-tube.com	Piqua	OH	45356	937-773-8550	773-8806	490
Jackson Typesetting Company Inc 1820 W Ganson St	Jackson	MI	49202	517-784-0576		781
Jackson (WY) Town Hall 150 E Pearl Ave *Web:* townofjackson.com	Jackson	WY	83001	307-733-3932	739-0919	337
Jackson Zoological Park 2918 W Capitol St *Web:* www.jacksonzoo.org	Jackson	MS	39209	601-352-2580	352-2594	823
Jackson's Bistro 601 S Harbor Island Blvd *Web:* www.jacksonsbistro.com	Tampa	FL	33602	813-277-0112		671
Jackson's Steakhouse 400 S Palafox St *Web:* greatsouthernrestaurants.com	Pensacola	FL	32502	850-469-9898		671
Jackson-Beldon Chamber of Commerce 5735 Wales Ave NW *TF:* 800-622-1893 ■ *Web:* www.jbcc.org	Jackson Township	OH	44646	330-833-4400	833-4456	139
Jackson-George Regional Library System 3214 S Pascagoula St *Web:* www.jgrls.org	Pascagoula	MS	39567	228-769-3060		434-3
Jackson-Madison County General Hospital 620 Skyline Dr *Web:* wth.org	Jackson	TN	38301	731-541-5000		374-3
Jackson-Madison County Library 433 E Lafayette St *Web:* www.jmclibrary.org	Jackson	TN	38301	731-425-8600	425-8609	434-3
Jacksonport State Park 1 Capitol Mall *TF:* 888-287-2757 ■ *Web:* www.arkansasstateparks.com	Newport	AR	72112	870-523-2143		565
Jacksonville Area Chamber of Commerce 310 E State St *TF:* 800-593 5678 ■ *Web:* www.jacksonvilleil.org	Jacksonville	IL	62650	217-243-5678		139
Jacksonville Bancorp Inc 1211 W Morton Ave *NASDAQ: JXSB* ■ *Web:* www.jacksonvillesavings.com	Jacksonville	IL	62650	217-245-4111		360-2
Jacksonville Chamber of Commerce 200 Dupree Dr *TF:* 877-815-3111 ■ *Web:* www.jacksonville-arkansas.com	Jacksonville	AR	72076	501-982-1511	982-1464	139
Jacksonville Chamber of Commerce Beaches Div 3 Independent Dr *Web:* www.myjaxchamber.com	Jacksonville	FL	32202	904-366-6600		139
Jacksonville City Hall 117 W Duval St Ste 400 *Web:* www.coj.net	Jacksonville	FL	32202	904-630-1776	630-2391	337
Jacksonville College 105 BJ Albritton Dr **Fax:* Admissions ■ *Web:* www.jacksonville-college.edu	Jacksonville	TX	75766	903-586-2518	586-0743*	162
Jacksonville Convention & Visitors Bureau 310 E State St *TF:* 800-593-5678 ■ *Web:* www.jacksonvilleil.org	Jacksonville	IL	62650	217-243-5678		206

Name / Address	City	State	ZIP	Phone	Fax	Class
Jacksonville Correctional Ctr 2268 E Morton Ave *TF:* 800-526-0844 ■ *Web:* illinois.gov	Jacksonville	IL	62650	217-245-1481		213
Jacksonville Independent School District PO Box 631 *TF:* 800-583-6908 ■ *Web:* www.jisd.org	Jacksonville	TX	75766	903-586-6511	586-3133	685
Jacksonville International Airport 2400 Yankee Clipper Dr *TF:* 800-554-1589 ■ *Web:* www.flyjacksonville.com	Jacksonville	FL	32218	904-741-4902	741-2224	27
Jacksonville Magazine 1261 King St *TF:* 800-962-0214 ■ *Web:* www.jacksonvillemag.com	Jacksonville	FL	32204	904-389-3622	389-3628	457-22
Jacksonville Municipal Stadium 1 EverBank Field Dr **Fax:* Mktg ■ *Web:* www.jaguars.com	Jacksonville	FL	32202	904-633-6000	633-6055*	720
Jacksonville Museum of Modern Art 333 N Laura St *Web:* www.mocajacksonville.org	Jacksonville	FL	32202	904-366-6911	366-6901	520
Jacksonville School District 117 516 Jordan St *Web:* jsd117.org	Jacksonville	IL	62650	217-243-9411		685
Jacksonville State University 700 Pelham Rd N **Fax:* Admissions ■ *TF:* 800-231-5291 ■ *Web:* www.jsu.edu	Jacksonville	AL	36265	256-782-5781	782-5953*	166
Jacksonville Steel Inc 310 W Dewitt Henry Dr	Beebe	AR	72012	501-882-3563		480
Jacksonville Symphony Orchestra (JSO) 300 W Water St Ste 200 *Web:* www.jaxsymphony.org	Jacksonville	FL	32202	904-354-5479		573-3
Jacksonville University 2800 University Blvd N **Fax:* Admissions ■ *TF:* 800-225-2027 ■ *Web:* www.ju.edu	Jacksonville	FL	32211	904-256-8000	256-7012*	166
Jacksonville Veterans Memorial Arena 300 A Philip Randolph Blvd *TF:* 800-745-3000 ■ *Web:* www.jaxevents.com	Jacksonville	FL	32202	904-630-3900	854-0601	720
Jacksonville Zoo & Gardens 370 Zoo Pkwy *TF:* 800-241-4113 ■ *Web:* www.jacksonvillezoo.org	Jacksonville	FL	32218	904-757-4463	757-4315	823
Jacksonville's Country WQIK 99.1 11700 Central Pkwy *Web:* 991wqik.iheart.com	Jacksonville	FL	32224	904-636-0507		645-79
Jacksonville/Onslow Chamber of Commerce 1099 Gum Branch Rd *Web:* www.jacksonvilleonline.org	Jacksonville	NC	28541	910-347-3141	347-4705	139
JACL (Japanese American Citizens League) 1765 Sutter St *TF:* 800-400-6633 ■ *Web:* www.jacl.org	San Francisco	CA	94115	415-921-5225	931-4671	48-14
Jaclyn Inc 197 W Spring Vly Ave *OTC: JCLY* ■ *Web:* www.jaclyninc.com	Maywood	NJ	07607	201-909-6000		430
Jacmel Jewelry Inc 1385 Broadway 8th Floor *TF:* 800-945-4300 ■ *Web:* www.jacmel.com	New York	NY	10018	800-945-4300		409
Jaco Electronics Inc 415 Oser Ave *OTC: JACO* ■ **Fax Area Code:* 631 ■ *TF:* 877-373-5226 ■ *Web:* www.jacoelect.com	Hauppauge	NY	11788	877-373-5226	231-1051*	246
Jaco Engineering 879 S E St *Web:* www.jacoengineering.com	Anaheim	CA	92805	714-991-1680		757
JACO Environmental Inc PO Box 14307	Mill Creek	WA	98082	425-398-6200		358
Jacob Group, The 6190 Virginia Pkwy One Jacob Pl Ste 100 *TF:* 800-875-8546 ■ *Web:* www.jacobgroup.com	Mckinney	TX	75071	214-544-9030		260
Jacob Holtz Co 10 Industrial Hwy MS-6 Airport Business Complex B *TF:* 800-445-4337 ■ *Web:* www.jacobholtz.com	Lester	PA	19029	215-423-2800	634-7454	350
Jacob K Javits Convention Ctr 655 W 34th St *Web:* www.javitscenter.com	New York	NY	10001	212-216-2000	216-2588	205
Jacob Leinenkugel Brewing Co 124 E Elm St *TF General:* 888-534-6437 ■ *Web:* www.leinie.com	Chippewa Falls	WI	54729	715-723-5558		102
Jacob Medinger & Finnegan LLP (JMF) 1270 Ave of the Americas *Web:* jmfnylaw.com	New York	NY	10020	212-524-5000		428
Jacob Securities Inc 199 Bay St Commerce Ct W PO Box 322 Ste 2901	Toronto	ON	M5L1G1	416-866-8300		401
Jacob Stern & Sons Inc 1464 E Valley Rd *TF Cust Svc:* 000-223-7054 ■ *Web:* www.jacobstern.com	Santa Barbara	CA	93108	805-565-1411		296-12
Jacob White Construction Co 2000 W Parkwood Ste 100 *TF:* 800-510-3111 ■ *Web:* www.jacobwhitecc.com	Friendswood	TX	77546	281-286-6666		186
Jacobi Medical Ctr 1400 Pelham Pkwy S *TF:* 800-698-4543 ■ *Web:* www.nychealthandhospitals.org	Bronx	NY	10461	718-918-5700		374-3
Jacobi Sales Inc 425 Main St NE PO Box 67 *TF:* 800-489-3617 ■ *Web:* www.jacobisales.com	Palmyra	IN	47164	812-364-6141	364-6157	274
Jaco-Bryant Printing LLC 4783 Hickory Hill Rd *Web:* www.jaco-bryant.com	Memphis	TN	38141	901-546-9600		627
Jacobs & Clevenger Inc 303 E Wacker Dr Ste 2030 *Web:* www.jacobsclevenger.com	Chicago	IL	60601	312-894-3000	894-3005	5
Jacobs Agency Inc 430 W Erie St Ste 403 *Web:* www.jacobsagency.com	Chicago	IL	60610	312-664-5000		7
Jacobs Engineering Group Inc 155 N Lake Ave PO Box 7084 *NYSE: JEC* ■ *TF:* 800-732-0330 ■ *Web:* www.jacobs.com	Pasadena	CA	91101	626-578-3500		261
Jacobs Entertainment Inc 17301 W Colfax Ave Ste 250 *Web:* jacobsentertainmentinc.com	Golden	CO	80401	303-215-5200		322
Jacobs Financial Group, The 20 Wind Trace Ct *Web:* www.thejacobsfinancialgroup.com	The Woodlands	TX	77381	281-298-6545		391-4
Jacobs Industries Inc 8096 Excelsior Blvd *Web:* www.jacobsinteractive.com	Hopkins	MN	55343	612-339-9500		360-3

	Phone	Fax	Class
Jacobs Management Group Inc 1420 Walnut St ... Philadelphia PA 19102 *TF:* 800-823-5100 ■ *Web:* www.jacobsmgt.com	215-732-6400		260
Jacobs Mechanical Inc 4500 W Mitchell Ave ... Cincinnati OH 45232 *Web:* jacobsmech.com	513-681-6800	681-6855	189-10
Jacobs Technology Inc 600 William Northern Blvd ... Tullahoma TN 37388 *TF:* 800-251-3540 ■ *Web:* www.jacobstechnology.com	931-455-6400		261
Jacobs Theatre 242 W 45th St ... New York NY 10036 *TF:* 800-447-7400 ■ *Web:* www.telecharge.com	212-239-6200		747
Jacobs Trading Co 8090 Excelsior Blvd ... Hopkins MN 55343 *TF:* 800-597-3886 ■ *Web:* www.jacobstrading.com	763-843-2000	843-2101	361
Jacobs Vehicle Systems Inc 22 E Dudley Town Rd ... Bloomfield CT 06002 *Web:* www.jacobsvehiclesystems.com	860-243-1441		60
Jacobsburg Environmental Education Ctr 835 Jacobsburg Rd ... Wind Gap PA 18091 *Web:* www.dcnr.state.pa.us	610-746-2801		565
Jacobsen 11108 Quality Dr ... Charlotte NC 28273 *TF:* 800-848-1636 ■ *Web:* www.jacobsen.com	704-504-6600	504-6661	429
Jacobsen Homes 600 Packard Ct ... Safety Harbor FL 34695 *TF:* 800-843-1559 ■ *Web:* www.jachomes.com	727-726-1138		505
Jacobson & Company Inc 1079 E Grand St PO Box 511 ... Elizabeth NJ 07207 *TF:* 800-480-3463 ■ *Web:* www.jacobsoncompany.com	908-355-5200	355-8680	189-9
Jacobson Companies Inc, The 1334 S Fifth Ave ... Yuma AZ 85364 *Web:* www.jacobsoncompanies.com	928-782-1801		656
Jacobson Floral Supply Inc 500 Albany St ... Boston MA 02118 *Web:* www.jacobsonfloral.com	617-426-4287		292
Jacobson Holman PLLC 400 Seventh St NW ... Washington DC 20004 *Web:* www.jhip.com	202-638-6666		428
Jacobson Plastics 1401 Freeman Ave ... Long Beach CA 90804 *Web:* www.jacobsonplastics.com	562-433-4911		608
Jacobson Rost Inc 233 N Water St Ste 6 ... Milwaukee WI 53202	414-220-4888		7
Jacobson, Hansen, Najarian & Mcquillan 1690 W Shaw Ave Ste 201 ... Fresno CA 93711	559-448-0400		428
Jacobus Wealth Management Inc 2323 N Mayfair Rd ... Milwaukee WI 53226 *Web:* www.jwmfamilyoffices.com	414-475-6565		401
Jacquelyn Wigs 15 W 37th St 4th Fl ... New York NY 10018 *TF:* 800-272-2424 ■ *Web:* www.jacquelynwigs.com	212-302-2266		348
Jacques Marchais Museum of Tibetan Art 338 Lighthouse Ave ... Staten Island NY 10306 *TF:* 800-348-9505 ■ *Web:* www.tibetanmuseum.org	718-987-3500		520
Jacques-Imo's Cafe 8324 Oak St ... New Orleans LA 70118 *Web:* jacques-imos.com	504-861-0886		671
Jacquette Consulting Inc 710 Providence Rd ... Malvern PA 19355 *Web:* www.jacquette.com	610-280-3911	280-3922	225
Jacquin Charles et Cie Inc 2633 Trenton Ave ... Philadelphia PA 19125	215-425-9300		80-1
Jacuzzi Brands Inc 13925 City Ctr Dr Ste 200 ... Chino Hills CA 91709 *Web:* www.jacuzzi.com	909-606-1416		401
JAD Business Services Inc PO Box 953 ... Shady Side MD 20764 *Web:* www.jadbsi.com	301-261-5538		113
Jadcore Inc 300 N Fruitridge ... Terre Haute IN 47803 *Web:* www.jadcore.com	812-234-2724		596
Jade Corp 3063 Philmont Ave ... Huntingdon Valley PA 19006 *Web:* www.jadecorp.com	215-947-3333		757
Jade Engineered Plastic Inc 121 Broadcommon Rd ... Bristol RI 02809 *TF:* 800-557-9155 ■ *Web:* www.jadeplastics.com	401-253-4440		326
Jade Garden Helena 3128 N Montana Ave ... Helena MT 59602 *Web:* jadegardenhelena.com	406-443-8899	443-8390	671
Jade Garden Restaurant 1200 Battlefield Blvd N Ste 119 ... Chesapeake VA 23320 *Web:* gojadegarden.com	757-436-1010		671
Jade Palace 906 W Seventh Ave ... Eugene OR 97402 *Web:* jadepalaceeugene.com	541-344-9523		671
Jade Palace 820 W Spring Creek Pkwy Ste 214 ... Plano TX 75023 *Web:* www.jadepalacechinese.com	972-424-5578		671
Jade Palace 1659 Rte 9 ... Wappingers Falls NY 12590 *Web:* www.jadepalacewappingersfalls.com	406-656-8888		671
Jade Travel Group 1650 Elgin Mills Rd E Unit 403 ... Richmond Hill ON L4S0B2 *TF:* 800-387-0387 ■ *Web:* www2.jadetours.com	905-787-9288	787-9299	760
Jadoo Power Systems Inc 181 Blue Ravine Rd Ste 120 ... Folsom CA 95630	916-608-9044		194
Jadtec Computer Group 1520 W Yale Ave ... Orange CA 92867 *Web:* www.jadtec.com	714-282-0828		175
JAE Electronics Inc 142 Technology Dr Ste 100 ... Irvine CA 92618 *TF:* 800-523-7278 ■ *Web:* www.jae.com	949-753-2600	753-2699	253
Jae Oregon Inc 11555 SW Leveton Dr ... Tualatin OR 97062 *Web:* jaeoregon.com	503-692-1333		596
Jaeckle Wholesale Inc 4101 Owl Creek Dr ... Madison WI 53718 *TF:* 800-236-7225 ■ *Web:* www.jaeckledistributors.com	608-838-5400		191-1
Jaekle Group Inc, The 1410 Highland Rd E ... Macedonia OH 44056 *TF:* 800-968-4332 ■ *Web:* www.jaeklegroup.com	330-405-9353		180
JAF Consulting Inc 6 Washington Ave ... Mullica Hill NJ 08062 *Web:* www.jafconsulting.com	856-241-1900		587
Jafco Foods 820 Turnpike St ... North Andover MA 01845 *TF:* 800-255-4256 ■ *Web:* www.jafcofoods.com	978-989-0012		345
Jaffe Communications Inc 312 North Ave E Ste 5 ... Cranford NJ 07016 *Web:* www.jaffecom.com	908-789-0700	292-1177	636
Jaffe Raitt Heuer & Weiss PC 27777 Franklin Rd Ste 2500 ... Southfield MI 48034 *Web:* www.jaffelaw.com	248-351-3000		428
Jaffrey-Rindge School District 81 Fitzgerald Dr Unit 2 ... Jaffrey NH 03452 *Web:* sau47.org	603-532-8100		685
Jafra Cosmetics International 2451 Townsgate Rd ... Westlake Village CA 91361 *TF:* 800-551-2345 ■ *Web:* www.jafra.com	805-449-3000		214
Jaftex Corp 49 W 37th St ... New York NY 10018	212-686-5194		594
JAG Advisors 9841 Clayton Rd ... Saint Louis MO 63124 *TF:* 800-966-4596 ■ *Web:* www.jaglynn.com	314-997-1277		528
Jagemann Stamping Co 5757 W Custer St ... Manitowoc WI 54220 *TF:* 888-337-7853 ■ *Web:* www.jagemann.com	920-682-4633		488
Jaguar Computer Systems Inc 4135 Indus Way ... Riverside CA 92503 *Web:* www.jaguar.net	951-273-7950	734-5615	175
Jaguar Design Studio Inc 9039 Soquel Dr ... Aptos CA 95003 *TF:* 800-411-7222 ■ *Web:* www.jaguardesignstudio.com	831-662-9991		344
Jai Transforme Salon 12730 Olive Blvd ... Saint Louis MO 63141 *Web:* www.jaitransformesalon.com	314-439-5542		77
Jailhouse Inn 13 Marlborough St ... Newport RI 02840 *Web:* www.jailhouse.com	401-847-4638		379
Jaipur Rugs Inc 2775 Pacific Dr ... Norcross GA 30071 *TF:* 888-676-7330 ■ *Web:* www.jaipurliving.com	404-351-2360		131
Jaipur, The 10922 Elm St ... Omaha NE 68144 *Web:* jaipurindianfood.com	402-392-7331		671
JAIR LYNCH Development Partners 1508 U St NW ... Washington DC 20009 *Web:* www.jairlynch.com	202-462-1092		653
Jajo Inc 131 N Rock Island ... Wichita KS 67202 *Web:* www.jajo.agency	316-267-6700		7
JAK Enterprises Inc 8309 N Knoxville Ave ... Peoria IL 61615 *TF:* 800-752-3295 ■ *Web:* www.bardoptical.com	309-692-8222		543
JaK's Grill 3701 NE 45th St ... Seattle WA 98105 *Web:* www.jaksgrill.com	206-985-8545		671
Jake & Telly's 2616 W Colorado Ave ... Colorado Springs CO 80904 *Web:* www.jakeandtellys.com	719-633-0406		671
Jake A Parrott Insurance Agency Inc 2508 N Herritage St ... Kinston NC 28501 *TF:* 800-727-7688 ■ *Web:* parrottins.com	252-523-1041		390
Jake's 2701 First Ave N ... Billings MT 59101 *Web:* jakesbillings.com	406-259-9375		671
Jake's Famous Crawfish 401 SW 12th Ave SW Stark ... Portland OR 97205 *TF:* 800-552-6379 ■ *Web:* www.mccormickandschmicks.com	503-226-1419	220-1856	671
Jake's Good Time Place 620 S Cleveland ... Pierre SD 57501 *Web:* dexknows.com	605-945-0485		671
Jake's Grill 611 SW Tenth Ave ... Portland OR 97205 *Web:* www.mccormickandschmicks.com	503-220-1850	226-8365	671
Jake's Seafood House Restaurant 29 Baltimore Ave ... Rehoboth Beach DE 19971 *Web:* www.jakesseafoodhouse.com	302-227-6237		671
Jake's Sports Cafe 5025 50th St ... Lubbock TX 79414 *Web:* www.jakes-sportscafe.com	806-687-5253		671
Jake's Tex-Mex Cafe 1710 Oak St ... Bakersfield CA 93301 *Web:* www.jakestexmex.com	661-322-6380	322-3731	671
Jaken Company Inc 14420 My ford rf Ste 150 ... Irvine CA 92606 *TF:* 800-401-7225 ■ *Web:* www.jaken.com	714-522-1700		206
Jakes Crane & Rigging Inc 6109 Dean Martin Dr ... Las Vegas NV 89118 *TF:* 800-872-5253 ■ *Web:* www.jakescrane.com	702-872-5253		190
JAKKS Pacific Inc 21749 Baker Pkwy ... Walnut CA 91789 *NASDAQ: JAKK* ■ *TF:* 877-875-2557 ■ *Web:* www.jakks.com	909-594-7771		762
Jakprints Inc 3133 Chester Ave ... Cleveland OH 44114 *Web:* www.jakprints.com	216-622-6360		627
Jalapeno Inferno 23587 N Scottsdale ... Scottsdale AZ 85255 *Web:* www.jalapenoinferno.com	480-585-6442		671
Jalapenos 85 Forest Dr ... Annapolis MD 21401 *Web:* jalapenosonline.com	410-266-7580		671
Jaleo 480 Seventh St NW ... Washington DC 20004 *Web:* www.jaleo.com	202-628-7949		671
JALPAK International Hawaii Inc 2270 Kalakaua Ave Ste 1600 ... Honolulu HI 96815	808-926-4500		760
JAM Productions Ltd 205 W Goethe ... Chicago IL 60610 *TF:* 800-745-3000 ■ *Web:* www.jamusa.com	312-440-9191		181
JAM'N 107.5 13333 SW 68th Pkwy Ste 310 ... Tigard OR 97223 *Web:* jamn1075.iheart.com	503-248-1075		645-128
JAMA (Japan Automobile Manufacturers Assn) 1050 17th St NW Ste 410 ... Washington DC 20036 *Web:* www.jama.org	202-296-8537	872-1212	49-21
JAMA (Journal of the American Medical Assn) PO Box 10946 ... Chicago IL 60654 *TF:* 800-262-2350 ■ *Web:* jama.jamanetwork.com	312-670-7827		457-16
Jamac Frozen Foods 570 Grand St ... Jersey City NJ 07302 *TF:* 800-631-0440 ■ *Web:* www.jamacfoods.com	201-333-6200		345
Jamaica 767 Third Ave 9th Fl ... New York NY 10017 *Web:* www.un.int	212-935-7509	935-7607	784
Jamaica Bay Riding Academy Inc 7000 Shore Pkwy ... Brooklyn NY 11234 *Web:* horsebackride.com	718-531-8949		148
Jamaica Chamber of Commerce 15711 Rockaway Blvd ... Jamaica NY 11434 *TF:* 800-315-4000 ■ *Web:* jamaicachambernyc.com	718-877-7704		139
Jamaica Embassy 1520 New Hampshire Ave NW ... Washington DC 20036 *Web:* www.embassyofjamaica.org	202-452-0660	452-0036	257
Jamaica Hospital Medical Ctr 8900 Van Wyck Expy ... Jamaica NY 11418 *Web:* www.jamaicahospital.org	718-206-6000		374-3
Jamaica Jamaica 4853 S Apex Hwy ... Durham NC 27713	919-544-1532		671

Name / Address	City	State	Zip	Phone	Fax	Class
Jamaica State Park 48 Salmon Hole Ln *Web:* www.vtstateparks.com	Jamaica	VT	05343	802-874-4600		565
Jamaica Tourist Board 5201 Blue Lagoon Dr Ste 670 *TF:* 800-526-2422 ■ *Web:* www.visitjamaica.com	Miami	FL	33126	305-665-0557		775
Jamak Fabrication Inc 1401 N Bowie Dr *TF:* 800-543-4747 ■ *Web:* www.jamak.com	Weatherford	TX	76086	817-594-8771	594-8324	677
Jamar Co 4701 Mike Colalillo Dr *TF:* 800-644-3624 ■ *Web:* www.jamarcompany.com	Duluth	MN	55807	218-628-1027	628-1174	189-10
Jamba Juice Co 6475 Christie Ave Ste 150 *Web:* www.jambajuice.com	Emeryville	CA	94608	510-596-0100		345
Jamco Aerospace Inc 121 E Industry Ct *Web:* www.jamco-aerospace.com	Deer Park	NY	11729	631-586-7900		454
Jamco America Inc 1018 80th St SW *Web:* www.jamco-america.com	Everett	WA	98203	425-347-4735	353-2343	22
Jamcracker Inc 4677 Old Ironsides Dr Ste 450 *Web:* www.jamcracker.com	Santa Clara	CA	95054	408-496-5500		39
James A Cummings Inc 3575 NW 53rd St	Fort Lauderdale	FL	33309	954-733-4211	485-9688	187
James A Garfield National Historic Site 8095 Mentor Ave *Web:* www.nps.gov/jaga	Mentor	OH	44060	440-255-8722	255-8545	564
James A Murphy & Son Inc 50 Colorado Ave *Web:* patch.com/attleboro	Warwick	RI	02886	508-761-5060		407
James A Normoyle Insurance Agency 669 Palmetto Ave Ste E	Chico	CA	95926	530-891-1122		390
James A Scott & Son Inc PO Box 10489 *TF:* 800-365-0101 ■ *Web:* www.scottins.com	Lynchburg	VA	24506	434-832-2100		391-4
James Alexander Corp 845 Route 94 *TF:* 800-424-9300 ■ *Web:* www.james-alexander.com	Blairstown	NJ	07825	908-362-9266		88
James Allyn Printing Inc 6575 Trinity Ct Ste B *Web:* www.jamesallyn.com	Dublin	CA	94568	925-828-5530		627
James Arthur Vineyards & Winery 2001 W Raymond Rd *Web:* www.jamesarthurvineyards.com	Raymond	NE	68428	402-783-5255		50-7
James Austin Co 115 Downieville Rd PO Box 827 *TF:* 800-245-1942 ■ *Web:* austinsbleach.com	Mars	PA	16046	724-625-1535	625-3288	151
James Avery Craftsman Inc 145 Avery Rd N *TF:* 800-283-1770 ■ *Web:* www.jamesavery.com	Kerrville	TX	78029	830-895-1122		409
James B Mcevoy CPA 280 N Bedford Rd *Web:* jmcevoycpa.com	Mt Kisco	NY	10549	914-241-0460		2
James Baird State Park 14 Maintenance Ln *Web:* parks.ny.gov/parks/101/details.aspx	Pleasant Valley	NY	12569	845-452-1489		565
James C Hailey & Co 7518 Hwy 70 S Ste 100 *Web:* jchengr.com	Nashville	TN	37221	615-883-4933	883-4937	261
James Candy Co 1519 Boardwalk *TF Orders:* 800-441-1404 ■ *Web:* www.jamescandy.com	Atlantic City	NJ	08401	609-344-1519	344-0246	296-8
James Chicago, The 55 E Ontario *TF:* 888-526-3778 ■ *Web:* www.jameshotels.com	Chicago	IL	60611	312-337-1000	337-7217	379
James City County PO Box 8784 *TF:* 800-275-2355 ■ *Web:* www.jamescitycountyva.gov	Williamsburg	VA	23187	757-253-6728	253-6833	338
James City Service Authority Water Treatment 101 Mounts Bay Rd *Web:* www.jamescitycountyva.gov/611/James-City-Service-Authority	Williamsburg	VA	23185	757-253-6800		104
James Coney Island Inc 1750 Stebbins Dr *TF:* 800-319-6410 ■ *Web:* www.jamesconeyisland.com	Houston	TX	77043	713-932-1500	932-0061	670
James Crabtree Correctional Ctr 216 N Murray St *Web:* www.ok.gov	Helena	OK	73741	580-852-3221		213
James Craft & Son Inc 2780 York Haven Rd PO Box 8 *TF:* 800-400-2420 ■ *Web:* www.jamescraftson.com	York Haven	PA	17370	717-266-6629	266-6623	189-10
James D Morrissey Inc 9119 Frankford Ave *TF:* 877-536-6857 ■ *Web:* www.jdm-inc.com	Philadelphia	PA	19114	215-357-5505	338-3225	188-4
James Davis 400 S Grove Pk Rd *TF:* 800-280-2347 ■ *Web:* jamesdavisstore.com	Memphis	TN	38117	901-767-4640		157-4
James E Conner Jr Plumbing 505 Rt 168 Stes B And C *Web:* jameseconnerjrplumbing.com	Turnersville	NJ	08012	856-784-0004		189-10
James E Raftery CPA PC 606 N Stapley Dr	Mesa	AZ	85203	480-835-1040		2
James E Roberts-obayashi Corp 20 Oak Ct *Web:* www.jerocorp.com	Danville	CA	94526	925-820-0600		190
James Farris Associates Ltd 909 NW 63rd St *TF:* 800-522-0761 ■ *Web:* www.jamesfarris.com	Oklahoma City	OK	73116	405-525-5061		260
James G Davis Construction Corp 12530 Parklawn Dr *Web:* www.davisconstruction.com	Rockville	MD	20852	301-881-2990	468-3918	186
James G Hardy & Co 24919 148th Rd	Jamaica	NY	11422	212-689-6680		361
James Gettys Hotel 27 Chambersburg St *TF:* 888-900-5275 ■ *Web:* www.jamesgettyshotel.com	Gettysburg	PA	17325	717-337-1334	334-2103	379
James Goodman Gallery 41 E 57th St Ste 802 *TF:* 800-586-3809 ■ *Web:* www.jamesgoodmangallery.com	New York	NY	10022	212-593-3737	980-0195	42
James Graham Brown Cancer Ctr 529 S Jackson St *TF:* 866-530-5516 ■ *Web:* www.kentuckyonehealth.org/browncancercenter	Louisville	KY	40202	502-562-4369		769
James Greene & Assoc Inc 275 W Kiehl Ave *TF:* 800-422-3384 ■ *Web:* jamesgreeneins.com	Sherwood	AR	72120	501-834-4001		390
James Group International 4335 W Ft St *Web:* www.jamesgroupintl.com	Detroit	MI	48209	313-841-0070		449
James Gutheim & Associates Inc 16400 Ventura Blvd Ste 312 *Web:* gutheim.com	Encino	CA	91436	818-784-7189		195
James H Drew Corp 8701 Zionsville Rd *Web:* jameshdrew.com	Indianapolis	IN	46268	317-876-3739	876-3829	188-4
James H Quillen Veterans Affairs Medical Ctr Corner of Lamont & Veterans Way *TF:* 877-573-3529 ■ *Web:* www.mountainhome.va.gov	Mountain Home	TN	37684	423-926-1171	979-3519	374-8
James H. Sloppy Floyd State Park 2800 Sloppy Floyd Lake Rd *Web:* www.gastateparks.org	Summerville	GA	30747	706-857-0826		565
James Hardie Bldg Products 26300 La Alameda Ave Ste 400 *TF:* 888-542-7343 ■ *Web:* www.jameshardie.com	Mission Viejo	CA	92691	866-302-3865		191-4
James Hoyer Newcomer & Smiljanich pa 3301 Thomasville Rd *Web:* www.jameshoyer.com	Tallahassee	FL	32308	850-325-2680		428
James Investment Research Inc 1349 Fairgrounds Rd *TF:* 800-995-2637 ■ *Web:* www.jamesfunds.com	Xenia	OH	45385	937-426-7640		401
James Irvine Foundation 1 Bush St Ste 800 *Web:* www.irvine.org	San Francisco	CA	94104	415-777-2244	777-0869	305
James J Hill House 240 Summit Ave *TF:* 888-727-8386 ■ *Web:* www.mnhs.org	Saint Paul	MN	55102	651-297-2555		50-3
James J Peters Veterans Affairs Medical Ctr 130 W Kingsbridge Rd *Web:* www.bronx.va.gov	Bronx	NY	10468	718-584-9000	741-4571	374-8
James J. Eagan Civic Center 1 James J Eagan Dr *Web:* www.florissantmo.com	Florissant	MO	63033	314-921-5700		720
James Jordan Middle School 7911 Winnetka Ave *Web:* www.jamesjordanms.com	Winnetka	CA	91306	818-882-2496		685
James Joyce Authentic Irish Pub 114 Eigth Ave SW *Web:* stthomasac.com	Calgary	AB	T2P1B3	403-262-0708		671
James K Polk Memorial State Historic Site 12031 Lancaster Hwy PO Box 475 *Web:* www.nchistoricsites.org	Pineville	NC	28134	704-889-7145	889-3057	50-3
James L Allen Ctr 2169 Campus Dr *TF:* 877-755-2227 ■ *Web:* www.kellogg.northwestern.edu	Evanston	IL	60208	847-467-7000	491-8002	377
James L Howard & Company Inc 10 Britton Dr *TF:* 800-252-8859 ■ *Web:* www.jameslhoward.com	Bloomfield	CT	06002	860-242-3581		350
James L Knight International Ctr 400 SE Second Ave *TF:* 800-745-3000 ■ *Web:* www.jlkc.com	Miami	FL	33131	305-416-5970	350-7910	572
James L Maher Center 120 Hillside Ave *Web:* www.mahercenter.org	Newport	RI	02840	401-846-0340		104
James L. Goodwin State Forest Goodwin Forest Conservation Education Ctr 23 Potter Rd *Web:* www.ct.gov	Hampton	CT	06226	860-455-9534	455-9857	565
James L. Taylor Manufacturing Co 108 Parker Ave *TF:* 800-952-1320 ■ *Web:* www.jamesltaylor.com	Poughkeepsie	NY	12601	845-452-3780	452-0764	821
James L. West Alzheimer Center 1111 Summit Ave *TF:* 800-508-9480 ■ *Web:* www.jameslwest.org	Fort Worth	TX	76102	817-877-1199		371
James Lane Air Conditioning Company Inc 5024 Old Jacksboro Hwy *TF:* 800-460-2204 ■ *Web:* www.jameslane.com	Wichita Falls	TX	76302	940-766-0244		610
James M Trotter Convention Ctr 402 Second Ave N	Columbus	MS	39701	662-328-4164		205
James M. Robb - Colorado River State Park PO Box 700 *Web:* cpw.state.co.us	Clifton	CO	81520	970-434-3388		565
James Machine Works LLC 1521 Adams St *TF:* 800-259-6104 ■ *Web:* www.jmwinc.net	Monroe	LA	71201	318-322-6104	388-4245	189-1
James Madison University 800 S Main St **Fax:* Admissions ■ *Web:* www.jmu.edu	Harrisonburg	VA	22807	540-568-6211	568-3332*	166
James Madison's Montpelier 13384 Laundry Rd *Web:* www.montpelier.org	Montpelier Station	VA	22957	540-672-2728		50-3
James Marine Inc (JMI) 4500 Clarks River Rd PO Box 2305 *Web:* www.jamesmarine.com	Paducah	KY	42002	270-898-7392		465
James McHugh Construction Co 1737 S Michigan Ave *TF:* 800-355-9401 ■ *Web:* www.mchughconstruction.com	Chicago	IL	60616	312-986-8000	431-8518	188-4
James Mulligan Printing Corp 1808 Washington Ave *TF:* 800-737-0874 ■ *Web:* mobile.weprint.com	St. Louis	MO	63103	314-621-0875		627
James Pate Philip State Park 2050 W Stearns Rd *Web:* www.dnr.state.il.us	Bartlett	IL	60103	847 608-3100		565
James Paton Memorial Hospital 125 Trans Canada Hwy *TF:* 800-611-7011 ■ *Web:* centralhealth.nl.ca	Gander	NL	A1V1P7	709-256-2500	256-7800	374-2
James Posey Assoc Inc 3112 Lord Baltimore Dr *Web:* www.jamesposey.com	Baltimore	MD	21244	410-265-6100		256
James R Mclauchlen Real Estate Inc 789 Hill St *Web:* mclauchlen.com	Southampton	NY	11968	631-283-0448		652
James R Swab 1707 Myrtle Rd	Silver Spring	MD	20902	301-681-7935		2
James Richardson International (JRI) 2800 One Lombard Pl *Web:* www.richardson.ca	Winnipeg	MB	R3B0X8	204-934-5961		275
James River Coal Co 901 E Byrd St Ste 1600 *TF:* 800-642-1687 ■ *Web:* www.jamesrivercoal.com	Richmond	VA	23219	804-780-3000		501
James River Convalescent Ctr 540 Aberthaw Ave *Web:* vahs.com	Newport News	VA	23601	757-595-2273		450

Name / Address	Phone	Fax	Class
James River Equipment 11047 Leadbetter Rd. Ashland VA 23005 *TF:* 800-872-2390 ■ *Web:* jamesriverequipment.com	804-798-6001		274
James Sewell Ballet 528 Hennepin Ave Ste 215 Minneapolis MN 55403 *Web:* www.jsballet.org	612-672-0480		573-1
James Skinner Baking Co 4657 G St Omaha NE 68117 *TF:* 800-358-7428 ■ *Web:* www.skinnerbaking.com	402-734-1672	734-0516	296-2
James Sprunt Community College 133 James Sprunt Dr Kenansville NC 28349 **Fax:* Admissions ■ *TF:* 800-774-9634 ■ *Web:* jamessprunt.edu	910-296-2400	296-1636*	162
James Steele Construction Co 1410 Sylvan St Saint Paul MN 55117 *Web:* www.jamessteeleconstruction.com	651-488-6755	488-4787	188-5
James Thompson & Company Inc 381 Pk Ave S # 718 New York NY 10016 *Web:* www.jamesthompson.com	212-686-4242	686-9528	208
James Tool Machine & Engineering Inc 130 Reep Dr Morganton NC 28655 *Web:* www.jamestool.com	828-584-8722		256
James V Brown Library of Williamsport & Lycoming County 19 E Fourth St Williamsport PA 17701 *Web:* www.jvbrown.edu	570-326-0536	326-1671	434-3
James W Bell Company Inc 1755 I Ave NE Cedar Rapids IA 52402 *Web:* jwbell.biz	319-362-1151	365-3649	358
James W Glover Ltd 248 Sand Island Access Rd Honolulu HI 96819 *TF:* 800-734-9181 ■ *Web:* www.gloverltd.com	808-591-8977		188-4
James Walker Co 7109 Milford Industrial Rd Baltimore MD 21215 *Web:* jameswalker.com	410-486-3950		470
James Walker Manufacturing Co 511 W 195th St Glenwood IL 60425 *Web:* www.jameswalker.biz	708-754-4020		326
James Whitcomb Riley Museum Home 528 Lockerbie St Indianapolis IN 46202 *TF:* 800-677-9800 ■ *Web:* www.rileykids.org	317-631-5885		520
James White Construction Company Inc 4156 Freedom Way Weirton WV 26062 *Web:* jameswhiteconstruction.com	304-748-8181	748-8183	188-10
James White's Fort 205 E Hill Ave Knoxville TN 37915 *Web:* jameswhitesfort.org	865-525-6514		520
James Wood Motors Inc 2111 US Hwy 287 S Decatur TX 76234 *TF:* 866-232-6058 ■ *Web:* www.jameswood.com	940-627-2177		57
James, McElroy & Diehl PA 600 S College St Charlotte NC 28202 *Web:* www.jmdlaw.com	704-372-9870		428
James, Stevens & Daniels Inc 1283 College Park Dr Dover DE 19904 *TF:* 800-305-0773 ■ *Web:* www.jsdinc.net	302-735-4020		160
James, The 300 W Tenth Ave Ste 519 Columbus OH 43210 *Web:* cancer.osu.edu	614-293-5066	293-3132	374-7
Jameson & Dunagan PC 5429 LBJ Fwy Ste 700 Dallas TX 75240 *Web:* www.jdlawtx.com	214-369-6422		428
Jameson Annex 1600 N Dr PO Box 5911 Sioux Falls SD 57117 *Web:* www.doc.sd.gov	605-367-5051	367-5585	213
Jameson Group 287 S Robertson Blvd Ste 474 Beverly Hills CA 90211 *TF:* 800-704-9115 ■ *Web:* www.thejamesongroup.com	310-289-5085		393
Jameson LLC 1451 Old N Main St Clover SC 29710 *Web:* www.jamesonllc.com	803-222-6400		253
Jameson Real Estate LLC 425 W N Ave Chicago IL 60610	312-751-0300		652
Jamestown Area Chamber of Commerce 120 Second St SE PO Box 1530 Jamestown ND 58402 *TF:* 800-882-2500 ■ *Web:* www.jamestownchamber.com	701-252-4830	952-4837	139
Jamestown Business College 7 Fairmount Ave PO Box 429 Jamestown NY 14702 *TF:* 877-557-2575 ■ *Web:* www.jbc.edu	716-664-5100	664-3144	800
Jamestown College 6000 College Ln Jamestown ND 58405 *TF:* 800-336-2554 ■ *Web:* www.uj.edu	701-252-3467	253-4318	166
Jamestown Community College 525 Faulkner St PO Box 20 Jamestown NY 14702 *TF:* 800-388-8557 ■ *Web:* www.sunyjcc.edu	716-338-1000		162
Cattaraugus County 260 N Union St PO Box 5901 Olean NY 14760 **Fax:* Admissions ■ *TF:* 800-388-9776 ■ *Web:* www.sunyjcc.edu	716-376-7500	376-7020*	162
Jamestown Livestock Auction 3443 82nd Ave SE Jamestown ND 58401 *Web:* www.jamestownlivestock.com	701-252-2111	252-1520	446
Jamestown Plastics Inc 8806 Highland Ave Brocton NY 14716 *Web:* www.jamestownplastics.com	716-792-4144	792-4154	602
Jamestown Promotions & Tourism Ctr 404 Louis L'Amour Ln Jamestown ND 58401 *TF:* 800-222-4766 ■ *Web:* discoverjamestownnd.com	701-251-9145	251-9146	206
Jamesville-Dewitt Central School Dist (Inc) 6845 Edinger Dr PO Box 606 Fayetteville NY 13066 *Web:* www.jamesvilledewitt.org	315-445-8340		685
Jamesway Incubator Co Inc 30 High Ridge Ct Cambridge ON N1R7L3 *TF:* 800-438-8077 ■ *Web:* www.jamesway.com	519-624-4646		273
Jamie Gibbs & Associates 120 W 73rd St Indianapolis IN 46260 *Web:* www.jamiegibbsassociates.com	917-862-5313		393
Jamie Whitten Delta States Research Ctr Experiment Stn Rd PO Box 225 Stoneville MS 38776 *Web:* www.ars.usda.gov	662-686-5265	686-5459	668
Jamison Bedding Inc PO Box 681948 Franklin TN 37068 *TF Cust Svc:* 800-255-1883 ■ *Web:* www.jamisonbedding.com	615-794-1883		471
Jamison Door Co 55 JV Jamison Dr Hagerstown MD 21740 **Fax Area Code:* 240 ■ *TF:* 800-532-3667 ■ *Web:* www.jamisondoor.com	301-733-3100	329-5155*	234
Jammin-FM 99.5 (Alt) 75153 Merle Dr Ste G Palm Desert CA 92211 *Web:* www.jammin995fm.com	760-568-4550		645-119

Name / Address	Phone	Fax	Class
Jampro Antennas Inc 6340 Sky Creek Dr Sacramento CA 95828 *TF:* 800-732-7665 ■ *Web:* www.jampro.com	916-383-1177	383-1182	647
JAMS/Endispute 500 N State College Blvd 14th Fl Orange CA 92868 *TF:* 800-352-5267 ■ *Web:* www.jamsadr.com	714-939-1300	939-8710	41
Jamsan Hotel Management Inc 440 Bedford St Lexington MA 02420 *TF:* 800-523-5549 ■ *Web:* www.jamsanhotels.com	781-863-8500		463
Jan Cos 35 Sockanosset Cross Rd Cranston RI 02920 *TF:* 888-693-6844 ■ *Web:* www.jancompanies.com	401-946-4000	946-4392	670
Jan Dils Attorneys at Law Lc 107 Lb And T Way Logan WV 25601 *TF:* 800-358-4383 ■ *Web:* www.jandils.com	304-831-0000		428
Jan Marini Skin Research Inc 6951 Via Del Oro San Jose CA 95119 *TF:* 800-347-2223 ■ *Web:* www.janmarini.com	408-362-0130	362-0140	214
Jan Packaging Inc 100 Harrison St Dover NJ 07801 *Web:* www.janpackaging.com	973-361-7200		311
Jan's Mountain Outfitters 1600 Pk Ave PO Box 280 Park City UT 84060 *TF:* 800-745-1020 ■ *Web:* www.jans.com	435-649-4949	649-7511	711
Jana Foods LLC 100 Wood Ave S Ste 206 Iselin NJ 08830 *Web:* www.janafoods.com	201-866-5001		297-8
Janalent Corp 7582 Las Vegas Blvd S Ste 580 Ste Las Vegas NV 89123 *TF:* 888-290-4870 ■ *Web:* www.janalent.com	888-290-4870		196
Janas Consulting 201 S Lake Ave Ste 302 Pasadena CA 91101 *TF:* 800-397-8865 ■ *Web:* www.janascorp.com	626-432-7000		708
Janazzo Services Corp 140 Norton St Rt 10 PO Box 469 Milldale CT 06467 *TF:* 800-297-3931 ■ *Web:* www.janazzo.com	860-621-7381	621-7529	189-10
Janco Supply Company Inc 723 N Highland Ave Aurora IL 60506	630-896-4651		366
Jancyn Inc 1100 Lincoln Ave Ste 367 San Jose CA 95125 **Fax Area Code:* 866 ■ *TF:* 800-339-2861 ■ *Web:* jancyn.com	800-339-2861	266-3140*	506
Jane Addams Hull-House Museum 800 S Halsted St Chicago IL 60607 *TF:* 800-625-2013 ■ *Web:* www.uic.edu	312-413-5353	413-2092	50-3
Jane Goodall Institute for Wildlife Research Education (JGI) 1595 Spring Hill Rd Ste 550 Vienna VA 22182 *TF:* 800-592-5263 ■ *Web:* www.janegoodall.org	703-682-9220	682-9312	48-3
Jane Rose Reporting 80 Fifth Ave New York NY 10011 *TF:* 800-825-3341 ■ *Web:* www.janerose.net/janeroseflash.swf	212-727-7773		445
Jane Rotrosen Agency 318 E 51st St New York NY 10022 *Web:* janerotrosen.com	212-593-4330	935-6985	444
Janell Inc 6130 Cornell Rd Cincinnati OH 45242 *TF:* 888-489-9111 ■ *Web:* www.janell.com	513-489-9111		358
Janes Island State Park 26280 Alfred Lawson Dr Crisfield MD 21817 *TF:* 877-620-8367 ■ *Web:* dnr2.maryland.gov	410-968-1565		565
Janesville Sand & Gravel Co (JSG) 1110 Harding St Janesville WI 53547 *TF:* 800-955-7702 ■ *Web:* www.jsandg.com	608-754-7701		503-4
Janesway Electronic Corp 404 N Terr Ave Mount Vernon NY 10552 *TF:* 800-431-1340 ■ *Web:* www.janesway.com	914-699-6710	699-6969	246
Janet Mcafee Real Estate 9889 Clayton Rd Saint Louis MO 63124 *TF:* 888-991-4800 ■ *Web:* www.janetmcafee.com	314-997-4800	997-0647	652
Janet's Antiques 2545 Central Ave Saint Petersburg FL 33713	727-823-5700		460
Janicki Industries Inc 1476 Moore St Sedro Woolley WA 98284 *Web:* www.janicki.com	360-856-5143		454
Jani-King International Inc 16885 Dallas Pkwy Addison TX 75001 *TF:* 800-526-4546 ■ *Web:* www.janiking.com	972-991-0900	991-5723	152
Janitronics Bldg Services 29 Sawyer Rd Waltham MA 02453 *TF:* 800-535-8285 ■ *Web:* www.janitronics.com	781-647-5570	893-5878	104
Janitronics Inc 1988 Central Ave Albany NY 12205 *Web:* www.janitronicsinc.com	518-456-8484		256
Jankins & Jablonski SC 15400 W Capitol Dr Brookfield WI 53005	262-781-2121		2
Janko Hospitality Llc 3050 Finley Rd Ste 300D-1 Downers Grove IL 60515 *Web:* www.jankohotels.com	630-434-9400		463
Jankovich Co, The Berth 74 San Pedro CA 90731 *TF:* 800-650-0200 ■ *Web:* www.jankovichcompany.com	310-547-3305		538
Janlynn Corp 2070 Westover Rd Chicopee MA 01022 *TF:* 800-445-5565 ■ *Web:* www.janlynn.com	413-206-0002		594
Janney Montgomery Scott LLC 1801 Market St Philadelphia PA 19103 *TF:* 800-526-6397 ■ *Web:* www.janney.com	215-665-6000		690
Jannus Inc (MSG) 1607 W Jefferson St Boise ID 83702 *Web:* www.jannus.org	208-336-5533	336-0880	48-17
Janoka Inc Dba The Medicine Shoppe 542 S Eufaula Ave Eufaula AL 36027	334-687-0021		237
Janos Technology LLC 55 Black Brook Rd Keene NH 03431 *Web:* www.janostech.com	603-757-0070		544
Janou Pakter Inc 108 W 39th St New York NY 10018 **Fax Area Code:* 310 ■ *Web:* www.janoupakter.com	212-989-1288	359-0232*	721
Jan-Pro Cleaning Systems Minneapolis 33 tenth Ave S Ste 200 Hopkins MN 55343 *Web:* twincities.jan-pro.com	952-238-1005		256
Jan-Pro International Inc (JPI) 2520 Northwinds Pkwy Ste 375 Alpharetta GA 30009 *TF:* 866-355-1064 ■ *Web:* www.jan-pro.com	678-336-1780		152
Janson Industries 1200 Garfield Ave SW Canton OH 44706 *TF:* 800-548-8982 ■ *Web:* www.jansonindustries.com	330-455-7029	455-5919	722
Janson Media Inc 118 Main St Tappan NJ 10983 *Web:* www.janson.com	845-359-8488		194
Janssen Clinic for Animals 1624 N High Point Rd Middleton WI 53562 *Web:* www.janssenclinic.com	608-836-0600		794

Name / Address	City	State	Zip	Phone	Fax	Class
Janssen Consulting Inc 1704 Mission Ave Ste 1 *Web:* www.janssenconsulting.com	Carmichael	CA	95608	916-716-2326		179
Janssen Pharmaceutica Inc 1125 Trenton-Harbourton Rd **Fax Area Code:* 609 ■ *TF:* 800-526-7736 ■ *Web:* www.janssen.com	Titusville	NJ	08560	908-218-6095	730-2378*	582
Jantek Industries 230 Rt 70 *TF:* 888-782-7937 ■ *Web:* jantekwindows.com	Medford	NJ	08055	609-654-1030	654-1083	234
Jantzen Beach SuperCenter 1405 Jantzen Beach Centre *TF:* 877-775-3462	Portland	OR	97217	877-775-3462		460
Janus Consulting Inc 14408 Ashleigh Greene Rd *Web:* janusconsulting.com	Boyds	MD	20841	301-515-9113		196
Janus Corp 1081 Shary Cir *Web:* www.januscorp.com	Concord	CA	94518	925-969-9200		186
Janus Henderson Investors 151 Detroit St *Web:* www.janus.com	Denver	CO	80206	303-333-3863		401
Janus Hotels & Resorts Inc 2300 Corporate Blvd NW Ste 232 *Web:* www.janushotels.com	Boca Raton	FL	33431	561-997-2325	997-5331	379
JANUS Research Group Inc 600 Ponder Pl Dr *Web:* janusresearch.com	Evans	GA	30809	706-364-9100		194
Japan 866 UN Plaza 2nd Fl *Web:* www.un.int	New York	NY	10017	212-223-4300	751-1966	784
Consulate General 3601 C St Ste 1300 *Web:* www.anchorage.us.emb-japan.go.jp	Anchorage	AK	99503	907-562-8424	562-8434	257
Consulate General 3438 Peachtree Rd Phipps Tower Ste 850 *Web:* www.atlanta.us.emb-japan.go.jp	Atlanta	GA	30326	404-240-4300	240-4311	257
Consulate General 1742 Nuuanu Ave *Web:* www.honolulu.us.emb-japan.go.jp	Honolulu	HI	96817	808-543-3111	543-3170	257
Consulate General 737 N Michigan Ave Ste 1100 *Web:* www.chicago.us.emb-japan.go.jp	Chicago	IL	60611	312-280-0400	280-9568	257
Consulate General 50 Fremont St Ste 2300 *Web:* www.sf.us.emb-japan.go.jp	San Francisco	CA	94105	415-777-3533	974-3660	257
Consulate General 1801 W End Ave Ste 900 *Web:* www.nashville.us.emb-japan.go.jp	Nashville	TN	37203	615-340-4300	340-4311	257
Consulate General 400 Renaissance Ctr Ste 1600 *Web:* www.detroit.us.emb-japan.go.jp	Detroit	MI	48243	313-567-0120	567-0274	257
Consulate General Wells Fargo Ctr 1300 SW Fifth Ave Ste 2700 *Web:* www.portland.us.emb-japan.go.jp	Portland	OR	97201	503-221-1811	224-8936	257
Consulate General 1225 17th St Ste 3000 *Web:* www.denver.us.emb-japan.go.jp	Denver	CO	80202	303-534-1151	534-3393	257
Consulate General 350 S Grand Ave Ste 1700 *Web:* www.la.us.emb-japan.go.jp	Los Angeles	CA	90071	213-617-6700	617-6727	257
Consulate General 299 Pk Ave 18th Fl *Web:* www.ny.us.emb-japan.go.jp	New York	NY	10171	212-371-8222	371-1294	257
Consulate General 601 Union St Ste 500 *Web:* www.seattle.us.emb-japan.go.jp	Seattle	WA	98101	206-682-9107	624-9097	257
Consulate General 80 SW Eigth St Brickell Bay View Ctr Ste 3200 *Web:* www.miami.us.emb-japan.go.jp	Miami	FL	33130	305-530-9090	530-0950	257
Consulate General 600 Atlantic Ave 22nd Fl *Web:* www.boston.us.emb-japan.go.jp	Boston	MA	02210	617-973-9772	542-1329	257
Japan Automobile Manufacturers Assn (JAMA) 1050 17th St NW Ste 410 *Web:* www.jama.org	Washington	DC	20036	202-296-8537	872-1212	49-21
Japan Canada Oil Sands Ltd 639-5th Ave SW Standard Life Bldg Ste 2300 *Web:* www.jacos.ca	Calgary	AB	T2P0M9	403-264-9046		536
Japan National Tourist Organization 707 Wilshire Blvd Ste 4325 *Web:* us.jnto.go.jp	Los Angeles	CA	90071	213-623-1952	623-6301	775
Japan National Tourist Organization 1 Grand Central Pl 60 E 42nd St Ste 448 *Web:* us.jnto.go.jp	New York	NY	10165	212-757-5640	307-6754	775
Japan Samurai 12233 Jefferson Ave *Web:* japansamurainn.com	Newport News	VA	23602	757-249-4400		671
Japan Society 333 E 47th St *Web:* www.japansociety.org	New York	NY	10017	212-832-1155	755-6752	48-14
Japan Telecom America Inc 100 Wall St Ste 1803 *Web:* www.jt-america.com	New York	NY	10005	212-422-4650		736
Japan Travel Bureau USA Inc 2 W 45th St Ste 305 *TF:* 800-235-3523 ■ *Web:* www.jtbusa.com	New York	NY	10019	212-698-4900	586-9686	771
Japanese American Citizens League (JACL) 1765 Sutter St *TF:* 800-400-6633 ■ *Web:* www.jacl.org	San Francisco	CA	94115	415-921-5225	931-4671	48-14
Japanese American National Museum 369 E First St *TF:* 800-461-5266 ■ *Web:* www.janm.org	Los Angeles	CA	90012	213-625-0414	625-0414	520
Japanese Chamber of Commerce & Industry of Chicago 541 N Fairbanks Ct Ste 2050 *Web:* jccc-chi.org/ja/ai1ec_event/environmentallaw	Chicago	IL	60611	312-245-8344	245-8355	138
Japanese Chamber of Commerce & Industry of Hawaii 714 Kanoelehua Ave *Web:* jccih.org	Hilo	HI	96720	808-934-0177	934-0178	138
Japanese Chamber of Commerce & Industry of New York Inc 145 W 57th St 6th Fl *Web:* www.jcciny.org	New York	NY	10019	212-246-8001	246-8002	138
Japanese Chamber of Commerce of Northern California 1875 S Grant St Ste 760 *Web:* www.jccnc.org	San Mateo	CA	94402	650-522-8500	522-8300	138
Japanese Cultural Ctr of Hawaii 2454 S Beretania St *Web:* www.jcch.com	Honolulu	HI	96826	808-945-7633	944-1123	520
Japanese Garden 611 SW Kingston Ave *TF:* 800-955-8352 ■ *Web:* www.japanesegarden.com	Portland	OR	97205	503-223-1321	223-8303	97
Japanese Kitchen 4024 N Mesa St	El Paso	TX	79902	915-533-4267		671
Japanese-American Museum 535 N Fifth St *Web:* www.jamsj.org	San Jose	CA	95112	408-294-3138	294-1657	520
Japango 1136 Pearl St *Web:* www.boulderjapango.com	Boulder	CO	80302	303-938-0330		671
Japan-US Friendship Commission 1201 15th St NW Ste 330 *Web:* www.jusfc.gov	Washington	DC	20005	202-653-9800	653-9802	340-20
Jaquith Industries Inc 600 E Brighton Ave *Web:* www.jaquith.com	Syracuse	NY	13210	315-478-5700	478-5707	697
JAR 8225 Beverly Blvd *Web:* www.thejar.com	Los Angeles	CA	90048	323-655-6566		671
Jarboe Sales Co 315 S 85th E Ave *Web:* www.jarboesales.com/JarboePublicSite	Tulsa	OK	74112	918-836-2511		80-3
Jarco Supply LLC 100 Ag Dr *Web:* jarcosupply.com	Youngsville	NC	27596	919-562-0123		191-1
Jarden Consumer Solutions 2381 Executive Ctr Dr *TF:* 800-777-5452 ■ *Web:* www.jardencs.com	Boca Raton	FL	33431	561-912-4100		37
Jarden Home Brands 14611 W Commerce Rd *TF Cust Svc:* 800-240-3340 ■ *Web:* www.jardenhomebrands.com	Daleville	IN	47334	765-557-3000		820
Jardine, Logan & O'Brien PLLP 8519 Eagle Point Blvd Ste 100 *Web:* www.jlolaw.com	Lake Elmo	MN	55042	651-290-6500		428
Jardiniere 300 Grove St *Web:* www.jardiniere.com	San Francisco	CA	94102	415-861-5555	861-5580	671
Jarecki Valves 6910 W Ridge Rd *Web:* jareckivalves.net	Fairview	PA	16415	814-474-2666	474-3645	789
Jared Coffin House 29 Broad St *TF Cust Svc:* 800-248-2405 ■ *Web:* www.jaredcoffinhouse.com	Nantucket	MA	02554	508-228-2400	228-8549	379
Jargon Software 708 N First St Ste 432 **Fax Area Code:* 866 ■ *Web:* www.jargonsoft.com	Minneapolis	MN	55401	952-426-0858	426-0858*	179
Jarlette Health Services 711 Yonge St *Web:* www.jarlette.com	Midland	ON	L4R2E1	705-549-4889	549-2494	463
Jaro Transportation Services Inc 975 Post Rd *TF:* 800-451-3447 ■ *Web:* www.jarotrans.com	Warren	OH	44483	330-393-5659	393-5906	780
JARP Industries Inc 1051 Pine St PO Box 923 *TF:* 800-558-5950 ■ *Web:* www.jarpind.com	Schofield	WI	54476	715-359-4241	355-4960	223
Jarrard Phillips Cate & Hancock Inc 219 Ward Cir *TF:* 888-844-6274 ■ *Web:* www.jarrardinc.com	Brentwood	TN	37027	312-419-0575		7
Jarrell Cove State Park 391 E Wingert Rd *Web:* www.parks.wa.gov	Shelton	WA	98584	360-426-9226		565
Jarrell Cove State Park E 391 Wingert Rd *Web:* www.parks.wa.gov	Shelton	WA	98584	360-426-9226		565
Jarrell Plantation State Historic Site 711 Jarrell Plantation Rd *Web:* www.gastateparks.org	Juliette	GA	31046	478-986-5172		565
Jarrett Industries of The Carolinas Inc 11511 Cronridge Dr *Web:* www.jarrettindustries.com	Owings Mills	MD	21117	410-581-0303		344
Jarrett Logistics Systems Inc 1347 N Main St *TF:* 800-872-9532 ■ *Web:* www.jarrettlogistics.com	Orrville	OH	44667	330-682-0099		449
Jarrow Formulas Inc 1824 S Robertson Blvd *TF:* 800-726-0886 ■ *Web:* www.jarrow.com	Los Angeles	CA	90035	310-204-6936	204-2520	799
J-Art Iron Co 9435 Jefferson Blvd *Web:* www.jartiron.com	Culver City	CA	90232	310-202-1126	202-1642	319-2
Jarvis Airfoil Inc 528 Glastonbury Tpke *Web:* www.jarvisairfoil.com	Portland	CT	06480	860-342-5000		22
Jarvis Caster Co 881 Lower Brownsville Rd *TF:* 800-995-9876 ■ *Web:* www.jarviscaster.com	Jackson	TN	38301	800-995-9876		350
Jarvis Christian College PO Box 1470 **Fax:* Admissions ■ *Web:* www.jarvis.edu	Hawkins	TX	75765	903-769-5700	769-1282*	166
Jarvis Press Inc, The 9112 Viscount Row *Web:* www.jarvispress.com	Dallas	TX	75247	214-637-2340		627
Jarvis Products Corp 33 Anderson Rd *Web:* www.jarvisproducts.com	Middletown	CT	06457	860-347-7271	347-6978	298
JAS (Jo-Ann Stores Inc) 5555 Darrow Rd *TF:* 888-739-4120 ■ *Web:* www.joann.com	Hudson	OH	44236	330-656-2600	463-6760	270
Jas Forwarding USA Inc 6165 Barfield Rd *Web:* jas.com	Atlanta	GA	30328	770-688-1206		311
Jas Net Consulting Inc 2053 Grant Rd Ste 321 *TF:* 800-433-5778 ■ *Web:* jasnetconsulting.com	Los Altos	CA	94024	408-257-3279		180
JASA (Jewish Assn for Services for the Aged) 247 W 37th St *Web:* www.jasa.org	New York	NY	10018	212-273-5272		48-6
JASCO Inc 28600 Mary's Ct *TF:* 800-333-5272 ■ *Web:* www.jascoinc.com	Easton	MD	21601	410-822-1220		407
Jasco Products Inc 10 E Memorial Rd *TF:* 800-654-8483 ■ *Web:* byjasco.com	Oklahoma City	OK	73114	405-752-0710	752-1537	246
Jasco Tools Inc 1390 Mt Read Blvd *Web:* www.jascotools.com	Rochester	NY	14606	585-254-7000		493
Jasculca/Terman & Assoc (JTPR) 730 N Franklin Ste 510 *Web:* www.jtpr.com	Chicago	IL	60654	312-337-7400		636
JASINT Consulting & Technologies LLC 6700 Alexander Bell Dr Ste 200 *Web:* www.jasint.com	Columbia	MD	21046	410-969-5573		180
Jasmine 1330 Niagara Falls Blvd *Web:* www.jasthai.com	Tonawanda	NY	14150	716-838-3011	332-0280	671

Name / Address	City	State	Zip	Phone	Fax	Class
Jasmine 4609 Convoy St	San Diego	CA	92111	858-268-0888		671
Web: jasmineseafood.com						
Jasmine 7231 Radio Rd	Naples	FL	34104	239-352-5528		671
Web: jasminechinesefood.com						
Jasmine Asian Cuisine						
9938 Bellaire Blvd Ste D	Houston	TX	77036	713-272-8188		671
Web: jasmineasianrestaurant.com						
Jasmine Engineering Inc						
115 E Travis St Ste 1020	San Antonio	TX	78205	210-227-3000		186
Web: www.jasmineengineering.com						
Jasmine Hill Gardens & Outdoor Museum						
3001 Jasmine Hill Rd	Wetumpka	AL	36093	334-567-6463		520
Web: www.jasminehill.org						
Jasmine's China Adventure Tours						
6044 Laguna Villa Way	Elk Grove	CA	95758	916-683-1790		760
Jason Inc						
411 E Wisconsin Ave Ste 2120	Milwaukee	WI	53202	414-277-9300		60
Web: www.jasoninc.com						
Jason Industrial Inc 340 Kaplan Dr	Fairfield	NJ	07004	973-227-4904	227-1651	370
Web: www.jasonindustrial.com						
Jason International Inc						
8328 MacArthur Dr	North Little Rock	AR	72118	501-771-4477	771-2333	375
TF: 800-255-5766 ■ *Web:* www.jasoninternational.com						
Jason McCoy Inc 41 E 57th St 11th Fl	New York	NY	10022	212-319-1996	319-4799	42
TF: 800-894-4548 ■ *Web:* www.jasonmccoyinc.com						
Jaspan Schlesinger Hoffman LLP						
300 Garden City Plaza	Garden City	NY	11530	516-746-8000		428
Web: www.jaspanllp.com						
Jasper County PO Box 1047	Bay Springs	MS	39422	601-764-3368	764-3999	338
Web: www.co.jasper.ms.us						
Jasper County 302 S Main St Rm 102	Carthage	MO	64836	417-358-0416	358-0415	338
Web: www.jaspercounty.org						
Jasper County 121 N Austin	Jasper	TX	75951	409-384-6226	384-7198	338
TF: 800-252-3439 ■ *Web:* www.co.jasper.tx.us						
Jasper County						
126 W Greene St Ste 18	Monticello	GA	31064	706-468-4900	468-4942	338
TF: 800-436-7442 ■ *Web:* jaspercountyga.org						
Jasper County 101 First St N	Newton	IA	50208	641-792-7016	792-1053	338
Web: www.co.jasper.ia.us						
Jasper County 204 W Washington St Ste 2	Newton	IL	62448	618-783-3124		338
Web: www.jaspercountyillinois.org/localgovernment.php						
Jasper County						
223 W Kellner Blvd Ste 204	Rensselaer	IN	47978	219-866-3080		338
Web: www.jaspercountyin.com						
Jasper County PO Box 248	Ridgeland	SC	29936	843-726-7710		338
Web: www.jaspercountychamber.com						
Jasper County Public Library						
208 W Susan St	Rensselaer	IN	47978	219-866-5881		434-3
Web: www.jasperco.lib.in.us						
Jasper County Rural Electric Membership Corp						
280 E 400 S	Rensselaer	IN	47978	219-866-4601	866-2199	245
TF: 888-866-7362 ■ *Web:* www.jasperremc.com						
Jasper Desk Co 415 E Sixth St	Jasper	IN	47546	812-482-4132	482-9552	319-1
TF Cust Svc: 800-365-7994 ■ *Web:* www.jasperdesk.com						
Jasper Engineering & Equipment Co						
3800 Fifth Ave W Ste1	Hibbing	MN	55746	218-262-3421		358
Web: www.jaspereng.com						
JASPER Engines & Transmissions						
815 Wernsing Rd PO Box 650	Jasper	IN	47547	812-482-1041	634-1820	60
TF: 800-827-7455 ■ *Web:* www.jasperengines.com						
Jasper Public Library 1116 Main St	Jasper	IN	47546	812-482-2712	482-7123	434-3
Jasper Rubber Products Inc						
1010 First Ave	Jasper	IN	47546	812-482-3242	482-0816	677
TF: 800-457-7457 ■ *Web:* www.jasperrubber.com						
Jasper Seating Company Inc						
Jasper Group 225 Clay St	Jasper	IN	47546	812-482-3204	482-1548	319-1
TF: 800-622-5661 ■ *Web:* www.jaspergroup.us.com						
Jasper State Recreation Site						
725 Summer St NE Ste C	Salem	OR	97301	541-937-1173		565
Web: www.oregonstateparks.org						
Jasper Wyman & Son PO Box 100	Milbridge	ME	04658	800-341-1758		315-1
TF Sales: 800-341-1758 ■ *Web:* www.wymans.com						
Jasper's 1201 W 103rd St	Kansas City	MO	64114	816-941-6600		671
TF: 800-810-3708 ■ *Web:* www.jasperskc.com						
Jasper-Newton Electric Co-op Inc (JNEC)						
812 S Margaret Ave	Kirbyville	TX	75956	409-423-2241		245
Web: www.jnec.com						
Jat Oil Inc 600 W Main St	Chattanooga	TN	37402	423-629-6611		579
Web: www.jatoil.com						
Jatco Inc 725 Zwissig Way	Union City	CA	94587	510-487-0888	487-1880	608
Web: www.jatco.com						
Jatheon Technologies Inc						
British Colonial Bldg 8 Wellington St E Mezzanine	Toronto	ON	M5E1C5	416-840-0418	849-9971	401
TF: 888-528-4366 ■ *Web:* www.jatheon.com						
Jatom Systems Inc						
99 Michael Cowpland Dr	Kanata	ON	K2M1X3	613-591-5910		224
JatoTech Ventures						
6300 Bridgepoint Pkwy	Austin	TX	78730	512-795-5860		792
Web: www.jatotech.com						
Java Dave's Executive Coffee Service						
6239 E 15th St	Tulsa	OK	74112	918-836-5570		113
TF: 800-725-7315 ■ *Web:* www.javadavescoffee.com						
Javan Engineering Inc						
465 Maryland Dr Ste 100	Ft Washington	PA	19034	215-654-7890		261
Web: javanengineering.com						
Javelina Partners 616 Texas St	Fort Worth	TX	76102	817-336-7109		652
Javier's Gourmet Mexicano						
4912 Cole Ave	Dallas	TX	75205	214-521-4211		671
Web: www.javiers.net						
Javiers 703 Washington Blvd	Ogden	UT	84404	801-393-4747		671
Web: javiersmexicanfood.com						
Javitch Block LLP						
700 Walnut St Ste 302	Cincinnati	OH	45202	513-744-9600	744-9602	428
TF: 800-837-0109 ■ *Web:* www.jbllc.com						
Javits Eric 433 Fifth Ave Fl 5	New York	NY	10016	212-213-4949		34
TF: 800-374-4287 ■ *Web:* www.ericjavits.com						
Jax Asphalt Co						
1800 Waterworks Rd	Mount Vernon	IL	62864	618-244-0500		46
JAX Chamber 3 Independent Dr	Jacksonville	FL	32202	904-366-6600		139
Web: www.myjaxchamber.com						
Jax Fish House 928 Pearl St	Boulder	CO	80302	303-444-1811		671
Web: jaxfishhouse.com/boulder						
Jax Fish House 1539 17th St	Denver	CO	80202	303-292-5767		671
Web: jaxfishhouse.com/denver						
Jax Kneppers Associates Inc						
2125 Ygnacio Valley Rd	Walnut Creek	CA	94598	925-933-3914		463
TF: 800-757-4025 ■ *Web:* www.jaxkneppers.com						
Jax Outdoor Gear						
1200 N College Ave	Fort Collins	CO	80524	970-221-0544		711
Web: www.jaxmercantile.com						
Jay Advertising Inc 170 Linden Oaks	Rochester	NY	14625	585-264-3600		7
Web: www.jayww.com						
Jay and Rose Phillips Family Foundation The						
615 First Ave NE Ste 330	Minneapolis	MN	55413	612-623-1654		303
Web: phillipsfamilymn.org						
Jay Cashman Inc 549 S St	Quincy	MA	02269	617-890-0600		194
Web: www.jaycashman.com						
Jay Cee Sales & Rivet Inc						
32861 Chesley Dr	Farmington	MI	48336	248-478-2150		351
TF: 800-521-6777 ■ *Web:* www.rivetsinstock.com						
Jay Cooke State Park 780 Hwy 210	Carlton	MN	55718	218-384-4610		565
Web: www.dnr.state.mn.us						
Jay County 120 N Ct St Ste 2	Portland	IN	47371	260-726-8080	726-2220	338
Web: www.co.jay.in.us						
Jay County Rural Electric Membership Corp						
484 S 200 W PO Box 904	Portland	IN	47371	260-726-7121	726-6240	245
TF: 800-835-7362 ■ *Web:* www.jayremc.com						
Jay Dee Contractors Inc						
38881 Schoolcraft Rd	Livonia	MI	48150	734-591-3400	464-6868	188-4
Web: www.jaydee.us						
Jay Electric Company Inc						
5300 E Lake Blvd	Birmingham	AL	35217	205-595-9910		463
Web: www.jayelectric.com						
Jay Franco & Sons Inc						
295 Fifth Ave 3rd Fl	New York	NY	10016	212-679-3022	685-4864	361
Web: www.jfranco.com						
Jay Packaging Group (JPG)						
100 Warwick Industrial Dr	Warwick	RI	02886	401-739-7200		88
Web: www.jaypack.com						
Jay Peak Resort 830 Jay Peak Rd	Jay	VT	05859	802-988-2611		669
TF: 800-451-4449 ■ *Web:* www.jaypeakresort.com						
Jay Roberts Jewelers 515 Rt 73 S	Marlton	NJ	08053	856-596-8600		410
TF: 888-828-8463 ■ *Web:* www.jayrobertsjewelers.com						
Jay Sons Screw Machine Products Inc						
197 Burritt St	Milldale	CT	06467	860-621-0141	621-0142	621
Web: www.jaysons.com						
Jay Wolfe Automotive Group						
1011 W 103rd St	Kansas City	MO	64114	816-943-6060		57
Web: www.jaywolfe.com						
Jay's Bistro 135 W Oak St	Fort Collins	CO	80524	970-482-1876	482-1897	671
Jay's Sporting Goods Inc						
8800 S Clare Ave	Clare	MI	48617	989-386-3475	386-3496	711
Web: www.jayssportinggoods.com						
Jayapal Pramila (Rep D - WA)						
319 Cannon HOB	Washington	DC	20515	202-225-3106	225-6197	342-2
Web: jayapal.house.gov						
Jayco Inc 903 S Main St	Middlebury	IN	46540	574-825-5861	825-7354	120
TF Cust Svc: 800-283-8267 ■ *Web:* www.jayco.com						
Jayde.com 2549 Richmond Rd 2nd Fl	Lexington	KY	40509	859-514-2720	219-0065	397
Web: www.jayde.com						
Jayhawk Bowling Supply Inc						
355 N Iowa St PO Box 685	Lawrence	KS	66044	785-842-3237	842-9667	710
TF: 800-255-6436 ■ *Web:* www.jayhawkbowling.com						
Jayhawk Pipeline LLC 2000 S Main St	McPherson	KS	67460	620-241-9270	241-9215	597
Web: www.jayhawkpl.com						
Jayman MasterBUILT Inc						
200 3132 - 118 Ave SE	Calgary	AB	T2Z3X1	403-258-3772		186
TF: 800-919-0204 ■ *Web:* www.jayman.com						
Jaymie Scotto & Associates LLC						
PO Box 20	Middlebrook	VA	24459	201-839-0177		636
TF: 866-695-3629 ■ *Web:* www.jaymiescotto.com						
Jaynes Corp 2906 Broadway NE	Albuquerque	NM	87107	505-345-8591	345-8598	186
Web: www.jaynescorp.com						
Jaypee International Inc						
30 S Wacker Dr Ste 1700	Chicago	IL	60606	312-655-7606		690
Web: www.jaypeeusa.com						
Jaypro Sports Inc 976 Hartford Tpke	Waterford	CT	06385	860-447-3001	444-1779	346
TF Cust Svc: 800-243-0533 ■ *Web:* www.jaypro.com						
Jayray Ads & Pr Inc 535 Dock St Ste 205	Tacoma	WA	98402	253-627-9128		7
Web: www.jayray.com						
Jayson Home & Garden						
1885 N Clybourn Ave	Chicago	IL	60614	773-248-8180		321
TF: 800-472-1885 ■ *Web:* jaysonhome.com						
JAZD Markets Inc 3 Dundee Pk Ste 102	Andover	MA	01810	978-470-4620		366
Jazz A Louisiana Kitchen 1421 Farnam St	Omaha	NE	68102	402-342-3662		671
Web: www.jazzkitchens.com						
Jazz Pharmaceuticals Inc						
3180 Porter Dr	Palo Alto	CA	94304	650-496-3777		582
TF: 866-997-3688 ■ *Web:* www.jazzpharma.com						
Jazz Restaurant 3703C 19th St	Lubbock	TX	79410	806-799-2124		671
Web: www.jazzkitchen.com						
Jazz Semiconductor Inc						
4321 Jamboree Rd	Newport Beach	CA	92660	949-435-8000		696
Web: www.jazzsemi.com						
Jazzeppi's 195 B Porter Ave	Biloxi	MS	39530	228-374-9660		671
Jazzercise Inc 2460 Impala Dr	Carlsbad	CA	92010	760-476-1750	602-7180	810
TF Cust Svc: 800-348-4748 ■ *Web:* www.jazzercise.com						
Jazziz Magazine						
2650 N Military Trail Ste 140	Boca Raton	FL	33431	561-893-6868	893-6867	457-9
TF: 888-852-9987 ■ *Web:* www.jazziz.com						
JazzTimes Magazine						
25 Braintree Hill Office Pk Ste 404	Braintree	MA	02184	617-706-9110	536-0102	457-9
Web: www.jazztimes.com						

Company / Address	City	State	ZIP	Phone	Fax	Class
JB Coxwell Contracting Inc 6741 Lloyd Rd W *TF:* 800-218-4424 ■ *Web:* www.jbcoxwell.com	Jacksonville	FL	32254	904-786-1120	783-2970	188-4
JB Goodwin Real Estate Company Inc 3933 Steck Ave Ste 110 *Web:* www.jbgoodwin.com	Austin	TX	78759	512-502-7800		652
JB Hunt Transport Services Inc 615 JB Hunt Corporate Dr *NASDAQ: JBHT* ■ *TF:* 800-643-3622 ■ *Web:* www.jbhunt.com	Lowell	AR	72745	479-820-0000		449
JB Martin Co 645 Fifth Ave Ste 400 *TF:* 800-223-0525 ■ *Web:* www.jbmartin.com	New York	NY	10022	212-421-2020	421-1460	745-1
J&B Medical Supply Co Inc 50496 W Pontiac Trail *TF:* 800-980-0047 ■ *Web:* www.jandbmedical.com	Wixom	MI	48393	800-737-0045		238
JB Nottingham & Company Inc Duraline Div 1731 Patterson Ave *Web:* jbn-duraline.com	DeLand	FL	32724	631-234-2002		815
JB Sandlin Cos 5137 Davis Blvd *TF:* 800-821-4663 ■ *Web:* sandlinhomes.com	Fort Worth	TX	76180	817-281-3509	656-0719	187
JB Smith Manufacturing Co 6618 Navigation Blvd *Web:* www.jbsmith.com	Houston	TX	77011	713-928-5711		595
Jb Wholesale Roofing & Bldg Supplies Inc 21524 Nordhoff St *Web:* www.jbroofing.com	Chatsworth	CA	91311	818-998-0440		191-3
JB&A Inc 5203 Leesburg Pk Ste 1401 *Web:* www.jb-a-inc.com	Falls Church	VA	22041	703-399-2850		194
Jbar A/C Inc 10221 Sweet Valley Dr *Web:* www.jbar-ac.com	Cleveland	OH	44125	216-447-4294		247
JBC Inc 1414 E 20th St Ste 6 *Web:* www.jbc1.com	Scottsbluff	NE	69361	308-635-0455		581
JBCConnect 3621 Hayden Ave *Web:* www.jbcconnect.com	Culver City	CA	90232	310-601-7231		260
JBCStyle Inc 108 W 39th St 7th Fl *Web:* www.jbcstyle.com	New York	NY	10018	212-355-3197		194
J-Berd Mechanical Contractors Inc 3308 Southway Dr **Fax Area Code:* 320 ■ *Web:* j-berd.com	St Cloud	MN	56301	701-664-8313	656-0312*	189-10
JBFCS (Jewish Board of Family & Children Services) 120 W 57th St *TF:* 888-523-2769 ■ *Web:* jewishboard.org	New York	NY	10019	212-582-9100	632-4495	48-6
Jbi Studios 21434 Wyandotte St *TF:* 800-263-2750 ■ *Web:* www.jbistudios.com	Canoga Park	CA	91303	818-592-0056		657
JBL Energy Partners LLC 23902 FM 2978 Ste B *Web:* www.jblenergypartners.com	Tomball	TX	77375	281-516-3137		536
JBL Enterprises International Inc 3219 Roymar Rd *TF:* 800-347-2822 ■ *Web:* www.jblspearguns.com	Oceanside	CA	92058	760-754-2727		454
JBL Professional 8500 Balboa Blvd *TF:* 800-852-5776 ■ *Web:* www.jblpro.com	Northridge	CA	91329	818-894-8850	830-1220	52
JBM Patrol & Protection Corp 3110 Kingsley Way *Web:* jbmpatrol.com	Madison	WI	53713	608-222-5156		693
JBMH (Joseph Brant Memorial Hospital) 1230 N Shore Blvd *TF:* 800-810-0000 ■ *Web:* www.josephbranthospital.ca	Burlington	ON	L7S1W7	905-632-3730	336-6480	374-2
JBoss Inc 3340 Peachtree Rd Ste 1200 *Web:* www.redhat.com	Atlanta	GA	30326	404-467-8555		177
JBRND 10525 Mopac Dr *Web:* www.jbrnd.com	San Antonio	TX	78217	210-590-3133		22
JBS Five Rivers Cattle Feeding LLC 1770 Promontory Cir *Web:* www.fiveriverscattle.com	Greeley	CO	80634	970-506-8363		473
JBS Group Inc 260 S Los Robles Ave Ste 217 *TF:* 800-348-8499 ■ *Web:* www.jbshotels.com	Pasadena	CA	91101	626-397-2886		393
JBS United Inc 4310 State Rd 38 W *TF:* 800-382-9909 ■ *Web:* www.jbsunited.com	Sheridan	IN	46069	317-758-4495		447
JBT (Jewelers Board of Trade) 95 Jefferson Blvd *Web:* www.jewelersboard.com	Warwick	RI	02888	401-467-0055	467-6070	49-4
JBW Entertainment LLC 2465 S Industrial Park Ave Ste 3 *Web:* www.koolpartyrentals.com	Phoenix	AZ	85282	623-434-8822		184
JC Blair Memorial Hospital 1225 Warm Springs Ave *TF:* 800-523-0300 ■ *Web:* www.jcblair.org	Huntingdon	PA	16652	814-643-2290		374-3
JC Evans Construction Company Inc 11230 Gold Express Dr Ste 310-325 *Web:* jc-evans.com	Gold River	CA	95670	916-858-8190		188-10
JC General Contractors Inc 8250 N Loop Dr	El Paso	TX	79907	915-598-8008		256
JC Higgins Corp 70 Hawes Way *Web:* www.jchigginscorp.com	Stoughton	MA	02072	781-341-1500	344-6075	189-10
JC Horizon Ltd 825 E State St *TF:* 800-743-3463 ■ *Web:* www.jchorizonltd.com	Ontario	CA	91761	626-446-1819		360-3
JC Jones & Associates LLC One Lockwood Dr Ste 310 *Web:* www.jcjones.com	Pittsford	NY	14534	585-899-4072		193
JC Newman Cigar Co 2701 16th St *Web:* www.cigarfamily.com	Tampa	FL	33605	813-248-2124	247-2135	756
JC Penney Co Inc 6501 Legacy Dr *NYSE: JCP* ■ *Web:* www.jcpenney.com	Plano	TX	75024	972-431-1000		229
JC Penney Optical Co 821 N Central Expy *TF:* 866-435-7111 ■ *Web:* www.jcpenneyoptical.com	Plano	TX	75075	972-516-1393		543
JC Raulston Arboretum North Carolina State University PO Box 7522 *TF:* 888-842-2442 ■ *Web:* www.ncsu.edu/jcraulstonarboretum	Raleigh	NC	27695	919-513-7457	515-5361	97
JC Resorts LLC 533 Coast Blvd S *Web:* www.jcresorts.com	La Jolla	CA	92037	858-605-2700		379
JC Smith Inc 345 Peat St *Web:* www.jcsmithinc.com	Syracuse	NY	13210	315-428-9903	428-9841	358
Jc Toys Group Inc 9590 NW 40th St Rd *Web:* www.jctoys.com	Doral	FL	33178	305-597-7801		787
JC Whitney 761 Progress Pkwy *TF:* 866-529-5530 ■ *Web:* www.jcwhitney.com	La Salle	IL	61301	866-529-5530		459
JCAHO (Joint Commission on Accreditation of Healthcare Organizations) 1 Renaissance Blvd *TF:* 800-994-6610 ■ *Web:* www.jointcommission.org	Oakbrook Terrace	IL	60181	630-792-5000	792-5005	48-1
Jcd Sports Group Inc 1300 Park of Commerce Ste 272 *Web:* www.jcdsportsgroup.com	Delray Beach	FL	33445	561-265-0255		720
JCG Technologies Inc 50 S Belcher Rd *Web:* jcgtech.com	Clearwater	FL	33765	727-461-3776		196
JCHS 1033 Massachusetts Ave *Web:* www.jchs.harvard.edu	Cambridge	MA	02138	617-495-7908	496-9957	634
JCI (Journal of Clinical Investigation) 15 Research Dr *Web:* www.jci.org	Ann Arbor	MI	48103	734-222-6050	222-6058	49-8
JCI (Junior Chamber International) 15645 Olive Blvd *TF:* 800-905-5499 ■ *Web:* www.jci.cc	Chesterfield	MO	63017	636-449-3100	449-3107	48-7
JCISD (Jackson County Intermediate School District) 6700 Browns Lake Rd *Web:* www.jcisd.org/site/default.aspx	Jackson	MI	49201	517-768-5200		685
JCJ (Jeter Cook & Jepson Architects Inc) 120 Huyshope Ave Ste 400 *Web:* www.jcj.com	Hartford	CT	06106	860-247-9226		261
JCM Associates Inc 301C Prince Georges Blvd *Web:* www.gojcm.com	Upper Marlboro	MD	20774	301-390-5500		35
JCM Engineering Corp 2690 E Cedar St *Web:* www.jcmcorp.com	Ontario	CA	91761	909-923-3730		256
Jcms Inc 1741 Whitehorse Mercerville Rd *TF:* 800-535-5198 ■ *Web:* www.jcms.com	Mercerville	NJ	08619	609-631-0700		196
JCN Construction Company Inc 155 Dow St *Web:* www.jcnconstruction.com	Manchester	NH	03101	603-624-7080		186
JCO Group Inc 360 Nueces St *Web:* jcogroup.com	Austin	TX	78701	512-246-9301		463
JCPL (Jackson County Public Library) 303 W Second St *Web:* www.myjclibrary.org	Seymour	IN	47274	812-522-3412	522-5456	434-3
JCS Consulting Group Inc 2775 Via De La Valle Ste 206 *Web:* jcsconsulting.com	San Diego	CA	92014	858-947-0101		631
JCSI Corporate Staffing 2 South St *TF:* 888-527-4462 ■ *Web:* www.jcsi.net	Grafton	MA	01519	774-760-1800		260
JD & Billy Hines Trucking Inc 407 Hines Blvd *Web:* www.hinestrucking.com	Prescott	AZ	71857	870-887-9400		311
JD Abrams LP 111 Congress Ave Ste 2400 *Web:* www.jdabrams.com	Austin	TX	78701	512-322-4000	322-4018	188-4
Jd Biggs & Associates Inc 12602 Bear Creek Terr *TF:* 800-506-5729 ■ *Web:* www.jdbiggs.com	Beltsville	MD	20705	410-322-8245		180
JD Calato Mfg Company Inc 4501 Hyde Pk Blvd *TF Cust Svc:* 800-358-4590 ■ *Web:* www.regaltip.com	Niagara Falls	NY	14305	716-285-3546	285-2710	527
JD Equipment Inc 1660 US 42 NE *TF:* 800-659-5646 ■ *Web:* www.jdequipment.com	London	OH	43140	614-879-6620		274
JD Events LLC 5520 Park Ave Ste 305 *Web:* www.jdevents.com	Trumbull	CT	06611	203-371-6322		195
JD Fields & Company Inc 55 Waugh Dr Ste 1250 *TF:* 800-950-7933 ■ *Web:* www.jdfields.com	Houston	TX	77007	281-558-7199		791
JD Ford & Company LLC 650 S Cherry St Ste 1200 *TF:* 888-999-9495 ■ *Web:* www.jdford.com	Denver	CO	80246	303-333-3673		690
JD Gould Co Inc 4707 Massachusetts Ave **Fax Area Code:* 317 ■ *TF:* 800-634-6853 ■ *Web:* www.gouldvalve.com	Indianapolis	IN	46218	800-634-6853	547-5234*	790
JD Heiskell & Co 1939 Hillman St *Web:* www.heiskell.com	Tulare	CA	93274	559-685-6100	686-8697	447
JD Long Masonry Inc 7044 Colchester Park Dr *Web:* www.jdlongmasonry.net/gallery.htm	Manassas	VA	20112	703-550-8880	730-5210	189-7
JD McCarty Ctr for Children with Developmental Disabilities 2002 E Robinson St *TF:* 800-777-1272 ■ *Web:* jdmc.org	Norman	OK	73071	405-307-2800	307-2801	374-1
JD Norman Industries Inc 787 W Belden Ave *Web:* www.jdnorman.com	Addison	IL	60101	630-458-3700		483
JD Power & Assoc 2625 Townsgate Rd Ste 100 *TF:* 800-274-5372 ■ *Web:* www.jdpower.com	Westlake Village	CA	91361	805-418-8000	418-8900	466
JD Squared Inc 2244 Eddie Williams Rd *Web:* www.jd2.com	Johnson City	TN	37601	423-979-0309		595
JD Streett & Company Inc 144 Weldon Pkwy *TF:* 800-899-6440 ■ *Web:* www.jdstreett.com	Maryland Heights	MO	63043	314-432-6600	432-4248	541
JDA Professional Services Inc 701 N Post Oak Rd Ste 610 *Web:* www.jdapsi.com	Houston	TX	77024	713-548-5400		260
JDA Software Group Inc 14400 N 87th St *NASDAQ: JDAS* ■ *Web:* www.jda.com	Scottsdale	AZ	85260	480-308-3000	308-3001	178-10
JDA Software Group Inc 1615 S Congress Ave Ste 100	Delray Beach	FL	33445	561-265-2700		178-1
J-dak Inc 6257 Hwy 76 E	Springfield	TN	37172	615-382-5651	382-5652	195
JDB Capital Partners LLC 20645 N Pima Rd Ste 110 *Web:* www.jdbcapital.com	Scottsdale	AZ	85255	480-502-9200		691
JDC (American Jewish Joint Distribution Committee) 711 Third Ave 10th Fl *Web:* www.jdc.org	New York	NY	10017	212-687-6200	370-5467	48-5
JDC Group Inc 990 Hammond Dr Ste 750 *Web:* www.jdc-group.com	Atlanta	GA	30328	404-601-3310		41
JDG (Justice Design Group) 500 S Grand Ave Ste 110 *Web:* www.jdg.com	Los Angeles	CA	90071	213-437-0102	437-0860	439

Phone Fax Class

JDH Pacific Inc 15301 S Blackburn Ave .... Norwalk CA 90650 562-926-8088 926-8066 492
Web: www.jdhpacific.com

JDi Data Corp
2400 E Commercial Blvd Ste 322 .... Fort Lauderdale FL 33308 954-938-9100 177
TF: 800-746-8307 ■ *Web:* www.jdidata.com

Jdk Consulting 4924 Balboa Blvd Ste 487 .... Encino CA 91316 818-705-8050 196
TF: 855-535-7877 ■ *Web:* www.jdkconsulting.com

Jdk Management Co Inc 1388 SR- 487 ...... Bloomsburg PA 17815 570-784-0111 784-4785 463
Web: www.jdkmgt.com

JDL Technologies Inc
5450 NW 33rd Ave Ft Lauderdale Commerce
Ste 106 .... Fort Lauderdale FL 33309 954-334-0650 393
Web: www.jdltech.com

Jdm & Associates Marketing Llc
3405 Park Pl .... Evanston IL 60201 847-570-9100 7
TF: 800-746-9462 ■ *Web:* www.jdmandassociates.com

Jdm Systems Consultants Inc
33117 Hamilton Ct .... Farmington Hills MI 48334 248-324-1937 225
Web: www.jdmconsulting.com

JDP Therapeutics Inc 823 Jays Dr .... Lansdale PA 19446 215-661-8557 743
Web: www.jdptherapeutics.com

JDR Microdevices Inc
229 Polaris Ave Ste 17 .... Mountain View CA 94043 650-625-1400 538-5005* 459
**Fax Area Code:* 800 ■ *TF:* 800-538-5000 ■ *Web:* www.jdr.com

JDRF (JDRF) 120 Wall St .... New York NY 10005 212-785-9500 785-9595 48-17
TF: 800-533-2873 ■ *Web:* www.jdrf.org

JE & LE Mabee Foundation Inc
401 S Boston Ave Ste 3001 .... Tulsa OK 74103 918-584-4286 305
Web: www.mabeefoundation.com

JE Adams Industries Ltd
1025 63rd Ave SW .... Cedar Rapids IA 52404 319-363-0237 54
TF: 800-553-8861 ■ *Web:* www.jeadams.com

JE Dunn Construction Co
1001 Locust St .... Kansas City MO 64106 816-474-8600 186
Web: www.jedunn.com

JE Herndon Company Inc
1020 J E Herndon Access Rd .... Kings Mountain NC 28086 704-739-4711 734-0621 745-8
TF: 800-277-0500 ■ *Web:* jeherndon.com

JE Sawyer & Company Inc
64 Glen St .... Glens Falls NY 12801 800-724-3983 612
TF: 800-724-3983 ■ *Web:* www.jesawyer.com

Jead Auto Supply Corp
1810 E Tremont Ave .... Bronx NY 10460 718-792-7113 61

Jean Brown Assoc Inc
1045 East 3900 South Ste 100 .... Salt Lake City UT 84124 801-261-2000 231
Web: www.jeanbrownresearch.com

Jean Coutu Group (PJC) Inc
530 Rue Beriault .... Longueuil QC J4G1S8 450-646-9760 237
TSE: PJC.A ■ *TF:* 800-361-4607 ■ *Web:* www.jeancoutu.com

Jean Georges 1 Central Pk W .... New York NY 10023 212-299-3900 671
Web: www.jean-georges.com

Jean Lafitte National Historical Park & Preserve
419 Decatur St .... New Orleans LA 70130 504-589-3882 589-3851 564
Web: www.nps.gov

Jean Mayer USDA Human Nutrition Research Ctr on Aging
711 Washington St .... Boston MA 02111 617-556-3000 556-3344 668
TF: 800-738-7555 ■ *Web:* hnrca.tufts.edu

Jean Paree Weegs Inc
4041 South 700 East Ste 2 .... Salt Lake City UT 84107 800-422-9447 348
TF Orders: 800-422-9447 ■ *Web:* www.jeanparee.com

Jean Simpson Personnel Services Inc
1318 Shreveport Barksdale .... Shreveport LA 71105 318-869-3494 721
Web: www.jeansimpson.com

Jean V Naggar Literary Agency Inc
216 E 75th St Ste 1E .... New York NY 10021 212-794-1082 444
Web: www.jvnla.com

Jeanes Hospital 7600 Central Ave .... Philadelphia PA 19111 215-728-2000 374-3
Web: www.jeanes.com

Jeans Warehouse Inc 2612 Waiwai Loop .... Honolulu HI 96819 808-839-2421 157-6
Web: jeanswarehousehawaii.com

Jeansonne & Remondet LLC
365 Canal St Ste 1600 .... New Orleans LA 70130 337-237-4370 428
TF: 800-446-2745 ■ *Web:* www.jeanrem.com

Jebco Industries Inc 111 Ellis Dr .... Barrie ON L4N8Z3 705-797-8888 480
Web: jebcoindustries.com

JEBCO Seismic LP
2450 Fondren Rd Ste 112 .... Houston TX 77063 713-975-0202 539
Web: www.jebcoseis.com

Jeckel Pork Farm Inc 600 N Sherman .... Delavan IL 61734 309-244-7281 10-6

Jedco Inc 1615 Broadway NW .... Grand Rapids MI 49504 616-459-5161 57
Web: jedco.us

Jedson Engineering 705 Central Ave .... Cincinnati OH 45202 513-965-5999 256
TF: 866-729-3945 ■ *Web:* www.jedson.com

Jeepnee Inc 511 Chabot Rd Ste 123 .... Pleasanton CA 12345 925-264-1213 260
Web: www.jeepnee.com

Jeeps Unlimited 4245 County Rd 6 .... Erie CO 80516 303-828-9020 62
Web: jeepsunlimited.net

Jeff Anderson Regional Medical Ctr
2124 14th St .... Meridian MS 39301 601-553-6000 374-3
Web: www.andersonregional.org

Jeff Cooper Inc 288 Wbury Ave .... Carle Place NY 11514 516-333-8200 411
Web: www.jeffcooperdesigns.com

Jeff Davis Bancshares Inc
507 N Main St PO Box 730 .... Jennings LA 70546 337-824-3424 824-7283 70
OTC: JDVB ■ *TF:* 800-789-5159 ■ *Web:* www.jdbank.com

Jeff Davis County 100 Ct Ave .... Fort Davis TX 79734 432-426-3251 338
Web: www.co.jeff-davis.tx.us

Jeff Flake (Sen R - AZ)
413 Russell Senate Office Bldg .... Washington DC 20510 202-224-4521 228-0515 342-2
Web: www.flake.senate.gov

Jeff Ruby's Steakhouse
700 Walnut St .... Cincinnati OH 45202 513-321-8080 671
Web: www.jeffruby.com

Jeff Scott & Assoc
2356 University Ave W Ste 400 .... St. Paul MN 55114 651-968-1457 4
Web: www.jeffscottandassociates.com

Jeff Zell Consultants Inc
1031 Fourth Ave .... Coraopolis PA 15108 412-262-2022 194
TF: 800-262-0058 ■ *Web:* www.jeffzell.com

Jeffboat LLC 1030 E Market St .... Jeffersonville IN 47130 812-288-1796 698

Jeffco Fibres Inc 12 Park St .... Webster MA 01570 508-943-0440 601
Web: www.jeffcofibres.com

Jefferds Corp 2070 Winfield Rd .... Saint Albans WV 25177 304-755-8111 385
TF: 888-848-6216 ■ *Web:* www.jefferds.com

Jefferies Group Inc
520 Madison Ave 10th Fl .... New York NY 10022 212-284-2300 690
NYSE: JEF ■ *TF:* 800-289-9999 ■ *Web:* www.jefferies.com

Jefferies Socks 2203 Tucker St .... Burlington NC 27215 336-226-7315 727-5502* 155-10
**Fax Area Code:* 800 ■ *TF:* 800-334-6831 ■ *Web:* www.jefferiessocks.com

Jeffers Inc
310 W Saunders Rd PO Box 100 .... Dothan AL 36301 334-793-6257 793-5179 578
TF: 800-533-3377 ■ *Web:* www.jefferspet.com

Jeffers, Danielson, Sonn & Aylward PS
2600 Chester Kimm Rd .... Wenatchee WA 98801 509-662-3685 428
Web: www.jdsalaw.com

Jefferson Area Local School District
906 W Main St .... West Jefferson OH 43162 614-879-7654 685
Web: www.west-jefferson.k12.oh.us

Jefferson Barracks County Park
345 N Dr .... Saint Louis MO 63125 314-615-8800 50-5

Jefferson Barracks National Cemetery
2900 Sheridan Rd .... Saint Louis MO 63125 314-845-8320 845-8355 136

Jefferson Ceramic Tile Company Inc
405 S Main St .... Jefferson WI 53549 920-674-5725 751

Jefferson Chamber of Commerce
3421 N Cswy Blvd Ste 203 .... Metairie LA 70002 504-835-3880 835-3828 139
Web: jeffersonchamber.org

Jefferson City Area Chamber of Commerce
213 Adams St .... Jefferson City MO 65101 573-634-3616 634-3805 139
TF: 866-223-6535 ■ *Web:* www.jcchamber.org

Jefferson City City Hall
320 E McCarty St .... Jefferson City MO 65101 573-634-6304 634-6329 337
Web: www.jeffersoncitymo.gov

Jefferson City Convention & Visitors Bureau
700 E Capitol Ave .... Jefferson City MO 65101 573-632-2820 638-4892 206
TF: 800-769-4183 ■ *Web:* www.visitjeffersoncity.com

Jefferson City Correctional Ctr
8200 No More Victims Rd .... Jefferson City MO 65101 573-751-3224 213
TF: 800-735-2966 ■ *Web:* mo.gov

Jefferson City National Cemetery
1024 E McCarty St .... Jefferson City MO 65101 314-845-8320 845-8355 136
TF: 877-907-8585 ■ *Web:* www.cem.va.gov/cems/nchp/jeffersoncity.asp

Jefferson City News Tribune
210 Monroe St .... Jefferson City MO 65101 573-636-3131 532-2
Web: www.newstribune.com

Jefferson College 1000 Viking Dr .... Hillsboro MO 63050 636-789-3951 789-5103* 162
**Fax:* Admissions ■ *Web:* www.jeffco.edu

Jefferson College of Health Sciences
101 Elm Ave SE .... Roanoke VA 24031 540-985-8483 224-6703 000
TF: 888-985-8483 ■ *Web:* www.jchs.edu

Jefferson Community & Technical College
109 E Broadway .... Louisville KY 40202 502-213-5333 213-2540* 162
**Fax:* Admissions ■ *TF:* 855-246-5282 ■ *Web:* www.jefferson.kctcs.edu

Jefferson Community College
1220 Coffeen St .... Watertown NY 13601 315-786-2200 786-2459 162
TF: 888-435-6522 ■ *Web:* www.sunyjefferson.edu

Jefferson County PO Box 1151 .... Beaumont TX 77704 409-835-8475 839-2394 338
Web: www.co.jefferson.tx.us

Jefferson County
716 Richard Arrington Jr Blvd N .... Birmingham AL 35203 205-325-5555 325-4860 338
Web: jeffconline.jccal.org

Jefferson County
102 S Monroe St PO Box H .... Boulder MT 59632 406-225-4020 225-4149 338
Web: www.jeffersoncounty-mt.gov

Jefferson County 155 Main St 2nd Fl .... Brookville PA 15825 814-849-3696 849-4084 338
TF: 800-852-8036 ■ *Web:* jeffersoncountypa.com

Jefferson County PO Box 208 .... Charles Town WV 25414 304-728-3215 338
Web: www.jeffersoncountywv.org

Jefferson County PO Box 890 .... Dandridge TN 37725 865-397-9642 397-0164 338
TF: 877-237-3847 ■ *Web:* www.jefferson-tn-chamber.org

Jefferson County 411 Fourth St .... Fairbury NE 68352 402-793-5585 338
Web: www.co.jefferson.ne.us

Jefferson County 51 W Briggs Ave .... Fairfield IA 52556 641-472-3454 472-9472 338
Web: www.jeffersoncountyiowa.com/court.htm

Jefferson County
1483 Main St PO Box 145 .... Fayette MS 39069 601-786-3021 786-6009 338
Web: jeffersoncountyms.gov

Jefferson County
100 Jefferson County Pkwy .... Golden CO 80419 303-279-6511 271-8197 338
Web: www.jeffco.us

Jefferson County 729 Maple St .... Hillsboro MO 63050 636-797-5466 797-5360 338
TF: 800-243-6060 ■ *Web:* www.jeffcomo.org

Jefferson County
320 S Main St Rm 109 .... Jefferson WI 53549 920-674-7140 338
Web: www.wisconline.com/counties/jefferson

Jefferson County 217 E Broad St .... Louisville GA 30434 478-625-3332 625-4007 338
TF: 800-247-1266 ■ *Web:* www.jeffersoncounty.org

Jefferson County 300 E Main St .... Madison IN 47250 812-265-8900 338
Web: jeffersoncounty.in.gov

Jefferson County 66 SE 'D' St Ste C .... Madras OR 97741 541-475-4451 325-5018 338
Web: www.co.jefferson.or.us

Jefferson County
300 Jefferson St PO Box 321 .... Oskaloosa KS 66066 785-863-2461 863-3135 338
TF: 800-201-4099 ■ *Web:* www.jfcountyks.com

Jefferson County
1820 Jefferson St .... Port Townsend WA 98368 360-385-9100 385-9382 338
TF: 800-385-8258 ■ *Web:* www.co.jefferson.wa.us

Jefferson County
210 Courthouse Way Ste 100 .... Rigby ID 83442 208-745-7756 745-9397 338
TF: 800-815-2666 ■ *Web:* www.co.jefferson.id.us

Jefferson County
301 Market St Courthouse .... Steubenville OH 43952 740-283-8500 283-8599 338
TF: 800-368-1019 ■ *Web:* www.jeffersoncountyoh.com

Jefferson County 175 Arsenal St .... Watertown NY 13601 315-785-3081 785-5145 338
Web: www.co.jefferson.ny.us

Jefferson County 220 N Main St Rm 103 .... Waurika OK 73573 580-228-2029 338

				Phone	Fax	Class
Jefferson County Chamber of Commerce 630 Market St	Steubenville	OH	43952	740-282-6226		139
TF: 800-304-3211 ■ *Web:* www.jeffersoncountychamber.com						
Jefferson County Chamber of Commerce 200 Potomac Blvd	Mount Vernon	IL	62864	618-242-5725	242-5130	139
TF: 800-792-8266 ■ *Web:* www.southernillinois.com						
Jefferson County Chamber of Commerce 201 E Washington St	Charles Town	WV	25414	304-725-2055		139
TF: 800-624-0577 ■ *Web:* www.jeffersoncountywvchamber.org						
Jefferson County Chamber of Commerce 532 Patriot Dr	Dandridge	TN	37725	865-397-9642	397-0164	139
TF: 877-237-3847 ■ *Web:* www.jefferson-tn-chamber.org						
Jefferson County Convention & Visitors Bureau 37 Washington Ct	Harpers Ferry	WV	25425	304-535-2627		206
TF: 866-435-5698 ■ *Web:* www.discoveritallwv.com						
Jefferson County Historical Society 228 Washington St	Watertown	NY	13601	315-782-3491	782-2913	520
Web: jeffersoncountyhistory.org						
Jefferson County Journal 1405 N Truman Blvd	Festus	MO	63028	636-937-9811	931-2638	532-4
TF: 800-365-0820 ■ *Web:* www.stltoday.com						
Jefferson County Kennel Club Inc 3079 N Jefferson St	Monticello	FL	32344	850-997-2561		642
TF: 800-224-9683 ■ *Web:* www.jckcgreyhounds.com						
Jefferson County Visitor's Bureau PO Box 274	Fairbury	NE	68352	402-729-3000		206
Web: www.visitoregontrail.org						
Jefferson Ctr 541 Luck Ave Ste 221	Roanoke	VA	24016	540-343-2624	343-3744	572
TF: 866-345-2550 ■ *Web:* www.jeffcenter.org						
Jefferson Davis Community College						
Atmore 6574 Hwy 21 N	Atmore	AL	36504	251-368-7610	368-7667	162
Web: www.jdcc.edu						
Brewton 220 Alco Dr	Brewton	AL	36426	251-867-4832	809-1596	162
Web: www.jdcc.edu						
Jefferson Davis County 1025 Third St PO Box 342	Prentiss	MS	39474	601-792-5903	792-0291	338
Web: www.jeffdavisms.com						
Jefferson Davis Electric Co-op 906 N Lake Arthur Ave PO Box 1229	Jennings	LA	70546	337-824-4330	824-8936	245
TF: 800-256-5332 ■ *Web:* www.jdec.org						
Jefferson Davis Memorial State Historic Site 338 Jeff Davis Pk Rd	Fitzgerald	GA	31750	229-831-2335		565
Web: www.gastateparks.org						
Jefferson Davis Parish Library 118 W Plaquemine St	Jennings	LA	70546	337-824-1210	824-5444	434-3
TF: 800-735-0746 ■ *Web:* www.jefferson-davis.lib.la.us						
Jefferson Davis Parish Schools 203 E Plaquemine St PO Box 640	Jennings	LA	70546	337-824-1834		685
Web: www.webserver.jeffersondavis.org						
Jefferson Electric Inc 9650 S Franklin Dr	Franklin	WI	53132	414-209-1620		767
Web: www.jeffersonelectric.com						
Jefferson Energy Co-op 3077 Hwy 17 PO Box 457	North Wrens	GA	30833	706-547-2167		245
TF: 877-533-3377 ■ *Web:* www.jeffersonenergy.com						
Jefferson Forwarding 2222 Jefferson St	Laredo	TX	78040	956-723-0111		311
Web: casaduana.com						
Jefferson Hotel 101 W Franklin St	Richmond	VA	23220	804-788-8000	225-0334	379
TF: 800-424-8014 ■ *Web:* jeffersonhotel.com						
Jefferson Hotel Washington Dc, The 1200 16th St NW	Washington	DC	20036	202-448-2300		707
TF: 877-313-9749 ■ *Web:* www.jeffersondc.com						
Jefferson Industries Corp 6670 Ohio 29	West Jefferson	OH	43162	614-879-5300		59
Jefferson Lake State Park 501 Township Rd 261A	Richmond	OH	43944	740-765-4459		565
Web: www.ohiodnr.com						
Jefferson Landing State Historic Site & Missouri State Museum 201 W Capitol	Jefferson City	MO	65101	573-751-2854		565
Web: mostateparks.com/park/missouri-state-museum						
Jefferson Mall 4801 Outerloop Rd	Louisville	KY	40219	502-968-4101		460
Web: www.shopjefferson-mall.com						
Jefferson Medical College of Thomas Jefferson University 1015 Walnut St	Philadelphia	PA	19107	215-955-6983	955-5151	167-2
TF: 800-533-3669 ■ *Web:* jefferson.edu/university/jmc						
Jefferson Memorial 701 E Basin Dr SW	Washington	DC	20242	202-426-6841	673-7747*	50-4
**Fax Area Code:* 912 ■ *Web:* www.nps.gov/thje						
Jefferson Millwork & Design 44098 Mercure Ci	Sterling	VA	20166	703 260-3370		499
Web: www.jeffersonmillwork.com						
Jefferson National Expansion Memorial 11 N Fourth St	Saint Louis	MO	63102	314-655-1700	655-1641	564
TF: 855-733-4522 ■ *Web:* www.nps.gov/jeff						
Jefferson Parish 200 Derbigny St Ste 3100	Gretna	LA	70053	504-364-2600		338
Web: www.jeffparish.net						
Jefferson Parish Library 4747 W Napoleon Ave	Metairie	LA	70001	504-838-1100	838-1110	434-3
TF: 800-945-6500 ■ *Web:* www.jefferson.lib.la.us						
Jefferson Partners LP 2100 E 26th St	Minneapolis	MN	55404	612-359-3400	359-3437	108
TF Cust Svc: 800-767-5333 ■ *Web:* www.jeffersonlines.com						
Jefferson Regional Medical Ctr (JRMC) Hwy 61 S PO Box 350	Crystal City	MO	63019	636-933-1000		374-3
TF: 800-318-2596 ■ *Web:* www.mercy.net						
Jefferson Regional Medical Ctr (JRMC) 1600 W 40th Ave	Pine Bluff	AR	71603	870-541-7100		374-3
Web: www.jrmc.org						
Jefferson Restaurant 1453 Richmond Rd	Williamsburg	VA	23185	757-229-2296		671
Jefferson Schools 2400 N Dixie Hwy	Monroe	MI	48162	734-289-5550		685
Web: www.jeffersonschools.org						
Jefferson State Community College 2601 Carson Rd	Birmingham	AL	35215	205-853-1200	856-6070*	162
**Fax:* Admissions ■ *TF:* 800-239-5900 ■ *Web:* www.jeffersonstate.edu						
Jefferson Urian Doane & Sterner Inc 651 N Bedford St Extn PO Box 830	Georgetown	DE	19947	302-856-3900		2
Web: www.juds.com						
Jefferson Valley Mall 650 Lee Blvd	Yorktown Heights	NY	10598	914-245-4688		460
Web: www.simon.com						
Jefferson Vineyards LP 1353 Thomas Jefferson Pkwy	Charlottesville	VA	22902	434-977-3042		80-3
Web: www.jeffersonvineyards.com						
Jefferson, The 900 N Taylor St	Arlington	VA	22203	703-516-9455		672
Web: www.sunriseseniorliving.com						
Jefferson-Madison Regional Library 201 E Market St	Charlottesville	VA	22902	434-979-7151	971-7035	434-3
TF: 866-979-1555 ■ *Web:* www.jmrl.org						
Jeffersontown Chamber of Commerce 10434 Watterson Tr	Jeffersontown	KY	40299	502-267-1674		139
Web: www.jtownchamber.com						
Jeffersonville Bancorp 4866 State Rt 52 PO Box 398	Jeffersonville	NY	12748	845-482-4000	482-3544	360-2
OTC: JFBC ■ *TF:* 800-472-3272 ■ *Web:* www.jeffbank.com						
Jeffrey Byrne & Assoc 4042 Central St	Kansas City	MO	64111	800-222-9233		41
TF: 800-222-9233 ■ *Web:* www.fundraisingjba.com						
Jeffrey Court Inc 620 Parkridge Ave	Norco	CA	92860	951-340-3383		191-1
Web: www.jeffreycourt.com						
Jeffrey D Stewart & Company CPA'S 6663 Western Row Rd	Mason	OH	45040	513-573-9600		2
Jeffrey Hale - St Brigid's Hospital 1250 ch Sainte-Foy	Quebec	QC	G1S2M6	418-684-5333	684-5333	374-2
TF: 888-984-5333 ■ *Web:* jhsb.ca						
Jeffrey M. Brown Assoc LLC 2337 Philmont Ave	Huntingdon Valley	PA	19006	215-938-5000		186
Web: www.jmbassociates.com						
Jeffrey Matthews Financial Group LLC, The 30B Vreeland Rd Ste 210	Florham Park	NJ	07932	973-805-6222		401
TF: 888-467-3636 ■ *Web:* www.jeffreymatthews.com						
Jeffrey Scott Agency Inc 670 P St	Fresno	CA	93721	559-268-9741		7
Web: jsaweb.com						
Jeffrey Slocum & Assoc Inc 43 Main St SE Ste 148	Minneapolis	MN	55414	612-338-7020		194
Jeffrey's Restaurant 1204 W Lynn St	Austin	TX	78703	512-477-5584		671
Web: www.jeffreysofaustin.com						
Jeffries Hakeem (Rep D - NY) 1607 Longworth HOB	Washington	DC	20515	202-225-5936		342-2
Web: jeffries.house.gov						
JEGI Capital LLC 150 E 52nd St 18th Fl	New York	NY	10022	212-754-0710		792
Web: www.jegi.com						
JEGS Performance Auto Parts 101 Jeg'S Pl	Delaware	OH	43015	614-294-5050		61
TF: 800-345-4545 ■ *Web:* www.jegs.com						
Jekyll Island Club Hotel 371 Riverview Dr	Jekyll Island	GA	31527	912-635-2600	635-2818	669
TF: 800-535-9547 ■ *Web:* www.jekyllclub.com						
Jekyll Island Convention Ctr 1 N Beachview Dr	Jekyll Island	GA	31527	912-635-5203		205
Web: www.jekyllisland.com						
Jel Sert Co Rt 59 & Conde St	West Chicago	IL	60185	630-876-4838		296-15
TF: 800-323-2592 ■ *Web:* www.jelsert.com						
Jeld-Wen Inc PO Box 1329	Klamath Falls	OR	97601	800-535-3936		499
TF: 800-535-3936 ■ *Web:* www.jeld-wen.com						
Jelliff Corp 354 Pequot Ave	Southport	CT	06890	203-259-1615	255-7908	688
TF: 800-243-0052 ■ *Web:* www.jelliff.com						
Jelly Belly Candy Co 1 Jelly Belly Ln	Fairfield	CA	94533	707-428-2800		296-8
TF: 800-323-9380 ■ *Web:* www.jellybelly.com						
Jellyvision Lab Inc, The 848 W Eastman St Ste 104	Chicago	IL	60642	312-266-0606		809
Web: www.jellyvision.com						
Jem Engineering LLC 8683 Cherry Ln	Laurel	MD	20707	301-317-1070		647
TF: 877-317-1070 ■ *Web:* www.jemengineering.com						
Jem Group LLC 509 N Second St	Harrisburg	PA	17101	717-238-7709		610
Web: www.jemgroup.net						
JEM Strapping Systems 116 Shaver St	Brantford	ON	N3T5M1	519-754-5432		656
TF: 877-536-6584 ■ *Web:* www.jemline.com						
Jemez Mountains Electric Co-op PO Box 128	Espanola	NM	87532	505-753-2105	753-6958	245
TF: 888-755-2105 ■ *Web:* www.jemezcoop.org						
Jen's Restaurant 701 W 36th Ave	Anchorage	AK	99503	907-561-5367		671
Web: www.jensrestaurant.com						
Jena Communications 125 Stokes Ave	Stroudsburg	PA	18360	800-367-5362		627
TF: 800-367-5362						
Jenco Productions Inc 401 South J St	San Bernardino	CA	92410	909-381-9453		88
Web: www.jencoproductions.com						
Jen-Coat Inc 132 N Elm St	Westfield	MA	01086	413-562-2315		555
Jendoco Construction Corp 2000 Lincoln Rd	Pittsburgh	PA	15235	412-361-4500		186
Web: www.jendoco.com						
Jenike & Johanson Inc 400 Business Park Dr	Tyngsboro	MA	01879	978-649-3300		261
Web: jenike.com						
Jenison Public Schools (JPS) 8375 20th Ave	Jenison	MI	49428	616-457-1402	457-8090	685
Web: www.jpsonline.org						
Jenken Biosciences Inc 2 Davis Dr Research Triangle Pk	Research Triangle Park	NC	27709	919-765-0032		231
Web: www.jenkenbio.com						
Jenkins & Wynne Inc 2655 Trenton Rd	Clarksville	TN	37040	931-647-3353		57
Web: www.jenkinsandwynne.com						
Jenkins Arboretum (JA) 631 Berwyn Baptist Rd	Devon	PA	19333	610-647-8870	647-6664	97
Web: www.jenkinsarboretum.org						
Jenkins Brick & Tile Company LLC 201 Sixth St N	Montgomery	AL	36104	334-834-2210		191-4
Web: www.jenkinsbrick.com						
Jenkins County 548 Cotton Ave	Millen	GA	30442	478-982-5595		338
TF: 800-262-0128 ■ *Web:* www.jenkinscountyga.com						

Phone | Fax | Class

Jenkins Electric Inc
5933 Brookshire Blvd — Charlotte NC 28216 — 800-438-3003 — 253
TF: 800-438-3003 ■ *Web:* www.jenkins.com

Jenkins Evan (Rep R - WV)
1609 Longworth HOB — Washington DC 20515 — 202-225-3452 — 225-9061 — 342-2
Web: evanjenkins.house.gov

Jenkins Fenstermaker PLLC
325 Eighth St — Huntington WV 25701 — 304-523-2100 — 428
TF: 866-617-4736 ■ *Web:* www.jenkinsfenstermaker.com

Jenkins Lynn (Rep R - KS)
1526 Longworth HOB — Washington DC 20515 — 202-225-6601 — 225-7986 — 342-2
Web: lynnjenkins.house.gov

Jenkins Mfg Company Inc
1608 Frank Akers Rd — Anniston AL 36207 — 256-831-7000 — 261-6116* — 236
**Fax Area Code:* 800 ■ *TF:* 800-633-2323 ■ *Web:* www.monarchwindows.com

Jenkins Oil Company Inc
1100 W Industrial Rd — Cedar City UT 84720 — 435-586-6931 — 579
Web: www.jenkins-oil.com

Jenkins Systems LLC 4336 Gateway Dr — Sheboygan WI 53081 — 920-452-2110 — 821
Web: www.jenkins-systems.com

Jenkins, Wilson, Taylor & Hunt PA
3015 Carrington Mill Blvd Ste 1200 — Durham NC 27707 — 919-493-8000 — 428
Web: www.jwth.com

Jenn's House Inc
3250 S Cedar Crest Blvd — Emmaus PA 18049 — 610-965-1777 — 372
Web: www.jennshouse.org

Jenner & Block LLP 353 N Clark St — Chicago IL 60654 — 312-222-9350 — 527-0484 — 428
Web: www.jenner.com

Jenness State Beach 2280 Ocean Blvd — Rye NH 03870 — 603-436-1552 — 565
Web: www.nhstateparks.org

Jennie Edmundson Hospital
933 E Pierce St — Council Bluffs IA 51503 — 712-396-6000 — 374-3
TF: 800-958-6498 ■ *Web:* www.bestcare.org

Jennie Stuart Medical Ctr
320 W 18th St PO Box 2400 — Hopkinsville KY 42241 — 270-887-0100 — 374-3
TF: 800-887-5762 ■ *Web:* www.jsmc.org

Jennie-O Turkey Store
2505 Willmar Ave SW — Willmar MN 56201 — 320-235-2622 — 619
TF: 800-621-3505 ■ *Web:* www.jennieo.com

Jennifer A Jones CPA Ltd
10615 Judicial Dr Ste 701 — Fairfax VA 22030 — 703-352-1587 — 2
Web: jajonescpa.com

Jennings & Assoc
2121 Palomar Airport Rd Ste 220 — Carlsbad CA 92011 — 760-431-7466 — 4
Web: jandacommunications.com

Jennings County PO Box 383 — Vernon IN 47282 — 812-352-3070 — 338
Web: jenningscounty-in.gov

Jennings County Chamber of Commerce
203 N State St PO Box 340 — North Vernon IN 47265 — 812-346-2339 — 139
TF: 866-382-4968 ■ *Web:* www.jenningscountychamber.com

Jennings County Schools
34 W Main St — North Vernon IN 47265 — 812-346-4483 — 685
TF: 866-346-3724 ■ *Web:* www.jenningscounty-in.gov

Jennings Environmental Education Ctr
2951 Prospect Rd — Slippery Rock PA 16057 — 724-794-6011 — 565
Web: www.dcnr.state.pa.us

Jennings International Corp
3 Blue Heron Dr — Collegeville PA 19426 — 610-831-1000 — 757
Web: www.jenningsinternational.com

Jennings Technology Co
970 McLaughlin Ave — San Jose CA 95122 — 408-292-4025 — 286-1789 — 203
TF: 800-292-4025 ■ *Web:* www.jenningstech.com

Jennmar Corp 258 Kappa Dr — Pittsburgh PA 15238 — 412-963-9071 — 963-9767 — 190
Web: www.jennmar.com

Jenny Jump State Forest 330 State Pk Rd — Hope NJ 07044 — 908-459-4366 — 565
Web: www.njparksandforests.org

Jenny Wiley State Resort Park
75 Theatre Ct — Prestonsburg KY 41653 — 800-325-0142 — 565
TF: 800-325-0142 ■ *Web:* www.parks.ky.gov

Jenpachi Japanese Steak House
3160 Wellner NE — Rochester MN 55906 — 507-292-1688 — 671
Web: jenpachisteakhouse.com

Jensen Arctic Museum 590 Church St W — Monmouth OR 97361 — 503-838-8468 — 838-8289 — 520
Web: wou.edu/president/advancement/jensen

Jensen Baird Gardner & Henry
10 Free St — Portland ME 04112 — 207-775-7271 — 428
Web: www.jensenbaird.com

Jensen Bridge & Supply Co
400 Stoney Creek Dr — Sandusky MI 48471 — 810-648-3000 — 648-3549 — 697
TF: 800-270-2852 ■ *Web:* www.jensenbridge.com

Jensen Builders Ltd 1175 S 32nd St — Fort Dodge IA 50501 — 515-573-3292 — 186
TF: 800-798-0001 ■ *Web:* www.jensenbuilders.com

Jensen Corp 1983 Concourse Dr — San Jose CA 95131 — 408-446-1118 — 446-4881 — 422
Web: www.jensencorp.com

Jensen Distribution Services
PO Box 3708 — Spokane WA 99220 — 800-234-1321 — 838-2432* — 351
**Fax Area Code:* 509 ■ *TF General:* 800-234-1321 ■ *Web:* www.jensenonline.com

Jensen Meat Company Inc 2525 Birch St — Vista CA 92081 — 760-727-6700 — 297-9
Web: www.jensenmeat.com

Jensen Mixers International Inc
5354 S Garnett Rd — Tulsa OK 74146 — 918-627-5770 — 190
Web: jensenmixers.com

Jensen Precast 625 Bergin Way — Sparks NV 89431 — 775-359-6200 — 359-1038 — 183
TF: 800-648-1134 ■ *Web:* www.jensenprecast.com

Jensen Tire & Auto 10609 I St — Omaha NE 68127 — 402-339-2917 — 62-5
Web: www.jensentireandauto.com

Jensen USA Inc 99 Aberdeen Loop — Panama City FL 32405 — 850-271-5959 — 14
Web: www.jensen-group.com

Jensen's Inc 715 W Jackson St — Shelbyville TN 37160 — 931-684-5021 — 685-9229 — 571
Web: jensensincorporated.com

Jensen-Alvarado Historic Ranch & Museum
4307 Briggs St — Riverside CA 92509 — 951-369-6055 — 520
TF: 800-234-7275 ■ *Web:* rivcoparks.org

Jenson USA Inc 1615 Eastridge Ave — Riverside CA 92507 — 909-947-9036 — 517
TF: 800-626-3440 ■ *Web:* www.jensonusa.com

Jentec Engineering Co
2820 E Coronado St — Anaheim CA 92806 — 714-632-6762 — 608

Jenzabar Inc
101 Huntington Ave Ste 2200 — Boston MA 02199 — 617-492-9099 — 492-9081 — 178-10
TF: 800-593-0028 ■ *Web:* www.jenzabar.com

Jeo Consulting Group Inc 142 W 11th St — Wahoo NE 68066 — 402-443-4661 — 256
Web: www.pdiowa.com

JEOL USA Inc 11 Dearborn Rd — Peabody MA 01960 — 978-535-5900 — 536-2205 — 419
Web: www.jeol.co.jp/en

Jeopardy Productions Inc
10202 Washington Blvd — Culver City CA 90232 — 310-244-8855 — 52
Web: www.jeopardy.com

JEPC (Jim Edgar Panther Creek State Fish & Wildlife Area)
10149 County Hwy 11 — Chandlerville IL 62627 — 217-452-7741 — 565
Web: www.dnr.illinois.gov/Parks/Pages/JimEdgarPantherCreek.aspx

Jeppesen Marine Inc
15242 NW Greenbrier Pkwy — Beaverton OR 97006 — 503-579-1414 — 390
Web: www.nobeltec.com

Jeppesen Sanderson Inc
55 Inverness Dr E — Englewood CO 80112 — 303-799-9090 — 328-4153 — 637-2
TF: 800-621-5377 ■ *Web:* ww1.jeppesen.com

Jepson Technologies Inc
14900 Ventura Blvd Ste 210 — Sherman Oaks CA 91403 — 818-990-0601 — 226
Web: jepsontech.com

Jerauld County
205 S Wallace — Wessington Springs SD 57382 — 605-539-1202 — 539-1203 — 338
Web: ujs.sd.gov/County_Information/jerauld.aspx

Jerdon Style LLC
1820 N Glenville Dr Ste 124 — Richardson TX 75081 — 972-690-4286 — 76
Web: www.jerdonstyle.com

Jeremiah's 1307 W 1200 S — Ogden UT 84404 — 801-394-3273 — 627-6579 — 671
Web: jeremiahsutah.com

Jergens Inc 15700 S Waterloo Rd — Cleveland OH 44110 — 877-486-1454 — 481-6193* — 493
**Fax Area Code:* 216 ■ *TF:* 800-537-4367 ■ *Web:* www.jergensinc.com

Jericho Road Ministries Inc
1090 Mondon Hill Rd — Brooksville FL 34601 — 352-799-2912 — 48-20
Web: www.jericho-road.net

Jerith Mfg Company Inc
14400 McNulty Rd — Philadelphia PA 19154 — 215-676-4068 — 676-9756 — 491
TF: 800-344-2242 ■ *Web:* www.jerith.com

Jernigan Oil Company Inc
415 E Main St PO Box 688 — Ahoskie NC 27910 — 252-332-2131 — 581
Web: www.jerniganoil.com

Jerome Cheese Co 547 W Nez Perce — Jerome ID 83338 — 208-324-8806 — 324-8892 — 296-5
TF: 800-757-7611 ■ *Web:* daviscofoods.com

Jerome County 300 N Lincoln Ave — Jerome ID 83338 — 208-644-2715 — 338
Web: jeromecountyid.us

Jerome County Fairgrounds 200 N Fir St — Jerome ID 83338 — 208-324-7209 — 642
Web: www.jeromecountyfair.com

Jerome State Historic Park
100 Douglas Rd — Jerome AZ 86331 — 928-634-5381 — 565
Web: www.azstateparks.com

Jerome's Furniture Warehouse
16960 Mesamint St — San Diego CA 92127 — 866-633-4094 — 753-0826* — 321
**Fax Area Code:* 858 ■ *TF:* 866-633-4094 ■ *Web:* www.jeromes.com

Jerry Brown Company Inc, The
2690 Prairie Rd — Eugene OR 97402 — 541-688-8211 — 579
Web: www.jbco.com

Jerry Bruckheimer Films
1631 Tenth St — Santa Monica CA 90404 — 310-664-6260 — 514
Web: www.jbfilms.com

Jerry G Williams & Sons Inc
524 Brogden Rd — Smithfield NC 27577 — 919-934-4115 — 683

Jerry Haag Motors Inc
1475 N High St — Hillsboro OH 45133 — 937-402-2090 — 57
Web: www.jerryhaagmotors.com

Jerry L Pettis Memorial Veterans Affairs Medical Ctr
11201 Benton St — Loma Linda CA 92357 — 909-825-7084 — 374-8
TF: 800-741-8387

Jerry Lipps Inc 3888 Nash Rd — Cape Girardeau MO 63702 — 573-335-8204 — 335-4483 — 780
TF: 800-325-3331 ■ *Web:* www.jerrylippsinc.com

Jerry Pate Turf & Irrigation Inc
301 Schubert Dr — Pensacola FL 32504 — 850-479-4653 — 484-8596 — 274
TF: 800-700-7004 ■ *Web:* www.jerrypate.com

Jerry Pittman & Associates Inc
12504 Hwy 57 — Vancleave MS 39565 — 228-826-9255 — 261
Web: www.jerrypittman.com

Jerry Sorbara Furs Inc
39 W 32nd St Ste 1400 — New York NY 10001 — 212-594-3897 — 155-7
Web: sorbarafur.com

Jerry Weintraub Productions
4000 Warner Blvd — Burbank CA 91522 — 818-954-2500 — 514

Jerry's Famous Deli Inc
12711 Ventura Blvd Ste 400 — Studio City CA 91604 — 818-766-8311 — 766-8315 — 670
Web: www.jerrysdeli.com

Jerry's Foods 5125 Vernon Ave S — Edina MN 55436 — 952-929-2685 — 345
Web: www.jerrysfoods.com

Jerry's Marine Service
100 SW 16th St — Fort Lauderdale FL 33315 — 800-432-2231 — 525-0361* — 770
**Fax Area Code:* 954 ■ **Fax:* Sales ■ *TF:* 800-432-2231 ■ *Web:* jms.qwik-order.com

Jerry's Sport Ctr Inc
100 Capital Rd — Jenkins Township PA 18640 — 800-234-2612 — 388-8452 — 710
TF: 800-234-2612 ■ *Web:* www.jerryssportscenter.com

Jerry's Supermarkets Inc
532 W Jefferson Blvd — Dallas TX 75208 — 214-941-8110 — 345
Web: www.supermarket.com

Jerry's Systems Inc
702 Russell Ave Ste 306 — Gaithersburg MD 20877 — 800-990-9176 — 670
TF: 800-990-9176 ■ *Web:* www.jerrysusa.com

Jersey Cape Realty Inc
739 Washington St — Cape May NJ 08204 — 609-884-5800 — 652
TF: 800-643-0043 ■ *Web:* www.jerseycaperealty.com

Jersey Cape Yachts Inc
2143 River Rd — Lower Bank NJ 08215 — 609-965-8650 — 965-7480 — 90
Web: www.jerseycapeyachts.com

Jersey City City Hall
280 Grove St — Jersey City NJ 07302 — 201-547-5000 — 547-5461 — 337
Web: www.cityofjerseycity.com

Jersey City Free Public Library
472 Jersey Ave — Jersey City NJ 07302 — 201-547-4501 — 547-4584 — 434-3
TF: 800-443-0315 ■ *Web:* jclibrary.org

Phone | Fax | Class

Jersey City Medical Ctr
355 Grand St ... Jersey City NJ 07302 201-915-2000 374-3
Web: www.barnabashealth.org
Jersey City Museum
350 Montgomery St ... Jersey City NJ 07302 201-413-0303 413-9922 520
Web: jerseycityonline.com
Jersey County 209 N State St ... Jerseyville IL 62052 618-498-5571 338
Web: www.jerseycounty.org
Jersey Journal
1 Harmon Plaza Ste 1010 ... Secaucus NJ 07094 201-653-1000 532-2
Web: www.jjournal.com
Jersey Precast Corp
853 Nottingham Way ... Hamilton Township NJ 08638 609-689-3700 183
Web: www.jerseyprecast.com
Jersey Shore Chamber of Commerce
2510 Belmar Blvd Ste I-20 ... Wall NJ 07719 732-280-8800 280-8505 139
Web: www.jerseyshorechambernj.com/kickoff.asp
Jersey Shore State Bank
300 Market St ... Williamsport PA 17701 570-322-1111 70
TF: 888-412-5772 ■ *Web:* www.jssb.com
Jersey Shore Steel Co
70 Maryland Ave PO Box 5055 ... Jersey Shore PA 17740 570-753-3000 753-3782 723
TF: 800-833-0277 ■ *Web:* www.jssteel.com
Jersey Shore University Medical Ctr
1945 Rt 33 ... Neptune NJ 07753 732-775-5500 751-5120 374-3
TF: 800-560-9990 ■ *Web:* www.jerseyshoreuniversitymedicalcenter.com
Jersey State Bank 1000 S State St ... Jerseyville IL 62052 618-498-6466 70
Web: jerseystatebank.com
Jerusalem Restaurant & Cafe
106 E Evergreen Blvd ... Vancouver WA 98660 360-906-0306 671
Web: thejerusalemcafe.com
Jervis B. Webb Co
34375 W 12 Mile Rd ... Farmington Hills MI 48331 248-553-1000 553-1228 483
Web: www.daifuku.com/us
Jes Search Firm Inc
1021 Stovall Blvd Ste 600 ... Atlanta GA 30319 404-812-0622 260
Web: www.jessearch.com
JESCO Inc 2020 McCullough Blvd ... Tupelo MS 38801 662-842-3240 186
Web: jescoinc.net
Jesco-Wipco Industries Inc
950 Anderson Rd PO Box 388 ... Litchfield MI 49252 517-542-2903 542-2501 286
TF: 800-455-0019 ■ *Web:* www.jescoonline.com
Jeskell Systems LLC
6201 chevy chase dr ... Laurel MD 20707 301-230-1533 463
Web: www.jeskell.com
Jeson Enterprises Inc 504 NE Fifth Ave ... Camas WA 98607 360-834-7728 761
Web: www.craftwarehouse.com
Jess & Jim's Steakhouse
517 E 135th St ... Kansas City MO 64145 816-941-9499 671
Web: www.jessandjims.com
Jess Dunn Correctional Ctr PO Box 316 ... Taft OK 74463 918-682-7841 682-4372 213
Web: www.ok.gov
Jessamine County 101 N Main St ... Nicholasville KY 40356 859-885-4161 338
Web: www.jessamineco.com
Jesse Duplantis Ministries
1973 Ormond Blvd ... Destrehan LA 70047 985-764-2000 48-20
Web: www.jdm.org
Jesse Engineering Co
1840 Marine View Dr ... Tacoma WA 98422 253-922-7433 922-1998 480
TF: 800-468-3595 ■ *Web:* www.jesseengineering.com
Jesse H Jones Hall for the Performing Arts
615 Louisiana St Ste 101 ... Houston TX 77002 713-227-3974 572
Web: www.houstontx.gov
Jessen Mfg
1409 W Beardsley Ave PO Box 1729 ... Elkhart IN 46515 574-295-3836 522-2962 621
Web: www.jessenmfg.com
Jessen Press Inc
3982 Alabama Ave S ... Minneapolis MN 55416 952-929-0346 627
Web: www.jessenpress.com
Jessica's Biscuit Mobile Book Fair
82 Needham St ... Newton MA 02461 617-965-0530 95
Jessie Lord Bakery LLC
21100 S Western Ave ... Torrance CA 90501 310-533-6010 68
Web: www.jessielordpies.com
Jessup Correctional Institution
7804 House of Correction Rd ... Jessup MD 20794 410-799-0100 213
Jestar Plumbing & Heating
23130 Ridge Rd ... Germantown MD 20876 301-353-1841 610
Jestine's Kitchen 251 Meeting St ... Charleston SC 29401 843-722-7224 671
Web: jestineskitchen.com
Jesuit Ctr for Spiritual Growth
501 N Church Rd ... Wernersville PA 19565 610-670-3642 673
TF: 800-273-8255 ■ *Web:* jesuitcenter.org
Jesuit Refugee Service North America (JRS)
1016 16th St NW Ste 500 ... Washington DC 20036 202-462-5200 48-5
Jesuit Retreat House
300 Manresa Way ... Los Altos CA 94022 650-917-4000 673
Web: www.jrclosaltos.org
Jesuit School of Theology at Berkeley
1735 LeRoy Ave ... Berkeley CA 94709 510-549-5000 841-8536 167-3
TF: 800-824-0122 ■ *Web:* www.scu.edu
Jesuit Spiritual Ctr
5361 S Milford Rd ... Milford OH 45150 513-248-3500 673
TF: 800-995-4863 ■ *Web:* www.jesuitspiritualcenter.com
Jet Aviation
112 Charles A Lindbergh Dr ... Teterboro NJ 07608 201-288-8400 462-4005 24
TF: 800-538-0832 ■ *Web:* www.jetaviation.com
JET Engineering Inc
1241 Park Pl NE Ste E ... Cedar Rapids IA 52402 319-294-6106 256
Web: www.jetinc.net
Jet Food Stores of Georgia
1106 S Harris St ... Sandersville GA 31082 478-552-2588 204
Jet Harbor Inc
2860 NW 59th St ... Fort Lauderdale FL 33309 954-772-2863 772-6510 63
TF: 800-760-0924 ■ *Web:* www.jetharbor.com
Jet Industries Inc
1935 Silverton Rd NE PO Box 7362 ... Salem OR 97303 503-363-2334 610
TF: 800-659-0620 ■ *Web:* jet.industries

Phone | Fax | Class

Jet International Company LLC
1811 Elmdale Ave ... Glenview IL 60026 847-657-8666 657-9197 770
Web: www.jetinternational.com
Jet Logistics Inc
2610 W Terminal Blvd ... Raleigh NC 27623 919-840-0555 196
Web: jetlogistics.us
Jet Parts Engineering Inc
4772 Ohio Ave S ... Seattle WA 98134 206-281-0963 256
Web: www.jetpartsengineering.com
Jet Professionals LLC
114 Charles A Lindbergh Dr Teterboro Airport
... Teterboro NJ 07608 800-441-6016 260
TF: 800-441-6016 ■ *Web:* www.jet-professionals.com
Jet Propulsion Laboratory (JPL)
4800 Oak Grove Dr ... Pasadena CA 91109 818-354-4321 668
Web: www.jpl.nasa.gov
Jet Rubber Company Inc
4457 Tallmadge Rd ... Rootstown OH 44272 330-325-1821 325-2876 676
Web: www.jetrubber.com
Jet Set Sports PO Box 366 ... Far Hills NJ 07931 908-766-1001 766-4646 707
Web: www.jetsetsports.com
Jet Source Inc
2056 Palomar Airport Rd ... Carlsbad CA 92011 760-438-0877 21
Web: www.jetsource.com
Jet Specialty Inc 211 Market Ave ... Boerne TX 78006 830-331-9457 538
Web: www.jetspecialty.com
Jet Star Inc 10825 Andrade Dr ... Zionsville IN 46077 317-873-4222 780
TF: 800-969-4222 ■ *Web:* www.jetstarinc.com
Jet X Aerospace 400 N York Rd ... Bensenville IL 60106 847-750-8888 57
Web: www.jetxaerospace.com
Jet's America Inc
37501 Mound Rd ... Sterling Heights MI 48310 586-268-5870 268-6762 670
Web: www.jetspizza.com
JetBlue Airways Corp
118-29 Queens Blvd ... Forest Hills NY 11375 718-286-7900 360-1
NASDAQ: JBLU ■ *TF:* 800-538-2583 ■ *Web:* www.jetblue.com
Jeter Cook & Jepson Architects Inc (JCJ)
120 Huyshope Ave Ste 400 ... Hartford CT 06106 860-247-9226 261
Web: www.jcj.com
Jetlease Inc 5718 Westheimer 17th Fl ... Houston TX 77057 713-952-5100 974-2813 21
Web: www.jetleaseinc.com
Jetline Engineering 15 Goodyear St ... Irvine CA 92618 949-951-1515 951-9237 811
Web: www.jetline.com
Jet-Lube Inc 4849 Homestead Rd Ste 232 ... Houston TX 77226 713-670-5700 678-4604 541
TF: 800-538-5823 ■ *Web:* www.jetlube.com
Jetstream Capital LLC
12 Cadillac Dr Ste 280 ... Brentwood TN 37027 615-425-3400 425-3401 401
TF: 800-432-1000 ■ *Web:* www.jetstreamcapital.com
Jetstream of Houston LLP
4930 Cranswick ... Houston TX 77041 713-462-7000 462-5387 790
TF: 800-231-8192 ■ *Web:* www.waterblast.com
JetSuite 18952 MacArthur Blvd ... Irvine CA 92612 866-779-7770 13
TF: 866-779-7770 ■ *Web:* www.jetsuite.com
Jetta Corp 425 Centennial Blvd ... Edmond OK 73013 405-340-6661 362
Web: www.jettacorp.com
Jetta Operating Company Inc
777 Taylor St Ft Worth Club Tower Ste P1 ... Fort Worth TX 76102 817-335-1179 539
TF: 800-455-3882 ■ *Web:* www.jettaoperating.com
Jeunesse Global LLC
650 Douglas Ave ... Altamonte Springs FL 32714 407-215-7414 76
Web: www.jeunesseglobal.com
Jewel Bako 239 E Fifth St ... New York NY 10003 212-979-1012 671
Web: www.jewelbakosushi.com
Jewel Box Theatre
3700 N Walker Ave ... Oklahoma City OK 73118 405-521-1786 572
Web: www.jewelboxtheatre.org
Jewel Case Corp 110 Dupont Dr ... Providence RI 02907 401-943-1400 943-1426 199
TF: 800-441-4447 ■ *Web:* www.jewelcase.com
Jewel Cave National Monument
11149 US Hwy 16 Bldg B-12 ... Custer SD 57730 605-673-2288 673-3294 564
Web: www.nps.gov
Jewel Date Co 84675 60th Ave ... Thermal CA 92274 760-399-4474 315-4
Web: www.shieldsdategarden.com
Jewel-Craft Inc 4122 Olympic Blvd ... Erlanger KY 41018 859-282-2400 411
TF: 800-525-5482 ■ *Web:* www.jewel-craft.com
Jewelers Board of Trade (JBT)
95 Jefferson Blvd ... Warwick RI 02888 401-467-0055 467-6070 49-4
Web: www.jewelersboard.com
Jewelers Inc, The 2400 Western Ave ... Las Vegas NV 89102 702-382-1234 410
TF: 800-561-3357 ■ *Web:* www.thejewelers.com
Jewelers of America (JA)
52 Vanderbilt Ave 19th Fl ... New York NY 10017 646-658-0246 658-0256 49-4
TF: 800-223-0673 ■ *Web:* www.jewelers.org
Jewelers Shipping Assn (JSA)
125 Carlsbad St ... Cranston RI 02920 401-943-6020 49-21
TF: 800-688-4572 ■ *Web:* www.jewelersshipping.com
Jewell Assoc Engineers Inc
560 Sunrise Dr ... Spring Green WI 53588 608-588-7484 261
Web: jewellassoc.com
Jewell Cemetery State Historic Site
c/o Rock Bridge Memorial State Pk
5901 S Hwy 163 ... Columbia MO 65203 573-449-7402 565
Web: www.mostateparks.com/jewellcem.htm
Jewell Instruments LLC
850 Perimeter Rd ... Manchester NH 03103 603-669-6400 669-5962 529
TF: 800-227-5955 ■ *Web:* jewellinstruments.com
Jewell Tool Technology
3129 State St ... Bettendorf IA 52722 563-355-5010 454
TF: 800-831-8665 ■ *Web:* www.jewellgroup.com
Jewel-Osco 150 Pierce Rd ... Itasca IL 60143 630-948-6000 410
Web: www.jewelosco.com
Jewelry Concepts Inc
41 Western Industrial Dr ... Cranston RI 02921 401-228-8586 410
Jewelry Fashions Inc 385 Fifth Ave ... New York NY 10016 212-889-4166 408
Web: www.robertrose.com
JewelryWeb.com Inc
98 Cuttermill Rd Ste 464 ... Great Neck NY 11021 516-482-3982 955-2520* 410
**Fax Area Code: 800* ■ *TF:* 800-955-9245 ■ *Web:* www.jewelryweb.com

Phone | Fax | Class

Jewett-Cameron Trading Company Ltd
32275 NW Hillcrest PO Box 1010 North Plains OR 97133 503-647-0110 647-2272 191-3
NASDAQ: JCTCF ■ *TF:* 800-547-5877 ■ *Web:* www.jewettcameron.com

Jewish Alcoholics Chemically Dependent Persons & Significant Others
135 W 50th St 6th Fl New York NY 10020 212-632-4600 399-3525 48-21
Web: jewishboard.org

Jewish Assn for Services for the Aged (JASA)
247 W 37th St New York NY 10018 212-273-5272 48-6
Web: www.jasa.org

Jewish Board of Family & Children Services (JBFCS)
120 W 57th St New York NY 10019 212-582-9100 632-4495 48-6
TF: 888-523-2769 ■ *Web:* jewishboard.org

Jewish Child Care Assn of New York
120 Wall St Fl 12 New York NY 10005 212-425-3333 147
Web: www.jccany.org

Jewish Community Centers Assn of North America
520 Eigth Ave New York NY 10018 212-532-4949 481-4174 48-20
Web: www.jcca.org

Jewish Heritage Ctr of Western Canada
C116-123 Doncaster St Winnipeg MB R3N2B2 204-477-7460 477-7465 50-2
Web: www.jhcwc.org

Jewish Home Lifecare 120 W 106th St New York NY 10025 212-870-5000 870-4715 450
TF: 800-544-0304 ■ *Web:* www.jewishhome.org

Jewish Hospital
4777 E Galbraith Rd Cincinnati OH 45236 513-686-3000 686-3003 374-3
Web: www.mercy.com/cincinnati/locations/hospitals/the-jewish-hospital

Jewish Hospital & St Mary's HealthCare
200 Abraham Flexner Way Louisville KY 40202 502-587-4011 374-5
TF: 800-451-3637

Jewish Museum 1109 Fifth Ave New York NY 10128 212-423-3200 423-3232 520
Web: www.thejewishmuseum.org

Jewish Museum of Florida
301 Washington Ave Miami Beach FL 33139 305-672-5044 672-5933 520
TF: 800-965-2030 ■ *Web:* jmof.fiu.edu

Jewish Museum of Maryland
15 Lloyd St Baltimore MD 21202 410-732-6400 732-6451 520
TF All: 800-235-4045 ■ *Web:* jewishmuseummd.org

Jewish National Fund (JNF) 42 E 69th St New York NY 10021 212-879-9300 48-20
TF: 800-542-8733 ■ *Web:* www.jnf.org

Jewish Press Inc 4915 16th Ave Brooklyn NY 11215 718-330-1100 532-3
TF: 800-992-1600 ■ *Web:* www.jewishpress.com

Jewish Publication Society
2100 Arch St 2nd Fl Philadelphia PA 19103 215-832-0600 568-2017 637-3
TF: 800-234-3151 ■ *Web:* jps.org

Jewish Reconstructionist Federation (JRF)
101 Greenwood Ave Jenkintown PA 19046 215-885-5601 885-5603 48-20
TF: 877-226-7573 ■ *Web:* archive.jewishrecon.org

Jewish Senior Services of Fairfield County Inc
175 Jefferson St Fairfield CT 06825 203-365-6400 374-8082 450
Web: jseniors.org

Jewish Telegraphic Agency
24 W 30th St 4th Fl New York NY 10001 212-643-1890 643-8499 530
Web: www.jta.org

Jewish Theological Seminary
3080 Broadway New York NY 10027 212-678-8832 166
Web: www.jtsa.edu

Jewish United Fund/Jewish Federation of Metropolitan Chicago (JUF)
30 S Wells St Chicago IL 60606 312-346-6700 444-2086 48-20
TF: 855-275-5237 ■ *Web:* www.juf.org

JewishCard 7360 Viewpoint Rd Aptos CA 95003 831-469-8883 662-2746 130
Web: www.jewishcard.com

Jews for Jesus 60 Haight St San Francisco CA 94102 415-864-2600 552-8325 48-20
TF: 800-366-5521 ■ *Web:* jewsforjesus.org

JF Ahern Co 855 Morris St Fond du Lac WI 54935 920-921-9020 921-8632 189-10
TF: 800-532-0155 ■ *Web:* www.jfahern.com

JF Drake State Technical College
3421 Meridian St N Huntsville AL 35811 256-539-8161 551-3142 800
TF: 888-413-7253 ■ *Web:* www.drakestate.edu

JF Electric Inc
100 Lakefront Pkwy PO Box 570 Edwardsville IL 62025 618-797-5353 189-4
Web: www.jfelectric.com

JF Fredericks Tool Company Inc
25 Spring Ln Farmington CT 06032 860-677-2646 454

JF O'Neill Packing Company Inc
3120 G St Omaha NE 68107 402-733-1200 473

JF Shea Company Inc Redding Div
17400 Clear Creek Rd Redding CA 96001 530-246-4292 503-5
TF: 800-685-6494 ■ *Web:* www.jfshea.com

JF Shea Construction Inc
655 Brea Canyon Rd Walnut CA 91789 909-594-9500 883-3371 188-4
TF: 888-779-7333 ■ *Web:* www.jfshea.com

JF Taylor Inc 21610 S Essex Dr Lexington Park MD 20653 301-862-3939 261
Web: jfti.com

JF White Contracting Co 10 Burr St Framingham MA 01701 508-879-4700 558-0460* 188-4
**Fax Area Code:* 617 ■ *TF:* 866-539-4400 ■ *Web:* www.jfwhite.com

JFC International Inc
7101 E Slauson Ave Los Angeles CA 90040 323-721-6100 721-6133 297-11
Web: www.jfc.com

JFE Steel Corp 350 Pk Ave 27th Fl New York NY 10022 212-310-9320 308-9292 723
Web: www.jfe-steel.co.jp

JFK (John F Kennedy International Airport)
150 Greenwich St New York NY 10007 212-435-7000 871-2343* 27
**Fax Area Code:* 201 ■ *Web:* www.panynj.gov/airports/jfk.html

JFK Johnson Rehabilitation Institute
65 James St Edison NJ 08818 732-321-7733 374-6
Web: www.jfkmc.org/clinical-services

JFK Medical Ctr 65 James St Edison NJ 08818 732-321-7000 374-3
TF: 800-283-1015 ■ *Web:* www.jfkmc.org

JFKL (John F Kennedy Library)
190 W 49th St Hialeah FL 33012 305-821-2700 818-9144 434-3
Web: www.hialeahfl.gov/library

Jfm Enterprises Inc
1301 W 22nd St Ste 1001 Oak Brook IL 60523 630-990-4555 787
Web: www.jfm.net

JFM Inc 4276 Lakeland Dr Flowood MS 39232 601-664-7177 204
Web: www.jfminc.net

JFP (Joyner Fine Properties)
2727 Enterprise Pkwy Richmond VA 23294 804-270-9440 967-2770 652
TF: 800-446-3858 ■ *Web:* www.joynerfineproperties.com

JFS Wealth Advisors LLC
1479 N Hermitage Rd Hermitage PA 16148 724-962-3200 401
Web: www.jfswa.com

Jfw Enterprises Inc
3350 Pawtucket Ave Riverside RI 02915 401-438-3030 177
Web: www.wallace1.com

JG Boswell Co 101 W Walnut St Pasadena CA 91103 626-583-3000 10-2
NYSE: BWEL

JG Tax Group
1430 S Federal Hwy Deerfield Beach FL 33441 866-477-5291 734
TF: 866-477-5291 ■ *Web:* www.jgtaxgroup.com

JG Van Holten & Son Inc
703 W Madison St PO Box 66 Waterloo WI 53594 920-478-2144 478-2316 296-19
TF: 800-970-9646 ■ *Web:* www.vanholtenpickles.com

JGA-Beacon Inc 2200 Cook Dr Atlanta GA 30340 770-246-3400 186
TF: 800-343-0839 ■ *Web:* www.jgacorp.com

JGB Enterprises Inc
115 Metropolitan Dr Liverpool NY 13088 315-451-2770 451-8503 370
Web: www.jgbhose.com

JGI (Jane Goodall Institute for Wildlife Research Education)
1595 Spring Hill Rd Ste 550 Vienna VA 22182 703-682-9220 682-9312 48-3
TF: 800-592-5263 ■ *Web:* www.janegoodall.org

JGPG (Joe Goode Performance Group)
499 Alabama St Ste 150 San Francisco CA 94110 415-561-6565 561-6562 573-1
TF: 800-838-3006 ■ *Web:* www.joegoode.org

JH Baxter & Co PO Box 5902 San Mateo CA 94402 650-349-0201 570-6878 818
TF: 800-556-1098 ■ *Web:* www.jhbaxter.com

JH Berra Construction Company Inc
5091 Baumgartner Rd Saint Louis MO 63129 314-487-5617 188-10
TF: 800-877-5617 ■ *Web:* www.jhberra.com

JH Fletcher & Co Inc 402 High St Huntington WV 25705 304-525-7811 525-3770 190
TF: 800-327-6203 ■ *Web:* www.jhfletcher.com

JH Industries Inc 1981 E Aurora Rd Twinsburg OH 44087 330-963-4105 963-4111 480
TF: 800-321-4968 ■ *Web:* www.copperloy.com

JH Kelly 821 Third Ave Longview WA 98632 360-423-5510 423-9170 189-10
Web: www.jhkelly.com

JH Larson Co 10200 51st Ave N Plymouth MN 55442 763-545-1717 545-1144 246
Web: www.jhlarson.com

JH Miles & Co Inc 902 S Hampton Ave Norfolk VA 23510 757-622-9264 285

JH Routh Packing Company Inc
4413 W Bogart Rd Sandusky OH 44870 419-626-2251 625-4782 473
TF: 800-446-6759 ■ *Web:* routhpacking.com

JH Technology Inc
5107 Lena Rd Unit 111 Bradenton FL 34211 941-758-7710 194
TF: 800-808-0300 ■ *Web:* www.jhtechnology.com

JH Walker Trucking Company Inc
152 N Hollywood Rd Houma LA 70364 985-868-8330 780
TF: 800-581-2600 ■ *Web:* www.jhwalkertrucking.com

JH Whitney & Co 130 Main St New Canaan CT 06840 203-716-6100 716-6122 792
Web: www.whitney.com

JH Williams Oil Company Inc
1237 E Twiggs St Tampa FL 33602 813-228-7776 224-9413 579
Web: www.jhwoil.com

JHCR (Jackson Hole Central Reservations)
140 E Broadway Ste 24 PO Box 2618 Jackson WY 83001 307-733-4005 733-1286 376
TF: 888-838-6606 ■ *Web:* www.jacksonholewy.com

JHE Production Group Inc
6427 Saddle Creek Ct Harrisburg NC 28075 704-455-8888 720
Web: www.gojhe.com

JHH (Johns Hopkins Health System)
600 N Wolfe St Baltimore MD 21287 410-955-5000 353
Web: www.hopkinsmedicine.org

JHL Industries 10012 Nevada Ave Chatsworth CA 91311 818-882-2233 882-4350 732
TF: 800-255-6636 ■ *Web:* www.jhlindustries.com

JHM Hotels Inc 60 Pointe Cir Greenville SC 29615 864-232-9944 248-1600* 379
**Fax:* PR ■ *Web:* www.jhmhotels.com

JHOC Inc 323 Cash Memorial Blvd Forest Park GA 30297 404-675-1950 311

JHPIEGO Corp 1615 Thames St Baltimore MD 21231 410-537-1800 463
Web: www.jhpiego.org

JHT Inc 2710 Discovery Dr Ste 100 Orlando FL 32826 407-381-7797 381-0017 463
Web: www.jht.com

JI Holcomb Observatory & Planetarium
4600 Sunset Ave Indianapolis IN 46208 317-940-8333 598
Web: www.butler.edu/holcomb-observatory

Jibe Consulting Inc
5000 Meadows Rd Ste 300 Lake Oswego OR 97035 503-274-0788 180
TF: 800-927-2363 ■ *Web:* www.jibeconsulting.com

Jibe Media Llc
774 South 300 West Unit B Salt Lake City UT 84101 801-433-5423 7
Web: jibemedia.com

Jibe Mobile Inc
990 N Rengstorff Ave Mountain View CO 94043 650-336-5423 387
Web: www.jibemobile.com

JibJab Media Inc 228 Main St Ste 4 Venice CA 90291 323-400-6307 33
Web: www.jibjab.com

Jiffy Lube PO Box 4427 Houston TX 77210 800-344-6933 62-5
TF: 800-344-6933 ■ *Web:* www.jiffylube.com

Jiffy-tite Company Inc
4437 Walden Ave Lancaster NY 14086 716-681-7200 350
Web: www.jiffy-tite.com

Jif-Pak Manufacturing Inc
1451 Engineer St Vista CA 92081 760-597-2665 601
TF: 800-777-6613 ■ *Web:* www.jifpak.com

JII (Jordan Industries Inc)
1751 Lake Cook Rd Ste 550 Deerfield IL 60015 847-945-5591 945-5698 185

JILA (JILA Science)
University of Colorado 440 UCB Boulder CO 80309 303-492-7789 492-5235 668
Web: jila.colorado.edu

JILA Science (JILA)
University of Colorado 440 UCB Boulder CO 80309 303-492-7789 492-5235 668
Web: jila.colorado.edu

Jill Newhouse Gallery 4 E 81st St New York NY 10028 212-249-9216 734-4098 42
Web: www.jillnewhouse.com

Jim & Jennie's Greek Village
3026 N 90th St Omaha NE 68134 402-571-2857 671
Web: jimandjennies.com

Jim 'N Nick's 7004 Charlotte Pk Nashville TN 37209 615-352-5777 671
Web: jimnnicks.com

Phone | Fax | Class

Jim Bishop Cabinets Inc
5640 Bell Rd. . . . . Montgomery AL 36116 800-410-2444 115
TF: 800-410-2444 ■ *Web:* www.bishopcabinets.com

Jim Edgar Panther Creek State Fish & Wildlife Area (JEPC)
10149 County Hwy 11 . . . . . Chandlerville IL 62627 217-452-7741 565
Web: www.dnr.illinois.gov/Parks/Pages/JimEdgarPantherCreek.aspx

Jim Ellis Auto Dealerships
5901 Peachtree Industrial Blvd S . . . . . Atlanta GA 30341 770-458-6811 57
Web: www.jimellis.com

Jim Henson's Creature Shop
1416 N LaBrea Ave. . . . . Hollywood CA 90028 323-802-1557 33
Web: www.creatureshop.com

Jim Hogg County 102 E Tilley St. . . . . Hebbronville TX 78361 361-527-3015 338

Jim Jordan & Assoc LP
12941 N Fwy Ste 226. . . . . Houston TX 77060 281-877-7009 466
Web: www.jordan-associates.com

Jim Marshall Insurance Inc
2084 Ninth St Ste D. . . . . Los Osos CA 93402 805-528-4739 390
Web: jimmarshallinsurance.com

Jim McKay Chevrolet Inc
3509 University Dr. . . . . Fairfax VA 22030 703-591-4800 57
Web: jimmckaychevrolet.com

Jim Neely's Interstate Barbeque
2265 S Third St . . . . . Memphis TN 38109 901-775-2304 775-3149 671
Web: www.interstatebarbecue.com

Jim Palmer Trucking Inc
9730 Derby Dr . . . . . Missoula MT 59808 406-721-5151 829-6271 780
TF: 888-698-3422 ■ *Web:* www.jimpalmertrucking.com

Jim Pattison Group
1067 W Cordova St Ste 1800. . . . . Vancouver BC V6C1C7 604-688-6764 687-2601 185
Web: www.jimpattison.com

Jim Walter Resources Inc
14730 Lock 17 Rd . . . . . Brookwood AL 35444 205-554-6450 501

Jim Wells County PO Box 1459 . . . . . Alice TX 78333 361-668-5702 338
Web: www.co.jim-wells.tx.us

Jim Whitten Roof Consultants LLC
Po Box 200925. . . . . Austin TX 78720 512-250-0999 463
Web: www.jimwhitten.com

Jim Wilson & Assoc Inc
2660 Eastchase Ln Ste 100. . . . . Montgomery AL 36117 334-260-2500 260-2533 655
Web: www.jwamalls.com

Jim's Downtown Steakhouse
110 SW Jefferson St. . . . . Peoria IL 61602 309-673-5300 673-9335 671
Web: www.jimssteakhouse.net

Jim's Farm Meat Inc 5881 N Winton Way . . . . . Winton CA 95388 209-358-3535 473

Jim's Restaurants
8520 Crownhill Blvd. . . . . San Antonio TX 78209 210-828-1493 822-8606 670
Web: www.jimsrestaurants.com

Jim's Seafood 950 Wilkinson Blvd . . . . . Frankfort KY 40601 502-223-7448 227-7419 671
Web: jimseafood1.wixsite.com

Jimbo's Jumbos Inc
185 Peanut Dr PO Box 465. . . . . Edenton NC 27932 919-482-2193 296-32
TF General: 800-334-4771

Jimbo's Pit BBQ 4103 W Kennedy Blvd. . . . . Tampa FL 33609 813-289-9724 289-1006 671
Web: www.jimbosbarbq.com

Jimcor Agency 60 Craig Rd. . . . . Montvale NJ 07645 201-573-8200 390
Web: jimcor.com

Jiminy Peak Mountain Resort LLC
37 Corey Rd . . . . . Hancock MA 01237 413-738-5500 707
TF: 800-835-2364 ■ *Web:* www.jiminypeak.com

Jimmie Davis State Park
1209 State Pk Rd . . . . . Chatham LA 71226 318-249-2595 565
TF: 888-677-2263 ■ *Web:* www.crt.state.la.us

Jimmy Bs Audiobooks 324 Ave I . . . . . Redondo Beach CA 90277 310-375-3134 95
Web: www.audiobooks.com

Jimmy Carter Library & Museum
441 Freedom Pkwy. . . . . Atlanta GA 30307 404-865-7100 865-7102 434-2
Web: www.jimmycarterlibrary.gov

Jimmy Carter National Historic Site
300 N Bond St . . . . . Plains GA 31780 229-824-4104 824-3441 564
Web: www.nps.gov/jica

Jimmy John's Franchise Inc
2212 Fox Dr . . . . . Champaign IL 61820 217-356-9900 359-2956 670
TF: 800-546-6904 ■ *Web:* www.jimmyjohns.com

Jimmy Kelly's 217 Louise Ave. . . . . Nashville TN 37203 615-329-4349 671
TF: 800-331-2123 ■ *Web:* www.jimmykellys.com

Jimmy Swaggart Ministries (JSM)
8919 World Ministry Blvd PO Box 262550. . . . . Baton Rouge LA 70810 225-768-8300 48-20
TF Orders: 800-288-8350 ■ *Web:* www.jsm.org

Jimmy's Family Steak House
1011 S Providence Rd . . . . . Columbia MO 65203 573-443-1796 671

Jim-n-Nick's 1908 11th Ave S. . . . . Birmingham AL 35205 205-320-1060 671
Web: jimnnicks.com

JIMO (Joint Institute for Marine Observations)
Scripps Institution of Oceanography UC San Diego
9500 Gilman Dr . . . . . La Jolla CA 92093 858-534-3624 668

Jims Place Grille
3660 S Houston Levee . . . . . Collierville TN 38017 901-861-5000 671
Web: jimsplacegrille.com

Jin Ju 5203 N Clark St. . . . . Chicago IL 60640 773-334-6377 6/1
Web: jinjurestaurant.com

Jinbeh 301 E Las Colinas Blvd . . . . . Irving TX 75039 972-869-4011 869-4311 671
TF: 800-315-2621 ■ *Web:* www.jinbeh.com

Jireh Metal Inc 3635 Nardin St. . . . . Grandville MI 49418 616-531-7581 295
Web: www.jirehmetal.com

Jiten Hotel Management Inc
495 Westgate Dr. . . . . Brockton MA 02301 508-427-1667 463
Web: www.jitenhotels.com

Jitlada 5233 1/2 W Sunset Blvd . . . . . Los Angeles CA 90027 323-667-9809 671
Web: jitladala.com

Jitney Trade Inc
360 St-Jacques St W Ste S-118. . . . . Montreal QC H2Y1P5 514-985-8080 691
Web: www.jitneytrade.com

Jivamukti Yoga Center Inc
841 Broadway Frnt 2. . . . . New York NY 10003 212-353-0214 148
Web: www.jivamuktiyoga.com

Jivaro Group Inc 5433 S Emporia Ct. . . . . Englewood CO 80111 303-740-0022 41

Jive Communications Inc
1275 W 1600 N Ste 100 . . . . . Orem UT 84057 866-768-5429 179
TF: 866-768-5429 ■ *Web:* jive.com

JJ Cassone Bakery Inc
202 S Regent St . . . . . Port Chester NY 10573 914-939-1568 345
Web: www.jjcassone.com

JJ Clarke Enterprises Inc
2905 N Charles St . . . . . Baltimore MD 21218 410-962-0241 652
Web: jjclarkeenterprises.com

J&J Foods Inc
1075 Jesse Jewell Pkwy SW. . . . . Gainesville GA 30501 770-287-7217 297-8
Web: www.jandjfoods.com

JJ Gumberg Company Inc
1051 Brinton Rd . . . . . Pittsburgh PA 15221 412-244-4000 655
Web: www.jjgumberg.com

JJ Haines & Company Inc
6950 Aviation Blvd . . . . . Glen Burnie MD 21061 800-922-9248 760-4045* 361
*Fax Area Code: 410 ■ *TF:* 800-922-9248 ■ *Web:* www.jjhaines.com

JJ Kane
8008 US Hwy 130 Bldg One Ste 214 . . . . . Delran NJ 08075 856-764-7163 138
Web: www.jjkane.com

JJ Keller & Assoc Inc
3003 Breezewood Ln PO Box 368. . . . . Neenah WI 54957 920-722-2848 727-7516* 637-11
*Fax Area Code: 800 ■ *TF:* 800-558-5011 ■ *Web:* www.jjkeller.com

JJ MacKay Canada Ltd
1342 Abercrombie Rd. . . . . New Glasgow NS B2H5C6 902-752-5124 770
TF: 888-462-2529 ■ *Web:* www.mackaymeters.com

JJ Neilson Arboretum
Ridgetown College
University of Guelph 120 Main St E . . . . . Ridgetown ON N0P2C0 519-674-1500 674-1515 97
Web: www.ridgetownc.uoguelph.ca/aboutus/arboretum.cfm

JJ Nichting Co Inc
1342 Pilot Grove Rd. . . . . Pilot Grove IA 52648 319-469-4461 469-4703 274
Web: jjnichting.com

JJ Powell Inc
109 W Presqueisle St. . . . . Philipsburg PA 16866 814-342-3190 579
TF: 800-432-0866 ■ *Web:* www.jjpowell.com

JJ Taylor Cos Inc 655 N AIA. . . . . Jupiter FL 33477 561-354-2900 81-1
Web: www.jjtaylor.com

JJ's Bistro de Paris
330 A1A N Ste 209. . . . . Ponte Vedra FL 32082 904-996-7557 671
Web: www.jjbistro.com

JJB Hilliard WL Lyons Inc
500 W Jefferson St. . . . . Louisville KY 40202 502-588-8400 585-8901* 690
*Fax: Hum Res ■ *TF:* 800-444-1854 ■ *Web:* www.hilliard.com

JJDS Environmental Inc
40 Woodview Dr. . . . . Doylestown PA 18901 267-880-2325 194
Web: www.jjdsenvironmental.com

JJJ Floor Covering Inc
4831 Passons Blvd Ste A. . . . . Pico Rivera CA 90660 562-692-9008 290
TF: 800-533-0472 ■ *Web:* www.jjjfloorcovering.com

JK Creative Printers & Mailing
2029 Hollister Whitney Pkwy Ste . . . . . Quincy IL 62305 217-222-5145 627
Web: www.jkcreative.com

JK Design Inc 465 Amwell Rd. . . . . Hillsborough NJ 08844 908-428-4700 344
Web: www.jkdesign.com

JK&B Capital
180 N Stetson Ave Ste 4500. . . . . Chicago IL 60601 312-946-1200 946-1103 792
Web: www.jkbcapital.com

JKL Technologies Inc
3245 Grande Vista Dr. . . . . Newbury Park CA 91320 805-375-5820 375-5830 180
Web: www.cos-jkl.com

JKM Consulting Inc PO Box 3250 . . . . . Oxford AL 36203 256-405-0613 463
Web: www.m2connections.com

JL Clark Mfg Co 923 23rd Ave . . . . . Rockford IL 61104 815-962-8861 124
TF: 877-482-5275 ■ *Web:* www.jlclark.com

JL Clark Mfg Co Lancaster Div
303 N Plum St. . . . . Lancaster PA 17602 717-392-4125 124
TF: 877-482-5275 ■ *Web:* www.jlclark.com

JL Darling LLC 2614 Pacific Hwy E . . . . . Tacoma WA 98424 253-922-5000 535
Web: www.riteintherain.com

JL Industries Inc
4450 W 78th St Cir. . . . . Bloomington MN 55435 952-835-6850 835-2218 286
TF: 800-554-6077 ■ *Web:* www.activarcpg.com

JL Media Inc 1600 Rt 22 E 2nd Fl . . . . . Union NJ 07083 908-687-8700 6
TF: 800-555-5595 ■ *Web:* www.jlmedia.com

JL Properties Inc 813 D St Ste 200 . . . . . Anchorage AK 99501 907-279-8068 652
Web: www.jlproperties.com

JL Richards & Assoc Ltd
864 Lady Ellen Pl . . . . . Ottawa ON K1Z5M2 613-728-3571 256
Web: www.jlrichards.ca

JLB Contracting LP
7151 Randol Mill Rd. . . . . Fort Worth TX 76120 817-261-2991 188-4

JLC Associates Inc
3198-A Airport Loop Dr . . . . . Costa Mesa CA 92626 714-241-4430 186
TF: 800-716-4408 ■ *Web:* www.jlcassoc.com

JLG Harvesting Inc 1450 S Atlantic Ave. . . . . Yuma AZ 85365 928-329-7548 11-1

JLG Industries Inc 1 JLG Dr. . . . . McConnellsburg PA 17233 717-485-5161 485-6417 190
Web: www.jlg.com

Jll Partners Inc
450 Lexington Ave 31st Fl . . . . . New York NY 10017 212-286-8600 405
Web: www.jllpartners.com

JLM Couture Inc
525 Seventh Ave Ste 1703 . . . . . New York NY 10018 212-221-8203 155-21
TF: 800-924-6475 ■ *Web:* www.jlmcouture.com

JLS Language Corp 135 Willow Rd. . . . . Menlo Park CA 94025 650-321-9832 768
Web: www.jls.com

JLS Mailing Services Inc
672 Crescent St . . . . . Brockton MA 02302 508-313-1000 5
TF: 866-557-6245 ■ *Web:* www.jlsms.com

JLS Security & Investigations Inc
5650 University Blvd SE. . . . . Albuquerque NM 87106 505-400-3840 693

JLSD (Jackson Local Schools District)
7602 Fulton Dr. . . . . Massillon OH 44646 330-830-8000 830-8008 186
Web: jackson.stark.k12.oh.us

JM Davis Arms & Historical Museum
330 N J M Davis Blvd. . . . . Claremore OK 74017 918-341-5707 341-5771 520
Web: www.thegunmuseum.com

JM DigitalWorks 2460 Impala Dr . . . . . Carlsbad CA 92010 760-476-1783 530

Company	Phone	Fax	Class
JM Family Enterprises Inc 100 Jim Moran Blvd .... Deerfield Beach FL 33442 *Web:* www.jmfamily.com	954-429-2000		57
JM Huber Corp 499 Thornall St 8th Fl .... Edison NJ 08837 **Fax:* Hum Res ■ *TF:* 877-418-0038 ■ *Web:* www.huber.com	732-549-8600	549-2239*	536
JM Manufacturing Company Inc 5200 W Century Blvd .... Los Angeles CA 90045 *TF:* 800-621-4404 ■ *Web:* www.jmeagle.com	800-621-4404		596
JM Search & Company Inc 1045 First Ave Ste 110 .... King Of Prussia PA 19406 *Web:* www.jmsearch.com	610-964-0200		194
JM Smith Corp 101 W Saint John St Ste 305 .... Spartanburg SC 29306 *TF:* 800-542-1216 ■ *Web:* www.jmsmithcorp.com	864-582-1216		238
JM Smucker Co 1 Strawberry Ln .... Orrville OH 44667 *NYSE:* SJM ■ *TF:* 888-550-9555 ■ *Web:* www.smuckers.com	330-682-3000		296-20
JM Smucker Pennsylvania Inc 300 Keck Ave .... New Bethlehem PA 16242	814-275-1323		296-20
JM Sorge Inc 57 Fourth St .... Somerville NJ 08876 *Web:* www.jmsorge.com	908-218-0066		192
JM Swank Co 395 Herky St .... North Liberty IA 52317 *TF:* 800-593-6333 ■ *Web:* www.jmswank.com	319-626-3683		297-8
JM Test Systems Inc 7323 Tom Dr .... Baton Rouge LA 70806 *TF:* 800-353-3411 ■ *Web:* www.jmtest.com	225-925-2029		743
JM Turner Engineering Inc 1325 College Ave .... Santa Rosa CA 95404 *TF:* 800-514-4220 ■ *Web:* www.jmteng.com	707-528-4503		256
JMA Energy Company LLC 1021 NW Grand Blvd .... Oklahoma City OK 73118 *Web:* www.jmaenergy.com	405-947-4322		536
JMA Information Technology Inc 10551 Barkley Ste 400 .... Overland Park KS 66212 *TF:* 800-767-3263 ■ *Web:* www.jmait.com	913-722-3252		180
JMA Railroad Supply Co 835 E Tenth St .... Seymour IN 47274 *Web:* www.jmarail.com	812-522-7200	522-1150	770
J-MacLumber Inc 4154 Faust St .... Bamberg SC 29003 *TF:* 800-282-9583 ■ *Web:* www.maclumber.com	803-245-1700	245-1701	661
J-Mar Enterprises Inc PO Box 4143 .... Bismarck ND 58502 *TF:* 800-446-8283 ■ *Web:* www.j-mar-enterprises.com	701-222-4518		780
JMC Communities 2201 Fourth St N Ste 200 .... Saint Petersburg FL 33704 *Web:* www.jmccommunities.com	727-823-0022		653
JMD Communications Inc 760 Calle Bolivar .... Santurce PR 00907 *Web:* www.jmdcom.com	787-728-3030		387
JMF (Jacob Medinger & Finnegan LLP) 1270 Ave of the Americas .... New York NY 10020 *Web:* jmfnylaw.com	212-524-5000		428
JMF Co 2735 62nd St Ct .... Bettendorf IA 52722 *TF:* 800-397-3739 ■ *Web:* www.jmfcompany.com	563-332-9200	332-9880	612
JMFA (M Floyd John & Assoc Inc) 125 N Burnett Dr .... Baytown TX 77520 **Fax Area Code:* 281 ■ *TF:* 800-809-2307 ■ *Web:* www.jmfa.com	800-809-2307	424-8864*	194
JMG Financial Group 2001 Butterfield Rd Ste 1400 .... Downers Grove IL 60515 *Web:* jmgfinancial.com	630-571-5252		401
JMG Realty Inc 5605 Glenridge Dr Ste 1010 .... Atlanta GA 30342 *Web:* www.jmgrealty.com	404-995-1111	995-1112	655
JMG Security Systems Inc 17150 Nowhope St Ste 109 .... Fountain Valley CA 92708 *TF:* 800-900-4564 ■ *Web:* www.jmgsecurity.com	714-545-8882		693
JMH (Johnson Memorial Hospital) 1125 W Jefferson St .... Franklin IN 46131 *Web:* www.johnsonmemorial.org	317-736-3300	736-2692	374-3
JMI (James Marine Inc) 4500 Clarks River Rd PO Box 2305 .... Paducah KY 42002 *Web:* www.jamesmarine.com	270-898-7392		465
JMK International 4800 Bryant Irvin Ct .... Fort Worth TX 76107	817-737-3703		360-3
JMK Nippon 2551 N Perryville Rd .... Rockford IL 61107 *Web:* jmkrockford.com	815-877-0505		671
Jmk Systems Solutions Inc 20 Broadway Ave .... Ipswich MA 01938 *Web:* www.jmkssi.com	978-356-8888		180
JML Care Ctr 184 Terr Heun Dr .... Falmouth MA 02540 *Web:* capecodhealth.org	508-457-4621	457-1218	450
JML Optical Industries Inc 820 Linden Ave .... Rochester NY 14625 *TF:* 800-621-2020 ■ *Web:* www.jmloptical.com	585-248-8900	248-8924	544
JMMC (John Muir Medical Ctr) 1601 Ygnacio Valley Rd .... Walnut Creek CA 94598 *TF:* 844-398-5376 ■ *Web:* www.johnmuirhealth.com	925-939-3000	308-8944	374-3
JMP Engineering Inc 4026 Meadowbrook Dr Unit 143 .... London ON N6L1C9 *TF:* 855-228-8668 ■ *Web:* www.jmpeng.com	519-652-2741		261
JMP IT Services 535 W 152 St .... New York NY 10031 *Web:* www.jmpits.com	646-397-8117		196
JMR Electronics Inc 8968 Fullbridht Ave .... Chatsworth CA 91311 *Web:* www.jmr.com	818-993-4801		254
Jms Elite 5900 Som Ctr Rd Ste 12 .... Willoughby OH 44094 *TF:* 800-870-2543 ■ *Web:* www.jmselite.com	440-943-9200		195
JMS North America Corp 22320 Foothill Blvd Ste 350 .... Hayward CA 94541 *Web:* www.jmsna.net	510-888-9090		729
JMS Southeast Inc 105 Temperature Ln .... Statesville NC 28677 *TF:* 800-873-1835 ■ *Web:* www.jms-se.com	704-873-1835		201
JMT (Johnson Mirmiran & Thompson) 72 Loveton Cir .... Sparks MD 21152 *TF:* 800-472-2310 ■ *Web:* www.jmt.com	410-329-3100	472-2200	261
JMT Consulting Group Inc 2200-2202 Route 22 .... Patterson NY 12563 *TF:* 888-368-2463 ■ *Web:* www.jmtconsulting.com	845-278-9262		528
JN Phillips Glass Company Inc 11 Wheeling Ave .... Woburn MA 01801 *Web:* www.jnphillips.com	781-939-3400		330
JNA Institute of Culinary Arts 1212 S Broad St .... Philadelphia PA 19146 *Web:* www.culinaryarts.com	215-468-8800	468-8838	163
JNBA Financial Advisors Inc 8500 Normandale Lake Blvd Ste 450 .... Minneapolis MN 55437 *Web:* jnba.com	952-844-0995		401
JNEC (Jasper-Newton Electric Co-op Inc) 812 S Margaret Ave .... Kirbyville TX 75956 *Web:* www.jnec.com	409-423-2241		245
JNF (Jewish National Fund) 42 E 69th St .... New York NY 10021 *TF:* 800-542-8733 ■ *Web:* www.jnf.org	212-879-9300		48-20
JNJ Express Inc 3935 Old Getwell Rd PO Box 30983 .... Memphis TN 38130 *TF:* 888-383-7157 ■ *Web:* www.jnjexpress.com	901-362-3444		780
JNJ Mobile Inc 186 S St .... Boston MA 02111 *Web:* www.jnjmobile.com	617-542-1614		387
JNK Securities Corp 902 Broadway 20th Fl .... New York NY 10010 *Web:* www.jnksecurities.com	212-885-6300		401
JNL Glass Inc 618 E Gutierrez St Ste B1 .... Santa Barbara CA 93103 *Web:* jnlglass.com	805-957-1685		329
Jo Daviess County 330 N Bench St .... Galena IL 61036 *TF:* 800-368-8683 ■ *Web:* www.jodaviess.org	815-777-0161	777-3688	338
Jo-Ad Industries Inc 31465 Stephenson Hwy .... Madison Heights MI 48071 *TF:* 800-331-8923 ■ *Web:* www.jo-ad.com	248-588-4810	588-3448	757
Joan C Edwards School of Medicine at Marshall University 1600 Medical Ctr Dr .... Huntington WV 25701 *TF:* 877-691-1600 ■ *Web:* jcesom.marshall.edu	304-691-1700	691-1726	167-2
Joan of Arc Academy 2221 Elmira Dr .... Ottawa ON K2C1H3 *Web:* joanofarcacademy.com	613-728-6364		685
Joan Shorenstein Ctr on the Press Politics & Public Policy 79 John F Kennedy St .... Cambridge MA 02138 *Web:* shorensteincenter.org	617-495-8269	495-8696	634
Jo-Ann Fabrics & Crafts 5555 Darrow Rd .... Hudson OH 44236 *TF:* 888-739-4120 ■ *Web:* www.joann.com	330-656-2600	463-6760	270
Jo-Ann Stores Inc (JAS) 5555 Darrow Rd .... Hudson OH 44236 *TF:* 888-739-4120 ■ *Web:* www.joann.com	330-656-2600	463-6760	270
Joanne Rile Artists Management Inc 93 York Rd Ste 222 .... Jenkintown PA 19046 *TF:* 800-650-0246 ■ *Web:* www.rilearts.com	215-885-6400		708
Joat Screen Printing 3601 W Parmer Ln .... Austin TX 78727	512-836-1300		627
Job Finders Employment Service Co 1729 W Broadway Ste 4 .... Columbia MO 65203 *Web:* www.jobfindersusa.com	573-446-4250		260
Job Performance Systems Inc 1240 N Pitt St Ste 200 .... Alexandria VA 22314 *Web:* www.jps-usa.com	703-683-5805		463
Job Shop Managers 28966 Hancock Pkwy .... Valencia CA 91355 *TF:* 800-243-2224 ■ *Web:* www.skmindustries.com	661-294-8373		350
Jobaline Inc 620 Kirkland Way Ste 208 .... Kirkland WA 98033 *Web:* www.jobaline.com	425-242-0866		387
Jobast Holdings Inc 377 Oak St Ste 402 .... Garden City NY 11530	516-997-4490		690
Jobbers Automotive Warehouse Inc 801 E Zimmerly St .... Wichita KS 67211 *Web:* www.jawinc.com	316-267-4393		61
Jobbers Meat Packing Company Inc 3336 Fruitland Ave .... Vernon CA 90058	323-588-9151		473
Jobboom Inc 800 rue du Sq Victoria Mezzanine - Bureau 5 .... Montreal QC H4Z0A3 *Web:* www.jobboom.com	514-504-2539		260
JobDig Inc 5051 Hwy 7 Ste 240 .... Saint Louis Park MN 55416 *Web:* www.jobdig.com	952-929-5627		260
JobDiva 116 John St Ste 1406 .... New York NY 10038 *TF:* 866-562-3482 ■ *Web:* www.jobdiva.com	866-562-3482		393
Jobe & Company Inc 9004 Yellow Brick Rd Ste F .... Rosedale MD 21237 *TF:* 855-805-2599 ■ *Web:* www.jobeandcompany.com	410-288-0560	285-8651	358
Jobe Hastings & Assoc CPA's 745 S Church St Ste 105 .... Murfreesboro TN 37133 *TF:* 866-207-2384 ■ *Web:* jobehastings.com	615-893-7777		2
Jobelephantcom Inc 5443 Fremontia Ln .... San Diego CA 92115 *TF:* 800-311-0563 ■ *Web:* www.jobelephant.com	619-795-0837		7
JobHive Inc 701 E Bridger Ave Ste 400 .... Las Vegas NV 89101 *TF:* 855-562-4483	855-562-4483		260
JobMonkey Inc 1409 Post Alley .... Seattle WA 98101 *TF:* 800-230-1095 ■ *Web:* www.jobmonkey.com	800-230-1095		260
Jobscope Corp 355 Woodruff Rd .... Greenville SC 29607 *TF:* 800-443-5794 ■ *Web:* www.jobscope.com	800-443-5794		178-11
JobsOhio 41 S High St Ste 1500 .... Columbus OH 43215 *TF:* 855-874-2530 ■ *Web:* jobs-ohio.com	614-224-6446		463
JobSync Inc 430 Colorado Ave Ste 302 .... Santa Monica CA 90401	310-394-8300		260
JobTarget LLC 225 State St Ste 300 .... New London CT 06320 *Web:* www.jobtarget.com	860-440-0635		260
JOC (Johnson Oil Company) 1918 Church St .... Gonzales TX 78629 *TF:* 800-284-2432 ■ *Web:* www.johnsonoilcompany.com	800-284-2432		579
Jo-Carroll Energy 793 US Hwy 20 W .... Elizabeth IL 61028 *TF:* 800-858-5522 ■ *Web:* www.jocarroll.com	815-858-2207	858-3731	245
Jockey Club, The 40 E 52nd St .... New York NY 10022 *Web:* www.jockeyclub.com	212-371-5970	371-6123	48-22
Jockey International Inc 2300 60th St PO Box 1417 .... Kenosha WI 53140 *TF:* 800-562-5391 ■ *Web:* www.jockey.com	800-562-5391		155-18
Jockey's Ridge State Park PO Box 592 .... Nags Head NC 27959 *Web:* www.jockeysridgestatepark.com	252-441-7132		565
Jockeys' Guild Inc 448 Lewis Hargett Cir Ste 220 .... Nicholasville KY 40503 *TF:* 866-465-6257 ■ *Web:* www.jockeysguild.com	859-523-5625	219-9892	48-22
Jocks & Jills Sports Grill 4109 S Stream Blvd .... Charlotte NC 28217 *Web:* www.jocks-frankies.com	704-423-0001		670

	Phone	Fax	Class
Jodon Engineering 62 Enterprise Dr. Ann Arbor MI 48103 *Web:* www.jodon.com	734-761-4044		425
Joe Allen 326 W 46th St. New York NY 10036 *Web:* www.joeallenrestaurant.com	212-581-6464		671
Joe Allen's Pit Bar-B-Que 301 S 11th St. Abilene TX 79602	325-672-6082		671
Joe Christensen Inc 1540 Adams St. Lincoln NE 68521 *Web:* jci.mightydrake.com/index.htm	402-476-7535	476-3094	626
Joe Gibbs Racing Inc 13415 Reese Blvd W. Huntersville NC 28078 *Web:* www.joegibbsracing.com	704-944-5000		642
Joe Goode Performance Group (JGPG) 499 Alabama St Ste 150. San Francisco CA 94110 *TF:* 800-838-3006 ■ *Web:* www.joegoode.org	415-561-6565	561-6562	573-1
Joe Holland Chevrolet Inc 210 Maccorkle Ave SW. South Charleston WV 25303 *TF:* 855-468-9491 ■ *Web:* www.joeholland.com	304-744-1561		57
Joe Krentzman & Son Inc 3175 Back Maitland Rd. Lewistown PA 17044 *TF:* 800-543-2000 ■ *Web:* www.krentzman.net	717-543-4000		686
Joe N Miles & Sons Inc 66 Miles Lumber Co Rd. Silver Creek MS 39663 *Web:* mileslumber.com	601-886-7844		683
Joe Roots Grill 2826 W Eigth St. Erie PA 16505	814-836-7668		671
Joe T Garcia's 2201 N Commerce St. Fort Worth TX 76164 *Web:* joetgarcias.com	817-626-4356		671
Joe Tahan's Furniture Liquidation Centers Inc 131 Henry St. Rome NY 13440 *TF:* 800-420-2337 ■ *Web:* www.tahans.com	315-339-2330		321
Joe Van Horn Chevrolet Inc PO Box 238. Plymouth WI 53073 *TF:* 800-236-1415 ■ *Web:* www.vanhornchev.com	920-893-6361		57
Joe Wheeler Electric Membership Corp PO Box 460. Trinity AL 35673 *TF:* 800-239-6518 ■ *Web:* www.jwemc.org	256-552-2300	355-0631	245
Joe Wheeler Resort Lodge & Convention Ctr 4401 McLean Dr. Rogersville AL 35652 *TF:* 800-544-5639 ■ *Web:* www.alapark.com/joewheeler	256-247-5461	247-5471	669
Joe's Crab Shack 6550 Marina Dr. Long Beach CA 90803 *Web:* joescrabshack.com	562-594-6551		671
Joe's Crab Shack 3320 Central Expy. Plano TX 75023 *Web:* joescrabshack.com	972-423-2800		671
Joe's Crab Shack 1568 Crossways Blvd. Chesapeake VA 23320 *Web:* joescrabshack.com	757-420-8330		671
Joe's Crab Shack 7646 E 61st St. Tulsa OK 74135 *Web:* joescrabshack.com	918-252-1010		671
Joe's Crab Shack 12011 Harbor Blvd. Garden Grove CA 92840 *Web:* www.joescrabshack.com	714-703-0505		671
Joe's Crab Shack 5802 W Loop S 289. Lubbock TX 79424 *Web:* www.joescrabshack.com	806-797-8600		671
Joe's Crab Shack 101 SE Columbia Way. Vancouver WA 98661 *Web:* joescrabshack.com	360-693-9211		671
Joe's Crab Shack 2288 N Garden St. Boise ID 83706 *Web:* www.joescrabshack.com	208-336-9370		671
Joe's Jeans Inc 2340 S Eastern Ave. Commerce CA 90040 *NASDAQ: JOEZ* ■ *TF:* 877-528-5637 ■ *Web:* www.joesjeans.com	323-837-3700		157-4
Joe's Seafood Prime Steak & Stone Crab 60 E Grand Ave. Chicago IL 60611 *Web:* www.leye.com	312-379-5637		671
Joe's Stone Crab 11 Washington Ave. Miami Beach FL 33139 *TF:* 800-780-2722 ■ *Web:* www.joesstonecrab.com	305-673-0365		671
Joel Lane House Museum & Gardens 728 W Hargett St. Raleigh NC 27603 *TF:* 800-514-3849 ■ *Web:* www.joellane.org	919-833-3431		520
Joerns Healthcare 5001 Joerns Dr. Stevens Point WI 54481 *TF:* 800-826-0270	800-826-0270	457-8827	319-3
Joes Sporting Goods - Ski Shop Inc 33 County Rd B E. Saint Paul MN 55117 *Web:* www.joessportinggoods.com	651-209-7800		711
Joester Loria Group Inc, The 30 Irving Pl 10th Fl. New York NY 10003 *Web:* joesterloriagroup.com	212-683-5150		226
JOEY Restaurants Rideau Centre Rideau St. Ottawa ON K1N9J7 *Web:* joeyrestaurants.com/menu	613-680-5639		671
Joey's Only Seafood Franchising Corp 514-42nd Ave SE. Calgary AB T2G1Y6 *TF:* 800-661-2123 ■ *Web:* www.joeys.ca	403-243-4584	243-8989	670
Joey's Restaurant 6594 Thompson Rd. Syracuse NY 13206 *Web:* joeysitalianrestaurant.com	315-432-0315		671
Joffrey Ballet of Chicago 10 E Randolph St. Chicago IL 60601 *Web:* joffrey.org	312-739-0120	739-0119	573-1
Joffrey's Coffee & Tea Co 3803 Corporex Pk Dr. Tampa FL 33619 *TF:* 800-458-5282 ■ *Web:* www.joffreys.com	813-250-0404		297-11
Johanna Foods Inc 20 Johanna Farm Rd PO Box 272. Flemington NJ 08822 *TF:* 800-727-6700 ■ *Web:* www.johannafoods.com	908-788-2200		296-20
Johanne's 196 S Indian Canyon Dr. Palm Springs CA 92262 *Web:* www.johannesrestaurants.com	760-778-0017		671
Johannes Flowers Inc 4990 Foothill Rd. Carpinteria CA 93013 *TF:* 800-365-9476 ■ *Web:* www.johannesflowers.com	805-684-5686	566-2199	369
Johannes Leonardo LLC 628 Broadway 6th FL. New York NY 10012 *Web:* www.johannesleonardo.com	212-462-8120		7
Johanson & Yau Accountancy Corp 160 W Santa Clara St Ste 900. San Jose CA 95113 *TF:* 800-681-1729 ■ *Web:* www.jyac.com	408-288-5111		41
Johanson Dielectrics 15191 Bledsoe St. Sylmar CA 91342 *Web:* www.johansondielectrics.com	818-364-9800		696
Johanson Mfg Corp 301 Rockaway Valley Rd. Boonton NJ 07005 **Fax:* Sales ■ *TF:* 800-477-1272 ■ *Web:* www.johansonmfg.com	973-334-2676	334-2954*	253
Johanson Transportation Service Inc 5583 E Olive Ave. Fresno CA 93727 *TF:* 800-742-2053 ■ *Web:* www.johansontrans.com	559-458-2200		311
John & Mable Ringling Museum of Art 5401 Bay Shore Rd. Sarasota FL 34243 *TF:* 800-975-3212 ■ *Web:* www.ringling.org	941-359-5700		520
John A Culhane CPA 755 Main St Bldg Ste 1. Monroe CT 06468 *Web:* culhanecpa.com	203-268-4431		2
John A Gupton College 1616 Church St. Nashville TN 37203 *Web:* guptoncollege.edu	615-327-3927	321-4518	800
John A Logan College 700 Logan College Rd. Carterville IL 62918	618-985-2828		162
John A Martin & Association Inc 950 S Grand Ave 4th Fl. Los Angeles CA 90015 *TF:* 800-776-2368 ■ *Web:* www.johnmartin.com	213-483-6490	483-3084	261
John A Penney Company Inc 270 Sidney St. Cambridge MA 02139	617-547-7744		189-4
John A Van Den Bosch Co 4511 Holland Ave. Holland MI 49424 *TF:* 800-968-6477 ■ *Web:* www.vbosch.com	800-968-6477		447
John A Volpe National Transportation Systems Ctr 55 Broadway. Cambridge MA 02142 *Web:* www.volpe.dot.gov	617-494-2000		668
John A. Minetto State Park c/o Burr Pond State Pk 385 Burr Mtn Rd. Torrington CT 06790 *Web:* www.ct.gov	860-482-1817		565
John Abbott College 21275 Ch Lakeshore Bureau 2000 Sainte-anne-de-bellevue QC H9X3L9 *Web:* www.johnabbott.qc.ca	514-457-6610	457-4730	166
John B Hynes Veterans Memorial Convention Ctr 900 Boylston St. Boston MA 02115 *TF:* 800-392-6089 ■ *Web:* massconvention.com	617-954-2000	954-2299	205
John B Malouf Inc 8201 Quaker Ave Ste 106. Lubbock TX 79424 *TF:* 800-658-9500 ■ *Web:* www.maloufs.com	806-794-9500		157-4
John B Sanfilippo & Son Inc 1703 N Randall Rd. Elgin IL 60123 *NASDAQ: JBSS* ■ *TF:* 800-874-8734 ■ *Web:* www.jbssinc.com	847-289-1800	289-1843	296-28
John Ball Zoological Garden 1300 W Fulton St. Grand Rapids MI 49504 *TF:* 800-645-3226 ■ *Web:* www.jbzoo.org	616-336-4301	336-3907	823
John Bean Co 309 Exchange Ave. Conway AR 72032 *TF:* 800-225-5786 ■ *Web:* www.johnbean.com	501-450-1500		60
John Bean Technologies Corp 70 W Madison Ste 4400. Chicago IL 60602 *Web:* www.jbtcorporation.com	312-861-5900		296
John Berggruen Gallery 228 Grant Ave. San Francisco CA 94108 *Web:* www.berggruen.com	415-781-4629	781-0126	42
John Boos & Co 3601 S Banker St PO Box 609. Effingham IL 62401 *TF:* 888-431-2667 ■ *Web:* www.johnboos.com	217-347-7701	347-7705	286
John Bouchard & Sons Co 1024 Harrison St. Nashville TN 37203 *Web:* www.jbouchard.com	615-256-0112		189-10
John Boyd Thacher State Park 1 Hailes Cave Rd. Voorheesville NY 12186 *TF:* 800-456-2267 ■ *Web:* parks.ny.gov/parks/128	518-872-1237	872-9133	565
John Brown Farm State Historic Site 115 John Brown Rd. Lake Placid NY 12946 *Web:* parks.ny.gov/historic-sites/29/details.aspx	518-523-3900		565
John Brown House Museum 52 Power St. Providence RI 02906 *Web:* www.rihs.org	401-273-7507		50-3
John Brown Ltd Inc 46 Grove St PO Box 296. Peterborough NH 03458 *TF:* 800-578-7947 ■ *Web:* www.johnbrownlimited.com	603-924-3834	924-7998	317
John Brown University 2000 W University St. Siloam Springs AR 72761 **Fax:* Admissions ■ *TF Admissions:* 877-528-4636 ■ *Web:* www.jbu.edu	479-524-9500	524-4196*	166
John Bryan State Park 3790 SR- 370. Yellow Springs OH 45387 *Web:* www.ohiodnr.com	937-767-1274		565
John Buck Co 225 W Washington St Ste 2300. Chicago IL 60606 *Web:* www.tjbc.com	312-993-9800		653
John Burns Construction Company Inc 17601 SW Hwy. Orland Park IL 60467 *Web:* www.jbconstructionco.com	708-326-3500		186
John C Dolph Co 320 New Rd. Monmouth Junction NJ 08852 *Web:* www.dolphs.com	732-329-2333		481
John C Flanagan House 942 NE Glen Oak Ave. Peoria IL 61603	309-674-1921		50-3
John C Hart Memorial Library 1130 E Main St. Shrub Oak NY 10588 *Web:* yorktownlibrary.org	914-245-5262	245-5936	434-3
John C Nordt Company Inc 1420 Coulter Dr NW. Roanoke VA 24012 *Web:* www.jcnordt.com	540-362-9717		409
John C Otto Company Inc, The 341 Shaker Rd. East Longmeadow MA 01028 *Web:* www.jco.com	413-525-4131		92
John C Proctor Endowment 2724 W Reservoir Blvd. Peoria IL 61615 *Web:* proctorplace.org	309-685-6580	566-4292	450
John C R Kelly Realty 3535 Blvd Of The Allies. Pittsburgh PA 15213 *Web:* jcrkelly.com	412-683-7300		652
John C. Heath, Attorney at Law PLLC 360 N Cutler Dr. Salt Lake City UT 84054 *TF:* 800-756-9681 ■ *Web:* www.lexingtonlaw.com	800-756-9681		428

	Phone	Fax	Class
John Callahan Agency Inc 294 New York Ave, Huntington NY 11743 *Web:* statefarm.com	631-271-1615		390
John Cannon Homes Inc 6710 Professional Pkwy W, Sarasota FL 34240 *Web:* www.johncannonhomes.com	941-924-5935	924-4129	187
John Carlo Inc 20848 Hall Rd, Clinton Township MI 48038	586-741 5302		188-4
John Carroll School, The 703 Churchville Rd, Bel Air MD 21014 *TF:* 800-422-0010 ■ *Web:* www.johncarroll.org	410-879-2480		685
John Carroll University 20700 N Pk Blvd, Cleveland OH 44118 **Fax:* Admissions ■ *TF:* 888-335-6800 ■ *Web:* www.jcu.edu	216-397-1886	397-4981*	166
John Chadds House 1736 N Creek Rd PO Box 27, Chadds Ford PA 19317 *Web:* www.chaddsfordhistory.org	610-388-7376	388-7480	50-3
John Cooper School 1 John Cooper Dr, The Woodlands TX 77381 *TF:* 800-295-1162 ■ *Web:* www.johncooper.org	281-367-0900		685
John Crane Canada Inc 423 Green Rd N, Stoney Creek ON L8E3A1 *Web:* www.johncrane.com	905-662-6191		326
John Crane Inc 6400 W Oakton St, Morton Grove IL 60053 *Web:* www.johncrane.com	847-967-2400	967-2400	326
John D & Catherine T MacArthur Foundation 140 S Dearborn St, Chicago IL 60603 *Web:* www.macfound.org	312-726-8000	920-6258	305
John D Archbold Memorial Hospital 915 Gordon Ave, Thomasville GA 31792 *TF:* 800-341-1009 ■ *Web:* www.archbold.org	229-228-2000		374-3
John d Miller Real Estate Investments LLC 1370 W SR- 89A Ste 17, Sedona AZ 86336 *Web:* johndmiller.com	928-254-0303		652
John D. MacArthur Beach State Park 10900 SR 703 (A1A), North Palm Beach FL 33408 *Web:* www.floridastateparks.org	561-624-6950		565
John D. Rockefeller Jr Memorial Parkway PO Box 170, Moose WY 83012 *Web:* www.nps.gov/jodr	307-739-3300	739-3438	564
John Daugherty Realtors 520 Post Oak Blvd 6th Fl, Houston TX 77027 *TF:* 800-231-2821 ■ *Web:* www.johndaugherty.com	713-626-3930	963-9588	652
John Day Co 6263 Abbott Dr, Omaha NE 68110 *TF:* 800-767-2273 ■ *Web:* www.johnday.com	402-455-8000		274
John Day Fossil Beds National Monument 32651 Hwy 19, Kimberly OR 97848 *Web:* www.nps.gov/joda	541-987-2333	987-2336	564
John Deere Coffeyville Works Inc 2624 N US Hwy, Coffeyville KS 67337 *TF:* 800-844-1337 ■ *Web:* www.deere.com	800-844-1337		620
John Deere Construction & Forestry 1515 Fifth Ave, Moline IL 61265 **Fax:* Cust Svc ■ *Web:* deere.com	309-765-0227	748-0117*	190
John Deere Credit Co 6400 NW 86th St, Johnston IA 50131 *TF:* 800-275-5322 ■ *Web:* www.deere.com/en_us/jdc	515-267-3000		216
John Deere Planetarium 820 38th St Augustana College, Rock Island IL 61201 *TF:* 800-798-8100 ■ *Web:* augustana.edu	309 794-7327	794-7564	598
John Deere Power Systems 3801 W Ridgeway Ave, Waterloo IA 50704 **Fax Area Code:* 319 ■ *TF:* 800-533-6446 ■ *Web:* www.deere.com	800-533-6446	292-5075*	262
John Deklewa & Sons Inc 1273 Washington Pk, Bridgeville PA 15017	412-257-9000		186
John Dickinson Plantation 340 Kitts Hummock Rd, Dover DE 19901 *Web:* history.delaware.gov	302-739-3277		50-3
John E Conner Museum 905 W Santa Gertrudis Ave 700 University Blvd, Kingsville TX 78363 *TF:* 800-726-8192 ■ *Web:* www.tamuk.edu/artsci/museum	361-593-2810	593-2112	520
John E Ernst 120 N 30th St Ste 103, Quincy IL 62301	217-223-4127		390
John E Green Co 220 Victor Ave, Highland Park MI 48203 *TF:* 800-571-8191 ■ *Web:* www.johnegreen.com	313-868-2400	868-0011	189-10
John E Jones Oil Co Inc 1016 S Cedar PO Box 546, Stockton KS 67669 *TF:* 800-323-9821 ■ *Web:* www.jonesoil.net	785-425-6746	425-6323	186
John E Koerner & Company Inc 4820 Jefferson Hwy, New Orleans LA 70121 **Fax Area Code:* 504 ■ *TF:* 800-333-1913 ■ *Web:* www.koerner-co.com	800-333-1913	734-0630*	297-11
John Evans' Sons Inc 1 Spring Ave PO Box 885, Lansdale PA 19446 *Web:* www.springcompany.com	215-368-7700	368-9019	719
John F Buchan Homes 2821 Northup Way Ste 100, Bellevue WA 98004 *Web:* www.buchan.com	425-827-2266		653
John F Kennedy Ctr for the Performing Arts 2700 F St NW, Washington DC 20566 *TF:* 800-444-1324 ■ *Web:* www.kennedy-center.org	202-416-8000	416-8205	572
John F Kennedy Hyannis Museum 397 Main St, Hyannis MA 02601 *Web:* jfkhyannismuseum.org	508-790-3077		520
John F Kennedy International Airport (JFK) 150 Greenwich St, New York NY 10007 **Fax Area Code:* 201 ■ *Web:* www.panynj.gov/airports/jfk.html	212-435-7000	871-2343*	27
John F Kennedy Library 500 Hoes Ln, Piscataway NJ 08854 *Web:* piscatawaylibrary.org	732-463-1633		434-3
John F Kennedy Library (JFKL) 190 W 49th St, Hialeah FL 33012 *Web:* www.hialeahfl.gov/library	305-821-2700	818-9144	434-3
John F Kennedy Memorial Hospital 47-111 Monroe St, Indio CA 92201 *Web:* www.jfkmemorialhosp.com	760-347-6191		374-3
John F Kennedy National Historic Site 83 Beals St, Brookline MA 02446 *Web:* www.nps.gov/jofi	617-566-7937	730-9884	564
John F Kennedy Presidential Library & Museum Columbia Pt, Boston MA 02125 *TF:* 866-535-1960 ■ *Web:* www.jfklibrary.org	617-514 1600	514-1652	434-2
John F Kennedy University 100 Ellinwood Way, Pleasant Hill CA 94523 **Fax:* Admissions ■ *TF:* 800-696-5358 ■ *Web:* www.jfku.edu	925-969-3300	969-3101*	166
John F Long Properties LLLP 1118 E Missouri Ave Ste A, Phoenix AZ 85014 **Fax Area Code:* 623 ■ *Web:* www.jflongproperties.com	602-272-0421	846-7208*	655
John F Otto Inc 1717 Second St, Sacramento CA 95811 *Web:* www.ottoconstruction.com	916-441-6870	441-6138	188-10
John F Sutherland & Assoc Ins Svcs Inc 6275 Lusk Blvd, San Diego CA 92121	858-535-1139		390
John F. Kennedy Space Ctr, Kennedy Space Center FL 32899 *TF:* 866-737-5235 ■ *Web:* www.nasa.gov/centers/kennedy	321-867-5000		668
John Fabick Tractor Co 1 Fabick Dr, Fenton MO 63026 *TF Cust Svc:* 800-845-9188 ■ *Web:* www.fabickcat.com	636-343-5900	343-4910	358
John G Riley Ctr/Museum of African American History & Culture 419 E Jefferson St, Tallahassee FL 32301 *Web:* www.rileymuseum.org	850-681-7881	681-7000	520
John G Shedd Aquarium 1200 S Lake Shore Dr, Chicago IL 60605 *Web:* www.sheddaquarium.org	312-939-2438		40
John Gallin & Son Inc 102 Madison Ave 9th Fl, New York NY 10016 *Web:* www.gallin.com	212-252-8900		186
John Gerlach & Co LLP 37 W Broad St Ste 530, Columbus OH 43215 *Web:* www.johngerlach.com	614-224-2164	224-1391	2
John Gorrie Museum State Park 46 Sixth St PO Box 267, Apalachicola FL 32320 *Web:* www.floridastateparks.org	850-653-9347		565
John H Hampshire Inc 320 W 24th St, Baltimore MD 21211 *TF:* 800-638-0076 ■ *Web:* www.jhhampshire.com	410-366-8900	467-7391	189-2
John Hancock Financial Services Inc 601 Congress St, Boston MA 02210 **Fax:* PR ■ *Web:* www.johnhancock.com	617-663-2400	663-4790*	360-4
John Hancock Funds 601 Congress St, Boston MA 02210 *TF:* 800-338-8080 ■ *Web:* www.jhinvestments.com	617-375 1500		528
John Hancock Life Insurance Co 1 John Hancock Way Ste 1700, Boston MA 02117 *TF:* 800-248-6110 ■ *Web:* www.johnhancock.com	617-572-6000		391-2
John Hancock New York 100 Summit Lake Dr, Valhalla NY 10595 *TF:* 800-732-5543 ■ *Web:* www.johnhancock.com	877-391-3748		391-2
John Harris-Simon Cameron Mansion, The 219 S Front St, Harrisburg PA 17104 *TF:* 800-732-0099 ■ *Web:* www.dauphincountyhistory.org	717-233-3462	233-6059	50-3
John Harvard's Brew House 33 Dunster St, Cambridge MA 02138 *Web:* www.johnharvards.com	617-868-3585	868-4341	670
John Heinz Institute of Rehabilitation Medicine 150 Mundy St Ste 3, Wilkes-Barre PA 18702 *Web:* allied-services.org	570-826-3800		374-6
John Henry Co 5800 W Grand River Ave, Lansing MI 48906 **Fax Area Code:* 800 ■ *TF:* 800-748-0517 ■ *Web:* www.jhc.com	517-323-9000	968-5646*	626
John Henry Foster Minnesota Inc 3103 Mike Collins Dr, Eagan MN 55121 *Web:* www.jhfoster.com	651-452-8452		172
John Henry's Cafe 1785 E Tahquitz Canyon Way, Palm Springs CA 92262 *Web:* johnhenryscafe.com	760-327-7667		671
John Hersey High School 1900 E Thomas St, Arlington Heights IL 60004 *Web:* jhhs.d214.org	847-718-4800		685
John Hine Mazda Inc 1545 Camino Del Rio S, San Diego CA 92108 *Web:* www.johnhine.com	619-297-4251		57
John Hoadley & Sons Inc 672 Union St, Rockland MA 02370 *Web:* hoadleyandsons.com	781-878-8098		189-10
John Hofmeister & Son Inc 2386 S Blue Island Ave, Chicago IL 60608 *Web:* www.hofhaus.com	773-847-0700		296-26
John Holmlund Nursery LLC 29285 SE Hwy 212, Boring OR 97009 *Web:* www.jhnsy.com	503-663-6650		192
John Hsu Capital Group Inc 747 Third Ave 26th Fl, New York NY 10017 *Web:* www.johnhsucapital.com	212-223-7515		401
John J Adams Die Corp 10 Nebraska St, Worcester MA 01604	508-757-3894		455
John J Campbell Company Inc 6012 Resources Dr, Memphis TN 38134 *TF:* 800-592-4709 ■ *Web:* www.campbellroofing.com	901-372-8400		189-12
John J Enoch Inc 2400 york rd, Lutherville timonium MD 21093 *Web:* www.enochoffice.com	410-561-7600		23
John J Pershing Veterans Affairs Medical Ctr 1500 N Westwood Blvd, Poplar Bluff MO 63901 *TF:* 888-557-8262 ■ *Web:* www.poplarbluff.va.gov	573-686-4151	778-4559	374-8
John J Smith Masonry Co 9200 Green Pk Rd, Saint Louis MO 63123 *Web:* www.smithmasonry.com	314-894-9500	894-1172	189-7
John James Audubon Museum 3100 US Hwy 41 N, Henderson KY 42419	270-826-2247		520
John James Audubon State Park 3100 US Hwy 41 N, Henderson KY 42419 *Web:* www.parks.ky.gov	270-826-2247		565
John Jasperse Co 140 Second Ave Ste 501, New York NY 10003 *Web:* www.johnjasperse.org	212-375-8283		573-1
John Jay Homestead State Historic Site PO Box 832, Katonah NY 10536 *TF:* 800-456-2267 ■ *Web:* parks.ny.gov/historic-sites/4/details.aspx	914-232-5651		565
John Johnson Co 274 S Waterman St, Detroit MI 48209 *TF:* 800-991-1394 ■ *Web:* www.johnjohnsonco.com	313-496 0600	496-0252	733
John Kautz Farms 5490 E Bear Oak Rd, Lodi CA 95240	209-334-4786		315-5
John Keal Music Company Inc 819 Livingston Ave, Albany NY 12206 *Web:* www.myjohnkeal.com	518-482-4405		526

				Phone	Fax	Class
John Knox Village 651 SW Sixth St *TF:* 800-998-5669 ■ *Web:* www.johnknoxvillage.com	Pompano Beach	FL	33060	800-998-5669		672
John Knox Village of the Rio Grande Valley 1300 S Border Ave *TF:* 800-245-6526 ■ *Web:* johnknoxvillagergv.com	Weslaco	TX	78596	956-968-4575		672
John L Wortham & Son LP 2727 Allen Pkwy *Web:* www.worthaminsurance.com	Houston	TX	77019	713-526-3366		390
John Lance Ford Inc 23775 Ctr Ridge Rd *Web:* autonationfordwestlake.com	Westlake	OH	44145	440-871-8600		57
John Leslie Consulting 20 Souhegan St *Web:* www.jlc.net	Milford	NH	03055	603-673-6132		196
John Levy Consulting 505 Mesa Rd Ste 1 *Web:* johnlevyconsulting.com	Point Reyes Station	CA	94956	415-663-1818		463
John Lilley Correctional Ctr 105150 N 3670 Rd Hwy 62 E 407971 *Web:* www.ok.gov	Boley	OK	74829	918-667-3381	667-3959	213
John Lyman Ctr for the Performing Arts 501 Crescent St *Web:* tickets.southernct.edu	New Haven	CT	06515	203-392-6154	946-2998	572
John M Browning Firearms Museum 2501 Wall Ave *Web:* theunionstation.org	Ogden	UT	84401	801-393-9886		520
John m Hartel & Company Inc 144 N Kinderkamack Rd *Web:* jmhartel.com	Montvale	NY	07645	845-735-3666		38
John M. Campbell & Co 1215 Crossroads Blvd *TF:* 800-821-5933 ■ *Web:* www.jmcampbell.com	Norman	OK	73072	405-321-1383		261
John Manlove Marketing & Communications 5125 Preston Ave *Web:* johnmanlove.com	Pasadena	TX	77505	281-668-9826		627
John Marshall House, The 818 E Marshall St *Web:* preservationvirginia.org	Richmond	VA	23219	804-648-7998	648-5880	50-3
John Marshall Law School 315 S Plymouth Ct *Web:* www.jmls.edu	Chicago	IL	60604	312-427-2737		167-1
John Masters Organic Hair Care Inc 77 Sullivan St *Web:* www.johnmasters.com	New York	NY	10012	212-343-9590		77
John Matouk Company Inc 118 W 22nd S 9th Fl *Web:* www.matouk.com	New York	NY	10011	212-683-9242		361
John Mcclaren Chevrolet Inc 1015 E Mcgregor Dr *Web:* johnmcclarenchevrolet.com	Mcgregor	TX	76657	254-840-3261		57
John Michael Kohler Arts Center 608 New York Ave *TF:* 800-457-9497 ■ *Web:* www.jmkac.org	Sheboygan	WI	53081	920-458-6144		520
John Morgan Mclachlan Agency, The 75 E Main St	Somerville	NJ	08876	908-526-4600		390
John Morrell & Co 805 E Kemper Rd *TF:* 800-722-1127 ■ *Web:* www.johnmorrell.com	Cincinnati	OH	45246	513-346-3540		473
John Muir Medical Ctr (JMMC) 1601 Ygnacio Valley Rd *TF:* 844-398-5376 ■ *Web:* www.johnmuirhealth.com	Walnut Creek	CA	94598	925-939-3000	308-8944	374-3
John Muir National Historic Site 4202 Alhambra Ave *Web:* www.nps.gov	Martinez	CA	94553	925-228-8860	228-8192	564
John Nuzzo 7428 W Belmont *Web:* johnnuzzo.com	Chicago	IL	60634	773-889-3900		390
John Paul Jones State Historic Site c/o Bureau of Parks & Lands *TF:* 800-452-1942 ■ *Web:* maine.gov/dacf/parks/index.shtml	Bangor	ME	04401	207-941-4014	941-4222	565
John Paul Mitchell Systems 1888 Century Park E ste 1600 *TF Cust Svc:* 800-793-8790 ■ *Web:* www.paulmitchell.com	Los Angeles	CA	90067	800-793-8790		214
John Paul Pet Salon 27762 Antonio Pkwy *TF:* 855-577-7669 ■ *Web:* johnpaulpetsalon.com	Ladera Ranch	CA	92694	855-577-7669	329-5779	794
John Peter Smith Hospital 1500 S Main St *Web:* www.jpshealthnet.org	Fort Worth	TX	76104	817-702-3431		374-3
John Portman & Assoc Inc 303 Peachtree Ctr Ave Ste 575 *Web:* www.portmanusa.com	Atlanta	GA	30303	404-614-5555		321
John Q Hammons Hotel Management LLC 300 S John Q Hammons Pkwy #900 *Web:* www.jqhhotels.com	Springfield	MO	65806	417-864-4300		379
John R Hess & Company Inc 400 Stn St PO Box 3615 *TF:* 800-828-4377 ■ *Web:* www.jrhessco.com	Cranston	RI	02910	401-785-9300	785-2510	146
John R Jurgensen Co 11641 Mosteller Rd *Web:* www.jrjnet.com	Cincinnati	OH	45241	513-771-0820		188-4
John R Manson Youth Institute 42 Jarvis St	Cheshire	CT	06410	203-806-2500	699-1845	412
John R Nalbach Engineering Co 621 E Plainfield Rd *Web:* www.nalbach.com	Countryside	IL	60525	708-579-9100	579-0122	547
John R Wald Company Inc 10576 Fairgrounds Rd *Web:* www.jrwald.com	Huntingdon	PA	16652	814-643-3908		295
John R White Company Inc PO Box 10043 *TF:* 800-245-1183 ■ *Web:* www.johnrwhite.com	Birmingham	AL	35202	205-595-8381	595-8386	146
John Randolph Medical Ctr 411 W Randolph Rd *Web:* hcavirginia.com	Hopewell	VA	23860	804-541-1600		374-3
John Roberts Co 9687 E River Rd *TF:* 800-551-1534 ■ *Web:* www.johnroberts.com	Coon Rapids	MN	55433	763-755-5500		627
John Rohrer Contracting Company Inc 2820 Roe Ln Bldg S *TF:* 800-255-6119 ■ *Web:* www.johnrohrercontracting.com	Kansas City	KS	66103	913-236-5005	236-7291	189-3
John S & James L Knight Foundation 200 S Biscayne Blvd Ste 3300 *Web:* www.knightfoundation.org	Miami	FL	33131	305-908-2600		305
John S Clark Co Inc 210 Airport Rd *Web:* www.jsclark.com	Mount Airy	NC	27030	336-789-1000		186
John S Knight Ctr 77 E Mill St *TF:* 800-245-4254 ■ *Web:* www.johnsknightcenter.org	Akron	OH	44308	330-374-8900		205
John Sakash Company Inc 700 Walnut St *TF:* 800-929-3940 ■ *Web:* www.johnsakash.com	Elmhurst	IL	60126	630-833-3940		492
John Simon Guggenheim Memorial Foundation 90 Pk Ave *TF:* 800-232-0960 ■ *Web:* www.gf.org	New York	NY	10016	212-687-4470	697-3248	305
John Snow Inc 44 Farnsworth St *Web:* www.jsi.com	Boston	MA	02210	617-482-9485	482-0617	194
John St 172 John St *Web:* www.johnst.com	Toronto	ON	M5T1X5	416-348-0048		7
John Steinbeck Library 350 Lincoln Ave *TF:* 800-806-4474 ■ *Web:* www.salinaspubliclibrary.org	Salinas	CA	93901	831-758-7311		434-3
John Stewart Company Inc 1388 Sutter St Fl 11 *Web:* www.jsco.net	San Francisco	CA	94109	415-345-4400		652
John T Cyr & Sons Inc 153 Gilman Falls Ave *TF:* 800-244-2335 ■ *Web:* johntcyrandsons.com	Old Town	ME	04468	207-827-2335	827-6763	109
John T Mather Memorial Hospital 75 N Country Rd *Web:* www.matherhospital.org	Port Jefferson	NY	11777	631-473-1320	476-2792	374-3
John Tanner State Park 354 Tanner's Beach Rd *Web:* www.gastateparks.org	Carrollton	GA	30117	770-830-2222		565
John Templeton Foundation 300 Conshohocken State Rd Ste 500 *Web:* www.templeton.org	West Conshohocken	PA	19428	610-941-2828	825-1730	305
John Tyler Community College 13101 Jefferson Davis Hwy **Fax:* Admissions ■ *TF:* 800-552-3490 ■ *Web:* www.jtcc.edu	Chester	VA	23831	804-796-4000	796-4362*	162
John U. Lloyd Beach State Park 6503 N Ocean Dr *Web:* www.floridastateparks.org	Dania	FL	33004	954-923-2833		565
John Volpi & Company Inc 5263 Northrup Ave *TF:* 800-288-3439 ■ *Web:* www.volpifoods.com	St Louis	MO	63110	314-772-8550		296-10
John W Bristol & Company Inc 48 Wall St 18th Fl *TF:* 800-935-9935 ■ *Web:* www.jwbristol.com	New York	NY	10005	212-389-5880		401
John W Danforth Co 300 Colvin Woods Pkwy *TF:* 800-888-6119 ■ *Web:* www.jwdanforth.com	Tonawanda	NY	14150	716-832-1940	832-2388	189-10
John W McDougall Company Inc (JWMCD) 3731 Amy Lynn Dr *TF:* 800-264-1122 ■ *Web:* www.jwmcd.com	Nashville	TN	37218	615-321-3900	329-9069	697
John W Stone Oil Distributor LLC 87 First St *TF:* 800-845-3401 ■ *Web:* www.stoneoil.com	Gretna	LA	70053	504-366-3401		579
John W. Kyle State Park 4235 State Pk Rd *Web:* www.mdwfp.com	Sardis	MS	38666	662-487-1345		565
John Waddell & Company CPAs 3416 American River Dr Ste A *Web:* jwaddell.com	Sacramento	CA	95864	916-488-2460		2
John Watson Chevrolet 3535 Wall Ave *TF:* 866-647-9930 ■ *Web:* www.johnwatsonchevrolet.com	Ogden	UT	84401	801-394-2611		57
John Wayne Airport 18601 Airport Way *Web:* www.ocair.com	Santa Ana	CA	92707	949-252-5200		27
John Wayne Birthplace & Museum 205 S John Wayne Dr *TF:* 877-462-1044 ■ *Web:* johnwaynebirthplace.museum	Winterset	IA	50273	515-462-1044		520
John Wieland Homes & Neighborhoods 4125 Atlanta Rd SE *TF:* 800-376-4663 ■ *Web:* www.jwhomes.com	Smyrna	GA	30080	770-996-2400	907-3481	653
John Wiley & Sons Inc 111 River St *NYSE: JW/A* ■ *TF Sales:* 800-225-5945 ■ *Web:* www.wiley.com	Hoboken	NJ	07030	201-748-6000	748-6088	637-2
John Wingate Weeks Historic Site 200 Weeks State Park Rd *Web:* www.nhstateparks.org	Lancaster	NH	03584	603-788-4004		565
John Wolf Florist 6228 Waters Ave *TF:* 800-944-6435 ■ *Web:* www.johnwolfflorist.com	Savannah	GA	31406	912-352-9843		292
John Wood Community College 1301 S 48th St **Fax:* Admissions ■ *Web:* www.jwcc.edu	Quincy	IL	62305	217-224-6500	641-4192*	162
Pittsfield 1308 W Washington St *Web:* www.jwcc.edu	Pittsfield	IL	62363	217-285-5319	641-4192	162
John Wornall House Museum 6115 Wornall Rd *TF:* 800-357-0909 ■ *Web:* wornallhouse.org	Kansas City	MO	64113	816-444-1858		520
John Zink Company LLC 11920 E Apache St *TF:* 800-421-9242 ■ *Web:* www.johnzink.com	Tulsa	OK	74116	918-234-1800	234-2700	357
John's Pass Village & Boardwalk 150 John's Pass Boardwalk Pl *TF:* 800-853-1536 ■ *Web:* www.johnspass.com	Madeira Beach	FL	33708	727-398-6577		50-6
JohnDow Industries Inc 151 Snyder Ave *TF:* 800-433-0708 ■ *Web:* johndow.com	Barberton	OH	44203	330-753-6895		54
John-Kenyon Eye Ctr 1305 Wall St *TF:* 800-342-5393 ■ *Web:* www.johnkenyon.com	Jeffersonville	IN	47130	800-342-5393		798
Johnnie Appleseed Visitor Ctr 1000 Rte 2 Westbound *Web:* www.appleseed.org	Lancaster	MA	01523	978-534-2302		138
Johnny Delmonico's 130 S Pinckney St *Web:* www.foodfightinc.com	Madison	WI	53703	608-257-8325		671
Johnny Janosik Inc 11151 Trussum Pond Rd *Web:* www.johnnyjanosik.com	Laurel	DE	19956	302-875-5955		321
Johnny Londoff Chevrolet Inc 1375 Dunn Rd	Florissant	MO	63031	314-262-4526		57

Name / Address	City	State	ZIP	Phone	Fax	Class
Johnny Quick Food Stores 1799 Bullard Ave *Web:* www.johnnyquik.com	Clovis	CA	93612	559-299-2443	299-2253	204
Johnny Rebs' Southern Roadhouse 4663 Long Beach Blvd *Web:* www.johnnyrebs.com	Long Beach	CA	90805	562-423-7327		671
Johnny Rockets 2 S Pointe Dr Ste 200 *TF:* 888-856-4669	Lake Forest	CA	92630	888-856-4669		671
Johnny V 625 E Las Olas Blvd *Web:* www.johnnyvlasolas.com	Fort Lauderdale	FL	33301	954-761-7920		671
Johnny's 4245 W Fourth St *Web:* johnnysristorante.com	Reno	NV	89523	775-747-4511		671
Johnny's Bar on Fulton 3164 Fulton Rd *TF:* 800-459-8860 ■ *Web:* johnnyscleveland.com	Cleveland	OH	44109	216-281-0055		671
Johnny's Cafe 4702 S 27th St *Web:* www.johnnyscafe.com	Omaha	NE	68107	402-731-4774		671
Johnny's Dock 1900 E D St *Web:* www.johnnysdock.com	Tacoma	WA	98421	253-627-3186		671
Johnny's Downtown 1406 W Sixth St *Web:* www.johnnyscleveland.com	Cleveland	OH	44113	216-623-0055		671
Johnny's Fine Foods Inc 319 E 25th St *TF General:* 800-962-1462 ■ *Web:* www.johnnysfinefoods.com	Tacoma	WA	98421	253-383-4597		296-37
Johnny's Half Shell 400 N Capitol St NW *Web:* www.johnnyshalfshell.net	Washington	DC	20001	202-737-0400		671
Johnny's Selected Seeds 955 Benton Ave *TF:* 877-564-6697 ■ *Web:* www.johnnyseeds.com	Winslow	ME	04901	207-861-3900	861-8363	694
Johnny's Stop n Shop 505 S Commercial St	Emporia	KS	66801	620-343-3803		297-8
Johns Dental Laboratory Inc 423 S 13th St *TF:* 800-457-0504 ■ *Web:* www.johnsdental.com	Terre Haute	IN	47807	812-232-6026		383
Johns Eastern Co Inc PO Box 110259 Lakewood Branch *TF General:* 877-326-5326 ■ *Web:* www.johnseastern.com	Sarasota	FL	34211	941-907-3100		390
Johns Greenhouse & Florist Shop 517 Copeland St *Web:* johnsgreenhouses-florist.com	Brockton	MA	02301	508-588-0955		292
Johns Hopkins Bayview Medical Ctr 4940 Eastern Ave *Web:* www.hopkinsmedicine.org	Baltimore	MD	21224	410-550-0100		374-3
Johns Hopkins Health System (JHH) 600 N Wolfe St *Web:* www.hopkinsmedicine.org	Baltimore	MD	21287	410-955-5000		353
Johns Hopkins Hospital 600 N Wolfe St *Web:* www.hopkinsmedicine.org	Baltimore	MD	21287	410-955-5000		374-3
Johns Hopkins University 3400 N Charles St *Web:* www.jhu.edu	Baltimore	MD	21218	410-516-8000	516-6025	166
Johns Hopkins University Applied Physics Laboratory 11100 Johns Hopkins Rd *TF:* 800-435-9294 ■ *Web:* www.jhuapl.edu	Laurel	MD	20723	240-228-5000	228-1093	668
Johns Hopkins University Press 2715 N Charles St *Fax: Orders ■ *TF Orders:* 800-537-5487 ■ *Web:* www.press.jhu.edu	Baltimore	MD	21218	410-516-6900	516-6998*	637-4
Johns Hopkins University School of Medicine 601 N Caroline St *Web:* www.hopkinsmedicine.org	Baltimore	MD	21205	410-955-3080	955-0026	167-2
Johns Hopkins University Sheridan Libraries 3400 N Charles St *Web:* www.library.jhu.edu	Baltimore	MD	21218	410-516-8335	516-5080	434-6
Johns Manville Corp 717 17th St PO Box 5108 *TF Prod Info:* 800-654-3103 ■ *Web:* www.jm.com	Denver	CO	80217	303-978-2000		389
JohnsByrne Co 6701 W Oakton St *TF:* 800-609-7079 ■ *Web:* www.johnsbyrne.com	Niles	IL	60714	847-583-3100		627
Johnson & Bell Ltd 33 W Monroe St Ste 2700 *Web:* johnsonandbell.com	Chicago	IL	60603	312-372-0770		428
Johnson & Johnson Consumer Products Co 199 Grandview Rd *TF:* 866-565-2229 ■ *Web:* www.johnsonsbaby.com	Skillman	NJ	08558	908-874-1000		214
Johnson & Johnson Development Corp 1 Johnson & Johnson Plaza *NYSE:* JNJ ■ *Web:* www.jnj.com	New Brunswick	NJ	08933	732-524-0400		792
Johnson & Johnson Inc 7101 Notre-Dame E *TF:* 800-361-8990 ■ *Web:* www.jnjcanada.com	Montreal	QC	H1N2G4	514-251-5100		214
Johnson & Johnson Vision Care Inc 7500 Centurion Pkwy *TF:* 800-843-2020 ■ *Web:* www.acuvueprofessional.com	Jacksonville	FL	32256	800-874-5278		542
Johnson & Jordan Inc 18 Mussey Rd *Web:* johnsonandjordan.net	Scarborough	ME	04074	207-883-8345		610
Johnson & Mackowiak 70 E Main St *Web:* jma-cpas.com	Fredonia	NY	14063	716-672-4770	679-1512	2
Johnson & Mock Attorneys at Law 307 N Oakland Ave *Web:* www.johnsonandmock.com	Oakland	NE	68045	402-685-5647		445
Johnson & Pace Inc 1201 W Loop 281 Ste 100 *Web:* www.johnsonpace.com	Longview	TX	75604	903-753-0663		261
Johnson & Quin Inc 7460 N Lehigh Ave *Web:* www.j-quin.com	Niles	IL	60714	847-588-4800		5
Johnson & Rountree Premium Inc 12835 Point Del Mar Way *Web:* www.jrpremium.com	Del Mar	CA	92014	858-259-5846		160
Johnson & Sheldon PC 500 S Taylor Plaza II Ste 200 *Web:* www.amacpas.com	Amarillo	TX	79105	806-371-7661		734
Johnson & Shute PS 11130 NE 33rd Pl *Web:* www.johnsonandshute.com	Bellevue	WA	98004	425-827-5755		2
Johnson & Wales University *Providence* 8 Abbott Pk Pl *TF:* 800-342-5598 ■ *Web:* www.jwu.edu	Providence	RI	02903	401-598-1000		166
Johnson & Wales University Charlotte 801 W Trade St *Fax: Admissions ■ *TF:* 866-598-2427 ■ *Web:* www.jwu.edu	Charlotte	NC	28202	980-598-1100	598-1111*	166
Johnson & Wales University Denver 7150 E Montview Blvd *TF:* 877-598-3368 ■ *Web:* www.jwu.edu	Denver	CO	80220	303-256-9300		166
Johnson & Wales University North Miami 1701 NE 127th St *Fax Area Code: 305 ■ *TF:* 866-598-3567 ■ *Web:* www.jwu.edu	North Miami	FL	33181	800-342-5598	892-7020*	166
Johnson Bank 4001 N Main St *Web:* johnsonbank.com	Racine	WI	53402	262-639-6010		70
Johnson Bill (Rep R - OH) 1710 Longworth HOB *Web:* billjohnson.house.gov	Washington	DC	20515	202-225-5705	225-5907	342-2
Johnson Brass & Machine Foundry Inc 270 N Mill St PO Box 80219 *Web:* www.johnsoncentrifugal.com	Saukville	WI	53080	262-377-9440	284-7066	308
Johnson Bros Bakery Supply 10731 N I-35 *Fax Area Code: 210 ■ *TF:* 877-446-2767 ■ *Web:* www.jbrosbakerysupply.com	San Antonio	TX	78233	800-590-2575	599-3102*	297-8
Johnson Bros Metal Forming Co 5744 McDermott Dr *TF:* 800-289-8739 ■ *Web:* www.johnsonrollforming.com	Berkeley	IL	60163	708-449-7050	449-0042	480
Johnson Bros Rubber Inc 42 W Buckeye St *TF:* 800-523-5474 ■ *Web:* www.johnsonbrosrubbercompany.com	West Salem	OH	44287	419-853-4122		677
Johnson Bros Wholesale Liquor Co 1999 ShepaRd Rd *Web:* www.johnsonbrothers.com	Saint Paul	MN	55116	651-649-5800		81-3
Johnson C Smith University 100 Beatties Ford Rd *Fax: Admissions ■ *TF Admissions:* 800-782-7303 ■ *Web:* www.jcsu.edu	Charlotte	NC	28216	704-378-1000	378-1242*	166
Johnson Carlier Inc 738 S 52nd St *Web:* www.johnsoncarlier.com	Tempe	AZ	85281	602-275-2222		780
Johnson City City Hall 601 E Main St *Web:* www.johnsoncitytn.com	Johnson City	TN	37601	423-434-6000	434-6205	337
Johnson City Medical Ctr 400 N State of Franklin Rd *Web:* www.mountainstateshealth.com	Johnson City	TN	37604	423-431-6111		374-3
Johnson City Press 204 W Main St *TF:* 800-949-3111 ■ *Web:* www.johnsoncitypress.com	Johnson City	TN	37604	423-929-3111	929-7484	532-2
Johnson City Public Library 100 W Millard St *Web:* www.jcpl.net	Johnson City	TN	37604	423-434-4450	434-4469	434-3
Johnson City Symphony Orchestra PO Box 533 *TF:* 800-852-3392 ■ *Web:* www.jcsymphony.com	Johnson City	TN	37605	423-926-8742	926-8979	573-3
Johnson City/Jonesborough/Washington County Chamber of Commerce 603 E Market St *Web:* www.johnsoncitytnchamber.com	Johnson City	TN	37601	423-461-8000	461-8047	139
Johnson College 3427 N Main Ave *Fax: Admissions ■ *TF:* 800-293-9675 ■ *Web:* www.johnson.edu	Scranton	PA	18508	570-342-6404	348-2181*	800
Johnson Concrete Co 217 Klumac Rd *Web:* www.johnsoncmu.com	Salisbury	NC	28145	704-636-5231		183
Johnson Contracting Company Inc 2750 Morton Dr *Web:* www.jccinc.com	East Moline	IL	61244	309-755-0601		189-10
Johnson Controls Fire & Security Solutions 5757 N Green Bay Ave PO Box 591 *Web:* www.johnsoncontrols.com/security	Milwaukee	WI	53201	414-524-1200		692
Johnson Controls Inc - YORK 5757 N Green Bay Ave *Web:* www.johnsoncontrols.com	Milwaukee	WI	53201	414-524-1200		15
Johnson Controls Inc Automotive Systems Group 49200 Halyard Dr *TF:* 800-257-6054 ■ *Web:* www.johnsoncontrols.com	Plymouth	MI	48170	734-254-5000		689
Johnson Controls Systems 9410 Bunsen Pkwy Ste 100-B *TF:* 800-765-7773 ■ *Web:* www.johnsoncontrols.com	Louisville	KY	40220	502-671-7300		202
Johnson County 76 N Main St *Web:* www.johnsoncountywyoming.org	Buffalo	WY	82834	307-684-7272	684-2708	338
Johnson County 215 Main St *Web:* local.arkansas.gov	Clarksville	AR	72830	479-754-2175		338
Johnson County 204 S Buffalo Ave *Web:* www.johnsoncountytx.org	Cleburne	TX	76033	817-556-6323		338
Johnson County 5 E Jefferson St 1st Fl *Web:* co.johnson.in.us	Franklin	IN	46131	317-346-4700	736-3749	338
Johnson County 913 S Dubuque St *TF:* 800-257-8563 ■ *Web:* www.johnson-county.com	Iowa City	IA	52240	319-356-6093	337-0495	338
Johnson County 222 W Main St *Web:* www.tn.gov	Mountain City	TN	37683	423-727-9633	727-7047	338
Johnson County 111 S Cherry St Ste 1200 *TF:* 800-766-3777 ■ *Web:* jocogov.org	Olathe	KS	66061	913-715-0775	715-0800	338
Johnson County 351 Broadway *Web:* www.co.johnson.ne.us	Tecumseh	NE	68450	402-335-6300	335-6311	338
Johnson County PO Box 96 *Web:* theviennatimes.com	Vienna	IL	62995	618-658-3611	658-9665	338
Johnson County 300 N Holden St	Warrensburg	MO	64093	660-747-6161		338
Johnson County 2557 E Elm St *TF:* 800-503-0204 ■ *Web:* www.johnsonco.org	Wrightsville	GA	31096	478-864-3484	864-1343	338
Johnson County Clerk 230 Ct St *Web:* johnsoncountyclerkky.com	Paintsville	KY	41240	606-789-2557		338
Johnson County Community College 12345 College Blvd *TF:* 866-896-5893 ■ *Web:* www.jccc.edu	Overland Park	KS	66210	913-469-8500	469-2524	162
Johnson County Library PO Box 2933 *Web:* www.jocolibrary.org	Shawnee Mission	KS	66201	913-826-4600		434-3
Johnson County Public Library 401 S State St *TF:* 800-272-3900 ■ *Web:* pageafterpage.org	Franklin	IN	46131	317-738-2833	738-9635	434-3
Johnson County Rural Electric Membership Corp 750 International Dr *TF:* 800-382-5544 ■ *Web:* www.jcremc.com	Franklin	IN	46131	317-736-6174		245
Johnson design Group Inc 1000 N Halsted Ste 204 *Web:* www.jdg1.com	Chicago	IL	60642	312-649-1650		466

Phone | Fax | Class

Johnson Eddie Bernice (Rep D - TX)
2468 Rayburn HOB ... Washington DC 20515 202-225-8885 226-1477 342-2
Web: ebjohnson.house.gov

Johnson Electric Coil Co 821 Watson St ... Antigo WI 54409 715-627-4367 623-2812 767
TF: 800-826-9741 ■ *Web:* www.johnsoncoil.com

Johnson Engineering Inc
2122 Johnson St ... Fort Myers FL 33901 239-334-0046 334-3661 256
TF: 866-367-4400 ■ *Web:* www.johnsonengineering.com

Johnson Fain 1201 N Broadway ... Los Angeles CA 90012 323-224-6000 224-6030 261
Web: www.johnsonfain.com

Johnson Farm Machinery Company Inc
38574 W Kentucky Ave ... Woodland CA 95695 530-662-1788 666-5585 273
Web: www.jfmco.com

Johnson Financial Group Inc
555 Main St Ste 400 ... Racine WI 53403 262-619-2790 360-2
Web: johnsonbank.com

Johnson Gas Appliance Co
520 E Ave NW ... Cedar Rapids IA 52405 319-365-5267 365-6282 318
TF: 800-553-5422 ■ *Web:* www.johnsongas.com

Johnson Golf Course Builders
497 Golf Rd ... South Sioux City NE 68776 402-494-4687 188-3

Johnson Group, The 436 Market St ... Chattanooga TN 37402 423-756-2608 4
Web: www.johngroup.com

Johnson Hall State Historic Site
139 Hall Ave ... Johnstown NY 12095 518-762-8712 565
Web: parks.ny.gov/historic-sites/10/details.aspx

Johnson Henry C "Hank" Jr (Rep D - GA)
2240 Rayburn Bldg ... Washington DC 20515 202-225-1605 226-0691 342-2
Web: hankjohnson.house.gov

Johnson Industries
5944 Peachtree Corners E ... Norcross GA 30071 770-441-1128 733-8010* 61
**Fax Area Code:* 866 ■ *Web:* www.teamji.com

Johnson Investment Counsel Inc
3777 W Fork Rd ... Cincinnati OH 45247 513-661-3100 401
TF: 800-541-0170 ■ *Web:* www.johnsoninv.com

Johnson Lambert & Company LLP
700 Spring Forest Rd ... Raleigh NC 27609 919-719-6400 2
Web: www.johnsonlambert.com

Johnson Level & Tool Mfg Company Inc
6333 W Donges Bay Rd ... Mequon WI 53092 262-242-1161 242-0189 758
TF: 800-535-4482 ■ *Web:* www.johnsonlevel.com

Johnson Lexus of Raleigh
5839 Capital Blvd ... Raleigh NC 27616 919-877-1800 57
Web: johnsonlexusraleigh.com

Johnson Litho Graphics of Eau Claire Ltd
2219 Galloway St ... Eau Claire WI 54703 715-832-3211 627
Web: www.johnsonlitho.com

Johnson March Systems Inc
220 Railroad Dr ... Ivyland PA 18974 215-364-2500 610
TF: 800-561-2831 ■ *Web:* www.johnsonmarch.com

Johnson Matthey 2001 Nolte Dr ... West Deptford NJ 08066 856-384-7000 143
Web: www.chemicals.matthey.com

Johnson Matthey Medical Products
1401 King Rd ... West Chester PA 19380 610-648-8000 648-8111 476
TF: 800-442-1405 ■ *Web:* www.jmmedical.com

Johnson Matthey Noble Metals
1401 King Rd ... West Chester PA 19380 610-648-8000 648-8105 482
Web: www.noble.matthey.com

Johnson Matthey Pharma Services Inc
25 Patton Rd ... Devens MA 01434 978-784-5000 784-5500 479
TF: 800-444-8544 ■ *Web:* www.jmpharmaservices.com

Johnson Memorial Hospital
201 Chestnut Hill Rd ... Stafford Springs CT 06076 860-684-4251 749-2201 374-3
Web: www.jmmc.com

Johnson Memorial Hospital (JMH)
1125 W Jefferson St ... Franklin IN 46131 317-736-3300 736-2692 374-3
Web: www.johnsonmemorial.org

Johnson Mike (Rep R - LA)
327 Cannon HOB ... Washington DC 20515 202-225-2777 342-2
Web: mikejohnson.house.gov

Johnson Mirmiran & Thompson (JMT)
72 Loveton Cir ... Sparks MD 21152 410-329-3100 472-2200 261
TF: 800-472-2310 ■ *Web:* www.jmt.com

Johnson Motors Inc 1891 Blinker Pkwy ... Du Bois PA 15801 814-371-4444 57
TF: 800-537-1768 ■ *Web:* www.johnsonauto.com

Johnson Nursery Corp
985 Johnson Nursery Rd ... Willard NC 28478 910-285-7861 293
TF: 800-624-8174 ■ *Web:* www.johnson-nursery.com

Johnson O'hare Company Inc
1 Progress Rd ... Billerica MA 01821 978-663-9000 262-2200 297-8
Web: www.johare.com

Johnson Oil Company (JOC)
1918 Church St ... Gonzales TX 78629 800-284-2432 579
TF: 800-284-2432 ■ *Web:* www.johnsonoilcompany.com

Johnson Oil Company of Gaylord
507 S Otsego Ave ... Gaylord MI 49734 989-732-2451 581
TF: 800-292-3941 ■ *Web:* www.johnsonspropane.com

Johnson Outdoors Inc 555 Main St ... Racine WI 53403 262-631-6600 631-6601 710
NASDAQ: JOUT ■ *TF:* 800-468-9716 ■ *Web:* www.johnsonoutdoors.com

Johnson Power Ltd 2530 Braga Dr ... Broadview IL 60155 708-345-4300 54
TF: 800-843-3211 ■ *Web:* www.johnsonpower.com

Johnson Press of America Inc
800 N Court St ... Pontiac IL 61764 815-844-5161 627
Web: jpapontiac.com

Johnson Public Library 274 Main St ... Hackensack NJ 07601 201-343-4169 343-1395 434-3
Web: www.bccls.org

Johnson Publishing Company Inc
200 S Michigan Ave ... Chicago IL 60604 312-322-9200 637-9
Web: www.johnsonpublishing.com

Johnson Refrigerated Truck Bodies
215 E Allen St ... Rice Lake WI 54868 715-234-7071 234-4628 516
TF Sales: 800-922-8360 ■ *Web:* www.johnsontruckbodies.com

Johnson Rice & Company LLC
639 Loyola Ave Ste 2775 ... New Orleans LA 70113 504-525-3767 194
Web: www.jrco.com

Johnson Ron (Sen R - WI)
328 Russell Bldg ... Washington DC 20510 202-224-5323 228-6965 342-2
Web: www.ronjohnson.senate.gov

Johnson Sam (Rep R - TX)
2304 Rayburn HOB ... Washington DC 20515 202-225-4201 342-2
Web: samjohnson.house.gov

Johnson Scale Company Inc
36 Stiles Ln ... Pine Brook NJ 07058 800-572-2531 882-8068* 684
**Fax Area Code:* 973 ■ *TF:* 800-572-2531 ■ *Web:* www.johnsonscale.net

Johnson School Bus Services Inc
2151 W Washington St PO Box 285 ... West Bend WI 53095 262-334-3146 334-8019 109
Web: www.johnsonschoolbus.com

Johnson Screens Inc
1950 Old Hwy 8 NW ... New Brighton MN 55112 651-636-3900 295
TF: 800-833-9473 ■ *Web:* www.water.bilfinger.com

Johnson Space Ctr 2101 NASA Pkwy ... Houston TX 77058 281-483-0123 668
Web: www.nasa.gov

Johnson Spellman & Assoc Inc
6991 Peachtree Industrial Blvd ... Norcross GA 30092 770-447-4555 261
Web: jsace.com

Johnson State College
337 College Hill ... Johnson VT 05656 802-635-2356 635-1230 166
TF: 800-635-2356 ■ *Web:* www.jsc.edu

Johnson Storage & Moving Co
221 Broadway ... Denver CO 80202 800-289-6683 519
TF: 800-289-6683 ■ *Web:* www.johnsonstorage.com

Johnson Supply Inc
10151 Stella Link Rd ... Houston TX 77025 713-830-2499 662-5519 612
TF: 800-833-5455 ■ *Web:* www.johnsonsupply.com

Johnson Technology Corp
2034 Latimer Dr ... Muskegon MI 49442 231-777-2685 454

Johnson University 7900 Johnson Dr ... Knoxville TN 37998 865-573-4517 251-2337 161
TF: 800-827-2122 ■ *Web:* www.johnsonu.edu

Johnson Victrola Museum 375 S New St ... Dover DE 19901 302-744-5055 520
Web: history.delaware.gov

Johnson Wholesale Floors Inc
1874 Defoor Ave NW ... Atlanta GA 30318 404-352-2700 131
TF: 800-345-9318 ■ *Web:* johnsonwholesalefloors.com

Johnson Window Films Inc
20655 Annalee Ave ... Carson CA 90746 310-631-6672 361
TF: 800-448-8468 ■ *Web:* www.johnsonwindowfilms.com

Johnson Youth Ctr 3252 Hospital Dr ... Juneau AK 99801 907-586-9433 463-4933 412
TF: 800-780-9972 ■ *Web:* dhss.alaska.gov

Johnson's Boiler & Control Inc
2440 S Gearhart Ave ... Fresno CA 93725 559-237-7772 612
TF: 800-800-3221 ■ *Web:* www.johnsonsboiler.com

Johnson's Garden Centers
2707 W 13th St ... Wichita KS 67203 316-942-1443 323
TF: 888-542-8463 ■ *Web:* www.johnsonsgarden.com

Johnson's Nursery Inc
W180 N 6275 Marcy Rd ... Menomonee Falls WI 53051 262-252-4988 252-4495 323
Web: www.johnsonsnursery.com

Johnson's Shut-Ins State Park
148 Taum Sauk Trl ... Middlebrook MO 63656 573-546-2450 565
Web: mostateparks.com

Johnson, Grossnickle & Associates LLC
29 S Park Blvd ... Greenwood IN 46143 317-215-2400 193
Web: www.jgacounsel.com

Johnsonite Inc 16910 Munn Rd ... Chagrin Falls OH 44023 440-543-8916 131
TF: 800-899-8916 ■ *Web:* www.johnsonite.com

Johnson-Laird Inc 850 NW Summit Ave ... Portland OR 97210 503-274-0784 180
Web: www.jli.com

JohnsonRauhoff 2525 Lake Pine Dr ... Saint Joseph MI 49085 269-428-3377 344
Web: www.johnson-rauhoff.com

Johnson-Sauk Trail State Park
28616 Sauk Trl Rd ... Kewanee IL 61443 309-853-5589 565
Web: www.dnr.illinois.gov/Parks/Pages/JohnsonSaukTrail.aspx

Johnsonville Sausage LLC
PO Box 906 ... Sheboygan Falls WI 53085 888-556-2728 296-26
TF: 888-556-2728 ■ *Web:* www.johnsonville.com

Johnsonville State Historic Park
90 Nell Beard Rd ... New Johnsonville TN 37134 931-535-2789 565
Web: tnstateparks.com

Johnstech International Corp
1210 New Brighton Blvd ... Minneapolis MN 55413 612-378-2020 378-2030 696
Web: www.johnstech.com

Johnston & Murphy Inc
1415 Murfreesboro Rd ... Nashville TN 37217 615-367-7168 301
TF: 800-424-2854 ■ *Web:* www.johnstonmurphy.com

Johnston Asset Management Corp
300 Atlantic St Ste 601 ... Stamford CT 06901 203-324-4722 401
Web: www.johnstonasset.com

Johnston Boiler Co 300 Pine St ... Ferrysburg MI 49409 616-842-5050 842-1854* 357
**Fax:* Cust Svc ■ *TF General:* 800-728-7511 ■ *Web:* www.johnstonboiler.com

Johnston Community College
245 College Rd ... Smithfield NC 27577 919-934-3051 989-7862* 162
**Fax:* Admissions ■ *TF:* 800-510-9132 ■ *Web:* johnstoncc.edu

Johnston Community School District
PO Box 10 ... Johnston IA 50131 515-278-0470 278-5884 685
Web: www.johnston.k12.ia.us

Johnston Correctional Institution
2465 US 70 W ... Smithfield NC 27577 919-934-8386 213

Johnston County
207 E Johnston St PO Box 1049 ... Smithfield NC 27577 919-989-5100 989-5179 338
Web: www.johnstonnc.com

Johnston County 403 W Main St ... Tishomingo OK 73460 405-379-5280 338
Web: oklahoma.usassessor.com

Johnston County Convention & Visitors Bureau
235 E Market St ... Smithfield NC 27577 919-989-8687 989-6295 206
TF: 800-441-7829 ■ *Web:* www.johnstoncountync.org

Johnston Lemon & Company Inc
1101 Vermont Ave NW Ste 800 ... Washington DC 20005 202-842-5500 690

Johnston Manufacturing Co
19406 E Parlier Ave ... Reedley CA 93654 559-638-2737 453

Johnston Memorial Hospital
509 N Bright Leaf Blvd ... Smithfield NC 27577 919-934-8171 374-3
Web: www.johnstonhealth.org

Johnston Paper Co 2 Eagle Dr ... Auburn NY 13021 315-253-8435 253-8744 559
TF: 800-800-7123 ■ *Web:* www.johnstonpaper.com

Johnston the Florist Inc
14179 Lincoln Way ... North Huntingdon PA 15642 412-751-2821 292
TF: 800-356-9371 ■ *Web:* www.johnstontheflorist.com

Phone | Fax | Class

Johnston's Trading Inc
11 N Pioneer Ave, Woodland CA 95776 — 530-661-6152 — 200
Web: johnstontrading.com

Johnston, Allison & Hord PA
1065 E Morehead St, Charlotte NC 28204 — 704-332-1181 — 428
TF: 800-473-9050 ■ *Web:* www.jahlaw.com

Johnstone Adams Bailey Gordon & Harris L L C
1 St Louis St 4th Fl, Mobile AL 36602 — 251-432-7682 — 445
Web: www.johnstoneadams.com

Johnstown Flood National Memorial
733 Lake Rd, South Fork PA 15956 — 814-495-4643 — 495-7463 — 564
Web: www.nps.gov/jofl

Johnstown Specialty Castings Inc
545 Central Ave, Johnstown PA 15902 — 814-535-9000 — 307
Web: whemco.com

Joie de Vivre Hospitality Inc
530 Bush St Ste 501, San Francisco CA 94108 — 415-835-0300 — 379
Web: www.jdvhotels.com

Joining Technologies Inc
17 Connecticut S Dr, East Granby CT 06026 — 860-653-0111 — 539
Web: www.joiningtech.com

Joint Base Myer 204 Lee Ave Bldg 59, Fort Myer VA 22211 — 703-696-0584 — 497-2
Web: www.army.mil

Joint Chiefs of Staff
Chairman
9999 Joint Chiefs of Staff Pentagon, Washington DC 20318 — 703-767-8267 — 340-3
Web: www.dtic.mil

Joint Commission on Accreditation of Healthcare Organizations (JCAHO)
1 Renaissance Blvd, Oakbrook Terrace IL 60181 — 630-792-5000 — 792-5005 — 48-1
TF: 800-994-6610 ■ *Web:* www.jointcommission.org

Joint Institute for Marine & Atmospheric Research
University of Hawaii at Manoa
1000 Pope Rd Marine Sciences Bldg 312, Honolulu HI 96822 — 808-956-8083 — 956-4104 — 668
Web: www.soest.hawaii.edu

Joint Institute for Marine Observations (JIMO)
Scripps Institution of Oceanography UC San Diego
9500 Gilman Dr, La Jolla CA 92093 — 858-534-3624 — 668

Joint Review Committee on Education in Radiologic Technology (JRCERT)
20 N Wacker Dr Ste 2850, Chicago IL 60606 — 312-704-5300 — 704-5304 — 48-1
Web: www.jrcert.org

Joint Review Committee on Educational Programs in Nuclear Medicine Technology, The (JRCNMT)
2000 W Danforth Rd Ste 130 203, Edmond OK 73003 — 405-285-0546 — 285-0579 — 48-1
Web: www.jrcnmt.org

Joint Technology Solution Inc
3919 Old Lee Hwy, Fairfax VA 22030 — 703-218-0372 — 180
Web: jointtechnologysolution.net

JoJo 160 E 64th St, New York NY 10021 — 212-223-5656 — 671
Web: jojorestaurantnyc.com

Jokake Construction Co
5013 E Washington St Ste 100, Phoenix AZ 85034 — 602-224-4500 — 187
Web: www.jokake.com

Jolera Inc 777 Richmond St W Unit 2, Toronto ON M6J0C2 — 416-410-1011 — 177
TF: 800-292-4078 ■ *Web:* www.jolera.com

Joliet Area Community Hospice
250 Water Stone Cir, Joliet IL 60431 — 815-740-4104 — 740-4107 — 371
TF: 800-360-1817 ■ *Web:* www.joliethospice.org

Joliet Avionics Inc
43w730 US Hwy 30, Sugar Grove IL 60554 — 630-584-3200 — 246
TF: 800-323-5966 ■ *Web:* www.jaair.com

Joliet Equipment Corp 1 Doris Ave, Joliet IL 60433 — 815-727-6606 — 727-6626 — 518
TF: 800-435-9350 ■ *Web:* www.joliet-equipment.com

Joliet Junior College 1215 Houbolt Rd, Joliet IL 60431 — 815-729-9020 — 280-2493* — 162
**Fax:* Admissions ■ *TF:* 800-636-9886 ■ *Web:* www.jjc.edu

Joliet Public Library 150 N Ottawa St, Joliet IL 60432 — 815-740-2660 — 740-6161 — 434-3
TF: 800-982-2787 ■ *Web:* jolietlibrary.org

Joliet Public School District 86
420 N Raynor Ave, Joliet IL 60435 — 815-740-3196 — 685
Web: www.joliet86.org

Joliet Region Chamber of Commerce & Industry
63 N Chicago St, Joliet IL 60432 — 815-727-5371 — 727-5374 — 139
Web: www.jolietchamber.com

Jolly Hotel Madison Towers
22 E 38th St, New York NY 10016 — 212-802-0600 — 447-0747 — 379
TF Resv: 888-726-0528 ■ *Web:* www.jollymadison.com

Jolly Roger Inn 640 W Katella Ave, Anaheim CA 92802 — 714-782-7500 — 379
TF: 888-296-5986 ■ *Web:* www.jollyrogerhotel.com

Jolt Consulting Group
112 Spring St Ste 301, Saratoga Springs NY 12866 — 877-249-6262 — 463
TF: 877-249-6262 ■ *Web:* www.joltconsultinggroup.com

Jomax Drilling (1988) Ltd
140 - 4 Ave SW Ste 1750, Calgary AB T2P3N3 — 403-265-5312 — 540
Web: www.jomax.ca

Jomax Recovery Services
9242 W Union Hills Dr Ste 102, Peoria AZ 85382 — 888-866-0721 — 866-0722* — 393
**Fax Area Code:* 602 ■ *TF:* 888-866-0721 ■ *Web:* jomaxrecovery.com

Jon Harvey Associates Inc
1300 N Federal Hwy Ste 104, Boca Raton FL 33432 — 561-368-5900 — 193
Web: www.jonharvey.com

Jon Lancaster Inc 3501 Lancaster Dr, Madison WI 53718 — 608-243-5500 — 57
Web: eastmadisontoyota.com

Jon Peddie Research Inc
4 Saint Gabrielle Ct, Tiburon CA 94920 — 415-435-9368 — 449
Web: www.jonpeddie.com

Jon Renau Collection
2510 Island View Way, Vista CA 92081 — 760-598-0067 — 348
TF: 800-462-9447 ■ *Web:* www.jonrenau.com

Jon's Nursery Inc 24546 Nursery Way, Eustis FL 32736 — 352-357-4289 — 292
TF: 800-322-4289 ■ *Web:* jonsnursery.com

Jonah Energy LLC
755 Mulberry Ave Ste 450, San Antonio TX 78212 — 210-375-3060 — 536
Web: jonahenergy.com

Jonah Group Ltd, The
461 King St W 3rd Fl, Toronto ON M5V1K4 — 416-304-0860 — 179
TF: 888-594-6260 ■ *Web:* www.jonahgroup.com

Jonal Laboratories Inc PO Box 743, Meriden CT 06450 — 203-634-4444 — 634-4448 — 677
Web: www.jonal.com

Jonar 55 Rue de Louvain W Ste 303, Montreal QC H2N1A4 — 514-335-5525 — 180
Web: www.jonar.com

Jonard Industries Corp
134 Marbledale Rd, Tuckahoe NY 10707 — 914-793-0700 — 793-4527 — 758
Web: www.jonard.com

Jonas Equities 725 Church Ave, Brooklyn NY 11218 — 718-871-6020 — 655
Web: www.jonasequities.com

Jonas Fitness Inc 16969 n texas ave, Webster TX 77598 — 800-324-9800 — 354
TF: 800-324-9800 ■ *Web:* www.jonasfitness.com

Jonathan Club Charitable Fund
545 S Figueroa St, Los Angeles CA 90071 — 213-624-0881 — 292
Web: www.jc.org

Jonathan Engineered Solutions
410 Exchange St Ste 200, Irvine CA 92602 — 714-665-4400 — 368-7002 — 350
Web: www.jonathanengr.com

Jonathan Lord Corp 87 Carlough Rd, Bohemia NY 11716 — 631-563-4445 — 297-8
TF: 800-814-7517 ■ *Web:* jonathanlord.com

Jonathan Louis International Ltd
544 W 130th St, Gardena CA 90248 — 323-770-3330 — 321
Web: www.jonathanlouis.net

Jonathan's Tucson Cork
6320 E Tanque Verde Rd, Tucson AZ 85715 — 520-296-1631 — 671
TF: 800-722-8848 ■ *Web:* www.jonathanscork.com

Jondo Ltd 22700 Savi Ranch Pkwy, Yorba Linda CA 92887 — 714-279-2300 — 627
Web: jondo.com

Jones & Frank Corp
1330 St Mary's St Ste 210, Raleigh NC 27605 — 919-838-7555 — 539
TF: 800-286-4133 ■ *Web:* www.jones-frank.com

Jones & Henry Engineers Ltd
3103 Executive Pkwy, Toledo OH 43606 — 419-473-9611 — 261
Web: jheng.com

Jones & Jones Inc
4500 N Tenth St Ste 90, McAllen TX 78504 — 956-687-1171 — 631-3345 — 229

Jones & Kolb
3475 Piedmont Rd NE Ste 100, Atlanta GA 30305 — 404-262-7920 — 2
Web: www.joneskolb.com

Jones & Roth PC 432 W 11th Ave, Eugene OR 97401 — 541-687-2320 — 485-0960 — 401
Web: www.jrcpa.com

Jones & Sons Inc PO Box 2057, Washington IN 47501 — 812-254-4731 — 254-3293 — 182
Web: www.jonesandsons.com

Jones & Vining Inc
1115 W Chestnut St, Brockton MA 02301 — 508-232-7470 — 232-7477 — 604
Web: www.jonesandvining.com

Jones Agency, The
303 N Indian Canyon Dr, Palm Springs CA 92262 — 760-325-1437 — 636
Web: www.jonesagency.com

Jones Apparel Group Inc Jones New York Collection Div
1411 Broadway, New York NY 10018 — 212-642-3860 — 155-21
TF: 888-880-8730 ■ *Web:* www.jny.com

Jones Beach State Park 1 Ocean Pkwy, Wantagh NY 11793 — 516-785-1600 — 565
Web: parks.ny.gov/parks/jonesbeach

Jones Cassity Inc 302 Pine Tree Rd, Longview TX 75604 — 903-759-0736 — 759-1406 — 364
Web: www.cassityjones.com

Jones College
5353 Arlington Expy, Jacksonville FL 32211 — 904-743-1122 — 166
TF: 800-331-0176 ■ *Web:* www.jones.edu

Jones Consulting Group LLC, The
12323 Waterstone Ln, Perrysburg OH 43551 — 248-677-2236 — 463
Web: www.jconsultants.net

Jones County 500 W Main St, Anamosa IA 52205 — 319-462-2282 — 338
TF: 800-622-3849 ■ *Web:* www.jonescountyiowa.org

Jones County PO Box 552, Anson TX 79501 — 325-823-3762 — 823-4223 — 338
Web: www.co.jones.tx.us

Jones County PO Box 1359, Gray GA 31032 — 478-986-6405 — 986-6462 — 338
Web: www.jonescountyga.org

Jones County PO Box 5279, Laurel MS 39441 — 601-649-3031 — 428-2047 — 338
Web: www.jonescounty.com

Jones County 310 Main St PO Box 448, Murdo SD 57559 — 605-669-2361 — 669-2641 — 338
Web: ujs.sd.gov/County_Information/jones.aspx

Jones County 410 Hwy 58 N, Trenton NC 28585 — 252-448-7571 — 371-9984* — 338
**Fax Area Code:* 412 ■ *Web:* www.jonescountync.gov

Jones County Junior College
900 S Ct St, Ellisville MS 39437 — 601-477-4000 — 477-4258* — 162
**Fax:* Admissions ■ *Web:* jcjc.edu

Jones CPA Group 749 Boush St, Norfolk VA 23510 — 757-627-7672 — 2
Web: stricklandandjones.com

Jones Cyber Solutions Ltd
9697 E Mineral Ave, Centennial CO 80112 — 303-784-3600 — 784-3797 — 178-7
Web: www.jonescyber.com

Jones Dairy Farm 800 Jones Ave, Fort Atkinson WI 53538 — 800-635-6637 — 296-26
TF: 800-635-6637 ■ *Web:* www.jonesdairyfarm.com

Jones Day 51 Louisiana Ave NW, Washington DC 20001 — 202-879-3939 — 626-1700 — 428
Web: www.jonesday.com

Jones Edmunds & Assoc Inc
730 NE Waldo Rd, Gainesville FL 32641 — 352-377-5821 — 377-3166 — 261
Web: www.jonesedmunds.com

Jones Environmental Inc
708 Milam St Ste 100, Shreveport LA 71101 — 318-226-8444 — 196
TF: 877-345-4534 ■ *Web:* www.jonesenvironmentalinc.com

Jones Eye Clinic
4405 Hamilton Blvd, Sioux City IA 51104 — 712-239-3937 — 239-1305 — 798
TF: 800-334-2015 ■ *Web:* joneseye.com

Jones Family Foundation
31021 Lakeview Ave, Red Wing MN 55066 — 651-388-7941 — 305
Web: www.jonesfamilyfoundation.org

Jones Gap State Park
303 Jones Gap Rd, Marietta SC 29661 — 864-836-3647 — 565
Web: www.southcarolinaparks.com

Jones Group Consulting
3824 Corrales Rd Ste 102, Corrales NM 87048 — 505-792-4070 — 463
Web: jonesgroupcrm.com

Jones Ham & Cluff P C
14475 SW Allen Blvd Ste A, Beaverton OR 97005 — 503-643-6333 — 2
Web: www.jonesandham.com

Jones Hamilton Co 30354 Tracy Rd, Walbridge OH 43465 — 419-666-9838 — 666-1817 — 143
TF: 888-858-4425 ■ *Web:* www.jones-hamilton.com

Jones Henle & Schunck
135 Town & Country Dr, Danville CA 94526 — 925-820-1821 — 2
Web: www.jhs.com

Name / Address	City	State	ZIP	Phone	Fax	Class
Jones Huyett Partners Inc 3200 SW Huntoon St *Web:* jhpadv.com	Topeka	KS	66604	785-228-0900		636
Jones Kohanski & Company LLP 6 Brookhill Sq S *Web:* jk-cpa.com	Sugarloaf	PA	18249	570-788-7000		2
Jones Lake State Park 4117 NC 242 Hwy *TF:* 800-277-9611 ■ *Web:* www.ncparks.gov	Elizabethtown	NC	28337	910-588-4550		565
Jones Lang LaSalle Inc 200 E Randolph Dr *NYSE: JLL* ■ *Web:* www.jll.com	Chicago	IL	60601	312-782-5800	782-4339	655
Jones Lang LaSalle IP Inc 200 E Randolph Dr *TF:* 800-282-5628 ■ *Web:* www.jll.com	Chicago	IL	60601	312-782-5800		655
Jones Library Inc 43 Amity St *Web:* www.joneslibrary.org	Amherst	MA	01002	413-259-3090	256-4096	434-3
Jones Metal Products Co 200 N Ctr St *TF:* 888-868-6535 ■ *Web:* www.jmpforming.com	West Lafayette	OH	43845	740-545-6381		757
Jones Metal Products Inc 3201 Third Ave *TF:* 800-967-1750 ■ *Web:* jonesmetalinc.com	Mankato	MN	56001	507-625-4436	625-2994	697
Jones Mobile Television 5200 Northshore Dr Ste F *Web:* jmtv.com	North Little Rock	AR	72118	501-376-1993		514
Jones Motor Group 654 Enterprise Dr *TF:* 800-825-6637 ■ *Web:* www.jonesmotor.com	Limerick	PA	19468	610-948-7900	948-5660	780
Jones Nale & Mattingly PLC 642 S Fourth Ave Ste 300 *Web:* www.jnmcpa.com	Louisville	KY	40202	502-583-0248		463
Jones Petroleum Company Inc 407 E Second St *Web:* www.jonespetroleum.com	Jackson	GA	30233	770-775-2386		581
Jones Printing Service Inc 931 Ventures Way *Web:* www.jones-printing.com	Chesapeake	VA	23320	757-436-3331		627
Jones Soda Co 66 S Hanford St Ste 150 *OTC: JSDA* ■ *Web:* www.jonessoda.com	Seattle	WA	98134	206-624-3357	624-6857	80-2
Jones Stephens 3249 Moody Pkwy *TF:* 800-355-6637 ■ *Web:* www.jonesstephens.com	Moody	AL	35004	800-355-6637	462-6991	610
Jones Walter B (Rep R - NC) 2333 Rayburn Bldg *Web:* jones.house.gov	Washington	DC	20515	202-225-3415		342-2
Jones, Allen & Fuquay LLP 8828 Greenville Ave *Web:* www.jonesallen.com	Dallas	TX	75243	214-343-7400		428
Jonesboro Regional Chamber of Commerce PO Box 789 *Web:* jonesborochamber.com	Jonesboro	AR	72403	870-932-6691	933-5758	139
Jonesboro Sun 518 Carson St *TF:* 800-237-5341 ■ *Web:* www.jonesborosun.com	Jonesboro	AR	72401	870-935-5525	935-5823	532-2
Jones-Onslow Electric Membership Corp 259 Western Blvd *TF:* 800-682-1515 ■ *Web:* www.joemc.com	Jacksonville	NC	28546	910-353-1940		245
JonesTrading Institutional Services LLC 32133 Lindero Canyon Rd Ste 208 *TF:* 800-367-3989 ■ *Web:* www.jonestrading.com	Westlake Village	CA	91361	818-991-5500		690
Jons International Market Place 5315 Santa Monica Blvd *Web:* www.jonsmarketplace.com	Los Angeles	CA	90029	323-460-4646		345
Joongang Daily News California Inc 690 Wilshire Pl *Web:* www.koreadaily.com	Los Angeles	CA	90005	213-368-2500		532-3
Jopari Solutions Inc 1855 Gateway Blvd Ste 500 *Web:* www.jopari.com	Concord	CA	94520	925-459-5200		317
JOPERD (Journal of Physical Education Recreation & Dance) 1900 Assn Dr *TF:* 800-213-7193 ■ *Web:* shapeamerica.org	Reston	VA	20191	703-476-3400	476-9527	457-8
Joplin Area Chamber of Commerce 320 E Fourth St *TF:* 800-544-3452 ■ *Web:* www.joplincc.com	Joplin	MO	64801	417-624-4150	624-4303	139
Joplin Convention & Visitors Bureau 222 W Third St *Web:* www.visitjoplinmo.com	Joplin	MO	64801	417-625-4789	624-7948	206
Joplin Globe 117 E Fourth St *TF:* 800-444-8514 ■ *Web:* www.joplinglobe.com	Joplin	MO	64801	417-623-3480	623-8598	532-2
Joplin Public Library 300 S Main St *TF:* 800-578-5284 ■ *Web:* www.joplinpubliclibrary.org	Joplin	MO	64801	417-623-7953	624-5217	434-3
Jordache Enterprises 1400 Broadway *Web:* www.jordache.com	New York	NY	10018	212-944-1330		155-11
Jordan *Embassy* 3504 International Dr NW *Web:* www.jordanembassyus.org	Washington	DC	20008	202-966-2664	966-3110	257
Jordan Advertising 3201 Quail Springs Pkwy Ste 100 *Web:* www.jordanet.com	Oklahoma City	OK	73134	405-840-3201		7
Jordan Education Media Inc 19105 Hilltop Rd *Web:* www.jordaneducationmedia.com	Lake Oswego	OR	97034	503-638-9200		195
Jordan Essentials 1106 eaglecrest st *TF:* 877-662-8669 ■ *Web:* www.jordanessentials.com	Nixa	MO	65714	877-662-8669		354
Jordan Hospital 275 Sandwich St *TF:* 800-256-7326 ■ *Web:* bidplymouth.org	Plymouth	MA	02360	508-746-2000		374-3
Jordan Industries Inc (JII) 1751 Lake Cook Rd Ste 550	Deerfield	IL	60015	847-945-5591	945-5698	185
Jordan Jim (Rep R - OH) 2056 Rayburn HOB *Web:* jordan.house.gov	Washington	DC	20515	202-225-2676	226-0577	342-2
Jordan Lake State Recreation Area 280 State Pk Rd *TF:* 877-722-6762 ■ *Web:* www.ncparks.gov	Apex	NC	27523	919-362-0586		565
Jordan Price Wall Gray Jones & Carlton PLLC 1951 Clark Ave *TF:* 800-304-6700 ■ *Web:* www.jordanprice.com	Raleigh	NC	27605	919-828-2501		428
Jordan Ramis 2 Ctrpointe Dr Ste 600 *Web:* www.jordanramis.com	Lake Oswego	OR	97035	503-598-7070		445
Jordan Schnitzer Museum of Art 1430 Johnson Ln *Web:* jsma.uoregon.edu	Eugene	OR	97403	541-346-3027	346-0976	520
Jordan Specialty Plastics Inc 1751 Lake Cook Rd	Deerfield	IL	60015	847-945-5591		604
Jordan Tourism Board (JTB) 1307 Dolley Madison Blvd Ste 2A *TF:* 877-733-5673 ■ *Web:* www.visitjordan.com	McLean	VA	22101	703-243-7404	243-7406	775
Jordan Valley Medical Ctr 3460 S Pioneer Pkwy	West Valley City	UT	84120	801-964-3100		374-3
Jordan'S Furniture Company Inc 450 Revolutionary Dr *Web:* jordans.com	E Taunton	MA	02718	508-828-4000		321
Jordanelle State Park SR 319 Ste 515 *Web:* www.stateparks.utah.gov	Heber City	UT	84032	435-649-9540		565
Jordano Electric Company Inc 200 Hudson St *Web:* www.jordanoelectric.com	Hackensack	NJ	07601	201-489-4800	489-5071	189-4
Jordano's Inc 550 S Patterson Ave *TF:* 800-325-2278 ■ *Web:* www.jordanos.com	Santa Barbara	CA	93111	805-964-0611	964-3821	297-8
Jorg's Cafe Vienna 1037 E 15th St *Web:* jorgscafevienna.com	Plano	TX	75074	972-509-5966		671
Jorge's Taco Garcia Mexican Cafe 1100 S Ross St *Web:* www.tacosgarcia.com	Amarillo	TX	79102	806-371-0411		671
Jorgensen Conveyors Inc 10303 N Baehr Rd *TF:* 800-325-7705 ■ *Web:* www.jorgensenconveyors.com	Mequon	WI	53092	262-242-3089	242-4382	207
Jorgensen Forge Corp 8531 E Marginal Way S *TF:* 800-231-5382 ■ *Web:* www.jorgensenforge.com	Tukwila	WA	98108	206-762-1100		483
Jorgensen Laboratories Inc 1450 Van Buren Ave *TF:* 800-525-5614 ■ *Web:* www.jorvet.com	Loveland	CO	80538	970-669-2500	663-5042	475
Jorgenson's 1720 11th Ave *Web:* www.jorgensons.com	Helena	MT	59601	406-442-6380		671
Jorgenson's Inn & Suites 1714 11th Ave *Web:* www.jorgensonsinn.com	Helena	MT	59601	406-442-1770		379
Jor-Mac Company Inc 155 E Main St *TF:* 800-242-7708 ■ *Web:* www.jor-mac.com	Lomira	WI	53048	920-269-8500		697
Jos A Bank Clothiers 500 Hanover Pk *TF Cust Svc:* 800-999-7472 ■ *Web:* www.josbank.com	Hampstead	MD	21074	410-239-2700		155-12
Josam Co 525 W US Hwy 20 **Fax Area Code:* 800 ■ *TF:* 800-365-6726 ■ *Web:* www.josam.com	Michigan City	IN	46360	219-872-5531	627-0008*	609
JOSE 93.9 5426 N Mesa St *Web:* www.jose939.com	El Paso	TX	79912	915-581-1126		645-53
Jose Matteo's Ballet Theatre 400 Harvard St *Web:* www.ballettheatre.org	Cambridge	MA	02138	617-354-7467		573-1
Joseph A Natoli Construction Corp 293 Changebridge Rd *Web:* www.jnatoli.com	Pine Brook	NJ	07058	973-575-1500	575-8216	186
Joseph A Paine Inc 4301 S Pine St Ste 26 *Web:* paineinsurance.com	Tacoma	WA	98409	253-472-3055		390
Joseph A. Schudt & Associates Inc 19350 S Harlem Ave *TF:* 800-948-8070 ■ *Web:* www.jaseng.com	Frankfort	IL	60423	708-720-1000		727
Joseph Blank Inc 62 W 47th St Ste 808 *TF:* 800-223-7666 ■ *Web:* www.josephblank.com	New York	NY	10036	212-575-9050	302-8521	411
Joseph Brant Memorial Hospital (JBMH) 1230 N Shore Blvd *TF:* 800-810-0000 ■ *Web:* www.josephbranthospital.ca	Burlington	ON	L7S1W7	905-632-3730	336-6480	374-2
Joseph C. Sansone Co 18040 Edison Ave *TF:* 800-394-0140 ■ *Web:* www.jcsco.com	Chesterfield	MO	63005	636-537-2700		317
Joseph Campione Garlic Bread 2201 W S Branch Blvd *Web:* www.josephcampione.com	Oak Creek	WI	53154	414-761-8944	761-2005	68
Joseph Construction Company Inc 203 Letterman Rd *Web:* www.josephconst.com	Knoxville	TN	37919	865-584-3945		186
Joseph Cory Holdings LLC 150 Meadowlands Pkwy 3rd Fl *TF:* 800-375-4585 ■ *Web:* www.corycompanies.com	Secaucus	NJ	07094	201-795-1000		360-3
Joseph Crnkovich Jr CPA 1053 Mclaughlin Run Rd	Bridgeville	PA	15017	412-257-0844		2
Joseph Davis State Park 4143 Lower River Rd *Web:* parks.ny.gov/parks/45/details.aspx	Lewiston	NY	14092	716-754-4596		565
Joseph Distel & Company Inc 5 Two Mile Rd *Web:* distelgroup.com	Farmington	CT	06032	860-677-6505		390
Joseph E. Ibberson Conservation Area c/o Little Buffalo State Pk 1579 State Pk Rd *Web:* www.dcnr.state.pa.us	Newport	PA	17074	717-567-9255		565
Joseph Freedman Co Inc 115 Stevens St Ste *Web:* www.josephfreedmanco.com	Springfield	MA	01104	413-781-4444		192
Joseph H. Stewart State Recreation Area 35251 Hwy 62 *TF:* 800-452-5687 ■ *Web:* www.oregonstateparks.org	Trail	OR	97541	541-560-3334		565
Joseph Harp Correctional Ctr 16161 Moffat Rd PO Box 548 *Web:* www.ok.gov	Lexington	OK	73051	405-527-5593	527-4841	213
Joseph J. Henderson & Son Inc 4288 Old Grand Ave *Web:* www.jjhenderson.com	Gurnee	IL	60031	847-244-3222	244-9572	187
Joseph Meyerhoff Symphony Hall 1212 Cathedral St *TF:* 877-276-1444 ■ *Web:* www.bsomusic.org	Baltimore	MD	21201	410-783-8100		572
Joseph Oat Corp 2500 Broadway *Web:* www.josephoat.com	Camden	NJ	08104	856-541-2900	541-0864	91
Joseph P Day Realty Corp 9 E 40th St *Web:* www.jpday.com	New York	NY	10016	212-889-7460		652
Joseph P O'Brien Agency Inc 454 New York Ave	Huntington	NY	11743	631-421-0505		390

Name / Address	City	State	Zip	Phone	Fax	Class
Joseph P. Carrara & Sons Inc 167 N Shrewsbury Rd *TF:* 800-292-7245 ■ *Web:* www.jpcarrara.com	North Clarendon	VT	05759	802-775-2301		183
Joseph Productions Inc 34525 Glendale St *Web:* www.jpitel.com	Livonia	MI	48150	734-266-0500		514
Joseph's Steakhouse 360 Fairfield Ave *Web:* www.josephssteakhouse.com	Bridgeport	CT	06604	203-337-9944		671
Joseph, Greenwald & Laake PA 6404 Ivy Ln Ste 400 *TF:* 877-412-7429 ■ *Web:* www.jgllaw.com	Rockville	MD	20770	301-220-2200		428
Josephine County 500 NW Sixth St *Web:* www.co.josephine.or.us	Grants Pass	OR	97526	541-474-5240	474-5246	338
Josephine County Fairgrounds 1451 Fairgrounds Rd *TF:* 800-773-1162 ■ *Web:* www.co.josephine.or.us	Grants Pass	OR	97527	541-476-3215	476-1027	642
Josephine County Library System 200 NW 'C' St PO Box 1684 *Web:* www.josephinelibrary.org	Grants Pass	OR	97526	541-476-0571		434-3
Josephine Tussaud Wax Museum 250 Central Ave *Web:* www.rideaduck.com	Hot Springs	AR	71901	501-623-5836		520
Josephine's 503 N Humphreys St *Web:* www.josephinesrestaurant.com	Flagstaff	AZ	86001	928-779-3400		671
Josephine's Personnel Services Inc 2158 Ringwood Ave *Web:* www.jps-inc.com	San Jose	CA	95131	408-943-0111		260
Joshen Paper & Packaging Company Inc 5808 Grant Ave *Web:* www.joshen.com	Cleveland	OH	44105	216-441-5600	441-7647	548
Joshua Tree National Park 74485 National Pk Dr *Web:* www.nps.gov	Twentynine Palms	CA	92277	760-367-5500	367-6392	564
Josie 2424 Pico Blvd	Santa Monica	CA	90405	310-581-9888		671
Joslin Diabetes Ctr 1 Joslin Pl *Web:* www.joslin.org	Boston	MA	02215	617-732-2400		668
Joslyn Art Museum 2200 Dodge St *TF:* 800-965-2030 ■ *Web:* www.joslyn.org	Omaha	NE	68102	402-342-3300	342-2376	520
Joslyn Castle 3902 Davenport St *Web:* www.joslyncastle.com	Omaha	NE	68131	402-595-2199		50-3
Joso's 202 Davenport Rd *Web:* josos.com	Toronto	ON	M5R1J2	416-925-1903	925-6567	671
Joss Cafe & Sushi Bar 195 Main St *TF:* 800-638-9192 ■ *Web:* josssushi.com	Annapolis	MD	21401	410-263-4688		671
Jostens Inc 3601 Minnesota Ave Ste 400 *TF:* 800-235-4774 ■ *Web:* www.jostens.com	Minneapolis	MN	55435	952-830-3300		409
Jottan Inc PO Box 166 *TF:* 800-364-4234 ■ *Web:* www.jottan.com	Florence	NJ	08518	609-447-6200	447-6200	189-12
Joule Inc 1245 Rt 1 S *TF:* 800-341-0341 ■ *Web:* www.jouleinc.com	Edison	NJ	08837	732-548-5444	494-6346	721
Joule Technologies Inc 4167 W Orleans St *Web:* www.jouletechnologies.com	Mchenry	IL	60050	815-759-0600		625
Journal & Courier 217 N Sixth St *TF News Rm:* 800-407-5813 ■ *Web:* www.jconline.com	Lafayette	IN	47901	765-423-5511		532-2
Journal & Topics Newspapers 622 Graceland Ave *TF:* 800-719-4881 ■ *Web:* www.journal-topics.com	Des Plaines	IL	60016	847-299-5511	298-8549	637-8
Journal Gazette 600 W Main St *TF:* 888-966-4532 ■ *Web:* www.journalgazette.net	Fort Wayne	IN	46802	260-461-8773	461-8648	532-2
Journal Graphics Inc 2840 NW 35th Ave *Web:* www.journalgraphics.com	Portland	OR	97210	503-790-9100	790-9043	637-8
Journal Inquirer 306 Progress Dr PO Box 510 *TF:* 800-237-3606 ■ *Web:* www.journalinquirer.com	Manchester	CT	06045	860-646-0500	646-9867	532-2
Journal Le Droit 47 Clarence St *TF:* 800-267-6961 ■ *Web:* www.lapresse.ca	Ottawa	ON	K1N9K1	613-562-0555		532-1
Journal Mississippi State Medical Assn 408 W PkwyPl *Web:* msmaonline.com	Ridgeland	MS	39157	601-853-6733		474
Journal News 228 Ct St *Web:* www.journal-news.com	Hamilton	OH	45011	513-863-8200	896-9489	532-2
Journal of Accountancy 220 Leigh Farm Rd *Fax Area Code: 919 ■ *TF:* 888-777-7077 ■ *Web:* www.journalofaccountancy.com	Durham	NC	27707	888-777-7077	419-5241*	457-5
Journal of Business 429 E Third Ave *Web:* www.spokanejournal.com	Spokane	WA	99202	509-456-5257	456-0624	457-5
Journal of Clinical Investigation (JCI) 15 Research Dr *Web:* www.jci.org	Ann Arbor	MI	48103	734-222-6050	222-6058	49-8
Journal of Financial Planning Assn 7535 E Hampden Ave Ste 600 *TF:* 800-322-4237 ■ *Web:* www.onefpa.org/journal/pages/default.aspx	Denver	CO	80231	303-759-4900	759-0749	457-5
Journal of Petroleum Technology 222 Palisades Creek Dr *TF:* 800-456-6863 ■ *Web:* www.spe.org	Richardson	TX	75080	972-952-9393	952-9435	457-21
Journal of Physical Education Recreation & Dance (JOPERD) 1900 Assn Dr *TF:* 800-213-7193 ■ *Web:* shapeamerica.org	Reston	VA	20191	703-476-3400	476-9527	457-8
Journal of Practical Nursing (JPN) 2071 N Bechtle Ave PMB 307 *TF:* 800-655-4845 ■ *Web:* www.napnes.org	Springfield	OH	45504	703-933-1003	940-4089	457-16
Journal of Property Management 430 N Michigan Ave *TF:* 800-837-0706 ■ *Web:* irem.org/home/pagenotfound	Chicago	IL	60611	800-837-0706	338-4736	457-5
Journal of Protective Coatings & Linings 2100 Wharton St Ste 310 *TF:* 800-837-8303 ■ *Web:* www.paintsquare.com	Pittsburgh	PA	15203	412-431-8300	431-5428	457-21
Journal of the American Dietetic Assn 1600 John F Kennedy Blvd *Fax Area Code: 212 ■ *TF:* 800-654-2452 ■ *Web:* jandonline.org	Philadelphia	PA	19103	800-654-2452	633-3820*	457-16
Journal of the American Medical Assn (JAMA) PO Box 10946 *TF:* 800-262-2350 ■ *Web:* jama.jamanetwork.com	Chicago	IL	60654	312-670-7827		457-16

Name / Address	City	State	Zip	Phone	Fax	Class
Journal of the American Pharmacists Assn 2215 Constitution Ave NW *TF:* 800-237-2742 ■ *Web:* www.pharmacist.com	Washington	DC	20037	202-628-4410	783-2351	457-16
Journal of the Kansas Bar Assn 1200 SW Harrison St *TF:* 800-928-3111 ■ *Web:* www.ksbar.org	Topeka	KS	66612	785-234-5696	234-3813	457-15
Journal of the Louisiana State Medical Society 6767 Perkins Rd Ste 100 *TF:* 800-375-9508 ■ *Web:* www.lsms.org	Baton Rouge	LA	70808	225-763-8500	768-5601	457-16
Journal of the Medical Assn of Georgia 1849 The Exchange Ste 200 *TF:* 800-282-0224 ■ *Web:* www.mag.org	Atlanta	GA	30339	678-303-9290	303-3732	457-16
Journal of the Mississippi State Medical Assn PO Box 2548 *Web:* www.msmaonline.com	Ridgeland	MS	39158	601-853-6733	853-6746	457-16
Journal of the Philosophy of Sport 1607 N Market St *TF:* 800-747-4457 ■ *Web:* www.humankinetics.com	Champaign	IL	61820	217-351-5076	351-1549	457-20
Journal of the San Juan Islands PO Box 519 *Web:* www.sanjuanjournal.com	Friday Harbor	WA	98250	360-378-5696		532-4
Journal Publishing Co 1242 S Green St *TF:* 800-264-6397 ■ *Web:* djournal.com	Tupelo	MS	38804	662-842-2611	842-2233	637-8
Journal Record Oklahoma City 101 N Robinson St Ste 101 *TF:* 800-451-9998 ■ *Web:* www.journalrecord.com	Oklahoma City	OK	73102	405-235-3100		532-2
Journal Times 212 Fourth St *TF:* 800-447-1339 ■ *Web:* www.journaltimes.com	Racine	WI	53403	262-634-3322	631-1780	532-2
Journal, The 207 W King St *Fax: PR ■ *TF:* 800-448-1895 ■ *Web:* www.journal-news.net	Martinsburg	WV	25402	304-263-8931	267-2903*	532-2
Journal-Patriot PO Box 70 *Web:* journalpatriot.com	North Wilkesboro	NC	28659	336-838-4117	838-9864	532-4
Journal-Standard 27 S State Ave *TF:* 800-325-6397 ■ *Web:* www.journalstandard.com	Freeport	IL	61032	815-232-1171	232-0105	532-2
Journey Group Inc 418 Fourth St NE *Web:* journeygroup.com	Charlottesville	VA	22902	434-961-2600		637-9
Journey Museum and Learning Ctr 222 New York St *Web:* www.journeymuseum.org	Rapid City	SD	57701	605-394-6923	394-6940	520
JourneyEd.com 80 E McDermott Dr *Fax Area Code: 866 ■ *TF:* 800-874-9001 ■ *Web:* www.journeyed.com	Allen	TX	75002	972-481-2000	362-2492*	174
Journyx Inc 7600 Burnet Rd Ste. 300 *TF:* 800-755-9878 ■ *Web:* www.journyx.com	Austin	TX	78757	512-834-8888		39
Jova Solutions 965 Mission St Ste 600 *Web:* www.jovasolutions.com	San Francisco	CA	94103	415-348-1400		463
JOWA USA Inc 59 Porter Rd *Web:* www.consiliumus.com	Littleton	MA	01460	978-486-9800		246
Joy Cone Co 3435 Lamor Rd *TF:* 800-242-2663 ■ *Web:* www.joycone.com	Hermitage	PA	16148	724-962-5747		296-9
Joy Dog Food PO Box 305 *Fax Area Code: 618 ■ *TF:* 800-245-4125 ■ *Web:* www.joypetfood.com	Pinckneyville	IL	62274	800-245-4125	357-3651*	578
Joy Equipment Protection Inc 5690 Casitas Pass Rd *Web:* joyequipment.com	Carpinteria	CA	93014	805-684-0805		189-10
Joy fm 93.3, The 1175 Senoia Rd *Web:* georgia.thejoyfm.com	Tyrone	GA	30290	770-487-4500		645
Joy Lucky 3467 Broadway	Grove City	OH	43123	614-277-0827		457-11
Joy of Tokyo 15 Pelham Rd Ste A *Web:* joyoftokyo.tv	Greenville	SC	29615	864-232-2888		671
Joy State Bank 101 W Main St *Web:* joystatebank.com	Joy	IL	61260	309-584-4146		360-2
Joyce David (Rep R - OH) 1124 Longworth HOB *Web:* joyce.house.gov	Washington	DC	20515	202-225-5731	225-3307	342-2
Joyce Florist 2729 S Hampton Rd *TF:* 800-527-1620 ■ *Web:* www.joyceflorist.com	Dallas	TX	75224	214-942-1776		292
Joyce Foundation 70 W Madison St Ste 2750 *Web:* www.joycefdn.org	Chicago	IL	60602	312-782-2464	782-4160	305
Joyce Honda 3166 SR- 10 *TF:* 844-332-5955 ■ *Web:* www.joycehonda.com	Denville	NJ	07834	973-361-3000		57
Joyce Koons Buick Gmc 10660 Automotive Dr *TF:* 866-755-0072 ■ *Web:* joycekoonsbuickgmc.com	Manassas	VA	20109	866-755-0072		516
Joyce Swanson CPA 6715 Grover St	Omaha	NE	68106	402-390-2722		2
Joyce Theatre Foundation 175 Eighth Ave *Web:* www.joyce.org	New York	NY	10011	212-691-9740		305
Joyce Windows 1125 Berea Industrial Pkwy *TF:* 800-824-7988 ■ *Web:* www.joycewindows.com	Berea	OH	44017	440-239-9100		234
Joyner Fine Properties (JFP) 2727 Enterprise Pkwy *TF:* 800-446-3858 ■ *Web:* www.joynerfineproperties.com	Richmond	VA	23294	804-270-9440	967-2770	652
Joyner Keeny & Assoc 1051 N Winstead Ave *Web:* joynerkeeny.com	Rocky Mount	NC	27804	252-977-3124		256
Joyva Corp 53 Varick Ave *Web:* www.joyva.com	Brooklyn	NY	11237	718-497-0170	366-8504	296-8
JP Carroll Company Inc 310 N Madison Ave *Web:* myhomepro.org	Los Angeles	CA	90004	323-660-9230		189-8
JP Coleman State Park 613 County Rd 321 *Web:* www.mdwfp.com/parkview/parks.asp?id=1814	Iuka	MS	38852	662-423-6515		565
JP Digital Imaging Inc 230 Polaris Ave *TF:* 800-391-4443 ■ *Web:* www.jpdigital.com	Mountain View	CA	94043	650-965-0803		225
JP Energy Partners LP 600 Las Colinas Blvd E Ste 2000 *Web:* www.jpenergypartners.com	Irving	TX	75039	972-444-0300		579
JP Everhart & Co 1840 N GreenvilleAve Ste 178	Richardson	TX	75081	678-546-5225		391-5
JP Flooring Systems Inc 9097 Union Centre Blvd *Web:* www.jpflooring.com	West Chester	OH	45069	513-346-4300		364

Company / Address	City	State	ZIP	Phone	Fax	Class
JP Graphics Inc 3001 E Venture Dr *Web:* www.jpinc.com	Appleton	WI	54911	920-733-4483		627
Jp Harvey Engineering Solutions 29 Kings Way *Web:* www.jphes.com	Hampton	VA	23669	757-722-7074		261
JP Maguire Assoc Inc 266 Brookside Rd *TF:* 877-576-2484 ■ *Web:* www.jpmaguire.com	Waterbury	CT	06708	203-755-2297	573-8547	83
JP Marketing 7589 N wilson St Ste 105 *Web:* jpmktg.com	Fresno	CA	93711	559-438-2180		195
Jp Mchale Pest Management Inc 241 Bleakley Ave *TF:* 800-479-2284 ■ *Web:* nopests.com	Buchanan	NY	10511	800-479-2284		577
JP Morgan Chase & Co 270 Pk Ave *TF:* 800-992-7169 ■ *Web:* www.jpmorganchase.com	New York	NY	10017	212-270-6000		70
JP Oil Company LLC 1604 W Pinhook Rd Ste 300 *TF:* 800-234-9703 ■ *Web:* www.jpoil.com	Lafayette	LA	70508	337-234-1170		536
JPG (Jay Packaging Group) 100 Warwick Industrial Dr *Web:* www.jaypack.com	Warwick	RI	02886	401-739-7200		88
JPI (Jan-Pro International Inc) 2520 Northwinds Pkwy Ste 375 *TF:* 866-355-1064 ■ *Web:* www.jan-pro.com	Alpharetta	GA	30009	678-336-1780		152
JPI Healthcare Solutions Inc 52 Newton Plaza *TF:* 800-214-1813 ■ *Web:* www.jpihealthcare.com	Plainview	NY	11803	516-513-1330		476
JPL (Jet Propulsion Laboratory) 4800 Oak Grove Dr *Web:* www.jpl.nasa.gov	Pasadena	CA	91109	818-354-4321		668
JPL Integrated Communictions Inc 471 Jplwick Dr *TF:* 800-421-7697 ■ *Web:* www.jplcreative.com	Harrisburg	PA	17111	717-558-8048		514
JPMorgan Fleming Asset Management PO Box 8528 *Fax Area Code: 816 ■ *TF:* 800-480-4111 ■ *Web:* am.jpmorgan.com	Boston	MA	02266	800-480-4111	471-3053*	401
JPMS Cox PLLC 11300 Cantrell Rd Ste 301 *Web:* www.jpmscox.com	Little Rock	AR	72212	501-227-5800	227-5851	2
JPN (Journal of Practical Nursing) 2071 N Bechtle Ave PMB 307 *TF:* 800-655-4845 ■ *Web:* www.napnes.org	Springfield	OH	45504	703-933-1003	940-4089	457-16
JPS (Jenison Public Schools) 8375 20th Ave *Web:* www.jpsonline.org	Jenison	MI	49428	616-457-1402	457-8090	685
JPS Industries Inc 55 Beattie Pl # 1510	Greenville	SC	29601	864-239-3900		191-4
JPW Riggers Inc 6376 Thompson Rd *Web:* www.jpwcompanies.com/jpw-riggers	Syracuse	NY	13206	315-432-1111		536
JR Barto Heating/Air- Conditioning/Sheet Metal Inc 300 N G St *Web:* jrbarto.com	Lompoc	CA	93436	805-736-5160		189-10
JR Filanc Construction Company Inc 740 N Andreasen Dr *TF:* 877-225-5428 ■ *Web:* www.filanc.com	Escondido	CA	92029	760-941-7130	941-3969	188-10
Jr Gales & Assoc Inc 2704 Brownsville Rd	Pittsburgh	PA	15227	412-885-8885		261
JR Jones Fixture Co 3216 Winnetka Ave N *Web:* jonesfixture.com	Minneapolis	MN	55427	763-544-4239	544-3106	286
JR Merritt Controls Inc 55 Sperry Ave *Web:* www.jrmerritt.com	Stratford	CT	06615	203-381-0100		203
JR O'Dwyer Co 271 Madison Ave 6th Fl *TF:* 866-395-7710 ■ *Web:* www.odwyerpr.com	New York	NY	10016	212-679-2471	683-2750	637-9
JR Pierce Plumbing Co 14481 Wicks Blvd *Web:* www.jrpierceplumbing.com	San Leandro	CA	94577	510-483-5473		189-10
JR Realty 101 E Horizon Dr *TF:* 800-541-6780 ■ *Web:* century21jrrealty.com	Henderson	NV	89015	702-564-5142		652
JR Simplot Co 999 W Main St Ste 1300 *TF:* 800-832-8893 ■ *Web:* www.simplot.com	Boise	ID	83702	208-336-2110		296-21
JR Watkins Inc 150 Liberty St PO Box 5570 *TF:* 800-243-9423 ■ *Web:* www.jrwatkins.com	Winona	MN	55987	507-457-3300	452-6723	366
JR's Texas Bar-B-Que 180 Otto Cir *Web:* www.jrtexasbbq.com	Sacramento	CA	95822	916-424-3520	424-9915	671
Jra Financial Advisors 7373 Kirkwood Ct Ste 300 *TF:* 800-278-5988 ■ *Web:* www.jrafinancial.com	Maple Grove	MN	55369	763-315-8000		401
JRCERT (Joint Review Committee on Education in Radiologic Technology) 20 N Wacker Dr Ste 2850 *Web:* www.jrcert.org	Chicago	IL	60606	312-704-5300	704-5304	48-1
JRCNMT (Joint Review Committee on Educational Programs in Nuclear Medicine Technology, The) 2000 W Danforth Rd Ste 130 203 *Web:* www.jrcnmt.org	Edmond	OK	73003	405-285-0546	285-0579	48-1
JRF (Jewish Reconstructionist Federation) 101 Greenwood Ave *TF:* 877-226-7573 ■ *Web:* archive.jewishrecon.org	Jenkintown	PA	19046	215-885-5601	885-5603	48-20
JRI (James Richardson International) 2800 One Lombard Pl *Web:* www.richardson.ca	Winnipeg	MB	R3B0X8	204-934-5961		275
JRI America Inc 277 Park Ave *Web:* www.jri-america.com	New York	NY	10172	212-224-4200		177
JRL Enterprises Inc 1820 St Charles Ave Ste 203 *Web:* www.icanlearn.com	New Orleans	LA	70130	504-263-1380		177
Jrm & Associates Inc 160 Cupped Oak Dr Ste A *TF:* 800-683-4579 ■ *Web:* www.jrmassociates.com	Stallings	NC	28104	704-882-2044		317
Jrm Consultants Inc PO Box 90310 *Web:* www.jrmconsultants.com	Santa Barbara	CA	93190	805-564-3119		180
JRM Industries Inc 1 Mattimore St *TF:* 800-533-2697 ■ *Web:* www.jrm.com	Passaic	NJ	07055	973-779-9340	779-8017	745-5
JRMC (Jefferson Regional Medical Ctr) Hwy 61 S PO Box 350 *TF:* 800-318-2596 ■ *Web:* www.mercy.net	Crystal City	MO	63019	636-933-1000		374-3
JRMC (Jefferson Regional Medical Ctr) 1600 W 40th Ave *Web:* www.jrmc.org	Pine Bluff	AR	71603	870-541-7100		374-3
JRN Inc 209 W Seventh St *Web:* kfc.com	Columbia	TN	38401	931-381-3000		670
JRS (Jesuit Refugee Service North America) 1016 16th St NW Ste 500	Washington	DC	20036	202-462-5200		48-5
JRSA (Justice Research & Statistics Assn) 720 Seventh St NW 3rd Fl *Web:* www.jrsainfo.org	Washington	DC	20001	202-842-9330	448-1723	49-10
JS Chinese 116 W Second St	Casper	WY	82601	307-577-0618		671
Js Dyer & Assoc Inc 8891 Research Dr	Irvine	CA	92618	949-296-8858		256
J&S Electronic Business System Inc 878 Jefferson St *Web:* www.jselectronics.com	Burlington	IA	52601	319-752-5603		175
JS McCormick Co 503 Hegner Way	Sewickley	PA	15143	412-794-6356		500
JS Paluch Company Inc 3708 River Rd Ste 400 *TF:* 800-621-5197 ■ *Web:* www.jspaluch.com	Franklin Park	IL	60131	847-678-9300		41
JS Woodhouse Company Inc 1314 Union St *TF:* 800-367-3599 ■ *Web:* www.jswoodhouse.com	West Springfield	MA	01090	413-736-5462	732-3786	274
JSA (Junior State of America) 400 S El Camino Real Ste 300 *TF:* 800-334-5353 ■ *Web:* www.jsa.org	San Mateo	CA	94402	650-347-1600	347-7200	48-11
JSA (Jewelers Shipping Assn) 125 Carlsbad St *TF:* 800-688-4572 ■ *Web:* www.jewelersshipping.com	Cranston	RI	02920	401-943-6020		49-21
Jsa Technologies 201 Main St Ste 1320 *TF:* 877-572-8324 ■ *Web:* www.jsatech.com	Fort Worth	TX	76102	877-572-8324		396
JSB Industries Inc 130 Crescent Ave *Web:* www.muffintown.com	Chelsea	MA	02150	617-846-1565		345
JSD Professional Services Inc 161 Horizon Dr Ste 101 *TF:* 800-437-2150 ■ *Web:* www.jsdinc.com	Verona	WI	53593	608-848-5060		727
JSG (Janesville Sand & Gravel Co) 1110 Harding St *TF:* 800-955-7702 ■ *Web:* www.jsandg.com	Janesville	WI	53547	608-754-7701		503-4
JSix Restaurant 616 J St *Web:* www.jsixrestaurant.com	San Diego	CA	92101	619-531-8744		671
JSJ Corp 700 Robbins Rd *TF:* 800-867-3208 ■ *Web:* www.jsjcorp.com	Grand Haven	MI	49417	616-842-6350	847-3112	319-1
Jsl Foods Inc 3550 Pasadena Ave *Web:* www.jslfoods.com	Los Angeles	CA	90031	323-223-2484		123
JSM (Jimmy Swaggart Ministries) 8919 World Ministry Blvd PO Box 262550 *TF Orders:* 800-288-8350 ■ *Web:* www.jsm.org	Baton Rouge	LA	70810	225-768-8300		48-20
JSMN International Inc 591 Summit Ave Ste 522 *Web:* www.jsmninc.com	Jersey City	NJ	07306	201-792-6800		260
JSO (Jacksonville Symphony Orchestra) 300 W Water St Ste 200 *Web:* www.jaxsymphony.org	Jacksonville	FL	32202	904-354-5479		573-3
Jsr Power Systems International Llc 5563 De Zavala Rd Ste 200 *Web:* jsrpsi.com	San Antonio	TX	78249	210-558-1943		226
JSSI 180 N Stetson 29th Fl *Web:* www.jetsupport.com	Chicago	IL	60601	312-644-4444		194
JST Enterprises 5120 Summerhill Rd *Web:* www.jstent.com	Texarkana	TX	75503	903-794-3743		2
JT Fennell Company Inc 1104 N Front St	Chillicothe	IL	61523	309-274-2145		492
JT Mega 4020 Minnetonka Blvd *Web:* www.jtmega.com	Minneapolis	MN	55416	952-929-1370		7
JT Schmid's Restaurant & Brewery 2610 E Katella Ave *Web:* www.jtschmidsrestaurants.com	Anaheim	CA	92806	714-634-9200	634-9200	671
JT Thorpe & Son Inc 1060 Hensley St *Web:* www.jtthorpe.com	Richmond	CA	94801	510-233-2500	233-2901	318
JTB (Jordan Tourism Board) 1307 Dolley Madison Blvd Ste 2A *TF:* 877-733-5673 ■ *Web:* www.visitjordan.com	McLean	VA	22101	703-243-7404	243-7406	775
Jtd Stamping Company Inc 403 Wyandanch Ave *Web:* www.jtdstamping.com	North Babylon	NY	11704	631-643-4144		488
JTech Communications Inc 6413 Congress Ave Ste 150 *TF:* 800-321-6221 ■ *Web:* www.jtech.com	Boca Raton	FL	33487	800-321-6221		735
JTEKT Corporation 29570 Clemens Rd *TF Cust Svc:* 800-263-5163 ■ *Web:* www.jtekt-na.com	Westlake	OH	44145	440-835-1000	835-9347	75
JTJ Commercial Interiors Inc 200 Shady Grove Rd *Web:* jtjcommercialinteriors.com	Nashville	TN	37214	615-872-9363		291
Jtl Technical Services LLC 113 Crosby Rd Ste 8 *TF:* 800-698-4004 ■ *Web:* www.jtltechnicalservices.com	Dover	NH	03820	603-834-6570		177
JTM Foods Inc 2126 E 33rd St *Web:* www.jjsbakery.net	Erie	PA	16510	814-899-0886		296-1
JTM Provisions Company Inc 200 Sales Dr *Web:* www.jtmfoodgroup.com	Harrison	OH	45030	513-367-4900		297-8
JTPR (Jasculca/Terman & Assoc) 730 N Franklin Ste 510 *Web:* www.jtpr.com	Chicago	IL	60654	312-337-7400		636
JTS Direct LLC 1180 Walnut Ridge Dr *Web:* www.jtsdirect.com	Hartland	WI	53029	262-369-9500		627
Juab County 160 N Main St *Web:* www.co.juab.ut.us	Nephi	UT	84648	435-623-3410		338
Juanita K Hammons Hall for the Performing Arts 901 S National Ave *TF:* 888-476-7849 ■ *Web:* www.hammonshall.com	Springfield	MO	65897	417-836-6776	836-6891	572
Juanita's Foods Inc PO Box 847 PO Box 847 *TF:* 800-303-2965 ■ *Web:* www.juanitasfoods.com	Wilmington	CA	90748	800-303-2965		296-36
J-U-B Engineers Inc 250 S Beechwood Ave Ste 201 *Web:* jub.com	Boise	ID	83709	208-376-7330		261

Phone | Fax | Class

Juban's 3739 Perkins Rd . . . Baton Rouge LA 70808 225-346-8422 387-2601 671
Web: www.jubans.com
Jubilee Christian Center
105 Nortech Pkwy. . . . San Jose CA 95134 408-262-0900 685
Web: jubilee.org
Jubilee College State Park
13921 W Rt 150 . . . Brimfield IL 61517 309-446-3758 446-3183 565
Web: www.dnr.illinois.gov/Parks/Pages/JubileeCollege.aspx
Jubilee Theatre 506 Main St . . . Fort Worth TX 76102 817-338-4204 573-4
Web: www.jubileetheatre.org
Jubitz Corp 33 NE Middlefield Rd . . . Portland OR 97211 503-283-1111 240-5834 324
TF: 800-523-0600 ■ *Web:* www.jubitz.com
Judaica Press Inc 123 Ditmas Ave. . . . Brooklyn NY 11218 718-972-6200 637-2
TF: 800-972-6201 ■ *Web:* www.judaicapress.com
Judd Wire Inc 124 Tpke Rd . . . Turners Falls MA 01376 413-863-4357 863-2305 814
TF Cust Svc: 800-545-5833 ■ *Web:* www.juddwire.com
Judge CR Magney State Park
4051 E Hwy 61 . . . Grand Marais MN 55604 218-387-3039 565
Web: www.dnr.state.mn.us
Judge Group Inc
300 Conshohocken State Rd Ste 300 . . West Conshohocken PA 19428 610-667-7700 667-1058 721
TF: 888-228-7162 ■ *Web:* www.judge.com
Judge Organization Companies, The
201A Export St . . . Newark NJ 07114 973-491-0600 41
Web: www.judgeorg.com
Judicare Wisconsin Inc Attys
401 Fifth St Ste 200 . . . Wausau WI 54403 715-842-1681 428
TF: 800-472-1638 ■ *Web:* www.judicare.org
Judicate West
1851 E First St Ste 1600. . . . Santa Ana CA 92705 714-834-1340 834-1344 41
TF: 800-488-8805 ■ *Web:* www.judicatewest.com
Judicial Conference of the US
One Columbus Cir NE . . . Washington DC 20544 202-502-2600 341
Web: www.uscourts.gov/judconf.html
Judicial Panel on Multidistrict Litigation
1 Columbus Cir NE Room G 255 N Lbby. . . . Washington DC 20544 202-502-2800 502-2888 341
Web: www.jpml.uscourts.gov
Judicial Watch Inc
425 Third St SW Ste 800 . . . Washington DC 20024 202-646-5172 646-5199 48-7
TF: 888-593-8442 ■ *Web:* www.judicialwatch.org
Judith Basin County
91 Third St N PO Box 339 . . . Stanford MT 59479 406-566-2277 338
Web: co.judith-basin.mt.us
Judson Center Inc 4410 W 13 Mile Rd. . . . Royal Oak MI 48073 248-549-4339 726
Web: www.judsoncenter.org
Judson College 302 Bibb St . . . Marion AL 36756 334-683-5110 166
TF Admissions: 800-447-9472 ■ *Web:* www.judson.edu
Judson Park 23600 Marine View Dr S . . . Des Moines WA 98198 206-824-4000 672
TF: 800-401-4113 ■ *Web:* www.judsonpark.com
Judson University 1151 N State St . . . Elgin IL 60123 847-628-2500 628-2526* 166
**Fax:* Admissions ■ *TF Admissions:* 800-879-5376 ■ *Web:* www.judsonu.edu
Judys Staffing Services Inc
3070 Harrodsburg Rd . . . Lexington KY 40503 859-223-5005 260
TF: 800-561-3357 ■ *Web:* www.judysstaffing.com
JUF (Jewish United Fund/Jewish Federation of Metropolitan Chicago)
30 S Wells St . . . Chicago IL 60606 312-346-6700 444-2086 48-20
TF: 855-275-5237 ■ *Web:* www.juf.org
JUGGLE Magazine
3315 E Russell Rd #A4 203 . . . Las Vegas NV 89120 702-798-0099 530
Web: www.juggle.org
Jugs Sports 11885 SW Herman Rd . . . Tualatin OR 97062 800-547-6843 691-1100* 710
**Fax Area Code:* 503 ■ *TF:* 800-547-6843 ■ *Web:* www.jugssports.com
Juice It Up! Franchise Corp
17915 Sky Pk Cir Ste J. . . . Irvine CA 92614 949-475-0146 475-0137 310
TF: 888-705-8423 ■ *Web:* www.juiceitup.com
Juice Studios 1648 Tenth St . . . Santa Monica CA 90404 310-460-7830 7
TF: 800-438-7325 ■ *Web:* www.juicestudios.tv
Juilliard School, The
Wallace Library 60 Lincoln Ctr Plaza. . . . New York NY 10023 212-799-5000 434-4
Web: juilliard.edu
Juju Inc 151 First Ave Ste 19 . . . New York NY 10003 212-537-3898 260
TF: 800-374-0119 ■ *Web:* www.juju.com
Jules 11805 Coastal Hwy . . . Ocean City MD 21842 410-524-3396 671
Web: ocjules.com
Jules Saint-Michel Luthier - Economuseum of Violin-Making
57 Ontario St W . . . Montreal QC H2X1Y8 514-288-4343 288-9296 520
Web: www.luthiersaintmichel.com
Jules Seltzer Assoc
9020 W Olympic Blvd. . . . Beverly Hills CA 90211 310-274-7243 274-7243 320
Web: www.julesseltzer.com
Julia Pfeiffer Burns State Park
52801 California SR 1 . . . Big Sur CA 93920 831-667-2315 565
Web: www.parks.ca.gov/default.asp?page_id=578
Julian Charter School Inc
1704 Cape Horn . . . Julian CA 92036 760-765-3847 685
TF: 866-853-0003 ■ *Web:* www.juliancharterschool.org
Julian F Keith Alcohol & Drug Abuse Treatment Ctr
201 Tabernacle Rd . . . Black Mountain NC 28711 828-257-6200 726
Julian J Rodriguez PA
2600 S Douglas Rd Ste 900 . . . Coral Gables FL 33134 305-445-0777 2
Web: jjrpa.net
Julian Tours 1721 Crestwood Dr . . . Alexandria VA 22302 703-379-2300 379-5030 760
TF: 800-541-7936 ■ *Web:* www.juliantours.com
Julian's 318 Broadway . . . Providence RI 02909 401-861-1770 671
Web: www.juliansprovidence.com
Juliano's 2912 Seventh Ave N . . . Billings MT 59101 406-248-6400 671
Web: wordpress.com
Julie Hat Co 5948 Industrial Blvd . . . Patterson GA 31557 912-647-2031 155-9
Julie Inc 3275 Executive Dr . . . Joliet IL 60431 815-741-5000 737
TF: 800-892-0123 ■ *Web:* www.illinois1call.com
Julie Morgenstern Enterprises LLC
850 Seventh Ave. . . . New York NY 10019 212-586-8084 194
Web: www.juliemorgenstern.com
Juliette Gordon Low Girl Scout National Ctr
10 E Oglethorpe Ave. . . . Savannah GA 31401 912-233-4501 50-3
Web: www.juliettegordonlowbirthplace.org
Julio's Barrio 10450 82nd Ave . . . Edmonton AB T6E2A2 780-431-0774 671
Web: www.juliosbarrio.com

Julio's Cafe Corona
8050 Gateway Blvd E . . . El Paso TX 79907 915-591-7676 592-1294 671
Web: julioscafecorona.com
Julio's Restaurant 54 State St . . . Montpelier VT 05602 802-229-9348 671
Web: www.julioscantina.com
Julius Koch USA Inc 387 Church St. . . . New Bedford MA 02745 508-995-9565 995-8434 745-5
TF Sales: 800-522-3652 ■ *Web:* www.jkusa.com
July Business Services
215 Mary Ave Ste 302 . . . Waco TX 76701 888-333-5859 41
TF: 888-333-5859 ■ *Web:* www.julyservices.com
Jumboshrimp Advertising Inc
544 Bryant St . . . San Francisco CA 94107 415-369-0500 7
Web: www.jumboshrimp.com
Jump Film Editing
625 Broadway Eighth Fl 8th Fl . . . New York NY 10012 212-228-7474 434-3
Web: www.nycjump.com
Jump River Electric Co-op PO Box 99 . . . Ladysmith WI 54848 715-532-5524 532-3065 245
TF: 866-273-5111 ■ *Web:* www.jrec.net
Jumping Brook Country Club
210 Jumping Brook Rd. . . . Neptune NJ 07753 732-922-8200 711
Web: www.jumpingbrookcc.com
JumpSport Inc 2055 S Seventh St Ste A . . . San Jose CA 95112 408-213-2551 41
TF: 888-567-5867 ■ *Web:* www.jumpsport.com
Jumpstart Automotive Media
550 Kearny St Ste 500 . . . San Francisco CA 94108 415-844-6300 317
Web: www.jumpstartautomotivegroup.com
JumpStart Partners Inc
3616 Far West Blvd Ste 117-294 . . . Austin TX 78731 512-576-9000 70
Web: www.jumpstartpartners.com
JumpStart Wireless Corp
566 SW 20th Ct Ste B. . . . Delray Beach FL 33445 561-243-4700 224
Web: www.jumpstartwireless.com
JumpstartMD 595 Price Ave Ste 200. . . . Redwood City CA 94063 650-701-1460 810
Web: www.jumpstartmd.com
Jun Japanese Restaurant
1760 Dublin Blvd . . . Colorado Springs CO 80918 719-531-9368 671
Junction City Area Chamber of Commerce
222 W Sixth St PO Box 26 . . . Junction City KS 66441 785-762-2632 139
TF: 800-909-3012 ■ *Web:* www.junctioncitychamber.org
Junction Networks Inc
55 Broad St 20th Fl. . . . New York NY 10004 800-801-3381 387
TF: 800-801-3381 ■ *Web:* www.onsip.com
Jundt Art Museum 202 E Cataldo Ave . . . Spokane WA 99258 509-313-6611 520
TF: 800-986-9585 ■ *Web:* www.gonzaga.edu
June Kelly Gallery
166 Mercer St # 3C . . . New York NY 10012 212-226-1660 42
TF: 800-925-8059 ■ *Web:* www.junekellygallery.com
Juneau Assoc Inc PC
2100 State St . . . Granite City IL 62040 618-877-1400 261
Web: jaipc.com
Juneau Chamber of Commerce
9301 Glacier Hwy Ste 110 . . . Juneau AK 99801 907-463-3488 463-3489 139
TF: 888-581-2201 ■ *Web:* www.juneauchamber.com
Juneau City & Borough 155 S Seward St . . . Juneau AK 99801 907-586-5278 586-5385 338
Web: www.juneau.org
Juneau Convention & Visitors Bureau
101 Egan Dr . . . Juneau AK 99801 907-586-1737 206
TF: 888-581-2201 ■ *Web:* www.traveljuneau.com
Juneau County 220 East State St Rm 112. . . . Mauston WI 53948 608-847-9300 338
Web: www.juneaucounty.com
Juneau Empire 3100 Ch Dr. . . . Juneau AK 99801 907-586-3740 586-9097 532-2
Web: juneauempire.com
Juneau Harbor 155 S Seward St . . . Juneau AK 99801 907-586-5255 586-2507 618
TF: 800-642-0066 ■ *Web:* www.juneau.org/harbors
Juneau International Airport
1873 Shell Simmons Dr Ste 200 . . . Juneau AK 99801 907-789-7821 789-1227 27
TF: 800-478-4176 ■ *Web:* www.juneau.org/airport
Juneau Public Libraries 292 Marine Way . . . Juneau AK 99801 907-586-5324 586-3419 434-3
TF: 800-478-4176 ■ *Web:* www.juneau.org
Juneau Symphony Orchestra
522 W Tenth St PO Box 21236 . . . Juneau AK 99802 907-586-4676 463-2555 573-3
Web: www.juneausymphony.org
Juneau-Douglas City Museum
114 W Fourth St . . . Juneau AK 99801 907-586-3572 586-3203 520
TF: 800-315-6608 ■ *Web:* www.juneau.lib.ak.us
Junex Inc 2795 Laurier Blvd Ste 200 . . . Quebec QC G1V4M7 418-654-9661 536
Web: www.junex.ca
Jungle Adventures
26205 E Colonial Dr . . . Christmas FL 32709 407-568-2885 823
TF: 877-424-2867 ■ *Web:* www.jungleadventures.com
Jungle Cat World Inc
3667 Concession Rd 6 . . . Orono ON L0B1M0 905-983-5016 983-9858 823
Web: www.junglecatworld.com
Jungle Gardens Hwy 329 . . . Avery Island LA 70513 337-369-6243 97
Web: www.junglegardens.org
Jungle Island 1111 Parrot Jungle Trl. . . . Miami FL 33132 305-400-7000 400-7290 823
TF: 800-901-8688 ■ *Web:* www.jungleisland.com
Jungle Theater 2951 Lindale Ave S . . . Minneapolis MN 55408 612-822-4002 572
Web: www.jungletheater.com
Juniata College 1700 Moore St . . . Huntingdon PA 16652 814-641-3000 641-3100* 166
**Fax:* Admissions ■ *TF:* 877-586-4282 ■ *Web:* www.juniata.edu
Juniata County 498 Jefferson St. . . . Mifflintown PA 17059 717-436-6378 436-7734 338
Web: www.co.juniata.pa.us
Juniata Fabrics Inc 1301 Broadway. . . . Altoona PA 16601 814-944-9381 745-1
Juniata Valley Area Chamber of Commerce
1 W Market St. . . . Lewistown PA 17044 717-248-6713 248-6714 139
Web: www.juniatarivervalley.org
Junior Achievement of Canada (JACAN)
1 Eva Rd Ste 218 . . . Toronto ON M9C4Z5 416-622-4602 622-6861 48-11
TF: 800-265-0699 ■ *Web:* jacanada.org
Junior Chamber International (JCI)
15645 Olive Blvd . . . Chesterfield MO 63017 636-449-3100 449-3107 48-7
TF: 800-905-5499 ■ *Web:* www.jci.cc
Junior State of America (JSA)
400 S El Camino Real Ste 300 . . . San Mateo CA 94402 650-347-1600 347-7200 48-11
TF: 800-334-5353 ■ *Web:* www.jsa.org
Junior's Bldg Materials Inc
7574 Battlefield Pkwy . . . Ringgold GA 30736 706-937-3400 364
Web: www.juniorsbuildingmaterials.com

Name / Address	City	State	ZIP	Phone	Fax	Class
Juniper Advisory LLC 191 N Wacker Dr Ste 900 *Web:* www.juniperadvisory.com	Chicago	IL	60606	312-506-3000		690
Juniper Industries Inc 72-15 Metropolitan Ave PO Box 148	Middle Village	NY	11379	718-326-2546	326-3786	697
Juniper Networks Inc 1194 N Mathilda Ave *NYSE:* JNPR ■ *TF:* 888-586-4737 ■ *Web:* www.juniper.net	Sunnyvale	CA	94089	408-745-2000	745-2100	176
Juniper Pharmaceuticals Inc 33 Arch St *NASDAQ:* CBRX ■ **Fax Area Code:* 973 ■ *TF:* 866-566-5636 ■ *Web:* www.juniperpharma.com	Boston	MA	02110	617-639-1500	994-3001*	582
Junipero Serra High School 31422 Camino Capistrano *Web:* serra.capousd.ca.schoolloop.com	San Juan Capistrano	CA	92675	949-489-7216		685
Junipero Serra Museum 2727 Presidio Dr *Web:* www.sandiegohistory.org	San Diego	CA	92103	619-232-6203		520
Junkermier Clark Campanella Stevens PC 501 Park Dr S Ste 100 *Web:* www.jccscpa.com	Great Falls	MT	59403	406-761-2820		2
JUNO Healthcare Staffing System Inc 4401 Wilshire Blvd Ste 230 *Web:* www.junohealthcare.com	Los Angeles	CA	90010	323-937-7210	937-4947	260
juno pacific 1100 McKinley St *Web:* www.junoinc.com	Anoka	MN	55303	763-703-5000		604
Jupiter Aluminum Corp 4825 Scott St *TF:* 800-392-7265 ■ *Web:* www.jupiteraluminum.com	Schiller Park	IL	60176	847-928-5930	928-0795	660
Jupiter Beach Resort 5 N A1A *TF:* 877-389-0571 ■ *Web:* www.jupiterbeachresort.com	Jupiter	FL	33477	561-746-2511		669
Jupiter Group, The 6565 W Loop S Ste 770 *Web:* www.jupgroup.com	Hamlin	TX	77401	832-778-1960		693
Jupiter Marine International Holdings 1103 12th AveEast *Web:* www.jupitermarine.com	Palmetto	FL	34221	941-729-5000		698
Jupiter Medical Ctr 1210 S Old Dixie Hwy *Web:* www.jupitermed.com	Jupiter	FL	33458	561-263-2234		374-3
Jupiter Realty Company LLC 401 Michigan Ave 13th Fl *Web:* www.jupiterrealty.com	Chicago	IL	60611	312-642-6000	642-2316	653
Jupitor Corporation USA 55 Fairbanks *Web:* www.jpus.com	Irvine	CA	92618	949-588-0505		21
Juran Institute Inc 160 Main St Ste 100 *TF:* 800-338-7726 ■ *Web:* www.juran.com	Southington	CT	06489	203-267-3445		113
Jurinnov Ltd The Idea Ctr 1375 Euclid Ave Ste 400 *Web:* www.jurinnov.com	Cleveland	OH	44115	216-664-1100		463
Jurupa Mountains Discovery Ctr 7621 Granite Hill Dr *TF:* 800-423-9986 ■ *Web:* www.jmdc.org	Riverside	CA	92509	951-685-5818	685-1240	50-2
Jury Research Institute 2617 Danville Blvd PO Box 100 *TF:* 800-233-5879 ■ *Web:* www.juryresearchinstitute.com	Alamo	CA	94507	925-932-5663	932-8409	445
Just Bagels Manufacturing Inc 527 Casanova St *Web:* www.justbagels.com	Bronx	NY	10474	718-328-9700	328-9997	297-8
Just Bead It 9514 Third Ave *Web:* www.justbeadit.net	Stone Harbor	NJ	08247	609-368-0400		411
Just Born Inc 1300 Stefko Blvd *TF:* 800-445-5787 ■ *Web:* www.justborn.com	Bethlehem	PA	18017	610-867-7568	867-3983	296-8
Just Desserts Inc 351 California St Ste 600 *Web:* www.justdesserts.com	San Francisco	CA	94104	510-567-2900		68
Just for Laughs Inc 2101 St-Laurent Blvd *Web:* www.hahaha.com	Montreal	QC	H2X2T5	514-845-3155	845-4140	514
Just For Wraps 5815 Smithway St *Web:* www.wrapper.com	Commerce	CA	90040	213-239-0503		157-6
Just Hair 1845 Eastwest Pkwy *Web:* www.justhair.mobi	Fleming Island	FL	32003	904-215-2995		77
Just Manufacturing Company Inc 9233 King St *TF:* 800-223-5529 ■ *Web:* www.justmfg.com	Franklin Park	IL	60131	847-678-5151		612
Just Packaging 450 Oak Tree Ave Ste 1 *Web:* www.justpackaging.com	South Plainfield	NJ	07080	908-753-6700		557
Just Service Inc 2940 N Clark St *Web:* www.justservice.com	Chicago	IL	60657	773-871-7171		175
Just Solutions Inc 7300 Pittsford Palmyra Rd (RT 31) PO Box 118 *Web:* www.justinc.com	Fairport	NY	14450	585-203-8910		175
justClick media Inc 16782-B Red Hill Ave *Web:* www.justclickmedia.com	Irvine	CA	92606	949-863-0066		5
Justia Inc 1380 Pear Ave Unit 2b *TF:* 800-300-0001 ■ *Web:* www.justia.com	Mountain View	CA	94043	650-810-1990		177
Justice Design Group (JDG) 500 S Grand Ave Ste 110 *Web:* www.jdg.com	Los Angeles	CA	90071	213-437-0102	437-0860	439
Justice in Aging (NSCLC) 1444 'I' St Ste 1100 *Web:* nsclc.org	Washington	DC	20005	202-289-6976		49-10
Justice Institute of British Columbia 715 McBride Blvd *Web:* www.jibc.bc.ca	New Westminster	BC	V3L5T4	604-525-5422		162
Justice Jim (R) 1900 Kanawha St *Web:* www.governor.wv.gov/Pages/default.aspx	Charleston	WV	25305	304-558-2000	342-7025	343
Justice Research & Statistics Assn (JRSA) 720 Seventh St NW 3rd Fl *Web:* www.jrsainfo.org	Washington	DC	20001	202-842-9330	448-1723	49-10
Justice Resource Institute Inc 160 Gould St Ste 300 *Web:* jri.org	Needham	MA	02494	781-559-4900		412
Justice Solutions of America Inc 467 Lake Howell Rd Stes 201-25 Ste *Web:* www.federalprisonconsultants.com	Maitland	FL	32751	386-341-9212		463
Justice Systems Inc 4600 McLeod NE *Web:* www.justicesystems.com	Albuquerque	NM	87109	505-883-3987	883-2845	177
Justifacts Credential Verification Inc 5250 Logan Ferry Rd *TF:* 800-356-6885 ■ *Web:* www.justifacts.com	Murrysville	PA	15668	412-798-4790		708
Justin Boot Co Inc 610 W Daggett St *TF Cust Svc:* 800-548-1021 ■ *Web:* www.justinboots.com	Fort Worth	TX	76104	817-332-4385		301
Justin Bradley 1725 I St NW Ste 300 *Web:* www.justinbradley.com	Washington	DC	20006	202-457-8400		721
Justin Electronics Corp 400 Oser Ave Ste 800 *Web:* www.justinelectronics.com	Hauppauge	NY	11788	631-951-4900	951-4747	246
Justin P. Wilson Cumberland Trail State Park 220 Pk Rd *TF:* 800-342-3145 ■ *Web:* tnstateparks.com/parks/contact/cumberland-trail	Caryville	TN	38555	423-566-2229	566-2290	565
Justiss Oil Company Inc 1120 E Oak St *TF:* 800-256-2501 ■ *Web:* www.justissoil.com	Jena	LA	71342	318-992-4111	992-7201	540
Justrite Manufacturing Co 2454 E Dempster St Ste 300 *TF:* 800-798-9250 ■ *Web:* www.justritemfg.com	Des Plaines	IL	60016	847-298-9250	298-9261	198
Just-Us Printers Inc 555 N Old Missouri Rd *Web:* www.just-usprinters.com	Springdale	AR	72764	479-751-0385		627
Justworks Inc 151 W 26th St Fl 12 *Web:* www.justworks.com	New York	NY	10001	646-663-1347		260
Juvenile Corrections Ctr-Nampa 1650 11th Ave N	Nampa	ID	83687	208-465-8443		412
Juvenile Corrections Ctr-Saint Anthony 2220 E 600 N PO Box 40	Saint Anthony	ID	83445	208-624-2100	624-0973	412
Juxtaposition Arts Inc 2007 Emerson Ave N *TF:* 800-774-2655 ■ *Web:* www.juxtaposition.org	Minneapolis	MN	55411	612-588-1148		520
JV Manufacturing Inc 1603 Burtner Rd	Natrona Heights	PA	15065	724-224-1704		386
JVA Inc 1319 Spruce St *Web:* www.jvajva.com	Boulder	CO	80302	303-444-1951		261
JVC Professional Products Co 1700 Valley Rd *TF:* 800-252-5722 ■ *Web:* www.pro.jvc.com/prof	Wayne	NJ	07470	973-317-5000	317-5030	52
Jviation Inc 35 S 400 W Ste 200 *Web:* jviation.com	St George	UT	84770	435-673-4677		261
JVKellyGroup Inc 145 E Main St *Web:* www.jvkg.com	Huntington	NY	11743	631-427-2888		196
Jvt Advisors 35 New England Business Ctr Dr Ste 210 *TF:* 800-546-6447 ■ *Web:* www.jvtadvisors.com	Andover	MA	01810	978-683-4555		631
JW Aluminum 435 Old Mt Holly Rd *TF Sales:* 877-586-5314 ■ *Web:* www.jwaluminum.com	Mount Holly	SC	29445	877-586-5314		485
JW Hampton Jr & Company Inc 161-15 Rockaway Blvd *Web:* jwhampton.com	Jamaica	NY	11434	718-276-0301		311
JW Jones Lumber Company Inc 1443 Northside Rd *TF:* 800-346-0473 ■ *Web:* mackeysferrysawmill.com	Elizabeth City	NC	27909	252-771-2497	771-8252	683
JW Jung Seed Co 335 S High St *TF:* 800-297-3123 ■ *Web:* www.jungseed.com	Randolph	WI	53956	800-297-3123	692-5864	694
JW Marriott Denver Cherry Creek Hotel 150 Clayton Ln *Web:* www.jwmarriottdenver.com	Denver	CO	80206	303-316-2700		378
JW Marriott Desert Ridge Resort & Spa 5350 E Marriott Dr *TF:* 800-845-5279 ■ *Web:* www.marriott.com/hotels/travel/phxdr	Phoenix	AZ	85054	480-293-5000	293-3600	669
JW Marriott Orlando Grande Lakes Resort 4040 Central Florida Pkwy *TF:* 800-576-5750 ■ *Web:* www.grandelakes.com	Orlando	FL	32837	407-206-2300	206-2301	669
JW Marriott Resort Las Vegas 221 N Rampart Blvd *TF:* 877-869-8777 ■ *Web:* www.marriott.com	Las Vegas	NV	89145	702-869-7777	869-7339	669
JW Mays Inc 9 Bond St *NASDAQ:* MAYS ■ *Web:* www.jwmays.com	Brooklyn	NY	11201	718-624-7400		655
J-W Operating Company Inc 15505 Wright Brothers Dr *Web:* www.jwenergy.com	Addison	TX	75001	972-233-8191		536
JW Pepper & Son Inc 2480 Industrial Blvd *TF:* 800-345-6296 ■ *Web:* www.jwpepper.com	Paoli	PA	19301	610-648-0500	993-0563	526
JW Peters Inc 500 W Market St *TF:* 866-265-7888 ■ *Web:* journaltimes.com	Burlington	WI	53105	262-806-9009		183
Jw Sieg & Co Inc 1180 Seminole Trl Ste 290	Charlottesville	VA	22901	434-244-5300	973-1209	80-3
JW Speaker Corp N 120 W 19434 Freistadt Rd PO Box 1011 *TF:* 800-558-7288 ■ *Web:* www.jwspeaker.com	Germantown	WI	53022	262-251-6660	251-2918	438
JW Starr Pass Resort & Spa 3800 W Starr Pass Blvd **Fax Area Code:* 817 ■ *TF:* 800-845-5279 ■ *Web:* www.marriott.com	Tucson	AZ	85745	520-792-3500	778-2049*	707
JW Wells State Park N/670 Hwy M 35 *Web:* www.michigandnr.com	Cedar River	MI	49887	906-863-9747		565
JW Williams Inc 2180 Renauna Ave	Casper	WY	82601	307-237-8345		539
JW Winco Inc 2815 S Calhoun Rd *TF:* 800-877-8351 ■ *Web:* www.jwwinco.com	New Berlin	WI	53151	262-786-8227		295
JWCI (Providence Health & Services) 2200 Santa Monica Blvd *TF:* 800-262-6259 ■ *Web:* california.providence.org/saint-johns	Santa Monica	CA	90404	310-582-7450	315-6148	668
JWF Industries 84 Iron St PO Box 1286 *TF:* 800-225-9359 ■ *Web:* www.jwfi.com	Johnstown	PA	15907	814-539-6922		811
JWMCD (John W McDougall Company Inc) 3731 Amy Lynn Dr *TF:* 800-264-1122 ■ *Web:* www.jwmcd.com	Nashville	TN	37218	615-321-3900	329-9069	697
JWS & Assoc Inc 10305 Latting Rd	Cordova	TN	38016	901-754-1239		256

	Phone	Fax	Class
JWV-NMI (National Museum of American Jewish Military History) 1811 R St NW ... Washington DC 20009 *Web:* www.nmajmh.org	202-265-6280	462-3192	520
Jyoti 2433 18th St NW ... Washington DC 20009 *Web:* jyotidc.com	202-518-5892	518-5892	671
Jzanus Healthcare Financial Service 170 Jericho Tpke ... Floral Park NY 11001 *Web:* jzanushomecare.com	516-437-4747	437-4902	196

K

	Phone	Fax	Class
K & H Printers-Lithographers Inc 7720 Hardeson Rd ... Everett WA 98203 *TF:* 800-451-5740 ■ *Web:* www.khprint.com	800-451-5740		627
K & K Die Inc 40700 Enterprise Dr ... Sterling Heights MI 48314 *Web:* www.kandkdie.com	586-268-8812		489
K & K Langham Ltd 11209 Metric Blvd Ste B ... Austin TX 78758 *Web:* www.austincountertops.com	512-835-5100	339-1796	724
K & K Veterinary Supply Inc 675 E Laura Ln ... Tontitown AR 72770 *Web:* www.kkvet.com	479-361-1516		584
K & L Microwave Inc 2250 Northwood Dr ... Salisbury MD 21801 *Web:* www.klmicrowave.com	410-749-2424		253
K & L Wine Merchants 855 Harrison St ... San Francisco CA 94107 *Web:* www.klwines.com	415-896-1734		443
K & M Machine-Fabricating Inc 20745 Michigan 60 ... Cassopolis MI 49031 *Web:* www.k-mm.com	269-445-2495		454
K & s Air Conditioning Inc 143 E Meats Ave ... Orange CA 92866 *Web:* www.kandsair.com	714-685-0077		610
K & S Contractors Supply Company Inc 1971 Gunnville Rd ... Lancaster NY 14086	716-759-6911		183
K A Hamilton & Assoc 159 Perry Hwy Ste 100 ... Pittsburgh PA 15229 *TF:* 800-746-4726 ■ *Web:* rcn.com	412-459-0122		260
K B L Design Center 6710 N Big Hollow Rd ... Peoria IL 61615 *Web:* www.kbldesign.com	309-692-8700		321
K B Recycling Inc PO Box 550 ... Canby OR 97013	503-266-7903		804
K Bell Plumbing & Heating Inc 3476 S 4600 S ... West Haven UT 84401 *Web:* kbellplumbing.com	801-731-6886		610
K D M Enterprise LLC 820 Commerce Pkwy ... Carpentersville IL 60110 *TF:* 877-591-9768 ■ *Web:* www.gokdm.com	847-783-0333		557
K G B Communictions L L C 3219 N Geronimo Ave ... Tucson AZ 85705 *Web:* www.kgbcommunications.com	520-743-3300		246
K L House Construction Company Inc 6409 Acoma Rd SE ... Albuquerque NM 87108 *Web:* www.klhouse.com	505-268-4361	268-9266	186
K Light Radio 98 - 1016 Komo Mai Dr ... Aiea HI 96701 *Web:* www.klight.org	808-524-1040		645
K Line America Inc 8730 Stony Pt Pkwy Ste 400 ... Richmond VA 23235 *TF:* 800-609-3221 ■ *Web:* www.kline.com	804-560-3600		313
K P Pharmaceutical Technology Inc 1212 W Rappel Ave ... Bloomington IN 47404 *Web:* www.kppt.com	812-330-8121	330-8363	582
K r Consulting Group Ltd 287 Burnside Ave ... Lawrence NY 11559 *Web:* krgroupny.com	516-837-0335		196
K Rcr Tv News Channel 7 Tv 755 Auditorium Dr ... Redding CA 96001 *TF:* 800-222-5727 ■ *Web:* www.krcrtv.com	530-243-7777		742
K Restaurant & Wine Bar 1710 Edgewater Dr ... Orlando FL 32804 *Web:* krestaurant.net	407-872-2332		671
K Wm Beach Mfg Company Inc 4655 Urbana Rd ... Springfield OH 45502 *Web:* www.kwmbeach.com	937-399-3838		326
K y Diamond Ltd 2645 Rue Diab ... St Laurent QC H4S1E7 *Web:* kydiamond.ca	514-333-5606	339-5493	697
K.D. Analytical Consulting Inc 4460 Linglestown Rd ... Harrisburg PA 17112 *Web:* www.kdanalytical.com	717-343-2984		196
K/E Electric Supply Co 146 N Groesbeck Hwy ... Mount Clemens MI 48043 *Web:* www.keelectric.com	586-469-3005	469-3006	203
K12 Inc 2300 Corporate Pk Dr ... Herndon VA 20171 *NYSE:* LRN ■ *TF:* 866-512-2273 ■ *Web:* www.k12.com	703-483-7000		685
K2 Bike 1600 Calebs Path Ext Ste 203 ... Hauppauge NY 11788 *Web:* www.ecycylesupply.com	631-780-5360	780-5358	82
K2 Communications 880 Apollo St Ste 239 ... El Segundo CA 90245 *Web:* k2communications.com	310-524-9100		225
K2 Engineering Services Inc 85 Rangeway Rd ... North Billerica MA 01862 *Web:* www.k2-eng.com	978-600-1333	600-1331	261
K2 Industrial Services 3838 N Sam Houston Parkway E Suite 285 ... Hammond IN 46320 **Fax Area Code:* 850 ■ *TF:* 800-347-4813 ■ *Web:* www.k2industrial.com	219-933-5300	477-8670*	189-8
K2 Partnering Solutions 100 Montgomery St Ste 2200 ... San Francisco CA 94104 *Web:* k2partnering.com	415-391-3804		193
K2 Project Control Systems 4330 E W Hwy Ste 320 ... Bethesda MD 20814 *Web:* www.k2consulting.com	301-656-2228		463
K2 Sports 4201 Sixth Ave S ... Seattle WA 98108 *TF:* 800-426-1617 ■ *Web:* www.k2sports.com	206-805-4800		710
K2Share LLC 1005 University Dr E ... College Station TX 77840 *Web:* k2share.com	979-260-0030		225
K3 Enterprises Inc 504 Cumberland St Ste 300 ... Fayetteville NC 28301 *Web:* www.k3-enterprises.com	910-307-3017		317
K-97 8882 170th St 2394 W Edmonton Mall ... Edmonton AB T5T4M2 *Web:* www.k97.fm	780-437-4996		645-52
K97 2650 Thousand Oaks Blvd Ste 4100 ... Memphis TN 38118 *Web:* k97fm.iheart.com	901-259-1300	259-6456	645-98
KA (Kraus-Anderson Co) 523 S Eigth St ... Minneapolis MN 55404 *Web:* www.krausanderson.com	612-332-7281	332-8739	185
K&A Tech Services 1215 Paramount Pkwy ... Batavia IL 60510 *Web:* karanet.com	630-879-1360		180
Kaady Car Washes 7400 SW Barbur Blvd ... Portland OR 97219 *Web:* www.kaady.com	503-246-7735		62-1
KAAL-TV Ch 6 (ABC) 1701 Tenth Pl NE ... Austin MN 55912 *Web:* www.kaaltv.com	507-437-6666	433-9560	741
KAAM-AM 770 (Nost) 3201 Royalty Row ... Irving TX 75062 *Web:* www.kaamradio.com	972-445-1700		645
Kaava Consulting Inc 15190 SW 136th St Ste 24 ... Miami FL 33196 *Web:* kaavainc.com	305-255-5151		196
Kaba Ilco Corp 400 Jeffreys Rd ... Rocky Mount NC 27804 *TF:* 800-334-1381 ■ *Web:* www.kaba-ilco.com	252-446-3321	446-4702	350
Kaba Mas 749 W Short St ... Lexington KY 40508 *Web:* www.mas-hamilton.com	859-253-4744		350
Kaback Enterprises Inc 45 W 25th St ... New York NY 10010 *Web:* www.kaback.com	212-645-5100		256
Kabam Inc 795 Folsom St Ste 600 ... San Francisco CA 94107 *Web:* kabam.com	415-391-0817		366
Kabana Inc 616 Indian School Rd NW ... Albuquerque NM 87102 *Web:* www.kabana.com	505-843-9330		411
KA-BAR Knives Inc 200 Homer St ... Olean NY 14760 *TF:* 800-282-0130 ■ *Web:* www.kabar.com	716-372-5952	790-7188	222
KABB-TV Ch 29 (Fox) 4335 NW Loop 410 ... San Antonio TX 78229 *TF:* 888-538-8541 ■ *Web:* www.foxsanantonio.com	210-366-1129	377-4758	741-116
KABC-AM 790 (N/T) 8965 Lindblade St ... Culver City CA 90232 *TF:* 800-222-5222 ■ *Web:* www.kabc.com	310-840-4900		645-92
KABC-TV Ch 7 (ABC) 500 Cir Seven Dr ... Glendale CA 91201	818-863-7777	863-7080	741
Kabel Business Services 1454 30th St Ste 105 ... West Des Moines IA 50266 *TF:* 800-300-9691 ■ *Web:* www.kabelbiz.com	515-224-9400	224-9256	113
KABF-FM 88.3 (Var) 2101 Main St # 200 ... Little Rock AR 72206 **Fax Area Code:* 504 ■ *Web:* www.kabf.org	501-372-6119	376-3952*	645-91
Kabinart Corp 3650 Trousdale Dr ... Nashville TN 37204	615-833-1961		115
Kable Link Communications 15273 Flight Path Dr ... Brooksville FL 34604 *Web:* www.kablelink.com	352-796-7639		116
Kable News Company Inc 14 Wall St Ste 4C ... New York NY 10005 *Web:* www.kablefulfillment.com	513-671-2800		96
Kabloee Design 8560 Cottonwood St NW Ste 100 ... Minneapolis MN 55443 *Web:* www.kabloee.com	763-785-9595		187
KaBloomcom Ltd 305 Harvard St ... Brookline MA 02446 *TF:* 800-522-5666 ■ *Web:* www.kabloom.com	617-730-9966		292
kabookaboo Marketing LLC 8385 NW 56th St ... Doral FL 33166 *Web:* www.kabookaboo.com	305-569-9154		195
Kabuki Japanese Restaurant 3539 E Foothill Blvd ... Pasadena CA 91107 *Web:* kabukirestaurants.com	253-474-1650		671
Kabuki Japanese Steak House 3503 Franklin Rd SW ... Roanoke VA 24014 *Web:* kabukiva.com	540-981-0222		671
Kabuki Japanese Steakhouse 8130 I 40 W ... Amarillo TX 79106 *TF:* 800-442-1162 ■ *Web:* kabukiromanza.com	806-358-7799		671
Kabul Afghan Cuisine 2301 N 45th St ... Seattle WA 98103 *Web:* www.kabulrestaurant.com	206-545-9000		671
Kabuto Inc 13158 Midlothian Tpke ... Midlothian VA 23113 *Web:* kabutorichmond.com	804-379-7979		671
Kabuto Sushi 5121 Geary Blvd ... San Francisco CA 94118	415-752-5652		671
KABX-FM 97.5 (Oldies) 1020 W Main St ... Merced CA 95340 *TF:* 800-350-3777 ■ *Web:* www.975kabx.com	209-723-2191	205-1013	645
KABZ-FM 103.7 (N/T) 2400 Cottondale Ln ... Little Rock AR 72202 *TF:* 800-477-1037 ■ *Web:* www.1037thebuzz.com	501-661-1037	664-5871	645-91
KAC (Kansas Assn of Counties) 300 SW Eigth St 3rd Fl ... Topeka KS 66603 *Web:* www.kansascounties.org	785-272-2585	272-3585	49-7
KAC (Korean American Coalition) 3727 W Sixth St Ste 305 ... Los Angeles CA 90020 *Web:* www.kacla.org	213-365-5999	380-7990	48-14
KACL-FM 98.7 (Oldies) 4303 Memorial Hwy ... Mandan ND 58554 *Web:* www.cool987fm.com	701-663-9898		645
KACU-FM 89.7 (NPR) 1925 Campus Ct ... Abilene TX 79699 *Web:* www.kacu.org	325-674-2441	674-2417	645-1
KACV-FM 90 (Alt) PO Box 447 ... Amarillo TX 79178 *TF:* 800-766-0176 ■ *Web:* www.kacvfm.org	800-766-0176		645-5
KACV-TV Ch 2 (PBS) PO Box 447 ... Amarillo TX 79178 *TF:* 800-638-9238 ■ *Web:* www.kacvtv.org	806-371-5222	371-5258	741-4
Kadant Black Clawson Inc 7312 Central Pk Blvd ... Mason OH 45040 *Web:* www.kadant.com	513-229-8100		556
Kadant Inc 1 Technology Pk Dr ... Westford MA 01886 *NYSE:* KAI ■ *TF:* 800-937-5449 ■ *Web:* www.kadant.com	978-776-2000	635-1593	556
Kaddis Mfg Corp 293 Patriot Wy PO Box 92985 ... Rochester NY 14692 *TF:* 800-394-5808 ■ *Web:* www.kaddis.com	585-464-9000	464-0008	621

	Phone	Fax	Class
KADI-FM 99.5 (Rel) 5431 W Sunshine St. . . . . Brookline Station MO 65619 *Web:* kadi.com	417-831-0995	831-4026	645
Kadlec Regional Medical Ctr 888 Swift Blvd . . . . Richland WA 99352 *TF:* 800-780-6067 ■ *Web:* www.kadlec.org	509-946-4611	942-2679	374-3
Kaena Point State Park 1151 Punchbowl St Rm 310. . . . . Honolulu HI 96813 *Web:* dlnr.hawaii.gov/dsp	808-587-0300		565
Kaepa USA Inc 9050 Autobahn Dr Ste 500 . . . . . . Dallas TX 75237 *TF:* 800-880-9200 ■ *Web:* www.kaepa.com	800-880-9200		301
Kaeser & Blair Inc 4236 Grissom Dr . . . . . . Batavia OH 45103 *TF:* 800-642-0790 ■ *Web:* kaeser-blair.com	800-642-0790		366
Kaeser Compressors Inc PO Box 946 . . . . Fredericksburg VA 22404 *Web:* www.kaeser.com	540-898-5500	898-5520	172
Kafafian Group Inc, The 2001 Rt 46 Ste 310. . . . . Parsippany NJ 07054 *Web:* www.kafafiangroup.com	973-299-0300	299-1002	734
KAFF-AM 930 (Ctry) 1117 W Rt 66. . . . . Flagstaff AZ 86001 *Web:* kaff.gcmaz.com	928-774-5231	779-2988	645-59
KAFF-FM 92.9 (Ctry) 1117 W Rt 66 . . . . Flagstaff AZ 86001 *Web:* kaff.gcmaz.com	928-774-5231	779-2988	645-59
KAFL Inc 85 Allen St Ste 300 . . . . Rochester NY 14608 *TF:* 800-272-6488 ■ *Web:* kafl.com	585-271-6400		390
KAFT-TV Ch 13 (PBS) 350 S Donaghey Ave . . . . . . Conway AR 72034 *TF:* 800-662-2386 ■ *Web:* www.aetn.org	501-682-2386	682-4122	741
KAG (Kenan Advantage Group Inc) 4366 Mt Pleasant St NW. . . . . North Canton OH 44720 *TF:* 800-969-5419 ■ *Web:* www.thekag.com	330-491-0474	409-2786	780
KAG West 4076 Seaport Blvd . . . . West Sacramento CA 95691 *TF:* 800-547-1587 ■ *Web:* www.thekag.com	916-371-8241	372-1760	780
Kagan 981 Calle Amanecer . . . . San Clemente CA 92673 *TF:* 800-933-2667 ■ *Web:* www.kaganonline.com	949-369-6310		530
Kagan Binder PLLC 221 Main St N Ste 200 . . . . Stillwater MN 55082 *Web:* www.kaganbinder.com	651-351-2900		428
Kagi Inc 1442-A Walnut St Ste 392 . . . . Berkeley CA 94709 *Web:* www.kagi.com	510-658-5244		387
Kagome Creative Foods LLC 710 N Pearl St . . . . Osceola AR 72370 *Web:* www.kagomeusa.com	870-563-2601		296-30
Kahala Corp 9311 E Via de Ventura . . . . Scottsdale AZ 85258 *Web:* www.blimpie.com	480-362-4800	362-4812	670
Kahala Hotel & Resort, The 5000 Kahala Ave. . . . . Honolulu HI 96816 *TF:* 800-367-2525 ■ *Web:* www.kahalaresort.com	808-739-8938		707
Kahala Mandarin Oriental Hotel Hawaii Resort 5000 Kahala Ave. . . . . Honolulu HI 96816 *TF:* 800-367-2525 ■ *Web:* www.kahalaresort.com	808-739-8888	739-8800	379
Kahala Travel 3838 Camino Del Rio N Ste 300. . . . . San Diego CA 92108 *TF:* 800-852-8338 ■ *Web:* www.kahalatravel.com	619-282-8300		772
Kahan Jewelry Corp 1156 Ave. . . . . New York NY 10036	212-719-1055		407
Kahiki Foods Inc 1100 Morrison Rd. . . . . Columbus OH 43230 *TF:* 855-524-4540 ■ *Web:* www.kahiki.com	614-322-3180		296-36
Kahler Grand Hotel, The 20 Second Ave SW Ste G13 . . . . Rochester MN 55902 *TF:* 800-533-1655 ■ *Web:* www.kahler.com	507-280-6200		671
Kahler Slater Inc 111 W Wisconsin Ave. . . . . Milwaukee WI 53203 *Web:* www.kahlerslater.com	414-272-2000		195
Kahn Consulting Inc PO Box 1045. . . . . Highland Park IL 60035 *Web:* www.kahnconsultinginc.com	847-266-0722		463
Kahn Litwin Renza & Company Ltd 951 N Main St . . . . Providence RI 02904 *TF:* 888-557-8557 ■ *Web:* www.kahnlitwin.com	401-274-2001		2
Kahn Lucas Lancaster Inc 112 W 34th St Ste 600 . . . . New York NY 10120 *Web:* www.kahnlucas.com	212-244-4500		155-4
Kahn Media Inc 11988 Challenger Ct Ste 102 . . . . Moorpark CA 93021 *Web:* www.kahnmedia.com	818-881-5246		636
Kahn Soares & Conway LLP 1415 L St Ste 400. . . . . Sacramento CA 95814 *TF:* 800-517-6222 ■ *Web:* www.ksclawyers.com	916-448-3826		428
Kahului Airport 1 Kahului Airport Rd. . . . . Kahului HI 96732 *TF:* 800-321-3712 ■ *Web:* www.hawaii.gov/ogg	808-872-3830	872-3829	27
Kahului Trucking & Storage Inc 140 Hobron Ave . . . . Kahului HI 96732 *TF:* 800-882-8811 ■ *Web:* kahuluitrucking.com	808-877-5001	877-0572	780
Kahuna Inc 555 Bryant St Ste 322 . . . . Palo Alto CA 94301 *TF:* 844-465-2486 ■ *Web:* www.kahuna.com	844-465-2486		387
KAI (Kingsway America Inc) 150 NW Pt Blvd . . . . Elk Grove Village IL 60007 *TF:* 800-232-0631 ■ *Web:* kaiadvantage.com	847-700-9100		360-4
Kai 20 Jay St Ste 530. . . . . Brooklyn NY 11201 *TF:* 888-832-7832 ■ *Web:* www.itoen.com	718-250-4000	246-1325	671
KAI USA ltd 18600 SW Teton Ave. . . . . Tualatin OR 97062 *Web:* kershaw.kaiusaltd.com	503-682-1966	682-7168	222
Kaiam Corp 39655 Eureka Dr. . . . . Newark CA 94560 *Web:* www.kaiam.com	510-226-8100	474-3155	735
KAIL-TV Ch 7 1066 E Shaw Ave. . . . . Fresno CA 93710 *Web:* www.kail.tv	559-230-1980	230-1981	741
Kailua Chamber of Commerce 600 Kailua Rd Ste 107 . . . . Kailua HI 96734 *TF:* 888-261-7997 ■ *Web:* kailuachamber.com	808-261-2727		139
KAIM-FM 95.5 (Rel) 1160 N King St . . . . Honolulu HI 96817 *Web:* www.thefishhawaii.com	808-296-3474		645-73
Kaine Tim (Sen D - VA) 231 Russell Senate Office Bldg. . . . . Washington DC 20510 *Web:* www.kaine.Senate.gov	202-224-4024	228-6363	342-2
Kairos Autonomi Inc 508 W 8360 S. . . . . Sandy UT 84070 *Web:* www.kairosautonomi.com	801-255-2950		647
Kaiser Air Cond & Sheet Metal Inc 600 Pacific Ave. . . . . Oxnard CA 93030 *Web:* kaiserac.com	805-988-1800		189-10
Kaiser Aluminum Canada Ltd 3021 Gore Rd . . . . London ON N5V5A9 *Web:* www.kaiseral.com	519-457-3610		492
Kaiser Aluminum Corp 27422 Portola Pkwy Ste 200. . . . . Foothill Ranch CA 92610 *TF Sales:* 800-873-2011 ■ *Web:* www.kaiseraluminum.com	949-614-1740	614-1930	485
Kaiser Assoc 1615 L St NW 13th Fl . . . . Washington DC 20036 *Web:* www.kaiserassociates.com	202-454-2000		194
Kaiser Financial Services 3087 Winch Rd. . . . . Springfield IL 62707 *Web:* www.kaiserfinancial.com	217-787-4845		251
Kaiser Foundation Health Plan Inc 1 Kaiser Plaza. . . . . Oakland CA 94612 **Fax Area Code:* 510 ■ *TF:* 800-464-4000 ■ *Web:* healthy.kaiserpermanente.org	408-972-3000	271-6493*	391-3
Kaiser Foundation Health Plan of Colorado 2500 S Havanna St. . . . . Aurora CO 80014 *TF:* 800-476-2167	800-476-2167		391-3
Kaiser Grille 205 S Palm Canyon Dr. . . . . Palm Springs CA 92262 *Web:* www.restaurantsofpalmsprings.com	760-323-1003		671
Kaiser Permanente 1 Kaiser Plaza 19th Fl. . . . . Oakland CA 94612 *Web:* healthy.kaiserpermanente.org	510-271-5953	271-6493	374-3
Kaiser Permanente 3495 Piedmont Rd NE 9 Piedmont Centery . . . . . . Atlanta GA 30305 *TF:* 800-611-1811 ■ *Web:* medicare.kaiserpermanente.org	404-364-7000		391-3
Kaiser Permanente 6041 Cadillac Ave. . . . . Los Angeles CA 90034 *TF:* 800-954-8000 ■ *Web:* healthy.kaiserpermanente.org	800-954-8000		374-3
Kaiser Permanente 3600 Broadway. . . . . Oakland CA 94611 *TF:* 800-464-4000 ■ *Web:* healthy.kaiserpermanente.org	510-752-1000		391-3
Kaiser Permanente Fontana Medical Center 9961 Sierra Ave . . . . Fontana CA 92335	909-427-5000		374-3
Kaiser Permanente Foundation Hospital 9400 E Rosecrans Ave . . . . Bellflower CA 90706 *TF:* 800-218-0594	510-271-5800	267-7524	374-3
Kaiser Permanente Harbor City Medical Ctr 25825 S Vermont Ave. . . . . Harbor City CA 90710 *TF:* 800-464-4000 ■ *Web:* healthy.kaiserpermanente.org	310-325-5111		374-3
Kaiser Permanente Hawaii 1292 Waianuenue Ave . . . . Hilo HI 96720 *TF:* 800-966-5955 ■ *Web:* kpinhawaii.com	808-334-4400		391-3
Kaiser Permanente Hayward Medical Ctr 27400 Hesperian Blvd . . . . Hayward CA 94545	510-454-1000		374-3
Kaiser Permanente Hospital 441 N Lakeview Ave . . . . Anaheim CA 92807 *TF:* 800-464-4000 ■ *Web:* healthy.kaiserpermanente.org	714-279-4000	279-5590	374-3
Kaiser Permanente Los Angeles Medical Ctr 4867 Sunset Blvd. . . . . Los Angeles CA 90027 *Web:* healthy.kaiserpermanente.org	323-783-4011		374-3
Kaiser Permanente Medical Center-South Sacramento 6600 Bruceville Rd . . . . Sacramento CA 95823 *TF:* 800-464-4000 ■ *Web:* mydoctor.kaiserpermanente.org	916-688-2000		374-3
Kaiser Permanente Medical Ctr 710 Lawrence Expy. . . . . Santa Clara CA 95051 *TF:* 800-464-4000 ■ *Web:* www.kaisersantaclara.org	408-851-1000		374-3
Kaiser Permanente Medical Ctr 3288 Moanalua Rd . . . . Honolulu HI 96819 *Web:* healthy.kaiserpermanente.org	808-432-8000		374-3
Kaiser Permanente Medical Ctr 1200 El Camino Real . . . . South San Francisco CA 94080 *TF:* 800-464-4000 ■ *Web:* healthy.kaiserpermanente.org	650-742-2000		374-3
Kaiser Permanente Medical Ctr San Francisco 2425 Geary Blvd. . . . . San Francisco CA 94115 *TF:* 800-464-4000 ■ *Web:* healthy.kaiserpermanente.org	415-833-2000		374-3
Kaiser Permanente Medicare 1 Kaiser Plaza 19th floor. . . . . Oakland CA 94612 *Web:* medicare.kaiserpermanente.org	510-271-5953	271-6493	374-3
Kaiser Permanente Northwest 500 NE Multnomah St Ste 100 . . . . Portland OR 97232 *TF:* 800-813-2000 ■ *Web:* healthy.kaiserpermanente.org	503-813-2000		391-3
Kaiser Permanente Panorama City Medical Ctr 13652 Cantara St . . . . Panorama City CA 91402 *Web:* healthy.kaiserpermanente.org	818-375-2000		374-3
Kaiser Permanente Parma Medical Ctr 12301 Snow Rd . . . . Cleveland OH 44130 *TF:* 800-686-7100 ■ *Web:* healthy.kaiserpermanente.org	216-362-2000		374-3
Kaiser Permanente Riverside Medical Ctr 10800 Magnolia Ave. . . . . Riverside CA 92505 *TF Cust Svc:* 800-464-4000 ■ *Web:* healthy.kaiserpermanente.org	951-353-2000	353-3055	374-3
Kaiser Permanente Walnut Creek Medical Ctr 1425 S Main St. . . . . Walnut Creek CA 94596 *TF:* 800-464-4000 ■ *Web:* mydoctor.kaiserpermanente.org	925-295-4000		374-3
Kaiser Systems Inc (KSI) 126 Sohier Rd . . . . Beverly MA 01915 *Web:* www.kaisersys.com	978-922-9300		253
Kaiser Ventures LLC 3633 Inland Empire Blvd Ste 480. . . . . Ontario CA 91764	909-483-8500		804
KaiserAir Inc 8735 Earhart Rd PO Box 2626 . . . . Oakland CA 94621 *TF:* 800-538-2625 ■ *Web:* www.kaiserair.com	510-569-9622	255-5017	13
Kaiser-Francis Oil Co 6733 S Yale Ave . . . . Tulsa OK 74136 *Web:* www.kfoc.net	918-494-0000		539
KAJN-FM 102.9 (Rel) 110 W Third St PO Box 1469. . . . . Crowley LA 70527 *TF:* 800-364-7238 ■ *Web:* www.kajn.com	337-783-1560	783-1674	645
KAKE-TV Ch 10 (ABC) 1500 NW St. . . . . Wichita KS 67203 *Web:* www.kake.com	316-943-4221	943-5374	741-142
Kakivik Asset Management LLC 560 E 34th Ave Ste 200 . . . . Anchorage AK 99503 *Web:* www.kakivik.com	907-770-9400	770-9450	567
Kakkis Everylife Foundation 77 Digital Dr Ste 210 . . . . Novato CA 94949 *Web:* everylifefoundation.org	415-884-0223		305
KAKM-TV Ch 7 (PBS) 3877 University Dr. . . . . Anchorage AK 99508 *TF:* 800-478-8255 ■ *Web:* www.alaskapublic.org	907-550-8400	550-8401	741-5
Kal Plastics 2050 E 48th St. . . . . Los Angeles CA 90058 *TF:* 800-321-3925 ■ *Web:* www.kal-plastics.com	323-581-6194	581-1805	602

Phone | Fax | Class

Kal Tire Ltd
1540 Kalamalka Lake Rd PO Box 1240 Vernon BC V1T6V2 250-542-2366 754
Web: www.kaltire.com

Kalahari Resorts
1305 Kalahari Dr. Wisconsin Dells WI 53965 608-254-5466 378
Web: www.kalahariresorts.com

Kalamata's 3764 Hillsboro Pike Nashville TN 37215 615-383-8700 671
Web: www.eatatkalamatas.com

Kalamazoo College 1200 Academy St Kalamazoo MI 49006 269-337-7166 337-7390* 166
**Fax:* Admissions ■ *TF Admissions:* 800-253-3602 ■ *Web:* www.kzoo.edu

Kalamazoo Community Foundation
151 S Rose St Ste 332 Kalamazoo MI 49007 269-381-4416 48-20
Web: www.kalfound.org

Kalamazoo County
201 W Kalamazoo Ave Kalamazoo MI 49007 269-383-8840 384-8143 338
Web: www.kalcounty.com

Kalamazoo County Convention & Visitors Bureau
141 E Michigan Ave Ste 100 Kalamazoo MI 49007 269-488-9000 488-0050 206
TF: 800-888-0509 ■ *Web:* www.discoverkalamazoo.com

Kalamazoo Gospel Mission
448 N Burdick St Kalamazoo MI 49007 269-345-2974 48-20
Web: kzoogospel.org

Kalamazoo Psychiatric Hospital
1312 Oakland Dr. Kalamazoo MI 49008 269-337-3000 374-5
TF: 888-509-7007 ■ *Web:* michigan.gov

Kalamazoo Public Library
315 S Rose St. Kalamazoo MI 49007 269-342-9837 434-3
Web: www.kpl.gov

Kalamazoo Speedway 7656 Ravine Rd Kalamazoo MI 49009 269-349-3978 515
Web: www.kalamazoospeedway.com

Kalamazoo Symphony Orchestra
359 S Kalamazoo Mall Ste 100 Kalamazoo MI 49007 269-349-7759 349-9229 573-3
Web: www.kalamazoosymphony.com

Kalamazoo Technical Furniture
6450 Vly Industrial Dr. Kalamazoo MI 49009 800-832-5227 420
TF: 800-832-5227 ■ *Web:* www.teclab.com

Kalamazoo Valley Community College
Arcadia Commons 202 N Rose St Kalamazoo MI 49007 269-373-7800 373-7892 162
Web: kvcc.edu
Texas Township 6767 W 'O' Ave. Kalamazoo MI 49003 269-488-4400 488-4161* 162
**Fax:* Admissions ■ *TF:* 800-221-2001 ■ *Web:* www.kvcc.edu

Kalamazoo Valley Plant Growers Cooperative Inc
8937 Krum Ave. Galesburg MI 49053 800-253-4898 342-1644* 186
**Fax Area Code:* 269 ■ *TF:* 800-253-4898 ■ *Web:* www.kvpg.com

Kalani Oceanside Retreat
12-6860 Kapoho Kalapana Rd Pahoa HI 96778 808-965-7828 965-0527 673
TF: 800-800-6886 ■ *Web:* www.kalani.com

Kalas Manufacturing Inc
167 Greenfield Rd. Lancaster PA 17601 717-336-5575 945-1002 813
Web: www.kalaswire.com

Kalaupapa National Historical Park
PO Box 2222 Kalaupapa HI 96742 808-567-6802 567-6729 564
Web: www.nps.gov

Kalba International Inc
116 McKinley Ave. New Haven CT 06515 203-397-2199 196
Web: www.kalbainternational.com

Kal-blue Reprographics Inc
914 E Vine St Kalamazoo MI 49001 269-349-8681 113
TF: 800-522-0541 ■ *Web:* www.kalblue.com

Kalcor Coatings Company Inc
37721 Stevens Blvd Willoughby OH 44094 440-946-4700 550
Web: www.kalcor.com

Kaleel Jamison Consulting Group Inc, The
5 Third St Ste 230 Troy NY 12180 518-271-7000 463
Web: www.kjcg.com

Kaleidescape 440 Potrero Ave Sunnyvale CA 94085 650-625-6100 52
Web: kaleidescape.com

Kaleidoscope
2500 Grand Blvd PO Box 419580 Kansas City MO 64108 816-274-8301 521
Web: hallmarkkaleidoscope.com

Kaleo Software Inc
2041 Rosecrans Ave Ste 245 El Segundo CA 90245 424-277-5597 387
TF: 888-937-8945 ■ *Web:* www.kaleosoftware.com

Kalfsbeek & Company Accountancy Corp
4529 Quail Lakes Dr Ste C Stockton CA 95207 209-235-1040 235-1044 2
Web: www.kalfsbeek.com

Kali's Mezze 1606 Thames St Baltimore MD 21231 410-563-7600 671
Web: www.kalismezze.com

Kalian Cos 225 Hwy 35 Navesink N Red Bank NJ 07701 732-741-0054 741-3404 187
Web: www.kalian.com

Kalibrate Technologies PLC
25B Hanover Rd Florham Park NJ 07932 973-549-1850 178-11
TF Cust Svc: 800-727-6774 ■ *Web:* www.kalibrate.com

Kalida Telephone Co
121 E Main St PO Box 267 Kalida OH 45853 419-532-3218 387
Web: www.kalidatel.com

Kalido 1 Wall St Ste 3 Burlington MA 01803 781-202-3200 178-1
TF: 866-466-3849 ■ *Web:* www.kalido.com

Kalinich Fence Company Inc
12223 Prospect Rd Strongsville OH 44149 440-238-6127 238-2178 279
Web: www.kalinichfenceco.com

Kalispell Area Chamber of Commerce
15 Depot Pk Kalispell MT 59901 406-758-2800 758-2805 139
TF: 800-872-2657 ■ *Web:* www.kalispellchamber.com

Kalispell Regional Medical Ctr
310 Sunnyview Ln Kalispell MT 59901 406-752-5111 374-3
TF: 800-228-1574 ■ *Web:* www.krh.org

Kalitta Charters LLC
843 Willow Run Airport Ypsilanti MI 48198 734-544-3400 21
TF: 800-525-4882 ■ *Web:* www.kalittacharters.com

Kalitta Flying Service
818 Willow Run Airport Ypsilanti MI 48198 734-484-0088 484-3640 12
TF: 800-521-1590 ■ *Web:* www.kalittaair.com

Kalkaska County 605 N Birch St. Kalkaska MI 49646 231-258-3336 338
Web: www.tcchamber.org

Kalkomey Enterprises Inc
14086 Proton Rd Dallas TX 75244 214-351-0461 95
TF: 800-830-2268 ■ *Web:* www.kalkomey.com

Kallista Inc 1227 N Eigth St Ste 2 Sheboygan WI 53081 920-457-4441 375
TF Cust Svc: 888-452-5547 ■ *Web:* www.kallista.com

Kallman & Company LLP
125 S Barrington Pl Los Angeles CA 90049 310-909-1900 2

Kallman Worldwide Inc 4 N St Ste 800 Waldwick NJ 07463 201-251-2600 206
TF: 877-492-7028 ■ *Web:* kallman.com

Kallo Inc 15 Allstate Pkwy Ste 600 Markham ON L3R5B4 416-246-9997 177
Web: www.kalloinc.ca

Kalman Floor Company Inc
1202 Bergen Pkwy Ste 110 Evergreen CO 80439 303-674-2290 674-1238 189-2
TF: 800-525-7840 ■ *Web:* kalmanfloor.com

Kalmanowitz & Lee CPAs Pllc
575 Eighth Ave Ste 1706 New York NY 10018 212-687-2628 2

Kalmar Investments Inc
Barley Mill House 3701 Kennett Pk Wilmington DE 19807 302-658-7575 401
Web: www.kalmarinvestments.com

Kalmar Nyckel Foundation
1124 E Seventh St Wilmington DE 19801 302-429-7447 429-0350 520
TF: 800-643-3779 ■ *Web:* www.kalmarnyckel.org

Kalmar RT Center LLC 103 Guadalupe Dr Cibolo TX 78108 210-599-6541 770
TF: 800-843-3625 ■ *Web:* www.kalmarrt.com

Kalmia Gardens of Coker College
1624 W Carolina Ave Hartsville SC 29550 843-383-8145 97
Web: www.coker.edu

Kalogridis International Ltd
4819 Maple Ave Dallas TX 75219 214-637-0519 21
Web: www.kalogridis.com

Kaloko-Honokohau National Historical Park
73-4786 Kanalani St Ste 14 Kailua-Kona HI 96740 808-329-6881 564
Web: www.nps.gov

Kalopa State Recreation Area
44 3480 Kalaniai Rd Honokaa HI 96727 808-961-9540 961-9599 565
Web: www.hawaii.gov

Kalos Therapeutics Inc
4370 La Jolla Village Dr Ste 400 San Diego CA 92122 850-552-6000 231
Web: www.kalostpx.com

Kalow Technologies Inc
238 Innovation Dr. North Clarendon VT 05759 802-775-4633 757
Web: www.kalowtech.com

Kalsec Inc 3713 W Main St Kalamazoo MI 49006 269-349-9711 382-3060 296-15
TF: 800-323-9320 ■ *Web:* www.kalsec.com

Kalsi Engineering Inc
745 Park Two Dr Sugar Land TX 77478 281-240-6500 240-0255 256
Web: www.kalsi.com

Kalt Manufacturing Co, The
36700 Sugar Ridge Rd North Ridgeville OH 44039 440-327-2102 757
Web: www.kaltmfg.com

Kalustyan Corp 855 Rahway Ave. Union NJ 07083 908-688-6111 123
Web: www.kalustyan.com

Kaluzny Bros Inc 1528 Mound Rd Rockdale IL 60436 815-744-1453 296-12

Kalwall Corp
1111 Candia Rd PO Box 237 Manchester NH 03105 603-627-3861 627-7905 608
TF: 800-258-9777 ■ *Web:* www.kalwall.com

KALW-FM 91.7 (NPR)
500 Mansell St. San Francisco CA 94134 415-841-4121 841-4125 645-145
Web: www.kalw.org

Kalypsys Inc 10420 Wateridge Cir. San Diego CA 92121 858-552-0674 583

Kam Companies Inc
3982 New Vision Dr Fort Wayne IN 46845 260-432-4432 175
Web: kamcompanies.com

Kam's 4500 Montrose Blvd Houston TX 77006 713-529-5057 529-5486 671
Web: kamscuisine.com

Kaman Aerospace Corp
Old Windsor Rd PO Box 2 Bloomfield CT 06002 860-242-4461 243-7514 20
Web: www.kaman.com

Kaman Corp PO Box 1 Bloomfield CT 06002 860-243-7100 185
NYSE: KAMN ■ *TF:* 866-450-3663 ■ *Web:* www.kaman.com

Kamatics Corp 1330 Blue Hills Ave. Bloomfield CT 06002 860-243-9704 243-7993 620
Web: www.kaman.com

Kamco Supply Corp of Boston
181 New Boston St. Woburn MA 01801 781-938-0909 191-1
Web: www.kamcoboston.com

KAMC-TV Ch 28 (ABC)
7403 S University Ave. Lubbock TX 79423 806-745-2345 748-2250 741-78
Web: everythinglubbock.com

KAMedData.com Inc
4400 Bayou Blvd Ste 12 Pensacola FL 32503 850-477-2475 194
Web: www.kameddata.com

Kamet Manufacturing Solutions
171 Commercial St. Sunnyvale CA 94086 408-522-8000 454
TF: 800-888-2089 ■ *Web:* www.kamet.com

Kamiya Biomedical Co 12779 Gateway Dr Seattle WA 98168 206-575-8068 575-8094 231
TF: 800-526-4925 ■ *Web:* www.kamiyabiomedical.com

Kamloops Chamber of Commerce
615 Victoria St Kamloops BC V2C2B3 250-372-7722 828-9500 137
Web: www.kamloopschamber.ca

Kamloops Daily News 393 Seymour St Kamloops BC V2C6P6 250-372-2331 532-1
Web: www.kamloopsnews.ca

KAMM Consulting Inc
1407 W Newport Ctr Dr Deerfield Beach FL 33442 954-949-2200 196
Web: www.kammconsulting.com

KaMMCO (Kansas Medical Mutual Insurance Co)
623 SW Tenth Ave Ste 200 Topeka KS 66612 785-232-2224 232-4704 391-5
TF: 800-232-2259 ■ *Web:* www.kammco.com

Kamminga & Roodvoets Inc
3435 Broadmoor Ave SE Grand Rapids MI 49512 616-949-0800 189-5

Kamon 2210 16th St Sacramento CA 95818 916-443-8888 671
Web: jensaisushi.com

Kamp Synergy 9434 N 107th St. Milwaukee WI 53224 414-354-6700 354-6701 639

Kampai Japanese Restaurant
2367 N Oxnard Blvd Oxnard CA 93036 805-983-3333 671

Kampgrounds of America Inc (KOA)
PO Box 30558 Billings MT 59114 888-562-0000 121
TF: 888-562-0000 ■ *Web:* www.koa.com

Kampi Components Co Inc
88 Canal Rd Fairless Hills PA 19030 215-736-2000 736-9000 770
Web: www.kampi.com

	Phone	Fax	Class
KAMR-TV Ch 4 (NBC) 1015 S Fillmore St........Amarillo TX 79101 *Web:* myhighplains.com	806-383-3321	220-0941	741-4
Kamsky Assoc Inc 563 Park Ave........New York NY 10065 *Web:* www.kamsky.com	212-317-1116		194
KANA Software Inc 840 W California Ave Ste 100........Sunnyvale CA 94086 *Fax Area Code: 408 ■ *Web:* www.kana.com	650-614-8300	736-7613*	178-7
Kanabec County 18 N Vine St........Mora MN 55051 *Web:* www.kanabeccounty.org	320-679-6466	679-6431	338
Kanaskat-Palmer State Park 32101 Kanaskat-Cumberland Rd........Ravensdale WA 98051 *Web:* www.parks.wa.gov	360-886-0148		565
Kanata Energy Group Ltd 1900 112 - Fourth Ave SW Sun Life Plz III - East Twr........Calgary AB T2P0H3 *TF:* 844-526-2822 ■ *Web:* www.kanataenergy.com	587-774-7000	774-6970	261
Kanatek Technologies Inc 359 Terry Fox Dr Ste 230........Kanata ON K2K2E7 *TF:* 800-526-2821 ■ *Web:* www.kanatek.com	613-591-1482		180
Kanawha County 409 Virginia St E........Charleston WV 25301 *Web:* www.kanawha.us	304-357-0130	357-0585	338
Kanawha Hospice Care 1606 Kanawha Blvd W........Charleston WV 25387 *TF:* 800-560-8523 ■ *Web:* www.hospicecarewv.org	304-768-8523		371
Kanawha Manufacturing Co 1520 Dixie St........Charleston WV 25311 *Web:* www.kanawhamfg.com	304-342-6127		234
Kanawha Scales & Systems Inc Rock Branch Industrial Pk 303 Jacobson Dr........Poca WV 25159 *TF:* 800-955-8321 ■ *Web:* www.kanawhascales.com	304-755-8321		361
Kanawha State Forest 7500 Kanawha State Forest Dr........Charleston WV 25314 *Web:* www.kanawhastateforest.com	304-558-3500		565
Kanawha Stone Company Inc 409 Jacobson Dr........Poca WV 25159 *Web:* www.kanawhastone.com	304-755-8271	755-8274	261
Kandiyohi County 400 Benson Ave SW PO Box 936........Willmar MN 56201 *Web:* www.co.kandiyohi.mn.us	320-231-6202	231-6263	338
Kane County 719 Batavia Ave Bldg A........Geneva IL 60134 *Web:* www.countyofkane.org	630-232-5930	232-9188	338
Kane County 78 S 100 E........Kanab UT 84741 *TF:* 800-733-5263 ■ *Web:* www.visitsouthernutah.com	435-644-5033		338
Kane Furniture Corp 5700 70th Ave N........Pinellas Park FL 33781 *Web:* www.kanesfurniture.com	727-545-9555		321
Kane Graphical Corp 2255 W Logan Blvd........Chicago IL 60647 *Fax Area Code: 773 ■ *TF:* 800-992-2921 ■ *Web:* www.kanegraphical.com	800-992-2921	384-1207*	344
Kane Manufacturing Corp 515 N Fraley St........Kane PA 16735 *TF:* 800-952-6399 ■ *Web:* www.kanesterling.com	814-837-6464		234
Kane Partners LLC 1816 W Point Pike Ste 221........Lansdale PA 19446 *TF:* 800-833-3810 ■ *Web:* www.kanepartners.net	215-699-5500		260
Kane Transport Inc 40925 403rd Ave........Sauk Centre MN 56378 *TF:* 800-892-8557 ■ *Web:* www.kanetransport.com	320-352-2762	352-6141	768
Kanebridge Corp 153 Bauer Dr........Oakland NJ 07436 *TF:* 888-222-9221 ■ *Web:* www.kanebridge.com	201-337-2300		350
Kanematsu USA Inc 500 Fifth Ave 29th Fl........New York NY 10110 *Web:* www.kanematsuusa.com	212-704-9400	704-9483	386
Kanequip Inc 1451 S Second Ave........Dodge City KS 67801 *TF:* 800-359-1108 ■ *Web:* kanequip.com	620-225-0016		429
Kaneva Inc 5901-C Peachtree Dunwoody Rd........Atlanta GA 30328 *Fax Area Code: 770 ■ *Web:* www.kaneva.com	678-367-0555	352-0077*	387
Kanguru Solutions 1360 Main St........Millis MA 02054 *TF Sales:* 888-526-4878 ■ *Web:* www.kanguru.com	508-376-4245	376-4462	173-8
Kanjoya Inc 456 Montgomery St Ste 500........San Francisco CA 94104 *Web:* www.experienceproject.com	650-745-1054		387
Kankakee Community College 100 College Dr........Kankakee IL 60901 *Fax: Admissions ■ *TF:* 800-526-0844 ■ *Web:* www.kcc.edu	815-802-8100	802-8101*	162
Kankakee County 189 E Ct St........Kankakee IL 60901 *Web:* www.co.kankakee.il.us	815-937-2990	939-8831	338
Kankakee Public Library 201 E Ct St........Kankakee IL 60901 *Web:* www.lions-online.org	815-939-4564		434-3
Kankakee River State Park 5314 W Rt 102 PO Box 37........Bourbonnais IL 60914 *Web:* www.dnr.illinois.gov/Parks/Pages/KankakeeRiver.aspx	815-933-1383		565
Kankakee Valley Construction Company Inc 4356 W SR 17........Kankakee IL 60901 *TF:* 800-800-7652 ■ *Web:* www.kvcci.com	815-937-8700	937-0402	188-4
Kanki Japanese House of Steaks 4500 Old Wake Forest Rd........Raleigh NC 27609 *Web:* www.kanki.com	919-782-9708	876-7699	671
Kanki Japanese House of Steaks 3504 Mt Moriah Rd........Durham NC 27707 *Web:* www.kanki.com	919-401-6908		671
Kann Enterprises Inc 209 Amendodge Dr........Shorewood IL 60404 *Web:* www.kannenterprises.com	815-609-7170		358
Kann Manufacturing Corp PO Box 400........Guttenberg IA 52052 *TF:* 800-806-5266 ■ *Web:* www.kannmfg.com	563-252-2035	252-3069	516
Kanomax Usa 250 W 57th St Ste 816........New York NY 10107 *Web:* kanomax-usa.com	212-489-3755		743
Kanopolis State Park 200 Horsethief Rd........Marquette KS 67464 *Web:* ksoutdoors.com/state-parks/locations/kanopolis	785-546-2565		565
Kanpai of Tokyo 2200 Hamilton Pl Blvd........Chattanooga TN 37421 *Web:* www.kanpaioftokyo.com	423-855-8204		671
Kanpai of Tokyo 533 Haywood Rd........Greenville SC 29607 *Web:* www.kanpaioftokyo.com	864-234-0334		671

	Phone	Fax	Class
Kansas			
Accountancy Board 900 SW Jackson St Ste 556........Topeka KS 66612 *Web:* www.ksboa.org	785-296-2162	291-3501	339-17
Aging Dept 503 S Kansas Ave........Topeka KS 66603 *Web:* www.kdads.ks.gov	785-296-4986		339-17
Agriculture Dept 900 SW Jackson Rm 456........Topeka KS 66612 *Web:* agriculture.ks.gov	785-296-3556	564-6777	339-17
Attorney General 120 SW Tenth Ave 2nd Fl........Topeka KS 66612 *TF:* 888-428-8436 ■ *Web:* ag.ks.gov	785-296-2215	296-6296	339-17
Banking Commissioner 700 SW Jackson St Ste 300........Topeka KS 66603 *Web:* www.osbckansas.org	785-296-2266	296-0168	339-17
Bill Status 300 SW Tenth Ave Ste 551-S........Topeka KS 66612 *Web:* www.kslegislature.org	785-296-2391	296-1153	433
Chief Legal Governor's Office 2nd Fl Capitol Bldg........Topeka KS 66612 *Web:* www.kansas.gov	785-368-8767		339-17
Commerce Dept 1000 SW Jackson St Ste 100........Topeka KS 66612 *Web:* www.kansascommerce.com	785-296-3481	296-5055	339-17
Conservation Commission 1320 Research Park Dr........Manhattan KS 66502 *Web:* agriculture.ks.gov	785-564-6620	564-6778	339-17
Consumer Protection Div 534 S Kansas Ave Ste 1210........Topeka KS 66603 *TF:* 800-452-6727 ■ *Web:* www.kansas.gov	785-296-5059	296-5563	339-17
Corp Commission 1500 SW Arrowhead Rd........Topeka KS 66604 *Web:* www.kcc.state.ks.us	785-271-3100	271-3354	339-17
Corrections Dept 714 SW Jackson Ste 300........Topeka KS 66612 *Web:* www.dc.state.ks.us	785-296-3317		339-17
Cosmetology Board 714 SW Jackson St Ste 100........Topeka KS 66603 *Web:* www.kansas.gov/kboc	785-296-3155	296-3002	339-17
Crime Victims Compensation Board 120 SW Tenth Ave 2nd Fl........Topeka KS 66612 *Web:* ag.ks.gov/victim-services/victim-compensation	785-296-2359	296-0652	339-17
Emergency Management Div 2800 SW Topeka Blvd........Topeka KS 66611 *Web:* www.kansas.gov	785-296-5059	646-1609	339-17
Governmental Ethics Commission 901 S Kansas Ave........Topeka KS 66612 *Web:* ethics.kansas.gov	785-296-4219	296-2548	265
Healing Arts Board 800 SW Jackson Lower Level Ste A........Topeka KS 66612 *TF:* 888-886-7205 ■ *Web:* www.ksbha.org	785-296-7413	368-7102	339-17
Health & Environment Dept 1000 SW Jackson St Ste 540........Topeka KS 66612 *Web:* www.kdheks.gov	785-296-0461	559-4269	339-17
Highway Patrol 122 SW Seventh St........Topeka KS 66603 *Web:* www.kansashighwaypatrol.org	785-296-6800		339-17
Historical Society 6425 SW Sixth Ave........Topeka KS 66615 *Web:* www.kshs.org	785-272-8681	272-8682	339-17
Housing Resources Corp 611 S Kansas Ave Ste 300........Topeka KS 66603 *Web:* www.kshousingcorp.org	785-217-2001	232-8084	339-17
Information Systems & Communications Div 900 SW Jackson........Topeka KS 66612 *Web:* da.ks.gov	785-296-2418	296-1168	339-17
Insurance Dept 420 SW Ninth St........Topeka KS 66612 *TF:* 800-432-2484 ■ *Web:* www.ksinsurance.org	785-296-3071	296-7805	339-17
Judicial Administrator 301 S W Tenth St Kansas Judicial Ctr........Topeka KS 66612 *Web:* www.kscourts.org	785-296-2256	296-7076	339-17
Legislature 300 SW Tenth Ave State Capitol Bldg........Topeka KS 66612 *Web:* www.kslegislature.org	785-296-2391	296-1153	339-17
Lieutenant Governor 300 SW Tenth Ave........Topeka KS 66612 *TF:* 800-766-3777 ■ *Web:* governor.kansas.gov	785-296-2214		339-17
Lottery 128 N Kansas Ave........Topeka KS 66603 *TF:* 800-544-9467 ■ *Web:* kslottery.com	785-296-5700		452
Motor Vehicles Div 915 SW Harrison St........Topeka KS 66612 *Web:* www.ksrevenue.org	785-296-3601		339-17
Real Estate Commission 120 SE Sixth Ave Ste 200 3 Townsite Plz........Topeka KS 66603 *Web:* www.accesskansas.org/krec	785-296-3411	296-1771	339-17
Regents Board 1000 S West Jackson St Ste 520........Topeka KS 66612 *Web:* www.kansasregents.org	785-430-4240	430-4233	339-17
Rehabilitation Services Div 915 SW Harrison Docking State Office Bldg 9th Fl N........Topeka KS 66612 *TF:* 866-213-9079 ■ *Web:* www.dcf.ks.gov	785-368-7471	368-7467	339-17
Revenue Dept 915 SW Harrison St........Topeka KS 66612 *Web:* www.ksrevenue.org	785-296-3909		339-17
Secretary of State 120 SW Tenth Ave 1st Fl........Topeka KS 66612 *Web:* www.kssos.org	785-296-4564	296-4570	339-17
Securities Commission 618 S Kansas Ave 2nd Fl........Topeka KS 66603 *Web:* www.ksc.ks.gov	785-296-3307	296-6872	339-17
Social & Rehabilitation Services Dept 915 SW Harrison St 6th Fl........Topeka KS 66612 *Web:* dcf.ks.gov	785-296-3959	296-2173	339-17
Supreme Court 301 SW Tenth Ave Rm 374........Topeka KS 66612 *Web:* kansas.gov	785-296-2256	296-7076	339-17
Technical Professions Board 900 SW Jackson St Ste 507........Topeka KS 66612 *Web:* www.ksbtp.ks.gov	785-296-3053	296-0167	339-17
Travel & Tourism Development Div 1020 S Kansas Ave Ste 200........Topeka KS 66612 *Web:* www.travelks.com	785-296-2009	296-6988	339-17
Veterans Affairs Commission 700 SW Jackson St Ste 701........Topeka KS 66603 *Web:* kcva.ks.gov	785-296-3976		339-17
Vital Statistics Div 1000 SW Jackson........Topeka KS 66612 *Web:* www.kdheks.gov/vital	785-296-1400		339-17

Phone | Fax | Class

Weights & Measures Div
Forbes Field Bldg 282 PO Box 19282 .... Topeka KS 66619 785-862-2415 339-17
Web: www.kansas.gov
Wildlife & Parks Dept
1020 S Kansas Ave Rm 200 .... Topeka KS 66612 785-296-2281 296-6953 339-17
Web: www.kdwpt.state.ks.us
Workers' Compensation Div
401 SW Topeka Blvd Ste 2 .... Topeka KS 66603 785-296-4000 296-0025 339-17
TF: 800-332-0353 ■ *Web:* www.dol.ks.gov

Kansas Action for Children Inc
720 SW Jackson St Ste 201 .... Topeka KS 66603 785-232-0550 533
Web: www.kac.org

Kansas African American Museum
601 N Water St .... Wichita KS 67203 316-262-7651 520
Web: tkaamuseum.org

Kansas Assn of Counties (KAC)
300 SW Eigth St 3rd Fl .... Topeka KS 66603 785-272-2585 272-3585 49-7
Web: www.kansascounties.org

Kansas Assn of Realtors
3644 SW Burlingame Rd .... Topeka KS 66611 785-267-3610 267-1867 656
TF: 800-366-0069 ■ *Web:* www.kansasrealtor.com

Kansas Aviation Museum
3350 S George Washington Blvd .... Wichita KS 67210 316-683-9242 683-0573 520
Web: www.kansasaviationmuseum.org

Kansas Bankers Surety Co
1220 SW Executive Dr .... Topeka KS 66615 785-228-0000 391-5

Kansas Bar Assn 1200 SW Harrison St .... Topeka KS 66612 785-234-5696 234-3813 72
TF: 800-928-3111 ■ *Web:* www.ksbar.org

Kansas Board of Regents, The
1000 SW Jackson St Ste 520 .... Topeka KS 66612 785-296-3421 296-0983 725
TF: 800-663 1662 ■ *Web:* www.kansasregents.org

Kansas Brick & Tile Inc
767 N US Hwy 281 .... Hoisington KS 67544 620-653-2157 653-7609 150
Web: www.kansasbrick.com

Kansas Building Systems Constructors Inc
1701 SW 41st St .... Topeka KS 66609 785-266-4222 610
Web: kbsci.com

Kansas Chamber of Commerce & Industry
835 SW Topeka Blvd .... Topeka KS 66612 785-357-6321 357-4732 140
TF: 800-221-8185 ■ *Web:* www.kansaschamber.org

Kansas Children's Service League (KCSL)
3545 SW 5th St .... Topeka KS 66606 785-274-3100 48-6
TF: 877-530-5275 ■ *Web:* www.kcsl.org

Kansas Christian Home 1035 SE Third St .... Newton KS 67114 316-283-6600 283-6375 672
TF: 800-733-0388 ■ *Web:* kschristianhome.org

Kansas City Art Institute
4415 Warwick Blvd .... Kansas City MO 64111 816-474-5224 802-3309 164
TF: 800-522-5224 ■ *Web:* www.kcai.edu

Kansas City Aviation Ctr Inc
15325 S Pflumm Rd .... Olathe KS 66062 913-782-0530 63
TF: 800-720-5222 ■ *Web:* www.kcac.com

Kansas City Board of Trade
4800 Main St Ste 303 .... Kansas City MO 64112 816-753-7500 691
Web: www.cmegroup.com

Kansas City Business Journal
1100 Main St Ste 210 .... Kansas City MO 64105 816-421-5900 472-4010 457-5
Web: www.bizjournals.com

Kansas City Chiefs 1 Arrowhead Dr .... Kansas City MO 64129 816-920-9300 920-4570 715-3
TF: 844-323-1227 ■ *Web:* www.chiefs.com

Kansas City Convention & Entertainment Centers
301 W 13th St .... Kansas City MO 64105 816-513-5000 205
TF: 800-767-7700 ■ *Web:* visitkc.com/convention-center/index.aspx

Kansas City Convention & Visitors Assn
1100 Main St Ste 2200 .... Kansas City MO 64105 816-221-5242 206
TF: 800-767-7700 ■ *Web:* www.visitkc.com

Kansas City Electrical Supply Co (KCES)
14851 W 99th St .... Lenexa KS 66215 913-563-7000 246
Web: www.kcelectricalsupply.com

Kansas City Hospice & Palliative Care
1500 Meadow Lake Pkwy Ste 100 .... Kansas City MO 64114 816-363-2600 523-0068 371
Web: www.kchospice.org

Kansas City International Airport
601 Brasilia Ave PO Box 20047 .... Kansas City MO 64153 816-243-5237 243-3171 27
TF: 800-433-7300 ■ *Web:* www.flykci.com

Kansas City Jazz Ambassadors (KCJA)
PO Box 36181 .... Kansas City MO 64171 816-888-4503 48-4
Web: www.kcjazzambassadors.com

Kansas City Kansas Community College
7250 State Ave .... Kansas City KS 66112 913-334-1100 288-7648* 162
**Fax:* Admissions ■ *TF:* 800-640-0352 ■ *Web:* www.kckcc.edu

Kansas City Kansas Convention & Visitors Bureau Inc
901 N Eigth St PO Box 171517 .... Kansas City KS 66117 913-321-5800 206
TF: 800-264-1563 ■ *Web:* www.visitkansascityks.com

Kansas City Kansas Public Library
625 Minnesota Ave .... Kansas City KS 66101 913-551-3280 434-3
Web: links.kckpl.org

Kansas City (KS) City Hall
701 N Seventh St .... Kansas City KS 66101 913-573-5000 573-5210 337
TF: 800-432-2484 ■ *Web:* www.wycokck.org

Kansas City Life Insurance Co
3520 Broadway .... Kansas City MO 64111 816-753-7000 753-4902 360-4
NASDAQ: KCLI ■ *TF:* 800-821-6164 ■ *Web:* www.kclife.com

Kansas City Missouri School District
1211 McGee St .... Kansas City MO 64106 816-418-7000 418-7766 685
Web: www.kcpublicschools.org

Kansas City (MO) City Hall
414 E 12th St .... Kansas City MO 64106 816-513-3360 513-3353 337
Web: www.kcmo.gov

Kansas City Peterbilt Inc
8915 Woodend Rd .... Kansas City KS 66111 913-441-2888 422-5029 62-5
TF: 800-489-1122 ■ *Web:* www.kcpete.com

Kansas City Power & Light Co
1200 Main .... Kansas City MO 64141 816-556-2200 654-1125 787
TF: 888-471-5275 ■ *Web:* www.kcpl.com

Kansas City Public Library, The (KCPL)
14 W Tenth St .... Kansas City MO 64105 816-701-3400 701-3401 434-3
Web: www.kclibrary.org

Kansas City Regional Assn of Realtors Inc, The
11150 Overbrook Rd Ste 100 .... Leawood KS 66211 913-498-1100 652
Web: www.kcrar.com

Kansas City Repertory Theatre
4949 Cherry St .... Kansas City MO 64110 816-235-2700 235-5508 749
TF: 800-745-3000 ■ *Web:* www.kcrep.org

Kansas City Royals
Kauffman Stadium 1 Royal Way .... Kansas City MO 64129 816-921-8000 921-5775 713
TF Sales: 800-676-9257 ■ *Web:* kansascity.royals.mlb.com

Kansas City Southern Railway Co
427 W 12th St .... Kansas City MO 64105 816-983-1303 648
TF: 800-468-6527 ■ *Web:* www.kcsouthern.com

Kansas City Star 1729 Grand Ave .... Kansas City MO 64108 877-962-7827 532-2
TF: 877-962-7827 ■ *Web:* www.kansascity.com

Kansas City Structural Steel Inc
3801 Raytown Rd .... Kansas City MO 64129 816-924-0977 492
TF: 800-381-5497 ■ *Web:* www.kcstructuralsteel.com

Kansas City Symphony
1703 Wyandotte Ste 200 .... Kansas City MO 64108 816-471-1100 471-0976 573-3
TF: 877-829-5590 ■ *Web:* www.kcsymphony.org

Kansas City Zoo 6800 Zoo Dr .... Kansas City MO 64132 816-595-1234 823
Web: www.kansascityzoo.org

Kansas Coliseum 1279 E 85th St N .... Park City KS 67147 316-440-0888 720
Web: www.kansascoliseum.com

Kansas Correctional Industries
PO Box 2 .... Lansing KS 66043 913-727-3249 727-2331 630
Web: kancorind.com

Kansas Cosmosphere & Space Ctr
1100 N Plum St .... Hutchinson KS 67501 620-662-2305 662-3693 521
TF: 800-397-0330 ■ *Web:* www.cosmo.org

Kansas Democratic Party
501 JEFFERSON St Ste 30 .... Topeka KS 66607 785-234-0425 234-8420 616-1
Web: www.ksdp.org

Kansas Expocentre 1 Expocentre Dr .... Topeka KS 66612 785-235-1986 235-2967 205
TF: 800-745-3000 ■ *Web:* www.ksexpo.com

Kansas Gas Service
7421 W 129th St .... Overland Park KS 66213 888-482-4950 787
TF: 888-482-4950 ■ *Web:* www.kansasgasservice.com

Kansas Health Foundation
309 E Douglas .... Wichita KS 67202 316-262-7676 305
TF: 800-373-7681 ■ *Web:* www.kansashealth.org

Kansas Living Magazine
2627 KFB Plaza .... Manhattan KS 66503 785-587-6000 587-6914 457-1
TF: 800-406-3053 ■ *Web:* www.kfb.org

Kansas Medical Mutual Insurance Co (KaMMCO)
623 SW Tenth Ave Ste 200 .... Topeka KS 66612 785-232-2224 232-4704 391-5
TF: 800-232-2259 ■ *Web:* www.kammco.com

Kansas Medical Society
623 SW Tenth Ave .... Topeka KS 66612 785-235-2383 235-5114 474
TF: 800-332-0156 ■ *Web:* kmsonline.org

Kansas Museum of History
6425 SW Sixth St .... Topeka KS 66615 785-272-8681 272-8682 520
TF: 800-279-3730 ■ *Web:* www.kshs.org

Kansas Pharmacists Assn
1020 SW Fairlawn Rd .... Topeka KS 66604 785-228-2327 585
TF: 888-792-6273 ■ *Web:* kansaspharmacistsassociation.wildapricot.org

Kansas Press Assn Inc
5423 SW Seventh St .... Topeka KS 66606 785-271-5304 271-7341 530
TF: 855-572-1863 ■ *Web:* www.kspress.com

Kansas Rehabilitation Hospital
1504 SW Eigth Ave .... Topeka KS 66606 785-235-6600 374-6
Web: www.kansasrehabhospital.com

Kansas Republican Party
2605 SW 21st St PO Box 4157 .... Topeka KS 66604 785-234-3456 228-0353 616-2
Web: www.ksgop.org

Kansas Sports Hall of Fame
515 S Wichita .... Wichita KS 67202 316-262-2038 522
Web: www.kshof.org

Kansas State Nurses Assn (KSNA)
1109 SW Topeka Blvd .... Topeka KS 66612 785-233-8638 233-5222 533
Web: www.ksnurses.com

Kansas State University
119 Anderson Hall .... Manhattan KS 66506 785-532-6250 532-6393* 166
**Fax:* Admissions ■ *TF Admissions:* 800-432-8270 ■ *Web:* www.k-state.edu

Kansas State University-Salina
Kansas State Polytechnic
2310 Centennial Rd .... Salina KS 67401 785-826-2640 166
Web: polytechnic.k-state.edu

Kansas Turnpike Authority (KTA)
9401 E Kellogg .... Wichita KS 67207 316-682-4537 271
Web: www.ksturnpike.com

Kansas University
Edwards 12600 Quivira Rd .... Overland Park KS 66213 913-897-8400 166
Web: www.edwardscampus.ku.edu

Kansas Venture Capital Inc (KVCI)
10601 Mission Rd Ste 250 .... Leawood KS 66206 913-262-7117 262-3509 402
Web: www.kvci.com

Kansas Veterinary Medical Assn
816 SW Tyler St Ste 200 .... Topeka KS 66612 785-233-4141 233-2534 795
TF: 888-545-5862 ■ *Web:* www.ksvma.org

Kansas Wesleyan University
100 E Claflin Ave .... Salina KS 67401 785-827-5541 827-0927* 166
**Fax:* Admissions ■ *TF:* 800-874-1154 ■ *Web:* www.kwu.edu

Kanson Electronics Inc
245 Forrest Ave .... Hohenwald TN 38462 931-796-3050 45
TF: 800-233-9354 ■ *Web:* www.issc-kanson.com

Kanstul Musical Instruments Inc
1332 S Claudina St .... Anaheim CA 92805 714-563-1000 526
Web: www.kanstul.com

Kantar Group 501 Kings Hwy E 4th Fl .... Fairfield CT 06825 203-330-5200 466

Kanto Corp 13424 N Woodrush Way .... Portland OR 97203 503-283-0405 240-0409 143
TF: 866-609-5571 ■ *Web:* www.kantocorp.com

Kantola Productions LLC
55 Sunnyside Ave .... Mill Valley CA 94941 415-381-9363 514
TF: 800-280-1180 ■ *Web:* www.kantola.com

KANU-FM 91.5 (NPR)
1120 W 11th St Kansas Public Radio .... Lawrence KS 66044 785-864-4530 645
TF: 888-577-5268 ■ *Web:* www.kansaspublicradio.org

Phone | Fax | Class

KANW-FM 89.1 (NPR)
2020 Coal Ave SE ... Albuquerque NM 87106 505-242-7163 645-4
Web: www.kanw.com
Kanzaki Specialty Papers
1 Monarch Pl Ste 800 ... Springfield MA 01144 888-526-9254 554
TF: 888-526-9254 ■ *Web:* www.kanzakiusa.com
Kao Specialties Americas LLC
243 Woodbine St PO Box 2316 ... High Point NC 27261 336-884-2214 884-8786 145
TF: 800-727-2214 ■ *Web:* chemical.kao.com
Kap Medical 1395 Pico St ... Corona CA 92881 951-340-4360 261
Web: www.kapmedical.com
KAP Project Services LTD
1200 Hwy 146 Ste 260 ... La Porte TX 77571 281-842-8333 180
Web: www.kap.us.com
Kapak Corp 5305 Parkdale Dr ... St Louis Park MN 55416 952-541-0730 596
Kapalua Villas, The 2000 Village Rd ... Lahaina HI 96761 808-665-9170 669
TF: 800-545-0018 ■ *Web:* www.outrigger.com
KAPCO Inc 1000 Badger Cir ... Grafton WI 53024 262-377-6500 483
Web: www.kapcoinc.com
KAPCO/VALTEC 3120 Enterprise St ... Brea CA 92821 714-223-5400 996-3490 770
Web: kapco-global.com
Kapitan Engineering Inc
802 Franklin St ... Sauk City WI 53583 608-643-6477 256
Web: kapitan-eng.com
Kaplan & Zubrin Inc 146 Kaighns Ave ... Camden NJ 08103 856-964-1083 296-19
Kaplan Computers LLC
61 Tolland Tpke ... Manchester CT 06042 860-643-6474 175
TF: 800-922-8014 ■ *Web:* kaplancomputers.com
Kaplan Devries Inc 1903 Ashwood Ct ... Greensboro NC 27455 336-288-8200 463
Web: www.kaplandevries.com
Kaplan Early Learning Co
1310 Lewisville-Clemmons Rd ... Lewisville NC 27023 336-766-7374 452-7526* 243
**Fax Area Code:* 800 ■ *TF:* 800-334-2014 ■ *Web:* www.kaplanco.com
Kaplan Inc
6301 Kaplan University Ave ... Fort Lauderdale FL 33309 954-515-3993 244
TF Cust Svc: 800-258-2432 ■ *Web:* www.kaplan.com
Kaplan Industries Inc
Route 73 & Morris Ave ... Maple Shade NJ 08052 856-779-8181 385
Web: www.kaplanindustries.com
Kaplan McLaughlin Diaz
222 Vallejo St ... San Francisco CA 94111 415-398-5191 261
Web: www.kmdarchitects.com
Kaplan Mrd Inc 31 Chesley Rd ... White Plains NY 10605 914-686-1450 466
Web: kaplanmrd.com
Kaplan Telephone Company Inc (KTC)
PO Box 369 ... Kaplan LA 70548 337-643-7171 643-6000 736
TF: 866-643-7171
Kaplan Trucking Co
6600 Bessemer Ave ... Cleveland OH 44127 216-341-3322 341-3348 780
TF: 800-352-2848 ■ *Web:* www.kaplantrucking.com
Kaplan University
6301 Kaplan University Ave ... Fort Lauderdale FL 33309 866-527-5268 588-4127* 800
**Fax Area Code:* 800 ■ *TF:* 866-527-5268 ■ *Web:* www.kaplanuniversity.edu
Kaplan University Lincoln 1821 K St ... Lincoln NE 68508 800-987-7734 800
TF: 800-987-7734 ■ *Web:* www.kaplanuniversity.edu
Kaplan University Omaha 5425 N 103rd St ... Omaha NE 68134 402-572-8500 800
TF: 800-987-7734 ■ *Web:* www.kaplanuniversity.edu
Kapp Construction Co
329 Mt Vernon Ave ... Springfield OH 45501 937-324-0134 324-3406 186
Web: www.kappconstruction.com
Kappa Alpha Order
115 Liberty Hall Rd PO Box 1865 ... Lexington VA 24450 540-463-1865 463-2140 48-16
Web: www.kappaalphaorder.org
Kappa Alpha Psi Fraternity Inc
2322-24 N Broad St ... Philadelphia PA 19132 215-228-7184 228-7181 48-16
Web: www.kappaalphapsi1911.com
Kappa Alpha Theta Fraternity
8740 Founders Rd ... Indianapolis IN 46268 317-876-1870 876-1925 48-16
TF: 800-526-1870 ■ *Web:* www.kappaalphatheta.org
Kappa Delta Pi
3707 Woodview Trace ... Indianapolis IN 46268 317-871-4900 704-2323 48-16
TF: 800-284-3167 ■ *Web:* www.kdp.org
Kappa Delta Sorority 3205 Players Ln ... Memphis TN 38125 901-748-1897 748-0949 48-16
TF: 800-536-1897 ■ *Web:* www.kappadelta.org
Kappa Kappa Gamma PO Box 38 ... Columbus OH 43216 614-228-6515 228-7809 48-16
TF: 866-554-1870 ■ *Web:* www.kappakappagamma.org
Kappa Sigma Fraternity
1610 Scottsville Rd ... Charlottesville VA 22902 434-295-3193 296-9557 48-16
Web: www.kappasigma.org
Kappe Associates Inc
100 Wormans Mill Ct ... Frederick MD 21701 301-846-0200 641
Web: www.kappe-inc.com
Kappes, Cassiday & Associates Inc
7950 Security Cir ... Reno NV 89506 775-972-7575 261
Web: kcareno.com
Kappler Inc
115 Grimes Dr PO Box 490 ... Guntersville AL 35976 256-505-4005 505-4151 576
TF: 800-600-4019 ■ *Web:* www.kappler.com
Kappy s Liquors 325 Bennett Hwy ... Malden MA 02148 781-321-1000 443
TF: 800-362-4429 ■ *Web:* www.kappys.com
KAPS-ALL Packaging Systems Inc
200 Mill Rd ... Riverhead NY 11901 631-727-0300 557
Web: www.kapsall.com
Kapstone 1101 Skokie Blvd Ste 300 ... Northbrook IL 60062 847-239-8800 745-3067* 557
**Fax Area Code:* 843 ■ *Web:* kapstonepaper.com
Kapstone Medical LLC
100 E South Main St ... Waxhaw NC 28173 704-843-7852 475
Web: www.kapstonemedical.com
KapStone Paper & Packaging Corp
1101 Skokie Blvd Ste 300 ... Northbrook IL 60062 847-239-8800 205-7551 557
NYSE: KS ■ *Web:* www.kapstonepaper.com
KapStone Paper and Packaging Corp
300 Fibre Way PO Box 639 ... Longview WA 98632 360-425-1550 638
TF: 800-933-7731 ■ *Web:* www.kapstonepaper.com
Kapta Inc 2220 1re Av ... Notre-dame-des-pins QC G0M1K0 418-774-5688 687
Web: kapta.ca
Kaptur Marcy (Rep D - OH)
2186 Rayburn Bldg ... Washington DC 20515 202-225-4146 225-7711 342-2
Web: www.kaptur.house.gov

Kar Laboratories Inc
4425 Manchester Rd ... Kalamazoo MI 49001 269-381-9666 743
Web: karlabs.com
Kar's Nuts 1200 E 14 Mile Rd ... Madison Heights MI 48071 800-527-6887 296-28
TF: 800-527-6887 ■ *Web:* www.karsnuts.com
Karaman Communications Inc
4424 Bragg Blvd Ste 101 ... Fayetteville NC 28303 910-222-1234 179
TF: 800-396-1911 ■ *Web:* www.karamancom.com
Karas & Karas Glass Company Inc
455 Dorchester Ave ... Boston MA 02127 617-268-8800 269-0536 189-6
TF: 800-888-1235 ■ *Web:* www.karasglass.com
Karavan Trailers Inc
100 Karavan Dr PO Box 27 ... Fox Lake WI 53933 920-928-6200 928-6201 763
Web: www.karavantrailers.com
Karbal, Cohen, Economou, Silk & Dunne LLC
150 S Wacker Dr Ste 1700 ... Chicago IL 60606 312-431-3700 428
TF: 800-973-1177 ■ *Web:* www.karballaw.com
Karbone 675 Third Ave Ste 3004 ... New York NY 10017 646-291-2900 219-7168 192
Web: www.karbone.com
Karbra Co 151 W 46th St 10th Fl ... New York NY 10036 212-736-9300 407
TF: 800-527-2721 ■ *Web:* karbra.com
Karcher Group Inc
14221a Willard Rd Ste 1500 ... Chantilly VA 20151 703-631-6626 180
Web: www.karchergroup.com
Kardex Systems Inc 114 Westview Ave ... Marietta OH 45750 740-374-9300 286
TF: 800-639-5805 ■ *Web:* www.kardex.com
Kardium Inc 12851 Rowan Pl Ste 100 ... Richmond BC V6V2K5 604-248-8891 723
TF: 800-567-2899 ■ *Web:* www.kardium.com
Karel Manufacturing Inc
16742 Pawlin Dr ... Schertz TX 78154 210-651-6643 480
Web: www.karelmfg.com
Karen Ann Quinlan Hospice
99 Sparta Ave ... Newton NJ 07860 973-383-0115 383-6889 371
TF: 800-882-1117 ■ *Web:* www.karenannquinlanhospice.org
KARE-TV Ch 11 (NBC)
8811 State Hwy 55 ... Golden Valley MN 55427 763-546-1111 741
Web: www.kare11.com
Karges Furniture Company Inc
4047 Eastern Ave SE ... Grand Rapids MI 49508 616-243-3676 286
Web: www.karges.com
Karges-Faulconbridge Inc
670 County Rd B W ... Saint Paul MN 55113 651-771-0880 261
Web: www.kaa-eng.com
Karl Chevrolet Accessories
1101 SE Oralabor Rd ... Ankeny IA 50021 515-299-4300 791
Web: www.karlchevrolet.com
Karl Ehmer Inc 48 S Ocean Ave ... Patchogue NY 11772 631-289-3448 296-26
TF: 800-325-0026 ■ *Web:* www.karlehmer.com
Karl Storz Endoscopy-america Inc
600 Corporate Pt ... Culver City CA 90230 310-338-8100 475
TF: 800-321-1304 ■ *Web:* www.karlstorz.com
Karl Storz Imaging Inc 175 Cremona Dr ... Goleta CA 93117 805-968-3568 544
TF: 800-796-8909 ■ *Web:* www.optronics.com
Karl Truman Law Office LLC
420 Wall St ... Jeffersonville IN 47130 812-282-8500 428
Web: www.trumanlaw.com
Karl Tyler Chevrolet Inc
3663 N Reserve ... Missoula MT 59808 406-721-2438 57
Web: gmofmontana.com
Karl W Richter Inc 350 Middlefield Rd ... Toronto ON M1S5B1 416-757-8951 351
TF: 077-597-8665 ■ *Web:* www.kwrtools.com
Karl's Transport Inc PO Box 333 ... Antigo WI 54409 715-623-2033 468
TF: 800-922-8707 ■ *Web:* www.karlstransport.com
Karla Colletto Swimwear Inc
319d Mill St NE ... Vienna VA 22180 703-281-3262 711
Web: www.karlacolletto.com
Karls Mechanical Contractors Inc
954 Forward Ave ... Chilton WI 53014 920-849-2050 189-10
Web: karlsmechanical.com
Karma 114 Chestnut St ... Philadelphia PA 19106 215-925-1444 671
Web: karmaphiladelphia.com
Karma Gaming International Inc
1498 Lower Water St ... Halifax NS B3J3R5 902-463-2280 387
KARMA Media Labs LLC
10215 Santa Monica Blvd ... Los Angeles CA 90067 310-722-7027 195
Web: www.karmamedialabs.com
Karman Rubber Co 2331 Copley Rd ... Akron OH 44320 330-864-2161 864-2124 677
Web: www.karman.com
Karmanos Cancer Institute Bone Marrow/Stem Cell Transplant Program
4100 John R St ... Detroit MI 48201 800-527-6266 769
TF: 800-527-6266 ■ *Web:* www.karmanos.org
Karnak Corp, The 330 Central Ave ... Clark NJ 07066 732-388-0300 388-9422 46
TF: 800-526-4236 ■ *Web:* www.karnakcorp.com
Karner Blue Marketing LLC
2 Nott Terr ... Schenectady NY 12308 518-935-4101 5
Web: www.karnerbluemarketing.com
Karnes County 210 W Calvert Ave ... Karnes City TX 78118 830-780-3938 780-4576 338
Web: www.co.karnes.tx.us
Karnes Electric Co-op Inc
1007 N Hwy 123 ... Karnes City TX 78118 830-780-3952 780-2347 245
TF: 888-807-3952 ■ *Web:* www.karnesec.org
Karns Quality Foods Ltd
6001 Allentown Blvd ... Harrisburg PA 17112 717-545-4731 345
Web: www.karns.com
Karo Group Inc
420 W Hastings St 2th FL ... Vancouver BC V6B1L1 403-266-4094 195
Web: www.karo.com
Karol Media
Hanover Industrial Estates
375 Stewart Rd ... Wilkes-barre PA 18706 570-822-8899 627
Karpel Computer Systems Inc
9717 Landmark Parkway Dr Ste 200 ... Saint Louis MO 63127 314-892-6300 892-8035 177
TF: 888-294-7886 ■ *Web:* www.karpel.com
Karpeles Manuscript Library
453 Porter Ave ... Buffalo NY 14201 716-885-4139 520
Web: www.rain.org/~karpeles
Karpeles Manuscript Library Museum
68 Spring St ... Charleston SC 29403 843-853-4651 853-4651 520
Web: www.rain.org

Phone Fax Class

Karpeles Manuscript Library Museum
101 W First St............................Jacksonville FL 32206 904-356-2992 520
TF: 800-584-4781 ■ *Web:* www.rain.org
Karpeles Manuscript Library Museum
407 S 'G' St.................................. Tacoma WA 98405 253-383-2575 520
TF: 800-764-2420 ■ *Web:* www.rain.org
Karpeles Manuscript Library Museum
902 E First St .... Duluth MN 55805 218-728-0630 520
Web: www.rain.org
Karr Barth Assoc Inc
40 Monument Rd .... Bala Cynwyd PA 19004 610-660-4459 401
Web: karr-barthassociates.com
Karrass Seminars
8370 Wilshire Blvd Fl 3 .... Beverly Hills CA 90211 323-951-7500 95
Web: www.karrass.com
Kartchner Caverns State Park
2980 Arizona 90............................ Benson AZ 85602 520-586-2283 565
Web: www.azstateparks.com
Kartemquin Films Ltd
1901 W Wellington Ave ....Chicago IL 60657 773-472-4366 472-3348 514
Web: www.kartemquin.com
Karthauser & Sons Inc
W 147 N 11100 Fond du Lac Ave........... Germantown WI 53022 262-255-7815 255-6920 293
TF: 800-338-8620 ■ *Web:* www.karthauser.net
Karuna Advisors LLP
1550 El Camino Real Ste 250.............. Menlo Park CA 94025 650-328-2758 734
Web: www.karunaadvisors.com
KARVY Global Services (US)
11 Broadway Ste 1568 ....New York NY 10004 212-267-4381 401
Web: www.karvyglobal.com
KAS Oriental Rugs Inc
62 Veronica Ave ....Somerset NJ 08873 800-967-4254 131
TF: 800-967-4254 ■ *Web:* www.kasrugs.com
Kasa Industrial Controls Inc
418 E Avo B .... Salina KS 67401 785-825-7181 825-1663 729
TF: 800-755-5272 ■ *Web:* www.kasacontrols.com
Kasco Fab Inc 4529 S Chestnut Ave............. Fresno CA 93725 559-442-1018 492
Kasco-Sharptech Corp
1569 Tower Grove Ave .... St. Louis MO 63110 314-771-1550 683
Web: www.kascosharptech.com
Kase Equipment Corp 7400 Hub Pkwy .... Valley View OH 44125 216-642-9040 628
Web: www.kaseequip.com
Kaseya Corp 400 Totten Pond Rd Ste 200.........Waltham MA 02451 877-926-0001 196
TF: 877-926-0001 ■ *Web:* www.kaseya.com
Kasgro Rail Corp 121 Rundle Rd ....New Castle PA 16102 724-658-9061 650
TF: 888-203-5580 ■ *Web:* www.kasgro.com
KASH-FM 107.5 (Ctry)
800 E Dimond Blvd Ste 3-370 ....Anchorage AK 99515 907-522-1515 743-5186 645-6
Web: kashcountry1075.iheart.com
Kashmir Fabrics + Furnishings
3191 Commonwealth Dr....................... Dallas TX 75247 214-631-8040 361
Web: www.kasmirfabrics.com
Kashrus Magazine PO Box 204 .... Brooklyn NY 11204 718-336-0544 336-8550 457 18
Web: www.kashrusmagazine.com
Kasich John (R) 77 S High St 30th Fl .... Columbus OH 43215 614-466-3555 466-9354 343
Web: governor.ohio.gov
Kaskaskia College 27210 College Rd .... Centralia IL 62801 618-545-3090 162
TF: 800-642-0859 ■ *Web:* kaskaskia.edu
Kaskaskia River State Fish & Wildlife Area
10981 Conservation Rd .... Baldwin IL 62217 618-785-2555 565
Web: dnr.illinois.gov/lands/Landmgt/PARKS/R4/kaskas.htm
KASL Consulting Engineers Inc
7777 Greenback Ln Ste 104 .... Citrus Heights CA 95610 916-722-1800 256
Web: www.kasl.com
Kaslen Textiles 6099 Triangle Dr ....Commerce CA 90040 323-588-7700 838-0346 746
TF: 800-777-5789 ■ *Web:* www.kaslentextiles.com
Kason Industries Inc 57 Amlajack Blvd.......... Newnan GA 30265 770-304-3000 251-4854 350
TF: 800-935-3550 ■ *Web:* www.kasonind.com
Kaspick & Co
203 Redwood Shores Pkwy Ste 300...... Redwood Shores CA 94065 650-585-4100 401
TF: 800-899-4766 ■ *Web:* www.kaspick.com
Kass Uehling Inc 333 Seventh Ave.............New York NY 10001 212-465-9206 344
Web: www.kassuehling.com
Kassbohrer All Terrain Vehicles Inc
8850 Double Diamond Pkwy .... Reno NV 89521 775-857-5000 857-5010 516
Web: www.pistenbully.com
Kastner & Partners 150 Pico Blvd..........Santa Monica CA 90405 310-458-2000 7
Web: www.kastnernetwork.us
KASW-TV Ch 61 (CW) 5555 N Seventh Ave........ Phoenix AZ 85013 480-661-6161 207-3327 741-99
KASY-TV Ch 50 (MNT)
13 Broadcast Plaza SW................... Albuquerque NM 87104 505-797-1919 741-3
KAT 103.7FM 5010 Underwood Ave ....Omaha NE 68132 402-561-2000 645-115
Web: thekat.iheart.com
Katahdin Iron Works State Historic Site
Peaks-Kenny State Park
401 State Park Rd ....Dover-Foxcroft ME 04426 207-564-2003 565
Web: maine.gov/dacf/mgs/index.shtml
Katahdin Paper Co 50 Main St...........East Millinocket ME 04430 207-723-5131 557
Katahdin Restaurant 27 Forest Ave.............Portland ME 04101 207-774-1740 774-1740 671
TF: 800-690-0415 ■ *Web:* www.katahdinrestaurant.com
Katalyst Data Management LLC
10311 Westpark Dr..........................Houston TX 77042 281-529-3200 539
TF: 855-529-6444 ■ *Web:* www.katalystdm.com
Katalyst Group Inc
15200 Sunset Blvd.................. Pacific Palisades CA 90272 323-327-5366 260
Web: www.katalystgroup.com
Katalyst Surgical LLC
754 Goddard Ave ....Chesterfield MO 63005 888-452-8259 690
TF: 888-452-8259 ■ *Web:* www.katalystsurgical.com
Kataman Metals LLC
7733 Forsyth Blvd Ste 300.................. St. Louis MO 63105 314-863-6699 791
TF: 800-678-4858 ■ *Web:* www.katamanmetals.com
KATB Life Changing Radio
6401 E Northern Lights Blvd................ Anchorage AK 99504 907-333-5282 645-6
Web: www.katb.org
Katcher Vaughn & Bailey Public Relations Inc
401 Church St Ste 2100..................... Nashville TN 37219 615-248-8202 636
Web: www.kvbpr.com

KATC-TV Ch 3 (ABC)
1103 Eraste Landry Rd .... Lafayette LA 70506 337-235-3333 741-70
Web: www.katc.com
Kate B Reynolds Charitable Trust
128 Reynolda Village .... Winston-Salem NC 27106 336-397-5500 723-7765 305
TF: 800-485-9080 ■ *Web:* www.kbr.org
Kate Spade 135 Fifth Ave...................... New York NY 10010 212-358-0420 349
TF: 866-999-5283 ■ *Web:* www.katespade.com
Katech Inc 24324 Sorrentino Ct............. Clinton Twp MI 48035 586-791-4120 247
Web: www.katechengines.com
Katecho Inc 4020 Gannett Ave.............. Des Moines IA 50321 515-244-1212 476
Web: www.katecho.com
Kater-Crafts Bookbinders Inc
4860 Gregg Rd .... Pico Rivera CA 90660 562-692-0665 692-7920 92
Web: www.katercrafts.com
Katharine Beecher
1250 Slate Hill Rd......................... Camp Hill PA 17011 800-233-7082 296-8
TF: 800-233-7082 ■ *Web:* www.padutchcandies.com
Katharine Ordway Preserve
4245 N Fairfax Dr Ste 100 .... Arlington VA 22203 203-226-4991 226-4807 50-5
TF: 800-628-6860 ■ *Web:* www.nature.org
Katherine Delmar Burke School
7070 California St...................... San Francisco CA 94121 415-751-0177 685
Web: www.kdbs.org
Katherine Shaw Bethea Hospital
403 E First St ....Dixon IL 61021 815-288-5531 285-5859 374-3
TF: 800-582-9731 ■ *Web:* www.ksbhospital.com
Kathoderay Media Inc
20 Country Estates Rd .... Greenville NY 12083 518-966-5600 344
Web: www.kathoderay.com
Kathrein Inc Scala Div 555 Airport Rd...........Medford OR 97504 541-779-6500 253
Web: www.kathrein.com
KATH-TV Ch 5 (NBC) 1107 W Eigth St.............Juneau AK 99801 907-586-8384 586-8394 741-67
Web: www.kath.tv
Kathy's Gazebo Cafe
4199 N Federal Hwy .... Boca Raton FL 33431 561-395-6033 671
Web: www.kathysgazebo.com
Kathy's House Inc 600 N 103 St............. Milwaukee WI 53226 414-453-8290 453-8292 372
Web: www.kathys-house.org
Katko John (Rep R - NY)
1620 Longworth HOB.....................Washington DC 20515 202-225-3701 225-4042 342-2
Web: katko.house.gov
Katmai Coastal Bear Tours PO Box 1503......... Homer AK 99603 907-235-8337 760
TF: 800-532-8338 ■ *Web:* www.katmaibears.com
Katmai National Park & Preserve
King Salmon Mall PO Box 7............... King Salmon AK 99613 907-246-3305 246-2116 564
Web: www.nps.gov/katm
KATN-TV Ch 2 (ABC)
516 Second Ave Ste 400.....................Fairbanks AK 99701 907-452-2125 741-47
Web: www.youralaskalink.com
Katonah Museum of Art Inc 134 Jay St .... Katonah NY 10536 914-232-9555 520
Web: www.katonahmuseum.org
KotoSushi 6340 NW Barry Rd................ Kansas City MO 64154 816-584-8883 671
Web: www.katosushi.com
KATP-FM 101.9 (Ctry) 6214 W 34th St ....Amarillo TX 79109 806-355-9777 645-5
Web: blakefm.com/help
KATT-FM 100.5 (Rock)
4045 NW 64th St Ste 600................ Oklahoma City OK 73116 405-607-2309 645-114
Web: www.katt.com
KATU-TV Ch 2 (ABC)
2153 NE Sandy Blvd..........................Portland OR 97232 503-231-4222 741-103
Web: www.katu.com
KATV-TV Ch 7 (ABC) 401 S Main St .... Little Rock AR 72201 501-324-7777 741-75
TF: 800-662-2386 ■ *Web:* www.katv.com
Katy Mills 5000 Katy Mills Cir...........................Katy TX 77494 281-644-5015 644-5001 460
Web: www.simon.com
Katz & Korin PC
The Emelie Bldg 334 N Senate Ave...........Indianapolis IN 46204 317-464-1100 428
TF: 800-464-2427 ■ *Web:* www.katzkorin.com
Katz Abosch Windesheim Gershman & Freedman PA
9690 Deereco Rd Ste 500............Lutherville Timonium MD 21093 410-828-2727 2
Web: www.katzabosch.com
Katz Cassidy An Accountancy Corp
11400 W Olympic Blvd Ste 1050 ....Los Angeles CA 90064 310-477-6300 734
Web: www.katzcassidy.com
Katz Goldstein & Warren PC
2345 Waukegan Rd Ste 150 ....Bannockburn IL 60015 847-317-9500 428
Web: kgwlaw.com
Katz Group
10104-103 Ave 1702 Bell Twr................. Edmonton AB T5J0H8 780-990-0505 237
Web: www.katzgroup.ca
Katz Law Office Ltd 2408 W Cermak Rd..........Chicago IL 60608 773-847-8982 428
TF: 800-352-3033 ■ *Web:* katzlawchicago.com
Katz Sapper & Miller
800 E 96th St Ste 500.....................Indianapolis IN 46240 317-580-2000 580-2117 2
Web: www.ksmcpa.com
Katzkin Leather Interiors Inc
6868 Acco St .... Montebello CA 90640 323-725-1243 453
Web: www.katzkin.com
Kaua'i Chamber of Commerce
2970 Kele St Ste 112 ....Lihue HI 96766 808-245-7363 245-8815 139
Web: www.kauaichamber.org
Kauai Builders Ltd 3988 Halau St ....Lihue HI 96766 808-245-2911 189-7
Kauai Commercial Company Inc
1811 Leleiona St..............................Lihue HI 96766 808-245-1985 780
Kauai Community College 2444 Dole St........... Lihue HI 96822 808-245-8311 245-8220 162
Web: www.kauai.hawaii.edu
Kauai County 4386 Rice St Ste 101................Lihue HI 96766 808-241-4800 241-6207 338
Web: www.kauai.gov
KAUAI KIAHUNA 2253 Poipu Rd Ste B..............Koloa HI 96756 808-742-6411 377
Web: kauai-kiahuna.com
Kauffman Stadium 1 Royal Way............ Kansas City MO 64129 512-434-1542 921-5775* 720
**Fax Area Code:* 816 ■ *TF:* 800-676-9257 ■ *Web:* kansascity.royals.mlb.com
Kauffman Tire Inc
2832 Anvil Block Rd........................ Ellenwood GA 30294 404-762-4944 755
TF: 800-364-4314 ■ *Web:* www.kauffmantire.com
Kauffmann & Assoc Pllc
4350 Brownsboro Rd Ste 170..................Louisville KY 40207 502-893-8067 2
Web: kaacpas.com

Phone | Fax | Class

Kaufman & Kabani
800 S Figueroa St Ste 900 ....Los Angeles CA 90017 213-488-6180 2
Web: kkcpa.com

Kaufman Borgeest & Ryan LLP
23975 Park Sorrento Ste 370................ Calabasas CA 91302 818-880-0993 428
Web: kbrlaw.com

Kaufman Bros LP 800 Third Ave 30th Fl.........New York NY 10022 212-292-8100 690
Web: www.kbro.com

Kaufman Company Inc 19 Walkhill Rd .... Norwood MA 02062 781-255-1000 41
TF: 800-338-8023 ■ *Web:* www.kaufmanco.com

Kaufman County 100 W Mulberry St .... Kaufman TX 75142 972-932-4331 338
Web: www.kaufmancounty.net

Kaufman Lynn Construction Inc
4850 T-Rex Ave Ste 300.................... Boca Raton FL 33431 561-361-6700 186
TF: 800-576-1372 ■ *Web:* www.kaufmanlynn.com

Kaufman Mfg Co
547 S 29th St PO Box 1056.................Manitowoc WI 54221 920-684-6641 686-4103 455
TF: 800-420-6641 ■ *Web:* www.kaufmanmfg.com

Kaufman Rossin & Co PA
2699 S Bayshore Dr .... Miami FL 33133 305-858-5600 856-3284 2
TF: 866-357-9634 ■ *Web:* www.kaufmanrossin.com

Kaumahina State Wayside
54 S High St Rm 101 .... Wailuku HI 96793 808-984-8109 984-8111 565
Web: dlnr.hawaii.gov/dsp

Kavaliro Staffing Services
12001 Research Pkwy Ste 344.................Orlando FL 32826 407-243-6006 260
TF: 800-562-1470 ■ *Web:* www.kavaliro.com

Kavanagh Associates
10585 Rookwood Dr.......................... San Diego CA 92131 858-549-6744 261
TF: 800-876-4766 ■ *Web:* kavassoc.com

Kavarna 143 N Broadway .... Green Bay WI 54303 920-430-3200 671
Web: www.kavarna.com

Kaveri Madras Cuisine
1148 Fulton Ave........................ Sacramento CA 95825 916-481-9970 671
Web: kaverimadrascuisine.com

Kavi Corp 225 SE Main St .... Portland OR 97214 503-234-4220 174
Web: www.kavi.com

Kavinoky Theatre 320 Porter Ave................Buffalo NY 14201 716-829-7668 572
Web: www.kavinokytheatre.com

Kavlico Corp 14401 Princeton Ave ....Moorpark CA 93021 805-523-2000 523-7125 472
Web: www.kavlico.com

Kawada Hotel 200 S Hill St.................Los Angeles CA 90012 213-621-4455 687-4455 379
TF: 800-752-9232 ■ *Web:* www.kawadahotel.com

Kawai America Corp
PO Box 9045 .... Rancho Dominguez CA 90224 310-631-1771 527
TF: 800-215-4334 ■ *Web:* www.kawaius.com

Kawailoa Development Company LP
1571 Poipu Rd Ste 307 PO Box 369...............Koloa HI 96756 808-742-6300 742-7197 379
Web: www.kawailoa.com

Kawaller & Company LLC 162 State St......... Brooklyn NY 11201 718-694-6270 463
Web: kawaller.com

Kawasaki Construction Machinery Copr of America
60 Amlajack Blvd .... Newnan GA 30265 770-499-7000 190
TF: 800-346-3169 ■ *Web:* www.kcmcorp.com

Kawasaki Heavy Industries USA Inc
60 E 42nd St Ste 2501 ....New York NY 10165 212-759-4950 759-6421 360-3
Web: www.khi.co.jp

Kawasaki Motors Corp USA
PO Box 25252 .... Santa Ana CA 92799 949-770-0400 460-5600 710
TF: 866-802-9381 ■ *Web:* www.kawasaki.com

Kawasaki Rail Car Inc
29 Wells Ave Bldg 4......................... Yonkers NY 10701 914-376-4700 650
Web: www.kawasakirailcar.com

Kawasaki Robotics Inc 28140 Lakeview Dr ....Wixom MI 48393 248-446-4100 446-4200 386
Web: robotics.kawasaki.com/en1

Kaweah Delta Hospital
400 W Mineral King Ave......................... Visalia CA 93291 559-624-2000 374-3
TF: 800-717-5670 ■ *Web:* www.kaweahdelta.org

Kawneer Company Inc 555 Guthridge Ct........ Norcross GA 30092 770-449-5555 734-1560 286
Web: www.kawneer.com

Kay & Associates Inc
165 N Arlington Heights Rd Ste 150.........Buffalo Grove IL 60089 847-255-8444 20
Web: www.kayinc.com

Kay Automotive Graphics
57 Kay Industrial Dr ....Lake Orion MI 48359 248-377-4999 377-2097 687
Web: www.kayautomotive.com

Kay Casto & Chaney PLLC
1500 Chase Tower 707 Virginia St E...........Charleston WV 25301 304-345-8900 428
Web: www.kaycasto.com

Kay Chemical Co 8300 Capital Dr............ Greensboro NC 27409 336-668-7290 225-3098* 151
**Fax Area Code:* 651 ■ *TF:* 877-315-1115 ■ *Web:* www.ecolab.com

Kay County 201 S Main St...................... Newkirk OK 74647 580-362-2565 362-3668 338
TF: 800-255-9456 ■ *Web:* www.courthouse.kay.ok.us

Kay Dee Designs Inc
177 Skunk Hill Rd....................... Hope Valley RI 02832 401-539-2400 539-2210 746
TF: 800-537-3433 ■ *Web:* www.kaydeedesigns.com

Kay Dee Feed Company Inc
1919 Grand Ave .... Sioux City IA 51106 712-277-2011 447
TF Cust Svc: 800-831-4815 ■ *Web:* kaydeefeed.com

Kay El Bar Guest Ranch PO Box 2480........ Wickenburg AZ 85358 928-684-7593 684-4497 239
TF: 800-684-7583 ■ *Web:* www.kayelbar.com

Kay Electric Co-op (KEC)
300 W Doolin Ave........................... Blackwell OK 74631 580-363-1260 363-2308 245
TF: 800-535-1079 ■ *Web:* www.kayelectric.coop

Kay Green Design Inc
668 Cherry St Suite A.................... Winter Park FL 32789 407-246-7155 426-7873 393
Web: www.kaygreendesign.com

Kay Jewelers 375 Ghent Rd........................Akron OH 44333 330-668-5000 410
TF: 800-681-8796 ■ *Web:* www.kay.com

Kay Manufacturing Co
602 State St .... Calumet City IL 60409 708-862-6800 862-8122 454
Web: www.kaymfg.com

Kay Park Recreation Corp
1301 Pine St.............................. Janesville IA 50647 800-553-2476 987-2900* 319-4
**Fax Area Code:* 319 ■ **Fax:* Cust Svc ■ *TF Cust Svc:* 800-553-2476 ■ *Web:* www.kaypark.com

Kay Toledo Tag Inc PO Box 5038................ Toledo OH 43612 419-729-5479 729-0315 627
TF: 800-822-8247 ■ *Web:* www.kaytag.com

Kaya 2000 Smallman St .... Pittsburgh PA 15222 412-261-6565 261-1526 671
Web: www.bigburrito.com

Kaya Assoc Inc
101 Quality Cir Ste 120 .... Huntsville AL 35806 256-382-8084 382-8089 194
Web: www.kayacorp.com

Kaydon Ring & Seal Inc
1600 Wicomico St ....Baltimore MD 21230 410-547-7700 576-9059 326
Web: www.skf.com

Kaye Personnel Inc
1868 Marlton Pike E.......................Cherry Hill NJ 08003 856-489-1200 260
Web: kayepersonnel.com

Kaye Rose & Partners Llp
1801 Century Park E Ste 1500 ....Los Angeles CA 90067 310-551-6555 445
Web: www.kayerose.com

Kayem Foods Inc 75 Arlington St............... Chelsea MA 02150 617-889-1600 296-26
TF: 800-426-6100 ■ *Web:* www.kayem.com

Kaye-Smith 4101 Oakesdale Ave SW..............Renton WA 98057 425-228-8600 110
TF: 800-822-9987 ■ *Web:* www.kayesmith.com

Kayhan International Ltd
1475 E Woodfield Rd Ste 104............. Schaumburg IL 60173 847-843-5060 320
TF: 800-937-8353 ■ *Web:* www.kayhan.com

Kayline Processing Inc 31 Coates St ....Trenton NJ 08611 609-695-1449 989-1094 600
Web: www.kayline.com

Kaylor Dental Laboratory Inc
619 N Florence St........................... Wichita KS 67212 316-943-3226 415
TF: 800-657-2549 ■ *Web:* www.kaylordental.com

Kayne Anderson Capital Advisors LP
1800 Ave of the Stars 3rd Fl ....Los Angeles CA 90067 310-282-7900 401
TF: 800-638-1496 ■ *Web:* www.kaynecapital.com

Kaytee Products Inc 521 Clay St...............Chilton WI 53014 920-849-2321 849-7044 578
TF: 800-529-8331 ■ *Web:* www.kaytee.com

KAYU-TV Ch 28 (Fox) 4600 S Regal St...........Spokane WA 99223 509-448-2828 741-127
Web: www.myfoxspokane.com

Kaz Home Environment 250 Tpke Rd....... Southborough MA 01772 508-490-7000 17
Web: www.kaz.com

KAZ Inc 250 Tpke Rd.................... Southborough MA 01772 800-477-0457 37
TF: 800-477-0457 ■ *Web:* www.kaz.com

Kaz Sushi Bistro 1915 I St NW .... Washington DC 20006 202-530-5500 671
Web: www.kazsushibistro.com

Kazak Composites Inc 10f Gill St .... Woburn MA 01801 781-932-5667 193
Web: plasan-na.com

Kazakhstan
Consulate 535 Fifth Ave 19th FL .... New York NY 10017 212-888-3024 370-6334* 257
**Fax Area Code:* 646 ■ *Web:* www.kazconsulny.org
Embassy 1401 16th St NW .... Washington DC 20036 202-232-5488 232-5845 257
Web: www.kazakhembus.com

Kazal Fire Protection Inc
3499 E 34th St ....Tucson AZ 85713 520-323-1518 610
Web: kazalfire.com

Kazan International Inc
190 Main St Ste 101 PO Box 571............ Gladstone NJ 07934 908-901-0900 260
Web: www.kazansearch.com

Kazan, McClain, Satterley & Greenwood
Jack London Market 55 Harrison St Ste 400.......Oakland CA 94607 877-995-6372 466
TF: 877-995-6372 ■ *Web:* www.kazanlaw.com

KAZI-FM 88.7 (Var) 8906 Wall St Ste 203 .... Austin TX 78754 512-836-9544 836-9563 645-14
Web: www.kazifm.org

Kazimierz World Wine Bar
7137 E Stetson Dr......................... Scottsdale AZ 85251 480-946-3004 671
Web: www.kazbar.net

KAZR-FM 103.3 (Rock)
1416 Locust St...........................Des Moines IA 50309 515-280-1350 280-3011 645-48
TF: 800-373-4930 ■ *Web:* www.lazer1033.com

KAZT-TV Ch 7 (Ind) 3211 Tower Rd............. Prescott AZ 86305 928-778-6770 741
TF: 800-264-5449 ■ *Web:* aztv.com

KB Electronics Inc
12095 NW 39th St .... Coral Springs FL 33065 954-346-4900 346-3377 203
TF: 800-221-6570 ■ *Web:* www.kbelectronics.com

KB Environmental Sciences Inc
9500 Koger Blvd N Ste 211 .... Saint Petersburg FL 33702 727-578-5152 192
Web: www.kbenv.com

KB Home 10990 Wilshire Blvd 7th Fl ....Los Angeles CA 90024 310-231-4000 231-4222 653
NYSE: KBH ■ *TF:* 800-304-0657 ■ *Web:* www.kbhome.com

K&B Industries
208 Rebecca's Pond Rd...................... Schriever LA 70395 985-868-6730 386
Web: www.kb-machine.com

KB International LLC
735 Broad St Ste 209 .... Chattanooga TN 37402 423-266-6964 146
Web: www.kbtech.com

KB Partners LLC
600 Central Ave Ste 390................. Highland Park IL 60035 847-681-1270 681-1370 792
Web: www.kbpartners.com

KBA Inc 11201 SE Eighth St Ste 160 ....Bellevue WA 98004 425-455-9720 261
Web: kbacm.com

KBA2 Inc 400 Treat Ave Ste E .... San Francisco CA 94110 415-528-5500 387
Web: www.crowdoptic.com

KBACE Technologies Inc 6 Trafalgar Sq .... Nashua NH 03063 603-821-7000 177
TF: 800-334-4470 ■ *Web:* www.kbace.com

KBAC-FM 98.1 (AAA)
2502 Camino Entrada Ste C ....Santa Fe NM 87507 505-988-5222 645 147
Web: www.santafe.com

Kbaer Design Center
1020 Michigan Ave.......................Sheboygan WI 53081 920-452-9666 610

KBAQ-FM 89.5 (Clas) 2323 W 14th St .... Tempe AZ 85281 480-833-1122 774-8475 645
TF: 800-776-1070 ■ *Web:* www.kbaq.org

KBBK-FM 107.3 (AC) 4343 'O' St .... Lincoln NE 68510 402-475-4567 645-90
Web: www.b1073.com

KBBO-FM 92.1 (AC) 833 Gambell St..........Anchorage AK 99501 907-344-4045 522-6053 645-6
Web: www.921bob.fm

KBBY-FM 95.1 (AC) 1376 Walter St .... Ventura CA 93003 805-642-8595 645
Web: www.951kbby.com

KBC Tools & Machinery Inc
6300 18 Mile Rd......................Sterling Heights MI 48314 586-979-0500 358
Web: www.kbctools.com

KBco The Polarized Lens Co
7328 S Revere Pkwy Unit 208................Centennial CO 80112 303-253-6600 543
Web: www.kbco.net

KBCO-FM 97.3 (AAA) 4695 S Monaco St.........Denver CO 80237 303-444-5600 645
Web: kbco.iheart.com

Name / Address	City	State	Zip	Phone	Fax	Class
KBCY-FM 99.7 (Ctry) 2525 S Danville Dr *Web:* www.kbcy.com	Abilene	TX	79605	325-793-9700	692-1576	645-1
KBEAR 104.1 301 Arctic Slope Ave Ste 200 *Web:* www.kbrj.com	Anchorage	AK	99518	907-344-9622		645-6
KBFB-FM 97.9 (Urban) 13760 Noel Rd Ste 1100 *TF:* 844-787-1979 ■ *Web:* thebeatdfw.com	Dallas	TX	75240	972-331-5400	331-5560	645-44
KBH Corp, The 395 Anderson Blvd *TF:* 800-843-5241 ■ *Web:* www.kbhequipment.com	Clarksdale	MS	38614	662-624-5471		273
KBHC (Kristin Brooks Hope Ctr) 1250 24th St NW Ste 300 *TF:* 800-784-2433 ■ *Web:* www.hopeline.com	Washington	DC	20037	202-536-3200	536-3206	48-17
KBHE-FM 89.3 (NPR) 555 N Dakota St PO Box 5000 *TF:* 800-456-0766 ■ *Web:* www.sdpb.org	Vermillion	SD	57069	605-677-5861	677-5010	645
KBHE-TV Ch 9 (PBS) 555 N Dakota St PO Box 5000 *Fax Area Code: 605 ■ *TF:* 800-333-0789 ■ *Web:* www.sdpb.org	Vermillion	SD	57069	800-333-0789	677-5010*	741
KBHK-TV Ch 44 (CW) 855 Battery St *Web:* cwsanfrancisco.cbslocal.com	San Francisco	CA	94111	415-765-8144		741-120
KBIA-FM 91.3 (NPR) 78 McReynolds Hall *TF:* 800-292-9136 ■ *Web:* www.kbia.org	Columbia	MO	65211	573-882-3431	882-2636	645
KBIQ-FM 102.7 (Rel) 7150 Campus Dr Ste 150 *Web:* www.kbiqradio.com	Colorado Springs	CO	80920	719-531-5438	531-5588	645-39
KBL Healthcare Ventures 150 W 56th St Ste 5901 *Web:* www.kblvc.com	New York	NY	10019	212-319-5555		792
KBLG-AM 910 (N/T) 2075 Central Ave Ste 5	Billings	MT	59102	406-652-5254		645-19
KBM Workspace 160 w santa clara st Ste 102 *Web:* www.kbmworkspace.com	San Jose	CA	95113	408-351-7100	938-0699	320
KBMCO (Keen Battle Mead & Co) 7850 NW 146th St Ste 200 PO Box 171870 *Web:* www.kbmco.com	Hialeah	FL	33016	305-558-1101	822-4722	391-4
KBME-TV Ch 3 (PBS) 207 N Fifth St *TF:* 800-359-6900 ■ *Web:* www.prairiepublic.org	Fargo	ND	58102	701-241-6900	239-7650	741-48
KBMY-TV Ch 17 (ABC) 301 Eighth St S *Web:* wday.com	Fargo	ND	58103	701-223-1700		741-16
KBNP-AM 1410 (N/T) 278 SW Arthur St *TF:* 888-214-9237 ■ *Web:* www.kbnp.com	Portland	OR	97201	503-223-6769		645-128
K-Bob's USA Inc 135 W Palace Ave Ste 300 *Web:* k-bobs.com	Santa Fe	NM	87501	505-982-3438		670
KBOO-FM 90.7 (Var) 20 SE Eighth Ave	Portland	OR	97214	503-231-8032		645-128
KBR Inc 601 Jefferson St *TF:* 800-203-1112 ■ *Web:* www.kbr.com	Houston	TX	77002	713-753-2000		261
KBR Rural Public Power District 374 N Pine St PO Box 187 *TF:* 800-672-0009 ■ *Web:* kbrpower.com	Ainsworth	NE	69210	402-387-1120		245
KBS 160 Varick St Fl 4 *Web:* www.kbsp.com	New York	NY	10013	212-633-0080		4
KBSX-FM 91.5 (NPR) 1910 University Dr *Web:* www.boisestatepublicradio.org	Boise	ID	83725	208-426-3663	344-6631	645-22
KBT Inc 3885 W Michigan St *TF:* 800-860-9455	Sidney	OH	45365	800-860-9455		685
KBTC-TV Ch 28 (PBS) 2320 S 19th St *TF:* 888-596-5282 ■ *Web:* www.kbtc.org	Tacoma	WA	98405	253-680-7700	680-7725	741-123
KBTS Technologies Inc 41461 W 11 Mile Rd *Web:* kbtstech.com	Novi	MI	48375	248-374-1230		196
KBUE-FM 105.5 (Span) 1845 Empire Ave	Burbank	CA	91504	818-729-5300		645
kbull 98.1 Fm 595 E Plumb Ln *Web:* www.nashfm981.com	Reno	NV	89502	775-789-6700	789-6767	645-133
KBXL-FM 94.1 (Rel) 1440 S Weideman Ave *TF:* 877-207-2276 ■ *Web:* www.941thevoice.com	Boise	ID	83709	208-377-3790	377-3792	645-22
KBXX-FM 97.9 (Urban) 24 Greenway Plaza Ste 900 *TF:* 888-407-4747 ■ *Web:* theboxhouston.com	Houston	TX	77046	713-623-2108		645-75
KBYU-TV Ch 11 (PBS) 2000 Ironton Blvd Brigham Young University *TF:* 800-298-5298 ■ *Web:* www.kbyutv.org	Provo	UT	84606	801-422-8450	422-8478	741
KBYZ-FM 96.5 (CR) 4303 Memorial Hwy *TF:* 888-663-9650 ■ *Web:* www.965thefox.com	Mandan	ND	58554	701-663-9600		645
KBZN-FM 97.9 (NAC) 257 East 200 South Ste 400 *Web:* www.kbzn.com	Salt Lake City	UT	84111	801-364-9836	364-8068	645-142
KBZY-AM 1490 (AC) 2659 Commercial St SE Ste 204 *TF:* 800-350-5390 ■ *Web:* www.kbzy.com	Salem	OR	97302	503-362-1490	362-6545	645-128
KC Electric Assn 422 Third Ave *TF:* 800-700-3123 ■ *Web:* www.kcelectric.coop	Hugo	CO	80821	719-743-2431	743-2396	245
KC Hilites Inc PO Box 155 *Web:* kchilites.com	Williams	AZ	86046	928-635-2607	635-2486	438
KC Jones Plating Co 2845 E Ten Mile Rd *Web:* www.kcjplating.com	Warren	MI	48091	586-755-4900		481
Kc Pharmaceuticals Inc 3201 Producer Way *Web:* kc-ph.com	Pomona	CA	91768	909-598-9499		231
Kc Robotics Inc 9000 Le Saint Dr *Web:* www.kcrobotics.com	West Chester	OH	45014	513-860-4442		358
Kc Sign Express Inc 5033 Mackey St *TF:* 800-654-5717 ■ *Web:* kcsignexpress.com	Shawnee	KS	66203	913-432-2500		8
KCAL-FM 96.7 (Rock) 1940 Orange Tree Ln Ste 200 *TF:* 800-996-9591 ■ *Web:* www.kcalfm.com	Redlands	CA	92374	909-793-3554		645-135
KCAL-TV Ch 9 (Ind) 4200 Radford Ave *Web:* losangeles.cbslocal.com	Studio City	CA	91604	818-655-2000		741
KCAQ-FM 104.7 (CHR) 2284 S Victoria Ave Ste 2G *TF:* 877-440-1047 ■ *Web:* q959.fm/contacts	Ventura	CA	93003	805-289-1400		645
KCB 117 E Colorado Blvd Ste 400 *Web:* www.kcbm.com	Pasadena	CA	91105	626-356-0944		194

Name / Address	City	State	Zip	Phone	Fax	Class
KCBD-TV Ch 11 (NBC) 5600 Ave A *Web:* www.kcbd.com	Lubbock	TX	79404	806-744-1414	749-1111	741-78
KCBI-FM 90.9 (Rel) 750 NSt Paul St *Web:* www.kcbi.org	Dallas	TX	76011	817-792-3800		645
KCBS-AM 740 (N/T) 865 Battery St *Web:* sanfrancisco.cbslocal.com	San Francisco	CA	94111	415-765-8758	765-8935	645-145
KCBS-TV Ch 2 (CBS) 4200 Radford Ave *Web:* losangeles.cbslocal.com	Studio City	CA	91604	818-655-2000		741
Kcc Contractor Inc 2664 E Kearney St *Web:* www.killco.com	Springfield	MO	65803	417-883-1204	887-7338	186
KCC Transport Systems Inc 311 W Artesia Blvd *Web:* www.kccusa.com	Compton	CA	90220	310-764-5933		311
KCCI-TV Ch 8 (CBS) 888 Ninth St *Web:* www.kcci.com	Des Moines	IA	50309	515-247-8888		741-40
KCCK-FM 88.3 (Jazz) 6301 Kirkwood Blvd SW *TF:* 800-798-0313 ■ *Web:* www.kcck.org	Cedar Rapids	IA	52404	319-398-5446		645-29
KCCN-FM 100.3 (CHR) 900 Ft St Ste 700 *Web:* kccnfm100.com	Honolulu	HI	96813	808-275-1000		645-73
KCCR-AM 1240 106 W Capitol Ave *TF:* 800-456-0766 ■ *Web:* www.todayskccr.com	Pierre	SD	57501	605-224-1240	945-4270	645-124
KCD Financial Inc 3061 Allied St Ste B *Web:* www.kcdfinancial.com	Green Bay	WI	54304	920-347-3400		401
KCEC-TV Ch 50 (Uni) 777 Grant St 5th Fl *TF:* 800-420-2757 ■ *Web:* www.entravision.com	Denver	CO	80203	303-832-0050	832-3410	741-39
KCEP-FM 88.1 (Urban) 330 W Washington Ave *Web:* kcep.power88lv.com	Las Vegas	NV	89106	702-648-0104		645-88
KCES (Kansas City Electrical Supply Co) 14851 W 99th St *Web:* www.kcelectricalsupply.com	Lenexa	KS	66215	913-563-7000		246
KCET-TV Ch 28 (PBS) 2900 W Alameda Ave *Web:* www.kcet.org	Burbank	CA	91505	747-201-5238		741-76
KCF Technologies Inc 336 S Fraser St *Web:* www.kcftech.com	State College	PA	16801	814-867-4097		261
KCFR-FM 90.1 (NPR) 7409 S Alton Ct *TF:* 800-722-4449 ■ *Web:* www.cpr.org	Centennial	CO	80112	303-871-9191	733-3319	645
KCFX-FM 101.1 (CR) 5800 Foxridge Dr 6th Fl *Web:* www.101thefox.net	Mission	KS	66202	913-514-3000		645
KCG Inc 15720 W 108th St Ste 100 *Web:* www.rewmaterials.com	Lenexa	KS	66219	913-438-4142		347
KCHZ-FM 95.7 (CHR) 5800 Foxridge Dr Fl 6 *Web:* www.957thevibe.com	Mission	KS	66202	913-514-3000		645
KCI 101 495 Benham St *Web:* kc101.iheart.com	Hamden	CT	06514	203-281-9600		645
KCI Aviation 2100 Aviation Way *Web:* www.kciaviation.com	Bridgeport	WV	26330	304-842-3591		317
KCI Construction Co 10315 Lake Bluff Dr *Web:* www.kciconstruction.com	St. Louis	MO	63123	314-894-8888		186
KCI Medical Canada Inc 75 Courtneypark Dr W Unit No 2 *TF:* 800-668-5403 ■ *Web:* www.kci-medical.ca	Mississauga	ON	L5W0E3	905-565-7187		475
KCI Technologies Inc 936 Ridgebrook Rd *TF:* 800-572-7496 ■ *Web:* kci.com	Sparks	MD	21152	410-316-7800		261
KCIT-TV Ch 14 (Fox) 1015 S Fillmore St *Web:* www.myhighplains.com	Amarillo	TX	79101	806-383-3321	322-0123	741-4
KCJA (Kansas City Jazz Ambassadors) PO Box 36181 *Web:* www.kcjazzambassadors.com	Kansas City	MO	64171	816-888-4503		48-4
KCK Chamber 727 Minnesota Ave *Web:* www.kckchamber.com	Kansas City	KS	66101	913-371-3070	371-3732	139
KCKC-FM 102.1 (AC) 508 Westport Rd Ste 202 *Web:* kc1021.com	Kansas City	MO	64111	816-753-4000		645-83
KCLB-FM 93.7 (Rock) 1321 N Gene Autry Trl *TF:* 800-827-2946 ■ *Web:* 937kclb.com	Palm Springs	CA	92262	760-322-7890		645-119
KCLR-FM 99.3 (Ctry) 3215 Lemone Industrial Blvd Ste 200 *TF:* 800-455-5257 ■ *Web:* www.clear99.com	Columbia	MO	65201	573-875-1099		645
KCLU-FM 88.3 (NPR) 60 W Olsen Rd Ste 4400 *Web:* www.kclu.org	Thousand Oaks	CA	91360	805-493-3900		645
KCM Investment Advisors LLC 750 Lindaro St Ste 250 *TF:* 888-287-5555 ■ *Web:* www.kcmadvisors.com	San Rafael	CA	94901	415-461-7788		401
KCMO-AM 710 (N/T) 5800 Foxridge Dr 6th Fl *Web:* www.kcmotalkradio.com	Mission	KS	66202	913-514-3000		645
KCMO-FM 94.9 (Oldies) 5800 Foxridge Dr 6th Fl *Web:* www.949kcmo.com	Mission	KS	66202	913-514-3000		645
KCMQ-FM 96.7 (CR) 3215 Lemone Industrial Blvd Ste 200 *TF:* 800-455-1967 ■ *Web:* www.kcmq.com	Columbia	MO	65201	573-875-1099		645
KCMS-FM 105.3 (Rel) 19319 Fremont Ave N *Web:* www.spirit1053.com	Shoreline	WA	98133	206-546-7350		645-150
KCOS-TV Ch 13 (PBS) 9050 Viscount Blvd Ste A-440 *TF:* 800-683-1899 ■ *Web:* www.kcostv.org	El Paso	TX	79925	915-590-1313	594-5394	741-43
KCPL (Kansas City Public Library, The) 14 W Tenth St *Web:* www.kclibrary.org	Kansas City	MO	64105	816-701-3400	701-3401	434-3
KCPQ-TV Ch 13 (Fox) 1813 Westlake Ave N *TF:* 800-245-6397 ■ *Web:* q13fox.com	Seattle	WA	98109	206-674-1313		741-123

Name / Address	City	State	Zip	Phone	Fax	Class
KCPT-TV Ch 19 (PBS) 125 E 31st St TF: 800-343-4727 ■ Web: www.kcpt.org	Kansas City	MO	64108	816-756-3580		741-68
KCRA-TV Ch 3 (NBC) 3 Television Cir Web: www.kcra.com	Sacramento	CA	95814	916-446-3333		741-113
KCRG-TV Ch 9 (ABC) 501 Second Ave SE TF: 800-332-5443 ■ Web: www.kcrg.com	Cedar Rapids	IA	52401	319-398-8393		741-23
KCRW-FM 89.9 (NPR) 1900 Pico Blvd TF: 877-527-9227 ■ Web: www.kcrw.com	Santa Monica	CA	90405	310-450-5183	450-7172	645
KCSA Public Relations Worldwide 880 Third Ave # 6 Web: www.kcsa.com	New York	NY	10022	212-682-6300		636
KCSD-FM 90.9 (NPR) 555 N Dakota St PO Box 5000 TF: 800-456-0766 ■ Web: www.sdpb.org	Vermillion	SD	57069	605-677-5861	677-5010	645
KCSL (Kansas Children's Service League) 3545 SW 5th St TF: 877-530-5275 ■ Web: www.kcsl.org	Topeka	KS	66606	785-274-3100		48-6
KCSM-FM 91.1 (Jazz) 1700 W Hillsdale Blvd TF: 800-488-6689 ■ Web: www.kcsm.org	San Mateo	CA	94402	650-574-6586		645
KCSP-AM 610 (Sports) 7000 Squibb Rd TF: 800-234-6860 ■ Web: 610sports.com	Mission	KS	66202	913-744-3600		645
KCTR-FM 102.9 (Ctry) 27 N 27th St 23rd Fl Web: catcountry1029.com	Billings	MT	59101	406-248-7827	252-9577	645-19
KCTS-TV Ch 9 (PBS) 401 Mercer St TF: 800-443-9991 ■ Web: kcts9.org	Seattle	WA	98109	206-728-6463	443-6691	741-123
KCTV-TV Ch 5 (CBS) 4500 Shawnee Mission Pkwy TF: 800-767-7700 ■ Web: www.kctv5.com	Fairway	KS	66205	913-677-5555	677-7243	741
KCUR-FM 89.3 (NPR) 4825 Troost Ave Ste 202 TF: 855-778-5437 ■ Web: www.kcur.org	Kansas City	MO	64110	816-235-1551	235-2864	645-83
KCVB (Kingsport Convention & Visitors Bureau) 400 Clinchfield St Ste 100 TF: 800-743-5282 ■ Web: www.visitkingsport.com	Kingsport	TN	37660	423-392-8820	392-8833	206
KCWC-TV Ch 4 (PBS) 2660 Peck Ave TF: 800-495-9788 ■ Web: wyomingpbs.org	Riverton	WY	82501	307-856-6944	856-3893	741
KCWE-TV Ch 29 (CW) 6455 Winchester Ave Web: www.kmbc.com/kcwe/index.html	Kansas City	MO	64133	816-221-2900		741-68
KCWY-TV Ch 13 (NBC) 141 Progress Cir Web: kcwy13.com	Mills	WY	82644	307-577-0013	577-5251	741
KCXX-FM 103.9 (Alt) 242 E Airport Dr Ste 106 Web: www.x1039.com	San Bernardino	CA	92408	909-890-5904	890-9035	645-135
KCYY-FM 100.3 (Ctry) 8122 Datapoint Dr Ste 600 Web: www.y100fm.com	San Antonio	TX	78229	210-615-5400		645-143
K&D Pratt Group Inc 126 Glencoe Dr TF: 800-563-9595 ■ Web: www.kdpratt.com	Mount Pearl	NL	A1N4S9	709-722-5690	722-6975	791
KD Scientific Inc 84 October Hill Rd Web: www.kdscientific.com	Holliston	MA	01746	508-429-6809		475
KDAQ-FM 89.9 (NPR) 8675 Youree Dr TF: 800-552-8502 ■ Web: www.redriverradio.org	Shreveport	LA	71115	318-798-0102	798-0107	645-151
KDAR-FM 98.3 (Rel) 500 E Esplanade Dr Web: 983fmtheword.com	Oxnard	CA	93036	805-485-8881		645-118
KDB-FM 93.7 (Clas) 414 E Cota St Web: www.kdb.com	Santa Barbara	CA	93101	805-966-4131	966-4788	645
KDC Technologies 27201 Tourney Rd Ste 201 TF: 877-532-1112 ■ Web: www.kdctechnologies.com	Valencia	CA	91355	877-532-1112		196
KDDB-FM 102.7 (CHR) 1000 Bishop St Ste 200 Web: www.1027dabomb.net	Honolulu	HI	96813	808-947-1500		645-73
KDDI America Inc 825 Third Ave Ste 3 Web: us.kddi.com	New York	NY	10022	212-295-1200	295-1080	736
K-Dee Supply Inc 621 E Lake St	Lake Mills	WI	53551	920-648-5188	648-8138	779
KDF Electronic & Vacuum Services Inc 10 Volvo Dr Web: www.kdf.com	Rockleigh	NJ	07647	201-784-5005		695
KDFW FOX 4 400 N Griffin St TF: 800-677-5339 ■ Web: www.fox4news.com	Dallas	TX	75202	214-720-4444	720-3263	741-37
KDGI (Kuhlmann Design Group Inc) 66 Progress Pkwy Web: www.kdginc.com	Maryland Heights	MO	63043	314-434-8898		261
KDI Capital Partners LLC 4101 Lake Boone Trl Ste 218 Web: www.kdicapitalpartners.com	Raleigh	NC	27607	919-573-4124		401
KDIndustries 1525 E Lake Rd TF: 800-840-9577 ■ Web: www.kold-draft.com	Erie	PA	16511	814-453-6761	455-6336	664
KDKS-FM 102.1 (Urban) 208 N Thomas Dr Web: www.kdks.fm	Shreveport	LA	71107	318-222-3122		645-151
KDLT-TV Ch 46 (NBC) 3600 S Westport Ave TF: 800-727-5358 ■ Web: kdlt.com	Sioux Falls	SD	57106	605-361-5555	361-3982	741-125
KDM Signs Inc 10450 N Medallion Dr TF: 855-232-7799 ■ Web: www.kdmpop.com	Cincinnati	OH	45241	855-232-7799		627
KDND-FM 107.9 (CHR) 5345 Madison Ave Web: www.endonline.com	Sacramento	CA	95841	916-334-7777		645-140
KDNL-TV Ch 30 (ABC) 1215 Cole St TF: 800-365-0820 ■ Web: www.abcstlouis.com	Saint Louis	MO	63106	314-436-3030		741-114
KDON-FM 102.5 (CHR) 903 N Main St TF: 888-558-5366 ■ Web: kdon.iheart.com	Salinas	CA	93906	831-755-8181		645
KDOT-FM 104.5 (Rock) 690 East Plumb Ln Web: www.kdot.com	Reno	NV	89502	775-329-9261	323-1450	645-133
KDR (National Fraternity of Kappa Delta Rho) 331 S Main St TF: 800-536-5371 ■ Web: www.kdr.com	Greensburg	PA	15601	724-838-7100	838-7101	48-16
KDR Supply Inc PO Box 10130 Web: www.kdrsupply.com	Liberty	TX	77575	936-336-6267	336-1034	358
KDRK-FM 93.7 (Ctry) 1601 E 57th Ave Web: www.937thecat.com	Spokane	WA	99223	509-448-1000	448-7015	645-154
KDSM-TV Ch 17 (Fox) 4023 Fleur Dr TF: 800-642-6140 ■ Web: www.kdsm17.com	Des Moines	IA	50321	515-287-1717	287-0064	741-40
KDSU-FM 91.9 (NPR) 207 Fifth St N TF: 800-359-6900 ■ Web: www.prairiepublic.org	Fargo	ND	58102	701-241-6900	239-7651	645-58
Kdt Solutions Inc 1256 Fifth St Web: www.kdtsolutions.com	West Palm Beach	FL	33409	561-688-9399		175
KDTX-TV Ch 58 (TBN) 2900 W Airport Fwy Web: www.tbn.org	Irving	TX	75062	972-313-1333		741
KDUK-FM 104.7 (CHR) 1500 Valley River Dr Ste 350 Web: www.kduk.com	Eugene	OR	97401	541-284-3600		645-55
KDVR-TV Ch 31 (Fox) 100 E Speer Blvd Web: kdvr.com	Denver	CO	80203	303-595-3131		741-39
KDWB-FM 101.3 (CHR) 1600 Utica Ave S Ste 500 (Fl 5) Web: kdwb.iheart.com	St. Louis Park	MN	55416	952-417-3000	417-3001	645-101
KDWN-AM 720 (N/T) 2920 S Durango Dr Web: www.kdwn.com	Las Vegas	NV	89117	702-730-0300	736-8447	645-88
Kea Lani Spa at the Fairmont Kea Lani Maui 4100 Wailea Alanui Dr TF: 800-659-4100 ■ Web: www.fairmont.com	Maui	HI	96753	808-875-2229	875-1200	707
KEA News 401 Capital Ave TF: 800-231-4532 ■ Web: www.kea.org	Frankfort	KY	40601	502-875-2889	227-8062	457-8
Keadle Lumber Enterprises Inc 889 Railroad St Web: www.keadlelumber.com	Thomaston	GA	30286	706-647-8982		683
KEAG-FM 97.3 301 Arctic Slope Ave Ste 200 Web: www.kool973.com	Anchorage	AK	99518	907-344-9622		645-6
Keais Records Service Inc 1010 Lamar 18th Fl TF: 800-467-0822 ■ Web: keais.com	Houston	TX	77002	713-224-6865		41
Keaiwa Heiau State Recreation Area 1151 Punchbowl St Rm 310 PO Box 621 Web: www.hawaii.gov	Honolulu	HI	96813	808-483-2511		565
Kealakekua Bay State Historical Park PO Box 936 Web: www.hawaii.gov	Hilo	HI	96721	808-974-6200		565
Kean University 1000 Morris Ave Kean Hall *Fax: Admissions ■ TF: 800-882-1037 ■ Web: www.kean.edu	Union	NJ	07083	908-737-7100	737-7105*	166
Keane Care Inc 8383 158th Ave NE Ste 100 *Fax Area Code: 425 ■ TF: 800-426-2675 ■ Web: www.nttdataltc.com	Redmond	WA	98052	800-426-2675	307-2220*	178-11
Keane Circuits Inc 341 Avondale Ave Web: www.keanecircuits.com	Haddonfield	NJ	08033	856-795-1181		256
Keane Inc 210 Porter Dr Ste 315	San Ramon	CA	94583	925-838-8600		225
KEAN-FM 105.1 (Ctry) 3911 S First St TF: 800-588-5326 ■ Web: www.keanradio.com	Abilene	TX	79605	325-676-5326		645-1
Kear IT Inc 1510-H Caton Ctr Dr TF: 877-532-7481 ■ Web: www.kearit.com	Baltimore	MD	21227	877-532-7481		393
Kearfott Guidance & Navigation Corp 1150 McBride Ave TF: 800-669-6801 ■ Web: www.kearfott.com	Little Falls	NJ	07424	973-785-6000	785-6025	529
Kearney Area Chamber of Commerce 1007 Second Ave PO Box 607 TF: 800-227-8340 ■ Web: www.kearneycoc.org	Kearney	NE	68848	308-237-3101	237-3103	139
Kearney County 424 N Colorado Ave TF: 800-368-8683 ■ Web: www.kearneycounty.ne.gov	Minden	NE	68959	308-832-2723	832-2729	338
Kearney Electric Inc 3609 E Superior Ave Web: www.kearneyaz.com	Phoenix	AZ	85040	602-437-0235		189-4
Kearney Hub 13 E 22Nd PO Box 1988 TF: 800-950-6113 ■ Web: www.kearneyhub.com	Kearney	NE	68847	308-237-2152		530
Kearney Mansion Museum 7160 W Kearney Blvd Web: www.valleyhistory.org	Fresno	CA	93706	559-441-0862	441-1372	520
Kearney Public Library & Information Ctr 2020 First Ave Web: www.cityofkearney.org	Kearney	NE	68847	308-233-3282	233-3291	434-3
Kearny County PO Box 86 Web: www.kearnycountykansas.com	Lakin	KS	67860	620-355-6422	355-7382	338
Kearny FSB 120 Passaic Ave *Fax Area Code: 201 ■ TF: 800-273-3406 ■ Web: www.kearnybank.com	Fairfield	NJ	07004	973-244-4500	991-6713*	70
Kearny Public Library 318 Kearny Ave Web: www.kearnylibrary.org	Kearny	NJ	07032	201-998-2666	998-1141	434-3
Kearny Steel Container Corp 401 S St TF: 800-406-9377 ■ Web: www.kearnysteel.com	Newark	NJ	07105	973-589-2070		100
Keating & Co LLC 285 W Broadway Ste 460 Web: www.keatingco.com	New York	NY	10013	212-925-6900		636
Keating Bldg Corp 1600 Arch St Ste 300 Web: www.tutorperinibuilding.com	Philadelphia	PA	19103	610-668-4100		186
Keating Daniel J Co 134 N Narberth Ave Web: www.djkeating.com	Narberth	PA	19072	610-664-4550		186
Keating Hotel, The 432 F St TF: 800-544-4479 ■ Web: www.thekeating.com	San Diego	CA	92101	619-814-5700		378
Keating Muething & Klekamp Pll 1 E Fourth St Ste 1400 Web: www.kmklaw.com	Cincinnati	OH	45202	513-579-6400	579-6457	428
Keating Technologies Inc 25 Royal Crest Court Ste 120 TF: 877-532-8464 ■ Web: www.keating.com	Markham	ON	L3R9X4	905-479-0230		463
Keating William (Rep D - MA) 2351 Rayburn HOB Web: keating.house.gov	Washington	DC	20515	202-225-3111	225-5658	342-2
Keats, Connelly & Associates LLC 3336 N 32nd St Ste 100 TF: 800-678-5007 ■ Web: www.keatsconnelly.com	Phoenix	AZ	85018	602-955-5007		401
Kebs Inc 2116 Haslett Rd TF: 800-246-6735 ■ Web: www.kebs.com	Haslett	MI	48840	517-339-1014		261

Name / Address	City	State	ZIP	Phone	Fax	Class
KEC (Kay Electric Co-op)						
300 W Doolin Ave	Blackwell	OK	74631	580-363-1260	363-2308	245
TF: 800-535-1079 ■ *Web:* www.kayelectric.coop						
KEC (Kiamichi Electric Co-op Inc)						
966 SW Hwy 2 PO Box 340	Wilburton	OK	74578	918-465-2338		245
TF: 800-888-2731 ■ *Web:* www.kiamichielectric.org						
Kec Engineering 200 N Sherman Ave	Corona	CA	92882	951-734-3010		261
TF: 800-368-4778 ■ *Web:* www.kecengineering.com						
Keck School of Medicine of the University of Southern California						
1975 Zonal Ave KAM 100	Los Angeles	CA	90089	323-442-1100		167-2
Web: www.usc.edu						
k-eCommerce 666 St-Martin W Blvd Ste 330	Laval	QC	H7M5G4	514-973-2510		387
Web: www.k-ecommerce.com						
Keddeg Co 10700 Pflumm Rd	Lenexa	KS	66215	913-492-1222		21
Web: www.keddeg.com						
Keds Corp 1400 Industries Rd	Richmond	IN	47374	800-680-0966	446-1339	301
TF: 800-680-0966 ■ *Web:* www.keds.com						
KEDT						
4455 S Padre Island Dr Ste 38	Corpus Christi	TX	78411	361-855-2213	855-3877	645-43
TF: 800-307-5338 ■ *Web:* www.kedt.org						
KEDT-TV Ch 16 (PBS)						
4455 S Padre Island Dr Ste 38	Corpus Christi	TX	78411	361-855-2213	855-3877	741-36
TF: 800-307-5338 ■ *Web:* www.kedt.org						
Ke-e Grill 17940 N Military Trl	Boca Raton	FL	33496	561-995-5044		671
Web: wix.com						
Keeco LLC 30736 Wiegman Rd	Hayward	CA	94544	510-324-8800		361
Web: keecohome.com						
Keefe Bruyette & Woods Inc						
787 Seventh Ave The Equitable Bldg 4th Fl	New York	NY	10019	212-887-7777		690
Web: www.kbw.com						
Keefe McCullough & Co LLP Certified Public Accountants						
6550 N Federal Hwy Ste 410	Fort Lauderdale	FL	33308	954-771-0896	938-9353	2
Web: www.kmccpa.com						
Keefe Real Estate 1155 E Geneva St	Delavan	WI	53115	262-728-8757		652
TF: 800-690-2292 ■ *Web:* www.keeferealestate.com						
Keegan & Coppin Company Inc						
1355 N Dutton Ave	Santa Rosa	CA	95401	707-528-1400		652
Web: www.keegancoppin.com						
Keek Inc 1 Eglinton E Ste 500	Toronto	ON	M4P3A1	416-639-5335		809
Web: www.k.to						
Keel Point Advisors LLC						
8065 Leesburg Pk Ste 300	Vienna	VA	22182	703-807-2020		194
TF: 800-310-4191 ■ *Web:* www.keelpoint.com						
Keeler Motor Car Co						
1111 Troy Schenectady Rd	Latham	NY	12110	518-785-4197		57
TF: 800-474-4197 ■ *Web:* www.keeler.com						
Keeley Investment Corp						
401 S La Salle St Ste 1201	Chicago	IL	60605	312-786-5000	786-5002	169
TF: 800-533-5344 ■ *Web:* www.keeleyfunds.com						
Keeling Co PO Box 15310	North Little Rock	AR	72231	501-945-4511		612
TF: 800-343-9464 ■ *Web:* www.keelingcompany.com						
Keen Battle Mead & Co (KBMCO)						
7850 NW 146th St Ste 200 PO Box 171870	Hialeah	FL	33016	305-558-1101	822-4722	391-4
Web: www.kbmco.com						
Keen Compressed Gas Company Inc						
4063 New Castle Ave	New Castle	DE	19720	302-594-4545		385
Web: www.keengas.com						
Keen Technical Solutions LLC						
800 Cottageview Dr Ste 1042	Traverse City	MI	49684	888-675-7772		192
TF: 888-675-7772 ■ *Web:* www.keen-minds.com						
Keenan & Assoc						
2355 Crenshaw Blvd Ste 200 PO Box 4328	Torrance	CA	90501	310-212-3344	212-0300	390
TF: 800-654-8102 ■ *Web:* www.keenan.com						
Keenan Agency Inc, The						
6805 Avery Muirfield Dr Ste 200	Dublin	OH	43016	614-764-7000		390
Web: keenanins.com						
Keene Promotions Inc						
450 Lexington St Ste 1	Auburndale	MA	02466	617-243-0101		636
Web: www.keenepromostore.com						
Keene Publishing Corp PO Box 546	Keene	NH	03431	603-352-1234	352-0437	637-8
TF: 800-765-9994 ■ *Web:* www.sentinelsource.com						
Keene State College 229 Main St	Keene	NH	03435	603-352-1909	358-2767*	166
*Fax: Admissions ■ *TF:* 800-572-1909 ■ *Web:* www.keene.edu						
Keene Valley Video Inc						
1948 nys Rt 73	Keene Valley	NY	12943	518-576-4510		116
Web: www.kvvi.net						
Keeneland Association Inc						
4201 Versailles Rd	Lexington	KY	40510	859-254-3412		446
TF: 800-456-3412 ■ *Web:* www.keeneland.com						
Keeney Manufacturing Co						
1170 Main St	Newington	CT	06111	860-666-3342	665-0374*	609
*Fax: Cust Svc ■ *TF Cust Svc:* 800-243-0526 ■ *Web:* www.keeneymfg.com						
Keeney, Waite & Stevens						
402 W Broadway Ste 1820	San Diego	CA	92101	619-238-1661		428
Web: www.keenlaw.com						
Keenpac North America Ltd						
25 Main St Ste 3	Goshen	NY	10924	845-291-8680		791
TF: 800-843-5325 ■ *Web:* keenpac.com						
Keep America Beautiful Inc						
1010 Washington Blvd	Stamford	CT	06901	203-659-3000		48-7
Web: www.kab.org						
Keep Me in Stitches						
14833 N Dale Mabry Hwy	Tampa	FL	33618	813-908-3889		711
TF: 800-845-8723 ■ *Web:* www.kmisinc.com						
Keepers International Inc						
9420 Eton Ave	Chatsworth	CA	91311	818-407-5332		155-10
Kees Inc 400 Industrial Dr	Elkhart Lake	WI	53020	920-876-3391		697
Web: www.kees.com						
Keesal Young & Logan						
400 Oceangate PO Box 1730	Long Beach	CA	90801	562-436-2000	436-7416	428
Web: www.kyl.com						
Keesler Federal Credit Union						
PO Box 7001	Biloxi	MS	39534	228-385-5500	385-5535	219
TF: 888-533-7537 ■ *Web:* www.kfcu.org						
Keeton's Office & Art Supply Co						
817 Manatee Ave W	Bradenton	FL	34205	941-747-2995		535
Web: www.keetonsonline.com						
Keewaydin State Park						
46165 NYS Rt 12 PO Box 247	Alexandria Bay	NY	13607	315-482-3331		565
Web: parks.ny.gov/parks/24/details.aspx						
Keg Steakhouse 10100 Shellbridge Way	Richmond	BC	V6X2W7	604-276-0242	276-2681	670
Web: www.kegsteakhouse.com						
KEG Steakhouse & Bar						
7104 MacLeod Trl S	Calgary	AB	T2H0L3	403-253-2534		671
Web: www.kegsteakhouse.com						
Keg Steakhouse & Bar						
859 W John Carpenter Fwy	Irving	TX	75039	972-556-9188		671
Web: www.kegsteakhouse.com						
Keg, The 560 King St W Second Fl	Toronto	ON	M5V0L5	416-695-2400		671
Web: www.kegsteakhouse.com						
KEGA-FM 101.5 (Ctry)						
50 West Broadway Ste 200	Salt Lake City	UT	84101	801-524-2600		645-142
TF: 866-551-1015 ■ *Web:* www.1015theeagle.com						
Kegans State Jail 707 Top St	Houston	TX	77002	713-224-6584		213
Web: tdcj.state.tx.us						
Kegel's Produce Inc						
2851 Old Tree Dr	Lancaster	PA	17603	717-392-6612		297-7
TF: 800-535-3435 ■ *Web:* kegels.com						
Kegels German Inn						
5901 W National Ave	Milwaukee	WI	53214	414-257-9999		671
Web: kegelsinn.com						
Kegerreis Outdoor Advertising LLC						
1310 Lincoln Way E	Chambersburg	PA	17202	717-263-6700		8
TF: 800-745-4166 ■ *Web:* www.kegerreis.com						
Kegler, Brown, Hill & Ritter Company LPA						
65 E State St Capitol Sq Ste 1800	Columbus	OH	43215	614-462-5400		428
Web: www.keglerbrown.com						
Kegworkscom 1460 Military Rd	Buffalo	NY	14217	716-856-9675		321
Web: www.kegworks.com						
Kehoe Component Sales Inc 34 Foley Dr	Sodus	NY	14551	800-228-7223		246
TF: 800-228-7223 ■ *Web:* www.paceelectronics.com						
Kehoe Custom Wood Designs Inc						
1320 N Miller St Ste D	Anaheim	CA	92806	714-993-0444		321
Web: kehoecustomwood.com						
Kehrer Saltzman & Associates LLC						
9218 Skipaway Dr	Waxhaw	NC	28173	704-243-4512		463
Web: kehrerbielan.com						
Keidel Supply Co						
1150 Tennessee Ave	Cincinnati	OH	45229	513-351-1600	351-9649	612
Web: www.keidel.com						
Keifer's 710 Poplar Blvd	Jackson	MS	39202	601-355-6825		671
Keiger Printing Co						
3735 Kimwell Dr	Winston-Salem	NC	27103	336-760-0099		627
Web: keiger.com						
Keiler & Co 304 Main St	Farmington	CT	06032	860-677-8821		4
Keilson-Dayton Co 107 Commerce Park Dr	Dayton	OH	45404	937-236-1070	236-2124	756
TF: 800-759-3174 ■ *Web:* keilsondayton.com						
Keim Lumber Company Inc						
4465 State Rt 557 PO Box 40	Charm	OH	44617	330-893-2251		752
TF: 800-362-6682 ■ *Web:* www.keimlumber.com						
Keim T S Inc						
1249 N Ninth St PO Box 226	Sabetha	KS	66534	800-255-2450		700
TF: 800-255-2450 ■ *Web:* keimts.com						
Keir Surgical Ltd						
408 E Kent Ave S Ste 120	Vancouver	BC	V5X2X7	604-261-9596		475
TF: 800-663-4525 ■ *Web:* www.keirsurgical.com						
Keiro Services 325 S Boyle Ave	Los Angeles	CA	90033	323-980-7555		463
Web: www.keiro.org						
Keiser University						
Daytona Beach						
1800 Business Pk Blvd	Daytona Beach	FL	32114	386-274-5060	274-2725	800
Web: www.keiseruniversity.edu						
Fort Lauderdale						
1500 W Commercial Blvd	Fort Lauderdale	FL	33309	954-776-4456	771-4894	800
TF: 800-749-4456 ■ *Web:* www.keiseruniversity.edu						
Melbourne 900 S Babcock St	Melbourne	FL	32901	321-409-4800	725-3766	800
TF: 888-534-7379 ■ *Web:* www.keiseruniversity.edu						
Sarasota 6151 Lake Osprey Dr	Sarasota	FL	34240	941-907-3900	907-2016	800
TF: 866-534-7372 ■ *Web:* www.keiseruniversity.edu						
Keith & Schnars PA						
6500 N Andrews Ave	Fort Lauderdale	FL	33309	954-776-1616	771-7690	261
Web: www.keithandschnars.com						
Keith A Shibou CPA Accountancy Corp						
1900 E Tahquitz Canyon Way	Palm Springs	CA	92262	760-325-1214		2
Keith County 511 N Spruce St Rm 205	Ogallala	NE	69153	308-284-7776	284-3922	338
Web: www.keithcountyne.gov						
Keith d Weiner & Associates Co Lpa						
75 Public Sq Ste 400	Cleveland	OH	44113	216-771-6500		445
Web: www.weinerlaw.com						
Keith Smith Company Inc						
130 K-Tech Ln PO Box 3800	Hot Springs	AR	71914	501-760-0100	760-9199	447
Web: www.keith-smith.com						
Keith Titus Corp PO Box 920	Weedsport	NY	13166	315-834-6681		780
TF: 800-233-2126 ■ *Web:* www.pagetrucking.com						
Keith Watson Productions Inc						
2425 NW 71st Pl	Gainesville	FL	32653	352-264-8812		33
TF: 800-584-1709 ■ *Web:* www.keithwatsonproductions.com						
Keithly-Williams Seeds Inc						
420 Palm Ave	Holtville	CA	92250	760-356-5533		694
TF: 800-533-3465 ■ *Web:* www.keithlywilliams.com						
Keizer Chamber of Commerce						
980 Chemawa Rd NE	Keizer	OR	97303	503-393-9111		139
Web: www.keizerchamber.com						
Keizer Heritage Museum						
980 Chemawa Rd NE	Keizer	OR	97303	503-393-9660	393-0209	520
Web: www.keizerheritage.org						
Kejr Inc 1835 Wall St	Salina	KS	67401	785-825-1842		407
TF: 800-436-7762 ■ *Web:* geoprobe.com						
Kek Associates Inc 100 Josons Dr	Rochester	NY	14623	585-424-3380		463
TF: 800-624-5234 ■ *Web:* kekdesign.com						
Keker & Van Nest LLP						
633 Battery St	San Francisco	CA	94111	415-391-5400		428
Web: www.keker.com						
Kelchner Inc 50 Advanced Dr	Springboro	OH	45066	937-704-9890		193
TF: 800-252-1542 ■ *Web:* www.kelchner.com						

Entry	City	State	ZIP	Phone	Fax	Class
Kelco Management & Development Inc 1020 Oriental Gardens Rd. *Web:* www.kelcohotels.com	Jacksonville	FL	32207	904-858-9919		707
Kelcourt Plastics Inc 1000 Calle Recodo *Web:* www.kelcourt.com	San Clemente	CA	92673	949-361-0774		608
Kele Inc PO Box 34817 *Web:* www.kele.com	Memphis	TN	38184	901-382-4300		62
Kell Partners 303 camp craft rd. *Web:* www.kellpartners.com	Austin	TX	78746	512-850-5355		225
Kell's 112 SW Second Ave *TF:* 800-231-2603 ■ *Web:* www.kellsirish.com	Portland	OR	97204	503-227-4057		671
Kell, Alterman & Runstein LLP 520 SW Yamhill St Ste 600 *TF:* 800-905-4676 ■ *Web:* www.kelrun.com	Portland	OR	97204	503-222-3531		428
Kellam Berg Engineering & Surveys Ltd 5800 1a St SW *Web:* www.kellamberg.com	Calgary	AB	T2H0G1	403-640-0900		261
Kelleher Associates LLC 1255 Drummers Ln Four Glenhardie Corporate Ctr Ste 103 *Web:* www.kelleherllc.com	Wayne	PA	19087	610-293-1115		390
Kellen Co National Press Bldg 529 14th St NW Ste 750 *Web:* www.kellencompany.com	Washington	DC	20045	202-591-2438		47
Keller & Heckman LLP 1001 G St NW Ste 500w *Web:* www.khlaw.com	Washington	DC	20001	202-434-4100	434-4646	428
Keller America Inc 813 Diligence Dr Ste 120 *Web:* www.kelleramerica.com	Newport News	VA	23606	757-596-6680		201
Keller Army Community Hospital 900 Washington Rd *TF:* 800-552-2907 ■ *Web:* kach.amedd.army.mil	West Point	NY	10996	845-938-7992		374-4
Keller Assoc Engineering Inc 131 SW Fifth Ave *Web:* www.kellerassociates.com	Meridian	ID	83642	208-288-1992		256
Keller Augusta Partners LLC 45 Newbury St Ste 204 *Web:* www.kelleraugusta.com	Boston	MA	02116	617-247-0505		260
Keller Equipment Supply Ltd 1228 26 Ave SE *TF:* 800-746-6646 ■ *Web:* www.keller.ca	Calgary	AB	T2G5S2	403-243-8666		579
Keller Fay Group LLC 65 Church St 3rd Fl *TF:* 800-273-8439 ■ *Web:* www.kellerfay.com	New Brunswick	NJ	08901	732-846-6800		463
Keller Grain & Feed Inc 7977 Main St *Web:* www.kellergrain.com	Greenville	OH	45331	937-448-2284		276
Keller Group Inc, The 1 Northfield Plaza Ste 510 *Web:* www.kellergroupinc.com	Northfield	IL	60093	847-446-7550	446-9384	360-3
Keller Inc N216 State Rd 55 *TF:* 800-236-2534 ■ *Web:* www.kellerbuilds.com	Kaukauna	WI	54130	920-766-5795		186
Keller Laboratories Inc 160 Larkin Williams Industrial Ct *TF:* 800-325-3056 ■ *Web:* www.kellerlab.com	Fenton	MO	63026	636-600-4200		418
Keller Schroeder & Assoc Inc 4920 Carriage Dr *Web:* kellerschroeder.com	Evansville	IN	47715	812-474-6825		177
Keller Supply Company Inc 3209 17th Ave W **Fax:* Acctg ■ *TF:* 800-285-3302 ■ *Web:* www.kellersupply.com	Seattle	WA	98119	206-285-3300	283-8668*	612
Keller Technology Corp 2320 Military Rd *Web:* www.kellertechnology.com	Tonawanda	NY	14150	716-693-3840		454
Keller Williams Realty Inc 807 Las Cimas Pkwy Ste 200 *Web:* www.kw.com	Austin	TX	78746	512-327-3070	328-1433	310
Kellermeyer Bergensons Services LLC 1575 Henthorne Dr *Web:* www.kbs-services.com	Maumee	OH	43537	419-867-4300		192
Kellerstrass Oil Co 1500 W 2550 S *Web:* www.kellerstrassoil.com	Ogden	UT	84401	801-392-9516	392-9589	581
Kelley & Ferraro LLP Ernst & Young Tower 950 Main Ave *TF:* 800-398-1795 ■ *Web:* www.kelley-ferraro.com	Cleveland	OH	44114	216-202-3450		428
Kelley Advertising Co 818 Fulton St *Web:* kellyadvertising.com	Fort Wayne	OK	46802	260-426-1843		7
Kelley Bean Company Inc 2407 Cir Dr *TF:* 800-637-5843 ■ *Web:* www.kelleybean.com	Scottsbluff	NE	69361	308-635-6438	635-7345	275
Kelley Blue Book Company Inc 195 Technology Dr *TF:* 800-258-3266 ■ *Web:* www.kbb.com	Irvine	CA	92618	949-770-7704	837-1904	58
Kelley Dewatering & Construction Co 5175 Clay Ave SW *TF:* 800-968-1170 ■ *Web:* www.kelleydewatering.com	Wyoming	MI	49548	616-538-8010	538-0708	189-15
Kelley Drye & Warren LLP 101 Pk Ave *TF:* 800-973-1177 ■ *Web:* www.kelleydrye.com	New York	NY	10178	212-808-7800	808-7897	428
Kelley Executive Partners 1275 E Tenth St *Web:* www.kelley.iu.edu	Bloomington	IN	47405	812-855-0229		41
Kelley Foods of Alabama Inc 1697 Lower Curtis Rd *Web:* www.kelleyfoods.com	Elba	AL	36323	334-897-5761		297-8
Kelley Library 234 Main St *Web:* www.kelleylibrary.org	Salem	NH	03079	603-898-7064		434-3
Kelley Manufacturing Co 80 Vernon Dr PO Box 1467 *TF:* 800-444-5449 ■ *Web:* www.kelleymfg.com	Tifton	GA	31793	229-382-9393	382-5259	273
Kelley Technical Coatings Inc 1445 S 15th St PO Box 3726 *Web:* www.kelleytech.com	Louisville	KY	40201	502-636-2561		550
Kelliher Samets Volk 212 Battery St *Web:* www.ksvc.com	Burlington	VT	05401	802-862-8261		395
Kellmark Corp 2501 Ada Dr *Web:* www.kellmark.net	Elkhart	IN	46514	574-264-9695		627
Kellogg Co 1 Kellogg Sq PO Box 3599 *NYSE:* K ■ *TF Cust Svc:* 800-962-1413 ■ *Web:* www.kelloggs.com	Battle Creek	MI	49016	269-961-2000		296-4
Kellogg Community College 450 N Ave **Fax:* Admissions ■ *TF:* 800-621-7440 ■ *Web:* kellogg.edu	Battle Creek	MI	49017	269-965-3931	966-4089*	162
Kellogg Garden Products 350 W Sepulveda Blvd *TF:* 800-232-2322 ■ *Web:* www.kellogggarden.com	Carson	CA	90745	800-232-2322		280
Kellogg Hotel & Conference Ctr 219 S Harrison Rd Michigan State University Campus *TF:* 800-875-5090 ■ *Web:* kelloggcenter.com	East Lansing	MI	48824	517-432-4000	353-1872	379
Kellogg Marine Supply Inc 5 Enterprise Dr **Fax Area Code:* 800 ■ *TF:* 800-243-9303 ■ *Web:* www.kelloggmarine.com	Old Lyme	CT	06371	860-434-6002	628-1304*	770
Kellogg, Huber, Hansen, Todd, Evans & Figel PLLC Sumner Sq 1615 M St NW Ste 400 *Web:* www.kellogghansen.com	Washington	DC	20036	202-326-7900	326-7999	428
Kelloggauto Supply 502 S Edgemoor St *TF:* 800-227-2669 ■ *Web:* www.poormanautosupply.com	Wichita	KS	67218	316-682-4525		791
Kellogg-Hubbard Library 135 Main St *Web:* www.kellogghubbard.org	Montpelier	VT	05602	802-223-3338	223-3338	434-3
Kell-Strom Tool Co 214 Church St *TF:* 800-851-6851 ■ *Web:* www.kell-strom.com	Wethersfield	CT	06109	860-529-6851	257-9694	757
Kellwood Co 600 Kellwood Pkwy *Web:* www.kellwood.com	Chesterfield	MO	63017	314-576-3100		155-21
Kelly Aerospace 1404 E S Blvd *TF:* 888-461-6077 ■ *Web:* www.kellyaerospace.com	Montgomery	AL	36116	334-286-8551	227-8596	247
Kelly Box & Packaging Corp 2801 Covington Rd *Web:* www.kellybox.com	Fort Wayne	IN	46802	260-432-4570		100
Kelly Collins & Gentry Inc 1700 N Orange Ave Ste 400 *Web:* kcgcorp.com	Orlando	FL	32804	407-898-7858		256
Kelly Computer Systems 1060 La Avenida St *Web:* www.kelly.com	Mountain View	CA	94043	650-960-1010		177
Kelly Dunn & Nestor 921 Bergen Ave	Jersey City	NJ	07306	201-795-1122		2
Kelly Home Care Services Inc 999 W Big Beaver Rd *TF:* 800-755-8636 ■ *Web:* homehealthcareagencies.com	Troy	MI	48084	248-362-4444		363
Kelly Inns Ltd 3205 W Sencore Dr *TF:* 800-635-3559 ■ *Web:* www.kellyinns.com	Sioux Falls	SD	57107	605-965-1440	965-1450	379
Kelly Law Registry Inc 999 W Big Beaver Rd *Web:* www.kellyservices.us	Troy	MI	48084	248-362-4444		721
Kelly Manufacturing Co 555 S Topeka St *Web:* www.kellymfg.com	Wichita	KS	67202	316-265-6868	265-6687	529
Kelly Mike Law Group LLC 500 Taylor St Ste 400 *TF:* 866-692-0123 ■ *Web:* www.mklawgroup.com	Columbia	SC	29201	803-726-0123		428
Kelly Mike (Rep R - PA) 1707 Longworth Bldg *Web:* kelly.house.gov	Washington	DC	20515	202-225-5406	225-3103	342-2
Kelly Paper Co 288 Brea Canyon Rd **Fax Area Code:* 909 ■ *TF:* 800-675-3559 ■ *Web:* www.kellypaper.com	Walnut	CA	91789	800-675-3559	859-8903*	553
Kelly Pipe Company LLC 11680 Bloomfield Ave *TF:* 800-305-3559 ■ *Web:* www.kellypipe.com	Santa Fe Springs	CA	90670	562-868-0456	863-4695	595
Kelly Press Inc 1701 Cabin Branch Dr *TF:* 888-535-5940 ■ *Web:* www.thekellycompanies.com	Cheverly	MD	20785	301-386-2800		627
Kelly Robin (Rep D - IL) 1239 Longworth HOB *Web:* robinkelly.house.gov	Washington	DC	20515	202-225-0773	225-4583	342-2
Kelly Ryan Equipment Co 900 Kelly Ryan Dr *TF:* 800-640-6967 ■ *Web:* www.kryan.com	Blair	NE	68008	402-426-2151	426-2186	273
Kelly Sauder Rupiper Equipment LLC 805 E Howard St *Web:* www.ksrequipment.com	Pontiac	IL	61764	815-842-1149		274
Kelly Services Inc 999 W Big Beaver Rd *NASDAQ:* KELYA ■ *Web:* www.kellyservices.com	Troy	MI	48084	248-362-4444		721
Kelly Systems Inc 422 N Western Ave *TF:* 800-258-8237 ■ *Web:* www.kellytubesystems.com	Chicago	IL	60612	312-733-3224	733-6971	470
Kelly Trent (Rep R - MS) 1721 Longworth HOB *Web:* trentkelly.house.gov	Washington	DC	20515	202-225-4306	225-3549	342-2
Kelly Waters Inc 5 Clementine Pk *Web:* kellywaters.com	Dorchester Center	MA	02124	617-282-3620		652
Kelly's Caribbean Bar Grill & Brewery 301 Whitehead St *TF:* 800-507-9955 ■ *Web:* www.kellyskeywest.com	Key West	FL	33040	305-293-8484	296-0047	671
Kelly's Janitorial Service Inc 228 Hazel Ave *TF:* 800-227-0366 ■ *Web:* www.kellysjanitorial.com	Trenton	NJ	08638	609-771-0365		256
Kelly's Pipe & Supply Co Inc 2124 Industrial Rd *Web:* www.kellyspipe.com	Las Vegas	NV	89102	702-382-4957	382-4879	612
Kelly's Pub & Eatery 1802 Cedar Ave *Web:* kpehotwings.com	Scranton	PA	18505	570-346-9758		671
Kelly-Moore Paint Company Inc 987 Commercial St *TF:* 800-874-4436 ■ *Web:* www.kellymoore.com	San Carlos	CA	94070	650-592-8337		550
Kellys Roast Beef Inc 605 Broadway Ste 300	Saugus	MA	01906	781-284-9129		670
Kelly-Strayhorn Theater 5941 Penn Ave *TF:* 800-421-9512 ■ *Web:* www.kelly-strayhorn.org	Pittsburgh	PA	15206	412-363-3000		573-1
KELO-AM 1320 (N/T) 500 S Phillips Ave *Web:* kelo.com	Sioux Falls	SD	57104	605-336-1320	336-0415	645-152

Phone | Fax | Class

KELO-FM 92.5 (AC)
500 S Phillips Ave .... Sioux Falls SD 57104 605-331-5350 336-0415 645-152
Web: www.kelofm.com
KELO-TV Ch 11 (CBS)
501 S Phillips Ave .... Sioux Falls SD 57104 605-336-1100 741-125
TF: 800-888-5356 ■ *Web:* www.keloland.com
Kelowna Chamber of Commerce
544 Harvey Ave........ Kelowna BC V1Y6C9 250-861-3627 861-3624 137
Web: www.kelownachamber.org
Kelowna General Hospital (KGH)
2268 Pandosy St .... Kelowna BC V1Y1T2 250-862-4000 862-4020 374-2
TF: 888-877-4442 ■ *Web:* www.interiorhealth.ca
KELP-AM 1590 (Rel) 6900 Commerce St .... El Paso TX 79915 915-779-0016 779-6641 645-53
TF: 800-658-6299 ■ *Web:* www.kelpradio.com
Kelsan Technologies Corp
1140 W 15th St........ North Vancouver BC V7P1M9 604-984-6100 770
TF: 800-255-4500 ■ *Web:* www.kelsan.com
Kelser Corp 111 Roberts St Ste D .... East Hartford CT 06108 860-528-9819 291-9088 225
TF: 800-647-5316 ■ *Web:* www.kelsercorp.com
Kelsey Construction Inc
306 E Princeton St .... Orlando FL 32804 407-898-4101 186
Web: www.kelseyconstruction.com
Kelsey Museum of Archaeology
434 S State St University of Michigan .... Ann Arbor MI 48109 734-763-3559 763-8976 520
TF: 800-562-3559 ■ *Web:* www.lsa.umich.edu/kelsey
Kelsey National Corp
3030 S Bundy Dr .... Los Angeles CA 90066 310-390-1000 390
TF: 800-366-5656 ■ *Web:* kelsey.com
Kelseyville Unified School District
4410 Konocti Rd........ Kelseyville CA 95451 707-279-1511 685
Web: www.kusd.lake.k12.ca.us
Kelso & Company Inc
320 Pk Ave 24th Fl .... New York NY 10022 212-751-3939 690
Web: www.kelso.com
Kelso Longview Chamber of Commerce
1563 Olympia Way........ Longview WA 98632 360-423-8400 423-0432 139
Web: www.kelsolongviewchamber.org
Kelso-Burnett Co
5200 Newport Dr .... Rolling Meadows IL 60008 847-259-0720 259-0839 189-4
Web: www.kelso-burnett.com
Keltic Transportation Inc
90 MacNaughton Ave Caledonia Industrial Pk .... Moncton NB E1H3L9 506-854-1233 314
TF: 888-854-1233 ■ *Web:* www.keltictransportation.com
Kelton House Museum & Garden
586 E Town St........ Columbus OH 43215 614-464-2022 520
TF: 800-746-7644 ■ *Web:* www.keltonhouse.com
Kelty 6235 Lookout Rd .... Boulder CO 80301 800-535-3589 504-2745 64
TF: 800-423-2320 ■ *Web:* www.kelty.com
KELYN Group LLC, The
137 Stone Root Ln Ste 1........ Concord MA 01742 978-369-7000 287-5309 195
Kelyniam Global Inc 97 River Rd........ Canton CT 06019 800-280-8192 250
TF: 800-280-8192 ■ *Web:* www.kelyniam.com
KEM Electric Co-op Inc 107 S Broadway .... Linton ND 58552 701-254-4666 254-4975 245
TF: 800-472-2673 ■ *Web:* www.kemelectric.com
Kem Krest Corp 3221 Magnum Dr .... Elkhart IN 46516 574-389-2650 311
Web: www.kemkrest.com
Kemark Financial Services Inc
1 Blue Hill Plaza 11th Fl........ Pearl River NY 10965 845-620-9300 620-9340 180
Web: www.kemarkfinancial.com
KEMCO Industries LLC 70 Keyes Ct........ Sanford FL 32773 407-322-1230 203
TF: 800-299-8598 ■ *Web:* www.kemco.com
Kemco Systems Inc 11500 47th St N........ Clearwater FL 33762 727-573-2323 573-2346 427
TF: 800-633-7055 ■ *Web:* www.kemcosystems.com
Kemeny Overseas Products Corp
The Civic Opera Bldg 20 N Wacker Dr Ste 1028.... Chicago IL 60606 312-857 0844 492
Web: www.kemenyoverseas.com
Kemerer Museum of Decorative Arts
427 N New St .... Bethlehem PA 18018 610-868-6868 520
Web: historicbethlehem.org
KEMET Corp PO Box 5928........ Greenville SC 29606 864-963-6300 253
NYSE: KEM ■ *Web:* www.kemet.com
Kemin Industries Inc 2100 Maury St........ Des Moines IA 50317 515-559-5100 559-5232 447
TF: 800-777-8307 ■ *Web:* www.kemin.com
Kemlon Products & Development Co
1424 N Main St .... Pearland TX 77581 281-997-3300 997-1300 641
Web: www.kemlon.com
Kemoll's 211 N Broadway........ Saint Louis MO 63102 314-421-0555 671
Web: www.kemolls.com
Kemp & Smith LLP 221 N Kansas Ste 1700 .... El Paso TX 79901 915-533-4424 546-5360 428
Web: www.kempsmith.com
Kemp Bros. Construction Inc
10135 Geary Ave .... Santa Fe Springs CA 90670 562-236-5000 186
Web: www.kempbros.com
Kempe Children's Ctr 13123 E 16th Ave .... Aurora CO 80045 303-864-5300 864-5302 48-6
Web: www.kempe.org
Kemper Arena & American Royal Centers
1701 American Royal Ct........ Kansas City MO 64102 816-221-5242 720
TF: 800-767-7700 ■ *Web:* www.visitkc.com
Kemper County PO Box 188........ De Kalb MS 39328 601-743-2460 524-0000* 338
**Fax Area Code:* 490 ■ *Web:* countycriminal.com/court-records
Kemper Equipment Inc
5051 Horseshoe Pk .... Honey Brook PA 19344 610-273-2066 273-3537 385
Web: www.kemperequipment.com
Kemper Lesnik Communications
500 Skokie Blvd 4th Fl........ Northbrook IL 60062 847-850-1818 559-0406 636
Web: www.kemperlesnik.com
Kemper Museum of Contemporary Art
4420 Warwick Blvd........ Kansas City MO 64111 816-753-5784 753-5806 520
Web: www.kemperart.org
Kempf House Museum 312 S Div St .... Ann Arbor MI 48104 734-994-4898 520
TF: 800-264-8330 ■ *Web:* www.kempfhousemuseum.org
KemPharm Inc
2656Crosspark Rd Ste 100........ Coralville IA 52241 319-665-2575 665-2577 668
Web: www.kempharm.com
Kemps LLC 1270 Energy Ln .... Saint Paul MN 55108 651-379-6500 296-27
TF: 800-322-9566 ■ *Web:* kemps.com
Kempsmith Machine Co 1819 S 71st St .... Milwaukee WI 53214 414-256-8160 476-0564 556
Web: www.kempsmith-dl.com

Phone | Fax | Class

Kempton Group, The
2 Garfield Pl Ste 1003........ Cincinnati OH 45202 513-651-5556 651-5574 195
Web: tkg-marketing.com
Kemron Environmental Services Inc
8521 Leesburg Pike Ste 175........ Vienna VA 22182 703-893-4106 893-1741 192
TF: 888-429-3516 ■ *Web:* kemron.com
Kemtah Group Inc
7601 Jefferson St NE Ste 120........ Albuquerque NM 87109 505-346-4900 180
TF: 877-753-6824 ■ *Web:* www.kemtah.com
Kemwel Inc 39 Commercial St........ Portland ME 04102 207-842-2285 842-2286 126
TF: 800-678-0678 ■ *Web:* www.kemwel.com
Ken & Sue's 636 Main Ave........ Durango CO 81301 970-385-1810 671
Web: www.kenandsues.com
Ken Bettridge Distributing Inc
386 N 100 W .... Cedar City UT 84721 435-586-2411 581
TF: 800-532-6457 ■ *Web:* www.kboil.net
Ken Blanchard Companies Inc, The
125 State Pl .... Escondido CA 92029 760-839-8070 194
Web: www.kenblanchard.com
Ken Brady Construction Company Inc
4001 Turnagain Blvd........ Anchorage AK 99517 907-243-4604 186
Web: www.kenbrady.com
Ken Clark International Inc
2000 Lenox Dr Ste 200........ Lawrenceville NJ 08648 609-308-5200 193
Web: www.kenclark.com
Ken Cook Co
9929 W Silver Springs Dr........ Milwaukee WI 53225 414-466-6060 637-11
Web: www.kencook.com
Ken Creative Inc
1500 Park Ave Ste 200........ Emeryville CA 94608 510-879-7977 195
TF: 800-462-3277 ■ *Web:* kencreative.com
Ken Fowler Motors 1265 Airport Pk Blvd........ Ukiah CA 95482 707-468-0101 462-2475 57
TF: 800-287-0107 ■ *Web:* www.fowlerautocenter.com
Ken Garff Automotive Group
405 S Main St........ Salt Lake City UT 84111 801-257-3400 57
TF: 888-630-6838 ■ *Web:* www.kengarff.com
Ken Garner Manufacturing - Rho Inc
1201 E 28th St # B........ Chattanooga TN 37404 423-698-6200 261
TF: 888-454-7207 ■ *Web:* www.kgarnermfg.com
Ken Grody Ford 6211 Beach Blvd .... Buena Park CA 90621 714-521-3110 57
Web: www.kengrody.com
Ken Jones Tire Inc 73 Chandler St........ Worcester MA 01609 508-755-5255 755-4397 755
TF: 800-225-9513 ■ *Web:* www.kenjones.com
Ken Leiner Associates Inc
10401 Connecticut Ave Ste 140 .... Kensington MD 20895 301-933-8800 193
Web: itsearch.com
Ken Nunn Law Office
104 S Franklin Rd........ Bloomington IN 47404 812-332-9451 428
TF: 800-487-8669 ■ *Web:* kennunn.com
Ken Stewart's Grille 1970 W Market St........ Akron OH 44313 330-867-2555 671
Web: kenstewarts.com
Ken Ton Fabricators Inc 2505 Main St........ Buffalo NY 14214 716-832-1200 321
Web: www.kentonfab.com
Ken Wilson Ford Inc 760 Champion Dr........ Canton NC 28716 828-648-2313 57
Web: www.kenwilsonford.net
Ken's 1108 Murfreesboro Pk........ Nashville TN 37217 615-321-2444 671
Web: www.kensushi.com
Ken's Flower Shop
140 W S Boundary St........ Perrysburg OH 43551 419-874-1333 292
TF: 800-253-0100 ■ *Web:* www.kensflowers.com
Ken's Foods Inc 1 D'Angelo Dr........ Marlborough MA 01752 508-229-1100 296-19
Web: www.kensfoods.com
Kenai Drilling Ltd
6430 Cat Canyon Rd........ Santa Maria CA 93454 805-937-7871 540
Web: www.kenaidrilling.com
Kenai Peninsula Borough
144 N Binkley St........ Soldotna AK 99669 907-262-4441 338
Web: www.kpb.us
Kenall Mfg 1020 Lakeside Dr........ Gurnee IL 60031 847-360-8200 360-1781 430
TF: 800-453-6255 ■ *Web:* www.kenall.com
Kenan Advantage Group Inc (KAG)
4366 Mt Pleasant St NW........ North Canton OH 44720 330-491-0474 409-2786 780
TF: 800-969-5419 ■ *Web:* www.thekag.com
Kenan Transport Co
100 Europa Ctr Ste 320 .... Chapel Hill NC 27517 919-967-8221 929-5295 780
TF: 866-821-3444 ■ *Web:* thekag.com
KenCast Inc 290 Harbor Dr .... Stamford CT 06902 203-359-6984 116
Web: www.kencast.com
Kenco Group Inc 2001 Riverside Dr .... Chattanooga TN 37406 800-758-3289 449
TF: 800-758-3289 ■ *Web:* www.kencogroup.com
Kencoil Inc 2805 Engineers Rd .... Belle Chasse LA 70037 504-394-4010 518
TF: 800-221-8577 ■ *Web:* www.kencoil.com
Kencove Farm Fence Inc
344 Kendall Rd........ Blairsville PA 15717 800-536-2683 191-1
TF: 800-536-2683 ■ *Web:* www.charleskendall.com
KenCraft Manufacturing Inc
4155 Dixie Inn Rd........ Wilson NC 27893 252-291-0271 90
Web: www.kencraftboats.com
KenCrest Services Inc
502 W Germantown Pk Ste 200 .... Plymouth Meeting PA 19462 610-825-9360 48-15
Web: www.kencrest.org
Kenda USA 7095 Americana Pkwy .... Reynoldsburg OH 43068 614-866-9803 866-9805 755
TF: 866-536-3287 ■ *Web:* www.kendatire.com
Kendal at Hanover 80 Lyme Rd .... Hanover NH 03755 603-643-8900 643-7099 672
TF: 800-457-6833 ■ *Web:* kah.kendal.org
Kendal at Ithaca 2230 N Triphammer Rd........ Ithaca NY 14850 607-266-5300 266-5353 672
TF: 800-253-6325 ■ *Web:* www.kai.kendal.org
Kendal at Oberlin 600 Kendal Dr .... Oberlin OH 44074 800-548-9469 672
TF Mktg: 800-548-9469 ■ *Web:* www.kao.kendal.org
Kendal Crosslands Communities
1109 E Baltimore Pk........ Kennett Square PA 19348 610-388-1441 388-5503 672
TF: 800-216-1920 ■ *Web:* kcc.kendal.org
Kendall & Davis Company Inc
3668 S Geyer Rd Ste 100 .... St. Louis MO 63127 866-675-3755 260
TF: 866-675-3755 ■ *Web:* www.kendallanddavis.com
Kendall College 900 N Branch St........ Chicago IL 60642 312-752-2000 163
TF: 888-905-3632 ■ *Web:* www.kendall.edu

Phone | Fax | Class

Kendall College of Art & Design of Ferris State University
17 Fountain St NW ... Grand Rapids MI 49503 616-451-2787 831-9689 166
TF: 800-676-2787 ■ Web: www.kcad.edu

Kendall County 201 E San Antonio St ... Boerne TX 78006 830-249-9343 249-1763 338
Web: www.co.kendall.tx.us

Kendall County 111 W Fox St ... Yorkville IL 60560 630-553-4104 553-4119 338
Web: www.co.kendall.il.us

Kendall Electric Inc
131 Grand Trunk Ave ... Battle Creek MI 49037 269-965-6897 246
TF: 800-632-5422 ■ Web: www.kendallelectric.com

Kendall News Gazette
6796 SW 62nd Ave ... South Miami FL 33143 305-669-7355 532-4
Web: www.communitynewspapers.com

Kendall Packaging Corp
10335 N Port Washington Rd ... Mequon WI 53092 262-404-1200 404-1221 600
TF: 800-237-0951 ■ Web: www.kendallpkg.com

Kendall Regional Medical Ctr
11750 SW 40th St ... Miami FL 33175 305-223-3000 374-3
Web: www.kendallmed.com

Kendall Toyota 10943 S Dixie Hwy ... Miami FL 33156 305-665-6581 57
Web: www.kendalltoyota.com

Kendall's Brasserie & Bar
135 N Grand Ave ... Los Angeles CA 90012 213-972-7322 671
Web: www.patinagroup.com/kendallsbrasserie

Kendall/Hunt Publishing Co
4050 Westmark Dr PO Box 1840 ... Dubuque IA 52002 563-589-1000 772-9165* 637-2
*Fax Area Code: 800 ■ *Fax: Cust Svc ■ TF Cust Svc: 800-228-0810 ■ Web: www.kendallhunt.com

Kendall-Jackson Wine Estates Ltd
425 Aviation Blvd ... Santa Rosa CA 95403 707-544-4000 80-3
TF: 800-769-3649 ■ Web: www.kj.com

Kendle International Inc
441 Vine St 1200 Carew Twr ... Cincinnati OH 45202 513-381-5550 381-5870 668
TF: 800-733-1572 ■ Web: www.kendle.com

Kendra Scott Design Inc
1400 S Congress Ave Ste A-170 ... Austin TX 78704 866-677-7023 411
TF: 866-677-7023 ■ Web: www.kendrascott.com

Kenedy County 139 N Main ... Sarita TX 78385 361-294-5785 294-5788 338
Web: www.co.kenedy.tx.us

Kenefick & Company CPA'S PA
2809 Cavan Ct ... Charlotte NC 28270 704-544-6757 2
Web: kenefickandco.com

Kenergy Corp 6402 Old Corydon Rd ... Henderson KY 42419 270-826-3991 826-3999 245
TF: 800-844-4832 ■ Web: www.kenergycorp.com

KENI-AM 650 (N/T)
800 E Dimond Blvd Ste 3-370 ... Anchorage AK 99515 907-522-1515 743-5186 645-6
Web: 650keni.iheart.com

Kenilworth Aquatic Gardens
1550 Anacostia Ave NE ... Washington DC 20019 202-426-6905 426-5991 97
TF: 877-642-4743 ■ Web: www.nps.gov/keaq

Kenlake State Resort Park
542 Kenlake Rd ... Hardin KY 42048 270-474-2211 565
TF: 800-325-0143 ■ Web: www.parks.ky.gov/findparks/resortparks/kl

Kenlee Precision Corp
1701 Inverness Ave ... Baltimore MD 21230 410-525-3800 646-3278 621
TF: 800-969-5278 ■ Web: www.kenlee.com

Ken-Mac Metals Inc
17901 Englewood Dr ... Cleveland OH 44130 440-234-7500 234-4459 492
TF: 800-831-9503 ■ Web: www.tkmna.com

Kenmar Corp
17515 W 9 Mile Rd Ste 1200 ... Southfield MI 48075 248-424-8200 61
Web: www.ekenmar.com

Kenmode Tool & Engineering Co
820 W Algonquin Rd ... Algonquin IL 60102 847-658-5041 658-9150 757
Web: kenmode.com

Kenmore Air Harbor Inc
6321 NE 175th St ... Kenmore WA 98028 425-486-1257 25
TF: 866-435-9524 ■ Web: www.kenmoreair.com

Kenmore Camera Inc
18031 67th Ave NE PO Box 82467 ... Kenmore WA 98028 425-485-7447 119
TF: 888-485-7447 ■ Web: www.kenmorecamera.com

Kenmore Construction Co Inc
700 Home Ave ... Akron OH 44310 330-762-9373 762-2135 186
Web: www.kenmorecompanies.com

Kenmore Mercy Hospital
2950 Elmwood Ave ... Kenmore NY 14217 716-706-2112 447-6090 374-3
Web: www.chsbuffalo.org/body.cfm?id=49

Kenmore-Town of Tonawanda Chamber of Commerce
3411 Delaware Ave ... Kenmore NY 14217 716-874-1202 874-3151 139
TF: 888-710-6626 ■ Web: www.ken-ton.org

Kennametal 1662 MacMillan Park Dr ... Fort Mill SC 29707 724-539-5000 493
NYSE: KMT ■ TF Cust Svc: 800-446-7738 ■ Web: www.kennametal.com

Kennametal Inc 2879 Aero Pk Dr ... Traverse City MI 49686 231-946-2100 946-3025* 1
NYSE: KMT ■ *Fax: Sales ■ TF: 800-662-2131 ■ Web: www.kennametal.com

Kennebec County 125 State St ... Augusta ME 04330 207-622-0971 623-4083 338
Web: www.kennebeccounty.org

Kennebec Savings Bank
150 State St PO Box 50 ... Augusta ME 04332 207-622-5801 626-2858 70
TF: 888-303-7788 ■ Web: www.kennebecsavings.bank

Kennebec Telephone Company Inc
220 S Main St ... Kennebec SD 57544 605-869-2220 869-2221 736
TF: 888-868-3390 ■ Web: www.kennebectelephone.com

Kennebec Valley Chamber of Commerce
21 University Dr ... Augusta ME 04330 207-623-4559 626-9342 139
TF: 800-205-5615 ■ Web: www.augustamaine.com

Kennebec Valley Community College
92 Western Ave ... Fairfield ME 04937 207-453-5000 453-5010 162
TF: 800-528-5882 ■ Web: www.kvcc.me.edu

Kennecott Uranium Co NW Of Rawlins ... Rawlins WY 82301 307-328-1476 502

Kennedy & Coe LLC 3030 Cortland Cir ... Salina KS 67401 785-825-1561 825-5371 2
Web: www.kcoe.com

Kennedy Anthony M
US Supreme Ct Bldg 1 1st St NE ... Washington DC 20543 202-479-3000 479-3472 341-4
TF: 800-772-1213 ■ Web: www.supremecourt.gov

Kennedy Consulting Ltd
205 E University Ave ... Georgetown TX 78626 512-864-2833 261
Web: www.kcitx.com

Kennedy Ctr Opera House Orchestra
John F Kennedy Ctr for the Performing Arts
2700 F St NW ... Washington DC 20566 800-444-1324 416-8205* 573-3
*Fax Area Code: 202 ■ TF: 800-444-1324 ■ Web: www.kennedy-center.org

Kennedy Health System-Cherry Hill
2201 Chapel Ave W ... Cherry Hill NJ 08002 856-488-6500 488-6526 374-3
TF: 866-224-0264 ■ Web: www.kennedyhealth.org

Kennedy III Joseph P (Rep D - MA)
434 Cannon HOB ... Washington DC 20515 202-225-5931 225-0182 342-2
Web: kennedy.house.gov

Kennedy John (Sen R - LA)
383 Russell Senate Office Bldg ... Washington DC 20510 202-224-4623 228-0447 342-2
Web: www.kennedy.senate.gov

Kennedy Krieger Institute
707 N Broadway ... Baltimore MD 21205 443-923-9200 374-1
TF: 800-873-3377 ■ Web: www.kennedykrieger.org

Kennedy Manufacturing Co
1260 Industrial Dr ... Van Wert OH 45891 419-238-2442 238-5644 488
TF: 800-413-8665 ■ Web: buykennedy.com

Kennedy Office Supply
4211-A Atlantic Ave ... Raleigh NC 27604 919-878-5400 790-9649 535
TF: 800-733-9401 ■ Web: kennedyoffice.com

Kennedy Tank & Mfg Company Inc
833 E Sumner Ave ... Indianapolis IN 46227 317-787-1311 480
Web: www.kennedytank.com

Kennedy Tool & Die Inc
325 W Main St ... Birdsboro PA 19508 610-582-8735 757
Web: www.ktdmold.com

Kennedy Valve 1021 E Water St ... Elmira NY 14902 607-734-2211 734-3288 789
TF: 800-782-5831 ■ Web: www.kennedyvalve.com

Kennedy Wholesale Inc
16014 Adelante St ... Irwindale CA 91706 818-241-9977 241-3046 297-3
TF: 877-292-2639 ■ Web: www.kennedywholesale.com

Kennedy's at Stone Creek
2560 Stone Creek Blvd ... Urbana IL 61802 217-384-8111 671

Kennedy/Jenks Consultants
303 Second St Ste 300 S ... San Francisco CA 94107 415-243-2150 896-0999 261
Web: www.kennedyjenks.com

Kennedy-King College
6301 S Halsted St ... Chicago IL 60621 773-602-5000 162
TF: 800-798-8100 ■
Web: www.ccc.edu/colleges/kennedy/pages/default.aspx

Kennedy-Wilson Inc
151 S El Camino Dr Ste 700 ... Beverly Hills CA 90212 310-887-6400 887-3410 51
Web: kennedywilson.com

Kenner Planetarium & MegaDome Cinema
2020 Fourth St Rivertown ... Kenner LA 70062 504-468-7231 598
Web: www.kenner.la.us

Kennerley Spratling Inc
2116 Farallon Dr ... San Leandro CA 94577 510-351-8230 352-9240 604
TF: 800-523-5474 ■ Web: ksplastic.com

Kennesaw Mountain National Battlefield Park
900 Kennesaw Mtn Dr ... Kennesaw GA 30152 770-427-4686 528-8398 564
Web: www.nps.gov

Kennesaw State University
1000 Chastain Rd ... Kennesaw GA 30144 770-423-6000 420-4435* 166
*Fax: Admissions ■ Web: www.kennesaw.edu

Kenneth Clark Company Inc
10264 Baltimore National Pk ... Ellicott City MD 21042 410-465-5116 195
TF: 866-999-5116 ■ Web: www.kennethclark.com

Kenneth Cole Productions Inc
603 W 50th St ... New York NY 10019 212-265-1500 315-8279* 301
NYSE: KCP ■ *Fax: Cust Svc ■ TF: 800-536-2653 ■ Web: www.kennethcole.com

Kenneth Delarbre & Company PA
1618 S Highland Ave ... Clearwater FL 33756 727-585-4708 2

Kenneth Hahn State Recreation Area
c/o Angeles District Office ... Los Angeles CA 90056 323-298-3660 565
Web: www.parks.ca.gov/default.asp?page_id=612

Kenneth Honey Rubenstein Juvenile Center
141 Forestry Camp Rd ... Davis WV 26260 304-259-5241 259-4851 412
Web: www.djs.wv.gov

Kenneth Rainin Foundation
155 Grand Ave Ste 1000 ... Oakland CA 94612 510-625-5200 303
Web: www.krfoundation.org

Kenneth Shuler School of Cosmetology & Hair Design Inc
449 Saint Andrews Rd ... Columbia SC 29210 803-772-6042 77
TF: 800-232-2774 ■ Web: www.kennethshuler.com

Kennetic Productions Inc
25 N Market St Ste 117 ... Jacksonville FL 32202 904-372-8570 514
Web: www.kenneticproductions.com

Kennewick Computer Co
2290 Robertson Dr ... Richland WA 99354 509-371-0600 175
TF: 800-735-6860 ■ Web: www.gopositive.com

Kennewick General Hospital (KGH)
900 S Auburn St ... Kennewick WA 99336 509-586-6111 374-3
Web: www.trioshealth.org

Kenney & Assoc
1754 N Washington St ... Naperville IL 60563 630-505-4333 390

Kenney Machinery Corp
8420 Zionsville Rd ... Indianapolis IN 46268 317-872-4793 429
Web: kenneymachinery.com

Kenney Mfg Co 1000 Jefferson Blvd ... Warwick RI 02886 401-739-2200 87
TF Cust Svc: 800-753-6639 ■ Web: www.kenney.com

Kennickell Printing Co
1700 E President St ... Savannah GA 31404 800-673-6455 627
TF: 800-673-6455 ■ Web: www.kennickell.com

Kennicott Bros 452 N Ashland Ave ... Chicago IL 60622 312-492-8200 293
TF: 866-346-2826 ■ Web: www.kennicott.com

Kennies Market Inc 217 W Middle St ... Gettysburg PA 17325 717-334-2179 345
Web: www.kenniesmarket.com

Kenny Construction Co
2215 Sanders Rd Ste 400 ... Northbrook IL 60062 831-724-1011 272-5421* 186
*Fax Area Code: 847 ■ TF: 800-211-4226 ■ Web: www.graniteconstruction.com

Kenny The Printer 17931 Sky Park Cir ... Irvine CA 92614 949-250-3212 627
TF: 800-583-2679 ■ Web: www.kennytheprinter.com

Kennywood Park
4800 Kennywood Blvd ... West Mifflin PA 15122 412-461-0500 32
Web: www.kennywood.com

Name / Address	City	State	Zip	Phone	Fax	Class
KENO-AM 1460 (Sports) 8755 W Flamingo Rd	Las Vegas	NV	89147	702-247-1460		645-88
Kenona Industries Inc 3044 Wilson Dr NW *Web:* www.kenona.com	Grand Rapids	MI	49534	616-735-6228		454
Kenora Daily Miner & News 33 Main St S PO Box 1620 *Web:* www.kenoradailyminerandnews.com	Kenora	ON	P9N3X7	807-468-5555	468-4318	532-1
Kenora District Services Board 211 Princess St *Web:* kdsb.on.ca	Dryden	ON	P8N3L5	807-223-2100		30
Kenosha Area Chamber of Commerce 600 52nd St Ste 130 *TF:* 800-273-1002 ■ *Web:* www.kenoshaareachamber.com	Kenosha	WI	53140	262-654-1234	654-4655	139
Kenosha Area Convention & Visitors Bureau 812 56th St *TF:* 800-654-7309	Kenosha	WI	53140	262-654-7307	654-0882	206
Kenosha County 1010 56th St *Web:* www.kenoshacounty.org	Kenosha	WI	53140	262-653-2552	653-2564	338
Kenosha Medical Ctr 6308 Eigth Ave *TF:* 800-994-6610 ■ *Web:* www.uhsi.org	Kenosha	WI	53143	262-656-2011		374-3
Kenosha Metal Products Inc 8121 - 104th St *Web:* www.kenosha-metal.com	Pleasant Prairie	WI	53158	262-947-8840		488
Kenosha News 5800 Seventh Ave *TF:* 800-292-2700 ■ *Web:* www.kenoshanews.com	Kenosha	WI	53140	262-657-1000	657-8455	532-2
Kenosha Public Library 7979 38th Ave *Web:* www.mykpl.info	Kenosha	WI	53142	262-564-6100	564-6370	434-3
Kenosha Public Museum 5500 First Ave *TF:* 888-258-9966 ■ *Web:* www.kenosha.org	Kenosha	WI	53140	262-653-4140	653-4437	520
Kenrick-Glennon Seminary 5200 Glennon Dr *Web:* www.kenrick.edu	Saint Louis	MO	63119	314-792-6100	792-6500	167-3
Kenron Industrial A/C Inc 299 Gregory St *Web:* kenron.com	Rochester	NY	14620	585-442-5000		189-10
Kens Reproductions Lllp 2220 Curtis St *Web:* www.kensrepro.com	Denver	CO	80205	303-297-9191		113
Kensey Nash Corp 735 Pennsylvania Dr *NASDAQ: KNSY* ■ *TF General:* 800-322-2885 ■ *Web:* dsm.com/markets/medical/en_us/home.html	Exton	PA	19341	484-713-2100	713-2900	476
Kensico Capital Management Corp 55 RailRoad Ave 2nd Fl *Web:* www.kensicocapital.com	Greenwich	CT	06830	203-862-5800	862-5801	401
Kensico Cemetery Inc, The 273 Lakeview Ave *Web:* www.kensico.org	Valhalla	NY	10595	914-949-0347		510
Kensington Community Church 1825 E Sq Lake Rd *Web:* kensingtonchurch.org	Troy	MI	48085	248-786-0600		48-20
Kensington Computer Products Group 333 Twin Dolphin Dr 6th Fl *TF:* 800-535-4242 ■ *Web:* www.kensington.com	Redwood Shores	CA	94065	650-572-2700		173-1
Kensington Furniture & Mattress 200 Tilton Rd *Web:* www.kensingtonfurniture.com	Northfield	NJ	08225	609-241-9102		321
Kensington Hotel, The 3500 S State St *TF Orders:* 800-344-7020 ■ *Web:* www.kcourtaa.com	Ann Arbor	MI	48108	734-761-7800		379
Kensington Park Hotel 450 Post St *TF:* 800-553-1900 ■ *Web:* www.kensingtonparkhotel.com	San Francisco	CA	94102	415-788-6400		379
Kensington Publishing Corp 119 W 40th St *TF:* 800-221-2647 ■ *Web:* www.kensingtonbooks.com	New York	NY	10018	212-407-1500	935-0699	637-2
Kensington Realty Advisors Inc 100 N Riverside Plaza Ste 2300 *Web:* www.kra-net.com	Chicago	IL	60606	312-993-7800		652
Kensington Riverside Inn 1126 Memorial Dr NW *TF:* 877-313-3733 ■ *Web:* www.kensingtonriversideinn.com	Calgary	AB	T2N3E3	403-228-4442	228-9608	379
Kensington Valley Chamber of Commerce 58000 Grand River Ave *Web:* www.southlyonchamber.com	New Hudson	MI	48165	248-617-3075		139
KENS-TV Ch 5 (CBS) 5400 Fredericksburg Rd *Web:* www.kens5.com	San Antonio	TX	78229	210-366-5000		741-116
Kent Area Chamber of Commerce 138 E Main St Ste 102 *TF:* 800-648-6342 ■ *Web:* www.kentbiz.com	Kent	OH	44240	330-673-9855		139
Kent Chamber of Commerce 524 W Meeker St Ste 1 *TF:* 800-321-2808 ■ *Web:* www.kentchamber.com	Kent	WA	98032	253-854-1770	854-8567	139
Kent Corp 4446 Pinson Valley Pkwy *Web:* www.kentcorp.com	Birmingham	AL	35215	205-853-3420		286
Kent County 400 High St *Web:* www.kentcounty.com	Chestertown	MD	21620	410-778-7435	778-7482	338
Kent County 555 S Bay Rd *Web:* www.co.kent.de.us	Dover	DE	19901	302-744-2305	736-2279	338
Kent County 300 Monroe Ave NW *Web:* www.accesskent.com	Grand Rapids	MI	49503	616-632-7640	632-7645	338
Kent County PO Box 9 *Web:* kentcountysherifftx.com	Jayton	TX	79528	806-237-3801		338
Kent County Library 2319 S Dupont Hwy *Web:* www.co.kent.de.us	Dover	DE	19901	302-698-6440	698-6441	434-3
Kent District Library 814 W River Ctr Dr NE *TF:* 877-243-2466 ■ *Web:* www.kdl.org	Comstock Park	MI	49321	616-784-2007	647-3908	434-3
Kent Elastomer Products Inc 1500 St Claire Ave *TF Cust Svc:* 800-331-4762 ■ *Web:* www.kentelastomer.com	Kent	OH	44240	330-673-1011	673-1351	676
Kent Falls State Park c/o Macedonia Brook State Pk 159 Macedonia Brook Rd *Web:* www.ct.gov	Kent	CT	06757	860-927-3238		565
Kent General Hospital 640 S State St *TF:* 888-761-8300 ■ *Web:* www.bayhealth.org	Dover	DE	19901	302-674-4700		374-3
Kent Hospital 455 Toll Gate Rd *TF:* 800-892-9291 ■ *Web:* www.kentri.org	Warwick	RI	02886	401-737-7000		374-3
Kent Quality Foods Inc 703 Leonard St NW *TF:* 800-748-0141 ■ *Web:* www.kqf.com	Grand Rapids	MI	49504	800-748-0141		296-26
Kent School PO Box 2006 *TF:* 800-538-5368 ■ *Web:* www.kent-school.edu	Kent	CT	06757	860-927-6111	927-6109	622
Kent Scientific Corp 1116 Litchfield St *TF:* 800-710-9863 ■ *Web:* www.kentscientific.com	Torrington	CT	06790	860-626-1172		407
Kent Security Services Inc 14600 Biscayne Blvd *TF:* 800-273-5368 ■ *Web:* www.kentsecurity.com	North Miami Beach	FL	33181	305-919-9400		693
Kent Sporting Goods Company Inc 433 Pk Ave S *TF:* 800-938-4646 ■ *Web:* www.kentwatersports.com	New London	OH	44851	419-929-7021	929-1769	710
Kent State University 800 E Summit St PO Box 5190 **Fax:* Admissions ■ *TF:* 800-988-5368 ■ *Web:* www.kent.edu	Kent	OH	44242	330-672-2121	672-2499*	166
Ashtabula 3300 Lake Rd W **Fax:* Admissions ■ *TF:* 800-988-5368 ■ *Web:* www.kent.edu/ashtabula	Ashtabula	OH	44004	440-964-3322	964-4269*	162
East Liverpool 400 E Fourth St *Web:* www.kent.edu	East Liverpool	OH	43920	330-385-3805		166
Geauga 14111 Claridon-Troy Rd **Fax:* Admissions ■ *Web:* www.kent.edu/geauga	Burton	OH	44021	440-834-4187	834-8846*	162
Libraries 1125 Risman Dr **Fax:* Admin ■ *Web:* www.library.kent.edu	Kent	OH	44242	330-672-3456	672-4811*	434-6
Salem 2491 SR-45 S **Fax:* Admissions ■ *Web:* www.kent.edu/columbiana	Salem	OH	44460	330-332-0361	337-4122*	166
Stark 6000 Frank Ave NW **Fax:* Admissions ■ *TF:* 800-988-5368 ■ *Web:* www.kent.edu/stark	North Canton	OH	44720	330-499-9600	499-0301*	166
Trumbull Campus 4314 Mahoning Ave NW **Fax:* Admissions ■ *TF:* 800-988-5368 ■ *Web:* www.kent.edu/trumbull	Warren	OH	44483	330-847-0571	675-8888*	166
Tuscarawas 330 University Dr NE **Fax:* Admissions ■ *TF:* 800-988-5368 ■ *Web:* www.kent.edu/tusc	New Philadelphia	OH	44663	330-339-3391	339-3321*	166
Kent State University Museum PO Box 5190 *TF:* 800-988-5368 ■ *Web:* www.kent.edu	Kent	OH	44242	330-672-3450	672-3218	520
Kent Supply Co 50 Jon Barrett Rd *TF:* 800-536-8636 ■ *Web:* www.kentsupply.com	Patterson	NY	12563	845-878-6940		612
Kent Sussex Industries Inc 301 N Rehoboth Blvd *TF:* 800-937-9696 ■ *Web:* www.ksiinc.org	Milford	DE	19963	302-422-4014		88
Kent Wool 671 Runnymede Rd *Web:* www.kentwool.com	Pickens	SC	29671	864-878-6367	878-2723	745-9
Kent, The 1131 Collins Ave *Web:* www.thekenthotel.com	Miami Beach	FL	33139	305-604-5068		379
Kentec Communications Inc 710 W Main St *Web:* kci.net	Sterling	CO	80751	970-522-8107		736
Kentec Medical Inc 17871 Fitch *TF:* 800-825-5996 ■ *Web:* www.kentecmedical.com	Irvine	CA	92614	949-863-0810	833-9730	475
Kentfield Rehabilitation Hospital 1125 Sir Francis Drake Blvd *Web:* www.kentfieldrehab.com	Kentfield	CA	94904	415-456-9680		374-6
Kenton County 303 Ct St *TF:* 800-282-9181 ■ *Web:* www.kentoncounty.org	Covington	KY	41011	859-392-1600		338
Kenton County Public Library 502 Scott Blvd *Web:* www.kentonlibrary.org	Covington	KY	41011	859-962-4060	962-4096	434-3
Kenton Groupcom LLC 4454 Fairway Oaks Dr Ste 400 *Web:* www.kentongroup.com	Mulberry	FL	33860	651-451-3465		196
Ken-Tool Co 768 E N St **Fax Area Code:* 800 ■ *TF:* 800-872-4929 ■ *Web:* www.kentool.com	Akron	OH	44305	330-535-7177	872-4929*	758
Ken-Tron Manufacturing Inc PO Box 21250 *TF:* 800-872-9336 ■ *Web:* www.ken-tron.com	Owensboro	KY	42304	270-684-0431		488
Kents Hill School 1614 Main St *Web:* www.kentshill.org	Kents Hill	ME	04349	207-685-4914		622
Kentuck Museum 503 Main Ave *Web:* kentuck.org	Northport	AL	35476	205-758-1257		520
Kentucky						
Accountancy Board 332 W Broadway Ste 310 *Web:* www.cpa.ky.gov	Louisville	KY	40202	502-595-3037	595-4500	339-18
Aging Services Office 275 E Main St Ste 3E-E *Web:* www.chfs.ky.gov/dail	Frankfort	KY	40621	502-564-6930	564-4595	339-18
Arts Council 500 Mero St 21st Fl Capital Plaza Tower *Web:* www.artscouncil.ky.gov	Frankfort	KY	40601	502-564-3757		339-18
Attorney General State Capitol Bldg 700 Capitol Ave Ste 120 *Web:* www.e-archives.ky.gov	Frankfort	KY	40601	502-696-5300	564-2894	339-18
Bill Status 702 Capitol Ave Rm 405F *Web:* kentuckyhouserepublicans.org	Frankfort	KY	40601	502-564-8100		433
Child Support Div 730 Schenkel Ln *TF:* 800-248-1163 ■ *Web:* www.chfs.ky.gov	Frankfort	KY	40601	800-248-1163		339-18
Consumer Protection Div 1024 Capital Ctr Dr Ste 200 *TF:* 888-432-9257 ■ *Web:* www.ag.ky.gov	Frankfort	KY	40601	502-696-5389	573-8317	339-18
Corrections Dept 275 E Main St PO Box 2400 *Web:* www.corrections.ky.gov	Frankfort	KY	40602	502-564-4726	564-5037	339-18
Crime Victims Compensation Board 130 Brighton Pk Blvd *TF:* 800-469-2120 ■ *Web:* www. cvcb.ky.gov	Frankfort	KY	40601	502-573-2290	573-4817	339-18
Department of Revenue 501 High St PO Box 68 *Web:* www.revenue.ky.gov	Frankfort	KY	40601	502-564-4581	564-3875	339-18
Economic Development Cabinet 500 Mero St *Web:* www.thinkkentucky.com	Frankfort	KY	40601	502-564-7670		339-18
Education Dept 300 Sower Blvd 5th Fl *Web:* www.education.ky.gov/KDE	Frankfort	KY	40601	502-564-4770		339-18
Education Professional Standards Board 100 Airport Dr 3rd Fl *Web:* www.kyepsb.net	Frankfort	KY	40601	502-564-4606		339-18

	City	State	ZIP	Phone	Fax	Class
Emergency Management Div 100 Minuteman Pkwy **Fax Area Code: 502 ■ TF: 800-255-2587 ■ Web: www.kyem.ky.gov*	Frankfort	KY	40601	800-255-2587	607-1614*	339-18
Finance & Administration Cabinet Capitol Annex Rm 383 *Web:* www.finance.ky.gov	Frankfort	KY	40601	502-564-4240	564-6785	339-18
Fish & Wildlife Resources Dept 1 Sportsman's Ln *TF:* 800-858-1549 ■ *Web:* fw.ky.gov	Frankfort	KY	40601	502-564-3400	564-9845	339-18
General Assembly 700 Capitol Ave State Capitol Bldg *TF:* 800-372-7181 ■ *Web:* www.lrc.state.ky.us	Frankfort	KY	40601	502-564-8100		339-18
Governor 700 Capital Ave Ste 100 *Web:* www.governor.ky.gov	Frankfort	KY	40601	502-564-2611	564-2517	339-18
Governor's Office for Technology 101 Cold Harbor Dr *Web:* www.got.state.ky.us	Frankfort	KY	40601	502-564-1201		339-18
Hairdressers & Cosmetologists Board 111 St James Ct Ste A	Frankfort	KY	40601	502-564-4262	564-0481	339-18
Health & Family Services Cabinet 275 E Main St 5th Fl W *TF:* 800-372-2973 ■ *Web:* www.chfs.ky.gov	Frankfort	KY	40621	502-564-7042	564-7091	339-18
Higher Education Assistance Authority PO Box 798 *TF:* 800-928-8926 ■ *Web:* www.kheaa.com	Frankfort	KY	40602	800-928-8926		725
Historical Society 100 W Broadway *TF:* 877-444-7867 ■ *Web:* www.history.ky.gov	Frankfort	KY	40601	502-564-1792		339-18
Horse Racing Authority 4063 Iron Works Pkwy Bldg B *Web:* khrc.ky.gov	Lexington	KY	40511	859-246-2040	246-2039	712
Housing Corp 1231 Louisville Rd *TF:* 800-633-8896 ■ *Web:* www.kyhousing.org	Frankfort	KY	40601	502-564-7630		339-18
Insurance Dept 215 W Main St *TF:* 800-595-6053 ■ *Web:* insurance.ky.gov	Frankfort	KY	40601	502-564-3630		339-18
Labor Cabinet 1047 Old US Hwy 127 S Ste 4 *Web:* www.labor.ky.gov	Frankfort	KY	40601	502-564-3070		339-18
Legislative Ethics Commission 22 Mill Creek Pk *Web:* www.klec.ky.gov	Frankfort	KY	40601	502-573-2863	573-2929	265
Lieutenant Governor State Capitol Bldg 700 Capitol Ave Ste 142 *Web:* www.ltgovernor.ky.gov	Frankfort	KY	40601	502-564-2611		339-18
Lottery Corp 1011 W Main St *TF:* 800-937-8946 ■ *Web:* www.kylottery.com	Louisville	KY	40202	502-560-1500		452
Medical Licensure Board 310 Whittington Pkwy Ste 1B *Web:* www.kbml.ky.gov	Louisville	KY	40222	502-429-7150	429-7158	339-18
Parks Dept 2 Hudson Hollow Rd Unit 1 *Web:* Www.parks.ky.gov	Frankfort	KY	40601	502-564-2172		339-18
Parole Board PO Box 2400 *Web:* justice.ky.gov	Frankfort	KY	40602	502-564-3620	564-8995	339-18
Postsecondary Education Council 1024 Capital Ctr Dr Ste 320 *Web:* www.cpe.ky.gov	Frankfort	KY	40601	502-573-1555	573-1535	339-18
Real Estate Commission (KREC) 10200 Linn Stn Rd Ste 201 *TF General:* 888-373-3300 ■ *Web:* www.krec.ky.gov	Louisville	KY	40223	502-429-7250	429-7246	339-18
Secretary of State The Capitol Bldg 700 Capital Ave Ste 152 *Web:* www.sos.ky.gov	Frankfort	KY	40601	502-564-3490	564-5687	339-18
State Government Information 229 W Main St Ste 400 *Web:* kentucky.gov	Frankfort	KY	40601	502-875-3733	875-3722	339-18
Supreme Court 700 Capitol Ave Rm 235 *Web:* apps.courts.ky.gov	Frankfort	KY	40601	502-564-5444		339-18
Travel and Tourism Dept 500 Mero St Ste 2200 *TF:* 800-225-8747 ■ *Web:* www.kentuckytourism.com	Frankfort	KY	40601	502-564-4930	564-5695	339-18
Treasury 1050 US Hwy 127 S Ste 100 *Web:* www.kytreasury.com	Frankfort	KY	40601	502-564-4722	564-6545	339-18
Vehicle Regulation Div 200 Mero St 3rd Fl *Web:* drive.ky.gov	Frankfort	KY	40601	502-564-7000	564-6403	339-18
Veterans Affairs Dept (KDVA) 1111B Louisville Rd *TF:* 800-572-6245 ■ *Web:* www.veterans.ky.gov	Frankfort	KY	40601	502-564-9203	564-9240	339-18
Vital Statistics Div 275 E Main St Ste 1EA *Web:* www.chfs.ky.gov	Frankfort	KY	40621	502-564-4212		339-18
Vocational Rehabilitation Dept 275 E Main St *TF:* 800-372-7172 ■ *Web:* ovr.ky.gov	Frankfort	KY	40601	502-564-4440	564-6745	339-18
Kentucky Assn of Realtors 2801 Palumbo Dr Ste 202 *TF:* 800-264-2185 ■ *Web:* www.kyrealtors.com	Lexington	KY	40509	859-263-7377	263-7565	656
Kentucky Bank PO Box 157 *TF:* 800-467-1939 ■ *Web:* www.kybank.com	Paris	KY	40362	859-987-1795		70
Kentucky Bankers Assn 600 W Main St Ste 400 *TF:* 800-392-4045 ■ *Web:* www.kybanks.com	Louisville	KY	40202	502-582-2453		533
Kentucky Bar Assn 514 W Main St *Web:* www.kybar.org	Frankfort	KY	40601	502-564-3795	564-3225	72
Kentucky Chamber of Commerce 464 Chenault Rd *TF:* 800-533-0127 ■ *Web:* www.kychamber.com	Frankfort	KY	40601	502-695-4700		140
Kentucky Christian University 100 Academic Pkwy **Fax:* Admissions ■ *TF Admissions:* 800-522-3181 ■ *Web:* www.kcu.edu	Grayson	KY	41143	606-474-3000	474-3155*	166
Kentucky Concrete Inc 3600 Leitchfield Rd *Web:* www.kyconcrete.com	Cecilia	KY	42724	270-737-8296		182
Kentucky Correctional Industries 1041 Leestown Rd *TF:* 800-828-9524 ■ *Web:* www.kci.ky.gov	Frankfort	KY	40601	502-573-1040	573-1050	630
Kentucky Correctional Institution for Women 3000 Ash Ave *TF:* 877-687-6818 ■ *Web:* corrections.ky.gov	Pewee Valley	KY	40056	502-241-8454	243-0079	213

	City	State	ZIP	Phone	Fax	Class
Kentucky Ctr for African American Heritage 1701 W Muhammad Ali Blvd *Web:* www.kcaah.org	Louisville	KY	40203	502-583-4100		50-2
Kentucky Ctr for, The Performing Arts, The 501 W Main St *TF:* 800-775-7777 ■ *Web:* www.kentuckycenter.org	Louisville	KY	40202	502-562-0100		572
Kentucky Democratic Party 190 Democrat Dr *TF:* 800-995-3386 ■ *Web:* www.kydemocrat.com	Frankfort	KY	40601	502-695-4828	695-7629	616-1
Kentucky Dept for Libraries & Archives 300 Coffee Tree Rd *TF:* 800-372-2968 ■ *Web:* www.kdla.ky.gov	Frankfort	KY	40602	502-564-8300	564-5773	434-5
Kentucky Derby Museum 704 Central Ave *TF:* 800-593-3729 ■ *Web:* www.derbymuseum.org	Louisville	KY	40208	502-637-1111	636-5855	520
Kentucky Downs LLC 5629 Nashville Rd *Web:* www.kentuckydowns.com	Franklin	KY	42135	270-586-7778		642
Kentucky Educational Television (KET) 600 Cooper Dr *TF:* 800-432-0951 ■ *Web:* www.ket.org	Lexington	KY	40502	859-258-7000	258-7399	632
Kentucky Electric Steel LLC 2704 S Big Run Rd W *TF:* 800-333-3012 ■ *Web:* www.kentuckyelectricsteel.com	Ashland	KY	41102	606-929-1200	929-1219	723
Kentucky Enquirer 226 Grandview Dr *Web:* www.kentucky.gov	Covington	KY	41017	859-578-5500		532-2
Kentucky Fair & Expo Ctr 937 Phillips Ln *Web:* www.kyfairexpo.org	Louisville	KY	40209	502-367-5000	367-5139	720
Kentucky Farm Bureau Mutual Insurance Co 9201 Bunsen Pkwy *Web:* kyfb.com	Louisville	KY	40220	502-495-5000		391-4
Kentucky Highlands Investment Corp 362 Old Whitley Rd PO Box 1738 *Web:* www.khic.org	London	KY	40743	606-864-5175	864-5194	402
Kentucky Horse Park 4089 Iron Works Pkwy *TF:* 800-678-8813 ■ *Web:* www.kyhorsepark.com	Lexington	KY	40511	859-233-4303	254-0253	823
Kentucky Hospital Assn 2501 Nelson Miller Pkwy Ste 200 *TF:* 800-945-4542 ■ *Web:* www.kyha.com	Louisville	KY	40223	502-426-6220		533
Kentucky International Convention Ctr 221 S Fourth St *TF:* 800-701-5831 ■ *Web:* www.kyconvention.org	Louisville	KY	40202	502-595-4381		205
Kentucky Medical Assn 9300 Shelbyville Rd Ste 850 *Web:* www.kyma.org	Louisville	KY	40222	502-426-6200	426-6877	474
Kentucky Military History Museum 125 E Main St *Web:* www.history.ky.gov	Frankfort	KY	40601	502-564-1792		520
Kentucky Mountain Bible College 855 Hwy 541 *TF:* 800-879-5622 ■ *Web:* www.kmbc.edu	Jackson	KY	41339	606-693-5000		161
Kentucky Museum of Art & Craft 715 W Main St *Web:* www.kmacmuseum.org	Louisville	KY	40202	502-589-0102		50-2
Kentucky National Insurance Co 2709 Old Rosebud Rd *Web:* www.kynatins.com	Lexington	KY	40509	859-367-5200		390
Kentucky New Era Inc PO Box 729 *Web:* www.kentuckynewera.com	Hopkinsville	KY	42241	270-886-4444		532-3
Kentucky Oil & Refining Co 156 Kentucky Oil Village *Web:* www.teamkore.com	Betsy Layne	KY	41605	606-478-9501		581
Kentucky Opera Assn 323 W Broadway Ste 601 *Web:* www.kyopera.org	Louisville	KY	40202	502-584-4500		573-2
Kentucky Organ Donor Affiliates (KODA) 10160 Linn Station Rd *TF:* 800-525-3456 ■ *Web:* www.kyorgandonor.org	Louisville	KY	40223	502-581-9511	589-5157	545
Kentucky Pharmacists Assn 1228 US 127 S *TF:* 800-922-1557 ■ *Web:* kphanet.org	Frankfort	KY	40601	502-227-2303	227-2258	585
Kentucky Press Assn 101 Consumer Ln *TF Cust Svc:* 800-264-5721 ■ *Web:* www.kypress.com	Frankfort	KY	40601	502-223-8821	226-3867	624
Kentucky Republican Party PO Box 1068 *Web:* www.rpk.org	Frankfort	KY	40602	502-875-5130	223-5625	616-2
Kentucky Science and Technology Corp 200 W Vine St Ste 420 *Web:* www.kstc.com	Lexington	KY	40507	859-233-3502		244
Kentucky Simpson County Clerk 103 W Cedar St *Web:* simpsoncountyclerk.ky.gov/Pages/default.aspx	Franklin	KY	42134	270-586-8161	586-6464	338
Kentucky Speedway 1 Speedway Blvd *TF Resv:* 888-652-7223 ■ *Web:* www.kentuckyspeedway.com	Sparta	KY	41086	859-567-3400	647-4307	515
Kentucky State Reformatory 3001 W Hwy 146 *Web:* corrections.ky.gov	LaGrange	KY	40032	502-222-9441		213
Kentucky State University 400 E Main St **Fax:* Admissions ■ *TF Admissions:* 800-325-1716 ■ *Web:* www.kysu.edu	Frankfort	KY	40601	502-597-6000	597-5814*	166
Kentucky Steel Center Inc 1101 Mayde Rd *Web:* www.kentuckysteel.com	Berea	KY	40403	859-986-0572		492
Kentucky Symphony Orchestra 540 Linden Ave PO Box 72810 *Web:* www.kyso.org	Newport	KY	41072	859-431-6216	431-3097	573-3
Kentucky Theater 214 E Main St *TF:* 800-845-3959 ■ *Web:* www.kentuckytheater.com	Lexington	KY	40507	859-231-7924		572
Kentucky Trailer 7201 Logistics Dr *TF:* 888-598-7245 ■ *Web:* www.kytrailer.com	Louisville	KY	40258	502-637-2551	636-3675	779
Kentucky Trailer Technologies 1240 N Pontiac Trial *TF:* 866-638-6080 ■ *Web:* www.kytrailer.com	Walled Lake	MI	48390	248-960-9700		779
Kentucky Veterinary Medical Assn 108 Consumer Ln *TF:* 800-552-5862 ■ *Web:* www.kvma.org	Frankfort	KY	40601	502-226-5862	226-6177	795
Kentucky Wesleyan College 3000 Frederica St **Fax:* Admissions ■ *TF Admissions:* 800-999-0592 ■ *Web:* www.kwc.edu	Owensboro	KY	42301	270-852-3120	852-3133*	166

Phone | Fax | Class

Kentuky Blood Center
3121 Beaumont Centre Cir .... Lexington KY 40513 859-276-2534 233-4166 89
TF: 800-775-2522 ■ Web: www.kybloodcenter.org

Kentwood Office Furniture Inc
3063 Breton Rd SE .... Grand Rapids MI 49512 616-957-2320 320
TF: 877-698-6250 ■ Web: www.kentwoodoffice.com

Kentwood Public Schools
5820 Eastern Ave SE .... Grand Rapids MI 49508 616-455-4400 455-4476 685
Web: www.kentwoodps.org

Kenvirons Inc 452 Versailles Rd .... Frankfort KY 40601 502-695-4357 695-4363 261
Web: www.kenvirons.com

Kenwal Steel Corp 8223 W Warren Ave .... Dearborn MI 48126 313-739-1000 739-1001 492
Web: www.kenwal.com

Kenway Corp 681 Riverside Dr .... Augusta ME 04330 207-622-6229 596
Web: www.kenway.com

Kenway Distributors Inc
6320 Strawberry Ln .... Louisville KY 40214 502-367-2201 368-5519 406
TF: 800-292-9478 ■ Web: www.kenway.net

Kenwel Printers Inc
4272 Indianola Ave .... Columbus OH 43214 614-261-1011 627
Web: kenwelprinters.com

Kenwood 75 Varney Pl .... San Francisco CA 94107 415-957-5333 514
Web: www.kenwoodx.com

Kenwood Towne Centre
7875 Montgomery Rd .... Cincinnati OH 45236 513-745-9100 460
Web: www.kenwoodtownecentre.com

Kenwood USA Corp
2201 E Dominguez St .... Long Beach CA 90810 310-639-9000 647
TF: 800-536-9663 ■ Web: www.kenwoodusa.com

Kenworth Northwest Inc
20220 International Blvd S .... SeaTac WA 98198 206-433-5911 878-7676 57
TF: 800-562-0060 ■ Web: www.kenworthnorthwest.com

Kenworth of Indianapolis Inc
2929 S Holt Rd .... Indianapolis IN 46241 317-247-8421 241-5742 57
TF: 800-827-8421 ■ Web: www.palmertrucks.com

Kenworth Sales Co
2125 Constitution Blvd .... West Valley City UT 84119 801-487-4161 780
TF General: 800-222-7831 ■ Web: www.kenworthsalesco.com

Kenworth Truck Co 10630 NE 38th Pl .... Kirkland WA 98033 425-828-5000 516
Web: www.kenworth.com

Kenya 866 UN Plaza Rm 304 .... New York NY 10017 212-421-4741 784
Web: www.kenyaun.org

Kenya Embassy 2249 R St NW .... Washington DC 20008 202-387-6101 462-3829 257
Web: www.kenyaembassy.com

Kenya Tourism Board
6033 W Century Blvd Ste 900 .... Los Angeles CA 90045 310-649-7718 914-6946* 775
*Fax Area Code: 952 ■ TF: 800-223-6486 ■ Web: www.magicalkenya.com

Kenyon College 103 College Dr .... Gambier OH 43022 740-427-5000 427-5770 166
TF: 800-848-2468 ■ Web: www.kenyon.edu

Kenyon Industries Inc 36 Sherman Ave .... Kenyon RI 02836 401-364-3400 364-6130 745-7
TF: 800-247-6658 ■ Web: www.brookwoodcos.com

Kenyon Plastering Inc
4001 W Indian School Rd .... Phoenix AZ 85019 602-233-1191 278-6801 550
TF: 800-949-4319 ■ Web: www.kenyonweb.com

Kenyon Press Inc
1 Kenyon Press Dr PO Box 710 .... Sherburne NY 13460 607-674-9066 627
Web: www.kenyonpress.net

Kenzer Group LLC 1 Penn Plaza .... New York NY 10119 212-308-4300 266
TF: 800-981-3849 ■ Web: www.kenzer.com

KEO Cutters Inc 25040 Easy St .... Warren MI 48089 586-771-2050 771-2062 493
TF: 888-390-2050 ■ Web: www.keocutters.com

Keo's 2028 Kuhio Ave .... Honolulu HI 96815 808-951-9355 671
Web: www.keosthaicuisine.com

KEOGH Consulting Inc
10217 Brecksville Rd Ste 101 .... Brecksville OH 44141 440-526-2002 196
Web: www.keogh1.com

Keokuk Area Chamber of Commerce
329 Main St .... Keokuk IA 52632 319-524-5055 524-5016 139
Web: www.keokukchamber.wildapricot.org

Keokuk Area Hospital 1600 Morgan St .... Keokuk IA 52632 319-524-7150 524-5317 374-3
Web: www.keokukhealthsystems.org

Keokuk County 101 S Main St .... Sigourney IA 52591 641-622-2210 622-2171 338
Web: www.keokukcountyia.com

Keokuk National Cemetery 1701 J St .... Keokuk IA 52632 309-782-2094 524-8118* 136
*Fax Area Code: 319 ■ TF: 800-273-8255 ■ Web: www.cem.va.gov/cems/nchp/keokuk.asp

Keowee-Toxaway State Natural Area
108 Residence Dr .... Sunset SC 29685 864-868-2605 565
Web: www.southcarolinaparks.com

Kepco Inc 131-38 Sanford Ave .... Flushing NY 11355 718-461-7000 767-1102 253
TF: 800-526-2324 ■ Web: www.kepcopower.com

Kepler Group LLC 6 E 32nd St 9th Fl .... New York NY 10016 646-524-6896 5
Web: www.keplergrp.com

Kepner Plastics Fabricators Inc
3131 Lomita Blvd .... Torrance CA 90505 310-325-3162 326-8560 600
Web: www.kepnerplastics.com

Kepner Products Co
995 N Ellsworth Ave .... Villa Park IL 60181 630-279-1550 279-9669 790
Web: www.kepner.com

Kepner-Tregoe Inc PO Box 704 .... Princeton NJ 08542 609-921-2806 497-0130 194
TF: 800-537-6378 ■ Web: www.kepner-tregoe.com

Keppel Union School District
PO Box 186 .... Pearblossom CA 93553 661-944-2155 944-2933 685
Web: www.keppel.k12.ca.us

Keppler Speakers Bureau
3030 Clarendon Blvd 7th Fl .... Arlington VA 22201 703-516-4000 516-4819 708
TF: 800-463-4693 ■ Web: www.kepplerspeakers.com

Kepware Inc 400 Congress St 4th Fl .... Portland ME 04101 207-775-1660 177
Web: www.kepware.com

Ker & Downey Inc 6703 Hwy Blvd .... Katy TX 77494 281-371-2500 371-2514 760
TF: 800-423-4236 ■ Web: www.kerdowney.com

KERA-FM 90.1 (NPR)
3000 Harry Hines Blvd .... Dallas TX 75201 214-871-1390 754-0635 645-44
TF: 800-456-5372 ■ Web: www.kera.org

KERAMIDA Inc 401 N College Ave .... Indianapolis IN 46202 317-685-6600 192
TF: 800-508-8034 ■ Web: keramida.com

Kerasotes ShowPlace Theatres LLC
1011 S Delano Ct .... Chicago IL 60605 312-447-6304 748
Web: showplaceicon.com

KERA-TV Ch 13 (PBS)
3000 Harry Hines Blvd .... Dallas TX 75201 214-871-1390 741-37
TF: 800-683-1899 ■ Web: www.kera.org

Keres Consulting Inc
5600 Wymng Blvd 225 .... Albuquerque NM 87109 505-837-2104 196
Web: www.keresnm.com

Kerite Co 49 Day St .... Seymour CT 06483 203-888-2591 888-1987 813
TF: 800-777-7483 ■ Web: www.kerite.com

Kerkau Manufacturing Co
1321 S Valley Ctr Dr .... Bay City MI 48706 989-686-0350 686-0399 483
TF: 800-248-5060 ■ Web: www.kerkau.com

Kerkstra Precast Inc 3373 Busch Dr .... Grandville MI 49418 616-224-6176 106
TF: 800-434-5830 ■ Web: www.kerkstra.com

Kerley & Sears Inc
4331 Cement Valley Rd .... Midlothian TX 76065 972-775-3902 791
TF: 800-346-4381 ■ Web: www.kerleyandsears.net

Kerley Ink Engineers Inc
2700 S 12th Ave .... Broadview IL 60155 708-344-1295 865-5759 388
TF: 800-359-5679 ■ Web: www.kerleyink.com

Kerlin Capital Group LLC
624 S Grand Ave Ste 2450 .... Los Angeles CA 90071 213-627-3300 627-2134 401
Web: www.kerlincapital.com

Kern Community College District
2100 Chester Ave .... Bakersfield CA 93301 661-336-5100 167
Web: www.kccd.edu

Kern County
1115 Truxtun Ave 5th Fl .... Bakersfield CA 93301 661-868-3198 868-3190 338
TF: 800-735-2929 ■ Web: www.co.kern.ca.us

Kern County Board of Trade
2101 Oak St .... Bakersfield CA 93301 661-868-5376 868-5376 139
TF General: 800-787-9920 ■ Web: www.visitkern.com

Kern County High School District
5801 Sundale Ave .... Bakersfield CA 93309 661-827-3100 827-3300 685
Web: www.kernhigh.org

Kern County Museum
3801 Chester Ave .... Bakersfield CA 93301 661-437-3330 520
Web: www.kcmuseum.org

Kern Health Systems
9700 Stockdale Hwy .... Bakersfield CA 93311 661-664-5000 231
TF: 888-466-2219 ■ Web: www.kernfamilyhealthcare.com

Kern Medical Ctr
1700 Mt Vernon Ave .... Bakersfield CA 93306 661-326-2000 326-2969* 374-3
*Fax: Admitting ■ Web: www.kernmedical.com

Kern Oil & Refining Co
7724 E Panama Ln .... Bakersfield CA 93307 661-845-0761 579
Web: www.kernoil.com

Kern Organization Inc
20955 Warner Ctr Ln .... Los Angeles CA 91367 818-703-8775 195
Web: kernagency.com

Kern River Gas Transmission Co
2755 E Cottonwood Pkwy Ste 300 .... Salt Lake City UT 84121 801-937-6000 325
TF: 800-420-7500 ■ Web: www.kernrivergas.com

Kern Schools Federal Credit Union
PO Box 9506 .... Bakersfield CA 93389 661-833-7900 219
TF: 800-221-3311 ■ Web: www.kcfcu.org

Kern Steel Fabrication Inc
627 Williams St .... Bakersfield CA 93305 661-327-9588 480
TF: 800-404-5376 ■ Web: kernsteel.com

Kern Valley Museum
49 Big Blue Rd PO Box 651 .... Kernville CA 93238 760-376-0083 520
TF: 800-545-2433 ■ Web: kernvalleymuseum.org

Kernan Hospital 2200 Kernan Dr .... Baltimore MD 21207 410-448-2500 374-6
Web: umrehabortho.org

Kerneos Inc 1316 Priority Ln .... Chesapeake VA 23324 757-494-1947 135
Web: www.kerneosinc.com

Kernodle Clinic Inc
1234 Huffman Mill Rd .... Burlington NC 27215 336-538-1234 374-3
Web: kernodle.duhs.duke.edu

Kerns Manufacturing Corp
37-14 29th St .... Long Island NY 11101 718-784-4044 786-0534 488
Web: www.kernsmfg.com

Kernutt Stokes LLP 1600 Executive Pkwy .... Eugene OR 97401 541-687-1170 2
Web: kernuttstokes.com

KERO-TV Ch 23 (ABC) 321 21st St .... Bakersfield CA 93301 661-637-2323 323-5538* 741-10
*Fax: News Rm ■ TF: 800-275-0764 ■ Web: www.turnto23.com

Kerr County 700 Main St Rm 122 .... Kerrville TX 78028 830-792-2255 895-1861 338
Web: www.co.kerr.tx.us

Kerr Energy Companies LLC
3400 Louisiana St .... Houston TX 77002 281-216-5089 536
Web: www.kerrenergycompanies.com

Kerr Lake State Recreation Area
6254 Satterwhite Pt Rd .... Henderson NC 27537 252-438-7791 565
Web: www.ncparks.gov

Kerr Lakeside Inc 26841 Tungsten Rd .... Euclid OH 44132 216-261-2100 261-9798 621
TF: 800-487-5377 ■ Web: www.kerrlakeside.com

Kerr Pump & Supply
12880 Cloverdale St .... Oak Park MI 48237 248-543-3880 543-3236 641
TF: 800-482-8259 ■ Web: www.kerrpump.com

Kerrington Group Inc
24 S fifth St .... Fernandina Beach FL 32034 904-491-1411 180
TF: 800-582-0828 ■ Web: www.kerringtongroup.com

Kerrville Area Chamber of Commerce
1700 Sidney Baker St Ste 100 .... Kerrville TX 78028 830-896-1155 896-1175 139
Web: www.kerrvilletx.com

Kerrville Bus Co 1 S Main St .... Del Rio TX 78840 830-775-7515 107
TF: 800-474-3352 ■ Web: www.iridekbc.com

Kerrville Convention & Visitors Bureau
2108 Sidney Baker St .... Kerrville TX 78028 830-792-3535 792-3230 206
TF: 800-221-7958 ■ Web: www.kerrvilletexascvb.com

Kerrville National Cemetery
3600 Memorial Blvd .... Kerrville TX 78028 210-820-3891 820-3445 136
TF: 800-273-8255 ■ Web: www.cem.va.gov

Kerrville State Hospital
721 Thompson Dr .... Kerrville TX 78028 830-896-2211 792-4926 374-5
TF: 888-963-7111 ■ Web: www.dshs.texas.gov/mhhospitals/kerrvillesh

Kerry Group LLC, The 44 Soccer Park Rd .... Fenton MO 63026 636-203-5550 184
Web: www.kerrygroup.net

Phone | Fax | Class

Kerry's Nursery Inc
21840 SW 258th St .... Homestead FL 33031 800-331-9127 369
TF: 800-331-9127 ■ *Web:* www.kerrys.com

Kerrytown Concert House
415 N Fourth Ave .... Ann Arbor MI 48104 734-769-2999 572
TF: 800-585-3737 ■ *Web:* www.kerrytownconcerthouse.com

Kershaw Correctional Institution
4848 Gold Mine Hwy .... Kershaw SC 29067 803-896-3301 213
Web: www.doc.sc.gov

Kershaw County 1121 Broad St Rm 202 .... Camden SC 29020 803-425-7226 425-6044 338
Web: www.kershaw.sc.gov

Kershaw County Chamber of Commerce
607 S Broad St .... Camden SC 29020 803-432-2525 432-4181 139
TF: 800-968-4037 ■ *Web:* www.kershawcountychamber.org

Kershaw County School District
2029 W DeKalb St .... Camden SC 29020 803-432-8416 425-8918 685
Web: www.kcsdschools.net

KershawHealth Medical Center
1315 Roberts St .... Camden SC 29020 803-432-4311 374-3
Web: www.kershawhealth.org

Kershaw-Ryan State Park PO Box 985 .... Caliente NV 89008 775-726-3564 565
Web: parks.nv.gov/parks/kershaw-ryan-state-park

Kerton Group 8032 Canyon Creek Cir .... Pleasanton CA 94588 408-935-8702 193
Web: kertongroup.com

Kerusso Activewear Inc
402 Hwy 62 Spur .... Berryville AR 72616 870-423-6242 687
TF: 800-424-0943 ■ *Web:* www.kerusso.com

Keryx Biopharmaceuticals Inc
1 Marina Park Dr 20th Fl .... Boston MA 02210 617-466-3500 466-3501 582
NASDAQ: KERX ■ *TF:* 800-903-0247 ■ *Web:* www.keryx.com

Kerzner International Ltd
1000 S Pine Island Rd Ste 800 .... Plantation FL 33324 954-809-2000 132
Web: www.kerzner.com

Kesler-Schaefer Auto Auction Inc
5333 W 46th St PO Box 53203 .... Indianapolis IN 46254 317-297-2300 297-6234 516
TF: 800-959-5722 ■ *Web:* www.ksaa1.com

Kesner, Godes & Morrissey LLC
15 Pacella Park Dr Ste 200 .... Randolph MA 02368 781-961-2900 961-2927 2
Web: www.kgmcpa.com

KESQ-TV Ch 3 (ABC)
42650 Melanie Pl .... Palm Desert CA 92211 760-318-8528 343-7480 741
TF: 888-776-8538 ■ *Web:* www.kesq.com

Kesselman Jones
3411 Candelaria Rd NE Ste G .... Albuquerque NM 87107 505-266-3461 195
TF: 866-219-4582 ■ *Web:* www.kessjones.com

Kesselrun 8215 Roswell Rd Ste 925 .... Atlanta GA 30350 770-640-9100 463

Kessington Aerospace
1020 County Rd 6 W .... Elkhart IN 46514 574-266-4500 266-8899 454
Web: www.kessington.com

Kessler & Assoc Inc
31800 NW Hwy .... Farmington Hills MI 48334 248-855-4224 855-4405 194
Web: www.kesslercpa.com

Kessler Crane Inc
1901 Western Ave Ste .... Plymouth IN 46563 574-936-3341 344
Web: www.kesslercrane.com

Kessler Industries
8600 Gateway Blvd E .... El Paso TX 79907 915-591-8161 598-7353 319-2
Web: www.kesslerind.com

Kessler International
45 Rockefeller Plaza Ste 2000 .... New York NY 10111 212-286-9100 730-2433 400
TF: 800-932-2221 ■ *Web:* www.investigation.com

Kessler Orlean Silver & Company PC
1101 Lake Cook Rd Ste C .... Deerfield IL 60015 847-580-4100 2
Web: koscpa.com

Kessler Sign Co 5804 Poe Ave .... Dayton OH 45414 937-898-0633 701
TF: 800-686-1870 ■ *Web:* www.kesslersignco.com

Kessler's Food & Liquor
615 Sixth Ave SE .... Aberdeen SD 57401 605-225-1692 345
Web: kesslersgrocery.com

Kessler's Inc 1201 Hummel Ave .... Lemoyne PA 17043 717-763-7162 763-4982 296-26
TF: 800-382-1328 ■ *Web:* www.kesslerfoods.com

Kester Inc 800 W Thorndale Ave .... Itasca IL 60143 630-616-4000 616-4044 145
TF: 800-253-7837 ■ *Web:* www.kester.com

Kestrel Labs Inc 3133 Indian Rd Ste K .... Boulder CO 80301 303-544-0660 177
Web: www.kestrellabs.com

Keswick Hall 701 Club Dr .... Keswick VA 22947 434-979-3440 977-4171 379
TF: 888-778-2565 ■ *Web:* www.keswick.com

Keswick Multi-Care Ctr
700 W 40th St .... Baltimore MD 21211 410-235-8860 662-4324 450
TF: 800-706-0766 ■ *Web:* choosekeswick.org

KET (Kentucky Educational Television)
600 Cooper Dr .... Lexington KY 40502 859-258-7000 258-7399 632
TF: 800-432-0951 ■ *Web:* www.ket.org

KET 600 Cooper Dr .... Lexington KY 40502 859-258-7000 258-7399 741
TF: 800-432-0951 ■ *Web:* www.ket.org

Ketcher & Co Inc 1717 E 5th .... North Little Rock AR 72114 501-372-5216 189-12
Web: ketcherco.com

Ketchikan Correctional Ctr
1201 Schoenbar Rd .... Ketchikan AK 99901 907-228-7350 225-7031 213
Web: www.correct.state.ak.us

Ketchikan Gateway Borough
1900 First Ave Ste 115 .... Ketchikan AK 99901 907-228-6604 338
Web: www.borough.ketchikan.ak.us

Ketchikan Integrated Support Command
1300 Stedman St .... Ketchikan AK 99901 907-228-0340 158
Web: www.uscg.mil

Ketchikan Ports & Harbors Dept
2933 Tongass Ave .... Ketchikan AK 99901 907-228-5632 618
Web: www.ktn-ak.us

Ketchikan Visitors Bureau
131 Front St .... Ketchikan AK 99901 907-225-6166 225-4250 206
TF: 800-770-3300 ■ *Web:* www.visit-ketchikan.com

Ketchmark & Assoc Inc 145 Tower Dr .... Burr Ridge IL 60527 630-850-7774 261

Ketchum 1285 Ave of the Americas .... New York NY 10019 646-935-3900 636
Web: www.ketchum.com

KETC-TV Ch 9 (PBS) 3655 Olive St .... Saint Louis MO 63108 314-512-9000 512-9005 741-114
TF: 855-482-5382 ■ *Web:* ninenet.org

Ketek Industries Ltd
20204 - 110 Ave NW .... Edmonton AB T5S1X8 780-447-5050 539
Web: www.ketek.ca

KETG-TV Ch 9 (PBS) 350 S Donaghey Ave .... Conway AR 72034 501-682-2386 682-4122 741
TF: 800-662-2386 ■ *Web:* www.aetn.org

KETH-TV Ch 14 (TBN)
10902 S Wilcrest Dr .... Houston TX 77099 281-561-5828 741-60
Web: myedutv.org

KETS-TV Ch 2 (PBS) 350 S Donaghey Ave .... Conway AR 72034 501-682-2386 682-4122 741
TF: 800-662-2386 ■ *Web:* www.aetn.org

Kett Engineering Corp
15500 Erwin St Ste 1029 .... Van Nuys CA 91411 818-908-5388 743
TF: 877-372-6799 ■ *Web:* www.ketteng.com

Kettering University
1700 University Ave .... Flint MI 48504 810-762-9500 762-9837 166
TF: 800-955-4464 ■ *Web:* www.kettering.edu

Kettering-Moraine-Oakwood Area Chamber of Commerce
2977 Far Hills Ave .... Kettering OH 45419 937-299-3852 299-3851 139
TF: 800-621-8931 ■ *Web:* www.kmo-coc.org

Kettle Creek State Park
97 Kettle Creek Pk Ln .... Renovo PA 17764 570-923-6004 565
Web: www.dcnr.state.pa.us

Kettle Moraine Correctional Institution
PO Box 31 .... Plymouth WI 53073 920-526-3244 526-9320 213
Web: doc.wi.gov

Kettle Moraine State Forest - Northern Unit
N1765 Hwy G .... Campbellsport WI 53010 262-626-2116 565
Web: www.dnr.wi.gov

Kettle Moraine State Forest - Pike Lake Unit
3544 Kettle Moraine Rd .... Hartford WI 53027 262-670-3400 670-3411 565
Web: dnr.wi.gov

Kettle Moraine State Forest Southern Unit
S91 W39091 Hwy 59 .... Eagle WI 53119 262-594-6200 565
Web: dnr.wi.gov/newurl.html

Kettle Moraine State Forest-Lapham Peak Unit
W329 N846 County Hwy C .... Delafield WI 53018 262-646-4421 565
Web: dnr.wi.gov

Kettler 8255 Greensboro Dr Ste 200 .... McLean VA 22102 703-641-9000 641-9630 653
Web: www.kettler.com

Kettletown State Park
1400 Georges Hill Rd .... Southbury CT 06488 203-264-5678 565
Web: www.ct.gov

KETV-TV Ch 7 (ABC) 2665 Douglas St .... Omaha NE 68131 402-345-7777 741-94
TF: 800-279-5388 ■ *Web:* www.ketv.com

Keuka College 141 Central Ave .... Keuka Park NY 14478 315-279-5254 536-5386* 166
**Fax: Admissions* ■ *TF Admissions:* 866-632-9992 ■ *Web:* www.keuka.edu

Keuka Lake State Park
3560 Pepper Rd .... Keuka Park NY 14478 315-536-3666 565
Web: parks.ny.gov/parks/67/hunting.aspx

Keurig Green Mountain Inc
33 Coffee Ln .... Waterbury VT 05676 831-633-6300 159

Keurig Inc 53 S Ave .... Burlington MA 01867 866-901-2739 102
TF: 866-901-2739 ■ *Web:* www.keurig.com

Kevin Ahrenholz Law Firm
620 Lafayette St Ste 300 .... Waterloo IA 50703 319-433-0754 445
Web: beecherlaw.com

Kevin Guest House 782 Ellicott St .... Buffalo NY 14203 716-882-1818 882-1291 372
Web: www.kevinguesthouse.com

Kevin J Goering CPA Pa
2201 W 25th St .... Lawrence KS 66047 785-832-8300 2
Web: goeringcpa.com

KEVN Black Hills Fox
2001 Skyline Dr .... Rapid City SD 57701 605-394-7777 747-7791* 741-106
**Fax Area Code: 202* ■ *Web:* www.blackhillsfox.com

Kewanna Metal Specialties Inc (KMS)
419 W Main St .... Kewanna IN 46939 574-653-2554 653-2556 73
Web: www.kmswire.com

Kewaunee County 613 Dodge St .... Kewaunee WI 54216 920-388-7144 338
Web: www.kewauneeco.org

Kewaunee Fabrications LLC
520 N Main St .... Kewaunee WI 54216 920-388-2000 388-0263 454
TF: 800-450-7260 ■ *Web:* www.kewauneefabrications.com

Kewaunee Scientific Corp
2700 W Front St PO Box 1842 .... Statesville NC 28687 704-873-7202 873-5160* 420
NASDAQ: KEQU ■ **Fax: Sales* ■ *TF:* 800-824-6626 ■ *Web:* www.kewaunee.com

Keweenaw Bay Indian Community
16429 Bear Town Rd .... Baraga MI 49908 906-353-6623 452
Web: www.kbic-nsn.gov

Keweenaw Bay Ojibwa Community College
111 Beartown Rd .... Baraga MI 49908 906-353-4600 353-8107 165
Web: www.kbocc.org

Keweenaw County 902 College Ave .... Houghton MI 49931 906-482-5240 338
Web: www.keweenaw.org

Keweenaw Financial Corp 235 Quincy St .... Hancock MI 49930 906-482-0404 482-4403 360-2
TF: 866-482-0404 ■ *Web:* www.snb-t.com

Keweenaw National Historical Park
25970 Red Jacket Rd PO Box 471 .... Calumet MI 49913 906-337-3168 337-3169 564
Web: www.nps.gov

Keweenaw Research Ctr
1400 Townsend Dr 1400 Townsend Dr .... Houghton MI 49931 906-487-2750 487-2202 668
Web: www.mtukrc.org

KEWF-FM Radio Billings, LLC
222 N 32nd St 10th Fl .... Billings MT 59101 406-238-1000 238-1038 645-19
Web: www.985thewolf.com

Kewin Consulting 62 Twenty Seventh St .... Toronto ON M8W2X4 416-802-2526 463
TF: 800-873-9118 ■ *Web:* www.kewin.ca

KEX-AM 1190 (N/T)
13333 SW 68th Pkwy Ste 310 .... Poland OR 97223 503-323-6400 645-128
Web: 1190kex.iheart.com

Key Arena 305 Harrison St .... Seattle WA 98109 206-684-7202 720
Web: www.seattlecenter.com

Key Bank 65 Dutch Hill Rd .... Orangeburg NY 10962 800-539-2968 70
TF Cust Svc: 800-539-2968 ■ *Web:* www.key.com

Key Bellevilles Inc 100 Key Ln .... Leechburg PA 15656 724-295-5111 492
TF: 800-245-3600 ■ *Web:* www.keybellevilles.com

Key Blue Prints Inc
195 E Livingston Ave .... Columbus OH 43215 614-225-7787 113
Web: www.key-evidence.com

Name / Address	City	State	Zip	Phone	Fax	Class
Key Cadillac Inc 6825 York Ave S *Web:* keycadillac.com	Edina	MN	55435	952-920-4300		57
Key Club International 3636 Woodview Trace *TF:* 800-549-2647 ■ *Web:* www.keyclub.org	Indianapolis	IN	46268	317-875-8755	879-0204	48-15
Key Computing 85 Sea Ln *Web:* keycomputing.com	Farmingdale	NY	11735	631-264-0660		225
Key Construction Inc 741 W Second *Web:* www.keyconstruction.com	Wichita	KS	67203	316-263-9515		186
Key Container Corp 21 Campbell St *TF:* 800-343-8811 ■ *Web:* www.keycontainercorp.com	Pawtucket	RI	02861	401-723-2000	725-5980	100
Key Corporate Services LLC 9746 Olympia Dr *TF:* 800-288-9748 ■ *Web:* kcsllc.net	Fishers	IN	46037	317-598-1950		260
Key Curriculum Press 1150 65th St *Fax Area Code: 800 ■ *TF:* 800-338-3987 ■ *Web:* www.keycurriculum.com	Emeryville	CA	94608	510-595-7000	541-2442*	637-2
Key Energy 2210 W Broadway *Web:* www.keyenergy.com	Sweetwater	TX	79556	325-236-6611		780
Key Equipment Finance 1000 S McCaslin Blvd *TF:* 888-301-6238 ■ *Web:* www.keyequipmentfinance.com	Superior	CO	80027	888-301-6238		216
Key Event Group LLC, The 3815 Hilldale Dr *TF:* 800-657-6910 ■ *Web:* www.nashvilledmc.com	Nashville	TN	37215	615-352-6900	385-4976	184
Key Events Inc 657 Mission St Ste 202 *Web:* www.keyevents.com	San Francisco	CA	94105	415-695-8000		179
Key Fasteners Corp 525 Key Way Dr *Web:* adamswells.com	Berne	IN	46711	260-589-2626		351
Key Fire Hose Corp (KFH) PO Box 7107 *TF:* 800-447-5666 ■ *Web:* keyhose.com	Dothan	AL	36302	334-671-5532		370
Key Food Stores Co-op Inc 1200 S Ave *Web:* keyfood.com	Staten Island	NY	10314	718-370-4200		297-8
Key Handling Systems Inc 137 W Commercial Ave *Web:* www.keyhandling.com	Moonachie	NJ	07074	201-933-9333		470
Key Industries Inc 400 Marble Rd *TF:* 800-835-0365 ■ *Web:* www.keyapparel.com	Fort Scott	KS	66701	620-223-2000		155-19
Key Information Systems Inc 30077 Agoura Ct 1st Fl *TF:* 877-442-3249 ■ *Web:* www.keyisit.com	Agoura Hills	CA	91301	818-992-8950	992-8970	178-11
Key Largo Chamber of Commerce 106000 Overseas Hwy *Web:* keylargochamber.org	Key Largo	FL	33037	305-451-1414	451-4726	139
Key Largo Grande Resort & Beach Club 97000 S Overseas Hwy *TF Resv:* 888-871-3437 ■ *Web:* www.keylargoresort.com	Key Largo	FL	33037	305-852-5553		669
Key Largo Marriott Bay Resort 103800 Overseas Hwy *TF Resv:* 888-731-9056 ■ *Web:* www.marriottkeylargo.com	Key Largo	FL	33037	305-453-0000		669
Key Lime Air Corp 13252 E Control Tower Rd *TF:* 888-870-9626 ■ *Web:* www.keylimeair.com	Englewood	CO	80112	303-768-9626		13
Key Lime Inn 725 Truman Ave *TF:* 800-549-4430 ■ *Web:* www.historickeywestinns.com	Key West	FL	33040	305-294-5229	294-9623	379
Key Magazine Inc PO Box 111266 *TF:* 888-807-2757 ■ *Web:* www.keymemphis.com	Memphis	TN	38111	901-458-3912	458-5723	457-22
Key Polymer Corp 17 Shepherd St *Web:* www.keypolymer.com	Lawrence	MA	01843	978-683-9411	686-7729	3
Key Safety Systems Inc 7000 Nineteen Mile Rd *OTC: BDTTZ* ■ *Web:* www.keysafetyinc.com	Sterling Heights	MI	48314	586-726-3800		678
Key Software Systems LLC 5100 Belmar Blvd *TF:* 800-220-0779 ■ *Web:* www.keysoftwaresystems.com	Farmingdale	NJ	07727	732-409-6068		180
Key Speakers Bureau Inc 3500 E Coast Hwy Ste 6 *TF:* 800-675-1175 ■ *Web:* www.keyspeakers.com	Corona del Mar	CA	92625	949-675-7856	675-1478	708
Key Technology Inc 150 Avery St *NASDAQ: KTEC* ■ *TF:* 877-341-5668 ■ *Web:* www.key.net	Walla Walla	WA	99362	509-529-2161	527-1331	298
Key Tronic Corp 4424 N Sullivan Rd *NASDAQ: KTCC* ■ *Web:* www.keytronic.com	Spokane	WA	99214	509-928-8000	927-5555	253
Key West Aloe 13095 N Telecom Pkwy *TF:* 800-445-2563 ■ *Web:* www.keywestaloe.com	Tampa	FL	33637	800-445-2563		214
Key West Aquarium 1 Whitehead St *TF:* 888-544-5927 ■ *Web:* www.keywestaquarium.com	Key West	FL	33040	305-296-2051		40
Key West Art & Historical Society 281 Front St *Web:* www.kwahs.com	Key West	FL	33040	305-295-6616		520
Key West Boats Inc 593 Ridgeville Rd PO Box 399 *Web:* www.keywestboatsinc.com	Ridgeville	SC	29472	843-873-0112	821-6334	90
Key West Botanical Garden 5210 College Rd *Web:* keywest.garden	Key West	FL	33040	305-296-1504	296-2242	97
Key West Citizen 3420 Northside Dr *Web:* www.keysnews.com	Key West	FL	33040	305-292-7777		532-2
Key West City Hall 3132 Flagler Ave *TF:* 800-955-8770 ■ *Web:* www.cityofkeywest-fl.gov	Key West	FL	33040	305-809-3700	809-3833	337
Key West International Airport 3491 S Roosevelt Blvd *TF:* 800-327-1390 ■ *Web:* keywestinternationalairport.com	Key West	FL	33040	305-809-5200		27
Key West Key 726 Passover Ln *Fax Area Code: 305 ■ *TF:* 800-881-7321 ■ *Web:* www.keywestkey.com	Key West	FL	33040	800-881-7321	294-2974*	376
Key West Lighthouse & Keepers Quarters Museum 938 Whitehead St *TF:* 800-786-5445 ■ *Web:* www.kwahs.org	Key West	FL	33040	305-294-0012	294-0012	520
Key West Technologies LLC 101 N Clematis St Ste 308	West Palm Beach	FL	33401	561-282-6160		463
Key West Visitors Ctr 510 Greene St 1st Fl *TF General:* 800-533-5397 ■ *Web:* www.keywestchamber.org	Key West	FL	33040	305-294-2587	294-7806	206
Key: This Week in Chicago Magazine 222 W Ontario St Ste 420 *TF:* 877-866-0966 ■ *Web:* www.keymagazinechicago.com	Chicago	IL	60654	312-943-0838	664-6113	457-22
Key2 Consulting LLC 11555 Medlock Bridge Rd *Web:* www.key2consulting.com	Johns Creek	GA	30097	770-402-6938		631
Keya Paha County PO Box 349 *Web:* www.co.keya-paha.ne.us	Springview	NE	68778	402-497-3791	497-3799	338
Keyano College 8115 Franklin Ave *TF:* 800-251-1408 ■ *Web:* www.keyano.ca	Fort Mcmurray	AB	T9H2H7	780-791-4800		95
Keyboard Magazine 28 E 28th St 12th Fl *Fax Area Code: 555 ■ *TF Cust Svc:* 800-483-2433 ■ *Web:* www.keyboardmag.com	New York	NY	10016	212-378-0400	555-4564*	457-9
Keybridge Medical Revenue Management 2348 Baton Rouge Ave *Web:* www.keybridgemed.com	Lima	OH	45805	419-993-2900		160
Keybridge Research LLC 3050 K St NW Ste 220 *Web:* keybridgedc.com	Washington	DC	20007	202-965-9480		466
Keycentrix LLC 2420 N Woodlawn Bldg 500 *Web:* www.keycentrix.com	Wichita	KS	67220	316-262-2231		177
Keycom Communications 1144 Solana Ave *TF:* 800-780-3631 ■ *Web:* www.keycom.net	Winter Park	FL	32789	407-949-0600		225
KeyCorp 127 Public Sq *NYSE: KEY* ■ *TF:* 800-539-9055 ■ *Web:* www.key.com	Cleveland	OH	44114	216-689-8481		360-2
Keydata International Inc 201 Cir Dr N Ste 101	Piscataway	NJ	08854	732-868-0588		173-2
Keyes Coverage Inc 5900 Hiatus Rd *Web:* keyescoverage.com	Tamarac	FL	33321	954-724-7000		390
Keyes Packaging Group Inc 3715 State Hwy *Web:* www.keyespackaging.com	Wenatchee	WA	98807	509-663-8537		601
Keyes Toyota 5855 Van Nuys Blvd *TF:* 844-781-4304 ■ *Web:* www.keyestoyota.com	Van Nuys	CA	91401	844-781-4304	781-4304	57
KEYE-TV Ch 42 (CBS) 10700 Metric Blvd *TF:* 800-621-3362 ■ *Web:* www.keyetv.com	Austin	TX	78758	512-835-0042	490-2111	741-9
Keyhole State Park 22 Marina Rd *Web:* wyoparks.state.wy.us	Moorcroft	WY	82721	307-756-3596		565
KeyImpact Sales & Systems Inc 1701 Crossroads Dr *TF:* 800-955-0600 ■ *Web:* www.kisales.com	Odenton	MD	21113	800-955-0600		691
Keylogic Systems Inc 3168 Collins Ferry Rd *Web:* keylogic.com	Morgantown	WV	26505	304-296-9100		225
Keymarket Communications 1370 Wash Pke Ste 406	Bridgeville	PA	15017	740-676-5661		645
KEYN-FM 103.7 (Oldies) 9111 E Douglas Ste 130 *TF:* 800-618-8255 ■ *Web:* www.keyn.com	Wichita	KS	67208	316-685-2121		645-175
Keynote Systems Inc 777 Mariners Island Blvd *NASDAQ: KEYN* ■ *TF:* 888-539-7978 ■ *Web:* www.keynote.com	San Mateo	CA	94404	650-403-2400	403-5500	178-7
KeyPoint Credit Union 2805 Bowers Ave *TF:* 888-255-3637 ■ *Web:* www.kpcu.com	Santa Clara	CA	95051	408-731-4100	731-4485	219
Keys Printing Co 1004 Keys Dr *Web:* www.keysprinting.com	Greenville	SC	29615	864-288-6560		627
Keyser & Miller Ford Inc 8 E Main St *Web:* www.keysermillerford.com	Collegeville	PA	19426	610-489-9366		57
Keyser Bros Cadillac Inc 4130 Sheridan Dr	Williamsville	NY	14221	716-568-7045		57
Keysource Group Inc, The 1920 Georgetown Rd Ste C *TF:* 800-225-0385 ■ *Web:* www.thekeysource.com	Hudson	OH	44236	330-342-4630		196
Keysource Medical Inc 7820 Palace Dr *Web:* www.keysourcemedical.com	Cincinnati	OH	45249	513-469-7881		231
Keyston Bros 2001 Academy Way Ste A *TF:* 800-453-1112 ■ *Web:* www.keystonbros.com	Sacramento	CA	95815	916-927-5851		594
Keystone Adjustable Cap Co 1591 Hylton Rd *Web:* www.beringer.net	Pennsauken	NJ	08110	856-663-5740		557
Keystone Aerial Surveys Inc 9800 Ashton Rd *Web:* kasurveys.com	Philadelphia	PA	19114	215-677-3119		727
Keystone Aniline Corp 2501 W Fulton St *TF:* 800-522-4393 ■ *Web:* www.dyes.com	Chicago	IL	60612	312-666-2015	666-8530	143
Keystone Automotive Operations Inc 44 Tunkhannock Ave *TF:* 800-521-9999 ■ *Web:* www.keystoneautomotive.com	Exeter	PA	18643	570-655-4514	603-2003	61
Keystone Builders Resource Group Inc 1207 Roseneath Rd *Web:* www.keybuild.com	Richmond	VA	23230	804-358-5768		653
Keystone Cable Corp 8200 Lynch Rd *Web:* www.keystonecable.net	Detroit	MI	48234	313-924-9720	924-0050	815
Keystone Capital Corporation 12230 El Camino Real Ste 230 *Web:* www.keystonecapcorp.com	San Diego	CA	92130	858-348-4405	348-4405	401
Keystone Capital Inc 155 N Wacker Dr Ste 4150 *Web:* www.keystonecapital.com	Chicago	IL	60606	312-219-7900		401
Keystone Chevrolet Inc 8700 Charles Page Blvd *Web:* www.keystonechevrolet.com	Sand Springs	OK	74063	918-932-1706		516
Keystone Clearwater Solutions LLC 34 Northeast Dr *Web:* www.keystoneclear.com	Hershey	PA	17033	717-508-0550		539
Keystone College 1 College Green *Fax: Admissions ■ *TF:* 800-824-2764 ■ *Web:* keystone.edu	La Plume	PA	18440	570-945-5141	945-7916*	166
Keystone Consolidated Industries Inc 7000 SW Adams St *Fax Area Code: 309 ■ *TF Sales:* 800-447-6444 ■ *Web:* www.redbrand.com	Peoria	IL	61641	800-447-6444	697-7120*	813
Keystone Ctr 2001 Providence Ave *TF:* 800-558-9600 ■ *Web:* www.keystonecenter.net	Chester	PA	19013	610-876-9000	876-5441	726
Keystone Ctr 1628 St John Rd *Web:* www.keystone.org	Keystone	CO	80435	970-513-5800	262-0152	634
Keystone Dental Inc 144 Middlesex Tpke *TF:* 866-902-9272 ■ *Web:* www.keystonedental.com	Burlington	MA	01803	781-328-3490		228

Phone | Fax | Class

Keystone Electrical Manufacturing Co
2511 Bell Ave, Des Moines IA 50321 — 515-283-2567 | 283-0418 | 729
Web: www.keystoneemc.com

Keystone Electronics Corp
31-07 20th Rd, Astoria NY 11105 — 718-956-8900 | 956-9040 | 350
TF: 800-221-5510 ■ *Web:* www.keyelco.com

Keystone Engineering 6310 Sidney St, Houston TX 77021 — 713-747-1478 | | 621
Web: www.keystoneeng.com

Keystone Equities Group, The
1003 B Egypt Rd, Oaks PA 19456 — 610-415-6300 | | 194
TF: 800-715-9905 ■ *Web:* www.keystoneequities.com

Keystone Folding Box Company Inc
367 Verona Ave, Newark NJ 07104 — 973-483-1054 | | 561
Web: www.keyboxco.com

Keystone Food Products Inc PO Box 326, Easton PA 18044 — 610-258-0888 | 250-0721 | 296-35
Web: www.keystonesnacks.com

Keystone Foods
905 Airport Rd Ste 400, West Chester PA 19380 — 610-668-6700 | | 296-26
Web: www.keystonefoods.com

Keystone Forging Co
215 Duke St PO Box 269, Northumberland PA 17857 — 570-473-3524 | 473-7273 | 483
TF: 800-453-1724 ■ *Web:* www.keystoneforging.com

Keystone Friction Hinge Co
520 Matthews Blvd, South Williamsport PA 17702 — 570-323-9479 | 326-0217 | 488
Web: kfhinge.com

Keystone Fruit Marketing
11 N Carlisle St Ste 102 PO Box 189, Greencastle PA 17225 — 717-597-2112 | 597-4096 | 194
Web: www.keystonefruit.com

Keystone Honing Co
1000 Industrial Dr, Titusville PA 16354 — 814-827-9641 | | 454

Keystone Industries
480 S Democrat Rd, Gibbstown NJ 08027 — 856-663-4700 | | 475
TF: 800-333-3131 ■ *Web:* www.keystoneindustries.com

Keystone Information Systems
1000 S Lenola Rd, Maple Shade NJ 08052 — 856-722-0700 | | 225
TF: 800-735-4862 ■ *Web:* www.keyinfosys.com

Keystone Learning Systems LLC
6030 Daybreak Cir Ste A150 116, Clarksville MD 21029 — 410-800-4000 | 422-7015* | 513
**Fax Area Code:* 866 ■ *TF:* 800-949-5590 ■ *Web:* www.keystonelearning.com

Keystone Lodge & Spa 22010 US Hwy 6, Keystone CO 80435 — 970-496-3000 | | 379
TF: 800-354-4386 ■ *Web:* keystoneresort.com

Keystone Marketing
709 N Main St, Winston-salem NC 27101 — 336-724-9899 | | 195
Web: www.keystonemarketing.net

Keystone Millbrook
3540 Jefferson Hwy, Grand Ledge MI 48837 — 517-627-4078 | | 627
Web: www.keystonemillbrook.com

Keystone Outdoors
186 Path Valley Rd, Fort Loudon PA 17224 — 717-369-2970 | | 791
Web: www.keystonecountrystore.com

Keystone Payroll
355 Colonnade Blvd Ste C, State College PA 16803 — 814-234-2272 | | 2
TF: 877-717-2272 ■ *Web:* www.keystonepayroll.com

Keystone Powdered Metal Co
251 State St, Saint Marys PA 15857 — 814-781-1591 | | 485
Web: www.keystonepm.com

Keystone Pretzels 124 W Airport Rd, Lititz PA 17543 — 888-572-4500 | 560-2241* | 296-9
**Fax Area Code:* 717 ■ *TF:* 888-572-4500 ■ *Web:* www.keystonepretzels.com

Keystone Printing Ink Co
2700 Roberts Ave, Philadelphia PA 19129 — 215-228-8100 | | 388
Web: www.keystoneink.com

Keystone Profiles Ltd
220 Seventh Ave, Beaver Falls PA 15010 — 724-506-1500 | | 492
TF: 800-777-1533 ■ *Web:* www.keystoneprofiles.com

Keystone Property Group Inc
1 Presidential Blvd Ste 300, Bala Cynwyd PA 19004 — 610-980-7000 | | 652
TF: 866-980-1818 ■ *Web:* www.keystonepropertygroup.com

Keystone Quality Transport Co
1260 E Woodland Ave, Springfield PA 19064 — 610-604-1421 | | 30
Web: keystonequalitytransport.com

Keystone Resort 21996 Hwy 6 PO Box 38, Keystone CO 80435 — 970-754-0001 | | 669
TF: 877-625-1556 ■ *Web:* www.keystoneresort.com

Keystone Retaining Wall Systems Inc
4444 W 78th St, Minneapolis MN 55435 — 952-897-1040 | | 724
TF: 800-747-8971 ■ *Web:* www.keystonewalls.com

Keystone RV Co
2642 Hackberry Dr PO Box 2000, Goshen IN 46527 — 574-535-2100 | | 120
TF: 866-425-4369 ■ *Web:* www.keystonerv.com

Keystone School District 451 Huston Ave, Knox PA 16232 — 814-797-5921 | | 685
Web: www.keyknox.com

Keystone Shipping Co
1 Bala Plaza E Ste 600, Bala Cynwyd PA 19004 — 610-617-6800 | 617-6899 | 312
Web: www.keyship.com

Keystone Sporting Arms LLC
155 Sodom Rd, Milton PA 17847 — 570-742-2777 | | 807
TF: 800-742-0455 ■ *Web:* www.keystonesportingarmsllc.com

Keystone State Park
1926 S Hwy 151, Sand Springs OK 74063 — 918-865-4991 | 865-2083 | 565
TF: 800-654-8240 ■ *Web:* www.travelok.com/listings/view.profile/id.4163

Keystone State Park 1150 Keystone Pk Rd, Derry PA 15627 — 724-668-2939 | | 565
Web: www.dcnr.state.pa.us

Keytroller LLC
3907 W Martin Luther King Blvd, Tampa FL 33614 — 813-877-4500 | | 203
TF: 800-760-0924 ■ *Web:* www.keytroller.com

KEYW Corp 7740 Milestone Pkwy Ste 400, Hanover MD 21076 — 443-733-1600 | | 177
TF: 800-340-1001 ■ *Web:* www.keywcorp.com

Keywell LLC 1035 Commercial Dr, Matthews NC 28104 — 708-608-8020 | | 686
Web: www.keywell.com

Keyword Connects LLC 241 Crescent St, Waltham MA 02453 — 781-899-3675 | | 195
Web: www.keywordconnects.com

KEYY-AM 1450 (Rel) 307 S 1600 W, Provo UT 84601 — 801-374-5210 | | 645
Web: www.keyradio.org

Kezber i Solution 2685 Rue Hertel, Sherbrooke QC J1J2J4 — 819-566-6900 | | 180
Web: www.kezber.com

KEZI-TV Ch 9 (ABC) PO Box 7009, Eugene OR 97408 — 541-485-5611 | 686-8004 | 741-45
Web: www.kezi.com

KEZK-FM 102.5 (AC)
1220 Olive St 3rd Fl, Saint Louis MO 63103 — 314-531-1025 | | 645-141
Web: kezk.cbslocal.com

Phone | Fax | Class

KEZN-FM 103.1 (AC)
72-915 Parkview Dr, Palm Desert CA 92260 — 760-340-9383 | | 645

KF Industries Inc
1500 SE 89th St, Oklahoma City OK 73149 — 405-631-1533 | 631-5034 | 789
TF: 800-398-2493 ■ *Web:* circorenergy.com

KF Jacobsen & Co
4315 SE McLoughlin Blvd, Portland OR 97202 — 503-239-5532 | | 188-4

KFAN-AM 1130 (Sports)
1600 Utica Ave S Ste 400, Minneapolis MN 55416 — 952-417-3000 | | 645-101
Web: kfan.iheart.com

KFAQ-AM 1170 (N/T) 4590 E 29th St, Tulsa OK 74114 — 918-743-7814 | | 645-168
Web: www.1170kfaq.com

KFAR 660 AM 529 Fifth Ave Ste 200, Fairbanks AK 99701 — 907-451-5910 | 451-5999 | 645-57
Web: www.kfar660.com

KFAT-FM 92.9 (Urban) 833 Gambell, Anchorage AK 99501 — 907-344-4045 | 522-6053 | 645-6
Web: 929kfat.com

KFAX-AM 1100 (Rel) 39138 Fremont Blvd, Fremont CA 94538 — 510-713-1100 | | 645
Web: www.kfax.com

KFBB-TV 3200 Old Havre Hwy, Black Eagle MT 59414 — 406-453-4377 | | 741
Web: www.kfbb.com

KFBC-AM 1240 (N/T) 1806 Capitol Ave, Cheyenne WY 82001 — 307-634-4462 | 632-8586 | 645-35
Web: www.kfbcradio.com

KFBK-AM 1530 (N/T)
1545 River Park Dr Ste 500, Sacramento CA 95815 — 916-929-5325 | | 645-140
Web: kfbk.iheart.com

KFBX-AM 970 (N/T) 546 Ninth Ave, Fairbanks AK 99701 — 907-450-1000 | 450-1092 | 645-57
Web: 970kfbx.iheart.com

KFBZ-FM 105.3 (AC)
9111 E Douglas Ste 130, Wichita KS 67207 — 316-685-2121 | | 645-175
Web: www.1053thebuzz.com

KFC Corp 1441 Gardiner Ln, Louisville KY 40213 — 920-923-2321 | | 670
TF: 800-225-5532 ■ *Web:* www.kfc.com

KFDA-TV Ch 10 (CBS) 7900 Broadway, Amarillo TX 79105 — 806-383-1010 | | 741-4
Web: www.newschannel10.com

KFDI-FM 101.3 (Ctry)
4200 N Old Lawrence Rd, Wichita KS 67219 — 316-838-9141 | | 645-175
Web: www.kfdi.com

KFDM-TV Channel 6 2955 I-10 E, Beaumont TX 77702 — 409-892-6622 | | 116
Web: www.kfdm.com

KFG Resources Ltd 150-A Providence Rd, Natchez MS 39120 — 601-446-5219 | | 538
Web: www.kfgresources.com

KFGO-AM 790 (N/T) 1020 25th St S, Fargo ND 58103 — 701-237-5346 | | 645-58
TF: 800-838-3006 ■ *Web:* www.kfgo.com

KFH (Key Fire Hose Corp) PO Box 7107, Dothan AL 36302 — 334-671-5532 | | 370
TF: 800-447-5666 ■ *Web:* keyhose.com

KFH-AM 1240 (N/T)
9111 E Douglas Ste 130, Wichita KS 67207 — 316-685-2121 | | 645-175
Web: www.kfhradio.com

KFI-AM 640 (N/T)
3400 W Olive Ave Ste 550, Burbank CA 91505 — 818-559-2252 | | 645
Web: kfiam640.iheart.com

KFIS-FM 104.1 (Rel)
6400 SE Lake Rd Ste 350, Portland OR 97222 — 503-786-0600 | | 645-128
Web: www.thefishportland.com

K-Five Construction Corp
999 Oakmont Plaza Dr, Lemont IL 60439 — 630-257-5600 | 257-6788 | 188-4
Web: k-five.com

KFJM-FM 90.7 (AAA) 207 N Fifth St, Fargo ND 58102 — 701-241-6900 | 239-7650 | 645
TF: 800-366-6888 ■ *Web:* www.prairiepublic.org

KFKF-FM 94.1 (Ctry)
508 Westport Rd Ste 202, Kansas City MO 64111 — 816-753-4000 | | 645-83
Web: www.kfkf.com

Kfm International Industries
14145 Proctor Ave Ste 7, La Puente CA 91746 — 626-369-9566 | | 358

KFMA-FM Radio 3871 N Commerce Dr, Tucson AZ 85705 — 520-407-4500 | | 645-167
TF: 800-638-8791 ■ *Web:* www.kfma.com

KFMB-AM 760 (N/T) 7677 Engineer Rd, San Diego CA 92111 — 858-292-7600 | | 645-144
TF: 800-760-5362 ■ *Web:* www.760kfmb.com

KFMB-FM 100.7 (AC) 7677 Engineer Rd, San Diego CA 92111 — 858-571-8888 | | 645-144
Web: www.kfmbfm.com

KFMB-TV Ch 8 (CBS) 7677 Engineer Rd, San Diego CA 92111 — 858-571-8888 | 560-0627 | 741-119
Web: www.cbs8.com

KFME-TV Ch 13 (PBS) 207 N Fifth St, Fargo ND 58102 — 701-241-6900 | 239-7650 | 741-48
TF: 800-359-6900 ■ *Web:* www.prairiepublic.org

KFMR Katz Ferraro McMurtry PC
300 Benedum-Trees Bldg 223 Fourth Ave, Pittsburgh PA 15222 — 412-485-6700 | | 2
Web: www.kfmr.com

KFMX-FM 94.5 (Rock)
4413 82nd St Ste 300, Lubbock TX 79424 — 806-798-7078 | 798-7052 | 645-94
TF: 800-776-1070 ■ *Web:* www.kfmx.com

KFNW-FM 97.9 (Rel) 5702 52nd Ave S, Fargo ND 58104 — 701-282-5910 | | 645-58
TF: 800-728-5697 ■ *Web:* www.life979.com

KFOG-FM 104.5 (CH)
750 Battery St 3rd Fl, San Francisco CA 94111 — 415-995-6800 | | 645-145
Web: www.kfog.com

KForce Government Soultions
2750 Prosperity Ave Ste 300, Fairfax VA 22031 — 703-245-7350 | 245-7560 | 180
TF: 800-200-7465 ■ *Web:* www.kforcegov.com

Kforce Inc 1001 E Palm Ave, Tampa FL 33605 — 813-552-5000 | 552-1482 | 721
NASDAQ: KFRC ■ *TF:* 877-453-6723 ■ *Web:* www.kforce.com

KFOR-TV Ch 4 (NBC)
444 E Britton Rd, Oklahoma City OK 73114 — 405-424-4444 | | 741-93
Web: www.kfor.com

K-Four Systems LLC
1660 Washington St, Holliston MA 01746 — 774-233-0697 | | 196
Web: kfoursystems.com

KFOX-TV Ch 14 (Fox)
200 S Alto Mesa St, El Paso TX 79912 — 915-833-8585 | 833-8973 | 741-43
Web: www.kfoxtv.com

KFPX-TV Ch 39 (I) 4570 114th St, Urbandale IA 50322 — 515-331-3939 | | 741

KFRG-FM 95.1 (Ctry)
900 E Washington St Ste 315, Colton CA 92324 — 909-825-9525 | 825-0441 | 645
TF: 888-431-3764 ■ *Web:* kfrog.cbslocal.com

KFRR-FM 104.1 (Rock) 1066 E Shaw Ave, Fresno CA 93710 — 559-230-0104 | | 645-64
Web: newrock1041.fm

KFRX-FM 106.3 (CHR)
3800 Cornhusker Hwy, Lincoln NE 68504 — 402-466-1234 | | 645-90
TF: 800-523-9101 ■ *Web:* www.kfrxfm.com

Name / Address	City	State	Zip	Phone	Fax	Class
Kfs Inc 1840 W Airfield Dr *TF:* 800-364-4115 ■ *Web:* www.kfsinc.com	Dallas	TX	75261	817-488-4115	488-4350	24
KFSI-FM 92.9 (Rel) 4016 28th St SE *TF:* 800-889-9508 ■ *Web:* www.kfsi.org	Rochester	MN	55904	507-289-8585	529-4017	645-137
KFSM-TV Ch 5 (CBS) 318 N 13th St *Web:* 5newsonline.com	Fort Smith	AR	72902	479-783-3131	783-3295	741-50
KFSN-TV Ch 30 (ABC) 1777 G St *TF:* 800-423-3030 ■ *Web:* abc30.com	Fresno	CA	93706	559-442-1170		741-52
KFTI-AM 1070 (Ctry) 4200 N Old Lawrence Rd *Web:* www.kfdi.com	Wichita	KS	67219	316-838-9141		645-175
KFTV-TV Ch 21 (Uni) 601 W Univision Plaza *TF:* 866-783-2645 ■ *Web:* www.univision.com/fresno/kftv	Fresno	CA	93704	559-222-2121		741-52
KFTX-FM 97.5 (Ctry) 1520 S Port Ave *TF:* 800-259-1061 ■ *Web:* www.kftx.com	Corpus Christi	TX	78405	361-883-5987	883-3648	645-43
KFWB-AM 980 (N/T) 5777 W Century Blvd Ste 1110 *Web:* www.kfwb.radio.net	Los Angeles	CA	90045	408-440-0851		645-92
KFXA-TV Ch 28 (Fox) 600 Old Marion Rd NE *TF:* 800-222-5426 ■ *Web:* cbs2iowa.com	Cedar Rapids	IA	52402	800-642-6140		741-23
KFXS-FM 100.3 (CR) 660 Flormann St Ste 100 *Web:* www.foxradio.com	Rapid City	SD	57701	605-394-4487	343-9012	645-132
KFYO-AM 790 (N/T) 4413 82nd St Ste 300 *TF:* 800-687-0790 ■ *Web:* www.kfyo.com	Lubbock	TX	79424	806-798-7078		645-94
KFYR-TV Ch 5 (NBC) 200 N Fourth St *Web:* www.kfyrtv.com	Bismarck	ND	58501	701-255-5757	255-8220	741-16
KGA-AM 1510 (N/T) 1601 E 57th Ave *Web:* www.1510kga.com	Spokane	WA	99223	509-448-1000	448-7015	645-154
KGAB-AM 650 (N/T) 1912 Capitol Ave Ste 300 *Web:* www.kgab.com	Cheyenne	WY	82001	307-632-4400		645-35
KGAN-TV Ch 2 (CBS) 600 Old Marion Rd NE *TF:* 800-642-6140 ■ *Web:* www.cbs2iowa.com	Cedar Rapids	IA	52402	319-395-9060	395-0987	741-23
KGBT-TV Ch 4 (CBS) 9201 W Expy 83 *Web:* www.valleycentral.com	Harlingen	TX	78552	956-366-4444	366-4494	741
KGET-TV Ch 17 (NBC) 2120 L St *TF:* 800-879-8542 ■ *Web:* www.kerngoldenempire.com	Bakersfield	CA	93301	661-283-1700		741-10
KGFE-TV Ch 2 (PBS) 207 N Fifth St *TF:* 800-359-6900 ■ *Web:* www.prairiepublic.org	Fargo	ND	58102	701-241-6900	239-7650	741-48
KGFM-FM 101.5 (AC) 1400 Easton Dr Ste 144-B *Web:* www.kgfm.com	Bakersfield	CA	93309	661-328-1410	328-0873	645-15
KGGI-FM 99.1 (CHR) 2030 Iowa Ave Ste 100 **Fax: Sales* ■ *TF:* 866-991-5444 ■ *Web:* 991kggi.iheart.com	Riverside	CA	92507	951-684-1991	486-7335*	645-135
KGH (Kelowna General Hospital) 2268 Pandosy St *TF:* 888-877-4442 ■ *Web:* www.interiorhealth.ca	Kelowna	BC	V1Y1T2	250-862-4000	862-4020	374-2
KGH (Kennewick General Hospital) 900 S Auburn St *Web:* www.trioshealth.org	Kennewick	WA	99336	509-586-6111		374-3
KGNC-FM 97.9 (Ctry) 3505 Olsen Blvd Ste 117 *TF:* 800-460-9226 ■ *Web:* www.kgncfm.com	Amarillo	TX	79109	806-355-9801		645-5
KGNU-FM 88.5 (Var) 4700 Walnut St *TF:* 800-737-3030 ■ *Web:* www.kgnu.org	Boulder	CO	80301	303-449-4885		645
KGNZ-FM 88.1 (Rel) 542 Butternut St *TF:* 800 588 8801 ■ *Web:* www.kgnz.com	Abilene	TX	79602	325-673-3045	672-7938	645-1
KGO-TV Ch 7 (ABC) 900 Front St	San Francisco	CA	94111	415-954-7842	954-7377	741-120
KGOU-FM 106.3 (NPR) 860 Van Vleet Oval Rm 300 *TF:* 866 533-2470 ■ *Web:* www.kgou.org	Norman	OK	73019	405-325 3388	325 7129	645
KGPE CBS47 5035 E McKinley Ave *Web:* www.yourcentralvalley.com	Fresno	CA	93727	559-222-2411		741-52
KGPR-FM 89.9 (NPR) 2100 16th Ave S Rm G118 *Web:* www.kgpr.org	Great Falls	MT	59405	406-268-3739	268-3736	645
KGRT-FM 103.9 (Ctry) 1355 California St PO Box 968 *Web:* www.kgrt.com	Las Cruces	NM	88001	575-525-9298		645
KGS Steel Inc 3725 Pine Ln *TF:* 800-533-3846 ■ *Web:* www.kgssteel.com	Bessemer	AL	35022	205-425-0800		492
KGSR-FM 93.3 (Urban) 8309 N IH-35 *Web:* www.kgsr.com	Austin	TX	78753	512-832-4000	832-4071	645-14
KGTV-TV Ch 10 (ABC) 4600 Airway *TF:* 800-799-8881 ■ *Web:* www.10news.com	San Diego	CA	92102	619-237-1010	527-0369	741-119
KGUN-TV Ch 9 (ABC) 7280 E Rosewood St *Web:* www.kgun9.com	Tucson	AZ	85710	520-722-5486	733-7050	741-137
KGWC-TV Ch 14 (CBS) 1856 Skyview Dr	Casper	WY	82601	307-234-1111	234-4005	741-22
KGWN-TV Ch 5 (CBS) 2923 E Lincolnway *TF:* 800-929-0132 ■ *Web:* www.kgwn.tv	Cheyenne	WY	82001	307-634-7755		741-28
KGW-TV Ch 8 (NBC) 1501 SW Jefferson St *TF:* 800-669-9777 ■ *Web:* www.kgw.com	Portland	OR	97201	503-226-5000		741-103
KGY-FM 96.9 (Ctry) 1700 Marine Dr NE *Web:* www.kgyradio.com	Olympia	WA	98501	360-943-1240		645
KHAFRA Engineering Consultants Inc 225 Peachtree St NE Ste 1600 *Web:* www.khafra.com	Atlanta	GA	30303	404-525-2120		256
Khan's Mongolian Barbecue 500 E 78th St *Web:* www.khansmongolianbarbecue.com	Richfield	MN	55423	612-861-7991		671
Khanna Ro (Rep D - CA) 513 Cannon HOB *Web:* khanna.house.gov	Washington	DC	20515	202-225-2631		342-2
KHAY-FM 100.7 (Ctry) 1376 Walter St *Web:* www.khay.com	Ventura	CA	93003	805-642-8595		645
Khazana 10177 107th St *Web:* www.khazana.ab.ca	Edmonton	AB	T5J1J5	780-702-0330		671
KHBS-TV Ch 40 (ABC) 2415 N Albert Pike *TF General:* 855-253-7122 ■ *Web:* www.4029tv.com	Fort Smith	AR	72904	479-783-4040	785-5375	741-50
Higher Education Assistance Authority PO Box 798 *TF:* 800-928-8926 ■ *Web:* www.kheaa.com	Frankfort	KY	40602	800-928-8926		725
Khemia Software Co 33080 Industrial Rd *Web:* khemia.com	Livonia	MI	48150	734-513-9940		179
KHET-TV Ch 11 (PBS) 2350 Dole St *Web:* www.pbshawaii.org	Honolulu	HI	96822	808-973-1000	973-1090	741-59
KHFM-FM 95.5 (Clas) 4125 Carlisle Blvd NE *Web:* www.classicalkhfm.com	Albuquerque	NM	87107	505-878-0980		645-4
KHIT-FM 106.9 (CHR) 4590 E 29th St *Web:* www.khits.com	Tulsa	OK	74114	918-743-7814		645-168
KHMX-FM 96.5 (CHR) 24 Greenway Plaza Ste 1900 *Web:* mix965houston.cbslocal.com	Houston	TX	77046	713-212-5965		645-75
KHNL-TV Ch 8 (NBC) 420 Waiakamilo Rd Ste 205 *Web:* www.hawaiinewsnow.com	Honolulu	HI	96817	808-847-3246	845-3616	741-59
KHOC-FM 102.5 (AC) 218 N Wolcott St **Fax Area Code:* 307	Casper	WY	82601	617-822-9600	473-7461*	645-28
Khong Guan Corp 30068 Eigenbrodt Way *TF:* 877-889-8968 ■ *Web:* kgcusa.squarespace.com	Union City	CA	94587	510-487-7800	487-0301	195
KHON-TV Ch 2 (Fox) 88 Piikoi St *TF:* 877-926-8300 ■ *Web:* www.khon2.com	Honolulu	HI	96814	808-591-4278	593-2418	741-59
Khoury Inc 1129 Webster Ave PO Box 1746 *TF:* 800-725-6765 ■ *Web:* www.khouryinc.com	Waco	TX	76703	254-754-5481	754-1606	319-1
KHOU-TV Ch 11 (CBS) 1945 Allen Pkwy *Web:* www.khou.com	Houston	TX	77019	713-526-1111		741-60
KHOZ-FM 102.9 (Ctry) 1111 Radio Ave *TF:* 800-553-6103 ■ *Web:* www.1029thez.com	Harrison	AR	72601	870-741-2301		645
KHQ-TV Ch 6 (NBC) 1201 W Sprague Ave *Web:* www.khq.com	Spokane	WA	99201	509-448-6000	448-4644	741-127
KHRI (Kresge Hearing Research Institute) 4605 Medical Science Unit *Web:* medicine.umich.edu	Ann Arbor	MI	48109	734 764 8110	764 0014	668
KHS & S Contractors Inc 5422 Bay Ctr Dr Ste 200 *TF:* 888-448-5477 ■ *Web:* www.khss.com	Tampa	FL	33609	813-628-9330	628-4339	189-9
KHTH-FM 101.7 (AC) 1410 Neotomas Ave Ste 200 *Web:* hot1017.com	Santa Rosa	CA	95405	707-543-0100	571-1097	645-74
KHTK-AM 1140 (Sports) 5244 Madison Ave *TF:* 800-920-1140 ■ *Web:* sacramento.cbslocal.com	Sacramento	CA	95841	916-338-9200		645-140
KHTS-FM 93.3 (CHR) 9660 Granite Ridge Dr Ste 100 *Web:* channel933.iheart.com	San Diego	CA	92123	858-292-2000	294-2916	645-144
KHVH-AM 830 (N/T) 650 Iwilei Rd Ste 400 *TF:* 844-289-7234 ■ *Web:* khvhradio.iheart.com	Honolulu	HI	96817	808-550-9200		645-73
KHYT-FM 107.5 (CR) 575 W Roger Rd *Web:* www.khit1075.com	Tucson	AZ	85705	520-887-1000		645-167
KI 1330 Bellevue St *TF:* 800-424-2432 ■ *Web:* ki.com	Green Bay	WI	54302	920-468-8100	468-0280	319-1
Ki Ho Military Acquisition Consulting Inc 5501 Backlick Rd *Web:* www.kihomac.com	Springfield	VA	22151	703-960-5450		256
KI Industries Inc 5540 McDermott Dr *Web:* www.kiindustries.com	Berkeley	IL	60163	708-449-1990	449-1997	604
KIAK-FM 102.5 (Ctry) 546 Ninth Ave *Web:* kiak.iheart.com	Fairbanks	AK	99701	907-450-1000	457-2128	645-57
Kiamichi Electric Co-op Inc (KEC) 966 SW Hwy 2 PO Box 340 *TF:* 800-888-2731 ■ *Web:* www.kiamichielectric.org	Wilburton	OK	74578	918-465-2338		245
Kiawah Island Golf Resort 1 Sancturay Beach Dr **Fax: Resv* ■ *TF Resv:* 800-654-2924 ■ *Web:* www.kiawahresort.com/golf	Kiawah Island	SC	29455	843-768-2121	768-2736*	669
Kibble Equipment 1150 S Victory Dr *TF:* 800-624-8983 ■ *Web:* www.kibbleeq.com	Mankato	MN	56001	507-387-8201	388-3565	358
Kibel Green Inc 2001 Wilshire Blvd Ste 420 *Web:* kginc.com	Santa Monica	CA	90403	310-829-0255		463
Kibow Biotech Inc 4781 W Chester Pike Newtown Business Ctr *TF:* 888-271-2560 ■ *Web:* www.kibowbiotech.com	Newtown Square	PA	19073	610-353-5130		231
KIBZ-FM 104.1 (Rock) 3800 Cornhusker Hwy *Web:* www.kibz.com	Lincoln	NE	68504	402-466-1234		645-90
Kice Industries Inc 5500 N Mill Heights Dr *TF:* 877-289-5423 ■ *Web:* www.kice.com	Wichita	KS	67219	316-744-7151	744-7355	207
Kichler Lighting 7711 E Pleasant Valley Rd PO Box 318010 *TF:* 866-558-5706 ■ *Web:* www.kichler.com	Cleveland	OH	44131	866-558-5706		439
Kickapoo Cavern State Park PO Box 705 *Web:* tpwd.texas.gov/state-parks/kickapoo-cavern	Brackettville	TX	78832	830-563-2342		565
Kickapoo State Recreation Area 10906 Kickapoo Pk Rd *Web:* www.dnr.illinois.gov/Parks/Pages/Kickapoo.aspx	Oakwood	IL	61858	217-442-4915		565
Kickapoo Traditional Tribe Of Texas 2212 Rosita Valley Rd *Web:* kickapootexas.org	Eagle Pass	TX	78852	830-773-2105		132
Kickerillo Cos 1306 S Fry Rd **Fax Area Code:* 281 ■ *Web:* www.kickerillo.com	Katy	TX	77450	713-951-0666	492-2018*	186
Kickhaefer Mfg Co (KMC) 1221 S Pk St PO Box 348 *TF:* 800-822-6080 ■ *Web:* www.kmcstampings.com	Port Washington	WI	53074	262-377-5030	284-9774	488
KickStart Alliance PO Box 705 *Web:* www.kickstartall.com	Los Altos	CA	94023	650-464-7663		463
KICT-FM 95.1 (Rock) 4200 N Old Lawrence Rd *Web:* www.t95.com	Wichita	KS	67219	316-838-9141		645-175
KICU-TV Ch 36 (Ind) KTUV Fox 2 *Web:* www.ktvu.com	San Jose	CA	95131	408-953-3636		741

Name / Address	City	State	Zip	Phone	Fax	Class
Kid to Kid 1244 Township Line Rd *Web:* www.kidtokid.com	Drexel Hill	PA	19026	610-446-2544		310
Kidango Inc 44000 Old Warm Springs Blvd *TF:* 800-262-4252 ■ *Web:* www.kidango.org	Fremont	CA	94538	408-258-3710		305
KidCo Inc 1013 Technology Way *TF:* 800-553-5529 ■ *Web:* www.kidco.com	Libertyville	IL	60048	847-549-8600	549-8660	64
Kidd & Company LLC 1455 E Putnam Ave *Web:* www.kiddcompany.com	Old Greenwich	CT	06870	203-661-0070		690
Kidd Kraddick in The Morning 220 Las Colinas Blvd E Ste C- 210 *TF:* 800-543-3548 ■ *Web:* www.kiddlive.com	Irving	TX	75039	972-432-9094		645-10
Kidde Aerospace 4200 Airport Dr NW *Fax: Hum Res ■ *Web:* utcaerospacesystems.com	Wilson	NC	27896	252-237-7004	246-7181*	283
Kidde-Fenwal Inc 400 Main St *TF Hum Res:* 800-872-6527 ■ *Web:* www.kidde-fenwal.com	Ashland	MA	01721	508-881-2000		202
Kidder County 120 E Broadway Kidder County Courthouse *TF:* 800-352-0867 ■ *Web:* ndcourts.gov	Steele	ND	58482	701-475-2632	475-2202	338
Kiddesigns Inc 1299 Main St *Web:* www.kiddesigns.com	Rahway	NJ	07065	732-574-9000		246
Kidron Auction Inc 4885 Kidron Rd *TF:* 800-589-9749 ■ *Web:* kidronauction.com	Kidron	OH	44636	330-857-2641	698-3088	446
Kidron Inc 13442 Emerson Rd *TF:* 800-321-5421 ■ *Web:* www.kidron.com	Kidron	OH	44636	330-857-3011	857-8451	516
Kids Cancer Care Foundation of Alberta 609 14 St NW *Web:* www.kidscancercare.ab.ca	Calgary	AB	T2N2A1	403-216-9210		305
Kids Help Phone 300-439 University Ave *TF:* 800-268-3062 ■ *Web:* www.kidshelpphone.ca	Toronto	ON	M5G1Y8	416-586-5437		138
Kids II 555 N Point Ctr E Ste 600 *TF:* 800-230-8190 ■ *Web:* www.kidsii.com	Alpharetta	GA	30022	770-751-0442	751-0543	64
Kids Play Today LLC 837 Route 6 Unit 5 *TF:* 800-401-8314 ■ *Web:* www.kidsplaytoday.com	Shohola	PA	18458	570-296-2313		31
KidsPeace Orchard Hills Campus 5300 Kids Peace Dr *TF:* 800-257-3223 ■ *Web:* www.kidspeace.org	Orefield	PA	18069	800-257-3223		374-1
Kieckhafer & Co 6201 Oak Canyon Dr *Web:* www.ksandco.com	Irvine	CA	92618	949-250-3900		138
Kieckhafer Dietzler & Hauser LLP 627 Elm St *Web:* kdhcpa.com	West Bend	WI	53095	262-334-2341		2
Kiefer Specialty Flooring Inc 2910 Falling Waters Blvd *TF:* 800-322-5448 ■ *Web:* kieferusa.com	Lindenhurst	IL	60046	847-245-8450		361
Kieffer & Company Inc 3322 Washington Ave *TF:* 800-458-4394 ■ *Web:* www.kieffersigns.com	Sheboygan	WI	53081	800-458-4394		701
Kiefner & Assoc Inc 585 Scherers Ct *Web:* www.kiefner.com	Worthington	OH	43085	614-888-8220		256
Kieft Bros Inc 837 S Riverside Dr *TF:* 800-701-8456 ■ *Web:* www.kieftbros.com	Elmhurst	IL	60126	630-832-8090	834-5765	183
Kiely and Assoc 329 Leroi Rd *Web:* www.kielyandassociates.com	Pittsburgh	PA	15208	412-243-2019		41
Kiemle & Hagood Co 601 W Main Ave Ste 400 *Web:* www.khco.com	Spokane	WA	99201	509-838-6541		652
Kien Giang 5825 Charlotte Pk	Nashville	TN	37209	615-353-1250		671
Kier & Wright Civil Engineers 2850 Collier Canyon Rd *Web:* kierwright.com	Livermore	CA	94551	925-245-8788		261
Kierland Commons 15205 N Kierland Blvd Ste 150 *Web:* www.kierlandcommons.com	Scottsdale	AZ	85254	480-348-1577		460
Kieve Camp 42 Kieve Rd *Web:* kievewavus.org	Nobleboro	ME	04555	207-563-5172		239
Kiewit Corp 3555 Farnam St *Fax: Hum Res ■ *TF:* 800-901-1087 ■ *Web:* www.kiewit.com	Omaha	NE	68131	402-342-2052	271-2829*	188-4
Kiewit Energy Co 10740 N Gessner Rd Ste 400 *Web:* kiewit.com	Houston	TX	77064	281-517-8900		610
KIFI-TV Ch 8 (ABC) 1915 N Yellowstone Hwy *Web:* www.localnews8.com	Idaho Falls	ID	83401	208-525-8888	522-1930	741-101
Kight Home Ctr 5521 Oak Grove Rd *Web:* www.kighthomecenter.com	Evansville	IN	47715	812-479-8281		191-3
Kightlinger Motors Inc 358 Rt 6 W *Web:* kightlingermotor.com	Coudersport	PA	16915	814-274-9660		57
Kigre Inc 100 Marshland Rd *Web:* www.kigre.com	Hilton Head Island	SC	29926	843-681-5800	681-4559	425
Kihuen Ruben J (Rep D - NV) 313 Cannon HOB *Web:* kihuen.house.gov	Washington	DC	20515	202-225-9894		342-2
KIII-TV Ch 3 (ABC) 5002 S Padre Island Dr *TF:* 800-882-9539 ■ *Web:* www.kiiitv.com	Corpus Christi	TX	78411	361-986-8300		741-36
KIIM-FM 99.5 (Ctry) 575 W Roger Rd *TF:* 800-505-0098 ■ *Web:* www.kiimfm.com	Tucson	AZ	85705	520-880-5446	887-6397	645-167
KIIS-FM 102.7 (CHR) 3400 W Olive Ave Ste 550 *Web:* kiisfm.iheart.com	Burbank	CA	91505	818-559-2252	940-1027	645
KIIX-AM 1410 (Sports) 4270 Byrd Dr *Web:* kiixcountry.iheart.com	Loveland	CO	80538	970-461-2560		645
KIK Custom Products 2730 Middlebury St *TF:* 800-479-6603 ■ *Web:* www.kikcorp.com	Elkhart	IN	46516	574-295-0000	296-1700	145
KIK Pool Additives Inc 5160 E Airport Dr *TF:* 800-745-4536 ■ *Web:* www.kem-tek.com	Ontario	CA	91761	909-390-9912	390-9911	145
Kiki's Bistro 900 N Franklin St *Web:* www.kikisbistro.com	Chicago	IL	60610	312-335-5454		671
Kikiriki 215 Market St *Web:* kikirikirestaurant.com	Paterson	NJ	07505	973-225-0336		671
Kikkoman Foods Inc N 1365 Six Corners Rd *Web:* www.kikkoman.com	Walworth	WI	53184	262-275-6181	275-9452	296-19
KIKN-FM 100.5 (Ctry) 5100 S Tennis Ln *Web:* www.kikn.com	Sioux Falls	SD	57108	605-361-0300		645-152
Kiko's 5514 Everhart Rd *Web:* kikosmexicanfood.com	Corpus Christi	TX	78411	361-991-1211		671
Kiku 225 W Station Square Dr *Web:* kikupittsburgh.net	Pittsburgh	PA	15219	412-765-3200		671
Kiku Obata & Co 6161 Delmar Blvd Ste 200 *Web:* www.kikuobata.com	Saint Louis	MO	63112	314-361-3110		344
Kikusui America Inc 1633 Bayshore Hwy Ste 331 *TF:* 877-876-2807 ■ *Web:* www.kikusuiamerica.com	Burlingame	CA	94010	650-259-5900		246
KIKU-TV 737 Bishop St Ste 1430 *Web:* www.kikutv.com	Honolulu	HI	96813	808-847-2021	841-3326	741-59
Kikyo Sushi & Seafood Bistro 3706 Riverside Dr	Upper Arlington	OH	43221	614-457-5277		671
Kilby Correctional Facility 12201 Wares Ferry Rd *Web:* doc.alabama.gov	Montgomery	AL	36117	334-215-6600		213
Kildair Service Ltee 92 Delangis Rd *TF:* 800-668-8091 ■ *Web:* www.kildair.com	St-paul De Joliette	QC	J0K3E0	450-756-8091		579
Kildee Daniel (Rep D - MI) 227 Cannon Bldg *Web:* dankildee.house.gov	Washington	DC	20515	202-225-3611		342-2
Kildeer Countryside Community Consolidated School District 96 1050 Ivy Hall Ln *Web:* www.kcsd96.org	Buffalo Grove	IL	60089	847-459-4260	459-2344	780
Kildonan School 425 Morse Hill Rd *Web:* www.kildonan.org	Amenia	NY	12501	845-373-8111	373-2004	622
Kilen Woods State Park 50200 860th St *Web:* www.dnr.state.mn.us	Lakefield	MN	56150	507-831-2900		565
Kilgore College 1100 Broadway *TF:* 800-275-8777 ■ *Web:* www.kilgore.edu	Kilgore	TX	75662	903-984-8531		162
Kilgore Flares Co LLC 155 Kilgore Dr *Web:* www.kilgoreflares.com	Toone	TN	38381	731-658-5231		268
Kilgore-Lewis House, The 560 N Academy St *TF:* 800-777-1004 ■ *Web:* www.kilgore-lewis.org	Greenville	SC	29601	864-232-3020		50-3
Kilian Community College 300 E Sixth St *Fax: Admissions ■ *TF:* 800-888-1147 ■ *Web:* www.kilian.edu	Sioux Falls	SD	57103	605-221-3100	336-2606*	162
Kil-Kare Speedway 1166 Dayton-Xenia Rd *TF:* 800-305-5202 ■ *Web:* www.kilkare.com	Xenia	OH	45385	937-429-2961		515
Kilkenny's Irish Pub & Eatery 1413 E 15th St *Web:* www.tulsairishpub.com	Tulsa	OK	74120	918-582-8282	582-3931	671
Kill Kare State Park 2714 Hathaway Point Rd *Web:* www.vtstateparks.com/htm/killkare.htm	St Albans	VT	05481	802-524-6021		565
Killam Oil Co 4320 University Blvd *Web:* www.killamco.com	Laredo	TX	78041	956-724-7141		538
Killdeer Mountain Manufacturing Inc (KMM) 233 Rodeo Dr *Web:* www.kmmnet.com	Killdeer	ND	58640	701-764-5651	764-5427	625
Killeen Civic & Conference Ctr & Visitors Bureau 3601 S WS Young Dr *Web:* www.visitkilleen.com	Killeen	TX	76542	254-501-3888		206
Killeen Daily Herald 1809 Florence Rd PO Box 1300 *Web:* www.kdhnews.com	Killeen	TX	76540	254-634-2125	200-7640	532-2
Killeen Dynamic Designs Inc 2100 E Stan Schlueter Loop Ste F *Web:* www.dynamicdesignsinc.com	Killeen	TX	76542	254-628-8272		687
Killens Pond State Park 5025 Killens Pond Rd *Web:* www.destateparks.com	Felton	DE	19943	302-284-4526	284-4694	565
Killer Dana Surf Shop 24621 Del Prado *Web:* www.killerdana.com	Dana Point	CA	92629	949-489-8380		711
Killian Jensen & Davis Pc Martin Cheryl 202 N Seventh St *TF:* 800-820-3097 ■ *Web:* www.killianlaw.com	Grand Junction	CO	81501	970-241-0707		428
Killington 4763 Killington Rd *TF:* 800-621-6867 ■ *Web:* www.killington.com	Killington	VT	05751	802 422 6200	422 6113	669
Killington Grand Resort Hotel & Conference Ctr 4763 Killington Rd *TF:* 800-621-6867 ■ *Web:* www.killington.com	Killington	VT	05751	802-422-5001		379
Killion Industries Inc 1380 Poinsettia Ave *TF:* 800-421-5352 ■ *Web:* www.killionindustries.com	Vista	CA	92081	760-727-5102	727-5108	286
Kilmer Derek (Rep D - WA) 1520 Longworth HOB *Web:* kilmer.house.gov	Washington	DC	20515	202-225-5916		342-2
Kilmer, Voorhees & Laurick PC 732 NW 19th Ave *TF:* 800-218-0302 ■ *Web:* www.kilmerlaw.com	Portland	OR	97209	503-224-0055		428
KILO-FM 94.3 (Rock) 1805 E Cheyenne Rd *TF General:* 800-727-5456 ■ *Web:* kilo943.com	Colorado Springs	CO	80905	719-634-4896	634-5837	645-39
Kilopass Technology Inc 2895 Zanker Rd *Web:* www.kilopass.com	San Jose	CA	95134	408-980-8808		696
Kilpatrick Life Insurance Co 1818 Marshall St *Web:* www.klic.com	Shreveport	LA	71101	318-222-0555		391-2
Kilpatrick Townsend & Stockton LLP 1100 Peachtree St *Web:* www.kilpatricktownsend.com	Atlanta	GA	30309	404-815-6500	815-6555	428
Kilroy Realty Corp 12200 W Olympic Blvd Ste 200 *NYSE:* KRC ■ *Web:* www.kilroyrealty.com	Los Angeles	CA	90064	310-481-8400	481-6501	655

Phone | Fax | Class

Kilwins Quality Confections Inc (KQC)
1050 Bay View Rd. Petoskey MI 49770 888-454-5946 123
TF: 888-454-5946 ■ *Web:* www.kilwins.com

Kim Davidson Aviation Inc
2701 Airport Ave. Santa Monica CA 90405 310-391-6293 359
Web: www.kdasmo.com

Kim Engineering Inc
11900 Baltimore Ave Ste F Beltsville MD 20705 240-542-4238 391-6790 256
Web: www.kimengineering.com

Kim Hotstart Manufacturing Co
5723 E Alki Ave. Spokane WA 99212 509-536-8660 15
TF: 800-224-5550 ■ *Web:* www.hotstart.com

Kim Lighting Inc
16555 E Gale Ave PO Box 60080 City of Industry CA 91745 626-968-5666 968-5716 439
Web: www.kimlighting.com

Kim Phung 7601 N Lamar Blvd Ste I Austin TX 78752 512-451-2464 671
Web: kplamar.com

Kimal Lumber Co 400 Riverview Dr. Nokomis FL 34275 941-484-9721 484-9593 191-3
Web: www.kimallumber.com

Kimball County 114 E Third St Kimball NE 69145 308-235-2241 235-3654 338
TF: 800-369-2850 ■ *Web:* www.co.kimball.ne.us

Kimball Electronics 13700 Reptron Blvd. Tampa FL 33626 813-814-5000 625

Kimball Electronics Group
1205 Kimball Blvd Jasper IN 47549 812-634-4200 625
Web: www.kimballelectronics.com

Kimball Genetics Inc
8490 Upland Dr Ste 100 Englewood CO 80112 800-444-9111 415
TF: 800-444-9111 ■ *Web:* www.kimballgenetics.com

Kimball Hospitality 1180 E 16th St Jasper IN 47549 276-666-8933 319-3
TF: 800-634-9510 ■ *Web:* www.kimballhospitality.com

Kimball International Inc
1600 Royal St Jasper IN 47549 812-482-1600 185
NASDAQ: KBAL ■ *TF:* 800-482-1616 ■ *Web:* www.kimball.com

Kimball Medical Ctr 600 River Ave Lakewood NJ 08701 732-363-1900 374-3
Web: www.barnabashealth.org

Kimball Midwest 4800 Robert Rd. Columbus OH 43228 614-219-6100 219-6101 385
TF: 800-233-1294 ■ *Web:* www.kimballmidwest.com

Kimball Office Furniture Co
1600 Royal St. Jasper IN 47549 800-482-1818 482-8300* 319-1
**Fax Area Code:* 812 ■ *TF:* 800-482-1818 ■ *Web:* www.kimballoffice.com

Kimball Property Maintenance
12717 S 125 E Draper UT 84020 801-571-3351 776
TF: 800-561-3357 ■ *Web:* kimballpm.com

Kimball Terrace Inn
10 Huntington Rd Northeast Harbor ME 04662 207-276-3383 379
TF: 800-454-6225 ■ *Web:* www.kimballterraceinn.com

Kimball Union Academy 7 Campus Ctr Dr Meriden NH 03770 603-469-2000 469-2040 622
Web: www.kua.org

Kimball, Tirey & St. John LLP
7676 Hazard Ctr Dr Ste 900 San Diego CA 92108 619-234-1690 428
TF: 800-519-3602 ■ *Web:* www.kts-law.com

Kimball-Jenkins Estate 266 N Main St. Concord NH 03301 603-225-3932 225-9288 50-3
Web: www.kimballjenkins.com

Kimbell Art Museum
3333 Camp Bowie Blvd Fort Worth TX 76107 817-332-8451 877-1264 520
Web: www.kimbellart.org

Kimber Manufacturing Inc
555 Taxter Rd Ste 235 Elmsford NY 10523 406-758-2222 326
TF: 888-243-4522 ■ *Web:* www.kimberamerica.com

Kimber Resources Inc
800 W Pender St Ste 220 Vancouver BC V6C2V6 604-669-2251 502
Web: invecture.com

Kimberly Crest House & Gardens
1325 Prospect Dr Redlands CA 92373 909-792-2111 798-1716 50-3
TF: 800-350-7551 ■ *Web:* www.kimberlycrest.org

Kimberly Hotel 145 E 50th St New York NY 10022 212-755-0400 355-4318 379
TF: 800-683-0400 ■ *Web:* www.kimberlyhotel.com

Kimberly-Clark Corp 351 Phelps Dr. Irving TX 75038 972-281-1200 558
NYSE: KMB ■ *TF:* 888-525-8388 ■ *Web:* www.kimberly-clark.com

Kimble Chase Life Science & Research Products LLC
1022 Spruce St. Vineland NJ 08362 856-692-8500 419
Web: www.kimble-chase.com

Kimble Companies Inc
3596 State Rt 39 NW Dover OH 44622 800-201-0005 787
TF: 800-201-0005 ■ *Web:* www.kimblecompanies.com

Kimble County 501 Main St Courthouse Junction TX 76849 325-446-3353 446-2986 338
TF: 800-772-1213 ■ *Web:* www.co.kimble.tx.us

Kimbro Oil Company Inc
2200 Clifton Ave. Nashville TN 37203 615-320-7484 579
Web: www.kimbrooil.com

Kimco Realty Corp
3333 New Hyde Pk Rd New Hyde Park NY 11042 516-869-9000 655
NYSE: KIM ■ *TF:* 800-645-6292 ■ *Web:* www.kimcorealty.com

Kimco Staffing Services Inc
17872 Cowan Ave. Irvine CA 92614 949-752-6996 721
TF: 800-649-5627 ■ *Web:* kimco.com

Kimley-Horn & Associates Inc
3001 Weston Pkwy Cary NC 27513 919-677-2000 194
Web: www.kimley-horn.com

Kimmel & Associates Inc 25 Page Ave. Asheville NC 28801 828-251-9900 193
TF: 800-561-3357 ■ *Web:* www.kimmel.com

Kimmel Ctr for the Performing Arts
1500 Walnut St Fl 17 Philadelphia PA 19102 215-790-5800 790-5801 572
Web: www.kimmelcenter.org

Kimmins Contracting Corp
1501 Second Ave Tampa FL 33605 813-248-3878 579-1081 188-10
TF: 800-594-7396 ■ *Web:* www.kimmins.com

Kimmons Investigative Services Inc
3033 Chimney Rock Ste 200 Houston TX 77056 713-532-5881 266-4002 693
TF: 800-681-5046 ■ *Web:* www.kimmonsinv.com

KiMo Theater 423 Central Ave NW Albuquerque NM 87102 505-768-3522 572
TF: 800-659-8331 ■ *Web:* kimotickets.com

Kimoto Tech Inc PO Box 1783 Cedartown GA 30125 770-748-2643 748-2648 600
TF: 888-546-6861 ■ *Web:* www.kimototech.com

Kimpton Hotel & Restaurant Group
422 SW Broadway Portland OR 97205 503-228-1212 228-3598 379
TF: 800-263-2305 ■ *Web:* www.hotelvintage-portland.com

Phone | Fax | Class

Kimpton Hotel & Restaurant Group LLC
222 Kearny St Ste 200 San Francisco CA 94108 415-397-5572 379
TF: 800-546-7866 ■ *Web:* www.kimptonhotels.com

Kimray Inc 52 NW 42nd St. Oklahoma City OK 73118 405-525-6601 525-7520 790
Web: www.kimray.com

KIMT-TV Ch 3 (CBS)
112 N Pennsylvania Ave Mason City IA 50401 641-423-2540 423-9309 741
TF: 800-323-4883 ■ *Web:* www.kimt.com

Kimwood Corp 77684 Oregon 99. Cottage Grove OR 97424 541-942-4401 942-0719 821
TF: 800-942-4401 ■ *Web:* www.kimwood.com

Kin Communications Inc
736 Granville St Ste 100 Vancouver BC V6Z1G3 604-684-6730 224
TF: 866-684-6730 ■ *Web:* www.kincommunications.com

Kin On Health Care Ctr
4416 S Brandon St Seattle WA 98118 206-721-3630 371
Web: kinon.org

Kin's Wok
4001 Virginia Beach Blvd Virginia Beach VA 23452 757-340-6898 671
Web: kinswokvb.com

Kinamed Inc 820 Flynn Rd. Camarillo CA 93012 805-384-2748 476
TF: 800-827-5775 ■ *Web:* www.kinamed.com

Kinark Child 500 Hood Rd Ste 200 Markham ON L3R9Z3 905-474-9595 393
TF: 800-230-8533 ■ *Web:* www.kinark.on.ca

Kinaxis 700 Silver Seven Rd. Ottawa ON K2V1C3 613-592-5780 592-0584 178-10
TF General: 877-546-2947 ■ *Web:* www.kinaxis.com

Kincaid Coach Lines Inc
9207 Woodend Rd Kansas City KS 66111 913-441-6200 441-0068 760
TF: 800-998-1901 ■ *Web:* www.kincaidcoach.com

Kincaid Grill 6700 Jewel Lake Rd Anchorage AK 99502 907-243-0507 243-5110 671
Web: www.kincaidgrill.com

Kincaid Lake State Park
565 Kincaid Pk Rd Falmouth KY 41040 859-654-3531 565
Web: www.parks.ky.gov

Kincaid's Fish Chop & Steak House
1050 Ala Moana Blvd Honolulu HI 96814 808-591-2005 671
Web: www.kincaids.com

Kincannon & Reed LLC
40 Stoneridge Dr Ste 101 Waynesboro VA 22980 540-941-3460 193
Web: www.krsearch.com

Kincardine Cable TV Ltd
223 Bruce Ave. Kincardine ON N2Z2P2 519-396-8880 116
TF: 800-265-3064 ■ *Web:* www.tnt21.com

Kinco Constructors LLC
12600 Lawson Rd. Little Rock AR 72210 501-225-7606 186
TF: 800-264-1023 ■ *Web:* www.kincoconstructors.com

Kinco International 4286 NE 185th Dr. Portland OR 97230 800-547-8410 536-4905 155-8
TF General: 800-547-8410 ■ *Web:* www.kinco.com

KINC-TV Ch 15 (Uni)
500 Pilot Rd Ste D Las Vegas NV 89119 702-434-0015 434-0527 741-72
Web: www.entravision.com

Kind Ron (Rep D - WI)
1502 Longworth Bldg Washington DC 20515 202-225-5506 225-5739 342-2
Web: kind.house.gov

Kinder Morgan
1001 Louisiana St Ste 1000 Houston TX 77002 713-369-9000 230-5675 325
NYSE: KMI ■ *TF:* 800-247-4122 ■ *Web:* www.kindermorgan.com

Kinder Morgan Bulk Terminals Inc
7116 Hwy 22 Sorrento LA 70778 225-675-5387 465
TF: 800-232-1627 ■ *Web:* www.kindermorgan.com

Kinder Morgan Energy Partners LP
500 Dallas St Ste 1000 Houston TX 77002 713-369-9000 514-6401* 325
NYSE: KMI ■ **Fax Area Code:* 403 ■ **Fax:* Hum Res ■ *TF:* 866-208-3372 ■ *Web:* www.kindermorgan.com

Kinder Morgan Inc KN Energy Retail Div
370 Van Gordon St Lakewood CO 80228 303-989-1740 707
TF: 800-232-1627 ■ *Web:* www.kindermorgan.com

Kinder Morgan Management LLC
500 Dallas St 1 Allen Ctr Ste 1000 Houston TX 77002 713-369-9000 325
NYSE: KMI ■ *TF:* 800-781-4152 ■ *Web:* www.kindermorgan.com

KinderCare Learning Centers LLC
650 NE Holladay St Ste 1400 Ste 1400 Portland OR 97232 800-633-1488 872-1427* 148
**Fax Area Code:* 503 ■ *TF:* 800-633-1488 ■ *Web:* www.kindercare.com

Kinderdance International Inc
5238 Valleypointe Pkwy Roanoke VA 24019 321-984-4448 310
TF: 800-554-2334 ■ *Web:* www.kinderdance.com

Kindred Healthcare Inc
700 W Sixth Ave Anchorage AK 99501 907-397-8909 374-7
Web: khparkview.com

Kindred Healthcare Inc
7710 Rialto Blvd Ste 150 Austin TX 78735 512-288-0859 301-4821 374-7
TF: 866-546-3733 ■ *Web:* www.kindredatlanta.com

Kindred Healthcare Inc
680 S Fourth Ave Louisville KY 40202 502-596-7300 353
NYSE: KND ■ *TF:* 800-545-0749 ■ *Web:* www.kindredhealthcare.com

Kindred Hospice
190 Bilmar Dr Ste 200 Pittsburgh PA 15205 412-494-5500 450
TF: 866-546-3733 ■ *Web:* www.kindredhospitalpittsburgh.com

Kindred Hospital - Saint Louis
4930 Lindell Blvd Saint Louis MO 63108 314-361-8700 361-1210 374-3
Web: www.kindredstlouis.com

Kindred Hospital Dallas
9525 Greenville Ave Dallas TX 75243 214-355-2600 355-2630 374-7
Web: www.khdallas.com

Kindred Hospital Fort Worth
815 Eigth Ave Fort Worth TX 76104 817-332-4812 332-8843 450
Web: kindredfortworth.com

Kindred Hospital Fort Worth Southwest
7800 Oakmont Blvd Fort Worth TX 76132 817-346-0094 263-4071 374-7
TF: 800-359-7412 ■ *Web:* www.kindredhospitalfwsw.com

Kindred Hospital Greensboro
2401 Southside Blvd Greensboro NC 27406 336-271-2800 271-2734 450
TF: 877-836-2671 ■ *Web:* www.khgreensboro.com

Kindred Hospital Kansas City
8701 Troost Ave Kansas City MO 64131 816-995-2000 995-2171 374-7
TF: 800-545-0749 ■ *Web:* www.kindredhospitalkc.com

Kindred Hospital Louisville
1313 St Anthony Pl. Louisville KY 40204 502-587-7001 587-0060 374-3
TF: 800-648-6057 ■ *Web:* www.kindredlouisville.com

Name / Address	City	State	Zip	Phone	Fax	Class
Kindred Hospital Philadelphia 6129 Palmetto St *TF*: 800-654-5988 ■ *Web*: www.kindredphila.com	Philadelphia	PA	19111	215-722-8555	725-8998	450
Kindred Partners LLC 535 Mission St 22nd Fl Ste 2250 *Web*: www.kindredpartners.com	San Francisco	CA	94105	650-573-5500		652
Kindred Transitional Care & Rehabilitation - Greenbriar 55 Harris Rd *TF*: 800-272-3900 ■ *Web*: www.greenbriarterrace.com	Nashua	NH	03062	603-888-1573	888-5089	450
Kindred Transitional Care and Rehabilitation 160 Main St *Web*: www.harringtonrehab.com	Walpole	MA	02081	508-660-3080		450
Kindred Transitional Care and Rehabilitation 75 McMillen Dr **Fax Area Code*: 502 ■ *Web*: www.newarkhealthcare.com	Newark	OH	43055	740-344-0357	596-4095*	450
Kinecta Federal Credit Union 1440 Rosecrans Ave PO Box 10003 *TF*: 800-854-9846 ■ *Web*: www.kinecta.org	Manhattan Beach	CA	90266	310-643-5400		219
Kinectrics Inc 800 Kipling Ave *Web*: www.kinectrics.com	Toronto	ON	M8Z5G5	416-207-6000		261
Kinefac Corp 156 Goddard Memorial Dr *Web*: www.kinefac.com	Worcester	MA	01603	508-754-6891	756-5342	456
KINE-FM 105.1 (AC) 900 Ft St Ste 700 *TF*: 800-922-0204 ■ *Web*: hawaiian105.com	Honolulu	HI	96813	808-275-1000		645-73
Kinemetrics Inc 222 Vista Ave *Web*: www.kinemetrics.com	Pasadena	CA	91107	626-795-2220		472
Kinemotive Corp 222 Central Ave *TF*: 800-334-3035 ■ *Web*: www.kinemotive.com	Farmingdale	NY	11735	631-249-6440		407
Kinesis Corp 22030 20th Ave SE Ste 102 *TF*: 800-454-6374 ■ *Web*: www.kinesis-ergo.com	Bothell	WA	98021	425-402-8100	402-8181	173-1
Kinetek Inc 1751 Lake Cook Rd ArborLake Ctr Ste 550 *Web*: www.kinetekinc.com	Deerfield	IL	60015	847-267-4473		518
Kinetic Books Company Inc 2003 Western Ave Ste 100 *Web*: www.kineticbooks.com	Seattle	WA	98121	206-448-1141		95
Kinetic Cafe Inc 934 - 1 Yonge St *Web*: www.kineticcafe.com	Toronto	ON	M5E1E5	416-899-0761		463
Kinetic Instrument Inc 17 Berkshire Blvd *TF*: 800-233-2346 ■ *Web*: www.kineticinc.com	Bethel	CT	06801	203-743-0080		228
Kinetic Systems Inc 20 Arboretum Rd *Web*: www.kineticsystems.com	Boston	MA	02131	617-522-8700		256
Kinetic The Technology Agency 200 Distillery Commons Ste 200 *Web*: kinetictms.com	Louisville	KY	40206	502-719-9500		592
Kinetico Inc 10845 Kinsman Rd **Fax Area Code*: 440 ■ *TF*: 800-944-9283 ■ *Web*: www.kinetico.com	Newbury	OH	44065	800-944-9283	564-9541*	806
Kineticorp 6070 Greenwood Plaza Blvd Ste 200 *Web*: www.kineticorp.com	Greenwood Village	CO	80111	303-733-1888		743
Kinetics Mechanical Service Inc 6691 Brisa St *Web*: www.kms-inc.com	Livermore	CA	94550	925-245-6200		610
Kinetix Technology Ctr 400 Murray St *Web*: www.kbisp.com	Alexandria	LA	71301	318-487-8200		396
King & I 545 Broadbridge Rd *Web*: www.kingandict.com	Bridgeport	CT	06610	203-374-2081		671
King & I 3157 S Grand Ave *Web*: kingandistl.squarespace.com	Saint Louis	MO	63118	314-771-1777		671
King & I, The 830 N Old World Third St *Web*: www.kingandirestaurant.com	Milwaukee	WI	53203	414-276-4181		671
King & Partners Plc 170 College Ave Ste 230 *Web*: www.king-partners.com	Holland	MI	49423	616-355-0400		428
King & Prince Beach & Golf Resort 201 Arnold Rd *TF*: 800-342-0212 ■ *Web*: www.kingandprince.com	Saint Simons Island	GA	31522	912-638-3631	638-7699	669
King & Prince Seafood Corp 1 King & Prince Blvd *TF*: 800-841-0205 ■ *Web*: www.kpseafood.com	Brunswick	GA	31520	912-265-5155		296-14
King & Queen County 242 Allens Cir Ste L PO Box 177 *Web*: www.kingandqueenco.net	King & Queen Court House	VA	23085	804-785-5975	785-5999	338
King & Schickli PLLC 800 Corporate Dr Ste 200 *TF*: 888-364-5712 ■ *Web*: www.iplaw1.net	Lexington	KY	40503	859-274-4287	252-0779	428
King & Spalding 1180 Peachtree St NE *Web*: www.kslaw.com	Atlanta	GA	30309	404-572-4600	572-5100	428
KING 5 Television 333 Dexter Ave N *TF*: 877-564-2261 ■ *Web*: www.king5.com	Seattle	WA	98109	206-448-5555	448-4525	741-123
KING AEROSPACE Inc 4444 Westgrove *Web*: www.kingaerospaceinc.com	Addison	TX	75001	972-248-4886		21
King Agency Inc, The 3 N Lombardy St *Web*: thekingagency.com	Richmond	VA	23220	804-249-7500		4
King Angus S Jr (Sen I - ME) 133 Hart Senate Office Bldg *Web*: www.king.senate.gov	Washington	DC	20510	202-224-5344		342-2
King Architectural Metals Inc PO Box 271169 *TF*: 800-542-2379 ■ *Web*: kingmetals.com	Dallas	TX	75227	800-542-2379		491
King Arthur Flour Co Inc, The 135 Rt 5 S *Web*: www.kingarthurflour.com	Norwich	VT	05055	802-649-3361	649-3365	68
King Arts Complex, The 867 Mt Vernon Ave *Web*: kingartscomplex.com	Columbus	OH	43203	614-645-5464	645-0672	50-2
King Buffet 2727 Bell Rd	Montgomery	AL	36117	334-273-8883		671
King Business Interiors Inc 6155 Huntley Rd Ste D *Web*: www.kbiinc.com	Columbus	OH	43229	614-430-0020		317
King City Union Elementary School District 800 Broadway St *Web*: www.kcusd.org	King City	CA	93930	831-385-1144		685
King College 1350 King College Rd *TF Admissions*: 800-362-0014 ■ *Web*: www.king.edu	Bristol	TN	37620	423-652-4861		166
King County PO Box 66 *Web*: www.tdcj.state.tx.us	Guthrie	TX	79236	806-596-4470		338
King County 401 Fifth Ave Ste 800 *TF*: 800-325-6165 ■ *Web*: www.kingcounty.gov	Seattle	WA	98104	206-296-1586	296-0194	338
King County Dept of Transportation 201 S Jackson St *Web*: www.kingcounty.gov	Seattle	WA	98104	206-684-1481	684-1224	468
King County Library System 960 Newport Way NW *Web*: www.kcls.org	Issaquah	WA	98027	425-369-3224		434-3
King Craft Co 142 N Main St *Web*: www.kingcraftco.com	Herkimer	NY	13350	315-866-5500	866-8062	44
King Ctr, The 449 Auburn Ave NE *Web*: www.thekingcenter.org	Atlanta	GA	30312	404-526-8900		48-8
King David's 129 Marshall St *Web*: www.kingdavids.com	Syracuse	NY	13210	315-471-5000		671
King Electrical Manufacturing Co 9131 Tenth Ave S *TF*: 800-603-5464 ■ *Web*: www.king-electric.com	Seattle	WA	98108	206-762-0400	763-7738	37
King Engineering Assoc Inc 4921 Memorial Hwy Ste 300 *Web*: www.kingengineering.com	Tampa	FL	33634	813-880-8881		261
King Engineering Corp 3201 S State St *TF Cust Svc*: 800-242-8871 ■ *Web*: www.king-gage.com	Ann Arbor	MI	48106	734-662-5691	662-6652	18
King Estate Winery 80854 Territorial Rd *TF*: 800-884-4441 ■ *Web*: www.kingestate.com	Eugene	OR	97405	541-942-9874	942-9867	50-7
King Features Syndicate Inc 300 W 57th St **Fax Area Code*: 646 ■ *TF*: 800-708-7311 ■ *Web*: www.kingfeatures.com	New York	NY	10019	212-969-7550	280-1550*	530
King Fuels Inc 14825 Willis St *Web*: www.king fuels.com	Houston	TX	77039	281-449-9975		579
King George County 9483 Kings Hwy Ste 3 *Web*: www.king-george.va.us	King George	VA	22485	540-775-3322	775-5466	338
King George Hotel 334 Mason St *Web*: www.kinggeorge.com	San Francisco	CA	94102	415-781-5050		378
King Hickory Furniture Co 1820 Main Ave SE *Web*: www.kinghickory.com	Hickory	NC	28602	828-322-6025		319-2
King Industries Inc 1 Science Rd *TF*: 800-431-7900 ■ *Web*: www.kingindustries.com	Norwalk	CT	06852	203-866-5551	866-1268	145
King Instrument Company Inc 12700 Pala Dr *Web*: www.kinginstrumentco.com	Garden Grove	CA	92841	714-891-0008		201
King Kamehameha V - Judiciary History Ctr 417 S King St *Web*: jhchawaii.net	Honolulu	HI	96813	808-539-4999		520
King Kamehameha's Kona Beach Hotel 75-5660 Palani Rd *TF*: 800-367-2111 ■ *Web*: www.konabeachhotel.com	Kailua-Kona	HI	96740	808-329-2911	329-4602	379
King Koil Licensing Company Inc 7501 S Quincy St Ste 130 *TF*: 800-525-8331 ■ *Web*: www.kingkoil.com	Willowbrook	IL	60527	800-525-8331		471
King Kullen Grocery Company Inc 185 Central Ave *Web*: www.kingkullen.com	Bethpage	NY	11714	516-733-7100		345
King Machine & Tool Co 1237 Sanders Ave SW *Web*: www.kmtco.com	Massillon	OH	44647	330-833-7217		295
King Milling Co 115 S Broadway St *Web*: www.kingmilling.com	Lowell	MI	49331	616-897-9264		296-23
King Mountain State Recreation Site Mile 76 Glenn Hwy 33915 N Glenn Hwy *Web*: dnr.alaska.gov	Palmer	AK	99645	907-240-9797		565
King Nummy Trail Camp Ground 205 Rt 47 S *Web*: kingnummytrail.com	Cape May Court House	NJ	08210	609-465-4242		239
King Nut Co 31900 Solon Rd *TF*: 800-860-5464 ■ *Web*: www.kingnut.com	Solon	OH	44139	440-248-8484	248-0153	296-28
King of Prussia Mall 160 N Gulph Rd *TF*: 877-746-6642 ■ *Web*: simon.com/mall/king-of-prussia-mall	King of Prussia	PA	19406	610-265-5727	265-1640	460
King Pacific Lodge PO Box 31878 *TF*: 855-825-9378	Steveston	BC	V7E0B5	604-503-5474		379
King Pete (Rep R - NY) 339 Cannon Bldg *Web*: peteking.house.gov	Washington	DC	20515	202-225-7896	226-2279	342-2
King Plastic Corp 1100 N Toledo Blade Blvd *TF*: 800-780-5502 ■ *Web*: www.kingplastic.com	North Port	FL	34288	941-493-5502	497-3274	608
King Plastics Inc 840 N Elm St *TF*: 800-363-9822 ■ *Web*: www.kingplastics.com	Orange	CA	92867	714-997-7540	997-0491	607
King Precision Glass Inc 177 S Indian Hill Blvd *Web*: www.kingprecisionglass.com	Claremont	CA	91711	909-626-3526	625-0173	332
King Ranch Inc 3 Riverway Ste 1600 *Web*: www.king-ranch.com	Houston	TX	77056	832-681-5700		10-1
King Relocation Services 13535 Larwin Cir *TF*: 800-854-3679 ■ *Web*: www.kingcompaniesusa.com	Santa Fe Springs	CA	90670	800-854-3679		519
King Sash & Door Inc 2799 Hope Church Rd *Web*: www.kingsashanddoor.com	Winston-Salem	NC	27127	336-774-3071		236
King Signs & Graphics 3858 Jackson River Rd	Monterey	VA	24465	540-468-2932		701
King Steve (Rep R - IA) 2210 Rayburn Bldg *Web*: steveking.house.gov	Washington	DC	20515	202-225-4426	225-3193	342-2
King Stringfellow Group 2105 Laurel Bush Rd Ste 200 *Web*: stringfellowgroup.net	Bel Air	MD	21015	443-640-1030	640-1031	47
King Taco Restaurants Inc 1118 Cypress Ave *Web*: www.kingtaco.com	Los Angeles	CA	90065	323-223-2595		670

				Phone	Fax	Class
King Tiger Martial Arts Inc 13401 New Hampshire Ave *Web:* kingtigermartialarts.com	Colesville	MD	20904	301-989-2400		148
King Tut's Grill 4132 Martin Mill Pk	Knoxville	TN	37920	865-573-6021		671
King William County 351 Courthouse Ln Ste 201 *Web:* www.kingwilliamcounty.us	King William	VA	23086	804-769-4947	769-4971	338
King William Historic District 122 Madison St *TF:* 800-745-3000 ■ *Web:* kwfair.org	San Antonio	TX	78204	210-271-3247		50-3
King Wire Partitions Inc 6044 N Figueroa St *TF:* 800-789-9608 ■ *Web:* www.kingwireusa.com	Los Angeles	CA	90042	323-256-4848		688
King Wok 712 Main St	Paterson	NJ	07503	973-881-8818		671
King's 3310 Central Ave	Hot Springs	AR	71913	501-318-1888		671
King's Academy Inc, The 8401 Belvedere Rd *TF:* 800-245-3200 ■ *Web:* www.tka.net	West Palm Beach	FL	33411	561-686-4244		685
King's Chapel 58 Tremont St *Web:* kings-chapel.org	Boston	MA	02108	617-227-2155	227-4101	50-1
King's College 133 N River St *Fax: Admissions ■ *TF:* 800-955-5777 ■ *Web:* www.kings.edu	Wilkes-Barre	PA	18711	570-208-5858	208-5971*	166
King's College & Seminary 14344 Sherman Way *Web:* www.tku.edu	Van Nuys	CA	91405	818-779-8505		161
King's College Library 322 Lamar Ave *TF:* 800-768-2255 ■ *Web:* www.kingscollegecharlotte.edu	Charlotte	NC	28204	704-372-0266		166
King's Command Foods Inc 7622 S 188th St *Web:* www.kingscommand.com	Kent	WA	98032	425-251-6788	251-0523	296-26
King's County Market 13735 Roundlake Blvd *Web:* kingscountymarket.com	Andover	MN	55304	763-422-1768		297-8
King's Daughters Medical Ctr 2201 Lexington Ave *TF:* 888-377-5362 ■ *Web:* www.kingsdaughtershealth.com	Ashland	KY	41101	606-408-8999		374-3
King's Daughters Medical Ctr 427 Hwy 51 N *Web:* www.kdmc.org	Brookhaven	MS	39601	601-833-6011		374-3
King's Daughters' Hospital 1373 E State Rd 62 *Web:* www.kdhmadison.org	Madison	IN	47250	812-801-0800	801-0680	374-3
King's Fish House 100 W Broadway *Web:* www.kingsfishhouse.com	Long Beach	CA	90802	562-432-7463	435-6143	671
King's Head Pub 120 King St *Web:* www.kingshead.ca	Winnipeg	MB	R3B1H9	204-957-7710		671
King's Heating & Sheet Metal Inc 137 S Work St *Web:* www.kings-heating.com	Falconer	NY	14733	716-665-3102		697
King's Jewelry & Loan 800 S Vermont Ave *TF:* 800-378-1111 ■ *Web:* www.kingspawn.com	Los Angeles	CA	90005	213-383-5555		410
King's Material Inc 650 12th Ave SW *TF:* 800-332-5298 ■ *Web:* www.kingsmaterial.com	Cedar Rapids	IA	52404	319-363-0233	366-0249	183
King's Medical Co 1094 Georgetown Rd *Web:* www.kingsmedical.com	Hudson	OH	44236	330-653-3968	656-0600	264-4
King's Palace Cafe 162 Beale St	Memphis	TN	38103	901-521-1851		671
King's Seafood Co 3185 Airway Ave *Web:* www.kingsseafood.com	Costa Mesa	CA	92626	714-432-0400		670
King's University College 9125 50th St *TF:* 800-661-8582 ■ *Web:* kingsu.ca	Edmonton	AB	T6B2H3	780-465-3500	465-3534	785
King, Krebs & Jurgens PLLC 201 St Charles Ave 45th Fl *Web:* www.kingkrebs.com	New Orleans	LA	70170	504-582-3800		428
Kingbridge Centre, The 12750 Jane St *TF:* 800-827-7221 ■ *Web:* www.kingbridgecentre.com	King City	ON	L7B1A3	905-833-3086	833-3075	377
KingChapman 3355 W Alabama St Ste 1255 *Web:* www.kcbcg.com	Houston	TX	77098	713-223-7233		194
Kingdom Come State Park 502 Pk Rd *Web:* www.parks.ky.gov	Cumberland	KY	40823	606-589-2479		565
Kingdom Inc 719 Lambs Creek Rd *Web:* www.kingdom.com	Mansfield	PA	16933	570-662-7515		174
Kingery & Crouse PA 2801 W Busch Blvd Ste 200 *Web:* www.tampacpa.com	Tampa	FL	33618	813-874-1280		2
Kingery Construction Co 201 N 46th St *Web:* www.kccobuilders.com	Lincoln	NE	68503	402-465-4400		196
Kingery Printing Co 3012 S Banker PO Box 727 *Web:* www.kingeryprinting.com	Effingham	IL	62401	217-347-5151		627
Kingfish Grill 252 Yacht Club Dr *Web:* www.kingfishgrill.com	Saint Augustine	FL	32084	904-824-2111		671
Kingfisher Bar & Grill 2564 E Grant Rd *Web:* www.kingfishertucson.com	Tucson	AZ	85716	520-323-7739	795-7810	671
Kingfisher County 301 N Main St	Kingfisher	OK	73750	405-375-3705		338
KING-FM 98.1 (Clas) 10 Harrison St Ste 100 *TF:* 800-448-4663 ■ *Web:* www.king.org	Seattle	WA	98109	206-691-2981	691-2982	645-150
Kingman Area Chamber of Commerce 120 W Andy Devine Ave *Web:* www.kingmanchamber.com	Kingman	AZ	86401	928-753-6253	753-1049	139
Kingman County 130 N Spruce St *Web:* kingmancoks.com	Kingman	KS	67068	620-532-2521		338
Kingman Group Corp, The 14010 Live Oak Ave *Web:* www.kingman.com	Baldwin Park	CA	91706	626-430-2300		360-3
Kingman Museum 175 Limit St *Web:* www.kingmanmuseum.org	Battle Creek	MI	49037	269-965-5117		520
Kingman Regional Medical Ctr (KRMC) 3269 Stockton Hill Rd *TF:* 877-757-2101 ■ *Web:* www.azkrmc.com	Kingman	AZ	86409	928-757-2101		374-3
King-o'rourke Cadillac Inc 756 Smithtown Byp *Web:* kingorourkeautogroup.com	Smithtown	NY	11787	631-724-4700	724-4784	57
Kings Aire Inc 1035 Kessler Dr *Web:* kingsaire.com	El Paso	TX	79907	915-592-2997		189-10
Kings Beach State Recreation Area c/o Sierra District Office PO Box 266 *Web:* www.parks.ca.gov/default.asp?page_id=511	Tahoma	CA	96142	530-525-7232		565
Kings County 360 Adams St Rm 189 *Web:* www.nycourts.gov/courts/2jd/kingsclerk	Brooklyn	NY	11201	347-404-9772		338
Kings County 680 Campus Dr *Web:* www.countyofkings.com	Hanford	CA	93230	559-582-3211	582-6639	338
Kings County Hospital Ctr 451 Clarkson Ave *Web:* www1.nyc.gov	Brooklyn	NY	11203	718-245-3131		374-3
Kings County Library 401 N Douty St *TF:* 800-984-4636 ■ *Web:* www.kingscountylibrary.org	Hanford	CA	93230	559-582-0261	583-6163	434-3
Kings Credit Services 510 N Douty St *TF:* 800-366-0950 ■ *Web:* www.kingscredit.com	Hanford	CA	93230	559-587-4200		160
Kings Dominion 16000 Theme Pkwy *Web:* www.kingsdominion.com	Doswell	VA	23047	804-876-5000	876-5864	32
Kings Family Restaurants 1820 Lincoln Hwy *Web:* www.kingsfamily.com	North Versailles	PA	15137	412-823-0324		670
Kings Gap Environmental Education & Training Ctr 500 Kings Gap Rd *Web:* www.dcnr.state.pa.us	Carlisle	PA	17015	717-486-5031		565
Kings Head British Pub 6460 US Hwy 1 N *Web:* kingsheadbritishpub.com	Saint Augustine	FL	32095	904-823-9787		671
Kings Island Resort & Conference Ctr 5691 Kings Island Dr	Mason	OH	45040	513-398-0115		379
Kings Liquor Inc 2810 W Berry St *Web:* www.kingsliquor.com	Fort Worth	TX	76109	817-923-3737		443
Kings Mountain National Military Park 2625 Pk Rd *Web:* www.nps.gov	Blacksburg	SC	29702	864-936-7921	936-9897	564
Kings Mountain State Park 1277 Pk Rd *Web:* www.southcarolinaparks.com	Blacksburg	SC	29702	803-222-3209	222-6948	565
Kings Oil Tools Inc PO Box 441 *Web:* www.kingsoiltools.com	San Ardo	CA	93450	831-627-2581		536
Kings Super Markets Inc 700 Lanidex Plaza *TF:* 800-325-4647 ■ *Web:* kingsfoodmarkets.com	Parsippany	NJ	07054	800-325-4647		297-8
Kingsboro Psychiatric Ctr 681 Clarkson Ave *TF:* 800-597-8481 ■ *Web:* www.omh.ny.gov	Brooklyn	NY	11203	800-597-8481		374-5
Kingsborough Community College 2001 Oriental Blvd *Web:* www.kbcc.cuny.edu	Brooklyn	NY	11235	718-368-5000		162
Kingsbrook Jewish Medical Ctr 585 Schenectady Ave *TF:* 800-906-9762 ■ *Web:* www.kingsbrook.org	Brooklyn	NY	11203	718-604-5000	604-5243	374-3
Kingsburg Apple Packers Inc 10363 E Davis Ave PO Box 38 *Web:* www.kingsburgorchards.com	Kingsburg	CA	93631	559-897-5132	897-4532	11-1
Kingsbury Corp 15 Business Center Dr *Web:* www.optimation.us	Swanzey	NH	03446	603-352-5212		697
Kingsbury County 202 Second St SE *Web:* ujs.sd.gov	De Smet	SD	57231	605-854-3811	854-9080	338
Kingsbury Electric Co-op Inc 511 US Hwy 14	De Smet	SD	57231	605-854-3522		245
Kingsbury Inc 10385 Drummond Rd *TF Sales:* 866-581-5464 ■ *Web:* www.kingsbury.com	Philadelphia	PA	19154	215-824-4000	824-4999	620
Kingsbury Printing Co Mount Royal Plaza State Rte 9 *Web:* www.kingsburyprinting.com	Queensbury	NY	12804	518-747-6606	747-8852	627
Kingsdale Capital Markets Inc 55 University Ave Ste M002 *Web:* www.kingsdalecapital.com	Toronto	ON	M5J2H7	416-867-4550		690
Kingsdown Inc 126 W Holt St *TF Cust Svc:* 800-354-5464 ■ *Web:* www.kingsdown.com	Mebane	NC	27302	919-563-3531		471
Kingsgate Marriott Conference Ctr at the University of Cincinnati 151 Goodman St *TF:* 800-228-9290 ■ *Web:* www.marriott.com/hotels/travel/cvgkg	Cincinnati	OH	45219	513-487-3800	487-3810	377
Kingsland Bay State Park 787 Kingsland Bay State Pk Rd *Web:* www.vtstateparks.com	Ferrisburgh	VT	05456	802-877-3445		565
Kingsley Consulting Group Ltd 701 Papworth Ave Ste 207 *Web:* kingsleygroup.com	Metairie	LA	70005	504-834-6484		196
Kingsley Plantation 11676 Palmetto Ave *TF:* 877-874-2478 ■ *Web:* www.nps.gov/timu	Jacksonville	FL	32226	904-251-3537	251-3577	520
Kingsley-Bate Ltd 7200 Gateway Ct *Web:* www.kingsleybate.com	Manassas	VA	20109	703-361-7000		319-4
Kingsmill Resort & Spa 1010 Kingsmill Rd *TF:* 800-832-5665 ■ *Web:* www.kingsmill.com	Williamsburg	VA	23185	757-253-1703	253-8246	669
Kingsport Area Chamber of Commerce 151 E Main St *Web:* www.kingsportchamber.org	Kingsport	TN	37660	423-392-8800		139
Kingsport Convention & Visitors Bureau (KCVB) 400 Clinchfield St Ste 100 *TF:* 800-743-5282 ■ *Web:* www.visitkingsport.com	Kingsport	TN	37660	423-392-8820	392-8833	206
Kingsport Public Library 400 Broad St *Web:* www.kingsportlibrary.org	Kingsport	TN	37660	423-224-2559		434-3
Kingsport Times-News 701 Lynn Garden Dr *TF:* 800-251-0328 ■ *Web:* www.timesnews.net	Kingsport	TN	37660	423-246-8121	392-1385	532-2
Kingston Cos 477 Shoup Ave *Web:* kingstoncorp.com	Idaho Falls	ID	83402	208-522-2365	522-7488	11-1
Kingston National Bank 2 N Main St PO Box 613 *TF:* 800-337-4562 ■ *Web:* www.kingstonnationalbank.com	Kingston	OH	45644	740-642-2191		70

Name / Address	City	State	Zip	Phone	Fax	Class
Kingston Oil Supply Corp 2926 Rt 32 N	Saugerties	NY	12477	845-247-2200	246-0207	316
TF: 800-755-6726 ■ *Web:* www.koscocomfort.com						
Kingston State Park 124 Main St	Kingston	NH	03848	603-642-5471		565
Web: www.nhstateparks.org						
Kingston Technology Co 17600 Newhope St	Fountain Valley	CA	92708	714-435-2600	435-2699	288
TF: 800-835-6575 ■ *Web:* www.kingston.com						
Kingston Whig-Standard, The 6 Cataraqui St	Kingston	ON	K7L4Z7	613-544-5000	530-4122	532-1
Web: www.thewhig.com						
Kingstone Companies Inc 1154 Broadway	Hewlett	NY	11557	516-374-7600	295-7216	391-4
NASDAQ: KINS ■ *Web:* www.kingstonecompanies.com						
Kingsville Chamber of Commerce 635 E King Ave # 124	Kingsville	TX	78363	361-592-6438	592-0866	139
Web: www.kingsville.org						
Kingsway America Inc (KAI) 150 NW Pt Blvd	Elk Grove Village	IL	60007	847-700-9100		360-4
TF: 800-232-0631 ■ *Web:* kaiadvantage.com						
Kingsway Arms Retirement Residences Inc 208 Evans Ave Ste 115	Toronto	ON	M8Z1J7	647-288-2942		672
Kingsway Charities 1119 Commonwealth Ave	Bristol	VA	24201	276-466-3014	466-0955	48-20
TF: 800-321-9234 ■ *Web:* www.kingswaycharities.org						
Kingsway Christian School 7979 E County Rd 100 N	Avon	IN	46123	317-272-2227		623
Web: www.kingswaychurch.org						
Kingsway College School 4600 Dundas St W	Etobicoke	ON	M9A1A5	416-234-5073		685
Web: www.kcs.on.ca						
Kingsway Financial Services Inc 45 St Clair Ave W Ste 400	Toronto	ON	M4V1K9	416-848-1171	848-1171	391-4
NYSE: KFS ■ *Web:* www.kingsway-financial.com						
Kingswood Senior Living Community 10000 Wornall Rd	Kansas City	MO	64114	816-942-0994		672
Web: kingswoodretirementliving.com						
Kingwood College 20000 Kingwood Dr	Kingwood	TX	77339	281-312-1600	312-1456	162
TF: 800-883-7939 ■ *Web:* www.lonestar.edu/kingwood.htm						
Kingwood Ctr 50 Trimble Rd	Mansfield	OH	44906	419-522-0211		97
Web: www.kingwoodcenter.org						
Kingwood Medical Ctr 22999 US Hwy 59	Kingwood	TX	77339	281-348-8000		374-3
Web: www.kingwoodmedical.com						
Kinkaid Lake State Fish & Wildlife Area 52 Cinder Hill Dr	Murphysboro	IL	62966	618-684-2867		565
Web: dnr.illinois.gov/Lands/Landmgt/PARKS/R5/Kinkaid.htm						
Kinkaid School, The 201 Kinkaid School Dr	Houston	TX	77024	713-782-1640		623
Web: www.kinkaid.org						
KINK-FM 101.9 (AAA) 1211 SW Fifth Ave Ste 600	Portland	OR	97204	503-517-6000		645-128
Web: www.kink.fm						
Kinloch Consulting Group Inc 25 Melville Park Rd Ste 260	Melville	NY	11747	631-773-6600		535
Web: www.kinlochcg.com						
Kinney & Lange PA 312 S Third St	Minneapolis	MN	55415	612-339-1863		428
Web: www.kinney.com						
Kinney Brick Co 100 Prosperity Rd PO Box 1804	Albuquerque	NM	87103	505-877-4550		150
TF: 800-464-4605 ■ *Web:* kinneybrickco.com						
Kinney Construction Services Inc 121 E Birch Ave Ste 100	Flagstaff	AZ	86001	928-779-2820		186
Web: www.kinneyconstruction.net						
Kinney County 501 S Ann St	Brackettville	TX	78832	830-563-2521		338
Web: www.co.kinney.tx.us						
Kinney Drugs Inc 520 E Main St	Gouverneur	NY	13642	315-287-3600		237
Web: www.kinneydrugs.com						
Kinney Electrical Manufacturing Co 678 Buckeye St	Elgin	IL	60123	847-742-9600		580
TF: 800-544-7375 ■ *Web:* www.kinneyelectric.com						
Kinnickinnic State Park W11983 820th Ave	River Falls	WI	54022	715-425-1129	425-0010	565
Web: dnr.wi.gov						
Kinnucan's 1199 S Donahue Dr Ste F	Auburn	AL	36832	334-887-6100		711
Web: www.kinnucans.com						
Kino Flo Inc 2840 N Hollywood Way	Burbank	CA	91505	818-767-6528		362
Web: www.kinoflo.com						
Kino International Corp 333 W 39th St Rm 503	New York	NY	10018	212-629-6880	714-0871	511
TF: 800-562-3330 ■ *Web:* www.kinolorber.com						
Kinokuniya Book Stores of America Company Ltd 1581 Webster St	San Francisco	CA	94115	415-673-7431		95
Web: www.kinokuniya.com						
Kinokuniya Bookstores 1073 Ave of the Americas	New York	NY	10018	212-869-1700	869-1703	95
Web: www.kinokuniya.co.jp						
Kinray Inc 152-35 Tenth Ave	Whitestone	NY	11357	718-767-1234	767-4706	238
TF: 800-854-6729 ■ *Web:* www.kinray.com						
Kinross Correctional Facility 16770 S Watertower Dr	Kincheloe	MI	49788	906-495-2282		213
TF: 800-326-4537 ■ *Web:* www.michigan.gov/corrections						
Kinross Gold Corp 25 York St 17th Fl	Toronto	ON	M5J2V5	416-365-5123	363-6622	502
NYSE: KGC ■ *TF:* 866-561-3636 ■ *Web:* www.kinross.com						
Kinross Gold USA Inc 5370 Kietzke Ln Ste 102	Reno	NV	89511	775-829-1000		502
TF: 800-521-6342 ■ *Web:* kinross.com						
Kinsail Corp 1420 Beverly Rd Ste 150	Mclean	VA	22101	703-994-4194		225
TF: 800-323-8819 ■ *Web:* www.kinsail.com						
Kinsbursky Brothers Inc 125 E Commercial	Anaheim	CA	92801	714-738-8516		196
TF: 800-548-8797 ■ *Web:* www.kinsbursky.com						
Kinseth Hotel Corp 2 Quail Creek Cir	North Liberty	IA	52317	319-626-5600		379
Web: www.kinseth.com						
Kinseth Plumbing & Heating Inc 148 E Main St	Belmond	IA	50421	641-444-4428		189-10
Web: kinsethplumbing.com						
Kinsey & Kinsey Inc 26 N Park Blvd	Glen Ellyn	IL	60137	630-858-4866		180
Web: kinsey.com						
Kinsley & Assoc 5401 S Prince St Ste 107	Littleton	CO	80120	303-798-3664		196
TF: 800-433-3755 ■ *Web:* kinsleyassociates.com						
Kinsley & Sons Inc 24 S Church St Ste A	Union	MO	63084	800-468-4428		409
TF General: 800-468-4428 ■ *Web:* www.gothic-jewelry.com						
Kinsley Construction Inc 1110 E Princess St	York	PA	17403	717-741-3841		186
Web: www.kinsleyconstruction.com						
Kinsman Robinson Galleries 108 Cumberland St	Toronto	ON	M5R1A6	416-964-2374	964-9042	42
Web: www.kinsmanrobinson.com						
Kinston-Lenoir County Chamber of Commerce 301 N Queen St	Kinston	NC	28501	252-527-1131	527-1914	139
Web: www.kinstonchamber.com						
Kintetsu International 1290 Ave Ste 900	New York	NY	10104	212-259-9600	259-9625	771
Web: www.kintetsu.com						
Kintetsu World Express USA Inc 1 Jericho Plaza Ste 100	Jericho	NY	11753	516-933-7100	933-7731	449
TF: 800-275-4045 ■ *Web:* www.kweusa.com						
Kintronic Laboratories Inc 144 Pleasant Grove Rd	Bluff City	TN	37618	423-878-3141		647
TF: 800-341-9678 ■ *Web:* www.kintronic.com						
Kinyo Company Inc 14235 Lomitas Ave	La Puente	CA	91746	626-333-3711	961-9114	173-5
TF: 800-735-4696 ■ *Web:* www.kinyo.com						
Kinze Manufacturing Inc 2172 M Ave	Williamsburg	IA	52361	319-668-1300		273
TF: 800-791-6476 ■ *Web:* kinze.com						
Kinzelman Art Consulting Llc 3909 Main St	Houston	TX	77002	713-533-9923		196
Web: www.kinzelmanart.com						
Kinzie Hotel 20 W Kinzie St	Chicago	IL	60654	312-395-9000		379
TF: 877-262-5341 ■ *Web:* kinziehotel.com						
Kinzinger Adam (Rep R - IL) 2245 Rayburn HOB	Washington	DC	20515	202-225-3635	226-3521	342-2
Web: kinzinger.house.gov						
Kinzua Bridge State Park c/o Bendigo State Pk 533 State Pk Rd	Johnsonburg	PA	15845	814-965-2646		565
Web: www.dcnr.state.pa.us						
KIOA-FM 93.3 (Oldies) 1416 Locust St	Des Moines	IA	50309	515-280-1350	280-3011	645-48
TF: 877-984-8786 ■ *Web:* www.kioa.com						
Kiolbassa Provision Co 1325 S Brazos St	San Antonio	TX	78207	210-226-8127		296-26
Web: www.kiolbassa.com						
KIOS-FM 91.5 (NPR) 3230 Burt St	Omaha	NE	68131	402-557-2777	557-2559	645-115
Web: www.kios.org						
Kiosk Information Systems Inc (KIS) 346 S Arthur Ave	Louisville	CO	80027	303-466-5471	466-6730	614
TF General: 800-509-5471 ■ *Web:* kiosk.com						
Kiowa County 1305 Goff	Eads	CO	81036	719-438-5421		338
Web: onlinedmv.com						
Kiowa County 211 E Florida Ave	Greensburg	KS	67054	620-723-3366	723-3234	338
TF: 800-262-8683 ■ *Web:* kiowacountyks.org						
Kiowa County 302 N Lincoln	Hobart	OK	73651	580-726-5286		338
Kip Inc 25740 Washington Ave	Murrieta	CA	92562	951-698-7890		188-10
Web: www.kipincorporated.com						
Kipany Productions Ltd 32 E 39th St	New York	NY	10016	212-883-8300		737
Web: www.kipany.com						
Kipe Technology Resources 14725 SW Millikan Way	Beaverton	OR	97006	503-590-7000		260
Web: www.kipetech.com						
Kipin Industries Inc 4194 Green Garden Rd	Aliquippa	PA	15001	724-495-6200	495-2219	189-16
Kiplinger Agriculture Letter 1729 H St NW	Washington	DC	20006	202-887-6400	778-8976	531-13
TF: 800-544-0155 ■ *Web:* www.kiplinger.com						
Kipp Foundation 135 Main St Ste 1700	San Francisco	CA	94105	415-399-1556		194
TF: 866-345-5477 ■ *Web:* www.kipp.org						
KippsDeSanto & Co 8000 Towers Crescent Dr Ste 1200	Tysons Corner	VA	22182	703-442-1400		690
Web: www.kippsdesanto.com						
KIPR-FM 92.3 (Urban) 700 Wellington Hills Rd	Little Rock	AR	72211	501-401-0200		645-91
Web: www.power923.com						
Kiptopeke State Park 3540 Kiptopeke Dr	Cape Charles	VA	23310	757-331-2267		565
Web: www.dcr.virginia.gov/state-parks/kiptopeke#general_information						
Kiran's Houston 2925 Richmond Ave	Houston	TX	77098	713-960-8472		671
Web: www.kiranshouston.com						
Kirby Agri Inc 500 Running Pump Rd PO Box 6277	Lancaster	PA	17607	717-299-2541	293-9306	280
TF: 800-745-7524 ■ *Web:* www.kirbyagri.com						
Kirby Bates Assoc 150 Monument Rd Ste 207 PMB 0035	Bala Cynwyd	PA	19004	610-667-1800		463
Web: www.kirbybates.com						
Kirby Bldg Systems Inc 124 Kirby Dr	Portland	TN	37148	615-325-4165		105
TF: 800-348-7799 ■ *Web:* www.kirbybuildingsystems.com						
Kirby Co 1920 W 114th St	Cleveland	OH	44102	216-228-2400	529-6146	788
TF: 800-437-7170 ■ *Web:* www.kirby.com						
Kirby Electric Inc 415 Northgate D	Warrendale	PA	15086	724-772-1800	772-2227	189-4
TF: 800-767-3263 ■ *Web:* www.kirbyelectricinc.com						
Kirby Foods Inc 4102-B Fieldstone Rd	Champaign	IL	61826	217-352-2600	352-9394	345
Web: www.kirbyfoods.com						
Kirby Mfg Inc 484 S Hwy 59	Merced	CA	95341	209-723-0778	723-3941	273
Web: www.kirbymfg.com						
Kirby Noonan Lance & Hoge LLP 350 Tenth Ave Ste 1300	San Diego	CA	92101	619-231-8666		428
Web: www.knlh.com						
Kirby Risk Corp 1815 Sagamore Pkwy N	Lafayette	IN	47904	765-448-4567		246
TF: 800-825-7877 ■ *Web:* www.kirbyrisk.com						
Kirby's Steakhouse 123 N Loop 1604 E	San Antonio	TX	78232	210-404-2221	404-2225	671
Web: www.kirbyssteakhouse.com						

Phone Fax Class

Kirila Contractors Inc
505 Bedford Rd PO Box 179 Brookfield OH 44403 330-448-4055 186
Web: www.kirila.com

Kiriu USA Corp
359 Mitch Mcconnell Way Bowling Green KY 42101 270-843-4160 518
Web: www.kiriu-usa.com

Kirk Co 201 St Helens Ave Tacoma WA 98402 800-426-8482 96
TF: 800-426-8482 ■ *Web:* www.kirktrees.com

Kirk Rankin Law Office
11501 Georgia Ave Ste 210 Silver Spring MD 20902 301-933-4648 428
Web: kirkrankin.com

Kirk Rudy Inc 125 Lorraine Pkwy Woodstock GA 30188 770-427-4203 427-4036 547
TF: 800-897-1910 ■ *Web:* www.kirkrudy.com

Kirk Williams Company Inc
2734 Home Rd Grove City OH 43123 614-875-9023 697
TF: 800-816-0705 ■ *Web:* www.kirkwilliamsco.com

Kirk's Folly 236 Chapman St Providence RI 02905 401-941-4300 408
Web: www.kirksfolly.com

Kirkegaard & Perry Laboratories Inc
910 Clopper Rd Gaithersburg MD 20878 301-948-7755 948-0169 231
TF: 800-638-3167 ■ *Web:* www.kpl.com

Kirkendall Public Library
1210 NW Prairie Ridge Dr Ankeny IA 50023 515-965-6460 289-9122 434-3
Web: www.ankenyiowa.gov

Kirkham Hardwoods Inc
3956 S State Rd 63 Terre Haute IN 47802 812-232-0624 683

Kirkham Michael Inc 12700 W Dodge Rd Omaha NE 68154 402-393-5630 255-3850 261
Web: www.kirkham.com

Kirkham's Outdoor Products
3125 S State St Salt Lake City UT 84115 801-486-4161 711
TF: 800-453-7756 ■ *Web:* www.kirkhams.com

Kirkhill Manufacturing Co
12023 Woodruff Ave Downey CA 90241 562-803-1117 803-3117 677
Web: www.rubbersales.com

Kirkhill-TA Co 300 E Cypress St Brea CA 92821 714-529-4901 529-0775 677
Web: www.esterline.com

Kirkland & Ellis LLP
200 E Randolph Dr Chicago IL 60601 312-861-2000 861-2200 428
TF: 800-647-7600 ■ *Web:* www.kirkland.com

Kirkland Correctional Institution
4344 Broad River Rd Columbia SC 29210 803-896-1521 896-1766 213
Web: doc.sc.gov

Kirkland's Inc 5310 Maryland Way Brentwood TN 37027 877-541-4855 362
NASDAQ: KIRK ■ *TF:* 877-541-4855 ■ *Web:* www.kirklands.com

Kirkpatrick Concrete Co
2000-A Southbridge Pkwy Ste 610 Birmingham AL 35209 205-423-2600 621-0952 182
Web: nationalcement.com

Kirkpatrick Phillips & Miller
1445 E Republic Rd Springfield MO 65804 417-882-4300 882-4343 2
Web: www.kpmcpa.com

Kirkridge Retreat & Study Ctr
2495 Fox Gap Rd Bangor PA 18013 610-588-1793 588-8510 673
TF: 800-231-2222 ■ *Web:* www.kirkridge.org

Kirksey 6909 Portwest Dr Houston TX 77024 713-850-9600 261
Web: www.kirksey.com

Kirkwood 904 Main St Wilmington MA 01887 978-658-4200 658-5547 627
Web: www.kirkwoodprinting.com

Kirkwood Bank & Trust Co
2911 N 14th St Bismarck ND 58503 701-258-6550 70
TF: 800-492-4955 ■ *Web:* kirkwoodbank.com

Kirkwood Community College
6301 Kirkwood Blvd SW Cedar Rapids IA 52404 319-398-5411 162
TF: 800-332-2055 ■ *Web:* www.kirkwood.edu

Kirkwood Digital 55 Sixth Rd Woburn MA 01801 781-938-6164 174
Web: kirkwooddigital.com

Kirkwood Industries Inc
1239 Rockside Rd Parma OH 44134 216-267-6200 351-3141 518
Web: www.kirkwoodholding.com

Kirkwood Library 6000 Kirkwood Hwy Wilmington DE 19808 302-995-7663 995-7687 434-3
TF: 888-352-7722 ■ *Web:* www.nccde.org

Kirkwood Mountain Resort LLC
1501 Kirkwood Meadows Dr Kirkwood CA 95646 209-258-6000 378
Web: www.kirkwood.com

Kirkwood Public Library
140 E Jefferson Ave Kirkwood MO 63122 314-821-5770 822-3755 434-3
Web: www.kirkwoodpubliclibrary.org

Kirkwood School District R-7 Inc
11289 Manchester Rd Kirkwood MO 63122 314-213-6100 984-0002 685
Web: www.kirkwoodschools.org

Kirkwood-Des Peres Area Chamber of Commerce
108 W Adams Ave Louis MO 63122 314-821-4161 821-5229 139
Web: www.kirkwooddesperes.com

Kirlin Co 3401 E Jefferson Ave Detroit MI 48207 313-259-6400 259-3121 439
Web: www.kirlinlighting.com

KIRO-FM 97.3 (N/T)
1820 Eastlake Ave E Seattle WA 98102 206-726-7000 645-150
TF: 800-756-5476 ■ *Web:* www.mynorthwest.com

KIRO-TV Ch 7 (CBS) 2807 Third Ave Seattle WA 98121 206-728-7777 741-123
Web: www.kiro7.com

Kirr Marbach & Co Investment Management
621 Washington St Columbus IN 47201 812-376-9444 401
TF: 800-808-9444 ■ *Web:* www.kirrmar.com

Kirsh Foundry Inc 125 Rowell St Beaver Dam WI 53916 920-887-0395 492
Web: www.kirshfoundry.com

Kirtland Air Force Base
2000 Wyoming Blvd SE Ste A-1 Kirtland AFB NM 87117 505-846-5991 497-1
TF: 877-246-1453 ■ *Web:* www.kirtland.af.mil

Kirtland Capital Partners
3201 Enterprise Pkwy Ste 200 Beachwood OH 44122 216-593-0100 593-0240 792
Web: www.kirtlandcapital.com

Kirtland Community College
10775 N St Helen Rd Roscommon MI 48653 989-275-5000 275-6789 162
TF: 866-632-9992 ■ *Web:* www.kirtland.edu

Kirtley Technology Corp
9s531 Wilmette Ave Darien IL 60561 630-512-0213 225
TF: 888-757-0778 ■ *Web:* kirtleytech.com

Kirtley-Cole Associates LLC
2820 Oakes Ave Ste B Everett WA 98201 425-609-0400 609-0410 186
Web: www.kirtley-cole.com

Kirwan Surgical Products Inc
180 Enterprise Dr Marshfield MA 02050 781-834-9500 476
TF: 888-547-9267 ■ *Web:* www.ksp.com

KIS (Kiosk Information Systems Inc)
346 S Arthur Ave Louisville CO 80027 303-466-5471 466-6730 614
TF General: 800-509-5471 ■ *Web:* kiosk.com

Kisco Senior Living LLC
5790 Fleet St Ste 300 Carlsbad CA 92008 760-804-5900 804-5909 450
Web: kiscoseniorliving.com

Kish Bancorp Inc
4255 E Main St PO Box 917 Belleville PA 17004 717-935-2191 70
OTC: KISB ■ *TF:* 888-554-4748 ■ *Web:* www.kishbank.com

Kishimoto.Gordon.Dalaya PC
1300 Wilson Blvd Ste 250 Rosslyn VA 22209 202-338-3800 393
Web: www.kgdarchitecture.com

Kishwaukee College 21193 Malta Rd Malta IL 60150 815-825-2086 825-2306 162
TF: 888-656-7329 ■ *Web:* www.kishwaukeecollege.edu

Kishwaukee Community Hospital
1 Kish Hospital Dr DeKalb IL 60115 815-756-1521 753-5661* 374-3
**Fax Area Code: 888* ■ *TF:* 800-397-1521 ■ *Web:* www.kishhealth.org

Kisinger Campo & Assoc Corp
201 N Franklin St Ste 400 Tampa FL 33602 813-871-5331 871-5135 261
Web: kisingercampo.com

Kiska Construction Corp USA
43-10 11th St 2nd Floor Long Island NY 11101 718-943-0400 943-0401 188-4
Web: www.kiskagroup.com

Kiski School 1888 Brett Ln Saltsburg PA 15681 724-639-3586 639-8596 622
TF: 877-547-5448 ■ *Web:* www.kiski.org

Kislak Company Inc, The
1000 Rt 9 N Woodbridge NJ 07095 732-750-3000 652
Web: kislakrealty.com

Kislak Organization, The
7900 Miami Lakes Dr W Miami Lakes FL 33016 305-364-4100 509
Web: www.kislak.com

Kisma Preserve PO Box 81 Mount Desert ME 04660 207-667-3244 823
Web: www.kismapreserve.org

KISQ-FM 98.1 (Urban AC)
340 Townsend St 4th Fl San Francisco CA 94107 415-975-5555 645-145
Web: 981thebreeze.iheart.com

Kiss 95.7 10 Columbus Blvd Hartford CT 06106 860-723-6000 645-72
Web: kiss957.iheart.com

Kiss 98.1 808 E Sprague Ave Spokane WA 99202 509-242-2400 242-1160 645-154
Web: kiss981.iheart.com

Kiss 99.9 194 NW 187th St Miami Fl 33169 305-654-1700 654-1715 645-99
TF: 866-954-0999 ■ *Web:* wkis.cbslocal.com

KISS Country 93.7
6341 Westport Ave Shreveport LA 71129 318-688-1130 645-151
Web: mykisscountry937.com

KISS FM 96.1 5010 Underwood Ave Omaha NE 68132 402-558-9696 645-115
Web: 961kissonline.iheart.com

KISS FM 96.9 6214 W 34th St Amarillo TX 79109 806-355-9777 645-5
Web: kissfm969.com

Kiss the Cook Restaurant
72 Church St Burlington VA 05401 802-863-4226 671
TF: 888-658-5477 ■ *Web:* www.kissthecook.net

KISS-FM 99.5 (Rock)
8122 Datapoint Dr Ste 600 San Antonio TX 78229 210-615-5400 615-5331 645-143
TF: 855-787-2227 ■ *Web:* www.kissrocks.com

Kissimmee Prairie Preserve State Park
33104 NW 192 Ave Okeechobee FL 34972 863-462-5360 565
Web: www.floridastateparks.org

Kissimmee Utility Authority Inc (KUA)
1701 W Carroll St Kissimmee FL 34741 407-933-7777 787
TF: 877-582-7700 ■ *Web:* www.kua.com

Kissimmee/Osceola County Chamber of Commerce
1425 E Vine St Kissimmee FL 34744 407-847-3174 870-8607 139
TF: 800-447-8206 ■ *Web:* www.kissimmeechamber.com

Kissinger & Fellman PC
3773 Cherry Creek N Dr Denver CO 80209 303-320-6100 428
Web: www.kandf.com

Kistler Instrument Corp
75 John Glenn Dr Amherst NY 14228 716-691-5100 691-5226 472
Web: www.kistler.com

Kistler-Morse Corp
150 Venture Blvd Spartanburg SC 29306 864-574-2763 574-8063 201
TF: 800-426-9010 ■ *Web:* www.kistlermorse.com

Kistner Concrete Products Inc
8713 Read Rd East Pembroke NY 14056 585-762-8216 762-8315 183
TF: 800-809-2801 ■ *Web:* www.kistner.com

KISU-FM 91.1 (NPR)
Idaho State University 921 S Eigth Ave Pocatello ID 83209 208-282-2475 645-126
Web: www.isu.edu/kisufm

KISU-TV Ch 10 (PBS)
921 S Eighth Ave Stop 8111 Pocatello ID 83209 208-282-2857 741-101
TF: 800-543-6868 ■ *Web:* www.idahoptv.org

KISW-FM 99.9 (Rock)
1100 Olive Way Ste 1650 Seattle WA 98101 206-285-7625 215-9355 645-150
Web: www.kisw.com

Kit Carson County
251 16th St # 103 Burlington CO 80807 719-346-8638 346-7242 338
Web: www.kitcarsoncounty.org

KIT HomeBuilders West LLC
1124 Garber St Caldwell ID 83605 208-454-5000 106
TF: 800-859-0347 ■ *Web:* www.kitwest.com

Kitamura Machinery of USA Inc
78 Century Dr Wheeling IL 60090 847-520-7755 520-7763 455
Web: www.kitamura-machinery.com

Kitano New York 66 Pk Ave E 38th St New York NY 10016 212-885-7000 885-7100 379
TF: 800-548-2666 ■ *Web:* www.kitano.com

Kitch Drutchas Wagner Valitutti & Sherbrook Pc
1 Woodward Ave Ste 2400 Detroit MI 48226 313-965-7900 428
Web: www.kitch.com

Kitchell Corp 1707 E Highland Ave Phoenix AZ 85016 602-264-4411 186
Web: www.kitchell.com

Kitchen & Bath Design Studio
914 S Kerr Ave Wilmington NC 28403 910-332-4656 362
TF: 800-696-3464 ■ *Web:* www.kandbgalleries.com

Name / Address	City	State	ZIP	Phone	Fax	Class
Kitchen & Bath Studios Inc 7001 Wisconsin Ave *Web:* kitchenbathstudios.com	Chevy Chase	MD	20815	301-657-1636		362
Kitchen 24 1608 N Cahuenga Blvd *Web:* www.kitchen24.info	Los Angeles	CA	90028	323-465-2424		362
Kitchen Academy 6370 W Sunset Blvd *TF:* 888-370-7589 ■ *Web:* www.chefs.edu	Hollywood	CA	90028	866-548-2223		163
Kitchen Art The Store for Cook 1550 Win Hentschel Blvd *Web:* k-art.com	West Lafayette	IN	47906	765-497-3878		361
Kitchen Collection Inc 71 E Water St *TF General:* 888-548-2651 ■ *Web:* www.kitchencollection.com	Chillicothe	OH	45601	740-773-9150		362
Kitchen Craft Cabinetry 1180 Springfield Rd *Web:* www.kitchencraft.com	Winnipeg	MB	R2C2Z2	204-224-3211		115
Kitchen Craft International 4129 United Ave *Web:* www.cookforlife.com	Mount Dora	FL	32757	352-483-7600		362
Kitchen Fantasy 27576 Ynez Rd Ste H9 *TF:* 800-561-3357 ■ *Web:* www.kitchenfantasy.com	Temecula	CA	92591	951-693-4264	693-4265	362
Kitchen Kompact Inc 911 E 11th St *Web:* www.kitchenkompact.com	Jeffersonville	IN	47130	812-282-6681	282-7880	115
Kitchen Restaurant, The 2225 Hurley Way *Web:* thekitchenrestaurant.com	Sacramento	CA	95825	916-568-7171		671
Kitchen Supply Co 5300 St Charles Rd *Web:* www.kitchensupply.com	Berkeley	IL	60130	708-240-8100		362
Kitchen Tune-Up 813 Cir Dr *TF:* 800-333-6385 ■ *Web:* www.kitchentuneup.com	Aberdeen	SD	57401	605-225-4049		189-11
Kitchen, The 4348 Fountain Ave *Web:* www.thekitchen.la	Los Angeles	CA	90029	323-664-3663		671
Kitchen-Quip Inc 405 E Marion St *Web:* www.kqcasting.com	Waterloo	IN	46793	260-837-8311	837-7919	308
Kitchens Bros Manufacturing Co 4854 Reed Town Rd	Utica	MS	39175	601-885-6001		683
Kitchin Neal Webb Webb & Futrell pa Attys 111 E Washington St *Web:* kitchinlaw.com	Rockingham	NC	28379	910-997-2206		445
Kitcho 1415 Timberlane Rd Ste 121 *TF:* 800-628-2866 ■ *Web:* www.kitchorestaurant.com	Tallahassee	FL	32312	850-893-7686		671
KITCO Fiber Optics Inc 5269 Cleveland St *TF:* 866-643-5220 ■ *Web:* www.kitcofo.com	Virginia Beach	VA	23462	757-518-8100		610
Kitco Inc 1625 N Mountain Springs Pkwy *Web:* www.kitcodefense.com	Springville	UT	84663	801-489-2000		22
Kite Realty Group Trust 30 S Meridian St Ste 1100 *NYSE:* KRG ■ *TF:* 888-577-5600 ■ *Web:* www.kiterealty.com	Indianapolis	IN	46204	317-577-5600	577-5605	654
Kitsap County 614 Div St MS 4 *Web:* www.kitsapgov.com	Port Orchard	WA	98366	360-337-7146	337-4632	338
Kitsap Memorial State Park 202 NE Pk St *Web:* www.parks.wa.gov	Poulsbo	WA	98370	360-779-3205		565
Kitsap Mental Health Services 5455 Almira Dr NE *Web:* www.kitsapmentalhealth.org	Bremerton	WA	98311	360-405-4010		450
Kitsap Regional Library 1301 Sylvan Way *TF:* 877-883-9900 ■ *Web:* www.krl.org	Bremerton	WA	98310	360-405-9100	405-9156	434-3
Kitsap Sun 545 Fifth St *TF:* 888-377-3711 ■ *Web:* www.kitsapsun.com	Bremerton	WA	98337	360-377-3711		532-2
KITS-FM 105.3 (Alt) 865 Battery St *TF:* 800-696-1053 ■ *Web:* live105.cbslocal.com	San Francisco	CA	94111	800-696-1053		645-145
KITSON 115 S Robertson Blvd	Los Angeles	CA	90048	310-859-2652		292
Kitt Peak National Observatory 950 N Cherry Ave *TF:* 888-809-4012 ■ *Web:* www.noao.edu/kpno	Tucson	AZ	85719	520-318-8600	318-8724	598
Kittatinny Valley State Park PO Box 621 *TF:* 800-473-0363 ■ *Web:* www.njparksandforests.org	Andover	NJ	07821	973-786-6445		565
Kittelson & Associates Inc 610 SW Alder Ste 700 *TF:* 800-746-9554 ■ *Web:* www.kittelson.com	Portland	OR	97205	503-228-5230		261
Kittery Trading Post 301 US 1 *Fax Area Code: 207 ■ *TF:* 888-587-6246 ■ *Web:* www.kitterytradingpost.com	Kittery	ME	03904	603-334-1157	439-8001*	157-2
Kittitas County 205 W Fifth Ave Ste 108 *Web:* www.co.kittitas.wa.us	Ellensburg	WA	98926	509-962-7508	962-7679	338
Kittle's Home Furnishings Center Inc 8600 Allisonville Rd *Web:* www.kittles.com	Indianapolis	IN	46250	317-849-5300		321
Kittredge Equipment Co Inc 100 Bowles Rd *TF:* 800-423-7082 ■ *Web:* www.kittredgeequipment.com	Agawam	MA	01001	413-304-4100	786-7086	300
Kittson County 410 Fifth St SE Ste 214 *Web:* www.visitnwminnesota.com	Hallock	MN	56728	218-843-2655		338
Kitty Askins Hospice Ctr 107 Handley Pk Ct *TF:* 800-692-4442 ■ *Web:* www.3hc.org	Goldsboro	NC	27534	919-735-5887	735-5948	371
Kitty Hawk Kites Inc 306 West Lake Dr Unit K *Web:* www.kittyhawk.com	Kill Devil Hills	NC	27948	252-441-4127		711
KITV-TV Ch 4 (ABC) 801 S King St *Web:* www.kitv.com	Honolulu	HI	96813	808-535-0240	536-8993	741-59
Kiva Kitchen & Bath Holdings LLC 6225 Burnet Rd	Austin	TX	78757	512-454-4526	406-0900	362
Kivell, Rayment & Francis PC 7666 E 61st St Ste 550 *TF:* 800-699-5893 ■ *Web:* www.kivell.com	Tulsa	OK	74133	918-254-0626		428
KIVI-TV Ch 6 (ABC) 1866 E Chisholm Dr *Web:* www.kivitv.com	Nampa	ID	83687	208-336-0500	381-6682	741
Kivort Steel 380 Hudson River Rd *TF:* 800-462-2616 ■ *Web:* www.kivortsteel.com	Waterford	NY	12188	518-590-7233	235-2042	492
Kiwanis International Foundation 3636 Woodview Trace *TF:* 800-549-2647 ■ *Web:* www.kiwanis.org	Indianapolis	IN	46268	317-875-8755	879-0204	305
Kiwash Electric Co-op Inc 120 W First St PO Box 100 *TF:* 888-832-3362 ■ *Web:* www.kiwash.coop	Cordell	OK	73632	580-832-3361		245
Kiwi Coders Corp 265 E Messner Dr *Web:* www.kiwicoders.com	Wheeling	IL	60090	847-541-4511		627
Kiwi Ii Construction Inc 28177 Keller Rd *TF:* 877-465-4942 ■ *Web:* www.kiwiconstruction.com	Murrieta	CA	92563	951-301-8975		186
Kiwi Partners Inc 30 Soundview Ln *Web:* www.kiwipartners.com	Port Washington	NY	11050	516-767-6678		2
Kiwibox Media Inc 330 W 38th St Ste 1602 *Web:* www.kiwibox.com	New York	NY	10018	212-239-8210		387
KIXI-AM 880 (Nost) 3650 131st Ave SE Ste 550 *TF:* 866-880-5494 ■ *Web:* www.kixi.com	Bellevue	WA	98006	425-562-8964	653-1088	645
Kizan International Inc 100 W Hill Dr *Web:* www.louisraphael.com	Brisbane	CA	94005	415-468-7360		157-3
KiZan Technologies LLC 1831 Williamson Ct *Web:* www.kizan.com	Louisville	KY	40223	502-327-0333		180
Kizer Pharmacy LLC 1117 S Miles Ave Ste 1	Union City	TN	38261	731-885-2226		237
KIZN-FM 92.3 (Ctry) 1419 W Bannock St *TF:* 800-529-5264 ■ *Web:* www.kizn.com	Boise	ID	83702	208-336-3670	336-3734	645-22
KJ Quinn & Co Inc 34 Folly Mill Rd	Seabrook	NH	03874	603-474-5753		550
KJAQ-FM 96.5 (Var) 1000 Dexter Ave N Ste 100 *TF:* 866-416-5225 ■ *Web:* jackseattle.cbslocal.com	Seattle	WA	98109	206-805-1100		645-150
KJB Security Products Inc 841-B Fessiers Pkwy *TF:* 800-590-4272 ■ *Web:* www.kjbsecurity.com	Nashville	TN	37210	615-620-1370		246
KJCB-AM 770 (Urban) 604 St John St	Lafayette	LA	70501	337-233-4262		645-86
KJCE-AM 1370 (N/T) 4301 Westbank Dr *Web:* www.talkradio1370am.com	Austin	TX	78746	512-327-9595	329-6252	645-14
Kjeldsen Sinnock & Neudeck Inc 711 N Pershing Ave *Web:* www.ksninc.com	Stockton	CA	95203	209-946-0268		256
Kjellstrom & Lee Inc 1607 Ownby Ln *TF:* 800-729-2012 ■ *Web:* www.kjellstromandlee.com	Richmond	VA	23220	804-288-0082	285-4288	186
KJJY-FM 92.5 (Ctry) 4143 109th St *Web:* 925nashicon.com	Urbandale	IA	50322	515-331-9200		645
KJKJ-FM 107.5 (Rock) 505 University Ave *Web:* kjkj.iheart.com	Grand Forks	ND	58203	701-746-1417		645-65
KJLA-TV Ch 57 (Ind) 2323 Corinth Ave *TF:* 800-588-5788 ■ *Web:* www.kjla.com	Los Angeles	CA	90064	310-943-5288	943-5299	741-76
KJLH-FM 102.3 (Urban) 161 N La Brea Ave *Web:* www.kjlhradio.com	Inglewood	CA	90301	310-330-2200		645
KJR-AM 950 (Sports) 645 Elliott Ave W Ste 400 *TF:* 800-829-0950 ■ *Web:* sportsradiokjr.iheart.com	Seattle	WA	98119	206-494-2000		645-150
KJRH-TV Ch 2 (NBC) 3701 S Peoria Ave *TF:* 800-727-5574 ■ *Web:* www.kjrh.com	Tulsa	OK	74105	918-743-2222	748-1436	741-138
KJSR-FM 103.3 (CR) 7136 S Yale Ave Ste 500 *Web:* 1033theeagle.com	Tulsa	OK	74136	918-493-3434	493-2376	645-168
KJUD-TV Ch 8 (ABC) 2700 E Tudor Rd *TF:* 877-304-1313 ■ *Web:* www.youralaskalink.com	Anchorage	AK	99507	907-561-1313		741-67
KJWL-FM 99.3 (Nost) 1415 Fulton Ave *Web:* www.kjwl.com	Fresno	CA	93721	559-497-5118	497-9760	645-64
KJZZ-FM 91.5 (NPR) 2323 W 14th St *Web:* kjzz.org	Tempe	AZ	85281	480-834-5627	774-8475	645
KJZZ-TV Ch 14 (Ind) 301 West South Temple *Web:* www.kjzz.com	Salt Lake City	UT	84101	801-537-1414		741-115
KK Audio Inc 12620 Raymer St	North Hollywood	CA	91605	818-765-2921		52
KKBQ-FM 92.9 (Ctry) 1990 Post Oak Blvd Ste 2300 *TF:* 877-745-6591 ■ *Web:* www.thenew93q.com	Houston	TX	77056	713-963-1200		645-75
KKBR-FM 97.1 (Oldies) 27 N 27th St 23rd Fl *Web:* popcrush971.com	Billings	MT	59101	406-245-9700		645-19
KKCB-FM 105.1 (Ctry) 14 E Central Entrance *Web:* www.kkcb.com	Duluth	MN	55811	218-727-4500		645-51
KKCT-FM 97.5 (CHR) 4303 Memorial Hwy *TF:* 800-850-7676 ■ *Web:* www.hot975fm.com	Mandan	ND	58554	701-250-6602	250-6632	645-21
KKDA-FM 104 621 NW Sixth St *Web:* www.myk104.com	Grand Prairie	TX	75050	972-263-9911		645-44
KKDO-FM 94.7 (NAC) 5345 Madison Ave *Web:* www.radio947.net	Sacramento	CA	95841	916-334-7777		645-140
KKE Architects Inc 300 First Ave N	Minneapolis	MN	55401	612-339-4200		261
KKFI-FM 90.1 (Var) 3901 Main St Ste 203 *TF:* 888-931-0901 ■ *Web:* www.kkfi.org	Kansas City	MO	64111	816-931-3122	931-7078	645-83
KKFM-FM 98.1 (CR) 6805 Corporate Dr Ste 130 *Web:* www.kkfm.com	Colorado Springs	CO	80919	719-593-2700	593-2727	645-39
KKFS-FM 103.9 (Rel) 1425 River Pk Dr Ste 520 *Web:* www.1039thefish.com	Sacramento	CA	95815	916-924-0710		645-140
KKHR-FM 106.3 (Span) 402 Cypress St *Web:* www.radioabilene.com	Abilene	TX	79601	325-672-5442		645-1
KKHT-FM 100.0 (Rel) 6161 Savoy Dr Ste 1200 *Web:* www.kkht.com	Houston	TX	77036	713-260-3600		645-75
KKLS-FM 104.7 (CHR) 5100 S Tennis Ln *Web:* www.hot1047.com	Sioux Falls	SD	57108	605-361-0300		645-152

Name / Address	City	State	Zip	Phone	Fax	Class
KKLZ-FM 96.3 2920 S Durango Dr Ste 800 — *Web:* www.963kklz.com	Las Vegas	NV	89117	702-730-0300	736-8447	645-08
KKMG-FM 98.9 (CHR) 6805 Corporate Dr Ste 130 — *Web:* www.989magicfm.com	Colorado Springs	CO	80919	719-593-2700	593-2727	645-39
KKMJ-FM 95.5 (AC) *Majic 95.5* 4301 Westbank Dr Escalade B Third Fl — *Web:* www.majic.com	Austin	TX	78746	512-327-9595		645-14
KKMK-FM 93.9 (AC) 660 Flormann St Ste 100 — *Web:* schurz.com	Rapid City	SD	57709	605-343-6161	343-9012	645-132
KKND-FM 102.9 (Urban) 201 St Charles Ave Ste 201 — *Web:* www.power1029.com	New Orleans	LA	70170	504-581-7002	566-4857	645-110
KKNU-FM 93.3 (Ctry) 925 Country Club Rd Ste 200 — *TF:* 800-285-2895 ■ *Web:* kknu.fm	Eugene	OR	97401	541-484-9400	344-9424	645-55
KKO & Associates LLC 5 Vine St — *TF:* 800-556-7345 ■ *Web:* kko.com	Andover	MA	01810	978-475-4079		463
KKOL-FM 107.9 (Oldies) 1160 N King St 2nd Fl — *Web:* 1079koolgold.com	Honolulu	HI	96817	808-533-0065		645-73
KKPT-FM 94.1 (CR) 2400 Cottondale Ln — *TF:* 800-844-0094 ■ *Web:* www.point941.com	Little Rock	AR	72202	501-664-9410		645-91
KKR Asset Management LLC 555 California St Ste 5000 — *Web:* kkr.com	San Francisco	CA	94104	415-315-3620	391-3077	654
KKSS-FM 97.3 (CHR) 8009 Marble Ave NE — *Web:* www.univision.com/albuquerque/kkss	Albuquerque	NM	87110	505-254-7110		645-4
KKTV-TV Ch 11 (CBS) 3100 N Nevada Ave — *TF:* 800-222-8477 ■ *Web:* www.kktv.com	Colorado Springs	CO	80907	719-634-2844	634-3741	741-32
KKVV-AM 1060 (Rel) 3185 S Highland Dr Ste 13 — *Web:* www.kkvv.com	Las Vegas	NV	89109	702-731-5588		645-88
KKYX-AM 680 (Ctry) 8122 Datapoint Dr Ste 600 — *Web:* www.kkyx.com	San Antonio	TX	78229	210-615-5400		645-143
KKZX-FM 98.9 (CR) 808 E Sprague Ave — *Web:* 989kkzx.iheart.com	Spokane	WA	99202	509-242-2400	242-1160	645-154
KL Communications Inc 50 English Plaza Ste 6B — *Web:* klcommunications.com	Red Bank	NJ	07701	732-224-9991		466
K&L Freight Management Inc 745 S Rohlwing Rd — *TF:* 800 770-9007 ■ *Web:* www.kandlfreight.com	Addison	IL	60101	630-607-1500		311
K&L Gates LLP 210 Sixth Ave — *TF:* 800-452-8260 ■ *Web:* www.klgates.com	Pittsburgh	PA	15222	412-355-6500	355-6501	428
KL Industries Inc 1790 Sun Dolphin Dr — *TF:* 800-733-2727 ■ *Web:* www.klindustries.com	Muskegon	MI	49444	231-733-2725	730 4502	710
KLA Laboratories Inc 6800 Chase Rd — *Web:* www.klalabs.com	Dearborn	MI	48126	313-846-3800		179
KlaasKids Foundation PO Box 925 — *Web:* www.klaaskids.org	Sausalito	CA	94966	415-331-6067		48-6
Klaff's Inc 28 Washington St — *Web:* www.klaffs.com	South Norwalk	CT	06854	203-866-1603		361
Klafter's Inc 216 N Beaver St — *TF:* 800-922-1233 ■ *Web:* www.klafters.com	New Castle	PA	16101	800-922-1233		756
Klamath Boat Co 5199 Fulton Dr Ste I — *Web:* www.klamathboats.com	Fairfield	CA	94534	707-643-0447		90
Klamath Community College 7390 S Sixth St — *Web:* www.klamathcc.edu/Home	Klamath Falls	OR	97603	541-882-3521	885-7758	162
Klamath County 305 Main St — *TF:* 800-377-6094 ■ *Web:* www.klamathcounty.org	Klamath Falls	OR	97601	541-883-5134	883-5165	338
Klamath County Chamber of Commerce 205 Riverside Dr — *Web:* www.klamath.org	Klamath Falls	OR	97601	541-884-5193	884-5195	139
Klamath County Library 126 S Third St — *Web:* klamathlibrary.org	Klamath Falls	OR	97601	541-882-8894	882-6166	434-3
Klamath County Museum 1451 Main St — *Web:* museum.klamathcounty.org	Klamath Falls	OR	97601	541-882-1000		520
KLAQ-FM 95.5 (Rock) 4180 N Mesa St — *TF:* 844-305-6210 ■ *Web:* www.klaq.com	El Paso	TX	79902	915-880-4955	532-3334	645-53
Klasky Csupo Inc 1238 N Highland Ave — *Web:* www.klaskycsupo.com	Hollywood	CA	90038	323-468-3020	468-3021	33
Klass Ingredients Inc 3885 N Buffalo St — *TF:* 800-662-6577 ■ *Web:* www.klassingredients.com	Orchard Park	NY	14127	716-662-6665	662-0285	345
Klassen Corp 2021 Westwind Dr — *Web:* www.klassencorp.com	Bakersfield	CA	93301	661-324-3000		186
KLAT-AM 1010 (Span N/T) 5100 SW Fwy — *TF:* 800-646-6779 ■ *Web:* corporate.univision.com	Houston	TX	77056	713-407-1415	407-1400	645-75
KLA-Tencor Corp 1 Technology Dr — *NASDAQ: KLAC* ■ *TF:* 800-600-2829 ■ *Web:* www.kla-tencor.com	Milpitas	CA	95035	408-875-3000	875-4144	248
Klatzkin & Company Jr CPA's 1670 Whitehorse Hamilton Sq Rd — *Web:* www.klatzkin.com	Hamilton	NJ	08690	609-890-9189		2
Klauber Bros Inc 980 Ave of the Americas 2nd Fl — *Web:* www.klauberlace.com	New York	NY	10018	212-686-2531	481-7194	745-4
Klauer Manufacturing Co 1185 Roosevelt Ext PO Box 59 — *Web:* www.klauer.com	Dubuque	IA	52004	563-582-7201	582-2022	697
Klaus Cos 8400 N Allen Rd — *TF:* 800-545-5287 ■ *Web:* www.klausco.com	Peoria	IL	61615	309-691-4840		38
Klaussner Home Furnishings 405 Lewallen Rd — *Web:* www.klaussner.com	Asheboro	NC	27205	336-625-6174		319-2
KLAZ-FM 105.9 (CHR) 125 Corporate Terr — *Web:* www.klaz.com	Hot Springs	AR	71913	501-525-4600	525-4344	645-74
KLBB-AM 1220 (Nost) 104 N Main St — *TF:* 800-620-3370 ■ *Web:* www.klbbradio.com	Stillwater	MN	55082	651-439-5006		645
KLBJ-AM 590 (N/T) 8309 N IH-35 — *Web:* www.newsradioklbj.com	Austin	TX	78753	512-836-0590		645-14
KLBJ-FM 93.7 (Rock) 8309 N IH-35 — *Web:* www.klbjfm.com	Austin	TX	78753	512-832-4000	832-4081	645-14
KLBK-TV Ch 13 (CBS) 7403 S University Ave — *Web:* everythinglubbock.com	Lubbock	TX	79423	806-745-2345	748-2250	741-78
KLCA-FM 96.5 (Alt) 961 Matley Ln Ste 120 — *TF:* 855-354-9111 ■ *Web:* www.alice965.com	Reno	NV	89502	775-829-1964	825-3183	645-133
KLCC-FM 89.7 (NPR) 4000 E 30th Ave — *TF:* 800-922-3682 ■ *Web:* www.klcc.org	Eugene	OR	97401	541-463-6000	463-6046	645-55
KLCS-TV Ch 58 (PBS) 1061 W Temple St — *Web:* www.klcs.org	Los Angeles	CA	90012	213-241-4000	481-1019	741-76
KLDJ-FM 101.7 (Oldies) 14 E Central Entrance — *Web:* www.kool1017.com	Duluth	MN	55811	218-727-5665		645-51
klean image 13498 Pond Springs Rd — *Web:* www.kleanimage.com	Austin	TX	78729	512-258-7003		256
Klean Industries Inc 349 W Georgia St Ste 3038 — *Web:* www.kleanindustries.com	Vancouver	BC	V6B3X5	604-637-9609		192
Kleber & Assoc 1215 Hightower Trial Bldg C — *Web:* www.kleberandassociates.com	Atlanta	GA	30350	770-518-1000		4
Kleberg County PO Box 1327 — *Web:* www.co.kleberg.tx.us	Kingsville	TX	78364	361-595-8548	593-1355	338
Kleen Air Service Corp 5354 N Northwest Hwy — *Web:* www.kleenair.com	Chicago	IL	60630	773-631-0007		612
Kleen Polymers Inc 145 Rainbow St — *Web:* www.kleenpolymers.com	Wadsworth	OH	44281	330 336-4212		256
Kleen Test Products Inc 1611 Sunset Rd — *TF:* 800-634-7328 ■ *Web:* www.kleentest.com	Port Washington	WI	53074	262-284-6600	284-6623	558
KLEEN-TEX Industries Inc 101 N Greenwood St Ste C — *Web:* www.kleen-tex.com	LaGrange	GA	30240	706-882-0111		508
Kleer Corp 19925 Stevens Creek Blvd Ste 111 — *Web:* www.kleer.com	Cupertino	CA	95014	408 973-7255		696
Kleet Lumber Company Inc 777 Pk Ave — *TF:* 800-696-5533 ■ *Web:* www.kleet.com	Huntington	NY	11743	631-427-7060	427-4384	191-3
Klehm Arboretum & Botanic Garden 2715 S Main St — *Web:* www.klehm.org	Rockford	IL	61102	815-965-8146	965-5914	97
Klein & Company Corporate Housing Services Inc 914 Washington Ave — *TF:* 800-208-9826 ■ *Web:* www.kleinandcompany.com	Golden	CO	80401	303-796-2100	796-2101	210
Klein & Hoffman Inc 150 S Wacker Dr — *Web:* kleinandhoffman.com	Chicago	IL	60606	312-251-1900		261
Klein Electronics Inc 349 N Vinewood St — *TF:* 800-959-2899 ■ *Web:* www.headsetusa.com	Escondido	CA	92029	760-781-3220		647
Klein Financial Inc 1550 Audubon Rd — *Web:* kleinbank.com	Chaska	MN	55318	952-448-2484		70
Klein Independent School District 7200 Spring Cypress Rd — *TF:* 888-703-0083 ■ *Web:* www.kleinisd.net	Spring	TX	77379	832-249-4000		685
Klein Managment Systems Inc 259 S Middletown Rd — *Web:* kleinmgmt.com	Nanuet	NY	10954	845-623-7778		225
Klein Steel Service 105 Vanguarden Pkwy — *TF Cust Svc:* 800-477-6789 ■ *Web:* www.kleinsteel.com	Rochester	NY	14606	585-328-4000	328-0470	492
Klein Tools Inc 450 Bond St — *TF Cust Svc:* 800-553-4676 ■ *Web:* www.kleintools.com	Lincolnshire	IL	60069	800-553-4676		758
Kleiner Perkins Caufield & Byers (KPCB) 2750 Sand Hill Rd — *Web:* www.kpcb.com	Menlo Park	CA	94025	650-233-2750	233-0300	792
Kleinfeld, Kaplan & Becker LLP 1140 19th St NW Ste 900 — *Web:* www.kkblaw.com	Washington	DC	20036	202-223-5120		428
Kleingers Group Inc, The 6305 Centre Park Dr — *Web:* kleingers.com	West Chester	OH	45069	513-779-7851		261
Kleinhans Music Hall 3 Symphony Cir — *TF:* 800-745-3000 ■ *Web:* www.kleinhansbuffalo.org	Buffalo	NY	14201	716-883-3560		572
Kleinknecht Electric Company Inc 252 W 37th St Ste 1402 — *Web:* www.kecny.com	New York	NY	10018	212-728-1800		189-4
Kleinpeter Farms Dairy LLC 14444 Airline Hwy — *Web:* www.kleinpeterdairy.com	Baton Rouge	LA	70817	225-753-2121		296-27
Kleinschmidt Inc 450 Lake Cook Rd — *TF:* 800-824-2330 ■ *Web:* www.kleinschmidt.com	Deerfield	IL	60015	847-945-1000	945-4619	39
Kleiss Gears 390 Industrial Ave — *Web:* www.kleissgears.com	Grantsburg	WI	54840	715-463-5995		608
Klement Sausage Co Inc 207 E Lincoln Ave — *Web:* www.klements.com	Milwaukee	WI	53207	414-744-2330	744-2438	296-26
Klemmer & Associates Leaders 1340 commerce st — *TF:* 800-577-5447 ■ *Web:* www.klemmer.com	Petaluma	CA	94954	707-559-7722		463
Klenda Austerman LLC 1600 Epic Ctr 301 N Main St — *Web:* klendalaw.com	Wichita	KS	67202	316-267-0331		428
Klewin Construction Inc 444 Brickell Ave Ste 900 — *Web:* www.klewin.com	Miami	FL	33131	305-709-0700	709-0715	256
KLFC-FM 88.1 (Rel) 205 W Atlantic St — *TF:* 877-410-8592 ■ *Web:* www.klfcradio.com	Branson	MO	65616	417-334-5532	335-2437	645-24

Phone Fax Class

KLFY-TV Ch 10 (CBS)
1808 Eraste Landry Rd Lafayette LA 70506 337-981-4823 741-70
Web: www.klfy.com

KLG Advisors 399 Park Ave 11th Fl New York NY 10022 212-514-4600 463
Web: www.klgadvisors.com

KLH Audio Systems 11131 Dora St Sun Valley CA 91352 818-767-2843 52
Web: www.klhaudio.com

Klickitat County
205 S Columbus Ave Rm 204 Goldendale WA 98620 509-773-5744 773-4559 338
Web: www.klickitatcounty.org

Klick-lewis Inc 720 E Main St Palmyra PA 17078 717-838-1353 57
Web: www.klicklewiscars.com

Kliemann Bros Heating & Air Conditioning Inc
4703 116th St E Tacoma WA 98446 253-537-0655 610
Web: kliemannbros.com

KLIK-AM 1240 (N/T)
1002 Diamond Ridge Ctr Ste 400 Jefferson City MO 65109 573-893-5100 645-80
Web: www.klik1240.com

Kliklok-Woodman USA
5224 Snapfinger Woods Dr Decatur GA 30035 770-981-5200 987-7160 547
TF: 800-621-4170 ■ *Web:* www.kliklokwoodman.com

Klikwood Corp
5224 Snapfinger Woods Dr Decatur GA 30035 770-981-5200 547
TF: 800-621-4170 ■ *Web:* www.kliklokwoodman.com

Kline & Company Inc
35 Waterview Blvd Ste 305 Parsippany NJ 07054 973-435-6262 435-6291 194
TF: 800-290-5214 ■ *Web:* www.klinegroup.com

Kline & Specter A Professional Corp
1525 Locust St 19th Fl Philadelphia PA 19102 215-772-1000 428
TF: 800-243-1100 ■ *Web:* www.klinespecter.com

Kline Hawkes & Co
11726 San Vicente Blvd Ste 300 Los Angeles CA 90049 310-442-4700 103

Kline Process Systems Inc
625 Spring St Ste 200 Reading PA 19610 610-371-0200 180
Web: www.kpsnet.com

Kline Scott Visco Commercial Real Estate Inc
117 W Patrick St Frederick MD 21701 301-694-8444 652
Web: klinescottvisco.com

Klinedinst Law 801 K St Fl 28 Sacramento CA 95814 916-444-7573 428
Web: www.klinedinstlaw.com

Klingberg Family Centers Inc
370 Linwood St New Britain CT 06052 860-224-9113 48-15
TF: 877-696-6775 ■ *Web:* www.klingberg.org

Klinge Corp 4075 E Market St York PA 17402 717-840-4500 539
TF: 800-581-8533 ■ *Web:* www.klingecorp.com

Klingelhofer Corp 165 Mill Ln Mountainside NJ 07092 908-232-7200 232-1841 455
TF: 800-879-5546 ■ *Web:* www.klingelhofer.com

Klingher Nadler LLP
580 Sylvan Ave Ste Ma Englewood Cliffs NJ 07632 201-731-3025 2
Web: klinghernadler.com

Klink Citrus Assn 32921 Rd 159 Ivanhoe CA 93235 559-798-1881 11-1

Klinke Bros Ice Cream Co
2450 Scaper Cove Memphis TN 38114 901-743-8250 296-25

Klipsch LLC 137 Hempstead 278 Hope AR 71801 888-250-8561 777-6753* 52
*Fax Area Code: 870 ■ *TF:* 888-250-8561 ■ *Web:* www.klipsch.com

Klitzberg Associates Inc
600 Alexander Rd Princeton NJ 08540 609-452-2888 528
Web: klitzbergfundsolutions.com

KLJ Computer Solutions Inc
115 Joseph Zatzman Dr Dartmouth NS B3B1N3 888-455-5669 179
TF: 888-455-5669 ■ *Web:* www.venueclaims.com

KLJC-FM 88.5 (Rel)
8717 W 110th St Ste 480 Overland Park KS 64147 913-451-8850 645-83
Web: life885.com

KLKN-TV Ch 8 (ABC) 3240 S Tenth St Lincoln NE 68502 402-434-8000 436-2236 741-74
Web: www.klkntv.com

KLLL-FM 96.3 (Ctry)
33 Briercroft Office Pk Lubbock TX 79412 806-762-3000 645-94
Web: www.klll.com

KLLM Inc 135 Riverview Dr Richland MS 39218 800-925-1000 780
TF: 800-925-5556 ■ *Web:* www.kllm.com

KLM Mechanical Service Inc
PO Box 35121 Louisville KY 40232 502-955-2062 189-10
TF: 866-466-4438 ■ *Web:* klm-mechanical.com

KLM Creative Inc
520 Townsend St San Francisco CA 94103 415-503-4150 195
Web: klmcreative.com

KLMP-FM 88.3
1853 Fountain Plaza Dr Rapid City SD 57702 605-342-6822 342-0854 645-132
Web: www.klmp.com

Kln Klein Product Development Inc
19787 56 Ave Langley BC V3A3X8 604-530-1491 196
Web: klnklein.com

KLN Steel Products Co 2 Winnco Dr San Antonio TX 78218 210-227-4747 227-4047 319-3
TF: 800-624-9101 ■ *Web:* www.kln.com

KLO-AM 1430 (N/T)
257 East 200 South Ste 400 Salt Lake City UT 84111 801-364-9836 645-142
TF: 866-627-1430 ■ *Web:* www.kloradio.com

Klobuchar Amy (Sen D - MN)
302 Hart Bldg Washington DC 20510 202-224-3244 228-2186 342-2
Web: www.klobuchar.senate.gov

Klochko Equipment Rental Company Inc
2782 Corbin Ave Melvindale MI 48122 313-386-7220 386-2530 264-3
TF: 800-783-7368 ■ *Web:* www.klochko.com

Klockner Pentaplast of America Inc
3585 Klockner Rd PO Box 500 Gordonsville VA 22942 540-832-3600 832-5656 599
Web: www.kpfilms.com

Kloepfer Concrete & Paving Co
505 E Ellis PO Box 840 Paul ID 83347 208-438-4525 438-5030 182
Web: www.kloepfer.com

Klondike Cheese Co W7839 Hwy 81 Monroe WI 53566 608-325-3021 296-5
Web: www.klondikecheese.com

Klondike Gold Rush National Historical Park - Seattle Unit
319 Second Ave S Seattle WA 98104 206-220-4240 564
Web: www.nps.gov

Klondike PROMOTIONS
1900 w benson blvd Anchorage AK 99517 907-274-3535 7
Web: www.klondikeadv.com

Kloppenberg & Co 2627 W Oxford Ave Englewood CO 80110 303-761-1615 789-1741 664
TF: 800-346-3246 ■ *Web:* www.kloppenberg.com

KLOS-FM 95.5 (CR)
3321 S La Cienega Blvd Los Angeles CA 90016 310-840-4828 645-92
TF: 800-955-5567 ■ *Web:* www.955klos.com

Klosterman Baking Company Inc
4760 Paddock Rd Cincinnati OH 45229 513-242-1004 296-1
TF: 877-301-1004 ■ *Web:* www.klostermanbakery.com

Klotz Assoc Inc 1160 Dairy Ashford St Houston TX 77079 281-589-7257 261
Web: www.klotz.com

KLPB-TV Ch 24 (PBS)
7733 Perkins Rd Baton Rouge LA 70810 225-767-5660 741-13
TF: 800-272-8161 ■ *Web:* www.lpb.org

KLPX-FM 96.1 (Rock) 3871 N Commerce Dr Tucson AZ 85705 520-407-4500 645-167
TF: 800-745-3000 ■ *Web:* www.klpx.com

KLRN-TV Ch 9 (PBS)
501 Broadway St San Antonio TX 78215 210-270-9000 270-9078 741-116
TF: 800-627-8193 ■ *Web:* www.klrn.org

KLRU-TV Ch 18 (PBS) 2504-B Whitis Ave Austin TX 78712 512-471-4811 475-9090 741-9
TF: 800-239-5233 ■ *Web:* www.klru.org

KLS Professional Advisors Group LLC
1325 Avenue of the Americas 14th Fl New York NY 10019 212-355-0346 355-0413 41
Web: www.klsadvisors.com

KLTS-TV Ch 24 (PBS)
7733 Perkins Rd Baton Rouge LA 70810 225-767-5660 767-4299 741-13
Web: www.lpb.org

KLTY-FM 94.9 (Rel)
6400 N Beltline Rd Ste 120 Irving TX 75063 972-870-9949 645
Web: www.klty.com

Kluane National Park & Reserve of Canada
PO Box 5495 Haines Junction YT Y0B1L0 867-634-7250 634-7208 563
TF: 877-852-3100 ■ *Web:* www.pc.gc.ca

Kluber Lubrication North America LP
32 Industrial Dr Londonderry NH 03053 603-647-4104 647-4106 541
TF: 800-447-2238 ■ *Web:* www.klueber.com

Kluge & Co 810 Seventh Ave Ste 29 New York NY 10019 212-606-4400 185

Klune Industries Inc
7323 Coldwater Canyon Ave North Hollywood CA 91605 818-503-8100 198
TF: 800-537-1085 ■ *Web:* www.klunev.com

KLUV-FM 98.7 (Oldies)
4131 N Central Expy Ste 1000 Dallas TX 75204 214-525-7000 645-44
TF: 855-987-5588 ■ *Web:* kluv.cbslocal.com

KLUX-FM 89.5 (AC)
1200 Lantana St Corpus Christi TX 78407 361-289-6437 289-1420 645-43
Web: www.goccn.org

KLVX-TV Ch 10 (PBS) 3050 E Flamingo Las Vegas NV 89121 702-799-1010 741-72
TF: 800-638-9238 ■ *Web:* www.vegaspbs.org

KM Fabrics Inc 2 Waco St Greenville SC 29611 864-295-2550 295-3356 745-1
TF: 800-845-1896

KM Ng Assoc Inc 6243 Ih 10 W San Antonio TX 78201 210-736-6623 261

K&M Printing Company Inc
1410 N Meacham Rd Schaumburg IL 60173 847-884-1100 627
Web: www.kmprinting.com

K&M Technology Group LLC
10077 Grogan's Mill Rd Ste 300 The Woodlands TX 77380 281-298-6900 261
Web: www.kmtechnology.com

K&M Tire Inc
965 Spencerville Rd PO Box 279 Delphos OH 45833 419-695-1061 754
TF: 877-879-5407 ■ *Web:* www.kmtire.com

Km2 Solutions LLC
100 Park Ave Ste 1600 New York NY 10017 404-848-8886 463
Web: www.km2solutions.com

KMA One 6815 Meadowridge Ct Alpharetta GA 30005 770-886-4000 366
TF: 888-500-2536 ■ *Web:* www.kmaone.com

KMA Sunbelt Trading Corp
3696 Ulmerton Rd Clearwater FL 33762 727-572-7258 411
Web: www.shopidc.com

K-Mac Enterprises Inc PO Box 6538 Fort Smith AR 72906 479-646-2053 646-8748 670
TF: 800-947-9277 ■ *Web:* www.kmaccorp.com

KMAJ-AM 1440 (N/T)
825 S Kansas Ave Ste 100 Topeka KS 66612 785-272-2122 272-6219 645-164
TF: 877-297-1077 ■ *Web:* www.kmaj.com

KMAJ-FM 107.7 (AC)
825 S Kansas Ave Ste 100 Topeka KS 66612 785-272-2122 272-6219 645-164
TF: 877-297-1077 ■ *Web:* www.kmaj.com

KMAX-TV Ch 31 (CBS)
2713 Kovr Dr West Sacramento CA 95605 916-374-1313 374-1304 741
TF: 800-374-8813 ■ *Web:* sacramento.cbslocal.com

KMBC-TV Ch 9 (ABC)
6455 Winchester Ave Kansas City MO 64133 816-221-9999 741-68
Web: www.kmbc.com

KMBH-TV Ch 60 (PBS)
1701 Tennessee St Harlingen TX 78550 956-421-4111 741

KMBR-FM 95.5 (Rock) 750 Dewey Blvd Ste 1 Butte MT 59701 406-494-4442 645
Web: www.955kmbr.com

KMBZ-AM 980 (N/T) 7000 Squibb Rd Mission KS 66202 913-744-3600 645
TF: 800-767-7700 ■ *Web:* www.kmbz.com

KMC (Kickhaefer Mfg Co)
1221 S Pk St PO Box 348 Port Washington WI 53074 262-377-5030 284-9774 488
TF: 800-822-6080 ■ *Web:* www.kmcstampings.com

KMC (Knapp Medical Ctr)
1401 E Eigth St PO Box 1110 Weslaco TX 78596 956-968-8567 374-3
Web: www.knappmed.org

KMC Controls Inc
19476 Industrial Dr New Paris IN 46553 574-831-5250 831-5252 202
TF: 877-444-5622 ■ *Web:* www.kmc-controls.com

KMC Exim Corp
1 Harbor Park Dr Port Washington NY 11050 516-621-6565 237

KMCI-TV Ch 38 (Ind) 4720 Oak St Kansas City MO 64112 816-753-4141 741-68
Web: www.kshb.com

KMCO LLC 16503 Ramsey Rd Crosby TX 77532 281-328-3501 328-9528 145
Web: kmcollc.com

KMDL-FM 97.3 (Ctry)
1749 Bertrand Dr Lafayette LA 70506 337-233-6000 645-86
TF: 800-324-1108 ■ *Web:* 973thedawg.com

KME Fire Apparatus 68 Sicker Rd Latham NY 12110 518-785-0900 785-1794 516
Web: kmefire.com

Kmea 964 Fifth Ave San Diego CA 92101 619-342-7377 194
TF: 800-559-5529 ■ *Web:* www.kmea.net

				Phone	Fax	Class
KMEZ-FM 106.7 (Oldies) 201 St Charles Ave Ste 201 *Web:* www.oldschool1067.com	New Orleans	LA	70170	504-581-7002		645-110
KMFC-FM 92.1 (Rel) 1249 E Hwy 22	Centralia	MO	65240	573-682-5525		645
KMG-Bernuth Inc 9555 W Sam Houston Pkwy S Ste 600 *Web:* kmgchemicals.com	Houston	TX	77099	713-600-3800		146
KMGE-FM 94.5 (AC) 925 Country Club Rd Ste 200 *Web:* 945mixfm.com	Eugene	OR	97401	541-484-9400	344-9424	645-55
KMGH-TV Ch 7 (ABC) 123 E Speer Blvd *TF:* 800-824-3463 ■ *Web:* www.thedenverchannel.com	Denver	CO	80203	303-832-7777	832-0119	741-39
KMGi Corp 4501 Seventh Ave N *Web:* www.kmgi.com	Saint Petersburg	FL	33713	727-322-9596		463
KMGL-FM 104.1 (AC) 400 E Britton Rd *TF:* 800-286-1025 ■ *Web:* www.magic104.com	Oklahoma City	OK	73114	405-478-5104		645-114
KMGN-FM 93.9 (CR) 1117 W Rt 66 *Web:* 939themountain.gcmaz.com	Flagstaff	AZ	86001	928-774-5231	779-2988	645-59
KMGV-FM 97.9 (Oldies) 1071 W Shaw Ave *Web:* www.mega979.com	Fresno	CA	93711	559-490-5800	490-4199	645-64
KMH Cardiology & Diagnostic Centres 2075 Hadwen Rd *Web:* www.kmhlabs.com	Mississauga	ON	L5K2L3	905-855-1860		415
KMHK FM 28 N 27th St Crowne Plaza 23rd Fl *Web:* kmhk.com	Billings	MT	59101	406-294-1037		645-19
KMI Diagnostics Inc 8201 Central Ave NE Ste P *TF:* 888-564-3424 ■ *Web:* www.kmidiagnostics.com	Minneapolis	MN	55432	763-231-3313	780-2988	231
KMIR-TV Ch 6 (NBC) 72920 Parkview Dr *TF:* 800-243-9352 ■ *Web:* kmir.com	Palm Desert	CA	92260	760-568-3636		741
KMIZ-TV Ch 17 (ABC) 501 Business Loop 70 E *TF:* 800-345-4109 ■ *Web:* www.abc17news.com	Columbia	MO	65201	573-449-0917	875-7078	741
Kmj Consulting Inc 120 E Lancaster Ave Ste 105 *Web:* www.kmjinc.com	Ardmore	PA	19003	610-896-1996		261
KMJ Corbin & Co 555 Anton Blvd Ste 1000 *Web:* www.corbincocpa.com	Costa Mesa	CA	92626	714-380-6565		734
KMJ-AM 580 (N/T) 1071 W Shaw Ave *TF:* 800-776-5858 ■ *Web:* kmjnow.com	Fresno	CA	93711	559-490-5800	490-5878	645-64
KMJ-FM 105.9 1071 W Shaw Ave *TF:* 800-491-1899 ■ *Web:* www.kmjnow.com	Fresno	CA	93711	559-490-5800	490-5878	645-64
KMLO-FM 100.7 (Ctry) 214 W Pleasant Dr *TF:* 800-658-5439 ■ *Web:* www.drgnews.com	Pierre	SD	57501	605-224-8686	224-8984	645-124
KMM (Killdeer Mountain Manufacturing Inc) 233 Rodeo Dr *Web:* www.kmmnet.com	Killdeer	ND	58640	701-764-5651	764-5427	625
Kmm Technologies Inc 2525 Emerson Dr Ste 101 *Web:* kmmtechnologies.com	Frederick	MD	21702	240-206-2321		261
KMOD-FM 97.5 (Rock) 2625 S Memorial Dr *Web:* kmod.iheart.com	Tulsa	OK	74129	918-388-5100		645-168
KMOS-TV Ch 6 (PBS) University of Central Missouri *Fax Area Code: 660 ■ *TF:* 800-753-3436 ■ *Web:* www.kmos.org	Warrensburg	MO	64093	800-753-3436	543-8863*	741
KMOV-TV Ch 4 (CBS) 1 Memorial Dr *Web:* www.kmov.com	Saint Louis	MO	63102	314-621-4444	621-4775	741-114
KMP Designs Inc 7145 W Credit Ave Ste 101 *Web:* www.kmpdesigns.com	Mississauga	ON	L5N6J7	905-812-5635		180
KMPH-TV Ch 26 (Fox) 5111 E McKinley Ave *TF:* 800-101-2045 ■ *Web:* kmph-kfre.com	Fresno	CA	93727	559-453-8850	255-9626	741-52
KMRY-AM 1450 (Nost) 1957 Blairs Ferry Rd NE *TF:* 800-320-2796 ■ *Web:* www.kmryradio.com	Cedar Rapids	IA	52402	319-393-1450	393-1407	645-29
KMS (Kewanna Metal Specialties Inc) 419 W Main St *Web:* www.kmswire.com	Kewanna	IN	46939	574-653-2554	653-2556	73
Kms Business Products Corp 3010 E Cervantes St *Web:* www.kmsbusiness.com	Pensacola	FL	32503	850-433-1131		180
Kms Consulting Services Inc 92 Broadway Ste 206 *Web:* kmssolutions.com	Greenlawn	NY	11740	631-912-0200		196
KMS Solutions LLC 205 S Whiting St Ste 400 *Web:* www.kmssol.com	Alexandria	VA	22304	703-823-8405		261
KMSP-TV Ch 9 (Fox) 11358 Viking Dr *Web:* www.fox9.com	Eden Prairie	MN	55344	952-944-9999		741
Kmtelecom 18 Second Ave NW *TF:* 888-232-3796 ■ *Web:* www.kmtel.com	Kasson	MN	55944	507-634-2511		116
KMTG (Kronick Moskovitz Tiedemann & Girard) 400 Capitol Mall Fl 27 *Web:* www.kmtg.com	Sacramento	CA	95814	916-321-4500	321-4555	428
KMUW-FM 89.1 (NPR) 3317 E 17th St N *Web:* www.kmuw.org	Wichita	KS	67208	316-978-6789	978-3946	645-175
KMW Ltd PO Box 327 *TF:* 800-445-7388 ■ *Web:* www.kmwloaders.com	Sterling	KS	67579	620-278-3641	278-2388	273
KMXB-FM 94.1 (AC) 7255 S Tenaya Way Ste 100 *TF:* 866-438-0220 ■ *Web:* mix941fm.cbslocal.com	Las Vegas	NV	89113	702-257-9400	257-2936	645-88
KMXC-FM 97.3 (AC) 5100 S Tennis Ln *Web:* www.mix97-3.com	Sioux Falls	SD	57108	605-361-0300		645-152
KMXJ-FM 94.1 (AC) 6214 W 34th St *Web:* www.mix941kmxj.com	Amarillo	TX	79109	806-355-9777		645-5
KMXS-FM 103.1 (AC) 301 Arctic Slope Ave *Web:* www.kmxs.com	Anchorage	AK	99518	907-344-9622		645-6
KMXV-FM 93.3 (CHR) 508 Westport Rd Ste 202 *Web:* www.mix93.com	Kansas City	MO	64111	816-753-4000		645-83
KMXZ-FM 94.9 7280 E Rosewood *Web:* www.mixfm.com	Tucson	AZ	85710	520-722-5486		645-167
KMYS-TV Ch 35 (MNT) 4335 NW Loop 410 *Fax: News Rm ■ *Web:* www.kmys.tv	San Antonio	TX	78229	210-366-1129	377-4758*	741-116
KMYX-FM 92.5 (Span) 4300 Stine Rd Ste 209 *Web:* campesina.net/bakersfield/bakersfield-radio	Bakersfield	CA	93313	661-837-0745	837-1612	645-15
KNA Structural Engineers 9931 Muirlands Blvd *Web:* www.knaconsulting.com	Irvine	CA	92618	949-462-3200		261
Knaack Manufacturing Co 420 E Terra Cotta Ave *TF:* 800-456-7865 ■ *Web:* www.knaack.com	Crystal Lake	IL	60014	815-459-6020	459-9097	488
Knack Systems LLC 1 Woodbridge Ctr Ste 335 *Web:* www.knacksystems.com	Woodbridge	NJ	07095	732-596-0110		196
Knape & Vogt Manufacturing Co 2700 Oak Industrial Dr NE *TF:* 800-253-1561 ■ *Web:* www.knapeandvogt.com	Grand Rapids	MI	49505	616-459-3311	459-3290	350
Knapheide Mfg Co 1848 Westphalia Strasse PO Box 7140 *Web:* www.knapheide.com	Quincy	IL	62305	217-222-7131		516
Knapp & Associates International 712 Executive Dr *Web:* www.knappinternational.com	Princeton	NJ	08540	609-921-3478		463
Knapp Medical Ctr (KMC) 1401 E Eigth St PO Box 1110 *Web:* www.knappmed.org	Weslaco	TX	78596	956-968-8567		374-3
Knappen Milling Co 110 S Water St *TF:* 800-562-7736 ■ *Web:* www.knappen.com	Augusta	MI	49012	269-731-4141		296-23
Knaster Technology Group, The 6500 S Quebec St Ste 300 *Web:* www.theknastergroup.com	Centennial	CO	80111	303-796-7626		525
KNAT-TV Ch 23 (TBN) 1510 Coors Blvd NW *Web:* www.tbn.org	Albuquerque	NM	87121	505-836-6585		741-3
Knauf Insulation 1 Knauf Dr *TF:* 800-825-4434 ■ *Web:* www.knaufinsulation.com	Shelbyville	IN	46176	317-398-4434	398-3675	389
KNAU-FM 88.7 (NPR) PO Box 5764 PO Box 5764 *TF:* 800-523-5628 ■ *Web:* www.knau.org	Flagstaff	AZ	86011	928-523-5628	523-7647	645-59
KNBA-FM 90.3 (NPR) 3600 San Geronimo Dr Ste 480 *TF:* 800-996-2848 ■ *Web:* www.knba.org	Anchorage	AK	99508	907-793-3500	793-3536	645-6
KNBN-TV Ch 27 (NBC) 2424 S Plaza Dr *Web:* www.newscenter1.tv	Rapid City	SD	57701	605-355-0024	355-9274	741-106
KNDD-FM 107.7 (Alt) 1100 Olive Way Ste 1650 *TF:* 800-749-9490 ■ *Web:* www.1077theend.com	Seattle	WA	98101	206-421-1077		645-150
KNDR-FM 104.7 (Rel) 1400 NE Third St *TF:* 800-767-5095 ■ *Web:* www.kndr.fm	Mandan	ND	58554	701-663-2345	663-2347	645
KNDX-TV Ch 26 (Fox) 3130 E Broadway Ave	Bismarck	ND	58501	701-355-0026		741-16
Knecht's Auto Parts 3400 Main St *Web:* www.knechts.com	Springfield	OR	97478	541-746-4446		54
Knepper Press 2251 Sweeney Dr *Web:* www.knepperpress.com	Clinton	PA	15026	724-899-4200	899-1331	627
Knew Deal Inc 1528 Woodward Ave 4th Fl *Web:* www.stik.com	Detroit	MI	48226	313-373-7844		387
KNF Flexpak Corp 734 W Penn Pk *TF:* 800-755-1942 ■ *Web:* www.knfcorporation.com	Tamaqua	PA	18252	570-386-3550		601
Knf Neuberger Inc Two Black Forest Rd *TF:* 800-766-7000 ■ *Web:* www.knf.com	Trenton	NJ	08691	609-890-8600	890-2838	420
Knichel Logistics LP 5347 William Flynn Hwy 2nd Fl *TF:* 888-386-7450 ■ *Web:* www.knichellogistics.com	Gibsonia	PA	15044	724-449-3300		311
Knickerbocker on, The Lake, The 1028 E Juneau Ave *Web:* www.knickerbockeronthelake.com	Milwaukee	WI	53202	414-276-8500	276-3668	379
Knickerbocker Partition Corp 193 Hanse Ave PO Box 690 *Web:* www.knickerbockerpartition.com	Freeport	NY	11520	516-546-0550	546-0549	286
Knickerbocker Russell Company Inc 4759 Campbells Run *Web:* bignick.biz	Pittsburgh	PA	15205	412-494-9233	787-7991	385
Knife & Fork Inn, The 3600 Atlantic Ave *Web:* www.knifeandforkinn.com	Atlantic City	NJ	08401	609-344-1133	344-3533	671
Knife River Corp 1150 W Century Ave *TF:* 800-982-5339 ■ *Web:* www.kniferiver.com	Bismarck	ND	58506	701-530-1400	530-1451	135
Knife River Corp - North Central 4787 Shadow Wood Dr NE	Sauk Rapids	MN	56379	320-251-9472		182
Knife River Indian Villages National Historic Site 564 County Rd 37 PO Box 9 *TF:* 866-705-5711 ■ *Web:* www.nps.gov	Stanton	ND	58571	701-745-3300	745-3708	564
Knight & Carver Yachtcenter Inc 1313 Bay Marina Dr	National City	CA	91950	619-336-4141		90
Knight Cap, The 320 E Michigan Ave *TF:* 800-725-5960 ■ *Web:* www.theknightcap.com	Lansing	MI	48933	517-484-7676		671
Knight Capital Group Inc 545 Washington Blvd *NYSE:* KCG ■ *TF:* 800-544-7508 ■ *Web:* www.kcg.com	Jersey City	NJ	07310	201-222-9400		690
Knight Dental Group 3659 Tampa Rd *TF:* 800-359-2043 ■ *Web:* www.knightdentalgroup.com	Oldsmar	FL	34677	813-854-3333		415
Knight Electronics Inc 10557 Metric Dr *TF:* 800-323-2439 ■ *Web:* www.orionfans.com	Dallas	TX	75243	214-340-0265		194
Knight Enterprises Inc 6056 Ulmerton Rd *Web:* www.knight-enterprises.com	Clearwater	FL	33760	727-524-6235		116
Knight Facilities Management Inc 5360 Hampton Pl *Web:* www.knightfm.com	Saginaw	MI	48604	989-793-8820	399-9096	194
Knight Feedlot Inc 1768 Ave J	Lyons	KS	67554	620-257-5106		10-1
Knight Global 2705 Commerce Pkwy *Web:* www.knight-ind.com	Auburn Hills	MI	48326	248-377-4950	377-2135	207

Listing	Phone	Fax	Class
Knight Hawk Coal LLC 500 Cutler-Trico Rd .... Percy IL 62272 *TF:* 855-611-2625 ■ *Web:* www.knighthawkcoal.com	618-426-3662		501
Knight Inlet Grizzly Bear Adventure Tours 8841 Driftwood Rd .... Black Creek BC V9J1A8 *TF:* 800-888-2535 ■ *Web:* www.grizzlytours.com	250-337-1953	337-1914	760
Knight Island State Park 1 Knight Island .... North Hero VT 05474 *Web:* www.vtstateparks.com/htm/knightisland.htm	802-524-6353		565
Knight Paper Box Company Inc 4651 W 72nd St .... Chicago IL 60629 *TF:* 800-585-2035 ■ *Web:* knightpack.com	773-585-2035	585-3824	101
Knight Printing LLC 16 S 16th St .... Fargo ND 58103 *Web:* www.knightprinting.com	701-235-1121		627
Knight Publishing Co 600 S Tryon St .... Charlotte NC 28202 *TF:* 800-332-0686 ■ *Web:* www.charlotteobserver.com	704-358-5000		637-8
Knight Rifles 213 Dennis st Athens .... Athens TN 37303 *TF:* 866-518-4181 ■ *Web:* www.knightrifles.com	866-518-4181		284
Knight Security Systems LLC 10105 Technology Blvd W Ste 100 .... Dallas TX 75220 *TF:* 800-642-1632 ■ *Web:* www.knightsecurity.com	214-350-1632		693
Knight Sky LLC 7470-F New Technology Way .... Frederick MD 21703 *Web:* www.knight-sky.com	240-252-1950		647
Knight Steve (Rep R - CA) 1023 Longworth HOB .... Washington DC 20515 *Web:* knight.house.gov	202-225-1956		342-2
Knight Transportation Inc 5601 W Buckeye Rd .... Phoenix AZ 85043 *NYSE: KNX* ■ *TF:* 800-489-2000 ■ *Web:* www.knighttrans.com	602-269-2000	269-8409	780
Knight's Action Park & Caribbean Water Adventure 1700 Recreation Dr .... Springfield IL 62711 *Web:* www.knightsactionpark.com	217-546-8881		32
Knight's Armament Co 701 Columbia Blvd .... Titusville FL 32780 *Web:* www.knightarmco.com	321-607-9900		807
Knight's Steak House 2324 Dexter Ave .... Ann Arbor MI 48103 *Web:* www.knightsrestaurants.com	734-665-8644		671
Knight-Abbey Commercial Prntrs 315 Caillavet St .... Biloxi MS 39530	228-374-3298		627
Knighthawk Engineering Inc 17625 El Camino Real Ste 412 .... Houston TX 77058 *Web:* www.knighthawk.com	281-282-9200		256
Knights Apparel Inc 5475 N Blackstone Rd .... Spartanburg SC 29303 *Web:* futurespark.com	864-587-9690		442
Knights of Columbus 1 Columbus Plaza .... New Haven CT 06510 *TF Cust Svc:* 800-380-9995 ■ *Web:* www.kofc.org	203-752-4000		48-15
Knightsbridge Asset Management LLC 660 Newport Ctr Dr Ste 460 .... Newport Beach CA 92660 *Web:* www.knightsb.com	949-644-4444		401
Knippelmier Chevrolet Inc 1811 E Hwy 62 E .... Blanchard OK 73010 *TF:* 877-644-7255 ■ *Web:* knippelmier.com	877-644-7255		57
KNIS-FM 91.3 (Rel) PO Box 21888 .... Carson City NV 89721 *TF:* 800-541-5647 ■ *Web:* www.pilgrimradio.com	775-883-5647		645-133
Knit Rite Inc 120 Osage Ave .... Kansas City KS 66105 *TF:* 800-821-3094 ■ *Web:* www.knitrite.com	913-281-4600	281-5455	476
Knitney Lines Inc 411 Gilligan St .... Scranton PA 18508 *TF General:* 866-564-8639 ■ *Web:* www.knitneylines.com	570-457-5060	457-6725	311
Knitting Guild of America, The (TKGA) 1100-H Brandywine Blvd .... Zanesville OH 43701 *Web:* www.tkga.com	740-452-4541	452-2552	48-18
KNIX-FM 102.5 (Ctry) 4686 E Van Buren St Ste 300 .... Phoenix AZ 85008 *Web:* knixcountry.iheart.com	602-374-6000		645-123
KNLJ-TV Ch 25 (Ind) 311 W Dunklin .... Jefferson City MO 65101 *Web:* www.knlj.tv	573-896-5105		741-65
KNME-TV Ch 5 (PBS) 1130 University Blvd NE University of New Mexico .... Albuquerque NM 87102 *TF:* 800-328-5663 ■ *Web:* www.newmexicopbs.org	505-277-2121		741-3
KNML-AM 610 (Sports) 500 Fourth St NW 5th Fl .... Albuquerque NM 87102 *TF:* 888-922-0610 ■ *Web:* www.610knml.com	505-767-6700	767-6711	645-4
Knob Hill Inn 960 N Main St PO Box 1327 .... Ketchum ID 83340 *TF:* 800-526-8010 ■ *Web:* www.knobhillinn.com	208-726-8010		379
Knob Noster State Park 873 SE 10th .... Knob Noster MO 65336 *Web:* www.mostateparks.com	660-563-2463		565
Knock Inc 1315 Glenwood Ave .... Minneapolis MN 55405 *Web:* www.knockinc.com	612-333-6511		514
Knockout Pest Control Inc 1009 Front St .... Uniondale NY 11553 *TF:* 800-244-7378 ■ *Web:* www.knockoutpest.com	516-489-7817	489-4348	577
Knoebels Amusement Resort 391 Knoebels Blvd .... Elysburg PA 17824 *TF:* 800-487-4386 ■ *Web:* www.knoebels.com	570-672-2572		32
Knoll Inc 1235 Water St .... East Greenville PA 18041 *NYSE: KNL* ■ *TF Cust Svc:* 800-343-5665 ■ *Web:* www.knoll.com	215-679-7991		319-1
Knollwood 6200 Oregon Ave NW .... Washington DC 20015 *TF:* 800-541-4255 ■ *Web:* www.armydistaff.org	202-541-0400		672
Knoodle 4450 N 12th St Ste 120 .... Phoenix AZ 85014 *Web:* www.knoodleshop.com	602-530-9900		7
Knopf Automotive 93 Shrewsbury Ave .... Red Bank NJ 07701 *Web:* www.mmknopf.com	732-212-0444	212-0443	61
Knopp Inc 1307 66th St .... Emeryville CA 94608 *TF:* 800-227-1848 ■ *Web:* www.knoppinc.com	510-653-1661	653-2202	248
Knorr Assoc Inc 10 Pk Pl PO Box 400 .... Butler NJ 07405 *Web:* www.knorrassociates.com	973-492-8500	492-0453	178-10
Knorr Beeswax Products Inc 14906 Via De La Valle .... Del Mar CA 92014 *TF:* 800-807-2337 ■ *Web:* www.knorrbeeswax.com	760-431-2007	431-8977	122
Knot Inc, The 195 Broadway 6th Fl .... New York NY 10013 **Fax Area Code:* 302 ■ *Web:* www.xogroupinc.com	212-219-8555	655-5049*	171
Knott House Museum 301 E Pk Ave .... Tallahassee FL 32301 *TF:* 800-628-2866 ■ *Web:* museumoffloridahistory.com	850-922-2459		520
Knott Laboratory LLC 7185 S Tucson Way .... Englewood CO 80112 *Web:* www.knottlab.com	303-925-1900		261
Knott's Berry Farm 8039 Beach Blvd .... Buena Park CA 90620 *TF:* 800-742-6427 ■ *Web:* www.knotts.com	714-220-5200	220-5124	32
Knott's Berry Farm Resort 7675 Crescent Ave .... Buena Park CA 90620 *TF:* 866-752-2444 ■ *Web:* www.knotts.com	714-995-1111	220-5124	669
Knott's Soak City San Diego 8039 Beach Blvd .... Buena Park CA 90620 *Web:* www.knotts.com	714-220-5200		32
Knouse Foods Co-op Inc 800 Peach Glen-Idaville Rd .... Peach Glen PA 17375 *Web:* www.knouse.com	717-677-8181	677-7069	296-20
Knovalent 3135 S State St Ste 300 .... Ann Arbor MI 48108 *Web:* www.knovalent.com	734-996-8300		178-10
Knovation Inc 3630 Park 42 Dr Ste 170F .... Cincinnati OH 45241 *Web:* www.nettrekker.com	513-731-4090		180
Know Before You Go Reservations 8000 International Dr .... Orlando FL 32819 *TF:* 800-749-1993 ■ *Web:* www.knowbeforeugo.com	407-352-9813		376
Know It All Intelligence Group 1950 St Rd Ste 402 .... Bensalem PA 19020 *Web:* www.screenmyapplicants.com	215-245-1975		196
Knowcean Consulting Inc 10605 Stapleford Hall Dr .... Potomac MD 20854 *Web:* www.knowceanconsulting.com	240-672-1699		177
KnowEm LLC 58 Phoenix Ave .... Morristown NJ 07753 *TF:* 800-691-5669 ■ *Web:* www.knowem.com	800-691-5669		5
Knowledge Anywhere Inc 3015 112th Ave NE Ste 210 .... Bellevue WA 98004 *Web:* www.knowledgeanywhere.com	425-454-4454		194
Knowledge Information Solutions Inc 2877 Guardian Ln Ste 201 .... Virginia Beach VA 23452 *TF:* 877-547-7248 ■ *Web:* www.kisinc.net	757-463-0033	463-3971	179
Knowledge Relay LLC 5836 Corporate Ave Ste 130 .... Cypress CA 90630 *Web:* www.knowledgerelay.com	714-761-6760		177
Knowledge Reservoir LLC 1800 W Loop S Ste 1000 .... Houston TX 77027 *Web:* www.knowledge-reservoir.com	713-586-5950		174
Knowledge Systems & Research Inc 120 Madison St 15th Fl .... Syracuse NY 13202 *Web:* www.ksrinc.com	315-470-1350		668
Knowledge Works Inc 5750 Old Orchard Rd Ste 250 .... Skokie IL 60077 **Fax Area Code:* 847 ■ *TF:* 866-825-3400 ■ *Web:* www.paynetonline.com	866-825-3400	965-9828*	466
KnowledgeBank 20365 Exchange St .... Ashburn VA 20147 *Web:* www.knowledgebank.us.com	703-448-8070		194
Knowles - Mcniff 12862 Garden Grove Blvd Ste C .... Garden Grove CA 92843 *TF:* 800-820-5254 ■ *Web:* www.knowles-mcniff.us	800-820-5254		177
Knowles Corp 1151 Maplewood Dr .... Itasca IL 60143 *Web:* www.knowlesinc.com	630-250-5100	250-0575	253
KnowX LLC 730 Peachtree St .... Atlanta GA 30308	404-541-0220		635
Knox College 59 St George St .... Toronto ON M5S2E6 *Web:* www.utoronto.ca	416-978-4500	971-2133	167-3
Knox College 2 E S St .... Galesburg IL 61401 **Fax:* Admissions ■ *Web:* www.knox.edu	309-341-7000	341-7806*	166
Knox Community Hospital 1330 Coshocton Rd .... Mount Vernon OH 43050 *Web:* www.kch.org	740-393-9000		374-3
Knox County PO Box 196 .... Benjamin TX 79505 *Web:* www.knoxcountytexas.org	940-459-2441	459-2005	338
Knox County 206 Main St .... Center NE 68724 *Web:* www.co.knox.ne.us	402-288-5604	288-5605	338
Knox County 200 S Cherry St .... Galesburg IL 61401 *TF:* 800-916-3330 ■ *Web:* www.knoxcountyil.com	309-343-3121		338
Knox County 400 W Main St Ste 603 .... Knoxville TN 37902 *Web:* www.knoxcounty.org	865-215-2534	215-2038	338
Knox County 117 E High St Ste 161 .... Mount Vernon OH 43050 *Web:* www.co.knox.oh.us	740-393-6703	393-6705	338
Knox County 62 Union St .... Rockland ME 04841 *Web:* knoxcountymaine.gov	207-594-0420	594-0443	338
Knox County 316 Main St .... Vincennes IN 47591 *Web:* www.knoxcountychamber.com	812-882-6440		338
Knox County Convention & Visitors Bureau 107 S Main St .... Mount Vernon OH 43050 *TF:* 800-837-5282 ■ *Web:* www.visitknoxohio.org	740-392-6102	392-7840	206
Knox County Health Dept 11660 Upper Gilchrist Rd .... Mount Vernon OH 43050 *TF:* 800-243-7703 ■ *Web:* www.knoxhealth.com	740-392-2200		804
Knox County Public Library 502 N Seventh St .... Vincennes IN 47591 *Web:* www.kcpl.lib.in.us	812-886-4380		434-3
Knox Machine Company Inc 936 Eastern Rd .... Warren ME 04864 *Web:* www.knoxmachine.com	207-273-2296		454
Knox McLaughlin Gornall & Sennett PC 120 W Tenth St .... Erie PA 16501 *TF:* 800-939-9886 ■ *Web:* kmgslaw.com	814-459-2800		428
Knox News Radio 1185 Ninth St NE .... Thompson ND 58278 *Web:* www.knoxradio.com	701-775-4611	772-0540	645
Knox Nursery Inc 940 Avalon Rd .... Winter Garden FL 34787 *TF:* 800-441-5669 ■ *Web:* www.knoxnursery.com	800-441-5669		369
Knox School 541 E Long Beach Rd .... Saint James NY 11780 *Web:* www.knoxschool.org	631-686-1600	686-1650	622
Knox Services 2250 Fourth Ave .... San Diego CA 92101 *TF:* 800-995-6694 ■ *Web:* www.knoxservices.com	619-233-9700		627
Knox's Headquarters State Historic Site 289 Old Forge Hill Rd .... Vails Gate NY 12584 *Web:* parks.ny.gov/historic-sites/5/details.aspx	845-561-5498		565
Knoxville Area Chamber Partnership 17 Market Sq Ste 201 .... Knoxville TN 37902 *TF:* 800-727-8045 ■ *Web:* www.knoxvillechamber.com	865-637-4550	523-2071	139

Name / Address	City	State	Zip	Phone	Fax	Class
Knoxville City Hall 400 W Main St *Web:* www.knoxvilletn.gov	Knoxville	TN	37902	865-215-2000	215-2085	337
Knoxville Civic Auditorium/Coliseum 500 Howard Baker Jr Ave *TF:* 877-995-9961 ■ *Web:* www.knoxvillecoliseum.com	Knoxville	TN	37915	865-215-8900	215-8989	572
Knoxville Convention Ctr 701 Henley St *Web:* www.kccsmg.com	Knoxville	TN	37902	865-522-5669	329-0422	205
Knoxville Hospital & Clinics 1002 S Lincoln St *Web:* www.knoxvillehospital.org	Knoxville	IA	50138	641-842-2151		363
Knoxville Locomotive Works 300 W Quincy Ave *Web:* knoxvillelocomotiveworks.com	Knoxville	TN	37917	865-522-7078		41
Knoxville Museum of Art 1050 World Fair Pk Dr *TF:* 800-732-6845 ■ *Web:* www.knoxart.org	Knoxville	TN	37916	865-525-6101	546-3635	520
Knoxville National Cemetery 939 Tyson St NW *Web:* www.cem.va.gov/cems/nchp/knoxville.asp	Knoxville	TN	37917	423-855-6590	855-6597	136
Knoxville News-Sentinel 2332 News Sentinel Dr **Fax:* Edit ■ *TF:* 800-237-5821 ■ *Web:* www.knoxnews.com	Knoxville	TN	37921	865-521-8181	342-8635*	532-2
Knoxville Opera Co 612 E Depot Ave *Web:* www.knoxvilleopera.com	Knoxville	TN	37917	865-524-0795	524-7384	573-2
Knoxville Symphony Orchestra 100 S Gay St Ste 302 *TF:* 800-845-5665 ■ *Web:* www.knoxvillesymphony.com	Knoxville	TN	37902	865-523-1178	546-3766	573-3
Knoxville Tourism & Sports Corp 301 S Gay St *TF:* 800-727-8045 ■ *Web:* visitknoxville.com	Knoxville	TN	37902	865-523-7263		206
Knoxville Wholesale Furniture Co Inc 410 N Peters Rd *Web:* www.knoxvillewholesalefurniture.com	Knoxville	TN	37922	865-671-5300		321
Knoxville Zoological Gardens Inc 3500 Knoxville Zoo Dr *Web:* www.zooknoxville.org	Knoxville	TN	37914	865-637-5331		823
KNPB-TV Ch 5 (PBS) 1670 N Virginia St *TF:* 800-726-3178 ■ *Web:* www.knpb.org	Reno	NV	89503	775-784-4555	784-1438	741-107
KNPR-FM 89.5 (NPR) 1289 S Torrey Pines Dr *TF:* 888-258-9895 ■ *Web:* www.knpr.org	Las Vegas	NV	89146	702-258-9895	258-5646	645-88
KNRK-FM 94.7 (Alt) 0700 SW Bancroft St *TF:* 800-777-0947 ■ *Web:* www.947.fm	Portland	OR	97239	503-733-5470		645-128
KNS Cos Inc 475 Randy Rd *Web:* www.knscompanies.com	Carol Stream	IL	60188	630-665-9010	665-1819	481
KNSD-TV Ch 39 (NBC) 225 Broadway *Web:* www.nbcsandiego.com	San Diego	CA	92101	619-231-3939		741-119
KNSS-AM 98.7/1330 2120 N Woodlawn St Ste 352 *Web:* www.knssradio.com	Wichita	KS	67207	316-685-2121		645-175
KNST-AM 3202 N Oracle Rd *Web:* knst.iheart.com	Tucson	AZ	85705	520-618-2100		645-167
KNTV-TV Ch 11 (NBC) 2450 N First St *Web:* www.nbcbayarea.com	San Jose	CA	95131	408-432-6221		741
Knudson-Smith Engineering Inc 2525 W Greenway Rd Ste 302	Phoenix	AZ	85023	602-347-7447		256
Knupp & Watson Inc 5201 Old Middleton Rd *Web:* kw2madison.com	Madison	WI	53705	608-232-2300	232-2301	7
KNUS-AM 710 (N/T) 3131 S Vaughn Way Ste 601 *Web:* www.710knus.com	Aurora	CO	80014	303-750-5687		645
Knutson Construction Services Inc 7515 Wayzata Blvd *Web:* www.knutsonconstruction.com	Minneapolis	MN	55426	763-546-1400		186
Knutte & Assoc PC 7900 S Cass Ave *Web:* www.knutte.com	Darien	IL	60561	630-960-3317		2
KNVA-TV Ch 54 (CW) 908 W ML King Jr Blvd *Web:* www.thecwaustin.com	Austin	TX	78701	512-478-5400	476-1520	741-9
KNWA-TV Ch 51 (NBC) 609 W Dickson St 3rd Flr *Web:* www.nwahomepage.com	Fayetteville	AR	72701	479-571-5100		741
KNWI-FM 107.1 (Rel) 3737 Woodland Ave Ste 300 *Web:* life1071.com	West Des Moines	IA	50266	515-327-1071		645
KNX-AM 1070 (N/T) 5670 Wilshire Blvd Ste 200 *Web:* losangeles.cbslocal.com	Los Angeles	CA	90036	323-569-1070		645-92
KNXT-TV Ch 49 (Ind) 1550 N Fresno St *Web:* www.knxt.tv	Fresno	CA	93703	559-488-7440	488-7444	741-52
KNXV-TV Ch 15 (ABC) 515 N 44th St *TF:* 800-222-4357 ■ *Web:* www.abc15.com	Phoenix	AZ	85008	602-273-1500		741-99
KNZR-AM 1560 (N/T) 3651 Pegasus Dr Ste 107 *Web:* www.knzr.com	Bakersfield	CA	93308	661-393-1900		645-15
KO Prime 90 Tremont St *TF:* 866-906-9090 ■ *Web:* www.ninezero.com	Boston	MA	02108	617-772-0202	772-5810	671
KOA (Kampgrounds of America Inc) PO Box 30558 *TF:* 888-562-0000 ■ *Web:* www.koa.com	Billings	MT	59114	888-562-0000		121
KOA Speer Electronics Inc 199 Bolivar Dr *Web:* www.evalue-tech.com	Bradford	PA	16701	814-362-5536		253
Koa Trading Co 2975 Aukele St	Lihue	HI	96766	808-245-6961		297-8
KOA-AM 850 (N/T) 4695 S Monaco Ave *Web:* koanewsradio.iheart.com	Denver	CO	80237	303-713-8000		645-47
KOAA-TV Ch 5/30 (NBC) 2200 Seventh Ave *Web:* www.koaa.com	Pueblo	CO	81003	719-544-5781	295-6677	741
KOAT-TV Ch 7 (ABC) 3801 Carlisle Blvd NE *TF:* 877-871-0165 ■ *Web:* www.koat.com	Albuquerque	NM	87107	505-884-7777		741-3
Kobayashi Travel Service 650 Iwilei Rd *Web:* www.kobay.com	Honolulu	HI	96817	808-593-9387		345
Kobayashi, Sugita & Goda LLP, Attorneys at Law 999 Bishop St Ste 2600 *Web:* www.ksglaw.com	Honolulu	HI	96813	808-535-5700		428
Kobe Japanese Steak House 3214 Electric Rd *Web:* www.kobesteakhouse.com	Roanoke	VA	24018	540-776-0008		671
Kobe Japanese Steakhouse Inc 468 W Hwy 436 *Web:* www.kobesteakhouse.com	Altamonte Springs	FL	32714	407-862-6099		670
Kobe Sportswear Inc 791 Tapscott Rd *Web:* kobesportswear.com	Scarborough	ON	M1X1A2	416-754-7024		442
Kobe Steaks Nashville 210 25th Ave N Ste 100 *Web:* www.kobesteaks.net	Nashville	TN	37203	615-327-9081		671
Kobe Steel Ltd 535 Madison Ave *Web:* www.kobelco.co.jp	New York	NY	10022	212-751-9400	355-5564	723
Kobelco Compressors (America) Inc 3000 Hammond Ave *Web:* www.kobelcocompressors.com	Elkhart	IN	46516	574-295-3145	293-1641	14
Kobelco Construction Machinery America LLC 501 Richardson Rd SE *Web:* www.kobelco-usa.com	Calhoun	GA	30701	706-629-5572		41
Kobelco Stewart Bolling Inc (KSBI) 1600 Terex Rd *TF:* 800-464-0064 ■ *Web:* www.ksbiusa.com	Hudson	OH	44236	330-655-3111	655-2982	386
Kobelt Manufacturing Company Ltd 8238 129th St *Web:* www.kobelt.com	Surrey	BC	V3W0A6	604-572-3935	590-8313	203
Koberg Beach State Recreation Site 725 Summer St NE Ste C *TF:* 800-551-6949 ■ *Web:* oregonstateparks.org	Salem	OR	97301	503-986-0707		565
KOB-TV Ch 4 (NBC) 4 Broadcast Plaza SW *Web:* www.kob.com	Albuquerque	NM	87104	505-243-4411	764-2522	741-3
Kobuk Valley National Park PO Box 1029 *Web:* www.nps.gov/kova	Kotzebue	AK	99752	907-442-3890	442-8316	564
Kobussen Buses Ltd W914 County Rd CE *TF:* 800-447-0116 ■ *Web:* www.kobussen.com	Kaukauna	WI	54130	920-766-0606	766-0797	109
KOCB-TV Ch 34 (CW) 1228 E Wilshire Blvd *Web:* www.cwokc.com	Oklahoma City	OK	73111	405-843-2525	478-4343	741-93
Koch & Company Inc 1809 North St *Web:* www.kochandco.com	Seneca	KS	66538	785-336-6022		115
Koch Air LLC 1900 W Lloyd Expy *Web:* www.kochair.com	Evansville	IN	47744	812-962-5200	962-5306	612
Koch Bros 325 Grand Ave *TF:* 800-944-5624 ■ *Web:* www.kochbros.com	Des Moines	IA	50309	515-283-2451		535
Koch Chemical Technology Group LLC 4111 E 37th St N *Web:* www.kochind.com/IndustryAreas/process.aspx	Wichita	KS	67220	316-828-5500		318
Koch Development Co 222 S Central Ave Ste 1100 *Web:* www.kochdevelopment.com	St Louis	MO	63105	314-333-5624		205
Koch Enterprises Inc 14 S 11th Ave *Web:* www.kochenterprises.com	Evansville	IN	47712	812-465-9800	465-9613	185
KOCH EYE Assoc 566 Toll Gate Rd *Web:* kocheye.com	Warwick	RI	02886	401-738-4800		374-3
Koch Family Children's Museum of Evansville 22 SE Fifth St *Web:* www.cmoekids.org	Evansville	IN	47708	812-464-2663	477-4339	521
Koch Filter Corp 625 W Hill St *TF:* 800-757-5624 ■ *Web:* www.kochfilter.com	Louisville	KY	40208	502-634-4796	637-2280	18
Koch Foods Inc 1300 Higgins Rd Ste 100 *TF:* 800-837-2778 ■ *Web:* www.kochfoods.com	Park Ridge	IL	60068	847-384-5940		619
Koch Foods of Mississippi LLC 4688 Highway 80 E	Morton	MS	39117	601-732-8911		619
Koch Foundation Inc 4421 NW 39th Ave Bldg 1 Ste 1 *Web:* www.thekochfoundation.org	Gainesville	FL	32606	352-373-7491		304
Koch Group & Company LLP 333 Seventh Ave Rm 8 *Web:* www.kgcpas.com	New York	NY	10001	212-631-0700		2
Koch Heat Transfer Company LP 12602 FM 529 *Web:* www.kochheattransfer.com	Houston	TX	77041	713-466-3535		91
Koch Industries Inc PO Box 2256 *Web:* www.kochind.com	Wichita	KS	67201	316-828-3756		185
Koch Knight LLC 5385 Orchard View Dr SE *Web:* www.kochknight.com	Canton	OH	44730	330-488-1651		751
Koch Membrane Systems Inc 850 Main St *TF:* 888-677-5624 ■ *Web:* www.kochmembrane.com	Wilmington	MA	01887	978-694-7000	657-5208	386
Koch Mineral Services LLC 4111 E 37th St N	Wichita	KS	67220	316-828-5500	828-6997	169
Koch Modular Process Systems LLC 45 Eisenhower Dr *Web:* www.modularprocess.com	Paramus	NJ	07652	201-267-8670		420
Koch Nitrogen Co 4111 E 37th St N *Web:* www.kochind.com	Wichita	KS	67220	316-828-5500		280
Koch Specialty Plant Services 12221 E Sam Houston Pkwy N *TF:* 800-765-9177 ■ *Web:* www.kochservices.com	Houston	TX	77044	713-427-7700	427-7747	539
Koch Supply & Trading LP 4111 E 37th St N *Web:* www.kochoil.com	Wichita	KS	67220	713-544-4123		391-4
Kocher Flower Growers 950 Brittany Rd	Encinitas	CA	92024	760-436-1458		369
Koch-Glitsch Inc 4111 E 37th St N *Web:* www.koch-glitsch.com	Wichita	KS	67220	316-828-5110	828-5263	386
KOCO-TV Ch 5 (ABC) 1300 E Britton Rd *TF:* 800-464-7928 ■ *Web:* www.koco.com	Oklahoma City	OK	73131	405-478-3000		741-93
Kocour Co 4800 S St Louis Ave *Web:* www.kocour.net	Chicago	IL	60632	773-847-1111	847-3399	500
KOCP-FM 95.9 (CR) 2284 S Victoria Ave	Ventura	CA	93003	805-339-9590		645

Phone | Fax | Class

KODA (Kentucky Organ Donor Affiliates)
10160 Linn Station Rd .... Louisville KY 40223 502-581-9511 589-5157 545
TF: 800-525-3456 ■ *Web:* www.kyorgandonor.org

Kodiak Electric Assn Inc
515 E Marine Way.. Kodiak AK 99615 907-486-7700 245
Web: www.kodiakelectric.com

Kodiak Island Borough 710 Mill Bay Rd .... Kodiak AK 99615 907-486-9300 338
Web: www.kodiakak.us

Kodiak Venture Partners
Wellesley Office Park 80 William St
Ste 260.. Wellesley MA 02481 781-672-2500 672-2501 792
Web: www.kodiakvp.com

KODS-FM 103.7 (Oldies)
961 Matley Ln Ste 120 .... Reno NV 89502 775-829-1964 825-3183 645-133
TF: 855-354-9111 ■ *Web:* www.river1037.com

KODZ-FM 99.1 (CR) 1465 W Seventh Ave.......... Eugene OR 97401 541-284-3600 645-55
Web: www.kool991.com

Koegel Meats Inc 3400 W Bristol Rd............... Flint MI 48507 810-238-3685 238-2467 296-26
TF: 800-678-1962 ■ *Web:* www.koegelmeats.com

Koehler Instrument Company Inc
1595 Sycamore Ave .... Bohemia NY 11716 631-589-3800 743
Web: www.koehlerinstrument.com

Koehler Lighting Products
380 Stewart Rd .... Hanover Township PA 18706 570-825-1900 825-7108 439
TF Cust Svc: 800-788-1696 ■ *Web:* www.flashlight.com

Koellmann Gear Corp 8 Industrial Pk........... Waldwick NJ 07463 201-447-0200 709
Web: www.koellmann.com

Koenig Jacobsen LLP 16300 Bake Pkwy........... Irvine CA 92618 949-756-0700 428
TF: 800-726-0126 ■ *Web:* kjattorneys.com

Koeppel Direct Inc
16200 Dallas Pkwy Ste 270 .... Dallas TX 75248 972-732-6110 7
Web: koeppeldirect.com

Koerner Distributors Inc
1305 W Wabash St PO Box 67 .... Effingham IL 62401 217-347-7113 347-8736 81-1
Web: www.koernerdistributor.com

Koerner Ford of Syracuse Inc
805 W Genesee St .... Syracuse NY 13204 315-474-4275 57
Web: www.koernerford.net

Koers-turgeon Consulting Service Inc
2000 Ridgeview Rd.................................. Salina KS 67401 785-825-8192 196
TF: 800-557-7509 ■ *Web:* beef4u.com

Koeze Co PO Box 9470.................... Grand Rapids MI 49509 800-555-9688 817-0147* 296-8
**Fax Area Code:* 866 ■ *TF:* 800-555-9688 ■ *Web:* www.koeze.com

Kofax PLC 15211 Laguna Canyon Rd.............. Irvine CA 92618 949-783-1000 727-3144 178-8
Web: www.kofax.com

Koger Ctr for the Arts
1051 Greene St............................. Columbia SC 29201 803-777-7500 777-9774 572
TF: 800-231-2222 ■ *Web:* www.kogercenterforthearts.com

Koger/Air Corp PO Box 2098................ Martinsville VA 24113 276-638-8821 151
TF: 800-368-2096 ■ *Web:* www.kogerair.com

KOGO-AM 600 (N/T)
9660 Granite Ridge Dr Ste 100.............. San Diego CA 92123 858-292-2000 645-144
Web: kogo.iheart.com

Kohala Historical Sites State Monument
Kalanimoku Bldg1151 Punchbowl St........... Honolulu HI 96813 808-974-6200 565
Web: dlnr.hawaii.gov/dsp

Kohala Spa 69-425 Waikoloa Beach Dr.......... Waikoloa HI 96738 808-886-2828 886-2953 706
Web: www.kohalaspa.com

Kohl & Frisch Ltd 7622 Keele St................ Concord ON L4K2R5 800-265-2520 231
TF: 800-265-2520 ■ *Web:* www.kohlandfrisch.com

Kohl's Corp
N 56 W 17000 Ridgewood Dr.......... Menomonee Falls WI 53051 262-703-7000 229
NYSE: KSS ■ *TF:* 855-564-5705 ■ *Web:* www.kohls.com

Kohlberg Capital Corp
295 Madison Ave 6th Fl .... New York NY 10017 212-455-8300 983-7654 690
Web: www.kohlbergcapital.com

Kohler Canada Company Hytec Plumbing Products Div
4150 Spallumcheen Dr........................ Armstrong BC V0E1B6 250-546-3067 546-3170 610
TF: 800-871-8311 ■ *Web:* www.hytec.ca

Kohler Co Inc 444 Highland Dr.................. Kohler WI 53044 920-457-4441 459-1826* 185
**Fax:* Mktg ■ *TF:* 800-456-4537 ■ *Web:* kohler.com

Kohler Engines 444 Highland Dr................ Kohler WI 53044 920-457-4441 459-1826* 262
**Fax:* Sales ■ *TF:* 800-544-2444 ■ *Web:* power.kohler.com/na-en/engines

Kohler Waters Spa 444 Highlands Dr.......... Kohler WI 53044 920-457-7777 707
TF: 866-928-3777 ■ *Web:* www.americanclubresort.com

Kohler-Andrae State Park
1020 Beach Pk Ln.......................... Sheboygan WI 53081 920-451-4080 451-4086 565
Web: dnr.wi.gov/topic/parks/name/kohlerandrae

KOHL-FM 89.3 (CHR) 43600 Mission Blvd........ Fremont CA 94539 510-659-6221 659-6001 645
TF: 800-870-6397 ■ *Web:* www.kohlradio.com

Kohli & Kaliher Assoc Inc
2244 Baton Rouge Ave .... Lima OH 45805 419-227-1135 261
Web: kohlikaliher.com

Kohll's Pharmacy & Homecare Inc
12759 Q St.................................. Omaha NE 68137 402-895-6812 238
Web: www.kohlls.com

Kohltech International Ltd
583 MacElmon Rd .... Debert NS B0M1G0 902-662-3100 752
TF: 800-565-4396 ■ *Web:* www.kohltech.com

Kohn Pedersen Fox Assoc PC
11 W 42nd St .... New York NY 10036 212-977-6500 956-2526 261
Web: www.kpf.com

Kohnami 313 S Guadalupe St.................... Santa Fe NM 87501 505-984-2002 671
Web: kohnamisantafe.com

Kohner Mann & Kailas SC
Washington Bldg 4650 N Port Washington Rd... Milwaukee WI 53212 414-962-5110 428
Web: www.kmksc.com

Kohnstamm Communications
400 Robert St N Ste 1450.................. Saint Paul MN 55101 651-228-9141 636
Web: kohnstamm.com

Kohrs Lonnemann Heil Engineers Psc
1538 Alexandria Pk........................ Ft Thomas KY 41075 859-442-8050 261

KOI Auto Parts
2701 Spring Grove Ave..................... Cincinnati OH 45225 513-357-2400 723-9204 54
TF: 800-354-0408 ■ *Web:* www.koiautoparts.com

Koibito 1707 Harrison Ave NW.................. Olympia WA 98502 360-352-4751 671
Web: koibitosushi.com

Koike Aronson Inc
635 W Main St PO Box 307 .... Arcade NY 14009 585-492-2400 457-3517 455
TF: 800-252-5232 ■ *Web:* www.koike.com

KOIN-TV Ch 6 (CBS)
222 SW Columbia St .... Portland OR 97201 503-464-0600 741-103
Web: www.koin.com

KoinzMedia Inc
1851 McCarthy Blvd Ste 101 .... Milpitas CA 95035 408-434-5927 387
Web: www.rewardspay.com

Kois Bros Equipment Company Inc
5200 Colorado Blvd .... Commerce CO 80022 303-298-7370 386
TF: 800-672-6010 ■ *Web:* www.koisbrothers.com

KOIT-FM 96.5 (AC)
201 Third St Ste 1200................. San Francisco CA 94103 415-777-0965 645-145
Web: www.koit.com

Kojak's House of Ribs 2808 W Gandy Blvd........ Tampa FL 33611 813-837-3774 671
Web: kojaksbbq.net

Koji 17 Asylum St .... Hartford CT 06103 860-247-5654 671

Koji Osakaya 606 SW Broadway .... Portland OR 97205 503-294-1169 671
Web: www.koji.com

Kokee State Park 3060 Eiwa St Rm 306........... Lihue HI 96766 808-274-3444 565
Web: dlnr.hawaii.gov/dsp/parks/kauai/kokee-state-park

KOKH-TV Ch 25 (Fox)
1228 E Wilshire Blvd .... Oklahoma City OK 73111 405-843-2525 478-4343 741-93
Web: www.okcfox.com

KOKI-TV Ch 23 (Fox) 2625 S Memorial Dr .... Tulsa OK 74129 918-491-0023 741-138
Web: www.fox23.com

Kokkari Estiatorio
200 Jackson St...................... San Francisco CA 94111 415-981-0983 982-0983 671
Web: www.kokkari.com

KoKo Fitness Inc
300 Ledgewood Pl Ste 200.................. Rockland MA 02370 781-753-9495 354
Web: www.kokofitclub.com

Koko Inn 5201 Ave Q .... Lubbock TX 79412 806-747-2591 379

Kokomo Opalescent Glass Co
1310 S Market St .... Kokomo IN 46902 765-457-8136 459-5177 329
TF: 877-475-6329 ■ *Web:* www.kog.com

Kokomo Tribune (KT)
300 N Union St PO Box 9014................ Kokomo IN 46901 765-459-3121 854-6733 532-2
TF: 800-382-0696 ■ *Web:* www.kokomotribune.com

Kokomo/Howard County Chamber of Commerce
325 N Main St .... Kokomo IN 46901 765-457-5301 452-4564 139
Web: greaterkokomo.com

Kokomo-Howard County Public Library
220 N Union St............................ Kokomo IN 46901 765-457-3242 457-3683 434-3
TF: 800-837-0971 ■ *Web:* www.kokomo.lib.in.us

Kokosing Construction Company Inc
17531 Waterford Rd PO Box 226 .... Fredericktown OH 43019 740-694-6315 694-1481 188-4
TF: 800-800-6315 ■ *Web:* www.kokosing.biz

Kokusai Semiconductor Equipment Corp
2460 N First St Ste 290 .... San Jose CA 95131 408-456-2750 456-2760 695
TF: 800-800-5321 ■ *Web:* www.ksec.com

KOKY-FM 102.1 (Urban)
700 Wellington Hills Rd .... Little Rock AR 72211 501-401-0200 645-91
Web: www.koky.com

KOKZ-FM 105.7 (Oldies)
514 Jefferson St .... Waterloo IA 50701 319-234-2200 645
TF: 800-845-1955 ■ *Web:* 1057kokz.com

KOLA-FM 99.9 (Clas)
1940 Orange Tree Ln Ste 200................ Redlands CA 92374 909-793-3554 645
TF: 800-996-9591 ■ *Web:* www.kolafm.com

Kolar Corp 412 S Washington Ste 200.......... Royal Oak MI 48067 248-543-0500 261
Web: kolarcorp.com

Kolberg-Pioneer Inc 700 W 21st St............. Yankton SD 57078 605-665-9311 207

Kolcraft Enterprises Inc
10832 NC Hwy 211 E .... Aberdeen NC 28315 910-944-9345 471
TF Cust Svc: 800-453-7673 ■ *Web:* www.kolcraft.com

KOLD-TV Ch 13 (CBS)
7831 N Business Pk Dr........................ Tucson AZ 85743 520-744-1313 744-5235 741-137
TF: 800-564-6253 ■ *Web:* www.tucsonnewsnow.com

Kolene Corp 12890 Westwood Ave .... Detroit MI 48223 313-273-9220 273-5207 145
TF: 800-521-4182 ■ *Web:* www.kolene.com

Koler Wealth Management 6400 Pearl Rd........ Parma OH 44130 440-884-7042 401
TF: 800-529-2007 ■ *Web:* www.kolerfinancialgroup.com

Kolkhorst Petroleum Co
1685 E Washington........................ Navasota TX 77868 936-825-6868 870-3355 316
TF: 800-548-6671 ■ *Web:* www.kolkhorst.com

Kollabra 2422 Lindbergh St .... Auburn CA 95602 530-887-1258 195
Web: www.kollabra.com

Koller & Company LLP
206 S Iowa Ave.......................... Washington IA 52353 319-653-6561 2
Web: kollerandcompany.com

Koller Craft Plastic Products
1400 S Old Hwy PO Box 718 .... Fenton MO 63026 636-343-9220 343-1034 661
Web: www.koller-craft.com

Kollmann Monumental Works Inc
1915 W Div St .... Saint Cloud MN 56301 320-251-8010 724
TF: 800-659-8010 ■ *Web:* www.kollmann.com

Kollmorgen Corp 203A W Rock Rd.............. Radford VA 24141 540-633-3545 731-5647 518
Web: www.kollmorgen.com

Kollmorgen Corp Electro-Optical Div
50 Prince St .... NorthHampton MA 01060 413-586-2330 586-1324* 544
**Fax:* Sales ■ *Web:* www2.l-3com.com

Kollsman Inc 220 Daniel Webster Hwy .... Merrimack NH 03054 603-889-2500 529
TF: 800-772-9603 ■ *Web:* www.elbitsystems-us.com

Kolltan Pharmaceuticals Inc
300 George St Ste 530...................... New Haven CT 06511 203-773-3000 231
Web: www.kolltan.com

Kolmar Americas Inc
10 Middle St PH.......................... Bridgeport CT 06604 203-873-2051 169
Web: www.kolmargroup.com

Kolmar Laboratories Inc
20 W King St .... Port Jervis NY 12771 845-856-5311 214
Web: www.kolmar.com

KOLN-TV Ch 10 (CBS) 840 N 40th............... Lincoln NE 68503 402-467-4321 467-9210 741-74
TF: 800-475-1011 ■ *Web:* www.1011now.com

Kolomoki Mounds State Historic Park
205 Indian Mounds Rd...................... Blakely GA 39823 229-724-2150 565
Web: www.gastateparks.org

	Phone	Fax	Class
Kolosso Toyota 3000 W Wisconsin Ave ... Appleton WI 54914	920-738-3666		57
TF: 877-756-2297 ■ *Web:* www.kolossotoyota.com			
Kolossos Printing Inc			
2055 W Stadium Blvd ... Ann Arbor MI 48103	734-994-5400		627
TF: 800-928-2086 ■ *Web:* kolossosprinting.com			
KOLO-TV Ch 8 (ABC) 4850 Ampere Dr ... Reno NV 89502	775-858-8888	858-8855*	741-107
*Fax: News Rm ■ *Web:* www.kolotv.com			
Kolpak 2915 Tennessee Ave N ... Parsons TN 38363	731-847-5328	847-5387	664
TF: 800-826-7036 ■ *Web:* www.kolpak.com			
Kolpin Powersports 9955 59th Ave N ... Plymouth MN 55442	920-928-3118	928-3687*	710
*Fax: Cust Svc ■ *TF:* 877-956-5746 ■ *Web:* www.kolpin.com/powersports			
KOLR-TV Ch 10 (CBS) 2650 E Div St ... Springfield MO 65803	417-862-1010	831-4209	741-130
Web: ozarksfirst.com			
Kolstad Company Inc 8501 Naples St NE ... Blaine MN 55449	763-792-1033		62-5
TF: 800-233-7560 ■ *Web:* www.kolstadco.com			
Kom International			
300 St-Sacrement Ste 307 ... Montreal QC H2Y1X4	514-849-4000	849-8888	449
Web: www.komintl.com			
KOMA-FM 92.5 (Oldies)			
400 E Britton Rd ... Oklahoma City OK 73114	405-478-5104		645-114
Web: www.komaradio.com			
Komar Industries Inc			
4425 Marketing Pl ... Groveport OH 43125	614-836-2366		454
TF: 800-331-0183 ■ *Web:* www.komarindustries.com			
Komatsu America Industries LLC			
1701 W Golf Rd Ste 300 ... Rolling Meadows IL 60008	847-437-3888	437-1811	386
Web: www.komatsupress.com			
Komax Corp			
1100 Corporate Grove Dr ... Buffalo Grove IL 60089	847-537-6640		454
Web: www.komaxusa.com			
Kombi Ltd 6 Thompson Dr ... Essex Junction VT 05452	802-879-3369		195
Web: www.kombicanada.com			
Komegashi 103 Montgomery St ... Jersey City NJ 07302	201-433-4567		671
Web: www.komegashi.com			
Komet Of America Inc			
2050 Mitchell Blvd ... Schaumburg IL 60193	847-923-8400	865-6638*	621
*Fax Area Code: 800 ■ *TF:* 800-865-6638 ■ *Web:* www.komet.com			
Komi 1509 17th St NW ... Washington DC 20036	202-332-9200	330-5909	671
Web: www.komirestaurant.com			
Kominiarek Bressler Harvick & Gudmundson LLC			
33 N Dearborn St Ste 1310 ... Chicago IL 60602	312-322-1111	782-1432	428
Web: www.kbhglaw.com			
Komisar Brady & Company LLP			
135 S 84th St Ste 200 ... Milwaukee WI 53214	414-271-3966		2
Web: www.komisarbrady.com			
Komline-Sanderson Engineering Corp			
12 Holland Ave ... Peapack NJ 07977	908-234-1000	234-9487	386
TF: 800-225-5457 ■ *Web:* www.komline.com			
Komo Machine Inc 1 Gusmer Dr ... Lakewood NJ 08701	732-719-6222		683
TF: 800-255-5670 ■ *Web:* www.komo.com			
KOMO-AM 1000 (N/T)			
140 Fourth Ave N Ste 340 ... Seattle WA 98109	206-404-4000		645-150
Web: www.komonews.com			
KOMO-TV Ch 4 (ABC) 140 Fourth Ave N ... Seattle WA 98109	206-404-4000	404-4422	741-123
Web: www.komonews.com			
KOMP-FM 92.3 (Rock)			
8755 W Flamingo Rd ... Las Vegas NV 89147	702-876-3692		645-88
Web: www.komp.com			
KomTeK Technologies 40 Rockdale St ... Worcester MA 01606	508-853-4500	853-2753	483
TF: 800-458-9887 ■ *Web:* www.komtektech.com			
KOMU-TV Ch 8 (NBC) 5550 Hwy 63 S ... Columbia MO 65201	573-884-6397		741
TF: 800-286-3932 ■ *Web:* www.komu.com			
Kona Grill & Sushi Bar			
7014 E Camelback Rd ... Scottsdale AZ 85251	480-429-1100		671
Web: konagrill.com			
Kona Grill Inc			
7150 E Camelback Rd Ste 220 ... Scottsdale AZ 85251	480-922-8100	991-6811	670
NASDAQ: KONA ■ *TF:* 866-328-5662 ■ *Web:* www.konagrill.com			
Kona International Airport			
73-200 Kupipi St ... Kailua-Kona HI 96740	808-327-9520	838-8067	27
TF: 800-321-3712 ■ *Web:* www.hawaii.gov/koa			
Kona Jack's Fish Market & Sushi Bar			
9419 N Meridian St ... Indianapolis IN 46260	317-843-1609	571-6987	671
Web: jacksarebetter.net			
Kona Kai Resort			
1551 Shelter Island Dr ... San Diego CA 92106	619-221-8000		379
TF: 800-566-2524 ■ *Web:* www.resortkonakai.com			
Kona Sports Ctr 103 E Rio Grande Ave ... Wildwood NJ 08260	609-522-7899		711
Web: www.konasurfco.com			
Kona-Kohala Chamber of Commerce			
75-5737 Kuakini Hwy Ste 208 ... Kailua-Kona HI 96740	808-329-1758	329-8564	139
TF: 800-353-5846 ■ *Web:* www.kona-kohala.com			
Konami Gaming Inc 585 Trade Ctr Dr ... Las Vegas NV 89119	702-616-1400		322
TF: 866-544-7568 ■ *Web:* www.gaming.konami.com/corporate/home.aspx			
Konarka Technologies Inc			
116 John St Third Fl Ste 12 ... Lowell MA 01852	978-569-1400		610
Konecranes America 7300 Chippewa Blvd ... Houston TX 77086	281-445-2225	445-9355	470
TF: 800-231-0241 ■ *Web:* www.konecranesusa.com			
KONE-FM 101.1 (Rock)			
33 Briercroft Office Pk ... Lubbock TX 79412	806-762-3000		645-94
Web: www.rock101.fm			
Koneta Inc 1400 Lunar Dr ... Wapakoneta OH 45895	419-739-4200	739-4247	676
TF: 800-331-0775 ■ *Web:* knrubber.com			
Kongregate Inc			
660 Mission St Ste 400 ... San Francisco CA 94105	415-618-0087		637-10
Web: www.kongregate.com			
Kongsberg Maritime Inc			
5373 W Sam Houston Pkwy N Ste 200 ... Houston TX 77041	713-329-5580	329-5581	647
TF: 800-947-7737 ■ *Web:* www.km.kongsberg.com			
KONG-TV Ch 16 (Ind) 333 Dexter Ave N ... Seattle WA 98109	206-448-5555	448-4525	741-123
Web: www.king5.com			
Koni Ameri Tech Services Inc			
15 Serina Dr ... Plainsboro NJ 08536	732-226-0727		177
Web: www.katsi.com			
KONI North America			
1961-A International Way ... Hebron KY 41048	859-586-4100	334-3340	60
TF: 800-965-5664 ■ *Web:* www.koni-na.com			
Koniag Services Inc			
4100 Lafayette Dr Ste 303 ... Chantilly VA 20151	703-488-9300		225
Web: www.ksikoniag.com			
Konica Minolta Business Solutions USA Inc			
100 Williams Dr ... Ramsey NJ 07446	201-825-4000		589
Web: www.kmbs.konicaminolta.us			
Konica Minolta Medical Imaging			
411 Newark Pompton Tpke ... Wayne NJ 07470	973-633-1500	523-7408	382
Web: konicaminolta.us			
Konicom Inc 1819 J St ... Sacramento CA 95811	916-441-7373		175
TF: 800-293-0703 ■ *Web:* www.konicom.com			
Konocti Harbor Resort & Spa			
8727 Soda Bay Rd ... Kelseyville CA 95451	707-279-4281		378
Web: www.konoctiharbor.com			
Konop Cos 1725 Industrial Dr ... Green Bay WI 54302	920-468-8517		296-34
TF: 800-770-0477 ■ *Web:* www.konopcompanies.com			
Konrad Group Inc 445 King St W 3rd Fl ... Toronto ON M5V1K4	416-551-3684		631
Web: www.konradgroup.com			
Konsultek 2230 Point Blvd Ste 800 ... Elgin IL 60123	847-426-9355		251
Web: www.konsultek.com			
Konsyl Pharmaceuticals Inc			
8050 Industrial Pk Rd ... Easton MD 21601	410-822-5192		582
TF: 800-356-6795 ■ *Web:* www.konsyl.com			
Kontek Industries Inc			
1200 Dawson Rd ... New Madrid MO 63869	573-748-5561		106
Web: www.kontekindustries.com			
Kontiki Beach Resort			
2290 N Fulton Beach Rd ... Rockport TX 78382	361-729-2318	729-3212	378
TF: 800-388-0649 ■ *Web:* www.kontikibeach.com			
Kontos Inc Dba Alexander'S Pharmacy			
505 Nashua Rd ... Dracut MA 01826	978-957-0330		237
Kontron Mobile Computing Inc			
7631 Anagram Dr ... Eden Prairie MN 55344	952-974-7000		173-2
TF: 880-343-5396 ■ *Web:* kontron.com			
Koochiching County			
715 Fourth St ... International Falls MN 56649	218-283-1152	283-1151	338
Web: www.co.koochiching.mn.us			
KOOL 105.5			
3071 Continental Dr ... West Palm Beach FL 33407	561-616-6600	616-6677	645-173
TF: 888-415-1055 ■ *Web:* 1055online.iheart.com			
KOOL-FM 100.7 (Oldies)			
3911 S First St ... Abilene TX 79605	325-676-5100		645-1
Web: koolfmabilene.com			
KOOL-FM 94.5 (Oldies)			
840 N Central Ave ... Phoenix AZ 85004	602-260-9494	440-6530	645-123
TF: 800-222-4357 ■ *Web:* kool.cbslocal.com			
Kooltronic Inc			
30 Pennington-Hopewell Rd ... Pennington NJ 08534	609-466-3400	466-1114	14
Web: www.kooltronic.com			
Koonce Securities Inc			
6550 Rock Spring Dr Ste 600 ... Bethesda MD 20817	301-897-9700		401
TF: 800-368-2806 ■ *Web:* www.koonce.net			
Koons Ford of Annapolis Inc			
2540 Riva Rd ... Annapolis MD 21401	410-224-2100		57
TF: 888-313-5524 ■ *Web:* www.koonsford.com			
Koontz-Wagner Electric Company Inc			
3801 Voorde Dr ... South Bend IN 46628	574-232-2051		189-4
TF: 800-345-2051 ■ *Web:* www.koontz-wagner.com			
Koopman Lumber Company Inc			
665 Church St ... Whitinsville MA 01588	508-234-4545		752
TF: 800-836-4545 ■ *Web:* www.koopmanlumber.com			
Koopman Ostbo Inc 412 NW Eighth Ave ... Portland OR 97209	503-223-2168		4
Web: koopmanostbo.com			
Koops Inc 987 Productions Ct ... Holland MI 49423	616-395-0230		261
Web: koops.com			
Kooser State Park 943 Glades Pk ... Somerset PA 15501	814-445-8673		565
Web: www.dcnr.state.pa.us			
Kootenai County			
451 N Government Way ... Coeur d'Alene ID 83814	208-446-1000	446-1188	338
TF: 800-325-7940 ■ *Web:* www.co.kootenai.id.us			
Kootenai Electric Co-op Inc			
2451 W Dakota Ave ... Hayden ID 83835	208-765-1200	772-5858	245
TF: 800-240-0459 ■ *Web:* www.kec.com			
Kootenay Boundary Regional Hospital			
1200 Hospital Bench ... Trail BC V1R4M1	250-368-3311		374-2
TF: 800-739-7367 ■ *Web:* www.interiorhealth.ca			
Kootenay Savings Financial			
300 - 1199 Cedar Ave ... Trail BC V1R4B8	250-368-2686		401
Web: www.kscu.com			
Koozoo Inc 880 Harrison St ... San Francisco CA 94107	415-778-6374		387
Kopachuck State Park			
10712 56th St NW ... Gig Harbor WA 98335	253-265-3606		565
Web: www.parks.wa.gov			
Kop-Coat Inc			
436 Seventh Ave 1850 Koppers Bldg ... Pittsburgh PA 15219	412-227-2426	227-2618	550
TF: 800-221-4466 ■ *Web:* www.kop-coat.com			
Kope & Associates LLC			
3900 Market St Ste 201 ... Camp Hill PA 17011	717-761-7573		428
Web: www.kopelaw.com			
Kopf Builders Inc			
420 Avon Belden Rd ... Avon Lake OH 44012	440-933-6908	933-6956	187
TF: 888-933-5673 ■ *Web:* www.kopf.net			
Kopin Corp 125 N Dr ... Westborough MA 01581	508-870-5959		696
NASDAQ: KOPN ■ *Web:* www.kopin.com			
Koplar Communications International Inc			
50 Maryland Dr Ste 300 ... Saint Louis MO 63108	314-345-1000		224
Web: www.koplar.com			
KOPN-FM 89.5 (Var) 915 E Broadway ... Columbia MO 65201	573-874-1139	499-1662	645
TF: 800-895-5676 ■ *Web:* www.kopn.org			
Kopp Drug 1405 13th Ave ... Altoona PA 16601	814-949-9512		237
Kopp Funds 7701 France Ave S ... Minneapolis MN 55435	952-841-0480		528
Koppers Inc 436 Seventh Ave ... Pittsburgh PA 15219	412-227-2001	227-2333	818
NYSE: KOP ■ *TF:* 800-385-4406 ■ *Web:* www.koppers.com			
KOPX-TV Ch 62 (I)			
13424 Railway Dr ... Oklahoma City OK 73114	405-478-9562		741-93
Web: ionmedia.tv			
Kor Electronics 10855 Business Ctr Dr ... Cypress CA 90630	714-898-8200		529
Web: www.mrcy.com			

	Phone	Fax	Class
KOR Water Inc 95 Enterprise Ste 310 ..... Aliso Viejo CA 92656 *TF:* 877-708-7567 ■ *Web:* www.korwater.com	714-708-7567		124
Koral Industries Inc 1504 S Kaufman St ..... Ennis TX 75119 *TF:* 800-627-2441 ■ *Web:* www.koralco.com	972-875-6555	875-9558	375
Korber Hats Inc 394 Kilburn St ..... Fall River MA 02724 *TF Cust Svc:* 800-428-9911 ■ *Web:* korberhats.com	508-672-7033	673-0762	155-9
Kord Technologies Inc 1101 Mcmurtrie Dr NW Bldg A ..... Huntsville AL 35806 *Web:* kordtechnologies.com	256-489-2346		177
Kordes Retreat Ctr 841 E 14th St ..... Ferdinand IN 47532 *TF:* 800-880-2777 ■ *Web:* www.thedome.org	812-367-2777		673
Kore Inc 355 Madison Ave ..... Morristown NJ 07960 *Web:* www.korecorp.com	973-883-0308		535
KORE Telematics Inc 3700 Mansell Rd Ste 250 ..... Alpharetta GA 30022 *Web:* www.koretelematics.com	203-478-5281		387
Korea House 2598 Royal Ln ..... Dallas TX 75229 *Web:* www.koreahousedallas.com	972-243-0434		671
Korea House 6410 Charlotte Pk Ste 108 ..... Nashville TN 37209	615-352-2790		671
Korea National Tourism Organization 2 Executive Dr Ste 750 ..... Fort Lee NJ 07024 *TF:* 800-868-7567 ■ *Web:* english.visitkorea.or.kr	201-585-0909	585-9041	775
Korea Republic of 335 E 45th St ..... New York NY 10017 *Web:* www.un.int	212-439-4000	986-1083	784
Consulate General 3243 Wilshire Blvd ..... Los Angeles CA 90010 *Web:* south-korea.embassy-online.net	213-385-9300	385-1849	257
Consulate General 460 Pk Ave ..... New York NY 10022	646-674-6000		257
Consulate General 2033 Sixth Ave Ste 1125 ..... Seattle WA 98121	206-441-1011		257
Consulate General 2756 Pali Hwy ..... Honolulu HI 96817 *Web:* usa-honolulu.mofat.go.kr	808-595-6109	595-3046	257
Consulate General 455 N City Front Plaza Dr NBC Tower Ste 2700 .. Chicago IL 60611 *Web:* usa-chicago.mofa.go.kr/english/am/usa-chicago/main	312-822-9485	822-9849	257
Korea Times Los Angeles Inc, The 4525 Wilshire Blvd ..... Los Angeles CA 90010 *Web:* www.koreatimes.com	323-692-2000		532-3
Korean Air 6101 W Imperial Hwy ..... Los Angeles CA 90045 *TF:* 800-438-5000 ■ *Web:* www.koreanair.com	310-417-5200		25
Korean Air Skypass 1813 Wilshire Blvd Ste 300 ..... Los Angeles CA 90057 *TF:* 800-438-5000 ■ *Web:* www.koreanair.com	213-484-1900		26
Korean American Coalition (KAC) 3727 W Sixth St Ste 305 ..... Los Angeles CA 90020 *Web:* www.kacla.org	213-365-5999	380-7990	48-14
Korean Barbeque Swan 2061 N Oxnard Blvd ..... Oxnard CA 93036	805-278-9611		671
Korean Chamber of Commerce 3435 Wilshire Blvd Ste 2450 ..... Los Angeles CA 90010	213-480-1115		138
Korean Chamber of Commerce & Industry in the USA Inc 460 Pk Ave Ste 410 ..... New York NY 10022 *Web:* www.kocham.org	212-644-0140	644-9106	138
Korean House 3219 Snyder Ave ..... Cheyenne WY 82001	307-638-7938		671
Korean Palace 2297A Stevens Creek Blvd ..... San Jose CA 95128	408-947-8600		671
Korean War Veterans Memorial 900 Ohio Dr SW 900 Ohio Dr SW ..... Washington DC 20024 *Web:* www.nps.gov/kowa	202-426-6841		50-4
Ko-Rec-Type 67 Kent Ave ..... Brooklyn NY 11249	718-782-2601		628
Korein Tillery LLC 505 N Seveth St Ste 3600 ..... Saint Louis MO 63101 *Web:* www.koreintillery.com	314-241-4844		445
Koren Rogers 4 W Red Oak Ln Ste 312 ..... White Plains NY 10604 *Web:* www.korenrogers.com	914-686-5800		260
Koreshan State Historic Site 3800 Corkscrew Rd ..... Estero FL 33928 *Web:* www.floridastateparks.org	239-992-0311	992-1607	565
Korey Kay & Partners 130 Fifth Ave ..... New York NY 10011 *TF:* 800-264-8590 ■ *Web:* www.koreykay.com	212-620-4300		4
Korg USA Inc 316 S Service Rd ..... Melville NY 11747 *Web:* www.korg.com	631-390-6500	390-6501	527
Kor-it Inc 1964 Auburn Blvd ..... Sacramento CA 95815 *TF:* 888-727-4560 ■ *Web:* www.kor-it.com	888-727-4560		190
Korman Healthcare LLC 5783 W Erie St ..... Chandler AZ 85226 *TF:* 800-250-4346 ■ *Web:* www.kormanhealthcare.com	480-365-0222		363
Korn Consulting Group Inc 151 E 83rd St Apt 4ab ..... New York NY 10028 *Web:* www.kornconsulting.com	212-734-6200		196
Korn/Ferry International 1900 Ave of the Stars Ste 2600 ..... Los Angeles CA 90067 *NYSE: KFY* ■ *TF:* 877-345-3610 ■ *Web:* www.kornferry.com	310-552-1834	553-6452	266
Korney Board Aids Sporting 312 Harrison Ave ..... Roxton TX 75477 *TF:* 800-842-7772 ■ *Web:* www.kbacoach.com	903-346-3269		711
Kornhauser Health Sciences Library *University of Louisville* 500 S Preston St ..... Louisville KY 40292 *Web:* www.louisville.edu	502-852-5771	852-1631	434-1
Kornit Digital North America Inc 10541 n commerce st ..... Mequon WI 53092 *Web:* www.kornit.com	262-518-0200		627
Kornitzer Capital Management Inc 5420 W 61st Pl ..... Mission KS 66205 *Web:* www.kornitzercapitalmanagement.com	913-677-7778		401
Korns Galvanizing Co 75 Bridge St ..... Johnstown PA 15902 *Web:* kornsgalvanizing.com	814-535-3293		481
Kornylak Corp 400 Heaton St ..... Hamilton OH 45011 *TF:* 800-837-5676 ■ *Web:* www.kornylak.com	513-863-1277	863-7644	470
Korsch America Inc 18 Bristol Dr ..... South Easton MA 02375 *TF:* 800-567-7241 ■ *Web:* www.korschamerica.com	508-238-9080		111
Korshak Kracoff Kong & Sugano LLP 1640 S Sepulveda Blvd Ste 520 ..... Los Angeles CA 90025 *Web:* www.kkks.com	310-996-2340		428

	Phone	Fax	Class
Korte Co, The 9225 W Flamingo Rd Ste 100 ..... Las Vegas NV 89147 *Web:* www.korteco.com	702-228-9551	228-5852	186
Korth Companies Inc, The 9101 Gaither Rd ..... Gaithersburg MD 20877 *Web:* www.korthcos.com	301-921-9500		186
Kortick Manufacturing Co 2230 Davis Ct ..... Hayward CA 94545 *TF:* 800-329-1900 ■ *Web:* www.kortick.com	510-856-3600		816
Kosakura & Assoc 3 Holland ..... Irvine CA 92618 *TF:* 800-681-5922 ■ *Web:* www.kosakura.com	949-529-3400	529-3411	233
Kosciusko County 121 N Lake St ..... Warsaw IN 46580 *TF:* 800-840-8757 ■ *Web:* www.kcgov.com	574-372-2331		338
Kosciusko County Rural Electric Membership Corp 370 S 250 E ..... Warsaw IN 46582 *Web:* kremc.com	574-267-6331		245
KOSCVB (Saint Tammany Parish Tourist & Convention Commission) 111 Capital Dr ..... Warsaw IN 46582 *TF:* 800-800-6090 ■ *Web:* visitkosciuskocounty.org	574-269-6090	269-2405	206
Koshii Maxelum America Inc 12 Van Kleeck Dr ..... Poughkeepsie NY 12602 *Web:* www.kmamax.com	845-471-0500		499
Koshin America Corp 1218 Remington Rd ..... Schaumburg IL 60173 *TF:* 800-634-4092 ■ *Web:* koshinamerica.com	847-310-0740		641
KOSI-FM 101(AC) 7800 E Orchard Rd Ste 400 ..... Greenwood Village CO 80237 *Web:* www.kosi101.com	303-967-2700		645-47
Kositzka Wicks & Co 5500 Cherokee Ave Ste 400 ..... Alexandria VA 22312 *Web:* www.kwccpa.com	703-642-2700		2
Koski Research Inc 7 joost ave Ste 301 ..... San Francisco CA 94131 *Web:* www.koskiresearch.com	415-334-3400		463
Koskoff, Koskoff & Bieder PC 350 Fairfield Ave ..... Bridgeport CT 06604 *Web:* www.koskoff.com	203-583-8634		428
Kosmos Energy LLC 8176 Park Ln Ste 500 ..... Dallas TX 75231 *Web:* www.kosmosenergy.com	214-445-9600		536
Koss Construction Co 5830 SW Drury Ln ..... Topeka KS 66604 *Web:* kossconstruction.com	785-228-2928	228-2927	188-4
Koss Corp 4129 N Port Washington Ave ..... Milwaukee WI 53212 *NASDAQ: KOSS* ■ *TF:* 800-872-5677 ■ *Web:* www.koss.com	414-964-5000	964-8615	52
Koss Industrial Inc 1943 Commercial Way ..... Green Bay WI 54311 *TF:* 800-844-6261 ■ *Web:* www.kossindustrial.com	920-469-5300		296
Kossuth County 114 W State St ..... Algona IA 50511 *TF:* 800-672-3093 ■ *Web:* www.co.kossuth.ia.us	515-295-2718	295-3071	338
Koss-Winn Bancshares Inc 101 N Main St ..... Buffalo Center IA 50424	641-562-2696		360-2
Kosta's Cafe 4621 W Pk Blvd Ste 100 ..... Plano TX 75093 *Web:* www.kostascafe.com	972-596-8424		671
Koster Industries Inc 40 Daniel St Ste 2 ..... Farmingdale NY 11735 *Web:* www.kosterindustries.com	631-454-1766		41
KOST-FM 103.5 (AC) 3400 W Olive Ave ..... Burbank CA 91505 *Web:* kost1035.iheart.com	818-559-2252	260-9961	645
Kota 518 St Joseph St ..... Rapid City SD 57701	605-342-2000		738
KOTA-TV Ch 3 (ABC) 518 St Joseph St ..... Rapid City SD 57701 *TF:* 866-558-4554 ■ *Web:* www.kotatv.com	605-342-2000		741-106
Kotecki Rock of Ages Memorials 3636 Pearl Rd ..... Cleveland OH 44109 *Web:* www.koteckifamilymemorials.com	216-749-2880		724
Kotin, Crabtree & Strong LLP 1 Bowdoin Sq ..... Boston MA 02114 *Web:* www.kcslegal.com	617-227-7031		428
Kotler Marketing Group 925 15th St NW Ste 400 ..... Washington DC 20005 *Web:* www.kotlermarketing.com	202-331-0555		195
Kotobuki 457 Summer St ..... Stamford CT 06901 *Web:* www.kotobukijapaneserestaurant.com	203-359-4747	357-7522	671
Kotobuki 721 W 21st St ..... Norfolk VA 23517 *Web:* kotobukisushibar.com	757-628-1025		671
Kotter International 5 Bennett St ..... Cambridge MA 02138 *TF:* 855-400-4712 ■ *Web:* www.kotterinternational.com	617-600-6787		463
Kotzebue Electric Assn Inc PO Box 44 ..... Kotzebue AK 99752 *Web:* www.kea.coop	907-442-3491	442-2482	245
Kountry Folks 3653 La Sierra Ave ..... Riverside CA 92505 *Web:* www.kountry.com	951-354-0437	354-7728	671
Koury Engineering & Testing Inc 14280 Euclid Ave ..... Chino CA 91710 *Web:* www.kouryengineering.com	310-851-8685		365
KOUT-FM 98.7 (Ctry) 660 Flormann St Ste 100 ..... Rapid City SD 57701 *TF:* 800-456-0766 ■ *Web:* www.katradio.com	605-343-6161	343-9012	645-132
Kovack Securities Inc 6451 N Federal Hwy # 1201 Ste 1201 ..... Fort Lauderdale FL 33308 *TF:* 800-711-4078 ■ *Web:* www.kovacksecurities.com	954-782-4771	943-7331	690
Kovak Likly Communications 23 Hubbard Rd ..... Wilton CT 06897 *TF:* 800-332-1088 ■ *Web:* www.klcpr.com	203-762-8833		636
Kovalsky-Carr Electric Supply Company Inc 208 St Paul St ..... Rochester NY 14604 *Web:* www.kovalskycarr.com	585-325-1950	546-6904	246
KovalWilliamson 11208 47th Ave W ..... Mukilteo WA 98275 *Web:* www.kwawest.com	425-347-4249		361
Kovash & Dasovick PC 148 W First St ..... Dickinson ND 58601	701-483-1156		2
Kovasys Inc 1800-500 Pl d'Armes ..... Montreal QC H2Y2W2 *TF:* 888-568-2747 ■ *Web:* www.kovasys.com	888-568-2747		260
Kovatch Castings Inc 3743 Tabs Dr ..... Uniontown OH 44685 *Web:* www.kovatchcastings.com	330-896-9944		492
Kovel/Fuller LLC 9925 Jefferson Blvd ..... Culver City CA 90232 *Web:* www.kovelfuller.com	310-841-4444	841-4599	4
Kovensky Daniels 1250 Connecticut Ave NW Ste 200 ..... Washington DC 20036 **Fax Area Code:* 413 ■ *Web:* www.kovdan.com	202-261-3555	832-1838*	266

Name / Address	City	State	Zip	Phone	Fax	Class
Kowa Pharmaceuticals America Inc 530 Industrial Park Blvd *Web:* www.kowapharma.com	Montgomery	Al	36117	334-288-1288		231
Kowal & Associates Inc 620 Massachusetts Ave *Web:* www.kowalassociates.com	Cambridge	MA	02139	617-577-0700	577-0500	737
Kowalski Companies Inc 1261 Grand Ave *Web:* www.kowalskis.com	St. Paul	MN	55105	651-698-3366		345
Kowalski Heat Treating Co 3611 Detroit Ave *Web:* www.khtheat.com	Cleveland	OH	44113	216-631-4411		484
Kowalski Sausage Company Inc 2270 Holbrook Ave *Web:* www.kowality.com	Hamtramck	MI	48212	313-873-8200		296-26
Koyo Restaurant 2275 East 33rd South *Web:* www.koyoslc.com	Salt Lake City	UT	84109	801-466-7111		671
Koza Inc 2910 S Main St *TF:* 800-594-5555 ■ *Web:* www.kozas.com	Pearland	TX	77581	281-485-1462		627
Kozeny-Wagner Inc 951 W Outer Rd *TF:* 800-872-7878 ■ *Web:* www.kozenywagner.com	Arnold	MO	63010	636-296-2012		194
KOZK-TV Ch 21 (PBS) 901 S National Ave *TF:* 866-684-5695 ■ *Web:* www.optv.org	Springfield	MO	65897	417-836-3500	836-3569	741-130
Kozy Heat Fireplace 204 Industrial Park Rd	Lakefield	MN	56150	507-662-6641		361
Kozy's Restaurant 3510 Loop Rd *Web:* www.killionrestaurants.com	Tuscaloosa	AL	35404	205-556-4112		671
KOZZ-FM 105.7 (CR) 2900 Sutro St *Web:* www.kozzradio.com	Reno	NV	89512	775-329-9261	323-1450	645-133
KP Tissue Inc 1900 Minnesota Crt Ste 200 *Web:* www.kptissueinc.com	Mississauga	ON	L5N5R5	905-812-6900		787
K-Paul's Louisiana Kitchen 416 Chartres St *TF:* 800-672-6124 ■ *Web:* www.kpauls.com	New Orleans	LA	70130	504-596-2530		671
KPAZ-TV Ch 21 (TBN) 3551 E McDowell Rd *TF:* 800-447-7235 ■ *Web:* www.tbn.org	Phoenix	AZ	85008	602-273-1477		741-99
KPBS-FM 89.5 (NPR) San Diego State University 5200 Campanile Dr *TF:* 888-399-5727 ■ *Web:* www.kpbs.org	San Diego	CA	92182	619-265-6438	594-3812	645-144
KPBS-TV Ch 15 (PBS) 5200 Campanile Dr *TF:* 888-399-5727 ■ *Web:* www.kpbs.org	San Diego	CA	92182	619-594-1515	594-3812	741-119
KPCB (Kleiner Perkins Caufield & Byers) 2750 Sand Hill Rd *Web:* www.kpcb.com	Menlo Park	CA	94025	650-233-2750	233-0300	792
KPCC-FM 89.3 (NPR) 1570 E Colorado Blvd *TF:* 800-222-5222 ■ *Web:* www.scpr.org	Pasadena	CA	91106	626-585-7000	585-7916	645
KPDQ-FM 93.9 (Rel) 6400 SE Lake Rd Ste 350 *TF:* 800-845-2162 ■ *Web:* www.kpdq.com	Portland	OR	97222	503-786-0600		645-128
KPDX-TV Ch 49 (MNT) 14975 NW Greenbrier Pkwy *TF:* 866-906-1249 ■ *Web:* www.kptv.com	Beaverton	OR	97006	503-906-1249	548-6920	741
KPEL-AM 1420 (Sports) 1749 Bertrand Dr *TF:* 800-324-1108 ■ *Web:* espn1420.com	Lafayette	LA	70506	337-233-6000		645-86
KPEL-FM 105.1 (N/T) 1749 Bertrand Dr *TF:* 800-324-1108 ■ *Web:* www.kpel965.com	Lafayette	LA	70506	337-233-6000		645-86
KPFF Consulting Engineers Inc 1601 Fifth Ave Ste 1600 *Web:* www.kpff.com	Seattle	WA	98101	206-622-5822		261
KPFX-FM 107.9 (CR) 2720 Seventh Ave S *Web:* www.1079thefox.com	Fargo	ND	58103	701-237-4500	235-9082	645-58
KPG PS 3131 Elliott Ave Ste 400 *Web:* www.kpg.com	Seattle	WA	98121	206-286-1640		256
KPIG-FM 107.5 (AAA) 1110 Main St Ste 16 *Web:* www.kpig.com	Watsonville	CA	95076	831-722-9000		645
Kpit Infosystems Inc 33 Wood Ave S Ste 720 *Web:* www.kpit.com	Iselin	NJ	08830	732-321-0921		177
KPLC-TV Ch 7 (NBC) 320 Div St *Web:* www.kplctv.com	Lake Charles	LA	70601	337-439-9071	437-7600	741
KPLM-FM 106.1 (Ctry) 75153 Merle Dr Ste G *TF:* 800-872-7245 ■ *Web:* www.thebig106.com	Palm Desert	CA	92211	760-568-4550		645-119
KPLO-FM 94.5 (Ctry) 214 W Pleasant Dr *TF General:* 800-658-5439 ■ *Web:* www.drgnews.com	Pierre	SD	57501	605-224-8686	224-8984	645-124
KPLO-TV Ch 6 (CBS) 501 S Phillips Ave *TF:* 800-888-5356 ■ *Web:* www.keloland.com	Sioux Falls	SD	57104	605-336-1100		741
KPLZ-FM 101.5 (AC) 140 Fourth Ave N Ste 340 *TF:* 888-821-1015 ■ *Web:* www.star1015.com	Seattle	WA	98109	206-404-4000	404-1015	645-150
KPM VIPER Consulting LLC South Shore Executive Park 10 Forbes Rd *Web:* www.kpm-us.com	Braintree	MA	02184	781-380-3520		260
KPMG International Co-op 345 Park Ave *Web:* corporatefinance.kpmg.us	New York	NY	10154	212-758-9700		70
KPMG LLP 333 Base St Ste 4600 *Web:* www.kpmg.com	Toronto	ON	M5H2S5	416-777-8500	777-8818	194
KPMG LLP US 3 Chestnut Ridge Rd *Web:* www.kpmg.com	Montvale	NJ	07645	201-307-7000		2
KPNT-FM 105.7 (Alt) 401 S 18th St *Web:* 1057thepoint.com	Saint Louis	MO	63103	314-231-1057	621-3000	645-141
KPRC AM 950 2000 W Loop S Ste 300 *Web:* www.kprcradio.com	Houston	TX	77027	713-212-8000		645-75
KPRC-TV Ch 2 (NBC) 8181 SW Fwy *Web:* www.click2houston.com	Houston	TX	77074	713-222-2222	771-4930	741-60
KPRO-AM 1570 (Rel) 7351 Lincoln Ave *TF:* 800-325-3535 ■ *Web:* kpro1570.com	Riverside	CA	92504	951-688-1570	688-7009	645-135
KPRS Construction Services Inc 2850 Saturn St *Web:* www.kprsinc.com	Brea	CA	92821	714-672-0800	672-0871	186
KPRS-FM 103.3 (Urban) 11131 Colorado Ave *Web:* www.kprs.com	Kansas City	MO	64137	816-763-2040	966-1055	645-83
KPRX-FM 89.1 (NPR) 2589 Alluvial Ave *Web:* www.kvpr.org	Clovis	CA	93611	559-862-2480	862-2715	645-64
KPS3 Inc 50 W Liberty St Ste 640 *Web:* kps3.com	Reno	NV	89501	775-686-7439		7
KPSI-AM 920 (N/T) 2100 Tahquitz Canyon Way *Web:* www.newstalk920.com	Palm Springs	CA	92262	760-325-2582		645-119
KPSI-FM 100.5 (AC) 1321 N Gene Autry Trail *Web:* www.mix1005.fm	Palm Springs	CA	92262	760-323-1005		645-119
KPTK-AM 1090 (N/T) 1000 Dexter Ave N Ste 100 *Web:* seattle.cbslocal.com	Seattle	WA	98109	206-805-1100	805-0915	645-150
KPTM 42.2 FM 4625 Farnam St *Web:* www.fox42kptm.com	Omaha	NE	68132	402-554-4282		741-94
KPTS-TV Ch 8 (PBS) 320 W 21 St *TF:* 800-794-8498 ■ *Web:* www.kpts.org	Wichita	KS	67203	316-838-3090	838-8586	741-142
KPTV-TV Ch 12 (Fox) 14975 NW Greenbrier Pkwy *TF:* 866-906-1249 ■ *Web:* www.kptv.com	Beaverton	OR	97006	503-906-1249	548-6920	741
KPVI-TV Ch 6 (NBC) 902 E Sherman St *Web:* www.kpvi.com	Pocatello	ID	83201	208-232-6666	233-6678	741-101
KPVU-FM 91.3 (NPR) Prairie View A & M University MS 1415 *TF:* 877-241-1752 ■ *Web:* pvamu.edu/auxiliaryservices/kpvu	Prairie View	TX	77446	936-261-3750	261-3769	645
KPXD-TV Ch 68 (I) 600 Six Flags Dr Ste 652	Arlington	TX	76011	817-633-6843	633-3176	741
KPXE-TV Ch 50 (I) 4220 Shawnee Mission Pkwy Ste 110 B **Fax Area Code:* 646 ■ *TF:* 888-467-2988 ■ *Web:* ionmedia.com	Fairway	KS	66205	212-757-3100	597-5903*	741
KPXO-TV Ch 66 (I) 875 Waimanu St Ste 630 *TF:* 888-467-2988 ■ *Web:* ionmedia.tv	Honolulu	HI	96813	808-591-1275		741-59
KPXR-TV Ch 47 1957 Blairs Ferry Rd NE *Web:* www.iontelevision.com	Cedar Rapids	IA	52402	319-378-1260		741-23
KQBR-FM 99.5 (Ctry) 4413 82nd St Ste 300 *Web:* lonestar995fm.com	Lubbock	TX	79424	806-798-7078		645-94
KQC (Kilwins Quality Confections Inc) 1050 Bay View Rd *TF:* 888-454-5946 ■ *Web:* www.kilwins.com	Petoskey	MI	49770	888-454-5946		123
KQCA-TV Ch 58 (MNT) 3 Television Cir *TF:* 800-872-7245 ■ *Web:* www.kcra.com	Sacramento	CA	95814	916-446-3333		741-113
KQCH-FM 94.1 (CHR) 10714 Mockingbird Dr *Web:* www.channel941.com	Omaha	NE	68127	402-938-9400		645-115
KQED Inc 50 W San Fernando St Ste 110 *Web:* www.kqed.org	San Jose	CA	95131	415-864-2000		741
KQED-FM 88.5 (NPR) 2601 Mariposa St *TF:* 800-723-3566 ■ *Web:* www.kqed.org	San Francisco	CA	94110	415-864-2000		645-145
KQED-TV Ch 9 (PBS) 2601 Mariposa St *TF:* 866-573-3123 ■ *Web:* www.kqed.org	San Francisco	CA	94110	415-864-2000	553-2254	741-120
KQRC-FM 98.9 (Rock) 7000 Squibb Rd *Web:* www.989therock.com	Mission	KS	66202	913-744-3600		645
KQRS-FM 92.5 (CR) 2000 SE Elm St *Web:* www.92kqrs.com	Minneapolis	MN	55414	612-617-4000		645-101
KQUS-FM 97.5 (Ctry) 125 Corporate Terr *Web:* www.myhotsprings.com	Hot Springs	AR	71913	501-525-9700		645-74
KQV-AM 1410 (N/T) 650 Smithfield St Ste 620 *TF:* 888-272-7229 ■ *Web:* www.kqv.com	Pittsburgh	PA	15222	412-562-5900	562-5903	645-125
KQXR-FM 100.3 (Rock) 5257 Fairview Ave *TF:* 800-505-3967 ■ *Web:* www.xrock.com	Boise	ID	83706	208-344-3511	947-6765	645-22
K&R Negotiation Associates LLC 908 Ethan Allen Hwy *Web:* www.negotiators.com	Ridgefield	CT	06877	203-431-7693		196
KRA International LLC 1810 Clover Rd *TF:* 800-301-4961 ■ *Web:* www.krainternational.com	Mishawaka	IN	46545	574-259-3550	255-1079	247
KRAB-FM 106.1 (Rock) 1100 Mohawk St Ste 280 *Web:* krab.iheart.com	Bakersfield	CA	93309	661-322-9929		645-15
Krabloonik 4250 Divide Rd PO Box 5517 *Web:* www.krabloonik.com	Snowmass Village	CO	81615	970-923-3953		671
Krack Corp 1300 N Arlington Heights Rd Ste 130 *Web:* www.krack.com	Itasca	IL	60143	630-629-7500	250-3537	14
Kraemer Bros Inc 925 Pk Ave *TF:* 800-223-3557 ■ *Web:* www.kraemerbrothers.com	Plain	WI	53577	608-546-2411	546-2509	186
Kraft Chemical Co 1975 N Hawthorne Ave *TF:* 800-345-5200 ■ *Web:* www.kraftchemical.com	Melrose Park	IL	60160	708-345-5200	345-4005	146
Kraft Fluid Systems Inc 14300 Foltz Pkwy *TF:* 800-257-1155 ■ *Web:* www.kraftfluid.com	Strongsville	OH	44149	440-238-5545		641
Kraft Foods North America Inc 3 Lakes Dr *NASDAQ:* KHC ■ *TF:* 800-732-0330 ■ *Web:* www.kraftheinzcompany.com	Northfield	IL	60093	847-646-2000		296-5
Kraft Hat Manufacturers Inc 725 Whittier St *TF:* 800-237-2267 ■ *Web:* www.krafthat.com	Bronx	NY	10474	845-735-6200	735-2299	155-9
Kraft Power Corp 199 Wildwood Ave *TF:* 800-969-6121 ■ *Web:* www.kraftpower.com	Woburn	MA	01801	781-938-9100	933-7812	518
KraftCPAs Pllc 555 Great Cir Rd *Web:* kraftcpas.com	Nashville	TN	37228	615-242-7351		2
Kraft-Engel Management 15233 Ventura Blvd Ste 200 *Web:* www.kraft-engel.com	Sherman Oaks	CA	91403	818-380-1918		731

Listing	Phone	Fax	Class
Kraftmaid Cabinetry Inc 15535 S State Ave PO Box 1055............ Middlefield OH 44062 *TF:* 888-562-7744 ■ *Web:* www.kraftmaid.com	888-562-7744		115
Kraftube Inc 925 E Church Ave................Reed City MI 49677 *Web:* www.kraftube.com	231-832-5562	832-2937	595
Kraftware Corp 270 Cox St......................Roselle NJ 07203 *TF Cust Svc:* 800-221-1728 ■ *Web:* www.kraftwarecorp.com	800-221-1728		607
Kraken Oil & Gas LLC 9821 Katy Fwy Ste 460......................Houston TX 77024 *Web:* www.krakenoil.com	713-360-7705		536
Kramer Accountancy Corp 120 N Topanga Canyon Blvd Ste 111..........Topanga CA 90290 *Web:* kramercpa.com	310-455-9300		2
KRAMER aerotek Inc 580 Utica Ave.............. Boulder CO 80304 *TF:* 800-677-1997 ■ *Web:* www.krameraerotek.com	303-247-1762		196
Kramer Fiduciary Services 1500 Ardmore Blvd Ste 205................. Pittsburgh PA 15221 *Web:* kramerfiduciary.com	412-351-2150		2
Kramer Gehlen & Associates Inc 400 Columbia St Ste 240.................. Vancouver WA 98660 *Web:* kramer-gehlen.com	360-693-1621		261
Kramer Graphics Inc 2408 W Dorothy Ln ....Dayton OH 45439 *TF:* 800-933-8453 ■ *Web:* www.kramergraphics.com	937-296-9600		781
Kramer Laboratories Inc 400 University Dr Ste 400................. Coral Gables FL 33134 *TF:* 800-824-4894 ■ *Web:* www.kramerlabs.com	305-223-1287	223-5510	582
Kramer, Dillof, Livingston & Moore 217 Broadway Fl 10.........................New York NY 10007 *Web:* kdlm.com	212-267-4177		428
Kramig Insulation 323 S Wayne Ave .... Cincinnati OH 45215 *TF:* 888-579-0079 ■ *Web:* www.kramiginsulation.com	513-761-4010		189-9
Krannert Art Museum & Kinkead Pavilion 500 E Peabody Dr........................ Champaign IL 61820 *Web:* www.kam.uiuc.edu	217-333-1861		520
Krannert Ctr for the Performing Arts 500 S Goodwin Ave ....Urbana IL 61801 *TF:* 800-527-2849 ■ *Web:* www.krannertcenter.com	217-333-6700	244-0810	572
Krasl Art Center 707 Lake Blvd............. Saint Joseph MI 49085 *Web:* krasl.org	269-983-0271		522
Kraton Performance Polymers Inc 15710 John F Kennedy Blvd Ste 300............Houston TX 77032 *NYSE:* KRA ■ *TF:* 800-457-2866 ■ *Web:* www.kraton.com	281-504-4950	504-4743	605-2
Kratos Analytical Inc 100 Red Schoolhouse Rd Bldg A......... Chestnut Ridge NY 10977 *Web:* www.kratos.com	845-426-6700		407
Kratos Defense & Security Solutions Inc 4820 Eastgate Mall Ste 200 .... San Diego CA 92121 *TF:* 877-548-7911 ■ *Web:* www.kratosdefense.com	858-332-3700	812-7301	261
Kratos Defense & Security Solutions, Inc. 3061 Industry Dr...........................Lancaster PA 17603 *Fax: Sales ■ *Web:* www.kratosmed.com/page/moved/herley	717-397-2777	397-7079*	504
Kraus & Naimer 760 New Brunswick Rd.......... Somerset NJ 08873 *Web:* www.krausnaimer.com	732-560-1240	560-8823	729
Kraus Global Inc 25 Paquin Rd................Winnipeg MB R2J3V9 *TF:* 800-325-3010 ■ *Web:* www.krausglobal.com	204-663-3601		358
Kraus Manning Inc 7233 Lake Ellenor Dr ....Orlando FL 32809 *Web:* www.kraus-manning.com	407-251-0085		194
Kraus USA Inc 160 Amsler Ave ....Shippenville PA 16254 *Web:* www.krausflooring.com	814-226-9300		361
Kraus-Anderson Co (KA) 523 S Eigth St..........................Minneapolis MN 55404 *Web:* www.krausanderson.com	612-332-7281	332-8739	185
Kraus-Anderson Insurance 420 Gateway Blvd.......................... Burnsville MN 55337 *Web:* www.kainsurance.com	952-707-8200	890-0535	390
Kraus-Anderson Realty Co 4210 W Old Shakopee Rd................. Bloomington MN 55437 *Web:* www.krausanderson.com	952-881-8166		655
Krause Gentle Corp 6400 Westown Pkwy..................West Des Moines IA 50266 *Web:* www.kumandgo.com	515-226-0128		204
Kraushaar Galleries Inc 15 E 71 St Ste 2B ....New York NY 10021 *TF:* 800-291-2513 ■ *Web:* www.kraushaargalleries.com	212-288-2558		42
Kravco Co 234 Mall Blvd............. King of Prussia PA 19406 *Web:* www.kravco.com	610-854-2800		655
Kravet Fabrics Inc 8687 Melrose Ave Ste B624............West Hollywood CA 90069 *Web:* www.kravetcanada.com	310-659-7100		321
Krazan & Assoc Inc 215 W Dakota Ave .... Clovis CA 93612 *Web:* www.krazan.com	559-348-2200	348-2201	261
KRBC-TV Ch 9 (NBC) 4510 S 14th St .... Abilene TX 79605 *Web:* www.bigcountryhomepage.com	325-692-4242		741-1
KRBE-FM 104.1 (CHR) 9801 Westheimer Rd Ste 700.................Houston TX 77042 *TF:* 888-955-2993 ■ *Web:* www.krbe.com	713-266-1000	954-2344	645-75
KRCB FM 5850 Labath Ave..................... Rohnert Park CA 94928 *TF:* 800-656-4673 ■ *Web:* www.krcb.org	707-584-2020		645-10
KRCC-FM 91.5 (NPR) 912 N Weber St..................... Colorado Springs CO 80903 *TF:* 800-748-2727 ■ *Web:* www.krcc.org	719-473-4801	473-7863	645-39
KRCG-TV Ch 13 (CBS) 10188 Old Hwy 54 N ....New Bloomfield MO 65063 *TF:* 800-773-6180 ■ *Web:* krcgtv.com	573-896-5144	896-5193	741
KRCS-FM 93.1 (CHR) 660 Flormann St Ste 100 .... Rapid City SD 57701 *Web:* www.hot931.com	605-343-6161		645-132
Kream & Kream 536 Broad St Ste 5 .... East Weymouth MA 02189 *Web:* www.kreamandkream.com	781-331-9333		428
Kreamer Feed Inc PO Box 38........................Kreamer PA 17833 *TF:* 800-767-4537 ■ *Web:* www.kreamerfeed.com	570-374-8148	374-2007	276
Kreate & Print Inc 14 Central St............... Norwood MA 02062 *Web:* www.kreateandprint.com	781-255-0505		627
Kreative Carriers Transportation & Logistic Services 61 Bluewater Rd .... Bedford NS B4B1G8 *TF:* 888-274-2444 ■ *Web:* www.kreativecarriers.com	888-274-2444		314
Krech Ojard & Assoc PA 227 W First St Ste 200..........................Duluth MN 55802 *Web:* www.krechojard.com	218-727-3282	727-1216	256
Kreeger Museum, The 2401 Foxhall Rd NW.........................Washington DC 20007 *Web:* www.kreegermuseum.org	202-338-3552	337-3051	520
Kreher Steel Company LLC 1550 N 25th Ave.........................Melrose Park IL 60160 *Fax Area Code: 708 ■ *TF:* 800-323-0745 ■ *Web:* www.kreher.com	800-323-0745	345-8293*	492
Krehling Industries Inc 1399 Hagy Way...........................Harrisburg PA 17110 *TF:* 800-839-1654 ■ *Web:* www.krehlingcountertops.com	717-232-7936	236-8810	182
Kreider Ayers & Assoc Inc 1130 Patterson Ave SW ....Roanoke VA 24016	540-343-7612		189-10
Kreider Corp 2000 S Yellow Springs St..................Springfield OH 45506 *Web:* www.kreidercorp.com	937-325-8787		483
Kreider Farms 1461 Lancaster Rd..............Manheim PA 17545 *TF:* 888-665-4415 ■ *Web:* www.kreiderfarms.com	717-665-4415	665-9614	10-3
Kreinik Manufacturing Company Inc 1708 Gihon Rd..........................Parkersburg WV 26101 *TF:* 800-537-2166 ■ *Web:* www.kreinik.com	304-422-8900		711
Kreis Enderle 8225 Moorsbridge Rd............. Portage MI 49024 *Web:* www.kreisenderle.com	269-324-3000		428
Kreis Johnson Construction 160 Village St..........................Birmingham AL 35242 *Web:* www.johnsonkreis.com	205-981-9030		186
Kreis' Restaurant 535 S Lindbergh Blvd..................... Saint Louis MO 63131 *Web:* www.kreissteakhouse.com	314-993-0735		671
Kreisler Industrial Corp 180 Van Riper Ave ....Elmwood Park NJ 07407 *Web:* www.kreislermfg.com	201-791-0700	791-8015	21
Kreisler Mfg Corp 180 Van Riper Ave ....Elmwood Park NJ 07407 *TF:* 888-750-5834 ■ *Web:* www.kreislermfg.com	201-791-0700	791-8015	21
Krell Industries Inc 45 Connair Rd ....Orange CT 06477 *Web:* www.krellonline.com	203-799-9954	799-9796	52
Krell Institute 1609 Golden Aspen Dr.............. Ames IA 50010 *Web:* www.krellinst.org	515-956-3696		196
Kremblas Foster Phillips & Pollick 7632 Slate Ridge Blvd .... Reynoldsburg OH 43068 *TF:* 800-759-8840 ■ *Web:* ohiopatent.com	614-575-2100		428
Kremer & Associates Inc 6400 Brooktree Ct Ste 240....................Wexford PA 15090 *Web:* www.kremerassociates.com	724-934-0808		463
KREM-TV Ch 2 (CBS) 4103 S Regal St ....Spokane WA 99223 *TF:* 888-404-3922 ■ *Web:* www.krem.com	509-448-2000		741-127
Krengel Enterprises 121 Fulton St Ste 2..........................New York NY 10038 *Web:* reviews.birdeye.com	212-227-1877		467
Kresge Foundation 3215 W Big Beaver Rd........... Troy MI 48084 *TF:* 800-537-9946 ■ *Web:* www.kresge.org	248-643-9630		305
Kresge Hearing Research Institute (KHRI) 4605 Medical Science Unit.................. Ann Arbor MI 48109 *Web:* medicine.umich.edu	734-764-8110	764-0014	668
Kress Corp 227 W Illinois St ....Brimfield IL 61517 *Web:* www.kresscarrier.com	309-446-3395	446-9625	190
Kress Employment Screening 320 Westcott St Ste 108........................Houston TX 77007 *TF:* 888-636-3693 ■ *Web:* www.kressinc.com	713-880-3693	880-3694	635
Krestmark Industries Lp 3950 Bastille Rd .... Dallas TX 75212 *Web:* www.krestmark.com	214-237-5055		234
Kretschmar & Smith Inc 6293 Pedley Rd .... Riverside CA 92509 *TF:* 800-364-2059 ■ *Web:* kandsmasonry.com	951-361-1405		189-7
Kretz Lumber Company Inc W11143 County Hwy G .... Antigo WI 54409 *Web:* www.kretzlumber.com	715-623-5410		683
Kreuzberger & Associates 1000 Fourth St ....San Rafael CA 94901 *Web:* www.kreuzberger.com	415-459-2300		260
KRGV-TV Ch 5 (ABC) 900 E Expy PO Box 5 ....Weslaco TX 78596 *Web:* www.krgv.com	956-968-5555	973-5016	741
Krieg DeVault Alexander & Capehart 1 Indiana Sq Ste 2800 ....Indianapolis IN 46204 *Web:* www.kriegdevault.com	317-636-4341	636-1507	428
Krieger Specialty Products Co 4880 Gregg Rd .... Pico Rivera CA 90660 *TF:* 866-203-5060 ■ *Web:* www.kriegerproducts.com	562-695-0645	692-0146	234
Kring & Chung LLP 38 Corporate Pk............. Irvine CA 92606 *TF:* 800-605-0777 ■ *Web:* www.kringandchung.com	949-261-7700		428
Kring Point State Park 25950 Kring Pt Rd .... Redwood City NY 13679 *Web:* parks.ny.gov/parks/14/details.aspx	315-482-2444		565
Kripalu Ctr for Yoga & Health 57 Interlaken Rd..........................Stockbridge MA 01262 *TF:* 800-741-7353 ■ *Web:* www.kripalu.org	413-448-3400	448-3384	706
Kris Way Truck Leasing Inc 43 Hemco Rd Ste 1.......................South Portland ME 04106 *Web:* www.kris-way.com	207-799-8593	799-8657	778
KrisDee & Associates Inc 755 Schneider Dr .... South Elgin IL 60177 *Web:* www.krisdee.com	847-608-8300		295
Krise Bus Service Inc 119 Bus Ln......... Punxsutawney PA 15767	814-938-6200		109
Krishnamoorthi Raja (Rep D - IL) 515 Cannon HOB ....Washington DC 20515 *Web:* krishnamoorthi.house.gov	202-225-3711		342-2
Krishnamurti Foundation of America 134 Besant Rd .... Ojai CA 93023 *Web:* kfa.org	805-646-2726		305
Krispy Kreme Doughnuts Corp 370 Knollwood St Ste 500 .... Winston-Salem NC 27103 *NYSE:* KKD ■ *TF:* 800-457-4779 ■ *Web:* www.krispykreme.com	336-725-2981		68
Krist Oil Co 303 Selden Rd.......................Iron River MI 49935 *TF:* 800-722-6691 ■ *Web:* www.kristoil.com	906-265-6144		345
Kristal Graphics 6029 Reseda Blvd..............Tarzana CA 91356 *Web:* www.kristalgraphics.net	818-342-7822		627

Name / Address	City	State	Zip	Phone	Fax	Class
Kristin Brooks Hope Ctr (KBHC) 1250 24th St NW Ste 300 *TF:* 800-784-2433 ■ *Web:* www.hopeline.com	Washington	DC	20037	202-536-3200	536-3206	48-17
KRIS-TV Ch 6 (NBC) 301 Artesian St *Web:* www.kristv.com	Corpus Christi	TX	78401	361-886-6100		741-36
KRIV-TV Ch 26 (Fox) 4261 SW Fwy **Fax:* News Rm ■ *Web:* www.fox26houston.com	Houston	TX	77027	713-479-2600	479-2859*	741-60
KRK Capital Partners 638 Fifth St NE *Web:* www.krkcapitalpartners.com	Washington	DC	20002	202-747-6565	747-6535	192
KRKA-FM 107.9 (Urban) 1749 Bertrand Dr *Web:* 1079ishot.com	Lafayette	LA	70506	337-233-6000		645-86
KRKS-FM 94.7 (Rel) 3131 S Vaughn Way *Web:* 947fmtheword.com	Aurora	CO	80014	303-750-5687	696-8063	645
KRKX-FM 94.1 (CR) 2075 Central Ave *Web:* www.941ksky.com	Billings	MT	59102	406-248-7777		645-19
KRLD-AM 1080 (N/T) 4131 N Central Expy Ste 100 *Web:* dfw.cbslocal.com	Dallas	TX	75204	214-525-7000		645-44
Krm Information Services Inc 200 Spring St *TF:* 800-775-7654 ■ *Web:* www.krm.com	Eau Claire	WI	54703	800-775-7654		242
KRMA-TV Ch 6 (PBS) 1089 Bannock St *TF:* 800-274-6666 ■ *Web:* www.rmpbs.org	Denver	CO	80204	303-892-6666	620-5600	741-39
KRMC (Kingman Regional Medical Ctr) 3269 Stockton Hill Rd *TF:* 877-757-2101 ■ *Web:* www.azkrmc.com	Kingman	AZ	86409	928-757-2101		374-3
KRMD-FM 101.1 (Ctry) 270 Plaza Loop *Web:* www.krmd.com	Bossier City	LA	71111	318-549-8500	549-8505	645
KRMG-AM 740 (N/T) 7136 S Yale Ave Ste 500 *TF:* 055-297-9090 ■ *Web:* www.krmg.com	Tulsa	OK	74136	918-493-7400	493-2376	645-168
KRNO-FM 106.9 (AC) 961 Matley Ln Ste 120 *Web:* 1069morefm.com	Reno	NV	89502	775-829-1964	825-3183	645-133
KROC-AM 1340 (N/T) 122 SW Fourth St *TF:* 800-889-9508 ■ *Web:* www.krocam.com/info/contact_us.php	Rochester	MN	55902	507-286-1010		645-137
Krochet Kids International 1630 Superior Ave Unit C *Web:* www.krochetkids.org	Costa Mesa	CA	92627	949-791-2560		305
KROD-AM 600 (N/T) 4180 N Mesa St *Web:* www.krod.com	El Paso	TX	79902	915-880-5763		645-53
Kroeschell Inc 3222 N Kennicott Ave *Web:* www.kroeschell.com	Arlington Heights	IL	60004	312-649-7980		261
Kroff Inc 1 N Shore Ctr Ste 450 12 Federal St *TF:* 800-424-9300 ■ *Web:* www.kroff.com	Pittsburgh	PA	15212	412-321-9800		146
Kroger Co 1014 Vine St *NYSE:* KR ■ *TF:* 800-576-4377 ■ *Web:* www.kroger.com	Cincinnati	OH	45202	513-762-4000		345
Krohn Conservatory 1501 Eden Pk Dr *Web:* www.cincinnatiparks.com	Cincinnati	OH	45202	513-421-5707		520
Krohn Industries Inc PO Box 98 *TF:* 800-526-6299 ■ *Web:* www.krohnindustries.com	Carlstadt	NJ	07072	201-933-9696	933-9684	407
Krohne Inc 7 Dearborn Rd *Web:* www.krohne.com	Peabody	MA	01960	978-535-6060		639
Kroll Background America Inc 100 Centerview Dr Ste 300 *TF:* 800-697-7189 ■ *Web:* www.kroll.com	Nashville	TN	37214	615-320-9800		635
Kroll Direct Marketing Inc 3914 Netherlee Way *Web:* www.krolldirect.com	Wellington	FL	33449	609-275-2900		5
Kroll Inc 600 Third Ave *TF:* 800-675-3772 ■ *Web:* www.kroll.com	New York	NY	10016	212-593-1000	593-2631	194
Kroll Ontrack Inc 9023 Columbine Rd *TF:* 800-872-2599 ■ *Web:* www.krollontrack.com	Eden Prairie	MN	55347	952-937-5161	937-5750	178-12
Krolls West 1990 S Ridge Rd *Web:* www.krollswest.com	Green Bay	WI	54304	920-497-1111		671
Krome Communications Inc 307 Fourth Ave *Web:* www.krome.com	Pittsburgh	PA	15222	412-471-0840		636
Kromet International Inc 200 Sheldon Dr *Web:* www.kromet.com	Cambridge	ON	N1R7K1	519-623-2511		488
Kromite LLC 243 N Union St Ste 117 *Web:* www.kromite.com	Lambertville	NJ	08530	267-983-6305		463
Krone North America 3363 Miac Cove *Web:* www.krone-northamerica.com	Memphis	TN	38118	901-842-6011		273
Kroner Publications Inc 1123a W Pk Ave	Niles	OH	44446	330-544-5500	544-5511	532-2
Krones Inc 9600 S 58th St PO Box 321801 **Fax:* Cust Svc ■ *TF:* 800-752-3787 ■ *Web:* www.krones.com	Franklin	WI	53132	414-409-4000	409-4100*	547
Kronick Moskovitz Tiedemann & Girard (KMTG) 400 Capitol Mall Fl 27 *Web:* www.kmtg.com	Sacramento	CA	95814	916-321-4500	321-4555	428
Kronos Inc 297 Billerica Rd *TF:* 888-293-5549 ■ *Web:* www.kronos.com	Chelmsford	MA	01824	978-250-9800	367-5900	178-11
Kronos Products Inc 1 Kronos Dr *TF:* 800-621-0099 ■ *Web:* kronosfoodscorp.com	Glendale Heights	IL	60139	800-621-0099		296-26
Kronos Worldwide Inc 5430 LBJ Fwy Ste 1700 *NYSE:* KRO ■ *TF:* 800-866-5600 ■ *Web:* www.kronostio2.com	Houston	TX	75240	281-423-3300	423-3258	145
Kropp Equipment Inc 1020 Kennedy Ave *TF:* 866-402-2222 ■ *Web:* www.kroppequipment.com	Schererville	IN	46375	866-402-2222		23
Kropp Forge 5301 W Roosevelt Rd **Fax:* Sales ■ *Web:* www.kroppforge.com	Cicero	IL	60804	708-652-6691	652-9144*	483
KROQ-FM 106.7 (Alt) 5901 Venice Blvd *TF:* 800-520-1067 ■ *Web:* kroq.cbslocal.com	Los Angeles	CA	90034	323-930-1067		645-92
Krove Corp 10180 Reflections Blvd *Web:* www.kroveonline.com	Sunrise	FL	33351	954-741-2972		180
KROX-AM 1260 (Var) 208 S Main St *TF:* 800-222-2537 ■ *Web:* www.kroxam.com	Crookston	MN	56716	218-281-1140	281-5036	645

Name / Address	City	State	Zip	Phone	Fax	Class
KROX-FM 101.5 (Alt) 8309 N IH-35 *Web:* www.101x.com	Austin	TX	78753	512-832-4000	832-4071	645-14
Kroy LLC 3830 Kelley Ave *TF Cust Svc:* 888-888-5769 ■ *Web:* www.kroy.com	Cleveland	OH	44114	216-426-5600	426-5601	173-6
Krozak Information Technologies Inc 201 Linton Knoll Ct *Web:* www.krozak.com	Silver Spring	MD	20904	301-384-4340		396
KRQE-TV Ch 13 (CBS) 13 Broadcast Plaza SW *TF:* 800-283-4227 ■ *Web:* www.krqe.com	Albuquerque	NM	87104	505-243-2285		741-3
KRQQ-FM 93.7 (CHR) 3202 N Oracle Rd *Web:* krq.iheart.com	Tucson	AZ	85705	520-618-2100		645-167
KRRO-FM 103.7 (Rock) 500 S Phillips Ave *TF:* 800-283-4867 ■ *Web:* www.krro.com	Sioux Falls	SD	57104	605-331-5350	336-0415	645-152
KRRQ-FM 95.5 (Urban) 202 Galbert Rd *Web:* www.krrq.com	Lafayette	LA	70506	337-232-1311		645-86
Krt Marketing Inc 3685 Mt Diablo Blvd Ste 255 *TF:* 800-261-1537 ■ *Web:* www.krtmarketing.com	Lafayette	CA	94549	925-284-0444		195
KRTH-FM 101.1 (Oldies) 5670 Wilshire Blvd Ste 200 *TF:* 800-232-5784 ■ *Web:* kearth101.cbslocal.com	Los Angeles	CA	90036	323-936-5784	933-6072	645-92
KRTR-FM 96.3 (AC) 900 Ft St Ste 700 *TF:* 800-669-1010 ■ *Web:* krater963.com	Honolulu	HI	96813	808-275-1000		645-73
KRTV-TV Ch 3 (CBS) PO Box 2989 *Web:* www.krtv.com	Great Falls	MT	59403	406-791-5400		741-54
KRTY-FM 95.3 (Ctry) 750 Story Rd *TF:* 800-373-3891 ■ *Web:* www.krty.com	San Jose	CA	95122	408-293-8030		645-146
Kruckeberg Botanic Garden 20312 15th Ave NW *Web:* www.kruckeberg.org	Shoreline	WA	98177	206-546-1281		97
Krueger Associates Inc 105 Commerce Dr *TF:* 800-637-1306 ■ *Web:* www.nfsrv.com	Aston	PA	19014	610-532-4700		225
Krueger Engineering & Manufacturing Co 12001 Hirsch Rd PO Box 11308 *TF:* 800-552-2975 ■ *Web:* www.kemco.net	Houston	TX	77293	281-442-2537	442-6668	91
Krueger Sheet Metal Co 731 N Superior St *TF:* 800-765-9055 ■ *Web:* kruegersheetmetal.com	Spokane	WA	99202	509-489-0221	489-6539	697
Krueger Wholesale Florist Inc 10706 Tesch Ln *Web:* kruegerwholesale.com	Rothschild	WI	54474	715-359-7202		292
Krueger-Gilbert Health Physics Inc 1118 Baldwin Mll Rd PO Box 410 *TF:* 800-735-2258 ■ *Web:* kruegergilbert.com	Jarrettsville	MD	21084	410-692-9806		194
Kruepke Trucking Inc 2881 Hwy P *TF Cust Svc:* 800-798-5000 ■ *Web:* kruepketrucking.com	Jackson	WI	53037	262-677-3155	677-3206	780
KRUF-FM 94.5 (CHR) 6341 W Port Ave *Web:* k945.com	Shreveport	LA	71129	318-688-1130		645-151
Kruger Inc 3285 Ch Bedford *Web:* www.kruger.com	Montreal	QC	H3S1G5	514-737-1131	343-3124	557
Kruger Street Toy & Train Museum 144 Kruger St *TF:* 877-242-8133 ■ *Web:* www.toyandtrain.com	Wheeling	WV	26003	304-242-8133	242-1925	520
Kruggel Lawton & Company LLC 210 S Michigan St Ste 200 *Web:* klcpas.com	South Bend	IN	46601	574-289-4011		2
Krugliak, Wilkins, Griffiths & Dougherty Co 4775 Munson St NW *Web:* www.kwgd.com	Canton	OH	44735	330-497-0700		428
Krung Thai 642 S Winchester Blvd *Web:* www.originalkrungthai.com	San Jose	CA	95128	408-260-8224		671
Kruse Adhesive Tape Inc 1610 E McFadden Ave *TF:* 800-992-7702 ■ *Web:* www.krusetape.com	Santa Ana	CA	92705	714-640-2130	640-2134	732
Krusinski Construction Co 2107 Swift Dr *Web:* www.krusinski.com	Oak Brook	IL	60523	630-573-7700		186
KRVK-FM 107.9 (Rock) 150 N Nichols Ave *TF:* 800-442-2256 ■ *Web:* www.theriver1079.com	Casper	WY	82601	307-266-5252		645-28
Krvn Transmitter 1007 Plum Crk Pkwy PO Box 880 *Web:* www.krvn.com	Lexington	NE	68850	308-324-2371		645-10
KRW Consulting Group LLC 1881 Commerce Dr Ste 111 *Web:* www.krweng.com	Elk Grove Village	IL	60007	847-734-0128		196
KRWG-FM 90.7 (NPR) 2915 McFie Cir PO Box 30001 *Web:* krwg.org	Las Cruces	NM	88003	575-646-2222	646-1974	645
KRXI-TV Ch 11 (Fox) 1790 Vassar St *Web:* www.foxreno.com	Reno	NV	89502	775-856-1100	324-3404	741-107
KRXO-FM 107.7 (CR) 400 E Britton Rd *Web:* www.krxo.com	Oklahoma City	OK	73114	405-478-5104		645-114
Kryptonite Kollectibles 1441 Plainfield Ave *TF:* 877-646-1728 ■ *Web:* www.kryptonitekollectibles.com	Janesville	WI	53545	877-646-1728		791
Krystal Klear Water Systems 10502 W 150th St *Web:* krystalklearh2o.com	Overland Park	KS	66221	913-897-6571		610
K&S (Kulicke & Soffa Industries Inc) 1005 Virginia Dr *NASDAQ:* KLIC ■ *Web:* www.kns.com	Fort Washington	PA	19034	215-784-6000	784-6001	695
KS 107.5 4700 S Syracuse St Ste 1050 *Web:* www.ks1075.com	Denver	CO	80111	303-228-1075		645
KS Energy Services LLC 19705 W Lincoln Ave *Web:* www.ksenergyservices.com	New Berlin	WI	53146	262-574-5100		261
KS Industries LP 6205 District Blvd *Web:* www.ksindustrieslp.com	Bakersfield	CA	93313	661-617-1700		256
KSA Engineers Inc 140 E Tyler St Ste 600 Ste 600 *TF:* 877-572-3647 ■ *Web:* www.ksaeng.com	Longview	TX	75601	903-236-7700	236-7779	261
KSAB-FM 501 Tupper Ln *Web:* ksabfm.iheart.com	Corpus Christi	TX	78417	361-289-0111	289-5035	645-43

	Phone	Fax	Class
KSAN-FM 107.7 (Alt) 750 Battery St 3rd Fl. . . . San Francisco CA 94105 *TF:* 888-303-2663 ■ *Web:* www.1077thebone.com	415-995-6800		645-145
KSAS-TV Ch 24 (Fox) 316 NW St . . . Wichita KS 67203 *Web:* www.foxkansas.com	316-942-2424	942-8927	741-142
KSAT-TV Ch 12 (ABC) 1408 N St Mary's St . . . San Antonio TX 78215 *Web:* www.ksat.com	210-351-1200		741-116
KSAZ-TV Ch 10 (Fox) 511 W Adams St. . . . Phoenix AZ 85003 *TF:* 888-369-4762 ■ *Web:* fox10phoenix.com	602-257-1234		741-99
KSBI (Kobelco Stewart Bolling Inc) 1600 Terex Rd. . . . Hudson OH 44236 *TF:* 800-464-0064 ■ *Web:* www.ksbiusa.com	330-655-3111	655-2982	386
KSBJ Educational Foundation Inc 1722 Treble Dr . . . Humble TX 77338 *TF:* 800-446-5725 ■ *Web:* www.ksbj.org	281-446-5725	540-2198	116
KSBW-TV Ch 8 (NBC) 238 John St . . . Salinas CA 93901 *Web:* www.ksbw.com	831-758-8888	424-3750	741
Ksby-Tv 1772 Calle Joaquin . . . San Luis Obispo CA 93405 *Web:* www.ksby.com	805-541-6666		116
KSC Adv & PR 40 Sarasota Ctr Blvd Ste 107 . . . Sarasota FL 34240 *Web:* kscadvpr.com	941-906-1555		4
KSC Industries Inc 881 Kuhn Dr Ste 200 . . . Chula Vista CA 91914 *Web:* www.kscind.com	619-671-0110	671-0330	52
KSCI-TV Ch 18 (Ind) 1990 S Bundy Dr Ste 850. . . . Los Angeles CA 90025 *Web:* www.la18.tv	310-478-1818	479-8118	741-76
KSCW-TV Ch 33 (CW) 2815 E 37th St N. . . . Wichita KS 67219 *Web:* kwch.com	316-838-1212		741-142
KSDK-TV Ch 5 (NBC) 1000 Market St . . . Saint Louis MO 63101 *Web:* www.ksdk.com	314-421-5055		741-114
KSDS-FM 88.3 (Jazz) 1313 Pk Blvd . . . San Diego CA 92101 *Web:* www.jazz88.org	619-388-3037	388-3928	645-144
KSED-FM 107.5 (Ctry) 2409 N Fourth St Ste 101. . . . Flagstaff AZ 86004 *Web:* www.koltcountry.com	928-779-1177	774-5179	645-59
KSEE-TV Ch 24 (NBC) 5035 E McKinley Ave . . . Fresno CA 93727 *TF:* 800-234-5733 ■ *Web:* www.yourcentralvalley.com	559-222-2411		741-52
KSEV-AM 700 (N/T) 11451 Katy Fwy Ste 215. . . . Houston TX 77079 *Web:* www.ksevradio.com	281-588-4800		645-75
KSFY-TV Ch 13 (ABC) 300 N Dakota Ave Ste 100 . . . Sioux Falls SD 57104 *Web:* www.ksfy.com	605-336-1300		741-125
KSGN-FM 89.7 (Rel) 2048 Orange Tree Ln Ste 200. . . . Redlands CA 92374 *TF:* 888-897-5746 ■ *Web:* www.ksgn.com	909-583-2150	583-2170	645-135
KSHB-TV Ch 41 (NBC) 4720 Oak St. . . . Kansas City MO 64112 *TF:* 800-222-1222 ■ *Web:* www.kshb.com	816-753-4141		741-68
KSI (Kaiser Systems Inc) 126 Sohier Rd. . . . Beverly MA 01915 *Web:* www.kaisersys.com	978-922-9300		253
KSII-FM 93.1 (AC) 4180 N Mesa St. . . . El Paso TX 79902 *Web:* kisselpaso.com	915-544-9300	532-3334	645-53
KSKA-FM 91.1 (NPR) 3877 University Dr . . . Anchorage AK 99508 *TF:* 800-478-8255 ■ *Web:* www.alaskapublic.org	907-550-8400		645-6
KSKN-TV Ch 22 (CW) 4103 S Regal St . . . Spokane WA 99223 *TF:* 888-404-3922 ■ *Web:* www.krem.com	509-448-2000		741-127
KSKS-FM 93.7 (Ctry) 1071 W Shaw Ave. . . . Fresno CA 93711 *TF:* 800-767-5477 ■ *Web:* www.ksks.com	559-490-5800		645-64
KSKY-AM 660 (N/T) 6400 N Beltline Rd Ste 110. . . . Irving TX 75063 *TF:* 800-941-7326 ■ *Web:* www.660amtheanswer.com	972-870-9949		645
KSL Media Inc 387 Park Ave S . . . New York NY 10016 *Web:* www.kslmedia.com	212-352-5800		195
KSL RADIO & TV 55 N 300 W. . . . Salt Lake City UT 84101 *Web:* www.ksl.com	801-575-5555		645-142
KSL Resorts 50-905 Avenida Bermudas. . . . La Quinta CA 92253 *Web:* www.kslresorts.com	760-564-8000		378
KSL-AM 1160 (N/T) 55 N Third W . . . Salt Lake City UT 84180 *Web:* www.ksl.com	801-575-7600		645-142
KSLA-TV Ch 12 (CBS) 1812 Fairfield Ave. . . . Shreveport LA 71101 *TF:* 800-444-5752 ■ *Web:* www.ksla.com	318-222-1212	677-6703	741-124
KSLR-AM 630 (Rel) 9601 McAllister Fwy Ste 1200 . . . San Antonio TX 78216 *Web:* am630theword.com	210-344-8481	340-1213	645-143
KSL-TV Ch 5 (NBC) PO Box 1160 . . . Salt Lake City UT 84110 *TF:* 800-862-9098 ■ *Web:* www.ksl.com	801-575-5555	575-5560	741-115
KSLX-FM 100.7 (CR) 4343 E Camelback Rd Ste 200 . . . Phoenix AZ 85018 *Web:* kslx.com	602-260-1007		645-123
KSM Industries Inc N 115 W 19025 Edison Dr . . . Germantown WI 53022 *Web:* www.ksmindustries.com	262-251-9510	251-4865	697
KSM Technology Partners LLC 2650 Eisenhower Ave . . . Norristown PA 19403 *Web:* ksmpartners.com	610-628-0550		177
KSME-FM 96.1 (CHR) 4270 Byrd Dr. . . . Loveland CO 80538 *TF:* 877-498-9600 ■ *Web:* kissfmcolorado.iheart.com	970-461-2560		645
KSMO-TV Ch 62 (MNT) 4500 Shawnee Mission Pkwy. . . . Fairway KS 66205 *TF:* 800-593-2222 ■ *Web:* www.kctv5.com	913-677-5555		741
KSMQ-TV Ch 15 (PBS) 2000 Eigth Ave NW. . . . Austin MN 55912 *TF:* 800-658-2539 ■ *Web:* www.ksmq.org	507-481-2095		741
KSMS-FM 90.5 (NPR) Missouri State University 901 S National . . . Springfield MO 65897 *TF:* 800-767-5768 ■ *Web:* www.ksmu.org	417-836-5878	836-5889	645-157
KSMU-FM 91.1 (NPR) Missouri State University 901 S National Ave. . . . Springfield MO 65897 *TF:* 800-767-5768 ■ *Web:* www.ksmu.org	417-836-5878	836-5889	645-157
KSNA (Kansas State Nurses Assn) 1109 SW Topeka Blvd. . . . Topeka KS 66612 *Web:* www.ksnurses.com	785-233-8638	233-5222	533
KSNT-TV Ch 27 (NBC) 6835 NW Hwy 24. . . . Topeka KS 66618 *TF:* 800-222-8477 ■ *Web:* ksnt.com	785-582-4000		741-135
KSNW-TV 833 N Main St. . . . Wichita KS 67203 *TF:* 800-432-3924 ■ *Web:* www.ksn.com	316-265-3333	292-1195	741-142
KSON-FM 97.3 (Ctry) 1615 Murray Canyon Rd Ste 710 . . . San Diego CA 92108 *TF:* 800-243-1973 ■ *Web:* www.kson.com	619-291-9797	543-1353	645-144
KSOO-AM 1140 (N/T) 5100 S Tennis Ln . . . Sioux Falls SD 57108 *Web:* www.ksoo.com	605-361-0300		645-152
KSOP-AM 1370 (Ctry) 1285 West 2320 South. . . . Salt Lake City UT 84119 *Web:* www.cc1370.com	801-972-1043	974-0868	645-142
KSOP-FM 104.3 (Ctry) 1285 W 2320 S. . . . West Valley City UT 84119 *Web:* www.ksopcountry.com	801-972-1043		645-142
k-Space Associates Inc 2182 Bishop Cir E . . . Dexter MI 48130 *Web:* www.k-space.com	734-426-7977		419
KSPR-TV Ch 33 (ABC) 1359 St Louis St. . . . Springfield MO 65802 *TF:* 877-248-6922 ■ *Web:* www.kspr.com	417-831-1333		741-130
KSPS Public TV 3911 S Regal St. . . . Spokane WA 99223 *TF:* 800-735-2377 ■ *Web:* www.ksps.org	509-443-7800		741-127
KSPW-FM 96.5 (CHR) 2330 W Grand St . . . Springfield MO 65802 *Web:* www.power965.com	417-865-6614	865-9643	645-157
KSSK-FM 92.3 (AC) 650 Iwilei Rd Ste 400 . . . Honolulu HI 96817 *Web:* ksskradio.iheart.com	808-550-9200		645-73
K-State Libraries 1117 Mid-Campus Dr N. . . . Manhattan KS 66506 *Web:* www.lib.k-state.edu	785-532-3014	532-7415	434-6
KSTP-AM 1500 (N/T) 3415 University Ave . . . Saint Paul MN 55114 *TF:* 877-615-1500 ■ *Web:* www.1500espn.com	651-646-8255		645-101
KSTP-FM 94.5 (AC) 3415 University Ave . . . Minneapolis MN 55414 *TF:* 800-603-6000 ■ *Web:* www.ks95.com	651-642-4141	647-2904	645-101
KSTP-TV Ch 5 (ABC) 3415 University Ave W. . . . Saint Paul MN 55114 *TF:* 800-895-1999 ■ *Web:* www.kstp.com	651-646-5555	642-4409	741-84
KSTU-TV Ch 13 (Fox) 5020 Amelia Earhart Dr. . . . Salt Lake City UT 84116 *TF:* 800-408-3178 ■ *Web:* fox13now.com	801-536-1313		741-115
KSTX-FM 89.1 (NPR) 8401 Datapoint Dr Ste 800 . . . San Antonio TX 78229 *TF:* 800-622-8977 ■ *Web:* www.tpr.org	210-614-8977	614-8983	645-143
KSTZ-FM 102.5 (AC) 1416 Locust St . . . Des Moines IA 50309 *Web:* www.star1025.com	515-280-1350	280-3011	645-48
KSUA-FM 91.5 (Alt) PO Box 750113 . . . Fairbanks AK 99775 *Web:* www.ksuaradio.com	907-474-7054		645-57
KSVI-TV Ch 6 (ABC) 445 S 24th St W . . . Billings MT 59102 *TF:* 800-679-1877 ■ *Web:* www.yourbigsky.com	406-652-4743	652-6963	741-14
KSWB-TV Ch 5 (Fox) 7191 Engineer Rd . . . San Diego CA 92111 **Fax:* News Rm ■ *Web:* www.fox5sandiego.com	858-492-9269	268-0401*	741-119
KSWD-FM 100.3 (Rock) 5900 Wilshire Blvd Ste 1900 . . . Los Angeles CA 90036 *TF:* 888-696-1003 ■ *Web:* www.thesoundla.com	323-634-1800		645-92
K-Swiss Inc 31248 Oak Crest Dr . . . Westlake Village CA 91361 *NASDAQ: KSWS* ■ *TF:* 800-938-8000 ■ *Web:* www.kswiss.com	818-706-5100		301
KSWV-AM 810 (Span) 102 Taos St . . . Santa Fe NM 87505 *TF:* 800-873-3372 ■ *Web:* santafenewmexican.com	505-983-3303		645-147
K-Systems Inc 2104 Aspen Dr. . . . Mechanicsburg PA 17055 *TF:* 800-221-0204 ■ *Web:* www.ksystemsinc.com	717-795-7711		178-1
KT (Kokomo Tribune) 300 N Union St PO Box 9014. . . . Kokomo IN 46901 *TF:* 800-382-0696 ■ *Web:* www.kokomotribune.com	765-459-3121	854-6733	532-2
KT Consulting Inc 4435 E Chandler Blvd. . . . Phoenix AZ 85048 *Web:* ktc-inc.com	480-538-2668	538-2686	809
K&T Switching Services Inc 3901 Colorado Ave. . . . Sheffield Village OH 44054 *Web:* www.ktswitching.com	440-949-1910		393
KT's Kitchens Inc 1065 E Walnut St Ste C . . . Carson CA 90746 *Web:* www.ktskitchens.com	310-764-0850		296-19
KTA (Kansas Turnpike Authority) 9401 E Kellogg . . . Wichita KS 67207 *Web:* www.ksturnpike.com	316 682 4537		271
KTA Super Stores 321 Keawe St . . . Hilo HI 96720 *Web:* ktastores.com	808-935-3751		345
KTAB-TV Ch 32 (CBS) 4510 S 14th St. . . . Abilene TX 79605 *Web:* www.bigcountryhomepage.com	325-695-2777	695-9922	741-1
KTAL-TV Ch 6 (NBC) 3150 N Market St . . . Shreveport LA 71107 **Fax Area Code:* 903 ■ *Web:* www.arklatexhomepage.com	318-629-6000	334-0288*	741-124
KTAR-FM 98.7 7740 N 16th St Ste 200. . . . Phoenix AZ 85020 *Web:* ktar.com	602-274-6200		645-123
Kta-Tator Inc 115 Technology Dr. . . . Pittsburgh PA 15275 *TF:* 800-582-4243 ■ *Web:* ktagage.com	412-788-1300		261
KTBN-TV Ch 40 (TBN) 2442 Michelle Dr. . . . Tustin CA 92780 *TF:* 888-731-1000 ■ *Web:* www.tbn.org	714-832-2950		741
KTBS-TV Ch 3 (ABC) 312 E Kings Hwy . . . Shreveport LA 71104 *TF:* 866-543-3296 ■ *Web:* www.ktbs.com	318-861-5800	219-4601	741-124
KTBU-TV Ch 55 (Ind) 7007 NW 77th Ave . . . Miami FL 33166 *NASDAQ: SBSA* ■ *Web:* www.spanishbroadcasting.com	305-441-6901	883-3375	741-82
KTBY-TV Ch 4 (Fox) 2700 E Tudor Rd. . . . Anchorage AK 99507 *TF:* 877-304-1313 ■ *Web:* www.youralaskalink.com	907-561-1313		741-5
KTC (Kaplan Telephone Company Inc) PO Box 369 . . . Kaplan LA 70548 *TF:* 866-643-7171	337-643-7171	643-6000	736
KTC Media Group 9891 Hamilton Ave. . . . Huntington Beach CA 92646 *TF:* 800-788-8165 ■ *Web:* www.ktcmediagroup.com	714-378-1660		5
KTCI-TV Ch 17 (PBS) 172 E Fourth St. . . . Saint Paul MN 55101 *Web:* www.tpt.org	651-222-1717		741-84

	Phone	Fax	Class
KTCL-FM 93.3 (Alt) 4695 S Monaco St .... Denver CO 80237 *Web:* area93.iheart.com	303-713-8000		645-47
KTCO-FM 98.9 (Ctry) 715 E Central Entrance .... Duluth MN 55811 *Web:* katcountry989.com	218-722-4321	722-5423	645-51
KTCS-FM 99.9 (Ctry) 5304 Hwy 45 E .... Fort Smith AR 72916 *Web:* www.ktcs.com	479-646-6151		645-61
KTDO-TV Ch 48 (Tele) 10033 Carnegie Ave .... El Paso TX 79925	915-591-9595		741-43
KTDY-FM 99.9 (AC) 1749 Bertrand Dr .... Lafayette LA 70506 *TF:* 800-324-1108 ■ *Web:* 999ktdy.com	337-233-6000		645-86
KTEP-FM 88.5 (NPR) 500 W University Ave Cotton Memorial Bldg Ste 203 .... El Paso TX 79968 *Web:* www.ktep.org	915-747-5152		645-53
KTHR 9323 E 37th St N .... Wichita KS 67226	316-436-1073		645-175
KTHT-FM 1990 Post Oak Blvd Ste 2300 .... Houston TX 77056 *TF:* 877-745-6591 ■ *Web:* www.countrylegends971.com	713-963-1200	622-5457	645-75
KTHV-TV Ch 11 (CBS) 720 S Izard St .... Little Rock AR 72201 *TF:* 800-621-3362 ■ *Web:* www.thv11.com	501-376-1111	376-1645	741-75
KTIK-AM 1350 (Sports) 1419 W Bannock St .... Boise ID 83702 *TF:* 866-296-1350 ■ *Web:* www.ktik.com	208-336-3670		645-22
KTKZ-AM 1380 (N/T) 1425 River Pk Dr Ste 520 .... Sacramento CA 95815 *TF:* 888-923-1380 ■ *Web:* www.am1380theanswer.com	916-924-0710	924-1587	645-140
KTLA-TV Ch 5 (CW) 5800 W Sunset Blvd .... Los Angeles CA 90028 *Web:* ktla.com	323-460-5500	460-5333	741-76
KTMD-TV Ch 47 (Tele) 1235 N Loop W Ste 125 .... Houston TX 77008 *Web:* www.telemundohouston.com	713-974-4848		741-60
KTMY-FM 107.1 (N/T) 3415 University Ave .... St. Paul MN 55114 *Web:* www.mytalk1071.com	651-642-4107	647-2904	645
KTNL-TV Ch 13 (CBS/I) 520 Lake St .... Sitka AK 99835	907-747-5749		741
KTNV-TV Ch 13 (ABC) 3355 S Valley View Blvd .... Las Vegas NV 89102 *Web:* www.ktnv.com	702-876-1313	876-2237	741-72
KTOK-AM 1000 (N/T) 1900 NW Expy Ste 1000 .... Oklahoma City OK 73118 *TF:* 844-289-7234 ■ *Web:* ktok.iheart.com	405-841-0200	858-5333	645-114
KTOM-FM 92.7 (Ctry) 903 N Main St .... Salinas CA 93906 *TF General:* 800-660-5866 ■ *Web:* ktom.iheart.com	831-755-8181		645
KTOO-FM 104.3 (NPR) 360 Egan Dr .... Juneau AK 99801 *TF:* 800-239-5233 ■ *Web:* www.ktoo.org	907-586-1670		645-82
KTOO-TV Ch 3 (PBS) 360 Egan Dr .... Juneau AK 99801 *TF:* 800-239-5233 ■ *Web:* www.ktoo.org	907-586-1670		741-67
KTRC-AM 1260 (N/T) 2502 Camino Entrada Ste C .... Santa Fe NM 87507 *TF:* 888-321-5123 ■ *Web:* www.santafe.com/ktrc	505-471-1067		645-147
KTRK-TV Ch 13 (ABC) 3310 Bissonnet St .... Houston TX 77005 *Web:* abc13.com	713-666-0713		741-60
KTRS-AM 550 (N/T) 638 Westport Plaza .... Saint Louis MO 63146 *TF:* 888-550-5877 ■ *Web:* www.ktrs.com	314-453-5500	453-9704	645-141
KTRS-FM 104.7 (CHR) 150 N Nichols Ave .... Casper WY 82601 *TF:* 800-442-2256 ■ *Web:* www.kisscasper.com	307-266-5252		645-28
KTSA-AM 550 (N/T) 4050 Eisenhauer Rd .... San Antonio TX 78218 *Web:* www.ktsa.com	210-654-5100		645-143
KTSC-TV Ch 8 (PBS) 2200 Bonforte Blvd .... Pueblo CO 81001 *Web:* www.rmpbs.org	719-543-8800	549-2208	741
KTSD-FM 91.1 (NPR) 555 N Dakota St PO Box 5000 .... Vermillion SD 57069 *TF:* 800-456-0766 ■ *Web:* www.sdpb.org	605-677-5861	677-5010	645
KTSD-TV Ch 10 (PBS) 555 N Dakota St PO Box 5000 .... Vermillion SD 57069 **Fax Area Code:* 605 ■ *TF:* 800-333-0709 ■ *Web:* www.sdpb.org	800-333-0789	677-5010*	741
KTSF-TV Ch 26 (Ind) 100 Valley Dr .... Brisbane CA 94005 *TF:* 800-772-1213 ■ *Web:* www.ktsf.com	415-468-2626	467-7559	741
KTSM-AM 690 (N/T) 4045 N Mesa St .... El Paso TX 79902 *Web:* ktsmradio.iheart.com	915-351-5400		645-53
KTTC-TV Ch 10 (NBC) 6301 Bandel Rd NW .... Rochester MN 55901 *TF:* 800-288-1656 ■ *Web:* www.kttc.com	507-288-4444	288-6324	741-110
KTTS-FM 94.7 (Ctry) 2330 W Grand St .... Springfield MO 65802 *TF:* 800-621-3362 ■ *Web:* www.ktts.com	417-865-6614	865-9643	645-157
KTTV-TV Ch 11 (Fox) 1999 S Bundy Dr .... Los Angeles CA 90025 *Web:* www.foxla.com	310-584-2000		741-76
KTTW-TV Ch 7 (Fox) 2817 W 11th St .... Sioux Falls SD 57104 *Web:* www.kttw.com	605-338-0017	338-7173	741-125
KTTZ-TV *Texas Tech University* 17th & Indiana .... Lubbock TX 79409 *Web:* www.kttz.org	806-742-2209	742-1274	741-78
KTU 103.5 32 Ave of the Americas .... New York NY 10013 *Web:* www.ktu.com	212-377-7900		645-111
K-Tube Technologies 13400 Kirkham Way .... Poway CA 92064 *TF:* 800-394-0058 ■ *Web:* www.k-tube.com	858-513-9229	513-9459	477
KTUL-TV Ch 8 (ABC) PO Box 8 .... Tulsa OK 74101 *Web:* www.ktul.com	918-445-8888		741-138
KTUU-TV Ch 2 (NBC) 501 E 40th Ave Ste 220 .... Anchorage AK 99503 *Web:* www.ktuu.com	907-762-9202	561-0874	741-5
KTVA-TV Ch 11 (CBS) 1001 Northway Dr St 202 .... Anchorage AK 99508 *TF:* 800-408-3178 ■ *Web:* www.ktva.com	907-274-1111	334-9427	741-5
KTVB-TV Ch 7 (NBC) 5407 Fairview .... Boise ID 83706 *TF:* 800-537-8939 ■ *Web:* www.ktvb.com	208-375-7277		741-17
KTVF-TV Ch 11 (NBC) 3650 Braddock St .... Fairbanks AK 99701 *Web:* www.webcenter11.com	907-458-1800	458-1820	741-47
KTVH 100 W Lyndale Ave Ste A .... Helena MT 59601 *Web:* www.ktvh.com	406-457-1212		741-58
KTVK-TV Ch 3 (Ind) 5555 N Seventh Ave .... Phoenix AZ 85013 *Web:* www.azfamily.com	602-207-3333	207-3477	741-99

	Phone	Fax	Class
KTVN-TV Ch 2 (CBS) 4925 Energy Way .... Reno NV 89502 *Web:* www.ktvn.com	775-858-2222	861-4298	741-107
KTVQ-TV Ch 2 (CBS) 3203 Third Ave N .... Billings MT 59101 *TF:* 800-908-4490 ■ *Web:* www.ktvq.com	406-252-5611	252-9938	741-14
KTVT-TV Ch 11 (CBS) 5233 Bridge St .... Fort Worth TX 76103 *Web:* dfw.cbslocal.com	817-451-1111		741-37
KTVU-TV Ch 2 (Fox) 2 Jack London Sq .... Oakland CA 94607 *Web:* www.ktvu.com	510-834-1212		741
KTWB-FM 101.9 (Ctry) 500 S Phillips Ave .... Sioux Falls SD 57104 *TF:* 888-293-2832 ■ *Web:* www.ktwb.com	605-331-5350	336-0415	645-152
KTWO-AM 1030 (Ctry) 150 N Nichols Ave .... Casper WY 82601 *Web:* www.k2radio.com	307-266-5252	235-9143	645-28
KTWO-TV Ch 2 (ABC) 1896 Skyview Dr .... Casper WY 82601 *Web:* www.k2tv.com	307-237-3711	234-9866	741-22
KTWU-TV Ch 11 (PBS) 1700 College .... Topeka KS 66621 *TF:* 800-866-5898 ■ *Web:* www.ktwu.org	785-670-1111	670-1112	741-135
KTXL-TV Ch 40 (Fox) 4655 Fruitridge Rd .... Sacramento CA 95820 *Web:* www.fox40.com	916-454-4422		741-113
KTXR-FM 101.3 (AC) 3000 E Chestnut Expy .... Springfield MO 65806 *TF General:* 855-586-8852 ■ *Web:* 1013theoutlaw.com	417-862-3751	869-7675	645-157
KTXS-TV Ch 12 (ABC) 4420 N Clack St .... Abilene TX 79601 **Fax:* News Rm ■ *TF:* 800-672-5897 ■ *Web:* www.ktxs.com	325-677-2281	672-5307*	741-1
KTXY-FM 106.9 (AC) 3215 Lemone Industrial Blvd Ste 200 .... Columbia MO 65201 *TF:* 800-500-9107 ■ *Web:* www.y107.com	573-875-1099		645
KUA (Kissimmee Utility Authority Inc) 1701 W Carroll St .... Kissimmee FL 34741 *TF:* 877-582-7700 ■ *Web:* www.kua.com	407-933-7777		787
KUAC FM/TV PO Box 755620 .... Fairbanks AK 99775 *TF:* 800-727-6543 ■ *Web:* kuac.org	907-474-7491	474-5064	632
KUAC-FM 89.9 (NPR) 312 Tanana Dr Ste 202 PO Box 755620 .... Fairbanks AK 99775 *TF:* 800-727-6543 ■ *Web:* www.kuac.org	907-474-7491	474-5064	645-57
KUAC-TV Ch 9 (PBS) University of Alaska PO Box 755620 .... Fairbanks AK 99775 *TF:* 800-727-6543 ■ *Web:* kuac.org	907-474-7491	474-5064	741-47
KUAD-FM 99.1 (Ctry) 600 Main St .... Windsor CO 80550 **Fax Area Code:* 970 ■ *TF:* 800-500-2599 ■ *Web:* www.k99.com	800-500-2599	686-7491*	645
KUAF 91.3 Public Radio 9 S School Ave .... Fayetteville AR 72701 *TF:* 800-522-5823 ■ *Web:* kuaf.com	479-575-2556	575-8440	645
Kuakini Health System 347 N Kuakini St .... Honolulu HI 96817 *Web:* www.kuakini.org	808-536-2236	547-9547	374-3
KUAT-FM 90.5 (Clas) PO Box 210067 .... Tucson AZ 85719 *Web:* radio.azpm.org/classical	520-621-5828		645-167
Kubera Partners LLC 1475 Franklin Ave Garden City .... New York NY 11530 *Web:* www.kuberapartners.com	212-202-7657		401
Kuberre Systems Inc 805 TurnPk St .... North Andover MA 01845 *TF:* 866-582-3773 ■ *Web:* www.kuberresystems.com	978-203-0453		809
Kubin-Nicholson Corp 8440 N 87th St .... Milwaukee WI 53224 *TF:* 800-858-9557 ■ *Web:* www.kubin.com	414-586-4300	586-6802	8
Kubisys 200 Wanaque Ave Ste 201 .... Pompton Lakes NJ 07442 *Web:* www.kubisys.com	973-513-9350		41
KUBL-FM 93.3 (Ctry) 434 Bearcat Dr .... Salt Lake City UT 84115 *Web:* www.kbull93.com	801-485-6700		645-142
Kubo's Sushi Bar & Grill 2414 University Blvd 200 .... Houston TX 77005 *Web:* www.kubos-sushi.com	713-528-7878		671
Kuboo Inc Ste 101 7740 E Evans Rd .... Scottsdale AZ 85260 *Web:* www.safecom.net	480-385-3893		224
Kubota Tractor Corp 3401 Del Amo Blvd .... Torrance CA 90503 *TF:* 888-458-2682 ■ *Web:* www.kubota.com	310-370-3370		273
Kubotek USA 2 Mt Royal Ave Ste 500 .... Marlborough MA 01752 *TF:* 800-372-3872 ■ *Web:* kubotek3d.com	508-229-2020	229-2121	178-5
KUBRA Data Transfer Ltd 5050 Tomken Rd .... Mississauga ON L4W5B1 *TF:* 800-766-6616 ■ *Web:* www.kubra.com	905-624-2220		177
Kucera International Inc 38133 Western Pkwy .... Willoughby OH 44094 *TF:* 800-527-3762 ■ *Web:* www.kucerainternational.com	440-975-4230		13
Kuck Mechanical Contractors Inc 395 W 67th St PO Box 388 .... Loveland CO 80538 *Web:* www.kuckmechanical.com	970-461-3553		610
Kucker & Bruh Llp 747 Third Ave .... New York NY 10017 *Web:* kbllp.com	212-869-5030		445
KUCR-FM 88.3 (Var) 691 W Linden St .... Riverside CA 92507 *Web:* www.kucr.org	951-827-3737	827-3240	645-135
Kuczmarski & Assoc 2001 N Halsted Ste 201 .... Chicago IL 60614 *Web:* www.kuczmarski.com/contact-2	312-988-1539		195
KUED-TV Ch 7 (PBS) 101 Wasatch Dr Rm 215 .... Salt Lake City UT 84112 *TF:* 800-477-5833 ■ *Web:* www.kued.org	801-581-7777	585-5096	741-115
KUEHNE + NAGEL INC 10 Exchange Pl .... Jersey City NJ 07302 *Web:* www.kn-portal.com	201-413-5500	413-5777	449
KUER-FM 90.1 (NPR) 101 S Wasatch Dr .... Salt Lake City UT 84112 *Web:* www.kuer.org	801-581-6625		645-142
Kuert Concrete Inc 3402 Lincoln Way W .... South Bend IN 46628 *TF:* 800-377-3877 ■ *Web:* www.kuert.com	574-232-9911	232-9977	182
Kuest Corp PO Box 33007 .... San Antonio TX 78265 *Web:* www.kuestcorp.com	210-655-1220	655-1220	697
Kugler Co 209 W Third St PO Box 1748 .... McCook NE 69001 *TF:* 800-445-9116 ■ *Web:* www.kuglercompany.com	308-345-2280	345-7756	276
KUGN-AM 590 (N/T) 1200 Executive Pkwy Ste 440 .... Eugene OR 97401 *Web:* www.kugn.com	541-284-8500	485-0969	645-55
KUHF-FM 88.7 (Clas) 4343 Elgin St 3rd Fl .... Houston TX 77204 *TF:* 877-252-0436 ■ *Web:* www.houstonpublicmedia.org	713-748-8888		645-75

Company	City	State	Zip	Phone	Fax	Class
Kuhl Corp 39 Kuhl Rd PO Box 26 *TF:* 800-780-5266 ■ *Web:* www.kuhlcorp.com	Flemington	NJ	08822	908-782-5696	782-2751	298
Kuhlman Corp 1845 Indian Woods Cir *TF:* 800-669-3309 ■ *Web:* www.kuhlman-corp.com	Maumee	OH	43537	419-897-6000	897-6061	182
Kuhlman Inc N 56 W 16865 Ridgewood Dr *Web:* www.kuhlmaninc.com	Menomonee Falls	WI	53051	262-252-9400		189-10
Kuhlmann Design Group Inc (KDGI) 66 Progress Pkwy *Web:* www.kdginc.com	Maryland Heights	MO	63043	314-434-8898		261
Kuhn & Company CPAs 1730 Park St *Web:* kuhnandcompany.com	Naperville	IL	60563	630-416-7700		2
Kuhn & Wittenborn Advertising 2405 Grand Blvd *Web:* kuhnwitt.com	Kansas City	MO	64108	816-471-7888		7
Kuhn Flowers Inc 3802 Beach Blvd *TF:* 800-458-5846 ■ *Web:* kuhnflowers.com	Jacksonville	FL	32207	904-398-8601		292
Kuhn Honda 2522 N Dale Mabry Hwy *Web:* www.kuhnhonda.com	Tampa	FL	33607	813-872-4816		54
Kuhn Knight Inc 1501 W Seventh Ave PO Box 0167 *Web:* www.kuhnnorthamerica.com	Brodhead	WI	53520	608-897-2131	897-2561	273
Kuhn Rikon Corp 16 Digital Dr Ste 220 *Web:* ch.kuhnrikon.com	Novato	CA	94949	415-883-1101	883-5985	362
Kuhns Brothers 558 Lime Rock Rd *Web:* www.kuhnsbrothers.com	Lakeville	CT	06039	860-435-7000		401
KUHT-TV Ch 8 (PBS) 4343 Elgin St *Web:* houstonpublicmedia.org	Houston	TX	77204	713-748-8888		741-60
Kuka Assembly & Test 5675 Dixie Hwy *Web:* www.kuka-at.com	Saginaw	MI	48601	989-777-2111	777-5620	248
Kuka Systems Corp North America 6600 Center Dr *Web:* www.kuka-systems.com/usa_nao/en	Sterling Heights	MI	48312	586-795-2000		494
Kula Hospital 100 Keokea Pl *TF:* 800-845-6733 ■ *Web:* www.hhsc.org	Kula	HI	96790	808-878-1221	878-1791	450
Kulicke & Soffa Industries Inc (K&S) 1005 Virginia Dr *NASDAQ: KLIC* ■ *Web:* www.kns.com	Fort Washington	PA	19034	215-784-6000	784-6001	695
Kuljian Corp 1880 JF Kennedy Blvd *Web:* www.kuljian.com	Philadelphia	PA	19103	215-243-1900	243-1942	261
KULL-FM 92.5 (Oldies) 3911 S First St *Web:* mix925abilene.com	Abilene	TX	79605	325-676-7711		645-1
KULR-TV Ch 8 (NBC) 2045 Overland Ave *Web:* www.kulr8.com	Billings	MT	59102	406-656-8000	652-8207	741-14
Kultur International Films Ltd PO Box 755 *TF:* 888-329-2580 ■ *Web:* kulturvideo.com	Forked River	NJ	08731	888-329-2580		513
Kulzer GmbH 99 Business Park Dr *Web:* heraeus-kulzer-us.com	Armonk	NY	10504	914-219-9000		228
Kumagoro Restaurant 533 W Fourth Ave	Anchorage	AK	99501	907-272-9905		671
Kumar & Assoc Inc 2390 S Lipan St *Web:* kumarusa.com	Denver	CO	80223	303-742-9700		261
Kumbrabow State Forest PO Box 65 *Web:* kumbrabow.com	Huttonsville	WV	26273	304-335-2219		565
KUMD-FM 103.3 (Var) 1201 ordean Ct 130 Humanities Bldg Rm 130 *Web:* www.kumd.org	Duluth	MN	55812	218-726-7181	726-6571	645-51
Kumho Tire USA Inc 10299 Sixth St *TF:* 800-445-8646 ■ *Web:* www.kumhotireusa.com	Rancho Cucamonga	CA	91730	909-428-3999		755
Kumon North America Inc 300 Frank W Burr Blvd Glenpointe Ctr E Ste 6 *TF:* 800-222-6284 ■ *Web:* www.kumon.com	Teaneck	NJ	07666	201-928-0444	928-0044	148
KUMU-FM 94.7 (AC) 1000 Bishop St Ste 200 *Web:* www.kumu.com	Honolulu	HI	96813	808-947-1500		645-73
Kunath Karren Rinne & Atkin LLC 1000 Second Ave Ste 4000 *Web:* www.kkra.com	Seattle	WA	98104	206-621-7400		405
Kuni Automotive Group 17800 SE Mill Plain Blvd Ste 190 *Web:* www.kuniauto.com	Vancouver	WA	98683	360-553-7350		57
KUNM-FM 89.9 (NPR) 1University of New Mexico MSC 06 3520 *TF:* 877-277-4806 ■ *Web:* www.kunm.org	Albuquerque	NM	87131	505-277-4806	277-6393	645-4
Kuno Creative Group LLC 36901 American Wy Ste 2A *TF:* 800-303-0806 ■ *Web:* www.kunocreative.com	Avon	OH	44011	800-303-0806		4
Kuntz Electroplating Inc 851 Wilson Ave *Web:* www.kuntz.com	Kitchener	ON	N2C1J1	519-893-7680	893-5431	481
Kuntzman Trucking Inc 13515 Oyster Rd *TF:* 800-362-9779 ■ *Web:* www.kmantrucking.com	Alliance	OH	44601	330-821-9160	821-9163	780
KUOW-FM 94.9 (NPR) 4518 University Way NE Ste 310 *TF:* 800-289-5869 ■ *Web:* www.kuow.org	Seattle	WA	98105	206-543-2710	543-2720	645-150
KUPD-FM 97.9 (Rock) 1900 W Carmen St *Web:* www.98kupd.com	Tempe	AZ	85283	480-838-0400		645
Kupferle Foundry Co, The 2511 N Ninth St *Web:* hydrants.com	Saint Louis	MO	63102	314-231-8738		789
KUPX-TV Ch 16 (I) 466C Lawndale Dr *TF:* 888-467-2988 ■ *Web:* www.stationindex.com/tv/callsign/KUPX	Salt Lake City	UT	84115	801-474-0016	463-9667	741-115
Kurama Seafood & Steakhouse 3644 Chapel Hill Blvd *TF:* 800-442-1162 ■ *Web:* www.kuramadurham.com	Durham	NC	27707	919-489-2669	489-4400	671
Kuraray America Inc 2625 Bay Area Blvd Ste 600 *TF:* 800-423-9762 ■ *Web:* www.kuraray.us.com	Houston	TX	77058	713-495-7342		745-1
Kuratur Inc 68 White St Ste 7-315 **Fax Area Code: 503*	Red Bank	NJ	07701	732-676-3183	212-0446*	387
KURB-FM 98.5 (AC) 700 Wellington Hills Rd *Web:* www.b98.com	Little Rock	AR	72211	501-401-0200		645-91
Kuriyama of America Inc 360 E State Pkwy *TF:* 800-800-0320 ■ *Web:* www.kuriyama.com	Schaumburg	IL	60173	847-755-0360	885-0996	191-2
KURL-AM 730 (Rel) 636 Haugen St *Web:* www.kurlradio.com	Billings	MT	59101	406-245-3121	245-0822	645-19
Kurlan & Associates Inc 114 Turnpike Rd *Web:* www.salesdevelopmentspecialists.com	Westborough	MA	01581	508-389-9350		194
Kurman Communications Inc 345 N Canal St Ste 1404 *TF:* 800-460-5657 ■ *Web:* kurman.com	Chicago	IL	60606	312-651-9000		636
Kurt J Lesker Co 1925 Rt 51 *Web:* www.lesker.com	Jefferson Hills	PA	15025	412-387-9200		419
Kurt Manufacturing Co 5280 Main St NE *TF:* 800-458-7855 ■ *Web:* www.kurt.com	Minneapolis	MN	55421	763-572-1500		454
Kurt Orban Partners LLC 111 Anza Blvd Ste 350 *TF:* 800-877-3830 ■ *Web:* www.kurtorbanpartners.com	Burlingame	CA	94010	650-579-3959		360-3
Kurt S Adler Inc 122 E 42nd St *Web:* www.kurtadler.com	New York	NY	10168	212-924-0900		328
Kurt Salmon Assoc Inc 1355 Peachtree St NE Ste 900 *Web:* www.kurtsalmon.com	Atlanta	GA	30309	404-892-0321		194
Kurt Versen Co 1 Paragon Dr *Web:* www.kurtversen.com	Montvale	NJ	07645	201-664-8200	664-4801	439
Kurt Weiss Greenhouses Inc 95 Main St *Web:* www.kurtweiss.com	Center Moriches	NY	11934	631-878-2500	878-2553	369
Kurtz & Hornak PA 354 N Ave E	Cranford	NJ	07016	908-276-3380		2
Kurtz Bros Company Inc 400 Reed St PO Box 392 *TF:* 800-252-3811 ■ *Web:* www.kurtzbros.com	Clearfield	PA	16830	814-765-6561	765-8690	86
Kurtzon Lighting Inc 1420 S Talman Ave *TF:* 800-837-8937 ■ *Web:* www.kurtzon.com	Chicago	IL	60608	773-277-2121	277-9164	439
Kuruma Zushi 7 E 47th St 2nd Fl *Web:* kurumazushi.com	New York	NY	10017	212-317-2802	317-2803	671
Kurz Electric Solutions Inc 1325 McMahon Dr *TF:* 800-776-3629 ■ *Web:* www.kurz.com	Neenah	WI	54956	920-886-8200	886-8201	709
Kurz Transfer Products Lp 3200 Woodpark Blvd *Web:* www.kurzusa.com	Charlotte	NC	28206	704-927-3700		658
Kurz-Kasch Inc 199 E State St *Web:* www.kurz-kasch.com	Newcomerstown	OH	43832	740-498-8343		596
KUSA-TV Ch 9 (NBC) 500 Speer Blvd *Web:* www.9news.com	Denver	CO	80203	303-871-9999	698-4700	741-39
KUSC-FM 91.5 (Clas) 1149 S Hill St Ste H100 PO Box 7913 *TF:* 877-587-2227 ■ *Web:* www.kusc.org	Los Angeles	CA	90015	213-225-7400	225-7410	645-92
KUSD-TV Ch 2 (PBS) 555 N Dakota St PO Box 5000 **Fax Area Code: 605* ■ *TF:* 800-333-0789 ■ *Web:* www.sdpb.org	Vermillion	SD	57069	800-333-0789	677-5010*	741
Kusel Equipment Co 820 W St *Web:* www.kuselequipment.com	Watertown	WI	53094	920-261-4112		429
KUSI-TV Ch 51 (Ind) 4575 Viewridge Ave *Web:* www.kusi.com	San Diego	CA	92123	858-571-5151		741-119
KUSM-TV Ch 9 (PBS) Visual Communications Bldg Rm 183 *TF:* 800-426-8243 ■ *Web:* www.montanapbs.org	Bozeman	MT	59717	406-994-3437	994-6545	741
KUSP-FM 88.9 (NPR) 203 Eigth Ave *TF:* 800-655-5877 ■ *Web:* www.kusp.org	Santa Cruz	CA	95062	831-476-2800		645
Kussmaul Electronics Company Inc 170 Cherry Ave *TF:* 800-346-0857 ■ *Web:* www.kussmaul.com	West Sayville	NY	11796	631-567-0314		256
Kuster Ann (Rep D - NH) 137 Cannon Bldg *Web:* kuster.house.gov	Washington	DC	20515	202-225-5206	225-2946	342-2
Kuster Co 2900 E 29th St *Web:* www.kusterco.com	Long Beach	CA	90806	562-595-0661		407
Kustoff David (Rep R - TN) 508 Cannon HOB *Web:* kustoff.house.gov	Washington	DC	20515	202-225-4714		342-2
Kustom Fit/Hi-Tech Seating 8990 Atlantic Ave *Web:* www.kustomfit.com	South Gate	CA	90280	323-564-4481		689
Kustom Fl LLC 265 Hunt Park Cv *TF:* 866-679-0699 ■ *Web:* www.kustom.us	Longwood	FL	32750	866-679-0699		186
Kutak Rock LLP 1650 Farnam St *Web:* www.kutakrock.com	Omaha	NE	68102	402-346-6000	346-1148	428
Kutchins, Robbins, & Diamond Ltd 1101 Perimter Dr Ste 760 *Web:* krdcpas.com	Schaumburg	IL	60173	847-240-1040		2
KUT-FM 90.5 (NPR) 300 W Dean Keeton *Web:* www.kut.org	Austin	TX	78712	512-471-1631	471-3700	645-14
Kutir Corp 37600 Central Ct Ste 280 *Web:* www.kutirtech.com	Newark	CA	94560	510-402-4526		180
Kutoka Interactive Inc 225 Roy E Ste 100 *TF:* 877-858-8652 ■ *Web:* www.kutoka.com	Montreal	QC	H2W1M5	514-849-4800	849-9182	7
KUTV-TV Ch 2 (CBS) 299 S Main St Ste 150 **Fax:* News Rm ■ *Web:* www.kutv.com	Salt Lake City	UT	84111	801-839-1234	839-1235*	741-115
Kutztown University 15200 Kutztown Rd *TF:* 877-628-1915 ■ *Web:* www.kutztown.edu	Kutztown	PA	19530	610-683-4000	683-1375	166
Kuukpik Corp PO Box 89187 *TF:* 866-480-6220 ■ *Web:* www.kuukpik.com	Nuiqsut	AK	99789	907-480-6220		345
KUVI-TV Ch 45 (MNT) 5801 Truxtun Ave *Web:* www.45kuvi.com	Bakersfield	CA	93309	661-334-2600		741-10
KUVO-FM 89.3 (Jazz) 2900 Welton St Ste 200 *TF:* 800-574-5886 ■ *Web:* www.kuvo.org	Denver	CO	80205	303-480-9272		645-47
Kuwait 321 E 44th St *Web:* www.kuwaitmission.com	New York	NY	10017	212-973-4300		784

Name / Address	City	State	ZIP	Phone	Fax	Class
Kuwait Airways Oasis Club 400 Kelby St	Fort Lee	NJ	07024	201-582-9222		26
TF: 800-458-9248 ■ *Web:* www.kuwaitairways.com						
Kuwait Embassy 2940 Tilden St NW	Washington	DC	20008	202-966-0702	966-0517	257
Web: www.kuwaitembassy.us						
KUWC-FM 91.3 (NPR) 1000 E University Ave	Laramie	WY	82071	307-766-1121		645
TF: 800-342-5996 ■ *Web:* www.uwyo.edu						
KUWJ-FM 90.3 (NPR) 1000 E University Ave	Laramie	WY	82071	307-766-4240	766-6184	645
TF: 800-729-5897 ■ *Web:* www.wyomingpublicmedia.org						
KUWS-FM 91.3 (NPR) 1805 Catlin Ave	Superior	WI	54880	715-394-8530		645
Kuyper College 3333 E Beltline Ave NE	Grand Rapids	MI	49525	616-222-3000	222-3045	161
TF: 800-511-3749 ■ *Web:* www.kuyper.edu						
Kuzmich Law Firm Pc 335 W Main St	Lewisville	TX	75057	972-434-1555		428
TF: 800-371-8751 ■ *Web:* www.kuzmichlaw.com						
KUZZ AM 55 FM 107.9 3223 Sillect Ave	Bakersfield	CA	93308	661-326-1011	328-7503	645-15
Web: www.kuzzradio.com/home.shtml						
KVAL Inc 825 Petaluma Blvd S	Petaluma	CA	94952	707-762-7367	762-0621	821
TF: 800-553-5825 ■ *Web:* www.kvalinc.com						
KVAL-TV 4575 Blanton Rd	Eugene	OR	97405	541-342-4961	342-2635	741-45
Web: www.kval.com						
K-VA-T Food Stores Inc PO Box 1158	Abingdon	VA	24212	276-623-5100		345
TF: 800-826-8451 ■ *Web:* www.foodcity.com						
KVCI (Kansas Venture Capital Inc) 10601 Mission Rd Ste 250	Leawood	KS	66206	913-262-7117	262-3509	402
Web: www.kvci.com						
KVCR-FM 91.9 (NPR) 701 S Mt Vernon Ave	San Bernardino	CA	92410	909-384-4444	885-2116	645-135
TF: 877-582-7288 ■ *Web:* www.kvcr.org						
KVDA-TV Ch 60 (Tele) 6234 San Pedro Ave	San Antonio	TX	78216	210-340-8860		741-116
KVEA-TV Ch 52 (Tele) 3000 W Alameda Ave	Burbank	CA	91523	202-237-2280		741
Web: www.telemundo52.com						
KVEG-FM 97.5 (Urban) 3999 Las Vegas Blvd S Ste K	Las Vegas	NV	89119	702-736-6161		645-88
TF: 800-273-8255 ■ *Web:* www.kvegas.com						
KVEO-TV Ch 23 (NBC) 394 N Expy	Brownsville	TX	78521	956-544-2323	544-4636	741-19
Web: www.rgvproud.com						
KVH Industries Inc 50 Enterprise Ctr	Middletown	RI	02842	401-847-3327	849-0045	529
NASDAQ: KVHI ■ *Web:* www.kvh.com						
KVI-AM 570 (N/T) 140 Fourth Ave N Ste 340	Seattle	WA	98109	206-404-4000	404-3648	645-150
TF: 888-312-5757 ■ *Web:* www.kvi.com						
KVIA-TV Ch 7 (ABC) 4140 Rio Bravo St	El Paso	TX	79902	915-496-7777	532-0505*	741-43
**Fax:* News Rm ■ *TF:* 800-433-7300 ■ *Web:* www.kvia.com						
Kvichak Marine Industries 469 NW Bowdoin Pl	Seattle	WA	98107	206-545-8485	545-3504	698
Web: www.kvichak.com						
KVIE-TV Ch 6 (PBS) 2030 W El Camino Ave	Sacramento	CA	95833	916-929-5843		741-113
TF: 800-347-5843 ■ *Web:* www.kvie.org						
KVK-TECH Inc 110 Terry Dr Ste 200	Newtown	PA	18940	215-579-1842		231
Web: www.kvktech.com						
KVLC-FM 101.1 (Oldies) 101 Perkins Dr	Las Cruces	NM	88005	575-527-1111		645
TF: 877-527-1011 ■ *Web:* www.101gold.com						
KVLY-TV Ch 11 (NBC) 1350 21st Ave S	Fargo	ND	58103	701-237-5211	232-0493	741-48
TF: 800-450-5844 ■ *Web:* www.valleynewslive.com						
KVOA-TV Ch 4 (NBC) 209 W Elm PO Box 5188	Tucson	AZ	85703	520-792-2270	620-1309	741-137
Web: www.kvoa.com						
KVOC 218 N Wolcott St	Casper	WY	82601	307-265-1984		643
KVOC-AM 1230 (Nost) 218 N Wolcott St	Casper	WY	82601	307-265-1984		645-28
KVOO-FM 98.5 (Ctry) 4590 E 29th St	Tulsa	OK	74114	918-743-7814		645-168
Web: www.kvoo.com						
KVOR-AM 740 (N/T) 6805 Corporate Dr Ste 130	Colorado Springs	CO	80919	719-540-0740	540-0740	645-39
Web: www.kvor.com						
KVOX-FM 99.9 (Ctry) 1020 S 25th St	Fargo	ND	58103	701-241-9936		645-58
Web: www.froggyweb.com						
KVPR-FM 89.3 (NPR) 2589 Alluvial Ave	Clovis	CA	93611	559-862-2480	862-2715	645-64
Web: www.kvpr.org						
KVS Information Systems Inc 821 Maple Rd	Williamsville	NY	14221	716-626-1976		177
Web: www.kvsinfo.com						
KVUE-TV Ch 24 (ABC) 3201 Steck Ave	Austin	TX	78757	512-459-6521	533-2233*	741-9
**Fax:* News Rm ■ *Web:* www.kvue.com						
KVVU-TV Ch 5 (Fox) 25 TV 5 Dr	Henderson	NV	89014	702-435-5555	451-4220	741
Web: www.fox5vegas.com						
KW Automotive North America Inc 300 W Pontiac Way	Clovis	CA	93612	800-445-3767	876-2259*	350
**Fax Area Code:* 559 ■ *TF:* 800-445-3767 ■ *Web:* www.kwsuspensions.com						
Kw Engineering 287 17th St Ste 300	Oakland	CA	94612	510-834-6420		463
Web: www.kw-engineering.com						
KW International Inc 18655 S Bishop Ave	Carson	CA	90746	310-354-6944		311
TF: 800-318-7281 ■ *Web:* www.kwinternational.com						
KW Property Management LLC 8200 NW 33rd St Ste 300	Miami	FL	33122	305-476-9188		652
Web: kwpmc.com						
K&W Tire Company Inc 735 N Prince St	Lancaster	PA	17603	717-397-3596		755
TF: 800-732-3563 ■ *Web:* www.kwtire.com						
KWAM-AM 990 (N/T) 5495 Murray Rd	Memphis	TN	38119	901-261-4200	261-4210	645-98
Web: www.kwam990.com						
Kwame Building Group Inc, The 1204 Washington Ave 200	Saint Louis	MO	63103	314-862-5344		196
Web: www.kwamebuildinggroup.com						
KWBY-AM 940 (Span) 1665 James St	Woodburn	OR	97071	503-981-9400		645-128
Web: lapantera940.com						
KWCG Inc 5471 Kearny Villa Rd Ste 300	San Diego	CA	92123	877-464-5924		260
TF: 877-464-5924 ■ *Web:* www.kwcg.us						
KWCH-TV Ch 12 (CBS) 2815 E 37th St N	Wichita	KS	67219	316-838-1212		741-142
Web: www.kwch.com						
KWD Manufacturing Co 2230 W Southcross Blvd	San Antonio	TX	78211	210-924-5999		470
KWEB-AM 1270 (Sports) 1530 Greenview Dr SW Ste 200	Rochester	MN	55902	507-288-3888	288-7815	645-137
Web: fan1270.iheart.com						
KWEN-FM 95.5 (Ctry) 7136 S Yale Ave Ste 500	Tulsa	OK	74136	918-493-7400		645-168
Web: www.k95tulsa.com						
KWHB-TV Ch 47 (Ind) 8835 S Memorial Dr	Tulsa	OK	74133	918-254-4701	254-5614	741-138
Web: kwhb.lesea.com						
KWHE-TV 14 1188 Bishop St Ste 502	Honolulu	HI	96813	808-538-1414	526-0326	741-59
TF: 800-218-1414 ■ *Web:* kwhe.lesea.com						
KWHL-FM 106.5 (Rock) 301 Arctic Slope Ave	Anchorage	AK	99518	907-344-9622		645-6
Web: www.kwhl.com						
KWHN-AM 1320 (N/T) 311 Lexington Ave	Fort Smith	AR	72901	479-782-8888	785-5946	645-61
Web: kwhn.iheart.com						
KWIC-FM 99.3 (Oldies) 825 S Kansas Ave Ste 100	Topeka	KS	66612	785-272-2122	272-6219	645-164
TF: 844-366-8993 ■ *Web:* www.eagle993.com						
Kwik Goal Ltd 140 Pacific Dr	Quakertown	PA	18951	215-536-2200	778-8869*	710
**Fax Area Code:* 800 ■ *TF:* 800-531-4252 ■ *Web:* www.kwikgoal.com						
Kwik Industries Inc 4725 Nall Rd	Dallas	TX	75244	972-458-9761	458-0948	711
Web: kwikind.com						
Kwik Kafe Company Inc 204 Furnace St	Bluefield	VA	24605	276-322-4691		366
TF: 800-533-4066 ■ *Web:* www.kwikkafeco.com						
Kwik Kopy Corp 12715 Telge Rd	Cypress	TX	77429	281-256-4100		627
Web: www.iced.net						
Kwik Kopy Printing Canada Corp 1550-16th Ave Bldg D	Richmond Hill	ON	L4B3K9	416-798-7007		627
Web: www.kkpcanada.ca						
Kwik Lok Corp 2712 S 16th Ave PO Box 9548	Yakima	WA	98909	509-248-4770	457-6531	298
TF: 800-688-5945 ■ *Web:* www.kwiklok.com						
Kwik Trip Inc 1626 Oak St PO Box 2107	La Crosse	WI	54602	608-781-8988	781-7517	204
TF: 800-305-6666 ■ *Web:* www.kwiktrip.com						
Kwik-Covers LLC 811 Ridge Rd	Webster	NY	14580	585-787-9620		362
TF: 866-586-9620 ■ *Web:* kwikcovers.com						
Kwiksew 3000 N Washington Ave	Minneapolis	MN	55411	612-521-7651		568
Web: kwiksew.mccall.com						
Kwik-Wall Co 1010 E Edwards St	Springfield	IL	62703	217-522-5553	522-1170	286
TF: 800-280-5945 ■ *Web:* www.kwik-wall.com						
KWIN-FM 97.7 (CHR) 3127 Transworld Dr Ste 270	Stockton	CA	95206	209-507-8500		645-159
TF: 800-585-5946 ■ *Web:* www.kwin.com						
KWJ Engineering Inc 8430 Central Ave Ste C	Newark	CA	94560	510-794-4296	574-8341	692
TF: 800-472-6626 ■ *Web:* www.kwjengineering.com						
KWJJ-FM 99.5 (Ctry) 0700 SW Bancroft St	Portland	OR	97239	503-733-9653	223-6909	645-128
TF: 866-239-9653 ■ *Web:* www.thewolfonline.com						
KWKB-TV Ch 20 (CW) 1547 Baker Ave	West Branch	IA	52358	319-643-5952	643-3124	741
Kwm Gutterman 795 S Larkin Ave	Rockdale	IL	60436	815-725-0206		358
Web: kwmgutterman.com						
KWMU-FM 90.7 (NPR) 3651 Olive St	Saint Louis	MO	63108	314-516-5968		645-141
TF: 866-240-5968 ■ *Web:* www.kwmu.org						
KWNR-FM 95.5 (Ctry) 2880 Meade Ave Ste 250	Las Vegas	NV	89102	702-238-7300	732-4890	645-88
Web: 955thebull.iheart.com						
KWOF-FM 92.5 (Ctry) 720 S Colorado Blvd	Denver	CO	80246	303-832-5665		645-47
Web: www.925thewolf.com						
KWPX-TV Ch 33 (I) 8112-C 304th Ave SE PO Box 426	Preston	WA	98050	212-757-3100	597-5903*	741
**Fax Area Code:* 646 ■ *TF:* 888-467-2988 ■ *Web:* ionmedia.com						
KWS Mfg Company Ltd 3041 Conveyor Dr	Burleson	TX	76028	817-295-2247	447-8528	207
TF: 800-543-6558 ■ *Web:* www.kwsmfg.com						
KWTV-TV Ch 9 (CBS) 7401 N Kelley Ave	Oklahoma City	OK	73111	405-843-6641	841-9989	741-93
TF: 888-550-5988 ■ *Web:* www.news9.com						
KWWL-TV Ch 7 (NBC) 500 E Fourth St	Waterloo	IA	50703	319-291-1200	291-1255	741
TF: 800-947-7746 ■ *Web:* www.kwwl.com						
KWYB-TV Ch 18 (ABC) 3825 Harrison Ave	Butte	MT	59701	406-782-7185	723-9269	741
Web: www.abcfoxmontana.com						
KWYE-FM 101.1 (CHR) 1071 W Shaw Ave	Fresno	CA	93711	559-490-5800		645-64
TF: 800-345-9101 ■ *Web:* www.y101hits.com						
KWYR-FM 93.7 (AC) PO Box 491	Winner	SD	57580	605-842-3333	842-3875	645
TF: 800-388-5997 ■ *Web:* www.kwyr.com						
KWYY-FM 95.5 (Ctry) 150 N Nichols Ave	Casper	WY	82601	307-266-5252		645-28
TF: 800-339-4673 ■ *Web:* www.mycountry955.com						
KX Systems Inc 530 Lytton St 2nd Fl	Palo Alto	CA	94301	650-798-5155		387
Web: www.kx.com						
KX Technologies LLC 55 Railroad Ave	West Haven	CT	06516	203-799-9000	799-7000	806
Web: www.kxtech.com						
KXAN News 908 W Martin Luther King Jr Bl	Austin	TX	78701	512-476-3636		741-9
TF: 800-843-5678 ■ *Web:* www.kxan.com						
KXAS-TV Ch 5 (NBC) 3900 Barnett St	Fort Worth	TX	76103	817-429-5555	654-6325	741-37
TF: 800-654-6385 ■ *Web:* www.nbcdfw.com						
KXFG-FM 92.9 (Ctry) 900 E Washington St Ste 315	Colton	CA	92324	909-825-9525		645
TF: 888-431-3764 ■ *Web:* kfrog.cbslocal.com						
KXJB-TV Ch 4 (CBS) 1350 21st Ave S	Fargo	ND	58103	701-237-5211	232-0493	741-48
TF: 877-571-0774 ■ *Web:* www.valleynewslive.com						
KXKC-FM 99.1 (Ctry) 202 Galbert Rd	Lafayette	LA	70506	337-920-5952		645-86
Web: www.nashfm991.com						
KXKL-FM 105 (Oldies) 720 S Colorado Blvd Ste 1200 N	Denver	CO	80246	303-832-5665		645-47
Web: www.kool105.com						
KXLF-TV Ch 4 (CBS) 1003 S Montana St	Butte	MT	59701	406-496-8400	782-8906	741
Web: www.kxlf.com						

	Phone	Fax	Class
KXLM-FM 102.9 (Span) 200 S Ste 400 Oxnard CA 93030 Web: www.radiolazer.com	805-240-2070	240-5960	645-118
KXLN-TV Ch 45 (Uni) 5100 SW Fwy Houston TX 77056 TF: 800-442-7189 ■ Web: www.univision.com/houston/kxln	713-662-4545	965-2604	741-60
KXLT-TV Ch 47 (Fox) 6301 Bandel Rd NW Rochester MN 55901 TF: 800-452-4368 ■ Web: www.myfox47.com	507-252-4747	252-5050	741-110
KXLY-AM 920 (N/T) 500 W Boone Ave Spokane WA 99201 Web: www.kxly.com	509-324-4000		645-154
KXLY-TV Ch 4 (ABC) 500 W Boone Ave Spokane WA 99201 Web: www.kxly.com	509-324-4000		741-127
KXNT-AM 840 (N/T) 7255 S Tenaya Way Ste 100 Las Vegas NV 89113 Web: lasvegas.cbslocal.com	702-889-7300		645-88
KXOJ-FM 100.9 (Rel) 2448 E 81st St Ste 5500 Tulsa OK 74137 Web: www.kxoj.com	918-492-2660		645-168
KXPR-FM 88.9 (Clas) 7055 Folsom Blvd Sacramento CA 95826 TF: 877-480-5900 ■ Web: www.capradio.org	916-278-8900	278-8989	645-140
KXRB-AM 1000 (Ctry) 5100 S Tennis Ln Sioux Falls SD 57108 Web: www.kxrb.com	605-361-0300		645-152
KXRM-TV Ch 21 (Fox) 560 Wooten Rd Colorado Springs CO 80915 TF: 800-317-6701 ■ Web: www.fox21news.com	719-596-2100	591-4180	741-32
KXSC-FM 104.9 (Alt) PO Box 6375 Artesia CA 90702 TF: 888-966-5332 ■ Web: www.kdfc.com	415-546-8710		645-146
KXTE-FM 107.5 (Alt) 7255 S Tenaya Way Ste 100 Las Vegas NV 89113 Web: x1075lasvegas.cbslocal.com	702-257-1075	889-7555	645-88
KXT-FM 91.7 (Rel) 3000 Harry Hines Blvd Dallas TX 75201 Web: kxt.org	214-871-1390	754-0635	645-44
KXTX-TV Ch 39 (Tele) 4805 Amon Carter Blvd Fort Worth TX 76155 TF: 877-266-8365 ■ Web: www.telemundodallas.com	877-266-8365		741-37
KXVO-TV Ch 15 (CW) 4625 Farnam St Omaha NE 68132 Web: cw15kxvo.com/station/contact	402-554-1500	554-4290	741-94
KXXO-FM 96.1 (AC) 119 NE Washington St Olympia WA 98501 Web: www.mixx96.com	360-943-9937	352-3643	645
KXXR-FM 93.7 (Rock) 2000 SE Elm St Minneapolis MN 55414 TF: 800-244-1111 ■ Web: www.93x.com	612-617-4000	676-8292	645-101
Ky-ani Sun Inc 1070 Riverwalk Dr Ste 350 Idaho Falls ID 83402 Web: www.kyani.net	208-529-9872		195
Kyanite Mining Corp 30 Willis Mtn Ln Dillwyn VA 23936 Web: www.kyanite.com	434-983-2085		503-2
KYB America LLC 140 N Mitchell Ct Addison IL 60101 Web: www.kyb.com	630-620-5555		61
KYBB-FM 102.7 (CR) 5100 S Tennis Ln Sioux Falls SD 57108 Web: www.b1027.com	605-361-0300		645-152
KYCC-FM 90.1 (Rel) 9019 W Ln Stockton CA 95210 TF: 800-654-5254 ■ Web: www.kycc.org	209-477-3690	477-2762	645-159
KYCK-FM 97.1 (Ctry) 1185 Ninth St NE Thompson ND 58278 TF: 800-244-1111 ■ Web: www.97kyck.com	701-775-4611	772-0540	645
KYD Inc 2949 Koapaka St Honolulu HI 96819 TF: 800-275-8777 ■ Web: www.kydinc.com	808-836-3221	833-8995	65
KYE Systems Corp 1301 NW 84th Ave Ste 127 Doral FL 33126 Web: www.geniusnet.com	305-468-9250	468-9251	173-1
Kyfi Inc 4300 Fern Valley Rd Louisville KY 40219 Web: www.kyfi.com	502-810-9800		311
KYGO-FM 98.5 (Ctry) 7800 E OrchaRd Rd Ste 400 Greenwood Village CO 80111 Web: www.kygo.com	303-321-0950		645
KYIS-FM 98.9 (AC) 4045 NW 64th St Ste 600 Oklahoma City OK 73116 Web: www.kyis.com	405-848-0100		645-114
KYKN-AM 1430 (N/T) PO Box 1430 Salem OR 97308 Web: www.kykn.com	503-390-3014	390-3728	645-128
Kyle Busch Motorsports Inc 351 Mazeppa Rd Mooresville NC 28115 Web: www.kylebuschmotorsports.com	704-662-0000		642
Kyma 3085 Piedmont Rd Atlanta GA 30305 Web: www.buckheadrestaurants.com	404-262-0702		671
Kyma Technologies Inc 8829 Midway W Rd Raleigh NC 27617 Web: www.kymatech.com	919-789-8880		696
KYMX-FM 96.1 (AC) 280 Commerce Cir Sacramento CA 95815 Web: kymx.cbslocal.com	916-923-6800		645-140
Kyne Communications Inc 252 W 37th St Ste 500E New York NY 10018 Web: www.kyne.com	212-594-5500		5
Kynikos Associates LP 20 W 55th St 8th Fl New York NY 10019 Web: www.kynikos.com	212-649-0200		41
Kyocera Communications Inc 9520 Towne Centre Dr San Diego CA 92121 TF: 800-349-4188 ■ Web: www.kyoceramobile.com	858-882-1400		647
Kyocera Industrial Ceramics Corp 5713 E Fourth Plain Rd Vancouver WA 98661 TF: 888-955-0800 ■ Web: americas.kyocera.com	360-696-8950	696-9804	249
Kyocera International Inc 8611 Balboa Ave San Diego CA 92123 TF: 877-248-4237 ■ Web: global.kyocera.com	858-576-2600	569-9412	360-3
Kyocera Mita Corp 225 Sand Rd PO Box 40008 Fairfield NJ 07004 Web: www.kyoceradocumentsolutions.com	973-808-8444		589
Kyocera Solar Inc 7812 E Acoma Dr Ste 2 Scottsdale AZ 85260 TF: 800-544-6466 ■ Web: www.kyocerasolar.com	480-948-8003	483-6431	696
Kyocera Tycom Corp 3565 Cadillac Costa Mesa CA 92626 TF: 800-823-7284 ■ Web: www.kyoceratycom.com	714-428-3600	428-3605	455
Kyoto 4920 Prytania St New Orleans LA 70115 Web: kyotonola.com	504-891-3644		671
Kyoto Japanese Steak House & Sushi Bar 1412 Greenbrier Pkwy Chesapeake VA 23320 Web: kyotochesapeakeva.com	757-420-0950		671
Kyo-Ya Company Ltd 2255 Kalakaua Ave Honolulu HI 96815 Web: kyoyahotelsandresorts.com	808-931-8600		378
Kyra InfoTech Inc 4454 Florida National Dr Lakeland FL 33813 TF: 800-550-1877 ■ Web: kyrasolutions.com/index.htm	863-686-2271		196
Kyron Inc 139 Forest Ave Palo Alto CA 94301 Web: kyron.com	650-888-3608		466
KYS 700 E Market St Jeffersonville IN 47130 Web: www.kys-marlago.com	812-282-2660		90
Kysela Pere Et Fils Ltd 331 Victory Rd Winchester VA 22602 Web: www.kysela.com	540-722-9228		80-3
Kysor Panel Systems 4201 N Beach St Fort Worth TX 76137 TF: 800-633-3426 ■ Web: kpsglobal.com	817-281-5121	281-5521	664
Kysor Warren Corp 5201 Transport Blvd Columbus GA 31907 TF: 800-866-5596 ■ Web: www.kysorwarren.com	706-568-1514		610
KYTV-TV Ch 3 (NBC) PO Box 3500 Springfield MO 65808 TF: 888-476-6988 ■ Web: www.ky3.com	417-268-3000		741-130
Kytx-Tv Cbs 19 2211 Ese Loop 323 Tyler TX 75701 Web: www.cbs19.tv	903-581-2211		116
KYUR-TV Ch 13 (ABC) 2700 E Tudor Rd Anchorage AK 99507 TF: 877-304-1313 ■ Web: www.youralaskalink.com	907-561-1313	561-8934	741-5
KYW-NEWSRADIO 1060 (N/T) 1555 Hamilton St 6th Fl Philadelphia PA 19130 Web: philadelphia.cbslocal.com	215-238-1060	977-5646	645-122
KYW-TV Ch 3 (CBS) 1555 Hamilton St Philadelphia PA 19130 Web: philadelphia.cbslocal.com	215-977-5333	977-5658	741-98
KYXY-FM 96.5 (AC) 8033 Linda Vista Rd San Diego CA 92111 TF: 888-560-9650 ■ Web: kyxy.cbslocal.com	858-571-7600	571-0326	645-144
Kyyba Inc 28230 Orchard Lake Rd Ste 130 Farmington Hills MI 48334 Web: www.kyyba.com	248-813-9665		177
KZBD-FM 105.7 (Rock) 1601 E 57th Ave Spokane WA 99223 Web: www.1057nowfm.com	509-448-1000		645-154
KZBQ-FM 93.7 (Ctry) PO Box 97 Pocatello ID 83204 TF: 800-234-1290 ■ Web: www.kzbq.com	208-234-1290	234-9451	645-126
KZEL-FM 96.1 (CR) 1200 Executive Pkwy Ste 440 Eugene OR 97401 Web: www.96kzel.com	541-284-8500		645-55
KZF Design Inc 700 Broadway St Cincinnati OH 45202 Web: www.kzf.com	513-621-6211		256
KZFM-FM 95.5 (CHR) 2117 Leopard St Corpus Christi TX 78408 Web: www.hotz95.com	361-883-3516		645-43
KZHT-FM 97.1 (CHR) 2801 S Decker Lake Dr Salt Lake City UT 84119 TF: 800-888-8499 ■ Web: 971zht.iheart.com	801-908-1300		645-142
KZIA-FM 102.9 (CHR) 1110 26th Ave SW Cedar Rapids IA 52404 Web: www.kzia.com	319-363-2061		645-29
KZII-FM 102.5 (CHR) 4413 82nd St Ste 300 Lubbock TX 79424 Web: 1025kiss.com	806-798-7078	798-7052	645-94
KZLT-FM 104.3 (AC) 1185 Ninth St NE Thompson ND 58278 Web: www.1043citiesfm.com	701-775-4611	772-0540	645-65
KZNS-AM 1280 (Sports) 301 W South Temple Salt Lake City UT 84101 TF: 855-340-9663 ■ Web: www.1280thezone.com	801-325-2043		645-142
KZOK-FM 102.5 (CR) 1000 Dexter Ave N Seattle WA 98109 TF: 800-252-1025 ■ Web: kzok.cbslocal.com	206-421-1025		645-150
KZON-FM 101.5 (Urban) 840 N Central Ave Phoenix AZ 85004 Web: live1015phoenix.cbslocal.com	602-452-1000		645-123
KZRK-FM 107.9 (Rock) 301 S Polk St Ste 100 Amarillo TX 79101 Web: www.amarillosrockstation.com	806-342-5200		645-5
KZTV-TV Ch 10 (CBS) 301 Artesian St Corpus Christi TX 78401 *Fax: News Rm ■ TF: 800-222-5426 ■ Web: www.kztv10.com	361-883-7070	884-8111*	741-36

L

	Phone	Fax	Class
L & B Realty Advisors LLP 8750 N Central Expy Ste 800 Dallas TX 75231 Web: www.lbgroup.com	214-989-0800		655
L & D Mail Masters Inc 110 Security Pkwy New Albany IN 47150 Web: www.ldmailmasters.com	812-981-7161		5
L & E Meridan 7400 Fullerton Rd Springfield VA 22153 TF: 800-723-2386 ■ Web: www.l-e.com	703-913-0300		225
L & H Boats Inc 3350 SE Slater St Stuart FL 34997 Web: www.lhboats.com	772-288-2291		90
L & H Industrial 913 L J Ct Gillette WY 82718 Web: www.lnh.net	307-682-7238		709
L & H Packing Co 647 Steves Ave San Antonio TX 78210 Web: www.lhpacking.com	210-532-3241		473
L & J Cafe 3622 E Missouri St El Paso TX 79903 Web: landjcafe.com	915-566-8418		671
L & L Hawaiian Barbecue 931 University Ave Ste 202 Honolulu HI 96826 Web: www.hawaiianbarbecue.com	808-951-9888		670
L & L Manufacturing Co 815 N Nash St El Segundo CA 90245	310-615-0000		155-3
L & L Nursery Supply Co Inc 2552 Shenandoah Way San Bernardino CA 92407 TF: 800-624-2517 ■ Web: www.llsupply.net	909-591-0461		293

Company	City	State	ZIP	Phone	Fax	Class
L & L Products Inc 160 McLean Dr TF: 800-631-0096 ■ Web: www.llproducts.com	Romeo	MI	48065	586-336-1700	336-1699	3
L & L Redi Mix 1939 Rt 206 Web: www.llredimix.com	Southampton	NJ	08088	609-859-2271		182
L & L Wings Inc 666 Broadway 2nd Fl Web: www.wingsbeachwear.com	New York	NY	10012	212-481-8299		157-6
L & M Botruc Rental Inc 18692 W Main St TF: 800-256-1186 ■ Web: www.botruc.com	Galliano	LA	70354	985-475-5733	475-5669	314
L & m Mail Service Inc 2452 Truax Blvd TF: 800-507-7070 ■ Web: www.lmmailservice.com	Eau Claire	WI	54703	715-836-0138		5
L & M Office Furniture Inc 4444 S 91st E Ave TF: 800-561-3357 ■ Web: www.l-mofficefurn.com	Tulsa	OK	74145	918-664-1010		321
L & M Radiator Inc 1414 E 37th St TF: 800-346-3500 ■ Web: www.mesabi.com	Hibbing	MN	55746	218-263-8993		61
L & M Technologies Inc 4209 Balloon Pk Rd NE Web: www.lmtechnologies.com	Albuquerque	NM	87109	505-343-0200	343-0300	271
L & N Federal Credit Union 9265 Smyrna Pkwy TF: 800-443-2479 ■ Web: www.lnfcu.com	Louisville	KY	40229	502-368-5858		219
L & R Manufacturing Co 577 Elm St Web: www.lrultrasonics.com	Kearny	NJ	07032	201-991-5330	991-5870	782
L & S Packing Company Inc 101 Central Ave TF: 800-447-1718 ■ Web: www.lspacking.com	E. Farmingdale	NY	11735	800-447-1718		123
L & S Truck Ctr of Appleton Inc 330 N Bluemound Dr TF: 888-617-3140 ■ Web: www.lstruck.com	Appleton	WI	54914	920-749-1700	749-0818	57
L & W Engineering Inc 107 Industrial Pkwy Web: www.lw-eng.com	Middlebury	IN	46540	574-825-5351		256
L & W Group Inc 30845 Huntwood Ave	Hayward	CA	94544	510-475-0111		297-8
L A Gear Inc 844 Moraga Dr TF: 800-252-4327 ■ Web: www.lagear.com	Los Angeles	CA	90049	310-889-3499		301
L a Party Rents Inc 13520 Saticoy St Web: lapartyrents.com	Van Nuys	CA	91402	818-989-4300		129
L a Tews Realty Inc 13011 Lazdins Cir Web: www.latews.com	Cypress	TX	77429	281-807-3444		652
L B L Group 3631 S Harbor Blvd Ste 200 TF: 800-451-8037 ■ Web: www.lblgroup.com	Santa Ana	CA	92704	657-232-0500		690
L b L Strategies Ltd 6321 N Avondale Ave Ste 214 Web: lblstrategies.com	Chicago	IL	60631	773-774-0240		195
L B Plastics Inc PO Box 907 TF: 800-752-7739 ■ Web: www.lbplastics.com	Mooresville	NC	28115	704-663-1543	664-2989	610
L b Property Management 4730 Woodman Ave Ste 200 TF: 888-400-7080	Sherman Oaks	CA	91423	888-400-7080		652
L Bornstein & Co Inc 321 Washington St	Somerville	MA	02143	617-776-3555		361
L Brands Inc 3 Limited Pkwy NYSE: LTD ■ Web: lb.com	Columbus	OH	43230	614-415-7000		157-6
L C Industries 1 Signature Dr	Hazlehurst	MS	39083	601-894-1771		508
L Catterton 599 W Putnam Ave Web: www.catterton.com	Greenwich	CT	06830	203-629-4901	629-4903	792
L D Reeves & Associates Inc 1889 Manzana Ave TF: 800-325-6000 ■ Web: www.ldreeves.com	Punta Gorda	FL	33950	941-575-3555		196
L E Coppersmith Inc 525 S Douglas St TF: 888-827-4388 ■ Web: www.coppersmith.com	El Segundo	CA	90245	310-607-8000	607-8001	311
L E Peabody & Assoc Inc 1501 Duke St Ste 200 Web: www.lepeabody.com	Alexandria	VA	22314	703-836-0100	836-0285	194
L f L Veritas LLC 1086 Teaneck Rd Ste 2C Web: www.lflveritas.com	Teaneck	NJ	07666	201-833-2266		2
L Frankel Packing Company Inc 230 N Peoria St	Chicago	IL	60607	312-421-3200		473
L H Carbide Corp 4420 Clubview Dr Web: www.lhindustries.com	Fort Wayne	IN	46804	260-432-5563	432-2503	488
L H Stamping Corp 4708 Clubview Dr Web: www.lhindustries.com/lh-stamping	Fort Wayne	IN	46804	260-432-9372		488
L H Thomson Company Inc, The 7800 NE Industrial Blvd Web: www.lhthomson.com	Macon	GA	31216	478-788-5052		483
L Kelley Construction Co 2901 Falling Springs Rd Web: www.lkeeley.com	Sauget	IL	62206	314-421-5933		186
L L Pelling Co 1425 W Penn St PO Box 230 Web: www.llpelling.com	North Liberty	IA	52317	319-626-4600	626-4605	186
L m Engineering Inc 2720 Intertech Dr Web: cybozone.com	Youngstown	OH	44509	330-270-2400		261
L M Scofield Co 6533 Bandini Blvd TF: 800-800-9900 ■ Web: www.scofield.com	Los Angeles	CA	90040	323-720-3000		183
L Peres & Assoc Inc 525 River Rd Web: lperes.com	Edgewater	NJ	07020	201-943-7717		652
L S Technologies LLC 4150 Rock Mtn Rd	Fallbrook	CA	92028	760-731-2320		179
L Salon & Color Group 223 S San Mateo Dr	San Mateo	CA	94401	650-342-6668		77
L Suzio Concrete Company Inc 975 Westfield Rd TF: 888-789-4626 ■ Web: www.suzioyorkhill.com	Meriden	CT	06450	203-237-8421	238-9177	182
L Tech Network Services Inc 9926 Pioneer Blvd Ste 101 Web: www.ltechnet.com	Santa Fe Springs	CA	90670	562-222-1121		225
L Thorn Co Inc 6000 Grant Line Rd TF: 800-662-4594 ■ Web: www.lthorn.com	New Albany	IN	47150	812-246-4461	246-2678	191-1
L' Appartement Hotel 455 Sherbrooke W TF: 800-363-3010 ■ Web: www.appartementhotel.com	Montreal	QC	H3A1B7	514-284-3634	287-1431	379
L'Absinthe Restaurant 227 E 67th St	New York	NY	10065	212-794-4950		671
L'Academie de Cuisine Inc 16006 Industrial Dr TF: 800-664-2433 ■ Web: www.lacademie.com	Gaithersburg	MD	20877	301-670-8670		163
L'Acadie-Nouvelle 476 St-Pierre W TF: 800-561-2255 ■ Web: www.acadienouvelle.com	Caraquet	NB	E1W1B7	506-727-4444	727-7620	532-1
L'Alouette 787 Massachusetts 28 Web: www.lalouettebistro.com	Harwich Port	MA	02646	508-430-0405		671
L'Amante 126 College St	Burlington	VT	05401	802-863-5200		671
L'Angolo Ristorante 1415 Porter St Web: www.salentorestaurant.com	Philadelphia	PA	19145	215-389-4252		671
L'Atelier 1739 Pearl St Web: www.latelierboulder.com	Boulder	CO	80302	303-442-7233		671
L'Auberge de Sedona 301 L'Auberge Ln TF: 855-905-5745 ■ Web: www.lauberge.com	Sedona	AZ	86336	928-282-1661	282-2885	671
L'Auberge Del Mar 1540 Camino del Mar PO Box 2889 TF: 800-245-9757 ■ Web: www.laubergedelmar.com	Del Mar	CA	92014	858-259-1515	755-4940	669
L'Echaude 73 Rue Sault-au-Matelot St Web: www.echaude.com	Quebec	QC	G1K3Y9	418-692-1299		671
L'Enfant Plaza Hotel 480 L'Enfant Plaza SW Web: www.hiltondcnationalmall.com	Washington	DC	20024	202-484-1000	646-4456	379
L'Entrecote Saint Jean 1080 St Jean St Web: www.entrecotesaintjean.com	Quebec	QC	G1R1S4	418-694-0234		671
L'Entrecote St-Jean 2022 Peel St Web: www.lentrecotestjean.com	Montreal	QC	H3A2W5	514-281-6492		671
L'Ermitage Beverly Hills Hotel 9291 Burton Way TF: 877-235-7582 ■ Web: www.viceroyhotelsandresorts.com	Beverly Hills	CA	90210	310-278-3344	278-8247	379
L'Escale 500 Steamboat Rd Web: www.lescalerestaurant.com	Greenwich	CT	06830	203-661-4600		671
L'Espalier 774 Bayleston St Web: www.lespalier.com	Boston	MA	02199	617-262-3023		671
L'Estaminet 1340 Fleury E Web: www.lestaminet.ca	Montreal	QC	H2C1R3	514-389-0596		671
L'etoile 22 N Water St Web: www.letoile.net	Edgartown	MA	02539	508-627-5187		671
L'Etoile 1 S Pinckney St Web: www.letoile-restaurant.com	Madison	WI	53703	608-251-0500	251-7577	671
L'Express 3927 St Denis St Web: restaurantlexpress.com	Montreal	QC	H2W2M4	514-845-5333		671
L'Garde Inc 15181 Woodlawn Ave Web: www.lgarde.com	Tustin	CA	92780	714-259-0771	259-7822	504
L'Horizon Resort & Spa 1050 E Palm Canyon Dr Web: www.thehorizonhotel.com	Palm Springs	CA	92264	760-323-1858		378
L'Hotel du Vieux-Quebec 1190 St Jean St TF: 800-361-7787 ■ Web: www.hvq.com	Quebec	QC	G1R1S6	418-692-1850		379
L'Hotel Quebec 3115 des Hotels Ave TF: 800-567-5276 ■ Web: www.hotelsjaro.com	Sainte-Foy	QC	G1W3Z6	418-658-5120	658-4504	379
L'Italiano 701 Barksdale Blvd Web: litalianorestaurant.webs.com	Bossier City	LA	71111	318-747-7777		671
L'Opera 101 Pine Ave TF: 800-437-2934 ■ Web: www.lopera.com	Long Beach	CA	90802	562-491-0066		671
L'Oreal USA 575 Fifth Ave TF: 800-322-2036 ■ Web: www.lorealusa.com	New York	NY	10017	212-818-1500		214
l'Usine Tactic Inc 127e rue E Ste 2030 Web: www.samplingproduct.com	Saint George	QC	G5Y2W8	418-227-4279		627
L. G. Jordan Oil Company Inc 314 N Hughes St Web: www.lgjordanoil.com	Apex	NC	27502	919-362-8388		579
L. H. P. Transportation Services Inc 2032 E Kearney Ste 213 TF: 800-642-1035 ■ Web: www.lhp-transport.com	Springfield	MO	65803	417-865-7577		311
L. J. Rogers Inc 421 Currant Rd Web: www.ljrogers.com	Fall River	MA	02720	508-672-8888		311
L. J. Thalmann Co 3132 Lake Ave Web: www.chaletnursery.com	Wilmette	IL	60091	847-256-0561	256-4978	323
L. M. s Technical Services Inc 21 Grand Ave Web: www.lmstech.com	Farmingdale	NY	11735	631-694-2034		175
L. Patrick Mulligan & Associates LPA 28 N Wilkinson St Web: www.patrickmulligan.com	Dayton	OH	45402	937-228-9790		428
L. Roy Papp & Associates LLP 2201 E Camelback Rd Ste 227B Web: www.roypapp.com	Phoenix	AZ	85016	602-956-0980		401
L.A. Hotel Downtown, The 333 S Figueroa St TF: 800-325-3535 ■ Web: www.thelahotel.com	Los Angeles	CA	90071	213-617-1133		707
L2 Consulting Services Inc 2100 E Hwy 290 Web: www.l2aviation.com	Dripping Springs	TX	78620	512-894-3414		256
L2 Inc 155 Wooster St Second Fl Ste Web: www.l2inc.com	New York	NY	10012	646-525-4153		466
L-3 1355 Bluegrass Lakes Pkwy Web: www.l-3com.com	Alpharetta	GA	30004	770-752-7000	752-5525	253
L-3 90 Nemco Way TF: 877-282-1168 ■ Web: www.l-3com.com	Ayer	MA	01432	978-568-5100	772-7581	647
L-3 Avionics Systems 5353 52nd St SE TF: 800-253-9525 ■ Web: www.l-3avionics.com	Grand Rapids	MI	49512	616-949-6600		529
L-3 Communications Corp Aviation Recorders Div 6000 Fruitville Rd TF: 877-726-2228 ■ Web: www.l-3ar.com	Sarasota	FL	34232	941-371-0811	377-5598	529
L-3 Communications Corp Communication Systems East Div 1 Federal St TF: 800-339-6197 ■ Web: www2.l-3com.com/cs-east	Camden	NJ	08103	856-338-3000	338-6014	529
L-3 Communications Corp Randtron Antenna Systems Div 130 Constitution Dr TF Sales: 866-900-7270 ■ Web: www2.l3t.com/randtron	Menlo Park	CA	94025	650-326-9500	326-1033	529
L-3 Communications Holdings Inc 640 North 2200 West PO Box 16850 Web: www2.l3t.com/csw	Salt Lake City	UT	84116	801-594-2000	594-3572	529

				Phone	Fax	Class
L-3 Communications Integrated Systems 1309 Ridge Rd Ste 401 *TF:* 877-282-1168 ■ *Web:* www.l3t.com/business-segments/communication-systems	Rockwall	TX	75087	903-455-3450	457-4413	22
L-3 Communications Telemetry East Div 1515 Grundy's Ln *TF:* 800-351-8483 ■ *Web:* www.l3t.com	Bristol	PA	19007	267-545-7000		647
L-3 Communications Telemetry West Div 9020 Balboa Ave *TF:* 800-351-8483 ■ *Web:* www2.l-3com.com/trf	San Diego	CA	92123	858-694-7500	694-7538	647
L-3 Electrodynamics Inc 3975 McMann Rd **Fax Area Code:* 847 ■ *Web:* www2.l3t.com/edi	Cincinnati	OH	45245	513-943-2000	660-1751*	248
L-3 Fuzing & Ordnance Systems 3975 Mcmann Rd	Cincinnati	OH	45245	513-943-2000		21
L-3 Ocean Systems 15825 Roxford St *Web:* l-3mps.com/OceanSystems	Sylmar	CA	91342	818-367-0111		529
L3 Payments LLC 850 Hampshire Rd Ste S *Web:* www.l3payments.com	Westlake Village	CA	91361	805-449-1191		463
L3 Stratis 941 mercantile dr Ste L	Hanover	MD	21076	410-684-3019		693
L3 Technologies Inc 600 Third Ave *Web:* www.l3t.com	New York	NY	10016	212-697-1111	490-0731	24
L-3 Vertex Aerospace Llc 555 Industrial Dr S *Web:* www2.l3t.com/vertex	Madison	MS	39110	601-607-6288		449
La 105.9 4745 N Seventh St Ste 140 *Web:* www.univision.com/musica	Phoenix	AZ	85014	602-308-7900	308-7979	645-123
La Barca 2414 S Vermont Ave	Los Angeles	CA	90007	323-735-6567		671
La Beau Bros Inc 295 N Harrison Ave *TF:* 800-747-9519 ■ *Web:* www.labeautrucks.com	Kankakee	IL	60901	815-933-5519	933-4366	57
La Bella Italia 402 York St *Web:* labellaitalia.com	Gettysburg	PA	17325	717-334-1978		671
La Bella Strings 256 Broadway *Web:* www.labella.com	Newburgh	NY	12550	845-562-4400		527
La Belle Dodge Chrysler Jeep Inc 501 S Main St *TF:* 800-226-1193 ■ *Web:* www.labelledodgechryslerjeep.com	Labelle	FL	33935	863-675-2701		57
La Bergerie 218 N Lee St *Web:* www.labergerie.com	Alexandria	VA	22314	703-683-1007	519-6114	671
La Bodega 703 SW Blvd *Web:* labodegakc.com	Kansas City	MO	64108	816-472-8272		671
La Cabana 312 E Fourth Ave *Web:* alaskalacabana.com	Anchorage	AK	99501	907-272-0135		671
La Cabanita 3447 N Verdugo Rd *Web:* cabanitarestaurant.com	Glendale	CA	91208	818-957-2711		671
La Caille at Quail Run 9565 Wasatch Blvd *Web:* www.lacaille.com	Sandy	UT	84092	801-942-1751	944-8990	671
La Calhene Inc 1325 Field Ave S *Web:* getinge.com/nuclear	Rush City	MN	55069	320-358-4713	358-4713	18
La Camarilla Racquet Fitness & Swim Club 5320 E Shea Blvd *Web:* www.lacamarilla.com	Scottsdale	AZ	85254	480-998-3388		77
La Canada Flowers 5971 University Ave Ste 312 *TF:* 800-472-9149 ■ *Web:* www.lacanadaflowers.com	San Diego	CA	92115	619-582-5021		292
La Canasta Mexican Food Products Inc 3101 W Jackson *Web:* www.la-canasta.com	Phoenix	AZ	85009	602-269-7721		123
La Capitol Federal Credit Union PO Box 3398 *TF:* 800-522-2748 ■ *Web:* www.lacapfcu.org	Baton Rouge	LA	70821	225-342-5055	342-9135	219
LA Care Health Plan 555 W Fifth St 29th Fl *TF:* 888-839-9909 ■ *Web:* www.lacare.org	Los Angeles	CA	90013	213-694-1250		391-3
La Carreta Mexican Restaurant 35 Manchester Rd Ste 5A *Web:* lacarretamex.com	Derry	NH	03038	603-421-0091		671
La Causa Inc PO Box 4188 *Web:* www.lacausa.org	Milwaukee	WI	53204	414-647-8750		48-8
La Cazuela Mexican Grill 1401 E Ftification St *Web:* lacazuela.com	Jackson	MS	39202	601-353-3014		671
La Cena Fine Foods Ltd 4 Rosol Ln *Web:* www.lacenafoods.com	Saddle Brook	NJ	07663	201-797-4600		345
La Chambre de Commerce de Drummond 234 Rue St Marcel CP 188 *Web:* www.ccid.qc.ca	Drummondville	QC	J2B6V7	819-477-7822	477-2823	137
La Chaumiere Restaurant 139 17th Ave SW *Web:* www.lachaumiere.ca	Calgary	AB	T2S0A4	403-228-5689	228-4448	671
La Chinita 1451 N Broadway St *Web:* www.lachinitamexicanrestaurant.com	Wichita	KS	67214	316-267-1552	267-7097	671
La Chronique 104 Ave Laurier Ouest *Web:* www.lachronique.qc.ca	Montreal	QC	H2T2N7	514-271-3095		671
La Cie Canada Tire Inc 21500 Transcanadienne *TF:* 888-267-5097 ■ *Web:* www.cdatire.com	Baie-D'Urfe	QC	H9X4B7	514-457-0155		754
La Cie Ltd 22985 NW Evergreen Pkwy *Web:* www.lacie.com	Hillsboro	OR	97124	503-844-4500		173-8
La Cita Country Club 777 Country Club Dr *Web:* www.lacitacc.com	Titusville	FL	32780	321-383-2582		669
La Citadelle International Academy of Arts & Science 36 Scarsdale Rd *Web:* www.lacitadelleacademy.com	North York	ON	M3B2R7	416-385-9685		685
La Cite collegiale 801 promenade de l'Aviation *Web:* www.collegelacite.ca	Ottawa	ON	K1K4R3	613-742-2483		165
La Clef De Sol Inc 840 Bouvier *Web:* www.laclefdesol.com	Quebec	QC	G2J1A3	418-627-0840		246
La Colombe 554 Duluth E *Web:* lacolomberestaurant.com	Montreal	QC	H2L1A9	514-849-8844		671
La Colombe D'Or Inn 3410 Montrose Blvd *TF:* 800-447-3372 ■ *Web:* www.lacolombedor.com	Houston	TX	77006	713-469-4750	524-8923	379
La Colonial Tortilla Products Inc 543 Monterey Pass Rd	Monterey Park	CA	91754	626-289-3647		123
La Corporation D'urgences-Sant, 3232 Rue Belanger *Web:* www.urgences-sante.qc.ca	Montreal	QC	H1P0A4	514-723-5600		314
La Costa 1600 E Second St *Web:* webs.com	Casper	WY	82601	307-235-6599		671
La Cote d'Or Cafe 6876 Lee Hwy *Web:* www.lacotedorarlington.com	Arlington	VA	22213	703-538-3033	573-0409	671
La Cremaillere 73 rue Sainte-Anne	Quebec	QC	G1R3X4	418-692-2216		671
La Crepe Nanou 1410 Robert St *Web:* www.lacrepenanou.com	New Orleans	LA	70115	504-899-2670		671
La Crete Sawmills Ltd Hwy 697 S PO Box 1090 *Web:* lacretesawmills.com	La Crete	AB	T0H2H0	780-928-2292		683
La Crosse Area Convention & Visitors Bureau 410 Veterans Memorial Dr *TF:* 800-658-9424 ■ *Web:* www.explorelacrosse.com	La Crosse	WI	54601	608-782-2366	782-4082	206
La Crosse County 400 N Fourth St Rm 1210 *Web:* www.co.la-crosse.wi.us	La Crosse	WI	54601	608-785-9581	785-9741	338
La Crosse County Library 103 State St *Web:* www.lacrossecountylibrary.org	Holmen	WI	54636	608-526-9600		434-3
La Crosse Ctr 300 Harborview Plaza *TF:* 800-745-3000 ■ *Web:* www.lacrossecenter.com	La Crosse	WI	54601	608-789-7400	789-7444	205
La Crosse Graphics Inc 3025 East Ave S *TF:* 800-832-2503 ■ *Web:* www.lacrossegraphics.com	La Crosse	WI	54601	608-788-2500		627
La Crosse Public Library 800 Main St *Web:* www.lacrosselibrary.org	La Crosse	WI	54601	608-789-7100	789-7106	434-3
La Crosse Tribune 401 N Third St **Fax:* Edit ■ *TF:* 800-262-0420 ■ *Web:* www.lacrossetribune.com	La Crosse	WI	54601	608-782-9710	782-9723*	532-2
La Cucina Sul Mare 237 Main St *Web:* www.lacucinasulmare.com	Falmouth	MA	02540	508-548-5600		671
La Cueva 9742 E Colfax Ave *Web:* www.lacueva.net	Aurora	CO	80010	303-367-1422		671
LA Darling Co 1401 Hwy 49B *TF:* 800-682-5730 ■ *Web:* www.ladarling.com	Paragould	AR	72450	870-239-9564		286
La Dolce Vita 17546 Woodward *Web:* ldvrestaurant.net	Detroit	MI	48203	313-865-0331		671
La Duni Latin Cafe 4264 Oak Lawn Ave *Web:* www.laduni.com	Dallas	TX	75219	214-520-7300	520-7390	671
La Famiglia 8 S Front St *Web:* www.lafamiglia.com	Philadelphia	PA	19106	215-922-2803		671
La Familia Restaurant 841 Foch St	Fort Worth	TX	76107	817-870-2002		671
La Fenice 319 King St W *Web:* www.lafenice.ca	Toronto	ON	M5V1J5	416-585-2377		671
La Fiesta Brava 6168 Hwy 49 N	Hattiesburg	MS	39401	601-584-9484		671
La Fiesta Grande 314 Versailles Rd	Frankfort	KY	40601	502-695-8378		671
La Fiesta Mexican Restaurant 9513 NW 39th Ave *Web:* www.lafiestagainesville.com	Gainesville	FL	32606	352-335-8484	332-0878	671
La Financiere Agricole Du Quebec 1400 Blvd Guillaume-Couture *Web:* www.fadq.qc.ca	Levis	QC	G6W8K7	418-838-5602		403
LA Fitness International 2880 Michelle Dr *Web:* www.lafitness.com	Irvine	CA	92606	714-505-8958		354
La Fleur 2285 Lincoln Hwy E Continental Inn *Web:* www.continentalinn.com/lafleur.asp	Lancaster	PA	17602	717-299-0421		671
La Fogata 2427 Vance Jackson Rd *Web:* www.lafogata.com	San Antonio	TX	78213	210-340-1337		671
La Folie 2316 Polk St *Web:* www.lafolie.com	San Francisco	CA	94109	415-776-5577	776-3431	671
La Follette Utilities Board 302 N Tennessee Ave PO Box 1411 *TF:* 800-352-1340 ■ *Web:* www.lub.org	La Follette	TN	37766	423-562-3316	566-0580	245
La Fonda 1900 N Second St *Web:* lafondaflg.com	Flagstaff	AZ	86004	928-779-0296		671
La Fonda 100 E San Francisco St *TF:* 800-523-5002 ■ *Web:* www.lafondasantafe.com	Santa Fe	NM	87501	505-982-5511	988-2952	379
La Fontaine Bleue Inc 7514 S Ritchie Hwy *Web:* www.lafontainebleu.com	Glen Burnie	MD	21061	410-760-4115		671
La Foret 21747 Bertram Rd *Web:* www.laforetrestaurant.com	San Jose	CA	95120	408-997-3458		671
La Fortaleza Inc 501 N Ford Blvd *Web:* www.la-fortaleza.com	Los Angeles	CA	90022	323-261-1211		345
La Fuente 625 S Fifth St	Milwaukee	WI	53204	414-271-8595		671
LA Fuess Partners Inc 3333 Lee Pkwy Ste 300 *Web:* www.lafp.com	Dallas	TX	75219	214-871-7010		256
La Gran Plaza 4200 S Fwy Ste 2500 *Web:* www.lagranplazamall.com	Fort Worth	TX	76115	817-922-8888		460
La Gran Tapa 611 B St *Web:* www.lagrantapa.com	San Diego	CA	92101	619-234-8272		671
La Grand Industrial Supply Co 2620 SW First Ave *Web:* lagrandindustrial.net	Portland	OR	97201	503-224-5800		679
La Grande FM 107.5 *CBS Radio Dallas* 4131 N Central Expy Ste 1000 *Web:* lagrande1075.cbslocal.com	Dallas	TX	75204	214-525-7000		645-44
La Grande-Union County Chamber of Commerce 102 Elm St *TF:* 800-848-9969 ■ *Web:* www.unioncountychamber.org	La Grande	OR	97850	541-963-8588	963-3936	139
La Grenouille 3 E 52nd St *Web:* www.la-grenouille.com	New York	NY	10022	212-752-1495		671
La Griglia 2002 W Gray St *Web:* www.lagrigliarestaurant.com	Houston	TX	77019	713-526-4700		671
La Grolla 815 Cote d'Abraham *Web:* www.restaurantlagrolla.com	Quebec	QC	G1R1A4	418-529-8107		671
La Grolla 452 Selby Ave *Web:* lagrollastpaul.com	Saint Paul	MN	55102	651-221-1061		671
La Grotta 2637 Peachtree Rd *Web:* www.la-grotta.com	Atlanta	GA	30305	404-231-1368		671

Name / Address	City	State	ZIP	Phone	Fax	Class
La Habra Area Chamber of Commerce 321 E La Habra Blvd *Web:* www.lahabrachamber.com	La Habra	CA	90631	562-697-1704	697-8359	139
La Habra City School District (LHCSD) 500 N Walnut St	La Habra	CA	90631	562-690-2305		186
La Habra Products Inc 4125 E La Palma Ave Ste 250 *TF:* 866-516-0061 ■ *Web:* www.lahabrastucco.com	Anaheim	CA	92807	714-778-2266	774-2079	500
La Hacienda 515 S Pk St	Madison	WI	53715	608-255-8227		671
La Hacienda Treatment Ctr 145 La Hacienda Way *TF:* 800-749-6160 ■ *Web:* www.lahacienda.com	Hunt	TX	78024	830-238-4222	238-3120	726
LA Hearne Company Inc 512 Metz Rd *Web:* www.hearneco.com	King City	CA	93930	831-385-5441	385-4377	11-1
La Isla 611 W Pk Row	Arlington	TX	76010	817-460-1180		671
La Jolla Beach & Tennis Club 2000 Spindrift Dr *TF:* 888-828-0948 ■ *Web:* www.ljbtc.com	La Jolla	CA	92037	858-454-7126	456-3805	669
La Jolla Bioengineering Institute 505 Coast Blvd S Ste 411 *Web:* www.ljbi.org	La Jolla	CA	92037	858-456-7505		261
La Jolla Light Newspaper 565 Pearl St Ste 300 *TF:* 800-691-0952 ■ *Web:* www.lajollalight.com	La Jolla	CA	92037	858-459-4201		532-3
La Jolla Nursing & Rehabilitation Ctr 2552 Torrey Pines Rd *TF:* 800-861-0086 ■ *Web:* covenantcare.com	La Jolla	CA	92037	858-453-5810	452-4301	450
La Jolla Pharmaceutical Co 10182 Telesis Ct 6th Fl *TF:* 800-732-0330 ■ *Web:* lajollapharmaceutical.com	San Diego	CA	92121	858-207-4264		85
La Jolla Playhouse PO Box 12039 *Web:* www.lajollaplayhouse.org	La Jolla	CA	92039	858-550-1070	550-1075	573-4
La Jolla Sports Club Inc 7825 Fay Ave *Web:* www.lajollasportsclub.com	La Jolla	CA	92037	858-456-2595		194
La Jolla Town Council 1150 Silverado St Ste 2131 *TF:* 800-727-4777 ■ *Web:* lajollatowncouncil.org	La Jolla	CA	92037	858-454-1444		139
La Lanterna 23 Grey Oaks Ave *Web:* www.lalanterna.com	Yonkers	NY	10710	914-476-3060	375-3008	671
LA Law Library 301 301 W First St *TF:* 800-426-1917 ■ *Web:* www.lalawlibrary.org	Los Angeles	CA	90012	213-785-2529		445
La Leche League International Inc (LLLI) 957 N Plum Grove Rd *TF:* 800-525-3243 ■ *Web:* www.lalecheleague.org	Schaumburg	IL	60173	847-519-7730	969-0460	48-17
La Ley 107.9 150 N Michigan Ave Ste 1040 **Fax:* PR ■ *Web:* laley1079.lamusica.com	Chicago	IL	60601	312-920-9500	920-9515*	645-36
La Loggia 68 W Flagler St *Web:* laloggia.org	Miami	FL	33130	305-373-4800		671
LA Louver Inc 45 N Venice Blvd *Web:* www.lalouver.com	Venice	CA	90291	310-822-4955	821-7529	42
La Lumiere School 6801 N Wilhelm Rd *Web:* www.lalumiere.org	La Porte	IN	46350	219-326-7450	325-3185	622
La Madeleine de Corps Inc 12201 Merit Dr Ste 900 *Web:* www.lamadeleine.com	Dallas	TX	75251	214-696-6962		671
La Marche Mfg Co 106 Bradrock Dr *TF:* 888-232-9562 ■ *Web:* www.lamarchemfg.com	Des Plaines	IL	60018	847-299-1188	299-3061	253
La Margarita Co 545 Ferry St SE *TF:* 800-291-6730 ■ *Web:* lamargaritasalem.com	Salem	OR	97301	503-362-8861		671
La Mariposa Nursing & Rehab 1244 Travis Blvd	Fairfield	CA	94533	707-422-7750		450
La Medusa 4857 Rainier Ave S *Web:* www.lamedusarestaurant.com	Seattle	WA	98118	206-723-2192		671
LA MEGA 106.1 122 Green St Ste 2L *Web:* www.megaworcester.com	Worcester	MA	01604	508-791-2111	752-6897	645-179
La Mer 1840 Rcn,L,vesque Est *Web:* lamer.ca	Montreal	QC	H2K4P1	514-522-3003	522-0467	671
La Mesa Rv Ctr Inc 7430 Copley Pk Pl *TF Sales:* 800-496-8778 ■ *Web:* www.lamesarv.com	San Diego	CA	92111	858-874-8000	874-8029	57
La Mesa-Spring Valley School District 4750 Date Ave *Web:* www.lmsvsd.k12.ca.us	La Mesa	CA	91941	619-668-5700		685
La Michoacana Meat Market Inc 4717 Telephone Rd *Web:* www.lamichoacanameatmarket.com	Houston	TX	77087	713-645-4202		345
La Minestra 106 E Dakota Ave *Web:* www.laminestra.com	Pierre	SD	57501	605-224-8090		671
LA Models 7700 Sunset Blvd *TF:* 800-556-6335 ■ *Web:* www.latalent.com	Los Angeles	CA	90046	323-436-7700		506
La Opinion 700 S Flower St Ste 3000 *Web:* www.laopinion.com	Los Angeles	CA	90017	213-622-8332		532-2
La Palma Intercommunity Hospital 7901 Walker St *TF:* 800-994-6610 ■ *Web:* www.lapalmaintercommunityhospital.com	La Palma	CA	90623	714-670-7400		374-3
La Pastaia 233 W Santa Clara St *TF:* 800-843-3700 ■ *Web:* www.destinationhotels.com/la-pastaia-restaurant	San Jose	CA	95113	408-286-1000		671
La Paz *La PazMexican Restaurant* 321 N Cotner Blvd *Web:* www.getintolapaz.com	Lincoln	NE	68505	402-466-9111		671
La Paz County 1108 S Joshua Ave *Web:* www.co.la-paz.az.us	Parker	AZ	85344	928-669-6115	669-9709	338
La Paz Regional Hospital Inc 1200 W Mohave Rd *Web:* www.lapazhospital.org	Parker	AZ	85344	928-669-9201		374-3
La Pensione Hotel 606 W Date St *TF:* 800-232-4683 ■ *Web:* www.lapensionehotel.com	San Diego	CA	92101	619-236-8000	236-8088	379
La Perla Cafe 5912 W Glendale Ave	Glendale	AZ	85301	623-939-7561		671
La Petite Bretonne Inc 1210 Boul Mich Le-Bohec *TF:* 800-361-3381 ■ *Web:* www.petitebretonne.com	Blainville	QC	J7C5S4	450-435-3381	435-0944	297-8
La Petite Folie 1504 E 55th St *Web:* www.lapetitefolie.com	Chicago	IL	60615	773-493-1394		671
La Petite France 3177 Glendale-Milford Rd *TF:* 800-261-8586 ■ *Web:* www.lapetitefrance.biz	Evendale	OH	45241	513-733-8383	733-0038	671
La Pinata Mexican Food Restaurant 5521 N Seventh Ave *Web:* lapinatarestaurantaz.com	Phoenix	AZ	85013	602-279-1763		671
LA Pipeline Rental & Industrial Supply LLC 3210 E Napoleon St *Web:* www.lapipelinerentals.com	Sulphur	LA	70663	337-533-8184		190
La Plata County 1060 E Second Ave Ste 134 *Web:* www.co.laplata.co.us	Durango	CO	81301	970-382-6280		338
La Plata Electric Assn Inc 45 Stewart St *TF:* 888-839-5732 ■ *Web:* www.lpea.com	Durango	CO	81303	970-247-5786	247-2674	245
La Playa Beach & Golf Resort 9891 Gulf Shore Dr *TF:* 800-237-6883 ■ *Web:* www.laplayaresort.com	Naples	FL	34108	239-597-3123	597-6278	669
La Porte County 813 Lincolnway *TF:* 800-654-3441 ■ *Web:* www.laportecounty.org	La Porte	IN	46350	219-326-6808		338
La Porte County Public Library 904 Indiana Ave *Web:* www.laportelibrary.org	La Porte	IN	46350	219-362-6156		434-3
La Porte Hospital (LPH) 1007 Lincolnway PO Box 250 *TF:* 800-235-6204 ■ *Web:* www.iuhealth.org/laporte	La Porte	IN	46350	219-326-1234	325-5403	374-3
La Porte-Bayshore Chamber of Commerce 712 W Fairmont Pkwy *Web:* www.laportechamber.org	La Porte	TX	77571	281-471-1123	471-1710	139
La Posada at Park Centre 350 E Morningside Rd *Web:* posadalife.org	Green Valley	AZ	85614	520-648-8131		672
La Posada de Santa Fe Resort & Spa 330 E Palace Ave **Fax Area Code:* 970 ■ *TF:* 866-280-3810 ■ *Web:* rockresorts.com	Santa Fe	NM	87501	505-986-0000	476-7425*	660
La Posada Hotel & Suites 1000 Zaragoza St *TF Resv:* 800-444-2099 ■ *Web:* www.laposada.com	Laredo	TX	78040	956-722-1701		379
La Preferida Inc 3400 W 35th St *Web:* www.lapreferida.com	Chicago	IL	60632	773-254-7200		297-8
La Quinta Inn & Suites Secaucus Meadowlands 350 Lighting Way *TF General:* 800-753-3757 ■ *Web:* www.lq.com/en/findandbook/hotel-details.7719.html	Secaucus	NJ	07094	201-863-8700	863-6209	379
La Quinta Resort & Club 49-499 Eisenhower Dr *Web:* www.laquintaresort.com	La Quinta	CA	92253	760-564-4111		669
La Reina Inc 316 N Ford Blvd *TF:* 800-367-7522 ■ *Web:* www.lareinainc.com	Los Angeles	CA	90022	323-268-2791		296-36
La Roche College 9000 Babcock Blvd *TF Admissions:* 800-838-4572 ■ *Web:* www.laroche.edu	Pittsburgh	PA	15237	412-367-9300		166
LA Rockler Fur Co 16 N Fourth St *Web:* rocklerfur.com	Minneapolis	MN	55401	612-332-8643		155-7
La Rockola 96.7FM 3101 W Fifth St *Web:* larockola967.estrellatv.com	Santa Ana	CA	92703	714-554-5000		645
La Rosa Del Monte Express Inc 1133-35 Tiffany St *TF:* 800-452-7072 ■ *Web:* www.larosadelmonte.com	Bronx	NY	10459	718-991-3300	893-1948	780
La Rustica 4100 Beach Dr SW	Seattle	WA	98116	206-932-3020		671
La Salle County 101 Courthouse Sq Ste 107 *Web:* www.co.la-salle.tx.us	Cotulla	TX	78014	830-879-4432	483-5101	338
La Salle University 1900 W Olney Ave **Fax:* Admissions ■ *TF:* 800-328-1910 ■ *Web:* www.lasalle.edu	Philadelphia	PA	19141	215-951-1500	951-1656*	166
La Salsa Fresh Mexican Grill 9311 E Via De Ventura *TF:* 866-452-7257 ■ *Web:* lasalsa.com	Scottsdale	AZ	85258	866-452-4252		670
La Scala of Little Italy 1012 Eastern Ave *Web:* www.lascaladining.com	Baltimore	MD	21202	410-783-9209	783-5949	671
La Scogliera Restaurant 474 River Rd *TF:* 800-442-1162 ■ *Web:* www.lascoglierarestaurant.com	Shelton	CT	06484	203-922-1179	922-1176	671
La Senorita 2706 Lake Lansing Rd *Web:* www.lasenorita.com	Lansing	MI	48912	517-485-0166		671
La Sierra University 4500 Riverwalk Pkwy *TF:* 800-874-5587 ■ *Web:* www.lasierra.edu	Riverside	CA	92515	951-785-2000	785-2901	166
La Sirena 6316 S Dixie Hwy *Web:* www.lasirenaonline.com	West Palm Beach	FL	33405	561-585-3128		671
La Sportiva North America Inc 3850 Frontier Ave Ste 100 *Web:* www.sportiva.com	Boulder	CO	80301	303-443-8710		301
LA STAGE Alliance 4200 Chevy Chase Dr *Web:* www.lastagealliance.com	Los Angeles	CA	90039	213-614-0556		720
La Strada 345 N Virginia St *Web:* eldoradoreno.com	Reno	NV	89501	775-348-9297		671
La Tapatia Tortilleria Inc 104 E Belmont Ave *Web:* www.tortillas4u.com	Fresno	CA	93701	559-441-1030	441-1712	296-36
La Tavola 248 Albemarle St *Web:* www.la-tavola.com	Baltimore	MD	21202	410-685-1859		671
La Tavola Trattoria 992 Virginia Ave *Web:* www.latavolatrattoria.com	Atlanta	GA	30306	404-873-5430		671
La Tercera Elementary School 1600 Albin Way *Web:* lt.oldadobe.org	Petaluma	CA	94954	707-765-4303		685
La Tolteca 3048 Richmond Rd	Williamsburg	VA	23185	757-253-2939		671
La Touraine Inc 625 Broadway Ste 700 *TF:* 800-893-8871 ■ *Web:* latouraineinc.com	San Diego	CA	92101	800-893-8871		225
La Trattoria 524 Duval St *Web:* www.latrattoria.us	Key West	FL	33040	305-296-1075		671
La Trattoria 522 Moosic St *Web:* thelatrattoria.com	Scranton	PA	18505	570-961-1504		671
La Traviata 314 Congress Ave *Web:* latraviata.net	Austin	TX	78701	512-479-8131		671

Phone | Fax | Class

La Traviata Restaurant
301 N Cedar Ave. Long Beach CA 90802 562-432-8022 671
Web: www.latraviata301.com

La Tribune 1950 Rue Roy Sherbrooke QC J1K2X8 819-564-5450 532-1
Web: www.lapresse.ca

La Valencia Hotel 1132 Prospect St. La Jolla CA 92037 858-454-0771 379
Web: www.lavalencia.com

La Valle Food Co
235 Murray Hill Pkwy East Rutherford NJ 07073 201-939-0005 345
Web: www.lavalleus.com

La Verne Chamber of Commerce
2078 Bonita Ave La Verne CA 91750 909-593-5265 139
Web: www.lavernechamber.org

La Veta/Cuchara Chamber of Commerce
132 W Ryus Ave La Veta CO 81055 719-742-3676 139
TF: 866-277-5550 ■ *Web:* www.lavetacucharachamber.com

La Vida Llena
10501 Lagrima de Oro NE Albuquerque NM 87111 505-293-4001 672
TF: 800-922-1344 ■ *Web:* www.lavidallena.com

La Vie Parisienne Corp
1837 Lincoln Blvd Santa Monica CA 90404 310-392-8428 411
Web: lavieparisienne.com

La Villita Historic Arts Village
418 Villita St. San Antonio TX 78205 210-207-8614 50-2

La Vina Winery 4201 S Hwy 28 La Union NM 88021 575-882-7632 50-7
TF: 800-545-9011 ■ *Web:* lavina.wolfep.com

La Vision
1394 Indian Trail - Lilburn Rd Ste 202 Norcross GA 30093 770-963-7521 963-7218 532-2
Web: www.lavisionnewspaper.com

La Vita E Bella 2411 Second Ave Seattle WA 98121 206-441-5322 671
Web: www.lavitaebella.us

LA Weekly 6715 Sunset Blvd Los Angeles CA 90028 866-789-6188 465-3220* 532-5
**Fax Area Code:* 323 ■ *TF:* 866-789-6188 ■ *Web:* www.laweekly.com

Lab Fabricators Co 1802 E 47th St Cleveland OH 44103 216-431-5444 420
Web: www.labfabricators.com

Lab Lite Llc 8 S Main St. New Milford CT 06776 860-355-8817 809
Web: www.lablite.com

Lab Products Inc 742 Sussex Ave Seaford DE 19973 302-628-4300 628-4309 73
TF: 800-526-0469 ■ *Web:* www.labproductsinc.com

Lab School of Washington, The
4759 Reservoir Rd NW Washington DC 20007 202-965-6600 685
TF: 800-505-3312 ■ *Web:* www.labschool.org

LabAnswer Government LLC
2277 Plaza Dr Ste 275 Sugar Land TX 77479 713-982-8030 809
Web: www.labanswer.com

LaBarge Coating LLC
211 N Broadway Ste 3050 Saint Louis MO 63102 314-646-3400 539
TF: 866-992-4191 ■ *Web:* www.labargecoating.com

Labat-Anderson Inc
8000 Westpark Dr Ste 400 Mclean VA 22102 703-506-9600 196
Web: www.labat.com

Labatt Breweries of Canada
207 Queen's Quay W Ste 299 Toronto ON M5J1A7 416-361-5050 102
TF Cust Svc: 800-268-2337 ■ *Web:* www.labatt.com

Labatt Food Service
4500 Industry Pk Dr San Antonio TX 78218 210-661-4216 661-0973 297-8
Web: www.labattfood.com

Labcon North America Inc
3700 Lkeville Hwy Petaluma CA 94954 707-766-2100 766-2199 419
TF: 800-227-1466 ■ *Web:* www.labcon.com

Labconco Corp 8811 Prospect Ave Kansas City MO 64132 816-333-8811 363-0130 420
TF Cust Svc: 800-821-5525 ■ *Web:* www.labconco.com

Label Graphics Company Inc
1225 Carnegie St Ste 104B Rolling Meadows IL 60008 847-454-1005 454-1008 413
TF: 800-635-6482 ■ *Web:* labelgraphicscompany.com

Label Impression Inc
1831 W Sequoia Ave. Orange CA 92868 714-634-3466 627
TF: 800-324-7770 ■ *Web:* www.labelimpressions.com

Label Printers Lp, The
1710 N Landmark Rd Aurora IL 60506 630-897-6970 627
TF: 800-229-9549 ■ *Web:* www.thelabelprinters.com

Label Systems Inc 4111 Lindbergh Dr Addison TX 75001 972-387-4512 627
TF: 800-220-9552 ■ *Web:* www.labelsystemsinc.com

Label Technology Inc 2050 Wardrobe Ave. Merced CA 95341 209-384-1000 627
TF: 800-388-1990 ■ *Web:* www.labeltech.com

Label Works 2025 Lookout Dr North Mankato MN 56003 800-522-3558 553-8698 627
TF: 800-522-3558 ■ *Web:* www.navitor.com

Label-Aire Inc 550 Burning Tree Rd Fullerton CA 92833 714-449-5155 526-0300 547
Web: www.label-aire.com

LaBella Associates PC
300 State St Ste 201 Rochester NY 14614 585-454-6110 261
Web: www.labellapc.com

LaBelle Management Inc
405 S Mission Rd Mount Pleasant MI 48858 989-772-2902 773-7521 670
Web: www.labellemgt.com

Labelmaster Co 5724 N Pulaski Rd. Chicago IL 60646 773-478-0900 413
TF: 800-621-5808 ■ *Web:* www.labelmaster.com

Labeltape Inc 5100 Beltway Dr SE Caledonia MI 49316 616-698-1830 698-7831 413
TF: 800-928-4537 ■ *Web:* www.labeltape-inc.com

Labenz & Assoc LLC
4535 Normal Blvd Ste 195 Lincoln NE 68506 402-437-8383 2
Web: labenz.com

Labette Bank 4th & Huston PO Box 497 Altamont KS 67330 620-784-5311 70
TF: 800-711-5311 ■ *Web:* www.labettebank.com

Labette Community College
200 S 14th St Parsons KS 67357 620-421-6700 421-0180* 162
**Fax:* Admissions ■ *TF:* 888-522-3883 ■ *Web:* www.labette.cc.ks.us

Labette County 501 Merchant St. Oswego KS 67356 620-795-2138 795-2928 338
Web: www.labettecounty.com

LabOne Inc 10101 Renner Blvd Lenexa KS 66219 913-888-1770 418
TF: 800-646-7788 ■ *Web:* www.labone.com

Labor Finders International Inc
11426 N Jog Rd Palm Beach Gardens FL 33418 561-627-6507 721
TF: 800-864-7749 ■ *Web:* www.laborfinders.com

Labor Law Center Inc
12534 Vly view st Garden Grove CA 92845 800-745-9970 138
TF: 800-745-9970 ■ *Web:* www.laborlawcenter.com

Labor Racketeering & Fraud Investigations Office
200 Constitution Ave NW Rm S5014 Washington DC 20210 202-693-5100 340-15
Web: www.oig.dol.gov/olrfi.htm

Laboratoire Du-var Inc
1460 Rue Graham-Bell Boucherville QC J4B6H5 450-641-4740 231
Web: www.du-var.com

Laboratory Corp of America Holdings
358 S Main St. Burlington NC 27215 336-584-5171 418
NYSE: LH ■ *TF:* 800-334-5161 ■ *Web:* www.labcorp.com

Laboratory for Laser Energetics
250 E River Rd Rochester NY 14623 585-275-5101 275-5960 668
Web: www.lle.rochester.edu

Laboratory Institute of Merchandising
12 E 53rd St New York NY 10022 212-752-1530 166
TF: 800-677-1323 ■ *Web:* www.limcollege.edu

Laborchex Co, The
2506 Lakeland Dr Ste 200 Jackson MS 39232 601-664-6760 844-2722* 635
**Fax Area Code:* 800 ■ *TF:* 800-880-0366 ■ *Web:* www.laborchex.com

Laborers National Pension Fund
14140 Midway Rd Ste 105 Dallas TX 75244 972-233-4458 528
Web: www.lnpf.org

Laborers' International Union of North America
905 16th St NW Washington DC 20006 202-737-8320 737-2754 414
TF: 800-548-6242 ■ *Web:* www.liuna.org

Laborie Medical Technologies Inc
6415 Northwest Dr Unit 11 Mississauga ON L4V1X1 905-612-1170 476
Web: www.laborie.com

LaborVoices Inc 10 Rollins Rd Ste 221 Millbrae CA 94030 925-456-4574 463
Web: www.laborvoices.com

Laboure College 303 Adams St. Milton MA 02186 617-322-3575 690-3730 800
TF: 800-877-1600 ■ *Web:* www.laboure.edu

Labov & Beyond Inc 609 E Cook Rd. Fort Wayne IN 46825 260-497-0111 7
Web: labov.com

Labovitz Enterprises
227 W First St Missabe Building Ste 950 Duluth MN 55802 218-727-7765 727-7362 707
Web: www.labovitzenterprises.com

Labrada Nutrition
403 Century Plaza Dr Ste 440 Houston TX 77073 800-832-9948 209-2135* 799
**Fax Area Code:* 281 ■ *TF:* 800-832-9948 ■ *Web:* www.labrada.com

Labrador Raul R (Rep R - ID)
1523 Longworth Bldg Washington DC 20515 202-225-6611 225-3029 342-2
Web: labrador.house.gov

Labrie Environmental Group
175 du Pont Saint-Nicolas QC G7A2T3 418-831-8250 831-5255 516
TF: 800-463-6638 ■ *Web:* www.labriegroup.com

LabRoots Inc
18340 Yorba Linda Blvd Ste 107 Yorba Linda CA 92886 714-463-4673 395
Web: labroots.com

LABS Inc 6933 S Revere Pkwy Centennial CO 80112 720-528-4750 528-4786 417
TF: 866-393-2244 ■ *Web:* www.labs-inc.org

Labsphere Inc 231 Shaker St. North Sutton NH 03260 603-927-4266 407
Web: www.labsphere.com

Labstat International ULC
262 Manitou Dr Kitchener ON N2C1L3 519-748-5409 743
Web: www.labstat.com

Labware Inc 3 Mill Rd Ste 102 Wilmington DE 19806 302-658-8444 658-7894 178-10
Web: www.labware.com

Lac Courte Oreilles Ojibwa Community College
13466 W Trepania Rd Hayward WI 54843 715-634-4790 634-5049* 165
**Fax:* Admissions ■ *TF:* 888-526-6221 ■ *Web:* www.lco.edu

Lac qui Parle County (LQP) 600 Sixth St Madison MN 56256 320-598-7444 598-3125 338
TF: 800-438-0576 ■ *Web:* www.lqpco.com

Lac Qui Parle State Park
14047 20th St NW St. Paul MN 55155 651-296-6157 734-4452* 565
**Fax Area Code:* 320 ■ *Web:* www.dnr.state.mn.us

Lacasse & Weston Inc
203 Anderson St Ste 201 Portland ME 04101 207-773-7711 261
Web: www.lacwes.com

Lace For Less Inc 1500 Main Ave Ste 3 Clifton NJ 07011 973-478-2955 478-8746 745-4
TF: 800-533-5223 ■ *Web:* www.parislace.com

Lacera Rajco International
375 County Ave Ste 653 Secaucus NJ 07094 201-583-0303 361

Lacey Drug Company Inc 4797 S Main St. Acworth GA 30101 770-974-3131 237
Web: laceydrug.com

Lacey Milling Co 217 W Fifth St. Hanford CA 93230 559-584-6634 296-23

Lacey Museum 829 1/2 Lacey St SE Lacey WA 98503 360-438-0209 520
Web: ci.lacey.wa.us

Lacey-Thurston County Chamber of Commerce
8300 Quinault Dr NE # A Lacey WA 98516 360-491-4141 139
Web: www.laceysschamber.com

Lachine General Hospital 650 16th Ave Lachine QC H8S3N5 514-934-1934 374-2

Lachman Consultant Services Inc
1600 Stewart Ave Ste 604 Westbury NY 11590 516-222-6222 194
Web: www.lachmanconsultants.com

Lachman Imports Inc
230 Fifth Ave Ste 900 New York NY 10001 212-532-1030 237
Web: www.guinotusa.com

Laciny Bros Inc 6622 Vernon Ave Saint Louis MO 63130 314-862-8330 697
Web: www.lacinybros.com

Lackawanna College 501 Vine St Scranton PA 18509 570-961-7810 162
TF: 877-346-3552 ■ *Web:* facebook.com/lackawanna

Lackawanna County 436 Spruce St Scranton PA 18503 570-963-6723 963-6387 338
TF: 800-963-0602 ■ *Web:* www.lackawannacounty.org

Lackawanna County Convention & Visitors Bureau
99 Glenmaura National Blvd Moosic PA 18507 570-496-1701 206
TF: 800-229-3526 ■ *Web:* www.visitnepa.org

Lackawanna State Park
1839 Abington Rd. North Abington Township PA 18414 570-945-3239 565
Web: www.dcnr.state.pa.us

Lackey Hershman LLP
3102 Oak Lawn Ave Ste 777 Dallas TX 75219 214-560-2201 428
TF: 800-764-9502 ■ *Web:* www.lhlaw.net

Lackmann Culinary Services
303 Crossways Pk Dr Woodbury NY 11797 516-364-2300 299

Lacks Enterprises
5460 Cascade Rd SE Grand Rapids MI 49546 616-949-6570 604
Web: www.lacksenterprises.com

Company / Address	City	State	Zip	Phone	Fax	Class
Lacks Valley Stores Ltd 1300 San Patricia St TF: 800-870-6999 ■ Web: www.lacks.com	Pharr	TX	78577	956-702-3361	782-5740	321
Laclede Chain Manufacturing Company LLC 1549 Fenpark Dr Web: www.lacledechain.com	Fenton	MO	63026	636-680-2320		492
Laclede County 200 N Adams Ave TF: 800-815-2666 ■ Web: www.lacledecountymissouri.org	Lebanon	MO	65536	417-532-5471	588-9288	338
Laclede Electric Co-op 1400 E Rt 66 TF: 800-299-3164 ■ Web: www.lacledeelectric.com	Lebanon	MO	65536	417-532-3164		245
Laclede Gas Co 720 Olive St TF: 800-887-4173 ■ Web: www.lacledegas.com	Saint Louis	MO	63101	314-342-0500		787
Laclede Inc 2103 E University Dr Web: www.laclede.com	Rancho Dominguez	CA	90220	310-605-4280		743
Laclede's Landing 710 N Second St Web: lacledeslanding.com	Saint Louis	MO	63102	314-241-5875		50-6
Laco Woodworks Inc 100 Airpark Industrial Rd	Alabaster	AL	35007	205-664-2986		200
La-Co/Markal Co 1201 Pratt Blvd *Fax Area Code: 800 ■ TF: 800-621-4025 ■ Web: www.laco.com	Elk Grove Village	IL	60007	847-956-7600	448-5436*	467
Lacombe Hospital & Care Ctr 5430 47th Ave TF: 800-291-2782 ■ Web: www.albertahealthservices.ca	Lacombe	AB	T4L1G8	403-782-3336	782-2818	374-2
Lacroix at the Rittenhouse 210 W Rittenhouse Sq Web: www.rittenhousehotel.com	Philadelphia	PA	19103	215-790-2533		671
LaCroix Precision Optics 50 LaCroix Dr Web: www.lacroixoptical.com	Batesville	AR	72501	870-698-1881		544
Lacrosse Fairgrounds Speedway N 4985 Cty Rd M Web: www.lacrossespeedway.com	West Salem	WI	54669	608-786-1525	786-1524	515
LaCrosse Footwear Inc 17634 NE Airport TF Cust Svc: 800-323-2668 ■ Web: lacrossefootwear.com	Portland	OR	97230	800-323-2668		301
Lacrosse Hall of Fame & Museum 113 W University Pkwy Web: www.uslacrosse.org	Baltimore	MD	21210	410-235-6882	366-6735	520
Lacrosse Unlimited Inc 59 Gilpin Ave Web: www.lacrosseunlimited.com	Hauppauge	NY	11788	631-582-2500		711
Lacy Construction Co 3356 W Old Hwy 30 P O Box 188 Web: www.lacygc.com	Grand Island	NE	68801	308-384-2866		186
Lacy Katzen LLP 130 E Main St 2nd Fl TF: 800-608-3333 ■ Web: www.lacykatzen.com	Rochester	NY	14604	585-454-5650		428
Lad Global Enterprises Inc 1309 S Fountain Dr Web: www.lad-global.com	Olathe	KS	66061	913-768-0888		787
Lad Lake Inc W350s1401 Waterville Rd TF: 877-965-2131 ■ Web: www.ladlake.org	Dousman	WI	53118	262-965-2131		148
Ladas & Parry LLP 1040 Ave of the Americas Web: www.ladas.com	New York	NY	10018	212-708-1800	246-8959	428
Ladco Company Ltd 200-40 Lakewood Blvd Web: www.ladco.mb.ca	Winnipeg	MB	R2J2M6	204-982-5900		186
Ladd-Peebles Stadium 1621 Virginia St TF: 800-957-3676 ■ Web: www.laddpeeblesstadium.com	Mobile	AL	36604	251-208-2500	208-2514	720
Ladenburg Thalmann Financial Services Inc 4400 Biscayne Blvd 12th Fl NYSE: LTS ■ *Fax Area Code: 305 ■ TF: 800-523-8425 ■ Web: www.ladenburg.com	Miami	FL	33137	212-409-2000	572-4199*	690
Ladew Topiary Gardens 3535 Jarettsville Pk Web: www.ladewgardens.com	Monkton	MD	21111	410-557-9466	557-7763	97
Ladies Auxiliary VFW Magazine 406 W 34th St Web: www.ladiesauxvfw.org	Kansas City	MO	64111	816-561-8655	931-4753	457-10
Ladies Professional Golf Assn (LPGA) 100 International Golf Dr Web: www.lpga.com	Daytona Beach	FL	32124	386-274-6200	274-1099	48-22
Lado International College 401 Ninth St NW Ste C100 TF: 800-281-7710 ■ Web: lado.edu	Washington	DC	20004	202-223-0023	337-1118	423
Lady & Sons, The 102 W Congress St Web: www.ladyandsons.com	Savannah	GA	31401	912-233-2600	233-8283	671
Lady Bird Johnson Wildflower Ctr 4801 LaCrosse Ave TF: 877-945-3357 ■ Web: www.wildflower.org	Austin	TX	78739	512-292-4200	232-0156	97
Lady Falconburgh's Barley Exchange 640 Main Ave	Durango	CO	81301	970-382-9664		671
Lady Grace Stores Inc 139 Endicott St Ste 1 *Fax Area Code: 800 ■ TF: 800-922-0504 ■ Web: www.ladygrace.com	Denvers	MA	01923	781-569-0727	437-9123*	157-6
Lady of America Franchise Corp 500 E Broward Blvd Ste 1650 Web: www.ladyofamerica.com	Fort Lauderdale	FL	33394	954-217-8660		354
Lady of The Sea General Hospital (LOSGH) 200 W 134th Pl Web: www.losgh.org	Cut Off	LA	70345	985-632-6401		374-3
Laerdal Medical Corp 167 Myers Corners Rd PO Box 1840 TF: 800-227-1143 ■ Web: www.laerdal.com	Wappingers Falls	NY	12590	845-297-7770		475
Laetitia Vineyards & Winery Inc 453 Laetitia Vineyard Dr TF: 888-809-8463 ■ Web: www.laetitiawine.com	Arroyo Grande	CA	93420	805-481-1772	481-6920	80-3
Lafarge North America Inc 8700 W Bryn Mawr Ave Ste 300 TF: 800-451-8346 ■ Web: www.lafarge-na.com	Chicago	VA	60631	703-480-3600	480-3899	135
Lafayette Antique Market 3108 Johnston St Web: lafayetteantiquemarket.com	Lafayette	LA	70503	337-981-9884		460
Lafayette College 730 High St *Fax: Admissions ■ Web: www.lafayette.edu	Easton	PA	18042	610-330-5000	330-5355*	166
Lafayette College Skillman Library 710 Sullivan Rd Web: library.lafayette.edu	Easton	PA	18042	610-330-5151	252-0370	434-6
Lafayette Consolidated Government 705 W University Ave PO Box 4017-C Web: www.lafayettegov.org	Lafayette	LA	70506	337-291-8200		338
Lafayette Convention & Visitors Commission 1400 NW Evangeline Thwy TF: 800-346-1958 ■ Web: www.lafayettetravel.com	Lafayette	LA	70501	337-232-3737	232-0161	206
Lafayette Copier Service & Sales 310 Farabee Dr TF: 800-877-3171 ■ Web: lafayettecopier.com	Lafayette	IN	47905	765-446-2230		535
Lafayette County 626 Main St PO Box 40 Web: www.co.lafayette.wi.gov	Darlington	WI	53530	608-776-4850	776-8893	338
Lafayette County 1001 Main St Web: www.lafayettecountymo.com	Lexington	MO	64067	660-259-4315	259-6109	338
Lafayette County 300 N Lamar Blvd Web: www.lafayettecoms.com	Oxford	MS	38655	662-236-2717	234-5402	338
Lafayette Data Systems Llc 605 S Buchanan St Web: www.lafayettedata.com	Lafayette	LA	70501	337-261-8999		180
Lafayette Federal Credit Union (Inc) 3535 University Blvd W TF: 800-888-6560 ■ Web: www.lfcu.org	Kensington	MD	20895	301-929-7990		219
Lafayette General Medical Ctr 1214 Coolidge Blvd Web: lafayettegeneral.com	Lafayette	LA	70505	337-289-7991		374-3
Lafayette Glass Company Inc 2841 Teal Rd TF: 800-382-7862 ■ Web: www.lafayetteglass.com	Lafayette	IN	47905	765-474-1402		189-6
Lafayette Hill Studios 651 Germantown Pk Web: www.lafayette.com	Lafayette Hill	PA	19444	610-828-1142		590
Lafayette Hotel 600 St Charles Ave TF: 800-366-2743 ■ Web: www.lafayettehotelneworleans.com	New Orleans	LA	70130	504-524-4441		379
Lafayette Hotel 101 Front St TF: 800-331-9336 ■ Web: www.lafayettehotel.com	Marietta	OH	45750	740-373-5522		379
Lafayette Hotel & Suites San Diego 2223 El Cajon Blvd TF: 800-468-3531 ■ Web: www.lafayettehotelsd.com	San Diego	CA	92104	619-296-2101	296-0512	379
Lafayette Life Insurance Co 400 Broadway *Fax Area Code: 513 ■ TF: 800-443-8793 ■ Web: www.llic.com	Cincinnati	OH	45202	800-443-8793	362-4900*	391-2
Lafayette Museum 1122 Lafayette St TF: 800-346-1958 ■ Web: lafayettetravel.com	Lafayette	LA	70501	337-234-2208	234-2208	520
Lafayette Natural History Museum & Planetarium 433 Jefferson St Web: www.lafayettesciencemuseum.org	Lafayette	LA	70501	337-291-5544		598
Lafayette Parish Public Library 301 W Congress St Web: lafayettepubliclibrary.org	Lafayette	LA	70501	337-261-5787	261-5782	434-3
Lafayette Parish School System 113 Chaplin Dr Web: www.lpssonline.com	Lafayette	LA	70508	337-521-7000		685
Lafayette Park Hotel 3287 Mt Diablo Blvd TF: 855-382-8632 ■ Web: www.lafayetteparkhotel.com	Lafayette	CA	94549	925-283-3700		379
Lafayette Quality Products 111 Farabee Dr Web: lqp-mfg.com	Lafayette	IN	47905	765-447-3108		482
Lafayette Regional Airport 222 Tower Dr Web: www.lftairport.com	Lafayette	LA	70508	337-266-4400		27
Lafayette Steel Erector Inc 313 Westgate Rd TF: 877-234-9435 ■ Web: www.l-s-e.com	Lafayette	LA	70506	337-234-9435	234-0217	189-14
Lafayette Venetian Blind Inc 3000 Klondike Rd PO Box 2838 TF: 800-342-5523 ■ Web: www.lafvb.com	West Lafayette	IN	47996	800-342-5523		87
Lafayette Wood-Works Inc 3004 Cameron St TF: 800-960-3311 ■ Web: www.lafwoodworks.com	Lafayette	LA	70506	337-233-5250	233-1147	499
LaFayette-Walker County Library 305 S Duke St Web: www.chrl.org	La Fayette	GA	30728	706-638-2992		434-3
Lafayette-West Lafayette Chamber of Commerce 337 Columbia St Web: www.greaterlafayettecommerce.com	Lafayette	IN	47902	765-742-4044	742-6276	139
Lafayette-West Lafayette Convention & Visitors Bureau 301 Frontage Rd TF: 800-872-6648 ■ Web: www.homeofpurdue.com	Lafayette	IN	47905	765-447-9999	447-5062	206
Lafferty Chevrolet 829 W St Rd Web: www.laffertychevy.com	Warminster	PA	18974	215-259-5817		57
Lafitte Cork & Capsule Inc 45 Executive Ct TF: 800-326-3264 ■ Web: www.lafitte-usa.com	Napa	CA	94558	707-258-2675		279
Laflamme Doors & Windows Corp 39 Industrielle TF: 800-463-1922 ■ Web: www.laflamme.com	St. Apollinaire	QC	G0S2E0	800-463-1922		499
Lafontaine Honda 2245 S Telegraph Rd TF: 866-567-5088 ■ Web: lafontainehonda.com	Dearborn	MI	48124	866-567-5088		57
LaForce inc 41 E 11th St 6th Fl Web: www.laforce-stevens.com	New York	NY	10003	212-367-8008		636
LaForce Inc 1060 W Mason St TF: 800-236-8858 ■ Web: www.laforceinc.com	Green Bay	WI	54303	920-497-7100	497-4955	234
Lafourche Chamber of Commerce, The 107 W 26th St Web: www.lafourchechamber.com	Larose	LA	70373	985-693-6700	693-6702	139
Lafourche Parish 402 Green St PO Box 5548 TF: 800-834-8832 ■ Web: www.lafourchegov.org	Thibodaux	LA	70302	985-446-8427	446-8459	338
Lafourche Sugars Corp 141 Lake Leighton Quarters Rd	Thibodaux	LA	70301	985-447-3210		296-38
LaFrance Corp 1 LaFrance Way PO Box 5002 Web: www.lafrancecorp.com	Concordville	PA	19331	610-361-4300	361-4301	701
LaFrance Equipment Corp 516 Erie St TF: 800-873-8808 ■ Web: www.lafrance-equipment.com	Elmira	NY	14904	607-733-5511	733-0482	679

Name / Address	City	State	Zip	Phone	Fax	Class
Lafromboise Communications Inc 321 N Pearl St *TF:* 800-356-4404 ■ *Web:* www.chronline.com	Centralia	WA	98531	360-736-3311		532-3
LAG (Lupient Automotive Group Inc) 7100 Wayzata Blvd Ste 600 *Web:* www.lupient.com	Minneapolis	MN	55426	763-546-2222		57
Lago Mar Resort & Club 1700 S Ocean Ln *TF:* 855-209-5677 ■ *Web:* www.lagomar.com	Fort Lauderdale	FL	33316	954-678-3915		669
Lagoon & Pioneer Village 375 N Lagoon Dr *TF:* 800-748-5246 ■ *Web:* www.lagoonpark.com	Farmington	UT	84025	801-451-8000		32
LaGrange College 601 Broad St **Fax:* Admissions ■ *TF Admissions:* 800-593-2885 ■ *Web:* www.lagrange.edu	LaGrange	GA	30240	706-880-8000	880-8005*	166
LaGrange County 114 W Michigan St *Web:* lagrangecounty.org	LaGrange	IN	46761	260-499-6300		338
LaGrange County Chamber of Commerce 901 S Detroit St Ste A *TF:* 800-898-6679 ■ *Web:* www.lagrangechamber.org	LaGrange	IN	46761	260-463-2443	463-2683	139
LaGrange County Public Library 203 W Spring St *Web:* www.lagrange.lib.in.us	LaGrange	IN	46761	260-463-2841		434-3
LaGrange County Rural Electric Membership Corp 1995 E US Hwy 20 *TF:* 877-463-7165 ■ *Web:* www.lagrangeremc.com	LaGrange	IN	46761	260-463-7165	463-4329	245
Lagrange Products Inc 607 S Wayne St *TF:* 800-369-6978 ■ *Web:* www.lagrangeproducts.com	Fremont	IN	46737	260-495-3025		770
LaGrange-Troup County Chamber of Commerce 111 Bull St *Web:* www.lagrangechamber.com	LaGrange	GA	30240	706-884-8671	882-8012	139
LaGuardia Community College 31-10 Thomson Ave **Fax:* Admissions ■ *Web:* www.laguardia.edu/home	Long Island	NY	11101	718-482-5000	609-2033*	162
Laguna Beach Chamber of Commerce 357 Glenneyre St *TF:* 800-854-2324 ■ *Web:* www.lagunabeachchamber.org	Laguna Beach	CA	92651	949-494-1018		139
Laguna Beach Visitors & Conference Bureau 381 Forest Ave *TF:* 800-877-1115 ■ *Web:* visitlagunabeach.com	Laguna Beach	CA	92651	949-497-9229		206
Laguna Brisas 1600 S Coast Hwy *Web:* www.lagunabrisas.com	Laguna Beach	CA	92651	949-497-7272		379
Laguna Cliffs Marriott Resort 25135 Pk Lantern *TF:* 800-545-7483 ■ *Web:* www.lagunacliffs.com	Dana Point	CA	92629	949-661-5000	661-5358	669
Laguna College of Art & Design 2222 Laguna Canyon Rd *TF:* 800-255-0762 ■ *Web:* www.lcad.edu	Laguna Beach	CA	92651	949-376-6000	376-6009	166
Laguna Development Corp I-40 W Exit 140 14500 Central Ave SW *Web:* www.lagunadevcorp.com	Albuquerque	NM	87121	505-352-7866		579
Laguna Honda Hospital & Rehabilitation Ctr 375 Laguna Honda Blvd *Web:* www.lagunahonda.org	San Francisco	CA	94116	415-759-2300	759-2374	374-6
Laguna Niguel Chamber of Commerce 28062 Forbes Rd Ste C *Web:* www.lnchamber.com	Laguna Niguel	CA	92677	949-363-0136	363-9026	139
Laguna Playhouse, The 606 Laguna Canyon Rd PO Box 1747 *Web:* www.lagunaplayhouse.com	Laguna Beach	CA	92651	949-497-2787	497-6948	749
Lahaina Shores Beach Resort 475 Front St *TF:* 866-934-9176 ■ *Web:* www.lahainashores.com	Lahaina	HI	96761	866-934-9176		378
Lahey Clinic Foundation Inc 41 Mall Rd *TF:* 800-524-3955 ■ *Web:* www.lahey.org	Burlington	MA	01805	781-744-8000		374-3
Lahontan State Recreation Area 16799 Lahontan Dam *Web:* www.parks.nv.gov	Fallon	NV	89406	775-577-2226		565
LaHood Darin (Rep R - IL) 1424 Longworth HOB *Web:* lahood.house.gov	Washington	DC	20515	202-225-6201	225-9249	342-2
LAI (Language Automation Inc) 1660 S Amphlett Blvd Ste 106 *Web:* www.lai.com	San Mateo	CA	94402	650-571-7877		178-7
Lai Wah Heen 108 Chestnut St *Web:* laiwahheen.com	Toronto	ON	M5G1R3	416-977-9899		671
Laibe Corp 1414 Bates St *TF:* 800-942-3388 ■ *Web:* www.laibecorp.com	Indianapolis	IN	46201	317-231-2250		492
Laico's 67 Terhune Ave *Web:* www.laicosjc.com	Jersey City	NJ	07305	201-434-4115		671
Laidlaw Carriers Bulk LP 240 Universal Rd *Web:* www.laidlaw.ca	Woodstock	ON	N4S0A9	519-539-0471		314
Laie Point State Wayside 55-001 Naupaka St *Web:* www.hawaiistateparks.org	Laie	HI	96762	808-587-0300		565
Laika 22990 NW Bennett St *Web:* www.laika.com	Hillsboro	OR	97124	503-225-1130		33
Laingsburg Community School District 205 S Woodhull Rd *Web:* www.laingsburg.k12.mi.us	Laingsburg	MI	48848	517-651-2705	651-9075	685
Laipac Technology Inc 20 Mural St Unit 5 *Web:* www.laipac.com	Richmond Hill	ON	L4B1K3	905-762-1228		246
Laird & Co 1 LaiRd Rd *TF:* 877-438-5247 ■ *Web:* www.lairdandcompany.com	Scobeyville	NJ	07724	732-542-0312	542-2244	80-1
Laird Noller Ford Inc 2245 SW Topeka Blvd *TF:* 877-803-1859 ■ *Web:* www.nollerford-topeka.com	Topeka	KS	66611	785-235-9211		516
Laird Norton Tyee 801 Second Ave Ste 1600 *TF:* 800-426-5105 ■ *Web:* lairdnortonwm.com	Seattle	WA	98104	206-464-5100		401
Laird Partners LLC 475 Tenth Ave 7th Fl *Web:* www.lairdandpartners.com	New York	NY	10018	212-478-8181		4
Laird Plastics Inc 6800 Broken Sound Pkwy Ste 150 *TF:* 800-243-9696 ■ *Web:* www.lairdplastics.com	Boca Raton	FL	33487	561-443-9100	443-9108	603
LAITEK Inc 18101 Martin Ave *TF:* 800-713-4556 ■ *Web:* www.laitek.com	Homewood	IL	60430	708-799-5000		177
Laitram LLC 200 Laitram Ln *TF:* 800-535-7631 ■ *Web:* www.laitram.com	Harahan	LA	70123	504-733-6000	733-2143	529
Lake & Cobb Plc 1095 W Rio Salado Pkwy Ste 206 *Web:* www.lakeandcobb.com	Tempe	AZ	85281	602-523-3000		445
Lake Afton Public Observatory 1845 Fairmount *Web:* www.webs.wichita.edu/lapo	Wichita	KS	67260	316-978-7827	978-3350	598
Lake Agassiz Regional Library (LARL) 118 Fifth St S PO Box 900 *TF:* 800-247-0449 ■ *Web:* www.larl.org	Moorhead	MN	56560	218-233-3757	233-7556	434-3
Lake Ahquabi State Park 1650 118th Ave *Web:* www.iowadnr.gov	Indianola	IA	50125	515-961-7101		565
Lake Air 7709 Winpark Dr *TF:* 888-785-2422 ■ *Web:* www.lakeairmetals.com	Minneapolis	MN	55427	763-546-0994	546-4469	489
Lake Air Metal Products 385 90th Ave NW *Web:* www.lakeairmetals.com/lakeairmetals/lahome.html	Coon Rapids	MN	55433	763-785-2429		697
Lake Aleknagik State Recreation Site 550 W Seventh Ave Ste 1380 *Web:* www.dnr.alaska.gov	Anchorage	AK	99501	907-842-2641		565
Lake Anita State Park 55111 750th St *Web:* www.iowadnr.gov	Anita	IA	50020	712-762-3564		565
Lake Anna State Park 6800 Lawyers Rd *Web:* www.dcr.virginia.gov/state-parks/lake-anna#general_information	Spotsylvania	VA	22553	540-854-5503		565
Lake Area Technical Institute 230 11th St NE PO Box 730 *TF:* 800-657-4344 ■ *Web:* lakeareatech.edu	Watertown	SD	57201	605-882-5284	882-6299	162
Lake Arrowhead Resort & Spa 27984 Hwy 189 *Web:* www.lakearrowheadresort.com	Lake Arrowhead	CA	92352	909-336-1511	744-3088	669
Lake Arrowhead State Park 229 Pk Rd 63 *Web:* tpwd.texas.gov/state-parks/lake-arrowhead	Wichita Falls	TX	76310	940-528-2211		565
Lake Austin Spa Resort 1705 S Quinlan Pk Rd *TF:* 800-847-5637 ■ *Web:* www.lakeaustin.com	Austin	TX	78732	512-372-7380	266-1572	707
Lake Avenue Cafe 394 S Lake Ave *Web:* www.lakeavenuecafe.com	Duluth	MN	55802	218-722-2355		671
Lake Avenue Community Foundation Inc 712 E Villa St *Web:* www.lakeavefoundation.org	Pasadena	CA	91101	626-449-4960		305
Lake Bank Shares Inc 437 Bridge Ave	Albert Lea	MN	56007	507-373-1481		70
Lake Barkley State Resort Park 3500 State Pk Rd *TF:* 800-325-1708 ■ *Web:* parks.ky.gov/findparks/resortparks/lb	Cadiz	KY	42211	800-325-1708		565
Lake Barkley Tourist Commission 82 Days Inn Dr *Web:* www.lakebarkley.org	Kuttawa	KY	42055	270-388-5300		206
Lake Bemidji State Park 500 Lafayette Rd *Web:* www.dnr.state.mn.us	St. Paul	MN	55155	651-296-6157	296-6047	565
Lake Bistineau State Park 103 State Park Rd *TF:* 888-677-2478 ■ *Web:* www.crt.state.la.us	Doyline	LA	71023	318-745-3503		565
Lake Bluff Public Library 123 E Scranton Ave *Web:* lakeblufflibrary.org	Lake Bluff	IL	60044	847-234-2540		435
Lake Bob Sandlin State Park 341 State Pk Rd 2117 *Web:* tpwd.texas.gov/state-parks/lake-bob-sandlin	Pittsburg	TX	75686	903-572-5531		565
Lake Book Manufacturing Inc 2085 N Cornell Ave *Web:* www.lakebook.com	Melrose Park	IL	60160	708-345-7000	345-1544	92
Lake Breeze Motel Resort 9000 Congdon Blvd *TF:* 800-738-5884 ■ *Web:* www.lakebreeze.com	Duluth	MN	55804	218-525-6808	525-2986	669
Lake Bronson State Park County Hwy 28 *Web:* www.dnr.state.mn.us	Lake Bronson	MN	56734	218-754-2200	754-6141	565
Lake Brownwood State Park 200 Hwy Pk Rd 15 *Web:* tpwd.texas.gov/state-parks/lake-brownwood	Lake Brownwood	TX	76801	325-784-5223		565
Lake Bruin State Park 201 State Pk Rd *TF:* 888-677-2784 ■ *Web:* www.crt.state.la.us	Saint Joseph	LA	71366	318-766-3530		565
Lake Buena Vista Factory Stores 15657 S Apopka Vineland Rd Sr 535 *Web:* www.lbvfs.com	Orlando	FL	32821	407-238-9301		460
Lake Carlos State Park 2601 County Rd 38 NE *Web:* www.dnr.state.mn.us	Carlos	MN	56319	320-852-7200		565
Lake Carmi State Park 460 Marsh Farm Rd *TF Resv:* 888-409-7579 ■ *Web:* www.vtstateparks.com	Enosburg Falls	VT	05450	802-933-8383		565
Lake Cascade State Park 970 Dam Rd *TF:* 866-634-3246 ■ *Web:* www.parksandrecreation.idaho.gov	Cascade	ID	83611	208-382-6544		565
Lake Catherine Footwear 3770 Malvern Rd PO Box 6048 *TF:* 800-819-1901 ■ *Web:* munroshoes.com	Hot Springs	AR	71901	800-819-1901		301
Lake Catherine State Park 1200 Catherine Pk Rd *Web:* www.arkansasstateparks.com	Hot Springs	AR	71913	501-844-4176		565
Lake Champlain Maritime Museum 4472 Basin Harbor Rd *TF:* 800-468-5227 ■ *Web:* www.lcmm.org	Vergennes	VT	05491	802-475-2022	475-2953	520
Lake Champlain Regional Chamber of Commerce 60 Main St Ste 100 *TF:* 877-686-5253 ■ *Web:* www.vermont.org	Burlington	VT	05401	802-863-3489	863-1538	139
Lake Charles American Press Inc PO Box 2893 *TF:* 800-737-2283 ■ *Web:* www.americanpress.com	Lake Charles	LA	70602	337-433-3000	494-4008	637-8

Name / Address	City	State	ZIP	Phone	Fax	Class
Lake Charles Civic Ctr 900 Lakeshore Dr TF: 888-620-1749 ■ Web: www.cityoflakecharles.com	Lake Charles	LA	70601	337-491-1256	491-1534	572
Lake Charles Memorial Health System (LCMH) 1701 Oak Pk Blvd TF: 800-494-5264 ■ Web: www.lcmh.com	Lake Charles	LA	70601	337-494-3000		374-3
Lake Charles State Park 3705 Hwy 25 Web: www.arkansasstateparks.com/lakecharles	Powhatan	AR	72458	870-878-6595		565
Lake Chelan National Recreation Area 810 State Rt 20 Web: www.nps.gov/lach	Sedro Woolley	WA	98284	360-854-7200	856-1934	564
Lake Chelan State Park 7544 S Lakeshore Dr Web: www.parks.wa.gov	Chelan	WA	98816	509-687-3710		565
Lake Chicot State Park 2542 Hwy 257 TF: 800-264-2430 ■ Web: www.arkansasstateparks.com	Lake Village	AR	71653	870-265-5480		565
Lake City Chamber of Commerce 12345 30th Ave NE Ste FG TF: 800-624-3555 ■ Web: www.lakecitychamber.org	Seattle	WA	98125	206-363-3287		139
Lake City Correctional Facility 7906 E US Hwy 90 TF: 800-656-4673 ■ Web: www.cca.com	Lake City	FL	32055	386-755-3379	752-7202	213
Lake City/Columbia County Chamber of Commerce 162 S Marion Ave Web: www.lakecitychamber.com	Lake City	FL	32025	386-752-3690	755-7744	139
Lake Claiborne State Park 225 State Pk Rd TF: 888-677-2524 ■ Web: www.crt.state.la.us	Homer	LA	71040	318-927-2976		565
Lake Clark National Park & Preserve 240 W Fifth Ave Ste 236 TF: 800-365-2267 ■ Web: www.nps.gov	Anchorage	AK	99501	907-644-3626	644-3810	564
Lake Cochrane Recreation Area 3454 Edgewater Dr Web: gfp.sd.gov/state-parks/directory/lake-cochrane	Gary	SD	57237	605-882-5200		565
Lake Colorado City State Park 4582 FM 2836 Web: tpwd.texas.gov/state-parks/lake-colorado-city	Colorado City	TX	79512	325-728-3931		565
Lake Compounce Family Theme Park 822 Lake Ave Web: www.lakecompounce.com	Bristol	CT	06010	860-583-3300	589-7974	32
Lake Corpus Christi State Park 23194 Pk Rd 25 Web: tpwd.texas.gov/state-parks/lake-corpus-christi	Mathis	TX	78368	361-547-2635		565
Lake Correctional Institution 19225 US Hwy 27 Web: dc.state.fl.us	Clermont	FL	34711	352-394-6146		213
Lake Cos Inc, The 2980 Walker Dr Web: www.lakeco.com	Green Bay	WI	54311	920-406-3030	406-3040	174
Lake Country Foods Inc 132 S Concord Rd Web: www.lcfoods.com	Oconomowoc	WI	53066	262-567-5521		578
Lake Country Power 2810 Elida Dr *Fax Area Code: 218 ■ TF: 800-421-9959 ■ Web: www.lakecountrypower.com	Grand Rapids	MN	55744	800-421-9959	326-8136*	245
Lake County 895 Michigan Ave PO Box 130 TF: 800-245-3240 ■ Web: www.lakecountymichigan.com	Baldwin	MI	49304	231-745-4331		338
Lake County 2293 N Main St TF: 800-340-8155 ■ Web: www.lakecountyin.org	Crown Point	IN	46307	219-755-3535		338
Lake County 255 N Forbes St Web: www.co.lake.ca.us	Lakeport	CA	95453	707-263-2371	263-2207	338
Lake County 513 Ctr St Web: www.lakecountyor.org	Lakeview	OR	97630	541-947-6006	947-6015	338
Lake County PO Box 917 Web: www.lakecountyco.com	Leadville	CO	80461	719-486-1410	486-3972	338
Lake County 200 E Ctr St Web: www.lake.sd.gov	Madison	SD	57042	605-256-5644	256-5080	338
Lake County 25 N Pk Pl TF: 800-899-5253 ■ Web: www.lakecountyohio.org	Painesville	OH	44077	440-350-2500		338
Lake County 550 W Main St Web: lakecountyfl.gov	Tavares	FL	32778	352-742-4102		338
Lake County 601 Third Ave Web: www.co.lake.mn.us	Two Harbors	MN	55616	218-834-8300	834-8360	338
Lake County 18 N County St TF: 800-367-5690 ■ Web: www.lakecountyil.gov	Waukegan	IL	60085	847-377-2000		338
Lake County Chamber of Commerce 5221 Grand Ave Web: www.lakecountychamber.com	Gurnee	IL	60031	847-249-3800		139
Lake County Convention & Visitors Bureau 5465 W Grand Ave Ste 100 TF: 800-525-3669 ■ Web: www.visitlakecounty.org	Gurnee	IL	60031	847-662-2700	662-2702	206
Lake County Courthouse 106 Fourth Ave E Web: www.lakemt.gov	Polson	MT	59860	406-883-7215		338
Lake County Educational Service Ctr 8221 Auburn Rd Web: www.lcesc.k12.oh.us	Concord Township	OH	44077	440-350-2563		242
Lake County Forest Preserve District 2000 N Milwaukee Ave Web: www.lcfpd.org	Libertyville	IL	60048	847-367-6640	367-6649	302
Lake County Library 1425 N High St TF: 800-525-3743 ■ Web: library.co.lake.ca.us	Lakeport	CA	95453	707-263-8817		434-3
Lake County Press Inc 98 Noll St Web: www.lakecountypress.com	Waukegan	IL	60085	847-336-4333		627
Lake County Public Library 1919 W 81st Ave TF: 800-448-3543 ■ Web: lcplin.org	Merrillville	IN	46410	219-769-3541	769-0690	434-3
Lake Court Medical Supplies Inc 27733 Groesbeck Hwy Web: www.lakecourt.com	Roseville	MI	48066	586-771-3100		41
Lake Cumberland Regional Hospital 305 Langdon St Web: lakecumberlandhospital.com	Somerset	KY	42503	606-679-7441	678-9919	374-3
Lake Cumberland State Resort Park 5465 State Pk Rd Web: www.state.ky.us	Jamestown	KY	42629	270-343-3111	343-5510	669
Lake D'Arbonne State Park 3628 Evergreen Rd TF: 888-677-5200 ■ Web: www.crt.state.la.us	Farmerville	LA	71241	318-368-2086		565
Lake Dardanelle State Park 100 State Park Dr Web: www.arkansasstateparks.com	Russellville	AR	72802	479-967-5516		565
Lake Darling State Park 111 Lake Darling Rd Web: www.iowadnr.gov	Brighton	IA	52540	319-694-2323		565
Lake Data Center Inc 800 Lloyd Rd Web: www.lakedata.com	Wickliffe	OH	44092	440-944-2020		225
Lake Easton State Park 150 Lake Easton State Pk Rd Web: www.parks.wa.gov	Easton	WA	98925	509-656-2230		565
Lake Elmo State Park 2300 Lake Elmo Dr Web: stateparks.mt.gov	Billings	MT	59105	406-247-2955		565
Lake Elsinore Valley Chamber of Commerce 132 W Graham Ave Web: www.lakeelsinorechamber.com	Lake Elsinore	CA	92530	951-245-8848	245-9127	139
Lake EMS 2761 W Old US Hwy 441 TF: 800-756-7233 ■ Web: www.lakeems.org	Mount Dora	FL	32757	352-383-4554		30
Lake Erie Beach Hotels 8696 E Lake Rd TF: 888-558-8439 ■ Web: www.lakeviewerie.com	Erie	PA	16511	814-899-6948		379
Lake Erie College 391 W Washington St *Fax: Admissions ■ TF: 800-533-4996 ■ Web: www.lec.edu	Painesville	OH	44077	440-375-7050	375-7005*	166
Lake Erie Construction Co 25 S Norwalk Rd TF: 800-362-1343 ■ Web: lec-co.com	Norwalk	OH	44857	419-668-3302		188-4
Lake Erie Electric Inc 25730 First St TF: 800-800-9818 ■ Web: www.lakeerieelectric.com	Westlake	OH	44145	440-835-5565	835-5688	189-4
Lake Erie Frozen Foods Co 1830 Orange Rd TF: 800-766-8501 ■ Web: www.leffco.net	Ashland	OH	44805	419-289-9204		345
Lake Erie Graphics Inc 5372 W 130th St TF: 888-293-7397 ■ Web: www.lakeeriegraphics.com	Brook Park	OH	44142	216-265-7575		627
Lake Erie Shores & Islands Welcome Ctr 770 SE Catawba Rd TF: 800-441-1271 ■ Web: www.shoresandislands.com	Port Clinton	OH	43452	419-734-4386	734-9798	206
Lake Erie Speedway 10700 Delmas Dr Web: www.lakeeriespeedway.com	North East	PA	16428	814-725-3303	725-3353	642
Lake Erie State Park 5838 Route 5 Web: parks.ny.gov/parks/129/details.aspx	Brocton	NY	14716	716-792-9214		565
Lake Eufaula State Park HC 60 PO Web: www.travelok.com	Checotah	OK	74426	918-689-7337		565
Lake Forest Academy 1500 W Kennedy Rd Web: www.lfanet.org	Lake Forest	IL	60045	847-234-3210		622
Lake Forest College 555 N Sheridan Rd TF: 800-828-4751 ■ Web: www.lakeforest.edu	Lake Forest	IL	60045	847-234-3100	735-6271	166
Lake Forest Hospital 660 N Westmoreland Rd Web: www.lakeforesthospital.com	Lake Forest	IL	60045	847-234-5600		374-3
Lake Fort Smith State Park PO Box 4 Web: www.arkansasstateparks.com	Mountainburg	AR	72946	479-369-2469		565
Lake Francis State Park 439 River Rd Web: www.nhstateparks.org	Pittsburg	NH	03592	603-538-6965		565
Lake Frierson State Park 7904 Hwy Web: www.arkansasstateparks.com	Jonesboro	AR	72401	870-932-2615		565
Lake Gogebic State Park N9995 State Hwy M-64 Web: www.michigandnr.com	Marenisco	MI	49947	906-842-3341		565
Lake Granbury Area Chamber of Commerce 3408 E Hwy 377 Web: www.granburychamber.com	Granbury	TX	76049	817-573-1622	573-0805	139
Lake Greenwood State Recreation Area 302 State Pk Rd TF: 866-345-7275 ■ Web: www.southcarolinaparks.com	Ninety Six	SC	29666	864-543-3535		565
Lake Griffin State Park 3089 US 441-27 Web: www.floridastateparks.org	Fruitland Park	FL	34731	352-360-6760		565
Lake Group Media Inc 1 Byram Brook Pl TF: 800-829-0422 ■ Web: www.lakegroupmedia.com	Armonk	NY	10504	914-925-2400	925-2499	5
Lake Hartwell State Recreation Area 19138 S Hwy 11 Ste A Web: www.southcarolinaparks.com	Fair Play	SC	29643	864-972-3352		565
Lake Havasu Area Chamber of Commerce 314 London Bridge Rd TF: 800-307-3610 ■ Web: www.havasuchamber.com	Lake Havasu City	AZ	86403	928-855-4115	680-0010	139
Lake Havasu State Park 699 London Bridge Rd Web: golakehavasu.com	Lake Havasu City	AZ	86403	928-855-2784		565
Lake Haven Utility District 31627-1st Ave S PO Box 4249 Web: www.lakehaven.org	Federal Way	WA	98063	253-941-1516		787
Lake Herman State Park 23409 State Pk Dr Web: gfp.sd.gov	Madison	SD	57042	605-256-5003		565
Lake Hiddenwood Recreation Area c/o W Whitlock Recreation Area 16157A W Whitlock Rd Web: www.gfp.sd.gov	Gettysburg	SD	57442	605-765-9410		565
Lake Hills Golf Club Inc 1930 Clubhouse Way Web: www.lakehillsgolf.com	Billings	MT	59105	406-252-9244		354
Lake Hope State Park 27331 State Rt 278 Web: parks.ohiodnr.gov/lakehope	McArthur	OH	45651	740-596-4938		565
Lake Houston Area Chamber of Commerce, The 110 W Main St Web: www.lakehouston.org	Humble	TX	77338	281-446-2128	446-7483	139
Lake Hudson Recreation Area 5505 Morey Hwy Web: www.michigandnr.com	Clayton	MI	49235	517-445-2265		565
Lake Immunogenics Inc 348 Berg Rd *Fax Area Code: 585 ■ TF: 800-648-9990 ■ Web: www.lakeimmunogenics.com	Ontario	NY	14519	800-648-9990	265-2306*	584

Name / Address	City	State	Zip	Phone	Fax	Class
Lake James State Park 6883 NC Hwy 126 PO Box 340	Nebo	NC	28761	828-584-7728		565
Web: www.ncparks.gov/lake-james-state-park						
Lake Junaluska Assembly Lake Junaluska Conference Retreat Ctr 689 N Lakeshore Dr	Lake Junaluska	NC	28745	828-452-2881		48-20
TF: 800-482-1442 ■ *Web:* www.lakejunaluska.com						
Lake Kegonsa State Park 2405 Door Creek Rd	Stoughton	WI	53589	608-873-9695	873-0674	565
TF General: 888-947-2757 ■ *Web:* dnr.wi.gov						
Lake Keomah State Park 2720 Keomah Ln	Oskaloosa	IA	52577	641-673-6975	673-0647	565
Web: www.iowadnr.gov						
Lake Kissimmee State Park 14248 Camp Mack Rd	Lake Wales	FL	33898	863-696-1112		565
Web: www.floridastateparks.org						
Lake Land College 5001 Lake Land Blvd	Mattoon	IL	61938	217-234-5253	234-5390*	162
**Fax:* Admissions ■ *Web:* www.lakelandcollege.edu						
Lake Lanier Islands Resort 7000 Holiday Rd	Buford	GA	30518	770-945-8787		669
TF: 800-840-5253 ■ *Web:* www.lanierislands.com						
Lake Lawn Resort 2400 E Geneva St	Delavan	WI	53115	262-728-7950		669
TF: 800-338-5253 ■ *Web:* www.lakelawnresort.com						
Lake Le-Aqua-Na State Recreation Area 8542 N Lake Rd	Lena	IL	61048	815-369-4282		565
Web: www.dnr.illinois.gov/Parks/Pages/LakeLeAquaNa.aspx						
Lake Lincoln State Park 2573 Sunset Dr	Wesson	MS	39191	601-643-9044		565
Web: reserveamerica.com						
Lake Logan State Park 20160 State Rd 664 20160 State Rd 664	Logan	OH	43138	740-385-6842		565
Web: www.dnr.state.oh.us						
Lake Loramie State Park 4401 Ft Loramie Swanders Rd	Minster	OH	45865	937-295-2011		565
Web: www.ohiodnr.com						
Lake Louisa State Park 7305 US Hwy 27	Clermont	FL	34714	352-394-3969		565
Web: www.floridastateparks.org						
Lake Louise Inn 210 Village Rd PO Box 209	Lake Louise	AB	T0L1E0	403-522-3791	522-2018	379
TF: 800-661-9237 ■ *Web:* www.lakelouiseinn.com						
Lake Louise State Park c/o Forestville/Mystery Cave State Pk 21071 County 118	Preston	MN	55965	507-352-5111	352-5113	565
Web: www.dnr.state.mn.us						
Lake Lowndes State Park 3319 Lake Lowndes Rd	Columbus	MS	39702	662-328-2110		565
Web: www.mdwfp.com						
Lake Lure Inn & Spa, The 2771 Memorial Hwy	Lake Lure	NC	28746	828-625-2525		379
TF: 888-434-4970 ■ *Web:* www.lakelure.com						
Lake Lurleen State Park 13226 Lake Lurleen Rd	Coker	AL	35452	205-339-1558	339-8885	565
TF: 800-760-4089 ■ *Web:* www.alapark.com						
Lake Macbride State Park 3525 Hwy 382 NE	Solon	IA	52333	319-624-2200	624-2188	565
Web: www.iowadnr.gov						
Lake Manatee State Park 20007 Hwy 64 E	Bradenton	FL	34212	941-741-3028		565
Web: www.floridastateparks.org						
Lake Manawa State Park 1100 S Shore Dr	Council Bluffs	IA	51501	712-366-0220	366-0474	565
Web: www.iowadnr.gov						
Lake Maria State Park 11411 Clementa Ave NW	Monticello	MN	55362	763-878-2325		565
Web: www.dnr.state.mn.us						
Lake Mary Ronan State Park 490 N Meridian Rd	Kalispell	MT	59901	406-752-5501		565
Web: www.fwp.mt.gov						
Lake McConaughy State Recreation Area 1450 Hwy 61N	Ogallala	NE	69153	308-284-8800		565
Web: outdoornebraska.gov						
Lake Mead National Recreation Area 601 Nevada Hwy	Boulder City	NV	89005	702-293-8990	293-8936	564
Web: www.nps.gov						
Lake Merced Golf & Country Club 2300 Junipero Serra Blvd	Daly City	CA	94015	650-755-2233		354
TF: 800-488-5869 ■ *Web:* www.lmgc.org						
Lake Meredith National Recreation Area 419 E Broadway	Fritch	TX	79036	806-857-3151	857-2319	564
Web: www.nps.gov/lamr						
Lake Merritt, The 1800 Madison St	Oakland	CA	94612	510-903-3600		379
Web: www.thelakemerritt.com						
Lake Metigoshe State Park 2 Lake Metigoshe State Pk	Bottineau	ND	58318	701-263-4651		565
Web: www.parkrec.nd.gov/parks/lmsp/lmsp.html						
Lake Michigan College 2755 E Napier Ave	Benton Harbor	MI	49022	269-927-1000	927-6875*	162
**Fax:* Admissions ■ *TF:* 800-252-1562 ■ *Web:* www.lakemichigancollege.edu						
Bertrand Crossing 1905 Foundation Dr	Niles	MI	49120	269-695-1391		162
TF: 800-252-1562 ■ *Web:* www.lakemichigancollege.edu						
South Haven 125 Veterans Blvd	South Haven	MI	49090	269-639-8442		162
TF: 800-252-1562 ■ *Web:* www.lakemichigancollege.edu						
Lake Michigan Mailers 3777 Sky King Blvd	Kalamazoo	MI	49009	269-383-9333		5
Web: www.lakemichiganmailers.com						
Lake Milton State Park 16801 Mahoning Ave	Lake Milton	OH	44429	330-654-4989		565
Web: www.ohiodnr.com						
Lake Minatare State Recreation Area PO Box 188	Minatare	NE	69356	308-783-2911		565
Web: outdoornebraska.gov						
Lake Mineral Wells State Park & Trailway 100 Pk Rd 71	Mineral Wells	TX	76067	940-328-1171		565
Web: tpwd.texas.gov/state-parks/lake-mineral-wells						
Lake Mission Viejo Assn 22555 Olympiad Rd	Mission Viejo	CA	92692	949-770-1327		533
Web: lakemissionviejo.org						
Lake Morey Resort 1 Clubhouse Rd	Fairlee	VT	05045	802-333-4311		669
TF: 800-423-1211 ■ *Web:* www.lakemoreyresort.com						
Lake Murphysboro State Park 52 Cinder Hill Dr	Murphysboro	IL	62966	618-684-2867		565
Web: dnr.illinois.gov/Lands/Landmgt/PARKS/R5/MURPHYSB.HTM						
Lake Murray Resort Park 3323 Lodge Rd	Ardmore	OK	73401	580-223-6600	326-2670	669
TF: 800-622-6317 ■ *Web:* www.travelok.com						
Lake Murray State Park 900 N Stiles Ave	Oklahoma City	OK	73152	800-652-6552		565
TF: 800-652-6552 ■ *Web:* www.travelok.com						
Lake Natoma Ltd 702 Gold Lake Dr	Folsom	CA	95630	916-932-2769		707
Web: www.lakenatomainn.com						
Lake Norman Chamber of Commerce 19900 W Catawba Ave Ste 101	Cornelius	NC	28031	704-892-1922	892-5313	139
TF: 800-305-2508 ■ *Web:* www.lakenormanchamber.org						
Lake Norman Regional Medical Ctr 171 Fairview Rd	Mooresville	NC	28117	704-660-4000		374-3
TF: 800-443-9354 ■ *Web:* www.lnrmc.com						
Lake Norman State Park 159 Inland Sea Ln	Troutman	NC	28166	704-528-6350		565
Web: ncparks.gov						
Lake of the Ozarks Convention & Visitors Bureau 5815 Hwy 54 PO Box 1498	Osage Beach	MO	65065	573-348-1599	348-2293	206
TF: 800-386-5253 ■ *Web:* www.funlake.com						
Lake of the Ozarks State Park PO Box 170	Kaiser	MO	65047	573-348-2694		565
Web: www.mostateparks.com						
Lake of the Torches Resort Casino 510 Old Abe Rd	Lac du Flambeau	WI	54538	715-588-7070		133
TF: 800-258-6724 ■ *Web:* www.lakeofthetorches.com						
Lake of the Woods County 206 Eigth Ave SE	Baudette	MN	56623	218-634-2836	634-2509	338
TF: 800-368-8683 ■ *Web:* www.co.lake-of-the-woods.mn.us						
Lake of the Woods District Hospital (LWDH) 21 Sylvan St	Kenora	ON	P9N3W7	807-468-9861	468-3939	374-2
TF: 800-445-1822 ■ *Web:* www.lwdh.on.ca						
Lake of Three Fires State Park 2303 Lake Rd	Bedford	IA	50833	712-523-2700	523-3104	565
Web: www.iowadnr.gov						
Lake Ogallala State Recreation Area 1450 Hwy 61N	Ogallala	NE	69153	308-284-8800		565
Web: outdoornebraska.gov/lakeogallala						
Lake Oroville State Recreation Area 917 Kelly Ridge Rd	Oroville	CA	95966	530-538-2219		565
Web: www.parks.ca.gov/default.asp?page_id=462						
Lake Oswego Chamber of Commerce 242 B Ave	Lake Oswego	OR	97034	503-636-3634	636-7427	139
TF: 800-518-0760 ■ *Web:* www.lake-oswego.com						
Lake Oswego Public Library 706 Fourth St	Lake Oswego	OR	97034	503-636-7628	635-4171	434-3
TF: 800-965-9324 ■ *Web:* www.ci.oswego.or.us						
Lake Ouachita State Park 5451 Mtn Pine Rd	Mountain Pine	AR	71956	501-767-9366		565
Web: www.arkansasstateparks.com						
Lake Owyhee State Park 725 Summer St NE Ste C	Salem	OR	97301	503-986-0707		565
TF: 800-551-6949 ■ *Web:* oregonstateparks.org						
Lake Park Retirement Residences 1850 Alice St	Oakland	CA	94612	510-835-5511		672
TF: 866-384-3130 ■ *Web:* www.lakeparkretirement.org						
Lake Perris State Recreation Area 17801 Lake Perris Dr	Perris	CA	92571	951-657-0676		565
Web: www.parks.ca.gov						
Lake Placid Convention & Visitors Bureau 2608 Main St	Lake Placid	NY	12946	518-523-2445	523-2605	206
TF: 800-447-5224 ■ *Web:* www.lakeplacid.com						
Lake Placid Lodge 144 Lodge Way	Lake Placid	NY	12946	518-523-2700	523-1124	379
TF: 877-523-2700 ■ *Web:* www.lakeplacidlodge.com						
Lake Poinsett Recreation Area 46109 202nd St	Bruce	SD	57220	605-627-5441		565
Web: sd.gov						
Lake Poinsett State Park 5752 State Pk Ln	Harrisburg	AR	72432	870-578-2064		565
Web: www.arkansasstateparks.com						
Lake Powell Resorts & Marinas 100 Lakeshore Dr	Page	AZ	86040	888-896-3829	326-2670*	669
**Fax Area Code:* 580 ■ *TF:* 800-622-6317 ■ *Web:* www.travelok.com						
Lake Printing Company Inc 6815 Hwy 54	Osage Beach	MO	65065	573-346-0600		627
TF: 800-466-3361 ■ *Web:* www.lakeprinting.com						
Lake Pueblo State Park 640 Pueblo Reservoir Rd	Pueblo	CO	81005	719-561-9320		565
Web: cpw.state.co.us						
Lake Quassapaug Park 2132 Middlebury Rd	Middlebury	CT	06762	203-758-2913		31
TF: 800-367-7275 ■ *Web:* www.quassy.com						
Lake Quinault Lodge 345 S Shore Rd	Quinault	WA	98575	360-288-2900	288-2901	669
TF: 800-562-6672 ■ *Web:* www.olympicnationalparks.com						
Lake Region Co-op Electrical Assn 1401 S Broadway PO Box 643	Pelican Rapids	MN	56572	218-863-1171	863-1172	245
TF: 800-552-7658 ■ *Web:* www.lrec.coop						
Lake Region Electric Assn Inc 1212 Main St	Webster	SD	57274	605-345-3379	345-4442	245
TF: 800-657-5869 ■ *Web:* www.lakeregion.coop						
Lake Region Electric Co-op Inc 516 S Lake Region Rd	Hulbert	OK	74441	918-772-2526		245
TF: 800-364-5732 ■ *Web:* www.lrecok.coop						
Lake Region Hospital 712 S Cascade St	Fergus Falls	MN	56537	218-736-8000		374-3
TF: 800-439-6424 ■ *Web:* www.lrhc.org						
Lake Region Packing Assn Inc 1293 S Duncan Dr	Tavares	FL	32778	352-343-3111		11-1
Lake Region State College 1801 College Dr N	Devils Lake	ND	58301	701-662-1600	662-1581*	162
**Fax:* Admissions ■ *TF:* 800-443-1313 ■ *Web:* www.lrsc.edu/discover-lrsc/visit-lrsc						
Lake Regional Health System 54 Hospital Dr	Osage Beach	MO	65065	573-348-8000		374-3
Web: www.lakeregional.com						
Lake Roosevelt National Recreation Area 1008 Crest Dr	Coulee Dam	WA	99116	509-633-9441	633-9332	564
Web: www.nps.gov						

	Phone	Fax	Class
Lake Saint Catherine State Park 3034 VT Rt 30 S Poultney VT 05764 *Web:* www.vtstateparks.com	802-287-9158		565
Lake Saint George State Park 278 Belfast Augusta Rd Liberty ME 04949 *Web:* www.maine.gov	207-589-4255		565
Lake Sammamish State Park 2000 NW Sammamish Rd Issaquah WA 98027 *TF:* 888-226-7688 ■ *Web:* www.parks.wa.gov	425-649-4275		565
Lake Scott State Park 520 W Scott Lake Dr Scott City KS 67871 *Web:* www.kansastravel.org	620-872-2061		565
Lake Seminole Square 8333 Seminole Blvd Seminole FL 33772 *TF:* 866-785-9025 ■ *Web:* brookdale.com/lake-seminole-square.aspx	727-228-7312		672
Lake Shaftsbury State Park 262 Shaftsbury State Pk Rd Shaftsbury VT 05262 *Web:* www.vtstateparks.com	802-375-9978		565
Lake Shetek State Park 163 State Pk Rd Currie MN 56123 *Web:* www.dnr.state.mn.us	507-763-3256		565
Lake Shore Athletic Club Inc 2401 NW 94th St Vancouver WA 98665 *Web:* www.lsac.com	360-574-1991		354
Lake Shore Bancorp Inc 128 E Fourth St Dunkirk NY 14048 *NASDAQ: LSBK* ■ *Web:* www.lakeshoresavings.com	716-366-4070	366-2965	71
Lake Shore Cryotronics 575 McCorkle Blvd Westerville OH 43082 *TF:* 877-969-0010 ■ *Web:* www.lakeshore.com	614-891-2243	818-1600	201
Lake Shore Industries Inc (LSI) 1817 Poplar St PO BOX 3427 Erie PA 16508 **Fax Area Code:* 814 ■ *TF:* 800-458-0463 ■ *Web:* www.lsisigns.com	800-458-0463	453-4293*	701
Lake Shore Railway Museum 31 Wall St North East PA 16428 *TF:* 800-945-0340 ■ *Web:* lakeshorerailway.com	814-725-1911	725-1911	520
Lake Shore Securities Lp 401 S La Salle St Ste 1000 Chicago IL 60605 *TF:* 000-289-9999 ■ *Web:* www.lakeshoresecurities.com	312-663-1307		690
Lake Somerville State Park 14222 Pk Rd 57 Somerville TX 77879 *Web:* tpwd.texas.gov/state-parks/lake-somerville	979-535-7763		565
Lake State Railway Co 750 N Washington Ave Saginaw MI 48607 *Web:* www.lsrc.com	989-393-9800	757-2134	648
Lake Sunapee Bank 9 Main St PO Box 29 Newport NH 03773 *TF:* 800-281-5772 ■ *Web:* www.lakesunbank.com	603-863-5772		360-2
Lake Superior College 2101 Trinity Rd Duluth MN 55811 **Fax:* Admissions ■ *TF:* 800-432-2884 ■ *Web:* lsc.edu	218-733-7600	733-5945*	162
Lake Superior Ind Sch Dist 381 1640 2 Hwy Two Harbors MN 55616 *TF:* 888-878-0136 ■ *Web:* www.isd381.k12.mn.us	218-834-8201	834-8239	685
Lake Superior Maritime Visitors Ctr 600 Lake Ave S Duluth MN 55802 *TF:* 800-430-5884 ■ *Web:* www.lsmma.com	218-727-2497		520
Lake Superior Railroad Museum 506 W Michigan St Duluth MN 55802 *TF:* 800-372-6437 ■ *Web:* www.lsrm.org	218-727-8025		520
Lake Superior State University 650 W Easterday Ave Sault Sainte Marie MI 49783 **Fax:* Admissions ■ *TF Admissions:* 888-800-5778 ■ *Web:* www.lssu.edu	906-632-6841	635-6696*	166
Lake Superior Zoo 7210 Fremont St Duluth MN 55807 *TF:* 800-642-6377 ■ *Web:* lszooduluth.org	218-730-4500	723-3750	823
Lake Sylvia State Park PO Box 701 Montesano WA 98563 *Web:* www.parks.wa.gov	360-249-3621		565
Lake Taghkanic State Park 1528 Rt 82 Ancram NY 12502 *Web:* parks.ny.gov/parks/38/hunting.aspx	518-851-3631	851-3633	565
Lake Tahoe Chamber of Commerce 169 Hwy 50 Stateline NV 89449 *Web:* www.tahoechamber.org	775-588-1728	588-1941	139
Lake Tahoe Community College 1 College Dr South Lake Tahoe CA 96150 **Fax:* Admissions ■ *TF:* 800-877-1466 ■ *Web:* www.ltcc.edu	530-541-4660	542-1781*	162
Lake Tahoe Horizon Casino Resort 50 Hwy 50 Stateline NV 89449 *Web:* www.tropicanacasinos.com	775-588-6211		132
Lake Tahoe Nevada State Park PO Box 8867 Incline Village NV 89452 *Web:* www.parks.nv.gov	775-831-0494	831-2514	565
Lake Tahoe Visitors Authority 3066 Lake Tahoe Blvd South Lake Tahoe CA 96150 *TF:* 800-288-2463 ■ *Web:* www.tahoesouth.com	530-544-5050		206
Lake Tarleton State Park 949 Rt 25C Piermont NH 03779 *Web:* www.nhstateparks.org	603-823-7722		565
Lake Tawakoni Regional Chamber of Commerce 100 W Hwy 276 West Tawakoni TX 75474 *Web:* www.laketawakonichamber.org	903-447-3020		139
Lake Tawakoni State Park 10822 Fm 2475 Wills Point TX 75169 *Web:* tpwd.texas.gov/state-parks/lake-tawakoni	903-560-7123		565
Lake Taylor Transitional Hospital 1309 Kempsville Rd Norfolk VA 23502 *TF:* 800-842-8275 ■ *Web:* www.laketaylor.org	757-461-5001	461-4282	374-7
Lake Texana State Park 46 Pk Rd 1 Edna TX 77957 *Web:* tpwd.texas.gov	361-782-5718		565
Lake Thompson Recreation Area 21176 Flood Club Rd Lake Preston SD 57249 *TF:* 800-710-2267 ■ *Web:* gfp.sd.gov	605-847-4893		565
Lake Thunderbird State Park 13101 Alameda Dr Norman OK 73026 *Web:* www.travelok.com	405-360-3572	366-8150	565
Lake Travis Independent School District 3322 Ranch Rd 620 S Austin TX 78738 *Web:* www.laketravis.txed.net	512-533-6000	533-6001	685
Lake Union Drydock Co 1515 Fairview Ave E Seattle WA 98102 *TF:* 800-323-8416 ■ *Web:* ludd.com	206-323-6400		698
Lake Vermillion Recreation Area 26140 451st Ave Canistota SD 57012	605-296-3643		565

	Phone	Fax	Class
Lake View Cemetery 12316 Euclid Ave Cleveland OH 44106 *Web:* lakeviewcemetery.com	216-421-2665	421-2415	520
Lake Villa Illinois Public Library District 1001 E Grand Ave Lake Villa IL 60046 *Web:* www.lvdl.org	847-356-7711		434-3
Lake Waccamaw State Park 1866 State Pk Dr Lake Waccamaw NC 28450 *Web:* www.ncparks.gov	910-646-4748		565
Lake Walcott State Park 959 E Minidoka Dam Rupert ID 83350 *Web:* www.parksandrecreation.idaho.gov	208-436-1258		565
Lake Wales Area Chamber of Commerce 340 W Central Ave Lake Wales FL 33859 *TF:* 800-365-6380 ■ *Web:* www.lakewaleschamber.com	863-676-3445	676-3446	139
Lake Wapello State Park 15248 Campground Rd Drakesville IA 52552 *TF:* 866-495-4868 ■ *Web:* www.iowadnr.gov	641-722-3371		565
Lake Wappapello State Park Hwy 172 Williamsville MO 63967 *Web:* www.mostateparks.com	573-297-3232		565
Lake Waramaug State Park 30 Lake Waramaug Rd New Preston CT 06777 *Web:* www.ct.gov	860-868-2592		565
Lake Warren State Park 1079 Lake Warren Rd Hampton SC 29924 *Web:* www.southcarolinaparks.com	803-943-5051		565
Lake Washington School District 414 16250 NE 74th St PO Box 97039 Redmond WA 98073 *Web:* www.lwsd.org	425-936-1200	936-1213	685
Lake Wateree State Recreation Area 881 State Pk Rd Winnsboro SC 29180 *Web:* www.southcarolinaparks.com	803-482-6401	482-6126	565
Lake Wenatchee State Park 21588 A Hwy 207 Leavenworth WA 98826 *Web:* www.parks.wa.gov	509-763-3101		565
Lake White State Park 2767 SR- 551 Waverly OH 45690 *Web:* www.ohiodnr.com	740-493-2212		565
Lake Whitney State Park PO Box 1175 Whitney TX 76692 *Web:* tpwd.texas.gov/state-parks/lake-whitney	254-694-3793		565
Lake Wilderness Arboretum 22520 SE 248th St PO Box 72 Maple Valley WA 98038 *Web:* www.lakewildernessarboretum.org	253-293-5103		97
Lake Winnepesaukah Amusement Park 1730 Lakeview Dr Rossville GA 30741 *Web:* www.lakewinnie.com	706-866-5681		32
Lake Winnipesaukee Golf Club Llc 1 Lake Winnipesaukee Dr New Durham NH 03855 *TF:* 800-325-4434 ■ *Web:* www.lwgcnh.com	603-569-3055		671
Lake Wissota State Park 18127 County Hwy O Chippewa Falls WI 54729 *TF:* 800-847-9367 ■ *Web:* dnr.wi.gov	715-382-4574	382-5187	565
Lake Wister State Park 25567 US Hwy 270 Wister OK 74966 *TF:* 800-622-6317 ■ *Web:* www.travelok.com	918-655-7212	655-7274	565
Lake Worth Herald/Coastal & Greenacres Observer 1313 Central Terr Lake Worth FL 33460 *Web:* www.lwherald.com	561-585-9387		532-4
Lake Worth Independent School District (LWISD) 6805 Telephone Rd Lake Worth TX 76135 *Web:* www.lwisd.org	817-306-4200	237-2583	685
Lake Worth Public Library 15 N 'M' St Lake Worth FL 33460 *Web:* www.lakeworth.org	561-533-7354	586-1651	434-3
Lake Wyola State Park 94 Lake View Rd Shutesbury MA 01072 *Web:* www.mass.gov	413-367-0317		565
Lake Zurich Area Chamber of Commerce 444 S Rand Rd Ste 308 Lake Zurich IL 60047 *Web:* www.lzacc.com	847-438-5572	438-5574	139
Lakefield College School 4391 County Rd 29 Lakefield ON K0L2H0	705-652-3324		622
Lakefront Lines Inc 13315 Brookpark Rd Brook Park OH 44142 *TF:* 800-543-9912 ■ *Web:* www.lakefrontlines.com	216-267-8810		760
Lakehead University 955 Oliver Rd Thunder Bay ON P7B5E1 *Web:* www.lakeheadu.ca	807-343-8110	343-8023	785
Lakeland Animal Nutrition 2801 S Combee Rd Lakeland FL 33803	863-665-5722		447
Lakeland Area Chamber of Commerce 35 Lake Morton Dr Lakeland FL 33801 *Web:* www.lakelandchamber.com	863-688-8551	683-7454	139
Lakeland Bancorp Inc 250 Oak Ridge Rd Oak Ridge NJ 07438 *NASDAQ: LBAI* ■ *TF:* 866-224-1379 ■ *Web:* www.lakelandbank.com	973-697-2000	697-8385	360-2
Lakeland College PO Box 359 Sheboygan WI 53082 **Fax:* Admissions ■ *TF:* 800-569-2166 ■ *Web:* www.lakeland.edu	920-565-2111	565-1215*	166
Lakeland Community College 7700 Clocktower Dr Kirtland OH 44094 **Fax:* Admissions ■ *TF:* 800-589-8520 ■ *Web:* lakelandcc.edu	440-525-7000	525-7651*	162
Lakeland Correctional Facility 141 First St Coldwater MI 49036 *TF:* 800-326-4537 ■ *Web:* www.michigan.gov/corrections	517-278-6942		213
Lakeland Financial Corp 202 E Ctr St Warsaw IN 46580 *NASDAQ: LKFN* ■ *TF:* 800-827-4522 ■ *Web:* www.lakecitybank.com	574-267-6144		360-2
Lakeland Industries Inc 701-7 Koehler Ave Ronkonkoma NY 11779 *NASDAQ: LAKE* ■ *TF:* 800-645-9291 ■ *Web:* www.lakeland.com	631-981-9700	981-9751	576
Lakeland Medical Center-Niles 31 N St Joseph Ave Niles MI 49120 *TF:* 800-968-0115 ■ *Web:* www.lakelandhealth.org	269-683-5510	683-2337	374-3
Lakeland Plastics Inc (LP) 1550 McCormick Blvd Mundelein IL 60060 *TF:* 800-454-4006 ■ *Web:* www.lakelandplastics.com	847-680-1550	680-1595	599
Lakeland Public Library 100 Lake Morton Dr Lakeland FL 33801 *Web:* www.lakelandgov.net/library/home.aspx	863-834-4270		434-3
Lakeland Regional Health 1324 Lakeland Hills Blvd Lakeland FL 33805 *Web:* mylrh.org	863-687-1100		374-3

Name / Address	City	State	Zip	Phone	Fax	Class
Lakeland Regional Library 318 Williams Ave *Web:* www.lakelandregionallibrary.ca	Killarney	MB	R0K1G0	204-523-4949	523-7460	436
Lakeland Surgical & Diagnostic Center LLP 1315 N Florida Ave *Web:* www.lsdc.net	Lakeland	FL	33805	863-683-2268		418
Lakeland Tool & Engineering Inc 2939 Sixth Ave	Anoka	MN	55303	763-422-8866		604
Lakeland Village Beach & Mountain Resort 3535 Lake Tahoe Blvd *TF:* 888-484-7094 ■ *Web:* lakeland--village.com	South Lake Tahoe	CA	96150	530-544-1685		669
Lakelands Concrete Products Inc 7520 E Main St *Web:* www.lakelandsconcrete.com	Lima	NY	14485	585-624-1990		183
Lakelands Trail State Park 8555 Silver Hill Rd 8555 Silver Hill Rt 1 *Web:* www.michigan.gov	Pinckney	MI	48169	734-426-4913		565
Lakeline Mall 11200 Lakeline Mall Dr *TF:* 800-408-8424 ■ *Web:* www.simon.com	Cedar Park	TX	78613	512-257-7467	257-0522	460
Lakepoint Resort State Park 104 Lakepoint Dr *TF:* 800-544-5253 ■ *Web:* www.alapark.com	Eufaula	AL	36027	334-687-8011	687-3273	565
Lakeport Regional Chamber of Commerce 875 Lakeport Blvd PO Box 295 *TF:* 866-525-3767 ■ *Web:* www.lakecochamber.com	Lakeport	CA	95453	707-263-5092	263-5104	139
Lakeport State Park 7605 Lakeshore Rd *Web:* www.michigandnr.com	Saint Clair	MI	48059	810-327-6224		565
Lakeridge Health Bowmanville 47 Liberty St S *TF:* 800-387-0073 ■ *Web:* www.lakeridgehealth.on.ca	Bowmanville	ON	L1C2N4	905-623-3331	743-5943	374-2
Lakeridge Health Oshawa 1 Hospital Ct *TF:* 866-338-1778 ■ *Web:* www.lakeridgehealth.on.ca	Oshawa	ON	L1G2B9	905-576-8711		374-2
Lakes Area Chamber of Commerce 305 N Pontiac Trl Ste B *Web:* www.lakesareachamber.com	Walled Lake	MI	48390	248-624-2826	624-2892	139
Lakes Area Co-op 459 Third Ave SE PO Box 247 *TF:* 866-346-5601 ■ *Web:* lakesareacoop.com	Perham	MN	56573	218-346-6240	346-6241	276
Lakes Gas Co 655 S Lake St *Web:* www.lakesgasco.com	Forest Lake	MN	55025	651-464-3345		316
Lakes Mall LLC, The 5600 Harvey St *Web:* www.thelakesmall.com	Muskegon	MI	49444	231-798-7104		710
Lakes Region Chamber 383 S Main St *Web:* lakesregionchamber.org	Laconia	NH	03246	603-524-5531		139
Lakes Region Community College (LRCC) 379 Belmont Rd *TF:* 800-357-2992 ■ *Web:* www.lrcc.edu	Laconia	NH	03246	603-524-3207	524-8084	162
Lakes Region General Hospital 80 Highland St *TF:* 800-327-0464 ■ *Web:* www.lrgh.org	Laconia	NH	03246	603-524-3211	527-2887	374-3
Lakeshirts Inc 750 Randolph Rd *TF:* 800-627-2780 ■ *Web:* www.lakeshirts.com	Detroit Lakes	MN	56501	218-847-2171		61
Lakeshore Chamber of Commerce 5246 Hohman Ave Ste 100 *Web:* www.lakeshorechamber.com	Hammond	IN	46320	219-931-1000	937-8778	139
Lakeshore Display Company Inc 2031 Washington Ave PO Box 983 *Web:* www.lakeshoredisplay.com	Sheboygan	WI	53081	920-457-3695	457-5673	233
Lakeshore Entertainment Corp 9268 W Third St *Web:* www.lakeshoreentertainment.com	Beverly Hills	CA	90210	310-867-8000		514
Lakeshore General Hospital (LGH) 160 Stillview Ste 1249 *Web:* www.fondationlakeshore.ca	Pointe-Claire	QC	H9R2Y2	514-630-2081	630-2873	374-2
Lakeshore Golf and Rv Resort 100 Silver Creek Trl *Web:* www.golfatthelakes.com	Wentworth	SD	57075	605-483-3800		121
Lakeshore Learning Materials 2695 E Dominguez St *TF:* 800-778-4456 ■ *Web:* www.lakeshorelearning.com	Carson	CA	90895	800-778-4456	537-5403	534
Lakeshore Staffing Inc 1 N Franklin St *Web:* www.livinglakeshore.com	Chicago	IL	60606	312-251-7575		721
Lakeshore State Park 2300 N Martin Luther King Jr Dr *Web:* dnr.wi.gov	Milwaukee	WI	53212	414-263-8500		565
Lakeshore Technical College 1290 N Ave *TF:* 888-468-6582 ■ *Web:* www.gotoltc.edu	Cleveland	WI	53015	920-693-1000	693-3561	800
Lakeshores Library System (LLS) 725 Cornerstone Crossing Ste C *Web:* www.lakeshores.lib.wi.us	Waterford	WI	53185	262-514-4500		434-3
Lakeside Bank 55 W Wacker Dr *TF:* 866-892-1572 ■ *Web:* www.lakesidebank.com	Chicago	IL	60601	312-435-5100		70
Lakeside Beach State Park Rt 18 *Web:* www.nysparks.com/parks/info.asp?parkid=8	Waterport	NY	14571	585-682-4888		565
Lakeside Behavioral Health System 2911 Brunswick Rd *TF:* 800-232-5253 ■ *Web:* lakesidebhs.com	Memphis	TN	38133	901-377-4700		374-5
Lakeside Capital Management LLC 50 S Sixth St Ste 1460 *TF:* 800-446-3655 ■ *Web:* www.gmbmezz.com	Minneapolis	MN	55402	612-243-4400		401
Lakeside Chamber of Commerce 9924 Vine St *TF:* 800-411-7343 ■ *Web:* lakesidechamber.org	Lakeside	CA	92040	619-561-1031	561-7951	139
Lakeside Foods Inc 808 Hamilton St *TF:* 800-466-3834 ■ *Web:* www.lakesidefoods.com	Manitowoc	WI	54220	920-684-3356	686-4033	296-20
Lakeside Industries Inc 6505 226th Pl SE # 200 *Web:* lakesideindustries.com	Issaquah	WA	98027	425-313-2600	313-2620	188-4
Lakeside Inn 100 N Alexander St *TF:* 800-556-5016 ■ *Web:* www.lakeside-inn.com	Mount Dora	FL	32757	352-383-4101	385-1615	379
Lakeside International LLC 11000 W Silver Spring Rd *TF:* 800-236-0444 ■ *Web:* www.lakesidetrucks.com	Milwaukee	WI	53225	414-353-4800	353-2743	57
Lakeside Lutheran High School 231 Woodland Beach Rd *TF:* 800-838-3006 ■ *Web:* www.llhs.org	Lake Mills	WI	53551	920-648-2321		685
Lakeside Mall 14000 Lakeside Cir *TF:* 800-992-9500 ■ *Web:* www.shop-lakesidemall.com	Sterling Heights	MI	48313	586-247-1590		460
Lakeside Manufacturing Inc 4900 W Electric Ave *TF:* 800-558-8565 ■ *Web:* www.elakeside.com	West Milwaukee	WI	53219	414-902-6400	902-6446	319-1
Lakeside Medical Center Inc 129 Sixth Ave SE *TF:* 800-333-2433 ■ *Web:* lmc-pcac.com	Pine City	MN	55063	320-629-2542		371
Lakeside Oil Company Inc 555 W Brown Deer Rd Ste 200 *Web:* lakesideoil.com	Milwaukee	WI	53217	414-540-4000		579
Lakeside Plastics Inc 450 W 33rd Ave *Web:* www.lakesideplastics.net	Oshkosh	WI	54902	920-235-3620	235-6545	608
Lakeside Process Controls Ltd 2475 Hogan Dr *TF:* 800-265-1005 ■ *Web:* www.lakesidecontrols.ca	Mississauga	ON	L5N0E9	905-629-9340		111
Lakeside Shopping Ctr 3301 Veterans Memorial Blvd *Web:* www.lakesideshopping.com	Metairie	LA	70002	504-835-8000		460
Lakeside Technologies LLC 7500 W 160th St *Web:* www.lakesidetechnologies.com	Stilwell	KS	66085	913-956-4170		463
Lakeside Toyota 3701 N Cswy Blvd *TF Sales:* 877-512-8274 ■ *Web:* www.lakesidetoyota.com	Metairie	LA	70002	504-833-3311		57
Lake-Sumter State College 9501 US Hwy 441 *Web:* www.lssc.edu	Leesburg	FL	34788	352-787-3747		162
South Lake 1250 N Hancock Rd *Web:* lssc.edu	Clermont	FL	34711	352-243-5722	243-0117	162
Sumter 1405 CR 526A *Web:* lssc.edu	Sumterville	FL	33585	352-568-0001	568-7515	162
Lakeview College of Nursing 903 N Logan Ave *Web:* www.lakeviewcol.edu	Danville	IL	61832	217-443-5238		166
Lakeview Construction Inc 10505 Corp Dr Ste 200 *Web:* www.lvconstruction.com	Pleasant Prairie	WI	53158	262-857-3336	857-3424	186
Lakeview Forge Co 1725 Pittsburgh Ave *Web:* lakeviewforge.com	Erie	PA	16505	814-454-4518	455-5875	483
Lakeview Golf Resort & Spa 1 Lakeview Dr *TF:* 800-624-8300 ■ *Web:* www.lakeviewresort.com	Morgantown	WV	26508	304-594-1111		669
Lakeview Hospital 630 E Medical Dr *TF:* 800-260-4854 ■ *Web:* www.lakeviewhospital.com	Bountiful	UT	84010	801-299-2200		374-3
Lakeview Industries Inc 1225 Lakeview Dr *Web:* www.lakeviewindustries.com	Chaska	MN	55318	952-368-3500		326
Lakeview Medical Ctr 1100 N Main St *Web:* www.lakeviewmedical.com	Rice Lake	WI	54868	715-234-1515		374-3
Lakeview Professional Services Inc 104 S Maple St *TF:* 800-287-1371 ■ *Web:* www.lakeviewpro.com	Corona	CA	92880	951-371-3390		196
Lakeview Regional Medical Ctr 95 Judge Tanner Blvd *TF:* 866-452-5384 ■ *Web:* www.lakeviewregional.com	Covington	LA	70433	985-867-3800		374-3
Lakeview Shock Incarceration Ctr 9300 Lake Ave PO Box T *Web:* ncjrs.gov	Brocton	NY	14716	716-792-7100		213
Lakeville Area Chamber of Commerce & Convention & Visitors Bureau 19950 Dodd Blvd Ste 101 *Web:* www.lakevillechamber.org	Lakeville	MN	55044	952-469-2020	469-2028	139
Lakeway Container Inc 5715 Superior Dr *Web:* www.lakewaycontainer.com	Morristown	TN	37814	423-581-2164		100
Lakeway Inn & Resort 101 Lakeway Dr *TF:* 800-525-3929 ■ *Web:* www.lakewayresortandspa.com	Austin	TX	78734	512-261-6600		377
Lakeway Regional Hospital (LRH) 726 McFarland St	Morristown	TN	37814	423-522-6000		374-3
Lakewold Gardens 12317 Gravelly Lake Dr SW *TF:* 888-858-4106 ■ *Web:* lakewoldgardens.org	Lakewood	WA	98499	253-584-4106	584-3021	97
Lakewood Chamber of Commerce 4650 Steilacoom Blvd SW Ste 109 *Web:* lakewood-chamber.com	Lakewood	WA	98499	253-582-9400	581-5241	139
Lakewood Chamber of Commerce 24 Lakewood Ctr Mall *Web:* www.lakewoodchamber.com	Lakewood	CA	90712	562-531-9733		139
Lakewood Chamber of Commerce 16017 Detroit Ave *Web:* www.lakewoodchamber.org	Lakewood	OH	44107	216-226-2900	226-1340	139
Lakewood Ctr Mall 500 Lakewood Ctr *Web:* www.shoplakewoodcenter.com	Lakewood	CA	90712	562-633-0437		460
Lakewood Health System 49725 County 83 *TF:* 800-525-1033 ■ *Web:* lakewoodhealthsystem.com	Staples	MN	56479	218-894-1515		363
Lakewood Hospital 14519 Detroit Ave *TF:* 866-588-2264 ■ *Web:* my.clevelandclinic.org	Lakewood	OH	44107	216-521-4200		374-3
Lakewood Manor 1900 Lauderdale Dr *TF:* 866-521-9100 ■ *Web:* lakewoodwestend.org	Richmond	VA	23238	804-740-2900		672
Lakewood Public Library 15425 Detroit Ave *Web:* lakewoodpubliclibrary.org	Lakewood	OH	44107	216-226-8275	521-4327	434-3
Lakewood Regional Medical Ctr 3700 S St *TF:* 800-743-6333 ■ *Web:* www.lakewoodregional.com	Lakewood	CA	90712	562-531-2550		374-3
Lakewood Shores Resort 7751 Cedar Lake Rd *TF:* 800-882-2493 ■ *Web:* www.lakewoodshores.com	Oscoda	MI	48750	989-739-2073		669
Lakewood United Methodist Church of North Little Rock 1922 Topf Rd *Web:* www.expandingthelight.org	North Little Rock	AR	72116	501-753-6186		48-20
Lakewoods Resort & Lodge 21540 County Hwy M *Web:* lakewoodsresort.com	Cable	WI	54821	715-794-2561		379

Phone | Fax | Class

Lakin General Corp 2044 N Dominick St ....Chicago IL 60614 773-871-6675 755
Web: www.lakincorp.com
Lakin Spears LLP
2400 Geng Rd Ste 110 ....Palo Alto CA 94303 650-328-7000 428
Web: www.lakinspears.com
Lakin Tire West Inc
15305 Spring Ave....................Santa Fe Springs CA 90670 562-802-2752 802-7584 755
TF: 800-488-2752 ■ *Web:* www.lakintire.com
Lakorn Thai Restaurant
470 S Main St...........................Manchester NH 03102 603-626-4545 671
Web: lakornthainh.com
Lala Rokh 97 Mt Vernon St.....................Boston MA 02108 617-720-5511 671
Web: www.lalarokh.com
LallyPak Inc 1209 Central Ave..................Hillside NJ 07205 908-351-4141 351-4411 548
TF: 800-523-8484 ■ *Web:* www.lallypak.com
Laloux 250 Pine Ave E.......................Montreal QC H2W1P3 514-287-9127 671
Web: www.laloux.com
Lam 103.7 355 So 'A' St Ste 103 ....Oxnard CA 93030 805-385-5656 385-5690 645-118
Web: www.lam1037.com
LAM Design Associates Inc
409 Manville Rd ....Pleasantville NY 10570 914-773-7600 344
TF: 800-620-1233 ■ *Web:* www.lamdesign.com
Lam Research Corp 4650 Cushing Pkwy.........Fremont CA 94538 510-572-0200 695
NASDAQ: LRCX ■ *TF:* 800-526-7678 ■ *Web:* lamresearch.com
LaMalfa Doug (Rep R - CA)
322 Cannon HOB ....Washington DC 20515 202-225-3076 342-2
Web: lamalfa.house.gov
Lamamco Drilling Co
4444 E 146th St N M ....Skiatook OK 74070 918-396-3020 538
Web: www.lamamco.net
Lamar & Wallace Inc
7000 Old Landover Rd ....Landover MD 20785 301-772-2400 499
Web: www.lamarandwallace.com
Lamar Adv Co 5321 Corporate Blvd..........Baton Rouge LA 70808 225-926-1000 8
NASDAQ: LAMR ■ *TF:* 800-235-2627 ■ *Web:* www.lamar.com
Lamar Community College 2401 S Main St ....Lamar CO 81052 719-336-2248 336-2400* 162
**Fax:* Admissions ■ *TF:* 800-968-6920 ■ *Web:* lamarcc.edu
Lamar County
408 Thomaston St Ste E....................Barnesville GA 30204 770-358-5146 358-5149 338
TF: 800-436-7442 ■ *Web:* www.lamarcountyga.com
Lamar County 119 N Main St Rm 109..............Paris TX 75460 903-737-2420 782-1100 338
Web: www.co.lamar.tx.us
Lamar County 403 Main St.....................Purvis MS 39475 601-794-8504 794-1049* 338
**Fax:* Administration ■ *Web:* www.lamarcountyms.gov/11/index.php
Lamar County Chamber of Commerce
1125 Bonham St..............................Paris TX 75460 903-784-2501 784-2503 139
TF: 800-727-4789 ■ *Web:* www.paristexas.com
Lamar electric Cooperative
1485 N Main St PO BOX 580....................Paris TX 75460 903-784-4303 784-7084 245
TF: 800-344-8377 ■ *Web:* www.lamarelectric.com
Lamar Plastic Packaging Ltd
216 N Main St ....Freeport NY 11520 516-378-2500 378-6192 602
TF: 800-780-4707 ■ *Web:* lamarplastics.net
Lamar Soutter Library 55 N Lake Ave ....Worcester MA 01655 508-856-6099 856-5899 434-1
Web: library.umassmed.edu
Lamar State College
Orange 410 Front St ....Orange TX 77630 409-883-7750 882-3055* 162
**Fax:* Admissions ■ *TF:* 800-477-5872 ■ *Web:* www.lsco.edu
Port Arthur PO Box 310....................Port Arthur TX 77641 409-983-4921 984-6025* 162
**Fax:* Admissions ■ *TF:* 800-477-5872 ■ *Web:* lamarpa.edu
Lamar University
4400 ML King Jr Pkwy ....Beaumont TX 77710 409-880-7011 880-8463 166
Web: www.lamar.edu
Lamart Corp 16 Richmond St....................Clifton NJ 07015 973-772-6262 772-3673 599
TF: 800-228-4535 ■ *Web:* www.lamartcorp.com
Lamartek Inc 175 NW Washington St...........Lake City FL 32055 386-752-1087 755-0613 710
TF Orders: 800-495-1046 ■ *Web:* www.diverite.com
Lamaze International
2025 M St NW Ste 800....................Washington DC 20036 202-367-1128 367-2128 49-8
TF: 800-368-4404 ■ *Web:* www.lamaze.org
Lamb & Barnosky LLP
534 Broadhollow Rd Ste 210 PO Box 9034 ....Melville NY 11747 631-694-2300 428
TF: 800-973-1177 ■ *Web:* www.lambbarnosky.com
Lamb County 100 Sixth St....................Littlefield TX 79339 806-385-4222 338
Lamb County Electric Co-op
2415 S Phelps Ave ....Littlefield TX 79339 806-385-5191 385-5197 245
Web: www.lcec.coop
Lamb McErlane PC
24 E Market St PO Box 565 ....West Chester PA 19381 610-430-8000 428
TF: 800-678-3276 ■ *Web:* www.lambmcerlane.com
Lamb Weston Inc 8701 W Gage Blvd ....Kennewick WA 99336 509-735-4651 296-21
Web: www.lambweston.com
Lamb's Tire & Automotive
2100 Kramer Ln ....Austin TX 78758 512-257-2350 62-5
Web: www.lambstire.com
Lambda Legal Defense & Education Fund
120 Wall St Ste 1500 ....New York NY 10005 212-809-8585 809-0055 48-8
TF: 866-542-8336 ■ *Web:* www.lambdalegal.org
Lambda Research Corp 25 Porter Rd ....Littleton MA 01460 978-486-0766 177
Web: lambdares.com
Lambda Solutions Inc
1700 Seventh Ave Ste 1200 ....Seattle WA 98104 604-398-0162 242
TF: 877-700-1118 ■ *Web:* www.lambdasolutions.net
Lambda Technologies
3929 Virginia Ave.........................Cincinnati OH 45227 513-561-0883 743
TF: 800-883-0851 ■ *Web:* www.lambdatechs.com
Lambeau Field Atrium
1265 Lombardi Ave........................Green Bay WI 54304 920-569-7500 569-7301 720
TF: 866-752-1265 ■ *Web:* www.packers.com
Lambent Technologies Corp
3938 Porett Dr ....Gurnee IL 60031 847-244-3410 146
Web: www.lambentcorp.com
Lambert Buick Pontiac-Gmc Truck Inc
2409 Front St ....Cuyahoga Falls OH 44221 330-923-9771 57
Web: lambertgm.com
Lambert Consulting Group Inc
8699 Craigston Ct ....Dublin OH 43017 614-792-6582 196
TF: 800-438-7325 ■ *Web:* lambertconsultinggroup.com
Lambert Saint Louis International Airport
10701 Lambert International Blvd
PO Box 10212 ....Saint Louis MO 63145 314-426-8000 426-1221 27
TF: 855-787-2227 ■ *Web:* www.flystl.com
Lambert's Cafe Inc 2305 E Malone ....Sikeston MO 63801 573-471-4261 471-7563 670
TF: 800-455-2855 ■ *Web:* www.throwedrolls.com
Lamborn Doug (Rep R - CO)
2402 Rayburn Bldg.......................Washington DC 20515 202-225-4422 226-2638 342-2
Web: lamborn.house.gov
Lambs & Ivy Inc
2040-2042 E Maple Ave ....El Segundo CA 90245 310-322-3800 361
Web: lambsivy.com
Lamb-Star Engineering LP
5700 W Plano Pkwy Ste 1000....................Plano TX 75093 214-440-3600 256
Web: www.lamb-star.com
Lambton College of Applied Arts & Technology, The
1457 London Rd............................Sarnia ON N7S6K4 519-542-7751 162
Web: www.lambtoncollege.ca
Lambuth University 705 Lambuth Blvd ....Jackson TN 38301 731-427-4725 422-2169* 166
**Fax:* Admissions ■ *TF:* 800-526-2305 ■ *Web:* memphis.edu
Lamcom Technologies inc
2330 Rue Masson.........................Montreal QC H2G2A6 514-271-2891 627
TF: 800-361-0378 ■ *Web:* www.lamcom.ca
Lamcraft Partition Company Inc
1231 County Rd 4781..........................Boyd TX 76023 940-433-5857 608
Lamers Bus Lines Inc 2407 S Pt Rd...........Green Bay WI 54313 920-496-3600 496-3611 107
TF: 800-236-1240 ■ *Web:* www.golamers.com
Lamesa Independent School District
212 N Houston ....Lamesa TX 79331 806-872-5461 872-6220 685
Web: www.lamesaisd.net
Lamesa National Bank, The
602 S First St ....Lamesa TX 79331 806-872-5457 70
Lamey-Wellehan Inc 940 Turner St ....Auburn ME 04210 207-784-6595 784-9650 301
TF: 800-370-6900 ■ *Web:* www.lwshoes.com
Lamiglas Inc 1400 Atlantic Ave ....Woodland WA 98674 360-225-9436 225-5050 710
Web: www.lamiglas.com
Laminar Consulting Services
424 S Olive St.............................Orange CA 92866 888-531-9995 196
TF: 888-531-9995 ■ *Web:* www.laminarconsulting.com
Lamin-Art Inc 1670 Basswood Rd...........Schaumburg IL 60173 847-860-4300 596
Web: www.laminart.com
Laminate Technologies Inc 161 Maule Rd.........Tiffin OH 44883 800-231-2523 817
TF: 800-231-2523 ■ *Web:* www.lamtech.net
Laminated Wood Systems Inc (LWS)
1327 285th Rd PO Box 386 ....Seward NE 68434 800-949-3526 643-4374* 817
**Fax Area Code:* 402 ■ *TF:* 800-949-3526 ■ *Web:* www.lwsinc.com
Laminating Company of America
20322 Windrow Dr.......................Lake Forest CA 92630 949-587-3300 599
Web: www.lcoa.com
Laminating Services Inc
4700 Robards Ln ....Louisville KY 40218 502-458-2614 596
Web: www.versawallcovering.com
Lamination Depot Inc
1505 E McFadden Ave ....Santa Ana CA 92705 714-954-0632 535
TF: 800-925-0054 ■ *Web:* www.laminationdepot.com
Lamination Specialties Corp
235 N Artesian Ave.........................Chicago IL 60612 312-243-2181 243-2873 767
TF: 800-734-7338 ■ *Web:* www.laminationspecialties.com
Laminations 3010 E Venturo Dr...............Appleton WI 54911 920-831-0596 548
TF: 800-925-2626 ■ *Web:* www.laminationsonline.com
Laminations Inc 101 Power Blvd ....Archbald PA 18403 570-876-8199 596
Web: www.laminations.com
Laminators Inc 3255 Penn St ....Hatfield PA 19440 215-723-8107 721-4669 817
TF: 877-663-4277 ■ *Web:* www.laminatorsinc.com
Laminex Inc 4209 Pleasant Rd.................Fort Mill SC 29708 704-679-4170 627
Web: www.laminex.com
Lamitech Inc 322 Half Acre Rd ....Cranbury NJ 08512 609-860-8037 561
Web: www.lamitech.com
Lammes Candies Since 1885 Inc
PO Box 1885 ....Austin TX 78767 512-310-2223 238-2019 296-8
TF: 800-252-1885 ■ *Web:* www.lammes.com
Lamms Machine Inc 3216 Berger St ....Allentown PA 18103 610-797-2023 454
Web: www.lammsmachine.com
Lamoille County PO Box 455 ....Morrisville VT 05661 802-888-5640 851-1136 338
Web: www.lamoilleeconomy.org
Lamoille Home Health & Hospice
54 Farr Ave..............................Morrisville VT 05661 802-888-4651 363
TF: 800-543-1624 ■ *Web:* www.lhha.org
Lamoine State Park 23 State Pk Rd.............Lamoine ME 04605 207-667-4778 565
Web: www.maine.gov
Lamons Gasket Co 7300 Airport Blvd............Houston TX 77061 713-222-0284 547-9502* 326
TF: 800-231-6906 ■ *Web:* www.lamonsgasket.com
Lamont Engineers 548 Main St ....Cobleskill NY 12043 518-234-4028 234-4613 194
TF: 800-882-9721 ■ *Web:* www.lamontengineers.com
Lamont Ltd 1530 Bluff Rd...................Burlington IA 52601 319-753-5131 753-0946 319-2
TF: 800-553-5621 ■
Web: www.lamonthome.com/7les1xn325ooeaai5xdzealg2mitl6
Lamont, Hanley & Associates Inc
1138 Elm St ....Manchester NH 03105 603-625-5547 160
TF: 800-639-2204 ■ *Web:* www.lhainc.com
Lamont-Doherty Earth Observatory
61 Route 9w ....Palisades NY 10964 845-359-2900 359-2931 668
TF: 800-968-4332 ■ *Web:* www.ldeo.columbia.edu
Lamothe House Hotel
621 Esplanade Ave ....New Orleans LA 70116 800-535-7815 302-2019* 379
**Fax Area Code:* 504 ■ *TF:* 800-535-7815 ■ *Web:* www.frenchquarterguesthouses.com
LaMotte Co 802 Washington Ave.............Chestertown MD 21620 410-778-3100 778-6394 419
TF: 800-344-3100 ■ *Web:* www.lamotte.com
LaMoure County PO Box 217 ....La Moure ND 58458 701-883-5301 338
Web: www.lamourend.com
Lamp Post Inn 2424 E Stadium Blvd ....Ann Arbor MI 48104 734-971-8000 971-7483 379
Web: www.lamppostinn.com
Lamp, Rynearson & Associates Inc
14710 W Dodge Rd Ste 100.....................Omaha NE 68154 402-496-2498 727
TF: 800-488-5275 ■ *Web:* www.lra-inc.com
Lampasas County 409 S Pecan St ....Lampasas TX 76550 512-556-8271 556-8270 338
Web: www.co.lampasas.tx.us

Name / Address	Phone	Fax	Class
Lampasas Isd 207 W Eigth St .... Lampasas TX 76550 *Web:* www.lisdtx.org/index.cfm	512-556-6224	556-8711	186
Lampert Yards Inc 1850 Como Ave .... Saint Paul MN 55108 *Web:* lampertlumber.com	651-695-3600		364
Lamphere Schools 31201 Dorchester Ave. .... Madison Heights MI 48071 *Web:* www.lampereschools.org	248-589-1990	589-2618	685
Lamplight Farms Inc W140 N4900 Lilly Rd .... Menomonee Falls WI 53051 *TF Cust Svc:* 888-473-1088 ■ *Web:* www.tikibrand.com	262-781-9590		439
Lamplighter Financial LLC 1260 Lake Blvd Ste 240 .... Davis CA 95616 *Web:* www.lamplighterfinancial.com	415-484-6190		463
Lamplighter Inn & Suites South 1772 S Glenstone Ave. .... Springfield MO 65804 *TF:* 800-345-8082 ■ *Web:* www.lamplighter-sgf.com	417-882-1113		379
Lampo Group Inc, The 1749 Mallory Ln. .... Brentwood TN 37027 *Web:* www.daveramsey.com	615-371-8881		401
Lamppost Pizza Franchise Corp 3002 Dow Ave. .... Tustin CA 92780 *Web:* www.lamppost-backstreet.com	714-731-6171		670
Lamps Plus Inc 20250 Plummer St. .... Chatsworth CA 91311 *TF:* 800-782-1967 ■ *Web:* lampsplus.com	800-782-1967		362
Lampton-Love Inc PO Box 1607 .... Jackson MS 39215 *Web:* www.lamptonlove.com	601-939-8304	939-8309	787
Lamsco West Inc 24823 Anza Dr .... Santa Clarita CA 91355 *Web:* www.shimtechgroup.com	661-295-8620	295-8626	599
Lamson & Goodnow Mfg Co 45 Conway St .... Shelburne Falls MA 01370 *TF:* 800-872-6564 ■ *Web:* www.lamsonsharp.com	413-625-0201		222
Lamson, Dugan & Murray LLP 10306 Regency Pkwy Dr. .... Omaha NE 68114 *Web:* www.ldmlaw.com	402-397-7300		428
Lamvin Inc 4675 N Ave .... Oceanside CA 92056 *TF:* 800-446-6329 ■ *Web:* www.lamvin.com	760-806-6400	806-3200	608
Lan Assoc Engineering Planning Architecture Surveying Inc 445 Godwin Ave Ste 9 .... Midland Park NJ 07432 *Web:* www.lan-nj.com	201-447-6400		256
Lan Pan Asian Cafe 8332 S Dixie Hwy. .... Miami FL 33143 *Web:* lanpanasian.com	305-661-8141		671
Lanair Group LLC 620 N Brand Blvd 6th Fl .... Glendale CA 91203 *Web:* www.lanairgroup.com	323-512-7363		180
Lanamark Inc 100 King St W Ste 5600 .... Toronto ON M5X1C9 *Web:* www.lanamark.com	416-342-1960	342-1961	179
Lanaux & Felger CPAs Apc 5779 Hwy 311 .... Houma LA 70360	985-851-0883		2
Lancair International Inc 250 SE Timber Ave .... Redmond OR 97756 *Web:* lancair.com	541-923-2233		21
Lancaster Archery Supply Inc 2195a Old Phila Pk. .... Lancaster PA 17602 *TF:* 800-829-7408 ■ *Web:* www.lancasterarchery.com	800-829-7408		711
Lancaster Barnstormers & Keystone Baseball 650 N Prince St .... Lancaster PA 17603 *Web:* www.lancasterbarnstormers.com	717-509-4487		713
Lancaster Bible College 901 Eden Rd .... Lancaster PA 17601 *TF:* 800-544-7335 ■ *Web:* www.lbc.edu	717-569-7071	560-8213	161
Lancaster Brewing Co 302 N Plum St. .... Lancaster PA 17602 *Web:* www.lancasterbrewing.com	717-391-6258	391-6015	671
Lancaster Chamber of Commerce & Industry PO Box 1558 .... Lancaster PA 17608 *Web:* lancasterchamber.com	717-397-3531	293-3159	139
Lancaster City School District 345 E Mulberry St. .... Lancaster OH 43130 *Web:* www.lancaster.k12.oh.us	740-687-7300		685
Lancaster Colony Corp 37 W Broad St .... Columbus OH 43215 *NASDAQ: LANC* ■ *Web:* www.lancastercolony.com	614-224-7141		185
Lancaster Commercial Products Inc 2353 Westbrooke Dr. .... Columbus OH 43228 *TF:* 844-324-1444 ■ *Web:* www.lccpinc.com	614-263-2850		300
Lancaster County 150 N Queen St .... Lancaster PA 17603 *Web:* www.co.lancaster.pa.us	717-299-8000	293-7208	338
Lancaster County PO Box 1809 .... Lancaster SC 29721 *Web:* mylancastersc.org	803-285-1581		338
Lancaster County 8265 Mary Ball Rd. .... Lancaster VA 22503 *Web:* www.courts.state.va.us	804-462-5611	462-9978	338
Lancaster County 575 S Tenth St Rm 108 .... Lincoln NE 68508 *Web:* www.lancaster.ne.gov	402-441-7481	441-8728	338
Lancaster County Chamber of Commerce PO Box 430 .... Lancaster SC 29721 *TF:* 800-532-0335 ■ *Web:* www.lancasterchambersc.org	803-283-4105	286-4360	139
Lancaster County Library 313 S White St .... Lancaster SC 29720 *Web:* www.lanclib.org	803-285-1502	285-6004	434-3
Lancaster County's Historical Society & President James Buchanan's Wheatland 230 N President Ave .... Lancaster PA 17603 *Web:* www.lancasterhistory.org	717-392-4633	293-2739	50-3
Lancaster DHIA 1592 Old Line Rd. .... Manheim PA 17545 *Web:* www.lancasterdhia.com	717-665-5960		368
Lancaster Eagle-Gazette 138 W Chestnut St .... Lancaster OH 43130 *TF:* 877-513-7355 ■ *Web:* www.lancastereaglegazette.com	740-654-1321		532-2
Lancaster Farming PO Box 609 .... Ephrata PA 17522 *TF:* 800-638-6693 ■ *Web:* www.lancasterfarming.com	717-626-1164	733-6058	532-4
Lancaster General Hospital 555 N Duke St .... Lancaster PA 17604 *Web:* www.lancastergeneralhealth.org	717-544-5511	544-5966	374-3
Lancaster Group Inc, The 3411 Richmond Ave Ste 460 .... Houston TX 77046 *Web:* www.lancaster.com	713-224-6000		378
Lancaster Host Resort 2300 Lincoln Hwy E .... Lancaster PA 17602 *TF Resv:* 800-233-0121 ■ *Web:* www.lancasterhost.com	717-299-5500		669
Lancaster Hotel 701 Texas St .... Houston TX 77002 *TF:* 800-231-0336 ■ *Web:* www.thelancaster.com	713-228-9500	223-4528	379
Lancaster Knives Inc 165 Ct St .... Lancaster NY 14086 *TF:* 800-869-9666 ■ *Web:* www.lancasterknives.com	716-683-5050	683-5068	493
Lancaster Newspapers Inc 8 W King St PO Box 1328 .... Lancaster PA 17603 *Web:* www.lancasteronline.com	717-291-8811	291-8728	637-8
Lancaster Pollard Investment Advisory Group 65 E State St Ste 1600 .... Columbus OH 43215 *TF:* 800-428-3320 ■ *Web:* www.lancasterpollard.com	614-224-8800		401
Lancaster Public Library 125 N Duke St .... Lancaster PA 17602 *Web:* lancasterpubliclibrary.org	717-394-2651	394-3083	434-3
Lancaster Pump Co 1340 Manheim Pk .... Lancaster PA 17601 *TF:* 800-442-0786 ■ *Web:* www.lancasterpump.com	717-397-3521	392-0266	806
Lancaster Regional Medical Ctr 1500 Highland Dr. .... Lititz PA 17543 *Web:* www.lancastermedicalcenters.com	717-625-5000	625-5672	374-3
Lancaster Regional Medical Ctr 250 College Ave .... Lancaster PA 17603 *TF:* 877-456-9617 ■ *Web:* www.lancastermedicalcenters.com	717-291-8211		374-3
Lancaster Sales Co 1375 Old Logan Rd Rt 33S .... Lancaster OH 43130	740-653-5334		229
Lancaster Systems Inc 411 Theodore Fremd Ave .... Rye NY 10580 *Web:* www.lancastersys.com	914-967-5700		180
Lancaster Theological Seminary 555 W James St .... Lancaster PA 17603 *TF:* 800-393-0654 ■ *Web:* www.lancasterseminary.edu	717-393-0654	393-4254	167-3
Lancaster Toyota Inc 5270 Manheim Pk .... East Petersburg PA 17520 *TF:* 888-424-1295 ■ *Web:* www.lancastertoyota.com	888-424-1295		57
Lancaster-Fairfield County Chamber of Commerce 109 N Broad St Ste 100 .... Lancaster OH 43130 *Web:* www.lancoc.org	740-653-8251	653-7074	139
Lance Camper Mfg Corp 43120 Venture St .... Lancaster CA 93535 *Web:* www.lancecamper.com	661-949-3322	949-1262	120
Lance Leonard (Rep R - NJ) 2352 Rayburn HOB .... Washington DC 20515 *Web:* lance.house.gov	202-225-5361	225-9460	342-2
Lance Soll & Lunghard LLP 203 N Brea Blvd Ste 203 .... Brea CA 92821 *Web:* www.lslcpas.com	714-672-0022		2
Lancer Corp 6655 Lancer Blvd. .... San Antonio TX 78219 *TF:* 800-729-1500 ■ *Web:* www.lancercorp.com	210-310-7000	310-7250	664
Lancer Industries Inc 450 Lexington Ave Ste 3350 .... New York NY 10017	212-286-8600		360-3
Lancer Label 301 S 74th St .... Omaha NE 68114 *TF Cust Svc:* 800-228-7074 ■ *Web:* www.lancerlabel.com	800-228-7074		413
Lancer Orthodontics Inc 1493 Poinsettia Bldg 143 .... Vista CA 92081 *NYSE: LANZ* ■ *TF Cust Svc:* 800-854-2896 ■ *Web:* www.lancerortho.com	760-744-5585	598-0418	228
Lancet Capital 245 First St Ste 1800 .... Cambridge MA 02142 *Web:* www.lancetcapital.com	617-444-8582	444-8405	792
Lancet Software Development Inc 11980 Portland Ave S .... Burnsville MN 55337 *Web:* www.lancetdatasciences.com	952-230-7360		177
Lancia Homes 9430 Lima Rd. .... Fort Wayne IN 46818 *Web:* www.lanciahomes.com	260-489-4433		653
Lancore Technologies 11211 Richmond Ave .... Houston TX 77082 *TF:* 866-492-5800 ■ *Web:* www.lancoretech.com	281-493-5850		177
Lancs Industries Holdings LLC 12704 NE 124th St Ste 36 40 .... Kirkland WA 98034 *Web:* www.lancsindustries.com	425-823-6634		596
Land & Legal Solutions Inc 300 S Hamilton Ave .... Greensburg PA 15601 *TF:* 800-245-7900	724-853-8992	853-3221	178-10
Land Coast Insulation Inc 4017 Second St PO Box 14110 .... New Iberia LA 70560 *TF:* 800-333-9424	337-367-7741	367-7744	189-9
Land Design Consultants Inc 2700 E Foothill Blvd .... Pasadena CA 91107 *Web:* ldcla.com	626-578-7000		261
Land Development Consultants Inc 14201 NE 200th St Ste 100 .... Woodinville WA 98072 *Web:* ldccorp.com	425-806-1869		261
Land Home Financial Services Inc 1355 Willow Way Ste 250 .... Concord CA 94520 *Web:* lhfs.com	925-338-8200		652
Land Information Access Association Land Information Access Association 324 Munson Ave .... Traverse City MI 49686 *TF:* 800-687-5171 ■ *Web:* www.liaa.org	231-929-3696		41
Land Line Magazine 1 NW Oodia Dr PO Box 1000 .... Grain Valley MO 64029 *TF:* 800-444-5791 ■ *Web:* www.landlinemag.com	816-229-5791	443-2227	457-21
Land O'Frost Inc 16850 Chicago Ave .... Lansing IL 60438 *Web:* www.landofrost.com	708-474-7100		473
Land O'Lakes Inc Dairyman's Div 400 S 'M' St .... Tulare CA 93274 *TF:* 800-328-4155 ■ *Web:* landolakesinc.com	559-687-8287		296-27
Land O'Lakes Inc Western Feed Div 4001 Lexington Ave N. .... Arden Hills MN 55126 *TF:* 800-328-9680 ■ *Web:* www.landolakesinc.com	800-328-9680		447
Land of the Yankee Fork State Park PO Box 1086 .... Challis ID 83226 *Web:* www.parksandrecreation.idaho.gov	208-879-5244	879-5243	565
Land Rover North America Inc 555 MacArthur Blvd .... Mahwah NJ 07430 *TF:* 800-637-6837 ■ *Web:* www.landrover.com	800-637-6837		59
Land Rover of Calgary 175 Glendeer Cir SE .... Calgary AB T2H2V4 *Web:* landrovercalgary.com	403-255-1994		57
Land Title Guarantee Co Inc 3033 E First Ave Ste 600 Ste 600 .... Denver CO 80206 *Web:* www.ltgc.com	303-321-1880		390
Land Trust Alliance (LTA) 1660 L St NW Ste 1100 .... Washington DC 20036 *Web:* www.landtrustalliance.org	202-638-4725	638-4730	48-13

Phone | Fax | Class

Landa & Assoc Inc
5128 E Thomas Rd Ste 100 ... Phoenix AZ 85018 602-443-5515 256
Web: www.landaandassociates.com

Landaal Packaging Systems Inc
3256 B Iron St ... Burton MI 48529 800-616-6619 100
TF: 800-616-6619 ■ *Web:* www.landaal.com

Landaas & Co
411 E Wisconsin Ave 20th Fl ... Milwaukee WI 53202 414-223-1099 401
TF: 800-236-1096 ■ *Web:* www.landaas.com

Landair Corp 1110 Myers St ... Greeneville TN 37743 888-526-3247 780
TF: 888-526-3247 ■ *Web:* www.landair.com

LandaJob
222 W Gregory Blvd Ste 304 ... Kansas City MO 64114 816-523-1881 195
TF: 800-931-8806 ■ *Web:* www.landajobnow.com

Landau Bldg Co 9855 Rinaman Rd ... Wexford PA 15090 724-935-8800 935-6510 186
Web: www.landau-bldg.com

Landau Uniforms Inc
8410 W Sandidge Rd ... Olive Branch MS 38654 662-895-7200 155-19
TF General: 800-238-7513 ■ *Web:* www.landau.com

Landauer Inc 2 Science Rd ... Glenwood IL 60425 708-755-7000 755-7016 576
NYSE: LDR ■ *TF:* 800-323-8830 ■ *Web:* www.landauer.com

Landavazo Bros Inc 29280 Pacific St ... Hayward CA 94544 510-581-7104 189-3

Landec Ag LLC 201 N Michigan St ... Oxford IN 47971 765-385-1000 280
TF: 800-241-7252 ■ *Web:* incotec.com

Landec Corp 3603 Haven Ave ... Menlo Park CA 94025 650-306-1650 605-2
NASDAQ: LNDC ■ *Web:* www.landec.com

Landel Telecom 142 Martinvale Ln ... San Jose CA 95119 855-624-5284 387
TF: 855-624-5284 ■ *Web:* www.landel.com

Lander County
315 S Humboldt St ... Battle Mountain NV 89820 775-635-5738 338
TF: 800-288-2020 ■ *Web:* landercountynv.org

Lander University 320 Stanley Ave ... Greenwood SC 29649 864-388-8307 388-8125* 166
**Fax:* Admissions ■ *TF Admissions:* 800-922-1117 ■ *Web:* www.lander.edu

Landers Premier Flooring Inc
2601 Mchale Ct Ste 140 ... Austin TX 78758 512-873-9470 290
Web: landerspremierflooring.com

Landesa 1424 Fourth Ave Ste 300 ... Seattle WA 98101 206-528-5880 305
Web: www.landesa.org

Landice Inc 111 Canfield Ave ... Randolph NJ 07869 973-927-9010 476
TF: 800-526-3423 ■ *Web:* www.landice.com

Landings Club Inc 71 Green Island Rd ... Savannah GA 31411 912-598-8050 354
TF: 800-841-7011 ■ *Web:* www.landingsclub.com

Landings Yacht Golf and Tennis Club Inc, The
4420 Flagship Dr ... Fort Myers FL 33919 239-482-3211 706
Web: www.landingsygtc.com

Landini Bros 115 King St ... Alexandria VA 22314 703-836-8404 549-3596 671
Web: www.landinibrothers.com

Landis Arboretum
174 Lape Rd PO Box 186 ... Esperance NY 12066 518-875-6935 97
Web: www.landisarboretum.org

Landis Block Co
711 N County Line Rd PO Box 64418 ... Souderton PA 18964 215-723-5506 723-5500 183
TF: 800-255-1727 ■ *Web:* www.landisbc.com

Landis Computer 1120 Division Hwy ... Ephrata PA 17522 717-733-0793 624
Web: landiscomputer.com

Landis Construction LLC
8300 Earhart Blvd Ste 300 PO Box 4278 ... New Orleans LA 70118 504-833-6070 833-6662 186
TF: 800-880-3290 ■ *Web:* www.landisllc.com

Landis Corp 6446 Fairway Ave SE ... Salem OR 97306 503-584-1576 261
Web: landisconsulting.com

Landis Gyr Inc 2800 Duncan Rd ... Lafayette IN 47904 765-742-1001 742-0936 248
TF: 888-390-5733 ■ *Web:* www.landisgyr.com

Landis Supermarket Inc
2685 County Line Rd ... Telford PA 18969 215-723-1157 345
Web: www.landismarket.com

Landiscor 7310 N 16th St Ste 275 ... Phoenix AZ 85020 602-248-8989 727
TF: 866-221-0578 ■ *Web:* www.landiscor.com

Landmann Wire Rope Products Inc
1818 Gilbreth Rd Ste 148 ... Burlingame CA 94010 650-777-4210 492
Web: www.landmannwire.com

Landmark Aviation 4360 Agar Dr ... Richmond BC V7B1A3 604-279-9922 279-9942 63
TF: 888-298-7326 ■ *Web:* www.landmarkaviation.com

Landmark Aviation
1500 City West Blvd Ste 600 ... Houston TX 77042 713-895-9243 690-9553 63
Web: www.landmarkaviation.com

Landmark Bank 801 E Broadway ... Columbia MO 65201 573-499-7333 70
Web: landmarkbank.com

Landmark Building Maintenance Inc
1725 W 17th St ... Tempe AZ 85281 480-303-0244 104
Web: www.landmarkcleaning.com

Landmark College 19 River Rd S ... Putney VT 05346 802-387-4767 162
Web: landmark.edu

Landmark Community Newspapers Inc
601 Taylorsville Rd ... Shelbyville KY 40065 502-633-4334 633-4447 637-8
TF: 800-939-9322 ■ *Web:* www.lcni.com

Landmark Construction Group Inc
300 NW 61st St Ste 100 ... Oklahoma City OK 73118 405-843-8041 780
Web: landmarkokc.com

Landmark Consultants Inc
141 Ninth St ... Steamboat Springs CO 80477 970-871-9494 261
Web: www.landmark-co.com

Landmark Credit Union
5445 S Westridge Dr PO Box 510910 ... New Berlin WI 53151 262-796-4500 782-3422 219
TF: 800-801-1449 ■ *Web:* www.landmarkcu.com

Landmark Equipment Company Inc
1309 Haltom Rd ... Fort Worth TX 76117 972-579-9999 429
Web: www.landmarkeq.com

Landmark Financial Group LLC
181 Old Post Rd ... Southport CT 06890 203-254-8422 251
TF: 800-437-4214 ■ *Web:* landmark-mortgage.com

Landmark Ford Inc 12000 SW 66th Ave ... Tigard OR 97223 503-639-1131 516
Web: www.landmarkford.com

Landmark Hotel Group LLC
4453 Bonney Rd ... Virginia Beach VA 23462 757-213-4380 378
TF: 800-448-2786 ■ *Web:* www.landmarkhotelgroup.com

Landmark Imaging Medical Group Inc
11620 Wilshire Blvd Ste 100 ... Los Angeles CA 90025 310-914-7336 415
Web: www.landmarkimaging.com

Landmark Industries Ltd
11111 Wilcrest Green Dr Ste 100 Ste 100 ... Houston TX 77042 713-789-0310 789-2907 316
Web: www.landmarkindustries.com

Landmark Inn 230 N Front St ... Marquette MI 49855 906-228-2580 228-5676 379
TF General: 888-752-6362 ■ *Web:* www.thelandmarkinn.com

Landmark Inn State Historic Site
402 E Florence St ... Castroville TX 78009 830-931-2133 565
Web: www.thc.texas.gov

Landmark International Trucks Inc
4550 Rutledge Pk ... Knoxville TN 37914 865-637-4881 780
TF: 800-968-9999 ■ *Web:* www.landmarktrucks.com

Landmark Lincoln-Mercury Inc
5000 S Broadway ... Englewood CO 80113 303-761-1560 57
TF: 888-318-9692 ■ *Web:* landmarklincoln.com

Landmark Manufacturing Corp
28100 Quick Ave ... Gallatin MO 64640 660-663-2185 663-2417 697
Web: www.landmarkfab.com

Landmark Medical Ctr 115 Cass Ave ... Woonsocket RI 02895 401-769-4100 374-3
TF: 800-494-8100 ■ *Web:* www.landmarkmedical.org

Landmark on the Park
160 Central Pk W ... New York NY 10023 212-971-5353 50-1
Web: www.landmarkonthepark.org

Landmark Parking Inc 33 S Gay St ... Baltimore MD 21202 410-837-5600 562
Web: landmarkparking.com

Landmark Plastic Corp 1331 Kelly Ave ... Akron OH 44306 330-785-2200 785-9200 608
TF: 800-242-1183 ■ *Web:* www.landmarkplastic.com

Landmark Protection Inc
675 N First St Ste 800 ... San Jose CA 95112 408-293-6300 693
Web: www.landmarkprotection.com

Landmark Realty LLC
2205 Beckett St ... Bossier City LA 71111 318-747-0052 652
Web: www.landmarkrealty.org

Landmark Resort 7643 Hillside Rd ... Egg Harbor WI 54209 920-868-3205 868-2569 669
TF: 800-273-7877 ■ *Web:* www.thelandmarkresort.com

Landmark Resort
1501 S Ocean Blvd ... Myrtle Beach SC 29577 843-448-9441 669
TF: 800-845-0658 ■ *Web:* www.landmarkresort.com

Landmark School
429 Hale St PO Box 227 ... Prides Crossing MA 01965 978-236-3010 927-7268 622
TF: 866-333-0859 ■ *Web:* www.landmarkschool.org

Landmark Staffing Resources Inc
2901 E Enterprise Ave Ste 600 ... Appleton WI 54913 920-731-3130 260
Web: www.landmarkstaffing.com

Landmark Structures LP
1665 Harmon Rd ... Fort Worth TX 76177 817-439-8888 439-9001 188-10
TF: 800-888-6816 ■ *Web:* www.teamlandmark.com

Landmark Testing & Engineering
795 E Factory Dr ... St George UT 84790 435-986-0566 261
Web: landmarktesting.com

Landmark Theaters
2222 S Barrington Ave ... Los Angeles CA 90064 310-473-6701 748
TF Cust Svc: 888-724-6362 ■ *Web:* www.landmarktheatres.com

Landmark Theatre 362 S Salina St ... Syracuse NY 13202 315-475-7979 572
Web: www.landmarktheatre.org

Landmark Tours Inc
4001 Stinson Blvd Ste 430 ... Minneapolis MN 55421 651-490-5408 760
TF: 888-231-8735 ■ *Web:* gowithlandmark.com

Landmark Volunteers 800 N Main St ... Sheffield MA 01257 413-229-0255 48-7

Landoll Corp 1900 North St ... Marysville KS 66508 785-562-5381 321-3865* 470
**Fax Area Code:* 888 ■ **Fax:* Sales ■ *TF Cust Svc:* 800-446-5175 ■ *Web:* www.landoll.com

Landor Assoc Ltd 1001 Front St ... San Francisco CA 94111 415-365-1700 195
TF: 888-252-6367 ■ *Web:* www.landor.com

Landpoint Surveys Inc
611 El Dorado Rd ... Magnolia AR 71753 870-234-6384 727
TF: 800-348-5254 ■ *Web:* www.landpoint.net

Landrum & Shouse LLP
220 W Main St Ste 800 ... Lexington KY 40507 502-589-7616 428
Web: www.landrumshouse.com

Landrum's Homestead & Village
1356 Hwy 15 S ... Laurel MS 39443 601-649-2546 520
TF: 800-257-1136 ■ *Web:* landrums.com

Landry harris & Co
600 Jefferson St Ste 200 ... Lafayette LA 70501 337-266-2150 266-2151 390
Web: www.landryharris.com

Landry's Restaurants Inc
1510 W Loop S ... Houston TX 77027 713-850-1010 670
TF: 800-552-6379 ■ *Web:* www.landrysinc.com

Landry's Seafood House
2900 W Missouri Hwy 76 ... Branson MO 65616 417-339-1010 671
Web: www.landrysseafood.com

Landry's Seafood House
6801 Gateway Blvd W ... El Paso TX 79925 915-779-2900 671
Web: www.landrysseafood.com

Lands' End Inc 1 Lands' End Ln ... Dodgeville WI 53595 800-963-4816 459
TF Orders: 800-963-4816 ■ *Web:* www.landsend.com

Landsberg Orora
1640 S Greenwood Ave ... Montebello CA 90640 323-832-2000 559
TF Cust Svc: 888-526-3723 ■ *Web:* www.landsberg.com

Landsby, The 1576 Mission Dr Ofc ... Solvang CA 93463 805-688-3121 378
TF: 800-457-5373 ■ *Web:* www.thelandsby.com

Landscape Concepts Management
31745 Alleghany Rd ... Grayslake IL 60030 847-223-3800 223-0169 422
TF: 866-655-3800 ■ *Web:* www.landscapeconcepts.com

Landscape Development Inc
28447 Witherspoon Pkwy ... Valencia CA 91355 661-295-1970 295-1969 422
Web: www.landscapedevelopment.com

Landscape Structures Inc
601 Seventh St S ... Delano MN 55328 763-972-3391 972-3185 346
TF: 800-328-0035 ■ *Web:* www.playlsi.com

Landscapes Unlimited LLC
1201 Aries Dr ... Lincoln NE 68512 402-423-6653 423-4487 188-3
Web: www.landscapesunlimited.com

Landsford Canal State Park 2051 Pk Dr ... Catawba SC 29704 803-789-5800 565
Web: www.southcarolinaparks.com

Landshark Inc PO Box 1791 ... Boulder CO 80306 303-494-1229 652

Landstar Express America Inc
13410 Sutton Pk Dr S ... Jacksonville FL 32224 904-398-9400 398-9400* 780
**Fax:* Hum Res ■ *TF:* 800-872-9400 ■ *Web:* www.Landstar.com

Name / Address	City	State	Zip	Phone	Fax	Class
Landstar Inway Inc 13410 Sutton Pk Dr S	Jacksonville	FL	61102	800-872-9400		780
TF: 800-435-7352 ■ *Web:* landstar.com						
Landstar Logistics Inc 13410 Sutton Pk Dr S	Jacksonville	FL	32224	904-398-9400		449
TF: 800-872-9400 ■ *Web:* www.landstar.com						
LandTek Group Inc, The 235 County Line Rd	Amityville	NY	11701	631-691-2381		188
Web: www.landtekgroup.com						
Lane & Waterman LLP 220 N Main St Ste 600	Davenport	IA	52801	563-324-3246	324-1616	428
Web: www.l-wlaw.com						
Lane Aviation Corp 4389 International Gateway	Columbus	OH	43219	614-237-3747	231-4741*	63
**Fax:* Cust Svc ■ *TF:* 800-848-6263 ■ *Web:* www.laneaviation.com						
Lane Bryant Inc 3344 Morse Crossing Rd	Columbus	OH	43219	954-970-2205		157-6
TF Cust Svc: 866-886-4731 ■ *Web:* www.lanebryant.com						
Lane College 545 Ln Ave	Jackson	TN	38301	731-426-7500	426-7559*	166
**Fax:* Admissions ■ *TF Admissions:* 800-960-7533 ■ *Web:* www.lanecollege.edu						
Lane Community College 4000 E 30th Ave	Eugene	OR	97405	541-463-3000	463-3995*	162
**Fax:* Admissions ■ *TF:* 800-321-2211 ■ *Web:* www.lanecc.edu						
Cottage Grove 1275 S River Rd	Cottage Grove	OR	97424	541-463-4202		162
Web: www.lanecc.edu						
Florence 3149 Oak St	Florence	OR	97439	541-997-8444	997-8448	162
TF: 800-222-3290 ■ *Web:* www.lanecc.edu						
Lane Construction Company Inc 1 Indian Rd	Denville	NJ	07834	973-586-2700	586-2965	188-4
Web: www.thelanegroup.us						
Lane Construction Corp 90 Fieldstone Ct	Cheshire	CT	06410	203-235-3351	237-4260	188-4
TF: 800-999-1018 ■ *Web:* www.laneconstruct.com						
Lane Conveyors & Drives Inc 15 Industrial Plaza	Brewer	ME	04412	207-989-4560		480
Web: lane.us.com						
Lane County PO Box 290	Dighton	KS	67839	620-397-2802	397-2802	338
Web: www.kansastreasurers.org						
Lane County 125 E Eigth Ave	Eugene	OR	97401	541-682-4203	682-4616	338
TF: 800-281-2800 ■ *Web:* www.lanecounty.org						
Lane Electric 787 Bailey Hill Rd PO Box 21410	Eugene	OR	97402	541-484-1151	484-7316	245
Web: www.laneelectric.com						
Lane Engineering LLC 117 Bay St	Easton	MD	21601	410-822-8003		261
TF: 800-638-1196 ■ *Web:* www.leinc.com						
Lane Events Ctr 796 W 13th Ave	Eugene	OR	97402	541-682-4292	682-3614	205
Web: www.atthefair.com						
Lane Gorman Trubitt LLP 2626 Howell St Ste 700	Dallas	TX	75204	214-871-7500	871-0011	2
Web: www.lgt-cpa.com						
Lane Group LLC, The 14-25 Plaza Rd	Fair Lawn	NJ	07410	201-398-9230		196
Web: www.tlgmeetings.com						
Lane Medical Library Stanford University Medical Ctr 300 Pasteur Dr Rm L-109	Stanford	CA	94305	650-723-6831	725-7471	434-1
Web: www.lane.stanford.edu						
Lane Memorial Blood Bank 2211 Willamette St	Eugene	OR	97405	541-484-9111	484-6976	89
Web: lanebloodcenter.org						
Lane Press Inc 87 Meadowland Dr PO Box 130	Burlington	VT	05402	802-863-5555		627
TF: 800-733-3740 ■ *Web:* www.lanepress.com						
Lane Public Library 300 N Third St	Hamilton	OH	45011	513-894-7156		434-3
Web: www.lanepl.org						
Lane Punch Corp 281 Ln Pkwy	Salisbury	NC	28146	704-633-3900	227-6725*	757
**Fax Area Code:* 800 ■ *Web:* www.lanepunch.com						
Lane Regional Medical Ctr 6300 Main St	Zachary	LA	70791	225-658-4000	658-4287	374-3
TF: 800-994-6610 ■ *Web:* www.lanermc.org						
Lane Steel Co Inc 4 River Rd	McKees Rocks	PA	15136	412-777-1700		492
Web: www.lanesteel.com						
Lane Supply Inc 120 Fairview	Arlington	TX	76010	817-261-9116	275-1660	579
Web: www.lanesupplyinc.com						
Lane's End 1500 Midway Rd PO Box 626	Versailles	KY	40383	859-873-7300	873-3746	368
Web: www.lanesend.com						
LANE4 Property Group Inc 4705 Central St	Kansas City	MO	64112	816-960-1444		652
Web: www.lane4group.com						
Lane-Scott Electric Co-op Inc 410 S High	Dighton	KS	67839	620-397-5327		245
TF: 800-407-2217 ■ *Web:* www.lanescott.coop						
LaneTerralever 725 W McDowell Rd	Phoenix	AZ	85007	602-258-5263		466
Web: terralever.com						
Laney College 900 Fallon St	Oakland	CA	94607	510-834-5740		162
Web: laney.edu						
Laney's Inc 55 27 St S	Fargo	ND	58103	701-237-0543		787
Web: www.laneysinc.com						
Lang Asset Management Inc 171 Village Pkwy NE Bldg 8A	Marietta	GA	30067	404-256-4100	256-1473	194
Web: www.langasset.com						
Lang Dental Manufacturing Co 175 Messner Dr	Wheeling	IL	60090	847-215-6622		228
TF: 800-222-5264 ■ *Web:* www.langdental.com						
Lang Diesel Inc 1366 Toulon Ave	Hays	KS	67601	785-735-2651		429
Web: langdieselinc.com						
Lang Naturals Inc 20 Silva Ln	Middletown	RI	02842	401-848-7700		297-8
Web: www.langnaturals.com						
Lang Realty 2901 Clint Moore Rd Ste 9	Boca Raton	FL	33496	561-998-0100		652
Web: www.langrealty.com						
Lang Richert & Patch 5200 N Palm Ave 4th Fl	Fresno	CA	93704	559-228-6700	228-6727	41
Web: www.lrp.org						
Lang Stone Co Inc 707 Short St	Columbus	OH	43215	614-235-4099		191-1
Web: www.langstone.com						
Langan Engineering & Environmental Services Inc 300 Kimball Dr 4th Fl	Elmwood Park	NJ	07054	973-560-4900	560-4901	261
Web: www.langan.com						
Langara College 100 W 49th Ave	Vancouver	BC	V5Y2Z6	604-323-5511		162
Web: langara.ca						
Langdale Forest Products Co 1202 Madison Hwy	Valdosta	GA	31603	229-333-2500	333-2533	683
Web: www.langdaleforest.com						
Langdon & Company LLP 223 Us 70 Hwy E Ste 100	Garner	NC	27529	919-662-1001		2
TF: 800-222-3454 ■ *Web:* www.langdoncpa.com						
Langdon Hall Country House Hotel & Spa 1 Langdon Dr	Cambridge	ON	N3H4R8	519-740-2100	740-8161	379
TF: 800-268-1898 ■ *Web:* www.langdonhall.ca						
Langdon Wilson Architecture Planning Interiors 1055 Wilshire Blvd Ste 1500	Los Angeles	CA	90017	213-250-1186	482-4654	261
Web: www.langdonwilson.com						
Lange Graphics Inc 1360 S Lipan St	Denver	CO	80223	303-777-1737		627
Web: www.langegraphics.com						
Langer Inc 2905 Veterans' Memorial Hwy	Ronkonkoma	NY	11779	800-645-5520		477
TF: 800-645-5520 ■ *Web:* www.langerbiomechanics.com						
Langers Juice Company Inc 16195 Stephens St	City of Industry	CA	91745	626-336-3100	961-2021	296-20
Web: www.langers.com						
Langevin Jim (Rep D - RI) 2077 Rayburn HOB	Washington	DC	20515	202-225-2735	225-5976	342-2
Web: langevin.house.gov						
Langevin Pierre Dr 2705 Laurier Blvd	Quebec	QC	G1V4G2	418-656-4141		374-2
Langham Boston, The 250 Franklin St	Boston	MA	02110	617-451-1900	423-2844	379
TF: 800-791-7781 ■ *Web:* www.langhamhotels.com						
Langhorne Carpet Co 201 W Lincoln Hwy PO Box 7175	Penndel	PA	19047	215-757-5155	757-2212	131
TF: 800-372-6274 ■ *Web:* www.langhornecarpets.com						
Langlade County 800 Clermont St	Antigo	WI	54409	715-627-6200	627-6303	338
Web: www.co.langlade.wi.us						
Langley Air Force Base 49 Spruce St	Langley AFB	VA	23665	757-764-1110	764-3315*	497-1
**Fax:* Library ■ *Web:* www.jble.af.mil						
Langley Chamber of Commerce 8047 199 St Ste 207	Langley	BC	V2Y0E2	604-530-6656		137
Web: www.langleychamber.com						
Langley Federal Credit Union 1055 W Mercury Blvd	Hampton	VA	23666	757-827-7200	825-7557	219
TF: 800-826-7490 ■ *Web:* www.langleyfcu.org						
Langley Memorial Hospital 22051 Fraser Hwy	Langley	BC	V3A4H4	604-534-4121	534-8283	374-2
Web: www.fraserhealth.ca						
Langley Porter Psychiatric Institute 401 Parnassus Ave	San Francisco	CA	94143	415-476-7000	476-7320	374-5
TF: 877-382-4357 ■ *Web:* psych.ucsf.edu						
Langley Recycling 503 SE Branner St	Topeka	KS	66607	785-234-2691		686
Web: kcscrapyard.com						
Langley Research Ctr 8 Lindbergh Wy	Hampton	VA	23681	757-864-1000		668
Web: www.nasa.gov/centers/langley						
Langley Speedway 11 Dale Lemonds Dr	Hampton	VA	23666	757-865-7223		515
Web: www.langley-speedway.com						
Langlois Co 10810 San Sevaine Way	Mira Loma	CA	91752	951-360-3900		296-16
TF: 800-962-5993 ■ *Web:* www.langloiscompany.com						
Lang-Mekra North America LLC 101 Tillessen Blvd	Ridgeway	SC	29130	803-337-5264	337-5265	332
TF: 888-635-7248 ■ *Web:* www.lang-mekra.com						
Langston Construction Company Inc 125 Langston Rd	Piedmont	SC	29673	864-295-9156		186
Web: www.langstonconstr.com						
Langston Cos Inc 1760 S Third St	Memphis	TN	38109	901-774-4440		67
TF: 800-627-5224 ■ *Web:* langstonbag.com						
Langston University 2013 Langston University PO Box 1500	Langston	OK	73050	877-466-2231		166
TF: 877-466-2231 ■ *Web:* www.langston.edu						
Langstons Co 2034 NW Seventh St	Oklahoma City	OK	73106	405-235-9536		229
TF: 800-658-2831 ■ *Web:* www.langstons.com						
Langtech Systems Consulting Inc 733 Frnt St Ste 110	San Francisco	CA	94111	415-364-9600		809
TF: 800-480-8488 ■ *Web:* www.langtech.com						
Language Academy 200 S Andrews Ave Ste 401	Fort Lauderdale	FL	33301	954-462-8373	462-3738	423
Web: www.languageacademy.com						
Language Automation Inc (LAI) 1660 S Amphlett Blvd Ste 106	San Mateo	CA	94402	650-571-7877		178-7
Web: www.lai.com						
Language Co 189 W 15th St	Edmond	OK	73013	405-715-9996	715-1116	423
Web: www.thelanguagecompany.com						
Language Door LLC 18103 Sky Park Cir Ste D2	Irvine	CA	92614	310-826-4140		423
Web: www.languagedoor.com						
Language Engineering Co 135 Beaver St Ste 204	Waltham	MA	02452	781-642-8900		178-3
TF: 888-366-4532 ■ *Web:* www.lec.com						
Language Exchange International 500 NE Spanish River Blvd Ste 19	Boca Raton	FL	33431	561-368-3913		423
Web: www.languageexchange.com						
Language Line Services 1 Lower Ragsdale Dr Bldg 2	Monterey	CA	93940	800-752-6096		768
TF: 800-752-6096 ■ *Web:* www.languageline.com						
Language Pacifica 585 Glenwood Ave	Menlo Park	CA	94025	650-321-1840		423
TF: 800-818-9128 ■ *Web:* www.languagepacifica.com						
Language Plus Inc 4110 Rio Bravo Ste 202	El Paso	TX	79902	915-544-8600		423
Web: www.languageplus.com						
Language Scientific 10 Cabot Rd Ste 209	Medford	MA	02155	617-621-0940		393
Web: www.languagescientific.com						
Language Services Associates Inc 455 Business Ctr Dr - Ste 100	Horsham	PA	19044	800-305-9673		768
TF: 800-305-9673 ■ *Web:* www.lsaweb.com						
Language Studies Canada 124 Eglinton Ave W Ste 400	Toronto	ON	M4R2G8	416-488-2200	488-2225	423
Web: www.ecenglish.com						
Language World Services Inc 7220 Fair Oaks Blvd Ste D	Carmichael	CA	95608	916-333-5247		768
Web: www.languageworldservices.com						

Name / Address	City	State	Zip	Phone	Fax	Class
Languages Canada 5886 169 A St *Fax Area Code: 888 ■ TF: 888-277-0522 ■ Web: www.languagescanada.ca	Surrey	BC	V3S6Z8	604-574-1532	277-0522*	49-5
Lanham Brothers General Contractors 2119 W Third St Web: www.lanhambros.com	Owensboro	KY	42301	270-683-4591		186
Lanier & Assoc Consulting Engi Neers Inc 4101 Magazine St Web: lanier-engineers.com	New Orleans	LA	70115	504-895-0368		261
Lanier County 56 W Main St Ste 9 TF: 800-436-7442 ■ Web: www.laniercountyboc.com	Lakeland	GA	31635	229-482-2088		338
Lanier County Board of Education 247 S Hwy 221 Web: www.lanier.k12.ga.us	Lakeland	GA	31635	229-482-3966	482-3020	685
Lanier Ford Shaver & Payne PC 2101 W Clinton Ave Ste 102 TF: 800-826-2433 ■ Web: www.lanierford.com	Huntsville	AL	35805	256-535-1100		428
Lanier Health Services (LHS) 4800 48th St *Fax: Admissions ■ Web: www.lanierhospital.com	Valley	AL	36854	334-756-1400	756-6698*	374-3
Lanier Law Group PA 600 S Duke St Web: lanierlawgroup.com	Durham	NC	27701	919-682-2111		428
Lanier Parking Solutions 233 Peachtree St NE Web: www.lanierparking.com	Atlanta	GA	30303	404-881-6076	881-6077	562
Lanigan, Ryan, Malcolm & Doyle PC 555 Quince Orchard Rd Ste 600 Web: lrmd-cpa.com	Gaithersburg	MD	20878	301-258-8900		2
Lank Oil Co 2203 W McNab Rd Web: lankoil.com	Pompano Bch	FL	33069	954-978-6600	974-0854	579
Lankenau Medical Ctr 100 E Lancaster Ave Web: www.mainlinehealth.org/locations/lankenau-medical-center	Wynnewood	PA	19096	484-476-2000		374-3
Lankford James (Sen R - OK) 316 Hart Senate Office Bldg Web: www.lankford.senate.gov	Washington	DC	20510	202-224-5754		342-2
Lankota Inc 270 Westpark Ave TF: 866-526-5682 ■ Web: www.lankota.com	Huron	SD	57350	605-352-4550		57
LANL (Los Alamos National Laboratory) PO Box 1663 TF: 877-723-4101 ■ Web: www.lanl.gov	Los Alamos	NM	87545	505-667-7000		668
Lanlogic Inc 248 Rickenbacker Cir Web: www.lanlogic.com	Livermore	CA	94551	925-273-2300		196
Lanly Co, The 26201 Tungsten Rd Web: www.lanly.com	Cleveland	OH	44132	216-731-1115	731-7900	318
Lanman Oil Co Inc PO Box 108 TF: 800-677-2819 ■ Web: www.lanmanoil.com	Charleston	IL	61920	800-677-2819		579
Lanmark Engineering & Surveying Inc 9330 Vanguard Dr Ste 131	Anchorage	AK	99507	907-562-6050		256
Lanmark Staffing Co 1002 Green Ave Web: lanmarkstaffing.com	Orange	TX	77630	409-886-7676		193
Lannett Company Inc (LCI) 13200 Townsend Rd NYSE: LCI ■ TF: 800-325-9994 ■ Web: www.lannett.com	Philadelphia	PA	19154	215-333-9000	333-9004	479
Lanni Restifo LLC 16-00 NJ-208	Fair Lawn	NJ	07410	201-797-1600		2
Lanning's 826 N Cleveland-Massillon Rd Web: www.lannings-restaurant.com	Akron	OH	44333	330-666-1159		671
Lanny's Alta Cocina Mexicana 3405 W Seventh St Web: www.lannyskitchen.com	Fort Worth	TX	76107	817-850-9996		671
LANSA Inc 3010 Highland Pkwy Ste 275 TF: 800-457-4083 ■ Web: www.lansa.com	Downers Grove	IL	60515	630-874-7000	874-7001	178-2
Lansberg, Gersick & Associates LLC 100 Whitney Ave Apt 1 Web: www.lgassoc.com	New Haven	CT	06510	203-497-0055		195
Lansco Colors 1 Blue Hill Plaza 11th Fl PO Box 1685 TF: 800-526-2783 ■ Web: www.pigments.com	Pearl River	NY	10965	845-507-5942	735-2787	550
Lansdale School of Business 290 Wissahickon Ave TF: 800-219-0486 ■ Web: www.lsb.edu	North Wales	PA	19454	215-699-5700	699-8770	800
Lansdale Semiconductor Inc 5245 S 39th St Web: www.lansdale.com	Phoenix	AZ	85040	602-438-0123	438-0138	695
Lansdowne Resort 44050 Woodridge Pkwy TF: 877-513-8400 ■ Web: www.destinationhotels.com/lansdowne-resort	Leesburg	VA	20176	703-729-8400	729-4096	377
Lansdowne-Moody Company LP 8445 E Fwy TF: 800-441-9474 ■ Web: www.lmtractor.com	Houston	TX	77029	713-672-8366		274
Lanshack.com 155 Meadow Rd Ste 100 TF: 800-925-3380 ■ Web: www.lanshack.com	Clark	NJ	07066	732-396-3600		116
Lansing Art Gallery 119 N Washington Sq TF: 800-372-8460 ■ Web: www.lansingartgallery.org	Lansing	MI	48933	517-374-6400		50-2
Lansing Bldg Products 8501 Sanford Dr Web: lansingbp.com	Richmond	VA	23228	804-266-8893	264-2124	191-4
Lansing Chamber of Commerce 3330 181st Pl Ste 103 Web: www.chamberoflansing.com	Lansing	IL	60438	708-474-4170		139
Lansing City Hall 124 W Michigan Ave 9th Fl Web: www.lansingmi.gov	Lansing	MI	48933	517-483-4131	377-0068	337
Lansing City Market 325 City Market Dr Web: www.lansingcitymarket.com	Lansing	MI	48912	517-483-7460	483-7462	460
Lansing Community College 419 N Washington Sq TF: 800-644-4522 ■ Web: www.lansing.cc.mi.us	Lansing	MI	48933	517-483-1957	483-9668	162
Lansing Ctr 333 E Michigan Ave TF: 800-514-3849 ■ Web: www.lansingcenter.com	Lansing	MI	48933	517-483-7400	483-7439	205
Lansing Ice & Fuel Co 911 Ctr St TF: 800-678-7230 ■ Web: propanefuellansing.com	Lansing	MI	48906	517-372-3850		316
Lansing Regional Chamber of Commerce 500 E Michigan Ave Ste 200 Web: www.lansingchamber.org	Lansing	MI	48912	517-487-6340	484-6910	139
Lansing State Journal 120 E Lenawee St TF: 800-234-1719 ■ Web: www.lansingstatejournal.com	Lansing	MI	48919	517-377-1000		532-2
Lansing Symphony Orchestra (LSO) 501 S Capitol Ave Ste 400 TF: 800-434-3913 ■ Web: www.lansingsymphony.org	Lansing	MI	48933	517-487-5001	487-0210	573-3
Lansing Tool & Engineering Inc 1313 S Waverly Rd TF: 800-440-3967 ■ Web: www.lansingtool.com	Lansing	MI	48917	517-372-2550		757
Lansmont Corp Ryan Ranch Research Pk 17 Mandeville Ct TF: 800-526-7666 ■ Web: www.lansmont.com	Monterey	CA	93940	831-655-6600		344
LANSolutions LLC 6359 Nancy Ridge Dr Web: www.lansolutions.net	San Diego	CA	92121	858-587-8000		196
Lantal Textiles Inc 1300 Langenthal Dr PO Box 965 TF: 800-334-3309 ■ Web: www.lantal.com	Rural Hall	NC	27045	336-969-9551		745-1
Lantana Communications Corp 1700 Tech Centre Pkwy Ste 100 TF: 800-345-4211 ■ Web: www.lantanacom.com	Arlington	TX	76014	800-345-4211		45
Lantec Products Inc 5302 Derry Ave Ste G TF: 800-392-7621 ■ Web: www.lantecp.com	Agoura Hills	CA	91301	818-707-2285		601
Lantech Inc 11000 Bluegrass Pkwy TF: 800-866-0322 ■ Web: www.lantech.com	Louisville	KY	40299	502-815-9109		547
Lantech LLC 1783 Tribute Rd Ste C TF: 800-600-2282 ■ Web: www.lantechllc.com	Sacramento	CA	95815	916-564-5455		180
Lanter Delivery Systems Inc 1 Caine Dr Web: www.lanterdeliverysystems.com	Madison	IL	62060	618-452-5300	452-5931	780
Lanterman Developmental Ctr 3530 Pomona Blvd TF: 800-838-9237 ■ Web: www.dds.ca.gov	Pomona	CA	91769	909-595-1221	598-4352	230
Lantern Lodge Motor Inn 411 N College St TF: 800-262-5564 ■ Web: www.thelanternlodge.com	Myerstown	PA	17067	717-866-6536	866-8857	379
Lantheus Medical Imaging Inc 331 Treble Cove Rd Bldg 200-2 Web: www.lantheus.com	North Billerica	MA	01862	978-667-9531		231
Lantronix Inc 167 Technology Dr NASDAQ: LTRX ■ TF Orders: 800-526-8766 ■ Web: www.lantronix.com	Irvine	CA	92618	949-453-3990	450-7249	735
Lantz Security Systems Inc 43440 Sahuayo St Web: www.lantzsecurity.com	Lancaster	CA	93535	661-949-3565		693
Lanxess Corp 111 RIDC Pk W Dr TF: 800-526-9377 ■ Web: www.lanxess.com	Pittsburgh	PA	15275	412-809-1000		605-3
LanXpert Corp 605 Market St Ste 410 TF: 888-499-1703 ■ Web: www.intivix.com	San Francisco	CA	94105	415-543-1033		177
Lanz & Mcardle Agency Inc 1022 17th Ave	Monroe	WI	53566	608-325-9126		390
Lanz Cabinet Shop Inc 3025 W Seventh Pl TF: 800-788-6332 ■ Web: www.lanzcabinets.com	Eugene	OR	97402	541-485-4050		301
Lanza Group LLC 1710 Defoor Ave NW PH 2 Penthouse 2	Atlanta	GA	30318	404-350-0200		636
Lao Laan-Xang 1146 Williamson St Web: www.laolaan-xang.com	Madison	WI	53703	608-280-0104		671
Lao People's Democratic Republic 317 E 51st St Web: www.un.int	New York	NY	10022	212-832-2734	750-0039	704
Lao People's Democratic Republic Embassy 2222 S St NW Web: www.laoembassy.com	Washington	DC	20008	202-332-6416	332-4923	257
Lapakahi State Historical Park 75 Aupuni St Rm 204 Web: dlnr.hawaii.gov	Hilo	HI	96721	808-327-4958		565
Lapeer Area Chamber of Commerce 108 W Pk St Web: www.lapeerareachamber.org	Lapeer	MI	48446	810-664-6641	664-4349	139
Lapeer County 255 Clay St Web: lapeercountyweb.org	Lapeer	MI	48446	810-667-0356		338
Lapeer Industries Inc 400 Mccormick Dr Web: www.lapeerind.com	Lapeer	MI	48446	810-664-1816		480
Lapeer Regional Hospital 1375 N Main St TF: 888-327-0671 ■ Web: www.mclaren.org	Lapeer	MI	48446	810-667-5500	667-5582	374-3
Lapels Dry Cleaning 962 Washington St TF: 866-695-2735 ■ Web: lapelsdrycleaning.com	Hanover	MA	02339	781-829-9935	829-9546	426
Lapham-Hickey Steel Corp 5500 W 73rd St TF: 800-323-8443 ■ Web: www.lapham-hickey.com	Chicago	IL	60638	708-496-6111	496-8504	492
Lapham-Patterson House State Historic Site 626 N Dawson St Web: www.gastateparks.org	Thomasville	GA	31792	229-225-4004		565
LaPine State Park 15800 State Recreation Rd TF: 800-551-6949 ■ Web: oregonstateparks.org	La Pine	OR	97739	800-551-6949		565
Lapiz Hispanic Marketing 35 W Wacker Dr Fl Twelve Web: www.lapizusa.com	Chicago	IL	60601	312-220-5000		7
Laplaca Cohen Adv Inc 43 W 24th St Fl 10 Web: www.laplacacohen.com	New York	NY	10010	212-675-4106		4
LapLink Software Inc 600 108th Ave NE Ste 610 TF: 800-343-8080 ■ Web: www.laplink.com	Bellevue	WA	98004	425-952-6000	952-6002	178-12
Lapmaster International LLC 501 W Algonquin Rd TF: 877-352-8637 ■ Web: www.lapmaster-wolters.com	Mount Prospect	IL	60056	224-659-7101		491
LaPolla Industries Inc 15402 Vantage Pkwy E Ste 322 OTC: LPAD ■ Web: lapolla.com/investor-relations	Houston	TX	77032	281-219-4700		3
Laporte & Assoc Inc 5515 SE Milwaukie Ave Web: laporte-insurance.com	Portland	OR	97202	503-239-4116		390
LaPorte County Convention & Visitors Bureau 4073 S Franklin St TF: 800-634-2650 ■ Web: www.michigancitylaporte.com	Michigan City	IN	46360	219-872-5055		206
LAPP Insulator Co 130 Gilbert St *Fax: Cust Svc ■ Web: www.lappinsulators.com	Le Roy	NY	14482	585-768-6221	768-6219*	249

Name / Address	City	State	ZIP	Phone	Fax	Class
Lapp, Fatch, Myers & Gallagher Accountants, PC 2401 Professional Pkwy *Web:* lfmgcpas.com	Santa Maria	CA	93455	805-934-0015		2
LaPrairie Crane 235 Front St Ste 209 *Web:* www.laprairiegroup.com	Tumbler Ridge	BC	V0C2W0	250-242-5561		261
Lar Lubovitch Dance Co 229 W 42nd St 8th Fl *Web:* www.lubovitch.org	New York	NY	10036	212-221-7909	221-7938	573-1
Larabida Children's Hospital 6501 S Promontory Dr E 65th St at Lk Michigan *Web:* www.larabida.org	Chicago	IL	60649	773-363-6700		374-1
Laramie Area Chamber of Commerce 800 S Third St *TF:* 866-876-1012 ■ *Web:* www.laramie.org	Laramie	WY	82070	307-745-7339	745-4624	139
Laramie County 309 W 20th St *Web:* laramiecountyclerk.com	Cheyenne	WY	82001	307-633-4264	633-4240	338
Laramie County Community College 1400 E College Dr **Fax:* Admissions ■ *TF:* 800-522-2993 ■ *Web:* www.lccc.cc.wy.us	Cheyenne	WY	82007	307-778-5222	778-1350*	162
Albany County 1125 Boulder Dr *TF:* 800-522-2993 ■ *Web:* www.lccc.wy.edu	Laramie	WY	82070	307-721-5138		162
Laramie County Public Library 2200 Pioneer Ave *TF:* 800-348-5194 ■ *Web:* www.lclsonline.org	Cheyenne	WY	82001	307-634-3561	634-2082	434-3
Laramie Plains Museum 603 E Ivinson St *Web:* www.laramiemuseum.org	Laramie	WY	82070	307-742-4448		520
Laramie River Dude Ranch 25777 County Rd 103 *TF:* 800-551-5731 ■ *Web:* www.lrranch.com	Jelm	WY	82063	970-435-5716		239
Larcan Inc 228 Ambassador Dr	Mississauga	ON	L5T2J2	905-564-9222		647
Larch Corrections Ctr 15314 NE Dole Valley Rd *Web:* doc.wa.gov	Yacolt	WA	98675	360-260-6300		213
Larchmont Engineering & Irrigation Co 11 Larchmont Ln PO Box 66 *TF:* 877-862-2550 ■ *Web:* www.larchmont-eng.com	Lexington	MA	02420	781-862-2550	862-0173	274
Larco 210 NE Tenth Ave *TF Cust Svc:* 800-523-6996 ■ *Web:* larco.com	Brainerd	MN	56401	218-829-9797	829-0139	253
Lard Oil Company Inc 914 Florida Blvd SW *TF:* 800-738-7738 ■ *Web:* www.lardoil.com	Denham Springs	LA	70726	225-664-3311		579
Laredo Community College (LCC) W End Washington St *Web:* www.laredo.edu	Laredo	TX	78040	956-722-0521	721-5493	162
Laredo Energy Arena 6700 Arena Blvd *TF:* 800-745-3000 ■ *Web:* www.learena.com	Laredo	TX	78041	956-791-9192	523-7777	720
Laredo Energy LP 840 W Sam Houston Pkwy N Ste 400 *Web:* www.laredoenergy.com	Houston	TX	77024	713-600-6000		580
Laredo Medical Ctr (LMC) 1700 E Saunders Ave *Web:* www.laredomedical.com	Laredo	TX	78041	956-796-5000		374-3
Laredo Morning Times 111 Esperanza Dr *TF:* 800-232-7907 ■ *Web:* www.lmtonline.com	Laredo	TX	78041	956-728-2500		532-2
Laredo Public Library 1120 E Calton Rd *Web:* www.laredolibrary.org	Laredo	TX	78041	956-795-2400	795-2403	434-3
Laredo's 694 S Whitney Way *Web:* laredosrestaurante.com	Madison	WI	53711	608-278-0585		671
Laredo-Webb County Chamber of Commerce 2310 San Bernardo Ave *TF:* 800-292-2122 ■ *Web:* www.laredochamber.com	Laredo	TX	78042	956-722-9895	791-4503	139
Largo Medical Ctr - Indian Rocks Rd Campus 2025 Indian Rocks Rd	Largo	FL	33774	727-588-5200		374-3
Larimer County 1 Old Town Sq *TF:* 800-772-7858 ■ *Web:* www.larimer.org	Fort Collins	CO	80524	970-498-7860	498-7906	338
Larimer Square 1430 Larimer St No 200 *Web:* www.larimersquare.com	Denver	CO	80202	303-534-2367		50-6
Lario Oil & Gas Co 301 S Market St *Web:* lariooil.com	Wichita	KS	67202	316-265-5611	265-5610	536
LaRiviere, Grubman PC 200 Sky Park Dr *Web:* www.lgpatlaw.com	Monterey	CA	93940	831-649-8800	649-8000	428
Lark Builders Inc 409 Dixon St *TF:* 800-841-7844 ■ *Web:* www.larkbuilders.com	Vidalia	GA	30474	912-538-1888		105
Lark Technologies Inc 2570 El Camino Real Ste 100 *Web:* www.lark.com	Mountain View	CA	94040	818-294-0888		743
Larkin Enterprises Inc 317 W Broadway PO Box 405 *TF:* 800-990-5418 ■ *Web:* larkinent.com	Lincoln	ME	04457	207-794-8700		188
Larkin Hoffman Daly & Lindgren Ltd 8300 Norman Center Dr Ste 1000 *Web:* larkinhoffman.com	Minneapolis	MN	55437	952-835-3800	896-3333	445
Larkin's on the River 318 S Main St *Web:* www.larkinsontheriver.com	Greenville	SC	29601	864-467-9777		671
Larksfield Place 7373 E 29th St N *TF:* 866-232-8484 ■ *Web:* www.larksfieldplace.org	Wichita	KS	67226	316-858-3910	636-5790	672
Larkspur Landing 550 W Hamilton Ave *Web:* www.larkspurhotels.com	Campbell	CA	95008	408-364-1514		379
Larkspur Restaurant & Grill 904 E Douglas St *Web:* www.larkspuronline.com	Wichita	KS	67202	316-262-5275	262-1292	671
LARL (Lake Agassiz Regional Library) 118 Fifth St S PO Box 900 *TF:* 800-247-0449 ■ *Web:* www.larl.org	Moorhead	MN	56560	218-233-3757	233-7556	434-3
Larmar Industries 3700 S County Rd W # 1295 *Web:* www.larmarindustries.com	Odessa	TX	79765	432-561-8700		358
Larned Juvenile Correctional Facility 1301 Kansas Hwy 264	Larned	KS	67550	620-285-0300		412
LARON Inc 4255 Santa Fe Dr *TF:* 800-248-3430 ■ *Web:* www.laron.com	Kingman	AZ	86401	928-757-8424		256
LaRosa's Inc 2334 Boudinot Ave *Web:* www.larosas.com	Cincinnati	OH	45238	513-347-5660		670
Larrabee State Park 245 Chuckanut Dr *TF:* 888-226-7688 ■ *Web:* parks.state.wa.us	Bellingham	WA	98229	360-676-2093		565
Larrabee Ventures Inc 15165 Ventura Blvd Ste 450 *TF:* 800-748-6123 ■ *Web:* www.larrabeeventures.com	Sherman Oaks	CA	91403	818-789-6020		194
Larry Associates Inc 6136 170th St Ste M1 *Web:* www.accountingbylarry.com	Fresh Meadows	NY	11365	718-321-0384		2
Larry Blumberg & Associates Inc 2733 Ross Clark Cir *Web:* lbaproperties.com	Dothan	AL	36301	334-793-6855		707
Larry Green Chevrolet Oldsmobile & Geo Inc 2050 Rodeo Dr *Web:* larrygreenchevrolet.com	Cottonwood	AZ	86326	928-634-2227		57
Larry H Miller Group 9350 S 150 E Ste 1000 *Web:* www.lhm.com	Sandy	UT	84070	801-563-4100		185
Larry Hopkins Honda 1048 W El Camino Real *TF:* 888-809-1033 ■ *Web:* www.larryhopkinshonda.com	Sunnyvale	CA	94087	888-809-1033		57
Larry M Jacobs & Assoc Inc 328 E Gadsden *Web:* lmj-a.com	Pensacola	FL	32501	850-434-0846		261
Larry Murphy Insurance Agency Inc 113 E Grand *Web:* larrymurphyinsurance.com	Ponca City	OK	74601	580-767-1520		390
Larry Roesch Chrysler-jeep-dodge LLC 200 W Grand Ave *Web:* www.larryroesch.com	Elmhurst	IL	60126	630-333-9121		57
Larry Snyder & Company Inc 4820 N Towne Centre Dr *Web:* lscinc.com	Ozark	MO	65721	417-887-6897		261
Larry's Main Entrance 1964 W Market St	Akron	OH	44313	330-864-8162		671
Larsen Design Office Inc 7101 York Ave S Ste 120 *Web:* www.larsen.com	Minneapolis	MN	55435	952-835-2271		344
Larsen Farms 2650 N 2375 E *TF Sales:* 800-767-6104 ■ *Web:* www.larsenfarms.com	Hamer	ID	83425	208-662-5501		296-18
Larsen Mfg LLC 1201 Allanson Rd *Web:* www.larsenmfg.net	Mundelein	IL	60060	847-970-9600		483
Larsen Pomada Literary Agents 1029 Jones St *Web:* www.larsenpomada.com	San Francisco	CA	94109	415-673-0939		444
Larsen Rick (Rep D - WA) 2113 Rayburn HOB *Web:* larsen.house.gov	Washington	DC	20515	202-225-2605	225-4420	342-2
Larsen Supply Company Inc 12055 E Slauson Ave PO Box 4388 *Web:* www.lasco.net	Santa Fe Springs	CA	90670	562-698-0731		612
Larson Berg & Perkins Pllc 105 N Third St *Web:* www.lbplaw.com	Yakima	WA	98901	509-457-1515		428
Larson Boats 700 Paul Larson Memorial Dr *TF General:* 800-220-6262 ■ *Web:* www.larsonboats.com	Little Falls	MN	56345	320-632-5481		90
Larson Contracting Inc 508 W Main St *TF:* 800-765-1426 ■ *Web:* www.larsoncontracting.com	Lake Mills	IA	50450	641-592-5800	592-8610	189-3
Larson Data Communications Inc 220 S Kimball St PO Box 96 *Web:* larsondata.com	Mitchell	SD	57301	605-996-5521		224
Larson Davis Inc 3425 Walden Ave *Web:* www.larsondavis.com	Depew	NY	14043	716-926-8243		201
Larson Design Group Inc 1000 Commerce Park Dr 2nd Fl Ste 201 *TF:* 877-323-6603 ■ *Web:* www.larsondesigngroup.com	Williamsport	PA	17701	570-323-6603	323-9902	261
Larson Engineering Inc 3524 Labore Rd *Web:* larsonengr.com	White Bear Lake	MN	55110	651-481-9120		261
Larson Hardware Manufacturing Co PO Box E *Web:* www.larsonhardware.com	Sterling	IL	61081	815-625-0503	625-8786	350
Larson John B (Rep D - CT) 1501 Longworth Bldg *Web:* www.larson.house.gov	Washington	DC	20515	202-225-2265	225-1031	342-2
Larson King LLP 30 E Seventh St Ste 2800 *TF:* 877-373-5501 ■ *Web:* www.larsonking.com	Saint Paul	MN	55101	651-312-6500	312-6618	428
Larson Manufacturing Co 2333 Eastbrook Dr *TF Cust Svc:* 888-483-3768 ■ *Web:* www.larsondoors.com	Brookings	SD	57006	605-692-6115		235
Larson Tool & Stamping Co 90 Olive St *Web:* www.larsontool.com	Attleboro	MA	02703	508-222-0897	226-7407	488
Larson-Danielson Construction Company Inc 302 Tyler St *TF:* 800-676-2127 ■ *Web:* www.ldconstruction.com	La Porte	IN	46350	219-362-2127		186
Larson-Juhl 3900 Steve Reynolds Blvd **Fax Area Code:* 770 ■ **Fax:* Hum Res ■ *TF:* 800-221-4123 ■ *Web:* www.larsonjuhl.com	Norcross	GA	30093	800-221-4123	279-5297*	309
Larson-Juhl Us LLC 22 Industrial Park Dr Ste B *Web:* www.larsonjuhl.com	Waldorf	MD	20602	301-870-5900		200
Larta Institute 606 S Olive St Ste 650 *TF:* 800-829-4933 ■ *Web:* www.larta.org	Los Angeles	CA	90014	213-694-2826		196
Larue Coffee 2631 S 156th Cir *TF:* 800-658-4498 ■ *Web:* www.laruecoffee.com	Omaha	NE	68130	402-333-9099		297-8
LaRue County 209 W High St *Web:* www.laruecounty.org	Hodgenville	KY	42748	270-358-3544	358-4528	338
Larwin Co 16633 Ventura Blvd Ste 1300	Encino	CA	91436	818-986-8890		41
Lary Archer & Associates Inc 1348 Palo Pinto Hwy *Web:* www.archerassoc.com	Palo Pinto	TX	76484	940-682-4069	659-4071	538
Larzelere Picou Wells Simpson Lonero LLC 2 Lakeway Ctr 3850 N Causeway Blvd Ste 1100 *Web:* lpwsl.com	Metairie	LA	70002	504-834-6500		445

				Phone	Fax	Class
Las Animas County 200 E First St Rm 204 *Web:* www.lasanimascounty.net	Trinidad	CO	81082	719-846-2981	845-2591	338
Las Casitas Village & Golden Door Spa 1000 El Conquistador Ave *Web:* www.lascasitasvillage.com	Fajardo	PR	00738	787-863-1000		669
Las Casuelas Terraza 222 S Palm Canyon Dr *Web:* lascasuelas.com	Palm Springs	CA	92262	760-325-2794		671
Las Cruces Bulletin 1740-A Calle de Mercado *Web:* www.lascrucesbulletin.com	Las Cruces	NM	88005	575-524-8061	526-4621	532-4
Las Cruces City Hall 200 N Church St *Web:* www.las-cruces.org	Las Cruces	NM	88001	575-541-2000	541-2117	337
Las Cruces Community Theatre 313 N Downtown Mall *Web:* www.lcctnm.org	Las Cruces	NM	88001	575-523-1200		572
Las Cruces Convention & Visitors Bureau 211 N Water St *TF:* 800-429-9488 ■ *Web:* www.lascrucescvb.org	Las Cruces	NM	88001	575-541-2444	541-2164	206
Las Cruces International Airport 8990 Zia Blvd *TF:* 800-428-4322 ■ *Web:* www.las-cruces.org	Las Cruces	NM	88007	575-541-2471		27
Las Cruces Museum of Natural History PO Box 20000 *Web:* www.las-cruces.org	Las Cruces	NM	88004	575-532-3372		520
Las Cruces Public Schools 505 S Main St Ste 249 *Web:* www.lcps.k12.nm.us	Las Cruces	NM	88001	575-527-5800		685
Las Cruces Sun-News 256 W Las Cruces Ave *TF:* 877-827-7200 ■ *Web:* www.lcsun-news.com	Las Cruces	NM	88005	575-541-5400	541-5498	532-2
Las Cruces Symphony Orchestra 1075 N Horseshoe Cir *TF:* 800-545-9011 ■ *Web:* www.lascrucessymphony.com	Las Cruces	NM	88003	575-646-3709	646-1086	573-3
LAS Enterprises Inc 2413 L & A Rd *TF:* 800-264-1527 ■ *Web:* lashome.com	Metairie	LA	70001	504-887-1515		187
Las Margaritas 123 S Industrial Rd	Tupelo	MS	38801	662-844-7399		671
Las Margaritas Restaurante 1999 W Fourth Ave *Web:* www.lasmargaritas.com	Vancouver	BC	V6J1M7	604-734-7117	734-3528	671
Las Olas Beauty 1503 E Las Olas Blvd	Fort Lauderdale	FL	33301	954-779-2616		77
Las Palmas Medical Ctr 1801 N Oregon St *Web:* www.laspalmasdelsolhealthcare.com	El Paso	TX	79902	915-521-1200		374-3
Las Positas College 3033 Collier Canyon Rd *Web:* www.laspositascollege.edu	Livermore	CA	94551	925-424-1000	443-0742	162
Las Vegas 51s, The 850 Las Vegas Blvd N *Web:* www.milb.com/index.jsp	Las Vegas	NV	89101	702-386-7200		354
Las Vegas Athletic Club 2655 S Maryland Pkwy Ste 201 *Web:* www.lvac.com	Las Vegas	NV	89109	702-734-8944		354
Las Vegas Chamber of Commerce 575 Symphony Park Ave Ste 100 *TF:* 800-468-7272 ■ *Web:* www.lvchamber.com	Las Vegas	NV	89105	702-641-5822	735-0406	139
Las Vegas City Hall 495 S Main St *Web:* www.lasvegasnevada.gov	Las Vegas	NV	89101	702-229-6011	386-9108	337
Las Vegas Color Graphics Inc 4265 W Sunset Rd *Web:* www.lasvegascolor.com	Las Vegas	NV	89118	702-617-9000		174
Las Vegas Convention & Visitors Authority 3150 Paradise Rd *TF:* 877-847-4050 ■ *Web:* www.lvcva.com	Las Vegas	NV	89109	702-892-0711	837-0315	206
Las Vegas Cuban Cuisine 2807 E Oakland Pk Blvd *Web:* www.lasvegascubancuisine.com	Fort Lauderdale	FL	33306	954-564-1370		671
Las Vegas Events 770 E Warm Springs Rd Ste 140 *Web:* lasvegasevents.com	Las Vegas	NV	89119	702-260-8605		317
Las Vegas Floral & Plant Wholesale 2404 We *TF:* 800-747-5449 ■ *Web:* floracouture.com	Las Vegas	NV	89102	702-221-1220		292
Las Vegas Motor Speedway 7000 Las Vegas Blvd N *TF:* 800-644-4444 ■ *Web:* www.lvms.com	Las Vegas	NV	89115	702-644-4444		515
Las Vegas Natural History Museum 900 Las Vegas Blvd N *TF:* 800-675-3267 ■ *Web:* www.lvnhm.org	Las Vegas	NV	89101	702-384-3466		520
Las Vegas Paving Corp 4420 S Decatur Blvd *Web:* www.lasvegaspaving.com	Las Vegas	NV	89103	702-251-5800		188-4
Las Vegas Premium Outlets 875 S Grand Central Pkwy *Web:* www.premiumoutlets.com	Las Vegas	NV	89106	702-474-7500		460
Las Vegas Presort LLC 3655 E Patrick Ln Ste 300 *Web:* lasvegaspresort.com	Las Vegas	NV	89120	702-320-0450		317
Las Vegas Review-Journal 1111 W Bonanza Rd PO Box 70 *Web:* www.reviewjournal.com	Las Vegas	NV	89106	702-383-0211	383-4676	532-2
Las Vegas Sands Corp 3355 Las Vegas Blvd S *NYSE: LVS* ■ *Web:* www.sands.com	Las Vegas	NV	89109	702-414-1000		379
Las Vegas Sun 2360 Corporate Cir *Web:* www.lasvegassun.com	Henderson	NV	89074	702-385-3111	383-7264	532-2
Lasalle College High School Endowment 8605 Cheltenham Ave *Web:* www.lschs.org	Wyndmoor	PA	19038	215-233-2911		305
LaSalle County 707 E Etna Rd *TF:* 800-247-5243 ■ *Web:* www.lasallecounty.org	Ottawa	IL	61350	815-433-3366	433-9522	338
LaSalle Grill 115 W Colfax Ave *TF:* 800-382-9323 ■ *Web:* www.lasallegrill.com	South Bend	IN	46601	574-288-1155		671
LaSalle Hotel 120 S Main St *Web:* www.lasalle-hotel.com	Bryan	TX	77803	979-822-2000		379
LaSalle Hotel Properties 3 Bethesda Metro Ctr Ste 1200 *NYSE: LHO* ■ *Web:* www.lasallehotels.com	Bethesda	MD	20814	301-941-1500	941-1553	379
LaSalle Lake State Fish & Wildlife Area 2660 E 2350th Rd *Web:* www.stateparks.com	Marseilles	IL	61341	815-357-1608		565
Lasalle Management Company LLC 192 Bastille Ln *Web:* lasallecorrections.com	Ruston	LA	71270	318-232-1500		271
LaSalle Parish PO Box 1288 *Web:* www.lpgov.org	Jena	LA	71342	318-992-2101	992-2103	338
Lasalle St Securities LLC 940 N Industrial Dr *Web:* www.lasallest.com	Elmhurst	IL	60126	630-600-0500		690
LaSalle Systems Leasing Inc 6111 N River Rd *Web:* www.elasalle.com	Rosemont	IL	60018	847-823-9600	823-1646	264-1
LASCCO (Los Angeles Smoking & Curing Co) 1100 W Ewing St *TF:* 800-365-8950 ■ *Web:* www.oceanbeauty.com	Seattle	WA	98119	206-285-6800		296-13
Lasco Fittings Inc 414 Morgan St PO Box 116 *TF:* 800-776-2756 ■ *Web:* www.lascofittings.com	Brownsville	TN	38012	731-772-3180	772-0835	596
Lasco Foods Inc 4553 Gustine Ave *Web:* www.lascofoods.com	St Louis	MO	63116	314-832-1906		297-8
Lasell College 1844 Commonwealth Ave **Fax:* Admissions ■ *TF Admissions:* 888-222-5229 ■ *Web:* www.lasell.edu	Newton	MA	02466	617-243-2225	243-2380*	166
Laser & Computer Options Inc 3758 E Grove St *Web:* www.laseroptionsinc.com	Phoenix	AZ	85040	480-968-8440		175
Laser 101.7 1530 Greenview Dr SW Ste 200 *Web:* laser1017.iheart.com	Rochester	MN	55902	507-288-3888	288-7815	645-137
Laser App Software Inc 3190 Shelby St Ste D 100 *Web:* www.laserapp.com	Ontario	CA	91764	909-985-2174		177
Laser Cutting Services Inc 12475 SW Herman Rd *Web:* www.lasercuttingservices.com	Tualatin	OR	97062	503-612-8311		697
Laser Diode Inc 4 Olsen Ave *Web:* www.laserdiode.com	Edison	NJ	08820	732-549-9001	906-1559	696
Laser Excel N6323 Berlin Rd *TF:* 800-285-6544 ■ *Web:* www.laserexcel.com	Green Lake	WI	54941	920-294-6544	294-6588	454
Laser Institute of America (LIA) 13501 Ingenuity Dr Ste 128 *TF:* 800-345-2737 ■ *Web:* www.lia.org	Orlando	FL	32826	407-380-1553	380-5588	49-19
Laser Print Plus Inc 1261 First St S Ext Ste A *TF:* 800-522-9085 ■ *Web:* www.laserprintplus.com	Columbia	SC	29209	803-695-7090		627
Laser Pros International 1 International Ln *TF:* 888-558-5277 ■ *Web:* www.laserpros.com	Rhinelander	WI	54501	715-369-5995	369-5910	174
Laser Quest Inc 3415 American Dr *TF:* 888-288-2001 ■ *Web:* www.laserquest.com	Mississauga	ON	L4U1TA	888-288-2001		31
Laser Reproductions Inc 950E Taylor Sta Rd	Gahanna	OH	43230	614-552-6905		627
Laser Technologies Inc 1120 N Frontenac Rd *Web:* lasertechnologiesinc.com	Naperville	IL	60563	630-761-1200		454
Laser Technology Inc 7070 S Tucson Way *TF:* 800-280-6113 ■ *Web:* www.lasertech.com	Englewood	CO	80112	303-649-1000	649-9710	495
Laser Tek Services Inc 742 19th St N *Web:* www.lasertekservices.com	Fargo	ND	58102	701-239-4033		179
Laserage Technology Corp 3021 N Delany Rd *Web:* www.laserage.com	Waukegan	IL	60087	847-249-5900	336-1103	476
LaserBand LLC 120 S Central Ave Ste 450	St. Louis	MO	63105	314-726-1060		475
LaserCard Corp 1875 N Shoreline Blvd *TF:* 800-237-7769 ■ *Web:* www.hidglobal.com	Mountain View	CA	94043	650-969-4428	969-3140	658
Lasercycle USA Inc 528 S Taylor Ave *TF:* 866-666-7776 ■ *Web:* www.lasercycleusa.com	Louisville	CO	80027	303-666-7776		589
Laserdome 2050 Auction Rd *TF:* 800-223-8963 ■ *Web:* laserdome.com	Manheim	PA	17545	717-492-0002		31
Laserflex Corp, The 3649 Parkway Ln *Web:* www.laserflex-inc.com	Hilliard	OH	43026	614-850-9600		454
LaserGen Inc 8052 El Rio St *Web:* www.lasergen.com	Houston	TX	77054	713-747-3380		743
Lasergraphics Inc 4 Squire Rd *TF:* 800-220-6262 ■ *Web:* www.laserg.com	Revere	MA	02151	781-289-2022	289-2027	781
LaserMax Corp 3495 Winton Pl *TF:* 800-527-3703 ■ *Web:* www.lasermax.com	Rochester	NY	14623	585-272-5420		544
Laserscope 3070 Orchard Dr *TF:* 800-878-3399 ■ *Web:* fundinguniverse.com	San Jose	CA	95134	408-943-0636		424
Lasership Inc 1912 Woodford Rd *TF:* 800-832-5660 ■ *Web:* www.lasership.com	Vienna	VA	22182	703-761-9030		41
LaserSight Technologies Inc 10244 E Colonial Dr Unit 201	Winter Park	FL	32817	407-678-9900	678-9981	424
LaserVue Eye Ctr 3540 Mendocino Ave Ste 200 *TF:* 888-527-3745 ■ *Web:* www.laservue.com	Santa Rosa	CA	95403	707-522-6200		798
Lashbrook Designs 131 E 13065 S *TF:* 888-252-7388 ■ *Web:* lashbrookdesigns.com	Draper	UT	84020	888-252-7388		411
Lashly & Baer PC 714 Locust St *Web:* www.lashlybaer.com	St. Louis	MO	63101	314-621-2939		428
Lasko Metal Products Inc 820 Lincoln Ave *TF:* 800-233-0268 ■ *Web:* www.laskoproducts.com	West Chester	PA	19380	610-692-7400	696-4648	37
LasscoWizer Inc 485 Hague St *TF:* 800-854-6595 ■ *Web:* www.lasscowizer.com	Rochester	NY	14606	585-436-1934	464-8665	629
Lassen Canyon Nursery Inc 1300 Salmon Creek Rd *Web:* www.lassencanyonnursery.com	Redding	CA	96003	530-223-1075		275
Lassen Community College 478-200 Hwy 139 PO Box 3000 **Fax:* Admissions ■ *TF:* 800-461-9389 ■ *Web:* www.lassencollege.edu	Susanville	CA	96130	530-257-6181	257-8964*	162

Name / Address	City	State	Zip	Phone	Fax	Class
Lassen County 220 S Lassen St Ste 5	Susanville	CA	96130	530-251-8217	257-3480	338
TF: 800-894-7761 ■ *Web:* www.lassencounty.org						
Lassen County Chamber of Commerce 75 N Weatherlow St	Susanville	CA	96130	530-257-4323		139
Web: www.lassencountychamber.org						
Lassen Land Co 320 E S St	Orland	CA	95963	530-865-7676		10-10
Lassen Volcanic National Park 38050 Hwy 36 E PO Box 100	Mineral	CA	96063	530-595-4480	595-3262	564
TF: 800-427-7623 ■ *Web:* www.nps.gov/lavo						
Lassen's Health Food 2150 Thousand Oaks Blvd	Thousand Oaks	CA	91362	805-495-2609		297
Web: www.lassens.com						
Lassiter-Taylor Law Firm, The 6215 Claret Dr	Jacksonville	FL	32210	904-779-5585		428
Web: www.lassiterlawyers.com						
Lassonde Pappas 1 Colons Dr Ste 200	Carneys Point	NJ	08069	856-455-1000	455-8746	296-20
TF: 800-257-7019 ■ *Web:* lassondepappas.com						
LassoSoft LLC PO Box 33	Manchester	WA	98353	954-302-3526	302-3526	178-7
TF: 888-286-7753 ■ *Web:* www.lassosoft.com						
Lassus BROS Handy Dandy 1800 Magnavox Way	Fort Wayne	IN	46804	260-436-1415		204
Web: www.lassus.com						
Lassus Bros Oil Inc 1800 Magnavox Way	Fort Wayne	IN	46804	260-436-1415		324
Web: lassus.com						
Lassus Wherley & Associates Pc 1 Academy St	New Providence	NJ	07974	908-464-0102		463
Web: www.lassuswherley.com						
Lastick Furniture Inc 269 E High St	Pottstown	PA	19464	610-323-4000		321
TF: 800-208-4240 ■ *Web:* www.lastickfurniture.com						
Lasting Impressions Inc 7406 43rd Ave NE	Marysville	WA	98270	360-659-1255		627
TF: 866-859-7625 ■ *Web:* www.lastingimp.com						
Lasting Legacy Ltd 812 Busse Hwy	Park Ridge	IL	60068	847-685-8402		690
Web: raymondjames.com						
LastMinuteTravel.com Inc 220 E Central Pkwy Ste 4000	Altamonte Springs	FL	32701	407-667-8700		773
TF: 800-442-0568 ■ *Web:* www.lastminutetravel.com						
Lastrapes Spangler & Pacheco 333 Rio Rancho Dr NE Ste 401	Rio Rancho	NM	87174	505-892-3607		445
TF: 800-876-6227 ■ *Web:* www.lsplegal.com						
Lasvegastickets.com 5030 Paradise Rd Ste B108	Las Vegas	NV	89119	702-597-1588		376
TF: 800-597-7469 ■ *Web:* lasvegastickets.com						
Latah County 522 S Adams St PO Box 8068	Moscow	ID	83843	208-882-8580	883-7203	338
TF: 800-815-2666 ■ *Web:* www.latah.id.us						
Latah Creek Winery 13030 E Indiana Ave	Spokane	WA	99216	509-926-0164		50-7
TF: 800-528-2427 ■ *Web:* www.latahcreek.com						
Latex Construction Co PO Box 917	Conyers	GA	30012	770-760-0820	760-0852	188-10
Web: www.latexconstruction.com						
Latham & Phillips Ophthalmic Products Inc 2300 SW Blvd	Grove City	OH	43123	614-871-6200		544
Web: lpoproducts.com						
Latham & Watkins LLP 885 Third Ave	New York	NY	10022	212-906-1200	751-4864	428
TF: 800-858-9616 ■ *Web:* www.lw.com						
Latham Hotel, The 135 S 17th St Ste 300	Philadelphia	PA	19103	610-557-1655	568-0505*	379
**Fax Area Code:* 215 ■ *TF:* 877-528-4261						
Latham Seed Co 131 180th St	Alexander	IA	50420	641-692-3258	692-3250	694
TF: 877-465-2842 ■ *Web:* www.lathamseeds.com						
Lathem Time Corp 200 Selig Dr SW	Atlanta	GA	30336	404-691-0400	252-2208*	111
**Fax Area Code:* 800 ■ *TF:* 800-241-4990 ■ *Web:* www.lathem.com						
Lathrop & Clark LLP 740 Regent St Ste 400	Madison	WI	53715	608-257-7766		317
TF: 800-254-7766 ■ *Web:* www.boardmanclark.com						
Lathrop Co 460 W Dussel Dr	Maumee	OH	43537	419-893-7000		186
Web: www.turnerconstruction.com						
Lathrop State Park 70 County Rd 502	Walsenburg	CO	81089	719-738-2376		565
Web: cpw.state.co.us						
Laticrete International Inc 91 Amity Rd	Bethany	CT	06524	203-393-0010	393-1684	3
TF: 800-243-4788 ■ *Web:* www.laticrete.com						
Latigo Partners LP 450 Park Ave Ste1200	New York	NY	10022	212-754-1610		194
Web: www.latigopartners.com						
Latigo Petroleum Inc 15 W Sixth St Ste 900	Tulsa	OK	74119	918-513-4570		538
Web: www.laredopetro.com						
Latigo Ranch PO Box 237	Kremmling	CO	80459	970-724-9008		239
Web: www.latigotrails.com						
Latimer County 109 N Central St Rm 109	Wilburton	OK	74578	918-465-3450	465-4005	338
Web: www.latimer.okcountytreasurers.com						
Latimer, Biaggi, Rachid, & Godreau LLP Firstbank Bldg 1519 Ponce de Leon Ave Ste 1205	San Juan	PR	00902	787-724-0230		428
Web: www.lbrglaw.com						
Latin Business Assn (LBA) 120 S San Pedro St Ste 530	Los Angeles	CA	90012	213-628-8510	628-8519	49-12
TF: 866-924-9757 ■ *Web:* lbausa.com						
Latin Chamber of Commerce 300 N 13th St	Las Vegas	NV	89101	702-385-7367	385-2614	139
Web: www.lvlcc.com						
Latin Chamber of Commerce of the US (CAMACOL) 1417 W Flagler St	Miami	FL	33135	305-642-3870		138
Web: www.camacol.org						
Latin King 2200 Hubbell Ave	Des Moines	IA	50317	515-266-4466		671
Web: www.tursislatinking.com						
Latin Press Inc 2455 SW 27th Ave	Miami	FL	33145	305-285-3133		637-9
Web: www.latinpressinc.com						
Latin School of Chicago 59 W N Blvd	Chicago	IL	60610	312-582-6000		623
Web: www.latinschool.org						
Latina Media Ventures LLC 120 Broadway 34th Fl	New York	NY	10271	212-642-0200	575-3088	457-11
TF: 888-489-7753 ■ *Web:* www.latina.com						
Latina Restaurant & Pizzeria 1370 W Bristol Rd	Flint	MI	48507	810-767-8491		671
Web: latinarestaurant.com						
Latino Book & Family Festival (LBFF) 3445 Catalina Dr	Carlsbad	CA	92010	858-603-8680		281
Latino Cultural Ctr 2600 Live Oak St	Dallas	TX	75204	214-671-0045	670-0633	50-2
Web: www.dallasculture.org						
Latitude 41 50 N Third St	Columbus	OH	43215	614-233-7541		671
Web: www.latitude41restaurant.com						
Latitude Consulting Group Inc 100 E Michigan Ave Ste 200	Saline	MI	48176	888-577-2797		463
TF: 888-577-2797 ■ *Web:* www.latitudecg.com						
Lat-Lon LLC 2300 S Jason St	Denver	CO	80223	303-937-7406		770
Web: www.lat-lon.com						
LaTolteca 2209 Concord Pk	Wilmington	DE	19803	302-778-4646		671
Web: authenticmex.com						
Latorra Paul & Mccann Inc 120 E Washington St University Bldg 10th Fl	Syracuse	NY	13202	315-476-1646		4
Web: www.lpm-adv.com/Home.aspx						
LatPro Inc 3980 N Broadway Ste 103-147	Boulder	CO	80304	954-727-3844		393
Web: www.latpro.com						
Latrobe Area Chamber of Commerce PO Box 463	Latrobe	PA	15650	724-537-2671	537-2690	139
Web: www.latrobelaurelvalley.org						
Latrobe Brewing Co 100 33rd St	Latrobe	PA	15650	724-537-5545		102
Web: www.rollingrock.com						
Latt Maxcy Corp 21299 US Hwy 27	Lake Wales	FL	33859	863-679-6700		652
Web: www.lattmaxcy.com						
Latta Harris Hanon & Penningroth LLP 2730 Naples Ave SW Ste 101	Iowa City	IA	52240	319-358-0520		2
Web: lattaharris.com						
Latta Robert E (Rep R - OH) 2448 Rayburn HOB	Washington	DC	20515	202-225-6405		342-2
Web: latta.house.gov						
Latta's School Supply 1502 Fourth Ave	Huntington	WV	25701	304-523-8400	525-5038	535
TF: 800-624-3501 ■ *Web:* www.lattas.com						
Latter & Blum Inc 430 Notre Dame St	New Orleans	LA	70130	504-525-1311	569-9336	652
Web: www.latterblum.com						
Latter Day Saints Business College 95 North 300 West	Salt Lake City	UT	84101	801-524-8100	524-1900	800
TF: 800-999-5767 ■ *Web:* www.ldsbc.edu						
Lattice Inc 1751 S Naperville Rd Ste 100	Wheaton	IL	60189	630-949-3250		178-12
TF Sales: 800-444-4309 ■ *Web:* www.lattice.com						
Lattice Semiconductor Corp 5555 NE Moore Ct	Hillsboro	OR	97124	503-268-8000	268-8347	696
NASDAQ: LSCC ■ *TF:* 800-528-8423 ■ *Web:* www.latticesemi.com						
Lattice3d 582 Market St Ste 1215	San Francisco	CA	94104	415-274-1670		177
TF: 800-600-2248 ■ *Web:* www.lattice3d.com						
Lattimore Black Morgan & Cain PC 5250 Virginia Way	Brentwood	TN	37027	615-377-4600		2
Web: www.lbmc.com						
Latva Machine Inc 744 John Stark Hwy	Newport	NH	03773	603-863-5155		454
Web: www.latva.com						
Latvia 333 E 50th St	New York	NY	10022	212-838-8877	838-8920	784
Web: mfa.gov.lv						
Latvia Embassy 2306 Massachusetts Ave NW	Washington	DC	20008	202-328-2840	328-2860	257
Web: www.mfa.gov.lv						
Laucks Testing Laboratories Inc 940 S Harney St	Seattle	WA	98108	206-767-5060	767-5063	743
Web: pacelabs.com						
Lauderdale County PO Box 1059	Florence	AL	35631	256-760-5750		338
TF: 800-535-9410 ■ *Web:* www.lauderdalecountyonline.com						
Lauderdale County 410 Constitution Ave 11th Fl	Meridian	MS	39301	601-482-9746		338
Web: www.lauderdalecounty.org						
Lauderdale County 123 S Jefferson St	Ripley	TN	38063	731-635-9541		338
Web: www.lauderdalecountytn.org						
Laughing Elephant 3645 Interlake Ave N	Seattle	WA	98103	800-354-0400		130
TF: 800-354-0400 ■ *Web:* www.laughingelephant.com						
Laughing Loon 344 GaRdiner Rd	Jefferson	ME	04348	207-549-3531		710
TF: 800-497-0010 ■ *Web:* www.laughingloon.com						
Laughing Planet Cafe 322 E Kirkwood Ave	Bloomington	IN	47408	812-323-2233		671
Web: thelaughingplanetcafe.com						
Laughing Seed Cafe 40 Wall St	Asheville	NC	28801	828-252-3445		671
Web: laughingseed.com						
Laughlin Air Force Base 561 Liberty Dr Ste 3	Laughlin AFB	TX	78843	830-298-5988		497-1
TF: 866-966-1020 ■ *Web:* www.laughlin.af.mil						
Laughlin Memorial Hospital 1420 Tusculum Blvd	Greeneville	TN	37745	423-787-5000	787-5083	374-3
TF: 800-852-7157 ■ *Web:* www.laughlinmemorial.org						
Laughlin River Lodge. 2700 S Casino Dr	Laughlin	NV	89029	702-298-2242		133
Laughlin/Constable Inc 207 E Michigan St	Milwaukee	WI	53202	414-272-2400	272-3056	4
Web: www.laughlin.com						
LaughStub LLC 2038 Armacost Ave	Los Angeles	CA	90025	800-927-0939		387
TF: 800-927-0939 ■ *Web:* www.laughstub.com						
Laumeier Sculpture Park & Museum 12580 Rott Rd	Saint Louis	MO	63127	314-615-5278		520
Web: laumeiersculpturepark.org						
Launch 2 W 45th St Fl 9	New York	NY	10036	212-845-5800		195
Web: www.321launch.com						
Launch Agency LP 4100 Midway Rd Ste 2110	Carrollton	TX	75007	972-818-4100		4
TF: 866-427-5013 ■ *Web:* launchagency.com						
Launch Dynamic Media 1103 Rocky Dr Ste 202	Reading	PA	19609	610-898-1330		180
Web: launchdm.com						
Launch Incentives Inc 224 Greenfield Ave Ste B	San Anselmo	CA	94960	415-457-1701		232
TF: 800-555-5555 ■ *Web:* www.launchincentives.com						

	Phone	Fax	Class
Launch Pad 18130 Jorene Rd, Odessa FL 33556 *TF:* 888-920-3450 ■ *Web:* www.launchpadonline.com	888-920-3450		179
Launchpad 119 W 24th St, New York NY 10010 *Web:* www.lpnyc.com	212-303-7650		4
Laura Davidson Public Relations Inc 72 Madison Ave Fl 11 8th Fl, New York NY 10016 *Web:* www.ldpr.com	212-696-0660		636
Laura Ingalls Wilder Museum & Home 3068 Hwy A, Mansfield MO 65704 *TF:* 877-924-7126 ■ *Web:* www.lauraingallswilderhome.com	877-924-7126		520
Laura S. Walker State Park 5653 Laura Walker Rd, Waycross GA 31503 *Web:* www.gastateparks.org	912-287-4900		565
Lauralee G Westine pa 800 Tarpon Woods Blvd Ste E1, Palm Harbor FL 34685 *Web:* lauraleewestine.com	727-773-2221		445
Lauran Technology Corp 1 Hamilton Ave, Cranford NJ 07016	908-276-6262		180
Laurdan Associates Inc 10220 River Rd Ste 201, Potomac MD 20854 *Web:* www.laurdan.com	301-299-4117		195
Laureate Education Inc 650 S Exeter St, Baltimore MD 21202 *TF:* 866-452-8732 ■ *Web:* www.laureate.net	410-843-6100		242
Laurel County 101 S Main St Rm 203, London KY 40741 *Web:* laurelcountyclerk.com	606-864-5158		338
Laurel Ctr 125 Holly Rd, Hamburg PA 19526 *Web:* genesishcc.com	610-562-2284		450
Laurel Grocery Co Inc 129 Barbourville Rd, London KY 40744 *Fax Area Code: 606 ■ *TF:* 800-467-6601 ■ *Web:* laurelgrocery.com	800-467-6601	878-9361*	297-8
Laurel Highland Total Communications Inc 4157 Main St, Stahlstown PA 15687 *TF:* 800-660-2215 ■ *Web:* www.lhtc.co	724-593-2411		224
Laurel Highlands Chamber of Commerce 537 W Main St, Mount Pleasant PA 15666 *Web:* www.westmorelandchamber.com	724-547-7521		139
Laurel Highlands School District (LHSD) 304 Bailey Ave, Uniontown PA 15401	724-437-2821		685
Laurel Highlands Visitors Bureau 120 E Main St, Ligonier PA 15658 *TF:* 800-333-5661 ■ *Web:* www.laurelhighlands.org	724-238-5661	238-3673	206
Laurel Hill State Park 1454 Laurel Hill Pk Rd, Somerset PA 15501 *Web:* www.dcnr.state.pa.us	814-445-7725		565
Laurel Inn 444 Presidio Ave, San Francisco CA 94115 *TF:* 800-552-8735 ■ *Web:* jdvhotels.com	415-346-7431		379
Laurel Lake Retirement Community 200 Laurel Lake Dr, Hudson OH 44236 *Fax Area Code: 330 ■ *TF:* 866-650-2100 ■ *Web:* laurellake.org	866-650-2100	655-1738*	672
Laurel Lodge Enterprises Inc 1909 Harper Rd, Beckley WV 25801 *Web:* lleinc.com	304-255-0228		379
Laurel Mountain State Park c/o Linn Run, Rector PA 15677 *Web:* www.dcnr.state.pa.us	724-238-6623		565
Laurel Outlook, The 415 E Main PO Box 278, Laurel MT 59044 *Web:* www.laureloutlook.com	406-628-4412		532-3
Laurel Park Rt 198 & Racetrack Rd PO Box 130, Laurel MD 20724 *Fax Area Code: 410 ■ *TF:* 800-638-1859 ■ *Web:* www.laurelpark.com	301-725-0400	792-7775*	642
Laurel Regional Hospital (LRH) 7300 Van Dusen Rd, Laurel MD 20707 *Web:* dimensionshealth.org	301-725-4300	497-7953	374-3
Laurel Rehabilitation Services 216 Haddon Ave Ste 702, Westmont NJ 08108 *Web:* laurelrehab.com	856-869-7360		363
Laurel Ridge State Park 1117 Jim Mtn Rd, Rockwood PA 15557 *Web:* www.dcnr.state.pa.us	724-455-3744		565
Laurel Summit State Park PO Box 50, Rector PA 15677 *Web:* www.dcnr.state.pa.us	724-238-6623		565
Laurel Theatre 1538 Laurel Ave, Knoxville TN 37916 *Web:* www.jubileearts.org	865-522-5851		572
Laurel-Jones County Library 530 Commerce St, Laurel MS 39440 *Web:* www.laurel.lib.ms.us	601-428-4313		434-3
Laurels of University Park, The 2420 Pemberton Rd, Richmond VA 23233 *Web:* www.laurelsofuniversitypark.com	804-747-9200	747-1574	450
Laurelville Mennonite Church Ctr 941 Laurelville Ln, Mount Pleasant PA 15666 *TF:* 800-839-1021 ■ *Web:* www.laurelville.org	724-423-2056	423-2096	673
Lauren Engineers & Constructors Inc 901 S First St, Abilene TX 79602 *TF:* 800-948-0142 ■ *Web:* www.laurenec.com	325-670-9660	670-9663	261
Lauren Mfg 2228 Reiser Ave SE, New Philadelphia OH 44663 *TF:* 800-683-0676 ■ *Web:* www.lauren.com	330-339-3373	339-1515	677
Lauren Rogers Museum of Art 565 N Fifth Ave, Laurel MS 39440 *Web:* www.lrma.org	601-649-6374	649-6379	520
Lauren Spencer Inc 40 Clairedan Dr, Powell OH 43065 *Web:* www.lauren-spencer.com	614-888-7773		410
Laurence Miller Gallery 20 W 57th St, New York NY 10019 *Web:* www.laurencemillergallery.com	212-397-3930	397-3932	42
Laurens County 117 E Jackson St, Dublin GA 31040 *TF:* 800-656-2298 ■ *Web:* www.laurenscoga.org	478-272-4755	272-3895	338
Laurens County 100 Hillcrest Sq # B, Laurens SC 29360 *Web:* www.laurenscountysc.org	864-984-3538	984-3726	338
Laurens County Board of Education 467 Firetower Rd, Dublin GA 31021 *Web:* www.lcboe.net	478-272-4767	277-2619	685
Laurens County Chamber of Commerce 291 Professional Pk Rd, Clinton SC 29325 *Web:* www.laurenscounty.org	864-833-2716	939-0016	139
Laurens County Library 1017 W Main St, Laurens SC 29360 *Web:* www.lcpl.org	864-681-7323	681-0598	434-3
Laurens Electric Co-op Inc 2254 S Carolina 14, Laurens SC 29360 *TF:* 800-942-3141 ■ *Web:* laurenselectric.com	800-942-3141		245
Laurent Clerc National Deaf Education Ctr 800 Florida Ave NE, Washington DC 20002 *Web:* www.gallaudet.edu	202-651-5050	651-5708	48-17
Laurentian Bank of Canada 1981 McGill College Ave, Montreal QC H3A3K3 *TSE: LB* ■ *TF:* 800-252-1846 ■ *Web:* www.laurentianbank.ca	514-284-4500	284-3988	70
Laurentian Bank Securities Inc 1981 McGill College Ave Ste 100, Montreal QC H3A3K3 *TF:* 888-350-8577 ■ *Web:* www.vmbl.ca	514-350-2800		401
Laurentian University 935 Ramsey Lake Rd, Sudbury ON P3E2C6 *TF:* 800-461-4030 ■ *Web:* www.laurentian.ca	705-675-1151		785
Lauretano Sign Group 1 Tremco Dr, Terryville CT 06786 *Web:* www.lauretano.com	860-582-0233		701
Laurie Raphael 117 Dalhousie St, Quebec QC G1K9C8 *TF:* 877-876-4555 ■ *Web:* www.laurieraphael.com	418-692-4555	692-4175	671
Laurier House National Historic Site 335 Laurier Ave E, Ottawa ON K1N6R4 *Web:* www.pc.gc.ca/eng/lhn-nhs/on/laurier/index.aspx	613-992-8142	947-4851	563
Laurin Publishing Co Inc 100 West St, Pittsfield MA 01202 *TF:* 877-422-7300 ■ *Web:* www.photonics.com	413-499-0514	442-3180	637-9
Laurinburg/Scotland County Area Chamber of Commerce 606 Atkinson St, Laurinburg NC 28352 *Web:* www.laurinburgchamber.com	910-276-7420	277-8785	139
Lauritzen Gardens Omaha's Botanical Ctr 100 Bancroft St, Omaha NE 68108 *Web:* www.lauritzengardens.org	402-346-4002	346-8948	97
LAURUS Systems Inc 3460 Ellicott Ctr Dr Ste 101, Ellicott City MD 21043 *TF:* 800-274-4212 ■ *Web:* www.laurussystems.com	410-465-5558		196
Laury's 350 MacCorkle Ave SE, Charleston WV 25314 *Web:* www.laurysrestaurant.com	304-343-0055	343-0078	671
LAUSD (Los Angeles Unified School District) 333 S Beaudry Ave, Los Angeles CA 90017 *TF:* 877-772-6273 ■ *Web:* home.lausd.net	213-241-1000		685
Lauterbach Group Inc W222 N5710 Miller Way, Sussex WI 53089 *TF Sales:* 800-841-7301 ■ *Web:* www.lauterbachgroup.com	262-820-8130	820-1806	554
Lautze & Lautze Cpas & Financial Consultant 111 W SAINT JOHN St Ste 1010, San Francisco CA 95113 *Web:* www.lautze.com	669-232-9500		344
Laux & Co 672 W Liberty St, Medina OH 44256 *Web:* www.lauxco.com	330-721-0100		690
Laux Sporting Goods Inc 25 Pineview Dr, Amherst NY 14228 *TF:* 800-526-8788 ■ *Web:* www.lauxsportinggoods.com	716-691-3367	691-4393	711
Lava Beds National Monument 1 Indian Well Headquarters, Tulelake CA 96134 *TF:* 866-705-5711 ■ *Web:* www.nps.gov/labe	530-260-0537		564
Lava Hot Springs State Foundation 430 E Main St PO Box 669, Lava Hot Springs ID 83246 *TF:* 800-423-8597 ■ *Web:* www.lavahotsprings.com	208-776-5221		50-5
Lavaca County 412 N Texana, Hallettsville TX 77964 *Web:* www.co.lavaca.tx.us	361-798-3612	798-1610	338
Laval Chamber of Commerce 1555 boul Chomedey Ste 200, Laval QC H7V3Z1 *Web:* www.ccilaval.qc.ca	450-682-5255	682-5735	137
Laval University 2325 Rue University, Quebec QC G1V0A6 *TF:* 877-785-2825 ■ *Web:* www2.ulaval.ca	418-656-2131	656-5216	785
Lavanture Products Co 22825 Gallatin Way, Elkhart IN 46514 *TF:* 800-348-7625 ■ *Web:* www.lavanture.com	574-264-0658	264-6601	600
Lavelle Industries Inc 665 McHenry St, Burlington WI 53105 *TF:* 800-528-3553 ■ *Web:* www.lavelle.com	262-763-2434	763-5607	677
LaVelle Vineyards 89697 Sheffler Rd, Elmira OR 97437 *Web:* www.lavellevineyards.com	541-935-9406		50-7
Lavelle's Bistro 575 First Ave, Fairbanks AK 99701 *Web:* www.lavellesbistro.com	907-450-0555		671
Lavendou 19009 Preston Rd Ste 200, Dallas TX 75252 *TF:* 800-546-6508 ■ *Web:* www.lavendou.com	972-248-1911	248-1660	671
LaVERDAD Hispanic Marketing Solutions 7817 Cooper Rd, Cincinnati OH 45242 *TF:* 800-994-3318 ■ *Web:* www.laverdadmarketing.com	513-891-1430		195
Lavery Chevrolet-Buick Inc 1096 W State St, Alliance OH 44601 *Web:* laveryauto.com	330-823-1100		57
LaVezzi Precision Inc 999 Regency Dr, Glendale Heights IL 60139 *TF:* 800-323-1772 ■ *Web:* www.lavezzi.com	630-582-1230	582-1238	454
Lavidge Co, The 2777 E Camelback Rd Ste 300, Phoenix AZ 85016 *Web:* www.lavidge.com	480-998-2600		7
Lavigne Oil Company LLC 11203 Proverbs Ave, Baton Rouge LA 70816 *TF:* 800-349-0170 ■ *Web:* www.lavigneoil.com	800-349-0170		538
Lavin O'Neil Ricci Cedrone & Disipio 190 N Independence Mall W, Philadelphia PA 19106 *Web:* www.lavin-law.com	215-627-0303	627-2551	428
Lavine Lofgren Morris & Engelberg CPAs 4180 La Jolla Village Dr Ste 300, La Jolla CA 92037 *Web:* www.llme.com	858-455-0898		2
Lavipharm Laboratories Inc 69 Princeton - Hightstown Rd, East Windsor NJ 08520 *Web:* www.lavipharm.com	609-469-5949		743
Lavista Assoc Inc 3105 Northwoods Pl, Norcross GA 30071 *Web:* www.lavista.com	770-448-6400		194
Law Bulletin Publishing Co 415 N State St, Chicago IL 60654 *Web:* www.lawbulletin.com	312-644-7800	644-4255	637-8
Law Company Inc, The 345 Riverview St, Wichita KS 67203 *Web:* www.law-co.com	316-268-0200	268-0210	186
Law Elder Law 2275 Church Rd, Aurora IL 60502 *TF:* 800-310-3100 ■ *Web:* lawelderlaw.com	630-585-5200		687

	Phone	Fax	Class
Law Enforcement Assoc Corp (LEA) 120 Penmarc Dr Ste 125 .... Raleigh NC 27616 *OTC:* LAWEQ ■ *TF:* 800-354-9669 ■ *Web:* www.leacorp.com	919-872-6210	872-6431	52
Law Enforcement Technology Magazine 1233 Janesville Ave .... Fort Atkinson WI 53538 *TF:* 800-547-7377 ■ *Web:* www.officer.com	800-547-7377		457-5
Law Engine 7660-H Fay Ave Ste 342 .... La Jolla CA 92037 *TF:* 800-894-2889 ■ *Web:* www.thelawengine.com	858-456-1234	454-3375	397
Law Office of John M Boyko 21250 Hawthorne Ste 730 .... Torrance CA 90503 *Web:* www.lawofficejohnschwartz.com	424-999-5579		41
Law Officer's Bulletin 610 Opperman Dr .... Eagan MN 55123 *TF:* 800-344-5008 ■ *Web:* legalsolutions.thomsonreuters.com	651-687-7000		531-2
Law Offices of Howard N Sobel PA, The 507 Kresson Rd PO Box 1525 .... Voorhees NJ 08043 *Web:* sobellaw.com	856-424-6400		428
Law Society of Manitoba 219 Kennedy St .... Winnipeg MB R3C1S8 *Web:* www.lawsociety.mb.ca	204-942-5571		428
Law Weathers & Richardson Pc 333 Bridge St NW .... Grand Rapids MI 49504 *Web:* www.varnumlaw.com/law-weathers	616-336-6000		428
Lawes Coal Company Inc Sycamore Ave PO Box 258 .... Shrewsbury NJ 07702 *Web:* www.lawescompany.com	732-741-6300		316
Lawgical Inc 11693 San Vicente Blvd Ste 910 .... Los Angeles CA 90049 *TF:* 800-811-4458 ■ *Web:* corp.lawgical.com	800-811-4458		195
Lawler Direct Mail 10300 Drummond Rd Ste 200 .... Philadelphia PA 19154 *TF:* 800-522-9085 ■ *Web:* www.lawlerdirect.com	215-824-3290		5
Lawler Foods Ltd Inc PO Box 2558 .... Humble TX 77347 *TF:* 800-541-8285 ■ *Web:* www.lawlers.com	281-446-0059	446-3806	296-1
Lawler Foundry Corp 4908 Powell Ave S .... Birmingham AL 35222 *Web:* www.lawlerfoundry.com	205-595-0596		492
Lawler Manufacturing Corp 7 Kilmer Ct .... Edison NJ 08817 *TF:* 800-259-2204 ■ *Web:* www.lawlercorp.com	732-777-2040	777-4828	14
Lawler-Wood LLC 900 S Gay St .... Knoxville TN 37902 *Web:* www.lawlerwood.com	865-637-7777		652
Lawley Service Insurance 361 Delaware Ave .... Buffalo NY 14202 *TF Cust Svc:* 800-860-5741 ■ *Web:* www.lawleyinsurance.com	716-849-8618	849-8291	390
Lawman Heating & Cooling Inc PO Box 599 .... Sackets Harbor NY 13685 *Web:* www.lawmanhc.com	315-646-2919		189-10
Lawn & Golf Supply Co Inc 647 Nutt Rd PO Box 447 .... Phoenixville PA 19460 *TF:* 800-793-1872 ■ *Web:* www.lawn-golf.com	610-933-5801	933-8890	429
Lawn Dawg Inc 39 Simon St, Unit 14 .... Nashua NH 03060 *TF:* 888-925-3294 ■ *Web:* www.lawndawg.com	888-993-3294		776
Lawn Doctor Inc 142 SR 34 .... Holmdel NJ 07733 *TF:* 800-845-0580 ■ *Web:* www.lawndoctor.com	800-845-0580		577
Lawn Equipment Parts Co 1475 River Rd PO Box 466 .... Marietta PA 17547 *TF:* 800-365-3726 ■ *Web:* lepco.com	717-426-5200	426-5201	429
Lawn-Boy Inc 8111 S Lyndale Ave .... Bloomington MN 55420 *Web:* www.lawnboy.com	952-888-8801		429
Lawndale Art & Performance Ctr 4912 Main St .... Houston TX 77002 *Web:* lawndaleartcenter.org	713-528-5858	528-4140	520
Lawndale Logistics 1239 12th Ave .... Grafton WI 53024 *TF:* 800-843-9992 ■ *Web:* www.lawndalelogistics.com	262-375-3684		314
Lawnwood Regional Medical Ctr (LRMC) 1700 S 23rd St .... Fort Pierce FL 34950 *Web:* www.lawnwoodmed.com	772-461-4000		374-3
Lawrence & Memorial Hospital 365 Montauk Ave .... New London CT 06320 *TF:* 800-579-3341 ■ *Web:* www.lmhospital.org	860-442-0711		374-3
Lawrence & Schiller Inc 3932 S Willow Ave .... Sioux Falls SD 57105 *Web:* www.l-s.com	605-338-8000		4
Lawrence Academy Powderhouse Rd PO Box 992 .... Groton MA 01450 *Web:* www.lacademy.edu	978-448-6535	448-9208	622
Lawrence Behr Assoc Inc 3400 Tupper Dr .... Greenville NC 27834 *TF:* 800-522-4464 ■ *Web:* www.lbagroup.com/associates	252-757-0279	752-9155	196
Lawrence Berkeley National Laboratory (LBNL) 1 Cyclotron Rd .... Berkeley CA 94720 *Web:* www.lbl.gov	510-486-4000	486-7000	668
Advanced Light Source 1 Cyclotron Rd Lawrence Berkeley National Laboratory .... Berkeley CA 94720 *Web:* www-als.lbl.gov	510-486-7745	486-4773	668
Lawrence Brenda (Rep D - MI) 1213 Longworth HOB .... Washington DC 20515 *Web:* lawrence.house.gov	202-225-5802	226-2356	342-2
Lawrence Companies (LTS) 872 Lee Hwy .... Roanoke VA 24019 **Fax Area Code:* 540 ■ *TF:* 800-336-9626 ■ *Web:* www.lawrencecompanies.com	800-336-9626	966-4555*	780
Lawrence Construction Company Inc 9002 N Moore Rd .... Littleton CO 80125 *Web:* lawrence-construction.com	303-791-5642	791-5647	188-4
Lawrence County 916 15th St Ste 31 .... Bedford IN 47421 *Web:* www.bedfordonline.com	812-275-7543	278-8845	338
Lawrence County 90 Sherman St .... Deadwood SD 57732 **Fax:* Acctg ■ *Web:* www.lawrence.sd.us	605-578-1941	578-1065*	338
Lawrence County 111 S Fourth St Ste 11 .... Ironton OH 45638 *Web:* www.lawrencecountyohio.org	740-533-4355		338
Lawrence County 240 W Gaines St .... Lawrenceburg TN 38464 *Web:* lawcotn.org	931-762-7700		338
Lawrence County 12521 Hwy 157 Ste L .... Moulton AL 35650 *Web:* www.lawrencealabama.com	256-974-1658	974-2400	338
Lawrence County 1 Courthouse Sq PO Box 188 .... Mount Vernon MO 65712 *Web:* lawrencecountymoassessor.com	417-466-2831	466-3931	338
Lawrence County County Courthouse 430 Court St .... New Castle PA 16101 *TF:* 855-564-6116 ■ *Web:* www.co.lawrence.pa.us	724-658-2541	652-9646	338

	Phone	Fax	Class
Lawrence County 315 W Main .... Walnut Ridge AR 72476 *TF:* 800-621-4000 ■ *Web:* www.lawrencecountysheriffsoffice.com	870-886-2525		338
Lawrence County Chamber of Commerce 138 W Washington St .... New Castle PA 16101 *TF:* 800-377-3539 ■ *Web:* www.lawrencecountychamber.org	724-654-5593	654-3330	139
Lawrence County Public Library 519 E Gaines St .... Lawrenceburg TN 38464 *TF:* 800-200-0017 ■ *Web:* lawrencecountytn.gov	931-762-4627	766-1597	434-3
Lawrence County Public Library 401 College St .... Moulton AL 35650	256-974-0883		434-3
Lawrence County Tennessee Chamber of Commerce 25B Public Sqr PO Box 86 .... Lawrenceburg TN 38464 *TF:* 877-388-4911 ■ *Web:* www.selectlawrence.com	931-762-4911	762-3153	139
Lawrence County Tourist Promotion Agency 229 S Jefferson St .... New Castle PA 16101 *TF:* 888-284-7599 ■ *Web:* www.visitlawrencecounty.com	724-654-8408	654-2044	206
Lawrence Equipment Inc 2034 Peck Rd .... El Monte CA 91733 *TF:* 800-423-4500 ■ *Web:* www.lawrenceequipment.com	626-442-2894	350-5181	298
Lawrence Foods Inc 2200 Lunt Ave .... Elk Grove Village IL 60007 *TF:* 800-323-7848 ■ *Web:* www.lawrencefoods.com	847-437-2400	437-2567	296-20
Lawrence General Hospital 1 General St .... Lawrence MA 01842 *Web:* www.lawrencegeneral.org	978-683-4000		374-3
Lawrence Green Fire Protection 18323 Weaver St .... Detroit MI 48228	313-835-5800		610
Lawrence Hall Chevrolet Inc 1385 S Danville Dr .... Abilene TX 79605 *TF:* 877-215-4703 ■ *Web:* www.lawrencehall.com	325-695-8800		57
Lawrence Heritage State Park 1 Jackson St .... Lawrence MA 01840 *Web:* www.mass.gov	978-794-1655		565
Lawrence Hospital 55 Palmer Ave .... Bronxville NY 10708 *Web:* nyplawrence.org	914-787-1000		374-3
Lawrence Journal-World 645 New Hampshire PO Box 888 .... Lawrence KS 66044 *TF:* 800-578-8748 ■ *Web:* www2.ljworld.com	785-843-1000	843-4512	637-8
Lawrence L Lee Scouting Museum 571 Holt Ave .... Manchester NH 03109 *Web:* www.scoutingmuseum.org	603-669-8919		520
Lawrence Livermore National Laboratory (LLNL) 7000 E Ave PO Box 808 .... Livermore CA 94550 *TF:* 800-356-4872 ■ *Web:* www.llnl.gov	925-422-1100	422-1370	668
Lawrence Memorial Hospital (LMH) 325 Maine St .... Lawrence KS 66044 *TF:* 800-749-4144 ■ *Web:* www.lmh.org	785-505-5000		374-3
Lawrence Memorial Hospital of Medford 170 Governors Ave .... Medford MA 02155 *TF:* 800-540-9191 ■ *Web:* www.hallmarkhealth.org	781-306-6000		374-3
Lawrence Paper Co 2801 Lakeview Rd .... Lawrence KS 66049 *TF:* 800-535-4553 ■ *Web:* www.lpco.net	785-843-8111		100
Lawrence Printing Co 400 Stribling Ave PO Box 886 .... Greenwood MS 38935 *Web:* www.laprico.com	662-453-6301		627
Lawrence Public Library 707 Vermont St .... Lawrence KS 66044 *Web:* www.lawrence.lib.ks.us	785-843-3833	843-3368	434-3
Lawrence Public Schools 110 McDonald Dr .... Lawrence KS 66044 *TF:* 800-772-1213 ■ *Web:* www.usd497.org	785-832-5000	832-5016	685
Lawrence Ragan Communications Inc 316 N Michigan Ave Ste 400 .... Chicago IL 60601 *TF:* 800-878-5331 ■ *Web:* www.ragan.com	312-960-4100	960-4106	531-3
Lawrence Ragan Communications Inc 111 E Wacker Dr Ste 500 .... Chicago IL 60601 **Fax Area Code:* 312 ■ *TF:* 800-878-5331 ■ *Web:* www.ragan.com	800-493-4867	960-4106*	637-9
Lawrence Ripak Company Inc 165 Field St .... West Babylon NY 11704 *Web:* www.ripak.com	631-694-1818		794
Lawrence Screw Products Inc 7230 W Wilson Ave .... Harwood Heights IL 60706 *Web:* www.lawrencescrew.com	708-867-5150	867-7052	278
Lawrence Service Co 1405 Xenium Ln N Ste 250 .... Plymouth MN 55441 *TF:* 800-328-3967 ■ *Web:* www.lmsvc.com	763-383-5700		463
Lawrence Technological University 21000 W 10-Mile Rd .... Southfield MI 48075 **Fax:* Admissions ■ *TF:* 800-225-5588 ■ *Web:* www.ltu.edu	248-204-3160	204-3188*	166
Lawrence Tractor Company Inc 2530 E Main St .... Visalia CA 93292 *Web:* www.lawrencetractor.com	559-734-7406	734-8325	274
Lawrence University 115 S Drew St .... Appleton WI 54911 *TF:* 800-432-5427 ■ *Web:* www.lawrence.edu	920-832-7000	832-6782	166
Lawrence University Mudd Library 711 E Boldt Way .... Appleton WI 54911 *TF:* 800-432-5427 ■ *Web:* www.lawrence.edu/library	920-832-6750	832-6967	434-6
Lawrenceburg Medical Supply Inc 753 W Broadway .... Lawrenceburg KY 40342	502-839-4557		238
Lawrenceville Correctional Ctr 1607 Planters Rd .... Lawrenceville VA 23868 *Web:* vadoc.virginia.gov	434-848-9349		213
Lawrenceville School 2500 Main St PO Box 6008 .... Lawrenceville NJ 08648 *TF:* 800-735-2030 ■ *Web:* www.lawrenceville.org	609-896-0400	895-2217	622
Lawrimore Communications Inc 1320 Fillmore Ave Unit 312 .... Charlotte NC 28203 *TF:* 800-438-7325 ■ *Web:* www.lciweb.com	704-332-4344		195
Lawry's Restaurants Inc 234 E Colorado Blvd Ste 500 .... Pasadena CA 91101 *TF:* 888-552-9797 ■ *Web:* www.lawrysonline.com	626-440-5234		670
Lawry's the Prime Rib 100 E Ontario St .... Chicago IL 60611 *Web:* www.lawrysonline.com	312-787-5000		671
Lawry's the Prime Rib 100 N La Cienega Blvd .... Beverly Hills CA 90211 *TF:* 877-529-7984 ■ *Web:* www.lawrysonline.com	310-652-2827	657-5463	671
Lawson & Weitzen LLP 88 Black Falcon Ave .... Boston MA 02210 *Web:* www.lawson-weitzen.com	617-439-4990		428

Phone | Fax | Class

Lawson Al (Rep D - FL)
1337 Longworth HOB Washington DC 20515 202-225-0123 225-2256 342-2
Web: lawson.house.gov

Lawson Health Research Institute Inc
268 Grosvenor St London ON N6A4V2 519-646-6005 415
Web: www.lawsonresearch.ca

Lawson Kroeker Investment Management Inc
450 Regency Pkwy Ste 410 Omaha NE 68114 402-392-2606 401
Web: www.lawsonkroeker.com

Lawson Lundell LLP
925 W Georgia St Cathedral Pl Ste 1600 Vancouver BC V6C3L2 604-685-3456 428
TF: 800-668-8661 ■ *Web:* www.lawsonlundell.com

Lawson Mechanical Contractors
6090 S Watt Ave Sacramento CA 95829 916-381-5000 381-5073 189-10
TF: 800-886-8442 ■ *Web:* www.lawsonmechanical.com

Lawson Products Inc
1666 E Touhy Ave Des Plaines IL 60018 847-827-9666 827-1525* 385
**Fax:* Sales ■ *TF:* 800-323-5922 ■ *Web:* www.lawsonproducts.com

Lawson State Community College
Bessemer 1100 Ninth Ave SW Bessemer AL 35022 205-925-2515 929-3598 800
TF: 800-373-4879 ■ *Web:* www.lawsonstate.edu

Lawson-Fisher Associates PC
525 W Washington Ave Ste 200 South Bend IN 46601 574-234-3167 261
Web: lawson-fisher.com

Lawson-Hemphill Inc
1658 G A R Hwy Ste 6 Swansea MA 02777 508-679-5364 679-5396 744
Web: www.lawsonhemphill.com

Lawton & Cates SC 10 E Doty St Ste 400 Madison WI 53703 608-282-6200 428
TF: 800-900-4539 ■ *Web:* www.lawtoncates.com

Lawton Constitution, The
102 SW Third St Lawton OK 73501 580-353-0620 532-2
Web: www.swoknews.com

Lawton Correctional Facility
8607 SE Flower Mound Rd Lawton OK 73501 580-351-2778 213

Lawton Group, The
4747 Viewridge Ave Ste 210 San Diego CA 92123 858-569-6260 260
Web: www.tlcstaffing.com

Lawton Industries Inc 4353 Pacific St Rocklin CA 95677 916-624-7895 624-7898 386
TF: 800-692-2600 ■ *Web:* www.lawtonindustries.com

Lawton Public Library 110 SW Fourth St Lawton OK 73501 580-581-3450 248-0243 434-3
TF: 855-895-8064 ■ *Web:* www.cityof.lawton.ok.us

Lawton's Drug Stores Ltd
236 Brownlow Ave Ste 270 Dartmouth NS B3B1V5 902-468-1000 231
TF: 866-990-1599 ■ *Web:* www.lawtons.ca

Lawyer Referral Service
123 Remsen St Brooklyn NY 11201 718-624-0843 428
TF: 800-342-8011 ■ *Web:* www.brooklynbar.org

Lawyers Aid Service Inc
408 W 17th St Ofc 101 Austin TX 78701 512-474-2002 445
Web: lawyersaidservice.com

Lawyers Diary & Manual
890 Mtn Ave Ste 300 New Providence NJ 07974 973-642-1440 642-4280* 637-2
**Fax:* Cust Svc ■ *TF:* 800-444-4041 ■ *Web:* www.lawdiary.com

Lawyers for Civil Justice (LCJ)
1140 Connecticut Ave NW Ste 503 Washington DC 20036 202-429-0045 429-6982 49-10
Web: www.lfcj.com

Lawyers Group Advertising Inc
631 S Tenth St Las Vegas NV 89101 702-382-5613 445
Web: lawyersgroup.com

Lawyers Weekly Inc 10 Milk St Ste 1000 Boston MA 02108 617-451-7300 532-3
TF: 800-444-5297 ■ *Web:* www.masslawyersweekly.com

Lawyers' Committee for Civil Rights Under Law
1401 New York Ave NW Ste 400 Washington DC 20005 202-662-8600 783-0857 49-10
TF: 888-299-5227 ■ *Web:* www.lawyerscommittee.org

Lawyers' Travel Service 71 Fifth Ave New York NY 10003 800-431-1112 771
TF General: 800-431-1112 ■ *Web:* www.lawyerstravel.com

Lawyers.com
Martindale-Hubbell 121 Chanlon Rd New Providence NJ 07974 908-464-6800 171
TF: 800-526-4902 ■ *Web:* www.lawyers.com

LAX Coastal Area Chamber of Commerce
9100 S Sepulveda Blvd Ste 210 Los Angeles CA 90045 310-645-5151 645-0130 139
Web: laxcoastal.com

Layer 3 Communications LLC
1450 Oakbrook Dr Ste 900 Norcross GA 30093 770-225-5300 225-5298 252
TF: 877-221-3924 ■ *Web:* www.layer3com.com

Layer 3 Technologies Inc
1645 Lyell Ave Ste 200 Rochester NY 14606 585-254-1966 196
Web: layer3direct.com

LayerZero Power Systems Inc
1500 Danner Dr Aurora OH 44202 440-399-9000 729
Web: www.layerzero.com

Laylalina Restaurant
5216 Wilson Blvd Arlington VA 22205 703-525-1170 671
Web: layalinarestaurant.com

Layne 4520 N State Rd 37 Orleans IN 47452 812-865-3232 865-3075 188-10
TF All: 855-529-6301 ■ *Web:* www.layne.com

Layser's Flowers Inc
501 W Washington Ave Myerstown PA 17067 717-866-5746 866-6099 369
Web: www.laysersflowers.com

Layton Manufacturing Corp
825 Remsen Ave Brooklyn NY 11236 718-498-6000 14
TF: 800-545-8002 ■ *Web:* www.laytonmfg.com

LAZ Parking Ltd 15 Lewis St Hartford CT 06103 860-522-7641 562
Web: www.lazparking.com

Lazar Equipment Ltd
520 Ninth St W Meadow Lake SK S9X1H1 306-236-5222 274
Web: www.lazarequipment.com

Lazard 30 Rockefeller Plaza New York NY 10112 212-632-6000 690
NYSE: LAZ ■ *TF:* 866-867-4070 ■ *Web:* www.lazard.com

Lazard Funds
30 Rockefeller Plaza 57th Fl New York NY 10112 800-823-6300 528
TF: 800-823-6300 ■ *Web:* lazardnet.com/us/mutual-funds/open-end-funds

Lazare Kaplan International Inc
19 W 44th St 16th Fl New York NY 10036 212-764-7201 407
OTC: LKII ■ *Web:* www.lazarediamonds.com

La-Z-Boy Inc 1284 N Telegraph Rd Monroe MI 48162 734-242-1444 457-2005* 319-2
NYSE: LZB ■ **Fax:* Sales ■ *TF:* 800-375-6890 ■ *Web:* www.la-z-boy.com

Lazbro Inc 12840 Bonaparte Ave Los Angeles CA 90066 310-989-6111 7
Web: www.lazbro.com

Lazear Capital Partners Ltd
401 N Front St Ste 350 Columbus OH 43215 614-221-1616 691
Web: www.lazearcapital.com

Lazega Law
13499 Biscayne Blvd Ste 107 North Miami FL 33181 754-263-4252 445
Web: lazegalaw.com

Lazenby & Associates Inc
10300ÿWÿCharelstonÿBlvdÿ ste 13-467 Las Vegas NV 89135 702-498-8506 401
Web: www.lazenbyassociates.com

Lazer Grant Inc 309 Mcdermot Ave Winnipeg MB R3A1T3 204-942-0300 957-5611 2
TF: 800-220-0005 ■ *Web:* www.lazergrant.ca

Lazer Inc
973 Pinebrook Knolls Dr Winston-Salem NC 27105 336-744-8047 92
Web: www.lazerinc.com

Lazlo's Brewery & Grill
210 N Seventh St Lincoln NE 68508 402-434-5636 434-3291 671
Web: lazlosbreweryandgrill.com

Lazo Technologies Inc
611 W Mockingbird Ln Dallas TX 75247 214-652-9898 246
TF: 800-213-8175 ■ *Web:* www.lazotech.com

Lazorpoint LLC
737 Bolivar Rd Ste 800 Cleveland OH 44115 216-325-5200 196
Web: www.lazorpoint.com

Lazy Acres Market 302 Meigs Rd Santa Barbara CA 93109 805-564-4410 345
Web: www.lazyacres.com

Lazy K Bar Ranch PO Box 1550 Big Timber MT 59011 406-537-9450 239
Web: lkbranch.com

Lazy L & B Ranch 1072 E Fork Rd Dubois WY 82513 307-455-2839 455-2849 239
TF Cust Svc: 800-453-9488 ■ *Web:* www.lazylb.com

Lazzari Fuel Company LLC
11 Industrial Way Brisbane CA 94005 415-467-2970 316
TF: 800-242-7265 ■ *Web:* www.lazzari.com

LB Foster Co 415 Holiday Dr Pittsburgh PA 15220 800-255-4500 650
NASDAQ: FSTR ■ *TF:* 800-255-4500 ■ *Web:* www.lbfoster.com

LB Furniture Industries LLC
99 S Third St Hudson NY 12534 518-828-1501 319-3
TF: 800-221-8752 ■ *Web:* www.lbempire.com

LB Sales Assoc LLC 50 Plant St New London CT 06320 860-437-3953 362

Lb Steel LLC 15700 Lathrop Ave Harvey IL 60426 708-331-2600 331-8500 454
Web: www.lbsteel.com

L&B Transport LLC
708 US190 PO Box 74870 Port Allen LA 70767 225-387-0894 449
TF: 800-545-9401 ■ *Web:* www.landbtransport.com

LB White Company Inc
W 6636 LB White Rd Onalaska WI 54650 608-783-5691 783-6115 357
TF: 800-345-7200 ■ *Web:* www.lbwhite.com

LBA (Latin Business Assn)
120 S San Pedro St Ste 530 Los Angeles CA 90012 213-628-8510 628-0519 49-12
TF: 866-924-9757 ■ *Web:* lbausa.com

LBA Group Inc 3400 Tupper Dr Greenville NC 27834 252-757-0279 752-9155 261
TF: 800-522-4464 ■ *Web:* www.lbagroup.com

LBC (Lexington Ballet Co)
161 N Mill St Lexington KY 40507 859-233-3925 573-1
Web: www.lexingtonballet.org

LBC Houston 11666 Port Rd Seabrook TX 77586 281-474-4433 291-3428 581
Web: www.lbctt.com

LBCH (Louisiana Baptist Children's Home Inc)
7200 DeSiard St Monroe LA 71203 318-343-2244 48-15
TF: 877-345-7411 ■ *Web:* www.lbch.org

LBFF (Latino Book & Family Festival)
3445 Catalina Dr Carlsbad CA 92010 858-603-8680 281

LBI Eyewear 20801 Nordhoff St Chatsworth CA 91311 818-407-1890 407-1895 542
TF Cust Svc: 800-423-5175 ■ *Web:* www.lbieyewear.com

LBi Software Inc 7600 Jericho Tpke Woodbury NY 11797 516-921-1500 177
Web: www.lbisoftware.com

LBIW Inc 2020 W 14th St Long Beach CA 90813 562-432-5451 723

LBJ Library & Museum 2313 Red River St Austin TX 78705 512-721-0216 721-0170 434-2
TF: 800-874-6451 ■ *Web:* www.lbjlibrary.org

LBL Architects Inc
1106 W Randol Mill Rd Ste 300 Arlington TX 76012 817-265-1510 393
Web: www.lblarchitects.com

LBM (Lloyd Bilyeu McLellan Construction Company Inc)
11421 Blankenbaker Access Dr Louisville KY 40299 502-452-1151 454-0291 186
Web: www.lbmconstructionco.com

LBNL (Lawrence Berkeley National Laboratory)
1 Cyclotron Rd Berkeley CA 94720 510-486-4000 486-7000 668
Web: www.lbl.gov

LBO Holding Inc Route 302 Bartlett NH 03812 603-374-2368 378
Web: www.attitash.com

LBP Manufacturing Inc
1325 S Cicero Ave Cicero IL 60804 708-652-5600 557
TF: 800-545-6200 ■ *Web:* www.lbpmfg.com

LBS (Library Binding Service)
1801 Thompson Ave Des Moines IA 50316 515-262-3191 262-4091* 92
**Fax Area Code:* 800 ■ *TF:* 800-247-5323 ■ *Web:* www.lbsbind.com

LBSO (Long Beach Symphony Orchestra)
249 E Ocean Blvd Ste 200 Long Beach CA 90802 562-436-3203 491-3599 573-3
Web: longbeachsymphony.org

LBT Inc 11502 "I" St Omaha NE 68137 402-333-4900 333-0685 779
TF: 888-528-7278 ■ *Web:* www.lbt-inc.com

LBU Inc 217 Brook Ave Passaic NJ 07055 973-773-4800 67
Web: www.lbuinc.com

LC Doane Co
110 Pond Meadow Rd PO Box 700 Ivoryton CT 06442 860-767-8295 767-1397 439
TF: 800-447-5006 ■ *Web:* www.lcdoane.com

Lc Engineers Inc
1471 Pinewood St Bldg 3 Rahway NJ 07065 732-340-9190 261
Web: www.lcengineers.com

LC Industries
2781 Katherine Wy Elk Grove Village IL 60007 312-455-0500 453
Web: lewisnclark.com

LC King Mfg Company Inc 24 Seventh St Bristol TN 37620 423-764-5188 764-6809 155-19
TF: 800-826-2510 ■ *Web:* lcking.com

LC Risq 555 Saturn Blvd Ste B143 San Diego CA 92154 310-406-5684 988-2913 466
Web: www.lcrisq.com

LC Sciences LLC
2575 W Bellfort St Ste 270 Houston TX 77054 713-664-7087 668
Web: www.lcsciences.com

Company / Address	Phone	Fax	Class
LC Walker Arena & Conference Ctr 955 Fourth St ... Muskegon MI 49440 *Web:* www.lcwalkerarena.com	231-724-5225		720
LC Whitford Company Inc 164 N Main St ... Wellsville NY 14895 *TF:* 800-321-3602 ■ *Web:* www.lcwhitford.com	585-593-3601	593-1876	188-4
LCA-Vision Inc 7840 Montgomery Rd ... Cincinnati OH 45236 *NASDAQ: LCAV* ■ *TF:* 800-688-4550 ■ *Web:* www.lasikplus.com	513-792-9292		798
LCB Assoc Inc 388 17th St Ste 200 ... Oakland CA 94612 *Web:* www.lcbassociates.com	510-763-7016		652
LCC (Laredo Community College) W End Washington St ... Laredo TX 78040 *Web:* www.laredo.edu	956-722-0521	721-5493	162
LCC International Inc 7900 Westpark Dr Ste A300 ... McLean VA 22102 *Web:* www.lcc.com	703-873-2000	873-2100	735
LCCC (Loudon County Chamber of Commerce) 318 Angel Row ... Loudon TN 37774 *Web:* www.loudoncountychamberofcommerce.com	865-458-2067	458-1206	139
LCCR (Leadership Conference on Civil Rights) 1629 K St NW Ste 1000 ... Washington DC 20006 *TF:* 888-460-0813 ■ *Web:* www.civilrights.org	202-466-3311	466-3435	48-8
LCD Lighting Inc 37 Robinson Blvd ... Orange CT 06477 *TF:* 800-826-9465 ■ *Web:* www.light-sources.com	203-795-1520	795-2874	437
LCEC 4980 Bayline Dr ... North Fort Myers FL 33917 *TF:* 800-282-1643 ■ *Web:* www.lcec.net	239-995-2121	995-7904	245
LCG Assoc Inc 400 Galleria Pkwy SE ... Atlanta GA 30339 *Web:* www.lcgassociates.com	770-644-0100	644-0105	401
LCG Inc 6000 Executive Blvd Ste 410 ... Rockville MD 20852 *Web:* www.lcgsystems.com	301-984-4004		177
LCH Paper Tube & Core Co 11930 Larc Industrial Blvd ... Burnsville MN 55337 *TF:* 800-472-3477 ■ *Web:* www.lchpapertube.com	952-358-3587	224-0087	125
LCI (Lannett Company Inc) 13200 Townsend Rd ... Philadelphia PA 19154 *NYSE: LCI* ■ *TF:* 800-325-9994 ■ *Web:* www.lannett.com	215-333-9000	333-9004	479
LCI Graphics Inc 2400 Main St Ext Ste 8 ... Sayreville NJ 08872 *Web:* www.lcigraphics.com	973-893-2913		627
LCJ (Lawyers for Civil Justice) 1140 Connecticut Ave NW Ste 503 ... Washington DC 20036 *Web:* www.lfcj.com	202-429-0045	429-6982	49-10
LCME (Liaison Committee on Medical Education) 330 N Wabash Ave Ste 39300 ... Chicago IL 60611 *Web:* www.lcme.org	312-464-4933		48-1
LCMH (Lake Charles Memorial Health System) 1701 Oak Pk Blvd ... Lake Charles LA 70601 *TF:* 800-494-5264 ■ *Web:* www.lcmh.com	337-494-3000		374-3
LCMS (Lutheran Church Missouri Synod) 1333 S Kirkwood Rd ... Saint Louis MO 63122 *TF:* 888-843-5267 ■ *Web:* www.lcms.org	314-965-9000		48-20
Lcms Foundation 361 Beaumont Hwy ... Lebanon CT 06249 *Web:* www.lfnd.org	860-450-0943		303
LCNB National Bank 3209 W Galbraith Rd ... Cincinnati OH 45239 *TF:* 800-344-2265 ■ *Web:* www.lcnb.com	513-932-1414		70
Lco Casino Lodge & Convention Center 13767 W County Rd B ... Hayward WI 54843 *Web:* lcocasino.com	715-634-5643		452
L-Com Inc 45 Beechwood Dr ... North Andover MA 01845 *Web:* www.l-com.com	978-682-6936		253
LCOR Inc 850 Cassatt Rd Ste 300 ... Berwyn PA 19312 *Web:* www.lcor.com	610-251-9110	408-4420	653
LCPS (Lenoir County Public School) 2017 W Vernon Ave PO Box 729 ... Kinston NC 28504 *TF:* 888-684-8404 ■ *Web:* www.lcpsnc.org	252-527-1109	527-6884	685
Lcptracker Inc 200 E Chapman Ave Ste D ... Orange CA 92866 *TF:* 800-378-0915 ■ *Web:* www.lcptracker.com	714-669-0052		179
LCS (Leon County Schools) 2757 W Pensacola St ... Tallahassee FL 32303 *Web:* www.leonschools.net	850-487-7100		685
LCS Precision Molding Inc 119 S Second St ... Waterville MN 56096 *Web:* www.lcsplastics.com	507-362-8685		608
LCS Technologies Inc 11230 Gold Express Dr Ste 310-140 ... Gold River CA 95670 *TF:* 855-277-5527 ■ *Web:* www.lcs-technologies-inc.com	855-277-5527		624
LCT Transportation Services 26444 County Rd 33 ... Okahumpka FL 34762 *Web:* citysearch.com/guide/orlando-fl-metro	352-326-8900		780
LD Amory & Co Inc 101 S King St ... Hampton VA 23669 *TF:* 800-272-2728 ■ *Web:* virginiaseafood.org	757-722-1915	723-1184	297-5
LD Systems LP 407 Garden Oaks ... Houston TX 77018 *TF:* 800-416-9327 ■ *Web:* www.ldsystems.com	713-695-9400		179
LD Telecommunications Inc 2121 Ponce de leon Blvd Ste 2000 ... Coral Gables FL 33134 *Web:* www.nexogy.com	305-358-8952		387
LDA (Learning Disabilities Assn of America) 4156 Library Rd ... Pittsburgh PA 15234 *TF:* 888-300-6710 ■ *Web:* ldaamerica.org	412-341-1515	344-0224	48-17
LDCI (Louis Dreyfus Co) 355 S Ninth St ... Winter Garden FL 34787 *Web:* www.ldcom.com	407-656-1000	656-1229	296-21
LDI Industries 1864 Nage Ave ... Manitowoc WI 54220 *Web:* www.ldi-industries.com	920-682-6877	684-7210	790
LDI Ltd 54 Monument Cir Ste 800 ... Indianapolis IN 46204 *Web:* www.ldiltd.com	317-237-5400	237-2280	185
LDI Mechanical Inc 1587 Bentley Dr ... Corona CA 92879	951-340-9685		610
LDK Solar Tech USA Inc 1290 Oakmead Pkwy Ste 306 ... Sunnyvale CA 94085 *Web:* www.ldksolar.com	408-245-0858		612
Ldm Technologies Inc 2500 Executive Hills Dr ... Auburn Hills MI 48326	248-858-2800		247
LDP Inc 75 Kiwanis Blvd PO Box O ... West Hazleton PA 18201 *TF:* 800-522-8413 ■ *Web:* www.leaderservices.com	800-522-8413		178-3
LDR Industries Inc 600 N Kilbourn Ave ... Chicago IL 60624 *TF:* 800-545-5230 ■ *Web:* www.ldrind.com	773-265-3000	265-3130	609
LDRR (Louisiana & Delta Railroad Inc) 402 W Washington St ... New Iberia LA 70560 *Web:* www.gwrr.com	337-364-9625		648
LDS Group, The PO Box 83480 ... Baton Rouge LA 70884 *Web:* www.theldsgroup.com	225-769-9923		391-2
LDS Hospital 8th Ave & C St ... Salt Lake City UT 84143 *TF:* 888-301-3880 ■ *Web:* intermountainhealthcare.org	801-408-1100		374-3
Le Baluchon 3550 chemin des Trembles ... Saint-Paulin QC J0K3G0 *TF:* 800-789-5968 ■ *Web:* www.baluchon.com	819-268-2555		707
Le Bas International 16152 Beach Blvd ... Huntington Beach CA 92467 *Web:* www.lebas.com	805-593-0510	593-0509	21
Le Bistro 4626 N Federal Hwy ... Lighthouse Point FL 33064 *Web:* www.lebistrorestaurant.com	954-946-9240		671
Le Bleu Corp 3134 Cornatzer Rd ... Advance NC 27006 *TF:* 800-854-4471 ■ *Web:* www.lebleu.com	800-854-4471		805
Le Boulanger Inc 305 N Mathilda ... Sunnyvale CA 94085 *Web:* www.leboulanger.com	408-774-9000		68
Le Chamois 4557 Blackcomb Way ... Whistler BC V0N1B4 *TF:* 888-621-1177 ■ *Web:* www.lechamoiswhistler.com	604-932-8700		379
Le Cheval Restaurant 1007 Clay St ... Oakland CA 94607 *Web:* www.lecheval.co	510-763-8495		671
Le Cirque 3600 Las Vegas Blvd S ... Las Vegas NV 89109 *TF:* 888-987-6667 ■ *Web:* www.bellagio.com	702-693-7111	693-8585	671
Le Colonial 937 N Rush St ... Chicago IL 60611 *Web:* www.lecolonialchicago.com	312-255-0088	255-1108	671
Le Continental 26 rue St-Louis ... Vieux-Quebec QC G1R3Y9 *TF:* 800-267-8687 ■ *Web:* www.restaurantlecontinental.com	418-694-9995		671
LE Cooke Co 26333 Rd 140 ... Visalia CA 93292 *Web:* lecooke.com	559-732-9146		461
Le Coq Au Vin 4800 S Orange Ave ... Orlando FL 32806 *TF:* 800-745-3000 ■ *Web:* www.lecoqauvinrestaurant.com	407-851-6980		671
Le Cordon Bleu College of Culinary Arts *Atlanta* 1927 Lakeside Pkwy ... Tucker GA 30084 *TF:* 888-549-8222 ■ *Web:* www.chefs.edu	770-938-4711		163
Las Vegas 1451 Ctr Crossing Rd ... Las Vegas NV 89144 *TF:* 888-551-8222 ■ *Web:* www.chefs.edu	702-365-7690	365-7911	163
Le Creuset of America Inc 114 Bob Gifford Blvd ... Early Branch SC 29916	803-943-4308	943-4510	486
Le Devoir 1265 Berri 8th Fl ... Montreal QC H2L4X4 *TF:* 800-463-7559 ■ *Web:* www.ledevoir.com	514-985-3333	985-3360	532-1
Le Fou Frog 400 E Fifth St ... Kansas City MO 64106 *Web:* www.lefoufrog.com	816-474-6060		671
Le Gourmand 4100 Fourth Ave S ... Seattle WA 98134 *Web:* www.legourmandseattle.com	206-588-9728		671
Le Groupe Genitique Inc 2655 Blvd du Royaume Faubourg Sagamie Ste 480 ... Jonquiere QC G7S4S9 *Web:* www.genitique.com	418-548-4626		196
LE Johnson Products Inc 2100 Sterling Ave ... Elkhart IN 46516 *TF:* 800-837-5664 ■ *Web:* www.johnsonhardware.com	574-293-5664	294-4697	350
LE Jones Co 1200 34th Ave ... Menominee MI 49858 *Web:* www.lejones.com	906-863-4411		128
Le Languedoc Bistro 24 Broad St ... Nantucket MA 02554 *Web:* languedocbistro.com	508-228-2552		671
Le Lapin Saute 52 ru du Petit-Champlain ... Ville de Quebec QC G1K4H4 *Web:* www.lapinsaute.com	418-692-5325		671
Le Mars Insurance Co PO Box 1608 ... Le Mars IA 51031 *TF:* 800-545-6480 ■ *Web:* www.lemm.com	800-545-6480		390
Le Mas Des Oliviers Restaurant 1216 Rue Bishop ... Montreal QC H3G2E3 *Web:* www.lemasdesoliviers.ca	514-861-6733		671
Le Meridian 20 Sidney St ... Cambridge MA 02139 *TF:* 800-543-4300 ■ *Web:* starwoodhotels.com	617-577-0200		379
Le Meridien Chambers Minneapolis 901 Hennepin Ave ... Minneapolis MN 55403 *TF General:* 877-782-0116 ■ *Web:* www.lemeridienchambers.com	612-767-6900		379
Le M,ridien Dallas, The Stoneleigh 2927 Maple Ave ... Dallas TX 75201 *Web:* lemeridiendallasstoneleigh.com	214-871-7111		379
Le M,ridien Delfina Santa Monica 530 W Pico Blvd ... Santa Monica CA 90405 *TF:* 888-627-8532 ■ *Web:* www.lemeridiendelfina.com	310-399-9344		379
Le Merigot - A JW Marriott Beach Hotel & Spa 1740 Ocean Ave ... Santa Monica CA 90401 *TF:* 888-539-7899 ■ *Web:* www.marriott.com	310-395-9700	395-9200	379
Le Meritage at the Maison Dupuy 1001 Rue Toulouse ... New Orleans LA 70112 *Web:* www.maisondupuy.com	504-522-8800		671
Le Montrose Suite Hotel 900 Hammond St ... West Hollywood CA 90069 *TF:* 800-776-0666 ■ *Web:* www.lemontrose.com	310-855-1115	657-9192	379
Le Moyne College 1419 Salt Springs Rd ... Syracuse NY 13214 **Fax:* Admissions ■ *TF Admissions:* 800-333-4733 ■ *Web:* www.lemoyne.edu	315-445-4100	445-4711*	166
Le Mridien Atlanta Perimeterrestaurant 111 Perimeter Ctr W ... Atlanta GA 30346 *Web:* www.lemeridienatlantaperimeter.com	770-396-6800		671
Le Nil Bleu 3706 St-Denis ... Montreal QC H2X3L7	514-285-4628		671
Le Nouvel Montreal Hotel & Spa 1740 Rene-Levesque Blvd W ... Montreal QC H3H1R3 *TF:* 800-363-6063 ■ *Web:* www.lenouvelhotel.com	514-931-8841	931-5581	379
Le Papillon 410 Saratoga Ave ... San Jose CA 95129 *Web:* www.lepapillon.com	408-296-3730	247-7812	671
Le Papillon on Front 69 Front St E ... Toronto ON M5E1B5 *Web:* papillononfront.com	416-367-0303		671
Le Parc Suite Hotel 733 NW Knoll Dr ... West Hollywood CA 90069 **Fax Area Code:* 310 ■ *TF Resv:* 800-864-8377 ■ *Web:* www.leparcsuites.com	877-591-9556	659-7812*	379
Le Parker Meridien Palm Springs 4200 E Palm Canyon Dr ... Palm Springs CA 92264 *Web:* www.starwoodhotels.com/lemeridien	760-770-5000	324-2188	669
Le Pavillon 45 San Marco Ave ... Saint Augustine FL 32084 *Web:* www.lepavillonstaugustine.com	904-824-6202		671

Name / Address	City	State	Zip	Phone	Fax	Class
Le Pavillon Hotel 833 Poydras St *Web:* www.lepavillon.com	New Orleans	LA	70112	504-581-3111	620-4130	379
Le Perigord 405 E 52nd St *Web:* www.leperigord.com	New York	NY	10022	212-755-6244		671
Le Petit Cafe 308 W Sixth St *Web:* lpc1977.com	Bloomington	IN	47404	812-334-9747		671
LE Phillips Memorial Public Library 400 Eau Claire St *Web:* www.ecpubliclibrary.info	Eau Claire	WI	54701	715-839-5004		434-3
Le Pichet 1933 First Ave *Web:* lepichetseattle.com	Seattle	WA	98101	206-256-1499		671
Le Port-Royal Hotel & Suites 144 St Pierre St *TF:* 866-417-2777 ■ *Web:* www.leportroyal.com	Quebec	QC	G1K8N8	418-692-2777	692-2778	379
Le Quotidien & Progres Dimanche 1051 boul Talbot *Web:* www.lapresse.ca	Chicoutimi	QC	G7H5C1	418-545-4474		532-1
Le Refuge Restaurant 127 N Washington St *Web:* www.lerefugealexandria.com	Alexandria	VA	22314	703-548-4661		671
Le Rendez-vous 3844 E Ft Lowell Rd *Web:* www.lerendez-vous.com	Tucson	AZ	85716	520-323-7373		671
Le Richelieu Hotel 1234 Chartres St *TF:* 800-535-9653 ■ *Web:* www.lerichelieuhotel.com	New Orleans	LA	70116	504-529-2492	524-8179	379
Le Saint Sulpice 414 Rue St Sulpice *TF General:* 877-785-7423 ■ *Web:* www.lesaintsulpice.com	Montreal	QC	H2Y2V5	514-288-1000	288-0077	379
Le Saint-Amour 48 rue Sainte-Ursule *Web:* www.saint-amour.com	Quebec	QC	G1R4E2	418-694-0667	694-0967	671
LE Schwartz & Son Inc 279 Reid St *TF:* 800-524-2421 ■ *Web:* www.leschwartz.com	Macon	GA	31206	478-745-6563	745-2711	189-12
Le Smith Co 1030 E Wilson St PO Box 766 *TF:* 888 637 6481 ■ *Web:* www.lesmith.com	Bryan	OH	43506	419-636-4555		350
Le Soleil 410 Boulevard Charest E *Web:* www.lapresse.ca	Ville de Qu,bec	QC	G1K8G3	418-686-3233		532-1
Le Sueur Cheese Company Inc 719 N Main St *TF:* 800-247-0871 ■ *Web:* daviscofoods.com	Le Sueur	MN	56058	507-665-3353	665-2820	296-5
Le Sueur County 88 S Pk Ave *Web:* www.co.le-sueur.mn.us	Le Center	MN	56057	507-357-2251	357-6375	338
Le Tourneau Plastics Inc 160 Charles St	Oconto	WI	54153	920-834-2777		596
Le Vallauris 385 W Tahquitz Canyon Way *Web:* www.palmsprings.com	Palm Springs	CA	92262	760-325-5059		671
Le Vieux Paris 170 W Camino Real	Boca Raton	FL	33432	561-368-7910		671
Le Yaca 1430 High St *Web:* leyacawilliamsburg.com	Williamsburg	VA	23185	757-220-3616		671
LEA (Law Enforcement Assoc Corp) 120 Penmarc Dr Ste 125 *OTC:* LAWEQ ■ *TF:* 800-354-9669 ■ *Web:* www.leacorp.com	Raleigh	NC	27616	919-872-6210	872-6431	52
Lea County 100 N Main St Ste 11 *TF:* 800-658-9955 ■ *Web:* www.leacounty.net	Lovington	NM	88260	575-396-8619	396-3293	338
LEA Group Holdings Inc 625 Cochrane Dr 9th Fl *Web:* www.lea.ca	Markham	ON	L3R9R9	905-470-0015		256
Lea Regional Medical Ctr 5419 N Lovington Hwy *TF:* 877-492-8001 ■ *Web:* www.learegionalmedical.com	Hobbs	NM	88240	575-492-5000	492-5505	374-3
Leach Botanical Garden 6704 SE 122 Ave PO Box 90667 *Web:* www.leachgarden.org	Portland	OR	97236	503-823-9503		97
Leach Enterprises 4304 II Rt 176 *Web:* www.leach-ent.com	Crystal Lake	IL	60014	815-459-6917		57
Leach Farms Inc W1102 Buttercup Ct PO Box 192 *Web:* www.leachfarms.com	Berlin	WI	54923	920-361-1880	361-4474	10-11
Leach International Corp 6900 Orangethorpe Ave *TF:* 800-232-7700 ■ *Web:* www.esterline.com	Buena Park	CA	90622	714-736-7598	739-1713	203
Lead Concepts Inc 1060 Texan Trail *Web:* www.leadconcepts.com	Grapevine	TX	76051	817-421-5803		463
Lead IT Corp 1999 Wabash Ave Ste 210 *Web:* www.leaditgroup.com	Springfield	IL	62704	217-726-7250		180
Lead Pulse Media 3535 hayden ave *TF:* 800-552-9000 ■ *Web:* www.leadpulsemedia.com	Culver City	CA	90232	310-439-2334		7
Lead Technologies Inc 1927 S Tryon St Ste 200 *TF:* 800-637-4699 ■ *Web:* www.leadtools.com	Charlotte	NC	28203	704-332-5532		177
LeadCreations com LLC 12717 W Sunrise Blvd Ste 312 *Web:* www.leadcreations.com	Ft Lauderdale	FL	33323	305-831-0999		195
LeadDog Marketing Group 440 Ninth Ave 17th Fl *Web:* www.leaddogmarketing.com	New York	NY	10001	212-488-6530		5
Leader & Berkon Llp 630 Third Ave Fl 17 *TF:* 800-330-5769 ■ *Web:* www.leaderberkon.com	New York	NY	10017	212-486-2400		445
Leader Business Systems 35436 Mound Rd *TF:* 800-510-4800 ■ *Web:* www.leaderbusiness.com	Sterling Heights	MI	48310	586-264-4908		525
Leader Capital Corp 919 N East 19th Ave Ste 200 *Web:* www.leadercapital.com	Portland	OR	97232	503-294-1010		690
Leader Engineering Fabrication Inc 695 Independence Dr *Web:* www.leaderengineeringfabrication.com	Napoleon	OH	43545	419-592-0008		757
Leader Global Technologies Inc 905 W 13th St *Web:* www.leadergt.com	Deer Park	TX	77536	281-542-0600		326
Leader Graphic Design Inc 5410 Newport Dr Ste 44 *Web:* www.leadergraphics.com	Rolling Meadows	IL	60008	847-564-5409		195
Leader Industries 10941 Weaver Ave *Web:* www.leader-ambulance.com	S El Monte	CA	91733	626-575-0880		59

Name / Address	City	State	Zip	Phone	Fax	Class
Leader Industries Inc 2509 Cruzen St *TF:* 800-388-3806 ■ *Web:* www.leaderindustries.com	Nashville	TN	37211	615-256-3500		697
Leader Newspapers 3500 T C Jester Blvd PO Box 924487 *Web:* theleadernews.com	Houston	TX	77292	713-686-8494	686-0970	532-4
Leader Promotions Inc 790 E Johnstown Rd *Web:* www.leaderpromos.com	Columbus	OH	43230	614-416-6565		4
Leader Union, The 229 S Fifth St *Web:* www.leaderunion.com	Vandalia	IL	62471	618-283-3374		637-8
Leader's Edge 2 Bala Plaza Ste 300 *Web:* www.the-leaders-edge.com	Bala Cynwyd	PA	19004	610-660-6684		41
Leaderpoint Llc 6045 Martway St Ste 108 *Web:* www.leaderpoint.biz	Mission	KS	66202	913-384-3212		193
Leaders Bank, The 2001 York Rd Ste 150 *Web:* leadersbank.com	Oak Brook	IL	60523	630-572-5323		70
Leaders Casual Furniture 6303 126th Ave *TF:* 800-665-5510 ■ *Web:* www.leadersfurniture.com	Largo	FL	33773	727-538-5577		321
Leaders LLC 2 Portland Fish Pier Ste 214 *TF:* 888-583-7770 ■ *Web:* www.leaders-llc.com	Portland	ME	04101	888-583-7770		690
LEADERS Magazine Inc 59 E 54Th St *Web:* www.leadersmag.com	New York	NY	10022	212-758-0740		41
Leadership Conference on Civil Rights (LCCR) 1629 K St NW Ste 1000 *TF:* 888-460-0813 ■ *Web:* www.civilrights.org	Washington	DC	20006	202-466-3311	466-3435	48-8
Leadership Directories Inc 104 Fifth Ave 3rd Fl *TF:* 800 627 0311 ■ *Web:* www.leadershipdirectories.com	New York	NY	10011	212-627-4140	645-0931	637-2
Leadership Journal 465 Gundersen Dr *TF:* 800-777-3136 ■ *Web:* christianitytoday.com/le	Carol Stream	IL	60188	630-260-6200		457-5
Leadership Management Inc 4567 Lake Shore Dr *TF:* 800-876-2389 ■ *Web:* www.lmi-world.com	Waco	TX	76710	254-776-2060	772-9588	765
Leadership Performance Sustainability Laboratories 4647 Hugh Howell Rd **Fax Area Code:* 770 ■ *TF:* 800-241-8334 ■ *Web:* www.lpslabs.com	Tucker	GA	30084	800-241-8334	243-8899*	541
Leadership Public Schools 344 Thomas L Berkley Way *Web:* www.leadps.org	Oakland	CA	94612	510-830-3780	225-2575	685
Leader-Telegram 701 S Farwell St **Fax:* Edit ■ *TF:* 800-236-8808 ■ *Web:* www.leadertelegram.com	Eau Claire	WI	54701	715-833-9200	858-7308*	532-2
Leading Age 2519 Connecticut Ave NW *TF:* 866-898-2624 ■ *Web:* www.leadingage.org	Washington	DC	20008	202-783-2242	783-2255	48-6
Leading Authorities Inc 1990 M St Ste 800 *TF:* 800-773-2537 ■ *Web:* www.leadingauthorities.com	Washington	DC	20036	202-783-0300	783-0301	708
Leading Hotels of the World 485 Lexington Ave Ste 401 *TF:* 800-745-8883 ■ *Web:* www.lhw.com	New York	NY	10017	212-515-5600		376
Leading Industry Inc 1151 Pacific Ave *Web:* www.ldind.com	Oxnard	CA	93033	805-385-4100		596
Leading Lady 24050 Commerce Pk *TF Cust Svc:* 800-321-4804 ■ *Web:* www.leadinglady.com	Beachwood	OH	44122	216-464-5490		155-18
Leading Market Technologies Inc 58 Winter St 5th Fl *TF:* 800-961-8948 ■ *Web:* www.lmtech.com	Boston	MA	02108	617-494-4747		204
Leading Systems Technologies Inc 2721 Prosperity Ave Ste 100 *Web:* www.leadingsystemstechnologies.com	Fairfax	VA	22031	703-204-0404		463
Leading Technology Composites Inc 2626 W May *TF:* 800-347-1200 ■ *Web:* www.ltc-ltc.com	Wichita	KS	67213	316-944-0011		504
LeadingResponse LLC 1820 Preston Park Blvd Ste 2200 *Web:* leadingresponse.com	Plano	TX	06901	201-387-7272		5
Leadman Electronic USA Inc 382 Laurelwood Dr *TF:* 877-532-3626 ■ *Web:* www.leadman.com	Santa Clara	CA	95054	408-738-1751	738-2620	174
LeadMD Inc 9383 E Bahia Dr Ste 225 *TF:* 800-255-3847 ■ *Web:* www.leadmd.com	Scottsdale	AZ	85260	480-278-7205		195
LeadMinders LLC 1643 VIVIAN ST *Web:* www.leadminders.com	Longmont	CO	80501	720-552-5650		5
LeadRival 1207 S White Chapel Blvd Ste 250 *TF:* 800-332-8017 ■ *Web:* www.leadrival.com	Southlake	TX	76092	800-332-8017		5
LeadScope Inc 1393 Dublin Rd *Web:* www.leadscope.com	Columbus	OH	43215	614-675-3730		177
LeadSwell PO Box 170432 *Web:* www.leadswell.com	San Francisco	CA	94117	415-518-6701		317
Leadtek Research Inc 910 Auburn Ct *Web:* www.leadtek.com	Fremont	CA	94538	510-490-8076		625
Leaf Chronicle Co 200 Commerce St *Web:* www.theleafchronicle.com	Clarksville	TN	37040	931-552-1808		637-8
LEAF Financial Corp 1 Commerce Sq 2005 Market St 15th Fl *TF:* 800-819-5556 ■ *Web:* LEAFFinancial.com	Philadelphia	PA	19103	800-819-5556		23
Leaf, Miele, Manganelli, Fortunato & Engel 310 Passaic Ave *Web:* www.leafsaltzman.com	Fairfield	NJ	07004	973-808-9500		2
League for Innovation in the Community College 4505 E Chandler Blvd Ste 250 *Web:* www.league.org	Phoenix	AZ	85048	480-705-8200	705-8201	48-11
League of American Bicyclists 1612 K St NW Ste 800 *Web:* www.bikeleague.org	Washington	DC	20006	202-822-1333	822-1334	48-22
League of American Orchestras 33 W 60th St 5th Fl *Web:* www.americanorchestras.org	New York	NY	10023	212-262-5161	262-5198	48-4
League of Conservation Voters 1920 L St NW Ste 800 *Web:* www.lcv.org	Washington	DC	20036	202-785-8683	835-0491	48-7

	Phone	Fax	Class
League of Kansas Municipalities 300 SW Eighth Ave Ste 100 .... Topeka KS 66603 *TF:* 800-445-5588 ■ *Web:* lkm.org	785-354-9565		533
League of Resident Theatres (LORT) 1501 Broadway Ste 1801 .... New York NY 10036 *Web:* www.lort.org	212-944-1501		48-4
League of Women Voters (LWV) 1730 M St NW Ste 1000 .... Washington DC 20036 *Web:* www.lwv.org	202-429-1965	429-0854	48-7
League to Save Lake Tahoe 2608 Lake Tahoe Blvd .... South Lake Tahoe CA 96150 *TF:* 877-277-6583 ■ *Web:* www.keeptahoeblue.org	530-541-5388	541-5454	48-13
Leahi Hospital 3675 Kilauea Ave .... Honolulu HI 96816 *TF:* 800-845-6733 ■ *Web:* www.hhsc.org	808-733-8000	733-7914	374-7
Leahy Patrick J (Sen D - VT) 437 Russell Bldg .... Washington DC 20510 *Web:* www.leahy.senate.gov	202-224-4242	224-3479	342-2
Leaktite Corp 40 Francis St .... Leominster MA 01453 *TF:* 800-392-0039 ■ *Web:* www.leaktite.com	978-537-8000	534-3539	608
Leam Drilling Systems Inc 2027a Airport Rd .... Conroe TX 77301 *TF:* 800-426-5349 ■ *Web:* leam.net	800-426-5349		539
Leamington District Chamber of Commerce 318 Erie St S .... Leamington ON N8H3C5 *TF:* 800-393-3769 ■ *Web:* www.leamingtonchamber.com	519-326-2721	326-3204	137
Lean Horizons Consulting LLC 79 Kingswood Dr .... South Glastonbury CT 06073 *Web:* www.leanhorizons.com	860-430-1174		538
Leanin' Tree Inc 6055 Longbow Dr .... Boulder CO 80301 *TF:* 800-525-0656 ■ *Web:* www.leanintree.com	800-525-0656		130
Leanin' Tree Museum of Western Art 6055 Longbow Dr .... Boulder CO 80301 *Fax Area Code: 303 ■ *TF:* 800-525-0656 ■ *Web:* www.leanintree.com	800-525-0656	530-5124*	520
LeanLogistics Inc 1351 S Waverly Rd .... Holland MI 49423 *TF:* 866-584-7280 ■ *Web:* www.leanlogistics.com	616-738-6400	738-6462	311
LEAP 2500 Technology Dr .... Louisville KY 40299 *Web:* www.leapagency.com	502-212-1390		5
Leap Group Llc, The 11 Waverly Rd .... San Anselmo CA 94960 *Web:* www.leapgroup.com	415-456-7404		317
Leap/Carpenter/Kemps Insurance Agency 3187 Collins Dr .... Merced CA 95348 *TF:* 800-221-0864 ■ *Web:* lckinsurance.com	209-384-0727		390
LeapFrog Enterprises Inc 6401 Hollis St Ste 100 .... Emeryville CA 94608 *NYSE:* LF ■ *TF:* 800-701-5327 ■ *Web:* leapfrog.com	510-420-5000		762
Leapfrog Services Inc 1190 W Druid Hills Dr Ste 200 .... Atlanta GA 30329 *Web:* leapfrogservices.com	404-870-2122	870-2123	180
LeapFrog Solutions Inc 3201 Jermantown Rd Ste 350 .... Fairfax VA 22030 *Web:* www.leapfrogit.com	703-273-7900		7
LeapFrog Systems Inc 1 International Pl 31st Fl .... Boston MA 02110 *Web:* www.leapfrogsystems.com	617-224-9700		177
Lear Capital Inc 1990 S Bundy Dr Ste 600 .... Los Angeles CA 90025 *TF:* 800-576-9355 ■ *Web:* www.learcapital.com	800-576-9355		251
Lear Corp 21557 Telegraph Rd .... Southfield MI 48033 *Web:* www.lear.com	248-447-1500		247
Lear Romec Crane Corp 241 S Abbe Rd PO Box 4014 .... Elyria OH 44036 *TF:* 800-601-3099 ■ *Web:* www.craneae.com	440-323-3211	322-3378	21
Leardon Boiler Works Inc 479 Walton Ave .... Bronx NY 10451	718-585-5314		189-10
Learfield Communications Inc 505 Hobbs Rd .... Jefferson City MO 65109 *Web:* www.learfield.com	573-893-7200		644
Learnframe Inc 9551 S 700 E .... Draper UT 84070	801-523-8000	523-8012	177
Learning Care Group Inc 21333 Haggerty Rd Ste 300 .... Novi MI 48375 *TF:* 877-817-3883 ■ *Web:* learningcaregroup.com	248-697-9000	697-9002	148
Learning Communications LLC 5520 Trabuco Rd .... Irvine CA 92620 *Fax Area Code: 949 ■ *TF:* 800-622-3610 ■ *Web:* www.learncom.com	800-622-3610	727-4323*	513
Learning Designs 614 Main St Ste 104 .... Park City UT 84060 *Web:* www.learningdesigns.com	435-645-9515		463
Learning Disabilities Assn of America (LDA) 4156 Library Rd .... Pittsburgh PA 15234 *TF:* 888-300-6710 ■ *Web:* ldaamerica.org	412-341-1515	344-0224	48-17
Learning Express Inc 29 Buena Vista St .... Devens MA 01434 *TF:* 888-725-8697 ■ *Web:* www.learningexpress.com	978-889-1000	889-1010	761
Learning Research & Development Ctr (LRDC) University of Pittsburgh 3939 O'Hara St .... Pittsburgh PA 15260 *TF:* 800-397-0071 ■ *Web:* www.lrdc.pitt.edu	412-624-7020	624-9149	668
Learning Resources 380 N Fairway Dr .... Vernon Hills IL 60061 *TF:* 800-222-3909 ■ *Web:* www.learningresources.com	847-573-8400	573-8425	243
Learning Source Ltd 644 Tenth St .... Brooklyn NY 11215 *Web:* www.learningsourceltd.com	718-768-0231	369-3467	94
Learning Systems Institute 4600 University Ctr .... Tallahassee FL 32306 *Web:* www.lsi.fsu.edu	850-644-2570		668
Learning Tree International Inc 1831 Michael Faraday Dr .... Reston VA 20190 *OTC:* LTRE ■ *TF Cust Svc:* 800-843-8733 ■ *Web:* www.learningtree.com	703-709-9119		764
Learning Unlimited 5810 E Skelly Dr Ste 500 .... Tulsa OK 74135 *TF:* 888-622-4203 ■ *Web:* learningunlimited.com	918-622-3292		463
Learning Works 181 Brackett St .... Portland ME 04102 *Web:* www.learningworks.me	207-775-0105		243
Learning Worlds Inc 2647 Broadway Ste 5W .... New York NY 10025 *Web:* learningworlds.com	212-725-0436		180
Learning Wrap-Ups Inc 1660 W Gordon Ave Ste 4 .... Layton UT 84041 *TF:* 800-992-4966 ■ *Web:* www.learningwrapups.com	801-497-0050	497-0063	243
Learning.Net 401 Glenneyre St Ste C .... Laguna Beach CA 92651 *Web:* www.learning.net	949-221-8600		463

	Phone	Fax	Class
LearnSpectrum 9912 Georgetown Pike Ste D203 .... Great Falls VA 22066 *TF:* 888-682-9485 ■ *Web:* www.learnspectrum.com	703-757-8200	757-8202	317
Lease Crutcher Lewis 2200 Western Ave Ste 500 .... Seattle WA 98121 *Fax Area Code: 202 ■ *Web:* www.lewisbuilds.com	206-622-0500	622-6451*	186
Lease Harbor LLC 414 N Orleans St Ste 602 .... Chicago IL 60654 *Web:* leaseharbor.com	312-494-9470		177
Lease Plan USA 1165 Sanctuary Pkwy .... Alpharetta GA 30004 *TF:* 888-536-4114 ■ *Web:* www.leaseplan.com	770-933-9090		289
LeaseQ LLC 100-D Office Tower Pk .... Woburn MA 01801 *TF:* 888-688-4519 ■ *Web:* www.leaseq.com	888-688-4519		393
Leaseteam Inc 4139 S 143rd Cir .... Omaha NE 68137 *Web:* leaseteam.com	402-493-3445		177
Leasing Assoc Inc 12600 N Featherwood Dr Ste 400 .... Houston TX 77034 *TF:* 800-449-4807 ■ *Web:* www.theleasingcompany.com	832-300-1300	300-1317	289
Leasing Technologies International Inc 221 Danbury Rd .... Wilton CT 06897 *TF:* 800-531-5086 ■ *Web:* www.ltileasing.com	203-563-1100	563-1112	264-1
Leason Ellis LLP 1 Barker Ave 5th Fl .... White Plains NY 10601 *Web:* www.leasonellis.com	914-821-9070		428
Leath Correctional Institution 2809 Airport Rd .... Greenwood SC 29649 *Fax Area Code: 803 ■ *Web:* doc.sc.gov	864-229-5709	896-1766*	213
Leath Furniture LLC 4370 Peachtree Rd .... Atlanta GA 30319 *Web:* www.leathfurniture.com	404-848-0880		321
Leatha's Bar-B-Que Inn 6374 US Hwy 98 .... Hattiesburg MS 39402	601-271-6003		671
Leather Bros Inc 1314 Nabholz Ave .... Conway AR 72034 *Web:* www.leatherbrothers.com	501-329-9471		432
Leather Creations Inc 2692 Peachtree Sq .... Atlanta GA 30360 *Web:* leathercreationsfurniture.com	678-584-1000		321
Leather Industries of America (LIA) 3050 K St NW Ste 400 .... Washington DC 20007 *TF:* 800-635-0617 ■ *Web:* www.leatherusa.com	202-342-8497	342-8583	49-4
Leather Specialty Co 1088 Business Ln .... Naples FL 34110	239-333-1000		453
Leathercraft PO Box 639 .... Conover NC 28613 *TF:* 800-627-1561 ■ *Web:* www.leathercraft-furniture.com	800-627-1561	627-1562	319-2
Leatherman Tool Group Inc 12106 NE Ainsworth Cir .... Portland OR 97220 *TF:* 800-847-8665 ■ *Web:* www.leatherman.com	503-253-7826	253-7830	758
Leatherock International Inc 5285 Lovelock St .... San Diego CA 92110 *TF:* 800-466-6667 ■ *Web:* www.leatherock.com	619-299-7625		432
Leatherup Com 955 Venice Blvd .... Los Angeles CA 90015 *TF:* 800-846-6010 ■ *Web:* www.leatherup.com	213-763-6185		225
Leavcon II Inc 108 American Ave .... Lansing KS 66043 *TF:* 800-633-1136 ■ *Web:* www.leavcon.com	913-351-1430		183
Leave No Trace Ctr for Outdoor Ethics Inc 1830 17th St .... Boulder CO 80302 *TF:* 800-332-4100 ■ *Web:* www.lnt.org	303-442-8222	442-8217	48-23
Leavell Insurance & Real Estate 117 E Broadway .... Hobbs NM 88240	575-393-2550		390
Leavenworth Convention & Visitors Bureau 100 N fifth St Rm 104 .... Leavenworth KS 66048 *TF:* 800-255-8070 ■ *Web:* www.visitleavenworthks.com	913-682-4113		206
Leavenworth County 300 Walnut St .... Leavenworth KS 66048 *TF:* 855-893-9533 ■ *Web:* www.leavenworthcounty.org	913-684-0421		338
Leavenworth National Cemetery 150 Muncie Rd .... Leavenworth KS 66048 *Web:* www.cem.va.gov/cems	913-758-4105	758-4136	136
Leavenworth Public Library 417 Spruce St .... Leavenworth KS 66048 *TF:* 800-829-3676 ■ *Web:* leavenworthpubliclibrary.org	913-682-5666	682-1248	434-3
Leavenworth-Jefferson Electric Co-op Inc 507 N Union St .... McLouth KS 66054 *TF:* 888-796-6111 ■ *Web:* www.ljec.coop	888-796-6111		245
Leavenworth-Lansing Area Chamber of Commerce 518 Shawnee St .... Leavenworth KS 66048 *TF:* 800-452-6727 ■ *Web:* www.llchamber.com	913-682-4112	682-8170	139
Leavitt Corp 100 Santilli Hwy .... Everett MA 02149 *TF:* 800-227-5980 ■ *Web:* teddie.com	617-389-2600	387-9085	296-28
leavitt group Enterprises 216 S 200 W .... Cedar City UT 84720 *TF:* 800-264-0085 ■ *Web:* www.leavitt.com	435-586-6553	586-1510	390
Leavitt Machinery & Rentals Inc 24389 Fraser Hwy .... Langley BC V2Z2L3 *TF:* 877-850-6499 ■ *Web:* www.leavittmachinery.com	604-607-4450		358
Leavitt Tube 1717 W 115th St .... Chicago IL 60643 *TF:* 800-532-8488 ■ *Web:* www.leavitt-tube.com	773-239-7700	239-1023	490
Lea-wayne Knitting Mills Inc 5937 Commerce Blvd .... Morristown TN 37814	423-586-7513		155-10
Lebanese Taverna 2641 Connecticut Ave NW .... Washington DC 20008 *Web:* www.lebanesetaverna.com	202-265-8681		671
Lebanese Taverna 2478 Solomons Island Rd Annapolis Harbour Ctr .... Annapolis MD 21401 *Web:* www.lebanesetaverna.com	410-897-1111		671
Lebanon 866 UN Plaza Rm 531-533 .... New York NY 10017	212-355-5460	838-2819	784
Consulate General 9 E 76th St .... New York NY 10021 *Web:* nylebcons.org	212-744-7905		257
Embassy 2560 28th St NW .... Washington DC 20008 *TF:* 800-845-8968 ■ *Web:* www.lebanonembassyus.org	202-939-6300	939-6324	257
Lebanon Area Chamber of Commerce 186 N Adams St .... Lebanon MO 65536 *TF:* 888-588-5710 ■ *Web:* www.lebanonmissouri.com	417-588-3256	588-3251	139
Lebanon Correctional Institution 3791 State Rt 63 PO Box 56 .... Lebanon OH 45036 *Web:* drc.ohio.gov/leci	513-932-1211	932-1320	213
Lebanon County 400 S Eigth St Rm 206 Municipal Bldg .... Lebanon PA 17042 *Web:* www.lebcounty.org	717-228-4444		338
Lebanon Daily News 718 Poplar St .... Lebanon PA 17042 *TF:* 800-457-5929 ■ *Web:* www.ldnews.com	717-272-5611	274-1608	532-2

Phone | Fax | Class

Lebanon High School 700 Holbrook Ave . . . . Lebanon OH 45036 513-934-5770 932-5906 685
Web: www.lebanonschools.org

Lebanon National Cemetery 20 Hwy 208. . . . . Lebanon KY 40033 270-692-3390 692-0018 136
Web: www.cem.va.gov

Lebanon Public Library 101 S Broadway. . . . . Lebanon OH 45036 513-932-2665 434-3
TF: 800-788-3600 ■ *Web:* www.lebanonlibrary.org

Lebanon Publishing Company Inc
402 N Cumberland St. . . . . Lebanon TN 37087 615-444-3952 532-3
Web: www.lebanondemocrat.com

Lebanon Seaboard Corp
1600 E Cumberland St . . . . Lebanon PA 17042 717-273-1685 280
TF: 800-233-0628 ■ *Web:* www.lebsea.com

Lebanon Valley Brethren Home
1200 Grubb Rd. . . . . Palmyra PA 17078 717-838-5406 672
Web: www.lvbh.org

Lebanon Valley Chamber of Commerce
604 Cumberland St. . . . . Lebanon PA 17042 717-273-3727 273-7940 139
Web: www.lvchamber.org

Lebanon Valley College
101 N College Ave . . . . Annville PA 17003 717-867-6181 867-6026* 166
**Fax:* Admissions ■ *TF:* 866-582-4236 ■ *Web:* www.lvc.edu

Lebanon-Wilson County Chamber of Commerce
149 Public Sq. . . . . Lebanon TN 37087 615-444-5503 443-0596 139
Web: www.lebanonwilsontnchamber.org

Lebanon-Wilson County Public Library
108 S Hatton Ave . . . . Lebanon TN 37087 615-444-0632 434-3
Web: www2.youseemore.com/lebanon-wilson/default.asp

LeBeouf Brothers Towing LLC
124 Dry Dock Rd . . . . Bourg LA 70343 985-594-6691 594-5253 465
Web: www.lebeouftowing.com

Lebhar-Friedman Inc 425 Pk Ave. . . . . New York NY 10022 212-756-5000 637-9

Leblon 106 S Holden Rd . . . . Greensboro NC 27407 336-294-2605 671
Web: leblonsteakhouse.com

Lebon Press Inc 73 Homestead Ave Ste . . . . Hartford CT 06112 860-278-6355 627
TF: 800-249-4066 ■ *Web:* www.lebonpress.com

Lebowitz Gould Design Inc
150 W 30th St 1202 . . . . New York NY 10001 212-695-5700 344
TF: 800-420-2337 ■ *Web:* lgd-inc.com

Lebus International Inc
215 Industrial Dr. . . . . Longview TX 75602 903-758-5521 757-7782 198
Web: www.lebus-intl.com

LEC (Lincoln Electric Co-op Inc)
500 Osloski Rd PO Box 628 . . . . Eureka MT 59917 406-889-3301 889-3874 245
TF: 800-442-2994 ■ *Web:* www.lincolnelectric.coop

LeCesse Development Corp
650 S Northlake Blvd Ste 450. . . . . Altamonte Springs FL 32701 407-645-5575 645-0553 653
Web: www.lecesse.com

LeChase Construction Services LLC
300 Trolley Blvd . . . . Rochester NY 14606 585-254-3510 186
Web: www.lechase.com

Lechler Inc 445 Kautz Rd. . . . . Saint Charles IL 60174 630-377-6611 444-7069* 487
**Fax Area Code:* 800 ■ *TF Cust Svc:* 800-777-2926 ■ *Web:* www.lechlerusa.com

Lechner Realty Group Inc
13421 Manchester Rd. . . . . Saint Louis MO 63131 314-909-8100 909-8105 652
Web: www.lechnerrealty.com

Leco Corp 3000 Lakeview Ave . . . . Saint Joseph MI 49085 269-985-5496 982-8977* 419
**Fax:* Sales ■ *TF:* 800-292-6141 ■ *Web:* www.leco.com

Leconte Wealth Management LLC
703 William Blount Dr . . . . Maryville TN 37801 865-379-8200 401
TF: 888-236-6630 ■ *Web:* lecontewealth.com

Lecoq Cuisine Corp 35 Union Ave . . . . Bridgeport CT 06607 203-334-1010 334-1800 297-11
Web: www.lecoqcuisine.com

LeCroy Corp
700 Chestnut Ridge Rd. . . . . Chestnut Ridge NY 10977 845-425-2000 425-8967 248
NASDAQ: LCRY ■ *TF:* 800-553-2769 ■ *Web:* teledynelecroy.com

Lectra USA Inc
889 Franklin Rd SE Bldg 100 . . . . Marietta GA 30067 770-422-8050 180
Web: www.lectra.com

Lectronix Inc 5858 Enterprise Dr. . . . . Lansing MI 48911 517-492-1900 494
Web: www.lectronix.biz

Lectrosonics Inc PO Box 15900. . . . . Rio Rancho NM 87174 505-892-4501 892-6243 52
TF: 800-821-1121 ■ *Web:* www.lectrosonics.com

LED Medical Diagnostics Inc
2 Ravinia Dr Unit 900 . . . . Atlanta GA 30346 604-434-4614 582
Web: www.leddental.com

LED Supply Co
747 Sheridan Blvd Unit 8E . . . . Lakewood CO 80214 877-595-4769 196
TF: 877-595-4769 ■ *Web:* ledsupplyco.com

Leda Corp 7080 Kearny Dr . . . . Huntington Beach CA 92648 714-841-7821 842-3683 625
Web: www.ledacorp.net

Ledalite Architectural Products
19750-92A Ave. . . . . Langley BC V1M3B2 604-888-6811 888-2003 439
TF: 800-665-5332 ■ *Web:* www.ledalite.com

Ledding Library 10660 SE 21st Ave . . . . Milwaukie OR 97222 503-786-7580 659-9497 434-3
TF: 800-701-8560 ■ *Web:* www.milwaukieoregon.gov

LEDdynamics Inc 44 Hull St. . . . . Randolph VT 05060 802-728-4533 362
Web: www.leddynamics.com

Lederle Machine Co 830 Jefferson St . . . . Pacific MO 63069 636-271-7200 514
Web: www.lederle.com

Ledge Light Technologies Inc
88D Howard St Ste D . . . . New London CT 06320 860-444-0138 444-0274 180
Web: www.ledgelight.com

Ledger Systems Inc 865 Laurel St . . . . San Carlos CA 94070 650-592-6211 175
Web: www.ledgersys.com

Ledger, The 300 W Lime St . . . . Lakeland FL 33815 863-802-7000 802-7809 532-2
TF: 888-431-7323 ■ *Web:* www.theledger.com

Ledges State Park 1515 P Ave. . . . . Madrid IA 50156 515-432-1852 565
Web: www.iowadnr.gov

LEDO Pizza System Inc
2001 Tidewater Colony Dr . . . . Annapolis MD 21401 410-721-6887 670

Ledoux & Company Inc 359 Alfred Ave . . . . Teaneck NJ 07666 201-837-7160 837-1235 743
Web: ledouxandcompany.com

Ledtronics Inc 23105 Kashiwa Ct . . . . Torrance CA 90505 310-534-1505 534-1424 437
TF: 800-579-4875 ■ *Web:* www.led.net

Leduc & Dexter Inc
2833A Dowd Dr PO Box 11157 . . . . Santa Rosa CA 95406 707-575-1500 610
Web: www.leducanddexterplumbing.com

Phone | Fax | Class

Ledwell & Son Enterprises
3300 Waco St . . . . Texarkana TX 75501 903-838-6531 831-2719* 779
**Fax:* Sales ■ *TF:* 888-533-9355 ■ *Web:* www.ledwell.com

Ledyard National Bank 320 Main St . . . . Norwich VT 05055 802-649-2050 649-2060 70
Web: www.ledyardbank.com

Lee & Assoc Commercial Real Estate Services Inc
13181 Crossroads Pkwy N Ste 300 . . . . City Of Industry CA 91746 562-699-7500 652
Web: www.lee-associates.com

Lee & Cates Glass Inc
5355 Shawland Rd . . . . Jacksonville FL 32254 904-358-8555 189-6
TF: 888-844-1989 ■ *Web:* www.leeandcatesglass.com

Lee & Hayes PLLC
601 W Riverside Ave Ste 1400 . . . . Spokane WA 99201 509-324-9256 428
Web: www.leehayes.com

Lee & Low Books Inc
95 Madison Ave Ste 1205. New York NY 10016 212-779-4400 95
Web: www.leeandlow.com

Lee Air Company Inc
7545 Wheatland Ave. . . . . Sun Valley CA 91352 818-767-0777 57
Web: www.leeairinc.com

Lee Arrendale State Prison
2023 Gainesville Hwy . . . . Alto GA 30510 706-776-4700 213
Web: dcor.state.ga.us

Lee Barbara (Rep D - CA)
2267 Rayburn Bldg. . . . . Washington DC 20515 202-225-2661 225-9817 342-2
Web: lee.house.gov

Lee Brass Co 1800 Golden Springs Rd . . . . Anniston AL 36207 800-876-1811 876-1800 308
TF General: 800-876-1811 ■ *Web:* www.leebrass.com

Lee Brick & Tile Co
3704 Hawkins Ave PO Box 1027 . . . . Sanford NC 27330 919-774-4800 774-7557 150
TF: 800-672-7559 ■ *Web:* www.leebrickonline.com

Lee Bros Foodservice Inc
660 E Gish Rd. . . . . San Jose CA 95112 408-275-0700 299
Web: www.leebros.com

Lee Burkhart Liu Inc
13335 Maxella Ave . . . . Marina del Rey CA 90292 310-829-2249 261

Lee Co 2 Pellitaug Rd PO Box 424 . . . . Westbrook CT 06498 860-399-6281 399-7058* 789
**Fax:* Sales ■ *TF:* 800-533-7584 ■ *Web:* www.theleeco.com

Lee Co Inc 331 Mallory Stn Rd. . . . . Franklin TN 37067 615-567-1000 189-10
TF: 800-600-5050 ■ *Web:* www.leecompany.com

Lee College 200 Lee Dr . . . . Baytown TX 77520 281-427-5611 425-6555 162
TF: 800-515-5419 ■ *Web:* www.lee.edu

Lee Company Inc 27 S 12th St . . . . Terre Haute IN 47807 812-235-8155 235-3587 320
Web: leecompanyinc.com

Lee Construction Co PO Box 7667 . . . . Charlotte NC 28241 704-588-5272 588-1535 188-4
Web: www.leecarolinas.com

Lee Correctional Institution
990 Wisacky Hwy . . . . Bishopville SC 29010 803-428-2800 896-1766 213

Lee County PO Box G. . . . . Beattyville KY 41311 606-464-4100 464-4145 338
Web: www.leecounty.ky.gov

Lee County 112 E Second St PO Box 329 . . . . Dixon IL 61021 815-288-3309 288-6492 338
Web: leecountyil.com

Lee County 933 Ave H . . . . Fort Madison IA 52627 319-372-6557 372-0200 338
Web: www.leecounty.org

Lee County PO Box 398 . . . . Fort Myers FL 33902 239-533-2236 338
Web: www.leegov.com

Lee County PO Box 419 . . . . Giddings TX 78942 979-542-3684 542-2623 338
Web: www.co.lee.tx.us

Lee County 110 Starksville Ave N. . . . . Leesburg GA 31763 229-759-6000 338
TF: 800-432-9630 ■ *Web:* www.lee.ga.us

Lee County 15 E Chestnut St . . . . Marianna AR 72360 870-295-7715 338
TF: 800-438-8683 ■ *Web:* lee.ark.org

Lee County 7992 Villanow Dr. . . . . Sanford NC 27332 919-718-4605 338
Web: www.leecountync.gov

Lee County 510 N Commerce St . . . . Tupelo MS 38804 662-841-9040 338
Web: www.leecosheriff.com

Lee County Library
2050 Central Ave . . . . Fort Myers FL 33901 239-479-4636 434-3
TF: 800-854-8195 ■ *Web:* www.leegov.com/library

Lee County Visitors & Convention Bureau
2201 Second St Ste 600. . . . . Fort Myers FL 33901 239-338-3500 334-1106 206
TF: 800-237-6444 ■ *Web:* www.fortmyers-sanibel.com

Lee Dan Communications Inc
155 Adams Ave. . . . . Hauppauge NY 11788 631-231-1414 231-1498 392
TF: 800-231-1414 ■ *Web:* www.leedan.com

Lee Davis Library 8060 Spencer Hwy . . . . Pasadena TX 77505 281-476-1850 434-3
Web: www.sanjac.edu

Lee Enterprises Inc
201 N Harrison St Ste 600 . . . . Davenport IA 52801 563-383-2100 637-8
NYSE: LEE ■ *Web:* www.lee.net

Lee Hecht Harrison LLC
50 Tice Blvd . . . . Woodcliff Lake NJ 07677 800-611-4544 193
TF: 800-611-4544 ■ *Web:* www.lhh.com

Lee Industries Inc 50 W Pine St. . . . . Philipsburg PA 16866 814-342-0461 342-5660 386
Web: www.leeind.com

Lee Jeans 9001 W 67th St . . . . Merriam KS 66202 913-384-4000 155-11
TF Cust Svc: 800-453-3348 ■ *Web:* www.lee.com

Lee Kennedy Company Inc
122 Quincy Shore Dr . . . . Quincy MA 02171 617-825-6930 186
Web: www.leekennedy.com

Lee Kum Kee Inc
14841 Don Julian Rd . . . . City of Industry CA 91746 626-709-1888 296-19
TF Orders: 800-654-5082 ■ *Web:* lkk.com

Lee Lewis Construction Inc
7810 Orlando Ave. . . . . Lubbock TX 79423 806-797-8400 797-8492 186
TF: 800-561-3357 ■ *Web:* www.leelewis.com

Lee Michaels Fine Jewelers Inc
7560 Corporate Blvd. . . . . Baton Rouge LA 70809 225-926-4644 926-9600 410
Web: lmfj.com

Lee Michaels Jewelers Inc
7560 Corporate Blvd. . . . . Baton Rouge LA 70809 225-926-4644 410
Web: www.lmfj.com

Lee Mike (Sen R - UT)
361A Russell Senate Office Bldg. . . . . Washington DC 20510 202-224-5444 228-1168 342-2
Web: www.lee.senate.gov

Lee Myles Auto Group 914 Fern Ave . . . . Reading PA 19607 800-533-6953 62-6
TF: 800-533-6953 ■ *Web:* www.leemyles.com

Name / Address	City	State	Zip	Phone	Fax	Class
Lee Oil Company Inc 1655 Bypass 35 *Web:* www.leeoilalvin.com	Alvin	TX	77511	281-331-3445		581
Lee Pharmaceuticals Inc 1434 Santa Anita Ave *OTC: LPHM*	South El Monte	CA	91733	626-442-3141	442-6994	214
Lee Printing Company Inc 3904 Leeland St *TF:* 800-329-6455 ■ *Web:* www.leeprintingco.com	Houston	TX	77003	713-227-5566		627
Lee Products Co 800 E 80th St *TF:* 800-989-3544 ■ *Web:* www.leeproducts.com	Bloomington	MN	55420	952-854-3544	854-7177	534
Lee Publications Inc 6113 State Hwy 5 *TF:* 800-836-2888 ■ *Web:* www.leepub.com	Palatine Bridge	NY	13428	518-673-3237	673-3245	637-8
Lee Richardson Zoo 312 E Finnup Dr *Web:* leerichardsonzoo.org	Garden City	KS	67846	620-276-1250	276-1259	823
Lee Silsby Compounding Pharmacy 3216 Silsby Rd *TF:* 800-918-8831 ■ *Web:* www.leesilsby.com	Cleveland Heights	OH	44118	216-321-4300		237
Lee Spring Company Inc 140 58th St Unit 3C *TF:* 800-110-2500 ■ *Web:* www.leespring.com	Brooklyn	NY	11220	718-236-2222	236-3919	719
Lee State Natural Area 487 Loop Rd *Web:* www.southcarolinaparks.com	Bishopville	SC	29010	803-428-5307		565
Lee State Prison 153 Pinewood Rd *Web:* dcor.state.ga.us	Leesburg	GA	31763	229-759-6453	759-3065	213
Lee Steel Corp 45525 Grand River Ave *Web:* www.leesteelcorp.com	Novi	MI	48374	313-925-2100		492
Lee Strasberg Theatre Institute, The 7936 Santa Monica Blvd *Web:* www.strasberg.com	West Hollywood	CA	90046	323-650-7777		166
Lee Supply Corp 6610 Guion Rd *TF:* 800-873-1103 ■ *Web:* leesupplycorp.com	Indianapolis	IN	46268	317-290-2500	290-2512	612
Lee University 1120 N Ocoee St **Fax:* Admissions ■ *TF:* 800-533-9930 ■ *Web:* www.leeuniversity.edu	Cleveland	TN	37311	423-614-8000	614-8533*	166
Lee's Cyclery 202 W Laurel St *Web:* www.leescyclery.com	Fort Collins	CO	80521	970-482-6006		711
Lee's Marketplace Inc 555 East 1400 North *Web:* www.leesmarketplace.com	Logan	UT	84341	435-755-5100		297-8
Lee's Morvillo Group 160 Niantic Ave *TF:* 800-821-1700 ■ *Web:* www.leesmfg.com	Providence	RI	02907	401-353-1740		407
Lee's Ready-Mix & Trucking Inc 1100 W John F Kennedy Dr	North Vernon	IN	47265	812-346-9767		135
Lee's Summit Chamber of Commerce 220 SE Main St *TF:* 888-816-5757 ■ *Web:* lschamber.com	Lees Summit	MO	64063	816-524-2424	524-5246	139
Leebaw Mfg Company Inc PO Box 553 *TF:* 800-841-8083 ■ *Web:* www.leebaw.com	Canfield	OH	44406	800-841-8083		470
Leeber Limited USA 115 Pencader Dr *Web:* www.leeber.com	Newark	DE	19702	302-733-0991		411
Leech Lake Area Chamber of Commerce 205 Minnesota Ave E *TF:* 800-833-1118 ■ *Web:* www.leech-lake.com	Walker	MN	56484	218-547-1313	547-1338	139
Leech Tishman Fuscaldo & Lampl LLC 525 William Penn Pl 28th Fl *Web:* www.leechtishman.com	Pittsburgh	PA	15219	412-261-1600		445
Leech Tool & Die Works Inc 13144 Dickson Rd *TF:* 800-523-5474 ■ *Web:* www.leechind.com	Meadville	PA	16335	814-336-2141	337-0354	757
Leeches USA Ltd 300 Shames Dr *TF:* 800-645-3569 ■ *Web:* www.leechesusa.com	Westbury	NY	11590	516-333-2570	997-4948	475
Leeco Steel LLC 1011 Warrenville Rd Ste 500 *TF:* 800-621-4366 ■ *Web:* www.leecosteel.com	Lisle	IL	60532	630-427-2100		791
Leed - Himmel Industries Inc 75 Leeder Hill Dr *Web:* www.leed-himmel.com	Hamden	CT	06517	203-287-6662		362
Leed Selling Tools Corp 9700 Hwy 57 *TF:* 855-687-5333 ■ *Web:* leedsamples.com	Evansville	IN	47725	812-867-4340		86
LEED Tool Corp PO Box 329 1352 Factory Dr *Web:* www.ces-wellsrvs.com	Fort Lupton	CO	80621	303-857-0876		538
Leedom & Associates LLC 3700 S Tamiami Trl *Web:* www.twentygroups.com	Sarasota	FL	34239	941-371-7999		463
Leeds Consulting Group Llc 1381 Bellewood Ln *Web:* www.leedscg.com	Freeland	WA	98249	360-331-5745		196
Leedy & Petzold Assoc LLC 12970 W Bluemound Rd	Elm Grove	WI	53122	262-860-1544		261
Leedy Manufacturing Co 210 Hall St SW *Web:* www.leedymfg.com	Grand Rapids	MI	49507	616-245-0517	245-3888	709
Lee-Fendall House Museum 614 Oronoco St *TF:* 800-388-9119 ■ *Web:* www.leefendallhouse.org	Alexandria	VA	22314	703-548-1789		520
Leehar Distributors Inc 701 Emerson Rd Ste 301 *TF:* 800-652-9550 ■ *Web:* www.ldirx.com	Creve Coeur	MO	63141	314-652-3121		194
Leelanau County 8527 E Government Ctr Dr *TF:* 866-256-9711 ■ *Web:* www.leelanau.cc	Suttons Bay	MI	49682	231-256-9824	256-0174	338
Leelanau Fruit Co 2900 SW Bay Shore Dr *TF:* 800-431-0718 ■ *Web:* www.leelanaufruit.com	Suttons Bay	MI	49682	231-271-3514	271-4367	296-21
Leelanau School 1 Old Homestead Rd *Web:* www.leelanau.org	Glen Arbor	MI	49636	231-334-5800	334-5898	622
Leelanau State Park 15310 N Lighthouse Pt Rd *Web:* www.michigandnr.com	Northport	MI	49670	231-386-5422		565
LeeMAH Electronics Inc 155 S Hill Dr *Web:* www.leemah.com	Brisbane	CA	94005	415-394-1288	433-2560	253
Leer LP 206 Leer St *TF Cust Svc:* 800-766-5337 ■ *Web:* www.leerinc.com	New Lisbon	WI	53950	608-562-7100	562-6022	664
Leerink Swann & Co 1 Federal St 37th Fl *TF:* 800-808-7525 ■ *Web:* www.leerink.com	Boston	MA	02110	800-808-7525		401
Leesburg Animal Park 19270 James Monroe Hwy *Web:* www.leesburganimalpark.com	Leesburg	VA	20175	703-433-0002		31
Leesburg Health & Rehabiltation LLC 715 E Dixie Ave	Leesburg	FL	34748	352-728-3020		450
Leesburg Public Library 100 E Main St *Web:* www.leesburgflorida.gov	Leesburg	FL	34748	352-728-9790	728-9794	434-3
Lees-McRae College 191 Main St W *TF:* 800-280-4562 ■ *Web:* www.lmc.edu	Banner Elk	NC	28604	828-898-5241		166
Leeson Canada Inc 320 Superior Blvd *TF:* 800-563-0949 ■ *Web:* www.leeson.ca	Mississauga	ON	L5T2N7	905-670-4770		111
Leeson Electric Corp 2100 Washington St *Web:* www.leeson.com	Grafton	WI	53024	262-377-8810		518
Leesta Industries Ltd 6 Plateau *Web:* www.leesta.com	Pointe-Claire	QC	H9R5W2	514-694-3930		21
Leesylvania State Park 2001 Daniel K Ludwig Dr	Woodbridge	VA	22191	703-730-8205		565
Leete Kosto & Wizner LLC 999 Asylum Ave Ste 202 *Web:* lkwvisa.com	Hartford	CT	06105	860-249-8100		428
Leevac Shipyards Inc 111 Bunge St	Jennings	LA	70546	337-824-2210	824-2970	698
Leevers Foods 501 Main St *Web:* www.leeversfoods.com	Cavalier	ND	58220	701-265-4011		345
Leevers Supermarkets Inc 2195 N Hwy 83 Unit AA *Web:* www.leevers.com	Franktown	CO	80116	303-814-8646		345
Leeward Community College 96-045 Ala Ike **Fax:* Admissions ■ *TF:* 888-442-4551 ■ *Web:* www.leeward.hawaii.edu	Pearl City	HI	96782	808-455-0011	454-8804*	162
Leewens Corp 630 Seventh Ave PO Box 2549 *Web:* www.leewens.com	Kirkland	WA	98033	425-827-7667		291
Lefere Forge & Machine Co 665 Hupp Ave *Web:* www.lefereforge.com	Jackson	MI	49203	517-784-7109	784-0929	483
Leff Electric 4700 Spring Rd *TF:* 800-686-5333 ■ *Web:* www.leffelectric.com	Cleveland	OH	44131	216-432-3000	432-0051	246
Leffler Accountancy Corp 16030 Ventura Blvd Ste 490	Encino	CA	91436	818-501-1181		2
Leffler Energy Inc 15 Mt Joy St *TF:* 800-984-1411 ■ *Web:* www.lefflerenergy.com	Mount Joy	PA	17552	800-984-1411		579
LeFiell Manufacturing Co 13700 Firestone Blvd *TF:* 800-451-5971 ■ *Web:* www.lefiell.com	Santa Fe Springs	CA	90670	562-921-3411		490
Lefler Engineering Inc 1651 Second St *Web:* leflerengineering.com	San Rafael	CA	94901	415-456-4220		261
LeFleur's Bluff State Park 2140 Riverside Dr *TF:* 800-237-6278 ■ *Web:* www.mdwfp.com	Jackson	MS	39202	601-987-3923		565
LeFlore County 100 S Broadway PO Box 100 *Web:* leflore.okcountytreasurers.com	Poteau	OK	74953	918-647-3525	647-7122	338
Leflore County PO Box 848 *Web:* www.greenwoodms.com	Greenwood	MS	38935	662-453-4152		338
Leflore County School District 1901 Hwy 82 W *Web:* www.lefcsd.org	Greenwood	MS	38930	662-453-8566		685
Left Bank 511 Rhode Island St *Web:* www.leftbankrestaurant.com	Buffalo	NY	14213	716-882-3509		671
Left Bank 377 Santana Row *Web:* www.leftbank.com	San Jose	CA	95128	408-984-3500	984-0300	671
Left Bank Books 399 N Euclid Ave *Web:* www.left-bank.com	Saint Louis	MO	63108	314-367-6731	367-3256	95
Left Bank Wine Co 4910 Triangle St *TF:* 800-905-6660 ■ *Web:* www.leftbankwine.com	Mc Farland	WI	53558	608-838-8400		443
Legacy Bank 1580 E Cheyenne Mtn Blvd *TF:* 866-627-0800 ■ *Web:* www.elegacybank.com	Colorado Springs	CO	80906	719-579-9150		70
Legacy Benefits Corp 350 Fifth Ave Ste 4320 *TF:* 800-875-1000 ■ *Web:* www.legacybenefits.com	New York	NY	10118	800-875-1000		796
Legacy Capital LLC 433 Metairie Rd Ste 405 *Web:* legacycapital.com	Metairie	LA	70005	504-837-3450		194
Legacy Classic Furniture Inc 2575 Penny Rd *Web:* www.legacyclassic.com	High Point	NC	27265	336-449-4600		321
Legacy Electronics Inc 1220 N Dakota St PO Box 348 *TF:* 888-466-3853 ■ *Web:* www.legacyelectronics.com	Canton	SD	57013	949-498-9600		174
Legacy Emanuel Hospital & Health Ctr 2801 N Gantenbein Ave *TF:* 888-598-4232 ■ *Web:* www.legacyhealth.org	Portland	OR	97227	503-413-2200	413-2428	374-3
Legacy Engineering LLC 18662 Macarthur Blvd Ste 457 *Web:* www.legacyeng.com	Irvine	CA	92612	949-794-5860		631
Legacy Golf Resort 6808 S 32nd St *TF:* 866-729-7182 ■ *Web:* www.shellhospitality.com	Phoenix	AZ	85042	602-305-5500		669
Legacy Good Samaritan Hospital 1015 NW 22nd Ave *TF:* 800-733-9959 ■ *Web:* www.legacyhealth.org	Portland	OR	97210	503-335-3500	413-6919	374-3
Legacy grain Coop 402 Walnut St PO Box 350 *Web:* www.legacygrain.com	Stonington	IL	62567	217-325-3211		10-5
Legacy Investments Inc 5910 N Central Expy	Dallas	TX	75206	214-750-1522		360-3
Legacy Meridian Park Hospital 19300 SW 65th Ave *TF:* 800-944-4773 ■ *Web:* www.legacyhealth.org	Tualatin	OR	97062	503-692-1212		374-3
Legacy Partners 1610 16th Ave S *Web:* www.legacy-fp.com	Nashville	TN	37212	615-292-5351		194

Name / Address	City	State	ZIP	Phone	Fax	Class
Legacy Partners Inc						
4000 E Third Ave Ste 600	Foster City	CA	94404	650-571-2250		390
Web: www.legacypartners.com						
Legacy Pharmaceutical Packaging LLC						
13333 Lakefront Dr	St. Louis	MO	63045	314-813-1555		583
Web: legacypackaging.com						
Legacy Property Group LLC						
300 Marietta St NW Ste 304	Atlanta	GA	30313	404-222-9100	222-9090	653
Web: www.legacyproperty.com						
Legacy Salmon Creek Hospital						
2211 NE 139th St	Vancouver	WA	98686	360-487-1000	487-3459	374-3
TF: 877-270-5566 ■ *Web:* www.legacyhealth.org						
Legacy Venture 180 Lytton Ave	Palo Alto	CA	94301	650-324-5980	324-5982	792
Web: www.legacyventure.com						
Legal & General America Inc						
1701 Research Blvd	Rockville	MD	20850	301-279-4800	294-6960*	360-4
**Fax:* Cust Svc ■ *TF:* 800-638-8428 ■ *Web:* www.lgamerica.com						
Legal Aid 126 W Adams St Fl 7	Jacksonville	FL	32202	904-356-8371		428
TF: 866-356-8371 ■ *Web:* www.jaxlegalaid.org						
Legal Aid Bureau Inc						
500 E Lexington St	Baltimore	MD	21202	410-951-7777		428
TF: 800-396-1274 ■ *Web:* www.mdlab.org						
Legal Aid Foundation of Los Angeles						
1550 W Eighth St	Los Angeles	CA	90017	323-801-7991	801-7945	428
Web: www.lafla.org						
Legal Aid of West Virginia Inc						
327 Ninth St	Parkersburg	WV	26101	304-485-7522		445
Web: www.wvlegalservices.org						
Legal Aid Society of Palm Beach County Inc						
423 Fern St Ste 200	West Palm Beach	FL	33401	561-655-8944		428
TF: 800-403-9353 ■ *Web:* www.legalaidpbc.org						
Legal Aid Society of San Mateo County, The						
330 Twin Dolphin Dr Ste 123	Redwood City	CA	94065	650-558-0915		428
Web: www.legalaidsmc.org						
Legal Club of America Corp						
7771 W Oakland Park Blvd Ste 217	Sunrise	FL	33351	954-377-0222		463
TF: 800-316-5387 ■ *Web:* www.legalclub.com						
Legal Cost Control Inc						
255 Kings Hwy E Ste 3	Haddonfield	NJ	08033	856-216-0800		445
TF: 800-774-5516 ■ *Web:* legalcost.com						
Legal Counsel for the Elderly						
601 E St NW	Washington	DC	20049	202-434-2170	434-6464	48-8
Web: www.aarp.org						
Legal Data Resources Inc						
2816 W Summerdale Ave	Chicago	IL	60625	773-561-2468		635
TF: 844-732-2437 ■ *Web:* www.ldrsearch.com						
Legal Interpreting Services Inc						
26 Court St Ste 1005	Brooklyn	NY	11242	718-237-8919		768
Web: www.lis-translations.com						
Legal Management: Journal of the Assn of Legal Administrators (ALA)						
75 Tri State International Ste 222	Lincolnshire	IL	60069	847-267-1252	267-1329	457-15
Web: www.alanet.org						
Legal Resources Inc						
2877 Guardian Ln Ste 101	Virginia Beach	VA	23452	757-498-1220	498-4114	260
TF: 800-728-5768 ■ *Web:* www.legalresources.com						
Legal Sea Foods						
2301 Jefferson Davis Hwy	Arlington	VA	22202	703-415-1200		671
Web: www.legalseafoods.com						
Legal Sea Foods 26 Pk Plaza	Boston	MA	02116	617-426-4444		671
Web: www.legalseafoods.com						
Legal Sea Foods Inc 1 Seafood Way	Boston	MA	02210	617-530-9000		670
Web: www.legalseafoods.com						
Legal Search 510 E 85th St Apt 9f	New York	NY	10028	212-472-3000		260
TF: 800-272-4615 ■ *Web:* www.legalsearchusa.com						
Legal Services Corp						
3333 K St NW 3rd Fl	Washington	DC	20007	202-295-1500	337-6797	340-20
Web: www.lsc.gov						
LegalEase Inc						
205 East 42nd St 20th Fl	New York	NY	10017	212-393-9070	580-4761*	635
**Fax Area Code:* 888 ■ *TF:* 800-393-1277 ■ *Web:* www.legaleaseinc.com						
Legend Data Systems Inc 18024 72nd Ave S	Kent	WA	98032	425-251-1670		45
TF: 866-371-1670 ■ *Web:* www.legendid.com						
Legend Energy Services LLC						
5801 Broadway Extn Ste 210	Oklahoma City	OK	73118	405-600-1264	608-8851	536
Web: www.legendenergyservices.com						
Legend Financial Advisors Inc						
5700 Corporate Dr Ste 350	Pittsburgh	PA	15237	412-635-9210		401
Web: www.legend-financial.com						
Legend Group Inc, The						
4600 E Park Dr Ste 300	Palm Beach Gardens	FL	33410	561-694-0110		194
Web: www.legendgroup.com						
Legend Homes Corp						
29256 SW Costa Cir E	Wilsonville	OR	97070	503-620-8080		653
Web: www.legendhomes.com						
Legend Power Systems Inc						
1480 Frances St	Vancouver	BC	V5L1Y9	604-420-1500	420-1533	767
TF: 866-772-8797 ■ *Web:* legendpower.com						
Legend Seeds Inc PO Box 241	De Smet	SD	57231	605-854-3346	854-3135	276
TF: 800-678-3346 ■ *Web:* www.legendseeds.net						
Legendary Marketing						
3729 S Lecanto Hwy	Lecanto	FL	34461	352-527-3553		195
TF: 800-827-1663 ■ *Web:* www.legendarymarketing.com						
Legendary Palace 708 Franklin St	Oakland	CA	94607	510-663-9188		671
Legendary Whitetails						
820 Enterprise Dr	Slinger	WI	53086	800-875-9453		361
TF: 800-875-9453 ■ *Web:* www.deergear.com						
Legends Brewhouse & Eatery						
2840 Shawano Ave	Green Bay	WI	54313	920-662-1111		671
Web: legendseatery.com						
Legends Furniture Inc						
10300 W Buckeye Rd	Tolleson	AZ	85353	623-931-6500		321
Web: legendsfurniture.com						
Legends Theater 1600 W Hwy 76	Branson	MO	65616	417-339-3003		572
TF: 800-374-7469 ■ *Web:* www.legendsinconcert.com						
Leger, The Research Intelligence Group						
507 Pl d'Armes Ste 700	Montreal	QC	H2Y2W8	514-982-2464		466
TF: 800-404-2464 ■ *Web:* leger360.com						
Legere Group Ltd PO Box 1527	Avon	CT	06001	860-674-0392	674-0469	115
Web: www.legeregroup.com						
Legg Company Inc 325 E Tenth St	Halstead	KS	67056	800-835-1003	835-3218*	370
**Fax Area Code:* 316 ■ *TF Sales:* 800-835-1003 ■ *Web:* www.leggbelting.com						
Legg Mason Inc (LMI)						
100 International Dr	Baltimore	MD	21202	410-539-0000		690
NYSE: LM ■ *TF:* 800-822-5544 ■ *Web:* www.leggmason.com						
Legg Mason Real Estate Investors Inc						
350 S Beverly Dr Ste 300	Beverly Hills	CA	90212	310-234-2100	234-2150	509
Web: www.lmrei.com						
Leggett & Platt Inc						
Number 1 Leggett Rd PO Box 757	Carthage	MO	64836	417-358-8131	358-6996	719
NYSE: LEG ■ *TF:* 800-888-4569 ■ *Web:* www.leggett.com						
Legion Lighting Company Inc						
221 Glenmore Ave	Brooklyn	NY	11207	718-498-1770	498-0128	439
TF: 800-453-4466 ■ *Web:* www.legionlighting.com						
Legion of Honor Museum						
100 34th Ave	San Francisco	CA	94121	415-750-3600		520
Web: legionofhonor.famsf.org						
Legion of Valor Museum						
2425 Fresno St at O St	Fresno	CA	93721	559-498-0510		520
Web: legionofvalor.org/museum						
Legion State Park						
635 Legion State Pk Rd	Louisville	MS	39339	662-773-8323		565
Web: www.mdwfp.com						
LEGO Systems Inc 555 Taylor Rd	Enfield	CT	06082	860-763-6731		762
TF: 877-518-5346 ■ *Web:* www.lego.com						
LEGOLAND California 1 Legoland Dr	Carlsbad	CA	92008	760-438-5346		32
TF: 877-534-6526 ■ *Web:* www.legoland.com						
LeGrand Hart 1055 Auraria Pkwy Ste 200	Denver	CO	80204	303-298-8470	298-8570	636
Web: www.legrandhart.com						
Legrand Johnson Construction Co						
1000 S Main St	Logan	UT	84321	435-752-2001		182
Legum & Norman Mid-West LLC						
4401 Ford Ave 12th Fl 12th Fl	Alexandria	VA	22302	703-600-6000	848-0982	393
Lehan Drugs Inc 1407 S Fourth St	Dekalb	IL	60115	815-758-0911		237
Web: lehandrugs.com						
Lehigh Acres Chamber of Commerce						
25 Homestead Rd N	Lehigh Acres	FL	33936	239-369-3322	368-0500	139
TF: 800-934-6489 ■ *Web:* www.lehighacreschamber.org						
Lehigh Asphalt Paving & Construction Co Inc						
1314 E Broad St	Tamaqua	PA	18252	570-668-4303	668-5910	188-4
TF: 877-222-5514 ■ *Web:* www.glasgowinc.com/subsidiaries.aspx						
Lehigh Carbon Community College						
4525 Education Pk Dr	Schnecksville	PA	18078	610-799-2121	799-1527	162
TF General: 800-414-3975 ■ *Web:* www.lccc.edu						
Morgan Ctr 234 High St	Tamaqua	PA	18252	570-668-6880	668-7296	162
TF: 800-424-2460 ■ *Web:* www.lccc.edu						
Lehigh County						
455 W Hamilton St Rm 132	Allentown	PA	18101	610-782-3148		338
TF: 800-370-2836 ■ *Web:* www.lehighcounty.org						
Lehigh County Museum						
432 W Walnut St	Allentown	PA	18102	610-435-1074		520
TF: 800-732-0999 ■ *Web:* www.lchs.museum						
Lehigh Fluid Power Inc						
1413 Route 179	Lambertville	NJ	08530	800-257-9515		641
TF: 800-257-9515 ■ *Web:* www.lehighfluidpower.com						
Lehigh Gorge State Park						
c/o Hickory Run State Park Complex						
3613 State Rt 534	White Haven	PA	18661	570-443-0400		565
Web: www.dcnr.state.pa.us						
Lehigh Heavy Forge Corp						
275 Emery St	Bethlehem	PA	18015	610-332-8100	332-8101	483
Web: www.lhforge.com						
Lehigh Inland Cement Ltd						
12640 Inland Way	Edmonton	AB	T5V1K2	780-420-2500	420-2550	135
TF Orders: 800-252-9304 ■ *Web:* www.lehighhansoncanada.com						
Lehigh Valley Dairies Inc						
880 Allentown Rd	Lansdale	PA	19446	215-855-8205		296-27
Web: www.lehighvalleydairyfarms.com						
Lehigh Valley Health Network						
700 E Broad St	Hazleton	PA	18201	570-501-4000	501-6971	374-3
TF: 800-528-1234 ■ *Web:* lvhn.org/hazleton						
Lehigh Valley Hospice						
2166 S 12th St Ste 401	Allentown	PA	18103	610-969-0300	969-0326	371
TF: 888-584-2273 ■ *Web:* www.lvhn.org						
Lehigh Valley International Airport						
3311 Airport Rd	Allentown	PA	18109	610-266-6000		27
TF: 800-359-5842 ■ *Web:* www.flylvia.com						
Lehigh Valley Plastics Inc						
187 N Commerce Way	Bethlehem	PA	18017	484-893-5500	893-5511	604
TF: 800-354-5344 ■ *Web:* www.lehighvalleyplastics.com						
Lehigh Valley Technologies Inc						
514 N 12th St	Allentown	PA	18102	610-782-9780		583
Web: www.lvtechinc.com						
Lehigh Valley Visitor Ctr						
840 Hamilton St Ste 200	Allentown	PA	18101	610-882-9200		206
TF: 800-747-0561 ■ *Web:* www.discoverlehighvalley.com						
Lehman College 250 Bedford Pk Blvd W	Bronx	NY	10468	718-960-8000	960-8712*	166
**Fax:* Admissions ■ *TF:* 800-311-5656 ■ *Web:* www.lehman.cuny.edu						
Lehman Hardware & Appliances Inc						
4779 Kidron Rd	Dalton	OH	44618	888-438-5346		393
TF: 888-438-5346 ■ *Web:* www.lehmans.com						
Lehman Trikes Inc 125 Industrial Dr	Spearfish	SD	57783	605-642-2111	642-1184	517
CVE: LHT ■ *TF:* 888-394-3357 ■ *Web:* www.lehmantrikes.com						
Lehner Screw Machine Co						
71 S River Rd	Munroe Falls	OH	44262	330-688-6616		454
Web: lehnerscrewmachine.com						
Lehr Construction Company Inc						
2115 Frederick Ave	Saint Joseph	MO	64501	816-232-4431		186
TF: 800-248-4327 ■ *Web:* www.lehrconstruction.com						
Lehr Middlebrooks & Vreeland PC						
2021 Third Ave N	Birmingham	AL	35203	205-326-3002		428
TF: 800-900-4250 ■ *Web:* www.lehrmiddlebrooks.com						
Leica Camera AG 1 Pearl Ct	Allendale	NJ	07401	800-222-0118	995-1686*	544
**Fax Area Code:* 201 ■ *TF:* 800-222-0118 ■ *Web:* us.leica-camera.com						
Leica Geosystems Inc						
3498 Kraft Ave SE	Grand Rapids	MI	49512	616-977-4189	942-4627	425
TF Sales: 800-367-9453 ■ *Web:* www.leica-geosystems.com						

Company / Address	City	State	ZIP	Phone	Fax	Class
Leica Microsystems Inc						
1700 Leider Ln	Buffalo Grove	IL	60089	847-405-0123		743
Web: www.leica-microsystems.com/contact/service						
Leick Furniture Inc 2219 S 19th St	Sheboygan	WI	53081	920-451-4060		321
Leidenheimer Baking Co						
1501 Simon Bolivar Ave	New Orleans	LA	70113	504-525-1575	525-1596	296-1
TF: 800-259-9099 ■ *Web:* www.leidenheimer.com						
Leigh Baldwin & Company LLC						
1 Hopper St Ste 1	Utica	NY	13501	315-734-1410		690
TF: 800-659-8044 ■ *Web:* www.leighbaldwin.com						
Leigh Bureau Inc						
92 E Main St Ste 200	Somerville	NJ	08876	908-253-8600		317
Web: www.leighbureau.com						
Leigh Fibers Inc 1101 Syphrit Rd	Wellford	SC	29385	864-439-4111	439-4116	745-8
TF: 800-274-7707 ■ *Web:* www.leighfibers.com						
Leight Sales Company Inc						
1051 E Artesia Blvd	Carson	CA	90746	310-223-1000		351
Leighton Group Inc 17781 Cowan St	Irvine	CA	92614	949-250-1421	250-1114	261
Web: www.leightongroup.com						
Leila Arboretum Society						
928 W Michigan Ave	Battle Creek	MI	49037	269-969-0270		97
Web: www.leilaarboretumsociety.org						
Leiss Tool & Die Co						
801 N Pleasant Ave	Somerset	PA	15501	814-444-1444	445-3456	454
Web: www.leiss.com						
Leisure and Recreation Concepts Inc						
2151 Ft Worth Ave	Dallas	TX	75211	214-942-4474		195
Web: larcinc.com						
Leisure Chateau Care Center Inc						
962 River Ave	Lakewood	NJ	08701	732-370-8600		371
TF: 800-822-0246 ■ *Web:* leisurechateau.com						
Leisure Fitness Inc						
231 Executive Dr Ste 15	Newark	DE	19702	302-224-5061		711
Web: www.leisurefitness.com						
Leisure Hotels LLC						
Leisure Hotel Corp						
8725 Rosehill Rd Ste 300	Lenexa	KS	66215	913-905-1460		379
Web: www.leisurehotel.com						
Leisure Living Management Inc						
3196 Kraft Ave SE Ste 200	Grand Rapids	MI	49512	616-464-1564		371
Web: www.leisure-living.com						
Leisure Pro 42 W 18th St	New York	NY	10011	212-645-1234		711
TF: 800-637-6880 ■ *Web:* www.leisurepro.com						
Leisure Sports Inc						
4670 Willow Rd Ste 110	Pleasanton	CA	94588	925-600-1966	600-1144	379
TF: 888-239-0930 ■ *Web:* www.leisuresportsinc.com						
Leisure Systems Inc						
502 TechneCenter Dr Ste D	Milford	OH	45150	513-831-2100	576-8670	121
TF: 866-928-9644 ■ *Web:* www.jellystonefranchise.com						
Leisure World of Maryland						
3701 Rossmoor Blvd	Silver Spring	MD	20906	301-598-1000		652
Web: www.leisureworldmaryland.com						
Leisure World Pool & Hearth Inc						
406 E 16th Ave	Kansas City	MO	64116	816-221-1731		361
Web: www.leisureworldkc.com						
Leitner Williams Dooley & Napolitan PLLC						
801 Broad St Third Fl	Chattanooga	TN	37402	423-265-0214		445
Web: www.leitnerfirm.com						
Leitz Music Company Inc						
508 Harrison Ave	Panama City	FL	32401	850-769-0111		526
TF: 800-747-9980 ■ *Web:* www.leitzmusic.com						
LeJeune Steel Co 118 W 60th St	Minneapolis	MN	55419	612-861-3321	861-2724	480
TF: 800-798-4504 ■ *Web:* www.lejeunesteel.com						
LEK Consulting 28 State St 16th Fl	Boston	MA	02109	617-951-9500	951-9392	194
TF: 800-929-4535 ■ *Web:* www.lek.com						
Lek Technology Consultants Inc						
12788 Gillard Rd	Winter Garden	FL	34787	407-877-6505		180
TF: 888-800-5447 ■ *Web:* lekcomp.com						
Lek's Taste of Thailand						
5421 Atlanta Hwy	Montgomery	AL	36109	334-244-8994		671
LEKTRO Inc 1190 SE Flightline Dr	Warrenton	OR	97146	503-861-2288		57
TF: 800-535-8767 ■ *Web:* www.lektro.com						
Leland Management Inc						
8009 S Orange Ave	Orlando	FL	32809	407-447-9955		463
Web: www.lelandmanagement.com						
Leland Stanford Mansion State Historic Park						
800 N St	Sacramento	CA	95814	916-324-0575		565
Leland, The 400 Bagley St	Detroit	MI	48226	313-962-2300		379
Web: theleland.net						
Le-Le 1012 S Martin Luther King Jr Way	Tacoma	WA	98405	253-572-9491		671
Web: lelerestaurant.com						
Lellyett & Rogers Services Company LLC						
1717 Lebanon Pk	Nashville	TN	37210	615-316-0780		627
Web: www.landrco.com						
Lemaire 101 W Franklin St	Richmond	VA	23220	804-649-4629		671
TF: 800-424-8014 ■ *Web:* www.lemairerestaurant.com						
LeMaitre Vascular Inc						
63 Second AVE	Burlington	MA	01803	781-221-2266		476
Web: www.lemaitre.com						
Leman USA Inc						
1860 Renaissance Blvd	Sturtevant	WI	53177	262-884-4700	884-4690	311
Web: us.leman.com						
LeMar Industries Corp						
2070 NE 60th Ave	Des Moines	IA	50313	515-266-7264		492
Web: www.lemarindustries.com						
Lematic Inc 2410 W Main St	Jackson	MI	49203	517-787-3301		362
TF: 800-297-8666 ■ *Web:* www.lematic.com						
Lemco Mills Inc 766 Koury Dr	Burlington	NC	27215	336-226-5548		155-10
Lemco Tool Corp						
1850 Metzger Ave	Cogan Station	PA	17728	570-494-0620	494-0860	454
TF: 800-233-8713 ■ *Web:* www.lemco-tool.com						
LeMessurier Consultants						
1380 Soldiers Field Rd	Boston	MA	02135	617-868-1200		261
TF: 800-640-3200 ■ *Web:* www.lemessurier.com						
Lemhi County 206 Courthouse Dr	Salmon	ID	83467	208-756-2815	756-8424	338
TF: 800-983-0937 ■ *Web:* www.lemhicountyidaho.org						
Lemhi Ventures Inc						
315 East Lake St Ste 304	Wayzata	MN	55391	952-908-9680		760
Web: www.lemhiventures.com						

Company / Address	City	State	ZIP	Phone	Fax	Class
Lemieux Bedard Communications Inc						
2665 King W Ste 315	Sherbrooke	QC	J1L2G5	819-823-0850		224
TF: 800-544-8614 ■ *Web:* www.lemieuxbedard.com						
Lemko Corp 1 Pierce Pl Ste 700	Itasca	IL	60143	630-948-3025		177
Web: www.lemkocorp.com						
Lemna Corporation Inc						
2445 Park Ave	Minneapolis	MN	55404	612-253-2000		612
Web: www.lemnatechnologies.com						
Lemon Creek Correctional Ctr						
2000 Lemon Creek Rd	Juneau	AK	99801	907-465-6200		213
Web: www.correct.state.ak.us						
Lemon Grass 238 W Jefferson St	Syracuse	NY	13202	315-475-1111		671
TF: 800-572-1111 ■ *Web:* www.lemongrasscny.com						
Lemon Grass 601 Munroe St	Sacramento	CA	95825	916-486-4891		671
Web: www.starginger.com						
Lemon Grass 331 Elgin St	Ottawa	ON	K2P1M5	613-233-5000		671
Web: www.ottawalemongrass.com						
Lemon Grass Restaurant						
212 Fourth Ave W	Olympia	WA	98501	360-705-1832		671
Lemon Peak Marketing Services						
500 W Putnam Ave Ste 400	Greenwich	CT	06831	888-253-7348		5
TF: 888-253-7348 ■ *Web:* www.lemonpeak.com						
Lemongrass 641 N High St	Columbus	OH	43215	614-224-1414	221-2535	671
Web: www.lemongrassfusion.com						
Lemongrass 1705 NE Couch St	Portland	OR	97232	503-231-5780		671
Lemongrass Thai Cuisine						
106 N Main St	Downtown Greenville	SC	29601	864-241-9988		671
Web: www.lemongrassthai.net						
LemonStand eCommerce Inc						
2416 Main St	Vancouver	BC	V5T3E2	604-558-0555		224
TF: 855-332-0555 ■ *Web:* lemonstand.com						
Lemont High School 800 Porter St	Lemont	IL	60439	630-257-5838		685
Web: lhs210.net						
Lenape Forged Products Corp						
1334 Lenape Rd	West Chester	PA	19382	610-793-5090	793-3070	483
Web: www.lenapeforge.com						
Lenape Resources Inc						
9489 Alexander Rd	Alexander	NY	14005	585-344-1200	344-3283	536
Web: www.lenaperesources.com						
Lenawee County 301 N Main St FL 2	Adrian	MI	49221	517-264-4599	264-4790	338
Web: www.lenawee.mi.us						
Lenawee County Library 4459 W US 223	Adrian	MI	49221	517-263-1011		434-3
Web: www.lenawee.lib.mi.us						
Lenawee Economic Development Corp						
5285 W US Hwy 223	Adrian	MI	49221	517-265-5141		139
Web: www.lenaweenow.org						
Lenco Inc - PMC 10240 Deer Pk Rd	Waverly	NE	68462	402-786-2000		604
Web: www.lencopmc.com						
Len-Co Lumber Corp 1445 Seneca St	Buffalo	NY	14210	716-822-0243	822-1821	364
TF: 800-258-4585 ■ *Web:* www.lencobuffalo.com						
Lend Lease Corp 200 Pk Ave 9th Fl	New York	NY	10166	212-592-6800	592-6988	186
Web: www.lendlease.com						
LendingTools.com Inc						
200 N Broadway Ste 700	Wichita	KS	67202	316-267-3200		174
TF: 800-453-9400 ■ *Web:* www.lendingtools.com						
LendingTree Inc 11115 Rushmore Dr	Charlotte	NC	28277	704-541-5351	541-1824	509
TF: 800-555-8733 ■ *Web:* www.lendingtree.com						
Lenel System International Inc						
1212 Pittsford-Victor Rd	Pittsford	NY	14534	585-248-9720	248-9185	178-12
Web: www.lenel.com						
Lenexa Convention & Visitors Bureau						
11180 Lackman Rd	Lenexa	KS	66219	913-888-1414	888-3770	206
Web: www.lenexa.org						
Lenexpo Inc						
1293 Mtn View Alviso Rd Ste A	Sunnyvale	CA	94089	408-962-0515		253
TF: 877-536-3976 ■ *Web:* www.atlona.com						
Lenning & Company Inc						
13924 Seal Beach Blvd Ste C	Seal Beach	CA	90740	562-594-9729		2
TF: 800-200-4829 ■ *Web:* lenning.com						
Lennon Weinberg Inc 514 W 25th St	New York	NY	10001	212-941-0012	929-3265	42
Web: www.lennonweinberg.com						
Lennox Industries Inc						
2100 Lake Pk Blvd	Richardson	TX	75080	800-953-6669		15
TF Cust Svc: 800-953-6669 ■ *Web:* www.lennox.com						
Lennox International Inc						
2140 Lake Pk Blvd	Richardson	TX	75080	972-497-5000	497-5292*	15
NYSE: LII ■ **Fax:* Mail Rm ■ *TF:* 800-953-6669 ■ *Web:* www.lennoxinternational.com						
Lenny's Franchisor LLC						
8295 Tournament Dr Ste 200	Memphis	TN	38125	901-753-4002		360-3
Web: www.lennys.com						
Lenoir City Public Library						
100 W Broadway	Lenoir City	TN	37771	865-986-3210		434-3
Web: www.lenoircitytn.gov						
Lenoir Community College PO Box 188	Kinston	NC	28502	252-527-6223	233-6879	162
TF: 866-866-2362 ■ *Web:* www.lenoircc.edu						
Lenoir County						
130 S Queen St PO Box 3289	Kinston	NC	28502	252-559-6450	559-6454	338
Web: www.co.lenoir.nc.us						
Lenoir County Public School (LCPS)						
2017 W Vernon Ave PO Box 729	Kinston	NC	28504	252-527-1109	527-6884	685
TF: 888-684-8404 ■ *Web:* www.lcpsnc.org						
Lenoir Empire Furniture						
1625 Cherokee Rd	Johnson City	TN	37604	423-929-7283	929-7040	320
Web: www.lenoirempirefurniture.com						
Lenoir Memorial Hospital						
100 Airport Rd	Kinston	NC	28501	252-522-7000		374-3
Web: www.lenoirmemorial.org						
Lenoir Mirror Company Inc						
401 Kincaid St	Lenoir	NC	28645	828-728-3271	728-5010	332
TF: 800-438-8204 ■ *Web:* www.lenoirmirror.com						
Lenoir-Rhyne University						
625 Seventh Ave NE	Hickory	NC	28601	828-328-7300	328-7378	166
TF: 800-277-5721 ■ *Web:* www.lr.edu						
Lenox Advisors Inc 530 Fifth Ave	New York	NY	10036	212-536-8700		401
Web: www.lenoxadvisors.com						
Lenox Corp PO Box 2006	Bristol	PA	19007	800-223-4311		730
TF: 800-223-4311 ■ *Web:* www.lenox.com						

Name / Address	City	State	Zip	Phone	Fax	Class
Lenox Group LLC, The						
3384 Peachtree Rd N E Ste 300	Atlanta	GA	30326	404-419-1660		690
Web: www.lenoxgroupllc.com						
Lenox Hill Hospital 100 E 77th St.	New York	NY	10075	212-434-2000		374-3
Web: www.northwell.edu						
Lenox Hill Radiology 61 E 77th St	New York	NY	10075	212-772-3111		415
Web: www.lenoxhillradiology.com						
Lenox Hotel 61 Exeter St	Boston	MA	02116	617-536-5300	267-1237	379
TF: 800-225-7676 ■ *Web:* www.lenoxhotel.com						
Lenox Hotel & Suites 140 N St	Buffalo	NY	14201	716-884-1700		379
Web: www.lenoxhotelandsuites.com						
Lenox Square Mall						
3393 Peachtree Rd NE	Atlanta	GA	30326	404-233-6767	233-7868	460
TF: 800-266-2278 ■ *Web:* www.simon.com						
Lenox Wealth Management Inc						
8044 Montgomery Rd Ste 170	Cincinnati	OH	45236	513-618-7080		401
Web: www.lenoxwealth.com						
LENSAR Inc 2800 Discovery Dr	Orlando	FL	32826	888-536-7271		475
TF: 888-536-7271 ■ *Web:* www.lensar.com						
LensCrafters Inc 4000 Luxottica Pl.	Mason	OH	45040	513-765-4321		543
TF: 877-753-6727 ■ *Web:* www.lenscrafters.com						
Lensic Performing Arts Ctr						
211 W San Francisco St	Santa Fe	NM	87501	505-988-7050	988-4370	572
TF: 800-242-4282 ■ *Web:* www.lensic.org						
Lenstec Inc						
1765 Commerce Ave N	St. Petersburg	FL	33716	727-571-2272		544
Web: www.lenstec.com						
LensVector Inc 677 Palomar Ave	Sunnyvale	CA	94085	408-542-0300		542
Web: www.lensvector.com						
Lentech Inc 4405 Westridge Ct NW	Albuquerque	NM	87114	505-217-9095		396
Web: www.lentechinc.com						
Lentros Engineering Inc 280 Eliot St	Ashland	MA	01721	508-881-1160		454
Web: www.lentros.com						
Lentz Milling Co 2045 N 11th St.	Reading	PA	19604	800-523-8132		805
TF: 800-523-8132 ■ *Web:* www.lentzmilling.com						
Lenze 630 Douglas St	Uxbridge	MA	01569	508-278-9100		709
TF: 800-217-9100 ■ *Web:* www.lenze.com/en-us/home						
Lenzi Martin Communications						
701 Hayes Ave	Oak Park	IL	60302	708-848-8404		636
Leo A Daly 8600 Indian Hills Dr	Omaha	NE	68114	402-391-8111	391-8111	261
Web: www.leoadaly.com						
Leo Burnett Company Inc						
35 W Wacker Dr	Chicago	IL	60601	312-220-5959		4
Web: www.leoburnett.com						
Leo Castelli Gallery 18 E 77th St.	New York	NY	10075	212-249-4470		42
Web: www.castelligallery.com						
LEO Events 265 S Front St	Memphis	TN	38103	901-766-1836		184
Web: www.leoevents.com						
Leo Pharma Inc						
123 Commerce Valley Dr E Ste 400	Thornhill	ON	L3T7W8	905-886-9822	886-6622	85
Web: www.leo-pharma.com						
Leo Wolleman Inc 45 W 45th St 10th Fl	New York	NY	10036	212-840-1881	869-4216	411
TF: 800-223-5667 ■ *Web:* www.leowolleman.com						
Leo's Foods Inc						
3200 Northern Cross Blvd	Fort Worth	TX	76137	817-834-3200		123
Leo's Ristorante 11 Leo Turo Wy	Worcester	MA	01604	508-753-9490		071
Web: www.leosristorante.net						
Leola Village Inn & Suites						
38 Deborah Dr	Leola	PA	17540	717-656-7002	656-7648	379
TF: 877-669-5094 ■ *Web:* www.theinnatleolavillage.com						
Leominster Credit Union						
20 Adams St	Leominster	MA	01453	978-537-8021		219
TF: 800-649-4646 ■ *Web:* www.leominstercu.com						
Leominster Public Library 30 W St.	Leominster	MA	01453	978-534-7522		434-3
TF: 800-733-1830 ■ *Web:* www.leominsterlibrary.org						
Leominster State Forest						
90 Fitchburg Rd Rt 31	Westminster	MA	01473	978-874-2303		565
Web: www.mass.gov						
Leon County PO Box 98	Centerville	TX	75833	903-536-2352		338
Web: www.co.leon.tx.us						
Leon County Public Library System						
200 W Pk Ave	Tallahassee	FL	32301	850-487-2665		434-3
Web: cms.leoncountyfl.gov/library						
Leon County Schools (LCS)						
2757 W Pensacola St	Tallahassee	FL	32303	850-487-7100		685
Web: www.leonschools.net						
Leon D. DeMatteis Construction						
820 Elmont Rd	Elmont	NY	11003	516-285-5500		186
Web: www.dematteisorg.com						
Leon Farmer & Co 100 Rail Ridge Rd	Athens	GA	30607	706-353-1166		81-1
TF: 800-926-0055 ■ *Web:* www.leonfarmer.com						
Leon Henry Inc						
200 N Central Ave Ste 220	Hartsdale	NY	10530	914-285-2256		5
Leon Max Inc 3100 New York Dr	Pasadena	CA	91107	626-797-9991		155-21
TF: 888-334-4629 ■ *Web:* www.maxstudio.com						
Leon Plastics Inc						
4901 Clay Ave SW	Grand Rapids	MI	49548	616-531-7970		604
Web: www.leonplastics.com						
Leon Regional Juvenile Detention Ctr						
2303 Ronellis Dr.	Tallahassee	FL	32310	850-488-7672	414-8780	412
Web: www.djj.state.fl.us						
Leon S McGoogan Library of Medicine						
University of Nebraska Medical Ctr						
42nd and Emile	Omaha	NE	68198	402-559-4000		434-1
TF: 866-800-5209 ■ *Web:* www.unmc.edu/library						
Leon's at Desert Princess						
28-555 Landau Blvd	Cathedral City	CA	92234	760-325-5002		671
Leon's Texas Cuisine Co						
2100 Redbud Blvd	McKinney	TX	75069	972-529-5050		296-36
TF: 800-527-1243 ■ *Web:* www.texascuisine.com						
Leona Group LLC 2125 University Pk Dr	Okemos	MI	48864	517-333-9030		242
TF: 800-656-6763 ■ *Web:* www.leonagroup.com						
Leonard 5275 Boul Wilfrid-hamel	Quebec	QC	G2E5M7	418-780-1706		396
Web: www.leonarddg.com						
Leonard Harrison State Park						
4797 Rt 660	Wellsboro	PA	16901	570-724-3061		565
Web: www.dcnr.state.pa.us						
Leonard Holding Company						
2001 S Laredo St	San Antonio	TX	78207	210-532-3241		473
Web: lhpacking.net						
Leonard Hutton Galleries						
790 Madison Ave Ste 506	New York	NY	10065	212-751-7373	832-2261	42
Web: www.leonardhuttongalleries.com						
Leonard Insurance Services Agency Inc						
4244 Mt Pleasant St NW	North Canton	OH	44720	330-266-1904		390
Web: leonardinsurance.com						
Leonard Masonry Inc 5925 Fee Fee Rd	Hazelwood	MO	63042	314-731-5500	731-3366	189-7
Web: www.leonardmasonry.com						
Leonard Paper Co 725 N Haven St	Baltimore	MD	21205	800-327-5547	563-0249*	559
**Fax Area Code:* 410 ■ *TF Cust Svc:* 800-327-5547 ■ *Web:* www.leonardpaper.com						
Leonard S. Fiore Inc						
5506 Sixth Ave Rear	Altoona	PA	16602	814-946-3686		186
Web: www.lsfiore.com						
Leonard Valve Co 1360 Elmwood Ave	Cranston	RI	02910	401-461-1200	941-5310	789
TF: 800-222-1208 ■ *Web:* www.leonardvalve.com						
Leonardo DRS						
2345 Crystal Dr Ste 1000	Arlington	VA	22202	703-416-8000		248
Web: www.drs.com						
Leonardo State Marina						
102 Concord Ave	Leonardo	NJ	07737	732-291-1333		565
Web: www.state.nj.us						
Leonardo's 706						
706 W University Ave	Gainesville	FL	32601	352-378-2001		671
Web: www.leonardosgainesville.com						
Leone Advertising						
2024 Santa Cruz Ave.	Menlo Park	CA	94025	650-854-5895		7
TF: 800-245-9278 ■ *Web:* leonead.com						
Leone Mcdonnell & Roberts pa Cpa						
5 Nelson St	Dover	NH	03820	603-749-2700		2
Web: www.lmrpa.com						
Leoni Wiring Systems Inc						
2861 N Flowing Wells Rd Ste 121	Tucson	AZ	85705	520-741-0895	741-0864	813
Web: www.leoni.com						
Leonie Industries LLC						
1235 S Clark St Ste 607	Arlington	VA	22202	703-685-6626	685-6627	5
Web: www.leoniegroup.com						
Leonis Partners 1 W Court Sq Ste 210	Atlanta	GA	30030	404-347-3992		528
TF: 800-459-1358 ■ *Web:* www.leonispartners.com						
Leonoro's Spaghetti House						
1507 Washington St E	Charleston	WV	25311	304-343-1851		671
Web: leonorosspaghettihouse.com						
Leopard Communications Inc						
555 17th St Ste 300	Denver	CO	80202	303-527-2900	530-3480	194
Web: www.leopard.com						
Leopardo Cos Inc						
5200 Prairie Stone Pkwy.	Hoffman Estates	IL	60192	847-783-3000	783-3001	186
Web: www.leopardo.com						
Leopold Ketel & Partners						
118 SW First Ave	Portland	OR	97204	503-295-1918		7
Web: www.leoketel.com						
LePage Paul (R) State House Stn Ste 1	Augusta	ME	04333	207-287-3531	287-1034	343
TF: 800-423-6900 ■ *Web:* www.maine.gov/governor						
Lepel Corp 200-G Executive Dr	Edgewood	NY	11717	631-586-3300	586-3232	318
Web: lepel.com						
Lepercq de Neuflize & Co						
156 W 56th St Ste 1204	New York	NY	10019	212-698-0700		690
Web: www.lepercq.com						
LePoldevin Rickinger Group, The						
245 S Executive Dr Ste 365	Brookfield	WI	53005	262-754-9550		7
Web: www.thelrgroup.com						
Leppo Inc PO Box 154	Tallmadge	OH	44278	330-633-3999	630-1599	264-3
TF: 800-453-7762 ■ *Web:* www.leppos.com						
Leprino Foods Co 1830 W 38th Ave	Denver	CO	80211	303-480-2600	480-2605	296-5
Web: www.leprinofoods.com						
Lerch Bates Inc						
8089 S Lincoln St Ste 300	Littleton	CO	80122	303-795-7956		261
TF: 800-409-5471 ■ *Web:* www.lerchbates.com						
Lerch Vinci & Higgins						
17-17 State Rt 208	Fair Lawn	NJ	07410	201-791-7100		2
Web: www.lvhcpa.com						
Lereta LLC 1123 Parkview Dr	Covina	CA	91724	800-537-3821		652
TF: 800-537-3821 ■ *Web:* www.lereta.com						
Lerman Senter PLLC						
2001 L St NW Ste 400	Washington	DC	20036	202-429-8970	293-7783	428
Web: www.lermansenter.com						
Lerner David Littenberg Krumholz & Mentlik						
600 South Ave W	Westfield	NJ	07090	908-654-5000		428
Web: www.lernerdavid.com						
Lerner Publishing Group						
1251 Washington Ave N	Minneapolis	MN	55401	800-328-4929	332-1132	637-2
TF: 800-328-4929 ■ *Web:* www.lernerbooks.com						
Lerner Research Institute						
9500 Euclid Ave	Cleveland	OH	44195	216-444-3900	444-3279	668
TF: 800-223-2273 ■ *Web:* www.lerner.ccf.org						
Lerner, Sampson & Rothfuss A Legal Professional Assn						
120 E Fourth St.	Cincinnati	OH	45202	513-241-3100		428
TF: 800-447-5375 ■ *Web:* www.lsrlaw.com						
Lernia Training Solutions						
3603 winding way	Newtown Square	PA	19073	610-356-1792		138
TF: 800-921-6955 ■ *Web:* www.lernia-ts.com						
Leroy & Clarkson 211 Centre St Rm 5I	New York	NY	10013	212-431-9291		344
Web: www.leroyandclarkson.com						
Leroy E Smith's Sons Inc						
4776 Old Dixie Hwy	Vero Beach	FL	32967	772-567-3421		315-2
TF: 800-435-5727 ■ *Web:* leroysmith.com						
Leroy Percy State Park						
1400 Highway 12 W	Hollandale	MS	38748	662-827-5436		565
Web: www.mdwfp.com						
LES (Loyd's Electric Supply Inc)						
838 Stonetree Dr.	Branson	MO	65616	417-334-2171	334-6635	246
TF: 800-492-4030 ■ *Web:* www.loydselectric.com						
LES (Licensing Executives Society)						
1800 Diagonal Rd Ste 280	Alexandria	VA	22314	703-836-3106	836-3107	49-18
Web: www.lesi.org						

	Phone	Fax	Class

Les Chaines Tele Astral
1800 Ave McGill College Bureau 1600 Montreal QC H3A3J6 514-938-3320 740
Web: www.bellmedia.ca

Les Chenets 2075 Rue Bishop Montreal QC H3G2G2 514-844-1842 671

Les entreprises energie Cardio
1040 Michele-Bohec Blvd Ste 300 Blainville QC J7C5E2 450-979-3613 354
Web: www.energiecardio.com

Les Folies 2552 Riva Rd Annapolis MD 21401 410-573-0970 671
Web: www.lesfoliesbrasserie.com

Les Howe Associates Inc
41 W High St East Hampton CT 06424 860-267-6651 7
TF: 888-800-5149 ■ *Web:* www.leshoweassociates.com

Les Mars Hotel 27 N St Healdsburg CA 95448 707-433-4211 433-4611 379
Web: www.hotellesmars.com

Les Meubles Saint Damase Inc
246 rue Principale St-Damase Comt St-damase QC J0H1J0 450-797-3702 361
Web: www.st-damase.com

Les Nomades 222 E Ontario St Chicago IL 60611 312-649-9010 649-0608 671
TF: 800-756-5784 ■ *Web:* www.lesnomades.net

Les Stanford Chevrolet Inc
21730 Michigan Ave Dearborn MI 48124 313-457-0364 57
TF: 800-836-0972 ■ *Web:* lesstanfordchevrolet.com

Les Suites Hotel Ottawa
130 Besserer St Ottawa ON K1N9M9 613-232-2000 232-1242 379
TF: 866-682-0879 ■ *Web:* www.les-suites.com

Les Trois Petits Cochons Inc
4223 First Ave 2nd Fl Brooklyn NY 11232 212-219-1230 941-9726 296-26
Web: www.3pigs.com

Les Wilkins & Assoc Inc
6850 35th Ave NE Seattle WA 98115 206-522-0908 522-5292 475
TF: 800-426-6634 ■ *Web:* www.leswilkins.com

Les Zygomates 129 S St Boston MA 02111 617-542-5108 671
Web: winebar129.com

Lesaffre Yeast Corp 7475 W Main St Milwaukee WI 53214 414-615-4094 296-42
TF Cust Svc: 800-770-2714 ■ *Web:* lesaffreyeast.com

LeSaint Logistics
868 W Crossroads Pkwy Romeoville IL 60446 630-243-5950 449
TF: 877-566-9375 ■ *Web:* www.lesaint.com

Lescarden Inc
420 Lexington Ave Ste 212 New York NY 10170 212-687-1050 85
Web: www.lescarden.com

Lesco Design & Mfg Company Inc
1120 Ft Pickens Rd Lagrange KY 40031 502-222-7101 261
Web: lescodesign.com

Lescure Company Inc
3667 Mt Diablo Blvd PO Box 968 Lafayette CA 94549 925-283-2528 610
Web: www.lescurecompany.com

LeSea Broadcasting Corp
61300 S Ironwood Rd South Bend IN 46614 574-291-8200 291-9043 738
TF: 800-365-3732 ■ *Web:* www.lesea.com

Lesic & Camper Communications
172 E State St Ste 410 Columbus OH 43215 614-224-0658 224
Web: www.lesiccamper.com

Lesley University 29 Everett St Cambridge MA 02138 617-868-9600 166
TF: 800-999-1959 ■ *Web:* www.lesley.edu

Leslie Controls Inc 12501 Telecom Dr Tampa FL 33637 813-978-1000 978-0984 789
TF: 800-323-8366 ■ *Web:* www.lesliecontrols.com

Leslie County PO Box 619 Hyden KY 41749 606-672-3200 672-7373 338
Web: www.lesliecounty.ky.gov

Leslie Lewis & Associates
247 Spring St Jeffersonville IN 47130 812-282-6606 393
Web: www.leslielewisdesign.com

Leslie Science & Nature Ctr
1831 Traver Rd Ann Arbor MI 48105 734-997-1553 997-1072 520
TF: 800-530-0741 ■ *Web:* lesliesnc.org

Leslie Tonkonow Artworks & Projects
535 W 22nd St 6th Fl New York NY 10011 212-255-8450 42
Web: www.tonkonow.com

Lesman Instrument Co
135 Bernice Dr Bensenville IL 60106 630-595-8400 595-2386 386
TF: 800-953-7626 ■ *Web:* www.lesman.com

Leson Chevrolet Co Inc
1501 Westbank Express Harvey LA 70058 504-366-4381 516
TF: 877-496-2420 ■ *Web:* lesonauto.com

Lesotho 204 E 39th St New York NY 10016 212-661-1690 682-4388 784
Web: www.un.int

Lesotho Embassy
2511 Massachusetts Ave NW Washington DC 20008 202-797-5533 234-6815 257
Web: www.lesothoemb-usa.gov.ls

Lesperance & Martineau
1440 Rue Sainte-catherine O Montreal QC H3G1R8 514-861-4831 428
TF: 888-273-8387 ■ *Web:* www.l-m.ca

Lessing-Flynn Adv Co
3106 Ingersoll Ave Des Moines IA 50312 515-274-9271 4
Web: www.lessingflynn.com

Lester Bldg Systems LLC
1111 Second Ave S Lester Prairie MN 55354 320-395-2531 106
TF: 800-826-4439 ■ *Web:* www.lesterbuildings.com

Lester Catalog Co 9850 Hillview Rd Newcastle CA 95658 530-823-0963 530

Lester Group, The
101 E Commonwealth Blvd Martinsville VA 24115 276-632-2195 752
Web: www.lestergroup.com

Lester Inc 19 Business Pk Dr Branford CT 06405 203-488-5265 483-0408 737
TF: 800-999-5265 ■ *Web:* www.lesterusa.com

Lester Lampert Corporate 7 E Huron St Chicago IL 60611 312-944-6888 410
Web: www.lesterlampert.com

Lester Lithograph Inc
1128 N Gilbert St Anaheim CA 92801 714-491-3981 627
Web: www.lesterlitho.com

Lester Sales Co Inc
4312 W Minnesota St Indianapolis IN 46241 317-244-7811 248-2369 246
TF: 888-963-6270 ■ *Web:* www.lestersalesco.com

Lester's Florist Inc 2100 Bull St Savannah GA 31401 912-233-6066 292
TF: 800-841-1103 ■ *Web:* www.lestersflorist.com

Let's Play
8300 S County Line Rd Oklahoma City OK 73169 405-261-6076 261-0328 181
Web: www.letsplaysoccer.com

Letcher County 156 Main St Ste 107 Whitesburg KY 41858 606-633-2129 633-7105 338
Web: letchercounty.ky.gov

Letchworth State Park
1 Letchworth State Pk Castile NY 14427 585-493-3600 565
Web: parks.ny.gov/parks/79/details.aspx

Letco Medical Inc 1316 Commerce Dr NW Decatur AL 35601 256-350-1297 583
TF: 800-239-5288 ■ *Web:* www.letcomedical.com

Lethbridge Chamber of Commerce
529 Sixth St S Ste 200 Lethbridge AB T1J2E1 403-327-1586 327-1001 137
Web: lethbridgechamber.com

Lethbridge Herald
504 - Seventh St S PO Box 670 Lethbridge AB T1J3Z7 403-328-4411 328-4536 532-1
Web: lethbridgeherald.com

Lethbridge Public Library
810 5 Ave S Lethbridge AB T1J4C4 403-380-7310 435
Web: www.lethlib.ca

Letica Corp 52585 Dequindre Rd Rochester MI 48307 248-652-0557 548
Web: www.letica.com

LeTip International Inc
4838 E Baseline Rd Ste 123 Mesa AZ 85206 480-264-4600 393
TF: 800-255-3847 ■ *Web:* www.letip.com

Letnan Industries Inc
6520 Arrow Dr Sterling Heights MI 48314 586-726-1155 247
Web: www.letnanind.com

LeTourneau University
2100 S Mobberly Ave Longview TX 75602 903-233-3000 233-4301* 166
**Fax:* Admissions ■ *TF:* 800-759-8811 ■ *Web:* www.letu.edu

Letsos Co
8435 Westglen Dr PO Box 36927 Houston TX 77063 713-783-3200 972-7880 186
Web: www.letsos.com

LetterLogic Inc 1209 Fourth Ave S Nashville TN 37210 615-783-0070 5
TF: 800-477-0180 ■ *Web:* www.letterlogic.com

Lettire Construction Corp
334-336 E 110th St New York NY 10029 212-996-6640 186
Web: lettire.com

Lettuce Entertain You Enterprises Inc
5419 N Sheridan Rd Chicago IL 60640 773-878-7340 670
Web: www.leye.com

Leucadia National Corp
520 Madison Ave New York NY 10022 212-460-1900 185
NYSE: LUK ■ *Web:* www.leucadia.com

Leucadia State Beach
948 Neptune Ave Encinitas CA 92024 760-633-2740 565
Web: www.parks.ca.gov/default.asp?page_id=661

Leunig's Bistro 115 Church St Burlington VT 05401 802-863-3759 671
Web: www.leunigsbistro.com

Leupold & Stevens Inc
14400 NW Greenbrier Pkwy Beaverton OR 97006 800-538-7653 544
TF: 800-538-7653 ■ *Web:* www.leupold.com

Leuthold Weeden Capital Management LLC
33 S Sixth St Ste 4600 Minneapolis MN 55402 612-332-9141 194
TF: 800-273-6886 ■ *Web:* www.leutholdfunds.com

Levasseur Dier & Associates Pc
3233 Coolidge Hwy Berkley MI 48072 248-586-1200 428
Web: ldalaw.com

Level 3 Communications Inc
1025 Eldorado Blvd Broomfield CO 80021 720-888-1000 394
NYSE: LVLT ■ *TF:* 877-453-8353 ■ *Web:* www.level3.com

Level 3 Post 2901 W Alameda Ave Burbank CA 91505 818-840-7200 512
Web: www.level3post.com

Level Agency 241 Fourth Ave Pittsburgh PA 15222 877-733-8625 5
TF: 877-733-8625 ■ *Web:* level.agency

Level Ii 774 Superior Ave San Leandro CA 94577 510-569-3299 463
Web: www.leveltwo.com

Level Up Analytics Inc
277 Castro St Mountain View CA 94041 650-386-5914 463

Levelfield.com Inc
11675 Jollyville Rd Ste 207 Austin TX 78759 512-401-9200 177
Web: www.levelfield.com

Levementum Inc
55 N Arizona Place# 203 Chandler AZ 85225 480-320-2500 196
Web: www.levementum.com

Levene Gouldin & Thompson Llp
450 Plaza Dr Vestal NY 13850 607-763-9200 445
Web: www.lgtllp.com

Levenger 420 S Congress Ave Delray Beach FL 33445 561-276-2436 243-3629 459
TF Cust Svc: 800-544-0880 ■ *Web:* www.levenger.com

Leventhal Ltd PO Box 564 Fayetteville NC 28302 800-847-4095 352-6635 155-19
TF General: 800-847-4095 ■ *Web:* www.leventhalltd.com

Lever Interactive Inc
701 Warrenville Rd Ste 200 Lisle IL 60532 630-435-6400 195
Web: www.leverinteractive.com

LeveragePoint Media Corp
111 Water St East Dundee IL 60118 847-437-5300 195
TF: 800-783-7171 ■ *Web:* www.leveragepointmedia.com

Levert Personnel Resources Inc
17 Frood Rd Sudbury ON P3C4Y9 705-525-8367 260
Web: www.levert.ca

Levi Jackson State Park
998 Levi Jackson Mill Rd London KY 40744 606-330-2130 565
Web: www.parks.ky.gov

Levi Ray & Shoup Inc
2401 W Monroe St Springfield IL 62704 217-793-3800 787-3286 178-1
Web: www.lrs.com

Levi Strauss & Co
1155 Battery St San Francisco CA 94111 415-501-6000 501-7112 155-11
TF: 866-290-6064 ■ *Web:* www.levistrauss.com

Leviathan Corp
55 Washington St Ste 457 Brooklyn NY 11201 718-701-5718 701-5745 386
Web: www.leviathancorp.com

LEVICK LLC 1900 M St NW Washington DC 20036 202-973-1300 636
Web: levick.com

Levin Furniture Co 5280 Rt 30 Greensburg PA 15601 724-834-3550 321
TF: 800-420-2337 ■ *Web:* www.levinfurniture.com

Levin Group Inc 10 New Plant Ct Owings Mills MD 21117 410-654-1234 463
Web: www.levingroup.com

Levin Sander (Rep D - MI)
1236 Longworth Bldg Washington DC 20515 888-810-3880 226-1033* 342-2
**Fax Area Code:* 202 ■ *TF:* 888-810-3880 ■ *Web:* levin.house.gov

Levin Tire Ctr 5713 Broadway Merrillville IN 46410 219-887-0531 57
Web: www.levintirecenter.com

Name / Address	City	State	Zip	Phone	Fax	Class
Levin, Swedler & Company Inc 3501 Embassy Pkwy Ste 200 *Web:* www.levinswedler.com	Akron	OH	44333	330-666-4199		2
Levindale Hebrew Geriatric Ctr & Hospital 2434 W Belvedere Ave *Web:* www.lifebridgehealth.org/levindale	Baltimore	MD	21215	410-601-2400		450
Levine Blaszak Block & Boothby LLP 2001 L St NW Ste 900 *Web:* www.lb3law.com	Washington	DC	20036	202-857-2550		428
Levine Builders 42-09 235th St *Web:* www.levinebuilders.com	Douglaston	NY	11363	212-400-9292		186
Levine Museum of the New South 200 E Seventh St *Web:* www.museumofthenewsouth.org	Charlotte	NC	28202	704-333-1887	333-1896	520
Levinson Axelrod 2 Lincoln Ct *Web:* njlawyers.com	Edison	NJ	08820	732-440-3089		445
Levinson Institute Inc 28 Main St Ste 100 *TF:* 800-290-5735 ■ *Web:* levinsonandco.com	Jaffrey	NH	03452	603-532-4700	532-4750	765
Levitt-Safety Ltd 2872 Bristol Cir *Web:* www.levitt-safety.com	Oakville	ON	L6H5T5	905 829-3299	829-2919	419
Levolor Kirsch Window Fashions 4110 Premier Dr *TF:* 800-752-9677 ■ *Web:* www.levolor.com	High Point	NC	27265	336-812-8181		87
Levy Affiliated Holdings LLC 201 Wilshire Blvd 2nd Fl *Web:* www.levyaffiliated.com	Santa Monica	CA	90401	310-395-5200		528
Levy County 355 S Ct St PO Box 310 *Web:* www.levycounty.org	Bronson	FL	32621	352-486-5218	486-5167	338
Levy Diamond Bello & Associates LLC 497 Bic Dr *Web:* www.ldbassociates.com	Milford	CT	06461	203-876-1000		317
Levy Economics Institute of Bard College Blithewood Rd Bard College *Web:* www.levyinstitute.org	Annandale-on-Hudson	NY	12504	845-758-7700	758-1149	634
Levy Home Entertainment LLC 1420 Kensington Rd Ste 300 *TF:* 800-549-5389 ■ *Web:* www.readerlink.com	Oak Brook	IL	60523	708-547-4400		530
Levy Restaurants 980 N Michigan Ave *Web:* www.levyrestaurants.com	Chicago	IL	60611	312-664-8200		670
Lew A. Cummings Company Inc 4 Peters Brook Dr *TF:* 800-647-0035 ■ *Web:* www.cummingsprinting.com	Hooksett	NH	03106	800-647-0035		627
Lew Edwards Group, The 5454 Broadway *Web:* lewedwardsgroup.com	Oakland	CA	94618	510-594-0224		196
Lew Jan Textile Corp 366 Veterans Memorial Hwy **Fax Area Code:* 631 ■ *TF:* 800-899-0531 ■ *Web:* www.lewjan.com	Commack	NY	11725	800-899-0531	543-0561*	594
LEWA Inc 132 Hopping Brook Rd *Web:* lewa-inc.com	Holliston	MA	01746	508-429-7403		641
LEWCO Inc 706 Lane St	Sandusky	OH	44870	419-625-4014		207
Lewcott Corp 86 Providence Rd *TF Sales:* 800-225-7725 ■ *Web:* barrday.com	Millbury	MA	01527	508-865-1791	865-0302	605-2
Lewellen Accountancy Corp 23521 Paseo De Valencia 205	Laguna Hills	CA	92653	949-859-4644		2
Lewer Agency Inc 4534 Wornall Rd **Fax Area Code:* 816 ■ *TF:* 800-821-7715 ■ *Web:* www.lewer.com	Kansas City	MO	64111	800-821-7715	561-6840*	300
Lewes Historical Society 110 Shipcarpenter St *Web:* www.historiclewes.org	Lewes	DE	19958	302-645-7670	645-2375	520
Lewin Group 3130 Fairview Pk Dr Ste 800 *TF:* 877-227-5042 ■ *Web:* www.lewin.com	Falls Church	VA	22042	703-269-5500	269-5501	194
Lewis & Assoc Insurance Brokers Inc 700 W Center Ave *Web:* since1927.com	Visalia	CA	93291	559-733-7272		390
Lewis & Clark Caverns State Park PO Box 489 *Web:* stateparks.mt.gov	Whitehall	MT	59759	406-287-3541		565
Lewis & Clark College 0615 SW Palatine Hill Rd **Fax:* Admissions ■ *TF Admissions:* 800-444-4111 ■ *Web:* www.lclark.edu	Portland	OR	97219	503-768-7040	768-7055*	166
Lewis & Clark College Watzek Library 0615 Palatine Hill Rd *TF:* 800-607-5501 ■ *Web:* library.lclark.edu	Portland	OR	97219	503-768-7270	768-7282	434-6
Lewis & Clark County 316 N Park Ave Rm 345 *Web:* www.lccountymt.gov	Helena	MT	59623	406-447-8200	447-8370	338
Lewis & Clark Law School 10015 SW Terwilliger Blvd **Fax:* Admissions ■ *Web:* www.lclark.edu	Portland	OR	97219	503-768-6600	768-6793*	167-1
Lewis & Clark Library 120 S Last Chance Gulch *TF:* 800-733-2767 ■ *Web:* www.lclibrary.org	Helena	MT	59601	406-447-1690	447-1687	434-3
Lewis & Clark National Historic Trail Interpretive Ctr 4201 Giant Springs Rd *Web:* www.fs.usda.gov/lcnf	Great Falls	MT	59405	406-727-8733	453-6157	50-5
Lewis & Clark Recreation Area 43349 SD Hwy 52 *Web:* lewisandclarkpark.com	Yankton	SD	57078	605-668-2985		565
Lewis & Clark State Historic Site 1 Lewis & Clark Trl *Web:* www.campdubois.com	Hartford	IL	62048	618-251-5811		50-3
Lewis & Clark State Park 21914 Pk Loop *Web:* www.lewisandclarktrail.com	Onawa	IA	51040	712-423-2829		565
Lewis & Clark State Park 801 Lake Crest Blvd *Web:* www.mostateparks.com	Rushville	MO	64484	816-579-5564		565
Lewis & Clark State Park 4583 Jackson Hwy *Web:* www.parks.wa.gov	Winlock	WA	98596	360-864-2643		565
Lewis & Clark State Recreation Area 54731 897 Rd *Web:* outdoornebraska.gov/lewisandclark	Crofton	NE	68730	402-388-4169		565
Lewis & Clark State Recreation Site 725 Summer St NE Ste C *TF:* 800-551-6949 ■ *Web:* oregonstateparks.org	Salem	OR	97301	503-986-0707		565
Lewis & Clark Trail Heritage Foundation 4201 Giant Springs Rd *TF:* 888-701-3434 ■ *Web:* www.lewisandclark.org	Great Falls	MT	59405	406-454-1234		48-23
Lewis & Clark Trail State Park 36149 Hwy 12 *Web:* www.parks.wa.gov	Dayton	WA	99328	509-337-6457		565
Lewis & Company PC 3804 Poplar Hill Rd Ste B	Chesapeake	VA	23321	757-638-4566		2
Lewis & Ellis Inc 2929 N Central Expy Ste 200 *Web:* www.lewisellis.com	Richardson	TX	75080	972-850-0850		196
Lewis & Kappes 1700 One American Sq Box 82053 *TF:* 800-388-1845 ■ *Web:* www.lewis-kappes.com	Indianapolis	IN	46282	317-639-1210		428
Lewis & Knopf CPAs PC 5206 Gateway Centre Ste 100 *TF:* 877-244-1787 ■ *Web:* www.lewis-knopf.com	Flint	MI	48507	810-238-4617		2
Lewis & Michael Inc 1827 Woodman Dr *TF:* 800-543-3524 ■ *Web:* atlaslm.com	Dayton	OH	45420	937-252-6683		186
Lewis & Raulerson Inc 1759 State St *Web:* www.lewisandraulerson.com	Waycross	GA	31501	912-283-5951	283-8281	316
Lewis Advertising Inc 1050 Country Club Rd *Web:* www.lewisadvertising.com	Rocky Mount	NC	27804	252-443-5131		7
Lewis Bakeries Inc 500 N Fulton Ave *Web:* lewisbakeries.net	Evansville	IN	47710	812-425-4642		296-1
Lewis Brisbois Bisgaard & Smith LLP 221 N Figueroa St Ste 1200 *Web:* lewisbrisbois.com	Los Angeles	CA	90012	213-250-1800	250-7900	428
Lewis Builders Inc 54 Sawyer Ave *Web:* www.lewisbuilders.com	Atkinson	NH	03811	603-362-5333	362-4936	187
Lewis Communications Inc 2030 First Ave N *Web:* www.lewiscommunications.com	Birmingham	AL	35203	205-980-0774		4
Lewis Contractors LLC 55 Gwynns Mill Ct *Web:* www.lewis-contractors.com	Owings Mills	MD	21117	410-356-4200		186
Lewis Corp 15136 W Hunziker Rd *Web:* www.lcorp.com	Pocatello	ID	83202	208-238-1202		697
Lewis County 7660 N State St *Web.* www.lewiscountyny.org	Lowville	NY	13367	315-376-5333	376-3768	338
Economic Development 106 N Ct St *Web:* www.lewiscountytn.com	Hohenwald	TN	38462	931-796-6012	796-6020	338
Lewis County Chamber of Commerce 7576 S State St *TF:* 800-724-0242 ■ *Web:* www.lewiscountychamber.org	Lowville	NY	13367	315-376-2213	376-0326	139
Lewis County Rural Electric Co-op 18256 Hwy 16 PO Box 68 *TF:* 888-454-4485 ■ *Web:* www.lewiscountyrec.org	Lewistown	MO	63452	573-215-4000		245
Lewis Critter Gitter 25 W Frnt St S *Web:* www.lewispestcontrol.net	Thomasville	AL	36784	334-636-4530		577
Lewis Direct Marketing 325 E Oliver St *TF:* 800-533-5394 ■ *Web:* www.lewisdirect.com	Baltimore	MD	21202	410-539-5100	685-5144	5
Lewis Drug Inc 4409 E 26th St *TF:* 800-723-3929 ■ *Web:* www.lewisdrug.com	Sioux Falls	SD	57103	605-367-2710	367-2070	237
Lewis Electric Supply Company Inc 1306 Second St PO Box 2237 *TF:* 800-239-0681 ■ *Web:* www.lesupply.com	Muscle Shoals	AL	35662	256-383-0681		246
Lewis Ford Sales Inc 3373 N College Ave PO Box 8430 *Web:* lewiscars.com	Fayetteville	AR	72703	479-442-5301		57
Lewis Ginter Botanical Garden 1800 Lakeside Ave *Web:* www.lewisginter.org	Richmond	VA	23228	804-262-9887	262-6329	97
Lewis Goetz & Company Inc 1571 Grandview Ave *TF:* 800-257-6239 ■ *Web:* www.lewis-goetz.com	Paulsboro	NJ	08066	856-579-1421	579-1429	385
Lewis Group 2766 Degen Dr *Web:* www.mcmillinrealty.com	Bonita	CA	91902	619-470-9110		652
Lewis Innovative Technologies Inc 110 Johnston St SE *Web:* lewisinnovative.com	Decatur	AL	35601	256-905-0775		261
Lewis J. Ort Library 1 Susan Eisel Dr *Web:* frostburg.edu/lewis-ort-library	Frostburg	MD	21532	301-687-4395	687-7069	434-6
Lewis Jason (Rep R - MN) 418 Cannon HOB *Web:* jasonlewis.house.gov	Washington	DC	20515	202-225-2271		342-2
Lewis John (Rep D - GA) 343 Cannon Bldg *Web:* johnlewis.house.gov	Washington	DC	20515	202-225-3801		342-2
Lewis Label Products 2300 Race St *TF:* 800-772-7728 ■ *Web:* www.lewislabel-products.com	Ft Worth	TX	76111	800-772-7728		548
Lewis Marine Supply Co Inc 220 SW 32nd St *Web:* www.lewismarine.com	Fort Lauderdale	FL	33315	954-523-4371		770
Lewis Media Partners LLC 500 Libbie Ave Ste 2-C *Web:* www.lewismediapartners.com	Richmond	VA	23226	804-741-7115		5
Lewis Military Museum PO Box 331001 *Web:* lewisarmymuseum.com	Lewis-McChord	WA	98433	253-967-7206		520
Lewis O Flom Lansing Public Library 2750 Indiana Ave *Web:* www.lansingpl.org	Lansing	IL	60438	708-474-2447	474-9466	434-3
Lewis Rice 600 Washington Ave Ste 2500 *Web:* www.lewisrice.com	St. Louis	MO	63101	314-444-7600		445
Lewis S. Mills High School 24 Lyon Rd *TF:* 800-673-2411 ■ *Web:* www.region10ct.org	Burlington	CT	06013	860-673-0423	673-9128	685
Lewis Tree Service Inc 300 Lucius Gordon Dr *TF:* 800-333-1593 ■ *Web:* www.lewistree.com	West Henrietta	NY	14586	585-436-3208	235-5864	776

				Phone	Fax	Class
Lewis University 1 University Pkwy Unit 297 *TF:* 800-897-9000 ■ *Web:* www.lewisu.edu	Romeoville	IL	60446	815-836-5250	836-5002	166
Lewis Wagner 501 Indiana Ave #200 *TF:* 800-237-0505 ■ *Web:* www.lewiswagner.com	Indianapolis	IN	46202	317-237-0500		428
Lewis Yockey & Brown Inc 505 N Main St *TF:* 800-338-3355 ■ *Web:* www.lybinc.com	Bloomington	IL	61701	309-829-2552		727
Lewis-Clark State College 500 Eigth Ave **Fax:* Admissions ■ *TF:* 800-933-5272 ■ *Web:* www.lcsc.edu	Lewiston	ID	83501	208-792-5272	792-2210*	166
Lewis-Gale Medical Ctr 1900 Electric Rd *TF:* 800-541-9992 ■ *Web:* lewisgale.com	Salem	VA	24153	540-776-4000	953-5372	374-3
Lewis-Goetz & Co Inc 650 Washington Rd Ste 210 *TF:* 800-989-0447 ■ *Web:* www.lewis-goetz.com	Pittsburgh	PA	15228	800-937-9070		385
Lewisohn Sales Company Inc 4001 Dell Ave *Web:* www.lewisohn.com	North Bergen	NJ	07047	201-864-0300		683
Lewiston City Library 428 Thain Rd *Web:* www.cityoflewiston.org	Lewiston	ID	83501	208-743-6519		434-3
Lewiston Morning Tribune PO Box 957 *Web:* www.lmtribune.com	Lewiston	ID	83501	208-743-9411	746-1185	532-2
Lewiston Public Library 200 Lisbon St *TF:* 800-866-5588 ■ *Web:* www.lplonline.org	Lewiston	ME	04240	207-513-3004		434-3
Lewiston Sales Inc 21241 Dutchmans Crossing Rd *TF:* 800-732-6334 ■ *Web:* www.lewistonsales.com	Lewiston	MN	55952	507-523-2112	523-2400	446
Lewistown Florist Store 129 S Main St Ste 200 *Web:* www.lewistownflorist.com	Lewistown	PA	17044	717-248-9683		292
Lewistown News-argus 521 W Main St PO Box 900 *TF:* 800-879-5627 ■ *Web:* www.lewistownnews.com	Lewistown	MT	59457	406-535-3401		532-3
Lewisville Chamber of Commerce 551 N Valley Pkwy *Web:* www.lewisvillechamber.org	Lewisville	TX	75067	972-436-9571	436-5949	139
Lewisville Public Library 1197 W Main St *Web:* www.cityoflewisville.com	Lewisville	TX	75067	972-219-3570	219-5094	434-3
LeWiz Communications Inc 1376 N Fourth St Ste 300 *Web:* www.lewiz.com	San Jose	CA	95112	408-452-9800		246
Lewnes' Steakhouse 401 Fourth St *TF:* 800-636-4462 ■ *Web:* www.lewnessteakhouse.com	Annapolis	MD	21403	410-263-1617		671
LexaMed Ltd 705 Front St *Web:* www.lexamed.net	Toledo	OH	43605	419-693-5307		463
Lexar Media Inc 47300 Bayside Pkwy *TF:* 877-747-4031 ■ *Web:* www.lexar.com	Fremont	CA	94538	510-413-1200		288
Lexel Corp 532 Broadhollow Rd Ste 125 *Web:* www.lexel.com	Melville	NY	11747	631-501-0700	501-1930	518
Lexel Imaging Systems Inc 1501 Newtown Pike *TF:* 800-397-8121 ■ *Web:* www.lexelimaging.com	Lexington	KY	40511	859-243-5500	243-5555	253
LexiCode 100 Executive Center Dr Ste 101 **Fax Area Code:* 803 ■ *TF:* 800-448-2633 ■ *Web:* www.lexicode.com	Columbia	SC	29210	800-448-2633	749-9788*	393
Lexicon Branding Inc 30 Liberty Ship Way Ste 3360 *TF:* 800-339-2861 ■ *Web:* www.lexiconbranding.com	Sausalito	CA	94965	415-332-1811	332-2528	195
Lexicon Group, The 1721 De La Vina St *Web:* www.lexicongroup.com	Santa Barbara	CA	93101	805-898-1943		226
Lexicon Inc 8900 Fourche Dam Pk *Web:* www.lexicon-inc.com	Little Rock	AR	72206	501-490-4200		480
Lexicon International Corp 1400A Adams Rd *TF:* 800-448-8201 ■ *Web:* lexicon-int.com	Bensalem	PA	19020	215-639-8220		387
Lexicon Marketing Corp 6380 Wilshire Blvd *Web:* www.lexiconmarketing.com	Los Angeles	CA	90048	323-782-7400		737
Lexicon Pharmaceuticals Inc 8800 Technology Forest Pl *NASDAQ: LXRX* ■ *TF:* 855-828-4651 ■ *Web:* www.lexpharma.com	The Woodlands	TX	77381	281-863-3000	863-8088	85
Lexinet Corp, The 701 N Union St *TF:* 800-767-1577 ■ *Web:* www.lexinetcorporation.com	Council Grove	KS	66846	620-767-7000		5
Lexington B & L Financial Corp 205 S 13th St PO Box 190 *Web:* www.bl-bank.com	Lexington	MO	64067	660-259-2247	259-2384	360-2
Lexington Ballet Co (LBC) 161 N Mill St *Web:* www.lexingtonballet.org	Lexington	KY	40507	859-233-3925		573-1
Lexington Building Supply Company Inc 1077 Eastland Dr *Web:* www.lbsco.net	Lexington	KY	40505	859-254-8836		499
Lexington Chamber of Commerce 1875 Massachusetts Ave *TF:* 800-832-3747 ■ *Web:* www.lexingtonchamber.org	Lexington	MA	02420	781-862-2480		139
Lexington Chamber of Commerce 311 W Main St *Web:* www.lexingtonsc.org	Lexington	SC	29072	803-359-6113	359-0634	139
Lexington City Board of Education 1010 Fair St *Web:* www.lexcs.org	Lexington	NC	27292	336-242-1527		685
Lexington College 310 S Peoria St	Chicago	IL	60607	312-226-6294		800
Lexington Convention Ctr 430 W Vine St *TF:* 800-223-1624 ■ *Web:* www.lexingtoncenter.com	Lexington	KY	40507	859-233-4567	253-2718	205
Lexington Corporate Properties Trust 1 Penn Plaza Ste 4015 *TF:* 800-850-3948 ■ *Web:* www.lxp.com	New York	NY	10119	212-692-7200	594-6600	655
Lexington Ctr Corp 430 W Vine St *TF:* 800-223-1624 ■ *Web:* www.lexingtoncenter.com	Lexington	KY	40507	859-233-4567	253-2718	655
Lexington Furniture Company Inc, The 3024 Blake James Dr	Lexington	KY	40509	859-254-4412		321
Lexington Health Care Center 17 Cornelia Dr	Lexington	NC	27292	336-242-1349		354
Lexington Herald-Leader 100 Midland Ave *TF:* 800-999-8881 ■ *Web:* www.kentucky.com	Lexington	KY	40508	859-231-3100		532-2
Lexington Home Brands 1300 National Hwy *TF:* 800-333-4300 ■ *Web:* www.lexington.com	Thomasville	NC	27360	336-474-5300		319-2
Lexington Hotel-George Washington Inn & Conference Ctr 500 Merrimac Trl	Williamsburg	VA	23185	757-259-5500		379
Lexington (Independent City) 300 E Washington St *Web:* lexingtonva.gov	Lexington	VA	24450	540-462-3700	463-5310	338
Lexington Insurance Company Inc 99 High St Fl 23 *TF:* 800-821-5100 ■ *Web:* www.lexingtoninsurance.com	Boston	MA	02110	617-330-1100		391-4
Lexington Investment Company Inc 2365 Harrodsburg Rd Ste B375 *TF:* 800-264-7073 ■ *Web:* www.lexinvest.com	Lexington	KY	40504	859-224-7073		690
Lexington Livestock Market Inc 300 Plum Creek Pkwy *Web:* www.lexlivestock.com	Lexington	NE	68850	308-324-4663		446
Lexington Manufacturing Inc 1330 115th Ave NW *Web:* www.lexingtonmfg.com	Minneapolis	MN	55448	763-754-9055		820
Lexington Market 400 W Lexington St *Web:* www.lexingtonmarket.com	Baltimore	MD	21201	410-685-6169		460
Lexington Medical Ctr 2720 Sunset Blvd *Web:* www.lexmed.com	West Columbia	SC	29169	803-791-2000		374-3
Lexington New York City, The 511 Lexington Ave 48th St *TF:* 800-223-4932 ■ *Web:* www.lexingtonhotelnyc.com	New York	NY	10017	212-755-4400		707
Lexington Opera House 401 W Short St *Web:* www.lexingtonoperahouse.com	Lexington	KY	40507	859-233-4567	253-2718	572
Lexington Philharmonic 161 N Mill St *TF:* 888-494-4226 ■ *Web:* www.lexphil.org	Lexington	KY	40507	859-233-4226	233-7896	573-3
Lexington Public Library 140 E Main St *Web:* www.lexpublib.org	Lexington	KY	40507	859-231-5504	231-5598	434-3
Lexington Public Library District 207 S Cedar St *TF:* 800-622-0034 ■ *Web:* lexington.lib.il.us	Lexington	IL	61753	309-365-7801		434-3
Lexington Realty Trust Inc 1 Penn Plaza Ste 4015 *Web:* www.lxp.com	New York	NY	10119	212-692-7200	594-6600	654
Lexington School District 4 607 E Fifth St *Web:* www.lexington4.net	Swansea	SC	29160	803-568-1000	568-1020	685
Lexington Steel Corp 5443 W 70th Pl *Web:* www.lexsteel.com	Bedford Park	IL	60638	708-594-9200		492
Lexington Technologies in 99 Rome St *Web:* lexingtontech.net	Farmingdale	NY	11735	631-755-8660		261
Lexington Theological Seminary 631 S Limestone St *TF:* 866-296-6087 ■ *Web:* www.lextheo.edu	Lexington	KY	40508	859-252-0361	281-6042	167-3
Lexington Veteran Affairs Medical Ctr 1101 Veterans Dr *TF:* 800-273-8255 ■ *Web:* www.lexington.va.gov	Lexington	KY	40502	859-233-4511		391-3
Lexington Visitors Ctr 401 W Main St Ste 104 *TF:* 800-845-3959 ■ *Web:* www.visitlex.com	Lexington	KY	40507	859-233-7299	254-4555	206
Lexington Wealth Management 12 Waltham St *Web:* www.lexingtonwealth.com	Lexington	MA	02421	781-860-7745		401
Lexington, The 1096 Grand Ave *Web:* www.snapagency.com	Saint Paul	MN	55105	651-222-5878		671
Lexington-Rockbridge County Chamber of Commerce 100 E Washington St *Web:* www.lexrockchamber.com	Lexington	VA	24450	540-463-5375		139
Lexipol LLC 6B Liberty Ste 200 *Web:* www.lexipol.com	Aliso Viejo	CA	92656	949-484-4444		194
LexisNexis Matthew Bender 744 Broad St *TF:* 800-252-9257 ■ *Web:* www.lexisnexis.com	Newark	NJ	07102	973-820-2000		637-2
LexJet Corp 1680 Fruitville Rd 3rd Fl *TF:* 800-453-9538 ■ *Web:* www.lexjet.com	Sarasota	FL	34236	941-330-1210		628
Lexmark Carpet Mills Inc 285 Kraft Dr *TF:* 800-871-3211 ■ *Web:* www.lexmarkcarpet.com	Dalton	GA	30721	800-871-3211		131
Lexmark International Inc 740 W New Cir Rd *NYSE: LXK* ■ *TF Cust Svc:* 800-539-6275 ■ *Web:* www.lexmark.com	Lexington	KY	40550	859-232-2000		173-6
Lextant Corp 250 S High St Ste 610 *Web:* www.lextant.com	Columbus	OH	43215	614-228-9711		180
Lextech Inc 202 Wilson Downing Rd *Web:* www.lextechky.com	Lexington	KY	40517	859-278-9230		180
Lexus of Memphis Inc 2600 Ridgeway Rd *Web:* lexusofmemphis.com	Memphis	TN	38119	901-362-8833		57
Lexy Pacific Corp 611 Vaqueros Ave *Web:* www.lexypacific.com	Sunnyvale	CA	94085	408-331-8818		174
Leyman Manufacturing Corp 10335 Wayne Ave *Web:* www.leymanlift.com	Cincinnati	OH	45242	513-891-6210		112
LFA (Lupus Foundation of America Inc) 2000 L St NW Ste 410 *TF:* 800-558-0121 ■ *Web:* www.lupus.org	Washington	DC	20036	202-349-1155	349-1156	48-17
LFCU (Lockheed Federal Credit Union) 2340 Hollywood Way *TF:* 800-328-5328 ■ *Web:* logixbanking.com	Burbank	CA	91505	818-565-2020		219
LFI Inc 271 US Hwy 46 Ste C101 *Web:* lfiincorporated.com	Fairfield	NJ	07004	973-882-0550		297-8
LFP Inc 8484 Wilshire Blvd Ste 900 *Web:* hustler.com	Beverly Hills	CA	90211	323-651-5400		637-9

	City	State	Zip	Phone	Fax	Class
LG Barcus & Sons Inc 1430 State Ave *TF:* 800-255-0180 ■ *Web:* www.barcus.com	Kansas City	KS	66102	913-621-1100	621-3288	188-2
LG Chem Power Inc 1857 Technology Dr *Web:* www.lgcpi.com	Troy	MI	48083	248-307-1800		192
LG Electronics USA Inc 1000 Sylvan Ave *TF Tech Supp:* 800-243-0000 ■ *Web:* www.lg.com	Englewood Cliffs	NJ	07632	201-816-2000		173-4
LG Everist Inc 300 S Phillips Ave Ste 200 *TF:* 800-843-7992 ■ *Web:* www.lgeverist.com	Sioux Falls	SD	57117	605-334-5000	334-3656	503-4
LG2 Environmental Solutions Inc 14785 Old St Augustine Rd Ste 4 *TF:* 800-435-0072 ■ *Web:* www.lg2es.com	Jacksonville	FL	32258	904-288-8631		652
LGB & Associates Inc 10400 Eaton Pl Ste 130 *Web:* www.lgb-inc.com	Fairfax	VA	22030	703-359-6950		177
LGH (Lakeshore General Hospital) 160 Stillview Ste 1249 *Web:* www.fondationlakeshore.ca	Pointe-Claire	QC	H9R2Y2	514-630-2081	630-2873	374-2
LGH (Lowell General Hospital) 295 Varnum Ave *TF:* 800-544-2424 ■ *Web:* www.lowellgeneral.org	Lowell	MA	01854	978-937-6000	937-6869	374-3
LGInternational 6700 SW Bradbury Ct *TF:* 800-345-0534 ■ *Web:* www.lgintl.com	Portland	OR	97224	503-620-0520	620-3296	413
LGL Group Inc, The 2525 Shader Rd *NYSE: LGL* ■ *Web:* www.lglgroup.com	Orlando	FL	32804	407-298-2000		185
LGPL (Los Gatos Public Library) 110 E Main St *Web:* www.losgatosca.gov	Los Gatos	CA	95030	408-354-8600	354-0578	434-3
LGS Technologies LP 2950 W Wintergreen Rd *Web:* www.lgstechnologies.com	Lancaster	TX	75134	972-224-9201		326
Lh Computer Services 12296 Wiles Rd *Web:* www.lhcomp.com	Coral Springs	FL	33321	954-752-5805		175
LH Frishkoff & Co 529 Fifth Ave Ste 901 *Web:* www.lhfrishkoff.com	New York	NY	10017	212-808-0070		2
LH Gault & Son Inc 11 Ferry Ln W *Web:* www.gaultenergy.com	Westport	CT	06880	203-227-5181		539
LH Lacy Co 1880 Crown Dr Ste 1200 *TF:* 800-280-2885 ■ *Web:* www.lhlacy.com	Dallas	TX	75234	214-357-0146	350-0662	188-4
LHB Inc 21 W Superior St Ste 500 *Web:* www.lhbcorp.com	Duluth	MN	55802	218-727-8446		261
LHC (Lutheran Medical Ctr) 150 55th St *TF:* 800-906-9762 ■ *Web:* lutheranhealthcare.org/main/home.aspx	Brooklyn	NY	11220	718-630-7000		374-3
LHC Group LLC 901 Hugh Wallis Rd S *NASDAQ: LHCG* ■ *TF:* 866-542-4768 ■ *Web:* www.lhcgroup.com	Lafayette	LA	70508	337-289-8100	289-8168	363
LHCSD (La Habra City School District) 500 N Walnut St	La Habra	CA	90631	562-690-2305		186
LHM Technologies Inc 446 Rowtree Dairy Rd *Web:* www.lhmtech.com	Woodbridge	ON	L4L8H2	905-856-2466		454
LHR 432 S Wabasha St Ste 100 *Web:* www.lodgohotolo.com	Saint Paul	MN	55107	651-340-1880		377
LHR Services & Equipment Inc lc-disc 4200 Fm 1128 Rd *TF:* 800-943-2324 ■ *Web:* www.lhrservices.com	Pearland	TX	77584	713-943-2324		608
LHS (Lanier Health Services) 4800 48th St **Fax:* Admissions ■ *Web:* www.lanierhospital.com	Valley	AL	36854	334-756-1400	756-6698*	374-3
LHS Productions Inc 260 Union St *Web:* www.videobankdigital.com	Northvale	NJ	07647	201-767-2002		177
LHSD (Laurel Highlands School District) 304 Bailey Ave	Uniontown	PA	15401	724-437-2821		685
LHUCA (Louise Hopkins Underwood Ctr for the Arts) 511 Ave K *Web:* www.lhuca.org	Lubbock	TX	79401	806-762-8606		50-2
LHV Power Corp 10221 Buena Vista Ave *Web:* www.lhvpower.com	Santee	CA	92071	619-258-7700		253
LHWH Advertising & PR 3005 Hwy 17 N Bypass *Web:* www.lhwh.com	Myrtle Beach	SC	29577	843-448-1123		7
Li Cor Inc PO Box 4425 *TF:* 800-447-3576 ■ *Web:* www.licor.com	Lincoln	NE	68504	402-467-3576	467-2819	419
Li'l Porgy's Bar-B-Q 1917 W Springfield Ave *Web:* www.lilporgysbbq.com	Champaign	IL	61821	217-398-8575		671
Li'l Thrift Food Marts Inc 1007 Arsenal Ave *TF:* 800-318-9806 ■ *Web:* www.shortstopfoodmarts.com	Fayetteville	NC	28305	910-433-4490		204
LIA (Laser Institute of America) 13501 Ingenuity Dr Ste 128 *TF:* 800-345-2737 ■ *Web:* www.lia.org	Orlando	FL	32826	407-380-1553	380-5588	49-19
LIA (Leather Industries of America) 3050 K St NW Ste 400 *TF:* 800-635-0617 ■ *Web:* www.leatherusa.com	Washington	DC	20007	202-342-8497	342-8583	49-4
Lia Auto Group, The 1258 Central Ave *TF:* 855-212-7985 ■ *Web:* www.liacars.com	Albany	NY	12205	855-212-7985		57
Liacouras Ctr 1776 N Broad St *TF:* 800-298-4200 ■ *Web:* www.liacourascenter.com	Philadelphia	PA	19121	215-204-2400		572
Liaison Committee on Medical Education (LCME) 330 N Wabash Ave Ste 39300 *Web:* www.lcme.org	Chicago	IL	60611	312-464-4933		48-1
Liaison Creative + Marketing 4302 Airport Blvd *Web:* www.liaisonresources.com	Austin	TX	78722	512-323-0550		260
Libbey Inc 300 Madison Ave PO Box 10060 *NYSE: LBY* ■ *TF:* 888-794-8469 ■ *Web:* www.libbey.com	Toledo	OH	43699	419-325-2100		334
Libby Hill Seafood Restaurants Inc 4517 W Market St *Web:* www.libbyhill.com	Greensboro	NC	27407	336-294-0505		670
Libby Laboratories Inc 1700 Sixth St *TF:* 800-843-2436 ■ *Web:* www.libbylabs.com	Berkeley	CA	94710	510-527-5400	527-8687	479
Libby Perszyk Kathman Holdings Inc 19 Garfield Pl *Web:* www.lpk.com	Cincinnati	OH	45202	513-241-6330		195

	City	State	Zip	Phone	Fax	Class
Liberal Area Chamber of Commerce PO Box 676 *Web:* www.liberalkschamber.com	Liberal	KS	67905	620-624-3855	624-8851	139
Liberal Party of Canada 81 Metcalfe St *TF:* 888-542-3725 ■ *Web:* www.liberal.ca	Ottawa	ON	K1P6M8	888-542-3725		615
Liberal R-II School District 104 N Payne *Web:* www.liberal.k12.mo.us	Liberal	MO	64762	417-843-2125		685
Embassy 5201 16th St NW *Web:* www.liberianembassyus.org	Washington	DC	20011	202-723-0437	723-0436	257
Liberman Broadcasting, INC 1845 Empire Ave *Web:* www.lbimedia.com	Burbank	CA	91504	818-729-5300		741
Libero & Kappel CPAs 57 Old Country Rd	Westbury	NY	11590	516-333-5511		2
Libertarian Party 2600 Virginia Ave NW Ste 200 *TF:* 800-735-1776 ■ *Web:* www.lp.org	Washington	DC	20037	202-333-0008	333-0072	616
Liberty Advisor Group LLC The Mercantile Exchange 30 S Wacker Dr 22nd Fl *Web:* www.libertyadvisorgroup.com	Chicago	IL	60606	312-869-9707		466
Liberty Bank 315 Main St *TF:* 800-622-6732 ■ *Web:* www.liberty-bank.com	Middletown	CT	06457	800-354-8950		70
Liberty Bank & Trust Co PO Box 60131 *TF:* 800-883-3943 ■ *Web:* www.libertybank.net	New Orleans	LA	70160	504-240-5100		70
Liberty Bell Ctr 6th & Market Sts *Web:* www.nps.gov	Philadelphia	PA	19106	215-965-2305	861-4950	50-4
Liberty Bell Equipment Corp 3201 S 76th St *TF:* 800-541-5827 ■ *Web:* www.medcotool.com	Philadelphia	PA	19153	215-492-6700		200
Liberty Bottle Co 2900 Sutherland Dr *Web:* www.libertybottles.com	Union Gap	WA	98903	509-834-6500	494-0189	124
Liberty Brass Turning Company Inc 1200 Shames Dr *TF:* 800-345-5939 ■ *Web:* www.libertybrass.com	Westbury	NY	11590	718-784-2911	784-2038	621
Liberty Carton Co 870 Louisiana Ave *Web:* www.libertycarton.com	Golden Valley	MN	55426	763-540-9600		100
Liberty Casting Company LLC 550 S Liberty Rd *TF:* 800-364-6038 ■ *Web:* www.libertycasting.com	Delaware	OH	43015	740-363-1941		492
Liberty Ch 1971 University Blvd *TF:* 800-332-1883 ■ *Web:* www.liberty.edu	Lynchburg	VA	24515	434-582-2000		740
Liberty Coating Company LLC 21 S Steel Rd *Web:* www.libertycoating.com	Morrisville	PA	19067	215-736-1111		481
Liberty Communications Business Office 413 N Calhoun St *Web:* www.libertycommunications.com	West Liberty	IA	52776	319-627-2145		387
Liberty Correctional Institution 11064 NW Dempsey Barron Rd *TF:* 800-543-5353 ■ *Web:* dc.state.fl.us	Bristol	FL	32321	850-643-9400	643-9412	213
Liberty County PO Box 523 *TF:* 800-760-2315 ■ *Web:* www.libertycountyflorida.com	Bristol	FL	32321	850-643-2360		338
Liberty County 112 N Main St *Web:* www.libertycounty.org	Hinesville	GA	31310	912-876-2164		338
Liberty County 1923 Sam Houston St *Web:* www.co.liberty.tx.us	Liberty	TX	77575	936-336-4600		338
Liberty County Chamber of Commerce 425 W Oglethorpe Hwy *TF:* 855-846-3940 ■ *Web:* www.libertycounty.org	Hinesville	GA	31313	912-368-4445	368-4677	139
Liberty Diversified International Inc 5600 Hwy 169 N *TF:* 800-421-1270 ■ *Web:* www.libertydiversified.com	New Hope	MN	55428	763-536-6600	536-6685	360-3
Liberty Drug & Surgical Inc 195 Main St *TF:* 877-816-0111 ■ *Web:* www.libertydrug.com	Chatham	NJ	07928	973-635-6200	635-6208	237
Liberty Falls State Recreation Site Mile 235 Edgerton Hwy *Web:* dnr.alaska.gov	Glennallen	AK	99588	907-823-2223		565
Liberty Forge Inc PO Box 1210 *TF:* 800-231-2377 ■ *Web:* www.libertyforgeinc.com	Liberty	TX	77575	800-231-2377		483
Liberty Fund Inc 8335 Allison Pt Trial Ste 300 *TF:* 800-955-8335 ■ *Web:* www.libertyfund.org	Indianapolis	IN	46250	317-842-0880	579-6060	305
Liberty Funds Group Inc 4711 Lakeside Dr	Colleyville	TX	76034	214-369-0500		528
Liberty Furniture Industries 6021 Greensboro Dr **Fax:* Cust Svc ■ *Web:* www.mylibertyfurniture.com	Atlanta	GA	30336	404-629-1003	629-0717*	319-1
Liberty Glass & Metal Industries Inc 339 Riverside Dr *Web:* www.lgminc.net	North Grosvenordale	CT	06255	860-923-3623		234
Liberty Global Inc 12300 Liberty Blvd *NASDAQ: LBTYA* ■ *Web:* www.libertyglobal.com	Englewood	CO	80112	303-220-6600		736
Liberty Group LLC 411 30th St 2nd Fl *TF:* 888-588-5818 ■ *Web:* www.libertygroupllc.com	Oakland	CA	94609	510-658-1880	658-1886	690
Liberty Hall Historic Site 202 Wilkinson St *TF:* 800-325-0063 ■ *Web:* www.libertyhall.org	Frankfort	KY	40601	502-227-2560		50-3
Liberty Hardware Mfg Corp 140 Business Pk Dr **Fax Area Code:* 336 ■ *TF:* 800-542-3789 ■ *Web:* www.libertyhardware.com	Winston-Salem	NC	27107	800-542-3789	769-1839*	350
Liberty Homes Inc 1101 Eisenhower Dr N *OTC: LIBHA* ■ *Web:* www.libertyhomesinc.com	Goshen	IN	46526	574-533-0431		505
Liberty Hospital 2525 Glenn Hendren Dr *TF:* 800-344-3829 ■ *Web:* www.libertyhospital.org	Liberty	MO	64068	816-781-7200	781-7550	374-3
Liberty Hotel, The 215 Charles St *Web:* www.libertyhotel.com	Boston	MA	02114	617-224-4000		378
Liberty House 76 Audrey Zapp Dr *Web:* www.libertyhouserestaurant.com	Jersey City	NJ	07305	201-395-0300		671

	Phone	Fax	Class
Liberty Independent School District 1600 Grand Ave .... Liberty TX 77575 *Web:* www.libertyisd.net	936-336-7213	336-2283	685
Liberty Industries Inc 130 E Cemetery Rd........................Fillmore IN 46128 *TF:* 800-446-1407 ■ *Web:* www.liberty-industries.com	765-246-4031		779
Liberty Industries LC 2855 Hwy 261 .... Newburgh IN 47630 *Web:* www.towerinnovations.net	812-853-0595		480
Liberty Institutional Review Board Inc 2024 Larchmont Dr..........................Deland FL 32724 *Web:* www.libertyirb.com	386-740-9278		474
Liberty Lane Service Company LLC Liberty Ln.................................. Hampton NH 03842 *Web:* www.latonaassociates.com	603-929-2600		401
Liberty Maritime Corp 1979 Marcus Ave Ste 200................Lake Success NY 11042 *Web:* libertygl.com	516-488-8800	488-8806	313
Liberty Media Holding Corp 12300 Liberty Blvd.......................Englewood CO 80112 *Web:* www.libertymedia.com	720-875-5400		360-3
Liberty Memorial Museum 100 W 26th St.......................... Kansas City MO 64108 *Web:* www.theworldwar.org	816-784-1918		520
Liberty Mountain Resort & Conference Ctr 78 Country Club Trl ....Carroll Valley PA 17320 *TF:* 800-548-8504 ■ *Web:* www.libertymountainresort.com	717-642-8282		669
Liberty Moving & Storage Inc 350 Moreland Rd .... Commack NY 11725 *Web:* www.libertymoving.com	631-234-3000		780
Liberty Mutual Group 175 Berkeley St............Boston MA 02116 *Web:* www.libertymutual.com	617-357-9500		391-4
Liberty Nursing & Rehabilitation Ctr 535 N 17th St...........................Allentown PA 18104 *Web:* heartland-manorcare.com	610-432-4351	435-4470	450
Liberty Oak Restaurant & Bar 100 W Washington St Ste D............... Greensboro NC 27401 *Web:* www.libertyoakrestaurant.com	336-273-7057		671
Liberty Paper Inc 13500 Liberty Ln .... Becker MN 55308 *Web:* www.libertycarton.com/?act=landing&cid=6	763-261-6100		548
Liberty Pioneer Energy Source Inc 1411 East 840 North.......................... Orem UT 84097 *Web:* www.libertypioneer.com	801-224-4771		540
Liberty Property Trust 500 Chesterfield Pkwy ....Malvern PA 19355 *NYSE: LPT* ■ *TF:* 800-732-0330 ■ *Web:* www.libertyproperty.com	610-648-1700	644-4129	655
Liberty Pumps Inc 7000 Apple Tree Ave...........Bergen NY 14416 *TF:* 800-543-2550 ■ *Web:* www.libertypumps.com	585-494-1817		641
Liberty Safe & Security Products Inc 1199 W Utah Ave ....Payson UT 84651 *TF:* 800-247-5625 ■ *Web:* www.libertysafe.com	801-925-1000	465-2712	487
Liberty Savings Bank FSB 3435 Airborne Rd Ste B .... Wilmington OH 45177 *TF:* 800-436-6300 ■ *Web:* www.libertysavingsbank.com	800-436-6300		70
Liberty Science Ctr Liberty State Pk 222 Jersey City Blvd..........Jersey City NJ 07305 *Web:* www.lsc.org	201-200-1000		520
Liberty Staffing LLC 550 Balmoral Cir N Ste 201 ....Jacksonville FL 32218 *Web:* www.libertystaffingllc.com	904-696-0285		260
Liberty State Park 200Morris Pesin Dr ....Jersey City NJ 07305 *Web:* www.njparksandforests.org/parks/liberty.html	201-915-3440	915-3408	565
Liberty Tax Service Inc 1716 Corporate Landing Pkwy .... Virginia Beach VA 23454 *TF Cust Svc:* 800-790-3863 ■ *Web:* www.libertytax.com	757-493-8855	493-0169	734
Liberty Throwing Company Inc 214 Pringle St.............................. Kingston PA 18704 *TF:* 800-827-8478 ■ *Web:* www.libertythrowing.com	570-287-1114	283-3531	745-9
Liberty Toyota Scion 4397 Rt 130 S .... Burlington NJ 08016 *TF:* 888-809-7798 ■ *Web:* www.libertytoyota.com	609-386-6300		516
Liberty Travel Inc 69 Spring St............... Ramsey NJ 07446 *TF:* 888-271-1584 ■ *Web:* www.libertytravel.com	888-271-1584		771
Liberty Tree Mall 100 Independence Way...................... Danvers MA 01923 *TF:* 877-746-6642 ■ *Web:* www.simon.com	978-777-0794	777-9857	460
Liberty University 1971 University Blvd .... Lynchburg VA 24502 **Fax Area Code: 800* ■ **Fax:* Admissions ■ *TF:* 800-543-5317 ■ *Web:* www.liberty.edu	434-582-2000	542-2311*	166
Liberty Vegetable Oil Co 15306 S Carmenita Rd .... Santa Fe Springs CA 90670 *Web:* www.libertyvegetableoil.com	562-921-3567		297-8
Liberty Wood Products 874 Iotla Church Rd .... Franklin NC 28734 *Web:* www.libertywoodproducts.net	828-524-7958	369-7652	819
Liberty-Dayton Area Chamber of Commerce 1801 Trinity St .... Liberty TX 77575 *Web:* www.libertydaytonchamber.com	936-336-5736	336-1159	139
Liberty-Eylau Independent School District 2901 Leopard Dr..........................Texarkana TX 75501 *Web:* www.leisd.net	903-832-1535	838-9444	685
Liberty-Pittsburgh Systems Inc 3498 Grand Ave .... Pittsburgh PA 15225	412-771-9900		110
LibertyTree 100 Swan Way.............. Oakland CA 94621 *TF:* 800-927-8733 ■ *Web:* www.independent.org	510-632-1366	568-6040	95
Libertyville District 70 1381 West Lake St .... Libertyville IL 60048 *Web:* www.d70.k12.il.us	847-362-9695	362-3003	685
Libertyville Bank & Trust Co 507 N Milwaukee Ave...................... Libertyville IL 60048 *Web:* www.libertyvillebank.com	847-367-6800		70
Libertyville Chevrolet Inc 1001 S Milwaukee Ave..................... Libertyville IL 60048 *TF Sales:* 877-520-1807 ■ *Web:* www.libertyvillechevrolet.com	847-362-1400		516
Libman Co 220 N Sheldon St.............. Arcola IL 61910 **Fax Area Code: 217* ■ *TF:* 877-818-3380 ■ *Web:* www.libman.com	877-818-3380	268-4168*	103
Libman Co, The 220 N Sheldon .... Arcola IL 61910 *Web:* www.libman.com	217-268-4200		103
Libra Industries Inc 7770 Div Dr ....Mentor OH 44060 *TF:* 800-825-1674 ■ *Web:* www.libraindustries.com	440-974-7770		625
Library & Information Technology Assn (LITA) 50 E Huron St............................... Chicago IL 60611 *TF:* 800-545-2433 ■ *Web:* www.ala.org	312-280-4270	280-3257	49-11
Library and Archives Canada 550 de la Cite Blvd .... Gatineau QC K1A0N4 *TF:* 800-461-8009 ■ *Web:* www.collectionscanada.ca	613-995-6274		434
Library Binding Service (LBS) 1801 Thompson Ave.......................Des Moines IA 50316 **Fax Area Code: 800* ■ *TF:* 800-247-5323 ■ *Web:* www.lbsbind.com	515-262-3191	262-4091*	92
Library Company of Philadelphia 1314 Locust St ....Philadelphia PA 19107 *Web:* www.librarycompany.org	215-546-3181	546-5167	434-4
Library Foundation of Hennepin County, The 300 Nicollet Mall ....Minneapolis MN 55401 *Web:* www.supporthclib.org	612-543-8100		434-3
Library Hotel 299 Madison Ave................New York NY 10017 *TF:* 877-793-7323 ■ *Web:* www.libraryhotel.com	212-983-4500		379
Library Journal 160 Varick St 11th Fl ....New York NY 10013 *TF:* 800-588-1030 ■ *Web:* lj.libraryjournal.com	646-380-0700	380-0756	457-8
Library Leadership & Management Assn (LLAMA) 50 E Huron St.............................Chicago IL 60611 *TF:* 800-545-2433 ■ *Web:* www.ala.org/llama	800-545-2433		49-11
Library of Congress (LOC) 101 Independence Ave SE...................Washington DC 20540 *TF:* 800-424-9530 ■ *Web:* www.loc.gov	202-707-5000		434-3
American Folklife Ctr 101 Independence Ave SE ....Washington DC 20540 *Web:* www.loc.gov/folklife	202-707-5510	707-2076	342
Congressional Research Service 101 Independence Ave SE ....Washington DC 20540 *Web:* www.loc.gov/crsinfo	202-707-5507		342
Law Library of Congress 101 Independence Ave SE.................Washington DC 20540 *TF:* 800-447-8737 ■ *Web:* loc.gov/law/index.html	202-707-5079	707-1820	342
National Library Service for the Blind & Physicall 1291 Taylor St NW.......................Washington DC 20542 *TF:* 888-657-7323 ■ *Web:* www.loc.gov/nls	202-707-5100	707-0712	342
US Copyright Office 101 Independence Ave SE.................Washington DC 20559 *TF:* 877-476-0778 ■ *Web:* www.copyright.gov	202-707-3000		342
Library of Hattiesburg Petal & Forrest County 329 Hardy St.............................. Hattiesburg MS 39401 *Web:* hatt.ent.sirsi.net/client/default2e	601-582-4461		434-3
Library of Michigan, The 702 W Kalamazoo St PO Box 30007............ Lansing MI 48909 *TF:* 800-726-7323 ■ *Web:* www.michigan.gov	517-373-1580	373-4480	434-5
Library of Rush University *Rush University Medical Ctr* 600 S Paulina St ....Chicago IL 60612 *Web:* rushu.libguides.com	312-942-7100		434-1
Library of Virginia 800 E Broad St............ Richmond VA 23219 *Web:* www.lva.virginia.gov	804-692-3500	692-3594	434-5
Library Reproduction Service 14214 S Figueroa St.......................Los Angeles CA 90061 *TF:* 800-255-5002 ■ *Web:* www.largeprintschoolbooks.com	800-255-5002		626
Library System of Lebanon County 125 N Seventh St ....Lebanon PA 17046 *Web:* lclibs.org	717-273-7624	273-2719	434-3
Library Theatre, The 200 Municipal Dr...........Hoover AL 35216 *Web:* www.thelibrarytheatre.com	205-444-7888		572
Liburdi Engineering Ltd 400 Hwy 6 N........... Dundas ON L9H7K4 *Web:* www.liburdi.com	905-689-0734		454
Libyan Arab Jamahiriya 309-315 E 48th St ....New York NY 10017 *TF:* 800-253-9646 ■ *Web:* www.un.org	212-752-5775	593-4787	784
Liccardi Ford Inc 1615 Rt 22 W ....Watchung NJ 07069 *Web:* liccardi.com	908-561-7500		57
Licensing Executives Society (LES) 1800 Diagonal Rd Ste 280 .... Alexandria VA 22314 *Web:* www.lesi.org	703-836-3106	836-3107	49-18
Licensing Resource Group LLC 442 Century Ln Ste 100 .... Holland MI 49423 *Web:* learfieldlicensing.com	616-395-0676		195
LICH (Long Island College Hospital) 339 Hicks St.............................. Brooklyn NY 11201 *TF:* 800-227-8922 ■ *Web:* www.downstate.edu/lich	718-780-1000	270-4775	374-3
Licher Direct Mail Inc 980 Seco St............Pasadena CA 91103 *TF:* 800-649-6277 ■ *Web:* www.licherdm.com	626-795-3333		5
Lichtenwald-Johnston Iron Works Corp 7840 Lehigh St........................ Morton Grove IL 60053 *Web:* lichtenwald-johnston.com	847-966-1100	966-1159	480
Lick Observatory 7281 Mt Hamilton Rd.....................Mt Hamilton CA 95140 *TF:* 800-866-1131 ■ *Web:* www.ucolick.org	408-274-5061		598
Licking County 20 S Second St..................Newark OH 43055 *Web:* www.lcounty.com	740-670-5110	670-5119	338
Licking County Chamber of Commerce 50 W Locust St.............................Newark OH 43055 *Web:* www.lickingcountychamber.com	740-345-9757	345-5141	139
Licking Memorial Hospital 1320 W Main St ....Newark OH 43055 *Web:* www.lmhealth.org	740-348-4000		374-3
Licking Valley Oil Inc PO Box 246................Butler KY 41006 *TF:* 800-899-9449 ■ *Web:* www.lvoinc.com	859-472-7111	472-7112	579
Licking Valley Rural Electric Co-op Corp 271 Main St ....West Liberty KY 41472 *TF:* 800-596-6530 ■ *Web:* lvrecc.com	606-743-3179	743-2415	245
LICT Corp 401 Theodore Fremd Ave............ Rye NY 10580 *TF:* 800-690-6903 ■ *Web:* www.lictcorp.com	914-921-8821	921-6410	736
Liddle & Robinson LLP 800 Third Ave Fl 8 ....New York NY 10022 *Web:* www.liddlerobinson.com	212-687-8500		428
LiDestri 815 Whitney Rd W..................... Fairport NY 14450 *Web:* www.lidestrifoods.com	585-377-7700	377-8150	296-20
Lidia's Italy 1400 Smallman St .... Pittsburgh PA 15222 *Web:* www.lidias-pittsburgh.com	412-552-0150		671
Lidia's Kansas City 101 W 22nd St .... Kansas City MO 64108 *TF:* 800-433-1426 ■ *Web:* www.lidias-kc.com	816-221-3722		671

Name / Address	City	State	ZIP	Phone	Fax	Class
Lido Beach Resort 700 Ben Franklin Dr *TF:* 800-441-2113 ■ *Web:* www.lidobeachresort.com	Sarasota	FL	34236	941-388-2161		707
Lido Van & Storage Co Inc 2152 Alton Pkwy Ste N **Fax Area Code:* 323	Irvine	CA	92606	949-863-9000	221-3479*	519
LidoChem Inc 20 Village Ct *Web:* www.lidochem.com	Hazlet	NJ	07730	732-888-8000	264-2751	146
Lieber Correctional Institution 136 Wilborn Ave *Web:* www.doc.sc.gov/institutions/lieber.jsp	Ridgeville	SC	29472	843-875-3332		213
Lieberman Ctr for Health & Rehabilitation 9700 Gross Pt Rd *Web:* cje.net	Skokie	IL	60076	847-674-7210		450
Lieberman Group LLC, The 223 NW Second St Ste 300 *Web:* www.ltnow.com	Evansville	IN	47708	812-434-6600		179
Lieberman Management Services Inc 230 W Monroe Ste 1550 **Fax Area Code:* 312 ■ *Web:* www.liebermanmanagement.com	Chicago	IL	60606	847-459-0000	553-1240*	463
Lieberman Productions 455 Ninth St *Web:* www.lieberman.com	San Francisco	CA	94103	415-955-0855		738
Lieberman Research 98 Cutter Mill Rd *Web:* www.liebermanresearch.com	Great Neck	NY	11021	516-829-8880	829-8880	466
Lieberman Software Corp 1900 Ave of the Stars Ste 425 *TF:* 800-829-6263 ■ *Web:* www.liebsoft.com	Los Angeles	CA	90067	310-550-8575		177
Liebherr-America Inc 4100 Chestnut Ave *Web:* liebherr.com	Newport News	VA	23607	757-245-5251		190
Liebherr-Canada Ltd 1015 Sutton Dr *Web:* www.liebherr.com	Burlington	ON	L7L5Z8	905-319-9222		690
Liechtenstein Embassy 2900 K St NW Ste 602B *Web:* www.liechtensteinusa.org	Washington	DC	20007	202-331-0590		257
Lied Ctr for Performing Arts 301 N 12th St *TF:* 800-432-3231 ■ *Web:* www.unl.edu	Lincoln	NE	68588	402-472-4700		572
Lied Discovery Children's Museum 360 Promenade Pl *TF:* 800-768-9653 ■ *Web:* www.discoverykidslv.org	Las Vegas	NV	89106	702-382-3445	382-0592	521
Lied Lodge & Conference Center 2700 Sylvan Rd *TF:* 800-546-5433 ■ *Web:* liedlodge.org	Nebraska City	NE	68410	402-873-8733		205
Lied's Landscape Design & Construction N120 W21350 Freistadt Rd *Web:* www.lieds.com/design	Germantown	WI	53022	262-255-4088		422
Liese Lumber Company Inc 319 E Main St *Web:* www.lieselumber.com	Belleville	IL	62220	618-234-0105		364
Lieu Ted (Rep D - CA) 233 Cannon HOB *Web:* lieu.house.gov	Washington	DC	20515	202-225-3976		342-2
Life 96.5 6300 S Tallgrass Ave *Web:* life965.fm	Sioux Falls	SD	57108	605-339-1270	339-1271	645-152
Life 97.3 1101 E Central Entrance *Web:* life973.com	Duluth	MN	55811	218-722-6700		645-51
Life Advantages LLC 600 First Ave N Ste 307 *Web:* www.lifeadvantages.com	St. Petersburg	FL	33701	727-381-9446		260
Life Alert 16027 Ventura Blvd *TF:* 800-920-3410 ■ *Web:* www.lifealert.com	Encino	CA	91436	818-700-7000		575
Life Baptist Church Mission Cottage 158 Sandy Acres Way	Saint Stephen	SC	29479	843-567-4775		48-20
Life Care Centers of America 3570 Keith St NW PO Box 3480 *Web:* www.lcca.com	Cleveland	TN	37312	423-472-9585	476-5974	451
Life Changing Radio 70 James St Ste 201 *Web:* lifechangingradio.com	Worcester	MA	01603	508-831-9863	831-7964	645-179
Life Cycle Engineering Inc 4360 Corporate Rd *Web:* lce.com	N Charleston	SC	29405	843-744-7110		261
Life Equity LLC 5611 Hudson Dr # 100 *Web:* www.lifeequity.net	Hudson	OH	44236	330-342-7772	342-7782	796
Life Flight Network LLC 22285 Yellow Gate Ln NE *TF:* 800-232-0911 ■ *Web:* www.lifeflight.org	Aurora	OR	97002	503-678-4364		13
Life Inc 2609 Royall Ave *Web:* www.lifeincorporated.com	Goldsboro	NC	27534	919-778-1900	778-1911	48-15
Life Insurance Co of Alabama 302 Broad St *TF:* 800-226-2371 ■ *Web:* www.licoa.com	Gadsden	AL	35901	256-543-2022		391-2
Life Measurement Inc 1850 Bates Ave *Web:* www.bodpod.com	Concord	CA	94520	925-676-6002		476
Life Medical Technologies Inc 3 Forest View Dr Hopewell Jct Hopewell Jct	East Fishkill	NY	12533	845-896-1230		743
Life of Learning Foundation 459 Galice Rd *Web:* guyfinley.org	Merlin	OR	97532	541-476-1200		48-20
Life of the South Insurance Co 10151 Deerwood Pk Blvd Bldg 100 *TF:* 800-888-2738 ■ *Web:* www.life-south.com	Jacksonville	FL	32256	904-350-9660		391-5
Life Outreach International 1801 W Euless Blvd *Web:* www.lifetoday.org	Euless	TX	76040	817-267-4211		48-20
Life Pacific College 1100 W Covina Blvd *TF:* 877-886-5433 ■ *Web:* www.lifepacific.edu	San Dimas	CA	91773	909-599-5433		161
Life Packaging Technology LLC 2751 Tern Cir Ste A **Fax Area Code:* 714 ■ *Web:* www.lifepackagingtechnology.com	Costa Mesa	CA	92626	949-395-8145	751-5027*	393
Life Partners Inc (LPI) 204 Woodhew Dr *TF:* 800-368-5569 ■ *Web:* www.lifepartnersinc.com	Waco	TX	76712	254-751-7797		796
Life Products Solutions Group Llc 7900 SW 57th Ave Ste 23 *TF:* 866-772-2370 ■ *Web:* www.lpsgroup.com	Miami	FL	33143	305-668-8780	668-8323	463
Life Radio Ministries Inc 100 S Hill St Ste 100 *Web:* www.wmvv.com	Griffin	GA	30223	770-229-2020		645-10
Life Sciences Greenhouse 225 Market St Ste 500 *Web:* www.lsgpa.com	Harrisburg	PA	17101	717-635-2100		792
Life Settlement Solutions Inc 9201 Spectrum Ctr Blvd Ste 105 *TF:* 800-762-3387 ■ *Web:* www.lss-corp.com	San Diego	CA	92123	858-576-8067	576-9329	796
Life Style Staffing 6765 W Greenfield Ave *TF:* 800-813-4874 ■ *Web:* www.lifestylestaffing.com	Milwaukee	WI	53214	414-475-0090		260
Life Systems Inc 515 Trade Ctr Blvd	Chesterfield	MO	63005	636-787-2100		475
Life Trust LLC 330 Madison Ave 6th Fl *Web:* www.life-trust.net	New York	NY	10017	212-653-0840	653-0844	796
Life University 1269 Barclay Cir *TF:* 800-543-3203 ■ *Web:* www.life.edu	Marietta	GA	30060	770-426-2884		166
Life's Doors Hospice 420 S Orchard St	Boise	ID	83705	208-344-6500	344-6590	371
Life's WORC 1501 Franklin Ave PO Box 8165 *Web:* www.lifesworc.org	Garden City	NY	11530	516-741-9000	741-5560	48-15
Life:WIRE Corp 129 Blantyre Ave Ste 200 *TF:* 888-738-4260 ■ *Web:* www.lifewiregroup.com	Toronto	ON	M1N2R6	888-738-4260	738-8981	177
Life-Assist Inc 11277 Sunrise Park Dr *TF:* 800-824-6016 ■ *Web:* www.life-assist.com	Rancho Cordova	CA	95742	800-824-6016		475
LifeBanc 4775 Richmond Rd *TF:* 888-558-5433 ■ *Web:* www.lifebanc.org	Cleveland	OH	44128	216-752-5433	751-4204	545
Lifeblood Mid-South Regional Blood Ctr 1040 Madison Ave *TF:* 888-543-3256 ■ *Web:* www.lifeblood.org	Memphis	TN	38104	901-522-8585		89
DeSoto Ctr 1040 Madison Ave *Web:* www.lifeblood.org	Memphis	TN	38104	901-271-1260		89
Lifecare Alliance 1699 W Mound St *Web:* www.lifecarealliance.org	Columbus	OH	43223	614-278-3130		363
LifeCare Health Partners 225 Penn Ave *Web:* lifecare-hospitals.com	Pittsburgh	PA	15221	412-247-2424	247-2333	374-7
LifeCare Solutions Inc 10119 Carroll Canyon Rd *Web:* www.lifecaresoln.com	San Diego	CA	92131	858-444-2800		363
LifeCell Corp 1 Millennium Way **Fax Area Code:* 908 ■ *TF:* 800-226-2714 ■ *Web:* www.lifecell.com	Branchburg	NJ	08876	800-226-2714	947-1089*	545
Lifechurch-tv 4600 E Second St *Web:* www.life.church	Edmond	OK	73034	405-478-5433		48 20
Lifecnter Plus Lf. Heath Fitnes 5133 Darrow Rd *Web:* www.lifecenterplus.com	Hudson	OH	44236	330-655-2377		354
LifeCore Biomedical LLC 3515 Lyman Blvd *TF Cust Svc:* 800-348-4368 ■ *Web:* www.lifecore.com	Chaska	MN	55318	952-368-4300	368-3411	85
LifeCourse Associates Inc 9080 Eaton Park Rd *TF:* 866-537-4999 ■ *Web:* www.lifecourse.com	Great Falls	VA	22066	866-537-4999		193
LifeFone 16 Yellowstone Ave *TF:* 888-687-0451 ■ *Web:* www.lifefone.com	White Plains	NY	10607	888-687-0451		575
LIFEFORCE USA 495 Raleigh Ave **Fax Area Code:* 800 ■ *TF:* 800-531-4877 ■ *Web:* lifeforce.net	El Cajon	CA	92020	858-218-3200	809-8208*	345
LifeLabs Inc 3680 Gilmore Way *Web:* www.lifelabs.com	Burnaby	BC	V5G4V8	604-431-5005		418
LifeLearn Inc 367 Woodlawn Rd W Unit 9 *TF:* 888-770-2218 ■ *Web:* www.lifelearn.com	Guelph	ON	N1H7K9	519-767-5043		242
Lifeline Data Centers LLC 401 N Shadeland Ave *Web:* www.lifelinedatacenters.com	Indianapolis	IN	46219	317-423-2591		225
Lifeline Foods LLC 2811 S 11th St Rd *Web:* www.lifeline-foods.com	Saint Joseph	MO	64503	816-279-1651		144
Lifeline Medical Assoc LLC 99 Cherry Hill Rd Ste 220 *TF:* 800-845-2785 ■ *Web:* www.lma-llc.com	Parsippany	NJ	07054	800-845-2785		374-3
Lifeline of Ohio 770 Kinnear Rd Ste 200 *TF:* 800-525-5667 ■ *Web:* www.lifelineofohio.org	Columbus	OH	43212	614-291-5667	291-0660	545
Lifeline Scientific Inc 1 Pierce Pl Ste 475W *TF:* 800-631-5590 ■ *Web:* lifeline-scientific.com	Itasca	IL	60143	847-294-0300		250
Lifeline Theatre 6912 N Glenwood Ave *TF:* 800-650-6449 ■ *Web:* www.lifelinetheatre.com	Chicago	IL	60626	773-761-4477	761-4582	572
Lifelink Foundation Inc 409 Bayshore Blvd *TF:* 800-262-5775 ■ *Web:* www.lifelinkfoundation.org	Tampa	FL	33606	813-253-2640		363
LifeLink Tissue Bank 9661 Delaney Creek Blvd *TF:* 800-683-2400 ■ *Web:* www.lifelinktissuebank.org	Tampa	FL	33619	813-886-8111	886-1851	545
Lifeloc Technologies Inc 12441 W 49th Ave Unit 4 *TF:* 800-722-4817 ■ *Web:* www.lifeloc.com	Wheat Ridge	CO	80033	303-431-9500		407
Lifelong Medical Care Inc PO Box 11247 *Web:* www.lifelongmedical.org	Berkeley	CA	94712	510-981-4100		374-3
LifeNet 1864 Concert Dr *TF:* 800-847-7831 ■ *Web:* www.lifenethealth.org	Virginia Beach	VA	23453	757-464-4761		545
LifeNet Health Northwest 501 SW 39th St *TF:* 800-847-7831 ■ *Web:* www.lifenethealth.org	Renton	WA	98057	425-981-8900		545
Lifenet Inc 6225 St Michaels Dr *TF:* 800-832-6395 ■ *Web:* www.lifenetems.org	Texarkana	TX	75503	903-832-8531		30
Lifepath Hospice 3010 W Azeele St *TF:* 800-209-2200 ■ *Web:* www.chaptershealth.org	Tampa	FL	33609	813-877-2200	872-7037	371
LifePics Inc 5777 Central Ave Ste 120 *Web:* www.lifepics.com	Boulder	CO	80301	303-413-9500		225
LifePlans Inc 51 Sawyer Rd Ste 340 *Web:* www.lifeplansinc.com	Waltham	MA	02453	781-893-7600	647-3552	194

	Phone	Fax	Class
LifePoint Health 330 Seven Springs Way .... Brentwood TN 37027 *NASDAQ: LPNT* ■ *TF:* 888-982-9144 ■ *Web:* www.lifepointhealth.net	615-920-7000		353
LifePoint Inc 164 Lott Ct Ste B .... West Columbia SC 29169	803-796-2195		269
Lifeport Inc 1610 Heritage St................. Woodland WA 98674 *Web:* www.lifeport.com	360-225-1212	225-1214	256
LifeRing Secular Recovery 1440 Broadway Ste 312 .... Oakland CA 94612 *TF:* 800-811-4142 ■ *Web:* www.lifering.org	510-763-0779	763-1513	48-21
LifeSafe Services LLC 5971 Powers Ave Ste 108.................Jacksonville FL 32217 *TF:* 800-968-5110 ■ *Web:* www.lifesafeservices.com	904-730-4800		194
Lifescale 1221 Chapala St Ste B .... Santa Barbara CA 93101 *Web:* www.lifescaleast.com	805-960-5100		407
Lifescan Canada Ltd 210-4321 Still Creek Dr ....Burnaby BC V5C6S7 *TF:* 800-663-5521 ■ *Web:* www.lifescan.com/company/world/canada	604-293-2266		476
LifeScan Inc 1000 Gibraltar Dr .... Milpitas CA 95035 *TF:* 800-227-8862 ■ *Web:* www.lifescan.com	408-263-9789		231
LifeScan Laboratory Inc 5255 W Golf............Skokie IL 60077 *TF:* 800-270-0037 ■ *Web:* lifescanlab.com	800-270-0037		415
LifeSensors Inc 271 Great Vly Pkwy Ste 100 .... Malvern PA 19355 *Web:* www.lifesensors.com	610-644-8845		668
LifeServe Blood Ctr 431 E Locust St .... Des Moines IA 50309 *TF:* 800-287-4903 ■ *Web:* www.lifeservebloodcenter.org	800-287-4903		89
LifeShare Blood Centers 8910 Linwood Ave .... Shreveport LA 71106 *TF:* 800-256-4483 ■ *Web:* www.lifeshare.org	318-222-7770		89
LifeShare Community Blood Services 105 Cleveland St ....Elyria OH 44035 *TF:* 800-317-5412 ■ *Web:* www.lifeshare.cc	440-322-5700	322-6240	89
LifeShare of the Carolinas 1200 Ridgefield Blvd Ste 150.................. Asheville NC 28806 *TF:* 800-932-4483 ■ *Web:* www.lifesharecarolinas.org	828-665-0107	665-4729	269
LifeShare Technologies LLC 2177 Intelliplex Dr Ste 150.................Shelbyville IN 46176 *Web:* www.lifesharetech.com	317-825-0320		387
LifeShare Transplant Donor Services of Oklahoma 4705 NW Expy ....Oklahoma City OK 73132 *TF:* 888-580-5680 ■ *Web:* www.lifeshareoklahoma.org	405-840-5551	840-9748	545
Lifesharing Community Organ & Tissue Donation 3465 Camino del Rio S Ste 410 .... San Diego CA 92108 *TF:* 866-797-2366 ■ *Web:* www.lifesharing.org	619-521-1983	521-2833	545
LifeSize Communications Inc 1601 S Mopac Expwy Ste 100 .... Austin TX 78746 *TF:* 877-543-3749 ■ *Web:* www.lifesize.com	512-347-9300	347-9301	52
Lifesize Entertainment & Releasing 194 Elmwood Dr Ste 2 ....Parsippany NJ 07054 *Web:* www.lifesizeentertainment.com	973-884-4884		511
LifeSource Blood Services 2764 Aurora Ave........................ Naperville IL 60540 *TF:* 877-543-3768 ■ *Web:* lifesource.org	877-543-3768		89
LifeSouth Community Blood Centers 4039 Newberry Rd ....Gainesville FL 32607 **Fax Area Code:* 352 ■ *TF:* 888-795-2707 ■ *Web:* www.lifesouth.org	888-795-2707	224-1650*	89
LifeSouth Community Blood Centers Atlanta 4891 Ashford Dunwoody Rd.................... Atlanta GA 30338 *TF:* 888-795-2707 ■ *Web:* lifesouth.org	404-329-1994		89
Lifespace Communities Inc 4201 Corporate Dr ....West Des Moines IA 50266 *Web:* www.lifespacecommunities.com	515-288-5805		672
Lifespire 350 Fifth Ave Ste 301 .... New York NY 10118 *TF:* 800-221-5594 ■ *Web:* www.lifespire.org	212-741-0100		48-17
Lifespring Inc 460 Spring St.............. Jeffersonville IN 47130 *TF:* 800-456-2117 ■ *Web:* lifespringhealthsystems.org	812-280-2080		353
Lifestar Response 3710 Commerce Dr Ste 1006................Halethorpe MD 21227 *Web:* www.lifestarcompanies.com	410-247-1178		30
Lifestream Inc PO Box 50487............. New Bedford MA 02745 *Web:* www.lifestreaminc.com	508-993-1991		48-15
Lifestyle Enterprises Inc 529 Townsend Ave ....High Point NC 27263 *Web:* www.lifestyle-datong.com	336-882-7900		321
LifeTech Capital 5200 Town Center Cir Ste 308 .... Boca Raton FL 33486 *Web:* www.lifetechcapital.com	561-395-1220		401
Lifetech Resources LLC 9540 Cozycroft Ave...................... Chatsworth CA 91311 *Web:* www.lifetechresources.com	818-885-1199		297-8
Lifetime Brands Inc 1000 Steward Ave....................... Garden City NY 11530 *NASDAQ: LCUT* ■ *TF:* 800-252-3390 ■ *Web:* www.lifetimebrands.com	516-683-6000		486
Lifetime Cabinet 601 Kellam Rd................. Dublin GA 31021 *Web:* www.lifetimecabinets.com	478-275-7457		115
Lifetime Care 3111 Winton Rd S..............Rochester NY 14623 *Web:* www.lifetimecare.org	585-214-1000		363
Lifetime Healthcare Cos, The 165 Ct St ....Rochester NY 14647 *Web:* www.lifethc.com	585-454-1700		360-4
Lifetime Nut Covers Inc 720 320th St............. Britt IA 50423 *Web:* lifetimenutcovers.com	641-565-3566		697
Lifetime Products Inc Freeport Ctr Bldg D-11 PO Box 160010.........Clearfield UT 84016 *TF:* 800-242-3865 ■ *Web:* www.lifetime.com	801-776-1532		710
Lifetime Recovery 10290 Southton Rd......................San Antonio TX 78223 *Web:* www.lifetimerecoverytx.org	210-633-0201		726
Lifetouch Church Directories 1371 Portland Way N .... Galion OH 44833 *TF:* 800-521-4611 ■ *Web:* www.lifetouch.com	419-468-4739		637-10
Lifeway Foods Inc 6431 W Oakton St...................... Morton Grove IL 60053 *NASDAQ: LWAY* ■ *TF:* 877-281-3874 ■ *Web:* lifewaykefir.com	847-967-1010	967-6558	296-27
Lifewings Partners LLC 9198 Crestwyn Hills Dr..................... Memphis TN 38125 *TF:* 800-290-9314 ■ *Web:* www.saferpatients.com	800-290-9314		463
Lift Agency Inc 205 Industrial Pkwy N Unit 1 .... Aurora ON L4G4C4 *Web:* www.getlift.com	647-684-3242		195
Lift Technologies Inc 7040 S Hwy 11.........................Westminster SC 29693 *TF:* 888-946-3330 ■ *Web:* www.lift-tekelecar.com	888-946-3330		358
Lift-All Company Inc 1909 McFarland Dr.......................Landisville PA 17538 **Fax:* Cust Svc ■ *TF:* 800-909-1964 ■ *Web:* www.lift-all.com	717-898-6615	898-1215*	470
Liftoff LLC 1667 Patrice Cir .... Crofton MD 21114 *Web:* www.liftofflearning.com	410-419-1591		177
Liftone 440 E Westinghouse Blvd.............. Charlotte NC 28273 *TF:* 855-543-8663 ■ *Web:* www.liftone.net	855-543-8663		470
Liftow Ltd 3150 American Dr.................. Toronto ON L4V1B4 *TF:* 866-465-4386 ■ *Web:* m.liftow.com	866-465-4386		358
Lifts West Condominium Resort Hotel PO Box 330 ....Red River NM 87558 *TF:* 800-221-1859 ■ *Web:* www.redrivernm.com/liftswest	505-754-2778	754-6617	669
Ligand Pharmaceuticals Inc 11085 N Torrey Pines Rd Ste 300............... La Jolla CA 92037 *NASDAQ: LGND* ■ *Web:* www.ligand.com	858-550-7500	550-7506	582
Ligature, The 4909 Alcoa Ave...............Los Angeles CA 90058 *TF:* 800-944-5440 ■ *Web:* www.theligature.com	323-585-6000		781
Light 103.9 FM, The 8001-101 Creedmoor Rd .... Raleigh NC 27613 *TF:* 877-310-9665 ■ *Web:* thelightnc.hellobeautiful.com	919-848-9736		645-131
Light Bistro 2801 Bridge Ave..................Cleveland OH 44113	216-771-7130		671
Light Brigade Inc, The 837 Industry Dr.............................. Tukwila WA 98188 *Web:* www.lightbrigade.com	206-575-0404		577
Light Engines LLC 29 Library Ln S .... Sturbridge MA 01566	508-347-0111		253
Light for Life Foundation International PO Box 644 ....Westminster CO 80036 *TF:* 800-273-8255 ■ *Web:* www.yellowribbon.org	303-429-3530	426-4496	48-17
Light Horse Tavern 199 Washington St.........................Jersey City NJ 07302 *Web:* www.lighthorsetavern.com	201-946-2028	946-2029	671
Light Impressions 100 Carlson Rd.............Rochester NY 14610 *TF:* 800-975-6429 ■ *Web:* www.lightimpressionsdirect.com	800-975-6429		628
Light Lines Inc 3337 Rauch St ....Houston TX 77029 *Web:* lightlines.net	713-673-7502		362
Light Metals Corp 2740 Prairie St SW ....Wyoming MI 49509 *TF:* 888-363-8257 ■ *Web:* www.light-metals.com	616-538-3030	538-2713	485
Light of Christ Rcssd 16 9301 19th Ave........................North Battleford SK S9A3N5 *Web:* www.loccsd.ca	306-445-6158		685
Light Sources Inc 37 Robinson Blvd ....Orange CT 06477 *TF:* 800-826-9465 ■ *Web:* www.light-sources.com	203-799-7877	795-5267	437
Light Styles Internet LLC 1843 S Broadway Ave Ste 104 .... Boise ID 83706 *Web:* www.lightingshowroom.com	208-433-3900		225
Lightburn 325 E Chicago St Ste 301........... Milwaukee WI 53202 *Web:* lightburn.co	414-347-1866		180
LightEdge Solutions Inc 215 Tenth St Ste 1000 ....Des Moines IA 50309 *TF:* 877-771-3343 ■ *Web:* www.lightedge.com	515-471-1000	471-1112	808
Lightel Technologies Inc 2210 Lind Ave SW Ste 100.....................Renton WA 98057 *Web:* www.lighteltech.com	425-277-8000		696
Lightfoot Air Conditioning & Refrigeration 1414 W Oak .... Palestine TX 75801 *Web:* lightfootair.com	903-723-2665		189-10
Lightfoot Capital Partners LP 725 Fifth Ave 19th Fl ....New York NY 10022 *TF:* 800-732-0330 ■ *Web:* www.lightfootcapital.com	212-993-1280		360-3
Lightfoot, Franklin & White LLC The Clark Bldg 400 20th St N..............Birmingham AL 35203 *Web:* www.lightfootlaw.com	205-581-0700		428
Lighthouse ArtCenter Gallery 373 Tequesta Dr .... Tequesta FL 33469 *Web:* www.lighthousearts.org	561-746-3101		50-2
Lighthouse Club Hotel 201 60th St...........Ocean City MD 21842 *TF:* 888-371-5400 ■ *Web:* fagers.com	410-524-5400		379
Lighthouse Computer Services Inc 6 Blackstone Valley Pl Ste 205................. Lincoln RI 02865 *TF:* 888-542-8030 ■ *Web:* www.lighthousecs.com	401-334-0799	334-0719	180
Lighthouse Electric Co-op PO Box 600 .... Floydada TX 79235 *Web:* www.lighthouse.coop	806-983-2814	983-2804	245
Lighthouse Field State Beach West Cliff Dr..............................Santa Cruz CA 95060 *Web:* www.parks.ca.gov/default.asp?page_id=550	831-429-2850		565
Lighthouse Hospice 1040 Kings Hwy N Ste 100.................Cherry Hill NJ 08034 *TF General:* 888-467-7423 ■ *Web:* www.lighthousehospice.net	856-414-1155	414-1313	371
Lighthouse Imaging LLC 765 Roosevelt Trail Ste 9 ....Windham ME 04062 *Web:* www.lighthouseoptics.com	207-893-8233	893-8245	544
Lighthouse Investment Partners LLC 3801 PGA Blvd Ste 500 .... Palm Beach Gardens FL 33410 *Web:* www.lighthousepartners.com	561-741-0820		401
Lighthouse Lodge & Suites 1150 Lighthouse Ave ....Pacific Grove CA 93950 *TF:* 800-858-1249 ■ *Web:* www.lighthouselodgecottages.com	800-858-1249		379
Lighthouse Travel & Tours 3561 Homestead Rd No 483................ Santa Clara CA 95051 *Web:* www.lighthouse-tours.com	408-260-5802		463
Lighting By Gregory LLC 158 Bowery ....New York NY 10012 *Web:* www.lightingbygregory.com	212-226-1276		362
Lighting Quotient, The 114 Boston Post Rd .... West Haven CT 06516 *Web:* www.thelightingquotient.com	203-931-4455	931-4464	439
Lighting Technology Services Inc 2801 Catherine Way .... Santa Ana CA 92705 *Web:* www.ltsinc.net	949-428-5040		104
Lighting Unlimited LLC 4211 Richmond Ave.........................Houston TX 77027 *Web:* www.lulighting.com	713-626-4025		361

	Phone	Fax	Class
Lighting Zone Inc 17354 Hawthorne Blvd Torrance CA 90504 *Web:* www.dreamonlighting.com	310-921-9495		362
Light-Life Foods Inc 153 Industrial Blvd Turners Falls MA 01376 *Web:* www.lightlife.com	413-774-9000		123
Lightner Electronics Inc 1771 Beaver Dam Rd Claysburg PA 16625 *TF:* 866-239-3888 ■ *Web:* www.lightnerelectronics.com	814-239-8323		186
Lightner Museum, The 75 King St Saint Augustine FL 32084 *Web:* www.lightnermuseum.org	904-824-2874		520
Lightning Energy Services LLC 104 Heliport Loop Rd PO Box 580 Bridgeport WV 26330	304-933-3544		536
Lightning Strike & Electric Shock Survivors International Inc (LSESSI) PO Box 1156 Jacksonville NC 28541 *Web:* www.lightning-strike.org	910-346-4708		48-21
Lightning Transportation Inc 16820 Blake Rd Hagerstown MD 21740 *TF:* 800-233-0624 ■ *Web:* www.lightningtrans.com	301-582-5700	582-5898	780
Lightopia LLC 1043 N Coast Hwy Laguna Beach CA 92651 *TF:* 800-377-5483 ■ *Web:* www.lightopiaonline.com	949-715-5575		196
Lightower Fiber Networks 80 Central St Boxborough MA 01719 *TF:* 888-583-4237 ■ *Web:* www.lightower.com	978-264-6000		736
LightPath Technologies Inc 2603 Challenger Tech Ct Ste 100 Orlando FL 32826 *NASDAQ: LPTH* ■ *Web:* lightpath.com	407-382-4003	382-4007	544
Lightriver Technologies Inc 2150 John Glenn Dre Ste 200 Concord CA 94520 *TF:* 888-544-4825 ■ *Web:* www.lightriver.com	941-552-9410		681
Lights of America 611 Reyes Dr Walnut CA 91789 *Web:* www.lightsofamerica.com	909-594-7883		439
LightSand Communications Inc 101 E Pk Blvd Ste 600 Plano TX 75074 *Web:* www.lightsand.com	972-516-3740	516-3741	176
Lightspeed Aviation Inc 6135 Jean Rd Lake Oswego OR 97035 *TF:* 800-332-2421 ■ *Web:* www.lightspeedaviation.com	503-968-3113		647
Lightspeed Venture Partners 2200 Sand Hill Rd Ste 100 Menlo Park CA 94025 *Web:* lsvp.com	650-234-8300	234-8333	792
Lightstone Group, The 460 Pk Ave Ste 1300 New York NY 10022 *Web:* www.lightstonegroup.com	212-616-9969		652
Lightwave Management Resources 4707 140th Ave N 316 Clearwater FL 33762 *TF:* 800-541-3891 ■ *Web:* www.sycoretech.com	727-507-0983		177
Lightwaves 2020 Inc 1323 Great Mall Dr Milpitas CA 95035 *Web:* www.lightwaves2020.com	408-503-8888		668
Lignite Energy Council 1016 E Owens Ave Bismarck ND 58502 *TF:* 800-932-7117 ■ *Web:* www.lignite.com	701-258-7117		138
Lignumvitae Key Botanical State Park Offshore Island Islamorada FL 33036 *Web:* www.floridastateparks.org/lignumvitaekey	305-664-2540		565
Ligon Industries LLC 1927 First Ave N 5th Fl Birmingham AL 35203 *Web:* www.ligonindustries.com	205-322-3302	322-3188	386
Lil Ray's 500A Courthouse Rd Gulfport MS 39507 *Web:* lilraysrestaurant.com	228-896-9601		671
Lil' Angels Photography 6831 Crumpler Blvd Ste 101 Olive Branch MS 38654 *Web:* lilangelsphoto.com	662-890-9103		310
Lil' Drug Store Products Inc 1201 Continental Pl NE Cedar Rapids IA 52402 *TF:* 800-553-5022 ■ *Web:* www.lildrugstore.com	800-553-5022		238
Lila Cockrell Theatre 900 E Market St San Antonio TX 78205 *Web:* www.sahbgcc.com	210-207-8500		572
Lilette 3637 Magazine St New Orleans LA 70115 *Web:* www.liletterestaurant.com	504-895-1636		671
Liliuokalani Trust 1100 Alakea St Ste 1100 Honolulu HI 96813 *Web:* www.onipaa.org	808-203-6150		305
Lilja Corp 229 Rickenbacker Cir Livermore CA 94551 *TF:* 800-654-4567 ■ *Web:* www.liljacorp.com	925-455-2300		256
Lilja Precision Rifle Barrel 81 Lower Lynch Creek Rd Plains MT 59859 *Web:* www.riflebarrels.com	406-826-3084		807
Lilker Associates Consulting Engineers PC 1001 Ave of the Americas Fl 9 New York NY 10018 *TF:* 800-356-8466 ■ *Web:* www.lilker.com	212-695-1000		261
Lilleys' Landing Resort 367 River Ln Branson MO 65616 *TF:* 866-545-5397 ■ *Web:* www.lilleyslanding.com	417-334-6380	334-6311	669
Lillian & Albert Small Jewish Museum 701 Third St NW Washington DC 20001 *Web:* www.loc.gov/rr/main/religion/jhw.html	202-789-0900	789-0485	520
Lillian August Designs Inc 32 Knight St Norwalk CT 06851 *Web:* www.lillianaugust.com	203-847-3314		361
Lillie's Asian Cuisine 129 E Fremont St Las Vegas NV 89101 *TF:* 800-634-3454 ■ *Web:* www.goldennugget.com/dining/lillies.asp	702-385-7111		671
Lilliputian Systems Inc 36 Jonspin Rd Wilmington MA 01887	978-203-1700		696
Lilly Endowment Inc 2801 N Meridian St Indianapolis IN 46208 *TF:* 800-952-2355 ■ *Web:* www.lillyendowment.org	317-924-5471	926-4431	305
Lilly Ventures 115 W Washington St Indianapolis IN 46204 *Web:* www.lillyventures.com	317-429-0140		792
Lilly's Bistro 1147 BaRdstown Rd Louisville KY 40204 *TF:* 800-863-7999 ■ *Web:* lillysbistro.com	502-451-0447		671
Lily Bay State Park 13 Myrle's Way Greenville ME 04441 *Web:* www.maine.gov	207-695-2700		565
Lily Transportation Corp 145 Rosemary St Needham MA 02494 *TF:* 800-248-5459 ■ *Web:* www.lily.com	800-248-5459		778
Lima Estates 411 N Middletown Rd Media PA 19063 *TF:* 888-398-2287 ■ *Web:* www.actsretirement.org	610-565-7020		672
Lima Memorial Hospital 1001 Bellefontaine Ave Lima OH 45804 *TF:* 877-362-5672 ■ *Web:* www.limamemorial.org	419-228-3335	226-5013	374-3
Lima News 3515 Elida Rd Lima OH 45807 *TF:* 800-686-9924 ■ *Web:* www.limaohio.com	419-223-1010	229-2926	532-2
Lima Public Library 650 W Market St Lima OH 45801 *Web:* www.limalibrary.com	419-228-5113		434-3
Lima/Allen County Chamber of Commerce 144 S Main St Ste 100 Lima OH 45801 *TF:* 800-233-5462 ■ *Web:* www.limachamber.com	419-222-6045	229-0266	139
Lima/Allen County Convention & Visitors Bureau 144 S Main St Ste 101 Lima OH 45801 *TF:* 888-222-6075 ■ *Web:* www.lima-allencvb.com	419-222-6075		206
Limbach 175 Titus Ave Ste 100 Warrington PA 18976 **Fax:* Cust Svc ■ *Web:* www.limbachinc.com	215-488-9700	488-9699*	189-10
Limbach Facility Services LLC 31 35th St Pittsburgh PA 15201 *TF:* 800-767-3263 ■ *Web:* www.limbachinc.com	412-359-2100	359-2235	189-10
Limco Airepair Inc 5304 S Lawton Ave Tulsa OK 74107 *TF:* 800-858-6287 ■ *Web:* www.limcoairepair.com	918-445-4300	445-2210	697
Lime Brokerage LLC 625 Broadway 12th Fl New York NY 10012 *Web:* www.limebrokerage.com	212-824-5000		690
Lime City Manufacturing Co 1470 Etna Ave Huntington IN 46750 *Web:* www.limecitymfg.com	260-356-6826		489
Lime Instruments LLC 1187 Brittmoore Rd Houston TX 77043 *Web:* www.limeinst.net	713-781-1883		201
Lime Kiln Point State Park 1567 Westside Rd Friday Harbor WA 98250 *Web:* www.parks.wa.gov	360-378-2044		565
Lime Lab Inc 650 Florida St Ste B San Francisco CA 94110 *Web:* www.lime-lab.com	415-643-5463		393
Lime Rock Park 60 White Hollow Rd Lakeville CT 06039 *TF:* 800-722-3577 ■ *Web:* limerock.com	860-435-5000	435-5010	515
Lime Street Cafe 951 S Durkin Dr Springfield IL 62704	217-793-1905		671
Limekiln State Park 1416 Ninth St Sacramento CA 94296 *Web:* www.parks.ca.gov/default.asp?page_id=577	916-653-6995		565
Limelight Communications Inc 2812 Roesh Way Vienna VA 22181 *Web:* www.limelight.com	703-242-4596		514
Limelight Theatre 11 Old Mission Ave Saint Augustine FL 32084 *TF:* 800-361-8388 ■ *Web:* www.limelight-theatre.org	904-825-1164		572
Limerick Traditional Public House 7304 MacLeod Trail SE Calgary AB T2H0L9 *Web:* calgarysbestpubs.com	403-252-9190	252-9174	671
Limestone College 1115 College Dr Gaffney SC 29340 *TF:* 800-795-7151 ■ *Web:* www.limestone.edu	864-489-7151		166
Limestone Correctional Facility 28779 Nick Davis Rd Harvest AL 35749	256-233-4600		213
Limestone County 100 S Clinton St Ste B Athens AL 35611 *Web:* limestonelicense.com	256-233-6430	233-6486	338
Limestone County School District 300 S Jefferson St Athens AL 35611 *Web:* www.lcsk12.org	256-232-5353	233-6461	685
Limestone Exploration II LLC 1100 W Wall St Midland TX 79701 *Web:* www.limestone2.com	432-687-4220		536
Limon Correctional Facility 49030 State Hwy 71 Limon CO 80826 *Web:* www.colorado.gov	719-775-9221	775-7607	213
Limon Dance Co 466 W 152nd St Fl 2 New York NY 10031 *Web:* www.limon.org	212-777-3353	777-4764	573-1
Limoneira Co 1141 Cummings Rd Santa Paula CA 93060 *NASDAQ: LMNR* ■ *TF:* 866-321-8953 ■ *Web:* www.limoneira.com	805-525-5541	525-8211	315-2
Limpert Bros Inc 202 NW Blvd PO Box 1480 Vineland NJ 08362 *TF:* 800-691-1353 ■ *Web:* www.limpertbrothers.com	856-691-1353	794-8968	296-15
LIMRA International Inc 300 Day Hill Rd Windsor CT 06095 *TF:* 800-235-4672 ■ *Web:* www.limra.com	860-688-3358	298-9555	49-9
Limra Trading 30 Mall Dr W Jersey City NJ 07310	201-792-7003		297-8
Limsky Kypriotis & Co 220 Ridgedale Ave Florham Park NJ 07932	973-822-3400		2
Lin Engineering Inc 16245 Vineyard Blvd Morgan Hill CA 95037 *Web:* www.linengineering.com	408-919-0200		256
Linak Us Inc 2200 Stanley Gault Pkwy Louisville KY 40223 *Web:* www.linak-us.com	502-253-5595	253-5596	223
Linamar Corp 287 Speedvale Ave W Guelph ON N1H1C5 *TSE: LNR* ■ *Web:* www.linamar.com	519-836-7550	824-8479	60
Linbeck Group LLC 3900 Essex Ln Ste 1200 Houston TX 77027 *Web:* www.linbeck.com	713-621-2350		186
Linc Services Mid-Atlantic LLC 3701 Saunders Ave Richmond VA 23227 *Web:* www.lincservice.com	804-254-5790		152
Lincare Holdings Inc 19387 US 19 N Clearwater FL 33764 *NASDAQ: LNCR* ■ *Web:* www.lincare.com	727-530-7700		363
Linch Capital LLC 3384 Peachtree Rd NW Ste 575 Atlanta GA 30326 *Web:* www.linchcapital.com	404-334-7047		691
Linchris Hotel Corp 269 Hanover St Hanover MA 02339 *Web:* www.linchris.com	781-826-8824	826-2411	463
Lincluden Investment Management 1275 N Service Rd W Ste 607 Oakville ON L6M3G4 *TF:* 800-532-7071 ■ *Web:* www.lincluden.com	905-825-9000		528
Lincoln Airport 2400 W Adams St Lincoln NE 68524 *TF:* 800-221-1212 ■ *Web:* www.lincolnairport.com	402-458-2480	458-2490	27

	Phone	Fax	Class
Lincoln Botanical Garden & Arboretum (BGA) University of Nebraska 1309 N 17th St........... Lincoln NE 68588 *TF:* 800-742-8800 ■ *Web:* www.unl.edu/bga	402-472-2679	472-9615	97
Lincoln Boyhood National Memorial 2916 E S St PO Box 1816..............Lincoln City IN 47552 *TF:* 800-445-9667 ■ *Web:* www.nps.gov/libo	812-937-4541	937-9929	564
Lincoln Builders Inc 1809 Northpointe Ste 201.....................Ruston LA 71270 *TF:* 800-320-1462 ■ *Web:* www.lincolnbuilders.com	318-255-3822		186
Lincoln Center Shops 374 Lincoln Centre......................... Stockton CA 95207 *Web:* www.lincolncentershops.com	209-477-4868		460
Lincoln Chamber of Commerce 1135 M St PO Box 83006.................... Lincoln NE 68508 *Web:* www.lcoc.com	402-436-2350	436-2360	139
Lincoln Children's Museum 1420 P St........ Lincoln NE 68508 *TF:* 800-423-8212 ■ *Web:* www.lincolnchildrensmuseum.org	402-477-4000	477-2004	521
Lincoln Children's Zoo 1222 S 27th St.......... Lincoln NE 68502 *Web:* www.lincolnzoo.org	402-475-6741	475-6742	823
Lincoln Christian College Seminary 100 Campus View Dr .... Lincoln IL 62656 *TF:* 888-522-5228 ■ *Web:* lincolnchristian.edu	217-732-3168		167-3
Lincoln City Hall 555 S Tenth St............. Lincoln NE 68508 *Web:* www.lincoln.ne.gov	402-441-7515	441-6533	337
Lincoln City Libraries 136 S 14th St........... Lincoln NE 68508 *Web:* www.lincolnlibraries.org	402-441-8500		434-3
Lincoln City Visitor & Convention Bureau 801 SW Hwy 101 Ste 401..................Lincoln City OR 97367 *TF:* 800-452-2151 ■ *Web:* www.oregoncoast.org	541-996-1274	994-2408	206
Lincoln College 300 Keokuk St................. Lincoln IL 62656 *TF:* 800-569-0556 ■ *Web:* www.lincolncollege.edu	217-732-3155	732-8859	162
Lincoln College of Technology 11194 E 45th Ave..........................Denver CO 80239 *TF:* 800-254-0547 ■ *Web:* www.lincolntech.edu/campus/denver-co	303-722-5724		800
Lincoln College of Technology 2410 Metro Centre Blvd...............West Palm Beach FL 33407 **Fax Area Code:* 850 ■ *TF:* 800-254-0547 ■ *Web:* www.lincolntech.edu	561-842-8324	245-3238*	800
Lincoln College of Technology 7225 Winton Dr Bldg 128..................Indianapolis IN 46268 **Fax Area Code:* 850 ■ *TF:* 800-228-6232 ■ *Web:* www.lincolntech.edu	317-632-5553	245-3238*	800
Lincoln Community Playhouse 2500 S 56th St.............................. Lincoln NE 68506 *Web:* www.lincolnplayhouse.com	402-489-7529	489-1035	572
Lincoln Contracting & Equipment Company Inc 2478 Lincoln Hwy........................ Stoystown PA 15563 *Web:* www.lincolncontracting.com	814-629-6641		480
Lincoln Contractors Supply Inc 11111 W Hayes Ave .... Milwaukee WI 53227 *Web:* www.lincolncontractorssupply.com	414-541-1327		358
Lincoln Controls Inc 55 W 39th St Rm 201 ....New York NY 10018 *Web:* www.lincolncontrolsinc.com	212-545-7705		400
Lincoln Convention & Visitors Bureau 1135 M St Ste 300........................... Lincoln NE 68508 *TF:* 800-423-8212 ■ *Web:* www.lincoln.org	402-434-5335	436-2360	206
Lincoln Correctional Ctr 1098 1350th St PO Box 549.................. Lincoln IL 62656 *Web:* illinois.gov	217-735-5411	735-5381	213
Lincoln Correctional Ctr 3216 W Van Dorn St PO Box 94661............. Lincoln NE 68522 *Web:* www.corrections.nebraska.gov	402-479-6175		213
Lincoln County PO Box 978 .... Brookhaven MS 39602 *TF:* 800-613-4667 ■ *Web:* brookhavenchamber.org	601-833-1411		338
Lincoln County 104 N Main St ....Canton SD 57013 **Fax:* Acctg ■ *TF:* 800-952-0123 ■ *Web:* www.lincolncountysd.org	605-764-2581	764-0134*	338
Lincoln County 300 Central Ave PO Box 338 .... Carrizozo NM 88301	575-648-2394		338
Lincoln County 811 Manvel Ave Rm 5 .... Chandler OK 74834	405-258-1264		338
Lincoln County 450 Logan St .... Davenport WA 99122 *Web:* www.co.lincoln.wa.us	509-725-1401		338
Lincoln County 112 Main St S................Fayetteville TN 37334 *Web:* www.lincolncountytngov.com	931-433-3045	433-9304	338
Lincoln County PO Box 497 ....Hamlin WV 25523 *TF:* 800-859-7375 ■ *Web:* www.lincolncountywv.org	304-824-7990	824-2444	338
Lincoln County 103 Third Ave..................... Hugo CO 80821 *TF:* 800-934-7128 ■ *Web:* www.lincolncountyco.us	719-743-2444	743-2524	338
Lincoln County 319 N Rebecca St............... Ivanhoe MN 56142 **Fax:* Acctg ■ *TF:* 800-438-0576 ■ *Web:* www.co.lincoln.mn.us	507-694-1529	694-1198*	338
Lincoln County 925 Sage Ave .... Kemmerer WY 83101 *TF:* 800-442-9001 ■ *Web:* www.lcwy.org	307-877-9056	877-3101	338
Lincoln County 512 California Ave .... Libby MT 59923 *TF:* 800-700-7345 ■ *Web:* www.lincolncountymt.us	406-293-7781	293-8577	338
Lincoln County 216 E Lincoln Ave.............. Lincoln KS 67455 *Web:* www.lincolncoks.com	785-524-4757	524-5008	338
Lincoln County 210 Humphrey St.............. Lincolnton GA 30817 *TF:* 800-533-3478 ■ *Web:* www.lcgagov.org	706-359-4444	359-4729	338
Lincoln County 115 W Main St.................Lincolnton NC 28092 *Web:* www.co.lincoln.nc.us	704-736-8471	736-8718	338
Lincoln County 1110 E Main St................. Merrill WI 54452 *Web:* www.co.lincoln.wi.us	715-536-6200		338
Lincoln County 225 W Olive St Rm 201 .... Newport OR 97365 *TF:* 800-735-2900 ■ *Web:* www.co.lincoln.or.us	541-265-4131	265-4950	338
Lincoln County 301 N Jeffers St .... North Platte NE 69101 *Web:* www.co.lincoln.ne.us	308-534-4350	535-3527	338
Lincoln County PO Box 17520 .... Reno NV 89511 *Web:* www.co.lincoln.nv.us	775-348-7299	348-7299	338
Lincoln County 111 W 'B' St Ste C .... Shoshone ID 83352 *TF:* 800-221-3295 ■ *Web:* www.lincolncountyid.us	208-886-7641	886-2798	338
Lincoln County 102 E Main St County Courthouse.............Stanford KY 40484 *Web:* www.lincolnky.com	606-365-2534	365-4514	338
Lincoln County 201 Main St.............................. Troy MO 63379 *Web:* lincolncountycollector.com/office-information	636-528-6300		338
Lincoln County PO Box 249 .... Wiscasset ME 04578 *Web:* www.lincolncountymaine.me	207-882-6311	882-4320	338
Lincoln County Convention & Visitor's Bureau 315 W Eugene Ave .... North Platte NE 69101 *TF:* 800-955-4528 ■ *Web:* www.visitnorthplatte.com	308-532-4729	532-5914	206

	Phone	Fax	Class
Lincoln Ctr Theater 150 W 65th St ....New York NY 10023 *TF:* 800-432-7250 ■ *Web:* www.lct.org	800-432-7250		749
Lincoln Educational Services 200 Executive Dr......................... West Orange NJ 07052 *NASDAQ: LINC* ■ *TF:* 800-254-0547 ■ *Web:* www.lincolntech.edu	973-736-9340		242
Suffield 8 PROGRESS DR .... Shelton CT 06484 *TF:* 800-254-0547 ■ *Web:* www.lincolntech.edu	203-929-0592		163
Lincoln Electric Co 22801 St Clair Ave ....Cleveland OH 44117 *TF:* 888-935-3878 ■ *Web:* www.lincolnelectric.com	216-481-8100	486-1751	811
Lincoln Electric Co-op Inc (LEC) 500 Osloski Rd PO Box 628.................... Eureka MT 59917 *TF:* 800-442-2994 ■ *Web:* www.lincolnelectric.coop	406-889-3301	889-3874	245
Lincoln Equities Group LLC 1 Meadowlands Plaza Ste 803 .... East Rutherford NJ 07073 *Web:* www.lincolnequities.com	201-460-3440		652
Lincoln FSB 1101 North St..................... Lincoln NE 68508 *TF:* 800-333-2158 ■ *Web:* www.lincolnfed.com	402-474-1400	474-1585	71
Lincoln General Insurance Co 3501 Concord Rd ....York PA 17402 *TF:* 800-876-3350 ■ *Web:* www.lincolngeneral.com	717-757-0000		390
Lincoln Heights Chamber of Commerce 2716 N Broadway Ste 210 ....Los Angeles CA 90031	323-221-6571		139
Lincoln Heritage Life Insurance Co PO Box 29045 ....Phoenix AZ 85038 *TF:* 800-433-8181 ■ *Web:* www.lhlic.com	602-808-0521	840-0969	391-2
Lincoln Heritage Life Insurance Co 4343 E Camelback Rd Ste 400 Ste 400...........Phoenix AZ 85018 *TF:* 800-438-7180 ■ *Web:* www.lhlic.com	602-957-1650	840-0969	391-2
Lincoln Heritage Public Library 105 N Wallace St ....Dale IN 47523 *Web:* www.lincolnheritage.lib.in.us	812-937-7170		434-3
Lincoln Highway Assn 136 N Elm St ....Franklin Grove IL 61031 *Web:* www.lincolnhighwayassoc.org	815-456-3030		48-23
Lincoln Hills School W4380 Copper Lake Rd ....Irma WI 54442 *Web:* doc.wi.gov	715-536-8386		412
Lincoln Home National Historic Site 413 S Eigth St................................Springfield IL 62701 *Web:* www.nps.gov	217-492-4241	492-4673	564
Lincoln Homestead State Park 5079 Lincoln Pk Rd ....Springfield KY 40069 *Web:* www.parks.ky.gov	859-336-7461		565
Lincoln Industrial Corp 5148 N Hanley Rd........................ Saint Louis MO 63134 **Fax Area Code:* 800 ■ **Fax:* Cust Svc ■ *TF:* 800-424-5359 ■ *Web:* www.lincolnindustrial.com	314-679-4200	424-5359*	386
Lincoln Journal-Star 926 P St................. Lincoln NE 68508 **Fax:* News Rm ■ *TF:* 800-742-7315 ■ *Web:* www.journalstar.com	402-475-4200	473-7291*	532-2
Lincoln Laboratory Massachusetts Institute of Technology 244 Wood St.................................Lexington MA 02421 *TF:* 800-445-8667 ■ *Web:* www.ll.mit.edu	781-981-5500		668
Lincoln Land Community College 5250 Shepherd Rd PO Box 19256 ....Springfield IL 62794 *TF:* 800-727-4161 ■ *Web:* www.llcc.edu	217-786-2200		162
Lincoln Land Oil Co PO Box 4307 ....Springfield IL 62708 *TF:* 800-238-4912 ■ *Web:* www.lincolnlandoil.com	217-523-5050	523-5001	316
Lincoln Laser Co 234 E Mohave St..............Phoenix AZ 85004 *Web:* www.lincolnlaser.com	602-257-0407		544
Lincoln Library 326 S Seventh St ....Springfield IL 62701 *TF:* 800-665-5576 ■ *Web:* www.lincolnlibrary.info	217-753-4900		434-3
Lincoln Machine Inc 6401 Cornhusker Hwy .... Lincoln NE 68507 *Web:* www.lincolnmachine.com	402-434-9140		454
Lincoln Manufacturing Inc 31209 FM 2978 Rd.......................... Magnolia TX 77354 *Web:* www.lincolnmanufacturing.com	281-252-9494		539
Lincoln Medical & Mental Health Ctr 234 E 149th St ....Bronx NY 10451 *Web:* nyc.gov	718-579-5016		374-3
Lincoln Memorial Garden & Nature Ctr 2301 E Lake Dr...........................Springfield IL 62712 *Web:* www.lincolnmemorialgarden.org	217-529-1111		50-5
Lincoln Memorial Shrine 125 W Vine St............................. Redlands CA 92373 *Web:* www.lincolnshrine.org	909-798-7632		50-4
Lincoln Memorial University 6965 Cumberland Gap Pkwy ....Harrogate TN 37752 *TF:* 800-325-0900 ■ *Web:* www.lmunet.edu	423-869-3611		166
Lincoln Military Housing 98 San Jacinto Rd......................... Oceanside CA 92058 *Web:* www.lincolnmilitary.com	760-430-5000		655
Lincoln Motor Company PO Box 6248 .... Dearborn MI 48126 *TF:* 800-521-4140 ■ *Web:* www.lincoln.com	800-521-4140		59
Lincoln National Corp (LNC) 150 N Radnor-Chester Rd......................Radnor PA 19087 *NYSE: LNC* ■ **Fax Area Code:* 215 ■ **Fax:* PR ■ *TF:* 877-275-5462 ■ *Web:* www.lfg.com	484-583-1400	448-3962*	360-4
Lincoln National Life Insurance Co 1300 S Clinton St........................ Fort Wayne IN 46802 *TF:* 800-454-6265 ■ *Web:* www.lfg.com	800-454-6265		391-2
Lincoln Parish 100 W Texas Ave .... Ruston LA 71270 *Web:* www.lincolnparish.org	318-251-5150		338
Lincoln Parish Library 910 N Trenton St..................................Ruston LA 71270 *Web:* www.mylpl.org	318-251-5030		434-3
Lincoln Park Chamber of Commerce 1925 N Clybourn Ave Ste 301 ....Chicago IL 60614 *Web:* www.lincolnparkchamber.com	773-880-5200	880-0266	139
Lincoln Park Hospital 550 W Webster Ave..........................Chicago IL 60614	773-883-2000		374-3
Lincoln Park Zoo 2001 N Clark St PO Box 14903 ....Chicago IL 60614 *Web:* www.lpzoo.org	312-742-2000	742-2299	823
Lincoln Property Co 2000 McKinney Ave Ste 1000................... Dallas TX 75201	214-740-3300		655
Lincoln Public Schools PO Box 82889........... Lincoln NE 68510 **Fax:* Hum Res ■ *TF:* 800-888-7828 ■ *Web:* www.lps.org	402-436-1000	436-1620*	685

Name / Address	City	State	ZIP	Phone	Fax	Class
Lincoln Rock State Park 13253 State Rt 2 *Web:* www.parks.wa.gov	East Wenatchee	WA	98802	509-884-8702		565
Lincoln Shoe Polish Co 172 Commercial St *Web:* www.lincolnshoepolish.com	Sunnyvale	CA	94086	408-732-5121		151
Lincoln Snacks Co 5020 S 19th St	Lincoln	NE	68512	402-328-9345		296-8
Lincoln Specialty Care Center 1128 Lincoln Mall Ste 100 *Web:* www.lincolndocs.com	Lincoln	NE	68501	402-436-2350		371
Lincoln Square Shopping Ctr 436 Lincoln Sq *Web:* www.lincolnsquarearlington.com	Arlington	TX	76011	817-461-7953		460
Lincoln State Park Hwy 162 PO Box 216 *TF:* 877-478-3657 ■ *Web:* www.in.gov	Lincoln City	IN	47552	812-937-4710		565
Lincoln Symphony Orchestra 233 S 13th St Ste 1702 *Web:* lincolnsymphony.org	Lincoln	NE	68508	402-476-2211		573-3
Lincoln Technical Institute 5151 Tilghman St *Web:* www.lincolntech.edu	Allentown	PA	18104	610-398-5300		800
Lincoln Technical Institute 9191 Torresdale Ave *Web:* www.lincolntech.edu	Philadelphia	PA	19136	215-335-0800		800
Lincoln Tomb Oak Ridge Cemetery 1500 Monument Ave *Web:* illinois.gov/ihpa	Springfield	IL	62702	217-782-2717		50-4
Lincoln Trail College 11220 State Hwy 1 *TF:* 866-582-4322 ■ *Web:* www.iecc.edu	Robinson	IL	62454	618-544-8657		162
Lincoln Trail State Park 16985 E 1350th Rd *Web:* www.dnr.illinois.gov/Parks/Pages/LincolnTrail.aspx	Marshall	IL	62441	217-826-2222		565
Lincoln Unified School District 2010 W Swain Rd *Web:* www.lusd.net	Stockton	CA	95207	209-953-8700		685
Lincoln University 820 Chestnut St B-7 Young Hall **Fax:* Admissions ■ *TF Admissions:* 800-521-5052 ■ *Web:* www.lincolnu.edu	Jefferson City	MO	65102	573-681-5599	681-5889*	166
Lincoln University 1570 Old Baltimore Pk PO Box 179 **Fax:* Admissions ■ *TF Admissions:* 800-790-0191 ■ *Web:* www.lincoln.edu	Lincoln University	PA	19352	484-365-8000	365-8109*	166
Lincoln University 401 15th St **Fax:* Admissions ■ *TF:* 888-810-9998 ■ *Web:* www.lincolnuca.edu	Oakland	CA	94612	510-628-8010	628-8012*	166
Lincoln Wood Products Inc 1400 W Taylor St PO Box 375 **Fax Area Code:* 715 ■ *TF:* 800-967-2461 ■ *Web:* www.lincolnwindows.com	Merrill	WI	54452	800-967-2461	536-7090*	236
Lincoln Woods State Park 2 Manchester Print Works Rd *Web:* www.riparks.com	Lincoln	RI	02865	401-723-7892	724-7951	565
Lincoln's New Salem State Historic Site 15588 History Ln *Web:* www.lincolnsnewsalem.com	Petersburg	IL	62675	217-632-4000	632-4010	520
Lincoln/Logan County Chamber of Commerce 1555 Fifth St *Web:* www.lincolnillinois.com	Lincoln	IL	62656	217-735-2385	735-9205	139
Lincoln-Herndon Law Offices State Historic Site 6th & Adams *Web:* illinois.gov/ihpa	Springfield	IL	62701	217-785-7289		50-3
Lincolnshire Management Inc 780 Third Ave 40th Fl *Web:* www.lincolnshiremgmt.com	New York	NY	10017	212-319-3633	755-5457	690
Lincolnton-Lincoln County Chamber of Commerce 101 E Main St *TF:* 800-222-1167 ■ *Web:* www.lincolnchambernc.org	Lincolnton	NC	28092	704-735-3096	735-5449	139
Lincolnville Telephone Co 133 Back Meadow Rd *Web:* www.lintelco.net	Nobleboro	ME	04555	207-763-9929		116
Lincoln-Way Central High School 1801 E Lincoln Hwy *Web:* www.lw210.org	New Lenox	IL	60451	815-462-2100		685
Lincus Inc 8950 S 52nd St Ste 415 *Web:* lincusenergy.com	Tempe	AZ	85284	480-598-8441	598-8485	261
Lind Jensen Sullivan & Peterson. A Professional Assn 1300 AT&T Tower 901 Marquette Ave S *Web:* www.lindjensen.com	Minneapolis	MN	55402	612-333-3637		428
Linda Hall Library 5109 Cherry St *TF:* 800-662-1545 ■ *Web:* www.lindahall.org	Kansas City	MO	64110	816-363-4600	926-8790	434-3
Linda's La Cantina 4721 E Colonial Dr *Web:* www.lindaslacantina.com	Orlando	FL	32803	407-894-4491	894-6415	671
Lindab Inc 2600 Airline Blvd *Web:* www.lindabusa.com	Portsmouth	VA	23701	757-488-1144		697
Lindal Cedar Homes Inc 4300 S 104th Pl *TF Prod Info:* 800-426-0536 ■ *Web:* www.lindal.com	Seattle	WA	98178	206-725-0900	725-1615	106
Lindamar Industries Inc 1603 Commerce Way *TF:* 800-235-1811 ■ *Web:* www.lindamarindustries.com	Paso Robles	CA	93446	805-237-1910		362
Lindar Corp 7789 Hastings Rd *Web:* www.lindarcorp.com	Baxter	MN	56425	218-829-3457		596
Lindblad Construction Co 717 E Cass St *Web:* www.lindbladconstruction.com	Joliet	IL	60432	815-726-6251	723-4907	189-3
Lindblad Expeditions 96 Morton St 9th Fl *TF:* 800-397-3348 ■ *Web:* www.expeditions.com	New York	NY	10014	212-765-7740	265-3770	760
Linde Hydraulics Corp 5089 W Western Reserve Rd *Web:* www.linde-hydraulics.com/en-gb	Canfield	OH	44406	330-533-6801		470
Lindeblad Piano Restoration 101 Us 46 *TF:* 888-587-4266 ■ *Web:* www.lindebladpiano.com	Pine Brook	NJ	07058	888-587-4266		527
Linden Bulk Transportation Company Inc 4200 Tremley Pt Rd *Web:* www.odysseylogistics.com/trucking/linden-bulk/?i=9	Linden	NJ	07036	908-862-3883		780
Linden Group Health Services Inc 2800 River Rd Ste 310 *Web:* www.lindengrouphealth.com	Des Plaines	IL	60018	847-294-0000		390
Linden Hall School for Girls 212 E Main St *TF:* 800-258-5778 ■ *Web:* www.lindenhall.org	Lititz	PA	17543	717-626-8512	627-1384	622
Linden Kildare 205 Kildare Rd *Web:* www.lkcisd.net	Linden	TX	75563	903-756-7071		685
Linden Lab 945 Battery St *TF:* 800-294-1067 ■ *Web:* www.lindenlab.com	San Francisco	CA	94111	415-243-9000		636
Linden Public Library 31 E Henry St *Web:* lindenpl.org	Linden	NJ	07036	908-298-3830		434-3
Linden Publishing 2006 S Mary St *TF Sales:* 800-345-4447 ■ *Web:* www.woodworkerslibrary.com	Fresno	CA	93721	559-233-6633	233-6933	637-2
Linden Row Inn 100 E Franklin St *TF:* 800-348-7424 ■ *Web:* www.lindenrowinn.com	Richmond	VA	23219	804-783-7000	648-7504	379
Linden Surfboards 1027 S Cleveland St *Web:* www.lindensurfboards.com	Oceanside	CA	92054	760-722-8956	722-8972	710
Linden Warehouse & Distribution Co Inc 1300 Lower Rd *TF:* 800-333-2855 ■ *Web:* www.lindencompanies.com	Linden	NJ	07036	908-862-1400	862-7539	780
Lindenmeyr Munroe 14 Research Pkwy *TF:* 800-842-8480 ■ *Web:* lindenmeyrmunroe.com	Wallingford	CT	06492	800-842-8480	890-3115	553
Lindenmeyr Munroe Central Central National-Gottesman Inc 3 Manhattanville Rd *TF:* 800-221-3042 ■ *Web:* www.cng-inc.com	Purchase	NY	10577	800-221-3042		553
Lindenmeyr Munroe Paper Corp 115 Moonachie Ave *TF:* 800-221-3042 ■ *Web:* www.lindenmeyr.com	Moonachie	NJ	07074	201-440-6491		553
Lindenwood University 209 S Kings Hwy **Fax:* Admissions ■ *TF:* 877-615-8212 ■ *Web:* www.lindenwood.edu	Saint Charles	MO	63301	636-949-2000	949-4989*	166
Linder & Associates Inc 840 N Main St PO Box 1202 *Web:* www.linderandassociates.com	Wichita	KS	67203	316-265-1616	265-8097	189-4
Linder Associates 7 E 14th St Apt 817 *Web:* www.srlinder.com	New York	NY	10003	212-645-7598		193
Linder Equipment Co 311 E Kern St *Web:* www.linderequipment.com	Tulare	CA	93274	559-685-5000		274
Lindey's 169 E Beck St *TF:* 800-695-6344 ■ *Web:* www.lindeys.com	Columbus	OH	43206	614-228-4343		671
Lindey's Prime Steak House 3600 N Snelling Ave *TF:* 866-491-0538 ■ *Web:* www.theplaceforsteak.com	Arden Hills	MN	55112	651-633-9813		671
LINDO Systems Inc 1415 N Dayton St *TF Sales:* 800-441-2378 ■ *Web:* www.lindo.com	Chicago	IL	60622	312-988-7422	988-9065	178-5
Lindquist & Vennum PLLP 4200 IDS Ctr 80 S Eighth St *TF:* 800 973 1177 ■ *Web:* www.lindquist.com	Minneapolis	MN	55402	612-371-3211		428
Lindquist Machine Corp 610 Baeten Rd *Web:* www.lmc-corp.com	Green Bay	WI	54304	920-713-4100	499-8482	454
Lindquist Steels Inc 1050 Woodend Rd **Fax Area Code:* 203 ■ *TF:* 800-243-9637 ■ *Web:* www.lindquiststeels.com	Stratford	CT	06615	800-243-9637	386 0132*	492
Lindquist Von Husen & Joyce LLP 90 New Montgomery St 11th Fl *Web:* lvhj.com	San Francisco	CA	94105	415-957-9999		2
Lindsay Cadillac Co 1525 Kenwood Ave *Web:* lindsaycars.com	Alexandria	VA	22302	703-998-6600		57
Lindsay Corp 2222 N 111th St *NYSE:* LNN ■ *TF:* 800-829-5300 ■ *Web:* www.lindsay.com	Omaha	NE	68164	402-829-6800	829-6834	273
Lindsay Hill Design C-5 Shipway Pl *Web:* lindsayhilldesign.com	Charlestown	MA	02129	617-886-0255		344
Lindsay Manufacturing Inc PO Box 1708 *TF:* 800-546-3729 ■ *Web:* www.lindsaymfg.com	Ponca City	OK	74602	580-762-2457	762-9547	788
Lindsay Stone & Briggs Inc 1 South Pinckney St Ste 500 *Web:* www.lsb.com	Madison	WI	53703	608-251-7070	251-8989	4
Lindsay Wildlife Museum 1931 First Ave *Web:* lindsaywildlife.org	Walnut Creek	CA	94597	925-627-2920		520
Lindsay Windows LLC 1995 Commerce Ln *Web:* www.lindsaywindows.com	North Mankato	MN	56003	507-625-4278		499
Lindsey & Company Inc 2302 Llama Dr *TF:* 800-890-7058 ■ *Web:* www.lindseysoftware.com	Searcy	AR	72143	501-268-5324		174
Lindsey & Company Inc 484 Boston Post Rd *Web:* www.lindseycompany.com	Darien	CT	06820	203-655-1590		260
Lindsey Office Furnishings 2223 First Ave N *Web:* www.lindseyof.com	Birmingham	AL	35203	205-251-9088		321
Lindsey State Jail 1620 FM 3344 *Web:* tdcj.state.tx.us	Jacksboro	TX	76458	940-567-2272	567-2292	213
Lindsey Wilson College 210 Lindsey Wilson St **Fax:* Admissions ■ *TF:* 800-264-0138 ■ *Web:* www.lindsey.edu	Columbia	KY	42728	270-384-2126	384-8591*	166
Lindstrand Balloons USA 11440 Dandar St *TF:* 800-397-1320 ■ *Web:* www.lindstrand.com	Galena	IL	61036	815-777-6006	777-6004	28
Lindstrom Sorenson & Assoc LLP 3815 N Mulford Rd *Web:* lsallp.com	Rockford	IL	61114	815-282-1288		2
Lindt & Sprungli USA 1 Fine Chocolate Pl *TF:* 877-695-4638 ■ *Web:* www.lindtusa.com	Stratham	NH	03885	603-778-8100		296-8
Lindy Property Management Co 207 Leedom St *Web:* www.lindyproperty.com	Jenkintown	PA	19046	215-886-8030		652
Line 6 26580 Agoura Rd *Web:* www.line6.com	Calabasas	CA	91302	818-575-3600	575-3601	52
Line Plot Productions LLC 146 Mt Auburn St	Cambridge	MA	02138	617-864-8300		514

Phone | Fax | Class

Line Systems Inc
1645 W Chester Pk ... West Chester PA 19382 610-355-9700 194
Web: www.linesystems.com

Lineage Capital LLC
399 Boylston St Ste 450 ... Boston MA 02116 617-778-0660 401
Web: www.lineagecap.com

Lineage Power Corp 601 Shiloh Rd ... Plano TX 75074 972-244-9288 787
TF: 877-546-3243 ■ *Web:* geindustrial.com/products/critical-power

Lineagen Inc
2677 E Parleys Way ... Salt Lake City UT 84109 801-931-6200 668
TF: 888-888-6736 ■ *Web:* www.lineagen.com

Linear Laboratories 42025 Osgood Rd ... Fremont CA 94539 510-226-0488 226-1112 201
TF: 800-536-0262 ■ *Web:* www.linearlabs.com

Linear Technology Corp
1630 McCarthy Blvd ... Milpitas CA 95035 408-432-1900 434-0507 696
NASDAQ: LLTC ■ *TF:* 888-500-6973 ■ *Web:* www.linear.com

Linebach - Funkhouser Inc
114 Fairfax Ave ... Louisville KY 40207 502-895-5009 261
Web: linebachfunkhouser.com

Linebaugh Public Library
105 W Vine St ... Murfreesboro TN 37130 615-893-4131 848-5038 434-3
Web: www.linebaugh.org

Linemark Printing Inc
501 Prince Georges Blvd ... Upper Marlboro MD 20774 301-925-9000 627
Web: www.linemark.com

Linemaster Switch Corp
29 Plaine Hill Rd ... Woodstock CT 06281 860-974-1000 974-3668* 485
*Fax Area Code: 800 ■ *TF:* 800-974-3668 ■ *Web:* www.linemaster.com

Linen Chest Inc
4455 AutoRt Des Laurentides ... Laval QC H7L5X8 514-341-7077 364
TF: 800-363-3832 ■ *Web:* www.linenchest.com

Linens of the Week
713 Lamont St NW ... Washington DC 20010 202-291-9200 442
Web: www.linensoftheweek.com

Lineo Group Ltd The
190 N Union St Ste 300 ... Akron OH 44304 330-475-1572 475-1573 636

Liner Products LLC 1468 W Hospital Rd ... Paoli IN 47454 812-723-0244 601
Web: www.linerproducts.com

LineStar Services Inc
4203 Montrose Blvd Ste 470 ... Houston TX 77006 832-830-8531 538
Web: www.linestar.com

Linetec 725 S 75th Ave ... Wausau WI 54401 715-843-4100 480
TF: 888-717-1472 ■ *Web:* www.linetec.com

Linfield College 900 SE Baker St ... McMinnville OR 97128 503-883-2213 883-2472* 166
*Fax: Admissions ■ *TF Admissions:* 800-640-2287 ■ *Web:* www.linfield.edu

Linfield Hunter & Junius
3608 18th St 200 ... Metairie LA 70002 504-833-5300 261
Web: www.lhjunius.com

Ling Shen Ching Tze Temple
17012 NE 40th Ct ... Redmond WA 98052 425-882-0916 50-1
Web: tbsseattle.org

Linger Peterson & Shrum
575 E Locust Ave Ste 308 ... Fresno CA 93720 559-438-8740 2
Web: www.lingercpa.com

Lingerie Outlet Store
3720 S Santa Fe Ave ... Vernon CA 90058 323-588-6917 157-6

Lingo Inc 7901 Jones Branch Dr Ste 900 ... Mclean VA 22102 888-546-4699 387
TF: 888-546-4699 ■ *Web:* www.lingo.com

Lingo Manufacturing Co
7400 Industrial Rd ... Florence KY 41042 859-371-2662 371-0283 233
TF Cust Svc: 800-354-9771 ■ *Web:* www.lingomfg.com

Lingo Media Corp
151 Bloor St W Ste 703 ... Toronto ON M5S1S4 416-927-7000 242
TF: 866-927-7011 ■ *Web:* www.lingomedia.com

Lingua School Inc
225 E Las Olas Blvd 6th Fl ... Fort Lauderdale FL 33301 954-577-9955 423
TF: 888-654-6482 ■ *Web:* www.linguaschool.com

Linguagraphics 194 Park Pl ... Brooklyn NY 11238 718-789-2782 196
Web: www.linguagraphics.com

Lingualinx Language Solutions Inc
433 River St ... Troy NY 12180 518-388-9000 768
Web: lingualinx.com

Linguistic Society of America (LSA)
1325 18th St NW Ste 211 ... Washington DC 20036 202-835-1714 835-1717 48-11
TF: 800-726-0479 ■ *Web:* www.linguisticsociety.org

Linguistics Systems Inc
201 Broadway ... Cambridge MA 02139 877-654-5006 528-7491* 768
*Fax Area Code: 617 ■ *TF:* 877-654-5006 ■ *Web:* www.linguist.com

Linick Group Inc, The
7 Putter Ln Linick Bldg ... Middle Island NY 11953 631-924-3888 195
Web: www.andrewlinickdirectmarketing.com

Linium LLC 187 Wolf Rd Ste 210 ... Albany NY 12205 518-689-3198 180
Web: www.linium.com

Linium Staffing LLC
124 Hebron Ave Eric Town Sq ... Glastonbury CT 06033 860-657-8971 260
Web: www.liniumrecruiting.com

Link America Inc 3002 Century Dr ... Rowlett TX 75088 800-318-4955 224
TF: 800-318-4955 ■ *Web:* www.linkam.com

Link Computer Corp Inc PO Box 250 ... Bellwood PA 16617 814-742-7700 742-7900 176
Web: www.linkcorp.com

Link Electronics Inc
2137 Rust Ave ... Cape Girardeau MO 63703 573-334-4433 116
TF: 800-776-4411 ■ *Web:* www.linkelectronics.com

Link Energy Inc 211 1500 14 St SW ... Calgary AB T3C1C9 855-444-5465 581
TF: 855-444-5465 ■ *Web:* www.linkenergy.com

Link Engineering Company Inc
43855 Plymouth Oaks Blvd ... Plymouth MI 48170 734-453-0800 472
Web: www.linkeng.com

Link Executive Search Inc
730 Second Ave S US Trust Bldg Ste 400 ... Minneapolis MN 55402 612-884-7000 260

Link Manufacturing Ltd
223 15th St NE ... Sioux Center IA 51250 712-722-4874 59
Web: www.linkmfg.com

Link Medical Computing Inc
1208 B VFW Pkwy Ste 103 ... Boston MA 02132 781-453-0300 180
Web: www.linkmed.com

Link Murrel & Co
18831 Bardeen Ave Ste 200 ... Irvine CA 92612 949-261-1120 2
Web: www.link-murrel.com

Link Solutions Inc
8251 Greensboro Dr 8th FL ... McLean VA 22102 703-707-6256 624
Web: www.linksol-inc.com

LINK Staffing Services Inc
1800 Bering Dr Ste 800 ... Houston TX 77057 713-784-4400 734
Web: www.linkstaffing.com

Link Technologies
9500 Hillwood Dr Ste 112 ... Las Vegas NV 89134 702-233-8703 261
Web: www.linktechconsulting.com

Link-Belt Construction Equipment Co
2651 Palumbo Dr ... Lexington KY 40583 859-263-5200 190
TF: 800-432-0913 ■ *Web:* www.linkbelt.com

Link-Burns Mfg Company Inc
253 American Way ... Voorhees NJ 08043 856-429-6844 697
TF: 800-457-4358 ■ *Web:* linkburns.com

Linkedin Corp 2029 Stierlin Ct ... Mountain View CA 94043 650-687-3600 736
Web: www.linkedin.com

Linkex Inc
2230 Lyndon B Johnson Fwy Ste 300 ... Dallas TX 75234 972-481-9900 311
TF: 800-319-6410 ■ *Web:* www.linkex.us

Linkfield & Cross Agency Inc
1600 E Beltline NE Ste 211 ... Grand Rapids MI 49525 616-447-2777 390

Linkous Construction Company Inc
1661 Aaron Brenner Dr Ste 207 ... Memphis TN 38120 901-754-0700 754-0302 360-2
Web: www.linkousconstruction.com

Links Magazine
10 Executive Park Rd ... Hilton Head Island SC 29928 843-842-6200 842-6233 457-20
Web: www.linksmagazine.com

Links Medical Products Inc
9247 Research Dr ... Irvine CA 92618 949-753-0001 476
Web: www.linksmed.com

Link-Systems International Inc
4515 George Rd Ste 340 ... Tampa FL 33634 813-674-0660 177
Web: www.link-systems.com

Linkus Enterprises Inc
5595 W San Madele Ave ... Fresno CA 93722 559-256-6600 681
TF: 888-854-6587 ■ *Web:* linkuscorp.com

Linn County 300 Fourth Ave SW ... Albany OR 97321 541-967-3802 338
Web: www.co.linn.or.us

Linn County 935 Second St SW ... Cedar Rapids IA 52404 319-892-5000 892-5009 338
Web: www.linncounty.org

Linn County 108 N High St ... Linneus MO 64653 660-895-5417 895-5527 338
Web: marcelinemo.us

Linn County PO Box 350 ... Mound City KS 66056 913-795-2660 795-2004 338
Web: www.linncountyks.com

Linn County Leader
107 N Main St PO Box 40 ... Brookfield MO 64628 660-258-7237 532-2
Web: www.linncountyleader.com

Linn County Rural Electric Co-op
5695 Rec Dr ... Marion IA 52302 319-377-1587 245
Web: www.linncountyrec.com

Linn Gear Co 100 N Eigth St PO Box 397 ... Lebanon OR 97355 541-259-1211 259-1299 620
TF: 800-547-2471 ■ *Web:* www.linngear.com

Linn Run State Park PO Box 50 ... Rector PA 15677 724-238-6623 565
Web: www.dcnr.state.pa.us

Linn-Benton Community College
6500 Pacific Blvd SW ... Albany OR 97321 541-917-4999 162
Web: www.linnbenton.edu

Linnie Thai Cuisine 1301 W Third Ave ... Spokane WA 99201 509-835-5800 671

Linnihan Foy Adv
615 First Ave NE Ste 320 ... Minneapolis MN 55413 612-331-3586 4
Web: www.linnihanfoy.com

Linon Home Dcor Products Inc
22 Jericho Tpke ... Mineola NY 11501 516-699-1000 362
Web: www.linon.com

Linowes & Blocher LLP
7200 Wisconsin Ave Ste 800 ... Bethesda MD 20814 301-654-0504 654-2801 428
Web: linowes-law.com

LINQ Services
1200 Steuart St Unit C3 ... Baltimore MD 21230 800-421-5467 387
TF: 800-421-5467 ■ *Web:* www.linqservices.com

Linq3 Technologies LLC
3060 Peachtree Rd NW Ste 1500 ... Atlanta GA 30305 678-666-4300 387
Web: www.linq3.com

LINQWARE Inc 6161 NE 175th St Ste 205 ... Kenmore WA 98028 585-563-1669 174
Web: www.lincware.com

Linscomb & Williams Inc
1400 Post Oak Blvd Ste 1000 ... Houston TX 77056 713-840-1000 401
TF: 800-960-1200 ■ *Web:* www.linscomb-williams.com

Linsly School 60 Knox Ln ... Wheeling WV 26003 304-233-3260 234-4614 622
TF: 866-648-1893 ■ *Web:* www.linsly.org

LinTech Global Inc
31600 W 13 Mile Rd Ste 122 ... Farmington Hills MI 48334 248-851-8877 180
Web: www.lintechglobal.com

Lintern Corp 8685 Stn St ... Mentor OH 44060 440-255-9333 255-6427 14
TF: 800-321-3638 ■ *Web:* www.lintern.com

Linville Caverns Inc 19929 US 221 N ... Marion NC 28752 800-419-0540 756-4171* 50-5
*Fax Area Code: 828 ■ *TF:* 800-419-0540 ■ *Web:* www.linvillecaverns.com

Linwood Care Center
201 New Rd & Central Ave ... Linwood NJ 08221 609-927-6131 450

Linwood Spiritual Ctr 50 Linwood Rd ... Rhinebeck NY 12572 845-876-4178 876-1920 673
Web: www.linwoodspiritualctr.org

Linx Partners LLC
100 Galleria Pkwy Ste 1150 ... Atlanta GA 30339 770-818-0335 403
Web: www.linxpartners.com

Linxx Security Inc
272 Bedix Rd Ste 220 ... Virginia Beach VA 23452 757-222-0300 393
Web: www.linxxsecurity.com

Linzer Products Corp
248 Wyandanch Ave ... West Babylon NY 11704 631-253-3333 103
Web: www.linzerproducts.com

Lion Apparel Inc 7200 Poe Ave Ste 400 ... Dayton OH 45414 937-898-1949 898-2848* 155-19
*Fax: Hum Res ■ *TF:* 800-548-6614 ■ *Web:* www.lionprotects.com

Lion Brand Yarn Co 135 Kero Rd ... Carlstadt NJ 07072 212-243-8995 745-9
TF: 800-795-5466 ■ *Web:* www.lionbrand.com

Lion Brewery Inc
700 N Pennsylvania Ave ... Wilkes-Barre PA 18705 570-823-8801 102
Web: www.lionbrewery.com

Name / Address	City	State	Zip	Phone	Fax	Class
Lion Bros Company Inc 300 Red Brook Blvd	Owings Mills	MD	21117	410-363-1000		258
TF Cust Svc: 800-365-6543 ■ *Web:* www.lionbrothers.com						
Lion Chemical Capital LLC 535 Madison Ave 4th Fl	New York	NY	10022	212-355-5500		405
Web: www.lionchemicalcapital.com						
Lion Country Safari 2003 Lion Country Safari Rd	Loxahatchee	FL	33470	561-793-1084	793-9603	823
Web: www.lioncountrysafari.com						
Lion Inc 200 Martin Ln Ste A	Elk Grove	IL	60007	872-228-5466		509
TF: 800-867-6320						
Lion Magazine 300 W 22nd St	Oak Brook	IL	60523	630-571-5466	571-8890	457-10
TF Circ: 800-710-7822 ■ *Web:* www.lionsclubs.org						
Lion Raisins 9500 S De Wols Ave PO Box 1350	Selma	CA	93662	559-834-6677	834-6622	315-5
Web: www.lionraisins.com						
Lion Ribbon 111 Eighth Ave	New York	NY	10011	212-255-4224		292
Web: www.artisticribbon.com						
Lion Supermarket 1710 Tully Rd	San Jose	CA	95122	408-238-4451		345
Web: www.lionsupermarket.com						
Lion World Travel 33 Kern Rd	Toronto	ON	M3B1S9	416-920-5466		774
TF: 800-387-2706 ■ *Web:* www.lionworldtravel.com						
Lionakis Beaumont Design Group Inc 1919 19th St	Sacramento	CA	95811	916-558-1900		261
Web: lionakis.com						
Lionbridge Technologies Inc 1050 Winter St Ste 2300	Waltham	MA	02451	781-434-6000	434-6034	768
NASDAQ: LIOX ■ *Web:* lionbridge.com						
Lionel .com LLC 26750 23 Mile Rd	Chesterfield	MI	48051	586-949-4100		762
TF: 800-454-6635 ■ *Web:* www.lionel.com						
Lionetti Assoc 450 S Front St	Elizabeth	NJ	07202	908-820-8800	820-8412	686
TF: 800-734-0910 ■ *Web:* www.lorcopetroleum.com						
Lionheart Publishing Inc 506 Roswell St	Marietta	GA	30060	888-303-5639		637-9
TF: 888-303-5639 ■ *Web:* lionheartpub.com						
Lions Eye Bank Alberta Society 7007 14th St SW	Calgary	AB	T2V1P9	403-943-3406		269
Lions Eye Bank for Long Island *North Shore University Hospital* 350 Community Dr	Manhasset	NY	11030	516-256-6990	256-6661	269
Web: www.northwell.edu						
Lions Eye Bank of Lexington 3290 Blazer Pkwy Ste 201	Lexington	KY	40509	859-323-6740		269
Web: www.mc.uky.edu						
Lions Eye Bank of Manitoba & Northwest Ontario Inc 691 Wolseley Ave	Winnipeg	MB	R3G1C3	204-788-8507		269
TF: 800-552-6820 ■ *Web:* www.eyebankmanitoba.com						
Lions Eye Bank of Nebraska Inc *University of Nebraska Medical Ctr* 985541 Nebraska Medical Ctr	Omaha	NE	68198	402-559-4039		269
TF: 800-225-7244 ■ *Web:* www.eyebanknebraska.org						
Lions Eye Bank of Northwest Pennsylvania Inc 5105 Richmond St	Erie	PA	16509	814-866-3545		269
Lions Eye Bank of Texas at Baylor College of Medicine *Dept of Opthalmology* 6565 Fannin St NC-205	Houston	TX	77030	713-798-4714	798-4645	269
Web: www.bcm.edu						
Lions Eye Bank of Wisconsin 2401 American Ln	Madison	WI	53704	608-233-2354		269
TF: 877-233-2354 ■ *Web:* lebw.org						
Lions Gate Entertainment Inc 2700 Colorado Ave Ste 200	Santa Monica	CA	90404	310-449-9200	255-3870	514
Web: www.lionsgate.com						
Lions Gate Hospital 231 E 15th St	North Vancouver	BC	V7L2L7	604-988-3131	984-5838	374-2
Web: www.vch.ca						
Lions Medical Eye Bank & Research Ctr of Eastern Virginia 600 Gresham Dr	Norfolk	VA	23507	800-453-6059	388-3744*	269
**Fax Area Code:* 757 ■ *TF:* 800-453-6059 ■ *Web:* www.lionseyebank.org						
Lionshare Leadership Group Inc 7065 Moores Ln Ste 200	Brentwood	TN	37027	615-377-4688		463
TF: 800-220-1691 ■ *Web:* lionshare.org						
Lionshare Marketing Inc 7830 Barton St	Overland Park	KS	66214	913-631-8400		195
TF: 800-928-0712 ■ *Web:* www.lionsharemarketing.com						
LIP (Long Island Philharmonic) 1 Huntington Quadrangle Ste 2C21	Melville	NY	11747	631-293-2223	293-2655	573-3
Web: www.liphilharmonic.com						
Lipantitlan State Historic Site c/o Lake Corpus Christi State Pk PO Box 1167	Mathis	TX	78368	361-547-2635		565
Web: tpwd.texas.gov/state-parks/lipantitlan						
Lipari Foods LLC 26661 Bunert Rd	Warren	MI	48089	586-447-3500		297-11
Web: liparifoods.com						
LiphaTech Inc 3600 W Elm St	Milwaukee	WI	53209	888-331-7900	247-8166*	85
**Fax Area Code:* 414 ■ *TF:* 888-331-7900 ■ *Web:* www.liphatech.com						
Lipinski Daniel (Rep D - IL) 2346 Rayburn HOB	Washington	DC	20515	202-225-5701	225-1012	342-2
Web: www.lipinski.house.gov						
Lipinski Landscape & Irrigation Contractors Inc 100 Sharp Rd	Marlton	NJ	08053	800-644-6035		422
TF: 800-644-6035 ■ *Web:* www.meritservicesolutions.com						
Lipman Hearne Inc 200 S Michigan Ave Ste 1600	Chicago	IL	60604	312-356-8000		317
Web: www.lipmanhearne.com						
Lippa Assoc Inc 3633 Camino Del Rio S 207	San Diego	CA	92108	619-283-2581		734
Lipparelli & Assoc Inc 517 Idaho St	Elko	NV	89801	775-738-7131		390
Web: progressive.com						
Lipper International Inc 235 Washington St	Wallingford	CT	06492	203-269-8588	284-8637	730
TF: 800-243-3129 ■ *Web:* www.lipperinternational.com						
Lippert Bros Inc 2211 E I-44 Service Rd PO Box 17450	Oklahoma City	OK	73136	405-478-3580	478-3301	186
Web: www.lippertbros.com						
Lippes Mathias Wexler Friedman LLP 665 Main St Ste 300	Buffalo	NY	14203	716-853-5100		428
Web: www.lippes.com						
Lippincott Marine 3420 Main St	Grasonville	MD	21638	410-827-9300		697
TF: 877-437-4193 ■ *Web:* www.lippincottmarine.com						
Lippincott Williams & Wilkins 530 Walnut St	Philadelphia	PA	19106	215-521-8300	521-8902	637-2
Web: www.lww.com						
Lippmann-Milwaukee Inc 3271 E Van Norman Ave	Cudahy	WI	53110	800-648-0486		190
TF: 800-648-0486 ■ *Web:* www.lippmann-milwaukee.com						
Lipscomb County PO Box 70	Lipscomb	TX	79056	806-862-3091	862-3004	338
Web: www.co.lipscomb.tx.us						
Lipscomb University 3901 Granny White Pk	Nashville	TN	37204	615-966-1000	966-1804*	166
**Fax:* Admissions ■ *TF:* 800-333-4358 ■ *Web:* www.lipscomb.edu						
Lipsey Logistics Worldwide LLC 1701 Oakbrook Dr	Norcross	GA	30093	678-336-1180		314
Lipsey Youngren Means Ogren & Sandberg LLP 525 B St Ste 1400	San Diego	CA	92101	619-234-0877	234-9319	2
Web: www.lymscpa.com						
Lipson, Neilson, Cole, Seltzer & Garin PC 3910 Telegraph Rd Ste 200	Bloomfield Hills	MI	48302	248-593-5000		428
Web: www.lipsonneilson.com						
Lipten Company LLC 28054 Ctr Oaks Ct	Wixom	MI	48393	248-374-8910	374-8906	385
TF: 800-860-0790 ■ *Web:* www.lipten.com						
Lipton Energy 458 S St	Pittsfield	MA	01201-8217	413-443-9191		580
Web: www.liptonenergy.com						
Lipton Law Center Pc 18930 W 10 Mile Rd	Southfield	MI	48075	248-557-1688		428
Web: www.liptonlaw.com						
Liquent Inc 101 Gibraltar Rd	Horsham	PA	19044	215-328-4444	328-4360	178-11
Web: parexel.com/liquent						
Liquid Adv Inc 499 Santa Clara Ave	Venice	CA	90291	310-450-2653		4
Web: www.liquidadvertising.com						
Liquid Agency Inc 448 S Market St	San Jose	CA	95113	408-850-8800		195
Web: www.liquidagency.com						
Liquid Controls LLC 105 Albrecht Dr	Lake Bluff	IL	60044	847-295-1050		201
Web: www.lcmeter.com						
Liquid Measurement Systems 141 Morse Dr PO Box 2070	Georgia	VT	05468	802-528-8100	528-8131	529
Web: www.liquidmeasurement.com						
Liquid Networx Inc PO Box 780099	San Antonio	TX	78278-0099	866-547-8439		196
TF: 866-547-8439 ■ *Web:* www.liquidnetworx.com						
Liquid Packaging Solutions 3999 E Hupp Rd Bldg R43	La Porte	IN	46350	219-393-3600		547
TF: 800-879-3337 ■ *Web:* www.liquidpackagingsolution.com						
Liquid Transport Corp 8470 Allison Pt Blvd Ste 400	Indianapolis	IN	46250	317-841-4200	841-8259	780
TF: 800-942-3175 ■ *Web:* www.liquidtransport.com						
Liquid Waste Technology 1750 Madison Ave	New Richmond	WI	54017	715-246-2888		190
Web: www.trashskimmer.com						
Liquidframeworks 24 E Greenway Plaza	Houston	TX	77046	713-552-9250		177
Web: liquidframeworks.com						
Liquidhub Inc 500 E Swedesford Rd Ste 300	Wayne	PA	19087	484-654-1400	654-1401	194
Web: www.liquidhub.com						
Liquidia Technologies Inc 419 Davis Dr Ste 100	Morrisville	NC	27560	919-328-4400		194
Web: www.liquidia.com						
Liquidity Services Inc 1920 L St NW 6th Fl	Washington	DC	20036	202-467-6868	467-5475	51
NASDAQ: LQDT ■ *TF:* 800-310-4604 ■ *Web:* www.liquidityservices.com						
Liquidmetal Coatings LLC 900 Rockmead Dr Ste 240	Kingwood	TX	77339	281-359-1283		481
Liquidmetal Technologies Inc (LQMT) 30452 Esperanza	Rancho Santa Margarita	CA	92688	949-635-2100	635-2188	482
OTC: LQMT ■ *TF:* 888-203-1112 ■ *Web:* www.liquidmetal.com						
Liquidnet Holdings Inc 498 Seventh Ave 15th Fl	New York	NY	10018	646-674-2000	674-2003	405
Web: www.liquidnet.com						
LiQuifix LLC 110 Lenox Ave	Stamford	CT	06906	203-653-4689		541
Web: www.liquifix.com						
Liquiflo Equipment Co 443 N Ave	Garwood	NJ	07027	908-518-0777	518-1847	641
Web: www.liquiflo.com						
Liquor Barn Inc 4301 Towne Ctr Dr	Louisville	KY	40241	502-426-4222		443
Web: www.liquorbarn.com						
Liquor Mart Inc 1750 15th St	Boulder	CO	80302	303-449-3374		443
TF: 800-597-4440 ■ *Web:* www.liquormart.com						
LiRo Group 3 Aerial Way	Syosset	NY	11791	516-938-5476		261
Web: www.liro.com						
LIRS (Lutheran Immigration & Refugee Service) 700 Light St	Baltimore	MD	21230	410-230-2700	230-2890	48-5
TF: 800-732-0999 ■ *Web:* www.lirs.org						
Lisa Motor Lines 1145 Empire Central Pl PO Box 655888	Dallas	TX	75247	214-630-8090		780
TF: 800-569-9200 ■ *Web:* www.ffeinc.com						
Lisega Inc 375 Lisega Blvd	Newport	TN	37821	423-625-2000		295
Web: www.lisega.de						
LISI Inc 1600 W Hillsdale Blvd	San Mateo	CA	94402	650-348-4131		390
TF: 800-930-5190 ■ *Web:* lisibroker.com						
Liskow & Lewis 701 Poydras St Ste 5000	New Orleans	LA	70139	504-581-7979		428
TF: 800-588-0046 ■ *Web:* www.liskow.com						
Lisle Convention & Visitors Bureau 925 Burlington Ave	Lisle	IL	60532	630-769-1000	769-1006	206
TF: 800-733-9811 ■ *Web:* stayinlisle.com						
Lisle Corp 813 E Main St	Clarinda	IA	51632	712-542-5101	542-6591	758
Web: www.lislecorp.com						
Lisle Library District 777 Front St	Lisle	IL	60532	630-971-1675		434-3
Web: www.lislelibrary.org						
Lisle Park District 1825 Short St	Lisle	IL	60532	630-964-3410		31
TF: 800-526-0854 ■ *Web:* www.lisleparkdistrict.org						
List Industries Inc 401 Jim Moran Blvd	Deerfield Beach	FL	33442	954-429-9155	428-3843	319-3
TF: 800-776-1342 ■ *Web:* www.listindustries.com						
Lista International Corp 106 Lowland St	Holliston	MA	01746	508-429-1350	429-0711	286
TF Cust Svc: 800-722-3020 ■ *Web:* www.listaintl.com						

Name / Address	City	State	Zip	Phone	Fax	Class
Listel Hotel, The 1300 Robson St.	Vancouver	BC	V6E1C5	604-684-8461	684-7092	379
TF: 800-663-5491 ■ *Web:* www.thelistelhotel.com						
Listengage.com 5 Edgell Rd Ste 30a	Framingham	MA	01701	508-935-2275		225
Web: www.listengage.com						
Lister-Petter Americas Inc						
815 E 56 Hwy	Olathe	KS	66061	913-764-3512	764-5493	385
Web: www.lister-petter.com						
Listo Pencil Corp 1925 Union St	Alameda	CA	94501	510-522-2910		571
TF: 800-547-8648 ■ *Web:* www.listo.com						
LITA (Library & Information Technology Assn)						
50 E Huron St.	Chicago	IL	60611	312-280-4270	280-3257	49-11
TF: 800-545-2433 ■ *Web:* www.ala.org						
Litchfield Beach & Golf Resort						
14276 Ocean Hwy.	Pawleys Island	SC	29585	843-237-3000	237-3282	669
TF: 888-734-8228 ■ *Web:* www.litchfieldbeach.com						
Litchfield County						
6 Titus Rd PO Box 396	Washington Depot	CT	06794	860-567-5060		338
Web: www.litchfieldcty.com						
Litchfield National Bank						
316 N State St.	Litchfield	IL	62056	217-324-6161		70
Web: www.ibanklnb.com						
Litchfield Park Recreation						
100 N Old Litchfield Rd	Litchfield Park	AZ	85340	623-935-9040		354
TF: 800-273-8255 ■ *Web:* www.litchfield-park.org						
Litchfield Plantation						
1 Avenue of Live Oaks.	Pawleys Island	SC	29585	843-543-3146		379
Web: www.litchfieldplantation.net						
Litco International Inc						
1 Litco Dr PO Box 150	Vienna	OH	44473	330-539-5433	539-5388	551
TF: 800-236-1903 ■ *Web:* www.litco.com						
Lite Access Technologies						
20678 Duncan Way Unit 5	Langley	BC	V3A7A3	604-247-4704		696
Web: www.liteaccess.com						
Lite Energy 780 Salaberry	Laval	QC	H7S1H3	450-668-9620	668-9625	439
Web: www.liteenergy.com						
Lite Metals Co 700 N Walnut St	Ravenna	OH	44266	330-296-6110		492
Web: www.litemetals.com						
Litecontrol 100 Hawks Ave	Hanson	MA	02341	781-294-0100	293-2849	439
Web: www.litecontrol.com						
LiteCure LLC 250 Corporate Blvd Ste B	Newark	DE	19702	302-709-0408		250
Web: www.litecure.com						
Litehaus Systems Inc						
7445 132nd St Ste 2010.	Surrey	BC	V3W1J8	866-771-0044		809
TF: 866-771-0044 ■ *Web:* www.litehaus360lease.com						
Litehouse Inc 1109 N Ella Ave.	Sandpoint	ID	83864	800-669-3169		296-19
TF: 800-669-3169 ■ *Web:* www.litehousefoods.com						
Litelab Corp 251 Elm St.	Buffalo	NY	14203	716-856-4491		362
TF: 800-238-4120 ■ *Web:* www.litelab.com						
Lite-On Trading USA Inc						
720 S Hillview Dr	Milpitas	CA	95035	408-946-4873	941-4597	173-4
Web: www.us.liteon.com						
Liter's Quarry Inc 5918 Haunz Ln.	Louisville	KY	40241	502-241-7637	241-9410	503-6
TF: 800-633-2602 ■ *Web:* www.litersinc.com						
Litera Corp 5000 Crossmill Rd.	Mcleansville	NC	27301	336-375-2991		177
Web: www.litera.com						
Literacy Council of Tyler						
1530 Loop 323 SSW Rm 120	Tyler	TX	75711	903-533-0330		242
Web: www.lcotyler.org						
Literacy Kansas City						
211 W Armour Blvd Fl 3.	Kansas City	MO	64111	816-333-9332		148
Web: literacykc.org						
Litetronics International Inc						
4101 W 123rd St	Alsip	IL	60803	708-389-8000	371-0627	437
TF: 800-860-3392 ■ *Web:* www.litetronics.com						
Lithgow Public Library 45 Winthrop St.	Augusta	ME	04330	207-626-2415		434-3
Web: www.lithgow.lib.me.us						
Lithia Motors Inc 360 E Jackson St	Medford	OR	97501	866-318-9660		57
NYSE: LAD ■ *TF:* 866-318-9660 ■ *Web:* www.lithia.com						
Litho Technical Services Inc						
1600 W 92nd St	Bloomington	MN	55431	952-888-7945		687
TF: 800-247-2751 ■ *Web:* lithotechusa.com						
Lithographix Inc						
12250 Crenshaw Blvd.	Hawthorne	CA	90250	323-770-1000	706-6574*	627
**Fax Area Code:* 310 ■ *Web:* www.lithographix.com						
Litho-Krome Co 5700 Old Brim Dr	Midland	GA	31820	706-562-7900		627
TF: 800-572-8028 ■ *Web:* www.lithokrome.com						
Litholink Corp						
2250 W Campbell Park Dr	Chicago	IL	60612	312-243-0600		415
Web: www.litholink.com						
Lithonia Lighting 1 Lithonia Way	Conyers	GA	30012	770-922-9000	483-2635	439
TF: 800-858-7763 ■ *Web:* www.lithonia.com						
Lith-O-Roll Corp 9521 Telstar Ave.	El Monte	CA	91731	626-579-0340		454
TF: 800-423-4176 ■ *Web:* www.lithoroll.com						
Lithotone Inc 1313 W Hively Ave	Elkhart	IN	46517	574-294-5521		627
Web: www.lithotone.com						
Lithtex Northwest LLC						
2000 Kentucky St Ste 6.	Bellingham	WA	98225	360-676-1977		627
TF: 800-246-1473 ■ *Web:* www.lithtexnw.com						
Lithtex Printing Solutions Inc						
6770 NW Century Blvd.	Hillsboro	OR	97124	503-641-5367		627
TF: 800-555-5555 ■ *Web:* www.lithtex.com						
Lithuania						
Consulate General						
420 Fifth Ave 3rd Fl	New York	NY	10018	212-354-7840	354-7911	257
Web: usa.mfa.lt						
Embassy 2622 16th St NW	Washington	DC	20009	202-234-5860	328-0466	257
Web: www.usa.mfa.lt						
Lithuanian Museum/Archives of Canada						
2185 Stavebank Rd.	Mississauga	ON	L5C1T3	416-533-3292		520
Web: www.klb.org						
Litigation Solution Inc, The						
901 Main St Ste C121	Dallas	TX	75202	303-820-2000		627
TF: 800-410-7066 ■ *Web:* www.lsilegal.com						
Lititz Mutual Insurance Co						
2 N Broad St PO Box 900	Lititz	PA	17543	717-626-4751	626-0970	391-4
TF: 800-626-4751 ■ *Web:* www.lititzmutual.com						
Litle & Co 900 Chelmsford St.	Lowell	MA	01851	978-275-6500		255
Web: www.litle.com						

Name / Address	City	State	Zip	Phone	Fax	Class
Litman Gregory Asset Management LLC						
100 Larkspur Landing Cir Ste 204	Larkspur	CA	94939	415-461-8999		401
Web: www.lginvestment.com						
Litman Gregory Research Inc						
100 Larkspur Landing Cir Ste 204	Larkspur	CA	94939	925-254-8999		401
TF: 800-960-0188 ■ *Web:* litmangregory.com						
Litronic 17861 Cartwright Rd	Irvine	CA	92614	949-851-1085	851-8588*	178-12
**Fax:* Sales ■ *Web:* www.litronic.com						
Littau Harvester Inc 855 Rogue Ave	Stayton	OR	97383	503-769-5953		274
TF: 866-262-2495 ■ *Web:* www.littauharvester.com						
Littelfuse Inc						
8755 W Higgins Rd Ste 500	Chicago	IL	60631	773-628-1000		729
NASDAQ: LFUS ■ *TF Sales:* 800-227-0029 ■ *Web:* www.littelfuse.com						
Littell LLC 1211 Tower Rd	Schaumburg	IL	60173	630-622-4700		492
Web: www.littell.com						
Little America Hotel & Resort Cheyenne						
2800 W Lincolnway	Cheyenne	WY	82009	307-775-8400	775-8425	379
TF: 800-445-6945 ■ *Web:* www.cheyenne.littleamerica.com						
Little America Hotel & Towers Salt Lake City						
555 S Main St.	Salt Lake City	UT	84101	801-258-6568	596-5911	379
TF: 800-453-9450 ■ *Web:* saltlake.littleamerica.com						
Little America Hotel Flagstaff						
2515 E Butler Ave	Flagstaff	AZ	86004	928-779-7900	779-7983	379
TF: 800-352-4386 ■ *Web:* flagstaff.littleamerica.com						
Little America Hotels & Resorts						
500 S Main St.	Salt Lake City	UT	84101	801-596-5700		379
TF: 800-281-7899 ■ *Web:* saltlake.littleamerica.com						
Little Apple Technologies						
112 S Broadway	Manhattan	MT	59741	406-284-3174		225
TF: 800-823-6766 ■ *Web:* littleappletech.com						
Little Bear Inn 1700 Little Bear Rd	Cheyenne	WY	82009	307-634-3684		671
Web: littlebearinn.com						
Little Beaver State Park						
1402 Grandview Rd	Beaver	WV	25813	304-763-2494		565
Web: www.littlebeaverstatepark.com						
Little Big Horn College						
8645 S Weaver Dr PO Box 370	Crow Agency	MT	59022	406-638-3100	638-3169	165
Web: www.lbhc.edu						
Little Bighorn Battlefield National Monument						
PO Box 39	Crow Agency	MT	59022	406-638-3214	638-2623	564
Web: www.nps.gov/libi						
Little Brown & Co 237 Pk Ave	New York	NY	10017	212-364-1100		637-2
TF Cust Svc: 800-759-0190 ■ *Web:* www.hachettebookgroup.com						
Little Buffalo State Park						
1579 State Pk Rd	Newport	PA	17074	717-567-9255		565
Web: www.dcnr.state.pa.us						
Little Caesars Inc 2211 Woodward Ave	Detroit	MI	48201	313-983-6000		670
TF: 800-722-3727 ■ *Web:* www.littlecaesars.com						
Little Caesars Pizza 2524 Third Line	Oakville	ON	L6M4Y7	905-825-0199		610
Web: littlecaesars.ca						
Little Co of Mary Hospital & Health Care Centers						
2800 W 95th St.	Evergreen Park	IL	60805	708-422-6200		374-3
Web: www.lcmh.org						
Little Company of Mary Home Based Services						
9800 SW Hwy.	Oak Lawn	IL	60453	708-229-4663	499-5975	371
TF: 800-252-2540 ■ *Web:* www.lcmh.org						
Little Cottage Cafe 2513 E Main Ave.	Bismarck	ND	58501	701-223-4949		671
Little Creek Casino Resort						
91 W State Rt 108	Shelton	WA	98584	360-427-7711		669
TF: 800-667-7711 ■ *Web:* www.little-creek.com						
Little Cypress-Mauriceville Cisd Inc						
6586 FM 1130	Orange	TX	77632	409-883-2232		685
Web: www.lcmcisd.org						
Little Door 8164 W Third St	Los Angeles	CA	90048	323-951-1210		671
Web: www.thelittledoor.com						
Little Dutch Boy Bakery Inc						
12349 S 970 E	Draper	UT	84020	801-571-3800		296-9
Little Earth Productions						
2400 Josephine St	Pittsburgh	PA	15203	412-471-0909		514
Web: www.littlearth.com						
Little Falls Granite Works						
10802 Hwy 10	Little Falls	MN	56345	800-862-2417		724
TF: 800-862-2417 ■ *Web:* lfgranite.com						
Little Falls Hospital						
140 Burwell St	Little Falls	NY	13365	315-823-1000		374-3
Web: www.bassett.org						
Little Flower Children & Family Services of New York						
2450 N Wading River Rd.	Wading River	NY	11792	631-929-6200		48-6
Web: www.littleflowerny.org						
Little Fountain Cafe						
2339 18th St NW	Washington	DC	20009	202-462-8100		671
Web: www.littlefountaincafe.com						
Little Friends Inc 140 N Wright St	Naperville	IL	60540	630-355-6533		685
Web: littlefriendsinc.org						
Little General Store Inc						
17 Yellow Wood Way	Beckley	WV	25801	304-253-9592		791
Web: lgstoreswv.com						
Little Gym International Inc						
7001 N Scottsdale Rd	Paradise Valley	AZ	85253	888-228-2878		354
TF General: 888-228-2878 ■ *Web:* www.thelittlegym.com						
Little Havana 1325 Key Hwy	Baltimore	MD	21230	410-837-9903		671
TF: 800-233-0828 ■ *Web:* www.littlehavanas.com						
Little India 330 E Sixth Ave	Denver	CO	80203	303-871-9777		671
Web: www.littleindiadenver.com						
Little Italy 2300 E 88th Ave	Anchorage	AK	99507	907-344-1515		671
Web: littleitalyalaska.com						
Little Italy's Trattoria						
901 Washington St.	Vancouver	WA	98660	360-737-2363		671
Web: www.littleitalystrattoria.com						
Little Kids Inc						
225 Chapman St Ste 202	Providence	RI	02905	401-454-7600		608
TF: 800-545-5437 ■ *Web:* www.littlekidsinc.com						
Little Lady Foods Inc						
2323 Pratt Blvd.	Elk Grove Village	IL	60007	847-631-3500		296-36
Web: www.littleladyfoods.com						
Little League Baseball Inc						
539 US Rt 15 Hwy PO Box 3485.	Williamsport	PA	17701	570-326-1921	326-1074	48-22
TF: 800-811-7443 ■ *Web:* www.littleleague.org						

Name / Address	City	State	ZIP	Phone	Fax	Class
Little Manatee River State Park 215 Lightfoot Rd *Web:* www.floridastateparks.org	Wimauma	FL	33598	813-671-5005		565
Little Manila Lumpia House 2124 Waldron Rd	Corpus Christi	TX	78418	361-937-5651		671
Little Moreau Recreation Area c/o Shadehill Recreation Area 19150 Summerville Rd *Web:* gfp.sd.gov/state-parks/directory/little-moreau	Shadehill	SD	57653	605-374-5114		565
Little Mountain Printing 234 E Rosebud Rd *Web:* littlemountainprinting.com	Myerstown	PA	17067	717-933-8091		627
Little Nell, The 675 E Durant Ave *TF:* 888-843-6355 ■ *Web:* www.thelittlenell.com	Aspen	CO	81611	970-920-4600		379
Little Nepal 925 Cortland Ave *Web:* www.littlenepalsf.com	San Francisco	CA	94110	415-643-3881	643-8088	671
Little Ocmulgee Electric Membership Corp 26 W Railroad Ave *TF:* 800-342-1290 ■ *Web:* www.littleocmulgeeemc.com	Alamo	GA	30411	912-568-7171		245
Little Ocmulgee State Park & Lodge 80 Live Oak Trail *Web:* littleocmulgeelodge.com	Helena	GA	31037	229-868-7474		565
Little Palm Island Resort & Spa 28500 Overseas Hwy *TF:* 800-343-8567 ■ *Web:* www.littlepalmisland.com	Little Torch Key	FL	33042	305-872-2524		669
Little Panda 1035 N Judge Ely Blvd *Web:* www.littlepandaonline.com	Abilene	TX	79601	325-670-9393		671
Little Pedersen Fankhauser LLP 901 Main St Ste 4110 *TF:* 800-447-5375 ■ *Web:* www.lpf-law.com	Dallas	TX	75202	214-573-2300		428
Little Pee Dee State Park 1298 State Pk Rd *TF:* 800-491-1764 ■ *Web:* www.southcarolinaparks.com	Dillon	SC	29536	843-774-8872		565
Little Pine State Park 4205 Little Pine Creek Rd *Web:* www.dcnr.state.pa.us	Waterville	PA	17776	570-753-6000		565
Little Pine State Park c/o Little Pine State Pk 4205 Little Pine Creek Rd *Web:* www.dcnr.state.pa.us	Waterville	PA	17776	570-753-6000		565
Little Planet Learning 2963 Foster Creighton Dr Ste *TF:* 800-388-1185 ■ *Web:* www.littleplanet.com	Nashville	TN	37204	615-259-3733		180
Little Priest Tribal College 601 E College Dr PO Box 270 *Web:* www.littlepriest.edu	Winnebago	NE	68071	402-878-2380	878-2355	165
Little Promise Keepers 12320 Cypress N Houston Rd	Cypress	TX	77429	281-807-0009		48-20
Little Rapids Corp 2273 Larsen Rd *Web:* www.littlerapids.com	Green Bay	WI	54303	920-496-3040		576
Little Red Services Inc 3700 Centerpoint Dr Ste 1300 *TF:* 800-764-3382 ■ *Web:* www.littleredservices.com	Anchorage	AK	99503	907-349-2931		539
Little Rhein Steakhouse 231 S Alamo St *Web:* www.littlerheinsteakhouse.com	San Antonio	TX	78205	210-225-2111	271-9180	671
Little River Canyon National Preserve 2141 Gault Ave N *Web:* www.nps.gov	Fort Payne	AL	35967	256-845-9605	997-9129	564
Little River Electric Co-op Inc (LRECI) PO Box 220 *TF:* 800-459-2141 ■ *Web:* www.lreci.coop	Abbeville	SC	29620	864-366-2141		245
Little River State Park 3444 Little River Rd *Web:* www.vtstateparks.com	Waterbury	VT	05676	802-244-7103		565
Little Rock Air Force Base 1250 Thomas Ave *TF:* 800-557-6815 ■ *Web:* www.littlerock.af.mil	Little Rock AFB	AR	72099	501-987-1110		497-1
Little Rock Central High School National Historic Site 2120 W Daisy L Gatson Bates Dr *Web:* www.nps.gov	Little Rock	AR	72202	501-374-1957	376-4728	564
Little Rock City Hall 500 W Markham St *Web:* www.littlerock.org	Little Rock	AR	72201	501-371-4770	371-4498	337
Little Rock National Cemetery 2523 Confederate Blvd *Web:* www.cem.va.gov	Little Rock	AR	72206	501-324-6401		136
Little Rock Regional Chamber of Commerce 1 Chamber Plaza *Web:* www.littlerockchamber.com	Little Rock	AR	72201	501-374-2001	374-6018	139
Little Rock School District 810 W Markham St **Fax:* Hum Res ■ *Web:* www.lrsd.org	Little Rock	AR	72201	501-447-1000	447-1162*	685
Little Rock Wastewater 11 Clearwater Dr *Web:* www.lrwu.com	Little Rock	AR	72204	501-376-2903	688-1409	804
Little Rock Zoo 1 Zoo Dr *Web:* www.littlerockzoo.com	Little Rock	AR	72205	501-666-2406	666-7040	823
Little Sahara State Park 101 Main St *Web:* www.travelok.com	Waynoka	OK	73860	580-824-1471	824-1472	565
Little Saigon 1106 E Colonial Dr *Web:* littlesaigonrestaurant.com	Orlando	FL	32803	407-423-8539		671
Little Savannah 3811 Clairmont Ave *Web:* www.birminghammenus.com	Birmingham	AL	35222	205-591-1119		671
Little Talbot Island State Park 12157 Heckscher Dr *TF:* 800-326-3521 ■ *Web:* www.floridastateparks.org/park/Little-Talbot-Island	Jacksonville	FL	32226	904-251-2320	251-2325	565
Little Thai Kitchen 1051 S Milton Rd	Flagstaff	AZ	86001	928-226-9422		671
Little Theatre of Alexandria 600 Wolfe St *Web:* www.thelittletheatre.com	Alexandria	VA	22314	703-683-5778	683-1378	572
Little Theatre of Norfolk 801 Claremont Ave *Web:* www.ltnonline.org	Norfolk	VA	23507	757-627-8551		572
Little Tikes Co, The 2180 Barlow Rd *TF Cust Svc:* 800-321-0183 ■ *Web:* www.littletikes.com	Hudson	OH	44236	800-321-0183		762
Little Tokyo 121B N Broadway *Web:* thegreenbaysushi.com	Green Bay	WI	54303	920-433-9323	433-9523	671
Little Valley Homes Inc 45225 Grand River Ave *Web:* www.lvhomes.net	Novi	MI	48375	231-775-8102		505
Little White House State Historic Site 401 Little White House Rd *TF:* 800-864-7275 ■ *Web:* gastateparks.org/info/littlewhite	Warm Springs	GA	31830	706-655-5870	655-5872	565
Littlefield Corp 2501 N Lamar Blvd *OTC: LTFD* ■ *Web:* www.littlefield.com	Austin	TX	78705	512-476-5141		322
Littlefield Feedyard Farm to Market 37	Littlefield	TX	79339	806-385-5141		10-1
Littlefield Oil Co 3403 Cavanaugh Rd *Web:* www.littlefieldcompanies.com	Fort Smith	AR	72908	479-646-0595		579
Littlejohn & Company LLC 8 Sound Shore Dr Ste 303 *Web:* www.littlejohnllc.com	Greenwich	CT	06830	203-552-3500	552-3550	403
Littler Mendelson PC 650 California St 20th Fl *TF:* 888-548-8537 ■ *Web:* www.littler.com	San Francisco	CA	94108	415-433-1940	399-8490	428
Littlestown Foundry Inc 150 Charles St PO Box 69 *TF:* 800-471-0844 ■ *Web:* www.littlestownfoundry.com	Littlestown	PA	17340	717-359-4141	359-5010	308
Littleton Adventist Hospital 7700 S Broadway *TF:* 800-390-4166 ■ *Web:* www.mylittletonhospital.org	Littleton	CO	80122	303-730-8900		374-3
Littleton Coin Company LLC 1309 Mt Eustis Rd *TF:* 800-645-3122 ■ *Web:* www.littletoncoin.com	Littleton	NH	03561	603-444-5386	444-0121	50-4
Litton Engineering Laboratories 200 Litton Dr Ste 200 *TF:* 800-821-8866 ■ *Web:* www.littonengr.com	Grass Valley	CA	95945	530-273-6176		454
Litton's Market & Restaurant & Bakery 2803 Essary Dr *Web:* www.littonsdirecttoyou.com/home.aspx	Knoxville	TN	37918	865-688-0429		671
Liturgical Publications Inc 2875 S James Dr *TF:* 800-876-4574 ■ *Web:* www.4lpi.com	New Berlin	WI	53151	262-785-1188		637-9
Live Auctioneers LLC 220 12th Ave 2nd Fl *Web:* www.liveauctioneers.com	New York	NY	10001	212-947-4428		317
Live centre speciality 1111 Gallagher Dr	Sherman	TX	75090	903-870-7000		374-3
Live Design 1166 Ave of the Americas 10th Fl **Fax Area Code:* 913 ■ *Web:* www.livedesignonline.com	New York	NY	10036	212-204-4272	514-3619*	457-9
Live Eyewear Inc 3490 Broad St *Web:* www.liveeyewear.com	San Luis Obispo	CA	93401	805-782-5070		543
Live Nation Inc 9348 Civic Ctr Dr *NYSE: LYV* ■ *Web:* www.livenation.com	Beverly Hills	CA	90210	310-867-7000		181
Live Oak County PO Box 280 *Web:* www.co.live-oak.tx.us	George West	TX	78022	361-449-2733		338
Live Oak Public Libraries 2002 Bull St *Web:* www.liveoakpl.org	Savannah	GA	31401	912-652-3600	652-3638	434-3
Live Wire Net 4577 Pecos St *TF:* 866-913-5221 ■ *Web:* www.livewirenet.com	Denver	CO	80211	303-458-5667		116
LiveBlock Auctions International Inc 2125 11th Ave Ste 200 *Web:* www.liveblockauctions.com	Regina	SK	S4P3X3	306-584-1383		809
LiveBridge Inc 7303 SE Lake Rd *Web:* www.livebridge.com	Portland	OR	97267	503-652-6000		737
Livecareer Inc 1432 Washington St *TF:* 800-652-8430 ■ *Web:* www.livecareer.com	San Francisco	CA	94109	800-652-8430		396
Livelogic L l c 13601 Preston Rd Ste 720e *Web:* www.livelogic.net	Dallas	TX	75240	972-385-8515		463
Livengrin Foundation 4833 Hulmeville Rd *TF:* 800-245-4746 ■ *Web:* www.livengrin.org	Bensalem	PA	19020	215-638-5200		726
LivePerson Inc 462 Seventh Ave 3rd Fl *NASDAQ: LPSN* ■ *Web:* www.liveperson.com	New York	NY	10018	212-609-4200	609-4201	39
LivePlanet Inc 2644 30th St *Web:* www.liveplanet.com	Santa Monica	CA	90405	310-664-2400		401
LiveRelay Inc 10815 Rancho Bernardo Rd Ste 300 *Web:* www.relaytv.com	San Diego	CA	92127	858-348-1710		387
Livermore Chamber of Commerce 2157 First St *TF:* 800-743-5000 ■ *Web:* www.livermorechamber.org	Livermore	CA	94550	925-447-1606	447-1641	139
Livermore Public Library 1188 S Livermore Ave *TF:* 800-735-2929 ■ *Web:* www.cityoflivermore.net	Livermore	CA	94550	925-373-5500		434-3
Livermore Valley Tennis Club II 2000 Arroyo Rd *Web:* www.lvtc.com	Livermore	CA	94550	925-443-7700		354
Livers Bronze Co 4621 E 75th Terr *TF:* 800-965-6360 ■ *Web:* www.liversbronze.com	Kansas City	MO	64132	816-300-2828	300-0864	491
Livesmart 360 LLC 6311 Porter Rd Ste 11	Sarasota	FL	34240	941-371-1010		225
Livestock Marketing Assn (LMA) 10510 N Ambassador Dr *TF:* 800-821-2048 ■ *Web:* www.lmaweb.com	Kansas City	MO	64153	816-891-0502	891-7108	48-2
LiveTechnology Holdings Inc 16 Sterling Lake Rd LiveTechnology Pk *Web:* www.livetechnology.com	Tuxedo Park	NY	10987	845-351-5100		180
Livewire LLC 4900 W Clay St *Web:* www.getlivewire.com	Richmond	VA	23230	804-937-9001		180
Livewire Printing Co 310 Second St *Web:* www.livewireprinting.com	Jackson	MN	56143	507-847-3771		627
LiveWorld Inc 4340 Stevens Creek Blvd Ste 101 *TF:* 800-301-9507 ■ *Web:* www.liveworld.com	San Jose	CA	95129	800-301-9507		7

Phone | Fax | Class

Living Assistance Services Inc
937 Haverford Rd Ste 200..................Bryn Mawr PA 19010 800-365-4189 310
TF: 800-365-4189 ■ *Web:* www.livingassistance.com
Living Bank PO Box 6725.....................Houston TX 77027 713-961-9431 961-0979 48-17
TF: 800-528-2971 ■ *Web:* www.livingbank.org
Living Classrooms Foundation
515 M St SE Ste 222....................Washington DC 20003 202-488-0627 521
Web: livingclassrooms.org
Living Color Enterprises Inc
6850 NW 12th Ave....................Fort Lauderdale FL 33309 954-970-9511 41
TF: 800-878-9511 ■ *Web:* www.livingcolor.com
Living Desert Zoo & Gardens
47900 Portola Ave.....................Palm Desert CA 92260 760-346-5694 568-9685 97
TF: 800-226-3369 ■ *Web:* www.livingdesert.org
Living Earth Crafts
3210 Executive Ridge Dr.......................Vista CA 92081 760-597-2155 76
TF: 800-358-8292 ■ *Web:* www.livingearthcrafts.com
Living Earth Technology Co
1901 California Crossing.....................Dallas TX 75220 972-869-4332 280
Web: www.livingearth.net
Living Faith Christian Church
19503 Business Ctr Dr....................Northridge CA 91324 818-709-8532 48-20
Web: living.org
Living History Farms 2600 111th St..........Urbandale IA 50322 515-278-5286 520
Web: www.lhf.org
Living Prairie Museum 2795 Ness Ave.........Winnipeg MB R3J3S4 204-832-0167 520
Web: www.winnipeg.ca/publicworks/parksOpenSpace/livingprairie
Living Room Realtors Inc
1401 NE Alberta St.........................Portland OR 97211 503-719-5588 652
Web: www.livingroomre.com
Living Spa at El Monte Sagrado
317 Kit Carson Rd............................Taos NM 87571 575-758-3502 737-2985 707
TF: 855-846-8267 ■ *Web:* www.elmontesagrado.com
Living Spaces Furniture LLC
14501 Artesia Blvd.......................La Mirada CA 90638 877-266-7300 321
TF: 877-266-7300 ■ *Web:* www.livingspaces.com
Livingston & Haven
11529 Wilmar Blvd PO Box 7207.............Charlotte NC 28273 704-588-3670 504-2530 385
TF: 800-835-4969 ■ *Web:* www.livhaven.com
Livingston County 6 Court St................Geneseo NY 14454 585-243-7000 338
Web: www.co.livingston.state.ny.us
Livingston County
200 E Grand River Ave.......................Howell MI 48843 517-546-0500 546-4354 338
Web: www.livgov.com
Livingston County 112 W Madison St...........Pontiac IL 61764 815-844-2006 842-1844 338
Web: livingstoncountyil.gov
Livingston County 335 Ct St................Smithland KY 42081 270-928-2162 928-2162 338
Web: www.livingstonco.ky.gov
Livingston County Chamber of Commerce
4635 Millennium Dr........................Geneseo NY 14454 585-243-2222 243-4824 139
TF: 800-538-7365 ■ *Web:* www.fingerlakeswest.com
Livingston County Daily Press & Argus
323 E Grand River Ave.......................Howell MI 48843 517-548-2000 637-8
TF: 888-999-1288 ■ *Web:* www.livingstondaily.com
Livingston Healtcare
320 Alpenglow Ln.........................Livingston MT 59047 406-222-3541 823-6499 374-3
Web: www.livingstonhealthcare.org
Livingston Memorial Visiting Nurse Assn Hospice
1996 Eastman Ave Ste 101....................Ventura CA 93003 805-642-1608 642-2320 371
TF: 800-830-8881 ■ *Web:* www.lmvna.org
Livingston Parish
20399 Government Blvd.....................Livingston LA 70754 225-686-4400 338
Web: www.livingstonparishla.gov
Livingston Parish Chamber of Commerce
PO Box 591...........................Denham Springs LA 70726 225-665-8155 665-2411 139
Web: www.livingstonparishchamber.org
Livingston Parish Library
20390 Iowa St PO Box 397..................Livingston LA 70754 225-686-2436 686-3888 434-3
TF: 800-227-2345 ■ *Web:* mylpl.info
Livingston Pipe & Tube Inc
1612 Rt 4 N..............................Staunton IL 62088 618-635-8700 492
TF: 800-548-7473 ■ *Web:* www.livingstonpipeandtube.com
Livingston Public Library
10 Robert H Harp Dr.......................Livingston NJ 07039 973-992-4600 434-3
Web: livingston.bccls.org
Livingston Regional Hospital
315 Oak St..............................Livingston TN 38570 931-823-5611 374-3
Web: mylivingstonhospital.com
Livingston Technologies
45 Horse Hill Rd Ste 105B................Cedar Knolls NJ 07927 973-322-5671 690
Livingstone College 701 W Monroe St.........Salisbury NC 28144 704-216-6963 216-6215 166
TF: 800-835-3435 ■ *Web:* www.livingstone.edu
Livingstone Partners LLC
443 N Clark Ste 200.........................Chicago IL 60654 312-670-5900 194
Web: www.livingstonepartners.com
Livingstone's Restaurant & Pub
831 E Fern Ave..............................Fresno CA 93728 559-485-5198 671
Web: towerdistrict.org
Livonia Chamber of Commerce
33233 5 Mile Rd.............................Livonia MI 48154 734-427-2122 427-6055 139
TF: 800-343-2076 ■ *Web:* www.livonia.org
Livonia Public Library
32777 Five Mile Rd..........................Livonia MI 48154 734-466-2491 458-6011 434-3
Web: livoniapubliclibrary.org
Liz Lerman Dance Exchange
7117 Maple Ave.........................Takoma Park MD 20912 301-270-6700 573-1
Web: www.danceexchange.org
Lizardos Engineering Assoc PC
200 Old Country Rd Ste 670.................Mineola NY 11501 516-484-1020 484-0926 187
Web: www.leapc.com
Lizzadro Museum of Lapidary Art
220 Cottage Hill Ave Wilder Pk...............Elmhurst IL 60126 630-833-1616 833-1225 520
Web: www.lizzadromuseum.org
LJ Gonzer Assoc Inc
14 Commerce Dr Ste 305.....................Cranford NJ 07016 908-709-9494 709-9077 721
Web: www.gonzer.com
LJ Kushner & Associates LLC
36 W Main St Ste 302.......................Freehold NJ 07728 732-577-8100 193
Web: ljkushner.com

Phone | Fax | Class

LJ Smith Co 35280 Scio-Bowerston Rd.........Bowerston OH 44695 740-269-2221 269-9047 499
Web: www.ljsmith.net
LJB Inc 2500 Newmark Dr...................Miamisburg OH 45342 937-259-5000 259-5100 261
TF: 866-552-3536 ■ *Web:* www.ljbinc.com
LJG Partners Inc 680 W Beech St.............San Diego CA 92101 619-232-3000 449
Web: www.ljg.com
LJM Engineering Group 439 Rt 46 E...........Rockaway NJ 07866 973-586-3004 261
LK Industries 1357 W Beaver St.............Jacksonville FL 32209 904-354-8882 298
TF: 800-531-4975 ■ *Web:* www.loadking.com
L-K Industries Inc 6952 Lawndale St............Houston TX 77023 713-926-2623 537
Web: www.lk-ind.com
L-K Marketing Group LLC 2421 Richards Dr........Waco TX 76710 254-741-1570 195
Web: www.lksupport.com
LKG Industries Inc
3660 Publisher's Dr........................Rockford IL 61109 815-874-2301 52
Lkh & s 54 W Hubbard St Ste 100................Chicago IL 60654 312-595-0200 7
Web: www.lkhs.com
LKM Industries Inc 44 Sixth Rd................Woburn MA 01801 781-935-9210 454
Web: www.lkm.com
LKQ Corp 500 W Madison St Ste 2800............Chicago IL 60661 312-621-1950 621-1969 61
NASDAQ: LKQX ■ *TF:* 877-557-2677 ■ *Web:* www.lkqcorp.com
LL Bean Inc 15 Casco St......................Freeport ME 04033 207-552-3080 552-3080 459
TF: 800-341-4341 ■ *Web:* www.llbean.com
L&L Foods Inc 333 N Euclid Way...............Anaheim CA 92801 714-254-1430 393
TF: 800-523-5030 ■ *Web:* llfoodsinc.com
LL Johnson Distributing Co
4700 Holly St................................Denver CO 80216 303-320-1270 429
Web: www.lljohnson.com
Ll Roberts Group
7475 Skillman St Ste 102c.....................Dallas TX 75231 214-221-6463 260
TF: 877-878-6463 ■ *Web:* www.llroberts.com
LL Smith Trucking Inc 711 Rail Rd.............Riverton WY 82501 307-856-2491 780
LLAMA (Library Leadership & Management Assn)
50 E Huron St................................Chicago IL 60611 800-545-2433 49-11
TF: 800-545-2433 ■ *Web:* www.ala.org/llama
Llano County PO Box 40......................Llano TX 78643 325-247-4455 247-2406 338
TF: 800-388-8075 ■ *Web:* www.co.llano.tx.us
Llano Estacado Winery 3426 E FM 1585........Lubbock TX 79404 806-745-2258 50-7
TF: 800-634-3854 ■ *Web:* www.llanowine.com
Llano National Bank 1001 Ford St..............Llano TX 78643 325-247-5701 70
Web: www.llanonationalbank.com
LLBL (Locke Lord Bissell & Liddell LLP)
2200 Ross Ave Ste 2200.......................Dallas TX 75201 214-740-8000 740-8000 428
Web: www.lockelord.com
LLEC (Lyon-Lincoln Electric Co-op Inc)
205 W Hwy 14 PO Box 639......................Tyler MN 56178 507-247-5505 245
TF: 800-927-6276 ■ *Web:* www.llec.coop
Llewellyn Johns Recreation Area
c/o Shadehill Recreation Area
19150 Summerville Rd.....................Shadehill SD 57653 605-374-5114 565
Web: gfp.sd.gov
Llewellyn Worldwide Inc
2143 Wooddale Dr.........................Woodbury MN 55125 651-291-1970 291-1908 637-2
TF: 800-843-6666 ■ *Web:* www.llewellyn.com
Llewelyn-davies Sahni International Inc
5120 Woodway Dr Ste 8010....................Houston TX 77056 713-850-1500 186
Web: www.theldnet.com
LLLI (La Leche League International Inc)
957 N Plum Grove Rd....................Schaumburg IL 60173 847-519-7730 969-0460 48-17
TF: 800-525-3243 ■ *Web:* www.lalecheleague.org
LLNL (Lawrence Livermore National Laboratory)
7000 E Ave PO Box 808....................Livermore CA 94550 925-422-1100 422-1370 668
TF: 800-356-4872 ■ *Web:* www.llnl.gov
Llorens Pharmaceuticals International Division
7080 NW 37th Ct............................Miami FL 33147 305-716-0595 414
TF: 866-595-5598 ■ *Web:* www.llorenspharm.com
Lloyd & McDaniel PLC
11405 Park Rd Ste 200.....................Louisville KY 40223 502-585-1880 428
TF: 866-548-2486 ■ *Web:* www.lloydmc.com
Lloyd Bilyeu McLellan Construction Company Inc (LBM)
11421 Blankenbaker Access Dr..............Louisville KY 40299 502-452-1151 454-0291 186
Web: www.lbmconstructionco.com
Lloyd Gray Whitehead & Monroe PC
2501 20th Pl S Ste 300...................Birmingham AL 35223 205-967-8822 428
TF: 800-967-7299 ■ *Web:* www.lgwmlaw.com
Lloyd Inc
604 W Thomas Ave PO Box 130...........Shenandoah IA 51601 712-246-4000 246-5245 584
TF: 800-831-0004 ■ *Web:* www.lloydinc.com
Lloyd Industries Inc
231 Commerce Dr...................Montgomeryville PA 18936 215-412-4445 697
Web: www.firedamper.com
Lloyd Laboratories Inc 24 Fitch Ct............Wakefield MA 01880 781-224-0083 145
Lloyd Pest Control Co Inc, The
1331 Morena Blvd Ste 300.................San Diego CA 92110 800-223-2847 577
TF: 800-223-2847 ■ *Web:* www.lloydpest.com
Lloyd Schuh Advertising Inc
2207 Cantrell Rd.........................Little Rock AR 72202 501-374-2332 195
TF: 866-572-6584 ■ *Web:* www.lscmarketing.com
Lloyd's America Inc
25 W 53rd St 14th Fl.......................New York NY 10019 212-382-4060 382-4070 391-7
Web: www.lloyds.com
Lloyd's Barbecue Co
1455 Mendota Heights Rd.............Mendota Heights MN 55120 651-688-6000 296-34
Web: hormel.com/brands/hormel-lloyds
Lloyd's Florist 9216 Preston Hwy..............Louisville KY 40229 502-968-5428 964-5696 292
TF: 800-264-1825 ■ *Web:* www.lloydsflorist.net
Lloyd's Register Americas Inc
1330 Enclave Pkwy Ste 200..................Houston TX 77077 281-398-7370 196
Web: www.cdlive.lr.org
LLS (Lakeshores Library System)
725 Cornerstone Crossing Ste C.............Waterford WI 53185 262-514-4500 434-3
Web: www.lakeshores.lib.wi.us
LM Capital Group LLC
750 B St Ste 3010.........................San Diego CA 92101 619-814-1401 401
TF: 800-877-7210 ■ *Web:* www.lmcapital.com
LMA (Livestock Marketing Assn)
10510 N Ambassador Dr....................Kansas City MO 64153 816-891-0502 891-7108 48-2
TF: 800-821-2048 ■ *Web:* www.lmaweb.com

	Phone	Fax	Class
LMC PO Box 428 Donalsonville GA 39845	229-524-2197	524-2531	298
TF: 800-332-8232 ■ *Web:* www.lmcarter.com			
LMC (Laredo Medical Ctr) 1700 E Saunders Ave Laredo TX 78041	956-796-5000		374-3
Web: www.laredomedical.com			
LMC Industries Inc 100 Manufacturers Dr Arnold MO 63010	636-282-8080	282-7114	489
Web: www.lmcindustries.com			
LMCG Investments LLC 200 Clarendon St 28th Fl Boston MA 02116	617-380-5600	380-5601	792
TF: 877-241-5191 ■ *Web:* www.lmcg.com			
Lmd 14409 Greenview Dr Ste 200 Laurel MD 20708	301-498-6656		195
TF: 800-874-2458 ■ *Web:* www.lmdagency.com			
Lme Consulting 4625 Ladera Way Carmichael CA 95608	916-601-1961		196
TF: 800-543-5073 ■ *Web:* www.lmeconsulting.net			
LMG Holdings Inc 4290 Glendale Milford Rd Blue Ash OH 45242	513-651-9560		407
Web: www.lifesafer.com			
LMG Inc 2350 Investors Row Orlando FL 32837	407-850-0505	438-8422	264-2
TF: 888-226-3100 ■ *Web:* www.lmg.net			
LMH (Lawrence Memorial Hospital) 325 Maine St Lawrence KS 66044	785-505-5000		374-3
TF: 800-749-4144 ■ *Web:* www.lmh.org			
LMI (Legg Mason Inc) 100 International Dr Baltimore MD 21202	410-539-0000		690
NYSE: LM ■ *TF:* 800-822-5544 ■ *Web:* www.leggmason.com			
Lmi Advertising 24e E Roseville Rd Lancaster PA 17601	717-569-8826		7
TF: 800-522-9967 ■ *Web:* lmiadvertising.com			
LMI Aerospace Inc (LMIA) 411 Fountain Lakes Blvd Saint Charles MO 63301	636-946-6525	949-1576	22
NASDAQ: LMIA ■ *Web:* www.lmiaerospace.com			
LMI Landscapes Inc 1437 Halsey Way Carrollton TX 75007	972-446-0020		422
Web: www.lmilandscapes.com			
LMI Packaging Solutions Inc 8911 102nd St Pleasant Prairie WI 53158	262-947-3300		627
TF: 800-208-3331 ■ *Web:* www.lmipackaging.com			
LMIA (LMI Aerospace Inc) 411 Fountain Lakes Blvd Saint Charles MO 63301	636-946-6525	949-1576	22
NASDAQ: LMIA ■ *Web:* www.lmiaerospace.com			
LMN Architects 801 Second Ave Ste 501 Seattle WA 98104	206-682-3460		261
Web: www.lmnarchitects.com			
Lmo Reps LLC 21 Roulston Rd Windham NH 03087	603-893-4178		2
Web: lmoreps.com			
LMS Reinforcing Steel Group Inc 6320 148th St Surrey BC V3S3C4	604-598-9930	598-9931	492
Web: www.lmsgroup.ca			
Lmt Mercer Group Inc 690 Puritan Ave Lawrenceville NJ 08648	609-989-0399		596
Web: www.lmtproducts.com			
Lmt USA Inc 1081 S Northpoint Blvd Waukegan IL 60085	630-969-5412	969-5492	386
Web: www.lmtfette.com			
Lmw Engineering Group LLC 2539 Brunswick Ave Linden NJ 07036	908-862-7600		261
TF: 800-580-1934 ■ *Web:* www.ftcny.com			
LN Curtis & Sons 1800 Peralta St Oakland CA 94607	510-839-5111	839-5325	679
TF: 800-443-3556 ■ *Web:* www.lncurtis.com			
L&N Enterprises Inc 5720 Daltry Ln Colorado Springs CO 80906	719-576-7925		443
LNC (Lincoln National Corp) 150 N Radnor-Chester Rd Radnor PA 19087	484-583-1400	448-3962*	360-4
NYSE: LNC ■ **Fax Area Code:* 215 ■ **Fax:* PR ■ *TF:* 877-275-5462 ■ *Web:* www.lfg.com			
LNI Custom Manufacturing Inc 12536 Chadron Ave Hawthorne CA 90250	310-978-2000		701
TF: 800-338-3387 ■ *Web:* www.lnisigns.com			
LNK International Inc 22 Arkay Dr Hauppauge NY 11788	631-435-3500		231
Web: www.lnkintl.com			
Lo Sole Mio 3001 S 32nd Ave Omaha NE 68105	402-345-5656		671
Web: www.losolemio.com			
Load Rite Trailers Inc 265 Lincoln Hwy Fairless Hills PA 19030	215-949-0500	949-1385	763
TF: 800-562-3783 ■ *Web:* www.loadrite.com			
Loadcraft Industries Inc 3811 N Bridge St Brady TX 76825	325-597-2911		779
TF: 800-803-0183 ■ *Web:* www.loadcraft.com			
Loadmaster Derrick & Equipment Inc 1084 Cruse Ave Broussard LA 70518	337-837-5429		539
Web: www.loadmasterderrick.com			
Loadmaster Universal Rigs Inc 6935 Brittmoore Rd Houston TX 77041	281-598-7240		256
Web: loadmasterur.com			
Loadstar Sensors Inc 48501 Warm Springs Blvd Ste 109 Fremont CA 94539	510-274-1872		407
TF: 800-344-3965 ■ *Web:* www.loadstarsensors.com			
Loaf N' Jug Mini Mart 442 Keeler Pkwy Pueblo CO 81001	719-948-3071		204
Web: www.loafnjug.com			
Loan Science PO Box 81671 Austin TX 78708	866-311-9450	646-4097*	215
**Fax Area Code:* 512 ■ *TF:* 866-311-9450 ■ *Web:* www.loanscience.com			
Loan Value Group LLC 47 W River Rd Ste C Rumson NJ 07760	732-741-7300		466
Web: www.loanvaluegroup.com			
loanDepot 26642 Towne Centre Dr Foothill Ranch CA 92610	888-337-6888		509
TF: 888-337-6888 ■ *Web:* www.loandepot.com			
LoBiondo Frank (Rep R - NJ) 2427 Rayburn Bldg Washington DC 20515	202-225-6572	225-3318	342-2
Web: lobiondo.house.gov			
Loblaw Cos Ltd 1 President's Choice Cir Brampton ON L6Y5S5	905-459-2500		345
TF: 888-495-5111 ■ *Web:* www.loblaw.ca/en.html			
Loblaws Inc 12 St Clair Ave E Toronto ON M4T1L7	416-960-8108		345
Web: www.loblaws.ca			
Loblolly Consulting Llc 506 Carolyn Ave Austin TX 78705	512-320-5421		196
TF: 800-527-4135 ■ *Web:* loblollyconsulting.com			
Lobob Laboratories Inc 1440 Atteberry Ln San Jose CA 95131	408-432-0580		543
Web: loboblabs.com			
Lobster Shop South 4015 Ruston Way Tacoma WA 98402	253-759-2165	752-9640	671
Web: wp.lobstershop.com			
Lobster Sports Inc 7340 Fulton Ave North Hollywood CA 91605	818-764-6000	764-6061	710
TF: 800-210-5992 ■ *Web:* www.lobstersports.com			
LoBue & Majdalany Management Group 572B Ruger St PO Box 29920 San Francisco CA 94129	415-561-6110	561-6120	47
TF: 800-820-4690 ■ *Web:* www.lm-mgmt.com			
LoBue Associates Inc 1771 E Flamingo Rd A219 Ste 219A89119 Las Vegas NV 89119	702-898-6940		463
Web: www.lobue.com			
LOC (Library of Congress) 101 Independence Ave SE Washington DC 20540	202-707-5000		434-3
TF: 800-424-9530 ■ *Web:* www.loc.gov			
LOC Enterprises LLC 7575 E Kemper Rd Cincinnati OH 45249	888-963-6320		195
TF: 888-963-6320 ■ *Web:* loccard.com/home.htm			
Loca Luna 3519 Old Cantrell Rd Little Rock AR 72202	501-663-4666	664-4176	671
TF: 800-208-6137 ■ *Web:* www.localuna.com			
Local Government Federal Credit Union 323 W Jones St Ste 600 Raleigh NC 27603	919-857-2150	755-0193	219
TF: 888-732-8562 ■ *Web:* www.lgfcu.org			
Local Investment Commission 3100 Broadway St Ste 1100 Kansas City MO 64111	816-889-5050		251
Web: www.kclinc.org			
Local Motion Inc 870 Kawaiahao St Honolulu HI 96813	808-523-7873		710
Web: www.localmotionhawaii.com			
Local, The 931 Nicollet Mall Minneapolis MN 55402	612-904-1000	904-1005	671
Web: www.the-local.com			
Local.com Corp 7555 Irvine Ctr Dr Irvine CA 92618	949-784-0800		175
TF: 800-651-9743 ■ *Web:* www.local.com			
LocalMemphis 2701 Union Ave Ext Memphis TN 38112	901-323-2430		741-81
Web: www.localmemphis.com			
Localstake 1010 Central Ave Ste C Indianapolis IN 46202	317-602-4790	602-4792	387
Web: www.localstake.com			
Localwineeventscom 2042 General Alexander Dr Malvern PA 19355	610-647-4888		443
Web: www.localwineevents.com			
Locanda Veneta 8638 W Third St Los Angeles CA 90048	310-274-1893	274-4217	671
Web: www.locandaveneta.net			
Locating Inc 4 Concourse Pkwy Ste 250 Atlanta GA 30328	678-461-3900	461-3902	261
Web: www.locatinginc.com			
Lochard Inc 903 Wapakoneta Ave Sidney OH 45365	937-492-8811		610
Web: www.lochard-inc.com			
Lochbridge One Campus Martius Detroit MI 48226	313-227-2621		196
Web: www.lochbridge.com			
Lochinvar Corp 300 Maddox Simpson Pkwy Lebanon TN 37090	615-889-8900	547-1000	36
TF: 800-722-2101 ■ *Web:* www.lochinvar.com			
Lochmueller Group 6200 Vogel Rd Evansville IN 47715	812-479-6200		256
TF: 800-423-7411 ■ *Web:* www.blainc.com			
Lochridge Group 420 Boylston St Boston MA 02116	617-267-5959		194
Lochsa Engineering Inc 6345 S Jones Blvd Ste 100 Las Vegas NV 89118	702-365-9312		261
TF: 866-606-9784 ■ *Web:* www.lochsa.com			
Lock Haven University 401 N Fairview St Lock Haven PA 17745	570-484-2011	484-2201*	166
**Fax:* Admissions ■ *Web:* www.lockhaven.edu			
Lock Joint Tube Inc 515 W Ireland Rd South Bend IN 46614	574-299-5326	299-3464*	490
**Fax:* Sales ■ *TF:* 800-257-6859 ■ *Web:* www.ljtube.com			
Lock Museum of America 230 Main St Rt 6 Rt 6 Terryville CT 06786	860-589-6359		520
Web: lockmuseumofamerica.org			
Lock Up Self Storage, The 800 Frontage Rd Northfield IL 60093	847-441-7477		803-3
Web: www.thelockup.com			
Lockard & Wechsler Inc 2 Bridge St Ste 200 Irvington NY 10533	914-591-6600		7
Web: www.lwdirect.com			
Lockard David 15 W Highland Ave Philadelphia PA 19118	215-753-0661		317
Web: davidlockard.com			
Locke Lord Bissell & Liddell LLP (LLBL) 2200 Ross Ave Ste 2200 Dallas TX 75201	214-740-8000	740-8000	428
Web: www.lockelord.com			
Locker's Florist 1640 S 83rd St West Allis WI 53214	414-276-7673		292
TF: 800-524-8727 ■ *Web:* www.lockersflorist.com			
Lockerly Arboretum 1534 Irwinton Rd Milledgeville GA 31061	478-452-2112	452-1020	97
Web: www.lockerly.org			
Lockformer Co 5480 Sixth St SW Cedar Rapids IA 52404	319-364-9181		456
Web: mestekmachinery.com			
Lockhart Cadillac Inc 9265 E 126th St Fishers IN 46038	317-644-2817		57
Web: www.lockhartcadillac.com			
Lockhart State Park 4179 State Pk Rd Lockhart TX 78644	512-398-3479		565
Web: tpwd.texas.gov/state-parks/lockhart			
Lockheed Federal Credit Union (LFCU) 2340 Hollywood Way Burbank CA 91505	818-565-2020		219
TF: 800-328-5328 ■ *Web:* logixbanking.com			
Lockheed Martin Aeronautics Co 1 Lockheed Blvd Fort Worth TX 76108	817-777-2000		20
Web: www.lockheedmartin.com			
Lockheed Martin Canada 3001 Solandt Rd Kanata ON K2K2M8	613-599-3270	599-3282	529
TF: 800-489-4518 ■ *Web:* www.lockheedmartin.com/canada			
Lockheed Martin Corp 6801 Rockledge Dr Bethesda MD 20817	301-897-6000		20
NYSE: LMT ■ *TF:* 866-562-2363 ■ *Web:* www.lockheedmartin.com			
Lockheed Martin Corp 5600 Sand Lake Rd Orlando FL 32819	407-356-2000		20
Web: www.kellyaviationcenter.com			
Lockheed Martin MS2 199 Borton Landing Rd Moorestown NJ 08057	856-722-4100		529
Web: lockheedmartin.com			
Lockheed Martin Sippican 7 Barnabas Rd Marion MA 02738	508-748-1160	748-3626	529
Web: www.sippican.com			
Lockheed Martin Space Systems Co Michoud Operations 13800 Old Gentilly Rd New Orleans LA 70129	504-257-3311		504
TF: 866-562-2363			
Lockheed Window Corp 925 S Main St PO Box 166 Pascoag RI 02859	401-568-3061	568-2273	234
TF: 800-537-3061 ■ *Web:* www.lockheedwindow.com			

	City	State	Zip	Phone	Fax	Class
Locklando Door & Millwork Inc 271 Southridge Industrial Dr	Tavares	FL	32778	352-343-6666		499
Lockmasters Security Institute 2101 John C Watts Dr *TF:* 800-654-0637 ■ *Web:* www.lockmasters.com	Nicholasville	KY	40356	859-885-6041		350
Lockport Optical 36 E Ave	Lockport	NY	14094	716-434-6900		543
Locks Gallery 600 Washington Sq S *Web:* www.locksgallery.com	Philadelphia	PA	19106	215-629-1000	629-3868	42
Lockton Cos 444 W 47th St Ste 900 *TF:* 800-442-7343 ■ *Web:* www.lockton.com	Kansas City	MO	64112	816-960-9000	960-9099	390
Lockwood Advisors Inc 760 Moore Rd *TF:* 800-200-3033 ■ *Web:* www.lockwoodadvisors.com	King Of Prussia	PA	19406	800-200-3033		69
Lockwood Andrews & Newnam Inc 2925 Briar Pk Dr *Web:* www.lan-inc.com	Houston	TX	77042	713-266-6900	266-2089	261
Lockwood Bros Inc 220 Salters Creek Rd *TF:* 800-554-4880 ■ *Web:* www.lockwoodbrothers.com	Hampton	VA	23661	757-722-1946		780
Lockwood International Inc 10203 Wallisville Rd *Web:* www.lockwoodint.com	Houston	TX	77013	713-675-8186	675-2733	194
Lockwood Kessler & Bartlett Inc 1 Aerial Way *Web:* www.lkbinc.com	Syosset	NY	11791	516-938-0600	931-6344	261
Lockwood Products Inc 5615 Willow Ln *TF:* 800-423-1625 ■ *Web:* www.loc-line.com	Lake Oswego	OR	97035	503-635-8113	635-2844	370
Lockwood-Mathews Mansion Museum 295 W Ave *Web:* www.ohwy.com	Norwalk	CT	06850	203-838-9799		520
Locordia Inc 16600 Sherman Way Ste 170 *TF:* 800-500-7090 ■ *Web:* www.locordia.com	Van Nuys	CA	91406	818-827-1328		317
Loctronix Corp 18815 139th Ave NE Ste C	Woodinville	WA	98072	425-307-3480		387
Locus Systems Inc 146 W Beaver Creek Rd Unit 1 *Web:* www.locussystems.com	Richmond Hill	ON	L4B1C2	905-948-0093		180
Locust Grove Historic Home 561 Blankenbaker Ln *TF:* 800-775-7777 ■ *Web:* www.locustgrove.org	Louisville	KY	40207	502-897-9845	897-0103	50-3
Locust Lake State Park 687 Tuscarora Pk Rd *Web:* www.dcnr.state.pa.us	Barnesville	PA	18214	570-467-2404		565
Locust Shade Park 4701 Locust Shade Dr *Web:* www.pwcparks.org	Triangle	VA	22172	703-221-8579		564
Locust Valley Central School District 22 Horse Hollow Rd *Web:* www.lvcsd.k12.ny.us	Locust Valley	NY	11560	516-277-5000		685
Lodal Inc 620 N Hooper St PO Box 2315 **Fax:* Orders ■ *TF:* 800-435-3500 ■ *Web:* www.lodal.com	Kingsford	MI	49802	906-779-1700	779-1160*	516
LoDan Electronics Inc 3311 N Kennicott Ave *TF:* 800-401-4995 ■ *Web:* www.lodanelectronics.com	Arlington Heights	IL	60004	847-398-5311	398-5340	816
Lodestar Research Corp 2400 Central Ave Ste P-5 *Web:* www.lodestar.com	Boulder	CO	80301	303-449-9691	449-3865	668
Lodgco Management LLC 5225 E Pickard Rd *TF:* 800-215-7780 ■ *Web:* lodgco.net	Mount Pleasant	MI	48858	989-773-2400		707
Lodge & Club at Ponte Vedra Beach 607 Ponte Vedra Blvd **Fax Area Code:* 904 ■ *TF:* 800-243-4304 ■ *Web:* www.pontevedra.com	Ponte Vedra Beach	FL	32082	888-839-9145	273-0210*	669
Lodge at Big Sky LLC, The 75 Sitting Bull Rd *TF:* 800-847-4868 ■ *Web:* www.lodgeatbigsky.com	Big Sky	MT	59716	406-995-7858		378
Lodge At Breckenridge, The 112 Overlook Dr *TF:* 800-736-1607 ■ *Web:* www.thelodgeatbreckenridge.com	Breckenridge	CO	80424	970-453-9300		379
Lodge at Koele 1 Keomoku Hwy *TF:* 800-321-4666 ■ *Web:* www.lodgeatkoele.com	Lanai City	HI	96763	808-565-4000		669
Lodge at Pebble Beach 1700 17-Mile Dr *TF:* 800-654-9300 ■ *Web:* www.pebblebeach.com	Pebble Beach	CA	93953	831-624-3811	625-8598	669
Lodge at Sonoma - A Renaissance Resort & Spa 1325 Broadway *TF:* 866-263-0758 ■ *Web:* www.marriott.com	Sonoma	CA	95476	707-935-6600	935-6829	669
Lodge at the Mountain Village 1415 Lowell Ave *TF:* 800-453-1360 ■ *Web:* visitparkcity.com	Park City	UT	84060	435-649-0800		379
Lodge at Tiburon, The 1651 Tiburon Blvd *TF:* 800-762-7770 ■ *Web:* www.lodgeattiburon.com	Tiburon	CA	94920	415-435-3133		378
Lodge At Torrey Pines, The 11480 N Torrey Pines Rd *Web:* www.lodgeattorreypines.com	La Jolla	CA	92037	858-453-4420		669
Lodge at Ventana Canyon - A Wyndham Luxury Resort 6200 N Clubhouse Ln *TF:* 800-828-5701 ■ *Web:* www.thelodgeatventanacanyon.com	Tucson	AZ	85750	520-577-1400		669
Lodge Casino 240 Main St PO Box 50 *Web:* www.thelodgecasino.com	Black Hawk	CO	80422	303-582-1771	582-6464	133
Lodge of Four Seasons 315 Four Seasons Dr PO Box 215 *TF Resv:* 888-265-5500 ■ *Web:* www.4seasonsresort.com	Lake Ozark	MO	65049	573-365-3000		669
Lodge on the Desert 306 N Alvernon Way *TF:* 877-498-6776 ■ *Web:* www.lodgeonthedesert.com	Tucson	AZ	85711	520-320-2000	327-5834	379
Lodgen, Lacher, Golditch, Sardi, Saunders, & Howard LLC 16530 Ventura Blvd Ste 305 *Web:* www.lgshcpa.com	Encino	CA	91436	818-783-0570		2
LodgeWorks LP 8100 E 22nd St Bldg 500 *Web:* www.lodgeworks.com	Wichita	KS	67226	316-681-5100	681-0905	379
Lodgian Inc 2002 Summit Blvd Ste 300 *NYSE: LGN*	Atlanta	GA	30319	404-364-9400	812-3102	379

	City	State	Zip	Phone	Fax	Class
Lodging Dynamics Hospitality Group LLC 5314 N River Run Dr Ste 310 *Web:* www.lodgingdynamics.com	Provo	UT	84604	801-919-3440		707
Lodging Hospitality Management Corp 111 W Port Plaza Ste 500 *Web:* www.lhmc.com	St Louis	MO	63146	314-434-9500		379
Lodging Media 385 Oxford Valley Rd Ste 420 *Web:* www.lodgingmagazine.com	Yardley	PA	19067	215-321-9662	321-5124	457-5
Lodi Conference & Visitors Bureau 115 S School St *TF:* 800-798-1810 ■ *Web:* www.visitlodi.com	Lodi	CA	95240	209-365-1195		206
Lodi District Chamber of Commerce 35 S School St *TF:* 800-860-7073 ■ *Web:* www.lodichamber.com	Lodi	CA	95240	209-367-7840	369-9344	139
Lodi Irrigation 1301 E Armstrong Rd *TF:* 800-634-7272 ■ *Web:* www.lodiirrigation.com	Lodi	CA	95242	800-634-7272		429
Lodi News-Sentinel 125 N Church St *Web:* www.lodinews.com	Lodi	CA	95240	209-369-2761	369-6706	532-2
Lodi Point State Marine Park c/o Sampson State Pk 6096 Rt 96A *Web:* www.nysparks.com/parks/info.asp?parkid=38	Romulus	NY	14541	315-585-6392		565
Lodi Public Library 201 W Locust St *Web:* www.lodilibraryfoundation.org	Lodi	CA	95240	209-333-5536		434-3
Lodolce Machine Coinc 196 Malden Tpke *Web:* www.lodolce.com	Saugerties	NY	12477	845-217-0983		567
Loeb & Loeb LLP 345 Park Ave *Web:* www.loeb.com	New York	NY	10154	212-407-4000	407-4990	2
Loeb Electric Co 1800 E Fifth Ave *Web:* www.loebelectric.com	Columbus	OH	43219	614-294-6351	294-7640	246
Loeb Enterprises LLC 712 Fifth Ave 14th Fl *Web:* www.loebenterprises.com	New York	NY	10019	646-442-5807		401
Loeb Equipment & Appraisal Co 4131 S State St *TF:* 800-560-5632 ■ *Web:* www.loebequipment.com	Chicago	IL	60609	773-548-4131		41
Loeb Properties Inc 825 Vly Brook Dr *Web:* www.loebproperties.com	Memphis	TN	38120	901-761-3333		652
Loeber Motors Inc 4255 W Touhy Ave *TF:* 888-211-4485 ■ *Web:* www.loebermotors.com	Lincolnwood	IL	60712	847-675-1000		57
Loebl Schlossman & Hackl Inc 233 N Michigan Ave Ste 3000 *Web:* www.lshdesign.com	Chicago	IL	60601	312-565-1800		186
Loebsack David (Rep D - IA) 1527 Longworth Bldg *Web:* loebsack.house.gov	Washington	DC	20515	202-225-6576	226-0757	342-2
Loeffel Steel Products PO Box 2100 *Web:* www.loeffelsteel.com	Barrington	IL	60011	847-382-6770	382-2487	492
Loeffler Randall Inc 525 Broadway 4th Fl *Web:* www.loefflerrandall.com	New York	NY	10012	212-226-8787		174
Loesel Schaaf Insurance Agency Inc 3537 W 12th St *TF:* 877-718-9935 ■ *Web:* lsinsure.com	Erie	PA	16505	814-833-5433		390
Loewinsohn Flegle Deary Simon LLP 12377 Merit Dr Ste 900 *Web:* lfdlaw.com	Dallas	TX	75251	214-572-1700		428
Loews Coronado Bay Resort 4000 Coronado Bay Rd *TF:* 855-905-6397 ■ *Web:* www.loewshotels.com/hotels/sandiego	Coronado	CA	92118	619-424-4000		669
Loews Corp 667 Madison Ave *Web:* www.loews.com	New York	NY	10065	212-521-2000		185
Loews Hotel 1000 1000 First Ave *TF:* 877-315-1088 ■ *Web:* www.hotel1000seattle.com	Seattle	WA	98104	206-957-1000	357-9457	379
Loews Hotels & Co 667 Madison Ave *TF:* 800-235-6397 ■ *Web:* www.loewshotels.com	New York	NY	10065	212-521-2000		379
Loews Madison Hotel 1177 15th St NW *TF:* 888-825-2436 ■ *Web:* loewshotels.com	Washington	DC	20005	202-862-1600		671
Loews Santa Monica Beach Hotel 1700 Ocean Ave *Web:* www.loewshotels.com/hotels/losangeles/default.asp	Santa Monica	CA	90401	310-458-6700		378
Loews Ventana Canyon Resort 7000 N Resort Dr *TF:* 800-234-5117 ■ *Web:* www.loewshotels.com	Tucson	AZ	85750	520-299-2020		669
Loffler Companies Inc 1101 E 78th St Ste 200 *Web:* www.loffler.com	Bloomington	MN	55420	952-925-6800		196
Lofgren Zoe (Rep D - CA) 1401 Longworth Bldg *Web:* lofgren.house.gov	Washington	DC	20515	202-225-3072		342-2
Loft Communications & Events Inc 27 Atlantic Ave *Web:* loftcommunications.com	Toronto	ON	M6K3E7	416-699-5638		224
Loft Restaurant, The 201 W Orange St *Web:* www.theloftlancaster.com	Lancaster	PA	17603	717-299-0661		671
Loftin Equipment Company Inc 12 N 45th Ave *TF:* 800-437-4376 ■ *Web:* www.loftinequip.com	Phoenix	AZ	85043	602-272-9466		536
Loftness Specialized Farm Equipment Inc 650 S Main St PO Box 337 *TF:* 800-828-7624 ■ *Web:* www.loftness.com	Hector	MN	55342	320-848-6266	848-6269	273
Lofton Label Inc 6290 Claude Way *TF:* 877-447-8118 ■ *Web:* www.loftonlabel.com	Inver Grove Heights	MN	55076	651-552-6257	457-3709	552-1
Lofts Hotel, The 55 E Nationwide Blvd *Web:* www.55lofts.com	Columbus	OH	43215	614-461-2663	461-2630	379
Loftus Engineering Inc 233 S Mccrea St Ste 700 *Web:* www.applied-e-s.com	Indianapolis	IN	46225	317-352-5822		194
Loftware Inc 166 Corporate Dr *TF:* 800-713-7278 ■ *Web:* www.loftware.com	Portsmouth	NH	03801	603-766-3630		177
Log Cabin 11 Lehoy Forest Dr *Web:* www.LogCabin1933.com	Leola	PA	17540	717-626-9999		671

Phone | Fax | Class

Log Cabin Homes Ltd
PO Drawer 1457 Rocky Mount NC 27802 252-454-1599 977-7511 106
Web: www.logcabinhomes.com

Log Cabin Village
2100 Log Cabin Village Ln Fort Worth TX 76109 817-392-5881 520
TF: 800-476-3263 ■ *Web:* www.logcabinvillage.org

Log Haven
6451 East Milcreek Canyon Salt Lake City UT 84109 801-272-8255 671
Web: www.log-haven.com

Log House Foods Inc
8711 Lyndale Ave S Bloomington MN 55420 763-546-8395 805
Web: www.loghousefoods.com

Logan Capital Management Inc
6 Coulter Ave Ste 2000 Ardmore PA 19003 800-215-1100 401
TF: 800-215-1100 ■ *Web:* www.logancapital.com

Logan Circle Partners LP
1717 Arch St Ste 1500 Philadelphia PA 19103 267-330-0000 401
Web: www.logancirclepartners.com

Logan Clay Products Co 201 S Walnut St Logan OH 43138 800-848-2141 385-9336* 150
**Fax Area Code:* 740 ■ *TF:* 800-848-2141 ■ *Web:* www.loganclaypipe.com

Logan Corp 555 Seventh Ave Huntington WV 25701 304-526-4700 526-4747 385
TF: 888-853-4751 ■ *Web:* www.logancorp.com

Logan Correctional Ctr 1096 1350th St Lincoln IL 62656 217-735-5581 735-1077 213
Web: www.illinois.gov

Logan County 117 E Columbus St Bellefontaine OH 43311 937-599-7283 599-7268 338
Web: www.co.logan.oh.us

Logan County 366 N Broadway Ave Booneville AR 72927 479-675-2951 338

Logan County
601 Broadway St PO Box 278 Lincoln IL 62656 217-732-4148 732-6064 338
Web: www.logancountyil.gov/index.php?lang=en

Logan County 300 Stratton St Logan WV 25601 304-792-8626 792-8511 338
Web: www.logancounty.wv.gov

Logan County 710 W Second St Oakley KS 67748 785-671-3216 671-0065 338
Web: kansastreasurers.org

Logan County
116 S Main St PO Box 358 Russellville KY 42276 270-726-2206 338
TF: 800-693-3299 ■ *Web:* www.loganchamber.com

Logan County 317 Main St PO Box 8 Stapleton NE 69163 308-636-2441 636-2678 338
Web: www.stapleton-ne.com

Logan County 315 Main St Ste 3 Sterling CO 80751 970-522-1544 522-2063 338
Web: www.colorado.gov

Logan County Chamber of Commerce
325 Stratton St PO Box 218 Logan WV 25601 304-752-1324 139
Web: www.logancountychamberofcommerce.com

Logan County Chamber of Commerce
116 S Main St Russellville KY 42276 270-726-2206 139
Web: www.loganchamber.com

Logan County Chamber of Commerce
100 S Main St Bellefontaine OH 43311 937-599-5121 599-2411 139
TF: 877-360-3608 ■ *Web:* www.logancountyohio.com

Logan County Co-op Power & Light Assn Inc
1587 County Rd 32 N Bellefontaine OH 43311 937-592-4781 592-5746 245
Web: www.logancounty.coop

Logan County District Library
220 N Main St Bellefontaine OH 43311 937-599-4189 599-5503 434-3
TF: 800-274-5515 ■ *Web:* www.logancountylibraries.org

Logan County Oklahoma
301 E Harrison Ste 102 Guthrie OK 73044 405-282-0266 282-0267 338
Web: logancountyok.com

Logan Library 255 N Main St Logan UT 84321 435-716-9123 434-3
Web: library.loganutah.org

Logan Machine Co 1405 Home Ave Akron OH 44310 330-633-6163 633-6362 454
Web: www.loganmachine.com

Logan Media Services LLC
1515 Elm Hill Pk Ste 205 Nashville TN 37210 615-361-8100 514
Web: www.loganmedia.net

Logan Regional Medical Ctr
20 Hospital Dr Logan WV 25601 304-831-1101 831-1871 374-3
TF: 888-982-9144 ■ *Web:* www.loganregionalmedicalcenter.com

Logan Simpson Design Inc
51 W Third St Ste 450 Tempe AZ 85281 480-967-1343 2
Web: www.logansimpson.com

Logan Square Aluminum Supply Inc
2500 N Pulaski Rd Chicago IL 60639 773-235-2500 234
Web: www.remodelerssupply.com

Logan Trucking Inc 3224 Navarre Rd SW Canton OH 44706 330-478-1404 478-6706 186
TF: 800-683-0142 ■ *Web:* www.logantrucking.com

Logan's Roadhouse
4249 Balmoral Dr SW Huntsville AL 35801 256-881-0584 671
Web: www.logansroadhouse.com

Logan's Roadhouse 6617 Lima Rd Fort Wayne IN 46818 260-487-9944 671
Web: www.logansroadhouse.com

LoganBritton Inc
1700 Park St Ste 111 Naperville IL 60563 800-362-4352 225
TF: 800-362-4352 ■ *Web:* www.loganbritton.com

Logan-Hocking County District Library
230 E Main St Logan OH 43138 740-385-2348 385-9093 434-3
TF: 800-654-8870 ■ *Web:* www.hocking.lib.oh.us

Logansport Financial Corp
723 E Broadway Logansport IN 46947 574-722-3855 722-3857 360-2
OTC: LOGN ■ *TF:* 800-541-9154 ■ *Web:* www.logansportsavings.com

Logansport Juvenile Correctional Facility
1118 S St Rd 25 Logansport IN 46947 574-753-7571 732-0729 412
TF: 800-800-5556 ■ *Web:* www.in.gov/idoc

Logansport/Cass County Chamber of Commerce
300 E Broadway Ste 103 Logansport IN 46947 574-753-6388 735-0909 139
TF: 800-886-3274 ■ *Web:* www.logan-casschamber.com

Logansport-Cass County Public Library
616 E Broadway Logansport IN 46947 574-753-6383 722-5889 434-3
Web: www.logan.lib.in.us

Logapps LLC
103 W Broad St Suit 250 Ste 250 Falls Church VA 22046 703-592-6362 463
Web: logapps.com

Logees Greenhouses Ltd 141 N St Danielson CT 06239 860-774-8038 192
TF: 888-330-8038 ■ *Web:* www.logees.com

Logfret Inc 6801 W Side Ave North Bergen NJ 07047 201-817-1140 311
Web: www.logfret.com

Logghe Stamping Co 16711 E 13-Mile Rd Fraser MI 48026 586-293-2250 489

Loggins Logistics Inc
5706 Commerce Sq Jonesboro AR 72401 870-932-9231 802-2190 449
Web: www.logginslogistics.com

Loghurst Western Reserve
3967 BoaRdman-Canfield Rd Canfield OH 44406 330-533-4330 50-3

Logic Choice Technologies LLC
950 E Haverford Rd Bryn Mawr PA 19010 610-525-1236 177
Web: www.logicchoice.com

Logic Devices Inc 1375 Geneva Dr Sunnyvale CA 94089 408-542-5400 542-0080 696
OTC: LOGC ■ *TF:* 800-233-2518 ■ *Web:* www.logicdevices.com

Logic PD Inc 6201 Bury Dr Eden Prairie MN 55346 952-941-8071 393
TF: 855-461-3802 ■ *Web:* www.logicpd.com

Logic Solutions Inc
2929 Plymouth Rd Ste 207 Ann Arbor MI 48105 734-930-0009 180
Web: www.logicsolutions.com

Logic Technologies Inc
117 Bellamy Pl Stockbridge GA 30281 770-389-4964 729
TF: 800-628-7813 ■ *Web:* logictechnologies.com

Logical Choice Technologies Inc
1045 Progress Cir Lawrenceville GA 30043 770-564-1044 174

Logical Images Inc
3445 Winton Pl Ste 240 Rochester NY 14623 585-427-2790 177
TF: 800-357-7611 ■ *Web:* www.logicalimages.com

Logical Innovations Inc
16902 El Camino Real Ste 3C Houston TX 77058 281-990-8560 177
Web: www.logical-i2.com

Logical It Solutions 157 Park St Ste 36 Bangor ME 04401 207-942-5487 809
Web: www.ameridyn.com

Logical Net Corp 1462 Erie Blvd Schenectady NY 12305 518-292-4500 387
TF: 800-600-0638 ■ *Web:* www.logical.net

Logical Solution Services Inc
200 Union Ave Lakehurst NJ 08733 732-657-7777 449
TF: 800-204-3622 ■ *Web:* www.solutionservices.us

Logicalis Inc
34505 W 12 Mile Rd Ste 210 Farmington Hills MI 48331 248-957-5600 180
Web: us.logicalis.com

LogiCan Technologies Inc
150 Karl Clark Rd Edmonton AB T6N1E2 780-450-4400 253
Web: www.logican.com

LogicData 10800 E Bethany Dr Ste 202 Aurora CO 80014 303-694-4400 463
Web: www.logicdata.com

Logicease Solutions Inc
1 Bay Plaza Ste 520 Burlingame CA 94010 650-373-1111 180
TF: 866-212-3273 ■ *Web:* complianceease.com

LogiCore Corp 1015 Henderson Rd NW Huntsville AL 35816 256-533-5789 63
Web: www.logicorehsv.com

Logicorps
35015 Automation Dr Clinton Township MI 48035 586-792-9900 177
TF: 800-433-5778 ■ *Web:* www.logicorps.com

LOGIKA Corp 3717 N Ravenswood Ave Chicago IL 60613 773-529-3482 529-3483 178-7
Web: www.logika.net

Logikal Solutions 3915 N 1800e Rd Herscher IL 60941 815-919-1593 180
Web: www.logikalsolutions.com

Logile Inc 1333 Corporate Dr Ste 310 Irving TX 75038 972-550-6000 194
Web: www.logile.com

Logility Inc 470 E Paces Ferry Rd Atlanta GA 30305 404-261-9777 264-5206 178-1
TF: 800-762-5207 ■ *Web:* www.logility.com

Login Consulting Services Inc
300 N Continental Blvd Ste 530 El Segundo CA 90245 310-607-9091 180
Web: www.loginconsult.com

Login Inc 4003 E Speedway Blvd Tucson AZ 85712 520-618-3000 225
Web: www.login.com

Logis Tech Inc
9450 Innovation Dr Ste 1 Manassas VA 20110 703-393-0122 472
Web: www.logis-tech.com

LogiSense Corp
278 Pinebush Rd Ste 102 Cambridge ON N1T1Z6 519-249-0508 177
Web: www.logisense.com

LogiSolve LLC 600 Inwood Ave N Ste 275 Oakdale MN 55128 763-383-1000 177
Web: www.logisolve.com

Logistic Dynamics Inc 1140 Wehrle Dr Amherst NY 14221 716-250-3477 314
TF: 800-554-3734 ■ *Web:* www.logisticdynamics.com

Logistic Professionals Inc
1920 Pennsylvania Ave Mcdonough GA 30253 770-692-0431 478
Web: www.logisticpros.com

Logistics Applications
2760 Eisenhower Ave Alexandria VA 22314 703-317-9800 271
Web: logapp.com

Logistics Capital & Strategy LLC
1110 N Glebe Rd Ste 250 Arlington VA 22201 703-276-9100 463
Web: www.logcapstrat.com

Logistics Management Resources Inc
4300 Crossings Blvd Prince George VA 23875 804-541-6193 180
Web: www.lmr-inc.com

Logistics Plus Inc 1406 Peach St Erie PA 16501 814-461-7600 461-7635 311
TF: 866-564-7587 ■ *Web:* www.logisticsplus.net

Logistics Store, The 26 Westwoods Dr Liberty MO 64068 816-781-0450 314
Web: www.thelogisticsstore.com

Logistics Value Integrations Inc
3828 Farr Oak Cir Fairfax VA 22030 703-934-4218 261

Logitech Inc 6505 Kaiser Dr Fremont CA 94555 510-795-8500 792-8901 173-1
TF Sales: 800-231-7717 ■ *Web:* www.logitech.com

Logitech WiLife 132 E 13065 S Ste 200 Draper UT 84020 801-316-4700 316-4701 693
Web: online.wilife.com

Logitek Electronic Systems Inc
5622 Edgemoor Dr Houston TX 77081 713-664-4470 647
TF: 877-231-5870 ■ *Web:* www.logitekaudio.com

Logitek Inc 110 Wilbur Pl Bohemia NY 11716 631-567-1100 567-1823 253
Web: www.naii.com

Logix Guru LLC
3821 Old William Penn Hwy Murrysville PA 15668 724-733-4500 177
TF: 800-446-0744 ■ *Web:* www.logixguru.com

Logo Inc 117 SE Pkwy Franklin TN 37064 615-261-2100 321
Web: www.logobrands.com

Logoly State Park PO Box 245 McNeil AR 71752 870-695-3561 565
Web: www.arkansasstateparks.com

LogoNation Inc PO Box 3847 Ste 102 Mooresville NC 28117 800-955-7375 627
TF: 800-955-7375 ■ *Web:* www.logonation.com

Phone | Fax | Class

Logos Bible Software
1313 Commercial St. Bellingham WA 98225 360-527-1700 178-9
Web: www.logos.com

Logos Christian College
6620 Southpoint Dr S Ste 200 Jacksonville FL 32216 904-745-3311 166
TF: 800-776-0127 ■ *Web:* www.logos.edu

Logos Evangelical Seminary
9358 Telstar Ave El Monte CA 91731 626-571-5110 571-5119 167-3
Web: www.les.edu/language/zh

Logoworks 1 State Street Plaza New York NY 10004 747-666-5646 627
Web: www.logoworks.com

Lohfeld Consulting Group Inc
940 S River Landing Rd Edgewater MD 21037 410-336-6264 196
Web: www.lohfeldconsulting.com

Lois Paul & Partners (LPP)
290 Congress St 6th Fl Boston MA 02210 617-986-5700 636
Web: www.lpp.com

Lois Pope LIFE Foundation
6274 Linton Blvd Ste 103 Delray Beach FL 33484 561-865-0955 305
Web: www.life-edu.org

Loki Systems Inc
1258-13351 Commerce Pkwy Richmond BC V6V2X7 604-249-5050 179
TF: 800-378-5654 ■ *Web:* www.lokisys.com

LOKRING Technology LLC
38376 Apollo Pkwy Willoughby OH 44094 440-942-0880 723
TF: 800-876-2323 ■ *Web:* www.lokring.com

Lola 2000 Fourth Ave Seattle WA 98121 206-441-1430 671
Web: www.tomdouglas.com

Lolita 900 Literary Rd Cleveland OH 44113 216-771-5652 671
Web: lolitarestaurant.com

LOMA 2300 Windy Ridge Pkwy Ste 600 Atlanta GA 30339 770-951-1770 984-0441 49-9
TF: 800-275-5662 ■ *Web:* www.loma.org

Loma Linda University
11234 Anderson St Loma Linda CA 92354 909-558-1000 166
TF: 800-872-1212 ■ *Web:* www.llu.edu

Loma Linda University Medical Ctr
11234 Anderson St Loma Linda CA 92354 909-558-4000 374-3
TF: 877-558-6248 ■ *Web:* lomalindahealth.org

Loma Linda University School of Medicine
11175 Campus St Loma Linda CA 92350 909-558-4467 167-2
TF: 800-422-4558 ■ *Web:* www.llu.edu/llu/medicine

Lomanco Inc 2101 W Main St Jacksonville AR 72076 501-982-6511 982-1258 14
TF: 800-643-5596 ■ *Web:* www.lomanco.com

Lomar Distributing 2500 Dixon St Des Moines IA 50316 515-244-3105 297-11

Lomax Consulting Group Llc The
1435 N Rt 9 Cape May Court House NJ 08210 609-465-9857 196
TF: 800-828-8312 ■ *Web:* lomaxconsulting.com

Lomax Cos, The
200 Highpoint Dr Ste 215 Chalfont PA 18914 215-822-1550 997-9582 655

Lombard Area Chamber of Commerce
10 Lilac Ln Lombard IL 60148 630-627-5040 627-5519 139
Web: www.lombardchamber.com

Lombard Co 4245 W 123rd St Alsip IL 60803 708-389-1060 389-7120 183
Web: lombardcompany.com

Lombardi Comprehensive Cancer Ctr at Georgetown University
3800 Reservoir Rd NW Washington DC 20007 202-444-2198 444-7338 374-7
Web: lombardi.georgetown.edu

Lombardi Contracting Corp
7744 Formula Pl San Diego CA 92121 858-566-0060 186

Lombardi Loper & Conant LLP
1999 Harrison St 26th Fl Oakland CA 94612 510-433-2600 445
Web: llcllp.com

Lombardi Sports Inc
1600 Jackson St San Francisco CA 94109 415-771-0600 711
Web: www.lombardisports.com

Lombardi's 401 Biscayne Blvd Miami FL 33132 888-286-3792 671
TF: 888-286-3792 ■ *Web:* www.lombardifamilyconcepts.com

Lombardia Capital Partners LLC
55 S Lake Ave Ste 200 Pasadena CA 91101 626-568-2792 796
Web: www.lombardiacapital.com

Lombardian 116 S Main St Lombard IL 60148 630-627-7010 627-7027 532-4
TF: 800-252-8980 ■ *Web:* lombardian.info

Lombardino's 2500 University Ave Madison WI 53705 608-238-1922 671
Web: www.lombardinos.com

Lombardo Insurance Agency
2096B Silas Deane Hwy Rocky Hill CT 06067 860-236-6064 390
Web: lombardo-ins.com

Lombardo's 216 Harrisburg Ave Lancaster PA 17603 717-394-3749 671
Web: www.lombardosrestaurant.com

Lombardy Hotel, The 111 E Fifth St New York NY 10022 212-753-8600 379
Web: www.lombardyhotel.com

Lomont Molding Imt
1516 E Mapleleaf Dr Mount Pleasant IA 52641 319-385-1528 601
TF: 800-776-0380 ■ *Web:* www.lomontimt.com

Lompoc Public Library 501 E N Ave Lompoc CA 93436 805-875-8775 434-3
TF: 800-340-1099 ■ *Web:* www.cityoflompoc.com

Lompoc Record, The 115 N H St Lompoc CA 93436 805-736-2313 532-3
TF: 800-831-2345 ■ *Web:* www.lompocrecord.com

Lompoc Unified School District
1301 N A St Lompoc CA 93436 805-742-3300 735-8452 685
Web: www.lusd.org

Lompoc Valley Chamber of Commerce & Visitors Bureau
PO Box 626 Lompoc CA 93438 805-736-4567 737-0453 139
TF: 800-240-0999 ■ *Web:* www.lompoc.com

Lon Musolf Distributing Inc
985 E Berwood Ave Vadnais Heights MN 55110 651-484-3020 683
Web: www.lonmusolf.com

London Broadcasting Co Inc
5052 Addison Cir Addison TX 75001 214-730-0151 514
Web: www.londonbroadcastingcompany.com

London Chamber of Commerce
244 Pall Mall St Ste 101 London ON N6A5P6 519-432-7551 432-8063 137
Web: www.londonchamber.com

London City School District 380 Elm St London OH 43140 740-852-5700 685
Web: www.london.k12.oh.us

London Company Investment Counsel, The
1801 Bayberry Ct Ste 301 Richmond VA 23226 804-775-0317 41
Web: www.tlcadvisory.com

London Computer Services
9140 Waterstone Blvd Cincinnati OH 45249 513-583-1482 179
TF: 800-669-0871 ■ *Web:* www.lcs.com

London Correctional Institution
1580 SR 56 London OH 43140 740-852-2454 845-3399 213
Web: www.drc.ohio.gov

London Drugs Ltd 12251 Horseshoe Way Richmond BC V7A4X5 604-272-7400 238
TF: 888-991-2299 ■ *Web:* www.londondrugs.com

London Economics International LLC
717 Atlantic Ave Ste 1A Boston MA 02111 617-933-7200 317
TF: 800-339-0260 ■ *Web:* www.londoneconomics.com

London Fischer LLP 59 Maiden Ln Fl 41 New York NY 10038 212-972-1000 445
Web: www.londonfischer.com

London Fog 1615 Kellogg Dr Douglas GA 31535 912-384-8189 155-5
TF: 877-588-8189 ■ *Web:* www.londonfog.com

London Free Press
369 York St PO Box 2280 London ON N6A4G1 519-679-1111 667-4528 532-1
TF: 866-541-6757 ■ *Web:* www.lfpress.com

London Grill 309 SW Broadway Portland OR 97205 503-228-2000 671
Web: www.coasthotels.com

London Health Sciences Centre
800 Commissioners Rd E PO Box 5010 London ON N6A5W9 519-685-8500 374-2
Web: www.lhsc.on.ca

London Health Sciences Centre Victoria Campus
800 Commissioners Rd E PO Box 5010 Stn B London ON N6A5W9 519-685-8500 667-6605 374-2
Web: www.lhsc.on.ca

London Life Insurance Co
255 Dufferin Ave London ON N6A4K1 519-432-5281 435-7679 391-2
TF: 800-990-6654 ■ *Web:* www.londonlife.com

London Luxury Bedding Inc
271 N Ave Ste 412 New Rochelle NY 10801 914-636-2100 321
Web: www.londonlux.com

London Machinery Inc
15790 Robin's Hill Rd London ON N5V0A4 519-963-2500 61
TF: 800-265-1098 ■ *Web:* www.lmi.ca

London Properties Ltd 6442 N Maroa Ave Fresno CA 93704 559-436-4000 652
Web: www.londonproperties.com

London West Hollywood Hotel
1020 N San Vicente Blvd West Hollywood CA 90069 866-282-4560 378
TF: 866-282-4560 ■ *Web:* www.thelondonwesthollywood.com

London/Laurel County Tourist Commission
140 Faith Assembly Church Rd London KY 40741 606-878-6900 877-1689 206
TF: 800-348-0095 ■ *Web:* www.laurelkytourism.com

Londrigan Potter & Randle P C
1227 S Seventh St Springfield IL 62703 217-544-9823 445
Web: lprpc.com

Lone Mountain Ranch
750 Lone Mtn Ranch Rd PO Box 160069 Big Sky MT 59716 406-995-4644 239
TF: 800-514-4644 ■ *Web:* www.lonemountainranch.com

Lone Mountain Sports Mountain Vlg. Big Sky MT 59716 406-995-4471 711
TF: 800-847-4868 ■ *Web:* www.lonemountainsports.net

Lone Oak First Baptist Church Inc
3601 Lone Oak Rd Paducah KY 42003 270-554-1441 48-20
Web: loneoakfbc.org

Lone Oak Fund LLC
11611 San Vincente Blvd Ste 640 Los Angeles CA 90049 310-826-2888 655
TF: 800-297-6061 ■ *Web:* www.loneoakfund.com

Lone Oak Lodge 2221 N Fremont St Monterey CA 93940 831-372-4924 372-4985 379
TF General: 800-283-5663 ■ *Web:* www.loneoaklodge.com

Lone Peak Labeling Systems Inc
1785 South 4490 West Salt Lake City UT 84106 801-975-1818 627
Web: www.lonepeaklabeling.com

Lone Pine State Park 490 N Meridian Kalispell MT 59901 406-752-5501 565
Web: www.fwp.mt.gov

Lone star 92.5
14001 N Dallas Pkwy Ste 300 Dallas TX 75240 214-866-8000 645-44
Web: www.lonestar925.com

Lone Star Abstract & Title Company Inc
600 N Loraine Midland TX 79701 432-683-1818 390
Web: lonestarabstract.com

Lone Star Circuits 901 Hensley Ln Wylie TX 75098 214-291-1427 291-1431 625
TF: 800-303-9266 ■ *Web:* lscpcbs.com

Lone Star Container Corp
700 N Wildwood Dr Irving TX 75061 800-552-6937 554-6081* 100
**Fax Area Code:* 972 ■ *TF:* 800-552-6937 ■ *Web:* www.lonestarcontainer.com

Lone Star Flight Museum
2002 Terminal Dr Galveston TX 77554 409-740-7722 740-7612 520
TF: 888-359-5736 ■ *Web:* www.lsfm.org

Lone Star Funds
2711 N Haskell Ave Ste 1700 Dallas TX 75204 214-754-8300 401
Web: www.lonestarfunds.com

Lone Star Legal Aid
1415 Fannin St Ste 300 Houston TX 77002 713-652-0077 428
TF: 800-204-2222 ■ *Web:* www.gclf.org

Lone Star Lions Eye Bank
102 E Wheeler PO Box 347 Manor TX 78653 512-457-0638 457-0658 269
TF: 800-977-3937 ■ *Web:* www.lsleb.org

Lone Star National Bank Shares Neveda
520 E Nolana Ave Ste 110 Mcallen TX 78504 956-682-1722 70
Web: www.lonestarnationalbank.com

Lone Star Park at Grand Prairie
1000 Lone Star Pkwy Grand Prairie TX 75050 972-263-7223 642
TF: 800-795-7223 ■ *Web:* www.lonestarpark.com

Lone Star Percussion 10611 Control Pl Dallas TX 75238 214-340-0835 526
TF: 866-792-0143 ■ *Web:* www.lonestarpercussion.com

Lone Star Railroad Contractors Inc
4201 S I-45 Ennis TX 75119 972-878-9500 188
TF: 800-838-7225 ■ *Web:* www.lonestarrailroad.com

Lone Star Steakhouse & Saloon Inc
5055 W Pk Blvd Ste 500 Plano TX 75093 972-295-8600 670
TF: 800-442-1162 ■ *Web:* www.lonestarsteakhouse.com

Lone Star Texas Grill
472 Morden Rd Ste 101 Oakville ON L6K3W4 905-845-5852 670
TF: 800-361-4004 ■ *Web:* www.lonestartexasgrill.com

Lone Wolf Mfg LLC
19321 Stuebner Airline Rd Spring TX 77379 281-370-3087 480
Web: lonewolfmfg.net

Name / Address	City	State	Zip	Phone	Fax	Class
Lone Wolf Real Estate Technologies Inc						
231 Shearson Crescent Ste 310	Cambridge	ON	N1T1J5	519-624-1236		179
Web: www.lwolf.com						
Lonely Planet Online 150 Linden St	Oakland	CA	94607	510-250-6400		773
TF: 800-275-8555 ■ *Web:* www.lonelyplanet.com						
Lonely Planet Publications						
50 Linden St	Oakland	CA	94607	510-893-8555	893-8572	637-2
TF: 800-275-8555 ■ *Web:* www.lonelyplanet.com						
lonelybrand LLC 118 W Kinzie St Fl 2	Chicago	IL	60654	312-880-7506		195
Web: www.lonelybrand.com						
Loners on Wheels (LOW)						
1795 O'Kelley Rd SE	Deming	NM	88030	575-544-7303		48-23
Web: www.lonersonwheels.com						
Lonesome Dove Western Bistro						
2406 N Main St	Fort Worth	TX	76164	817-740-8810		671
Web: www.lonesomedovebistro.com						
Lonesome Pine Regional Library						
124 Library Rd	Wise	VA	24293	276-328-8325		434-3
Web: lprlibrary.org						
Lonestar 98.7 6214 W 34th St	Amarillo	TX	79109	806-355-9777		645-5
TF: 866-930-5225 ■ *Web:* 987jackfm.com						
Lonestar Badge & Sign						
301 Quail Run	Martindale	TX	78655	512-357-2261		366
TF: 800-357-2686 ■ *Web:* lonestarbadge.com						
Lonestar Resources Inc						
509 Pecan Ste 200	Fort Worth	TX	76102	817-921-1889		536
TF: 800-671-7032 ■ *Web:* lonestarresources.com						
LoneStar West Inc						
RR 1 Box 1, Site 5	Sylvan Lake	AB	T4S1X6	403-887-2074		539
TF: 800-613-3995 ■ *Web:* www.lonestarwest.com						
Long & Foster Realtors						
14501 George Carter Way	Chantilly	VA	20151	703-653-8500		652
TF: 800-237-8800 ■ *Web:* www.longandfoster.com						
Long & McQuade Musical Instruments						
722 Rosebank Rd	Pickering	ON	L1W4B2	905-837-9785		526
Web: www.long-mcquade.com						
Long Beach Airport LGB						
4100 Donald Douglas Dr	Long Beach	CA	90808	562-570-2600	570-2601	27
TF: 800-331-1212 ■ *Web:* www.lgb.org						
Long Beach Area Chamber of Commerce						
1 World Trade Ctr Ste 206	Long Beach	CA	90831	562-436-1251	436-7099	139
Web: www.lbchamber.com						
Long Beach Arena 300 E Ocean Blvd	Long Beach	CA	90802	562-436-3636	436-9491	720
Web: longbeachcc.com						
Long Beach Chamber of Commerce						
350 National Blvd	Long Beach	NY	11561	516-432-6000	432-0273	139
Web: www.thelongbeachchamber.com						
Long Beach City College						
4901 E Carson St	Long Beach	CA	90808	562-938-4111	938-4858*	162
**Fax:* Admissions ■ *TF:* 888-442-4551 ■ *Web:* www.lbcc.edu						
Long Beach City Hall						
333 W Ocean Blvd	Long Beach	CA	90802	562-570-6101	570-6789	337
Web: www.longbeach.gov						
Long Beach Convention & Entertainment Ctr						
300 E Ocean Blvd	Long Beach	CA	90802	562-436-3636	436-9491	205
TF: 800-345-9845 ■ *Web:* www.longbeachcc.com						
Long Beach Convention & Visitors Bureau						
301 E Ocean Blvd	Long Beach	CA	90802	562-436-3645	435-5653	206
TF: 800-452-7829 ■ *Web:* www.visitlongbeach.com						
Long Beach Hose & Coupling Coinc						
1265 W 16th St	Long Beach	CA	90813	562-901-2970		790
Web: www.lbhose.com						
Long Beach Medical Ctr						
455 E Bay Dr	Long Beach	NY	11561	516-897-1000		374-3
TF: 800-804-5447 ■ *Web:* longbeachmedicalcenter.org						
Long Beach Memorial Medical Ctr						
2801 Atlantic Ave	Long Beach	CA	90806	562-933-2000		374-3
Web: www.memorialcare.org						
Long Beach Museum of Art						
2300 E Ocean Blvd	Long Beach	CA	90803	562-439-2119	439-3587	520
Web: www.lbma.org						
Long Beach Opera 507 Pacific Ave	Long Beach	CA	90802	562-432-5934	683-2109	573-2
Web: www.longbeachopera.org						
Long Beach Playhouse						
5021 E Anaheim St	Long Beach	CA	90804	562-494-1014		572
TF: 800-745-3000 ■ *Web:* www.lbplayhouse.org						
Long Beach Public Library						
101 Pacific Ave	Long Beach	CA	90822	562-570-7500	570-7408	434-3
TF: 800-923-1100 ■ *Web:* www.lbpl.org						
Long Beach Symphony Orchestra (LBSO)						
249 E Ocean Blvd Ste 200	Long Beach	CA	90802	562-436-3203	491-3599	573-3
Web: longbeachsymphony.org						
Long Beach Transit						
1963 E Anaheim St	Long Beach	CA	90813	562-591-2301		108
Web: www.lbtransit.com						
Long Billy (Rep R - MO)						
2454 Rayburn HOB	Washington	DC	20515	202-225-6536	225-5604	342-2
Web: long.house.gov						
Long Branch Free Public Library						
328 Broadway	Long Branch	NJ	07740	732-222-3900		434-3
TF: 800-323-5655 ■ *Web:* www.longbranchlib.org						
Long Branch Nature Ctr						
625 S Carlin Springs Rd	Arlington	VA	22204	703-228-6535		50-5
TF: 800-745-7433 ■ *Web:* arlingtonva.us						
Long Branch State Park						
28615 Visitor Ctr Rd	Macon	MO	63552	660-773-5229		565
Web: www.mostateparks.com						
Long Building Technologies Inc						
5001 S Zuni St	Littleton	CO	80120	303-975-2100		189-10
Web: long.com						
Long Business Systems Inc						
10749 Pearl Rd Ste 2A	Strongsville	OH	44136	440-846-8500		177
TF: 800-366-3836 ■ *Web:* www.lbsi.com						
Long Chilton LLP						
3125 Central Blvd	Brownsville	TX	78520	956-546-1655		2
Web: www.longchilton.com						
Long County 459 S McDonald St	Ludowici	GA	31316	912-545-2143	545-2150	338
Web: longcountyboc.com						
Long County Board of Education						
PO Box 428	Ludowici	GA	31316	912-545-2367	545-2380	685
Web: www.longcountyps.com						
Long Engineering Inc						
2550 Heritage Court Ste 100	Atlanta	GA	30339	770-951-2495		261
Web: www.longeng.com						
Long Farms Inc 2849 Lust Rd	Apopka	FL	32703	407-889-4141		10-11
Long Hollow Ranch 71105 Holmes Rd	Sisters	OR	97759	541-923-1901		239
TF: 877-923-1901 ■ *Web:* www.lhranch.com						
Long House Alaskan Hotel						
4335 Wisconsin St	Anchorage	AK	99517	907-243-2133		379
TF: 888-243-2133 ■ *Web:* www.longhousehotel.com						
Long House Reserve						
133 Hands Creek Rd	East Hampton	NY	11937	631-329-3568	329-4299	97
Web: longhouse.org						
Long International						
10029 Whistling Elk Dr	Littleton	CO	80127	303-972-2443		194
Web: www.long-intl.com						
Long Island Assn						
300 Broadhollow Rd Ste 110-W	Melville	NY	11747	631-493-3000	499-2194	139
Web: longislandassociation.org						
Long Island Baroque Ensemble						
154 W 123rd St	New York	NY	10027	212-222-5795		573-3
Web: www.libaroque.org						
Long Island Business News Inc						
2150 Smithtown Ave Ste 7	Ronkonkoma	NY	11779	631-737-1700		532-3
Web: www.libn.com						
Long Island Children's Museum						
11 Davis Ave	Garden City	NY	11530	516-224-5800	302-8188	521
Web: www.licm.org						
Long Island College Hospital (LICH)						
339 Hicks St	Brooklyn	NY	11201	718-780-1000	270-4775	374-3
TF: 800-227-8922 ■ *Web:* www.downstate.edu/lich						
Long Island Convention & Visitors Bureau & Sports Commission						
330 Motor Pkwy Ste 203	Hauppauge	NY	11788	877-386-6654	951-3439*	206
**Fax Area Code:* 631 ■ *TF:* 877-386-6654 ■ *Web:* www.discoverlongisland.com						
Long Island Fireproof Door Inc						
1105 Clintonville St	Whitestone	NY	11357	718-767-8800		499
Web: lifd.com						
Long Island Hotels LLC						
1757 Veteran'S Memorial Hwy Ste 22	Islandia	NY	11749	631-234-9700		379
Web: www.longislandhotelsllc.com						
Long Island MacArthur Airport						
100 Arrival Ave Ste 100	Ronkonkoma	NY	11779	631-467-3300	467-3348	27
TF: 888-542-4776 ■ *Web:* www.macarthurairport.com						
Long Island Museum of American Art History & Carriages						
1200 Rt 25A	Stony Brook	NY	11790	631-751-0066	751-0353	520
TF: 800-745-3000 ■ *Web:* www.longislandmuseum.org						
Long Island National Cemetery						
2040 Wellwood Ave	Farmingdale	NY	11735	631-454-4949	694-5422	136
Web: www.cem.va.gov/cems/nchp/longisland.asp						
Long Island Philharmonic (LIP)						
1 Huntington Quadrangle Ste 2C21	Melville	NY	11747	631-293-2223	293-2655	573-3
Web: www.liphilharmonic.com						
Long Island Pipe Supply Inc						
586 Commercial Ave	Garden City	NY	11530	516-222-8008		595
Web: www.lipipe.com						
Long Island Power Authority						
333 Earle Ovington Blvd Ste 403	Uniondale	NY	11553	516-222-7700	222-9137	787
TF Cust Svc: 877-275-5472 ■ *Web:* www.lipower.org						
Long Island Press						
575 Underhill Blvd Ste 210	Syosset	NY	11791	516-284-3300	284-3310	532-5
TF: 800-545-6683 ■ *Web:* www.longislandpress.com						
Long Island State Veterans Home						
100 Patriots Rd	Stony Brook	NY	11790	631-444-8500		793
Long Island University						
Brentwood 100 Second Ave	Brentwood	NY	11717	631-273-5112	273-3155	166
TF: 800-458-5398 ■ *Web:* www.liunet.edu						
Brooklyn 1 University Plaza	Brooklyn	NY	11201	718-488-1011	797-2399*	166
**Fax:* Admissions ■ *TF:* 800-548-7526 ■ *Web:* www.liu.edu						
Long John Silver's Restaurants Inc						
9505 Williamsburg Plaza	Louisville	KY	40222	502-815-6100		670
Web: www.ljsilvers.com						
Long Key State Park PO Box 776	Long Key	FL	33001	305-664-4815		565
Web: www.floridastateparks.org						
Long Lake State Recreation Area						
524 Panzer St PO Box 508	Bassett	NE	68714	402-684-2921		565
Web: outdoornebraska.gov/longlake						
Long Leaf Medical Treatment Ctr						
4761 Ward Blvd	Wilson	NC	27893	252-399-2112		450
Long Lines LLC						
501 Fourth St PO Box 67	Sergeant Bluff	IA	51054	712-271-4000		225
TF: 800-901-5004 ■ *Web:* www.longlines.com						
Long Painting Co 21414 68th Ave S	Kent	WA	98032	253-234-8050	234-0034	189-8
TF: 800-687-5664 ■ *Web:* www.longpainting.com						
Long Pine State Recreation Area						
524 Panzer St PO Box 508	Bassett	NE	68714	402-684-2921		565
Web: outdoornebraska.gov/longpine						
Long Point Capital Inc						
26700 Woodward Ave	Royal Oak	MI	48067	248-591-6000		796
Web: www.longpointcapital.com						
Long Point State Park - Finger Lakes						
2063 Lake Rd	Aurora	NY	13026	315-364-5637		565
Web: parks.ny.gov/parks/170/hunting.aspx						
Long Point State Park - Thousand Islands						
7495 State Pk Rd	Three Mile Bay	NY	13693	315-649-5258		565
Web: parks.ny.gov/parks/54/details.aspx						
Long Point State Park on Lake Chautauqua						
4459 Rt 430	Bemus Point	NY	14712	716-386-2722		565
Web: parks.ny.gov/parks/109/details.aspx						
Long Pond Ironworks State Park						
c/o Ringwood State Pk 1304 Sloatsburg Rd	Ringwood	NJ	07456	973-962-7031		565
TF: 800-852-7899 ■ *Web:* www.njparksandforests.org/parks/longpond.html						
Long Prairie Packing Co						
10 Riverside Dr	Long Prairie	MN	56347	320-732-2171	552-2107*	473
**Fax Area Code:* 651						
Long Term Solutions Inc						
235 W Central St	Natick	MA	01760	508-907-6290		363
TF: 800-839-6544 ■ *Web:* www.longtermsol.com						

Name / Address	City	State	Zip	Phone	Fax	Class
Long Trail Brewing Co 5520 Rt 4	Bridgewater Corners	VT	05035	802-672-5011	672-5012	102
TF: 800-767-7882 ■ *Web:* www.longtrail.com						
Long Valley Charter School 436 Susan Dr 965 PO Box 7	Doyle	CA	96109	530-827-2395		685
TF: 800-979-4436 ■ *Web:* www.longvalleycs.org						
Long View Systems Corp 250-2 St SW Ste 2100	Calgary	AB	T2P0C1	403-515-6900		174
TF: 866-515-6900 ■ *Web:* www.longviewsystems.com						
Long Wharf Theatre 222 Sargent Dr	New Haven	CT	06511	203-787-4282	776-2287	572
TF: 800-782-8497 ■ *Web:* www.longwharf.org						
Long Wholesale Distributors Inc 5173 Pioneer Rd	Meridian	MS	39301	601-482-3144		297-8
Web: www.longwholesale.com						
Longacre Theatre 220 W 48th St	New York	NY	10036	212-239-6200		747
TF: 800-447-7400 ■ *Web:* www.telecharge.com						
Longboard Restaurant & Pub 217 Main St	Huntington Beach	CA	92648	714-960-1896		671
TF: 800-326-3264 ■ *Web:* longboardpub.com						
Longboat Key Club 220 Sands Point Rd	Longboat Key	FL	34228	941-383-8821		669
TF: 800-237-8821 ■ *Web:* www.longboatkeyclub.com						
Longboat Observer 5570 Gulf of Mexico Dr	Longboat Key	FL	34228	941-383-5509		532-4
Web: www.yourobserver.com						
Longbottom Coffee & Tea Inc 4893 NW 235th Ave	Hillsboro	OR	97124	503-924-4470		805
Web: www.longbottomcoffee.com						
Longbranch Restaurant & Lounge 351 S Pierre St	Pierre	SD	57501	605-224-6166		671
Longfellow National Historic Site 105 Brattle St	Cambridge	MA	02138	617-876-4491	497-8718	564
TF: 800-315-4000 ■ *Web:* www.nps.gov/long						
Longfellow-Evangeline State Historic Site 1200 N Main St	Saint Martinville	LA	70582	337-394-3754		565
TF: 888-677-2900 ■ *Web:* www.crt.state.la.us						
Longhi's *Ala Moana Shopping Ctr* 1450 Ala Moana Blvd Ste 3001	Honolulu	HI	96814	808-947-9899		671
Longhorn BBQ 635 C St SW	Auburn	WA	98001	253-804-9600		671
Web: www.thelonghornbbq.com						
Longhorn Cavern State Park PO Box 732	Burnet	TX	78611	830-598-2283		565
Web: www.longhorncaverns.com						
Longhorn Imports Inc 2202 E Union Bower	Irving	TX	75061	972-721-9102	579-4890	311
TF: 800-641-8348 ■ *Web:* longhornimports.com						
Longhorn Recycling LP 5785 Fm 1346	San Antonio	TX	78220	210-661-2341		638
TF: 800-253-2687 ■ *Web:* www.longhornrecycling.com						
Longhorn Steakhouse 2400 N Monroe St	Tallahassee	FL	32303	850-385-4028		671
TF: 800-887-2968 ■ *Web:* www.longhornsteakhouse.com						
LongHorn Steakhouse 1000 Darden Ctr Dr	Orlando	FL	32837	888-221-0642		670
TF: 888-221-0642 ■ *Web:* www.longhornsteakhouse.com						
Longistics Transportation Inc 10900 World Trade Blvd	Raleigh	NC	27617	919-872-7626	872-2883	803-1
TF: 800-289-0082 ■ *Web:* www.longistics.com						
Longley Supply Company Inc 2018 Oleander Dr	Wilmington	NC	28403	910-762-7793	762-9178	612
TF: 800-561-3357 ■ *Web:* longleysupplycompany.com						
Longmont Area Chamber of Commerce 528 Main St	Longmont	CO	80501	303-776-5295	776-5657	139
Web: www.longmontchamber.org						
Longmont Public Library 409 Fourth Ave	Longmont	CO	80501	303-651-8470		434-3
Web: longmontcolorado.gov						
Longmont United Hospital (LUH) 1950 Mountain View Ave	Longmont	CO	80501	303-651-5111		374-3
Web: www.luhcares.org						
Longnecker & Associates 11011 Jones Rd Ste 200	Houston	TX	77070	281-378-1350		193
Web: www.longnecker.com						
Longos a fresh tradition 8800 Huntington Rd	Vaughan	ON	L4H3M6	905-264-4100		297-8
Web: www.longos.com						
Longs Human Resource Services 19 midtown park w	Mobile	AL	36606	251-476-4080		260
Web: www.longshrs.com						
Long-Stanton Manufacturing Co 9388 Sutton Pl	West Chester Township	OH	45011	513-874-8020		488
Web: www.longstanton.com						
Longsworth Law Offices LLC 7030 Pointe Inverness Way Ste 330	Fort Wayne	IN	46804	260-436-1555		428
Web: longsworthlaw.com						
Longue Vue House & Gardens 7 Bamboo Rd	New Orleans	LA	70124	504-488-5488	486-7015	520
TF: 800-476-9137 ■ *Web:* www.longuevue.com						
Longust Distributing Inc 2432 W Birchwood Ave	Mesa	AZ	85202	480-820-6244	352-0526*	361
**Fax Area Code:* 800 ■ *TF:* 800-352-0521 ■ *Web:* www.longust.com						
Longview News-Journal 320 E Methvin St	Longview	TX	75601	903-757-3311	757-3742*	532-2
**Fax:* News Rm ■ *TF:* 800-825-9799 ■ *Web:* www.news-journal.com						
Longview Partnership 410 N Center St	Longview	TX	75601	903-237-4000	237-4049	139
TF: 800-338-7232 ■ *Web:* www.longviewchamber.com						
Longview Public Library 1600 Louisiana St	Longview	WA	98632	360-442-5300	442-5954	434-3
Web: www.longviewlibrary.org						
Longview Public Library 222 W Cotton St	Longview	TX	75601	903-237-1351		434-3
Web: www.longviewtexas.gov/2163/library						
Longview Regional Medical Ctr 2901 N Fourth St	Longview	TX	75605	903-758-1818		374-3
Web: www.longviewregional.com						
Longview School District 2715 Lilac St	Longview	WA	98632	360-575-7000	575-7231	685
Web: www.longview.k12.wa.us						
Longview Solutions 65 Allstate Pkwy Ste 200	Markham	ON	L3R9X1	905-940-1510	940-8310	178-1
TF: 888-454-2549 ■ *Web:* www.longview.com						
Longview Wealth Management LLC 15268 Boulder Pointe Rd	Eden Prairie	MN	55347	952-906-1289		401
Web: www.longviewwealth.com						
Longwall Associates Inc 212 Kendall Ave	Chilhowie	VA	24319	276-646-2004		45
Web: www.longwall.com						
Longway Planetarium 1310 E Kearsley St	Flint	MI	48503	810-237-3400	237-3417	598
Web: www.sloanlongway.org						
Longwood Elastomers Inc 706 Green Valley Rd Ste 212	Greensboro	NC	27408	336-272-3710	272-3710	677
TF: 800-829-7231 ■ *Web:* www.longwoodindustries.com						
Longwood Foundation Inc 100 W Tenth St Ste 1109	Wilmington	DE	19801	302-654-2477		303
Web: longwoodfoundation.com						
Longwood Gardens 1001 Longwood Rd	Kennett Square	PA	19348	610-388-1000	388-5488	97
Web: longwoodgardens.org						
Longwood Management Corp 4032 Wilshire Blvd Ste 600	Los Angeles	CA	90010	213-389-6900		363
Longwood University 201 High St	Farmville	VA	23909	434-395-2060	395-2332*	166
**Fax:* Admissions ■ *TF:* 800-281-4677 ■ *Web:* www.longwood.edu						
Lonn Mfg Co Inc 5450 W 84th St	Indianapolis	IN	46268	317-897-1440	898-4561	151
Web: www.lonn.net						
Lonoke County 301 N Ctr St	Lonoke	AR	72086-0870	501-676-2368	676-3014	338
Web: www.lonokecircuitclerk.com						
Lonsdale Quay Hotel 123 Carrie Cates Ct	North Vancouver	BC	V7M3K7	604-986-6111		379
TF: 800-836-6111 ■ *Web:* www.lonsdalequayhotel.com						
Lonseal Inc 928 E 238th St	Carson	CA	90745	310-830-7111	830-9986	361
TF: 800-832-7111 ■ *Web:* www.lonseal.com						
Look Ahead Veterinary Services 1451 Clark Rd	Oroville	CA	95965	530-534-0722		794
TF: 800-947-1662 ■ *Web:* www.lookaheadvet.net						
Look Matters 1815 Rae St	Regina	SK	S4T2E3	306-757-4686		180
Web: lookmatters.com						
Lookout Inn 6901 Lookout Rd	Boulder	CO	80301	209-485-3365		379
TF: 877-234-4770 ■ *Web:* thelookoutboulder.com						
Lookout Mountain Youth Services Ctr 2901 Ford St	Golden	CO	80401	303-866-2471		412
Web: colorado.gov						
Loomis & Company CPA's LLP 267 E Campbell Ave Ste 200	Campbell	CA	95008	408-385-3400		2
Web: www.loomiscpas.com						
Loomis Agency LLC, The 17120 Dallas Pkwy Ste 200	Dallas	TX	75248	972-331-7000		7
TF: 800-908-5395 ■ *Web:* www.theloomisagency.com						
Loomis Armored US Inc 2500 Citywest Blvd Ste 900	Houston	TX	77042	713-435-6700		693
TF: 866-383-5069 ■ *Web:* www.loomis.us						
Loomis Chaffee School 4 Batchelder Rd	Windsor	CT	06095	860-687-6400	298-8756	622
Web: www.loomischaffee.org						
Loomis Co 850 N Pk Rd	Wyomissing	PA	19610	610-374-4040	374-6578	390
TF: 800-782-0392 ■ *Web:* www.loomisco.com						
Loomis Communities 246 N Main St	South Hadley	MA	01075	413-532-5325	532-8676	672
TF: 800-865-7655 ■ *Web:* www.loomiscommunities.org						
Loomis Fargo & Co 2500 Citywest Blvd Ste 900	Houston	TX	77042	713-435-6700		692
TF: 866-383-5069 ■ *Web:* www.loomis.us						
Loomis Group Inc 345 Spear St Ste 110	San Francisco	CA	94105	415-882-9494		5
Web: www.loomisgroup.com						
Loomis Sayles & Company Inc LP One Financial Ctr	Boston	MA	02111	800-633-3330		401
TF: 800-343-2029 ■ *Web:* www.loomissayles.com						
Loomis Sayles Funds 1 Financial Ctr	Boston	MA	02111	617-482-2450		528
TF: 800-633-3330 ■ *Web:* www.loomissayles.com						
Loon Energy Corp 1500-700 4 Ave SW	Calgary	AB	T2P3J4	403-264-8877		536
Web: www.loonenergy.com						
Looney Ricks Kiss Architects 175 Toyota Plaza Ste 600	Memphis	TN	38103	901-521-1440		261
Web: www.lrk.com						
Loop Capital Markets LLC 111 W Jackson Blvd Ste 1901	Chicago	IL	60604	312-913-4900		690
TF: 888-294-8898 ■ *Web:* www.loopcapital.com						
Loop Consulting Group 9485 SW 72nd St	Miami	FL	33173	305-444-3948		195
Loop Parking 1200 Washington Ave S Ste 150	Minneapolis	MN	55415	612-333-2293		562
Web: www.loopparking.com						
LOOP88 INC 1001 N 19th St Ste 930	Arlington	VA	22209	202-595-9545		5
Loop-Loc Ltd 390 Motor Pkwy	Hauppauge	NY	11788	631-582-2626	582-2636	733
TF: 800-562-5667 ■ *Web:* www.looploc.com						
Loopnet Inc 2100 E Rt 66	Glendora	CA	91740	626-803-5000		652
Web: loopnet.com						
LOPA (Louisiana Organ Procurement Agency) 3545 N I-10 Service Rd Ste 300	Metairie	LA	70002	800-521-4483		545
TF: 800-521-4483 ■ *Web:* www.lopa.org						
Lopata Flegel & Company LLP 600 Mason Ridge Ctr Dr Ste 100	Saint Louis	MO	63141	314-514-8881		2
Web: www.lopataflegel.com						
Lopez Foods Inc 6016 NW 120th Ct	Oklahoma City	OK	73162	405-603-7500		296-26
Web: www.lopezfoods.com						
Lopez Marketing Group Inc 11169 La Quinta Pl	El Paso	TX	79936	915-772-8018		7
TF: 800-438-7325 ■ *Web:* www.lopezgroup.com						
Lopez Mchugh LLP 1123 Admiral Peary Way	Philadelphia	PA	19112	215-952-6910		428
TF: 877-703-7070 ■ *Web:* lopezmchugh.com						
Lopez Negrete Communications Inc 3336 Richmond Ave Ste 200	Houston	TX	77098	713-877-8777		4
Web: www.lopeznegrete.com						
Lopez Research LLC 2269 Chestnut St	San Francisco	CA	94123	415-894-5781		466
Web: www.lopezresearch.com						

Phone | Fax | Class

Lopez State Jail 1203 El Cibolo Rd .... Edinburg TX 78542 956-316-3810 316-7447 213
Web: tdcj.state.tx.us

Lorain Correctional Institution
2075 Avon Belden Rd .... Grafton OH 44044 440-748-1049 748-2191 213
TF: 888-842-8464 ■ *Web:* drc.ohio.gov

Lorain County 225 Ct St .... Elyria OH 44035 440-329-5536 329-5404 338
TF: 800-750-0750 ■ *Web:* www.loraincounty.us

Lorain County Automotive Systems Inc
7470 Industrial Pkwy Dr .... Lorain OH 44053 440-960-7470 60
Web: www.camacollc.com

Lorain County Chamber of Commerce
226 Middle Ave. .... Elyria OH 44035 440-328-2550 328-2557 139
TF: 800-633-4766 ■ *Web:* www.loraincountychamber.com

Lorain County Community College
1005 N Abbe Rd .... Elyria OH 44035 440-365-5222 366-4167 162
TF: 800-995-5222 ■ *Web:* www.lorainccc.edu

Lorain County Visitors Bureau
8025 Leavitt Rd. .... Amherst OH 44001 440-984-5282 206
TF: 800-334-1673 ■ *Web:* www.visitloraincounty.com

Lorain Public Library System
351 W Sixth St .... Lorain OH 44052 440-244-1192 244-4888 434-3
TF: 800-687-5664 ■ *Web:* lorainpubliclibrary.org

Lorain-Medina Rural Electric Co-op Inc
22898 W Rd .... Wellington OH 44090 440-647-2133 647-4870 245
TF: 800-222-5673 ■ *Web:* www.lmre.org

Loral Space & Communications Ltd
600 Third Ave .... New York NY 10016 212-697-1105 529
NASDAQ: LORL ■ *Web:* www.loral.com

Loram Maintenance of Way
3900 Arrowhead Dr PO Box 188 .... Hamel MN 55340 763-478-6014 650
TF: 800-328-1466 ■ *Web:* www.loram.com

Loranger International Corp
817 Fourth Ave .... Warren PA 16365 814-723-2250 723-5391 695
Web: www.loranger.com

Lorann Oils 4518 Aurelius Rd .... Lansing MI 48910 517-882-0215 345
TF: 800-862-8620 ■ *Web:* www.lorannoils.com

Loras College 1450 Alta Vista St .... Dubuque IA 52001 563-588-7100 588-7119* 166
**Fax:* Admissions ■ *TF:* 800-245-6727 ■ *Web:* www.loras.edu

Lorber Greenfield & Polito LLP
13985 Stowe Dr .... Poway CA 92064 858-513-1020 428
TF: 800-659-8821 ■ *Web:* lorberlaw.com

Lorch Microwave Inc
1725 N Salisbury Blvd .... Salisbury MD 21802 410-860-5100 253
Web: www.lorch.com

Lord & Taylor 424 Fifth Ave .... New York NY 10018 212-391-3344 391-3262 229
TF: 800-223-7440 ■ *Web:* www.lordandtaylor.com

Lord Abbett & Co 90 Hudson St .... Jersey City NJ 07302 201-827-2000 401
TF: 888-522-2388 ■ *Web:* www.lordabbett.com

Lord Baltimore Properties
6225 Smith Ave Ste B100 .... Baltimore MD 21209 410-415-7638 580-9250 653

Lord Corp 111 Lord Dr .... Cary NC 27511 919-468-5979 3
TF: 877-275-5673 ■ *Web:* www.lord.com

Lord Electric Co Of Puerto Rico Inc
8 Simon Madera .... San Juan PR 00924 787-758-4040 787
Web: www.lordelectric.com

Lord Elgin Hotel 100 Elgin St .... Ottawa ON K1P5K8 613-235-3333 235-3223 379
TF: 800-267-4298 ■ *Web:* www.lordelginhotel.ca

Lord Fairfax Community College
Fauquier 6480 College St .... Warrenton VA 20187 540-351-1505 351-1530* 162
**Fax:* Admissions ■ *Web:* www.lfcc.edu
Middletown 173 Skirmisher Ln .... Middletown VA 22645 540-868-7000 868-7005* 162
**Fax:* Admissions ■ *TF:* 800-906-5322 ■ *Web:* www.lfcc.edu

Lord Nelson Hotel & Suites
1515 S Pk St. .... Halifax NS B3J2L2 902-423-6331 423-7148 379
TF: 800-565-2020 ■ *Web:* www.lordnelsonhotel.com

Lord of Life Lutheran Church Lcms
3601 W 15th St. .... Plano TX 75075 972-867-5588 48-20
Web: planolutheran.com

Lord Stanley Suites on the Park
1889 Alberni St. .... Vancouver BC V6G3G7 604-688-9299 688-9297 379
TF: 888-767-7829 ■ *Web:* www.lordstanley.com

Lord Whalen LLC
371 Van Ness Way Ste 110 .... Torrance CA 90501 310-676-3300 225
Web: www.institutionalriskanalytics.com

Lordco Parts Ltd
22866 Dewdney Trunk Rd .... Maple Ridge BC V2X3K6 604-467-1581 57
TF: 877-591-1581 ■ *Web:* www.lordco.com

LORE Product Design Engineering & Development Inc
36 Eglinton Ave W Ste 707 .... Toronto ON M4R1A1 416-489-9008 261
Web: www.designlore.com

Lorelei Personnel Inc
1 Aucr Ct .... East Brunswick NJ 00010 732-390-1170 260
TF: 800-591-0935 ■ *Web:* www.loreleipersonnel.com

Loren Cook Co 2015 E Dale St. .... Springfield MO 65803 417-869-6474 862-3820 18
Web: www.lorencook.com

Loren D Stark Company Inc
10750 Rockley Rd. .... Houston TX 77099 281-498-5777 463
Web: www.ldsco.com

Loren Hyundai Inc 1620 Waukegan Rd. .... Glenview IL 60025 224-766-7189 724-8429* 516
**Fax Area Code:* 847 ■ *Web:* www.lorenautogroup.com

Lorenz Corp 501 E Third St .... Dayton OH 45402 800-444-1144 223-2042* 637-7
**Fax Area Code:* 937 ■ *TF:* 800-444-1144 ■ *Web:* www.lorenz.com

Lorenzo State Historic Site
17 Rippleton Rd .... Cazenovia NY 13035 315-655-3200 565
Web: www.parks.ny.gov/historic-sites/15/details.aspx

Lorenzo's Bread Bistro
972 S Hebron Ave. .... Evansville IN 47714 812-475-9477 671
Web: lorenzosbistro.net

Lorenzo's Trattoria
1933 Edwards St. .... Saint Louis MO 63110 314-773-2223 671
Web: www.lorenzostrattoria.com

Loretto Hospital 645 S Central Ave. .... Chicago IL 60644 773-626-4300 374-3
Web: www.lorettohospital.org

LOREX Corp 3700 Koppers St Ste 504 .... Baltimore MD 21227 888-425-6739 693
TF: 888-425-6739 ■ *Web:* www.lorextechnology.com

Lorge & Lorge Law Firm
501 W Willow St. .... Bear Creek WI 54922 715-752-3304 428
TF: 800-529-2946 ■ *Web:* www.lawfirm.net

Lori Bonn Jewelery 114 Linden St .... Oakland CA 94607 877-507-4206 410
TF: 877-507-4206 ■ *Web:* www.loribonn.com

Lori Brock Children's Discovery Ctr
3801 Chester Ave .... Bakersfield CA 93301 661-437-3330 521

Lorin Industries 1960 S Roberts St .... Muskegon MI 49443 231-722-1631 481
TF: 800-654-1159 ■ *Web:* www.lorin.com

Loring Ward International Ltd
3055 Olin Ave Ste 2000 .... San Jose CA 95128 408-260-3100 194
Web: www.loringward.com

Loring, Wolcott & Coolidge Fiduciary Advisors LLP
230 Congress St. .... Boston MA 02110 617-523-6531 251
Web: www.lwcotrust.com

Loroco Industries Inc
5000 Creek Rd .... Cincinnati OH 45242 513-891-9544 891-9549 555
TF: 800-215-9474 ■ *Web:* www.lorocoindustries.com

Lorraine Gregory Communications Inc
110 Schmitt Blvd .... Farmingdale NY 11735 631-694-1500 694-1501 5
Web: lorrainegregory.com

Lorraine Travel Bureau Inc
377 Alhambra Cir .... Coral Gables FL 33134 305-446-4433 771
TF: 800-666-8911 ■ *Web:* www.lorrainetravel.com

LORT (League of Resident Theatres)
1501 Broadway Ste 1801 .... New York NY 10036 212-944-1501 48-4
Web: www.lort.org

LoRusso's Cucina 3121 Watson Rd .... Saint Louis MO 63139 314-647-6222 671
Web: www.lorussos.com

Lory State Park 708 Lodgepole Dr .... Bellvue CO 80512 970-493-1623 565
Web: cpw.state.co.us

Los Abrigados Resort 160 Portal Ln .... Sedona AZ 86336 928-282-1777 282-2614 669
TF: 877-374-2582 ■ *Web:* www.diamondresorts.com

Los Adaes State Historic Site
6354 Hwy 485 .... Robeline LA 71469 318-472-9449 565
TF: 888-677-5378 ■ *Web:* www.crt.state.la.us

Los Alamitos Medical Ctr
3751 Katella Ave .... Los Alamitos CA 90720 562-598-1311 371-3
Web: www.losalamitosmedctr.com

Los Alamitos Race Course
4961 Katella Ave. .... Los Alamitos CA 90720 714-820-2800 642
Web: www.losalamitos.com/laqhr

Los Alamitos Unified School District
10293 Bloomfield St. .... Los Alamitos CA 90720 562-799-4700 799-4711 685
Web: www.losal.org

Los Alamos Historical Museum
1050 Bathtub Row PO Box 43 .... Los Alamos NM 87544 505-662-6272 520
Web: www.losalamoshistory.org

Los Alamos National Laboratory (LANL)
PO Box 1663 .... Los Alamos NM 87545 505-667-7000 668
TF: 877-723-4101 ■ *Web:* www.lanl.gov

Los Alamos Technical Assoc Inc
6501 Americas Parkway NE Ste 200 .... Albuquerque NM 87110 505-662-9080 880-3560 192
TF: 800-952-5282 ■ *Web:* www.lata.com

Los Altos Chamber of Commerce
321 University Ave .... Los Altos CA 94022 650-948-1455 948-6238 139
TF: 800-829-1040 ■ *Web:* www.losaltoschamber.org

Los Altos Community Foundation
183 Hillview Ave. .... Los Altos CA 94022 650-949-5908 305
Web: www.losaltoscf.org

Los Altos Food Products Inc
450 N Baldwin Park Blvd .... City of Industry CA 91746 626-330-6555 330-6755 206-6
Web: www.losaltosfoods.com

Los Altos School District
201 Covington Rd. .... Los Altos CA 94024 650-947-1150 947-0118 685
Web: www.lasdschools.org

Los Altos Town Crier 138 Main St .... Los Altos CA 94022 650-948-9000 532-4
Web: losaltosonline.com

Los Amigos 2610 State Ave .... Kansas City KS 66102 913-281-4547 671

Los Amigos 1926 Atlantic Ave .... Atlantic City NJ 08401 609-344-2293 671
Web: www.losamigosrest.com

Los Amigos Mexican Restaurant
5935 Veterans Pkwy .... Columbus GA 31909 706-322-1993 671

Los Angeles Air Force Base
483 N Aviation Blvd Los Angeles AFB .... El Segundo CA 90245 310-653-1110 497-1
TF: 800-275-8777 ■ *Web:* www.losangeles.af.mil

Los Angeles Angels of Anaheim
Angel Stadium 2000 Gene Autry Way .... Anaheim CA 92806 714-940-2000 940-2205* 713
**Fax:* PR ■ *Web:* losangeles.angels.mlb.com

Los Angeles Area Chamber of Commerce
350 S Bixel St. .... Los Angeles CA 90017 213-580-7500 580-7511 139
TF: 800-331-7593 ■ *Web:* www.lachamber.com

Los Angeles Athletic Club
431 W Seventh St. .... Los Angeles CA 90014 213-625-2211 689-1194 379
TF: 800-421-8777 ■ *Web:* www.laac.com

Los Angeles Biomedical Research Institute
1124 W Carson St .... Torrance CA 90502 424-201-3000 222-3640* 668
**Fax Area Code:* 310 ■ *Web:* www.labiomed.org

Los Angeles Business Journal
5700 Wilshire Blvd Ste 170 .... Los Angeles CA 90036 323-549-5225 549-5255 457-5
Web: www.labusinessjournal.com

Los Angeles City College
855 N Vermont Ave. .... Los Angeles CA 90029 323-953-4000 953-4013* 162
**Fax:* Admissions ■ *TF:* 800-207-1710 ■ *Web:* www.lacitycollege.edu

Los Angeles City Hall
200 N Spring St Rm 360. .... Los Angeles CA 90012 213-473-3231 978-1027 337
Web: www.lacity.org

Los Angeles Clippers
Staples Ctr 1111 S Figueroa St Ste 1100 ...... Los Angeles CA 90015 213-742-7100 742-7550 714-1
TF: 855-895-0872 ■ *Web:* www.nba.com/clippers

Los Angeles Confidential Magazine
717 N Highland Ave Unit 10 .... Los Angeles CA 90038 310-289-7300 457-22
TF: 866-891-3144 ■ *Web:* www.la-confidential-magazine.com

Los Angeles Convention & Visitors Bureau
333 S Hope St 18th Fl .... Los Angeles CA 90071 213-624-7300 206
Web: www.discoverlosangeles.com

Los Angeles Convention Ctr
1201 S Figueroa St. .... Los Angeles CA 90015 213-741-1151 205
Web: www.lacclink.com

Los Angeles County
500 W Temple St. .... Los Angeles CA 90012 213-974-1311 680-1122 338
TF: 800-735-2929 ■ *Web:* www.lacounty.gov

Name / Address	City	State	ZIP	Phone	Fax	Class
Los Angeles County Arboretum & Botanic Garden 301 N Baldwin Ave *Web:* www.arboretum.org	Arcadia	CA	91007	626-821-3222	445-1217	97
Los Angeles County Fairplex 1101 W McKinley Ave *Web:* www.fairplex.com	Pomona	CA	91768	909-623-3111	865-3602	515
Los Angeles County Metropolitan Transportation Authority 1 Gateway Plaza *TF:* 800-621-7828 ■ *Web:* www.metro.net	Los Angeles	CA	90012	213-922-6000		468
Los Angeles County Museum of Art 5905 Wilshire Blvd *Web:* www.lacma.org	Los Angeles	CA	90036	323-857-6000	857-6212	520
Los Angeles County Public Library 7400 E Imperial Hwy *Web:* www.colapublib.org	Downey	CA	90242	562-940-8462	803-3032	434-3
Los Angeles Dodgers Dodger Stadium 1000 Elysian Pk Ave **Fax:* PR ■ *Web:* losangeles.dodgers.mlb.com	Los Angeles	CA	90012	323-224-1500	224-4294*	713
Los Angeles Downtown News 1264 W First St *TF:* 877-338-1010 ■ *Web:* www.ladowntownnews.com	Los Angeles	CA	90026	213-481-1448	250-4617	532-4
Los Angeles Federal Credit Union PO Box 53032 *TF:* 877-695-2328 ■ *Web:* www.lafcu.org	Los Angeles	CA	90053	818-242-8640	242-5812	219
Los Angeles Galaxy Home Depot Ctr 18400 Avalon Blvd Ste 200 *TF:* 877-342-5299 ■ *Web:* www.lagalaxy.com	Carson	CA	90746	310-630-2200	630-2250	717
Los Angeles Harbor College 1111 Figueroa Pl *Web:* www.lahc.cc.ca.us	Wilmington	CA	90744	310-233-4000	233-4223	162
Los Angeles International Short Film Festival 1610 Argyle Ave Ste 113 *Web:* www.lashortsfest.com	Hollywood	CA	90028	323-461-4400		282
Los Angeles Kings Staples Ctr 1111 S Figueroa St *TF:* 888-546-4752 ■ *Web:* kings.nhl.com	Los Angeles	CA	90015	213-742-7100		716
Los Angeles Lakers 555 N Nash St *TF:* 866-648-4668 ■ *Web:* www.nba.com/lakers	El Segundo	CA	90245	310-426-6000	426-6105	714-1
Los Angeles Lawyer Magazine 261 S Figueroa St	Los Angeles	CA	90012	213-627-2727		457-15
Los Angeles Lighting Manufacturing Company Inc 10141 Olney St *Web:* www.lalighting.com	El Monte	CA	91731	626-454-8300		362
Los Angeles Magazine 5900 Wilshire Blvd 10th Fl **Fax:* Edit ■ *TF Cust Svc:* 800-876-5222 ■ *Web:* www.lamag.com	Los Angeles	CA	90036	323-801-0100	801-0105*	457-22
Los Angeles Memorial Coliseum & Sports Arena 3939 S Figueroa St *Web:* www.lacoliseum.com	Los Angeles	CA	90037	213-747-7111		720
Los Angeles Mission College 13356 Eldridge Ave **Fax:* Admissions ■ *TF:* 800-854-7771 ■ *Web:* www.lamission.edu	Sylmar	CA	91342	818-364-7600	364-7806*	162
Los Angeles National Cemetery 950 S Sepulveda Blvd *Web:* www.cem.va.gov	Los Angeles	CA	90049	310-268-4494	268-3257	136
Los Angeles Opera 135 N Grand Ave Ste 327 *Web:* laopera.org	Los Angeles	CA	90012	213-972-7219	687-3490	573-2
Los Angeles Philharmonic Assn 151 S Grand Ave *TF:* 800-864-8377 ■ *Web:* www.laphil.com	Los Angeles	CA	90012	323-850-2000		573-3
Los Angeles Police Federal Credit Union PO Box 10188 *TF:* 877-695-2732 ■ *Web:* www.lapfcu.org	Van Nuys	CA	91410	818-787-6520		219
Los Angeles Poultry Company Inc 4816 Long Beach Ave *Web:* www.lapoultry.com	Los Angeles	CA	90058	323-232-1619		619
Los Angeles Public Library 630 W Fifth St *TF:* 800-427-8700 ■ *Web:* www.lapl.org	Los Angeles	CA	90071	213-228-7000	228-7369	434-3
Los Angeles School of Make-up Inc 129 S San Fernando Blvd *Web:* www.makeupschool.com	Burbank	CA	91502	818-729-9420		77
Los Angeles Smoking & Curing Co (LASCCO) 1100 W Ewing St *TF:* 800-365-8950 ■ *Web:* www.oceanbeauty.com	Seattle	WA	98119	206-285-6800		296-13
Los Angeles Southwest College 1600 W Imperial Hwy *Web:* www.lasc.edu	Los Angeles	CA	90047	323-241-5225		162
Los Angeles Sparks 865 S Figueroa St Ste 104 *TF:* 888-694-3278 ■ *Web:* www.wnba.com	Los Angeles	CA	90017	213-929-1300	929-1325	714-2
Los Angeles Times 111 W Wilson Ave Ste 200 *Web:* www.latimes.com/socal/burbank-leader	Glendale	CA	91203	818-637-3200	241-1975	532-4
Los Angeles Times 202 W First St *TF:* 800-528-4637 ■ *Web:* www.latimes.com	Los Angeles	CA	90012	213-237-5000	237-4712	532-2
Los Angeles Times Festival of Books Los Angeles Times 202 W First St *TF:* 800-528-4637 ■ *Web:* events.latimes.com	Los Angeles	CA	90012	213-237-2335		281
Los Angeles Times Orange County 1375 W Sunflower Ave *Web:* www.reptiland.com	Costa Mesa	CA	92626	714-966-5600		532-2
Los Angeles Times-Washington Post News Service Inc 1150 15th St NW *TF:* 800-627-1150 ■ *Web:* www.washingtonpost.com	Washington	DC	20071	202-334-6000		530
Los Angeles Trade Technical College 400 W Washington Blvd **Fax:* Admissions ■ *Web:* www.lattc.edu	Los Angeles	CA	90015	213-763-7000	763-5386*	162
Los Angeles Turf Club Inc 285 W Huntington Dr *Web:* www.santaanita.com	Arcadia	CA	91007	626-574-7223		642
Los Angeles Unified School District (LAUSD) 333 S Beaudry Ave *TF:* 877-772-6273 ■ *Web:* home.lausd.net	Los Angeles	CA	90017	213-241-1000		685
Los Angeles Valley College 5800 Fulton Ave *Web:* www.lavc.edu	Valley Glen	CA	91401	818-947-2600		162
Los Angeles Zoo & Botanical Gardens 5333 Zoo Dr *Web:* www.lazoo.org	Los Angeles	CA	90027	323-644-4200	662-9786	823
Los Arcos 2000 E Dowling St *Web:* www.losarcosmexicanrestaurant.net	Anchorage	AK	99507	907-562-0477		671
Los Arcos Mexican Grill 4120 Commercial St SE	Salem	OR	97302	503-581-2740		671
Los Baez 2920 Commercial St SE	Salem	OR	97302	503-363-3109		671
Los Banditos 1258 Main St *Web:* foodspot.com	Green Bay	WI	54302	920-432-9462		671
Los Banos California 645 Seventh St *Web:* www.losbanos.org	Los Banos	CA	93635	209-827-7034		685
Los Cerritos Ctr 239 Los Cerritos Ctr *Web:* www.shoploscerritos.com	Cerritos	CA	90703	562-860-0341		460
Los Compadres 2102 W Pensacola St *Web:* bestmexicanfoodtallahassee.com	Tallahassee	FL	32304	850-576-8946		671
Los Compas Cafe 603 S Nevarez St	Las Cruces	NM	88001	575-523-1778		671
Los Gatos Chamber of Commerce 349 N Santa Cruz Ave *Web:* www.losgatoschamber.com	Los Gatos	CA	95030	408-354-9300	399-1594	139
Los Gatos Hotel Corp 210 E Main St *TF:* 800-238-6111 ■ *Web:* hotellosgatos.com	Los Gatos	CA	95030	408-335-1700		378
Los Gatos Lodge Inc 50 Los Gatos Saratoga Rd *Web:* losgatoslodge.com	Los Gatos	CA	95032	408-354-3300		132
Los Gatos Meadows 110 Wood Rd *Web:* jtm-esc.org/lgm/index	Los Gatos	CA	95030	408-354-0211	354-4193	672
Los Gatos Public Library (LGPL) 110 E Main St *Web:* www.losgatosca.gov	Los Gatos	CA	95030	408-354-8600	354-0578	434-3
Los Gatos Research Inc 67 E Evelyn Ave Ste 3 *Web:* www.lgrinc.com	Mountain View	CA	94041	650-965-7772		256
Los Gatos Union Elementary School District 17010 Roberts Rd *Web:* www.lgusd.org	Los Gatos	CA	95032	408-335-2000		685
Los Medanos College 2700 E Leland Rd *TF:* 800-677-6337 ■ *Web:* www.losmedanos.edu	Pittsburg	CA	94565	925-439-2181	427-1599	162
Los Molcajetes 4320 Western Ctr Blvd *Web:* www.losmolcajetes.com	Fort Worth	TX	76137	817-306-9000	306-9033	671
Los Olivos Mexican Patio 7328 E Second St *Web:* losolivosrestaurants.com	Scottsdale	AZ	85251	480-946-2256		671
Los Rancheros 7250 Plantation Rd *Web:* larumbamexicanrestaurant.com	Pensacola	FL	32504	850-476-1623	476-5595	671
Los Robles Hospital & Medical Ctr (LRHMC) 215 W Janss Rd *Web:* www.losrobleshospital.com	Thousand Oaks	CA	91360	805-497-2727		374-3
Los Tarascos 622 S College Ave *Web:* lostarascos.com	Fort Collins	CO	80524	970-416-0265		671
Los Tarascos 1759 Skyland Blvd E	Tuscaloosa	AL	35404	205-553-8896		671
Los Willows Inn & Spa 530 Stewart Canyon Rd *Web:* www.loswillows.com	Fallbrook	CA	92028	760-731-9400		707
Losasso Adv Inc 4853 N Ravenswood Ave *Web:* www.losasso.com	Chicago	IL	60640	773-271-2100		4
Office of Student Financial Assistance 602 N Fifth St PO Box 91202 *TF:* 800-259-5626 ■ *Web:* www.osfa.la.gov	Baton Rouge	LA	70802	225-219-1012	208-1496	725
LOSGH (Lady of The Sea General Hospital) 200 W 134th Pl *Web:* www.losgh.org	Cut Off	LA	70345	985-632-6401		374-3
Losi 4710 E Guasti Rd *TF:* 888-899-5674 ■ *Web:* www.losi.com	Ontario	CA	91761	909-390-9595	390-5356	762
Lost City Museum of Archeology 721 S Moapa Valley Blvd *TF:* 800-326-6868 ■ *Web:* nvculture.org/museums	Overton	NV	89040	775-687-4810	687-4168	520
Lost Creek State Park 3201 Spurgin Rd *Web:* stateparks.mt.gov	Missoula	MT	59804	406-542-5500		565
Lost Dutchman State Park 6109 N Apache Tr *Web:* azstateparks.com	Apache Junction	AZ	85119	480-982-4485		565
Lost Nation Theater 39 Main St *Web:* www.lostnationtheater.org	Montpelier	VT	05602	802-229-0492		573-4
Lost Planet Editorial 113 Spring St Fl 4 *Web:* www.quakebasket.com	New York	NY	10012	212-226-5678		4
Lost Recovery Network Lrni 406 dixon st *TF:* 877-693-1456 ■ *Web:* www.lrni.com	Vidalia	GA	30474	912-537-3901		463
Lost River Career Co-op 600 Elm St Ste 1 *Web:* lostrivercareercoop.com	Paoli	IN	47454	812-723-4818		623
Lost River Caverns 726 Durham St PO Box M *TF:* 888-529-1907 ■ *Web:* www.lostcave.com	Hellertown	PA	18055	610-838-8767	838-2961	50-5
Lost River State Park 321 Pk Dr *Web:* www.lostriversp.com	Mathias	WV	26812	304-897-5372		565
Lost Valley Ranch 29555 Goose Creek Rd *Web:* ranchweb.com	Sedalia	CO	80135	303-647-2311		239
Losurdo Foods Inc 20 Owens Rd *Web:* www.losurdofoods.com	Hackensack	NJ	07601	201-343-6680	343-8078	297-11
Losvet Company LLC 260 S Beverly Dr Ste 301	Beverly Hills	CA	90212	310-273-5364		652
Lot 401 44 Hospital St	Providence	RI	02903	401-490-3980		671
Lotek Wireless Inc 115 Pony Dr *Web:* www.lotek.com	Newmarket	ON	L3Y7B5	905-836-6680	836-6455	256
Loteria! Grill 6333 W Third St *Web:* www.loteriagrill.com	Los Angeles	CA	90036	323-930-2211		671
Loth Inc 3574 E Kemper Rd *Web:* www.lothexperts.com	Cincinnati	OH	45241	513-554-4900	554-8700	320
Lotos Club, The 5 E 66th St *Web:* lotosclub.org	New York	NY	10065	212-737-7100		181

	City	State	ZIP	Phone	Fax	Class
Lotsa Helping Hands Inc 118 N Peoria St FL 3 *Web:* www.lotsahelpinghands.com	Chicago	IL	60607	301-942-6430		387
Lotspeich Co 16101 NW 54th Ave *TF:* 800-771-6001 ■ *Web:* www.lotspeich.com	Miami	FL	33014	305-624-7777	624-4517	189-9
Lott Oil Company Inc 1855 Hwy 1 *TF:* 800-284-2540 ■ *Web:* www.lottoil.com	Natchitoches	LA	71457	318-352-2055		581
Lott (TE) & Co 221 N Seventh St *Web:* www.telott.com	Columbus	MS	39701	662-328-5387		2
Lotte USA Inc 5243 Wayne Rd *Web:* koalasmarch-usa.com	Battle Creek	MI	49037	269-963-6664	963-6695	296-6
Lotus Cars USA Inc 2236 Northmont Pkwy *TF Cust Svc:* 800-245-6887 ■ *Web:* www.lotuscars.com	Duluth	GA	30043	770-476-6540		59
Lotus Communications Corp 3301 Barham Blvd Ste 200 *Web:* www.lotuscorp.com	Los Angeles	CA	90068	323-512-2225	512-2224	643
Lotus Garden 111 E Hospitality Ln *Web:* lotusgardensanbernardino.com	San Bernardino	CA	92408	909-381-6171		671
Lotus Garden 810 Charnelton St *Web:* lotusgardenveg.com	Eugene	OR	97401	541-344-1928		671
Lotus Hotels Inc 2525 San Pablo Dam Rd *TF:* 800-462-7424 ■ *Web:* www.lotushotels.com	San Pablo	CA	94806	925-979-5758		377
Lotus Inn 905 N Expy *Web:* lotuscafe.us	Brownsville	TX	78520	956-542-5715		671
Lotus of Siam 953 E Sahara Ave *Web:* lotusofsiamlv.com	Las Vegas	NV	89104	702-735-3033	735-3033	671
Lou & Mickey's 224 Fifth Ave *Web:* www.louandmickeys.com	San Diego	CA	92101	619-237-4900		671
Lou Bachrodt Auto Group 7070 Cherryvale N Blvd *TF:* 866-635-2349 ■ *Web:* www.bachrodt.com	Rockford	IL	61112	815-332-3000		57
Lou's Brews & BBQ Grill 21501 Brookhurst St *Web:* www.lousbbq.com	Huntington Beach	CA	92646	714-965-5200		671
LOUD Technologies Inc 16220 Wood Red Rd NE *OTC:* LTEC ■ *TF:* 866-858-5832 ■ *Web:* www.loudtechinc.com	Woodinville	WA	98072	425-892-6500		52
LOUD3R Inc 541 Avon Ave Ste 301	Pasadena	CA	91105	626-768-2023		5
Louddoor 1001 harden St Market Place Shopping Ctr Ste 203 *Web:* www.louddoor.com	Columbia	SC	29205	803-765-2995		463
Louden Tunneling Company Inc 103 Shaw Rd	Sterling	VA	20166	703-450-5656		610
Loudermilk Barry (Rep R - GA) 329 Cannon HOB *Web:* loudermilk.house.gov	Washington	DC	20515	202-225-2931	225-2944	342-2
Loudon County 100 River Rd *Web:* www.loudoncounty.org	Loudon	TN	37774	865-458-5411		338
Loudon County Chamber of Commerce (LCCC) 318 Angel Row *Web:* www.loudoncountychamberofcommerce.com	Loudon	TN	37774	865-458-2067	458-1206	139
Loudon Park National Cemetery 3445 Frederick Rd *Web:* www.cem.va.gov/cems/nchp/loudonpark.asp	Baltimore	MD	21228	410-644-9696	644-1563	136
Loudoun County 1 Harrison St SE PO Box 7000 *Web:* www.loudoun.gov	Leesburg	VA	20177	703-777-0200	777-0325	338
Loudoun County Chamber of Commerce 19301 Winmeade Dr Ste 210 *TF:* 800-905-4942 ■ *Web:* www.loudounchamber.org	Lansdowne	VA	20176	703-777-2176	777-1392	139
Loudoun County Public Library 380 Old Waterford Rd *Web:* www.library.loudoun.gov	Leesburg	VA	20176	703-777-0368	771-5620	434-3
Loudoun House 209 Castlewood Dr *Fax Area Code: 209 ■ *TF:* 866-945-7920 ■ *Web:* nps.gov	Lexington	KY	40505	859-254-7024	372-0739*	50-3
Loudoun Stairs Inc 341 N Maple Ave *Web:* www.loudounstairs.com	Purcellville	VA	20132	703-478-8800		499
Loudoun Times-Mirror 1602 Village Market Blvd SE Ste 360 *Web:* www.loudountimes.com	Leesburg	VA	20175	703-777-1111	771-1285	532-4
Loudspeaker Components Corp 7596 US Hwy 61 S *Web:* loudspeakercomponents.com	Lancaster	WI	53813	608-723-2127	723-7775	52
Louhelen Baha'i School 3208 S State Rd *TF:* 800-894-9716 ■ *Web:* louhelen.org	Davison	MI	48423	810-653-5033	653-7181	673
Louie's Backyard 700 Waddell Ave *Web:* www.louiesbackyard.com	Key West	FL	33040	305-294-1061		671
Louie's Finer Meats Inc Hwy 63 N 2025 Superior Ave *Web:* www.louiesfinermeats.com	Cumberland	WI	54829	715-822-4728	822-3150	296-26
Louis A Johnson Veterans Affairs Medical Ctr 1 Medical Ctr Dr *TF:* 800-733-0512 ■ *Web:* www.clarksburg.va.gov	Clarksburg	WV	26301	304-623-3461		374-8
Louis A Weiss Memorial Hospital 4646 N Marine Dr *TF:* 800-503-1234 ■ *Web:* weisshospital.com	Chicago	IL	60640	773-878-8700		374-3
Louis Allis Co 645 Lester Doss Rd *TF:* 800-927-5292 ■ *Web:* louisallis.com	Warrior	AL	35180	205-590-2986	590-1571	518
Louis Berger Group Inc 412 Mt Kemble Ave *Web:* www.louisberger.com	Morristown	NJ	07960	973-407-1000		261
Louis Berkman Co, The 330 N Seventh St *Web:* www.follansbeesteel.com	Steubenville	OH	43952	740-283-3722		697
Louis Boston 60 Northern Ave *Web:* www.louisboston.com	Boston	MA	02210	617-262-6100		157-3
Louis Calder Memorial Library University of Miami School of Medicine R-950 PO Box 016950 *Web:* calder.med.miami.edu	Miami	FL	33101	305-243-6648	325-9670	434-1
Louis D Brandeis School of Law at the Univeristy of Louisville 2301 S Third St *Web:* louisville.edu/law	Louisville	KY	40208	502-852-6358	852-0862	167-1
Louis Dreyfus Co (LDCI) 355 S Ninth St *Web:* www.ldcom.com	Winter Garden	FL	34787	407-656-1000	656-1229	296-21
Louis Ferre Inc 302 Fifth Ave Ste 10 *TF:* 800-695-1061 ■ *Web:* www.louisferre.com	New York	NY	10001	212-239-1600		348
Louis Glunz Beer Inc 7100 N Capitol Dr *TF:* 800-933-2500 ■ *Web:* www.glunzbeers.com	Lincolnwood	IL	60712	847-676-9500	675-5678	81-1
Louis Hornick & Co Inc 117 E 38th St *Web:* www.louishornick.com	New York	NY	10016	212-679-2448	779-7098	746
Louis M Gerson Company Inc 16 Commerce Blvd *TF:* 800-225-8623 ■ *Web:* www.gersonco.com	Middleboro	MA	02346	508-947-4000	947-5442	576
Louis M Martini Winery 254 S St Helena Hwy *TF:* 866-549-2582 ■ *Web:* www.louismartini.com	Saint Helena	CA	94574	866-549-2582		80-3
Louis Maull Co, The 219 N Market St *Web:* www.maull.com	Saint Louis	MO	63102	314-241-8410		296-20
Louis Padnos Iron & Metal Co PO Box 1979 *TF:* 800-442-3509 ■ *Web:* www.padnos.com	Holland	MI	49422	616-396-6521		686
Louis Plung & Company LLP 420 Ft Duquesne Blvd Ste 1900 *Web:* www.louisplung.com	Pittsburgh	PA	15222	412-281-8771		2
Louis Riel School Division 900 St Mary's Rd *TF:* 800-940-3447 ■ *Web:* www.lrsd.net	Winnipeg	MB	R2M3R3	204-257-7827		685
Louis Shanks of Texas 2930 W Anderson Ln *Web:* www.louisshanksfurniture.com	Austin	TX	78757	512-451-6501	451-6520	321
Louis Stokes Cleveland Veterans Affairs Medical Ctr 10701 E Blvd *TF:* 888-838-6446 ■ *Web:* www.cleveland.va.gov	Cleveland	OH	44106	216-791-3800		374-8
Louis Tussaud's Plaza Wax Museum & Ripley's Believe It or Not! Museum 301 Alamo Plaza *Web:* www.ripleys.com	San Antonio	TX	78205	210-224-9299		520
Louis Vuitton NA Inc 1 E 57th St *TF Cust Svc:* 866-884-8866 ■ *Web:* louisvuitton.com	New York	NY	10022	212-758-8877		157-6
Louis' Basque Corner 301 E Fourth St *Web:* louisbasquecorner.com	Reno	NV	89501	775-323-7203		671
Louisa County 1 Woolfolk Ave *Web:* www.louisacounty.com	Louisa	VA	23093	540-967-0401	967-3411	338
Louisa County 117 S Main St *Web:* www.louisacountyiowa.org	Wapello	IA	52653	319-523-4541	523-4542	338
Louisbourg Investments 770 Main St 10th Fl *Web:* www.louisbourg.net	Moncton	NB	E1C8L1	506-853-5410		528
Louisburg College 501 N Main St *Fax: Admissions ■ *TF:* 800-775-0208 ■ *Web:* www.louisburg.edu	Louisburg	NC	27549	919-496-2521	496-1788*	162
Louise Hopkins Underwood Ctr for the Arts (LHUCA) 511 Ave K *Web:* www.lhuca.org	Lubbock	TX	79401	806-762-8606		50-2
Louise Paris Ltd 1407 Broadway 14th Fl *Web:* www.louiseparis.com	New York	NY	10018	212-354-5411		360-3
Louisiana						
Agriculture & Forestry Dept 5825 Florida Blvd *TF:* 866-927-2476 ■ *Web:* www.ldaf.state.la.us	Baton Rouge	LA	70806	225-922-1234	922-1253	339-19
Arts Div PO Box 44247 *Web:* www.crt.state.la.us	Baton Rouge	LA	70804	225-342-8180	342-8173	339-19
Attorney General 1885 N Third St *Web:* www.ag.state.la.us	Baton Rouge	LA	70802	225-326-6079	326-6757	339-19
Board of Regents 1201 N Third St *Web:* www.regents.state.la.us	Baton Rouge	LA	70802	225-342-4253	342-6926	339-19
Certified Public Accountants Board 601 Poydras St Ste 1770 *Web:* www.cpaboard.state.la.us	New Orleans	LA	70130	504-566-1244	566-1252	339-19
Community Services Office 627 N Fourth St *Fax Area Code: 225 ■ *TF:* 888-524-3578 ■ *Web:* www.dss.state.la.us	Baton Rouge	LA	70802	888-524-3578	342-2268*	339-19
Consumer Protection Office 1885 N Third St *TF:* 800-351-4889 ■ *Web:* www.ag.state.la.us	Baton Rouge	LA	70804	225-326-6465	326-6499	339-19
Contractors Licensing Board 2525 Quail Dr *TF:* 800-256-1392 ■ *Web:* www.lslbc.louisiana.gov	Baton Rouge	LA	70808	225-765-2301	765-2431	339-19
Crime Victims Reparations Board Box 3133 *TF:* 888-684-2846 ■ *Web:* www.lcle.state.la.us	Baton Rouge	LA	70821	225-342-1749		339-19
Culture Recreation & Tourism Dept PO Box 94361 *Web:* www.crt.state.la.us	Baton Rouge	LA	70804	225-342-0880	342-3207	339-19
Education Dept PO Box 94064 *Fax Area Code: 225 ■ *TF:* 877-453-2721 ■ *Web:* www.louisianabelieves.com	Baton Rouge	LA	70804	877-453-2721	342-0193*	339-19
Environmental Quality Dept 602 N Fifth St *TF:* 866-896-5337 ■ *Web:* www.deq.louisiana.gov	Baton Rouge	LA	70802	225-219-5337		339-19
Ethics Board 617 N Third St LaSalle Bldg Ste 10-36 *TF:* 800-842-6630 ■ *Web:* www.ethics.la.gov	Baton Rouge	LA	70802	225-219-5600	381-7271	339-19
Financial Institutions Office PO Box 94095 *TF:* 888-525-9414 ■ *Web:* www.ofi.state.la.us	Baton Rouge	LA	70804	225-925-4660	925-4548	339-19
Health & Hospitals Dept PO Box 629 *Web:* www.dhh.state.la.us	Baton Rouge	LA	70821	225-342-9500	342-5568	339-19
Historic Preservation Div 1051 N Third St Rm 405 *Web:* www.crt.state.la.us	Baton Rouge	LA	70802	225-342-8160	219-9772	339-19
Homeland Security & Emergency Preparedness Office 7667 Independence Blvd *Web:* lerc.dps.louisiana.gov	Baton Rouge	LA	70806	225-925-7500	925-7501	339-19
Housing Finance Agency 2415 Quail Dr *TF:* 888-454-2001 ■ *Web:* www.lhfa.state.la.us	Baton Rouge	LA	70808	225-763-8700	763-8710	339-19

Name / Address	City	State	Zip	Phone	Fax	Class
Information Services Office						
1201 N Third St	Baton Rouge	LA	70802	225-342-9288	342-0902	339-19
TF: 844-692-8019 ■ *Web:* louisiana.gov						
Insurance Dept 1702 N Third Str	Baton Rouge	LA	70802	225-342-5900		339-19
TF: 800-259-5300 ■ *Web:* www.ldi.la.gov						
Judicial Administrators Office						
400 Royal St Ste 1190	New Orleans	LA	70130	504-310-2550		339-19
Web: www.lasc.org						
Legislature PO Box 94062	Baton Rouge	LA	70804	225-342-2456		339-19
TF: 800-256-3793 ■ *Web:* www.legis.state.la.us						
Lieutenant Governor						
1051 N Third St	Baton Rouge	LA	70802	225-342-7009	342-1949	339-19
Web: www.crt.state.la.us						
Lottery Corp 555 Laurel St	Baton Rouge	LA	70801	225-297-2000	297-2005	452
TF: 877-770-7867 ■ *Web:* louisianalottery.com						
Medical Examiners Board (LSBME)						
630 Camp St	New Orleans	LA	70130	504-568-6820	568-6880	339-19
Web: www.lsbme.louisiana.gov						
Natural Resources Dept						
PO Box 94396	Baton Rouge	LA	70804	225-342-8955	342-3442	339-19
Web: dnr.louisiana.gov						
Office of Student Financial Assistance						
602 N Fifth St PO Box 91202	Baton Rouge	LA	70802	225-219-1012	208-1496	725
TF: 800-259-5626 ■ *Web:* www.osfa.la.gov						
Office of the Governor						
PO Box 94004	Baton Rouge	LA	70804	225-342-7015	342-7099	339-19
TF: 866-366-1121 ■ *Web:* gov.louisiana.gov						
Public Safety & Corrections Dept						
504 Mayflower St PO Box 94304	Baton Rouge	LA	70804	225-342-6740	342-3095	339-19
Web: www.doc.louisiana.gov						
Public Service Commission						
PO Box 91154	Baton Rouge	LA	70821	225-342-4999	342-2831	339-19
TF: 800-256-2397 ■ *Web:* www.lpsc.org						
Racing Commission						
320 N Carrollton Ave Ste 2-B	New Orleans	LA	70119	504-483-4000	483-4898	712
Web: horseracing.louisiana.gov						
Rehabilitation Services						
627 N Fourth St	Baton Rouge	LA	70802	225-219-2943		339-19
Web: www.dss.louisiana.gov						
Revenue Dept						
617 N Third St PO Box 201	Baton Rouge	LA	70802	855-307-3893		339-19
TF: 855-307-3893 ■ *Web:* www.rev.state.la.us						
Secretary of State PO Box 94125	Baton Rouge	LA	70804	225-922-2880		339-19
Web: www.sos.la.gov						
State Parks Office PO Box 44426	Baton Rouge	LA	70804	225-342-8111	342-8107	339-19
TF: 877-226-7652 ■ *Web:* www.crt.state.la.us						
State Police						
7919 Independence Blvd	Baton Rouge	LA	70896	225-925-6006		339-19
Web: www.lsp.org						
Supreme Court						
400 Royal St Ste 4200	New Orleans	LA	70130	504-310-2300		339-19
Web: www.lasc.org						
Tourism Office						
1051 N Third Stt PO Box 94291	Baton Rouge	LA	70802	225-342-8100	342-1051	339-19
Web: www.crt.state.la.us						
Treasurer						
900 N Third St Fl 3 PO Box 44154	Baton Rouge	LA	70802	225-342-0010	342-0046	339-19
Web: www.treasury.state.la.us/default.aspx						
Veterans Affairs Dept						
PO Box 94095	Baton Rouge	LA	70804	225-219-5000	219-5590	339-19
TF: 877-432-8982 ■ *Web:* www.vetaffairs.la.gov						
Weights & Measures Div						
PO Box 3098	Baton Rouge	LA	70821	225-922-1380	923-4877	339-19
Web: vwwwprd.doa.louisiana.gov						
Wildlife & Fisheries Dept						
2000 Quail Dr	Baton Rouge	LA	70898	225-765-2800		339-19
TF: 800-256-2749 ■ *Web:* www.wlf.louisiana.gov						
Workers' Compensation Office						
PO Box 94040	Baton Rouge	LA	70804	225-342-8980	342-5665	339-19
Web: www.laworks.net/WorkersComp/OWC_MainMenu.asp						
Workforce Commission						
1001 N 23rd St	Baton Rouge	LA	70802	225-342-3111	342-7960	259
Web: www.laworks.net						
Louisiana & Delta Railroad Inc (LDRR)						
402 W Washington St	New Iberia	LA	70560	337-364-9625		648
Web: www.gwrr.com						
Louisiana Art & Science Museum						
100 S River Rd	Baton Rouge	LA	70802	225-344-5272	344-9477	520
TF: 800-527-6843 ■ *Web:* www.lasm.org						
Louisiana Assn For, The Blind, The						
1750 Claiborne Ave	Shreveport	LA	71103	318-635-6471	635-8902	552-2
TF: 877-913-6471 ■ *Web:* www.lablind.com						
Louisiana Assn of Business & Industry						
3113 Vly Creek Dr PO Box 80258	Baton Rouge	LA	70898	225-928-5388		140
TF: 888-816-5224 ■ *Web:* www.labl.org						
Louisiana Association of Educators						
8322 One Kalais Ave	Baton Rouge	LA	70809	225-343-9243	343-9272	457-8
TF: 800-256-4523 ■ *Web:* www.lae.org						
Louisiana Banker PO Box 2871	Baton Rouge	LA	70821	225-387-3282	343-3159	531-1
TF: 888-249-3050 ■ *Web:* www.lba.org						
Louisiana Baptist Children's Home Inc (LBCH)						
7200 DeSiard St	Monroe	LA	71203	318-343-2244		48-15
TF: 877-345-7411 ■ *Web:* www.lbch.org						
Louisiana Bistro 337 Dauphine St	New Orleans	LA	70112	504-525-3335		671
Web: louisianabistro.net						
Louisiana Chemical Equipment Company LLC						
7911 Wrenwood Ste A	Baton Rouge	LA	70896	225-923-3602		690
Web: www.lcec.com						
Louisiana Children's Museum						
420 Julia St	New Orleans	LA	70130	504-586-0725	529-3666	521
Web: www.lcm.org						
Louisiana College 1140 College Dr	Pineville	LA	71359	318-487-7011	487-7550*	166
**Fax:* Admissions ■ *TF:* 800-487-1906 ■ *Web:* www.lacollege.edu						
Louisiana Creole Gumbo Restaurant						
2051 Gratiot Ave	Detroit	MI	48207	313-567-1200		671
Web: www.detroitgumbo.com						
Louisiana Culinary Institute						
10550 Airline Hwy	Baton Rouge	LA	70816	877-533-3198	769-8792*	163
**Fax Area Code:* 225 ■ *TF:* 877-533-3198 ■ *Web:* lci.edu						
Louisiana Delta Community College						
7500 Millhaven Rd	Monroe	LA	71203	318-345-9000		162
TF: 866-500-5322 ■ *Web:* www.ladelta.edu						
Louisiana Democratic Party						
701 Government St	Baton Rouge	LA	70802	225-336-4155	336-0046	616-1
Web: louisianademocrats.org						
Louisiana Dental Assn						
7833 Office Pk Blvd	Baton Rouge	LA	70809	225-926-1986	926-1886	227
TF: 800-388-6642 ■ *Web:* www.ladental.org						
Louisiana Medical Mutual Insurance Co						
1 Galleria Blvd Ste 700	Metairie	LA	70001	800-452-2120	841-5300*	391-5
**Fax Area Code:* 504 ■ *TF:* 800-452-2120 ■ *Web:* www.lammico.com						
Louisiana Naval War Memorial						
305 S River Rd	Baton Rouge	LA	70802	225-342-1942	342-2039	520
TF: 800-955-6962 ■ *Web:* www.usskidd.com						
Louisiana Office Supply Co						
7643 Florida Blvd	Baton Rouge	LA	70806	225-927-1110	927-3085	535
Web: losco.com						
Louisiana Organ Procurement Agency (LOPA)						
3545 N I-10 Service Rd Ste 300	Metairie	LA	70002	800-521-4483		545
TF: 800-521-4483 ■ *Web:* www.lopa.org						
Louisiana Pharmacists Assn						
450 Laurel St Ste 1400	Baton Rouge	LA	70801	225-346-6883	344-1132	585
TF: 877-252-5100 ■ *Web:* www.louisianapharmacists.com						
Louisiana Philharmonic Orchestra						
1010 Common St Ste 2120	New Orleans	LA	70112	504-523-6530		573-3
Web: www.lpomusic.com						
Louisiana Plastic Industries Inc						
501 Downing Pines Rd	West Monroe	LA	71292	318-388-4562	387-5642	600
TF: 800-277-7491 ■ *Web:* laplastic.com						
Louisiana Public Broadcasting						
7733 Perkins Rd	Baton Rouge	LA	70810	225-767-5660	767-4299	632
TF: 800-973-7246 ■ *Web:* lpb.org						
Louisiana Purchase Restaurant						
10320 111th St NW	Edmonton	AB	T5K1M9	780-420-6779		671
TF: 800-231-5511 ■ *Web:* www.louisianapurchase.ca						
Louisiana Radio Network Inc						
10500 Coursey Blvd Ste 104	Baton Rouge	LA	70816	225-291-2727		116
Web: louisianaradionetwork.com						
Louisiana Republican Party						
530 Lake Land Rd	Baton Rouge	LA	70802	225-389-4495	389-4493	616-2
Web: www.lagop.com						
Louisiana Restaurant						
1708 Aliceanna St	Baltimore	MD	21231	410-327-2610		671
Web: www.louisianasrestaurant.com						
Louisiana Sports Hall of Fame						
500 Front St	Natchitoches	LA	71457	318-238-4255	238-4258	522
Web: www.lasportshall.com						
Louisiana State Arboretum						
1300 Sudie Lawton Ln	Ville Platte	LA	70586	337-363-6289		565
TF: 888-677-6100 ■ *Web:* www.crt.state.la.us						
Louisiana State Bar Assn (LSBA)						
601 St Charles Ave	New Orleans	LA	70130	504-566-1600	566-0930	72
TF: 800-421-5722 ■ *Web:* www.lsba.org						
Louisiana State Library						
701 N Fourth St	Baton Rouge	LA	70802	225-342-4915	219-4725	434-5
Web: www.state.lib.la.us						
Louisiana State Medical Society						
6767 Perkins Rd Ste 100	Baton Rouge	LA	70808	225-763-8500		474
TF: 800-375-9508 ■ *Web:* www.lsms.org						
Louisiana State Museum						
751 Chartres St	New Orleans	LA	70116	504-568-6968	568-4995	520
TF: 800-568-6968 ■ *Web:* www.crt.state.la.us						
Louisiana State Nurses Assn, The (LSNA)						
5713 Superior Dr Ste A-6	Baton Rouge	LA	70816	225-201-0993		533
TF: 800-457-6378 ■ *Web:* www.lsna.org						
Louisiana State Penitentiary						
17544 Tunica Trace	Angola	LA	70712	225-655-4411		213
TF: 800-259-3333 ■ *Web:* doc.la.gov						
Louisiana State University						
Alexandria 8100 US Hwy 71 S	Alexandria	LA	71302	318-445-3672	473-6418*	166
**Fax:* Admissions ■ *TF Admissions:* 888-473-6417 ■ *Web:* www.lsua.edu						
Baton Rouge 110 Thomas Boyd Hall	Baton Rouge	LA	70803	225-578-3202	578-4433*	166
**Fax:* Admissions ■ *TF:* 888-846-6810 ■ *Web:* www.lsu.edu						
Eunice PO Box 1129	Eunice	LA	70535	337-457-7311	550-1306*	162
**Fax:* Admissions ■ *TF:* 888-367-5783 ■ *Web:* www.lsue.edu						
Shreveport 1 University Pl	Shreveport	LA	71115	318-797-5000	797-5286*	166
**Fax:* Admissions ■ *Web:* www.lsus.edu						
Louisiana State University Health Sciences Ctr (LSUHSC)						
1501 Kings Hwy	Shreveport	LA	71130	318-675-5000		374-3
TF: 800-337-3627 ■ *Web:* www.lsuhscshreveport.edu						
Louisiana State University Museum of Art						
100 Lafayette St	Baton Rouge	LA	70801	225-389-7200		520
Web: www.lsumoa.org						
Louisiana State University Paul M Hebert Law Ctr						
Paul M Hebert Law Ctr	Baton Rouge	LA	70803	225-578-8646	578-8647	167-1
Web: www.law.lsu.edu						
Louisiana State University School of Medicine in New Orleans						
433 Bolivar St	New Orleans	LA	70112	504-568-6262	568-7701	167-2
Web: www.medschool.lsuhsc.edu						
Louisiana State University School of Medicine in Shreveport						
1501 Kings Hwy PO Box 33932	Shreveport	LA	71130	318-675-5000	675-5000	167-2
TF: 800-337-3627 ■ *Web:* www.sh.lsuhsc.edu						
Louisiana State University System						
125 E Boyd Dr	Baton Rouge	LA	70803	225-578-3357		786
TF: 800-234-5046						
Louisiana Tech University						
305 Wisteria St	Ruston	LA	71272	318-257-2000	257-2499*	166
**Fax:* Admissions ■ *TF Admissions:* 800-528-3241 ■ *Web:* www.latech.edu						
Louisiana Tech University Prescott Memorial Library						
PO Box 10408	Ruston	LA	71272	318-257-3555		434-6
Web: www.latech.edu/library						
Louisiana Valve Source Inc						
101 Metals Dr	Youngsville	LA	70592	337-856-9100		454
Web: www.lavalve.com						
Louisiana Veterinary Medical Assn						
8550 United Plaza Blvd Ste 1001	Baton Rouge	LA	70809	225-928-5862	408-4422	795
TF: 800-524-2996 ■ *Web:* www.lvma.org						

Name / Address	City	State	ZIP	Phone	Fax	Class
Louisiana War Veterans' Home 4739 Hwy 10 — *Web:* wwwprd.doa.louisiana.gov	Jackson	LA	70748	225-634-5265	634-4057	793
Louisiana-Pacific Corp 414 Union St Ste 2000 — *NYSE:* LPX ■ *TF:* 888-820-0325 ■ *Web:* www.lpcorp.com	Nashville	TN	37219	615-986-5600	986-5666	683
Louisville & Indiana Railroad Co 500 Willinger Ln — *Web:* www.anacostia.com	Jeffersonville	IN	47130	812-288-0940		649
Louisville & Jefferson County Convention & Visitors Bureau 401 W Main St Ste 2300 — *TF:* 800-626-5646 ■ *Web:* www.gotolouisville.com	Louisville	KY	40202	502-584-2121	584-6697	206
Louisville Athletic Club LLC 9565 Taylorsville Rd — *Web:* athleticclubs.org	Louisville	KY	40299	502-753-0999		354
Louisville Ballet 315 E Main St — *Web:* www.louisvilleballet.org	Louisville	KY	40202	502-583-3150	583-0006	573-1
Louisville Bedding Co 10400 Bunsen Way — *Web:* www.loubed.com	Louisville	KY	40299	502-491-3370		746
Louisville Bible College 8013 Damascus Rd	Louisville	KY	40228	502-231-5221		166
Louisville City Hall 601 W Jefferson St — *Web:* www.louisvilleky.gov	Louisville	KY	40202	502-574-1100		337
Louisville Eccentric Observer 607 W Main St Ste 001 — *Web:* www.leoweekly.com	Louisville	KY	40202	502-895-9770	895-9779	532-5
Louisville Free Public Library 301 York St — *Web:* www.lfpl.org	Louisville	KY	40203	502-574-1611		434-3
Louisville Golf Club Co 2320 Watterson Trail — *TF:* 800-456-1631 ■ *Web:* www.louisvillegolf.com	Louisville	KY	40299	502-491-5490	491-6189	710
Louisville International Airport 700 Administration Dr PO Box 9129 — *TF:* 800-433-7300 ■ *Web:* flylouisville.com	Louisville	KY	40209	502-368-6524	367-0199	27
Louisville Lumber & Millwork Co 1400 Lincoln Ave — *Web:* www.louisvillelumber.com	Louisville	KY	40213	502-459-8710		499
Louisville Magazine 137 W Muhammad Ali Blvd Ste 102 — *TF:* 866-832-0011 ■ *Web:* www.louisville.com	Louisville	KY	40202	502-625-0100	625-0109	457-22
Louisville Municipal School District 112 S Columbus Ave PO Box 909 — *Web:* www.louisville.k12.ms.us	Louisville	MS	39339	662-773-3411	773-4013	685
Louisville Orchestra 323 W Broadway Ste 700 — *Web:* www.louisvilleorchestra.org	Louisville	KY	40202	502-587-8681		573-3
Louisville Palace Theatre 625 S Fourth St — *TF:* 800-745-3000 ■ *Web:* www.louisvillepalace.com	Louisville	KY	40202	502-583-4555		572
Louisville Presbyterian Theological Seminary 1044 Alta Vista Rd — *TF:* 800-264-1839 ■ *Web:* www.lpts.edu	Louisville	KY	40205	502-895-3411	895-1096	167-3
Louisville Science Ctr 727 W Main St — *TF:* 800-591-2203 ■ *Web:* www.kysciencecenter.org	Louisville	KY	40202	502-561-6100	561-6145	520
Louisville Slugger Museum 800 W Main St — **Fax Area Code:* 502 ■ *TF:* 877-775-8443 ■ *Web:* www.sluggermuseum.com	Louisville	KY	40202	877-775-8443	585-1179*	522
Louisville State Recreation Area 15810 Hwy 50 — *Web:* outdoornebraska.gov/louisville	Louisville	NE	68037	402-234-6855		565
Louisville Technical Institute *Sullivan College of Technology & Design* 3901 Atkinson Sq Dr — *TF:* 800-844-6528 ■ *Web:* www.sctd.edu	Louisville	KY	40218	502-456-6509	456-2341	800
Louisville Zoo 1100 Trevilian Way — *TF:* 866-229-0502 ■ *Web:* www.louisvillezoo.org	Louisville	KY	40213	502-459-2181	459-2196	823
Louisville-Jefferson County 527 W Jefferson St — *Web:* www.louisvilleky.gov	Louisville	KY	40202	502-574-3427		338
Loup County PO Box 138 — *Web:* www.co.loup.ne.us	Taylor	NE	68879	308-942-6146	942-3103	338
Loup Public Power District (LPPD) 2404 15th St PO Box 988 — *TF:* 866-869-2087 ■ *Web:* www.loup.com	Columbus	NE	68602	402-564-3171	564-0970	245
Lourdes College 6832 Convent Blvd — **Fax:* Admissions ■ *TF:* 800-878-3210 ■ *Web:* www.lourdes.edu	Sylvania	OH	43560	419-885-5291	882-3987*	166
Lourdes Homecare & Hospice 2855 Jackson St — *TF:* 800-870-7460 ■ *Web:* www.elourdes.com	Paducah	KY	42003	270-444-2262		371
Lourdes Industries Inc 65 Hoffman Ave — *Web:* www.lourdesinc.com	Hauppauge	NY	11788	631-234-6600		789
Lourdes Medical Ctr 520 N Fourth Ave — *Web:* www.yourlourdes.com	Pasco	WA	99301	509-547-7704		374-3
Lourdes Medical Ctr of Burlington County 218 Sunset Rd — *Web:* www.lourdesnet.org	Willingboro	NJ	08046	609-835-2900		374-3
Lourdes-Noreen Mckeen Residence For Geriatric Care Inc 315 S Flagler Dr — *Web:* www.lourdesmckeen.org	West Palm Beach	FL	33401	561-655-8544		371
Loureiro Engineering Associates 100 Northwest Dr — *Web:* www.loureiro.com	Plainville	CT	06062	860-747-6181		727
Lou-Rich Inc 100 Commercial St — *Web:* www.lou-rich.com	Hayward	MN	56043	507-377-1400		454
Lou-Rich Machine Tool Inc 505 W Front St — *TF:* 800-893-3235 ■ *Web:* www.lou-rich.com	Albert Lea	MN	56007	507-377-8910	373-7110	757
Lous Clinical Laboratory Inc 635 N Grandview — *Web:* www.drug-screen.com	Odessa	TX	79761	432-332-9421		415
Loutit District Library 407 Columbus St — *Web:* www.loutitlibrary.org	Grand Haven	MI	49417	616-842-5560	847-0570	434-3

Name / Address	City	State	ZIP	Phone	Fax	Class
Love & Quiches Desserts 178 Hanse Ave — *TF:* 800-525-5251 ■ *Web:* www.loveandquiches.com	Freeport	NY	11520	516-623-8800		297-11
Love & War In Texas 601 E Plano Pkwy — *Web:* www.loveandwarintexas.com	Plano	TX	75074	972-422-6201	633-1225	671
Love Adv Inc 770 S Post Oak Ln Ste 101 — *Web:* www.loveadv.com	Houston	TX	77056	713-552-1055		4
Love Communications 546 South 200 West — *Web:* www.lovecomm.net	Salt Lake City	UT	84101	801-519-8880		636
Love County 405 W Main St Ste 203 — *TF:* 800-536-7134 ■ *Web:* love.okcounties.org	Marietta	OK	73448	580-276-3059		338
Love Envelopes Inc 10733 E Ute St — *TF:* 800-532-9747 ■ *Web:* www.loveenvelopes.com	Tulsa	OK	74116	918-836-3535	832-9978	263
Love Heating & Air Conditioning Inc 4115 E Tenth St — *Web:* love-hvac.com	Indianapolis	IN	46201	317-353-2141		610
Love Mia (Rep R - UT) 217 Cannon HOB — *Web:* love.house.gov	Washington	DC	20515	202-225-3011	225-5638	342-2
Love Scherle & Bauer PC 310 Grant St Ste 1020 — *Web:* lovescherlebauer.com	Pittsburgh	PA	15219	412-281-8270		2
Love Stores 144 W 72nd St	New York	NY	10023	212-877-5351		237
Love to Swim & Tumble School 15502 Huebner Rd Ste 111 — *Web:* www.love-to-swim.com	San Antonio	TX	78248	210-492-2606		711
Love's Travel Stops 10601 N Pennsylvania Ave — *TF:* 800-388-0983 ■ *Web:* www.loves.com	Oklahoma City	OK	73120	800-388-0983		204
Lovegreen Industrial Services Inc 2280 Sibley Ct — *TF:* 800-262-8284 ■ *Web:* www.lovegreen.com	Eagan	MN	55122	651-890-1166	890-8370	470
Lovejoy Hospice 939 SE Figth St	Grants Pass	OR	97526	541-474-1193		371
Lovejoy Inc 2655 Wisconsin Ave — *Web:* www.lovejoy-inc.com	Downers Grove	IL	60515	630-852-0500		620
Lovejoy Tool Company Inc 133 Main St — *TF:* 800-843-8376 ■ *Web:* www.lovejoytool.com	Springfield	VT	05156	802-885-2194	885-9511	493
Lovelace Medical Ctr 5400 Gibson Blvd SE — *TF:* 888-281-6531 ■ *Web:* www.lovelace.com	Albuquerque	NM	87108	505-727-8000	727-8000	374-3
Lovelace Respiratory Research Institute (LRRI) 2425 Ridgecrest Dr SE — *TF:* 800-700-1016 ■ *Web:* www.lrri.org	Albuquerque	NM	87108	505-348-9400		668
Loveland Chamber of Commerce 5400 Stone Creek Cir Ste 200 — *TF:* 800-216-0680 ■ *Web:* www.loveland.org	Loveland	CO	80538	970-667-6311	667-5211	139
Loveland Daily Reporter-Herald 201 E Fifth St — *TF:* 800-244-5613 ■ *Web:* www.reporterherald.com	Loveland	CO	80537	970-669-5050	667-1111	532-2
Loveland Ready Mix Concrete Inc 644 N County Rd 19 E	Loveland	CO	80537	970-667-1108		182
Loveland SC & Co 127 W Supawna Rd	Pennsville	NJ	08070	856-935-8100		312
Love-Less Ash Co 1285 E 650 S — *Web:* www.lovelessash.com	Price	UT	84501	435-637-5885		427
Lovelock Correctional Ctr 1200 Prison Rd — *Web:* doc.nv.gov	Lovelock	NV	89419	775-273-1300		213
Lovely Lane Museum 2200 St Paul St — *Web:* www.lovelylanemuseum.org	Baltimore	MD	21218	410-889-4458		520
Loveman Steel Corp 5455 Perkins Rd — *TF:* 800-568-3626 ■ *Web:* www.lovemansteel.com	Bedford Heights	OH	44146	800-568-3626		492
Loven Contracting Inc 1100 S Pinnacle St — *Web:* www.lovencontracting.com	Flagstaff	AZ	86001	928-774-9040		186
Lovers Key State Park 8700 Estero Blvd — *TF:* 800-326-3521 ■ *Web:* www.floridastateparks.org	Fort Myers Beach	FL	33931	239-463-4588	463-8851	565
Lovers Lane & Co 46750 Port St — *Web:* www.loverslane.com	Plymouth	MI	48170	734-414-0010		157-6
Loveshaw Corp 2206 Easton Tpke — *TF Cust Svc:* 800-747-1586 ■ *Web:* www.loveshaw.com	South Canaan	PA	18459	570-937-4921		547
Lovewell State Park 2446 250 Rd — *Web:* ksoutdoors.com/State-Parks/Locations/Lovewell	Webber	KS	66970	785-753-4971		565
Loving County 100 Bell St PO Box 194	Mentone	TX	79754	432-377-2441		338
Loving Hands Home Care Services Inc 1777 Hamilton Ave — *Web:* lovinghandshmcare.com	San Jose	CA	95125	408-266-8331		363
Lovio George Inc 681 W Forest Ave — *TF:* 800-874-2458 ■ *Web:* www.loviogeorge.com	Detroit	MI	48201	313-832-2210		636
Lovitt & Touche Inc 7202 E Rosewood St Ste 200 PO Box 32702 — *TF:* 800-426-2756 ■ *Web:* www.lovitt-touche.com	Tucson	AZ	85710	520-722-3000	722-7245	390
LOW (Loners on Wheels) 1795 O'Kelley Rd SE — *Web:* www.lonersonwheels.com	Deming	NM	88030	575-544-7303		48-23
Lowden State Park 1411 N River Rd — *Web:* www.dnr.illinois.gov/Parks/Pages/Lowden.aspx	Oregon	IL	61061	815-732-6828		565
Lowden-Miller State Forest 1365 W Castle Rock Rd — *Web:* www.dnr.illinois.gov/parks/pages/castlerock.aspx	Oregon	IL	61061	815-732-7329		565
Lowe Art Museum University of Miami 1301 Stanford Dr — *Web:* www6.miami.edu/lowe	Coral Gables	FL	33124	305-284-3535	284-2024	520
Lowe Boats 2900 Industrial Dr — *TF:* 800-641-4372 ■ *Web:* www.loweboats.com	Lebanon	MO	65536	417-532-9101	532-8991	90
Lowe Electric Supply Co 1525 Forsyth St PO Box 4767 — *TF:* 800-868-8661 ■ *Web:* www.loweelectric.com	Macon	GA	31208	478-743-8661	742-3374	246
Lowe Enterprises 11777 San Vicente Blvd Ste 900 — *TF:* 800-842-2252 ■ *Web:* www.loweenterprises.com	Los Angeles	CA	90049	310-820-6661	207-1132	655
Lowe Hauptman Ham & Berner LLP 2318 Mill Rd Ste 1400 — *TF:* 800-973-1177 ■ *Web:* www.ipfirm.com	Alexandria	VA	22314	703-684-1111		445

Name / Address	City	State	ZIP	Phone	Fax	Class
Lowe Products Company Inc 777 Potomac Farms Dr *Web:* www.lowe-products.com	Shepherdstown	WV	25443	304-876-2546		200
Lowe's 1804 Hall Ave *TF:* 800-234-5258 ■ *Web:* www.lowesmarket.com	Littlefield	TX	79339	806-385-3366	385-8629	345
Lowe's Cos Inc 1000 Lowe's Blvd *NYSE: LOW* ■ *TF:* 800-445-6937 ■ *Web:* www.lowes.com	Mooresville	NC	28117	704-758-1000		364
Lowe's Home Centers Inc PO Box 1111 *TF:* 800-445-6937 ■ *Web:* www.lowes.com	North Wilkesboro	NC	28656	800-445-6937		364
Lowell Correctional Institution-Women's Unit 11120 NW Gainesville Rd *Web:* dc.state.fl.us	Ocala	FL	34482	352-401-5301	401-5331	213
Lowell D Holmes Museum of Anthropology Neff Hall 1845 Fairmount PO Box 52 *Web:* webs.wichita.edu/anthropology	Wichita	KS	67260	316-978-3195	978-3351	520
Lowell Five Cent Savings Bank, The 1 Merrimack Plaza *Web:* www.lowellfive.com	Lowell	MA	01852	978-452-1300		70
Lowell General Hospital (LGH) 295 Varnum Ave *TF:* 800-544-2424 ■ *Web:* www.lowellgeneral.org	Lowell	MA	01854	978-937-6000	937-6869	374-3
Lowell Heritage State Park 160 Pawtucket Blvd	Lowell	MA	01854	978-458-8750		565
Lowell Inc 9425 83rd Ave N *Web:* www.lowellinc.com	Brooklyn Park	MN	55445	763-425-3355		567
Lowell Inn 102 N Second St *Web:* www.lowellinn.com	Stillwater	MN	55082	651-439-1100		379
Lowell Manufacturing Co 100 Integram Dr *TF:* 800-325-9660 ■ *Web:* www.lowellmfg.com	Pacific	MO	63069	636-257-3400	257-6606	52
Lowell National Historical Park 67 Kirk St *Web:* www.nps.gov	Lowell	MA	01852	978-970-5000		564
Lowell Observatory 1400 W Mars Hill Rd *TF:* 800-289-5898 ■ *Web:* www.lowell.edu	Flagstaff	AZ	86001	928-774-3358	774-6296	598
Lowell Sun Publishing Co 491 Dutton St **Fax:* Edit ■ *TF Cust Svc:* 800-359-1300 ■ *Web:* www.lowellsun.com	Lowell	MA	01854	978-458-7100	970-4600*	637-8
Lowe-Martin Company Inc 400 Hunt Club Rd *TF:* 866-521-9871 ■ *Web:* www.lmgroup.com	Ottawa	ON	K1V1C1	613-741-0962		225
Lowen Corp PO Box 1528 *TF:* 800-835-2365 ■ *Web:* www.lowen.com	Hutchinson	KS	67504	620-663-2161		627
Lowenstein Sandler PC 65 Livingston Ave St 2 *TF:* 800-973-1177 ■ *Web:* www.lowenstein.com	Roseland	NJ	07068	973-597-2500		428
Lowenstein-Yost Assoc Inc 121 W 27th St Ste 501 *Web:* www.lowensteinassociates.com	New York	NY	10001	212-206-1630	727-0280	444
Lowenthal Alan (Rep D - CA) 125 Cannon HOB *Web:* lowenthal.house.gov	Washington	DC	20515	202-225-7924	225-7926	342-2
Lower Bucks County Chamber of Commerce 409 Hood Blvd *TF:* 800-786-2234 ■ *Web:* www.lbccc.org	Fairless Hills	PA	19030	215-943-7400	943-7404	139
Lower Bucks Hospital 501 Bath Rd *Web:* www.lowerbuckshosp.com	Bristol	PA	19007	215-785-9200	785-9825	374-3
Lower Cape Fear Hospice & Life Care 1414 Physicians Dr *TF:* 800-733-1476 ■ *Web:* www.hospiceandlifecarecenter.org	Wilmington	NC	28401	910-796-7900	796-7901	371
Lower Chatanika River State Recreation Area c/o Northern Area Office 3700 Airport Way *Web:* www.dnr.alaska.gov	Fairbanks	AK	99709	907-269-8400		565
Lower Columbia College 1600 Maple St PO Box 3010 **Fax:* Admissions ■ *TF:* 866-900-2311 ■ *Web:* www.lowercolumbia.edu	Longview	WA	98632	360-442-2301	442-2379*	162
Lower East Side Business Improvement District 54 Orchard St *Web:* lowereastside.org	New York	NY	10002	212-226-9010		460
Lower East Side Tenement Museum National Historic Site 108 Orchard St *Web:* www.tenement.org	New York	NY	10002	212-431-0233	431-0402	520
Lower Fort Garry National Historic Site 5925 Hwy 9 *Web:* www.pc.gc.ca/eng/lhn-nhs/mb/fortgarry/index.aspx	Saint Andrews	MB	R1A4A8	204-785-6050	482-5887	563
Lower Keys Chamber of Commerce 31020 Overseas Hwy *TF:* 800-872-3722 ■ *Web:* www.lowerkeyschamber.com	Big Pine Key	FL	33043	305-872-2411	872-0752	139
Lower Keys Medical Ctr 5900 College Rd *TF:* 800-355-2470 ■ *Web:* www.lkmc.com	Key West	FL	33040	305-294-5531	294-8065	374-3
Lower Valley Energy 236 N Washington PO Box 188 *TF:* 800-882-5875 ■ *Web:* www.lvenergy.com	Afton	WY	83110	307-885-3175	885-5787	245
Lower Wekiva River Preserve State Park 1800 Wekiwa Cir *TF:* 800-326-3521 ■ *Web:* www.floridastateparks.org	Apopka	FL	32712	407-884-2008	884-2039	565
Lower White River Museum State Park 2009 Main St *Web:* www.arkansasstateparks.com	Des Arc	AR	72040	870-256-3711		565
Lower Yellowstone Rural Electric Assn Inc 3200 W Holly St PO Box 1047 *TF:* 844-441-5627 ■ *Web:* www.lyrec.com	Sidney	MT	59270	406-488-1602	488-6524	245
Lowes Food Stores Inc 1381 Old Mill Cir Ste 200 *TF:* 800-669-5693 ■ *Web:* www.lowesfoods.com	Winston-Salem	NC	27103	336-659-0180	768-4702	345
Lowes Wilshire Market 301 N Richman Ave	Fullerton	CA	92832	714-519-3249		297-8
Lowey Nita (Rep D - NY) 2365 Rayburn Bldg *Web:* lowey.house.gov	Washington	DC	20515	202-225-6506	225-0546	342-2
Lown Cardiovascular Research Foundation 21 Longwood Ave *Web:* lowninstitute.org	Brookline	MA	02446	617-992-9322		305
Lowndes County 1121 Main St	Columbus	MS	39701	662-329-5884		338
Lowndes County 325 W Savannah Ave *TF:* 800-829-3676 ■ *Web:* www.lowndescounty.com	Valdosta	GA	31601	229-671-2400	245-5222	338
Lowrance Electronics Inc 12000 E Skelly Dr *TF:* 800-628-4487 ■ *Web:* www.lowrance.com	Tulsa	OK	74128	918-437-6881		529
Lowrey Organ Co 989 AEC Dr *TF:* 800-451-5939 ■ *Web:* www.lowrey.com	Wood Dale	IL	60191	800-451-5939		527
Lowrider Magazine 2400 E Katella Ave 11th Fl *Web:* www.lowrider.com	Anaheim	CA	92806	714-939-2400		457-3
Lowry Park Zoo 1101 W Sligh Ave *Web:* www.lowryparkzoo.org	Tampa	FL	33604	813-935-8552	935-9486	823
Lowville Producers Dairy Co-op 7396 Utica Blvd *TF:* 800-342-3009 ■ *Web:* www.gotgoodcheese.com	Lowville	NY	13367	315-376-3921	376-3442	297-4
Loxcreen Co Inc, The 1630 Old Dunbar Rd PO Box 4004 *TF:* 800-330-5699 ■ *Web:* www.loxcreen.com	West Columbia	SC	29172	803-822-8200	822-8547	485
Loyal American Life Insurance Co *Great American Financial Resources Inc* PO Box 26580 *TF:* 800-315-5522 ■ *Web:* www.gafri.com	Austin	TX	78755	800-545-4269		391-2
Loyal Termite & Pest Control Company Inc 2610 E Parham Rd *Web:* www.loyalpest.com	Richmond	VA	23228	804-737-7777		577
LOYAL3 Holdings Inc 150 California St Ste 400 *Web:* www.loyal3.com	San Francisco	CA	94111	415-981-0700		387
Loyalist College Wallbridge-Loyalist Rd *TF:* 800-992-5866 ■ *Web:* www.loyalistcollege.com	Belleville	ON	K8N5B9	613-969-1913		162
Loyalist Group Ltd 1255 Bay St 8th Fl *TF:* 800-555-0888 ■ *Web:* www.loyalistgroup.com	Toronto	ON	M5R2A9	416-969-9800		242
Loyalty 360 Inc 4120 Dumont St *Web:* loyalty360.org	Cincinnati	OH	45226	513-800-0360		5
Loyalty Factor LLC 579 Sagamore Ave Unit 109 *Web:* www.loyaltyfactor.com	Portsmouth	NH	03801	603-334-3401		196
Loyalty Methods Inc 80 Yesler Way Ste 310 *TF:* 800-693-2040 ■ *Web:* www.loyaltymethods.com	Seattle	WA	98104	206-257-2111		463
LoyaltyExpress Inc 53 Commerce Way *TF:* 800-882-1844 ■ *Web:* www.loyaltyexpress.com	Woburn	MA	01801	781-938-1175		195
Loyd Keith Friedlander Partners Ltd 18 Prospect St	Huntington	NY	11743	631-424-2600		390
Loyd's Aviation 1601 Skyway Dr Ste 100 PO Box 80958 *TF:* 800-284-1334 ■ *Web:* www.bakersfieldjetcenter.com	Bakersfield	CA	93308	661-393-1334	393-0824	63
Loyd's Electric Supply Inc (LES) 838 Stonetree Dr *TF:* 800-492-4030 ■ *Web:* www.loydselectric.com	Branson	MO	65616	417-334-2171	334-6635	246
Loy-Lange Box Co 222 Russell Blvd *Web:* www.loylangebox.com	St. Louis	MO	63104	314-776-4712		100
Loyola Academy 1100 Laramie *TF:* 800-222-1222 ■ *Web:* www.goramblers.org	Wilmette	IL	60091	847-256-1100		685
Loyola College 4501 N Charles St **Fax:* Admissions ■ *TF:* 800-221-9107 ■ *Web:* www.loyola.edu	Baltimore	MD	21210	410-617-5012	617-2176*	166
Loyola Enterprises Inc 2984 S Lynnhaven Rd Ste 101 *TF:* 800-937-9021 ■ *Web:* www.loyola.com	Virginia Beach	VA	23452	757-498-6118		261
Loyola Marymount Law School 919 Albany St *Web:* www.lls.edu	Los Angeles	CA	90015	213-736-1000	736-6523	167-1
Loyola Marymount University 1 LMU Dr *TF:* 800-568-4636 ■ *Web:* www.lmu.edu	Los Angeles	CA	90045	310-338-2700	338-2797	166
Loyola Paper Co 951 W Lunt Ave	Elk Grove Village	IL	60007	847-956-7770		554
Loyola Retreat House 161 James St *Web:* www.loyola.org	Morristown	NJ	07960	973-539-0740	898-9839	673
Loyola University *Monroe Library* 6363 St Charles Ave *Web:* library.loyno.edu	New Orleans	LA	70118	504-864-7111	864-7247	434-6
New Orleans 6363 St Charles Ave **Fax:* Admissions ■ *TF Admissions:* 800-456-9652 ■ *Web:* www.loyno.edu	New Orleans	LA	70118	504-865-3240	865-3383*	166
Loyola University Chicago *Cudahy Library* 1032 W Sheridan Rd *Web:* libraries.luc.edu/cudahy	Chicago	IL	60660	773-508-2632		434-6
Lake Shore 6525 N Sheridan Rd *TF:* 800-262-2373 ■ *Web:* www.luc.edu	Chicago	IL	60626	773-508-3075	508-8926	166
School of Law 25 E Pearson St *TF:* 866-596-7890 ■ *Web:* www.luc.edu	Chicago	IL	60611	312-915-7120	915-7201	167-1
Water Tower 820 N Michigan Ave **Fax:* Admissions ■ *TF Admissions:* 800-262-2373 ■ *Web:* www.luc.edu	Chicago	IL	60611	312-915-6500	915-7216*	166
Loyola University Chicago Stritch School of Medicine 2160 S First Ave *Web:* www.meddean.luc.edu	Maywood	IL	60153	708-216-3229		167-2
Loyola University Medical Ctr 2160 S First Ave *TF:* 888-584-7888 ■ *Web:* www.luhs.org	Maywood	IL	60153	888-584-7888		374-3
Loyola University New Orleans College of Law 7214 St Charles Ave Campus Box 903 *Web:* www.law.loyno.edu	New Orleans	LA	70118	504-861-5550		167-1
Loysville Youth Development Ctr 10 Opportunity Dr	Loysville	PA	17047	717-789-3841		412
Lozano Caseworks Inc 242 W Hanna St	Colton	CA	92324	909-783-7530		321
Lozano Smith 7404 N Spalding Ave *TF:* 800-900-4250 ■ *Web:* www.lozanosmith.com	Fresno	CA	93720	559-431-5600		428
Lozier Corp 6336 John J Pershing Dr **Fax:* Cust Svc ■ *TF:* 800-228-9882 ■ *Web:* www.lozier.com	Omaha	NE	68110	402-457-8000	457-8297*	286
Lozier Group 1300 114th Ave SE Ste 100 *Web:* www.loziergroup.com	Bellevue	WA	98004	425-635-3922		653
Lozier's Box R Ranch 552 Willow Creek Rd PO Box 100 *TF:* 800-822-8466 ■ *Web:* www.boxr.com	Cora	WY	82925	307-367-4868	367-6260	239
LP (Lakeland Plastics Inc) 1550 McCormick Blvd *TF:* 800-454-4006 ■ *Web:* www.lakelandplastics.com	Mundelein	IL	60060	847-680-1550	680-1595	599

	Phone	Fax	Class
LP Amina Inc 13850 Ballantyne Corporate Pl Ste 125 .... Charlotte NC 28277 *Web:* www.lpamina.com	704-944-5425		192
LP Field 1 Titans Way .... Nashville TN 37213 *TF:* 800-745-3000 ■ *Web:* www.titansonline.com	615-565-4300		720
LPA Designs 21 Gregory Dr Ste 140 .... South Burlington VT 05403 *Web:* www.lpadesign.com	802-658-0038		407
LPA Inc 5161 California Ave Ste 100............... Irvine CA 92617 *Web:* www.lpainc.com	949-261-1001	260-1190	261
LPC 170 Woodside Ave P.O. Box 2608.......... Lewisburg TN 37091 *TF:* 800-559-1526 ■ *Web:* www.lewisburgprinting.com	800-559-1526		627
LPC Crude Oil Marketing LLC 408 W Wall .... Midland TX 79701 *Web:* lpccrude.com	432-682-8555		536
LPCH (Lucile Packard Children's Hospital) 725 Welch Rd .... Palo Alto CA 94304 **Fax:* Admitting ■ *TF:* 800-995-5724 ■ *Web:* stanfordchildrens.org	650-497-8000	497-8968*	374-1
LPCiminelli 2421 Main St .... Buffalo NY 14214 *Web:* www.lpciminelli.com	716-855-1200	854-6655	186
Lpd Music International Corp 32575 Industrial Dr................... Madison Heights MI 48071 *Web:* www.lpdmusic.com	248-585-9630		526
LPGA (Ladies Professional Golf Assn) 100 International Golf Dr .... Daytona Beach FL 32124 *Web:* www.lpga.com	386-274-6200	274-1099	48-22
LPH (La Porte Hospital) 1007 Lincolnway PO Box 250.................. La Porte IN 46350 *TF:* 800-235-6204 ■ *Web:* www.iuhealth.org/laporte	219-326-1234	325-5403	374-3
LPI (Life Partners Inc) 204 Woodhew Dr........... Waco TX 76712 *TF:* 800-368-5569 ■ *Web:* www.lifepartnersinc.com	254-751-7797		796
Lpi Group 253 62 Ave SE Ste 101................ Calgary AB T2H0R5 *Web:* www.lpi-group.com	403-735-0655		224
Lpit Solutions Inc 25 Commerce Ave SW Ste 200............ Grand Rapids MI 49503 *Web:* www.implanttracking.com	616-632-2222		177
LPL Financial Services 75 State St 22nd Fl.......................... Boston MA 02109 **Fax Area Code:* 858 ■ *TF:* 800-877-7210	800-877-7210	546-8324*	690
LPP (Lois Paul & Partners) 290 Congress St 6th Fl......................... Boston MA 02210 *Web:* www.lpp.com	617-986-5700		636
LPPD (Loup Public Power District) 2404 15th St PO Box 988.................... Columbus NE 68602 *TF:* 866-869-2087 ■ *Web:* www.loup.com	402-564-3171	564-0970	245
LPS Industries Inc 10 Caesar Pl.............. Moonachie NJ 07074 *TF Sales:* 800-275-6577 ■ *Web:* www.lpsind.com	201-438-3515		548
LQ Management LLC 909 Hidden Ridge Ste 600 .... Irving TX 75038 *TF:* 800-753-3757 ■ *Web:* www.lq.com	214-492-6600		379
La Quinta Inn & Suites 909 Hidden Ridge Ste 600.......................... Irving TX 75038 *TF:* 800-753-3757 ■ *Web:* www.lq.com	214-492-6600		379
LQM Petroleum Services Inc 80 Broadway.............................. Cresskill NJ 07626 *Web:* www.lqm.com	201-871-9010		579
LQMT (Liquidmetal Technologies Inc) 30452 Esperanza .... Rancho Santa Margarita CA 92688 *OTC: LQMT* ■ *TF:* 888-203-1112 ■ *Web:* www.liquidmetal.com	949-635-2100	635-2188	482
LQP (Lac qui Parle County) 600 Sixth St .... Madison MN 56256 *TF:* 800-438-0576 ■ *Web:* www.lqpco.com	320-598-7444	598-3125	338
L&R Security Services Inc 3930 Old Gentilly Rd .... New Orleans LA 70126 *Web:* www.lrsecurity.com	504-943-3191		400
LR Services 602 Hayden Cir .... Allentown PA 18109 *TF:* 888-675-9650 ■ *Web:* www.lrservices.com	610-266-2500	266-3100	13
LRCC (Lakes Region Community College) 379 Belmont Rd .... Laconia NH 03246 *TF:* 800-357-2992 ■ *Web:* www.lrcc.edu	603-524-3207	524-8084	162
LRDC (Learning Research & Development Ctr) University of Pittsburgh 3939 O'Hara St........ Pittsburgh PA 15260 *TF:* 800-397-0071 ■ *Web:* www.lrdc.pitt.edu	412-624-7020	624-9149	668
LRECI (Little River Electric Co-op Inc) PO Box 220 .... Abbeville SC 29620 *TF:* 800-459-2141 ■ *Web:* www.lreci.coop	864-366-2141		245
LRF (Lymphoma Research Foundation) 115 Broadway Ste 1301 .... New York NY 10006 *TF:* 800-500-9976 ■ *Web:* www.lymphoma.org	212-349-2910	349-2886	48-17
LRG Marketing Communications Inc 48 Burd St Ste105 .... Nyack NY 10960 *TF:* 800-714-0717 ■ *Web:* lrgmarketing.com	845-358-1801		195
LRH (Laurel Regional Hospital) 7300 Van Dusen Rd .... Laurel MD 20707 *Web:* dimensionshealth.org	301-725-4300	497-7953	374-3
LRH (Lakeway Regional Hospital) 726 McFarland St......................... Morristown TN 37814	423-522-6000		374-3
LRHMC (Los Robles Hospital & Medical Ctr) 215 W Janss Rd .... Thousand Oaks CA 91360 *Web:* www.losrobleshospital.com	805-497-2727		374-3
LRL Associates Ltd 5430 Canotek Rd............ Ottawa ON K1J9G2 *Web:* www.lrl.ca	613-842-3434		261
LRMC (Lawnwood Regional Medical Ctr) 1700 S 23rd St.......................... Fort Pierce FL 34950 *Web:* www.lawnwoodmed.com	772-461-4000		374-3
LRP 360 Hiatt Dr .... Palm Beach Gardens FL 33418 *TF:* 800-621-5463 ■ *Web:* www.lrp.com	561-622-6520	622-2423	531-1
LRP Publications 360 Hiatt Dr .... Palm Beach Gardens FL 33418 *TF:* 800-621-5463 ■ *Web:* www.lrp.com	561-622-6520	622-2423	637-2
LRRI (Lovelace Respiratory Research Institute) 2425 Ridgecrest Dr SE.................... Albuquerque NM 87108 *TF:* 800-700-1016 ■ *Web:* www.lrri.org	505-348-9400		668
LS Gallegos & Associates Inc 9137 E Mineral Cir Ste 220 .... Centennial CO 80112 *Web:* www.lsgallegos.com	303-790-8474		463
LS Starrett Co 121 Crescent St.................. Athol MA 01331 *NYSE: SCX* ■ *TF:* 800-482-8710 ■ *Web:* www.starrett.com	978-249-3551	249-8495	682

	Phone	Fax	Class
LS Tractor USA LLC 6900 Corporation Pkwy .... Battleboro NC 27809 *Web:* www.lstractorusa.com	252-984-0700		273
LS3P Assoc Ltd 205 1/2 King St.............. Charleston SC 29401 *Web:* www.ls3p.com	843-577-4444	722-4789	261
LSA (Linguistic Society of America) 1325 18th St NW Ste 211.................. Washington DC 20036 *TF:* 800-726-0479 ■ *Web:* www.linguisticsociety.org	202-835-1714	835-1717	48-11
LSA Assoc Inc 20 Executive Pk Ste 200............ Irvine CA 92614 *Web:* lsa.net	949-553-0666		193
LSB Industries Inc 16 S Pennsylvania Ave .... Oklahoma City OK 73107 *NYSE: LXU* ■ *TF:* 800-657-4428 ■ *Web:* www.lsbindustries.com	405-235-4546	235-5067	143
LSBA (Louisiana State Bar Assn) 601 St Charles Ave......................... New Orleans LA 70130 *TF:* 800-421-5722 ■ *Web:* www.lsba.org	504-566-1600	566-0930	72
LSC & LSC Digital 6 Trowbridge Dr PO Box 516 .... Bethel CT 06801 *Web:* www.listservices.com	203-743-2600		5
LSESSI (Lightning Strike & Electric Shock Survivors International Inc) PO Box 1156 .... Jacksonville NC 28541 *Web:* www.lightning-strike.org	910-346-4708		48-21
Lsg Solutions LLC 501 E 15th St Ste 200B....................... Edmond OK 73013 *Web:* www.lsgsolutions.com	405-285-2500		631
LSI (Lake Shore Industries Inc) 1817 Poplar St PO BOX 3427.................... Erie PA 16508 **Fax Area Code:* 814 ■ *TF:* 800-458-0463 ■ *Web:* www.lsisigns.com	800-458-0463	453-4293*	701
LSI Computer Systems Inc 1235 Walt Whitman Rd....................... Melville NY 11747 *Web:* www.lsicsi.com	631-271-0400	271-0405	696
LSI Corp of America Inc 704 W Main St .... Teutopolis IL 62467 *TF:* 800-541-3029 ■ *Web:* www.lsi-casework.com	763-559-4664	559-4395	599
LSI Industries Inc 10000 Alliance Rd .... Cincinnati OH 45242 *NASDAQ: LYTS* ■ *TF:* 800-436-7800 ■ *Web:* www.lsi-industries.com	513-793-3200	984-1335	439
LSI Robway Pty Ltd 9633 Zaka Rd .... Houston TX 77064 *Web:* www.loadsystems.com	281-664-1330		684
LSNA (Louisiana State Nurses Assn, The) 5713 Superior Dr Ste A-6................. Baton Rouge LA 70816 *TF:* 800-457-6378 ■ *Web:* www.lsna.org	225-201-0993		533
LSO (Lansing Symphony Orchestra) 501 S Capitol Ave Ste 400 .... Lansing MI 48933 *TF:* 800-434-3913 ■ *Web:* www.lansingsymphony.org	517-487-5001	487-0210	573-3
LSP Products Group Inc 3689 Arrowhead Dr....................... Carson City NV 89706 *TF:* 800-854-3215 ■ *Web:* www.lspproducts.com	800-854-3215	243-1777	608
LSQ Funding Group LC 2600 Lucien Way Ste 100.................... Maitland FL 32751 *TF:* 800-474-7606 ■ *Web:* www.lsq.com	800-474-7606		272
LSUHSC (Louisiana State University Health Sciences Ctr) 1501 Kings Hwy .... Shreveport LA 71130 *TF:* 800-337-3627 ■ *Web:* www.lsuhscshreveport.edu	318-675-5000		374-3
LT Apparel Group 100 W 33rd St Ste 1012..................... New York NY 10001 *Web:* www.lollytogs.com	212-502-6000	268-5160	155-4
LTA (Land Trust Alliance) 1660 L St NW Ste 1100 .... Washington DC 20036 *Web:* www.landtrustalliance.org	202-638-4725	638-4730	48-13
LTC Properties Inc 2829 Townsgate Rd Ste 350 .... Westlake Village CA 91361 *NYSE: LTC* ■ *Web:* www.ltcreit.com	805-981-8655	981-8663	654
LTC Roll & Engineering Co 23500 John Gorsuch Dr .... Clinton Township MI 48036 *Web:* www.ltcroll.com	586 465 1023		482
LTD Hospitality Group LLC 1564 Crossways Blvd..................... Chesapeake VA 23320 *Web:* ltdhospitality.com	757-420-0900		378
LTD Managemen 1230 Pottstown Pike Ste 6 .... Glenmoore PA 19343 *Web:* www.ltdmgmt.com	610-715-3710	458-8039	194
Lti Printing Inc 518 N Centerville Rd .... Sturgis MI 49091 *TF:* 800-592-6990 ■ *Web:* www.ltiprinting.com	269-651-7574		627
LTI Trucking Services Inc 411 N Tenth St Ste 500...................... St. Louis MO 63101 *TF:* 800-642-7222 ■ *Web:* www.ltitrucking.com	800-642-7222		314
LTK Engineering Services Inc 100 W Butler Ave .... Ambler PA 19002 *Web:* www.ltk.com	215-542-0700		434-3
LTL Consultants Ltd 1 Town Ctr Dr................ Oley PA 19547 *Web:* www.ltlconsultants.com	610-987-9290		261
LTS (Lawrence Companies) 872 Lee Hwy........ Roanoke VA 24019 **Fax Area Code:* 540 ■ *TF:* 800-336-9626 ■ *Web:* www.lawrencecompanies.com	800-336-9626	966-4555*	780
LTS Corp 7250 Woodmont Ave Ste 340........... Bethesda MD 20814	301-652-2121		248
Lts Lohmann Therapy Systems Corp 21 Henderson Dr .... West Caldwell NJ 07006 *Web:* www.ltslaminates.com	973-276-1583		583
LTS Wireless Inc 311 S LHS Dr .... Lumberton TX 77657 *TF:* 800-255-5471 ■ *Web:* www.ltswireless.com	409-755-4038	755-7409	170
LTVtrade LLC 501 Madison Ave Ste 501 .... New York NY 10022 *Web:* www.ltvtrade.com	212-616-4600		690
Lu'ma Native Housing Society 2960 Nanaimo St .... Vancouver BC V5N5G3 *Web:* lnhs.ca	604-876-0811		653
LUA (Lumbermen's Underwriting Alliance) 1905 NW Corporate Blvd Ste 110........... Boca Raton FL 33431 **Fax:* Hum Res ■ *TF:* 800-327-0630 ■ *Web:* www.lumbermensunderwriting.com	561-994-1900	997-9489*	391-4
Luan Enterprises 5624 W 79th St............... Burbank IL 60459 *Web:* www.alltite.com	708-423-4547		41
Lubar & Co 700 N Water St Ste 1200........... Milwaukee WI 53202 *Web:* www.lubar.com	414-291-9000	291-9061	792
Lubbock Avalanche-Journal 710 Ave J .... Lubbock TX 79401 *TF:* 800-692-4021 ■ *Web:* lubbockonline.com	806-762-8844	744-9603	532-2
Lubbock Chamber of Commerce 1500 Broadway Ste 101 .... Lubbock TX 79401 *Web:* www.lubbockchamber.com	806-761-7000	761-7013	139

Name / Address	City	State	ZIP	Phone	Fax	Class
Lubbock Christian University 5601 19th St.	Lubbock	TX	79407	806-720-7151	720-7162*	166
**Fax:* Admissions ■ *TF:* 800-933-7601 ■ *Web:* www.lcu.edu						
Lubbock City Hall 1625 13th St	Lubbock	TX	79401	806-775-3000	775-3002	337
TF: 800-882-3887 ■ *Web:* www.ci.lubbock.tx.us						
Lubbock Convention & Visitors Bureau 1500 Broadway St 6th Fl.	Lubbock	TX	79401	806-747-5232	747-1419	206
TF: 800-692-4035 ■ *Web:* www.visitlubbock.org						
Lubbock County 904 Broadway St Rm 207	Lubbock	TX	79401	806-775-1000	775-7950	338
Web: www.co.lubbock.tx.us						
Lubbock Memorial Arboretum 4111 University Ave	Lubbock	TX	79413	806-797-4520		97
TF: 800-692-4035 ■ *Web:* www.lubbockarboretum.org						
Lubbock Memorial Civic Ctr 1501 MacDavis Ln	Lubbock	TX	79401	806-775-2242	775-3240	205
Web: www.mylubbock.us						
Lubbock Municipal Auditorium/Coliseum 1501 Mac Davis Ln.	Lubbock	TX	79401	806-775-2242	775-3240	720
TF: 800-735-2989 ■ *Web:* www.mylubbock.us						
Lubbock National Bank 4811 50th St	Lubbock	TX	79414	806-792-1000	792-0976	70
Lubbock Preston Smith International Airport 5401 N Martin Luther King Blvd	Lubbock	TX	79403	806-775-2044		27
TF: 800-231-2222 ■ *Web:* www.mylubbock.us						
Lubbock Public Library 1306 Ninth St	Lubbock	TX	79401	806-775-2835		434-3
Web: www.mylubbock.us						
Lubbock Regional Mental Health Mental Retardation Center 1602 Tenth St	Lubbock	TX	79401	806-766-0310		371
TF: 800-687-7581 ■ *Web:* www.lubbockmhmr.org						
Lubbock-Cooper Independent School District 16302 Loop 493	Lubbock	TX	79423	806-863-2282		685
Web: www.lcisd.net						
Luber Bros Inc 5224 Bear Creek Ct	Irving	TX	75061	972-313-2020		274
TF: 800-375-8237 ■ *Web:* www.luber.com						
Luberski Inc 310 N Harbor Blvd Ste 205	Fullerton	CA	92832	714-680-3447		297-4
TF: 800-326-3220 ■ *Web:* www.hiddenvilla.com						
Lubitz Financial Group, The 9130 S Dadeland Blvd Ste 1625	Miami	FL	33156	305-670-4440		528
Web: www.lubitzfinancial.com						
Lubricating Specialties Co 8015 Paramount Blvd	Pico Rivera	CA	90660	562-776-4000		541
Web: www.lsc-online.com						
Lubrication Engineers Inc 300 Bailey Ave	Fort Worth	TX	76107	817-834-6321	228-1142*	541
**Fax Area Code:* 800 ■ **Fax:* Sales ■ *TF:* 800-537-7683 ■ *Web:* www.lelubricants.com						
Lubrication Technologies Inc 900 Mendelssohn Ave N.	Golden Valley	MN	55427	763-545-0707	545-9256	541
TF: 800-328-5573 ■ *Web:* www.lubetech.com						
Lubri-Lab Inc 1540 de Coulomb	Boucherville	QC	J4B8A3	450-449-1626	449-9174	541
TF: 888-449-1626 ■ *Web:* www.lubrilab.com						
Lubrizol Corp 29400 Lakeland Blvd	Wickliffe	OH	44092	440-943-4200		145
NYSE: LZ ■ *TF:* 800-380-5397 ■ *Web:* www.lubrizol.com						
Luburgh Inc 4174 E Pk	Zanesville	OH	43701	740-452-3668		189-5
Luby's Inc 13111 NW Fwy Ste 600	Houston	TX	77040	713-329-6800		670
NYSE: LUB ■ *TF:* 800-886-4600 ■ *Web:* www.lubys.com						
Luca d'Italia 711 Grant St	Denver	CO	80203	303-832-6600		671
Web: www.lucadenver.com						
Luca International Group LLC 39650 Liberty St Ste 410	Fremont	CA	94538	510-498-8829	498-1926	536
Lucano 1815 E Ave	Rochester	NY	14610	585-244-3460		671
Web: www.ristorantelucano.com						
Lucas Assoc Inc 3384 Peachtree Rd Ste 900	Atlanta	GA	30326	800-466-4489		721
TF: 800-515-0819 ■ *Web:* www.lucasgroup.com						
Lucas Color Card 4900 N Santa Fe Ave	Oklahoma City	OK	73118	405-524-1811		344
TF: 888-845-8227 ■ *Web:* lucascolorcard.com						
Lucas County 916 Braden St	Chariton	IA	50049	641-774-4411		338
Web: lucas.iowaassessors.com						
Lucas County 1 Government Ctr Ste 800	Toledo	OH	43604	419-213-4500	213-4532	338
Web: www.co.lucas.oh.us						
Lucas County Educational Service Ctr 2275 Collingwood Blvd	Toledo	OH	43620	419-245-4150	245-4186	449
Web: www.esclakeeriewest.org						
Lucas Engineering & Management Services Inc 3160 George Washington Way Ste 102	Richland	WA	99352	509-942-1080		194
Web: www.lucasinc.com						
Lucas Frank (Rep R - OK) 2405 Rayburn HOB	Washington	DC	20515	202-225-5565	225-8698	342-2
Web: lucas.house.gov						
Lucas Horsfall Murphy & Pindroh LLP 100 E Corson St Ste 200	Pasadena	CA	91103	626-744-5100		2
Web: www.lhmp.com						
Lucas Ltd 1200 Wilshire Blvd Ste 208	Los Angeles	CA	90017	213-240-5990		652
Lucas Newman Science & Technologies Inc 5403 Bluebird Trl	Stillwater	OK	74074	502-409-7231		192
Web: artlucas.org						
Lucas Oil Stadium 500 S Capitol Ave	Indianapolis	IN	46225	317-262-8600		720
Web: www.icclos.com						
Lucas Precision LP 13020 St Clair Ave	Cleveland	OH	44108	216-451-5588	451-5174	455
TF: 800-336-1262 ■ *Web:* www.lucasprecision.com						
Lucas Systems Inc 11279 Perry Hwy 4th Fl	Wexford	PA	15090	724-940-7000		177
TF: 800-852-3282 ■ *Web:* www.lucasware.com						
Lucasfilm Ltd PO Box 29901	San Francisco	CA	94129	415-623-1000		514
Web: www.lucasfilm.com						
Lucasfilm Ltd LucasArts Entertainment Div 1110 Gorgas St.	San Francisco	CA	94129	410-568-3670	662-1639*	178-6
**Fax Area Code:* 415 ■ *Web:* starwars.com/games-apps						
Lucas-Milhaupt Inc 5656 S Pennsylvania Ave	Cudahy	WI	53110	414-769-6000	769-1093	485
TF: 800-558-3856 ■ *Web:* www.lucasmilhaupt.com						
Lucca 226 Hanover St	Boston	MA	02113	617-742-9200		671
Web: www.luccaboston.com						
Lucca Restaurant & Bar 1615 J St	Sacramento	CA	95814	916-669-5300		671
Web: www.luccarestaurant.com						
Lucchese Boot Co 20 ZANE GREY	El Paso	TX	79906	888-582-1883		301
TF: 800-637-6888 ■ *Web:* www.lucchese.com						
Luce County 407 W Harrie St	Newberry	MI	49868	906-293-5521		338
Web: www.lucecountymi.com/#!92nd-district-court/c1j6s						
Luce, Schwab & Kase Inc 9 Gloria Ln	Fairfield	NJ	07007	973-227-4840		665
TF: 800-458-7329 ■ *Web:* www.lskair.com						
Lucent Capital Inc 9454 Wilshire Blvd Ste 525	Beverly Hills	CA	90212	310-876-8454		691
Web: www.lucentcapital.com						
Lucent Medical Systems Inc 821 Kirkland Ave Ste 100	Kirkland	WA	98033	425-822-3310		476
Web: www.lucentmedical.com						
Luci Ancora 2060 Randolph Ave	Saint Paul	MN	55105	651-698-6889		671
Web: luciancora.com						
Lucia's 1432 W 31st St	Minneapolis	MN	55408	612-825-1572		671
Web: www.lucias.com						
Lucid Fusion Inc 8935 Research Dr Ste 200	Irvine	CA	92618	949-502-7750		4
Web: www.lucidfusion.com						
Lucid Technology 1754 N Wilmot	Chicago	IL	60647	312-238-8976		180
Web: www.lucidtec.com						
Lucidview LLC 80 Rolling Links Blvd	Oak Ridge	TN	37830	865-220-8440		196
TF: 888-582-4384 ■ *Web:* www.lucidview.com						
Lucile Packard Children's Hospital (LPCH) 725 Welch Rd	Palo Alto	CA	94304	650-497-8000	497-8968*	374-1
**Fax:* Admitting ■ *TF:* 800-995-5724 ■ *Web:* stanfordchildrens.org						
Lucile's Famous Creole Seasonings 2124 14th St	Boulder	CO	80302	303-442-4743	939-9848	296-37
Web: www.luciles.com						
Lucille Lortel Theatre 121 Christopher St	New York	NY	10014	212-924-2817		572
Web: www.lortel.org						
Lucille Roberts Women's Gym 430 89th St	Brooklyn	NY	11209	718-680-8200		354
Web: www.lucilleroberts.com						
Lucille's Smokehouse Bar-B-Que 7411 Carson St	Long Beach	CA	90808	562-938-7427		671
Web: www.lucillesbbq.com						
Lucille's Stateside Bistro 4700 Camp Bowie Blvd	Fort Worth	TX	76107	817-738-4761		671
Web: lucilesstatesidebistro.com						
Lucius Beebe Memorial Library 345 Main St	Wakefield	MA	01880	781-246-6334	246-6385	434-3
Web: www.wakefieldlibrary.org						
Lucix Corp 800 Avenida Acaso	Camarillo	CA	93012	805-987-3677		253
Web: www.lucix.com						
Luckett & Farley Architects Engineers & Construction Managers Inc 737 S Third St	Louisville	KY	40202	502-585-4181		186
Web: www.luckett-farley.com						
Luckey Farmers Inc 1200 W Main St PO Box 217	Woodville	OH	43469	419-849-2711	849-2720	276
Web: www.luckeyfarmers.com						
Luckie & Co 600 Luckie Dr Ste 150	Birmingham	AL	35223	205-879-2121		4
Web: www.luckie.com						
Luckman Fine Arts Complex 5151 State University Dr	Los Angeles	CA	90032	323-343-6611		572
Web: www.luckmanarts.org						
Lucks Co, The 3003 S Pine St	Tacoma	WA	98409	253-383-4815	383-0071*	296-8
**Fax:* Orders ■ *TF:* 800-426-9778 ■ *Web:* www.lucks.com						
Lucky Chances Casino 1700 Hillside Blvd	Colma	CA	94014	650-758-2237		452
Web: www.grubgirl.com						
Lucky China Buffet 1102 NW Hwy	Garland	TX	75041	972-270-3430	270-8839	671
Lucky Eagle Casino 12888 188th Ave SW	Rochester	WA	98579	360-273-2000		133
TF: 800-720-1788 ■ *Web:* www.luckyeagle.com						
Lucky Fortune 1401 Lancaster Dr NE	Salem	OR	97301	503-399-9189		671
Web: www.luckyfortunechinesesalem.com						
Lucky Strike Lanes Orange 20 City Blvd W Ste G2	Orange	CA	92868	714-937-5263		99
Web: www.bowlluckystrike.com						
Lucor Inc 790 Pershing Rd	Raleigh	NC	27608	919-828-9511		62-5
Lucques 8474 Melrose Ave	Los Angeles	CA	90069	323-655-6277	655-3925	671
Web: www.lucques.com						
Lucta USA Inc Pine Meadow Corporate Ctr 950 Technology Way Ste 110	Libertyville	IL	60048	847-996-3400		447
TF: 800-323-5341 ■ *Web:* www.lucta.com						
Lucy Corr Village 6800 Lucy Corr Blvd	Chesterfield	VA	23832	804-748-1511	706-5572	450
Web: www.lucycorrvillage.com						
Lucy Craft Laney Museum 1116 Phillips St	Augusta	GA	30901	706-724-3576	724-3576	520
TF: 800-763-4222 ■ *Web:* www.lucycraftlaneymuseum.com						
Lucy Robbins Welles Library 95 Cedar St	Newington	CT	06111	860-665-8700	667-1255	434-3
TF: 800-842-1423 ■ *Web:* www.newingtonct.gov						
Lucy's Chinese Food 3330 S Campbell	Springfield	MO	65807	417-882-5383		671
Web: www.lucyschinesefood.com						
Ludeca Inc 1425 NW 88th Ave	Doral	FL	33172	305-591-8935		246
Web: www.ludeca.com						
Ludington State Park PO Box 709	Ludington	MI	49431	231-843-2423		565
Web: www.michigandnr.com						
Ludlow Composites Corp 2100 Commerce Dr	Fremont	OH	43420	800-628-5463	332-7776*	676
**Fax Area Code:* 419 ■ *TF:* 800-628-5463 ■ *Web:* www.ludlow-comp.com						
Ludlum Measurements Inc 501 Oak St	Sweetwater	TX	79556	325-235-5494	235-4672	472
TF: 800-622-0828 ■ *Web:* www.ludlums.com						
Ludowici Roof Tile Inc 4757 Tile Plant Rd PO Box 69	New Lexington	OH	43764	740-342-1995	342-0025	150
TF Cust Svc: 800-945-8453 ■ *Web:* www.ludowici.com						
Ludvik Electric Co 3900 S Teller St	Lakewood	CO	80235	303-781-9601		189-4
Web: www.ludvik.com						
Ludwig Buildings Inc 521 Timesaver Ave	Harahan	LA	70123	504-733-6260	733-7458	105
Web: ludwigbuildings.com						
Ludwig Von Mises Institute 518 W Magnolia Ave	Auburn	AL	36832	334-321-2100		166
Web: www.mises.org						

Name / Address	City	State	ZIP	Phone	Fax	Class
Lueder Construction Co 9999 J St Ste B	Omaha	NE	68127	402-339-1000		186
TF: 800-354-3988 ■ *Web:* www.lueder.com						
Luetkemeyer Blaine (Rep R - MO)						
2230 Rayburn HOB	Washington	DC	20515	202-225-2956	225-5712	342-2
Web: luetkemeyer.house.gov						
Lufkin Daily News 300 Ellis Ave	Lufkin	TX	75904	936-632-6631	632-6655	532-2
TF: 888-664-8792 ■ *Web:* www.lufkindailynews.com						
Lufkin Industries Inc						
4000 Monroe Rd	Farmington	NM	87401	505-566-9285		709
Web: www.lufkin.com						
Lufkin/Angelina County Chamber of Commerce						
1615 S Chestnut St	Lufkin	TX	75901	936-634-6644	634-8726	139
TF: 800-409-5659 ■ *Web:* www.lufkintexas.org						
Lugg and Lugg Law Offices						
350 E Water St Box 905	Lock Haven	PA	17745	570-748-2481		445
TF: 800-624-9060 ■ *Web:* lugglaw.com						
LUH (Longmont United Hospital)						
1950 Mountain View Ave	Longmont	CO	80501	303-651-5111		374-3
Web: www.luhcares.org						
Luhr Bros Inc 250 W Sand Bank Rd	Columbia	IL	62236	618-281-4106	281-4288	188-5
Web: www.luhr.com						
Luhring Augustine Gallery						
531 W 24th St	New York	NY	10011	212-206-9100	206-9055	42
TF: 800-944-8639 ■ *Web:* www.luhringaugustine.com						
Luigi Bormioli						
5 Walnut Grove Dr Ste 140	Horsham	PA	19044	215-672-7111		361
Web: www.luigibormioli.com						
Luigi Vitrone's Pastabilities						
415 N Lincoln St	Wilmington	DE	19805	302-656-9822		671
Web: www.ljv-pastabilities.com						
Luigi's 245 W Main St	Spokane	WA	99201	509-624-5226		671
Web: www.luigis-spokane.com						
Luigi's 947 S Tejon St	Colorado Springs	CO	80903	719-632-7339		671
Web: www.luigiscoloradosprings.com						
Luigi's 590 Broad St	Augusta	GA	30901	706-722-4056		671
Web: www.luigisinc.com						
Luigi's 2132 Davison Rd	Flint	MI	48506	810-234-9545		671
Web: luigissince1955.com						
Luigi's 1524 Valley Dr	Syracuse	NY	13207	315-492-9997		671
Luigi's 105 N Main St	Akron	OH	44308	330-253-2999		671
Web: luigisrestaurant.com						
Luigi's Italian Bistro						
2733 Mantiwoc Rd	Green Bay	WI	54311	920-468-4900		671
Web: luigisitalianbistro.com						
Luitpold Pharmaceuticals Inc						
1 Luitpold Dr PO Box 9001	Shirley	NY	11967	631-924-4000	924-1731	584
TF: 800-645-1706 ■ *Web:* www.luitpold.com						
Lujan Ben R (Rep D - NM)						
2231 Rayburn HOB	Washington	DC	20515	202-225-6190	226-1528	342-2
Web: lujan.house.gov						
Lujan Grisham Michelle (Rep D - NM)						
214 Cannon Bldg	Washington	DC	20515	202-225-6316	225-4975	342-2
Web: lujangrisham.house.gov						
LuK USA LLC 3401 Old Airport Rd	Wooster	OH	44691	330-264-4383		60
Web: www.schaeffler.us						
Lukas Partners Inc 11915 P St Ste 100	Omaha	NE	68137	402-895-2552		636
TF: 800-800-1439 ■ *Web:* www.lukaspartners.com						
Luke Air Force Base						
14185 W Falcon St	Luke AFB	AZ	85309	623-856-5853	856-6013	497-1
TF: 855-655-1004 ■ *Web:* www.luke.af.mil						
Luke Soules Acosta 2003 Rickety Ln Ste D	Tyler	TX	75703	903-561-4241		297-8
Lukins & Annis PS						
1600 WA Trust Financial Ctr 717 W Sprague Ave						
Ste 1600	Spokane	WA	99201	509-455-9555		428
Web: www.lukins.com						
Lula Westfield LLC						
451 LA 1005 PO Box 10	Paincourtville	LA	70391	985-369-6450	369-6139	296-38
Web: www.luwest.com						
Luling Independent School District						
212 E Bowie St	Luling	TX	78648	830-875-3191		685
Web: www.luling.txed.net						
Lumbee Enterprises Inc						
356 W Phillips Rd	Greer	SC	29650	864-989-0149		61
Web: www.lumbeena.com						
Lumbee River Electric Membership Corp						
PO Box 830	Red Springs	NC	28377	910-843-4131	843-6422	245
TF: 800-683-5571 ■ *Web:* www.lumbeeriver.com						
Lumber Industries Inc						
5809 Kennett Pk	Wilmington	DE	19807	302-655-9651		360-2
Lumber Liquidators Inc						
1455 VFW Pkwy	West Roxbury	MA	02132	617-327-1222	750-7802*	290
**Fax Area Code:* 978 ■ *TF:* 800-227-0332 ■ *Web:* www.lumberliquidators.com						
Lumber One Avon Inc						
101 Second St NW PO Box 7	Avon	MN	56310	320-356-7342		186
Web: www.lumber-one.com						
Lumber River State Park						
2819 Princess Ann Rd	Orrum	NC	28369	910-628-4564		565
TF: 800-277-9611 ■ *Web:* www.ncparks.gov/visit/parks/luri/main.php						
Lumber Specialties Ltd						
1700 Beltline Rd	Dyersville	IA	52040	563-875-2858		817
Web: www.lbrspec.com						
Lumberjack Building Centers						
3470 Pointe Tremble Rd	Algonac	MI	48001	810-794-4921		711
TF: 800-466-5164 ■ *Web:* www.lumber-jack.com						
Lumbermen's Merchandising Corp						
137 W Wayne Ave	Wayne	PA	19087	610-293-7000		191-3
Web: www.lmc.net						
Lumbermen's Underwriting Alliance (LUA)						
1905 NW Corporate Blvd Ste 110	Boca Raton	FL	33431	561-994-1900	997-9489*	391-4
**Fax:* Hum Res ■ *TF:* 800-327-0630 ■ *Web:* www.lumbermensunderwriting.com						
Lumberton Area Chamber of Commerce						
800 N Chestnut St	Lumberton	NC	28358	910-739-4750	671-9722	139
Web: www.lumbertonchamber.com						
Lumberton Area Visitors Bureau						
3431 Lackey St	Lumberton	NC	28360	910-739-9999		206
TF: 800-359-6971 ■ *Web:* www.lumberton-nc.com						
Lumberton Correctional Institution						
75 Legend Rd	Lumberton	NC	28359	910-618-5574		213
Web: www.ncdps.gov						
Lumberton Honda Mitsubishi Inc						
301 Wintergreen Dr	Lumberton	NC	28358	910-739-9871		516
TF: 855-712-9438 ■ *Web:* www.lumbertonhonda.com						
Lumec Inc 640 Blvd Cur-Boivin	Boisbriand	QC	J7G2A7	450-430-7040	430-1453	439
TF: 800-424-3996 ■ *Web:* www.lumec.com						
Lumed Science Inc 375 S Logan St	Denver	CO	80209	303-775-3762		743
Web: www.lumedscience.com						
Lumedx Corp 555 12th St Ste 2060	Oakland	CA	94607	510-419-1000	419-3699	178-10
TF: 800-966-0699 ■ *Web:* www.lumedx.com						
Lumedyne Technologies Inc						
9275 Sky Park Ct Ste 100	San Diego	CA	92123	858-560-5208		590
Web: www.omegasensors.com						
Lumen Legal 1025 N Campbell Rd	Royal Oak	MI	48067	248-597-0400	597-0410	721
TF: 877-933-1330 ■ *Web:* www.lumenlegal.com						
Lumen, The 6101 Hillcrest Ave	Dallas	TX	75205	214-219-2400	219-2402	379
TF: 800-908-1140 ■ *Web:* www.hotellumen.com						
Lumenera Corp 7 Capella Ct	Ottawa	ON	K2E8A7	613-736-4077		692
Web: www.lumenera.com						
Lumenis Ltd 2033 Gateway Pl Ste 200	San Jose	CA	95110	408-764-3000	764-3999	424
TF: 877-586-3647 ■ *Web:* www.lumenis.com						
Lumens Light & Living 2028 K St	Sacramento	CA	95811	916-444-5585		815
TF: 877-445-4486 ■ *Web:* www.lumens.com						
Lumension Security Inc						
8660 E Hartford Dr Ste 300	Scottsdale	AZ	85255	888-725-7828	970-6323*	225
**Fax Area Code:* 480 ■ *TF:* 888-725-7828 ■ *Web:* www.lumension.com						
LumenVox LLC 3615 Kearny Villa Rd	San Diego	CA	92123	858-707-7700		177
Web: www.lumenvox.com						
Lumex Inc 290 E Helen Rd	Palatine	IL	60067	847-359-2790		253
TF: 800-278-5666 ■ *Web:* www.lumex.com						
Lumicor Inc 1400 Monster Rd SW	Renton	WA	98057	425-255-4000		610
Web: www.lumicor.com						
Lumiere 1293 Washington St	Newton	MA	02465	617-244-9199	796-9178	671
Web: www.lumiererestaurant.com						
Lumina Foundation for Education						
30 S Meridian St Ste 700	Indianapolis	IN	46204	317-951-5300		305
TF: 800-834-5756 ■ *Web:* www.luminafoundation.org						
Luminaire (Miami) Inc 8950 NW 33rd St	Miami	FL	33172	305-437-7975		321
Web: www.luminaire.com						
Luminalt Energy Corp						
1320 Potrero Ave	San Francisco	CA	94110	415-641-4000		610
Web: www.luminalt.com						
Luminator 900 Klein Rd	Plano	TX	75074	972-424-6511	423-1540	438
TF: 800-388-8205 ■ *Web:* www.ltgglobal.com						
Luminex Corp 12212 Technology Blvd	Austin	TX	78727	512-219-8020	219-5195	419
NASDAQ: LMNX ■ *TF:* 888-219-8020 ■ *Web:* www.luminexcorp.com						
Luminex Molecular Diagnostics						
439 University Ave Ste 900	Toronto	ON	M5G1Y8	416-593-4323	593-1066	178-10
Web: www.luminexcorp.com						
Luminex Software Inc						
871 Marlborough Ave	Riverside	CA	92507	951-781-4100	781-4105	178-12
TF Sales: 888-586-4639 ■ *Web:* www.luminex.com						
Luminit LLC 1850 W 205th St	Torrance	CA	90501	310-320-1066		253
Web: www.luminitco.com						
Luminite Products Corp						
148 Commerce Dr	Bradford	PA	16701	814-817-1420		781
TF: 888-545-2270 ■ *Web:* luminite.com						
Lumisolution Inc 162 Av Du Sacre-Coeur	Quebec	QC	G1N2W2	418-522-5693		361
Web: lumisolution.com						
Lumitex Inc 8443 Dow Cir	Strongsville	OH	44136	440-243-8401	243-8402	729
TF: 800-969-5483 ■ *Web:* www.lumitex.com						
Lumitron Inc						
10503 Timberwood Cir Ste 120	Louisville	KY	40223	502-423-7225		358
Web: www.lumitron ir.com						
Lummus Corp						
225 Bourne Blvd PO Box 929	Savannah	GA	31408	912-447-9000	447-9250	744
TF: 800-458-6687 ■ *Web:* www.lummus.com						
Lummus Supply Co 1554 Bolton Rd NW	Atlanta	GA	30331	404-794-1501	794-4519	191-2
Web: www.lummus supply.com						
Lumos & Assoc Inc						
800 E College Pkwy	Carson City	NV	89706	775-883-7077	883-7114	261
TF: 800-621-7155 ■ *Web:* www.lumosinc.com						
Lumpkin County						
99 Courthouse Hill Ste A	Dahlonega	GA	30533	706-864-3742	864-4760	338
TF: 800-231-5543 ■ *Web:* www.lumpkincounty.gov						
Lums Pond State Park						
1068 Howell School Rd	Bear	DE	19701	302-368-6989		565
Web: www.destateparks.com						
Lumtron Technologies Inc						
820 E Terra Cotta Ave Ste 242	Crystal Lake	IL	60014	815-788-0088		180
Web: www.lumtron.com						
Lum-Yuen 3190 Portland Rd NE	Salem	OR	97303	503-581-2912		671
Web: lumyuensalem.com						
Luna 5620 S Perry St	Spokane	WA	99223	509-448-2383		671
TF: 800-669-7634 ■ *Web:* www.lunaspokane.com						
Luna Community College 366 Luna Dr	Las Vegas	NM	87701	505-454-2500	454-2519	162
TF: 800-588-7232 ■ *Web:* luna.edu						
Luna de Noche 7602 N Jupiter Rd	Garland	TX	75044	469-246-8271		671
Web: www.lunadenochetexmex.com						
Luna Garcia 201 San Juan Ave	Venice	CA	90291	310-396-8026		730
TF: 800-905-9975 ■ *Web:* www.lunagarcia.com						
Luna Maya 2010 Colley Ave and 21st St	Norfolk	VA	23517	757-622-6986		671
Web: www.lunamayarestaurant.com						
Luna Vineyards Inc 2921 Silverado Trl	Napa	CA	94558	707-255-5862		443
Web: www.lunavineyards.com						
Lunan Corp 414 N Orleans St Ste 402	Chicago	IL	60654	312-645-9898		670
Web: www.arbysrestaurants.com						
Lunar Cow 120 E Mill St Ste 415	Akron	OH	44308	330-253-9000		180
Web: www.lunarcow.com						
Lunarline Inc						
3300 N Fairfax Dr Ste 308	Arlington	VA	22201	571-481-9300		225
Web: www.lunarline.com						
Lunarpages. Inc 1360 N Hancock St	Anaheim	CA	92807	714-521-8150		463
Web: www.lunarpages.com						
Lund Food Holdings Inc 4100 W 50th St	Edina	MN	55424	952-927-3663	915-2600	345
Web: www.lundsandbyerlys.com						
Lund Industrial Group						
400 E Industrial Pk Rd	Holly Springs	MS	38635	662-252-2340	252-3352	273
Web: www.lundonline.com						

	Phone	Fax	Class
Lund International Holdings Inc			
4325 Hamilton Mill Rd Ste 400 Buford GA 30518	800-241-7219		60
TF: 800-241-7219 ■ *Web:* www.lundinternational.com			
Lund's Fisheries Inc 997 Ocean Dr Cape May NJ 08204	609-884-7600	884-0664	285
TF: 800-328-7687 ■ *Web:* www.lundsfish.com			
Lunda Construction Company Inc			
620 GebhaRdt Rd Black River Falls WI 54615	715-284-9491	284-9146	188-4
TF: 800-242-7113 ■ *Web:* www.lundaconstruction.com			
Lundbeck Canada Inc			
2600 Alfred-Nobel Blvd Ste 400 St Lauren QC H4S0A9	514-844-8515	844-5495	85
TF: 800-586-2325 ■ *Web:* www.lundbeck.com			
Lundberg Family Farms			
5370 Church St PO Box 369 Richvale CA 95974	530-882-4551		296-4
Web: www.lundberg.com			
Lundell Manufacturing Corp			
2700 Ranchview Ln Plymouth MN 55447	763-559-4114		326
Web: www.lundellmfg.com			
Lundquist Consulting Inc			
111 Anza Blvd Ste 310 Burlingame CA 94010	650-342-9486		196
Web: www.lundquistconsulting.com			
Lunenburg Correctional Ctr			
690 Falls Rd Victoria VA 23974	434-696-2045		213
Web: vadoc.virginia.gov			
Lunenburg County			
11413 Courthouse Rd Lunenburg VA 23952	434-696-2142		338
Web: www.lunenburgva.org			
Lunseth Plumbing & Heating Co			
1710 N Washington St Grand Forks ND 58203	701-772-6631		610
Web: www.dakotafire.com			
Luntz Global LLC 9165 Key Commons Ct Manassas VA 20110	571-299-2050		5
Web: www.luntzglobal.com			
Lupa Osteria Romana 170 Thompson St New York NY 10012	212-982-5089		671
Web: www.luparestaurant.com			
Lupient Automotive Group Inc (LAG)			
7100 Wayzata Blvd Ste 600 Minneapolis MN 55426	763-546-2222		57
Web: www.lupient.com			
Luppen & Hawley Inc 7400 14th Ave Sacramento CA 95820	916-456-7831		610
Web: www.luppenandhawleyinc.com			
Lupus Foundation of America Inc (LFA)			
2000 L St NW Ste 410 Washington DC 20036	202-349-1155	349-1156	48-17
TF: 800-558-0121 ■ *Web:* www.lupus.org			
Luquire George Andrews Inc			
4201 Congress St Ste 400 Charlotte NC 28209	704-552-6565	552-1972	4
Web: www.lgaadv.com			
Lurleen B Wallace Community College			
Andalusia			
1000 Dannelly Blvd PO Box 1418 Andalusia AL 36420	334-222-6591	881-2201*	162
**Fax:* Admissions ■ *TF:* 877-382-4357 ■ *Web:* www.lbwcc.edu			
MacArthur 1708 N Main St PO Box 910 Opp AL 36467	334-493-3573	493-7003	800
TF: 877-382-4357 ■ *Web:* www.lbwcc.edu			
Lusardi Construction Company Inc			
1570 Linda Vista Dr San Marcos CA 92078	760-744-3133	744-9064	186
Web: www.lusardi.com			
Luse Holdings Inc 3990 Enterprise Ct Aurora IL 60504	630-862-2600	862-2674	189-9
TF: 800-747-6422 ■ *Web:* luse.com			
Luseaux Laboratories Inc			
16816 S Gramercy Pl Gardena CA 90247	310-324-1555		151
TF: 800-424-9300 ■ *Web:* luseaux.com			
Lush Group Inc 28 Narragansett Ave Jamestown RI 02835	401-423-9111		41
Web: www.lgisoftware.com			
Luso-Americano Newspaper 66 Union St Newark NJ 07105	973-344-3200	344-4201	532-3
Web: www.lusoamericano.com			
Luster Products Inc 1104 W 43rd St Chicago IL 60609	773-579-1800	579-1912	214
TF: 800-621-4255 ■ *Web:* www.lusterproducts.com			
Lutamar Electrical Assemblies Inc			
8030 Ridgeway Ave Skokie IL 60076	847-679-5400		625
Lutco Bearings Inc 130 Higgins St Worcester MA 01606	508-756-6296		75
Web: www.lutco.com			
Lutco Inc 677 Cambridge St Worcester MA 01610	508-756-6296	799-6848	75
Web: www.lutco.com			
Lute Plumbing Supply Inc			
3920 US Hwy 23 Portsmouth OH 45662	740-353-7638		610
Web: www.lutesupply.com			
Luth Research Inc 1365 Fourth Ave San Diego CA 92101	619-234-5884		466
TF: 800-465-5884 ■ *Web:* www.luthresearch.com			
Luther Brookdale Chevrolet			
6701 Brooklyn Blvd Brooklyn Center MN 55429	612-424-7337		516
Web: www.brookdalechevrolet.com			
Luther Burbank Home & Gardens			
204 Santa Rosa Ave Santa Rosa CA 95404	707-524-5445		97
Web: www.lutherburbank.org			
Luther Burbank Savings			
804 Fourth St Santa Rosa CA 95404	707-578-9216	581-2102	70
TF: 888-205-6005 ■ *Web:* www.lutherburbanksavings.com			
Luther College 700 College Dr Decorah IA 52101	563-387-2000	387-2159*	166
**Fax:* Admissions ■ *TF:* 800-458-8437 ■ *Web:* www.luther.edu			
Luther Consulting LLC			
10435 Commerce Dr Ste 140 Carmel IN 46032	317-636-0282		196
TF: 866-517-6570 ■ *Web:* www.lutherconsulting.com			
Luther Luckett Correctional Complex			
Dawkins Rd PO Box 6 LaGrange KY 40031	502-222-0363	222-8112	213
TF: 800-511-1670 ■ *Web:* www.corrections.ky.gov			
Luther Manor 3131 Hillcrest Rd Dubuque IA 52001	563-588-1413		371
Web: www.luthermanor.com			
Luther Memorial Home 221 Sixth St SW Madelia MN 56062	507-642-3271		371
Web: www.luthermemorialhome.org			
Luther Rice College & Seminary			
3038 Evans Mill Rd Lithonia GA 30038	770-484-1204		166
Web: www.lutherrice.edu/index.cms			
Luther Seminary 2481 Como Ave Saint Paul MN 55108	651-641-3456	641-3425	167-3
TF: 800-588-4373 ■ *Web:* www.luthersem.edu			
Lutheran Church Missouri Synod (LCMS)			
1333 S Kirkwood Rd Saint Louis MO 63122	314-965-9000		48-20
TF: 888-843-5267 ■ *Web:* www.lcms.org			
Lutheran Church of Hope			
925 Jordan Creek Pkwy West Des Moines IA 50266	515-222-1520		48-20
Web: www.lutheranchurchofhope.org/west-des-moines			

	Phone	Fax	Class
Lutheran Community at Telford			
12 Lutheran Home Dr Telford PA 18969	215-723-9819	723-3623	672
TF: 877-343-7518 ■ *Web:* www.lctelford.org			
Lutheran Disaster Response			
8765 W Higgins Rd Chicago IL 60631	800-638-3522	380-2707*	48-5
**Fax Area Code:* 773 ■ *TF:* 800-638-3522 ■ *Web:* www.elca.org			
Lutheran Home at Hollidaysburg, The			
916 Hickory St Hollidaysburg PA 16648	814-696-4527		48-20
TF: 800-400-2285 ■ *Web:* www.alsm.org			
Lutheran Home of The Cannon Valley Inc			
900 Cannon Vly Dr Northfield MN 55057	507-645-9511		48-20
Web: www.northfieldretirement.org			
Lutheran Hospital 1730 W 25th St Cleveland OH 44113	216-696-4300		374-3
Web: my.clevelandclinic.org			
Lutheran Hospital of Indiana			
7950 W Jefferson Blvd Fort Wayne IN 46804	260-435-7001		374-3
TF: 800-444-2001 ■ *Web:* www.lutheranhospital.com			
Lutheran Immigration & Refugee Service (LIRS)			
700 Light St Baltimore MD 21230	410-230-2700	230-2890	48-5
TF: 800-732-0999 ■ *Web:* www.lirs.org			
Lutheran Life Villages			
6701 S Anthony Blvd Fort Wayne IN 46816	260-447-1591	447-7369	672
TF: 800-930-2562 ■ *Web:* www.lutheranlifevillages.org			
Lutheran Magazine 8765 W Higgins Rd Chicago IL 60631	800-638-3522	380-2409*	457-18
**Fax Area Code:* 773 ■ *TF:* 800-638-3522 ■ *Web:* www.livinglutheran.org			
Lutheran Medical Ctr (LHC) 150 55th St Brooklyn NY 11220	718-630-7000		374-3
TF: 800-906-9762 ■ *Web:* lutheranhealthcare.org/main/home.aspx			
Lutheran Metropolitan Ministry Admin			
1468 W 25th St Cleveland OH 44113	216-696-5507		48-20
Web: www.lutheranmetro.org			
Lutheran School of Theology at Chicago			
1100 E 55th St Chicago IL 60615	773-256-0700	256-0782	167-3
TF: 800-635-1116 ■ *Web:* www.lstc.edu			
Lutheran Social Services			
715 Falconer St Jamestown NY 14701	716-665-4905		450
Web: www.lutheran-jamestown.org			
Lutheran Social Services of Illinois			
1001 E Touhy Ave Ste 50 Des Plaines IL 60018	847-635-4600		48-15
TF: 888-671-0300 ■ *Web:* www.lssi.org			
Lutheran Theological Seminary			
114 Seminary Crescent Saskatoon SK S7N0X3	306-966-7850	966-7852	167-3
Web: www.usask.ca			
Lutheran Theological Seminary at Gettysburg			
61 Seminary Ridge Gettysburg PA 17325	717-334-6286	334-3469	167-3
TF: 800-658-8437 ■ *Web:* www.ltsg.edu			
Lutheran Theological Seminary at Philadelphia			
7301 Germantown Ave Philadelphia PA 19119	215-248-4616	248-4577	167-3
TF: 800-286-4616 ■ *Web:* www.ltsp.edu			
Luthi Machinery Co Inc 1 Atlas Ave Pueblo CO 81001	719-948-1110	948-4273	298
Web: www.luthi.com			
Lutonix Inc 9409 Science Ctr Dr New Hope MN 55428	763-445-2352		668
Web: www.lutonix.com			
Lutron Electronics Company Inc			
7200 Suter Rd Coopersburg PA 18036	610-282-6280	282-6253	203
TF Tech Supp: 800-523-9466 ■ *Web:* www.lutron.com			
Lutsen Resort 5700 W Hwy 61 PO Box 9 Lutsen MN 55612	218-663-7212		669
TF: 800-258-8736 ■ *Web:* www.lutsenresort.com			
Lutz & Carr 300 E 42nd St New York NY 10017	212-697-2299		2
Web: www.lutzandcarr.com			
Lutz Frey Corp 1195 Ivy Dr Lancaster PA 17601	717-898-6808		189-10
TF: 800-280-6794 ■ *Web:* www.freylutz.com			
Lutz, Daily & Brain LLC			
6400 Glenwood St Shawnee Mission KS 66202	913-831-0833		261
Web: www.ldbeng.com			
Luurtsema Sales Inc			
6672 Ctr Industrial Dr Jenison MI 49428	616-669-9301		292
Web: luurtsema.com			
Luv N' Care Ltd 3030 Aurora Ave Monroe LA 71201	800-588-6227		258
TF: 800-588-6227 ■ *Web:* www.nuby.com			
Luvata Appleton LLC 553 Carter Ct Kimberly WI 54136	920-749-3820	749-3850	485
TF: 866-488-0217 ■ *Web:* www.luvata.com			
Luvata Ohio Inc 1376 Pittsburgh Dr Delaware OH 43015	740-363-1981	363-3847	485
TF: 800-749-5510 ■ *Web:* www.luvata.com			
Luverne Truck Equipment Inc			
1200 Birch St Brandon SD 57005	605-582-7200		60
Web: www.luvernetruck.com			
Luverne Veterans Home			
1300 N Kniss Ave Luverne MN 56156	507-283-1100		793
TF: 800-627-3529 ■ *Web:* mn.gov			
Lux 5 Events			
4060 Campus Dr Ste 110 Newport Beach CA 92660	714-505-0050		193
Lux Art Institute			
1550 S El Camino Real Encinitas CA 92024	760-436-6611		520
TF: 800-745-3000 ■ *Web:* www.luxartinstitute.org			
Lux Bond & Green Inc			
46 Lasalle Rd West Hartford CT 06107	800-524-7336	521-8693*	410
**Fax Area Code:* 860 ■ *TF:* 800-524-7336 ■ *Web:* www.lbgreen.com			
Lux Scientiae Inc PO Box 326 Westwood MA 02090	800-441-6612		809
TF: 800-441-6612 ■ *Web:* luxsci.com			
Luxco 5050 Kemper Ave Saint Louis MO 63139	314-772-2626	772-6021	81-3
Web: www.luxco.com			
Luxe Bistro 47 York St Ottawa ON K1N5S7	613-241-8805		671
Web: www.luxebistro.com			
Luxe City Center Hotel			
1020 S Figueroa St Los Angeles CA 90015	213-748-1291		707
Web: www.luxecitycenter.com			
Luxe Hotel Rodeo Drive			
360 N Rodeo Dr Beverly Hills CA 90210	310-273-0300	859-8730	379
TF: 800-336-3745 ■ *Web:* www.luxehotels.com			
Luxe Hotel Sunset Blvd			
11461 Sunset Blvd Los Angeles CA 90049	310-476-6571	471-6310	379
TF: 800-468-3541 ■ *Web:* www.luxehotels.com			
Luxe Travel Management Inc			
16450 Bake Pkwy Ste 100 Irvine CA 92618	949-336-1000		772
Web: www.luxetm.com			
Luxe Worldwide Hotels			
11461 W Sunset Blvd Los Angeles CA 90049	310-440-3090		379
TF: 888-336-3745 ■ *Web:* www.luxehotels.com			

Phone | Fax | Class

Luxembourg
Consulate General 17 Beekman Pl. . . . New York NY 10022 212-888-6664 888-6116 257
Web: newyork-cg.mae.lu/en
Consulate General
1 Sansome St Ste 830 . . . San Francisco CA 94104 415-788-0816 788-0985 257
Web: sanfrancisco.mae.lu
Embassy 2200 Massachusetts Ave NW . . . Washington DC 20008 202-265-4171 328-8270 257
Web: washington.mae.lu

Luxfer Gas Cylinders
3016 Kansas Ave . . . Riverside CA 92507 951-684-5110 223
TF: 800-764-0366 ■ *Web:* luxfer.com

Luxo Corp 5 Westchester Plaza . . . Elmsford NY 10523 914-345-0067 345-0068* 439
*Fax: Sales ■ *TF:* 800-222-5896 ■ *Web:* glamox.com/luxous

Luxor Hotel & Casino
3900 Las Vegas Blvd S. . . . Las Vegas NV 89119 702-262-4000 262-4404 133
TF Resv: 800-288-1000 ■ *Web:* www.luxor.com

Luxour 2245 Delany Rd. . . . Waukegan IL 60087 847-244-1800 327-1698* 319-1
*Fax Area Code: 800 ■ *TF:* 800-323-4656 ■ *Web:* www.luxorfurn.com

Luxury Bath Technologies Corporate
1800 Industrial Dr. . . . Libertyville IL 60139 630-283-7545 362
Web: www.luxurybath.com

Luxury Link LLC
5200 W Century Blvd Ste 410. . . . Los Angeles CA 90045 310-215-8060 772
TF: 888-297-3299 ■ *Web:* www.luxurylink.com

Luxury Optical Holdings Inc
2651 N Crimson Canyon Dr Ste 200 . . . Las Vegas NV 89128 702-798-8638 544
Web: www.loholdings.com

Luxury Retreats International Inc
5530 St Patrick St Ste 2210 . . . Montreal QC H4E1A8 514-393-8844 505
TF: 877-993-0100 ■ *Web:* www.luxuryretreats.com

LUZ Inc 221 Main St Ste 1300. . . . San Francisco CA 94105 415-981-5890 393
Web: www.luz.com

Luzerne County 200 N River St . . . Wilkes-Barre PA 18711 570-825-1500 825-9343 338
Web: www.luzernecounty.org

Luzerne County Community College
1333 S Prospect St. . . . Nanticoke PA 18634 800-377-5222 740-0238* 162
*Fax Area Code: 570 ■ *Fax: Admissions ■ *TF:* 800-377-5222 ■ *Web:* www.luzerne.edu

Luzerne Optical Laboratories Ltd
180 N Wilkes Barre Blvd. . . . Wilkes-barre PA 18702 570-822-3183 237
Web: www.luzerneoptical.com

LV Lomas Ltd 99 Summerlea Rd . . . Brampton ON L6T4V2 905-458-1555 458-0722 146
TF: 800-575-3382 ■ *Web:* www.lvlomas.com

LVM Systems Inc 4262 E Florian Ave . . . Mesa AZ 85206 480-633-8200 177
Web: www.lvmsystems.com

LVM-JEGEL 1821 Albion Rd Unit 7 . . . Toronto ON M9W5W8 416-213-1060 261

LW Robbins Assoc 201 Summer St. . . . Holliston MA 01746 800-229-5972 317
TF: 800-229-5972 ■ *Web:* www.robbinskersten.com

LW Rozzo Inc 17200 Pines Blvd. . . . Pembroke Pines FL 33029 954-435-8501 436-6243 503-6

LWBJ Financial LLC
4200 University Ave Ste 410. . . . West Des Moines IA 50266 515-222-5600 463
Web: www.lwbj.com

LWDH (Lake of the Woods District Hospital)
21 Sylvan St. . . . Kenora ON P9N3W7 807-468-9861 468-3939 374-2
TF: 800-445-1822 ■ *Web:* www.lwdh.on.ca

LWISD (Lake Worth Independent School District)
6805 Telephone Rd. . . . Lake Worth TX 76135 817-306-4200 237-2583 685
Web: www.lwisd.org

Lwrc International LLC
815 Chesapeake Dr. . . . Cambridge MD 21613 410-901-1348 807
Web: www.lwrci.com

LWS (Laminated Wood Systems Inc)
1327 285th Rd PO Box 386 . . . Seward NE 68434 800-949-3526 643-4374* 817
*Fax Area Code: 402 ■ *TF:* 800-949-3526 ■ *Web:* www.lwsinc.com

LWV (League of Women Voters)
1730 M St NW Ste 1000. . . . Washington DC 20036 202-429-1965 429-0854 48-7
Web: www.lwv.org

LXE Inc 125 Technology Pkwy. . . . Norcross GA 30092 770-447-4224 447-4405 173-2
TF: 800-664-4593 ■ *Web:* www.honeywellaidc.com

LXR Luxury Resorts
501 E Camino Real Blvd. . . . Boca Raton FL 33432 561-447-5300 379
Web: www.luxuryresorts.com

Lyceum History Museum
201 S Washington St . . . Alexandria VA 22314 703-838-4994 838-4997 520
Web: www.alexandriava.gov/lyceum

Lyceum Kennedy French & American School
1 Cross Rd . . . Ardsley NY 10502 914-479-0722 196
TF: 800-944-7112 ■ *Web:* lyceumkennedy.org

Lyceum Theatre 149 W 45th St. . . . New York NY 10036 212-239-6200 747
TF: 800-432-7780 ■ *Web:* www.telecharge.com

Lychner State Jail 2350 Atascocita Rd. . . . Humble TX 77396 281-454-5036 213

Lycian Stage Lighting
1144 Kings Hwy PO Box D. . . . Sugar Loaf NY 10981 845-469-2285 469-5355 722
Web: www.lycian.com

Lyco Manufacturing Inc
115 Commercial Dr . . . Columbus WI 53925 920-623-4152 697
Web: www.lycomfg.com

Lycoming College 700 College Pl. . . . Williamsport PA 17701 570-321-4000 321-4317* 166
*Fax: Admissions ■ *TF:* 800-345-3920 ■ *Web:* www.lycoming.edu

Lycoming Engines 652 Oliver St. . . . Williamsport PA 17701 570-323-6181 529
TF: 800-258-3279 ■ *Web:* www.lycoming.com

Lycon Inc
1110 Harding St PO Box 427 . . . Janesville WI 53547 608-754-7701 754-8555 182
TF: 800-955-8758 ■ *Web:* www.lyconinc.com

LycoRed 377 Crane St. . . . Orange NJ 07050 973-882-0322 882-0323 479
TF: 877-592-6733 ■ *Web:* www.lycored.com

Lycos Inc 52 Second Ave . . . Waltham MA 02451 781-370-2700 397
Web: www.lycos.com

Lydall Inc 1 Colonial Rd. . . . Manchester CT 06042 860-646-1233 646-4917 561
NYSE: LDL ■ *Web:* www.lydall.com

Lyden Oil Company Inc
30692 Tracy Rd. . . . Walbridge OH 43465 419-666-1948 579
TF: 800-362-9410 ■ *Web:* www.lydenoilcompany.com

Lydig Construction Inc
11001 E Montgomery St. . . . Spokane WA 99206 509-534-0451 535-6622 186
Web: www.lydig.com

Lydon Co 143 St Clair Dr . . . Saint Simons Island GA 31522 912-638-0901 184

Lykes Cartage Company Inc
8606 Wall St Bldg 19 . . . Austin TX 78754 512-933-9060 314
Web: www.lykescartage.com

Lykes Insurance Inc 400 N Tampa St. . . . Tampa FL 33602 813-223-3911 391-4
Web: www.lykesinsurance.com

Lylab Technology Solutions Inc
526 Cumberland St. . . . Lebanon PA 17042 717-279-8595 196
Web: www.lylab.net

Lyle Co
3140 Gold Camp Dr Ste 30. . . . Rancho Cordova CA 95670 916-266-7000 196
Web: www.lyleco.com

Lyles-De Grazier Co
2050 N Stemmons Fwy Ste 7943 . . . Dallas TX 75207 214-747-3558 411
Web: www.lylesjewelry.com

Lyman Allyn Art Museum
625 Williams St . . . New London CT 06320 860-443-2545 442-1280 520
Web: www.lymanallyn.org

Lyman County PO Box 38 . . . Kennebec SD 57544 605-869-2247 338
TF: 800-368-8683 ■ *Web:* www.lymancounty.org

Lyman Lake State Park 11 US 180 . . . Saint Johns AZ 85936 928-337-4441 565
Web: www.azstateparks.com

Lyman Lumber Co 520 Third St Ste 200 . . . Excelsior MN 55331 952-470-3600 470-3670 191-3
Web: www.lymanlumber.com

Lyman Museum & Mission House
276 Haili St. . . . Hilo HI 96720 808-935-5021 969-7685 520
Web: www.lymanmuseum.org

Lyman Products Corp 475 Smith St. . . . Middletown CT 06457 860-632-2020 632-1699 284
TF: 800-225-9626 ■ *Web:* www.lymanproducts.com

Lyman Run State Park 454 Lyman Run Rd . . . Galeton PA 16922 814-435-5010 565
Web: www.dcnr.state.pa.us

Lyman-Richey Corp 4315 Cuming St. . . . Omaha NE 68131 402-558-2727 556-5171 191-1
TF: 800-537-2179 ■ *Web:* www.lymanrichey.com

Lymba Corp 1701 N Collins Blvd . . . Richardson TX 75080 972-680-0800 177
Web: www.lymba.com

Lyme Academy College of Fine Arts
84 Lyme St . . . Old Lyme CT 06371 860-434-5232 166
Web: www.lymeacademy.edu

Lymphoma Research Foundation (LRF)
115 Broadway Ste 1301 . . . New York NY 10006 212-349-2910 349-2886 48-17
TF: 800-500-9976 ■ *Web:* www.lymphoma.org

Lyna Manufacturing Inc
1125 15th St W. . . . North Vancouver BC V7P1M7 604-990-0988 754
TF: 800-993-4007 ■ *Web:* tirelyna.com

Lynair Inc 3515 Scheele Dr . . . Jackson MI 49202 517-787-2240 787-4521 223
Web: www.lynair.com

Lynbrook Glass & Architectural Metals Corp
941 Motor Pkwy . . . Hauppauge NY 11788 631-582-3060 582-3974 189-6
Web: www.lynbrookglass.com

Lynch Exhibits 7 Campus Dr. . . . Burlington NJ 08016 609-387-1600 239-1669 232
TF: 800-343-1666 ■ *Web:* www.lynchexhibits.com

Lynch Ford - Mt Vernon Inc
410 Hwy 30 SW . . . Mount Vernon IA 52314 319-895-8500 57
Web: www.lynchfordchevrolet.com

Lynch Livestock Co 331 Third St NW. . . . Waucoma IA 52171 563-776-3311 446
TF: 800-468-3178 ■ *Web:* www.lynchlivestock.com

Lynch Management Co
2165 River Blvd . . . Jacksonville FL 32204 904-387-1537 57

Lynch Metals Inc 1075 Lousons Rd. . . . Union NJ 07083 908-686-8401 791
TF: 888-272-9464 ■ *Web:* www.lynchmetals.com

Lynch Oil Company Inc
1244 E Carroll St . . . Kissimmee FL 34744 407-847-4161 316
Web: lynchoil.com

Lynch Stephen F (Rep D - MA)
2268 Rayburn HOB. . . . Washington DC 20515 202-225-8273 225-3984 342-2
Web: lynch.house.gov

Lynch, Traub, Keefe & Errante A Professional Corp
52 Trumbull St PO Box 1612 . . . New Haven CT 06510 203-787-0275 428
TF: 888-692-7403 ■ *Web:* www.ltke.com

Lynchburg College 1501 Lakeside Dr. . . . Lynchburg VA 24501 434-544-8100 544-8653* 166
*Fax: Admissions ■ *TF:* 800-426-8101 ■ *Web:* www.lynchburg.edu

Lynchburg Health & Rehabilitation Ctr
5615 Seminole Ave. . . . Lynchburg VA 24502 434-239-2657 450
Web: lynchburghealthrehab.com

Lynchburg (Independent City)
900 Church St . . . Lynchburg VA 24504 434-856-2489 847-1536 338
TF: 800-552-0962 ■ *Web:* www.lynchburgva.gov

Lynchburg Public Library
2315 Memorial Ave. . . . Lynchburg VA 24501 434-455-6300 434-3
Web: www.lynchburgpubliclibrary.org

Lynchburg Regional Chamber of Commerce
2015 Memorial Ave. . . . Lynchburg VA 24501 434-845-5966 522-9592 139
Web: www.lynchburgregion.org

Lynchburg Steel & Specialty Co
275 Francis Ave . . . Monroe VA 24574 434-929-0951 929-2613 723
Web: lynchburgsteel.com

Lynches River Electric Co-op Inc
1104 W McGregor St . . . Pageland SC 29728 843-672-6111 672-6118 245
TF: 800-922-3486 ■ *Web:* www.lynchesriver.com

Lynchval Systems Worldwide Inc
13921 Park Center Rd Ste 100 . . . Herndon VA 20171 703-709-1000 463
Web: www.lynchval.com

Lynco Flange & Fitting Inc
5114 Steadmont Dr. . . . Houston TX 77040 713-690-0040 61
Web: www.lyncoflange.com

Lynda.com Inc 6410 Via Real . . . Carpinteria CA 93013 805-477-3900 194
TF: 888-335-9632 ■ *Web:* www.lynda.com

Lynden Air Cargo LLC
6441 S Airpark Pl. . . . Anchorage AK 99502 907-243-7248 257-5124 12
TF: 888-243-7248 ■ *Web:* www.lynden.com

Lynden Door Inc 2077 Main St . . . Lynden WA 98264 360-354-5676 499
Web: www.lyndendoor.com

Lynden Inc
18000 International Blvd Ste 800 . . . Seattle WA 98188 206-241-8778 243-8415 311
TF: 888-596-3361 ■ *Web:* www.lynden.com

Lynden International Logistics Co
10 Corrine Ct . . . Vaughan ON L4K4T7 905-879-0114 449
Web: www.lynden.com/lilco

	Phone	Fax	Class
Lynden Transport Inc 3027 Rampart Dr .... Anchorage AK 99501 *Fax Area Code: 907 ■ TF: 800-327-9390 ■ Web: www.lynden.com	800-327-9390	257-5155*	780
Lynden Tribune 113 Sixth St .... Lynden WA 98264 Web: lyndentribune.com	360-354-4444		5
Lynde-Ordway Company Inc 3308 W Warner Ave .... Santa Ana CA 92704 TF: 800-762-7057 ■ Web: www.lynde-ordway.com	714-957-1311	433-2166	111
Lyndhurst 635 S Broadway .... Tarrytown NY 10591 Web: www.lyndhurst.org	914-631-4481		50-3
Lyndhurst Foundation 517 E Fifth St .... Chattanooga TN 37403 Web: www.lyndhurstfoundation.org	423-756-0767		305
Lyndon B. Johnson National Historical Park 100 Lady Bird Ln .... Johnson City TX 78636 Web: www.nps.gov/lyjo	830-868-7128	868-7863	564
Lyndon B. Johnson State Park & Historic Site PO Box 238 .... Stonewall TX 78671 Web: tpwd.texas.gov	830-644-2252		565
Lyndon Baines Johnson Memorial Grove on the Potomac Turkey Run Pk George Washington Memorial Pkwy . McLean VA 22101 Web: www.nps.gov/lyba	703-289-2500	289-2598	564
Lyndon Group LLC 220 Newport Ctr Dr Ste 11-529 .... Newport Beach CA 92660 TF: 800-900-1131 ■ Web: www.lyndon-group.com	949-494-7722		466
Lyndon State College 1001 College Rd PO Box 919 .... Lyndonville VT 05851 TF: 800-225-1998 ■ Web: www.lyndonstate.edu	802-626-6413	626-6335	166
Lyndon Steel Co 1947 Union Cross Rd .... Winston-Salem NC 27107 Web: www.lyndonsteel.com	336-785-0848		480
Lyn-Flex West Inc 405 Red Oak Rd PO Box 570 .... Owensville MO 65066 Web: www.lynflex.com	573-437-4125	437-2350	301
Lynn a Sylvester CPA PA 675 S Haywood St .... Waynesville NC 28786 Web: www.lascpa-nc.com	828-456-6505		2
Lynn Area Chamber of Commerce 583 Chestnut St Unit 8 .... Lynn MA 01901 TF: 800-617-4762 ■ Web: www.lynnareachamber.com	781-592-2900	592-2903	139
Lynn Blueprint & Supply Company Inc 328 Old Vine St .... Lexington KY 40507 Web: www.lynnimaging.com	859-255-1021		627
Lynn County PO Box 937 .... Tahoka TX 79373 Web: www.co.lynn.tx.us	806-561-4750	561-4988	338
Lynn Electronics Corp 154 Railroad Dr .... Ivyland PA 18974 TF: 800-624-2220 ■ Web: www.lynnelec.com	215-355-8200		253
Lynn Ladder & Scaffolding Company Inc 20 Boston St .... Lynn MA 01904 TF: 800-225-2510 ■ Web: www.lynnladder.com	781-598-6010	593-2915	421
Lynn Layton Chevrolet Inc 2416 Hwy 31 S .... Decatur AL 35601 Web: www.lynnlaytonchevrolet.com	256-274-4665		57
Lynn Meadows Discovery Ctr 246 Dolan Ave .... Gulfport MS 39507 Web: www.lmdc.org	228-897-6039	248-0071	521
Lynn Products Inc 2645 W 237th St .... Torrance CA 90505 Web: www.lynnprod.com	310-530-5966	530-8426	814
Lynn Public Library 5 N Common St .... Lynn MA 01902 Web: www.noblenet.org/lynn	781-595-0567	592-5050	434-3
Lynn Sign 8 Gleason St .... Andover MA 01810	978-470-1194		701
Lynn Todd m 12350 Jefferson Ave Ste 300 .... Newport News VA 23602 Web: www.pwhd.com	757-223-4573		428
Lynn University 3601 N Military Trl .... Boca Raton FL 33431 *Fax: Admissions ■ TF Admissions: 800-888-5966 ■ Web: www.lynn.edu	561-237-7900	237-7100*	166
Lynn Water & Sewer Commission 400 Parkland Ave .... Lynn MA 01905 TF: 800-870-9999 ■ Web: www.lynnwatersewer.org	781-596-2400		192
Lynn's Steakhouse 955 Dairy Ashford .... Houston TX 77079 Web: www.lynnssteakhouse.com	281-870-0807	870-0888	671
Lynnco Supply Chain Solutions Inc 2448 E 81St St Ste 2600 .... Tulsa OK 74137 TF: 866-872-3264 ■ Web: lynnco-scs.com	918-664-5540		314
Lynnhaven Fish House 2350 Starfish Rd .... Virginia Beach VA 23451 TF: 800-296-0800 ■ Web: www.lynnhavenfishhouse.net	757-481-0003		671
Lynnhaven House 2040 Potters Rd .... Virginia Beach VA 23454 Web: www.virginiabeachhistory.org	757-491-3490		50-3
Lynnhaven Mall 701 Lynnhaven Pkwy Ste 1068 .... Virginia Beach VA 23452 Web: www.lynnhavenmall.com	757-340-9340		460
Lynntech Inc 2501 Earl Rudder Fwy S Ste 100 .... College Station TX 77845 Web: www.lynntech.com	979-764-2200		201
Lynnwood Convention Center 3711 196th St SW .... Lynnwood WA 98036 TF: 800-778-7155 ■ Web: lynnwoodcc.com	425-778-7155		184
Lyntegar Electric Co-op Inc PO Box 970 .... Tahoka TX 79373 TF: 877-218-2308 ■ Web: lyntegar.coop	806-561-4588		245
LynuxWorks Inc 855 Embedded Way .... San Jose CA 95138 TF: 800-255-5969 ■ Web: lynx.com/index.php	408-979-3900	979-3920	178-10
Lynx Brand Fence Products 4330 76 Ave SE .... Calgary AB T2C2J2 TF: 800-665-5969 ■ Web: www.lynxfence.com	403-273-4821		191-1
Lynx Computer Technologies Inc 7 Bristol Ct .... Wyomissing PA 19610 TF: 800-331-5969 ■ Web: lynxnet.com	610-678-8131		180
Lynx Enterprises 724 E Grant Line Rd Ste B .... Tracy CA 95304 Web: lynxenterprises.com	209-833-3400		697
Lynx Equity Ltd 692 Queen St E Ste 205 .... Toronto ON M4M1G9 Web: www.lynxequity.com	416-323-3512		528
Lynx Grills Inc 5895 Rickenbacker Rd .... Commerce CA 90040 TF: 888-289-5969 ■ Web: www.lynxgrills.com	323-838-1770		362
Lynx Group Inc 2746 Front St NE .... Salem OR 97301 TF: 800-882-1844 ■ Web: www.lynxgroup.com	503-588-9339		627
Lynx Media Inc 12501 Chandler Blvd Ste 202 .... Valley Village CA 91607 TF: 800-451-5969 ■ Web: lynxmedia.com	818-761-5859		177
Lynx Studio Technology Inc 1048 Irvine Ave .... Newport Beach CA 92660 Web: www.lynxstudio.com	949-515-8265		526
Lyon & Billard Co, The 38 Gypsy Ln .... Meriden CT 06451	203-235-4487		191-3
Lyon & Healy Harps Inc 168 N Ogden Ave .... Chicago IL 60607 TF: 800-621-3881 ■ Web: www.lyonhealy.com	312-786-1881	226-1502	527
Lyon Advertising 600 Escarpment Blvd 745 28 .... Austin TX 78749 Web: www.lyonadvertising.com	512-480-5966		7
Lyon College 2300 Highland Rd .... Batesville AR 72501 TF: 800-423-2542 ■ Web: www.lyon.edu	870-793-9813		166
Lyon County 27 S Main St .... Yerington NV 89447 Web: www.lyoncounty.ky.gov	270-388-2331	388-0634	338
Lyon County 430 Commercial St .... Emporia KS 66801 Web: www.lyoncounty.org	620-341-4380		338
Lyon County 607 W Main St .... Marshall MN 56258 *Fax: Acctg ■ Web: www.lyonco.org	507-537-6722	537-6091*	338
Lyon County 206 S Second Ave .... Rock Rapids IA 51246 Web: www.lyoncountyiowa.com	712-472-8530		338
Lyon Rural Electric Co-op 116 S Marshall St .... Rock Rapids IA 51246 TF: 800-658-3976 ■ Web: www.lyonrec.coop	712-472-2506		245
Lyon Shipyard Inc PO Box 2180 .... Norfolk VA 23501 Web: www.lyonshipyard.com	757-622-4661		698
Lyon Veterinary Clinic 21188 Pontiac Trl .... South Lyon MI 48178 Web: lyonveterinaryclinic.com	248-486-8800		794
Lyon Work Space Products 420 N Main St .... Montgomery IL 60538 TF: 800-433-8488 ■ Web: www.lyonworkspace.com	630-892-8941	892-8966	286
Lyon-Coffey Electric Co-op Inc 1013 N 4th PO Box 229 .... Burlington KS 66839 TF: 800-748-7395 ■ Web: www.lyon-coffey.coop	620-364-2116		245
Lyondellbasell Industries Inc 1221 McKinney St LyondellBasell Tower Ste 700 .... Houston TX 77010 TF: 800-526-1072 ■ Web: www.lyondellbasell.com	713-309-7200		787
LyonHeart Communications Inc 220 E 42nd St 3rd Fl .... New York NY 10017	212-771-3000	771-3010	4
Lyon-Lincoln Electric Co-op Inc (LLEC) 205 W Hwy 14 PO Box 639 .... Tyler MN 56178 TF: 800-927-6276 ■ Web: www.llec.coop	507-247-5505		245
Lyons & Lyons Attorneys at Law 8310 Princeton Glendale Rd .... West Chester OH 45069 TF: 800-210-7239 ■ Web: www.lyonsandlyonslaw.com	513-777-2222		428
Lyons Company Inc 308 Samson St .... Glasgow KY 42141 Web: www.lyonscompany.com	270-651-2733		697
Lyons Doughty & Veldhuis PC 15 Ashley Pl Ste 2b .... Wilmington DE 19804 Web: www.ldvlaw.com	302-428-1670		445
Lyons Elementary School District 103 4100 Joliet Ave .... Lyons IL 60534 Web: www.sd103.com	708-783-4100		685
Lyons Magnus Inc 3158 E Hamilton Ave .... Fresno CA 93702 *Fax Area Code: 559 ■ TF: 800-344-7130 ■ Web: www.lyonsmagnus.com	800-344-7130	233-8249*	296-20
Lyons Tool & Die Company Inc, The 185 Research Pkwy .... Meriden CT 06450 Web: www.lyons.com	203-238-2689		697
LyonsHR 1941 Florence Blvd .... Florence AL 35630 Web: www.lyonshr.com	256-767-5900		260
Lyric Opera of Chicago 20 N Wacker Dr .... Chicago IL 60606 Web: www.lyricopera.org	312-332-2244	332-8120	573-2
Lyric Optical Company Wholsle 3533 Cardiff Ave .... Cincinnati OH 45209 TF: 800-543-7376 ■ Web: www.superoptical.com	513-321-2456		544
Lyric Theatre of Oklahoma 1727 NW 16th St .... Oklahoma City OK 73106 Web: www.lyrictheatreokc.com	405-524-9312	524-9316	573-4
Lyster Army Health Clinic Andrews Ave .... Fort Rucker AL 36362 TF: 800-261-7193 ■ Web: lyster.amedd.army.mil/sitepages/home.aspx	800-261-7193		374-4
Lytica Inc 308 Legget Dr Ste 200 .... Kanata ON K2K1Y6 Web: www.lytica.com	613-271-1414		463
Lytle Land & Cattle Co 1150 E S 11th St .... Abilene TX 79604 Web: www.lytlelandandcattle.com	325-677-1925		671
Lytmos Group Inc 400 SW Longview Blvd Ste 290 .... Lees Summit MO 64081 Web: www.lytmos.com	816-347-9449		708
Lytro 1300 Terra Bella Ave .... Mountain View CA 94043 Web: www.lytro.com	650-316-8888		224
Lytron Inc 55 Dragon Ct .... Woburn MA 01801 Web: www.lytron.com	781-933-7300		664
Lytton Gardens Inc 656 Lytton Ave .... Palo Alto CA 94301 Web: www.jtm-esc.org/lytton-gardens	650-617-7373	617-7415	793
Lyynks Inc 1812 W Burbank Blvd Unit 644 .... Burbank CA 91506 Web: lyynks.com	818-478-2260		177
LZ Truck Equipment Inc 1881 Rice St .... Saint Paul MN 55113 TF: 800-247-1082 ■ Web: www.lztruckequipment.com	651-488-2571	488-9857	516

M

Phone | Fax | Class

M & A Supply Company Inc
1540 Amherst Rd — Knoxville TN 37909 — 865-584-0510 — 612
Web: www.masupplycompany.com

M & A Technology Inc
2045 Chenault Dr — Carrollton TX 75006 — 972-490-5803 — 490-0616 — 174
TF: 800-225-1452 ■ *Web:* www.macomp.com

M & C Specialties Co 90 James Way — SouthHampton PA 18966 — 215-322-1600 — 322-1620 — 732
TF Cust Svc: 800-441-6996 ■ *Web:* www.mcspecialties.com

M & F Worldwide Corp 35 E 62nd St — New York NY 10065 — 212-572-8600 — 296-15
NYSE: MFW ■ *Web:* www.mandfworldwide.com

M & G Electronics Corp
889 Seahawk Cir — Virginia Beach VA 23452 — 757-468-6000 — 247

M & G Graphics 3500 W 38th St — Chicago IL 60632 — 773-247-1596 — 627
TF: 800-252-6793 ■ *Web:* m-g-graphics.com

M & G Industries Inc
85 Broadcommon Rd — Bristol RI 02809 — 401-253-0096 — 492
Web: www.m-gind.com

M & H Enterprises Inc
19450 Hwy 249 Ste 600 — Houston TX 77070 — 281-664-7222 — 261
Web: mhes.com

M & J Materials Inc
7561 Gadsden Hwy — Trussville AL 35173 — 205-655-7451 — 480

M & J Transportation
3536 Nicholson Ave — Kansas City MO 64120 — 816-231-6733 — 231-7645 — 449
TF: 866-298-3858 ■ *Web:* www.mjtransportationkc.com

M & K CPAs PLLC
4100 Nsam Houston Pkwy — Houston TX 77086 — 832-242-9950 — 2
TF: 866-770-5931 ■ *Web:* mkcpas.com

M & L Industries Inc 1210 St Charles St — Houma LA 70360 — 985-876-2280 — 872-9596 — 385
TF General: 800-969-0068 ■ *Web:* www.mlind.net

M & L Transit Systems Inc
60 Olympia Ave Ste 1 — Woburn MA 01801 — 781-938-8646 — 108
Web: www.mltsi.com

M & M Designs Inc
1981 Quality Blvd — Huntsville TX 77320 — 800-627-0656 — 295-9286* — 687
**Fax Area Code:* 936 ■ *TF:* 800-627-0656 ■ *Web:* www.m-mdesigns.com

M & M Industries Inc
316 Corporate Pl — Chattanooga TN 37419 — 423-821-3302 — 596
Web: www.ultimatepail.com

M & M Innovations
7424 Blythe Island Hwy — Brunswick GA 31523 — 912-265-7110 — 228
TF: 800-688-3384 ■ *Web:* www.drgeorges.com

M & M Pipeline Services LLC
274 Mt Moriah Rd — Eupora MS 39744 — 662-258-7101 — 539
Web: www.mmpipeline.com

M & M Supply Co
901 Peach Ave PO Box 548 — Duncan OK 73534 — 580-252-7879 — 252-7708 — 537
TF: 800-424-9300 ■ *Web:* www.mmsupply.com

M & p Export Management Corp
2329 Hwy 34 Ste 204 — Manasquan NJ 08736 — 732-223-0160 — 195
Web: mpexport.com

M & Q Plastic Products Inc
PO Box 180 Ste 206 — Schuylkill Haven PA 17972 — 570-385-4991 — 385-4954 — 604
Web: www.mqplastics.com

M & R Sales & Service Inc
1n 372 Main St — Glen Ellyn IL 60137 — 630-858-6101 — 858-6134 — 627
TF: 800-736-6431 ■ *Web:* www.mrprint.com

M & W Transportation Company Inc
1110 Pumping Sta Rd — Nashville TN 37210 — 615-256-5755 — 393
TF: 800-251-4209 ■ *Web:* www.mwlginc.com

M at Miranova 2 Miranova PL Ste 100 — Columbus OH 43215 — 614-629-0000 — 221-5020 — 671
TF: 877-491-1267 ■ *Web:* www.matmiranova.com

M B Klein Inc
243-A Cockeysville Rd Ste A — Cockeysville MD 21030 — 410-229-9995 — 761
Web: www.modeltrainstuff.com

M Block & Sons Inc
5020 W 73rd St — Bedford Park IL 60638 — 708-728-8400 — 728-0022 — 361
TF: 800-621-8845 ■ *Web:* www.mblock.com

M Booth & Assoc Inc
300 Pk Ave S 12th Fl — New York NY 10010 — 212-481-7000 — 636
Web: www.mbooth.com

M Box Design 9234 Deering Ave — Chatsworth CA 91311 — 818-700-7770 — 180
Web: www.mboxdesign.com

M C Electronics Inc 1891 Airway Dr — Hollister CA 95023 — 831-637-1651 — 45
Web: www.mcelectronics.com

M C Steel Inc
2 Braco International Blvd — Wilder Ky 41076 — 859-781-8600 — 492
Web: www.mcsteel.com

M Conley Co 1312 Fourth St SE — Canton OH 44707 — 330-456-8243 — 588-2572* — 559
**Fax:* Cust Svc ■ *TF:* 800-362-6001 ■ *Web:* www.mconley.com

M Corp 947 Enterprise Dr Loft C — Sacramento CA 95825 — 916-254-0355 — 463
Web: www.the-mcorp.com

M Cubed Technologies Inc 921 Main St — Monroe CT 06468 — 203-452-2333 — 452-2335 — 696
Web: www.mmmt.com

M Davis & Sons Inc 19 Germay Dr — Wilmington DE 19804 — 302-998-3385 — 610
TF: 800-913-2847 ■ *Web:* www.mdavisinc.com

M e Group Inc 2820 N 48th St Ste 200 — Lincoln NE 68504 — 402-464-3833 — 187
Web: www.megroup.com

M Ecker & Co 9525 W Bryn Mawr Ave — Rosemont IL 60018 — 847-994-6000 — 233-9715 — 189-9

M Eg Enterprises 262 W Broadway — Waukesha WI 53186 — 262-522-3220 — 226

M Floyd John & Assoc Inc (JMFA)
125 N Burnett Dr — Baytown TX 77520 — 800-809-2307 — 424-8864* — 194
**Fax Area Code:* 281 ■ *TF:* 800-809-2307 ■ *Web:* www.jmfa.com

M G America Inc 31 Kulick Rd — Fairfield NJ 07004 — 973-808-8185 — 358
Web: mgamerica.com

M G Credit Inc 5115 San Juan Ave — Jacksonville FL 32210 — 800-387-6503 — 160
TF: 800-387-6503 ■ *Web:* www.mgcredit.com

M Gibson Hotels Group
409 Montbrook Ln — Knoxville TN 37919 — 865-539-0588 — 378
Web: www.mgibsonhotels.com

M Gingerich Gereaux & Assoc
240 N Industrial Dr — Bradley IL 60915 — 815-939-4921 — 261

M Gottfried Roofing Inc
89 Research Dr — Stamford CT 06906 — 203-323-8173 — 189-12
Web: www.mgottfried.com

M Group Inc
187 S Old Woodward Ste 200 — Birmingham MI 48009 — 248-540-8843 — 360-3
Web: www.mgroupinc.com

M Holland 400 Skokie Blvd Ste 600 — Northbrook IL 60062 — 800-872-7370 — 603
TF: 800-872-7370 ■ *Web:* www.mholland.com

M K Products Inc 16882 Armstrong Ave — Irvine CA 92606 — 949-863-1234 — 474-1428 — 811
TF: 800-787-9707 ■ *Web:* www.mkprod.com

M K Smith Chevrolet 12845 Central Ave — Chino CA 91710 — 909-628-8961 — 628-6637 — 516
Web: www.mksmithchevrolet.com

M K Specialty Metal Fabricators
725 W Wintergreen Rd — Hutchins TX 75141 — 972-225-6562 — 697
TF: 866-814-4617 ■ *Web:* www.mkspecialty.com

M L S Data Management Solutions
6115 Camp Bowie Blvd Ste 200 — Fort Worth TX 76116 — 817-804-6900 — 463
TF: 800-454-0223 ■ *Web:* www.mlsc.com

M Lipsitz & Co Inc 100 Elm St — Waco TX 76704 — 254-756-6661 — 752-0175 — 686
Web: www.mlipsitzco.com

M N S Ltd 766 Pohukaina St — Honolulu HI 96813 — 808-591-2550 — 237
Web: www.abcstores.com

M Neils Engineering Inc
100 Howe Ave — Sacramento CA 95825 — 916-923-4400 — 261
Web: mneilsengineering.com

M R A Technologies 2502 Park Rd — Emerald Hills CA 94062 — 650-361-8140 — 180
Web: www.mra-tech.com

M R L Equipment Company Inc
PO Box 31154 — Billings MT 59107 — 406-869-9900 — 358
TF: 877-788-2907 ■ *Web:* www.markritelines.com

M Ramsey King Securities Inc
93 Tomlin Cir — Burr Ridge IL 60527 — 630-789-0607 — 690
Web: mramseyking.com

M Resort LLC, The
12300 Las Vegas Blvd S — Henderson NV 89044 — 702-797-1000 — 133
Web: www.themresort.com

M Rondano Inc 49 E Ave — Norwalk CT 06851 — 203-846-1577 — 846-9564 — 189-5
Web: www.rondano.com

M S Benbow & Associates Professional Engineering Corp
2450 Severn Ave — Metairie LA 70001 — 504-832-2000 — 261
Web: www.msbenbow.com

M Squared Engineering LLC
W62n215 Washington Ave — Cedarburg WI 53012 — 262-376-4246 — 261
Web: msquaredengineering.com

M Steinert & Sons Co 162 Boylston St — Boston MA 02116 — 617-426-1900 — 526
TF: 800-540-8157 ■ *Web:* www.msteinert.com

M Tm Molded Products 3370 Obco Ct — Dayton OH 45414 — 937-890-7461 — 361
Web: www.mtmcase-gard.com

M W Consulting Engineers LLC
222 Wall St Ste 200 — Spokane WA 99201 — 509-838-9020 — 261
Web: www.mwengineers.com

M Waterfront Grille
4300 Gulf Shore Blvd N — Naples FL 34103 — 239-263-4421 — 671
Web: www.mwaterfrontgrille.com

M. Braun Inc 14 Marin Way — Stratham NH 03885 — 603-773-9333 — 773-0008 — 419
Web: www.mbraun.com

M. H. Eby Inc PO Box 127 — Blue Bell PA 17506 — 717-354-4971 — 355-2114 — 516
TF: 800-292-4752 ■ *Web:* www.mheby.com

M. Lee Smith Publishers LLC
PO Box 5094 — Brentwood TN 37024 — 615-373-7517 — 627
TF: 800-274-6774 ■ *Web:* www.mleesmith.com

M.B. Kahn Construction Company Inc
101 Flintlake Rd — Columbia SC 29223 — 803-736-2950 — 186
Web: www.mbkahn.com

M.d.m. Commercial Enterprises Inc
1102 A1a N Ste 205 — Ponte Vedra FL 32082 — 800-359-6741 — 241-3133* — 38
**Fax Area Code:* 904 ■ *TF:* 800-359-6741 ■ *Web:* www.mdmcommercial.com

M.G. Newell Corp 301 Citation Ct — Greensboro NC 27409 — 336-393-0100 — 358
TF: 800-334-0231 ■ *Web:* www.mgnewell.com

M.H. Equipment Co
2001 E Hartman Rd — Chillicothe IL 61523 — 309-579-8020 — 358
TF: 888-564-2191 ■ *Web:* www.mhequipment.com

M.J. Harris Construction Services LLC
1 Riverchase Rdg — Birmingham AL 35244 — 205-380-6800 — 380-6801 — 186
Web: www.mjharris.com

M/A/R/C Research 1660 Westridge Cir — Irving TX 75038 — 972-983-0400 — 983-0444 — 466
TF: 800-884-6272 ■ *Web:* www.marcresearch.com

M/A-COM Technology Solutions Inc
100 Chelmsford St — Lowell MA 01851 — 978-656-2500 — 696
TF: 800-366-2266 ■ *Web:* macom.com

M/E Engineering PC
150 N Chestnut St — Rochester NY 14604 — 585-288-5590 — 288-0233 — 261
Web: www.meengineering.com

M/I Homes Inc 3 Easton Oval — Columbus OH 43219 — 614-418-8700 — 418-8080 — 653
NYSE: MHO ■ *TF:* 888-644-4111 ■ *Web:* www.mihomes.com

M1 Networks Inc 6019 Mcpherson Rd Ste 4 — Laredo TX 78041 — 956-718-1005 — 175
TF: 800-433-5778 ■ *Web:* m1networks.net

M-13 Construction Management LLC
775 W Spring Creek Pl — Springville UT 84663 — 801-489-3215 — 480
Web: www.m-13.com

M2 Global Inc 5714 Epsilon — San Antonio TX 78249 — 210-561-4800 — 561-4852 — 697
Web: www.m2global.com

M2 Logistics Inc 2413 Hazelwood Ln — Green Bay WI 54304 — 920-569-8800 — 463
TF: 800-391-5121 ■ *Web:* www.m2logistics.com

M2 Technology Inc
21702 Hardy Oak Ste 100 — San Antonio TX 78258 — 210-566-3773 — 566-3993 — 178-1
TF: 800-267-1760 ■ *Web:* www.m2ti.com

M2M Data Corp
345 Inverness Dr S Ste C-320 — Englewood CO 80112 — 303-768-0064 — 799-8828 — 177
Web: www.m2mdatacorp.com

M2M Datasmart Inc
2010 Jimmy Durante Blvd Ste 220 — Del Mar CA 92014 — 858-350-5855 — 387
Web: www.m2mdatasmart.com

m2m Imaging Corp
5247 Wilson Mills Rd Ste 252 — Cleveland OH 44143 — 440-684-9690 — 476
TF: 800-686-7826 ■ *Web:* www.m2mimaging.com

m2M Strategies LLC
33 Buford Village Way Ste 329 — Buford GA 30518 — 678-835-9080 — 466
TF: 800-345-1070 ■ *Web:* m2mstrategies.com

Phone | Fax | Class

M2ns Inc 6037 Frantz Rd Ste 103 Dublin OH 43017 614-798-5177 180
Web: www.m2ns.com

M2S Inc 12 Commerce Ave West Lebanon NH 03784 603-298-5509 298-5055 177
Web: www.m2s.com

M2SYS LLC
1050 Crown Pointe Pkwy Ste 850 Atlanta GA 30338 770-393-0986 400
TF: 800-356-7311 ■ *Web:* www.m2sys.com

M3 Capital Partners
150 S Wacker Dr 31st Fl Chicago IL 60606 312-499-8500 691
TF: 800-289-9999 ■ *Web:* www.mcp-llc.com

M3 Engineering & Technology Corp
2051 W Sunset Rd Tucson AZ 85704 520-293-1488 261
Web: m3eng.com

M3 Technology Inc 58 Sawgrass Dr Bellport NY 11713 631-205-0005 179
TF: 800-356-6599 ■ *Web:* www.m3-tec.com

M3 USA Corp 1215 17th St NW Ste 100 Washington DC 20036 202-293-2288 395
TF: 800-638-3030 ■ *Web:* usa.m3.com

M45 Marketing Services Inc
524 W Stephenson St Freeport IL 61032 815-297-0166 195
Web: m45.com

M5 Marketing Communications Inc
42 O'Leary Ave St. John's NL A1B4B7 709-753-5559 5
Web: www.m5.ca

M-5 Steel Manufacturing Inc
1450 Mirasol St Los Angeles CA 90023 323-263-9383 480
Web: www.m5steel.com

M80 Services Inc 2894 Rowena Ave Los Angeles CA 90039 323-436-6750 644-7801 366

MA (Marble Arms) 420 Industrial Pk Dr Gladstone MI 49837 906-428-3710 710
Web: www.marblearms.com

M&A Advisor LLC, The
108-18 Queens Blvd 2nd Fl Forest Hills NY 11375 718-997-7900 557
TF: 877-996-3743 ■ *Web:* www.maadvisor.com

MA Angeliades Inc 5-44 47th Ave Long Island NY 11101 718-786-5555 786-4700 186
Web: www.ma-angeliades.com

Ma Cher (usa) Inc
1518 Abbot Kinney Blvd Venice CA 90291 310-581-5222 636
Web: www.macher.com

Ma Engineers Inc
5160 Carroll Canyon Rd Ste 200 San Diego CA 92121 858-200-0030 261
Web: www.ma-engr.com

MA Gedney Co 2100 Stoughton Ave Chaska MN 55318 952-448-2612 448-1790 296-19
TF: 888-244-0653 ■ *Web:* www.gedneyfoods.com

Ma Industries Inc
303 Dividend Dr Peachtree City GA 30269 770-487-7761 596
Web: www.maind.com

MA Laboratories Inc
2075 N Capitol Ave San Jose CA 95132 408-941-0808 941-0909 174
Web: www.malabs.com

MA Mortenson Co 700 Meadow Ln N Minneapolis MN 55422 763-522-2100 186
Web: www.mortenson.com

MA Ogg Heating & Air Conditioning Inc
4721 Arrow Hwy Ste B Montclair CA 91763 909-624-8608 624-9326 189-10

MA Patout & Son Ltd
3512 J Patout Burns Rd Jeanerette LA 70544 337-276-4592 276-4247 296-38
Web: www.mapatout.com

MA Reich & Co Inc 481 Franklin St Buffalo NY 14202 716-856-4085 411

MAA (MAAC) 6584 Poplar Ave Memphis TN 38138 901-682-6600 682-6667 655
NYSE: MAA ■ *TF:* 866-620-1130 ■ *Web:* www.maac.com

MAA (Mathematical Assn of America)
1529 18th St NW Washington DC 20036 202-387-5200 265-2384 49-19
TF: 800-331-1622 ■ *Web:* www.maa.org

MAA FOCUS 1529 18th St NW Washington DC 20036 202-387-5200 265-2384 457-8
TF: 800-741-9415 ■ *Web:* maa.org/publications/periodicals/maa-focus

MAAC (MAA) 6584 Poplar Ave Memphis TN 38138 901-682-6600 682-6667 655
NYSE: MAA ■ *TF:* 866-620-1130 ■ *Web:* www.maac.com

MAAC Machinery Corp
590 Tower Blvd Carol Stream IL 60188 630-665-1700 111
TF: 800-588-6222 ■ *Web:* maacmachinery.com

Maaco LLC 440 S Church St Ste 700 Charlotte NC 28202 800-523-1180 62-4
TF: 800-523-1180 ■ *Web:* www.maaco.com

Maahs & Vanlahr PC
3911 Old Lee Hwy Ste 43E Fairfax VA 22030 703-691-8632 734
Web: maahsandvanlahrcpa.com

Maas Bros Construction Company Inc
410 Water Tower Ct Watertown WI 53094 920-261-1682 186
Web: www.maasbros.com

Maas-Hansen Steel Corp
2435 E 37th St PO Box 58364 Vernon CA 90058 323-586-0171 492
TF: 800-647-8335 ■ *Web:* www.maashansen.com

Maas-Rowe Carillons Inc
2255 Meyers Ave Escondido CA 92029 800-854-2023 747-2677* 527
**Fax Area Code: 760* ■ *TF:* 800-854-2023 ■ *Web:* www.maasrowe.com

Maax Corp 160 St Joseph Blvd Lachine QC H8S2L3 877-438-6229 610
TF: 888-957-7816 ■ *Web:* www.maax.com

Maax Spas (Arizona) Inc
25605 S Arizona Ave Chandler AZ 85248 480-895-0598 610
Web: www.colemanspas.com

Mabbett & Associates Inc 5 Alfred Cir Bedford MA 01730 781-275-6050 256
Web: www.mabbett.com

Mabel Bassett Correctional Ctr
29501 Kickapoo Rd McLoud OK 74851 405-964-3020 213

Mabiles Corner Pharmacy 100 Gulf St Coushatta LA 71019 318-932-5727 237

Mabis Healthcare Inc 1931 Norman Dr Waukegan IL 60085 800-526-4753 479-7968 475
TF: 800-526-4753 ■ *Web:* www.mabisdmi.com

Mabry House 1540 Irving Pl Shreveport LA 71101 318-227-1121 671

Mabuchi Motor America Corp
3001 W Big Beaver Rd Ste 328 Troy MI 48084 248-816-3100 816-3242 518
Web: www.mabuchi-motor.co.jp

MabVax Therapeutics Inc
11588 Sorrento Valley Rd Ste 20 San Diego CA 92121 858-259-9405 231
Web: www.mabvax.com

MAC (Monongalia Arts Ctr)
107 High St PO Box 239 Morgantown WV 26507 304-292-3325 292-3326 50-2
TF: 800-745-3000 ■ *Web:* www.monartscenter.com

Mac Cal Company Inc
1737 Junction Ave San Jose CA 95112 408-441-1435 697
TF: 800-642-2541 ■ *Web:* www.maccal.com

Phone | Fax | Class

Mac Haik Auto Group 11711 Katy Fwy Houston TX 77079 866-721-8619 57
TF: 866-721-8619 ■ *Web:* www.machaik.com

Mac Haik Ford Inc 10333 Katy Fwy Houston TX 77024 713-932-5000 57
Web: www.machaikford.com

Mac Machine Company Inc
7209 Rutherford Rd Baltimore MD 21244 410-944-6171 454
Web: www.macmachine.com

Mac Metal Products of Wisconsin Inc
W190 N11225 Carnegie Dr Germantown WI 53022 262-251-4890 567
Web: www.macmetal.com

Mac Metal Sales Inc 1650 W Hwy 80 Somerset KY 42503 606-678-8331 492
Web: www.macmetalsales.com

Mac Papers
3300 Phillips Hwy PO Box 5369 Jacksonville FL 32207 904-348-3300 553
TF: 800-622-2968 ■ *Web:* www.macpapers.com

Mac Pizza Management Inc
3104 Texas Ave S College Station TX 77845 979-695-9912 194
Web: www.macpizzamgmt.com

Mac Products Inc
60 Pennsylvania Ave PO Box 469 Kearny NJ 07032 973-344-0700 344-5368 203
Web: www.macproducts.net

MAC Publishing LLC
501 Second St San Francisco CA 94107 415-243-0505 637-9
Web: www.macworld.com

Mac Tools Inc 505 N Cleveland Ave Westerville OH 43082 614-755-7000 758
TF: 800-622-8665 ■ *Web:* www.mactools.com

Mac Trailer Mfg Inc
14599 Commerce St NE Alliance OH 44601 330-823-9900 823-0232 779
TF: 800-795-8454 ■ *Web:* www.mactrailer.com

Mac Valves Inc 30569 Beck Rd Wixom MI 48393 248-624-7700 624-0549 789
TF: 800-622-8587 ■ *Web:* www.macvalves.com

Mac's Convenience Stores Inc
305 Milner Ave Ste 400 4th Fl Toronto ON M1B3V4 800-268-5574 204
TF: 800-268-5574 ■ *Web:* www.macs.ca

Mac's Tire Recyclers Inc
2058 Highway 145 N Saltillo MS 38866 662-869-1860 755

Macabe Associates Inc, The
110 Union St Ste 310 Seattle WA 98101 206-382-0924 809
Web: www.macabe.com

Macadam Capital Partners
4800 SW Macadam Ave Ste 311 Portland OR 97239 503-225-0889 194
Web: www.macadamcapital.com

Macadamian Technologies Inc
165 Rue Wellington Gatineau QC J8X2J3 819-772-0300 463
TF: 877-779-6336 ■ *Web:* www.macadamian.com

Macalester College 1600 Grand Ave Saint Paul MN 55105 651-696-6357 696-6724* 166
**Fax: Admissions* ■ *TF Admissions:* 800-231-7974 ■ *Web:* www.macalester.edu

MacAllister Machinery Company Inc
7515 E 30th St Indianapolis IN 46219 317-545-2151 860-3310 358
TF: 800-382-1896 ■ *Web:* www.macallister.com

Macally USA Mace Group Inc
4601 E Airport Dr Ontario CA 91761 909-230-6888 230-6889 173-1
TF: 800-644-1132 ■ *Web:* www.macally.com

Macaluso's 1747 Alton Rd Miami Beach FL 33139 305-604-1811 671
Web: macalusosmiami.com

MacAndrews & Forbes Holdings Inc
35 E 62nd St New York NY 10065 212-572-8600 185
Web: www.macandrewsandforbes.com

Macaroni Joe's
1619 S Kentucky St Ste 1500-D Amarillo TX 79102 806-358-8990 671
Web: www.macaronijoes.com

Macaroni's
9315 Old Bustleton Ave Philadelphia PA 19115 215-464-3040 671
Web: macaronis.net

Macarthur Associated Consultants LLC
25 NW 146th St Ste 250E Oklahoma City OK 73013 405-848-2471 261
TF: 800-748-8276 ■ *Web:* www.macokc.com

MacArthur Co 2400 Wycliff St Saint Paul MN 55114 651-646-2773 191-4
TF: 800-777-7507 ■ *Web:* www.macarthurco.com

MacArthur Ctr 300 Monticello Ave Norfolk VA 23510 757-627-6000 460
Web: www.shopmacarthur.com

MacArthur Memorial Museum, The
198 Bank St Norfolk VA 23510 757-441-2965 441-5389 520
TF: 800-877-8339 ■ *Web:* macarthurmemorial.org

MacArthur Museum of Arkansas Military History
503 E Ninth St Little Rock AR 72202 501-376-4602 376-4593 520
Web: www.littlerock.org

MacArthur Place 29 E MacArthur St Sonoma CA 95476 707-938-2929 933-9833 379
TF: 800-722-1866 ■ *Web:* www.macarthurplace.com

MacArthur Tom (Rep R - NJ)
506 Cannon HOB Washington DC 20515 202-225-4765 225-0778 342-2
Web: macarthur.house.gov

Macatawa Bank Corp
10753 Macatawa Dr PO Box 3119 Holland MI 49424 616-820-1444 494-7644 360-2
NASDAQ: MCBC ■ *TF:* 877-820-2265 ■ *Web:* www.macatawabank.com

Macaulay-Brown Inc 4021 Executive Dr Dayton OH 45430 937-426-3421 426-5364 261
TF: 800-432-3421 ■ *Web:* www.macb.com

Macayo Mexican Restaurants
12637 S 48th St Phoenix AZ 85044 480-598-5101 670
Web: www.macayo.com

MacBride Museum 1124 First Ave Whitehorse YT Y1A1A4 867-667-2709 633-6607 520
TF: 800-894-9931 ■ *Web:* www.macbridemuseum.com

MACC (Murray Area Chamber of Commerce)
5250 S Commerce Dr Ste 180 Murray UT 84107 801-263-2632 263-8262 139
Web: www.murraychamber.org

MacCabe Electric Conductors Inc
426 Stump Rd PO Box 590 Montgomeryville PA 18936 215-368-9420 368-9220 470
Web: www.maccabeelectric.com

Maccabee 211 N First St Ste 425 Minneapolis MN 55401 612-337-0087 636
Web: www.maccabeegroup.com

Maccabi USA/Sports for Israel
1926 Arch St Ste 4R Philadelphia PA 19103 215-561-6900 561-5470 48-22
Web: www.maccabiusa.com

MacCormac College 29 E Madison St Chicago IL 60602 312-922-1884 922-4286 800
TF: 800-621-7740 ■ *Web:* www.maccormac.edu

MacCurrach Golf Construction Inc
3501 Faye Rd Jacksonville FL 32226 904-646-1581 188-3
TF: 800-553-1380 ■ *Web:* www.maccurrachgolf.com

Phone | Fax | Class

Macdac Engineering 27 Quality Ave .... Somers CT 06071 860-749-5544 177
Web: www.macdac.com

MacDermid Inc 245 Freight St .... Waterbury CT 06702 203-575-5700 145
TF: 800-328-2942 ■ Web: www.macdermid.com

MacDon Industries Ltd 680 Moray St .... Winnipeg MB R3J3S3 204-885-5590 832-7749 273
Web: www.macdon.com

MacDonald Dettwiler & Assoc Ltd
13800 Commerce Pkwy .... Richmond BC V6V2J3 604-278-3411 727
TSE: MDA ■ Web: www.mdacorporation.com

Macdonald Devin PC
3800 Renaissance Tower 1201 Elm St .... Dallas TX 75270 214-744-3300 428
TF: 800-973-1177 ■ Web: macdonalddevin.com

MacDonald Media LLC
185 Madidon Ave 4th Fl .... New York NY 10016 212-578-8735 6
Web: www.macdonaldmedia.com

Macdonald Realty
203 5188 Wminster Hwy .... Richmond BC V7C5S7 604-279-9822 652
TF: 877-278-3888 ■ Web: www.macrealty.com

MacDonald-Bedford LLC
2900 Main St Ste 200 .... Alameda CA 94501 510-521-4020 186
Web: www.macdonaldbedford.com

MacDonald-Miller Facility Solutions Inc
7717 Detroit Ave SE .... Seattle WA 98106 206-763-9400 189-10
TF: 800-962-5979 ■ Web: www.macmiller.com

MacDougall Correctional Institution
1153 E St S .... Suffield CT 06080 860-627-2100 627-2144 213
Web: ct.gov

MacDougall Correctional Institution
1516 Old GilliaRd Rd .... Ridgeville SC 29472 843-688-5251 213
Web: doc.sc.gov

MacDuffie School 66 School St .... Granby MA 01033 413-255-0000 622
Web: macduffie.org

Mace Security International Inc
240 Gibraltar Rd Ste 220 .... Horsham PA 19044 267-317-4009 692
OTC: MACE ■ Web: corp.mace.com

Macedonia 189 Liberty St NE .... Salem OR 97301 503-316-9997 316-9997 671
Web: reedoperahouse.com

Macedonia Brook State Park
159 Macedonia Brook Rd .... Kent CT 06757 860-927-4100 565
Web: www.ct.gov

Macedonian Tribune Museum
124 W Wayne St Ste 204 .... Fort Wayne IN 46802 260-422-5900 422-1348 520
Web: www.macedonian.org

MacElree Harvey Ltd
17 W Miner St .... West Chester PA 19381 610-436-0100 428
TF: 800-580-9136 ■ Web: www.macelree.com

Macera & Jarzyna LLP
1200-427 Laurier Ave W .... Ottawa ON K1R7Y2 613-238-8173 428
TF: 800-379-6668 ■ Web: www.macerajarzyna.com

Macerich Co, The
401 Wilshire Blvd Ste 700 .... Santa Monica CA 90401 310-394-6000 395-2791 655
NYSE: MAC ■ Web: www.macerich.com

MacEwan College 10700 104 Ave NW .... Edmonton AB T5J4S2 888-497-4622 162
TF: 888-497-4622 ■ Web: www.macewan.ca

MacEwen Petroleum Inc
18 Adelaide St PO Box 100 .... Maxville ON K0C1T0 613-527-2100 579
TF: 800-267-7175 ■ Web: www.macewen.ca

MacFarms of Hawaii LLC
89-406 Mamalahoa Hwy .... Captain Cook HI 96704 808-328-2435 328-8081 10-10
Web: www.macfarms.com

MACFS (Mid-America College of Funeral Science)
3111 Hamburg Pk .... Jeffersonville IN 47130 812-288-8878 288-5942 800
TF: 800-221-6158 ■ Web: www.mid-america.edu

Mac-Gray Corp 404 Wyman St Ste 400 .... Waltham MA 02451 781-487-7600 385
NYSE: TUC ■ TF: 800-622-4729 ■ Web: www.macgray.com

Mach 1 Development LLC
525 K E Market St Ste 296 .... Leesburg VA 20176 877-222-2968 349-1461* 196
*Fax Area Code: 703 ■ TF: 877-222-2968

Mach Industrial Group 6119 Fulton St .... Houston TX 77022 713-695-6000 595
Web: www.machindustrialgroup.com

Machaon Diagnostics Inc
3023 Summit St .... Oakland CA 94609 510-839-5600 418
TF: 800-566-3462 ■ Web: www.machaondiagnostics.com

Machias Savings Bank
4 Ctr St PO Box 318 .... Machias ME 04654 207-255-3347 255-3170 70
TF: 800-982-7179 ■ Web: www.machiassavings.bank

Machine Laboratory Inc 8040 Bond St .... Lenexa KS 66214 913-825-7400 480
Web: www.machlab.com

Machine Maintenance Inc
2300 Cassens Dr .... Fenton MO 63026 636-343-9970 190
TF: 800-325-3322 ■ Web: www.lubyequipment.com

Machine Shop Service Inc
202 Venture Blvd .... Houma LA 70360 985-876-6630 454
Web: www.msshouma.com

Machine Specialties Inc (MSI)
6511 Franz Warner Pkwy .... Whitsett NC 27377 336-603-1919 621
Web: www.machspec.com

Machine Specialty & Manufacturing Inc
215 Rousseau Rd .... Youngsville LA 70592 337-837-0020 837-0062 483
TF: 800-256-1292 ■ Web: www.machine-specialty.com

Machinery & Equipment Company Inc
3401 Bayshore Blvd .... Brisbane CA 94005 415-467-3400 358
TF: 800-227-4544 ■ Web: www.machineryandequipment.com

Machinery Dealers National Assn (MDNA)
315 S Patrick St .... Alexandria VA 22314 703-836-9300 836-9303 49-18
TF: 800-872-7807 ■ Web: www.mdna.org

Machinery Sales Co
17253 Chestnut St .... City of Industry CA 91748 626-581-9211 581-9277 385
TF: 800-588-8111 ■ Web: www.mchysales.com

Machinery Sales Company Inc
120 Webster Ave .... Memphis TN 38126 800-932-8376 526-2339* 821
*Fax Area Code: 901 ■ TF: 800-932-8376 ■ Web: machinery-sales.com

Machinery Systems Inc
614 E State Pkwy .... Schaumburg IL 60173 847-882-8085 882-2894 385
Web: www.machsys.com

Machinima Inc
8441 Santa Monica Blvd .... West Hollywood CA 90069 323-301-1529 177
TF: 800-328-2189 ■ Web: www.machinima.com

Machining Time Savers Inc
1338 S State College Pkwy .... Anaheim CA 92806 714-635-7373 358
TF: 800-375-5673 ■ Web: www.mtscnc.com

MACI (Michigan Automotive Compressor Inc)
2400 N Dearing Rd .... Parma MI 49269 517-796-3200 172
Web: www.michauto.com

Macina Bose Copeland & Assoc Inc
1035 Central Pkwy N .... San Antonio TX 78232 210-545-1122 261

Macintosh Engineering
2 Mill Rd Ste 100 .... Wilmington DE 19806 302-252-9200 261
Web: macintosheng.com

MacIntyre Assoc Inc
106 W State St .... Kennett Square PA 19348 610-925-5925 317
Web: www.macintyreassociates.com

Mack & Associates Ltd
100 N La Salle St Ste 2110 .... Chicago IL 60602 312-368-0677 390
Web: www.mackltd.com

Mack Avenue Records Ii LLC
19900 Harper Ave .... Harper Woods MI 48225 313-640-8414 657
Web: www.mackavenue.com

Mack Boring & Parts Co 2365 US Hwy 22 W .... Union NJ 07083 908-964-0700 964-8475 385
Web: www.mackboring.com

Mack Energy Co 1202 N Tenth St .... Duncan OK 73533 580-252-5580 536
Web: www.mackenergy.com

Mack Engineering Corp
3215 E 26th St .... Minneapolis MN 55406 612-721-2471 757
TF: 800-831-8587 ■ Web: www.mackengineering.com

Mack Hils Inc 544 North Ave .... Moberly MO 65270 660-263-7444 480
Web: www.mackhilsmetalfabrication.com

Mack Industries Inc
1321 Industrial Pkwy N Ste 500 .... Brunswick OH 44212 330-460-7005 183
Web: www.mackconcrete.com

Mack Manufacturing Inc
7205 Bellingrath Rd .... Theodore AL 36582 251-653-9999 190
Web: www.mackmfg.com

Mack Molding Company Inc
608 Warm Brook Rd .... Arlington VT 05250 802-375-2511 375-0792* 604
*Fax: Hum Res ■ Web: www.mack.com

Mack Prototype Inc 424 Main St .... Gardner MA 01440 978-632-3700 632-3777 602
Web: www.mackprototype.com

Mack Pump & Equipment Company Inc
12005 S Spaulding School Dr .... Plainfield IL 60585 815-439-2030 358
TF: 800-605-3848 ■ Web: www.mackpump.com

Mack Sign Advertising 893 Main St .... Wakefield MA 01880 617-387-1010 7
Web: www.battensign.com

MACK Technologies Inc 27 Carlisle Rd .... Westford MA 01886 978-392-5500 179
TF: 800-299-5605 ■ Web: www.macktech.com

MacKay & Somps (MSCE)
5142 Franklin Dr Ste B .... Pleasanton CA 94588 925-225-0690 225-0698 261
TF: 800-795-1747 ■ Web: www.msce.com

Mackay Communications Inc
3691 Trust Dr .... Raleigh NC 27616 281-478-6245 954-1707* 529
*Fax Area Code: 919 ■ TF: 888-798-7979 ■ Web: www.mackaycomm.com

Mackay Envelope Corp
2100 Elm St SE .... Minneapolis MN 55414 800-622-5299 263
TF: 800-622-5299 ■ Web: mackaymitchell.com

Mack-Cali Realty Corp 343 Thornall St .... Edison NJ 08837 732-590-1000 205-8237 655
NYSE: CLI ■ TF: 800-317-4445 ■ Web: www.mack-cali.com

MacKellar Assoc Inc
1729 Northfield Dr .... Rochester Hills MI 48309 248-335-4440 96
Web: www.mackellar.com

Mackenthun's 851 Marketplace Dr .... Waconia MN 55387 952-442-2512 345
Web: www.mackenthuns.com

Mackenzie Eason & Associates
3023 S University Dr Ste 230 .... Fort Worth TX 76109 817-922-9152 363
Web: mackenzieeason.com

Mackenzie Financial Corp
180 Queen St W .... Toronto ON M5V3K1 416-922-5322 922-5660 401
TF: 888-653-7070 ■ Web: www.mackenzieinvestments.com

Mackenzie House Museum 82 Bond St .... Toronto ON M5B1X2 416-392-6915 392-0114 520
TF: 800-668-2437 ■ Web: www.toronto.ca

MacKenzie's Chop House Restaurant
128 S Tejon St .... Colorado Springs CO 80903 719-635-3536 671
Web: www.mackenzieschophouse.com

MacKenzie-Childs LLC 3260 SR-90 .... Aurora NY 13026 315-364-7123 321
TF: 888-665-1999 ■ Web: www.mackenzie-childs.com

MacKerricher State Park
24100 MacKerricher Park Rd .... Fort Bragg CA 95437 707-964-9112 565
Web: www.parks.ca.gov/default.asp?page_id=436

Mackie Consultants LLC
9575 W Higgins Rd Ste 500 .... Rosemont IL 60018 847-696-1400 727
TF: 800-364-2059 ■ Web: www.mackieconsult.com

Mackie Group 933 Bloor St W .... Oshawa ON L1J5Y7 905-728-2400 314
TF: 800-565-4646 ■ Web: www.mackiegroup.com

Mackie Research Capital Corp
110 Nineth Ave SW 9th Fl .... Calgary AB T2P0T1 403-218-6375 218-6376 690
TF: 877-605-0909 ■ Web: secure.mackieresearch.com/jenningscapital.php

Mackie Research Capital Corp
199 Bay St Commerce Ct W Ste 4500 .... Toronto ON M5L1G2 416-860-7600 401
TF: 800-289-9999 ■ Web: www.mackieresearch.com

Mackinac County 100 S Marley St .... Saint Ignace MI 49781 906-643-7300 643-7302 338
Web: www.mackinaccounty.net

Mackinac Island Butterfly
6750 Mcgulpin St .... Mackinac Island MI 49757 906-847-3972 522
Web: www.originalbutterflyhouse.com

Mackinac Partners LLC
74 W Long Lake Rd Ste 205 .... Bloomfield Hills MI 48304 248-258-6900 401
Web: www.mackinacpartners.com

Mackinac Savings Bank FSB
2901-A N Military Trl .... West Palm Beach FL 33409 561-686-2352 70
Web: www.mackbank.com

Mackinaw Area Visitors Bureau
10800 US 23 .... Mackinaw City MI 49701 231-436-5664 436-5991 206
TF: 800-666-0160 ■ Web: www.mackinawcity.com

Mackinaw River State Fish & Wildlife Area
15470 Nelson Rd .... Mackinaw IL 61755 309-963-4969 565

Mackinaws Grill & Spirits
2925 Voyager Dr .... Green Bay WI 54311 920-406-8000 671
Web: www.mackinaws.com

	Phone	Fax	Class
MacKinnon Calderwood Advertising Inc 1555 Dundas St W .... Mississauga ON L5C1E3 *Web:* www.mackinnoncalderwood.com	905-281-6146		7
Mackinnon Transport Inc 405 Laird Rd .... Guelph ON N1G4P7 *TF:* 800-265-9394 ■ *Web:* www.mackinnontransport.com	519-821-2311	821-1834	803-1
Mackintire Insurance Agency Inc 11 W Main St .... Westborough MA 01581 *Web:* mackintire.com	508-366-6161		390
MacKissic Inc PO Box 111 .... Parker Ford PA 19457 *TF:* 800-348-1117 ■ *Web:* www.mackissic.com	610-495-7181	495-5951	429
Macklowe Properties 767 Fifth Ave .... New York NY 10153 *Web:* www.macklowe.com	212-265-5900	554-5895	655
Macks Prairie Wings 2335 Hwy 63 N .... Stuttgart AR 72160 *TF:* 800-658-3094 ■ *Web:* www.mackspw.com	870-673-6960		711
Macktown Living History 2221 Freeport Rd .... Rockton IL 61072 *Web:* www.macktownlivinghistory.com	815-624-4200		50-3
Macky Auditorium Concert Hall 285 UCB University Ave .... Boulder CO 80309 *Web:* www.colorado.edu	303-492-8423	492-1651	572
Macky's Bayside Bar & Grill 54th St on the Bay .... Ocean City MD 21842 *Web:* www.mackys.com	410-723-5565		671
Mac-Lander Inc 509 E Maple .... Milton IA 52570 *Web:* www.mac-lander.com	641-656-4271	656-4225	763
MacLaren Youth Correctional Facility 2630 N Pacific Hwy .... Woodburn OR 97071 *Web:* oregon.gov	503-981-9531	982-4439	412
Maclean Assoc LLC 1700 Boston Post Rd .... Guilford CT 06437 *TF:* 877-819-6922 ■ *Web:* www.landroverguilford.com	877-819-6922		57
MacLean Power Systems 11411 Addison St .... Franklin Park IL 60131 **Fax:* Sales ■ *TF:* 855-677-7447 ■ *Web:* www.macleanpower.com	847-455-0014	455-0029*	816
Maclean's Magazine 1 Mt Pleasant Rd 11th Fl .... Toronto ON M4Y2Y5 *TF:* 800-268-9119 ■ *Web:* macleans.ca	416-764-1300	764-1332	457-17
MacLean-Fogg Co 1000 Allanson Rd .... Mundelein IL 60060 *TF:* 800-323-4536 ■ *Web:* www.macleanfogg.com	847-566-0010		60
MacLellan Services Inc 3120 Wall St Ste 100 .... Lexington KY 40513 *Web:* www.maclellan-usa.com	859-219-5400		256
MacMicro Inc 29 Williamsburg Close .... Scarsdale NY 10583 *Web:* www.macmicro.com	914-472-8292		396
Macmillan Piper Inc 1509 Taylor Way .... Tacoma WA 98421 *Web:* www.macpiper.com	253-627-3767		549
MacMillan Sobanski & Todd LLC 1 Maritime Plaza 720 Water St 5th Fl .... Toledo OH 43604 *Web:* www.mstfirm.com	419-255-5900		445
MacMunnis Inc 1840 Oak Ave Ste 300 .... Evanston IL 60201 *Web:* www.macmunnis.com	847-316-1100		463
MacMurray College 447 E College Ave .... Jacksonville IL 62650 **Fax:* Admissions ■ *TF:* 800-252-7485 ■ *Web:* www.mac.edu	217-479-7056	291-0702*	166
MacNeal Hospital 3249 S Oak Pk Ave .... Berwyn IL 60402 *TF:* 888-622-6325 ■ *Web:* www.macneal.com	708-783-9100		374-3
MacNeil Lehrer Productions LLC 2700 Quincy St Ste 250 .... Arlington VA 22206 *Web:* www.macneil-lehrer.com	703-998-2170		514
MacNeill Engineering Company Inc 140 Locke Dr PO Box 735 .... Marlborough MA 01752 *TF:* 800-652-4267 ■ *Web:* www.champspikes.com	508-481-8830	303-4923	710
Macnica Americas Inc 380 Stevens Ave Ste 206 .... Solana Beach CA 92075 *TF:* 888-399-4937 ■ *Web:* www.macnica.com/web/americas	760-707-0120		246
MACo (Maryland Assn of Counties) 169 Conduit St .... Annapolis MD 21401 *Web:* www.mdcounties.org	410-269-0043	268-1775	49-7
Macomb Area Chamber of Commerce & Downtown Development Corp 214 N Lafayette St .... Macomb IL 61455 *Web:* www.macombareachamber.com	309-837-4855	837-4857	139
Macomb Area Convention & Visitors Bureau 201 S Lafayette St .... Macomb IL 61455 *TF:* 800-593-5678 ■ *Web:* www.makeitmacomb.com	309-833-1315	833-3575	206
Macomb Community College *Center* 44575 Garfield Rd .... Clinton Township MI 48038 **Fax:* Admissions ■ *TF:* 866-622-6621 ■ *Web:* www.macomb.edu	586-445-7999	286-4787*	162
South 14500 E 12-Mile Rd .... Warren MI 48088 **Fax:* Admissions ■ *TF:* 866-622-6621 ■ *Web:* www.macomb.edu	586-445-7000	445-7140*	162
Macomb Community Unit School District 185 323 W Washington St .... Macomb IL 61455 *Web:* www.medfd.org	309-833-4161		685
Macomb Correctional Facility 34625 26th Mile Rd .... New Haven MI 48048 *Web:* michigan.gov	586-749-4900		213
Macomb County 40 N Main St .... Mount Clemens MI 48043 *Web:* macombgov.org	586-469-5120		338
Macomb County 1 S Main 8th Floor .... Mount Clemens MI 48038 *Web:* www.makemacombyourhome.com	586-469-7001		434-3
Macomb County Chamber 28 First St Ste B .... Mount Clemens MI 48043 *TF:* 800-564-3136 ■ *Web:* macombcountychamber.com	586-493-7600	493-7602	139
Macomb County Chamber of Commerce 28 First St .... Mount Clemens MI 48043 *Web:* macombcountychamber.com	586-493-7600	493-7602	139
Macomb Daily 100 Macomb Daily Dr .... Mount Clemens MI 48043 *Web:* www.macombdaily.com	586-469-4510		532-2
Macomb Group Inc, The 6600 E 15 Mile Rd .... Sterling Heights MI 48312 *Web:* www.macombgroup.com	586-274-4100		492
Macomb Journal 203 N Randolph St .... Macomb IL 61455 *TF:* 800-747-5401 ■ *Web:* www.mcdonoughvoice.com	309-833-2114		532-2
Macomb Mall 32233 Gratiot Ave .... Roseville MI 48066 *Web:* www.shopmacombmall.com	586-293-7800		460
Macomb Reservation State Park 201 Campsite Rd .... Schuyler Falls NY 12985 *Web:* www.parks.ny.gov/parks/77/details.aspx	518-643-9952		565
Macon Centreplex Coliseum 200 Coliseum Dr .... Macon GA 31217 *TF:* 877-532-6144 ■ *Web:* www.maconcentreplex.org	478-751-9152	751-9154	720
Macon Cigar & Tobacco Company Inc 575 12th St .... Macon GA 31201 *Web:* www.mctweb.com	478-743-2236	744-0903	756
Macon City Auditorium 415 First St .... Macon GA 31201 *TF:* 877-532-6144 ■ *Web:* www.maconcentreplex.org	478-751-9152	751-9154	572
Macon City Hall 700 Poplar St .... Macon GA 31201 *Web:* www.maconbibb.us	478-751-7400		337
Macon County 141 S Main St Rm 104 .... Decatur IL 62523 *TF:* 800-368-8683 ■ *Web:* co.macon.il.us	217-424-1305	423-0922	338
Macon County 5 W Main St .... Franklin NC 28734 *Web:* www.maconnc.org	828-349-2025	349-2400	338
Macon County 201 County Courthouse .... Lafayette TN 37083 *Web:* www.maconcountytn.com	615-666-2363	666-5323	338
Macon County 410 N Missouri St Ste D .... Macon MO 63552 *TF:* 800-981-9409 ■ *Web:* www.maconcounty.org	660-385-5627		338
Macon County 121 S Sumter St .... Oglethorpe GA 31068 *Web:* www.maconcountyga.org	678-215-1705		338
Macon County 101 E Northside St Courthouse .... Tuskegee AL 36083 *Web:* alabama.travel	334-727-5120		338
Macon County Nursing Home District 701 Sunset Hills Dr .... Macon MO 63552 *TF:* 800-309-3282 ■ *Web:* www.lochhaven.com	660-385-3113		371
Macon Electric Co-op 31571 Bus Hwy 36 E PO Box 157 .... Macon MO 63552 *TF:* 800-553-6901 ■ *Web:* www.maconelectric.com	660-385-3157	385-3334	245
Macon Little Theater 4220 Forsyth Rd .... Macon GA 31210 *Web:* www.maconlittletheatre.org	478-477-3342		572
Macon Mall 3661 Eisenhower Pkwy .... Macon GA 31206 *Web:* maconmall.com	478-477-8840		460
Macon Resources Inc 2121 Hubbard Ave .... Decatur IL 62526 *Web:* www.maconresources.org	217-875-1910		488
Macon Road Barbecue 2703 Avalon Rd .... Columbus GA 31907	706-563-0542		671
Macon State College 100 College Stn Dr .... Macon GA 31206 **Fax:* Admissions ■ *TF:* 800-272-7619 ■ *Web:* www.mga.edu	478-471-2700	471-5343*	166
Warner Robins 100 University Blvd .... Warner Robins GA 31093 *Web:* www.mga.edu	478-929-6700	929-6726	166
Macon Symphony Orchestra 400 Poplar St .... Macon GA 31201 *Web:* www.maconsymphony.com	478-301-5300		573-3
Macon Telegraph 120 Broadway .... Macon GA 31201 *TF:* 800-679-6397 ■ *Web:* www.macon.com	478-744-4200	744-4385	532-2
Macon Water Authority 790 Second St PO Box 108 .... Macon GA 31202 *Web:* www.maconwater.org	478-464-5600	741-9146	806
Macon-Bibb County Convention/Visitors Bureau 450 Martin Luther King Jr Blvd .... Macon GA 31201 *TF:* 800-768-3401 ■ *Web:* www.maconga.org	478-743-1074	745-2022	206
Macoupin County 201 E Main .... Carlinville IL 62626 *Web:* www.macoupincountyil.gov	217-854-3214	854-7361	338
Macphail Center For Music - Minneapolis 501 S Second St .... Minneapolis MN 55401 *TF:* 800-767-9660 ■ *Web:* www.macphail.org	612-321-0100	321-9740	572
Macpherson Oil Co 100 Wilshire Ste 800 .... Santa Monica CA 90401 *Web:* www.macphersonenergy.com	310-452-3880		536
MacPherson's Inc 18551 Aurora Ave N Ste 300 .... Shoreline WA 98133 *TF:* 866-866-2323 ■ *Web:* www.macphersons.com	206-542-6363	542-6899	652
MacPractice Inc 233 N Eighth St Ste 300 .... Lincoln NE 68508 *TF:* 877-220-8418 ■ *Web:* www.macpractice.com	402-420-2430		174
Macquarie Infrastructure Company Inc 125 W 55th St .... New York NY 10019 *NYSE: MIC* ■ *Web:* www.macquarie.com	212-231-1000		70
Macquarium Intelligent Communications 1800 Peachtree St NW Ste 250 .... Atlanta GA 30309 *Web:* www.macquarium.com	404-554-4000		7
MacQue's 8101 Elder Creek Rd .... Sacramento CA 95824 *Web:* www.macques.com	916-381-4119		671
Macritchie Engineering Inc 197 Quincy Ave .... Braintree MA 02184 *Web:* macritchie.net	781-848-4464		261
Macro Engineering & Technology Inc 199 Traders Blvd E .... Mississauga ON L4Z2E5 *Web:* www.macroeng.com	905-507-9000		757
Macro Group Inc, The 1200 Washington Ave S Ste 350 .... Minneapolis MN 55415 *Web:* www.macrogroup.net	612-332-7880		177
Macro Management Service 800 Navarro St .... San Antonio TX 78205 *Web:* www.macromgt.com	210-226-1047		463
Macro Plastics Inc 2250 Huntington Dr .... Fairfield CA 94533 *Web:* www.macroplastics.com	707-437-1200		596
Macro Solutions 800 Maryland Ave NE Ste 900 .... Washington DC 20002 *Web:* www.macrosolutions.com	703-527-9400		177
Macrolink Inc 1500 N Kellogg Dr .... Anaheim CA 92807 *Web:* www.macrolink.com	714-777-8800		625
Macronix America Inc 680 N McCarthy Blvd .... Milpitas CA 95035 *Web:* www.macronix.com	408-262-8887	262-8810	696
MacroSoft Inc 2 Sylvan Way 3rd Fl .... Parsippany NJ 07054 *Web:* www.macrosoftinc.com	973-889-0500		195
Macrovision Inc 301 S Main St Ste 3w .... Doylestown PA 18901 *Web:* www.macrovis.com	215-348-1010		7
MACS (Mobile Air Conditioning Society Worldwide) 225 S Broad St .... Lansdale PA 19446 *TF:* 800-641-1133 ■ *Web:* www.macsw.org	215-631-7020	631-7017	49-21
Macs at Work Inc 775 Hartford Tpke .... Shrewsbury MA 01545 *Web:* www.macsatwork.com	508-845-0709		179
MACTE (Montessori Accreditation Council for Teacher Education) 420 Park St .... Charlottesville VA 22902 **Fax Area Code:* 888 ■ *Web:* www.macte.org	434-202-7793	525-8838*	48-1

	City	State	ZIP	Phone	Fax	Class
Mactus Group 4034 148th Ave NE Bldg K1 *TF:* 800-597-1686 ■ *Web:* www.mactusgroup.com	Redmond	WA	98052	425-883-3640		393
Macula Foundation Inc 210 E 64th St *TF:* 800-622-8524 ■ *Web:* www.maculafoundation.org	New York	NY	10065	212-605-3777		48-17
Macworld Magazine 501 Second St Ste 600 *TF Cust Svc:* 800-288-6848 ■ *Web:* www.macworld.com	San Francisco	CA	94107	415-243-0505		457-7
Macy's 400 Fifth Ave *TF:* 877-884-3751 ■ *Web:* www.macys.com	Pittsburgh	PA	15219	513-573-7912		229
Macy's 151 W 34th St *TF:* 800-243-0443 ■ *Web:* www.macys.com	New York	NY	10001	212-695-4400		229
Macy's 111 N State St *Web:* www.macys.com	Chicago	IL	60602	312-781-1000		229
Macy's Home Store 7 W Seventh St *Web:* www.macysinc.com	Cincinnati	OH	45202	212-695-4400		361
Macy's Inc 7 W Seventh St *NYSE: M* ■ *TF:* 800-261-5385 ■ *Web:* www.federated-fds.com	Cincinnati	OH	45202	513-579-7000		229
Mad 4 Marketing Inc 5255 NW 33rd Ave *Web:* www.mad4marketing.com	Fort Lauderdale	FL	33309	954-485-5448		7
Mad Catz Interactive Inc 7480 Mission Valley Rd Ste 101 *NYSE: MCZ* ■ *Web:* www.madcatz.com	San Diego	CA	92108	619-683-9830	683-9839	173-1
MAD DADS (Men Against Destruction Defending Against Drugs & Social Disorder Inc) 3026 Fourth Ave S *Web:* www.maddads.com	Minneapolis	MN	55408	612-822-0802	253-0663	48-6
Mad Dogg Athletics Inc 2111 Narcissus Ct *TF:* 800-847-7746 ■ *Web:* www.spinning.com	Venice	CA	90291	310-823-7008		711
Mad Greek 2466 Fairmount Blvd *Web:* www.madgreekcleveland.com	Cleveland Heights	OH	44106	216-421-3333		671
Mad House 240 Madison Ave 14th Fl *Web:* www.madhousenyc.com	New York	NY	10016	212-867-1615		512
Mad Mary's Steakhouse & Saloon 110 E Dakota Ave	Pierre	SD	57501	605-224-6469		671
Mad Platter, The 1239 Sixth Ave N *Web:* www.madplatternashville.com	Nashville	TN	37208	615-242-2563		671
Mad Science Group 8360 Bougainville St Ste 201 *TF:* 800-586-5231 ■ *Web:* www.madscience.org	Montreal	QC	H4P2G1	514-344-4181	344-6695	310
Mada Medical Products Inc 625 Washington Ave *TF:* 800-526-6370 ■ *Web:* www.madamedical.com	Carlstadt	NJ	07072	201-460-0454	460-3509	475
Madagascar 820 Second Ave Ste 800	New York	NY	10017	212-986-9491	986-6271	784
Madagascar Embassy 2374 Massachusetts Ave NW *Web:* www.madagascar-embassy.org	Washington	DC	20008	202-265-5525		257
Madam Mam's 2514 Guadalupe St *Web:* madammam.com	Austin	TX	78705	512-472-8306		671
Madame Claude Cafe 364 1/2 Fourth St *Web:* www.madameclaudecafe.com	Jersey City	NJ	07302	201-876-8800		671
Madame Tussauds New York Inc 234 W 42nd St Times Sq *TF:* 800-434-7894 ■ *Web:* www.madametussauds.com	New York	NY	10036	212-512-9600		520
Madame Walker Theatre Ctr 617 Indiana Ave *TF:* 800-225-0248 ■ *Web:* thewalkertheatre.org	Indianapolis	IN	46202	317-236-2099	236-2097	572
Madan Plastics Inc 370 North Ave *Web:* www.madanplastics.com	Cranford	NJ	07016	908-276-8484		596
MadCap Software Inc 7777 Fay Ave *Web:* www.madcapsoftware.com	La Jolla	CA	92037	858-320-0387		179
MADD (Mothers Against Drunk Driving) 511 E John Carpenter Fwy Ste 700 *TF:* 877-275-6233 ■ *Web:* www.madd.org	Irving	TX	75062	214-744-6233		48-6
Madden Communications Inc 901 Mittel Dr *Web:* www.madden.com	Wood Dale	IL	60191	630-787-2200		535
Madden Manufacturing Inc PO Box 387 **Fax:* Sales ■ *TF:* 800-369-6233 ■ *Web:* www.maddenmfg.com	Elkhart	IN	46515	574-295-4292	295-7562*	641
Madden's on Gull Lake 11266 Pine Beach Peninsula *TF:* 800-642-5363 ■ *Web:* www.maddens.com	Brainerd	MN	56401	218-829-2811		669
MaddenCo Inc 4847 E Virginia Ste G *TF:* 800-438-4487 ■ *Web:* www.maddenco.com	Evansville	IN	47715	812-474-6245		225
Maddock Douglas Inc 111 Adell Pl *TF:* 800-788-9041 ■ *Web:* www.maddockdouglas.com	Elmhurst	IL	60126	630-279-3939		7
Maddox Foundry & Machine Works Inc 13370 SW 170th St *Web:* www.maddoxfoundry.com	Archer	FL	32618	352-495-2121	495-3962	307
Maddox Metal Works Inc 4116 Bronze Way *Web:* www.maddoxmetalworks.com	Dallas	TX	75237	214-333-2311	337-8169	697
Madeira School 8328 Georgetown Pk *Web:* www.madeira.org	McLean	VA	22102	703-556-8200		622
Madelaine Chocolate Novelties Inc 9603 Beach Ch Dr *TF:* 800-322-1505 ■ *Web:* www.madelainechocolate.com	Rockaway Beach	NY	11693	718-945-1500	318-4607	296-8
Madeleine Crouch & Company Inc 14070 Proton Rd Ste 100 *Web:* www.madcrouch.com	Dallas	TX	75244	972-233-9107	490-4219	47
Maden Technologies 4601 N Fairfax Dr Ste 1030 *Web:* www.madentech.com	Arlington	VA	22203	703-940-3609		180
Mader News Inc 913 Ruberta Ave *Web:* www.madernews.com	Glendale	CA	91201	818-551-5000		532-3
Mader's German Restaurant 1041 N Old World Third St *Web:* www.madersrestaurant.com	Milwaukee	WI	53203	414-271-3377		671
Madera Community Hospital 1250 E Almond Ave *TF:* 800-431-8455 ■ *Web:* www.maderahospital.org	Madera	CA	93637	559-675-5555		374-3
Madera County 200 W Fourth St *TF:* 800-427-6897 ■ *Web:* www.madera-county.com	Madera	CA	93637	559-675-7703	673-3302	338
Madera County Library 121 N 'G' St *TF:* 800-799-7233 ■ *Web:* www.madera-county.com	Madera	CA	93637	559-675-7871		434-3

	City	State	ZIP	Phone	Fax	Class
Madera District Chamber of Commerce 120 NE St **Fax:* Acctg ■ *Web:* www.maderachamber.com	Madera	CA	93638	559-673-3563	673-5009*	139
Madera Unified School District 1902 HowaRd Rd *TF:* 800-322-6384 ■ *Web:* www.madera.k12.ca.us	Madera	CA	93637	559-675-4500	675-1186	685
Made-Rite Co PO Box 3283 *Web:* www.themade-ritecompany.com	Longview	TX	75606	903-753-8604	236-9743	81-2
MadeToOrder 1244-A Quarry Ln *TF:* 800-843-6243 ■ *Web:* www.madetoorder.com	Pleasanton	CA	94566	925-484-0600		7
Madewell Inc 486 Broadway *Web:* www.madewell.com	New York	NY	10013	212-226-6954		157-2
MadgeTech Inc 6 Warner Rd *TF:* 877-671-2885 ■ *Web:* www.madgetech.com	Warner	NH	03278	603-456-2011		256
Madias Bros Inc 12850 Evergreen Rd	Detroit	MI	48223	313-272-5330		189-8
Madico Inc 64 Industrial Pkwy *TF:* 800-456-4331 ■ *Web:* www.madico.com	Woburn	MA	01801	781-935-7850	935-6841	599
Madigan Army Medical Ctr 9040 Jackson Ave	Tacoma	WA	98431	253-968-1110		374-4
Madison & Associates Inc 4108 Holly Rd *TF:* 800-264-1170 ■ *Web:* www.tdmadison.com	Virginia Beach	VA	23451	757-425-9950		260
Madison Area Chamber of Commerce 301 E Main St *TF:* 800-559-2956 ■ *Web:* www.madisonindiana.com/chamber	Madison	IN	47250	812-265-3135	265-9784	139
Madison Area Technical College 1701 Wright St *TF:* 800-322-6282 ■ *Web:* www.madisoncollege.edu	Madison	WI	53704	608-246-6100	246-6880	800
Madison Ballet 160 Westgate Mall *Web:* www.madisonballet.org	Madison	WI	53711	608-278-7990		573-1
Madison Boulder Natural Area 473 Boulder Rd *Web:* www.nhstateparks.org	Madison	NH	03849	603-227-8745		565
Madison Buffalo Jump State Park 6990 Buffalo Jump Rd *Web:* www.fwp.mt.gov	Three Forks	MT	59752	406-994-4042		565
Madison Cable Corp 125 Goddard Memorial Dr *TF:* 877-623-4766 ■ *Web:* www.te.com	Worcester	MA	01603	508-752-2884	752-4230	814
Madison Capital Partners Corp 500 W Madison St Ste 3890 *Web:* madison.net	Chicago	IL	60661	312-277-0156	277-0163	403
Madison Chemical Company Inc 3141 Clifty Dr *Web:* madchem.com	Madison	IN	47250	812-273-6000	273-6002	151
Madison Children's Museum 100 N Hamilton St *Web:* www.madisonchildrensmuseum.org	Madison	WI	53703	608-256-6445		521
Madison City Hall 210 Martin Luther King Jr Blvd Rm 403 *TF:* 800-242-8511 ■ *Web:* www.cityofmadison.com	Madison	WI	53703	608-266-4611	267-8671	337
Madison Components LLC 1 Merrill Industrial Dr Ste 19	Hampton	NH	03842	603-758-1700		770
Madison Concourse Hotel & Governors Club 1 W Dayton St *TF:* 800-356-8293 ■ *Web:* www.concoursehotel.com	Madison	WI	53703	608-257-6000	257-5280	379
Madison Convention & Visitors Bureau 118 N Main St *TF:* 800-709-7406 ■ *Web:* www.madisonga.org	Madison	GA	30650	706-342-4454		206
Madison Correctional Facility 800 MSH Busstop Dr *Web:* in.gov	Madison	IN	47250	812-265-6154	265-2142	213
Madison Correctional Institution 382 SW MCI Way *Web:* dc.state.fl.us	Madison	FL	32340	850-973-5300		213
Madison Correctional Institution 1851 State Rt 56 PO Box 740 *Web:* drc.ohio.gov/maci	London	OH	43140	740-852-9777	852-3666	213
Madison County 16 E Ninth St *Web:* www.madisoncty.com	Anderson	IN	46016	765-641-9419	648-1375	338
Madison County 146 W Ctr St *TF:* 800-428-0584 ■ *Web:* www.madison-co.com	Canton	MS	39046	601-859-1177	859-5875	338
Madison County 91 Albany Ave *Web:* www.qpublic.net	Danielsville	GA	30633	706-795-6355	795-5715	338
Madison County 157 N Main St Ste 109 *Web:* www.co.madison.il.us	Edwardsville	IL	62025	618-692-6290	692-8903	338
Madison County 1 Courthouse Sq *Web:* madisoncountymo.us	Fredericktown	MO	63645	573-783-6544		338
Madison County 100 Northside Sq *TF:* 800-392-5658 ■ *Web:* madisoncountyal.gov	Huntsville	AL	35801	256-532-3492	532-6994	338
Madison County 201 Main St *Web:* madisoncogov.com	Huntsville	AR	72740	479-738-2747		338
Madison County 100 E Main St Ste 105 *Web:* www.co.madison.tn.us	Jackson	TN	38301	731-423-6022		338
Madison County 1 N Main St PO Box 618 *Web:* www.co.madison.oh.us	London	OH	43140	740-852-2972	845-1660	338
Madison County 248 SW Range Ave PO Box 237 *TF:* 877-272-3642 ■ *Web:* www.madisonfl.org	Madison	FL	32340	850-973-2788	973-8864	338
Madison County 1313 N Main St *TF:* 800-368-8683 ■ *Web:* www.madisoncountyne.com	Madison	NE	68748	402-454-3311		338
Madison County 110 N Main St *Web:* madisonva.com	Madison	VA	22727	540-948-4455		338
Madison County PO Box 142 *Web:* www.madisoncountync.org	Marshall	NC	28753	828-649-2531	649-0187	338
Madison County PO Box 389 *Web:* www.co.madison.id.us	Rexburg	ID	83440	208-359-6200	356-8396	338
Madison County 100 Wallace St PO Box 185 *Web:* madisoncountymt.gov	Virginia City	MT	59755	406-843-4230	843-5207	338
Madison County 138 N Ct St Bldg 4 PO Box 668 *Web:* madisoncounty.ny.gov	Wampsville	NY	13163	315-366-2261		338
Madison County 73 Jefferson St *TF:* 800-298-6119 ■ *Web:* www.madisoncounty.com	Winterset	IA	50273	515-462-1185		338

Company / Address	City	State	Zip	Phone	Fax	Class
Madison County Chamber of Commerce 618 Crescent Blvd Ste 101 *TF:* 800-342-2383 ■ *Web:* www.madisoncountychamber.com	Ridgeland	MS	39157	601-605-2554	605-2260	139
Madison County Healthcare System 300 Hutchings St *Web:* www.madisonhealth.com	Winterset	IA	50273	515-462-2373	462-5132	374-3
Madison Cutting Die Inc 2547 Progress Rd *TF:* 800-395-9405 ■ *Web:* www.mcd.net	Madison	WI	53716	608-221-3422		555
Madison Cutting Tools Inc 485 Narragansett Pk Dr *Web:* www.madisontools.com	Pawtucket	RI	02861	401-729-0400		493
Madison Dearborn Partners LLC (MDP) 70 W Madison Ste 4600 *Web:* www.mdcp.com	Chicago	IL	60602	312-895-1000	895-1001	792
Madison Electric Co 31855 Van Dyke Ave *Web:* www.madisonelectric.com	Warren	MI	48093	586-825-0200	825-0225	246
Madison Gas & Electric Co 133 S Blair St *TF:* 800-245-1125 ■ *Web:* www.mge.com	Madison	WI	53703	608-252-7000	252-7098	787
Madison Geology Museum 1215 W Dayton St *Web:* geoscience.wisc.edu/museum	Madison	WI	53706	608-262-2399		520
Madison Heights Public Library 240 W 13 Mile Rd *Web:* www.madison-heights.org/departments/library	Madison Heights	MI	48071	248-588-7763		434-3
Madison Heights-Hazel Park Chamber of Commerce (MHP) 939 E 12 Mile Rd *Web:* www.madisonheightschamber.com	Madison Heights	MI	48071	248-542-5010	542-6821	139
Madison Hotel 79 Madison Ave *Web:* www.madisonhotelmemphis.com	Memphis	TN	38103	901-333-1200	333-1210	379
Madison Hotel, The 1 Convent Rd *TF:* 800-526-0729 ■ *Web:* www.themadisonhotel.com	Morristown	NJ	07960	973-285-1800	540-8566	379
Madison Industries Inc of Georgia 1035 Iris Dr *Web:* www.madisonind.com	Conyers	GA	30094	770-483-4401	785-7967	105
Madison Investment Advisors Inc 550 Science Dr *TF:* 800-767-0300 ■ *Web:* www.madisonadv.com	Madison	WI	53711	608-274-0300		401
Madison Local Board of Education 1379 Grace St *Web:* www.madison-richland.k12.oh.us	Mansfield	OH	44905	419-589-2600		685
Madison Marquette 909 Montgomery St Ste 200 *Web:* www.madisonmarquette.com	San Francisco	CA	94133	415-277-6800		655
Madison Mechanical Inc 5621 Old Frederick Rd Ste 1 **Fax Area Code:* 650 ■ *Web:* www.madisonmechanical.net	Catonsville	MD	21784	617-661-8300	319-2221*	610
Madison Metropolitan School District 545 W Dayton St **Fax:* Hum Res ■ *TF:* 800-422-7128 ■ *Web:* www.madison.k12.wi.us	Madison	WI	53703	608-663-1879	204-0346*	685
Madison National Life Insurance Company Inc PO Box 5008 *TF:* 800-356-9601 ■ *Web:* www.madisonlife.com	Madison	WI	53705	608-830-2000	830-2700	391-2
Madison Newspapers Inc 1901 Fish Hatchery Rd *TF Sales:* 800-252-7723 ■ *Web:* host.madison.com	Madison	WI	53713	608-252-6200	252-6119	637-8
Madison Park Financial Corp 155 Grand Ave Ste 1025 *Web:* www.mpfcorp.com	Oakland	CA	94612	510-452-2944	452-2973	655
Madison Precision Products Inc 94 E 400 N *Web:* www.madisonprecision.com	Madison	IN	47250	812-273-4702	273-2451	308
Madison Public Library 201 W Mifflin St *Web:* www.madisonpubliclibrary.org	Madison	WI	53703	608-266-6300		434-3
Madison Rivergate Area Chamber of Commerce 301 Madison St *Web:* www.madisonrivergatechamber.com	Madison	TN	37115	615-865-5400		139
Madison Security Group Inc 31 Kirk St *TF:* 800-596-0754 ■ *Web:* www.madisonsg.com	Lowell	MA	01852	978-459-5911		693
Madison Square Garden Corp 4 Pennsylvania Plaza *Web:* www.thegarden.com	New York	NY	10001	212-465-6000		655
Madison Symphony Orchestra 201 State St *Web:* www.madisonsymphony.org	Madison	WI	53703	608-257-3734	280-6192	573-3
Madison Wood Preservers Inc 216 Oak Park Rd *TF:* 844-623-9663 ■ *Web:* www.madwood.com	Madison	VA	22727	844-623-9663		818
Madison's Cafe 216 Madison St *Web:* www.madisonscafe.com	Jefferson City	MO	65101	573-634-2988		671
Madison-Jefferson County Public Library 420 W Main St *Web:* www.mjcpl.org	Madison	IN	47250	812-265-2744		434-3
Madison-Kipp Corp 201 Waubesa St *TF:* 800-356-6148 ■ *Web:* www.madison-kipp.com	Madison	WI	53704	800-356-6148		308
Madisonville Community College 2000 College Dr **Fax:* Admissions ■ *TF:* 866-227-4812 ■ *Web:* www.madisonville.kctcs.edu	Madisonville	KY	42431	270-821-2250	824-1864*	162
Madisonville-Hopkins County Chamber of Commerce 15 E Ctr St *Web:* www.hopkinschamber.com	Madisonville	KY	42431	270-821-3435	821-9190	139
Madonna Rehabilitation Hospital 5401 S St *TF:* 800-676-5448 ■ *Web:* www.madonna.org	Lincoln	NE	68506	402-489-7102		374-6
Madonna University 36600 Schoolcraft Rd *TF:* 800-852-4951 ■ *Web:* www.madonna.edu	Livonia	MI	48150	734-432-5339	432-5424	166
Madras Pavilion 3910 Kirby Dr *Web:* madraspavilion.us	Houston	TX	77098	713-521-2617		671
Madsen Inc 2901 Springfield Rd *Web:* www.madseninc.com	Broomall	PA	19008	610-356-4800		115
Madsen Kneppers & Assoc Inc 100 Pringle Ave Ste 340 *Web:* mkainc.com	Walnut Creek	CA	94596	925-934-3235		261
Madwire 3420 E Harmony Rd *TF:* 855-773-8171 ■ *Web:* www.madwiremedia.com	Fort Collins	CO	80528	855-773-8171		7

Company / Address	City	State	Zip	Phone	Fax	Class
Maersk Inc 9300 Arrowpoint Blvd *Web:* maerskline.com	Charlotte	NC	28273	973-514-5000		313
Maersk Line Ltd 2510 Walmer Ave Ste C *Web:* www.maersklinelimited.com	Norfolk	VA	23513	757-857-4800		313
Maestro SVP 3615 St Laurent Blvd *Web:* www.maestrosvp.com	Montreal	QC	H2X1V5	514-842-6447		671
Maestro Technologies Inc 1471 Boul Lionel Boulet *Web:* www.maestro.ca	Varennes	QC	J3X1P7	514-990-0864		180
Maetta Sciences Inc 1585 Lionel-Boulet blvd Ste 109 *Web:* www.maetta.ca	Varennes	QC	J3X1P7	450-652-4200		477
MAF (Mission Aviation Fellowship) 112 N Pilatus Ln *TF:* 800-359-7623 ■ *Web:* www.maf.org	Nampa	ID	83687	208-498-0800	498-0801	48-20
Mafcote Industries Inc 108 Main St *TF Cust Svc:* 800-526-4280 ■ *Web:* www.mafcote.com	Norwalk	CT	06851	203-847-8500	849-9177	554
MAG (Medical Assn of Georgia) 1849 The Exchange Ste 200 *TF:* 800-282-0224 ■ *Web:* www.mag.org	Atlanta	GA	30339	678-303-9290	303-3732	474
Mag Instrument Inc 2001 S Hillman Ave *TF:* 800-289-6241 ■ *Web:* www.maglite.com	Ontario	CA	91761	909-947-1006	947-3116	439
Mag Usa Inc 105 Matthew Warren Dr	Clinton	TN	37716	865-259-0109		247
Maga Ltd 2610 Lake Cook Rd *TF:* 800-533-6242 ■ *Web:* magaltc.com	Riverwoods	IL	60015	847-940-8866		390
Magasin Latulippe 637 Rue Saint-vallier O *Web:* latulippe.com	Quebec	QC	G1N1C6	418-529-0024		711
Magavern Magavern & Grimm LLP 1100 Rand Bldg *Web:* www.magavern.com	Buffalo	NY	14203	716-856-3500		428
Magazine Publishers of America (MPA) 810 Seventh Ave 24th Fl *TF:* 800-234-3368 ■ *Web:* www.magazine.org	New York	NY	10019	212-872-3700	888-4217	49-16
Magazine Publishers of AmNAerica PAC 1211 Connecticut Ave NW Ste 610 *Web:* magazine.org	Washington	DC	20036	202-296-7277	296-0343	615
Magbee Contractors Supply 1065 Bankhead Hwy *Web:* www.magbee.com	Winder	GA	30680	678-425-2600	425-2602	191-3
Mage LLC 831 Beacon St Ste 310 *Web:* www.mageusa.com	Newton	MA	02459	617-244-8366		463
Magee Plastics Co 303 Brush Creek Rd *Web:* www.mageeplastics.com	Warrendale	PA	15086	724-776-2220		596
Magee Rehabilitation 1513 Race St *TF:* 800-966-2433 ■ *Web:* www.mageerehab.org	Philadelphia	PA	19102	215-587-3000	568-3736	374-6
Magee Resource Group LLC 920 Pierremont Rd *Web:* www.mageeresource.com	Shreveport	LA	71106	318-865-8411		463
Magee Thomson Investment Partners LLC 12531 High Bluff Dr Ste 120 *TF:* 800-521-9390 ■ *Web:* www.mageethomson.com	San Diego	CA	92130	858-350-5050		401
Magee-Womens Hospital 300 Halket St *Web:* www.upmc.com/locations/hospitals/Magee/Pages/default.aspx	Pittsburgh	PA	15213	412-641-1000		374-7
Magellan Aerospace 2320 Wedekind Dr *Web:* magellan.aero	Middletown	OH	45042	513-422-2751		22
Magellan Aerospace Corp 3160 Derry Rd E *TSE: MAL* ■ *Web:* www.magellan.aero	Mississauga	ON	L4T1A9	905-677-1889	677-5658	22
Magellan Development Group LLC 225 N Columbus Dr Ste 100 *Web:* www.magellandevelopment.com	Chicago	IL	60601	312-642-8869		653
Magellan Health Services Inc 55 Nod Rd *NASDAQ: MGLN* ■ *TF:* 800-424-4399 ■ *Web:* www.magellanhealth.com	Avon	CT	06001	860-507-1900	507-1990	462
Magellan Midstream Partners LP 1 Williams Ctr *NYSE: MMP* ■ *TF:* 800-574-6671 ■ *Web:* www.magellanlp.com	Tulsa	OK	74172	918-574-7000		597
Magellan Search Group Inc 620 W Germantown Pike Ste 300 *Web:* www.magellangroup.com	Plymouth Meeting	PA	19462	610-941-0100		193
Magellan Transport Logistics 2511 St Johns Bluff Rd Ste 107 *Web:* www.magellantransportlogistics.com	Jacksonville	FL	32246	904-620-0311		314
Magenium Solutions LLC 535 Pennsylvania Ave Ste 103 *Web:* www.magenium.com	Glen Ellyn	IL	60137	630-786-5900		180
Magenta Corp 15160 New Ave *Web:* www.magentallc.com	Lockport	IL	60441	773-777-5050		154
Maggiano's Little Italy 205 Northpark Ctr *Web:* www.maggianos.com	Dallas	TX	75225	214-360-0707		670
Maggiano's Little Italy 3550 E 86th St *Web:* www.maggianos.com	Indianapolis	IN	46240	317-814-0700		671
Maggiano's Little Italy 500 16th St *Web:* www.maggianos.com	Denver	CO	80202	303-260-7707		671
Maggiano's Little Italy Restaurant 2019 Post Oak Blvd *Web:* www.maggianos.com	Houston	TX	77056	713-961-2700		671
Maggie L Walker National Historic Site 600 N Second St *Web:* www.nps.gov/malw	Richmond	VA	23223	804-771-2017	771-2226	564
Maggie Valley Resort & Country Club 1819 Country Club Dr *TF:* 800-438-3861 ■ *Web:* www.maggievalleyclub.com	Maggie Valley	NC	28751	800-438-3861		669
Maggie's Kitchen 636 Bridge St NW	Grand Rapids	MI	49504	616-458-8583		671
Magic 101.1 FM 546 Ninth Ave *Web:* 101magic.iheart.com	Fairbanks	AK	99701	907-450-1000		645-57
Magic 107.3 KMJK-FM 5800 Foxridge Dr Ste 600 *Web:* www.magic1073.com	Mission	KS	66202	816-576-7107		645
Magic 590 6 Johnson Rd *Web:* albanymagic.com	Latham	NY	12110	518-786-6600		645

Company	Phone	Fax	Class
Magic 90.9 351 Tilghman Rd. Salisbury MD 21804 *Web:* mymagic989.iheart.com	410-742-1923		645
Magic Beans LLC 312 Harvard St. Brookline MA 02446 *TF:* 800-780-9949 ■ *Web:* www.mbeans.com	617-264-2326		761
Magic Castle Hotel 7025 Franklin Ave. Los Angeles CA 90028 *Web:* magiccastlehotel.com	323-851-0800		379
Magic House Saint Louis Children's Museum 516 S Kirkwood Rd. Saint Louis MO 63122 *TF:* 800-325-7962 ■ *Web:* www.magichouse.org	314-822-8900	822-8930	521
Magic Johnson Foundation Inc 9100 Wilshire Blvd Beverly Hills CA 90212 *Web:* magicjohnson.org	310-246-4400	786-8796	305
Magic Kingdom Park 1180 Seven Seas Dr Lake Buena Vista FL 32830 *Web:* disneyworld.disney.go.com/parks/magic-kingdom	407-824-4321		32
Magic Logix Inc 16610 Dallas Pkwy Ste 2200 Dallas TX 75248 *Web:* www.magiclogix.com	214-694-2162		195
Magic Metals Inc 3401 Bay St. Union Gap WA 98903 *Web:* www.magicmetals.com	509-453-1690		697
Magic Mountain Fun Centers 5890 Scarborough Blvd Columbus OH 43232 *Web:* www.magicmountainfuncenter.com	614-840-9600		31
Magic Novelty Inc 308 Dyckman St. New York NY 10034 *TF:* 800-561-3357 ■ *Web:* www.magicnovelty.com	212-304-2777	567-2809	407
Magic Plastics Inc 25215 Ave Stanford Valencia CA 91355 *TF:* 800-369-0303 ■ *Web:* www.magicplastics.com	661-257-4485		608
Magic Springs Theme Park & Crystal Falls Water Park 1701 E Grand Ave. Hot Springs AR 71901 *Web:* www.magicsprings.com	501-624-0100	318-5367	32
Magic Steel Sales LLC 4242 Clay Ave SW Grand Rapids MI 49540 *Web:* magicsteel.com	616-532-4071		492
Magic Tilt Trailers Inc 2161 Lions Club Rd Clearwater FL 33764 *Web:* www.boattrailers.com	727-535-5561		779
Magic Time Machine 8520 Crownhill Blvd. San Antonio TX 78209 *Web:* www.magictimemachine.com	210-828-1493		670
Magic Valley Electric Co-op Inc One 3/4 Mile W Hwy 83 PO Box 267 Mercedes TX 78570 *TF:* 866-225-5683 ■ *Web:* www.magval.com	866-225-5683		245
Magic Valley Newspapers 132 Fairfield St W. Twin Falls ID 83301 *TF:* 800-658-3883 ■ *Web:* www.magicvalley.com	208-733-0931	734-5538	637-8
Magic Valley Speedway 04N 150W Jerome Jerome ID 83338 *Web:* www.magicvalleyspeedway.com	208-734-3700	324-9616	515
Magicomm LLC 15 Alexander Rd. Billerica MA 01821	978-964-1900		195
Magid Glove & Safety Manufacturing Co 2060 N Kolmar Ave. Chicago IL 60639 *TF:* 800-444-8010 ■ *Web:* www.magidglove.com	773-384-2070	384-6677	155-8
Magil Construction Corp 1655 rue De Beauharnois Ouest Montreal QC H4N1J6 *Web:* www.magil.com	514-341-9899		186
MagiQ Technologies Inc 11 Ward St. Somerville MA 02143 **Fax Area Code:* 604 ■ *Web:* www.magiqtech.com	716-938-9175	688-6566*	743
Magis Group LLC, The 106 Brinker Rd Barrington IL 60010 *Web:* themagisgroup.com	847-756-4200		193
Magitech Corp 1500 Don Mills Rd Ste 702 North York ON M3B3K4 *Web:* www.ezgame.com	416-441-1933		179
Mag-Knight 18121 117th St SE Snohomish WA 98290 *Web:* www.mag-knight.com	360-805-0100	805-0811	517
Maglin Miskiv & Assoc CPA'S PA 299 Cherry Hill Rd Ste 100. Parsippany NJ 07054	973-263-3300		2
Magline Inc 1205 W Cedar St Standish MI 48658 **Fax Area Code:* 989 ■ *TF:* 800-624-5463 ■ *Web:* www.magliner.com	800-624-5463	879-5399*	470
Maglio & Company Whlse Fruits 4287 N Port Washington Rd. Milwaukee WI 53212 *Web:* www.maglioproduce.com	414-906-8800		260
Magmic 126 York St 4th Fl Ottawa ON K1N5T5 *Web:* www.magmic.com	613-241-3571		225
Magmotor Technologies Inc 10 Coppage Dr Worcester MA 01603 *Web:* www.inverpower.com	508-459-5991		253
Magna Chek Inc 32701 Edward Ave Madison Heights MI 48071 *TF:* 800-582-8947 ■ *Web:* www.magnachek.com	248-597-0089	597-0440	743
Magna Design Inc 12020 NE 26th PL. Bellevue WA 98005 *TF:* 800-426-1202 ■ *Web:* www.magnadesign.com	206-852-5282		319-1
MAGNA Global USA 100 W 33rd St 9th Fl. New York NY 10001 *Web:* www.magnaglobal.com	212-883-4751		6
Magna Group Inc, The 17-17 Rt 208 N Fair Lawn NJ 07410 *Web:* www.themagnagroup.com	201-652-8600		7
Magna International Inc 337 Magna Dr. Aurora ON L4G7K1 *TSE:* MG ■ *TF:* 800-377-5794 ■ *Web:* www.magna.com	905-726-2462	726-7164	60
Magna International of America 750 Tower Dr Troy MI 48098 *TF:* 800-436-7936 ■ *Web:* www.magna.com	248-631-1100		60
Magna IV 2401 Commercial Ln Little Rock AR 72206 *TF:* 800-946-2462 ■ *Web:* www.magna4.com	501-376-2397		627
Magna Machine & Tool Company Inc 3722 N Messick Rd New Castle IN 47362 *Web:* www.magnamachine.com	765-766-5388	766-5300	454
Magna Machine Co 11180 Southland Rd. Cincinnati OH 45240 *Web:* www.magna-machine.com	513-851-6900	851-6904	556
Magna Visual Inc 9400 Watson Rd Sappington MO 63126 **Fax Area Code:* 314 ■ *TF:* 800-843-3399 ■ *Web:* www.magnavisual.com	800-843-3399	843-0000*	534
Magnani & Associates Advertising Inc 200 S Michigan Ave Ste 500 Chicago IL 60604 *Web:* www.magnani.com	312-957-0770		195
Magnaserv Enterprises Inc 2862 SE Monroe St Stuart FL 34997 *Web:* www.magnaserv.com	772-219-2229		475

Company	Phone	Fax	Class
Magnatech Engineering 1204 Tonganoxie Rd. Tonganoxie KS 66086 *Web:* magnatechengineering.com	913-845-3553		207
Magnatech International Inc 17 E Meadow Ave Robesonia PA 19551 *TF:* 800-523-8193 ■ *Web:* magnatech-int.com	610-693-8866		111
Magnatex Inc 2520 Ridgemar Ct. Louisville KY 40207	502-493-0558		330
Magnatex Pumps Inc 3575 W 12th St Ste 208 Houston TX 77008 *Web:* www.magnatexpumps.com	719-329-0777		641
Magnatron Inc 225 S Peters Rd Knoxville TN 37923 *TF:* 800-583-0148 ■ *Web:* magnatron.com	865-769-2622		177
Magnaworks Technology Inc 36 Carlough Rd Bohemia NY 11716 *Web:* www.magnaworkstechnology.com	631-218-3431		458
Magneco/Metrel Inc 223 W I- Rd Addison IL 60101 *Web:* www.magneco-metrel.com	630-543-6660	543-1479	662
Magner Sanborn 111 N Post Ste 400 Spokane WA 99201 *Web:* www.magnersanborn.com	509-688-2200		7
magnes 2911 Russell St Berkeley CA 94705 *Web:* www.magnes.org	510-549-6950		520
Magnesita Refractories Co 425 S Salem Church Rd York PA 17408 **Fax:* Sales ■ *Web:* www.magnesita.com/?lang=en	717-792-3611	848-2294*	663
Magnesium Products of America Inc 2001 Industrial Dr (Island Cty Industrial Park) Eaton Rapids MI 48827 *Web:* www.meridian-mag.com/locations/?loc=3	517-663-2700		821
Magness Oil Co 167 Tucker Cemetary Rd. Gassville AR 72635 *TF:* 800-373-1542 ■ *Web:* www.magnessoil.com	870-425-4353		581
Magnet Schultz of America Inc 401 Plaza Dr Westmont IL 60559 *Web:* www.magnet-schultz.com	630-789-0600		203
Magnet Technology Inc 1599 Kingsview Dr Lebanon OH 45036 *Web:* www.magtech.cc	513-932-4416	932-4502	458
Magnetech Industrial Services Inc 800 Nave Rd SE Massillon OH 44646 *TF General:* 800-837-1614 ■ *Web:* www.magnetech.com	330-830-3500	830-3520	485
Magnetecs Corp 10524 La Cienega Blvd. Inglewood CA 90304 *Web:* www.magnetecs.com	310-670-7700		293
MagneTek Inc N49 W13650 Campbell Dr Menomonee Falls WI 53051 *NASDAQ:* MAG ■ *TF:* 800-288-8178 ■ *Web:* www.magnetek.com	800-288-8178	298-3503	253
Magneti Marelli Powertrain USA Inc 2101 Nash St Sanford NC 27330 *Web:* www.magnetimarelli.com	919-776-4111		60
Magnetic Analysis Corp 103 Fairview Park Dr Elmsford NY 10523 *TF:* 800-463-8622 ■ *Web:* www.mac-ndt.com	914-699-9450	703-3790	472
Magnetic Component Engineering Inc 2830 Lomita Blvd Torrance CA 90505 *TF:* 800-989-5656 ■ *Web:* www.mceproducts.com	800-989-5656		458
Magnetic Inspection Laboratory Inc 1401 Greenleaf Ave. Elk Grove Village IL 60007 *TF:* 800-543-3292 ■ *Web:* www.milinc.com	847-437-4488	437-4538	743
Magnetic Instrumentation Inc 8431 Castlewood Dr. Indianapolis IN 46250 *Web:* www.maginst.com	317-842-7500	849-7600	487
Magnetic Metals Corp 1900 Hayes Ave Camden NJ 08105 *TF:* 800-257-8174 ■ *Web:* www.magneticmetals.com	856-964-7842	963-8569	481
Magnetic Products Inc 683 Town Center Dr Highland MI 48357 *TF:* 800-544-5930 ■ *Web:* www.mpimagnet.com	800-544-5930		567
Magnetic Springs Water Co 1917 Joyce Ave. Columbus OH 43219 *TF:* 800-572-2990 ■ *Web:* www.magneticsprings.com	614-421-1780		297-8
Magnetrol International Inc 5300 Belmont Rd Downers Grove IL 60515 *TF:* 800-624-8765 ■ *Web:* magnetrol.com	630-969-4000	969-9489	201
Magnets Usa 817 Connecticut Ave NE. Roanoke VA 24012 *TF:* 800-869-7562 ■ *Web:* www.magnetsusa.com	800-869-7562		195
Magnets.com 51 Pacific Ave Ste 4 Jersey City NJ 07304 *TF:* 866-229-8237 ■ *Web:* www.magnets.com	866-229-8237		366
Magnetsigns Adv Inc 4225 38th St Camrose AB T4V3Z3 **Fax Area Code:* 780 ■ *TF:* 800-219-8977 ■ *Web:* www.magnetsigns.com	800-219-8977	672-8716*	310
Magni Group Inc 390 Pk St. Birmingham MI 48009 *Web:* www.magnicoatings.com	248-647-4500		550
Mag-Nif Inc 8820 E Ave. Mentor OH 44060 **Fax Area Code:* 440 ■ *TF:* 800-869-5463 ■ *Web:* www.magnif.com	800-869-5463	974-0449*	762
Magnifying Ctr 10086 W McNab Rd Tamarac FL 33321 *TF:* 800-364-1612 ■ *Web:* www.magnifyingcenter.com	954-722-1580		543
Magni-Industries Inc 2771 Hammond St. Detroit MI 48209 *Web:* magnicoatings.com	313-843-7855		550
Magnitude Capital LLC 200 Park Ave 56th Fl New York NY 10166 *Web:* www.magnitudecapital.com	212-915-3900		401
Magno International Lp 11014 NW 33rd St Ste 100. Doral FL 33172 *TF:* 800-866-5500 ■ *Web:* www.magnointl.com	305-392-4726		770
Magno Sound Inc 729 Seventh Ave Fl 2 New York NY 10019 *Web:* magnoscreening.com	212-302-2505		514
Magnode Corp 400 E State St Trenton OH 45067 *Web:* www.magnode.com	513-988-6351	988-6357	485
Magnolia Brush Mfg Ltd 1000 N Cedar PO Box 932 Clarksville TX 75426 **Fax Area Code:* 800 ■ *TF:* 800-248-2261 ■ *Web:* www.magnoliabrush.com	903-427-2261	427-5231*	103
Magnolia Cafe 2304 Lake Austin Blvd Austin TX 78703 *Web:* www.magnoliacafeaustin.com	512-478-8645		671
Magnolia Clipping Service 298 Commerce Pk Dr Ste A Ridgeland MS 39157 *Web:* www.magnoliaclips.com	601-856-0911		624
Magnolia Consulting LLC 5135 Blenheim Rd Charlottesville VA 22902 *TF:* 855-984-5540 ■ *Web:* www.magnoliaconsulting.org	434-984-5540		196

Name / Address	City	State	ZIP	Phone	Fax	Class
Magnolia Electric Power Assn PO Box 747 Web: mepcoop.com	McComb	MS	39649	601-684-4011	684-5535	245
Magnolia Estates 1511 Dulles Dr. Web: www.centralcontrolmgmt.com	Lafayette	LA	70506	337-216-0950		371
Magnolia Financial Inc 187 W Broad St TF: 866-573-0611 ■ Web: www.magfinancial.com	Spartanburg	SC	29306	864-573-9900	573-9912	272
Magnolia Forest Products Inc 13252 I- 55 S PO Box 99 *Fax Area Code: 601 ■ TF: 800-366-6374 ■ Web: www.magnoliaforest.com	Terry	MS	39170	800-366-6374	878-2590*	191-3
Magnolia Grange & Museum 10201 Iron Bridge Rd PO Box 40 Web: www.chesterfieldhistory.com	Chesterfield	VA	23832	804-796-7121	777-9643	520
Magnolia Hotel & Spa, The 623 Courtney St TF: 877-624-6654 ■ Web: www.magnoliahotel.com	Victoria	BC	V8W1B8	250-381-0999	381-0988	379
Magnolia Hotel Dallas 1401 Commerce St TF: 888-915-1110 ■ Web: www.magnoliahotels.com	Dallas	TX	75201	214-915-6500	253-0053	379
Magnolia Hotel Denver 818 17th St TF: 888-915-1110 ■ Web: www.magnoliahotels.com	Denver	CO	80202	303-607-9000	607-0101	379
Magnolia Hotel Houston 1100 Texas Ave TF: 888-915-1110 ■ Web: www.magnoliahotels.com	Houston	TX	77002	713-221-0011		379
Magnolia Manor Inc 2001 S Lee St Web: www.magnoliamanor.com	Americus	GA	31709	229-924-9352		450
Magnolia Metal Corp 10675 Bedford Ave Ste 200 TF: 800-228-4043 ■ Web: www.magnoliabronze.com	Omaha	NE	68134	402-455-8760	455-8762	308
Magnolia Mound Plantation 2161 Nicholson Dr Web: brec.org	Baton Rouge	LA	70802	225-343-4955		520
Magnolia Pictures LLC 49 W 27th St 7th Fl. Web: www.magpictures.com	New York	NY	10001	212-924-6701		748
Magnolia Plantation & Gardens 3550 Ashley River Rd TF: 800-367-3517 ■ Web: www.magnoliaplantation.com	Charleston	SC	29414	843-571-1266		97
Magnolia Regional Health Ctr 611 Alcorn Dr. Web: www.mrhc.org	Corinth	MS	38834	662-293-1000		374-3
Magnolia Springs State Park 1053 Magnolia Springs Dr Web: www.gastateparks.org	Millen	GA	30442	478-982-1660		565
Magnolia Steel Company Inc PO Box 5007 Web: www.magnoliasteel.com	Meridian	MS	39302	601-693-4301		480
Magnolia-Columbia County Chamber of Commerce 211 W Main St PO Box 866 Web: www.magnoliachamber.com	Magnolia	AR	71753	870-234-4352	234-9291	139
Magnotta Winery Corp 271 Chrislea Rd TF: 800-461-9463 ■ Web: www.magnotta.com	Vaughan	ON	L4L8N6	905-738-9463	738-5551	80-3
Magnum Hospitality 1515 Cass St Ste D. TF: 800-442-1162 ■ Web: www.magnumhospitality.com	Traverse City	MI	49684	231-932-1633		360-3
Magnum Hunter Resources 120 Prosperous Pl Ste 201 TF: 800-732-0330 ■ Web: www.magnumhunterresources.com	Lexington	KY	40509	859-263-3948		536
Magnum Integrated Technologies Inc 200 First Gulf Blvd TF: 800-830-0642 ■ Web: www.mit-world.com	Brampton	ON	L6W4T5	905-595-1998	455-0422	674
Magnum Machining Inc 20959 State Hwy 6 Web: www.magnummachining.com	Deerwood	MN	56444	218-534-3552		454
Magnum Magnetics Corp 801 Masonic Pk Rd TF: 800-258-0991 ■ Web: www.magnummagnetics.com	Marietta	OH	45750	740-373-7770	373-2880	458
Magnum Photos Inc 151 W 25th St Fl 5 Web: www.magnumphotos.com	New York	NY	10001	212-929-6000		592
Magnum Research Inc 7110 University Ave NE TF: 800-772-6168 ■ Web: www.magnumresearch.com	Minneapolis	MN	55432	763-574-1868		711
Magnum Staffing Services Inc 2900 Smith St Ste 250 Web: www.magnumstaffing.com	Houston	TX	77006	713-658-0068	523-3621	721
Magnus Equipment 4500 Beidler Rd TF: 800-456-6423 ■ Web: www.magnusequipment.com	Willoughby	OH	44094	440-942-8488		358
Magnus Mobility Systems Inc 2805 Barranca Pkwy TF: 800-858-7801 ■ Web: www.magnusinc.com	Irvine	CA	92606	714-771-2630	744-0134	350
Magnus-hitech Industries Inc 1605 Lake St. Web: www.magnushitech.com	Melbourne	FL	32901	321-724-9731		697
Magnuson Hotels PO Box 1434 Web: www.magnusonhotels.com	Spokane	WA	99210	509-747-8713		707
Magnussen Dealership Group 401 Burgess Dr Ste A	Menlo Park	CA	94025	650-327-4100		57
Magnussen Home Furnishings Ltd 66 Hincks St Web: www.magnussen.com	New Hamburg	ON	N3A2A3	519-662-3040		320
Magnusson Klemencic Assoc Inc 1301 Fifth Ave Ste 3200 Web: www.mka.com	Seattle	WA	98101	206-292-1200		261
Magoffin County 249 Mountain Pkwy Dr PO Box 430 Web: magoffincounty.ky.gov	Salyersville	KY	41465	606-349-2313		338
Magoffin Home State Historic Site 1120 Magoffin Ave Web: www.thc.texas.gov	El Paso	TX	79901	915-533-5147		565
Magoo's Automotive Consultants Inc 4580 Market St.	Ventura	CA	93003	805-676-3440		62
Magotteaux Inc 725 Cool Springs Blvd Ste 200 TF: 800-828-5360 ■ Web: www.magotteaux.com	Franklin	TN	37067	615-385-3055	297-6743	485
MagPortal.com PO Box 463 Web: www.magportal.com	Bryn Mawr	PA	19010	610-581-7702		397
Magpul Industries Corp 400 Young Ct Unit 1 TF: 800-694-5263 ■ Web: www.magpul.com	Erie	CO	80516	303-828-3460		807

Name / Address	City	State	ZIP	Phone	Fax	Class
Magtech Industries Corp 5625 Arville St Ste A. TF: 888-954-4481 ■ Web: www.magtechind.com	Las Vegas	NV	89118	702-364-9998		253
Magtrol Inc 70 Gardenville Pkwy W. TF: 800-828-7844 ■ Web: www.magtrol.com	Buffalo	NY	14224	716-668-5555	668-8705	620
Maguire Associates Inc 555 Virginia Rd 5 Concord Farms Ste 201 Web: www.maguireassoc.com	Concord	MA	01742	978-371-1775		466
Maguire Investments Inc 1862 S Broadway Ste 100 Web: www.maguireinvest.com	Santa Maria	CA	93454	805-922-6901		690
Maguire Iron Inc 1610 N Minnesota Ave Web: www.maguireiron.com	Sioux Falls	SD	57104	605-334-9749		480
MaguireZay LLC 17194 Preston Rd Ste 102-143 Web: maguirezay.com	Dallas	TX	75248	214-692-5002		463
Magyar Bancorp Inc 400 Somerset St. NASDAQ: MGYR ■ Web: www.magbank.com/home/home	New Brunswick	NJ	08901	732-342-7600		70
Magyar Bank 400 Somerset St TF: 800-472-3272 ■ Web: www.magbank.com	New Brunswick	NJ	08901	732-342-7600		70
MAH (Mount Auburn Hospital) 330 Mt Auburn St. Web: www.mountauburnhospital.org	Cambridge	MA	02138	617-492-3500		374-3
Mahaffey & Gore PC 300 NE First St. Web: www.mahaffeygorelaw.com	Oklahoma City	OK	73104	405-236-0478		428
Mahaffey Enterprises 3327 E Ridgeview St.	Springfield	MO	65804	417-883-9180		643
Mahaffey Theater for the Performing Arts 400 First St S TF: 800-435-7352 ■ Web: www.themahaffey.com	Saint Petersburg	FL	33701	727-892-5798	892-5897	572
Mahaffey's Quality Printing Inc 355 W Pearl St. Web: quality-printing.com	Jackson	MS	39203	601-353-9663		627
Mahanoy Area School District 1 Golden Bear Dr Web: www.mabears.net	Mahanoy City	PA	17948	570-773-3443		685
Mahar Tool Supply Co Inc 112 Williams St TF: 800-456-2427 ■ Web: www.mahartool.com	Saginaw	MI	48605	989-799-5530	799-0830	385
Maharaja 1550 N Farwell Ave	Milwaukee	WI	53202	414-276-2250		671
Maharaja Restaurant 6308 Hulen Bend Blvd Web: maharajadfw.com	Fort Worth	TX	76132	817-263-7156		671
Maharishi University of Management 1000 N Fourth St TF: 800-369-6480 ■ Web: www.mum.edu	Fairfield	IA	52557	641-472-1110	472-1179	166
Mahaska County 106 S First St Mahaska Courthouse Web: www.mahaskacounty.org	Oskaloosa	IA	52577	641-673-7786		338
Maher Duessel DL Clark Bldg 503 Martindale St Ste 600 Web: www.md-cpas.com	Pittsburgh	PA	15212	412-471-5500		466
Maher Terminals LLC 1210 Corbin St Web: www.maherterminals.com	Elizabeth	NJ	07201	908-527-8200		313
Maher, Guiley & Maher PA 631 W Morse Blvd Ste 200 Web: maherlawfirm.com	Winter Park	FL	32789	407-839-0866		428
MAHLE Industries Inc 2020 Sanford St TF: 888-255-1942 ■ Web: www.us.mahle.com	Muskegon	MI	49444	231-722-1300		128
Mahlum Architects Inc 71 Columbia 4th Fl. Web: www.mahlum.com	Seattle	WA	98104	206-441-4151	441-0478	261
Mahogany Grille 699 Main Ave. Web: www.mahoganygrille.com	Durango	CO	81301	970-247-4433	259-2208	671
Mahogany Prime Steak House 6823 S Yale Ave Web: www.mahogany.ehsrg.com	Tulsa	OK	74136	918-494-4043		671
Mahoney Assoc Inc 2455 E Sunrise Blvd Ste 300 Web: www.mahoneyandassociates.com	Fort Lauderdale	FL	33304	954-564-4300		194
Mahoney Institute of Neurological Sciences 3535 Market St Mezzanine Web: www.med.upenn.edu	Philadelphia	PA	19104	215-662-2560	349-8312	668
Mahoney Ulbrich Christiansen & Russ P A 30 E Plato Blvd Web: www.mucr.com	Saint Paul	MN	55107	651-227-6695		2
Mahoney's Garden Ctr 242 Cambridge St. TF: 800-341-6900 ■ Web: www.mahoneysgarden.com	Winchester	MA	01890	781-729-5900		323
Mahoning County 120 Market St TF: 800-548-7175 ■ Web: www.mahoningcountyoh.gov	Youngstown	OH	44503	330-740-2104	740-2105	338
Mahoning County Convention & Visitors Bureau 21 W Boardman St TF: 800-447-8201 ■ Web: www.youngstownlive.com	Youngstown	OH	44503	330-740-2130	740-2144	206
Mahr 1144 Eddy St Web: www.mahrfederal.com	Providence	RI	02905	401-784-3100	784-3246	201
Mahuta Tool Corp N118W19137 Bunsen Dr TF: 888-686-4940 ■ Web: www.mahutatool.com	Germantown	WI	53022	262-502-4100		757
MAI (Minuteman Aviation Inc) 5225 Hwy 10 W Web: www.minutemanaviation.com	Missoula	MT	59808	406-728-9363		63
MAI (Medical Action Industries Inc) 500 Expy Dr S. NASDAQ: MDCI ■ TF: 800-645-7042 ■ Web: www.medical-action.com	Brentwood	NY	11717	631-231-4600		477
MAI (Marketing Analysts Inc) 2000 Sam Rittenberg Blvd Ste 3007 Web: www.mairesearch.com	Charlotte	SC	29407	704-405-2150		466
Mai Thai 750 W Idaho St Web: www.maithaigroup.com	Boise	ID	83702	208-344-8424		671
Mai Village 394 University Ave	Saint Paul	MN	55103	651-290-2585		671
Maibec Inc 202 1984 Fifth St. TF: 800-363-1930 ■ Web: www.maibec.com	Levis	QC	G6W5M6	418-659-3323		683
Maid Brigade USA/Minimaid Canada 4 Concourse Pkwy Ste 200. TF: 866-800-7470 ■ Web: www.maidbrigade.com	Atlanta	GA	30328	770-551-9630		152

Name / Address	City	State	Zip	Phone	Fax	Class
Maida Development Co 201 S Mallory St	Hampton	VA	23663	757-723-0785	722-1194	253
Web: www.maida.com						
MaidPro Corp 180 Canal St	Boston	MA	02114	617-742-8787		310
TF: 888-624-3776 ■ *Web:* www.maidpro.com						
Maid-Rite Steak Company Inc						
105 Keystone Industrial Pk	Dunmore	PA	18512	570-343-4748	969-2878	296-26
TF: 800-233-4259 ■ *Web:* maidritesteak.com						
Maids International						
9394 W Dodge Rd Ste 140	Omaha	NE	68114	402-558-8600	558-4112	152
TF: 800-843-6243 ■ *Web:* www.maids.com						
Maidstone Hotel, The 207 Main St	East Hampton	NY	11937	631-324-5006		378
TF: 800-654-3131 ■ *Web:* www.themaidstone.com						
Maidstone State Park						
4858 Maidstone Lake Rd	Maidstone	VT	05905	802-676-3930		565
Web: www.vtstateparks.com						
Maier Markey & Justic LLP						
222 Bloomingdale Rd Ste 400	White Plains	NY	10605	914-644-9200		466
Web: mgroupusa.com						
Maier Siebel Baber						
80 E Sir Francis Drake Blvd	Larkspur	CA	94939	415-591-9900		655
Web: www.msb-realestate.com						
Mail America Communications Inc						
1174 Elkton Farm Rd	Forest	VA	24551	434-534-8000		5
Web: www.mail-america.com						
Mail Bag Inc 3030 Waterview Ave	Baltimore	MD	21230	410-565-5299	565-5017	5
Web: www.mailbaginc.com						
Mail Communications Group LLC						
4100 121st St	Des Moines	IA	50323	515-727-7700		627
Web: www.mailcommunicationsgroup.com						
Mail Contractors of America						
3809 Roundtop Dr N	Little Rock	AR	72117	501-280-0500		780
Mail Dispatch LLC						
9710 Distribution Ave	San Diego	CA	92121	800-275-0450		317
TF: 800-275-0450 ■ *Web:* www.maildispatch.com						
Mail Handling Inc						
7550 Corporate Way	Eden Prairie	MN	55344	952-975-5000		627
Web: www.mailhandling.com						
Mail Right Inc 4470 Yankee Hill Rd	Auburn	CA	95677	530-492-5147		5
Web: mailright.com						
Mail Shark 4125 New Holland Rd	Mohnton	PA	19540	610-621-2994		366
TF: 888-457-4275 ■ *Web:* www.themailshark.com						
Mail Source Inc 111 Boardwalk	Fall Creek	WI	54742	715-877-3711		5
TF: 800-275-8777 ■ *Web:* mailsourceinc.com						
Mail Stream Inc 125 Mason Cir Ste K	Concord	CA	94520	925-676-6711		627
Web: mail-stream.net						
Mail Unlimited Inc 4607 Metric Dr	Winter Park	FL	32792	407-657-9333		5
Web: mailunlimited.com						
Mailbox, The						
3515 W Market St Ste 200	Greensboro	NC	27403	336-854-0309	334-0298*	457-8
**Fax Area Code:* 800 ■ *Web:* www.themailbox.com						
Mailender Inc 9500 Glades Dr	Hamilton	OH	45011	513-942-5453		690
TF: 800-998-5453 ■ *Web:* www.mailender.com						
Mailer's Choice Inc						
1504 Elm Hill Pk	Nashville	TN	37210	615-883-0070		5
Web: www.mailerschoice.com						
Mailing Services of Pittsburgh Inc						
155 Commerce Dr	Freedom	PA	15042	724-774-3244		5
TF: 800-876-3211 ■ *Web:* msp-pgh.com						
Mailing Systems Inc						
2431 Mercantile Dr Ste A	Rancho Cordova	CA	95742	916-674-2035		5
TF: 877-577-2647 ■ *Web:* www.msimail.net						
Mailings Unlimited						
116 Riverside Industrial Pkwy	Portland	ME	04103	207-347-5000		5
TF: 800-773-7417 ■ *Web:* www.growwithmail.com						
Maillard Redwoods State Natural Reserve						
PO Box 440	Mendocino	CA	95460	707-937-5804	937-2953	565
Web: www.parks.ca.gov/default.asp?page_id=439						
Maillie LLP						
1521 Concord Pike Ste 301	Wilmington	DE	19803	302-358-2371		466
TF: 800-292-9507 ■ *Web:* www.maillie.com						
Mailman Research Ctr						
McLean Hospital 115 Mill St	Belmont	MA	02478	617-855-2000		668
TF: 800-333-0338 ■ *Web:* mcleanhospital.org/research/mrc						
Mailmark Enterprises LLC						
8587 Canoga Ave	Canoga Park	CA	91304	818-407-0660		5
TF: 800-334-8983 ■ *Web:* mailmark.com						
Mailrite Print & Mail Inc						
834 Striker Ave Ste C	Sacramento	CA	95834	916-927-6245		5
Web: www.mailritemail.com						
Mailroom Service Center Inc						
3075 Shattuck Rd	Saginaw	MI	48603	989-790-2166		5
Web: www.mailroomservicecenter.com						
Mailways Enterprises Inc						
6105 Factory Rd Ste 1	Crystal Lake	IL	60014	815-455-4850		5
Web: mailways.net						
Maimonides Medical Ctr (MMC)						
4802 Tenth Ave	Brooklyn	NY	11219	718-283-6000		374-3
Web: www.maimonidesmed.org						
Main & Sky Park City						
201 Heber Ave Main St	Park City	UT	84060	435-658-2500	615-6751	378
Web: www.skyparkcity.com						
Main Banc Inc						
2424 Louisiana Blvd NE	Albuquerque	NM	87110	505-880-1700		70
Web: mainbank.com						
Main Electric Supply Co						
6700 S Main St	Los Angeles	CA	90003	323-753-5131	753-7750	246
Web: www.mainelectricsupply.com						
Main Industries Inc 107 E St	Hampton	VA	23661	757-380-0180		313
Web: www.mainindustries.com						
Main Line 25 Penncraft Ave # 4	Chambersburg	PA	17201	717-263-0813		643
Web: mix95.com						
Main Line Chamber of Commerce						
175 Strafford Ave Ste 130	Wayne	PA	19087	610-687-6232	687-8085	139
Web: www.mlcc.org						
Main Line Supply Company Inc						
300 N Findlay St	Dayton	OH	45403	937-254-6910		358
TF: 800-561-3357 ■ *Web:* www.mainlinesupply.com						
Main Line Tire & Service						
102 Robbins Rd	Downingtown	PA	19335	610-514-3600		57
Web: unitedtire.com						
Main Moon 1760 Belmont Ave	Youngstown	OH	44504	330-743-1638		671
Main Source Bank 201 N Broadway	Greensburg	IN	47240	800-713-6083		70
TF: 800-713-6083 ■ *Web:* www.mainsourcebank.com						
Main Street Advisors LLC						
205 E Main St	Westminster	MD	21157	410-840-9200		401
Web: www.mainstadvisors.com						
Main Street America Group 55 W St	Keene	NH	03431	603-352-4000		391-4
TF: 800-258-5310 ■ *Web:* www.msagroup.com						
Main Street Capital Corp						
1300 Post Oak Blvd	Houston	TX	77056	713-350-6000	350-6042	405
NYSE: MAIN ■ *TF:* 800-966-1559 ■ *Web:* www.mainstcapital.com						
Main Street Chamber of Leake County, The						
PO Box 209	Carthage	MS	39051	601-267-9231		338
Web: www.leakems.com						
Main Street Gourmet Inc						
170 Muffin Ln	Cuyahoga Falls	OH	44223	330-929-0000		296-2
TF: 800-678-6246 ■ *Web:* www.mainstreetgourmet.com						
Main Street Grill & Bar						
118 Main St	Montpelier	VT	05602	802-223-3188		671
Web: www.neci.edu						
Main Street Grille 112 N Main St	Mishawaka	IN	46544	574-254-4995		671
Web: www.mainstgrille.com						
Main Street Media Group LLC						
6400 Monterey St	Gilroy	CA	95020	408-842-6400	842-1021	532-3
Main Street Radiology						
13625 37th Ave Fl 2	Flushing	NY	11354	718-428-1500		415
TF: 888-930-4674 ■ *Web:* www.mainstreetradiology.com						
Main Street Station Hotel & Casino						
200 N Main St	Las Vegas	NV	89101	702-387-1896		379
TF: 800-713-8933 ■ *Web:* www.mainstreetcasino.com						
Main-Care Energy PO Box 11029	Albany	NY	12211	800-542-5552	438-5991*	579
**Fax Area Code:* 518 ■ *TF:* 800-542-5552 ■ *Web:* www.maincareenergy.com						
Maine						
Administrative Office of the Cts						
PO Box 4820	Portland	ME	04112	207-822-0792		339-20
Web: courts.maine.gov						
Agriculture Dept 22 State House Stn	Augusta	ME	04333	207-287-3200	287-2400	339-20
Web: www.maine.gov						
Arts Commission 193 State St	Augusta	ME	04330	207-287-2724	287-2725	339-20
Web: mainearts.maine.gov						
Attorney General 6 State House Stn	Augusta	ME	04333	207-626-8800		339-20
Web: www.maine.gov						
Chief Medical Examiner						
37 State House Stn	Augusta	ME	04333	207-624-7180	624-7178	339-20
Web: www.maine.gov						
Child & Family Services Office						
2 Anthony Ave 11 State House Sta	Augusta	ME	04333	207-624-7900	287-5282	339-20
Web: maine.gov/dhhs/ocfs						
Conservation Dept 22 State House Stn	Augusta	ME	04333	207-287-3200	287-2400	339-20
Web: maine.gov/dacf						
Consumer Protection Unit						
85 Leighton Rd	Augusta	ME	04333	207-287-2923	287-4667	339-20
TF: 800-436-2131 ■ *Web:* www.maine.gov						
Corrections Dept						
25 Tyson Dr Third Fl 111 State House Stn	Augusta	ME	04333	207-287-2711	287-4370	339-20
Web: www.maine.gov						
Economic & Community Development Dept						
111 Sewall St Burton Cross Bldg 3rd Fl	Augusta	ME	04330	207-624-9800		339-20
Web: www.maine.gov						
Education Dept 23 State House Stn	Augusta	ME	04333	207-624-6600	624-6700	339-20
Web: www.maine.gov/education						
Elder Services Office 41 Anthony Ave	Augusta	ME	04333	207-287-9200		339-20
TF: 888-568-1112 ■ *Web:* www1.maine.gov/dhhs/oads						
Employment Services Bureau						
55 State House Stn	Augusta	ME	04330	207-623-7981	287-5933	259
TF: 888-457-8883 ■ *Web:* www.mainecareercenter.com						
Environmental Protection Dept						
17 State House Stn	Augusta	ME	04333	207-287-7688	287-7826	339-20
TF: 800-452-1942 ■ *Web:* www.maine.gov						
Finance Authority of Maine						
5 Community Dr PO Box 949	Augusta	ME	04332	207-623-3263	623-0095	725
TF: 800-228-3734 ■ *Web:* www.famemaine.com						
Financial Institutions Bureau						
36 State House Sta	Augusta	ME	04333	207-624-8570	624-8590	339-20
TF: 800-965-5235 ■ *Web:* www.maine.gov						
Governmental Ethics & Election Practices Com						
45 Memorial Cir	Augusta	ME	04330	207-287-4179	287-6775	265
Web: www.maine.gov						
Governor 1 State House Stn	Augusta	ME	04333	207-287-3531	287-1034	339-20
TF: 855-721-5203 ■ *Web:* www.maine.gov/governor						
Health Bureau 221 State St	Augusta	ME	04333	207-287-3707	287-3005	339-20
Web: www.maine.gov						
Historic Preservation Commission						
65 State House Stn	Augusta	ME	04333	207-287-2132		339-20
Web: www.maine.gov						
Housing Authority 353 Water St	Augusta	ME	04330	207-626-4600	626-4678	339-20
TF: 800-452-4668 ■ *Web:* www.mainehousing.org						
Human Services Dept						
221 State St 11 State House Sta	Augusta	ME	04333	207-287-3707		339-20
Web: www.maine.gov						
Information Services Bureau						
145 State House Stn	Augusta	ME	04333	207-624-8800	287-4563	339-20
Web: www.maine.gov						
Inland Fisheries & Wildlife Dept						
41 State House Stn	Augusta	ME	04333	207-287-8000	287-6395	339-20
Web: www.maine.gov						
Insurance Bureau 34 State House Stn	Augusta	ME	04333	207-624-8475	624-8599	339-20
TF: 800-300-5000 ■ *Web:* www.maine.gov/pfr/insurance						
Labor Dept 54 State House Sta	Augusta	ME	04333	207-623-7900		339-20
Web: www.state.me.us/labor						
Legislature 115 State House Stn	Augusta	ME	04333	207-287-1615	287-1621	339-20
Web: maine.gov/legis						
Licensure in Medicine Board						
161 Capitol St	Augusta	ME	04330	207-287-3601	287-6590	339-20
TF: 888-365-9964 ■ *Web:* www.docboard.org						

Phone | Fax | Class

Motor Vehicles Bureau
29 State House Stn .... Augusta ME 04333 207-624-9000 624-9013 339-20
Web: www.maine.gov/sos/bmv

Parks & Land Bureau
22 State House Stn .... Augusta ME 04333 207-287-3821 287-6170 339-20
Web: www.maine.gov

Parole Board 111 State House Stn. .... Augusta ME 04333 207-287-2711 287-4370 339-20
Web: www.maine.gov

Public Utilities Commission
18 State House Stn .... Augusta ME 04333 207-287-3831 287-1039 339-20
Web: www.maine.gov

Quality Assurance & Regulations Div
28 State House Stn .... Augusta ME 04333 207-287-3841 287-5576 339-20
Web: www.maine.gov

Rehabilitation Services Bureau
150 State House Stn .... Augusta ME 04333 800-698-4440 287-5292* 339-20
**Fax Area Code:* 207 ■ *TF:* 800-698-4440 ■ *Web:* www.maine.gov/rehab

Revenue Services 24 State House Stn .... Augusta ME 04333 207-287-2076 287-3618 339-20
Web: www.maine.gov

Secretary of State
148 State House Stn .... Augusta ME 04333 207-626-8400 287-8598 339-20
Web: www.maine.gov/sos

Securities Div 76 Northern Ave .... Gardiner ME 04345 207-624-8551 624-8590 339-20
TF: 877-624-8551 ■ *Web:* www.maine.gov

State Government Information
26 Edison Dr .... Augusta ME 04330 207-624-9494 339-20
TF: 888-577-6690 ■ *Web:* www.maine.gov

State Police
45 Commerce Dr 42 State House Station. .... Augusta ME 04333 207-624-7200 339-20
Web: www.maine.gov/dps/msp

Supreme Court 205 Newbury St Rm 139. .... Portland ME 04101 207-822-4286 339-20
Web: courts.maine.gov/maine_courts/supreme

Tourism Office 59 State House Sta. .... Augusta ME 04333 207-624-7483 624-6331* 339-20
**Fax Area Code:* 877 ■ *TF:* 888-624-6345 ■ *Web:* www.visitmaine.com

Transportation Dept
16 State House Stn .... Augusta ME 04333 207-624-3000 339-20
Web: www.maine.gov/mdot

University of Maine System Board of Trustees
16 Central St .... Bangor ME 04401 207-973-3211 973-3296 339-20
Web: www.maine.edu

Veterans' Services Bureau
117 State House Stn .... Augusta ME 04333 207-430-6035 626-4471 339-20
Web: www.maine.gov

Victims' Compensation Program
6 State House Sta. .... Augusta ME 04333 207-624-7882 624-7730 339-20
Web: www.maine.gov

Vital Records Office 220 Capitol St .... Augusta ME 04333 207-287-3181 339-20
TF: 888-664-9491 ■ *Web:* www.maine.gov/dhhs

Workers' Compensation Board
442 Civic Ctr Dr, 27 State House Stn Ste 100 ... Augusta ME 04333 207-287-3751 287-7198 339-20
TF: 888-801-9087 ■ *Web:* www.maine.gov

Maine Assn of Realtors
19 Community Dr .... Augusta ME 04330 207-622-7501 623-3590 656
Web: www.mainerealtors.com

Maine Biotechnology Services Inc
1037 R Forest Ave. .... Portland ME 04103 207-797-5454 797-5595 231
TF: 800-925-9476 ■ *Web:* www.mainebiotechnology.com

Maine Bucket Co 21 Fireslate Pl .... Lewiston ME 04240 207-784-6700 200
TF: 800-231-7072 ■ *Web:* mainebucket.com

Maine Central Institute
295 MAIN ST .... Pittsfield ME 04967 207-487-3355 487-3512 622
Web: www.mci-school.org

Maine Coast Heritage Trust
1 Bowdoin Mill Island Ste 201 .... Topsham ME 04086 207-729-7366 804
Web: www.mcht.org

Maine College of Art 522 Congress St .... Portland ME 04101 207-775-3052 772-5069 164
TF: 800-639-4808 ■ *Web:* www.meca.edu

Maine Correctional Ctr
17 Mallison Falls Rd. .... Windham ME 04062 207-893-7000 893-7001 213
Web: maine.gov

Maine Course Hospitality Group Inc
15 Main St Ste 210. .... Freeport ME 04032 207-865-6105 378
Web: www.mchg.com

Maine Democratic Party PO Box 5258. .... Augusta ME 04332 207-622-6233 622-2657 616-1
Web: www.mainedems.org

Maine Dental Assn 29 Assn Dr .... Manchester ME 04351 207-622-7900 227
Web: www.medental.org

Maine Educator Magazine
35 Community Dr. .... Augusta ME 04330 207-622-5866 457-8
TF: 800-332-8529 ■ *Web:* centralmaine.com

Maine Endwell Central School
712 Farm to Market Rd. .... Endwell NY 13760 607-754-1400 754-1650 685
Web: www.me.stier.org

Maine Folklife Ctr
5773 S Stevens Hall University of Maine .... Orono ME 04469 207-581-1891 581-1823 50-2
TF: 800-753-9044 ■ *Web:* www.umaine.edu/folklife

Maine General Medical Ctr (MGMC)
Augusta 361 Old Belgrade Rd .... Augusta ME 04330 207-626-1000 621-8801 374-3
TF: 800-266-6809 ■ *Web:* www.mainegeneral.org

Maine Historical Society
489 Congress St Maine Historical Society .... Portland ME 04101 207-774-1822 775-4301 520
Web: mainehistory.org

Maine Hospital Association
33 Fuller Rd .... Augusta ME 04330 207-622-4794 138
TF: 800-341-1650 ■ *Web:* themha.org

Maine Instrument Flight Inc
215 Winthrop St .... Augusta ME 04330 207-622-1211 622-7858 63
TF: 888-643-3597 ■ *Web:* www.maineinstrumentflight.com

Maine Lobster Direct 48 Union Wharf. .... Portland ME 04101 800-556-2783 297-5
TF: 800-556-2783 ■ *Web:* www.mainelobsterdirect.com

Maine Machine Products Co
79 Prospect Ave .... South Paris ME 04281 207-743-6344 454

Maine Mall 364 Maine Mall Rd .... South Portland ME 04106 207-774-0303 460
Web: www.mainemall.com

Maine Maritime Academy 66 Pleasant St. .... Castine ME 04420 207-326-4311 326-2515* 166
**Fax:* Admissions ■ *TF Admissions:* 800-464-6565 ■ *Web:* www.mainemaritime.edu

Maine Maritime Museum 243 Washington St .... Bath ME 04530 207-443-1316 443-1665 520
TF: 800-942-5313 ■ *Web:* mainemaritimemuseum.org

Maine Medical Assn 30 Assn Dr .... Manchester ME 04351 207-622-3374 622-3332 474
TF: 800-772-0815 ■ *Web:* www.mainemed.com

Maine Medical Ctr (MMC) 22 Bramhall St .... Portland ME 04102 207-662-0111 374-3
TF: 877-339-3107 ■ *Web:* mainehealth.org/maine-medical-center

Brighton Campus 335 Brighton Ave .... Portland ME 04102 207-775-4000 374-3
Web: mainehealth.org/maine-medical-center

Maine Narrow Gauge Railroad Museum
58 Fore St. .... Portland ME 04101 207-828-0814 520
Web: www.mainenarrowgauge.org

Maine Nurse Practitioners Association
11 Columbia St. .... Augusta ME 04330 207-621-0313 533
Web: www.mnpa.us

Maine Oxy 22 Albiston Way .... Auburn ME 04210 207-784-5788 784-5383 811
TF: 800-639-1108 ■ *Web:* www.maineoxy.com

Maine People's Alliance
27 State St Ste 44 .... Bangor ME 04401 207-990-0672 615
Web: mainepeoplesalliance.org

Maine Pharmacy Assn
127 Pleasant Hill Rd. .... Scarborough ME 04074 207-396-5340 585
Web: www.mparx.com

Maine Plastics Inc 1817 Kenosha Rd .... Zion IL 60099 847-379-9100 603
TF: 800-338-7728 ■ *Web:* www.maineplastics.com

Maine Pointe LLC
470 Atlantic Ave 4th Fl .... Boston MA 02210 617-273-8450 194
Web: www.mainepointe.com

Maine Potato Growers Inc
56 Parsons St. .... Presque Isle ME 04769 207-764-3131 764-8450 274
TF: 800-649-3358 ■ *Web:* www.mpgco-op.com

Maine Public Broadcasting Network (MPBN)
65 Texas Ave. .... Bangor ME 04401 207-941-1010 942-2857 632
TF: 800-884-1717 ■ *Web:* mainepublic.org

Maine Republican Party 9 Higgins St. .... Augusta ME 04330 207-622-6247 616-2
Web: www.mainegop.com

Maine State Ballet 348 US Rt 1 .... Falmouth ME 04105 207-781-7672 573-1
Web: www.mainestateballet.org

Maine State Bar Assn 124 State St .... Augusta ME 04330 207-622-7523 623-0083 72
TF: 800-475-7523 ■ *Web:* www.mainebar.org

Maine State Chamber of Commerce
125 Community Dr Ste 101 .... Augusta ME 04330 207-623-4568 622-7723 140
TF: 800-546-7866 ■ *Web:* www.mainechamber.org

Maine State Library
64 State House Stn .... Augusta ME 04333 207-287-5600 287-5615 434-5
TF: 800-427-8336 ■ *Web:* www.maine.gov

Maine State Museum 83 State House Stn .... Augusta ME 04333 207-287-2301 287-6633 520
TF: 800-686-7633 ■ *Web:* www.mainestatemuseum.org

Maine State Nurses Assn (MSNA)
160 Capitol St Ste 1 .... Augusta ME 04330 207-622-1057 623-4072 533
Web: www.nationalnursesunited.org

Maine Veterans Home-Bangor 44 Hogan Rd. .... Bangor ME 04401 207-942-2333 793
TF: 888-684-4665 ■ *Web:* mainevets.org

Maine Veterans Home-Caribou
163 Van Buren Rd Ste 2 .... Caribou ME 04736 207-498-6074 793
Web: mainevets.org

Maine Veterans Home-Scarborough
290 US Rt 1 .... Scarborough ME 04074 207-883-7184 793
Web: mainevets.org

Maine Veterans Home-South Paris
477 High St .... South Paris ME 04281 207-743-6300 793
Web: mainevets.org

Maine Veterans' Homes 310 Cony Rd .... Augusta ME 04330 207-622-2454 793
TF: 800-278-9494 ■ *Web:* mainevets.org

Maine Veterinary Medical Assn (MVMA)
97A Exchange St Ste 305 .... Portland ME 04101 800-448-2772 612-0941* 795
**Fax Area Code:* 888 ■ *TF:* 800-448-2772 ■ *Web:* netforum.avectra.com

Maine Windjammer Cruises PO Box 617 .... Camden ME 04843 207-236-2938 236-3229 220
TF: 800-736-7981 ■ *Web:* www.mainewindjammercruises.com

Maine Wood Concepts Inc
1687 New Vineyard Rd .... New Vineyard ME 04956 207-652-2441 820
TF: 800-374-6961 ■ *Web:* www.mainewoodconcepts.com

Mainebiz 48 Free St .... Portland ME 04101 207-761-8379 530
Web: www.mainebiz.biz

MaineHealth 110 Free St. .... Portland ME 04101 207-661-7001 363
Web: mainehealth.org

Mainelli Wagner & Associates Inc
6920 Van Dorn St Ste A .... Lincoln NE 68506 402-421-1717 261
Web: www.mwaeng.com

Maines Paper & Food Service Co
101 Broome Corporate Pkwy .... Conklin NY 13748 607-779-1200 297-8
TF: 800-366-3669 ■ *Web:* www.maines.net

Mainetti USA 300 Mac Ln .... Keasbey NJ 08832 201-215-2900 607
Web: www.mainetti.com

Mainland Medical Ctr
6801 Emmett Lowry Expy .... Texas City TX 77591 409-938-5000 374-3
Web: www.mainlandmedical.com

Mainland preparatory Academy
319 Newman Rd .... La Marque TX 77568 409-934-9100 934-9130 559
Web: mainland-classical.responsiveed.com

Mainline Information Systems Inc
1700 Summit Lake Dr. .... Tallahassee FL 32317 850-219-5000 180
TF: 866-490-6246 ■ *Web:* www.mainline.com

Mainline Printing Inc
3500 SW Topeka Blvd. .... Topeka KS 66611 785-233-2338 627
TF: 800-770-2055 ■ *Web:* www.mainlineprinting.com

Mains'l Services Inc
7000 78th Ave N. .... Brooklyn Park MN 55445 800-441-6525 363
TF: 800-441-6525 ■ *Web:* www.mainsl.com

Mainsail Partners
1 Front St Ste 3000. .... San Francisco CA 94111 415-391-3150 360-3
Web: www.mainsailpartners.com

Mainsaver Software LLC
10803 Thornmint Rd. .... San Diego CA 92127 858-674-8700 179
Web: www.mainsaver.com

MainScapes Inc
20400 New Hampshire Ave. .... Brinklow MD 20861 301-260-0190 776
Web: www.mainscapes.com

Mainship Corp 255 Diesel Rd .... St Augustine FL 32084 904-827-2007 90
TF: 800-771-5556 ■ *Web:* www.mainship.com

Phone | Fax | Class

MainSpring Inc
20010 Fisher Ave Ste E PO Box 505 .... Poolesville MD 20837 301-948-8077 180
Web: www.gomainspring.com

Mainstay Technologies
201 Daniel Webster Hwy .... Belmont NH 03220 603-524-4774 180
Web: www.mstech.com

Mainstream Data Inc
375 Chipeta Way Ste B .... Salt Lake City UT 84108 801-584-2800 387
Web: www.mainstreamdata.com

Mainstream Engineering Corp
200 Yellow Pl .... Rockledge FL 32955 321-631-3550 256
Web: www.mainstream-engr.com

Maintenx 2202 N Howard Ave .... Tampa FL 33607 855-751-0075 610
TF: 855-751-0075 ■ *Web:* maintenx.com

Mainthia Technologies Inc
7055 Engle Rd Ste 502 .... Cleveland OH 44130 440-816-0202 816-1121 271
Web: www.mainthia.com

Mairs & Power Funds
332 Minnesota St Ste W-1520 .... Saint Paul MN 55101 651-222-8478 528
TF: 800-304-7404 ■ *Web:* mairsandpower.com

Maison 140 Beverly Hills
140 Lasky Dr .... Beverly Hills CA 90212 310-281-4000 379
Web: maison140.com

Maison Carlos
3010 S Dixie Hwy .... West Palm Beach FL 33405 561-659-6524 671
Web: www.maisoncarlos.com

Maison Dupuy Hotel
1001 Toulouse St .... New Orleans LA 70112 504-586-8000 379
TF: 800-535-9177 ■ *Web:* www.maisondupuy.com

Maison Weiss
4500 I-55 at Highland Village .... Jackson MS 39211 601-981-4621 981-4671 157-6
TF: 800-283-9490 ■ *Web:* maisonweiss.com

Maisons Marques & Domaines USA Inc
383 Fourth St Ste 400 .... Oakland CA 94607 510-286-2000 81-3
Web: www.mmdusa.net

Maitland Area Chamber of Commerce
110 N Maitland Ave .... Maitland FL 32751 407-644-0741 539-2529 139
Web: www.maitlandchamber.com

Maitland Art Ctr 231 W Packwood Ave .... Maitland FL 32751 407-539-2181 316-5729* 50-2
**Fax Area Code:* 888 ■ *TF:* 800-435-7352 ■ *Web:* www.artandhistory.org

Maitland Primrose Group Inc
7220 N 16th St Ste c .... Phoenix AZ 85020 602-944-0046 514
Web: www.maitlandprimrose.com

Maize
Maize Restaurant 50 Pk Pl .... Newark NJ 07102 973-733-2202 671
Web: www.maizerestaurant.com

Majerle's Sports Grill 24 N Second St .... Phoenix AZ 85004 602-253-0118 671
Web: www.majerles.com

Majesco Entertainment Co
160 Raritan Ctr Pkwy .... Edison NJ 08837 732-225-8910 637-10
NASDAQ: COOL ■ *Web:* www.majescoent.com

MajescoMastek
105 Fieldcrest Ave Ste 208 .... Edison NJ 08837 732-590-6400 225
Web: www.majesco.com

Majestic Athletic Ltd
2320 Newlins Mill Rd .... Easton PA 18045 610-746-6800 442
Web: www.majesticathletic.com

Majestic Drug Company Inc
4996 Main St Rt 42 .... South Fallsburg NY 12779 845-436-0011 237
TF: 800-238-0220 ■ *Web:* www.majesticdrug.com

Majestic Hotel 528 W Brompton .... Chicago IL 60657 773-404-3499 379
Web: www.majestic-chicago.com

Majestic Industries Inc
15378 Hallmark Ct .... Macomb MI 48042 586-786-9100 697
Web: www.majesticind.net

Majestic Medical Solutions Inc
17424 Airline Hwy Ste 12 .... Prairieville LA 70769 225-677-9867 475
Web: majesticms.com

Majestic Metals Inc 7770 Washington St .... Denver CO 80229 303-288-6855 697
Web: majesticmetals.com

Majestic Realty Co
13191 Crossroads Pkwy N 6th Fl .... City of Industry CA 91746 562-692-9581 695-2329 655
Web: www.majesticrealty.com

Majestic Star Casino & Hotel
1 Buffington Harbor Dr .... Gary IN 46406 888-225-8259 133
TF: 888-225-8259 ■ *Web:* www.majesticstarcasino.com

Majestic Steakhouse 931 Broadway .... Kansas City MO 64105 816-221-1888 671
Web: www.majestickc.com

Majestic Steel USA
5300 Majestic Pkwy .... Cleveland OH 44146 440-786-2666 786-0576 492
TF: 800-321-5590 ■ *Web:* www.majesticsteel.com

Majestic Theatre 1925 Elm St Ste 500 .... Dallas TX 75201 214-670-3687 670-1404 572
TF: 800-255-5002 ■ *Web:* www.dallasculture.org/majestictheatre

Majestic Theatre 4120 Woodward Ave .... Detroit MI 48201 313-833-9700 572
Web: www.majesticdetroit.com

Majestic Theatre 245 W 44th St .... New York NY 10036 212-239-6200 747
TF: 800-447-7400 ■ *Web:* www.telecharge.com

Majestic Transportation
283 Lockhaven Ste 100 .... Houston TX 77073 281-869-8031 449
Web: www.majestictransportation.com

Majesty Hospitality Staffing
1720 Regal Row Ste 115 .... Dallas TX 75235 214-634-7508 260
Web: www.majestyhospitalitystaffing.com

Majic 102.3/92.7
8515 Georgia Ave 9th Fl .... Silver Spring MD 20910 301-306-1111 306-9540 645
Web: mymajicdc.hellobeautiful.com

Majic 105.7
6200 Oak Tree Blvd 4th Fl .... Cleveland OH 44131 216-520-2600 645
TF: 800-669-1057 ■ *Web:* wmji.iheart.com

Majic 107.5 101 Marietta St 12th Fl .... Atlanta GA 30303 404-765-9750 688-7686 645-10
Web: majicatl.com

Majic 107.5|97.5
101 Marietta St 12th Fl .... Atlanta GA 30303 404-765-9750 688-7686 645-10
Web: majicatl.hellobeautiful.com

Majilite Corp 1530 Broadway Rd .... Dracut MA 01826 978-441-6800 441-0835 594
Web: www.majilite.com

Majon International PO Box 6059 .... Los Osos CA 93412 805-528-2100 530
TF: 800-535-3212 ■ *Web:* www.majon.com

Major Brands Inc 6701 SW Ave .... St Louis MO 63143 314-645-1843 80-3
Web: www.majorbrands.com

Major County Economic Development
2004 Commerce St .... Fairview OK 73737 580-227-2512 338
Web: www.okmajordev.org

Major Custom Cable Inc 281 Lotus Dr .... Jackson MO 63755 800-455-6224 243-1365* 813
**Fax Area Code:* 573 ■ *TF:* 800-455-6224 ■ *Web:* www.majorcustomcable.com

Major Farms Inc 1060 Growers St .... Salinas CA 93901 831-422-9616 10-11

Major Fulfillment Inc
13707 S Figueroa St .... Los Angeles CA 90061 310-204-1874 5
TF: 800-466-4189 ■ *Web:* www.majorfulfillment.com

Major Hospital
150 W Washington St .... Shelbyville IN 46176 317-392-3211 374-3
Web: www.mymhp.org

Major Industries Inc 7120 Stewart Ave .... Wausau WI 54401 888-759-2678 697
TF: 888-759-2678 ■ *Web:* www.majorskylights.com

Major League Baseball (Office of the Commissioner)
245 Pk Ave 31st Fl .... New York NY 10167 212-931-7800 949-5654* 713
**Fax:* PR ■ *TF Cust Svc:* 866-800-1275 ■ *Web:* mlb.mlb.com

Major League Baseball Players Assn
12 E 49th St Ste 24 .... New York NY 10017 212-826-0808 752-4378 48-22
Web: mlbplayers.mlb.com/nasapp/mlb/pa

Major League Soccer (MLS)
420 Fifth Ave 7th Fl .... New York NY 10018 212-450-1200 717
TF: 800-658-0700 ■ *Web:* www.mlssoccer.com

Major Legal Services
4500 Rockside Rd Ste 210 .... Independence OH 44131 216-579-9782 721
Web: majorlegalservices.com

Major Lindsey & Africa
555 Montgomery St Ste 1500 .... San Francisco CA 94111 415-956-1010 398-2425 266
Web: www.mlaglobal.com

Major Pharmaceutical Co
31778 Enterprise Dr .... Livonia MI 48150 734-743-6161 582
TF: 800-875-0123 ■ *Web:* www.majorpharmaceuticals.com

Major Prime Plastics Inc
649 N Ardmore Ave .... Villa Park IL 60181 630-834-9400 600
Web: majorprime.com

Major Properties Real Estate
1200 W Olympic Blvd .... Los Angeles CA 90015 213-747-4151 749-7972 652
Web: www.majorproperties.com

Major Tool & Machine Inc
1458 E 19th St .... Indianapolis IN 46218 317-636-6433 634-9420 454
Web: www.majortool.com

Majors Plastics Inc 10117 I St .... Omaha NE 68127 402-331-1660 331-9041 608
Web: www.majorsplastics.com

Mak Design Build Inc 430 F St Ste B .... Davis CA 95616 530-750-2209 186
Web: www.makdesignbuild.com

Maka Beauty Systems
3959 E Speedway Blvd Ste 308 .... Tucson AZ 85712 520-322-6252 77
TF: 800-293-6252 ■ *Web:* www.maka.com

Makai Ocean Engineering Inc
41-305 Kalanianaole Hwy .... Waimanalo HI 96795 808-259-8871 256
Web: www.makai.com

Makarios Consulting Llc
1308 Summerhill Dr Ste .... Downingtown PA 19335 610-380-8735 196
Web: makariosconsulting.com

Make It Better LLC
1150 Wilmette Ave Ste J .... Wilmette IL 60091 847-256-4642 761
Web: www.makeitbetter.net

Make It Right Inc 55 E Huntington Dr .... Arcadia CA 91006 626-445-0366 186
Web: www.makeitright.net

Make It Work Inc
21 E Canon Perdido St Ste 209 .... Santa Barbara CA 93101 805-705-9371 809
Web: www.makeitwork.com

Make-A-Wish Foundation of America
4742 N 24th St Ste 400 .... Phoenix AZ 85016 602-279-9474 279-0855 48-5
TF: 800-722-9474 ■ *Web:* www.wish.org

MakeMusic! Inc
7615 Golden Triangle Dr Ste M .... Eden Prairie MN 55344 952-937-9611 937-9760 178-6
NASDAQ: MMUS ■ *TF:* 800-843-2066 ■ *Web:* www.makemusic.com

Maker Studios Inc
13428 Maxella Ave Ste 525 .... Los Angeles CA 90016 310-606-2182 195
Web: www.makerstudios.com

Maker's Mark Distillery Inc
3350 Burke Spring Rd .... Loretto KY 40037 270-865-2881 80-1
Web: www.makersmark.com

Making Waves Education Program
200 24th St .... Richmond CA 94804 510-237-3434 196
Web: www.making-waves.org

Makino 7680 Innovation Way .... Mason OH 45040 513-573-7200 573-7360 455
TF: 888-625-4661 ■ *Web:* www.makino.com

Makita USA Inc 14930 Northam St .... La Mirada CA 90638 714-522-8088 522-8133 759
TF: 800-462-5482 ■ *Web:* www.makitatools.com

Makor Solutions LLC
7430 W 27th St .... Minneapolis MN 55426 952-922-2975 196
Web: www.makorerp.com

Makoshika State Park PO Box 1242 .... Glendive MT 59330 406-377-6256 565
Web: www.fwp.mt.gov

Makoto 4822 MacArthur Blvd NW .... Washington DC 20007 202-298-6866 671
Web: makotorestaurantdc.com

Makovsky + Co 16 E 34th St .... New York NY 10016 212-508-9600 636
Web: www.makovsky.com

Makowski's Real Sausage Co
2710 S Poplar Ave .... Chicago IL 60608 312-842-5330 296-26
TF: 800-746-9554 ■ *Web:* realsausage.com

Makoy Center Inc 5462 Center St .... Hilliard OH 43026 614-777-1211 354
TF: 800-222-4655 ■ *Web:* www.makoy.com

Makray Manufacturing Co
4400 N Harlem Ave .... Norridge IL 60706 708-456-7100 604
Web: www.makray.com

Makro Technologies Inc
1 Washington Pk Ste 1502 .... Newark NJ 07102 973-481-0100 225
Web: www.makrotech.com

mal Energy International Inc, The
36 Bentley Ave .... Ottawa ON K2E6T8 613-723-6776 463
Web: www.thermalenergy.com

Malabar Farm State Park
4050 Bromfield Rd .... Lucas OH 44843 419-892-2784 892-3988 565
Web: www.ohiodnr.com

Listing	City	State	ZIP	Phone	Fax	Class
Malaco Music Group Inc 3023 W Northside Dr *TF Cust Svc:* 800-272-7936 ■ *Web:* www.malaco.com	Jackson	MS	39213	601-982-4522	982-4528	657
Malaekahana State Recreation Area PO Box 621 *Web:* dlnr.hawaii.gov	Honolulu	HI	96809	808-587-0300		565
Malaga Financial Corp 2514 Via Tejon *OTC:* MLGF ■ *TF:* 888-362-5242 ■ *Web:* www.malagabank.com	Palos Verdes Estates	CA	90274	310-375-9000	373-3615	360-2
Malaga Inn 359 Church St *TF:* 800-235-1586 ■ *Web:* malagainn.com	Mobile	AL	36602	251-438-4701	438-4701	379
Malaika Corp 3010 63rd Ave *Web:* www.malaikacorp.com	Hyattsville	MD	20785	240-235-6570		180
Malarkey Roofing Products PO Box 17217 *TF:* 800-545-1191 ■ *Web:* www.malarkeyroofing.com	Portland	OR	97217	503-283-1191	289-7644	46
Malawi 866 UN Plaza Ste 486 *Web:* www.un.int/malawi	New York	NY	10017	212-317-8738	317-8729	784
Malay Cafe 6003 NW Barry Rd	Kansas City	MO	64154	816-741-3616		671
Malaya 857 Collier Rd *Web:* malayaatlanta.com	Atlanta	GA	30318	404-609-9991		671
Malaysia 313 E 43rd St *Web:* www.un.int/malaysia	New York	NY	10017	212-986-6310	490-8576	784
Consulate General 777 S Figueroa St Ste 600 *Web:* www.kln.gov.my/web/usa_los-angeles/home	Los Angeles	CA	90017	213-892-1238		257
Embassy 3516 International Ct NW *TF:* 800-786-9199 ■ *Web:* www.kln.gov.my/web/usa_washington/home	Washington	DC	20008	202-572-9700	572-9882	257
Malaysia Airlines 100 N Sepulveda Blvd Ste 1710 *TF Resv:* 800-552-9264 ■ *Web:* www.malaysiaairlines.com	El Segundo	CA	90245	310-535-9288		25
Malbar Vision Ctr 409 N 78th St *TF:* 800-269-3666 ■ *Web:* www.malbar.com	Omaha	NE	68114	402-391-6600	493-4041	543
Malco Products Inc 14080 State Hwy 55 NW PO Box 400 *TF:* 800-328-3530 ■ *Web:* www.malcoproducts.com	Annandale	MN	55302	320-274-8246	274-2269	758
Malco Products Inc 361 Fairview Ave PO Box 892 *TF:* 800-253-2526 ■ *Web:* www.malcopro.com	Barberton	OH	44203	330-753-0361	753-2025	151
Malco Theatres Inc 5851 Ridgeway Ctr Pkwy *Web:* www.malco.com	Memphis	TN	38120	901-761-3480	681-2044	748
Malcolm Drilling Co Inc 3503 Breakwater Ct *Web:* www.malcolmdrilling.com	Hayward	CA	94545	510-780-9181	780-9167	188-2
Malcolm Wiener Ctr for Social Policy John F Kennedy School of Government Harvard Univer 79 John F Kennedy St *TF:* 866-845-6596 ■ *Web:* www.hks.harvard.edu	Cambridge	MA	02138	617-496-4082	496-9053	634
Malcolm X College 1900 W Jackson *TF:* 877-542-0285 ■ *Web:* www.ccc.edu/colleges/malcolm-x/Pages/default.aspx	Chicago	IL	60612	312-850-7000	850-7092	162
Malcom Randall VAMC NF/SGVHS 1601 SW Archer Rd **Fax:* Mail Rm ■ *TF:* 800-324-8387 ■ *Web:* www.va.gov/directory/guide/facility.asp?id=54	Gainesville	FL	32608	352-376-1611	374-6113*	374-8
Maldaner's 222 S Sixth St *TF:* 800-545-7300 ■ *Web:* www.maldaners.com	Springfield	IL	62701	217-522-4313		671
MALDEF (Mexican American Legal Defense & Educational Fund) 634 S Spring St *Web:* www.maldef.org	Los Angeles	CA	90014	213-629-2512	629-0266	48-14
Malden Chamber of Commerce 200 Pleasant St Ste 416 *TF:* 800-540-9191 ■ *Web:* www.maldenchamber.org	Malden	MA	02148	781-322-4500	322-4866	139
Malden Evening News 277 Commercial St	Malden	MA	02148	781-321-8000		532-2
Malden Public Library 36 Salem St *Web:* www.maldenpubliclibrary.org	Malden	MA	02148	781-324-0218	324-4467	434-3
Maldives 800 Second Ave Ste 400-E	New York	NY	10017	212-599-6194		784
Maldonado Nursery & Landscaping Inc 16348 Nacogdoches Rd *Web:* mnlsa.com	San Antonio	TX	78247	210-599-1219		776
Male Survivor 4768 BRdway Ste 527 *TF:* 800-738-4181 ■ *Web:* www.malesurvivor.org	New York	NY	10034	800-738-4181		48-17
Malema Engineering Corp 1060 S Rogers Cir *TF:* 800-637-6418 ■ *Web:* www.malema.com	Boca Raton	FL	33487	561-995-0595	995-0622	201
Maley & Wertz Inc 900 E Columbia St *Web.* www.maleyandwertz.com	Evansville	IN	47711	812-425-3358		683
Malheur County 251 B St W *Web:* www.malheurco.org	Vale	OR	97918	541-473-5151	473-5523	338
Mali Embassy 2130 R St NW *Web:* www.maliembassy.us	Washington	DC	20008	202-332-2249	332-6603	257
Mali Restaurant 961 Amsterdam Ave NE *Web:* www.malirestaurant.com	Atlanta	GA	30306	404-874-1411		671
Malibu Beach Inn 22878 Pacific Coast Hwy *Web:* www.malibubeachinn.com	Malibu	CA	90265	310-651-7777	456-1499	379
Malibu Boats LLC 5075 Kimberly Way *Web:* www.malibuboats.com	Loudon	TN	37774	209-383-7469		698
Malibu Chamber of Commerce 23805 Stuart Ranch Rd Ste 210 *TF:* 800-442-4988 ■ *Web:* www.malibu.org	Malibu	CA	90265	310-456-9025	456-0195	139
Malibu Creek State Park 1925 Las Virgenes Rd *Web:* www.parks.ca.gov/default.asp?page_id=614	Calabasas	CA	91302	818-880-0367		565
Malibu Grill 106 N Walnut St *Web:* www.malibugrill.net	Bloomington	IN	47404	812-332-4334	333-2282	671
Malibu Lagoon State Beach 23200 Pacific Coast Hwy *Web:* www.parks.ca.gov/default.asp?page_id=835	Malibu	CA	90265	310-457-8143		565
Malibu Technologies Inc 48700 Structural Dr *Web:* www.malibutech.com	Chesterfield	MI	48051	586-598-9900		196
Malin International Ship Repair & Drydock Inc 320 77th St Pier 41 *TF:* 800-527-3154 ■ *Web:* www.malinshiprepair.com	Galveston	TX	77554	409-740-3314		698
Mall at Cortana 9401 Cortana Pl *Web:* www.cortanamall.com	Baton Rouge	LA	70815	225-927-6747		460
Mall at Fairfield Commons 2727 Fairfield Commons *Web:* www.mallatfairfieldcommons.com	Beavercreek	OH	45431	937-427-4300		460
Mall at Greece Ridge, The 271 Greece Ridge Ctr Dr *Web:* www.themallatgreeceridge.com	Rochester	NY	14626	585-225-0430		460
Mall at Millenia 4200 Conroy Rd *Web:* www.mallatmillenia.com	Orlando	FL	32839	407-363-3555	363-6877	460
Mall at Robinson 100 Robinson Centre Dr *Web:* www.shoprobinsonmall.com	Pittsburgh	PA	15205	412-788-0816	788-1156	460
Mall at Short Hills 1200 Morris Tpke *Web:* www.shopshorthills.com	Short Hills	NJ	07078	973-376-7350		460
Mall at Wellington Green 10300 W Forest Hill Blvd *Web:* www.shopwellingtongreen.com	Wellington	FL	33414	561-227-6900		460
Mall Craft Inc 2225 N Windsor st *TF:* 800-400-7072 ■ *Web:* www.mallcraft.com	Altadena	CA	91001	626-398-3598		186
Mall del Norte 5300 San Dario *TF:* 800-326-3264 ■ *Web:* www.malldelnorte.com	Laredo	TX	78041	956-724-8191		460
Mall of America 60 E Broadway *Web:* www.mallofamerica.com	Bloomington	MN	55425	952-883-8810		460
Mall of Louisiana 6401 Bluebonnet Blvd *Web:* www.mallofIouisiana.com	Baton Rouge	LA	70836	225-761-7228		460
Mall Saint Matthews 5000 Shelbyville Rd *Web:* www.mallstmatthews.com	Louisville	KY	40207	502-893-0311		460
Mall Saint Vincent 1133 St Vincent Ave Ste 200 *Web:* www.mallstvincent.com	Shreveport	LA	71104	318-227-9880		460
Mallah Furman & Co Brickell Bay Office Tower 1001 Brickell Bay Dr Ste 1400 *Web:* www.mallahfurman.com	Miami	FL	33131	305-371-6200		2
Mallet & Company Inc 51 Arch St Ext *TF:* 800-245-2757 ■ *Web:* www.malletoil.com	Carnegie	PA	15106	412-276-9000	276-9002	296-23
Mallett Group Inc, The 566 Danbury Rd Ste 6 *Web:* www.mallettgroup.com	New Milford	CT	06776	860-350-0809		195
Malleys Chocolates 13400 Brookpark Rd **Fax Area Code:* 800 ■ *TF:* 800-275-6255 ■ *Web:* www.malleys.com	Cleveland	OH	44135	216-362-8700	211-0567*	296-8
Mallick Plumbing & Heating 8010 Cessna Ave *TF:* 888-805-3354 ■ *Web:* www.mallickplumbing.com	Gaithersburg	MD	20879	888-805-3354		610
Mallilo & Grossman 16309 Northern Blvd *TF:* 866-593-6274 ■ *Web:* www.malliloandgrossman.com	Flushing	NY	11358	718-461-6633		428
Mallin Casual Furniture 1 Minson Way *TF:* 800-251-6537 ■ *Web:* minson.com/mallin	Montebello	CA	90640	800-251-6537		319-4
Mallinckrodt Inc 675 McDonnell Blvd *TF:* 800-325-8888	Hazelwood	MO	63042	314-654-2000	654-6257	231
Mallof, Abruzino & Nash Marketing 765 Kimberly Dr *TF:* 800-438-7325 ■ *Web:* www.manmarketing.com	Carol Stream	IL	60188	630-929-5200		7
Mallorca 2228 E Carson St *Web:* mallorcarestaurantpgh.com	Pittsburgh	PA	15203	412-488-1818		671
Mallorca 1390 W Ninth St *Web:* www.clevelandmallorca.com	Cleveland	OH	44113	216-687-9494		671
Mallory & Church LLC 676 S Industrial Way	Seattle	WA	98108	206-587-2100		155-13
Mallory & Evans Inc 646 Kentucky St *Web:* www.malloryandevans.com	Scottdale	GA	30079	404-297-1000	297-1075	189-10
Mallory Capital Group LLC 19 Old King'S Hwy S Ste 14 *Web:* www.mallorycapital.com	Darien	CT	06820	203-655-1571		401
Mallory Safety & Supply Inc 1040 Industrial Way PO Box 2068 *Web:* www.malloryco.com	Longview	WA	98632	360-636-5750		535
Mallory Sonalert Products Inc 4411 S High School Rd *Web:* www.mallory-sonalert.com	Indianapolis	IN	46241	317-612-1000		791
Malloy Air East Inc Avenue B	WestHampton Beach	NY	11978	631-288-2917		63
Malloy Dan (D) 210 Capitol Avey **Fax Area Code:* 860 ■ *TF:* 800-406-1527 ■ *Web:* www.ct.gov/governor	Hartford	CT	06106	800-406-1527	524-7395*	343
Malmark Inc 5712 Easton Rd *Web:* www.malmark.com	Plumsteadville	PA	18949	215-766-7200		526
Malmberg Engineering Inc 550 Commerce Way *Web:* malmbergengineering.com	Livermore	CA	94551	925-606-6500		697
Malmstrom Air Force Base 21 77th St N Bldg 500 *Web:* www.malmstrom.af.mil	Malmstrom AFB	MT	59402	406-731-1110	731-2759	497-1
Malmstrom Air Force Base Museum & Air Park 341 Missile Wing/MU 21 77th St N Ste 144 *Web:* www.malmstrom.af.mil	Malmstrom AFB	MT	59402	406-731-2705	731-2769	520
Malnati Organization Inc 3685 Woodhead Dr *TF:* 800-568-8646 ■ *Web:* www.loumalnatis.com	Northbrook	IL	60062	847-562-1814		670
Malnove Inc 13434 F St *TF:* 800-228-9877 ■ *Web:* www.malnove.com	Omaha	NE	68137	402-330-1100	330-2941	101
Malolo Beverages & Supplies Ltd 120 Sand Island Access Rd *TF:* 800-247-5626 ■ *Web:* malolobeverages.com	Honolulu	HI	96819	808-845-4830	845-4835	81-2
Malone College 515 25th St NW **Fax:* Admissions ■ *TF:* 800-521-1146 ■ *Web:* www.malone.edu	Canton	OH	44709	330-471-8100	471-8149*	166
Malone's *Bluegrass Hospitality Group* 3347 Tates Creek Rd *Web:* www.bluegrasshospitality.com	Lexington	KY	40502	859-335-6500		671
MaloneBailey LLP 9801 Westheimer Rd Ste 1100 *Web:* www.malonebailey.com	Houston	TX	77042	713-343-4286		734

	City	State	Zip	Phone	Fax	Class
Maloney & Bell General Contractors Inc 3117 Fite Cir Ste 101 *Web:* www.maloneyandbell.com	Sacramento	CA	95827	916-687-8779	756-2402	186
Maloney & Kennedy Pllc 15 Dartmouth Dr Ste 203 *Web:* maloneyandkennedy.com	Auburn	NH	03032	603-624-8819		2
Maloney & Porcelli 37 E 50th St *Web:* www.maloneyandporcelli.com	New York	NY	10022	212-750-2233		671
Maloney Carolyn (Rep D - NY) 2308 Rayburn Bldg *Web:* maloney.house.gov	Washington	DC	20515	202-225-7944	225-4709	342-2
Maloney Sean Patrick (Rep D - NY) 1027 Longworth HOB *Web:* seanmaloney.house.gov	Washington	DC	20515	202-225-5441	225-3289	342-2
Maloney Security Inc 1055 Laurel St *Web:* www.maloneysecurityinc.com	San Carlos	CA	94070	650-593-0163	593-1101	693
Maloney Technical Products 1300 E Berry St *TF:* 800-231-7236 ■ *Web:* www.maloneytech.com	Fort Worth	TX	76119	817-923-3344	923-1339	596
Malouf Engineering International Inc 17950 Preston Rd Ste 720 *TF:* 800-649-2520 ■ *Web:* www.maloufengineering.com	Dallas	TX	75252	972-783-2578	783-2583	188-1
Malt Products Corp 88 Market St *TF:* 800-526-0180 ■ *Web:* www.maltproducts.com	Saddle Brook	NJ	07663	201-845-4420	845-0028	102
Malta 249 E 35th St *Web:* www.foreign.gov.mt	New York	NY	10016	212-725-2345		784
Malta Embassy 2017 Connecticut Ave NW *Web:* www.malta-citizenship.info	Washington	DC	20008	202-462-3611		257
Maltby Electric Supply Company Inc 336 Seventh St *TF:* 800-339-0668 ■ *Web:* maltbyelectric.com	San Francisco	CA	94103	415-863-5000	863-5011	246
Maltz Jupiter Theatre 1001 E Indiantown Rd *TF:* 800-445-1666 ■ *Web:* www.jupitertheatre.org	Jupiter	FL	33477	561-743-2666	743-0107	749
Maltz Sales Company Inc 67 Green St *TF:* 800-370-0439 ■ *Web:* www.maltzsales.com	Foxboro	MA	02035	508-203-2400		358
Malvern FSB Inc 42 E Lancaster Ave *Web:* www.malvernfederal.com	Paoli	PA	19301	610-644-9400		70
Malvern Institute 940 W King Rd *TF:* 888-643-3869 ■ *Web:* www.malverninstitute.com	Malvern	PA	19355	610-647-0330		726
Malvern Instruments Inc 117 Flanders Rd *Web:* www.malvern.com	Westborough	MA	01581	508-768-6400		419
Malvern Prep School 418 S Warren Ave *Web:* malvernprep.org	Malvern	PA	19355	484-595-1100		685
Malvern Systems Inc 81 Lancaster Ave Ste 219 *TF:* 800-296-9642 ■ *Web:* www.malvernsys.com	Malvern	PA	19355	800-296-9642		178-1
Malverne Union Free School District 12 301 Wicks Ln *Web:* www.malverne.k12.ny.us	Malverne	NY	11565	516-887-6400		685
Malwin Electronics Corp 52 E 22nd St *Web:* www.malwin.com	Paterson	NJ	07514	973-881-1500		703
MAM Global Financial Services 16161 Ventura Blvd *Web:* www.mamgfs.com	Encino	CA	91436	818-784-8752		691
Mama Carolla's Old Italian Restaurant 1031 E 54th St *Web:* www.mamacarollas.com	Indianapolis	IN	46220	317-259-9412		671
Mama DiMatteo's 34 Kennebec Pl *TF:* 800-246-5842 ■ *Web:* www.mamadimatteos.com	Bar Harbor	ME	04609	207-288-3666		671
Mama Inez 390 Yellowstone Ave *Web:* mamainezid.com	Pocatello	ID	83201	208-234-7674		671
Mama Ricotta's 601 S Kings Dr *Web:* www.mamaricottasrestaurant.com	Charlotte	NC	28204	704-343-0148	377-7461	671
Mama Tosca's 9000 Ming Ave Ste K2-K3 *Web:* www.mamatoscas.com	Bakersfield	CA	93311	661-831-1242		671
Mama's on the Half Shell 2901 O'Donnell St *Web:* www.mamasmd.com	Baltimore	MD	21224	410-276-3160		671
Mama's Royal Cafe 4012 Broadway *Web:* mamasroyalcafeoakland.com	Oakland	CA	94611	510-547-7600		671
MAMAC Systems Inc 8189 Century Blvd *TF:* 800-843-5116 ■ *Web:* www.mamacsys.com	Minneapolis	MN	55317	952-556-4900		201
Mamasan 2800 Monroe Ave *Web:* www.mamasans.com	Rochester	NY	14618	585-461-3290		671
Mamata Usa LLC 2275 Cornell Ave *Web:* www.mamatausa.com	Montgomery	IL	60538	630-801-2320		358
Mambo Sprouts Marketing Corp 923 Haddonfield Rd Ste 300 *Web:* www.mambosprouts.com	Cherry Hill	NJ	08002	856-833-1933		7
Mamco Corp 8630 Industrial Dr *Web:* www.mamcomotors.com	Franksville	WI	53126	262-886-9069	886-4639	518
Mamiye Bros Inc 1385 Broadway 18th Fl *Web:* mamiye.com	New York	NY	10018	212-279-4150	695-2659	155-16
Mamma 'Zu 501 S Pine St	Richmond	VA	23220	804-788-4205		671
Mamma DiSalvo's Italian Ristorante 1375 E Stroop Rd *Web:* www.mammadisalvo.com	Dayton	OH	45429	937-299-5831	299-1752	671
Mamma Grazzi's Kitchen 25 George St *TF:* 800-363-4465 ■ *Web:* www.mammagrazzis.com	Ottawa	ON	K1N8W5	613-241-8656	241-5738	671
Mamma Luisa 673 Thames St *Web:* www.mammaluisa.com	Newport	RI	02840	401-848-5257		671
Mamma Maria's 3 N Sq *Web:* www.mammamaria.com	Boston	MA	02113	617-523-0077		671
Mamma Mia's 420 W Francis Ave *Web:* mammamiaspokane.com	Spokane	WA	99205	509-467-7786		671
Mamma Mia's 128 N Mesquite St	Corpus Christi	TX	78401	361-883-3773		671
Mamma Ventura 13 Chambersburg St *Web:* mammaventuras.com	Gettysburg	PA	17325	717-334-5548	334-7231	671
Mammoet USA Inc 20525 Farm-to-Market Rd 521 *Web:* www.mammoet.com	Rosharon	TX	77583	281-369-2200		314
Mammoth Cave National Park 1 Mammoth Cave Pkwy PO Box 7 *TF:* 800-798-0560 ■ *Web:* www.nps.gov/maca	Mammoth Cave	KY	42259	270-758-2180	758-2349	564
Mammoth Inc 13200 Pioneer Trl Ste 150 *Web:* www.mammoth-inc.com	Chaska	MN	55318	952-358-6600	358-6700	14
Mammoth Mountain Resort 10001 Minaret Rd *TF:* 800-626-6684 ■ *Web:* www.mammothmountain.com	Mammoth Lakes	CA	93546	760-934-2571	934-0615	669
Mammoth Spring State Park PO Box 36 *Web:* www.arkansasstateparks.com	Mammoth Spring	AR	72554	870-625-7364		565
Mammoth Times, The PO Box 3929 *TF:* 800-427-7623 ■ *Web:* www.mammothtimes.com	Mammoth Lakes	CA	93546	760-934-3929	934-3951	532-4
Mamoun's Falafel Restaurant 85 Howe St *Web:* www.mamouns.com	New Haven	CT	06511	203-562-8444		671
Man Lift Mfg Co 5707 S Pennsylvania Ave *Web:* manliftmfg.com	Cudahy	WI	53110	414-486-1760		190
MAN Roland Inc 800 E Oak Hill Dr *Web:* manrolandsheetfed.com	Westmont	IL	60559	630-920-2000		629
Mana Products Inc 32-02 Queens Blvd *Web:* www.manaproducts.com	Long Island	NY	11101	718-361-2550		214
Manafort Bros Inc 414 New Britain Ave *Web:* www.manafort.com	Plainville	CT	06062	860-229-4853	747-4861	189-5
Managed Business Solutions 12325 Oracle Blvd Ste 200 *Web:* www.thinkmbs.com	Colorado Springs	CO	80921	719-314-3400	314-3499	180
Managed by Q Inc 161 Ave of the Americas 11th FL *Web:* www.managedbyq.com	New York	NY	10013	212-401-1982		393
Managed Care of America Inc 1910 Cochran Rd Ste 605 *TF:* 800-922-4966 ■ *Web:* www.mcoa.com	Pittsburgh	PA	15220	412-922-2803		390
Managed Funds Association 600 14th St NW Ste 900 *Web:* www.managedfunds.org	Washington	DC	20005	202-367-1140		533
Managed Health Network Inc 1600 Los Gamos Dr Ste 300 *TF:* 800-327-2133 ■ *Web:* www.mhn.com	San Rafael	CA	94903	800-327-2133		462
Managed HealthCare Northwest Inc 422 East Burnside St Suite 215 PO Box 4629 *TF:* 800-648-6356 ■ *Web:* www.mhninc.com	Portland	OR	97208	503-413-5800	413-5801	390
Management & Engineering Technologies International Inc (METI) 8600 Boeing Dr *Web:* www.meticorp.com	El Paso	TX	79925	915-772-4975	772-2253	463
Management Analysis Inc 2070 Chain Bridge Rd	Vienna	VA	22182	703-506-0505		177
Management Consulting Inc 1961 Diamond Springs Rd *TF:* 888-892-0787 ■ *Web:* www.manconinc.com	Virginia Beach	VA	23455	757-460-0879		261
Management Information Control Systems Inc (MICS) 2025 Ninth St *TF:* 800-838-6427 ■ *Web:* www.bissoftware.com	Los Osos	CA	93402	805-543-7000	543-0373	178-10
Management International Inc 1828 SE First Ave **Fax Area Code:* 800 ■ *TF:* 800-425-1995 ■ *Web:* www.currentreviews.com	Fort Lauderdale	FL	33316	954-763-8003	425-1995*	184
Management Network Group Inc (TMNG) 7300 College Blvd Ste 302 *NASDAQ: CRTN* ■ *TF:* 800-690-6903 ■ *Web:* cartesian.com	Overland Park	KS	66210	913-345-9315		196
Management Recruiters International Worldwide Inc 1717 Arch St 36th Fl *TF:* 800-875-4000 ■ *Web:* www.mrinetwork.com	Philadelphia	PA	19103	800-875-4000		266
Management Science Assoc Inc 6565 Penn Ave *Web:* www.msa.com	Pittsburgh	PA	15206	412-362-2000	363-5598	178-12
Management Solutions Plus Inc 9707 Key W Ave Ste 100 *Web:* www.mgmtsol.com	Rockville	MD	20850	301-258-9210	990-9771	47
Manager Tools LLC 5765-F Burke Centre Pkwy Ste 152 *Web:* www.manager-tools.com	Burke	VA	22015	571-336-6211		463
Manager's Intelligence Report (MIR) 316 N Michigan Ave Ste 400 **Fax Area Code:* 312 ■ *TF:* 800-878-5331 ■ *Web:* www.managersintelligencereport.biz	Chicago	IL	60601	800-878-5331	861-3592*	531-2
Managing Editor Inc 610 York Rd # 250 *TF:* 800-638-1214 ■ *Web:* www.maned.com	Jenkintown	PA	19046	215-886-5662	886-5681	178-10
Manahan Group, The 222 Capitol St Ste 400 *Web:* manahangroup.com	Charleston	WV	25301	304-343-2800		7
Manarin Investment Counsel Ltd 505 N 210th St *TF:* 800-397-1167 ■ *Web:* www.manarin.com	Omaha	NE	68022	402-330-1166		401
Manassas (Independent City) 9027 Ctr St *TF:* 800-552-7001 ■ *Web:* www.manassascity.org	Manassas	VA	20110	703-257-8200	335-0042	338
Manassas Park (Independent City) 1 Pk Ctr Ct *TF:* 800-222-1222 ■ *Web:* www.cityofmanassaspark.us	Manassas Park	VA	20111	703-335-8800	335-0053	338
Manatee Cafe 525 SR 16 Ste 106 Westgate Plz *Web:* www.manateecafe.com	Saint Augustine	FL	32084	904-826-0210	826-4080	671
Manatee Chamber of Commerce 222 Tenth St W *TF:* 800-297-3758 ■ *Web:* www.manateechamber.com	Bradenton	FL	34205	941-748-3411	745-1877	139
Manatee Community College *South* 8000 S Tamiami Tr *Web:* www.scf.edu	Venice	FL	34293	941-408-1300		162
Manatee Convention Ctr 1 Haben Blvd *TF:* 800-822-2017 ■ *Web:* www.bradentongulfislands.com	Palmetto	FL	34221	941-722-3244	729-1820	205
Manatee County 1112 Manatee Ave W *TF:* 800-292-3368 ■ *Web:* www.mymanatee.org	Bradenton	FL	34205	941-748-4501		338
Manatee County Port Authority 300 Tampa Bay Way *Web:* www.portmanatee.com	Palmetto	FL	34221	941-722-6621	729-1463	618

Phone | Fax | Class

Manatee County Public Library System
PO Box 1000 ... Bradenton FL 34206 941-748-4501 749-7191 434-3
Web: www.mymanatee.org

Manatee County Rural Health Services Inc (MCRHS)
12271 US Hwy 301 ... Parrish FL 34219 941-776-4000 374-3
Web: www.mcrhs.org

Manatee Memorial Hospital
206 Second St E ... Bradenton FL 34208 941-746-5111 745-6862 374-3
TF: 800-994-6610 ■ *Web:* www.manateememorial.com

Manatee Regional Juvenile Detention Ctr
1803 Fifth St W ... Bradenton FL 34205 941-741-3023 412
Web: manateeclerk.com

Manatee Springs Care & Rehab
5627 Ninth St E ... Bradenton FL 34203 941-753-8941 450
Web: manateespringsrehab.com

Manatee Springs State Park
11650 NW 115th St ... Chiefland FL 32626 352-493-6072 565
Web: www.floridastateparks.org

Manatee Technical Institute East Campus
6305 State Rd 70 E ... Bradenton FL 34203 941-752-8100 162
TF: 800-390-3948 ■ *Web:* www.manateetechnicalinstitute.org

Manatron Inc 510 E Milham Ave ... Portage MI 49002 269-567-2900 178-11
TF Cust Svc: 866-471-2900 ■ *Web:* tax.thomsonreuters.com

Manatt's Inc 1775 Old 6 Rd ... Brooklyn IA 52211 641-522-9206 522-5594 188-4
TF: 800-532-1121 ■ *Web:* www.manatts.com

Manatt, Phelps & Phillips
11355 W Olympic Blvd ... Los Angeles CA 90064 310-312-4000 428
Web: www.manatt.com

Mancha Development Co
2275 Sampson Ave Ste 201 ... Corona CA 92879 951-271-4100 670

Manchester Capital Management LLC
3657 Main St PO Box 416 ... Manchester VT 05254 802-362-4410 194
Web: www.mcmllc.com

Manchester City Hall
1 City Hall Plaza W wing ... Manchester NH 03101 603-624-6455 624-6481 337
Web: www.manchesternh.gov

Manchester City Library
405 Pine St ... Manchester NH 03104 603-624-6550 624-6559 434-3
Web: www.manchesternh.gov

Manchester College
604 E College Ave ... North Manchester IN 46962 260-982-5000 982-5239* 166
*Fax: Admissions ■ *TF Admissions:* 800-852-3648 ■ *Web:* www.manchester.edu

Manchester Community College
PO Box 1046 ... Manchester CT 06045 860-512-2800 512-3221* 162
*Fax: Admissions ■ *TF:* 888-999-5545 ■ *Web:* www.manchestercc.edu

Manchester Community College
1066 Front St ... Manchester NH 03102 603-206-8000 668-5354 162
TF: 800-924-3445 ■ *Web:* mccnh.edu

Manchester Ctr
1901 E Shields Ave Ste 203 ... Fresno CA 93726 559-227-1901 460
Web: www.manchester-center.com

Manchester Financial Inc
2815 Townsgate Rd Ste 100 ... Westlake Village CA 91361 805-495-4405 401
TF: 800-492-1107 ■ *Web:* www.mfinvest.com

Manchester Grand Hyatt San Diego
1 Market Pl ... San Diego CA 92101 619-232-1234 378
Web: manchester.grand.hyatt.com/en/hotel/home.html

Manchester Manor Health Care Ctr
385 W Ctr St ... Manchester CT 06040 860-646-0129 450
Web: www.manchestermanorct.com

Manchester Memorial Hospital
71 Haynes St ... Manchester CT 06040 860-646-1222 374-3
Web: www.manchestermemorial.org

Manchester Monarchs 555 Elm St ... Manchester NH 03101 603-626-7825 717
Web: www.manchestermonarchs.com

Manchester State Park
44500 Kinney Rd ... Manchester CA 95459 707-882-2463 565
Web: www.parks.ca.gov/default.asp?page_id=437

Manchester State Park
7767 E Hilldale ... Port Orchard WA 98366 360-871-4065 565

Manchester Tank
1000 Corp Centre Dr Ste 300 ... Franklin TN 37067 615-370-6300 370-6150 172
TF: 800-399-5628 ■ *Web:* www.mantank.com

Manchin Joe III (Sen D - WV)
306 Hart Bldg ... Washington DC 20510 202-224-3954 228-0002 342-2
Web: www.manchin.senate.gov

Mancini Duffy 275 Seventh Ave 19th Fl ... New York NY 10001 212-938-1260 393
Web: www.manciniduffy.com

Mancini Foods PO Box 157 ... Zolfo Springs FL 33890 800-741-1778 735-1172* 296-36
*Fax Area Code: 863 ■ *TF:* 800-741-1778 ■ *Web:* www.mancinifoods.com

Mancini's Char House
531 Seventh St W ... Saint Paul MN 55102 651-224-7345 671
Web: www.mancinis.com

Mancino Burfield Edgerton
12 Roszel Rd Ste C-101 ... Princeton NJ 08540 609-520-8400 260
Web: www.mbels.com

Mancom Manufacturing Inc
1335 Osprey Dr ... Ancaster ON L9G4V5 905-304-6141 711

Mancor Industries Inc 2485 Speers Rd ... Oakville ON L6L2X9 905-827-3737 295
Web: www.mancor.com

Mancos State Park 42545 County Rd N ... Mancos CO 81328 970-533-7065 565
Web: cpw.state.co.us

Mancuso Cheese Co 612 Mills Rd ... Joliet IL 60433 815-722-2475 722-1302 296-5
Web: mancusocheese.com

Mancy's 953 Phillips Ave ... Toledo OH 43612 419-476-4154 671
Web: www.mancys.com

Manda Fine Meats 2445 Sorrel Ave ... Baton Rouge LA 70802 225-344-7636 344-7647 297-9
TF: 800-343-2642 ■ *Web:* www.mandafinemeats.com

Manda Machine Co
2683 Myrtle Springs Ave ... Dallas TX 75220 214-352-5946 757
Web: www.mandamachine.com

Mandala Agency, The 2855 NW Crossing Dr ... Bend OR 97703 541-389-6344 7
Web: mandala.agency

Mandalay Bay Resort & Casino
3950 Las Vegas Blvd S ... Las Vegas NV 89119 702-632-7777 669
TF: 877-632-7800 ■ *Web:* www.mandalaybay.com

Mandalay Pictures
4751 Wilshire Blvd 3rd Fl ... Los Angeles CA 90010 323-549-4300 514
Web: www.mandalay.com

Mandarin 8 Clipper Crt ... Brampton ON L6W4T9 905-451-4100 456-3411 671
Web: www.mandarinrestaurant.com

Mandarin Garden 2394 S Oneida St ... Green Bay WI 54304 920-499-4459 671
Web: mandaringardengreenbay.com

Mandarin Garden 555 Chalkstone Ave ... Providence RI 02908 401-751-0144 671

Mandarin House
675 Yellowstone Ave Ste D ... Pocatello ID 83201 208-233-6088 671
Web: www.mandarinhouse.takeout1.com

Mandarin Kitchen
8766 Lyndale Ave S ... Bloomington MN 55420 952-884-5356 671

Mandarin Oriental Hotel Group (USA)
345 California St Ste 1250 ... San Francisco CA 94104 415-772-8800 782-3778 379
TF: 800-526-6566 ■ *Web:* www.mandarinoriental.com

Mandarin Oriental Miami
500 Brickell Key Dr ... Miami FL 33131 305-913-8288 379
TF: 800-526-6566 ■ *Web:* www.mandarinoriental.com

Mandarin Oriental New York
80 Columbus Cir ... New York NY 10023 212-805-8800 805-8888 379
TF: 866-801-8880 ■ *Web:* www.mandarinoriental.com

Mandarin Oriental San Francisco
222 Sansome St ... San Francisco CA 94104 415-276-9888 433-0289 379
TF: 800-526-6566 ■ *Web:* www.mandarinoriental.com

Mandarin Oriental Washington DC
1330 Maryland Ave SW ... Washington DC 20024 202-554-8588 379
TF: 888-888-1778 ■ *Web:* www.mandarinoriental.com

Mandarin Presbyterian Church Inc, The
11844 Mandarin Rd ... Jacksonville FL 32223 904-680-9944 48-20

Mandee Shop 275 W Rte 46 ... Totowa NJ 07512 973-256-7080 157-6
Web: www.mandee.com

Mandel Co 727 W Glendale Ave Ste 100 ... Milwaukee WI 53209 414-271-6970 627
TF: 800-888-6970 ■ *Web:* www.mandelcompany.com

Mandel Communications Inc
820 Bay Ave Ste 113 ... Capitola CA 95010 831-475-8202 765
Web: www.mandel.com

Mandel Metals Inc
11400 W Addison Ave ... Franklin Park IL 60131 847-455-6606 492
TF: 800-962-9851 ■ *Web:* www.mandelmetals.com

Mandel Scientific Company Inc
2 Admiral Pl ... Guelph ON N1G4N4 519-763-9292 763-2005 419
TF: 888-883-3636 ■ *Web:* www.mandel.ca

Mandel, Katz & Brosnan LLP
The Law Bldg 210 Rt 303 ... Valley Cottage NY 10989 845-639-7800 428
Web: www.mkbllp.com

Mandelbaum Commercial Real Estate
2502 N Clark St ... Chicago IL 60614 773-525-4700 656

Mandell School, The 795 Columbus Ave ... New York NY 10025 212-222-2925 685
Web: www.mandellschool.org

Manders Merighi Portadin Farrell Architects LLC
1138 E Chestnut Ave Bldg 4 ... Vineland NJ 08360 856-696-9155 261

MANDEX Inc
12500 Fair Lakes Cir Ste 125 ... Fairfax VA 22033 703-227-0900 227-0910 180
Web: www.mandex.com

Mandil Inc 846 Elati St ... Denver CO 80204 303-892-5805 393
Web: www.mandilinc.com

Mandli Communications Inc
4801 Tradewinds Pkwy ... Madison WI 53718 608-835-3500 180
TF: 888-545-2214 ■ *Web:* mandli.com

Mandrake Management Consultants
55 St Clair Ave W Ste 401 ... Toronto ON M4V2Y7 416-922-5400 193
TF: 888-778-7020 ■ *Web:* www.mandrake.ca

Manduka LLC 358 Coral Cir ... El Segundo CA 90245 310-426-1495 648-7968 361
Web: www.manduka.com

Mane Street Manor Hair Salon & Day Spa
1108 S Main St ... Hampstead MD 21074 410-239-1425 77
Web: manestreetmanorspa.com

Maneki 304 Sixth Ave S ... Seattle WA 98104 206-622-2631 671
Web: manekirestaurant.com

Manex Resource Group Inc
1100 - 1199 W Hastings St ... Vancouver BC V6E3T5 604-684-9384 194
TF: 888-456-1112 ■ *Web:* www.manexresourcegroup.com

Manga Hotels Inc 3279 Caroga Dr ... Mississauga ON L4V1A3 905-672-4821 707
Web: www.mangahotels.com

Mangan Holcomb Partners
2300 Cottondale Ln ... Little Rock AR 72202 501-376-0321 4
Web: www.manganholcomb.com

Manganaro Corp New England
52 Cummings Pk ... Woburn MA 01801 781-937-8880 937-8882 189-9
Web: www.manganaro.com

Mangia 81 Main St ... Annapolis MD 21401 410-268-1350 671
Web: mangiasannapolis.com

Mangia Mangia 900 Southard St ... Key West FL 33040 305-294-2469 671
Web: www.mangia-mangia.com

Mangiamo 2000 Main St ... Hilton Head Island SC 29926 843-682-2444 682-3355 671
Web: www.hhipizza.com

Mango Hair Salon 123 Libbie Ave ... Richmond VA 23226 804-285-2800 77
Web: mangosalon.com

Mango Tree 217 S Reynolds Rd ... Toledo OH 43615 419-536-2883 671
Web: mangotreedining.com

Mango's Thai Cuisine
4701 W Pk Blvd Ste 104 ... Plano TX 75093 972-599-0289 671
Web: www.mangothaicuisine.com

Mangoes 700 Duval St ... Key West FL 33040 305-292-4606 671
Web: www.keywestmangoes.com

Mangos Graphics Inc
1010 Spring Mill Ave Ste 200 ... Conshohocken PA 19428 610-296-2555 7
Web: mangos.agency

Mangos Restaurant & Lounge
904 E Las Olas Blvd ... Fort Lauderdale FL 33301 954-523-5001 671

Mangroves Bar & Grille 208 S Howard Ave ... Tampa FL 33606 813-258-3302 671
Web: www.mangroves-restaurants.com

Mangy Moose PO Box 590 ... Teton Village WY 83025 307-733-4913 671
TF: 800-247-8390 ■ *Web:* mangymoose.com

Manhasset Specialty Co
3505 Fruitvale Blvd ... Yakima WA 98902 509-248-3810 248-3834 527
TF: 800-795-0965 ■ *Web:* www.manhasset-specialty.com

Manhattan Area Chamber of Commerce
501 Poyntz Ave ... Manhattan KS 66502 785-776-8829 776-0679 139
TF: 800-759-0134 ■ *Web:* www.manhattan.org

Phone | Fax | Class

Manhattan Area Technical College
3136 Dickens ... Manhattan KS 66503 785-587-2800 162
TF: 800-352-7575 ■ *Web:* manhattantech.edu

Manhattan Assoc Inc
2300 Windy Ridge Pkwy 10th Fl ... Atlanta GA 30339 770-955-7070 955-0302 178-10
NASDAQ: MANH ■ *TF:* 877-756-7435 ■ *Web:* www.manh.com

Manhattan at Times Square Hotel, The
790 Seventh Ave ... New York NY 10019 212-581-3300 378
Web: www.manhattanhoteltimessquare.com

Manhattan Bagel Co Inc
555 Zang St Ste 300 ... Lakewood CO 80228 303-568-8000 68
Web: www.manhattanbagel.com

Manhattan Beach Chamber of Commerce
425 15th St ... Manhattan Beach CA 90266 310-545-5313 139
Web: manhattanbeachchamber.com

Manhattan Beach State Recreation Site
8845 Beach St ... Rockaway Beach OR 97136 503-368-5943 565
TF: 800-551-6949 ■ *Web:* oregonstateparks.org

Manhattan Beach Trading Inc
1926 E Maple Ave ... El Segundo CA 90245 310-647-4281 690
Web: www.mbtrading.com

Manhattan Chamber of Commerce
575 Fifth Ave 14th Fl ... New York NY 10017 212-479-7772 473-8074 139
Web: www.manhattancc.org

Manhattan Christian College
1415 Anderson Ave ... Manhattan KS 66502 785-539-3571 776-9251 161
TF: 877-246-4622 ■ *Web:* www.mccks.edu

Manhattan College
4513 Manhattan College Pkwy ... Bronx NY 10471 718-862-8000 862-8027* 166
**Fax:* Admissions ■ *TF:* 855-841-2843 ■ *Web:* www.manhattan.edu

Manhattan Convention & Visitors Bureau
501 Poyntz Ave ... Manhattan KS 66502 785-776-8829 776-0679 206
TF: 800-759-0134 ■ *Web:* www.manhattancvb.org

Manhattan Ctr Studios 311 W 34th St ... New York NY 10001 212-695-6600 572
Web: www.mcstudios.com

Manhattan Institute for Policy Research Inc
52 Vanderbilt Ave ... New York NY 10017 212-599-7000 599-3494 634
Web: www.manhattan-institute.org

Manhattan Media LLC
79 Madison Ave 16th Fl ... New York NY 10016 212-268-8600 268-0503 637-8
Web: www.manhattanmedia.com

Manhattan Neighborhood Network
537 W 59th St ... New York NY 10019 212-757-2670 116
Web: www.mnn.org

Manhattan Public Library
629 Poyntz Ave ... Manhattan KS 66502 785-776-4741 776-1545 434-3
Web: mhklibrary.org

Manhattan School of Music
120 Claremont Ave ... New York NY 10027 212-749-2802 749-3025* 166
**Fax:* Admissions ■ *Web:* www.msmnyc.edu

Manhattan Telecommunications Corp
55 Water St 32nd Fl ... New York NY 10041 212-607-2000 387
Web: www.mettel.net

Manhattan Theatre Club Inc
311 W 43rd St 8th Fl ... New York NY 10036 212-399-3000 749
Web: www.manhattantheatreclub.com

Manhattan Toy
300 First Ave N Ste 200 ... Minneapolis MN 55401 800-541-1345 64
TF: 800-541-1345 ■ *Web:* www.manhattantoy.com

Manhattanville College
2900 Purchase St ... Purchase NY 10577 914-323-5464 694-1732 166
TF: 800-328-4553 ■ *Web:* www.mville.edu

Manidokan Camp and Retreat Center
1600 Harpers Ferry Rd ... Knoxville MD 21758 301-834-7244 377
Web: www.manidokan.org

Manifest Solutions Corp
2035 Riverside Dr ... Upper Arlington OH 43221 614-930-2800 177
Web: www.manifestsc.com

Manifold Capital Corp
140 Broadway 47th Fl ... New York NY 10005 212-375-2000 375-2100 360-3
OTC: MANF ■ *Web:* www.aca.com

Manildra Group USA
4210 Shawnee Mission Pkwy Ste 312A .. Shawnee Mission KS 66205 913-362-0777 362-0052 296-23
TF: 800-323-8435 ■ *Web:* manildrausa.com

Manischewitz Company, The 80 Ave K ... Newark NJ 07105 201-553-1100 296-36
Web: www.rabfoodgroup.com

Manistee County Historical Museum
425 River St ... Manistee MI 49660 231-723-5531 520
TF: 800-841-4243 ■ *Web:* www.manisteemuseum.org

Manitex Inc 3000 S Austin Ave ... Georgetown TX 78626 512-942-3000 470
TF: 877-314-3390 ■ *Web:* www.manitex.com

Manitoba Agricultural Services Corp
Unit 100 - 1525 First St S ... Brandon MB R7A7A1 204-726-6850 316
Web: www.masc.mb.ca

Manitoba Chamber Orchestra
393 Portage Ave Portage Pl Unit Y300 ... Winnipeg MB R3B3H6 204-783-7377 783-7383 573-3
Web: www.themco.ca

Manitoba Chambers of Commerce, The
227 Portage Ave ... Winnipeg MB R3B2A6 204-948-0100 948-0110 137
TF: 877-444-5222 ■ *Web:* www.mbchamber.mb.ca

Manitoba Museum 190 Rupert Ave ... Winnipeg MB R3B0N2 204-956-2830 942-3679 520
TF: 800-633-8332 ■ *Web:* www.manitobamuseum.ca/main

Manitoba Sports Hall of Fame & Museum
145 Pacific Ave ... Winnipeg MB R3B2Z6 204-925-5600 522
Web: www.sportmanitoba.ca/hall-of-fame

Manitok Energy Inc
639 5 Ave SW Ste 2500 ... Calgary AB T2P0M9 403-984-1750 536
Web: www.manitokenergy.com

Manitou Cliff Dwellings Museum
10 Cliff Rd ... Manitou Springs CO 80829 719-685-5242 520
TF: 800-354-9971 ■ *Web:* www.cliffdwellingsmuseum.com

Manitou North America 6401 Imperial Dr ... Waco TX 76712 254-799-0232 470
Web: www.constructionequipment.com

Manitowoc Area Visitor & Convention Bureau
4221 Calumet Ave ... Manitowoc WI 54220 800-627-4896 206
TF: 800-627-4896 ■ *Web:* www.manitowoc.info

Manitowoc Beverage Equipment
2100 Future Dr ... Sellersburg IN 47172 812-246-7000 246-9922 298
TF: 800-367-4233 ■ *Web:* www.manitowocbeverage.com

Manitowoc Company Inc
2400 S 44th St ... Manitowoc WI 54220 920-684-4410 190
NYSE: MTW ■ *Web:* www.manitowoccranes.com/en

Manitowoc County
1010 S Eighth St 1st Fl Rm 115 ... Manitowoc WI 54220 920-683-4003 683-5180 338
Web: www.co.manitowoc.wi.us

Manitowoc Ice 2110 S 26th St ... Manitowoc WI 54220 920-682-0161 683-7589* 664
**Fax:* Sales ■ *TF:* 800-545-5720 ■ *Web:* www.manitowocice.com

Manitowoc-Calumet Library System
707 Quay St ... Manitowoc WI 54220 920-686-3010 434-3
TF: 800-627-4896 ■ *Web:* www.manitowoclibrary.org

Manitowoc-Two Rivers Area Chamber of Commerce
1515 Memorial Dr ... Manitowoc WI 54220 920-684-5575 684-1915 139
TF: 866-727-5575 ■ *Web:* chambermanitowoccounty.org

Mankato-Kasota Stone Inc
818 N Willow St ... Mankato MN 56001 507-625-2746 724
Web: www.mankato-kasota-stone.com

Manke Lumber Company Inc
1717 Marine View Dr ... Tacoma WA 98422 253-572-6252 383-2489 683
TF: 800-426-8488 ■ *Web:* www.mankelumber.com

Manko Window Systems Inc
800 Hayes Dr ... Manhattan KS 66502 785-776-9643 480
TF: 800-642-1488 ■ *Web:* www.mankowindows.com

Manley Deas & Kochalski LLC
PO Box 165028 ... Columbus OH 43216 614-220-5611 428
TF: 800-973-1177 ■ *Web:* mdk-llc.com

Manley Performance Engineering
1960 Swarthmore Ave ... Lakewood NJ 08701 732-905-3366 60
Web: manleyperformance.com

Man-maid Cleaning Services Inc
29 Fox Creek Dr ... Rehoboth Beach DE 19971 631-281-5308 104
Web: www.manmaidcleaning.com

Mann & Parker Lumber Company Inc, The
335 N Constitution Ave ... New Freedom PA 17349 717-235-4834 235-5547 499
TF: 800-632-9098 ■ *Web:* m-pgoldbrand.com

Mann Armistead & Epperson Ltd
119 Shockoe Slip ... Richmond VA 23219 804-644-1200 401
Web: www.maeltd.com

Mann Ctr for the Performing Arts
5201 Parkside Ave ... Philadelphia PA 19131 215-546-7900 546-9524 572
TF: 800-745-3000 ■ *Web:* www.manncenter.org

Mann Packing Co PO Box 690 ... Salinas CA 93902 800-285-1002 11-1
TF: 800-285-1002 ■ *Web:* www.veggiesmadeeasy.com

Mann Simons Cottage 1403 Richland St ... Columbia SC 29201 803-252-7742 929-7695 50-3
Web: www.historiccolumbia.org

Mann Urrutia Nelson CPA's & Assoc LLP
2901 Douglas Blvd Ste 290 ... Roseville CA 95661 916-774-4208 774-4230 2
Web: www.muncpas.com

Mann's Jewelers Inc 2945 Monroe Ave ... Rochester NY 14618 585-271-4000 410
TF: 800-828-6234 ■ *Web:* www.mannsjewelers.com

Manna House of Prayer
323 E Fifth St ... Concordia KS 66901 785-243-4428 673
Web: www.mannahouse.org

Manna Pro Corp
707 Spirit 40 Pk Dr Ste 150 ... Chesterfield MO 63005 800-690-9908 447
TF: 800-690-9908 ■ *Web:* www.mannapro.com

Mannatech Inc 600 S Royal Ln Ste 200 ... Coppell TX 75019 972-471-7400 471-8191 366
NASDAQ: MTEX ■ *Web:* us.mannatech.com

Manncorp Inc
1610 Republic Rd ... Huntingdon Valley PA 19006 215-830-1200 295
Web: www.manncorp.com

Mannes College of Music
150 W 85th St ... New York NY 10024 212-580-0210 580-1738* 166
**Fax:* Admissions ■ *Web:* www.newschool.edu

Mannik & Smith Group Inc
1800 Indian Wood Cir ... Maumee OH 43537 419-891-2222 261
TF: 888-891-6321 ■ *Web:* manniksmithgroup.com

Manning & Napier Advisors Inc
290 Woodcliff Dr ... Fairport NY 14450 585-325-6880 401
Web: www.manning-napier.com

Manning Elliott LLP
1050 W Pender St 11th Fl ... Vancouver BC V6E3S7 604-714-3600 2
Web: www.manningelliott.com

Manning Fulton & Skinner PA
3605 Glenwood Ave ... Raleigh NC 27612 919-787-8880 428
Web: www.manningfulton.com

Manning Lighting
1810 N Ave PO Box 1063 ... Sheboygan WI 53083 920-458-2184 458-2491 439
TF: 800-621-1348 ■ *Web:* www.manningltg.com

Manning Search Group Llc
1101 Saint Peters Howell Rd ... Saint Peters MO 63376 636-875-5080 260
Web: manningsearchgroup.com

Manning Selvage & Lee
375 Hudson St 14th Fl ... New York NY 10014 646-500-7600 636
Web: northamerica.mslgroup.com

Mannington Mills Inc
75 Mannington Mills Rd ... Salem NJ 08079 856-935-3000 291
TF Cust Svc: 800-356-6787 ■ *Web:* www.mannington.com

Mannix Architectural Window Products
345 Crooked Hill Rd ... Brentwood NY 11717 631-231-0800 231-0571 234
Web: mannixwindows.com

Mannix Mktg Inc 11 Broad St 3rd Fl ... Glens Falls NY 12801 518-743-9424 195
TF: 800-972-1229 ■ *Web:* www.mannixmarketing.com

MannKind Corp 28903 N Ave Paine ... Valencia CA 91355 661-775-5300 85
NASDAQ: MNKD ■ *Web:* www.mannkindcorp.com

Manns Bait Co 1111 State Docks Rd ... Eufaula AL 36027 800-841-8435 687-4352* 710
**Fax Area Code:* 334 ■ *TF:* 800-841-8435 ■ *Web:* www.mannsbait.com

Manny Silverman Gallery
619 N Almont Dr ... Los Angeles CA 90069 310-659-8256 659-1001 42
Web: mannysilvermangallery.com

Manny's Steak House
825 Marquette Ave ... Minneapolis MN 55403 612-339-9900 341-2373 671
Web: www.mannyssteakhouse.com

Manoir du Lac Delage 40 Ave du Lac ... Lac Delage QC G3C5C4 418-848-2551 848-1352 669
TF: 888-202-3242 ■ *Web:* www.lacdelage.com

Manoir-Papineau National Historic Site
500 Notre-Dame ... Montebello QC J0V1L0 819-423-6965 423-6455 563
Web: www.pc.gc.ca

Phone | Fax | Class

Manomet Center for Conservation Sciences
81 Stage Point Rd .... Manomet MA 02345 508-224-6521 41
Web: www.manomet.org

Manor College 700 Fox Chase Rd .... Jenkintown PA 19046 215-885-2360 576-6564* 162
**Fax:* Admissions ■ *Web:* www.manor.edu

Manor House 1001 Middleford Rd .... Seaford DE 19973 302-629-4593 672
TF: 800-775-4593 ■ *Web:* www.actsretirement.org

Manor House Inn 106 W St .... Bar Harbor ME 04609 207-288-3759 379
TF: 800-437-0088 ■ *Web:* www.barharbormanorhouse.com

Manor Park Inc 2208 N Loop 250 W .... Midland TX 79707 432-689-9898 694-2551 672
TF: 800-523-9898 ■ *Web:* www.manorparkinc.org

Manor Tool & Manufacturing Co
9200 Ivanhoe St .... Schiller Park IL 60176 847-678-2020 678-6937 454
TF: 800-532-2252 ■ *Web:* www.manortool.com

Manor Vail Lodge 595 E Vail Vly Dr .... Vail CO 81657 970-476-5000 669
TF: 800-950-8245 ■ *Web:* www.manorvail.com

Manora's Thai Cuisine
1600 Folsom St .... San Francisco CA 94103 415-861-6224 671
Web: www.manorathai.com

ManorCare Health Services - Arlington
550 S Carlin Springs Rd .... Arlington VA 22204 703-379-7200 450
Web: www.hcr-manorcare.com

ManorCare Health Services - Arlington Heights
715 W Central Rd .... Arlington Heights IL 60005 847-392-2020 392-0174 450
Web: www.heartland-manorcare.com/locations/manorcare-at-arlington-heights

ManorCare Health Services - Carrollwood
3030 W Bearss Ave .... Tampa FL 33618 813-968-8777 450
Web: www.hcr-manorcare.com

ManorCare Health Services - Fair Oaks
12475 Lee Jackson Memorial Hwy .... Fairfax VA 22033 703-352-7172 352-1455 450
Web: www.heartland-manorcare.com

ManorCare Health Services - Homewood
940 Maple Ave .... Homewood IL 60430 708-799-0244 799-1505 450
Web: www.heartland-manorcare.com

ManorCare Health Services - Mountainside
1180 Rt 22 W .... Mountainside NJ 07092 908-654-0020 450
TF: 800-366-1232 ■ *Web:* www.hcr-manorcare.com

ManorCare Health Services - North Olmsted
23225 Lorain Rd .... North Olmsted OH 44070 440-779-6900 450
Web: www.hcr-manorcare.com

ManorCare Health Services - Oak Lawn East
9401 S Kostner Ave .... Oak Lawn IL 60453 708-423-7882 423-7947 450
Web: www.heartland-manorcare.com

ManorCare Health Services - Rossville
6600 Ridge Rd .... Baltimore MD 21237 410-574-4950 391-4386 450
Web: www.heartland-manorcare.com

ManorCare Health Services - Ruxton
7001 N Charles St .... Towson MD 21204 410-821-9600 337-8313 450
Web: www.heartland-manorcare.com

Manorhouse Management Inc
706 Old Stream Rd .... Manakin Sabot VA 23103 804-784-7255 463
Web: www.manorhouseretirement.com

Manos Greek Restaurant & Bar
1701 Adams St .... Toledo OH 43604 419-244-4479 671
Web: www.manosgreekrestaurant.com

Manpower Demonstration Research Corp
16 E 34th St 19th Fl .... New York NY 10016 212-532-3200 684-0832 634
TF: 800-221-3165 ■ *Web:* www.mdrc.org

Manpower Inc.
8170 W Sahara Ave Ste 207 .... Las Vegas NV 89101 702-363-2626 363-0461 631
TF: 888-333-1597 ■ *Web:* www.manpowerlv.com

ManpowerGroup 100 Manpower Pl .... Milwaukee WI 53212 414-961-1000 721
NYSE: MAN ■ *Web:* www.manpower.us

Manroy USA LLC
201 Lonnie E Crawford Blvd .... Scottsboro AL 35769 256-259-9800 807
Web: www.manroy-usa.com

Mansermar Inc
2405 Satellite Blvd Ste 100 .... Duluth GA 30096 678-330-2000 652
Web: mansermar.com

Mansfield Correctional Institution
1150 N Main St PO Box 788 .... Mansfield OH 44901 419-525-4455 524-8022 213
Web: drc.ohio.gov/manci

Mansfield Hollow State Park
c/o Mashamoquet Brook State Pk
RFD Wolf Den Rd Ste 1 .... Pomfret Center CT 06259 860-928-6121 565
Web: www.ct.gov

Mansfield Industries Inc
1776 Harrington Memorial Rd .... Mansfield OH 44903 419-524-1300 350
Web: mansfieldec.com

Mansfield Motorsports Speedway
100 Crall Rd .... Mansfield OH 44903 419-524-0183 515
Web: www.mansfield-speedway.com

Mansfield Oil Co
1025 Airport Pkwy SW .... Gainesville GA 30501 800-695-6626 539
TF: 800-695-6626 ■ *Web:* mansfield.energy

Mansfield Plumbing Products Inc
150 E First St .... Perrysville OH 44864 419-938-5211 938-6234 611
TF: 877-850-3060 ■ *Web:* www.mansfieldplumbing.com

Mansfield State Historic Site
15149 Hwy 175 .... Mansfield LA 71052 318-872-1474 565
TF: 888-677-6267 ■ *Web:* www.crt.state.la.us

Mansfield University Alumni Hall .... Mansfield PA 16933 570-662-4000 662-4121 166
TF Admissions: 800-577-6826 ■ *Web:* www.mansfield.edu

Mansfield, The 12 W 44th St .... New York NY 10036 212-277-8700 764-4477 379
TF: 800-255-5167 ■ *Web:* www.mansfieldhotel.com

Mansfield/Richland County Convention & Visitors Bureau
124 N Main St .... Mansfield OH 44902 419-525-1300 524-7722 206
TF: 800-642-8282 ■ *Web:* www.destinationmansfield.com

Mansfield-Richland County Public Library
43 W Third St .... Mansfield OH 44902 419-521-3100 525-4750 434-3
TF: 877-795-2111 ■ *Web:* www.mrcpl.org

Manship House Museum
420 E Fortification St .... Jackson MS 39202 601-961-4724 520
Web: mdah.state.ms.us

Mansion at Griffin Gate
1800 Newtown Pk .... Lexington KY 40511 859-231-5100 288-6216 671
Web: www.mansionatgriffingate.com

Mansion on Forsyth Park
700 Drayton St .... Savannah GA 31401 912-238-5158 238-5146 379
TF: 888-213-3671 ■ *Web:* www.mansiononforsythpark.com

Mansion View Inn & Suites
529 S Fourth St .... Springfield IL 62701 217-544-7411 379
TF: 800-252-1083 ■ *Web:* www.mansionview.com

Manson Construction Co
5209 E Marginal Way S .... Seattle WA 98134 206-762-0850 764-8590 188-5
TF General: 800-352-0050 ■ *Web:* www.mansonconstruction.com

Mansour Travel Co
8383 Wilshire Blvd Ste 350 .... Beverly Hills CA 90211 310-276-2768 276-7638 772
Web: www.mansourtravel.com

Mansur's 5720 Corporate Blvd Ste A .... Baton Rouge LA 70808 225-923-3366 671
Web: www.mansursontheboulevard.com

Mantaline Corp 4754 E High St .... Mantua OH 44255 330-274-2264 274-8850 677
Web: www.mantaline.com

MANTEC Inc 600 N Hartley St Ste 100 .... York PA 17404 717-843-5054 138
TF: 800-343-6732 ■ *Web:* www.mantec.org

Mantec Services Inc 4400 24th Ave W .... Seattle WA 98199 206-285-5656 599
TF: 800-321-5253 ■ *Web:* www.mantecservicesinc.com

Manteca Chamber of Commerce
183 W N St Ste 6 .... Manteca CA 95336 209-823-6121 239-6131 139
Web: www.manteca.org

ManTech Advanced Systems International Inc
12015 Lee Jackson Hwy .... Fairfax VA 22033 703-218-6000 256
TF: 800-800-4857 ■ *Web:* www.mantech.com

ManTech International Corp
2250 Corporate Park Dr Ste 500 .... Herndon VA 20171 703-218-6000 809
Web: www.mcdonaldbradley.com

Mantel Machine Products Inc
W141 N9350 Fountain Blvd .... Menomonee Falls WI 53051 262-255-6780 255-9724 621
Web: www.mantelmachine.com

MantelsDirect 217 N Seminary St .... Florence AL 35630 888-493-8898 183
TF: 888-493-8898 ■ *Web:* www.mantelsdirect.com

Manteno High School 443 N Maple St .... Manteno IL 60950 815-928-7100 685
Web: www.manteno5.org

Manteo High School 829 Wingina St .... Manteo NC 27954 252-473-5841 685
Web: mhs.daretolearn.org

Mantey Heights Rehabilitation & Care Centre
2825 Patterson Rd .... Grand Junction CO 81506 970-242-7356 371
TF: 800-254-9442 ■ *Web:* www.fivestarseniorliving.com

Manth-Brownell Inc 1120 Fyler Rd .... Kirkville NY 13082 315-687-7263 687-6856 621
Web: www.manth.com

Mantis Technology Group Inc
12413 Willows Rd NE Ste 300 .... Kirkland WA 98034 425-250-0400 809
Web: www.mantis-tgi.com

Mantissa Corp 616 Pressley Rd .... Charlotte NC 28217 704-525-1749 358
Web: www.mantissacorporation.com

Manton Industrial Cork Products Inc
415 Oser Ave Unit U .... Hauppauge NY 11788 631-273-0700 273-0038 209
TF: 800-663-1921 ■ *Web:* www.mantoncork.com

Mantra Technologies
284 S Main St Ste 700 .... Alpharetta GA 30009 770-456-5652 180
Web: www.mantrasys.com

Mantros-Haeuser & Company Inc
1175 Post Rd E .... Westport CT 06880 203-454-1800 227-0558 550
TF General: 800-344-4229 ■ *Web:* www.mantrose.com

Mantua Mfg Co 7900 Northfield Rd .... Walton Hills OH 44146 800-333-8333 929-8014 319-2
TF Orders: 800-333-8333 ■ *Web:* www.bedframes.com

Mantz Automation Inc
1630 Innovation Way .... Hartford WI 53027 262-673-7560 697
Web: www.mantzautomation.com

Manual Woodworkers & Weavers Inc
3737 HowaRd Gap Rd .... Hendersonville NC 28792 828-692-7333 696-2961 746
TF: 800-542-3139 ■ *Web:* www.manualww.com

Manufactured Housing Enterprises Inc
09302 St Rt 6 Rt 6 .... Bryan OH 43506 419-636-4511 505
TF: 800-821-0220 ■ *Web:* www.mheinc.com

Manufactured Housing Institute (MHI)
2101 Wilson Blvd Ste 610 .... Arlington VA 22201 703-558-0400 558-0401 49-3
TF: 800-505-5500 ■ *Web:* www.manufacturedhousing.org

Manufactured Housing Institute PAC (MHI PAC)
1655 N Ft Myer Dr Ste 104 .... Arlington VA 22209 703-558-0400 558-0401 615
TF: 800-505-5500 ■ *Web:* www.manufacturedhousing.org

Manufacturers Alliance/MAPI Inc
1600 Wilson Blvd Ste 1100 .... Arlington VA 22209 703-841-9000 841-9514 49-12
Web: www.mapi.net

Manufacturers Chemicals LLC
4325 Old Tasso Rd .... Cleveland TN 37320 423-476-6518 131
Web: synalloychemicals.com

Manufacturers Industrial Group LLC
659 Natchez Trace Dr .... Lexington TN 38351 731-967-0001 968-3320 482
Web: www.migllc.com

Manufacturers' Lease Plans Inc
818 E Osborn Rd Ste 200 .... Phoenix AZ 85014 602-944-4411 944-4417 264-1
Web: www.leaseplans.com

Manufacturers' News Inc
1633 Central St .... Evanston IL 60201 847-864-7000 532-3
Web: www.manufacturersnews.com

Manufacturing & Design Technology Inc
1033a Cavalier Blvd .... Chesapeake VA 23323 757-485-8924 454
Web: www.m-d-t.com

Manufacturing Jewelers & Suppliers of America Inc (MJSA)
57 John L Dietsch Sq .... Attleboro MA 02763 401-274-3840 274-0265 49-4
TF: 800-444-6572 ■ *Web:* www.mjsa.org

Manufacturing Technology Inc (MTI)
1702 W Washington St .... South Bend IN 46628 574-233-9490 233-9489 811
Web: www.mtiwelding.com

Manulife Financial Corp
200 Bloor St E .... Toronto ON M4W1E5 416-926-3000 926-5410 360-4
NYSE: MFC ■ *TF:* 800-795-9767 ■ *Web:* www.manulife.com

Manulife Securities Inc
500-1235 N Service Rd W .... Oakville ON L6M2W2 905-469-2100 691
Web: www.manulife.ca

Manus & Assoc Literary Agency Inc
425 Sherman Ave Ste 200 .... Palo Alto CA 94306 650-470-5151 470-5159 444
Web: www.manuslit.com

Name / Address	City	State	Zip	Phone	Fax	Class
Manus Group, The 5000-18 Hwy 17, Ste D Web: www.themanusgroup.com	Fleming Island	FL	32003	904-264-5406		317
Manus Products of Minnesota Inc 866 Industrial Blvd Web: www.manus.net	Waconia	MN	55387	952-442-3323	442-3327	3
Manx, The 370 Elgin St Web: manxpub.com	Ottawa	ON	K2P1N1	613-231-2070		671
Manzama Inc 328 NW Bond St Ste 201 Web: www.manzama.com	Bend	OR	97701	541-701-2267		5
Manzanar National Historic Site 5001 Hwy 395 PO Box 426 Web: www.nps.gov/manz	Independence	CA	93526	760-878-2194	878-2949	564
Manzella Marketing Group 80 Sonwil Dr TF: 800-366-8573 ■ Web: manzellamarketing.com	Buffalo	NY	14225	716-681-6565		636
Manzi Metals Inc 15293 Flight Path Dr TF: 800-799-8211 ■ Web: www.manzimetals.com	Brooksville	FL	34604	352-799-8211		492
Manzi, Pino & Company PC 1895 Walt Whitman Rd - Ste 5 Web: manzipinocpa.com	Melville	NY	11747	631-420-5620		2
MAOF (Mexican-American Opportunity Foundation) 401 N Garfield Ave Web: www.maof.org	Montebello	CA	90640	323-890-9600	890-9637	48-14
MAP (Maryland Art Place) 218 W Saratoga St Web: www.mdartplace.org	Baltimore	MD	21201	410-962-8565		50-2
MAP (Mississippi Action For Progress Inc) 1751 Morson Rd TF: 800-924-4615 ■ Web: www.mapheadstart.org	Jackson	MS	39209	601-923-4100		147
Map Assoc Inc Dba North Star Engineering 111 Mission Ranch Blvd	Chico	CA	95926	530-893-1600		261
MAP International 4700 Glynco Pkwy TF: 800-225-8550 ■ Web: www.map.org	Brunswick	GA	31525	912-265-6010	265-6170	48-5
MAPEI Corp 1144 E Newport Ctr Dr TF: 800-426-2734 ■ Web: www.mapei.com	Deerfield Beach	FL	33442	954-246-8888	246-8800	3
Mapei Corp 530 Industrial Dr Web: www.mapei.com/US-EN	West Chicago	IL	60185	630-293-5800		3
Mapes Panels LLC 2929 Cornhusker Hwy PO Box 80069 TF: 800-228-2391 ■ Web: mapes.com	Lincoln	NE	68504	800-228-2391	737-6756	697
MAPFRE USA Corp 211 Main St TF: 800-922-8276 ■ Web: www.commerceinsurance.com	Webster	MA	01570	800-922-8276		391-4
Maple City Ice Co Inc 371 Cleveland Rd TF Cust Svc: 800-736-6091 ■ Web: www.maplecityice.net	Norwalk	OH	44857	419-668-2531		81-1
Maple City Rubber Co 55 Newton St TF: 800-841-9434 ■ Web: www.maplecityrubber.com	Norwalk	OH	44857	419-668-8261	668-1275	762
Maple Direct Inc 2349 Haddonfield Rd TF: 800 906 2753 ■ Web: www.mapledirect.com	Pennsauken	NJ	08110	856-488-4700		5
Maple Donuts Inc 3455 E Market St TF: 800-627-5348 ■ Web: www.mapledonuts.com	York	PA	17402	717-757-7826	755-8725	68
Maple Garden 5401 Ninth Ave S	Great Falls	MT	59405	406-727-0310		671
Maple Garden 1275 Alder St Web: www.eugenemaplegarden.com	Eugene	OR	97401	541-683-8128		671
Maple Grove Farms of Vermont 1052 Portland St TF: 800-525-2540 ■ Web: www.maplegrove.com	Saint Johnsbury	VT	05819	802-748-5141		296-39
Maple Grove Raceway 30 Stauffer Pk Ln TF: 877-814-2538 ■ Web: www.maplegroveraceway.com	Mohnton	PA	19540	610-856-9200	856-1601	515
Maple Hill Auto Group 5622 W Main St Web: www.maplehillauto.com	Kalamazoo	MI	49009	269-342-6600		57
Maple Hill Farm Bed & Breakfast Inn 11 Inn Rd TF: 800-622-2708 ■ Web: www.maplebb.com	Hallowell	ME	04347	207-622-2708	622-0655	379
Maple Hill Farms Inc 12 Burr Rd PO Box 767 Web: mhfct.com	Bloomfield	CT	06002	860-242-9689	243-2490	296-27
Maple Island Inc 2497 Seventh Ave E Ste 105 TF: 800-369-1022 ■ Web: www.maple-island.com	St Paul	MN	55109	651-773-1000		296-10
Maple Knoll Communities Inc 11100 Springfield Pk TF: 800-272-3900 ■ Web: www.mapleknoll.org	Cincinnati	OH	45246	513 782 2400		672
Maple Lake Ltd 60 Columbia Way Ste 502 Web: www.txtgroup.com	Markham	ON	L3R0C9	905-513-7480		196
Maple Lane Nursing & Retirement Home 60 Maple Ln	Barton	VT	05822	802-754-8575		793
Maple Lawn Homes 700 N Main St Web: www.maple-lawn.com	Eureka	IL	61530	309-467-2337		371
Maple Lawn Nursing Home 400 Seventh St TF: 800-255-4268 ■ Web: www.maplelawn.org	Fulda	MN	56131	507-425-2571		371
Maple Leaf Farms Inc PO Box 308 TF: 800-348-2812 ■ Web: www.mapleleaffarms.com	Milford	IN	46542	574-658-4121		10-8
Maple Leaf Foods Inc 30 St Clair Ave W Ste 1500 TSE: MFI ■ TF: 800-268-3708 ■ Web: www.mapleleaf.ca	Toronto	ON	M4V3A1	800-268-3708		296-26
Maple Press 480 Willow Springs Ln Web: www.maple-vail.com	York	PA	17406	717-764-5911	764-4702	626
Maple Ridge Farms Inc 975 S Park View Cir Web: www.mapleridge.com	Mosinee	WI	54455	715-693-4346		297-8
Maple Shade Mazda 2921 Rt 73 S Web: www.msmazda.com	Maple Shade	NJ	08052	856-667-8004		516
Maple Valley School District 11090 Nashville Hwy Web: www.mvs.k12.mi.us	Vermontville	MI	49096	517-852-9699		685
Maple Woods Community College 2601 NE Barry Rd Web: www.mcckc.edu	Kansas City	MO	64156	816-437-3000		162
Maplehurst Inc 50 Maplehurst Dr TF: 800-428-3200 ■ Web: www.maplehurstbakeries.com	Brownsburg	IN	46112	317-858-9000		296-2
Maples Gas Company Inc 101-65th Ave Web: www.maplesgas.com	Meridian	MS	39301	601-693-5115		581
Maples Industries Inc PO Box 40 Web: www.maplesrug.com	Scottsboro	AL	35768	256-259-1327	259-2072	131
Maplewood Barn Community Theatre Maplewood Barn PO Box 1704 Web: www.maplewoodbarn.com	Columbia	MO	65205	573-227-2276		572
Maplewood Investment Advisors Inc 8750 N Central Expy Ste 715 Web: www.maplewoodinvestments.com	Dallas	TX	75231	214-739-5677		401
Maplewood Nursing Home Inc 100 Daniel Dr Web: m.visitmaplewood.com	Webster	NY	14580	585-872-1800		371
Maplewood State Park 39721 Pk Entrance Rd Web: www.dnr.state.mn.us	Pelican Rapids	MN	56572	218-863-8383		565
MAPP (Mid-Atlantic Petroleum Properties LLC) 12311 Middlebrook Rd	Germantown	MD	20874	301-972-4116		579
Mapp Construction LLC 344 Third St Web: www.mappbuilt.com	Baton Rouge	LA	70801	225-757-0111		186
Mapp Kenneth (I) Government House 21-22 Kongens Gade Charlotte Amalie Web: governormapp.com	St. Thomas	VI	00802	340-774-0001	693-4374	343
Mapping Analytics LLC 120 Allens Creek Rd Ste 10 Web: www.mappinganalytics.com	Rochester	NY	14618	585-271-6490		195
MAPSYS Inc 920 Michigan Ave Web: www.mapsysinc.com	Columbus	OH	43215	614-224-5193	224-6048	176
MAQUET Cardiac Assist 15 Law Dr TF: 800-777-4222 ■ Web: ca.maquet.com	Fairfield	NJ	07004	973-244-6100		250
MAQUET Cardiovascular LLC 45 Barbour Pond Dr TF: 800-437-2437 ■ Web: www.maquet.com	Wayne	NJ	07470	973-709-7000		477
Maquet-Dynamed Inc 235 Shields Ct TF: 800-227-7215	Markham	ON	L3R8V2	905-752-3300		475
Maquoketa Caves State Park 10970 98th St Web: www.iowadnr.gov	Maquoketa	IA	52060	563-652-5833	652-0061	565
Maquoketa Valley Rural Electric Co-op 109 N Huber St TF: 800-927-6068 ■ Web: www.mvec.com	Anamosa	IA	52205	319-462-3542	462-3217	245
MAR Inc 1803 Research Blvd Ste 204 *Fax Area Code: 240 ■ Web: www.marinc.com	Rockville	MD	20850	301-231-0100	453-9871*	261
Mar West Real Estate Inc 1049 Camino Del Mar Ste 12 Web: marwestcommercial.com	Del Mar	CA	92014	858-775-4917		652
MARAD (Maritime Administration) 1200 New Jersey Ave SE TF Hotline: 800-996-2723 ■ Web: www.marad.dot.gov	Washington	DC	20590	202-366-5007		340-17
Maradyne Corp 4540 W 160th St TF: 800-537-7444 ■ Web: www.maradyne.com	Cleveland	OH	44135	216-362-0755		14
Marakon Associates Inc 1411 Bwy 35th fl Web: www.marakon.com	New York	NY	10018	212-520-7120		463
Marana Unified School District 6 11279 W Grier Rd Ste 127 Web: www.maranausd.org	Marana	AZ	85653	520-682-4757		685
Maranatha Baptist Bible College 745 W Main St *Fax: Admissions ■ TF: 800-622-2947 ■ Web: mbu.edu	Watertown	WI	53094	920-206-2330	261-9109*	166
Maranatha Bible Camp Inc 16800 E Maranatha Rd TF: 800-448-3000 ■ Web: www.maranathacamp.org	Maxwell	NE	69151	308 582 4513		239
Marantz America Inc 100 Corporate Dr Web: www.marantz.com	Mahwah	NJ	07430	201-762-6500	762-6670	52
Marathon Cheese Corp 304 E St PO Box 185 Web: www.mcheese.com	Marathon	WI	54448	715-443-2211		296-5
Marathon Coach 91333 Coburg Industrial Way TF: 800-234-9991 ■ Web: www.marathoncoach.com	Coburg	OR	97408	541-343-9991	343-2401	62-7
Marathon County 500 Forest St TF: 800-247-5645 ■ Web: www.co.marathon.wi.us	Wausau	WI	54403	715-261-1500	261-1515	338
Marathon County Public Library (MCPL) 300 N First St Web: www.mcpl.us	Wausau	WI	54403	715-261-7200	261-7204	434-3
Marathon Digital Services 716 W Pennway St TF: 877-568-1122 ■ Web: www.mysmartplans.com	Kansas City	MO	64108	816-221-7881		177
Marathon Electric Inc 100 E Randolf St PO Box 8003 TF: 800-616-7077 ■ Web: www.marathonelectric.com	Wausau	WI	54402	715-675-3311		518
Marathon Electrical Contractors Inc 614 38th St S Web: www.marathonelectrical.com	Birmingham	AL	35222	205-323-8500		189-4
Marathon Enterprises Inc 9 Smith St TF: 800-722-7388 ■ Web: sabrett.com	Englewood	NJ	07631	201-935-3330	935-5693	296-26
Marathon Equipment Co PO Box 1798 TF: 800-633-8974 ■ Web: www.marathonequipment.com	Vernon	AL	35592	205-695-9105	695-8813	386
Marathon Ethiopian Restaurant 130 Tenth St NW Web: www.marathonethiopianrestaurantcalgary.com	Calgary	AB	T2N1V3	403-283-6796		671
Marathon Oil Corp 5555 San Felipe St Web: www.marathonoil.com	Houston	TX	77056	713-629-6600		536
Marathon Petroleum LLC PO Box 1 TF: 866-462-7284 ■ Web: www.marathonpetroleum.com	Findlay	OH	45839	419-422-2121		46
Marathon Pipe Line LLC (MPL) 539 S Main St Web: www.marathonpipeline.com	Findlay	OH	45840	419-422-2121		597
Marathon Press Inc 1500 Sq Turn Blvd TF: 800-228-0629 ■ Web: www.marathonpress.com	Norfolk	NE	68701	402-371-5040		627
Marathon Special Products 13300 Van Camp Rd PO Box 468 Web: www.marathonsp.com	Bowling Green	OH	43402	419-352-8441	352-0875	729
MarathonFoto 3490 Martin Hurst Rd TF: 800-424-3686 ■ Web: www.marathonfoto.com	Tallahassee	FL	32312	972-330-7656		590
MarathonNorco Aerospace Inc 8301 Imperial Dr Web: www.mnaerospace.com	Waco	TX	76712	254-776-0650	776-6558	621

Name / Address	City	State	ZIP	Phone	Fax	Class
Maravia Corp of Idaho 602 E 45th St *TF:* 800-223-7238 ■ *Web:* www.maravia.com	Boise	ID	83714	208-322-4949	322-5016	710
Maravilla Foundation 5723 Union Pacific Ave.	Commerce	CA	90022	323-721-4162		305
Mar-Bal Inc 16930 Munn Rd *Web:* www.mar-bal.com	Chagrin Falls	OH	44023	440-543-7526	543-4374	599
Marberry Cleaners & Launderers 220 John St *Web:* www.marberrycleaners.com	North Aurora	IL	60542	630-897-0011		426
Marberry Machine Co 6210 Cunningham Rd. *Web:* www.marberrymachine.com	Houston	TX	77041	713-466-9666		454
Marble A D & Company Inc 375 E Elm St Ste 101 *Web:* www.admarble.com	Conshohocken	PA	19428	484-533-2500		463
Marble Arms (MA) 420 Industrial Pk Dr *Web:* www.marblearms.com	Gladstone	MI	49837	906-428-3710		710
Marble House 596 Bellevue Ave *Web:* www.newportmansions.org	Newport	RI	02840	401-847-1000	847-1361	50-3
Marble Institute of America (MIA) 28901 Clemens Rd Ste 100 *TF:* 800-433-4903 ■ *Web:* www.marble-institute.com	Westlake	OH	44145	440-250-9222	250-9223	49-3
Marble Systems Inc 2737 Dorr Ave *Web:* www.marblesystems.com	Fairfax	VA	22031	703-204-1818		191-1
Marblehead Lighthouse State Park 110 Lighthouse Dr *Web:* www.dnr.state.oh.us	Marblehead	OH	43440	419-734-4424		565
marblemedia Inc 74 Fraser Ave Ste 100 *TF:* 800-543-4512 ■ *Web:* www.marblemedia.com	Toronto	ON	M6K3E1	416-646-2711		225
Marbles Kids Museum 201 E Hargett St *TF:* 800-745-3000 ■ *Web:* www.marbleskidsmuseum.org	Raleigh	NC	27601	919-834-4040	834-3516	520
Marborg Industries 728 E Yanonali St *TF:* 800-798-1852 ■ *Web:* www.marborg.com	Santa Barbara	CA	93103	805-963-1852	962-0552	660
Marbridge Foundation Inc 2310 Bliss Spillar Rd *TF:* 800-252-8263 ■ *Web:* marbridge.org	Manchaca	TX	78652	512-282-1144		305
Marburger Farm Dairy Inc 1506 Mars Evans City Rd *TF:* 800-331-1295 ■ *Web:* www.marburgerdairy.com	Evans City	PA	16033	724-538-4800	538-3250	10-3
Marburn Academy 1860 Walden Dr *Web:* marburnacademy.org	Columbus	OH	43229	614-433-0822		148
Marc B Freedman CPA PC 215 W 95th St. *Web:* mbfcpa.com	New York	NY	10025	212-678-2418		2
Marc Bouwer 141 Fulton St 2nd Fl	New York	NY	10038	212-242-7510		277
Marc Jacobs International 72 Spring St *TF:* 877-707-6272 ■ *Web:* www.marcjacobs.com	New York	NY	10012	877-707-6272		277
MARC Promotions 7172 Lkview Pkwy W Dr	Indianapolis	IN	46268	317-290-3516		195
Marc Publishing Co 600 Germantown Pk *TF:* 800-432-5478 ■ *Web:* www.marcpub.com	Lafayette Hill	PA	19444	610-834-8585		637-6
MARC USA 225 W Stn Sq Dr Ste 500 *Web:* www.marcusa.com	Pittsburgh	PA	15219	412-562-2000	562-2022	4
Marca Hispanic LLC 1320 S Dixie Hwy *Web:* marcamiami.com	Coral Gables	FL	33146	305-665-5410		4
Marcari, Russotto, Spencer & Balaban PC 2443 Lynn Rd Ste 101 *Web:* www.donmarcari.com	Raleigh	NC	27613	919-787-9944		428
Marcegaglia USA Inc 1001 E Waterfront Dr *Web:* www.marcegaglia.com	Munhall	PA	15120	412-462-2185	462-6059	490
Marcel Media LLC 445 W Erie St Ste 200 *Web:* www.marceldigital.com	Chicago	IL	60654	312-255-8044		4
Marcel's 2401 Pennsylvania Ave NW *Web:* www.marcelsdc.com	Washington	DC	20037	202-296-1166		671
Marcella Restaurant 3507 Tully Rd.	Modesto	CA	95356	209-577-3777		671
March Associates Inc 601 Hamburg Tpke *Web:* www.marchassociates.com	Wayne	NJ	07470	973-904-0213		186
March Consulting Associates Inc 200 201 21st St E *Web:* www.marchconsulting.com	Saskatoon	SK	S7K0B8	306-651-6330		261
March Field Air Museum 22550 Van Buren Blvd *TF:* 800-440-5910 ■ *Web:* www.marchfield.org	Riverside	CA	92518	951-902-5949		520
March of Dimes Foundation 1275 Mamaroneck Ave *Web:* www.marchofdimes.org	White Plains	NY	10605	914-428-7100		48-17
Marchand's Bar & Grill 501 Fifth Ave NE Renaissance Vinoy Resort *Web:* www.marriott.com	Saint Petersburg	FL	33701	727-824-8072		671
Marchant Kenny (Rep R - TX) 2369 Rayburn HOB *Web:* marchant.house.gov	Washington	DC	20515	202-225-6605	225-0074	342-2
Marchant Schmidt Inc 24 W Larsen Dr. *Web:* www.marchantschmidt.net	Fond Du Lac	WI	54937	920-921-4760		492
Marche 296 E Fifth Ave. *Web:* www.marcherestaurant.com	Eugene	OR	97401	541-342-3612		671
Marche Akhavan 6170 Rue Sherbrooke O *Web:* akhavanfood.com	Montreal	QC	H4B1L8	514-485-4887		297-8
Marcheschi Plankis & Pogore 9951 W 190th St Ste A *Web:* mppcpa.com	Mokena	IL	60448	708-479-7333		2
Marchex Inc 520 Pike St Ste 2000 *NASDAQ: MCHX* ■ *TF:* 800-840-1012 ■ *Web:* www.marchex.com	Seattle	WA	98101	206-331-3300	331-3695	7
Marcive Inc 12100 Crownpoint Dr Ste 160 *TF:* 800-531-7678 ■ *Web:* www.marcive.com	San Antonio	TX	78233	210-646-6161		434-3
Marck Industries Inc 401 Main St E *Web:* www.marck.net	Cassville	MO	65625	417-847-5900		660
Marc-michaels Interior Design Inc 850 E Palmetto Park Rd *Web:* www.marc-michaels.com	Boca Raton	FL	33432	561-362-7037		393
Marco 4581 Forsyth Rd. *Web:* www.marcomacon.com	Macon	GA	31210	478-405-5660		671
Marco & Pepe 289 Grove St *Web:* www.marcoandpepe.com	Jersey City	NJ	07302	201-860-9688		671
Marco Beach Ocean Resort 480 S Collier Blvd *TF:* 800-715-8517 ■ *Web:* www.marcoresort.com	Marco Island	FL	34145	239-393-1400	393-1401	669
Marco Corp, The 470 Hardy Rd **Fax Area Code: 519* ■ *TF:* 888-636-6161 ■ *Web:* www.themarcocorporation.biz/marcohome	Brantford	ON	N3V6T1	888-636-6161	751-0561*	7
Marco Crane & Rigging Co 221 S 35th Ave *TF:* 800-668-2671 ■ *Web:* www.marcocrane.com	Phoenix	AZ	85009	602-272-2671	352-0413	264-3
Marco Enterprises Inc 3504 Watkins Ave *Web:* www.marcoenterprises.com	Landover	MD	20785	301-773-5656	773-0422	186
MARCO Global 7915 Tenth Ave S. *Web:* www.marcoglobal.com	Seattle	WA	98199	206-285-3200	282-8520	698
Marco Island Chamber of Commerce 1102 N Collier Blvd *TF:* 888-330-1422 ■ *Web:* www.marcoislandchamber.org	Marco Island	FL	34145	239-394-7549	394-3061	139
Marco Ophthalmic Inc 11825 Central Pkwy *Web:* www.marco.com	Jacksonville	FL	32224	904-642-9330		543
Marco Polo Global Restaurant 300 Liberty St SE	Salem	OR	97301	503-364-4833		671
Marco Polo Securities Inc 144 E 44th St 8th Fl *Web:* mpsecurities.com	New York	NY	10017	212-220-2700		690
Marco Promotional Products 2640 Commerce Dr **Fax Area Code: 866* ■ *TF:* 877-545-9322 ■ *Web:* www.marcopromotionalproducts.com	Harrisburg	PA	17110	877-545-9322	545-5672*	9
Marco Rubber 35 Woodworkers Way *TF:* 800-775-6525 ■ *Web:* www.marcorubber.com	Seabrook	NH	03874	603-468-3600		326
Marco's 1085 Niagara St *Web:* marcosbuffalo.com	Buffalo	NY	14213	716-882-5539		671
MARCOA Publishing Inc 9955 Black Mtn Rd *TF:* 800-854-2935 ■ *Web:* www.marcoa.com	San Diego	CA	92126	858-695-9600	695-9641	637-1
Marcole Enterprises Inc 2920 Camino Diablo Ste 200 *Web:* www.marcole.com	Walnut Creek	CA	94597	925-933-9792		177
Marcom Gurus 2083 Louise Ln *Web:* marcomgurus.com	Los Altos	CA	94024	650-564-0011		195
Marcus & Assoc Inc 1045 Mapunapuna St *Web:* www.marcusrealty.com	Honolulu	HI	96819	808-839-7446		652
Marcus & Pollack LLP 633 Third Ave 9th fl *Web:* marcuspollack.com	New York	NY	10017	212-490-2900		428
Marcus Bros Textiles Inc 980 Ave of the Americas *TF:* 800-548-8295 ■ *Web:* marcusfabrics.com	New York	NY	10018	212-354-8700		594
Marcus Corp 100 E Wisconsin Ave *NYSE: MCS* ■ *TF:* 800-468-9716 ■ *Web:* www.marcuscorp.com	Milwaukee	WI	53202	414-905-1000		379
Marcus Ctr for the Performing Arts 929 N Water St *TF:* 888-612-3500 ■ *Web:* www.marcuscenter.org	Milwaukee	WI	53202	414-273-7206		572
Marcus Errico Emmer & Brooks PC 45 Braintree Hill Pk Ste 107 *Web:* www.meeb.com	Braintree	MA	02184	781-843-5000		2
Marcus Evans Inc 455 N Cityfront Plaza Dr The NBC Tower 9th Fl *Web:* www.marcusevans.com	Chicago	IL	60611	312-540-3000		387
Marcus Group Inc, The 150 Clove Rd Ste 11 *TF:* 800-622-3542 ■ *Web:* www.marcusgroup.com	Little Falls	NJ	07424	973-890-9590		636
Marcus Hotels & Resorts 100 E Wisconsin Ave Ste 1950 *Web:* www.marcushotels.com	Milwaukee	WI	53202	414-905-1200	905-2250	379
Marcus Productions Inc 3107 Stirling Rd Ste 204 *Web:* www.marcusproductions.com	Fort Lauderdale	FL	33312	954-965-5295		513
Marcus Theatres Corp 100 E Wisconsin Ave Ste 2000 *TF Cust Svc:* 800-274-0099 ■ *Web:* marcustheatres.com	Milwaukee	WI	53202	414-905-1000		748
Marcus Whitman Hotel & Conference Center LLC 6 W Rose St *TF:* 800-523-2464 ■ *Web:* www.marcuswhitmanhotel.com	Walla Walla	WA	99362	509-525-2200		707
Marcy Correctional Facility 9000 Old River Rd	Marcy	NY	13403	315-768-1400		213
Mardel Inc 7727 SW 44th St *Web:* www.mardel.com	Oklahoma City	OK	73179	405-745-1300		685
Marden's 458 Kennedy Memorial Dr *Web:* www.mardenssurplus.com	Waterville	ME	04901	207-873-6112		791
Marden-Kane Inc 36 Maple Pl *Web:* www.mardenkane.com	Manhasset	NY	11030	516-365-3999		7
Mared Mechanical Contractors Corp 4230 W Douglas Ave *Web:* maredmechanical.com	Milwaukee	WI	53209	414-536-0411		189-10
Marek Bros Co 3701 Piney Woods *Web:* www.marekbros.com	Houston	TX	77018	713-681-9213	681-0446	189-9
Maren Engineering 111 W Taft Dr *TF:* 800-875-1038 ■ *Web:* marenengineering.com	South Holland	IL	60473	708-333-6250		261
Maren Group LLC 11th Fl 400 Madison Ave	New York	NY	10017	212-584-2340		70
Marena Studio 12W 23rd St *Web:* www.marenastudios.com	New York	NY	10010	212-243-3070		344
Marengo County 101 E Coats Ave. *Web:* www.marengocountyal.com	Linden	AL	36748	334-295-2200		338
Marenzana Group Inc 780 Third Ave	New York	NY	10017	212-735-0011		271
Mares America Corp 1 Selleck St *TF:* 800-874-3236 ■ *Web:* www.mares.com	Norwalk	CT	06855	203-855-0631		710
Marfield Corporate Stationery 1225 E Crosby Rd Ste B1 *Web:* www.marfield.com	Carrollton	TX	75006	972-245-9122		627
Marfood USA Inc 21655 Trolley Industrial Dr *Web:* marfoodusa.com	Taylor	MI	48180	313-292-4100		296-26

Name / Address	City	State	ZIP	Phone	Fax	Class
Margaret Chase Smith Policy Ctr University of Maine *TF:* 877-486-2364 ■ *Web:* www.umaine.edu	Orono	ME	04469	207-581-1648	581-1266	634
Margaret E Heggan Public Library 606 Delsea Dr *Web:* www.hegganlibrary.org	Sewell	NJ	08080	856-589-3334		434-3
Margaret Harwell Art Museum 421 N Main St *TF:* 800-793-0010 ■ *Web:* www.mham.org	Poplar Bluff	MO	63901	573-686-8002		520
Margaret Lewis Norrie State Park 9 Old Post Rd PO Box 308 *Web:* parks.ny.gov/parks/171/details.aspx	Staatsburg	NY	12580	845-889-4646	889-8321	565
Margaret Mary Community Hospital Inc 321 Mitchell Ave PO Box 226 *TF:* 800-562-5698 ■ *Web:* www.mmhealth.org	Batesville	IN	47006	812-934-6624	934-5373	374-3
Margaret Mitchell House 990 Peachtree St NE *TF:* 800-401-2407 ■ *Web:* atlantahistorycenter.com/mmh	Atlanta	GA	30309	404-249-7015		50-3
Margaret R Pardee Memorial Hospital 800 N Justice St *Web:* www.pardeehospital.org	Hendersonville	NC	28791	828-696-1000		374-3
Margaret Sanger Ctr International (MSCI) 26 Bleecker St *Web:* www.plannedparenthood.org	New York	NY	10012	212-965-7000	274-7299	48-6
Margaret Tietz Ctr for Nursing Care 164-11 Chapin Pkwy *Web:* www.margarettietz.org	Jamaica	NY	11432	718-298-7800		450
Margarita's 200 Griffin Rd Ste 1 *Web:* www.margs.com	Portsmouth	NH	03801	603-430-8905		671
Margaritas 390 Western Ave *Web:* www.margs.com	Augusta	ME	04330	207-622-7874		671
Margaritaville 500 Duval St *Web:* www.margaritavillekeywest.com	Key West	FL	33040	305-292-1435		671
Margate on Winnipesaukee, The 76 Lake St *Web:* www.themargate.com	Laconia	NH	03246	603-524-5210		669
Margaux Farm LLC 596 Moores Mill Rd PO Box 4220 *Web:* www.margauxfarm.com	Midway	KY	40347	859-846-4433	846-4486	368
Marge Carson Inc 9056 Garvey Ave *TF:* 800-318-9806 ■ *Web:* margecarson.com	Rosemead	CA	91770	626-571-1111		319-2
Marger Johnson & McCollom PC 210 S W Morrison St *Web:* techlaw.com	Portland	OR	97204	503-222-3613		428
Marglen Industries Inc 1748 WaRd Mtn Rd *Web:* www.marglen.us	Rome	GA	30161	706-295-5621		131
Margo Leavin Gallery 812 N Robertson Blvd *Web:* www.margoleavingallery.com	West Hollywood	CA	90069	310-273-0603	273-9131	42
Margolin Winer & Evens LLP 400 Garden City Plaza 5th Fl *Web:* www.mwellp.com	Garden City	NY	11530	516-747-2000	747-6707	2
Margolis Edelstein 170 S Independence Mall W The Curtis Ctr Ste 400E *Web:* www.margolisedelstein.com	Philadelphia	PA	19106	215-922-1100		428
Margot Cafe & Bar 1017 Woodland Ct *Web:* margotcafe.com	Nashville	TN	37206	615-227-4668		671
Marguerite Centre 700 Mackay St *Web:* www.margueritecentre.com	Pembroke	ON	K8A1G6	613-732-9925		673
Maria Collection, The 1048 N Pearl St *TF:* 800-707-7923 ■ *Web:* www.themariacollection.com	Bridgeton	NJ	08302	856-453-9523		410
Maria College 700 New Scotland Ave *Web:* mariacollege.edu	Albany	NY	12208	518-438-3111	453-1366	162
Maria Mitchell Assn Aquarium 4 Vestal St *Web:* mariamitchell.org	Nantucket	MA	02554	508-228-9198	228-1031	40
Maria Paonessa Moda 2000 1500 N Wells St 2	Chicago	IL	60610	312-994-6747		810
Maria Parham Medical Ctr 566 Ruin Creek Rd PO Box 59 *Web:* www.mariaparham.com	Henderson	NC	27536	252-438-4143		374-3
Maria's 337 Cumberland Ave *Web:* mariasrestaurant.com	Portland	ME	04101	207-772-9232		671
Maria's New Mexican Kitchen 555 W Cordova Rd *TF:* 800-523-5002 ■ *Web:* www.marias-santafe.com	Santa Fe	NM	87505	505-983-7929		671
Marian Community Hospital (MCH) 100 Lincoln Ave	Carbondale	PA	18407	570-281-1000		374-3
Marian Goodman Gallery 24 W 57th St *Web:* www.mariangoodman.com	New York	NY	10019	212-977-7160	581-5187	42
Marian Heath Greeting Cards Inc 9 Kendrick Rd *TF Sales:* 800-688-9998 ■ *Web:* www.marianheath.com	Wareham	MA	02571	508-291-0766	291-2976	130
Marian Koshland Science Museum 6th & E Sts NW *TF:* 888-567-4526 ■ *Web:* www.koshland-science-museum.org	Washington	DC	20001	202-334-1201	334-1548	520
Marian Medical Ctr 1400 E Church St *Web:* www.marianmedicalcenter.org	Santa Maria	CA	93454	805-739-3000		374-3
Marian University 3200 Cold Spring Rd **Fax:* Admissions ■ *TF Admissions:* 800-772-7264 ■ *Web:* www.marian.edu	Indianapolis	IN	46222	317-955-6038	955-6401*	166
Marian University 45 S National Ave *TF:* 800-262-7426 ■ *Web:* www.marianuniversity.edu	Fond du Lac	WI	54935	800-262-7426		166
Marianapolis Preparatory School 26 Chase Rd PO Box 304 *Web:* www.marianapolis.org	Thompson	CT	06277	860-923-9565	923-3730	622
Mariani & Reck LLC 83 Broad St *Web:* www.marianireck.com	New London	CT	06320	860-443-5023		428
Mariani Enterprises Inc 300 Rockland Rd *Web:* www.marianilandscape.com	Lake Bluff	IL	60044	847-234-2172		422
Mariani Nut Co 709 Dutton St *TF:* 800-680-1788 ■ *Web:* www.marianinut.com	Winters	CA	95694	530-662-3311	949-4042	11-1
Mariani Packing Company Inc 500 Crocker Dr *TF:* 800-231-1287 ■ *Web:* www.mariani.com	Vacaville	CA	95688	707-452-2800	452-2973	11-1
Marianjoy Rehabilitation Hospital 26 W 171 Roosevelt Rd *TF:* 800-462-2366 ■ *Web:* www.marianjoy.org	Wheaton	IL	60187	630-462-4000		374-6
Marianna Industries Inc 11222 "I" St *TF:* 800-228-9060 ■ *Web:* www.mariannaind.com	Omaha	NE	68137	402-593-0211		231
Mariano's Mexican Cuisine 2614 Majesty Dr *Web:* laharanch.com	Arlington	TX	76011	817-640-5118		671
Marianopolis College 4873 Av Westmount *Web:* www.marianopolis.edu	Westmount	QC	H3Y1X9	514-931-8792		166
Marias River Electric Co-op Inc PO Box 729 *Web:* www.mariasriverec.com	Shelby	MT	59474	406-434-5575		245
Maricich Brand Communications 18201 McDurmott W Ste A *Web:* www.maricich.com	Irvine	CA	92614	949-223-6455		4
Marick Group, The 9100 Rexis Ave Ste 100 *Web:* www.marickgroup.com	Perry Hall	MD	21128	410-258-2390	529-0065	809
Maricopa County 301 W Jefferson St 10th Fl *TF:* 800-370-4879 ■ *Web:* www.maricopa.gov	Phoenix	AZ	85003	602-506-3415	506-6402	338
Maricopa County Library District 2700 N Central Ave Ste 700 *TF:* 800-275-8777 ■ *Web:* www.mcldaz.org	Phoenix	AZ	85004	602-652-3000		434-3
Maricopa Medical Ctr 2601 E Roosevelt St *TF:* 866-749-2876 ■ *Web:* www.mihs.org	Phoenix	AZ	85008	602-344-5011	344-0719	374-3
Marie Callender Restaurant & Bakery 27101 Puerta Real Ste 200 *TF:* 800-776-7437 ■ *Web:* mariecallenders.com	Mission Viejo	CA	92691	800-776-7437		670
Marie Claire Magazine 300 W 57th St 34th Fl *TF:* 800-777-3287 ■ *Web:* www.marieclaire.com	New York	NY	10019	515-282-1607		457-11
Marie Joseph Spiritual Ctr 10 Evans Rd *Web:* www.mariejosephspiritual.org	Biddeford	ME	04005	207-284-5671	286-1371	673
Marie Livingston's Steakhouse & Saloon 2705 Apalachee Pkwy *Web:* marielivingstonsteakhouse.com	Tallahassee	FL	32301	850-562-2525		671
Marie Selby Botanical Gardens 811 S Palm Ave *Web:* www.selby.org	Sarasota	FL	34236	941-366-5731	366-9807	97
Maries County 211 Fourth St *Web:* mariesco.org	Vienna	MO	65582	573-422-3338		338
Marietta Area Chamber of Commerce 100 Front St Ste 200 *Web:* www.mariettachamber.com	Marietta	OH	45750	740-373-5176	373-7808	139
Marietta College 215 Fifth St **Fax:* Admissions ■ *TF Admissions:* 800-331-7896 ■ *Web:* www.marietta.edu	Marietta	OH	45750	740-376-4000	376-8888*	166
Marietta Conference Ctr & Resort 500 Powder Springs St **Fax Area Code:* 678 ■ *TF:* 888-685-2500 ■ *Web:* www3.hilton.com/en/index.html	Marietta	GA	30064	770-427-2500	819-3224*	377
Marietta Daily Journal 580 Fairground St *Web:* www.mdjonline.com	Marietta	GA	30060	770-428-9411	428-7945	532-2
Marietta Drapery & Window Coverings Company Inc 22 Trammel St PO Box 569 **Fax:* Mktg ■ *TF:* 800-241-7974 ■ *Web:* www.mariettadrapery.com	Marietta	GA	30064	800-241-7974	824-9456*	746
Marietta Hospitality 37 Huntington St **Fax:* Cust Svc ■ *TF:* 800-950-7772 ■ *Web:* www.mariettahospitality.com	Cortland	NY	13045	607-753-6746	756-0658*	9
Marietta Memorial Hospital 401 Matthew St *TF:* 800-523-3977 ■ *Web:* mhsystem.org	Marietta	OH	45750	740-374-1400	374-1787	374-3
Marietta National Cemetery 500 Washington Ave **Fax Area Code:* 770 ■ *TF:* 866-236-8159 ■ *Web:* www.cem.va.gov	Marietta	GA	30060	866-236-8159	479-9311*	136
Marigold Cafe 4605 Centennial Blvd *Web:* marigoldcoloradosprings.com	Colorado Springs	CO	80919	719-599-4776		671
Marijuana Anonymous World Services (MAWS) PO Box 7807 *TF:* 800-766-6779 ■ *Web:* www.marijuana-anonymous.org	Torrance	CA	90504	800-766-6779		48-21
Marilyn Model Agency 32 Un Sq E PH *Web:* www.marilynagency.com	New York	NY	10003	212-260-6500		506
Marimba One Inc 901 O St Ste D *TF:* 888-990-6663 ■ *Web:* www.marimbaone.com	Arcata	CA	95521	707-822-9570		527
Marimon Business Systems Inc 7300 N Gessner *Web:* www.marimoninc.com	Houston	TX	77040	713-856-2000		535
Marin Academy 1600 Mission Ave *Web:* www.ma.org	San Rafael	CA	94901	415-453-4550		685
Marin Charter & Tours 8 Lovell Ave *Web:* www.marinairporter.com	San Rafael	CA	94901	415-256-8830	256-8839	107
Marin Christian Academy 1370 S Novato Blvd *Web:* visitmca.org	Novato	CA	94947	415-892-5713		148
Marin Community Foundation 5 Hamilton Landing Ste 200 *TF:* 800-273-6222 ■ *Web:* www.marincf.org	Novato	CA	94949	415-464-2500	464-2555	303
Marin Convention & Visitors Bureau 1 Mitchell Blvd Ste B *TF:* 866-925-2060 ■ *Web:* www.visitmarin.org	San Rafael	CA	94903	415-925-2060	925-2063	206
Marin County 3501 Civic Ctr Dr *TF:* 800-648-0600 ■ *Web:* www.marincounty.org	San Rafael	CA	94903	415-499-6450		338
Marin County Free Library 3501 Civic Ctr Dr Ste 414 *Web:* marinlibrary.org	San Rafael	CA	94903	415-499-3220		434-3
Marin General Hospital 250 Bon Air Rd *TF:* 888-996-9644 ■ *Web:* www.maringeneral.org	Greenbrae	CA	94904	415-925-7000	925-7317	374-3
Marin Independent Journal 150 Alameda Del Prado *TF:* 877-229-8655 ■ *Web:* www.marinij.com	Novato	CA	94949	415-883-8600	883-5458	532-2

Name / Address	City	State	ZIP	Phone	Fax	Class
Marin Investments Ltd						
700 W Georgia St Ste 3010	Vancouver	BC	V7Y1B6	604-687-1450		360-3
Web: www.marin.ca						
Marin Mountain Bikes Inc						
265 Bel Marin Keys Blvd	Novato	CA	94949	415-382-6000		711
TF: 800-876-9840 ■ *Web:* www.marinbikes.com						
Marin Suites Hotel LLC						
45 Tamal Vista Blvd	Corte Madera	CA	94925	415-924-3608		378
TF: 800-362-3372 ■ *Web:* www.marinsuites.com						
Marin Symphony						
4340 Redwood Hwy Ste 409C	San Rafael	CA	94903	415-479-8100		573-3
Web: www.marinsymphony.org						
Marina Care Center						
5240 Sepulveda Blvd	Culver City	CA	90230	310-391-7266		371
Web: www.marinacare.com						
Marina Chamber of Commerce PO Box 425	Marina	CA	93933	831-384-0155		139
Web: www.marinachamber.com						
Marina Civic Ctr 8 Harrison Ave	Panama City	FL	32401	850-763-4696		572
TF: 800-622-5025 ■ *Web:* www.marinaciviccenter.com						
Marina Deck 306 Dorchester St	Ocean City	MD	21842	410-289-4411		671
Web: www.marinadeckrestaurant.com						
Marina Del Mar Resort & Marina						
527 Caribbean Dr	Key Largo	FL	33037	305-451-4107	451-1891	379
Web: www.marinadelmarkeylargo.com						
Marina Del Rey Hospital						
4650 Lincoln Blvd	Marina del Rey	CA	90292	310-823-8911		374-3
TF: 888-600-5600 ■ *Web:* www.marinahospital.com						
Marina del Rey Hotel						
13534 Bali Way	Marina Del Rey	CA	90292	310-301-1000		707
Web: www.marinadelreyhotel.com						
Marina Graphic Ctr 12901 Cerise Ave	Hawthorne	CA	90250	310-970-1777		627
TF: 800-974-5777 ■ *Web:* marinagraphics.com						
Marina Inn at Grande Dunes						
8121 Amalfi Pl	Myrtle Beach	SC	29572	843-913-1333	913-1334	379
TF Resv: 877-913-1333 ■ *Web:* www.marinainnatgrandedunes.com						
Marina State Beach						
c/o Monterey District 2211 Garden Rd	Monterey	CA	93940	831-649-2836	647-6239	565
Web: www.parks.ca.gov						
Marinco 2655 Napa Valley Corp Dr	Napa	CA	94558	707-226-9600		815
TF: 800-307-6702 ■ *Web:* www.marinco.com						
Marine 3280 Russell Rd	Quantico	VA	22134	800-627-4632		340-7
TF: 800-627-4632 ■ *Web:* www.marines.com						
Marine Bank of Champaign-Urbana						
2434 Village Green Pl	Champaign	IL	61822	217-239-0100		70
Web: www.ibankmarine.com						
Marine Biological Laboratory (MBL)						
7 MBL St	Woods Hole	MA	02543	508-548-3705	540-6902	668
TF: 800-222-1222 ■ *Web:* www.mbl.edu						
Marine Corps Air Station Beaufort						
PO Box 55001	Beaufort	SC	29904	843-228-7121	228-6005	497-3
Web: www.beaufort.marines.mil						
Marine Corps Air Station Yuma						
Shaw Ave Bldg 980	Yuma	AZ	85369	928-269-2252	269-3282	497-3
Web: www.mcasyuma.marines.mil/Contact-Us						
Marine Corps Assn (MCA) PO Box 1775	Quantico	VA	22134	703-640-6161	640-0823	48-19
TF: 800-336-0291 ■ *Web:* www.mca-marines.org						
Marine Corps Base Hawaii						
PO Box 63002	Kaneohe Bay	HI	96863	808-257-8457	257-1259	497-3
Web: www.mcbhawaii.marines.mil						
Marine Corps Base Quantico						
3250 Catlin Ave	Quantico	VA	22134	703-784-2121		497-3
TF: 800-268-3710 ■ *Web:* www.quantico.marines.mil						
Marine Corps Community Services						
3044 Catlin Ave	Quantico	VA	22134	703-784-3809		229
Web: www.usmc-mccs.org						
Marine Corps Recruit Depot San Diego						
1600 Henderson Ave	San Diego	CA	92145	619-524-1011		497-3
Web: www.marines.mil						
Marine Corps Reserve Association						
8626 Lee Hwy Ste 205	Fairfax	VA	22031	703-207-0626		138
TF: 800-717-0060 ■ *Web:* www.nationalmcla.org						
Marine Depot 14271 Corporate Dr	Garden Grove	CA	92843	800-566-3474		770
TF: 800-566-3474 ■ *Web:* www.marinedepot.com						
Marine Engineers' Beneficial Assn (MEBA)						
444 N Capitol St NW Ste 800	Washington	DC	20001	202-638-5355	638-5369	414
Web: mebaunion.org						
Marine Environmental Research Institute (MERI)						
55 Main St PO Box 1652	Blue Hill	ME	04614	207-374-2135		668
Web: www.meriresearch.org						
Marine Environmental Services Inc						
3301 Ballard Ave	Portsmouth	VA	23701	757-465-3993		698
Web: www.mesincorporated.com						
Marine Exhaust Systems of Alabama Inc						
757 Nichols Ave	Fairhope	AL	36532	251-928-1234	928-1234	454
TF: 800-237-3160 ■ *Web:* www.mesamarine.com						
Marine Hydraulics International Inc (MHI)						
543 E Indian River Rd	Norfolk	VA	23523	757-545-6400	545-8169	698
Web: www.mhi-shiprepair.com						
Marine Mammal Commission						
4340 E W Hwy Ste 700	Bethesda	MD	20814	301-504-0087	504-0099	340-20
Web: www.mmc.gov						
Marine Mammal Stranding Ctr						
3625 Brigantine Blvd	Brigantine	NJ	08203	609-266-0538		520
Web: www.mmsc.org						
Marine Military Academy Air Wing Inc						
320 Iwo Jima Blvd	Harlingen	TX	78550	956-423-6006		685
Web: www.mma-tx.org						
Marine Petroleum Trust						
2911 Turtle Creek Blvd Ste 850	Dallas	TX	75219	800-758-4672		675
NASDAQ: MARPS ■ *TF:* 800-758-4672 ■ *Web:* www.marps-marine.com						
Marine Power Holding LLC						
17506 Marine Power Industrial Pk	Ponchatoula	LA	70454	985-386-2081		262
Web: www.marinepowerusa.com						
Marine Room, The 2000 Spindrift Dr	La Jolla	CA	92037	858-459-7222	551-4673	671
TF: 866-644-2351 ■ *Web:* www.marineroom.com						
Marine Safety Corp						
5050 Industrial Rd PO Box 465	Wall	NJ	07719	732-938-5668	938-4839	90
Web: marinesafetycorporation.com						
Marine Science Institute						
University of California	Santa Barbara	CA	93106	805-893-4093	893-8062	668
Web: www.msi.ucsb.edu						
Marine Surf Waikiki Hotel						
364 Seaside Ave	Honolulu	HI	96815	808-779-3261		379
Web: www.waikikiview.com						
Marine Systems Corp						
70 Fargo St Seaport Ctr	Boston	MA	02210	617-542-3345	542-2461	261
Web: www.mscorp.net						
Marine Systems Inc 116 Capital Blvd	Houma	LA	70360	985-223-7100		698
Web: www.kirbycorp.com						
Marine Toys for Tots Foundation						
18251 Quantico Gateway Dr	Triangle	VA	22172	703-640-9433	649-2054	48-5
Web: www.toysfortots.org						
Marineland 7657 Portage Rd	Niagara Falls	ON	L2E6X8	905-356-9565	374-6652	32
Web: www.marinelandcanada.com						
Marineland of Florida						
9600 Ocean Shore Blvd	Saint Augustine	FL	32080	904-471-1111	471-1111	40
TF: 877-933-3402 ■ *Web:* www.marineland.net						
Marinelife Ctr of Juno Beach						
14200 US Hwy 1 Loggerhead Pk	Juno Beach	FL	33408	561-627-8280	627-8305	40
TF: 800-843-5451 ■ *Web:* www.marinelife.org						
Mariner Partners						
1 Germain St 18th Fl	Saint John	NB	E2L4V1	506-642-9000		463
Web: www.marinerpartners.com						
Mariner Wealth Advisors						
1 Giralda Farms Ste 130	Madison	NJ	07940	800-364-2468		194
TF: 800-364-2468 ■ *Web:* www.marinerwealthadvisors.com						
Mariner's Inn, The						
5339 Lighthouse Bay Dr	Madison	WI	53704	608-246-3120		671
Web: marinersmadison.com						
Mariner's Point Resort of Cape Cod						
425 Grand Ave	Falmouth	MA	02540	508-457-0300		379
Web: www.marinerspointresort.com						
Mariners' Museum 100 Museum Dr	Newport News	VA	23606	757-596-2222		520
TF: 800-581-7245 ■ *Web:* marinersmuseum.org						
Marines Memorial Theatre						
609 Sutter St	San Francisco	CA	94102	415-447-0188		572
Web: marinesmemorialtheatre.com						
Marinette County 1926 Hall Ave	Marinette	WI	54143	715-732-7406	732-7532	338
TF: 800-236-6681 ■ *Web:* www.marinettecounty.com						
Marinette Marine Corp 1600 Ely St	Marinette	WI	54143	715-735-9341	735-3516*	698
**Fax:* Cust Svc ■ *Web:* marinettemarine.com						
Marinette School District						
2139 Pierce Ave	Marinette	WI	54143	715-735-1400		685
Web: www.marinette.k12.wi.us						
Marino Tom (Rep R - PA)						
2242 Rayburn HOB	Washington	DC	20515	202-225-3731	225-9594	342-2
Web: marino.house.gov						
Marino/Ware Industries Inc						
400 Metuchen Rd	South Plainfield	NJ	07080	908-757-9000		190
Web: www.marinoware.com						
Marinsa Miami Corp 12250 SW 133 Ct	Miami	FL	33186	305-252-0118		311
Web: marinsa.com						
Marinus Pharmaceuticals Inc						
21 Business Park Dr	Branford	CT	06405	203-315-0566		668
Web: www.marinuspharma.com						
Mario Industries of Virginia Inc						
2490 Patterson Ave SW PO Box 3190	Roanoke	VA	24016	540-342-1111	345-4813	439
TF: 800-458-1244 ■ *Web:* www.marioindustries.com						
Mario Pastega Guest House						
3505 NW Samaritan Dr	Corvallis	OR	97330	541-768-4650		372
TF: 800-863-5241 ■ *Web:* www.samhealth.org						
Mario's 4222 Second Ave	Detroit	MI	48201	313-832-1616		671
Web: www.mariosdetroit.com						
Mario's Italian Restaurant						
1298 Main St	Dubuque	IA	52001	563-556-9424		671
Web: mariosofdubuque.com						
Mario's Mexican Food & Cantina						
15964 Springdale St	Huntington Beach	CA	92649	714-894-2896		671
Web: mariosmexicanfoodcantina.com						
Mario's Peruvian 5786 Melrose Ave	Los Angeles	CA	90038	323-466-4181		671
Mario's Place 3646 Mission Inn Ave	Riverside	CA	92501	951-684-7755		671
TF: 800-359-2464 ■ *Web:* www.mariosplace.com						
Mario's Via Abruzzi 2740 Monroe Ave	Rochester	NY	14618	585-271-1111		671
Web: www.mariosit.com						
Marion Area Chamber of Commerce						
267 W Ctr St Ste 100	Marion	OH	43302	740-382-2181	387-7722	139
TF: 800-371-6688 ■ *Web:* www.marionareachamber.org						
Marion Body Works Inc						
211 W Ramsdell St PO Box 500	Marion	WI	54950	715-754-5261	754-5776	516
Web: www.marionbody.com						
Marion Ceramics Inc PO Box 1134	Marion	SC	29571	843-423-1311	423-1515	150
TF: 800-845-4010 ■ *Web:* www.marionceramics.com						
Marion Chamber of Commerce						
1225 Sixth Ave Ste 100	Marion	IA	52302	319-377-6316		139
Web: www.cedarrapids.org						
Marion Correctional Institution						
PO Box 57	Marion	OH	43302	740-382-5781	382-0595	213
TF: 800-237-3454 ■ *Web:* ohio.gov						
Marion County 250 Broad St	Columbia	MS	39429	601-731-5972		338
Marion County 200 Jackson St	Fairmont	WV	26554	304-367-5410	366-6532	338
Web: www.marioncountywv.com						
Marion County 132 Military St Ste 204	Hamilton	AL	35570	205-921-7451		338
Web: marioncountyalabama.org						
Marion County						
200 E Washington St Ste W122	Indianapolis	IN	46204	317-327-4740		338
TF: 800-913-6050 ■ *Web:* www.indy.gov						
Marion County						
1 Courthouse Sq PO Box 789	Jasper	TN	37347	423-942-2552		338
Web: www.marioncountytn.net						
Marion County 102 W Austin St	Jefferson	TX	75657	903-665-3971		338
Web: www.co.marion.tx.us						
Marion County 214 E Main St	Knoxville	IA	50138	641-828-2257		338
Web: www.redrockarea.com						
Marion County						
223 N Spalding Ave Ste 201	Lebanon	KY	40033	270-692-2651	692-9487	338
TF: 800-843-9214 ■ *Web:* www.marioncounty.ky.gov						

Phone | Fax | Class

Marion County 200 S Third St Ste 104 .... Marion KS 66861 620-382-2185 382-3420 338
TF: 800-305-8851 ■ Web: www.marioncoks.net
Marion County 100 N Main St. .... Marion OH 43302 740-223-4270 338
Web: www.co.marion.oh.us
Marion County 103 W Ct St. .... Marion SC 29571 843-423-8225 423-8306 338
Web: www.marionsc.org
Marion County 100 S Main St Ste 107 .... Palmyra MO 63461 573-769-2549 769-4312 338
Marion County 118 Cross Creek Blvd. .... Salem IL 62881 618-548-3878 548-3866 338
TF: 800-362-7257 ■ Web: www.marioncountyhealthdept.org
Marion County
555 Court St NE Ste 5232 PO Box 14500. .... Salem OR 97301 503-588-5225 373-4408 338
Web: www.co.marion.or.us
Marion County Board of Education Inc
200 Gaston Ave. .... Fairmont WV 26554 304-367-2100 685
Web: www.marionboe.com
Marion County Chamber of Commerce
110 Adams St. .... Fairmont WV 26554 304-363-0442 363-0480 139
Web: www.marionchamber.com
Marion County Development Partnership (MCDP)
412 Courthouse Sq PO Box 272. .... Columbia MS 39429 601-736-6385 736-6392 139
Web: www.mcdp.info
Marion County Historical Society Museum (MCHS)
260 12th St SE .... Salem OR 97301 503-364-2128 520
Web: www.marionhistory.org
Marion County International Raceway
2303 Richwood-LaRue Rd .... La Rue OH 43332 740-499-3666 499-2185 515
Web: www.mcir.com
Marion County Library System (MCL)
101 E Ct St. .... Marion SC 29571 843-423-8300 423-8302 434-3
Web: www.marioncountylibrary.org
Marion County Medical Ctr
2829 E Hwy 76 .... Mullins SC 29574 843-431-2000 374-3
TF: 800-499-5849 ■ Web: www.carolinashospitalmarion.com
Marion Ctr Area School District
PO Box 156 .... Marion Center PA 15759 724-397-5551 685
Web: www.mcasd.net
Marion General Hospital (MGH)
441 N Wabash Ave .... Marion IN 46952 765-660-6000 651-7351 374-3
Web: www.mgh.net
Marion General Hospital (MGH)
1000 McKinley Pk Dr .... Marion OH 43302 740-383-8400 374-3
Web: www.ohiohealth.com
Marion J Mohr Memorial Library
1 Memorial Ave. .... Johnston RI 02919 401-231-4980 231-4984 434-3
Web: www.mohrlibrary.org
Marion Military Institute
1101 Washington St .... Marion AL 36756 334-683-2322 162
TF: 800-664-1842 ■ Web: www.marionmilitary.edu
Marion National Cemetery
1700 E 38th St .... Marion IN 46953 765-674-0284 674-4521 136
Web: www.cem.va.gov
Marion Plywood Corp
222 S Parkview Ave PO Box 497 .... Marion WI 54950 715-754-5231 754-2582 613
Web: www.marionplywood.com
Marion Public Library 1095 Sixth Ave. .... Marion IA 52302 319-377-3412 377-0113 434-3
TF: 800-367-3388 ■ Web: www.marionpubliclibrary.org
Marion Regional Healthcare Systems
2829 E Hwy 76 .... Mullins SC 29574 843-464-0533 793
Web: www.marioncountyhfoundation.org
Marion Regional Juvenile Detention Ctr
3040 NW Tenth St. .... Ocala FL 34475 352-732-1450 412
Marion Star, The 163 E Center St. .... Marion OH 43302 740-387-0400 532-2
TF: 877-987-2782 ■ Web: www.marionstar.com
Marion Technical College
1467 Mt Vernon Ave. .... Marion OH 43302 740-389-4636 389-6136 800
TF: 800-772-1213 ■ Web: www.mtc.edu
Marion/Walthall Correctional Facility
503 S Main St. .... Columbia MS 39429 601-736-3621 736-4473 213
Marion-Grant County Chamber of Commerce
215 S Adams St .... Marion IN 46952 765-664-5107 668-5443 139
Web: www.marionchamber.org
Marion-Grant County Convention & Visitors Bureau
428 S Washington St Ste 261. .... Marion IN 46953 765-668-5435 668-5424 206
TF: 800-662-9474 ■ Web: www.showmegrantcounty.com
Mariplast North America Inc
365 Business Pkwy. .... Greer SC 29651 864-989-0560 989-0561 608
Web: www.mariplast.com
Mariposa 1450 Ala Moana Blvd .... Honolulu HI 96814 808-951-3420 671
Web: neimanmarcus.com
Mariposa County
5100 Bullion St PO Box 784. .... Mariposa CA 95338 209-966-3222 966-5147 338
TF: 800-549-6741 ■ Web: www.mariposacounty.org
Mariposa Horticultural Enterprises Inc
15529 Arrow Hwy .... Irwindale CA 91706 626-960-0196 422
Web: mariposa-ca.com
Maris West & Baker Inc
18 Northtown Dr. .... Jackson MS 39211 601-977-9200 4
Web: www.mwb.com
Mariscal Weeks Mcintyre & Friedlander Pa
2901 N Central Ave. .... Phoenix AZ 85012 602-285-5000 428
Web: www.dickinson-wright.com
Marisco Ltd 91-607 Malakole Rd. .... Kapolei HI 96707 808-682-1333 698
Web: www.marisco.net
Mariscos La Playa 537 W Cordova Rd. .... Santa Fe NM 87505 505-982-2790 671
Marisol 5834 High Point Rd .... Greensboro NC 27407 336-852-3303 671
Web: www.themarisol.com
Marist College 3399 N Rd. .... Poughkeepsie NY 12601 845-575-3000 575-3215 166
TF: 800-436-5483 ■ Web: www.marist.edu
Maritech Resources Inc
24955 I-45 N .... The Woodlands TX 77380 281-364-4343 536
Web: www.maritechresources.com
Maritime Administration (MARAD)
1200 New Jersey Ave SE. .... Washington DC 20590 202-366-5807 340-17
TF Hotline: 800-996-2723 ■ Web: www.marad.dot.gov
Div of Gulf Operations
500 Poydras St Ste 1223. .... New Orleans LA 70130 504-589-2000 589-6559 340-17
Web: www.marad.dot.gov
National Maritime Resource & Education Ctr (NMREC)
1200 New Jersey Ave SE .... Washington DC 20590 202-366-9595 340-17
Web: www.marad.dot.gov
US Merchant Marine Academy
300 Steamboat Rd .... Kings Point NY 11024 516-773-5387 773-5509 340-17
TF: 866-546-4778 ■ Web: www.usmma.edu
Maritime Administration Regional Offices
Great Lakes Region PO Box 1156 .... Chicago IL 60690 312-353-1032 353-1036 340-17
Web: www.marad.dot.gov
North Atlantic Region
1 Bowling Green Rm 418. .... New York NY 10004 212-668-3330 668-3382 340-17
Web: www.marad.dot.gov
Western Region
201 Mission St Ste 2200. .... San Francisco CA 94105 415-744-3125 744-2576 340-17
Web: marad.dot.gov
Maritime Aquarium at Norwalk
10 N Water St .... Norwalk CT 06854 203-852-0700 838-5416 40
TF: 800-200-2882 ■ Web: www.maritimeaquarium.org
Maritime Broadcasting System (MBS)
90 Lovett Lake Crt. .... Halifax NS B3S0H6 902-425-1225 423-2093 643
Web: www.mbsradio.com
Maritime Company For Navigation, The
249 Shipyard Blvd .... Wilmington NC 28412 910-343-8900 311
TF: 800-742-5877 ■ Web: themaritimecompany.com
Maritime Energy Inc
234 Pk St PO Box 485 .... Rockland ME 04841 207-594-4487 579
TF: 800-333-4489 ■ Web: www.maritimeenergy.com
Maritime Helicopters 3520 Faa Rd .... Homer AK 99603 907-235-7771 313
TF: 800-230-3843 ■ Web: www.maritimehelicopters.com
Maritime Museum of San Diego
1492 N Harbor Dr. .... San Diego CA 92101 619-234-9153 234-8345 520
Web: www.sdmaritime.org
Maritime Museum of the Atlantic
1675 Lower Water St. .... Halifax NS B3J1S3 902-424-7490 424-0612 520
Maritime Paper Products Ltd
25 Borden Ave PO Box 668 .... Dartmouth NS B2Y3Y9 902-468-5353 554
TF: 800-565-5353 ■ Web: www.maritimepaper.com
Maritime Travel Inc
202-2000 Barrington St Cogswell Tower .... Halifax NS B3J3K1 902-420-1554 775
TF: 800-593-3334 ■ Web: www.maritimetravel.ca
Maritz Canada Inc 6900 Maritz Dr .... Mississauga ON L5W1L8 905-696-9400 466
TF: 844-277-2663 ■ Web: aworldmoreloyal.com
Maritz Inc 1375 N Hwy Dr .... Fenton MO 63099 636-827-4000 466
Web: www.maritz.com
MaritzCX Research LLC 1355 N Hwy Dr .... Fenton MO 63099 385-695-2940 466
TF: 877-462-7489 ■ Web: www.maritzcx.com
Mar-Jac Poultry Inc
1020 Aviation Blvd PO Box 1017 .... Gainesville GA 30501 770-531-5007 619
TF: 800-226-0561 ■ Web: www.marjacpoultry.com
MarJam Supply Co Inc 20 Rewe St .... Brooklyn NY 11211 718-388-6465 989-0029 364
TF All: 800-848-8407 ■ Web: www.marjam.com
Marjon Specialty Foods Inc
3508 Sydney Rd .... Plant City FL 33566 813-752-3482 345
Web: www.marjonspecialtyfoods.com
Marjorie Barrick Museum
4505 S Maryland Pkwy. .... Las Vegas NV 89154 702-895-3381 895-5737 520
TF: 877-895-0334 ■ Web: www.unlv.edu/barrickmuseum
Marjorie Kinnan Rawlings Historic State Park
18700 S County Rd 325 .... Cross Creek FL 32640 352-466-3672 565
Web: www.floridastateparks.org
Marjorie McNeely Conservatory at Como Park
1225 Estabrook Dr .... Saint Paul MN 55103 651-487-8201 97
Web: www.comozooconservatory.org
Mark Andy Inc
18081 Chesterfield Airport Rd .... Chesterfield MO 63005 636-532-4433 532-4701* 629
*Fax: Cust Svc ■ TF: 800-700-6275 ■ Web: www.markandy.com
Mark Anthony Brewing Inc
300 W Hubbard St Ste 301. .... Chicago IL 60654 312-202-1712 77
Web: www.mabrewing.com
Mark Architectural Lighting
3 Kilmer Rd. .... Edison NJ 08817 732-985-2600 985-8441 439
Web: www.marklighting.com
Mark Asset Management Corp
667 Madison Ave 9th Fl .... New York NY 10065 212-372-2500 401
Web: markasset.com
Mark Bailey & Co Ltd
1495 Ridgeview Dr Ste 200 .... Reno NV 89519 775-332-4200 2
Web: www.markbaileyco.com
Mark C Pope Associates
2215 Birmingham Dr .... Albany GA 31705 229-435-2473 770
TF: 800-237-8274 ■ Web: www.markcpope.com
Mark Cerrone Inc
2368 Maryland Ave. .... Niagara Falls NY 14305 716-282-5244 186
TF: 855-250-7739 ■ Web: markcerrone.com
Mark Chevrolet Inc 33200 Michigan Ave. .... Wayne MI 48184 734-629-4964 57
Web: www.markchevrolet.com
Mark Harris Plumbing Company Inc
1830 Gillespie Way Ste 104 .... El Cajon CA 92020 619-596-9470 610
Web: mhp-co.com
Mark Hershey Farms Inc
479 Horseshoe Pk .... Lebanon PA 17042 717-867-4624 867-4313 447
TF: 888-801-3301 ■ Web: www.markhersheyfarms.com
Mark IV Capital Inc
100 Bayview Cir Ste 4500. .... Newport Beach CA 92660 949-509-1444 41
TF: 800-868-8482 ■ Web: www.markiv.com
Mark Line Industries Inc
51687 County Rd 133 PO Box 277. .... Bristol IN 46507 574-825-5851 825-9139 505
Web: www.marklineindustries.com
Mark Morris Dance Group
3 Lafayette Ave .... Brooklyn NY 11217 718-624-8400 624-8900 573-1
TF: 800-957-1046 ■ Web: www.markmorrisdancegroup.org
Mar-K Quality Parts LLC
6625 W Wilshire Blvd. .... Oklahoma City OK 73132 405-721-7945 54
Web: mar-k.com
Mark Sand & Gravel Co
525 Kennedy Pk Rd PO Box 458. .... Fergus Falls MN 56537 218-736-7523 736-2647 503-4
TF: 800-427-8316 ■ Web: www.marksandgravel.com

Company / Address	City	State	ZIP	Phone	Fax	Class
Mark Scott Construction 2835 Contra Costa Blvd; *Web:* www.msconstruction.com	Pleasant Hill	CA	94523	925-944-0502		378
Mark Siegel Associates Inc 236 Auburndale Ave; *Web:* msasolutions.net	Newton	MA	02466	617-527-0519		393
Mark Spencer Hotel 409 SW 11th Ave; *TF:* 800-548-3934 ■ *Web:* www.markspencer.com	Portland	OR	97205	503-224-3293	223-7848	379
Mark Steel Corp 1230 West 200 South; *Web:* www.marksteel.net	Salt Lake City	UT	84104	801-521-0670	303-2040	480
Mark Thomas & Company Inc 2290 N First St Ste 304; *Web:* www.markthomas.com	San Jose	CA	95131	408-453-5373		261
Mark Thomas Motors Inc 2315 Santiam Hwy; *Web:* www.markthomasmotors.com	Albany	OR	97321	541-967-9105		57
Mark Travel Corp 8907 N Port Washington Rd; *Web:* www.marktravel.com	Milwaukee	WI	53217	414-228-7472		771
Mark Trece Inc 2001 Stockton Rd; *Web:* www.marktrece.com	Joppa	MD	21085	410-879-0060	879-3438	781
Mark Twain Birthplace State Historic Site 37352 Shrine Rd; *Web:* mostateparks.com	Florida	MO	65283	573-565-3449		565
Mark Twain Hotel 225 NE Adams St; *TF:* 866-325-6351 ■ *Web:* www.marktwainhotel.com	Peoria	IL	61602	309-676-3600	636-6118	379
Mark Twain House & Museum 351 Farmington Ave; *Web:* www.marktwainhouse.org	Hartford	CT	06105	860-247-0998		520
Mark Twain State Park 20057 State Pk Rd; *Web:* www.mostateparks.com	Stoutsville	MO	65283	573-565-3440		565
Mark Twain State Park & Soaring Eagles Golf Course 201 Middle Rd; *Web:* parks.ny.gov/golf-courses/3/details.aspx	Horseheads	NY	14845	607-739-0034		565
Mark Vii Equipment 5981 Tennyson St; *Web:* www.markvii.net	Arvada	CO	80003	303-423-4910		427
Mark Young Construction Inc 7200 Miller Pl; *Web:* www.markyoungconstruction.com	Frederick	CO	80504	303-776-1449	776-1729	685
Mark's Plumbing Parts 3312 Ramona Dr; *TF:* 800-772-2347 ■ *Web:* www.markspp.com	Fort Worth	TX	76116	817-731-6211		612
Mark's Work Warehouse 1035 64th Ave SE Ste 30; *TF:* 800-663-6275 ■ *Web:* marks.com	Calgary	AB	T2H2J7	403-255-9220	255-6005	157-5
Mark/Space Softworks 1999 S Bascom Ave Ste 325; *Web:* www.markspace.com	Campbell	CA	95008	408-293-7299	293-7298	178-7
Mark-10 Corp 11 Dixon Ave; *Web:* www.mark-10.com	Copiague	NY	11726	631-842-9200		201
Markal Finishing Corp 400 Bostwick Ave; *Web:* markalfinishing.com	Bridgeport	CT	06605	203-384-8219	336-1231	555
Mark-Costello Co, The 1145 E Dominguez St; *Web:* www.mark-costello.com	Carson	CA	90746	310-637-1851	762-2330	386
Mar-kee Consulting Group Inc 26248 Equity Dr; *Web:* www.markeegroup.com	Daphne	AL	36526	251-621-7010		196
Markel Corp 435 School Ln; **Fax:* Sales ■ *Web:* www.markelcorporation.com	Plymouth Meeting	PA	19462	610-272-8960	270-3138*	605-2
Markel Corp 4521 Highwoods Pkwy; *NYSE: MKL* ■ **Fax Area Code:* 855 ■ *TF:* 877-566-6323 ■ *Web:* markelinsurance.com	Glen Allen	VA	23060	800-431-1270	662-7535*	360-4
Markel Corp 222 S 15th St StE Ste 1500N; **Fax Area Code:* 866 ■ *TF:* 888-500-3344 ■ *Web:* www.markelinsurance.com/smallbusiness	Omaha	NE	68102	888-500-3344	338-2667*	391-4
Markel Specialty Commercial 4600 Cox Rd; **Fax Area Code:* 804 ■ *TF:* 800-416-4364 ■ *Web:* www.markelinsurance.com	Glen Allen	VA	23060	800-416-4364	527-7915*	391-4
Markem-Imaje Inc 5448 Timberlea Blvd; *TF:* 800-267-5108 ■ *Web:* www.markem-imaje.com	Mississauga	ON	L4W2T7	800-267-5108		358
Markent Personnel Inc 121 E Conant St; *Web:* www.markentpersonnel.com	Portage	WI	53901	608-742-7300		175
Marker 32 14549 Beach Blvd; *Web:* www.marker32.com	Jacksonville	FL	32250	904-223-1534		671
Marker Seven 701 Sutter St Fl 5; *TF:* 800-874-2458 ■ *Web:* www.markerseven.com	San Francisco	CA	94109	415-447-2841		396
Marker's Restaurant 153 Plaza II Harborside Financial Ctr; *Web:* www.markersrestaurant.com	Jersey City	NJ	07311	201-433-6275	433-0399	671
Market America Inc 1302 Pleasant Ridge Rd; *TF:* 866-420-1709 ■ *Web:* www.marketamerica.com	Greensboro	NC	27409	336-605-0040	605-0041	114
Market Basket Inc, The 813 Franklin Lakes Rd; *TF:* 800-472-5970 ■ *Web:* www.marketbasket.com	Franklin Lakes	NJ	07417	201-891-2000		345
Market Builder Inc, The 5135 E Ingram St; *TF:* 800-655-0441 ■ *Web:* www.themarketbuilder.com	Mesa	AZ	85205	480-707-0444		396
Market Connections 82 Patton Ave Ste 710; *Web:* www.mktconnections.com	Asheville	NC	28801	828-398-5250		195
Market Contractors 10250 NE Marx St; *TF:* 800-876-9133 ■ *Web:* www.marketcontractors.com	Portland	OR	97220	503-255-0977	262-4280	186
Market Creation Group LLC 201 Milwaukee St Ste 200; *Web:* www.marketcreationgroup.com	Denver	CO	80206	303-325-7423		196
Market Data Retrieval 6 Armstrong Rd; *TF:* 800-333-8802 ■ *Web:* www.schooldata.com	Shelton	CT	06484	203-926-4800	926-0784	5
Market Decisions LLC 75 Washington Ave Ste 206; *TF:* 800-293-1538 ■ *Web:* www.marketdecisions.com	Portland	ME	04101	207-767-6440		466
Market Force Information Inc 371 Centennial Pkwy Ste 210; *Web:* www.marketforce.com	Louisville	CO	80027	303-402-6920		196
Market Forge Industries Inc 35 Garvey St; **Fax Area Code:* 800 ■ *TF:* 866-698-3188 ■ *Web:* www.mfii.com	Everett	MA	02149	617-387-4100	227-2659*	298
Market Grocery Co 16 Forest Pkwy Bldg K; *Web:* www.marketgrocery.com	Forest Park	GA	30297	404-361-8620	361-3773	345
Market Hall Foods 5655 College Ave Ste 201; *Web:* www.rockridgemarkethall.com	Oakland	CA	94618	510-250-6000		345
Market Metrics Inc 53 State St Ste 6; *Web:* www.marketmetrics.com	Boston	MA	02109	617-376-0550		194
Market of Choice 1475 Siskiyou Blvd; *Web:* www.marketofchoice.com	Ashland	OR	97520	541-488-2773		297-8
Market One Builders Inc 926 J St; *Web:* www.m1b.com	Sacramento	CA	95814	916-928-7474		186
Market Pavilion Hotel 225 E Bay St; *TF:* 877-440-2250 ■ *Web:* www.marketpavilion.com	Charleston	SC	29401	843-723-0500	723-4320	379
Market Place, The 20 Wall St; *Web:* www.marketplace-restaurant.com	Asheville	NC	28801	828-252-4162	253-3120	671
Market Scan Information Systems Inc 811 Camarillo Springs Ste B; *TF:* 800-658-7226 ■ *Web:* www.marketscan.com	Camarillo	CA	93012	800-658-7226		178-10
Market Semiotics PO Box 1457; *Web:* www.marketsemiotics.com	Castleton	VT	05735	802-273-3800		297-8
Market Share Inc 2001 Tarob Ct; *Web:* www.getmarketshare.com	Milpitas	CA	95035	408-262-0677		8
Market Square Travel LLC 13756 83rd Way N; *Web:* www.tvlleaders.com	Maple Grove	MN	55369	763-231-8870		772
Market Strategies Inc 17430 College Pkwy; *TF:* 800-420-9366 ■ *Web:* www.marketstrategies.com	Livonia	MI	48152	734-542-7600	542-7620	466
Market Street Broiler 48 W Market St; *Web:* marketstreetgrill.com	Salt Lake City	UT	84101	801-322-4668	531-0730	671
Market Street Cafe 1 N Forest Beach Blvd; *Web:* www.marketstreetcafe.com	Hilton Head Island	SC	29928	843-686-4976		671
Market Street Consulting Group Inc 6965 El Camino Real Ste 105599; **Fax Area Code:* 888 ■ *Web:* www.marketstreetfs.com	Carlsbad	CA	92009	760-518-2310	621-5904*	691
Market Street Oyster Bar 54 W Market St; *Web:* marketstreetgrill.com	Salt Lake City	UT	84101	801-531-6044	531-0730	671
Market Street Partners LLC 477 Pacific Ave; *TF:* 800-368-1217 ■ *Web:* www.marketstreetpartners.com	San Francisco	CA	94133	415-445-3240		401
Market Street Trust Co 80 E Market St Ste 300; *Web:* www.marketstreettrust.com	Corning	NY	14830	607-962-6876		528
Market Track LLC 233 S Wacker Dr Ste 1801; *Web:* www.markettrack.com	Chicago	IL	60606	312-529-5102		466
Market Traders Institute 400 Colonial Ctr Pkwy Ste 350; *TF:* 800-866-7431 ■ *Web:* www.markettraders.com	Lake Mary	FL	32746	407-740-0900		528
Market Transport Ltd 110 N Marine Dr; *TF:* 800-547-0781 ■ *Web:* markettransport.com	Portland	OR	97217	503-283-2405		780
Market Velocity Inc 1305 Mall of Georgia Blvd Ste 190; *Web:* www.marketvelocity.com	Buford	GA	30519	770-325-6300		387
Market Wire Inc 100 N Sepulveda Blvd Ste 325; *TF General:* 800-774-9473 ■ *Web:* www.marketwired.com	El Segundo	CA	90245	310-765-3200	765-3297	530
Market, The 2628 S Glenstone Ave	Springfield	MO	65804	417-889-1145		460
MarketAxess Holdings Inc 299 Pk Ave 10th Fl; *NASDAQ: MKTX* ■ *Web:* www.marketaxess.com	New York	NY	10171	212-813-6000	813-6390	178-4
MarketBridge Inc 4350 East-West Hwy 6th Fl; *TF:* 888-468-6658 ■ *Web:* www.market-bridge.com	Bethesda	MD	20814	240-752-1800		195
MarketCounsel LLC 61 W Palisade Ave; *TF:* 800-441-1219 ■ *Web:* www.marketcounsel.com	Englewood	NJ	07631	201-705-1200		261
Marketech 7915 Westglen Dr; *Web:* www.marketechcorp.com	Houston	TX	77063	713-667-7778		463
Marketechs Exhibit Design 3425 Woodbridge Cir; *TF:* 800-648-8479 ■ *Web:* www.marketechs.com	York	PA	17406	717-764-2588		232
MarketFrames Group LLC 5331 SW Macadam Ave Ste 357; *Web:* www.marketframes.com	Portland	OR	97239	503-892-0160		45
Marketing & Planning Systems 501 Boylston St Ste 6101; *Web:* www.millwardbrownanalytics.com	Boston	MA	02116	617-598-5300		466
Marketing Analysts Inc (MAI) 2000 Sam Rittenberg Blvd Ste 3007; *Web:* www.mairesearch.com	Charlotte	SC	29407	704-405-2150		466
Marketing Directions 28005 Clemens Rd; *Web:* ideaswithapoint.com	Westlake	OH	44145	440-835-5550		4
Marketing Drive LLC 800 Connecticut Ave; *Web:* www.matchmg.com	Norwalk	CT	06854	203-857-6100		5
Marketing Evolution Inc 122 E 42nd St Ste 4500; *Web:* www.marketingevolution.com	New York	NY	10168	646-651-4300		809
Marketing General Inc 625 N Washington St Ste 450; *Web:* www.marketinggeneral.com	Alexandria	VA	22314	703-739-1000		195
Marketing Innovators International Inc 9701 W Higgins Rd; **Fax Area Code:* 847 ■ *TF:* 800-543-7373 ■ *Web:* www.marketinginnovators.com	Rosemont	IL	60018	800-543-7373	696-3194*	384
Marketing Library Services 143 Old Marlton Pk; *TF:* 800-300-9868 ■ *Web:* www.infotoday.com/mls	Medford	NJ	08055	609-654-6266	654-4309	531-10
Marketing Management Group Inc 561 Seventh Ave 17th Fl; *Web:* www.mmgus.com	New York	NY	10018	212-768-9660		195
Marketing News 311 S Wacker Dr Ste 5800; *TF:* 800-262-1150 ■ *Web:* www.ama.org	Chicago	IL	60606	312-542-9000	922-3763	457-5

Company / Address	City	State	ZIP	Phone	Fax	Class
Marketing Resource Group Inc (MRG) 225 S Washington Sq. *TF:* 800-928-2086 ■ *Web:* mrgmi.com	Lansing	MI	48933	517-372-4400	372-4045	5
Marketing Results 2900 W Horizon Ridge Pkwy Ste 200 *Web:* www.marketingresults.net	Henderson	NV	89052	702-361-3850		195
Marketing Support Inc 200 E Randolph Dr Ste 5000 *TF:* 800-908-5395 ■ *Web:* agencymsi.com	Chicago	IL	60601	312-565-0044	946-6100	4
Marketing Werks Inc 130 E Randolph St. *Web:* www.marketingwerks.com	Chicago	IL	60601	312-228-0800	228-0801	194
Marketing Workshop Inc 3725 Da Vinci Ct *Web:* www.mwshop.com	Norcross	GA	30092	770-449-6767		466
MarketingProfs LLC 419 N Larchmont Blvd #295 *TF:* 866-557-9625 ■ *Web:* www.marketingprofs.com	Los Angeles	CA	90004	866-557-9625		195
Marketingworks Inc 7000 Romaine St *Web:* www.marketingworksagency.com	Los Angeles	CA	90038	323-436-2000		224
Marketlab Inc 6850 Southbelt Dr **Fax Area Code:* 616 ■ *TF:* 866-237-3722 ■ *Web:* marketlab.com	Caledonia	MI	49316	866-237-3722	656-2475*	475
MarketLauncher Inc 1800 Pembroke Dr Ste 300. *TF:* 800-901-3803 ■ *Web:* www.marketlauncher.com	Orlando	FL	32810	800-901-3803		7
Marketleap Inc 359 Texas St	San Francisco	CA	94107	415-642-7779		631
MarketLeverage LLC 171 English Landing Dr Ste 215 *TF:* 888-653-8372 ■ *Web:* www.marketleverage.com	Kansas City	MO	64152	888-653-8372		5
Marketocracy Inc 1208 W Magnolia Ste 236 **Fax Area Code:* 888 ■ *TF:* 877-462-4180 ■ *Web:* www.marketocracy.com	Fort Worth	TX	76104	877-462-4180	777-6181*	401
Marketplace Mall 1 Miracle Mile Dr *Web:* www.themarketplacemall.com	Rochester	NY	14623	585-424-6220	427-2745	460
MarketPro Inc 53 Perimeter Ctr E Ste 200 *Web:* marketproinc.com	Atlanta	GA	30346	404-222-9992		260
MarketResearch.com 11200 Rockville Pk Ste 504 *Web:* www.marketresearch.com	Rockville	MD	20852	240-747-3000	747-3004	387
Marketri LLC 58 Charter Oak Dr. *Web:* www.marketri.com	Doylestown	PA	18901	215-489-5563		463
Marketsmith Inc 2 Wing Dr *TF:* 800-242-4349 ■ *Web:* www.marketsmithinc.com	Cedar Knolls	NJ	07927	973-889-0006		5
Marketstar Corp 2475 Washington Blvd. *Web:* www.marketstar.com	Ogden	UT	84401	801-393-1155	393-4115	721
MarketVision Research Inc 10300 Alliance Rd Ste 200 *TF:* 800-232-4250 ■ *Web:* www.mv-research.com	Cincinnati	OH	45242	513-791-3100	794-3500	466
Marketware Inc 7070 Union Park Ctr Ste 300 *TF:* 800-777-6368 ■ *Web:* marketware.com	Midvale	UT	84047	801-944-4230		225
Marketwell Inc 230 Park Ave Ste 1000. *Web:* marketwell.com	New York	NY	10169	646-435-5987		463
MarketWise Solutions Inc 4843 W 106th St. *Web:* www.marketwisesolutions.com	Zionsville	IN	46077	317-873-6976		195
Markey Edward J (Sen D - MA) 255 Dirksen Senate Office Bldg *Web:* www.markey.senate.gov	Washington	DC	20510	202-224-2742		342-2
Markey Machinery Company Inc 7266 Eigth Ave S *TF:* 800-637-3430 ■ *Web:* www.markeymachinery.com	Seattle	WA	98108	206-622-4697		770
Markham Board of Trade 80 F Centurian Dr Ste 206 *Web:* www.markhamboard.com	Markham	ON	L3R8C1	905-474-0730	474-0685	137
Markham Contracting Company Inc 22820 N 19th Ave. *Web:* www.markhamcontracting.com	Phoenix	AZ	85027	623-869-9100		189-5
Markham Regional Arboretum 1202 La Vista Ave. *Web:* www.markhamarboretum.org	Concord	CA	94521	925-681-2968		97
Markham Stouffville Hospital *Markham* 381 Church St PO Box 1800 *Web:* www.msh.on.ca	Markham	ON	L3P7P3	905-472-7000	472-7086	374-2
Markham Street Grill & Pub 11321 W Markham St Ste 6 *Web:* markhamstreetpub.com	Little Rock	AR	72211	501-224-2010		671
Markitects Inc 107 W Lancaster Ave Ste 203 *TF:* 800-695-4570 ■ *Web:* www.markitects.com	Wayne	PA	19087	610-687-2200		195
Markland Industries Inc 1111 E McFadden Ave *Web:* www.marklandindustries.com	Santa Ana	CA	92705	714-245-2850		481
Markley Enterprise Inc 800 Lillian St. *Web:* www.markleyent.com	Elkhart	IN	46516	574-295-4195		687
Markley Motors 3325 S College Ave *Web:* www.markleymotors.com	Fort Collins	CO	80525	970-226-2214		57
Markon Inc 400 S Maple Ave Ste 230 *TF:* 800-677-3693 ■ *Web:* www.markonsolutions.com	Falls Church	VA	22046	703-884-0030		463
Markon NSI PO Box 83 Ste 202 *Web:* www.educationaltechnology.com	Bellmore	NY	11710	516-221-8440		52
Markpoint Venture Partners 15770 Dallas Pkwy Ste 800 *Web:* www.markpt.com	Dallas	TX	75248	972-490-1976	490-1980	792
Markraft Cabinets Inc 2705 Castle Creek Ln *Web:* www.markraft.com	Wilmington	NC	28401	910-762-1986	762-1985	191-3
Marks Brothers Inc 12265 SE 282nd Ave *Web:* www.marks-brothers.com	Boring	OR	97009	503-663-0211		454
Marks Group P C 45 E city ave *TF:* 888-224-0649 ■ *Web:* www.marksgroup.net	Bala Cynwyd	PA	19004	888-224-0649		196
Marks Metal Technology Inc 10300 SE Jennifer St *Web:* www.marksmetal.com	Clackamas	OR	97015	503-656-0901		492
Marks Nelson Vohland & Campbel 7701 College Blvd Ste 150 *Web:* www.marksnelsoncpa.com	Overland Park	KS	66210	913-498-9000		41
Marks Paneth & Shron LLP 685 Third Ave *Web:* www.markspaneth.com	New York	NY	10017	212-503-8800	503-8800	2
Marks Toy Museum 915 Second St *Web:* www.marxtoymuseum.com	Moundsville	WV	26041	304-845-6022		520
Marksmen Energy Inc 368 Sunmills Dr SE *Web:* www.marksmenenergy.com/s/home.asp	Calgary	AB	T2X3H6	403-265-7270		539
Markstein Beverage Co 505 S Pacific St *Web:* www.marksteinbeer.com	San Marcos	CA	92078	760-744-9100		81-1
Marksville State Historic Site 837 ML King Dr *TF:* 888-253-8954 ■ *Web:* www.crt.state.la.us	Marksville	LA	71351	318-253-8954		565
MarkWest Energy Partners LP 1515 Arapahoe St Tower 1 Ste 1600 *NYSE: MWE* ■ *TF:* 800-730-8388 ■ *Web:* www.markwest.com	Denver	CO	80202	303-925-9200	290-8769	597
Markwins International Corp 22067 Ferrero Pkwy *Web:* www.markwins.com	Walnut	CA	91789	909-595-8898		214
Markwort Sporting Goods Co 1101 Research Blvd *TF:* 800-669-6626 ■ *Web:* markwort.com	St. Louis	MO	63132	314-652-8935		711
Marky's 1000 NW 159 Dr *Web:* www.markys.com	Miami Gardens	FL	33169	305-758-9288		297
Marla Junes Clothing Company Inc 207 SE Ct Ave. *Web:* marlajunes.com	Pendleton	OR	97801	541-276-0778		157-6
Marland Clutch 2032 VALLEYDALE Rd **Fax Area Code:* 877 ■ *TF:* 800-216-3515 ■ *Web:* www.marland.com	Birmingham	AL	35244	800-216-3515	216-3001*	620
Marlboro College 2582 S Rd PO Box A *TF:* 800-343-0049 ■ *Web:* www.marlboro.edu	Marlboro	VT	05344	802-257-4333	451-7555	166
Marlboro College Graduate Ctr PO Box A *TF:* 800-343-0049 ■ *Web:* www.marlboro.edu	Marlboro	VT	05344	802-258-9200		166
Marlboro County PO Box 419 *Web:* www.marlborocounty.sc.gov	Bennettsville	SC	29512	843-479-5600	479-5639	338
Marlboro County Library 203 Fayetteville Ave *Web:* www.edelmanpubliclibrary.org	Bennettsville	SC	29512	843-479-5630	479-5645	434-3
Marlboro Wire 2403 N 24th St *Web:* www.marlborowire.com	Quincy	IL	62305	217-224-7989	224-7990	73
Marlborough Hills Healthcare Ctr 121 Northboro Rd E	Marlborough	MA	01752	508-485-4040		450
Marlborough Public Library 35 W Main St *TF:* 800-592-2000 ■ *Web:* www.marlborough-ma.gov	Marlborough	MA	01752	508-624-6900	485-1494	434-3
Marlborough Public Schools (MPS) 17 Washington St *Web:* www.mps-edu.org	Marlborough	MA	01752	508-460-3509		186
Marlborough Regional Chamber of Commerce 11 Florence St *TF:* 800-508-2265 ■ *Web:* www.marlboroughchamber.org	Marlborough	MA	01752	508-485-7746	481-1819	139
Mar-Lee Cos 55 Marshall St *Web:* www.mar-leecompanies.com	Leominster	MA	01453	978-534-8305		604
Marlen International Inc 4780 NW 41st St Ste 100 **Fax Area Code:* 913 ■ *TF:* 800-862-7536 ■ *Web:* www.marlen.com	Riverside	MO	64150	800-862-7536	888-6440*	298
Marlex Pharmaceuticals 50 Mccullough Dr. *Web:* www.marlexpharm.com	New Castle	DE	19720	302-328-3355		583
Marley Engineered Products 470 Beauty Spot Rd E *TF:* 800-452-4179 ■ *Web:* www.marleymep.com	Bennettsville	SC	29512	843-479-4006	479-8912	37
Marley Precision Inc 455 Fritz Keiper Blvd	Battle Creek	MI	49037	269-963-7374		247
Marley's Island Grille 35 Office Pk Rd *Web:* marleyshhi.com	Hilton Head Island	SC	29928	843-686-5800		671
Marlin Alliance 3990 Old Town Ave Ste C-205 *TF:* 800-897-8049 ■ *Web:* themarlinalliance.com	San Diego	CA	92110	619-450-1717		463
Marlin Business Services Inc 300 Fellowship Rd *NASDAQ: MRLN* ■ *TF:* 888-479-9111 ■ *Web:* www.marlinfinance.com	Mount Laurel	NJ	08054	888-479-9111	479-1100	264-2
Marlin Central Monitoring LLC 3600 Commerce Pl Ste 201 *TF:* 866-383-0333	Kissimmee	FL	34742	866-383-0333	383-0334	693
Marlin Environmental Inc 3935 Commerce Dr *Web:* marlinenv.com	Saint Charles	IL	60174	630-444-1933		196
Marlin Firearms Co PO Box 1871 **Fax Area Code:* 336 ■ *TF Cust Svc:* 800-544-8892 ■ *Web:* www.marlinfirearms.com	Madison	NC	27025	800-544-8892	548-7801*	284
Marlin Network Inc 1200 E Woodhurst Bldg V *TF:* 800-261-1537 ■ *Web:* marlinco.com	Springfield	MO	65804	417-885-4500		7
Marlin Steel Wire Products 2640 Merchant Dr. *Web:* www.marlinwire.com	Baltimore	MD	21230	410-644-7456		490
Marlo Furniture Company Inc 3300 Marlo Ln *Web:* www.marlofurniture.com	Forestville	MD	20747	301-735-2000		321
Marlo Plastic Products Inc 289 SR- 33 Ste 12 *Web:* marloplasticproducts.com	Manalapan Township	NJ	07726	732-792-1988		196
Marlow Industries Inc 10451 Vista Pk Rd *TF:* 877-627-5691 ■ *Web:* www.marlow.com	Dallas	TX	75238	214-340-4900	340-7728	253
Marman Industries Inc 1701 Earhart. *Web:* marman.com	La Verne	CA	91750	909-392-2136		711
Marmaxx Group 770 Cochituate Rd. *Web:* www.tjx.com	Framingham	MA	01701	508-390-1000		156
Marmen Inc 845 Berlinguet St. *Web:* www.marmeninc.com	Trois-rivieres	QC	G8T8N9	819-379-0453		454
Marmik Oil Co 200 N Jefferson Ave. *Web:* www.marmikoil.com	El Dorado	AR	71730	870-862-8546		539

Phone | Fax | Class

Marmol Radziner & Associates AIA
12210 Nebraska Ave. Los Angeles CA 90025 310-826-6222 321
Web: www.marmol-radziner.com

Marmon Group LLC, The
181 W Madison St 26th Fl Chicago IL 60602 312-372-9500 845-5305 185
Web: www.marmon.com

Marmon/Keystone Corp PO Box 992 Butler PA 16003 724-283-3000 283-0558 492
TF: 800-544-1748 ■ *Web:* www.marmonkeystone.com

Marmon-Herrington Co
13001 Magisterial Dr Louisville KY 40223 502-253-0277 253-0317 60
TF: 800-227-0727 ■ *Web:* marmon-herrington.com

MARN (Massachusetts Assn of Registered Nurses)
PO Box 285 Milton MA 02186 617-990-2856 533
Web: anamass.org

Marne Construction Inc 748 N Poplar St Orange CA 92868 714-935-0995 186
TF: 800-559-5529 ■ *Web:* www.marneconstruction.com

Marnell Companies LLC
222 Via Marnell Way Las Vegas NV 89119 702-739-2000 195
Web: www.marnellcompanies.com

Marnen Mioduszewski Bordonaro Wagner & Sinnott LLC
516 W Tenth St Erie PA 16502 814-874-3460 428
TF: 800-201-3187 ■ *Web:* mmbwslaw.com

Maron Hotel & Suites 42 Lake Ave Ext Danbury CT 06811 203-791-2200 379
Web: www.maronhotel.com

Maron Products Inc
1301 Industrial Dr. Mishawaka IN 46544 574-259-1971 488
Web: www.maronproducts.com

Maroon Inc 1390 Jaycox Rd. Avon OH 44011 440-937-1000 937-1001 146
TF General: 877-627-6661 ■ *Web:* maroongroupllc.com

Maroosh 223 Valencia Ave Coral Gables FL 33134 305-476-9800 671
Web: www.maroosh.com

Marotta Controls Inc
78 Boonton Ave PO Box 427 Montville NJ 07045 973-334-7800 334-1219 789
TF: 888-627-6882 ■ *Web:* www.marotta.com

Marouch 4905 Santa Monica Blvd Los Angeles CA 90029 323-662-9325 664-4229 671
Web: www.marouchrestaurant.com

Marox Corp 373 Whitney Ave. Holyoke MA 01040 413-536-1300 534-1829 621
TF: 800-964-1395 ■ *Web:* www.marox.com

Marposs Corp
3300 Cross Creek Pkwy Auburn Hills MI 48326 248-370-0404 472
TF: 888-627-7677 ■ *Web:* www.marposs.com

Marq Packaging Systems Inc
3801 W Washington Ave. Yakima WA 98903 509-966-4300 557
TF: 800-998-4301 ■ *Web:* www.marq.net

Marquand Books Inc
1402 Third Ave Ste 300 Seattle WA 98101 206-624-2030 344
Web: luciamarquand.com

Marquardt & Company
161 Ave of the Americas New York NY 10013 212-645-7200 536-0282 553

Marquardt Switches Inc 2711 US 20 Cazenovia NY 13035 315-655-8050 655-8042 203
Web: us.marquardt.com

Marque Millennium Capital Management LLC
850 Third Ave 13th Fl New York NY 10022 212-759-6801 401
Web: www.marqmil.com

Marquee Energy Ltd
500 Fourth Ave SW Ste 1700 Calgary AB T2P2V6 403-384-0000 539
Web: www.marquee-energy.com

Marquee Fire Protection
710 W Stadium Ln Sacramento CA 95834 916-641-7997 610
Web: www.marqueefire.com

MarQueen Hotel 600 Queen Anne Ave N. Seattle WA 98109 206-282-7407 283-1499 379
Web: www.marqueen.com

Marquesa Hotel 600 Fleming St Key West FL 33040 305-292-1919 294-2121 379
TF: 800-869-4631 ■ *Web:* www.marquesa.com

Marquette 8140 Township Line Rd Indianapolis IN 46260 317-875-9700 672
TF: 800-874-7317 ■ *Web:* www.marquetteseniorliving.org

marquette 1600 W 82nd St Ste 250 Bloomington MN 55431 952-703-7474 216
Web: www.marqcfi.com

Marquette Asset Management
60 S Sixth St Ste 3900 Minneapolis MN 55402 612-661-3770 401
TF: 866-661-3770 ■ *Web:* www.marquetteam.com

Marquette Bank 10000 W 151st St Orland Park IL 60462 708-226-8026 70
TF: 888-254-9500 ■ *Web:* www.emarquettebank.com

Marquette Branch Prison
1960 US Hwy 41 S Marquette MI 49855 906-226-6531 226-6557 213
Web: www.michigan.gov/corrections

Marquette Commercial Finance
1600 W 82nd St Ste 250 Bloomington MN 55431 952-703-7474 703-1692 216
Web: www.marqtransfinance.com

Marquette Country Convention & Visitors Bureau
117 W Washington St Marquette MI 49855 906-228-7749 206
TF: 800-544-4321 ■ *Web:* www.travelmarquettemichigan.com

Marquette County 234 W Baraga Ave Marquette MI 49855 906-225-8151 225-8155 338
Web: www.co.marquette.mi.us

Marquette County
77 W Park St PO Box 129 Montello WI 53949 608-297-9136 338
Web: www.co.marquette.wi.us

Marquette General Hospital
580 W College Ave Marquette MI 49855 906-228-9440 225-3084 374-3
Web: www.mgh.org

Marquette Hotel, The
710 Marquette Ave Minneapolis MN 55402 612-333-4545 288-2188 379

Marquette Partners LP
801 W Adams Ste 500 Chicago IL 60607 312-224-2400 690
Web: www.marquettepartners.com

Marquette Public Service Garage
919 W Baraga Ave Marquette MI 49855 906-662-4395 57
Web: www.publicservicegarage.com

Marquette Savings Bank 920 Peach St Erie PA 16501 814-455-4481 453-5345 70
TF: 866-672-3743 ■ *Web:* www.marquettesavings.com

Marquette Tool & Die Co
3185 S KingsHwy Blvd Saint Louis MO 63139 314-771-8509 771-7964 489
Web: www.marquettetool.com

Marquette Transportation Company LLC
150 Ballard Cir Paducah KY 42001 800-456-9404 314
TF: 800-456-9404 ■ *Web:* www.marquettetrans.com

Marquette Transportation Company LLC
5525 Mounes St New Orleans LA 70123 504-733-5845 465
TF: 800-735-5845 ■ *Web:* www.marquettetrans.com

Marquette University
1217 W Wisconsin Ave Milwaukee WI 53233 414-288-7302 288-3764* 166
**Fax:* Admissions ■ *TF Admissions:* 800-222-6544 ■ *Web:* www.marquette.edu

Marquette University Law School
1215 W Michigan St Milwaukee WI 53233 414-288-7090 288-6403 167-1
Web: www.law.marquette.edu

Marquette University Raynor Memorial Library
1355 W Wisconsin Ave Milwaukee WI 53233 414-288-7556 288-5324 434-6
TF: 800-876-1715 ■ *Web:* www.marquette.edu/library

Marquez Bros International Inc
5801 Rue Ferrari San Jose CA 95138 408-960-2700 960-3213 297-8
TF: 800-858-1119 ■ *Web:* www.marquezbrothers.com

MarquipWardUnited 1300 N Airport Rd Phillips WI 54555 715-339-2191 339-4469 556
Web: www.marquipwardunited.com

Marquis Consulting Services Inc
2914 Independence Dr Fort wayne IN 46808 260-497-6437 818-2027 463
Web: www.marquis-id.com

Marquis Energy LLC
11953 Prairie Industrial Pkwy Hennepin IL 61327 815-925-7300 580
Web: www.marquisgrain.com

Marquis Software Development Inc
1611 Jaydell Cir Ste G Tallahassee FL 32308 850-877-8864 177
Web: marquisware.com

Marquis Spas Corp 596 Hoffman Rd Independence OR 97351 503-838-0888 838-3849 375
TF: 800-275-0888 ■ *Web:* www.marquisspas.com

Marquis Who's Who
300 Connell Dr Ste 2000 Berkeley Heights NJ 07922 908-673-1000 673-1189 637-2
TF: 800-473-7020 ■ *Web:* www.marquiswhoswho.com

Marrakech 1833 Fulton Ave Sacramento CA 95825 916-486-1944 671
Web: www.marrakechrestaurant.com

Marrakech Express Inc
720 Wesley Ave Ste 10 Tarpon Springs FL 34689 727-942-2218 627
TF: 800-880-4571 ■ *Web:* www.marrak.com

Marrakesh 517 S Leithgow St Philadelphia PA 19147 215-925-5929 671
Web: marrakesheastcoast.com

Marriner Marketing Communications Inc
6731 Columbia Gateway Dr Ste 250 Columbia MD 21046 410-715-1500 7
TF: 800-268-6475 ■ *Web:* www.marriner.com

Marrinson Senior Care Residences
1701 NE 26th St Wilton Manors FL 33305 954-566-8353 371
Web: www.marrinson.com

Marriott Charleston Hotel
170 Lockwood Blvd Charleston SC 29403 843-723-3000 723-0276 379
TF: 888-236-2427 ■ *Web:* www.marriott.com

Marriott Columbus 800 Front Ave Columbus GA 31901 706-324-1800 576-4413 379
TF: 800-455-9261 ■ *Web:* www.marriott.com

Marriott International Inc
11966 El Camino Real San Diego CA 92130 888-236-2427 369-6066* 671
**Fax Area Code:* 858 ■ *TF:* 888-236-2427 ■ *Web:* marriott.com/hotel-restaurants
ExecuStay Corp 2222 Corinth Ave. Los Angeles CA 90064 800-990-9292 210
TF: 800-990-9292 ■ *Web:* www.execustay.com
Ritz-Carlton Hotel Co LLC
4445 Willard Ave Ste 800 Chevy Chase MD 20815 301-547-4700 379
TF: 800-241-3333 ■ *Web:* www.ritzcarlton.com

Marriott Kaua'i Resort & Beach Club
3610 Rice St Kalapaki Beach Lihue HI 96766 808-245-5050 245-5049 669
TF: 800-220-2925 ■ *Web:* www.marriott.com

Marriott Montgomery Prattville at Capitol Hill
2500 Legends Cir Prattville AL 36066 334-290-1235 290-2222 377
TF Resv: 800-593-6429 ■ *Web:* www.marriott.com

Marriott Theatre in Lincolnshire
10 Marriott Dr Lincolnshire IL 60069 847-634-0200 572
Web: www.marriotttheatre.com

Marriott Vacation Club International
6649 Westwood Blvd Ste 500 Orlando FL 32821 407-206-6000 753
TF: 800-307-7312 ■ *Web:* www.marriottvacationclub.com

Marrone, Robinson, Frederick & Foster
111 N First St Ste 300 Burbank CA 91502 818-841-1144 428
Web: www.mrfflaw.net

Marrs Electric Inc PO Box 690296 Tulsa OK 74169 918-437-5802 438-3563 189-4
Web: www.marrselectric.com

Mars 800 High St Hackettstown NJ 07840 908-850-1753 296-8
Web: www.mars.com

Mars & Co 124 Mason St Greenwich CT 06830 203-629-9292 629-9432 194
Web: www.marsandco.com

Mars Adv Company Inc
25200 Telegraph Rd Southfield MI 48034 248-936-2200 4
TF: 800-270-3538 ■ *Web:* themarsagency.com

Mars Electric Co 6655 Beta Dr Willoughby OH 44143 440-946-2250 946-3214 246
Web: www.mars-electric.com

Mars Hill College 100 Athletics St Mars Hill NC 28754 828-689-1219 166
Web: marshilllions.com

Mars Hill Productions Inc
4711 Lexington Blvd. Missouri City TX 77459 281-403-1463 403-4463 514
Web: www.mars-hill.org

Mars Inc 6885 Elm St McLean VA 22101 703-821-4900 448-9678 185
Web: www.mars.com

Mars Stout Inc 4500 Majestic Dr Missoula MT 59808 406-721-6280 737
TF: 800-451-6277 ■ *Web:* www.marsstout.com

Mars Supermarkets Inc
9627 Philadelphia Rd Rosedale MD 21237 410-590-0500 345
Web: www.marsfood.com

Marsh & Mclennan Agency
250 Pehle Ave Saddle Brook NJ 07663 800-642-0106 795-0931* 390
**Fax Area Code:* 866 ■ *TF:* 800-669-6330 ■ *Web:* www.mma-ne.com

Marsh & McLennan Cos Inc
1166 Ave of the Americas New York NY 10036 212-345-5000 360-3
NYSE: MMC ■ *TF:* 866-374-2662 ■ *Web:* www.mmc.com

Marsh Bellofram Corp
8019 Ohio River Blvd Newell WV 26050 304-387-1200 387-1212 201
TF: 800-727-5646 ■ *Web:* www.marshbellofram.com

Marsh Berry & Company Inc
4420 Sherwin Rd Willoughby OH 44094 440-354-3230 194
TF: 800-426-2774 ■ *Web:* www.marshberry.com

Marsh Creek State Park 675 Pk Rd Downingtown PA 19335 610-458-5119 565
Web: www.dcnr.state.pa.us

Marsh Electronics Inc
1563 S 101st St Milwaukee WI 53214 414-475-6000 771-2847 246
TF Cust Svc: 800-926-2774 ■ *Web:* www.marshelectronics.com

Name / Address	City	State	Zip	Phone	Fax	Class
Marsh Fischmann & Breyfogle LLP						
8055 E Tufts Ave Ste 450	Denver	CO	80237	303-770-0051		428
TF: 800-333-7173 ■ *Web:* www.mfblaw.com						
Marsh Furniture Co PO Box 870	High Point	NC	27261	336-884-7363	884-3553	115
Web: www.marshfurniture.com						
Marsh Industries Inc						
49680 Leona Dr	Chesterfield	MI	48051	586-949-9300	949-1290	326
Web: www.marshindustries.com						
Marsh Ridge Resort						
4815 Old US Hwy 27 S	Gaylord	MI	49735	989-732-5552		669
Web: www.marshridge.com						
Marsh Saldana						
1166 Ave of the Americas New York	New York	NY	10036	787-721-2600		390
Web: latinamerica.marsh.com						
Marsh's Edge						
136 Marsh's Edge Ln	St. Simons Island	GA	31522	912-291-2000		371
TF: 800-715-4225 ■ *Web:* marshs-edge.com						
Marshad Technology Group						
99 Hudson St Fl 5	New York	NY	10013	212-925-8656		4
Web: www.marshad.com						
Marshal Mize Ford Inc						
5348 Hwy 153	Chattanooga	TN	37343	888-633-5038		57
TF: 888-633-5038 ■ *Web:* marshalmizeford.net						
Marshall & Bruce Printing Co						
689 Davidson St	Nashville	TN	37213	615-256-3661	256-6803	92
Web: www.marbruco.com						
Marshall & Sterling Inc						
110 Main St	Poughkeepsie	NY	12601	845-454-0800	454-0880	390
TF: 800-333-3766 ■ *Web:* marshallsterling.com						
Marshall & Stevens Inc						
601 S Figueroa St Ste 2301	Los Angeles	CA	90017	213-612-8000	612-8010	194
TF: 800-950-9588 ■ *Web:* www.marshall-stevens.com						
Marshall & Sullivan Inc						
1109 First Ave Ste 200	Seattle	WA	98101	206-621-9014		401
TF: 800-735-7290 ■ *Web:* www.msinvest.com						
Marshall Adv & Design						
2729 Bristol St	Costa Mesa	CA	92626	714-545-5757		4
Marshall Air Systems Inc						
419 Peachtree Dr S	Charlotte	NC	28217	704-525-6230		697
Web: www.marshallair.com						
Marshall Area Convention & Visitors Bureau						
317 W Main St	Marshall	MN	56258	507-532-4484	532-4485	206
TF: 800-581-0081 ■ *Web:* www.marshall-mn.org						
Marshall Communications Corp						
20098 Ashbrook Pl Ste 260	Ashburn	VA	20147	571-223-2010		194
Web: www.marshallcomm.com						
Marshall County 1101 Main St	Benton	KY	42025	270-527-4750		338
Web: www.marshallcounty.net						
Marshall County						
911 Vander Horck PO Box 130	Britton	SD	57430	605-448-5213	448-5201	338
Web: ujs.sd.gov/County_Information/marshall.aspx						
Marshall County 424 Blount Ave	Guntersville	AL	35976	256-571-7701		338
TF: 800-476-3939 ■ *Web:* www.marshallco.org						
Marshall County 520 J M Ash Dr	Holly Springs	MS	38635	662-252-3916	252-7160	338
Web: marshallcoms.com						
Marshall County						
122 N Prairie St PO Box 328	Lacon	IL	61540	309-246-6325	246-3667	338
Web: www.marshallcountyillinois.com						
Marshall County						
1 E Main St 3rd Fl	Marshalltown	IA	50158	641-754-6355	754-6349	338
Web: www.co.marshall.ia.us						
Marshall County 1201 Broadway	Marysville	KS	66508	785-562-5361	562-5262	338
Web: ks-marshall.manatron.com						
Marshall County PO Box 459	Moundsville	WV	26041	304-845-1220	845-5891	338
TF: 800-642-9066 ■ *Web:* www.marshallcountywv.org						
Marshall County 211 W Madison St	Plymouth	IN	46563	574-936-8922	936-8893	338
Web: www.co.marshall.in.us						
Marshall County 208 E Colvin Ave	Warren	MN	56762	218-745-4851		338
TF: 800-228-0296 ■ *Web:* www.visitnwminnesota.com						
Marshall County Chamber of Commerce						
609 Jefferson Ave	Moundsville	WV	26041	304-845-2773	845-2773	139
TF: 800-642-9066 ■ *Web:* www.marshallcountychamber.com						
Marshall County Chamber of Commerce						
17 US Hwy 68 W	Benton	KY	42025	270-527-7665	527-9193	139
TF: 800-626-2250 ■ *Web:* www.marshallcounty.net						
Marshall County Correctional Facility						
833 W St	Holly Springs	MS	38635	662-274-0225		213
Marshall County Library						
109 E Gholson Ave	Holly Springs	MS	38635	662-252-3823	252-3066	434-3
TF: 800-844-8418 ■ *Web:* www.marshall.lib.ms.us						
Marshall County REMC						
11299 12th Rd PO Box 250	Plymouth	IN	46563	574-936-3161	935-4162	245
Web: www.marshallremc.com						
Marshall Dennehey Warner Coleman & Goggin						
1845 Walnut St	Philadelphia	PA	19103	215-575-2600	575-0856	428
TF: 800-220-3308 ■ *Web:* www.marshalldennehey.com						
Marshall Durbin Co						
2830 Commerce Blvd	Birmingham	AL	35210	205-380-3251		619
TF Sales: 800-245-8204 ■ *Web:* www.marshalldurbin.com						
Marshall Furniture Inc 999 Anita Ave	Antioch	IL	60002	847-395-9350		321
Web: www.marshallfurniture.com						
Marshall Gold Discovery State Historic Park						
310 Back St PO Box 265	Coloma	CA	95613	530-622-3470		565
Web: www.parks.ca.gov/default.asp?page_id=484						
Marshall Graphics Systems						
210 Hill Ave	Brentwood	TN	37210	615-399-8896	399-8898	387
Web: www.marshallgraphics.com						
Marshall Hotels & Resorts Inc						
1315 S Division St	Salisbury	MD	21804	410-749-8464		378
Web: www.marshallhotels.com						
Marshall Independent School District (Inc)						
1305 E Pinecrest Dr	Marshall	TX	75670	903-927-8701	935-0203	685
Web: www.marshallisd.com						
Marshall Islands						
800 Second Ave 18th Fl	New York	NY	10017	212-983-3040		784
Marshall Islands Embassy						
2433 Massachusetts Ave NW	Washington	DC	20008	202-234-5414	232-3236	257
TF: 800-860-8610 ■ *Web:* www.rmiembassyus.org						
Marshall Medical Ctr South (MMCS)						
2505 US Hwy 431	Boaz	AL	35957	256-593-8310		374-3
Web: www.mmcenters.com/facilities/marshall-medical-south						
Marshall Memorial Library						
110 S Diamond Ave	Deming	NM	88030	575-546-9202		434-3
Marshall Middle School						
401 S Saratoga St	Marshall	MN	56258	507-537-6938		685
Web: www.marshall.k12.mn.us/site/Default.aspx?PageID=875						
Marshall Music Co						
4555 Wilson Ave SW Ste 1	Grandville	MI	49418	616-530-7700		526
TF: 800-242-4705 ■ *Web:* www.marshallmusic.com						
Marshall Public Library						
113 S Garfield Ave	Pocatello	ID	83204	208-232-1263		434-3
Web: www.marshallpl.org						
Marshall Public Library						
300 S Alamo St	Marshall	TX	75670	903-935-4465		434-3
Web: marshalltexas.net						
Marshall Retail Group 5385 Wynn Rd	Las Vegas	NV	89118	702-385-5233		157-6
TF: 800-713-0915 ■ *Web:* www.marshallretailgroup.com						
Marshall Roger (Rep R - KS)						
312 Cannon HOB	Washington	DC	20515	202-225-2715		342-2
Web: marshall.house.gov						
Marshall Screw Products Co						
3820 Chandler Dr NE	Minneapolis	MN	55421	800-321-6727		454
TF: 800-321-6727 ■ *Web:* www.marshallmfg.com						
Marshall Square Mall						
720 University Ave	Syracuse	NY	13210	315-422-3234		460
Marshall State Fish & Wildlife Area						
236 State Rt 26	Lacon	IL	61540	309-246-8351		565
Marshall Truss Systems Inc						
200 S 11th St	Marshall	MN	56258	507-537-0581		817
Web: www.marshalltruss.com						
Marshall University						
1 John Marshall Dr	Huntington	WV	25755	304-696-3170	696-3135*	100
**Fax:* Admissions ■ *TF:* 800-642-3463 ■ *Web:* www.marshall.edu						
Marshall V Miller & Company Pc						
4929 Main St	Kansas City	MO	64112	816-561-4999		428
Web: www.millerco.com						
Marshalls Inc 770 Cochituate Rd	Framingham	MA	01701	508-390-1000		157-2
TF: 888-627-7425 ■ *Web:* www.marshallsonline.com						
Marshalltown Area Chamber of Commerce						
709 S Ctr St PO Box 1000	Marshalltown	IA	50158	641-753-6645	752-8373	139
TF: 800-725-5301 ■ *Web:* www.marshalltown.org						
Marshalltown Co 104 S Eigth Ave	Marshalltown	IA	50158	641-753-5999	753-6341	758
TF: 800-888-0127 ■ *Web:* www.marshalltown.com						
Marshalltown Community College						
3700 S Ctr St	Marshalltown	IA	50158	641-844-5708	752-8149	162
TF: 866-622-4748 ■ *Web:* mcc.iavalley.edu						
Marshalltown Public Library						
105 W Boone St	Marshalltown	IA	50158	641-754-5738	754-5708	434-3
Web: www.marshalltownlibrary.org						
Marsh-Billings-Rockefeller National Historical Park						
54 Elm St	Woodstock	VT	05091	802-457-3368	457-3405	564
Web: www.nps.gov						
Marshfield Convention & Visitors Bureau						
700 S Central Ave PO Box 868	Marshfield	WI	54449	715-384-3454	387-8925	206
TF: 800-422-4541 ■ *Web:* www.marshfieldchamber.com						
Marshfield Public Library						
211 E Second St	Marshfield	WI	54449	715-387-8494		434-3
Web: www.marshfieldlibrary.org						
Marson & Marson Lumber Inc						
PO Box 218	Leavenworth	WA	98826	509-548-5829	548-6372	364
Web: www.marsonandmarson.com						
Marston House Museum & Gardens						
3525 Seventh Ave	San Diego	CA	92103	619-297-9327		50-3
TF: 800-577-6679 ■ *Web:* www.sohosandiego.org						
Marston Keyser Associates Inc						
160 Pacific Ave Ste 204	San Francisco	CA	94111	415-398-3050		196
TF: 800-366-1178 ■ *Web:* www.keysermarston.com						
Marstons Mills Public Library						
2160 Main St	Marstons Mills	MA	02648	508-428-5175	420-5194	434-3
Web: www.mmpl.org						
Marsulex Environmental Technology						
200 N Seventh St	Lebanon	PA	17046	717-274-7000	274-7103	18
Web: www.met.net						
MARTA (Metropolitan Atlanta Rapid Transit Authority)						
2424 Piedmont Rd NE	Atlanta	GA	30324	404-848-5000		468
Web: www.itsmarta.com						
Martec Group Inc, The						
105 W Adams St Ste 2125	Chicago	IL	60603	312-606-9690		668
TF: 888-811-5755 ■ *Web:* www.martecgroup.com						
Martec Ltd 1888 Brunswick St Ste 400	Halifax	NS	B3J3J8	902-425-5101		256
Web: www.martec.com						
Martec USA LLC 1800 N Topping Ave	Kansas City	MO	64120	816-241-4144		583
Martech Medical Products Inc						
1500 Delp Dr	Harleysville	PA	19438	215-256-8833	256-8837	477
Web: www.martechmedical.com						
Martek Biosciences Corp						
6480 Dobbin Rd	Columbia	MD	21045	410-740-0081		85
Web: www.lifesdha.com						
Marten Law 1191 Second Ave Ste 2200	Seattle	WA	98101	206-292-2600		428
Web: www.martenlaw.com						
Marten Transport Ltd 129 Marten St	Mondovi	WI	54755	715-926-4216	926-5609	780
NASDAQ: MRTN ■ *TF:* 800-395-3000 ■ *Web:* www.marten.com						
Martenson & Eisele Inc 1377 Midway Rd	Menasha	WI	54952	920-731-0381		261
Web: www.martenson-eisele.com						
Martha Stewart Living Magazine						
601 W 26th St 9th Fl	New York	NY	10001	800-999-6518		457-11
TF: 800-999-6518 ■ *Web:* www.marthastewart.com						
Martha Washington Hotel & Spa, The						
150 W Main St	Abingdon	VA	24210	276-628-3161	628-8885	379
TF: 888-999-8078 ■ *Web:* www.themartha.com						
Martha's Vineyard & Nantucket Reservations						
73 Lagoon Pond Rd	Vineyard Haven	MA	02568	508-693-7200		376
Web: www.mvreservations.com						
Martha's Vineyard Museum						
59 School St PO Box 1310	Edgartown	MA	02539	508-627-4441	627-4436	520
Web: www.mvmuseum.org						

Name / Address	City	State	ZIP	Phone	Fax	Class
Martha's Vineyard Preservation Trust 99 Main St PO Box 5277 *Web:* www.mvpreservation.org	Edgartown	MA	02539	508-627-4440	627-8088	50-1
Martha's Vineyard Regional Transit Authority 11 A St MV Business Pk *Web:* www.vineyardtransit.com	Edgartown	MA	02539	508-693-9440	693-9953	108
Martha's Vineyard Savings Bank 78 Main St PO Box 1069 *Web:* mvbank.com	Edgartown	MA	02539	508-627-4266		71
Martin & Bayley Inc 1311 A W Main *TF:* 800-876-2511 ■ *Web:* www.martinandbayley.com	Carmi	IL	62821	618-382-2334		345
Martin & Kieklak Law Firm 2059 N Green Acres Rd *TF:* 800-633-2160 ■ *Web:* www.martinlawpartners.com	Fayetteville	AR	72703	479-442-2244		445
Martin & Martin Certified Public Accountants Ltd 1001 W Hawthorn Dr *Web:* mmcpasltd.com	Itasca	IL	60143	847-250-5074	250-5105	2
Martin Agency Inc 1 Shockoe Plaza *Web:* www.martinagency.com	Richmond	VA	23219	804-698-8000	698-8001	4
Martin Allgeier & Assoc Inc 7231 E 24th St *Web:* www.amce.com	Joplin	MO	64804	417-680-7200		186
Martin Archery Inc 3134 Heritage Rd *TF:* 800-694-9494 ■ *Web:* www.martinarchery.com	Walla Walla	WA	99362	509-529-2554	529-2186	710
Martin Army Community Hospital 6600 Van Aalst Blvd *Web:* www.martin.amedd.army.mil	Fort Benning	GA	31905	762-408-2604		374-4
Martin Asphalt Co 3 Riverway Ste 400 *TF:* 800-662-0987 ■ *Web:* www.themartincompanies.com	South Houston	TX	77056	713-350-6800		46
Martin Automatic Inc 1661 Northrock Ct *Web:* www.martinauto.com	Rockford	IL	61103	815-654-4800	654-4810	203
Martin Automotive Group 12101 W Olympic Blvd *Web:* martinautogroup.com	Los Angeles	CA	90064	310-622-9334	622-9334	57
Martin Automotive Group Inc 1048 Ashley St Ste 401 *Web:* www.martingp.com	Bowling Green	KY	42103	270-783-8080	783-4347	57
Martin Avenue Pharmacy 1247 Rickert Dr *Web:* www.critterchronicle.com	Naperville	IL	60540	630-355-6400		237
Martin Aviation 19300 Ike Jones Rd *Web:* martin-aviation.com	Santa Ana	CA	92707	714-210-2945	557-0637	24
Martin Bontempo Matacera Bartlett Inc 212 W State St *Web:* www.mbiglückshaw.com	Trenton	NJ	08608	609-392-3100		636
Martin Cabinet Inc 336 S Washington St *TF:* 800-750-5769 ■ *Web:* martincabinet.com	Plainville	CT	06062	860-747-5769	747-9595	115
Martin Capital Management LLP 300 NIBCO Pkwy Ste 301 *Web:* www.mcmadvisors.com	Elkhart	IN	46516	574-293-2077		401
Martin Chevrolet 23505 Hawthorne Blvd *Web:* www.martinchevrolet.com	Torrance	CA	90505	310-378-0211		516
Martin Chevrolet Sales Inc 8800 Gratiot Rd *Web:* www.martincars.net	Saginaw	MI	48609	989-607-0584		516
Martin Community College 1161 Kehukee Pk Rd *TF:* 800-488-4101 ■ *Web:* www.martin.cc.nc.us	Williamston	NC	27892	252-792-1521	792-0826	162
Martin County 201 Lake Ave Ste 201 **Fax:* Acctg ■ *Web:* www.co.martin.mn.us	Fairmont	MN	56031	507-238-3211	238-3259*	338
Martin County PO Box 460 *Web:* peoplesmart.com	Inez	KY	41224	606-298-2810	298-0143	338
Martin County 129 Main St	Shoals	IN	47581	812-247-3651		338
Martin County 301 N St Peter St *Web:* www.martincountytexas.us	Stanton	TX	79782	432-756-3336	607-2992	338
Martin County 2401 SE Monterey Rd *Web:* www.martin.fl.us	Stuart	FL	34996	772-288-5400	288-5548	338
Martin County 305 E Main St PO Box 308 *Web:* www.martincountyncgov.com	Williamston	NC	27892	252-792-2515		338
Martin County Chamber of Commerce 415 E Blvd *Web:* martincountync.com	Williamston	NC	27892	252-792-4131	792-1013	139
Martin County Public Library 2401 SE Monterey Rd *Web:* www.martin.fl.us	Stuart	FL	34996	772-288-5702	219-4959	434-3
Martin County Travel & Tourism Authority 100 E Church St PO Box 382 *TF:* 800-776-8566 ■ *Web:* www.visitmartincounty.com	Williamston	NC	27892	252-792-6605		206
Martin County West High School 16 W Fifth St *TF:* 800-352-7550 ■ *Web:* martin.k12.mn.us	Sherburn	MN	56171	507-764-4661		685
Martin Creek Lake State Park 9515 CR 2181D *Web:* tpwd.texas.gov	Tatum	TX	75691	903-836-4336		565
Martin Decker Totco Inc 1200 Cypress Creek Rd	Cedar Park	TX	78613	512-340-5000		537
Martin Dies Jr State Park 634 Private Rd 5025 *Web:* tpwd.texas.gov	Jasper	TX	75951	409-384-5231		565
Martin Door Manufacturing Inc 2828 South 900 West *TF:* 800-388-9310 ■ *Web:* www.martindoor.com	Salt Lake City	UT	84119	801-973-9310	688-8182	364
Martin Eagle Oil Company Inc 2700 James St *TF:* 800-316-6148 ■ *Web:* www.martineagle.com	Denton	TX	76205	940-383-2351	382-9342	579
Martin Engineering 1 Martin Pl *TF:* 800-544-2947 ■ *Web:* www.martin-eng.com	Neponset	IL	61345	309-594-2384	594-2432	207
Martin Enterprises Inc 4315 Meyer Rd *Web:* truckdriver.com	Fort Wayne	IN	46806	260-447-5591		780
Martin Furniture 2345 Britannia Blvd **Fax Area Code:* 619 ■ *TF Cust Svc:* 800-268-5669 ■ *Web:* www.martinfurniture.com	San Diego	CA	92154	800-268-5669	671-5199*	319-1
Martin Glass Co 25 Ctr Plaza *TF:* 800-325-1946 ■ *Web:* www.martinglass.net	Belleville	IL	62220	618-277-1946		62-2
Martin Group LLC, The 477 Main St *Web:* tmgbrandfuel.com	Buffalo	NY	14203	716-853-2757		195
Martin Health System (MMHS) 200 SE Hospital Ave PO Box 9010 *TF:* 844-630-4968 ■ *Web:* www.martinhealth.org	Stuart	FL	34994	772-287-5200		374-3
Martin Investment Management LLC 1560 Sherman Ave Ste 1250 *Web:* www.martin-investments.com	Evanston	IL	60201	847-424-9124		195
Martin Iron Works Inc 530 E Fourth St *Web:* www.martinironworks.net	Reno	NV	89512	775-329-8631		480
Martin K. Eby Construction Co 610 N Main Ste 500 Ste 500 *TF:* 800-253-7156 ■ *Web:* www.ebycorp.com	Wichita	KS	67203	316-268-3500	268-3649	188-4
Martin Kilpatrick Table Tennis 4482 Technology Dr NW *Web:* www.butterflyonline.com	Wilson	NC	27896	252-291-4770		711
Martin Luther College 1995 Luther Ct **Fax:* Admissions ■ *TF:* 877-652-1995 ■ *Web:* www.mlc-wels.edu	New Ulm	MN	56073	507-354-8221	354-8225*	166
Martin Luther King Jr Arena 301 W Oglethorpe Ave *Web:* www.savannahga.gov	Savannah	GA	31401	912-651-6550	651-6552	720
Martin Luther King Jr Memorial Library (MLK) 901 G St NW *Web:* www.dclibrary.org	Washington	DC	20001	202-727-0321		434-3
Martin Luther King Jr National Historic Site 450 Auburn Ave NE *Web:* www.nps.gov/malu	Atlanta	GA	30312	404-331-5190	730-3112	564
Martin Marietta Magnesia Specialties Inc 8140 Corporate Dr Ste 220 *TF:* 800-648-7400 ■ *Web:* www.magnesiaspecialties.com	Baltimore	MD	21236	410-780-5500	780-5777	143
Martin Marietta Materials Inc 2710 Wycliff Rd *NYSE: MLM* ■ *Web:* www.martinmarietta.com	Raleigh	NC	27607	919-781-4550		503-5
Martin Mechanical Design Inc 702 28th Ave N Ste 200	Fargo	ND	58102	701-293-7957		261
Martin Memorial Library 159 E Market St *Web:* www.yorklibraries.org	York	PA	17401	717-846-5300	848-2330	434-3
Martin Methodist College 433 W Madison St **Fax:* Admissions ■ *TF:* 800-467-1273 ■ *Web:* www.martinmethodist.edu	Pulaski	TN	38478	931-363-9804	363-9803*	166
Martin Midstream Partners LP 4200 Stone Rd *NASDAQ: MMLP* ■ *TF:* 800-256-6644 ■ *Web:* martinmidstream.com	Kilgore	TX	75662	903-983-6200		579
Martin Park Nature Ctr 5000 W Memorial Rd *Web:* okc.gov/parks/martin%5fpark	Oklahoma City	OK	73142	405-297-3882		50-5
Martin Partners LLC 224 S Michigan Ave Ste 620 *Web:* www.martinpartners.com	Chicago	IL	60604	312-922-1800		193
Martin Petersen Company Inc 9800 55th St *Web:* www.mpcmech.com	Kenosha	WI	53144	262-658-1326	658-1048	189-10
Martin Resource Management Corp (MRMC) PO Box 191 *TF:* 888-334-7473 ■ *Web:* www.martinmidstream.com	Kilgore	TX	75663	903-983-6200	983-6271	316
Martin Rosol Inc 45 Grove St *TF:* 800-937-2682 ■ *Web:* martinrosolsinc.com	New Britain	CT	06053	860-223-2707		296-26
Martin Sprocket & Gear Inc 3100 Sprocket Dr *Web:* www.martinsprocket.com	Arlington	TX	76015	817-258-3000	258-3333	620
Martin Supply Co 200 Appleton Ave *TF:* 800-828-8116 ■ *Web:* www.martinsupply.com	Sheffield	AL	35660	256-383-3132	383-3136	385
Martin Thomas Inc 42 Riverside Dr **Fax Area Code:* 866 ■ *Web:* www.martinthomas.com	Barrington	RI	02806	401-245-8500	899-2710*	4
Martin Trucking Inc 1015 W City Limits St	Hugoton	KS	67951	620-544-4920		780
Martin University 2171 Avondale Pl *Web:* www.martin.edu	Indianapolis	IN	46218	317-543-3235		166
Martin Van Buren National Historic Site 1013 Old Post Rd *Web:* www.nps.gov	Kinderhook	NY	12106	518-758-9689	758-6986	564
Martin Wells Industries 5886 Compton Ave *TF:* 800-421-6000	Los Angeles	CA	90001	323-581-6266	589-2334	128
Martin Wheel Company Inc 342 W Ave *TF:* 800-462-7846 ■ *Web:* www.martinwheelco.com	Tallmadge	OH	44278	330-633-3278	633-3303	754
Martin Yale Industries Inc 251 Wedcor Ave *TF:* 800-225-5644 ■ *Web:* www.martinyale.com	Wabash	IN	46992	260-563-0641	563-4575	111
Martin's Famous Pastry Shoppe Inc 1000 Potato Roll Ln *TF Cust Svc:* 800-548-1200 ■ *Web:* potatorolls.com	Chambersburg	PA	17201	717-263-9580		296-1
Martin's Marketplace 130 Tichenal Way *TF:* 800-961-0162 ■ *Web:* martinsmarketplace.com	Cashmere	WA	98815	509-782-3801	782-2212	345
Martin's Potato Chips Inc 5847 Lincoln Hwy W PO Box 28 *TF:* 800-272-4477 ■ *Web:* www.martinschips.com	Thomasville	PA	17364	717-792-3565	792-4906	296-35
Martin, Disiere, Jefferson & Wisdom LLP 808 Travis St # 1800 Houston Tx *Web:* www.mdjwlaw.com	Houston	TX	77002	512-610-4400		428
Martin, Harding & Mazzotti LLP 1222 Troy-Schenectady Rd *TF:* 800-529-1010 ■ *Web:* www.1800law1010.com	Niskayuna	NY	12309	518-862-1200		428
Martin, Leigh, Laws & Fritzlen Professional Corp 1044 Main St Ste 900 *TF:* 800-280-2832 ■ *Web:* www.martinleigh.com	Kansas City	MO	64105	816-221-1430		428
Martin, Shudt, Wallace, DiLorenzo & Johnson 258 Hoosick St Ste 201 *TF:* 800-979-3658 ■ *Web:* www.martinshudt.com	Troy	NY	12180	518-272-6565		428
Martin/F Weber Co 2727 Southampton Rd *TF:* 800-876-8076 ■ *Web:* www.weberart.com	Philadelphia	PA	19154	215-677-5600	677-3336	43
Martin`s Abattoir & Wholesale Meats Inc 1600 Martin Rd	Godwin	NC	28344	910-567-6102		296-26

Name / Address	City	State	ZIP	Phone	Fax	Class
Martina's Flowers & Gifts 3925 Washington Rd *TF:* 800-927-1204 ■ *Web:* www.martinas.com	Augusta	GA	30907	706-863-7172		292
MartinAire Aviation LLC 4553 Glenn Curtiss Dr *TF:* 866-557-1861 ■ *Web:* www.martinaire.com	Addison	TX	75001	972-349-5700	349-5750	12
Martinak State Park 137 Deep Shore Rd *Web:* dnr2.maryland.gov	Denton	MD	21629	410-820-1668		565
Martin-Baker America Inc 423 Walters Ave *Web:* www.martin-baker.com	Johnstown	PA	15904	814-262-9325		529
Martindale Electric Co 1375 Hird Ave *TF:* 800-344-9191 ■ *Web:* www.martindaleco.com	Cleveland	OH	44107	216-521-8567	521-9476	518
Martindale-Hubbell 121 Chanlon Rd Ste 110 *TF:* 800-526-4902 ■ *Web:* www.martindale.com	New Providence	NJ	07974	800-526-4902		387
Martinez & Turek Inc 300 S Cedar Ave *Web:* www.martinezandturek.com	Rialto	CA	92376	909-820-6800		454
Martinez Area Chamber of Commerce 603 Marina Vista *TF:* 877-855-5506 ■ *Web:* www.martinezchamber.com	Martinez	CA	94553	925-228-2345	228-2356	139
Martinez Susana (R) State Capitol 4th Fl *Web:* www.governor.state.nm.us	Santa Fe	NM	87501	505-476-2200	476-2226	343
Martinez Unified School District 921 Susana St *Web:* www.martinezusd.net	Martinez	CA	94553	925-335-5800		685
Martin-Harris Construction Co 3030 S Highland Dr *TF:* 800-364-2059 ■ *Web:* www.martinharris.com	Las Vegas	NV	89109	702-385-5257	474-8257	186
Martini Iosue & Akpovi CPAs 16830 Ventura Blvd Ste 415 *TF:* 800-829-1040 ■ *Web:* www.miacpas.com	Encino	CA	91436	818-789-1179		734
Martini Modern Italian 445 N High St *Web:* www.martinimodernitalian.com	Columbus	OH	43215	614-224-8259	224-8780	671
Martinique Bistro 5908 Magazine St *Web:* www.martiniquebistro.com	New Orleans	LA	70115	504-891-8495		671
Martinique Promotion Bureau 825 Third Ave 29th Fl *Web:* www.martinique.org	New York	NY	10022	212-838-6887		775
Martinizing Dry Cleaning 8944 Columbia Rd Ste J *TF:* 800-827-0207 ■ *Web:* www.martinizing.com	Loveland	OH	45140	800-827-0207		310
MartinLogan Ltd 2101 Delaware St *Web:* www.martinlogan.com	Lawrence	KS	66046	785-749-0133	749-5320	52
Martino-White Printing 543 N Central Ave *Web:* www.martinowhite.com	Atlanta	GA	30354	404-768-8708		627
Martinsburg-Berkeley County Chamber of Commerce 198 Viking Way *TF:* 800-332-9007 ■ *Web:* www.berkeleycounty.org	Martinsburg	WV	25401	304-267-4841	263-4695	139
Martinsburg-Berkeley County Public Library 101 W King St *Web:* martinsburg.lib.wv.us	Martinsburg	WV	25401	304-267-8933	267-9720	434-3
Martinsville Bulletin PO Box 3711 *TF:* 800-234-6575 ■ *Web:* www.martinsvillebulletin.com	Martinsville	VA	24115	276-638-8801		532-2
Martinsville (Independent City) PO Box 1112 *Web:* www.martinsville-va.gov	Martinsville	VA	24114	276-403-5106	403-5280	338
Martinsville Speedway PO Box 3311 *Fax Area Code: 276 ■ *TF:* 877-722-3849 ■ *Web:* www.martinsvillespeedway.com	Martinsville	VA	24115	877-722-3849	956-2820*	515
Martinsville-Henry County Chamber of Commerce 115 Broad St *TF:* 800-811-6302 ■ *Web:* www.martinsville.com	Martinsville	VA	24112	276-632-6401	632-5059	139
Martin-Williams Adv 150 S Fifth st Ste 900 *TF:* 800-632-1388 ■ *Web:* www.martinwilliams.com	Minneapolis	MN	55402	612-340-0800		4
Marton Precision Manufacturing LLC 1365 S Acacia Ave *Web:* www.martoninc.com	Fullerton	CA	92831	714-808-6523		454
Martopia Inc 805 E Main St Ste H *Web:* www.martopia.com	Saint Charles	IL	60174	630-587-9944		466
Martori Farms 7332 E Butherus Dr *Web:* www.martorifarms.com	Scottsdale	AZ	85260	480-998-1444		315-4
Martrex Inc 1107 Hazeltine Blvd Ste 535 *TF:* 800-328-3627 ■ *Web:* www.martrexinc.com	Minnetonka	MN	55345	952-933-5000	933-1889	276
Martronic Engineering Inc 80 W Cochran St Ste B *TF:* 800-960-0808 ■ *Web:* meilaser.com	Simi Valley	CA	93065	805-583-0808		261
Marts & Lundy Inc 1200 Wall St W *TF:* 800-526-9005 ■ *Web:* www.martsandlundy.com	Lyndhurst	NJ	07071	201-460-1660	460-0680	787
Marty Franich Ford Lincoln 550 Auto Ctr Dr *Fax Area Code: 831 ■ *TF:* 888-442-9037 ■ *Web:* www.franichford.com	Watsonville	CA	95076	888-442-9037	722-1853*	57
Martz First Class Coach Company Inc 4783 37th St N *TF:* 800-282-8020 ■ *Web:* www.martzfirstclass.com	Saint Petersburg	FL	33714	727-526-9086	522-5548	107
Martz Plumbing & Heating Inc 216 W Fifth St	Waynesboro	PA	17268	717-762-6115		189-10
Martz Supply Co 5330 Pecos St *TF:* 800-456-4672 ■ *Web:* www.martzsupply.com	Denver	CO	80221	303-421-6665		612
Martz Trailways 239 Old River Rd *Web:* www.martztrailways.com	Wilkes-Barre	PA	18702	570-821-3838		108
Marubeni America Corp 375 Lexington Ave *TF:* 800-483-6000 ■ *Web:* www.marubeni-usa.com	New York	NY	10017	212-450-0100	450-0700	169
Marucco, Stoddard, Ferenbach & Walsh Inc 3445 Liberty Dr *Web:* www.msfw.com	Springfield	IL	62704	217-698-3535		180
Maruichi American Corp 11529 Greenstone Ave *TF:* 800-654-5495 ■ *Web:* www.macsfs.com	Santa Fe Springs	CA	90670	562-903-8600		492
Maruji & Raines PS 775 S Main St Ste A *Web:* www.mrcpas.com	Colville	WA	99114	509-684-5289		2
Maruka USA Inc 400 Commons Way *TF:* 800-631-0426 ■ *Web:* www.marukausa.com	Rockaway	NJ	07866	973-983-1000		386
Marukai Wholesale Mart 2310 Kamehameha Hwy *Web:* www.marukaihawaii.com	Honolulu	HI	96819	808-845-5051		812
Maruson Technology Corp 18557 Gale Ave *TF:* 888-627-8766 ■ *Web:* marusonusa.com	City Of Industry	CA	91748	626-912-8388		767
Marvair 156 Seedling Dr *Web:* www.marvair.com	Cordele	GA	31015	229-273-3636	273-5154	14
Marval Industries Inc 315 Hoyt Ave *TF:* 800-446-1800 ■ *Web:* www.marvalindustries.com	Mamaroneck	NY	10543	914-381-2400	381-2259	605-2
Marvel Abrasive Products Inc 6230 S Oak Pk Ave *TF:* 800-621-0673 ■ *Web:* www.marvelabrasives.com	Chicago	IL	60638	800-621-0673	701-0187	1
Marvel Aero International Inc 21 Rancho Cir	Lake Forest	CA	92630	949-829-8031		771
Marvel Consultants Inc 28601 Chagrin Blvd Ste 210 *TF:* 800-338-1257 ■ *Web:* www.marvelconsultants.com	Cleveland	OH	44122	216-292-2855	292-7207	631
Marvel Group Inc 3843 W 43rd St *Fax: Cust Svc ■ *TF Cust Svc:* 800-621-8846 ■ *Web:* www.marvelgroup.com	Chicago	IL	60632	800-621-8846	237-0358*	319-1
Marvel Mfg Company Inc 3501 Marvel Dr *TF:* 800-472-9464 ■ *Web:* www.marvelsaws.com	Oshkosh	WI	54902	920-236-7200	236-7209	682
Marvell Semiconductor Inc 5488 Marvell Ln *TF Cust Svc:* 855-627-8355 ■ *Web:* www.marvell.com	Santa Clara	CA	95054	408-222-2500		176
Marvell Technology Group Ltd 5488 Marvell Ln *NASDAQ: MRVL* ■ *Web:* www.marvell.com	Santa Clara	CA	95054	408-222-2500	988-8279	696
Marvelwood School 476 Skiff Mountain Rd *Web:* marvelwood.org	Kent	CT	06757	860-927-0047		622
Marvin & Company PC 11 British American Blvd *Web:* marvincpa.com	Latham	NY	12110	518-785-0134		2
Marvin & Palmer Assoc Inc 200 Bellevue Pky Ste 220 *Web:* www.marvinandpalmer.com	Wilmington	DE	19809	302-573-3570		401
Marvin Engineering Co 261 W Beach Ave *Web:* www.marvingroup.com	Inglewood	CA	90302	310-674-5030	673-9472	807
Marvin F Poer & Company Inc 12700 Hillcrest Rd Ste 125 *Web:* www.mfpoer.com	Dallas	TX	75230	972-770-1100		194
Marvin Groves Electric Company Inc 506 Seventh St *Web:* www.marvingroveselectric.com	Wichita Falls	TX	76301	940-767-2711		610
Marvin Huffaker Consulting Inc 1311 W Chandler Blvd Ste 160 *TF:* 888-690-0013 ■ *Web:* www.redjuju.com	Chandler	AZ	85224	480-988-7215		196
Marvin K. Brown Auto Ctr Inc 1441 Camino Del Rio S *Web:* www.mkb.com	San Diego	CA	92108	619-291-2040		57
Marvin W Foote Youth Services Ctr 13500 E Fremont Pl *TF:* 800-970-3468 ■ *Web:* www.colorado.gov	Englewood	CO	80112	303-534-3468	768-7516	412
Marvin Windows & Doors PO Box 100 *TF:* 888-537-7828 ■ *Web:* www.marvin.com	Warroad	MN	56763	218-386-1430		236
Marvin Windows & Doors 2020 Silver Bell Rd Ste 15 *Web:* www.marvin.com	St Paul	MN	55122	651-452-3039		499
Marwit Capital LLC 100 Bayview Cir Ste 550 *TF:* 800-880-7293 ■ *Web:* www.marwit.com	Newport Beach	CA	92660	949-861-3636	861-3637	402
Marwood Group LLC 733 Third Ave 11th Fl *Web:* www.marwoodgroup.com	New York	NY	10017	212-532-3651		390
Marx | Okubo Associates Inc 455 Sherman St Ste 200 *Web:* www.marxokubo.com	Denver	CO	80203	303-861-0300		261
Marx Bros Cafe 627 W Third Ave *TF:* 800-245-2527 ■ *Web:* www.marxcafe.com	Anchorage	AK	99501	907-278-2133	258-6279	671
Marx Layne & Co 31420 NW Hwy *Web:* www.marxlayne.com	Farmington Hills	MI	48334	248-855-6777		636
Mary Ann Liebert Publishers Inc 140 Huguenot St 3rd Fl *TF:* 800-654-3237 ■ *Web:* www.liebertpub.com	New Rochelle	NY	10801	914-740-2100	740-2101	637-9
Mary Ann's Baking Co 8371 Carbide Ct *Web:* maryannsbaking.com	Sacramento	CA	95828	916-681-7444		296-1
Mary Baldwin College 318 Prospect St PO Box 1500 *TF Admissions:* 800-468-2262 ■ *Web:* www.marybaldwin.edu/about-us/contact	Staunton	VA	24401	540-887-7019		166
Mary Black Memorial Hospital 1700 Skylyn Dr *TF:* 800-439-4590 ■ *Web:* www.maryblackhealthsystem.com	Spartanburg	SC	29307	864-573-3000		374-3
Mary Bridge Children's Hospital & Health Ctr 317 Martin Luther King Jr Way *TF:* 800-552-1419 ■ *Web:* www.multicare.org	Tacoma	WA	98405	253-403-1400	403-1247	374-1
Mary Cheney Library 586 Main St *Web:* library.townofmanchester.org	Manchester	CT	06040	860-643-2471		434-3
Mary Fisher Design LLC 1731 Emerson St *Web:* www.maryfisherdesign.com	Jacksonville	FL	32207	904-398-3699		395
Mary Free Bed Rehabilitation Hospital 235 Wealthy St SE *TF:* 800-528-8989 ■ *Web:* www.maryfreebed.com	Grand Rapids	MI	49503	616-242-0300		374-6
Mary Greeley Medical Ctr 1111 Duff Ave *Web:* www.mgmc.org	Ames	IA	50010	515-239-2011		374-3
Mary H Weirton Public Library 3442 Main St *TF:* 800-774-2429 ■ *Web:* www.weirton.lib.wv.us	Weirton	WV	26062	304-797-8510	797-8526	434-3
Mary Immaculate Hospital 2 Bernardine Dr *Web:* www.bonsecours.com/hampton-roads	Newport News	VA	23602	757-886-6000		374-3

Name / Address	Phone	Fax	Class
Mary Institute & Saint Louis Country Day School 101 N Warson Rd........................ Saint Louis MO 63124 *Web:* www.micds.org	314-993-5100		623
Mary Jane Thurston State Park 1466 State Rt 65..............................McClure OH 43534 *TF:* 866-644-6727 ■ *Web:* www.dnr.state.oh.us	419-832-7662		565
Mary Jurek Design Inc 2301 W 205th St Unit 114 ....Torrance CA 90501 *Web:* maryjurekdesign.com	310-533-1196		393
Mary Kay Inc PO Box 799045.................. Dallas TX 75379 *TF Cust Svc:* 800-627-9529 ■ *Web:* www.marykay.com	972-687-6300		214
Mary Lanning Memorial Hospital 715 N St Joseph Ave........................ Hastings NE 68901 *TF:* 800-269-0473 ■ *Web:* www.marylanning.org	402-463-4521		374-3
Mary Mahoney's 110 Rue Magnolia...............Biloxi MS 39530 *Web:* www.marymahoneys.com	228-374-0163		671
Mary Maxim Inc 2001 Holland Ave PO Box 5019.............Port Huron MI 48061 *TF:* 800-962-9504 ■ *Web:* www.marymaxim.com	810-987-2000	987-5056	459
Mary Maxim Ltd 75 Scott Ave...................... Paris ON N3L3G5 *TF:* 888-442-2266 ■ *Web:* www.marymaxim.ca	888-442-2266		761
Mary McLeod Bethune Council House National Historic Site 1318 Vermont Ave NW...................Washington DC 20005 *Web:* www.nps.gov/mamc	202-673-2402	673-2414	564
Mary Pomerantz Advertising 300 Raritan Ave....................... Highland Park NJ 08904 *Web:* www.marypomerantzadvertising.com	732-214-9600		7
Mary Rutan Hospital 205 E Palmer Rd....................... Bellefontaine OH 43311 *Web:* www.maryrutan.org	937-592-5015	592-0207	374-7
Mary Ryan Gallery 515 W 26th St ....New York NY 10001 *Web:* www.maryryangallery.com	212-397-0669		42
Mary Todd Lincoln House 578 W Main St..............................Lexington KY 40507 *TF:* 800-755-6956 ■ *Web:* www.mtlhouse.org	859-233-9999		50-3
Mary Washington Hospice 5012 Southpoint Pkwy..................Fredericksburg VA 22407 *TF:* 800-257-1667 ■ *Web:* www.marywashingtonhealthcare.com	540-741-1667		371
Mary Washington Hospital 1001 Sam Perry Blvd ....Fredericksburg VA 22401 *TF:* 800-395-2455 ■ *Web:* www.marywashingtonhealthcare.com	540-741-1100	310-0100	374-3
Mary-Anne Martin Fine Art 23 E 73rd St 4th Fl.........................New York NY 10021 *Web:* www.mamfa.com	212-288-2213	861-7656	42
Maryanov Madsen Gordon & Campbell CPA 801 E Tahquitz Canyon Way Ste 200 PO Box 1826 ....Palm Springs CA 92262 *Web:* www.mmgcpa.com	760-320-6642	327-6854	401
Marycrest Assisted Living 2850 Columbine Rd..........................Denver CO 80221 *Web:* www.marycrest.org	303-433-0282		673
Marycrest Manor 15475 Middlebelt Rd...........Livonia MI 48154 *Web:* www.trinityhealthseniorcommunities.org/marycrest	734-743-4000		672
Marygrove College 8425 W McNichols Rd .... Detroit MI 48221 **Fax:* Admissions ■ *TF Admissions:* 866-313-1927 ■ *Web:* www.marygrove.edu	313-927-1200	927-1399*	166
Maryhill State Park 50 Hwy 97 .... Goldendale WA 98620	509-773-5007		565
Maryland			
Administrative Office of the Courts 580 Taylor Ave........................... Annapolis MD 21401 *Web:* www.courts.state.md.us	410-260-1400		339-21
Aging Dept 301 W Preston St Ste 1007.........Baltimore MD 21201 *TF:* 800-243-3425 ■ *Web:* www.aging.maryland.gov	410-767-1100	333-7943	339-21
Agriculture Dept 50 Harry S Truman Pkwy .... Annapolis MD 21401 *Web:* mda.maryland.gov	410-841-5700	841-5914	339-21
Assessments & Taxation Dept 301 W Preston St.........................Baltimore MD 21201 *TF:* 888-246-5941 ■ *Web:* www.dat.state.md.us	410-767-1184		339-21
Business & Economic Development Dept 217 E Redwood St.......................Baltimore MD 21202 *Web:* business.maryland.gov	410-767-6300		339-21
Chief Medical Examiner 900 W Baltimore St......................Baltimore MD 21223 *Web:* dhmh.maryland.gov	410-333-3250	333-3063	339-21
Court of Appeals 361 Rowe Blvd............ Annapolis MD 21401 *TF:* 800-926-2583 ■ *Web:* www.courts.state.md.us/coappeals	410-260-1500		339-21
Criminal Injuries Compensation Board 6776 Reisterstown Rd Ste 206............Baltimore MD 21215 *TF:* 888-679-9347 ■ *Web:* msa.maryland.gov	410-585-3010	764-3815	339-21
Department of Budget & Management 45 Calvert St .... Annapolis MD 21401 *TF:* 800-705-3493 ■ *Web:* dbm.maryland.gov	800-705-3493		339-21
Dept of Legislative Services 90 State Cir .... Annapolis MD 21401 *TF:* 800-492-7122 ■ *Web:* www.dls.state.md.us	410-946-5400	946-5508	433
Education Dept 200 W Baltimore St..............Baltimore MD 21201 *TF:* 888-246-0016 ■ *Web:* www.marylandpublicschools.org	410-767-0100		339-21
Emergency Management Agency 5401 Rue St Lo Dr.................... Reisterstown MD 21136 *TF:* 877-636-2872 ■ *Web:* mema.state.md.us	410-517-3600	517-3610	339-21
Environment Dept 1800 Washington Blvd...................Baltimore MD 21230 *TF:* 800-633-6101 ■ *Web:* www.mde.state.md.us	410-537-3000		339-21
Ethics Commission 45 Calvert St .... Annapolis MD 21401 *TF:* 877-669-6085 ■ *Web:* ethics.maryland.gov	410-260-7770	260-7746	265
Financial Regulation Div 500 N Calvert St Ste 402...............Baltimore MD 21202 *TF:* 888-784-0136 ■ *Web:* www.dllr.state.md.us	410-230-6100	333-0475	339-21
Fisheries Service 580 Taylor Ave............. Annapolis MD 21401 *TF:* 877-620-8367 ■ *Web:* www.dnr.state.md.us/fisheries	410-260-8281	260-8279	339-21
General Assembly 90 State Cir .... Annapolis MD 21401 *Web:* www.mlis.state.md.us	410-841-3000	841-3850	339-21
Governor State House 100 State Cir .... Annapolis MD 21401 *TF:* 800-811-8336 ■ *Web:* governor.maryland.gov	410-974-3901	974-3275	339-21
Health & Mental Hygiene Dept 201 W Preston St 5th Fl..................Baltimore MD 21201 *Web:* dhmh.maryland.gov	410-767-6500		339-21
Higher Education Commision 839 Bestgate Rd Ste 400..................Baltimore MD 21201 *TF:* 800-974-0203 ■ *Web:* www.mhec.state.md.us	410-260-4500	260-3200	339-21
Historical & Cultural Programs Div 100 Community Pl 3rd Fl ....Crownsville MD 21032 *Web:* www.marylandhistoricaltrust.net	410-514-7648	514-7678	339-21
Housing & Community Development Dept 7800 Harkins Rd ....Lanham MD 21032 *TF:* 800-756-0119 ■ *Web:* www.dhcd.state.md.us	301-429-7400		339-21
Insurance Administration 200 St Paul Pl Ste 2700..................Baltimore MD 21202 *TF:* 800-492-6116 ■ *Web:* www.mdinsurance.state.md.us	410-468-2000	468-2020	339-21
Labor & Industry Div 1100 N Eutaw St Rm 606..................Baltimore MD 21201 *TF:* 888-257-6674 ■ *Web:* www.dllr.state.md.us	410-767-2241	767-2986	339-21
Motor Vehicle Administration 6601 Ritchie Hwy NE..................Glen Burnie MD 21062 *TF:* 800-950-1682 ■ *Web:* www.mva.maryland.gov	410-768-7000		339-21
Natural Resources Dept 580 Taylor Ave.......................... Annapolis MD 21401 *TF:* 877-620-8367 ■ *Web:* dnr2.maryland.gov	877-620-8367		339-21
Parole & Probation Div 6776 Reisterstown Rd ....Baltimore MD 21215 *Web:* msa.maryland.gov	410-585-3500		339-21
Physician Quality Assurance Board 4201 Patterson Ave ....Baltimore MD 21215 *TF:* 800-492-6836 ■ *Web:* www.mbp.state.md.us	410-764-4777	358-2252	339-21
Public Service Commission 6 St Paul St 16th Fl ....Baltimore MD 21202 *TF:* 800-492-0474 ■ *Web:* www.psc.state.md.us	410-767-8000	333-6495	339-21
Racing Commission 500 N Calvert St Rm 201.................Baltimore MD 21202 *Web:* www.dllr.state.md.us	410-230-6330		339-21
Secretary of State 16 Francis St.............. Annapolis MD 21401 *Web:* www.sos.state.md.us	410-974-5521	974-5190	339-21
Securities Div 200 St Paul Pl.................Baltimore MD 21202 *TF:* 888-743-0023 ■ *Web:* www.oag.state.md.us/Securities	410-576-6360		339-21
Social Services Administration 311 W Saratoga St.........................Baltimore MD 21201 *Web:* www.dhr.state.md.us	410-767-7216		339-21
State Arts Council 175 W Ostend St Ste E....................Baltimore MD 21230 *Web:* www.msac.org	410-767-6555	333-1062	339-21
State Athletic Commission 500 N Calvert St Rm 304.................Baltimore MD 21202 *Web:* www.dllr.state.md.us/license/ath	410-230-6223	333-6314	712
State Forest & Park Service 580 Taylor Ave Rm E-3 .... Annapolis MD 21401 *TF Campground Resv:* 800-830-3974 ■ *Web:* dnr2.maryland.gov	410-260-8186	260-8191	339-21
State Government Information State House .... Annapolis MD 21401 *Web:* www.maryland.gov	410-974-3901		339-21
State Lottery 1800 Washington Blvd Ste 330............Baltimore MD 21230 *TF:* 800-201-0108 ■ *Web:* www.mdlottery.com	410-230-8800		452
State Police 1201 Reisterstown Rd ....Pikesville MD 21208 *TF:* 800-525-5555 ■ *Web:* www.mdsp.org	410-653-4200		339-21
Teacher Certification & Accreditation Div 200 W Baltimore St ....Baltimore MD 21201 *TF:* 888-246-0016 ■ *Web:* www.marylandpublicschools.org	410-767-0412		339-21
Tourism Development Office 401 E Pratt Str 14th Fl...................Baltimore MD 21202 *TF:* 877-333-4455 ■ *Web:* visitmaryland.org	410-767-3400		339-21
Treasurer 80 Calvert St Rm 109.............. Annapolis MD 21401 *TF:* 800-974-0468 ■ *Web:* www.treasurer.state.md.us	410-260-7533		339-21
Veterans Affairs Dept 31 Hopkins Plaza Rm 1231 ....Baltimore MD 21201 *TF:* 800-446-4926 ■ *Web:* veterans.maryland.gov	410-230-4444		339-21
Vital Records Div 6764-B Reisterstown Rd ....Baltimore MD 21215 *TF:* 800-832-3277 ■ *Web:* www.dhmh.maryland.gov	410-764-3038		339-21
Weights & Measures Section 50 Harry S Truman Pkwy .... Annapolis MD 21401 *Web:* mda.maryland.gov	410-841-5790	841-2765	339-21
Workers' Compensation Commission 10 E Baltimore St.........................Baltimore MD 21202 *TF:* 800-492-0479 ■ *Web:* www.wcc.state.md.us	410-864-5100		339-21
Workforce Development Div 1100 N Eutaw St Rm 616..................Baltimore MD 21201 *Web:* www.dllr.state.md.us/employment	410-767-2173	767-2986	259
Maryland & Virginia Milk Producers Co-op Assn Inc 1985 Isaac Newton Sq W ....Reston VA 20190 *TF:* 800-552-1976 ■ *Web:* www.mdvamilk.com	703-742-6800	742-7459	297-4
Maryland Art Place (MAP) 218 W Saratoga St ....Baltimore MD 21201 *Web:* www.mdartplace.org	410-962-8565		50-2
Maryland Assn of Counties (MACo) 169 Conduit St........................... Annapolis MD 21401 *Web:* www.mdcounties.org	410-269-0043	268-1775	49-7
Maryland Assn of Realtors 2594 Riva Rd .... Annapolis MD 21401 **Fax Area Code:* 301 ■ *TF:* 800-638-6425 ■ *Web:* www.mdrealtor.org	410-841-6080	261-8369*	656
Maryland Bar Journal 520 W Fayette St...........................Baltimore MD 21201 *TF:* 800-492-1964 ■ *Web:* www.msba.org/departments	410-685-7878	685-1016	457-15
Maryland Bartending Academy 209 New Jersey Ave NE ....Glen Burnie MD 21060 *Web:* www.marylandbartending.com	410-787-0020		800
Maryland Beachcomber 12417 Ocean Gateway Ste A-7..............Ocean City MD 21842 *Web:* www.mddcpress.com	410-213-9442		532-4
Maryland Ceramic & Steatite Company Inc PO Box 527 .... Bel Air MD 21014 *Web:* www.marylandceramic.com	410-838-4114	457-4333	249
Maryland Chamber of Commerce 60 W St Ste 100......................... Annapolis MD 21401 *Web:* www.mdchamber.org	410-269-0642	269-5247	140

Phone | Fax | Class

Maryland Composition Co
14880 Sweitzer Rd .... Laurel MD 20707 240-295-5674 781
Web: ags.com

Maryland Cork Co Inc
505 Blue Ball Rd PO Box 126.................. Elkton MD 21922 410-398-2955 392-9433 209
TF: 800-662-2675 ■ *Web:* www.marylandcork.com

Maryland Correctional Adjustment Ctr
401 E Madison St..........................Baltimore MD 21202 410-539-5445 213

Maryland Correctional Enterprises (MCE)
7275 Waterloo Rd.............................Jessup MD 20794 410-540-5454 540-5570 630
TF: 800-735-2258 ■ *Web:* mce.md.gov

Maryland Correctional Institution for Women (MCI-W)
7943 Brockbridge Rd ....Jessup MD 20794 410-379-3800 213

Maryland Correctional Institution-Hagerstown
18601 Roxbury Rd .... Hagerstown MD 21746 301-733-2800 790-4939 213
Web: msa.maryland.gov

Maryland Correctional Training Ctr
18800Roxbury Rd........................ Hagerstown MD 21746 240-420-1601 213
Web: dbm.maryland.gov

Maryland Federation of Art Cir Gallery (MFA)
18 State Cir.............................. Annapolis MD 21401 410-268-4566 50-2
Web: www.mdfedart.com

Maryland Film Festival 34 E 25th St...........Baltimore MD 21218 410-752-8083 282
Web: www.mdfilmfest.com

Maryland Gazette 2000 Capital Dr............ Annapolis MD 21401 410-268-5000 268-4643 532-4
TF: 800-557-2068 ■ *Web:* www.capitalgazette.com

Maryland General Hospital
827 Linden Ave...........................Baltimore MD 21201 410-225-8000 374-3
Web: ummidtown.org

Maryland Hall for the Creative Arts
801 Chase St .... Annapolis MD 21401 410-263-5544 263-5114 572
TF: 866-438-3808 ■ *Web:* www.marylandhall.org

Maryland Health Enterprises Inc
3300 N Ridge Rd Ste 390.................. Ellicott City MD 21043 410-750-7500 194
Web: www.lorienhealth.com

Maryland Heights Chamber of Commerce
547 W Port Plaza .... Saint Louis MO 63146 314-576-6603 576-6855 139
Web: www.mhcc.com

Maryland Historical Society Museum & Library
201 W Monument St........................Baltimore MD 21201 410-685-3750 385-2105 520
TF: 800-537-5487 ■ *Web:* www.mdhs.org

Maryland Inn 16 Church Cir .... Annapolis MD 21401 410 263 2641 268 3613 379
TF: 800-847-8882 ■ *Web:* www.historicinnsofannapolis.com

Maryland Institute College of Art
1300 W Mt Royal Ave......................Baltimore MD 21217 410-669-9200 225-2337 164
Web: www.mica.edu

Maryland Jockey Club of Baltimore City Inc
5201 Park Heights Ave ....Baltimore MD 21215 410-542-9400 642
Web: www.marylandracing.com

Maryland Library Assn (MLA)
1401 Hollins St...........................Baltimore MD 21223 410-947-5090 947-5089 435
TF: 800-433-3243 ■ *Web:* www.mdlib.org

Maryland Match Corp 605 Alluvion St ....Baltimore MD 21230 410-752-8164 752-3441 469
TF: 800-423-0013 ■ *Web:* www.marylandmatch.com

Maryland Midland Railway Inc
40 N Main St .... Union Bridge MD 21791 410-775-7718 649

Maryland Municipal League Insurance Agency Inc
1212 W St Ste 100 .... Annapolis MD 21401 410-268-5514 533
TF: 800-492-7121 ■ *Web:* www.mdmunicipal.org

Maryland Nurses Assn (MNA)
21 Governor's Ct Ste 195 ....Baltimore MD 21244 410-944-5800 533
Web: www.marylandrn.org

Maryland Paper Company LP
16144 Elliott Pkwy .... Williamsport MD 21795 301 223 6550 557
Web: www.marylandpaper.com

Maryland Pharmacists Assn
9115 Guilford Rd Ste 200...................Columbia MD 21046 410-727-0746 727-2253 585
Web: www.marylandpharmacist.org

Maryland Plastics Inc
251 E Central Ave.......................Federalsburg MD 21632 410-754-5566 607
TF Cust Svc: 800-544-5582 ■ *Web:* www.marylandplastics.com

Maryland Precision Spring Co
8900 Kelso Dr...........................Baltimore MD 21221 410-391-7400 687-9223 719
TF: 800-237-5225 ■ *Web:* www.mw-ind.com

Maryland Public Interest Research Group (MaryPIRG)
3121 St Paul St Ste 26.......................Baltimore MD 21218 410-467-0439 366 2051 633
Web: www.marylandpirg.org

Maryland Public Television (MPT)
11767 Owings Mills Blvd................. Owings Mills MD 21117 410-581-4201 581-4338 632
TF: 800-223-3678 ■ *Web:* www.mpt.org

Maryland Renaissance Festival
PO Box 315 ....Crownsville MD 21032 410-266-7304 573-1508 149
TF: 800-296-7304 ■ *Web:* www.rennfest.com

Maryland Republican Party
69 Franklin St .... Annapolis MD 21401 410-263-2125 616-2
Web: www.mdgop.org

Maryland Science Ctr 601 Light St............Baltimore MD 21230 410-685-2370 545-5974 520
Web: www.mdsci.org

Maryland State Bar Assn Inc
520 W Fayette St.........................Baltimore MD 21201 410-685-7878 685-1016 72
TF: 800-492-1964 ■ *Web:* www.msba.org

Maryland State Dental Assn
6410 Dobbin Rd ....Columbia MD 21045 410-964-2880 964-0583 227
TF: 800-621-8099 ■ *Web:* www.msda.com

Maryland State Medical Society
1211 Cathedral St.........................Baltimore MD 21201 410-539-0872 547-0915 474
TF: 800-492-1056 ■ *Web:* www.medchi.org

Maryland Symphony Orchestra, The
30 W Washington St..................... Hagerstown MD 21740 301-797-4000 797-2314 573-3
Web: www.marylandsymphony.org

Maryland Theatre 21 S Potomac St.......... Hagerstown MD 21740 301-790-3500 791-6114 572
TF: 800-895-2785 ■ *Web:* www.mdtheatre.org

Maryland Thermoform Corp
2717 Wilmarco Ave.........................Baltimore MD 21223 410-947-5063 596
Web: www.mdthermo.com

Maryland Transit Administration (MTA)
6 St Paul St..............................Baltimore MD 21202 410-539-5000 333-4810 468
Web: www.mta.maryland.gov

Maryland Veterinary Medical Assn
8015 Corporate Dr Ste A..................Baltimore MD 21236 410-931-3332 931-2060 75
TF: 888-884-6862 ■ *Web:* www.mdvma.org

Maryland Zoo in Baltimore
1876 Mansion House Dr....................Baltimore MD 21217 410-396-7102 83
Web: marylandzoo.org

Marylhurst University
17600 Pacific Hwy 43 PO Box 261............Marylhurst OR 97036 503-636-8141 635-6585* 66
**Fax:* Admissions ■ *TF:* 800-634-9982 ■ *Web:* www.marylhurst.edu

Marymount Hospital
12300 McCracken Rd..................Garfield Heights OH 44125 216-581-0500 587-8882 74-3
TF: 800-801-2273 ■ *Web:* my.clevelandclinic.org

Marymount Manhattan College
221 E 71st St ....New York NY 10021 212-517-0400 517-0448 66
TF: 866-667-6572 ■ *Web:* www.mmm.edu

Marymount University
2807 N Glebe Rd ....Arlington VA 22207 703-522-5600 522-0349 66
TF: 800-548-7638 ■ *Web:* www.marymount.edu

MaryPIRG (Maryland Public Interest Research Group)
3121 St Paul St Ste 26......................Baltimore MD 21218 410-467-0439 366-2051 33
Web: www.marylandpirg.org

Marysville House 153 Main St............... Marysville MT 59640 406-443-6677 71

Maryvale Hospital 5102 W Campbell Ave .... Phoenix AZ 85031 623-848-5000 74-3
Web: www.abrazohealth.com

Maryville College
502 E Lamar Alexander Pkwy ....Maryville TN 37804 865-981-8000 981-8005* 166
**Fax:* Admissions ■ *TF:* 800-597-2687 ■ *Web:* www.maryvillecollege.edu

Marywood University Arboretum
2300 Adams Ave...........................Scranton PA 18509 570-348-6218 97
TF: 866-279-9663 ■ *Web:* www.marywood.edu

Marzano 516 Garfield St S .... Tacoma WA 98444 253-537-4191 671
Web: www.dinemarzano.com

MAS Capital Inc
2715 Coney Island Ave...................... Brooklyn NY 11235 866-553-7493 091
TF: 866-553-7493 ■ *Web:* www.mascapital.com

MAS (Farmhouse) 39 Downing St..............New York NY 10014 212-255-1790 255-0279 671
Web: masfarmhouse.com

Masa
10 Columbus Cir Time Warner Ctr 4th Fl ....New York NY 10019 212-823-9800 671
Web: www.masanyc.com

Masa's Restaurant 648 Bush St........... San Francisco CA 94108 415-989-7154 671
Web: www.masasrestaurant.com

Maschmeyer Concrete Company of Florida
1142 Watertower Rd ....Lake Park FL 33403 561-844-9994 182
Web: www.maschmeyer.com

Maschoff Design Engineering Inc
1325 Kenilworth Dr....................... Woodbury MN 55125 651-578-3565 261
Web: www.mdeeng.com

Masco Cabinetry LLC 5353 W US 223............ Adrian MI 49221 517-263-0771 115
TF: 866-850-8557 ■ *Web:* www.merillat.com

Masco Corp 21001 Van Born Rd ....Taylor MI 48180 313-274-7400 792-4177 609
NYSE: MAS ■ *TF:* 888-627-6397 ■ *Web:* www.masco.com

Mascott Equipment Company Inc
435 NE Hancock St..........................Portland OR 97212 503-282-2587 480
Web: www.mascottec.com

Maser Consulting PA
331 Newman Springs Rd Ste203 ....Red Bank NJ 07701 732-383-1950 383-1984 261
Web: www.maserconsulting.com

Masergy Communications Inc
2740 N Dallas Pkwy Ste 260.....................Plano TX 75093 214-442-5700 442-5756 224
TF: 866-588-5885 ■ *Web:* www.masergy.com

Mash Studios Inc
2611 W Exposition Blvd ....Los Angeles CA 90018 310-313-4700 321
Web: mashstudios.com

Mashamoquet Brook State Park
147 Wolf Den Dr.....................Pomfret Center CT 06259 860-928-6121 565
Web: www.ct.gov

Mashwork Inc 85 BRd St 18th Fl.............. New York NY 10004 646-201-9124 466
Web: canvs.tv

Masimo Corp 40 Parker .... Irvine CA 92618 949-297-7000 250
TF: 800-326-4890 ■ *Web:* www.masimo.com

Mask-Off Company Inc 345 W Maple Ave....... Monrovia CA 91016 626-359-3261 359-7160 3
Web: www.mask-off.com

Masland Carpets Inc
716 Bill Myles Dr .... Saraland AL 36571 800-633-0468 131
TF: 800-633-0468 ■ *Web:* www.maslandcarpets.com

Maslon Edelman Borman & Brand LLP
3300 Wells Fargo Ctr 90 S Seventh St ....Minneapolis MN 55402 612-672-8200 428
Web: www.maslon.com

Maslow Media Group Inc, The
2233 Wisconsin Ave NW Ste 400............ Washington DC 20007 202-965-1100 514
TF: 800-337-1629 ■ *Web:* www.maslowmedia.com

Mason & Blair LLC
1762 Technology Dr Ste 206 ....San Jose CA 95110 408-436-6300 260
Web: www.masonblair.com

Mason & Hamlin Piano Co
35 Duncan St .... Haverhill MA 01830 978-374-8888 374-8080 527
Web: www.masonhamlin.com

Mason Assocaites Inc
170 Us Rt 1 Ste 280 ....Falmouth ME 04105 207-347-3557 180
Web: www.masonassociates.com

Mason City Area Chamber of Commerce
25 W State St .... Mason City IA 50401 641-423-5724 423-5725 139
Web: www.masoncityia.com

Mason City Convention & Visitors Bureau
2021 Fourth St SW Hwy 122 W .... Mason City IA 50401 641-422-1663 206
TF: 800-423-5724 ■ *Web:* www.visitmasoncityiowa.com

Mason City Public Library
225 Second St SE......................... Mason City IA 50401 641-421-3668 423-2615 434-3
TF: 800-532-1531 ■ *Web:* www.mcpl.org

Mason City School District 211 NE St........... Mason OH 45040 513-398-0474 780
Web: www.masonohioschools.com

Mason Contractors Assn of America (MCCA) (MCAA)
1481 Merchant Dr.......................... Algonquin IL 60102 224-678-9709 678-9714 49-3
TF: 800-536-2225 ■ *Web:* www.masoncontractors.org

Mason Corp 123 W Oxmoor Rd ....Birmingham AL 35209 205-942-4100 480
TF: 800-868-4100 ■ *Web:* www.masoncorp.com

Mason County 125 N Plum ....Havana IL 62644 309-543-6661 543-2085 338
Web: www.masoncountyil.org

Name / Address	City	State	ZIP	Phone	Fax	Class
Mason County 304 E Ludington Ave	Ludington	MI	49431	231-843-8202	843-1972	338
Web: www.masoncounty.net						
Mason County PO Box 702	Mason	TX	76856	325-347-5253	347-6868	338
Web: www.co.mason.tx.us						
Mason County						
81 East Wilburs Way PO Box 787	Shelton	WA	98584	360-426-8729	427-0319	338
Mason County 200 Sixth St	Point Pleasant	WV	25550	304-675-1110	675-4982	338
Web: www.masoncounty.wv.gov						
Mason County						
419 N Fourth St PO Box 340	Shelton	WA	98584	360-427-9670		338
Web: www.co.mason.wa.us						
Mason County Area Chamber of Commerce						
305 Main St	Point Pleasant	WV	25550	304-675-1050	675-1601	139
Web: www.masoncountychamber.org						
Mason County Public Library						
508 Viand St	Point Pleasant	WV	25550	304-675-0894	675-0895	434-3
Web: masoncounty.lib.wv.us						
Mason Horvath Inc						
999 Canada Pl Ste 404	Vancouver	BC	V6C3E2	604-899-9498		774
Web: www.masonhorvath.com						
Mason Inc 23 Amity Rd	Bethany	CT	06524	203-393-1101		5
Web: www.mason-madison.com						
Mason Industries Inc 350 Rabro Dr	Hauppauge	NY	11788	631-348-0282		472
Web: www.mason-ind.com						
Mason Jar, The						
2925 W Colorado Ave	Colorado Springs	CO	80904	719-632-4820		671
Web: www.masonjarcolorado.com						
Mason Mfg LLC 1645 N Railroad Ave	Decatur	IL	62524	217-422-2770		361
Web: www.masonmfg.com						
Mason Neck State Park 7301 High Pt Rd	Lorton	VA	22079	703-490-4979		565
Web: www.dcr.virginia.gov/state-parks/mason-neck						
Mason Structural Steel Inc						
7500 Northfield Rd	Walton Hills	OH	44146	440-439-1040		362
TF: 800-686-1223 ■ Web: www.masonsteel.com						
Mason Wells						
411 E Wisconsin Ave Ste 1280	Milwaukee	WI	53202	414-727-6400	727-6410	402
Web: www.masonwells.com						
Mason Wells Biomedical Fund						
411 E Wisconsin Ave Ste 1280	Milwaukee	WI	53202	414-727-6400	727-6410	792
Web: www.masonwells.com						
Mason West Inc 1601 E Miraloma Ave	Placentia	CA	92870	714-630-0701		358
Web: www.masonwest.com						
Mason, Griffin & Pierson PC						
101 Poor Farm Rd	Princeton	NJ	08540	609-921-6543		428
Web: www.mgplaw.com						
MasonBaronet Inc						
1801 N Lamar St Ste 250	Dallas	TX	75202	214-954-0316		7
Web: www.masonbaronet.com						
Mason-Dixon Historical Park						
79 Buckeye Rd	Core	WV	26541	304-879-4101		50-4
Masonic 22 Masonic Ave	Wallingford	CT	06492	203-679-5900		450
Web: masonicare.org						
Masonic Service Assn of North America (MSANA)						
8120 Fenton St Ste 203	Silver Spring	MD	20910	301-588-4010	608-3457	48-15
TF: 855-476-4010 ■ Web: www.msana.com						
Masonic Temple Theatre 500 Temple St	Detroit	MI	48201	313-832-7100		572
Web: www.themasonic.com						
Masonic Villages Of Pennsylvania						
One Masonic Dr	Elizabethtown	PA	17022	717-367-1121		793
TF: 800-462-7664 ■ Web: masonicvillages.org/elizabethtown						
Masonic, The 1111 California St	San Francisco	CA	94108	415-776-7457		205
Web: sfmasonic.com						
Masonite International Corp						
201 N Franklin St Ste 300	Tampa	FL	33602	813-877-2726	739-0204	236
TF: 800-895-2723 ■ Web: www.masonite.com						
Masonite Primeboard Inc						
2441 15th St N	Wahpeton	ND	58075	701-642-1152		819
Masonry Arts Inc 2105 Third Ave N	Bessemer	AL	35020	205-428-0780		189-7
Web: www.masonryarts.com						
Masonry Reinforcing Corp of America						
400 Roundtree Rd	Charlotte	NC	28224	704-525-5554		480
Web: www.wirebond.com						
Masonry Technology Inc						
24235 Electric St	Cresco	IA	52136	563-547-1122		608
Web: iqpowertools.com/product-category/tec-connect						
Maspeth Federal Savings 56-18 69th St	Maspeth	NY	11378	718-335-1300	446-3671	70
TF: 888-558-1300 ■ Web: www.maspethfederal.com						
Masraff's 1753 S Post Oak Ln	Houston	TX	77056	713-355-1975	355-1965	671
Web: www.masraffs.com						
Mass Bay Commuter Railroad Co 89 S St	Boston	MA	02111	617-222-8001		546
Mass Connections Inc						
13131 E 166th St	Cerritos	CA	90703	562-365-0200		195
Mass Media Inc 883 Patriot Dr	Moorpark	CA	93021	805-531-9399		225
Web: www.massmedia.com						
Mass Movement Inc 65 Green St Ste 1	Foxboro	MA	02035	508-543-2073		711
Web: www.massmovement.com						
Mass Precision Sheetmetal Inc						
2110 Oakland Rd	San Jose	CA	95131	408-954-0200	954-0288	488
Web: www.massprecision.com						
Massa Products Corp 280 Lincoln St	Hingham	MA	02043	781-749-4800		668
TF: 800-962-7543 ■ Web: www.massa.com						
Massa's 1160 Smith St	Houston	TX	77002	713-650-0837		671
Web: www.massas.com						
Massachusetts						
Agricultural Resources Dept						
251 Cswy St Ste 500	Boston	MA	02114	617-626-1700	626-1850	339-22
Web: www.mass.gov/eea/agencies/agr						
Attorney General 1 Ashburton Pl	Boston	MA	02108	617-727-2200		339-22
Web: www.mass.gov						
Banks Div 1000 Washington St FL 10	Boston	MA	02118	617-956-1500	956-1599	339-22
TF: 800-495-2265 ■ Web: www.mass.gov						
Business Development Office						
10 Pk Plaza Ste 5220	Boston	MA	02116	617-973-8600	973-8554	339-22
Web: www.mass.gov						
Child Support Enforcement Div						
51 Sleeper St 4th Fl	Boston	MA	02205	617-660-1234	626-3894	339-22
TF: 800-332-2733 ■ Web: www.mass.gov						
Correction Dept 50 Maple St Ste 3	Milford	MA	01757	508-422-3300	422-3386	339-22
Web: www.mass.gov						
Cultural Council 10 St James Ave 3rd Fl	Boston	MA	02116	617-858-2700	727-0044	339-22
TF: 800-232-0960 ■ Web: www.massculturalcouncil.org						
Department of Elementary and Secondary Education						
350 Main St	Malden	MA	02148	781-338-3000		339-22
Web: www.doe.mass.edu						
Emergency Management Agency						
400 Worcester Rd	Framingham	MA	01702	508-820-2000	820-2030	339-22
Web: www.mass.gov						
Environmental Protection Dept						
1 Winter St	Boston	MA	02108	617-292-5500		339-22
Web: mass.gov/eea/agencies/massdep						
Executive Office of Transportation						
10 Pk Plaza Ste 3170	Boston	MA	02116	617-973-7000	973-8031	339-22
TF: 800-219-9936 ■ Web: www.massdot.state.ma.us						
Fish & Game Dept 251 Cswy St Ste 400	Boston	MA	02114	617-626-1500	626-1505	339-22
Web: mass.gov/eea/pagenotfound.html						
General Court State House	Boston	MA	02133	617-722-2000		339-22
Web: malegislature.gov						
Governor						
State House Executive Office Rm 280	Boston	MA	02133	617-725-4005	727-9725	339-22
TF: 888-870-7770 ■ Web: www.mass.gov						
Higher Education Board						
1 Ashburton Pl Rm 1401	Boston	MA	02108	617-994-6950	727-6397	339-22
Web: www.mass.edu						
Historical Commission						
220 William T Morrissey Blvd	Boston	MA	02125	617-727-8470	727-5128	339-22
Web: www.sec.state.ma.us						
Housing & Community Development Dept						
100 Cambridge St Ste 300	Boston	MA	02114	617-573-1100	573-1120	339-22
Web: mass.gov/hed/economic/eohed/dhcd						
Housing Finance Agency 1 Beacon St	Boston	MA	02108	617-854-1000	854-1029	339-22
TF: 800-882-1154 ■ Web: www.masshousing.com						
Information Technology Div						
1 Ashburton Pl Rm 804	Boston	MA	02108	617-626-4400	626-4411	339-22
Web: www.mass.gov						
Insurance Div						
1000 Washington St Ste 810	Boston	MA	02118	617-521-7794	753-6830	339-22
TF: 877-563-4467 ■ Web: mass.gov/ocabr/government/oca-agencies/doi-lp						
Medical Examiner 720 Albany St	Boston	MA	02118	617-267-6767	266-6763	339-22
TF: 800-962-7877 ■ Web: www.mass.gov						
Mental Health Dept 25 Staniford St	Boston	MA	02114	617-626-8000		339-22
TF: 800-221-0053 ■ Web: www.mass.gov/eohhs/gov/departments/dmh						
Parole Board 12 Mercer Rd	Natick	MA	01760	508-650-4500	650-4599	339-22
TF: 888-298-6272 ■ Web: mass.gov/eopss/agencies/parole-board						
Professional Licensure Div						
1000 Washington St Ste 710	Boston	MA	02118	617-727-3074	727-1944	339-22
Web: mass.gov/ocabr/government/oca-agencies/dpl-lp						
Public Health Dept 250 Washington St	Boston	MA	02108	617-624-6000		339-22
Web: mass.gov/eohhs/gov/departments/dph						
Public Protection & Advocacy Bureau						
100 Cambridge St	Boston	MA	02114	617-727-2200		339-22
Web: www.sec.state.ma.us						
Public Utilities Dept 1 S Stn	Boston	MA	02110	617-305-3500		339-22
Web: www.mass.gov/eea						
Registry of Motor Vehicles						
PO Box 55891	Boston	MA	02205	617-351-4500		339-22
Web: www.massrmv.com						
Rehabilitation Commission						
27 Wormwood St Ste 600	Boston	MA	02210	617-204-3600		339-22
Web: www.mass.gov						
Revenue Dept PO Box 7010	Boston	MA	02204	617-887-6436		339-22
TF: 800-392-6089 ■ Web: www.mass.gov/dor						
Secretary of the Commonwealth						
State House Rm 337	Boston	MA	02133	617-727-9180	742-4722	339-22
Web: www.sec.state.ma.us						
Securities Div 1 Ashburton Pl 17th Fl	Boston	MA	02108	617-727-3548	248-0177	339-22
TF: 800-269-5428 ■ Web: www.sec.state.ma.us/sct						
Standards Div 1 Ashburton Pl Rm 1115	Boston	MA	02108	617-727-3480		339-22
Web: www.mass.gov						
State Boxing Commission						
1 Ashburton Pl Rm 1301	Boston	MA	02108	617-727-3200		712
Web: www.mass.gov/mbc						
State Ethics Commission						
1 Ashburton Pl Rm 619	Boston	MA	02108	617-371-9500	723-5851	265
Web: www.mass.gov/ethics						
State Lottery Commission						
60 Columbian St	Braintree	MA	02184	781-849-5555	849-5546	452
Web: www.masslottery.com						
State Parks & Recreation Div						
251 Cswy St Ste 900	Boston	MA	02114	617-626-1250	626-1351	339-22
Web: mass.gov						
State Police Dept 470 Worcester Rd	Framingham	MA	01702	508-820-2300	820-2211	339-22
Web: www.mass.gov						
State Racing Commission						
1 Ashburton Pl 11th Fl	Boston	MA	02108	617-727-2581	994-6024	712
Web: www.mass.gov						
Supreme Judicial Ct						
1 Pemberton Sq Ste 2500	Boston	MA	02108	617-557-1000		339-22
Web: www.mass.gov/courts						
Transitional Assistance Dept						
600 Washington St	Boston	MA	02111	617-348-8400		339-22
Web: www.mass.gov/eohhs/gov/departments/dta						
Travel & Tourism Office						
10 Pk Plaza Ste 4510	Boston	MA	02116	617-973-8500	973-8525	339-22
TF: 800-227-6277 ■ Web: www.massvacation.com						
Treasurer State House Rm 227	Boston	MA	02133	617-367-6900		339-22
Web: mass.gov/treasury						
Veterans' Services Dept						
600 Washington St 7th Fl	Boston	MA	02111	617-210-5480	210-5755	339-22
Web: www.mass.gov/veterans						
Victim Compensation & Assistance Div						
1 Ashburton Pl 19th Fl	Boston	MA	02108	617-727-2200		339-22
Web: www.mass.gov						
Vital Records & Statistics Registry						
150 Mt Vernon St 1st Fl	Dorchester	MA	02125	617-740-2600		339-22
Web: www.mass.gov						

Phone | Fax | Class

Workforce Development Dept
1 Ashburton Pl Rm 107 .... Boston MA 02108 617-727-4100 727-5514 259
Web: www.mass.gov

Massachusetts Assn of Realtors
256 Second Ave .... Waltham MA 02451 781-890-3700 890-4919 656
TF: 800-725-6272 ■ *Web:* www.marealtor.com

Massachusetts Assn of Registered Nurses (MARN)
PO Box 285 .... Milton MA 02186 617-990-2856 533
Web: anamass.org

Massachusetts Bar Assn 20 W St .... Boston MA 02111 617-338-0500 72
Web: mass.gov

Massachusetts Bay Community College
Framingham 19 Flagg Dr .... Framingham MA 01702 508-270-4000 872-4067 162
Web: www.massbay.edu
Wellesley Hills 50 Oakland St .... Wellesley Hills MA 02481 781-239-3000 239-1047 162
TF: 800-233-3182 ■ *Web:* www.massbay.edu

Massachusetts Bay Transportation Authority (MBTA)
10 Pk Plaza Ste 3910 .... Boston MA 02116 617-222-5000 222-3340* 468
**Fax:* Mktg ■ *Web:* www.mbta.com

Massachusetts Board of Library Commissioners
98 N Washington St .... Boston MA 02114 617-725-1860 725-0140 434-5
TF: 800-952-7403 ■ *Web:* mblc.state.ma.us

Massachusetts Capital Resource Co
420 Boylston St 5th Fl .... Boston MA 02116 617-536-3900 792
Web: www.masscapital.com

Massachusetts College of Art
621 Huntington Ave .... Boston MA 02115 617-879-7222 879-7250 166
TF: 800-834-3242 ■ *Web:* www.massart.edu

Massachusetts College of Liberal Arts
375 Church St .... North Adams MA 01247 413-662-5000 662-5179 166
Web: www.mcla.edu

Massachusetts College of Pharmacy & Health Sciences
179 Longwood Ave .... Boston MA 02115 617-732-2850 732-2110 166
TF: 800-225-5506 ■ *Web:* www.mcphs.edu

Massachusetts Correctional Industries
1 Industries Dr Bldg A PO Box 188 .... Norfolk MA 02056 508-850-1070 850-1091 630
TF: 800-222-2211 ■ *Web:* www.mass.gov

Massachusetts Correctional Institution-Cedar Junction
2405 Main St .... Walpole MA 02071 508-668-2100 213
Web: www.mass.gov

Massachusetts Correctional Institution-Framingham
PO Box 9007 .... Framingham MA 01704 508-532-5100 213
Web: www.mass.gov

Massachusetts Correctional Institution-Plymouth (MCI)
1 Bumps Pond Rd .... South Carver MA 02366 508-291-2441 213
Web: www.mass.gov

Massachusetts Democratic Party
11 Beacon St Ste 410 .... Boston MA 02108 617-939-0800 616-1
Web: www.massdems.org

Massachusetts Dental Society
2 Willow St Ste 200 .... Southborough MA 01745 508-480-9797 480-0002 227
TF: 800-342-8747 ■ *Web:* www.massdental.org

Massachusetts Eye & Ear 243 Charles St .... Boston MA 02114 617-523-7900 374-7
TF: 800-841-2900 ■ *Web:* www.masseyeandear.org

Massachusetts General Hospital
55 Fruit St .... Boston MA 02114 617-726-2000 374-3
Web: www.massgeneral.org

Massachusetts Growth Capital Corp (MGCC)
529 Main St Schrafft Ctr Ste 1M10 .... Charlestown MA 02129 617-523-6262 523-7676 792
Web: www.massgcc.com

Massachusetts Historical Society, The
1154 Boylston St .... Boston MA 02215 617-646-0500 520
Web: www.masshist.org

Massachusetts Hospital School
3 Randolph St .... Canton MA 02021 781-828-2440 821-4086 374-1
Web: www.prhc.us

Massachusetts Institute of Technology
77 Massachusetts Ave .... Cambridge MA 02139 617-253-1000 258-8304 166
TF: 800-556-3656 ■ *Web:* www.web.mit.edu

Massachusetts Maritime Academy
101 Academy Dr .... Buzzards Bay MA 02532 508-830-5000 830-5077* 166
**Fax:* Admissions ■ *TF Admissions:* 800-544-3411 ■ *Web:* www.maritime.edu

Massachusetts Medical Society (MMS)
860 Winter St .... Waltham MA 02451 781-893-4610 893-8009 474
TF: 800-322-2303 ■ *Web:* www.massmed.org

Massachusetts National Cemetery
Conery Ave .... Bourne MA 02532 508-563-7113 564-9946 136
TF: 800-827-1000 ■ *Web:* www.cem.va.gov

Massachusetts Nurses Assn (MNA)
340 Tpke St .... Canton MA 02021 781-821-4625 821-4445 533
TF: 800-882-2056 ■ *Web:* www.massnurses.org

Massachusetts Pharmacists Assn
500 W Cummings Pk Ste 3475 .... Woburn MA 01801 781-933-1107 585
TF: 888-772-7227 ■ *Web:* netforum.avectra.com

Massachusetts Port Authority
1 Harborside Dr Ste 200S .... East Boston MA 02128 617-568-7300 618
Web: www.massport.com

Massachusetts Public Interest Research Group (MASSPIRG)
44 Winter St 4th Fl .... Boston MA 02108 617-292-4800 292-4800 633
Web: www.masspirg.org

Massachusetts Republican State Committee
85 Merrimac St Ste 400 .... Boston MA 02114 617-523-5005 616-2
Web: www.massgop.com

Massachusetts Society of Certified Public Accountants
105 Chauncy St 10th Fl .... Boston MA 02111 617-556-4000 2
TF: 800-392-6145 ■ *Web:* www.mscpaonline.org

Massachusetts Symphony Orchestra
Tuckerman Hall Po Box 20070 .... Worcester MA 01602 508-754-1234 752-3671 573-3
Web: www.masymphony.org/mso/Home.html

Massachusetts Veterinary Medical Assn
163Lakeside Ave .... Marlborough MA 01752 508-460-9333 460-9969 795
TF: 800-272-1813 ■ *Web:* www.massvet.org

Massacre Rocks State Park
3592 N Pk Ln .... American Falls ID 83211 208-548-2672 565
Web: parksandrecreation.idaho.gov

Massanutten Military Academy
614 S Main St .... Woodstock VA 22664 540-459-2167 459-5421 622
TF: 877-466-6222 ■ *Web:* www.militaryschool.com

Phone | Fax | Class

Massanutten Regional Library
174 S Main St .... Harrisonburg VA 22801 540-434-4475 434-3
TF: 800-552-7001 ■ *Web:* www.mrlib.org

Massanutten Resort
1822 Resort Dr .... McGaheysville VA 22840 540-289-9441 289-6981 669
Web: www.massresort.com

Massaro Properties LLC
120 Delta Dr .... Pittsburgh PA 15238 412-963-2800 652
Web: www.massaroproperties.com

Massasoit Community College
1 Massasoit Blvd .... Brockton MA 02302 508-588-9100 427-1255* 162
**Fax:* Admissions ■ *TF:* 800-434-6000 ■ *Web:* www.massasoit.edu

Massasoit State Park
Middleboro Ave .... East Taunton MA 02718 508-822-7405 565
Web: www.mass.gov

massAV 3 Radcliff Rd .... Tewksbury MA 01803 800-423-7830 232
TF: 800-423-7830 ■ *Web:* www.massav.com

Massey Cancer Ctr
Virginia Commonwealth University
401 College St PO Box 980037 .... Richmond VA 23298 804-828-0450 828-8453 668
TF: 877-462-7739 ■ *Web:* www.massey.vcu.edu

Massey Hall 178 Victoria St .... Toronto ON M5B1T7 416-872-4255 572
Web: www.masseyhall.com

Massey Knakal Realty Services Inc
275 Madison Ave 3rd Fl .... New York NY 10016 212-696-2500 652
Web: www.masseyknakal.com

Massey Services Inc
315 Groveland St E .... Orlando FL 32804 407-645-2500 577
TF: 888-262-7739 ■ *Web:* www.masseyservices.com

Massey Theatre 735 Eighth Ave .... New Westminster BC V3M2R2 604-517-5900 749
Web: vcn.bc.ca

Massie Thomas (Rep R - KY)
2453 Rayburn HOB .... Washington DC 20515 202-225-3465 342-2
Web: massie.house.gov

Massillon Area Chamber of Commerce
137 Lincoln Way E .... Massillon OH 44646 330-833-3146 833-8944 139
Web: www.massillonohchamber.com

Massillon City School District
207 Oak Ave SE .... Massillon OH 44646 330-830-3900 685
Web: www.massillonschools.org

Massimo's 5200 Mowry Ave .... Fremont CA 94538 510-792-2000 792-7041 671
Web: www.massimos.com

Massini Group
1323 NE Orenco Stn Pkwy Ste 300 .... Hillsboro OR 97124 503-640-9800 195
Web: www.massini-group.com

Massive Audio 2261 S Atlantic Blvd .... Commerce CA 90040 323-262-2262 57
Web: www.massiveaudio.com

Massive Prints Inc
2035 Vista Bella Way Rancho Dominguez .... Compton CA 90220 310-667-8991 195
Web: www.massiveinc.com

Massman Automation Designs LLC
1010 E Lake St .... Villard MN 56385 320-554-3611 547
Web: www.massmanllc.com

Massman Construction Co
4400 W 109th St .... Overland Park KS 66211 913-291-2600 291-2601 188-5
Web: www.massman.net

MassMutual Ctr 1277 Main St .... Springfield MA 01103 413-787-6610 787-6645 205
TF: 800-639-8602 ■ *Web:* www.massmutualcenter.com

MassMutual PAC 1295 State St .... Springfield MA 01111 413-788-8411 615
TF: 800-272-2216 ■ *Web:* www.massmutual.com/pac

Massoud Furniture Manufacturing Inc
8351 Moberly Ln .... Dallas TX 75227 214-388-8655 321
TF: 800-762-2797 ■ *Web:* www.massoudfurniture.com

MASSPIRG (Massachusetts Public Interest Research Group)
44 Winter St 4th Fl .... Boston MA 02108 617-292-4800 292-4800 633
Web: www.masspirg.org

MassTech Inc
6992 Columbia Gateway Dr .... Columbia MD 21046 443-539-1758 419
Web: www.apmaldi.com

MAST Biosurgery Inc
6749 Top Gun St Ste 108 .... San Diego CA 92121 858-550-8050 475
Web: www.mastbio.com

Mast Brian (Rep R - FL)
2182 Rayburn HOB .... Washington DC 20515 202-225-3026 225-8398 342-2
Web: mast.house.gov

Mast Drug Company Inc
1910 Ross Mill Rd .... Henderson NC 27537 252-438-3112 237
Web: www.mastdrug.com

Mast General Store Inc
721 S Second St .... Clinton IA 52732 563-242-5702 206
TF: 800-579-2294 ■ *Web:* www.clintoniowatourism.com

Mast General Store Inc
3565 Nc Hwy 194 S .... Banner Elk NC 28604 828-963-6511 229
Web: www.mastgeneralstore.com

Mast Hill Consulting Inc
15 Mast Hill Rd .... Hingham MA 02043 781-741-5200 463
Web: www.masthillconsulting.com

MAST Vacation Partners Inc
635 Butterfield Rd Ste 150 .... Oakbrook Terrace IL 60181 630-889-9817 889-9832 772
Web: www.mvptravel.com

MasTec Inc 800 Douglas Rd 12th Fl .... Coral Gables FL 33134 305-599-1800 406-1960 188-1
NYSE: MTZ ■ *TF:* 800-531-5000 ■ *Web:* www.mastec.com

Master Appliance Corp 2420 18th St .... Racine WI 53403 262-633-7791 633-9745 759
TF: 800-558-9413 ■ *Web:* www.masterappliance.com

Master Automatic Inc
40485 Schoolcraft Rd .... Plymouth MI 48170 734-414-0500 454
Web: www.masterautomatic.com

Master Bond Inc 154 Hobart St .... Hackensack NJ 07601 201-343-8983 3
Web: www.masterbond.com

Master Brewers Assn of the Americas (MBAA)
3340 Pilot Knob Rd .... Saint Paul MN 55121 651-454-7250 49-6
TF: 800-328-7560 ■ *Web:* www.mbaa.com

Master Cutlery Inc 700 Penhorn Ave .... Secaucus NJ 07094 201-271-7600 271-7666 222
TF: 888-271-7229 ■ *Web:* www.mastercutlery.com

Master Design Co 789 State Rt 94 E .... Fulton KY 42041 270-838-7060 838-7060 65
Web: www.masterdesign.org

Master Finish Co
2020 Nelson SE PO Box 7505 .... Grand Rapids MI 49510 877-590-5819 245-0039* 481
**Fax Area Code:* 616 ■ *TF:* 877-590-5819 ■ *Web:* www.masterfinishco.com

Company	Address	City	State	Zip	Phone	Fax	Class	Notes
Master Graphics LLC	1100 S Main St	Rochelle	IL	61068	815-562-5800	562-6600	627	*Web:* www.mg-printing.com
Master Halco Inc	3010 Lyndon B Johnson Fwy Ste 800	Dallas	TX	75234	972-714-7300	542-8488*	279	*Fax Area Code: 800 ■ *Fax: Cust Svc ■ *TF:* 800-883-8384 ■ *Web:* www.masterhalco.com
Master Industries Inc	14420 Myford Rd	Irvine	CA	92606	714-918-4650		710	*Web:* www.masterindustries.com
Master Klean Janitorial Inc	2149 S Clermont St	Denver	CO	80222	303-753-6084		104	*TF:* 800-659-3999 ■ *Web:* www.masterklean.com
Master Lock Company LLC	137 W Forest Hill Ave PO Box 927	Oak Creek	WI	53154	800-464-2088	308-9245	350	*TF:* 800-464-2088 ■ *Web:* www.masterlock.com
Master Machine & Tool Company Inc	5857 Jefferson Ave	Newport News	VA	23605	757-245-6653		757	*TF:* 800-232-6133 ■ *Web:* www.master-machine.com
Master Magnetics Inc	747 S Gilbert St	Castle Rock	CO	80104	303-688-3966		295	*TF:* 800-525-3536 ■ *Web:* www.magnetsource.com
Master Manufacturing Co Inc	4703 Ohara Dr	Evansville	IN	47711	812-425-1561	425-4320	172	
Master Marine Inc	14284 Shell Belt Rd	Bayou La Batre	AL	36509	251-824-4151		698	*Web:* www.mastermarineinc.com
Master Mark Plastics	210 Ampe Dr	Paynesville	MN	56362	320-243-7318		429	*TF Cust Svc:* 800-535-4838 ■ *Web:* www.mastermark.com
Master Mechanical Inc	820 Greenbrier Cir Ste 11	Chesapeake	VA	23320	757-424-5013		698	*Web:* www.mastermechanical.com
Master Metal Products Co	495 Emory St	San Jose	CA	95110	408-275-1210	275-0523	482	*TF:* 800-488-6903 ■ *Web:* www.mastermetalproducts.com
Master Molded Products Corp	1000 Davis Rd	Elgin	IL	60123	847-695-9700	695-9707	604	*TF:* 800-634-7821 ■ *Web:* www.mastermolded.com
Master Package Corp	200 Madson St	Owen	WI	54460	715-229-2156		125	*TF:* 800-396-8425 ■ *Web:* www.masterpackage.com
Master Pitching Machine	4200 NE Birmingham Rd	Kansas City	MO	64117	816-452-0228	452-7581	710	*Web:* www.masterpitch.com
Master Precision Machining Inc	2199 Ronald St	Santa Clara	CA	95050	408-727-0185		757	*Web:* master-precision.com
Master Print Inc	8401 Terminal Rd	Newington	VA	22122	703-550-9555	550-9673	627	*Web:* www.master-print.com
Master Solutions Inc	20 Wolf Bridge Rd	Carlisle	PA	17013	717-243-6849		207	*Web:* www.mastersi.com
Master Spas Inc	6927 Lincoln Pkwy	Fort Wayne	IN	46804	260-436-9100		375	*TF:* 800-860-7727 ■ *Web:* www.masterspas.com
MASTER Teacher Inc, The	2600 Leadership Ln	Manhattan	KS	66505	800-669-9633		528	*TF:* 800-669-9633 ■ *Web:* www.masterteacher.com
Master Translating Services Inc	10651 N Kendall Dr Ste 220	Miami	FL	33176	305-279-2484		768	*Web:* www.mastertranslating.com
Master's College	21726 Placerita Canyon Rd	Santa Clarita	CA	91321	661-259-3540	288-1037*	166	*Fax: Admissions ■ *TF:* 800-568-6248 ■ *Web:* www.masters.edu
Master-Bilt Products	908 Hwy 15 N	New Albany	MS	38652	662-534-9061	534-6049	14	*TF:* 800-647-1284 ■ *Web:* www.master-bilt.com
MasterCard Inc	2000 Purchase St	Purchase	NY	10577	914-249-2000		215	*NYSE: MA* ■ *TF:* 800-100-1087 ■ *Web:* www.mastercard.us/en-us.html
Masterchem Industries LLC	3135 Old Hwy M	Imperial	MO	63052	866-774-6371		550	*TF:* 866-774-6371 ■ *Web:* www.kilz.com
Mastercoil Spring	4010 Albany	McHenry	IL	60050	815-344-0051	344-0071	719	*TF:* 800-854-2025 ■ *Web:* www.mastercoil.com
Mastercool Usa Inc	1 Aspen Dr	Randolph	NJ	07869	973-252-9119		787	*Web:* www.mastercool.com
MasterCraft Boat Co	100 Cherokee Cove Dr	Vonore	TN	37885	423-884-2221	884-2295	90	*TF:* 800-443-8774 ■ *Web:* mastercraft.com
Mastercraft Engineering Inc	323 Southwell Blvd	Tifton	GA	31794	229-386-1858		488	*Web:* www.mastercraftengineering.com
Mastercraft Industries Inc	777 S St	Newburgh	NY	12550	845-565-8850	565-9392	115	*TF:* 800-835-7812 ■ *Web:* mastercraftusa.com
Mastercraft Mold Inc	3301 W Vernon Ave	Phoenix	AZ	85009	602-484-4520		596	
Masterdrive	15659 E Hinsdale Dr	Centennial	CO	80112	303-627-4447		507	*Web:* www.masterdrive.com
Masterfile Corp	3 Concorde Gate 4th Fl	Toronto	ON	M3C3N7	416-929-3000		589	*TF:* 800-387-9010 ■ *Web:* www.masterfile.com
MasterGraphics Inc	2979 Triverton Pike Dr	Madison	WI	53711	608-256-4884		174	*TF:* 800-873-7238 ■ *Web:* www.mastergraphics.com
Masterit LLC	8024 Stage Hills Blvd Ste 101	Memphis	TN	38133	901-377-7891		175	*Web:* www.master-it.com
Master-Lee Energy Services Corp	5631 Route 981	Latrobe	PA	15650	724-539-8060		104	*TF:* 800-662-4493 ■ *Web:* www.masterlee.com
Masterloy Products Ltd	5663 Doncaster Rd	Ottawa	ON	K1G3N4	613-822-1010		492	*TF:* 800-424-9300 ■ *Web:* www.masterloy.com
Masterman's LLP	11 C St	Auburn	MA	01501	800-525-3313		45	*TF:* 800-525-3313 ■ *Web:* www.mastermans.com
Mastermedia LLC	1908 Coney Island Ave Ste 200	Brooklyn	NY	11230	800-318-1368	504-4000*	177	*Fax Area Code: 718 ■ *TF:* 800-318-1368 ■ *Web:* www.mastermediallc.com
Mastermind LP	2134 Queen St E	Toronto	ON	M4E1E3	416-699-3797		95	*TF:* 888-388-0000 ■ *Web:* www.mastermindtoys.com
Masterpiece International Ltd	39 Broadway 14th Fl	New York	NY	10006	212-825-4800	825-7010	311	*Web:* www.masterpieceintl.com
Masters & Assoc Insurance Inc	24 E Linden Ave	Miamisburg	OH	45343	937-866-3361		390	*Web:* mastersins.com
Masters Academy of Central Florida Inc, The	1500 Lukas Ln	Oviedo	FL	32765	407-971-2221		685	
Masters Advisors Inc	480 New Holland Ave Ste 7201	Lancaster	PA	17602	717-581-1323		463	*TF:* 800-571-1323 ■ *Web:* www.mastersadvisors.com
Masters Gallery Foods Inc	328 County Hwy PP PO Box 170	Plymouth	WI	53073	920-893-8431		297-4	*TF General:* 800-236-8431 ■ *Web:* www.mastersgalleryfoods.com
Masters Gallery Ltd	2115 Fourth St SW	Calgary	AB	T2S1W8	403-245-2064	244-1636	42	*TF:* 866-245-0616 ■ *Web:* www.mastersgalleryltd.com
Masters Inc	5741 NW Cornelius Pass Rd	Hillsboro	OR	97124	503-531-3308	531-9153	229	*TF:* 877-652-5656
Masters Pharmaceutical Inc	11930 Kemper Springs Dr	Cincinnati	OH	45240	513-354-2690		238	*Web:* mastersrx.com
Masters School, The	49 Clinton Ave	Dobbs Ferry	NY	10522	914-479-6400	693-1230	622	*Web:* www.mastersny.org
Masters' Supply Inc	4505 Bishop Ln	Louisville	KY	40218	800-388-6353		612	*TF:* 800-388-6353 ■ *Web:* www.masterssupply.net
Masterson Company Inc	4023 W National Ave	Milwaukee	WI	53215	414-647-1132	647-1170	296-8	*TF:* 800-558-0990 ■ *Web:* www.mastersoncompany.com
Mastertech Services Inc	691 Corporate Cir	Golden	CO	80401	303-278-7300		260	*Web:* www.mastertechservices.com
Masterword Services, International Inc	303 Stafford St	Houston	TX	77079	281-589-0810		768	*TF:* 866-716-4999 ■ *Web:* www.masterword.com
Masterwork Electronics Inc	630 Martin Ave	Rohnert Park	CA	94928	707-588-9906	588-9908	625	*Web:* www.masterworkelectronics.com
Masterworks	19265 Powder Hill Pl NE	Poulsbo	WA	98370	360-394-4300		5	*Web:* www.masterworks.com
Mastics-moriches-shirley Community Library	407 William Floyd Pkwy	Shirley	NY	11967	631-399-1511		434-3	*Web:* www.communitylibrary.org
Masto Public Relations Inc	1811 Western Ave	Albany	NY	12203	518-786-6488		636	*Web:* mastopr.com
Mastodon State Historic Site	1050 Charles J Becker Dr	Imperial	MO	63052	636-464-2976		565	*TF:* 800-334-6946 ■ *Web:* www.mostateparks.com
Mastro Graphic Arts Inc	67 Deep Rock Rd	Rochester	NY	14624	585-436-7570		687	*Web:* www.mastrographics.com
Mastro's Steakhouse	246 N Canon Dr	Beverly Hills	CA	90210	310-888-8782		671	*Web:* mastrosrestaurants.com
Mat & Naddie's Restaurant	937 Leonidas St	New Orleans	LA	70118	504-861-9600		671	*Web:* www.matandnaddies.com
MATA (Memphis Area Transit Authority)	1370 Levee Rd	Memphis	TN	38108	901-722-7100	722-7123	468	*Web:* www.matatransit.com
Matador Resources Co	5400 Lyndon B Johnson Fwy Ste 1500	Dallas	TX	75240	972-371-5200		536	*TF:* 800-368-5948 ■ *Web:* www.matadorresources.com
Matagorda County	1700 Seventh St Rm 202	Bay City	TX	77414	979-244-7680	244-7688	338	*TF:* 800-806-8333 ■ *Web:* www.co.matagorda.tx.us
Matagorda Island Wildlife Management Area	1700 Seventh St	Bay City	TX	77414	979-244-7670		565	*Web:* tpwd.texas.gov
Matan Companies LLLP	4600 Wedgewood Blvd Ste A	Frederick	MD	21703	301-694-9200		528	*TF:* 800-431-2584 ■ *Web:* www.mataninc.com
Matandy Steel & Metal Products LLC	1200 Central Ave	Hamilton	OH	45011	513-844-2277		295	*Web:* www.matandy.com
Matanuska Glacier State Recreation Site	c/o Mat-Su/CB Area Office 7278 E Bogard Rd	Wasilla	AK	99654	907-745-3975		565	*Web:* dnr.alaska.gov
Matanuska Telephone Assn Inc	1740 S Chugach St	Palmer	AK	99645	907-745-3211		736	*TF:* 800-478-3211 ■ *Web:* www.mta-telco.com
Matanuska Valley Fcu	1020 S Bailey St	Palmer	AK	99645	907-745-4891		219	*Web:* mvfcu.coop
Matanuska-Susitna Borough	350 E Dahlia Ave	Palmer	AK	99645	907-745-4801	745-9845	338	*Web:* matsugov.us
Matawan-Aberdeen Chamber of Commerce	201 Broad St PO Box 522	Matawan	NJ	07747	732-290-1125	290-1125	139	*Web:* macocnj.com
Match Eyewear LLC	1600 Shames Dr	Westbury	NY	11590	516-877-0170		535	*Web:* www.matcheyewear.com
MatchCraft Inc	2701 Ocean Park Blvd Ste 220	Santa Monica	CA	90405	310-314-3320		7	*TF:* 888-502-7238 ■ *Web:* www.matchcraft.com
Matchless Metal Polish Co	840 W 49th Pl	Chicago	IL	60609	773-924-1515	924-5513	151	*TF:* 800-323-9732 ■ *Web:* www.matchlessmetal.com
Matco Electric Corp	3913 Gates Rd	Vestal	NY	13850	607-729-4921	729-0932	189-4	*TF:* 800-441-4181 ■ *Web:* www.matcoelectric.com
Matco Tools	4403 Allen Rd	Stow	OH	44224	330-926-5332		758	*TF:* 866-289-8665 ■ *Web:* www.matcotools.com
Matco-Norca Inc	Rt 22	Brewster	NY	10509	845-278-7570		610	*TF:* 800-431-2082 ■ *Web:* www.matco-norca.com
Matcor Automotive	401 S Steele St	Ionia	MI	48846	616-527-4050		489	
Matcor Metal Fabrication Inc	1021 W Birchwood St	Morton	IL	61550	309-266-7176		697	*Web:* www.matcor-matsu.com
Mate Precision Tooling Inc	1295 Lund Blvd	Anoka	MN	55303	763-421-0230	421-0285	757	*TF:* 800-328-4492 ■ *Web:* www.mate.com
Matec Instrument Cos Inc	56 Hudson St	Northborough	MA	01532	508-393-0155		360-2	*Web:* www.matec.com

Company / Address	City	State	ZIP	Phone	Fax	Class
Matech Advanced Materials Inc 31304 Via Colinas Ste 102 — *Web:* www.matech.us	Westlake Village	CA	91362	818-991-8500		743
Matelski Lumber Co 2617 M 75 S — *TF:* 800-920-0642 ■ *Web:* www.matelskilumbercompany.com	Boyne Falls	MI	49713	231-549-2780		279
Matenaer Corp 810 Schoenhaar Dr — *TF:* 800-254-0873 ■ *Web:* www.matenaer.com	West Bend	WI	53090	262-338-0700		492
Mater Dei Academy 3695 Elm St — *Web:* materdei.biz	Whitehall	OH	43213	614-231-1984	516-0481	41
Material & Contract Services LLC 5820 Stoneridge Mall Rd — *TF:* 866-772-9250 ■ *Web:* www.macservices.us	Pleasanton	CA	94588	925-460-0397		463
Material Handling Equipment Distributors Assn (MHEDA) 201 US Hwy 45 — *Web:* www.mheda.org	Vernon Hills	IL	60061	847-680-3500	362-6989	49-13
Material Handling Industry of America (MHIA) 8720 Red Oak Blvd Ste 201 — *TF:* 800-345-1815 ■ *Web:* www.mhi.org	Charlotte	NC	28217	704-676-1190	676-1199	49-13
Material Handling Products Corp 6601 Joy Rd — *TF:* 866-980-4788 ■ *Web:* www.mhpcorp.com	East Syracuse	NY	13057	315-437-2891		770
Material Motion Inc 203 Rio Cir — *Web:* www.materialmotion.com	Decatur	GA	30030	404-237-6127		358
Material Sciences Corp (MSC) 2200 E Pratt Blvd — *NASDAQ: MASC* ■ **Fax Area Code: 847* ■ *Web:* www.materialsciencescorp.com	Elk Grove Village	IL	60007	734-207-4444	439-0737*	481
Materials and Electrochemical Research Corp 7960 S Kolb Rd — *Web:* www.mercorp.com	Tucson	AZ	85706	520-574-1980		261
Materials Engineer & Testing 125 Valley Ct — *Web:* www.meandt.com	Oak Ridge	TN	37830	865-482-7762		743
Materials Innovation Technologies LLC 320 Rutledge Rd — *Web:* www.emergingmit.com	Fletcher	NC	28732	828-651-9646		791
Materials Mktg Ltd 120 W Josephine St — *Web:* www.mstoneandtile.com	San Antonio	TX	78212	210-731-8453		191-1
Materials Properties Council (MPC) PO Box 201547 — *Web:* www.forengineers.org/mpc	Shaker Heights	OH	44122	216-658-3847	658-3854	49-19
Materials Research Society (MRS) 506 Keystone Dr — *TF:* 800-732-0999 ■ *Web:* www.mrs.org	Warrendale	PA	15086	724-779-3003	779-8313	49-19
Materials Transportation Co (MTC) 1408 S Commerce PO Box 1358 — *TF:* 800-433-3110 ■ *Web:* www.gomtc.com	Temple	TX	76503	254-298-2900		386
Materion Corp 6070 Parkland Blvd — *NYSE: MTRN* ■ *TF:* 800-321-2076 ■ *Web:* www.materion.com	Mayfield Heights	OH	44124	216-486-4200	383-4091	502
Materion Technical Materials 5 Wellington Rd — *Web:* www.materion.com/technicalmaterials	Lincoln	RI	02865	401-333-1700		567
Materna Medical Inc 2500 Grant Rd — *Web:* www.maternamedical.com	Mountain View	CA	94040	415-254-1031		475
Math Teachers Press Inc 4850 Park Glen Rd — *Web:* www.movingwithmath.com	St Louis Park	MN	55416	952-545-6535		196
Mathematica Inc PO Box 2393 — *Web:* www.mathematica-mpr.com	Princeton	NJ	08543	609-799-3535	799-0005	634
Mathematical Assn of America (MAA) 1529 18th St NW — *TF:* 800-331-1622 ■ *Web:* www.maa.org	Washington	DC	20036	202-387-5200	265-2384	49-19
Matheny Medical & Educational Ctr 65 Highland Ave — *Web:* www.matheny.org	Peapack	NJ	07977	908-234-0011	719-2137	374-7
Matheny Sears Linkert & Jaime LLP 3638 American River Dr — *Web:* www.mathenysears.com	Sacramento	CA	95864	916-978-3434		428
Mather & Company CPAs LLC 9100 Shelbyville Rd — *Web:* matherandcompany.com	Louisville	KY	40222	502-429-0800		2
Mather Economics LLC 43 Woodstock St Historic Roswell District — *Web:* www.mathereconomics.com	Roswell	GA	30075	770-993-4111		196
Mather Group LLC, The Oakbrook Ter Tower One Tower Ln Ste 1820 — *TF:* 800-832-6669 ■ *Web:* www.themathergroup.com	Oakbrook Terrace	IL	60181	630-537-1080		528
Matherly Mechanical Contractors LLC 1520 Ocama Blvd PO Box 30889 — *Web:* www.matherlymech.com	Midwest City	OK	73140	405-737-3488		610
Mathers Museum of World Cultures 416 N Indiana Ave — *Web:* indiana.edu	Bloomington	IN	47408	812-855-6873	855-0205	520
Matheson Tri-Gas Inc 959 Rt 46 E — *TF:* 800-424-9300 ■ *Web:* www.mathesongas.com	Parsippany	NJ	07054	973-257-1100		143
Matheson Trucking Inc 9785 Goethe Rd — *TF:* 800-455-7678 ■ *Web:* www.mathesoninc.com	Sacramento	CA	95827	916-685-2330		780
Matheus Lumber 15800 Woodinville-Redmond Rd NE — *TF:* 800-284-7501 ■ *Web:* www.matheuslumber.com	Woodinville	WA	98072	425-489-3000	822-4028	191-3
Mathew Zechman Company Inc 152 Resar Ct	Elyria	OH	44035	440-366-2442		756
Mathews Assoc Inc 220 Power Ct — *TF:* 800-871-5262 ■ *Web:* www.maifl.com	Sanford	FL	32771	407-323-3390	323-3115	74
Mathews Bros Co 22 Perkins Rd — *TF:* 800-615-2004 ■ *Web:* www.mathewsbrothers.com	Belfast	ME	04915	207-338-6490	338-6300	236
Mathews Co 500 Industrial Ave — *TF:* 800-323-7045 ■ *Web:* www.mathewscompany.com	Crystal Lake	IL	60012	815-459-2210	459-5889	273
Mathews County 10622 Buckley Hall Rd PO Box 463 — *Web:* co.mathews.va.us	Mathews	VA	23109	804-725-2550	725-7456	338
Mathews Inc 919 River Rd — *Web:* www.mathewsinc.com	Sparta	WI	54656	608-269-2728		711
Mathews Jewelers 126 Strickland Dr — *Web:* mathewsjewelers.com	Orange	TX	77630	409-886-7233		327
Mathias Ham House Historic Site 350 E Third St — *TF:* 800-226-3369 ■ *Web:* www.rivermuseum.com	Dubuque	IA	52001	563-557-9545		50-3
Mathiowetz Construction Co 30676 County Rd 24 — *Web:* www.mathiowetzconst.com	Sleepy Eye	MN	56085	507-794-6953	794-3514	186
Mathis Bros Furniture Inc 6611 S 101 St E Ave — *TF Cust Svc:* 800-329-3434 ■ *Web:* www.mathisbrothers.com	Tulsa	OK	74133	918-461-7700		321
Mathis-Akins Concrete Block Co Inc 130 Lower Elm St	Macon	GA	31206	478-746-5154		183
Mathnasium LLC 5120 W Goldleaf Cir Ste 300 — *TF:* 877-601-6284 ■ *Web:* www.mathnasium.com	Los Angeles	CA	90056	323-421-8000		310
Mathtech Inc 6402 Arlington Blvd Ste 1200 — *Web:* mathtechinc.com	Falls Church	VA	22042	703-875-8866		225
Mathworks Inc 3 Apple Hill Dr — *Web:* in.mathworks.com	Natick	MA	01760	508-647-7000	647-7001	178-5
Mathy Construction Co Inc 920 Tenth Ave N PO Box 189 — *Web:* mathy.com	Onalaska	WI	54650	608-783-6411	783-4311	188-4
Mathys Potestio LLC 917 SW Oak St N Pacific Bldg Ste 313 — *Web:* www.mathys-potestio.com	Portland	OR	97205	503-489-7396		260
Mati Therapeutics Inc 4317 Dunning Ln — *Web:* www.matitherapeutics.com	Austin	TX	78746	512-329-6360		475
Matich Corp 1596 Harry Sheppard Blvd — *TF:* 800-404-4975 ■ *Web:* www.matichcorp.com	San Bernardino	CA	92408	909-382-7400		188-4
Matik Inc 33 Brook St — *TF:* 800-245-1628 ■ *Web:* www.matik.com	West Hartford	CT	06110	860-232-2323		535
Matis Warfield Inc 10540 York Rd Ste M — *Web:* matiswarfield.com	Cockeysville	MD	21030	410-683-7004		261
Matlab Inc 1112 Nc Hwy 49 S — *Web:* www.matlabinc.com	Asheboro	NC	27205	336-629-4161		608
MATLET Group LLC 60 Delta Dr — *Web:* www.thematletgroup.com	Pawtucket	RI	02860	401-834-3007		627
MatlinPatterson Global Advisers LLC 520 Madison Ave 35 FL — *Web:* www.matlinpatterson.com	New York	NY	10022	212-651-9500		401
Matlock Adv & Public Relations 107 Luckie St — *Web:* www.matlock-adpr.com	Atlanta	GA	30303	404-872-3200		4
Matmoncom 303 W Capitol Ave Ste 150 — *Web:* www.matmon.com	Little Rock	AR	72201	501-375-4999		396
Matot Inc 2501 Van Buren St — *TF:* 800-369-1070 ■ *Web:* www.matot.com	Bellwood	IL	60104	708-547-1888	547-1608	256
Matous Construction Ltd 8602 State Hwy 317 — *Web:* www.matousconstruction.com	Belton	TX	76513	254-780-1400	780-2599	186
Matric Group LLC 2099 Hill City Rd — *TF:* 800-462-8742 ■ *Web:* www.matricgroup.com	Seneca	PA	16346	814-677-0716		393
Matricis Informatique Inc 1425 Rene-Levesque Blvd W Ste 240 — *Web:* matricis.com	Montreal	QC	H3G1T7	514-394-0011		180
Matrix 2 Inc 1903 NW 97th Ave — *Web:* www.matrix2advertising.com	Miami	FL	33172	305-591-7672		344
Matrix Capital Advisors LLC 200 S Wacker Dr Ste 680 — *Web:* matrixcapital.com	Chicago	IL	60606	312-612-6100		401
Matrix Companies, The 7162 Reading Rd Ste 250 — *TF:* 877-550-7973 ■ *Web:* www.matrixtpa.com	Cincinnati	OH	45237	513-351-1222		393
Matrix Composites Inc 275 Barnes Blvd — *Web:* www.matrixcomp.com	Rockledge	FL	32955	321-633-4480		256
Matrix Computer Solutions Inc 3001 Bridgeway Ste K314 — *TF:* 800-433-5778 ■ *Web:* www.matrixcomp.net	Sausalito	CA	94965	415-331-3600		261
Matrix Design Group Inc 1601 Blake St Ste 200 — *Web:* www.matrixdesigngroup.com	Denver	CO	80202	303-572-0200		261
Matrix Energy Services Inc 3221 Ramos Cir — *TF:* 800-556-2123 ■ *Web:* www.matrixescorp.com	Sacramento	CA	95827	916-363-9283		256
Matrix Engineering Pllc 112 Walter Jetton Blvd — *Web:* matrixengineer.com	Paducah	KY	42001	270-442-5600		261
Matrix Fitness Systems Corp 1600 Landmark Dr — *Web:* www.matrixfitness.com	Cottage Grove	WI	53527	608-839-8686		354
Matrix Hotel 10640-100 Ave — *TF:* 866-465-8150 ■ *Web:* www.matrixedmonton.com	Edmonton	AB	T5J3N8	780-429-2861		379
Matrix Imaging Solutions Inc 6341 Inducon Dr — *Web:* www.matriximaging.com	Sanborn	NY	14132	716-504-9700		627
Matrix Integration LLC 417 Main St — *TF:* 800-264-1550 ■ *Web:* www.matrixintegration.com	Jasper	IN	47546	812-634-1550		180
Matrix Iv Inc 610 E Judd St — *Web:* www.matrixiv.com	Woodstock	IL	60098	815-338-4500		608
Matrix Partners 1000 Winter St Ste 4500 — *Web:* www.matrixpartners.com	Waltham	MA	02451	781-890-2244	890-2288	792
Matrix Publishing Services 36 N Highland Ave — *Web:* matrix508.com	York	PA	17404	717-764-9673	764-9672	781
Matrix Realty Group LLC 2066 Ridge Rd — *Web:* www.matrixrealtygroup.com	Homewood	IL	60430	708-799-3600		652
Matrix Service Co 5100 E Skelly Dr 74135 — *NASDAQ: MTRX* ■ **Fax Area Code: 918* ■ *TF:* 866-367-6879 ■ *Web:* www.matrixservice.com	Tulsa	OK	74135	866-367-6879	838-8810*	539
Matrix Systems Inc 1041 Byers Rd — *TF:* 800-562-8749 ■ *Web:* www.matrixsys.com	Miamisburg	OH	45342	937-438-9033	438-0900	692
Matrix Technologies Corp 22 Friars Dr — *Web:* www.matrixtechcorp.com	Hudson	NH	03051	603-595-0505		419

	Phone	Fax	Class
Matrix Technologies Inc 1760 Indian Wood Cir. Maumee OH 43537 *Web:* matrixti.com	419-897-7200		180
Matrix Tool Inc 4976 Franklin Ave Fairview PA 16415 *Web:* www.matrixtoolinc.com	814-474-5531		596
Matrox Electronic Systems Ltd 1055 St Regis Blvd. Dorval QC H9P2T4 *TF:* 800-361-1408 ■ *Web:* www.matrox.com	514-822-6000	822-6363	173-5
MATRRIX Energy Technologies 808 - Fourth Ave SW Ste 350 Calgary AB T2P3E8 *Web:* www.matrrix.com	403-984-5042		540
Mats Inc 37 Shuman Ave Stoughton MA 02072 *Web:* www.matsinc.com	781-344-1536		131
Matson & Cuprill LLC 7361 Kemper Rd Ste B Cincinnati OH 45249 *Web:* matsonandcuprill.com	513-563-7526		390
Matson Logistics Inc 555 12th St Oakland CA 94607 *TF:* 800-762-8766 ■ *Web:* www.matson.com	510-628-4000		449
Matson Lumber Company Inc 132 Main St Brookville PA 15825 *Web:* www.matsonlumber.com	814-849-5334	849-3811	683
Matson Navigation Co 555 12th St Oakland CA 94607 *TF Cust Svc:* 800-462-8766 ■ *Web:* www.matson.com	510-628-4000	628-7380	312
Matsu Japanese Restaurant 18035 Beach Blvd. Huntington Beach CA 92648 *TF:* 800-632-1698 ■ *Web:* matsusogood.com	714-848-4404	842-4049	671
Matsuhisa 303 E Main St. Aspen CO 81611 *Web:* www.matsuhisarestaurants.com	970-544-6628		671
Matsuhisa Beverly Hills 129 N La Cienega Blvd Beverly Hills CA 90211 *Web:* www.nobumatsuhisa.com	310-659-9639	659-0492	671
Matsui Doris O (Rep D - CA) 2311 Rayburn HOB Washington DC 20515 *Web:* matsui.house.gov	202-225-7163	225-0566	342-2
Matsui International Company Inc 1501 W 178th St. Gardena CA 90248 *TF:* 800-359-5679 ■ *Web:* www.matsui-color.com	310-767-7812	767-7836	388
Matsui Nursery Inc 1645 Old Stage Rd Salinas CA 93908 *TF:* 800-793-6433 ■ *Web:* www.matsuinursery.com	831-422-6433	422-2387	369
Matsuo Industries USA Inc 408 Municipal Dr Jefferson City TN 37760	865-475-9085		54
Matsuri Restaurant 1105 S Charles St. Baltimore MD 21230 *Web:* www.matsuri-restaurant.com	410-752-8561		671
Matt Blatt Inc 501 Delsea Dr N. Glassboro NJ 08028 *TF:* 877-462-5288 ■ *Web:* www.mattblatt.com	856-881-0444		57
Matt Brewing Co 811 Edward St. Utica NY 13502 *TF:* 800-428-1150 ■ *Web:* www.saranac.com	315-624-2400	624-2452	102
Matt Castrucci Auto Mall of Dayton 3013 Mall Pk Dr Dayton OH 45459 *TF:* 855-204-5293 ■ *Web:* www.mattcastrucciautomall.com	855-204-5293		516
Matt Construction Corp 9814 Norwalk Blvd Ste 100 Santa Fe Springs CA 90670 *TF:* 800-927-4817 ■ *Web:* www.mattconstruction.com	562-903-2277		196
Matt Swanson's School of Golf 6224 Theall Rd Houston TX 77066 *Web:* swingpure.com	713-413-4484		148
Matt's Building Materials 404 E Expy 83 Pharr TX 78577 *Web:* www.mattsbuildingmaterials.com	956-787-5561		191-3
Matt's in the Market 94 Pike St Ste 32 Seattle WA 98101 *Web:* www.mattsinthemarket.com	206-467-7909		671
Mattatuck Museum of the Mattatuck Historical Society 144 W Main St Waterbury CT 06702 *Web:* www.mattmuseum.org	203-753-0381	756-6283	520
Mattel Inc 333 Continental Blvd El Segundo CA 90245 *NASDAQ: MAT* ■ *TF:* 800-524-8697 ■ *Web:* www.mattel.com	310-252-2000		762
Matter Communications Inc 50 Water St Mill No 3 The Tannery Newburyport MA 01950 *Web:* www.matternow.com	978-518-4547		463
Mattern & Craig Inc 701 First St SW Roanoke VA 24016 *Web:* matternandcraig.com	540-345-9342		261
Mattersight Corp 200 S Wacker Ste 3100 Chicago IL 60606 **Fax Area Code:* 312 ■ *TF:* 877-235-6925 ■ *Web:* www.mattersight.com	877-235-6925	454-3501*	463
Matthaei Botanical Gardens 1800 N Dixboro Rd Ann Arbor MI 48105 *TF:* 800-666-8693 ■ *Web:* www.lsa.umich.edu/mbg	734-647-7600	998-6205	97
Matthew Hall Lumber Co 127 Sixth Ave N Saint Cloud MN 56303 *Web:* www.mathewhall.com	320-252-1920		364
Matthew Marks Gallery 523 W 24th St. New York NY 10011 *Web:* www.matthewmarks.com	212-243-0200		42
Matthew's 2107 Hendricks Ave Jacksonville FL 32207 *Web:* www.matthewsrestaurant.com	904-396-9922		671
Matthews Book Co 11559 Rock Island Ct Maryland Heights MO 63043 *TF:* 800-633-2665 ■ *Web:* www.matthewsbooks.com	314-432-1400	432-7044	95
Matthews Carter & Boyce PC 12500 Fair Lakes Cir Ste 260 Fairfax VA 22033 *Web:* www.mcb-cpa.com	703-218-3600	218-1808	2
Matthews Construction Company Inc 210 First Ave S Conover NC 28613 *Web:* www.matthewsconstruction.com	828-464-7325	465-6747	186
Matthews Currie Ford Company Inc 130 N Tamiami Trl. Nokomis FL 34275 *TF:* 855-491-3131 ■ *Web:* www.matthewscurrie.com	941-488-6787		57
Matthews Group Inc, The 400 Lake St Bryan TX 77801 *Web:* www.thematthewsgroup.com	979-823-3600		4
Matthews International Corp Marking Products Div 6515 Penn Ave Pittsburgh PA 15206 *TF:* 800-775-7775 ■ *Web:* www.matthewsmarking.com	412-665-2500	665-2550	467
Matthews Mfg 41 Branch St Saint Louis MO 63147	314-231-4900		610
Matthews Opera House 612 Main St. Spearfish SD 57783 *Web:* www.matthewsopera.com	605-642-7973		572
Matthews Pierce & Lloyd Inc 830 Walker Rd Ste 12 Dover DE 19904 *TF:* 800-267-4026 ■ *Web:* mpli.net	302-678-5500		160
Matthews Studio Equipment Group 2405 W Empire Ave Burbank CA 91504 **Fax Area Code:* 323 ■ *TF:* 800-237-8263 ■ *Web:* www.msegrip.com	818-843-6715	849-1525*	591
Matthews-Hargreaves Chevrolet Co 2000 E12 Mile Rd Royal Oak MI 48067 *Web:* www.mhchevy.com	248-398-8800		516
Matthiessen State Park PO Box 509 Utica IL 61373 *Web:* www.stateparks.com/matthiessen.html	815-667-4868		565
Matthijssen Inc 14 Rt 10 East Hanover NJ 07936 *TF:* 800-845-2200 ■ *Web:* www.mattnj.com	973-887-1100	887-2453	175
Mattingly Lumber & Millwork Inc 410 E St Madison IL 62040 *Web:* www.mattinglylumber.com	636-343-3877		191-3
Mattioni LLP 1316 Kings Hwy Swedesboro NJ 08085 *Web:* www.mattioni.com	856-241-9779		428
Mattracks Systems 202 Cleveland Ave E Karlstad MN 56732 *TF:* 877-436-7800 ■ *Web:* www.mattracks.com	218-436-7000		370
Mattress Firm Inc 5815 Gulf Fwy Houston TX 77023 *TF:* 800-821-6621 ■ *Web:* www.mattressfirm.com	713-923-1090		362
Mattsco Supply Co 1111 N 161st E Ave Tulsa OK 74116 *Web:* www.mattsco.org	918-836-0451		492
Mattson Resources Inc 7994 Swamp Flower Dr E Jacksonville FL 32244	904-772-6506		652
Mattson Spray Equipment 230 W Coleman St Rice Lake WI 54868 *TF:* 800-877-4857 ■ *Web:* www.mattsonspray.com	715-234-1617	236-7032	172
Mattson Technology Inc 47131 Bayside Pkwy Fremont CA 94538 *NASDAQ: MTSN* ■ *TF:* 800-315-6607 ■ *Web:* www.mattson.com	510-657-5900	492-5911	695
Matuba 2930 McKinley Ave South Bend IN 46615	574-251-0674		671
Maturehealth Communications 502 Centennial Ave Cranford NJ 07016 *TF:* 800-730-3930 ■ *Web:* www.maturehealth.com	908-709-8080		195
Maude Cobb Convention Ctr 100 Grand Blvd PO Box 1952 Longview TX 75604 *Web:* www.longviewtexas.gov	903-237-1230		205
Maude Kerns Art Ctr 1910 E 15th Ave Eugene OR 97403 *TF:* 800-422-7558 ■ *Web:* www.mkartcenter.org	541-345-1571	345-6248	50-2
Maudslay State Park 74 Curzon Mill Rd Newburyport MA 01950 *Web:* www.mass.gov	978-465-7223		565
Maui Beach Hotel Inc 170 Kaahumanu Ave Kahului HI 96732 *Web:* www.mauibeachhotel.net	808-877-0051		378
Maui County 200 S High St Wailuku HI 96793 *TF:* 800-272-0117 ■ *Web:* www.co.maui.hi.us	808-270-7748	270-7171	338
Maui Divers of Hawaii 1520 Liona St Honolulu HI 96814 *TF:* 800-462-4454 ■ *Web:* www.mauidivers.com	808-946-7979		409
Maui Jim Inc 721 Wainee St Lahaina HI 96761 *TF:* 888-352-2001 ■ *Web:* www.mauijim.com	808-661-8841	661-0351	542
Maui Land & Pineapple Company Inc 120 Kane St PO Box 187 Kahului HI 96733 *TF:* 800-356-2017 ■ *Web:* www.mauiland.com	808-877-3351		315-4
Maui Memorial Hospital 221 Mahalani St Wailuku HI 96793 *Web:* www.mmmc.hhsc.org	808-244-9056	242-2443	374-3
Maui News 100 Mahalani St. Wailuku HI 96793 **Fax:* Edit ■ *TF:* 888-683-1115 ■ *Web:* www.mauinews.com	808-244-3981	242-9087*	532-2
Maui Ocean Ctr 192 Maalaea Rd. Wailuku HI 96793 *TF:* 800-350-5634 ■ *Web:* www.mauioceancenter.com	808-270-7000	270-7070	40
Maui Soda & Ice Works Ltd 918 A Lower Main St Wailuku HI 96793 *Web:* www.roselani.com	808-244-7951		805
Maui Tacos International Inc 2001 Palmer Ave Ste 105 Larchmont NY 10538 *TF:* 866-388-3758 ■ *Web:* www.mauitacos.com	866-388-3758		670
Maui Time Weekly 33 N Market St Ste 201 Wailuku HI 96793 *Web:* www.mauitime.com	808-244-0777		532-5
Maui Wowi Hawaiian Coffees & Smoothies 9311 E Via de Ventura Scottsdale AZ 85258 *Web:* www.mauiwowi.com	480-362-4800		310
Mauldin & Jenkins Certified Public Accountants LLC 200 Galleria Pkwy SE Atlanta GA 30339 **Fax Area Code:* 229 ■ *TF:* 800-277-0080 ■ *Web:* www.mjcpa.com	770-955-8600	446-3664*	2
Maule Air Inc 2099 GA Hwy 133 S Moultrie GA 31788 *Web:* www.mauleairinc.com	229-985-2045	890-2402	20
Maumee Bay Lodge & Conference Ctr 1750 Pk Rd Ste 2 Oregon OH 43616 *TF:* 800-282-7275 ■ *Web:* www.maumeebaystateparklodge.com	419-836-1466	836-2438	379
Maumee Bay State Park 1400 State Pk Rd Oregon OH 43616 *Web:* www.ohiodnr.com	419-836-7758	836-8711	565
Maumee Valley Fabricators 4801 Bennett Rd Toledo OH 43612 *Web:* www.maumeevalleyfab.com	419-476-1411		492
Mauna Kea Beach Hotel 62-100 Maunakea Beach Dr Island of Hawaii HI 96743 *TF:* 866-977-4589 ■ *Web:* www.princeresortshawaii.com	808-882-7222	882-5700	669
Mauna Lani Bay Hotel & Bungalows 68-1400 Mauna Lani Dr Kohala Coast HI 96743 *TF:* 800-367-2323 ■ *Web:* www.maunalani.com	808-885-6622	881-7000	669
Mauna Loa Macadamia Nut Corp 16-701 Macadamia Rd Keaau HI 96749 *TF Cust Svc:* 888-628-6256 ■ *Web:* www.maunaloa.com	808-966-8618		10-10
Maupin Travel Inc 510 Daniels St Raleigh NC 27605 *TF:* 800-786-2738 ■ *Web:* www.maupintravel.com	919-821-2146	829-0232	771
Maupintour Inc 2690 Weston Rd Ste 200 Weston FL 33331 *TF:* 800-255-4266 ■ *Web:* www.maupintour.com	954-653-3820	888-9082	760
Maur Hill-Mount Academy 1000 Green St. Atchison KS 66002 *Web:* www.maurhillmountacademy.com	913-367-5482	367-5096	622
Maurey Manufacturing Corp 410 Industrial Pk Rd Holly Springs MS 38635 **Fax Area Code:* 662 ■ *TF:* 800-284-2161 ■ *Web:* www.maurey.biz	800-284-2161	252-6364*	620
Maurice Electrical Supply Co 500 Penn St NE Washington DC 20002 *Web:* www.mauriceelectric.com	202-675-9400		246
Maurice K. Goddard State Park 684 Lake Wilhelm Rd Sandy Lake PA 16145 *Web:* www.dcnr.state.pa.us	724-253-4833		565

Name / Address	City	State	ZIP	Phone	Fax	Class
Maurice M Pine Free Public Library 10-01 Fair Lawn Ave *Web:* www.fairlawnlibrary.org	Fair Lawn	NJ	07410	201-796-3400		434-3
Maurice Pincoffs Company Inc 1235 N Loop W Ste 510 PO Box 920919 *Web:* www.pincoffs.com	Houston	TX	77008	713-681-5461	681-8521	485
Maurice Vaughan Furniture Co 610 E Stuart Dr *Web:* www.mauricevaughaninc.com	Galax	VA	24333	276-236-9781		321
Maurice's Gourmet Barbeque PO Box 6847 *TF:* 800-628-7423 ■ *Web:* www.piggiepark.com	West Columbia	SC	29171	803-791-5887	791-8707	296-19
Maurices Inc 105 W Superior St *TF:* 866-977-1542 ■ *Web:* www.maurices.com	Duluth	MN	55802	218-727-8431	720-2102	157-4
Mauritania 116 E 38th St *Web:* www.un.int	New York	NY	10016	212-252-0113	252-0175	784
Mauritania Embassy 2129 Leroy Pl NW *TF:* 800-860-8610 ■ *Web:* www.mauritaniaembassy.com	Washington	DC	20008	202-232-5700		257
Mauritius 211 E 43rd St	New York	NY	10017	212-949-0190		784
Mauritius Embassies 1709 N St NW *TF:* 800-860-8610 ■ *Web:* www.maurinet.com/embasydc.html	Washington	DC	20036	202-244-1491	966-0983	257
Mauritzon Inc 3939 W Belden Ave *TF:* 800-621-4352 ■ *Web:* www.mauritzononline.com	Chicago	IL	60647	773-235-6000		733
Maury Alliance 106 W Sixth St *TF:* 800-562-8732 ■ *Web:* www.mauryalliance.com	Columbia	TN	38401	931-388-2155	380-0335	139
Maury County 106 W Sixth St PO Box 1076 *Web:* www.mauryalliance.com	Columbia	TN	38402	931-388-2155		338
Maury Regional Hospital 1224 Trotwood Ave *Web.* www.mauryregional.com	Columbia	TN	38401	931-381-1111		374-3
Mauser USA LLC 35 Cotters Ln *Web:* www.mausergroup.com	Brunswick	IL	60440	732-353-7100	651-9777	608
Mautino Distributing Co 500 N Richards St	Spring Valley	IL	61362	815-664-4311	664-2224	81-1
Mautino State Fish & Wildlife Area 16006-875 E St *Web:* www.dnr.state.il.us	Sheffield	IL	61361	815-454-2328		565
Maven Engineering Corp 15946 Derwood Rd *Web:* www.mavencorporation.com	Rockville	MD	20855	301-519-3400		529
Maven Group LLC, The 320 N Salem St Ste 204 *TF:* 800-343-6612 ■ *Web:* www.themavengroup.com	Apex	NC	27502	919-386-1010		260
MavenWire LLC 630 Freedom Business Ctr 3rd Fl *TF:* 866-343-4870 ■ *Web:* www.perfitcomputer.com	King Of Prussia	PA	19406	866-343-4870		463
Maverick Arms Inc Industrial Blvd *Web:* www.mavericksarms.com	Eagle Pass	TX	78852	830-773-9007		807
Maverick Boat Company Inc 3207 Industrial 29th St *Web:* www.maverickboats.com	Fort Pierce	FL	34946	772-465-0631	489-2168	90
Maverick Construction Corp 1 Westinghouse Plaza *TF:* 800-255-1997 ■ *Web:* www.maverickcorporation.com	Boston	MA	02136	617-361-6700		256
Maverick County 1508 Las Quintas Blvd *Web:* co.maverick.tx.us	Eagle Pass	TX	78852	830-757-9201	752-1664	338
Maverick Directional Services 25615 Oakhurst Dr *TF:* 866-459-0233 ■ *Web:* www.maverickdirectional.com	Spring	TX	77386	281-364-1212		540
Maverick Enterprises Inc 751 E Gobbi St *Web:* www.maverickcaps.com	Ukiah	CA	95482	707-463-5591		297-8
Maverick Media Inc 123 W 17th St *Web:* www.ncnewspress.com	Syracuse	NE	68446	402-269-2135		637-8
Maverick Mesa Computer Specialties Inc 10814 W Orangewood Ave *Web:* mavmesa.com	Glendale	AZ	85307	623-872-1296		180
Maverick Oilfield Services Ltd PO Box 597 3808 - 52 Ave *TF:* 800-490-7192 ■ *Web:* mavoil.com	Provost	AB	T0B3S0	780-753-2992		538
Maverick Technologies 265 Admiral Trost Rd PO Box 470 *TF:* 888-917-9109 ■ *Web:* www.mavtechglobal.com	Columbia	IL	62236	618-281-9100	281-9191	178-1
Maverick USA Inc 13301 Valentine Rd *TF:* 800-289-6600 ■ *Web:* www.maverickusa.com	North Little Rock	AR	72117	501-955-1255	955-4670	780
Maverik Inc 880 W Center St *TF Cust Svc:* 800-789-4455 ■ *Web:* www.maverik.com	North Salt Lake	UT	84054	801-936-5573		204
Maveron LLC 411 First Ave S Ste 600 *Web:* www.maveron.com	Seattle	WA	98104	206-288-1700		792
Mavro Imaging LLC 22 maple tree dr *Web:* www.mavroimaging.com	Westampton	NJ	08060	609-265-3803		138
Mawer Investment Management Ltd 517 - Tenth Ave S W Ste 600 *TF:* 800-889-6248 ■ *Web:* www.mawer.com	Calgary	AB	T2R0A8	800-889-6248		528
Mawicke & Goisman SC 1509 N Prospect Ave *Web:* mawickelaw.com	Milwaukee	WI	53202	414-224-0600		428
MAWS (Marijuana Anonymous World Services) PO Box 7807 *TF:* 800-766-6779 ■ *Web:* www.marijuana-anonymous.org	Torrance	CA	90504	800-766-6779		48-21
Mawson & Mawson Inc 1800 Old Lincoln Hwy PO Box 248 *TF:* 800-262-9766 ■ *Web:* www.mawsonandmawson.com	Langhorne	PA	19047	215-750-1100		780
Max & Erma's 3750 W Market St *Web:* maxandermas.com	Fairlawn	OH	44333	330-666-1002		671
Max & Erma's Restaurant 1500 N Military Hwy *Web:* www.maxandermas.com	Norfolk	VA	23502	757-282-2004		671
Max Arnold & Sons LLC 702 N Main St *Web:* www.maxfuel.net	Hopkinsville	KY	42240	270-885-8488		581
Max Auto Supply Co 1101 Monroe St	Toledo	OH	43604	419-243-7281		54
Max Credit Union 400 Eastdale Cir *TF:* 800-776-6776 ■ *Web:* www.mymax.com	Montgomery	AL	36117	334-260-2600		70
Max Downtown 185 Asylum St *TF:* 800-442-1162 ■ *Web:* www.maxrestaurantgroup.com	Hartford	CT	06103	860-522-2530	246-5279	671
Max Environmental Technologies Inc 1815 Washington Rd *TF:* 800-851-7845 ■ *Web:* www.maxenvironmental.com	Pittsburgh	PA	15241	412-343-4900		196
Max Group Corp 17011 Green Dr *TF:* 800-256-9040 ■ *Web:* www.maxgroup.com	City of Industry	CA	91745	626-935-0050	935-0056	174
Max Hansen & Son Inc 200 Industrial Rd	San Carlos	CA	94070	650-595-5841		652
Max International Converters Inc 2360 Dairy Rd *TF:* 800-233-0222 ■ *Web:* www.maxintl.com	Lancaster	PA	17601	800-233-0222		554
Max It Group Inc 715 Rt 10 E Ste 205 *Web:* www.maxitgroupinc.com	Randolph	NJ	07869	973-343-2951		180
Max J. Kuney Co 120 N Ralph St PO Box 4008 *Web:* www.maxkuney.com	Spokane	WA	99220	509-535-0651	534-6828	186
Max Leather Group Inc 1415 Redfern Ave	Far Rockaway	NY	11691	718-471-3300	471-3707	155-2
Max Levy Autograph Inc 2710 Commerce Way *TF:* 800-798-3675 ■ *Web:* www.maxlevy.com	Philadelphia	PA	19154	215-842-3675		481
Max Machinery Inc 33A Healdsburg Ave *TF:* 800-321-2260 ■ *Web:* www.maxmachinery.com	Healdsburg	CA	95448	707-433-2662	433-1818	495
Max Media LLC 900 Laskin Rd *Web:* www.maxmediallc.com	Virginia Beach	VA	23451	757-437-9800		116
Max Technical Training 4900 Pkwy Dr Ste 160 *TF:* 866-595-6863 ■ *Web:* www.maxtrain.com	Mason	OH	45040	513-322-8888		196
MAX Technologies Inc 2051 Victoria Ave *TF:* 800-361-1629 ■ *Web:* www.maxt.com	Saint-Lambert	QC	J4S1H1	450-443-3332	443-1618	668
Max Tool Inc 119b Citation Ct *TF:* 800-783-6298 ■ *Web:* www.maxtoolinc.com	Birmingham	AL	35209	205-942-2466		351
Max's Allegheny Tavern 537 Suismon St *Web:* www.maxsalleghenytavern.com	Pittsburgh	PA	15212	412-231-1899		671
Max's Grille 404 Plaza Real *Web:* www.maxsgrille.com	Boca Raton	FL	33432	561-368-0080		671
Max's of Manila 313 W Broadway *Web:* www.maxschicken.com	Glendale	CA	91204	818-637-7751		671
Max's Oyster Bar 964 Farmington Ave *Web:* www.maxrestaurantgroup.com	West Hartford	CT	06107	860-236-6299	233-6969	671
Max's Tavern 1000 W Columbus Blvd *Web:* www.maxrestaurantgroup.com/tavern	Springfield	MA	01105	413-746-6299		671
MaxBotix Inc 13860 Shawkia Dr *Web:* www.maxbotix.com	Brainerd	MN	56401	218-454-0766	454-0768	693
MaxBounty Inc PO Box 17039 *Web:* www.maxbounty.com	Ottawa	ON	K4A4W8	613-834-3955		393
Maxcel Co 13601 Preston Rd E Twr Ste 935 *Web:* www.maxcel.net	Dallas	TX	75240	972-644-0880	680-2488	384
Maxcess International Corp 222 W Memorial Rd *Web:* www.maxcessintl.com	Oklahoma City	OK	73114	405-755-1600		201
Maxcess International, Inc. 222 W Memorial Rd *TF:* 800-333-3433 ■ *Web:* www.maxcessintl.com	Oklahoma City	OK	73114	405-755-1600	755-8425	203
Maxco Inc 836 Centennial Way Ste 170	Lansing	MI	48917	517-575-6603	575-6496	360-3
Maxcomm Inc 5671 S Redwood Rd Ste 20 *Web:* www.maxcomminc.com	Salt Lake City	UT	84123	801-631-0890		260
Maxell Corp of America 3 Garret Mountain Plaza 3rd Fl Ste 300 *Web:* www.maxell-usa.com	Woodland Park	NJ	07424	973-653-2400		658
Maxi Foods LLC 8616 California Ave *Web:* www.maxifoods.com	Riverside	CA	92504	951-688-0538		297-8
Maxi Volt Corporation Inc 800 S Rusk St *Web:* www.maxivolt.com	Amarillo	TX	79106	806-371-0722		580
Maxim Crane Works 1225 Washington Pk *TF:* 877-629-5438 ■ *Web:* www.cranerental.com	Bridgeville	PA	15017	412-504-0200	504-0126	264-3
Maxim Group LLC 405 Lexington Ave *TF:* 800-724-0761 ■ *Web:* www.maximgrp.com	New York	NY	10174	212-895-3500		401
Maxim Integrated 6440 Oak Canyon Ste 100 *Web:* www.maximintegrated.com	Irvine	CA	92618	714-508-8800		696
Maxim Integrated Products Inc 120 San Gabriel Dr *NASDAQ:* MXIM ■ *TF:* 888-629-4642 ■ *Web:* www.maximintegrated.com	Sunnyvale	CA	94086	408-737-7600	737-7194	696
Maxim Partners LLC 105 E First St Ste 203 *Web:* www.maximpartnersllc.com	Hinsdale	IL	60521	630-206-4040		528
Maxim Technologies Inc 1607 Derwent Way *TF:* 800-663-9925 ■ *Web:* www.maxim-technologies.com	Delta	BC	V3M6K8	800-663-9925		151
Maxima Technologies Stewart Warner 1811 Rohrerstown Rd *TF:* 800-676-1837 ■ *Web:* www.maximatecc.com	Lancaster	PA	17601	717-581-1000	569-7247	495
Maxime 1131 St Mary's Rd *Web:* maximesrestaurant.ca	Winnipeg	MB	R2M3T9	204-257-1521		671
Maximizer Software Inc 1090 W Pender St 10th Fl *TF:* 800-804-6299 ■ *Web:* www.maximizer.com	Vancouver	BC	V6E2N7	604-601-8000		180
Maximum Insights Inc 17295 Chesterfield Airport Rd Ste 200	Chesterfield	MO	63005	314-878-8700		177
Maximum Marketing Services Inc 833 W Jackson Blvd *Web:* www.maxmarketing.com	Chicago	IL	60607	312-226-4111		636
Maximum Potential Inc 2854 Hwy 55 Ste 150 *Web:* www.maximumpotential.com	Saint Paul	MN	55121	651-452-8256		463
Maximum Quality Foods Inc 3351 Tremley Pt Rd *Web:* www.maximumqualityfoods.com	Linden	NJ	07036	908-474-0003	474-1320	299
Maximus Federal Services Inc 3750 Monroe Ave Ste 702 *Web:* www.medicareappeal.com	Pittsford	NY	14534	585-348-3300		449

Company / Address	Phone	Fax	Class
MAXIMUS Inc 1891 Metro Center Dr .... Reston VA 20190 *NYSE: MMS* ■ *Web:* www.maximus.com	703-251-8500	251-8240	194
Maxitrol Co 23555 Telegraph Rd PO Box 2230 .... Southfield MI 48033 *TF:* 800-463-6727 ■ *Web:* www.maxitrol.com	248-356-1400	356-0829	201
Maxland International Inc 9457 Rush St .... South El Monte CA 91733 *TF:* 800-376-2886 ■ *Web:* www.maxland.com	626-443-2443		787
MaxLinear Inc 2051 Palomar Airport Rd Ste 100 .... Carlsbad CA 92011 *NYSE: MXL* ■ *TF:* 888-505-4369 ■ *Web:* www.maxlinear.com	760-692-0711	444-8598	695
Maxmedia Inc 2160 Hills Ave Ste A .... Atlanta GA 30318 *Web:* www.maxmedia.com	404-564-0063		5
MAXON COMPUTER Inc 2640 Lavery Ct Ste A .... Newbury Park CA 91320 *TF:* 877-264-6283 ■ *Web:* www.maxon.net	805-376-3333		177
Maxon Corp 201 E 18th St PO Box 2068 .... Muncie IN 47307 *Web:* www.maxoncorp.com	765-284-3304	286-8394	789
Maxon Furniture Inc 660 SW 39th St Ste 150 .... Renton WA 98057 *TF Cust Svc:* 800-876-4274 ■ *Web:* www.maxonfurniture.com	800-876-4274	257-2635	319-1
Maxon Industries Inc 11921 Slauson Ave .... Santa Fe Springs CA 90670 **Fax Area Code: 888* ■ *TF:* 800-227-4116 ■ *Web:* www.maxonlift.com	562-464-0099	771-7713*	470
Maxor National Pharmacy Services Corp 320 S Polk St Ste 100 .... Amarillo TX 79101 *TF:* 800-658-6146 ■ *Web:* www.maxor.com	806-324-5400	324-5495	586
Max-Pak LLC 2808 New Tampa Hwy .... Lakeland FL 33815 *Web:* www.maxpak.cc	863-682-0123		559
MaxPoint Interactive Inc 3020 Carrington Mill Blvd Ste 300 .... Morrisville NC 27560 *TF:* 800-916-9960 ■ *Web:* www.maxpoint.com	800-916-9960		177
Maxs Bistro 1784 W Bullard Ave .... Fresno CA 93711 *Web:* www.maxsbistro.com	559-439-6900	439-7206	671
Maxson & Assoc Accountancy Corp 6700 E Pacific Coast Hwy .... Long Beach CA 90803 *Web:* maxson-accounting.com	562-594-4681		2
Maxson Automatic Machinery Co 70 Airport Rd .... Westerly RI 02891 *Web:* www.maxsonautomatic.com	401-596-0162	596-1050	556
Maxsys 173 Dalhousie St .... Ottawa ON K1N7C7 *TF:* 800-429-5177 ■ *Web:* maxsys.ca	613-562-9943		260
Maxtec 2305 South 1070 West .... Salt Lake City UT 84119 *TF:* 800-748-5355 ■ *Web:* www.maxtec.com	801-266-5300	973-6090	476
Maxtex Inc 3620 Francis Cir .... Alpharetta GA 30004 *TF:* 800-241-1836 ■ *Web:* www.maxtexinc.com	770-772-6757		361
MaxTool 5798 Ontario Mills Pkwy .... Ontario CA 91764 *TF:* 800-629-3325 ■ *Web:* www.maxtool.com	909-568-2800		351
MaxTradeIn.com LLC 9102 N Meridian St Ste 450 .... Indianapolis IN 46260	317-218-3612		387
Maxum LLC 1307 Tool Dr .... New Iberia LA 70560 *Web:* www.maxumllc.com	337-364-9526		260
Maxus Group Inc 345 Seventh Ave Fl 4 .... New York NY 10001 *TF:* 800-359-0077 ■ *Web:* maxusgroup.com	212-823-2010		260
Maxus Realty Trust Inc 104 Armour Rd PO Box 34729 .... North Kansas City MO 64116 *OTC: MRTI* ■ *TF:* 800-937-5449 ■ *Web:* www.mrti.com	816-303-4500	221-1829	655
MaxVal Group Inc 2251 Grant Rd .... Los Altos CA 94024 *TF:* 800-421-2154 ■ *Web:* www.maxval.com	650-472-0644		226
MaxVision Corp 495 Production Ave .... Madison AL 35758 *TF:* 800-533-5805 ■ *Web:* www.maxvision.com	256-772-3058	772-3078	173-2
Maxwell Air Force Base 55 Le May Plaza S .... Maxwell AFB AL 36112 *TF:* 877-353-6807 ■ *Web:* www.maxwell.af.mil	334-953-2014		497-1
Maxwell Davidson Gallery 724 Fifth Ave 4th Fl .... New York NY 10001 *Web:* www.davidsongallery.com	212-759-7555	759-5824	42
Maxwell Geoservices 1168 Hamilton St .... Vancouver BC V6B2S2 *Web:* maxwellgeoservices.com	604-678-3298		177
Maxwell Hardwood Flooring 190 Wilson Mill Rd .... Monticello AR 71655 *Web:* www.maxwellhardwoodflooring.com	870-367-2436		106
Maxwell Locke & Ritter LLP 401 Congress Ave Ste 1100 .... Austin TX 78701 *Web:* www.mlrpc.com	512-370-3200		734
Maxwell Museum of Anthropology University of New Mexico .... Albuquerque NM 87131 *TF:* 800-821-7443 ■ *Web:* www.unm.edu	505-277-4405	277-1547	520
Maxwell Noll Inc 600 S Lake Ave Ste 502 .... Pasadena CA 91106 *Web:* www.maxnoll.com	626-796-7133		428
Maxwell Sensors Inc 10020 Pioneer Blvd Ste 103 .... Santa Fe Springs CA 90670 *Web:* www.maxwellsensors.com	562-801-2088		743
Maxwell Silverman's Toolhouse Lincoln Sq .... Worcester MA 01608 *Web:* www.maxwellmaxine.com	508-755-1200	753-8217	671
Maxwell Technologies Inc 5271 Viewridge Ct Ste 100 .... San Diego CA 92123 *NASDAQ: MXWL* ■ *TF:* 877-511-4324 ■ *Web:* www.maxwell.com	858-503-3300	503-3301	253
Maxwell's 1 Wall St .... Morgantown WV 26505	304-292-0982		671
Maxwelton Braes Golf Resort 7670 Hwy 57 .... Baileys Harbor WI 54202 *TF:* 800-707-6660 ■ *Web:* maxweltonbraes.com	920-839-2321		669
Maxxam 335 LaiRd Rd Unit 2 .... Guelph ON N1G4P7 *TF:* 877-706-7678 ■ *Web:* www.maxxam.ca	877-706-7678		417
MAXXAM Inc 1330 Post Oak Blvd Ste 2000 .... Houston TX 77056 *OTC: MAXX* ■ *Web:* charleshurwitz.com	713-975-7600		185
Maxxon Corp 920 Hamel Rd .... Hamel MN 55340 *TF:* 800-356-7887 ■ *Web:* www.maxxon.com	763-478-9600		135
MaxYield Co-op 313 Third Ave NE PO Box 49 .... West Bend IA 50597 *TF:* 800-383-0003 ■ *Web:* www.maxyieldcooperative.com	515-887-7211	887-7291	275
Maxymillian Technologies Inc 1801 E St .... Pittsfield MA 01201 *Web:* www.maxymillian.com	413-499-3050	443-0511	192
Maxzone Vehicle Lighting Corp 15889 Slover Ave Ste A .... Fontana CA 92337 *Web:* www.maxzone.com	909-822-3288	822-3399	61
May & Co 110 Monument Pl .... Vicksburg MS 39180 *Web:* www.maycpa.com	601-636-4762		2
May Adv 718 Washington Ave N Ste 306 .... Minneapolis MN 55401 *Web:* www.mayads.com	612-332-2450		4
May Cocagne & King Pc 1353 E Mound Rd Ste 300 .... Decatur IL 62526 *Web:* www.mckcpa.com	217-762-3136		2
May Dragon 4848 Beltline Rd .... Dallas TX 75254 *Web:* www.maydragon.com	972-392-9998	490-5023	671
May Institute Inc 41 Pacella Pk Dr .... Randolph MA 02368 *TF:* 800-778-7601 ■ *Web:* www.mayinstitute.org	781-440-0400		48-6
May Memorial Library 342 S Spring St .... Burlington NC 27215 *Web:* www.alamancelibraries.org	336-229-3588	229-3592	434-3
May National Assoc 995 Towbin Ave .... Lakewood NJ 08701 *Web:* www.maynational.com	973-473-3330		3
May Supply Company Inc 1775 Erickson Ave .... Harrisonburg VA 22801 *TF:* 800-296-9997 ■ *Web:* www.maysupply.com	540-433-2611		612
May Tool & Mold Company Inc 2922 Wheeling Ave .... Kansas City MO 64129 *Web:* www.mayinc.com	816-923-6262	923-6277	757
May Trucking Co 4185 Brooklake Rd .... Salem OR 97303 *TF:* 800-547-9169 ■ *Web:* www.maytrucking.com	503-393-7030		780
May, Adam, Gerdes & Thompson LLP 503 S Pierre St .... Pierre SD 57501 *TF:* 800-636-8803 ■ *Web:* www.magt.com	605-224-8803		428
Maya Overseas Foods Inc 151 Fulton Ave .... Maspeth NY 11378 *Web:* www.mayafoods.com	718-894-5145	894-5178	297-8
Maybank Industries LLC 525 E Bay St .... Charleston SC 29403	843-278-0339		175
Maybelline New York 575 Fifth Ave PO Box 1010 .... New York NY 10017 *TF:* 800-944-0730 ■ *Web:* www.maybelline.com	800-944-0730		214
Mayberry Fine Art Inc 212 Mcdermot Ave .... Winnipeg MB R3B0S3 *TF:* 877-871-9261 ■ *Web:* www.mayberryfineart.com	204-255-5690		42
Maybury State Park 20145 Beck Rd .... Northville MI 48167 *Web:* www.michigandnr.com	248-349-8390		565
Mayco Industries LLC 18 W Oxmoor Rd .... Birmingham AL 35209 *TF:* 800-749-6061 ■ *Web:* www.maycoindustries.com	205-942-4242	945-8704	697
Mayco International LLC 42400 Merrill Rd .... Sterling Heights MI 48314 *Web:* maycointernational.com	586-803-6000		60
Mayday Manufacturing Co 3100 Jim Christal Rd .... Denton TX 76207 *Web:* www.maydaymfg.com	940-898-8301	898-8305	22
Mayer Bros Apple Products Inc 3300 Transit Rd .... West Seneca NY 14224 *TF:* 800-696-2928 ■ *Web:* www.mayerbrothers.com	716-668-1787	668-2437	296-20
Mayer Electric Supply Co 3405 Fourth Ave S .... Birmingham AL 35222 *TF:* 866-637-1255 ■ *Web:* www.mayerelectric.com	205-583-3500	322-2625	246
Mayer Industries Inc 3777 Industrial Blvd .... Orangeburg SC 29116 *Web:* mayerind.com	803-536-3500	536-2545	744
Mayer Laboratories Inc 1950 Addison St Ste 101 .... Berkeley CA 94704 *Web:* www.mayerlabs.com	510-229-5300		743
Mayer Pollock Steel Corp Industrial Hwy .... Pottstown PA 19464 *Web:* www.mayerpollock.com	610-323-5500	323-5506	686
Mayer, Shanzer, & Mayer PC 918 Maple St .... Conshohocken PA 19428 *Web:* www.msmpc.com	610-828-0200		2
Mayers Electric Company Inc 4004 Erie Ct .... Cincinnati OH 45227 *Web:* mayerselectriccompany.com	513-272-2900	272-2904	189-4
Mayes County 1 Court Pl .... Pryor OK 74361 *Web:* mayes.okcounties.org	918-825-2426		338
Mayesh Wholesale Florist Inc 5401 W 104th St .... Los Angeles CA 90045 *TF:* 888-462-9374 ■ *Web:* www.mayesh.com	310-348-4921		292
Mayfair Hotel 1256 W Seventh St .... Los Angeles CA 90017 *Web:* www.mayfairla.com	213-632-1200		378
Mayfair Hotel & Spa 3000 Florida Ave .... Coconut Grove FL 33133 *TF:* 800-433-4555 ■ *Web:* www.mayfairhotelandspa.com	305-441-0000	447-9173	379
Mayfair Infants Group 100 W 33rd St Ste 813 .... New York NY 10001 *TF:* 800-989-9499 ■ *Web:* tawil.com	212-279-3211		155-4
Mayfair Mall 2500 N Mayfair Rd .... Milwaukee WI 53226 *Web:* www.mayfairmall.com	414-771-1300		460
Mayfield & Associates 12452 Highway 49 N Ste B .... Gulfport MS 39503 *Web:* www.mayfieldis.com	228-896-1555		390
Mayfield Fund 2484 Sand Hill Rd Quadrus Complex .... Menlo Park CA 94025 *Web:* www.mayfield.com	650-854-5560	854-5712	792
Mayfield Paper Co 1115 S Hill St .... San Angelo TX 76903 *TF:* 800-725-1441 ■ *Web:* www.mayfieldpaper.com	325-653-1444		559
Mayfield Transfer Company Inc 3200 West Lake St .... Melrose Park IL 60160 *TF:* 800-222-2959 ■ *Web:* www.mfld.net	708-681-4440	681-4483	780
Mayfield-Graves County Chamber of Commerce 201 E College St .... Mayfield KY 42066 *Web:* www.mayfieldchamber.com	270-247-6101		139
Mayflower Inn 118 Woodbury Rd .... Washington CT 06793 *TF:* 800-585-7198 ■ *Web:* gracehotels.com/mayflower	860-868-9466	868-1497	379
Mayflower Park Hotel 405 Olive Way .... Seattle WA 98101 *TF:* 800-426-5100 ■ *Web:* www.mayflowerpark.com	206-623-8700	382-6996	379

	Phone	Fax	Class
Mayflower Retirement Community 1620 Mayflower Ct .... Winter Park FL 32792 *TF:* 800-228-6518 ■ *Web:* www.themayflower.com	407-672-1620	671-6336	672
Mayflower Tours Inc 1225 Warren Ave PO Box 490 .... Downers Grove IL 60515 *TF:* 800-323-7604 ■ *Web:* www.mayflowertours.com	630-435-8500	960-3575	760
Mayflower Transit LLC 1 Mayflower Dr .... Fenton MO 63026 *TF:* 800-325-9970 ■ *Web:* www.mayflower.com/moving	636-305-4000		519
Mayflower Vehicle System 55 N Garfield St .... Norwalk OH 44857	419-668-8132		516
Mayflowers Software 44 Stoneymeade Wy .... Acton MA 01720 *Web:* www.maysoft.com	978-635-1700		178-1
Mayfran International Inc 6650 Beta Dr. .... Cleveland OH 44143 *Web:* www.mayfran.com	440-461-4100	461-5565	207
Mayhew Steel Products Inc 199 Industrial Blvd .... Turners Falls MA 01376 *TF:* 800-872-0037 ■ *Web:* www.mayhew.com	413-863-4860	863-8464	758
Maykadeh 470 Green St. .... San Francisco CA 94133 *Web:* www.maykadehrestaurant.com	415-362-8286		671
Mayland Community College 200 Mayland Dr PO Box 547 .... Spruce Pine NC 28777 **Fax:* Admissions ■ *TF:* 800-462-9526 ■ *Web:* www.mayland.edu	828-765-7351	765-0728*	162
Mayline Group 619 N Commerce St PO Box 728 .... Sheboygan WI 53082 *TF:* 800-822-8037 ■ *Web:* www.mayline.com	920-457-5537	457-7388	319-1
Maymead Inc 1995 Roan Creek Rd .... Mountain City TN 37683 *Web:* www.maymead.com	423-727-2000		188-4
Maymont 2201 Shields Dr .... Richmond VA 23220 *Web:* www.maymont.org	804-358-7166	358-9994	520
Maynard Furniture Company Inc 725 Anderson St. .... Belton SC 29627 *TF:* 800-420-0249 ■ *Web:* www.maynardshomefurnishings.com	864-338-7751		321
Maynard Steel Casting Co 2856 S 27th St .... Milwaukee WI 53215 *Web:* www.maynardsteel.com	414-385-6500	645-7378	307
Maynards Industries Ltd 1837 Main St .... Vancouver BC V5T3B8 *Web:* www.maynards.com	604-876-6787		459
Mayo Aviation Inc 7735 S Peoria St. .... Englewood CO 80112 *TF:* 800-525-0194 ■ *Web:* www.mayoaviation.com	303-792-4020		13
Mayo Civic Ctr 30 Civic Ctr Dr SE. .... Rochester MN 55904 *TF:* 800-422-2199 ■ *Web:* www.mayociviccenter.com	507-328-2220	328-2221	205
Mayo Clinic 4500 San Pablo Rd .... Jacksonville FL 32224 *TF:* 888-255-4458 ■ *Web:* www.mayoclinic.org	904-992-9992		379
Mayo Clinic 200 First St SW .... Rochester MN 55905 *Web:* mayoclinic.org	507-284-2511	284-0161	374-3
Mayo Clinic Health Letter 200 First St NW .... Rochester MN 55905 *TF:* 800-291-1128 ■ *Web:* store.mayoclinic.com	800-291-1128		531-8
Mayo Clinic Health System Austin 1000 First Dr NW .... Austin MN 55912 *TF:* 888-609-4065 ■ *Web:* mayoclinichealthsystem.org	507-433-7351		374-3
Mayo Clinic Health System Southwest Minnesota 1025 Marsh St .... Mankato MN 56001 *TF:* 800-327-3721 ■ *Web:* mayoclinichealthsystem.org	507-625-4031		374-3
Mayo Clinic Hospital 5777 E Mayo Blvd .... Phoenix AZ 85054 *TF:* 888-266-0440 ■ *Web:* mayoclinic.org/patient-visitor-guide	480-342-2000		374-3
Mayo Clinic Proceedings Magazine 200 First St SW Siebens Bldg 7-70 .... Rochester MN 55905 *TF Cust Svc:* 800-654-2452 ■ *Web:* www.mayoclinicproceedings.org	507-284-2094	284-0252	457-16
Mayo Clinic: Benavente Luis A MD 200 SW First St .... Rochester MN 55905 *Web:* www.mayoclinic.org	507-284-2511	284-0161	353
Mayo Collaborative Services Inc 3050 Superior Dr NW. .... Rochester MN 55901 *TF:* 800-533-1710 ■ *Web:* www.mayomedicallaboratories.com	507-266-5700		415
Mayo Foundation for Medical Education & Research 1221 Whipple St PO Box 4105 .... Eau Claire WI 54702 *Web:* mayoclinichealthsystem.org	715-838-3219		374-3
Mayo Knitting Mills Inc 2204 Austin St PO Box 160 .... Tarboro NC 27886 *Web:* mayoknitting.com	252-823-3101	823-0368	155-10
Mayo Manufacturing Corp 4101 Terry St .... Texarkana TX 75501 *Web:* www.mayofurniture.com	903-838-0518	838-4531	321
Mayo Medical School 200 First St SW .... Rochester MN 55905 *Web:* www.mayo.edu/mms	507-284-2511	284-2634	167-2
Mayport Coast Guard Base 4200 Ocean St .... Atlantic Beach FL 32233 *Web:* www.uscg.mil	904-564-7500		158
Mays Chemical Company Inc 5611 E 71st St .... Indianapolis IN 46220 *TF:* 800-833-2661 ■ *Web:* www.mayschem.com	317-842-8722		146
MayStreet LLC 135 W 26th St. .... New York NY 10001 *Web:* www.maystreet.com	212-600-1639		196
Maysville Community & Technical College 1755 US 68 .... Maysville KY 41056 *Web:* www.maysville.kctcs.edu	606-759-7141	759-5818	162
Maytag Aircraft Corp 6145 Lehman Dr Ste 300 .... Colorado Springs CO 80918 *TF:* 800-525-0194 ■ *Web:* www.maytagaircraft.com	719-593-1600		359
Maytag Appliances 403 W Fourth St N .... Newton IA 50208 *TF Cust Svc:* 800-344-1274 ■ *Web:* www.maytag.com	800-344-1274		36
Maytag Dairy Farms Inc 2282 E Eighth St N .... Newton IA 50208 *Web:* iowabackroads.com	641-792-1133		10-3
Maytex Mills Inc 261 Fifth Ave 17th Fl .... New York NY 10016 *Web:* www.maytex.com	212-684-1191		361
Mayville Engineering Company Inc 715 S St .... Mayville WI 53050 *Web:* www.mecinc.com	920-387-4500	387-2682	190
Mayville Products Corp 403 Degner Ave .... Mayville WI 53050 *TF:* 800-558-7297 ■ *Web:* optimastantron.com/en/optima-stantron	920-387-3000		697
Mayville Savings Bank 200 S Main St .... Mayville WI 53050 *Web:* mayvillesavings.com	920-387-2310		70
Mayville State University 330 Third St NE .... Mayville ND 58257 **Fax Area Code:* 701 ■ **Fax:* Admissions ■ *TF:* 800-437-4104 ■ *Web:* leightoninteractive.com	800-437-4104	788-4748*	166
Mayway Corp 1338 Mandela Pkwy .... Oakland CA 94607 *Web:* mayway.com	510-208-3113		297
Maywood Park 8600 W N Ave. .... Melrose Park IL 60160 *Web:* www.maywoodpark.com	708-343-4800		642
Maywood Public Library 121 S Fifth Ave .... Maywood IL 60153 *Web:* www.maywoodlibrary.org	708-343-1847	343-2115	434-3
Maz Mezcal Inc 316 E 86th St .... New York NY 10028 *Web:* mazmezcal.com	212-472-1599		670
Mazama Capital Management Inc 1 S W Columbia St Ste 1500 .... Portland OR 97258 *Web:* www.mazamacap.com	503-221-8725		401
Mazany Office Interiors 428 Livingston Ave. .... Jamestown NY 14701 *TF:* 800-585-5957 ■ *Web:* www.mazanyoffice.com	716-487-1617		320
Mazars Harel Drouin LLP 215 Saint Jacques Bureau 1200 .... Montreal QC H2Y1M6 *Web:* www.mazars.ca	514-845-9253		194
Mazatlan 211 N 70th St .... Lincoln NE 68505	402-464-7201		671
Mazda Knoxville 8814 Kingston Pk .... Knoxville TN 37923 *Web:* www.mazdaknoxville.com	865-690-9395		57
Mazda North American Operations 7755 Irvine Center Dr PO Box 19734 .... Irvine CA 92623 *TF Cust Svc:* 800-222-5500 ■ *Web:* www.mazdausa.com	949-727-1990		59
Mazda of Roswell 11185 Alpharetta Hwy .... Roswell GA 30076 *Web:* mazdaofroswell.com	770-993-6999		57
Mazel & Company Inc 4300 W Ferdinand St .... Chicago IL 60624 *TF:* 800-525-4023 ■ *Web:* www.mazelandco.com	773-533-1600	533-9490	492
Mazon Assoc Inc 800 W Airport Fwy Ste 900 .... Irving TX 75062 *TF:* 800-442-2740 ■ *Web:* mazonfactoring.com	972-554-6967	554-0951	272
Mazonia-Braidwood State Fish & Wildlife Areas PO Box 126 .... Braceville IL 60407 *Web:* www.dnr.illinois.gov/Parks/Pages/Mazonia-Braidwood.aspx	815-237-0063		565
Mazuma Credit Union 9300 Troost Ave .... Kansas City MO 64131 *Web:* mazuma.org	816-361-4194		219
Mazursky Constantine LLC 999 Peachtree St Ste 1500 .... Atlanta GA 30309 *Web:* www.mazconlaw.com	404-888-8820		428
Mazza 1515 S 1500 E .... Salt Lake City UT 84105 *Web:* www.mazzacafe.com	801-484-9259	484-4277	671
Mazza Gallerie 5300 Wisconsin Ave NW .... Washington DC 20015 *Web:* www.mazzagallerie.com	202-966-6114		460
Mazza Vineyards 11815 E Lake Rd .... North East PA 16428 *TF:* 800-796-9463 ■ *Web:* enjoymazza.com/mazza-vineyards	814-725-8695	725-3948	50-7
Mazzella Lifting Technologies 21000 Aerospace Pkwy .... Cleveland OH 44142 *TF:* 800 362 4601 ■ *Web:* www.mazzellacompanies.com/mazzellalifting	440-239-7000	239-7010	470
Mazzeo Agency 54 Shrewsbury Ave Ste C .... Red Bank NJ 07701 *Web:* www.mazzeoagency.com	732-268-7545		390
Mazzetta Co 1990 St Johns Ave .... Highland Park IL 60035 *Web:* www.mazzetta.com	847-433-1150		297-5
Mazzo Energy 139 Van Winkle Ave .... Garfield NJ 07026 *Web:* mazzoenergy.com	973-473-5181		316
Mazzone & Associates Inc 75 Fourteenth St NE Office Tower at the Four Seaso Ste 2800 .... Atlanta GA 30309 *Web:* www.globalmna.com	404-931-8545		194
Mazzotta, Sherwood & Vagianelis, P.C. 9 Washington Sq Washington Ave Ext .... Albany NY 12205 *Web:* www.msvlawfirm.com	518-452-0941		428
Mb Bark LLC 100 Bark Mulch Dr .... Auburn ME 04210 *Web:* www.mbbarkllc.com	207-786-0600		200
Mb Consulting Group Inc 225 S Meramec Ave Ste 621t .... Saint Louis MO 63105 *TF:* 855-622-4911 ■ *Web:* www.contactmb.com	314-725-3584		193
MB Financial Inc 6111 N River Rd .... Rosemont IL 60018 *NASDAQ: MBFI* ■ *TF:* 888-422-6562 ■ *Web:* www.mbfinancial.com	888-422-6562		360-2
MB Haynes Corp 187 Deaverview Rd .... Asheville NC 28806 *Web:* www.mbhaynes.com	828-254-6141	253-8136	189-7
MB Industries Inc 9205 Rosman Hwy .... Rosman NC 28772 *Web:* www.m-bindustries.com	828-862-4201	862-4297	744
MBA (Military Benefit Assn) 14605 Avion Pkwy PO Box 221110 .... Chantilly VA 20153 *TF:* 800-336-0100 ■ *Web:* www.militarybenefit.org	703-968-6200	968-6423	48-19
MBA (Mortgage Bankers Assn) 1919 M St NW 5th Fl .... Washington DC 20036 **Fax:* Cust Svc ■ *TF:* 800-793-6222 ■ *Web:* www.mba.org	202-557-2700	721-0245*	49-2
MBA Construction 298 W Bridge St .... Blackfoot ID 83221 *Web:* www.mbaconstruction.net	208-785-7171		186
MBA Polymers Inc 500 W Ohio Ave .... Richmond CA 94804 *Web:* www.mbapolymers.com	510-231-9031		601
Mba Surety Agency Inc 207 E Capitol Ave .... Jefferson City MO 65101 *Web:* www.mobankers.com	573-636-2142		69
MBAA (Master Brewers Assn of the Americas) 3340 Pilot Knob Rd .... Saint Paul MN 55121 *TF:* 800-328-7560 ■ *Web:* www.mbaa.com	651-454-7250		49-6
MBAF 1450 Brickell Ave 18th Fl .... Miami FL 33131 *TF:* 800-239-3843 ■ *Web:* www.mbafcpa.com	305-373-5500	373-0056	2
Mbb Enterprises 3352 W Grand Ave. .... Chicago IL 60651 *Web:* www.mbbmasonry.com	773-278-7100		358
MBC (Memorial Blood Centers) 737 Pelham Blvd .... Saint Paul MN 55114 *TF Cust Svc:* 888-448-3253 ■ *Web:* www.mbc.org	651-332-7000	332-7001	89
MBC (Mc Kenzie Banking Co) 676 N Main St .... McKenzie TN 38201 *Web:* www.foundationbank.org	731-352-2262	352-7778	70
Mbc Computer Service Inc 11134 Downs Rd .... Pineville NC 28134 *TF:* 800-532-6096 ■ *Web:* www.mbcservice.com	704-525-7590		685

Name / Address	City	State	ZIP	Phone	Fax	Class
MBDA (Minority Business Development Agency) 1401 Constitution Ave NW *TF:* 800-735-2258 ■ *Web:* www.mbda.gov	Washington	DC	20230	202-482-1940		340-2
MBF Clearing Corp 1 N End Ave World Financial Ctr Ste 1201 *Web:* www.mbfcc.com	New York	NY	10282	212-845-5000		691
MBFI (Miami Book Fair International) 300 NE Second Ave Freedom Twr, 7th Fl *Web:* www.miamibookfair.com	Miami	FL	33132	305-237-3258		281
MBG Technologies Inc 1105 Pittsburgh St PO Box 2024 *Web:* mbgtech.com	Newport Beach	CA	15204	724-274-7741		528
MBH Architects 960 atlantic ave *Web:* www.mbharch.com	Alameda	CA	94501	510-865-8663	865-1611	261
MBI Direct Mail 710 W New Hampshire Ave *TF:* 800-359-4780 ■ *Web:* www.mbidirectmail.com	Deland	FL	32720	386-736-9998	736-1100	7
MBI Inc 47 Richards Ave *TF:* 800-922-6918 ■ *Web:* www.mbi-inc.com	Norwalk	CT	06857	203-853-2000		459
MBI International 3815 Technology Blvd *Web:* www.mbi.org	Lansing	MI	48910	517-337-3181	337-2122	668
MBIA Inc 113 King St *NYSE: MBI* ■ *TF:* 800-468-9716 ■ *Web:* www.mbia.com	Armonk	NY	10504	914-273-4545		360-4
MBIA Insurance Corp 113 King St *TF:* 800-468-9716 ■ *Web:* www.mbia.com	Armonk	NY	10504	914-273-4545		391-5
MBK Senior Living Ltd 4 Park Plaza Ste 400 *Web:* www.mbkseniorliving.com	Irvine	CA	92614	949-242-1400		371
MBL (Marine Biological Laboratory) 7 MBL St *TF:* 800-222-1222 ■ *Web:* www.mbl.edu	Woods Hole	MA	02543	508-548-3705	540-6902	668
MBL International Corp 4 H Constitution Way *TF:* 800-200-5459 ■ *Web:* www.mblintl.com	Woburn	MA	01801	781-939-6964		194
MBM (MBM Corp) 3134 Industry Dr *TF Cust Svc:* 800-223-2508 ■ *Web:* www.mbmcorp.com	North Charleston	SC	29418	843-552-2700	552-2974	111
MBM Corp (MBM) 3134 Industry Dr *TF Cust Svc:* 800-223-2508 ■ *Web:* www.mbmcorp.com	North Charleston	SC	29418	843-552-2700	552-2974	111
Mbm Corp 2641 Meadowbrook Rd *Web:* www.mbmcorp.com	Rocky Mount	NC	27801	252-450-6100		805
MBN Corp 812 Memorial Dr NW *Web:* www.middlefield.com	Calgary	AB	T2N3C8	403-269-2100		403
MBNA (Monument Builders of North America) 136 S Keowee St **Fax Area Code: 937* ■ *TF:* 800-233-4472 ■ *Web:* www.monumentbuilders.org	Dayton	OH	45402	800-233-4472	222-5794*	49-3
MBO Partners Inc 13454 Sunrise Vly Dr Ste 300 *Web:* www.mbopartners.com	Herndon	VA	20171	703-793-6000		387
Mbox Communications LLC 1319 Wisconsin Ave NW *Web:* www.mboxcommunications.com	Washington	DC	20007	202-536-4903		33
MBP (McDonough Bolyard Peck Inc) 3040 Williams Dr Williams Plaza 1 Ste 300 *TF:* 800-898-9088 ■ *Web:* www.mbpce.com	Fairfax	VA	22031	703-641-9088	641-8965	261
MBS (Maritime Broadcasting System) 90 Lovett Lake Crt *Web:* www.mbsradio.com	Halifax	NS	B3S0H6	902-425-1225	423-2093	643
MBS Assoc Inc 7800 E Kemper Rd Ste 160 *TF:* 888-469-9301 ■ *Web:* www.mbsassociates.com	Cincinnati	OH	45249	513-645-1600		261
MBS Outsourcing 1201 Oakridge Dr Ste 320 *Web:* www.mbsoutsourcing.com	Fort Collins	CO	80525	970-224-1016		463
MBS Textbook Exchange Inc 2711 W Ash St *TF Cust Svc:* 800-325-0530 ■ *Web:* www.mbsbooks.com	Columbia	MO	65203	573-445-2243		96
MBT Financial Corp 102 E Front St *NASDAQ: MBTF* ■ *TF:* 800-321-0032 ■ *Web:* www.mbandt.com	Monroe	MI	48161	734-241-3431		360-2
MBTA (Massachusetts Bay Transportation Authority) 10 Pk Plaza Ste 3910 **Fax: Mktg* ■ *Web:* www.mbta.com	Boston	MA	02116	617-222-5000	222-3340*	468
MBTC (Mifflinburg Bank & Trust Co) 250 E Chestnut St PO Box 186 *TF:* 888-966-3131 ■ *Web:* www.mbtc.com	Mifflinburg	PA	17844	570-966-1041		70
MC & A Inc 615 Piikoi St Ste 1000 *TF General:* 877-589-5589 ■ *Web:* www.mcahawaii.com	Honolulu	HI	96814	808-589-5500	589-5501	771
Mc Carty Printing Corp 246 E Seventh St *TF:* 800-298-9688 ■ *Web:* www.mccartyprinting.com	Erie	PA	16503	814-454-6337		627
Mc Dermott Auto Group 655 Main St *Web:* mcdermottauto.com	East Haven	CT	06512	203-466-1000		516
MC Dixon Lumber Company Inc 605 W Washington St *Web:* www.dixonlumber.com	Eufaula	AL	36027	334-687-8204	687-8208	683
Mc Donnell Boehnen Hulbert & Berghoff LLP 1136 Water St *Web:* www.mbhb.com	Port Townsend	WA	98368	360-379-6514		445
Mc Donough Engineering Corp 5625 Schumacher Ln *Web:* www.mectx.com	Houston	TX	77057	713-975-9990		261
MC Gill Corp 4056 Easy St *Web:* www.thegillcorp.com	El Monte	CA	91731	626-443-6094	350-5880	22
Mc Glaughlin Oil Co, The 3750 E Livingston Ave *TF:* 800-839-6589 ■ *Web:* www.mcglaughlinoil.com	Columbus	OH	43227	614-231-2518		579
Mc Kenzie Banking Co (MBC) 676 N Main St *Web:* www.foundationbank.org	McKenzie	TN	38201	731-352-2262	352-7778	70
MC Machinery Systems Inc 1500 Michael Dr *Web:* www.mcmachinery.com	Wood Dale	IL	60191	630-860-4210		491
Mc Pherson Plastics Inc PO Box 58 *Web:* www.mcpherson-plastics.com	Otsego	MI	49078	269-694-9487	694-6662	608
M&C Saatchi LA Inc 2032 Broadway *Web:* mcsaatchi-la.com	Santa Monica	CA	90404	310-401-6070		7
MC Sign Company Inc 8959 Tyler Blvd *TF:* 800-627-4460 ■ *Web:* www.mcsign.com	Mentor	OH	44060	440-209-6200		701
MC Software LLC 2225 Washington Blvd	Ogden	UT	84401	801-621-3900		178-11
MC Sports 3070 Shaffer Ave SE *TF:* 800-626-1762 ■ *Web:* www.mcsports.com	Grand Rapids	MI	49512	616-942-2600	942-2786	711
MC Squared Inc 17 Harbourton Ridge Dr *Web:* www.mcsqd.com	Pennington	NJ	08534	609-474-8100		261
MC10 Inc 10 Maguire Rd Bldg 3 1st Fl *Web:* www.mc10inc.com	Cambridge	MA	02421	617-234-4448		253
Mc2 Executive Search Inc PO Box 452 *Web:* www.mc2execsearch.com	Washington Crossing	PA	18977	215-504-5488		193
MC2 Inc 1106 S First St *Web:* www.mc2wi.com	Milwaukee	WI	53204	414-276-2200		179
MCA (Medical Ctr of Aurora) 1501 S Potomac St *Web:* www.auroramed.com	Aurora	CO	80012	303-695-2600		374-3
MCA (Medical City Arlington) 3301 Matlock Rd *Web:* www.medicalcenterarlington.com	Arlington	TX	76015	817-465-3241	472-4878	374-3
MCA (Marine Corps Assn) PO Box 1775 *TF:* 800-336-0291 ■ *Web:* www.mca-marines.org	Quantico	VA	22134	703-640-6161	640-0823	48-19
MCAA (Mason Contractors Assn of America (MCCA)) 1481 Merchant Dr *TF:* 800-536-2225 ■ *Web:* www.masoncontractors.org	Algonquin	IL	60102	224-678-9709	678-9714	49-3
MCAA (Mechanical Contractors Assn of America) 1385 Piccard Dr *TF:* 800-556-3653 ■ *Web:* www.mcaa.org	Rockville	MD	20850	301-869-5800	990-9690	49-3
mcaConnect LLC 8055 E Tufts Ave Ste 1300 *TF:* 866-662-0669 ■ *Web:* www.mcaconnect.net	Denver	CO	80237	866-662-0669		196
MCAD Technologies Inc 7450 W Alaska Dr *TF:* 800-693-9000 ■ *Web:* www.mcad.com	Lakewood	CO	80226	303-969-8844		180
McAdams Graphics Inc 7200 S First St *Web:* www.mcadamsgraphics.com	Oak Creek	WI	53154	414-768-8080	768-8099	626
McAfee & Taft A Professional Corp 2 Leadership Sq 211 N Robinson Ste 1000 *TF:* 800-235-9621 ■ *Web:* www.mcafeetaft.com	Oklahoma City	OK	73102	405-235-9621		428
McAfee Inc 2821 Mission College Blvd *TF Cust Svc:* 888-847-8766 ■ *Web:* www.mcafee.com	Santa Clara	CA	95054	408-988-3832	970-9727	178-12
McAfee Tool & Die Inc 1717 Boettler Rd *Web:* www.mcafeetool.com	Uniontown	OH	44685	330-896-9555	896-9549	757
Mcairlaid's Inc 180 Corporate Dr	Rocky Mount	VA	24151	540-352-5050		548
McAlester Regional Health Ctr 1 Clark Bass Blvd *Web:* www.mrhcok.com	McAlester	OK	74501	918-426-1800		374-3
McAllen Chamber of Commerce 1200 Ash Ave *TF:* 800-786-9199 ■ *Web:* mcallen.org	McAllen	TX	78501	956-682-2871	687-2917	139
McAllen Medical Ctr 301 W Expy 83 *TF:* 800-994-6610 ■ *Web:* www.southtexashealthsystem.com	McAllen	TX	78503	956-632-4000		374-3
McAllen Memorial Library 601 N Main St *Web:* www.mcallenlibrary.net	McAllen	TX	78501	956-688-3300		434-3
McAllister House Museum 423 N Cascade Ave *TF:* 800-367-9723 ■ *Web:* www.mcallisterhouse.org	Colorado Springs	CO	80903	719-635-7925		520
McAllister Towing & Transportation Co Inc 17 Battery Pl Ste 1200 *TF:* 888-764-5980 ■ *Web:* www.mcallistertowing.com	New York	NY	10004	212-269-3200	509-1147	465
McAlpin Industries Inc 255 Hollenbeck St *TF:* 800-388-2148 ■ *Web:* www.mcalpin-ind.com	Rochester	NY	14621	585-266-3060	266-8091	488
McAndrews Held & Malloy 500 W Madison St 34th Fl *Web:* www.mcandrews-ip.com	Chicago	IL	60661	312-775-8000	775-8100	428
McAninch Corp 4001 Delaware Ave *TF:* 800-381-5497 ■ *Web:* www.mcaninchcorp.com	West Des Moines	IA	50313	515-267-2500	267-2550	189-5
MCAP Financial Corp 1140 W Pender St Ste 1400 *TF:* 800-977-5877 ■ *Web:* mcap.com	Vancouver	BC	V6E4G1	604-681-8805		217
MCAP Service Corp 400-200 King St W *TF:* 800-387-4405 ■ *Web:* www.mcap.com	Toronto	ON	M5H3T4	416-598-2665		652
mCapitol Management 1341 G St NW Ste 700 *Web:* www.mcapitol.com	Washington	DC	20005	202-296-5354		393
McArdle Laboratory for Cancer Research University of Wisconsin Dept of Oncology 1111 Highland Ave *Web:* mcardle.oncology.wisc.edu	Madison	WI	53705	608-262-2177	262-2824	668
McArthur-Burney Falls Memorial State Park c/o Northern Buttes District Office 400 Glen Dr *Web:* www.parks.ca.gov/?page_id=455	Oroville	CA	95966	530-538-2200		565
McAuliffe Terry (D) PO Box 1475 *Web:* governor.virginia.gov	Richmond	VA	23218	804-786-1201	371-0038	343
MCB Printing Inc 230 Walnut Hill Ln *Web:* www.mcbprinting.com	Havertown	PA	19083	610-446-6011	446-6013	626
McBee Assoc Inc 997 Old Eagle School Rd Ste 205 *TF:* 800-767-6203 ■ *Web:* www.mcbeeassociates.com	Wayne	PA	19087	610-964-9680		194
McBride & Assoc Inc 1633 Normandy Ct Ste A-200 *Web:* www.mcbridemanagement.com	Lincoln	NE	68512	402-476-3852	476-6547	47
McBride & Son Inc 16091 Swingley Ridge Rd Ste 300 *Web:* www.mcbridehomes.com	Chesterfield	MO	63005	636-537-2000	537-2546	187
McBride Associates Inc 1701 Pennsylvania Ave NW Ste 300 *Web:* www.mcbrideassociates.com	Washington	DC	20006	202-349-3663		463
McBride Construction Resources Inc 224 Nickerson St *Web:* www.mcbrideconstruction.com	Seattle	WA	98109	206-283-7121	284-5670	186

Phone | Fax | Class

MCC (Mini-Cassia Chamber of Commerce)
1177 Seventh St .... Heyburn ID 83336 208-679-4793 679-4794 139
Web: www.minicassiachamber.com

MCC (Mennonite Central Committee)
21 S 12th St PO Box 500 .... Akron PA 17501 717-859-1151 859-2171 48-5
TF: 888-563-4676 ■ *Web:* www.mcc.org

Mcc International Inc
110 Centrifugal Ct .... Mcdonald PA 15057 724-745-0300 308
Web: www.millercentrifugal.com

Mcc Planners Inc
290 N Queen St Ste 208 .... Toronto ON M9C5L2 416-621-6622 317
TF: 800-565-2724 ■ *Web:* mccplanners.com

McCabe Hamilton & Renny Company Ltd (MHR)
1130 N Nimitz Hwy Rm A265 .... Honolulu HI 96817 808-524-3255 545-3101 465
TF: 800-462-8848 ■ *Web:* www.mhrhawaii.com

McCabe Software Inc
3300 N Ridge Rd .... Ellicott City MD 21043 410-381-3710 178-12
TF: 800-638-6316 ■ *Web:* www.mccabe.com

Mccabes Quality Carpet & Linoleum Inc
101 Genesee St .... Marquette MI 49855 906-228-8821 290
Web: mccabesflooring.com

Mccaffery Interests Inc
875 N Michigan Ave Ste 1800 .... Chicago IL 60611 312-944-3777 652
Web: www.mccafferyinterests.com

McCain Engineering Inc
2002 Mccain Pkwy .... Pelham AL 35124 205-663-0123 612
Web: www.mccainengineering.com

McCain Foods Ltd 181 Bay St Ste 3600 .... Toronto ON M5J2T3 416-955-1700 296-21
TF: 800-938-7799 ■ *Web:* www.mccain.com

McCain Foods USA Inc 2275 Cabot Dr .... Lisle IL 60532 800-938-7799 296-21
TF: 800-938-7799 ■ *Web:* www.mccainusa.com

McCain John (Sen R - AZ)
218 Russell Senate Office Bldg .... Washington DC 20510 202-224-2235 228-2862 342-2
Web: www.mccain.senate.gov

McCain Mall
3929 Mccain Blvd .... North Little Rock AR 72116 501-758-6317 758-0131 460
Web: www.simon.com/mall

Mccall & Almy Inc
1 Post Office Sq Ste 2800 .... Boston MA 02109 617-542-4141 652
Web: mccallalmy.com

McCall & Associates Inc
3308 Country Club Rd .... Valdosta GA 31605 229-242-2551 256
Web: www.mccallinc.com

McCall Aviation 300 Deinhard Ln .... McCall ID 83638 208-634-7137 634-3917 63
TF: 800-992-6559 ■ *Web:* www.mccallaviation.com

McCall Handling Co 8801 Wise Ave .... Dundalk MD 21222 410-388-2600 385
TF: 888-870-0685 ■ *Web:* www.mccallhandling.com

McCall Oil & Chemical Corp
5480 NW Front Ave .... Portland OR 97210 503-221-6400 579
TF: 800 622 2558 ■ *Web:* www.mccalloil.com

McCall Patterns Magazine
120 Broadway .... New York NY 10271 800-782-0323 457-14
TF: 800-782-0323 ■ *Web:* www.mccall.com

McCall Service Inc
2861 College St .... Jacksonville FL 32205 904-389-5561 389-3212 577
TF: 800-342-6948 ■ *Web:* www.mccallservice.com

McCall's Quilting Magazine
741 Corporate Cir Ste A .... Golden CO 80401 303-215-5600 457-14
TF: 800-944-0736 ■ *Web:* www.mccallsquilting.com

McCallie Assoc Inc
3906 Raynor Pkwy Ste 200 .... Bellevue NE 68123 402-291-2203 291-8221 178-11
Web: www.mccallie.com

McCallie School 500 Dodds Ave .... Chattanooga TN 37404 423-624-8300 493-5426 622
TF: 800-234-2163 ■ *Web:* www.mccallie.org

McCalls Dam State Park
17215 Buffalo Rd .... Mifflinburg PA 17844 570-966-1455 565
Web: www.dcnr.state.pa.us

McCallum Printing Group Inc
11755 108 Ave Northwest .... Edmonton AB T5H1B8 780-455-8885 627
Web: www.mcprint.ca

McCallum Theatre
73000 Fred Waring Dr .... Palm Desert CA 92260 760-340-2787 779-9445 572
TF: 866-889-2787 ■ *Web:* www.mccallumtheatre.com

Mccallum, Hoaglund, Cook & Irby LLP
905 Montgomery Hwy Ste 201 .... Vestavia AL 35216 205-824-7767 428
TF: 866-974-8145 ■ *Web:* www.mhcilaw.com

McCamly Plaza Hotel
50 Capital Ave SW .... Battle Creek MI 49017 269-963-7050 379
TF: 800-337-0300 ■ *Web:* www.mccamlyplaza.com

Mccann Plastics Inc
5600 Mayfair Rd .... North Canton OH 44720 330-499-1515 596
Web: www.mccannplastics.com

McCann Realty Partners LLC
2520-B Gaskins Rd .... Richmond VA 23238 804-290-8870 652
Web: www.mrpapts.com

Mccann Systems LLC 290 Fernwood Ave .... Edison NJ 08837 732-346-9600 196
Web: www.mccannsystems.com

McCann WorldGroup Inc 622 Third Ave .... New York NY 10017 646-865-2000 5
Web: www.mccannworldgroup.com

McCann's Engineering & Manufacturing Co
4570 W Colorado Blvd .... Los Angeles CA 90039 818-637-7200 637-7222 664
TF: 800-423-2429 ■ *Web:* www.manitowocbeverage.com

McCarl's Inc 1413 Ninth Ave .... Beaver Falls PA 15010 724-843-5660 843-3180 189-10
Web: www.mccarl.com

McCarran International Airport
5757 Wayne Newton Blvd PO Box 11005 .... Las Vegas NV 89119 702-261-5211 597-9553 27
TF: 888-261-4414 ■ *Web:* www.mccarran.com

McCarter Theatre 91 University Pl .... Princeton NJ 08540 609-258-6500 497-0369 749
Web: www.mccarter.org

McCarthy Beach State Park
7622 McCarthy Beach Rd .... Side Lake MN 55781 218-254-7979 565
Web: www.dnr.state.mn.us

McCarthy Bldg Cos Inc
1341 N Rock Hill Rd .... Saint Louis MO 63124 314-968-3300 186
Web: www.mccarthy.com

McCarthy Improvement Company Inc
5401 Victoria Ave .... Davenport IA 52807 563-359-0321 188-4
Web: www.mccarthyimprovement.com

McCarthy Kevin (Rep R - CA)
2421 Rayburn Bldg .... Washington DC 20515 202-225-2915 225-2908 342-2
Web: kevinmccarthy.house.gov

Mccarthy Print Inc
1804 Chicon St Ste 106 .... Austin TX 78702 512-479-8938 627
TF: 800-594-0954 ■ *Web:* www.mccarthyprint.com

McCarty Equipment Co Ltd
1103 Industrial Blvd .... Abilene TX 79602 325-691-5558 386
Web: www.mccartyequipment.com

Mccarys Jewelers Inc
1409 E 70th St Ste 118 .... Shreveport LA 71105 318-798-3050 410
Web: mccarys.com

McCaskill Claire (Sen D - MO)
503 Hart Senate Office Bldg .... Washington DC 20510 202-224-6154 228-6326 342-2
Web: www.mccaskill.senate.gov

McCaul Michael T (Rep R - TX)
2001 Rayburn Bldg .... Washington DC 20515 202-225-2401 225-5955 342-2
Web: mccaul.house.gov

Mc-Caulou's Inc 3512 Mt Diablo Blvd .... Lafayette CA 94549 925-283-3380 229
TF: 800-585-1244 ■ *Web:* www.mccaulous.com

McClain County
121 N Second St Ste 206 PO Box 629 .... Purcell OK 73080 405-527-6561 338
Web: www.mcclain-co-ok.us

McClancy Seasoning Co 1 Spice Rd .... Fort Mill SC 29707 803-548-2366 345
TF: 800-843-1968 ■ *Web:* www.mcclancy.com

McClard's Bar-B-Q
505 Albert Pike Rd .... Hot Springs AR 71901 501-623-9665 671
TF: 866-622-5273 ■ *Web:* www.mcclards.com

McClarin Plastics Inc
15 Industrial Dr .... Hanover PA 17331 717-637-2241 606
TF: 800-233-3189 ■ *Web:* www.mcclarinplastics.com

McClatchy Newspapers 2100 Q St .... Sacramento CA 95816 916-321-1000 321-1869 637-8
TF: 866-807-2200 ■ *Web:* www.mcclatchy.com

McClellan Park LLC
3140 Peacekeeper Way .... Mcclellan CA 95652 916-965-7100 10-3
Web: www.mcclellanpark.com

McClelland Oilfield Rentals Ltd
8720-110 St .... Grande Prairie AB T8V8K1 780-539-3656 540
TF: 866-539-3656 ■ *Web:* www.mcclellandoilfieldrentals.com

McClenahan Bruer
1200 NW Naito Pkwy Ste 100 .... Portland OR 97209 503-546-1000 7
Web: www.mcbru.com

Mccleskey Mills Inc 197 Rhodes St .... Smithville GA 31787 229-846-4110 275
Web: www.mccleskeymills.com

McClintock Tom (Rep R - CA)
2312 Rayburn HOB .... Washington DC 20515 202-225-2511 225-5444 342-2
Web: mcclintock.house.gov

McClinton Chevrolet Co
1325 Seventh St .... Parkersburg WV 26101 304-699-2478 516
Web: mcclintonchevrolet.com

McClone Agency Inc 150 Main St Ste 300 .... Menasha WI 54952 920-725-3232 390

McCloskey Motors Inc
6710 N Academy Blvd .... Colorado Springs CO 80918 719-594-9400 57
TF: 877-389-6671 ■ *Web:* www.bigjoeauto.com

McClung Cos Inc 550 Commerce Ave .... Waynesboro VA 22980 540-949-8139 344
Web: www.mcclungco.com

McClure Co 4101 N Sixth St .... Harrisburg PA 17110 717-232-9743 189-10
TF: 800-382-1319 ■ *Web:* www.mcclureco.com

McClure Engineering Associates Inc
4700 Kennedy Dr .... East Moline IL 61244 309-792-9305 261
Web: www.mcclureengineering.com

McClure Oil Corp
Junction of Hwys 35 and 37 PO Box 1750 .... Marion IN 46952 765-674-9771 677-3223 579
Web: in.mcclureoil.net

McClure Oil Corp 530 Friend Way .... Lebanon IN 46052 765-482-0005 324
Web: www.mcclureoilcorp.com

McCluskey Chevrolet Inc
9673 Kings Automall Dr .... Cincinnati OH 45249 513-761-1111 516
Web: www.mccluskeychevrolet.com

McCollister's Transportation Group Inc
1800 Rt 130 N .... Burlington NJ 08016 609-386-0600 386-5608 519
TF: 800-257-9595 ■ *Web:* www.mccollisters.com

McCollum Betty (Rep D - MN)
2256 Rayburn HOB .... Washington DC 20515 202-225-6631 225-1968 342-2
Web: mccollum.house.gov

McCombs Energy Ltd
5599 San Felipe Ste 1200 .... Houston TX 77056 713-621-0033 536
Web: www.mccombsenergy.com

McCone County 1004 C Ave PO Box 199 .... Circle MT 59215 406-485-3505 485-2689 338
Web: mcconecountymt.com

McCone Electric Co-op Inc 110 Main St .... Circle MT 59215 406-485-3430 245
TF: 800-684-3605 ■ *Web:* www.mcconeelectric.coop

McConkey 1615 Puyallup St PO Box 1690 .... Sumner WA 98390 253-863-8111 863-5833 199
TF: 800-426-8124 ■ *Web:* www.mcconkeyco.com

McConnaughhay Duffy Coonrad Pope & Weaver PA
1709 Hermitage Blvd Ste 200 .... Tallahassee FL 32308 850-222-8121 428
Web: www.mcconnaughhay.com

McConnell Air Force Base
57837 Coffeyville St Ste 271 .... McConnell AFB KS 67221 316-759-6100 497-1
TF: 877-272-7337 ■ *Web:* www.mcconnell.af.mil

McConnell Jones Lanier & Murphy LLP
The Lakes On Post Oak 3040 Post Oak Blvd
Ste 1600 .... Houston TX 77056 713-968-1600 2
TF: 866-908-4650 ■ *Web:* www.mcconnelljones.com

McConnell Mitch (Sen R - KY)
317 Russell Bldg .... Washington DC 20510 202-224-2541 224-2499 342-2
Web: www.mcconnell.senate.gov

McConnell State Recreation Area
8800 McConnell Rd .... Ballico CA 95303 209-394-7755 565
Web: www.parks.ca.gov/default.asp?page_id=554

McConnell Valdes 270 Munz Rivera Ave .... Hato Rey PR 00918 787-759-9292 445
Web: www.mcvpr.com

McCook Community College
1205 E Third St .... McCook NE 69001 308-345-8100 345-8180* 162
*Fax: Admissions ■ *TF:* 800-658-4348 ■ *Web:* www.mpcc.edu

McCook County 130 W Essex PO Box 504 .... Salem SD 57058 605-425-2781 425-3144 338
TF: 800-231-8346 ■ *Web:* www.mccookcountysd.com

Name / Address	City	State	Zip	Phone	Fax	Class
McCook Public Power District 1510 N Hwy 83 *TF:* 800-658-4285 ■ *Web:* www.mppdonline.com	McCook	NE	69001	308-345-2500	345-4772	245
Mccool Carlson Green Inc 421 W First Ave Ste 300 *Web:* mcgalaska.com	Anchorage	AK	99501	907-563-8474		261
McCord Museum of Canadian History 690 Sherbrooke St W *Web:* www.mccord-museum.qc.ca/en	Montreal	QC	H3A1E9	514-398-7100	398-5045	520
Mccormack Guyette & Assoc PC 66 Grove St *Web:* cpa-vermont.com	Rutland	VT	05701	802-775-3221		2
McCormick & Co Inc 18 Loveton Cir *NYSE: MKC* ■ *Web:* www.mccormickcorporation.com	Sparks	MD	21152	410-771-7244		296-37
McCormick & Company Inc McCormick Flavor Div 226 Schilling Cir *TF:* 800-322-7742 ■ *Web:* www.mccormickforchefs.com	Hunt Valley	MD	21031	800-322-7742		296-37
McCormick & Company Inc US Consumer Products Div 211 Schilling Cir *TF:* 800-342-5283 ■ *Web:* www.mccormick.com	Hunt Valley	MD	21031	410-527-6000		296-37
McCormick & Schmick's 448 W 47th St *Web:* www.mccormickandschmicks.com	Kansas City	MO	64112	816-531-6800		671
McCormick & Schmick's 9114 Strada Pl *Web:* www.mccormickandschmicks.com	Naples	FL	34108	407-226-6515		671
McCormick & Schmick's 1 S Broad St *Web:* www.mccormickandschmicks.com	Philadelphia	PA	19107	215-568-6888	568-2066	671
McCormick & Schmick's 190 Marietta St NW *Web:* www.mccormickandschmicks.com	Atlanta	GA	30303	404-521-1236	521-1237	671
McCormick & Schmick's 800 Nicollet Mall *Web:* www.mccormickandschmicks.com	Minneapolis	MN	55402	612-338-3300		671
McCormick & Schmick's 200 S Tryon St *TF:* 800-552-6379 ■ *Web:* www.mccormickandschmicks.com	Charlotte	NC	28202	704-377-0201	377-0208	671
McCormick & Schmick's 335 Hughes Ctr Dr *Web:* www.mccormickandschmicks.com	Las Vegas	NV	89169	702-836-9000	836-9500	671
McCormick & Schmick's 2010B Crystal Dr *Web:* www.mccormickandschmicks.com	Arlington	VA	22202	703-413-6400	413-7118	671
McCormick & Schmick's Harborside 0309 SW Montgomery **Fax Area Code:* 614 ■ *TF Resv:* 888-262-4386 ■ *Web:* www.mccormickandschmicks.com	Portland	OR	97201	503-220-1865	476-3663*	671
Mccormick Armstrong Company Inc 1501 E Douglas *Web:* www.mcaprint.com	Wichita	KS	67211	316-264-1363		627
McCormick Correctional Institution 386 Redemption Way *Web:* doc.sc.gov	McCormick	SC	29899	864-443-2114	443-2114	213
McCormick County 133 S Mine St Rm 102 *TF:* 800-827-1000 ■ *Web:* www.mccormickcountysc.org	McCormick	SC	29835	864-852-2231		338
McCormick Distilling Co Inc 1 McCormick Ln *Web:* www.mccormickdistilling.com	Weston	MO	64098	816-640-2276		80-1
McCormick Group Inc, The 1440 Central Park Blvd Ste 207 *TF:* 800-264-1170 ■ *Web:* www.mccormickgroup.com	Fredericksburg	VA	22401	540-786-9777		463
McCormick Ingredients 18 Loveton Cir *TF:* 800-632-5847 ■ *Web:* www.mccormick.com	Sparks	MD	21152	410-771-7301		296-37
McCormick Place 2301 S Lake Shore Dr *TF:* 800-995-3579 ■ *Web:* www.mccormickplace.com	Chicago	IL	60616	312-791-7000	791-6543	205
McCormick Taylor & Assoc Inc 2001 Market St 10th Fl *Web:* www.mccormicktaylor.com	Philadelphia	PA	19103	215-592-4200	592-0682	261
McCormick Theological Seminary 5460 S University Ave *TF:* 800-228-4687 ■ *Web:* www.mccormick.edu	Chicago	IL	60615	773-947-6300	288-2612	167-3
McCormick's Creek State Park 250 McCormick's Creek Rd *Web:* www.in.gov	Spencer	IN	47460	812-829-2235		565
McCormick's Enterprises Inc 216 W Campus Dr Ste 101 *Web:* www.mccormicksnet.com	Arlington Heights	IL	60004	847-398-8680		711
McCormick's Fish House & Bar 722 Fourth Ave *Web:* www.mccormickandschmicks.com	Seattle	WA	98104	206-682-3900		671
McCorvey Sheet Metal Works LP 8610 Wallisville Rd *TF:* 800-580-7545 ■ *Web:* www.mccorvey.com	Houston	TX	77029	713-672-7545	672-0509	697
McCourt Equipment Company Inc 60 K St Ste 2 *Web:* www.mccourtconstruction.com	Boston	MA	02127	617-269-2330		188-4
McCourt Label Co 20 Egbert Ln *TF:* 800-458-2390 ■ *Web:* www.mccourtlabel.com	Lewis Run	PA	16738	814-362-3851	362-4156	413
McCowan Design & Mfg Ltd 1760 Birchmount Rd *Web:* www.mccowan.ca	Toronto	ON	M1P2H7	416-291-7111		535
McCown De Leeuw & Co (MDC) 950 Tower Ln Ste 800 *Web:* www.mdcpartners.com	Foster City	CA	94404	650-854-6000	854-0853	405
Mccown Gordon Construction LLC 422 Admiral Blvd *Web:* www.mccowngordon.com	Kansas City	MO	64106	816-960-1111		186
Mccoy Miller LLC 1110 Di Dr *Web:* www.mccoymiller.com	Elkhart	IN	46514	574-970-6799		59
McCoy's Bldg Supply 1350 IH 35 N *Web:* www.mccoys.com	San Marcos	TX	78666	512-353-5400		364
McCoy-Ellison Inc 1107 Curtis St *Web:* www.mccoymachinery.com	Monroe	NC	28111	704-289-5413	283-0480	744
Mc-Coy-Mills 700 W Commonwealth *TF Sales:* 888-434-3145 ■ *Web:* www.mccoymillsford.com	Fullerton	CA	92832	888-434-3145		516
McCracken County 301 S Sixth St *Web:* www.mccrackenky.com	Paducah	KY	42003	270-444-4707		338
McCracken County Public Library 555 Washington St *TF:* 866-829-7532 ■ *Web:* www.mclib.net	Paducah	KY	42003	270-442-2510		434-3
McCracken Financial Solutions Corp 8 Suburban Park Dr *TF:* 800-426-9990 ■ *Web:* www.mccrackenfs.com	Billerica	MA	01821	978-439-9000		180
McCrady's 2 Unity Alley *TF:* 800-831-3490 ■ *Web:* www.mccradysrestaurant.com	Charleston	SC	29401	843-577-0025		671
McCranie, Sistrunk, Anzelmo, Hardy, McDaniel & Welch LLC 909 Poydras St Ste 1000 *TF:* 800-977-8810 ■ *Web:* www.mcsalaw.com	New Orleans	LA	70112	504-831-0946		428
Mccraw Oil Company Inc 2207 N Ctr St *Web:* www.mccrawoil.com	Bonham	TX	75418	903-583-7481		581
McCray Lumber Co 10741 El Monte Ln *Web:* www.mccraylumber.com	Overland Park	KS	66211	913-341-6900		191-3
McCrea Equipment Company Inc 4463 Beech Rd *TF:* 800-597-0091 ■ *Web:* mccreaway.com	Temple Hills	MD	20748	301-423-4585		189-10
McCreary County Tourist Commission PO Box 699 *Web:* www.mccrearycounty.com	Whitley City	KY	42653	606-376-3008		338
McCrometer Inc 3255 W Stetson Ave *TF:* 800-220-2279 ■ *Web:* www.mccrometer.com	Hemet	CA	92545	951-652-6811	652-3078	201
McCrone Assoc Inc 850 Pasquinelli Dr *Web:* www.mccrone.com/materials-analysis	Westmont	IL	60559	630-887-7100	887-7417	668
McCrone Inc 20 Ridgely Ave *Web:* mccrone-engineering.com	Annapolis	MD	21401	410-267-8621		261
McCrory Construction 522 Lady St *Web:* www.mccroryconstruction.com	Columbia	SC	29201	803-799-8100	254-9800	685
McCroskey State Park McCroskey State Pk *Web:* www.visitidaho.org	Farmington	ID	99128	208-686-1308		565
McCullagh Coffee 245 Swan St *TF:* 800-753-3473 ■ *Web:* www.mccullaghcoffee.com	Buffalo	NY	14204	800-753-3473		296-7
McCulloch County 199 Courthouse Sq Rm 103 *Web:* co.mcculloch.tx.us	Brady	TX	76825	325-597-0733	597-0606	338
McCullough & Assoc 1746 NE Expy PO Box 29803 *TF:* 800-969-1606 ■ *Web:* www.mccanda.com	Atlanta	GA	30329	404-325-1606	329-0208	146
McCullough & Associates LLC 101 California St Ste 3260 *Web:* www.macinv.com	San Francisco	CA	94111	415-956-8700		401
Mccullough Industries Inc 13047 County Rd 175 *Web:* www.mcculloughind.com	Kenton	OH	43326	419-673-0767		697
McCune Foundation 3 PPG Pl Ste 400 *Web:* www.mccune.org	Pittsburgh	PA	15222	412-644-8779	644-8059	305
McCurtain County PO Box 1078 *Web:* okcountyrecords.com	Idabel	OK	74745	580-286-2370		338
McCutchen Group LLC 925 Fourth Ave Ste 2288 *Web:* www.mccutchengroup.com	Seattle	WA	98104	206-816-6850	816-6830	401
MCD Innovations 3303 N MCDonald St *TF:* 800-804-1757 ■ *Web:* www.mcdinnovations.com	Mckinney	TX	75071	972-548-1850		499
McDade-Woodcock Inc 2404 Claremont Ave NE PO Box 11592 *Web:* mwieic.com	Albuquerque	NM	87107	505-884-0155		203
McDanel Advanced Ceramic Technologies LLC 510 Ninth Ave *Web:* www.ceramics.com/vesuvius	Beaver Falls	PA	15010	724-843-8300		663
McDaniel College 2 College Hill **Fax:* Admissions ■ *TF Admissions:* 800-638-5005 ■ *Web:* www.mcdaniel.edu	Westminster	MD	21157	410-857-2230	857-2757*	166
McDaniel Motor Co 1111 Mt Vernon Ave *TF:* 877-362-0288 ■ *Web:* mcdanieltoyota.com	Marion	OH	43302	740-389-2355		516
Mcdaniel Tech Services Inc 2005 N Yellowood Ave *Web:* www.mcdanieltsi.com	Broken Arrow	OK	74012	918-294-1628		261
Mcdaniels Marketing Communications 11 Olt Ave *TF:* 866-431-4230 ■ *Web:* www.mcdanielsmarketing.com	Pekin	IL	61554	309-346-4230		195
McDantim Inc 750 Shepard Way *TF:* 888-735-5607 ■ *Web:* mcdantim.com	Helena	MT	59601	406-442-5153	442-5154	789
Mcdermott & Bull Executive Search 2 Venture Ste 100 *Web:* mbsearch.com	Irvine	CA	92618	949-753-1700		260
Mcdermott & Miller Pc 13616 California St Ste 300 **Fax Area Code:* 402 ■ *Web:* www.mmcpas.com	Omaha	NE	68154	308-234-5565	496-2711*	196
McDermott International Inc 757 N Eldridge Pkwy *NYSE: MDR* ■ *Web:* www.mcdermott.com	Houston	TX	77079	281-870-5000		188-5
McDermott Will & Emery 444 West Lake St *Web:* www.mwe.com	Chicago	IL	60606	312-372-2000	984-7700	428
McDevitt Trucks Inc 1 Mack Ave PO Box 4640 *TF:* 800-370-6225 ■ *Web:* www.mctrucks.com	Manchester	NH	03108	603-668-1700	668-1865	57
MCDI (Medical Care Development International) 8401 Colesville Rd Ste 425 *TF:* 800-427-7566 ■ *Web:* www.mcd.org	Silver Spring	MD	20910	301-562-1920	562-1921	48-5
McDill Associates 4800 Leapfrog Ln *Web:* jacobsheart.org	Soquel	CA	95073	831-462-3198		195
McDill Design 626 N Water St Ste 2 *Web:* www.mcdilldesign.com	Milwaukee	WI	53202	414-277-8111		344
Mcdivitt Law Firm 19 E Cimarron St *Web:* mcdivittlaw.com	Colorado Springs	CO	80903	303-426-4878		428
McDonald Carano Wilson LLP 100 W Liberty St 10th Fl *TF:* 800-872-3862 ■ *Web:* www.mcdonaldcarano.com	Reno	NV	89505	775-788-2000		41
McDonald County 602 Main St PO Box 606 *Web:* www.mcdonaldcountygov.com	Pineville	MO	64856	417-223-7523	223-2881	338
McDonald Information Service Inc 215 14th St *Web:* www.callmis.com	Jersey City	NJ	07310	201-659-2600		194

Name / Address	City	State	Zip	Phone	Fax	Class
McDonald Oil Company Inc 1700 Lukken Indus Dr W *Web:* www.mcdonaldoil.com	Lagrange	GA	30240	706-884-6191		443
McDonald Partners LLC 959 W St Clair Ave *Web:* www.mcdonald-partners.com	Cleveland	OH	44113	216-912-0567		194
McDonald Publishing 567 Hanley Industrial Ct *TF:* 800-722-8080 ■ *Web:* www.mcdonaldpublishing.com	Saint Louis	MO	63144	314-781-7400	781-7480	243
McDonald Technologies International Inc 2310 McDaniel Dr *Web:* www.mcdonald-tech.com	Carrollton	TX	75006	972-421-4100		625
McDonald Theatre 1010 Willamette St *Web:* www.mcdonaldtheatre.com	Eugene	OR	97401	541-345-4442		572
McDonald Wholesale Co 2350 W Broadway St *TF:* 877-722-5503 ■ *Web:* www.mcdonaldwhsl.com	Eugene	OR	97402	541-345-8421	345-7146	297-3
McDonald's Corp 1 McDonald's Plaza *NYSE: MCD* ■ *TF:* 800-244-6227 ■ *Web:* www.mcdonalds.com	Oak Brook	IL	60523	630-623-3000		670
McDonald's Restaurants of Canada Ltd PO Box 61023 *TF:* 888-424-4622 ■ *Web:* www.mcdonalds.ca	Winnipeg	MB	R3M3X8	416-443-1000	446-3443	670
McDonnell Investment Management LLC 18W140 Butterfield Rd Ste 1200 *TF:* 800-862-4863 ■ *Web:* www.mcdmgmt.com	Oak Brook	IL	60181	630-684-8600		401
McDonough Bolyard Peck Inc (MBP) 3040 Williams Dr Williams Plaza 1 Ste 300 *TF:* 800-898-9088 ■ *Web:* www.mbpce.com	Fairfax	VA	22031	703-641-9088	641-8965	261
McDonough Manufacturing Co 2320 Melby St PO Box 510 *TF:* 800-553-0182 ■ *Web:* www.mcdonough-mfg.com	Eau Claire	WI	54702	715-834-7755	834-3968	821
McDonough Museum of Art 525 Wick Ave *Web:* web.ysu.edu	Youngstown	OH	44502	330-941-1400		520
McDonough Power Co-op 1210 W Jackson St *Web:* mcdonoughpower.com	Macomb	IL	61455	309-833-2101		245
McDougal & Sons 305 Olds Stn Rd	Wenatchee	WA	98801	509-662-2136		315-3
Mcdougall & Duval Adv Inc 24 Millyard Ste 8 *Web:* mcdougallduval.com	Amesbury	MA	01913	978-388-3100		4
McDougall Gauley 500-616 Main St *TF:* 800-994-3337 ■ *Web:* www.mcdougallgauley.com	Saskatoon	SK	S7H0J6	306-653-1212		428
McDowell & Assoc Inc 21355 Hatcher Ave *Web:* www.mcdowasc.com	Ferndale	MI	48220	248-399-2066		256
McDowell County 60 E Court St *Web:* www.mcdowellgov.com	Marion	NC	28752	828-652-7121		338
McDowell County 90 Wyoming St Ste 201 *Web:* www.mcdowellcounty.wv.gov	Welch	WV	24801	304-436-8548	436-8572	338
McDowell County Chamber of Commerce 1170 W Tate St *TF:* 800-996-6277 ■ *Web:* www.mcdowellchamber.com	Marion	NC	28752	828-652-4240	659-9620	139
McDowell County Public Library 90 W Ct St *Web:* www.main.nc.us	Marion	NC	28752	828-652-3858	652-2098	434-3
McDowell County Schools 334 S Main St *Web:* www.mcdowell.k12.nc.us	Marion	NC	28752	828-652-4535		434-3
McDowell County Tourism Development Authority 91 S Catawba Ave *TF:* 888-233-6111 ■ *Web:* blueridgetravelers.com	Old Fort	NC	28762	828-668-4282		206
Mcdowell Group Inc 9360 Glacier Hwy Ste 201 *Web:* www.mcdowellgroup.net	Juneau	AK	99801	907-586-6126		195
McDowell Public Library 90 Howard St *Web:* mcdowell.lib.wv.us	Welch	WV	24801	304-436-3070	436-8079	434-3
Mcdowell Rice Smith & Buchanan PC 605 W 47th St Ste 350 *Web:* www.mcdowellrice.com	Kansas City	MO	64112	816-753-5400		428
McDowell Technical Community College 54 College Dr **Fax:* Admissions ■ *Web:* www.mcdowelltech.edu	Marion	NC	28752	828-652-6021	652-1014*	162
McDowell-Craig Office Furniture 13146 Firestone Blvd *Web:* www.mcdowellcraig.com	Norwalk	CA	90650	562-921-4441		319-1
MCDP (Marion County Development Partnership) 412 Courthouse Sq PO Box 272 *Web:* www.mcdp.info	Columbia	MS	39429	601-736-6385	736-6392	139
McDuffie County PO Box 158 *Web:* www.dca.state.ga.us	Thomson	GA	30824	404-679-4940		338
MCE (Maryland Correctional Enterprises) 7275 Waterloo Rd *TF:* 800-735-2258 ■ *Web:* mce.md.gov	Jessup	MD	20794	410-540-5454	540-5570	630
MCE (Medical Ctr Enterprise) 400 N Edwards St *TF:* 800-994-6610 ■ *Web:* www.mcehospital.com	Enterprise	AL	36330	334-347-0584		374-3
MCE Technologies LLC 30 Hughes Ste 203 *TF:* 800-500-0622 ■ *Web:* www.mcetech.com	Irvine	CA	92618	949-458-0800		95
McEachin A Donald (Rep R - VA) 314 Cannon HOB *Web:* mceachin.house.gov	Washington	DC	20515	202-225-6365		342-2
McEagle Properties LLC 1001 Boardwalk Springs Pl	O'Fallon	MO	63368	636-561-9300		652
MCEER 212 Ketter Hall *Web:* www.mceer.buffalo.edu	Buffalo	NY	14260	716-645-3391	645-3733	668
Mcelrath Geyer Sandler & Fisher 1500 Quail St Ste 450	Newport Beach	CA	92660	949-252-0252		2
Mcelroy & Associates Inc 1164 George Ln	Naperville	IL	60540	630-355-3151		195
McElroy Deutsch & Mulvaney LLP PO Box 2075 *Web:* www.mdmc-law.com	Morristown	NJ	07962	973-993-8100	425-0161	428
McElroy Manufacturing Inc 833 N Fulton Ave *Web:* www.mcelroy.com	Tulsa	OK	74115	918-836-8611		454
McElroy Metal Inc 1500 Hamilton Rd *TF:* 800-562-3576 ■ *Web:* www.mcelroymetal.com	Bossier City	LA	71111	318-747-8097	747-8657	480
McElroy Truck Lines Inc 111 80 Spur PO Box 104 *TF:* 800-992-7863 ■ *Web:* www.mcelroytrucklines.com	Cuba	AL	36907	205-392-5579	392-7992	449
McElvaine Investment Management Ltd Ste 219 2187 Oak Bay Ave Ste 219 *Web:* mcelvaine.com	Victoria	BC	V8R1G1	250-708-8345		528
Mcenearney Assoc Inc 109 S Pitt St *TF:* 877-624-9322 ■ *Web:* www.mcenearney.com	Alexandria	VA	22314	703-549-9292		652
McEntire Produce Inc 2040 American Italian Way *TF:* 800-845-2334 ■ *Web:* www.mcentireproduce.com	Columbia	SC	29209	803-799-3388		10-11
MCESI (Mid-Coast Electric Supply Inc) 1801 Stolz St PO Box 2505 *Web:* www.mcesi.com	Victoria	TX	77901	361-575-6311	575-5515	246
MCF Systems Atlanta Inc 5353 Snapfinger Woods Dr	Decatur	GA	30035	770-593-9434		660
Mcf Technology Solutions LLC 30400 Detroit Rd *TF:* 800-867-1389 ■ *Web:* www.mcftech.com	Westlake	OH	44145	440-201-6050		225
McFarland & Company Inc 960 NC Hwy 88 W PO Box 611 *TF:* 800-253-2187 ■ *Web:* www.mcfarlandbooks.com	Jefferson	NC	28640	336-246-4460		637-2
McFarland Cascade 1640 E Marc St PO Box 1496 *TF Cust Svc:* 800-426-8430 ■ *Web:* www.ldm.com	Tacoma	WA	98421	253-572-3033	627-0764	818
McFarlane Inc 3473 N Washington St *TF:* 800-273-9071 ■ *Web:* mcfarlane-e3.com	Grand Forks	ND	58203	701-772-9511		697
McFarlane Mfg Company Inc 1259 Water St PO Box 100 *TF:* 800-627-8569 ■ *Web:* www.mcfarlanes.net	Sauk City	WI	53583	608-643-3321	643-2309	276
McFarling Foods Inc 333 W 14th St *TF:* 800-495-7222 ■ *Web:* www.mcfarling.com	Indianapolis	IN	46202	317-635-2633		345
McFoster's Natural Kind Cafe 302 S 38th St *Web:* mcfosters.com	Omaha	NE	68131	402-345-7477		671
MCG Architecture 111 Pacifica Ste 280 *Web:* www.mcgarchitecture.com	Irvine	CA	92618	949-553-1117		261
MCG Capital Corp 1001 19th St N 10th fl *NASDAQ: MCGC*	Arlington	VA	22209	703-247-7500		792
MCG Global LLC 300 Long Beach Blvd Ste 13 *Web:* www.mcgglobal.com	Stratford	CT	06615	203-386-0615		403
McGard LLC 3875 California Rd *TF:* 800-444-5847 ■ *Web:* www.mcgard.com	Orchard Park	NY	14127	716-662-8980	662-8985	61
McGarrah Jessee LP 205 Brazos *Web:* www.mc-j.com	Austin	TX	78701	512-225-2000		7
Mcgarry Bair Pc 32 Market Ave SW Ste 500 *TF:* 800-973-1177 ■ *Web:* www.mcgarrybair.com	Grand Rapids	MI	49503	616-742-3500		428
McGean-Rohco Inc 2910 Harvard Ave *TF Orders:* 800-932-7006 ■ *Web:* www.mcgean.com	Cleveland	OH	44105	216-441-4900	441-1377	145
McGee Company Inc 1140 S Jason St *Web:* www.mcgeecompany.com	Denver	CO	80223	303-777-2615		172
McGee Creek State Park 576-A S McGee Creek Dam Rd *Web:* www.travelok.com	Atoka	OK	74525	580-889-5822	889-7868	565
MCGG (Morrow County Grain Growers Inc) 350 N Main St *TF:* 800-452-7396 ■ *Web:* www.mcgg.net	Lexington	OR	97839	541-989-8221	989-8229	10-5
McGhee Tyson Airport 2055 Alcoa Hwy *Web:* flyknoxville.com	Alcoa	TN	37701	865-342-3000	342-3050	27
McGiffert & Associates LLC 2814 Stillman Blvd *TF:* 800-625-9576 ■ *Web:* www.mcgiffert.com	Tuscaloosa	AL	35401	205-759-1521		256
McGill Airflow Corp 900 Pinder Ave **Fax Area Code:* 614 ■ *Web:* www.mcgillairflow.com	Grinnell	IA	50112	641-236-1580	829-1291*	697
McGill Buckley Inc 2206 Anthony Ave *TF:* 800-544-8614 ■ *Web:* www.mcgillbuckley.com	Ottawa	ON	K2B6V2	613-728-4199		7
McGill Hose & Coupling Inc 41 Benton Dr PO Box 408 *TF:* 800-669-1467 ■ *Web:* www.mcgillhose.com	East Longmeadow	MA	01028	413-525-3977		385
McGill Inc 131 E Prairie St *Web:* www.mcgillinc.com	Marengo	IL	60152	815-568-7244		534
McGill Maintenance Partnership Ltd 6402 E Hwy 332 *Web:* www.mcgillmaintenance.com	Freeport	TX	77542	979-233-5438		454
McGill Smith Punshon Inc 3700 Park 42 Dr Ste 190B *TF:* 800-759-8065 ■ *Web:* www.mcgillsmithpunshon.com	Cincinnati	OH	45241	513-759-0004		261
McGill University 845 Sherbrooke St W **Fax:* Admissions ■ *TF:* 800-606-8734 ■ *Web:* www.mcgill.ca	Montreal	QC	H3A2T5	514-398-4455	398-8939*	785
McGill University Life Sciences Library & Osler Library of the History of Medicine 3655 Sir William Osler *Web:* www.mcgill.ca	Montreal	QC	H3G1Y6	514-398-4475		434-1
McGill's 1560 E 21st St *Web:* dinemcgills.com	Tulsa	OK	74114	918-742-8080		671
McGillicuddy's Irish Pub 14 Langdon St *TF:* 800-896-8939 ■ *Web:* mcgillicuddysvt.com	Montpelier	VT	05862	802-223-2721		671
Mcginnis Inc 502 Second St Ext *Web:* www.mcginnisinc.com	South Point	OH	45680	740-377-4391		698
Mcginnis Lochridge & Kilgore LLP 600 Congress Ave *Web:* www.mcginnislaw.com	Austin	TX	78701	512-495-6000	495-6093	428
McGinnis Meadows Cattle & Guest Ranch 6220 Mcginnis Meadows Rd *Web:* www.mmgranch.net	Libby	MT	59923	406-293-5000		239
Mcgohan Brabender Inc 3931 S Dixie Dr *Web:* www.mcgohanbrabender.com	Dayton	OH	45439	937-293-1600		390
Mcgoodwin Williams & Yates Inc (MWY) 302 E Millsap Rd *Web:* www.mwyusa.com	Fayetteville	AR	72703	479-443-3404	443-4340	261
McGough Construction Co Inc 2737 Fairview Ave N *TF:* 800-552-7670 ■ *Web:* www.mcgough.com	Saint Paul	MN	55113	651-633-5050	633-5673	186

Phone Fax Class

McGovern James (Rep D - MA)
438 Cannon Bldg .... Washington DC 20515 202-225-6101 225-5759 342-2
Web: mcgovern.house.gov

Mcgowan Hood & Felder LLC
1517 Hampton St .... Columbia SC 29201 803-779-0100 428
TF: 888-800-2455 ■ *Web:* www.mcgowanhood.com

McGowan-Stauffer Inc 1400 Stn St. .... Coraopolis PA 15108 412-264-3500 189-5
TF: 800-771-3244 ■ *Web:* www.mcgowan-stauffer.com

McGowen Hurst Clark & Smith PC
1601 West Lakes Pkwy Ste 300 .... West Des Moines IA 50266 515-288-3279 2
Web: www.mhcscpa.com

McGraphics Inc 601 Hagan St .... Nashville TN 37203 615-242-8779 555

McGrath Auto Group
4610 Ctr Pt Rd NE .... Cedar Rapids IA 52402 888-902-8414 57
TF: 888-902-8414 ■ *Web:* www.mcgrathauto.com

McGrath RentCorp
5700 Las Positas Rd .... Livermore CA 94551 925-606-9200 453-3200 505
NASDAQ: MGRC ■ *TF:* 800-962-4284 ■ *Web:* www.mgrc.com

McGrath's Fish House
1036 Vly River Way .... Eugene OR 97401 541-342-6404 671
Web: www.mcgrathsfishhouse.com

McGrath's Pub & Restaurant
202 Locust St .... Harrisburg PA 17101 717-232-9914 671
Web: mcgrathspub.net

McGraw Wentworth Inc
3331 W Big Beaver Rd Ste 200 .... Troy MI 48084 248-822-8000 463
Web: www.mcgrawwentworth.com

McGraw-Hill Education 8787 Orion Pl .... Columbus OH 43240 800-334-7344 243
TF: 800-334-7344 ■ *Web:* www.mheducation.com

McGraw-Hill Education
1221 Ave of the Americas P.O. Box 182605ÿ .... New York NY 10020 212-512-2000 637-2
NYSE: MHFI ■ *Web:* www.mcgraw-hill.com

McGraw-Hill Higher Education Group
1333 Burr Ridge Pkwy .... Burr Ridge IL 60527 630-789-4000 637-2
TF: 800-634-3963 ■ *Web:* www.mheducation.com/highered/home-guest.html

McGraw-Hill Professional Publishing Group
2 Penn Plaza 11th Fl .... New York NY 10121 877-833-5524 637-2
TF: 877-833-5524 ■ *Web:* www.mhprofessional.com

Mcgreal & Company PC 5740 W 95th St .... Oak Lawn IL 60453 708-422-8600 2
Web: mcgreal.com

McGregor & Company LLP
1190 Blvd NE .... Orangeburg SC 29115 803-536-1015 2
Web: mcgregorcpa.com

McGregor Industries Inc 46 Line St .... Dunmore PA 18512 570-343-2436 343-4915 491
TF: 800-326-6786 ■ *Web:* www.mcgregorindustries.com

McGregor Metalworking Cos
2100 S Yellow Springs St .... Springfield OH 45506 937-325-5561 256
Web: mcgregormetal.com

McGriff Seibels & Williams Inc
2211 Seventh Ave S .... Birmingham AL 35233 205-252-9871 581-9293 390
TF: 800-476-2211 ■ *Web:* www.mcgriff.com

McGuffin Creative Group
566 W Adams St Ste 440 .... Chicago IL 60661 312-715-9812 5
Web: mcguffincg.com

McGuire
W194 N11481 McCormick Dr PO Box 309 .... Germantown WI 53022 518-828-7652 255-9399* 470
**Fax Area Code:* 262 ■ *TF:* 800-624-8473 ■ *Web:* www.wbmcguire.com

McGuire Air Force Base
2901 Falcon Ln
Rm 235 .... Joint Base McGuire-Dix-Lakehurst NJ 08641 609-754-2104 754-6999 497-1
Web: www.jointbasemdl.af.mil

McGuire Cadillac Inc 910 Rt 1 N .... Woodbridge NJ 07095 866-552-4208 326-0385* 516
**Fax Area Code:* 732 ■ *TF:* 866-552-4208 ■ *Web:* www.mcguirecadillac.com

McGuire Craddock & Strother P C
2501 N Harwood St Ste 1800 .... Dallas TX 75201 214-954-6800 445
Web: www.mcslaw.com

McGuire Furniture Co
1201 Bryant St .... San Francisco CA 94103 415-626-1414 864-8593 319-2
TF: 800-662-4847 ■ *Web:* www.mcguirefurniture.com

McGuire Manufacturing
60 Grandview Ct .... Cheshire CT 06410 203-699-1801 612
TF: 800-676-1832 ■ *Web:* www.mcguiremfg.com

Mcguire Peck & Co 630 Silver St .... Agawam MA 01001 413-789-2551 2

McGuire's Irish Pub
600 E Gregory St .... Pensacola FL 32502 850-433-6789 671
Web: www.mcguiresirishpub.com

McGuires Motor Inn
120 S Telegraph Rd .... Waterford MI 48328 248-682-5100 378
Web: www.mcguiresmotorinn.com

McGuireWoods LLP
901 E Cary St 1 James Ctr .... Richmond VA 23219 804-775-1000 775-1061 428
TF: 877-712-8778 ■ *Web:* www.mcguirewoods.com

McGuyer Homebuilders Inc (MHI)
7676 Woodway Ste 104 .... Houston TX 77063 713-952-6767 952-5637 653
Web: www.mcguyerhomebuilders.com

MCH (Medical Ctr Hospital)
500 W Fourth St .... Odessa TX 79761 432-640-6000 374-3
Web: www.medicalcenterhealthsystem.com

MCH (Marian Community Hospital)
100 Lincoln Ave .... Carbondale PA 18407 570-281-1000 374-3

MCH Inc 601 E Marshall St .... Sweet Springs MO 65351 660-335-6373 366
Web: www.mchdata.com

McHale & Slavin PA
2855 PGA Blvd .... Palm Beach Gardens FL 33410 561-625-6575 428
TF: 800-201-3187 ■ *Web:* www.mchaleslavin.com

McHenry Area Chamber of Commerce
1257 N Green St .... McHenry IL 60050 815-385-4300 385-9142 139
TF: 800-374-8373 ■ *Web:* www.mchenrychamber.com

McHenry County 407 Main St S Rm 201 .... Towner ND 58788 701-537-5724 338
Web: www.mchenrycountynd.com

McHenry County 2200 N Seminary Ave .... Woodstock IL 60098 815-334-4000 334-8727 338
Web: www.co.mchenry.il.us

McHenry County College
8900 US Hwy 14 .... Crystal Lake IL 60012 815-455-3700 455-3766 162
TF: 888-977-4847 ■ *Web:* www.mchenry.edu

McHenry Creative Services Inc
345 Main St .... Harleysville PA 19438 215-513-0251 514
Web: www.mchenrycreative.com

McHenry Museum 1402 'I' St .... Modesto CA 95354 209-577-5235 520
Web: www.mchenrymuseum.org

McHenry Patrick T (Rep R - NC)
2334 Rayburn HOB .... Washington DC 20515 202-225-2576 225-0316 342-2
Web: mchenry.house.gov

McHenry Public Library District
809 N Front St .... Mchenry IL 60050 815-385-0036 434-3
Web: mchenrylibrary.org

McHenry Savings Bank 353 Bank Dr .... McHenry IL 60050 815-385-3000 385-4433 70
Web: www.mchenrysavings.com

McHone Metal Fabricators Inc
10300 County Rd 304 .... Terrell TX 75160 972-524-7775 697
Web: www.kwikbilt.com

MCHS (Marion County Historical Society Museum)
260 12th St SE .... Salem OR 97301 503-364-2128 520
Web: www.marionhistory.org

MCI (Massachusetts Correctional Institution-Plymouth)
1 Bumps Pond Rd .... South Carver MA 02366 508-291-2441 213
Web: www.mass.gov

MCI Inc 26 First Ave N .... Waite Park MN 56387 320-227-4061 290
Web: www.mcicarpetonewaitepark.com

MCI Optonix LLC
2020 Contractors Rd Ste 8 .... Sedona AZ 86336 800-678-6649 682-4079* 475
**Fax Area Code:* 928 ■ *TF:* 800-678-6649 ■ *Web:* www.mcio.com

McIlhenny Co Hwy 329 .... Avery Island LA 70513 337-365-8173 296-19
TF Orders: 800-634-9599 ■ *Web:* www.tabasco.com

McInnis Brothers Construction Inc
119 Pearl St .... Minden LA 71055 318-377-6134 256
Web: www.mcinnisbrothers.com

McIntire Co 745 Clark Ave .... Bristol CT 06010 860-585-0050 314-4500 18
TF: 800-437-9247 ■ *Web:* www.mcintireco.com

Mcintosh & Associates LLC
1955 Lakeway Dr Ste 270b .... Lewisville TX 75057 214-488-2321 463
TF: 800-982-9614 ■ *Web:* mcintoshassociates.com

McIntosh County 112 First St NE .... Ashley ND 58413-7009 701-328-7300 328-7308 338
Web: www.ndaco.org

McIntosh County PO Box 584 .... Darien GA 31305 912-437-6671 437-6416 338
Web: georgia.gov

McIntosh County
110 N First St PO Box 107 .... Eufaula OK 74432 918-689-2611 689-3611 338
Web: mcintosh.oklahoma.usassessor.com

McIntosh County Board of Education
200 Pine St .... Darien GA 31305 912-437-6645 685
Web: www.mcintosh.k12.ga.us

McIntosh Laboratory Inc
2 Chambers St .... Binghamton NY 13903 607-723-3512 724-0549 52
TF: 800-538-6576 ■ *Web:* mcintoshlabs.com

McIntosh Woods State Park
1200 E Lake St .... Ventura IA 50482 641-829-3847 565
Web: www.iowadnr.gov

McIntyre Assoc 5 Essex Ct .... Farmington CT 06032 860-284-1000 260
Web: www.mcassoc.com

McIntyre Elwell & Strammer General Contractors Inc
1645 Barber Rd .... Sarasota FL 34240 941-377-6800 186
Web: www.mesgc.com

McIver's Grant Public Library
410 W Court St .... Dyersburg TN 38024 731-285-5032 434-3
Web: www.dyersburgdyercolibrary.com

MCI-W (Maryland Correctional Institution for Women)
7943 Brockbridge Rd .... Jessup MD 20794 410-379-3800 213

Mckay Brothers LLC 2355 broadway .... Oakland CA 94612 312-948-9188 736
Web: www.mckay-brothers.com

McKay Nursery Company Inc
750 S Monroe St PO Box 185 .... Waterloo WI 53594 920-478-2121 478-3615 323
TF: 800-236-4242 ■ *Web:* www.mckaynursery.com

McKay Press Inc 7600 W Wackerly Rd .... Midland MI 48642 989-631-2360 627
Web: mckaypress.com

McKay-Cocker Construction Ltd
1665 Oxford St E .... London ON N5Y5R9 519-451-5270 186
Web: www.mckaycocker.com

McKay-Dee Hospital Ctr
4401 Harrison Blvd .... Ogden UT 84403 801-627-2800 374-3
Web: www.intermountainhealthcare.org

McKean County 500 W Main St .... Smethport PA 16749 814-887-5571 887-2242 338
TF: 800-482-1280 ■ *Web:* www.mckeancountypa.org

McKechnie Vehicle Components (MVC)
27087 Gratiot Ave Fl 2 .... Roseville MI 48066 586-491-2600 489
Web: www.mvcusa.com

McKee Botanical Garden 350 US 1 .... Vero Beach FL 32962 772-794-0601 794-0602 97
Web: www.mckeegarden.org

McKee Foods Corp PO Box 750 .... Collegedale TN 37315 423-238-7111 296-1
TF Cust Svc: 800-522-4499 ■ *Web:* www.mckeefoods.com

McKee Gallery 745 Fifth Ave 4th Fl .... New York NY 10151 212-688-5951 752-5638 42
Web: www.mckeegallery.com

McKee Group
940 W Sproul Rd Ste 301 .... Springfield PA 19064 610-604-9800 653
Web: www.mckeebuilders.com

McKee Medical Ctr 2000 N Boise Ave .... Loveland CO 80538 970-669-4640 635-4112 374-3
Web: www.bannerhealth.com

McKee Surfaces PO Box 230 .... Muscatine IA 52761 563-263-2421 264-5365 594
TF Cust Svc: 800-553-9662 ■ *Web:* www.mckeesurfaces.com

McKee Wallwork Cleveland LLC
1030 18th St NW .... Albuquerque NM 87104 505-821-2999 4
Web: mckeewallwork.com

McKee, Voorhees & Sease PLC
801 Grand Ste 3200 .... Des Moines IA 50309 515-288-3667 428
Web: www.ipmvs.com

Mckeever Enterprises Inc
4216 S Hocker Dr .... Independence MO 64055 816-478-3095 345

Mckeil Marine Ltd 208 Hillyard St .... Hamilton ON L8L6B6 905-528-4780 313
TF: 800-454-4780 ■ *Web:* www.mckeil.com

McKellar & Co 311 E Rose Ln .... Phoenix AZ 85012 602-277-1800 277-0429 792

McKelvie's 1680 Lower Water St .... Halifax NS B3J2Y3 902-421-6161 671
Web: www.mckelvies.com

McKendree College 701 College Rd .... Lebanon IL 62254 618-537-4481 537-6496* 166
**Fax:* Admissions ■ *TF:* 800-232-7228 ■ *Web:* www.mckendree.edu

Name / Address	City	State	Zip	Phone	Fax	Class
McKendrick's Steak House 4505 Ashford Dunwoody Rd *Web:* www.mckendricks.com	Atlanta	GA	30346	770-512-8888		671
Mckenna & Assoc PC 1515 S Washington St *Web:* mckennaandassociates.net	Grand Forks	ND	58206	701-772-4819		2
Mckenna Distribution & Warehousing 1260 Lkshore Rd E *TF:* 800-561-4997 ■ *Web:* www.mckennalogistics.ca	Mississauga	ON	L5E3B8	905-274-1234		205
McKenna Pro Imaging 2815 Falls Ave. *TF General:* 800-238-3456 ■ *Web:* www.mckennapro.com	Waterloo	IA	50701	319-235-6265	235-1121	588
McKenna Storer 33 N LaSalle St Ste 1400 *Web:* mckenna-law.com	Chicago	IL	60602	312-558-3900		428
McKenney's Inc 1056 Moreland Industrial Blvd SE *TF:* 877-440-4204 ■ *Web:* www.mckenneys.com	Atlanta	GA	30316	404-622-5000		189-10
Mckenneys Air Conditioning Inc 2323 R St *Web:* mckenneysair.com	Bakersfield	CA	93301	661-327-4037		610
McKenzie County PO Box 699 *TF:* 800-701-2804 ■ *Web:* county.mckenziecounty.net	Watford City	ND	58854	701-444-2804		338
McKenzie Electric Co-op Inc PO Box 649 *TF:* 800-584-9239 ■ *Web:* www.mckenzieelectric.com	Watford City	ND	58854	701-444-9288	444-3002	245
Mckenzie Lake Lawyers LLP 300 Dundas St *TF:* 800-261-4844 ■ *Web:* www.mckenzielake.com	London	ON	N6B1T6	519-672-5666		428
McKenzie Tank Lines Inc 1966 Commonwealth Ln. *TF:* 800-828-6495 ■ *Web:* www.mckenzietank.com	Tallahassee	FL	32303	850-576-1221		780
McKenzie Valve & Machining LLC 146 Airport Rd *Web:* www.mckenzievalve.com	McKenzie	TN	38201	731-352-5027	352-3029	789
McKenzie-Willamette Hospital 1460 G St *TF:* 800-227-2345 ■ *Web:* www.mckweb.com	Springfield	OR	97477	541-726-4400		374-3
McKeon Door Co 44 Sawgrass Dr *TF:* 800-266-9392 ■ *Web:* www.mckeondoor.com	Bellport	NY	11713	631-803-3000	803-3030	234
McKesson Corp 1 Post St *NYSE:* MCK ■ *TF:* 800-482-3784 ■ *Web:* www.mckesson.com	San Francisco	CA	94104	415-983-8300		360-3
McKesson Information Solutions 5995 Windward Pkwy *Web:* mckesson.com	Alpharetta	GA	30005	404-338-6000		178-10
McKesson Medical Group Extended Care 8121 Tenth Ave N **Fax Area Code:* 763 ■ *TF:* 800-328-8111 ■ *Web:* www.mbbnet.umn.edu	Golden Valley	MN	55427	800-328-8111	595-6677*	475
McKesson Medical-Surgical 8741 Landmark Rd *TF:* 800-446-3008 ■ *Web:* www.mckesson.com	Richmond	VA	23228	415-983-8300		475
McKesson Pharmaceutical 1 Post St *TF:* 800-571-2889 ■ *Web:* www.mckesson.com	San Francisco	CA	94104	415-983-8300		587
McKey Perforating Company Inc 3033 S 166th St *TF:* 800-345-7373 ■ *Web:* www.mckeyperforatedmetal.com	New Berlin	WI	53151	202-780-2700		198
McKibbon Hospitality 5315 Avion Park Dr Ste 120 *Web:* www.mckibbonhotels.com	Tampa	FL	33607	813-241-2399		379
McKim & Creed PA 243 N Front St. *Web:* www.mckimcreed.com	Wilmington	NC	28401	910-343-1048	251-8282	261
McKing Consulting Corp 2810 Old Lee Hwy Ste 250 *TF:* 800-496-2996 ■ *Web:* www.mcking.com	Fairfax	VA	22031	703-204-2385		196
McKinley Air Transport Inc 5430 Lauby Rd *TF General:* 800-225-6446 ■ *Web:* mckinleyair.com	North Canton	OH	44720	330-499-3316	499-0444	24
McKinley Capital Management LLC 3301 C St Ste 500 *Web:* www.mckinleycapital.com	Anchorage	AK	99503	907-563-4488		401
McKinley County 207 W Hill Ave *Web:* www.co.mckinley.nm.us	Gallup	NM	87301	505-863-6866	863-1419	338
McKinley David (Rep R - WV) 2239 Rayburn HOB *Web:* mckinley.house.gov	Washington	DC	20515	202-225-4172	225-7564	342-2
McKinley Equipment Corp 17611 Armstrong Ave *TF:* 800-770-6094 ■ *Web:* www.mckinleyequipment.com	Irvine	CA	92614	949-261-9222		385
McKinley Grand Hotel 320 Market Ave S *TF:* 844-378-9476 ■ *Web:* www.mckinleygrandhotel.com	Canton	OH	44702	330-454-5000		379
Mckinley Marketing Partners Inc 111 Franklin St *Web:* mckinleymarketingpartners.com	Alexandria	VA	22314	703-836-4445		195
McKinney 318 Blackwell St *Web:* www.mckinney.com	Durham	NC	27701	919-313-0002		4
Mckinney & Company Inc 100 S Railroad Ave *Web:* mckinney-usa.com	Ashland	VA	23005	804-798-1451		261
McKinney Avenue Contemporary (The MAC) 3120 McKinney Ave *Web:* www.the-mac.org	Dallas	TX	75204	214-953-1212		50-2
McKinney Chamber of Commerce 2150 S Central Expy # 150 *Web:* www.mckinneychamber.com	McKinney	TX	75070	972-542-0163	548-0876	139
McKinney Falls State Park 5808 McKinney Falls Pkwy. *Web:* tpwd.texas.gov	Austin	TX	78744	512-243-1643		565
Mckinney Petroleum Equipment Inc 3926 Halls Mill Rd *TF:* 800-476-7867 ■ *Web:* mckinneypetroleum.com	Mobile	AL	36693	251-661-8800		358
McKinsey & Company Inc 55 E 52nd St *Web:* www.mckinsey.com	New York	NY	10022	212-446-7000	446-8575	194
McKinstry Co 5005 Third Ave S. *TF:* 800-669-6223 ■ *Web:* www.mckinstry.com	Seattle	WA	98134	206-762-3311	762-2624	189-10
McKissock LP 218 Liberty St. *TF:* 800-328-2008 ■ *Web:* www.mckissock.com	Warren	PA	16365	814-723-6979		177
McKnight Foundation 710 Second St S Ste 400 *Web:* www.mcknight.org	Minneapolis	MN	55401	612-333-4220	332-3833	305

Name / Address	City	State	Zip	Phone	Fax	Class
McKnight's Long-Term Care News 900 Skokie Blvd *TF:* 800-558-1703 ■ *Web:* www.mcknights.com	Northfield	IL	60062	847-559-2884		637-9
McKonly & Asbury LLP 415 Fallowfield Rd *Web:* www.macpas.com	Camp Hill	PA	17011	717-761-7910		2
MCL (Marion County Library System) 101 E Ct St *Web:* www.marioncountylibrary.org	Marion	SC	29571	843-423-8300	423-8302	434-3
MCL (Monmouth County Library) 125 Symmes Rd *Web:* www.monmouthcountylib.org	Manalapan	NJ	07726	732-431-7220		434-3
MCL (Mercer County Library System) 2751 Brunswick Pk *Web:* www.mcl.org	Lawrenceville	NJ	08648	609-882-9246		434-3
MCL (Morris County Library) 30 E Hanover Ave *Web:* www.gti.net/mocolib1	Whippany	NJ	07981	973-285-6930		434-3
MCL Inc 501 S Woodcreek Rd. *TF Support:* 800-743-4625 ■ *Web:* www.mcl.com	Bolingbrook	IL	60440	630-759-9500	759-5018	647
McLain Plumbing & Electrical Service Inc 107 Magnolia St *Web:* www.mclaininc.com	Philadelphia	MS	39350	601-656-6333		610
McLanahan Corp 200 Wall St *Web:* www.mclanahan.com	Hollidaysburg	PA	16648	814-695-9807		492
McLane Company Inc 4747 McLane Pkwy *TF:* 800-299-1401 ■ *Web:* www.mclaneco.com	Temple	TX	76504	254-771-7500	771-7244	297-8
McLane Foodservice Inc 2085 Midway Rd. **Fax Area Code:* 254 ■ *TF:* 800-299-1401 ■ *Web:* www.mclaneco.com	Carrollton	TX	75006	972-364-2000	771-7244*	297-8
McLane Manufacturing Inc 7110 E Rosecrans Ave *Web:* mclanemower.com	Paramount	CA	90723	562-633-8158		429
McLaren Performance Technologies Inc 32233 W Eight Mile Rd. *Web:* www.linamar.com	Livonia	MI	48152	248-477-6240		261
McLaren Regional Medical Ctr 401 S Ballenger Hwy *Web:* www.mclaren.org	Flint	MI	48532	810-342-2000	342-2428	374-3
McLarty Associates 900 17th St NW Ste 800 *Web:* www.maglobal.com	Washington	DC	20006	202-419-1420		463
McLaughlin & Moran Inc 40 Slater Rd *Web:* www.mclaughlinmoran.com/index.php	Cranston	RI	02920	401-463-5454	463-3770	81-1
McLaughlin Body Co 2430 River Dr *Web:* www.mclbody.com	Moline	IL	61265	309-762-7755	762-7807	516
Mclaughlin Group Inc 2006 Perimeter Rd *Web:* www.mightymole.com	Greenville	SC	29605	864-277-5870		190
McLaughlin Research Corp 132 Johnnycake Hill Rd *TF:* 800-556-7154 ■ *Web:* www.mrcds.com	Middletown	RI	02842	401-849-4010		261
McLaughlin Youth Ctr 2600 Providence Dr *TF:* 800-478-2221 ■ *Web:* dhss.alaska.gov	Anchorage	AK	99508	907-261-4399	261-4308	412
Mclean 75 great pond rd. *Web:* www.mcleancare.org	Simsbury	CT	06070	860-658-3700		793
McLean & Partners Wealth Management Ltd 801 Tenth Ave S W *Web:* www.mcleanpartners.com	Calgary	AB	T2R0B4	403-234-0005		528
McLean Contracting Co 6700 McLean Way *TF:* 800-677-1997 ■ *Web:* mcleancont.com	Glen Burnie	MD	21060	410-553-6700	553-6718	188-10
McLean County 115 E Washington St Rm 102 *Web:* www.mcleancountyil.gov	Bloomington	IL	61701	309-888-5190	888-5932	338
McLean County 210 Main St PO Box 127 *Web:* www.mcleancounty.ky.gov	Calhoun	KY	42327	270-273-3213	273-9965	338
McLean County 712 Fifth Ave *Web:* www.mcleancountynd.gov	Washburn	ND	58577	701-462-8541	462-8212	338
McLean County Chamber of Commerce 2203 E Empire St *Web:* www.mcleancochamber.org	Bloomington	IL	61704	309-829-6344	827-3940	139
McLean Electric Co-op Inc 4031 Hwy 37 Bypass NW *TF:* 800-263-4922 ■ *Web:* www.mcleanelectric.com	Garrison	ND	58540	701-463-2291		245
McLean Hospital 115 Mill St *TF:* 800-333-0338 ■ *Web:* mcleanhospital.org	Belmont	MA	02478	617-855-2000		374-5
Mclean Implement Inc 793 Illinois Rte 130 *TF:* 888-720-4440 ■ *Web:* www.mcleanimp.com	Albion	IL	62806	618-445-3676	445-2846	57
McLean Inc 3409 E Miraloma Ave *TF Cust Svc:* 800-451-2424 ■ *Web:* mcleaninc.com	Anaheim	CA	92806	714-996-5451	996-5453	455
Mclean Packaging Corp 1000 Thomas Busch Memorial Hwy *Web:* www.mcleanpackaging.com	Pennsauken	NJ	08110	856-359-2600		100
Mclean School of Maryland Inc, The 8224 Lochinver Ln *Web:* www.mcleanschool.org	Potomac	MD	20854	301-299-8277		685
McLellan Botanicals 2352 San Juan Rd **Fax Area Code:* 415 ■ *TF:* 800-467-2443 ■ *Web:* www.taisucoamerica.com	Aromas	CA	95004	800-467-2443	543-6836*	369
Mclellan Creative 695 Mistletoe Rd Ste M2 *Web:* www.mclellancreative.com	Ashland	OR	97520	541-488-2270		195
McLellan Equipment Inc 251 Shaw Rd **Fax Area Code:* 650 ■ *TF:* 800-848-8449 ■ *Web:* mclellanindustries.com	South San Francisco	CA	94080	800-848-8449	589-7398*	190
Mclendon Hardware Inc 440 Rainier Ave S *Web:* www.mclendons.com	Renton	WA	98057	425-235-3555		351
McLennan Community College 1400 College Dr **Fax:* Admissions ■ *TF:* 866-339-5555 ■ *Web:* www.mclennan.edu	Waco	TX	76708	254-299-8000	299-8694*	162
McLennan County 501 Washington Ave *Web:* www.co.mclennan.tx.us	Waco	TX	76701	254-757-5078	757-5146	338
McLennan County Electric Co-op 1111 Johnson Dr PO Box 357 *TF:* 800-840-2957 ■ *Web:* www.hotec.coop	McGregor	TX	76657	254-840-2871	840-4250	245

	Phone	Fax	Class
McLennan Ross LLP 600 W Chambers 12220 Stony Plain Rd ... Edmonton AB T5N3Y4 *TF:* 800-567-9200 ■ *Web:* www.mross.com	780-482-9200		428
McLeod Co-op Power Assn 1231 Ford Ave N ... Glencoe MN 55336 *TF:* 800-494-6272 ■ *Web:* www.mcleodcoop.com	320-864-3148	864-4850	245
McLeod County 830 11th St ... Glencoe MN 55336 *TF:* 800-657-3717 ■ *Web:* www.co.mcleod.mn.us	320-864-5551		338
McLeod Express LLC 5002 Cundiff Ct ... Decatur IL 62526 *TF General:* 800-709-3936 ■ *Web:* www.mcleodexpress.com/default.asp	800-709-3936		685
McLeod Hospice 1203 E Cheves St ... Florence SC 29506 *TF:* 800-768-4556 ■ *Web:* www.mcleodhealth.org	843-777-2564		371
Mcleod Insurance Inc 14425 N Seventh St Ste 100 ... Phoenix AZ 85022 *Web:* mcleodinsinc.com	602-843-0005		390
McLeod Medical Ctr Dillon 301 E Jackson St ... Dillon SC 29536 *TF:* 800-994-6610 ■ *Web:* www.mcleodhealth.org	843-774-4111		374-3
McLeod Optical Company Inc 50 Jefferson Park Rd ... Warwick RI 02888 *TF:* 800-766-2769 ■ *Web:* www.mcleodoptical.com	401-467-3000		543
McLeod Regional Medical Ctr 555 E Cheves St ... Florence SC 29506 *TF:* 800-994-6610 ■ *Web:* www.mcleodhealth.org	843-777-2000		374-3
McLeod Software Corporation Inc 2550 Acton Rd PO Box 43200 ... Birmingham AL 35243 *Web:* www.mcleodsoftware.com	205-823-5100		177
MCLNO (University Hospital) 2021 Perdido St ... New Orleans LA 70112 *TF:* 800-960-7705 ■ *Web:* www.lsuhospitals.org	504-903-3000		374-3
McLoone 75 Sumner St ... La Crosse WI 54603 *TF:* 800-624-6641 ■ *Web:* www.mcloone.com	608-784-1260	782-3711	701
McLure Hotel, The 1200 Market St ... Wheeling WV 26003	304-232-0300		379
MCM Construction Inc 6413 32nd St PO Box 620 ... North Highlands CA 95660 *TF:* 800-599-6996 ■ *Web:* www.mcmconstructioninc.com	916-334-1221	334-8355	188-4
MCM Elegante Suites 4250 Ridgemont Dr ... Abilene TX 79606 *TF:* 888-897-9644 ■ *Web:* www.mcmelegantesuites.com	325-698-1234	698-2771	379
MCM Management Corp 35980 Woodward Ave Ste 210 ... Bloomfield Hills MI 48304 *Web:* www.mcmmanagement.com	248-932-9600		667
MCM Services Group 1300 Corporate Ctr Curve ... Eagan MN 55121 *TF:* 888-507-6262 ■ *Web:* www.mcmservicesgroup.com	888-507-6262		196
Mcmahon Assoc Inc 425 Commerce Dr Ste 200 ... Fort Washington PA 19034 *Web:* mcmahonassociates.com	215-283-9444		261
McMahon Group 1445 McMahon Dr ... Neenah WI 54956 *Web:* www.mcmgrp.com	920-751-4200	751-4284	261
Mcmahon Group Inc 670 Mason Ridge Ctr Dr Ste 220 ... Saint Louis MO 63141 *TF:* 800-365-2498 ■ *Web:* www.mcmahongroup.com	314-744-5040		196
Mcmahon Publishing Group 545 W 45th St ... New York NY 10036 *TF:* 800-872-5652 ■ *Web:* www.mcmahonmed.com	212-957-5300		418
McManis & Monsalve Associates 100 State St Ste 103 ... Erie PA 16507 **Fax Area Code:* 866 ■ *Web:* mcmanis-monsalve.com	814-454-4000	438-2210*	463
McManis Faulkner Fairmont Plaza 50 W San Fernando St 10th Fl ... San Jose CA 95113 *TF:* 800-767-3263 ■ *Web:* www.mcmanislaw.com	408-279-8700		428
McManus Wealth Building & Management 1930 17th St Ste 210 ... Boulder CO 80302 *Web:* www.mcmanusandyou.com	303-544-0355		194
McMaster Henry (R) 1205 Pendleton St ... Columbia SC 29201 *Web:* governor.sc.gov	803-734-2100	734-5167	343
McMaster University 1280 Main St W ... Hamilton ON L8S4L8 *TF:* 800-238-1623 ■ *Web:* www.mcmaster.ca	905-525-9140	527-1105	785
McMaster University Health Sciences Library 1200 Main St W ... Hamilton ON L8N3Z5 *Web:* hsl.mcmaster.ca	905-525-9140	528-3733	434-1
MCMC LLC 300 Crown Colony Dr Ste 203 ... Quincy MA 02169 *TF:* 800-326-5496 ■ *Web:* www.mcmcllc.com	617-375-7700		317
McMenamins 430 N Killingsworth ... Portland OR 97217 *TF:* 800-669-8610 ■ *Web:* www.mcmenamins.com	503-223-0109	294-0837	102
McMenamins on the Columbia 1801 S Access Rd ... Vancouver WA 98661 *TF:* 800-669-8610 ■ *Web:* mcmenamins.com	360-699-1521		671
Mcmillan & Terry pa 6101 Carnegie Blvd Ste 310 ... Charlotte NC 28209 *TF:* 800-837-3031 ■ *Web:* mplawcarolinas.com	704-552-9997		428
McMillan Electric Co 400 Best Rd ... Woodville WI 54028 *Web:* www.mcmillanelectric.com	715-698-2488		518
McMillan Memorial Library 490 E Grand Ave ... Wisconsin Rapids WI 54494 *Web:* www.mcmillanlibrary.org	715-423-1040	423-2665	434-3
Mcmillen Engineering Inc 115 Wayland Smith Dr ... Uniontown PA 15401 *Web:* mcmilleng.com	724-439-8110		261
McMinn County 5 S Hill St Ste A ... Athens TN 37303 *Web:* mcminncountytn.gov	423-745-4440	744-1657	338
McMinnville Public Library 225 NW Adams St ... McMinnville OR 97128 *Web:* www.maclibrary.org	503-435-5555		434-3
McMinnville-Warren County Chamber of Commerce 110 S Ct Sq ... McMinnville TN 37110 *TF:* 800-933-3909 ■ *Web:* www.warrentn.com	931-473-6611	473-4741	139
McMorgan & Co LLC 1 Front St Ste 500 ... San Francisco CA 94111 *Web:* www.nylinvestments.com	415-788-9300		401
McMorris Rodgers Cathy (Rep R - WA) 1314 Longworth HOB ... Washington DC 20515 *Web:* mcmorris.house.gov	202-225-2006	225-3392	342-2
McMullen Oil Co Inc 11965 49th St N ... Clearwater FL 33762 *Web:* www.mcmullenoil.com	727-573-0016		316
McMurry Ready Mix Co 5684 Old W Yellowstone Hwy ... Casper WY 82604 *Web:* www.mcmurryreadymix.com	307-473-9581	235-0144	188-4
McMurry University 1400 Sayles Blvd ... Abilene TX 79697 *TF:* 800-460-2392 ■ *Web:* www.mcm.edu	325-793-4700		166
McMurry University Jay-Rollins Library 1400 Sayles Blvd ... Abilene TX 79697 *Web:* www.mcm.edu/newsite/web/library	325-793-4692		434-6
MCN Healthcare Inc 1777 S Harrison St Ste 405 ... Denver CO 80210 *Web:* www.mcnhealthcare.com	303-762-0778		507
McNair McLemore Middlebrooks & Company LLP 389 Mulberry St ... Macon GA 31202 *Web:* www.mmmcpa.com	478-746-6277		2
McNairy County County Courthouse 170 W Ct Ave Rm 104 ... Selmer TN 38375 *Web:* www.mcnairycountytn.com	731-645-3511	646-1414	338
McNally Group 5445 DTC Pkwy P4 ... Greenwood Village CO 80111 *Web:* www.mcnally-group.com	303-846-3035		21
McNally Industries LLC 340 W Benson Ave ... Grantsburg WI 54840 *TF:* 800-366-1410 ■ *Web:* www.northern-pump.com	715-463-8300		641
McNally International Inc 1855 Barton St E ... Hamilton ON L8H2Y7 *Web:* www.mcnallycorp.com	905-549-6561		188
McNally Robinson Booksellers Inc 1120 Grant Ave ... Winnipeg MB R3M2A6 *TF:* 800-561-1833 ■ *Web:* www.mcnallyrobinson.com	204-475-0483		95
McNally Smith College of Music Foundation 19 Exchange St E ... Saint Paul MN 55101 *TF:* 800-594-9500 ■ *Web:* www.mcnallysmith.edu	651-361-3320		166
McNally Temple Associates Inc 1817 Capitol Ave ... Sacramento CA 95811 *Web:* www.mcnallytemple.com	916-447-8186		636
Mcnamara Financial Services Inc Marshfield Professional Ctr 1020 Plain St Ste 200 ... Marshfield MA 02050 *Web:* www.mcnamarafinancial.com	781-834-2010		251
McNaughton & Gunn Inc 960 Woodland Dr ... Saline MI 48176 **Fax Area Code:* 800 ■ *Web:* www.mcnaughton-gunn.com	734-429-5411	677-2665*	626
McNaughton-McKay Electric Company Inc 1357 E Lincoln Ave ... Madison Heights MI 48071 *Web:* www.mc-mc.com	248-399-7500	399-6828	246
MCNB Bank & Trust Co PO Box 549 ... Welch WV 24801 *TF:* 800-532-9553 ■ *Web:* www.mcnbbanks.com	304-436-4112		70
MCNC Inc 3021 E Cornwallis Rd PO Box 12889 ... Research Triangle Park NC 27709 *Web:* www.mcnc.org	919-248-1900		387
McNeal Enterprises Inc 2031 Ringwood Ave ... San Jose CA 95131 *TF:* 800-562-6325 ■ *Web:* www.mcnealplasticmachining.com	408-922-7290	922-7299	602
McNear Brick & Block 1 McNear BrickyaRd Rd PO Box 151380 ... San Rafael CA 94901 *TF:* 888-442-6811 ■ *Web:* www.mcnear.com	415-453-7702	453-3141	150
McNeece Brothers Oil Company Inc 691 E Heil Ave ... El Centro CA 92243 *TF:* 877-782-6543 ■ *Web:* www.mcneecebros.com	760-352-4721		579
McNeel International Corp 5401 W Kennedy Blvd ... Tampa FL 33609	813-286-8680		600
McNeely Pigott & Fox 611 Commerce St Ste 2800 ... Nashville TN 37203 *TF:* 800-818-6953 ■ *Web:* www.mpf.com	615-259-4000	259-4040	636
McNees Wallace & Nurick LLC 125 N Washington Ave ... Scranton PA 18503 *Web:* www.mcneeslaw.com	570-209-7220		428
McNeese State University 4205 Ryan St ... Lake Charles LA 70609 **Fax:* Admissions ■ *TF:* 800-622-3352 ■ *Web:* www.mcneese.edu	337-475-5000	475-5151*	166
McNeil & NRM Inc 96 E Crosier St ... Akron OH 44311 *TF:* 800-669-2525 ■ *Web:* www.mcneilnrm.com	330-253-2525	253-7022	386
Mcneills Furniture & Appliance of Denton Inc 104 W Oak ... Denton TX 76201 *Web:* mcneillsappliance.com	940-382-6932		321
McNeilus Cos Inc 524 County Rd 34 E PO Box 70 ... Dodge Center MN 55927 *TF:* 800-265-1098 ■ *Web:* www.mcneiluscompanies.com	507-374-6321	374-6394	516
Mcnerney & Associates Inc 440 Northland Blvd ... Cincinnati OH 45240 *Web:* www.pjmcnerney.com	513-825-5547		627
McNerney Jerry (Rep D - CA) 2265 Rayburn HOB ... Washington DC 20515 *Web:* mcnerney.house.gov	202-225-1947	225-4060	342-2
McNichols Co 9401 Corporate Lake Dr ... Tampa FL 33634 **Fax Area Code:* 813 ■ *TF:* 877-884-4653 ■ *Web:* www.mcnichols.com	877-884-4653	243-1888*	492
McNinch House 511 N Church St ... Charlotte NC 28202 *Web:* www.mcninchhouserestaurant.com	704-332-6159		671
McNulty's Tea & Coffee Company Inc 109 Christopher St ... New York NY 10014 *TF:* 800-356-5200 ■ *Web:* www.mcnultys.com	212-242-5351		159
McNutt Service Group Inc 39 Loop Rd ... Arden NC 28704 *Web:* www.mcnuttservicegroup.com	828-212-4292		189-10
M-CON Products Inc 2150 Richardson Side Rd ... Carp ON K0A1L0 *TF:* 800-267-5515 ■ *Web:* www.mconproducts.com	613-831-1736	831-2048	183
MCP Industries Inc Mission Clay Products Div 708 S Temescal St Ste 101 ... Corona CA 92879 *Web:* www.mcpind.com	951-736-1881	549-8280	150
McPherson College PO Box 1402 ... McPherson KS 67460 **Fax:* Admissions ■ *TF:* 800-365-7402 ■ *Web:* www.mcpherson.edu	620-242-0400	241-8443*	166
McPherson Companies Inc, The 5051 Cardinal St ... Trussville AL 35173 *TF:* 800-688-6199 ■ *Web:* www.mcphersonoil.com	205-661-4400		581
McPherson Concrete Storage Systems Inc 116 N Augustus St ... Mcpherson KS 67460 *Web:* www.mcphersonconcrete.com	620-241-4362		186
McPherson County 706 Main St PO Box 248 ... Leola SD 57456 *Web:* ujs.sd.gov/County_Information/mcpherson.aspx	605-439-3361	439-3297	338

Phone | Fax | Class

McPherson County
117 N Maple Courthouse PO Box 425 .... McPherson KS 67460 620-241-3656 241-1168 338
TF: 800-368-8683 ■ *Web:* www.mcphersoncountyks.us

McPhie Cabinetry 435 E Main St............. Bozeman MT 59715 406-586-1708 321
Web: www.mcphiecabinetry.com

MCPL (Marathon County Public Library)
300 N First St.............................. Wausau WI 54403 715-261-7200 261-7204 434-3
Web: www.mcpl.us

McQ Inc 1551 Forbes St..................Fredericksburg VA 22405 540-373-2374 256
TF: 866-373-2374 ■ *Web:* www.mcqinc.com

McQuade & Bannigan Inc 1300 Stark St........... Utica NY 13502 315-724-7119 358
Web: www.mqb.com

MCR American Pharmaceuticals Inc
16255 Aviation Loop.......................Brooksville FL 34604 352-754-8587 231
Web: www.mcramerican.com

MCR LLC 2010 Corporate Ridge Ste 350........... McLean VA 22102 703-506-4600 506-8601 261
Web: www.mcri.com

MCR Safety 5321 E Shelby Dr................. Memphis TN 38118 901-795-5810 999-3908* 155-8
**Fax Area Code:* 800 ■ **Fax:* Sales ■ *TF:* 800-955-6887 ■ *Web:* www.mcrsafety.com

MCR Technologies 6 Greenwood St............Wakefield MA 01880 781-245-6644 535
TF: 800-328-9901 ■ *Web:* www.mcrtechnologies.com

McRae Industries Inc PO Box 1239 ....Mount Gilead NC 27306 910-439-6147 439-4190 185
Web: www.mcraeindustries.com

MCRD Parris Island
283 Blvd de France...................... Parris Island SC 29905 843-228-2111 228-2122 497-3
Web: www.mcrdpi.marines.mil

McREL (Mid-Continent Research for Education & Learning)
4601 DTC Blvd Ste 500 ....Denver CO 80237 303-337-0990 337-3005 668
Web: www.mcrel.org

MCRHS (Manatee County Rural Health Services Inc)
12271 US Hwy 301...........................Parrish FL 34219 941-776-4000 374-3
Web: www.mcrhs.org

McRoberts Protective Agency Inc
87 Nassau St ....New York NY 10038 212-425-6500 693
TF: 800-866-7233 ■ *Web:* www.mcroberts1876.com

Mcruer & & Associates Cpas
1251 NW Briarcliff Pkwy Ste 100 .... Kansas City MO 64116 816-741-7882 2
Web: kccpa.com

MCS (Metropolitan Construction Services LLC)
2803 Butterfield Rd Ste 100 .... Oak Brook IL 60523 630-691-7200 691-7234 685
Web: www.metroconstructionllc.com

Mcs Advertising 4110 Progress Blvd Ste 1c..........Peru IL 61354 815-224-3011 261
Web: www.mcsadv.com

MCS Financial Advisors
360 E Tenth Ave Ste 200......................Eugene OR 97401 541-345-7023 401
Web: www.mcsfa.com

MCS Healthcare Public Relations
1420 US Hwy 206 Ste 100................ Bedminster NJ 07921 908-234-9900 470-4490 636
TF: 800-421-0837 ■ *Web:* www.mcspr.com

MCS Referral & Resources Inc
6101 Gentry Ln...........................Baltimore MD 21210 410-889-6666 889-4944 48-17
TF: 800-526-7234 ■ *Web:* www.mcsrr.org

McSally Martha (Rep R - AZ)
1029 Longworth House Office Bldg ....Washington DC 20515 202-225-2542 225-0378 342-2
Web: mcsally.house.gov

Mcsd Studio 514 W 43rd St................Indianapolis IN 46208 317-926-0773 657
Web: mcsdstudio.com

McShan Lumber Company Inc PO Box 27 ....McShan AL 35471 205-375-6277 375-2773 752
TF: 800-882-3712 ■ *Web:* www.mcshanlumber.com

McStain Neighborhoods
7100 N Broadway Ste 5-H ....Denver CO 80221 303-494-5900 653
TF: 800-570-2289 ■ *Web:* www.mcstain.com

Mcswain & Co PS
612 Woodland Sq Loop SE Ste 300 ....Lacey WA 98503 360-357-9304 2
TF: 800-282-1301 ■ *Web:* mcswaincpa.net

McSweeney & Assoc A Professional Corp
350 Crown Point Cir Ste 200 ....Grass Valley CA 95945 530-272-5555 2
Web: mcsweeneyandassociates.com

Mcsweeney & Ricci Insurance Agency Inc
420 Washington St.......................... Braintree MA 02184 781-848-8600 390
Web: mcsweeneyricci.com

MCT Industries Inc
7451 Pan American Fwy.................. Albuquerque NM 87109 505-345-8651 779
TF: 800-876-8651 ■ *Web:* www.mct-ind.com

MCT Transportation LLC
1600 E Benson Rd ....Sioux Falls SD 57104 605-339-8400 339-8407 780
TF Cust Svc: 800-843-9904 ■ *Web:* mcttrans.com

MCT Worldwide LLC
121 S Figth St Ste 960....................Minneapolis MN 55402 612-436-3240 436-3242 695
Web: www.mct.com

McTeague Higbee Case Cohen Whitney & Toker PA
4 Union Pk.............................. Topsham ME 04086 207-725-5581 428
TF: 800-482-0958 ■ *Web:* www.me-law.com

Mctish Kunkel & Assoc
3500 Winchester Rd.......................Allentown PA 18104 610-841-2700 261
Web: mctish.com

McTurbine Inc
401 Junior Beck Dr.....................Corpus Christi TX 78405 361-851-1290 790
TF: 800-352-0050 ■ *Web:* www.mcturbine.com/contact.shtml

MCUA (Middlesex County Utilities Authority Inc)
2571 Main St PO Box 159 ....Sayreville NJ 08872 732-721-3800 721-0206 787
Web: www.mcua.com

Mcube Investment Technologies LLC
5240 Tennyson Pkwy Ste 102........................Plano TX 75024 972-608-9919 796
TF: 800-519-3100 ■ *Web:* www.mcubeit.com

MCVB (Merced Conference & Visitors Bureau)
710 W 16th St.......................... Merced CA 95340 209-384-2791 206
TF: 800-446-5353 ■ *Web:* visitmerced.travel

MCVB (Middletown Convention-Visitors)
4935 Riverview Ave .... Middletown OH 45042 513-422-3030 206
Web: gettothebc.com

McVean Trading & Investments LLC
850 Ridge Lake Blvd Ste One............... Memphis TN 38120 901-761-8400 791
TF: 800-374-1937 ■ *Web:* www.mcvean.com

Mcveigh & Mangum Engineering Inc
9133 Rg Skinner Pkwy ....Jacksonville FL 32256 904-483-5200 261
Web: mcveighmangum.com

McVeigh Associates Ltd
275 Dixon Ave ....Amityville NY 11701 631-789-8833 196
TF: 800-726-5655 ■ *Web:* www.mcveigh.com

McWane Inc 2900 Hwy 280 Ste 300 ....Birmingham AL 35223 205-414-3100 414-3170 595
TF: 800-634-4746 ■ *Web:* www.mcwane.com

McWane Science Ctr 200 19th St N ....Birmingham AL 35203 205-714-8300 714-8400 520
Web: www.mcwane.org

Mcwhirter Realty Partners LLC Formerly Mcwhirter Realty Corp
300 Galleria Pkwy Ste 300 ....Atlanta GA 30339 770-955-2000 652
Web: mcwrealty.com

McWilliams Forge Company Inc
387 Franklin Ave..........................Rockaway NJ 07866 973-627-0200 625-9316 483
Web: www.mcwilliamsforge.com

MD Anderson Cancer Ctr
1515 Holcombe Blvd ....Houston TX 77030 713-792-2121 374-7
TF: 800-889-2094 ■ *Web:* www.mdanderson.org

MD Atkinson Company Inc
1401 19th St Ste 400 ....Bakersfield CA 93301 661-334-4800 652
Web: www.mdatkinson.com

M-D Bldg Products Inc
4041 N Santa Fe Ave....................Oklahoma City OK 73118 405-528-4411 234
TF Cust Svc: 800-654-8454 ■ *Web:* mdbuildingproducts.com

MD Buyline 2711 N Haskell Ave Ste 1450 .... Dallas TX 75204 800-375-5463 532-3
TF: 800-375-5463 ■ *Web:* www.mdbuyline.com

MD Helicopters Inc 4555 E Mcdowell Rd........... Mesa AZ 85215 480-346-6344 25
Web: www.mdhelicopters.com

MD Management Inc
5201 Johnson Dr Ste 100.....................Mission KS 66205 913-831-2996 652
Web: www.mdmgt.com

MD Physician Services Inc
1870 Alta Vista Dr...........................Ottawa ON K1G6R7 613-731-4552 528
TF: 800-267-4022 ■ *Web:* mdm.ca

M&D Printing 616 University Ave ....Henry IL 61537 309-364-3957 627
TF: 888-242-7552 ■ *Web:* www.mdprint.com

MD Sass Investor Services Inc
1185 Ave of the Americas 18th Fl..............New York NY 10036 212-730-2000 764-0381 401
Web: www.mdsass.com

MDA (Muscular Dystrophy Assn)
3300 E Sunrise Dr ....Tucson AZ 85718 520-529-2000 48-17
TF: 800-572-1717 ■ *Web:* www.mda.org

MDA Engineering Inc 1415 Holland Rd..........Maumee OH 43537 419-893-3141 261

MDA Geospatial Services International
13800 Commerce Pkwy .... Richmond BC V6V2J3 604-244-0400 393
Web: mdacorporation.com/geospatial/international

MDA Information Systems LLC
820 W Diamond Ave Ste 300 .... Gaithersburg MD 20878 240-833-8200 833-8201 261
TF: 800-642-1687 ■ *Web:* www.mdaus.com

MDA Leadership Consulting Inc
150 S Fifth St ....Minneapolis MN 55402 612-332-8182 463
Web: www.mdaleadership.com

MDAH (Mississippi Dept of Archives & History)
200 N St ....Jackson MS 39201 601-576-6876 576-6964 520
Web: mdah.state.ms.us

MDC (McCown De Leeuw & Co)
950 Tower Ln Ste 800......................Foster City CA 94404 650-854-6000 854-0853 405
Web: www.mdcpartners.com

MDC Holdings Inc
4350 S Monaco St Ste 500 ....Denver CO 80237 303-773-1100 771-3461 360-3
NYSE: MDC ■ *TF:* 888-500-7060 ■ *Web:* www.richmondamerican.com

MDC Systems Inc
37 N Valley Rd 3 Sta Sq Ste 100.................. Paoli PA 19301 610-640-9600 186
TF: 888-632-9977 ■ *Web:* www.mdcsystems.com

M-DCPS (Miami-Dade County Public Schools)
1450 NE Second Ave .... Miami FL 33132 305-995-1000 685
TF: 800-955-5504 ■ *Web:* www.dadeschools.net

MD&E Inc
5805 State Bridge Rd Ste G-371............Johns Creek GA 30097 678-291-9690 317
Web: www.mdeclarity.com

MDI (Molecular Devices Inc)
1311 Orleans Dr .... Sunnyvale CA 94089 408-747-1700 747-3601 419
TF: 800-635-5577 ■ *Web:* www.moleculardevices.com

MDI Achieve
10900 Hampshire Ave S Ste 100 .... Bloomington MN 55438 952-995-9800 995-9735 178-10
TF: 800-869-1322 ■ *Web:* www.matrixcare.com

Mdi Imaging & Mail Llc
21955 Cascades Pkwy .... Sterling VA 20166 703-433-1200 7
TF: 800-328-2725 ■ *Web:* mdimail.biz

MDI Security Systems Inc
12500 Network Dr Ste 303 ....San Antonio TX 78249 210-477-5400 477-5401 692
TF: 866-435-7634 ■ *Web:* www.mdisecure.com

MDI Worldwide
38271 W 12-Mile Rd .... Farmington Hills MI 48331 248-553-1900 488-5700* 233
**Fax:* Sales ■ *TF Sales:* 800-228-8925 ■ *Web:* www.mdiworldwide.com

Mdic Investment Advisory Service LLC
116 Kraft Ave Ste8 .... Bronxville NY 10708 914-793-4095 251
Web: www.mdicinc.com

MDL Doors Inc 42918-B Cranbrook Rd...........Brussels ON N0G1H0 519-887-6974 601
Web: www.mdldoors.com

Mdl Enterprise Inc 9888 SW Fwy..............Houston TX 77074 713-771-6350 180
TF: 800-879-0840 ■ *Web:* www.mdlent.com

MDNA (Machinery Dealers National Assn)
315 S Patrick St .... Alexandria VA 22314 703-836-9300 836-9303 49-18
TF: 800-872-7807 ■ *Web:* www.mdna.org

MDP (Madison Dearborn Partners LLC)
70 W Madison Ste 4600.......................Chicago IL 60602 312-895-1000 895-1001 792
Web: www.mdcp.com

Mdr Associates Inc
6486 Little Falls Dr.......................San Jose CA 95120 408-927-8302 809
Web: mdrandassociates.com

Mdr Fitness Corp 14101 NW Fourth St........... Sunrise FL 33325 954-845-9500 354
TF: 800-637-8227 ■ *Web:* www.mdr.com

MDRT (Million Dollar Round Table)
325 W Touhy Ave ....Park Ridge IL 60068 847-692-6378 518-8921 49-9
Web: www.mdrt.org

MDS (Mennonite Disaster Service)
583 Airport Rd ....Lititz PA 17543 717-735-3536 48-5
TF: 800-241-8111 ■ *Web:* www.mds.mennonite.net

	Phone	Fax	Class
MDS Aero Support Corp 1220 Old Innes Rd Ste 200.................... Ottawa ON K1B3V3 *TF:* 800-465-7447 ■ *Web:* mdsaero.com	613-744-7257		256
MDS Builders of Texas Inc 3910 S IH 35 Frontage Rd Ste 110.............. Austin TX 78704 *Web:* www.mdsbuilders.com	512-851-1133		186
MDSL 1410 Broadway Ste 2101................ New York NY 10018 *Web:* www.mdsl.com	212-201-6199		387
MDT Advisors Inc 125 High St Oliver St Tower Ste 2100............ Boston MA 02110 *TF:* 800-685-4277 ■ *Web:* www.federatedinvestors.com	617-235-7100	235-7199	792
MDT Labor LLC 2325 Paxton Church Rd Ste B .... Harrisburg PA 17110 *TF:* 888-454-9202 ■ *Web:* www.mdttechnical.com	888-454-9202		260
MDTA (Miami-Dade Transit) 701 NW First Ct....... Miami FL 33136 **Fax Area Code:* 786 ■ *TF:* 800-955-5504 ■ *Web:* miamidade.gov	305-468-5402	469-5580*	468
MDU (Montana-Dakota Utilities Co) 400 N Fourth St .... Bismarck ND 58501 *TF:* 800-638-3278 ■ *Web:* www.montana-dakota.com	701-222-7900		787
MDU Communications International Inc 60 D Commerce Way.............................. Totowa NJ 07512 *OTC: MDTV* ■ *TF:* 866-286-9638 ■ *Web:* mymdu.com	973-237-9499	237-9243	681
MDU Resources Group Inc 1200 W Century Ave PO Box 5650............ Bismarck ND 58506 *NYSE: MDU* ■ *TF:* 866-760-4852 ■ *Web:* www.mdu.com	701-530-1000		185
MDX Medical Inc 210 Clay Ave Ste 140......... Lyndhurst NJ 07071 *Web:* www.vitals.com	201-842-0760		363
Me Cos Inc 635 Brooksedge Blvd .... Westerville OH 43081	614-818-4900		652
M-E Engineers Inc 10055 W 43rd Ave .... Wheat Ridge CO 80033 *Web:* www.me-engineers.com	303-421-6655		261
ME Heuck Co 1600 Beech St.................. Terre Haute IN 47804 *TF Cust Svc:* 866-634-3825 ■ *Web:* www.heuck.com	812-238-5000		486
ME Tile 447 Atlas Dr.......................... Nashville TN 37211 *TF:* 888-348-8453 ■ *Web:* www.metile.com	888-348-8453		751
MEA Advisors LLC Graybar Bldg Ste 300 420 Lexington Ave......... New York NY 10170 *Web:* www.meaadvisorsllc.com	212-249-2239		70
Mea Mft 1232 E Sixth Ave .... Helena MT 59601 *TF:* 800-735-1246 ■ *Web:* www.mea-mft.org	406-365-4015		474
MEA Voice Magazine 1216 Kendale Blvd PO Box 2573 .... East Lansing MI 48826 *TF:* 800-292-1934 ■ *Web:* www.mea.org	517-332-6551	337-5414	457-8
Mead & Hunt Inc 6501 Watts Rd.............. Madison WI 53719 *Web:* www.meadhunt.com	608-273-6380		261
Mead Clark Lumber Co 2667 Dowd Dr PO Box 529.................. Santa Rosa CA 95407 *TF:* 800-585-9663 ■ *Web:* www.meadclark.com	707-576-3333	523-0350	191-3
Mead Fluid Dynamics Inc 4114 N Knox Ave .... Chicago IL 60641 *TF Cust Svc:* 877-632-3872 ■ *Web:* www.mead-usa.com	773-685-6800	685-7002	790
Mead Jewelers Inc 1309 13th St............. Woodward OK 73801 *Web:* meadjewelers.com	580-256-6373		410
Mead Johnson Nutritionals 2701 Patriot Blvd 4th Fl .... Glenview IL 60026 *TF:* 800-231-5469 ■ *Web:* www.meadjohnson.com	847-832-2420		296-10
Mead Matthew (R) State Capitol Bldg Rm 124 .... Cheyenne WY 82002 *Web:* governor.wyo.gov	307-777-7434	632-3909	343
Mead Metals Inc 555 Cardigan Rd.............. St. Paul MN 55126 *TF:* 800-992-1484 ■ *Web:* www.meadmetals.com	651-484-1400		492
Mead O'brien Inc 1429 Atlantic Ave .... North Kansas City MO 64116 *TF:* 800-892-2769 ■ *Web:* www.meadobrien.com	816-471-3993		112
Mead Public Library 710 N Eigth St........... Sheboygan WI 53081 *TF:* 800-441-4563 ■ *Web:* www.meadpl.org	920-459-3400	459-0204	434-3
Mead School District 2323 E Farwell Rd........... Mead WA 99021 *Web:* www.mead354.org	509-465-6000	465-6020	685
Mead Westvaco Office Products Group 4751 Hempstead Station Dr .... Dayton OH 45429	937-495-6323		304
Meade Auto Group 45001 Northpointe Blvd......... Utica MI 48315 *Web:* meadelexus.com/v2	586-726-7900		57
Meade County 516 Hillcrest Dr............ Brandenburg KY 40108 *Web:* kentucky.gov/pages/pagenotfounderror.aspx	270-422-2152		338
Meade County PO Box 278..................... Meade KS 67864 *TF:* 800-368-8683 ■ *Web:* www.meadeco.org	620-873-8700	873-8713	338
Meade County 1425 Sherman St PO Box 939 .... Sturgis SD 57785 *TF:* 800-952-3696 ■ *Web:* www.meadecounty.org	605-347-2356	347-3526	338
Meade County Rural Electric Co-op Corp 1351 Kentucky 79....................... Brandenburg KY 40108 *Web:* www.mcrecc.com	270-422-2162	422-4705	245
Meade Electric Company Inc 9550 W 55th St Ste A................... Countryside IL 60525 *Web:* www.meadeelectric.com	708-588-2500	588-2501	189-4
Meade Instruments Corp 27 Hubble............. Irvine CA 92618 *NASDAQ: MEAD* ■ *TF:* 800-626-3233 ■ *Web:* www.meade.com	949-451-1450	451-1460	544
Meade State Park 13051 V Rd.................. Meade KS 67864 *Web:* www.stateparks.com	620-873-2572		565
Meaden Precision Machined Products Co 16W210 83rd St............................. Burr Ridge IL 60527 *Web:* www.meaden.com	630-655-0888	655-3012	621
Meador Staffing Services Inc 722 Fairmont Pkwy Ste A.................. Pasadena TX 77504 *TF:* 800-332-3310 ■ *Web:* www.meador.com	713-941-0616		260
Meadow Brook Dairy 2365 Buffalo Rd............. Erie PA 16510 *Web:* www.meadowbrookdairy.com	814-899-3191		296-27
Meadow Burke LLC 531 S US Hwy 301 .... Tampa FL 33619 *Web:* www.meadowburke.com	813-248-1944		191-1
Meadow Farms Sausage Co 6215 S Western Ave...................... Los Angeles CA 90047 *Web:* meadowfarmssausage.com	323-752-2300		296-26
Meadow Gold Dairy 55 S Wakea Ave............ Kahului HI 96732 *Web:* www.lanimoo.com	808-877-5541		10-3
Meadow Green Nursing & Rehabilitation Ctr 45 Woburn St................................ Waltham MA 02452 *Web:* www.meadowgreen.org	781-899-8600		450

	Phone	Fax	Class
Meadow Lake Resort 100 St Andrews Dr.................. Columbia Falls MT 59912 *TF:* 800-321-4653 ■ *Web:* www.meadowlake.com	406-892-8700	892-8731	669
Meadow Valley Corp 3333 E Camelback Rd Ste 240................. Phoenix AZ 85018	602-437-5400		188-4
Meadow View Nursing Center 1404 Hay St........ Berlin PA 15530 *Web:* meadowview.net	814-267-4212		371
Meadow Wind Health Care Center Inc 300 23rd St NE............................ Massillon OH 44646 *TF:* 800-272-1711 ■ *Web:* www.meadowwind.net	330-833-2026		371
Meadowbrook Insurance Group Inc 26255 American Dr........................ Southfield MI 48034 *NYSE: MIG* ■ *TF:* 800-482-2726 ■ *Web:* www.meadowbrookinsgrp.com	248-358-1100	358-1614	360-4
Meadowlands Exposition Ctr 355 Plaza Dr............................... Secaucus NJ 07094 *Web:* www.mecexpo.com	201-330-7773	330-1172	205
Meadowlands Racetrack 50 Rt 120 .... East Rutherford NJ 07073 *TF:* 800-227-4480 ■ *Web:* www.meadowlandsracetrack.com	201-843-2446		642
Meadowlands Regional Chamber of Commerce 201 Rt 17 .... Rutherford NJ 07070 *Web:* www.meadowlands.org	201-939-0707	939-0522	139
Meadowlark Botanical Gardens 9750 Meadowlark Gardens Ct.................. Vienna VA 22182 *Web:* www.novaparks.com	703-255-3631		97
Meadowmere Resort 74 Main St.............. Ogunquit ME 03907 *TF:* 800-633-8718 ■ *Web:* www.meadowmere.com	207-646-9661		378
Meadowood 3205 Skippack Pike PO Box 670 .... Worcester PA 19490 *TF:* 800-930-7275 ■ *Web:* www.meadowood.net	610-584-1000	584-3645	672
Meadowood Napa Valley 900 Meadowood Ln .... Saint Helena CA 94574 *TF:* 800-458-8080 ■ *Web:* www.meadowood.com	707-963-3646	963-3532	669
Meadowood Retirement Community 2455 Tamarack Trl....................... Bloomington IN 47408 *Web:* www.fivestarseniorliving.com	812-336-7060		672
Meadowridge School 12224 240 St.......... Maple Ridge BC V4R1N1 *Web:* www.meadowridge.bc.ca	604-467-4444		685
Meadows & Ohly LLC Two Sun Ct Ste 350....... Norcross GA 30092 *Web:* www.meadowsandohly.com	678-282-0220		205
Meadows Farms Inc 43054 John Mosby Hwy..................... Chantilly VA 20152 *Web:* www.meadowsfarms.com	703-327-3940		323
Meadows Field Airport 3701 Wings Way Ste 300.................. Bakersfield CA 93308 *Web:* www.meadowsfield.com	661-391-1800	391-1801	27
Meadows Foundation Inc 3003 Swiss Ave........ Dallas TX 75204 *TF:* 800-826-9431 ■ *Web:* www.mfi.org	214-826-9431	827-7042	305
Meadows Mark (Rep R - NC) 1024 Longworth HOB.................... Washington DC 20515 *Web:* meadows.house.gov	202-225-6401	226-6422	342-2
Meadows Museum 5900 Bishop Blvd .... Dallas TX 75205 *Web:* www.meadowsmuseumdallas.org	214-768-2516	768-1688	520
Meadows Museum of Art at Centenary College 2911 Centenary Blvd .... Shreveport LA 71104 *TF:* 800-234-4448 ■ *Web:* www.centenary.edu/meadows	318-869-5169		520
Meadows Office Furniture Co 71 W 23rd St .... New York NY 10010 *Web:* meadowsofficeinteriors.com	212-741-0333	741-0303	319-3
Meadows Psychiatric Ctr 132 The Meadows Dr...................... Centre Hall PA 16828 *TF:* 800-641-7529 ■ *Web:* www.themeadows.net	814-364-2161		374-5
Meadows Racetrack 210 Racetrack Rd....... Washington PA 15301 *TF:* 800-804-0468 ■ *Web:* www.meadowsgaming.com	724-225-9300		642
Meadows Regional Medical Ctr (MRMC) 1 Meadows Pkwy .... Vidalia GA 30474 *TF:* 800-382-4023 ■ *Web:* www.meadowsregional.org	912-535-5555		374-3
Meadows Urquhart Acree & Cook LLP 1802 Bayberry Court Ste 102 .... Richmond VA 23226 *Web:* www.muacllp.com	804-249-5786		734
Meadowview Psychiatric Hospital 595 County Ave .... Secaucus NJ 07094 *Web:* hudsoncountynj.org	201-319-3660		374-5
Meadowview Regional Medical Ctr (MRMC) 989 Medical Pk Dr .... Maysville KY 41056 *Web:* www.meadowviewregional.com	606-759-5311		374-3
Meadville Forging Co 15309 Baldwin St PO Box 459 .... Meadville PA 16335 *TF:* 800-444-5427 ■ *Web:* www.meadforge.com	814-332-8200	333-4657	483
Meadville Lombard Theological School 5701 S Woodlawn Ave .... Chicago IL 60637 **Fax Area Code:* 312 ■ *TF:* 800-848-0979 ■ *Web:* www.meadville.edu	773-256-3000	327-7002*	167-3
Meadville Medical Ctr (MMC) 751 Liberty St.............................. Meadville PA 16335 *TF:* 800-254-5164 ■ *Web:* www.mmchs.org	814-333-5000		374-3
Meadville Tribune 947 Federal Ct .... Meadville PA 16335 *TF:* 800-879-0006 ■ *Web:* www.meadvilletribune.com	814-724-6370	724-8755	532-2
Meadville-Western Crawford County Chamber of Commerce 908 Diamond Pk........................... Meadville PA 16335 *TF:* 800-315-5721 ■ *Web:* www.meadvillechamber.com	814-337-8030	337-8022	139
Meadwestvaco Calmar Inc 11901 Grandview Rd .... Grandview MO 64030	816-986-6000		596
MEAG Power 1470 Riveredge Pkwy NW............ Atlanta GA 30328 *TF:* 800-333-6324 ■ *Web:* www.meagpower.org	770-563-0300		787
Meagher County 15 W Main St .... White Sulphur Springs MT 59645 *TF:* 800-332-2272 ■ *Web:* meaghercounty.mt.gov	406-547-3612	547-3388	338
Meaher State Park 5200 Battleship Pkwy.................... Spanish Fort AL 36577 *TF:* 800-252-7275 ■ *Web:* www.alapark.com	251-626-5529	626-5529	565
Meakwan 230 Third Ave.................. Chula Vista CA 91910 *Web:* www.meakwanthaicuisine.com	619-426-5172		671
Mealey's Furniture Inc 908 W St Rd......... Warminster PA 18974 *Web:* www.mealeysfurniture.com	215-672-1333		321
Meals on Wheels Inc of Tarrant County Endowment Fund 320 S Fwy................................ Fort Worth TX 76104 *Web:* mealsonwheels.org	817-336-0912		305

Company / Address	City	State	ZIP	Phone	Fax	Class
Means Industries Inc 3715 E Washington Rd *TF:* 800-869-1433 ■ *Web:* www.meansindustries.com	Saginaw	MI	48601	989-754-1433	754-1103	489
Mears Group Inc 4500 N Mission Rd *TF:* 800-632-7727 ■ *Web:* www.mears.net	Rosebush	MI	48878	989-433-2929	433-2199	188-10
Mears Transportation Group 324 W Gore St *TF:* 800-759-5219 ■ *Web:* www.mearstransportation.com	Orlando	FL	32806	407-422-4561	422-6923	441
Mearthane Products Corp 16 W Industrial Dr *Web:* www.mearthane.com	Cranston	RI	02921	401-612-3086		596
Mease Dunedin Hospital 601 Main St	Dunedin	FL	34698	727-733-1111		374-3
Mease Manor Retirement Living 700 Mease Plaza *TF:* 800-561-3357 ■ *Web:* www.measemanor.com	Dunedin	FL	34698	727-738-3000		672
Measurement Group LLC, The 5757 Uplander Way Ste 200 *Web:* www.themeasurementgroup.com	Culver City	CA	90230	310-216-1800		196
Measurement Systems Intl Inc 14240 Interurban Ave S Ste 200 *Web:* www.msiscales.com	Tukwila	WA	98168	206-433-0199		770
Measurement Technology Group Inc 1310 Emerald Rd *Web:* www.redsealmeasurement.com	Greenwood	SC	29646	864-223-1212		407
Measurement Technology Northwest Inc 4211 24th Ave W *TF:* 800-932-3500 ■ *Web:* www.mtnw-usa.com	Seattle	WA	98199	206-634-1308		201
Meat & Potatoes 649 Penn Ave *Web:* meatandpotatoespgh.com	Pittsburgh	PA	15222	412-325-7007		671
Meb Management services 1215 E Missouri Ave *Web:* mebapts.com	Phoenix	AZ	85014	602-279-5515		652
MEBA (Marine Engineers' Beneficial Assn) 444 N Capitol St NW Ste 800 *Web:* mebaunion.org	Washington	DC	20001	202-638-5355	638-5369	414
MEC Dynamics Corp 90 Rose Orchard Way *Web:* www.mecdynamics.com	San Jose	CA	95134	408-428-9427		743
MECA Sportswear 1120 Townline Rd *TF:* 800-729-6322 ■ *Web:* www.mecasportswear.com	Tomah	WI	54660	608-374-6450	374-6405	155-5
Mecanex USA Inc 119 White Oak Dr *Web:* www.mecanexusa.com	Berlin	CT	06037	860-828-6531		770
Mecanica Solutions Inc 6300 Cote-de-Liesse Ste 200 *TF:* 800-567-4223 ■ *Web:* www.mecanicasolutions.com	Montreal	QC	H4T1E3	514-340-1818		261
Meccon Industries Inc 2703 Bernice Rd *Web:* www.meccon.com	Lansing	IL	60438	708-474-8300	474-9550	189-10
Mecham Co, The 4107 S Forest Meadows *Web:* www.mechamcompany.com	Spokane	WA	99206	509-922-0535		41
Mechancial Service Corp 41 S Jefferson Rd *Web:* mscnj.com	Whippany	NJ	07981	973-884-5000		189-10
Mechanical Construction Company LLC 3001 17th St *Web:* www.bernhardmcc.com	Metairie	LA	70002	504-833-8291		189-10
Mechanical Contractor 4165 Brunswick Rd	Memphis	TN	38133	901-730-4799		186
Mechanical Contractors Assn of America (MCAA) 1385 Piccard Dr *TF:* 800-556-3653 ■ *Web:* www.mcaa.org	Rockville	MD	20850	301-869-5800	990-9690	49-3
Mechanical Design Systems Inc 6302 Aaron Ln *Web:* www.mds-hvac.com	Clinton	MD	20735	301-877-9600		610
Mechanical Products Co 1112 N Garfield St *Web:* www.mechprod.com	Lombard	IL	60148	630-953-4100		729
Mechanical Rubber Products Corp 77 Forester Ave *Web:* mechanicalrubber.com	Warwick	NY	10990	845-986-2271		677
Mechanical Servants Inc 2755 Thomas St *TF:* 800-351-2000 ■ *Web:* www.cvalet.com	Melrose Park	IL	60160	800-351-2000		238
Mechanical Services Inc 400 Presumpscot St *Web:* www.mechanicalservices.com	Portland	ME	04103	207-774-1531		610
Mechanical Supply Co 1001 Crews Rd *Web:* www.mechsupply.com	Matthews	NC	28105	704-847-9641		612
Mechanical Systems of Dayton 4401 Springfield St *TF:* 800-254-9455 ■ *Web:* www.msdinc.net	Dayton	OH	45431	937-254-3235		610
Mechanical Technology Inc 325 Washington Sq Ste 3 *NASDAQ: MKTY* ■ *TF:* 800-937-5449 ■ *Web:* www.mechtech.com	Albany	NY	12205	518-533-2200	218-2500	668
Mechanics Hall 321 Main St *Web:* www.mechanicshall.org	Worcester	MA	01608	508-752-5608	754-8442	572
Mechanics Savings Bank 100 Minot Ave PO Box 400 *TF:* 877-886-1020 ■ *Web:* www.mechanicssavings.com/home/home	Auburn	ME	04210	207-786-5700	786-5709	70
Mechanicsburg Area School District (Inc) 100 E Elmwood Ave 2nd Fl *Web:* www.mbgsd.org	Mechanicsburg	PA	17055	717-691-4500		685
Mechanicsville Local 6400 Mechanicsville Tpke *TF:* 800-468-3382 ■ *Web:* www.richmond.com	Mechanicsville	VA	23111	804-746-1235	730-0476	532-4
Mechatronics Inc 8152 304th Ave SE PO Box 5012 *Web:* www.mechatronics.com	Preston	WA	98050	425-222-5900		75
Mech-Tronics Corp 1635 N 25th Ave *Web:* www.mech-tronics.com	Melrose Park	IL	60160	708-344-9823	344-0067	697
Mecklenburg County 393 Washington St PO Box 530 *Web:* www.mecklenburgva.com	Boydton	VA	23917	434-738-6191	738-6861	338
Mecklenburg County 600 E Fourth St 11th Fl Charlotte-Mecklenburg Government Ctr *TF:* 800-323-8603 ■ *Web:* charmeck.org	Charlotte	NC	28202	704-336-2472	336-5887	338
Mecklenburg Electric Co-op 11633 Hwy Ninety Two *TF:* 800-989-4161 ■ *Web:* www.meckelec.org	Chase City	VA	23924	434-372-6100		245
Meckley Services Inc 5701 General Washington Dr Ste O *TF:* 877-632-5539 ■ *Web:* www.meckleyservices.com	Alexandria	VA	22312	703-333-2040		610
Meckley's Limestone Products Inc 1543 State Rt 225 *TF:* 800-326-9467 ■ *Web:* www.meckleys.com	Herndon	PA	17830	570-758-3011	758-2400	503-5
Meclabs LLC 1300 Marsh Landing Pkwy Ste 106 *TF:* 800-517-5531 ■ *Web:* www.meclabs.com	Jacksonville Beach	FL	32250	800-517-5531		138
Meco Corp 1500 Industrial Rd *TF:* 800-251-7558 ■ *Web:* www.meco.net	Greeneville	TN	37745	423-639-1171	639-1055	319-3
Meco Inc 2121 S Main St	Paris	IL	61944	217-465-7575		21
Mecor Inc 1567 Elmhurst Rd *Web:* mecor.net	Elk Grove Village	IL	60007	847-690-0777		358
Mecosta County 400 Elm St *Web:* www.co.mecosta.mi.us	Big Rapids	MI	49307	231-796-2505	592-0121	338
Mecosta County Area Chamber of Commerce 246 N State St *Web:* www.mecostacounty.com	Big Rapids	MI	49307	231-796-7649	796-1625	139
Mecosta-Osceola Intermediate School District 15760 190th Ave *TF:* 877-211-5253 ■ *Web:* www.moisd.org	Big Rapids	MI	49307	231-796-3543		685
MECS Inc 14522 S Outer 40 Rd *Web:* www.mecsglobal.com	Chesterfield	MO	63017	314-275-5700	275-5701	188-7
MecSoft Corp 18019 Sky Park Cir Ste KL *Web:* www.mecsoft.com	Irvine	CA	92614	949-654-8163		225
Med 4 Home Inc 10800 N Congress Ave *Web:* www.med4home.com	Kansas City	MO	64153	816-801-7400		475
Med Fusion LLC 2501 S State Hwy 121 Business Ste 1100 *TF:* 800-426-8157 ■ *Web:* www.medfusionservices.com	Lewisville	TX	75067	972-966-7000		415
Med Legal Consulting Source Inc 201 S Santa Fe Ave Ste 100 *Web:* elevateservices.com	Los Angeles	CA	90012	213-347-0203		196
Med Pro Health Care Staffing 5608 Princeton Ave *TF:* 800-264-1170 ■ *Web:* www.medprostaffing.com	Columbus	GA	31904	706-322-7085		193
Med Shield Inc 2424 E 55th St *TF:* 800-272-5454 ■ *Web:* www.medshield.com	Indianapolis	IN	46220	317-613-3700		160
Med Team Home Health Care 131 S Beckham Ave *TF:* 800-825-2873 ■ *Web:* med-team.com	Tyler	TX	75702	903-592-9747		363
Meda Ltd 1575 Lauzon Rd *TF:* 888-518-6332 ■ *Web:* www.medagroup.com	Windsor	ON	N8S3N4	519-944-7221		256
MedaCheck LLC 602 Main St Ste 401 *Web:* www.medacheck.com	Cincinnati	OH	45202	513-488-1111		475
Medaille College 18 Agassiz Cir **Fax:* Admissions ■ *TF:* 800-292-1582 ■ *Web:* www.medaille.edu	Buffalo	NY	14214	716-880-2200	880-2007*	166
Medaire Inc 4722 N 24th St Ste 450 *Web:* www.medaire.com	Phoenix	AZ	85016	480-333-3700		477
Medallion Athletic Products Inc 150 River Park Rd *TF:* 888-000-3412 ■ *Web:* www.medallionathletics.com	Mooresville	NC	28117	704-660-3000		711
Medallion Cabinetry 2222 Camden Ct *TF:* 800-543-4074 ■ *Web:* www.medallioncabinetry.com	Oak Brook	IL	60523	800-476-4181		115
Medallion Financial Corp 3000 W County Rd 42 Ste 301 *Web:* www.medallionfinancial.com	Burnsville	MN	55337	952-831-2025	831-2945	403
Medallion Financial Corp 437 Madison Ave 38th Fl *NASDAQ: TAXI* ■ **Fax:* PR ■ *TF:* 877-633-2554 ■ *Web:* www.medallionfinancial.com	New York	NY	10022	212-328-2100	328-2121*	216
Medallion Industries Inc 3221 NW Yeon Ave *Web:* www.medallionindustries.com	Portland	OR	97210	503-221-0170		499
Medallion Laboratories 9000 Plymouth Ave N *TF:* 800-245-5615 ■ *Web:* www.medallionlabs.com	Minneapolis	MN	55427	763-764-4453	764-4010	192
MedAltus 944 College Park Rd Ste B *TF:* 800-393-3848 ■ *Web:* www.medaltus.com	Summerville	SC	29486	800-393-3848		395
Medarray Inc 3915 research park dr *TF:* 800-345-3148 ■ *Web:* www.permselect.com	Ann Arbor	MI	48108	734-769-1066		476
Medart Inc 124 Manufacturers Dr *TF Cust Svc:* 800-888-7181 ■ *Web:* www.medartinc.com	Arnold	MO	63010	636-282-2300		385
MedAvail Technologies Inc 6665 Millcreek Dr Unit No1 *Web:* www.medavail.com	Mississauga	ON	L5N5M4	905-812-0023		475
MedAvante Inc 100 American Metro Blvd Ste 106 *Web:* www.medavante.com	Hamilton	NJ	08619	609-528-9400		582
Medbuy Corp 4056 Meadowbrook Dr Unit 135 *TF:* 800-837-8958 ■ *Web:* www.medbuy.ca	London	ON	N6L1E4	519-652-1688		317
Medcare Products Inc 151 E Cliff Rd *TF:* 800-695-4479 ■ *Web:* medcarelifts.com	Burnsville	MN	55337	952-894-7076		475
MedCAREERS Group Inc 758 E Bethel School Rd *Web:* www.medcareersgroup.com	Coppell	TX	75019	972-393-5892		395
Medcenter One Hospital 300 N Seventh St *TF:* 800-932-8758 ■ *Web:* bismarck.sanfordhealth.org	Bismarck	ND	58501	701-323-6000		374-3
Medco Enterprises Inc 3530 Wayne Ave	Bronx	NY	10467	718-655-1700		463
Medco Health Solutions Inc 100 Parsons Pond Dr *NYSE: MHS* ■ *TF:* 800-732-0330 ■ *Web:* www.express-scripts.com	Franklin Lakes	NJ	07417	201-269-3400		586
Medco Services Inc 7037 Madison Pike Ste 105 *Web:* www.extendedearlyout.com	Huntsville	AL	35805	256-665-9194		160
Medcom Inc 6060 Phyllis Dr *TF:* 800-541-0253 ■ *Web:* www.medcomrn.com	Cypress	CA	90630	800-877-1443		33
Medcom Trainex 6060 Phyllis Dr **Fax Area Code:* 714 ■ *TF Cust Svc:* 800-877-1443 ■ *Web:* www.medcomrn.com	Cypress	CA	90630	800-877-1443	898-4852*	513
Medcor Inc 4805 W Prime Pkwy *TF:* 877-696-6775 ■ *Web:* www.medcor.com	McHenry	IL	60050	815-363-9500	363-9696	463

	Phone	Fax	Class
MedCost Benefit Services LLC 165 Kimel Park Dr .... Winston-salem NC 27103 *Web:* www.medcost.com	336-774-4400		390
MEDCURE Inc 1811 NE Sandy Blvd.............Portland OR 97230 *TF:* 866-560-2525 ■ *Web:* www.medcure.org	503-257-9100	257-9100	363
MedDirect Inc 3200 Broadmoor Ave SE.................Grand Rapids MI 49512	616-940-0500		509
MEDecision Inc 550 E Swedesford Rd Ste 220.................. Wayne PA 19087 *Web:* www.medecision.com	610-540-0202	540-0270	178-10
Medeco Security Locks Inc 3625 Alleghany Dr .... Salem VA 24153 **Fax Area Code:* 800 ■ *TF:* 800-839-3157 ■ *Web:* www.medeco.com	540-380-5000	421-6615*	350
Medefis Inc 10826 Old Mill Rd Suitte 101..................Omaha NE 68154 *Web:* www.medefis.com	402-393-6333		463
Medegen Medical Products LLC 209 Medegen Dr........................... Gallaway TN 38036	901-867-2951		596
MED-EL Corp 2511 Old Cornwallis Rd Ste 100............... Durham NC 27713 *Web:* www.medel.com	919-572-2222		475
Medela Inc 1101 Corporate Dr................ Mchenry IL 60050 *TF:* 800-435-8316 ■ *Web:* www.medela.us	815-363-1166		684
MedeliaCommunications LLC 2029 Taft St..............................Hollywood FL 33020	954-922-0846		195
Medelis Inc 5870 FLwring Sage Ct Ste 200.......... Reno NV 89511 *Web:* www.medelis.com	775-851-9460		743
Medexcel USA Inc 484 Temple Hill Rd......................New Windsor NY 12553 *TF:* 800-563-6384 ■ *Web:* www.medexcelusa.com	845-565-3700		463
MedExpert International Inc 1300 Hancock St .... Redwood City CA 94063 *TF:* 800-999-1999 ■ *Web:* www.medexpert.com	650-326-6000		194
Med-Fit Systems Inc 3553 Rosa Way .... Fallbrook CA 92028 *Web:* www.medfitsystems.com	760-723-9618		475
Medflow Inc 2100 Redford Rd Ste 100 .... Charlotte NC 28211 *TF:* 844-366-5129 ■ *Web:* eyecareleaders.com/medflow	844-366-5129		179
Medford Care Center 185 Tuckerton Rd ....Medford NJ 08055 *Web:* www.medfordcare.com	856-983-8500		371
Medford Chamber of Commerce 1 Shipyard Way Ste 302......................Medford MA 02155 *Web:* medfordchamberma.com	781-396-1277	396-1278	139
Medford Leas 1 Medford Leas Way.............Medford NJ 08055 *TF:* 800-331-4302 ■ *Web:* www.medfordleas.org	609-654-3000		672
Medford Mail Tribune PO Box 1108 ....Medford OR 97501 *Web:* www.mailtribune.com	541-776-4411	858-5126	532-2
Medford Public Library 111 High St............Medford MA 02155 *TF:* 800-447-8844 ■ *Web:* www.medfordlibrary.org	781-395-7950	391-2261	434-3
Medford Township Board of Education 128 Rt 70 Ste 1................................Medford NJ 08055 *Web:* www.medford.k12.nj.us	609-654-6416	654-7436	685
Medgar Evers College 1650 Bedford Ave......................... Brooklyn NY 11225 **Fax:* Admissions ■ *TF:* 866-277-5719 ■ *Web:* www.mec.cuny.edu	718-270-4900	270-6411*	166
MedGyn Products Inc 100 W Industrial Rd .... Addison IL 60101 *TF:* 800-451-9667 ■ *Web:* www.medgyn.com	630-627-4105		608
Media 100 Inc 450 Donald Lynch Blvd.................. Marlborough MA 01752 *TF:* 888-772-6747 ■ *Web:* www.media100.com	508-460-1600	460-8627	178-8
Media Breakaway LLC 1490 W 121st Ave Ste 201................Westminster CO 80234 *Web:* www.mediabreakaway.com	303-464-8164	464-8218	194
Media Brokers International Inc 555 N Point Ctr E Ste 700.................. Alpharetta GA 30022-8268 **Fax Area Code:* 678 ■ *TF:* 866-514-1620 ■ *Web:* www.media-brokers.com	866-514-1620	514-6299*	6
Media Business Corp 1810 Platte St............Denver CO 80202 *Web:* mediabiz.com	303-271-9960		637-9
Media Buying Services Inc 4545 E Shea Blvd Ste 162 ....Phoenix AZ 85028 *TF:* 888-996-2232 ■ *Web:* www.mediabuyingservices.com	602-996-2232		4
Media Convergence Group Inc 904 Elm St Ste 208........................Columbia MO 65201 *Web:* www.newsy.com	573-442-4557		387
Media Cybernetics Inc 4340 E W Hwy Ste 400...................... Bethesda MD 20814 *TF Sales:* 800-263-2088 ■ *Web:* www.mediacy.com	301-495-3305	495-5964	178-10
Media Excel Inc 8834 N Capital of Texas Hwy Ste 270............. Austin TX 78759 *Web:* www.mediaexcel.com	512-502-0034		177
Media Financial Management Assn (MFM) 550 W Frontage Rd Ste 3600 ....Northfield IL 60093 *Web:* www.bcfm.com	847-716-7000	716-7004	49-14
Media Fusion Inc 4951 Century St............ Huntsville AL 35816 *Web:* www.fusiononline.com	256-532-3874		7
Media General Inc 333 E Franklin St.......... Richmond VA 23219 *NYSE: MEG* ■ *Web:* www.media-general.com	804-649-6000		637-8
Media Imagery 7905 Browning Rd Ste 218................Pennsauken NJ 08109 *Web:* www.mediaimagery.com	856-317-0990		514
Media Industry Newsletter (MIN) 110 William St 11th Fl......................New York NY 10038 **Fax Area Code:* 212 ■ *TF:* 888-707-5814 ■ *Web:* www.minonline.com	888-707-5814	621-4879*	531-11
Media Law Reporter 1801 S Bell St............... Arlington VA 22202 *TF:* 800-372-1033 ■ *Web:* www.bna.com/media-law-reporter-p5934	800-372-1033		531-11
Media Law Resource Ctr (MLRC) 266 W 37th St Ste 20......................New York NY 10018 *Web:* www.medialaw.org	212-337-0200		49-10
Media Logic USA LLC 59 Wolf Rd .... Albany NY 12205 *TF:* 866-353-3011 ■ *Web:* medialogic.com	518-456-3015	456-4279	4
Media Relations Report 316 N Michigan Ave Ste 400 ....Chicago IL 60601 *TF:* 800-878-5331 ■ *Web:* www.ragan.com	312-960-4100	960-4106	531-11
Media Sciences International Inc 203 Ridge Rd .... Goshen NY 10924 *Web:* www.mediasciences.com	201-677-9311		627
Media Services 500 S Sepulveda Blvd 4th Fl................Los Angeles CA 90049 *TF:* 800-738-0409 ■ *Web:* www.media-services.com	310-440-9600		570
Media Services Ltd 2510 W Dunlap Ave Ste 250..................Phoenix AZ 85021 *Web:* www.msgl.com	602-674-5800		514
Media Space Solutions 5600 Rowland Rd Ste 170 .... Minnetonka MN 55343 *TF:* 888-672-2100 ■ *Web:* www.mediaspacesolutions.com	612-253-3900	454-2848	6
Media Storm LLC 99 Washington St......................South Norwalk CT 06854 *Web:* www.mediastorm.biz	203-852-8001		4
Media Talent Group 9200 Sunset Blvd Ste 550 ....West Hollywood CA 90069	310-275-7900		731
Media Temple Inc 8520 National Blvd Bldg A...............Culver City CA 90232 *TF:* 877-578-4000 ■ *Web:* www.mediatemple.net	877-578-4000		395
Media Two Interactive LLC 111 E Hargett St Ste 200..................... Raleigh NC 27601 *Web:* www.mediatwo.net	919-553-1246		4
Media Watch PO Box 618...................Santa Cruz CA 95061 *TF:* 800-631-6355 ■ *Web:* www.mediawatch.com	831-423-6355		48-8
Media Works Ltd 1425 Clarkview Rd Ste 500...................Baltimore MD 21209 *TF:* 800-214-5034 ■ *Web:* www.medialtd.com	443-470-4400		6
Media/Professional Insurance Inc 1201 Walnut Ste 1800 ....Kansas City MO 64106 *TF:* 866-282-0565 ■ *Web:* www.axiscapital.com	816-471-6118	471-6119	391-5
Media3 Technologies LLC 33 Riverside Dr N River Commerce Pk......... Pembroke MA 02359 *TF:* 800-903-9327 ■ *Web:* www.media3.net	781-826-1213	826-1513	808
Mediabidscom Inc 448 Main St................Winsted CT 06098 *TF:* 800-989-0406 ■ *Web:* www.mediabids.com	860-379-9602		7
MediaBrains Inc 720 Goodlette Rd N Ste 400.....................Naples FL 34102 *Web:* www.mediabrains.com	239-594-3200		395
MediaChoice LLC 3701 Bee Caves Rd Ste 101 .... Austin TX 78746 *Web:* www.mediachoice.com	512-693-9905		8
Mediacom Communications Corp 100 Crystal Run Rd....................... Middletown NY 10941 *TF General:* 800-479-2082 ■ *Web:* mediacomcable.com	845-695-2600		116
Mediaedge:cia LLC 825 Seventh Ave...........New York NY 10019 *Web:* www.mecglobal.com	212-474-0000		6
Mediafour Corp 1101 Fifth St...........West Des Moines IA 50265 *Web:* www.mediafour.com	515-225-7409	225-6370	178-12
Mediagrif Interactive Technologies Inc 1111 St-Charles St W E Tower Ste 255......... Longueuil QC J4K5G4 *TSE: MDF* ■ *TF:* 877-677-9088 ■ *Web:* www.mediagrif.com	450-449-0102	449-8725	178-1
Medialets Inc 80 Eighth Ave 5th Fl.............New York NY 10014 **Fax Area Code:* 646	212-300-5670	569-3199*	387
Media-Max Inc 12 N Washington St .... Montoursville PA 17754 *Web:* www.mediamaxinc.net	570-368-7633		4
MediaNews Group Inc 101 W Colfax Ave ....Denver CO 80202 *Web:* digitalfirstmedia.com	303-954-6360		637-8
MediaPro Inc 20021 120th Ave NE Ste 102 ....Bothell WA 98011 *TF:* 800-726-6951 ■ *Web:* www.mediapro.com	425-483-4700		180
Mediaspot Inc 1550 Bayside Dr ....Corona Del Mar CA 92625 *Web:* www.mediaspot.com	949-721-0500		6
Mediassociates Inc 75 Glen Rd.............Sandy Hook CT 06482 *Web:* www.mediassociates.com	203-797-9500	797-1400	7
MediaTech Capital Partners LLC 70 E 55th St 21st Fl ....New York NY 10022 *TF:* 800-654-8471 ■ *Web:* www.mediatechcapital.com	212-759-3022		360-3
Mediatech Institute of Austin 4719 s congress ave.......................... Austin TX 78745 *TF:* 866-498-1122 ■ *Web:* mediatech.edu	512-447-2002		162
MediaTek USA Inc 120 Presidential Way .... Woburn MA 01801 *Web:* www.mediatek.com	781-503-8000		360-3
MediaTracks Communications 2250 E Devon Ave Ste 151 .... Des Plaines IL 60018 *Web:* www.mediatracks.com	847-299-9500	299-9501	646
Medic Rescue 313 Bridge St.................... Beaver PA 15009 *Web:* www.medicrescue.org	724-728-3620		30
MEDICA 401 Carlson Pkwy .... Minnetonka MN 55305 *TF Cust Svc:* 800-952-3455 ■ *Web:* www.medica.com	952-992-2900		391-3
Medica Corp 5 Oak Park Dr.................... Bedford MA 01730 *TF:* 800-777-5983 ■ *Web:* www.medicacorp.com	781-275-4892		476
Medical Action Industries Inc (MAI) 500 Expy Dr S.............................Brentwood NY 11717 *NASDAQ: MDCI* ■ *TF:* 800-645-7042 ■ *Web:* www.medical-action.com	631-231-4600		477
Medical Analysis Systems Inc 46360 Fremont Blvd..............................Fremont CA 94538 *TF:* 800-232-3342 ■ *Web:* www.thermofisher.com	510-979-5000	979-5002	231
Medical Assn of Georgia (MAG) 1849 The Exchange Ste 200......................Atlanta GA 30339 *TF:* 800-282-0224 ■ *Web:* www.mag.org	678-303-9290	303-3732	474
Medical Associates Healthcare 911 Carter St NW ....Elkader IA 52043 *TF:* 800-648-6868 ■ *Web:* www.mahealthcare.com	563-245-1717		543
Medical Assurance Inc 100 Brookwood Pl Ste 300.................Birmingham AL 35209 *TF Cust Svc:* 800-282-6242 ■ *Web:* www.proassurance.com	205-877-4400		391-5
Medical Benefits Mutual Life Insurance Co 1975 Tamarack Rd ....Newark OH 43058 *TF:* 800-423-3151 ■ *Web:* www.medben.com	740-522-8425		391-3
Medical Billing Concepts Inc 16001 Ventura Blvd Ste 135.....................Encino CA 91436 *Web:* www.medbillconcepts.com	818-817-9832		2
Medical Billing Unlimited Inc 5959 Gateway Blvd W Ste 120 .... El Paso TX 79925 *Web:* mbuinc.com	915-779-1716		2
Medical Care Development International (MCDI) 8401 Colesville Rd Ste 425 ....Silver Spring MD 20910 *TF:* 800-427-7566 ■ *Web:* www.mcd.org	301-562-1920	562-1921	48-5

	Phone	Fax	Class
Medical Center Pharmacy 2401 N Ocoee St....Cleveland TN 37311 *TF:* 877-753-9555 ■ *Web:* www.medicalcenterrx.com	423-476-5548		237
Medical City Arlington (MCA) 3301 Matlock Rd....Arlington TX 76015 *Web:* www.medicalcenterarlington.com	817-465-3241	472-4878	374-3
Medical City Denton 3535 S I-35 E....Denton TX 76210 *Web:* www.dentonregional.com	940-384-3535	384-4702	374-3
Medical City Hospital 7777 Forest Ln....Dallas TX 75230 *Web:* www.medicalcityhospital.com	972-566-7000		374-3
Medical City Las Colinas 6800 N MacArthur Blvd....Irving TX 75039 *Web:* www.lascolinasmedical.com	972-969-2000	969-2080	374-3
Medical City McKinney 4500 Medical Ctr Dr....McKinney TX 75069 *Web:* www.medicalcenterofmckinney.com/home	972-547-8000		374-3
Medical city plano 3901 W 15th St....Plano TX 75075 *Web:* www.themedicalcenterofplano.com	972-596-6800		374-3
Medical Clinic of North Texas 9003 Airport Fwy Ste 300....North Richland TX 76180 *Web:* www.mcnt.com	817-514-5200		374-2
Medical Coaches Inc 399 County Hwy 58....Oneonta NY 13820 *Web:* www.medcoach.com	607-432-1333	432-8190	516
Medical College of Wisconsin 8701 Watertown Plank Rd....Milwaukee WI 53226 *Web:* www.mcw.edu	414-456-8296	456-6506	167-2
Medical Communications Media Inc 17 Blacksmith Rd Ste 100....Newtown PA 18940 *Web:* cmecorner.com	267-364-0556		194
Medical Components Inc 1499 Delp Dr....Harleysville PA 19438 *Web:* www.medcompnet.com	215-256-4201		476
Medical Cost Management Corp 105 W Adams St Ste 2200....Chicago IL 60603 *TF:* 800-367-9938 ■ *Web:* www.medicalcost.com	312-236-2694		363
Medical Ctr Enterprise (MCE) 400 N Edwards St....Enterprise AL 36330 *TF:* 800-994-6610 ■ *Web:* www.mcehospital.com	334-347-0584		374-3
Medical Ctr for Federal Prisoners Springfield 1900 W Sunshine St....Springfield MO 65807 *TF:* 877-623-8426 ■ *Web:* www.bop.gov	417-862-7041	837-1717	212
Medical Ctr Hospital (MCH) 500 W Fourth St....Odessa TX 79761 *Web:* www.medicalcenterhealthsystem.com	432-640-6000		374-3
Medical Ctr of Aurora (MCA) 1501 S Potomac St....Aurora CO 80012 *Web:* www.auroramed.com	303-695-2600		374-3
Medical Ctr of South Arkansas 700 W Grove St....El Dorado AR 71730 *TF:* 800-285-1131 ■ *Web:* www.themedcenter.net	870-863-2000	863-5442	374-3
Medical Ctr of Southeast Texas, The 2555 Jimmy Johnson Blvd....Port Arthur TX 77640 *Web:* www.medicalcentersetexas.com	409-724-7389		374-3
Medical Ctr, The 250 Pk St....Bowling Green KY 42101 *Web:* www.mcbg.org	270-700-2660		374-3
Medical Ctr, The 710 Center St....Columbus GA 31901 *TF:* 800-476-7378 ■ *Web:* www.columbusregional.com	706-571-1000	571-1216	374-3
Medical Depot Inc 99 Seaview Blvd....Port Washington NY 11050 *Web:* www.drivemedical.com	516-998-4600		477
Medical Designs LLC 1210 W 18th St Ste 104....Sioux Falls SD 57104 *Web:* www.medicaldesignsllc.com	605-376-6008		476
Medical Devices Inc 4500 140th Ave N Ste 101....Clearwater FL 33762 *Web:* www.mdevicesinc.com	727-451-7160		582
Medical Diagnostic Laboratories LLC 2439 Kuser Rd....Hamilton NJ 08690 *TF:* 877-269-0090 ■ *Web:* www.mdlab.com	609-570-1000		418
Medical Doctor Assoc 4775 Peachtree Industrial Blvd Ste 300....Norcross GA 30092 **Fax Area Code:* 770 ■ *TF:* 800-780-3500 ■ *Web:* www.mdainc.com	800-780-3500	246-0882*	194
Medical Education Technologies Inc (METI) 6300 Edgelake Dr....Sarasota FL 34240 *TF:* 866-462-7920 ■ *Web:* www.caehealthcare.com	941-377-5562		250
Medical Extrusion Technologies Inc 26608 Pierce Cir....Murrieta CA 92562 *Web:* www.medicalextrusion.com	951-698-4346		596
Medical Eye Bank of Florida 2902 N Orange Ave....Orlando FL 32804	407-422-2020		269
Medical Eye Bank of Maryland 815 Pk Ave....Baltimore MD 21201 *TF:* 800-756-4824 ■ *Web:* www.tbionline.org	410-752-2020		269
Medical Eye Bank of West Virginia 3 Courtney Dr....Charleston WV 25304	304-926-9200		269
Medical Eye Services Inc 345 Baker St E....Costa Mesa CA 92626 *TF:* 800-877-6372 ■ *Web:* www.mesvision.com	714-619-4660		390
Medical Genetics Consultants 819 DeSoto St....Ocean Springs MS 39564 **Fax Area Code:* 228 ■ *TF:* 800-362-4363 ■ *Web:* www.legalgenetics.com	800-362-4363	872-1893*	417
Medical Graphics Corp 350 Oak Grove Pkwy....Saint Paul MN 55127 *NASDAQ: ANGN* ■ *TF:* 800-950-5597 ■ *Web:* mgcdiagnostics.com	651-484-4874	379-8227	250
Medical Group Management Assn (MGMA) 104 Inverness Terr E....Englewood CO 80112 *TF:* 877-275-6462 ■ *Web:* www.mgma.com	303-799-1111		49-8
Medical Indicators 16 Thomas J Rhodes Industrial Dr....Hamilton NJ 08619 *Web:* medicalindicators.com	609-737-1600	587-8635	475
Medical Information Technology Inc 1 Meditech Cir....Westwood MA 02090 *Web:* ehr.meditech.com	781-821-3000	821-2199	178-10
Medical Information Technology Inc Meditech Cir....Westwood MA 02090 *Web:* ehr.meditech.com	781-821-3000		177
Medical Instrument Development Laboratories Inc 557 McCormick St....San Leandro CA 94577 *TF:* 800-929-5227 ■ *Web:* www.midlabs.com	510-357-3952		415
Medical International Technology Inc 1872 Beaulac Ville Saint-Laurent....Montreal QC H4R2E7 *Web:* www.mitcanada.ca	514-339-9355		476
Medical Knowledge Systems Inc 440 Burrough Ste 130....Detroit MI 48202	313-483-0955		176
Medical Learning Inc 287 E Sixth St Ste 400....St. Paul MN 55101 *Web:* www.medlearn.com	651-292-3400		196
Medical Lette, The 1000 Main St....New Rochelle NY 10801 *Web:* secure.medicalletter.org	914-235-0500		434-3
Medical Library Assn (MLA) 65 E Wacker Pl Ste 1900....Chicago IL 60601 *TF:* 800-523-1850 ■ *Web:* www.mlanet.org	312-419-9094	419-8950	49-11
Medical Linen Service Inc 290 S Maple Ave....South San Francisco CA 94080 *Web:* www.completelinen.com	650-873-1221		442
Medical Management Specialists 4100 Embassy Dr SE Ste 200....Grand Rapids MI 49546 *TF:* 888-707-2684 ■ *Web:* www.mms.med.pro	616-975-1845		2
Medical Metrics Inc 2121 Sage Rd Ste 300....Houston TX 77056 *Web:* www.medicalmetrics.com	713-850-7500		363
Medical Mutual Group 700 Spring Forest Rd....Raleigh NC 27609 *TF:* 800-662-7917 ■ *Web:* www.medicalmutualgroup.com	919-872-7117	878-7550	391-5
Medical Mutual Insurance Company of Maine 1 City Ctr Ste 9....Portland ME 04112 *TF:* 800-942-2791 ■ *Web:* www.medicalmutual.com	207-775-2791	775-6576	391-5
Medical Mutual Liability Insurance Society of Maryland 225 International Cir PO Box 8016....Hunt Valley MD 21030 *TF:* 800-492-0193 ■ *Web:* www.medicalmutualofmd.com	410-785-0050	785-2631	391-5
Medical Mutual of Ohio 2060 E Ninth St....Cleveland OH 44115 **Fax:* Hum Res ■ *TF:* 800-700-2583 ■ *Web:* www.medmutual.com	216-687-7000	687-6585*	391-3
Medical Park Pharmacy Inc 301 Penny Ln....Morehead City NC 28557 *Web:* www.medicalparkpharmacy.net	252-726-0777		237
Medical Practice Partners 29 Naek Rd....Vernon Rockville CT 06066 *Web:* www.healthwisema.com	860-872-2289		734
Medical Priority Consultants Inc 139 E S Temple St....Salt Lake City UT 84111 *Web:* www.prioritydispatch.net	801-363-9127		179
Medical Products Laboratories Inc 9990 Global Rd....Philadelphia PA 19115 *TF:* 800-523-0191 ■ *Web:* www.mplusa.com	215-677-2700	677-7736	582
Medical Properties Trust Inc 1000 Urban Ctr Dr Ste 501....Birmingham AL 35242 *NYSE: MPW* ■ *Web:* www.medicalpropertiestrust.com	205-969-3755		654
Medical Protective Co 5814 Reed Rd....Fort Wayne IN 46835 **Fax Area Code:* 800 ■ *TF:* 800-463-3776 ■ *Web:* www.medpro.com	260-485-9622	398-6726*	391-5
Medical Research Law & Policy Report 1801 S Bell St....Arlington VA 22202 *TF:* 800-372-1033 ■ *Web:* www.bna.com/medical-research-law-p0700	800-372-1033		531-7
Medical Resources Inc 1455 Broad St....Bloomfield NJ 07003	973-707-1100	707-1118	383
Medical Risk Managers Inc 1170 Ellington Rd....South Windsor CT 06074 *Web:* www.mrm-mgu.com	860-732-3248		390
Medical Services of America Inc (MSA) 171 Monroe Ln....Lexington SC 29072 *TF:* 800-845-5850 ■ *Web:* www.msa-corp.com	803-957-0500		363
Medical Society of Virginia 2924 Emerywood Pkwy Ste 300....Richmond VA 23294 *TF:* 800-746-6768 ■ *Web:* www.msv.org	804-353-2721	355-6189	474
Medical Specialties Managers Inc 1 City Blvd W Ste 1100....Orange CA 92868 *Web:* www.msmnet.com	714-571-5000		196
Medical Staffing Associates Inc 6731 Whittier Ave 3rd Fl....McLean VA 22101 **Fax Area Code:* 703 ■ *TF:* 800-235-5105 ■ *Web:* www.medstaffer.com	800-235-5105	893-7358*	721
Medical Staffing Network Holdings Inc 901 Yamato Rd Ste 110....Boca Raton FL 33431 *TF:* 800-676-8326 ■ *Web:* www.msnhealth.com	800-676-8326		721
Medical Strategic Planning Inc 5 Shelbern Dr....Lincroft NJ 07738 *TF:* 800-605-2665 ■ *Web:* www.medsp.com	732-219-5090		463
Medical Tactile Inc 5757 Century Blvd Ste 600....Los Angeles CA 90045 *Web:* www.medicaltactile.com	310-641-8228		476
Medical Teams International (MTI) PO Box 10....Portland OR 97207 *TF:* 800-959-4325 ■ *Web:* www.medicalteams.org	503-624-1000	624-1001	48-5
Medical Treatment Systems Inc 6300 Westgate Rd Ste A....Raleigh NC 27617	919-782-9050		475
Medical University of South Carolina (MUSC) 171 Ashley Ave....Charleston SC 29425 *Web:* academicdepartments.musc.edu	843-792-1414		167-2
Medical University of South Carolina 41 Bee St PO Box 175....Charleston SC 29425 **Fax:* Admissions ■ *TF:* 800-424-6872 ■ *Web:* www.musc.edu	843-792-3281	792-3764*	166
Blood & Marrow Transplant Program 86 Jonathan Lucas St....Charleston SC 29425 *Web:* www.muschealth.org/index.html	843-792-9300		769
Medical University of South Carolina Children's Hospital 165 Ashley Ave....Charleston SC 29425 *Web:* www.musckids.org	843-792-2300		374-1
MedicAlert Foundation International 5226 Pirrone Ct....Salida CA 95368 **Fax Area Code:* 209 ■ *TF Cust Svc:* 800-432-5378 ■ *Web:* www.medicalert.org	800-432-5378	669-2495*	48-17
Medicalodges Inc 201 W Eighth St....Coffeyville KS 67337 *TF:* 800-782-0120 ■ *Web:* www.medicalodges.com	800-782-0120		793
MedicaMetrix Inc 1 Old Sudbury Rd....Wayland MA 01778 *TF:* 800-236-1900 ■ *Web:* www.medicametrix.com	617-694-1713		475
Medicap Pharmacies Inc 1 Rider Trail Plaza Dr....Earth City MO 63045 *TF:* 800-407-8055 ■ *Web:* www.medicap.com	314-993-6000		237

	Phone	Fax	Class
MediCapture Inc 580 W Germantown Pk Ste 103 .... Plymouth Meeting PA 19462 *TF:* 800-932-5676 ■ *Web:* www.medicapture.com	610-238-0700		475
Medicare Compliance Alert 11300 Rockville Pk Ste 1100 .... Rockville MD 20852 *TF:* 800-929-4824	301-287-2700	816-8945	531-7
Medicare Payment Advisory Comm 601 New Jersey Ave NW.................. Washington DC 20001 *Web:* www.medpac.gov	202-220-3700		434-3
Medicare Rights Ctr (MRC) 520 Eigth Ave N Wing 3rd Fl .... New York NY 10018 *TF Hotline:* 800-333-4114 ■ *Web:* www.medicarerights.org	212-869-3850	869-3532	48-17
Medicat LLC Sandy Springs 1100 Johnson Ferry Rd Ste LL75.... Atlanta GA 30342 *Web:* www.medicat.com	404-252-2295		179
Medicatech USA Inc 50 Maxwell Ave .... Irvine CA 92618 *TF:* 800-817-5030 ■ *Web:* www.medicatechusa.com	949-679-2881		476
Medicine & Health/Rhode Island Magazine 405 Promenade St Ste A.................... Providence RI 02908 *Web:* www.rimed.org	401-331-3207		457-16
Medicine Creek State Recreation Area 40611 Rd 728............................ Cambridge NE 69022 *Web:* outdoornebraska.gov/medicinecreek	308-697-4667		565
Medicine Hat & District Chamber of Commerce 413 Sixth Ave SE .... Medicine Hat AB T1A2S7 *Web:* www.medicinehatchamber.com	403-527-5214	527-5182	137
Medicine Hat Regional Hospital 666 Fifth St SW .... Medicine Hat AB T1A4H6 *Web:* albertahealthservices.ca	403-529-8000	529-8998	374-2
Medicine Lodge Memorial Hospital 710 N Walnut St..................... Medicine Lodge KS 67104 *Web:* www.mlmh.net	620-886-3771		371
Medicine Lodge State Archaeological Site Hwy 31.................................. Hyattville WY 82428 *Web:* wyoparks.state.wy.us	307-469-2234		565
Medicine Online Inc 18800 Delaware St Ste 650........... Huntington Beach CA 92648 *Web:* www.medicineonline.com	714-848-0444	242-1484	356
Medicine Rocks State Park PO Box 1630 .... Miles City MT 59301 *Web:* fwp.mt.gov	406-234-0926		565
Medicines Co 8 Sylvan Way .... Parsippany NJ 07054 *NASDAQ: MDCO* ■ *TF:* 800-388-1183 ■ *Web:* www.themedicinescompany.com	973-290-6000	656-9898	85
Medicis Pharmaceutical Corp 7720 N Dobson Rd....................... Scottsdale AZ 85256 *TF Cust Svc:* 866-246-8245 ■ *Web:* valeant.com	800-321-4576		582
Medico Group 1515 S 75th St.................. Omaha NE 68124 *TF:* 800-228-6080 ■ *Web:* gomedico.com	402-391-6900		391-2
Medico Industries Inc 1500 Hwy 315 .... Wilkes-Barre PA 18702 *TF:* 800-633-0027 ■ *Web:* medicoind.com	570-825-7711	824-1169	264-3
Medicomp Inc 600 Atlantis Rd .... Melbourne FL 32904 *TF:* 800-234-3278 ■ *Web:* www.medicompinc.com	321-794-3811		639
MediConnect Global Inc 10897 S Riverfront Pkwy Ste 500.......... South Jordan UT 84095 *TF:* 800-489-8710 ■ *Web:* www.mediconnect.net	801-545-3700		225
Medicount Management Inc 10361 Spartan Dr...................... Cincinnati OH 45215 *TF:* 800-962-1484 ■ *Web:* www.medicount.com	513-772-4465		41
Medicus Healthcare Solutions LLC 7 Industrial Way Unit 5 Ste 5 .... Salem NH 03079 *TF:* 855-301-0563 ■ *Web:* www.medicushcs.com	855-301-0563		193
Mediderm Laboratories 9840- 9842 Alburtis Ave............... Santa Fe Springs CA 90670 *Web:* www.medidermstore.com	562-944-2211		231
Medieval Academy of America, The 17 Dunster St Ste 202...................... Cambridge MA 02138 *TF:* 800-937-5300 ■ *Web:* www.medievalacademy.org	617-491-1622	492-3303	48-11
Medifast Inc 11445 Cronhill Dr............ Owings Mills MD 21117 *NYSE: MED* ■ *TF:* 800-209-0878 ■ *Web:* www.medifast1.com	800-209-0878		296-11
MediGene Inc 10650 Scripps Ranch Blvd Ste 206 .... San Diego CA 92131 *Web:* www.medigene.com	858-586-2240		85
Medi-Globe Corp 110 W Orion St Ste 136 .... Tempe AZ 85283 *Web:* www.mediglobe.com	480-897-2772		475
MediGrafix Inc 9 Fairway Ln Ste C .... Blythewood SC 29016 **Fax Area Code:* 888 ■ *TF:* 888-744-1301 ■ *Web:* www.medi-grafix.com	803-261-6387	744-1301*	478
Medigroup Services Corp 1360 S Fifth St Ste 334..................... St. Charles MO 63301 *TF:* 800-331-0500 ■ *Web:* www.medigroup.com	636-947-7555		475
MediLodge Group, The 64500 Van Dyke .... Washington MI 48095 *Web:* www.lcsnet.com	586-752-5008		194
Medilodge of Monroe LLC 481 Village Green Ln .... Monroe MI 48162 *TF:* 800-465-3203 ■ *Web:* www.medilodge.com	734-242-6282		371
MediMedia ManagedÿMarkets 780 Township Line Rd .... Yardley PA 19067 *TF:* 800-643-7226 ■ *Web:* www.medimedia.com	267-685-2300		457-13
MedImpact Healthcare Systems Inc 10680 Treena St Ste 500.................... San Diego CA 92131 *TF:* 800-788-2949 ■ *Web:* www.medimpact.com	858-566-2727		586
Medin Corp 90 Dayton Ave Bldg 16C............ Passaic NJ 07055 *TF:* 800-922-0476 ■ *Web:* www.medin.com	973-779-2400		476
Medina County 1100 16th St................... Hondo TX 78861 *Web:* www.medinacountytexas.org	830-741-6000	741-6015	338
Medina County District Library 210 S Broadway .... Medina OH 44256 *Web:* www.mcdl.info	330-725-0588	725-2053	434-3
Medina Electric Co-op Inc PO Box 370 .... Hondo TX 78861 **Fax Area Code:* 830 ■ *TF:* 866-632-3532 ■ *Web:* www.medinaec.org	866-632-3532	426-2796*	245
MedInformatix Inc 5777 W Century Blvd Ste 1700............. Los Angeles CA 90045 *Web:* www.medinformatix.com	310-348-7367		174
Medinox Inc 6120 Paseo Del Norte Ste B-2 .... Carlsbad CA 92011	760-603-8989		231
Medi-Nuclear Corp Inc 4610 Littlejohn St...................... Baldwin Park CA 91706 *TF:* 800-321-5981 ■ *Web:* www.medinuclear.com	626-960-9822		476
Mediostream Inc 4962 El Cmno Real 201 .... Los Altos CA 94022 *Web:* www.mediostream.com	650-625-8900		658
Med-I-Pant Inc 9100 Ray Lawson Blvd.......... Montreal QC H1J1K8 *Web:* www.mipinc.info	514-356-1224		476
Mediplay Inc 526 Pylon Dr .... Raleigh NC 27606 *TF:* 800-537-3238 ■ *Web:* mediplay.com	919-341-8582		195
Medirect Inc 36380 Garfield Rd Ste 7 .... Clinton Township MI 48035 *TF:* 800-915-7727 ■ *Web:* www.medirectinc.com	586-792-7777		180
MediRevv Inc 2600 University Pkwy .... Coralville IA 52241 *TF:* 888-665-6310 ■ *Web:* www.medirevv.com	888-665-6310		196
Medisolv Inc 10420 Little Patuxent Pkwy Ste 400 .... Columbia MD 21044 *Web:* www.medisolv.com	443-539-0505		196
Medison Econet Corp 8085 NW 90th St .... Medley FL 33166	305-599-7161	599-7144	475
Medistar Home Health 347 Moreau St .... Marksville LA 71351	318-253-0014		363
Medisys for Physicians Inc 7201 Halcyon Summit Dr.................. Montgomery AL 36117 *TF:* 800-333-4747 ■ *Web:* www.medisysinc.com	334-277-6201		179
Medisys Health Network Inc 8900 Van Wyck Expy .... Jamaica NY 11418 *Web:* medisyshealth.org	718-206-6000		360-3
Meditech Communications Inc 533 Phalen Blvd.......................... Saint Paul MN 55130 *Web:* www.gomeditech.com	651-636-7350		514
Mediteranno Restaurant 2900 S State St............................ Ann Arbor MI 48108 *Web:* mediterrano.com	734-332-9700		671
Mediterranean Bistro 1712 N 120th St........... Omaha NE 68154 *Web:* www.medbistro.com	402-493-3080		671
Mediterranean Cuisine 4111 N Mesa St......... El Paso TX 79902	915-542-1012		671
Mediterranean Grill 42 S Pk Ave................ Helena MT 59601 *Web:* www.mediterraneangrillhelena.com	406-495-1212		671
Mediterranean Inn 425 Queen Anne Ave N......................... Seattle WA 98109 *Web:* www.mediterranean-inn.com	206-428-4700		379
Mediterranean Shipping Company (USA) Inc 420 Fifth Ave 37th St 8th Fl .... New York NY 10018 *Web:* www.msc.com/usa	212-764-4800		770
Mediterraneo 1970 Main St .... Sarasota FL 34236 *Web:* mediterraneorest.com	941-365-4122	954-0106	671
Medium Blue Search Engine Marketing 670 Eleventh St, NW............................ Atlanta GA 30318 *TF:* 800-942-1304 ■ *Web:* www.mediumblue.com	404-525-4420		463
MediUSA L P 6481 Franz Warner Pkwy .... Whitsett NC 27377 *TF:* 800-633-6334 ■ *Web:* www.mediusa.com	336-449-4440		156
Medivance Inc 321 S Taylor Ave Ste 200 .... Louisville CO 80027 *Web:* www.medivance.com	303-926-1917		476
Medivation Inc 235 E 42nd St 3rd Fl .... New York NY 10017 *NASDAQ: MDVN* ■ *TF:* 800-879-3477 ■ *Web:* www.medivation.com	212-733-2323		582
MediVista Media LLC 1100 Spring St Ste 750 .... Atlanta GA 30309 *Web:* www.everwell.com	404-817-7767		708
Mediware Information Systems Inc 11711 W 79th St.............................. Lenexa KS 66214 *NASDAQ: MEDW* ■ *TF:* 800-255-0026 ■ *Web:* www.mediware.com	913-307-1000	307-1111	178-11
Medix 222 S Riverside Plaza Ste 2120 .... Chicago IL 60606 *Web:* medixteam.com	312-487-5800	877-5613	260
Medix Specialty Vehicles Inc 3008 Mobile Dr .... Elkhart IN 46514 *Web:* www.medixambulance.com	574-266-0911		59
Medizone International Inc 4000 Bridgeway Ste 401..................... Sausalito CA 94965 *Web:* www.medizoneint.com	415-331-0303		477
MedjetAssist 3500 Colonnade Pkwy Ste 500 PO Box 43099. .Birmingham AL 35243 *TF:* 800-527-7478 ■ *Web:* www.medjetassist.com	205-595-6626	595-6658	30
Medler Eelectric Company Inc 2155 Redman Dr.............................. Alma MI 48801 **Fax Area Code:* 989 ■ *TF:* 800-229-5740 ■ *Web:* www.medlerelectric.com	800-229-5740	463-4522*	249
Medley 220 Humboldt Ct .... Sunnyvale CA 94089 *Web:* medley.com	408-745-5555		5
Medley Material Handling Company Inc 4201 Will Rogers Pkwy.................. Oklahoma City OK 73108 *TF:* 800-643-5424 ■ *Web:* www.medleycompany.com	405-946-3453		358
Medley Steel & Supply Inc 9925 NW 116th Way.......................... Medley FL 33178 *Web:* www.medleysteel.com	305-863-7480		492
Medliance 1839 S Alma School Rd Ste 230 .... Mesa AZ 85210 *Web:* www.medliance.com	480-784-6335		463
Medline Industries Inc 1 Medline Pl........... Mundelein IL 60060 *TF Cust Svc:* 800-633-5463 ■ *Web:* www.medline.com	847-949-5500	643-3295	576
MedlinePlus National Library of Medicine 8600 Rockville Pk.......................... Bethesda MD 20894 *TF:* 888-346-3656 ■ *Web:* medlineplus.gov	301-594-5983	402-1384	356
Medlink Corp 10393 San Diego Mission Rd Ste 120 .... San Diego CA 92108 *TF:* 800-452-2400 ■ *Web:* www.medlink.com	619-640-4660		194
Medmart Inc 10780 Reading Rd .... Cincinnati OH 45241 *TF:* 888-260-4430 ■ *Web:* medmartonline.com	888-260-4430		196
MedMatica Consulting Associates 18 Barrington Ln.................... Chester Springs PA 19425 *TF:* 800-999-1950 ■ *Web:* www.medmatica.com	610-827-1356		177
MedMeme LLC 501 Seventh Ave Ste 508 .... New York NY 10018 *Web:* www.medmeme.com	212-725-5990		237
MEDNOVUS Inc 664 Hymettus Ave............. Leucadia CA 92024 *TF:* 800-788-6617 ■ *Web:* www.mednovus.com	760-390-1410		476
Medoc Mountain State Park 1541 Medoc State Pk Rd .... Hollister NC 27844 *Web:* www.ncparks.gov	252-586-6588		565
MEDomics LLC 426 N San Gabriel Ave .... Azusa CA 91702 *Web:* www.medomics.com	626-804-3645		415
Medone Surgical Inc 670 Tallevast Rd........... Sarasota FL 34243 *TF:* 866-633-6631 ■ *Web:* www.medone.com	941-359-3129		476

Phone | Fax | Class

Medpace Medical Device Inc
3787 95th Ave NE Ste 100 ....Minneapolis MN 55014 612-234-8500 743
Web: www.medpace.com

MedPlast Inc 405 W Geneva Dr.................. Tempe AZ 85282 480-553-6400 601
Web: medplastgroup.com

MedPlus Inc 4690 Pkwy Dr..................... Mason OH 45040 513-229-5500 229-5505 178-10
TF: 800-444-6235 ■ *Web:* questdiagnostics.com

Med-Plus Medical Supplies
17 Vanderbilt Ave .... Brooklyn NY 11205 718-222-4416 419
TF: 888-433-2300 ■ *Web:* www.medexsupply.com

MedPoint Digital Inc
909 Davis St Ste 500 .... Evanston IL 60201 847-869-4700 4
Web: www.medpt.com

Medpoint Search 4011 Garrott St...............Houston TX 77006 713-524-4443 260
Web: www.medpointsearch.com

MedPointe Pharmaceuticals
265 Davidson Ave Ste 300 ....Somerset NJ 08873 732-564-2200 582
Web: meda.us

MEDport LLC 23 Acorn St....................Providence RI 02903 401-273-0444 273-0630 477

MedPricer 2346 Boston Post Rd Unit 2...........Guilford CT 06437 203-453-4554 453-4558 225
TF: 888-453-4554 ■ *Web:* www.medpricer.com

Medquest Assoc Inc
3480 Preston Ridge Rd Ste 600 .... Alpharetta GA 30005 678-992-7200 383
Web: www.mqimaging.com

Medrec Inc 85 NE Loop 410 Ste 610..........San Antonio TX 78216 210-494-2343 545-1657 260

MedReview Inc
1 Seaport Plaza 199 Water St 27th Fl ....New York NY 10038 212-897-6000 533
TF: 800-400-9916 ■ *Web:* www.medreview.us

Med-RT
27758 Santa Margarita Pkwy .... Mission Viejo CA 92691 949-502-2800 393
Web: www.med-rt.com

MedRx Inc 1200 Starkey Rd Ste 105 ....Largo FL 33771 727-584-9600 476
TF: 888-392-1234 ■ *Web:* www.medrx-usa.com

MedSafe 4200 Underwood Rd ....La Porte TX 77571 281-476-5392 475
Web: www.gosafe.com

MedShape Inc
1575 Northside Dr NW Ste 440 ....Atlanta GA 30318 404-249-9155 477
Web: www.medshape.com

MedSignals Corp 217 Alamo Plaza...........San Antonio TX 78205 210-222-2067 475
TF: 800-438-1277 ■ *Web:* www.medsignals.com

Med-Staff Oklahoma LLC
8321 E 61st St Ste 221..........................Tulsa OK 74133 918-317-0270 804-4937* 363
*Fax Area Code: 866

MedStar Health
10980 Grantchester Way......................Columbia MD 21044 410-772-6500 353
TF: 877-772-6505 ■ *Web:* www.medstarhealth.org

MedSupply 5850 E Shields Ave Ste 105.......... Fresno CA 93727 559-292-1540 475
TF: 800-889-9081 ■ *Web:* www.gomedsupply.net

Med-Tech Resource Inc 29485 Airport Rd ....Eugene OR 97402 888-627-7779 525
TF: 888-627-7779 ■ *Web:* www.gomed-tech.com

MedTel.com Inc 353 Third Ave Ste 19 ....New York NY 10010 212-777-7722 224
Web: www.medtel.com

MedTera Solutions
40 W 37th St Ste 1203 ....New York NY 10018 212-400-2130 5
Web: www.medterasolutions.com

MEDTOX Diagnostics Inc
1230 Anthony Rd ....Burlington NC 27216 336-226-6311 286-6222* 231
*Fax Area Code: 651 ■ *TF:* 800-334-1116 ■ *Web:* www.medtox.com

MEDTOX Scientific Inc
402 W County Rd D .... Saint Paul MN 55112 651-636-7466 416
NASDAQ: MTOX ■ *TF:* 800-832-3244 ■ *Web:* www.medtox.com

Medtronic Inc
710 Medtronic Pkwy NE....................Minneapolis MN 55432 763-514-4000 514-4879 250
NYSE: MDT ■ *TF Cust Svc:* 800-328-2518 ■ *Web:* www.medtronic.com

Medtronic MiniMed Inc
18000 Devonshire St ....Northridge CA 91325 800-646-4633 477
TF: 800-646-4633 ■ *Web:* www.medtronicdiabetes.com

Medtronic Neurosurgery 125 Cremona Dr .... Goleta CA 93117 800-633-8766 476
TF Cust Svc: 800-468-9710 ■ *Web:* medtronic.com

Medtronic of Canada Ltd
99 Hereford St ....Brampton ON L6Y0R3 905-826-6020 826-6620 250
TF: 800-268-5346 ■ *Web:* www.medtronic.com

Medtronic Perfusion Systems
7611 Northland Dr .... Brooklyn Park MN 55428 763-391-9000 250
TF: 800-328-3320 ■ *Web:* www.medtronic.com

Medtronic Powered Surgical Solutions
4620 N Beach St..........................Fort Worth TX 76137 817-788-6400 477
TF: 800-643-2773 ■ *Web:* www.medtronic.com

Medtronic Surgical Technologies
6743 Southpoint Dr N.....................Jacksonville FL 32216 904-296-9600 477
TF: 800-874-5797 ■ *Web:* www.medtronic.com

Medullan Inc
625 Mt Auburn St Ste 201 ....Cambridge MA 02138 617-547-0273 180
Web: www.medullan.com

Meduri Farms Inc 12375 Smithfield Rd .... Dallas OR 97338 503-623-0308 296-19
Web: www.medurifarms.com

Medusind 6115 Camp Bowie Ste 260.............Fort Worth TX 76116 817-570-5102 899-7771* 371
*Fax Area Code: 866 ■ *Web:* www.medusind.com

Medusind Solutions Inc
31103 Rancho Viejo Rd Ste 2150..... San Juan Capistrano CA 92675 877-741-4573 463
TF: 877-741-4573 ■ *Web:* www.medusind.com

MedValue Offshore Solutions Inc
1415 W 22nd St Tower Fl Regency Towers ...... Oak Brook IL 60523 630-299-7370 624
TF: 800-544-7521 ■ *Web:* www.medvaluebpo.com

Medvantx Inc 5626 Oberlin Dr Ste 110......... San Diego CA 92121 858-625-2990 625-2999 721
TF: 866-744-0621 ■ *Web:* www.medvantx.com

Medve Group Inc
8390 Delmar Blvd Fl 1 .... Saint Louis MO 63124 314-569-0004 652
Web: www.medve.com

Medved Autoplex
11001 W I-70 Frontage Rd N .... Wheat Ridge CO 80033 303-421-0100 57
Web: www.medved.com

Medved Chevrolet Inc
11001 W I-70 Frontage Rd N .... Wheat Ridge CO 80033 303-421-0100 57
Web: medved.com

Medway Country Manor 115 Holliston St........Medway MA 02053 508-533-6634 793
Web: www.medwaymanor.com

Medway Plastics Corp
2250 Cherry Industrial Cir ....Long Beach CA 90805 562-630-1175 596
Web: www.medwayplastics.com

Medweb 667 Folsom St .... San Francisco CA 94107 415-541-9980 194
Web: www.medweb.com

Medwig & Co 401 Wood St...................Pittsbugh PA 15222 412-562-9061 2

MedX Health Corp
1495 Bonhill Rd Unit 1................... Mississauga ON L5T1M2 905-670-4428 250
Web: www.medxhealth.com

Mee Industries Inc
16021 Adelante St .... Irwindale CA 91702 626-359-4550 14
TF: 800-732-5364 ■ *Web:* www.meefog.com

Meeder Equipment Co
12323 Sixth St ....Rancho Cucamonga CA 91739 909-463-0600 463-0102 357
TF: 800-423-3711 ■ *Web:* www.meeder.com

Meehan Pat (Rep R - PA)
2305 Rayburn HOB........................Washington DC 20515 202-225-2011 226-0280 342-2
Web: meehan.house.gov

Meehleis Modular Buildings Inc
1303 E Lodi Ave ....Lodi CA 95240 209-334-4637 186
TF: 800-860-7073 ■ *Web:* www.meehleis.com

Meeker Co-op Light & Power Assn
1725 E US Hwy 12 PO Box 68 .... Litchfield MN 55355 320-693-3231 693-2980 245
TF: 800-232-6257 ■ *Web:* www.meeker.coop

Meeker County 325 N Sibley Ave .... Litchfield MN 55355 320-693-5200 338
TF: 800-232-6257 ■ *Web:* www.co.meeker.mn.us

Meeker Mansion 312 Spring St .... Puyallup WA 98372 253-848-1770 520
Web: www.meekermansion.org

Meeks PO Box 1746........................Springfield MO 65804 417-521-2801 236
Web: meeks.com

Meeks Gregory W (Rep D - NY)
2234 Rayburn Bldg.......................Washington DC 20515 202-225-3461 226-4169 342-2
Web: meeks.house.gov

Meeman-Shelby Forest State Park
910 Riddick Rd............................ Millington TN 38053 901-876-5215 565
Web: www.state.tn.us

Meer.net LLC 202 S Randolph Ave ....Elkins WV 26241 304-636-5722 387

Meers Engineering Inc
209 S Danville Dr Ste B 200................... Abilene TX 79605 325-691-1200 691-1206 261
Web: www.meersengineering.com

Meet Minneapolis
250 Marquette Ave Ste 1300................Minneapolis MN 55401 612-767-8000 206
TF: 800-445-7412 ■ *Web:* www.minneapolis.org

Meeting Alliance LLC
Bank Plaza 14 Main St ....Robbinsville NJ 08691 609-208-1908 184
Web: www.meetingalliance.com

Meeting Connection Inc, The
6373 Meadow Glen Dr N ....Westerville OH 43082 614-898-9361 184
TF: 800-398-2568 ■ *Web:* www.the-meeting-connection.com

Meeting House, The
5885 Robert Oliver Pl.......................Columbia MD 21045 410-730-4090 720
TF: 800-494-8497 ■ *Web:* www.themeetinghouse.org

Meeting Incentive Experts
61 W 15th St Ste 301 ....Chicago IL 60605 312-842-3600 463
Web: www.miexperts.com

Meeting Masters 107 Oakmont Rd..........Mount Laurel NJ 08054 856-787-9590 196
Web: meetingmastersinc.com

Meeting Matters Inc
11 Dougal Ln ....East Northport NY 11731 631-368-2082 463
Web: meeting-matters.com

Meeting Professionals International (MPI)
2711 Lyndon B Johnson Fwy Ste 600............. Dallas TX 75234 972-702-3053 702-3065 49-12
TF: 866-318-2743 ■ *Web:* www.mpiweb.org

Meeting Services Unlimited
135 S Mitthoeffer Rd.......................Indianapolis IN 46229 317-841-7171 184
Web: www.meetingservicesunlimited.com

Meeting Solutions Llc 593 N Wolf Rd.......... Wheeling IL 60090 847-808-1818 463
TF: 800-345-8082 ■ *Web:* www.associationandmeetingsolutions.com

Meeting Street Inn 173 Meeting St ....Charleston SC 29401 843-723-1882 379
TF: 800-842-8022 ■ *Web:* www.meetingstreetinn.com

Meeting Systems Inc
600 N Curtis Rd Ste 170.......................... Boise ID 83706 208-288-0290 463
TF: 800-587-2201 ■ *Web:* www.meetingsystems.com

MeetingOne Corp
501 S Cherry St One Cherry Ctr Ste 1000 ....Denver CO 80246 303-623-2530 387
Web: www.meetingone.com

Meetings & Conventions Magazine
100 Lighting Way...........................Secaucus NJ 07094 201-902-2000 457-5
Web: www.meetings-conventions.com

Meetings & Incentives Group
21760 Stevens Creek Blvd ....Cupertino CA 95014 408-973-1915 184
Web: www.migr.com

Meetings and Events International
1314 Burch Dr .... Evansville IN 47725 812-471-3000 463
Web: www.meintl.com

MeetMe Inc 100 Union Sq Dr .... New Hope PA 18938 215-862-1162 395
Web: www.meetme.com

MEG Energy Corp 1500 520 - 3 Ave SW.......... Calgary AB T2P0R3 403-770-0446 536
Web: www.megenergy.com

Mega Care 1883 Whitney Mesa Dr.............Henderson VA 89014 626-382-9492 793
TF: 888-883-6342 ■ *Web:* www.megacare.com

Mega Force Staffing Services Inc
1001 Hay St ....Fayetteville NC 28305 910-484-5313 260
Web: www.megaforce.com

Mega Group Inc 720-1st Ave N............... Saskatoon SK S7K6R9 306-242-7366 41
TF: 800-265-9030 ■ *Web:* www.megagroup.ca

Megadoor Inc
611 Hwy 74 S Ste 100 .... Peachtree City GA 30269 770-631-9086 234
Web: www.megadoor.com

Megadyne Medical Products Inc
11506 S State St.............................. Draper UT 84020 801-576-9669 476
TF: 800-747-6110 ■ *Web:* www.megadyne.com

MegaFab PO Box 457........................ Hutchinson KS 67504 620-663-1127 456
TF: 800-338-5471 ■ *Web:* www.megafab.com

MEGA-FM 94.9 (Span CHR)
7601 Riviera Blvd ....Miramar FL 33023 954-862-2000 832-3149* 645
*Fax Area Code: 210 ■ *TF:* 877-599-2946 ■ *Web:* mega949.iheart.com

	Phone	Fax	Class
MegaPath Inc 6800 Koll Ctr Pkwy Ste 200 ... Pleasanton CA 94566 *TF:* 800-917-9188 ■ *Web:* www.megapath.com	925-201-2500		225
Megaplexus Corp 214 California St ... Newton MA 02458 *Web:* www.megaplexus.com	617-244-4405		196
Mega-Pro International Inc 251 W Hilton Dr ... Saint George UT 84770 *TF:* 800-541-9469 ■ *Web:* www.mega-pro.com	435-673-1001	673-1007	799
Megaputer Intelligence Inc 1600 W Bloomfield Rd Ste E ... Bloomington IN 47403 *Web:* www.megaputer.com	812-330-0110	330-0150	178-10
Megastar Financial Corp 1080 Cherokee St ... Denver CO 80204 *TF:* 800-218-1415 ■ *Web:* www.libertyhomefinancial.com	303-321-8800		401
Megatech Corp 525 Woburn St ... Tewksbury MA 01876 *Web:* www.megatechcorp.com	978-937-9600		766
Megatran Electric Ltd 860 Lucien Beaudin ... St. Jean-sur-richelieu QC J2X5V5	450-346-6622		767
Megawatt Daily 2 Penn Plaza 25th Fl ... New York NY 10121 **Fax Area Code:* 800 ■ *TF:* 800-752-8878 ■ *Web:* platts.com/products/megawatt-daily	212-904-3070	752-8878*	531-5
Megger 4271 Bronze Way ... Dallas TX 75237 *TF:* 800-723-2861 ■ *Web:* www.megger.com	214-333-3201	331-7399	248
Meggitt Safety Systems Inc 1915 Voyager Ave ... Simi Valley CA 93063 *Web:* www.meggitt.com	805-584-4100	578-3400	283
Meggitt Training Systems Inc 296 Brogdon Rd ... Suwanee GA 30024 *TF:* 800-813-9046 ■ *Web:* www.meggitttrainingsystems.com	678-288-1090	288-1515	703
Megu 355 W 16th St ... New York NY 10011	212-885-9400		671
Meguiar's Inc 17991 Mitchell S ... Irvine CA 92614 *TF Cust Svc:* 800-347-5700 ■ *Web:* www.meguiars.com	949-752-8000	752-5784	151
Meharry Medical College Library 1005 DB Todd Blvd ... Nashville TN 37208 *Web:* www.mmc.edu	615-327-6318		434-1
Meherrin Agricultural & Chemical Co Inc 413 Main St ... Severn NC 27877 *TF:* 800-775-0333 ■ *Web:* meherrinag.com	252-585-1744	585-1718	276
Mehling & Associates Inc 9846 Hwy 31 E ... Tyler TX 75705 *Web:* www.athomehealth.org	903-592-8001		363
Mehlville School District 3120 Lemay Ferry Rd ... Saint Louis MO 63125 *Web:* www.mehlvilleschooldistrict.com	314-467-5000		186
Mehron Inc 100 Red Schoolhouse Rd Ste C2 ... Spring Valley NY 10977 *TF:* 800-332-9955 ■ *Web:* www.mehron.com	845-426-1700		237
Mehta Tech Inc 208 N 12th Ave ... Eldridge IA 52748 *Web:* www.mehtatech.com	563-285-9151		639
Mei Ji Sushi 454 River Ave ... Winnipeg MB R3L0C6	204-284-3996		671
MEI Real Estate Services 5757 W Century Blvd Ste 605 ... Los Angeles CA 90045 *Web:* www.meirealty.com	310-258-0444		652
MEI Technologies Inc 18050 Saturn Ln Ste 300 ... Houston TX 77058 *Web:* www.meitechinc.com	281-283-6200		261
Meier Enterprises Inc 12 W Kennewick Ave ... Kennewick WA 99336 *TF:* 800-239-7589 ■ *Web:* meierinc.com	509-735-1589		261
Meier Supply Company Inc 530 Bloomingburg Rd ... Middletown NY 10940 *TF:* 800-418-3216 ■ *Web:* www.meiersupply.com	845-733-5666		610
Meier Tool & Engineering Inc 875 Lund Blvd ... Anoka MN 55303 *Web:* www.meiertool.com	763-427-6275		488
Meier's Wine Cellars Inc 6955 Plainfield Rd ... Cincinnati OH 45236 *TF:* 800-229-9813 ■ *Web:* www.meierswinecellars.com	513-891-2900	891-6370	80-3
Meigs County *Economic Development Office* 238 W Main St ... Pomeroy OH 45769 *Web:* www.meigscountyohio.com	740-992-3034	992-7942	338
Meijer Inc 2929 Walker Ave NW ... Grand Rapids MI 49544 *TF:* 800-543-3704 ■ *Web:* www.meijer.com	616-453-6711		345
Meiji Corp 660 Fargo Ave ... Elk Grove Village IL 60007 *Web:* www.meijicorp.com	847-364-9333		57
Meisel 2019 McKenzie Dr ... Carrollton TX 75006 *TF:* 800-527-5186 ■ *Web:* www.meisel.com	214-688-4950	688-4950	588
Meisner & Associates Pc 30200 Telegraph Rd Ste 467 ... Bingham Farms MI 48025 *TF:* 800-470-4433 ■ *Web:* meisner-law.com	248-644-4433		428
Meisner Electric Inc 220 NE First St ... Delray Beach FL 33444 *Web:* www.mei.cc	561-278-8362	278-8397	189-4
Meissner Tierney Fisher & Nichols S.C 111 E Kilbourn Avc 19th Fl ... Milwaukee WI 53202 *Web:* www.mtfn.com	414-273-1300		428
Meister Media Worldwide 37733 Euclid Ave ... Willoughby OH 44094 *TF Orders:* 800-572-7740 ■ *Web:* www.meistermedia.com	440-942-2000	942-0662	637-9
Meister Seelig & Fein LLP 125 Park Ave 7th Fl ... New York NY 10017 *Web:* www.meisterseelig.com	212-655-3500		445
Mej Personal Business Services Inc 245 E 116th St ... New York NY 10029 *TF:* 866-418-3836 ■ *Web:* www.mejpbs.com	212-426-6017		113
Mejia Technologies Ltd 2189 Spinningwheel Ln ... Cincinnati OH 45244 *Web:* www.mejiatechnologies.com	513-231-1920		809
Mekanika Inc 3998 FAU Blvd Ste 210 ... Boca Raton FL 33431 *Web:* www.mekanika.com	561-210-5671		177
Mekanism Inc 640 Second St Fl 3 ... San Francisco CA 94107 *TF:* 800-230-2050 ■ *Web:* www.mekanism.com	415-908-4000		7
Meketa Investment Group 100 Lowder Brook Dr Ste 1100 ... Westwood MA 02090 *Web:* www.meketagroup.com	781-471-3500		796
Mekong 6004 W Broad St ... Richmond VA 23230 *Web:* mekongisforbeerlovers.com	804-288-8929		671
Mekong 125 Columbia St NW ... Olympia WA 98501	360-352-9620		671
Mekong 637 Somerset St W ... Ottawa ON K1R5K3 *Web:* www.mekong.ca	613-237-7717		671
Mel Bay Publications Inc 1734 Gilsinn Ln ... Fenton MO 63026 *TF:* 800-863-5229 ■ *Web:* www.melbay.com	636-257-3970	257-5062	637-2
Mel Fisher Maritime Museum 200 Greene St ... Key West FL 33040 *TF:* 800-434-1399 ■ *Web:* www.melfisher.org	305-294-2633		520
Mel Foster Company Inc 7566 Market Pl Dr ... Eden Prairie MN 55344 *Web:* melfoster.com	952-941-9790		360-3
Mel Rapton Inc 3630 Fulton Ave ... Sacramento CA 95821 *TF:* 800-529-3053 ■ *Web:* www.melraptonhonda.com	916-482-5400		516
Mel Trotter Ministries 363 E State St ... Belding MI 48809 *Web:* meltrotter.org	616-794-9844		48-20
Mel Wheeler Inc 3934 Electric Rd Ste 107 ... Roanoke VA 24018 *Web:* melwheelerinc.com	540-774-9200		643
Melaleuca Inc 3910 S Yellowstone Hwy ... Idaho Falls ID 83402 **Fax Area Code:* 888 ■ *TF Sales:* 800-282-3000 ■ *Web:* www.melaleuca.com	208-522-0700	528-2090*	366
Melanson Company Inc, The 353 W St ... Keene NH 03431 *Web:* www.melanson.com	603-352-4232		697
Melanson Heath & Company PC 102 Perimeter Rd ... Nashua NH 03063 *Web:* melansonheath.com	603-882-1111		2
Melbourne Greyhound Park 1100 N Wickham Rd ... Melbourne FL 32935 *Web:* www.mgpark.com	321-259-9800		642
Melbourne Regional Chamber of East Central Florida 1005 E Strawbridge Ave ... Melbourne FL 32901 *TF:* 800-288-2020 ■ *Web:* melbourneregionalchamber.com	321-724-5400	725-2093	206
Mele & Co 2007 Beechgrove Pl ... Utica NY 13501 *TF:* 800-635-6353 ■ *Web:* www.melejewelrybox.com	315-733-4600	733-3183	200
MELE Associates Inc 11 Taft Court Ste 101 ... Rockville MD 20850 *Web:* www.meleassociates.com	240-453-6990		463
Mele Printing Company LLC 619 N Tyler St ... Covington LA 70433 *TF:* 800-463-3339 ■ *Web:* www.meleprinting.com	985-893-9522		113
Melges Boatworks Inc PO Box 1 ... Zenda WI 53195 *Web:* www.melges.com	262-275-1110	275-8012	90
Melick-Tully & Assoc PC 117 Canal Rd ... South Bound Brook NJ 08880 *Web:* melick-tully.com	732-356-3400		261
Meli-Melo 362 Greenwich Ave ... Greenwich CT 06830 *Web:* melimelogreenwich.com	203-629-6153		671
Melin Tool Co 5565 Venture Dr Unit C ... Cleveland OH 44130 **Fax Area Code:* 800 ■ *TF:* 800-521-1078 ■ *Web:* www.endmill.com	216-362-4230	521-1558*	493
Melissa DATA Corp 22382 Avenida Empresa ... Rancho Santa Margarita CA 92688 *Web:* www.melissadata.com	949-858-3000		225
Melissa's/World Variety Produce Inc 5325 S Soto St ... Vernon CA 90058 *TF:* 800-588-0151 ■ *Web:* www.melissas.com	800-588-0151		297-7
Melisse 1104 Wilshire Blvd ... Santa Monica CA 90401 *Web:* www.melisse.com	310-395-0881		671
Melitta Canada Inc 50 Ronson Dr Unit 150 ... Toronto ON M9W1B3 *TF:* 800-565-4882 ■ *Web:* www.melitta.ca	800-565-4882		296-7
Melitta USA Inc 13925 58th St N ... Clearwater FL 33760 *Web:* www.melitta.com	727-535-2111		548
Mel-Kay Electric Company Inc 1511 N Garvin St ... Evansville IN 47711 *Web:* www.mel-kayelectric.com	812-423-1128		787
Mellano & Co 766 Wall St ... Los Angeles CA 90014 *TF:* 888-635-5266 ■ *Web:* www.mellano.com	213-622-0796		292
Mellette County S First & McKinley St PO Box 257 ... White River SD 57579 *Web:* ujs.sd.gov/County_Information/mellette.aspx	605-259-3230	259-3030	338
Melling Tool Co 2620 Saradan St PO Box 1188 ... Jackson MI 49204 *Web:* www.melling.com	517-787-8172	787-5304	60
MeLLmo Inc 120 S Sierra Ave ... Solana Beach CA 92075 *TF:* 800-642-7676 ■ *Web:* www.roambi.com	858-847-3272		174
Mellon Capital Management Corp 50 Fremont St Ste 3900 ... San Francisco CA 94105 *Web:* www.mcm.com	415-546-6056	777-5699	401
Mellor Engineering Inc 887 N 100 E Ste 1 ... Lehi UT 84043 *Web:* mellorengineering.com	801-768-0658		261
Mellott Manufacturing Co 13156 Long Ln ... Mercersburg PA 17236 *Web:* www.mellottmfg.com	717-369-3125		454
Melloul-Blamey Construction Ltd 55 Commerce Ctr ... Greenville SC 29615 *Web:* www.melloul.com	864-627-0302	627-0804	780
Melloy Nissan 7707 Lomas Blvd NE ... Albuquerque NM 87110 *Web:* www.melloynissan.com	505-265-8721		57
Mellwood Arts & Entertainment Ctr 1860 Mellwood Ave ... Louisville KY 40206 *Web:* www.mellwoodartcenter.com	502-895-3650		50-6
Melnor Inc 109 Tyson Dr ... Winchester VA 22603 **Fax Area Code:* 888 ■ *TF:* 877-283-0697 ■ *Web:* www.melnor.com	540-722-5600	411-2500*	429
Meloon Foundries Inc 1841 Lemoyne Ave ... Syracuse NY 13208 *Web:* www.meloon.com	315-454-3231		492
Melo-Tone Vending Inc 130 Broadway ... Somerville MA 02145 *Web:* melo-tone-vending-inc.placestars.com	617-666-4900		55
Melrath Gasket 1500 John F Kennedy Blvd Ste 200 ... Philadelphia PA 19102	215-223-6000		326
Melrose Cafe & Bar 730 17th Ave SW ... Calgary AB T2S0B7 *Web:* www.melrosecalgary.com	403-228-3566		671
Melrose Chamber of Commerce 1 W Foster St ... Melrose MA 02176 *TF:* 800-272-3900 ■ *Web:* www.melrosechamber.org	781-665-3033		139
Melrose Hotel Washington DC, The 2430 Pennsylvania Ave NW ... Washington DC 20037 *TF:* 800-635-7673 ■ *Web:* www.melrosehoteldc.com	202-955-6400		378
Melrose Public Library 69 W Emerson St ... Melrose MA 02176 *TF:* 800-733-2767 ■ *Web:* www.melrosepubliclibrary.org	781-665-2313		434-3

Listing	City	State	ZIP	Phone	Fax	Class
Melrose-Wakefield Hospital 585 Lebanon St *Web:* www.hallmarkhealth.org	Melrose	MA	02176	781-979-3000		374-3
Melting Pot of Ahwatukee, The 3626 E Ray Rd *Web:* www.meltingpot.com	Phoenix	AZ	85044	480-704-9206	704-2973	671
Melting Pot of Annapolis, The 2348 Solomons Island Rd *TF:* 800-783-0867 ■ *Web:* www.meltingpot.com	Annapolis	MD	21401	410-266-8004	266-8431	671
Melting Pot of Arlington, The 1110 N Glebe Rd *Web:* www.meltingpot.com	Arlington	VA	22201	703-243-4490	243-4547	671
Melting Pot of Charlotte, The 901 S Kings Dr Ste 140B *TF:* 800-783-0867 ■ *Web:* www.meltingpot.com	Charlotte	NC	28204	704-334-4400	334-0535	671
Melting Pot of Columbia, The 1410 Colonial Life Blvd *TF:* 800-783-0867 ■ *Web:* www.meltingpot.com	Columbia	SC	29210	803-731-8500	731-8569	671
Melting Pot of Greensboro, The 2045 S Hurstbourne Pkwy *Web:* www.meltingpot.com	Louisville	NC	27408	502-491-3125		671
Melting Pot of Indianapolis, The 5650 E 86th St Ste A *TF:* 800-783-0867 ■ *Web:* www.meltingpot.com	Indianapolis	IN	46250	317-841-3601	841-1207	671
Melting Pot of Miami, The 11520 Sunset Dr *Web:* www.meltingpot.com	Miami	FL	33173	305-279-8816	598-8931	671
Melting Pot of Pensacola, The 418 Gregory St Ste 500 *TF:* 800-783-0867 ■ *Web:* www.meltingpot.com	Pensacola	FL	32502	850-438-4030	433-7664	671
Melting Pot of Raleigh, The 3100 Wake Forest Rd *Web:* www.meltingpot.com	Raleigh	NC	27609	919-878-0477	878-0815	671
Melting Pot of Richmond, The 9704 Gayton Rd *Web:* www.meltingpot.com	Richmond	VA	23233	804-741-3120	741-2781	671
Melting Pot of San Antonio, The 14855 Blanco Rd Ste 110 *TF:* 800-783-0867 ■ *Web:* www.meltingpot.com	San Antonio	TX	78216	210-479-6358	479-8106	671
Melting Pot of Tampa, The 13164 N Dale Mabry Hwy *TF:* 800-783-0867 ■ *Web:* www.meltingpot.com	Tampa	FL	33618	813-962-6936	963-0125	671
Melting Pot of Virginia Beach, The 1564 Laskin Rd *Web:* www.meltingpot.com	Virginia Beach	VA	23451	757-425-3463		671
Melting Pot Restaurants Inc 8810 Twin Lakes Blvd *TF:* 800-783-0867 ■ *Web:* www.meltingpot.com	Tampa	FL	33614	813-881-0055		670
Melting Pot ST Petersburg, The 2221 Fourth St N *Web:* www.meltingpot.com	Saint Petersburg	FL	33704	727-895-6358	894-7383	671
Melting Pot, The 2727 N Monroe St *Web:* www.meltingpot.com	Tallahassee	FL	32303	850-386-7440		671
Melting Pot, The 5001 N Kings Hwy *Web:* www.meltingpot.com	Myrtle Beach	SC	29577	843-692-9003	692-9004	671
Melting Pot, The 166 Second Ave N *Web:* www.meltingpot.com	Nashville	TN	37201	615-742-4970	726-6328	671
Melting Pot, The 1601 Concord Pike Ste 43-47 Independence Mall *TF:* 800-783-0867 ■ *Web:* www.meltingpot.com	Wilmington	DE	19803	302-652-6358	652-8101	671
Melting Pot, The 5294 Corporate Blvd *Web:* www.meltingpot.com	Baton Rouge	LA	70808	225-928-5677	928-5622	671
Melting Pot, The 80 S Ninth St *Web:* www.meltingpot.com	Minneapolis	MN	55402	612-338-9900	312-2855	671
Melting Pot, The 2828 Wolfcreek Pkwy *Web:* www.meltingpot.com	Memphis	TN	38133	901-380-9500		671
Melting Pot, The 2121 Pacific Ave *Web:* www.meltingpot.com	Tacoma	WA	98402	253-535-3939		671
Meltmedia 1255 W Rio Salado Pkwy Ste 209 *Web:* www.meltmedia.com	Tempe	AZ	85281	602-340-9440		196
Melton Machine & Control Co 6350 Bluff Rd *Web:* www.meltonmachine.com	Washington	MO	63090	636-239-7765		811
Melton Truck Lines Inc 808 N 161 E Ave *TF General:* 800-635-8669 ■ *Web:* www.meltontruck.com	Tulsa	OK	74116	918-234-8000	270-9401	780
Meltzer Lippe Goldstein & Schissel LLP 190 Willis Ave *Web:* www.mlg.com	Mineola	NY	11501	516-747-0300		428
Melvindale-Northern Allen Park Public Schools 18530 Prospect St *Web:* www.melnapschools.com	Melvindale	MI	48122	313-389-3300	389-3312	685
Melvyn's 200 W Ramon Rd *Web:* www.inglesideinn.com	Palm Springs	CA	92264	760-325-2323		671
Melwood Horticultural Training Center In 5606 Dower House Rd *Web:* www.melwood.org	Upper Marlboro	MD	20772	301-599-8000		260
MEMA (Motor & Equipment Manufacturers Assn) 10 Laboratory Dr	Research Triangle Park	NC	27709	919-549-4800		49-21
Member One Federal Credit Union 202 Fourth NE *Web:* memberonefcu.com	Roanoke	VA	24016	540-982-8811		219
MemberPlanet Inc 23224 Crenshaw Blvd *Web:* www.memberplanet.com	Torrance	CA	94065	916-445-1254		387
Members Trust Co 14025 Riveredge Dr Ste 280 *TF:* 888-727-9191 ■ *Web:* www.memberstrust.com	Tampa	FL	33637	813-631-9191		70
MembersFirst Inc 321 Commonwealth Rd *TF:* 800-528-4290 ■ *Web:* www.membersfirst.com	Wayland	MA	01778	508-653-3399		177
Membrane Technology & Research Inc 1360 Willow Rd Ste 103 *Web:* www.mtrinc.com	Menlo Park	CA	94025	650-328-2228	328-6580	668
MEMdata LLC 1601 Sebesta *Web:* www.memdata.com	College Station	TX	77845	979-695-1950		194
Memering Motorplex Inc 1949 Hart St *Web:* www.memeringmotorplex.com	Vincennes	IN	47591	812-882-5367		57
Memocast 1801 Bush St *Web:* www.memocast.com	San Francisco	CA	94109	415-673-5122		514
Memorial Art Gallery of the University of Rochester 500 University Ave *Web:* www.mag.rochester.edu	Rochester	NY	14607	585-276-8900		520
Memorial Blood Centers (MBC) 737 Pelham Blvd *TF Cust Svc:* 888-448-3253 ■ *Web:* www.mbc.org	Saint Paul	MN	55114	651-332-7000	332-7001	89
Memorial City Mall 303 Memorial City *Web:* memorialcity.com	Houston	TX	77024	713-464-8640	464-7845	460
Memorial Hall Library 2 N Main St *Web:* www.mhl.org	Andover	MA	01810	978-623-8400		434-3
Memorial Health Partners 4700 Waters Ave *TF:* 800-537-0690 ■ *Web:* www.memorialhealth.com	Savannah	GA	31404	912-350-8000	350-5976	391-3
Memorial Health Services Inc 7677 Center Ave *Web:* www.memorialcare.org	Huntington Beach	CA	92647	657-241-3680		353
Memorial Health University Medical Ctr 4700 Waters Ave *Web:* www.memorialhealth.com	Savannah	GA	31404	912-350-8000		374-3
Memorial Healthcare Ctr 826 W King St *TF:* 800-206-8706 ■ *Web:* www.memorialhealthcare.org	Owosso	MI	48867	989-723-5211		374-3
Memorial Hermann - Texas Medical Ctr 6411 Fannin St *Web:* www.memorialhermann.org	Houston	TX	77030	713-704-4000		374-3
Memorial Hermann Health Network Providers Inc 7737 SW Fwy Ste C98 *Web:* mhmd.memorialhermann.org	Houston	TX	77074	713-338-6464		225
Memorial Hermann Healthcare System 7600 Beechnut St *TF:* 000-777-6330 ■ *Web:* www.memorialhermann.org	Houston	TX	77074	713-456-4280		353
Memorial Hermann Katy Hospital 23900 Katy Fwy *Web:* memorialhermann.org/locations	Katy	TX	77494	281-644-7000		374-3
Memorial Hermann Memorial City Hospital 921 Gessner Rd **Fax Area Code:* 281 ■ *TF:* 800-526-2121 ■ *Web:* www.memorialhermann.org	Houston	TX	77024	713-242-3000	359-3340*	374-3
Memorial Hermann Prevention & Recovery Ctr (MHPARC) 3043 Gessner *TF:* 877-464-7272 ■ *Web:* parc.memorialhermann.org	Houston	TX	77080	713-939-7272	939-7272	374-5
Memorial Hermann Southwest Hospital 7600 Beechnut St *Web:* www.memorialhermann.org	Houston	TX	77074	713-456-5000		374-3
Memorial Hospital 4500 Memorial Dr *Web:* www.memhosp.com	Belleville	IL	62226	618-233-7750		374-3
Memorial Hospital 2525 Desales Ave *Web:* www.memorial.org	Chattanooga	TN	37404	423-495-2525		374-3
Memorial Hospital 325 S Belmont St *TF:* 800-436-4326 ■ *Web:* www.mhyork.org	York	PA	17405	717-843-8623	849-5329	374-3
Memorial Hospital 320 Hospital Dr *TF:* 800-932-0262 ■ *Web:* www.martinsvillehospital.com	Martinsville	VA	24115	276-666-7200	666-7600	374-3
Memorial Hospital & Health Care Ctr 800 W Ninth St *TF:* 800-852-7279 ■ *Web:* www.mhhcc.org	Jasper	IN	47546	812-996-2345		374-3
Memorial Hospital at Gulfport 4500 13th St *Web:* www.gulfportmemorial.com	Gulfport	MS	39501	228-867-4000		374-3
Memorial Hospital of Adel 706 N Parrish Ave	Adel	GA	31620	229-896-8000	896-8001	374-3
Memorial Hospital of Carbondale 405 W Jackson St *TF:* 800-457-1393 ■ *Web:* www.sih.net	Carbondale	IL	62902	618-549-0721	529-0449	374-3
Memorial Hospital of Rhode Island (MHRI) 111 Brewster St *TF:* 800-647-4362 ■ *Web:* www.mhri.org	Pawtucket	RI	02860	401-729-2000		374-3
Memorial Hospital of Salem County 310 Woodstown Rd *TF:* 800-753-3779 ■ *Web:* www.mhschealth.com	Salem	NJ	08079	856-935-1000		374-3
Memorial Hospital of Sweetwater County 1200 College Dr *TF General:* 866-571-0944 ■ *Web:* www.sweetwatermemorial.com	Rock Springs	WY	82901	307-362-3711		374-3
Memorial Hospital of Tampa 2901 W Swann Ave *Web:* www.memorialhospitaltampa.com	Tampa	FL	33609	813-873-6400		374-3
Memorial Hospital Pembroke (MHP) 7800 Sheridan St *Web:* www.mhs.net/locations/memorial-pembroke	Pembroke Pines	FL	33024	954-962-9650		374-3
Memorial Hospital West 703 N Flamingo Rd *Web:* www.mhs.net/locations/memorial-west	Pembroke Pines	FL	33028	954-436-5000		374-3
Memorial Investments Corp 110 The American Rd	Morris Plains	NJ	07950	973-538-2808		690
Memorial Lake State Park 18 Boundary Rd *Web:* www.dcnr.state.pa.us	Grantville	PA	17028	717-865-6470		565
Memorial Medical Ctr 1086 Franklin St *TF:* 800-441-2555 ■ *Web:* www.conemaugh.org	Johnstown	PA	15905	814-534-9000		374-3
Memorial Medical Ctr 2450 S Telshor Blvd *Web:* www.mmclc.org	Las Cruces	NM	88011	575-522-8641		374-3
Memorial Medical Ctr 701 N First St *Web:* www.memorialmedical.com	Springfield	IL	62781	217-788-3000		374-3
Memorial Medical Ctr (MMC) 1700 Coffee Rd *TF:* 800-477-2258 ■ *Web:* www.memorialmedicalcenter.org	Modesto	CA	95355	209-526-4500		374-3
Memorial Medical Ctr 1615 Maple Ln *TF:* 888-868-9292 ■ *Web:* www.ashlandmmc.com	Ashland	WI	54806	715-685-5500	685-7504	374-3
Memorial MRI & Diagnostic 1241 Campbell Rd *Web:* www.memorialdiagnostic.com	Houston	TX	77055	713-461-3399		383
Memorial North Park Hospital 2051 Hamill Rd *Web:* www.memorial.org	Hixson	TN	37343	423-495-7100		374-3

Name / Address	City	State	Zip	Phone	Fax	Class
Memorial Regional Hospital 3501 Johnson St *Web:* www.mhs.net/locations/memorial-regional	Hollywood	FL	33021	954-987-2000		374-3
Memorial Sloan-Kettering Cancer Ctr 1275 York Ave. *TF:* 800-525-2225 ■ *Web:* www.mskcc.org	New York	NY	10065	212-639-2000		374-7
Memphis 201 N Broadway *Web:* memphiscafe.com	Santa Ana	CA	92701	714-564-1064		671
Memphis Area Transit Authority (MATA) 1370 Levee Rd *Web:* www.matatransit.com	Memphis	TN	38108	901-722-7100	722-7123	468
Memphis Botanic Garden 750 Cherry Rd *Web:* www.memphisbotanicgarden.com	Memphis	TN	38117	901-636-4100	682-1561	97
Memphis Brooks Museum of Art 1934 Poplar Ave Overton Pk. *Web:* www.brooksmuseum.org	Memphis	TN	38104	901-544-6200	725-4071	520
Memphis Business Journal 80 Monroe Ave Ste 600 *Web:* www.bizjournals.com	Memphis	TN	38103	901-523-1000	526-5240	457-5
Memphis City Board of Education 2597 Avery Ave. *Web:* www.memphis.edu/cepr	Memphis	TN	38112	901-416-5300	416-5578	685
Memphis City Hall 125 N Main St *Web:* www.cityofmemphis.org	Memphis	TN	38103	901-576-6500		337
Memphis College of Art 1930 Poplar Ave *TF:* 800-727-1088 ■ *Web:* www.mca.edu	Memphis	TN	38104	901-272-5100	272-5158	164
Memphis Convention & Visitors Bureau 47 Union Ave *TF:* 888-633-9099 ■ *Web:* www.memphistravel.com	Memphis	TN	38103	901-543-5300	543-5350	206
Memphis Cook Convention Ctr 3205 Elvis Presley Blvd *Web:* www.memphistravel.com	Memphis	TN	38116	901-543-5333		205
Memphis Cotton Exchange, The 65 Union Ave Mezzanine. *Web:* www.memphiscottonmuseum.org	Memphis	TN	38103	901-531-7826		520
Memphis Flyer 460 Tennessee St *TF:* 877-292-3804 ■ *Web:* www.memphisflyer.com	Memphis	TN	38103	901-521-9000	521-0129	532-5
Memphis Grizzlies FedExForum 191 Beale St. *Web:* www.nba.com/grizzlies	Memphis	TN	38103	901-205-1234	205-1235	714-1
Memphis International Airport 2491 Winchester Rd Ste 113 *Web:* www.flymemphis.com	Memphis	TN	38116	901-922-8000	922-8099	27
Memphis Light Gas & Water (MLGW) 220 S Main St. *Web:* www.mlgw.com	Memphis	TN	38103	901-528-4011		787
Memphis Magazine 460 Tennessee St Ste 200. *TF:* 800-288-9999 ■ *Web:* www.memphismagazine.com	Memphis	TN	38103	901-521-9000	521-0129	457-22
Memphis National Cemetery 3568 Townes Ave *Web:* www.cem.va.gov	Memphis	TN	38122	901-386-8311	382-0750	136
Memphis Pink Palace Museum 3050 Central Ave *TF:* 800-979-3370 ■ *Web:* www.memphismuseums.org	Memphis	TN	38111	901-636-2362	320-6391	520
Memphis Rock 'n' Soul Museum 191 Beale St. *Web:* www.memphisrocknsoul.org	Memphis	TN	38103	901-205-2533	205-2534	520
Memphis Symphony Orchestra 585 S Mendenhall Rd *Web:* www.memphissymphony.org	Memphis	TN	38117	901-537-2525	537-2550	573-3
Memphis Theological Seminary 168 E Pkwy S *Web:* www.memphisseminary.edu	Memphis	TN	38104	901-458-8232	452-4051	167-3
Memphis Zoo 2000 Prentiss Pl *Web:* www.memphiszoo.org	Memphis	TN	38112	901-333-6500	333-6501	823
Memry Corp 3 Berkshire Blvd *TF:* 866-466-3679 ■ *Web:* www.memry.com	Bethel	CT	06801	203-739-1100	798-6606	485
MEMS Optical Inc 205 Import Cir. *Web:* www.memsoptical.com	Huntsville	AL	35806	256-859-1886		542
Memsic Inc 1 Tech Dr Ste 325. *Web:* www.memsic.com	Andover	MA	01810	978-738-0900		696
MEMStaff Inc 8 Pine St. *Web:* www.memstaff.com	Newburyport	MA	01950	617-996-9263		226
Men Against Destruction Defending Against Drugs & Social Disorder Inc (MAD DADS) 3026 Fourth Ave S *Web:* www.maddads.com	Minneapolis	MN	55408	612-822-0802	253-0663	48-6
Men's Fitness Magazine 1 Pk Ave 3rd Fl *Web:* www.mensfitness.com	New York	NY	10016	212-223-8811		457-13
Men's Health Magazine 400 S Tenth St *TF:* 800-666-2303 ■ *Web:* www.menshealth.com	Emmaus	PA	18098	610-967-5171		457-13
Men's Journal LLC 1290 Ave of the Americas 2nd Fl *TF:* 800-677-6367 ■ *Web:* www.mensjournal.com	New York	NY	10104	800-677-6367		457-11
Men's Wearhouse Inc 6380 Rogerdale Rd. *NYSE: MW* ■ *TF:* 877-986-9669 ■ *Web:* www.menswearhouse.com	Houston	TX	77072	281-776-7000	776-7038	157-3
Mena Hospital Commission 311 Morrow St N *TF:* 800-394-6185 ■ *Web:* www.menaregional.com	Mena	AR	71953	479-394-2534		363
Mena Tours and Travel Inc 5209 N Clark St *Web:* www.mena.travel	Chicago	IL	60640	733-275-2125		377
Menara 41 E Gish Rd *Web:* menara41.com	San Jose	CA	95112	408-453-1983		671
Menard Correctional Ctr 711 Kaskaskia St	Menard	IL	62259	618-826-5071		213
Menard County 102 S Seventh St PO Box 465 *Web:* www.menardcountyil.com	Petersburg	IL	62675	217-632-3201		338
Menard County Texas PO Box 1038 *Web:* co.menard.tx.us	Menard	TX	76859	325-396-4682	396-2047	338
Menard Electric Co-op 14300 State Hwy 97 PO Box 200 *TF:* 800-872-1203 ■ *Web:* www.menard.com	Petersburg	IL	62675	217-632-7746		245
Menard Inc 5101 Menard Dr *Web:* www.menards.com	Eau Claire	WI	54703	715-876-5911	876-2868	364
Menardi 1 Maxwell Dr *TF:* 800-321-3218 ■ *Web:* menardifilters.com	Trenton	SC	29847	803-663-6551	663-4029	67
Menas Realty Co 4990 Mission Blvd *Web:* www.menas.com	San Diego	CA	92109	619-276-5169		652
Menasha Corp 1645 Bergstrom Rd *TF:* 800-558-5073 ■ *Web:* www.menasha.com	Neenah	WI	54956	920-751-1000		100
Menasha Packaging Co 1645 Bergstrom Rd. *TF:* 800-558-5073 ■ *Web:* www.menasha.com	Neenah	WI	54956	920-751-1000	751-1075	100
Menasha Public Library 440 First St. *Web:* www.menashalibrary.org	Menasha	WI	54952	920-967-3690	967-5159	434-3
Menasha Rand Group 3 Ethel Rd Ste 301	Edison	NJ	08817	732-287-2525		195
Menasha Utilities 321 Milwaukee St PO Box 340 *Web:* www.menashautilities.com	Menasha	WI	54952	920-967-3400	967-3441	787
MENC: NA for Music Education 1806 Robert Fulton Dr *TF:* 800-336-3768 ■ *Web:* nafme.org	Reston	VA	20191	703-860-4000	860-1531	49-5
Menches Tool & Die Inc 30995 San Benito St. *TF:* 877-592-2328 ■ *Web:* www.menches.com	Hayward	CA	94544	510-476-1160		697
Mended Hearts Inc, The 8150 N Central Expy M2075. *TF:* 888-432-7899 ■ *Web:* www.mendedhearts.org	Dallas	TX	75206	214-296-9252	295-9552	48-17
Mendenhall Plantation 603 W Main St PO Box 512 *Web:* www.mendenhallhomeplace.com	Jamestown	NC	27282	336-454-3819		50-3
Mendes & Mount LLP 750 Seventh Ave *Web:* www.mendes.com	New York	NY	10019	212-261-8000		428
Mendocino Brewing Co 455 Kunzler Ranch Rd *Web:* www.mendobrew.com	Ukiah	CA	95482	707-462-1697	462-1699	102
Mendocino Coast Botanical Gardens 18220 N Hwy 1 *Web:* www.gardenbythesea.org	Fort Bragg	CA	95437	707-964-4352	964-3114	97
Mendocino Coast Chamber of Commerce 217 S Main St PO Box 1141 *TF:* 800-382-7244 ■ *Web:* www.mendocinocoast.com	Fort Bragg	CA	95437	707-961-6300	964-2056	139
Mendocino Coast District Hospital 700 River Dr *Web:* www.mcdh.org	Fort Bragg	CA	95437	707-961-1234		374-3
Mendocino College 1000 Hensley Creek Rd **Fax:* Admissions ■ *Web:* www.mendocino.edu	Ukiah	CA	95482	707-468-3000	468-3430*	162
Mendocino County 501 Low Gap Rd Rm 1020. *Web:* www.mendocinocounty.org	Ukiah	CA	95482	707-463-4376	463-4257	338
Mendocino County Library 105 N Main St. *Web:* www.mendocinocounty.org	Ukiah	CA	95482	707-234-2874	463-5472	434-3
Mendocino Headlands State Park 1416 Ninth St *Web:* www.parks.ca.gov/default.asp?page_id=442	Sacramento	CA	95814	707-937-5804		565
Mendocino Hotel & Garden Suites 45080 Main St *Web:* www.mendocinohotel.com	Mendocino	CA	95460	707-937-0511		379
Mendocino Redwood Company LLC 850 Kunzler Ranch Rd *TF:* 800-547-9520 ■ *Web:* www.hrcllc.com	Ukiah	CA	95482	707-463-5110		752
Mendocino Wine Co 501 PaRducci Rd. *TF:* 800-362-9463 ■ *Web:* www.mendocinowineco.com	Ukiah	CA	95482	707-463-5350	462-7260	80-3
Mendocino Woodlands State Park 39350 Little Lake Rd. *Web:* www.parks.ca.gov	Mendocino	CA	95460	707-937-5755		565
Mendon Truck Leasing & Rental 8215 Foster Ave *TF:* 800-724-9886 ■ *Web:* www.mendonleasing.com	Brooklyn	NY	11236	718-209-9886		778
Mendota Mental Health Institute 301 Troy Dr. *TF:* 800-323-8942 ■ *Web:* www.dhs.wisconsin.gov	Madison	WI	53704	608-301-1000	301-1358	374-5
Mendoza Ribas Farinas & Assoc 6265 Executive Blvd	Rockville	MD	20852	301-468-8882		261
Me-N-Ed's-Bullard/West 1731 W Bullard Ave Ste 101. *Web:* www.meneds.com	Fresno	CA	93711	559-431-7331		670
Menendez Robert (Sen D - NJ) 528 Hart Bldg *Web:* menendez.senate.gov	Washington	DC	20510	202-224-4744	228-2197	342-2
Meng Grace (Rep D - NY) 1317 Longworth Bldg. *Web:* meng.house.gov	Washington	DC	20515	202-225-2601	225-1589	342-2
Mengel Metzger Barr & Company LLP 100 Chestnut St Ste 1200. *Web:* www.mengelmetzgerbarr.com	Rochester	NY	14604	585-423-1860		734
Menger Hotel 204 Alamo Plaza *TF:* 800-345-9285 ■ *Web:* www.mengerhotel.com	San Antonio	TX	78205	210-223-4361	228-0022	379
Menifee County Clerk PO Box 123 *TF:* 800-368-8683 ■ *Web:* www.menifeecountyclerk.com	Frenchburg	KY	40322	606-768-3512	768-6738	338
Menifee Valley Chamber of Commerce 29683 New Hub Dr Ste C *Web:* www.menifeevalleychamber.com	Menifee	CA	92586	951-672-1991		139
Menil Collection 1515 Sul Ross St. *Web:* www.menil.org	Houston	TX	77006	713-525-9400	525-9444	520
Menke Marking Devices 13253 Alondra Blvd *TF:* 800-231-6023 ■ *Web:* www.menkemarking.com	Santa Fe Springs	CA	90670	562-921-1380	921-1184	467
Menk-USA LLC 2207 Enterprise Dr *Web:* www.menk-usa.com	Sterling	IL	61081	815-626-9730		567
Menlo College 1000 El Camino Real. *TF:* 800-556-3656 ■ *Web:* www.menlo.edu	Atherton	CA	94027	650-543-3753	543-4496	166
Menlo Park Chamber of Commerce 1100 Merrill St. *TF:* 800-660-4287 ■ *Web:* www.menloparkchamber.com	Menlo Park	CA	94025	650-325-2818	325-0920	139
Menlo Park Public Library 800 Alma St *Web:* menlopark.org/389/Library	Menlo Park	CA	94025	650-330-2500	327-7030	434-3
Menlo Scientific Ltd 5161 Rain Cloud Dr *Web:* www.menloscientific.com	Richmond	CA	94803	510-758-9014		196
Menlo Ventures 2884 Sand Hill Rd Ste 100 *Web:* www.menlovc.com	Menlo Park	CA	94025	650-854-8540	854-7059	792
Mennel Milling Co 128 W Crocker St. *TF:* 800-688-8151 ■ *Web:* www.mennel.com	Fostoria	OH	44830	419-435-8151	436-5150	296-23

Phone Fax Class

Mennello Museum of American Folk Art
900 E Princeton St .... Orlando FL 32803 407-246-4278 246-4329 520
Web: www.mennellomuseum.com

Mennen Medical Corp
950 Industrial Hwy .... SouthHampton PA 18966 215-259-1020 250
Web: www.mennenmedical.com

Mennie's Machine Co (MMC)
Rt 71 & Mennie Dr PO Box 110 .... Mark IL 61340 815-339-2226 339-6550 621
Web: www.mennies.com

Menninger Clinic 12301 Main St .... Houston TX 77035 713-275-5000 275-5107 374-5
TF: 800-351-9058 ■ *Web:* www.menningerclinic.com

Menno Village 2075 Scotland Ave .... Chambersburg PA 17201 717-262-2373 672
Web: www.mennohaven.org

Mennonite Brethren Biblical Seminary
4824 E Butler Ave .... Fresno CA 93727 559-453-2000 167-3
TF: 800-251-6227 ■
Web: www.fresno.edu/programs-majors/biblical-seminary

Mennonite Central Committee (MCC)
21 S 12th St PO Box 500 .... Akron PA 17501 717-859-1151 859-2171 48-5
TF: 888-563-4676 ■ *Web:* www.mcc.org

Mennonite Disaster Service (MDS)
583 Airport Rd .... Lititz PA 17543 717-735-3536 48-5
TF: 800-241-8111 ■ *Web:* www.mds.mennonite.net

Mennonite Economic Development Associates of Canada
155 Frobisher Dr Ste I-106 .... Waterloo ON N2V2E1 519-725-1633 393
Web: www.meda.org

Mennonite Friendship Communities
600 W Blanchard Rd .... South Hutchinson KS 67505 620-663-7175 672
TF: 800-897-6991 ■ *Web:* www.mennofriend.com

Mennonite Home 1520 Harrisburg Pk .... Lancaster PA 17601 717-393-1301 48-15
Web: www.mennonitehome.org

Mennonite Savings & Credit Union (Ontario) Ltd
1265 Strasburg Rd .... Kitchener ON N2R1S6 519-746-1010 403
Web: kitchenerhills.com

Mennonite Village 5353 Columbus St SE .... Albany OR 97322 541-928-7232 917-1399 672
TF: 800-211-2713 ■ *Web:* www.mennonitevillage.org

Menominee County PO Box 279 .... Keshena WI 54135 715-799-3311 338
Web: www.wisconline.com/counties/menominee

Menominee County 839 Tenth Ave .... Menominee MI 49858 906-863-9968 863-8839 338
Web: www.menomineecounty.com

Menominee Hotel PO Box 760 .... Keshena WI 54135 715-799-3600 378
TF: 800-343-7778 ■ *Web:* www.menomineecasinoresort.com

Menominee Tribal Enterprises PO Box 10 .... Neopit WI 54150 715-756-2311 683
Web: www.mtewood.com

Menomonee Falls Chamber of Commerce
N91 W17271 .... Menomonee Falls WI 53051 262-251-2430 139
Web: www.fallschamber.com

Menomonee Falls Public Library
W156 N8436 Pilgrim Rd .... Menomonee Falls WI 53051 262-532-8900 532-8939 434-3
Web: www.menomoneefallslibrary.org

Menomonie Public Library
600 Wolske Bay Rd .... Menomonie WI 54751 715-232-2164 232-2324 434-3
Web: www.menomonielibrary.org

Menorah Medical Ctr
5721 W 119th St .... Overland Park KS 66209 913-498-6000 374-3
TF: 800-766-3777 ■ *Web:* www.menorahmedicalcenter.com

Menshen Packaging USA Inc
21 Industrial Pk .... Waldwick NJ 07463 201-445-7436 557
Web: www.menshenusa.com

Mensor Corp 201 Barnes Dr .... San Marcos TX 78666 512-396-4200 396-1820 201
Web: www.mensor.com

Mental Health America (MHA)
2000 N Beauregard St 6th Fl .... Alexandria VA 22311 703-684-7722 684-5968 48-17
TF Help Line: 800-969-6642 ■ *Web:* mentalhealthamerica.net

Mental Health Institute
2277 Iowa Ave .... Independence IA 50644 319-334-2583 374-5
Web: independenceia.com

Mentholatum Company Inc
707 Sterling Dr .... Orchard Park NY 14127 716-677-2500 582
TF: 800-688-7660 ■ *Web:* www.mentholatum.com

Mentis Group
8330 Lyndon B Johnson Fwy Ste 450 .... Dallas TX 75243 214-691-7800 180
Web: www.mentis-group.com

MENTISoftware Solutions LLC
3 Columbus Cir FL 15 .... New York NY 10019 212-861-2235 387
Web: www.mentisoftware.com

Mentor Chamber of Commerce
6972 Spinach Dr .... Mentor OH 44060 440-255-1616 255-1717 139
Web: www.mentorchamber.org

Mentor Corp 201 Mentor Dr .... Santa Barbara CA 93111 805-879-6000 477
NASDAQ: MENT ■ *TF:* 800-525-0245 ■ *Web:* www.mentorwwllc.com

Mentor Graphics Corp
8005 SW Boeckman Rd .... Wilsonville OR 97070 503-685-7000 685-1204 178-5
NASDAQ: MENT ■ *TF:* 800-592-2210 ■ *Web:* www.mentor.com

Mentor Group Inc, The
1775 E Palm Canyon Dr Ste 110-132 .... Palm Springs CA 92264 760-325-6411 656

MENTOR Network, The
313 Congress St 5th Fl .... Boston MA 02210 617-790-4800 790-4848 462
TF: 800-388-5150 ■ *Web:* www.thementornetwork.com

Mentor Public Schools 6451 Center St .... Mentor OH 44060 440-255-4444 685
TF: 800-447-0529 ■ *Web:* www.mentorschools.net

MENTOR/National Mentoring Partnership
201 South St Ste 615 .... Boston MA 02111 703-224-2200 226-2581 48-6
TF: 877-333-2464 ■ *Web:* www.mentoring.org

Mentoring USA 115 E 13th St .... New York NY 10003 212-400-7000 400-7005 48-6
Web: www.helpusa.org

MentorMate LLC 3036 Hennepin Ave .... Minneapolis MN 55408 612-823-4000 177
Web: www.mentormate.com

Mentus
6755 Mira Mesa Blvd Ste 123-137 .... San Diego CA 92121 858-455-5500 344
Web: www.mentus.com

Menusoft Systems Corp
7370 Steel Mill Dr .... Springfield VA 22150 703-912-3000 177
Web: www.digitaldining.com

Menzner Lumber & Supply Co
PO Box 217 .... Marathon WI 54448 800-257-1284 443-3798* 499
**Fax Area Code:* 715 ■ *TF:* 800-257-1284 ■ *Web:* www.menznerhardwoods.com

MEP Associates 2720 Arbor Ct .... Eau Claire WI 54701 715-832-5680 186
Web: www.mepassociates.com

MEP Consulting Engineers Inc
2928 Story Rd W Ste A .... Las Colinas TX 75038 972-870-9060 186
Web: www.mepce.com

Mepkin Abbey Botanical Garden
1098 Mepkin Abbey Rd .... Moncks Corner SC 29461 843-761-8509 761-6719 97
Web: www.mepkinabbey.org

MEPS Real-Time Inc
6451 El Camino Real Ste C .... Carlsbad CA 92009 760-448-9500 448-9599 475
Web: www.mepsrealtime.com

Meramec Group Inc 338 Ramsey St .... Sullivan MO 63080 573-468-3101 860-3101 301
Web: www.meramec.com

Meramec State Park 115 Meramec Pk Dr .... Sullivan MO 63080 573-468-6072 565
Web: www.mostateparks.com

Meramec Valley Bank
199 Clarkson Rd .... Ellisville MO 63011 636-230-3500 230-3191 70
Web: www.meramecvalleybank.com

Meramec Valley R-3 School District
126 N Payne St .... Pacific MO 63069 636-271-1400 271-1406 685
TF: 866-632-9992 ■ *Web:* www.mvr3.k12.mo.us

Mercadien Group
3625 Quakerbridge Rd Ste D .... Hamilton Township NJ 08619 609-689-9700 838-3331 401
Web: www.mercadien.com

Mercado Latino Inc
245 Baldwin Park Blvd .... Industry CA 91746 626-333-6862 805
Web: www.mercadolatinoinc.com

Mercana Growth Partners
390 Bay St Ste 1706 .... Toronto ON M5H2Y2 416-947-1300 70
Web: www.mercanagrowth.com

Mercantil Commercebank Holding Corp
220 Alhambra Cir .... Coral Gables FL 33134 305-629-1212 460-4010* 360-2
**Fax:* Cust Svc ■ *Web:* www.mercantilbank.com

Mercantile Bank
200 N 33rd St PO Box 3455 .... Quincy IL 62305 217-223-7300 360-2
NYSE: MBCA ■ *TF:* 800-405-6372 ■ *Web:* www.mercantilebk.com

Mercantile Bank Corp
310 Leonard St NW .... Grand Rapids MI 49504 616-406-3000 360-2
NASDAQ: MBWM ■ *TF:* 888-345-6296 ■ *Web:* www.mercbank.com

Mercato 111 Market St NW .... Olympia WA 98501 360-528-3663 671
Web: www.mercatoristorante.com

Mercator Asset Management LP
1314 E Las Olas Blvd Ste 1233 .... Fort Lauderdale FL 33301 561-361-1079 368-8010 690
Web: www.mercatorasset.com

Mercator Transport Group Corp
Ste 220 8200 Boul Decarie Ste 220 .... Montreal QC H4T1M4 514-874-1616 449
Web: www.corpgmt.com

Mercatus Energy Advisors LLC
708 Main St Ste 880 .... Houston TX 77002 713-970-1003 463
TF: 800-867-2617 ■ *Web:* www.mercatusenergy.com

Merce Cunningham Dance Co
130 W 56TH St Ste 707 .... New York NY 10019 212-255-8240 573-1
Web: www.mercecunningham.org

Merced College 3600 M St .... Merced CA 95348 209-384-6000 384-6339* 162
**Fax:* Admissions ■ *TF:* 800-784-2433 ■ *Web:* www.mccd.edu

Merced Conference & Visitors Bureau (MCVB)
710 W 16th St .... Merced CA 95340 209-384-2791 206
TF: 800-446-5353 ■ *Web:* visitmerced.travel

Merced County 2222 M St .... Merced CA 95340 209-385-7434 385-7375 338
Web: www.co.merced.ca.us

Merced County Chamber of Commerce
860 W 18th St .... Merced CA 95340 209-722-3864 139

Merced County Library 2100 O St .... Merced CA 95340 209-385-7643 726-7912 434-3
TF: 866-249-0773 ■ *Web:* www.co.merced.ca.us

Merced Irrigation District PO Box 2288 .... Merced CA 95344 209-722-5761 722-6421 186
Web: mercedid.com

Merced Sun-Star 3033 N G St .... Merced CA 95340 209-722-1511 532-2
TF: 800-540-4203 ■ *Web:* www.mercedsunstar.com

Merced Transportation Co
300 Grogan Ave .... Merced CA 95341 209-384-2575 108

Mercedes Distribution Center Inc
Brooklyn Navy Yard 63 Flushing Ave Ste 340 .... Brooklyn NY 11205 718-534-3000 637-9
Web: www.mdist.com

Mercedes Restaurants Inc
2402 W Nebraska Ave .... Peoria IL 61604 309-676-6443 670
Web: mercedesrestaurants.com

Mercedes Textiles Ltd
5838 Cypihot St .... Ville Saint Laurent QC H4S1Y5 514-335-4337 335-9633 678
Web: www.mercedestextiles.com

Mercedes-Benz Canada Inc
98 Vanderhoof Ave .... Toronto ON M4G4C9 416-425-3550 57
Web: www.mercedes-benz.ca

Mercedes-Benz Financial Services USA LLC
PO Box 685 .... Roanoke TX 76262 800-654-6222 267-6745* 217
**Fax Area Code:* 877 ■ *TF:* 800-654-6222 ■ *Web:* www.mbfs.com

Mercedes-Benz of Caldwell
1230 Bloomfield Ave .... Fairfield NJ 07004 973-227-3600 575-7835 57
Web: www.mbofcaldwell.com

Mercedes-Benz Of Cincinnati
8727 Montgomery Rd .... Cincinnati OH 45236 513-984-9000 516
Web: www.mbcincy.com

Mercedes-Benz of San Francisco
500 Eigth St .... San Francisco CA 94103 415-673-2000 57
TF: 877-554-6016 ■ *Web:* www.sfbenz.com

Mercedes-Benz Superdome
PO Box 52439 .... New Orleans LA 70152 504-587-3663 720
Web: www.mbsuperdome.com

Mercedes-Benz U.S. International Inc
1 Mercedes Dr .... Vance AL 35490 205-507-2252 59
TF: 888-286-8762 ■ *Web:* www.mbusi.com

Mercedes-Benz USA LLC 1 Mercedes Dr .... Montvale NJ 07645 201-573-0600 59
TF Cust Svc: 800-367-6372 ■ *Web:* www.mbusa.com

Mercedes-Benz USA LLC
11850 Bel-Red Rd .... Bellevue WA 98005 425-455-8535 516
Web: www.mercedesbenzofbellevue.com

Mercedes-Benz USA LLC
4500 Stevens Creek Blvd .... San Jose CA 95129 408-641-4610 57
Web: mbofstevenscreek.com

Mercer Arboretum & Botanic Gardens
22306 Aldine Westfield Rd .... Humble TX 77338 281-443-8731 97
TF: 877-321-2652 ■ *Web:* www.hcp4.net/mercer

Company	Phone	Fax	Class
Mercer Canyons Inc 46 Sonova Rd .... Prosser WA 99350 *Web:* mercercanyons.com	509-894-4773		10-4
Mercer Construction Company Inc 42690 Rio Nedo Way Ste D .... Temecula CA 92590 *Web:* www.mercerconstruction.com	951-296-0111		186
Mercer County PO Box 66 .... Aledo IL 61231 *TF:* 800-368-8683 ■ *Web:* www.mercercountyil.org	309-582-7021	582-7022	338
Mercer County 220 W Livingston St Rm A201 .... Celina OH 45822 *TF:* 800-686-1093 ■ *Web:* www.mercercountyohio.org	419-586-3178	586-1699	338
Mercer County 124A S Main St .... Harrodsburg KY 40330 *Web:* www.merceronline.com	859-734-2365		338
Mercer County 109 Courthouse .... Mercer PA 16137	724-662-3800	662-2096	338
Mercer County 621 Commerce St PO Box 4088 .... Bluefield WV 24701 *TF:* 800-221-3206 ■ *Web:* www.visitmercercounty.com	304-325-8438	324-8483	338
Mercer County PO Box 39 .... Stanton ND 58571 *TF:* 800-441-2649 ■ *Web:* www.mercercountynd.com	800-441-2649		338
Mercer County PO Box 8068 .... Trenton NJ 08650 *Web:* www.nj.gov/counties/mercer	609-585-6200	989-1111	338
Mercer County Community College PO Box B .... Trenton NJ 08690 *TF:* 800-982-9491 ■ *Web:* www.mccc.edu	609-586-4800		162
Kerney Ctr N Broad & Academy St .... Trenton NJ 08608 *TF:* 800-982-9491 ■ *Web:* www.mccc.edu	609-586-4800		162
West Windsor 1200 Old Trenton Rd .... West Windsor NJ 08550 **Fax:* Admissions ■ *TF:* 800-982-9491 ■ *Web:* www.mccc.edu	609-586-4800	570-3861*	162
Mercer County Convention & Visitors Bureau 621 Commerce St .... Bluefield WV 24701 *TF:* 800-221-3206 ■ *Web:* www.visitmercercounty.com	304-325-8438	324-8483	206
Mercer County Joint Township Community Hospital 800 W Main St .... Coldwater OH 45828 *TF:* 888-844-2341 ■ *Web:* www.mercer-health.com	419-678-2341		374-3
Mercer County Library System (MCL) 2751 Brunswick Pk .... Lawrenceville NJ 08648 *Web:* www.mcl.org	609-882-9246		434-3
Mercer County State Bancorp Inc 3279 S Main St .... Sandy Lake PA 16145 *Web:* www.mcsbank.bank	724-376-7015		780
Mercer Engineering & Research 135 Osigian Blvd .... Warner Robins GA 31088 *TF:* 877-650-6372 ■ *Web:* www.merc-mercer.org	478-953-6800		138
Mercer Forge Corp 200 Brown St .... Mercer PA 16137	724-662-2750	662-5642	483
Mercer Global Advisors Inc 1801 E Cabrillo Blvd .... Santa Barbara CA 93108 *TF:* 800-258-1559 ■ *Web:* www.merceradvisors.com	800-898-4642		401
Mercer Hotel 147 Mercer St .... New York NY 10012 *TF:* 888-918-6060 ■ *Web:* www.mercerhotel.com	212-966-6060	965-3838	379
Mercer Inc 1166 Ave of the Americas .... New York NY 10036 *TF:* 800-732-0330 ■ *Web:* www.mercer.com	212-345-5000	345-7414	194
Mercer Industries Inc 10760 SW Denney Rd .... Beaverton OR 97008 *Web:* www.mercerwindows.com	503-526-3650		480
Mercer International 14900 Interurban Ave S Ste 282 .... Seattle WA 98168 *Web:* www.mercerint.com	604-684-1099		638
Mercer Kitchen 99 Prince St .... New York NY 10012 *Web:* www.jean-georges.com	212-966-5454		671
Mercer Lime & Stone Co 50 Abele Rd Ste 1006 .... Bridgeville PA 15017 *Web:* www.mercerlime.com	412-220-0316	220-0347	440
Mercer LLC 400 W Market St .... Louisville KY 40202 *TF:* 800-333-3070 ■ *Web:* www.mercer.com	502-561-4500	561-4747	193
Mercer Metals 1249 Ave R .... Grand Prairie TX 75050 *Web:* www.mercermetals.com	972-790-1576		492
Mercer Morgan 8350 E Raintree Dr .... Scottsdale AZ 85260 *TF:* 800-383-4542 ■ *Web:* mercermorgan.com	480-281-1833		260
Mercer Museums 84 S Pine St .... Doylestown PA 18901 *Web:* www.mercermuseum.org	215-345-0210		520
Mercer Rubber Co 350 Rabro Dr .... Hauppauge NY 11788 *Web:* www.mercer-rubber.com	631-582-1524	348-0279	370
Mercer Transportation Co 1128 W Main St PO Box 35610 .... Louisville KY 40232 *TF:* 800-626-5375 ■ *Web:* www.mercer-trans.com	502-584-2301		780
Mercer University 1400 Coleman Ave .... Macon GA 31207 *TF:* 800-637-2378 ■ *Web:* www.mercer.edu	478-301-2650		166
Cecil B Day 3001 Mercer University Dr .... Atlanta GA 30341 *TF:* 800-840-8577 ■ *Web:* www.mercer.edu	678-547-6089	547-6367	166
Jack Tarver Library 1501 Mercer University Dr .... Macon GA 31207 *Web:* libraries.mercer.edu	478-301-2961	301-2252	434-6
Mercer Wrecking Recycling Corp 1519 Calhoun St .... Trenton NJ 08638 *Web:* mercergroup.com	609-393-6775		189-16
Mercersburg Academy 300 E Seminary St .... Mercersburg PA 17236 *TF:* 800-588-2550 ■ *Web:* www.mercersburg.edu	717-328-6173		622
Mercersburg Printing 9964 Buchanan Trl W .... Mercersburg PA 17236 *TF:* 800-955-3902 ■ *Web:* www.mercersburg.net	717-328-3902		627
Merchant & Evans Inc 308 Connecticut Dr .... Burlington NJ 08016 *TF:* 800-257-6215 ■ *Web:* www.ziprib.com	609-387-3033		480
Merchant & Gould 3200 IDS Ctr 80 S Eighth St .... Minneapolis MN 55402 *Web:* www.merchantgould.com	612-332-5300		428
Merchant Energy Partners 10901 W Toller Dr Ste 200 .... Littleton CO 80127 *Web:* mehllc.com	720-351-4000		538
Merchant Factors Corp 1441 Broadway 22nd Fl .... New York NY 10018 *TF All:* 800-970-9997 ■ *Web:* www.merchantfactors.com	212-840-7575	869-1752	272
Merchant Law Group LLP 2401 Saskatchewan Dr Saskatchewan Dr Plaza ..... Regina SK S4P4H8 *TF:* 888-567-7777 ■ *Web:* www.merchantlaw.com	306-359-7777		41
Merchant One Payment Systems Inc 524 Arthur Godfrey Rd 3rd Fl .... Miami Beach FL 33140 *TF:* 800-610-4189 ■ *Web:* www.merchantone.com	800-610-4189		95
Merchant, The 279 Grove St .... Jersey City NJ 07302 *Web:* www.themerchantnj.com	201-200-0202		671
MerchantCircle Inc 201 Main St Ste 100 .... Los Altos CA 94022 *Web:* www.merchantcircle.com	650-352-1335		387
Merchants & Medical Credit Corporation Inc 6324 Taylor Dr .... Flint MI 48507 *TF:* 800-562-0273 ■ *Web:* www.mermed.com	810-239-3030		160
Merchants Automotive Group Inc 1278 Hooksett Rd .... Hooksett NH 03106 *Web:* www.merchantsauto.com	603-669-4100		57
Merchants Bancshares Inc 1013 Centre Rd .... Wilmington DE 19805 *NASDAQ: MBVT* ■ *TF:* 800-322-5222 ■ *Web:* www.mbvt.com	802-658-3400		360-2
Merchants Building Maintenance 606 Monterey Pass Rd .... Monterey Park CA 91754 *TF:* 800-560-6700 ■ *Web:* www.mbmonline.com	800-560-6700		177
Merchants Co 1100 Edwards St .... Hattiesburg MS 39401 *TF:* 800-451-8346 ■ *Web:* merchantsfoodservice.com	601-583-4351	582-5333	297-8
Merchants Credit Bureau 955 Green St .... Augusta GA 30901 *TF:* 800-426-5265 ■ *Web:* www.mcbusa.com	706-823-6246	823-6253	218
Merchants Grocery Co 800 Maddox Dr PO Box 1268 .... Culpeper VA 22701 *TF:* 877-897-9893 ■ *Web:* www.merchants-grocery.com	540-825-0786	825-9016	345
Merchants Insurance Group 250 Main St .... Buffalo NY 14202 *TF:* 800-462-1077 ■ *Web:* merchantsgroup.com	716-849-3333	849-3246	391-4
Merchants Metals Inc 900 Ashwood Pkwy Ste 600 .... Atlanta GA 30338 *TF:* 800-272-6171 ■ *Web:* www.merchantsmetals.com	770-960-2880		279
Merchants National Bank of Bangor Inc 25 Broadway PO Box 227 .... Bangor PA 18013 *TF:* 877-678-6622 ■ *Web:* www.merchantsbangor.com	610-588-0981		70
Merchants Overseas Inc 41 Bassett St .... Providence RI 02903	401-331-5603		411
Merchants Paper Co 4625 SE 24th Ave .... Portland OR 97202 *TF:* 800-605-6301 ■ *Web:* merchantspaper.com	503-235-2171		557
Merchants Solutions International 19252 S Blackhawk Pkwy Unit 75 .... Mokena IL 60448 **Fax Area Code:* 517 ■ *TF:* 800-485-2630	800-485-2630	882-4030*	112
Merck & Company Inc 1 Merck Dr PO Box 100 .... Whitehouse Station NJ 08889 *NYSE: MRK* ■ *TF Cust Svc:* 800-672-6372 ■ *Web:* www.merck.com	908-423-1000		582
Merco Group Inc, The 7711 N 81st St .... Milwaukee WI 53223	414-365-2600		360-3
Merco Inc 1117 Rt 31 S .... Lebanon NJ 08833 *TF:* 800-589-5704 ■ *Web:* www.mercoinc.com	908-730-8622	730-6472	188-4
Mercom Capital Group LLC 6836 Bee Cave Rd Ste 238 .... Austin TX 78746 *Web:* www.mercomcapital.com	512-215-4452		796
Mercom Inc 313 Commerce Dr .... Pawleys Island SC 29585 *TF:* 877-223-8330 ■ *Web:* www.mercomcorp.com	843-979-9957		180
Merco-Savory Inc 1111 N Hadley Rd .... Fort Wayne IN 46804 *TF Cust Svc:* 800-547-2513 ■ *Web:* www.mercoproducts.com	260-459-8200	436-0735	298
Mercury Air Group Inc 2780 Skypark Dr .... Torrance CA 90505 *Web:* mercuryair.com	310-827-2737	827-8921	24
Mercury Aircraft Inc 17 Wheeler Ave .... Hammondsport NY 14840 *Web:* www.mercurycorp.com	607-569-4200	569-4306	697
Mercury Casualty Co 555 W Imperial Hwy .... Brea CA 92821 **Fax Area Code:* 323 ■ **Fax:* Hum Res ■ *Web:* mercuryinsurance.com	714-671-6600	857-7116*	391-4
Mercury Communication Partners 13414 Watertown Plank Rd .... Elm Grove WI 53122 *Web:* www.mercuryww.com	262-782-4637		7
Mercury Instruments Inc 3940 Virginia Ave .... Cincinnati OH 45227 *Web:* www.mercuryinstruments.com	513-272-1111		153
Mercury Insurance Co 555 W Imperial Hwy .... Brea CA 92821	714-671-6600		391-4
Mercury Insurance Group 4484 Wilshire Blvd .... Los Angeles CA 90010 *NYSE: MCY* ■ *TF:* 800-956-3728 ■ *Web:* www.mercuryinsurance.com	323-937-1060	857-7116	391-4
Mercury International 20 Alice Agnew Dr .... North Attleboro MA 02763 *Web:* mercuryfootwear.com	508-699-9000		301
Mercury Investment Management LLC 88 Union Ctr Ste 1150 .... Memphis TN 38103 *Web:* www.mercuryprop.com	901-521-4200		401
Mercury Lighting Products Company Inc 20 Audrey Pl .... Fairfield NJ 07004 *TF:* 800-637-2584 ■ *Web:* www.mercltg.com	973-244-9444	244-9522	439
Mercury Luggage Manufacturing Co 4843 Victor St .... Jacksonville FL 32207 *Web:* www.mercuryluggage.com	904-482-0091	733-9671	453
Mercury Mambo 1107 S Eighth St .... Austin TX 78704 *Web:* www.mercurymambo.com	512-447-4440		344
Mercury Marine Ltd 8698 Escarpment Way .... Milton ON L9T0M1	905-636-1705		690
Mercury Medical 11300 49th St N .... Clearwater FL 33762 *TF:* 800-237-6418 ■ *Web:* www.mercurymed.com	727-573-0088	571-3922	476
Mercury Paper Inc 495 Radio Sta Rd .... Strasburg VA 22657 *Web:* www.mercurypaper.com	540-465-7700		557
Mercury Pen Company Inc 245 Eastline Rd .... Ballston NY 12019 *Web:* www.mercurypen.com	518-899-9653	899-9657	571
Mercury Plastics Inc 15760 Madison Rd .... Middlefield OH 44062 *Web:* www.mercuryplastics.com	440-632-5281		326
Mercury Press Inc 1910 S Nicklas St .... Oklahoma City OK 73128 *TF:* 800-423-5984 ■ *Web:* www.mercurypressinc.com	405-682-3468		627
Mercury Public Affairs 137 Fifth Ave Ste 3 .... New York NY 10010 *TF:* 800-325-4151 ■ *Web:* www.mercuryllc.com	212-681-1380		636
Mercury Systems Inc 267 Lowell Rd Ste 101 .... Hudson NH 03051 *NASDAQ: MRCY* ■ *Web:* rf.mrcy.com	603-546-4100		735
Mercury Tube Products 3211 W Bear Creek Dr .... Englewood CO 80110 *Web:* merctube.com	303-761-1835	781-7307	490

Name / Address	Phone	Fax	Class
Mercury Wire Products Inc 1 Mercury Dr ... Spencer MA 01562 *Web:* www.mercurywire.com	508-885-6363		813
Mercury Wireless LLC 2825 se california ave ... Topeka KS 66605 *TF:* 800-354-4915 ■ *Web:* www.mercurywireless.com	800-354-4915		736
Mercury Z 1150 SE Maynard Rd Ste 140 ... Cary NC 27511 *TF:* 877-548-4052 ■ *Web:* www.mercuryz.com	877-548-4052		196
Mercury, The 24 N Hanover St ... Pottstown PA 19464 *Web:* www.pottsmerc.com	610-323-3000		532-2
Mercury, The 11909 Preston Rd Ste 1418 ... Dallas TX 75240 *Web:* www.themercurydallas.com	972-960-7774		671
MercuryCSC 109 N Rouse ... Bozeman MT 59715 *Web:* www.mercurycsc.com	406-586-2280		7
Mercy 1235 E Cherokee ... Springfield MO 65804 *TF:* 800-909-8326 ■ *Web:* www.mercy.net	417-820-2000	820-6996	374-3
Mercy 615 S New Ballas Rd ... Saint Louis MO 63141 *TF:* 800-318-2596 ■ *Web:* www.mercy.net	314-251-6000		374-3
Mercy College 555 Broadway ... Dobbs Ferry NY 10522 **Fax:* Admissions ■ *TF:* 800-637-2969 ■ *Web:* www.mercy.edu	914-693-4500	674-7382*	166
Manhattan 66 W 35th St ... New York NY 10001 *TF:* 800-637-2969 ■ *Web:* www.mercy.edu	212-615-3300		166
White Plains 277 Martine Ave Ste 201 ... White Plains NY 10601 *TF:* 888-464-6737 ■ *Web:* www.mercy.edu	914-948-3666		166
Yorktown Heights 2651 Strang Blvd ... Yorktown Heights NY 10598 **Fax:* Admissions ■ *TF:* 877-637-2946 ■ *Web:* www.mercy.edu	914-245-6100	962-0931*	166
Mercy College of Ohio 2221 Madison Ave ... Toledo OH 43604 *TF:* 888-806-3729 ■ *Web:* www.mercycollege.edu	419-251-1313		507
Mercy Ctr 2300 Adeline Dr ... Burlingame CA 94010 *Web:* www.mercy-center.org	650-340-7474	340-1299	673
Mercy Ctr at Madison 167 Neck Rd ... Madison CT 06443 *Web:* www.mercybythesea.org	203-245-0401	245-8718	673
Mercy Ctr for Healing the Whole Person 520 W Buena Ventura ... Colorado Springs CO 80907 *Web:* www.mercycenter.com	719-633-2302	633-1031	673
Mercy Flights Inc 2020 Milligan Way ... Medford OR 97504 *TF:* 800-903-9000 ■ *Web:* www.mercyflights.com	541-858-2600		30
Mercy General Health Partners *Muskegon Campus* 1500 E Sherman Blvd ... Muskegon MI 49444 *TF:* 800-368-4125 ■ *Web:* www.mercyhealthmuskegon.com	231-672-2000		374-3
Mercy General Hospital 4001 J St ... Sacramento CA 95819 *TF:* 888-800-7688 ■ *Web:* hospitals.dignityhealth.org	916-453-4545		374-3
Mercy health 3131 Queen City Ave ... Cincinnati OH 45238 *Web:* e-mercy.com	513-389-5000	389-5201	374-3
Mercy Health Ctr (MHC) 4300 W Memorial Rd ... Oklahoma City OK 73120 *Web:* www.mercy.net	405-755-1515		374-3
Mercy Health Ctr Fort Scott 401 Woodland Hills Blvd ... Fort Scott KS 66701 *TF:* 800-464-7942 ■ *Web:* mercy.net	620-223-2200	223-5327	374-3
Mercy Health System of Northwest Arkansas 2710 Rife Medical Ln ... Rogers AR 72758 *Web:* www.mercy.net	479-338-8000		374-3
Mercy Home Care & Medical Supplies Inc 2001 McDonald Ave ... Brooklyn NY 11223 *Web:* www.mercymedsupplies.com	718-376-3131		690
Mercy Hospice 281 Enterprise Ct Ste 200 ... Bloomfield Hills MI 48302	248-452-5300		371
Mercy Hospice of Horry County PO Box 50640 ... Myrtle Beach SC 29579	843-236-2282	347-5535	371
Mercy Hospital 800 Mercy Dr ... Council Bluffs IA 51503 *Web:* chihealth.com	712-328-5000		374-3
Mercy Hospital 3663 S Miami Ave ... Miami FL 33133 *Web:* www.mercymiami.com	305-854-4400		374-3
Mercy Hospital 144 State St ... Portland ME 04101 *TF:* 800-293-6583 ■ *Web:* www.mercyhospital.org	207-879-3000		374-3
Mercy Hospital 4050 Coon Rapids Blvd ... Coon Rapids MN 55433 *Web:* www.allinahealth.org	763-236-6000		374-3
Mercy Hospital & Medical Ctr (MHMC) 2525 S Michigan Ave ... Chicago IL 60616 *Web:* www.mercy-chicago.org	312-567-2000		374-3
Mercy Hospital & Trauma Ctr 1000 Mineral Point Ave ... Janesville WI 53548 *TF:* 800-756-4147 ■ *Web:* www.mercyhealthsystem.com	608-756-6000		374-3
Mercy Hospital Anderson 7500 State Rd ... Cincinnati OH 45255 *Web:* e-mercy.com	513-624-4500		374-3
Mercy Hospital Cadillac 400 Hobart St ... Cadillac MI 49601 *Web:* www.munsonhealthcare.org	231-876-7473		374-3
Mercy Hospital of Buffalo 565 Abbott Rd ... Buffalo NY 14220 *TF:* 800-804-5447 ■ *Web:* www.chsbuffalo.org	716-826-7000		374-3
Mercy Hospital of Philadelphia 501 S 54th St ... Philadelphia PA 19143 *Web:* www.mercyhealth.org	215-748-9000		374-3
Mercy Hospitals of Bakersfield Truxtun Campus (MHB) 2215 Truxtun Ave ... Bakersfield CA 93301 *Web:* www.mercybakersfield.org	661-632-5000		374-3
Mercy Housing Inc 1999 Broadway Ste 1000 ... Denver CO 80202 *TF:* 866-338-0557 ■ *Web:* www.mercyhousing.org	303-830-3300		187
Mercy Iowa City 500 E Market St ... Iowa City IA 52245 *TF:* 800-637-2942 ■ *Web:* www.mercyiowacity.org	319-339-0300	339-3788	374-3
Mercy Medical Center 1000 N Village Ave ... Rockville Centre NY 11570 *Web:* mercymedicalcenter.chsli.org	516-705-2525	705-1406	374-3
Mercy Medical Center North Iowa 1000 Fourth St SW ... Mason City IA 50401 *TF:* 800-297-4719 ■ *Web:* www.mercynorthiowa.com	641-428-6208		371
Mercy Medical Ctr (MMC) 801 Fifth St ... Sioux City IA 51102 *TF:* 800-352-3559 ■ *Web:* www.mercysiouxcity.com	712-279-2010	279-2034	374-3
Mercy Medical Ctr 271 Carew St ... Springfield MA 01104 *Web:* www.mercycares.com	413-748-9000		374-3
Mercy Medical Ctr 1111 Sixth Ave ... Des Moines IA 50314 *TF:* 800-637-2993 ■ *Web:* www.mercydesmoines.org	515-247-3121		374-3
Mercy Medical Ctr (MMC) 345 St Paul Pl ... Baltimore MD 21202 *TF:* 800-636-3729 ■ *Web:* www.mdmercy.com	410-332-9000		374-3
Mercy Medical Ctr 701 Tenth St SE ... Cedar Rapids IA 52403 *Web:* www.mercycare.org	319-398-6011	398-6912	374-3
Mercy Medical Ctr 1320 Mercy Dr NW ... Canton OH 44708 *TF:* 800-223-8662 ■ *Web:* www.cantonmercy.org	330-489-1000		374-3
Mercy Medical Ctr 1010 Third Springs Blvd ... Durango CO 81301 *TF:* 800-345-2516 ■ *Web:* www.mercydurango.org	970-247-4311		374-3
Mercy Medical Ctr 250 Mercy Dr ... Dubuque IA 52001 *Web:* www.mercydubuque.com	563-589-8000	589-8073	374-3
Mercy Medical Ctr (MMC) 500 S Oakwood Rd ... Oshkosh WI 54904 *TF:* 800-894-9327 ■ *Web:* www.affinityhealth.org	920-223-2000		374-3
Mercy Medical Ctr Hospice 7568 Whipple Ave NW ... Canton OH 44720 *Web:* cantonmercy.org	330-492-8803	649-4399	371
Mercy Medical Ctr Merced Community Campus 333 Mercy Ave ... Merced CA 95340 *Web:* www.mercymercedcares.org	209-564-5000		374-3
Mercy Medical Ctr North Iowa 1000 Fourth St SW ... Mason City IA 50401 *TF:* 800-433-3883 ■ *Web:* www.mercynorthiowa.com	641-428-7000		374-3
Mercy Memorial Health Ctr (MMHC) 1011 14th Ave NW ... Ardmore OK 73401 *TF:* 888-637-2937 ■ *Web:* www.mercy.net	580-223-5400		374-3
Mercy Memorial Hospital (MMH) 718 N Macomb St ... Monroe MI 48162 *Web:* www.mercymemorial.org	734-240-8400		374-3
Mercy Regional Medical Ctr 3700 Kolbe Rd ... Lorain OH 44053 *Web:* www.mercyonline.org	440-960-4000		374-3
Mercy San Juan Medical Ctr 6501 Coyle Ave ... Carmichael CA 95608 *TF:* 888-800-7688 ■ *Web:* hospitals.dignityhealth.org	916-537-5000		374-3
Mercy Southwest Hospital 400 Old River Rd ... Bakersfield CA 93311	661-663-6000		374-3
Mercy St Anne Hospital 3404 W Sylvania Ave ... Toledo OH 43623 *Web:* www.mercyweb.org	419-407-2663	407-3889	374-3
Mercy St Theresa Center Inc 7010 Rowan Hill Dr ... Cincinnati OH 45202 *Web:* www.catholiccincinnati.org	513-271-7010		793
Mercy Suburban Hospital (MSH) 2701 De Kalb Pk ... Norristown PA 19401 *Web:* www.mercyhealth.org/suburban	610-278-2000		374-3
Mercy Surgical Dressing Group Inc 4 Zesta Dr ... Pittsburgh PA 15205	412-788-5200		475
MercyCare Insurance Company Inc 580 N Washington St PO Box 550 ... Janesville WI 53547 *Web:* www.mercycarehealthplans.com	608-752-3431		390
Mercyhurst College 501 E 38th St ... Erie PA 16546 **Fax:* Admissions ■ *TF:* 800-825-1926 ■ *Web:* www.mercyhurst.edu	814-824-2202	824-3634*	166
Mercy-USA for Aid & Development Inc (M-USA) 44450 Pinetree Dr Ste 201 ... Plymouth MI 48170 *TF:* 800-556-3729 ■ *Web:* www.mercyusa.org	734-454-0011	454-0303	48-5
Meredith & Jeannie Ray Cancer Ctr 255 N 30th St ... Laramie WY 82072 *TF:* 800-854-1115 ■ *Web:* www2.ivinsonhospital.org	307-742-7586	742-0286	374-3
Meredith College 3800 Hillsborough St ... Raleigh NC 27607 **Fax:* Admissions ■ *TF All:* 800-637-3348 ■ *Web:* www.meredith.edu	919-760-8581	760-2348*	166
Meredith Corp 1716 Locust St ... Des Moines IA 50309 *NYSE: MDP* ■ *Web:* www.meredith.com	515-284-3000		637-9
Meredith Enterprises Inc 3000 Sand Hill Rd Bldg 2 Ste 120 ... Menlo Park CA 94025 *Web:* www.meredithreit.com	650-233-7140		654
Meredith Long & Co 2323 San Felipe ... Houston TX 77019 *Web:* www.meredithlonggallery.com	713-523-6671	523-2355	42
Meredith O'Donnell Inc 1751 Post Oak Blvd ... Houston TX 77056 *Web:* www.meredithodonnell.com	713-526-7332		321
Meredith Village Savings Bank (MVSB) 24 State Rt 25 PO Box 177 ... Meredith NH 03253 *TF:* 800-922-6872 ■ *Web:* www.mvsb.com	603-279-7986	279-5710	70
Meredith-Webb Printing Company Inc 334 N Main St ... Burlington NC 27217 *Web:* www.meredithwebb.com	336-228-8378		627
Mereen-Johnson Machine Co 4401 Lyndale Ave N ... Minneapolis MN 55412 *TF:* 888-465-7297 ■ *Web:* www.mereen-johnson.com	612-529-7791	529-0120	821
Merfish Pipe & Supply Co PO Box 15879 ... Houston TX 77220 *TF:* 800-869-5731 ■ *Web:* www.merfish.com	713-869-5731	867-0738	492
Merge Helathcare 350 N Orleans St 1st Fl ... Chicago IL 60654 *TF:* 877-446-3743 ■ *Web:* www.merge.com	312-565-6868	565-6870	382
Mergenet Solutions Inc 6601 Lyons Rd Ste B1-B4 ... Coconut Creek FL 33073 *Web:* www.mergenetsolutions.com	561-208-3770		475
Mergent FIS Inc 580 Kingsley Pk Dr ... Fort Mill SC 29715 **Fax Area Code:* 704 ■ *TF:* 800-342-5647 ■ *Web:* www.mergent.com	800-342-5647	559-6945*	637-10
Mergent Inc 477 Madison Ave Ste 410 ... New York NY 10022 *TF:* 800-937-1398 ■ *Web:* www.mergent.com	212-413-7700	413-7670	637-9
Mergenthaler Transfer & Storage 1414 N Montana Ave ... Helena MT 59601 *TF General:* 800-826-5463 ■ *Web:* www.mergenthaler.net	406-442-9470	442-4340	780
Mergers & Acquisitions Law Report 1801 S Bell St ... Arlington VA 22202 *TF:* 800-372-1033 ■ *Web:* www.bna.com/mergers-acquisitions-law-p5940	800-372-1033		531-7
Mergers & Acquisitions Magazine 1 State Street Plaza 27th FL ... New York NY 10004 *TF Cust Svc:* 866-596-7456 ■ *Web:* www.themiddlemarket.com	212-803-8200		457-5
Mergon Corp 5350 Old Pearman Dairy Rd ... Anderson SC 29625 *Web:* mergon.com/contact-us/us	864-222-0422		596
Merhaba 2801 W Ball Rd ... Anaheim CA 92804 *Web:* merhabarestaurant.com	714-826-8859		671

	Phone	Fax	Class
MERI (Marine Environmental Research Institute)			
55 Main St PO Box 1652 .... Blue Hill ME 04614	207-374-2135		668
Web: www.meriresearch.org			
Meri Meri 63 Leonard St .... Belmont MA 02478	617-484-5571		130
TF: 800-638-2881			
Merial 20201 Clark Graham Ave.............. Baie-d'urfe QC H9X4B6	888-637-4251		582
TF: 888-637-4251 ■ *Web:* ca.merial.com			
Merial Ltd 3239 Satellite Blvd Bldg 500............ Duluth GA 30096	678-638-3000		584
TF: 888-637-4251 ■ *Web:* www.merial.com			
Meriam Process Technologies Inc			
10920 Madison Ave .... Cleveland OH 44102	216-281-1100		407
TF: 800-255-3924 ■ *Web:* www.meriam.com			
Merical Inc 233 E Bristol Ln .... Orange CA 92865	714-283-9551		583
Web: www.merical.com			
Mericle Commercial Real Estate Services			
100 Baltimore Dr .... Wilkes-Barre PA 18702	570-823-1100	823-0300	655
Web: www.mericle.com			
Mericon Industries Inc			
8819 N Pioneer Rd .... Peoria IL 61615	309-693-2150		583
TF: 800-242-6464 ■ *Web:* www.mericon-industries.com			
Meriden Manufacturing Inc PO Box 694........ Meriden CT 06450	203-237-7481	235-3146	488
Web: www.meridenmfg.com			
Meriden Public Library 105 Miller St .... Meriden CT 06450	203-238-2344	238-3647	434-3
Web: meridenlibrary.org			
Meridian Aerospace Group Ltd			
3796 Vest Mill Rd..................... Winston-Salem NC 27106	336-765-5560		770
Web: airunion.us			
Meridian Associates Inc			
1 E Erie St Ste 240 .... Chicago IL 60611	312-335-8050		196
Web: www.meridianai.com			
Meridian Auto Parts			
10211 Pacific Mesa Blvd Ste 404............. San Diego CA 92121	800-874-1974		54
TF: 800-874-1974 ■ *Web:* www.meridianautoparts.com			
Meridian Bioscience Inc			
3471 River Hills Dr....................... Cincinnati OH 45244	513-271-3700	272-5421	231
NASDAQ: VIVO ■ *TF Cust Svc:* 800-543-1980 ■ *Web:* www.meridianbioscience.com			
Meridian Capital LLC			
1809 Seventh Ave Ste 1330 .... Seattle WA 98101	206-623-4000	623-8221	690
Web: www.meridianllc.com			
Meridian Chamber of Commerce			
215 E Franklin Rd.......................... Meridian ID 83642	208-888-2817	888-2682	139
TF: 866-833-3330 ■ *Web:* www.meridianchamber.org			
Meridian Community College			
910 Hwy 19 N.............................. Meridian MS 39307	601-483-8241		162
TF: 800-622-8431 ■ *Web:* www.mcc.cc.ms.us			
Meridian Display & Merchandising Inc			
162 York Ave E .... St Paul MN 55117	651-227-3020		5
TF: 800-786-2501 ■ *Web:* www.meridiandisplay.com			
Meridian Equity Partners Inc			
40 Wall St Ste 1704 .... New York NY 10005	212-500-6650		690
Web: meptraders.com			
Meridian Foods 201 W 1100 N..................... Eaton IN 47338	765-396-3344		296-18
Meridian Gold Co 9670 Gateway Dr Ste 200......... Reno NV 89521	775-850-3777	249-6189*	502
**Fax Area Code:* 888			
Meridian Graphics Inc 2652 Dow Ave............. Tustin CA 92780	949-833-3500		627
Web: www.mglitho.com			
Meridian Health System Inc			
1967 Hwy 34, Bldg C, Ste 104 .... Wall NJ 07719	800-560-9990		363
TF: 800-560-9990 ■ *Web:* www.meridianhealth.com			
Meridian Institute 105 Village Pl................. Dillon CO 80435	970-513-8340		196
Web: www.merid.org			
Meridian IQ			
11501 Outlook St Ste 500.................. Overland Park KS 66211	877-246-4909	696-7501*	449
**Fax Area Code:* 913 ■ *TF:* 877-246-4909 ■ *Web:* www2.miq.com			
Meridian Lightweight Technologies Inc			
25 MacNab Ave............................ Strathroy ON N7G4H6	519-246-9600	245-6605	295
Web: www.meridian-mag.com			
Meridian Mall 1982 W Grand River Ave .... Okemos MI 48864	517-349-2031		460
Web: www.meridianmall.com			
Meridian Mattress Factory Inc			
200 Rubush Rd............................ Meridian MS 39301	601-693-3875		471
Web: mermat.com			
Meridian Medical Technologies Inc			
6350 Stevens Forest Rd Ste 301.............. Columbia MD 21046	443-259-7800	259-7801	476
TF: 800-638-8093 ■ *Web:* www.meridianmeds.com			
Meridian Midwest Payment			
402 S Patterson Ave.......................... Joplin MO 64801	887-916-1846		225
Web: meridian-midwest.com			
Meridian Mobile Home Park Spaces & Rentals			
1801 Meridian St Ofc 18..................... Nashville TN 37207	615-227-1159		505
Meridian One Corp			
5775 General Washington Dr .... Alexandria VA 22312	703-461-5200		195
Web: www.meridianone.com			
Meridian Plaza Resort			
2310 N Ocean Blvd..................... Myrtle Beach SC 29577	843-626-4734	497-5717	379
TF: 888-590-0801 ■ *Web:* www.meridianplaza.com			
Meridian Products Inc			
124 Earland Dr Bldg 2 .... New Holland PA 17557	717-355-7700		115
Web: www.meridianproduct.com			
Meridian Specialty Yarns Inc			
312 Colombo St SW.......................... Valdese NC 28690	828-874-2151	874-3780	745-9
TF: 800-331-4762 ■ *Web:* www.msyg.com			
Meridian Star Inc 814 22nd Ave............... Meridian MS 39301	601-693-1551	485-1275	637-8
TF Cust Svc: 800-232-2525 ■ *Web:* www.meridianstar.com			
Meridian State Park 173 Pk Rd 7 .... Meridian TX 76665	254-435-2536		565
Web: tpwd.texas.gov			
Meridian Surveys Ltd			
355 16th St W......................... Prince Albert SK S6V3V6	306-764-9229		466
Web: www.meridiansurveys.ca			
Meridian Technology Group Inc			
12909 SW 68th Pkwy Ste 340 .... Portland OR 97223	503-697-1600		177
TF: 800-755-1038 ■ *Web:* www.meridiangroup.com			
Meridian Title Corp			
202 S Michigan St .... South Bend IN 46601	574-232-5845		391-6
TF: 800-777-1574 ■ *Web:* www.meridiantitle.com			
Meridian West Consultants LLC			
7603 S Main St............................. Midvale UT 84047	801-542-7082		261
Web: www.meridian-west.com			
Meridian/Lauderdale County Tourism Bureau			
212 Constitution Ave .... Meridian MS 39301	601-482-8001	486-4988	206
TF: 888-868-7720 ■ *Web:* www.visitmeridian.com			
Meridian-Baseline State Park			
16345 McClure Rd.......................... Chelsea MI 48118	734-475-8307		565
Web: www.michigandnr.com			
Meridican Incentive Consultants			
16 Esna Park Dr Ste 103.................... Markham ON L3R5X1	905-477-7700		772
Web: www.meridican.com			
Merin Hunter Codman Inc			
1601 Forum Pl Ste 200............... West Palm Beach FL 33401	561-471-8000		652
Web: www.mhcreal.com			
Meringcarson 1700 I St 2nd Fl .... Sacramento CA 95811	916-441-0571		7
Web: www.meringcarson.com			
Merion Mercy Academy			
511 Montgomery Ave .... Merion Station PA 19066	610-664-6655		685
TF: 800-352-7550 ■ *Web:* www.merion-mercy.com			
Merion Publications Inc			
2900 Horizon Dr...................... King of Prussia PA 19406	610-278-1400	278-1425	637-9
TF: 800-355-1088 ■ *Web:* www.advanceweb.com			
Merisant Worldwide Inc			
125 S Wacker Dr Ste 3150 .... Chicago IL 60606	312-840-6000		296-38
Web: www.merisant.com			
Meristem LLP			
601 Carlson Pkwy Ste 800 .... Minnetonka MN 55305	952-835-2577		41
Web: www.meristemfw.com			
Merit Accounting And Financial Services			
2201 Broadway........................... North Bend OR 97459	973-331-5600		401
Merit Brass Co 1 Merit Dr................... Cleveland OH 44143	216-261-9800		595
TF: 800-375-8181 ■ *Web:* www.meritbrass.com			
Merit Electric Company Inc			
6520 125th Ave N............................. Largo FL 33773	727-536-5945	536-9014	189-4
TF: 800-330-5945 ■ *Web:* www.meritelectricco.com			
Merit Electrical Inc			
17723 Airline Hwy .... Prairieville LA 70769	225-673-8850	673-8838	189-4
Web: www.meritelectrical.com			
Merit Gage Inc			
3954 Meadowbrook Rd St. Louis Park .... Minneapolis MN 55426	952-935-0113	935-2641	454
Web: www.meritgage.com			
Merit Gear Corp 810 Hudson St .... Antigo WI 54409	715-623-2307		454
Web: www.meritgear.com			
Merit Health Biloxi 150 Reynoir St .... Biloxi MS 39530	228-432-1571	436-1205	374-3
TF: 800-664-8031 ■ *Web:* www.merithealthbiloxi.com			
Merit Health Gilmore Memorial (GMRMC)			
1105 Earl Frye Blvd .... Amory MS 38821	662-256-7111		374-3
TF: 800-636-7622 ■ *Web:* www.merithealthgilmore.com			
Merit Health Rankin			
350 Crossgates Blvd........................ Brandon MS 39042	601-825-2811	824-8519	374-3
Web: www.merithealthrankin.com			
Merit Health River Region			
2100 Hwy 61 N.......................... Vicksburg MS 39183	601-883-5000	883-5196	374-3
Web: www.riverregion.com			
Merit Health Wesley 5001 Hardy St .... Hattiesburg MS 39402	601-268-8000		374-3
TF: 877-456-9617 ■ *Web:* www.wesley.com			
Merit Marketing Inc 741 S Campbell Ave......... Tucson AZ 85719	520-624-8211		195
Web: meritmarketinginc.com			
Merit Medical Systems Inc			
1600 W Merit Pkwy .... South Jordan UT 84095	801-253-1600	253-1652	476
NASDAQ: MMSI ■ *TF:* 800-356-3748 ■ *Web:* www.merit.com			
Merit Network Inc			
1000 Oakbrook Dr Ste 200................. Ann Arbor MI 48104	734-764-9430	527-5790	171
Web: www.merit.edu			
Merit Solutions Inc			
1749 S Naperville Rd Ste 200................ Wheaton IL 60189	630-614-7133		196
Web: meritsolutions.com			
Merit Systems Protection Board (MSPB)			
1615 M St NW .... Washington DC 20419	202-653-7200	653-7130	340-20
TF: 800-209-8960 ■ *Web:* www.mspb.gov			
Merit Systems Protection Board Regional Offices (MSPB)			
Atlanta Region			
401 W Peachtree St NW 10th Fl............... Atlanta GA 30308	404-730-2755	730-2767	340-20
TF: 800-209-8960 ■ *Web:* www.mspb.gov			
Central Region			
230 S Dearborn St 31st Fl .... Chicago IL 60604	312-353-2923	886-4231	340-20
TF: 800-424-9121 ■ *Web:* www.mspb.gov			
Denver Field Office			
165 S Union Blvd Ste 318 .... Lakewood CO 80228	303-969-5101		340-20
TF: 800-209-8960 ■ *Web:* www.mspb.gov			
New York Field Office			
26 Federal Plaza Rm 3137-A .... New York NY 10278	212-264-9372		340-20
Web: www.mspb.gov			
Northeastern Region			
1601 Market St Ste 1700................ Philadelphia PA 19103	215-597-9960	597-3456	340-20
Web: mspb.gov			
Washington (DC) Region			
1800 Diagonal Rd Ste 205................ Alexandria VA 22314	703-756-6250	756-7112	340-20
Web: www.mspb.gov			
Western Region			
201 Mission St Ste 2310............. San Francisco CA 94105	415-904-6772	904-0580	340-20
Web: www.mspb.gov			
Merit Travel Group Inc 111 Peter St .... Toronto ON M5V2H1	416-364-3775		771
TF: 866-341-1777 ■ *Web:* www.merit.ca			
Merit USA 620 Clark Ave .... Pittsburg CA 94565	800-445-6374	427-6427*	492
**Fax Area Code:* 925 ■ *TF:* 800-445-6374 ■ *Web:* www.meritsteel.com			
Meritage 70 Rowes Wharf .... Boston MA 02110	617-439-3995		671
Web: www.meritagetherestaurant.com			
Meritage at the Claremont			
41 Tunnel Rd.............................. Berkeley CA 94705	510-549-8510		671
Web: www.fairmont.com/claremont-berkeley			
Meritage Homes Corp			
17851 N 85th St Ste 300 .... Scottsdale AZ 85255	480-515-8100		653
NYSE: MTH ■ *Web:* www.meritagehomes.com			
Meritage Hospitality Group Inc			
3310 Eagle Park Dr Ste 205 .... Grand Rapids MI 49525	616-776-2600		670
OTC: MHGU ■ *TF:* 800-937-5449 ■ *Web:* www.meritagehospitality.com			
Meritage Midstream Services LLC			
1331 Seventeenth St Ste 1100 .... Denver CO 80202	303-551-8150		539
Web: www.meritagemidstream.com			

Phone | Fax | Class

Meritage Portfolio Management Inc
7500 College Blvd Ste 1212 .... Overland Park KS 66210 913-345-7000 401
TF: 800-486-6468 ■ *Web:* www.meritageportfolio.com

MeriTec Services Inc
12770 Cimarron Path Ste 118 .... San Antonio TX 78249 210-694-4635 225
Web: www.meritecservices.com

Meritech Inc
4577 Hinckley Industrial Pkwy .... Cleveland OH 44109 216-459-8333 179
Web: www.meritechinc.com

Meritide Inc 2685 Patton Rd .... Saint Paul MN 55113 651-255-7300 809
Web: www.meritide.com

Merits Health Products Inc
730 NE 19th Pl .... Cape Coral FL 33909 239-772-0579 477
TF: 800-963-7487 ■ *Web:* www.meritshealth.com

Merittech LLC
6700 Kirkville Rd Bldg B Ste 105 .... East Syracuse NY 13057 315-234-4545 180

Meritus Health
11116 Medical Campus Rd .... Hagerstown MD 21742 301-790-8000 374-3
TF: 800-735-2258 ■ *Web:* www.meritushealth.com

Meriwest Credit Union PO Box 530953 .... San Jose CA 95153 877-637-4937 363-3330* 219
**Fax Area Code:* 408 ■ *TF:* 877-637-4937 ■ *Web:* www.meriwest.com

Meriwether Capital LLC
30 Rockefeller Plaza Rm 5600 .... New York NY 10112 212-649-5890 41
Web: www.meriwethercapital.net

Meriwether County
17234 Roosevelt Hwy Bldg B .... Greenville GA 30222 706-672-1314 672-9544 338
Web: meriwethercountyga.gov

Meriwether County Schools
2100 Gaston St PO Box 70 .... Greenville GA 30222 706-672-4297 685
Web: www.mcssga.org

Meriwether Godsey Inc
4944 Old Boonsboro Rd .... Lynchburg VA 24503 434-384-3663 77
TF: 800-308-4842 ■ *Web:* www.merig.com

Merix Financial Inc
390 Bay St 18th Fl Ste 500 .... Toronto ON M5H2Y2 877-637-4914 509
TF: 877-637-4914 ■ *Web:* www.merixfinancial.com

Merkle Group Inc
7001 Columbia Gateway Dr .... Columbia MD 21046 443-542-4000 542-4758 636
Web: www.merkleinc.com

Merkle Inc
50 Chestnut Ridge Rd Ste. 120 .... Montvale NJ 07645 201-571-2000 195
Web: www.merkleinc.com

Merkle Wildlife Sanctuary
580 Taylor Ave .... Annapolis MD 21401 877-620-8367 565
TF: 877-620-8367 ■ *Web:* dnr2.maryland.gov

Merkle-Korff Industries Inc
25 NW Pt Blvd Ste 900 .... Elk Grove Village IL 60007 847-439-3760 439-3963 518
Web: www.merkle-korff.com

Merkley & Partners
200 Varick St 12th Fl .... New York NY 10014 212-805-7500 4
TF: 800-438-7325 ■ *Web:* www.merkleyandpartners.com

Merkley Jeff (Sen D - OR)
313 Hart Bldg .... Washington DC 20510 202-224-3753 228-3997 342-2
Web: www.merkley.senate.gov

Merle Boes Inc 11372 E Lakewood Blvd .... Holland MI 49424 616-392-7036 579
TF: 800-545-0706 ■ *Web:* www.merleboes.com

Merle Hay Mall 3800 Merle Hay Rd .... Des Moines IA 50310 515-276-8551 276-9227 460
Web: www.merlehaymall.com

Merle Norman Cosmetics Inc
9130 Bellanca Ave .... Los Angeles CA 90045 310-641-3000 214
TF: 800-421-6648 ■ *Web:* www.merlenorman.com

Merle's Automotive Supply Inc
33 W University Blvd .... Tucson AZ 85705 520-622-3526 54
TF: 800-546-6040 ■ *Web:* www.merlesauto.com

Merlex Stucco Co
2911 N Orange-Olive Rd .... Orange CA 92865 714-637-1700 637-4865 500
Web: www.merlex.com

Merlin Corp 3815 E Main St .... Saint Charles IL 60174 630-513-8200 513-1388 310
TF: 800-652-9910 ■ *Web:* www.merlins.com

Merlin Law Group PA
777 S Harbour Island Blvd .... Tampa FL 33602 813-229-1000 41
TF: 800-993-4601 ■ *Web:* www.merlinlawgroup.com

Merlin Petroleum Company Inc
235 Post Rd W .... Westport CT 06880 203-227-3200 539
Web: www.merlinpetroleum.com

Merlino Foods 4100 Fourth Ave S .... Seattle WA 98134 206-723-4700 138
Web: www.merlino.com

MerlinOne Inc 17 Whitney Rd .... Quincy MA 02169 617-328-6645 226
Web: www.merlinone.com

Merlo on Maple 16 W Maple St .... Chicago IL 60610 312-335-8200 335-8205 671
Web: www.merlochicago.com

Merlot Marketing 4430 Duckhorn Dr .... Sacramento CA 95834 916-285-9835 7
TF: 800-873-5673 ■ *Web:* www.merlotmarketing.com

Mermaid Manufacturing
2651 Park Windsor Dr Ste 203 .... Fort Myers FL 33901 239-418-0535 14
TF: 800-330-3553 ■ *Web:* www.mmair.com

Mermet Lake State Fish & Wildlife Area
1812 Grinnell Rd .... Belknap IL 62908 618-524-5577 565
Web: www.dnr.illinois.gov/parks/pages/mermetlake.aspx

Merollis Chevrolet Sales & Service Inc
21800 Gratiot Ave .... Eastpointe MI 48021 586-775-8300 57
Web: www.merollischevy.com

Merrell Footwear
9341 Courtland Dr NE .... Rockford MI 49351 616-866-5500 866-5625 301
TF Cust Svc: 800-288-3124 ■ *Web:* www.merrell.com/us/en

Merriam-Webster Inc PO Box 281 .... Springfield MA 01102 413-734-3134 731-5979 637-2
TF Cust Svc: 800-828-1880 ■ *Web:* www.merriam-webster.com

Merrick & Co 2450 S Peoria St .... Aurora CO 80014 303-751-0741 751-2581 261
TF: 800-544-1714 ■ *Web:* www.merrick.com

Merrick County
1510 18th St PO Box 27 .... Central City NE 68826 308-946-2881 946-2332 338
Web: www.merrickcounty.ne.gov

Merrick Engineering Inc 1275 Quarry St .... Corona CA 92879 951-737-6040 608
Web: www.merrickengineering.com

Merrick House 907 Coral Way .... Coral Gables FL 33134 305-460-5361 50-3
Web: coralgables.com

Merrick Industries Inc
10 Arthur Dr .... Lynn Haven FL 32444 850-265-3611 265-9768* 684
**Fax:* Hum Res ■ *TF:* 800-345-8440 ■ *Web:* www.merrick-inc.com

Merrick Inn, The 1074 Merrick Dr .... Lexington KY 40502 859-269-5417 671
TF: 800-734-5611 ■ *Web:* themerrickinn.com

Merrick State Park S2965 Sr 35 .... Fountain City WI 54629 608-687-4936 565
Web: dnr.wi.gov

Merrick Towle Associates Inc
5801-F Ammendale Rd .... Beltsville MD 20705 301-974-6000 5
Web: www.merricktowle.com

Merrick's Inc
2415 Parview Rd PO Box 620307 .... Middleton WI 53562 608-831-3440 836-8943 447
TF: 800-637-7425 ■ *Web:* www.merricks.com

Merrigan Brandt Ostenso & Cambre pa
25 Ninth Ave N .... Hopkins MN 55343 952-933-2390 428
TF: 800-770-7008 ■ *Web:* merriganlaw.com

Merrill Area Chamber of Commerce
705 N Ctr Ave .... Merrill WI 54452 715-536-9474 539-2043 139
TF: 877-907-2757 ■ *Web:* www.merrillchamber.org

Merrill Auditorium 20 Myrtle St .... Portland ME 04101 207-842-0800 842-0810 572
Web: tickets.porttix.com

Merrill Corp 1 Merrill Cir .... Saint Paul MN 55108 651-646-4501 627
TF: 800-688-4400 ■ *Web:* www.merrillcorp.com

Merrill Corporation 1 Merrill Cir .... St. Paul MN 55108 651-646-4501 387
TF: 888-311-4100 ■ *Web:* www.merrillcorp.com

Merrill Iron & Steel Inc
900 Alderson St .... Schofield WI 54476 715-355-8924 480
Web: www.merrilliron.com

Merrill Manufacturing Co
315 Flindt Dr .... Storm Lake IA 50588 712-732-2760 789
Web: www.merrillmfg.com

Merrill Mfg Corp 236 S Genesee St .... Merrill WI 54452 715-536-5533 536-5590 811
TF: 888-662-9473 ■ *Web:* www.merrill-mfg.com

Merrill Tool & Machine Co Inc
21659 Gratiot Rd .... Merrill MI 48637 989-643-7981 643-7975 494
Web: www.merrilltool.com

Merrill's Packaging Inc
1529 Rollins Rd .... Burlingame CA 94010 650-259-5959 596
Web: www.merrills.com

Merrill-Stevens Dry Dock Company Inc
1270 NW 11th St .... Miami FL 33125 305-324-5211 698
Web: www.merrill-stevensyachts.com

Merrimac Industries Inc
41 Fairfield Pl .... West Caldwell NJ 07006 973-575-1300 575-0531* 253
**Fax:* Sales ■ *Web:* www.craneae.com

Merrimac Tile Company Inc
18 Tsienneto Rd .... Derry NH 03038 603-432-2544 191-1
Web: www.merrimactile.com

Merrimack College 315 Tpke St .... North Andover MA 01845 978-837-5000 837-5133* 166
**Fax:* Admissions ■ *TF:* 800-433-3243 ■ *Web:* www.merrimack.edu

Merrimack Repertory Theatre
132 Warren St .... Lowell MA 01852 978-654-7550 654-7575 749
Web: www.mrt.org

Merrimack Valley Chamber of Commerce
264 Essex St .... Lawrence MA 01840 978-686-0900 794-9953 139
TF: 800-966-3375 ■ *Web:* www.merrimackvalleychamber.com

Merrimack Valley Distributing Co
50 Prince St .... Danvers MA 01923 978-777-2213 774-7487 81-1
TF: 800-331-2829 ■ *Web:* mvdc.com

Merrimack Valley Hospice
360 Merrimack St Bldg 9 .... Lawrence MA 01843 800-933-5593 552-4401* 371
**Fax Area Code:* 978 ■ *TF:* 800-933-5593 ■ *Web:* www.homehealthfoundation.org

Merrion Group LLC 210 Elmer St .... Westfield NJ 07090 908-654-0033 690
Web: www.merriongroup.net

Merrion Oil & Gas 610 Reilly Ave .... Farmington NM 87401 505-324-5300 536
Web: www.merrion.bz

Merrithew Corp 2200 Yonge St Ste 500 .... Toronto ON M4S2C6 416-482-4050 787
TF: 800-910-0001 ■ *Web:* www.merrithew.com

Merritt Bros Lumber Co Inc
5400 E Hwy 54 .... Athol ID 83801 208-683-3321 683
Web: www.merrittbros.com

Merritt Capital Management Inc
30 Western Ave Ste 101 .... Gloucester MA 01930 978-282-0035 401
Web: www.merrittcapitalmanagement.com

Merritt College 12500 Campus Dr .... Oakland CA 94619 510-531-4911 162
Web: www.merritt.edu

Merritt Environmental Consulting Corp
77 Arkay Dr .... Hauppauge NY 11788 631-617-6200 261
Web: merrittec.com

Merritt Equipment Co 9339 Hwy 85 .... Henderson CO 80640 303-289-2286 288-6127 779
TF: 800-634-3036 ■ *Web:* www.merrittequipment.com

Merritt Interpreting Services
3626 N Hall St Ste 504 .... Dallas TX 75219 214-969-5585 768
TF: 866-761-2585 ■ *Web:* www.mis-interpreting.com

Merritt Museum of Anthropology
12500 Campus Dr .... Oakland CA 94619 510-531-4911 520
Web: merritt.edu

Merritt Properties LLC
2066 Lord Baltimore Dr .... Baltimore MD 21244 410-298-2600 298-9644 655
Web: www.merrittproperties.com

Merritt Reservoir State Recreation Area
420 E First St .... Valentine NE 69201 402-376-3320 565
Web: outdoornebraska.gov/merrittreservoir

Merritt Technical Associates Inc
114 Saint Johns Rd .... Wilton CT 06897 203-834-0010 225
Web: www.merritt-tech.com

Merritt's Boat & Engine Works Inc
2931 NE 16th St .... Pompano Beach FL 33062 954-943-6250 90
Web: www.merrittboat.com

Merriweather Post Pavilion (MPP)
10475 Little Patuxent Pkwy .... Columbia MD 21044 410-715-5550 715-5560 572
TF: 877-435-9849 ■ *Web:* www.merriweathermusic.com

Merry Maids
3839 Forrest Hill-Irene Rd .... Memphis TN 38125 800-798-8000 597-8140* 152
**Fax Area Code:* 901 ■ *TF:* 800-798-8000 ■ *Web:* www.merrymaids.com

Merry Rama Insurance 4236 County Hwy 18 .... Delhi NY 13753 607-746-2226 746-2911 391-1
Web: www.cattlexchange.com/insurance.htm

Merry X-Ray Corp
4444 Viewridge Ave Ste A .... San Diego CA 92123 858-565-4472 475
Web: www.merryxray.com

	Phone	Fax	Class
Mersana Therapeutics Inc 840 Memorial Dr ... Cambridge MA 02139 *Web:* www.mersana.com	617-498-0020		668
Mersen Inc 374 Merrimac St ... Newburyport MA 01950 *TF:* 800-388-5428 ■ *Web:* www.mersen.com	978-462-6662	462-7934	729
Mersen USA BN Corp 400 Myrtle Ave ... Boonton NJ 07005 **Fax Area Code:* 973 ■ *TF General:* 800-526-0877 ■ *Web:* www.mersen.com	800-526-0877	334-6394*	127
Mershon Ctr 1501 Neil Ave ... Columbus OH 43201 *Web:* mershoncenter.osu.edu	614-292-1681	292-2407	634
Mersoft Corp 7007 College Blvd Ste 350 ... Overland Park KS 66211 *Web:* www.mersoft.com	913-871-6200		177
Mert's Heart & Soul 214 N College St ... Charlotte NC 28202 *Web:* www.uptown2go.com	704-342-4222		671
Mertz Mfg Inc 1701 N Waverly St ... Ponca City OK 74601 *Web:* www.mertzok.com	580-762-5646	767-8411	273
Meruelo Construction 9550 Firestone Blvd Ste 105 ... Downey CA 90241 *Web:* merueloenterprises.com	562-745-2300		787
Mervis Diamond Corp 1900 Mervis Way Tyson's Corner ... Vienna VA 22182 *TF:* 800-437-5683 ■ *Web:* www.mervisdiamond.com	703-448-9000		410
Mervis Industries Inc 3295 E Main St ... Danville IL 61834 *Web:* www.mervis.com	217-442-5300	477-9245	686
MERX Networks Inc 6 Antares Dr Phase II Unit 103 ... Ottawa ON K2E8A9 *TF:* 800-964-6379 ■ *Web:* www.merx.com	613-727-4900		387
Merz Group, The 1570 Mcdaniel Dr ... West Chester PA 19380 *TF:* 800-600-9900 ■ *Web:* www.themerzgroup.com	610-429-3160		7
Mesa 85 Fifth Ave 6th Fl ... New York NY 10003 *Web:* www.mesaglobal.com	212-792-3950		70
Mesa Arizona Temple 101 S LeSueur ... Mesa AZ 85204 *TF:* 855-537-4357 ■ *Web:* www.lds.org/church/temples	480-833-1211	827-2828	50-1
Mesa Arts Ctr 1 E Main St PO Box 1466 ... Mesa AZ 85201 *Web:* www.mesaartscenter.com	480-644-6501	644-6503	50-2
Mesa Assoc Inc PO Box 196 ... Madison AL 35758 *Web:* www.mesainc.com	256-258-2100	258-2103	261
Mesa Chamber of Commerce 165 N Centennial Way ... Mesa AZ 85201 *Web:* www.mesachamber.org	480-969-1307	827-0727	139
Mesa Citrus Growers Assn 254 W Broadway Rd ... Mesa AZ 85210	480-964-8615		11-1
Mesa City Hall PO Box 1466 ... Mesa AZ 85211 *TF:* 866-406-9659 ■ *Web:* www.mesaaz.gov	480-644-2221	644-2821	337
Mesa Community College 1833 W Southern Ave ... Mesa AZ 85202 *TF:* 866-532-4983 ■ *Web:* mesacc.edu	480-461-7000		162
Red Mountain 7110 E McKellips Rd ... Mesa AZ 85207 *TF:* 866-532-4983 ■ *Web:* mesacc.edu	480-654-7200	654-7379	162
Mesa Convention Ctr 263 N Ctr St ... Mesa AZ 85201 *Web:* mesaaz.gov/business/mesa-convention-center	480-644-2178	644-2617	205
Mesa County PO Box 20000 ... Grand Junction CO 81502 *Web:* www.mesacounty.us	970-244-1800	256-1588	338
Mesa Equipment & Supply Co 7100 Second St NW ... Albuquerque NM 87107 *Web:* mesaequipment.com	505-345-0284		358
Mesa Fully Formed Inc 1111 S Sirrine ... Mesa AZ 85210 *Web:* www.mesa.org	480-834-9331		115
Mesa Grande School Elementary School 9172 Third Ave ... Hesperia CA 92345 *Web:* www.mesagrandeelementary.org	760-244-3709		685
Mesa Historical Museum 51 E Main St PO Box 582 ... Mesa AZ 85201 *Web:* www.valleyhistoryinc.com	480-835-7358		520
Mesa Industries Inc 1726 S Magnolia Ave ... Monrovia CA 91016 *Web:* www.mesaetp.com	626-359-9361	359-7985	326
Mesa Laboratories Inc 12100 W Sixth Ave ... Lakewood CO 80228 *NASDAQ: MLAB* ■ *TF Sales:* 800-992-6372 ■ *Web:* www.mesalabs.com	303-987-8000	987-8989	475
Mesa Mechanical Inc 3514 Pinemont Dr ... Houston TX 77018 *Web:* www.mesamechanical.com	713-681-5300	681-6675	610
Mesa Products Inc 4445 S 74th E Ave ... Tulsa OK 74145 *Web:* www.mesaproducts.com	918-627-3188		690
Mesa Public Library 64 E First St ... Mesa AZ 85201 *Web:* www.mesalibrary.org	480-644-3100		434-3
Mesa State College 1100 N Ave ... Grand Junction CO 81501 **Fax:* Admissions ■ *TF:* 800-982-6372 ■ *Web:* coloradomesa.edu	970-248-1020	248-1973*	166
Mesa Systems Inc 681 Railroad Blvd ... Grand Junction CO 81505 *TF:* 800-654-3225 ■ *Web:* www.mesasystemsinc.com	970-241-6450		360-2
Mesabi Range Community & Technical College 1100 Industrial Pk Dr PO Box 648 ... Eveleth MN 55734 *TF:* 800-657-3860 ■ *Web:* www.mr.mnscu.edu	218-741-3095	744-7466	162
Mesalands Community College 911 S Tenth St ... Tucumcari NM 88401 *Web:* www.mesalands.edu	575-461-4413		162
Mesch, Clark & Rothschild PC 259 N Meyer Ave ... Tucson AZ 85701 *Web:* www.mcrazlaw.com	520-624-8886		428
Mesco Bldg Solutions 5244 Bear Creek Ct ... Irving TX 75061 *TF:* 800-556-3726 ■ *Web:* www.mescobuildingsolutions.com	214-687-9999	687-9736	105
MESDA (Museum of Early Southern Decorative Arts) 924 S Main St ... Winston-Salem NC 27101 *Web:* www.mesda.org	336-721-7360	721-7367	520
Mesh Dynamics Inc 2953 Bunker Hill Ln Ste 400 ... Santa Clara CA 95054 *Web:* www.meshdynamics.com	408-373-7700		647
Mesh Systems LLC 12400 N Meridian St Ste 175 ... Carmel IN 46032 *TF:* 800-867-1389 ■ *Web:* www.mesh-systems.com	317-661-4800		387
Mesilla Valley Hospice 299 Montana Ave ... Las Cruces NM 88005 *TF:* 800-400-2820 ■ *Web:* www.mvhospice.org	575-525-5757	527-2204	371
Mesilla Valley Kitchen 2001 E Lohman ... Las Cruces NM 88001 *Web:* www.mesillavalleykitchen.com	575-523-9311		671
Mesilla Valley Mall 700 S Telshor Blvd ... Las Cruces NM 88011 *Web:* www.mesillavalleymall.com	575-522-1001	522-0956	460
Mesirow Financial Inc 350 N Clark St ... Chicago IL 60654 **Fax:* Hum Res ■ *TF:* 888-681-0082 ■ *Web:* www.mesirowfinancial.com	312-595-6000	595-4246*	690
Mesirow Financial Insurance Services Div 353 N Clark St ... Chicago IL 60654 *TF:* 800-453-0600 ■ *Web:* www.mesirowfinancial.com	312-595-6200		390
Mesirow Financial Private Equity 350 N Clark St ... Chicago IL 60654 *TF:* 800-453-0600 ■ *Web:* www.mesirowfinancial.com	312-595-6000	595-4246	792
Mesker Park Zoo 1545 Mesker Pk Dr ... Evansville IN 47720 *Web:* meskerparkzoo.com	812-435-6143	435-6140	823
Mesko Glass & Mirror Company Inc 801 Wyoming Ave ... Scranton PA 18509 *TF:* 800-982-4055 ■ *Web:* www.mesko.com	570-346-0777		330
Meskwaki Bingo Hotel Casino 1504 305th St ... Tama IA 52339 *TF:* 800-728-4263 ■ *Web:* www.meskwaki.com	800-728-4263		133
MesoCoat Inc 24112 Rockwell Dr ... Euclid OH 44117 *Web:* www.mesocoat.com	216-453-0866		481
Mesotec Inc 4705 Boul de Portland ... Sherbrooke QC J1L0H3 *Web:* www.mesotec.ca	819-822-2777	822-4117	21
Mesquite Chamber of Commerce 617 N Ebrite St ... Mesquite TX 75149 *Web:* www.mesquitechamber.com	972-285-0211	285-3535	139
Mesquite Championship Rodeo Inc 1818 Rodeo Dr ... Mesquite TX 75149 *TF:* 800-745-3000 ■ *Web:* www.mesquiterodeo.com	972-285-8777		671
Mesquite Public Library 300 W Grubb Dr ... Mesquite TX 75149 *TF:* 800-772-1213 ■ *Web:* www.cityofmesquite.com	972-216-6220	216-6740	434-3
Messa & Associates PC 123 S 22nd St ... Philadelphia PA 19103 *Web:* messalaw.com	215-568-3500		428
MessageBank LLC 250 W 57Th St Ste 1001 ... New York NY 10107 *TF:* 800-989-8001 ■ *Web:* www.messagebank.com	212-333-9300		387
MessageSolution Inc 1851 McCarthy Blvd Ste 105 ... Milpitas CA 95035 *Web:* www.messagesolution.com	408-383-0100		225
Messaging Architects 180 Peel St Ste 333 ... Montreal QC H3C2G7 *TF:* 866-497-0101 ■ *Web:* www.netmail.com	514-392-9220		179
Messaging Solutions LLC 8203 Shoregrove Dr Ste 200 ... Humble TX 77346 *Web:* www.messagingsolutions.com	281-852-1301	661-1160	435
Messe Frankfurt Inc 1600 Parkwood Cir Ste 615 ... Atlanta GA 30339 *Web:* us.messefrankfurt.com	770-984-8016	984-8023	822
Messenger, The 713 Central Ave ... Fort Dodge IA 50501 *TF:* 800-622-6613 ■ *Web:* www.messengernews.net	515-573-2141	574-4529	532-2
Messenger, The PO Box 727 ... Troy AL 36081 *Web:* www.troymessenger.com	334-566-4270		532-2
Messenger-Inquirer 1401 Fredrica St ... Owensboro KY 42301 *TF:* 800-633-2008 ■ *Web:* www.messenger-inquirer.com	270-926-0123	686-7868	532-2
Messer Construction Co 5158 Fishwick Dr ... Cincinnati OH 45216 *Web:* www.messer.com	513-242-1541	242-6467	186
Messer Luke (Rep R - IN) 1230 Longworth HOB ... Washington DC 20515 *Web:* messer.house.gov	202-225-3021		342-2
Messerli & Kramer PA 1400 Fifth St Towers 100 S Fifth St ... Minneapolis MN 55402 *Web:* www.messerlikramer.com	612-672-3600	672-3777	428
Messiah College PO Box 3005 ... Grantham PA 17027 **Fax:* Admissions ■ *TF:* 800-233-4220 ■ *Web:* www.messiah.edu	717-691-6000	796-5374*	166
Messiah Lutheran Church 303 Rt- 101 PO Box 488 ... Amherst NH 03031 *Web:* www.messiahnh.org	603-673-2011		48-20
Messiah Village 100 Mt Allen Dr Ofc ... Mechanicsburg PA 17055 *Web:* messiahlifeways.org	717-790-8232		48-20
Messina & Company LLC 1615 Pontiac Ave ... Cranston RI 02920	401-463-6800		2
Mesta Electronics Inc 11020 Parker Dr ... North Huntingdon PA 15642 *TF:* 800-535-6798 ■ *Web:* www.mesta.com	412-754-3000		767
Mestek Inc 260 N Elm St ... Westfield MA 01085 *Web:* www.mestek.com	413-568-9571		14
Mestel & Company Inc 575 Madison Ave Ste 3000 ... New York NY 10022 *Web:* www.mestel.com	646-356-0500	356-0545	266
Education Trust PO Box 30198 ... Lansing MI 48909 *TF General:* 800-638-4543 ■ *Web:* www.setwithmet.com	517-335-4767	373-6967	725
Met Hotel Troy, The 5500 Crooks Rd ... Troy MI 48098 *Web:* www.themettroy.com	248-879-2100		377
Met One Instruments Inc 1600 Washington Blvd ... Grants Pass OR 97526 *Web:* www.metone.com	541-471-7111		407
Met Weld International LLC 5727 Ostrander Rd ... Altamont NY 12009 *Web:* www.metweldintl.com	518-765-2318		454
Meta Environmental Inc 100 Truck Hill Rd ... Fairport MA 14450 *Web:* metaenv.com	585-364-0728		261
Meta Manufacturing Corp 8901 Blue Ash Rd ... Cincinnati OH 45242 *Web:* metamfg.com	513-793-6382		757
Meta Pharmaceutical Services LLC 482 Norristown Rd Ste 200 ... Blue Bell PA 19422 *TF:* 800-927-9801 ■ *Web:* www.metapharm.net	610-834-9988		583
Meta Solutions Inc 63 Grove St ... Somerville NJ 08876 *Web:* www.metasol.com	908-791-1900		196
Meta5 Inc 122 W Main St Ste 204 ... Babylon NY 11702 *Web:* www.meta5.us	631-587-6800		393
Metabo Corp 1231 Wilson Dr ... West Chester PA 19380 *Web:* metabo.us	610-436-5900		350

Phone | Fax | Class

Metabolic Maintenance Products Inc
68994 N Pine St .... Sisters OR 97759 541-549-7800 345
Web: www.metabolicmaintenance.com

Metabolon Inc
3410 Industrial Blvd Ste 103 .... West Sacramento CA 95691 916-371-7974 668
Web: www.lipomics.com

MetaDesign North America
615 Battery St 6th Fl .... San Francisco CA 94111 415-627-0790 7
Web: www.metadesign.com

Metadyne Inc Fox Chase Dr PO Box 328 .... Towanda PA 18848 570-265-6963 567
Web: www.towandametadyne.com

Metafile Information Systems Inc
3428 Lakeridge Pl NW .... Rochester MN 55901 507-286-9232 286-9065 178-11
TF Sales: 800-638-2445 ■ *Web:* metaviewer.com

Metairie Bank & Trust Co
3344 Metairie Rd .... Metairie LA 70001 504-834-6330 70
Web: www.metairiebank.com

Metairie Park Country Day School Alumni Assn
300 Park Rd .... Metairie LA 70005 504-837-5204 685
Web: mpcds.com

Metal & Wire Products Co
1065 Salem Pkwy .... Salem OH 44460 330-332-9448 492
Web: www.metalandwire.com

Metal Arts Finishing Inc
1001 S Lake St .... Aurora IL 60506 630-892-6744 481

Metal Box International
11600 W King St .... Franklin Park IL 60131 847-455-8500 488
Web: edsal.com

Metal Cladding Inc 230 S Niagara St .... Lockport NY 14094 800-432-5513 439-4010* 481
**Fax Area Code:* 716 ■ *TF:* 800-432-5513 ■ *Web:* www.metalcladding.com

Metal Coatings Corp 3700 Dunvale Rd .... Houston TX 77063 713-977-0123 977-0824 481
Web: www.metcoat.com

Metal ComponentsLLC
3281 Roger B Chaffee Memorial Blvd SE .... Grand Rapids MI 49548 616-252-1900 488
Web: metalcompinc.com

Metal Craft Machine & Engineering Inc
13760 Business Ctr Dr .... Elk River MN 55330 763-441-1855 454
Web: www.metal-craft.com

Metal Culverts Inc
2107 Rear Missouri Blvd .... Jefferson City MO 65109 573-636-7312 295
TF: 800-694-2958 ■ *Web:* www.metalculverts.com

Metal Cutting Corp 89 Commerce Rd .... Cedar Grove NJ 07009 973-239-1100 239-6651 455
TF: 800-783-6382 ■ *Web:* www.metalcutting.com

Metal Edge Magazine
333 Seventh Ave Ste 1100 .... New York NY 10001 212-780-3500 457-9

Metal Exchange Corp
111 W Port Plaza Ste 350 .... Saint Louis MO 63146 314-434-3500 434-2196 686
TF: 800-440-3110 ■ *Web:* www.metalexchangecorp.com

Metal Fabricating Corp
10408 Berea Rd .... Cleveland OH 44102 216-631-2480 631-2453 482
Web: www.metalfabricatingcorp.com

Metal Flow Corp 11694 James St .... Holland MI 49424 616-392-7976 392-5814 488
Web: www.metalflow.com

Metal Forming & Coining Corp (MFC)
1007 Illinois Ave .... Maumee OH 43537 419-893-8748 483
Web: www.mfccorp.com

Metal Forms Corp 3334 N Booth St .... Milwaukee WI 53212 414-964-4550 697
Web: www.metalforms.com

Metal Improvement Company LLC
80 Rt 4 E Ste 310 .... Paramus NJ 07652 201-843-7800 843-3460 484
Web: cwst.com

Metal Management Mississippi Inc
304 W Bankhead St .... New Albany MS 38652 662-534-3004 660
TF: 800-446-0244 ■ *Web:* www.simsmm.com

Metal Marketplace International (MMI)
718 Sansom St .... Philadelphia PA 19106 215-592-8777 592-8195 411
TF: 800-523-9191 ■ *Web:* www.metalmarketplace.com

Metal Master Sales Corp
1159 N Main St .... Glendale Heights IL 60139 630-858-4750 256
Web: www.metalmaster.com

Metal Masters Inc
3825 Crater Lake Hwy .... Medford OR 97504 541-779-1049 186
TF: 800-866-9437 ■ *Web:* www.metalmasters-inc.com

Metal Powder Industries Federation (MPIF)
105 College Rd E .... Princeton NJ 08540 609-452-7700 987-8523 49-13
TF: 800-237-7600 ■ *Web:* www.mpif.org

Metal Seal & Products Inc
4323 Hamann Pkwy .... Willoughby OH 44094 440-946-8500 247
Web: www.metalseal.com

Metal Spinners Inc 800 Growth Pkwy .... Angola IN 46703 260-665-2192 483
Web: www.metalspinners.com

Metal Standard Corp 286 Hedcor St .... Holland MI 49423 616-396-4890 697
Web: www.metalstd.com

Metal Supermarkets IP Inc
520 Abilene Dr 2nd Fl .... Mississauga ON L5T2H7 905-362-8226 492
TF: 866-867-9344 ■ *Web:* www.metalsupermarkets.com

Metal Technologies of Murfreesboro Inc
314 W Broad St .... Murfreesboro NC 27855 252-398-4041 757
TF: 800-624-3279 ■ *Web:* www.metaltechnc.com

Metal Textiles 970 New Durham Rd .... Edison NJ 08818 732-287-0800 287-8546* 688
**Fax:* Sales ■ *Web:* www.metaltextiles.com

Metal Trades Inc PO Box 129 .... Hollywood SC 29449 843-889-6441 697
Web: www.metaltrades.com

Metalcare Group Inc
291 Macalpine Cres .... Fort Mcmurray AB T9H4Y4 780-715-1889 365
Web: metalcare.com

Metalcraft of Mayville Inc
1000 Metalcraft Dr .... Mayville WI 53050 920-387-3150 492
Web: www.mtlcraft.com

Metalcraft Technologies Inc
526 N Aviation Way .... Cedar City UT 84720 435-586-3871 586-0289 697
Web: www.metalcraft.net

Metal-Era Inc 1600 Airport Rd .... Waukesha WI 53188 800-558-2162 697
TF: 800-558-2162 ■ *Web:* www.metalera.com

Metalex Corp
1530 Artaius Pkwy PO Box 399 .... Libertyville IL 60048 847-362-8300 362-7939 723
TF: 800-323-0792 ■ *Web:* www.metlx.com

Metalex Manufacturing Inc
5750 Cornell Rd .... Cincinnati OH 45242 513-489-0507 489-1020 454
Web: www.metalexmfg.com

Metal-Fab Inc 3025 May St .... Wichita KS 67213 316-943-2351 943-2717 697
TF: 800-835-2830 ■ *Web:* www.mtlfab.com

Metalforms Manufacturing Inc
7218 Garth St .... Beaumont TX 77705 409-842-1626 842-1503 91
Web: www.metalformsltd.com

Metalico Annaco Inc 943 Hazel St .... Akron OH 44305 330-376-1400 376-9696 686
TF: 800-966-1499 ■ *Web:* www.metalico.com

Metalink Technologies Inc
417 Wayne Ave PO Box 1124 .... Defiance OH 43512 419-782-3472 224
TF: 888-999-8002 ■ *Web:* www.metalink.net

Metalist International Inc
1159 S Pennsylvania Ave .... Lansing MI 48912 517-371-2940 371-3027 483
Web: www.metalist.com

Metallic Arts Inc 914 N Lake Rd .... Spokane WA 99212 509-489-7173 483-1759 777
TF: 800-541-3200 ■ *Web:* www.geminisignproducts.com

Metallics Inc
W7274 County Hwy Z PO Box 99 .... Onalaska WI 54650 608-781-5200 781-2254 702
TF: 800-280-0780 ■ *Web:* www.metallics.net

Metallized Carbon Corp 19 S Water St .... Ossining NY 10562 914-941-3738 941-4050 620
Web: www.metcar.com

Metalloid Southwest
1829 Norman Dr .... Jacksonville TX 75766 903-589-3933 579
Web: metalloidcorp.com

Metallurgical Products Co
810 Lincoln Ave PO Box 598 .... West Chester PA 19381 610-696-6770 430-8431 485
TF: 800-659-4672 ■ *Web:* www.metprodco.com

Metallurgical Technologies Inc PA
160 Bevan Dr .... Mooresville NC 28115 704-663-5108 415
Web: www.met-tech.com

MetaLogix Inc
9789 Charlotte Hwy Ste 400-142 .... Fort Mill SC 29707 704-543-1616 177
Web: www.metalogixinc.com

Metalor Electrotechnics
1003 Corporate Ln .... Export PA 15632 724-733-8332 733-8341 815
Web: www.metalor.com

MetaLPlate Galvanizing LP
1120 39th St N .... Birmingham AL 35234 205-595-4703 481
Web: www.metalplate.com

Metals Service Ctr Institute (MSCI)
4201 Euclid Ave .... Rolling Meadows IL 60008 847-485-3000 485-3001 49-18
TF: 800-634-2358 ■ *Web:* www.msci.org

Metals Technology Corp
120 N Schmale Rd .... Carol Stream IL 60188 630-221-2500 484
Web: metalstechnology.com

Metals Week 2 Penn Plaza .... New York NY 10121 800-752-8878 531-13
TF: 800-752-8878 ■ *Web:* www.platts.com

Metalsco Inc 1828 Craig Rd .... Saint Louis MO 63146 314-997-5200 997-5921 686
TF: 800-325-7042 ■ *Web:* www.metalsco.com

Metaltech Inc 206 Prospect Ave .... Kirkwood MO 63122 314-965-4550 697

Metaltech Service Center Inc
9915 Monroe .... Houston TX 77075 713-991-5100 492
TF: 800-644-1204 ■ *Web:* www.metaltechsc.com

Metal-Tronics Inc 126 Merrimack St .... Lawrence MA 01843 978-659-6960 488
Web: www.metaltronics.com

Metalworking Group Inc
9070 Pippin Rd .... Cincinnati OH 45251 513-521-4114 521-2816 487
TF: 800-476-9409 ■ *Web:* www.metalworkinggroup.com

Metalworking Lubricants Co
25 Silverdome Industrial Pk .... Pontiac MI 48342 248-332-3500 332-4959 541
TF: 800-394-5494 ■ *Web:* www.metalworkinglubricants.com

Metalworks Inc 902 E Fourth St .... Ludington MI 49431 231-845-5136 845-1043 697
TF: 800-580-9902 ■ *Web:* metalworks1.com

Metalworx Inc 340 Deming Way .... Summerville SC 29483 843-402-0999 697
Web: www.metalworxinc.com

MetaMetrics Inc
1000 Park Forty Plaza Dr Ste 120 .... Durham NC 27713 919-547-3400 242
Web: www.lexile.com

Metamora-Hadley Recreation Area
3871 Herd Rd .... Metamora MI 48455 810-797-4439 565
Web: www.michigandnr.com

Metaops Inc 30425 Munger Dr .... Livonia MI 48154 734-425-1455 396
Web: www.metaops.com

MetaOption LLC
574 Newark Ave Ste 210 .... Jersey City NJ 07306 201-377-3150 196
Web: www.metaoption.com

MetaResponse Group Inc
700 W Hillsboro Blvd Ste 4-107 .... Deerfield Beach FL 33441 954-360-0644 5
Web: www.metaresponse.com

Metasense Inc
403 Commerce Ln Ste 5 .... West Berlin NJ 08091 856-873-9950 225
Web: www.metasenseusa.com

MetaStat Inc 27 Drydock Ave 2nd fl .... Boston MA 02210 973-744-7618 250
Web: www.metastat.com

Metasys Technologies Inc
3460 Summit Ridge Pkwy Ste 401 .... Duluth GA 30096 678-218-1600 260
TF: 800-447-2446 ■ *Web:* www.metasysinc.com

Metasystems Inc
13700 State Rd Ste 1 .... North Royalton OH 44133 440-526-1454 463
TF: 800-788-5253 ■ *Web:* www.metasystems.com

Metcalfe County 100 E Stockton .... Edmonton KY 42129 270-432-4821 338
Web: www.metcalfecountyclerk.com

Metcalfe Group Inc, The
30405 Solon Rd Unit 5 .... Solon OH 44139 440-349-5995 393
Web: www.metcalfegroup.com

Metcalfe Realty & Auction Company Inc
100 Castle Ridge Dr .... Edmonton KY 42129 270-432-7355 652
Web: metcalferealty.net

Metcam Inc 305 Tidwell Cir .... Alpharetta GA 30004 770-475-9633 442-3425 697
TF: 888-394-9633 ■ *Web:* www.metcam.com

Met-Chem Canada Inc
555, Blvd Rene-Levesque Ouest 3e etage .... Montreal QC H2Z1B1 514-288-5211 261
TF: 800-461-4094 ■ *Web:* www.met-chem.com

Metco Industries Inc
1241 Brusselles St .... St Mary PA 15857 814-781-3630 487
Web: www.metcopm.com

Name / Address	City	State	ZIP	Phone	Fax	Class
Metco Landscape Inc 2200 Rifle St. Web: www.metcolandscape.com	Aurora	CO	80011	303-421-3100		776
Met-Con Construction Inc 15760 Acorn Trl TF: 800-222-6060 ■ Web: www.met-con.com	Faribault	MN	55021	507-332-2266		186
Met-Con Inc 465 Canaveral Groves Blvd Web: www.metconinc.com	Cocoa	FL	32926	321-632-4880	639-0158	480
Metcut Research Inc 3980 Rosslyn Dr. TF: 877-847-1985 ■ Web: www.metcut.com	Cincinnati	OH	45209	513-271-5100	271-9511	743
Metem Corp 700 Parsippany Rd Web: www.metem.com	Parsippany	NJ	07054	973-887-6635	887-1755	386
Meteor Crater & Museum of Astrogeology Exit 233 Off I-40 Meteor Crater Rd *Fax Area Code: 928 ■ TF: 800-289-5898 ■ Web: www.meteorcrater.com	Winslow	AZ	86047	800-289-5898	289-2598*	520
Meteor Express Inc PO Box 248 Web: www.meteorx.com	Scottsboro	AL	35768	256-218-3000		449
Meteorcomm LLC 1201 SW Seventh St Web: www.meteorcomm.com	Renton	WA	98057	253-872-2521	872-7662	224
Metex Inc 789 Don Mills Rd Ste 218 TF: 866-817-8137 ■ Web: www.metex.com	North York	ON	M3C1T5	416-203-8388		764
Metglas Inc 440 Allied Dr TF: 800-581-7654 ■ Web: www.metglas.com	Conway	SC	29526	843-349-7319	349-6815	485
Methane Specialists 621 Via Alondra Ste 611 Web: methanespecialists.com	Camarillo	CA	93012	805-987-5356		261
Methanex Corp 1800 Waterfront Centre 200 Burrard St. TSE: MX ■ TF: 800-661-8851 ■ Web: www.methanex.com	Vancouver	BC	V6C3M1	604-661-2600	661-2676	144
Methanol Institute (MI) 4100 Fairfax Dr Ste 740 Web: www.methanol.org	Arlington	VA	22203	703-248-3636	248-3997	48-12
Methapharm Inc 11772 W Sample Rd. TF: 800-287-7686 ■ Web: www.methapharm.com	Coral Springs	FL	33065	954-341-0795		238
Method Inc 585 Howard St Ground Fl. Web: www.method.com	San Francisco	CA	94105	415-901-6300		7
Methode Electronics Inc 7401 W Wilson Ave NYSE: MEI ■ TF: 877-316-7700 ■ Web: www.methode.com	Chicago	IL	60706	708-867-6777	867-6999	253
Methodist Alliance Hospice 6400 Shelby View Dr Ste 101 TF: 800-541-8277 ■ Web: www.methodisthealth.org	Memphis	TN	38134	901-516-1999		371
Methodist Charlton Medical Ctr 3500 W Wheatland Rd Web: methodisthealthsystem.org	Dallas	TX	75237	214-947-7777		374-3
Methodist Dallas Medical Ctr 1441 N Beckley Ave Web: www.methodisthealthsystem.org	Dallas	TX	75203	214-947-8181		374-3
Methodist ElderCare Services 5155 N High St. TF: 855-636-2225 ■ Web: www.wesleyridge.com/wesleyglen_home.aspx	Columbus	OH	43214	614-396-4990	436-6012	672
Methodist Health Care System 6565 Fannin St. TF: 877-726-9362 ■ Web: www.houstonmethodist.org	Houston	TX	77030	713-790-3311		353
Methodist Healthcare Inc 1265 Union Ave TF: 800-222-1222 ■ Web: www.methodisthealth.org	Memphis	TN	38104	901-516-7000		353
Methodist Healthcare Ministries of South Texas Inc 4507 Medical Dr. TF: 800-959-6673 ■ Web: www.mhm.org	San Antonio	TX	78229	210-692-0234	614-7563	353
Methodist Hospital 1305 N Elm St. TF: 888-318-1498 ■ Web: www.methodisthospital.net	Henderson	KY	42420	270-827-7700		374-3
Methodist Hospital 6500 Excelsior Blvd TF: 800-994-6610 ■ Web: www.parknicollet.com	Minneapolis	MN	55426	952-993-5000		374-3
Methodist Hospital 600 Grant St Web: www.methodisthospitals.org	Gary	IN	46402	219-886-4000		374-3
Methodist Hospital 1701 N Senate Blvd PO Box 1367 TF: 800-899-8448 ■ Web: www.iuhealth.org/methodist	Indianapolis	IN	46202	317-962-2000	962-0304	374-3
Methodist Hospital 6565 Fannin St. Web: www.houstonmethodist.org	Houston	TX	77030	713-790-3311	441-7465	374-3
Methodist Hospital 8109 Fredericksburg Rd TF: 800-333-7333 ■ Web: sahealth.com	San Antonio	TX	78229	210-575-0355	575-6292	374-3
Methodist Hospital 2301 S Broad St Web: hospitals.jefferson.edu/methodist	Philadelphia	PA	19148	215-952-9000		374-3
Methodist Hospital of Chicago (MHC) 5025 N Paulina St. TF: 800-222-1222 ■ Web: www.methodistchicago.org	Chicago	IL	60640	773-271-9040		374-3
Methodist Hospital of Sacramento 7500 Hospital Dr TF: 888-800-7688 ■ Web: hospitals.dignityhealth.org	Sacramento	CA	95823	916-423-3000		374-3
Methodist Hospital of Southern California 300 W Huntington Dr TF: 888-388-2838 ■ Web: www.methodisthospital.org	Arcadia	CA	91007	626-898-8000		374-3
Methodist Hospital South (MHS) 1300 Wesley Dr TF: 800-222-1222 ■ Web: www.methodisthealth.org/methodist	Memphis	TN	38116	901-516-3700		374-3
Methodist Hospital System, The 6447 Main St Web: www.houstonmethodist.org	Houston	TX	77030	713-790-3333		374-3
Methodist Hospitals of Dallas 1441 N Beckley Ave TF: 800-725-9664 ■ Web: www.methodisthealthsystem.org	Dallas	TX	75203	214-947-8181		353
Methodist Medical Ctr of Illinois 221 NE Glen Oak Ave Web: unitypoint.org/peoria	Peoria	IL	61636	309-672-5522		374-3
Methodist Medical Ctr of Oak Ridge 990 Oak Ridge Tpke Web: www.mmcoakridge.com	Oak Ridge	TN	37831	865-835-1000		374-3
Methodist North Hospital 3960 New Covington Pk. Web: www.methodisthealth.org	Memphis	TN	38128	901-516-5200		374-3

Name / Address	City	State	ZIP	Phone	Fax	Class
Methodist Rehabilitation Ctr 1350 E Woodrow Wilson Dr TF: 800-223-6672 ■ Web: www.methodistonline.org	Jackson	MS	39216	601-981-2611		374-6
Methodist Retirement Communities 1440 Lake Front Cir Ste 110. Web: www.mrcaff.org	The Woodlands	TX	77380	281-363-2600		371
Methodist Richardson Medical Ctr 401 W Campbell Rd Web: methodisthealthsystem.org	Richardson	TX	75080	972-498-4000		374-3
Methodist Senior Services 300 Airline Rd. *Fax Area Code: 601 ■ Web: www.mss.org	Columbus	MS	39702	662-327-6716	482-5567*	672
Methodist Theological School in Ohio 3081 Columbus Pk. TF: 800-333-6876 ■ Web: www.mtso.edu	Delaware	OH	43015	740-363-1146	362-3135	167-3
Methodist University 5400 Ramsey St *Fax: Admissions ■ TF: 800-488-7110 ■ Web: www.methodist.edu	Fayetteville	NC	28311	910-630-7000	630-7285*	166
Methods Machine Tools Inc 65 Union Ave TF: 877-668-4262 ■ Web: www.methodsmachine.com	Sudbury	MA	01776	978-443-5388		358
Meth-Wick Community 1224 13th St NW Web: www.methwick.org	Cedar Rapids	IA	52405	319-365-9171		672
METI (Management & Engineering Technologies International Inc) 8600 Boeing Dr Web: www.meticorp.com	El Paso	TX	79925	915-772-4975	772-2253	463
METI (Medical Education Technologies Inc) 6300 Edgelake Dr TF: 866-462-7920 ■ Web: www.caehealthcare.com	Sarasota	FL	34240	941-377-5562		250
Metis Communications Inc 294 Washington St Ste 607 Web: metiscomm.com	Boston	MA	02108	617-236-0500		636
Metis Strategy LLC 6900 Wisconsin Ave Ste 300 Web: www.metisstrategy.com	Bethesda	MD	20815	301-893-4610		463
Met-L-Flo Inc 720 Heartland Dr Unit S Web: www.metlflo.com	Sugar Grove	IL	60554	630-409-9860		463
MetLife Foundation 27-01 Queens Plaza N TF: 800-638-5433 ■ Web: www.metlife.com	Long Island	NY	11101-4007	800-638-5433		304
MetLife Inc 200 Pk Ave NYSE: MET ■ TF: 800-638-5433 ■ Web: global.metlife.com	New York	NY	10166	212-578-2211		391-2
Metl-Saw Systems Inc 2950 Bay Vista Ct Web: www.metlsaw.com	Benicia	CA	94510	707-746-6200	746-5085	455
Metl-Span LLC 1720 Lakepointe Dr Ste 101 TF: 877-585-9969 ■ Web: www.metlspan.com	Lewisville	TX	75057	972-221-6656	420-9382	105
MetoKote Corp 1340 Neubrecht Rd. Web: www.metokote.com	Lima	OH	45801	419-996-7800	996-7801	481
Metompkin Bay Oyster Co 101 N 11th St Ste 105 Web: www.metompkinseafood.com	Crisfield	MD	21817	410-968-0660	968-0670	296-14
Metpar Corp 95 State St. Web: www.metpar.com	Westbury	NY	11590	516-333-2600	333-2618	286
Met-Pro Corp Duall Div 1550 Industrial Dr. Web: www.cecoenviro.com/hee-duall	Owosso	MI	48867	989-725-8184	725-8188	18
Met-Pro Corp Fybroc Div 700 Emlen Way. TF: 800-392-7621 ■ Web: www.mp-gps.com	Telford	PA	18969	215-723-8155	723-2197	641
Met-Pro Corp Sethco Div 800 Emlen Way. TF: 800-645-0500 ■ Web: www.mp-gps.com	Telford	PA	18969	215-799-2577	799-0920	641
Metra Electronics Corp 460 Walker St TF Sales: 800-221-0932 ■ Web: www.metraonline.com	Holly Hill	FL	32117	386-257-1186	255-3965	52
MetraPark 308 Sixth Ave N TF: 800-366-8538 ■ Web: www.metrapark.com	Billings	MT	59101	406-256-2400		205
MetraTech Corp 200 W St. Web: www.metratech.com	Waltham	MA	02451	781-839-8300	839-8301	39
Metrex Research Corp 1717 W Collins Ave TF: 800-424-9300 ■ Web: www.metrex.com	Orange	CA	92867	714-516-7788		228
Metric Machining Co 1425 S Vineyard Ave. Web: www.metricorp.com	Ontario	CA	91761	909-947-9222	923-1796	621
Metric Precision Machine & Engineering LLC 350 W Compton Blvd Web: metric-precision.com	Gardena	CA	90248	310-515-2584		256
Metric Products Inc 4630 Leahy St. TF: 800-713-7278 ■ Web: www.metric-products.com	Culver City	CA	90232	310-815-9000		34
Metric Stream Inc 2600 E Bayshore Rd TF: 800-417-4370 ■ Web: www.metricstream.com	Palo Alto	CA	94303	650-620-2900	565-8542	178-7
Metrican Stamping LLC 101 Warren G Medley Dr	Dickson	TN	37055	615-446-1018		489
Metrics Contract Services Inc 1240 Sugg Pkwy. Web: www.metricsinc.com	Greenville	NC	27834	252-752-3800	758-8522	668
MetriTech Inc 4106 Fieldstone Rd Web: www.metritech.com	Champaign	IL	61826	217-398-4868		94
Metrix Instrument Co 8824 Fallbrook Dr. TF: 800-638-7494 ■ Web: www.metrixvibration.com	Houston	TX	77064	713-461-2131	559-9417	472
Metrix Marketing Inc 40 Wildbriar Rd Web: www.metrix-marketing.com	Rochester	NY	14623	585-334-0890		195
Metro - Sales Inc 1640 E 78th St TF: 800-862-7414 ■ Web: www.metrosales.com	Minneapolis	MN	55423	612-861-4000	866-8069	112
Metro 1 120 NE 27 St Ste 200 Web: www.metro1.com	Miami	FL	33137	305-571-9991	571-9661	224
Metro Atlanta Chamber of Commerce 235 International Blvd NW TF: 800-897-1910 ■ Web: www.metroatlantachamber.com	Atlanta	GA	30303	404-880-9000		139
Metro Aviation Inc 1214 Hawn Ave PO Box 7008 Web: www.metroaviation.com	Shreveport	LA	71137	318-222-5529	222-0503	30

Name / Address	City	State	Zip	Phone	Fax	Class
Metro Bench Advertisers 3014 W Horatio St	Tampa	FL	33609	813-872-8502		8
Web: www.metrobench.com						
Metro Business Systems 2950 Kaverton Rd	District Heights	MD	20747	301-967-8758		535
Web: www.mbs-copiers.com						
Metro Creative Graphics Inc 519 Eigth Ave	New York	NY	10018	212-947-5100		344
TF: 800-223-1600 ■ *Web:* mcg.metrocreativeconnection.com						
Metro Development Group 2502 N Rocky Point Dr Ste 1050	Tampa	FL	33607	813-288-8078		653
Web: metrodevelopmentgroup.com						
Metro ECSU 2 Pine Tree Dr Ste 101	Arden Hills	MN	55112	612-638-1500		242
Web: www.ecsu.k12.mn.us						
Metro Energy Group 1011 Hudson Ave	Ridgefield	NJ	07657	201-941-3470		316
TF: 800-951-2941 ■ *Web:* www.metroenergynj.com						
Metro Express Transportation Services Inc 875 Fee Fee Rd	St. Louis	MO	63043	314-993-1511		311
TF: 800-805-0073 ■ *Web:* www.metroexpressinc.com						
Metro Fabricating Inc 1650 Tech Dr	Bay City	MI	48706	989-667-8100		729
Web: www.metrofab.com						
Metro Flag 353 Richard Mine Rd Ste 100	Wharton	NJ	07885	973-366-1776	366-0956	287
TF: 800-515-7840 ■ *Web:* nationalflag.com						
Metro Ford Inc 9000 NW Seventh Ave	Miami	FL	33150	305-751-9711		57
Web: www.metrofordmiami.com						
Metro Fuel Oil Corp 500 Kingsland Ave	Brooklyn	NY	11222	718-383-1400		539
TF: 800-542-5552 ■ *Web:* metroenergy.com						
Metro Health Hospital 5900 Byron Ctr Ave.	Wyoming	MI	49519	616-252-7200	252-0630	374-3
TF: 800-968-0051 ■ *Web:* www.metrohealth.net						
Metro Hvac Mechanical Contractor Inc 7802 Norris Fwy	Knoxville	TN	37938	865-922-5912		610
Metro Jackson Convention & Visitors Bureau 111 E Capitol St Ste 102	Jackson	MS	39202	601-960-1891	960-1827	206
TF: 800-354-7606 ■ *Web:* www.visitjackson.com						
Metro Label Group Inc 999 Progress Ave	Toronto	ON	M1B6J1	416-292-6600		88
TF: 800-668-4405 ■ *Web:* www.metrolabel.com						
Metro Machine & Engineering Corp 8001 Wallace Rd	Eden Prairie	MN	55344	952-937-2800	937-2374	547
Web: www.metromachine.com						
Metro Machine Works 11977 Harrison Rd	Romulus	MI	48174	734-941-4571		21
Web: www.metromachineworks.net						
Metro Mailing Service Inc 4251 Gateway Park Blvd	Sacramento	CA	95834	916-928-0801		5
Web: www.mmsmail.com						
Metro Materials Inc 2174 E Person Ave	Memphis	TN	38114	901-324-3894		182
Metro Mechanical Contractors Inc 1200 SW 24th St	Newcastle	OK	73065	405-387-3930		610
Metro Metals Northwest 5611 NE Columbia Blvd	Portland	OR	97218	503-287-8861	287-5569	686
TF: 800-610-5680 ■ *Web:* www.metrometalsnw.com						
Metro Mold & Design Inc 20600 County Rd 81	Rogers	MN	55374	763-428-8310		757
Web: www.metromold.com						
Metro News Services 160 Dalton Dr	Desoto	TX	75115	972-230-4277		530
Metro North Chamber of Commerce 14583 Orchard Pkwy Ste 300	Westminster	CO	80023	303-288-1000	227-1050	139
Web: www.metronorthchamber.com						
Metro Packaging & Imaging Inc 5 Haul Rd	Wayne	NJ	07470	973-709-9100		557
Web: metro-pi.com						
Metro Parks 1069 W Main St Unit A	Westerville	OH	43081	614-891-0700		564
TF: 800-524-3492 ■ *Web:* www.metroparks.net						
Metro Pavia Health System Inc MaraMar Plaza Bldg Avenida San Patricio Ste 950-960	Guaynabo	PR	00968	888-882-0882		363
TF: 888-882-0882 ■ *Web:* www.metropavia.com						
Metro Pictures Gallery 519 W 24th St	New York	NY	10011	212-206-7100	337-0070	42
Web: metropicturesgallery.com						
Metro Ready Mix Concrete Inc 1136 Second Ave N	Nashville	TN	37208	615-255-1900		182
Web: www.mrm1.com						
Metro Recycling Co Inc 2424 Beekman St	Cincinnati	OH	45214	513-294-8711		660
Metro Santa Cruz 550 S First St	San Jose	CA	95113	408-298-8500		532-5
Web: www.metroactive.com						
Metro Silicon Valley 550 S First St	San Jose	CA	95113	408-298-8000	298-0602	532-5
TF: 800-831-2345 ■ *Web:* www.metroactive.com						
Metro South Chamber of Commerce 60 School St	Brockton	MA	02301	508-586-0500	587-1340	139
TF: 877-777-4414 ■ *Web:* www.metrosouthchamber.com						
Metro South Medical Ctr 12935 S Gregory St	Blue Island	IL	60406	708-597-2000		374-3
Web: www.metrosouthmedicalcenter.com						
Metro Storage LLC 13528 Boulton Blvd	Lake Forest	IL	60045	847-235-8900		803-3
Web: www.metrostorage.com						
Metro Supermarkets 156 Main St S	Brampton	ON	L6W2C9	905-459-6212		297-8
Web: metro.ca						
Metro Teleproductions Inc 2425 L St NW Ste 224	Washington	DC	20037	301-608-9077	608-9078	514
Web: www.mtitv.com						
Metro Times 733 St Antoine St	Detroit	MI	48226	313-961-4060	961-6598	532-5
TF: 866-687-8683 ■ *Web:* www.metrotimes.com						
Metro Toronto Convention Centre 255 Front St W	Toronto	ON	M5V2W6	416-585-8000	585-8262*	205
**Fax:* Hum Res ■ *TF:* 800-422-7969 ■ *Web:* www.mtccc.com						
Metro Transit 200 NE 21st St	Oklahoma City	OK	73105	405-522-8000	297-2111	468
Web: www.okladot.state.ok.us						
Metro Transit 200 Ilsley Ave	Dartmouth	NS	B3B1V1	902-490-4000	490-6688	468
TF: 800-835-6428 ■ *Web:* www.halifax.ca/metrotransit						
Metro Transit 560 Sixth Ave N	Minneapolis	MN	55411	612-349-7400		468
Web: www.metrotransit.org						
Metro Travel & Tours 9298 Central Ave NE Ste 222	Minneapolis	MN	55434	763-784-0560		772
Web: metrotravel.biz						
Metro Truck Body Inc 1201 W Jon St	Torrance	CA	90502	310-532-5570	532-0754	516
Web: www.metrotruckbody.com						
Metro Waste Authority 300 E Locust St Ste 100	Des Moines	IA	50309	515-244-0021	244-9477	804
Web: www.mwatoday.com						
Metro Web Corp 5901 Tonnelle Ave	North Bergen	NJ	07047	201-553-0700		627
Web: www.metrowebnj.com						
Metro West Ambulance Service Inc 5475 NE Dawson Creek Dr	Hillsboro	OR	97124	503-648-6658		30
TF: 800-752-9422 ■ *Web:* www.metrowest.fm						
Metro West Chamber of Commerce 1671 Worcester Rd Ste 201	Framingham	MA	01701	508-879-5600	875-9325	139
TF: 866-709-9401 ■ *Web:* www.metrowest.org						
Metro Wine Bar & Bistro 6418 N Western Ave	Oklahoma City	OK	73116	405-840-9463		671
TF: 800-225-5652 ■ *Web:* www.metrowinebar.com						
Metro Wire & Cable Co 6636 Metropolitan Pkwy	Sterling Heights	MI	48312	586-264-3050	264-7390	246
TF: 800-633-1432 ■ *Web:* www.metrowire.net						
Metro! 14 Campbell Ave SE	Roanoke	VA	24011	540-345-6645		671
Web: www.metroroanoke.com						
MetroActive Publishing Inc 550 S First St	San Jose	CA	95113	408-298-8000	298-0602	637-8
TF: 800-831-2345 ■ *Web:* www.metroactive.com						
Metro-Can Construction Ltd 10470 152 St Ste 520	Surrey	BC	V3R0Y3	604-583-1174		261
Web: www.metrocan.com						
Metrocast Cablevision of New Hampshire LLC 9 Apple Rd	Belmont	NH	03220	603-524-4425		116
Web: www.metrocast.com						
Metroclean Commercial Building Services Inc 9000 SW Fwy Ste 412	Houston	TX	77074	713-255-0100		104
Web: www.metrocleanonline.com						
Metro-Clean Corp 936 W Greenfield Ave	Milwaukee	WI	53204	414-671-6660		256
Metrocrest Chamber of Commerce 5100 Belt Line Rd Ste 430	Dallas	TX	75254	469-587-0420	587-0428	139
Web: www.metrocrestchamber.com						
Metro-Goldwyn-Mayer Studios Inc (MGM) 245 N Beverly Dr	Beverly Hills	CA	90210	310-449-3000		514
Web: www.mgm.com						
MetroHartford Alliance 31 Pratt St 5th Fl.	Hartford	CT	06103	860-525-4451	293-2592	139
Web: www.metrohartford.com						
MetroHealth Medical Ctr 2500 MetroHealth Dr	Cleveland	OH	44109	216-778-7800		374-3
TF: 800-554-5251 ■ *Web:* www.metrohealth.org						
Metroland 523 Western Ave Ste 1	Albany	NY	12203	518-463-2500		532-5
Metroland Media Group Ltd 3125 Wolfedale Rd	Mississauga	ON	L5C1W1	905-281-5656		532-3
Web: www.metroland.com						
Metrolina Expo Trade Ctr 7100 Statesville Rd	Charlotte	NC	28269	704-596-4650		205
Web: www.metrolinatradeshowexpo.com						
Metrolina Greenhouses Inc 16400 Huntersville-Concord Rd	Huntersville	NC	28078	704-875-1371	875-0741	369
TF: 800-543-3915 ■ *Web:* www.metrolinagreenhouses.com						
Metrolina Steel Inc 2601 Westinghouse Blvd	Charlotte	NC	28273	704-598-7007		492
Web: www.metrolinasteel.com						
MetroList Services Inc 1164 W National Dr Ste 60	Sacramento	CA	95834	916-922-7584		656
Web: www.metrolistmls.com						
Metromedia Energy Inc 6 Industrial Way W	Eatontown	NJ	07724	732-542-7575	542-8655	787
Web: www.metromediaenergy.com						
Metromont Corp PO Box 2486	Greenville	SC	29602	844-882-4015	295-0295*	183
**Fax Area Code:* 864 ■ *TF:* 888-295-0383 ■ *Web:* www.metromont.com						
Metromont Corp 2802 White Horse Rd	Greenville	SC	29611	864-605-5000		183
Web: www.metromont.com						
Metron Inc 1505 W Third Ave	Denver	CO	80223	303-592-1903	534-1947	201
Web: www.metroninc.com						
Metroplex Hospital 2201 S Clear Creek Rd	Killeen	TX	76549	254-526-7523	526-3483	374-3
TF: 800-926-7664 ■ *Web:* www.mplex.org						
Metropolis Cafe 584 Tremont St	Boston	MA	02118	617-247-2931		671
Web: www.metropolisboston.com						
Metropolis Coffee Company LLC 1039 W Granville Ave Ste 1041	Chicago	IL	60660	773-764-0400		297-8
Web: metropoliscoffee.com						
Metropolis Magazine 205 Lexington Ave 17th Fl	New York	NY	10016	212-627-9977		457-2
TF: 800-344-3046 ■ *Web:* www.metropolismag.com						
Metropolitan Alloys Corp 17385 Ryan Rd	Detroit	MI	48212	313-366-4443		492
Web: www.metroalloys.com						
Metropolitan Atlanta Rapid Transit Authority (MARTA) 2424 Piedmont Rd NE	Atlanta	GA	30324	404-848-5000		468
Web: www.itsmarta.com						
Metropolitan Ceramics 1201 Millerton St SE	Canton	OH	44707	800-325-3945		751
TF: 800-325-3945 ■ *Web:* www.metroceramics.com						
Metropolitan College of New York 431 Canal St	New York	NY	10013	212-343-1234	625-2072*	166
**Fax:* Admissions ■ *Web:* www.mcny.edu						
Metropolitan Communications 309 Commerce Dr Ste 100	Exton	PA	19341	610-363-5858		647
Web: www.mcsradio.com						
Metropolitan Community College PO Box 3777	Omaha	NE	68103	402-457-2400		162
TF: 800-228-9553 ■ *Web:* www.mccneb.edu						
Elkhorn Valley 829 N 204th	Elkhorn	NE	68022	402-289-1200		162
Web: www.mccneb.edu						
Metropolitan Community College Blue River 20301 E 78 Hwy	Independence	MO	64057	816-220-6500	220-6577*	162
**Fax:* Admissions ■ *TF:* 800-622-2070 ■ *Web:* www.mcckc.edu						
Metropolitan Community College Longview 500 SW Longview Rd	Lees Summit	MO	64081	816-672-2000		162
Web: www.mcckc.edu						

	Phone	Fax	Class
Metropolitan Community College Penn Valley			
3201 SW Trafficway ... Kansas City MO 64111	816-759-4000	759-4161	162
TF: 866-676-6224 ■ *Web:* www.mcckc.edu			
Metropolitan Construction Services LLC (MCS)			
2803 Butterfield Rd Ste 100 ... Oak Brook IL 60523	630-691-7200	691-7234	685
Web: www.metroconstructionllc.com			
Metropolitan Correctional Ctr			
Chicago 71 W Van Buren St ... Chicago IL 60605	312-322-0567	322-1120	212
TF: 877-623-8426 ■ *Web:* www.bop.gov			
New York 150 Pk Row ... New York NY 10007	646-836-6300	836-7751	212
Web: www.bop.gov/locations/institutions/nym/index.jsp			
Metropolitan Glass Inc			
6400 Franklin St ... Denver CO 80229	303-853-4527		186
Web: www.metroglass.com			
Metropolitan Grill			
2931 E Battlefield ... Springfield MO 65804	417-889-4951		671
TF: 800-225-6343 ■ *Web:* metropolitan-grill.com			
Metropolitan Grill 820 Second Ave ... Seattle WA 98104	206-624-3287	389-0042	671
Web: www.themetropolitangrill.com			
Metropolitan Halifax Chamber of Commerce			
656 Windmill Rd Ste 200 ... Dartmouth NS B3B1B8	902-468-7111	468-7333	137
Web: www.halifaxchamber.com			
Metropolitan Health Networks Inc			
777 Yamato Rd Ste 510 ... Boca Raton FL 33431	561-805-8500		463
NYSE: MDF ■ *Web:* www.metcare.com			
Metropolitan Hotel Vancouver			
645 Howe St ... Vancouver BC V6C2Y9	604-687-1122		379
TF: 800-667-2300 ■ *Web:* www.metropolitan.com/vanc			
Metropolitan Indianapolis Public Broadcasting Corp			
1401 N Meridian St ... Indianapolis IN 46202	317-636-2020		632
TF: 800-456-0766 ■ *Web:* www.wfyi.org			
Metropolitan Methodist Hospital			
1310 McCullough Ave ... San Antonio TX 78212	210-757-2200		374-3
TF: 800-553-6321 ■ *Web:* sahealth.com			
Metropolitan Milwaukee Assn of Commerce			
756 N Milwaukee St ... Milwaukee WI 53202	414-287-4100	271-7753	139
TF: 855-729-1300 ■ *Web:* www.mmac.org			
Metropolitan Museum of Art			
1000 Fifth Ave ... New York NY 10028	212-535-7710		520
TF: 800-468-7386 ■ *Web:* www.metmuseum.org			
Metropolitan Nashville Airport Authority			
1 Terminal Dr Ste 501 ... Nashville TN 37214	615-275-1675		27
TF: 800-628-6800 ■ *Web:* www.flynashville.com			
Metropolitan Nashville Public Schools (MNPS)			
2601 Bransford Ave ... Nashville TN 37204	615-259-8531	214-8890	685
TF: 800-848-0298 ■ *Web:* www.mnps.org			
Metropolitan National Bank			
501 Main St ... Pine Bluff AR 71601	870-541-1000		70
Web: simmonsfirst.com			
Metropolitan Opera			
65th St & Broadway ... New York NY 10023	212-799-3100		573-2
Web: metopera.org			
Metropolitan Plant & Flower Exchange			
2125 Fletcher Ave ... Fort Lee NJ 07024	201-944-1050		292
TF: 800-638-7613 ■ *Web:* www.metroplantexchange.com			
Metropolitan Poultry & Seafood Co			
1920 Stanford Ct ... Landover MD 20785	301-772-0060	772-1013	297-10
TF: 800-522-0060 ■ *Web:* www.metropoultry.com			
Metropolitan State College of Denver			
Student Success Bldg 890 Auraria Pkwy Ste 140 ... Denver CO 80204	303-556-5740	556-2720*	166
**Fax:* Admissions ■ *Web:* www.msudenver.edu			
Metropolitan State Hospital			
11401 Bloomfield Ave ... Norwalk CA 90650	562-863-7011		374-5
Web: dsh.ca.gov			
Metropolitan State University			
700 E Seventh St ... Saint Paul MN 55106	651-793-1300	793-1310*	166
**Fax:* Admissions ■ *TF:* 888-234-2690 ■ *Web:* www.metrostate.edu			
Metropolitan Steel Industries Inc			
601 Fritztown Rd ... Reading PA 19608	610-678-6411		480
Web: www.metropolitan-steel.com			
Metropolitan Theaters Corp			
8727 W Third St ... Los Angeles CA 90048	310-858-2800		748
Web: www.metrotheatres.com			
Metropolitan Transit Authority of Harris County			
1900 Maine ... Houston TX 77002	713-739-4000	739-4096	468
TF: 800-844-0046 ■			
Web: ridemetro.org/news/emergencyalerts/default.aspx			
Metropolitan Trucking Inc (MRTK)			
299 Market St ... Saddle Brook NJ 07663	800-967-3278	843-6179*	449
**Fax Area Code:* 201 ■ *TF:* 800-967-3278 ■ *Web:* www.mtrk.com			
Metropolitan Vacuum Cleaner Co Inc			
1 Ramapo Ave PO Box 149 ... Suffern NY 10901	845-357-1600	357-1640	788
TF: 800-822-1602 ■ *Web:* www.metrovacworld.com			
Metropower Inc 798 21st Ave ... Albany GA 31706	229-432-7345		189-4
Web: www.metropower.com			
Metrosonics 1060 Corporate Ctr Dr ... Oconomowoc WI 53066	262-567-9157	567-4047	472
TF: 800-245-0779 ■ *Web:* 3m.com			
MetroStage 1201 N Royal St ... Alexandria VA 22314	703-548-9044	548-9089	572
TF: 800-494-8497 ■ *Web:* www.metrostage.org			
MetroStar Systems Inc			
1856 Old Reston Ave Ste 100 ... Reston VA 20190	703-481-9581		177
TF: 800-576-9956 ■ *Web:* www.metrostarsystems.com			
Metrotech Corp 3251 Olcott St ... Santa Clara CA 95054	408-734-1400	734-1415	472
TF: 800-446-3392 ■ *Web:* www.vivax-metrotech.com			
Metrovision Production Group LLC			
508 W 24th St ... New York NY 10011	212-989-1515		738
TF: 800-242-2424 ■ *Web:* www.metrovision-nyc.com			
MetroWest Daily News			
33 New York Ave ... Framingham MA 01701	508-626-4412	626-4400*	532-2
**Fax:* News Rm ■ *TF:* 800-624-7355 ■ *Web:* www.metrowestdailynews.com			
MetroWest Medical Ctr			
115 Lincoln St ... Framingham MA 01702	508-383-1000	383-1344	374-3
TF: 800-872-5473 ■ *Web:* www.mwmc.com			
Leonard Morse Campus 67 Union St ... Natick MA 01760	508-650-7000		374-3
TF: 800-872-5473 ■ *Web:* www.mwmc.com			
Metrus Group Inc 953 Route 202 ... Somerville NJ 08876	908-231-1900		463
Web: www.metrus.com			
Met-scan Canada Ltd 30 Kern Rd Ste 104 ... Toronto ON M3B1T1	416-391-2200		261
Web: www.met-scan.com			

	Phone	Fax	Class
Metso Automation 44 Bowditch Dr ... Shrewsbury MA 01545	508-852-0200		789
Web: www.maxcontrols.com			
Metso Paper USA Inc 25 Beloit St ... Aiken SC 29805	803-293-2100		556
Web: www.metso.com			
Metson Marine Inc			
2060 Knoll Dr Ste 100 ... Ventura CA 93003	805-658-2628		667
TF: 800-900-6387 ■ *Web:* www.metsonmarine.com			
Metterra Hotel on Whyte			
10454 82nd Ave ... Edmonton AB T6E4Z7	780-465-8150		379
TF: 866-465-8150 ■ *Web:* www.metterra.com			
Metters Industries Inc			
8200 Greensboro Dr Ste 500 ... McLean VA 22102	703-821-3300	821-3996	180
Web: www.metters.com			
Mettler Electronics Corp			
1333 S Claudina St ... Anaheim CA 92805	714-533-2221		477
TF: 800-854-9305 ■ *Web:* www.mettlerelectronics.com			
Mettler-Toledo International Inc			
5 Barr Rd ... Ithaca NY 14850	800-836-0836	266-5478*	684
**Fax Area Code:* 607 ■ *TF:* 800-836-0836 ■ *Web:* mt.com/hi-speed			
Mettler-Toledo International Inc			
1900 Polaris Pkwy ... Columbus OH 43240	614-438-4511		419
Web: www.mt.com			
Metz Beverage Company Inc			
302 N Custer St ... Sheridan WY 82801	307-674-4818		81-2
Metzgar Conveyor Co Inc			
901 Metzgar Dr NW ... Comstock Park MI 49321	616-784-0930	784-4100	207
TF: 888-266-8390 ■ *Web:* www.metzgarconveyors.com			
Metzger's German Restaurant			
305 N Zeeb Rd ... Ann Arbor MI 48103	734-668-8987		671
Web: www.metzgers.net			
Meux Home Museum 1007 R St ... Fresno CA 93721	559-233-8007		520
Web: www.meux.mus.ca.us			
Mevion Medical Systems Inc			
300 Foster Sreet ... Littleton MA 01460	978-540-1500		723
Web: www.mevion.com			
Mewbourne Oil Company Inc			
3901 S Broadway Ave ... Tyler TX 75701	903-561-2900		536
Web: mewbourne.net			
Mews Restaurant & Cafe			
429 Commercial St ... Provincetown MA 02657	508-487-1500	487-3700	671
Web: mews.com			
Mexco Energy Corp			
214 W Texas Ave Ste 1101 PO Box 10502 ... Midland TX 79701	432-682-1119	682-1123	536
NYSE: MXC ■ *Web:* www.mexcoenergy.com			
MexGrocer.com LLC			
4060 Morena Blvd Ste C ... San Diego CA 92117	858-270-0577		387
Web: www.mexgrocer.com			
Mexicali Blues 2933 Wilson Blvd ... Arlington VA 22201	703-812-9352		671
Web: www.mexicali-blues.com			
Mexican Accent LLC			
16675 W Glendale Dr ... New Berlin WI 53151	262-784-4422		123
Mexican American Legal Defense & Educational Fund (MALDEF)			
634 S Spring St ... Los Angeles CA 90014	213-629-2512	629-0266	48-14
Web: www.maldef.org			
Mexican Heritage Corp			
1700 Alum Rock Ave ... San Jose CA 95116	408-794-6240		522
Web: mhcviva.org			
Mexican Museum			
Fort Mason Ctr 2 Marina Blvd Bldg D ... San Francisco CA 94123	415-202-9700		520
TF: 800-843-5200 ■ *Web:* www.mexicanmuseum.org			
Mexican Post 3100 Naamans Rd ... Wilmington DE 19810	302-478-3939	478-5599	671
Web: www.mexicanpost.com			
Mexican Restaurants Inc			
1135 Edgebrook St ... Houston TX 77034	713-943-7574	300-5859*	670
OTC: CASA ■ **Fax Area Code:* 832			
Mexican Village 814 Main Ave ... Fargo ND 58103	701-293-0120		671
Web: www.mexicanvillage.com			
Mexican-American Opportunity Foundation (MAOF)			
401 N Garfield Ave ... Montebello CA 90640	323-890-9600	890-9637	48-14
Web: www.maof.org			
Mexic-Arte Museum 419 Congress Ave ... Austin TX 78701	512-480-9373		520
TF: 800-731-7469 ■ *Web:* www.mexic-artemuseum.org			
Mexico 3810 Ventor Ave ... Atlantic City NJ 08401	609-344-0366		671
Web: mexicorestaurantbar.com			
Consulate General 800 Brazos St Ste 330 ... Austin TX 78701	512-478-2866	478-8008	257
Web: www.sre.gob.mx			
Consulate General 1010 Eigth St ... Sacramento CA 95814	916-441-3287		257
Web: www.mexico.us/consulate.htm			
Consulate General			
910 E San Antonio Ave ... El Paso TX 79901	915-533-3644	532-7163	257
Web: www.sre.gob.mx			
Consulate General 127 Navarro St ... San Antonio TX 78205	210-227-9145		257
Consulate General 1612 Farragut St ... Laredo TX 78040	956-723-0990	723-1741	257
Web: www.sre.gob.mx			
Consulate General			
5350 Leesdale Dr Ste 100 ... Denver CO 80246	303-331-1110	331-0169	257
Web: consulmex.sre.gob.mx/denver			
Consulate General 204 S Ashland Ave ... Chicago IL 60607	312-738-2383		257
Consulate General 27 E 39th St ... New York NY 10016	212-217-6400		257
Web: www.consulmexny.org			
Consulate General 4506 Carolinas St ... Houston TX 77004	713-271-6800	271-3201	257
TF: 877-639-4835 ■ *Web:* www.sre.gob.mx			
Consulate General			
1911 Pennsylvania Ave NW ... Washington DC 20006	202-728-1600		257
Web: embamex2.sre.gob.mx/eua/index.php/es			
Consulate General 532 Folsom St ... San Francisco CA 94105	415-354-1700		257
Web: consulmex.sre.gob.mx/sanfrancisco			
Consulate General of Mexico in Nogals			
571 N Grand Ave ... Nogales AZ 85621	520-287-2521	287-3175	257
Web: www.sre.gob.mx			
Embassy 1911 Pennsylvania Ave NW ... Washington DC 20006	202-728-1600		257
Web: embamex.sre.gob.mx			
Mexico Lindo 3635 Dutch Village Rd ... Halifax NS B3N2S4	902-445-0996		671
Web: www.mexicolindo.ca			
Mexico Plastics Company (Inc)			
2000 W Blvd ... Mexico MO 65265	800-325-0216		66
TF: 800-325-0216 ■ *Web:* www.continentalproducts.com			

Phone | Fax | Class

Mexico Tourism Board (CSTM)
225 N Michigan Ave Ste 1800 ... Chicago IL 60601 800-446-3942 775
TF General: 800-446-3942 ■ *Web:* www.visitmexico.com

Mexico Tourism Board
4507 San Jacinto St ... Houston TX 77004 713-772-2581 775
TF: 800-446-3942 ■ *Web:* www.visitmexico.com

Mexico Tourism Board 1399 SW First Ave ... Miami FL 33130 786-621-2909 775
TF: 800-446-3942 ■ *Web:* www.visitmexico.com

Mexico Tourism Board
152 Madison Ave Ste 1800 ... New York NY 10016 212-308-2110 775
TF: 800-446-3942 ■ *Web:* www.visitmexico.com

Meydenbauer Ctr 11100 NE Sixth St ... Bellevue WA 98004 425-637-1020 637-0166 205
Web: www.meydenbauer.com

Meyenberg PO Box 934 ... Turlock CA 95381 800-891-4628 668-4977* 296-10
**Fax Area Code:* 209 ■ *TF:* 800-891-4628 ■ *Web:* meyenberg.com

Meyer & Lundahl 2345 W Lincoln St ... Phoenix AZ 85009 602-254-9286 189-2
Web: www.meyerandlundahl.com

Meyer & Najem Inc
11787 Lantern Rd Ste 100 ... Fishers IN 46038 317-577-0007 577-0286 186
TF: 888-578-5131 ■ *Web:* www.meyer-najem.com

Meyer Assoc Inc 14 Seventh Ave N ... Saint Cloud MN 56303 320-259-4000 259-4044 737
TF: 800-676-9233

Meyer Brothers Building Company Inc
800 E 101st Terr Ste 120 ... Kansas City MO 64131 816-246-4800 104
Web: www.meyerbro.com

Meyer Communications Inc
3000 E Chestnut Expy ... Springfield MO 65802 417-862-3751 645-10
Web: radiospringfield.com

Meyer Corp 1 Meyer Pl ... Vallejo CA 94590 707-551-2800 551-2953* 486
**Fax:* PR ■ *TF Cust Svc:* 800-888-3883 ■ *Web:* www.meyer.com

Meyer Crest Ltd 725 Folger Ave ... Berkeley CA 94710 510-845-1077 845-1544 379
Web: www.meyercrest.com

Meyer East Gallery 225 Canyon Rd ... Santa Fe NM 87501 505-983-1434 42
TF: 800-779-7387 ■ *Web:* www.meyergalleries.com

Meyer Jabara Hotels
1001 Belvedere Rd Ste 407 S ... West Palm Beach FL 33406 561-689-6602 689-4363 379
TF: 877-696-8671 ■ *Web:* www.meyerjabarahotels.com

Meyer Machine Company Inc
3528 Fredericksburg Rd PO Box 5460 ... San Antonio TX 78201 210-736-1811 298
Web: www.meyer-industries.com

Meyer Manufacturing Corp
County Hwy A W 574 W Ctr Ave PO Box 405 ... Dorchester WI 54425 715-654-5132 273
TF: 800-325-9103 ■ *Web:* www.meyermfg.com

Meyer May House
450 Madison Ave SE ... Grand Rapids MI 49503 616-246-4821 50-3
TF: 800-585-3737 ■ *Web:* meyermayhouse.steelcase.com

Meyer Memorial Trust
425 NW Tenth Ave Ste 400 ... Portland OR 97209 503-228-5512 305
Web: www.mmt.org

Meyer Plastics Inc
5167 E 65th St ... Indianapolis IN 46220 317-259-4131 602
TF: 800-968-4131 ■ *Web:* www.meyerplastics.com

Meyer Products 18513 Euclid Ave ... Cleveland OH 44112 216-486-1313 486-1321* 190
**Fax:* Sales ■ *TF:* 800-232-6950 ■ *Web:* www.meyerproducts.com

Meyer Sound Laboratories Inc
2832 San Pablo Ave ... Berkeley CA 94702 510-486-1166 486-8356 52
Web: www.meyersound.com

Meyer Steel Drum Inc
3201 S Millard Ave ... Chicago IL 60623 773-376-8376 198
Web: www.meyersteeldrum.com

Meyer Tool Inc 3055 Colerain Ave ... Cincinnati OH 45225 513-853-4400 454
Web: www.meyertool.com

Meyer Truck Equipment
196 W State Rd 56 ... Jasper IN 47546 812-695-3451 516
Web: www.meyertruckeq.com

Meyer Unkovic & Scott LLP
535 Smithfield St Ste 1300 ... Pittsburgh PA 15222 412-456-2800 456-2864 428
Web: www.muslaw.com

Meyercord Revenue Inc
475 Village Dr ... Carol Stream IL 60188 630-682-6200 627
TF: 800-937-8864 ■ *Web:* meyercord.com

Meyerland Plaza 420 Meyerland Plaza ... Houston TX 77096 713-349-0245 600-1017 460
TF: 888-675-2275

Meyers Printing Cos Inc, The
7277 Boone Ave N ... Minneapolis MN 55428 763-533-9730 627
Web: www.meyers.com

Meyocks Group Inc, The
6800 Lake Dr Ste 150 ... West Des Moines IA 50266 515-225-1200 7
TF: 800-261-1537 ■ *Web:* www.meyocks.com

Meziere Enterprises Inc
220 S Hale Ave ... Escondido CA 92029 760-746-3273 481
TF: 800-208-1755 ■ *Web:* www.meziere.com

Mezzanotte Bistro 50 Murray St ... Ottawa ON K1N9M5 613-562-3978 671
Web: www.mezzanotte-bistro.com

MFA (Maryland Federation of Art Cir Gallery)
18 State Cir ... Annapolis MD 21401 410-268-4566 50-2
Web: www.mdfedart.com

MFA Inc 201 Ray Young Dr ... Columbia MO 65201 573-874-5111 876-5505 276
Web: mfa-inc.com

MFA Mortgage Investments Inc
350 Pk Ave 20th Fl ... New York NY 10022 212-207-6400 207-6420 654
Web: www.mfafinancial.com

MFA Oil Co 1 Ray Young Dr ... Columbia MO 65205 573-442-0171 581
TF: 800-366-0200 ■ *Web:* www.mfaoil.com

MFC (Metal Forming & Coining Corp)
1007 Illinois Ave ... Maumee OH 43537 419-893-8748 483
Web: www.mfccorp.com

MFJ Enterprises Inc
300 Industrial Pk Rd ... Starkville MS 39759 662-323-5869 323-6551 647
TF: 800-647-1800 ■ *Web:* www.mfjenterprises.com

Mflex (Multi-Fineline Electronix Inc)
3140 E Coronado St ... Anaheim CA 92806 714-238-1488 253
NASDAQ: MFLX ■ *Web:* www.mflex.com

MFM (Media Financial Management Assn)
550 W Frontage Rd Ste 3600 ... Northfield IL 60093 847-716-7000 716-7004 49-14
Web: www.bcfm.com

MFour Mobile Research Inc
19800 MacArthur Blvd Ste 700 ... Irvine CA 92612 714-754-1234 224
Web: mfour.com

MFR Consultants Inc
128 Chestnut St ... Philadelphia PA 19106 215-238-9270 195
Web: www.mfrconsultants.com

MFS Investment Management
500 Boylston St ... Boston MA 02116 617-954-5000 954-6621 401
TF: 877-960-6077 ■ *Web:* www.mfs.com

MFX Solutions Inc
1050 17th St NW Ste 550 ... Washington DC 20036 202-527-9947 401
Web: www.mfxsolutions.com

MG Design Assoc Corp
8778 100th St ... Pleasant Prairie WI 53158 262-947-8890 232
Web: www.mgdesign.com

Mg International Inc
90 International Pkwy ... Dallas GA 30157 770-505-0004 601

MG Maher & Company Inc
365 Canal St Ste 1600 ... New Orleans LA 70130 504-581-3320 314
TF: 800-837-1063 ■ *Web:* www.mgmaher.com

MG Mechanical Contracting Inc
1513 Lamb Rd ... Woodstock IL 60098 815-334-9450 610
Web: www.mgmechanical.com

MG Oil Inc 1002 W Main St ... Rapid City SD 57701 605-342-0527 579
Web: www.mgoil.com

Mg Scientific Inc
8500 107th St ... Pleasant Prairie WI 53158 262-947-7000 535
TF: 800-343-8338 ■ *Web:* www.mgscientific.com

MG Studios Inc
2005 Tree Fork Ln Ste 113 ... Longwood FL 32750 407-679-9291 514

MGA Entertainment Inc
16300 Roscoe Blvd Ste 150 ... Van Nuys CA 91406 818-894-2525 761
TF: 800-222-4685 ■ *Web:* www.mgae.com

MGBW (Mitchell Gold & Bob Williams Co)
135 One Comfortable Pl ... Taylorsville NC 28681 828-632-9200 632-2693 319-2
TF: 000-789-5401 ■ *Web:* www.mgbwhome.com

MGCC (Massachusetts Growth Capital Corp)
529 Main St Schrafft Ctr Ste 1M10 ... Charlestown MA 02129 617-523-6262 523-7676 792
Web: www.massgcc.com

Mge Engineering Inc
7415 Greenhaven Dr ... Sacramento CA 95831 916-421-1000 261
TF: 800-755-3354 ■ *Web:* www.mgeeng.com

MGH (Marion General Hospital)
441 N Wabash Ave ... Marion IN 46952 765-660-6000 651-7351 374-3
Web: www.mgh.net

MGH (Marion General Hospital)
1000 McKinley Pk Dr ... Marion OH 43302 740-383-8400 374-3
Web: www.ohiohealth.com

MGH Adv Inc
100 Painters Mill Rd Ste 600 ... Owings Mills MD 21117 410-902-5000 4
Web: www.mghus.com

MGH Institute of Health Professions Inc
Charlestown Navy Yard 36 First Ave ... Boston MA 02129 617-726-2947 166
Web: www.mghihp.edu

MGI Coutier 603 W Seventh St ... Cadillac MI 49601 231-775-6571 775-8731 677
Web: mgicoutier.com

MGM (Metro-Goldwyn-Mayer Studios Inc)
245 N Beverly Dr ... Beverly Hills CA 90210 310-449-3000 514
Web: www.mgm.com

MGM Grand Detroit 1777 Third St ... Detroit MI 48226 313-465-1400 133
TF: 877-888-2121 ■ *Web:* www.mgmgranddetroit.com

MGM Grand Hotel & Casino
3799 Las Vegas Blvd S ... Las Vegas NV 89109 702-891-1111 891-3036 669
TF: 877-880-0880 ■ *Web:* www.mgmgrand.com

MGM Industries Inc
287 Freehill Rd ... Hendersonville TN 37075 615-824-6572 390
TF: 800-476-5584 ■ *Web:* www.mgmindustries.com

MGM Transformer Co 5701 Smithway St ... Commerce CA 90040 323-726-0888 726-8224 767
TF: 800-423-4366 ■ *Web:* www.mgmtransformer.com

MGMA (Medical Group Management Assn)
104 Inverness Terr E ... Englewood CO 80112 303-799-1111 49-8
TF: 877-275-6462 ■ *Web:* www.mgma.com

MGMC (Maine General Medical Ctr)
Augusta 361 Old Belgrade Rd ... Augusta ME 04330 207-626-1000 621-8801 374-3
TF: 800-266-6809 ■ *Web:* www.mainegeneral.org

MGP Ingredients Inc
100 Commercial St PO Box 130 ... Atchison KS 66002 913-367-1480 367-0192 296-23
NASDAQ: MGPI ■ *TF:* 800-255-0302 ■ *Web:* www.mgpingredients.com

MGQ & Associates Inc
3104 N Armenia Ave Ste 4 ... Tampa FL 33607 813-877-8895 186
TF: 800-340-3866 ■ *Web:* www.mgqassociates.com

Mgs Inc 178 Muddy Creek Church Rd ... Denver PA 17517 717-336-7528 336-0514 91
TF: 800-952-4228 ■ *Web:* www.mgsincorporated.com

Mgs Machine Corp 9900 85th Ave N ... Maple Grove MN 55369 763-425-8808 547
Web: www.mgsmachine.com

MGS Services LLC
18775 N Frederick Ave Ste E ... Gaithersburg MD 20879 301-330-9793 539
TF: 877-647-4255 ■ *Web:* www.mgsservices.com

MGT of America Inc 516 N Adams St ... Tallahassee FL 32301 850-386-3191 385-4501 194
Web: www.mgtconsulting.com

MH (Milford Hospital) 300 Seaside Ave ... Milford CT 06460 203-876-4000 876-4220 374-3
Web: www.milfordhospital.org

MH King Co 1032 Idaho Ave ... Burley ID 83318 208-678-7181 229
Web: kingsdiscount.com

M&h Plastics Inc 485 Brooke Rd ... Winchester VA 22603 540-504-0030 358
Web: www.mhplastics.com

MHA (Mental Health America)
2000 N Beauregard St 6th Fl ... Alexandria VA 22311 703-684-7722 684-5968 48-17
TF Help Line: 800-969-6642 ■ *Web:* mentalhealthamerica.net

Mha an Association of Montana Health Care Providers
1720 Ninth Ave ... Helena MT 59601 406-442-1911 533
TF: 800-351-3551 ■ *Web:* mtha.org

MHB (Mercy Hospitals of Bakersfield Truxtun Campus)
2215 Truxtun Ave ... Bakersfield CA 93301 661-632-5000 374-3
Web: www.mercybakersfield.org

MHC (Mercy Health Ctr)
4300 W Memorial Rd ... Oklahoma City OK 73120 405-755-1515 374-3
Web: www.mercy.net

MHC (Methodist Hospital of Chicago)
5025 N Paulina St ... Chicago IL 60640 773-271-9040 374-3
TF: 800-222-1222 ■ *Web:* www.methodistchicago.org

Phone | Fax | Class

MHC Engineers Inc 150 Eighth St .... San Francisco CA 94103 415-512-7141 261
Web: mhcengr.com

MHC Kenworth
1524 N Corrington Ave.................... Kansas City MO 64120 816-483-7035 778
TF: 888-259-4826 ■ *Web:* mhc.com

MHD Enterprises 9715 Burnet Rd #125 .... Austin TX 78758 512-992-2565 449
Web: www.mhdenterprises.com

MHE (University of Maryland Shore Medical Ctr)
219 S Washington St .... Easton MD 21601 410-822-1000 763-7051 374-3
Web: www.umshoreregional.org

MHEDA (Material Handling Equipment Distributors Assn)
201 US Hwy 45.......................... Vernon Hills IL 60061 847-680-3500 362-6989 49-13
Web: www.mheda.org

MHF Inc 2328 Evans City Rd.................. Zelienople PA 16063 724-452-3900 311
Web: mhftrans.com

MHG (MHG Hotels)
1220 Brookville Way...................... Indianapolis IN 46239 317-356-4000 356-4004 463
Web: www.mhghotelsllc.com

MHG Hotels (MHG)
1220 Brookville Way...................... Indianapolis IN 46239 317-356-4000 356-4004 463
Web: www.mhghotelsllc.com

MHG of Pensacola, Florida LLC
481 Creighton Rd .... Pensacola FL 32504 850-484-7022 484-7044 707
Web: www.mckibbon.com

MHI (Manufactured Housing Institute)
2101 Wilson Blvd Ste 610 .... Arlington VA 22201 703-558-0400 558-0401 49-3
TF: 800-505-5500 ■ *Web:* www.manufacturedhousing.org

MHI (Marine Hydraulics International Inc)
543 E Indian River Rd.......................... Norfolk VA 23523 757-545-6400 545-8169 698
Web: www.mhi-shiprepair.com

MHI (McGuyer Homebuilders Inc)
7676 Woodway Ste 104 .... Houston TX 77063 713-952-6767 952-5637 653
Web: www.mcguyerhomebuilders.com

MHI PAC (Manufactured Housing Institute PAC)
1655 N Ft Myer Dr Ste 104.................... Arlington VA 22209 703-558-0400 558-0401 615
TF: 800-505-5500 ■ *Web:* www.manufacturedhousing.org

MHIA (Material Handling Industry of America)
8720 Red Oak Blvd Ste 201 .... Charlotte NC 28217 704-676-1190 676-1199 49-13
TF: 800-345-1815 ■ *Web:* www.mhi.org

MHM Services Inc
1593 Spring Hill Rd Ste 600...................... Vienna VA 22182 703-749-4600 749-4604 463
TF: 800-416-3649 ■ *Web:* www.mhm-services.com

MHMC (Mercy Hospital & Medical Ctr)
2525 S Michigan Ave......................... Chicago IL 60616 312-567-2000 374-3
Web: www.mercy-chicago.org

MHNet Behavioral Health
9606 N MoPac Exwy Ste 600 .... Austin TX 78759 888-646-6889 462
TF: 888-646-6889 ■ *Web:* www.mhnet.com

MHP (Madison Heights-Hazel Park Chamber of Commerce)
939 E 12 Mile Rd .... Madison Heights MI 48071 248-542-5010 542-6821 139
Web: www.madisonheightschamber.com

MHP (Memorial Hospital Pembroke)
7800 Sheridan St .... Pembroke Pines FL 33024 954-962-9650 374-3
Web: www.mhs.net/locations/memorial-pembroke

MHPARC (Memorial Hermann Prevention & Recovery Ctr)
3043 Gessner................................ Houston TX 77080 713-939-7272 939-7272 374-5
TF: 877-464-7272 ■ *Web:* parc.memorialhermann.org

MHR (McCabe Hamilton & Renny Company Ltd)
1130 N Nimitz Hwy Rm A265 .... Honolulu HI 96817 808-524-3255 545-3101 465
TF: 800-462-8848 ■ *Web:* www.mhrhawaii.com

MHRI (Memorial Hospital of Rhode Island)
111 Brewster St .... Pawtucket RI 02860 401-729-2000 374-3
TF: 800-647-4362 ■ *Web:* www.mhri.org

MHS (Methodist Hospital South)
1300 Wesley Dr .... Memphis TN 38116 901-516-3700 374-3
TF: 800-222-1222 ■ *Web:* www.methodisthealth.org/methodist

MHW Ltd 1129 Northern Blvd Ste 312 .... Manhasset NY 11030 516-869-9170 80-3
Web: www.mhwltd.com

MI (Methanol Institute)
4100 Fairfax Dr Ste 740 .... Arlington VA 22203 703-248-3636 248-3997 48-12
Web: www.methanol.org

Mi Casa 9200 Glacier Hwy .... Juneau AK 99801 907-789-3636 671

Mi Casita 3600 Bonney Rd................ Virginia Beach VA 23452 757-463-3819 671
Web: micasitamexican.com

Mi Nidito Restaurant 1813 S Fourth Ave.......... Tucson AZ 85713 520-622-5081 671
Web: www.minidito.net

Mi Pueblito Beauty Salon
4534 E Tropicana Ave......................... Las Vegas NV 89121 702-433-6435 77

Mi Pueblo IV 2419 W Jefferson Blvd........... Fort Wayne IN 46802 260-432-8462 671

Mi Ranchito Cafe 425 S Ctr St................ Stockton CA 95203 209-946-9257 671

Mi Tierra Mexican Restaurant
27 Mellichamp Dr Unit 101 .... Bluffton SC 29910 843-757-7200 671
Web: www.mitierrabluffton.com

MI Windows & Doors LLC 650 W Market St .... Gratz PA 17030 717-365-3300 365-0940 234
Web: miwindows.com

mi9 retail 12000 Biscayne Blvd Ste 600 .... Miami FL 33181 786-577-3200 177
Web: mi9retail.com

MIA (Marble Institute of America)
28901 Clemens Rd Ste 100 .... Westlake OH 44145 440-250-9222 250-9223 49-3
TF: 800-433-4903 ■ *Web:* www.marble-institute.com

Miami Air International Inc
5000 NW 36 St Ste 307 .... Miami FL 33122 305-876-3600 13
Web: www.miamiair.com

Miami Beach Botanical Garden
2000 Convention Ctr Dr.................. Miami Beach FL 33139 305-673-7256 97
Web: www.mbgarden.org

Miami Beach Chamber of Commerce
1920 Meridian Ave 3rd Fl.................. Miami Beach FL 33139 305-672-1270 538-4336 139
TF: 800-501-0401 ■ *Web:* www.miamibeachchamber.com

Miami Beach Convention Ctr
1901 Convention Ctr Dr.................... Miami Beach FL 33139 786-276-2600 673-7435* 205
**Fax Area Code:* 305 ■ *Web:* www.miamibeachconvention.com

Miami Beach Resort & Spa
4833 Collins Ave .... Miami Beach FL 33140 305-532-3600 669
TF: 866-765-9090 ■ *Web:* www.miamibeachresortandspa.com

Miami Book Fair International (MBFI)
300 NE Second Ave Freedom Twr, 7th Fl .... Miami FL 33132 305-237-3258 281
Web: www.miamibookfair.com

Miami Children's Hospital
3100 SW 62nd Ave........................... Miami FL 33155 305-666-651[illegible]
TF: 800-432-6837 ■ *Web:* www.nicklauschildrens.org/home

Miami Children's Museum
980 MacArthur Cswy .... Miami FL 33132 305-373-5437 373-543[illegible]
Web: www.miamichildrensmuseum.org

Miami City Ballet
2200 Liberty Ave......................... Miami Beach FL 33139 305-929-7000 573-[illegible]
TF: 877-929-7010 ■ *Web:* www.miamicityballet.org

Miami City Hall 3500 Pan American Dr............ Miami FL 33133 305-250-5400 250-5410 337
Web: www.ci.miami.fl.us

Miami Coast Guard Air Station
Opa Locka Airport 14750 NW 44th Ct.......... Opa Locka FL 33054 305-953-2130 158
Web: www.uscg.mil

Miami Corp, The
720 Anderson Ferry Rd..................... Cincinnati OH 45238 513-451-6700 594
TF: 800-543-0448 ■ *Web:* www.miamicorp.com

Miami Correctional Facility
3038 W 850 S.............................. Bunker Hill IN 46914 765-689-8920 689-7479 213
TF: 800-451-6028 ■ *Web:* in.gov

Miami County 201 S Pearl St Ste 102.............. Paola KS 66071 913-294-3976 294-9544 338
TF: 800-669-8683 ■ *Web:* www.miamicountyks.org

Miami County 25 N Broadway .... Peru IN 46970 765-472-3901 472-1778 338
Web: miamicountyin.gov

Miami County 201 W Main St .... Troy OH 45373 937-335-1920 338
Web: www.co.miami.oh.us

Miami County Chamber of Commerce
13 E Main St................................... Peru IN 46970 765-472-1923 472-7099 139
TF: 800-521-9945 ■ *Web:* www.miamicochamber.com

Miami Dade College
Homestead 500 College Terr Rm A230 .... Homestead FL 33030 305-237-5555 237-5019* 162
**Fax:* Admissions ■ *Web:* www.mdc.edu/homestead
Kendall 11011 SW 104th St.................... Miami FL 33176 305-237-2000 162
Web: www.mdc.edu/kendall
Medical Ctr 950 NW 20th St .... Miami FL 33127 305-237-4100 162
Web: www.mdc.edu/medical
North 11380 NW 27th Ave..................... Miami FL 33167 305-237-1000 162
Web: www.mdc.edu/north
North-Hialeah Ctr 1780 W 49th St............. Hialeah FL 33012 305-237-8700 162
Web: www.mdc.edu
Wolfson 300 NE Second Ave................... Miami FL 33132 305-237-3000 162
Web: www.mdc.edu/wolfson

Miami Direct Inc 8200 NW 41 St Ste 225.......... Miami FL 33166 305-597-3998 317
Web: www.gbm.net

Miami Dolphins 7500 SW 30th St.................. Davie FL 33314 305-943-8000 715-3
Web: www.miamidolphins.com

Miami Film Festival 300 NE Second Ave.......... Miami FL 33132 305-237-3456 282
Web: www.miamifilmfestival.com

Miami Heart Institute
4701 N Meridian Ave .... Miami Beach FL 33140 305-676-6408 374-7
Web: www.msmc.com

Miami Heat
American Airlines Arena 601 Biscayne Blvd........ Miami FL 33132 786-777-1000 777-1615 714-1
Web: www.nba.com

Miami Industrial Trucks Inc
2830 E River Rd .... Dayton OH 45439 937-293-4194 358
Web: www.mitlift.com

Miami International Airport
2261 NW 66th Ave Bldg 702 Ste 217 .... Miami FL 33122 305-876-7000 876-8077 27
TF: 800-825-5642 ■ *Web:* www.miami-airport.com

Miami International Airport Hotel
NW 20th St & Le Jeune Rd .... Miami FL 33122 305-871-4100 871-0800 379
TF: 800-327-1276 ■ *Web:* usmia2.webhotel.microsdc.us

Miami International University of Art & Design
1501 Biscayne Blvd .... Miami FL 33132 305-428-5700 374-5933 164
TF: 800-225-9023 ■ *Web:* www.artinstitutes.edu/miami

Miami Machine Corp 4251 Riverside Dr .... Overpeck OH 45055 513-863-6707 821
Web: www.miamimachine.com

Miami New Times 2800 Biscayne Blvd............ Miami FL 33137 305-576-8000 571-7677 532-5
Web: www.miaminewtimes.com

Miami Parking System 190 NE Third St .... Miami FL 33132 305-373-6789 562
Web: miamiparking.com

Miami Project to Cure Paralysis
1095 NW 14th Terr Lois Pope LIFE Ctr............ Miami FL 33136 305-243-6001 243-6017 668
TF General: 800-782-6387 ■ *Web:* www.themiamiproject.org

Miami Seaquarium 4400 Rickenbacker Cswy....... Miami FL 33149 305-361-5705 361-6077 40
Web: www.miamiseaquarium.com

Miami Symphony Orchestra, The (MISO)
10689 N Kendall Dr Ste 307 .... Miami FL 33176 305-275-5666 573-3
Web: www.miamisymphony.org

Miami Today 710 Brickell Ave .... Miami FL 33131 305-358-2663 358-4811 532-4
Web: www.miamitodaynews.com

Miami University 501 E High St .... Oxford OH 45056 513-529-1809 529-1550* 166
**Fax:* Admissions ■ *TF:* 866-426-4643 ■ *Web:* miamioh.edu
Hamilton 1601 University Blvd .... Hamilton OH 45011 513-785-3000 162
Web: www.ham.miamioh.edu
Middletown 4200 E University Blvd.......... Middletown OH 45042 513-727-3200 166
Web: www.mid.muohio.edu

Miami Valley Child Development Centers
215 Horace St................................ Dayton OH 45402 937-226-5664 148
Web: www.mvcdc.org

Miami Valley Family Care Center
922 W Riverview Ave .... Dayton OH 45402 937-223-7217 726
Web: www.cssmv.org

Miami Valley Hospital 1 Wyoming St .... Dayton OH 45409 937-208-8000 374-3
TF All: 800-544-0630 ■ *Web:* www.miamivalleyhospital.org

Miami Valley Steel Service Inc
201 Fox Dr..................................... Piqua OH 45356 937-773-7127 492
Web: www.miamivalleysteel.com

Miami-Cass County Rural Electric Membership Corp
3086 W 100 N PO Box 168......................... Peru IN 46970 765-473-6668 473-8770 245
TF General: 800-844-6668 ■ *Web:* mcremc.coop

Miami-Dade Chamber of Commerce
11380 NW 27th Ave Ste 1328.................... Miami FL 33167 305-751-8648 139
Web: www.m-dcc.org

Miami-Dade County
111 NW First St Ste 220........................ Miami FL 33128 305-375-5218 338
Web: www.miamidade.gov

Name / Address	City	State	Zip	Phone	Fax	Class
Miami-Dade County Auditorium 2901 W Flagler St	Miami	FL	33135	305-547-5414		572
Miami-Dade County Public Schools (M-DCPS) 1450 NE Second Ave *TF:* 800-955-5504 ■ *Web:* www.dadeschools.net	Miami	FL	33132	305-995-1000		685
Miami-Dade Transit (MDTA) 701 NW First Ct **Fax Area Code: 786* ■ *TF:* 800-955-5504 ■ *Web:* miamidade.gov	Miami	FL	33136	305-468-5402	469-5580*	468
Miami-Luken Inc 265 S Pioneer Blvd *Web:* www.miamiluken.com	Springboro	OH	45066	937-743-7775		238
MIB Inc 50 Braintree Hill Pk *Web:* www.mib.com	Braintree	MA	02184	781-751-6000		225
Miba Bearings Us LLC 5037 N SR-60 NW *Web:* www.miba.com/Engine_Bearings-Sites-Miba_Bearings_US,83,en.html	Mcconnelsville	OH	43756	740-962-4242		247
MIBRO Group 111 Sinnott Rd *TF:* 866-941-9006 ■ *Web:* www.mibro.com	Toronto	ON	M1L4S6	416-285-9000		758
MIC (Micro Instrument Corp) 1199 Emerson St PO Box 60619 *TF:* 800-200-3150 ■ *Web:* www.microinst.com	Rochester	NY	14606	585-458-3150		454
MIC (Motorcycle Industry Council) 2 Jenner St Ste 150 *TF:* 800-352-6232 ■ *Web:* www.mic.org	Irvine	CA	92618	949-727-4211	727-3313	49-21
Mic Industries Inc 11911 Freedom Dr *Web:* www.micindustries.com	Reston	VA	20190	703-318-1900		190
Mic Mac Mall 21 MicMac Blvd *Web:* www.micmacmall.com	Dartmouth	NS	B3A4N3	902-463-5891	469-5268	460
MIC Services Insurance Inc 170 Kinnelon Rd - Ste 11 *Web:* micinsurance.com	Kinnelon	NJ	07405	973-492-2828		390
MICA (Mortgage Insurance Cos of America) 1425 K St NW Ste 210 *Web:* usmi.org	Washington	DC	20005	202-682-2683		49-9
Mica Corp 5750 N Riverside Dr	Fort Worth	TX	76137	817-847-6121	847-6831	188-4
MIcah Group 389 Waller Ave Ste 210 *TF:* 877-260-7760 ■ *Web:* www.micahgroup.com	Lexington	KY	40504	859-260-7760		192
Micato Safaris 15 W 26th St 11th Fl *TF:* 800-642-2861 ■ *Web:* www.micato.com	New York	NY	10010	212-545-7111	545-8297	760
Mice Groups Inc, The 1730 S Amphlett Blvd Ste 100 *Web:* www.micegroups.com	San Mateo	CA	94402	650-655-4800		193
Miceli Dairy Products 2721 E 90th St *Web:* www.miceli-dairy.com	Cleveland	OH	44104	216-791-6222		296-5
Michael Allen Co 9 Old Kings Hwy S *Web:* www.michaelallencompany.com	Darien	CT	06820	203-662-5100		195
Michael Angelo's Gourmet Foods Inc 200 Michael Angelo Way *TF:* 877-482-5426 ■ *Web:* www.michaelangelos.com	Austin	TX	78728	512-218-3500		296-36
Michael Anthony's Cucina Italiana 37 New Orleans Rd Ste L *Web:* www.michael-anthonys.com	Hilton Head Island	SC	29928	843-785-6272		671
Michael Baker Corp 500 Grant St Ste 5400 *NYSE: BKR* ■ *TF:* 800-553-1153 ■ *Web:* www.mbakercorp.com	Pittsburgh	PA	15219	412-918-4000		261
Michael Best & Friedrich LLP 100 E Wisconsin Ave Ste 3300 *TF:* 800-973-1177 ■ *Web:* www.michaelbest.com	Milwaukee	WI	53202	414-271-6560		41
Michael Bossy Group 251 James St *Web:* www.bnggroup.ca	Delhi	ON	N4B2B2	519-582-1280		2
Michael Brandman Associates 220 Commerce Ste 200 *TF:* 888-826-5814 ■ *Web:* www.firstcarbonsolutions.com	Irvine	CA	92602	714-508-4100		196
Michael C Carlos Museum 571 S Kilgo St *Web:* www.carlos.emory.edu	Atlanta	GA	30322	404-727-4282	727-4292	520
Michael C. Fina Corporate Sales 3301 Hunters Point Ave *TF:* 800-999-3462 ■ *Web:* www.mcfrecognition.com	Long Island	NY	11101	800-999-3462		193
Michael Day Enterprises PO Box 151 *Web:* www.mdayinc.com	Wadsworth	OH	44282	330-335-5100		605-2
Michael Foods Inc 301 Carlson Pkwy Ste 400 *TF:* 800-328-5474 ■ *Web:* www.michaelfoods.com	Minnetonka	MN	55305	952-258-4000		619
Michael Gibson Gallery 157 Carling St *TF:* 866-644-2766 ■ *Web:* www.gibsongallery.com	London	ON	N6A1H5	519-439-0451		42
Michael J Fox Foundation for Parkinson's Research Grand Central Stn PO Box 4777 *TF:* 800-708-7644 ■ *Web:* www.michaeljfox.org	New York	NY	10163	800-708-7644		305
Michael J Liccar & Co 231 s la salle st *TF:* 800-922-6604 ■ *Web:* www.liccar.com	Chicago	IL	60604	312-922-6600	922-0315	2
Michael J O'Connor & Associates LLC 608 W Oak St *TF:* 800-518-4529 ■ *Web:* www.oconnorlaw.com	Frackville	PA	17931	570-874-3300		445
Michael Jordan's Steak House 23 Vanderbilt Ave *Web:* michaeljordansnyc.com	New York	NY	10017	212-655-2300		671
Michael Kors 11 W 42nd St *Web:* www.michaelkors.com	New York	NY	10036	212-201-8100		277
Michael Lewis Co 8900 W 50th St *Web:* www.mlco.com	McCook	IL	60525	708-688-2200	688-2880	86
Michael Mina 3600 Las Vegas Blvd S *Web:* michaelmina.net/restaurants/locations/mmlv.php	Las Vegas	NV	89109	702-693-7223		671
Michael P Randolph 1001 E Wt Harris Blvd *Web:* agents.allstate.com	Charlotte	NC	28213	704-549-1710		390
Michael Quinlan Inc 3752 N Lowell	Chicago	IL	60641	773-286-6237		317
Michael R Rubenstein & Assoc 12527 New Brittany Blvd *TF:* 888-616-1222 ■ *Web:* mrubensteincpa.com	Fort Myers	FL	33907	239-489-4443		2
Michael Raiser Associates Inc 500 Valley Rd Ste 106 *TF:* 800-561-3357 ■ *Web:* teammra.com	Wayne	NJ	07470	973-305-0011		463
Michael Ramey & Assoc Inc PO Box 744 **Fax Area Code: 925* ■ *TF:* 800-321-0505 ■ *Web:* www.rameypi.com	Danville	CA	94526	800-321-0505	820-8082*	400
Michael Roberts Auto Sales 9051 SR- 2830	Maceo	KY	42355	270-264-7100		57
Michael Rosenfeld Gallery 100 Eleventh Ave *Web:* www.michaelrosenfeldart.com	New York	NY	10011	212-247-0082	247-0402	42
Michael S Kaslik PC 1123 Vesper Rd	Ann Arbor	MI	48103	734-995-4455		2
Michael Taylor Designs Inc 135 Rhode Island St *Web:* www.michaeltaylordesigns.com	San Francisco	CA	94103	415-558-9940		321
Michael Thomas Furniture Inc 100 E Newberry Ave *Web:* themtcompany.com	Liberty	NC	27298	336-622-3075		319-2
Michael W Middleton PC (MWMPC) 3330 Longmire Dr *Web:* www.mwmpc.com	College Station	TX	77845	979-695-2726	695-2754	787
Michael Weining Inc 124 Crosslake Pk Dr PO Box 3158 *TF:* 877-548-0929 ■ *Web:* www.weinigusa.com	Mooresville	NC	28117	704-799-0100	799-7400	821
Michael Werner Gallery 4 E 77th St 2nd Fl *Web:* www.michaelwerner.com	New York	NY	10075	212-988-1623	988-1774	42
Michael West & Assoc 5356 Clayton Rd Ste 216 *Web:* westfinancial.net	Concord	CA	94521	925-676-7437		734
Michael's 9777 Las Vegas Blvd S *TF:* 866-796-7111 ■ *Web:* www.southpointcasino.com	Las Vegas	NV	89183	702-796-7111		671
Michael's 532 Margaret St *Web:* www.michaelskeywest.com	Key West	FL	33040	305-295-1300		671
Michael's Finer Meats & Seafoods 3775 Zane Trace Dr *TF:* 800-282-0518 ■ *Web:* www.michaelsmeats.com	Columbus	OH	43228	614-527-4900	527-4520	297-9
Michael's New York 24 W 55th St *Web:* www.michaelsnewyork.com	New York	NY	10019	212-767-0555		671
Michael's on East 1212 E Ave S *Web:* bestfood.com	Sarasota	FL	34239	941-366-0007	953-3463	671
Michael's Transportation Service Inc 140 Yolano Dr *TF Cust Svc:* 800-295-2448 ■ *Web:* bustransportation.com	Vallejo	CA	94589	707-643-2099	643-1906	109
Michael-David Winery 4580 W Hwy 12 *TF:* 888-707-9463 ■ *Web:* www.michaeldavidwinery.com	Lodi	CA	95242	209-368-7384	368-5801	50-7
Michaels Creative Jewelry 4843 E Ray Rd *Web:* www.michaelscreative.com	Phoenix	AZ	85044	480-598-0306		410
Michaels Group Homes 10 Blacksmith Dr Ste 1 *Web:* www.michaelsgroup.com	Mechanicville	NY	12118	518-899-6311	899-6260	187
Michaels Stores Inc 8000 Bent Branch Dr *TF Cust Svc:* 800-642-4235 ■ *Web:* www.michaels.com	Irving	TX	75063	972-409-1300		45
Michalik & Daniels LLC 934 Western Ave	Pittsburgh	PA	15233	412-322-2662		2
Michaud Cooley Erickson & Assoc Inc 1200 Metropolitan Ctr Ste 1200 *Web:* www.michaudcooley.com	Minneapolis	MN	55402	612-339-4941	339-8354	261
Michbi Doors Inc 75 Emjay Blvd *TF:* 800-854-4541 ■ *Web:* www.michbidoors.com	Brentwood	NY	11717	631-231-9050		499
Michel's 2895 Kalakaua Ave Colony Surf Hotel *Web:* www.michelshawaii.com	Honolulu	HI	96815	808-923-6552	926-6063	671
Michelangelo 420 W Magee Rd *Web:* www.michelangelotucson.com	Tucson	AZ	85704	520-297-5775		671
Michelangelo Ristorante 420 W Magee Rd *Web:* www.michelangelotucson.com	Tucson	AZ	85704	520-297-5775		671
Michelin North America (Canada) Inc 2500 Boulevard Daniel-Johnson Ste 500 *Web:* www.michelin.ca	Laval	QC	H7T2P6	450-978-4700		755
Michelin North America Inc 1 PkwyS PO Box 19001 **Fax:* Cust Svc ■ *TF Cust Svc:* 866-866-6605 ■ *Web:* www.michelin.com	Greenville	SC	29615	864-458-5000	458-6359*	754
Michelina's 3241 E Shea Blvd *Web:* www.michelinasrestaurant.com	Phoenix	AZ	85028	602-996-8977		671
Michelinos 3615 Rutherglen St	El Paso	TX	79925	915-592-1700		671
Michell Consulting Group Inc 8240 NW 52nd Terr Ste 410 *TF:* 800-442-5011 ■ *Web:* www.michellgroup.net	Doral	FL	33166	305-592-5433		196
Michelle's 194 Main St *Web:* www.ivymanor.com	Bar Harbor	ME	04609	207-288-2138		671
Michelman Inc 9080 Shell Rd *TF:* 800-333-1723 ■ *Web:* www.michelman.com	Cincinnati	OH	45236	513-793-7766	793-2504	550
Michels Corp 817 W Main St *TF:* 877-297-8663 ■ *Web:* www.michels.us	Brownsville	WI	53006	920-583-3132	583-3429	188-10
Michels Plumbing & Heating 36354 Priestap St	Richmond	MI	48062	586-727-4636		610
Michel-Schlumberger Partners LP 4155 Wine Creek Rd *TF:* 800-447-3060 ■ *Web:* www.michelschlumberger.com	Healdsburg	CA	95448	707-433-7427		80-3
Michelson Laboratories Inc 6280 Chalet Dr *Web:* michelsonlab.com	Commerce	CA	90040	562-928-0553		743
Michener Institute for Applied 222 Saint Patrick St *TF:* 800-387-9066 ■ *Web:* www.michener.ca	Toronto	ON	M5T1V4	416-596-3101		685
Michiana Health Information Network Llc 220 W Colfax Ave, Ste 300 *TF:* 800-814-6446 ■ *Web:* www.mhin.org	South Bend	IN	46601	574-968-1001		624
Aging Services Office 201 N Washington Sq Ste 920 *Web:* leadingagemi.org	Lansing	MI	48933	517-323-3687		339-23
Michigan						
Arts & Cultural Affairs Council 300 N Washington Sq *Web:* www.michigan.gov	Lansing	MI	48913	517-241-3972		339-23
Attorney General 525 W Ottawa St *TF:* 877-765-8388 ■ *Web:* www.michigan.gov	Lansing	MI	48909	517-373-1110	373-3042	339-23
Career Education & Workforce Programs 201 N Washington Sq Victor Office Center *TF:* 888-253-6855 ■ *Web:* www.michigan.gov/mdcd	Lansing	MI	48913	517-335-5858	373-0314	339-23
Child Support Office 235 S Grand Ave PO Box 30037 *TF:* 866-661-0005 ■ *Web:* www.michigan.gov/dhs	Lansing	MI	48933	866-661-0005		339-23

				Phone	Fax	Class
Civil Rights Dept 110 W Michigan Ave Ste 800 Capitol Tower Bldg *Web:* www.michigan.gov/mdcr	Lansing	MI	48933	517-241-6300	335-3882	339-23
Civil Service Dept Capitol Commons Ctr 400 S Pine St *TF:* 800-788-1766 ■ *Web:* www.michigan.gov	Lansing	MI	48913	517-373-3030	373-7690	339-23
Community Health Dept Capitol View Bldg 201 Townsend St *Web:* www.michigan.gov/mdch	Lansing	MI	48913	517-373-3740		339-23
Consumer Protection Div PO Box 30213 *TF:* 877-765-8388 ■ *Web:* www.michigan.gov/ag	Lansing	MI	48909	517-373-1140	241-3771	339-23
Corrections Dept 206 E Michigan Ave Grandview Plaza PO Box 30003 *Web:* www.michigan.gov/corrections	Lansing	MI	48909	517-335-1426		339-23
Crime Victims Services Commission 320 S Walnut St Garden Level Lewis Cass Bldg *TF:* 877-251-7373 ■ *Web:* www.michigan.gov	Lansing	MI	48933	517-373-7373	373-2439	339-23
Driver & Vehicle Bureau 7064 Crowner Dr *Web:* www.michigan.gov/sos	Lansing	MI	48918	517-322-1460	322-5458	339-23
Drug Control Policy Office 320 S Walnut St Lewis Cass Bldg 5th Fl *Web:* www.michigan.gov/mdch	Lansing	MI	48913	517-373-4700	241-2199	339-23
Economic Development Corp (MEDC) 300 N Washington Sq *Fax Area Code: 517 ■ *TF:* 888-522-0103 ■ *Web:* www.michiganbusiness.org	Lansing	MI	48913	888-522-0103	241-3683*	339-23
Education Dept 608 W Allegan St PO Box 30008 *Web:* www.michigan.gov	Lansing	MI	48909	517-373-3324		339-23
Education Trust PO Box 30198 *TF General:* 800-638-4543 ■ *Web:* www.setwithmet.com	Lansing	MI	48909	517-335-4767	373-6967	725
eLibrary Information 702 W Kalamazoo St PO Box 30007 *TF:* 877-479-0021 ■ *Web:* www.michigan.gov	Lansing	MI	48909	517-373-4331		339-23
Emergency Management & Homeland Security Div PO Box 30636 *Web:* michigan.gov	Lansing	MI	48909	517-332-2521	333-4987	339-23
Environmental Quality Dept 3423 N Logan St *Web:* www.michigan.gov	Lansing	MI	48906	517-373-7917		339-23
Financial & Insurance Regulation 530 W Allegan St *TF:* 877-999-6442 ■ *Web:* www.michigan.gov	Lansing	MI	48909	517-373-0220	335-4978	339-23
Gaming Control Board 3062 W Grand Blvd Ste L-700 *Web:* www.michigan.gov/mgcb	Detroit	MI	48202	313-456-4100	456-4200	339-23
Governor PO Box 30013 *Web:* www.michigan.gov/gov	Lansing	MI	48909	517-373-3400	335-6863	339-23
Human Services Dept 235 S Grand Ave PO Box 30037 *Web:* www.michigan.gov/dhs	Lansing	MI	48909	517-373-2035	335-6101	339-23
Labor & Economic Growth Dept 611 W Ottawa St *Web:* www.michigan.gov	Lansing	MI	48933	517-373-1820	373-2129	339-23
Lieutenant Governor PO Box 30013 *Web:* www.michigan.gov/ltgov	Lansing	MI	48909	517-373-3400		339-23
Management & Budget Dept 320 S Walnut St PO Box 30026 *Web:* www.michigan.gov/dmb	Lansing	MI	48909	517-241-5545	373-7268	339-23
Military & Veterans Affairs Dept 3411 N ML King Blvd *Web:* www.michigan.gov/dmva	Lansing	MI	48906	517-481-8000		339-23
Parks & Recreation Div PO Box 30257 *TF Campground Resv:* 800-447-2757 ■ *Web:* www.michigan.gov/dnr	Lansing	MI	48909	517-284-7275	373-4625	339-23
Public Service Commission 7109 W Saginaw Hwy *Web:* www.michigan.gov/mpsc	Lansing	MI	48917	517-241-6180	284-8304	339-23
Secretary of State 430 W Allegan St 4th Fl *Web:* www.michigan.gov	Lansing	MI	48918	517-373-2510		339-23
State Court Administrator 925 W Ottawa St *Web:* courts.mi.gov	Lansing	MI	48919	517-373-0128	373-9831	339-23
State Historic Preservation Office 702 W Kalamazoo St PO Box 30740 *Web:* www.michigan.gov	Lansing	MI	48909	517-373-1630	335-0348	339-23
State Housing Development Authority PO Box 30044 *Web:* www.michigan.gov/mshda	Lansing	MI	48909	517-373-8370	335-4797	339-23
State Lottery 101 E Hillsdale St PO Box 30023 *TF:* 844-887-6836 ■ *Web:* www.michigan.gov/lottery	Lansing	MI	48909	517-335-5756	335-5644	452
State Police Dept 7150 Harrison Dr *Web:* www.michigan.gov/msp	East Lansing	MI	48821	517-332-2521	336-6255	339-23
Student Financial Services Bureau Austin Bldg 430 W Allegan *TF:* 888-447-2687 ■ *Web:* www.michigan.gov/mistudentaid	Lansing	MI	48922	888-447-2687		725
Supreme Court 925 W Ottawa St *Web:* courts.mi.gov	Lansing	MI	48909	517-373-0120		339-23
Transportation Dept PO Box 30050 *Web:* www.michigan.gov/mdot	Lansing	MI	48909	517-373-2090		339-23
Travel Michigan 300 N Washington Sq *TF:* 888-784-7328 ■ *Web:* www.michigan.org	Lansing	MI	48913	517-335-4590		339-23
Treasurer 430 W Allegan St *Web:* www.michigan.gov/treasury	Lansing	MI	48922	517-373-3200		339-23
Unemployment Insurance Agency Cadillac Pl Ste 11-500 *Web:* www.michigan.gov/uia	Detroit	MI	48202	313-456-2400	456-2424	339-23
Vital Records Div 201 Townsend St Capitol View Bldg 3rd Fl *Web:* www.michigan.gov/mdch	Lansing	MI	48913	517-335-8656		339-23
Wildlife Div PO Box 30444 4th Fl PO Box 30444 *Web:* www.michigan.gov/dnr	Lansing	MI	48909	517-284-9453		339-23
Workers Compensation Agency 2501 Woodlake Cir *TF:* 888-396-5041 ■ *Web:* www.michigan.gov/wca	Okemos	MI	48864	517-284-8902		339-23
Michigan Arc Products Corp 2040 Austin Dr *Web:* www.micharc.com	Troy	MI	48083	248-740-8066		358
Michigan Assn of Realtors 720 N Washington Ave *TF:* 800-454-7842 ■ *Web:* www.mirealtors.com	Lansing	MI	48906	517-372-8890	334-5568	656
Michigan Association of Insurance Agents 1141 Centennial Way *Web:* www.michagent.org	Lansing	MI	48917	517-323-9473		138
Michigan Automotive Compressor Inc (MACI) 2400 N Dearing Rd *Web:* www.michauto.com	Parma	MI	49269	517-796-3200		172
Michigan Bankers Assn 507 S Grand Ave *TF:* 800-368-7764 ■ *Web:* www.mibankers.com	Lansing	MI	48933	517-485-3600		138
Michigan Bar Journal 306 Townsend St *TF:* 888-726-3678 ■ *Web:* www.michbar.org/journal	Lansing	MI	48933	517-346-6300	482-6248	457-15
Michigan Blood 4005 Orchard Dr *TF:* 866-642-5663 ■ *Web:* www.miblood.org	Midland	MI	48670	989-839-3490		89
Michigan Blueberry Growers Assn 4726 County Rd 215 *TF:* 800-654-1152 ■ *Web:* www.blueberries.com	Grand Junction	MI	49056	269-434-6791		315-1
Michigan Boating Industries Assn 32398 5 Mile Rd *Web:* www.mbia.org	Livonia	MI	48154	734-261-0123		533
Michigan Bulb Co PO Box 4180 *Web:* www.michiganbulb.com	Lawrenceburg	IN	47025	513-354-1498	354-1499	323
Michigan Chamber of Commerce 600 S Walnut St *TF:* 800-748-0266 ■ *Web:* www.michamber.com	Lansing	MI	48933	517-371-2100	371-7224	140
Michigan Chandelier Company Inc 20855 Telegraph Rd *Web:* www.michand.com	Southfield	MI	48033	248-353-0510	353-0973	246
Michigan City Area Chamber of Commerce 200 E Michigan Blvd *Web:* www.michigancitychamber.com	Michigan City	IN	46360	219-874-6221	873-1204	139
Michigan Community Blood Centers 1036 Fuller Ave NE *TF:* 866-642-5663 ■ *Web:* www.miblood.org	Grand Rapids	MI	49503	616-774-2300		89
Michigan Community Blood Centers Northwest 2575 Aero Pk Dr *TF General:* 866-642-5663 ■ *Web:* www.miblood.org	Traverse City	MI	49686	231-935-3030		89
Michigan Democratic Party 606 Townsend St *Web:* www.michigandems.com	Lansing	MI	48933	517-371-5410	371-2056	616-1
Michigan Dental Assn 3657 Okemos Rd Ste 200 *Fax: PR ■ *TF:* 800-589-2632 ■ *Web:* www.smilemichigan.com	Okemos	MI	48864	517-372-9070	372-0008*	227
Michigan Drill Corp North 1863 Larch Wood *Web:* www.michigandrill.com	Troy	MI	48083	248-689-5050		454
Michigan Extruded Aluminum Corp 205 Watts Rd *TF:* 800-866-2227 ■ *Web:* www.extrude.net	Jackson	MI	49203	517-764-5400		492
Michigan Federation of Teachers 2661 E Jefferson Ave *TF:* 800-638-8868 ■ *Web:* www.mftsrp.org	Detroit	MI	48207	313-393-2200		414
Michigan Fluid Power Inc 4556 Spartan Industrial Dr SW *TF:* 800-635-0289 ■ *Web:* www.mifp.com	Grandville	MI	49418	616-538-5700	538-0888	386
Michigan Historical Museum 702 W Kalamazoo St *Web:* michigan.gov	Lansing	MI	48915	517-373-3559	241-3647	520
Michigan Instruments Inc 4717 Talon Ct SE *Web:* www.michiganinstruments.com	Grand Rapids	MI	49512	616-554-9696		476
Michigan Insurance Co 1700 E Beltline NE PO Box 152120, Ste 100 *TF:* 888-606-6426 ■ *Web:* www.michiganinsurance.com	Grand Rapids	MI	49515	888-606-6426		390
Michigan International Speedway 12626 US 12 *TF:* 800-354-1010 ■ *Web:* www.mispeedway.com	Brooklyn	MI	49230	517-592-6666	592-3848	515
Michigan Jewish Institute 25401 Coolidge Hwy *TF:* 888-463-6654 ■ *Web:* www.mji.edu	Oak Park	MI	48237	248-414-6900		166
Michigan Language Ctr 309 S State St *Web:* www.englishclasses.com	Ann Arbor	MI	48107	734-663-9415	663-9623	423
Michigan Manufacturers Association, The 620 S Capitol Ave *TF:* 800-253-9039 ■ *Web:* mimfg.org	Lansing	MI	48901	517-372-5900		138
Michigan Maple Block Co 1420 Standish Ave	Petoskey	MI	49770	231-347-4170		820
Michigan Masonic Home 1200 Wright Ave *TF:* 800-321-9357 ■ *Web:* masonicpathways.com	Alma	MI	48801	989-463-3141		672
Michigan Mfg Technology Ctr 47911 Halyard Dr *Fax Area Code: 734 ■ *TF:* 888-414-6682 ■ *Web:* www.the-center.org	Plymouth	MI	48170	888-414-6682	451-4201*	668
Michigan Milk Producers Assn 41310 Bridge St *Web:* www.mimilk.com	Novi	MI	48375	248-474-6672	474-0924	296-27
Michigan Millers Mutual Insurance Co 2425 E Grand River Ave PO Box 30060 *TF:* 800-888-1914 ■ *Web:* www.mimillers.com	Lansing	MI	48912	800-888-1914		391-4
Michigan Municipal League 1675 Green Rd PO Box 1487 *TF:* 800-653-2483 ■ *Web:* www.mml.org	Ann Arbor	MI	48105	734-662-3246	662-8083	48-5
Michigan Nurses Assn (MNA) 2310 Jolly Oak Rd *TF:* 888-646-8773 ■ *Web:* www.minurses.org	Okemos	MI	48864	517-349-5640	349-5818	533
Michigan Opera Theatre 1526 Broadway *Web:* michiganopera.org	Detroit	MI	48226	313-961-3500	237-3412	573-2
Michigan Out-of-Doors Magazine (MOOD) 2101 Wood St PO Box 30235 *TF:* 800-777-6720 ■ *Web:* www.mucc.org	Lansing	MI	48912	517-371-1041		457-22

Phone | Fax | Class

Michigan Paving & Materials Co
1100 Market Ave SW ... Grand Rapids MI 49503 616-459-9545 188-4
Web: www.michiganpaving.com

Michigan Pharmacists Assn
408 Kalamazoo Plaza ... Lansing MI 48933 517-484-1466 484-4893 585
TF: 800-227-2345 ■ *Web:* www.michiganpharmacists.org

Michigan Production Machining Inc
16700 23 Mile Rd ... Macomb MI 48044 586-228-9700 454
Web: www.michpro.com

Michigan Public Media
535 W William St Ste 110 ... Ann Arbor MI 48103 734-764-9210 632
Web: www.michiganradio.org

Michigan Reformatory 1727 Bluewater Hwy ... Ionia MI 48846 616-527-2510 213
Web: www.michigan.gov/corrections

Michigan Republican State Committee
520 Seymour Ave ... Lansing MI 48933 517-487-5413 487-0090 616-2
Web: www.migop.org

Michigan Schools & Government Credit Union
40400 Garfield Rd ... Clinton Township MI 48038 586-263-8800 219

Michigan Society of Association Executives
1350 Haslett Rd ... East Lansing MI 48823 517-332-6723 533
Web: www.msae.org

Michigan Spring & Stamping LLC
2700 Wickham Dr ... Muskegon MI 49441 231-755-1691 755-3449 719
Web: www.msands.com

Michigan Stadium
1201 S Main St University of Michigan ... Ann Arbor MI 48104 734-647-2583 764-3221 720
TF: 866-296-6849 ■ *Web:* www.mgoblue.com

Michigan State Industries
5656 S Cedar St ... Lansing MI 48909 517-373-4277 630
Web: www.michigan.gov

Michigan State Medical Society
120 W Saginaw St ... East Lansing MI 48823 517-337-1351 337-2490 474
TF: 800-482-4881 ■ *Web:* www.msms.org

Michigan State University
250 Hannah Admin Bldg ... East Lansing MI 48824 517-355-1855 353-1647 166
TF: 800-500-1554 ■ *Web:* www.msu.edu

Michigan State University College of Human Medicine
965 Fee Rd Rm A-110 ... East Lansing MI 48824 517-353-1730 355-0342 167-2
Web: www.humanmedicine.msu.edu

Michigan State University College of Law
368 Law College Bldg ... East Lansing MI 48824 517-432-6810 432-0098* 167-1
**Fax:* Admissions ■ *TF:* 800-844-9352 ■ *Web:* www.law.msu.edu

Michigan State University Library
366 W Circle Dr ... East Lansing MI 48824 517-353-8700 432-1191 434-6
TF: 800-500-1554 ■ *Web:* www.lib.msu.edu

Michigan State University Museum
W Cir Dr ... East Lansing MI 48824 517-355-2370 432-2846 520
TF: 800-354-1010 ■ *Web:* museum.msu.edu

Michigan State University Press
1405 S Harrison Rd
Ste 25 Manly Miles Bldg ... East Lansing MI 48823 517-355-9543 432-2611 637-4
Web: msupress.org

Michigan Sugar Company Inc
2600 S Euclid Ave ... Bay City MI 48706 989-686-0161 671-3695 296-38
Web: www.michigansugar.com

Michigan Technological University
1400 Townsend Dr ... Houghton MI 49931 906-487-2335 487-2125* 166
**Fax:* Admissions ■ *TF:* 888-688-1885 ■ *Web:* www.mtu.edu

Michigan Theater 603 E Liberty St ... Ann Arbor MI 48104 734-668-8397 668-7136 572
TF: 800-745-3000 ■ *Web:* www.michtheater.org

Michigan Theological Seminary
41550 E Ann Arbor Trail ... Plymouth MI 48170 734-207-9581 207-9582 167-3
TF: 800-356-6639 ■ *Web:* www.moody.edu

Michigan Veterinary Medical Assn (MVMA)
2144 Commons Pkwy ... Okemos MI 48864 517-347-4710 347-4666 795
TF: 800-869-1100 ■ *Web:* www.michvma.org

Michigan Wheel Corp
1501 Buchanan Ave SW ... Grand Rapids MI 49507 616-452-6941 247-0227 386
TF: 800-369-4335 ■ *Web:* www.miwheel.com

Michigan Women's Historical Ctr & Hall of Fame
213 W Main St ... Lansing MI 48933 517-484-1880 372-0170 520
Web: www.michiganwomenshalloffame.org

Michigan's Adventure Inc
4750 Whitehall Rd ... Muskegon MI 49445 231-766-3377 31
TF: 800-243-7280 ■ *Web:* www.miadventure.com

Micke Grove Zoo 11793 N Micke Grove Rd ... Lodi CA 95240 209-953-8840 331-7271 823
Web: www.sjgov.org/mgzoo

Mickey & Mooch The other Joint
8128 Providence Rd Ste 1200 ... Charlotte NC 28277 704-752-8080 671
Web: www.mickeyandmooch.com

Mickey Casanova & Sack
1735 - 28th St ... Bakersfield CA 93301 661-325-9451 2

Mickey Mantle's Steakhouse
7 Mickey Mantle Dr ... Oklahoma City OK 73104 405-272-0777 232-7111 671
Web: mickeymantlesteakhouse.com

Mickey Thompson Tires 4600 Prosper Dr ... Stow OH 44224 330-928-9092 754
TF: 800-222-9092 ■ *Web:* www.mickeythompsontires.com

Mickey Truck Bodies Inc
1305 Trinity Ave ... High Point NC 27261 336-882-6806 779
TF: 800-334-9061 ■ *Web:* www.mickeybody.com

Mickey's CMB BBQ
1622 Pk Ave ... Hot Springs National Park AR 71901 501-624-1247 671
Web: www.mickeysbbq.net

Mickey's Linen & Towel Supply
4601 W Addison St ... Chicago IL 60641 773-545-7211 545-9111 442
Web: mickeyslinen.com

Mickle Wagner Coleman Inc
3434 Country Club Ave ... Fort Smith AR 72903 479-649-8484 261
TF: 800-901-4079 ■ *Web:* www.mwc-engr.com

Mico Inc 1911 Lee Blvd ... North Mankato MN 56003 507-625-6426 625-3212 386
TF: 800-477-6426 ■ *Web:* www.mico.com

Mico Industries Inc 2929 32nd St ... Kentwood MI 59512 616-245-6426 245-2661 61
Web: www.micoindustries.com

Mi-Co LLC 4601 Creekstone Dr Ste 102 ... Durham NC 27703 919-485-4819 177
Web: www.mi-corporation.com

MiCocina 509 Main St ... Fort Worth TX 76102 817-877-3600 671
Web: micocinarestaurants.com

Micor Industries Inc
1314 A State Docks Rd ... Decatur AL 35601 256-560-0770 621
Web: www.micorind.com

Micro 100 Tool Corp 1410 E Pine Ave ... Meridian ID 83642 208-888-7310 888-2106 493
TF: 800-421-8065 ■ *Web:* www.micro100.com

Micro Abrasives Corp
720 Southampton Rd ... Westfield MA 01085 413-562-3641 1
Web: www.microgrit.com

Micro Care Corp
595 John Downey Dr ... New Britain CT 06051 860-827-0626 827-8105 151
TF: 800-638-0125 ■ *Web:* www.microcare.com

Micro Com Systems Ltd
8527 Eastlake Dr ... Burnaby BC V5A4T7 604-872-6771 872-2533 496
Web: www.microcomsys.com

Micro Control Co 7956 Main St NE ... Minneapolis MN 55432 763-786-8750 248
TF: 800-328-9923 ■ *Web:* www.microcontrol.com

Micro Craft Inc 207 Big Springs Ave ... Tullahoma TN 37388 931-455-2617 20
Web: www.microcraft.aero

Micro Electronics Inc 4119 Leap Rd ... Hilliard OH 43026 614-850-3000 850-3001 173-2
TF: 800-207-3434 ■ *Web:* www.microcenter.com

Micro Electronics, Inc.
2701 Charter St Ste A ... Columbus OH 43228 614-326-8500 173-2
TF: 877-636-9793 ■ *Web:* www.microcenter.com

Micro Express Inc 8 Hammond Dr Ste 105 ... Irvine CA 92618 949-460-9911 269-3070 173-2
TF: 800-989-9900 ■ *Web:* www.microexpress.net

Micro Force Inc
505 Jericho Tpke ... Huntington Station NY 11746 631-421-1030 180
Web: micro-force.com

Micro Instrument Corp (MIC)
1199 Emerson St PO Box 60619 ... Rochester NY 14606 585-458-3150 454
TF: 800-200-3150 ■ *Web:* www.microinst.com

Micro Lithography Inc 1257 Elko Dr ... Sunnyvale CA 94089 408-747-1769 201
Web: www.mliusa.com

Micro Logic Corp 666 Godwin Ave ... Midland Park NJ 07432 201-962-7510 178-12
Web: www.mlclog.com

Micro Machine Company LLC
2429 N Burdick ... Kalamazoo MI 49007 269-388-2440 454
TF: 800-290-1347 ■ *Web:* www.micromachineco.com

Micro Matic USA Inc
10726 N Second St ... Machesney Park IL 61115 815-968-7557 968-0363* 664
**Fax:* Sales ■ *TF:* 866-291-5756 ■ *Web:* www.micromatic.com

Micro Mech Inc 33 Tpke Rd ... Ipswich MA 01938 978-356-2966 127

Micro Plastics Inc
11 Industry Ln Hwy 178 N PO Box 149 ... Flippin AR 72634 870-453-2261 453-8676 608
TF: 800-466-1467 ■ *Web:* secure.microplastics.com

Micro Powders Inc
580 White Plains Rd ... Tarrytown NY 10591 914-793-4058 472-7098 145
TF: 800-424-9300 ■ *Web:* www.micropowders.com

Micro Precision Calibration Inc
22835 Industrial Pl ... Grass Valley CA 95949 530-268-1860 743
Web: www.microprecision.com

Micro Precision Inc
1102 Windham Rd ... South Windham CT 06266 860-423-8334 454
Web: www.micro-precision.com

Micro Source Inc 655 Fairfield Ct ... Ann Arbor MI 48108 734-669-8833 180
Web: www.microsrc.com

Micro Stamping Corp 140 Belmont Dr ... Somerset NJ 08873 732-302-0800 302-0436 488
Web: www.microstamping.com

Micro Strategies Inc
1140 Parsippany Blvd ... Denville NJ 07054 888-467-6588 625-5130* 177
**Fax Area Code:* 973 ■ *TF:* 888-467-6588 ■ *Web:* www.microstrat.com

Micro Surface Engr Inc
1550 E Slauson Ave ... Los Angeles CA 90011 323-582-7348 582-0934 485
TF: 800-322-5832 ■ *Web:* www.precisionballs.com

Micro Surface Finishing Products Inc
1217 W Third St ... Wilton IA 52778 563-732-3240 1
TF: 800-225-3006 ■ *Web:* www.micro-surface.com

Micro Systems Engineering Inc
6024 SW Jean Rd Ste B4 ... Lake Oswego OR 97035 503-635-4016 696
Web: www.biotronik.com

Micro Technology Concepts (MTC)
17837 Rowland St ... City Of Industry CA 91748 626-839-6800 174
Web: www.mtcusa.com

Micro/Sys Inc 3730 Pk Pl ... Montrose CA 91020 818-244-4600 244-4246 173-2
Web: www.embeddedsys.com

MicroAire Surgical Instruments Inc
3590 Grand Forks Blvd ... Charlottesville VA 22911 800-722-0822 476
TF: 800-722-0822 ■ *Web:* www.microaire.com

Microalloying International Inc
9977 W Sam Houston Pkwy N Ste 140 ... Houston TX 77064 281-664-0150 664-0153 463
Web: www.microalloying.com

Microbac Laboratories Inc
101 Bellevue Rd Ste 301 ... Pittsburgh PA 15229 412-459-1060 743
Web: microbac.com

Microbest Inc
670 Captain Neville Dr ... Waterbury CT 06705 203-597-0355 621
Web: www.microbest.com

Microbial Insights Inc
2340 Stock Creek Blvd ... Rockford TN 37853 865-573-8188 743
Web: www.microbe.com

MicroBilt Corp
1640 Airport Rd Ste 115 ... Kennesaw GA 30144 800-884-4747 178-10
TF: 800-884-4747 ■ *Web:* www.microbilt.com

Microbiology & Quality Associates Inc
2341 Stanwell Dr ... Concord CA 94520 925-270-3800 463
Web: microqa.com

MicroBiz Corp
655 Oak Grove Ave Ste 493 Ste 493 ... Menlo Park CA 94025 702-749-5353 178-1
TF: 800-937-2289 ■ *Web:* www.microbiz.com

Microboard Processing Inc
36 Cogwheel Ln ... Seymour CT 06483 203-881-4300 625
Web: www.microboard.com

Microboards Technology LLC
8150 Mallory Ct PO Box 846 ... Chanhassen MN 55317 952-556-1600 556-1620 173-8
TF: 800-646-8881 ■ *Web:* www.microboards.com

Microbrush International Ltd
1376 Cheyenne Ave ... Grafton WI 53024 262-375-4011 228
Web: www.microbrush.com

Company	City	State	ZIP	Phone	Fax	Class
Microcast Technologies Corp (MTC) 1611 W Elizabeth Ave *Web:* www.mtcnj.com	Linden	NJ	07036	908-523-9503	523-0910	481
Microcheck Inc 142 Gould Rd *Web:* www.microcheck.com	Northfield	VT	05663	802-485-6600		794
Microchem Corp 90 Oak St *Web:* www.microchem.com	Newton	MA	02464	617-965-5511	965-5818	145
Microchip Technology Inc 2355 W Chandler Blvd *NASDAQ: MCHP* ■ **Fax Area Code:* 602 ■ *Web:* www.microchip.com	Chandler	AZ	85224	480-792-7200	687-4646*	696
Micro-Clean Inc 177 N Commerce Way *TF:* 800-523-9852 ■ *Web:* www.microcln.com	Bethlehem	PA	18017	610-867-5302		743
Micro-coax Inc 206 Jones Blvd *TF:* 800-223-2629 ■ *Web:* www.micro-coax.com	Pottstown	PA	19464	610-495-0110	495-6656	253
Microcomputer Applications Inc 1025 W Seventh Ave *Web:* www.keylok.com	Denver	CO	80204	720-904-2252		637-10
Microcredit Summit 440 First St NW Ste 460 *Web:* www.microcreditsummit.org	Washington	DC	20001	202-637-9600		533
Microdea Inc 85 Enterprise Blvd Ste 407 *Web:* www.microdea.com	Markham	ON	L6G0B5	905-881-6071		179
Microdynamics Group 1400 Shore Rd *Web:* www.microdg.com	Naperville	IL	60563	630-527-8400		393
Microdyne Plastics Inc 1901 E Cooley Dr *Web:* www.microdyneplastics.com	Colton	CA	92324	909-503-4010	503-4011	608
Microelectronic Modules Corp 2601 S Moorland Rd *Web:* www.mefas.com	New Berlin	WI	53151	262-782-5626		696
Microfibres Inc 1 Moshassuck St PO Box 1208 *Web:* www.microfibres.com	Pawtucket	RI	02862	401-725-4883	722-8520	745-7
Microflex Corp 2301 Robb Dr *Web:* microflexpublic-ansellhealthcare.msappproxy.net	Reno	NV	89523	775-746-6600		476
Microflex Inc 1800 N US Hwy 1 *TF:* 800-856-4580 ■ *Web:* www.microflexinc.com	Ormond Beach	FL	32174	386-677-8100		295
MicroFluidic Systems 1252 Quarry Ln Ste B	Pleasanton	CA	94566	510-354-0400		743
Microfluidics International Corp 90 Glacier Dr Ste 1000 *TF:* 800-370-5452 ■ *Web:* www.microfluidicscorp.com	Westwood	MA	02090	617-969-5452	965-1213	298
Microgauge Inc 7350 Kensington Rd *Web:* muellerindustriesipd.com/category/microgauge	Brighton	MI	48116	248-446-3720		454
Microgreen Polymers Inc 7220 201St St NE *Web:* www.microgreeninc.com	Arlington	WA	98223	360-435-7400		596
MicroGroup Inc 7 Industrial Pk Rd *TF:* 800-255-8823 ■ *Web:* www.microgroup.com	Medway	MA	02053	508-533-4925	533-5691	595
Microintegration Inc 460 stull st Ste 200 *Web:* www.microintegration.net	South Bend	IN	46601	574-256-6777		177
Microland Electronics Corp 1883 Ringwood Ave *Web:* www.microlandusa.com	San Jose	CA	95131	408-441-1688	441-1767	174
Microlife USA Inc 1617 Gulf to Bay Blvd Second Fl Ste B *TF:* 888-314-2599 ■ *Web:* www.microlifeusa.com	Clearwater	FL	33755	727-451-0484		476
Microline Surgical Inc 800 Cummings Ctr Ste 157-X *Web:* www.microlinesurgical.com	Beverly	MA	01915	978-922-9810		476
MicroLink Devices Inc 6457 W Howard St *Web:* www.mldevices.com	Niles	IL	60714	847-588-3001		696
Microlink Enterprise Inc 20955 Pathfinder Rd Ste 100 *TF:* 800-829-3688 ■ *Web:* www.microlinkenterprise.com	Diamond Bar	CA	91765	562-205-1888	205-1886	178-1
Microlog Corp 401 Professional Dr Ste 125 *Web:* www.mlog.com	Gaithersburg	MD	20879	301-540-5500		735
MicroLumen Inc 1 Microlumen Way *TF:* 800-968-9014 ■ *Web:* www.microlumen.com	Oldsmar	FL	34677	813-886-1200		476
Microlynx Systems Ltd 1925 18 Ave NE Ste 107 *TF:* 866-835-4332 ■ *Web:* www.microlynxsystems.com	Calgary	AB	T2E7T8	403-275-7346		261
MicroMass Communications Inc 100 Regency Forest Dr Ste 400 *Web:* www.micromass.com	Cary	NC	27518	919-851-3182	851-3188	178-11
Micromatic LLC 525 Berne St *TF:* 800-333-5752 ■ *Web:* www.micromaticllc.com	Berne	IN	46711	260-589-2136	589-8966	223
Micromatic Spring & Stamping Company Inc 45 N Church St *Web:* www.micromaticspring.com	Addison	IL	60101	847-671-6600	671-3452	719
Micro-Matics Corp 8050 Ranchers Rd *Web:* www.micro-matics.com	Fridley	MN	55432	763-780-2700	780-2706	621
microMEDIA Imaging Systems Inc 300-2 Rte 17 S Ste 4 **Fax Area Code:* 516 ■ *Web:* www.imagingservices.com	Lodi	NJ	07644	973-685-5164	355-0316*	496
Micromeritics Instrument Corp 1 Micromeritics Dr *TF:* 800-229-5052 ■ *Web:* www.micromeritics.com	Norcross	GA	30093	770-662-3620	662-3696	419
Micrometals Inc 5615 E La Palma Ave *TF:* 800-356-5977 ■ *Web:* www.micrometals.com	Anaheim	CA	92807	714-970-9400		767
MicroMetl Corp 3035 N Shadeland Ave Ste 300 *TF:* 800-662-4822 ■ *Web:* www.micrometl.com	Indianapolis	IN	46226	800-662-4822		664
Micromidas Inc 930 Riverside Pkwy Ste 10 *Web:* www.micromidas.com	West Sacramento	CA	95605	916-231-9329		192
MicroMod Automation Inc 75 Town Centre Dr *TF:* 800-480-1975 ■ *Web:* www.micmod.com	Rochester	NY	14623	585-321-9200		201
Micron Industries Corp 1211 22nd St Ste 200 *Web:* micronpower.com	Oak Brook	IL	60523	630-516-1222		45
Micron Laser Technology Inc 22750 NW Wagon Way *Web:* www.micronlaser.com	Hillsboro	OR	97124	503-439-9000		625
Micron Optics Inc 1852 Century Pl NE *TF:* 800-837-0864 ■ *Web:* www.micronoptics.com	Atlanta	GA	30345	404-325-0005		407
Micron Technology Inc 8000 S Federal Way *NASDAQ: MU* ■ *TF:* 888-363-2589 ■ *Web:* www.micron.com	Boise	ID	83707	208-368-4000	368-4617	625
Micron Technology Inc SpecTek Div 8000 S Federal Way PO Box 6 *Web:* www.spectek.com	Boise	ID	83707	208-363-5716		625
Micronesia 300 E 42nd St Ste 1600 *TF:* 800-469-4828 ■ *Web:* www.fsmgov.org/fsmun	New York	NY	10017	212-697-8370	697-8295	784
Consulate 1725 N St NW Ste 910 *TF:* 877-730-9753 ■ *Web:* www.fsmembassydc.org	Washington	DC	20036	202-223-4383	223-4391	257
Micronics Inc 8463 154th Ave NE Bldg G *TF:* 800-321-1924 ■ *Web:* micronics.net	Redmond	WA	98052	425-895-9197		743
Micropac Industries Inc 905 E Walnut St *OTC: MPAD* ■ *Web:* www.micropac.com	Garland	TX	75040	972-272-3571	487-6918	696
Micropace EP Inc 3205 W Warner Ave *TF:* 800-594-7836 ■ *Web:* www.micropaceep.com	Santa Ana	CA	92704	714-258-7025		476
MicroPact 12901 Worldgate Dr Ste 800 *TF:* 866-346-9492 ■ *Web:* www.micropact.com	Herndon	VA	20170	703-709-6110	709-6118	177
Microphase Corp 587 Connecticut Ave *Web:* www.microphase.com	Norwalk	CT	06854	203-866-8000		735
Microphor Inc 452 E Hill Rd *TF Orders:* 800-358-8280 ■ *Web:* www.wabtec.com/business-units/microphor	Willits	CA	95490	707-459-5563	459-6617	611
MicroPlanet Technology Corp 15530 Woodinville-Redmond Rd NE Ste B100 *Web:* www.microplanet.com	Woodinville	WA	98072	425-984-2740		253
Micro-Poise Measurment Systems LLC 1624 Englewood Ave *TF:* 800-428-3812 ■ *Web:* www.micropoise.com	Akron	OH	44305	330-784-1251	798-0250	386
MicroPRINT 335 Bear Hill Rd *Web:* www.mprint.com	Waltham	MA	02451	781-890-7500		627
Microprocessor Report 355 Chesley Ave **Fax Area Code:* 650 ■ *TF:* 800-413-2881 ■ *Web:* www.linleygroup.com	Mountain View	CA	94040	408-270-3772	745-1490*	531-3
Micropump Inc 1402 NE 136th Ave *TF Sales:* 800-222-9565 ■ *Web:* www.micropump.com	Vancouver	WA	98684	360-253-2008	253-8294	641
MicroRam Electronics Inc 222 Dunbar Ct *TF:* 800-642-7671 ■ *Web:* www.microram.com	Oldsmar	FL	34677	813-854-5500		246
Microsearch 3903 Stoney Brook Dr *Web:* www.microsearch.com	Houston	TX	77063	713-988-2818		52
Microsemi Corp 2381 Morse Ave *NASDAQ: MSCC* ■ *TF:* 800-713-4113 ■ *Web:* www.microsemi.com	Irvine	CA	92614	949-221-7100	756-0308	696
Microsemi Corp-Scottsdale 8700 E Thomas Rd	Scottsdale	AZ	85251	480-941-6300		696
Microsemi-RFIS 1000 Avenida Acaso *TF:* 800-390-3232 ■ *Web:* www.microsemi.com	Camarillo	CA	93012	805-388-1345	484-2191	735
MicroSense LLC 205 Industrial Ave E *Web:* www.microsense.net	Lowell	MA	01852	978-843-7673		407
Microserv Computer Techs Inc 1808 E 17th St *TF:* 866-988-7164 ■ *Web:* risebroadband.com	Idaho Falls	ID	83404	866-988-7164		180
Microserve 276 Fifth Ave Ste 1011 *Web:* www.mserve.com	New York	NY	10001	212-683-2811		808
Microsmarts LLC 600 Holiday Plaza Dr Ste 545 *Web:* microsmartsllc.com	Matteson	IL	60443	708-748-7558		177
Microsoft Corp 1 Microsoft Way *NASDAQ: MSFT* ■ *TF:* 800-642-7676 ■ *Web:* www.microsoft.com	Redmond	WA	98052	425-882-8080	936-7329	178-1
Microsoft Great Plains Business Solutions 3900 Great Plains Dr S *TF:* 888-477-7877 ■ *Web:* www.microsoft.com	Fargo	ND	58104	701-281-6500		178-1
Microsonic Systems Inc 76 Bonaventura Dr *Web:* www.microsonics.com	San Jose	CA	95134	408-844-4980		419
Microspace Communications Corp 3100 Highwoods Blvd Ste 120 *TF:* 800-200-0014 ■ *Web:* www.microspace.com	Raleigh	NC	27604	919-850-4500	850-4518	681
Micro-Star Int'l Co.,Ltd 901 Canada Ct *Web:* msicomputer.com	City of Industry	CA	91748	626-913-0828		625
MicroStrategy 1850 Towers Crescent Plaza *NASDAQ: MSTR* ■ *TF:* 888-266-0321 ■ *Web:* www.microstrategy.com	Tysons Corner	VA	22182	703-848-8600	848-8610	178-11
Microsystems 3025 Highland Pkwy Ste 450 *Web:* www.microsystems.com	Downers Grove	IL	60515	630-598-1100		178-1
Microtech Computers Inc 4921 Legends Dr *Web:* www.microtechcomp.com	Lawrence	KS	66049	785-841-9513		173-2
Micro-Tech Consultants Inc 1686 Jessica Pl *Web:* www.micro-techco.com	Santa Rosa	CA	95403	707-575-4820		466
microtek 10900 183rd St Ste 290 *Web:* www.microtekusa.com	Cerritos	CA	90703	310-687-5800		173-7
Microtel Inn & Suites 11274 S Fortuna Rd *TF:* 800-465-4329 ■ *Web:* www.underhilltransfer.com	Yuma	AZ	85367	928-345-1777		378
Microthermics Inc 3216 Wellington Ct Ste 101 *TF:* 800-466-2369 ■ *Web:* www.microthermics.com	Raleigh	NC	27615	919-878-8045		296
Microtrac Inc 215 Keystone Dr *Web:* www.microtrac.com	Montgomeryville	PA	18936	215-619-9920		419
Micro-Tronics Inc 2905 S Potter Dr *Web:* www.micro-tronics.com	Tempe	AZ	85282	602-437-8995	431-9480	454
Micro-Tube Fabricators Inc 250 Lackland Dr *TF:* 800-323-9732 ■ *Web:* hhmtf.com	Middlesex	NJ	08846	732-469-7420	469-4314	476
MicroVention Inc 1311 Valencia Ave *TF:* 800-990-8368 ■ *Web:* www.microvention.com	Tustin	CA	92780	714-247-8000		477
MicroVision Development Inc 5541 Fermi Ct Ste 120 *TF:* 800-998-4555 ■ *Web:* www.mvd.com	Carlsbad	CA	92008	760-438-7781	438-7406	178-8
Microvision Inc 6222 185th Ave NE Ste 100 *NASDAQ: MVIS* ■ *Web:* www.microvision.com	Redmond	WA	98052	425-936-6847	882-6600	544

Company / Address	City	State	ZIP	Phone	Fax	Class
MicroVote General Corp 6366 Guilford Ave *TF:* 800-257-4901 ■ *Web:* www.microvote.com	Indianapolis	IN	46220	317-257-4900	254-3269	801
Micro-vu Corp 7909 Conde Ln *Web:* www.microvu.com	Windsor	CA	95492	707-838-6272		493
Microwave Applications Group 3030 Industrial Pkwy *Web:* magsmx.com	Santa Maria	CA	93455	805-928-5711		225
Microwave Engineering Corp 1551 Osgood St *Web:* www.microwaveeng.com	North Andover	MA	01845	978-685-2776	975-4363	253
Microwave Filter Company Inc 6743 Kinne St *TF:* 800-448-1666 ■ *Web:* www.microwavefilter.com	East Syracuse	NY	13057	315-438-4700		253
Microwave Networks Inc 4000 Greenbriar Ste 100A *Web:* www.microwavenetworks.com	Stafford	TX	77477	281-263-6500		647
Microway Inc 12 RichaRds Rd. *Web:* www.microway.com	Plymouth	MA	02360	508-746-7341	746-4678	173-2
Microwest Software Systems Inc 10981 San Diego Mson Rd Ste 210 *TF:* 800-969-9699 ■ *Web:* www.microwestsoftware.com	San Diego	CA	92108	619 280 0440		100
Microworks 359 Kent St Ste 301 *TF:* 877-232-3859 ■ *Web:* www.microworks.ca	Ottawa	ON	K2P0R6	613-232-3859		180
MICS (Management Information Control Systems Inc) 2025 Ninth St *TF:* 800-838-6427 ■ *Web:* www.bissoftware.com	Los Osos	CA	93402	805-543-7000	543-0373	178-10
Mid America Computer Corp PO Box 700 *TF:* 800-622-2502 ■ *Web:* www.maccnet.com	Blair	NE	68008	402-426-6222	533-5369	225
Mid America Motorworks 17082 N US Hwy 45 PO Box 1368 *TF:* 866-350-4543 ■ *Web:* www.mamotorworks.com	Effingham	IL	62401	217-540-4200	540-4800	61
Mid American Growers Inc 14240 Greenhouse Ave	Granville	IL	61326	815-339-0831		369
Mid American Products Inc 1623 Wildwood Ave	Jackson	MI	49202	517-789-8116		596
Mid Atlantic Center for The Arts 1048 Washington St *TF:* 800-275-4278 ■ *Web:* www.capemaymac.org	Cape May	NJ	08204	609-884-5404		520
Mid Atlantic Printers Ltd 503 Third St *TF:* 888-231-3175 ■ *Web:* www.mapl.net	Altavista	VA	24517	434-369-6633		532-3
Mid City Steel Fabricating Inc 115 Buchner Pl *Web:* www.mid-citysteel.com	La Crosse	WI	54603	608-782-0770		492
Mid Coast Hospital 123 Medical Ctr Dr *TF:* 800-994-6610 ■ *Web:* www.midcoasthealth.com	Brunswick	ME	04011	207-729-0181	721-1230	374-3
Mid Columbia Lumber & Box Company Inc 380 NW Adler *Web:* www.mid-columbialumber.com	Madras	OR	97741	541-475-7241		683
Mid Country Financial Corp PO Box 4164 *Web:* www.midcountryfinancial.com	Macon	GA	31208	478-746-8222		360-2
Mid Michigan Community College (MMCC) 1375 S Clare Ave *Web:* www.midmich.edu	Harrison	MI	48625	989-386-6622	386-6613	162
Mid Ohio Energy Co-op Inc 555 W Franklin St *TF:* 888-382-6732 ■ *Web:* www.midohioenergy.com	Kenton	OH	43326	419-673-7289	673-8388	245
Mid Ohio Regional Planning Commission 111 Liberty St Ste 100 *TF:* 800-750-0750 ■ *Web:* morpc.org	Columbus	OH	43215	614-228-2663		463
Mid Pacific Testing & Inspection Inc 94-547 Ukee St #200, *Web:* www.midpacifictesting.com	Waipahu	HI	96797	808-676-2720		794
Mid Peninsula Endoscopy Center 50 S San Mateo Dr Ste 400	San Mateo	CA	94401	650-373-1970		463
Mid Penn Bancorp Inc 349 Union St *NASDAQ:* MPB ■ *TF:* 866-642-7736 ■ *Web:* midpennbank.com	Millersburg	PA	17061	717-692-2133		360-2
Mid Pines Inn & Golf Club 1010 Midland Rd *TF:* 800-747-7272 ■ *Web:* www.pineneedles-midpines.com	Southern Pines	NC	28387	910-692-2114	692-5349	669
Mid Rivers Mall 1600 Mid Rivers Mall *Web:* www.shopmidriversmall.com	Saint Peters	MO	63376	636-970-2610		460
Mid Seven Transportation Co 2323 Delaware Ave *Web:* www.mid7.com	Des Moines	IA	50317	515-266-5181		780
Mid South Lumber Inc 1115 C St *Web:* www.mid-southlumber.com	Meridian	MS	39301	601-483-4389		683
Mid South Sales Inc 243 County Rd 414 *Web:* midsouthsales.com/index.php	Jonesboro	AR	72404	870-933-6457	933-0446	579
Mid South Steel Inc 15 Welborn St *TF:* 800-255-5213 ■ *Web:* www.midsouthsteelinc.com	Pelham	AL	35124	205-663-1750		492
Mid State Sales Inc 1101 Gahanna Pkwy *Web:* www.midstate-sales.com	Columbus	OH	43230	614-864-1811		755
Mid State Trading Co 2525 Trenton Ave	Williamsport	PA	17701	570-326-9431		686
Mid Valley Agricultural Services Inc 16401 E Hwy 26 PO Box 593 *Web:* www.midvalleyag.com	Linden	CA	95236	209-931-7600	931-0747	10-4
Mid Valley Chamber of Commerce 7120 Hayvenhurst Ave Ste 114 *Web:* www.sanfernandovalleychamber.com	Van Nuys	CA	91406	818-989-0300	989-3836	139
Mid Valley Industries 1151 Delanglade St *Web:* www.mvii.com	Kaukauna	WI	54130	920-759-0314		454
Mid Valley School District 52 Underwood Rd *Web:* www.mvsd.us	Throop	PA	18512	570-307-1150		186
Mid West Products Inc PO Box 301 *TF:* 800-303-4312 ■ *Web:* www.lambertmfg.com	Phillipsburg	OH	45354	937-337-3641		429
Mid Wisconsin Federated Library System 112 Clinton St	Horicon	WI	53032	920-485-0833		434-3
Mid Yellowstone Elec Co-Op Inc 203 Elliott	Hysham	MT	59038	406-342-5521		245
MID-AM Bldg Supply Inc 1615 Omar Bradley Dr PO Box 645 *TF:* 800-892-5850 ■ *Web:* www.midambuilding.com	Moberly	MO	65270	660-263-2140		191-3
Midamar Corp PO Box 218 *TF:* 800-362-3711 ■ *Web:* www.midamar.com	Cedar Rapids	IA	52406	319-362-3711	362-4111	297-9
Mid-America Cabinet Inc 20980 Marion Lee Rd *TF:* 800-754-4111 ■ *Web:* www.midamericacabinets.com	Gentry	AR	72734	479-736-2671	736-8086	115
Mid-America Charter Lines 2513 E Higgins Rd *TF:* 800-323-0312 ■ *Web:* bus-charter.com	Elk Grove Village	IL	60007	847-437-3779		107
Mid-America Christian University 3500 SW 119th St **Fax:* Admissions ■ *TF:* 888-888-2341 ■ *Web:* www.macu.edu	Oklahoma City	OK	73170	405-691-3800	692-3165*	166
Mid-America College of Funeral Science (MACFS) 3111 Hamburg Pk. *TF:* 800-221-6158 ■ *Web:* www.mid-america.edu	Jeffersonville	IN	47130	812-288-8878	288-5942	800
Midamerica Hotels Corp 105 S Mt Auburn Rd *TF:* 888-866-4326 ■ *Web:* www.midamcorp.com	Cape Girardeau	MO	63703	573-334-0546		378
Mid-America Machining Inc 11530 Brooklyn Rd *TF:* 800-704-1078 ■ *Web:* www.mid-americamachining.com	Brooklyn	MI	49230	517-592-8988		454
Mid-America Merchandising Inc 204 W Third St *TF:* 800-333-6737 ■ *Web:* www.mmipromo.com	Kansas City	MO	64105	816-471-5600	842-0952	9
Midamerica National Bancshares 100 W Elm St *TF:* 877-647-5050 ■ *Web:* www.midnatbank.com	Canton	IL	61520	309-647-5000	647-8551	70
MidAmerica Nazarene University 2030 E College Way **Fax:* Admissions ■ *TF:* 800-800-8887 ■ *Web:* www.mnu.edu	Olathe	KS	66062	913-782-3750	971-3481*	166
Mid-America Precision Products LLC 1927 W Fourth St *TF:* 800-781-0112 ■ *Web:* www.midampp.com	Joplin	MO	64801	417-623-2285		234
Mid-America Publishing Corp 9 Second St NW *TF:* 800-558-1244 ■ *Web:* www.hamptonchronicle.com	Hampton	IA	50441	641-456-2585	456-2587	637-8
Mid-America Radio Group 1639 Burton Ln. *Web:* www.wcbk.com	Martinsville	IN	46151	765-342-3394	342-5020	643
Mid-America Reformed Seminary 229 Seminary Dr. *TF:* 888-440-6277 ■ *Web:* www.midamerica.edu	Dyer	IN	46311	219-864-2400	864-2410	167-3
Mid-America Rehabilitation Hospital 5701 W 110th St *TF:* 800-325-3591 ■ *Web:* midamericarehabhospital.com	Overland Park	KS	66211	913-491-2400		374-6
Mid-America Science Museum 500 Mid-America Blvd *Web:* www.midamericamuseum.org	Hot Springs	AR	71913	501-767-3461		520
Mid-America Steel Drum Co Inc 8570 S Chicago Rd *Web:* www.midamericasteeldrum.com	Oak Creek	WI	53154	414-762-1114	762-1623	198
Mid-America Transplant Services (MTS) 1110 Highlands Plaza Dr E Ste 100 *TF:* 888-376-4854 ■ *Web:* www.midamericatransplant.org	Saint Louis	MO	63110	314-735-8200		545
Mid-American Coaches Inc 4530 Hwy 47 *TF:* 866-944-8687 ■ *Web:* www.mid-americancoaches.com	Washington	MO	63090	866-944-8687		760
MidAmerican Energy Holdings Co 666 Grand Ave PO Box 657 *TF:* 888-427-5632 ■ *Web:* www.midamerican.com	Des Moines	IA	50303	712-277-7475		360-5
Midas Hospitality LLC 1804 Borman Cir Dr Ste 100 *Web:* www.midashospitality.com	St. Louis	MO	63146	314-692-0100		378
Midas International Corp 1300 Arlington Heights Rd *TF:* 800-621-8545 ■ *Web:* www.midas.com	Itasca	IL	60143	630-438-3000	438-3700	62-3
Mid-Atlantic Christian Universit 715 N Poindexter St *TF:* 866-996-6228 ■ *Web:* www.macuniversity.edu	Elizabeth City	NC	27909	252-334-2070	334-2071	161
Mid-Atlantic Clearing House Association Inc, The 1344 Ashton Rd Ste 202 *TF:* 800-500-0100 ■ *Web:* www.macha.org	Hanover	MD	21076	410-859-0090		507
Mid-Atlantic Diamond Ventures 1801 Liacouras Walk 503 Alter Hall *Web:* www.fox.temple.edu	Philadelphia	PA	19122	215-204-3082		734
Mid-Atlantic PenFed Realty Berkshire Hathaway HomeServices (PCR) 3050 Chain Bridge Rd *TF:* 866-225-5778 ■ *Web:* www.penfedrealty.com	Fairfax	VA	22030	703-691-7653	691-7662	655
Mid-Atlantic Petroleum Properties LLC (MAPP) 12311 Middlebrook Rd	Germantown	MD	20874	301-972-4116		579
MidCap Advisors LLC 1556 Third Ave Ste 410 *Web:* www.midcapadvisors.com	New York	NY	10128	212-722-5683	722-6861	390
Mid-Carolina Electric Co-op Inc PO Box 669 *TF Cust Svc:* 888-813-8000 ■ *Web:* www.mcecoop.com	Lexington	SC	29071	803-749-6555		245
Mid-Carolina Steel & Recycling Company Inc 7425 Fairfield Rd *Web:* www.mid-carolinasteel.com	Columbia	SC	29203	803-786-9888		480
Mid-Central Educational Cooperative Office 612 Main Ave *Web:* midcentral-coop.org	Platte	SD	57369	605-337-2636		685
Mid-City Electrical Construction 1099 Sullivant Ave *TF:* 800-306-7172 ■ *Web:* www.midcityelectric.com	Columbus	OH	43223	614-221-5153		189-4
Mid-City Motor World 4800 N Hwy 101 *Web:* midcitymotorworld.com	Eureka	CA	95503	707-443-4871		57
Mid-City Transit Corp 518 State Rt 17M *Web:* www.midcitytransit.com	Middletown	NY	10940	845-343-4702		108
Midco Connections Inc 4901 E 26th St *TF:* 800-843-8800 ■ *Web:* www.midcoconnections.com	Sioux Falls	SD	57110	605-330-4125		393
MidCoast Capital 259 N Radnor-Chester Rd Ste 210 *Web:* www.midcoastcapital.com	Radnor	PA	19087	610-687-8580	971-2154	792

	Phone	Fax	Class
Mid-Coast Electric Supply Inc (MCESI) 1801 Stolz St PO Box 2505 .... Victoria TX 77901 *Web:* www.mcesi.com	361-575-6311	575-5515	246
Mid-Columbia Bus Co PO box 1108 .... Pendleton OR 97801 *Web:* www.midcobus.com	541-278-1444		109
Mid-Columbia Libraries 405 S Dayton St .... Kennewick WA 99336 *TF:* 800-237-1233 ■ *Web:* www.midcolumbialibraries.org	509-586-3156		434-3
Midcom Data Technologies Inc 33493 W 14 Mile Rd Ste 150 .... Farmington Hills MI 48331 *Web:* www.midcomdata.com	248-661-0100		246
MIDCON Data Services Inc 401 W 33rd St .... Edmond OK 73013 *Web:* www.midcondata.com	405-478-1234		539
Mid-Con Energy Partners LP 2501 N Harwood St Ste 2410 .... Dallas TX 75201 *TF:* 800-364-2274 ■ *Web:* www.midconenergypartners.com	918-743-7575		536
Midcontinent Airport 2173 Air Cargo Rd .... Wichita KS 67209 *TF:* 800-628-6800 ■ *Web:* www.flywichita.com	316-946-4700	946-4793	27
Midcontinent Communications PO Box 5010 .... Sioux Falls SD 57117 *TF:* 800-888-1300 ■ *Web:* www.midco.com	605-274-9810		116
Mid-Continent Engineering Inc 405 35th Ave NE .... Minneapolis MN 55418 *Web:* www.mid-continent.com	612-781-0260	782-1320	697
Mid-Continent Group 1437 S Boulder Ave W PO Box 1409 .... Tulsa OK 74119 *TF:* 800-722-4994 ■ *Web:* www.mcg-ins.com	918-587-7221		391-4
Mid-Continent Public Library 15616 E 24 Hwy .... Independence MO 64050 *TF:* 800-318-2596 ■ *Web:* www.mymcpl.org	816-836-5200	521-7253	434-3
Mid-Continent Research for Education & Learning (McREL) 4601 DTC Blvd Ste 500 .... Denver CO 80237 *Web:* www.mcrel.org	303-337-0990	337-3005	668
Mid-Continent Safety 8225 E 35th St N .... Wichita KS 67226 *TF General:* 800-776-0956 ■ *Web:* www.midsafe.com/store/index.cfm	316-522-0900		679
Mid-Continent University 99 Powell Rd E .... Mayfield KY 42066 *Fax: Admissions ■ *TF:* 888-628-4723 ■ *Web:* www.midcontinent.edu	270-247-8521	247-3115*	166
Mid-Continental Restoration Company Inc 401 E Hudson Rd PO Box 429 .... Fort Scott KS 66701 *TF:* 800-835-3700 ■ *Web:* www.midcontinental.com	620-223-3700	223-5052	189-7
Mid-Delta Health Systems Inc 405 N Hayden St .... Belzoni MS 39038 *TF:* 800-543-9055 ■ *Web:* www.middelta.com	662-247-1254		371
Middle Atlantic Products Inc 300 Fairfield Rd .... Fairfield NJ 07004 *Web:* www.middleatlantic.com	973-839-1011		697
Middle Bass Island State Park 1719 Fox Rd .... Middle Bass Island OH 43446 *TF:* 866-644-6727 ■ *Web:* parks.ohiodnr.gov	419-285-0311		565
Middle Country Public Library 101 Eastwood Blvd .... Centereach NY 11720 *Web:* www.mcplibrary.org	631-585-9393		434-3
Middle Fork State Fish & Wildlife Area 10906 Kickapoo Pk Rd .... Oakwood IL 61858 *Web:* www.dnr.illinois.gov/Parks/Pages/MiddleFork.aspx	217-442-4915		565
Middle Georgia College 1100 Second St SE .... Cochran GA 31014 *TF:* 800-548-4221 ■ *Web:* www.mga.edu	478-934-6221		162
Middle Georgia Electric Membership Corp 600 Tippettville Rd .... Vienna GA 31092 *TF:* 800-342-0144 ■ *Web:* mgemc.com	229-268-2671		245
Middle Georgia Regional Airport 1000 Airport Dr .... Macon GA 31216 *Web:* iflymacon.com	478-788-3760		27
Middle Georgia Regional Library System 1180 Washington Ave .... Macon GA 31201 *Web:* maconbibb.us	478-751-7400		434-3
Middle River Aircraft Systems (MRAS) 103 Chesapeake Pk Plaza .... Baltimore MD 21220 *TF:* 877-432-3272 ■ *Web:* www.mras-usa.com	410-682-1500	682-1230	22
Middle States Commission on Higher Education 3624 Market St .... Philadelphia PA 19104 *Fax Area Code: 215 ■ *TF:* 800-621-7440 ■ *Web:* www.msche.org	267-284-5000	662-5501*	49-5
Middle Tennessee Electric Membership Corp 555 New Salem Rd .... Murfreesboro TN 37129 *Web:* www.mtemc.com	615-890-9762	494-1012	245
Middle Tennessee Mental Health Institute 221 Stewarts Ferry Pike .... Nashville TN 37214 *TF:* 800-770-8277 ■ *Web:* tn.gov	615-902-7400	741-8953	374-5
Middle Tennessee Natural Gas Utility District (MTNG) 1036 W Broad St PO Box 670 .... Smithville TN 37166 *TF:* 800-880-6373 ■ *Web:* www.mtng.com	615-597-4300	597-6331	787
Middle Tennessee State University 1301 E Main St .... Murfreesboro TN 37132 *Fax: Admissions ■ *TF Admissions:* 877-444-6878 ■ *Web:* www.mtsu.edu	615-898-2300	898-5478*	166
Middlebridge Mktg Inc 1525 Old Louisquisset Pk .... Lincoln RI 02865	401-728-0040		76
Middleburgh Telephone Co, The 103 Cliff St .... Middleburgh NY 12122 *Web:* www.midtel.net	518-827-5211		116
Middlebury College 131 S Main St .... Middlebury VT 05753 *Fax: Admissions ■ *TF:* 877-214-3330 ■ *Web:* www.middlebury.edu	802-443-3000	443-2056*	166
Middlebury College Library 110 Storrs Ave .... Middlebury VT 05753 *TF:* 800-829-1040 ■ *Web:* www.middlebury.edu	802-443-5494	443-5698	434-6
Middlebury Community Schools 57853 Northridge Dr .... Middlebury IN 46540 *TF:* 866-632-9992 ■ *Web:* www.mcsin-k12.org	574-825-9425		685
Middlebury Hardwood Products Inc 101 Joan Dr PO Box 1429 .... Middlebury IN 46540 *Web:* mhpi.us	574-825-9524		499
Middlebury National Corp PO Box 189 .... Middlebury VT 05753 *OTC:* MDVT ■ *Web:* nbmvt.com	802-388-4982		70
Middleby Corp 1400 Toastmaster Dr .... Elgin IL 60120 *NASDAQ:* MIDD ■ *TF:* 800-331-5842 ■ *Web:* www.middleby.com	847-741-3300	741-0015	298

	Phone	Fax	Class
Middlefield Plastics Inc PO Box 708 .... Middlefield OH 44062 *Web:* www.middlefieldplastics.com	440-834-4638		608
Middlesboro Appalachian Regional Hospital 3600 W Cumberland Ave .... Middlesboro KY 40965 *TF:* 800-335-0657 ■ *Web:* arh.org/locations/middlesboro.aspx	606-242-1100	248-1018	374-3
Middlesboro Coca-Cola Bottling Works Inc 1324 Cumberland Ave .... Middlesboro KY 40965 *TF:* 800-442-0102 ■ *Web:* www.mccbw.com	877-692-4679		80-2
Middlesboro Independent School 220 N 20th St .... Middlesboro KY 40965 *Web:* mboro.k12.ky.us	606-242-8800	242-8805	780
Middlesex Community College 590 Springs Rd .... Bedford MA 01730 *Fax Area Code: 781 ■ *TF:* 800-818-3434 ■ *Web:* www.middlesex.mass.edu	978-656-3370	280-3603*	162
Middlesex Community College 100 Training Hill Rd .... Middletown CT 06457 *Fax: Admissions ■ *TF:* 800-818-5501 ■ *Web:* mxcc.edu	860-343-5800	344-7488*	162
Middlesex County 56 Paterson St .... New Brunswick NJ 08901 *Web:* www.judiciary.state.nj.us	732-519-3200		338
Middlesex Judicial District including Superior Court 1 Ct St .... Middletown CT 06457 *Web:* www.jud.ct.gov	860-343-6400	343-6423	338
Middlesex County Chamber of Commerce 393 Main St .... Middletown CT 06457 *Web:* www.middlesexchamber.com	860-347-6924	346-1043	139
Middlesex County College 2600 Woodbridge Ave PO Box 3050 .... Edison NJ 08818 *Fax: Admissions ■ *TF:* 888-442-4551 ■ *Web:* middlesexcc.edu	732-548-6000	906-7728*	162
Middlesex County Educational Service Commission 1660 Stelton Rd .... Piscataway NJ 08854 *Web:* www.mresc.k12.nj.us	732-777-9848		685
Middlesex County Regional Chamber of Commerce 109 Church St .... New Brunswick NJ 08901 *TF:* 800-595-4849 ■ *Web:* www.mcrcc.org	732-745-8090	745-8098	139
Middlesex County Utilities Authority Inc (MCUA) 2571 Main St PO Box 159 .... Sayreville NJ 08872 *Web:* www.mcua.com	732-721-3800	721-0206	787
Middlesex County Vocational & Technical High Schools PO Box 1070 .... East Brunswick NJ 08816 *Web:* www.mcvts.net	732-257-3300		685
Middlesex Gases & Technologies Inc 292 Second St PO Box 490249 .... Everett MA 02149 *TF:* 800-649-6704 ■ *Web:* www.middlesexgases.com	617-387-5050		791
Middlesex Hospital 28 Crescent St .... Middletown CT 06457 *TF:* 800-548-2394 ■ *Web:* www.middlesexhospital.org	860-358-6000	358-2626	374-3
Middlesex Mutual Assurance Co 213 Ct St PO Box 891 .... Middletown CT 06457 *TF:* 800-622-3780 ■ *Web:* www.middleoak.com	800-622-3780		391-4
Middlesex Research Mfg Company Inc 27 Apsley St .... Hudson MA 01749 *TF:* 800-424-5188 ■ *Web:* www.middlesexresearch.com	978-562-3697	562-7446	745-2
Middlesex Savings Bank 120 Flanders Rd .... Westborough MA 01581 *TF:* 877-463-6287 ■ *Web:* www.middlesexbank.com	508-653-0300		70
Middlesex School 1400 Lowell Rd .... Concord MA 01742 *Web:* www.mxschool.edu	978-369-2550	287-4759	622
Middlesex Water Co 1500 Ronson Rd PO Box 1500 .... Iselin NJ 08830 *NASDAQ:* MSEX ■ *TF:* 800-549-3802 ■ *Web:* middlesexwater.com	732-634-1500	638-7515	787
Middlesex West Chamber of Commerce 179 Great Rd Ste 104B .... Acton MA 01720 *TF:* 800-439-0183 ■ *Web:* www.mwcoc.com	978-263-0010	264-0303	139
Middleton & Company Inc 600 Atlantic Ave 18th Fl .... Boston MA 02210 *TF:* 800-357-5101 ■ *Web:* www.middletonco.com	617-357-5101		41
Middleton & Reutlinger 401 S Fourth St Ste 2600 .... Louisville KY 40202 *Web:* www.middletonlaw.com	502-584-1135	561-0442	445
Middleton Cross Plains Area School District 7106 S Ave .... Middleton WI 53562 *Web:* www.mcpasd.k12.wi.us	608-829-9000		685
Middleton Place 4300 Ashley River Rd .... Charleston SC 29414 *TF:* 800-782-3608 ■ *Web:* www.middletonplace.org	843-556-6020	766-4460	671
Middleton Public Library 7425 Hubbard Ave .... Middleton WI 53562 *Web:* www.midlibrary.org	608-831-5564	836-5724	434-3
Middleton Village Nursing & Rehabilitation Ctr 6201 Elmwood Ave .... Middleton WI 53562	608-831-8300		450
Middletown & Hummelstown Rr Co 136 Brown St .... Middletown PA 17057 *Web:* www.mhrailroad.com	717-944-4435		649
Middletown Area School District (Inc) 55 W Water St .... Middletown PA 17057 *Web:* www.raiderweb.org	717-948-3300	948-3329	685
Middletown City School 1515 Girard Ave .... Middletown OH 45044 *Web:* middletowncityschools.com	513-423-0781	420-4579	685
Middletown Convention-Visitors (MCVB) 4935 Riverview Ave .... Middletown OH 45042 *Web:* gettothebc.com	513-422-3030		206
Middletown Public Library 125 S Broad St .... Middletown OH 45044 *Web:* www.midpointelibrary.org	513-424-1251		434-3
Middletown Township Library 55 New Monmouth Rd .... Middletown NJ 07748 *Web:* www.mtpl.org	732-671-3700	671-5839	434-3
Middleville Tool & Die Co 1900 Patterson .... Middleville MI 49333 *Web:* www.mtd-inc.com	269-795-2824		488
Middough Assoc Inc 1901 E 13th St .... Cleveland OH 44114 *Fax: Hum Res ■ *Web:* www.middough.com	216-367-6000	367-6020*	261
Mide Technology Corp 200 Boston Ave .... Medford MA 02155 *Web:* mide.com	781-306-0609		261
Mid-East Career & Technology Centers 400 RichaRds Rd .... Zanesville OH 43701 *Web:* www.mid-east.k12.oh.us	740-454-0101	454-0731	685

Company	City	State	Zip	Phone	Fax	Class
Midego Inc 4710 Olley Ln *Web:* midego.publishpath.com	Fairfax	VA	22032	571-331-4158		196
MidFirst Bank PO Box 76149 **Fax:* Cust Svc ■ *TF:* 888-643-3477 ■ *Web:* www.midfirst.com	Oklahoma City	OK	73147	405-767-7000	840-0862*	70
Midhattan Woodworking Corp 3130 Bordentown Ave. *Web:* www.midhattan.com	Old Bridge	NJ	08857	732-727-3020		499
Mid-Hudson Civic Ctr 14 Civic Ctr Plaza *Web:* www.midhudsonciviccenter.org	Poughkeepsie	NY	12601	845-454-5800		572
Mid-Hudson Library System 103 Market St *TF:* 800-336-6997 ■ *Web:* www.midhudson.org	Poughkeepsie	NY	12601	845-471-6060		434-3
MidHudson Regional Hospital 241 N Rd *Web:* www.midhudsonregional.org	Poughkeepsie	NY	12601	845-483-5000		374-3
Midi Inc 125 Sandy Dr *TF:* 800-519-4627 ■ *Web:* www.midi-inc.com	Newark	DE	19713	302-824-4736		476
Midian Electronic Comm Systems 2302 E 22nd St *TF:* 800-643-4267 ■ *Web:* www.midians.com	Tucson	AZ	85713	520-884-7981		647
MIDIOR Consulting Inc 22 Putnam Ave *Web:* www.midior.com	Cambridge	MA	02139	617-864-8813		463
MIDJersey Chamber of Commerce 1A Quakerbridge Plaza Dr Ste 2 *Web:* www.midjerseychamber.org	Hamilton	NJ	08619	609-689-9960		139
Mid-Kansas Co-op Assn (MKC) PO Box D *TF:* 800-864-4428 ■ *Web:* mkcoop.com	Moundridge	KS	67107	620-345-6361		48-2
Midkiff, Muncie & Ross PC 300 Arboretum Pl Ste 420 *Web:* www.midkifflaw.com	Richmond	VA	23236	804-560-9600		428
Mid-Lakes Distributing Inc 1029 W Adams St *TF:* 888-733-2700 ■ *Web:* www.mid-lakes.com	Chicago	IL	60607	312-733-1033	733-1721	612
Midland Area Chamber of Commerce 300 Rodd St Ste 101 *TF:* 800-715-0074 ■ *Web:* www.macc.org	Midland	MI	48640	989-839-9901	835-3701	139
Midland Area Community Foundation 76 Ashman Cir *Web:* www.midlandfoundation.org	Midland	MI	48640	989-839-9661		305
Midland Asphalt Materials Inc 640 Young St *Web:* www.midlandasphalt.com	Tonawanda	NY	14150	716-692-0730	692-0613	46
Midland by AMC, The 1228 Main St *TF:* 800-653-8000 ■ *Web:* www.midlandkc.com	Kansas City	MO	64105	816-283-9900		572
Midland Chamber of Commerce 109 N Main St *TF:* 800-624-6435 ■ *Web:* www.midlandtxchamber.com	Midland	TX	79701	432-683-3381	686-3556	139
Midland College 3600 N Garfield St **Fax:* Admissions ■ *TF:* 800-474-7164 ■ *Web:* www.midland.edu	Midland	TX	79705	432-685-4500	685 6480*	162
Midland Community Healthcare Services 2502 Delano Ave Ste 1090 *Web:* www.midlandchs.com	Midland	TX	79701	432-699-3817	570-4286	463
Midland County 220 W Ellsworth St *Web:* www.co.midland.mi.us	Midland	MI	48640	989-832-6739	832-6680	338
Midland County 500 N Loraine St *Web:* www.co.midland.tx.us	Midland	TX	79701	432-688-4401	688-4926	338
Midland County Convention & Visitors Bureau 300 Rodd St Ste 101 *TF:* 800-444-9979 ■ *Web:* www.macc.org	Midland	MI	48640	989-839-0340	835-3701	206
Midland County Public Library 301 W Missouri Ave *TF:* 800-491-4636 ■ *Web:* www.co.midland.tx.us	Midland	TX	79701	432-688-4320	688-4939	434-3
Midland Ctr for the Arts Inc 1801 W St Andrews Rd *TF:* 800-523-7649 ■ *Web:* www.mcfta.org	Midland	MI	48640	989-631-5930	631-7890	520
Midland Daily News 124 McDonald St *TF:* 877-411-2762 ■ *Web:* www.ourmidland.com	Midland	MI	48640	989-835-7171	835-6991	532-2
Midland Engineering 52369 SR 933 N *Web:* www.midlandengineering.com	South Bend	IN	46637	574-272-0200	272-7400	189-12
Midland High School 615 W Missouri Ave *TF:* 866-632-9992 ■ *Web:* www.midlandisd.net	Midland	TX	79701	432-240-1000		685
Midland Hospice Care 200 SW Frazier Cir *TF:* 800-491-3691 ■ *Web:* www.midlandcareconnection.org	Topeka	KS	66606	785-232-2044	232-5567	371
Midland Industries Inc 1424 N Halsted St *TF:* 800-662-8228 ■ *Web:* www.zincbig.com	Chicago	IL	60642	312-664-7300	664-7371	485
Midland Information Resources Co 5440 Corporate Pk Dr *TF:* 800-232-3696 ■ *Web:* elandersamericas.com/pages/redirect.aspx	Davenport	IA	52807	563-359-3696	359-1333	627
Midland Instruments Ltd 20 Ed Connelly Dr Huronia Airport *Web:* www.midlandinstruments.com	Tiny	ON	L0L2J0	705-527-4447		647
Midland International Airport 9506 Laforce Blvd PO Box 60305 *TF:* 800-973-2867 ■ *Web:* www.midlandinternational.com	Midland	TX	79711	432-560-2200		27
Midland Iron & Steel Corp 3301 Fourth Ave *Web:* midlanddavis.com	Moline	IL	61265	309-764-6723	764-6729	686
Midland Machinery Company Inc 101 Cranbrook Ext *Web:* www.midlandmachinery.com	Tonawanda	NY	14150	716-692-1200		190
Midland Manufacturing 101 E County Line Rd *Web:* www.midlandmfgco.com	Monroe	IA	50170	641-259-2625	259-3216	98
Midland Memorial Hospital 2200 W Illinois Ave *TF:* 800-833-2916 ■ *Web:* www.midland-memorial.com	Midland	TX	79701	432-685-1111		374-3
Midland Metal Products 1200 W 37th St *Web:* www.midlandmetalproducts.com	Chicago	IL	60609	773-927-5700		454
Midland Mortgage Co 999 NW Grand Blvd Ste 100 **Fax Area Code:* 405 ■ **Fax:* Cust Svc ■ *TF:* 800-654-4566 ■ *Web:* www.mymidlandmortgage.com	Oklahoma City	OK	73118-6077	800-654-4566	767-5500*	509
Midland National Bank 527 N Main *TF:* 800-810-9457 ■ *Web:* www.midland.bank	Newton	KS	67114	316-283-1700	283-3813	70
Midland National Life Insurance Co 1 Sammons Plaza *TF:* 800-923-3223 ■ *Web:* midlandnational.com	Sioux Falls	SD	57193	605-335-5700	335-3621	391-2
Midland Packaging & Display Inc 3545 Nicholson Rd *TF:* 800-745-9353 ■ *Web:* midlandpkg.com	Franksville	WI	53126	262-886-8851		100
Midland Paper 101 E Palatine Rd *TF:* 800-323-8522 ■ *Web:* www.midlandpaper.com	Wheeling	IL	60090	847-777-2700	777-2552	553
Midland Power Co-op 1005 E Lincolnway PO Box 420 *TF:* 800-833-8876 ■ *Web:* www.midlandpower.coop	Jefferson	IA	50129	515-386-4111	386-2385	245
Midland Radio Corp 5900 Parretta Dr *Web:* midlandusa.com	Kansas City	MO	64120	816-241-8500	241-5713	35
Midland Reporter-Telegram PO Box 1650 *TF:* 800-542-3952 ■ *Web:* mrt.com	Midland	TX	79702	432-682-5311	570-7650	532-2
Midland School 5100 Figueroa Mtn Rd PO Box 8 *Web:* www.midland-school.org	Los Olivos	CA	93441	805-688-5114	686-2470	622
Midland Stamping & Fabricating 9521 W Ainslie St *TF:* 800-532-2252 ■ *Web:* midlandstamping.com	Schiller Park	IL	60176	847-678-7573		488
Midland University 900 N Clarkson St **Fax:* Admissions ■ *Web:* my.midlandu.edu	Fremont	NE	68025	402-941-6270	941-6513*	166
Midlands Business Journal 1324 S 119th St *TF:* 800-694-5455 ■ *Web:* www.mbj.com	Omaha	NE	68144	402-330-1760	758-9315	457-5
Midlands Technical College PO Box 2408 **Fax:* Admissions ■ *TF:* 800-922-8038 ■ *Web:* www.midlandstech.edu	Columbia	SC	29202	803-738-1400	790-7524*	162
Midlantic Marketing 117 Commons Ct *Web:* www.midlantic.net	Chadds Ford	PA	19317	610-361-0500		195
Midlothian Public Library 14701 Kenton Ave *Web:* www.midlothianlibrary.org	Midlothian	IL	60445	708-535-2027		435
Mid-Maine Chamber of Commerce 50 Elm St *Web:* www.midmainechamber.com	Waterville	ME	04901	207-873-3315	877-0087	139
MidMark Capital 177 Madison Ave *Web:* www.midmarkcapital.com	Morristown	NJ	07960	973-971-9960	971-9963	401
Midmark Corp 60 Vista Dr *TF:* 800-643-6275 ■ *Web:* www.midmark.com	Versailles	OH	45380	937-526-3662		476
MidMichigan Home Care 3007 N Saginaw Rd *TF:* 800-852-9350 ■ *Web:* www.midmichigan.org	Midland	MI	48640	989-633-1400		371
Mid-Michigan Industries Inc (MMI) 2426 Pkwy Dr *Web:* www.mmionline.com	Mount Pleasant	MI	48858	989-773-6918	773 1317	193
MidMichigan Medical Ctr 4005 Orchard Dr *Web:* www.midmichigan.org	Midland	MI	48670	989 839 3000		374-3
Midnight Oil 3000 W Vanowen St Ste 101 *Web:* www.midnightoilcreative.com	Burbank	CA	91505	818-295-6300		344
Midnight Rose Hotel & Casino 256 E Bennett Ave *TF:* 800-635-5825 ■ *Web:* triplecrowncasinos.com	Cripple Creek	CO	80813	719 689 2446		133
Midnight Sun Adventure Travel 1027 Pandora Ave *TF:* 800-255-5057 ■ *Web:* www.midnightsuntravel.com	Victoria	BC	V8V3P6	250-480-9409	483-7422	760
Mid-Ohio Aviation 6250 N Honeytown Rd *TF:* 800-669-4243 ■ *Web:* www.midohioaviation.com	Smithville	OH	44677	330 669 2671		63
Mid-Ohio Sports Car Course 7721 Steam Corners Rd PO Box 3108 *TF:* 800-643-6446 ■ *Web:* www.midohio.com	Lexington	OH	44904	419-884-4000		515
Mid-Pacific Institute 2445 Kaala St *Web:* www.midpac.edu	Honolulu	HI	96822	808 973-5000		622
Mid-Park Inc 1021 Salt River Rd *Web:* www.mid-park.com	Leitchfield	KY	42754	270-259-3152		488
MidPenn Legal Services 213 A N Front St *Web:* www.midpenn.org	Harrisburg	PA	17101	717-234-0492		428
Midpoint National 1263 SW Blvd	Kansas City	KS	66103	913-362-7400		463
Midrange Software Inc 12716 Riverside Dr *TF:* 800-737-6766 ■ *Web:* www.midrangesoftware.com	Studio City	CA	91607	818-762-8539		178-10
Midrange Solutions Inc 20 Hillside Ave *TF:* 800-882-4008 ■ *Web:* www.midrangeusa.com	Springfield	NJ	07081	973-912-7050		196
Midrex Technologies 2725 Water Ridge Pkwy Ste 100 *Web:* www.midrex.com	Charlotte	NC	28217	704-373-1600	373-1611	261
MidSouth Bancorp Inc 102 Versailles Blvd *NYSE: MSL* ■ *TF:* 800-213-2265 ■ *Web:* www.midsouthbank.com	Lafayette	LA	70501	337-237-8343		360-2
Mid-South Bldg Supply Inc 7940 Woodruff Ct *Web:* www.msbs.net	Springfield	VA	22151	703-321-8500	321-9308	191-3
Mid-South Community College 2000 W Broadway **Fax:* Admissions ■ *TF:* 866-733-6722 ■ *Web:* www.asumidsouth.edu	West Memphis	AR	72301	870-733-6722	733-6719*	162
Mid-South Engineering Co 1658 Malvern Ave *Web:* www.mseco.com	Hot Springs	AR	71901	501-321-2276		256
Mid-south Health Systems 102 SW Larkspur Dr *TF:* 800-542-1031 ■ *Web:* www.mshs.org	Walnut Ridge	AR	72476	870-886-7924		726
Mid-South Wire Company Inc 1070 Visco Dr *TF:* 800-714-7800 ■ *Web:* www.midsouthwire.com	Nashville	TN	37210	615-743-2850	256-5836	813
Midstate College 411 W Northmoor Rd *TF:* 800-251-4299 ■ *Web:* www.midstate.edu	Peoria	IL	61614	309-692-4092	692-3893	800
Midstate Construction Corp 1180 Holm Rd *Web:* www.midstateconstruction.com	Petaluma	CA	94954	707-762-3200	762-0700	186
Mid-State Contracting LLC 2001 County Hwy U *TF:* 800-236-2500 ■ *Web:* www.midstatecontracting.com	Wausau	WI	54402	715-675-2388	675-6971	189-10

Name / Address	City	State	ZIP	Phone	Fax	Class
Mid-State Correctional Facility PO Box 216 *Web:* www.prisontalk.com	Marcy	NY	13403	315-768-8581		213
Midstate Electric Co-op Inc 16755 Finley Butte Rd *TF:* 800-722-7219 ■ *Web:* www.midstateelectric.coop	La Pine	OR	97739	541-536-2126	536-1423	245
Mid-State Equipment Inc W 1115 Bristol Rd *TF:* 877-677-4020 ■ *Web:* www.midstateequipment.com	Columbus	WI	53925	920-623-4020	623-4500	274
Midstate Financial Corp 1 E Main St PO Box 230	Brownsburg	IN	46112	317-852-2268		70
Mid-State Machine & Fabricating Corp 2730 Mine and Mill Rd *Web:* www.midstatefl.com	Lakeland	FL	33801	863-665-6233		295
Mid-State Machine Products Inc 83 Verti Dr *Web:* hnprecision.com	Winslow	ME	04901	207-873-6136		757
Mid-State Petroleum Inc 4192 Mendenhall Oaks Pkwy *Web:* www.mid-statepetroleum.com	High Point	NC	27265	336-841-3000		581
Mid-States Bolt & Screw Co 4126 Somers Dr **Fax Area Code:* 810 ■ *TF:* 800-482-0867 ■ *Web:* www.midstatesbolt.com	Burton	MI	48529	800-482-0867	744-3798*	278
Mid-States Packaging Inc 12163 State Rte 274 *TF:* 800-944-8511 ■ *Web:* www.midstatespackaging.com	Lewistown	OH	43333	937-843-3243	843-4378	547
Mid-States Screw Corp 1817 18th Ave *TF:* 888-354-6772 ■ *Web:* www.midstatesscrew.com	Rockford	IL	61104	815-397-2440	398-1047	278
Mid-States Supply Co 1716 Guinotte Ave *TF:* 800-825-1410 ■ *Web:* www.midcoonline.com	Kansas City	MO	64120	816-842-4290	842-3630	612
Midtex Oil LP 3455 IH 35 S *Web:* midtexoil.com	New Braunfels	TX	78132	830-625-4214		324
Midtown Cafe 102 19th Ave S *Web:* www.midtowncafe.com	Nashville	TN	37203	615-320-7176		671
Midtown Cafe & Dessertery 151 S Stratford Rd *Web:* www.midtowncafews.com	Winston-Salem	NC	27104	336-724-9800	724-9830	671
Midtown Educational Foundation 718 S Loomis St *Web:* midtown-metro.org	Chicago	IL	60607	312-738-8300		242
Midtown Electric Supply Corp 157 W 18th St *Web:* www.midtownelectric.com	New York	NY	10011	212-255-3388	255-3177	246
Midtown Hotel 220 Huntington Ave *TF:* 800-343-1177 ■ *Web:* www.midtownhotel.com	Boston	MA	02115	617-262-1000	262-8739	379
Midtown Printing LLC 2115 59th St *TF:* 800-882-1844 ■ *Web:* www.modernlitho.com	St. Louis	MO	63110	314-781-6505		627
Mid-valley Distributors Inc 3886 E Jensen Ave *TF:* 800-268-7021 ■ *Web:* www.mvdinc.com	Fresno	CA	93725	559-485-2660		619
Midway Auto Supply Inc 1101 S Hampton Rd *Web:* www.midwayautosupply.com	Dallas	TX	75208	214-943-4341		54
Midway College 512 E Stephens St **Fax:* Admissions ■ *TF:* 800-755-0031 ■ *Web:* midway.edu	Midway	KY	40347	859-846-5346	846-5787*	166
Midway Dental Supply Inc 701 N Michigan St *TF:* 800-372-4346 ■ *Web:* www.midwaydental.com	Lakeville	IN	46536	574-784-2533		475
Midway Displays Inc 6554 S Austin Ave *Web:* www.midwaydisplays.com	Bedford Park	IL	60638	708-563-2323		8
Midway Grinding Inc 1451 Lunt Ave *Web:* www.midwaygrinding.com	Elk Grove Village	IL	60007	847-439-7424		454
Midway Industrial Supply Inc 51 Wurz Ave *TF:* 800-333-0598 ■ *Web:* www.midway.ws	Utica	NY	13502	315-797-6660		385
Midway Mall 3343 Midway Mall *Web:* www.midwaymallshopping.com	Elyria	OH	44035	440-324-5749		460
Midway Products Group Inc 1 Lyman E Hoyt Dr **Fax:* Sales ■ *TF:* 800-543-0283 ■ *Web:* www.midwayproducts.com	Monroe	MI	48161	734-241-7242	384-0811*	489
Midway Speedway 22301 Hwy B *TF:* 800-478-7688 ■ *Web:* www.lebanonmidwayspeedway.com	Lebanon	MO	65536	417-588-4430		515
Midway Village Museum 6799 Guilford Rd *Web:* www.midwayvillage.com	Rockford	IL	61107	815-397-9112	397-9156	520
Midwesco Filter Resources Inc 309 N BraddockÿSt *TF:* 800-336-7300 ■ *Web:* www.midwesco-tdcfilter.com	Winchester	VA	22601	540-773-4780		18
Midwest Acoust-A-Fiber Inc 759 Pittsburgh Dr *Web:* www.acoust-a-fiber.com	Delaware	OH	43015	740-369-3624		247
Midwest Action Cycle Inc 251 Host Dr *Web:* www.midwestactioncycle.com	Lake Geneva	WI	53147	262-249-0600	249-0608	61
Midwest Aero Support Inc 1303 Turret Dr *Web:* www.midwestaerosupport.com	Machesney Park	IL	61115	815-398-9202		443
Midwest Ambulance Service of Iowa 2535 106th St *Web:* www.midwestambulance.com	Des Moines	IA	50322	515-222-2222		30
Midwest America Federal Credit Union 1104 Medical Pk Dr *TF:* 800-348-4738 ■ *Web:* www.mwafcu.org	Fort Wayne	IN	46825	260-482-3334		219
Midwest Associates of Colleges Employers 100 E Grand Ave Ste 330 *Web:* www.nalmco.org	Des Moines	IA	50309	515-243-2360		166
Midwest Automotive Inc 1065 Lee St *Web:* midwestautomotiveinc.com	Des Plaines	IL	60016	847-827-8400		54
Midwest Bank 105 E Soo St PO Box 40 *TF:* 877-365-5155 ■ *Web:* www.midwestbank.net	Parkers Prairie	MN	56361	218-338-6054	338-5070	70
Midwest Bio-systems Inc 28933 35 E St *TF:* 877-649-2114 ■ *Web:* www.midwestbiosystems.com	Tampico	IL	61283	815-438-7200		429
Midwest Canvas Corp 4635 West Lake St *Web:* www.midwestcanvas.com	Chicago	IL	60644	773-287-4400		733
Midwest Cast Stone Inc 1610 State Ave *Web:* www.midwestcaststone.com	Kansas City	KS	66102	913-371-3300		183
Midwest City Chamber of Commerce 5905 Trosper Rd *Web:* www.midwestcityok.com	Midwest City	OK	73110	405-733-3801		139
Midwest Clinical Laboratories 3267 S 16th St	Milwaukee	WI	53215	414-647-5505		418
Midwest Commercial Interiors 987 SW Temple *Web:* www.midwestcommercialinteriors.com	Salt Lake City	UT	84101	801-505-4288		319-1
Midwest Communications Inc 904 Grand Ave **Fax:* Hum Res ■ *TF:* 877-945-4236 ■ *Web:* www.mwcradio.com	Wausau	WI	54403	715-842-1437	842-7061*	643
Midwest Consulting Group 5605 N MacArthur Blvd *Web:* www.mcginfo.com	Irving	TX	75038	972-910-9200		463
Midwest Control Products Corp 590 E Main St *Web:* www.midwestcontrol.com	Bushnell	IL	61422	309-772-3163	772-2266	620
Midwest Corporate Aviation 3512 N Webb Rd *TF:* 800-435-9622 ■ *Web:* www.midwestaviation.com	Wichita	KS	67226	316-636-9700	636-9747	63
Midwest Dental Equipment Services & Supplies 2700 Commerce St **Fax Area Code:* 888 ■ *TF:* 800-766-2025 ■ *Web:* www.mwdental.com	Wichita Falls	TX	76301	800-766-2025	551-3514*	228
Midwest Designer Supply Inc N30 W22377 Green Rd Ste C *TF:* 888-523-2611 ■ *Web:* www.midwestdesignersupply.com	Waukesha	WI	53186	888-523-2611		361
Midwest Direct 2222 W 110th St *Web:* www.mw-direct.com	Cleveland	OH	44102	216-251-2500		7
Midwest Drywall Company Inc 1351 S Reca Ct *Web:* www.mwdw.com	Wichita	KS	67209	316-722-9559	722-9682	189-9
Midwest Elastomers Inc 700 Industrial Dr PO Box 412 *TF:* 877-786-3539 ■ *Web:* www.midwestelastomers.com	Wapakoneta	OH	45895	419-738-8844		605-3
Midwest Electric Co-op Corp 104 Washington Ave *TF:* 800-451-3691 ■ *Web:* www.midwestecc.com	Grant	NE	69140	308-352-4356	352-4957	245
Midwest Employers Casualty Co 14755 N Outer 40 Dr Ste 300 *TF:* 877-975-2667 ■ *Web:* www.mwecc.com	Chesterfield	MO	63017	636-449-7000	449-7199	391-4
Midwest Energy Co-op 901 E State St *TF:* 800-492-5989 ■ *Web:* www.teammidwest.com	Cassopolis	MI	49031	800-492-5989		245
Midwest Energy Inc 1330 Canterbury Dr *TF:* 800-222-3121 ■ *Web:* www.mwenergy.com	Hays	KS	67601	785-625-3437	625-1494	245
Midwest Express Inc 11590 Township Rd 157 *Web:* www.midwestexpressgroup.com	East Liberty	OH	43319	937-642-0335		54
Mid-West Fabricating Co 313 N Johns St *Web:* www.midwestfab.com	Amanda	OH	43102	740-969-4411	969-4433	113
Midwest Family Broadcasting 2453 E Elm St *Web:* www.mwfmarketing.fm	Springfield	MO	65802	417-886-5677	886-2155	643
Midwest Fasteners Inc 450 Richard St *Web:* www.midwestfasteners.com	Miamisburg	OH	45342	937-866-0463		350
Midwest Federal Savings & Loan Assn of St Joseph 1901 Frederick Ave	St Joseph	MO	64501	816-233-5148		70
Midwest Feeders Inc 5013 13 Rd *Web:* www.midwest-feeders.com	Ingalls	KS	67853	620-335-5790		10-1
Midwest Folding Products Inc 1414 S Western Ave *TF:* 800-621-4716 ■ *Web:* www.midwestfolding.com	Chicago	IL	60608	312-666-3366	666-2606	319-3
Mid-West Forge Corp 17301 St Clair Ave *Web:* www.mid-westforge.com	Cleveland	OH	44110	216-481-3030	481-7288	483
Midwest Gun & Supply Inc 16 E Peoria	Paola	KS	66071	913-557-4867		711
Midwest Hardwood Corp 9540 83rd Ave N *TF:* 800-788-5568 ■ *Web:* www.midwesthardwood.com	Maple Grove	MN	55369	763-425-8700	391-6740	683
Midwest Helicopter Airways Inc 525 Executive Dr *TF:* 800-323-7609 ■ *Web:* www.midwesthelicopters.com	Willowbrook	IL	60527	630-325-7860	325-3313	359
MIDWEST Homes for Pets 3142 S Cowan Rd PO Box 1031 *TF:* 800-428-8560 ■ *Web:* www.midwesthomes4pets.com	Muncie	IN	47302	765-289-3355	289-6524	578
Midwest Industrial Metal Fabrication 281 Thurman Poe Way *Web:* www.midwestindustrialcoatings.com	Huntington	IN	46750	260-356-5262		567
Midwest Industries Inc 122 E State Hwy 175 *TF:* 800-859-3028 ■ *Web:* www.shorelandr.com	Ida Grove	IA	51445	712-364-3365	364-3361	763
Midwest Institute For Clinical Research Inc 8803 N Meridian St *TF:* 800-422-6237 ■ *Web:* micr.com	Indianapolis	IN	46260	317-705-7050		743
Midwest Instrument Company Inc 541 Industrial Dr *Web:* www.minco.net	Hartland	WI	53029	262-367-7384		201
Midwest International Standard Products Inc 105 Stover Rd *Web:* www.midwestmagic.com	Charlevoix	MI	49720	231-547-4000	547-9453	18
Midwest Iron & Metal Co Inc 700 S Main St *Web:* www.midwestironandmetal.com	Hutchinson	KS	67501	620-662-0551	662-1413	492
Midwest Janitorial Service 2831 Falls Ave *Web:* midwestjanitorialservice.com	Waterloo	IA	50701	319-233-6787		104
Midwest Laboratories Inc 13611 B St *Web:* www.midwestlabs.com	Omaha	NE	68144	402-334-7770		743
Midwest Land & Cattle Company Inc 503 N Mur-Len Rd	Olathe	KS	66062	913-782-6677		446
Midwest Library Service Inc 11443 St Charles Rock Rd *TF:* 800-325-8833 ■ *Web:* www.midwestls.com	Bridgeton	MO	63044	314-739-3100	739-1326	96

				Phone	Fax	Class
Midwest Livestock Systems Inc 3600 N Sixth St *Web:* www.midwestlivestock.com	Beatrice	NE	68310	402-223-5281		446
Midwest Living Magazine 1716 Locust St *TF:* 800-678-8093 ■ *Web:* www.midwestliving.com	Des Moines	IA	50309	515-247-2982		457-22
Midwest Manufacturing Inc 5311 Kane Rd *TF:* 800-826-7126 ■ *Web:* www.midwestmanufacturing.com	Eau Claire	WI	54703	715-876-5555		815
Midwest Manufacturing Resources Inc 1993 Case Pkwy N *TF:* 800-833-0246 ■ *Web:* www.hfomidwest.com	Twinsburg	OH	44087	330-405-4227		791
Mid-West Marketing Inc 239 Hwy 61 *TF:* 800-662-7538 ■ *Web:* mwmktg.espwebsite.com	Bloomsdale	MO	63627	573-483-2577	483-9747	366
Midwest Materials Inc 3687 Shepard Rd *Web:* www.midwestmaterials.com	Perry	OH	44081	440-259-5200		492
Midwest Mechanical Group 801 Parkview Blvd *TF:* 800-214-3680 ■ *Web:* www.midwestmech.com	Lombard	IL	60148	630-850-2300	655-0730	189-10
Midwest Medical Insurance Holding Co 7650 Edinborough Way Ste 400 *TF:* 800-328-5532 ■ *Web:* www.mmicgroup.com	Minneapolis	MN	55435	952-838-6700		177
Midwest Memorial Group LLC 31300 Southfield Rd Ste 1 *Web:* midwestmemorialgroup.com	Beverly Hills	MI	48025	248-290-0338		510
Midwest Metal Products Co 2100 W Mt Pleasant Rd *TF:* 888-741-1044 ■ *Web:* www.midwestmetal.com	Muncie	IN	47302	888-741-1044		480
Midwest Minerals Inc 709 N Locust St PO Box 412 *Web:* www.midwestminerals.com	Pittsburg	KS	66762	620-231-8120	235-0840	503-5
Midwest Motor Express Inc 5015 E Main Ave *TF:* 800-741-4097 ■ *Web:* www.mmeinc.com	Bismarck	ND	58502	701-223-1880	224-1405	780
Midwest Mountaineering Inc 309 Cedar Ave S *TF:* 800-524-0820 ■ *Web:* www.midwestmtn.com	Minneapolis	MN	55454	612-339-3433		711
Midwest Plan Service 122 Davidson Hall ISU *TF:* 800-562-3618 ■ *Web:* www-mwps.sws.iastate.edu	Ames	IA	50011	515-294-4337	294-9589	637-2
Midwest Plastic Components 7309 W 27th St *TF:* 800-243-3221 ■ *Web:* spectrumplasticsgroup.com	Minneapolis	MN	55426	952-929-3312	929-8404	604
Midwest Pro Painting Inc 12845 Farmington Rd *TF:* 800-860-6757 ■ *Web:* www.mpp-inc.com	Livonia	MI	48150	734-427-1040	427-0209	189-8
Midwest Products & Engineering Inc 10597 W Glenbrook Ct *Web:* www.mpe-inc.com	Milwaukee	WI	53224	414-355-0310		198
Midwest Products Company Inc 400 S Indiana St **Fax:* Sales ■ *TF Orders:* 800-348-3497 ■ *Web:* www.midwestproducts.com	Hobart	IN	46342	219-942-1134	947-2347*	762
Midwest Products Finishing Company Inc 6194 Section Rd *Web:* www.midwestecoat.com	Ottawa Lake	MI	49267	734-856-5200	856-7267	481
Midwest Quality Gloves Inc 835 Industrial Rd *TF:* 800-821-3028 ■ *Web:* www.midwestglove.com	Chillicothe	MO	64601	660-646-2165	646-6933	155-8
Midwest Railcar Repair Inc 25965 482nd Ave *Web:* www.mwrail.com	Brandon	SD	57005	605-582-8300		366
Midwest Reliability Organization 380 Saint Peter St Ste 800 *Web:* www.midwestreliability.org	Saint Paul	MN	55102	651-855-1760		533
Midwest Research Institute (MRI) 425 Volker Blvd *Web:* www.mriglobal.org	Kansas City	MO	64110	816-753-7600		668
Midwest Sales & Service Inc 917 S Chapin St *TF:* 800-772-7262 ■ *Web:* midwestsales.org	South Bend	IN	46601	574-287-3365		38
Midwest Screw Products Inc 34700 Lakeland Blvd *Web:* www.midwestllc.com	Eastlake	OH	44095	440-951-2333	951-2336	621
Midwest Specialized Transportation Inc 4515 Hwy 63 N PO Box 6418 *TF:* 800-927-8007 ■ *Web:* www.midspec.com	Rochester	MN	55906	507-424-4838	228-6859	449
Midwest Sports Supply Inc 11613 Reading Rd *TF:* 800-334-4580 ■ *Web:* www.midwestsports.com	Cincinnati	OH	45241	513-956-4900		711
Mid-West Spring & Stamping Co 1404 Joliet Rd Unit C *TF:* 800-619-0909 ■ *Web:* www.mwspring.com	Romeoville	IL	60446	630-739-3800		719
Midwest Steel & Equipment Company Inc 9825 Moers Rd *TF:* 800-777-9378 ■ *Web:* www.midwest-steel.com	Houston	TX	77075	713-991-7843	991-4745	189-16
Mid-West Steel Bldg Co 7301 Fairview *TF:* 800-777-9378 ■ *Web:* www.mid-weststeel.com	Houston	TX	77041	713-466-7788		105
Midwest Steel Inc 2525 E Grand Blvd *TF:* 800-261-6270 ■ *Web:* www.midweststeel.com	Detroit	MI	48211	313-873-2220	873-2222	189-14
Midwest Steeplejacks Inc 133 W Main Ave Ste 201 *Web:* www.midweststeeplejacks.com	West Fargo	ND	58078	701-241-7040	298-8485	480
Midwest Supplies 5825 Excelsior Blvd *Web:* www.midwestsupplies.com	St Louis Park	MN	55416	952-562-5300		298
Midwest Systems 5911 Hall St *TF:* 800-383-6281 ■ *Web:* www.mwsystems.com	Saint Louis	MO	63147	314-389-6280	389-9443	779
Midwest Telemark International Inc 112 Main St West *Web:* www.mtind.com	Mohall	ND	58761	701-756-6483		393
Mid-West Terminal Warehouse Company Inc 1700 Universal Ave *Web:* www.mwtco.com	Kansas City	MO	64120	816-231-8811	231-0020	803-1
Midwest Tile & Concrete Products Inc 4309 Webster Rd *TF:* 800-359-4701 ■ *Web:* www.midwesttile.net	Woodburn	IN	46797	260-749-5173	493-2477	183
Midwest Tool & Cutlery Co Inc 1210 Progress St PO Box 160 *TF:* 800-782-4659 ■ *Web:* www.midwestsnips.com	Sturgis	MI	49091	269-651-7964	651-4412	222
Midwest Tool & Engineering Co 112 Webster St *Web:* www.themidwesttool.com	Dayton	OH	45402	937-224-0756	224-0757	757
Midwest Towers Inc 1156 Hwy 19 E *TF:* 800-900-2190 ■ *Web:* www.midwesttowers.com	Chickasha	OK	73018	405-224-4622	224-4625	14
Midwest Trading Horticultural Supplies Inc 48w805 Il Rt 64 *TF:* 800-546-9522 ■ *Web:* www.midwest-trading.com	Maple Park	IL	60151	630-365-1990		292
Midwest Truck & Auto Parts Inc 1001 W Exchange *TF:* 800-934-2727 ■ *Web:* www.midwesttruck.com	Chicago	IL	60609	773-247-3400	579-3788	61
Mid-West Truckers Assn Inc 2727 N Dirksen Pkwy *Web:* mid-westtruckers.com	Springfield	IL	62702	217-525-0310	525-0342	49-21
Midwest Walnut 1914 Tostevin *TF:* 800-592-5688 ■ *Web:* www.midwestwalnut.com	Council Bluffs	IA	51503	712-325-9191	325-0156	448
Midwest Wire Products Inc 800 Woodward Heights *TF:* 800-989-9881 ■ *Web:* www.midwestwire.com	Ferndale	MI	48220	248-399-5100	542-7104	73
Midwest Wire Products Inc PO Box 770 *TF:* 800-445-0225 ■ *Web:* www.wireforming.com	Sturgeon Bay	WI	54235	920-743-6591	743-3777	488
Midwestern Baptist Theological Seminary 5001 N Oak Trafficway *TF:* 800-944-6287 ■ *Web:* www.mbts.edu	Kansas City	MO	64118	816-414-3700		167-3
Midwestern Industries Inc 915 Oberlin Rd SW *TF Cust Svc:* 877-474-9464 ■ *Web:* www.midwesternind.com	Massillon	OH	44647	330-837-4203	837-4210	190
Midwestern Intermediate Unit Iv 453 Maple St *TF:* 800-942-8035 ■ *Web:* www.miu4.org/site/default.aspx?pageid=1	Grove City	PA	16127	724-458-6700	458-5083	685
Midwestern Manufacturing Company Inc 2119 S Union Ave *Web:* www.sidebooms.com	Tulsa	OK	74107	918-858-4200		537
Midwestern Regional Medical Ctr (MRMC) 2520 Elisha Ave *TF:* 800-615-3055 ■ *Web:* www.cancercenter.com	Zion	IL	60099	847-872-4561		374-7
Midwestern State University 3410 Taft Blvd **Fax:* Admissions ■ *TF Admissions:* 800-842-1922 ■ *Web:* www.mwsu.edu	Wichita Falls	TX	76308	940-397-4000	397-4672*	166
MidWestOne Bank 102 S Clinton St PO Box 1700 *NASDAQ: MOFG* ■ *TF Cust Svc:* 800-247-4418 ■ *Web:* ir.midwestone.com	Iowa City	IA	52240	319-356-5800	356-5849	360-2
Midwood Ambulance & Oxygen Service Inc 2593 W 13th St *TF:* 800-934-7704 ■ *Web:* www.midwoodambulance.com	Brooklyn	NY	11223	718-645-1000		30
Mid-York Library System 1600 Lincoln Ave *Web:* catalog.midyork.org/client/en_US/default	Utica	NY	13502	315-735-8328	735-0943	434-3
Miele Inc 9 Independence Way *TF:* 800-843-7231 ■ *Web:* www.miele.com	Princeton	NJ	08540	609-419-9898	419-4298	36
Miers Insurance Inc 2222 S 12th St *Web:* miersinsurance.com	Allentown	PA	18103	610-797-7900		390
MIF (Milk Industry Foundation) 1250 H St NW Ste 900 *Web:* www.idfa.org	Washington	DC	20005	202-737-4332	331-7820	48-2
Mifflin County 20 N Wayne St *TF:* 800 872 7245 ■ *Web:* www.co.mifflin.pa.us	Lewistown	PA	17044	717-248-6733	248-3695	338
Mifflin County School District 201 Eigth St *Web:* www.mcsdk12.org	Lewistown	PA	17044	717-248-0148		685
Mifflinburg Bank & Trust Co (MBTC) 250 E Chestnut St PO Box 186 *TF:* 888-966-3131 ■ *Web:* www.mbtc.com	Mifflinburg	PA	17844	570-966-1041		70
Mig Communications 800 Hearst Ave *TF:* 800-790-8444 ■ *Web:* www.migcom.com	Berkeley	CA	94710	510-845-7549		224
Mighty Distributing System of America Inc 650 Engineering Dr *TF:* 800-829-3900 ■ *Web:* www.mightyautoparts.com	Norcross	GA	30092	770-448-3900	446-8627	61
Mighty Eighth Air Force Museum 175 Bourne Ave *Web:* www.mightyeighth.org	Pooler	GA	31322	912-748-8888	748-0209	520
Migrant Legal Action Program (MLAP) 1001 Connecticut Ave NW Ste 915 *Web:* www.mlap.org	Washington	DC	20036	202-775-7780		48-8
Migration & Refugee Services US Conference of Catholic Bishops 3211 Fourth St NE	Washington	DC	20017	202-541-3000		48-5
Migratory Bird Conservation Commission 5275 Leesburg Pike *Web:* www.fws.gov	Falls Church	VA	22203	703-358-1716		340-20
Migu Press Inc 260 Ivyland Rd *TF:* 800-882-1844 ■ *Web:* www.migupress.com	Warminster	PA	18974	215-957-9763		627
Miguel's 7555 Pacific Ave	Stockton	CA	95207	209-951-1931		671
Mihlfeld & Assoc Inc 2841 E Division St *Web:* www.mihlfeld.com	Springfield	MO	65803	417-831-6727		311
MII (Mitcham Industries Inc) 8141 Hwy 75 S PO Box 1175 *NASDAQ: MIND* ■ **Fax:* Sales ■ *Web:* www.mitchamindustries.com	Huntsville	TX	77340	936-291-2277	295-1922*	264-3
Mii Amo at Enchantment Resort 525 Boynton Canyon Rd *TF:* 888-749-2137 ■ *Web:* www.miiamo.com	Sedona	AZ	86336	928-203-8500	282-9249	707
MII Life Inc 1750 Yankee Doodle Rd *Web:* www.selectaccount.com	Eagan	MN	55121	651-662-5065		463
Mijac Alarm 9339 Charles Smith Ave Ste 100 *TF:* 800-982-7612 ■ *Web:* www.mijacalarm.com	Rancho Cucamonga	CA	91730	909-982-7612		693
Mi-Jack Products Inc 3111 W 167th St *Web:* www.mi-jack.com	Hazel Crest	IL	60429	708-596-5200		190
Mika Meyers PLC 900 Monroe Ave NW *Web:* www.mmbjlaw.com	Grand Rapids	MI	49503	616-632-8000		445
Mikado 3971 28th St SE *Web:* mikadogr.com	Grand Rapids	MI	49512	616-285-7666		671
Mikado Japanese Restaurant 895 S College Mall Rd *Web:* www.btownmenus.com	Bloomington	IN	47401	812-333-1950		671

Phone | Fax | Class

Mikado Japanese Restaurant
148 S Illinois St .... Indianapolis IN 46225 317-972-4180 671
Web: indymikado.com

Mikado Ryotei 9033 Research Blvd. .... Austin TX 78758 512-833-8188 671
Web: mikadoaustin.com

MIKAL Salon & Spa Software
4382 Mt Carmel Tobasco .... Cincinnati OH 45244 513-528-5100 177
Web: www.mikal.com

Mikan Associates Consulting
141 W Jackson Blvd Ste 1520 .... Chicago IL 60604 847-613-6010 463
TF: 888-902-1970 ■ *Web:* www.mikanassociates.com

Mikart Inc 1750 Chattahoochee Ave NW .... Atlanta GA 30318 404-351-4510 350-0432 582
Web: www.mikart.com

Mikasa Sports Usa Inc 1821 Kettering .... Irvine CA 92614 949-863-1588 711
Web: www.mikasasports.com

Mikata Japanese Steakhouse
5300 Sidney Simons Blvd .... Columbus GA 31904 706-327-5100 671
Web: www.mikatasteakhouse.com

Mikato Japanese Steak House
1092 S Ponce de Leon Blvd .... Saint Augustine FL 32084 904-824-7064 671
Web: mymikato.com

Mike Anderson's Seafood
1031 W Lee Dr .... Baton Rouge LA 70820 225-766-7823 671
Web: www.mikeandersons.com

Mike Calvert Toyota Inc 2333 S Loop W .... Houston TX 77054 713-558-8100 57
Web: mikecalverttoyota.com

Mike Castrucci Ford Sales Inc
1020 State Rt 28 .... Milford OH 45150 513-831-7010 831-6239 516
TF: 855-823-5631 ■ *Web:* www.mikecastruccifordmilford.com

Mike Collins & Associates Inc
6048 Century Oaks Dr .... Chattanooga TN 37416 423-892-8899 175
TF: 800-347-6950 ■ *Web:* www.mcollins.com

Mike Davis & Associates Inc
15505 Long Vista Dr # 200. .... Austin TX 78728 512-836-8442 344
TF: 888-836-8442 ■ *Web:* www.imagecraftexhibits.com

Mike Ditka's Restaurants
100 E Chestnut St. .... Chicago IL 60611 312-587-8989 671
Web: www.ditkasrestaurants.com

Mike Durfee State Prison
1412 Wood St. .... Springfield SD 57062 605-369-2201 369-2813 213
Web: doc.sd.gov

Mike Ferry Organization, The
7220 S Cimarron Rd Ste 300 .... Las Vegas NV 89113 702-982-6260 260
TF: 800-448-0647 ■ *Web:* www.mikeferry.com

Mike Moss Agency Inc
803 S Dogwood .... Siloam Springs AR 72761 479-524-5111 390
TF: 800-447-0163 ■ *Web:* mossins.com

Mike Murach & Assoc Inc 4340 N Knoll .... Fresno CA 93722 559-440-9071 440-0963 637-2
TF: 800-221-5528 ■ *Web:* www.murach.com

Mike Reed Chevrolet
1559 E Oglethorpe .... Hinesville GA 31313 877-228-3943 57
TF: 877-228-3943 ■ *Web:* mikereedchevy.com

Mike Roess Gold Head Branch State Park
6239 SR 21. .... Keystone Heights FL 32656 352-473-4701 565
Web: www.floridastateparks.org

Mike Rose's Auto Body Inc
2260 Via de Marcardos. .... Concord CA 94520 925-689-1739 689-0991 62-4
TF: 855-340-1739 ■ *Web:* mikesautobody.com

Mike Savoie Chevrolet Inc PO Box 520 .... Troy MI 48084 248-643-8000 649-3007 57
Web: www.mikesavoie.com

Mike Shannon's
871 S Arbor Vitae Ste 101 .... Edwardsville MO 62025 618-655-9911 671
Web: www.mikeshannonsgrill.com

Mike's Archery Center Inc
413 Franklin Ave NE .... Saint Cloud MN 56304 320-251-2242 711
TF: 800-658-3094 ■ *Web:* www.mikesarcherycenter.com

Mike's Famous Harley-Davidson of Groton
951 Bank St .... New London CT 06320 860-574-9200 520
Web: www.mikesfamous.com

Miken Builders Inc
32782 Cedar Dr Unit 1 .... Millville DE 19967 302-537-4444 537-4525 685
TF: 800-888-7501 ■ *Web:* www.mikenbuilders.com

Miken Sales Inc 539 S Mission Rd. .... Los Angeles CA 90033 323-266-2560 266-2580 157-6
Web: mikenusa.com

Mike-Sell's Potato Chip Co
333 Leo St PO Box 115 .... Dayton OH 45404 937-228-9400 461-5707 296-35
TF: 800-257-4742 ■ *Web:* www.mike-sells.com

Miki Japanese Restaurant
106 S First St .... Ann Arbor MI 48104 734-665-8226 671

Mikimoto (America) Company Ltd
730 Fifth Ave. .... New York NY 10019 212-457-4500 411
TF: 844-341-0579 ■ *Web:* www.mikimotoamerica.com

Mikimoto's 1212 N Washington St .... Wilmington DE 19801 302-656-8638 671
Web: www.mikimotos.com

MikiSushi 180 Leveland Ln .... Modesto CA 95350 209-524-3555 671

Mikro Systems Inc
1180 Seminole Trl Ste 220 .... Charlottesville VA 22901 434-244-6480 261
Web: www.mikrosystems.com

Mikros Engineering Inc
8755 Wyoming Ave N. .... Brooklyn Park MN 55445 763-424-4642 261
TF: 800-394-5499 ■ *Web:* www.mikros.com

Mikros Systems Corp
707 Alexander Rd Ste 208 Ste 208 .... Princeton NJ 08540 609-987-1513 529
Web: www.mikrossystems.com

Mikuni American Corp
8910 Mikuni Ave. .... Northridge CA 91324 818-885-1242 993-6877 60
Web: www.mikuni.com

Mil Corp 4000 Mitchellville Rd. .... Bowie MD 20716 301-805-8500 805-8505 177
Web: www.milcorp.com

Mila Displays Inc
1315B Broadway Ste 108 .... Hewlett NY 11557 516-791-2643 5
TF: 800-295-6452 ■ *Web:* www.miladisplays.com

Milacron Inc 3010 Disney St. .... Cincinnati OH 45209 513-487-5000 386
Web: www.milacron.com

Milaeger's Inc 4838 Douglas Ave .... Racine WI 53402 262-639-2040 681-6192 323
TF: 800-669-1229 ■ *Web:* www.milaegers.com

Milam County 107 W Main St .... Cameron TX 76520 254-697-7049 697-7055 338
TF: 800-299-2437 ■ *Web:* www.milamcounty.net

Phone | Fax | Class

Milam's Market
11 N Royal Poinciana Blvd Ste 100 .... Miami Springs FL 33166 305-884-4870 345
Web: www.milamsmarkets.com

Milan Engineering Inc
925 S Semoran Blvd. .... Winter Park FL 32792 407-678-2055 186

Milan Express Company Inc
1091 Kefauver Dr .... Milan TN 38358 731-686-7428 780
TF: 800-231-7303 ■ *Web:* www.milanexpress.com

Milan Hill State Park 427 Milan Hill Rd .... Milan NH 03588 603-449-2429 565
Web: www.nhstateparks.org

Milan Salami Company Inc 1155 67th St .... Oakland CA 94608 510-654-7055 296-26

Milan Tool Corp 8989 Brookpark Rd .... Cleveland OH 44129 216-661-1078 350
Web: milantool.com

Milbank Mfg Company Inc
4801 Deramus Ave .... Kansas City MO 64120 816-483-5314 483-6357 697
Web: www.milbankworks.com

Milbank Tweed Hadley & McCloy LLP
1 Chase Manhattan Plaza .... New York NY 10005 212-530-5000 530-5219 428
TF: 800-229-0543 ■ *Web:* www.milbank.com

Milbar Hydro-Test Inc 651 Aero Dr .... Shreveport LA 71107 318-227-8210 222-2558 539
TF: 800-259-8210 ■ *Web:* www.milbarhydro-test.com

Milber Makris Plousadis & Seiden LLP
3 Barker Ave 6th Fl .... White Plains NY 10601 914-681-8700 681-8709 445
Web: milbermakris.com

Milco Industries Inc
550 E Fifth St .... Bloomsburg PA 17815 570-784-0400 387-8433 155-15
Web: milcotextile.com

Milco Manufacturing Co
2147 E 10-Mile Rd .... Warren MI 48091 586-755-7320 755-7442 811
Web: www.milcomfg.com

Mildred High School
5475 S US Hwy 287 .... Corsicana TX 75109 903-872-6505 685
Web: www.mildredisd.org

Mildred's Big City Food
3445 W University Ave .... Gainesville FL 32607 352-371-1711 671
Web: www.mildredsbigcityfood.com

Mile High Racing & Entertainment/Mile High
10750 E Iliff Ave .... Aurora CO 80014 303-751-5918 642
Web: www.mihiracing.com

Mile High Shooting Accessories LLC
3731 Monarch St .... Erie CO 80516 303-255-9999 225
TF: 877-871-9990 ■ *Web:* milehighshooting.com

Mile High United Way Inc 2505 18th St .... Denver CO 80211 303-433-8383 455-6462 48-15
Web: www.unitedwaydenver.org

Mile Marker International Inc
2121 BLOUNT Rd .... Pompano Beach FL 33069 800-886-8647 61
TF: 800-886-8647 ■ *Web:* milemarker.com

Milender White Construction Co
12655 W 54th Dr .... Arvada CO 80002 303-216-0420 186
Web: www.milenderwhite.com

MileNorth Chicago Hotel
166 E Superior St .... Chicago IL 60611 312-787-6000 707
Web: www.milenorthhotel.com

Miles & More PO Box 946. .... Santa Clarita CA 91380 800-581-6400 244-4950* 26
**Fax Area Code:* 661 ■ *TF:* 800-581-6400 ■ *Web:* www.miles-and-more.com

Miles & Stockbridge P C
100 Light St .... Baltimore MD 21202 410-727-6464 445
Web: www.milesstockbridge.com

Miles Chemical Co 12801 Rangoon St. .... Arleta CA 91331 818-504-3355 146
Web: www.mileschemical.com

Miles City Livestock Commission
337 I-94 Bus Loop .... Miles City MT 59301 406-234-1790 446
Web: www.milescitylivestock.com

Miles College
5500 Myron Massey Blvd. .... Fairfield AL 35064 205-929-1000 929-1627* 166
**Fax:* Admissions ■ *TF Admissions:* 800-445-0708 ■ *Web:* www.miles.edu

Miles Community College
2715 Dickinson St .... Miles City MT 59301 406-874-6100 874-6283* 162
**Fax:* Admissions ■ *TF:* 800-541-9281 ■ *Web:* www.milescc.edu

Miles Kimball Co 250 City Ctr Bldg .... Oshkosh WI 54906 920-231-3800 231-6942 459
TF Cust Svc: 855-202-7394 ■ *Web:* www.mileskimball.com

Miles Media Group Inc
6751 Professional Pkwy W Ste 200 .... Sarasota FL 34240 941-342-2300 637-9
TF: 888-232-2499 ■ *Web:* www.see-florida.com

Miles Sand & Gravel Company Inc
400 Valley Ave NE. .... Puyallup WA 98372 253-833-3705 833-3746 503-4
Web: miles.rocks

Miles Technologies Inc
300 W Route 38 .... Moorestown NJ 08057 856-439-0999 180
TF: 800-496-8001 ■ *Web:* www.milestechnologies.com

MilesTek Corp 1506 I-35 W .... Denton TX 76207 940-484-9400 194
TF: 800-958-5173 ■ *Web:* www.milestek.com

Milestone Contractors LP
3410 S 650 E .... Elizabethtown IN 47232 812-579-5248 579-6703 188-4
TF: 800-377-7727 ■ *Web:* www.milestonelp.com

Milestone Growth Fund
250 Second Ave S Ste 106 .... Minneapolis MN 55401 612-338-0090 403
Web: www.milestonegrowth.com

Milestone Hospitality Management LLC
717 Light St .... Baltimore MD 21230 561-981-8828 707
Web: www.milestonehotels.com

Milestone Investments Inc
315 Manitoba Ave Ste 310 .... Wayzata MN 55391 952-476-8516 401
Web: www.milestoneusa.com

Milestone Partners LLC
6047 Tyvola Glen Cir .... Charlotte NC 28217 704-414-6532 691
Web: www.milestonex.com

Milestone Retirement Communities LLC
201 NE Park Plaza Dr Ste 105. .... Vancouver WA 98684 360-882-4500 371
Web: www.milestoneretirement.com

Milestone Scientific Inc
220 S Orange Ave. .... Livingston NJ 07039 973-535-2717 535-2829 477
OTC: MLSS ■ *TF:* 800-862-1125 ■ *Web:* www.milestonescientific.com

Milestone Technologies Inc
3101 Skyway Ct .... Fremont CA 94539 877-651-2454 393
TF: 877-651-2454 ■ *Web:* www.milestonepowered.com

Milestone Venture Partners
551 Madison Ave 7th Fl .... New York NY 10022 212-223-7400 792
Web: www.milestonevp.com

Name / Address	City	State	Zip	Phone	Fax	Class
Milford Area Chamber of Commerce 258 Main St *Web:* www.milfordchamber.org	Milford	MA	01757	508-473-6700	473-8467	139
Milford Bank 33 Broad St *TF:* 800-340-4862 ■ *Web:* www.milfordbank.com	Milford	CT	06460	203-783-5700		70
Milford Chamber of Commerce 5 Broad St *Web:* www.milfordct.com	Milford	CT	06460	203-878-0681	876-8517	139
Milford Daily News Co 197 Main St *Web:* www.milforddailynews.com	Milford	MA	01757	508-634-7522	634-7514	637-8
Milford Exempted Village School District 1039 St Rt 28 *Web:* www.milfordschools.org	Milford	OH	45150	513-831-9690	831-3208	685
Milford Federal Savings & Loan Assn 246 Main St *TF:* 800-478-6990 ■ *Web:* www.milfordfederal.com	Milford	MA	01757	508-634-2500		71
Milford Historical Society 124 E Commerce St Ste 2 *Web:* www.milfordhistory.org	Milford	MI	48381	248-685-7308		520
Milford Hospital (MH) 300 Seaside Ave *Web:* www.milfordhospital.org	Milford	CT	06460	203-876-4000	876-4220	374-3
Milford Markets Inc PO Box 7812 *TF:* 800-746-7748 ■ *Web:* www.shoprite.com	Edison	NJ	08818	800-746-7748		345
Milford Mirror 1000 Bridgeport Ave *TF Advertisement:* 800-372-2790 ■ *Web:* www.milfordmirror.com	Shelton	CT	06484	203-402-2315		532-4
Milford National Bank & Trust Co, The 300 E Main St *Web:* www.milfordnationalonline.com	Milford	MA	01757	508-634-4100	634-4107	70
Milford Public Library 57 New Haven Ave	Milford	CT	06460	203-783-3290		434-3
Milford Regional Medical Ctr 14 Prospect St *Web:* www.milfordregional.org	Milford	MA	01757	508-473-1190		374-3
Milford State Park 3612 State Pk Rd *Web:* ksoutdoors.com/State-Parks/Locations/Milford	Milford	KS	66514	785-238-3014		565
Milford Town Library 80 Spruce St *Web:* www.milfordtownlibrary.org	Milford	MA	01757	508-473-2145		434-3
Milford-Miami Township Chamber of Commerce 983 Lila Ave *TF:* 800-837-3200 ■ *Web:* www.milfordmiamitownship.com	Milford	OH	45150	513-831-2411	831-3547	139
Milgo Industrial Inc 68 Lombardi St *TF:* 800-424-3996 ■ *Web:* www.milgo-bufkin.com	Brooklyn	NY	11222	718-388-6476	963-0614	491
Milgram & Company Ltd 400 - 645 Wellington *TF:* 800-879-6144 ■ *Web:* www.milgram.com	Montreal	QC	H3C0L1	514-288-2161		314
Milgro Nursery LLC 1085 Victoria Ave	Oxnard	CA	93030	805-985-0855		292
Milhouse Engineering & Construction Inc 60 E Van Buren St Ste 1501 *Web:* milhouseinc.com	Chicago	IL	60605	312 987-0061		261
Milian & Swain Associates Inc 2025 SW 32nd Ave *Web:* www.milianswain.com	Miami	FL	33145	305-441-0123		261
Milieu Landscaping 48 E Hintz Rd *Web:* www.milieu-design.com	Wheeling	IL	60090	847-465-1160		317
Milio's Sandwiches 901 Deming Way Ste 202 *Web:* www.milios.com	Madison	WI	53717	608-662-3000	662-3001	670
Military & Aerospace Electronics Magazine PO Box 3425 *Web:* www.militaryaerospace.com	Northbrook	IL	60065	847-559-7330	763-9607	457-12
Military Advantage Inc 799 Market St Ste 700 *Web:* www.military.com	San Francisco	CA	94103	415-820-3434	820-0552	171
Military Affairs 3000 Monroe Ave NW	Grand Rapids	MI	49505	616-364-5300		793
Military Benefit Assn (MBA) 14605 Avion Pkwy PO Box 221110 *TF:* 800-336-0100 ■ *Web:* www.militarybenefit.org	Chantilly	VA	20153	703-968 6200	968-6423	48-19
Military Engineer Magazine 607 Prince St *TF Cust Svc:* 800-336-3097 ■ *Web:* www.same.org	Alexandria	VA	22314	703-549-3800	684-0231	457-12
Military Officers Assn of America (MOAA) 201 N Washington St *TF:* 800 234 6622 ■ *Web:* www.moaa.org	Alexandria	VA	22314	703-549-2311		48-19
Military Personnel Services Corp 6066 Leesburg Pk *Web:* www.mpscrc.com	Falls Church	VA	22041	571-481-4000		177
Military Sales & Service Co 5301 S Westmoreland Rd *Web:* mssco.com	Dallas	TX	75237	214-330-4621	330-1740	195
Military Sealift Command 2000 W Marine View Dr Washington Navy Yard	Everett	WA	98207	425-304-4851		340-6
Milk Industry Foundation (MIF) 1250 H St NW Ste 900 *Web:* www.idfa.org	Washington	DC	20005	202-737-4332	331-7820	48-2
Milk Products LLC PO Box 150 *TF:* 800-657-0793 ■ *Web:* www.milkproductsinc.com	Chilton	WI	53014	920-849-2348	849-9014	296-10
Milk Specialties Co 7500 Flying Cloud Dr Ste 500 *TF:* 800-323-4274 ■ *Web:* www.milkspecialties.com	Eden Prairie	MN	55344	952-942-7310		447
Milkco Inc 220 Deaverview Rd *TF:* 800-842-8021 ■ *Web:* www.milkco.com	Asheville	NC	28806	828-254-9560		296-27
Milken Community High School 15800 Zeldins Way *Web:* www.milkenschool.org	Los Angeles	CA	90049	310-440-3500		685
Milken Family Foundation 1250 Fourth St *Web:* www.mff.org	Santa Monica	CA	90401	310-570-4800	570-4801	305
Milken Institute 1250 Fourth St *Web:* www.milkeninstitute.org	Santa Monica	CA	90401	310-570-4600	570-4601	634
Milkshake Media LP 2210 S Congress Ave *Web:* www.milkshakemedia.com	Austin	TX	78704	512-474-7777		344
Mill & Timber Products Ltd 12770- 116th Ave *TF:* 800-663-9844 ■ *Web:* www.millandtimber.com	Surrey	BC	V3V7H9	604-580-2781		683
Mill City Museum 704 S Second St *TF:* 800-657-3773 ■ *Web:* www.millcitymuseum.org	Minneapolis	MN	55401	612-341-7555		520
Mill Creek Carpet & Tile Co 6845 E 41st St *TF:* 800-262-4990 ■ *Web:* www.millcreekcarpet.com	Tulsa	OK	74145	918-621-4000		290
Mill Creek Mall 654 Millcreek Mall *TF:* 800-615-3535 ■ *Web:* www.millcreekmall.net	Erie	PA	16565	814-868-9000	864-1193	460
Mill Hill Historic Park & Museum 2 East Wall St *Web:* www.norwalkhistoricalsociety.org	Norwalk	CT	06851	203-846-0525		50-3
Mill Mountain Theatre 1 Market Sq *Web:* www.millmountain.org	Roanoke	VA	24011	540-342-5740		572
Mill Neck Manor School for The Deaf 40 Frost Mill Rd *Web:* millneck.org	Mill Neck	NY	11765	516-922-3818		768
Mill Ridge Farm 2800 Bowman Mill Rd *TF:* 800-950-6397 ■ *Web:* www.millridge.com	Lexington	KY	40513	859-231-0606	255-6010	368
Mill River Lumber Ltd 2639 Middle Rd *Web:* www.millriverlumber.com	Clarendon	VT	05759	802-775-0032		683
Mill Springs National Cemetery 9044 W Hwy 80 *Web:* www.cem.va.gov/cems/nchp/millsprings.asp	Nancy	KY	42544	859-885-5727	887-4860	136
Mill Steel Co 5116 36th St SE **Fax Area Code:* 616 ■ *TF:* 800-247-6455 ■ *Web:* www.millsteel.com	Grand Rapids	MI	49512	800-247-6455	977-9411*	723
Mill Street Inn 75 Mill St *TF:* 800-392-1316 ■ *Web:* www.millstreetinn.com	Newport	RI	02840	401-849-9500	848-5131	379
Mill Supply Div 266 Morse St *TF General:* 888-585-9354 ■ *Web:* www.millsupplydiv.com	Hamden	CT	06517	203-777-7668		87
Mill Valley Film Festival (MVFF) 1001 Lootens Pl Ste 220 *Web:* www.mvff.com	San Rafael	CA	94901	415-383-5256	383-8606	282
Mill Valley Inn 165 Throckmorton Ave *TF:* 855-334-7946 ■ *Web:* www.marinhotels.com	Mill Valley	CA	94941	415-389-6608	389-5051	379
Mill Valley Public Library 375 Throckmorton Ave *Web:* www.millvalleylibrary.org	Mill Valley	CA	94941	415-389-4292	388-8929	434-3
Mill's Tavern 101 N Main St *Web:* www.millstavernrestaurant.com	Providence	RI	02903	401-272-3331		671
Mill33 Inc 848 Elm St Ste 301 *TF:* 888-603-2336	Manchester	NH	03101	888-603-2336		195
Millard County 765 S Hwy 99 Ste 6 *Web:* www.millardcounty.com	Fillmore	UT	84631	435-743-5227		338
Millard County Chronicle Progress 40 N 300 W *Web:* millardccp.com	Delta	UT	84624	435-864-2400		532-4
Millard Fillmore Gates Cir Hospital 726 Exchange St *Web:* www.kaleidahealth.org	Buffalo	NY	14210	716-859-8000		374-3
Millard Lumber Inc 12900 I St PO Box 45445 *TF:* 800-228-9260 ■ *Web:* millardlumber.com	Omaha	NE	68145	402-896-2800	896-2865	191-3
Millard Manufacturing Corp 10602 Olive St *Web:* www.millardmfg.com	Omaha	NE	68128	402-331-8010		207
Millard Refrigerated Services Inc 4715 S 132nd St *Web:* www.millardref.com	Omaha	NE	68137	402-896-6600		449
Millard, Rouse & Rosebrugh LLP 96 Nelson St *Web:* www.millards.com	Brantford	ON	N3T5N3	519-863-3557		2
Millbrook Capital Management Inc 570 Lexington Ave 46th Fl *Web:* www.millcap.com	New York	NY	10022	212-586-4333		401
Millbrook School 131 Millbrook School Rd *Web:* www.millbrook.org	Millbrook	NY	12545	845 677-8261	677-1265	622
Millburn Township New Jersey Board Education 434 Millburn Ave *Web:* www.millburn.org	Millburn	NJ	07041	973-376-3600		685
Millburn Veterinary Hospital 147 Millburn Ave *TF:* 800-365-8295 ■ *Web:* millburnvet.com	Millburn	NJ	07041	973-467-1700		794
Millcraft Investments 95 W Beau St Ste 600 *Web:* www.millcraftinv.com	Washington	PA	15301	724-229-8800	229-8800	190
Millcraft Paper Co 6800 Grant Ave *TF:* 800-860-2482 ■ *Web:* www.millcraft.com	Cleveland	OH	44105	216-441-5500		553
Mille Lacs Band of Ojibwe 43408 Oodena Dr *TF:* 800-709-6445 ■ *Web:* millelacsband.com	Onamia	MN	56359	320-532-4181	532-7505	132
Mille Lacs County 635 Second St SE *Web:* www.co.mille-lacs.mn.us	Milaca	MN	56353	320-983-8313	983-8384	338
Mille Lacs Electric Co-op PO Box 230 *TF:* 800-450-2191 ■ *Web:* www.mlecmn.net	Aitkin	MN	56431	218-927-2191	927-6822	245
Mille Lacs Health System 200 Elm St N *TF:* 877-535-3154 ■ *Web:* www.mlhealth.org	Onamia	MN	56359	320-532-3154		374-3
Mille Lacs Kathio State Park 15066 Kathio State Pk Rd *Web:* www.dnr.state.mn.us	Onamia	MN	56359	320-532-3523		565
Milledgeville-Baldwin County Chamber of Commerce 130 S Jefferson St *Web:* milledgevillega.com	Milledgeville	GA	31061	478-453-9311		139
Millenium Aviation 2365 Bernville Rd Reading Regional Airport *TF:* 800-366-9419 ■ *Web:* www.majets.com	Reading	PA	19605	610-372-4728	374-7580	63
Millenium Challenge Corp 875 15th St NW *Web:* www.mcc.gov	Washington	DC	20005	202-521-3600		340-20
Millenium Home Health Care Inc 370 Reed Rd Ste 319 *TF:* 800-518-3639 ■ *Web:* www.mhomehealth.com	Broomall	PA	19008	610-543-4126		363
Millenium Products Inc 6346 Heron Pkwy *Web:* www.milleniumproducts.net	Clarkston	MI	48346	239-877-6811		183
Millennium 580 Geary St *TF:* 800-847-5949 ■ *Web:* www.millenniumrestaurant.com	San Francisco	CA	94102	415-345-3900		671
Millennium Airship Inc Bremerton National Airport PO Box 1972 *Web:* www.millenniumairship.com	Belfair	WA	98528	360-674-2488	674-2494	28

Name / Address	City	State	ZIP	Phone	Fax	Class
Millennium Bankshares Corp 21430 Cedar Dr Ste 200 *OTC: MBVA*	Sterling	VA	20164	703-464-0100		360-2
Millennium Broadway Hotel New York 145 W 44th St *TF:* 800-622-5569 ■ *Web:* www.millenniumhotels.com	New York	NY	10036	212-768-4400	768-0847	377
Millennium Dental Technologies Inc 10945 South St Ste 104-A *Web:* www.lanap.com	Cerritos	CA	90703	562-860-2908		250
Millennium Foods 7796 Moller Rd *Web:* www.mfoodsindy.com	Indianapolis	IN	46268	317-334-7744		123
Millennium Forge Inc 990 W Ormsby Ave *Web:* www.millenniumforge.com	Louisville	KY	40210	502-635-3350	635-3028	483
Millennium Industrial Tires LLC 433 Lane Dr *Web:* www.millenniumtire.com	Florence	AL	35630	256-764-2900		754
Millennium Line X & Truck Accessories 905 N Raceway Rd *Web:* www.millenniumlinings.com	Indianapolis	IN	46234	317-209-8000		54
Millennium Management LLC 666 Fifth Ave *Web:* www.mlp.com	New York	NY	10103	212-841-4100		690
Millennium Marking Co 2600 Greenleaf Ave *Web:* www.millmarking.com	Elk Grove Village	IL	60007	847-806-1750		534
Millennium Pharmaceuticals Inc 40 Lansdowne St *Web:* www.takedaoncology.com	Cambridge	MA	02139	617-679-7000		85
Millennium Resort Scottsdale McCormick Ranch 7401 N Scottsdale Rd **Fax Area Code:* 480 ■ *TF:* 800-243-1332 ■ *Web:* millenniumhotels.com	Scottsdale	AZ	85253	716-681-2400	991-5572*	669
Miller & Chevalier Chartered 655 15th St NW Ste 900 *TF:* 866-628-4282 ■ *Web:* www.millerchevalier.com	Washington	DC	20005	202-626-5800	626-5801	428
Miller & Co LLC 9700 W Higgins Rd Ste 1000 *TF:* 800-727-9847 ■ *Web:* www.millerandco.com	Rosemont	IL	60018	847-696-2400	696-2419	500
Miller & Company Plc 900 S Shackleford Rd Ste 100 *Web:* millercocpas.net	Little Rock	AR	72211	501-221-3343		2
Miller & Holmes Inc 2311 O'Neil Rd *Web:* mhgas.com	Hudson	WI	54016	715-377-1730		204
Miller & Long Concrete Construction Inc 7101 Wisconsin Ave *Web:* www.millerandlong.com	Bethesda	MD	20814	301-657-8000	657-8610	189-3
Miller & Luring Company LPa 314 W Main St *TF:* 800-381-9680 ■ *Web:* www.millerluring.com	Troy	OH	45373	937-339-2627		428
Miller & Martin PLLC 832 Georgia Ave Volunteer Bldg Ste 1000 *TF:* 800-447-5375 ■ *Web:* www.millermartin.com	Chattanooga	TN	37402	423-756-6600		428
Miller & Miller Accountancy Corp 1320 E Shaw Ave Ste 167 *Web:* millermillerpc.com	Fresno	CA	93710	559-225-6211		2
Miller & Smith Cos 8401 Greensboro Dr Ste 300 *Web:* www.millerandsmith.com	McLean	VA	22102	703-821-2500		653
Miller Bonded Inc 4538 Mcleod Rd NE *Web:* millerbonded.com	Albuquerque	NM	87109	505-881-0220		610
Miller Brooks Inc 11712 N Michigan Rd *Web:* millerbrooks.com	Zionsville	IN	46077	317-873-8100		4
Miller Bros Express LC 560 W 400 NorNth *Web:* www.mbexlc.com	Hyrum	UT	84319	435-245-6025		449
Miller Brothers Contractors Inc 990 Cattleman Rd *Web:* www.millerbrosinc.com	Sarasota	FL	34232	941-371-4162		183
Miller Buettner & Parrott Inc 1515 S Meridian Rd	Rockford	IL	61102	815-986-0059		390
Miller Canfield Paddock & Stone PLC 150 W Jefferson Ave Ste 2500 *Web:* www.millercanfield.com	Detroit	MI	48226	313-963-6420	496-7500	428
Miller Chemical & Fertilizer Corp 120 Radio Rd PO Box 333 *TF:* 800-233-2040 ■ *Web:* www.millerchemical.com	Hanover	PA	17331	717-632-8921		280
Miller Compressing Co 1640 W Bruce St	Milwaukee	WI	53204	414-671-5980	671-7191	686
Miller Consolidated Industries Inc 2221 Arbor Blvd *TF:* 800-589-4133 ■ *Web:* www.millerconsolidated.com	Dayton	OH	45439	937-294-2681		484
Miller Container Corp 3402 78th Ave W *TF:* 800-654-2699 ■ *Web:* www.millercontainer.com	Rock Island	IL	61201	309-787-6161		100
Miller Cooper & Company Ltd 1751 Lake Cook Rd Ste 400 *Web:* www.millercooper.com	Deerfield	IL	60015	847-205-5000		2
Miller County 400 Laurel St Rm 105 *TF:* 800-482-8998 ■ *Web:* www.millercountyar.org	Texarkana	AR	71854	870-774-1501		338
Miller County 2001 Missouri 52 *TF:* 800-737-4145 ■ *Web:* millercountymissouri.org	Tuscumbia	MO	65082	573-369-1900		338
Miller Drug Inc 210 State St *Web:* www.millerdrug.com	Bangor	ME	04401	207-947-8369		231
Miller Electric Co 2251 Rosselle St *TF Sales:* 877-540-2160 ■ *Web:* www.mecojax.com	Jacksonville	FL	32204	904-388-8000	389-8653	189-4
Miller Electric Mfg Co 1635 W Spencer St **Fax:* Sales ■ *TF:* 888-843-7693 ■ *Web:* www.millerwelds.com	Appleton	WI	54914	920-734-9821	735-4134*	811
Miller Energy Inc 3200 S Clinton Ave *TF:* 800-631-5454 ■ *Web:* www.millerenergy.com	South Plainfield	NJ	07080	908-755-6700		177
Miller Engineering Co 1616 S Main St *TF:* 800-626-9799 ■ *Web:* mecogroup.com	Rockford	IL	61102	815-963-4878		189-10
Miller Engineers & Scientists 5308 S 12th St *TF:* 800-969-7013 ■ *Web:* www.startwithmiller.com	Sheboygan	WI	53081	920-458-6164		261
Miller Environmental Services Inc 401 Navigation Blvd *TF:* 800-929-7227 ■ *Web:* www.millerenviro.com	Corpus Christi	TX	78408	361-289-9800		63
Miller Giangrande LLP 915 W Imperial Hwy *Web:* mngcpa.com	Brea	CA	92821	714-494-2200		2
Miller Heiman Inc 10509 Professional Cir Ste 100 *Web:* www.millerheimangroup.com	Reno	NV	89521	775-827-4411		195
Miller Industries Inc 7 Canal St	Lisbon Falls	ME	04252	207-353-4371		746
Miller Industries Inc 8503 Hilltop Dr *NYSE: MLR* ■ *TF:* 800-292-0330 ■ *Web:* www.millerind.com	Ooltewah	TN	37363	423-238-4171	238-5371	516
Miller International Inc Rocky Mountain Clothing Co Div 8500 Zuni St *Web:* www.rockymountainclothing.com	Denver	CO	80260	303-428-5696		155-20
Miller J Walter Company Brass Foundry 411 E Chestnut St *Web:* www.jwaltermiller.com	Lancaster	PA	17602	717-392-7428		492
Miller Johnson Snell & Cummiskey PLC 250 Monroe Ave NW Ste 800 PO Box 306 *TF:* 800-772-1213 ■ *Web:* www.millerjohnson.com	Grand Rapids	MI	49503	616-831-1700	831-1701	428
Miller Jones Recruiting Inc 235 W Giaconda Way Ste 215 *TF:* 800-264-1170 ■ *Web:* millerjonesrecruiting.com	Tucson	AZ	85704	520-206-9300		260
Miller Jordan Middle School 700 N Mccullough St *Web:* mjms.sbcisd.net	San Benito	TX	78586	956-361-6650		685
Miller Kaplan Arase & Company LLP 4123 Lankershim Blvd *Web:* www.millerkaplan.com	Hollywood	CA	91602	818-769-2010		2
Miller Law Firm Pc, The 950 W University Dr Ste 300 *Web:* www.millerlawpc.com	Rochester	MI	48307	248-841-2200		428
Miller Livestock Markets Inc 100 Sale Barn Rd *Web:* millerlivestockinc.com	Dequincy	LA	70633	337-786-2995		446
Miller Machinery & Supply Co 127 NE 27th St	Miami	FL	33137	305-573-1300		274
Miller Memorial Community 360 Broad St *TF:* 800-227-3449 ■ *Web:* www.millercommunity.org	Meriden	CT	06450	203-237-8815		450
Miller Metal Fabricators Inc 345 National Ave	Staunton	VA	24401	540-886-5575		480
Miller Metals Service Corp 2400 Bond St *Web:* www.millermetals.com	University Park	IL	60484	708-534-7200		492
Miller Morton Caillat & Nevis LLP 50 W San Fernando St Ste 1300 *Web:* www.millermorton.com	San Jose	CA	95113	408-292-1765		445
Miller Motorcars Inc 342 W Putnam Ave *Web:* www.millermotorcars.com	Greenwich	CT	06830	203-629-3890		57
Miller Nash LLP 3400 US Bancorp Tower *Web:* www.millernash.com	Portland	OR	97204	503-224-5858		428
Miller Oil Co 1000 E City Hall Ave *Web:* www.milleroil.com	Norfolk	VA	23504	757-695-3143	625-0528	579
Miller Oil Company Inc 4504 Bells Ln *Web:* www.mocgas.com	Louisville	KY	40211	502-772-1722		579
Miller Outdoor Theatre 6000 Hermann Pk Dr **Fax Area Code:* 713 ■ *Web:* www.milleroutdoortheatre.com	Houston	TX	77030	281-823-9103	942-0863*	572
Miller Pacific Engineering Group 504 Redwood Blvd Ste 220 *Web:* www.millerpac.com	Novato	CA	94947	415-382-3444		261
Miller Packing Co 1122 Industrial Way PO Box 1390 *TF:* 800-624-2328 ■ *Web:* www.millerhotdogs.com	Lodi	CA	95241	209-339-2310		296-26
Miller Paint Company Inc 12812 NE Whitaker Way *Web:* www.millerpaint.com	Portland	OR	97230	503-255-0190	255-0192	550
Miller Pipeline Corp 8850 Crawfordsville Rd *TF:* 800-428-3742 ■ *Web:* www.millerpipeline.com	Indianapolis	IN	46234	317-293-0278	293-8502	188-10
Miller Products Company Inc 2511 S Tricenter Blvd *TF:* 800-782-7437 ■ *Web:* www.millerproducts.com	Durham	NC	27713	919-313-2100	313-2101	576
Miller Russell H. Law Offices 20 Park Rd Ste E *Web:* www.millerpoliticallaw.com	Burlingame	CA	94010	650-401-8735		428
Miller Saint Nazianz Inc 511 E Main St *TF:* 800-247-5557 ■ *Web:* www.millerstn.com	Saint Nazianz	WI	54232	920-773-2121	773-1200	273
Miller School 1000 Samuel Miller Loop *Web:* millerschoolofalbemarle.org	Charlottesville	VA	22903	434-823-4805	823-6617	622
Miller Staffing 2525 Rt 130 Bldg A	Cranbury	NJ	08512	609-395-1800		260
Miller State Park 13 Miller Park Rd *Web:* www.nhstateparks.org	Peterborough	NH	03458	603-924-3672		565
Miller Stratvert PA 500 Marquette Ave NW Ste 1100 *Web:* www.mstlaw.com	Albuquerque	NM	87125	505-842-1950		428
Miller Studio 734 Fair Ave NW *TF:* 800-332-0050 ■ *Web:* miller-studio.com	New Philadelphia	OH	44663	330-339-1100		500
Miller Supply Inc 29902 Avenida de las Banderas *TF:* 888-240-9237 ■ *Web:* www.millersupplyinc.com	Rancho Santa Margarita	CA	92688	888-240-9237		553
Miller Systems Inc 175 Portland St 5th fl *Web:* www.millersystems.com	Boston	MA	02114	617-266-4200		113
Miller Technical Services Inc 7444 Haggerty Rd *Web:* www.mtsmedicalmfg.com	Canton	MI	48187	734-738-1970		492

				Phone	Fax	Class
Miller Thomson LLP Scotia Plaza 40 King St W Ste 5800 *TF:* 888-762-5559 ■ *Web:* www.millerthomson.com	Toronto	ON	M5H3S1	416-595-8500		41
Miller Transfer 3833 State Rt 183 *TF:* 800-832-5660 ■ *Web:* www.millertransfer.com	Rootstown	OH	44272	330-325-2521		207
Miller Transporters Inc 5500 Hwy 80 W *TF Cust Svc:* 800-645-5378 ■ *Web:* www.millert.com	Jackson	MS	39209	601-922-8331	923-2535	780
Miller Travel Services Inc 4380 W 12th St *TF:* 800-989-8747 ■ *Web:* www.millertravel.com	Erie	PA	16505	814-833-8888		771
Miller Valentine Group 4000 Miller Valentine Ct *TF:* 877-684-7687 ■ *Web:* www.mvg.com	Dayton	OH	45439	937-293-0900	299-1564	655
Miller Zell 6100 Fulton Industrial Blvd SW *Web:* www.millerzell.com	Atlanta	GA	30336	404-691-7400	699-2189	393
Miller's Carpet One 15615 Hwy 99 *Web:* www.carpetone.com	Lynnwood	WA	98087	425-312-6259		290
Miller's Crossing 52 S Pk Ave *Web:* www.millerscrossing.biz	Helena	MT	59601	406-442-3290		671
Miller's Health Systems Inc 1690 S County Farm Rd *Web:* www.millershealthsystems.com	Warsaw	IN	46581	574-267-7211	267-4908	793
Miller's Honey Co Inc 3000 SW Temple *Web:* www.millerhoney.com	Salt Lake City	UT	84115	801-486-8479	486-8494	296-24
Miller's Merry Manor 612 E 11th St *Web:* millersmerrymanor.com	Rushville	IN	46173	765-932-4127	932-3054	450
Miller's Merry Manor 1500 Grant St *Web:* www.millersmerrymanor.com	Huntington	IN	46750	260-356-5713	356-8671	450
Miller's Merry Manor 200 26th St *TF:* 800-254-9442 ■ *Web:* www.millersmerrymanor.com	Logansport	IN	46947	574-722-4006		450
Miller's Presort Inc 1147 Sweitzer Ave *TF:* 800-706-6245 ■ *Web:* millerspresort.com	Akron	OH	44301	330-434-9200		5
Millerbernd Manufacturing Co 622 Sixth St S *Web:* www.millerberndmfg.com	Winsted	MN	55395	320-485-2111		723
Miller-Bradford & Risberg Inc W250 N6851 Hwy 164 *Web:* www.miller-bradford.com	Sussex	WI	53089	262-246-5700		358
Miller-Davis Co 1029 Portage St *Web:* www.miller-davis.com	Kalamazoo	MI	49001	269-345-3561		186
Miller-Eads Company Inc 4125 N Keystone Ave *TF:* 800-530-0684 ■ *Web:* www.miller-eads.com	Indianapolis	IN	46205	317-545-7101	545-4660	787
Miller-Green Financial Group 600 Travis St Ste 5900 *Web:* www.miller-green.com	Houston	TX	77380	281-364-9100	364-9101	401
Miller-Keystone Blood Ctr 1465 Vly Ctr Pkwy *TF:* 800-223-6667 ■ *Web:* www.hcsc.org	Bethlehem	PA	18017	610-691-5850		89
Miller-Leaman 800 Orange Ave *TF:* 800-881-0320 ■ *Web:* www.millerleaman.com	Daytona Beach	FL	32114	386-248-0500		697
Miller-Lewis Benefit Consultants 121 E Sixth Ave *TF:* 800-734-3198 ■ *Web:* miller-lewis.com	Lancaster	OH	43130	740-654-4055	687-2236	390
Millers Artist Supplies Co 33332 W 12 Mile Rd	Farmington Hills	MI	48334	248-489-8070		45
Millers First Insurance Co 111 E Fourth St	Alton	IL	62002	618-463-3636		391-4
Millers Forge Inc 1411 Capital Ave *Web:* www.millersforge.com	Plano	TX	75074	972-422-2145	881-0639	222
Miller-Stephenson Chemical Co 55 Backus Ave *TF Tech Supp:* 800-992-2424 ■ *Web:* www.miller-stephenson.com	Danbury	CT	06810	203-743-4447	791-8702	145
Millersville University of Pennsylvania PO Box 1002 PO Box 1002 *TF:* 800-682-3648 ■ *Web:* www.millersville.edu	Millersville	PA	17551	717-872-3011	871-2147	166
Millersylvania State Park 12245 Tilley Rd S *Web:* www.parks.wa.gov	Olympia	WA	98512	360-753-1519		565
Miller-Thomas-Gyekis Inc 3341 Stafford St	Pittsburgh	PA	15204	412-331-4610		189-12
Millerton Lake State Recreation Area 5290 Millerton Rd *Web:* www.parks.ca.gov/default.asp?page_id=587	Friant	CA	93626	559-822-2332		565
Millet Learning Ctr 3660 Southfield Dr *Web:* www.sisd.cc	Saginaw	MI	48601	989-777-2520		685
Millet the Printer Inc 1000 S Ervay St *Web:* www.millettheprinter.com	Dallas	TX	75201	214-741-3602		627
Millford Farm 377 Weisenberger Mill Rd PO Box 4351 *Web:* www.millford.com	Midway	KY	40347	859-846-4705	846-4226	368
Millhopper Veterinary Medical Center 4209 Northwest 37th Pl *Web:* millhoppervet.com	Gainesville	FL	32606	352-373-8055		794
Millicent Library 45 Ctr St *Web:* www.millicentlibrary.org	Fairhaven	MA	02719	508-992-5342	993-7288	434-3
Millie & Severson Inc 3601 Serpentine Dr *Web:* www.mandsinc.com	Los Alamitos	CA	90720	562-493-3611		186
Millie's 2603 E Main St *Web:* www.milliesdiner.com	Richmond	VA	23223	804-643-5512	648-4321	671
Milligan & Higgins Maple Ave PO Box 506 *Web:* www.milligan1868.com	Johnstown	NY	12095	518-762-4638	762-7039	296-22
Milligan College PO Box 500 *TF:* 800-262-8337 ■ *Web:* www.milligan.edu	Milligan College	TN	37682	423-461-8730		166
Milligan News Co Inc 150 N Autumn St *Web:* www.milligannews.com	San Jose	CA	95110	408-286-7604		96
Milliken & Co 920 Milliken Rd **Fax:* Hum Res ■ *Web:* www.milliken.com/en-us/Pages/default.aspx	Spartanburg	SC	29303	864-503-2020	503-2100*	745-1
Milliken & Co KEX Div PO Box 1926 MS 801 **Fax:* Cust Svc ■ *TF:* 800-241-4826 ■ *Web:* www.millikencarpet.com	Spartanburg	SC	29304	706-880-5511	880-5358*	131
Milliken & Co's Live Oak Plant 300 Industrial Dr *TF:* 800-241-8666 ■ *Web:* www.milliken.com	La Grange	GA	30240	800-241-8666		131

				Phone	Fax	Class
Milliken Millwork Inc 6361 Sterling Dr N *TF:* 800-686-9218 ■ *Web:* www.millikenmillwork.com	Sterling Heights	MI	48312	586-264-0950	264-5430	499
Milliken Millwork Inc 172 Plummer Rd *TF:* 800-452-0251 ■ *Web:* www.millikenmillwork.com	Sidman	PA	15955	800-452-0251		191-3
Millikin University 1184 W Main St *TF:* 800-373-7733 ■ *Web:* www.millikin.edu	Decatur	IL	62522	217-424-6211		166
Milliman USA 1301 Fifth Ave Ste 3800 *Web:* in.milliman.com	Seattle	WA	98101	206-624-7940		194
Milliner & Associates LLC 4181 E 96th St Ste 120 *TF:* 800-832-8268 ■ *Web:* www.millinerandassoc.com	Indianapolis	IN	46240	317-218-1195		260
Million Air 4300 Westgrove Dr *TF:* 800-248-1602 ■ *Web:* www.millionair.com	Addison	TX	75001	972-248-1600	733-5803	63
Million Air Interlink Inc 8501 Telephone Rd **Fax Area Code:* 866 ■ *TF:* 888-589-9059 ■ *Web:* www.millionair.com	Houston	TX	77061	713-640-4000	283-8274*	24
Million Dollar Baby 841 Washington Blvd *Web:* www.milliondollarbaby.com	Montebello	CA	90640	323-728-8988		319-2
Million Dollar Round Table (MDRT) 325 W Touhy Ave *Web:* www.mdrt.org	Park Ridge	IL	60068	847-692-6378	518-8921	49-9
Milliron Industries Inc 2375 Springmill Rd *Web:* millironautoparts.com	Mansfield	OH	44903	419-747-4566		61
Millitech Inc 29 Industrial Dr E *Web:* www.millitech.com	NorthHampton	MA	01060	413-582-9620		647
Millman Search Group Inc 11419 Cronridge Dr Ste 17 *TF:* 800-906-0044 ■ *Web:* www.millmansearch.com	Owings Mills	MD	21117	410-902-6600		95
Mill-Max Mfg Corp 190 Pine Hollow Rd *TF:* 800-333-4237 ■ *Web:* www.mill-max.com	Oyster Bay	NY	11771	516-922-6000	922-9253	815
Millogic Ltd 89 Cambridge St *Web:* millogic.com	Burlington	MA	01803	339-234-5700		261
Mill-Rite Woodworking Company Inc 6401 47th St N *Web:* www.mill-rite.com	Pinellas Park	FL	33781	727-521-1644		499
Millrock *RiverRun Commercial* 4660 Early Rd *Web:* www.riverruncommercial.com	Mt. Crawford	VA	22841	540-437-3458		286
Mill-Rose Co 7995 Tyler Blvd *TF:* 800-321-3533 ■ *Web:* www.millrose.com	Mentor	OH	44060	440-255-9171	255-5039	103
Millrun Tours Inc 424 Madison Ave 12th Fl *Web:* www5.millrun.com	New York	NY	10017	212-486-9840	223-8129	16
Mills & Assoc Inc 3242 Henderson Blvd	Tampa	FL	33609	813-876-5869		261
Mills & Murphy Software Systems Inc 618 94th Ave N *TF:* 800-745-4712 ■ *Web:* www.millsmur.com	Saint Petersburg	FL	33702	727-577-1236		180
Mills at Jersey Gardens, The 651 Kapkowski Rd *TF:* 877-789-2327 ■ *Web:* www.simon.com/mall/the-mills-at-jersey-gardens	Elizabeth	NJ	07201	908-354-5900		460
Mills College 5000 MacArthur Blvd **Fax:* Admissions ■ *TF Admissions:* 877-746-4557 ■ *Web:* www.mills.edu	Oakland	CA	94613	510-430-2135	430-3314*	166
Mills County 418 Sharp St County Courthouse *Web:* www.millscoia.us	Glenwood	IA	51534	712-527-4880		338
Mills County PO Box 646 *Web:* www.co.mills.tx.us	Goldthwaite	TX	76844	325-648-2711	648-3251	338
Mills House Hotel 115 Meeting St *TF:* 800-874-9600 ■ *Web:* www.millshouse.com	Charleston	SC	29401	843-577-2400		379
Mills Iron Works Inc 14834 Maple Ave **Fax Area Code:* 310 ■ *TF:* 800-421-2281 ■ *Web:* www.millsiron.com	Gardena	CA	90248	323-321-6520	532-0470*	505
Mills James Inc 3545 Fishinger Blvd *TF:* 800-937-4249 ■ *Web:* www.mjp.com	Columbus	OH	43026	614-777-9933		514
Millsap Fuel Distributors Ltd 905 Ave P S *TF:* 800-667-9767 ■ *Web:* millsapfuels.ca	Saskatoon	SK	S7M2X3	306-244-7916		580
Millsaps College 1701 N State St **Fax:* Admissions ■ *TF Admissions:* 800-352-1050 ■ *Web:* www.millsaps.edu	Jackson	MS	39210	601-974-1000	974-1059*	166
Millsite State Park Ferron Canyon Rd PO Box 1343 *TF:* 800-322-3770 ■ *Web:* stateparks.utah.gov	Huntington	UT	84528	435-384-2552		565
Millstone Medical Outsourcing LLC 580 Commerce Dr *Web:* www.millstonemedical.com	Fall River	MA	02720	508-679-8384	679-8414	195
Milltech Manufacturing Co 537 Easy St *TF:* 800-472-4643 ■ *Web:* www.milltechmfg.com	Garland	TX	75042	972-276-1786		454
Milluzzo & Company PC 182 Kelsey St	Newington	CT	06111	860-667-9991		2
Millville Chamber of Commerce 4 City Pk Dr *TF:* 800-984-3272 ■ *Web:* www.millville-nj.com	Millville	NJ	08332	856-825-2600	825-5333	139
Millville/Bridgeton News 100 E Commerce St *Web:* www.nj.com	Bridgeton	NJ	08302	856-451-1000	455-3098	532-2
Millward Brown Group 33 Bloor St E Ste 701 *Web:* www.millwardbrown.com	Toronto	ON	M4W3H1	203-330-2581		466
Millward Brown IntelliQuest 11 Madison Ave 12th Fl *Web:* www.millwardbrown.com	New York	NY	10010	212-548-7200	548-7201	466
Millwood Inc 33 Stiles Ln *Web:* www.millwoodinc.com	North Haven	CT	06473	203-248-7902		200
Millwood State Park 1564 Hwy 32 E *Web:* www.arkansasstateparks.com	Ashdown	AR	71822	870-898-2800		565
Milne Fruit Products Inc 804 Bennett Ave *TF:* 800-962-7663 ■ *Web:* www.milnefruit.com	Prosser	WA	99350	509-786-2611	786-4915	296-21
Milne Public Library 1095 Main St *Web:* www.milnelibrary.org	Williamstown	MA	01267	413-458-5369	458-3085	434-3
Milner Hotel Boston 813 S Flower St *TF:* 877-645-6377 ■ *Web:* www.milner-hotels.com	Los Angeles	CA	90017	617-426-6220	350-0360	379

	Phone	Fax	Class
Milner Technologies Inc 5125 Peachtree Industrial Blvd .... Norcross GA 30092 TF: 800-592-3766 ■ Web: www.milnertechnologies.com	770-734-5300		178-1
Milnot Co 105 Washington Ave .... Seneca MO 64865 Web: www.milnotmilk.com	417-776-2243		619
Milo McIver State Park 24101 SE Entrance Rd .... Estacada OR 97023 Web: www.oregonstateparks.org	503-630-7150		565
Milo's Restaurant 2870 S Philo Rd .... Urbana IL 61802 TF: 800-369-6151 ■ Web: www.milosurbana.com	217-344-8946	344-8922	671
Milos 5357 du Parc Ave .... Montreal QC H2V4G9 Web: www.milos.ca	514-272-3522		671
Mil-Pac Technology 1672 Main St Ste E-254 .... Ramona CA 92065 Web: milpac.com	760-788-3030		177
Milpitas Post 59 Marylinn Dr .... Milpitas CA 95035 TF: 800-870-6397 ■ Web: www.mercurynews.com	408-262-2454	263-9710	532-4
Milport Enterprises Inc 2829 S Fifth Ct .... Milwaukee WI 53207 Web: www.milport.com	414-769-7350	769-0167	146
Milrose Consultants Inc 498 Seventh Ave .... New York NY 10018 TF: 800-806-7129 ■ Web: www.milrose.com	212-643-4545		365
Milsco Mfg Co 1301 W Canal St .... Milwaukee WI 53233 Web: www.milsco.com	414-354-0500	354-0508	689
Miltenyi Biotec Inc 2303 Lindbergh St .... Auburn CA 95602 Web: www.miltenyibiotec.com	530-888-8871		743
Miltex Inc 589 Davies Dr .... York PA 17402 TF: 866-854-8400 ■ Web: www.miltex.com	717-840-9335		228
Milton & Hattie Kutz Home Inc, The 704 River Rd .... Wilmington DE 19809 TF: 800-372-2022 ■ Web: kutzhome.org	302-764-7000		371
Milton Academy 170 Centre St .... Milton MA 02186 Web: www.milton.edu	617-898-1798		622
Milton CAT 554 Maple St .... Hopkinton NH 03229 TF: 800-473-5298 ■ Web: www.miltoncat.com	603-746-4611		358
Milton Chamber of Commerce 251 Main St E Ste 104 .... Milton ON L9T1P1 Web: miltonchamber.ca	905-878-0581	878-4972	137
Milton Hershey School PO Box 830 .... Hershey PA 17033 TF: 800-322-3248 ■ Web: www.mhskids.org	717-520-2100	520-2117	622
Milton Industries Inc 4500 W Cortland .... Chicago IL 60639 Web: www.miltonindustries.com	773-235-9400		153
Milton Martin Toyota 2350 Browns Bridge Rd .... Gainesville GA 30504 Web: www.miltonmartintoyota.com	770-532-4355		57
Milton Public Library 476 Canton Ave .... Milton MA 02186 Web: www.miltonlibrary.org	617-698-5757		434-3
Milton Roy USA 201 Ivyland Rd .... Ivyland PA 18974 Web: www.miltonroy.com	215-441-0800	441-8620	640
Milton State Park Bridge Ave .... Sunbury PA 17801 Web: www.dcnr.state.pa.us/stateparks/parks/milton.aspx	570-988-5557		565
Milton Sternberger Co, The 1230 N Watkins .... Memphis TN 38108 Web: www.sternberger.com	901-276-7733		683
Milton Transportation Inc 5505 State Rt 405 PO Box 355 .... Milton PA 17847 Web: www.miltontrans.com	570-742-8774	742-2856	780
Miltons Inc 250 Granite St .... Braintree MA 02184 TF: 888-645-8667 ■ Web: www.miltons.com	781-848-1880		157-3
MILVETS Systems Technology Inc 11825 High Tech Ave Ste 150 .... Orlando FL 32817 Web: www.milvets.com	407-207-2242		180
Milwaukee Academy of Science 2000 W Kilbourn Ave .... Milwaukee WI 53233 Web: milwaukeeacademyofscience.org	414-933-0302		165
Milwaukee Area Technical College 700 W State St .... Milwaukee WI 53233 TF: 866-211-3380 ■ Web: www.matc.edu	414-297-6600	297-6496	800
Milwaukee Art Museum 700 N Art Museum Dr .... Milwaukee WI 53202 TF: 877-638-7620 ■ Web: www.mam.org	414-224-3200	271-7588	520
Milwaukee Athletic Club 758 N Broadway .... Milwaukee WI 53202 Web: www.macwi.org	414-273-5080		354
Milwaukee Ballet 504 W National Ave .... Milwaukee WI 53204 Web: www.milwaukeeballet.org	414-643-7677	649-4066	573-1
Milwaukee Bearing & Machining Inc W134N5235 Campbell Dr .... Menomonee Falls WI 53051 Web: www.milwaukeebearing.com	262-783-1100		757
Milwaukee Brewers Miller Pk 1 Brewers Way .... Milwaukee WI 53214 TF: 877-722-6458 ■ Web: milwaukee.brewers.mlb.com	414-902-4452	902-4588	713
Milwaukee Bucks Bradley Ctr 1001 N Fourth St .... Milwaukee WI 53203 Web: www.nba.com	414-227-0500		714-1
Milwaukee Catholic Home 2330 & 2462 N Prospect Ave .... Milwaukee WI 53211 Web: www.milwaukeecatholichome.org	414-224-9700	224-1666	672
Milwaukee Chamber Theatre 158 N Broadway Broadway Theatre Ctr .... Milwaukee WI 53202 Web: www.chamber-theatre.com	414-276-8842	277-4477	572
Milwaukee Chop House 633 N Fifth St .... Milwaukee WI 53203 Web: chophouse411.com/chophouse_location_mch.asp	414-226-2467		671
Milwaukee City Hall 200 E Wells St .... Milwaukee WI 53202 Web: www.city.milwaukee.gov	414-286-2200	286-3191	337
Milwaukee Coast Guard Base 2420 S Lincoln Memorial Dr .... Milwaukee WI 53207 TF: 866-772-8724 ■ Web: www.uscg.mil	414-747-7100	747-7108	158
Milwaukee County 901 N Ninth St .... Milwaukee WI 53233 TF: 877-652-6377 ■ Web: county.milwaukee.gov	414-278-4143	223-1379	338
Milwaukee County Mental Health Complex 9455 Watertown Plank Rd .... Milwaukee WI 53226 Web: www.county.milwaukee.gov	414-257-6995		374-5
Milwaukee County Transit System 1942 N 17th St .... Milwaukee WI 53205 *Fax: Hum Res ■ TF: 800-947-3529 ■ Web: www.ridemcts.com	414-343-1700	343-1787*	468
Milwaukee Courier, The 2003 W Capitol Dr .... Milwaukee WI 53206 Web: milwaukeecourieronline.com	414-449-4860	906-5383	532-4
Milwaukee Electric Tool Corp 13135 W Lisbon Rd .... Brookfield WI 53005 *Fax Area Code: 800 ■ *Fax: Orders ■ TF: 800-729-3878 ■ Web: www.milwaukeetool.com	262-781-3600	638-9582*	759
Milwaukee Gear Co 5150 N Port Washington Rd .... Milwaukee WI 53217 Web: www.regalpts.com/brands/milwaukeegear/Pages/milwaukeegear.aspx	414-962-3532	962-2774	709
Milwaukee Institute of Art & Design 273 E Erie St .... Milwaukee WI 53202 *Fax: Admissions ■ TF: 888-749-6423 ■ Web: www.miad.edu	414-276-7889	291-8077*	166
Milwaukee Jewish Federation Inc 1360 N Prospect Ave .... Milwaukee WI 53202 Web: milwaukeejewish.org	414-390-5700		522
Milwaukee Magazine 126 N Jefferson St .... Milwaukee WI 53202 TF: 800-662-4818 ■ Web: www.milwaukeemag.com	414-273-1101		457-22
Milwaukee Malleable & Grey Iron Works 2773 S 29th St .... Milwaukee WI 53201 Web: milwtool.com	414-645-0200		307
Milwaukee Protestant Home For The Aged 2505 E Bradford Ave .... Milwaukee WI 53211 Web: eastcastleplace.com	414-219-1398		371
Milwaukee Public Library 814 W Wisconsin Ave .... Milwaukee WI 53233 TF: 866-947-7363 ■ Web: www.mpl.org	414-286-3000	286-2798	434-3
Milwaukee Public Museum 800 W Wells St .... Milwaukee WI 53233 Web: www.mpm.edu	414-278-2728		520
Milwaukee Public Schools 5225 W Vliet St .... Milwaukee WI 53208 *Fax: Hum Res ■ Web: mps.milwaukee.k12.wi.us/en/home.htm	414-475-8393	475-8722*	685
Milwaukee Repertory Theater 108 E Wells St .... Milwaukee WI 53202 TF: 800-403-9898 ■ Web: www.milwaukeerep.com	414-224-1761	224-9097	573-4
Milwaukee Rescue Mission 830 n 19th st .... Milwaukee WI 53233 TF: 800-950-9675 ■ Web: www.milmission.org	414-344-2211		764
Milwaukee School of Engineering 1025 N Broadway St .... Milwaukee WI 53202 *Fax: Admissions ■ TF: 800-332-6763 ■ Web: www.msoe.edu	414-277-6763	277-7475*	166
Milwaukee Symphony Orchestra 1101 N Market St STE 100 .... Milwaukee WI 53202 TF: 888-367-8101 ■ Web: milwaukee.broadway.com	414-273-7121		573-3
Milwaukee Valve Company Inc 16550 W Stratton Dr .... New Berlin WI 53151 TF: 800-348-6544 ■ Web: www.milwaukeevalve.com	262-432-2800	432-2801	789
Milwaukee Wave LLC 510 W Kilbourn Ave .... Milwaukee WI 53203 TF: 800-745-3000 ■ Web: www.milwaukeewave.com	414-224-9283	224-9290	717
Milwhite Inc 5487 S Padre Island Hwy .... Brownsville TX 78521 TF: 800-442-0082 ■ Web: www.milwhite.com	956-547-1970	547-1999	503-2
Milyli Inc 415 n sangamon st .... Chicago IL 60642 Web: www.milyli.com	312-265-0136		138
mImage Inc, The PO Box 27168 .... Salt Lake City UT 84127 Web: www.thermimage.com	801-207-8281		743
Mimaki USA Inc 150 Satellite Blvd NE Ste A .... Suwanee GA 30024 Web: www.mimakiusa.com	678-730-0170		174
MIMC (Mobile Infirmary Medical Ctr) 5 Mobile Infirmary Cir .... Mobile AL 36607	251-435-2400		374-3
MiMedx Group Inc 1775 W Oak Commons Ct NE .... Marietta GA 30062 TF: 888-543-1917 ■ Web: www.mimedx.com	888-543-1917		476
Mimi's Cafe 7450 W Bell Rd .... Glendale AZ 85308 Web: www.mimiscafe.com	623-979-4500		671
Mimic Technologies Inc 811 First Ave Ste 408 .... Seattle WA 98104 TF: 800-918-1670 ■ Web: www.mimicsimulation.com	206-923-3337		177
MIMICS Inc 2620 Dakota NE .... Albuquerque NM 87110 Web: www.mimics.com	505-332-9220		177
Mimma's Cafe 1307 E Brady St .... Milwaukee WI 53202 Web: www.mimmas.com	414-271-7337		671
Mimosa Grill 327 S Tryon St .... Charlotte NC 28202 Web: www.harpersgroup.com	704-343-0700		671
Mims Meat Company Inc 12634 E Farway .... Houston TX 77015	713-453-0151		296-26
MIN (Media Industry Newsletter) 110 William St 11th Fl .... New York NY 10038 *Fax Area Code: 212 ■ TF: 888-707-5814 ■ Web: www.minonline.com	888-707-5814	621-4879*	531-11
Minact Inc 5220 Keele St .... Jackson MS 39206 Web: www.minact.com	601-362-1631	362-5771	764
Minas Energy Positive Solutions 3 Bedford Hills Rd .... Bedford NS B4A1J5 Web: www.minas.ns.ca	902-835-7100	835-8062	557
Minato Auto LLC Dba Toyota of Portsmouth 150 Greenleaf Ave .... Portsmouth NH 03801	603-431-6100		57
Minco Manufacturing Inc 855 Aeroplaza Dr .... Colorado Springs CO 80916 Web: www.mincomfg.com	719-550-1223		591
Minco Products Inc 7300 Commerce Ln NE .... Minneapolis MN 55432 *Fax: Sales ■ Web: www.minco.com	763-571-3121	571-0927*	201
Minco Tool & Mold Co 5690 Webster St .... Dayton OH 45414 TF: 800-367-4720 ■ Web: www.mincogroup.com	937-890-7905		711
Mincron Software Systems 333 N Sam Houston Pkwy E Ste 1100 .... Houston TX 77060 Web: www.mincron.com	281-999-7010		178-11
Mind Drivers LLC The Mill 381 Brinton Lake Rd .... Thornton PA 19373	610-361-1000		196
Mind Gym (USA) Inc 9 E 37th St .... New York NY 10016 Web: us.themindgym.com	646-649-4333		242
Mind Your Business Inc (myb) 305 Eighth Ave E .... Hendersonville NC 28792 TF: 888-758-3776	888-869-2462		260
Mindbody Online 4051 Broad St Ste 220 .... Sn Luis Obisp CA 93401 TF: 877-755-4279 ■ Web: www.mindbodyonline.com	877-755-4279		396

Name / Address	City	State	ZIP	Phone	Fax	Class
MindEdge Inc 271 Waverley Oaks Rd *Web:* www.mindedge.com	Waltham	MA	02452	781-250-1805		397
Minden Medical Ctr 1 Medical Plaza *Web:* www.mindenmedicalcenter.com	Minden	LA	71055	318-377-2321		374-3
Mindex Technologies Inc 3495 Winton Pl. *Web:* mindex.com	Rochester	NY	14623	585-424-3590		177
Mindfinders Inc 1200 18th St NW Ste 550 *Web:* www.themindfinders.com	Washington	DC	20036	202-400-2602		177
Mindgrub Technologies LLC 1215 E Ft Ave Ste 200 *TF:* 855-646-3472 ■ *Web:* www.mindgrub.com	Baltimore	MD	21230	410-988-2444		4
Mindgruve Inc 1018 Eight Ave *Web:* mindgruve.com	San Diego	CA	92101	619-757-1325		624
Mindjet Corp 1160 Battery St E 4th Fl *TF:* 877-646-3538 ■ *Web:* www.mindjet.com	San Francisco	CA	94111	415-229-4200	229-4201	178-12
Mindlance Inc 80 River St Fl 4 *Web:* www.mindlance.com	Hoboken	NJ	07030	201-386-5400	386-0553	194
MindLeaders.com Inc 5500 Glendon Ct Ste 200 **Fax Area Code:* 614	Dublin	OH	43016	506-462-1397	781-6510*	764
MindPlay Educational Software 4400 E Broadway Blvd Ste 206 *TF:* 800-221-7911 ■ *Web:* www.mindplay.com	Tucson	AZ	85711	520-888-1800	888-7904	178-3
Mindpower Inc 337 Georgia Ave SE *Web:* www.mindpowerinc.com	Atlanta	GA	30312	404-581-1991		7
Mindray DS USA Inc 800 MacArthur Blvd *Web:* www.mindraynorthamerica.com	Mahwah	NJ	07430	201-995-8000		476
Minds Eye Entertainment Ltd 480 Henderson Dr *Web:* www.mindseyepictures.com	Regina	SK	S4N6E3	306-359-7618		614
Mindseeker 20130 Lakeview Ctr Plaza *Web:* www.mindseeker.com	Ashburn	VA	20147	571-313-5950		260
Minds-Eye-View Inc 103 Remsen St Ste 201 *Web:* www.ipix.com	Cohoes	NY	12047	518-237-1975		178-8
MindShare 498 Seventh Ave *Web:* www.mindshareworld.com	New York	NY	10018	212-297-7000		4
MindSnacks Inc 1479 Folsom St *Web:* www.mindsnacks.com	San Francisco	CA	94103	415-400-4626		387
MindSpark International Inc 1205 Peachtree Pkwy Ste 1204 *TF:* 888-820-3616 ■ *Web:* www.mindsparkit.com	Cumming	GA	30041	888-820-3616		196
Mindspeed Technologies Inc 4000 MacArthur Blvd *NASDAQ: MSPD* ■ *Web:* macom.com	Newport Beach	CA	92660	949-579-3000		696
Mindstorm Communications Group Inc 10316 Feld Farm Ln Ste 200 *Web:* www.gomindstorm.com	Charlotte	NC	28210	704-331-0870		4
Mindstream LLC 2872 NE 25th Ct **Fax Area Code:* 866 ■ *Web:* mindstreamstudio.com	Fort Lauderdale	FL	33305	954-594-2601	990-5622*	463
MindTouch Inc 401 W A St *Web:* www.mindtouch.com	San Diego	CA	92101	619-795-8459		177
Mindways Software Inc 3001 S Lamar Blvd Ste 302 *Web:* www.qct.com	Austin	TX	78704	512-912-0871		476
Mindwrap Inc 492 Blackwell Rd Ste 202 *TF:* 800-573-1874 ■ *Web:* www.mindwrap.com	Warrenton	VA	20186	540-347-2552		180
Mine & Mill Industrial Supply Company Inc 2500 S Combee Rd *TF:* 800-282-8489 ■ *Web:* www.minemill.com	Lakeland	FL	33801	863-665-5601		186
Mine Development Assoc 210 S Rock Blvd *Web:* www.mda.com	Reno	NV	89502	775-856-5700		261
Mine Kill State Park PO Box 923 Route 30 *Web:* parks.ny.gov/parks/165/details.aspx	North Blenheim	NY	12131	518-827-6111		565
Mine Safety & Health Administration (MSHA) 1100 Wilson Blvd *TF:* 800-746-1553 ■ *Web:* www.msha.gov	Arlington	VA	22209	202-693-9400	693-9401	340-15
Coal Mine Safety & Health Office 1100 Wilson Blvd *Web:* www.msha.gov/programs/coal.htm	Arlington	VA	22209	202-693-9500		340-15
Metal & Non-Metal Mine Safety & Health Office 1100 Wilson Blvd *Web:* www.msha.gov/programs/metal.htm	Arlington	VA	22209	202-693-9600	693-9601	340-15
National Mine Health & Safety Academy 1301 Airport Rd *Web:* www.msha.gov	Beaver	WV	25813	304-256-3100	256-3324	340-15
MineAfrica Inc 769 Euclid Ave *Web:* www.mineafrica.com	Toronto	ON	M6G2V3	416-588-7749		5
MinePAC 101 Constitution Ave NW Ste 500 E *Web:* nma.org	Washington	DC	20001	202-463-2625	463-2666	615
Miner County 217 S Main St PO Box 129 *TF:* 800-383-8000 ■ *Web:* www.minercountybank.com	Howard	SD	57349	605-772-4561		338
Miner Elastomer Products Corp 1200 E State St *Web:* www.minerelastomer.com	Geneva	IL	60134	630-232-3000	232-3172	604
Miner Enterprises Inc 1200 E State St *TF:* 888-822-5334 ■ *Web:* www.minerent.com	Geneva	IL	60134	630-232-3000	232-3055	650
Miner'S Inc 5065 Miller Trunk Hwy *Web:* superonefoods.com	Hermantown	MN	55811	218-729-5882		345
Miner, Barnhill & Galland PC 14 W Erie St *Web:* www.lawmbg.com	Chicago	IL	60654	312-751-1170		428
Mineral Area College 5270 Frat River Rd PO Box 1000 **Fax:* Admissions ■ *Web:* www.mineralarea.edu	Park Hills	MO	63601	573-431-4593	518-2166*	162
Mineral Area Regional Medical Ctr (WARMC) 1212 Weber Rd Ste 302	Farmington	MO	63640	573-756-4581		374-3
Mineral County 1201 N Main St PO Box 70 *Web:* www.colorado.gov/mineralcountycolorado	Creede	CO	81130	719-658-2575	658-2764	338
Mineral County 150 Armstrong St *Web:* www.mineralcountywv.com	Keyser	WV	26726	304-788-5150	788-4100	338
Mineral County 300 River St PO Box 396 *Web:* www.co.mineral.mt.us	Superior	MT	59872	406-822-3577	822-3579	338
Mineral County Chamber of Commerce 40 1/2 N Main St *Web:* www.mineralchamber.com	Keyser	WV	26726	304-788-2513		139
Mineral Daily News Tribune Inc 24 Armstrong St *TF:* 800-733-9694 ■ *Web:* www.newstribune.info	Keyser	WV	26726	304-788-3333		637-8
Mineral Labs Inc 309 Pkwy Dr *Web:* minerallabs.com	Salyersville	KY	41465	606-349-6145		743
Mineral Mound State Park 48 Finch Ln *Web:* www.parks.ky.gov	Eddyville	KY	42038	270-388-3673		565
Mineral Resources International 2720 Wadman Dr *TF:* 800-731-7866 ■ *Web:* www.mineralresourcesint.com	Ogden	UT	84401	801-731-7040	731-7985	297-8
Mineral Wells Area Chamber of Commerce 511 E Hubbard St *TF:* 800-252-6989 ■ *Web:* www.mineralwellstx.com	Mineral Wells	TX	76067	940-325-2557	328-0850	139
Minerals Management Service 1849 C St NW Ste 4210 *TF:* 800-200-4853 ■ *Web:* www.doi.gov	Washington	DC	20240	202-208-3985	208-7242	340-13
Minerals Metals & Materials Society (TMS) 184 Thorn Hill Rd *TF:* 800-759-4867 ■ *Web:* www.tms.org	Warrendale	PA	15086	724-776-9000	776-3770	49-13
Minerals Research Inc 4620 S Coach Dr *Web:* www.mrrinc.com	Tucson	AZ	85714	520-837-9289		191-1
Minerals Technologies Inc 405 Lexington Ave *Web:* mineralstech.com	New York	NY	10174	212-878-1800		663
Minerals Technologies Inc 622 Third Ave 38th Fl *NYSE: MTX* ■ *Web:* www.mineralstech.com	New York	NY	10017	212-878-1831		143
Miner-Dederick Construction LLP 1532 Peden	Houston	TX	77006	713-529-3001		360-2
Minergy Corp 1512 S Commercial St *Web:* www.minergy.com	Neenah	WI	54956	920-727-1919	727-1418	660
Minerva & D'agostino PC 107 S Central Ave *Web:* mindaglaw.com	Valley Stream	NY	11580	516-872-7400		428
Minerva Networks Inc 2150 Gold St *TF:* 800-806-9594 ■ *Web:* www.minervanetworks.com	Santa Clara	CA	95002	408-567-9400	567-0747	647
Minerva's 301 S Phillips Ave *Web:* www.minervas.net	Sioux Falls	SD	57104	605-334-0386	334-9585	671
Minerva's 2111 N Lacrosse St *Web:* minervas.net	Rapid City	SD	57701	605-394-9505		671
Mines of Spain State Recreation Area 8991 Bellevue Heights *Web:* www.iowadnr.gov	Dubuque	IA	52003	563-556-0620	556-8474	565
Mines Press Inc, The 231 Croton Ave *TF:* 800-447-6788 ■ *Web:* www.minespress.com	Cortlandt Manor	NY	10567	914-788-1698		627
Ming Court 9188 International Dr *TF:* 800-333-3333 ■ *Web:* www.ming-court.com	Orlando	FL	32819	407-351-9988		671
Ming Garden 1250 Shreveport Barksdale Hwy	Shreveport	LA	71104	318-861-2741		671
Ming Wah 1618 W Third Ave	Spokane	WA	99201	509-455-9474		671
Ming's 2330 S Carson St *Web:* officialmobilesite.com	Carson City	NV	89701	775-887-8878		671
Ming's Cuisine 514 Cahaba Pk Cir *Web:* mingsmenu.com	Birmingham	AL	35242	205-991-3803		671
Mingan Archipelago National Park Reserve of Canada 1340 de la Digue St *TF:* 877-737-3783 ■ *Web:* www.pc.gc.ca/pn-np/qc/mingan/index.aspx	Havre Saint-Pierre	QC	G0G1P0	418-538-3331	538-3595	563
Mingei International Museum of Folk Art 1439 El Prado *Web:* www.mingei.org	San Diego	CA	92101	619-239-0003	239-0605	520
Mingo County PO Box 1197 *Web:* mingocountywv.com	Williamson	WV	25661	304-235-0378		338
Mings Garden Chinese Restaurant 1741 Eastern Bypass *Web:* www.mingsgardenmontgomery.com	Montgomery	AL	36117	334-277-8188		671
Minh's 2500 Wilson Blvd *Web:* minhdcrestaurant.com	Arlington	VA	22201	703-525-2828	525-2829	671
Minhas Craft Brewery 1208 14th Ave *Web:* www.minhasbrewery.com	Monroe	WI	53566	608-325-3191		102
Miniature Museum of Greater Saint Louis 4746 Gravois Ave *Web:* www.miniaturemuseum.org	Saint Louis	MO	63116	314-832-7790		520
Miniature Precision Components Inc 820 Wisconsin St *Web:* www.mpc-inc.com	Walworth	WI	53184	262-275-5791	275-6346	599
Mini-Cassia Chamber of Commerce (MCC) 1177 Seventh St *Web:* www.minicassiachamber.com	Heyburn	ID	83336	208-679-4793	679-4794	139
Mini-Circuits Laboratories Inc 13 Neptune Ave *TF:* 800-654-7949 ■ *Web:* www.minicircuits.com	Brooklyn	NY	11235	718-934-4500	332-4661	696
Minidoka County 715 G St PO Box 368 *Web:* www.minidoka.id.us	Rupert	ID	83350	208-436-7111	436-0737	338
Minidoka National Historic Site PO Box 570 *Web:* www.nps.gov/miin	Hagerman	ID	83332	208-933-4127	837-4857	564
Minier Financial Inc 101 S Main PO Box 800 *Web:* firstfarmers.com	Minier	IL	61759	309-392-2623		70
Minimus LLC 2610 Conejo Spectrum St *Web:* www.minimus.biz	Newbury Park	CA	91320	805-480-1415		7
Mining Journal PO Box 430 *Web:* www.miningjournal.net	Marquette	MI	49855	906-228-2500	228-2617	532-2
Minisink Valley Central School District PO Box 217 Rte 6 *Web:* www.minisink.com	Slate Hill	NY	10973	845-355-5100		685
Ministries Today Magazine 600 Rinehart Rd *Web:* ministrytodaymag.com	Lake Mary	FL	32746	407-333-0600		457-18

Name / Address	Phone	Fax	Class
Ministry of Tourism of Dominican Republic			
848 Brickell Ave .... Miami FL 33131	305-358-2899		775
TF: 888-358-9594 ■ *Web:* godominicanrepublic.com			
Ministry Partners Investment Company LLC			
915 W Imperial Hwy Ste 120 .... Brea CA 92821	714-671-5720		217
Web: www.ministrypartners.org			
Ministry Saint Joseph's Hospital (MSJH)			
611 St Joseph Ave .... Marshfield WI 54449	715-387-1713		374-3
TF: 800-888-4755 ■ *Web:* www.ministryhealth.org/sjh/home.nws			
Minitab Inc			
Quality Plaza 1829 Pine Hall Rd .... State College PA 16801	814-238-3280		178-10
TF: 800-448-3555 ■ *Web:* www.minitab.com			
Minka Group 1151 W Bradford Ct .... Corona CA 92882	951-735-9220		439
TF: 800-221-7977 ■ *Web:* www.minkagroup.net			
Minkin Chandler Corp 15400 Oakwood Dr ...... Romulus MI 48174	734-229-9200		686
Web: minkinchandler.weebly.com			
Minmetals Inc 120 Schor Ave........ Leonia NJ 07605	201-809-1898		492
Web: usa.minmetals.com.cn			
Minn-Dak Farmers Co-op			
7525 Red River Rd .... Wahpeton ND 58075	701-642-8411		296-38
Web: www.mdfarmerscoop.com			
Minn-Dak Growers Ltd			
4034 40th Ave N........ Grand Forks ND 58203	701-746-7453	780-9050	10-5
Web: www.minndak.com			
Minn-Dak Yeast Company Inc			
18175 Red River Rd W .... Wahpeton ND 58075	701-642-3300	642-1908	296-42
TF: 800-348-0991 ■ *Web:* www.dakotayeast.com/home.html			
Minneapolis City Hall			
350 S Fifth St .... Minneapolis MN 55415	612-673-3000	673-3812	337
TF: 800-569-4287 ■ *Web:* www.ci.minneapolis.mn.us			
Minneapolis College of Art & Design			
2501 Stevens Ave........ Minneapolis MN 55404	612-874-3760	874-3701	164
TF: 800-874-6223 ■ *Web:* www.mcad.edu			
Minneapolis Community & Technical College			
1501 Hennepin Ave........ Minneapolis MN 55403	612-659-6200	659-6210*	162
**Fax:* Admissions ■ *TF:* 800-247-0911 ■ *Web:* www.minneapolis.edu			
Minneapolis Convention Ctr			
1301 Second Ave S........ Minneapolis MN 55403	612-335-6000	335-6757	205
TF: 800-438-5547 ■ *Web:* www.minneapolis.org			
Minneapolis Foundation			
80 S Eigth St 800 IDS Ctr........ Minneapolis MN 55402	612-672-3878	672-3846	303
TF: 866-305-0543 ■ *Web:* www.minneapolisfoundation.org			
Minneapolis Grain Exchange			
400 S Fourth St 130 Grain Exchange Bldg ..... Minneapolis MN 55415	612-321-7101	339-1155	691
TF: 800-827-4746 ■ *Web:* www.mgex.com			
Minneapolis Institute of Arts			
2400 Third Ave S .... Minneapolis MN 55404	612-870-3000	870-3004	520
TF: 888-642-2787 ■ *Web:* new.artsmia.org			
Minneapolis Northwest			
6200 Shingle Creek Pkwy Ste 130 .... Brooklyn Center MN 55430	763-852-7500		206
TF: 800-541-4364 ■ *Web:* www.minneapolisnorthwest.com			
Minneapolis Public Schools			
3345 Chicago Ave........ Minneapolis MN 55407	612-668-0000	668-0525	685
TF: 800-543-7709 ■ *Web:* www.mpls.k12.mn.us			
Minneapolis Regional Chamber of Commerce			
81 S Ninth St Ste 200........ Minneapolis MN 55402	612-370-9100	370-9195	139
Web: www.minneapolischamber.org			
Minneapolis/St Paul International Film Festival			
125 SE Main St Ste 341 .... Minneapolis MN 55414	612-331-7563		282
Minneapolis/St. Paul City Pages			
401 N Third St Ste 550........ Minneapolis MN 55401	612-375-1015	372-3737	532-5
TF: 844-387-6962 ■ *Web:* www.citypages.com			
Minneapolis-Saint Paul Business Journal			
333 S Seventh St Ste 350........ Minneapolis MN 55402	612-288-2100	288-2121	457-5
Web: www.bizjournals.com/twincities			
Minneapolis-Saint Paul Magazine			
220 S Sixth St Ste 500 .... Minneapolis MN 55402	612-339-7571	339-5806	457-22
TF: 800-999-5589 ■ *Web:* www.mspmag.com			
Minnehaha Academy			
3100 W River Pkwy........ Minneapolis MN 55406	612-729-8321		685
Web: www.minnehahaacademy.net			
Minnehaha County 415 N Dakota Ave .... Sioux Falls SD 57104	605-367-4206	367-8314	338
Web: www.minnehahacounty.org			
Minneopa State Park 54497 Gadwall Rd........ Mankato MN 56001	507-389-5464		565
Web: www.dnr.state.mn.us			
Minnesota			
Aging Board 540 Cedar St........ Saint Paul MN 55155	651-431-2500		339-24
TF: 800-882-6262 ■ *Web:* www.mnaging.org			
Arts Board 400 Sibley St Ste 200 .... Saint Paul MN 55101	651-215-1600	215-1602	339-24
TF: 800-866-2787 ■ *Web:* www.arts.state.mn.us			
Attorney General			
445 Minnesota St Ste 1400........ Saint Paul MN 55101	651-296-3353		339-24
TF: 800-657-3787 ■ *Web:* www.ag.state.mn.us			
Bill Status-Senate			
100 Rev Dr Martin Luther King Junior Blvd			
.... Saint Paul MN 55155	651-296-2146		433
Web: www.house.leg.state.mn.us			
Campaign Finance & Public Disclosure Boa			
658 Cedar St Ste 190........ Saint Paul MN 55155	651-296-5148	296-1722	265
TF: 800-657-3889 ■ *Web:* www.cfboard.state.mn.us			
Child Support Enforcement Div			
444 Lafayette Rd N........ Saint Paul MN 55164	651-431-2000	431-7670	339-24
TF: 800-747-5484 ■ *Web:* mn.gov			
Commerce Dept			
85 Seventh Pl E Ste 500 .... Saint Paul MN 55101	651-539-1500		339-24
TF: 800-657-3602 ■ *Web:* mmd.admin.state.mn.us			
Corrections Dept			
1450 Energy Pk Dr Ste 200 .... Saint Paul MN 55108	651-361-7200	642-0223	339-24
Web: www.corr.state.mn.us			
Department of Education			
1500 Hwy 36 W........ Roseville MN 55113	651-582-8200		339-24
Web: education.state.mn.us			
Department of Public Safety			
444 Minnesota St........ Saint Paul MN 55101	651-201-7000		339-24
TF: 800-657-3787 ■ *Web:* www.dps.mn.gov			
Driver & Vehicle Services Div			
445 Minnesota St........ Saint Paul MN 55101	651-201-7000	296-3141	339-24
Web: dps.mn.gov/divisions/dvs/Pages/default.aspx			
Employment & Economic Development Dept (DEED)			
1st National Bank Bldg 332 Minnesota St			
Ste E200 .... Saint Paul MN 55101	651-259-7114		339-24
TF: 800-657-3858 ■ *Web:* mn.gov/deed			
Enterprise Technology Office			
658 Cedar St........ Saint Paul MN 55155	651-296-8888		339-24
Web: www.mmb.state.mn.us			
Fish & Wildlife Div			
500 Lafayette Rd PO Box 25 .... Saint Paul MN 55155	651-259-5096		339-24
Web: www.dnr.state.mn.us			
Governor			
130 State Capitol			
75 Rev Dr Martin Luther King Jr Blvd .... Saint Paul MN 55155	651-201-3400	797-1850	339-24
TF: 800-657-3717 ■ *Web:* mn.gov			
Health Dept 625 Robert St N .... Saint Paul MN 55164	651-201-4545	201-4606	339-24
TF: 888-345-0823 ■ *Web:* www.health.state.mn.us			
Historical Society			
345 Kellogg Blvd W........ Saint Paul MN 55102	651-259-3000		339-24
TF: 800-657-3773 ■ *Web:* www.mnhs.org			
Homeland Security & Emergency Management Div			
445 Minnesota St Ste 223 .... Saint Paul MN 55101	651-201-7400	296-0459	339-24
Web: dps.mn.gov/divisions/hsem			
Housing Finance Authority			
400 Sibley St Ste 300 .... Saint Paul MN 55101	651-296-7608		339-24
TF: 800-657-3769 ■ *Web:* www.mnhousing.gov			
Human Services Dept			
444 Lafayette Rd .... Saint Paul MN 55155	651-431-2000		339-24
Web: mn.gov			
Labor & Industry Dept			
443 Lafayette Rd N........ Saint Paul MN 55155	651-284-5005	284-5727	339-24
TF: 800-342-5354 ■ *Web:* www.doli.state.mn.us			
Legislature			
75 Rev D rMartin Luther King Jr Blvd			
Rm 231 .... Saint Paul MN 55155	651-296-0504	296-6511	339-24
TF: 888-234-1112 ■ *Web:* www.leg.state.mn.us			
Medical Practice Board			
2829 University Ave SE Ste 500........ Minneapolis MN 55414	612-617-2130	617-2166	339-24
TF: 800-657-3709 ■ *Web:* mn.gov			
Natural Resources Dept			
500 Lafayette Rd .... Saint Paul MN 55155	651-296-6157		339-24
TF: 888-646-6367 ■ *Web:* www.dnr.state.mn.us			
Office of Higher Education			
1450 Energy Pk Dr Ste 350 .... Saint Paul MN 55108	651-642-0567	642-0675	725
TF: 800-657-3866 ■ *Web:* www.ohe.state.mn.us			
Parks & Recreation Div			
500 Lafayette Rd .... Saint Paul MN 55155	651-259-5300		339-24
TF: 888-646-6367 ■ *Web:* dnr.state.mn.us/contact/index.html			
Public Utilities Commission			
121 Seventh Pl E Ste 350 .... Saint Paul MN 55101	651-296-7124		339-24
TF: 800-657-3782 ■ *Web:* mn.gov/puc			
Revenue Dept 600 N Roberts St........ Saint Paul MN 55101	651-556-3000		339-24
TF: 800-657-3666 ■ *Web:* www.revenue.state.mn.us			
Secretary of State			
100 Rev Dr Martin Luther King Jr Blvd			
Ste 100 .... Saint Paul MN 55103	651-201-1342	215-0682	339-24
Web: www.sos.state.mn.us			
State Court Administrator			
25 Rev Dr Martin Luther King Jr Blvd			
Rm 135 .... Saint Paul MN 55155	651-296-2474	297-5636	339-24
Web: www.mncourts.gov			
State Lottery 2645 Long Lake Rd........ Roseville MN 55113	651-635-8273		452
TF: 800-333-4673 ■ *Web:* www.mnlottery.com			
Supreme Court			
25 Rev Dr Martin Luther King Jr Blvd .... Saint Paul MN 55155	651-297-1000		339-24
Transportation Dept			
395 John Ireland Blvd .... Saint Paul MN 55155	651-296-3000		339-24
TF: 800-657-3774 ■ *Web:* www.dot.state.mn.us			
Veterans Affairs Dept			
20 W 12th St Room 206 .... Saint Paul MN 55155	651-296-2562		339-24
Web: mn.gov			
Weights & Measures Div			
14305 Southcross Dr W Ste 150........ Burnsville MN 55306	651-539-1555		339-24
Workers" Compensation Div			
443 Lafayette Rd .... Saint Paul MN 55155	651-284-5005		339-24
TF: 800-342-5354 ■ *Web:* www.dli.mn.gov			
Minnesota Assn of Realtors			
5750 Lincoln Dr........ Minneapolis MN 55436	952-935-8313		656
TF: 800-862-6097 ■ *Web:* www.mnrealtor.com			
Minnesota Ballet 301 W First St Ste 800........ Duluth MN 55802	218-529-3742	529-3744	573-1
TF: 800-627-3529 ■ *Web:* www.minnesotaballet.org			
Minnesota Chamber of Commerce			
400 Robert St N Ste 1500........ Saint Paul MN 55101	651-292-4650	292-4656	140
TF: 800-821-2230 ■ *Web:* www.mnchamber.com			
Minnesota Chemical Co			
2285 Hampden Ave........ Saint Paul MN 55114	651-646-7521	649-1101	427
TF: 800-328-5689 ■ *Web:* www.minnesotachemical.com			
Minnesota Children's Museum			
10 W Seventh St........ Saint Paul MN 55102	651-225-6000	225-6006	521
Web: www.mcm.org			
Minnesota Commercial Railway			
508 Cleveland Ave N........ Saint Paul MN 55114	651-646-2010	646-8337	651
Web: mnnr.net			
Minnesota Correctional Facility-Fairbault			
1101 Linden Ln .... Faribault MN 55021	507-334-0700		213
TF: 800-657-3830 ■ *Web:* www.doc.state.mn.us			
Minnesota Correctional Facility-Lino Lakes			
7525 Fourth Ave........ Lino Lakes MN 55014	651-717-6100		213
Minnesota Correctional Facility-Moose Lake			
1000 Lake Shore Dr .... Moose Lake MN 55767	218-485-5000		213
Minnesota Correctional Facility-Rush City			
7600 525th St........ Rush City MN 55069	320-358-0400		213
Minnesota Correctional Facility-Shakopee			
1010 W Sixth Ave........ Shakopee MN 55379	952-496-4440		213
Web: www.doc.state.mn.us			
Minnesota Correctional Facility-Stillwater			
970 Picket St N........ Bayport MN 55003	651-779-2700		213
Minnesota Corrugated Box Inc			
2200 YH Hanson Ave .... Albert Lea MN 56007	507-373-5006		100
Web: www.mcbox.com			

Phone | Fax | Class

Minnesota Dance Theatre
528 Hennepin Ave 6th Fl . . . Minneapolis MN 55403 — 612-338-0627 — 573-1
Web: www.mndance.org

Minnesota Dental Assn
1335 Industrial Blvd Ste 200 . . . Minneapolis MN 55413 — 612-767-8400 767-8500 — 227
TF: 800-950-3368 ■ *Web:* www.mndental.org

Minnesota Discovery Ctr
1005 Discovery Dr . . . Chisholm MN 55719 — 218-254-7959 254-7971 — 520
TF: 800-372-6437 ■ *Web:* www.mndiscoverycenter.com

Minnesota Diversified Products Inc
9091 County Rd 50 . . . Rockford MN 55373 — 763-477-5854 477-5863 — 601
Web: www.diversifoam.com

Minnesota Educator Magazine
41 Sherburne Ave . . . Saint Paul MN 55103 — 651-227-9541 292-4802 — 457-8
TF: 800-652-9073 ■ *Web:* educationminnesota.org

Minnesota Elevator Inc
19336 607th Ave . . . Mankato MN 56001 — 507-245-3060 245-3956 — 256
Web: meielevatorsolutions.com

Minnesota Eye Consultants PA
710 E 24th St Ste 100 . . . Minneapolis MN 55404 — 612-813-3600 813-3601 — 798
TF: 800-526-7632 ■ *Web:* www.mneye.com

Minnesota Historical Society History Ctr Museum
345 Kellogg Blvd W . . . Saint Paul MN 55102 — 651-259-3001 296-1004 — 520
TF: 800-657-3773 ■ *Web:* www.mnhs.org

Minnesota Knitting Mills
1450 Mendota Heights Rd . . . Saint Paul MN 55120 — 651-452-2240 — 745-4
TF: 800-438-5800 ■ *Web:* www.mnknit.com

Minnesota Landscape Arboretum
3675 Arboretum Dr . . . Chaska MN 55318 — 952-443-1400 443-2521 — 97
Web: www.arboretum.umn.edu

Minnesota Lawyers Mutual Insurance Co
333 S Seventh St Ste 2200 . . . Minneapolis MN 55402 — 800-422-1370 305-1510 — 390
TF: 800-422-1370 ■ *Web:* www.mlmins.com

Minnesota Library Assn (MLA)
1821 University Ave W Ste S256 . . . Saint Paul MN 55104 — 651-999-5343 — 435
Web: www.mnlibraryassociation.org

Minnesota Lions Eye Bank
1000 Westgate Dr Ste 260 . . . Saint paul MN 55114 — 612-625-5159 — 269
TF Cust Svc: 866-887-4448 ■ *Web:* www.mnlionseyebank.org

Minnesota Lynx
600 First Ave N Target Ctr . . . Minneapolis MN 55403 — 612-673-1600 673-8407 — 714-2
Web: www.wnba.com/lynx

Minnesota Medical Assn
1300 Godward St NE Ste 2500 . . . Minneapolis MN 55413 — 612-378-1875 — 474
Web: www.mnmed.org

Minnesota Multi Housing Services Inc
1600 W 82nd St Ste 110 . . . Bloomington MN 55431 — 952-854-8500 — 138
TF: 800-967-4222 ■ *Web:* www.mmha.com

Minnesota Nurses Assn (MNA)
345 Randolph Ave Ste 200 . . . Saint Paul MN 55102 — 651-414-2800 — 533
TF: 800-536-4662 ■ *Web:* www.mnnurses.org

Minnesota Opera 620 N First St . . . Minneapolis MN 55401 — 612-333-2700 333-0869 — 573-2
TF: 800-676-6737 ■ *Web:* www.mnopera.org

Minnesota Orchestra
1111 Nicollet Mall Orchestra Hall . . . Minneapolis MN 55403 — 612-371-5600 371-7170 — 573-3
TF: 800-292-4141 ■ *Web:* www.minnesotaorchestra.org

Minnesota Pharmacists Assn (MPhA)
1935 W County Rd B2 . . . Roseville MN 55113 — 651-697-1771 697-1776 — 585
TF: 800-451-8349 ■ *Web:* www.mpha.org

Minnesota Power 30 W Superior St . . . Duluth MN 55802 — 218-722-2625 720-2795 — 787
TF: 800-228-4966 ■ *Web:* www.mnpower.com

Minnesota Public Radio (MPR)
480 Cedar St . . . Saint Paul MN 55101 — 651-290-1212 — 632
TF: 800-228-7123 ■ *Web:* www.mpr.org

Minnesota Republican Party
2200 E Franklin Ave Ste 201 . . . Minneapolis MN 55404 — 651-222-0022 — 616-2
Web: www.mngop.com

Minnesota Rubber & Plastics
1100 Xenium Ln N . . . Minneapolis MN 55441 — 952-927-1400 927-1470 — 604
TF: 800-927-1422 ■ *Web:* www.mnrubber.com

Minnesota State Bar Assn
600 Nicollet Mall Ste 380 . . . Minneapolis MN 55402 — 612-333-1183 333-4927 — 72
TF: 800-882-6722 ■ *Web:* www.mnbar.org

Minnesota State Community & Technical College
Detroit Lakes 900 Hwy 34E . . . Detroit Lakes MN 56501 — 218-846-3700 846-3794 — 162
TF: 800-492-4836 ■ *Web:* www.minnesota.edu
Fergus Falls 1414 College Way . . . Fergus Falls MN 56537 — 218-736-1500 736-1510* — 162
*Fax: Admissions ■ *TF:* 877-450-3322 ■ *Web:* www.minnesota.edu
Moorhead 1900 28th Ave S . . . Moorhead MN 56560 — 218-299-6500 — 162
TF: 800-426-5603 ■ *Web:* www.minnesota.edu

Minnesota State University
Mankato 122 Taylor Ctr . . . Mankato MN 56001 — 507-389-1822 389-1511 — 166
TF Admissions: 800-722-0544 ■ *Web:* www.mnsu.edu
Moorhead 1104 Seventh Ave S . . . Moorhead MN 56563 — 218-477-2161 — 166
TF: 800-593-7246 ■ *Web:* www.mnstate.edu

Minnesota State University Mankato
Memorial Library
601 Maywood Ave PO Box 8419 . . . Mankato MN 56002 — 507-389-5952 389-5155 — 434-6
TF: 800-722-0544 ■ *Web:* www.lib.mnsu.edu

Minnesota State University Moorhead Regional Science Ctr
1104 Seventh Ave S . . . Moorhead MN 56563 — 218-477-2920 477-4372 — 520
TF: 800-593-7246 ■ *Web:* www.mnstate.edu/regsci

Minnesota Supply Company Inc
6470 Flying Cloud Dr . . . Eden Prairie MN 55344 — 952-828-7300 828-7301 — 385
TF: 800-869-1028 ■ *Web:* www.mnsupply.com

Minnesota Timberwolves
Target Ctr 600 First Ave N . . . Minneapolis MN 55403 — 612-673-1600 673-1699 — 714-1
TF: 855-895-0872 ■ *Web:* www.nba.com

Minnesota Transportation Museum
193 E Pennsylvania Ave . . . Saint Paul MN 55130 — 651-228-0263 — 520
Web: transportationmuseum.org

Minnesota Twins 1 Twins Way . . . Minneapolis MN 55403 — 612-375-1366 — 713
TF: 800-338-9467 ■ *Web:* minnesota.twins.mlb.com

Minnesota Valley Co-op Light & Power Assn
501 S First St . . . Montevideo MN 56265 — 320-269-2163 269-2302 — 245
TF: 800-247-5051 ■ *Web:* www.mnvalleyrec.com

Minnesota Valley Electric Co-op
125 Minnesota Vly Electric Dr PO Box 77024 . . . Jordan MN 55352 — 952-492-2313 492-8281 — 245
TF: 800-282-6832 ■ *Web:* www.mvec.net

Minnesota Valley State Recreation Area
19825 Park Blvd . . . Jordan MN 55352 — 651-259-5774 — 565
Web: www.dnr.state.mn.us

Minnesota Veterans Home-Fergus Falls
1821 N Pk St . . . Fergus Falls MN 56537 — 218-736-0400 — 793
TF: 800-642-6143 ■ *Web:* mn.gov

Minnesota Veterans Home-Minneapolis
5101 Minnehaha Ave . . . Minneapolis MN 55417 — 612-721-0600 — 793
TF: 877-838-6757 ■ *Web:* mn.gov

Minnesota Veterans Home-Silver Bay
45 Banks Blvd . . . Silver Bay MN 55614 — 218-226-6300 — 793
TF: 877-729-8387 ■ *Web:* mn.gov

Minnesota Veterinary Medical Assn
101 Bridgepoint Way Ste 100 . . . South Saint Paul MN 55075 — 651-645-7533 645-7539 — 795
Web: www.mvma.org

Minnesota Vikings 9520 Viking Dr . . . Eden Prairie MN 55344 — 952-828-6500 828-6540 — 715-3
TF: 877-722-6458 ■ *Web:* www.vikings.com

Minnesota Visiting Nurse Agency
2000 Summer St . . . Minneapolis MN 55413 — 612-617-4600 617-4782 — 363
Web: www.mvna.org

Minnesota West Community & Technical College
1450 Collegeway . . . Worthington MN 56187 — 507-372-3400 372-5803* — 162
*Fax: Admissions ■ *TF:* 800-657-3966 ■ *Web:* www.mnwest.edu

Minnesota Wild 317 Washington St . . . Saint Paul MN 55102 — 651-602-6000 222-1055 — 716
Web: wild.nhl.com

Minnesota Wing Commemorative Air Force Museum
310 Airport Rd Hanger 3 . . . South Saint Paul MN 55075 — 651-455-6942 — 520
Web: www.cafmn.org

Minnesota Wire & Cable Co
1835 Energy Park Dr . . . Saint Paul MN 55108 — 651-642-1800 — 815
TF: 800-258-6922 ■ *Web:* www.mnwire.com

Minnesota Womens Press Inc
771 Raymond Ave . . . Saint Paul MN 55114 — 651-646-3968 — 532-3
Web: www.womenspress.com

Minnesota Zoo 13000 Zoo Blvd . . . Apple Valley MN 55124 — 952-431-9200 431-9300 — 823
TF: 800-366-7811 ■ *Web:* mnzoo.org

Minnesuing Acres
8084 E Minnesuing Acres Dr . . . Lake Nebagamon WI 54849 — 715-374-2262 — 317
Web: www.minnesuingacres.com

Minnetonka Public School Service Ctr
5621 County Rd 101 . . . Minnetonka MN 55345 — 952-401-5000 401-5093 — 685
Web: www.minnetonkaschools.org

Minnetronix Inc 1635 Energy Park Dr . . . St Paul MN 55108 — 651-917-4060 — 261
Web: minnetronix.com

Minnewaska Area High School
25122 State Hwy 28 . . . Glenwood MN 56334 — 320-239-4820 — 685
TF: 800-222-1222 ■ *Web:* www.minnewaska.k12.mn.us

Minnie's 107 McHenry Ave . . . Modesto CA 95354 — 209-524-4621 524-6043 — 671
Web: minnies.58-s.com

Minnotte Corp Minnotte Sq . . . Pittsburgh PA 15220 — 412-922-1633 — 307
Web: www.minnotte.com

Minnow Project a Creative Lab
815 O St Ste 3 . . . Lincoln NE 68508 — 402-475-3322 — 4
Web: www.minnowproject.com

Minnpar LLC 5273 Program Ave . . . Mounds View MN 55112 — 612-379-0606 — 61
TF: 800-889-3382 ■ *Web:* www.minnpar.com

Minntech Corp 14605 28th Ave N . . . Minneapolis MN 55447 — 763-553-3300 553-3387 — 476
TF: 800-328-3345 ■ *Web:* www.medivators.com

Minnwest Bank
14820 Highway 7 Ste 200 . . . Minnetonka MN 55345 — 952-230-9800 — 360-3
Web: www.minnwest.com

Minor League Baseball
9550 16th St N . . . Saint Petersburg FL 33716 — 727-822-6937 821-5819 — 48-22
Web: www.milb.com

Minor Rubber Company Inc
49 Ackerman St . . . Bloomfield NJ 07003 — 973-338-6800 893-1399 — 677
TF: 800-433-6886 ■ *Web:* www.minorrubber.com

Minor Tire & Wheel Company Inc
3512 Sixth Ave SE . . . Decatur AL 35603 — 256-353-4957 — 54
TF: 800-633-3936 ■ *Web:* www.visionwheel.com

Minority Alliance Capital LLC
6960 Orchard Lake Rd Ste 306 . . . West Bloomfield MI 48322 — 248-855-8660 — 69
Web: www.mac-leasing.com

Minority Business Development Agency (MBDA)
1401 Constitution Ave NW . . . Washington DC 20230 — 202-482-1940 — 340-2
TF: 800-735-2258 ■ *Web:* www.mbda.gov

Minority Business Development Agency Regional Offices
Atlanta Region 75 Fifth St NW Ste 300 . . . Atlanta GA 30308 — 404-894-2096 — 340-2
Web: www.mbda.gov
Chicago Region 105 W Adams St Ste 2300 . . . Chicago IL 60603 — 312-353-0182 — 340-2
TF: 888-324-1551 ■ *Web:* www.mbda.gov
Dallas Region
1401 constitution Ave NW Rm 726 . . . Washington DC 20230 — 214-767-8001 — 340-2
Web: www.mbda.gov
New York Region
26 Federal Plaza Ste 3720 . . . New York NY 10278 — 212-264-3262 — 340-2
TF: 800-833-9282 ■ *Web:* www.mbda.gov
San Francisco Region
1401 Constitution Ave . . . Washington DC 20230 — 202-482-1940 — 340-2
TF: 800-903-7227 ■ *Web:* www.mbda.gov

Minot Air Force Base 201 Summit Dr . . . Minot AFB ND 58705 — 701-723-6212 — 497-1
Web: www.minot.af.mil

Minot Area Chamber of Commerce
1020 20th Ave SW . . . Minot ND 58701 — 701-852-6000 838-2488 — 139
TF: 800-829-1040 ■ *Web:* www.minotchamber.org

Minot Convention & Visitors Bureau
1020 S Broadway . . . Minot ND 58701 — 701-857-8206 857-8228 — 206
TF: 800-264-2626 ■ *Web:* www.visitminot.org

Minot Daily News 301 Fourth St SE . . . Mohall ND 58761 — 701-857-1900 857-1907 — 532-2
Web: www.minotdailynews.com

Minot Public Library 516 Second Ave SW . . . Minot ND 58701 — 701-852-1045 852-2595 — 434-3
TF: 800-843-9948 ■ *Web:* www.minotlibrary.org

Minot Public School District 1
215 Second St SE . . . Minot ND 58701 — 701-857-4400 857-4432 — 685
Web: minot.k12.nd.us

Minot State University
500 University Ave W . . . Minot ND 58707 — 701-858-3000 858-3888 — 166
TF: 800-777-0750 ■ *Web:* www.minotstateu.edu

Name / Address	Phone	Fax	Class
Minot State University Bottineau 105 Simrall Blvd. . . . . Bottineau ND 58318 *Fax: Admissions ■ *TF:* 800-542-6866 ■ *Web:* dakotacollege.edu	701-228-5451	228-5499*	162
MinoTech Engineering Inc JRD Technology Ctr 242 Sturbridge Rd . . . . . Charlton MA 01507 *TF:* 800-421-1327 ■ *Web:* www.minotecheng.com	978-474-8034		466
Minova USA Inc 150 Carley Ct . . . . . Georgetown KY 40324 *TF:* 800-626-2948 ■ *Web:* www.minovaglobal.com	502-863-6800	863-6805	605-2
Minskoff Theatre 200 W 45th St . . . . . New York NY 10036 *TF:* 800-714-8452 ■ *Web:* minskofftheatre.com	212-869-0550		747
Minson Corp 1 Minson Way. . . . . Montebello CA 90640 *TF:* 800-251-6537 ■ *Web:* www.minson.com	323-513-1041		319-4
Minster Bank 95 W Fourth St . . . . . Minster OH 45865 *Web:* www.minsterbank.com	419-628-2351		70
Minster Machine Co 240 W Fifth St PO Box 120. . . . . Minster OH 45865 *Web:* www.minster.com	419-628-2331	628-3517	456
Mint Magazine Inc 6960 Bonneval Rd Ste 102. . . . . Jacksonville FL 32216 *Web:* mintmag.com	904-281-8800		5
Mint Museum of Art 2730 Randolph Rd. . . . . Charlotte NC 28207 *Web:* www.mintmuseum.org	704-337-2000	337-2101	520
Mint Restaurant & Bar 816 N Russell St. . . . . Portland OR 97227 *Web:* www.mintand820.com	503-284-5518		671
Mint Turbines LLC 2915 N State Hwy 99 . . . . . Stroud OK 74079 *TF:* 800-284-0606 ■ *Web:* www.mintturbines.com	918-968-9561		21
Minter Field Air Museum 401 Vultee St PO Box 445 . . . . . Shafter CA 93263 *Web:* www.minterfieldairmuseum.com	661-393-0291	393-3296	520
Mintie Corp 1114 San Fernando Rd. . . . . Los Angeles CA 90065 *TF:* 800-964-6843 ■ *Web:* www.mintie.com	323-225-4111		35
Minto Rentals In Ottawa 185 Lyons St N . . . . . Ottawa ON K1R5W4 *TF:* 800-267-3377 ■ *Web:* www.minto.com	613-232-2200	232-6962	379
Mintz & Hoke Inc 40 Tower Ln . . . . . Avon CT 06001 *TF:* 800-678-0473 ■ *Web:* www.mintz-hoke.com	860-678-0473		7
Mintz Levin Cohn Ferris Glovsky & Popeo PC 1 Financial Ctr . . . . . Boston MA 02111 *TF:* 800-962-4284 ■ *Web:* www.mintz.com	617-542-6000	542-2241	428
Minus Forty Technologies Corp 30 Armstrong Ave. . . . . Georgetown ON L7G4R9 *TF:* 800-800-5706 ■ *Web:* www.minusforty.com	905-702-1441		665
Minute Maid Park 501 Crawford St . . . . . Houston TX 77002 *TF:* 877-927-8767 ■ *Web:* houston.astros.mlb.com	713-259-8000	259-8981	720
Minute Man National Historical Park 174 Liberty St. . . . . Concord MA 01742 *Web:* www.nps.gov	978-369-6993	318-7800	564
Minute Men Staffing Services 3740 Carnegie Ave . . . . . Cleveland OH 44115 *TF:* 877-873-8856 ■ *Web:* www.minutemeninc.com	216-426-9675	426-2246	721
Minuteman Aviation Inc (MAI) 5225 Hwy 10 W . . . . . Missoula MT 59808 *Web:* www.minutemanaviation.com	406-728-9363		63
Minuteman Group Inc 35 Bedford St Ste 2. . . . . Lexington MA 02420 *Web:* www.minuteman-group.com	781-861-7493		177
Minuteman International Inc 111 S Rohlwing Rd. . . . . Addison IL 60101 *TF:* 800-323-9420 ■ *Web:* www.minutemanintl.com	630-627-6900	627-1130	386
Minuteman Missile National Historic Site 21280 SD Hwy 240. . . . . Philip SD 57567 *Web:* www.nps.gov	605-433-5552	433-5558	564
Minuteman Press International Inc 61 Executive Blvd . . . . . Farmingdale NY 11735 *TF:* 800-645-3006 ■ *Web:* www.minutemanpress.com	631-249-1370	249-5618	310
Minuteman Regional High School 758 Marrett Rd . . . . . Lexington MA 02421 *TF:* 800-962-2973 ■ *Web:* www.minuteman.org	781-861-6500		685
Minuteman Senior Services 26 Crosby Dr . . . . . Bedford MA 01730 *Web:* www.minutemansenior.org	781-272-7177		672
Minuteman Trucks Inc 2181 Providence Hwy. . . . . Walpole MA 02081 *TF:* 800-231-8458 ■ *Web:* www.minutemantrucks.com	508-668-3112		780
Minvalco Inc 3340 Gorham Ave . . . . . Minneapolis MN 55426 *TF:* 800-642-9090 ■ *Web:* minvalco.com	952-920-0131		612
Minwax Co 10 Mountainview Rd. . . . . Upper Saddle River NJ 07450 *TF:* 800-523-9299 ■ *Web:* www.minwax.com	800-523-9299		550
MinXray Inc 3611 Commercial Ave . . . . . Northbrook IL 60062 *TF:* 800-221-2245 ■ *Web:* www.minxray.com	847-564-0323		475
Mio 2930 Arbutus St . . . . . Vancouver BC V6J3Y9 *TF:* 877-770-1116 ■ *Web:* www.mioglobal.com	604-224-9184		475
Mio Sushi 2271 NW Johnson St. . . . . Portland OR 97210 *Web:* www.miosushi.com	503-221-1469		671
MIPS Technologies Inc 955 E Arques Ave . . . . . Sunnyvale CA 94085 *NASDAQ: MIPS* ■ *Web:* www.imgtec.com	408-530-5000		696
MIR (Manager's Intelligence Report) 316 N Michigan Ave Ste 400 . . . . . Chicago IL 60601 *Fax Area Code: 312 ■ *TF:* 800-878-5331 ■ *Web:* www.managersintelligencereport.biz	800-878-5331	861-3592*	531-2
Mira Godard Gallery 22 Hazelton Ave . . . . . Toronto ON M5R2E2 *Web:* www.godardgallery.com	416-964-8197	964-5912	42
MIRA Mobile Television Inc 25749 SW Canyon Creek Rd Ste 100. . . . . Wilsonville OR 97070	503-464-0900		514
Mira Monte Inn & Suites 69 Mt Desert St. . . . . Bar Harbor ME 04609 *Fax Area Code: 207 ■ *TF:* 800-553-5109 ■ *Web:* www.miramonte.com	800-553-5109	288-3115*	379
Mira Vista Diagnostics LLC 4705 Decatur Blvd Ste 300. . . . . Indianapolis IN 46241 *Web:* www.miravistalabs.com	317-856-2681		743
Mirabeau Park Hotel 1100 N Sullivan Rd. . . . . Spokane Valley WA 99037 *TF:* 866-584-4674 ■ *Web:* www.mirabeauparkhotel.com	509-924-9000	922-4965	379
Mirabile Investment Corp 1900 Whitten Rd. . . . . Memphis TN 38133 *Web:* www.mic-memphis.com	901-324-0450		670
Mirabito Fuel Group Inc 49 Ct St PO Box 5306. . . . . Binghamton NY 13902 *TF:* 800-934-9480 ■ *Web:* mirabito.com	607-352-2800	584-5130	316
Miracell Botanicals 921 N 1430 W. . . . . Orem UT 84057 *Web:* www.miracell.com	801-434-8165		77
Miracle Healthcare 4322 N Hamilton Rd Ste H. . . . . Gahanna OH 43230 *TF:* 844-560-7775 ■ *Web:* www.miraclehealthcare.com	614-237-7702	235-5383	363
Miracle Method US Corp 4239 N Nevada Ave Ste 115 . . . . . Colorado Springs CO 80907 *TF:* 800-444-8827 ■ *Web:* www.miraclemethod.com	719-594-9091		189-11
Miracle Mile Shops at Planet Hollywood 3663 Las Vegas Blvd S. . . . . Las Vegas NV 89109 *TF:* 888-800-8284 ■ *Web:* www.miraclemileshopslv.com	702-866-0703		50-6
Miracle Recreation Equipment Co 878 Hwy 60 . . . . . Monett MO 65708 *TF:* 800-523-4202 ■ *Web:* miracle-recreation.com	417-235-6917		346
Miracle-Ear Inc 5000 Cheshire Pkwy N. . . . . Minneapolis MN 55446 *TF:* 800-464-8002 ■ *Web:* www.miracle-ear.com	800-464-8002		477
Miracles Can Happen Inc 1600 Church Ave . . . . . Brooklyn NY 11226	718-693-3400		260
Miraco Inc 102 Maple St. . . . . Manchester NH 03103 *Web:* www.miracoinc.com	603-665-9449		359
MiraCosta College *Oceanside* 1 Barnard Dr Ste 7 . . . . . Oceanside CA 92056 *Fax: Admissions ■ *TF:* 888-201-8480 ■ *Web:* www.miracosta.edu	760-757-2121	795-6626*	162
San Elijo 3333 Manchester Ave. . . . . Cardiff CA 92007 *TF:* 888-201-8480 ■ *Web:* www.miracosta.cc.ca.us	760-944-4449	634-7875	162
Mirage Productions Inc 111 Spring St. . . . . Newton NJ 07860 *TF:* 800-477-3456 ■ *Web:* www.mirageproductions.com	973-300-9477		514
Mirage, The 3400 Las Vegas Blvd S . . . . . Las Vegas NV 89109 *TF:* 800-627-6667 ■ *Web:* www.mirage.com	702-791-7111	791-7414	669
Miragee Corp 2512 Merriwood Dr. . . . . Louisville KY 40299 *Web:* www.miragee.com	502-266-8768		180
Miragen Therapeutics Inc 6200 Lookout Rd Ste 100. . . . . Boulder CO 80301 *Web:* www.miragentherapeutics.com	303-531-5952		231
Mirai Sushi 2020 W Div St. . . . . Chicago IL 60622 *Web:* www.miraisushi.com	773-862-8500		671
Miramar Hospitality Consulting 1100 Lincoln Ave Ste 105. . . . . Los Altos CA 94022 *Web:* www.miramarhospitality.com	650-941-5202		196
Miramar-Pembroke Pines Regional Chamber of Commerce 10100 Pines Blvd 4th Fl. . . . . Pembroke Pines FL 33026 *Web:* www.miramarpembrokepines.org	954-432-9808	432-9193	139
Miramax Film NY LLC 2540 Colorado Ave Ste 100E . . . . . Santa Monica CA 90404 *TF:* 800-547-0007 ■ *Web:* www.miramax.com	310-409-4321		514
Miramichi Chamber of Commerce 120 Newcastle Blvd Ste 2 PO Box 342 . . . . . Miramichi NB E1N3A7 *Web:* www.miramichichamber.com	506-622-5522	622-5959	137
Miramont Castle Museum 9 Capitol Hill Ave . . . . . Manitou Springs CO 80829 *TF:* 888-685-1011 ■ *Web:* www.miramontcastle.org	719-685-1011	685-1985	520
Miramonte Resort & Spa 45000 Indian Wells Ln . . . . . Indian Wells CA 92210 *TF:* 800-237-2926 ■ *Web:* www.miramonteresort.com	760-341-2200		669
Mirari Biosciences Inc 9610 Medical Ctr Dr Ste 240 . . . . . Rockville MD 20850	240-447-6456		231
Miratek Corp Inc 8201 Lockheed Dr Ste 218. . . . . El Paso TX 79925 *Web:* miratek.us	915-772-2852		194
Miratel Solutions Inc 2501 Steeles Ave W . . . . . North York ON M3J2P1 *TF:* 866-647-2835 ■ *Web:* www.miratelinc.com	416-650-7850		737
Miraval AZ Resort & Spa 5000 E Via Estancia Miraval . . . . . Tucson AZ 85739 *Fax Area Code: 520 ■ *TF:* 800-232-3969 ■ *Web:* www.miravalresorts.com	800-232-3969	825-5163*	706
Mirbeau Inn & Spa 851 W Genesee St . . . . . Skaneateles NY 13152 *TF:* 877-647-2328 ■ *Web:* www.mirbeau.com	315-685-5006		379
Mircom Technologies Ltd 25 Interchange Way . . . . . Vaughan ON L4K5W3 *TF:* 888-660-4655 ■ *Web:* www.mircom.com	905-660-4655	660-4113	693
Miria Systems Inc 2570 Blvd of the Generals Ste 222 . . . . . Norristown PA 19403 *TF:* 800-450-3133 ■ *Web:* www.miriasystems.com	484-446-3300		177
Miriam Hospital, The 164 Summit Ave. . . . . Providence RI 02906 *Web:* www.miriamhospital.org	401-793-2500		374-3
Miriam Shiell Fine Art Ltd 16-A Hazelton Ave . . . . . Toronto ON M5R2E2 *TF:* 800-555-5621 ■ *Web:* www.miriamshiell.com	416-925-2461	925-2471	42
Mirick O'Connell Demaillie & Lougee LLP 1700 Bank of Boston Tower 100 Frnt . . . . . Worcester MA 01608 *Web:* www.mirickoconnell.com	508-791-8500		167
Mirixa Corp 11600 Sunrise Vly Dr Ste 100 . . . . . Reston VA 20191 *TF:* 800-541-2905 ■ *Web:* www.mirixa.com	703-683-1955		612
Miro Spanish Grille 12239 N Community House Rd . . . . . Charlotte NC 28277 *Web:* www.mirospanishgrille.com	704-540-7374		671
Miron Construction Co Inc 1471 McMahon Dr. . . . . Neenah WI 54956 *TF:* 800-871-1668 ■ *Web:* miron-construction.com	920-969-7000	969-7393	186
Mirror Image Internet Inc 2 Highwood Dr. . . . . Tewksbury MA 01876 *TF:* 800-353-2923 ■ *Web:* www.mirror-image.com	781-376-1100	376-1110	178-7
Mirror Lake Inn Resort & Spa 77 Mirror Lake Dr. . . . . Lake Placid NY 12946 *Web:* www.mirrorlakeinn.com	518-523-2544	523-2871	707
Mirror Lake State Park E10320 Fern Dell Rd. . . . . Baraboo WI 53913 *Web:* dnr.wi.gov	608-254-2333		565
Mirror Show Management Inc 855 Hard Rd. . . . . Webster NY 14580 *TF:* 800-247-4302 ■ *Web:* www.mirrorshow.com	585-232-4020		184

Phone | Fax | Class

Mirrorball Group LLC 134 w 25th st .... New York NY 10001 212-604-9988 636
Web: www.mirrorball.com

Mirrotek International LLC
90 Dayton Ave. .... Passaic NJ 07055 973-472-1400 544
TF: 888-659-3030 ■ *Web:* www.mirrotek.com

Mirus International Inc
31 Sun Pac Blvd .... Brampton ON L6S5P6 905-494-1120 767
TF: 888-866-4787 ■ *Web:* www.mirusinternational.com

MIRUS Restaurant Solutions
820 Gessner Rd Ste 1600 .... Houston TX 77024 713-468-7300 196
Web: www.mirus.com

Mirwec Film Inc 601 S Liberty Dr .... Bloomington IN 47403 812-331-7194 600
Web: www.mirwecfilm.com

MIS Inc 222 W Highland Dr .... Lakeland FL 33813 863-669-1100 196
TF: 800-288-8221 ■ *Web:* www.mis-inc.net

MIS Training Institute LLC
153 Cordaville Rd Ste 200 .... Southborough MA 01772 508-879-7999 177
Web: www.misti.com

Misa Metal Fabricating Inc
7101 International Dr .... Louisville KY 40258 502-933-5555 480
Web: www.misametalfab.com

MISA Metal Processing of Tennessee Inc
104 Western Dr .... Portland TN 37148 615-325-5454 690
Web: www.misa.com

Misaki Japanese Steak House
8207 Kingston Pk .... Knoxville TN 37919 865-691-3121 671

Misaki Seafood & Steak House of Japan
3104 Bristol Hwy .... Johnson City TN 37601 423-282-5451 671

Misaki Sushi 379 W Main St .... Hyannis MA 02601 508-771-3771 671
Web: www.misakisushi.com

Misco Home and Garden
100 S Washington Ave .... Dunellen NJ 08812 732-752-7500 292
Web: www.miscohomeandgarden.com

Mise En Place 442 W Kennedy Blvd .... Tampa FL 33606 813-254-5373 671
Web: miseonline.com

Misericordia Community Hospital & Health Ctr
16940 87th Ave. .... Edmonton AB T5R4H5 780-735-2000 374-2

Misericordia Nursing & Rehabilitation Center
998 S Russell St .... York PA 17402 717-755-1964 371
Web: mn-rc.org

Misericordia University 301 Lake St. .... Dallas PA 18612 570-674-6400 675-2441* 166
**Fax:* Admissions ■ *TF:* 866-262-6363 ■ *Web:* www.misericordia.edu

Mishawaka-Penn-Harris Public Library Indiana
209 Lincoln Way E .... Mishawaka IN 46544 574-259-5277 435
TF: 800-622-4970 ■ *Web:* mphpl.org

Miskelly Furniture 101 Airport Rd .... Jackson MS 39208 601-939-6288 321
TF: 888-939-6288 ■ *Web:* www.miskellys.com

MISO (Miami Symphony Orchestra, The)
10689 N Kendall Dr Ste 307 .... Miami FL 33176 305-275-5666 573-3
Web: www.miamisymphony.org

Misonix Inc 1938 NEW Hwy .... Farmingdale NY 11735 631-694-9555 250
TF: 800-694-9612 ■ *Web:* www.misonix.com

MISource Inc 11940 Sheldon Rd .... Tampa FL 33626 813-286-9888 260
Web: www.misource.net

Miss Elaine Inc 8430 Valcour Ave. .... Saint Louis MO 63123 314-631-1900 155-15
TF: 800-458-1422 ■ *Web:* www.misselaine.com

MISS Foundation PO Box 5333 .... Peoria AZ 85385 623-979-1000 48-21
TF: 888-455-0477 ■ *Web:* www.missfoundation.org

Miss Hall's School 492 Holmes Rd .... Pittsfield MA 01201 413-443-6401 622
Web: www.misshalls.org

Miss Paige Ltd
8430 W Bryn Mawr Ste 625 .... Chicago IL 60631 773-693-0480 693-9071 631
Web: www.jobgiraffe.com

Miss Porter's School 60 Main St .... Farmington CT 06032 860-409-3530 622
Web: www.porters.org/page

Miss Universe LP
1370 Ave of the Americas 16th Fl .... New York NY 10019 212-373-4999 315-5378 181
Web: www.missuniverse.com

Missaukee County
111 S Canal PO Box 800 .... Lake City MI 49651 231-839-4967 839-3684 338
Web: www.missaukee.org

MISSCO Contract Sales
2001 Airport Rd Ste 102 PO Box 321400 .... Flowood MS 39232 601-987-8600 487-2800 320
Web: www.missco.com

Mission Ambulance 1055 E Third St .... Corona CA 92879 800-899-9100 30
TF: 800-899-9100 ■ *Web:* www.missionambulance.com

Mission American Kitchen
77 S Seventh St .... Minneapolis MN 55402 612-339-1000 339-8700 671
Web: www.missionamerican.com

Mission Aviation Fellowship (MAF)
112 N Pilatus Ln .... Nampa ID 83687 208-498-0800 498-0801 48-20
TF: 800-359-7623 ■ *Web:* www.maf.org

Mission Basilica San Diego de Alcala
10818 San Diego Mission Rd .... San Diego CA 92108 619-283-7319 283-7762 520
Web: www.missionsandiego.com

Mission Bell Manufacturing Inc
16100 Jacqueline Ct .... Morgan Hill CA 95037 408-778-2036 499
TF: 800-317-6150 ■ *Web:* www.missionbell.com

Mission Benefits Inc
256 Gibraltar Dr Ste 104 .... Sunnyvale CA 94089 408-734-0438 193
Web: www.missionbenefits.com

Mission Beverage Co
550 S Mission Rd .... Los Angeles CA 90033 323-266-6238 81-1

Mission Bicycles Inc
766 Valencia St .... San Francisco CA 94110 415-683-6166 711
Web: missionbicycle.com

Mission Chamber of Commerce
202 W Tom Landry St .... Mission TX 78572 956-585-2727 585-3044 139
TF: 800-827-8298 ■ *Web:* www.missionchamber.com

Mission City Federal Credit Union
1391 Franklin St .... Santa Clara CA 95050 408-244-5818 219
Web: missioncityfcu.org

Mission College
3000 Mission College Blvd .... Santa Clara CA 95054 408-988-2200 980-8980* 162
**Fax:* Admissions ■ *TF:* 800-242-8721 ■ *Web:* missioncollege.edu

Mission Creative 140 E Ninth St .... Dubuque IA 52001 563-583-0853 7
Web: www.missioncreative.biz

Mission Critical Technologies Inc
2041 Rosecrans Ave .... El Segundo CA 90245 310-246-4455 177
Web: www.mctinc.net

Mission Cultural Ctr for Latino Arts
2868 Mission St .... San Francisco CA 94110 415-821-1155 648-0933 50-2
Web: www.missionculturalcenter.org

Mission Dolores 3321 16th St .... San Francisco CA 94114 415-621-8203 621-2294 50-1
Web: www.missiondolores.org

Mission Essential Personnel LLC
4343 Easton Commons Ste 100 .... Columbus OH 43219 614-416-2345 766
TF: 888-542-3447 ■ *Web:* www.missionessential.com

Mission Federal Credit Union
PO Box 919023 .... San Diego CA 92121 858-524-2850 219
TF: 800-500-6328 ■ *Web:* www.missionfed.com

Mission Foods
1159 Cottonwood Ln Ste 200 .... Irving TX 75038 972-232-5000 296-35
TF: 800-443-7994 ■ *Web:* www.missionfoodservice.com

Mission Golf Cars
18865 Redland Rd .... San Antonio TX 78259 210-545-7868 57
TF: 800-324-7868 ■ *Web:* www.missiongolfcars.com

Mission Hospice Inc of San Mateo County
1670 S Amphlett Blvd Ste 300 .... San Mateo CA 94402 650-554-1000 554-1001 371
TF: 800-227-2345 ■ *Web:* www.missionhospice.org

Mission Hospital Regional Medical Ctr Inc
27700 Medical Ctr Rd .... Mission Viejo CA 92691 949-364-1400 374-3
Web: www.mission4health.com

Mission Hospital-St Joseph Campus
428 Biltmore Ave .... Asheville NC 28801 828-213-1111 374-3
Web: mission-health.org

Mission Houses Museum 553 S King St .... Honolulu HI 96813 808-447-3910 545-2280 520
Web: www.missionhouses.org

Mission Inn 3649 Mission Inn Ave .... Riverside CA 92501 951-784-0300 683-1342 379
TF: 800-843-7755 ■ *Web:* www.missioninn.com

Mission Inn Museum 3696 Main St .... Riverside CA 92501 951-788-9556 341-6574 520
Web: missioninnmuseum.org

Mission Inn Resort & Club
10400 County Rd 48 .... Howey in the Hills FL 34737 352-324-3101 669
TF: 800-874-9053 ■ *Web:* www.missioninnresort.com

Mission Laboratories
2433 Birkdale St .... Los Angeles CA 90031 323-223-1405 223-9968 151
TF: 800-535-5053 ■ *Web:* www.missionlabs.net

Mission Landscape Services Inc
536 E Dyer Rd .... Santa Ana CA 92707 800-545-9963 668-0119* 422
**Fax Area Code:* 714 ■ *TF:* 800-545-9963 ■ *Web:* www.missionlandscape.com

Mission Memorial Hospital
7324 Hurd St .... Mission BC V2V3H5 604-826-6261 826-9513 374-2
TF: 800-663-3333 ■ *Web:* www.fraserhealth.ca

Mission Mill Museum 1313 Mill St SE .... Salem OR 97301 503-585-7012 50-3
TF: 800-551-6949 ■ *Web:* willametteheritage.org

Mission of Nombre de Dios & Shrine of Our Lady of La Leche
27 Ocean Ave .... Saint Augustine FL 32084 904-824-2809 50-1
TF: 800-342-6529 ■ *Web:* www.missionandshrine.org

Mission Petroleum Carriers Inc
8450 Mosley .... Houston TX 77075 713-943-8250 468
TF: 800-737-9911 ■ *Web:* www.mipc.com

Mission Pharmacal PO Box 786099 .... San Antonio TX 78278 210-696-8400 696-6010 582
TF: 800-531-3333 ■ *Web:* missionpharmacal.com

Mission Pharmacy Services LLC
201 N Jefferson St Ste 300 .... Kittanning PA 16201 866-579-3181 237
TF: 877-758-2039 ■ *Web:* www.missionpharmacy.com

Mission Point Mackinac Island
1 Lakeshore Dr .... Mackinac Island MI 49757 231-331-3419 669
TF: 800-833-7711 ■ *Web:* www.missionpoint.com

Mission Pools of Escondido
755 W Grand Ave .... Escondido CA 92025 760-743-2605 728
Web: www.missionpools.com

Mission Produce Inc
2500 Vineyard Ave Ste 300 .... Oxnard CA 93036 805-981-3650 315-4
Web: www.worldsfinestavocados.com

Mission Regional Chamber of Commerce
34033 Lougheed Hwy .... Mission BC V2V5X8 604-826-6914 826-5916 137
Web: www.missionchamber.bc.ca

Mission Regional Medical Ctr
900 S Bryan Rd .... Mission TX 78572 956-323-9000 323-1360 374-3
Web: missionrmc.org

Mission Road Pharmacy Inc
1155 N Mission Rd .... Los Angeles CA 90033 323-227-4646 237

Mission Rubber Co 1660 Leeson .... Corona CA 92879 951-736-1343 677
Web: www.missionrubber.com

Mission San Fernando Rey De Espana
15151 San Fernando Mission Blvd .... Mission Hills CA 91345 818-361-0186 50-1
Web: missiontour.org

Mission San Jose 701 E Pyron Ave .... San Antonio TX 78214 210-922-0543 50-1
Web: www.nps.gov

Mission San Luis Apalachee
2100 W Tennessee St .... Tallahassee FL 32304 850-245-6406 488-6186 50-3
TF: 800-301-8009 ■ *Web:* www.missionsanluis.org

Mission San Luis Rey de Francia
4050 Mission Ave .... Oceanside CA 92057 760-757-3651 757-4613 50-1
TF: 800-356-3247 ■ *Web:* www.sanluisrey.org

Mission Search International Inc
2203 N Lois Ave Ste 1225 .... Tampa FL 33607 813-870-9500 870-9051 193
Web: www.missionsearch.com

Mission Springs Community Church of Fremont Inc
48989 Milmont Dr .... Fremont CA 94538 510-490-0446 48-20
Web: msccfremont.org

Mission Stucco Company Inc
7751 70th St .... Paramount CA 90723 562-634-1400 634-4440 500
TF: 800-678-0738 ■ *Web:* missionstucco.net

Mission Tejas State Park
120 State Pk Rd 44 .... Grapeland TX 75844 936-687-2394 565
Web: tpwd.texas.gov

Mission Trail Waste Systems
1060 Richard Ave .... Santa Clara CA 95050 408-727-5365 427
Web: www.missiontrail.com

Mission Valley Ford Truck Sales Inc
780 E Brokaw Rd .... San Jose CA 95112 408-933-2300 436-0313 57
TF: 888-284-7471 ■ *Web:* missionvalleykubota.com

Name / Address	City	State	ZIP	Phone	Fax	Class
Mission Ventures 9255 Towne Ctr Dr Ste 350 *Web:* www.missionventures.com	San Diego	CA	92121	858-350-2100		792
Mission Wealth Management LLC 1123 Chapala St 3rd Fl *TF:* 888-642-7221 ■ *Web:* www.missionwealthmanagement.com	Santa Barbara	CA	93101	805-882-2360		401
Mission, The 304 E Onondaga St *Web:* themissionrestaurant.com	Syracuse	NY	13202	315-475-7344		671
Mission1st Group Inc Princeton Forrestal Village 155 Village Blvd Ste 203 *Web:* www.mission1st.com	Princeton	NJ	08540	609-520-1900		463
Missionary Oblates 327 Oblate Dr *Web:* www.oblatemissions.com	San Antonio	TX	78216	210-349-1475		148
Mississauga Board of Trade 77 City Centre Dr Ste 701 *Web:* www.mbot.com	Mississauga	ON	L5B1M5	905-273-6151	273-4937	137
Mississinewa Lake 4673 S 625 E *Web:* www.in.gov	Peru	IN	46970	765-473-6528		565
Mississippi						
Administrative Office of the Courts 450 High St Gartin Justice Bldg PO Box 117 *Web:* courts.ms.gov	Jackson	MS	39205	601-576-4630	576-4639	339-25
Archives & History Dept 200 N St PO Box 571 *Web:* www.mdah.state.ms.us	Jackson	MS	39201	601-576-6850		339-25
Arts Commission 501 NW St Ste 1101-A *Web:* www.arts.state.ms.us	Jackson	MS	39201	601-359-6030	359-6008	339-25
Banking & Consumer Finance Dept PO Box 12129 *TF:* 800-844-2499 ■ *Web:* www.dbcf.state.ms.us	Jackson	MS	39236	601-321-6901	321-6933	339-25
Bill Status PO Box 2611 *Web:* billstatus.ls.state.ms.us	Jackson	MS	39215	601-359-2420		433
Child Support Enforcement Div 750 N State St *TF:* 877-882-4916 ■ *Web:* www.childsupporthq.com/mississippi-child-support-collection.html	Jackson	MS	39202	601-359-4861		339-25
Contractors Board 2679 Crane Ridge Dr Ste C *TF:* 800-880-6161 ■ *Web:* msboc.us	Jackson	MS	39216	601-354-6161	354-6715	339-25
Corrections Dept 633 N State St *Web:* www.mdoc.state.ms.us	Jackson	MS	39202	601-359-5600	359-5719	339-25
Development Authority 501 NW St *TF:* 800-360-3323 ■ *Web:* www.mississippi.org	Jackson	MS	39201	601-359-3449	359-2832	339-25
Education Dept 359 N West St Ste 270	Jackson	MS	39201	601-359-3513		339-25
Emergency Management Agency One Mema Dr PO Box 5644 *TF:* 800-222-6362 ■ *Web:* www.msema.org	Pearl	MS	39288	601-933-6362	933-6800	339-25
Employment Security Commission 1235 Echelon Pkwy PO Box 1699 *TF:* 888-844-3577 ■ *Web:* www.mdes.ms.gov	Jackson	MS	39215	601-321-6000	321-6004	259
Enviromental Quality Dept 515 E Amite St *TF:* 888-786-0661 ■ *Web:* www.deq.state.ms.us	Jackson	MS	39201	601-961-5611	961-5171	339-25
Ethics Commission 660 North St Ste 100-C *Web:* www.ethics.state.ms.us	Jackson	MS	39202	601-359-1285	359-1292	265
Family & Children Services Div 750 N State St *TF:* 800-345-6347	Jackson	MS	39202	601-359-4500		339-25
Finance & Administration Dept 501 NW St Ste 1301 Woolfolk Bldg *Web:* www.dfa.state.ms.us	Jackson	MS	39201	601-359-3402	359-2405	339-25
Governor PO Box 139 *Web:* www.governorbryant.ms.gov	Jackson	MS	39205	601-359-3150	359-3741	339-25
Health Dept PO Box 1700 *Web:* www.msdh.state.ms.us	Jackson	MS	39215	601-576-7400		339-25
Higher Learning Institutions Board of Trustees 3825 Ridgewood Rd *Web:* www.ihl.state.ms.us	Jackson	MS	39211	601-432-6198	432-6972	339-25
Historic Preservation Div PO Box 571 *Web:* www.mdah.ms.gov/new/preserve/state-historic-preservation-office	Jackson	MS	39205	601-576-6850	576-6955	339-25
Home Corp 735 Riverside Dr *Web:* www.mshomecorp.com	Jackson	MS	39202	601-718-4642	718-4643	339-25
Human Services Dept 750 N State St *Web:* www.mdhs.state.ms.us	Jackson	MS	39202	601-359-4500		339-25
Information Technology Services Dept 301 N Lamar St Ste 508 *Web:* www.its.ms.gov	Jackson	MS	39201	601-359-1395	354-6016	339-25
Insurance Dept 1001 Woolfolk State Office Bldg 501 NW St 501 N West St *TF:* 800-562-2957 ■ *Web:* www.mid.ms.gov	Jackson	MS	39201	601-359-3569		339-25
Legislature PO Box 1018 PO Box 1018 *Web:* billstatus.ls.state.ms.us	Jackson	MS	39215	601-359-3770	359-2775	339-25
Medical Licensure Board 1867 Crane Ridge Dr Ste 200-B *Web:* www.msbml.ms.gov	Jackson	MS	39216	601-987-3079	987-4159	339-25
Motor Vehicle Commission 1755 Lelia Dr Ste 200 *Web:* www.mmvc.state.ms.us	Jackson	MS	39236	601-987-3995	987-3997	339-25
Parole Board 660 N St Ste 100 A *Web:* www.mpb.state.ms.us	Jackson	MS	39202	601-576-3520	576-3528	339-25
Public Accountancy Board (MSBPA) 5 Old River Pl Ste 104 *Web:* www.msbpa.ms.gov	Jackson	MS	39202	601-354-7320	354-7290	339-25
Public Health Statistics Bureau 571 Stadium Dr PO Box 1700 *Web:* www.msdh.state.ms.us/phs	Jackson	MS	39215	601-206-8200	206-8272	339-25
Public Service Commission PO Box 1174 *Web:* www.psc.state.ms.us	Jackson	MS	39215	601-961-5434	961-5469	339-25
Real Estate Commission 4780 I-55 N LeFleur's Bluff Tower Ste 300 *Web:* www.mrec.state.ms.us	Jackson	MS	39211	601-321-6970	321-6955	339-25
Rehabilitation Services Dept 1281 Highway 51 PO Box 1698 *TF:* 800-443-1000 ■ *Web:* www.mdrs.ms.gov	Madison	MS	39110	800-443-1000		339-25
Securities Div 401 Mississippi St *Web:* www.sos.ms.gov	Jackson	MS	39201	601-359-1334	359-9070	339-25
State Government Information 200 S Lamar St Ste 800 *TF:* 877-290-9487 ■ *Web:* www.ms.gov	Jackson	MS	39201	601-351-5023		339-25
State Medical Examiner PO Box 958 *Web:* www.dps.state.ms.us	Jackson	MS	39205	601-987-1212		339-25
Supreme Court PO Box 117 *Web:* courts.ms.gov	Jackson	MS	39205	601-359-3694	359-2407	339-25
Treasury Dept 501 N West St Ste 1101	Jackson	MS	39205	601-359-3600		339-25
Veterans Affairs Board (MSVAB) PO Box 5947 *Web:* www.vab.ms.gov	Pearl	MS	39288	601-576-4850	576-4868	339-25
Weights & Measures Div 121 N Jefferson St *TF:* 800-551-1830	Jackson	MS	39201	601-359-1100	354-6290	339-25
Wildlife Fisheries & Parks Dept 1505 Eastover Dr *Web:* www.mdwfp.com	Jackson	MS	39211	601-432-2400		339-25
Worker's Compensation Commission 1428 Lakeland Dr *TF:* 866-473-6922 ■ *Web:* www.mwcc.state.ms.us	Jackson	MS	39216	601-987-4200		339-25
Mississippi Action For Progress Inc (MAP) 1751 Morson Rd *TF:* 800-924-4615 ■ *Web:* www.mapheadstart.org	Jackson	MS	39209	601-923-4100		147
Mississippi Agriculture & Forestry Museum/National Agricultural Aviation Museum 1150 Lakeland Dr *TF:* 800-844-8687 ■ *Web:* www.mdac.ms.gov	Jackson	MS	39216	601-359-1100	982-4292	520
Mississippi Arts Ctr 201 E Pascagoula St Ste 102 *Web:* www.arts.state.ms.us	Jackson	MS	39201	601-359-6030		50-2
Mississippi Assn of Realtors 4274 Lakeland Dr PO Box 321000 *TF:* 800-747-1103 ■ *Web:* www.msrealtors.org	Jackson	MS	39232	601-932-9325	932-0382	656
Mississippi Authority for Educational Television 3825 Ridgewood Rd *TF:* 800-850-4406 ■ *Web:* www.mpbonline.org	Jackson	MS	39211	601-432-6565	432-6311	632
Mississippi Bar 643 N State St *TF:* 800-682-6423 ■ *Web:* www.msbar.org	Jackson	MS	39202	601-948-4471	355-8635	72
Mississippi Blood Services 115 Tree St *TF:* 888-902-5663 ■ *Web:* www.msblood.com	Flowood	MS	39232	601-981-3232		89
Mississippi Business Journal 200 N Congress St *Web:* www.msbusiness.com	Jackson	MS	39201	601-364-1000	364-1007	457-5
Mississippi Coast Coliseum & Convention Ctr 2350 Beach Blvd *TF:* 800-726-2781 ■ *Web:* mscoastcoliseum.com	Biloxi	MS	39531	228-594-3700	594-3812	205
Mississippi College 200 S Capitol St *TF:* 800-738-1236 ■ *Web:* www.mc.edu	Clinton	MS	39056	601-925-3000		166
Mississippi College School of Law 151 E Griffith St *Web:* www.law.mc.edu	Jackson	MS	39201	601-925-7100		167-1
Mississippi County 200 W Walnut St Rm 204 *TF:* 800-455-5600 ■ *Web:* www.mcagov.com	Blytheville	AR	72315	870-763-3212	838-7784	338
Mississippi County 200 N Main St *TF:* 800-368-8683 ■ *Web:* www.misscomo.net	Charleston	MO	63834	573-683-2146	683-6071	338
Mississippi County Electric Co-op 510 N Broadway St *TF:* 800-439-4563 ■ *Web:* www.mceci.com	Blytheville	AR	72315	870-763-4563		245
Mississippi Delta Community College PO Box 668 *Web:* www.msdelta.edu	Moorhead	MS	38761	662-246-6322		162
Mississippi Dental Assn 439 B katherine Dr Ste C *TF:* 800-562-2957 ■ *Web:* www.msdental.org	Flowood	MS	39232	601-664-9691		227
Mississippi Dept of Archives & History (MDAH) 200 N St *Web:* mdah.state.ms.us	Jackson	MS	39201	601-576-6876	576-6964	520
Mississippi Economic Council PO Box 23276 *TF:* 800-748-7626 ■ *Web:* www.msmec.com	Jackson	MS	39225	601-969-0022	353-0247	140
Mississippi Export Railroad Co 4519 McInnis Ave *Web:* mserailroad.com	Moss Point	MS	39563	228-475-3322	475-3337	648
Mississippi Gulf Coast Chamber of Commerce 11975-E Seaway Rd *TF:* 800-726-2781 ■ *Web:* www.mscoastchamber.com	Gulfport	MS	39503	228-604-0014	604-0105	139
Mississippi Gulf Coast Community College 51 Main St PO Box 548 *Fax: Admitting ■ *TF:* 866-735-1122 ■ *Web:* www.mgccc.edu	Perkinston	MS	39573	601-928-5211	928-6345*	162
Jackson County 2300 Hwy 90 PO Box 100 *TF:* 866-735-1122 ■ *Web:* www.mgccc.edu	Gautier	MS	39553	228-497-9602		162
Jefferson Davis 2226 Switzer Rd *Fax: Admissions ■ *TF:* 866-735-1122 ■ *Web:* www.mgccc.edu	Gulfport	MS	39507	228-896-3355	896-2520*	162
Mississippi Gulf Coast Convention & Visitors Bureau 2350 Beach Blvd Ste A *TF:* 888-467-4853 ■ *Web:* www.gulfcoast.org	Biloxi	MS	39531	228-896-6699		206
Mississippi Lawyer Magazine 643 N State St *TF:* 800-682-6423 ■ *Web:* www.msbar.org	Jackson	MS	39202	601-948-4471	355-8635	457-15
Mississippi Lions Eye Bank 431 Katherine Dr *Web:* www.mslionseyebank.org	Flowood	MS	39232	601-420-5739		269
Mississippi Magazine 5 Lakeland Cir PO Box 16445 *Web:* www.mismag.com	Jackson	MS	39216	601-982-8418	982-8447	457-22
Mississippi Market Natural Foods Coop 1500 W Seventh St *Web:* www.msmarket.coop	Saint Paul	MN	55102	651-690-0507		345
Mississippi Museum of Art 380 S Lamar St *TF:* 866-843-9278 ■ *Web:* www.msmuseumart.org	Jackson	MS	39201	601-960-1515	960-1505	520
Mississippi Museum of Natural Science 2148 Riverside Dr *TF:* 800-467-2757 ■ *Web:* www.mdwfp.com	Jackson	MS	39202	601-576-6000	354-7227	520
Mississippi Music Inc 222 N Main St *TF:* 800-844-5821 ■ *Web:* mississippimusic.net	Hattiesburg	MS	39401	800-844-5821		525

	Phone	Fax	Class
Mississippi National River & Recreation Area 111 E Kellogg Blvd Ste 105 Saint Paul MN 55101 *Web:* www.nps.gov/miss	651-290-4160	290-3214	564
Mississippi Nurses Assn (MNA) 31 Woodgreen Pl Madison MS 39110 *Web:* www.msnurses.org	601-898-0670	898-0190	533
Mississippi Opera PO Box 1551 Jackson MS 39215 *TF:* 800-305-7414 ■ *Web:* www.msopera.org	601-960-2300		573-2
Mississippi Palisades State Park 16327A IL Rt 84 Savanna IL 61074 *Web:* www.dnr.illinois.gov/Parks/Pages/MississippiPalisades.aspx	815-273-2731		565
Mississippi Petrified Forest 124 Forest Pk Rd Flora MS 39071 *Web:* www.mspetrifiedforest.com	601-879-8189		50-5
Mississippi Pharmacists Assn 341 Edgewood Terr Dr Jackson MS 39206 *TF:* 800-421-2408 ■ *Web:* www.mspharm.org	601-981-0416	981-0451	585
Mississippi Polymers Inc 2733 S Harper Rd Corinth MS 38834 *Web:* www.mississippipolymers.com	662-287-1401		600
Mississippi Prison Industries Corp 663 N State St Jackson MS 39202 *Web:* www.mpic.net	601-969-5750	969-5757	630
Mississippi Public Broadcasting 3825 Ridgewood Rd Jackson MS 39211 *Web:* www.mpbonline.org	601-432-6565		645-78
Mississippi Republican Party 415 Yazoo St PO Box 60 Jackson MS 39201 *Web:* www.msgop.org	601-948-5191	354-0972	616-2
Mississippi River Corp 30 Majorca Rd Natchez MS 39120 *Web:* www.msriver.com	601-445-0100		638
Mississippi River Museum 125 N Front St Memphis TN 38103 *TF:* 800-507-6507 ■ *Web:* www.mudisland.com	901-576-7241	576-6666	520
Mississippi River State Fish & Wildlife Area 17836 State Hwy 100 N Grafton IL 62037 *Web:* www.dnr.illinois.gov	618-376-3303		565
Mississippi Sports Hall of Fame & Museum 1152 Lakeland Dr Jackson MS 39216 *TF:* 800-280-3263 ■ *Web:* www.msfame.com	601-982-8264		522
Mississippi State Hospital PO Box 157A Whitfield MS 39193 *Web:* www.msh.state.ms.us	601-351-8000		374-5
Mississippi State Port Authority at Gulfport 2510 14th St Ste 1450 Gulfport MS 39501 *TF:* 877-881-4367 ■ *Web:* www.shipmspa.com	228-865-4300	865-4335	618
Mississippi State University PO Box 6305 Mississippi State MS 39762 *Fax: Admissions ■ *Web:* www.msstate.edu	662-325-2224	325-7360*	166
Mississippi State Veterans Affairs Board 310 Autumn Ridge Dr Kosciusko MS 39090	662-289-7809	289-7824	793
Mississippi State Veterans Home 120 Veterans Dr Oxford MS 38655 *Web:* caremississippi.org	662-236-7641		793
Mississippi State Veterans' Home Collins 3261 Hwy 49 S Collins MS 39428 *TF:* 877-203-5632 ■ *Web:* www.vab.ms.gov	601-765-0403		793
Mississippi Symphony Orchestra 201 E Pascagoula St Jackson MS 39201 *TF:* 800-305-7414 ■ *Web:* www.msorchestra.com	601-960-1565	960-1564	573-3
Mississippi Tank & Manufacturing Co 3000 W Seventh St Hattiesburg MS 39403 *Web:* www.mstank.com	601-264-1800	264-0769	91
Mississippi University for Women 1100 College St MUW-1613 Columbus MS 39701 *Fax: Admissions ■ *TF:* 877-462-8439 ■ *Web:* web3.muw.edu	662-329-4750	241-7481*	166
Mississippi Valley Equipment Company Inc 1198 Pershall Rd Saint Louis MO 63137 *TF:* 800-325-8001 ■ *Web:* www.mve-stl.com	314-869-8600	869-6862	358
Mississippi Valley Regional Blood Ctr 5500 Lakeview Pkwy Davenport IA 52807 *TF:* 800-747-5401 ■ *Web:* www.bloodcenter.org	563-359-5401	359-8603	89
Mississippi Valley State University 14000 Hwy 82 Itta Bena MS 38941 *TF:* 800-844-6885 ■ *Web:* www.mvsu.edu	662-254-9041	254-3759	166
Mississippi Valley Title Services Company 1022 Highland Colony Pkwy Ste 200 Ridgeland MS 39157 *TF:* 800-647-2124 ■ *Web:* www.mvt.com	601-969-0222	969-2215	391-6
Mississippi Veterans Memorial Stadium 2531 N State St Jackson MS 39216 *TF:* 800-745-3000 ■ *Web:* www.ms-veteransstadium.com	601-354-6021	354-6019	720
Mississippi Welders Supply Co 5150 W Sixth St Winona MN 55987 *TF:* 800-657-4422 ■ *Web:* www.mwsco.com	507-454-5231		386
Missman Inc 1011 27th Ave PO Box 6040 Rock Island IL 61201 *TF:* 800-969-3029 ■ *Web:* missman.com	309-788-7644	788-7691	261
Missoula Area Chamber of Commerce 825 E Front St Missoula MT 59802 *Web:* www.missoulachamber.com	406-543-6623		139
Missoula County 200 W Broadway St Missoula MT 59802 *Web:* www.missoulacounty.us	406-721-5700	258-4899	338
Missoula Electric Co-op Inc 1700 W Broadway Missoula MT 59808 *TF:* 800-352-5200 ■ *Web:* www.missoulaelectric.com	406-541-4433	541-6318	245
Missoula Federal Credit Union 3600 Brooks St Missoula MT 59801 *Web:* missoulafcu.org	406-523-3300		219
Missoula Independent 317 S Orange St Missoula MT 59801 *Web:* missoulanews.bigskypress.com	406-543-6609	543-4367	532-5
Missoula Public Library 301 E Main St Missoula MT 59802 *Web:* www.missoula.lib.mt.us	406-721-2665	728-5900	434-3
Missoulian PO Box 8029 Missoula MT 59807 *TF:* 800-366-7102 ■ *Web:* www.missoulian.com	406-523-5200	523-5294	532-2
Missouri			
Agriculture Dept 1616 Missouri Blvd PO Box 630 Jefferson City MO 65102 *Web:* mda.mo.gov	573-751-4211	751-1784	339-26
Arts Council 815 Olive St Ste 16 Saint Louis MO 63101 *Web:* www.missouriartscouncil.org	314-340-6845	340-7215	339-26
Attorney General 207 W High St PO Box 899 Jefferson City MO 65102 *TF:* 800-392-8222 ■ *Web:* www.ago.mo.gov	573-751-3321	751-0774	339-26
Child Support Enforcement Div 205 Jefferson St Fl 10 Jefferson City MO 65103 *TF:* 800-859-7999 ■ *Web:* www.dss.mo.gov/cse	573-522-8024		339-26
Conservation Dept 2901 W Truman Blvd Jefferson City MO 65109 *Web:* www.mdc.mo.gov	573-751-4115	751-4467	339-26
Consumer Protection Div 207 W High St PO Box 899 Jefferson City MO 65102 *TF:* 800-392-8222 ■ *Web:* www.ago.mo.gov/about-us/contact-us	573-751-3321	751-0774	339-26
Corrections Dept PO Box 236 Jefferson City MO 65102 *Web:* www.doc.mo.gov	573-522-1118		339-26
Crime Victims' Compensation Unit PO Box 1589 Jefferson City MO 65102 *Web:* www.dps.mo.gov	573-526-6006		339-26
Economic Development Dept 301 W High St Jefferson City MO 65102 *Web:* www.ded.mo.gov/Ded	573-522-4173	522-9462	339-26
Elementary & Secondary Education Dept 205 Jefferson St PO Box 480 Jefferson City MO 65101 *Web:* www.dese.mo.gov	573-751-4212		339-26
Emergency Management Agency 2302 Militia Dr PO Box 116 Jefferson City MO 65102 *Web:* www.sema.dps.mo.gov	573-526-9100	634-7966	339-26
Family Services Div PO Box 2320 Jefferson City MO 65102 *Web:* www.dss.mo.gov/fsd	573-751-3221		339-26
Finance Div Truman State Office Bldg Rm 630 Jefferson City MO 65102 *TF:* 888-246-7225 ■ *Web:* www.finance.mo.gov	573-751-3242	751-9192	339-26
General Assembly State Capitol Jefferson City MO 65101 *Web:* www.moga.mo.gov	573-751-4633		339-26
Governor 201 W Capitol Ave, Rm 216 PO Box 720 Jefferson City MO 65102 *Web:* www.governor.mo.gov	573-751-3222		339-26
Healing Arts Board 3605 Missouri Blvd PO Box 4 Jefferson City MO 65102 *Web:* www.pr.mo.gov	573-751-0098	751-3166	339-26
Health & Senior Services Dept 912 Wildwood PO Box 570 Jefferson City MO 65102 *Web:* www.health.mo.gov	573-751-6400	751-6010	339-26
Higher Education Dept 205 Jefferson St Jefferson City MO 65109 *TF:* 800-473-6757 ■ *Web:* www.dhe.mo.gov	573-751-2361	751-6635	339-26
Historical Preservation Office 1101 Riverside Dr Jefferson City MO 65101 *TF:* 800-361-4827 ■ *Web:* www.dnr.mo.gov	573-751-3443	522-6262	339-26
Housing Development Commission 3435 Broadway Kansas City MO 64105 *Web:* www.mhdc.com	816-759-6600		339-26
Insurance Dept 301 W High St Rm 530 Jefferson City MO 65101 *TF:* 800-726-7390 ■ *Web:* insurance.mo.gov	573-751-4126	751-1165	339-26
Labor & Industrial Relations Dept 3315 W Truman Blvd Rm 214 PO Box 599 Jefferson City MO 65102 *Web:* www.labor.mo.gov/lirc	573-751-2461	751-7806	339-26
Lieutenant Governor State Capitol Bldg Rm 224 Jefferson City MO 65101 *Web:* ltgov.mo.gov	573-751-4727	751-9422	339-26
Lottery 1823 Southridge Dr PO Box 1603 Jefferson City MO 65109 *TF:* 888-238-7633 ■ *Web:* www.molottery.com	573-751-4050	751-5188	452
Motor Vehicles & Drivers Licensing Div 301 W High St Jefferson City MO 65106 *Web:* dor.mo.gov	573-751-3505	751-2195	339-26
Natural Resources Dept 1101 Riverside Dr Jefferson City MO 65102 *TF Cust Svc:* 800-361-4827 ■ *Web:* www.dnr.mo.gov	573-751-3443		339-26
Professional Registration Div 3605 Missouri Blvd PO Box 1335 Jefferson City MO 65102 *TF:* 800-735-2466 ■ *Web:* www.pr.mo.gov	573-751-0293		339-26
Public Service Commission 200 Madison St PO Box 360 Jefferson City MO 65102 *TF:* 800-819-3180 ■ *Web:* www.psc.mo.gov	573-751-3234		339-26
Real Estate Commission 3605 Missouri Blvd PO Box 1339 Jefferson City MO 65102 *TF:* 800-735-2466 ■ *Web:* www.pr.mo.gov/realestate.asp	573-751-2628	751-2777	339-26
Revenue Dept 301 W High St Jefferson City MO 65101 *Web:* dor.mo.gov	573-526-3669		339-26
Secretary of State PO Box 778 Jefferson City MO 65102 *Web:* www.sos.mo.gov	573-751-4936		339-26
Securities Div 600 W Main St Rm 229 PO Box 1276 Jefferson City MO 65102 *TF:* 800-721-7996 ■ *Web:* s1.sos.mo.gov	573-751-4136		339-26
Social Services Dept Broadway State Office Bldg Jefferson City MO 65102 *Web:* www.dss.mo.gov	573-751-4815	751-3203	339-26
State Courts Administrator 2112 Industrial Dr Jefferson City MO 65110 *TF:* 888-541-4894 ■ *Web:* www.courts.mo.gov	888-541-4894		339-26
State Highway Patrol 1510 E Elm St Jefferson City MO 65101 *Web:* www.mshp.dps.missouri.gov	573-751-3313	751-9419	339-26
State Parks Div PO Box 176 Jefferson City MO 65102 *TF:* 800-334-6946 ■ *Web:* www.mostateparks.com	573-751-2479		339-26
Supreme Court 207 W High St Jefferson City MO 65101 *TF:* 888-541-4894 ■ *Web:* www.courts.mo.gov/page.jsp?id=27	573-751-4144		339-26
Tourism Div PO Box 1055 Jefferson City MO 65102 *TF:* 800-519-2100 ■ *Web:* www.visitmo.com	573-751-4133	751-5160	339-26
Transportation Dept 105 W Capitol Ave PO Box 270 Jefferson City MO 65102 *TF:* 888-275-6636 ■ *Web:* www.modot.org	573-751-2551	751-6555	339-26
Treasurer PO Box 210 Jefferson City MO 65102 *Web:* www.treasurer.mo.gov	573-751-8533	751-0343	339-26

Phone | Fax | Class

Veterans Commission
205 Jefferson St Fl 12 ... Jefferson City MO 65102 573-751-3779 339-26
TF: 866-838-4636 ■ *Web:* mvc.dps.mo.gov

Vital Records Bureau
930 Wildwood PO Box 570 ... Jefferson City MO 65102 573-751-6387 339-26
Web: www.sos.mo.gov

Vocational & Adult Education Div
3024 Dupont Cir PO Box 480 ... Jefferson City MO 65109 573-751-3251 751-1441 339-26
TF: 877-222-8963 ■ *Web:* dese.mo.gov/college-career-readiness

Weights & Measures Div
1616 Missouri Blvd PO Box 630 ... Jefferson City MO 65102 573-751-4316 339-26
Web: agriculture.mo.gov/weights

Workers Compensation Div
PO Box 58 ... Jefferson City MO 65102 573-751-4231 751-2012 339-26
TF: 800-775-2667 ■ *Web:* www.labor.mo.gov/DWC

Missouri Afl-cio
227 Jefferson St ... Jefferson City MO 65101 573-634-2115 414
TF: 800-486-1223 ■ *Web:* moaflcio.org

Missouri Assn of Realtors
2601 Bernadette Pl ... Columbia MO 65203 573-445-8400 445-7865 656
TF: 800-403-0101 ■ *Web:* www.missourirealtor.org

Missouri Athletic Club
405 Washington Ave ... Saint Louis MO 63102 314-231-7220 354
Web: www.mac-stl.org

Missouri Bank & Trust Co
1044 Main St ... Kansas City MO 64105 816-881-8200 70
Web: www.mobank.com

Missouri Baptist Hospital of Sullivan
751 Sappington Bridge Rd ... Sullivan MO 63080 573-468-4186 860-2696 374-3
TF: 800-939-2273 ■ *Web:* www.missouribaptistsullivan.org

Missouri Baptist Medical Ctr
3015 N Ballas Rd ... Saint Louis MO 63131 314-996-5000 374-3
TF: 800-392-0936 ■ *Web:* www.missouribaptist.org

Missouri Baptist University
1 College Pk Dr ... Saint Louis MO 63141 314-434-1115 434-7596 166
TF: 877-434-1115 ■ *Web:* www.mobap.edu

Troy/Wentzville Extension
75 College Campus Dr ... Moscow Mills MO 63362 636-366-4363 356-4119* 166
**Fax:* Admissions ■ *Web:* www.mobap.edu

Missouri Bar, The
326 Monroe St PO Box 119 ... Jefferson City MO 65102 573-635-4128 635-2811 72
TF: 888-253-6013 ■ *Web:* www.mobar.org

Missouri Botanical Garden
4344 Shaw Blvd ... Saint Louis MO 63110 314-577-5100 97
TF: 800-642-8842 ■ *Web:* www.missouribotanicalgarden.org

Missouri Chamber of Commerce
428 E Capitol Ave PO Box 149 ... Jefferson City MO 65102 573-634-3511 634-8855 140
TF: 800-956-2682 ■ *Web:* www.mochamber.com

Missouri Delta Medical Ctr
1019 N Main St ... Sikeston MO 63801 573-471-1600 374-3
Web: www.missouridelta.com

Missouri Democratic Party
300 St James St Ste 104 ... Columbia MO 65201 573-636-5241 634-8176 616-1
Web: missouridemocrats.org

Missouri Dental Assn
3340 American Ave ... Jefferson City MO 65109 573-634-3436 635-0764 227
TF: 800-688-1907 ■ *Web:* www.modental.org

Missouri Department of Corrections Medical Services Section
Division of Offender Rehabilitative Services
PO Box 236 ... Jefferson City MO 65102 573-751-6663 751-9197 630
TF Sales: 800-392-8486 ■ *Web:* www.doc.mo.gov

Missouri Eastern Correctional Ctr
18701 Old Hwy 66 ... Pacific MO 63069 636-257-3322 257-5296 213
TF: 800-735-2966 ■ *Web:* mo.gov

Missouri Enterprise
900 Innovation Dr Ste 300 ... Rolla MO 65401 800-956-2682 195
TF: 800-956-2682 ■ *Web:* www.missourienterprise.org

Missouri Fox Trotting Horse Breed Assn Inc
PO Box 1027 ... Ava MO 65608 417-683-2468 683-6144 48-3
Web: www.mfthba.com

Missouri Gas Energy 3420 Broadway ... Kansas City MO 64111 816-756-5252 787
TF: 800-582-1234 ■ *Web:* www.missourigasenergy.com

Missouri Headwaters State Park
1585 Trident Rd ... Three Forks MT 59752 406-994-4042 565
Web: www.stateparks.mt.gov

Missouri History Museum
5700 Lindell Blvd PO Box 11940 ... Saint Louis MO 63112 314-746-4599 454-3162 520
TF: 800-610-2094 ■ *Web:* www.mohistory.org

Missouri Home Therapy
11636 W Florissant Ave ... Saint Louis MO 63033 314-246-0137 726
Web: www.missourihometherapy.com

Missouri Lawyers Media
319 N Fourth St ... Saint Louis MO 63102 314-421-1880 421-0436 637-8
TF: 800-635-5297 ■ *Web:* www.molawyersmedia.com

Missouri Medicine Magazine
PO Box 1028 ... Jefferson City MO 65102 573-636-5151 636-8552 457-16
TF: 800-869-6762 ■ *Web:* www.msma.org

Missouri Metals LLC
9970 Page Boulvard ... St. Louis MO 63132 314-222-7100 697
Web: www.missourimetals.com

Missouri Mines State Historic Site
4000 Missouri 32 ... Park Hills MO 63601 573-431-6226 565
Web: www.mostateparks.com

Missouri Municipal League
1727 Southridge Dr ... Jefferson City MO 65109 573-635-9134 533
Web: www.mocities.com

Missouri National Recreational River
508 E Second St ... Yankton SD 57078 605-665-0209 665-4183 564
Web: www.nps.gov/mnrr

Missouri Nurses Assn (MONA)
1904 Bubba Ln PO Box 105228 ... Jefferson City MO 65110 573-636-4623 636-9576 533
Web: www.missourinurses.org

Missouri Office Systems & Supplies
941 W 141st Terr Ste B ... Kansas City MO 64145 816-761-5152 292

Missouri Pharmacy Assn
211 E Capitol Ave ... Jefferson City MO 65101 573-636-7522 636-7485 585
TF: 800-468-4672 ■ *Web:* www.morx.com

Missouri Protection & Advocacy Services
925 S Country Club Dr Ste 3 ... Jefferson City MO 65109 573-893-3333 41
Web: www.moadvocacy.org

Missouri Refractories Company Inc
1198 Mason Cir ... Pevely MO 63070 636-479-7770 751
Web: www.refractories.net

Missouri Rehabilitation Ctr
600 N Main St ... Mount Vernon MO 65712 417-466-3711 374-6
Web: www.muhealth.org

Missouri River Regional Library
214 Adams St ... Jefferson City MO 65101 573-634-2464 634-7028 434-3
TF: 800-949-7323 ■ *Web:* www.mrrl.org

Missouri School Boards Assn
2100 I-70 Dr SW ... Columbia MO 65203 573-445-9920 685
TF: 800-221-6722 ■ *Web:* www.msbanet.org

Missouri Slope Lutheran Care Center Foundation
2425 Hillview Ave ... Bismarck ND 58501 701-223-9407 48-20
Web: www.mslcc.com

Missouri Southern State University
3950 Newman Rd ... Joplin MO 64801 417-625-9300 659-4429 166
TF: 866-818-6778 ■ *Web:* www.mssu.edu

Missouri Sports Hall of Fame
3861 E Stan Musial Dr ... Springfield MO 65809 417-889-3100 889-2761 522
TF: 800-498-5678 ■ *Web:* www.mosportshalloffame.com

Missouri State Employees' Retirement System
907 Wildwood Dr ... Jefferson City MO 65109 573-632-6100 528
TF: 800-827-1063 ■ *Web:* www.mosers.org

Missouri State Library
600 W Main St ... Jefferson City MO 65101 573-751-3615 526-1142 434-5
Web: www.sos.mo.gov/library

Missouri State Medical Assn
113 Madison St ... Jefferson City MO 65101 573-636-5151 636-8552 474
TF: 800-869-6762 ■ *Web:* www.msma.org

Missouri State Museum
201 W Capitol ... Jefferson City MO 65101 573-751-2854 520
TF: 800-927-7294 ■ *Web:* mostateparks.com

Missouri State Teachers Assn
407 S Sixth St ... Columbia MO 65201 573-442-3127 443-5079 457-8
TF General: 800-392-0532 ■ *Web:* msta.org

Missouri State University (MSU)
901 S National Ave ... Springfield MO 65897 417-836-5000 836-6334 166
TF: 800-492-7900 ■ *Web:* www.missouristate.edu

Missouri Theatre 203 S Ninth St ... Columbia MO 65211 573-882-3781 572
Web: concertseries.missouri.edu

Missouri Tie LLC 8324 Highway 72 ... Bunker MO 63629 573-689-2040 683
Web: www.missouritie.com

Missouri University of Science & Technology
Rolla 1870 Miner Cir ... Rolla MO 65409 573-341-4111 341-4082* 166
**Fax:* Admissions ■ *TF:* 800-522-0938 ■ *Web:* www.mst.edu

Missouri Valley College
500 E College St ... Marshall MO 65340 660-831-4000 831-4233* 166
**Fax:* Admissions ■ *TF:* 800-999-8219 ■ *Web:* www.moval.edu

Missouri Valley Times-enterprise Inc
501 E Erie St ... Missouri Valley IA 51555 712-642-2791 532-3
Web: www.dcpostgazette.com

Missouri Veterans Home-Cape Girardeau
2400 Veterans Memorial Dr ... Cape Girardeau MO 63701 573-290-5870 290-5909 793
TF: 800-392-0210 ■ *Web:* www.mo.gov

Missouri Veterans Home-Mount Vernon
1600 S Hickory ... Mount Vernon MO 65712 417-466-7103 466-4040 793
TF: 800-735-2966 ■ *Web:* mvc.dps.mo.gov

Missouri Veterans Home-Saint James
620 N Jefferson St ... Saint James MO 65559 573-265-3271 793

Missouri Veterans Home-Saint Louis
10600 Lewis & Clark Blvd ... Saint Louis MO 63136 314-340-6389 340-6379 793
Web: mvc.dps.mo.gov

Missouri Veterinary Medical Assn
2500 Country Club Dr ... Jefferson City MO 65109 573-636-8612 659-7175 795
TF: 800-632-6900 ■ *Web:* movma.org

Missouri Western State University
4525 Downs Dr ... Saint Joseph MO 64507 816-271-4266 271-5833 166
TF: 800-662-7041 ■ *Web:* www.missouriwestern.edu

Missourian Publishing Co
14 W Main St ... Washington MO 63090 636-239-7701 239-0915 637-8
TF: 888-239-7701 ■ *Web:* www.emissourian.com

Mist Mobility Integrated Systems Technology Inc
3 Iber Rd ... Ottawa ON K2S1E6 613-723-0403 723-8925 21
Web: www.mmist.ca

Mister Car Wash 3101 E Speedway Blvd ... Tucson AZ 85716 520-615-4000 62-1
TF Cust Svc: 866-254-3229 ■ *Web:* www.mistercarwash.com

Mister Kleen Maintenance Company Inc
7302 Beulah St ... Alexandria VA 22315 703-719-6900 104
TF: 800-273-7991 ■ *Web:* www.misterkleen.com

Mister Money Investment
2057 Vermont Dr ... Fort Collins CO 80525 800-290-4598 490-2099* 141
**Fax Area Code:* 970 ■ *TF:* 888-336-0403 ■ *Web:* ww2.firstcash.com

Mister Safety Shoes Inc
6-2300 Finch Ave W ... Toronto ON M9M2Y3 416-746-3000 358
TF: 800-707-0051 ■ *Web:* www.mistersafetyshoes.com

Mistletoe State Park
3723 Mistletoe Rd ... Appling GA 30802 706-541-0321 565
Web: www.gastateparks.org

Mistral 223 Columbus Ave ... Boston MA 02116 617-867-9300 351-2601 671
Web: www.mistralbistro.com

Mistral Gagnant 160 St-Paul ... Quebec QC G1K3W1 418-692-4260 671
Web: mistralgagnant.ca

Misty Harbor & Barefoot Beach Resort
118 Weirs Rd ... Gilford NH 03249 603-293-4500 379
TF: 800-336-4789 ■ *Web:* www.mistyharbor.com

Misty's Steakhouse & Brewery
200 N 11th St ... Lincoln NE 68508 402-476-7766 671
Web: www.mistyslincoln.com

Misys International Banking Systems Inc
1180 Ave ... New York NY 10036 212-898-9500 177
Web: www.misys.com

MIT Holding Inc
37 W Fairmont Ave Ste 202 ... Savannah GA 31406 912-925-1905 582

Phone | Fax | Class

MIT International
77 Massachusetts Ave Cambridge TX 02139 617-253-1000 283-1190* 389
**Fax Area Code:* 480 ■ *TF General:* 800-228-9290 ■ *Web:* web.mit.edu

MIT Media Laboratory
Massachusetts Institute of Technology
77 Massachusetts Ave Cambridge MA 02139 617-253-5960 258-6264 668
Web: www.media.mit.edu

MIT Museum 265 Massachusetts Ave Cambridge MA 02139 617-253-4444 253-8994 520
TF: 800-228-9000 ■ *Web:* www.web.mit.edu

MIT Press, The 1 Rogers St Cambridge MA 02142 617-253-5646 253-1709 637-4
TF: 800-405-1619 ■ *Web:* www.mitpress.mit.edu

Mit Professionals Inc 523 Lovett Blvd Houston TX 77006 713-934-9700 196
Web: www.mitprof.com

MiTAC Digital Corp
471 El Camino Real Santa Clara CA 95050 408-615-5100 647
Web: www.magellangps.com

Mitcham Industries Inc (MII)
8141 Hwy 75 S PO Box 1175 Huntsville TX 77340 936-291-2277 295-1922* 264-3
NASDAQ: MIND ■ **Fax:* Sales ■ *Web:* www.mitchamindustries.com

Mitchco International Inc
4801 Sherburn Ln Louisville KY 40207 502-896-9653 896-2989 670
Web: www.mitchcointernational.com

Mitchel & Scott Machine Co
1841 Ludlow Ave Indianapolis IN 46201 317-639-5331 621
Web: www.mitsco.com

Mitchell & Resnikoff
8003 Old York Rd Elkins Park PA 19027 215-635-1000 7

Mitchell & Titus LLP
1 Battery Pk Plaza 27th Fl New York NY 10004 212-709-4500 709-4680 401
Web: www.mitchelltitus.com

Mitchell 1 14145 Danielson St Poway CA 92064 858-391-5000 746-8915* 637-11
**Fax:* Sales ■ *TF:* 888-724-6742 ■ *Web:* www.mitchell1.com

Mitchell Aircraft 1160 Alexander Ct Cary IL 60013 847-516-3773 770
Web: www.mitchellair.com

Mitchell and McCormick Inc
2165 W Park Ct Ste G Stone Mountain GA 30087 770-465-1511 180
Web: www.mandm.net

Mitchell Bank 1039 W Mitchell St Milwaukee WI 53204 414-645-0600 70
Web: www.mitchellbank.com

Mitchell Block, The 173 McDermot Ave Winnipeg MB R3B0S1 204-949-9032 671
Web: www.trevisirestaurant.com

Mitchell College 437 Pequot Ave New London CT 06320 860-701-5000 444-1209* 166
**Fax:* Admissions ■ *TF Admitting:* 800-443-2811 ■ *Web:* www.mitchell.edu

Mitchell Community College
500 W Broad St Statesville NC 28677 704-878-3200 878-0872 162
Web: www.mitchellcc.edu

Mitchell Company Inc, The
41 W I-65 Service Rd N Mobile AL 36608 251-380-2929 345-1264 653
Web: www.mitchellcompany.com

Mitchell County
26 Crimson Laurel Cir # 5 Bakersville NC 28705 828-688-2139 688-4443 338
TF: 800-222-1222 ■ *Web:* www.mitchellcounty.org

Mitchell County PO Box 190 Beloit KS 67420 785-738-3652 738-5524 338
Web: www.mcks.org

Mitchell County 26 N Ct St PO Box 187 Camilla GA 31730 229-336-2000 336-2003 338
TF: 800-427-2457 ■ *Web:* www.mitchellcountyga.net

Mitchell County Clerk of Court
508 State St Osage IA 50461 641-732-3726 338

Mitchell County Hospital Health Systems
400 W Eighth St P O Box 399 Beloit KS 67420 785-738-9590 363
Web: www.mchks.com

Mitchell Electric Membership Corp
475 Cairo Rd Camilla GA 31730 229-336-5221 336-7088 245
TF: 800-479-6034 ■ *Web:* www.mitchellemc.com

Mitchell Elementary School
14429 Condon Ave Lawndale CA 90260 310-676-6140 685
Web: www.lawndale.k12.ca.us

Mitchell Fuel Company Inc
1209 Sullivan Ave South Windsor CT 06074 860-644-2561 316
TF: 800-336-3762 ■ *Web:* www.mitchellfuel.com

Mitchell Furniture Systems Inc
1700 W St Paul Ave Milwaukee WI 53233 414-342-3111 319-3
TF: 800-290-5960 ■ *Web:* www.mitchell-tables.com

Mitchell Gallery of Flight
5300 S Howell Ave
General Mitchell International Airport Milwaukee WI 53207 414-747-5300 747-4525 520
Web: www.mitchellgallery.org

Mitchell Gold & Bob Williams Co (MGBW)
135 One Comfortable Pl Taylorsville NC 28681 828-632-9200 632-2693 319-2
TF: 800-789-5401 ■ *Web:* www.mgbwhome.com

Mitchell Golf Equipment Co
954 Senate Dr Dayton OH 45459 937-436-1314 711
TF: 800-437-1314 ■ *Web:* www.mitchellgolf.com

Mitchell Group The Consltnt
1816 11th St NW Washington DC 20001 202-745-1919 195
Web: www.the-mitchellgroup.com

Mitchell Industrial Tire Co
2915 Eigth Ave PO Box 71839 Chattanooga TN 37407 423-698-4442 697-7143* 754
**Fax:* Sales ■ *TF:* 800-251-7226 ■ *Web:* www.mitco.com

Mitchell International Inc
6220 Greenwich Dr San Diego CA 92122 858-368-7000 637-11
TF: 800-854-7030 ■ *Web:* www.mitchell.com

Mitchell Martin Inc
307 W 38th St Ste 1305 New York NY 10018 212-943-1404 355-0229* 631
**Fax Area Code:* 646 ■ *Web:* www.mitchellmartin.com

Mitchell Metal Products Inc
19250 Hwy 12 E PO Box 789 Kosciusko MS 39090 662-289-7110 289-7112 697
TF: 800-258-6137 ■ *Web:* www.mitchellmetal.net

Mitchell Paul (Rep R - MI)
211 Cannon HOB Washington DC 20515 202-225-2106 342-2
Web: mitchell.house.gov

Mitchell Plumbing & Heating Company Inc
801 N Rowley St 1328 Mitchell SD 57301 605-996-7583 189-10

Mitchell Rubber Products Inc
10220 San Sevaine Way Mira Loma CA 91752 800-453-7526 676
TF: 800-453-7526 ■ *Web:* www.mitchellrubber.com

Mitchell Selling Dynamics
1360 Puritan Ave Birmingham MI 48009 248-644-8092 463
TF: 800-328-9696 ■ *Web:* www.mitchellsell.com

Mitchell Supreme Fuel Co
532 Freeman St Orange NJ 07050 973-678-1800 672-0148 316
TF: 800-832-7090 ■ *Web:* www.supremeenergyinc.com

Mitchell Technical Institute
821 N Capital St Mitchell SD 57301 800-684-1969 995-3083* 162
**Fax Area Code:* 605 ■ *TF:* 800-684-1969 ■ *Web:* www.mitchelltech.edu

Mitchell Williams Selig Gates & Woodyard Pllc
425 W Capitol Ave Ste 1800 Little Rock AR 72201 501-688-8800 688-8807 428
Web: mitchellwilliamslaw.com

Mitchell's Fish Market
1245 Olentangy River Rd Columbus OH 43212 614-291-3474 671
Web: www.mitchellsfishmarket.com

Mitchell's Ocean Club
4002 Easton Stn Columbus OH 43219 614-416-2582 416-2800 671
Web: www.ocean-prime.com

Mitchell's Steakhouse 45 N Third St Columbus OH 43215 614-621-2333 671
Web: www.mitchellssteakhouse.com

Mitchell-Iness & Nash Gallery
1018 Madison Ave New York NY 10075 212-744-7400 744-7401 42
Web: www.miandn.com

Mitchells Family of Stores
270 Main St Huntington NY 11743 631-423-1660 157-3
Web: mitchellstores.com

Mitchells Salon & Day Spa
5901 E Galbraith Rd Cincinnati OH 45236 513-793-0900 77
Web: www.mitchellssalon.com

Mitchell-wayne Technologies
2901 Third Ave N Birmingham AL 35203 205-313-7500 180
Web: www.mitchellwaynetech.com

Mitee-bite Products Inc
PO Box 430 Center Ossipee NH 03814 603-539-4538 454
TF: 800-543-3580 ■ *Web:* www.miteebite.com

MiTek Canada Inc 100 Industrial Rd Bradford ON L3Z3G7 905-952-2900 952-2901 491
Web: www.mitek.ca

MiTek Industries Inc
14515 N Outer 40 Rd Ste 300 Chesterfield MO 63017 314-434-1200 434-5343 91
TF: 800-325-8075 ■ *Web:* mii.com

Mitek Systems Inc 600 B St Ste 100 San Diego CA 92101 619-269-6800 269-6801 178-8
Web: www.miteksystems.com

Mitel Networks Corp 350 Legget Dr Kanata ON K2K2W7 613-592-2122 735
TF: 800-722-1301 ■ *Web:* www.mitel.com

Mitem Corp 640 Menlo Ave Menlo Park CA 94025 650-323-1500 323-1511 178-12
TF Sales: 800 648 3660 ■ *Web:* www.mitem.com

MITIMCo Private Equity
238 Main St Ste 200 Cambridge MA 02142 617-253-4900 528
Web: www.mitimco.org

Mi-T-M Corp 8650 Enterprise Dr Peosta IA 52068 563-556-7484 198
Web: www.mitm.com

Mitographers Inc, The
4720 Fourth Ave N Sioux Falls SD 57104 605-336-1818 336-2007 687
TF: 800-221-6486 ■ *Web:* mito.com

MITRE Corp 202 Burlington Rd Bedford MA 01730 781-271-2000 668
Web: www.mitre.org

Mitsuba Bardstown Inc
901 Withrow Ct Bardstown KY 40004 502-348-3100 60
TF: 800-704-1078 ■ *Web:* www.americanmitsuba.com

Mitsubishi Caterpillar Forklift America Inc
2121 W Sam Houston Pkwy N Houston TX 77043 713 366 1000 365-1441 470
TF: 800-325-7425 ■ *Web:* www.mcfa.com

Mitsubishi Chemical Fp America Inc
401 Volvo Pkwy Chesapeake VA 23320 757-382-5750 234
Web: www.mitsubishichemical.com

Mitsubishi Corp
2800-200 Granville St Vancouver BC V6C1G6 604-654-8000 654-8222 59
Web: www.mitsubishicorp.com

Mitsubishi Digital Electronics America Inc
9351 Jeronimo Rd Irvine CA 92618 949-465-6000 52
TF: 800-332-2119 ■ *Web:* www.mitsubishi-tv.com

Mitsubishi Electric Automotive America Inc
4773 Bethany Rd Mason OH 45040 513-398-2220 398-1121 247
Web: www.meaa-mea.com

Mitsubishi Electric Power Products Inc
Thorn Hill Industrial Park 530 Keystone Dr
Warrendale PA 15086 724-772-2555 729
TF: 800-887-7830 ■ *Web:* www.meppi.com

Mitsubishi Estate NY Inc
1221 Avenue of the Americas New York NY 10020 212-698-2200 698-2211 653

Mitsubishi Heavy Industries America Inc
630 Fifth Ave Ste 2650 New York NY 10111 212-969-9000 262-2113 698
Web: www.mitsubishitoday.com

Mitsubishi International Corp
655 Third Ave New York NY 10017 212-605-2000 579
Web: www.mitsubishicorp.com

Mitsubishi Motors North America Inc
100 N Mitsubishi Motorway Normal IL 61761 309-888-8000 59
Web: www.mitsubishicars.com

Mitsubishi Polyester Film LLC
2001 Hood Rd Greer SC 29650 864-879-5000 879-5006* 600
**Fax:* Mktg ■ *TF:* 800-334-1934 ■ *Web:* www.m-petfilm.com

Mitsubishi Power Systems Inc
100 Colonial Ctr Pkwy Lake Mary FL 32746 407-688-6201 194
TF: 800-445-9723 ■ *Web:* www.mpshq.com

Mitsui & Co (USA) Inc 200 Pk Ave New York NY 10166 212-878-4000 878-4800 449
TF: 877-248-4237 ■ *Web:* www.mitsui.com/us

Mitsui Chemicals America Inc
800 Westchester Ave Rye Brook NY 10573 914-253-0777 253-0790* 144
**Fax:* PR ■ *TF:* 800-972-7252 ■ *Web:* www.mitsuichemicals.com

Mitsui Foods International
35 Maple St Norwood NJ 07648 201-750-0500 750-0150 297-11
Web: www.mitsuifoods.com

Mitsui Fudosan America Inc
1251 Ave of the Americas Ste 800 New York NY 10020 212-403-5600 652
Web: www.mfamerica.com

Mitsumi Electronics Corp
40000 Grand River Ave
Novi Technology Ctr Ste 200 Novi MI 48375 248-426-8448 173-8
Web: www.mitsumi.com

Mitsven Surfboards 1157 Cushman Ave San Diego CA 92110 619-299-7873 710
TF: 800-561-3357 ■ *Web:* mitsvensurfboards.com

Name / Address	City	State	Zip	Phone	Fax	Class
Mitternight Boiler Works Inc 5301 Highway 43 N PO Box 489 *Web:* www.mitternight.com	Satsuma	AL	36572	251-675-2550	675-2671	91
Mittler Corp 10 Cooperative Way *TF:* 800-467-2464 ■ *Web:* www.mittlerbros.com	Wright City	MO	63390	636-745-7757		454
Mity-Lite Inc 1301 W 400 N *TF:* 800-909-8034 ■ *Web:* www.mitylite.com	Orem	UT	84057	801-224-0589	224-6191	319-3
MIX 2020 Pennsylvania Ave NW Ste 353 *Web:* www.mixmarket.org	Washington	DC	20006	202-659-9094		530
Mix 100 720 S Colorado Blvd Ste 1200N *Web:* www.mix100.com	Denver	CO	80246	303-832-5665		645-47
MIX 108 14 E Central Entrance *Web:* www.mix108.com	Duluth	MN	55811	218-727-4500		645-51
MIX 93.1 1331 Main St 4th Fl *TF:* 888-293-9310 ■ *Web:* mix931.iheart.com	Springfield	MA	01103	413-781-1011		645-156
MIX 93.5 3807 Brandon Ave Ste 2350 *Web:* sunny935.iheart.com	Roanoke	VA	24018	540-725-1220	725-1245	645-136
Mix 94.7 4301 Westbank Dr Escalade B Third Fl *Web:* www.mix947.com	Austin	TX	78746	512-327-9595		645-14
Mix 96.9 8402 Memorial Pkwy SW *Web:* www.mix969huntsville.com	Huntsville	AL	35802	256-885-9797	885-9796	645-76
Mix 97.3 1015 Main St *Web:* mix973wheeling.iheart.com	Wheeling	WV	26003	304-232-1170	234-0041	645-174
Mix Pacific Rim 1001 E University Ave	Las Cruces	NM	88001	575-532-2042		671
Mix Software Inc 1203 Berkeley Dr *TF:* 800-333-0330 ■ *Web:* www.mixsoftware.com	Richardson	TX	75081	972-231-0949		178-2
Mixamo Inc 2415 Third St Ste 239 *Web:* www.mixamo.com	San Francisco	CA	94107	415-255-7455		387
Mixcor Aggregates Inc 6303 43 St *Web:* www.mixcor.ca	Leduc	AB	T9E0G8	780-986-6721		191-1
Mixer Systems Inc 190 Simmons Ave *TF:* 800-756-4937 ■ *Web:* www.mixersystems.com	Pewaukee	WI	53072	262-691-3100		190
MIX-FM 101.9 (CR) 1020 25th St S *Web:* mixfargo.com/contact-us	Fargo	ND	58103	701-237-5346	235-4042	645-58
Mixology Wine Institute 77 W Broad St *Web:* mixologywine.com	Bethlehem	PA	18018	610-814-2900		800
Mixtec Group 9829 Blue Larkspur Ln *Web:* www.mixtec.net	Monterey	CA	93940	831-373-7077		41
Miya 68 Howe St *Web:* www.miyassushi.com	New Haven	CT	06511	203-777-9760		671
Miya Sushi 3222 SW 35th Blvd *Web:* miyasushi.net	Gainesville	FL	32608	352-335-3030		671
Miyabi 9732 N Kings Hwy *Web:* miyabimyrtlebeach.com	Myrtle Beach	SC	29572	843-449-9294	692-2274	671
Miyako 227 N Second St	Harrisburg	PA	17101	717-234-3250		671
Miyako Hotel Los Angeles 328 E First St *TF:* 800-228-6596 ■ *Web:* www.miyakoinn.com	Los Angeles	CA	90012	213-617-2000	617-2700	379
Miz Zips Cafe 2924 E Rt 66	Flagstaff	AZ	86004	928-526-0104		671
Mize Houser & Co 534 S Kansas Ave Ste 700 *Web:* www.mizehouser.com	Topeka	KS	66603	785-233-0536	233-1078	178-7
Mizel Museum of Judaica 400 S Kearney St *Web:* www.mizelmuseum.org	Denver	CO	80224	303-394-9993	394-1119	520
Mizkan Americas Inc 1661 Feehanville Dr Ste 300 *TF:* 800-323-4358 ■ *Web:* www.mizkan.com	Mount Prospect	IL	60056	847-590-0059		296-41
Mizuho America 133 Brimbal Ave *Web:* mizuho.publishpath.com	Beverly	MA	01915	978-921-1718		476
Mizuho OSI Inc 30031 Ahern Ave *TF:* 800-777-4674 ■ *Web:* www.mizuhosi.com	Union City	CA	94587	510-429-1500		475
Mizuho Securities USA 1251 Sixth Ave *Web:* www.mizuhoamericas.com	New York	NY	10020	212-282-3000		690
Mizuna 214 N Howard St *Web:* www.mizuna.com	Spokane	WA	99201	509-747-2004		671
Mizuna 225 E Seventh Ave *Web:* www.mizunadenver.com	Denver	CO	80203	303-832-4778		671
Mizuno USA 4925 Avalon Ridge Pkwy *TF:* 800-966-1211 ■ *Web:* www.mizunousa.com	Norcross	GA	30071	770-441-5553		710
Mizzen Marketing Resources LLC 8195 Bramble Creek Ct *TF:* 800-238-7999 ■ *Web:* www.mizzenmarketing.com	Mansfield	TX	76063	817-477-1991		195
MJ Altman Cos Inc 205 S Magnolia Ave *TF:* 800-927-2655 ■ *Web:* mjaltman.com	Ocala	FL	34471	352-732-1112		160
MJ Celco Inc 3900 Wesley Terr *Web:* www.mjcelco.com	Schiller Park	IL	60176	847-671-1900		488
MJ Electric Inc PO Box 686 *Web:* www.mjelectric.com	Iron Mountain	MI	49801	906-774-8000	779-4217	189-4
Mj Insurance Inc 9225 Priority Way W Dr *Web:* mjinsurance.com	Indianapolis	IN	46240	317-805-7500		390
MJ Mechanical Services Inc 2040 Military Rd *Web:* www.mjmechanical.com	Tonawanda	NY	14150	716-874-9200		189-10
MJ Murdock Charitable Trust 703 Broadway St Ste 710 *Web:* murdocktrust.org	Vancouver	WA	98660	360-694-8415	694-1819	305
MJ Partners Inc 1433 43rd Ave *Web:* www.mjpartnersinc.com	Kenosha	WI	53144	262-553-9696		177
MJ Soffe Co 1 Soffe Dr *TF:* 888-257-8673 ■ *Web:* www.soffe.com	Fayetteville	NC	28312	888-257-8673		155-1
MJ Whitman LLC 622 Third Ave 32nd Fl *Web:* www.mjwhitman.com	New York	NY	10017	212-888-2290		401
MJH (Sentara Martha Jefferson Hospital) 500 Martha Jefferson Dr *TF:* 888-652-6663 ■ *Web:* www.sentara.com	Charlottesville	VA	22911	434-654-7000		374-3
MJL Enterprises LLC 2748 Sonic Dr *Web:* www.mjl-enterprises.com	Virginia Beach	VA	23453	757-963-8740		350
MJLF & Associates 300 First Stamford Pl *Web:* www.mjlf.com	Stamford	CT	06902	203-326-2800		770
MJM Creative Services Inc 71 Fifth Ave *Web:* www.mjmcreative.com	New York	NY	10003	212-924-7070		232
MJM Electric Co-op Inc (MJMEC) 264 NE St PO Box 80 *TF:* 800-648-4729 ■ *Web:* www.mjmec.coop	Carlinville	IL	62626	217-854-3137	854-3918	245
MJM Reynolda Laundromat 2802 Reynolda Rd	Winston-Salem	NC	27106	336-724-4242		671
MJMEC (MJM Electric Co-op Inc) 264 NE St PO Box 80 *TF:* 800-648-4729 ■ *Web:* www.mjmec.coop	Carlinville	IL	62626	217-854-3137	854-3918	245
Mjs Advertising Marketing Consulting LLC 301 Yamato Rd Ste 4100 *Web:* www.mjsadvertising.com	Boca Raton	FL	33431	561-443-0440		7
MJSA (Manufacturing Jewelers & Suppliers of America Inc) 57 John L Dietsch Sq *TF:* 800-444-6572 ■ *Web:* www.mjsa.org	Attleboro	MA	02763	401-274-3840	274-0265	49-4
MK Diamond Products Inc 1315 Storm Pkwy *TF:* 800-421-5830 ■ *Web:* www.mkdiamond.com	Torrance	CA	90501	310-539-5221	539-5158	682
MK Morse Co 1101 11th St SE *TF:* 800-733-3377 ■ *Web:* www.mkmorse.com	Canton	OH	44707	330-453-8187	453-1111	682
MK Tech Solutions Inc 12843 Covey Ln *Web:* www.mktechsolutions.com	Houston	TX	77099	281-564-8851		539
MKC (Mid-Kansas Co-op Assn) PO Box D *TF:* 800-864-4428 ■ *Web:* mkcoop.com	Moundridge	KS	67107	620-345-6361		48-2
Mkec Engineering Consultants Inc 411 N Webb Rd *Web:* mkec.com	Wichita	KS	67206	316-684-9600		261
MKM Partners LLC 300 First Stamford Pl E 4th Fl *Web:* www.mkmpartners.com	Stamford	CT	06902	203-861-9060		690
MKP communications Inc 5 E 16th St 3rd Fl *Web:* www.mkpteam.com	New York	NY	10003	212-983-5700		463
MKS Instruments Inc 2 Tech Dr Ste 201 *TF:* 800-428-9401 ■ *Web:* www.mksinst.com	Andover	MA	01810	978-645-5500	557-5100	201
MKTG Inc 32 Ave of the Americas 20th Fl *OTC:* CMKG ■ *TF:* 800-547-4742 ■ *Web:* www.mktg.com	New York	NY	10013	212-366-3400		4
ML Levin & Associates 4927 W 88TH ST	Prairie Village	KS	66207	913-226-8840		463
ML Macadamia Orchards LP 26-238 Hawaii Belt Rd *NYSE:* NNUT	Hilo	HI	96720	808-969-8057		10-10
ML McDonald LLC 50 Oakland St PO Box 315 *TF:* 800-733-6243 ■ *Web:* www.mlmcdonald.com	Watertown	MA	02471	617-923-0900	926-8418	189-8
M&I Professional Services Inc 7667 N Ave *Web:* www.mlproclean.com	Lemon Grove	CA	91945	619-469-1604		104
MLA (Music Library Assn) 8551 Research Way Ste 180 *TF:* 800-999-8558 ■ *Web:* www.musiclibraryassoc.org	Middleton	WI	53562	608-836-5825	831-8200	49-11
MLA (Maryland Library Assn) 1401 Hollins St *TF:* 800-433-3243 ■ *Web:* www.mdlib.org	Baltimore	MD	21223	410-947-5090	947-5089	435
MLA (Minnesota Library Assn) 1821 University Ave W Ste S256 *Web:* www.mnlibraryassociation.org	Saint Paul	MN	55104	651-999-5343		435
MLA (Medical Library Assn) 65 E Wacker Pl Ste 1900 *TF:* 800-523-1850 ■ *Web:* www.mlanet.org	Chicago	IL	60601	312-419-9094	419-8950	49-11
MLA (Modern Language Assn) 26 Broadway 3rd Fl *TF:* 800-323-4900 ■ *Web:* mla.org	New York	NY	10004	646-576-5000	458-0030	49-5
Mla General Contractor Inc PO Box 624 *Web:* mlacontractor.com	Fallbrook	CA	92088	760-723-0210		169
MLAP (Migrant Legal Action Program) 1001 Connecticut Ave NW Ste 915 *Web:* www.mlap.org	Washington	DC	20036	202-775-7780		48-8
MLB Advertising 182 N Franklin St *Web:* mlbadvertising.com	Wilkes-barre	PA	18701	570-824-1500		5
MLGW (Memphis Light Gas & Water) 220 S Main St *Web:* www.mlgw.com	Memphis	TN	38103	901-528-4011		787
MLK (Martin Luther King Jr Memorial Library) 901 G St NW *Web:* www.dclibrary.org	Washington	DC	20001	202-727-0321		434-3
MLMIA (Multi-Level Marketing International Assn) 119 Stanford Ct *Web:* www.mlmia.com	Irvine	CA	92612	949-854-0484		49-18
MLP Seating Corp 950 Pratt Blvd *TF:* 800-723-3030 ■ *Web:* www.mlpseating.com	Elk Grove Village	IL	60007	847-956-1700	956-1776	319-3
MLQ Attorney Services 2000 River Edge Pkwy Ste 885 *TF:* 800-446-8794 ■ *Web:* www.mlqattorneyservices.com	Atlanta	GA	30328	770-984-7007		635
MLRC (Media Law Resource Ctr) 266 W 37th St Ste 20 *Web:* www.medialaw.org	New York	NY	10018	212-337-0200		49-10
MLS (Major League Soccer) 420 Fifth Ave 7th Fl *TF:* 800-658-0700 ■ *Web:* www.mlssoccer.com	New York	NY	10018	212-450-1200		717
MLS (MLS Freight Logistics) 1802 S Expy 281 *Web:* mlsfreight.com	Edinburg	TX	78542	956-292-2700		311
MLS Freight Logistics (MLS) 1802 S Expy 281 *Web:* mlsfreight.com	Edinburg	TX	78542	956-292-2700		311
MLS Property Information Network Inc 904 Hartford Tpke *TF:* 800-695-3000 ■ *Web:* www.mlspin.com	Shrewsbury	MA	01545	508-845-1011		656
MLT Inc 700 Central Ave *TF:* 800-727-1111 ■ *Web:* www.mltvacations.com	Atlanta	GA	30354	404-559-2270		760
MLV & Co 1300 N17th St Ste 1400 *Web:* www.mlvco.com	Arlington	NY	22209	212-542-5880		690

Name / Address	City	State	Zip	Phone	Fax	Class
MM (Moderation Management Network Inc) 22 W 27th St. *Web:* www.moderation.org	New York	NY	10001	212-871-0974		48-21
MM Comfort Systems 18103 NE 68th St *Web:* mmcomfortsystems.com	Redmond	WA	98052	425-881-7920		189-10
MM Fowler Inc 4220 Neal Rd *TF:* 800-647-0766 ■ *Web:* familyfareconveniencestores.com	Durham	NC	27705	919-309-2925	309-9924	324
M&M Manufacturing Co 4001 Mark IV Pkwy *TF:* 866-706-3999 ■ *Web:* www.mmmfg.com	Fort Worth	TX	76106	817-336-2311		697
M&M Meat Shops 640 Trillium Dr PO Box 2488 *Web:* www.mmfoodmarket.com	Kitchener	ON	N2H6M3	519-895-1075		336
M&M Pump & Supply Inc 1125 Olivette Executive Pkwy Ste 110 *Web:* www.mandmpump.com	St. Louis	MO	63132	314-395-8122		358
M&M Refrigeration Inc 412 Railroad Ave. *Web:* www.mmrefrigeration.com	Federalsburg	MD	21632	410-754-8005		610
MM Systems Corp 50 MM Way *TF:* 800-241-3460 ■ *Web:* www.mmsystemscorp.com	Pendergrass	GA	30567	706-824-7500	824-7501	234
M&M Transport Services Inc 21 Mcgrath Hwy Ste 204 *Web:* www.mmtransport.com	Quincy	MA	02169	617-769-9370		311
MMA Capital Management LLC (MuniMae) 3600 O'Donnell St Ste 600 *OTC:* MMAB ■ *TF:* 855-650-6932 ■ *Web:* www.mmacapitalmanagement.com	Baltimore	MD	21224	443-263-2900		509
MMA Creative Inc 705 N Dixie Ave *TF:* 800-499-2332 ■ *Web:* www.mmacreative.com	Cookeville	TN	38501	931-528-8852		7
MMA Financial LLC 3600 O'Donnell St Ste 600 *Web:* www.mmacapitalmanagement.com	Baltimore	MD	21224	443-263-2900		401
Mmar Medical Group Inc 9619 Yupondale Dr. *TF:* 800-662-7633 ■ *Web:* www.mmarmedical.com	Houston	TX	77080	713-465-2003	465-2818	475
MMC (Maimonides Medical Ctr) 4802 Tenth Ave. *Web:* www.maimonidesmed.org	Brooklyn	NY	11219	718-283-6000		374-3
MMC (Maine Medical Ctr) 22 Bramhall St *TF:* 877-339-3107 ■ *Web:* mainehealth.org/maine-medical-center	Portland	ME	04102	207-662-0111		374-3
MMC (Mercy Medical Ctr) 801 Fifth St. *TF:* 800-352-3559 ■ *Web:* www.mercysiouxcity.com	Sioux City	IA	51102	712-279-2010	279-2034	374-3
MMC (Mercy Medical Ctr) 345 St Paul Pl. *TF:* 800-636-3729 ■ *Web:* www.mdmercy.com	Baltimore	MD	21202	410-332-9000		374-3
MMC (Mennie's Machine Co) Rt 71 & Mennie Dr PO Box 110 *Web:* www.mennies.com	Mark	IL	61340	815-339-2226	339-6550	621
MMC (Memorial Medical Ctr) 1700 Coffee Rd. *TF:* 800-477-2258 ■ *Web:* www.memorialmedicalcenter.org	Modesto	CA	95355	209-526-4500		374-3
MMC (Meadville Medical Ctr) 751 Liberty St *TF:* 800-254-5164 ■ *Web:* www.mmchs.org	Meadville	PA	16335	814-333-5000		374-3
MMC (Mercy Medical Ctr) 500 S Oakwood Rd *TF:* 800-894-9327 ■ *Web:* www.affinityhealth.org	Oshkosh	WI	54904	920-223-2000		374-3
MMC Corp 10955 Lowell Ste 350 *Web:* mmccorp1932.com	Overland Park	KS	66210	913-469-0101		189-10
MMC Group LLC 105 Decker Ct Ste 1100 *Web:* www.careerxroads.com	Irving	TX	75062	732-821-6652		194
MMC Materials Inc 1052 Highland Colony Pkwy Ste 201 *Web:* www.mmcmaterials.com	Ridgeland	MS	39157	601-898-4000		182
Mmc Systems Inc 44632 Guilford St, Ste 101 *Web:* www.mmcsystems.com	Ashburn	VA	20147	201-484-7966		260
MMCC (Mid Michigan Community College) 1375 S Clare Ave *Web:* www.midmich.edu	Harrison	MI	48625	989-386-6622	386-6613	162
MMCS (Marshall Medical Ctr South) 2505 US Hwy 431 *Web:* www.mmcenters.com/facilities/marshall-medical-south	Boaz	AL	35957	256-593-8310		374-3
MMD Equipment 121 High Hill Rd *TF:* 800-433-1382 ■ *Web:* www.mmdequipment.com	Swedesboro	NJ	08085	856-467-3200	467-5235	483
MMF Industries 1111 S Wheeling Rd *TF:* 800-323-8181 ■ *Web:* www.mmfind.com	Wheeling	IL	60090	800-323-8181		692
MMG Corp 1717 Olive St	Saint Louis	MO	63103	314-421-2182		155-13
MMG Corporate Communication Inc 515 W Loveland Ave. *Web:* www.mmgonline.com	Loveland	OH	45140	513-677-8787		514
MMG Insurance Co 44 Maysville St *Web:* www.mmgins.com	Presque Isle	ME	04769	207-764-6611		390
MMG Partners 1605 John St Ste 203A **Fax Area Code:* 212 ■ *Web:* www.mmgpartners.com	Fort Lee	NJ	07024	774-234-6647	709-9403*	463
MMG Ventures LP 826 E Baltimore St *TF:* 800-648-8533 ■ *Web:* www.mmgcapitalgroup.com	Baltimore	MD	21202	410-333-2548		403
MMG Works/Status Promotions 4601 Madison Ave **Fax Area Code:* 816 ■ *TF:* 800-945-4044 ■ *Web:* www.mmgworks.com	Kansas City	MO	64112	800-945-4044	472-7107*	9
MMG Worldwide 4601 Madison Ave. *Web:* www.mmgyglobal.com	Kansas City	MO	64112	816-472-5988		4
MMH (Mercy Memorial Hospital) 718 N Macomb St. *Web:* www.mercymemorial.org	Monroe	MI	48162	734-240-8400		374-3
MMHC (Mercy Memorial Health Ctr) 1011 14th Ave NW *TF:* 888-637-2937 ■ *Web:* www.mercy.net	Ardmore	OK	73401	580-223-5400		374-3
MMHS (Martin Health System) 200 SE Hospital Ave PO Box 9010 *TF:* 844-630-4968 ■ *Web:* www.martinhealth.org	Stuart	FL	34994	772-287-5200		374-3
MMI (Metal Marketplace International) 718 Sansom St *TF:* 800-523-9191 ■ *Web:* www.metalmarketplace.com	Philadelphia	PA	19106	215-592-8777	592-8195	411
MMI (Mid-Michigan Industries Inc) 2426 Pkwy Dr. *Web:* www.mmionline.com	Mount Pleasant	MI	48858	989-773-6918	773-1317	193
MMI Associates Inc 7406 Chapel Hill Rd Ste H *Web:* www.mmipublicrelations.com	Raleigh	NC	27607	919-233-6600		195
MMI Engineering 1111 Broadway 6th Fl. *Web:* www.mmiengineering.com	Oakland	CA	94607	510-836-3002	836-3036	256
MMI Hotel Group PO Box 320009 *Web:* mmihospitality.com	Jackson	MS	39232	601-936-3666	939-5685	379
Mmi Services Inc 4042 Patton Way *Web:* www.mmi-services.com	Bakersfield	CA	93308	661-589-9366		539
MML Bay State Life Insurance Co 100 Bright Meadow Blvd *Web:* www.massmutual.com	Enfield	CT	06082	860-562-1000		391-2
MML Investors Services Inc 1295 State St *TF:* 800-289-9999 ■ *Web:* www.mmlinvestors.com	Springfield	MA	01111	413-737-8400		390
MMR Group Inc 15961 Airline Hwy *TF:* 800-880-5090 ■ *Web:* www.mmrgrp.com	Baton Rouge	LA	70817	225-756-5090	753-7012	189-4
MMS (Massachusetts Medical Society) 860 Winter St *TF:* 800-322-2303 ■ *Web:* www.massmed.org	Waltham	MA	02451	781-893-4610	893-8009	474
MMS Education 105 TERRY DR Ste 120 *Web:* www.mmseducation.com	Newtown	PA	18940	215-579-8590		393
MM&T Packaging Co 8310 S Valley Hwy 400 *Web:* www.mmt.ca	Englewood	CO	80112	303-790-8023		627
M&N Trading LLC 952 West Lake St *Web:* www.mntrading.com	Chicago	IL	60607	312-568-5000	568-5010	194
MNA (Maryland Nurses Assn) 21 Governor's Ct Ste 195 *Web:* www.marylandrn.org	Baltimore	MD	21244	410-944-5800		533
MNA (Massachusetts Nurses Assn) 340 Tpke St *TF:* 800-882-2056 ■ *Web:* www.massnurses.org	Canton	MA	02021	781-821-4625	821-4445	533
MNA (Michigan Nurses Assn) 2310 Jolly Oak Rd *TF:* 888-646-8773 ■ *Web:* www.minurses.org	Okemos	MI	48864	517-349-5640	349-5818	533
MNA (Minnesota Nurses Assn) 345 Randolph Ave Ste 200 *TF:* 800-536-4662 ■ *Web:* www.mnnurses.org	Saint Paul	MN	55102	651-414-2800		533
MNA (Mississippi Nurses Assn) 31 Woodgreen Pl *Web:* www.msnurses.org	Madison	MS	39110	601-898-0670	898-0190	533
MNA (Montana Nurses Assn) 20 Old Montana State Hwy *Web:* www.mtnurses.org	Montana City	MT	59634	406-442-6710	442-1841	533
MNAP Medical Solutions Inc 9908 E Roosevelt Blvd *TF:* 888-674-4381 ■ *Web:* mnap.com	Philadelphia	PA	19115	215-464-3300		383
Mncl Inc 9810 E 42nd St Ste 223	Tulsa	OK	74146	918-728-6032		525
Mnemonics Inc 3900 Dow Rd *Web:* www.mnemonicsinc.com	Melbourne	FL	32934	321-254-7300		22
MNP LLP 715 Fifth Ave SW 7th Fl *Web:* www.mnp.ca	Calgary	AB	T2P2X6	403-444-0150		2
MNPS (Metropolitan Nashville Public Schools) 2601 Bransford Ave *TF:* 800-848-0298 ■ *Web:* www.mnps.org	Nashville	TN	37204	615-259-8531	214-8890	685
Mo Bio Laboratories Inc 2746 Loker Ave W Ste A *Web:* www.mobio.com	Carlsbad	CA	92010	760-929-9911		415
Mo Mo Sushi 1385 Fordham Dr.	Virginia Beach	VA	23464	757-366-3188		671
Mo's 1116 White St	Key West	FL	33040	305-296-8955		671
Mo's Restaurants 657 SW Bay Blvd. *Web:* www.moschowder.com	Newport	OR	97365	541-265-7512	265-9323	670
MoA (Museum of the Americas) 2500 NW 79th Ave Ste 104 *Web:* www.museumamericas.org	Doral	FL	33122	305-599-8089		520
MOAA (Military Officers Assn of America) 201 N Washington St *TF:* 800-234-6622 ■ *Web:* www.moaa.org	Alexandria	VA	22314	703-549-2311		48-10
Moag & Company LLC 323 W Camden St Ste 400 *Web:* www.moagandcompany.com	Baltimore	MD	21201	410-230-0105		690
Moai Technologies Inc 100 First Ave 9th Fl *TF:* 800-814-1548 ■ *Web:* www.moai.com	Pittsburgh	PA	15222	412-454-5550	454-5555	178-7
Mob Media Inc 27042 Towne Centre Dr Ste 260 *Web:* mobmedia.com	Foothill Ranch	CA	92610	949-222-0220		4
Moberg Research Inc 224 S Maple St. *Web:* www.moberg.com	Ambler	PA	19002	215-283-0860		476
Moberly Area Community College 101 College Ave *TF:* 800-622-2070 ■ *Web:* www.macc.edu	Moberly	MO	65270	660-263-4110	263-2406	162
Moberly Correctional Ctr 5201 S Morley *TF:* 800-905-5499 ■ *Web:* www.doc.mo.gov	Moberly	MO	65270	660-263-3778		213
Moberly Monitor Index/Gatehouse Media Inc 218 N Williams St. *Web:* www.moberlymonitor.com	Moberly	MO	65270	660-263-4123		532-3
Mobi PCS Inc 1467 S King St Ste B *Web:* www.mobipcs.com	Honolulu	HI	96814	808-723-1111		387
MOBI Wireless Management LLC 6100 W 96th St Ste 150 *TF:* 855-259-6624 ■ *Web:* mobiwm.com	Indianapolis	IN	46278	855-259-6624		196
Mobile Accord Inc 2150 W 29th Ave 2nd Fl *Web:* www.mobileaccord.com	Denver	CO	80211	303-531-5505		387
Mobile Air Conditioning Society Worldwide (MACS) 225 S Broad St *TF:* 800-641-1133 ■ *Web:* www.macsw.org	Lansdale	PA	19446	215-631-7020	631-7017	49-21
Mobile Area Chamber of Commerce 451 Government St *TF:* 800-422-6951 ■ *Web:* www.mobilechamber.com	Mobile	AL	36602	251-433-6951	432-1143	139
Mobile Area Education Foundation 605 Bel Air Blvd Ste 400 *TF:* 800-633-1508 ■ *Web:* maef.net	Mobile	AL	36606	251-476-0002		305
Mobile Botanical Gardens 5151 Museum Dr *Web:* www.mobilebotanicalgardens.org	Mobile	AL	36608	251-342-0555		97
Mobile City Hall 205 Government St *TF:* 800-957-3676 ■ *Web:* www.cityofmobile.org	Mobile	AL	36602	251-208-7411	208-7576	337

Name / Address	City	State	ZIP	Phone	Fax	Class
Mobile Climate Control Corp 17103 State Rd 4 E *TF:* 800-450-2211 ■ *Web:* www.mcc-hvac.com	Goshen	IN	46528	574-534-1516		14
Mobile Communication of Gwinnett Inc 2241 Tucker Industrial Rd *TF:* 800-749-7170 ■ *Web:* www.callmc.com	Tucker	GA	30084	770-963-3748		246
Mobile Concepts by Scotty Inc 480 Bessemer Rd *Web:* www.mobileconcepts.com	Mount Pleasant	PA	15666	724-542-7640		59
Mobile County 205 Government St *Web:* www.mobilecountyal.gov	Mobile	AL	36644	251-574-5077		338
Mobile County Public Schools 1 Magnum Pass PO Box 180069 *Fax: Hum Res ■ *TF:* 800-605-1033 ■ *Web:* www.mcpss.com	Mobile	AL	36618	251-221-4000	221-4545*	685
Mobile Electric Power Solutions Inc 2623 National Cir *Web:* www.meps.com	Garland	TX	75041	972-864-1015	271-0635	518
Mobile Fixture & Equipment Company Inc 1155 Montlimar Dr *TF:* 800-345-6458 ■ *Web:* www.mobilefixture.com	Mobile	AL	36609	251-342-0455		406
Mobile Gas Service Corp 2828 Dauphin St *Fax: Mktg ■ *TF:* 800-837-3374 ■ *Web:* www.mobile-gas.com	Mobile	AL	36606	251-476-8052	471-2588*	787
Mobile Id Solutions Inc 1574 N Batavia St Ste 1 *Web:* www.mobileidsolutions.com	Orange	CA	92867	714-922-1134		761
Mobile Infirmary Medical Ctr (MIMC) 5 Mobile Infirmary Cir	Mobile	AL	36607	251-435-2400		374-3
Mobile Life Support Services Inc 3188 Us Rt 9w *TF:* 800-209-8815 ■ *Web:* www.mobilelife.com	New Windsor	NY	12553	845-562-4368		30
Mobile Medical International Corp 2176 Portland St PO Box 672 *TF:* 800-692-5205 ■ *Web:* www.mobile-medical.com	St. Johnsbury	VT	05819	802-748-2322		475
Mobile Medical Lab Services 6312 Carolina Beach Rd	Wilmington	NC	28412	910-452-0093		416
Mobile Museum of Art 4850 Museum Dr *TF:* 800-222-7270 ■ *Web:* www.mobilemuseumofart.com	Mobile	AL	36608	251-208-5200		520
Mobile National Cemetery 1202 Virginia St *TF:* 800-827-1000 ■ *Web:* www.cem.va.gov	Mobile	AL	36604	850-453-4108	453-4635	136
Mobile Nations 3151 E Thomas St *TF:* 877-799-0143	Inverness	FL	34453	877-799-0143		157-5
Mobile Office Acquisition Corp 9155 Harrison Park Ct *Web:* www.pacvan.com	Indianapolis	IN	46216	317-489-5771	489-9971	256
Mobile One Courier Services Inc 1457 Miller Store Rd Ste 101 *Web:* www.mobileonecourier.com	Virginia Beach	VA	23455	757-622-9500		314
Mobile Opera Inc 257 Dauphin St *Web:* mobileopera.org	Mobile	AL	36602	251-432-6772	431-7613	573-2
Mobile Paint 4775 Hamilton Blvd *TF:* 800-621-6952 ■ *Web:* www.blpmobilepaint.com	Theodore	AL	36582	251-443-6110	408-0410	550
Mobile Parts Inc 2472 Evans Rd PO Box 327 *TF:* 800-461-4055 ■ *Web:* www.mobileparts.com	Val Caron	ON	P3N1P5	705-897-4955		358
Mobile Public Library 701 Government St *TF:* 877-322-8228 ■ *Web:* www.mobilepubliclibrary.org	Mobile	AL	36602	251-208-7073	208-7137	434-3
Mobile Regional Airport 8400 Airport Blvd *TF:* 800-357-5373 ■ *Web:* www.mobairport.com	Mobile	AL	36608	251-633-4510	639-7437	27
Mobile Smith 5400 Trinity Rd Ste 320 *TF:* 800-578-9000 ■ *Web:* www.mobilesmith.com	Raleigh	NC	27607	800-578-9000		39
Mobile Symphony PO Box 3127 *Web:* www.mobilesymphony.org	Mobile	AL	36652	251-432-2010		573-3
Mobile Technical Services 70 Old Bloomfield Ave *TF:* 800-408-6404 ■ *Web:* mtsnj.com	Pine Brook	NJ	07058	973-808-2882		180
Mobile Video Services Ltd 1620 I St NW Ste 1000 10th Fl *Web:* www.mobilevideo.net	Washington	DC	20006	202-331-8882		194
Mobile Zoo 15161 WaRd Rd W *Web:* www.mobilezoo.cc	Wilmer	AL	36587	251-649-1845		823
Mobile/Modular Express Inc 1301 Trimble Rd *Web:* www.mobilemodular.com	Edgewood	MD	21040	410-676-3700		505
MobileIQ Inc 4800 Baseline Rd Ste E104-247 *TF:* 866-261-8600 ■ *Web:* www.gomobileiq.com	Boulder	CO	80303	866-261-8600		387
Mobility Center Inc 6693 Dixie Hwy *TF:* 866-361-7559 ■ *Web:* www.myamigo.com	Bridgeport	MI	48722	989-777-0910		480
Mobilized Systems Inc 1032 Seabrook Way	Cincinnati	OH	45245	513-943-1111		779
Mobiquity Networks Inc 600 Old Country Rd Ste 541 *Web:* www.mobiquitynetworks.com	Garden City	NY	11530	516-256-7766		195
Mobis Alabama LLC 1395 Mitchell Young Rd	Montgomery	AL	36108	334-387-4800		247
Mobisante Inc 8201 164th Ave NE Ste 200 *Web:* www.mobisante.com	Redmond	WA	98052	425-605-0600		723
Mobium Creative Group 2000 S Merchandise Mart 17th FL *Web:* www.mobium.com	Chicago	IL	60604	312-422-8950		393
Mobius Executive Leadership 177 worcester st *TF:* 800-631-1463 ■ *Web:* www.mobiusleadership.com	Wellesley Hills	MA	02481	781-237-1362		138
Mobivity Inc 58 W Buffalo Ste 200 *TF:* 877-282-7660 ■ *Web:* mobivity.com	Chandler	AZ	85225	877-282-7660		5
Mobridge Regional Hospital Inc PO Box 580 *Web:* www.mobridgehospital.org	Mobridge	SD	57601	605-845-3692		374-3
Mobridge Tribune 1413 E Grand Xing *TF:* 800-594-9418 ■ *Web:* www.mobridgetribune.com	Mobridge	SD	57601	605-845-3646		532-3
Moc1 Solutions 2011 E Financial Way *Web:* moc1solutions.com	Glendora	CA	91741	626-610-1970		180
MOCAP Inc 409 Parkway Dr *TF:* 800-633-6775 ■ *Web:* www.mocap.com	Park Hills	MO	63601	314-543-4000	543-4111	608
MoCaro Industries Inc 2201 Mocaro Dr *TF:* 800-621-1711 ■ *Web:* www.mocaro.com	Statesville	NC	28677	704-878-6645	873-6139	745-4
Moccasin Bend Mental Health Institute 100 Moccasin Bend Rd *TF:* 800-560-5767 ■ *Web:* tn.gov	Chattanooga	TN	37405	423-265-2271	785-3333	374-5
Moccasin Creek State Park 3655 Hwy 197 *Web:* www.gastateparks.org	Clarkesville	GA	30523	706-947-3194		565
Moceri Development Corp 3005 University Dr *TF:* 800-732-5569 ■ *Web:* www.moceri.com	Auburn Hills	MI	48326	248-340-9400	340-9401	653
Mock Plumbing & Mechanical Inc PO Box 22456 *Web:* www.mocksavannah.com	Savannah	GA	31403	912-232-1104	232-6284	189-10
Mockler Beverage Co 11811 Reiger Rd *Web:* mocklerbeverage.com	Baton Rouge	LA	70809	225-408-4283		297-8
Mocon Inc 7500 Mendelssohn Ave N *NASDAQ: MOCO* ■ *Web:* www.mocon.com	Minneapolis	MN	55428	763-493-6370	493-6358	201
Moctezuma's 4102 S 56th St *Web:* www.moctezumas.com	Tacoma	WA	98409	253-474-5593		671
Mod43 Inc 7946 N Lilley Rd *TF:* 800-560-6256 ■ *Web:* mod43.com	Canton	MI	48187	734-416-1009		225
MODA Hotel 900 Seymour St *TF:* 877-683-5522 ■ *Web:* www.modahotel.ca	Vancouver	BC	V6B3L9	604-683-4251	683-0611	379
Modaexpress of USA Inc 900 Secaucus Rd Unit A *TF:* 800-832-5660 ■ *Web:* www.modaexpress.com	Secaucus	NJ	07094	201-325-8808		311
Modagrafics Inc 5300 Newport Dr *TF:* 800-424-3996 ■ *Web:* www.modagrafics.com	Rolling Meadows	IL	60008	847-392-3980		687
Modal Shop Inc, The 1776 Mentor Ave *TF:* 800-860-4867 ■ *Web:* www.modalshop.com	Cincinnati	OH	45212	513-351-9919		419
Modea Corp 902 Prices Fork Rd Ste 2100 *Web:* www.modea.com	Blacksburg	VA	24060	540-552-3210		7
Model Airplane News 20 Westport Rd *TF:* 800-988-6488 ■ *Web:* www.modelairplanenews.com	Wilton	CT	06897	203-431-9000		457-14
Model Cleaners Uniforms & Apparel LLC 100 Third St *TF:* 800-967-0800 ■ *Web:* www.modeluniforms.com	Charleroi	PA	15022	724-489-9553		426
Model Coverall Service Inc 100 28th St SE *TF:* 800-968-6491 ■ *Web:* www.modelcoverall.com	Grand Rapids	MI	49548	616-241-6491	241-0677	442
Model Electronics Inc 615 E Crescent Ave *TF:* 800-433-9657 ■ *Web:* www.modelelectronics.com	Ramsey	NJ	07446	800-433-9657		45
Model Rectifier Corp 80 Newfield Ave *Web:* www.modelrec.com	Edison	NJ	08837	732-225-2100		762
Modell's Sporting Goods 498 Seventh Ave 20th Fl *TF:* 800-275-6633 ■ *Web:* www.modells.com	New York	NY	10018	800-275-6633		157-5
Modellers LLC, The 6995 Union Park Ctr Ste 300 *Web:* www.themodellers.com	Salt Lake City	UT	84047	801-290-3800		466
Models & Tools 51400 Bellestri Ct *Web:* www.modelsandtools.com	Shelby Township	MI	48315	586-580-6900		697
Moderation Management Network Inc (MM) 22 W 27th St *Web:* www.moderation.org	New York	NY	10001	212-871-0974		48-21
Modern Abrasive Corp PO Box 219 *Web:* www.modernabrasive.com	Spring Grove	IL	60081	815-675-2352		1
Modern Aire Manufacturing Corp 7319 Lankershim Blvd *TF:* 866-731-2007 ■ *Web:* www.modernaire.com	North Hollywood	CA	91605	818-765-9870		198
Modern American Safety Training-mast 841 Alton Ave *Web:* www.mastohio.com	Columbus	OH	43219	614-252-0565		507
Modern Art Museum of Fort Worth 3200 Darnell St *TF:* 866-824-5566 ■ *Web:* themodern.org	Fort Worth	TX	76107	817-738-9215		520
Modern Automation Inc 134 Tennsco Dr *TF:* 800-921-9705 ■ *Web:* www.modernautomation.com	Dickson	TN	37055	615-446-1990		358
Modern Business Associates Inc 9455 Koger Blvd Ste 200 *Web:* www.mbahro.com	St. Petersburg	FL	33702	727-563-1500		631
Modern Cafe 337 13th Ave NE	Minneapolis	MN	55413	612-378-9882		671
Modern Chevrolet of Winston-Salem 5955 University Pkwy *TF General:* 888-306-0825 ■ *Web:* www.modernchevy.com	Winston-Salem	NC	27105	336-722-4191		57
Modern Comfort Systems Inc 100 Airport Dr *Web:* www.moderncomfortsystems.com	Westminster	MD	21157	410-876-2200		697
Modern Controls Inc 7 Bellecor Dr *Web:* www.moderncontrols.com	New Castle	DE	19720	302-325-6800		610
Modern Corp 4746 Model City Rd *TF:* 800-662-0012 ■ *Web:* www.moderncorporation.com	Model City	NY	14107	716-754-8226		804
Modern Dental Laboratory USA LLC 13228 SE 30th St Ste C-6 *TF:* 877-711-8778 ■ *Web:* www.moderndentalusa.com	Bellevue	WA	98005	877-711-8778		415
Modern Dispersions Inc 78 Marguerite Ave *Web:* www.moderndispersions.com	Leominster	MA	01453	978-534-3370	537-6065	605-2
Modern Distributors Inc 817 W Columbia St *TF:* 800-880-5543 ■ *Web:* teammodern.com	Somerset	KY	42501	606-679-1178		756
Modern Drop Forge Co 13810 S Western Ave *Web:* www.modernforge.com	Blue Island	IL	60406	708-388-1806	597-3633	483
Modern Earth 449 Provencher Blvd *TF:* 866-766-7640 ■ *Web:* www.modernearth.net	Winnipeg	MB	R2J0B8	204-885-2469		225
Modern Equipment Company Inc 6161 Abbott Dr PO Box 12278 *Web:* www.moderneq.com	Omaha	NE	68110	402-341-4939		567

Company / Address	City	State	ZIP	Phone	Fax	Class
Modern Exploration Inc 4900 Texoma Pkwy *Web:* www.modernexploration.com	Sherman	TX	75090	903-893-1129		536
Modern Farm Equipment Co 2929 N Bluff St *TF:* 800-807-5777 ■ *Web:* www.modernfarmequip.com	Fulton	MO	65251	573-642-5777		45
Modern Group Ltd 2501 Durham Rd *TF:* 800-223-3827 ■ *Web:* www.moderngroup.com	Bristol	PA	19007	215-943-9100	943-4978	385
Modern Group Ltd 1655 Louisiana St *TF Cust Svc:* 800-231-8198 ■ *Web:* www.modernusa.com	Beaumont	TX	77701	409-833-2665		273
MODERN Honolulu, The 1775 Ala Moana Blvd *Web:* www.themodernhonolulu.com	Honolulu	HI	96815	808-943-5800		707
Modern Ice Equipment & Supply Co 5709 Harrison Ave *TF:* 800-543-1581 ■ *Web:* www.modernice.com	Cincinnati	OH	45248	513-367-2101	367-5762	665
Modern Inc/Environmental & Wastewater 210 Durham Rd *TF:* 888-965-3227 ■ *Web:* www.modcon.com	Ottsville	PA	18942	610-847-5112	847-2468	183
Modern Industries Inc 613 W 11th St *Web:* modernind.com	Erie	PA	16501	814-455-8061	453-4382	484
Modern Language Assn (MLA) 26 Broadway 3rd Fl *TF:* 800-323-4900 ■ *Web:* mla.org	New York	NY	10004	646-576-5000	458-0030	49-5
Modern Machine & Engineering Corp 9380 Winnetka Ave N *TF:* 800-443-5117 ■ *Web:* www.mmcincmn.com	Brooklyn Park	MN	55445	612-781-3347	781-0030	621
Modern Machine & Tool Company Inc 11844 Jefferson Ave *TF:* 800-482-1835 ■ *Web:* www.mmtool.com	Newport News	VA	23606	757-873-1212		407
Modern Machine Shop Magazine 6915 Valley Ave *TF:* 800-950-8020 ■ *Web:* www.mmsonline.com	Cincinnati	OH	45244	513-527-8800	527-8801	457-21
Modern Management Inc 253 Commerce Dr Ste 105 *TF:* 800-323-1331 ■ *Web:* www.modernmanagement.com	Grayslake	IL	60030	847-945-7400		193
Modern Marketing Partners 1220 Iroquois Ave Ste 210 *Web:* www.modernmarketingpartners.com	Naperville	IL	60563	630-868-5060		7
Modern Medical Modalities Corp 439 Chestnut St *NYSE: MODM*	Union	NJ	07083	908-933-0216		264-4
Modern Office Methods Inc 4747 Lake Forest Dr *Web:* momnet.com	Cincinnati	OH	45242	513-791-0909		366
Modern Parking Inc 303 S Union Ave 1st Fl *Web:* www.modernparking.com	Los Angeles	CA	90017	213-482-8400		562
Modern Plastics Inc 88 Long Hill Cross Rd *TF:* 800-243-9696 ■ *Web:* www.modernplastics.com	Shelton	CT	06484	203-333-3128		601
Modern Press Inc 1 Colonie St *Web:* www.modernpress.com	Albany	NY	12207	518-434-2921		627
Modern Print Shop 508 Cortlandt St *Web:* modernprintshop.com	Houston	TX	77007	713-861-7262		627
Modern Process Equipment Inc 3125 S Kolin Ave *Web:* mpechicago.com	Chicago	IL	60623	773-254-3929		261
Modern Quilters Inc 62038 Minnesota Hwy 24 PO Box 66 *TF:* 800-290-9199 ■ *Web:* modernquilters.com	Litchfield	MN	55355	320-693-7987		34
Modern Technology Solutions Inc (MTSI) 5285 Shawnee Rd Ste 400 *Web:* www.mtsi-va.com	Alexandria	VA	22312	703-564-3800		261
Modern Tool Inc 1200 Northdale Blvd *Web:* www.mtoolinc.com	Coon Rapids	MN	55448	763-754-7337		697
Modern Track Machinery 1415 Davis Rd *Web:* www.geismar-mtm.com	Elgin	IL	60123	847-697-7510		770
Modern Transportation Service Inc 2605 Nicholson Rd *Web:* www.moderntrans.com	Sewickley	PA	15143	412-489-4800		449
Modern Videofilm Inc 2300 Empire Ave *Web:* www.mvf.com	Burbank	CA	91504	818-840-1700		512
Modern Way Printing & Fulfillment 8817 Production Ln *TF:* 800-603-5135 ■ *Web:* www.modernwayco.com	Ooltewah	TN	37363	423-238-4500		627
Modern Welding Company Inc 2880 New Hartford Rd *TF:* 800 922 1932 ■ *Web:* www.modweldco.com	Owensboro	KY	42303	270-685-4400	684-6972	91
Modern Wireless Inc 1163 N Patt St *Web:* www.modernwirelessusa.com	Anaheim	CA	92801	714-535-6399		736
Modern Woodcrafts LLC 72 NW Dr Farmington Industrial Pk *Web:* www.modernwoodcrafts.com	Plainville	CT	06062	860-677-7371		286
Modern Woodmen of America 1701 First Ave *TF:* 800-447-9811 ■ *Web:* www.modernwoodmen.org	Rock Island	IL	61201	309-786-6481	793-5547	391-2
Moderna Therapeutics Inc 320 Bent St *Web:* www.modernatx.com	Cambridge	MA	02141	617-714-6500		231
Moderne Glass Company Inc 1000 Industrial Blvd *TF:* 800-645-5131 ■ *Web:* www.glassamerica.com	Aliquippa	PA	15001	724-857-5700		330
Moderne Hotel, The 243 W 55th St *Web:* modernehotelnyc.com	New York	NY	10019	212-397-6767	397-8787	379
Modernfold Inc 215 W New Rd **Fax Area Code: 866* ■ *TF:* 800-869-9685 ■ *Web:* www.modernfold.com	Greenfield	IN	46140	800-869-9685	410-5016*	286
Modernism Inc 685 Market St Ste 290 *Web:* www.modernisminc.com	San Francisco	CA	94105	415-541-0461	541-0425	42
Modernism Magazine 199 George St *Web:* ragoarts.com	Lambertville	NJ	08530	609-397-4104		457-2
ModernThink LLC 4519 Weldin Rd *Web:* www.modernthink.com	Wilmington	DE	19803	302-764-4477		195
Modesto 5257 Shaw Ave *Web:* www.saucecafe.com/modesto	Saint Louis	MO	63110	314-772-8272		671
Modesto & Empire Traction Co 530 11th St *Web:* www.metrr.com	Modesto	CA	95354	209-524-4631	529-0336	648
Modesto Bee 1325 H St *TF:* 800-776-4233 ■ *Web:* www.modbee.com	Modesto	CA	95354	209-578-2000	578-2207	532-2
Modesto Centre Plaza 1000 L St *Web:* www.modestogov.com/prnd/facilities/mcp	Modesto	CA	95354	209-577-6444	544-6729	205
Modesto Chamber of Commerce 1114 J St *Web:* www.modchamber.org	Modesto	CA	95354	209-577-5757	577-2673	139
Modesto City Airport 617 Airport Way *Web:* www.modestogov.com	Modesto	CA	95354	209-577-5319	576-1985	27
Modesto City Hall PO Box 642 *Web:* www.modestogov.com	Modesto	CA	95353	209-577-5200	571-5152	337
Modesto City Schools 426 Locust St **Fax: Hum Res* ■ *TF:* 800-942-3767 ■ *Web:* www.mcs4kids.com/district	Modesto	CA	95351	209-576-4011	576-4846*	685
Modesto Convention & Visitors Bureau 1150 Ninth St Ste C *TF:* 888-640-8467 ■ *Web:* www.visitmodesto.com	Modesto	CA	95354	209-526-5588	526-5586	206
Modesto Junior College 435 College Ave **Fax: Admissions* ■ *TF:* 800-228-2262 ■ *Web:* www.mjc.edu	Modesto	CA	95350	209-575-6550	575-6859*	162
Modesto Symphony Orchestra 911 13th St *TF:* 877-488-3380 ■ *Web:* www.modestosymphony.org	Modesto	CA	95354	209-523-4156	523-0201	573-3
Modine Manufacturing Co 1500 De Koven Ave *NYSE: MOD* ■ *TF:* 800-828-4328 ■ *Web:* www.modine.com	Racine	WI	53403	262-636-1200	636-1424	15
Modineer Co 2190 Industrial Dr *Web:* www.modineer.com	Niles	MI	49120	269-683-2550		489
Modis Inc 10 Bay St 7th Floor *TF:* 800-842-5907 ■ *Web:* www.modis.com	Toronto	ON	M5J2R8	904-360-2300	360-2110	463
Modjeski & Masters Inc 100 Sterling Pkwy Ste 302 *TF:* 888-663-5375 ■ *Web:* www.modjeski.com	Mechanicsburg	PA	17050	717-790-9565	790-9564	261
Modo Inc 20325 NW von Neumann Dr Ste 170 *Web:* www.modocarts.com	Beaverton	OR	97006	503-690-1400		475
MOD-PAC Corp 1801 Elmwood Ave *NASDAQ: MPAC* ■ *TF Cust Svc:* 866-216-6193 ■ *Web:* www.modpac.com	Buffalo	NY	14207	716-873-0640	873-6008	101
Modrall Sperling Roehl Harris & Sisk P.a PO Box 2168 *Web:* www.modrall.com	Albuquerque	NM	87103	505-848-1800		428
Modspace Financial Services Canada Ltd 2300 N Park Dr *Web:* www.modspace.com/en-ca	Brampton	ON	L6S6C6	905-794-3900		194
Modtech Holdings Inc 1660 Chicago Ave Ste M-21 *Web:* www.modtech.com	Riverside	CA	92507	951-686-3633		106
Modulant Inc 5600 Tennyson Pkwy Ste 355 *Web:* www.modulant.com	Plano	TX	75024	843-743-2888		177
Modular Communications Systems 13309 Saticoy St *TF:* 800-266-5367 ■ *Web:* www.moducom.com	North Hollywood	CA	91605	818-764-1333		647
Modular Components National Inc 105 E Jarrettsville Rd PO Box 453 *Web:* www.modularcomp.com	Forest Hill	MD	21050	410-879-6553		625
Modular Connections LLC 1090 Industrial Blvd *TF:* 877-903-6335 ■ *Web:* www.modularconnections.com	Bessemer	AL	35022	205-980-4565		186
Modular Genius Inc 1201 S Mountain Rd *TF:* 000-420-1113 ■ *Web:* www.modulargenius.com	Joppa	MD	21085	888-420-1113		186
Modular Mining Systems 3289 E Hemisphere Loop *Web:* www.mmsi.com	Tucson	AZ	85706	520-746-9127		454
Modular One LLC 1884 Mines Rd *Web:* www.modularone.net	Pulaski	TN	38478	931-424-7306		106
Modular Process Control LLC 11477 Olde Cabin Rd Ste 300 *Web:* www.mpcenergyllc.com	Saint Louis	MO	63141	636-536-1000		463
Modular Systems Inc 169 Pk St *Web:* www.mod-eez.com	Fruitport	MI	49415	231-865-3167	865-6101	286
Moduline Industries Canada Ltd 1421 Brier Park Crescent NW *TF:* 800-658-5908 ■ *Web:* www.moduline.ca	Medicine Hat	AB	T1C1T8	403-527-1555		505
Modulis Inc 6250 Blvd Monk *Web:* www.modulis.com	Montreal	QC	H4E3H7	514-284-2020		224
Modus Furniture International 5410 McConnell Ave *Web:* www.modusfurniture.com	Los Angeles	CA	90066	310-827-2129		361
ModusLink Open Channel Solutions Inc 3 Allied Dr Ste 303	Dedham	MA	02026	781-407-3900	407-3939	809
Moe's Books 2476 Telegraph Ave *Web:* www.moesbooks.com	Berkeley	CA	94704	510-849-2087		95
Moe's Southwest Grill 6401 E Lloyd Expy *Web:* www.moes.com	Evansville	IN	47715	812-491-6637		671
Moelis & Co LLC 399 Pk Ave 5th Fl *Web:* www.moelis.com	New York	NY	10022	212-883-3800		69
Moeller Fine Art Ltd 35 E 64th St *Web:* www.moellerfineart.com	New York	NY	10065	212-644-2133	644-2134	42
Moeller Mfg Company Inc Aircraft Div 30100 Beck Rd *TF:* 800-321-8010 ■ *Web:* www.moelleraircraft.com	Wixom	MI	48393	248-960-3999	960-1593	21
Moeller Mfg Company Inc Punch & Die Div 43938 Plymouth Oaks Blvd *TF:* 800-521-7613 ■ *Web:* www.moellerpunch.com	Plymouth	MI	48170	734-416-0000	416-2200	757
Moen Inc 25300 Al Moen Dr **Fax Area Code: 800* ■ **Fax: Hum Res* ■ *TF Cust Svc:* 800-289-6636 ■ *Web:* www.moen.com	North Olmsted	OH	44070	440-962-2000	848-6636*	609
Moen Inc 101 Industrial Dr *Web:* www.moen.com	New Bern	NC	28562	252-638-3300		609
Moen Inc CSI Bath Accessories Div 25300 Al Moen Dr *TF:* 800-289-6636 ■ *Web:* www.moen.com	North Olmsted	OH	44070	440-962-2000	962-2145	609
Moet Hennessy USA 85 Tenth Ave *Web:* www.mhusa.com	New York	NY	10011	212-251-8200		81-3
Moews Seed Co PO Box 214 Route 89 S of Jct 89 & 71 *TF:* 800-663-9795 ■ *Web:* www.moews.com	Granville	IL	61326	815-339-2201		10-5

	Phone	Fax	Class
Moffat County 221 W Victory Way ... Craig CO 81625 *Web:* colorado.gov	970-824-9104	824-0351	338
Moffatt & Nichol Engineers 3780 Kilroy Airport Way # 750 ... Long Beach CA 90806 *TF:* 888-399-6609 ■ *Web:* www.moffattnichol.com	562-590-6500	590-6512	261
Moffatt Thomas Barrett Rock & Fields 101 S Capitol Blvd 10th Fl ... Boise ID 83702 *Web:* www.moffatt.com	208-345-2000		428
MoffettNathanson LLC 1180 Ave Of The Americas ... New York NY 10036 *Web:* www.moffettnathanson.com	212-519-0020		401
Moffitt Cancer Center University of S Florida 12902 Magnolia Dr ... Tampa FL 33612 **Fax Area Code:* 813 ■ *TF:* 800-456-3434 ■ *Web:* www.moffitt.org	888-663-3488	745-4064*	374-7
Moffitt Corp Inc 1351 13th Ave S Ste 130 ... Jacksonville Beach FL 32250 *TF:* 800-474-3267 ■ *Web:* www.moffittcorp.com	904-241-9944		256
Moffitt Genetics Corporation Inc 10902 N McKinley Dr ... Tampa FL 33612 *Web:* www.m2gen.com	813-745-4261		416
Mogas Industries 14330 E Hardy Rd ... Houston TX 77039 *Web:* www.mogas.com	281-449-0291		789
Mogg QuickSet 3650 Woodhead Dr ... Northbrook IL 60062 *Web:* www.tripods.com	847-498-0700	498-1258	591
MOGL Loyalty Services Inc 9645 Scranton Rd Ste 110 ... San Diego CA 92121 *TF:* 888-664-5669 ■ *Web:* www.mogl.com	888-664-5669		387
Mohair Council of America 233 W Twohig Rd ... San Angelo TX 76903 *TF:* 800-583-3161 ■ *Web:* www.mohairusa.com	325-655-3161		48-2
Mohan Group, The 2345 Stanfield Rd ... Mississauga ON L4Y3Y3 *Web:* www.mohangroup.com	416-255-2500		5
Mohave Community College *Bullhead City* 3400 Hwy 95 ... Bullhead City AZ 86442 *TF:* 866-664-2832 ■ *Web:* www.mohave.edu	928-758-3926	704-9460	162
Lake Havasu 1977 W Acoma Blvd ... Lake Havasu City AZ 86403 **Fax:* Admissions ■ *TF:* 866-664-2832 ■ *Web:* www.mohave.edu	928-855-7812	680-5955*	162
North Mohave PO Box 980 ... Colorado City AZ 86021 **Fax:* Admissions ■ *TF:* 800-678-3992 ■ *Web:* www.mohave.edu	928-875-2799	875-2831*	162
Mohave County 3269 N Burbank PO Box 7000 ... Kingman AZ 86409 *Web:* www.mohavecounty.us	928-692-5705	753-5103	338
Mohave County Fair Assn 2600 Fairgrounds Blvd ... Kingman AZ 86401 *Web:* www.mcfafairgrounds.org	928-753-2636	753-8383	642
Mohave Educational Services Cooperative Inc 625 E Beale St ... Kingman AZ 86401 *TF:* 800-742-2437 ■ *Web:* www.mesc.org	928-753-6945		434-3
Mohave Mental Health Clinic Inc 3505 Western Ave ... Kingman AZ 86409 *TF:* 888-757-8111 ■ *Web:* www.mmhc-inc.org	928-757-8111		726
Mohawk College 135 Fennell Ave W ... Hamilton ON L9C0E5 *Web:* www.mohawkcollege.ca	905-575-1212		162
Mohawk Council of Akwesasne PO Box 90 Po Box 579 ... Akwesasne QC H0M1A0 *TF:* 888-632-6273 ■ *Web:* www.akwesasne.ca	613-575-2250		685
Mohawk Doors 980 Pt Township Dr ... Northumberland PA 17857 *TF:* 888-676-6429 ■ *Web:* www.mohawkdoors.com	570-473-3557	473-3737	236
Mohawk Fine Papers Inc 465 Saratoga St ... Cohoes NY 12047 *TF:* 800-843-6455 ■ *Web:* www.mohawkconnects.com	518-237-1740	237-7394	552-2
Mohawk Industries Inc 160 S Industrial Blvd ... Calhoun GA 30703 *NYSE:* MHK ■ *TF:* 800-241-4494 ■ *Web:* www.mohawkind.com	706-629-7721		131
Mohawk Industries Inc Lees Carpets Div 160 S Industrial Blvd ... Calhoun GA 30701 *TF:* 800-241-4494 ■ *Web:* mohawkind.com/content.aspx?id=1785	706-629-7721		131
Mohawk Metal Co 30011 Leghorn Ave ... Eugene OR 97402 *Web:* www.mohawkmetal.com	541-744-3838		567
Mohawk State Forest 20 Mohawk Mtn Rd ... Goshen CT 06756 *Web:* www.ct.gov	860-491-3620		565
Mohawk Trail State Forest Cold River Rd ... Charlemont MA 01339	413-339-5504		565
Mohawk Valley Chamber of Commerce 200 Genesee St ... Utica NY 13502 *Web:* greateruticachamber.org	315-724-3151	724-3177	139
Mohawk Valley Community College 1101 Sherman Dr ... Utica NY 13501 *TF:* 800-733-6822 ■ *Web:* www.mvcc.edu	315-792-5400	792-5527	162
Mohawk Valley Library System 858 Duanesburg Rd ... Schenectady NY 12306 *Web:* www.mvls.info	518-355-2010		434-3
Mohawk Valley Psychiatric Ctr 1400 Noyes St ... Utica NY 13502 *TF:* 800-597-8481 ■ *Web:* omh.ny.gov	315-738-3800	738-4414	374-5
Mohegan Sun 1 Mohegan Sun Blvd ... Uncasville CT 06382 *Web:* www.wnba.com	860-862-4000	862-4010	714-2
Mohegan Sun Resort & Casino 1 Mohegan Sun Blvd ... Uncasville CT 06382 *TF:* 888-226-7711 ■ *Web:* www.mohegansun.com	860-862-8150		133
Mohegan Tribal Gaming Authority 1 Mohegan Sun Blvd ... Uncasville CT 06382 *TF:* 888-226-7711 ■ *Web:* www.mtga.com	888-226-7711		77
Mohican State Park 3116 SR- 3 ... Loudonville OH 44842 *Web:* www.ohiodnr.com	419-938-6222		565
Mohl Fur Company Inc 345 Seventh Ave 3rd Fl ... New York NY 10001	212-736-7676	629-4832	155-7
Mohonk Mountain House 1000 Mtn Rest Rd ... New Paltz NY 12561 *TF:* 800-772-6646 ■ *Web:* www.mohonk.com	845-255-1000		669
Mohr & Assoc Inc 1324 N Hearne Ave Ste 301 ... Shreveport LA 71107 *Web:* www.mohrandassoc.com	318-686-7190		261
Mohr Corp PO Box 1600 ... Brighton MI 48114 *TF:* 800-223-6647 ■ *Web:* www.mohrcorp.com	810-225-9494	225-4634	458
Mohr Davidow Ventures 777 Mariners Island Blvd Ste 550 ... San Mateo CA 94404 *Web:* www.mdv.com	650-854-7236	854-7365	792
Mohr Power Solar Inc 1452 Pomona Rd ... Corona CA 92882 *TF:* 800-637-6527 ■ *Web:* www.mohrpower.com	951-736-2000		610
Moishe's 6333 W Third St ... Los Angeles CA 90036 *Web:* moishes-la.com	323-936-4998		671
Moishes Steakhouse 3961 St Laurent Blvd ... Montreal QC H2W1Y4 *TF:* 800-235-6397 ■ *Web:* www.moishes.ca	514-845-3509		671
Moja Inc 7010 Infantry Ridge Rd Ste 104 ... Manassas VA 20109 *Web:* www.moja.net	703-369-4339		225
Mojave A Desert Resort 73721 Shadow Mtn Dr ... Palm Desert CA 92260 *TF Resv:* 800-391-1104 ■ *Web:* www.resortmojave.com	760-346-6121	674-9072	379
Mojave Copy & Printing Inc 12402 Industrial Blvd ... Victorville CA 92395 *Web:* www.mojavecopy.com	760-241-7898		627
Mojave Electric Inc 3755 W Hacienda Ave ... Las Vegas NV 89118	702-798-2970		189-4
Mojave National Preserve 2701 Barstow Rd ... Barstow CA 92311 *TF:* 800-444-7275 ■ *Web:* www.nps.gov/moja	760-252-6100	252-6174	564
Mojio Inc 1080 Howe St 9th Fl ... Vancouver BC V6Z2T1 *TF:* 855-556-6546 ■ *Web:* www.moj.io	855-556-6546		224
MoJiva Inc 136 Baxter St ... New York NY 10013 *Web:* www.mojiva.com	646-862-6201		387
Mojix Inc 11075 Santa Monica Blvd Ste 350 ... Los Angeles CA 90025 *Web:* www.mojix.com	310-479-9021		194
Mojo Interactive Inc 1080 Woodcock Rd Ste 108 ... Orlando FL 32803 *Web:* www.mojointeractive.com	407-206-0700		177
Mokara Hotel & Spa 212 W Crockett St ... San Antonio TX 78205 *TF:* 866-605-1212 ■ *Web:* www.omnihotels.com/hotels/san-antonio-mokara	210-396-5800		707
MOL (America) Inc 700 E Butterfield Rd Ste 150 ... Lombard IL 60148 *Web:* www.molpower.com	630-812-3700		711
Molalla Communications Co-op 211 Robbins St PO Box 360 ... Molalla OR 97038 *TF:* 800-332-2344 ■ *Web:* www.molalla.com	503-829-1100	829-7781	736
Mold Base Industries Inc 7501 Derry St ... Harrisburg PA 17111 **Fax Area Code:* 717 ■ *TF:* 800-241-6656 ■ *Web:* www.moldbase.com	800-241-6656	564-2250*	757
Mold Craft Inc 200 Stillwater Rd PO Box 458 ... Willernie MN 55090 *TF:* 800-947-8631 ■ *Web:* www.mold-craft.com	651-426-3216		711
Mold in Graphic Systems 999 Hwy 89 ... Clarkdale AZ 86324 *TF:* 800-297-6707 ■ *Web:* www.moldingraphics.com	928-634-8838		627
Mold Masters International Inc 7500 Clover Ave ... Mentor OH 44060 *Web:* www.moldmastersintl.com	440-953-0220	953-1016	757
Mold-A-Matic Corp 147 River St ... Oneonta NY 13820 *TF:* 866-886-2626 ■ *Web:* www.mamco-molding.com	607-433-2121	432-7861	757
Moldamatic LLC 29 Noeland Ave ... Penndel PA 19047 *Web:* www.moldamatic.com	215-757-4819		608
Molded Acoustical Products of Easton Inc 3 Danforth Dr ... Easton PA 18045 *Web:* mapeaston.com	610-253-7135	253-1664	389
Molded Devices Inc 6918 Ed Perkic St ... Riverside CA 92504 *Web:* moldeddevices.com	951-509-6918		608
Molded Fiber Glass Cos 2925 MFG Pl PO Box 675 ... Ashtabula OH 44005 *TF:* 800-860-0196 ■ *Web:* www.moldedfiberglass.com	440-997-5851	994-5162	604
Molded Fiber Glass Tray Co 6175 US Hwy 6 ... Linesville PA 16424 *TF Sales:* 800-458-6050 ■ *Web:* www.mfgtray.com	814-683-4500	683-4504	199
Molded Rubber & Plastic Corp 13161 W Glendale Ave ... Butler WI 53007 *Web:* www.mrpcorp.com	262-781-7122	781-5353	677
Moldex 823 Bessemer St ... Meadville PA 16335 *Web:* www.moldexcorp.com	814-337-3190		711
Moldex Metric Inc 10111 W Jefferson Blvd ... Culver City CA 90232 **Fax:* Sales ■ *TF:* 800-421-0668 ■ *Web:* www.moldex.com	310-837-6500	837-9563*	576
Molding Corp of America 10349 Norris Ave ... Pacoima CA 91331 *TF:* 800-423-2747 ■ *Web:* www.moldingcorp.com	818-890-7877	890-7885	604
Molding International & Engineering Inc 42136 Avenida Alvarado ... Temecula CA 92590	951-296-5010		256
Mold-masters Ltd 41 Todd Rd ... Georgetown ON L7G4R8 *Web:* moldmasters.com	905-702-8955		608
Moldova Embassy 2101 S St NW ... Washington DC 20008 *Web:* www.embassy.org	202-667-1130	667-2624	257
Mold-Rite Plastics LLC 1 Plant St ... Plattsburgh NY 12901 *TF:* 800-432-5277 ■ *Web:* www.mrpcap.com	518-561-1812		608
Moldtech Inc 1900 Commerce Pkwy ... Lancaster NY 14086 *Web:* www.moldtechrubber.com	716-685-3344		677
Mole Hollow Candles Ltd 208 Charlton Rd Rt 20 PO Box 223 ... Sturbridge MA 01566 **Fax Area Code:* 888 ■ *TF Cust Svc:* 800-445-6653 ■ *Web:* www.moleholl owcandles.com	800-445-6653	998-9292*	327
Mole Lake Casino Lodge & Conference Ctr 3084 State Hwy 55 ... Crandon WI 54520 *TF:* 800-236-9466 ■ *Web:* www.molelakecasino.com	715-478-3200		452
Molecular Devices Inc (MDI) 1311 Orleans Dr ... Sunnyvale CA 94089 *TF:* 800-635-5577 ■ *Web:* www.moleculardevices.com	408-747-1700	747-3601	419
Molecular Imaging Services Inc 10 Whitaker Ct ... Bear DE 19701 *TF:* 866-937-8855 ■ *Web:* www.mismedical.com	866-937-8855		415
Molecular Pathology Laboratory Network Inc 250 E Broadway ... Maryville TN 37804 *TF:* 800-932-2943 ■ *Web:* www.mplnet.com	865-380-9746	380-9191	417
Molecular Sciences Institute 2168 Shattuck Ave Ste 200 ... Berkeley CA 94704 *Web:* www.molsci.org	510-647-0690		743

Name / Address	City	State	Zip	Phone	Fax	Class
Moleculera Labs LLC 755 Research Pkwy Ste 410; *Web:* www.moleculeralabs.com	Oklahoma City	OK	73104	405-239-5250		415
Mole-Richardson Company Inc 937 N Sycamore Ave; *Web:* www.mole.com	Hollywood	CA	90038	323-851-0111	851-5593	439
Molex Inc 2222 Wellington Ct; *NASDAQ: MOLX* ■ *TF Cust Svc:* 800-786-6539 ■ *Web:* www.molex.com	Lisle	IL	60532	630-969-4550	969-1352	253
Moliga Lolo Matalasi (I) Executive Office Bldg 3rd Flr	Pago Pago	AS	96799	684-633-4116	633-2269	343
Molin Concrete Products Co 415 Lilac St; *TF:* 800-336-6546 ■ *Web:* www.molin.com	Lino Lakes	MN	55014	651-786-7722	786-0229	183
Molina Healthcare Inc 200 Oceangate Ste 100; *NYSE: MOH* ■ *TF:* 888-562-5442 ■ *Web:* www.molinahealthcare.com	Long Beach	CA	90802	562-435-3666		391-3
Molina's Ranch Restaurant 4090 E Eigth Ave; *Web:* www.molinasranchrestaurant.com	Hialeah	FL	33013	305-693-4440		671
Moline Dispatch Publishing Co 1720 Fifth Ave; *TF:* 800-660-2472 ■ *Web:* qconline.com	Moline	IL	61265	309-764-4344	797-0317	637-8
Moline Forge Inc 4101 Fourth Ave; *Web:* www.molineforge.com	Moline	IL	61265	309-762-5506		483
Moline Machinery LLC 114 S Central Ave; *TF:* 800-767-5734 ■ *Web:* www.moline.com	Duluth	MN	55807	218-624-5734		362
Molivos 2310 Guy; *Web:* molivos.ca	Montreal	QC	H3H2M2	514-846-8818		671
Molle Toyota Inc 601 W 103rd St; *TF:* 888-510-7705 ■ *Web:* www.molletoyota.com	Kansas City	MO	64114	816-942-5200		57
Mollenberg-Betz Inc 300 Scott St; *Web:* www.mollenbergbetz.com	Buffalo	NY	14204	716-614-7473		189-10
Moller International Inc 1222 Research Park Dr; *Web:* www.moller.com	Davis	CA	95618	530-756-5086		20
Mollidgewock State Park 1437 Berlin Rd; *TF:* 800-922-8825 ■ *Web:* www.nhstateparks.org	Errol	NH	03579	603-482-3373		565
Mollie's La Casita Restaurant 2006 Madison Ave; *Web:* www.mollyslacasita.com	Memphis	TN	38104	901-726-1873		671
Molloy College 1000 Hempstead Ave PO Box 5002; *TF Admissions:* 888-466-5569 ■ *Web:* www.molloy.edu	Rockville Centre	NY	11571	516-678-5000		166
Mollusk Surf Shop LLC 4500 Irving St; *Web:* mollusksurfshop.com	San Francisco	CA	94122	415-564-6300		711
Molly Brannigans 506 State St; *Web:* www.mollybrannigans.com	Erie	PA	16501	814-453-7800		671
Molly Brannigans 31 N Second St; *Web:* www.mollybrannigans.com	Harrisburg	PA	17101	717-260-9242		671
Molly Brown House 1340 Pennsylvania St; *Web:* www.mollybrown.org	Denver	CO	80203	303-832-4092		520
Molly Pitcher Inn 88 Riverside Ave; *Web:* www.mollypitcher-oysterpoint.com	Red Bank	NJ	07701	732-747-2500		379
Molly Stark State Park 705 Rt 9 E; *Web:* www.vtstateparks.com	Wilmington	VT	05363	802-464-5460		565
Molly's House 430 SE Osceola St; *Web:* www.mollyshouse.org	Stuart	FL	34994	772-223-6659	223-9990	372
Molo Oil Company Inc 123 Southern Ave; *TF:* 877-983-3761 ■ *Web:* www.molocompanies.com	Dubuque	IA	52003	563-557-7540		581
Molok North America Ltd 179 Norpark Ave; *TF:* 877-558-5576 ■ *Web:* molokna.com	Mount Forest	ON	N0G2L0	519-323-9909		38
Molon Motor & Coil Corp 300 N Ridge Ave; *TF:* 800-526-6867 ■ *Web:* www.molon.com	Arlington Heights	IL	60005	847-253-6000	259-5491	518
Moloney Electric Inc 35 Leading Rd; *Web:* www.moloney-electric.com	Toronto	ON	M9V4B7	416-534-9226		767
Moloney Securities Company Inc 13537 Barrett Pkwy Dr Ste 300; *Web:* www.moseco.com	Manchester	MO	63021	314-909-0600		390
Molpus Co, The 502 Vly View Dr PO Box 59; *TF:* 800-535-5434 ■ *Web:* www.molpus.com	Philadelphia	MS	39350	601-656-3373	656-4947	817
Molson Coors Brewing Co 1225 17th St Ste 3200; *NYSE: TAP* ■ *TF:* 800-645-5376 ■ *Web:* www.molsoncoors.com	Denver	CO	80202	303-927-2337		102
Molten (North America) Corp 1835 Industrial Dr; *Web:* www.moltencorp.com	Findlay	OH	45840	419-425-2700		677
Molycorp Inc 67750 Bailey Rd; *Web:* www.molycorp.com	Mountain Pass	CA	92366	760-856-2201	856-2253	502
Mom & Dad's 4175 Apalachee Pkwy; *Web:* www.momanddadstally.com	Tallahassee	FL	32311	850-877-4518		671
Momar Inc 1830 Ellsworth Industrial Dr; **Fax Area Code: 800* ■ *TF:* 800-556-3967 ■ *Web:* www.momar.com	Atlanta	GA	30318	404-355-4580	849-5684*	145
Moment Design 13 Crosby St 6th Fl; *Web:* www.momentdesign.com	New York	NY	10013	212-625-9744		180
Moment Magazine 4115 Wisconsin Ave NW Ste 10; *TF:* 800-777-1005 ■ *Web:* www.momentmag.com	Washington	DC	20016	202-363-6422	362-2514	457-18
Momenta Pharmaceuticals Inc 675 W Kendall St; *NASDAQ: MNTA* ■ *Web:* www.momentapharma.com	Cambridge	MA	02142	617-491-9700	621-0431	85
Momentum Bmw Ltd 10002 SW Fwy; *TF:* 800-731-8114 ■ *Web:* momentumbmw.net	Houston	TX	77074	800-731-8114		516
Momentum Capital Partners 1227 W Magnolia Ave Ste 300; *Web:* mocappartners.com	Fort Worth	TX	76104	817-920-7599		225
Momentum Engineering Company LLC 5225 Katy Fwy Ste 605; *Web:* momentumtx.com	Houston	TX	77007	713-910-8300		186
Momentum For Mental Health 438 N White Rd; *TF:* 800-273-8255 ■ *Web:* www.momentumformentalhealth.org	San Jose	CA	95127	408-254-6828		726
Momentum Healthware Inc 308-131 Provencher Blvd; *Web:* www.momentumhealthware.com	Winnipeg	MB	R2H0G2	204-231-3836		179
Momentum Inc 1520 Fourth Ave Ste 300; *TF:* 800-992-4978 ■ *Web:* www.momentumbuilds.com	Seattle	WA	98101	206-267-1900		226
Momentum Oil and Gas LLC 20445 Texas 249; *Web:* www.momentumog.com	Houston	TX	77070	832-698-5600		536
Momentum Systems Ltd 41 Twosome Dr Ste 9; *TF:* 800-279-1384 ■ *Web:* www.momsys.com	Moorestown	NJ	08057	856-727-0777	273-3765	178-7
Momentum Technologies Inc (MTI) 1507 Boettler Rd	Uniontown	OH	44685	330-896-5900	896-9943	603
Momentum Worldwide 250 Hudson St 2nd Fl; *Web:* www.momentumww.com	New York	NY	10013	646-638-5400		4
Momentummedia-mag Inc 31 Dutch Mill Rd; *Web:* momentummedia.com	Ithaca	NY	14850	607-257-6970		177
Momentus Media Inc 650 Alabama St; *Web:* momentusmedia.com	San Francisco	CA	94110	415-895-0571		5
Momo Automotive Accessories Inc 20512 Crescent Bay Ste 104; *TF:* 800-749-6666 ■ *Web:* www.momo.com	Lake Forest	CA	92630	949-380-7556		54
Momocho Mod Mex 1835 Fulton Rd; *Web:* www.momocho.com	Cleveland	OH	44113	216-694-2122		671
Mon Ami Gabi 2300 N Lincoln Pk W; *Web:* www.monamigabi.com	Chicago	IL	60614	773-348-8886		671
Mon Cheri Bridals LLC 1018 Whitehead Rd Extn; *Web:* www.moncheribridals.com	Trenton	NJ	08638	609-530-1900		594
MONA (Missouri Nurses Assn) 1904 Bubba Ln PO Box 105228; *Web:* www.missourinurses.org	Jefferson City	MO	65110	573-636-4623	636-9576	533
MONA 216 S Brand Blvd Ste 101; *Web:* www.neonmona.org	Glendale	CA	91204	818-696-2149		520
Mona Electric Group Inc 7915 Malcolm Rd; *Web:* www.getmona.com	Clinton	MD	20735	301-868-8400		189-4
Mona Lisa 1697 Corydon Ave; *Web:* www.monalisarestaurant.ca	Winnipeg	MB	R3N0K4	204-488-3684	489-1679	671
Monache High School 960 N Newcomb St; *Web:* mhs.portervilleschools.org	Porterville	CA	93257	559-782-7150		685
Monaco 866 UN Plaza Ste 520; *Web:* www.monaco-un.org	New York	NY	10017	212-832-0721	832-5358	784
Monaco Coach Corp 1031 US 224 E; *TF:* 877-466-6226 ■ *Web:* monacocoach.com	Decatur	IN	46733	877-466-6226		120
Monaco Enterprises Inc 14820 E Sprague Ave PO Box 14129; *Web:* www.monaco.com	Spokane	WA	99216	509-926-6277	924-4980	678
Monaco Government Tourist Office 565 Fifth Ave 23rd Fl; *TF:* 800-753-9696 ■ *Web:* www.visitmonaco.com	New York	NY	10017	212-286-3330		775
Monadnock Family Services 64 Main St Ste 201; *TF:* 800-852-3323 ■ *Web:* www.mfs.org	Keene	NH	03431	603-357-4400		726
Monadnock Paper Mills Inc 117 Antrim Rd; **Fax: Sales* ■ *TF Orders:* 800-221-2159 ■ *Web:* www.mpm.com	Bennington	NH	03442	603-588-3311	588-3158*	557
Monadnock State Park 116 Poole Rd; *Web:* www.nhstateparks.org	Jaffrey	NH	03452	603-532-8862		565
Monaghan Medical Corp 5 Latour Ave Ste 1600; *TF:* 800-833-9653 ■ *Web:* www.monaghanmed.com	Plattsburgh	NY	12901	518-561-7330		477
Monahans Sandhills State Park PO Box 1738; *Web:* tpwd.texas.gov/state-parks/monahans-sandhills	Monahans	TX	79756	432-943-2092		565
Monarch Beverage Co 1123 Zonolite Rd NE Ste 10	Atlanta	GA	30306	404-262-4040		80-2
Monarch Capital Management Inc 127 W Berry St Ste 402; *Web:* www.monarchcapitalmgmt.com	Fort Wayne	IN	46802	260-422-2765		401
Monarch Casino & Resort Inc 3800 S Virginia St; *NASDAQ: MCRI* ■ *TF:* 800-723-6500 ■ *Web:* www.monarchcasino.com	Reno	NV	89502	775-335-4600	332-9171	669
Monarch Cement Co 449 1200 St PO Box 1000; *OTC: MCEM* ■ *TF:* 800-545-1882 ■ *Web:* www.monarchcement.com	Humboldt	KS	66748	620-473-2222	473-2447	135
Monarch Construction Company Inc PO Box 12249; *TF:* 800-893-3665 ■ *Web:* www.monarchconstruction.cc	Cincinnati	OH	45212	513-351-6900	351-0979	186
Monarch Creative 309 N Water St Ste 360; *Web:* monarchcreative.net	Milwaukee	WI	53202	414-277-0077		7
Monarch Dental Corp 7989 Belt Line Rd Ste 90; *Web:* www.monarchdental.com	Dallas	TX	75248	972-702-9017		194
Monarch Hotel & Conference Ctr 12566 SE 93rd Ave; *TF:* 800-492-8700 ■ *Web:* www.monarchhotel.cc	Clackamas	OR	97015	503-652-1515	652-7509	379
Monarch Industries Inc 99 Main St; *Web:* www.monarchinc.com	Warren	RI	02885	401-247-5200		309
Monarch Instrument Inc 15 Columbia Dr; *TF:* 800-343-0499 ■ *Web:* www.monarchinstrument.com	Amherst	NH	03031	603-883-3390		201
Monarch Lathes 615 N Oaks Ave PO Box 4609; *TF:* 800-543-7666 ■ *Web:* www.monarchlathe.com	Sidney	OH	45365	937-492-4111	492-7958	455
Monarch Litho Inc 1501 Date St; *Web:* www.monarchlitho.com	Montebello	CA	90640	323-727-0300	720-1169	627
Monarch LLC 7050 N 76th St; *TF:* 800-444-0311 ■ *Web:* www.monarchcorp.com	Milwaukee	WI	53223	414-353-8820		480
Monarch Medical Imaging Equipment Inc 101 Ellis St; *Web:* www.monarchmedical.com	Staten Island	NY	10307	718-317-0124		475
Monarch Plastics Inc 1205 65th St; *TF:* 800-552-5790 ■ *Web:* www.monarch-plastics.com	Kenosha	WI	53143	262-652-4444		601
Monarch Recovery Management Inc 10965 Decatur Rd; *Web:* monarchrm.com	Philadelphia	PA	19154	215-281-7500		160

Phone | Fax | Class

Monarch Ski & Snowboard Area
1 Powder Pl .... Monarch CO 81227 719-530-5000 377
Web: www.skimonarch.com

Monarch Textile Rental Services Inc
2810 Foundation Dr .... South Bend IN 46628 574-233-9433 258
TF: 800-589-9434 ■ *Web:* www.monarchlinen.com

Monastery of Saint Gertrude
465 Keuterville Rd .... Cottonwood ID 83522 208-962-3224 962-7212 673
Web: www.stgertrudes.org

Moncla Marine LLC 2107 Carmel Dr .... Lafayette LA 70501 337-456-8799 536
Web: www.moncla.com

Moncove Lake State Park
695 Moncove Lake Access Rd .... Gap Mills WV 24941 304-772-3450 772-3450 565
Web: www.moncovelakestatepark.com

Moncton Flight College
1719 Champlain St.......................... Dieppe NB E1A7P5 506-857-3080 23
TF: 800-760-4632 ■ *Web:* www.mfc.nb.ca

Moncton Hospital, The
135 MacBeath Ave .... Moncton NB E1C6Z8 506-857-5111 857-5545 374-2
Web: horizonnb.ca

Moncton Museum 20 Mountain Rd .... Moncton NB E1C2J8 506-856-4383 522
TF: 800-363-4558 ■ *Web:* www.moncton.ca

Monday Magazine 818 Broughton St .... Victoria BC V8W1E4 250-382-6188 532-5
Web: www.mondaymag.com

Mondial International Corp
101 Secor Ln PO Box 8369 .... Pelham Manor NY 10803 914-738-7411 738-7521 360-3
Web: mondialgroup.com

Mondo Mannequins LLC 300 Karin Ln .... Hicksville NY 11801 516-935-7700 279-3300* 7
*Fax Area Code: 877 ■ *Web:* www.mondomannequins.com

Mondorf & Fenwick Pllc
523 Columbia Dr .... Johnson City NY 13790 607-797-4339 2
Web: mfcpas.com

Mondre Energy Inc
1800 John F Kennedy Blvd Ste 1504 .... Philadelphia PA 19103 215-988-0577 192
TF: 800-375-8181 ■ *Web:* www.mondreenergy.com

Mondrian Hotel
8440 Sunset Blvd.................... West Hollywood CA 90069 323-650-8999 650-5215 379
TF: 800-525-8029 ■ *Web:* www.morganshotelgroup.com

Monebo Technologies Inc
1800 Barton Creek Blvd .... Austin TX 78735 512-732-0235 732-0285 475
Web: www.monebo.com

Monel Inc 2770 NW 24th St..................... Miami FL 33142 305-635-7331 805
Web: www.monelgourmet.com

Monell Chemical Senses Ctr
3500 Market St.......................... Philadelphia PA 19104 267-519-4700 519-4805 668
TF: 800-732-0999

Moneris Solutions Corp
3300 Bloor St W............................ Toronto ON M8X2X2 416-734-1000 215
TF: 800-465-7166 ■ *Web:* www.moneris.com

Monett Speedway 685 Chapell Dr .... Monett MO 65708 417-236-0600 515
Web: www.monettspeedway.net

Monetta Family of Mutual Funds
1776A S Naperville Rd Ste 100............... Wheaton IL 60189 630-462-9800 528
TF: 800-241-9772 ■ *Web:* www.monetta.com

Monex Deposit Co 4910 Birch St.......... Newport Beach CA 92660 949-752-1400 411
Web: www.monex.com

Money & Politics Report
1801 S Bell St............................. Arlington VA 22202 800-372-1033 531-7
TF: 800-372-1033 ■ *Web:* www.bna.com/money-politics-report-p6103

Money Concepts International Inc
11440 N Jog Rd .... Palm Beach Gardens FL 33418 561-472-2000 690
Web: www.moneyconcepts.com

Money Mailer LLC
12131 Western Ave..................... Garden Grove CA 92841 714-889-3800 5
TF: 800-468-5865 ■ *Web:* www.moneymailer.com

Money Market Directories Inc
401 E Market St PO Box 1608 .... Charlottesville VA 22902 434-977-1450 979-9962 177
Web: marketintelligence.spglobal.com

Money Movers Inc PO Box 241 .... Sebastopol CA 95473 707-829-5557 251
TF: 800-861-5029 ■ *Web:* moneymovers.com

Money Tree Software Ltd
2430 NW Professional Wy .... Corvallis OR 97330 541-754-3701 738-6522 177
TF: 877-421-9815 ■ *Web:* www.moneytree.com

MoneyGram International Inc
2828 N Harwood Fl 15 .... Dallas TX 75201 800-666-3947 69
NASDAQ: MGI ■ *TF:* 800-666-3947 ■ *Web:* www.moneygram.com

Moneytree Inc 6720 Ft Dent Way .... Seattle WA 98188 206-246-3500 248-3400 69
TF: 877-613-6669 ■ *Web:* www.moneytreeinc.com

Mongolia 6 E 77th St .... New York NY 10075 212-861-9460 861-9464 784
Web: www.un.int/mongolia

Mongolia Embassy 2833 M St NW........... Washington DC 20007 202-333-7117 298-9227 257
Web: www.mongolianembassy.us

Mongolian Grill
4801 E Second St Ste 110 .... Casper WY 82609 307-473-1033 671

Mongolian Grill
1415 N Lacrosse St Ste 1 .... Rapid City SD 57701 519-645-6400 671
Web: mongoliangrill.com

Mongoose Atlantic Inc
61 Broadway Rm 3024 .... New York NY 10006 212-968-0196 194

Monic PO Box 2018 .... Boulder CO 80306 303-530-3050 208
Web: www.monic.com

Monical Pizza Corp 530 N Kinzie Ave .... Bradley IL 60915 815-937-1890 937-9828 670
TF: 800-929-3227 ■ *Web:* monicals.com

Monigle Associates Inc 150 Adams St.......... Denver CO 80206 303-388-9358 5
TF: 800-346-4710 ■ *Web:* www.monigle.com

Moniker Online Services LLC
20 SW 27th Ave Ste 201............. Pompano Beach FL 33069 800-688-6311 396
TF: 844-760-0251 ■ *Web:* www.moniker.com

Monin Inc 2100 Range Rd .... Clearwater FL 33765 727-461-3033 297-8
Web: www.monin.com

Moniteau County 200 E Main St.............. California MO 65018 573-796-4521 338

Monitor Clipper Partners LLC
116 Huntington Ave 9th Fl .... Boston MA 02116 617-638-1100 401
Web: www.monitorclipper.com

Monitor Elevator Products Inc
125 Ricefield Ln .... Hauppauge NY 11788 800-527-9156 256
TF: 800-527-9156 ■ *Web:* www.mcontrols.com

Monitor on Psychology
750 First Ave NE......................... Washington DC 20002 202-336-5500 457-16
Web: www.apa.org/monitor

Monitor, The 1400 E Nolana Loop.............. McAllen TX 78504 956-683-4000 683-4401 532-2
TF: 800-366-4343 ■ *Web:* www.themonitor.com

Monjunis 1315 Louisiana Ave .... Shreveport LA 71101 318-227-0847 671
Web: www.monjunis.com

Monkey Jungle 14805 SW 216th St .... Miami FL 33170 305-235-1611 823
Web: www.monkeyjungle.com

Monmouth Battlefield State Park
347 Freehold-Englishtown Rd .... Manalapan NJ 07726 732-462-9616 565
Web: www.njparksandforests.org/parks/monbat.html

Monmouth College 700 E Broadway Ave .... Monmouth IL 61462 309-457-2311 457-2141 166
TF: 888-827-8268 ■ *Web:* www.monmouthcollege.edu

Monmouth County 1 E Main St............... Freehold NJ 07728 732-431-7324 409-7566 338
Web: co.monmouth.nj.us/index.aspx

Monmouth County Library (MCL)
125 Symmes Rd......................... Manalapan NJ 07726 732-431-7220 434-3
Web: www.monmouthcountylib.org

Monmouth Historic Inn & Gardens
1358 John A Quitman Blvd.................... Natchez MS 39120 601-442-5852 446-7762 379
TF: 800-828-4531 ■ *Web:* www.monmouthhistoricinn.com

Monmouth Medical Ctr
300 Second Ave .... Long Branch NJ 07740 732-222-5200 374-3
TF: 888-724-7123 ■ *Web:* www.barnabashealth.org

Monmouth Park Racetrack
175 Oceanport Ave .... Oceanport NJ 07757 732-222-5100 571-5226 642
Web: www.monmouthpark.com

Monmouth Real Estate Investment Corp (MREIC)
3499 Rt 9 N Ste 3C........................ Freehold NJ 07728 732-577-9996 655
NASDAQ: MNR ■ *TF:* 800-937-5449 ■ *Web:* www.mreic.com

Monmouth University
400 Cedar Ave .... West Long Branch NJ 07764 732-571-3456 263-5166* 166
*Fax: Admissions ■ *TF:* 800-543-9671 ■ *Web:* www.monmouth.edu

Mono County PO Box 237.................. Bridgeport CA 93517 760-932-5530 932-5531 338
Web: www.monocounty.ca.gov

Mono Lake Tufa State Reserve
1 Visitor Ctr Dr......................... Lee Vining CA 93541 760-647-6331 565
Web: www.parks.ca.gov

Monobind Inc 100 N Pt Dr................. Lake Forest CA 92630 949-951-2665 951-3539 231
TF: 800-854-6265 ■ *Web:* www.monobind.com

Monocacy National Battlefield
5201 Urbana Pk .... Frederick MD 21704 301-662-3515 662-3420 564
Web: www.nps.gov

Monocacy River Natural Resources Management Area
c/o Seneca Creek State Pk
11950 Clopper Rd .... Gaithersburg MD 20878 301-924-2127 565
Web: dnr2.maryland.gov

Monoflo International Inc
882 Baker Ln .... Winchester VA 22603 540-665-1691 596
Web: www.miworldwide.com

Monogram Aerospace Fasteners
3423 S Garfield Ave .... Los Angeles CA 90040 323-722-4760 721-1851 278
Web: www.monogramaerospace.com

Monogram Biosciences Inc
345 Oyster Pt Blvd .... South San Francisco CA 94080 650-635-1100 419
TF: 800-777-0177 ■ *Web:* www.monogrambio.com

Monogram Center 437 Amboy Ave.......... Perth Amboy NJ 08861 732-442-1800 711
Web: www.monogramcenter.com

Monograms 5301 S Federal Cir................ Littleton CO 80123 866-270-9841 760
TF: 866-270-9841 ■ *Web:* monograms.com

Monolith Productions Inc
12131 113th Ave NE Ste 300 .... Kirkland WA 98034 425-739-1500 322
Web: www.lith.com

Monolithic Power Systems Inc (MPS)
6409 Guadalupe Mines Rd .... San Jose CA 95120 408-826-0600 696
NASDAQ: MPWR ■ *Web:* www.monolithicpower.com

Monona County 610 Iowa Ave.................. Onawa IA 51040 712-423-2491 338
TF: 800-326-7732 ■ *Web:* www.mononacounty.org

Monona Plumbing & Fire Protection Inc
3126 Watford Way .... Madison WI 53713 608-273-4556 610
Web: www.mononapfp.com

Monona Terrace Community & Convention Ctr
1 John Nolen Dr........................... Madison WI 53703 608-261-4000 261-4049 205
TF: 800-947-3529 ■ *Web:* www.mononaterrace.com

Monongahela Valley Hospital
1163 Country Club Rd .... Monongahela PA 15063 724-258-1000 258-1830 374-3
Web: www.monvalleyhospital.com

Monongalia Arts Ctr (MAC)
107 High St PO Box 239................. Morgantown WV 26507 304-292-3325 292-3326 50-2
TF: 800-745-3000 ■ *Web:* www.monartscenter.com

Monongalia County
243 High St Courthouse Rm 123 .... Morgantown WV 26505 304-291-7230 338
Web: www.co.monongalia.wv.us

Monongalia General Hospital
1200 JD Anderson Dr................... Morgantown WV 26505 304-598-1200 374-3
Web: mongeneral.com

MonoSol LLC 707 E 80th Pl Ste 301 .... Merrillville IN 46410 219-762-3165 601
Web: www.monosol.com

MonoSol Rx Inc 30 Technology Dr .... Warren NJ 07059 732-564-5000 231
Web: www.monosolrx.com

Monro Muffler Brake Inc
200 Holleder Pkwy .... Rochester NY 14615 585-647-6400 647-0945 62-3
NASDAQ: MNRO ■ *TF:* 800-876-6676 ■ *Web:* www.monro.com

Monroe Bank & Trust 102 E Front St............ Monroe MI 48161 734-241-3431 70
TF: 800-321-0032 ■ *Web:* www.mbandt.com

Monroe Chamber of Commerce
212 Walnut St Ste 100 .... Monroe LA 71201 318-323-3461 322-7594 139
TF: 888-677-5200 ■ *Web:* www.monroe.org

Monroe Chamber of Commerce & Industry
1505 Ninth St.............................. Monroe WI 53566 608-325-7648 328-2241 139
Web: www.monroechamber.org

Monroe Civic Ctr 401 Lea Joyner Expy........... Monroe LA 71201 318-329-2225 329-2548 205
Web: ci.monroe.la.us

Monroe Clinic Hospital 515 22nd Ave .... Monroe WI 53566 608-324-2000 374-3
TF: 800-338-0568 ■ *Web:* www.monroeclinic.org

Monroe College 2501 Jerome Ave .... Bronx NY 10468 718-933-6700 364-3552* 800
*Fax: Admissions ■ *TF:* 800-556-6676 ■ *Web:* www.monroecollege.edu

Name / Address	Phone	Fax	Class
Monroe Community College 1000 E Henrietta Rd .... Rochester NY 14623 *TF:* 800-875-6269 ■ *Web:* www.monroecc.edu	585-292-2000	292-3860	162
Monroe Community Hospital 435 E Henrietta Rd .... Rochester NY 14620 *Web:* www.monroehosp.org	585-760-6500		374-7
Monroe County 124 W Commerce St .... Aberdeen MS 39730 *TF:* 800-457-5351 ■ *Web:* www.gomonroe.org	662-369-6488	369-6489	338
Monroe County 10 Benton Ave E....... Albia IA 52531 *Web:* www.monroecoia.us	641-932-2180		338
Monroe County 301 N College Ave .... Bloomington IN 47404 *Web:* www.co.monroe.in.us	812-349-2600	349-2610	338
Monroe County 123 Madison St .... Clarendon AR 72029 *Web:* monroecounty.arkansas.gov	870-747-3632		338
Monroe County 38 W Main St PO Box 189....... Forsyth GA 31029 *TF:* 800-282-5852 ■ *Web:* www.monroecountygeorgia.com	478-994-7000	994-7294	338
Monroe County 1100 SimontonSt....... Key West FL 33040 *TF:* 800-429-4529 ■ *Web:* www.monroecounty-fl.gov	305-294-4641		338
Monroe County 103 College St S Ste 1 .... Madisonville TN 37354 *Web.* www.monroegovernment.org	423-442-2220	442-9542	338
Monroe County 106 E First St....... Monroe MI 48161 *TF:* 800-401-6402 ■ *Web:* www.co.monroe.mi.us	734-240-7020	240-7045	338
Monroe County PO Box 8 .... Monroeville AL 36461 *Web:* www.monroecountyal.com	251-743-4107	575-7934	338
Monroe County 300 N Main Rm 101....... Paris MO 65275 *Web:* www.monroecountycollector.com	660-327-4320	327-5063	338
Monroe County 202 S K St Rm 1 .... Sparta WI 54656 *Web:* www.co.monroe.wi.us	608-269-8705	269-8747	338
Monroe County 610 Monroe St....... Stroudsburg PA 18360 *Web:* www.pacourts.us	570-420-3400		338
Monroe County 200 N Main St Ste D....... Tompkinsville KY 42167 *Web:* monroecountyclerkky.com	270-487-5471	487-8821	338
Monroe County 216 Main St PO Box 350 .... Union WV 24983 *Web:* www.monroecountywv.net	304-772-3096	772-4191	338
Monroe County 100 S Main St .... Waterloo IL 62298 *Web:* monroecountyil.org	618-939-8681		338
Monroe County 101 N Main St Rm 12 .... Woodsfield OH 43793 *Web:* www.monroecountyohio.net	740-472-5181	472-2526	338
Monroe County Chamber of Commerce 1645 N Dixie Hwy Ste 20 .... Monroe MI 48162 *TF:* 855-386-1280 ■ *Web:* monroecountychamber.com	734-384-3366	384-3367	139
Monroe County Chamber of Commerce 124 W Commerce St....... Aberdeen MS 39730 *TF:* 800-457-5351 ■ *Web:* www.gomonroe.org	662-369-6488	369-6489	139
Monroe County Chamber of Commerce 520 Cook St Ste A .... Madisonville TN 37354 *TF:* 800-245-5428 ■ *Web:* www.monroecountychamber.org	423-442-4588	442-9016	139
Monroe County Community College 1555 S Raisinville Rd....... Monroe MI 48161 **Fax:* Admissions ■ *TF:* 877-937-6222 ■ *Web:* www.monroeccc.edu	734-242-7300	242-9711*	162
Monroe County Electric Power Assn 601 N Main St .... Amory MS 38821 *TF:* 866 656 2962	662-256-2962		245
Monroe County Historical Museum 126 S Monroe St .... Monroe MI 48161 *Web:* co.monroe.mi.us	734-240-7780		520
Monroe County History Ctr 202 E Sixth St....... Bloomington IN 47408 *Web:* monroehistory.org	812-332-2517	355-5593	520
Monroe County Intermediate School District 1101 S Raisinville Rd....... Monroe MI 48161 *Web:* www.monroeisd.us	734-242-5799		685
Monroe County Library System 3700 S Custer Rd....... Monroe MI 48161 *TF:* 800-462-2050 ■ *Web:* www.monroe.lib.mi.us	734-241-5277	241-4722	434-3
Monroe County Public Library 303 E Kirkwood Ave .... Bloomington IN 47408 *Web:* www.monroe.lib.in.us	812 349 3050	349-3051	434-3
Monroe County Public Library System 700 Fleming St....... Key West FL 33040 *TF:* 877-772-8346 ■ *Web:* keyslibraries.org	305-292-3595	295-3626	434-3
Monroe County Tourist Development Council 1201 White St Ste 102 .... Key West FL 33040 *TF:* 800-242-5229 ■ *Web:* www.fla-keys.com	305-296-1552	296-6962	206
Monroe County Water Authority 475 Norris Dr PO Box 10999 .... Rochester NY 14610 *TF:* 866-426-6292 ■ *Web:* www.mcwa.com	585-442-2000	442-0220	787
Monroe Electronics Inc 100 Housel Ave....... Lyndonville NY 14098 *TF:* 800-821-6001 ■ *Web:* www.monroe-electronics.com	585-765-2254	765-9330	248
Monroe Energy LLC 4101 Post Rd Trainer .... Trainer PA 19061 *TF:* 800-424-9300 ■ *Web:* www.monroe-energy.com	610-364-8000		579
Monroe Environmental Corp 810 W Front St....... Monroe MI 48161 *TF:* 800-992-7707 ■ *Web:* www.monroeenvironmental.com	734-242-7654	242-5275	386
Monroe Evening News 20 W First St....... Monroe MI 48161 *Web:* www.monroenews.com	734-242-1100		532-2
Monroe Financial Partners Inc 100 N Riverside Plaza Ste 1620 .... Chicago IL 60606 *TF:* 800-766-5560 ■ *Web:* www.monroefp.com	312-327-2530		194
Monroe Fluid Technology Inc 36 Draffin Rd .... Hilton NY 14468 *TF:* 800-828-6351 ■ *Web:* www.monroefluid.com	585-392-3434	392-2691	145
Monroe Hardware Co 101 N Sutherland Ave....... Monroe NC 28110 *TF:* 800-222-1974 ■ *Web:* www.monroehardware.com	704-289-3121	289-2838	351
Monroe Lake 4850 S State Rd 446 .... Bloomington IN 47401 *Web:* www.in.gov	812-837-9546		565
Monroe Litho Inc 39 Delevan St....... Rochester NY 14605 *TF:* 800-456-3337 ■ *Web:* www.monroelitho.com	585-454-3290		627
Monroe Medi-Trans Inc 1669 Lyell Ave .... Rochester NY 14606 *Web:* www.monroeambulance.com	585-454-6910		30
Monroe Oil Co 519 E Franklin St....... Monroe NC 28112 *TF General:* 800-452-2717 ■ *Web:* www.monroeoilco.com	704-289-5438		324

Name / Address	Phone	Fax	Class
Monroe School Transportation 970 Emerson St .... Rochester NY 14606 *TF:* 800-276-1169 ■ *Web:* monroeschooltrans.com	585-458-3230	458-9159	109
Monroe Shine & Company Inc 222 E Market St .... New Albany IN 47150 *Web:* www.monroeshine.com	812-945-2311		2
Monroe Table Co 316 N Walnut St .... Colfax IA 50054	515-674-3511		319-3
Monroe Title Insurance Corp 47 W Main St .... Rochester NY 14614 *TF:* 800-966-6763 ■ *Web:* www.monroetitle.com	585-232-4950	232-4988	391-6
Monroe Township Free Public Library 713 Marsha Ave .... Williamstown NJ 08094 *TF:* 800-635-4417 ■ *Web:* www.monroetpl.org	856-629-1212		434-3
Monroe Tractor & Implement Company Inc 1001 Lehigh Stn Rd .... Henrietta NY 14467 *TF:* 866-683-5338 ■ *Web:* www.monroetractor.com	585-334-3867	334-0001	358
Monroe Truck Equipment Inc 1051 W Seventh St....... Monroe WI 53566 *TF:* 800-356-8134 ■ *Web:* www.monroetruck.com	608-328-8127	328-4278	516
Monroe Wheelchair 388 Old Niskayuna Rd....... Latham NY 12110 *TF:* 888-546-8505 ■ *Web:* www.monroewheelchair.com	518-783-1653		476
Monroeville | Monroe County Chamber of Commerce 86 N Alabama Ave....... Monroeville AL 36460 *Web:* www.monroecountyal.com	251-743-2879	743-2189	139
Monroeville Area Chamber of Commerce 4268 Northern Pike....... Monroeville PA 15146 *TF:* 800-527-8941 ■ *Web:* www.monroevillechamber.com	412-856-0622	856-1030	139
Monroeville Mall 200 Mall Blvd....... Monroeville PA 15146 *TF:* 800-487-3247 ■ *Web:* www.monroevillemall.com	412-243-8511		460
Monroe-West Monroe Convention & Visitors Bureau 601 Constitution Dr PO Box 1436 .... West Monroe LA 71292 *TF:* 800-843-1872 ■ *Web:* www.monroe-westmonroe.org	318-387-5691	324-1752	206
Monrovia Chamber of Commerce 620 S Myrtle Ave .... Monrovia CA 91016 *TF:* 800-755-1515 ■ *Web:* www.monroviacc.com	626-358-1159	357-6036	139
Monrovia Public Library 321 S Myrtle Ave .... Monrovia CA 91016 *TF:* 877-322-8228 ■ *Web:* www.cityofmonrovia.org	626-256-8274	256-8255	434-3
Monrovia Unified School District 325 E Huntington Dr....... Monrovia CA 91016 *Web:* www.monroviaschools.net	626-471-2000		685
Monsieur Touton Selections of Massachusetts Ltd 230 Lowell St Ste 2i .... Wilmington MA 01887 *Web:* www.mtouton.com	978-657-0405		80-3
Monson Lake State Park 1690 15th St NE .... Sunburg MN 56289 *Web:* www.dnr.state.mn.us	320-366-3797		565
Monsoon Capital LLC 4720 Montgomery Ln Ste 410 .... Bethesda MD 20814 *Web:* www.monsooncapital.com	301-222-8000		194
Monsoon Inc 1250 45th St Ste 100 .... Emeryville CA 94608 *TF:* 800-520-2294 ■ *Web:* www.monsooncommerce.com	510-594-4500	652-2403	803-1
Monster Cable Products Inc 455 Valley Dr .... Brisbane CA 94005 *TF:* 877 800 8080 ■ *Web:* www.monsterproducts.com	415-840-2000		52
Monster Medic Inc 909 Perkins Dr .... Mukwonago WI 53149	262-363-3066		587
Mont Clare Elmwood Park Chamber of Commerce 11 Conti Pkwy .... Elmwood Park IL 60707 *Web:* grandchamber.org	708-456-8000	456-8680	139
Mont Eagle Mills Inc 804 W Main St....... Oblong IL 62449 *Web:* monteaglemills.com	618-592-4211		275
Mont Pelerin Capital LLC 660 Newport Ctr Dr Ste 1220 .... Newport Beach CA 92660 *Web:* www.montpelerincapital.com	949-706-6707		414
Montage Inc Washington Navy Yard .... Washington DC 20010 *Web:* www.montageinc.com/montage/montage.html	202-332-0186		186
Montage Resort & Spa 30801 S Coast Hwy .... Laguna Beach CA 92651 *TF:* 866-271-6953 ■ *Web:* montagehotels.com/lagunabeach	949-715-6000		669
Montague County PO Box 77....... Montague TX 76251 *Web:* www.co.montague.tx.us	940-894-2461	894-3110	338
Montalbano Lumber Company Inc 1309 Houston Ave .... Houston TX 77007 *Web:* www.montalbanolumber.com	713-228-9011	228-8222	364
Montalvan Sales Inc 2225 S Castle Harbour Pl....... Ontario CA 91761 *TF:* 800-454-1207 ■ *Web:* www.montalvans.com	909-930-5670		345
Montana			
Arts Council PO Box 202201....... Helena MT 59620 *TF:* 800-282-3092 ■ *Web:* www.art.mt.gov	406-444-6430	444-6548	339-27
Attorney General 215 N Sanders St Justice Bldg, 3rd Fl....... Helena MT 59620 *Web:* dojmt.gov/agooffice	406-444-2026	444-3549	339-27
Banking & Financial Institutions Div 301 S Park Ste 316 PO Box 200546 .... Helena MT 59620 *TF:* 800-914-8423 ■ *Web:* www.banking.mt.gov	406-841-2920	841-2930	339-27
Child & Family Services Div PO Box 8005 .... Helena MT 59604 *TF:* 866-820-5437 ■ *Web:* dphhs.mt.gov	406-841-2400	841-2487	339-27
Commerce Dept 301 S Pk Ave PO Box 200501 .... Helena MT 59601 *Web:* www.commerce.mt.gov	406-841-2700	841-2701	339-27
Commissioner of Political Practices 1205 Eigth Ave PO Box 202401....... Helena MT 59620 *Web:* www.politicalpractices.mt.gov	406-444-2942	444-1643	265
Community Development Div 301 S Pk Ave PO Box 200523 .... Helena MT 59620 *Web:* www.comdev.mt.gov	406-841-2770	841-2771	339-27
Consumer Protection Office 555 Fuller Ave....... Helena MT 59620 *TF:* 800-481-6896 ■ *Web:* dojmt.gov	406-444-4500	442-2174	339-27
Corrections Dept 5 S Last Chance Gulch PO Box 201301....... Helena MT 59620 *Web:* www.cor.mt.gov	406-444-3930	444-4920	339-27
Court Administration 301 S Park Rm 328 PO Box 203005 .... Helena MT 59620 *Web:* www.montanacourts.org	406-841-2950		339-27

Name / Address	City	State	Zip	Phone	Fax	Class
Department of Labor & Industry - Business Standard 301 S Pk Rm 430 PO Box 200513	Helena	MT	59620	406-841-2300		339-27
Web: www.bsd.dli.mt.gov						
Environmental Quality Dept PO Box 200901	Helena	MT	59620	406-444-2544		339-27
Web: montanatu.org						
Forensic Science Div 2679 Palmer St	Missoula	MT	59808	406-728-4970	549-1067	339-27
Web: dojmt.gov/crime						
Healthcare Licensing Bureau 301 S Pk Ave Rm 430	Helena	MT	59620	406-841-2303	841-2305	339-27
Web: mt.gov						
Higher Education Board of Regents 2500 Broadway St PO Box 203201	Helena	MT	59620	406-444-6570	444-1469	725
TF: 877-501-1722 ■ Web: www.mus.edu						
Highway Patrol Div 2550 Prospect Ave PO Box 201419	Helena	MT	59620	406-444-3780	444-4169	339-27
Web: dojmt.gov/highwaypatrol						
Historical Society 225 N Roberts St	Helena	MT	59601	406-442-4120		339-27
Web: helenamt.com						
Housing Div PO Box 200528	Helena	MT	59620	406-841-2840	841-2841	339-27
Web: www.housing.mt.gov						
Information Technology Services Div 125 N Roberts St PO Box 200113	Helena	MT	59620	406-444-2511	444-2701	339-27
TF: 800-628-4917 ■ Web: www.itsd.mt.gov						
Insurance Div 1315 E Lockey	Helena	MT	59604	406-444-3783		339-27
Web: uid.dli.mt.gov						
Labor & Industry Dept PO Box 1728	Helena	MT	59624	406-444-2840	444-1394	339-27
Web: www.dli.mt.gov						
Legislative Services 1301 E Sixth Ave PO Box 201706	Helena	MT	59620	406-444-3064	444-3036	433
Web: leg.mt.gov						
Lieutenant Governor PO Box 200801	Helena	MT	59620	406-444-3111	444-5529	339-27
Web: www.governor.mt.gov						
Motor Vehicle Div 302 N Roberts St, PO Box 201430	Helena	MT	59620	406-444-3933		339-27
Web: dojmt.gov/driving						
Natural Resources & Conservation Dept 1539 Eleventh Ave	Helena	MT	59601	406-444-2074	444-2684	339-27
Web: www.dnrc.mt.gov						
Office of Governor PO Box 200801	Helena	MT	59620	406-444-3111	444-5529	339-27
TF: 855-318-1330 ■ Web: www.governor.mt.gov						
Public Education Board 46 N Last Chance Gulch PO Box 200601	Helena	MT	59620	406-444-6576	444-0847	339-27
Web: bpe.mt.gov						
Public Health & Human Services Dept 111 N Sanders	Helena	MT	59604	406-444-5622	444-1970	339-27
Web: mt.gov						
Public Service Commission 1701 Prospect Ave PO Box 202601	Helena	MT	59620	406-444-6199	444-7618	339-27
Web: Www.psc.mt.gov						
Revenue Dept 125 N Roberts PO Box 5805	Helena	MT	59604	406-444-6900	444-3696	339-27
TF: 866-859-2254 ■ Web: revenue.mt.gov						
Secretary of State 1301 E Sixth Ave PO Box 202801	Helena	MT	59601	406-444-2034	444-3976	339-27
Web: www.sos.mt.gov						
Securities Dept 840 Helena Ave	Helena	MT	59601	406-444-2040	444-3497	339-27
TF: 800-332-6148 ■ Web: www.sao.mt.gov						
State Auditor Office 840 Helena Ave	Helena	MT	59601	406-444-2040	444-3497	339-27
Web: www.sao.mt.gov						
State Government Information PO Box 200113	Helena	MT	59620	406-444-2511	444-2701	339-27
Web: www.mt.gov						
State Legislature 1301 E Sixth Ave	Helena	MT	59620	406-444-3060	444-3036	339-27
Web: www.leg.mt.gov						
Supreme Court Justice Bldg 215 N Sanders St Rm 323	Helena	MT	59620	406-444-3858	444-5705	339-27
Web: courts.mt.gov						
Transportation Dept 2701 Prospect Ave PO Box 201001	Helena	MT	59620	406-444-6200		339-27
Web: www.mdt.mt.gov						
Victim Services Office 555 Fuller Ave PO Box 201410	Helena	MT	59601	406-444-1907	442-2174	339-27
TF: 800-498-6455 ■ Web: dojmt.gov/victims						
Vital Records Bureau 111 N Sanders St	Helena	MT	59604	406-444-4228		339-27
Web: montanagenealogy.com						
Weights & Measures Program PO Box 200516 PO Box 200513	Helena	MT	59620	406-443-8065	443-8163	339-27
Web: www.bsd.dli.mt.gov/bc/ms_index.asp						
Wildlife And Parks 1420 E Sixth Ave PO Box 200701	Helena	MT	59620	406-444-2535	444-4952	339-27
Web: www.fwp.mt.gov						
Worker's Compensation Ct 1625 11th Ave PO Box 537	Helena	MT	59624	406-444-7794	444-7798	339-27
Web: www.wcc.dli.mt.gov						
Montana Assn of Realtors 1 S Montana Ave Ste M1	Helena	MT	59601	406-443-4032	443-4220	656
TF: 800-477-1864 ■ Web: www.montanarealtors.org						
Montana Brewing Co 113 N 28th St	Billings	MT	59101	406-252-9200		671
Web: www.montanabrewingcompany.com						
Montana Chamber of Commerce 900 Gibbon St PO Box 1730	Helena	MT	59624	406-442-2405	442-2409	140
TF: 888-442-6668 ■ Web: www.montanachamber.com						
Montana Club 24 W Sixth Ave	Helena	MT	59601	406-442-5980		671
Web: www.mtclub.org						
Montana Coffee Traders Inc 5810 Hwy 93 S	Whitefish	MT	59937	406-862-7633	862-7680	159
TF: 800-345-5282 ■ Web: www.coffeetraders.com						
Montana Construction Corp Inc 80 Contant Ave	Lodi	NJ	07644	973-478-5200	478-7604	188-10
Web: www.montanaconstructioninc.com						
Montana Democratic Party PO Box 802	Helena	MT	59624	406-442-9520	442-9534	616-1
Web: www.montanademocrats.org						
Montana Dental Assn 17 1/2 S Last Chance Gulch PO Box 1154	Helena	MT	59624	406-443-2061	443-1546	227
TF: 800-257-4988 ■ Web: www.mtdental.com						
Montana Exploration Corp 144 4 Ave SW Ste 2300	Calgary	AB	T2P3N4	403-265-9091		536
TF: 800-713-7278 ■ Web: www.montanaexplorationcorp.com						
Montana Historical Society Museum 225 N Roberts St	Helena	MT	59620	406-444-2694	444-2696	520
TF: 800-243-9900 ■ Web: mhs.mt.gov						
Montana Idaho Log & Timber 1069 US Hwy 93 N	Victor	MT	59875	406-961-3092		106
TF: 800-600-8604 ■ Web: www.mtidlog.com						
Montana Lawyer Magazine 7 W Sixth Ave Ste 2B	Helena	MT	59601	406-442-7660	442-7763	457-15
TF: 888-385-9119 ■ Web: www.montanabar.org						
Montana Lottery 2525 N Montana Ave	Helena	MT	59601	406-444-5825	444-5830	452
TF: 800-425-1435 ■ Web: www.montanalottery.com						
Montana Manufacturing Extension Center 2310 University Way Bldg 2	Bozeman	MT	59715	406-994-3812		463
TF: 800-637-4634 ■ Web: www.montana.edu/mmec						
Montana Medical Assn 2021 11th Ave Ste 1	Helena	MT	59601	406-443-4000	443-4042	474
TF: 877-443-4000 ■ Web: www.mmaoffice.org						
Montana Nurses Assn (MNA) 20 Old Montana State Hwy	Montana City	MT	59634	406-442-6710	442-1841	533
Web: www.mtnurses.org						
Montana Public Radio 32 Campus Dr University of Montana	Missoula	MT	59812	406-243-4931	243-3299	632
TF: 800-325-1565 ■ Web: www.mtpr.org						
Montana Public Television 183 Visual Communications Bldg	Bozeman	MT	59717	866-832-0829	994-6545*	632
*Fax Area Code: 406 ■ TF: 800-426-8243 ■ Web: www.montanapbs.org						
Montana Rail Link Inc 101 International Way	Missoula	MT	59808	406-523-1500	523-1493	648
TF: 800-338-4750 ■ Web: www.montanarail.com						
Montana Refining Co 1900 Tenth St NE	Great Falls	MT	59404	317-328-5660	328-2359	580
TF: 800-437-3188 ■ Web: calumetspecialty.com						
Montana Republican Party PO Box 935	Helena	MT	59624	406-442-6469		616-2
Web: www.mtgop.org						
Montana River Outfitters 923 Tenth Ave N	Great Falls	MT	59401	406-761-1677		760
TF: 800-800-8218 ■ Web: www.montanariveroutfitters.com						
Montana Standard 25 W Granite St	Butte	MT	59701	406-496-5500	496-5551	532-2
TF: 800-877-1074 ■ Web: www.mtstandard.com						
Montana State Fair 400 Third St NW	Great Falls	MT	59404	406-727-8900	452-8955	642
Web: goexpopark.com						
Montana State Library (MSL) 1515 E Sixth Ave	Helena	MT	59620	406-444-3115		434-5
Web: home.msl.mt.gov						
Montana State Prison 400 Conley Lake Rd	Deer Lodge	MT	59722	406-846-1320		213
TF: 888-739-9122 ■ Web: www.cor.mt.gov						
Montana State University						
Billings 1500 University Dr	Billings	MT	59101	406-657-2011	657-2302*	166
*Fax: Admissions ■ TF: 800-565-6782 ■ Web: www.msubillings.edu						
Bozeman PO Box 172190	Bozeman	MT	59717	406-994-2452	994-7360*	166
*Fax: Admissions ■ TF Admissions: 888-678-2287 ■ Web: www.montana.edu						
Library Renne Library PO Box 173320	Bozeman	MT	59717	406-994-3171	994-2851	434-6
Web: www.lib.montana.edu						
Northern PO Box 7751	Havre	MT	59501	406-994-2452		166
TF: 800-662-6132 ■ Web: www.montana.edu						
Montana Stone Gallery LLC 6900 Kestrel Dr	Missoula	MT	59808	406-541-7625		189-7
Web: www.montanastonegallery.com						
Montana Sulphur & Chemical Co PO Box 31118	Billings	MT	59107	406-252-9324		145
Web: www.montanasulphur.com						
Montana Tech of the University of Montana 1300 W Pk St	Butte	MT	59701	406-496-4101	496-4710*	166
*Fax: Admissions ■ TF Admissions: 800-445-8324 ■ Web: www.mtech.edu						
Montana University System 2500 E Broadway St	Helena	MT	59601	406-444-6570		786
Web: www.mus.edu						
Montana Veterans Home 400 Veterans Dr	Columbia Falls	MT	59912	406-892-3256	892-0256	793
TF: 888-279-7532 ■ Web: dphhs.mt.gov						
Montana Veterinary Medical Assn PO Box 6322	Helena	MT	59604	406-447-4259		795
Web: www.mtvma.org						
Montana Wilderness Assn (MWA) 80 South Warren St	Helena	MT	59601	406-443-7350	443-0750	48-13
Web: www.wildmontana.org						
Montana Women's Prison 701 S 27th St	Billings	MT	59101	406-247-5100	247-5161	213
Web: mt.gov						
Montana Workforce Services Div 1315 E Lockey PO Box 1728	Helena	MT	59604	406-444-2648	444-3037	259
Web: wsd.dli.mt.gov						
Montana World Trade Ctr Gallagher Business Bldg Ste 257	Missoula	MT	59812	406-243-6982		822
TF: 800-930-7098 ■ Web: www.mwtc.org						
Montana-Dakota Utilities Co (MDU) 400 N Fourth St	Bismarck	ND	58501	701-222-7900		787
TF: 800-638-3278 ■ Web: www.montana-dakota.com						
Montara State Beach c/o Santa Cruz District Office 303 Big Trees Park Rd	Felton	CA	95018	650-726-8819		565
Web: www.parks.ca.gov/?page_id=532						
Montauk Downs State Park 50 S Fairview Ave	Montauk	NY	11954	631-668-3781		565
Web: parks.ny.gov/golf-courses/8/details.aspx						
Montauk Point State Park 2000 Montauk Hwy	Montauk	NY	11954	631-668-3781		565
Web: parks.ny.gov/parks/61/hunting.aspx						
Montauk State Park 345 County Rd 6670	Salem	MO	65560	573-548-2201		565
Web: www.mostateparks.com						
Montauk Yacht Club Resort & Marina 32 Star Island Rd	Montauk	NY	11954	631-668-3100		669
TF: 888-692-8668 ■ Web: www.montaukyachtclub.com						
MontaVista Software Inc 2929 Patrick Henry Dr	Santa Clara	CA	95054	408-572-8000	572-8005	174
TF: 888-624-4846 ■ Web: www.mvista.com						

Name / Address	City	State	Zip	Phone	Fax	Class
Montcalm Community College						
2800 College Dr	Sidney	MI	48885	989-328-2111	328-2950*	162
*Fax: Admissions ■ Web: www.montcalm.edu						
Montcalm County PO Box 368	Stanton	MI	48888	989-831-7339		338
Web: montcalm.org						
Montclair Art Museum 3 S Mtn Ave	Montclair	NJ	07042	973-746-5555	746-0536	520
TF: 800-732-6845 ■ Web: montclairartmuseum.org						
Montclair Chamber of Commerce						
5220 Benito St	Montclair	CA	91763	909-624-4569	625-2009	139
Web: www.montclairchamber.com						
Montclair Kimberley Academy, The						
201 Valley Rd	Montclair	NJ	07042	973-746-9800		164
Web: www.mka.org						
Montclair Plaza						
5060 Montclair Plaza Ln	Montclair	CA	91763	909-626-2442		460
TF: 800-531-9817 ■ Web: montclairplace.com						
Montclair Public Library						
50 S Fullerton Ave	Montclair	NJ	07042	973-744-0500		435
TF: 800-682-1707 ■ Web: www.montclairlibrary.org						
Montclair State University						
1 Normal Ave	Montclair	NJ	07043	973-655-4000	655-7700*	166
*Fax: Admissions ■ TF Admissions: 800-331-9205 ■ Web: www.montclair.edu						
Monte Carlo Inn-Airport Suites						
7035 Edwards Blvd	Mississauga	ON	L5T2H8	905-564-8500	564-8400	379
TF: 800-363-6400 ■ Web: www.montecarloinns.com						
Monte Carlo Resort & Casino						
3770 Las Vegas Blvd S	Las Vegas	NV	89109	702-730-7777	730-7200	669
TF: 800-311-8999 ■ Web: www.montecarlo.com						
Monte L Bean Life Science Museum						
Brigham Young University 645 E 1430 N	Provo	UT	84602	801-422-5051	422-0093	520
Web: mlbean.byu.edu						
Monte Package Company Inc						
3752 Riverside Rd	Riverside	MI	49084	269-849-1722	849-0185	200
TF: 800-653-2807 ■ Web: www.montepkg.com						
Monte R Lee & Co						
100 NW 63rd St Ste 100	Oklahoma City	OK	73116	405-842-2405		261
TF: 800-923-8726 ■ Web: www.mrleng.com						
Monte Sano State Park						
5105 Nolen Ave	Huntsville	AL	35801	256-534-3757	539-7069	565
TF: 800-252-7275 ■ Web: www.alapark.com						
Monte Vista Christian School						
2 School Way	Watsonville	CA	95076	831-722-8178	722-6003	622
Web: www.mvcs.org						
Monte Vista Fire Station						
3201 Central Ave NE	Albuquerque	NM	87106	505-255-2424		671
Web: montevistafirestation.com						
Monte Vista High School Keynoters						
3131 Stone Valley Rd	Danville	CA	94526	925-552-5530		685
Web: www.mvkeynoters.org						
Montebello Brands Inc						
1919 Willow Spring Ave	Baltimore	MD	21222	410-282-8800	282-8809	80-1
Montebello Chamber of Commerce						
109 N 19th St	Montebello	CA	90640	323-721-1153	721-7946	139
Web: www.montebellochamber.org						
Montebello Container Corp						
13220 Molette St	Santa Fe Springs	CA	90670	562-404-6221		100
Web: www.montcc.com						
Montebello on Academy, The						
10500 Academy Rd NE	Albuquerque	NM	87111	505-294-9944		672
Web: www.fivestarseniorliving.com						
Montebello Unified School District (MUSD)						
123 S Montebello Blvd	Montebello	CA	90640	323-887-7900		685
Web: www.montebello.k12.ca.us						
Montecito Bank & Trust						
1000 State St	Santa Barbara	CA	93101	805-963-7511		70
Web: montecito.bank						
Montecito Inn Inc						
1295 Coast Village Rd	Santa Barbara	CA	93108	805-969-7854		707
TF: 800-843-2017 ■ Web: www.montecitoinn.com						
Montefiore Medical Ctr 111 E 210th St	Bronx	NY	10467	718-920-4321		374-3
Web: www.montefiore.org						
Monteith Engineering Research Ctr						
North Carolina State University						
2410 Campus Shore Dr Centennial Campus	Raleigh	NC	27606	919-515-2030	515-5055	668
Web: www.ncsu.edu						
Montello Heel Mfg Inc 13 Emerson Ave	Brockton	MA	02301	508-586-0603		301
Web: www.montelloheel.com						
Montello Inc 6106 E 32nd Pl Ste 100	Tulsa	OK	74135	800-331-4628	665-1480*	145
*Fax Area Code: 918 ■ TF: 800-331-4628 ■ Web: www.montelloinc.com						
Montereau Inc 6800 S Granite Ave	Tulsa	OK	74136	918-495-1500		672
Web: www.montereau.net						
Monterey Bay Aquarium						
886 Cannery Row	Monterey	CA	93940	831-648-4800		40
TF: 866-963-9645 ■ Web: www.montereybayaquarium.org						
Monterey Bay Inn 242 Cannery Row	Monterey	CA	93940	831-373-6242	655-8174	379
TF: 800-424-6242 ■ Web: www.montereybayinn.com						
Monterey Bay Nursery Inc						
748 San Miguel Canyon Rd	Watsonville	CA	95077	831-724-6361		293
Web: www.montereybaynsy.com						
Monterey Boats 1579 SW 18th St	Williston	FL	32696	352-528-2628	529-2628	90
TF: 800-772-6287 ■ Web: www.montereyboats.com						
Monterey City Hall 580 Pacific St	Monterey	CA	93940	831-646-3935	646-3702	337
Web: www.monterey.org						
Monterey Conference Ctr						
1 Portola Plaza	Monterey	CA	93940	831-646-3770	646-3777	205
TF Sales: 800-742-8091 ■ Web: www.montereyconferencecenter.com						
Monterey County 168 W Alisal St	Salinas	CA	93901	831-755-5115	757-5792	338
TF: 800-994-9662 ■ Web: www.co.monterey.ca.us						
Monterey County Convention & Visitors Bureau						
PO Box 1770	Monterey	CA	93942	831-657-6400	648-5373	206
TF: 888-221-1010 ■ Web: www.seemonterey.com						
Monterey County Herald						
2200 Garden Rd	Monterey	CA	93940	831-372-3311	372-8401	532-2
TF: 800-688-1808 ■ Web: www.montereyherald.com						
Monterey County Weekly						
668 Williams Ave	Seaside	CA	93955	831-394-5656	394-2909	532-5
Web: www.montereycountyweekly.com						
Monterey Financial Services Inc						
4095 Avenida De La Plata	Oceanside	CA	92056	760-639-3500		393
TF: 800-456-2225 ■ Web: www.montereyfinancial.com						
Monterey Hotel 406 Alvarado St	Monterey	CA	93940	831-375-3184	373-2899	379
TF: 800-966-6490 ■ Web: www.montereyhotel.com						
Monterey International						
200 W Superior St Ste 202	Chicago	IL	60654	312-640-7500	640-7515	731
Web: www.montereyinternational.net						
Monterey Jet Center LLC						
300 Skypark Dr	Monterey	CA	93940	831-373-0100		63
TF: 800-679-2992 ■ Web: www.montereyjetcenter.com						
Monterey Maritime & History Museum						
5 Custom House Plaza	Monterey	CA	93940	831-372-2608		520
TF: 800-448-3883 ■ Web: museumofmonterey.org						
Monterey Mechanical Co						
8275 San Leandro St	Oakland	CA	94621	510-632-3173	632-0732	189-10
Web: www.montmech.com						
Monterey Mills Inc						
1725 E Delavan Dr	Janesville	WI	53546	608-754-2866	754-3750	745-4
TF: 800-255-9665 ■ Web: www.montereymills.com						
Monterey Museum of Art						
559 Pacific St	Monterey	CA	93940	831-372-5477	372-5680	520
Web: www.montereyart.org						
Monterey Mushrooms Inc						
260 Westgate Dr	Watsonville	CA	95076	831-763-5300	929-0271*	10-7
*Fax Area Code: 610 ■ TF: 800-333-6874 ■ Web: www.montereymushrooms.com						
Monterey Park Chamber of Commerce						
700 El Mercado Ave	Monterey Park	CA	91754	626-570-9429		139
Web: gmpkchamber.org						
Monterey Pasta Co 2315 Moore Ave	Fullerton	CA	92833	800-588-7782		296-31
TF: 800-588-7782 ■ Web: www.montereygourmetfoods.com						
Monterey Peninsula Airport						
200 Fred Kane Dr Ste 200	Monterey	CA	93940	831-648-7000	373-2625	27
TF: 800-252-7522 ■ Web: www.montereyairport.com						
Monterey Peninsula Artists/Paradigm						
404 W Franklin St	Monterey	CA	93940	831-375-4889		731
TF: 800-947-0651 ■ Web: www.paradigmagency.com						
Monterey Peninsula Chamber of Commerce						
30 Ragsdale Dr #200	Monterey	CA	93940	831-648-5360	649-3502	139
Web: www.montereychamber.com						
Monterey Peninsula College						
980 Fremont St	Monterey	CA	93940	831-646-4000	646-4015*	162
*Fax: Admissions ■ TF: 877-663-5433 ■ Web: www.mpc.edu						
Monterey Peninsula College Theatre						
980 Fremont St	Monterey	CA	93940	831-646-4213		572
Web: www.mpctheatreco.com						
Monterey Plaza Hotel & Spa						
400 Cannery Row	Monterey	CA	93940	877-862-7552		379
TF: 877-862-7552 ■ Web: montereyplazahotel.com						
Monterey Public Library						
625 Pacific St	Monterey	CA	93940	831-646-3932	646-5618	434-3
TF: 800-338-0505 ■ Web: www.monterey.org						
Monterey State Beach						
c/o Monterey District Office 2211 Garden Rd	Monterey	CA	93940	831-649-2836		565
Web: www.parks.ca.gov/default.asp?page_id=576						
Monterey State Historic Park						
20 Custom House Plaza	Monterey	CA	93940	831-649-7118		565
Web: www.parks.ca.gov						
Monterey Technologies Inc						
24600 Silver Cloud Court Ste 103	Monterey	CA	93940	831-648-0190		466
Web: www.montereytechnologies.com						
Monterey-Salinas Transit (MST)						
1 Ryan Ranch Rd	Monterey	CA	93940	831-899-2555		468
TF: 800-291-2877 ■ Web: www.mst.org						
Monteris Medical Inc						
16305 36th Ave N Ste 200	Plymouth	MN	55446	763-253-4710		475
Web: www.monteris.com						
Monterrey 3724 Battleground Ave	Greensboro	NC	27410	336-282-5588		671
TF: 800-344-2282 ■ Web: monterrey29.com						
Montesquieu Winery 8221 Arjons Dr	San Diego	CA	92126	800-860-2378		636
TF: 800-860-2378 ■ Web: www.montesquieu.com						
Montessori Accreditation Council for Teacher Education (MACTE)						
420 Park St	Charlottesville	VA	22902	434-202-7793	525-8838*	48-1
*Fax Area Code: 888 ■ Web: www.macte.org						
Montezuma Castle National Monument						
527 S Main St	Camp Verde	AZ	86322	928-567-5276	567-3597	564
Web: www.nps.gov/moca						
Montezuma County 109 W Main St	Cortez	CO	81321	970-565-8317	565-3420	338
Web: montezumacounty.org/web						
Montfort Bros Inc 44 Elm St	Fishkill	NY	12524	845-896-6225	896-0021	183
TF: 800-724-1777 ■ Web: www.montfortgroup.com						
Montfort Group, The 44 Elm St	Fishkill	NY	12524	845-896-6225	896-0021	183
TF: 800-724-1777 ■ Web: www.montfortgroup.com						
Montfort Hospital 713 Montreal Rd	Ottawa	ON	K1K0T2	613-746-4621	748-4914	374-2
TF: 866-670-4621 ■ Web: www.hopitalmontfort.com						
Montgomery Advertiser						
425 Molton St	Montgomery	AL	36104	334-262-1611		532-2
TF: 877-424-0007 ■ Web: www.montgomeryadvertiser.com						
Montgomery Area Chamber of Commerce						
41 Commerce St PO Box 79	Montgomery	AL	36104	334-834-5200	265-4745	139
Web: www.montgomerychamber.com						
Montgomery Area Chamber of Commerce Convention & Visitor Bureau						
300 Water St	Montgomery	AL	36104	334-261-1100		206
TF: 800-240-9452 ■ Web: www.visitingmontgomery.com						
Montgomery Aviation Corp						
4525 Selma Hwy	Montgomery	AL	36108	334-288-7334	288-7337	63
TF: 800-392-8044 ■ Web: www.montgomeryaviation.com						
Montgomery Ballet						
2101 E Blvd Ste 223	Montgomery	AL	36117	334-409-0522		573-1
Web: www.montgomeryballet.org						
Montgomery Bank						
1 Montgomery Bank Plaza PO Box 948	Sikeston	MO	63801	573-471-2275		70
TF: 800-455-2275 ■ Web: www.montgomerybank.com						
Montgomery Bell State Resort Park						
1020 Jackson Hill Rd	Burns	TN	37029	615-797-9052		565
TF: 800-250-8613 ■ Web: www.state.tn.us						
Montgomery Botanical Ctr						
11901 Old Cutler Rd	Miami	FL	33156	305-667-3800	661-5984	97
TF: 800-435-7352 ■ Web: www.montgomerybotanical.org						

Name / Address	City	State	Zip	Phone	Fax	Class
Montgomery City Hall 103 N Perry St. *Web:* www.montgomeryal.gov	Montgomery	AL	36104	334-625-4400		337
Montgomery City Planetarium 1010 Forest Ave	Montgomery	AL	36106	334-241-4799		598
Montgomery City-County Public Library 245 High St. *Web:* www.mccpl.lib.al.us	Montgomery	AL	36104	334-240-4999	240-4980	434-3
Montgomery College 3200 College Pk Dr. *Web:* www.lonestar.edu	Conroe	TX	77384	936-273-7000		162
Montgomery College Rockville 51 Mannakee St. *Web:* cms.montgomerycollege.edu	Rockville	MD	20850	301-279-5000		162
Montgomery Communications Inc 222 W Sixth St. *Web:* www.dailyu.com	Junction City	KS	66441	785-762-5000		532-3
Montgomery Community College Foundation Inc 1011 Page St. *TF:* 800-839-6222 ■ *Web:* www.montgomery.edu	Troy	NC	27371	910-576-6222		434-3
Montgomery County 755 Roanoke St Ste 2E. *TF:* 800-956-4237 ■ *Web:* www.montva.com	Christiansburg	VA	24073	540-382-6954	382-6943	338
Montgomery County 1 Millennium Plaza. *Web:* www.mcgtn.org	Clarksville	TN	37040	931-648-8482	553-5160	338
Montgomery County 20 Park St. *Web:* www.co.montgomery.ny.us	Fonda	NY	12068	518-853-4304	853-8220	338
Montgomery County 1 Courthouse Sq PO Box 595. *Web:* www.montgomeryco.com	Hillsboro	IL	62049	217-532-9530	532-9581	338
Montgomery County 101 S Lawrence St PO Box 1667. *Web:* www.mc-ala.org	Montgomery	AL	36102-1667	334-832-1210	832-2533	338
Montgomery County 723 N Sturgeon St. *Web:* www.montgomerycitymo.org	Montgomery City	MO	63361	573-564-3160	564-3802	338
Montgomery County 105 Highway 270 E.	Mount Ida	AR	71957	870-867-3521		338
Montgomery County 44 W Main St Fiscal Ct. *TF:* 800-465-9191 ■ *Web:* www.montgomerycounty.ky.gov	Mount Sterling	KY	40353	859-498-8707	498-1040	338
Montgomery County 310 W Broad St. *TF:* 800-888-4213 ■ *Web:* www.montgomerycountyga.gov	Mount Vernon	GA	30445	912-583-2363	583-2026	338
Montgomery County PO Box 311. *TF:* 800-932-4600 ■ *Web:* www.montcopa.org	Norristown	PA	19404	610-278-3346	278-5188	338
Montgomery County 105 Coolbaugh St. *Web:* www.montgomerycountyiowa.com	Red Oak	IA	51566	712-623-3180	623-6540	338
Montgomery County 101 Monroe St. *TF:* 800-950-1682 ■ *Web:* www.montgomerycountymd.gov	Rockville	MD	20850	240-777-2500	777-2517	338
Montgomery County 203 W Main St. *TF:* 800-682-2014 ■ *Web:* montgomery.ces.ncsu.edu	Troy	NC	27371	910-576-6011	576-2635	338
Montgomery County Chamber of Commerce 1520 N Franklin St. *Web:* www.montgomerycc.org	Christiansburg	VA	24073	540-382-3020		139
Montgomery County Chamber of Commerce 51 Monroe St Ste 1800. *Web:* www.montgomerycountychamber.com	Rockville	MD	20850	301-738-0015	738-8792	139
Montgomery County Chamber of Commerce 2 N Main St PO Box 836. *Web:* fultonmontgomeryny.org	Gloversville	NY	12078	518-725-0641	725-0643	139
Montgomery County Chamber of Commerce PO Box 200. *TF:* 800-841-4141 ■ *Web:* www.montgomerycountychamber.org	Eagleville	PA	19408	610-265-1776	265-0473	139
Montgomery County Community College *Central* 340 DeKalb Pk. **Fax:* Admitting ■ *TF:* 800-624-0756 ■ *Web:* mc3.edu	Blue Bell	PA	19422	215-641-6300	619-7188*	162
Pottstown 101 College Dr. *Web:* mc3.edu	Pottstown	PA	19464	610-718-1800	718-1999	162
Montgomery County Intermediate Unit 23 1605 W Main St Ste B. *Web:* www.mciu.org	Norristown	PA	19403	610-539-8550		193
Montgomery County Library 104 I-45 N. *Web:* www.countylibrary.org	Conroe	TX	77301	936-442-7712	788-8398	434-3
Montgomery County Mississippi Genealogy & History Network PO Box 71. *Web:* montgomery.msghn.org/addresses.html	Winona	MS	38967	662-283-2333		338
Montgomery County Pennsylvania PO Box 311. *Web:* www.montcopa.org	Norristown	PA	19404	610-278-3000		532-4
Montgomery County Visitors & Convention Bureau 218 E Pike St. *TF:* 800-866-3973 ■ *Web:* www.visitmoco.com	Crawfordsville	IN	47933	765-362-5200	362-5215	206
Montgomery County-Norristown Public Library 1001 Powell St. *Web:* mnl.mclinc.org	Norristown	PA	19401	610-278-5100	277-0344	434-3
Montgomery Gallery 406 Jackson St. *Web:* www.montgomerygallery.com	San Francisco	CA	94111	415-788-8300	788-5469	42
Montgomery General Hospital 18101 Prince Philip Dr. *Web:* www.medstarhealth.org	Olney	MD	20832	301-774-8882		374-3
Montgomery Hospice 1355 Piccard Dr Ste 100. *TF:* 800-994-6610 ■ *Web:* www.montgomeryhospice.org	Rockville	MD	20850	301-921-4400	921-4433	371
Montgomery Hospital 1301 Powell St. *Web:* www.montgomeryhospital.org	Norristown	PA	19401	610-270-2000		374-3
Montgomery Independent 141 Market Pl. *Web:* www.al.com	Montgomery	AL	36117	334-265-7323		532-4
Montgomery Industries International Inc 2017 Thelma St. *Web:* www.montgomeryindustries.com	Jacksonville	FL	32206	904-355-4055	355-0401	273
Montgomery Inn 9440 Montgomery Rd. *Web:* www.montgomeryinn.com	Montgomery	OH	45242	513-791-3482		671
Montgomery Investment Management Inc 6229 Executive Blvd. *Web:* www.miminvest.com	Rockville	MD	20852	301-897-9783		690
Montgomery Little & Soran PC 5445 Dtc Pkwy Ste 800. *Web:* www.montgomerylittle.com	Greenwood Village	CO	80111	303-773-8100		428
Montgomery Martin Contractors LLC 8245 Tournament Dr Ste 300. *Web:* www.montgomerymartin.com	Memphis	TN	38125	901-374-9400	374-9402	186
Montgomery Museum of Fine Arts 1 Museum Dr PO Box 230819. *Web:* www.mmfa.org	Montgomery	AL	36117	334-240-4333	240-4384	520
Montgomery Mutual Insurance Co 6230 Old Dobbin Ln Ste 200. **Fax:* Hum Res ■ *TF:* 800-561-0178	Columbia	MD	21045-5801	704-759-7661	544-2971*	391-4
Montgomery Public Schools 307 S Decatur St. *Web:* www.mps.k12.al.us	Montgomery	AL	36104	334-223-6700	269-3076	685
Montgomery Regional Airport 4445 Selma Hwy. *TF:* 800-433-7300 ■ *Web:* www.flymgm.com	Montgomery	AL	36108	334-281-5040	281-5041	27
Montgomery Regional Hospital 3700 S Main St. *TF:* 800-222-1222 ■ *Web:* lewisgale.com	Blacksburg	VA	24060	540-951-1111	953-5372	374-3
Montgomery Street Antique Mall 2601 Montgomery St. *Web:* www.montgomerystreetantiques.com	Fort Worth	TX	76107	817-735-9685		460
Montgomery Truss & Panel Inc 803 W Main St. *TF:* 800-942-8010 ■ *Web:* montgomerytruss.com	Grove City	PA	16127	724-458-7500	458-0765	817
Montgomery Woods State Reserve 15825 Orr Springs Rd. *Web:* www.parks.ca.gov/default.asp?page_id=434	Ukiah	CA	95482	707-937-5804		565
Montgomery Zoo 2301 Coliseum Pkwy. *Web:* www.montgomeryzoo.com	Montgomery	AL	36110	334-240-4900	240-4916	823
Montgomery-Floyd Regional Library 125 Sheltman St. *Web:* www.mfrl.org	Christiansburg	VA	24073	540-382-6965	382-6964	434-3
Monti Inc 4510 Reading Rd. *Web:* www.monti-inc.com	Cincinnati	OH	45229	513-761-7775	948-6858	816
Monticello 556 Dettor Rd Ste 107. *TF:* 800-243-0743 ■ *Web:* www.monticello.org	Charlottesville	VA	22903	434-984-9822		50-3
Monticello Central School District 237 Forestburgh Rd. *TF:* 866-805-0990 ■ *Web:* www.monticelloschools.net	Monticello	NY	12701	845-794-7700		685
Monticello Corp, The PO Box 190645. *Web:* www.thepapertiger.com	Atlanta	GA	30319	404-478-6413		525
Monticello Nursing & Rehabilitation Ctr 500 Pinehaven Dr. *Web:* monticellocampus.com	Monticello	IA	52310	319-465-5415		450
Monticello Spring Corp 3137 Freeman Rd PO Box 705. *TF:* 800-321-0746 ■ *Web:* www.monticellospring.com	Monticello	IN	47960	574-583-8090	583-9299	719
Montie Roland 2106 Jerimouth Dr. *Web:* www.montie.com	Apex	NC	27502	919-481-1845		196
Montien Thai Restaurant 63 Stuart St. *Web:* www.montien-boston.com	Boston	MA	02116	617-338-5600		671
Montini Catholic High School 19w070 16th St. *Web:* montini.org	Lombard	IL	60148	630-627-6930		685
Montlake Capital 1200 Fifth Ave Ste 1800. *Web:* www.montlakecapital.com	Seattle	WA	98101	206-956-0898	956-0863	792
Mont-Laurier Chamber of Commerce 385 Rue Du Pont 2E Etage. *Web:* www.ccmont-laurier.com	Mont-Laurier	QC	J9L3G9	819-623-3642	623-5220	137
Montlick & Associates PC 17 Executive Park Dr Ste 300. *Web:* www.montlick.com	Atlanta	GA	30329	404-529-6333		428
Montmarte 327 Seventh St SE. *Web:* montmartredc.com	Washington	DC	20003	202-544-1244		671
Montmorency County PO Box 789. *TF:* 800-396-9129 ■ *Web:* montmorencycountymichigan.us	Atlanta	MI	49709	989-785-8013	785-8014	338
Montour County 29 Mill St. *TF:* 800-632-9063 ■ *Web:* www.montourco.org	Danville	PA	17821	570-271-3010	271-3089	338
Montowese Health & Rehabilitation Ctr Inc 163 Quinnipiac Ave. *TF:* 800-272-3900 ■ *Web:* www.montowesehealth.com	North Haven	CT	06473	203-624-3303	787-9243	450
Montpelier City Hall 39 Main St. *Web:* montpelier-vt.org	Montpelier	VT	05602	802-223-9502	223-9519	337
Montpelier Glove Co Inc 129 N Main St. *TF:* 800-645-3931 ■ *Web:* www.montpeliergsp.com	Montpelier	IN	47359	765-728-2481		155-8
Montreal Alouettes 1260 boul Robert-Bourassa Ste 100. *Web:* www.montrealalouettes.com	Montreal	QC	H3B3B9	514-787-2525	871-2277	715-2
Montreal Botanical Garden 4101 Sherbrooke St E. *Web:* ville.montreal.qc.ca	Montreal	QC	H1X2B2	514-872-1400	872-1455	97
Montreal Canadiens Bell Centre 1260 de la Gauchetiere St W. **Fax:* PR ■ *TF:* 800-363-8162 ■ *Web:* canadiens.nhl.com	Montreal	QC	H3B5E8	514-989-2841	925-2144*	716
Montreal Exchange 800 Victoria Sq Third Fl PO Box 61. *TF:* 800-361-5353 ■ *Web:* www.m-x.ca	Montreal	QC	H4Z1A9	514-871-2424		691
Montreal Heart Institute 5000 Belanger St E. *TF:* 855-922-6387 ■ *Web:* www.icm-mhi.org	Montreal	QC	H1T1C8	514-376-3330	593-2540	374-2
Montreal Holocaust Memorial Centre 5151 Ch de la C(te-Sainte-Catherine. *Web:* museeholocauste.ca/fr	Montreal	QC	H3W1M6	514-345-2605	344-2651	520
Montreal Inn Beach Dr & Madison Ave. *TF:* 800-525-7011 ■ *Web:* montrealbeachresort.com	Cape May	NJ	08204	609-884-7011		669
Montreal International 380 Saint-Antoine St W Ste 8000. *Web:* www.montrealinternational.com	Montreal	QC	H2Y3X7	514-987-8191		463
Montreal Port Authority Port of Montreal Bldg 2100 Pierre-Dupuy Ave Wing 1. *Web:* www.port-montreal.com	Montreal	QC	H3C3R5	514-283-7011	283-0829	618

	Phone	Fax	Class
Montreal World Film Festival 1432 Rue de Bleury .... Montreal QC H3A2J1 *Web:* www.ffm-montreal.org	514-848-3883	848-3886	282
Montreat College 310 Gaither Cir PO Box 1267 .... Montreat NC 28757 *TF:* 800-622-6968 ■ *Web:* www.montreat.edu	828-669-8011	669-0120	166
Montrio 414 Calle Principal .... Monterey CA 93940 *Web:* www.montrio.com	831-648-8880		671
Montrose Chamber of Commerce 1519 E Main St .... Montrose CO 81401 *TF:* 800-923-5515 ■ *Web:* montrosechamber.com	970-249-5000	249-2907	139
Montrose County 161 S Townsend .... Montrose CO 81401 *Web:* www.co.montrose.co.us	970-249-3362	249-7761	338
Montrose County School District Re-1j Inc PO Box 10000 .... Montrose CO 81402 *Web:* www.mcsd.org	970-249-7726	249-7173	685
Montrose Historical & Telephone Pioneer Museum 144 E Hickory St .... Montrose MI 48457 *TF:* 800-686-1883 ■ *Web:* montrosemuseum.com	810-639-6644		520
Montrose Travel 2355 Honolulu Ave .... Montrose CA 91020 *TF:* 800-766-4687 ■ *Web:* www.montrosetravel.com	800-766-4687		771
Montrose Visitor & Convention Bureau 107 S Cascade Ave .... Montrose CO 81401 *TF:* 888-212-8294 ■ *Web:* www.visitmontrose.com	970-249-5000	964-4073	206
Montrusco Bolton Investments Inc 1501 McGill College Ave Ste 1200 .... Montreal QC H3A3M8 *TF:* 800-461-4551 ■ *Web:* www.montruscobolton.com	514-842-6464		528
Montserrat College of Art 23 Essex St .... Beverly MA 01915 *Fax: Admissions ■ *TF:* 800-836-0487 ■ *Web:* www.montserrat.edu	978-921-4242	921-4241*	166
Montserrat Jesuit Retreat House 600 N Shady Shores Dr PO Box 1390 .... Lake Dallas TX 75065 *TF:* 800-621-5197 ■ *Web:* www.montserratretreat.org	940-321-6020	321-6040	673
Montverde Academy 17235 Seventh St .... Montverde FL 34756 *Web:* www.montverde.org	407-469-2561	469-3711	622
Monument Builders of North America (MBNA) 136 S Keowee St .... Dayton OH 45402 *Fax Area Code: 937 ■ *TF:* 800-233-4472 ■ *Web:* www.monumentbuilders.org	800-233-4472	222-5794*	49-3
Monument Consulting LLC 3957 Westerre Pkwy Ste 330 .... Richmond VA 23233 *Web:* www.monumentconsulting.com	804-622-9992		463
Monument Hill & Kreische Brewery State Historic Sites 414 State Loop 92 .... La Grange TX 78945 *Web:* tpwd.texas.gov	979-968-5658		565
Monument Security Inc 5844 Price Ave .... Sacramento CA 95652 *TF:* 877-506-1755 ■ *Web:* monumentsecurity.com	916-564-4234		693
Monumental Sales Inc 537 22nd Ave N PO Box 667 .... Saint Cloud MN 56302 *TF:* 800-442-1660 ■ *Web:* www.sunburstmemorials.com	320-251-6585	251-6547	724
Monumental Sports & Entertainment LLC 601 F St NW .... Washington DC 20004 *Web:* www.monumentalsports.com	202-628-3200		717
MOOD (Michigan Out-of-Doors Magazine) 2101 Wood St PO Box 30235 .... Lansing MI 48912 *TF:* 800-777-6720 ■ *Web:* www.mucc.org	517-371-1041		457-22
Mood Media Corp 1703 W Fifth St Ste 600 .... Austin TX 78703 *Web:* www.moodmedia.com	512-380-8500		195
Moody Air Force Base 4343 George St Bldg 904 .... Moody AFB GA 31699 *Web:* www.moody.af.mil	229-257-3395		497-1
Moody Aldrich Partners LLC 18 Sewall St .... Marblehead MA 01945 *Web:* www.moodyaldrich.com	781-639-2750	639-2751	401
Moody Bible Institute 820 N La Salle St .... Chicago IL 60610 *Fax: Admissions ■ *TF:* 800-967-4624 ■ *Web:* www.moody.edu	312-329-4400	329-8955*	161
Moody County 101 E Pipestone Ave .... Flandreau SD 57028 *Web:* moodycounty.net	605-997-3181		338
Moody Dunbar Inc 2000 Waters Edge Dr Ste 21 .... Johnson City TN 37604 *TF:* 800-251-8202 ■ *Web:* moodydunbar.com	423-952-0100	952-0289	296-20
Moody Famiglietti & Andronico LLP 1 Highwood Dr .... Tewksbury MA 01876 *Web:* mfa-cpa.com	978-557-5300		734
Moody Foundation 2302 Post Office St Ste 704 .... Galveston TX 77550 *TF:* 800-421-9512 ■ *Web:* www.moodyf.org	409-797-1500		305
Moody Gardens Convention Ctr 7 Hope Blvd .... Galveston TX 77554 *TF:* 888-388-8484 ■ *Web:* www.moodygardenshotel.com	409-741-8484		205
Moody Global Ministries 820 N La Salle Blvd .... Chicago IL 60610 *Web:* moodyglobal.org	312-329-4000		644
Moody Medical Library 914 Market St .... Galveston TX 77555 *Fax Area Code: 832 ■ *TF:* 866-235-5223	409-772-2372	202-2689*	434-1
Moody Nolan Inc 300 Spruce St Ste 300 .... Columbus OH 43215 *Web:* www.moodynolan.com	614-461-4664		261
Moody Planetarium 3301 Fourth St Museum of Texas Tech University .... Lubbock TX 79409 *Web:* www.depts.ttu.edu/museumttu	806-742-2432	742-1136	598
Moody Rambin Interests 3003 W Alabama St .... Houston TX 77098 *Web:* www.moodyrambin.com	713-271-5900	773-5555	655
Moody's Corp 250 Greenwich St 7 World Trade Ctr .... New York NY 10007 *NYSE:* MCO ■ *Web:* www.moodys.com	212-553-0300		401
Moody's of Dayton Inc 4359 Infirmary Rd .... Miamisburg OH 45342 *Web:* www.moodysofdayton.com	937-859-4482		537
Moody-Price LLC 18320 Petroleum Dr .... Baton Rouge LA 70809 *Fax Area Code: 225 ■ *TF:* 800-272-9832 ■ *Web:* www.moodyprice.com	800-272-9832	763-6005*	386
Moog Animatics 3200 Patrick Henry Dr .... Santa Clara CA 95054 *Web:* www.animatics.com	408-748-8721		225
Moog Flo-Tork Inc 1701 N Main St PO Box 68 .... Orrville OH 44667 *TF:* 800-558-5950 ■ *Web:* flotork.com	330-682-0010	683-6857	223
Moog Inc Jamison Rd .... East Aurora NY 14052 *NYSE:* MOG/A ■ *TF:* 800-336-2112 ■ *Web:* www.moog.com	716-652-2000	687-4457	203
Moog Music Inc 160 Broadway St .... Asheville NC 28801 *Web:* www.moogmusic.com	828-251-0090		526
Moolenaar John (Rep R - MI) 117 Cannon HOB .... Washington DC 20515 *Web:* moolenaar.house.gov	202-225-3561	225-9679	342-2
Moon Distributors Inc 2800 Vance St .... Little Rock AR 72206 *TF:* 800-331-3005 ■ *Web:* moondist.com	501-375-8291		81-1
Moon Lake Electric Assn Inc 800 W Hwy 40 PO Box 278 .... Roosevelt UT 84066 *Web:* www.mleainc.com	435-722-5400		245
Moon Lake State Recreation Site c/o Northern Area Office 3700 Airport Way .... Fairbanks AK 99709 *Web:* www.dnr.alaska.gov	907-883-3686		565
Mooney & Thomas PC 2111 Plum St Ste 150 .... Aurora IL 60506 *Web:* mooneythomas.com	630-844-5272		2
Mooney Aircraft Corp 165 Al Mooney Rd .... Kerrville TX 78028 *TF:* 800-456-3033 ■ *Web:* www.mooney.com	800-456-3033		20
Mooney Alex (Rep R - WV) 1232 Longworth HOB .... Washington DC 20515 *Web:* mooney.house.gov	202-225-2711	225-7856	342-2
Mooney Farms 1220 Fortress St .... Chico CA 95973 *Web:* www.mooneyfarms.com	530-899-2661	899-7746	11-1
Mooney General Paper Co 1451 Chestnut Ave PO Box 3800 .... Hillside NJ 07205 *TF:* 800-882-8846 ■ *Web:* www.mooneygeneral.com	973-926-3800	926-0425	547
MoonFish 7525 W Sand Lake Rd .... Orlando FL 32819 *Web:* www.talkofthetownrestaurants.com	407-363-7262		671
Moon-matz Ltd 2902 S Sheridan Way Ste 300 .... Oakville ON L5G3H5 *Web:* moon-matz.com	905-274-7556	274-5382	261
Moonshine Patio Bar & Grill 303 Red River St .... Austin TX 78701 *Web:* www.moonshinegrill.com	512-236-9599		671
Moonstone Hotel Properties Inc 2905 Burton Dr .... Cambria CA 93428 *TF:* 800-656-6650 ■ *Web:* www.moonstonehotels.com	805-927-4200		707
Moonstruck Chocolate Co 6600 N Baltimore Ave .... Portland OR 97203 *TF:* 800-557-6666 ■ *Web:* www.moonstruckchocolate.com	503-247-3448	247-3450	296-8
Moonworks 1137 Park E Dr .... Woonsocket RI 02895 *TF:* 800-975-6666 ■ *Web:* www.moonworkshome.com	800-975-6666		752
Moore & Company PA 560 Riverside Dr Ste A-102 .... Salisbury MD 21801 *Web:* moore-company.com	410-749-3211		2
Moore & Neidenthal Inc 3034 N Wooster Ave .... Dover OH 44622 *TF:* 866-364-7774 ■ *Web:* mnpinnacle.com	330-364-7774		2
Moore & Scarry Advertising Inc 12601 Westlinks Dr Ste 7 .... Fort Myers FL 33913 *Web:* www.mooreandscarry.com	239-689-4000		7
Moore Bass Consulting Inc 805 N Gadsden St .... Tallahassee FL 32303 *Web:* moorebass.com	850-222-5678		261
Moore Chamber of Commerce 305 W Main St .... Moore OK 73160 *Web:* www.moorechamber.com	405-794-3400	794-8555	139
Moore College of Art & Design 20th St & the Pkwy .... Philadelphia PA 19103 *TF:* 800-523-2025 ■ *Web:* www.moore.edu	215-965-4000	568-8017	164
Moore Communications Group Inc 2011 Delta Blvd .... Tallahassee FL 32303 *Web:* www.moorecommgroup.com	850-224-0174		7
Moore Computing LLP 317 N 11th St Ste 200 .... Saint Louis MO 63101 *Web:* www.moorecomputing.com	314-621-5585		180
Moore County PO Box 905 .... Carthage NC 28327 *Web:* www.moorecountync.gov/administration	910-947-6363	947-1874	338
Moore County 715 S Dumas Ave Rm 304 .... Dumas TX 79029 *Web:* co.moore.tx.us	806-935-5654	935-9004	338
Moore County 196 Main St PO Box 206 .... Lynchburg TN 37352 *Web:* www.lynchburgtn.com	931-759-7346		338
Moore County Chamber of Commerce 10677 Hwy 15-501 .... Southern Pines NC 28387 *TF:* 800-346-5362 ■ *Web:* www.moorecountychamber.com	910-692-3926	692-0619	139
Moore Erection LP 19921 Fm 2252 .... Garden Ridge TX 78266 *Web:* melpsteel.com	210-648-7461		723
Moore Food Distributors Co 9910 Page Ave .... Saint Louis MO 63132 *TF:* 800-467-7878 ■ *Web:* www.moorefooddist.com	314-426-1300		297-7
Moore Group, The 407 W Bute St .... Norfolk VA 23510 *Web:* www.themooregroup.com	757-627-1015		764
Moore Gwen (Rep D - WI) 2252 Rayburn Bldg .... Washington DC 20515 *Web:* gwenmoore.house.gov	202-225-4572	225-8135	342-2
Moore Haven Correctional Facility PO Box 69 Moore Haven Correctional Facility .... Moore Haven FL 33471 *Web:* dc.state.fl.us	863-946-2420	946-3437	213
Moore Industries International Inc 16650 Schoenborn St .... North Hills CA 91343 *TF:* 800-999-2900 ■ *Web:* www.miinet.com	818-894-7111	891-2816	201
Moore Ingram Johnson & Steele LLP Emerson Overlook 326 Roswell Rd .... Marietta GA 30060 *TF:* 800-226-0793 ■ *Web:* www.mijs.com	770-429-1499		428
Moore J & Co 118 Naylon Ave .... Livingston NJ 07039 *Web:* www.jmoore.com	973-992-6970		189-10
Moore Lane Veterinary Hospital 30 Moore Ln .... Billings MT 59101 *Web:* www.yellowstonevalleyvet.com	406-252-4159		794
Moore Medical Corp 389 John Downey Dr .... New Britain CT 06050 *Fax Area Code: 800 ■ *TF Sales:* 800-234-1464 ■ *Web:* www.mooremedical.com	860-826-3600	944-6667*	475
Moore Memorial Public Library 1701 Ninth Ave N .... Texas City TX 77590 *Web:* www.texascity-library.org	409-643-5979	948-1106	434-3

Name / Address	City	State	ZIP	Phone	Fax	Class
Moore Oil Company Inc 4033 W Custer Ave *TF:* 800-279-2976 ■ *Web:* mooreoil.com	Milwaukee	WI	53209	414-462-3200		179
Moore Regional Hospital 155 Memorial Dr PO Box 3000 *TF:* 866-415-2778 ■ *Web:* www.firsthealth.org	Pinehurst	NC	28374	910-715-1000	428-1567	374-3
Moore Reichl & Baker P C 11200 Wheimer Ste 410 *Web:* mrbcpas.com	Houston	TX	77042	281-558-9800		2
Moore State Park Mill St *TF:* 800-437-5922 ■ *Web:* www.mass.gov	Paxton	MA	01612	508-792-3969		565
Moore Stephens Lovelace PA 1201 S Orlando Ave Ste 400 *TF:* 800-683-5401 ■ *Web:* www.mslcpa.com	Winter Park	FL	32789	407-740-5400	740-0012	2
Moore Supply Co 200 N Loop 336 W *Web:* www.mooresupply.com	Conroe	TX	77301	936-756-4445	441-8468	612
Moore Temporaries Inc 184 Pleasant Vly St *Web:* www.moorestaffing.com	Methuen	MA	01844	978-682-4994		260
Moore Tool Company Inc 800 Union Ave *Web:* www.mooretool.com	Bridgeport	CT	06607	203-366-3224		360-3
Mooreland Partners LLC 537 Steamboat Rd Ste 200 *Web:* www.moorelandpartners.com	Greenwich	CT	06830	203-629-4400		401
Moores Creek National Battlefield 40 Patriots Hall Dr *Web:* www.nps.gov	Currie	NC	28435	910-283-5591	283-5351	564
Moores Electrical & Mechanical PO Box 119 *TF:* 888-722-2712 ■ *Web:* www.mooreselectric.com	Altavista	VA	24517	434-369-4374	369-7402	186
Mooresville Graded School District 305 N Main St *TF:* 800-222-1222 ■ *Web:* www.mgsd.k12.nc.us	Mooresville	NC	28115	704-658-2530	663-3005	685
Mooresville Public Library 220 W Harrison St *Web:* www.mooresvillelib.org	Mooresville	IN	46158	317-831-7323	831-7383	434-3
Mooresville-South Iredell Chamber of Commerce 149 E Iredell Ave *TF:* 800-764-7113 ■ *Web:* www.mooresvillenc.org	Mooresville	NC	28115	704-664-3898	664-2549	139
Moorfeed Corp 1445 Brookville Way Ste R *Web:* www.moorfeed.com	Indianapolis	IN	46239	317-545-7171	542-7317	273
Mooring, The Sayer's Wharf *TF:* 800-228-9290 ■ *Web:* www.mooringrestaurant.com	Newport	RI	02840	401-846-2260		671
Moorings Park 120 Moorings Pk Dr *TF:* 866-802-4302 ■ *Web:* www.mooringspark.org	Naples	FL	34105	239-643-9111		672
Moorpark Chamber of Commerce 18 E High St *Web:* www.moorparkchamber.com	Moorpark	CA	93021	805-529-0322	529-5304	139
Moorpark College 7075 Campus Rd *Web:* moorparkcollege.edu	Moorpark	CA	93021	805-378-1400		162
Moors & Cabot Inc 111 Devonshire St *TF:* 800-426-0501 ■ *Web:* www.moorscabot.com	Boston	MA	02109	617-426-0500		405
Moose 96.3, The 833 Gambell St *Web:* themoose963.com	Anchorage	AK	99501	907-344-4045	522-6053	645-6
Moose Cafe 570 BrevaRd Rd *Web:* eatatthemoosecafe.com	Asheville	NC	28806	828-255-0920		671
Moose International Inc 155 S International Dr *TF:* 800-668-5901 ■ *Web:* www.mooseintl.org	Mooseheart	IL	60539	630-859-2000		48-15
Moose Jaw & District Chamber of Commerce 88 Saskatchewan St E *Web:* www.mjchamber.com	Moose Jaw	SK	S6H0V4	306-692-6414	694-6463	137
Moose Jaw Museum & Art Gallery 461 Langdon Crescent Pk *Web:* www.mjmag.ca	Moose Jaw	SK	S6H0X6	306-692-4471	694-8016	520
Moose Lake State Park 4252 County Rd 137 *Web:* www.dnr.state.mn.us	Moose Lake	MN	55767	218-485-5420		565
Moose Magazine 155 S International Dr *TF:* 800-544-4407 ■ *Web:* www.mooseintl.org/public/moose_magazine.aspx	Mooseheart	IL	60539	630-859-2000		457-10
Moose Point State Park 310 W Main St *Web:* www.maine.gov	Searsport	ME	04974	207-548-2882		565
Moose River Lumber Co Inc 432 Milo Rd *Web:* pleasantriverlumber.com	Dover-Foxcroft	ME	04426	207-564-8520	564-8259	683
Moose Travel Network 192 Spadina Ave Unit 408 *TF:* 888-244-6673 ■ *Web:* www.moosenetwork.com	Toronto	ON	M5T2C2	604-297-0255	297-0228	760
Moosylvania Marketin LC 7303 Marietta Ave *Web:* www.moosylvania.com	St. Louis	MO	63143	314-644-7900		195
Moot House 2626 S College Ave *Web:* www.themoothouse.com	Fort Collins	CO	80525	970-226-2121		671
Mopals Com Inc 109 Atlantic Ave *Web:* www.mopals.com	Toronto	ON	M6K1X4	416-362-4888		317
mopeutix Inc, The 9951 Businesspark Ave Ste B *Web:* thermopeutix.com	San Diego	CA	92131	858-549-1760		506
MOPS International 2370 S Trenton Way *TF General:* 888-910-6677 ■ *Web:* www.mops.org	Denver	CO	80231	303-733-5353	733-5770	48-6
Moquin Press Inc 555 Harbor Blvd *Web:* www.moquinpress.com	Belmont	CA	94002	650-592-0575		627
Morabito Baking Company Inc 757 Kohn St *TF:* 800-525-7747 ■ *Web:* www.morabito.com	Norristown	PA	19401	610-275-5419	275-0358	296-1
Moraine Hills State Park 1510 S River Rd *Web:* www.dnr.illinois.gov/Parks/Pages/MoraineHills.aspx	McHenry	IL	60051	815-385-1624		565
Moraine Park Technical College 235 N National Ave *TF:* 800-472-4554 ■ *Web:* www.morainepark.edu	Fond du Lac	WI	54935	920-922-8611	924-3421	800
Moraine State Park 225 Pleasant Valley Rd *Web:* www.dcnr.state.pa.us	Portersville	PA	16051	724-368-8811		565
Moraine Valley Community College 9000 W College Pkwy *Web:* www.morainevalley.edu	Palos Hills	IL	60465	708-974-4300		162
Moraine View State Recreation Area 27374 Moraine View Pk Rd *Web:* www.dnr.illinois.gov/Parks/Pages/MoraineView.aspx	Le Roy	IL	61752	309-724-8032		565
Morales Group Inc 5628 W 74th St *Web:* moralesgroup.net	Indianapolis	IN	46278	317-472-7600		260
Moran Environmental Recovery LLC 75-D York Ave *Web:* www.moranenvironmental.com	Randolph	MA	02368	781-815-1100		192
Moran Jerry (Sen R - KS) 521 Dirksen Senate Office Bldg *Web:* www.moran.senate.gov	Washington	DC	20510	202-224-6521	228-6966	342-2
Moran Printing Inc 5425 Florida Blvd *TF:* 800-211-8335 ■ *Web:* www.moranprinting.com	Baton Rouge	LA	70806	225-923-2550		626
Moran State Park 3572 Olga Rd *Web:* www.parks.wa.gov	Olga	WA	98279	360-376-2326		565
Moran Technology Consulting Llc 1215 Hamilton Ln Ste 200 *TF:* 888-699-4440 ■ *Web:* www.morantechnology.com	Naperville	IL	60540	888-699-4440		196
Moran Towing Corp 50 Locust Ave *Web:* www.morantug.com	New Canaan	CT	06840	203-442-2800		478
Morans Ground Beef Co 3425 E Vernon Ave *Web:* www.moransgroundbeef.com	Vernon	CA	90058	323-585-0068		473
Mora-San Miguel Electric Co-op Hwy 518 Main St *TF:* 800-421-6773 ■ *Web:* www.moraelectric.org	Mora	NM	87732	575-387-2205		245
Morasch Meats Inc 4050 NE 158th Ave *Web:* moraschmeats.com	Portland	OR	97230	503-257-9821		345
Moravek Biochemicals Inc 577 Mercury Ln *Web:* www.moravek.com	Brea	CA	92821	714-990-2018		143
Moravian College 1200 Main St **Fax:* Admissions ■ *TF:* 800-441-3191 ■ *Web:* www.moravian.edu	Bethlehem	PA	18018	610-861-1300	625-7930*	166
Moravian Hall Square 175 W N St *TF:* 800-496-1985 ■ *Web:* www.moravian.com	Nazareth	PA	18064	610-746-1000	746-1023	672
Moravian Manor 300 W Lemon St *Web:* www.moravianmanor.org	Lititz	PA	17543	717-626-0214		672
Moravian Theological Seminary 1200 Main St *TF:* 800-843-6541 ■ *Web:* www.moravianseminary.edu	Bethlehem	PA	18018	610-861-1516	861-1569	167-3
Moravian Village of Bethlehem 526 Wood St *Web:* www.moravianvillage.com	Bethlehem	PA	18018	610-625-4885		672
Morbark Inc 8507 S Winn Rd *TF:* 800-831-0042 ■ *Web:* www.morbark.com	Winn	MI	48896	989-866-2381		448
Morcom International Inc 3656 Centerview Dr Unit 1 *TF:* 800-955-2596 ■ *Web:* www.morcom.com	Chantilly	VA	20151	703-263-9305	263-9308	647
Morcon Construction Company Inc 5905 Golden Valley Rd *Web:* www.morcon.com	Golden Valley	MN	55422	763-546-6066		186
Mordecai Historic Park 1 Mimosa St *Web:* www.raleighnc.gov/mordecai	Raleigh	NC	27604	919-996-4364		50-3
Mordine & Company Dance Theatre 1016 N Dearborn Pkwy *Web:* www.mordine.org	Chicago	IL	60610	312-654-9540		573-1
MORE 104 KMYR 1416 Locust St *Web:* more1041.com	Des Moines	IA	50309	515-280-1350	280-3011	645-48
More Effective Consulting LLC 10 Chestnut Cir *Web:* www.moreeffective.com	Mont Vernon	NH	03057	603-801-3923		196
More Hawaii for Less 11 Ash Tree Ln *TF:* 800-967-6687 ■ *Web:* www.hawaii4less.com	Irvine	CA	92612	949-724-5050		771
More Media Group 1427 Goodman Ave *TF:* 800-435-9599 ■ *Web:* www.moremediagroup.com	Redondo Beach	CA	90278	310-991-9798		7
More Space Place Inc 5040 140th Ave N *TF:* 888-731-3051 ■ *Web:* www.morespaceplace.com	Clearwater	FL	33760	888-731-3051		361
Moreau Lake State Park 605 Old Saratoga Rd *Web:* parks.ny.gov/parks/150	Gansevoort	NY	12831	518-793-0511		565
Moreau-Grand Electric Co-op Inc 405 Ninth St *TF:* 800-952-3158 ■ *Web:* www.mge.coop	Timber Lake	SD	57656	605-865-3511		245
MoreDirect Inc 1001 Yamato Rd Ste 200 *TF:* 800-800-5555 ■ *Web:* www.moredirect.com	Boca Raton	FL	33431	561-237-3300		196
Morehead Memorial Hospital 117 E King's Hwy *TF:* 800-291-4020 ■ *Web:* www.morehead.org	Eden	NC	27288	336-623-9711	623-7660	374-3
Morehead Planetarium 250 E Franklin St UNC Chapel Hill CB 3480 *Web:* www.moreheadplanetarium.org	Chapel Hill	NC	27599	919-962-1236	962-1238	598
Morehead State University 100 Admissions Ctr **Fax:* Admissions ■ *TF:* 800-585-6781 ■ *Web:* www.moreheadstate.edu	Morehead	KY	40351	606-783-2000	783-5038*	166
Morehouse College 830 Westview Dr SW **Fax:* Admissions ■ *Web:* www.morehouse.edu	Atlanta	GA	30314	404-681-2800	572-3668*	166
Morehouse Foods Inc 760 Epperson Dr *TF:* 888-297-9800 ■ *Web:* www.morehousefoods.com	City of Industry	CA	91748	626-854-1655	854-1656	296-19
Morehouse Parish 100 E Madison Ave **Fax:* Morehouse Clerk of Court	Bastrop	LA	71220	318-281-4907	281-3775*	338
Morehouse School of Medicine 720 Westview Dr SW **Fax:* Admissions ■ *Web:* www.msm.edu	Atlanta	GA	30310	404-752-1500	752-1512*	167-2
Morehouse-COWLES 13930 Magnolia Ave *Web:* www.morehousecowles.com	Chino	CA	91710	909-627-7222		111
Morel Restaurant 3809 S Tuttle Ave *Web:* www.morelrestaurant.com	Sarasota	FL	34239	941-927-8716		671
Moreland & Altobelli Assoc Inc 2211 Beaver Ruin Rd Ste 190 *Web:* www.maai.net	Norcross	GA	30071	770-263-5945	263-0166	261

Phone | Fax | Class

Moreland Associates Corp
2532 Santa Clara Ave Ste 413 ... Alameda CA 94501 510-748-8146 463
Web: www.morelandassoc.com

Moreland Plaza Pharmacy Inc
827 W Moreland Blvd ... Waukesha WI 53188 262-542-4488 237

Morell Engineering 711 Hobbs St E ... Athens AL 35611 256-867-4957 261
Web: www.morellengineering.com

Morello Bistro 253 Greenwich Ave ... Greenwich CT 06830 203-661-3443 661-3588 671
Web: www.morellobistro.com

Morely Library 184 Phelps St ... Painesville OH 44077 440-352-3383 434-3
TF: 800-896-6446 ■ *Web:* www.morleylibrary.org

Moreno Valley Chamber of Commerce
12625 Frederick St ... Moreno Valley CA 92553 951-697-4404 697-0995 139
TF: 800-234-7275 ■ *Web:* www.movalchamber.org

Moreno Valley Mall
22500 Town Cir Ste 1206 ... Moreno Valley CA 92553 951-653-1177 460
TF: 800-593-6460 ■ *Web:* www.morenovalleymall.com

Moresatile Global Mktng Llc
4110 Milano Way ... Oceanside CA 92057 760-757-7676 193
TF: 800-438-7325 ■ *Web:* www.moresatile.com

Moresource Inc 401 Vandiver Dr ... Columbia MO 65202 573-443-1234 631
TF: 800-495-5678 ■ *Web:* www.moresource-inc.com

Moretrench American Corp
100 Stickle Ave ... Rockaway NJ 07866 973-627-2100 627-3950 189-5
Web: www.moretrench.com

Moretz Inc 514 W 21st St ... Newton NC 28658 828-464-0751 155-10
Web: b2b.goldtoemoretz.com

Morey Corp 100 Morey Dr ... Woodridge IL 60517 630-754-2300 253
Web: www.moreycorp.com

Morey's Piers & Raging Waters Waterparks
3501 Boardwalk ... Wildwood NJ 08260 609-522-3900 32
Web: www.moreyspiers.com

Morey's Seafood International LLC
1218 Hwy 10 S ... Motley MN 56466 218-352-6345 296-14
TF: 800-808-3474 ■ *Web:* www.moreys.com

Morga-Gallacher Inc
8707 Millergrove Dr ... Santa Fe Springs CA 90670 562-695-1232 151
Web: www.morgan-gallacher.com

Morgan & Co 1131 Glendon Ave ... Los Angeles CA 90024 310-208-3377 208-6920 410
TF: 800-458-4367 ■ *Web:* www.morganjewellers.com

Morgan & Myers
N 16 W 23233 Stone Ridge Dr Ste 200 ... Weukesha WI 53188 262-650-7260 636
Web: www.morganmyers.com

Morgan & Welsbrod
6800 W Loop S Ste 450 ... Bellaire TX 77401 713-838-0003 428
TF: 877-898-1581 ■ *Web:* www.morganweisbrod.com

Morgan Adhesives Co 4560 Darrow Rd ... Stow OH 44224 330-688-1111 688-2540 3
TF: 866-262-2822 ■ *Web:* www.mactac.com

Morgan Advanced Materials
7331 William Ave ... Allentown PA 18106 610-366-7100 411
Web: www.morgantechnicalceramics.com

Morgan Bldg Systems Inc
2800 McCree Rd ... Garland TX 75041 972-864-7300 106
TF: 800-935-0321 ■ *Web:* www.morganusa.com

Morgan Clarke Enterprises Inc
119 S Warren St ... Trenton NJ 08608 609-278-3500 463

Morgan Community College
920 Barlow Rd ... Fort Morgan CO 80701 970-542-3100 162
TF: 800-622-0216 ■ *Web:* www.morgancc.edu

Morgan Corporation
111 Morgan Way PO Box 588 ... Morgantown PA 19543 800-666-7426 516
TF: 800-666-7426 ■ *Web:* www.morgancorp.com

Morgan County
77 Fairfax St Ste 102 ... Berkeley Springs WV 25411 304-258-8547 258-8545 338
Web: www.morgancountywv.gov

Morgan County PO Box 668 ... Decatur AL 35602 256-351-4730 351-4738 338
Web: www.co.morgan.al.us

Morgan County
231 Ensign St PO Box 1399 ... Fort Morgan CO 80701 970-542-3521 542-3520 338
Web: www.co.morgan.co.us

Morgan County 300 W State St ... Jacksonville IL 62651 217-243-8581 243-8368 338
Web: www.morgancounty-il.com

Morgan County 150 E Washington St ... Madison GA 30650 706-342-0725 343-6450 338
Web: www.morganga.org

Morgan County 180 S Main St ... Martinsville IN 46151 765-342-1007 342-1111 338
TF: 800-382-9467 ■ *Web:* www.morgancounty.in.gov

Morgan County 358 E Main St ... McConnelsville OH 43756 740-962-2533 962-3316 338
Web: www.morgan.lib.oh.us

Morgan County PO Box 886 ... Morgan UT 84050 801-845-4011 829-6176 338
Web: www.morgan-county.net

Morgan County 100 E Newton St ... Versailles MO 65084 573-378-5436 378-5991 338
Web: morgan-county.org

Morgan County 415 N Kingston St ... Wartburg TN 37887 423-346-6288 338
Web: www.morgancountytn.gov

Morgan County
450 Prestonsburg St ... West Liberty KY 41472 606-743-3949 743-2111 338
Web: www.morgancounty.ky.gov

Morgan County Rural Electric Assn
20169 US Hwy 34 ... Fort Morgan CO 80701 970-867-5688 867-3277 245
TF: 877-495-6487 ■ *Web:* www.mcrea.org

Morgan County Schools
1325 Pt Mallard Pkwy ... Decatur AL 35601 256-353-6442 685
Web: www.morgank12.org

Morgan Creek Capital Management LLC
301 W Barbee Chapel Rd Ste 200 ... Chapel Hill NC 27517 919-933-4004 194
Web: www.morgancreekcap.com

Morgan Dempsey Capital Management LLC
111 Heritage Reserve Ste 200 ... Menomonee Falls WI 53051 414-319-1080 319-1087 401
Web: www.morgandempsey.com

Morgan Distributing Inc
3425 N 22nd St ... Decatur IL 62526 217-877-3570 579
Web: www.mdilubes.com

Morgan Fabrics Corp
4265 Exchange Ave ... Los Angeles CA 90058 323-583-9981 923-2352 413
Web: www.morganfabrics.com

Morgan Foods Inc 90 W Morgan St ... Austin IN 47102 812-794-1170 296-20
TF: 888-430-1780 ■ *Web:* www.morganfoods.com

Morgan Group Inc 5606 S Rice Ave ... Houston TX 77081 713-361-7200 361-7299 187
Web: www.morgangroup.com

Morgan Hill Chamber of Commerce
17485 Monterey St Ste 105 ... Morgan Hill CA 95037 408-779-9444 779-5405 139
Web: www.morganhill.org

Morgan Hill Plastics Inc
8118 Arroyo Cir ... Gilroy CA 95020 408-842-1322 842-1335 602
Web: morganhillplastics.net

Morgan Hunter Companies
7600 W 110th St ... Overland Park KS 66210 913-491-3434 260
TF: 800-917-6447 ■ *Web:* www.morganhunter.com

Morgan Jacoby Thurn Boyle & Assoc PA
700 20th St ... Vero Beach FL 32960 772-562-4158 734
Web: www.mjtbcpa.com

Morgan Lewis & Bockius LLP
1701 Market St ... Philadelphia PA 19103 215-963-5000 963-5001 428
TF: 866-963-7137 ■ *Web:* www.morganlewis.com

Morgan Lewis & Bockius LLP
1 Federal St ... Boston MA 02110 617-951-8000 428
Web: www.morganlewis.com

Morgan Linen Service Inc
145 Broadway Menands ... Albany NY 12204 518-465-3337 442
TF: 800-542-5793 ■ *Web:* www.morganlinenservice.com

Morgan Lumber Company Inc
628 Jeb Stuart Hwy ... Red Oak VA 23964 434-735-8151 683
Web: www.morganlumber.com

Morgan Marketing and Communications
690 Mill Hill Terr ... Southport CT 06890 203-255-4686 195
TF: 800-611-2470 ■ *Web:* morganmarketcomm.com

Morgan Meighen & Associates Ltd
10 Toronto St ... Toronto ON M5C2B7 416-366-2931 528
TF: 866-443-6097 ■ *Web:* www.mmainvestments.com

Morgan Melhuish Abrutyn
651 W Mt Pleasant Ave Ste 200 ... Livingston NJ 07039 973-994-2500 428
Web: www.morganlawfirm.com

Morgan Murphy Broadcasting Group
7025 Raymond Rd ... Madison WI 53719 608-271-4321 271-6111 738
Web: www.channel3000.com

Morgan Olson Corp 1801 S Nottawa Rd ... Sturgis MI 49091 269-659-0200 624-9005* 516
**Fax Area Code:* 800 ■ *TF:* 800-233-4823 ■ *Web:* www.morganolson.com

Morgan Park Academy 2153 W 111th St ... Chicago IL 60643 773-881-6700 148
TF: 800-741-6931 ■ *Web:* www.morganparkacademy.org

Morgan Printing Inc 402 Hill Ave ... Grafton ND 58237 701-352-0640 627
Web: www.morganprinting.com

Morgan Properties
500 W University Pkwy ... Baltimore MD 21210 410-467-9890 671
Web: www.morgan-properties.com/thecarlyle

Morgan Run Natural Environment Area
580 Taylor Ave ... Annapolis MD 21401 410-461-5005 565
TF: 800-830-3974 ■
Web: dnr.maryland.gov/publiclands/Pages/central/morganrun.aspx

Morgan Run Resort & Club
5690 Cancha de Golf ... Rancho Santa Fe CA 92091 858-756-2471 669
TF Resv: 800-378-4653 ■ *Web:* www.clubcorp.com

Morgan RV Resorts LLC
63 Putnam St Ste 201 ... Saratoga Springs NY 12866 518-615-0552 121

Morgan Samuels Co
6420 Wilshire Blvd Ste 1100 ... Los Angeles CA 90048 310-205-2200 193
TF: 800-451-9900 ■ *Web:* morgansamuels.com

Morgan Schaffer Systems Inc
8300, rue Saint-Patrick Bureau 150 LaSalle ... Montreal QC H8N2H1 514-739-1967 743
TF: 800-923-2999 ■ *Web:* www.morganschaffer.com

Morgan Scientific Inc 151 Essex St ... Haverhill MA 01832 978-521-4440 476
TF: 800-525-5002 ■ *Web:* www.morgansci.com

Morgan Services Inc
323 N Michigan Ave ... Chicago IL 60601 312-346-3181 346-0144 442
TF: 888-966-7426 ■ *Web:* www.morganservices.com

Morgan Stanley 1585 Broadway ... New York NY 10036 212-761-4000 690
NYSE: MS ■ *TF General:* 800-223-2440 ■ *Web:* www.morganstanley.com

Morgan Stanley Investment Management
1221 Ave of the Americas 5th Fl ... New York NY 10020 212-296-6600 452-0390* 690
**Fax Area Code:* 646 ■ *TF General:* 800-223-2440 ■ *Web:* www.morganstanley.com/im

Morgan Stanley Venture Partners
1585 Broadway 38th Fl ... New York NY 10036 212-761-4000 792
TF: 866-722-7310 ■ *Web:* www.morganstanley.com

Morgan State University
1700 E Cold Spring Ln ... Baltimore MD 21251 443-885-3333 885-8260* 166
**Fax:* Admissions ■ *TF:* 800-319-4678 ■ *Web:* www.morgan.edu

Morgan's Foods Inc
4829 Galaxy Pkwy Ste S ... Cleveland OH 44128 216-360-7500 670
TF: 800-869-8691 ■ *Web:* www.morgansfoods.com

MorganFranklin Corp
1753 Pinnacle Dr Ste 1200 ... Mclean VA 22102 703-564-7525 180
Web: www.morganfranklin.com

Morgan-Keller Inc
70 Thomas Johnson Dr Ste 200 ... Frederick MD 21702 301-663-0626 261
TF: 800-725-5051 ■ *Web:* www.morgankeller.com

Morgan-McClure Motorsports Inc
26502 Newbanks Rd ... Abingdon VA 24210 276-628-3683 787
Web: www.morgan-mcclure.com

Morgans Hotel 237 Madison Ave ... New York NY 10016 212-686-0300 779-8352 379
TF: 800-606-6090 ■ *Web:* www.morganshotelgroup.com

Morgans Hotel Group Co 475 Tenth Ave ... New York NY 10018 212-277-4100 532-0099* 379
NASDAQ: MHGC ■ **Fax Area Code:* 305 ■ *TF:* 800-606-6090 ■ *Web:* www.morganshotelgroup.com

Morganti Group Inc
100 Mill Plain Rd 4th Fl ... Danbury CT 06811 203-743-2675 830-4478* 186
**Fax:* Sales ■ *TF:* 800-239-5260 ■ *Web:* www.morganti.com

Morganton Honda 1600 Burkemont Ave ... Morganton NC 28655 828-437-3181 57
Web: morgantonhonda.com

Morgantown Area Chamber of Commerce
1029 University Ave Ste 101 ... Morgantown WV 26505 304-292-3311 296-6619 139
TF General: 800-618-2525 ■ *Web:* www.morgantownchamber.org

Morgantown City Hall 389 Spruce St ... Morgantown WV 26505 304-284-7439 337
Web: www.morgantownwv.gov

Morgantown Municipal Airport
100 Hartfield Rd ... Morgantown WV 26505 304-291-7461 27
Web: morgantownairport.com

Morgantown Printing & Binding LLC
915 Greenbag Rd ... Morgantown WV 26508 304-292-3368 627
Web: www.morgantownprinting.com

				Phone	Fax	Class
Morgantown Public Library						
373 Spruce St	Morgantown	WV	26505	304-291-7425	291-7437	434-3
Web: morgantown.lib.wv.us						
Morgenthaler 3200 Alpine Rd	Portola Valley	CA	94028	650-388-7600	388-7601	792
Web: www.morgenthaler.com						
Morgenthaler Ventures						
600 Superior Ave Ste 2500	Cleveland	OH	44114	216-416-7500		792
Web: www.morgenthaler.com						
Morgood Tools Inc 940 Millstead Way	Rochester	NY	14624	585-436-8828	436-2426	455
Web: www.morgood.com						
Mor-Gran-Sou Electric Co-op Inc						
202 Sixth Ave W	Flasher	ND	58535	701-597-3301		245
TF: 800-750-8212 ■ *Web:* www.morgransou.com						
Morguard Investments Ltd						
55 City Centre Dr Ste 800	Mississauga	ON	L5B1M3	905-281-3800		653
Web: www.morguard.com						
Mori Sushi 11500 W Pico Blvd	Los Angeles	CA	90064	310-479-3939		671
Web: www.morisushi.org						
Moriah School of Engelwood						
53 S Woodland St	Englewood	NJ	07631	201-567-0208		685
Web: www.moriahschool.org						
Moriah Shock Incarceration Correctional Facility						
75 Burhart Ln PO Box 999	Mineville	NY	12956	518-942-7561		213
Web: www.doccs.ny.gov						
Morikami Museum & Japanese Gardens						
4000 Morikami Pk Rd	Delray Beach	FL	33446	561-495-0233		520
TF: 800-564-9539 ■ *Web:* www.morikami.org						
Morimoto 723 Chestnut St	Philadelphia	PA	19106	215-413-9070		671
Web: www.morimotorestaurant.com						
Morin Brick Co						
130 Morin Brick Rd PO Box 1510	Auburn	ME	04210	207-784-9375	784-2013	150
Web: www.morinbrick.com						
Moritomo 32 Ft Eddy Rd	Concord	NH	03301	603-224-8363		671
Web: moritomonh.com						
Moritz Embroidery Works Inc, The						
405 Industrial Park Dr PO Box 187	Mount Pocono	PA	18344	570-839-9600	839-3031	258
TF: 800-533-4183 ■ *Web:* www.moritzembroidery.com						
Mork Process Inc 4278 Hudson Dr	Stow	OH	44224	330-928-3728		231
Web: www.morkusa.com						
Morlan & Associates Inc						
6625 McVey Blvd	Columbus	OH	43235	614-889-6152		767
TF: 800-336-4206 ■ *Web:* www.flex-core.com						
Morley 100 High Grove Blvd	Glendale Heights	IL	60139	847-639-4646	639-4723	527
TF: 800-284-5172 ■ *Web:* www.morleypedals.com						
Morley 4800 Rosebud Ln	Newburgh	IN	47630	812-464-9585	464-2514	261
Web: morleycorp.com						
Morley Candy Makers Inc						
23770 Hall Rd	Clinton Township	MI	48036	586-468-4300		296-8
TF: 800-651-7263 ■ *Web:* www.sanderscandy.com						
Morley Companies Inc 1 Morley Plaza	Saginaw	MI	48603	989-791-2550		775
Web: www.morleycompanies.com/home						
Morley Company Inc 2717 Schust	Saginaw	MI	48603	989-791-2565	497-1874	194
TF: 800-323-1492 ■ *Web:* www.morleycompanies.com/travel						
Morley Financial Services Inc						
1300 SW Fifth Ave Ste 3300	Portland	OR	97201	503-484-9300		401
TF: 800-548-4806 ■ *Web:* www.morley.com						
Morley Sales Company Inc						
119 N Second St	Geneva	IL	60134	630-845-8750	845-8749	297-5
Morley-Murphy Co						
200 S Washington St Ste 305	Green Bay	WI	54301	920-499-3171	499-9409	612
TF: 877-499-3171 ■ *Web:* www.morley-murphycompany.com						
Mormac Marine Group Inc						
1 Landmark Sq Ste 710	Stamford	CT	06901	203-977-8900		312
Mormon Battalion Visitors Ctr						
2510 Juan St	San Diego	CA	92110	619-298-3317		50-4
Web: lds.org						
Mormon Island State Recreation Area						
7425 S Hwy 281	Doniphan	NE	68832	308-385-6211		565
Web: outdoornebraska.gov/mormonisland						
Mormon Station State Historic Park						
PO Box 302	Genoa	NV	89411	775-782-2590		565
Web: parks.nv.gov						
Mormon Trail Ctr at Historic Winter Quarter						
3215 State St	Omaha	NE	68112	402-453-9372		50-4
Web: lds.org						
Morning Breeze Inc 950 N Lkview Dr	Greensburg	IN	47240	812-662-7778		793
Web: exceptionallivingcenters.com						
Morning Call PO Box 1260	Allentown	PA	10105	610-820-6500	820-6603	532-2
TF: 800-666-5492 ■ *Web:* www.mcall.com						
Morning Glory Cafe 450 Willamette St	Eugene	OR	97401	541-687-0709		671
Web: morninggloryeugene.squarespace.com						
Morning Glory Diner						
735 S Tenth St	Philadelphia	PA	19147	215-413-3999		671
Web: www.themorninggRorydiner.com						
Morning Journal 1657 Broadway Ave	Lorain	OH	44052	440-245-6901	245-6912	532-2
TF: 888-757-0727 ■ *Web:* www.morningjournal.com						
Morning News 310 S Dargan St	Florence	SC	29506	843-317-6397	317-7292	532-2
Web: www.scnow.com						
Morning News of Northwest Arkansas						
2560 N Lowell Rd	Springdale	AR	72764	479-751-6200	872-5055	532-2
Web: www.nwaonline.com						
Morning Sentinel 31 Front St	Waterville	ME	04901	207-873-3341	861-9191	532-2
TF: 800-287-1945 ■ *Web:* centralmaine.com						
Morningside College						
1501 Morningside Ave	Sioux City	IA	51106	712-274-5000	274-5101*	166
**Fax:* Admissions ■ *TF:* 800-831-0806 ■ *Web:* www.morningside.edu						
Morningside Equities Group Inc						
223 W Erie St 3rd Fl	Chicago	IL	60654	312-280-7770		653
Web: www.morningsideusa.com						
Morningside Ministries						
700 Babcock Rd	San Antonio	TX	78201	210-734-1000		48-20
Web: mmliving.org						
Morningside of Fullerton						
800 Morningside Dr	Fullerton	CA	92835	714-256-8000		672
TF: 800-803-7597 ■ *Web:* www.morningsideoffullerton.com						
Morningstar Inc 22 W Washington St	Chicago	IL	60602	312-696-6000	696-6009	401
NASDAQ: MORN ■ *TF Orders:* 800-735-0700 ■ *Web:* www.corporate.morningstar.com						
Mornington Communications Co-operative Ltd						
16 Mill St E	Milverton	ON	N0K1M0	519-595-8331		224
TF: 800-250-8750 ■ *Web:* mornington.ca						
Moro Bay State Park 6071 US Hwy 600	Jersey	AR	71651	870-463-8555		565
TF: 888-742-8701 ■ *Web:* www.arkansasstateparks.com						
Morocco						
Consulate General						
10 E 40th St 24th Fl	New York	NY	10016	212-758-2625	779-7441	257
TF: 800-787-8806 ■ *Web:* www.moroccanconsulate.com						
Embassy 1601 21st St NW	Washington	DC	20009	202-462-7979		257
Web: embassywashingtondc.com						
Moroch Partners 3625 N Hall St Ste 1100	Dallas	TX	75219	214-520-9700		4
Web: www.moroch.com						
Morongo Casino Resort & Spa						
49500 Seminole Dr	Cabazon	CA	92230	951-849-3080		669
TF: 800-252-4499 ■ *Web:* www.morongocasinoresort.com						
Moroni Feed Co 15 E 1900 S	Moroni	UT	84646	435-436-8225		447
Moroso Performance Products Inc						
80 Carter Dr	Guilford	CT	06437	203-453-6571	453-6906*	489
**Fax:* Cust Svc ■ *Web:* www.moroso.com						
MORPAC (Mortgage Bankers Assn PAC)						
1717 Rhode Island Ave NW 5th Fl	Washington	DC	20036	202-557-2700		615
Web: www.mba.org						
MORPACE International Inc						
31700 Middlebelt Rd Ste 200	Farmington Hills	MI	48334	248-737-5300	737-5326	466
Web: www.morpace.com						
Morphix Business Consulting						
PO Box 5217 Stn A	Calgary	AB	T2H1X3	403-520-7710		196
TF: 866-680-2503 ■ *Web:* www.morphix.biz						
Morphotek Inc 210 Welsh Pool Rd	Exton	PA	19341	610-423-6100		743
Web: www.morphotek.com						
MorphoTrak Inc						
113 S Columbus St 4th Fl	Alexandria	VA	22314	703-797-2600		84
TF: 800-601-6790 ■ *Web:* www.morphotrak.com						
MorphoTrust USA Inc 296 Concord Rd	Billerica	MA	01821	978-215-2400		692
TF: 888-245-1114 ■ *Web:* www.morphotrust.com						
Morrell Inc 333 Bald Mtn Rd	Auburn Hills	MI	48326	248-373-1600	373-0612	386
Web: www.morrell-group.com						
Morrill County 606 L St	Bridgeport	NE	69336	308-262-0860	262-1469	338
Web: www.co.morrill.ne.us						
Morrill Memorial Library						
33 Walpole St PO Box 220	Norwood	MA	02062	781-769-0200		434-3
Web: www.norwoodlibrary.org						
Morrill Motors Inc 229 S Main Ave	Erwin	TN	37650	888-743-7001		518
TF: 888-743-7001 ■ *Web:* www.morrillmotors.com						
Morrilton Packing Company Inc						
51 Blue Diamond Dr	Morrilton	AR	72110	501-354-2474	354-2283	473
TF: 800-264-2475 ■ *Web:* petitjeanmeats.com						
Morris & Assoc Inc 803 Morris Dr	Garner	NC	27529	919-582-9200	582-9100	664
Web: www.morris-associates.com						
Morris & Broms LLC						
900 Wellington Ave	Cranston	RI	02910	401-781-3134		567
Web: www.morrisandbroms.com						
Morris & Dickson Co Ltd 410 Kay Ln	Shreveport	LA	71115	318-797-7900		238
TF: 800-388-3833 ■ *Web:* www.morrisdickson.com						
Morris & Gwendolyn Cafritz Foundation						
1825 K St NW Ste 1400	Washington	DC	20006	202-223-3100	296-7567	305
Web: www.cafritzfoundation.org						
Morris & Mcdaniel Inc Consultants						
117 S Saint Asaph St	Alexandria	VA	22314	703-836-3600		195
Web: www.morrisandmcdaniel.com						
Morris Arboretum of the University of Pennsylvania						
100 E NW Ave	Philadelphia	PA	19118	215-247-5777		97
Web: www.business-services.upenn.edu/arboretum						
Morris Bean & Co 777 E Hyde Rd	Yellow Springs	OH	45387	937-767-7301		492
Web: www.morrisbean.com						
Morris Brown College						
643 Martin Luther King Jr Dr	Atlanta	GA	30314	404-739-1010		162
TF: 800-662-8925 ■ *Web:* www.morrisbrown.edu						
Morris Cerullo World Evangelism						
3545 Aero Ct Frnt	San Diego	CA	92123	858-277-2200		48-20
Web: www.mcwe.com						
Morris College 100 W College St	Sumter	SC	29150	803-934-3200	773-8241*	166
**Fax:* Admissions ■ *TF Admissions:* 866-853-1345 ■ *Web:* www.morris.edu						
Morris Communications Company LLC						
725 Broad St	Augusta	GA	30901	706-724-0851	828-3830	637-8
TF: 800-622-6358 ■ *Web:* www.morris.com						
Morris Costumes Inc 4300 Monroe Rd	Charlotte	NC	28205	704-333-4653	348-3032	155-6
TF: 000-334 2466 ■ *Web:* morriscostumes.com						
Morris County 501 W Main St	Council Grove	KS	66846	620-767-5533		338
Morris County 500 Broadnax St	Daingerfield	TX	75638	903-645-3911	645-5729	338
Web: www.co.morris.tx.us						
Morris County						
10 Court St PO Box 900	Morristown	NJ	07960	973-285-6000		338
Web: morriscountynj.gov						
Morris County Chamber of Commerce						
25 Lindsley Dr Ste 105	Morristown	NJ	07960	973-539-3882	539-3960	139
Web: www.morrischamber.org						
Morris County Library (MCL)						
30 E Hanover Ave	Whippany	NJ	07981	973-285-6930		434-3
Web: www.gti.net/mocolib1						
Morris Coupling Co 2240 W 15th St	Erie	PA	16505	814-459-1741	453-5155	490
TF: 800-426-1579 ■ *Web:* www.morriscoupling.com						
Morris Duffy Alonso & Faley						
2 Rector St 22nd Fl	New York	NY	10006	212-766-1888		428
Web: www.mdafny.com						
Morris Furniture Co Inc						
2377 Commerce Ctr Dr	Fairborn	OH	45324	937-874-7100		321
TF: 800-243-0000 ■ *Web:* morrisathome.com						
Morris Group Inc						
3 Office Pk Cir Ste 302	Mountain Brook	AL	35223	205-871-3500		186
Morris Herald-News 1804 N Division St	Morris	IL	60450	815-942-3221		532-3
TF: 800-397-9397 ■ *Web:* www.morrisherald-news.com						
Morris Hospital 150 W High St	Morris	IL	60450	815-942-2932	941-4363	374-3
TF: 877-743-3123 ■ *Web:* secure.morrishospital.org						
Morris Industries Inc						
777 Rt 23	Pompton Plains	NJ	07444	973-835-6600	835-1245	537
TF: 800-835-0777 ■ *Web:* www.morrispipe.com						

				Phone	Fax	Class
Morris Inn 130 Morris Inn University of Notre Dame *Web:* www.morrisinn.nd.edu	Notre Dame	IN	46556	574-631-2000		379
Morris J Golombeck Inc 960 Franklin Ave. *Web:* www.golombeckspice.com	Brooklyn	NY	11225	718-284-3505	693-1941	297-11
Morris K Udall Foundation 130 S Scott Ave *Web:* www.udall.gov	Tucson	AZ	85701	520-901-8500	670-5530	340-20
Morris Machine Company Inc 6480 S Belmont *Web:* www.morrismachine.com	Indianapolis	IN	46217	317-788-0371		454
Morris Material Handling Inc 315 W Forest Hill Ave *TF:* 800-933-3001 ■ *Web:* www.morriscranes.com	Oak Creek	WI	53154	414-764-6200	570-2779	470
Morris Multimedia Inc 27 Abercorn St *TF:* 800-533-1150 ■ *Web:* www.morrismultimedia.com	Savannah	GA	31401	912-233-1281	232-4639	637-8
Morris Murdock LLC 515 South 700 East Ste 1B *Web:* www.morrismurdock.com	Salt Lake City	UT	84102	801-483-6441		772
Morris Museum 6 Normandy Heights Rd *TF:* 800-590-4064 ■ *Web:* www.morrismuseum.org	Morristown	NJ	07960	973-971-3700		520
Morris Museum of Art 1 Tenth St. *TF:* 800-961-3119 ■ *Web:* www.themorris.org	Augusta	GA	30901	706-724-7501	724-7612	520
Morris Performing Arts Ctr 211 N Michigan St *TF:* 800-537-6415 ■ *Web:* www.morriscenter.org	South Bend	IN	46601	574-235-9190		572
Morris Polich & Purdy 1055 W Seventh St Ste 2400 *Web:* www.mpplaw.com	Los Angeles	CA	90017	213-891-9100	488-1178	428
Morris Printing Group 3212 Hwy 30 E. *TF:* 800-445-6621 ■ *Web:* www.morriscookbooks.com	Kearney	NE	68847	800-445-6621		627
Morris Products Inc 53 Carey Rd. *TF:* 888-777-6678 ■ *Web:* www.morrisproducts.com	Queensbury	NY	12804	518-743-0523		787
Morris School District 31 Hazel St *Web:* www.morrisschooldistrict.org	Morristown	NJ	07960	973-292-2300		685
Morris School District 54 54 White Oak Dr *Web:* www.morris54.org	Morris	IL	60450	815-942-0056	942-0240	780
Morris-Butler House Museum 1204 N Pk Ave *TF:* 800-450-4534 ■ *Web:* indianalandmarks.org	Indianapolis	IN	46202	317-636-5409		50-3
Morrisette Paper Company Inc 5925 Summit Ave *TF:* 800-822-8882 ■ *Web:* morrisette.com	Browns Summit	NC	27214	336-375-1515	621-0751	553
Morris-Jumel Mansion 65 Jumel Terr at 160th St *Web:* www.morrisjumel.org	New York	NY	10032	212-923-8008		520
Morrison & Foerster LLP 425 Market St *TF:* 800-952-5210 ■ *Web:* www.mofo.com	San Francisco	CA	94105	415-268-7000	268-7522	428
Morrison Agency Inc, The 3365 Piedmont Rd Ste 1400 Tower Walk at Tower Pl *Web:* www.morrisonagency.com	Atlanta	GA	30305	404-233-3405	261-8384	195
Morrison and Abraham Inc 322 N Main St Ste 6 *Web:* www.morrisonandabraham.com	Randolph	MA	02368	781-986-2100		7
Morrison Berkshire Inc 865 S Church St *Web:* www.morrisonberkshire.com	North Adams	MA	01247	413-663-6501		744
Morrison Bros Co 570 E Seventh St *TF:* 800-553-4840 ■ *Web:* www.morbros.com	Dubuque	IA	52001	563-583-5701	583-5028	537
Morrison Construction Co 1834 Summer St. *Web:* www.mcco.com	Hammond	IN	46320	219-932-5036	933-7302	189-10
Morrison Container Handling Solutions 335 W 194th St. *TF:* 800-369-2440 ■ *Web:* www.morrison-chs.com	Glenwood	IL	60425	708-756-6660		454
Morrison Correctional Institution 1573 McDonald Church Rd PO Box 169 *Web:* www.ncdps.gov	Hoffman	NC	28347	910-281-3161	281-3609	412
Morrison County 213 SE First Ave *TF:* 866-401-1111 ■ *Web:* www.co.morrison.mn.us	Little Falls	MN	56345	320-632-2941		338
Morrison County Record 216 SE First St *TF:* 888-637-2345 ■ *Web:* www.mcrecord.com	Little Falls	MN	56345	320-632-2345	632-2348	532-4
Morrison Enterprises 3303 W 12th St	Hastings	NE	68901	402-463-3191		10-4
Morrison Express Corp USA 2000 S Hughes Way *Web:* www.morrisonexpress.com	El Segundo	CA	90245	310-322-8999	322-6688	311
Morrison Hershfield Group Inc 125 Commerce Valley Dr W Ste 300 *TF:* 888-649-4730 ■ *Web:* www.morrisonhershfield.com	Markham	ON	L3T7W4	416-499-3110		261
Morrison Hospital Assn 6 Ter St *Web:* www.morrisonnh.org	Whitefield	NH	03598	603-837-2541		793
Morrison House 116 S Alfred St *TF:* 866-834-6628 ■ *Web:* www.morrisonhouse.com	Alexandria	VA	22314	703-838-8000		671
Morrison Industrial Equipment Co 1825 Monroe NW *Web:* www.morrison-ind.com	Grand Rapids	MI	49505	616-447-3800	361-0885	57
Morrison Institute of Technology 701 Portland Ave *Web:* www.morrisontech.edu	Morrison	IL	61270	815-772-7218	772-7584	800
Morrison Mahoney LLP 250 Summer St *Web:* www.morrisonmahoney.com	Boston	MA	02210	617-439-7500	439-7590	428
Morrison Management Specialists Inc 5801 Peachtree Dunwoody Rd *Web:* www.iammorrison.com	Atlanta	GA	30342	404-845-3330	845-3333	299
Morrison Milling Co 319 E Prairie St *TF:* 800-531-7912 ■ *Web:* morrisonmilling.com	Denton	TX	76201	940-387-6111		296-23
Morrison Scott Alan Law Offices of pa 141 W Patrick St Ste 300 *TF:* 866-220-5185 ■ *Web:* www.samlawoffice.com	Frederick	MD	21701	301-694-6262		428
Morrison Supply Company Inc 311 E Vickery Blvd *TF:* 800-451-9343 ■ *Web:* www.morsco.com	Fort Worth	TX	76104	817-870-2227		612
Morrison Terrebonne Lumber Center LLC 605 Barataria Ave *Web:* www.lumbercenter.com	Houma	LA	70360	985-879-1597		361
Morrison Textile Machinery Co 6044 Lancaster Hwy *Web:* www.morrisontexmach.com	Fort Lawn	SC	29714	803-872-4401		744
Morrison-Clark Historic Inn & Restaurant 1015 L St NW *TF:* 800-332-7898 ■ *Web:* www.morrisonclark.com	Washington	DC	20001	202-898-1200		379
Morrison-Knudsen Nature Ctr 600 S Walnut St	Boise	ID	83712	208-334-2225		50-5
Morrison-Maierle Inc 1 Engineering Pl *Web:* www.m-m.net	Helena	MT	59604	406-442-3050		261
Morrison-Rockwood State Park 18750 Lake Rd *Web:* www.dnr.illinois.gov/Parks/Pages/MorrisonRockwood.aspx	Morrison	IL	61270	815-772-4708		565
Morrissey Family Businesses Inc 5919 Spring Creek Rd *TF:* 800-942-0191 ■ *Web:* www.morrisseyfamily.com	Rockford	IL	61114	815-282-4600		734
Morrissey Hospitality Companies Inc 345 St Peter St Ste 2000 *Web:* www.morrisseyhospitality.com	Saint Paul	MN	55102	651-221-0815		707
Morrissey Inc 9304 Bryant Ave S *Web:* www.morrisseyinc.com	Bloomington	MN	55420	952-888-4675		488
Morrisson-Reeves Public Library 80 N Sixth St *Web:* mrlinfo.org	Richmond	IN	47374	765-966-8291	962-1318	434-3
Morristown Area Chamber of Commerce 825 W First N St *Web:* www.morristownchamber.com	Morristown	TN	37814	423-586-6382	586-6576	139
Morristown Drivers Service Inc PO Box 2158 *Web:* www.mdstrucking.com	Morristown	TN	37816	423-581-6048		780
Morristown Medical Ctr 100 Madison Ave *TF:* 877-310-7226 ■ *Web:* www.atlantichealth.org	Morristown	NJ	07960	973-971-5000		374-3
Morristown National Historical Park 30 Washington Pl *TF:* 800-275-4278 ■ *Web:* www.nps.gov/morr	Morristown	NJ	07960	973-543-4030	451-9212	564
Morristown Utility Systems PO Box 667 *Web:* www.morristownutilities.org	Morristown	TN	37815	423-586-4121	587-6590	787
Morristown-Hamblen Public Library 417 W Main St *Web:* morristownhamblenlibrary.org	Morristown	TN	37814	423-586-6410	587-6226	434-3
Morris-Union Jointure Commission 340 Central Ave *Web:* www.mujc.org	New Providence	NJ	07974	908-464-7625		685
Morrisville State College 80 Eaton St PO Box 901 *Fax: Admissions ■ *TF Admissions:* 800-258-0111 ■ *Web:* www.morrisville.edu	Morrisville	NY	13408	315-684-6000	684-6427*	166
Morro Bay State Park 60 State Park Rd *TF:* 800-777-0369 ■ *Web:* www.parks.ca.gov/?page_id=594	Morro Bay	CA	93442	800-777-0369		565
Morro Strand State Beach Morro Bay State Pk Rd Morro Bay State Pk Rd *Web:* www.parks.ca.gov/?page_id=23793	Morro Bay	CA	93442	805-772-2560		565
Morrow & Co LLC 470 W Ave *TF:* 800-662-5200 ■ *Web:* morrowco.com	Stamford	CT	06902	203-658-9400		401
Morrow Control & Supply Co 810 Marion Motley Ave NE *TF:* 800-362-9830 ■ *Web:* www.morrowcontrol.com	Canton	OH	44705	330-452-9791		612
Morrow County 100 Ct St PO Box 788 *Web:* www.co.morrow.or.us	Heppner	OR	97836	541-676-9061	676-9876	338
Morrow County 80 N Walnut St. *Web:* morrowcounty.info	Mount Gilead	OH	43338	419-947-4085		338
Morrow County Chamber of Commerce 17 1/2 W High St PO Box 174 *Web:* www.morrowchamber.org	Mount Gilead	OH	43338	419-946-2821		139
Morrow County Grain Growers Inc (MCGG) 350 N Main St *TF:* 800-452-7396 ■ *Web:* www.mcgg.net	Lexington	OR	97839	541-989-8221	989-8229	10-5
Morrow Enterprises 350 130th Ave *Web:* morrowent.com	Vero Beach	FL	32968	772-257-3300		328
Morrow Equipment Company LLC 3218 Pringle Rd SE PO Box 3306 *Web:* www.morrow.com	Salem	OR	97302	503-585-5721	363-1172	264-3
Morrow Mountain State Park 49104 Morrow Mtn Rd *Web:* www.ncparks.gov	Albemarle	NC	28001	704-982-4402		565
Morrow Realty Co Inc 809 22nd Ave *Web:* www.morrowrealty.com	Tuscaloosa	AL	35401	205-759-5781		652
Morrow Romine & Pearson Pc Atty 122 S Hull St *Web:* www.mrplaw.com	Montgomery	AL	36104	334-262-7707		445
Morrow-Meadows Corp 231 Benton Ct. *Web:* www.morrow-meadows.com	City of Industry	CA	91789	909-598-7700	598-3907	189-4
Morse Electric Inc 500 W S St. *Web:* www.themorsegroup.com	Freeport	IL	61032	815-266-4200	266-8900	189-4
Morse Industries Inc 25811 74th Ave S *TF:* 800-325-7513 ■ *Web:* www.morseindustries.com	Kent	WA	98032	800-325-7513		697
Morse Institute Library 14 E Central St *Web:* www.morseinstitute.org	Natick	MA	01760	508-647-6520		434-3
Morse Operations Inc 3790 W Blue Herron Blvd *TF:* 800-755-2593 ■ *Web:* www.edmorsehonda.com	Riviera Beach	FL	33404	800-755-2593		516
Morse, Barnes-Brown & Pendleton PC CityPoint 230 Third Ave 4th Fl *Web:* www.mbbp.com	Waltham	MA	02451	781-622-5930		428
MorseLife Inc 4847 Fred Gladstone Dr *TF:* 800-498-6937 ■ *Web:* www.morselife.org	West Palm Beach	FL	33417	561-471-5111		371
Morstan General Agency Inc 600 Community Dr PO Box 4500 *Web:* www.morstan.com	Manhasset	NY	11030	516-488-4747		390

Name / Address	City	State	Zip	Phone	Fax	Class
Mort Crim Communications Inc 155 W Congress Ste 501 *Web:* mccicorp.com	Detroit	MI	48226	313-481-4700		514
Mortara Instrument Inc 7865 N 86th St *TF:* 800-231-7437 ■ *Web:* www.mortara.com	Milwaukee	WI	53224	414-354-1600	354-4760	250
Mortech Manufacturing Inc 411 N Aerojet Ave *TF:* 800-410-0100 ■ *Web:* mortechmfg.com	Azusa	CA	91702	626-334-1471		406
Mortgage Bankers Assn (MBA) 1919 M St NW 5th Fl **Fax:* Cust Svc ■ *TF:* 800-793-6222 ■ *Web:* www.mba.org	Washington	DC	20036	202-557-2700	721-0245*	49-2
Mortgage Bankers Assn PAC (MORPAC) 1717 Rhode Island Ave NW 5th Fl *Web:* www.mba.org	Washington	DC	20036	202-557-2700		615
Mortgage Banking Solutions Frost Bank Tower 401 Congress Ave Ste 1540 *TF:* 800-476-0853 ■ *Web:* www.mortgagebankingsolutions.com	Austin	TX	78701	512-977-9900		463
Mortgage Builders Software 24370 NW Hwy Ste 200 *TF:* 800-850-8060 ■ *Web:* www.mortgagebuilder.com	Southfield	MI	48075	800-850-8060		178-10
Mortgage Guaranty Insurance Corp 270 E Kilbourn Ave *TF:* 800-558-9900 ■ *Web:* www.mgic.com	Milwaukee	WI	53202	414-347-6480		391-5
Mortgage Insurance Cos of America (MICA) 1425 K St NW Ste 210 *Web:* usmi.org	Washington	DC	20005	202-682-2683		49-9
Mortgage Intelligence Inc 5770 Hurontario St Ste 600 *Web:* www.mortgageintelligence.ca	Mississauga	ON	L5R3G5	905-283-3600		217
Mortgage Investors Group 8320 E Walker Springs Ln *TF:* 800-489-8910 ■ *Web:* www.migonline.com	Knoxville	TN	37923	865-691-8910	691-7714	509
Mortgage Returns 1335 Strassner Dr *Web:* www.web.mortgagereturns.com	St. Louis	MO	63144	314-989-9100		509
Mortgageflex Systems Inc 1200 Riverplace Blvd Ste 650 *TF General:* 800-326-3539 ■ *Web:* www.mortgageflex.com	Jacksonville	FL	32207	904-356-2490		177
Morton Arboretum 4100 Illinois Rt 53 *Web:* www.mortonarb.org	Lisle	IL	60532	630-968-0074		97
Morton Buildings Inc 380 Erie Ave PO Box 399 *TF:* 800-447-7436 ■ *Web:* www.mortonbuildings.com	Morton	IL	61550	309-263-3680	263-4573	105
Morton Capital Management 27200 Agoura Rd Ste 200 *Web:* www.mortoncapital.com	Calabasas	CA	91301	818-222-4727		401
Morton College 3801 S Central Ave **Fax:* Admitting ■ *Web:* www.morton.edu	Cicero	IL	60804	708-656-8000	656-9592*	162
Morton Community Bank 721 W Jackson St *Web:* hometownbanks.com	Morton	IL	61550	309-266-5337		70
Morton Consulting LLC 4701 Cox Rd *Web:* www.mortonconsulting.com	Glen Allen	VA	23060	804-290-4272		194
Morton County PO Box 1116 *Web:* www.mtcoks.com	Elkhart	KS	67950	620-697-2157	697-2159	338
Morton County 210 Second Ave NW *Web:* www.co.morton.nd.us	Mandan	ND	58554	701-667-3300		338
Morton Grove Pharmaceuticals Inc 6451 Main St **Fax Area Code:* 973 ■ *TF:* 800-346-6854 ■ *Web:* www.wockhardtusa.com	Morton Grove	IL	60053	847-967-5600	257-4978*	583
Morton Grove Public Library 6140 Lincoln Ave *TF:* 800-288-2020 ■ *Web:* www.mgpl.org	Morton Grove	IL	60053	847-965-4220	965-7903	434-3
Morton H Meyerson Symphony Ctr 2301 Flora St *Web:* www.dallasculture.org	Dallas	TX	75201	214-670-3600	670-4334	572
Morton High School 500 Champion Dr *Web:* mortonisd.net	Morton	TX	79346	806-266-5505		685
Morton Hospital & Medical Ctr 88 Washington St *Web:* www.mortonhospital.org	Taunton	MA	02780	508-828-7000		374-3
Morton Industries LLC 70 Commerce Dr *Web:* www.mortonwelding.com	Morton	IL	61550	309-263-2590		595
Morton Leben 270 N Ave	New Rochelle	NY	10801	914-636-1800		2
Morton Machining & Manufacturing Co 701 Flint Ave *Web:* www.mortonmachining.com	Morton	IL	61550	309-266-6551		454
Morton Plant Hospital 300 Pinellas St *TF:* 800-229-2273 ■ *Web:* www.baycare.org	Clearwater	FL	33756	727-462-7000		374-3
Morton Salt Inc 123 N Wacker Dr *TF:* 800-725-8847 ■ *Web:* www.mortonsalt.com	Chicago	IL	60606	312-807-2000		680
Morton's of Chicago 4 Ave Rd *Web:* www.mortons.com	Toronto	ON	M5R2E8	416-925-0648		671
Morton's the Steakhouse 300 S Charles St *Web:* www.mortons.com	Baltimore	MD	21201	410-547-8255	547-8244	671
Morton's the Steakhouse 285 J St *Web:* www.mortons.com	San Diego	CA	92101	619-696-3369		671
Morton's the Steakhouse 213 SW Clay St *Web:* www.mortons.com	Portland	OR	97201	503-248-2100		671
Morton's the Steakhouse 41 E Washington St *Web:* www.mortons.com	Indianapolis	IN	46204	317-229-4700		671
Morton's The Steakhouse 625 Liberty Ave *Web:* www.mortons.com	Pittsburgh	PA	15222	412-261-7141	261-7151	671
Morton's The Steakhouse 303 Peachtree Ctr Ave *Web:* www.mortons.com	Atlanta	GA	30308	404-577-4366		671
Morton's The Steakhouse 2222 McKinney Ave *Web:* www.mortons.com	Dallas	TX	75201	214-741-2277		671
Morton's The Steakhouse 1450 Ala Moana Blvd *Web:* www.mortons.com	Honolulu	HI	96814	808-949-1300		671
Morton's The Steakhouse 5000 Westheimer Rd *Web:* www.mortons.com	Houston	TX	77056	713-629-1946		671
Morton's the Steakhouse 435 S La Cienega Blvd *Web:* www.mortons.com	Los Angeles	CA	90048	310-246-1501		671
Morton's The Steakhouse 1200 Brickell Ave *Web:* www.mortons.com	Miami	FL	33131	305-400-9990		671
Morton's The Steakhouse 1511 Sixth Ave *Web:* www.mortons.com	Seattle	WA	98101	206-223-0550		671
Morton's the Steakhouse 1050 Connecticut Ave NW *Web:* www.mortons.com	Washington	DC	20036	202-955-5997		671
Morton's the Steakhouse 777 S Flagler Dr *Web:* www.mortons.com	West Palm Beach	FL	33401	561-835-9664		671
Morton's The Steakhouse 618 Church St *TF:* 800-297-3276 ■ *Web:* www.mortons.com	Nashville	TN	37219	615-259-4558	726-2760	671
Morton's The Steakhouse 400 Post St *Web:* www.mortons.com	San Francisco	CA	94102	415-986-5830		670
Morton's The Steakhouse 7600 Doctor Phillips Blvd *Web:* www.mortons.com	Orlando	FL	32819	407-248-3485		671
Morton's The Steakhouse 1411 Walnut St *Web:* www.mortons.com	Philadelphia	PA	19102	215-557-0724	557-9741	671
Morton's the Steakhouse 1050 N State St *Web:* www.mortons.com	Chicago	IL	60610	312-266-4820		671
Mortons the Steakhouse 1600 W Second St *Web:* www.mortons.com	Cleveland	OH	44113	216-621-6200		671
Morven Museum & Gardens 55 Stockton St *Web:* morven.org	Princeton	NJ	08540	609-924-8144		97
Morwear Manufacturing Inc 620 Lamar St *Web:* www.morwear.com	Los Angeles	CA	90031	323-222-7000		550
Mosaic Business Solutions LLC 3262 Superior Ln Ste 217	Bowie	MD	20715	301-464-2665		570
Mosaic Company Inc, The 555 S Renton Village Pl *Web:* www.themosaiccompany.com	Renton	WA	98057	425-254-1724		260
Mosaic Energy Ltd 606-4th St SW Ste 900 *TF:* 888-221-4420 ■ *Web:* mosaicenergy.ca	Calgary	AB	T2P1T1	403-699-7650		539
Mosaic Event Management Inc 67 Haight St *Web:* www.mosaicevents.com	San Francisco	CA	94102	415-908-2650		196
Mosaic Financial Partners Inc 140 Geary St 6th Fl *TF:* 800-677-6204 ■ *Web:* mosaicfp.com	San Francisco	CA	94108	415-788-1952		463
Mosaic Hotel 125 S Spalding Dr *TF:* 800-463-4466 ■ *Web:* www.mosaichotel.com	Beverly Hills	CA	90212	310-278-0303		379
Mosaic Records 35 Melrose Pl *Web:* www.mosaicrecords.com	Stamford	CT	06902	203-327-7111	323-3526	657
Moschip Semiconductor Technology USA 840 N Hillview Dr *Web:* www.moschip.com	Milpitas	CA	95035	408-737-7141	737-7708	696
Moscone Ctr 747 Howard St *TF:* 800-216-4916 ■ *Web:* www.moscone.com	San Francisco	CA	94103	415-974-4000	974-4073	205
Moscot Mobileyes Foundation Inc 118 Orchard St *Web:* www.moscot.com	New York	NY	10002	212-477-3796		543
Moscow Chamber of Commerce 411 S Main St *TF:* 866-770-2020 ■ *Web:* www.moscowchamber.com	Moscow	ID	83843	208-882-1800		139
Moscow on the Hill 371 Selby Ave *Web:* www.moscowonthehill.com	Saint Paul	MN	55102	651-291-1236		671
Mosebach Manufacturing Co 1417 Mclaughlin Run Rd *Web:* www.mosebachresistors.com	Pittsburgh	PA	15241	412-220-0200		203
Moseley Architects PC 3200 Norfolk St *Web:* www.moseleyarchitects.com	Richmond	VA	23230	804-794-7555	355-5690	186
Moseley Assoc Inc 82 Coromar Dr *Web:* www.moseleysb.com	Santa Barbara	CA	93117	805-968-9621	685-9638	647
Moseley Corp, The 31 Hayward St *Web:* www.moseleycorp.com	Franklin	MA	02038	508-520-4004		463
Moseley Technical Services Inc 7500 S Memorial Pkwy Ste 215-R *TF:* 800-897-7249 ■ *Web:* www.moseleytechnical.com	Huntsville	AL	35802	256-880-0446		261
Moseo Corp 2722 Elake Ave E *TF:* 800-741-0926 ■ *Web:* www.seniorhomes.com	Seattle	WA	98102	206-905-8774		387
Moser Corp 601 N 13th St *TF:* 800-632-4564 ■ *Web:* www.mosercorporation.com	Rogers	AR	72756	479-636-3481		321
Moses Anshell Inc 20 W Jackson St *Web:* mosesinc.com	Phoenix	AZ	85003	602-254-7312		4
Moses Greeley Parker Memorial Library 28 Arlington St *TF:* 800-660-2868 ■ *Web:* www.dracutlibrary.org	Dracut	MA	01826	978-454-5474	454-9120	434-3
Moses H Cone Memorial Hospital 1200 N Elm St *TF:* 866-391-2734 ■ *Web:* www.conehealth.com	Greensboro	NC	27401	336-832-7000		374-3
Moses Lake Area Chamber of Commerce 324 S Pioneer Way *TF:* 800-992-6234 ■ *Web:* www.moseslake.com	Moses Lake	WA	98837	509-765-7888		139
Moses Lake Industries Inc 8248 Randolph Rd NE *Web:* www.mlindustries.com	Moses Lake	WA	98837	509-762-5336	762-5981	145
Moses Taylor Hospital 700 Quincy Ave *Web:* commonwealthhealth.net	Scranton	PA	18510	570-340-2100		374-3
Moshannon Valley Economic Development Partnership 200 Shady Ln *Web:* www.mvedp.org	Philipsburg	PA	16866	814-342-2260	342-2878	139
Mosher Co 15 Exchange St *Web:* www.mocomfg.com	Chicopee	MA	01014	413-598-8341		1

Name / Address	City	State	Zip	Phone	Fax	Class
Mosholu Parkway Nursing & Rehabilitation Ctr 3356 Perry Ave	Bronx	NY	10467	718-655-3568		450
Mosites Rubber Company Inc PO Box 2115 *Web:* www.mositesrubber.com	Fort Worth	TX	76113	817-335-3451	870-1564	676
Mosquito Lake State Park 1439 State Rt 305 *Web:* www.ohiodnr.com	Cortland	OH	44410	330-637-2856		565
Mosquito Lake State Recreation Site 1439 State Rt 305	Cortland	OH	44410	330-637-2856		565
Moss Adams LLP 999 Third Ave Ste 2800 *Web:* www.mossadams.com	Seattle	WA	98104	206-302-6500		2
Moss Construction Management 2101 N Andrews Ave *TF:* 855-360-6677 ■ *Web:* mosscm.com	Fort Lauderdale	FL	33311	954-524-5678		610
Moss Inc PO Box 189 *TF:* 800-932-6677 ■ *Web:* www.mosssubstrates.com	Pasadena	MD	21123	410-768-3442	768-3971	231
Moss Landing State Beach c/o Monterey District Office 2211 Garden Rd www.parks.ca.gov/default.asp?page_id=574	Monterey	CA	93940	831-384-7695		565
Moss Mansion 914 Div St *TF:* 800-735-2635 ■ *Web:* www.mossmansion.com	Billings	MT	59101	406-256-5100		50-3
Moss Precision Inc 3200 Arden Rd *Web:* www.mossprecision.com	Hayward	CA	94545	510-785-2235		454
Moss Supply Company Inc 5001 N Graham St *TF:* 800-438-0770 ■ *Web:* www.mosssupply.com	Charlotte	NC	28269	704-596-8717	598-9012	234
Mossberg & Company Inc 301 E Sample St *TF:* 800-428-3340 ■ *Web:* www.mossbergco.com	South Bend	IN	46601	574-289-9253		626
Mossberg Industries Inc 204 N Second St *Web:* mossbergind.com	Garrett	IN	46738	260-357-5141	357-5144	601
Mosse & Mosse Insurance Associates LLC 50 Salem St Bldg B *TF:* 800-562-5261 ■ *Web:* www.mosseandmosse.com	Lynnfield	MA	01940	781-224-1700		390
Mosser Companies 308 Jessie St *TF:* 800-523-2222 ■ *Web:* www.mosserco.com	San Francisco	CA	94103	415-284-9000		463
Mosser Construction 122 S Wilson Ave *Web:* www.mosserconstruction.com	Fremont	OH	43420	419-334-3801		186
Mosser Hotel 54 Fourth St *TF:* 800-227-3804 ■ *Web:* www.themosser.com	San Francisco	CA	94103	415-986-4400		379
Mossman's Southwest 3610 Wible Rd *Web:* mossmanscatering.com	Bakersfield	CA	93309	661-832-5130	832-4783	671
MossWarner 33332 Valle Rd Ste 200 *Web:* mosswarner.com	San Juan Capistrano	CA	92675	949-429-2266		7
Mossy Motors Inc 1331 S Broad St *Web:* www.mossymotors.com	New Orleans	LA	70125	504-822-2050		57
Mosteller & Associates 2433 Morgantown Rd Ste 100 *Web:* www.mostellerhr.com	Reading	PA	19607	610-779-3870		195
MoSys Inc 3301 Olcott St *Web:* www.mosys.com	Santa Clara	CA	95054	408-418-7500		696
Mote Marine Laboratory 1600 Ken Thompson Pkwy *Web:* www.mote.org	Sarasota	FL	34236	941-388-4441	388-4312	668
Motel 6 Wichita 8302 E Kellogg Dr *TF:* 800-466-8356 ■ *Web:* www.motel6.com	Wichita	KS	67207	316-612-4646		370
Mother Bethel AME Church 419 S Sixth St *Web:* www.motherbethel.org	Philadelphia	PA	19147	215-925-0616	925-1402	50-1
Mother Frances Hospital 800 E Dawson St *Web:* tmfhc.org	Tyler	TX	75701	903-593-8441		374-3
Mother Jones Magazine 222 Sutter St Ste 600 *TF:* 800-438-6656 ■ *Web:* www.motherjones.com	San Francisco	CA	94108	415-321-1700	321-1701	457-17
Mother Lode Holding Co 189 Fulweiler Ave *Web:* placertitle.com	Auburn	CA	95603	530-887-2410		390
Mother Lode Internet 197A Mono Wy *Web:* www.motherlodeinternet.com	Sonora	CA	95370	209-536-5800		396
Mother Murphy's Labs Inc 2826 S Elm St PO Box 16846 *TF:* 800-849-1277 ■ *Web:* www.mothermurphys.com	Greensboro	NC	27416	336-273-1737	273-2615	296-15
Mother Neff State Park 1680 Texas 236 Hwy *Web:* tpwd.texas.gov/state-parks/mother-neff	Moody	TX	76557	254-853-2389		565
Mother of Good Counsel Home 6825 Natural Bridge Rd *TF:* 800-566-6150 ■ *Web:* mogch.org	St. Louis	MO	63121	314-383-4765		672
Mother's 33 Virginia Pl	Buffalo	NY	14202	716-882-2989		671
Mother's Bistro & Bar 212 SW Stark St *Web:* www.mothersbistro.com	Portland	OR	97204	503-464-1122		671
Mother's Market & Kitchen 1890 Newport Blvd *TF:* 800-595-6667 ■ *Web:* www.mothersmarket.com	Costa Mesa	CA	92627	949-631-4741		345
Mother's Polishes Waxes & Cleaners 5456 Industrial Dr *TF:* 800-221-8257 ■ *Web:* www.mothers.com	Huntington Beach	CA	92649	714-891-3364	893-1827	151
Motherhood Maternity 456 N Fifth St **Fax:* Cust Svc ■ *TF:* 800-291-7800 ■ *Web:* www.motherhood.com	Philadelphia	PA	19123	215-873-2200	625-3843*	157-6
Mothers Against Drunk Driving (MADD) 511 E John Carpenter Fwy Ste 700 *TF:* 877-275-6233 ■ *Web:* www.madd.org	Irving	TX	75062	214-744-6233		48-6
Mothers Supporting Daughters with Breast Cancer (MSDBC) 25235 Fox Chase Dr *Web:* www.mothersdaughters.org	Chestertown	MD	21620	410-778-1982	778-1411	48-17
Moti Mahal 1805 14 St SW *Web:* www.motimahal.ca	Calgary	AB	T2T3T1	403-228-9990		671
Motif Seattle 1415 Fifth Ave *TF:* 855-515-1144 ■ *Web:* www.motifseattle.com	Seattle	WA	98101	206-971-8000		707
Motion Analysis Corp 3617 Wwind Blvd *Web:* www.motionanalysis.com	Santa Rosa	CA	95403	707-579-6500		639
Motion Composites 160 Armand-Majeau Sud *Web:* www.motioncomposites.com	Saint-roch-de-l'achigan	QC	J0K3H0	450-588-6555		477
Motion Control Engineering Inc 11380 White Rock Rd *TF:* 800-444-7442 ■ *Web:* www.mceinc.com	Rancho Cordova	CA	95742	916-463-9200		256
Motion Dynamics Corp 5625 Airline Rd *Web:* www.motiondc.com	Fruitport	MI	49415	231-865-7400		492
Motion Envelope Inc 1455 Terre Colony Ct *Web:* i3plasticcards.com	Dallas	TX	75212	214-634-2131	634-2132	263
Motion Fitness LLC 1400 W Northwest Hwy *Web:* www.motionfitness.com	Palatine	IL	60067	847-963-8969		711
Motion Industries Inc 1605 Alton Rd *TF:* 800-526-9328 ■ *Web:* www.motionindustries.com	Birmingham	AL	35210	205-956-1122	951-1172	385
Motion Picture & Television Fund 23388 Mulholland Dr *TF:* 855-760-6783 ■ *Web:* www.mptf.com	Woodland Hills	CA	91364	855-760-6783		48-4
Motion Picture Assn (MPA) 15301 Ventura Blvd Bldg E Sherman Oaks *Web:* www.mpaa.org	Sherman Oaks	CA	91403	818-995-6600		48-4
Motion Picture Assn of America 1600 Eye St NW *Web:* www.mpaa.org	Washington	DC	20006	202-293-1966	296-7410	48-4
Motion Recruitment Partners 131 Clarendon St 3rd Fl *Web:* www.motionrecruitment.com	Boston	MA	02116	617-585-6500		721
Motion Specialties Inc 2720 12 St NE *TF:* 800-661-6672 ■ *Web:* www.motionspecialties.com	Calgary	AB	T2E7N4	403-247-2222		45
Motion Systems Corp 600 Industrial Way W *Web:* actuator.com	Eatontown	NJ	07724	732-222-1800	389-0101	220
Motion Tech Automation Inc 7166 Fourth St N *Web:* www.motiontech.com	St Paul	MN	55128	651-730-9010		815
MotionDSP Inc 700 Airport Blvd Ste 270 *Web:* www.motiondsp.com	Burlingame	CA	94010	650-288-1164		174
MotionPoint Corp Lyons Technology Ctr 4661 Johnson Rd Ste 14 *Web:* www.motionpoint.com	Coconut Creek	FL	33073	954-421-0890		768
Mo-Tires Ltd 2830 5 Ave N *TF:* 800-774-3888 ■ *Web:* www.mo-tires.com	Lethbridge	AB	T1H0P1	403-329-4533		393
Motista Inc 1777 Borel Pl Ste 500 *Web:* www.motista.com	San Mateo	CA	94402	650-204-7976		387
Motiva Enterprises LLC 700 Milam St *Web:* www.motiva.com	Houston	TX	77002	713-277-8000		580
MotivAction 16355 36th Ave N Ste 100 *TF:* 800-326-2226 ■ *Web:* www.motivaction.com	Minneapolis	MN	55446	763-412-3000		384
Motivano Inc 5810 W Cypress St Ste H *TF:* 866-664-4621 ■ *Web:* www.motivano.com	Tampa	FL	33607	866-664-4621		194
Motivating Graphics Inc 3100 Eagle Pkwy *Web:* www.motivatinggraphics.com	Fort Worth	TX	76177	817-491-4788		027
Motivation Through Incentives Inc 10400 W 103 St Ste 10 *TF:* 800-826-3464 ■ *Web:* www.mtievents.com	Overland Park	KS	66214	800-826-3464		384
Motive 2901 Blake St Ste 180 *Web:* thinkmotive.com	Denver	CO	80205	303-302-2100		195
Motive Entertainment Inc 1303 Oakgrove Pl *Web:* www.motivemarketing.biz	Westlake Village	CA	91362	805-778-1930		5
Motive Equipment Inc 8300 W Sleske Ct *Web:* www.motiveequipment.com	Milwaukee	WI	53223	414-446-3379		650
Motley County 701 Dundee Ave	Matador	TX	79244	806-347-2234	347-2220	338
Motley Fool Inc 2000 Duke St 4th Fl *TF:* 800-292-7677 ■ *Web:* www.fool.com	Alexandria	VA	22314	703-838-3665	254-1999	404
Motlow State Community College PO Box 8500 *TF:* 800-654-4877 ■ *Web:* www.mscc.edu	Lynchburg	TN	37352	931-393-1500		162
Moto Japanese Restaurant 2607 N Roan St	Johnson City	TN	37601	423-282-6686		671
Moto Mart 3301 hiawatha ave *Web:* www.mymotomart.com	Minneapolis	MN	55406	612-722-9665		324
Motor & Equipment Manufacturers Assn (MEMA) 10 Laboratory Dr	Research Triangle Park	NC	27709	919-549-4800		49-21
Motor Appliance Corp 601 International Ave *TF:* 800-622-3406 ■ *Web:* www.macmc.com	Washington	DC	63090	636-532-3406	532-4609	518
Motor Castings Co 1323 S 65th St *Web:* www.motorcastings.com	Milwaukee	WI	53214	414-476-1434	476-2845	307
Motor City Computer 1610 E Highwood Dr *TF:* 800-231-1127 ■ *Web:* www.motorcitycomputer.com	Pontiac	MI	48340	248-454-2000		393
Motor City Electric Co 9440 Grinnell St *Web:* www.mceco.com	Detroit	MI	48213	313-921-5300	921-5310	189-4
Motor Coach Industries International Co 1700 E Golf Rd Ste 300 *TF:* 800-743-3624 ■ *Web:* www.mcicoach.com	Schaumburg	IL	60173	847-285-2000		516
Motor Inn of Knoxville LLC 114 S Sixth St *Web:* motorinnautogroup.com	Estherville	IA	51334	712-362-5834		57
Motor Products Owosso Corp 201 S Delaney Rd **Fax Area Code:* 989 ■ *TF:* 800-248-3841 ■ *Web:* www.motorproducts.net	Owosso	MI	48867	800-248-3841	723-6035*	518
Motor Racing Network (MRN) 555 MRN Dr *Web:* www.mrn.com/?homepage=true	Concord	NC	28027	704-262-6700	262-6811	644
Motor Service Inc 130 Byassee Dr *TF:* 800-966-5080 ■ *Web:* www.motorserviceinc.net	Hazelwood	MO	63042	314-731-4111	731-1213	186
Motor Specialty Inc 2801-17 Lathrop Ave PO Box 081278 *Web:* www.motorspecialty.com	Racine	WI	53408	262-632-2794	632-8899	518

Name / Address	City	State	Zip	Phone	Fax	Class
Motor State Distributing 8300 Lane Dr *TF:* 800-772-2678 ■ *Web:* www.motorstate.com	Watervliet	MI	49098	269-463-4113		54
Motor Supply Company Bistro 920 Gervais St *TF:* 800-228-9290 ■ *Web:* www.motorsupplycobistro.com	Columbia	SC	29201	803-256-6687		671
Motor Trend Auto Shows Inc PO Box 4097 *Web:* www.motortrendautoshows.com	Harrisburg	PA	17111	717-566-6100		232
Motor Trend Magazine 6420 Wilshire Blvd 7th Fl *TF:* 800-800-6848 ■ *Web:* www.motortrend.com	Los Angeles	CA	90048	323-782-2000	782-2355	457-3
Motorad of America 6292 Walmore Rd *Web:* www.motoradusa.com	Niagara Falls	NY	14304	716-731-6442		54
Motorcar Parts & Accessories 2929 California St *TF:* 800-890-9988 ■ *Web:* www.motorcarparts.com	Torrance	CA	90503	310-212-7910	212-7581	247
Motorcars International 3015 E Cairo St *TF:* 866-970-6800 ■ *Web:* www.motorcars-intl.com	Springfield	MO	65802	417-831-9999	831-9995	57
MotorCity Casino Hotel 2901 Grand River Ave *TF:* 866-752-9622 ■ *Web:* www.motorcitycasino.com	Detroit	MI	48201	313-237-7711		133
Motorcycle Consumer News Magazine 3 Burroughs *TF:* 888-333-0354 ■ *Web:* www.mcnews.com/mcnews	Irvine	CA	92618	949-855-8822	855-0654	457-3
Motorcycle Hall of Fame Museum 13515 Yarmouth Dr *TF:* 800-262-5646 ■ *Web:* www.americanmotorcyclist.com	Pickerington	OH	43147	614-856-2222	856-2221	522
Motorcycle Industry Council (MIC) 2 Jenner St Ste 150 *TF:* 800-352-6232 ■ *Web:* www.mic.org	Irvine	CA	92618	949-727-4211	727-3313	49-21
MotorHome Magazine 2750 Park View Ct Ste 240 *TF Cust Svc:* 800-678-1201 ■ *Web:* www.motorhome.com	Oxnard	CA	93036	805-667-4100		457-22
Motorists Life Insurance Co 471 E Broad St *Web:* www.motoristsinsurancegroup.com	Columbus	OH	43215	614-225-8211	225-8365	391-2
Motorists Mutual Insurance Co 471 E Broad St **Fax Area Code:* 866 ■ *Web:* www.motoristsinsurancegroup.com	Columbus	OH	43215	614-225-8211	225-1889*	391-4
Motorlease Corp 1506 New Britain Ave *TF:* 800-243-0182 ■ *Web:* motorlease.com	Farmington	CT	06032	860-677-9711	674-8677	289
Motorola Foundation 1303 E Algonquin Rd *TF:* 800-262-8509 ■ *Web:* motorola.com	Schaumburg	IL	60196	847-576-5000		304
Motorola Mobility LLC 600 N US Hwy 45 *Web:* motorola-mobility-en-in.custhelp.com	Libertyville	IL	60048	847-523-5000		615
Motors Management Inc D/B/Atroy Honda 1835 Maplelawn	Troy	MI	48084	248-649-0202		57
Motor-Services Hugo Stamp Inc 3190 SW Fourth Ave *TF:* 800-622-6747 ■ *Web:* www.mshs.com	Fort Lauderdale	FL	33315	954-763-3660		757
Motorsports Hall of Fame of America (MSHFA) 1801 W International Speedway Blvd *Web:* www.mshf.com	Daytona Beach	FL	32114	248-349-7223		522
Motovan Corp 1391 Guy Lussac *TF:* 800-628-4040 ■ *Web:* www.motovan.com	Boucherville	QC	J4B7K1	450-449-3903		517
Motown Museum 2648 W Grand Blvd *TF:* 800-745-3000 ■ *Web:* www.motownmuseum.org	Detroit	MI	48208	313-875-2264	875-2267	520
Motrec Inc 200 rue Des PME St *Web:* www.motrec.com	Sherbrooke	QC	J1C0R2	819-846-2010		711
Motson Graphics Inc 1717 Bethlehem Pk *TF:* 800-972-1986 ■ *Web:* www.motson.com	Flourtown	PA	19031	215-233-0500	233-5014	687
Mott Corp 84 Spring Ln *TF:* 800-289-6688 ■ *Web:* www.mottcorp.com	Farmington	CT	06032	860-747-6333		476
Mott's LLP PO Box 869077 *TF Consumer Info:* 800-426-4891 ■ *Web:* www.motts.com	Plano	TX	75086	800-426-4891		296-20
MOTU Inc 1280 Massachusetts Ave *Web:* www.motu.com	Cambridge	MA	02138	617-576-2760	576-3609	178-9
Moulton Logistics Management 7850 Ruffner Ave *TF:* 800-808-3304 ■ *Web:* www.moultonlogistics.com	Van Nuys	CA	91406	800-808-3304		194
Moulton Seth (Rep D - MA) 1408 Longworth HOB *Web:* moulton.house.gov	Washington	DC	20515	202-225-8020	225-5915	342-2
Moultrie County 10 S Main St Ste 6 *Web:* moultriecountyil.com	Sullivan	IL	61951	217-728-4389	728-8178	338
Moultrie Feeders 150 Industrial Rd *TF:* 800-653-3334 ■ *Web:* www.moultriefeeders.com	Alabaster	AL	35007	205-664-6700		710
Moultrie News 134 Columbus St *Web:* www.moultrienews.com	Charleston	SC	29403	843-958-7489		532-4
Moultrie-Colquitt County Chamber of Commerce 116 First Ave SE *TF:* 888-408-4748 ■ *Web:* www.moultriechamber.com	Moultrie	GA	31768	229-985-2131		139
Moulures M Warnet Mouldings Inc 100 Rue Marius-Warnet *Web:* www.mwarnet.com	Blainville	QC	J7C5P9	450-437-1209	437-3679	752
Mound City National Cemetery Junction - Hwy 37 & 51 *Web:* www.cem.va.gov/cems/nchp/moundcity.asp	Mound City	IL	62963	314-845-8320	845-8355	136
Mound Correctional Facility 17601 Mound Rd *Web:* www.michigan.gov/corrections	Detroit	MI	48212	313-368-8300	368-8972	213
Mound Printing Company Inc 2455 Belvo Rd *Web:* www.moundprinting.com	Miamisburg	OH	45342	937-866-2872		627
Mound Technologies Inc 25 Mound Pk Dr *TF:* 800-788-1549 ■ *Web:* moundtechnologies.com	Springboro	OH	45066	937-748-2937	748-9763	480
Mounds State Park 4306 Mounds Rd *Web:* www.in.gov	Anderson	IN	46017	765-642-6627		565
Mount Airy News 319 N Renfro St *Web:* www.mtairynews.com	Mount Airy	NC	27030	336-786-4141	789-2816	532-2
Mount Allison University 62 York St *TF:* 800-244-8353 ■ *Web:* www.mta.ca	Sackville	NB	E4L1E2	506-364-2269	364-2272	785
Mount Aloysius College 7373 Admiral Perry Hwy *TF:* 888-823-2220 ■ *Web:* www.mtaloy.edu	Cresson	PA	16630	814-886-6383	886-6441	166
Mount Angel Seminary 1 Abbey Dr *TF:* 800-845-8272 ■ *Web:* www.mountangelabbey.org	Saint Benedict	OR	97373	503-845-3951		167-3
Mount Arlington Public Library 333 Howard Blvd *Web:* mountarlingtonlibrary.org	Mount Arlington	NJ	07856	973-398-1516	398-0171	434-3
Mount Auburn Hospital (MAH) 330 Mt Auburn St *Web:* www.mountauburnhospital.org	Cambridge	MA	02138	617-492-3500		374-3
Mount Bachelor Village Resort & Conference Ctr 19717 Mt Bachelor Dr *TF:* 800-547-5204 ■ *Web:* www.mtbachelorvillage.com	Bend	OR	97702	541-389-5900	388-7401	669
Mount Blue State Park 297 Center Hill Rd PO Box 610 *Web:* www.maine.gov	Weld	ME	04285	207-585-2261		565
Mount Calvary Retreat House 505 E Los Olivos *Web:* www.mount-calvary.org	Santa Barbara	CA	93105	805-682-4117		673
Mount Carmel Ctr 4600 W Davis St *Web:* www.mountcarmelcenter.org	Dallas	TX	75211	214-331-6224		673
Mount Carmel Public Utility Co 316 Market St PO Box 220 *TF:* 877-262-7036 ■ *Web:* www.mtcpu.com/home.php	Mount Carmel	IL	62863	618-262-5151		787
Mount Carmel Saint Ann's Hospital 500 S Cleveland Ave *TF:* 800-837-7555 ■ *Web:* www.mountcarmelhealth.com	Westerville	OH	43081	614-898-4000		374-3
Mount Carmel West Hospital 793 W State St *TF:* 800-346-1009 ■ *Web:* mountcarmelhealth.com	Columbus	OH	43222	614-234-5000	944-5070	374-3
Mount Clare Museum House 1500 Washington Blvd Carroll Pk *Web:* www.mountclare.org	Baltimore	MD	21230	410-837-3262	837-0251	520
Mount Clemens General Hospital 1000 Harrington Blvd *Web:* www.mclaren.org	Mount Clemens	MI	48043	586-493-8000		374-3
Mount Dora Farms 16398 Jacinto Ft Blvd *Web:* www.mountdorafarms.com	Houston	TX	77015	713-821-7439		315-4
Mount Everett State Reservation c/o Rd 3 E St	Mount Washington	MA	01258	413-528-0330		565
Mount Gilead State Park 4119 State Rt 95 *Web:* www.ohiodnr.com	Mount Gilead	OH	43338	419-946-1961		565
Mount Grace State Forest Winchester Rd *Web:* www.mass.gov	Warwick	MA	01378	978-544-3939		565
Mount Greylock State Reservation 30 Rockwell Rd *Web:* www.mass.gov	Lanesborough	MA	01237	413-499-4262		565
Mount Holyoke College 50 College St *TF:* 800-642-4483 ■ *Web:* www.mtholyoke.edu	South Hadley	MA	01075	413-538-2000	538-2409	166
Mount Hood Community College 26000 SE Stark St **Fax:* Admissions ■ *TF:* 800-232-4448 ■ *Web:* www.mhcc.edu	Gresham	OR	97030	503-491-6422	491-7388*	162
Mount Hood Equity Partners LP 4800 SW Meadows Rd Ste 300	Lake Oswego	OR	97035	503-639-0915		194
Mount Ida College 777 Dedham St **Fax:* Admissions ■ *Web:* www.mountida.edu	Newton Center	MA	02459	617-928-4500	928-4507*	166
Mount Jefferson State Natural Area 1481 Mt Jefferson State Park Rd *Web:* ncparks.gov	West Jefferson	NC	28694	336-246-9653		565
Mount Joy Wire Corp 1000 E Main St *TF:* 800-321-2305 ■ *Web:* www.mjwire.com	Mount Joy	PA	17552	717-653-1461		813
Mount Juliet Chamber of Commerce 46 W Caldwell St *Web:* www.mjchamber.org	Mount Juliet	TN	37122	615-758-3478	754-8595	139
Mount Kearsarge Indian Museum 18 Highlawn Rd PO Box 142 *Web:* indianmuseum.org	Warner	NH	03278	603-456-2600		520
Mount Laurel Library 100 Walt Whitman Ave *TF:* 888-576-5529 ■ *Web:* www.mtlaurel.lib.nj.us	Mount Laurel	NJ	08054	856-234-7319	234-6916	434-3
Mount Magazine State Park 16878 Hwy 309 S *Web:* www.arkansasstateparks.com	Paris	AR	72855	479-963 8502		565
Mount Marty College 1105 W Eigth St **Fax:* Admissions ■ *TF Admissions:* 800-658-4552 ■ *Web:* www.mtmc.edu	Yankton	SD	57078	605-668-1545	668-1508*	166
Mount Mary College 2900 N Menomonee River Pkwy **Fax:* Admissions ■ *TF Admissions:* 800-321-6265 ■ *Web:* www.mtmary.edu	Milwaukee	WI	53222	414-256-1219	256-0180*	166
Mount Mercy College 1330 Elmhurst Dr NE *TF:* 800-248-4504 ■ *Web:* www.mtmercy.edu	Cedar Rapids	IA	52402	319-368-6460	861-2390	166
Mount Miguel Covenant Village 325 Kempton St **Fax Area Code:* 617 ■ *TF:* 800-562-2734 ■ *Web:* www.mountmiguelcovenantvillage.org	Spring Valley	CA	91977	619-479-4790	565-3809*	672
Mount Mitchell State Park 2388 State Hwy 128 *Web:* www.ncparks.gov	Burnsville	NC	28714	828-675-4611		565
Mount Nebo State Park 16728 W State Hwy 155 *Web:* www.arkansasstateparks.com	Dardanelle	AR	72834	479-229-3655		565
Mount Nittany Medical Ctr 1800 E Pk Ave *TF:* 866-686-6171 ■ *Web:* www.mountnittany.org	State College	PA	16803	814-231-7000		374-3
Mount Olive Area Chamber of Commerce 123 N Ctr St *Web:* www.moachamber.com	Mount Olive	NC	28365	919-658-3113		139
Mount Olive Area Chamber of Commerce PO Box 192 *Web:* mountolivechambernj.com	Budd Lake	NJ	07828	908-509-1774		139

Phone | Fax | Class

Mount Olive College
634 Henderson St........................Mount Olive NC 28365 919-658-2502 658-9816* 166
*Fax: Admissions ■ TF: 800-653-0854 ■ Web: umo.edu

Mount Olive Correctional Complex
1 Mtnside Way..........................Mount Olive WV 25185 304-442-7213 213

Mount Olivet Careview Home
5517 Lyndale Ave S....................Minneapolis MN 55419 612-827-5677 371
Web: mtolivethomes.org

Mount Philo State Park
5425 Mt Philo Rd.........................Charlotte VT 05445 802-425-2390 565
Web: www.vtstateparks.com

Mount Pisgah Arboretum
34901 Frank Parrish Rd......................Eugene OR 97405 541-747-1504 741-4904 97
Web: mountpisgaharboretum.org

Mount Pisgah State Park 28 Entrance Rd...........Troy PA 16947 570-297-2734 565
Web: www.dcnr.state.pa.us

Mount Pleasant Public Library NY
350 Bedford Rd.........................Pleasantville NY 10570 914-769-0548 434-3
Web: www.mountpleasantlibrary.org

Mount Pleasant-Titus County Chamber of Commerce
1604 N Jefferson Ave.................Mount Pleasant TX 75455 903-572-8567 572-0613 139
Web: www.mtpleasanttx.com

Mount Prospect Chamber of Commerce
662 E NW Hwy......................Mount Prospect IL 60056 847-398-6616 398-6780 139
TF: 800-584-4452 ■ Web: www.mountprospectchamber.org

Mount Prospect Public Library
10 S Emerson St.....................Mount Prospect IL 60056 847-253-5675 434-3
Web: www.mppl.org

Mount Rainier National Park
55210 238th Ave E..........................Ashford WA 98304 360-569-2211 569-6519 564
Web: www.nps.gov/mora

Mount Regis Ctr 405 Kimball Ave................Salem VA 24153 877-217-3447 726
TF: 877-217-3447 ■ Web: www.mtregis.com

Mount Revelstoke National Park of Canada
PO Box 350...........................Revelstoke BC V0E2S0 250-837-7500 837-7536 563
TF: 866-787-6221 ■ Web: www.pc.gc.ca

Mount Royal College
4825 Mt Royal Gate SW.....................Calgary AB T3E6K6 403-440-6111 785
TF: 877-440-5001 ■ Web: www.mtroyal.ca

Mount Royal Printing Company Inc
6310 Blair Hill Ln.....................Baltimore MD 21209 410-296-1117 627
TF: 800-442-1162 ■ Web: mtroyalprinting.com

Mount Rushmore National Memorial
13000 Hwy 244 Bldg 31 Ste 1................Keystone SD 57751 605-574-2523 574-2307 564
Web: www.nps.gov

Mount Rushmore Society
711 N Creek Dr..........................Rapid City SD 57703 605-341-8883 341-0433 48-13
Web: www.mountrushmoresociety.com

Mount Saint Helens National Volcanic Monument
42218 NE Yale Bridge Rd.....................Amboy WA 98601 360-449-7800 449-7801 50-5
TF: 800-416-5615 ■ Web: www.fs.fed.us

Mount Saint Joseph Hospital
3080 Prince Edward St..................Vancouver BC V5T3N4 604-874-1141 374-2
Web: providencehealthcare.org

Mount Saint Mary College
330 Powell Ave..........................Newburgh NY 12550 845-569-3248 562-6762 166
TF: 888-937-6762 ■ Web: www.msmc.edu

Mount Saint Mary' s University
12001 Chalon Rd.......................Los Angeles CA 90049 310-954-4000 954-4259* 166
*Fax: Admissions ■ Web: www.msmu.edu

Mount Saint Mary's Hospital
5300 Military Rd..........................Lewiston NY 14092 716-297-4800 374-3
Web: www.chsbuffalo.org

Mount Saint Mary's University
16300 Old Emmitsburg Rd................Emmitsburg MD 21727 301-447-5214 447-5860* 166
*Fax: Admissions ■ TF Admissions: 800-448-4347 ■ Web: www.msmary.edu

Mount Saint Mary's University Doheny
10 Chester Pl.........................Los Angeles CA 90007 613-562-5353 162
Web: www.bkstr.com

Mount Saint Vincent University
166 Bedford Hwy............................Halifax NS B3M2J6 902-457-6117 457-6498 785
TF: 877-733-6788 ■ Web: www.msvu.ca

Mount San Jacinto College
1499 N State St.......................San Jacinto CA 92583 951-487-6752 654-6738* 162
*Fax: Admissions ■ TF: 800-624-5561 ■ Web: www.msjc.edu

Mount Shasta Resort
1000 Siskiyou Lake Blvd................Mount Shasta CA 96067 530-926-3030 926-0333 669
TF: 800-958-3363 ■ Web: www.mountshastaresort.com

Mount Sinai Hospital
600 University Ave..........................Toronto ON M5G1X5 416-596-4200 586-4807* 374-2
*Fax: PR ■ Web: www.mountsinai.on.ca

Mount Sinai Hospital Bone Marrow Transplant Program
19 E 98th St............................New York NY 10029 212-241-6021 769
TF: 866-682-9380 ■ Web: www.mountsinai.org

Mount Sinai Hospital Medical Ctr of Chicago
California Ave 15th St.......................Chicago IL 60608 773-542-2000 374-3
TF: 877-448-7848 ■ Web: www.sinai.org

Mount Sinai Medical Ctr
4300 Alton Rd.........................Miami Beach FL 33140 305-674-2121 374-3
Web: www.msmc.com

Mount Sinai Medical Ctr, The
1 Gustave L Levy Pl......................New York NY 10029 212-241-6500 731-3418 374-3
TF: 800-637-4624 ■ Web: www.mountsinai.org

Mount Sinai Memorial Park
5950 Forest Lawn Dr....................Los Angeles CA 90068 323-469-6000 510
TF: 800-600-0076 ■ Web: mountsinaiparks.org

Mount Sinai Queens 25-10 30th Ave.............Astoria NY 11102 718-932-1000 278-1786 374-3
TF: 800-968-7637 ■ Web: www.mshq.org

Mount st Louis Moonstone Ski Resort Ltd
24 Mt St Louis Rd W Rr 4..................Coldwater ON L0K1E0 905-856-4754 377
Web: www.skicanada.org

Mount Sugarloaf State Reservation
300 Sugarloaf St.....................South Deerfield MA 01373 413 665-2928 565
Web: www.mass.gov

Mount Sunapee State Park 1460 Rt 103.......Newbury NH 03255 603-763-5561 565
Web: www.nhstateparks.org

Mount Tom State Reservation
125 Resv Rd..............................Holyoke MA 01040 413-534-1186 565
Web: mass.gov

Mount Union College 1972 Clark Ave...........Alliance OH 44601 330-823-2590 823-5097* 166
*Fax: Admissions ■ TF Admissions: 800-334-6682 ■ Web: mountunion.edu

Mount Vernon & Knox County Public Library
201 N Mulberry St.....................Mount Vernon OH 43050 740-392-2665 434-3

Mount Vernon Chamber of Commerce
65 Haven Ave..........................Mount Vernon NY 10553 914-775-8127 699-0139 139

Mount Vernon City School Dist 80
2710 North St.........................Mount Vernon IL 62864 618-244-8080 449
Web: www.mtv80.org

Mount Vernon Hospital
12 N Seventh Ave.....................Mount Vernon NY 10550 914-664-8000 374-3

Mount Vernon Hotel Museum & Garden
421 E 61st St...............................New York NY 10065 212-838-6878 838-7390 520
Web: www.mvhm.org

Mount Vernon Mills Inc
503 S Main St PO Box 100...................Mauldin SC 29662 864-688-7100 745-1
Web: www.mvmills.com

Mount Vernon Nazarene University
800 Martinsburg Rd...................Mount Vernon OH 43050 740-392-6868 166
TF Admissions: 800-766-8206 ■ Web: www.mvnu.edu

Mount Vernon Public Library
28 S First Ave........................Mount Vernon NY 10550 914-668-1840 434-3
Web: mountvernonpubliclibrary.org

Mount Vernon Restaurant
3535 Broad St.........................Chattanooga TN 37409 423-266-6591 671

Mount Vernon-Knox County Chamber of Commerce
400 S Gay St..........................Mount Vernon OH 43050 740-393-1111 393-1590 139
Web: www.knoxchamber.com

Mount Vernon-Lee Chamber of Commerce
6911 Richmond Hwy Ste 320...............Alexandria VA 22306 703-360-6925 360-6928 139
TF: 800-628-8092 ■ Web: www.mtvernon-leechamber.org

Mount View Hotel & Spa
1457 Lincoln Ave...........................Calistoga CA 94515 707-942-6877 942-6904 379
TF: 800-816-6877 ■ Web: www.mountviewhotel.com

Mount View Youth Services Ctr
7862 W Mansfield Pkwy......................Denver CO 80235 303-987-4502 412
Web: www.colorado.gov

Mount Wachusett Community College
444 Green St................................Gardner MA 01440 978-632-6600 630-9554* 162
*Fax: Admissions ■ TF: 800-705-9692 ■ Web: mwcc.edu

Mount Washington Hotel & Resort
Rt 302................................Bretton Woods NH 03575 603-278-1000 669
TF: 800-314-1752 ■ Web: www.brettonwoods.com

Mount Washington Pediatric Hospital
1708 W Rogers Ave.......................Baltimore MD 21209 410-578-8600 374-1
TF: 800-463-6295 ■ Web: www.mwph.org

Mount Washington State Forest
Rd 3 E St.........................Mount Washington MA 01258 413-528-0330 565

Mount Yale Capital Group LLC
8000 Norman Ctr Dr Ste 630...............Minneapolis MN 55437 952-897-5390 194
Web: www.mtyale.com

Mountain Air Conditioning & Heating Corp
735 S Broadway...........................Hicksville NY 11801 516-935-0149 189-10

Mountain America Credit Union
PO Box 9001............................West Jordan UT 84084 801-325-6228 219
TF: 800-748-4302 ■ Web: www.macu.com

Mountain Boy Sledworks Inc
1070 Greene St...............................Silverton CO 81433 970-387-5077 761
TF: 800-333-1307 ■ Web: www.mountainboysleds.com

Mountain Cascade Inc PO Box 5050.........Livermore CA 94551 925-373-8370 188-10
Web: www.mountaincascade.com

Mountain Cement Co 5 Sand Creek Rd..........Laramie WY 82070 307-745-4879 742-4534 135
Web: www.mountaincement.com

Mountain Creek Resort 200 Rt 94.............Vernon NJ 07462 973-827-2000 669
Web: mountaincreek.com

Mountain Democrat 1360 Broadway..........Placerville CA 95667 530-622-1255 532-3
TF: 800-231-2222 ■ Web: www.mtdemocrat.com

Mountain Electric Co-op Inc
PO Box 180.............................Mountain City TN 37683 423-727-1800 727-1822 245
TF Cust Svc: 800-638-3788 ■ Web: www.mountainelectric.com

Mountain Empire Community College
3441 Mtn Empire Rd....................Big Stone Gap VA 24219 276-523-2400 523-8297* 162
*Fax: Admissions ■ TF: 800-981-0600 ■ Web: www.me.cc.va.us

Mountain Empire Family Medicine
31115 Hwy 94...............................Campo CA 91906 619-445-6200 354
Web: www.mtnhealth.org

Mountain Empire Oil Co
282 Christian Church Rd................Johnson City TN 37616 423-928-7241 579
Web: www.roadrunnermarkets.com

Mountain Empire Unified School District
3291 Buckman Springs Rd..................Pine Valley CA 91962 619-473-9022 685
Web: www.meusd.k12.ca.us

Mountain Equipment Co-operative
149 W Fourth Ave..........................Vancouver BC V5Y4A6 604-707-3300 711
TF: 800-722-1960 ■ Web: www.mec.ca

Mountain Fresh Supermarket
2203 SR- 118...........................Hunlock Creek PA 18621 570-477-2988 345

Mountain Haus 292 E Meadow Dr...............Vail CO 81657 970-476-2434 476-3007 379
TF: 800-237-0922 ■ Web: www.mountainhaus.com

Mountain High Resort
24510 State Hwy 2........................Wrightwood CA 92397 888-754-7878 132
TF: 888-754-7878 ■ Web: www.mthigh.com

Mountain Home Air Force Base
366 Gunfighter Ave Ste 314.........Mountain Home AFB ID 83648 208-828-6800 497-1
TF: 855-366-0140 ■ Web: www.mountainhome.af.mil

Mountain Home Area Chamber of Commerce
1023 Hwy 62..........................Mountain Home AR 72653 870-425-5111 425-4446 139
TF: 800-822-3536 ■ Web: www.enjoymountainhome.com

Mountain Home National Cemetery
53 Memorial Ave......................Mountain Home TN 37684 423-979-3535 979-3521 136
TF: 800-827-1000 ■ Web: www.cem.va.gov/cems/nchp/mountainhome.asp

Mountain Home News
195 S Third E St PO Box 1330...........Mountain Home ID 83647 208-587-3331 587-9205 637-8
Web: www.mountainhomenews.com

Mountain King 6950 Neuhaus St................Houston TX 77061 713-923-5807 10-11

Mountain Lake Hotel 115 Hotel Cir...........Pembroke VA 24136 540-626-7121 626-7172 379
TF: 800-346-3334 ■ Web: www.mtnlakelodge.com

Name / Address	City	State	ZIP	Phone	Fax	Class
Mountain Laurel Resort & Spa Rt 940 PO Box 9	White Haven	PA	18661	570-443-8411		669
TF: 888-243-9300 ■ *Web:* www.mountainlaurelresort.com						
Mountain Laurel Spa at Stonewall Resort 940 Resort Dr	Roanoke	WV	26447	304-269-8881		707
TF: 888-278-8150 ■ *Web:* www.stonewallresort.com						
Mountain Light Photography Inc 106 S Main St.	Bishop	CA	93514	760-873-7700	873-3980	593
TF: 800-877-8339 ■ *Web:* www.mountainlight.com						
Mountain Lion Foundation PO Box 1896	Sacramento	CA	95812	916-442-2666		48-3
TF: 800-319-7621 ■ *Web:* www.mountainlion.org						
Mountain Lion Inc PO Box 799	Pennington	NJ	08534	609-730-1665		94
Web: www.mtlioninc.net/Biography.html						
Mountain Lodge at Telluride 457 Mtn Village Blvd	Telluride	CO	81435	970-369-5000	369-4317	669
TF: 866-368-6867 ■ *Web:* www.mountainlodgetelluride.com						
Mountain Ltd 19 Yarmouth Dr Ste 301	New Gloucester	ME	04260	207-688-6200	688-6212	631
TF: 800-322-8627 ■ *Web:* www.mountainltd.com						
Mountain Manor of Paintsville 1025 Euclid Ave	Paintsville	KY	41240	606-789-5808		371
TF: 800-321-1245 ■ *Web:* www.mountainmanorofpaintsville.com						
Mountain Manor Treatment Ctr 9701 Keysville Rd.	Emmitsburg	MD	21727	301-447-2361		726
TF: 800-537-3422 ■ *Web:* www.mountainmanor.org						
Mountain Mission School 1760 Edgewater Dr	Grundy	VA	24614	276-935-2954		685
Web: mmskids.org						
Mountain Oasis 11 E Aspen Ave	Flagstaff	AZ	86001	928-214-9270		671
Mountain Parks Electric Inc 321 W Agate Ave.	Granby	CO	80446	970-887-3378	887-3996	245
TF: 877-887-3378 ■ *Web:* www.mpei.com						
Mountain Province Diamonds Inc 161 Bay St Ste 2315	Toronto	ON	M5J2S1	416-361-3562	603-8565	503-3
TSE: MPV ■ *Web:* www.mountainprovince.com						
Mountain Research LLC 825 25th St.	Altoona	PA	16601	814-949-2034		743
TF: 800-837-4674 ■ *Web:* www.mountainresearch.com						
Mountain Sky Guest Ranch PO Box 1219	Emigrant	MT	59027	406-333-4911		239
TF: 800-548-3392 ■ *Web:* www.mtnsky.com						
Mountain States Constructors Inc 3601 Pan American Rd NE	Albuquerque	NM	87107	505-292-0108		188-4
Mountain States Pipe & Supply Co 111 W Las Vegas St	Colorado Springs	CO	80903	719-634-5555	634-5551	612
TF: 800-777-7173 ■ *Web:* www.msps.com						
Mountain States Steel Inc 325 S Geneva Rd	Lindon	UT	84042	801-785-5085		492
TF: 800-227-8335 ■ *Web:* www.mssteel.com						
Mountain States Supply Inc 184 West 3300 South	Salt Lake City	UT	84115	801-484-8885		612
Web: www.mountainlandsupply.com						
Mountain Supply Co 2101 Mullan Rd	Missoula	MT	59808	406-543-8255		612
TF: 800-821-1646 ■ *Web:* www.mountainsupply.com						
Mountain Telephone Co 405 Main St	West Liberty	KY	41472	606-743-3121		387
TF: 800-939-3121 ■ *Web:* www.mrtc.com						
Mountain Thunder Lodge 50 Mountain Dr	Breckenridge	CO	80424	970-547-5650		652
Web: breckresorts.com						
Mountain Times PO Box 1815	Boone	NC	28607	828-264-6397	262-0282	532-4
TF: 800-829-4477 ■ *Web:* www.wataugademocrat.com/mountaintimes						
Mountain Tools Inc 225 Crossroads Blvd	Carmel	CA	93923	831-620-0911		711
Web: www.mtntools.com						
Mountain Top Arboretum Rt 23C Maude Adams Rd PO Box 379	Tannersville	NY	12485	518-589-3903		97
Web: www.mtarboretum.org						
Mountain Travel Sobek 1266 66th St Ste 4	Emeryville	CA	94608	510-594-6000	594-6001	760
TF: 888-831-7526 ■ *Web:* www.mtsobek.com						
Mountain V Oil & Gas Inc 415 Heliport Rd	Bridgeport	WV	26330	304-842-6320		536
Web: mountainvoilandgas.com						
Mountain Valley Bank 317 DAVIS Ave	Elkins	WV	26241	304-637-2265	637-2270	70
TF: 800-555-3503 ■ *Web:* www.mountainvalleybank.com						
Mountain Valley Farms & Lumber Inc 1240 Nawakwa Rd	Biglerville	PA	17307	717-677-6166	677-9283	551
Web: www.mtvalleyfarms.com						
Mountain Valley Spring Co 150 Central Ave	Hot Springs	AR	71901	501-624-1635		805
Web: www.mountainvalleyspring.com						
Mountain View College 4849 W Illinois Ave.	Dallas	TX	75211	214-860-8680	860-8570*	162
**Fax:* Admissions ■ *Web:* www.mountainviewcollege.edu/pages/default.aspx						
Mountain View Electric Assn Inc 1655 Fifth St PO Box 1600	Limon	CO	80828	719-775-2861	775-9513	245
TF: 800-388-9881 ■ *Web:* www.mvea.coop						
Mountain View Hospital 1000 East 100 North	Payson	UT	84651	801-465-7000		374-3
TF: 877-865-9738 ■ *Web:* www.mvhpayson.com						
Mountain View Public Library 585 Franklin St	Mountain View	CA	94041	650-903-6335	962-0438	434-3
TF: 800-984-4636 ■ *Web:* mountainview.gov						
Mountain View School District (MVSD) 3320 Gilman Rd	El Monte	CA	91732	626-652-4000		685
Web: www.mtviewschools.com						
Mountain View Youth Development Ctr 809 Peal Ln	Dandridge	TN	37725	865-397-0174		412
Mountain Villas 9525 W Skyline Pkwy	Duluth	MN	55810	218-624-5784		379
TF: 866-688-4552 ■ *Web:* www.mtvillas.com						
Mountain Xpress 2 Wall St Ste 211	Asheville	NC	28801	828-251-1333	251-1311	532-5
Web: mountainx.com						
Mountaineer Capital LP 305 Washington St W Ste 300	Charleston	WV	25302	304-347-7519	347-0072	792
Mountaineer Inn 3343 Mountain Rd.	Stowe	VT	05672	802-253-7525		378
Web: www.stowemountaineerinn.com						
Mountaineer Park Inc 1420 Mountaineer Cir.	New Cumberland	WV	26047	800-804-0468		132
TF: 800-804-0468 ■ *Web:* www.moreatmountaineer.com						
Mountaineers Books 1001 SW Klickitat Way Ste 201	Seattle	WA	98134	206-223-6303		95
TF: 800-553-4453 ■ *Web:* www.mountaineersbooks.org						
Mountaineers, The 7700 Sand Pt Way NE	Seattle	WA	98115	206-521-6000	523-6763	48-23
TF: 800-573-8484 ■ *Web:* www.mountaineers.org						
Mountainland Supply Co 1505 W 130 S	Orem	UT	84058	801-224-6050		612
Web: www.mtncom.net						
Mountainside Fitness 9745 W Happy Valley Rd	Peoria	AZ	85383	623-561-5525		354
Web: www.mountainsidefitness.com						
MountainView Hospital 3100 N Tenaya Way	Las Vegas	NV	89128	702-255-5000		374-3
Web: www.mountainview-hospital.com						
MountainView Regional Medical Ctr 4311 E Lohman Ave	Las Cruces	NM	88001	575-556-7600	556-7619	374-3
Web: www.mountainviewregional.com						
Mountainview Youth Correctional Facility 31 Petticoat Ln	Annandale	NJ	08801	908-638-6191		412
Mountainview Youth Development Ctr 1182 Dover Rd	Charleston	ME	04422	207-285-0880	285-0836	412
Web: maine.gov						
Mountaire Corp PO Box 1320	Millsboro	DE	19966	302-934-1100		447
TF: 877-887-1490 ■ *Web:* www.mountaire.com						
Mountaire Farms 17269 NC Hwy 71 N.	Lumber Bridge	NC	28357	910-843-5942		619
TF: 877-887-1490 ■ *Web:* www.mountaire.com						
Mountaire Farms of Delaware Inc 29005 John JWilliams Hwy	Millsboro	DE	19966	302-934-1100		619
Mountaire Farms of North Carolina 203 Morris Farm Rd	Candor	NC	27229	910-974-3232		447
TF: 800-331-9790 ■ *Web:* mountaire.com						
Mountrail County 101 N Main St	Stanley	ND	58784	701-627-4835		338
Web: www.co.mountrail.nd.us						
Mountrail-Williams Electric Co-op 218 58th St W PO Box 1346	Williston	ND	58802	701-577-3765	577-3777	245
TF: 800-279-2667 ■ *Web:* www.mwec.com						
Mounts Botanical Garden 531 N Military Trl	West Palm Beach	FL	33415	561-233-1757		97
TF: 888-800-5447 ■ *Web:* www.mounts.org						
Mountz Inc 1080 N 11th St	San Jose	CA	95112	408-292-2214		350
TF: 888-925-2763 ■ *Web:* www.mountztorque.com						
Moureaux Hauspy Design Inc 276 Rue St Jacques	Montreal	QC	H2Y1N3	514-844-3938		393
Web: provencherroy.ca						
Mouse River State Forest 307 - First St E	Bottineau	ND	58318	701-228-5422	228-5448	565
Web: www.ndsu.edu						
Mouser Custom Cabinetry 2112 N Hwy 31 W.	Elizabethtown	KY	42701	270-737-7477		115
TF: 800-345-7537 ■ *Web:* www.mousercc.com						
Mouser Electronics Corp 1000 N Main St	Mansfield	TX	76063	817-804-3888	804-3899	246
TF: 800-346-6873 ■ *Web:* mouser.in						
Mousetail Landing State Park 3 Campground Rd	Linden	TN	37096	731-847-0841		565
Web: www.state.tn.us						
Movado Group Inc 650 From Rd Ste 375	Paramus	NJ	07652	201-267-8000		153
NYSE: MOV ■ *Web:* www.movadogroupinc.com						
Move Networks Inc 796 E Utah Vly Dr	American Fork	UT	84003	801-756-5805		5
Move Your Mind a Fitness First 2100 Tremont Ctr	Columbus	OH	43221	614-486-0575		354
Movie Colony Hotel 726 N Indian Canyon Dr	Palm Springs	CA	92262	760-320-6340	320-1640	379
Web: www.moviecolonyhotel.com						
Movieland Wax Museum of the Stars 4848 Clifton Hill	Niagara Falls	ON	L2G3N4	905-358-3061		520
TF: 800-663-3301 ■ *Web:* www.cliftonhill.com						
Movies Unlimited Inc 3015 Darnell Rd	Philadelphia	PA	19154	630-919-2192		459
TF: 800-668-4344 ■ *Web:* www.moviesunlimited.com						
MovieTickets.com Inc 2255 Glades Rd Ste 100E	Boca Raton	FL	33431	561-322-3200		41
Web: www.movietickets.com						
Moving Off Campus LLC 5257 Shaw Blvd Ste 102	St. Louis	MO	63110	314-367-2456		5
Web: www.movingoffcampus.com						
Movius Interactive 11360 Lakefield Dr	Duluth	GA	30097	770-283-1000		735
Web: www.moviuscorp.com						
Mowat Mackie & Anderson LLP 1999 Harrison St Ste 1500	Oakland	CA	94612	510-893-1120		2
Web: www.mowat.com						
Mower County 201 First St NE	Austin	MN	55912	507-437-9535		338
Web: www.co.mower.mn.us						
Moxie Hair Salon 2649 Lyndale Ave S	Minneapolis	MN	55408	612-813-0330		77
Web: moxiesalon.com						
Moxie Java International LLC 4990 W Chinden Blvd.	Boise	ID	83714	208-322-7773		159
Web: moxiejava.com						
Moxie Pictures 18 E 16th St Fl 4	New York	NY	10003	212-807-6901		362
Web: www.moxiepictures.com						
Moximed Inc 26460 Corporate Ave Ste 100	Hayward	CA	94545	510-887-3300		477
Web: www.moximed.com						
Moxy Commerce Inc 965-A Detroit Ave	Concord	CA	94518	206-257-2121	277-1030*	5
**Fax Area Code:* 636						
Moyco Technologies Inc 200 Commerce Dr	Montgomeryville	PA	18936	215-855-4300		1
Moye's Pharmacy 4467 N Henry Blvd	Stockbridge	GA	30281	770-474-0704		237
TF: 800-579-7967 ■ *Web:* www.moyespharmacy.com						
Moyer & Son Inc 113 E Reliance Rd	Souderton	PA	18964	215-799-2000		447
TF: 866-669-3747 ■ *Web:* www.emoyer.com						
Moyno Inc 1895 W Jefferson St	Springfield	OH	45506	937-327-3111	327-3177*	641
**Fax:* Mktg ■ *TF:* 877-486-6966 ■ *Web:* www.moyno.com						
Mozambique 420 E 50th St	New York	NY	10022	212-644-6800	644-5972	784
Web: www.un.int						

Name / Address	City	State	Zip	Phone	Fax	Class
Mozambique Embassy 1525 New Hampshire Ave NW *Web:* www.embamoc-usa.org	Washington	DC	20036	202-293-7146		257
Mozingo Liquors Inc 120 S Sixth St	Hartsville	SC	29550	843-332-6554		443
MP Assoc Inc 1721 Boxelder St Ste 107 *Web:* www.mpassociates.com	Louisville	CO	80027	303-530-4562	530-4334	184
MP Biomedicals LLC 3 Hutton Ctr Dr Ste 100 *TF:* 800-633-1352 ■ *Web:* www.mpbio.com	Santa Ana	CA	92707	949-833-2500		477
MP Global Products Inc 2500 Old Hadar Rd *TF:* 888-379-9695 ■ *Web:* www.mpglobalproducts.com	Norfolk	NE	68701	402-379-9695		258
MP Husky Corp 204 Old Piedmont Hwy PO Box 16749 *TF:* 800-277-4810 ■ *Web:* www.mphusky.com	Greenville	SC	29605	864-234-4800	234-4822	816
MP Metal Products Inc W1250 Elmwood Ave *TF:* 800-824-6744 ■ *Web:* www.mpmetals.com	Ixonia	WI	53036	920-261-9650	261-9652	482
MP Pumps Inc 34800 Bennett Dr *TF:* 800-563-8006 ■ *Web:* www.mppumps.com	Fraser	MI	48026	586-293-8240	293-8469	641
MP2 Energy Texas LLC 21 Waterway Ave Ste 450 *Web:* www.mp2energy.com	The Woodlands	TX	77380	832-510-1030		466
MPA (Motion Picture Assn) 15301 Ventura Blvd Bldg E Sherman Oaks *Web:* www.mpaa.org	Sherman Oaks	CA	91403	818-995-6600		48-4
MPA (Magazine Publishers of America) 810 Seventh Ave 24th Fl *TF:* 800-234-3368 ■ *Web:* www.magazine.org	New York	NY	10019	212-872-3700	888-4217	49-16
Mpa Media 5406 Bolsa Ave *TF:* 800-324-7758 ■ *Web:* www.mpamedia.com	Huntington Beach	CA	92649	714-230-3150		463
Mpathix Inc 87 Skyway Ave Ste 200 *Web:* www.mpathix.com	Toronto	ON	M9W6R3	416-849-4210		387
MPBN (Maine Public Broadcasting Network) 65 Texas Ave *TF:* 800-884-1717 ■ *Web:* mainepublic.org	Bangor	ME	04401	207-941-1010	942-2857	632
MPC (Materials Properties Council) PO Box 201547 *Web:* www.forengineers.org/mpc	Shaker Heights	OH	44122	216-658-3847	658-3854	49-19
MPC Promotions 4300 Produce Rd PO Box 34336 **Fax Area Code:* 888 ■ *TF:* 800-331-0989 ■ *Web:* www.mpcpromotions.com	Louisville	KY	40232	502-451-4900	451-8475*	155-9
MPCA 10635 Santa Monica Blvd *Web:* mpcafilm.com	Los Angeles	CA	90025	310-319-9500	319-9501	514
MPD Inc 316 E Ninth St *TF:* 866-225-5673 ■ *Web:* www.mpdinc.com	Owensboro	KY	42303	270-685-6200		419
Mpe Engineering Ltd Ste 260 E Atrium 2635 37 Ave NE	Calgary	AB	T1Y5Z6	403-329-3442		261
MPEC (Multi-Purpose Events Ctr) 1000 Fifth St *TF:* 800-799-6732 ■ *Web:* www.wfmpec.com	Wichita Falls	TX	76301	940-716-5500		205
Mpell Solutions LLC 3142 Tiger Run Ct Ste 108 *Web:* www.mpellsolutions.com	Carlsbad	CA	92010	760-727-9600		195
MPhA (Minnesota Pharmacists Assn) 1935 W County Rd B2 *TF:* 800-451-8349 ■ *Web:* www.mpha.org	Roseville	MN	55113	651-697-1771	697-1776	585
Mphasis Corp 460 Pk Ave S Rm 1101 *Web:* www.mphasis.com	New York	NY	10016	212-686-6655		179
mphoria LLC 1245 Rosemont Dr *TF:* 888-415-4933	Indian Land	SC	29707	888-415-4933		5
MPI (Meeting Professionals International) 2711 Lyndon B Johnson Fwy Ste 600 *TF:* 866-318-2743 ■ *Web:* www.mpiweb.org	Dallas	TX	75234	972-702-3053	702-3065	49-12
MPI Group LLC, The 319 N Hills Rd *Web:* www.metalproductsinc.com	Corbin	KY	40701	606-523-0461		295
MPI Label Systems Inc 450 Courtney Rd *TF:* 800-423-0442 ■ *Web:* www.mpilabels.com	Sebring	OH	44672	330-938-2134	938-9878	413
MPI Media Group 16101 108th Ave *Web:* www.mpimedia.com	Orland Park	IL	60467	708-460-0555		511
MPI Technologies 37 E St *TF:* 888-674-8088 ■ *Web:* www.mpirelease.com	Winchester	MA	01890	781-729-8300	729-9093	600
MPIF (Metal Powder Industries Federation) 105 College Rd E *TF:* 800-237-7600 ■ *Web:* www.mpif.org	Princeton	NJ	08540	609-452-7700	987-8523	49-13
MPL (Marathon Pipe Line LLC) 539 S Main St *Web:* www.marathonpipeline.com	Findlay	OH	45840	419-422-2121		597
MPM Capital Offices 200 Clarendon St 54th Fl *TF:* 888-286-8010 ■ *Web:* www.mpmcapital.com	Boston	MA	02116	617-425-9200		792
MPM Medical Inc 2301 Crown Ct *TF:* 800-232-5512 ■ *Web:* www.mpmmedicalinc.com	Irving	TX	75038	972-893-4090		476
Mpo Videotronics Inc 5069 Maureen Ln *Web:* www.mpo-video.com	Moorpark	CA	93021	805-499-8513		233
mPower Software Services LLC 115 Pheasant Run Ste 110 *Web:* www.mpowerss.com	Newtown	PA	18940	215-497-9730		19
MPP (Merriweather Post Pavilion) 10475 Little Patuxent Pkwy *TF:* 877-435-9849 ■ *Web:* www.merriweathermusic.com	Columbia	MD	21044	410-715-5550	715-5560	572
MPR (Minnesota Public Radio) 480 Cedar St *TF:* 800-228-7123 ■ *Web:* www.mpr.org	Saint Paul	MN	55101	651-290-1212		632
Mpress Inc 4100 Howard Ave *Web:* www.mpressnow.com	New Orleans	LA	70125	504-524-8248		5
MPS (Monolithic Power Systems Inc) 6409 Guadalupe Mines Rd *NASDAQ: MPWR* ■ *Web:* www.monolithicpower.com	San Jose	CA	95120	408-826-0600		696
MPS (Marlborough Public Schools) 17 Washington St *Web:* www.mps-edu.org	Marlborough	MA	01752	508-460-3509		186
MPS Group Inc 2920 Scotten St **Fax Area Code:* 248 ■ *Web:* www.mpsgrp.com	Detroit	MI	48210	313-841-7588	489-0653*	192
MPS LORIA Financial Planners LLC 7500 S County Line Rd *Web:* www.mpsloria.com	Burr Ridge	IL	60527	630-887-4404		401
MPT (Maryland Public Television) 11767 Owings Mills Blvd *TF:* 800-223-3678 ■ *Web:* www.mpt.org	Owings Mills	MD	21117	410-581-4201	581-4338	632
MPW Industrial Services Group Inc 9711 Lancaster Rd SE *TF:* 800-827-8790 ■ *Web:* mpwservices.com	Hebron	OH	43025	740-929-1614	928-8140	152
MPX Geophysics Ltd Unit 14 25 Valleywood Dr *TF:* 800-672-4774 ■ *Web:* www.mpxgeophysics.com	Markham	ON	L3R5L9	905-947-1782		536
Mr Appliance Corp 304 E Church Ave **Fax Area Code:* 254 ■ *TF:* 888-998-2011 ■ *Web:* www.mrappliance.com	Killeen	TX	76541	888-998-2011	537-0745*	310
Mr B's Bistro 201 Royal St *TF:* 800-672-6124 ■ *Web:* www.mrbsbistro.com	New Orleans	LA	70130	504-523-2078	521-8304	671
Mr Button Products Inc 7840 Rockville Rd *TF:* 800-214-3545 ■ *Web:* www.mrbutton.com	Indianapolis	IN	46214	317-273-4333		627
Mr Crane Inc 647 N Hariton St *TF:* 800-598-3465 ■ *Web:* www.mrcrane.com	Orange	CA	92868	714-633-2100		190
MR Diamonds Inc 66 W 47th St Window 1A *Web:* mr-diamond-usa.com	New York	NY	10036	212-869-7202		411
Mr Friendly's New Southern Cafe 2001 Greene St *Web:* www.mrfriendlys.com	Columbia	SC	29205	803-254-7828	254-8219	671
Mr Goodcents Franchise Systems Inc 8997 Commerce Dr *TF:* 800-648-2368 ■ *Web:* goodcentssubs.com	DeSoto	KS	66018	800-648-2368		670
Mr Greek 1670 H Pass Rd	Biloxi	MS	39531	228-432-7888		671
Mr Handyman International LLC 3948 Ranchero Dr Ste 1C *TF Cust Svc:* 855-632-2126 ■ *Web:* www.mrhandyman.com	Ann Arbor	MI	48108	734-666-3021		310
Mr Hero Restaurants 7010 Engle Rd Ste 100 *TF:* 888-860-5082 ■ *Web:* www.mrhero.com	Middleburg Heights	OH	44130	440-625-3080		670
Mr Jim's Pizza Inc *Franchise Service Ctr* 2521 Pepperwood St *TF:* 800-583-5960 ■ *Web:* mrjims.pizza	Farmers Branch	TX	75234	972-267-5467		670
MR Label Inc 5018 Gray Rd *TF:* 888-522-3526 ■ *Web:* www.mrlabelco.com	Cincinnati	OH	45232	513-681-2088		627
Mr Mudd 5225 Wilshire Blvd Ste 604 *Web:* mrmudd.com	Los Angeles	CA	90036	323-932-5656		514
Mr Pickwick's 8620 Granville St	Vancouver	BC	V6P5A1	604-266-2340		671
Mr Powdrell's Barbeque House 11301 Central Ave NE *Web:* powdrellsbbq.webs.com	Albuquerque	NM	87123	505-298-6766		671
Mr Rooter Corp 1010 N University Parks Dr *TF:* 855-982-2028 ■ *Web:* www.mrrooter.com	Waco	TX	76707	254-340-1321	745-2501	189-10
M-R Sign Company Inc 1706 First Ave N *TF:* 800-231-5564 ■ *Web:* www.mrsigncompany.com	Fergus Falls	MN	56537	218-736-5681	736-4070	701
Mr Tire Auto Service Centers Inc 200 Holleder Pkwy *TF:* 800-876-6676 ■ *Web:* www.mrtire.com	Rochester	NY	14615	800-876-6676		62-5
Mr Transmission 9675 Yonge St 2nd Fl *TF:* 800-373-8432 ■ *Web:* www.mistertransmission.com	Richmond Hill	ON	L4C1V7	905-884-1511	884-4727	62-6
Mr Youth LLC 225 Park Ave S Fl 16 *Web:* www.mryouth.com	New York	NY	10003	212-779-8700		7
Mr.Clean Car Wash 2567 EW Conn SW *Web:* www.mrcleancarwash.com	Austell	GA	30106	770-222-5811		62-1
Mr.Copy Inc 5657 Copley Dr *Web:* www.mrc360.com	San Diego	CA	92111	858-573-6300		196
MRAS (Middle River Aircraft Systems) 103 Chesapeake Pk Plaza *TF:* 877-432-3272 ■ *Web:* www.mras-usa.com	Baltimore	MD	21220	410-682-1500	682-1230	22
Mrasek & Assoc PC 6193 Miller Rd Ste A1	Swartz Creek	MI	48473	810-635-2409		2
Mraz, Amerine & Associates Inc 1120 13th St Ste K *Web:* www.mrazamerine.com	Modesto	CA	95354	209-593-5870		528
MRB Partners Inc 2001 boul Robert-Bourassa Ste 810 *Web:* www.mrbpartners.com	Montreal	QC	H3A2A6	514-558-1515		401
MRC (Medicare Rights Ctr) 520 Eigth Ave N Wing 3rd Fl *TF Hotline:* 800-333-4114 ■ *Web:* www.medicarerights.org	New York	NY	10018	212-869-3850	869-3532	48-17
MRC Global Inc 2 Houston Ctr *TF:* 877-294-7574 ■ *Web:* www.mrcglobal.com/global region/default	Houston	TX	77010	877-294-7574		787
MRC Polymers Inc 3307 S Lawndale Ave *Web:* www.mrcpolymers.com	Chicago	IL	60623	773-890-9000	890-9007	605-2
MRCE (Mueser Rutledge Consulting Engineers) 14 Penn Plaza 225 W 34th St *Web:* www.mrce.com	New York	NY	10122	917-339-9300	339-9400	261
MREIC (Monmouth Real Estate Investment Corp) 3499 Rt 9 N Ste 3C *NASDAQ: MNR* ■ *TF:* 800-937-5449 ■ *Web:* www.mreic.com	Freehold	NJ	07728	732-577-9996		655
MRG (Marketing Resource Group Inc) 225 S Washington Sq *TF:* 800-928-2086 ■ *Web:* mrgmi.com	Lansing	MI	48933	517-372-4400	372-4045	5
MRI (Midwest Research Institute) 425 Volker Blvd *Web:* www.mriglobal.org	Kansas City	MO	64110	816-753-7600		668
MRI Flexible Packaging Co 122 Penns Trl *TF:* 800-448-8183 ■ *Web:* www.mriflex.com	Newtown	PA	18940	800-448-8183		627
MRI Group 2100 Harrisburg Pk *TF:* 888-674-1377 ■ *Web:* www.mrigroup.com	Lancaster	PA	17601	717-291-1016		415
Mri Technologies 17047 El Camino Real Ste 200 *Web:* mricompany.com	Houston	TX	77058	281-786-2004		175
MRM//McCANN 622 Third Ave *Web:* mrm-mccann.com/en/index.html	New York	NY	10017	646-865-6230		4
MRMC (Midwestern Regional Medical Ctr) 2520 Elisha Ave *TF:* 800-615-3055 ■ *Web:* www.cancercenter.com	Zion	IL	60099	847-872-4561		374-7

Phone | Fax | Class

MRMC (Martin Resource Management Corp)
PO Box 191 .... Kilgore TX 75663 903-983-6200 983-6271 316
TF: 888-334-7473 ■ *Web:* www.martinmidstream.com

MRMC (Meadows Regional Medical Ctr)
1 Meadows Pkwy .... Vidalia GA 30474 912-535-5555 374-3
TF: 800-382-4023 ■ *Web:* www.meadowsregional.org

MRMC (Meadowview Regional Medical Ctr)
989 Medical Pk Dr .... Maysville KY 41056 606-759-5311 374-3
Web: www.meadowviewregional.com

MRN (Motor Racing Network) 555 MRN Dr .... Concord NC 28027 704-262-6700 262-6811 644
Web: www.mrn.com/?homepage=true

Mrp LLC 1640 New Market Ave .... South Plainfield NJ 07080 732-968-6061 480

MRS (Materials Research Society)
506 Keystone Dr .... Warrendale PA 15086 724-779-3003 779-8313 49-19
TF: 800-732-0999 ■ *Web:* www.mrs.org

Mrs Clark's Foods 740 SE Dalbey Dr .... Ankeny IA 50021 515-299-6400 296-21
TF: 800-736-5674 ■ *Web:* www.mrsclarks.com

Mrs Gerrys Kitchen Inc
2110 Y H Hanson Ave .... Albert Lea MN 56007 507-373-6384 123
Web: www.mrsgerrys.com

Mrs Nelsons Library Service
1650 W Orange Grove Ave .... Pomona CA 91768 909-397-7820 95
TF: 800-875-9911 ■ *Web:* www.mrsnelsons.com

Mrs Ressler's Food Products Co
5501 Tabor Ave .... Philadelphia PA 19120 215-744-4700 744-4750 296-26
Web: www.ressler.com

Mrs Robino's Restaurant
520 N Union St .... Wilmington DE 19801 302-652-9223 671
Web: www.mrsrobinos.com

Mrs Stratton's Salads Inc
380 Industrial Ln .... Birmingham AL 35211 205-940-9640 297-8
Web: www.mrsstrattons.com

MRS Systems Inc
19000 33rd Ave W Ste 130 .... Seattle WA 98036 206-633-6145 177
TF: 800-253-4827 ■ *Web:* www.mrsys.com

MRTK (Metropolitan Trucking Inc)
299 Market St .... Saddle Brook NJ 07663 800-967-3278 843-6179* 449
**Fax Area Code:* 201 ■ *TF:* 800-967-3278 ■ *Web:* www.mtrk.com

MRU Instruments Inc
6699 Portwest Dr Ste 130 .... Houston TX 77024 713-426-3260 407
TF: 800-495-2919 ■ *Web:* www.mru-instruments.com

MRV Communications Inc
20415 Nordhoff St .... Chatsworth CA 91311 818-773-0900 773-0906 792
OTC: MRVC ■ *TF Sales:* 800-338-5316 ■ *Web:* www.mrv.com

Mrv Marketing Llc
31877 Del Obispo St Ste 203 .... San Juan Capo CA 92675 949-487-0550 195
Web: mrvdairysolutions.com

Ms Aerospace Inc 13928 Balboa Blvd .... Sylmar CA 91342 818-833-9095 833-9525 278
Web: www.msaerospace.com

MS Consultants Inc
333 E Federal St .... Youngstown OH 44503 330-744-5321 261
Web: www.msconsultants.com

Ms Dallas Reprographics Inc
2300 Reagan St .... Dallas TX 75219 214-521-7000 113
Web: www.msdallas.com

Ms Fitness Magazine PO Box 2490 .... White City OR 97503 541-830-0400 457-13
Web: www.msfitness.com

MS Foundation for Women
12 MetroTech Ctr 26th Fl .... Brooklyn NY 11201 212-742-2300 742-1653 48-24
Web: forwomen.org

MS Howells & Co
20555 N Pima Rd Ste 100 .... Scottsdale AZ 85255 480-563-2000 690
Web: www.mshowells.com

MS Kennedy Corp 4707 Dey Rd .... Liverpool NY 13088 315-701-6751 701-6752 253
Web: www.mskennedy.com

Ms Magazine 1600 Wilson Blvd Ste 801 .... Arlington VA 22209 703-522-4201 522-2219 457-11
TF: 866-672-6363 ■ *Web:* www.msmagazine.com

MS Technology Inc
137 Union Valley Rd .... Oak Ridge TN 37830 865-483-0895 261
Web: mstechnology.com

MS Willett Inc
220 Cockeysville Rd .... Cockeysville MD 21030 410-771-0460 771-6972 757
Web: www.mswillett.com

Ms. Bubbles Inc 2731 S Alameda St .... Los Angeles CA 90058 323-544-0300 239-9709* 155-3
**Fax Area Code:* 213 ■ *Web:* www.msbubbles.com

MSA (Medical Services of America Inc)
171 Monroe Ln .... Lexington SC 29072 803-957-0500 363
TF: 800-845-5850 ■ *Web:* www.msa-corp.com

MSA Aircraft Products Inc
10000 Iota Dr .... San Antonio TX 78217 210-590-6100 22
TF: 800-695-1212 ■ *Web:* www.msaaircraft.com

MSA architecture + design
360 22nd st Ste 800 .... Oakland CA 94612 415-541-0977 393
Web: www.msasf.com

MSA Consulting Inc
34200 Bob Hope Dr .... Rancho Mirage CA 92270 760-320-9811 261
Web: www.msaconsultinginc.com

MSA Professional Services Inc
1230 South Blvd .... Baraboo WI 53913 608-356-2771 261
TF: 800-362-4505 ■ *Web:* msa-ps.com

MSA Security 9 Murray St 2nd Fl .... New York NY 10007 212-509-1336 692
TF: 800-286-2000 ■ *Web:* www.msasecurity.net

MSANA (Masonic Service Assn of North America)
8120 Fenton St Ste 203 .... Silver Spring MD 20910 301-588-4010 608-3457 48-15
TF: 855-476-4010 ■ *Web:* www.msana.com

MSB Fairway Capital Partners
1800 St James Pl Ste 450 .... Houston TX 77056 713-622-9961 691
Web: www.msfairway.com

MSB Financial Corp (MSBF)
1902 Long Hill Rd .... Millington NJ 07946 908-647-4000 647-6196 70
NASDAQ: MSBF

MSBF (MSB Financial Corp)
1902 Long Hill Rd .... Millington NJ 07946 908-647-4000 647-6196 70
NASDAQ: MSBF

MSC (Material Sciences Corp)
2200 E Pratt Blvd .... Elk Grove Village IL 60007 734-207-4444 439-0737* 481
NASDAQ: MASC ■ **Fax Area Code:* 847 ■ *Web:* www.materialsciencescorp.com

MSC (Murray Supply Co)
102 W Third St .... Winston-Salem NC 27101 336-546-1780 245-0686 612
Web: www.murraysupply.com

MSC Cruises USA Inc
6750 N Andrews Ave Ste 100 .... Fort Lauderdale FL 33309 954-772-6262 220
TF: 800-665-4655 ■ *Web:* www.msccruisesusa.com/en-us/homepage.aspx

MSC Filtration Technologies
198 Freshwater Blvd .... Enfield CT 06082 860-745-7475 745-7477 806
TF Cust Svc: 800-237-7359 ■ *Web:* www.mscfiltertech.com

MSC Industrial Direct Co
75 Maxess Rd .... Melville NY 11747 516-812-2000 255-5067* 385
NYSE: MSM ■ **Fax Area Code:* 800 ■ *TF:* 800-645-7270 ■ *Web:* www.mscdirect.com

MSC.Software Corp
4675 MacArthur Crt .... Newport Beach CA 92660 714-540-8900 784-4056 178-5
Web: www.mscsoftware.com

MSCE (MacKay & Somps)
5142 Franklin Dr Ste B .... Pleasanton CA 94588 925-225-0690 225-0698 261
TF: 800-795-1747 ■ *Web:* www.msce.com

MSCI (Metals Service Ctr Institute)
4201 Euclid Ave .... Rolling Meadows IL 60008 847-485-3000 485-3001 49-18
TF: 800-634-2358 ■ *Web:* www.msci.org

MSCI (Margaret Sanger Ctr International)
26 Bleecker St .... New York NY 10012 212-965-7000 274-7299 48-6
Web: www.plannedparenthood.org

MSDBC (Mothers Supporting Daughters with Breast Cancer)
25235 Fox Chase Dr .... Chestertown MD 21620 410-778-1982 778-1411 48-17
Web: www.mothersdaughters.org

MSDSonline Inc 350 N Orleans Ste 950 .... Chicago IL 60654 312-881-2000 317
Web: www.msdsonline.com

MSE Express America Inc
2700 Delta Ln .... Elk Grove Village IL 60007 847-238-2600 311
Web: www.tasexpress.com

MSE Power Systems Inc
403 New Karner Rd .... Albany NY 12205 518-452-7718 261
Web: www.msepower.com

MSE Technology Applications Inc
200 Technology Way .... Butte MT 59701 406-494-7100 494-7230 743

MSF (Multiple Sclerosis Foundation)
6520 N Andrews Ave .... Fort Lauderdale FL 33309 954-776-6805 48-17
TF: 800-225-6495 ■ *Web:* www.msfocus.org

Msf Electric Inc
10455 Fountaingate Dr .... Stafford TX 77477 281-494-4700 189-4
TF: 866-366-7943 ■ *Web:* www.msfelectric.com

MSG (Jannus Inc) 1607 W Jefferson St .... Boise ID 83702 208-336-5533 336-0880 48-17
Web: www.jannus.org

MSG Network 2 Pennsylvania Plaza .... New York NY 10121 212-465-6741 740
Web: www.msgnetworks.com/index.html

MSH (Mercy Suburban Hospital)
2701 De Kalb Pk .... Norristown PA 19401 610-278-2000 374-3
Web: www.mercyhealth.org/suburban

MSHA (Mine Safety & Health Administration)
1100 Wilson Blvd .... Arlington VA 22209 202-693-9400 693-9401 340-15
TF: 800-746-1553 ■ *Web:* www.msha.gov

MSHFA (Motorsports Hall of Fame of America)
1801 W International Speedway Blvd .... Daytona Beach FL 32114 248-349-7223 522
Web: www.mshf.com

Mship Co 401 W A St Ste 2125 .... San Diego CA 92101 619-232-8937 698
Web: www.mshipco.com

MSI (Machine Specialties Inc)
6511 Franz Warner Pkwy .... Whitsett NC 27377 336-603-1919 621
Web: www.machspec.com

MSI Benefits Group Inc
245 Townpark Dr Ste 100 .... Kennesaw GA 30144 770-425-1231 425-4722 390
TF: 800-580-1629 ■ *Web:* www.msibenefitsgroup.com

MSI Data Systems
10033 N Port Washington Rd .... Mequon WI 53092 262-241-7800 177
Web: www.msidata.com

MSI General Corp PO Box 7 .... Oconomowoc WI 53066 262-367-3661 803-1
Web: www.msigeneral.com

MSI International Inc
650 Pk Ave .... King of Prussia PA 19406 610-265-2000 265-2213 266
TF: 800-927-0919 ■ *Web:* www.msimsi.com

MSI Inventory Service Corp
PO Box 320129 .... Flowood MS 39232 601-939-0130 939-0061 399
TF: 800-820-1460 ■ *Web:* www.msi-inv.com

Msi Tec Inc 8925 E Nichols Ave .... Centennial CO 80112 720-875-9835 180
TF: 866-397-7388 ■ *Web:* www.msitec.com

Msights Inc 9935 Rea Rd Ste D-301 .... Charlotte NC 28277 877-267-4448 809
TF: 877-267-4448 ■ *Web:* msights.com

MSJH (Ministry Saint Joseph's Hospital)
611 St Joseph Ave .... Marshfield WI 54449 715-387-1713 374-3
TF: 800-888-4755 ■ *Web:* www.ministryhealth.org/sjh/home.nws

MSK Precision Products Inc
10101 NW 67th St .... Tamarac FL 33321 954-776-0770 776-3780 621
TF: 800-992-5018 ■ *Web:* www.mskprecision.com

MSL (Montana State Library)
1515 E Sixth Ave .... Helena MT 59620 406-444-3115 434-5
Web: home.msl.mt.gov

MSM Industries Inc 802 Swan Dr .... Smyrna TN 37167 615-355-4355 355-6874 676
TF: 800-648-6648 ■ *Web:* www.msmind.com

MSM Transportation Inc
124 Commercial Rd .... Bolton ON L7E1K4 905-951-6800 311
TF: 800-667-4175

MSNA (Maine State Nurses Assn)
160 Capitol St Ste 1 .... Augusta ME 04330 207-622-1057 623-4072 533
Web: www.nationalnursesunited.org

MSP Corp
5910 Rice Creek Pkwy Ste 300 .... Shoreview MN 55126 651-287-8100 407
Web: www.mspcorp.com

MSPB (Merit Systems Protection Board)
1615 M St NW .... Washington DC 20419 202-653-7200 653-7130 340-20
TF: 800-209-8960 ■ *Web:* www.mspb.gov

MSPB (Merit Systems Protection Board Regional Offices)
Atlanta Region
401 W Peachtree St NW 10th Fl .... Atlanta GA 30308 404-730-2755 730-2767 340-20
TF: 800-209-8960 ■ *Web:* www.mspb.gov

Mspca Animal Shelter
1577 Falmouth Rd .... Centerville MA 02632 508-775-0940 794
Web: www.mspca.org

Name / Address	City	State	Zip	Phone	Fax	Class
Mspta 1715 Abbey Rd Ste B *TF:* 800-539-2346 ■ *Web:* mspta.net	East Lansing	MI	48823	517-336-7782		414
MSR Communications 832 Sansome St 2nd Fl *TF:* 866-247-6172 ■ *Web:* www.msrcommunications.com	San Francisco	CA	94111	415-989-9000		636
MSRB (Municipal Securities Rulemaking Board) 1900 Duke St Ste 600 *TF:* 888-475-8376 ■ *Web:* www.msrb.org	Alexandria	VA	22314	703-797-6600	797-6700	49-2
MSS Services Inc 14200 Schaeffer Rd *Web:* mssserv.com	Germantown	MD	20874	301-528-5531		463
MSS Technologies Inc 1555 E Orangewood Ave *TF:* 800-694-1302 ■ *Web:* www.msstech.com	Phoenix	AZ	85020	602-387-2100		180
MST (Monterey-Salinas Transit) 1 Ryan Ranch Rd *TF:* 800-291-2877 ■ *Web:* www.mst.org	Monterey	CA	93940	831-899-2555		468
MST Steel Corp 24417 Groesbeck Hwy *Web:* www.mststeel.com	Warren	MI	48089	586-773-5460		399
MSTV (Association for Maximum Service Television) 1776 Massachusetts Ave NW	Washington	DC	20036	202-861-0344		49-14
MSU (Missouri State University) 901 S National Ave *TF:* 800-492-7900 ■ *Web:* www.missouristate.edu	Springfield	MO	65897	417-836-5000	836-6334	166
MSU-DOE Plant Research Laboratory 612 Wilson Rd *Web:* prl.natsci.msu.edu	East Lansing	MI	48824	517-353-2270	353-9168	668
Msys Inc 140 Iowa Ln Ste 201 *Web:* www.msysinc.com	Cary	NC	27511	919-380-9783		193
M&T Bank 1 M & T Plaza 8th Fl *NYSE: MTB* ■ *TF:* 800-724-2440 ■ *Web:* www.mtb.com	Buffalo	NY	14203	716-842-4470		70
M&T Bank Stadium 1101 Russell St *Web:* www.baltimoreravens.com	Baltimore	MD	21230	410-261-7283		720
Mt Konocti Growers Inc 2550 Big Valley Rd *Web:* mtkonoctiwines.com	Kelseyville	CA	95451	707-279-4213		315-3
MT Mckinley Bank 500 Fourth Ave *Web:* mtmckinleybank.com	Fairbanks	AK	99701	907-452-1751		70
Mt Pleasant Central School District 825 Westlake Dr *Web:* www.mtplcsd.org	Thornwood	NY	10594	914-769-5500	769-3733	685
Mt Shasta Spring Water Company Inc 1878 Twin View Blvd *TF:* 800-922-6227 ■ *Web:* www.mtshastaspringwater.com	Redding	CA	96003	530-246-8800		366
Mt Street Michael High School 4300 Murdock Ave *Web:* mtstmichael.org	Bronx	NY	10466	718-515-6400		685
Mt. Lebanon School District 7 Horsman Dr *Web:* www.mtlsd.org	Pittsburgh	PA	15228	412-344-2000	344-2047	685
Mt. San Antonio College 1100 N Grand Ave *Web:* www.mtsac.edu	Walnut	CA	91789	909-594-5611		162
Mt. Vernon illinois 1100 Main St *Web:* www.mtvernon.com	Mount Vernon	IL	62864	618-242-5000	244-0746	206
MTA (Maryland Transit Administration) 6 St Paul St *Web:* www.mta.maryland.gov	Baltimore	MD	21202	410-539-5000	333-4810	468
MTA Today Magazine 20 Ashburton Pl *TF:* 800-392-6175 ■ *Web:* www.massteacher.org	Boston	MA	02108	617-878-8000	742-7046	457-8
MTC (Micro Technology Concepts) 17837 Rowland St *Web:* www.mtcusa.com	City Of Industry	CA	91748	626-839-6800		174
MTC (Microcast Technologies Corp) 1611 W Elizabeth Ave *Web:* www.mtcnj.com	Linden	NJ	07036	908-523-9503	523-0010	401
MTC (Materials Transportation Co) 1408 S Commerce PO Box 1358 *TF:* 800-433-3110 ■ *Web:* www.gomtc.com	Temple	TX	76503	254-298-2900		386
MTC Logistics 4851 Holabird Ave *Web:* mtccold.com	Baltimore	MD	21224	410-342-9300	522-1163	803-2
MTD Products Inc 5965 Grafton Rd *TF:* 800-800-7310 ■ *Web:* www.mtdproducts.com	Valley City	OH	44280	330-225-2600		429
MTE Consultants Inc 520 Bingemans Centre Dr *TF:* 800-387-9355 ■ *Web:* www.mte85.com	Kitchener	ON	N2B3X9	519-743-6500		196
MTE Corp PO Box 9013 *TF:* 800-455-4683 ■ *Web:* www.mtecorp.com	Menomonee Falls	WI	53051	262-253-0200	253-8222	767
Mte Hydraulics 4701 Kishwaukee St *Web:* www.mtehydraulics.com	Rockford	IL	61109	815-397-4701	399-5528	640
Mtech Mechanical Technologies Group Inc 12300 Pecos St *Web:* www.mtechg.com	Westminster	CO	80234	303-650-4000		610
Mthink 55 New Montgomery St Ste 617 *Web:* www.mthink.com	San Francisco	CA	94105	415-371-8800		4
MTI (Momentum Technologies Inc) 1507 Boettler Rd	Uniontown	OH	44685	330-896-5900	896-9943	603
MTI (Manufacturing Technology Inc) 1702 W Washington St *Web:* www.mtiwelding.com	South Bend	IN	46628	574-233-9490	233-9489	811
MTI (Medical Teams International) PO Box 10 *TF:* 800-959-4325 ■ *Web:* www.medicalteams.org	Portland	OR	97207	503-624-1000	624-1001	48-5
MTI America PO Box 667140 *TF:* 800-553-2155 ■ *Web:* www.mtiamerica.com	Pompano Beach	FL	33066	800-553-2155		393
Mti Electronics Inc W133 N5139 Campbell Dr *Web:* www.mtielectronics.com	Menomonee Falls	WI	53051	262-783-6080		625
MTI Inc 1050 NW 229th Ave *TF:* 888-684-0040 ■ *Web:* mobiletechinc.com	Hillsboro	OR	97124	503-648-6500		614
MTI Instruments Inc 325 Washington Ave Ext *TF:* 800-342-2203 ■ *Web:* www.mtiinstruments.com	Albany	NY	12205	518-218-2550		407
MTI Systems Inc 59 Interstate D *TF:* 800-644-4318 ■ *Web:* www.mtisystems.com	West Springfield	MA	01089	413-733-1972	739-9250	178-12
MTI-Milliren Technologies Inc 2 New Pasture Rd *Web:* www.mti-milliren.com	Newburyport	MA	01950	978-465-6064		253
MT&L Card Products & Fulfillment Services 2911 Kraft Dr *Web:* www.mtlcard.com	Nashville	TN	37204	615-254-9471		627
MTM Assn for Standards & Research 1111 E Touhy Ave Ste 280 **Fax Area Code: 847* ■ *TF:* 844-300-5355 ■ *Web:* www.mtm.org	Des Plaines	IL	60018	844-300-5355	299-3509*	49-19
MTM Publishing Inc 435 W 23rd St Ste 8C *Web:* www.mtmpublishing.com	New York	NY	10011	212-242-6930	242-6906	94
Mtm Recognition Corp 3201 SE 29th St *TF:* 877-686-7464 ■ *Web:* www.mtmrecognition.com	Oklahoma City	OK	73115	405-670-4545	672-1308	409
MTM Technologies Inc 1200 High Ridge Rd *OTC: MTMC* ■ *Web:* www.mtm.com	Stamford	CT	06905	203-975-3700		176
MTNA (Music Teachers NA) 441 Vine St Ste 3100 *TF:* 888-512-5278 ■ *Web:* www.mtna.org	Cincinnati	OH	45202	513-421-1420	421-2503	49-5
MTNG (Middle Tennessee Natural Gas Utility District) 1036 W Broad St PO Box 670 *TF:* 800-880-6373 ■ *Web:* www.mtng.com	Smithville	TN	37166	615-597-4300	597-6331	787
MTPB (Tourism Malaysia) 120 E 56th St 15th Fl *Web:* www.malaysia.travel/en/us	New York	NY	10022	212-754-1113		775
MtronPTI 1703 E Hwy 50 *TF:* 800-762-8800 ■ *Web:* www.mtronpti.com	Yankton	SD	57078	605-665-9321		253
MTS (Mid-America Transplant Services) 1110 Highlands Plaza Dr E Ste 100 *TF:* 888-376-4854 ■ *Web:* www.midamericatransplant.org	Saint Louis	MO	63110	314-735-8200		545
MTS (MTS Safety Products Inc) PO Box 204 *TF General:* 800-647-8168 ■ *Web:* www.mts-safety.com	Golden	MS	38847	800-647-8168	329-9687	576
MTS (Musical Theatre Southwest) 6320 Domingo Rd NE Ste B *Web:* www.musicaltheatresw.com	Albuquerque	NM	87108	505-265-9119		573-2
MTS Ambulance 2431 Greenup Ave *TF:* 800-598-3458 ■ *Web:* www.mtsambulance.com	Ashland	KY	41101	606-324-3286		30
MTS Consulting LLC 7444 Long Ave *Web:* www.mtsconsulting.com	Skokie	IL	60077	847-675-6666		734
MTS Safety Products Inc (MTS) PO Box 204 *TF General:* 800-647-8168 ■ *Web:* www.mts-safety.com	Golden	MS	38847	800-647-8168	329-9687	576
MTS Seating Inc 7100 Industrial Dr **Fax Area Code: 800* ■ *TF:* 800-329-0687 ■ *Web:* www.mtsseating.com	Temperance	MI	48182	734-847-3875	329-0687*	319-1
MTS Systems Corp 14000 Technology Dr *NASDAQ: MTSC* ■ *TF Cust Svc:* 800-328-2255 ■ *Web:* www.mts.com	Eden Prairie	MN	55344	952-937-4000	937-4515	472
MTSI (Modern Technology Solutions Inc) 5285 Shawnee Rd Ste 400 *Web:* www.mtsi va.com	Alexandria	VA	22312	703-564-3800		261
MTSI Inc 145 S State College Blvd Ste 180 *Web:* www.mtsiinc.com	Brea	CA	92821	714-257-1144	257-1654	647
MTT-S (IEEE Microwave Theory & Techniques Society) 5829 Bellanca Dr *TF:* 800-678-4333 ■ *Web:* www.mtt.org	Elkridge	MD	21075	410-796-5866		49-19
MTU Aero Engines North America Inc 795 Brook St Bldg 5 *Web:* www.mtu.de	Rocky Hill	CT	06067	860-258-9700	258-9797	21
MTU Onsite Energy Corp 100 Power Dr **Fax:* Sales ■ *TF:* 800-325-5450 ■ *Web:* www.mtuonsiteenergy.com	Mankato	MN	56001	507-625-7973	625-2968*	518
MTV Networks 1515 Broadway **Fax Area Code: 201* ■ *Web:* www.mtv.com	New York	NY	10036	212-846-6000	422-6630*	740
MTV Networks On Campus Inc (MTVU) 1515 Broadway 45th FL *TF:* 877-800-4483 ■ *Web:* www.mtvu.com	New York	NY	10036	877-800-4483		740
MTVU (MTV Networks On Campus Inc) 1515 Broadway 45th FL *TF:* 877-800-4483 ■ *Web:* www.mtvu.com	New York	NY	10036	877-800-4483		740
Mtw Solutions LLC 3236 W Edgewood Dr Ste D *TF:* 800-438-7325 ■ *Web:* www.mtwsolutions.com	Jefferson City	MO	65109	573-893-7997		180
Mu Du Noodles 1494 Cerrillos Rd *TF:* 800-727-5531 ■ *Web:* www.mudunoodles.com	Santa Fe	NM	87505	505-983-1411		671
Mu Lan 824 Juniper St NE *Web:* mulanatlanta.net	Atlanta	GA	30308	404-877-5797		671
Mu Net Inc 442 Marrett Rd *Web:* www.munet.com	Lexington	MA	02421	781-861-8644		625
Mu Phi Epsilon International Music Fraternity PO Box 1369 *TF:* 888-259-1471 ■ *Web:* www.muphiepsilon.org	Fort Collins	CO	80522	888-259-1471		48-16
Muckel Anderson CPAs 300 E Second St	Reno	NV	89501	775-686-3200		2
Mud Hole Custom Tackle Inc 400 Kane Ct *TF:* 866-790-7637 ■ *Web:* www.mudhole.com	Oviedo	FL	32765	407-447-7637		711
Mudd Advertising 915 Technology Pkwy	Cedar Falls	IA	50613	319-277-2003		5
Mudiam Inc 7100 regency Sq blvd *TF:* 888-306-2062 ■ *Web:* www.mudiaminc.com	Houston	TX	77036	713-484-7266		225
Mueller Brass Co 2199 Lapeer Ave **Fax Area Code: 616* ■ *TF:* 800-553-3336 ■ *Web:* muellerindustriesipd.com	Port Huron	MI	48060	810-987-7770	794-1214*	485
Mueller Co 500 W Eldorado St **Fax:* Cust Svc ■ *TF:* 800-423-1323 ■ *Web:* www.muellerflo.com	Decatur	IL	62522	217-423-4471	425-7537*	789
Mueller Graphic Supply Inc 11475 W Thdore Trcker Way *Web:* www.muellergraphics.com	Milwaukee	WI	53214	414-475-0990	475-0454	386
Mueller Inc 1913 Hutchins Ave *TF:* 877-268-3553 ■ *Web:* www.muellerinc.com	Ballinger	TX	76821	325-365-3555	365-8181	105
Mueller Industries Inc 8285 Tournament Dr Ste 150 *NYSE: MLI* ■ *TF:* 800-348-8464 ■ *Web:* www.muellerindustries.com	Memphis	TN	38125	901-753-3200	753-3251	485
Mueller Law Office, The 404 W Seventh St *Web:* themuellerlawoffice.com	Austin	TX	78701	512-478-1236		41
Mueller Metals LLC 2152 Schwartz Rd *Web:* www.muellermetals.com	San Angelo	TX	76904	325-651-9558		492
Mueller Planetarium University of Nebraska 210 Morrill Hall *TF:* 800-432-3216 ■ *Web:* www.spacelaser.com	Lincoln	NE	68588	402-472-2641		598

				Phone	Fax	Class
Mueller Plastics Corp 3070 E Cedar *TF:* 800-348-8464 ■ *Web:* www.muellerindustries.com	Ontario	CA	91761	909-930-2060	930-2070	596
Mueller Recreational Products Inc 4825 S 16th St *TF:* 800-925-7665 ■ *Web:* www.muellers.com	Lincoln	NE	68512	402-423-8888		711
Mueller Refrigeration LLC 121 Rogers St *Web:* www.muellerrefrigeration.com	Hartsville	TN	37074	615-374-2124	374-2080	789
Mueller Sports Medicine Inc 1 Quench Dr *Web:* www.muellersportsmed.com	Prairie Du Sac	WI	53578	608-643-8530		582
Mueller State Park ?21045 Hwy 67 S *Web:* cpw.state.co.us	Divide	CO	80814	719-687-2366		565
Mueller Steam Specialty 1491 NC Hwy 20 W *TF:* 800-334-6259 ■ *Web:* www.muellersteam.com	Saint Pauls	NC	28384	910-865-8241	865-8245	386
Muermann Engineering LLC 116 Fremont St *Web:* www.me-pe.com	Kiel	WI	53042	920-894-7800		261
Mueser Rutledge Consulting Engineers (MRCE) 14 Penn Plaza 225 W 34th St *Web:* www.mrce.com	New York	NY	10122	917-339-9300	339-9400	261
Muffuletta Cafe 2260 Como Ave *Web:* www.muffuletta.com	Saint Paul	MN	55108	651-644-9116	644-5329	671
Muhammad Ali Ctr 144 N Sixth St *Web:* www.alicenter.org	Louisville	KY	40202	502-584-9254	589-4905	520
Muhlenberg College 2400 Chew St *Web:* muhlenberg.edu	Allentown	PA	18104	484-664-3100	664-3234	166
Muhlenberg County PO Box 137 *Web:* www.muhlenbergcounty.ky.gov	Greenville	KY	42345	270-338-2520	338-6116	338
Muhlenberg Regional Medical Ctr Park Ave & Randolph Rd *TF:* 800-247-9580 ■ *Web:* jfkmc.org/jfk-muhlenberg-campus	Plainfield	NJ	07060	908-668-2000		374-3
Mui Scientific 145 Traders Blvd E *TF:* 800-303-6611 ■ *Web:* muiscientific.com	Mississauga	ON	L4Z3L3	905-890-5525		476
Muir Enterprises Inc 3575 West 900 South PO Box 26775 *Fax: Sales ■ *TF:* 877-268-2002 ■ *Web:* www.coppercanyonfarms.com	Salt Lake City	UT	84104	801-363-7695	322-1640*	297-7
Muir Glen Organic PO Box 9452 *Fax Area Code: 763 ■ *TF:* 800-832-6345 ■ *Web:* www.muirglen.com	Minneapolis	MN	55440	800-832-6345	764-8330*	296-20
Muir Woods National Monument 1 Muir Woods Rd *Web:* www.nps.gov/muwo	Mill Valley	CA	94941	415-388-2596	389-6957	564
Mukwonago Area School District 385 County Rd NNE *Web:* www.masd.k12.wi.us	Mukwonago	WI	53149	262-363-6300	363-6272	685
Mulberry Metal Products Inc 2199 Stanley Terr *Web:* www.mulberrymetal.com	Union	NJ	07083	908-688-8850	688-7294	816
Mule Creek State Prison 4001 Hwy 104 *TF:* 877-256-6877 ■ *Web:* cdcr.ca.gov	Ione	CA	95640	209-274-4911	274-4861	213
Mule Lighting Inc 46 Baker St *TF:* 800-556-7690 ■ *Web:* www.mulelighting.com	Providence	RI	02905	401-941-4446	941-2929	439
Mulgrew Aircraft Components Inc 1810 S Shamrock Ave *TF:* 800-600-0134 ■ *Web:* www.mulgrewaircraft.com	Monrovia	CA	91016	626-256-1375		454
Mulherin, Rehfeldt & Varchetto PC 211 S Wheaton Ave Ste 200 *Web:* www.mrvlaw.com	Wheaton	IL	60187	630-653-9300		428
Mulhern Belting Inc 148 Bauer Dr *TF:* 800-253-6300 ■ *Web:* www.mulhernbelting.com	Oakland	NJ	07436	201-337-5700	337-6540	370
Mull Group Inc 1025 Main St *Web:* www.mullindustries.com	Wheeling	WV	26003	304-232-2520		492
Mullan Enterprises Inc 2330 W Joppa Rd Ste 210 *Web:* www.mullancontr.com	Lutherville	MD	21093	410-494-9200		655
Mullaney's Harp & Fiddle 2329 Penn Ave *TF:* 800-561-3357 ■ *Web:* www.harpandfiddle.com	Pittsburgh	PA	15222	412-642-6622		671
Mullen 40 Broad St *Web:* us.mullenlowe.com	Boston	MA	02109	617-226-9000	226-9100	4
Mullen & Filippi LLP 1601 Response Rd Ste 300 *Web:* www.mulfil.com	Sacramento	CA	95815	916-442-4503		428
Mullen Guitar Company Inc 11906 County Rd Mm *Web:* www.mullenguitars.com	Flagler	CO	80815	970-664-2518		526
Muller Engineering Company Inc 777 S Wadsworth Blvd *Web:* www.mullereng.com	Lakewood	CO	80226	303-988-4939		261
Muller Inc 2800 Grant Ave *Web:* mullerbev.com	Philadelphia	PA	19114	215-676-7575	698-0414	81-1
Muller Martini Mailroom Systems Inc 40 Rabro Dr *Web:* www.mullermartini.com/ms	Hauppauge	NY	11788	631-582-4343		547
Muller Media Conversions Inc 21 Locust St *TF:* 800-314-8972 ■ *Web:* mullermedia.com	Manhasset	NY	11030	516-833-3067		396
Muller Muller Richmond Harms Myers & Sgroi Atty 33233 Woodward Ave *TF:* 800-711-0023 ■ *Web:* www.mullerfirm.com	Birmingham	MI	48009	248-645-2440		428
Muller Systems Corp 926 Juliana Dr *TF:* 800-668-6954 ■ *Web:* www.mullersys.com	Woodstock	ON	N4V1B9	519-421-1800		180
Mullin Hoard & Brown LLP Amarillo National Plaza Two Ste 800 500 S Taylor Lobby Box Ste 213 *Web:* www.mullinhoard.com	Amarillo	TX	79101	806-372-5050		428
Mullin Markwayne (Rep R - OK) 1113 Longworth HOB *Web:* mullin.house.gov	Washington	DC	20515	202-225-2701	225-3038	342-2
Mullinix Packages Inc 3511 Engle Rd *Web:* www.mullinixpackages.com	Fort Wayne	IN	46809	260-747-3149	747-1598	604
Mullins Ctr 200 Commonwealth Ave University of Massachusetts *TF:* 800-946-4452 ■ *Web:* www.mullinscenter.com	Amherst	MA	01003	413-545-3001		720
Mullins Food Products Inc 2200 S 25th Ave *Web:* www.mullinsfood.com	Broadview	IL	60155	708-344-3224	344-0153	296-20
MultAlloy Inc 8511 Monroe St *TF:* 800-568-9551 ■ *Web:* www.multalloy.com	Houston	TX	77061	800-568-9551		492
Multax Systems Inc 505 N Sepulveda Blvd Ste 7 *TF:* 800-888-0199 ■ *Web:* www.multax.net	Manhattan Beach	CA	90266	310-379-8398	379-1142	261
Multi Dimensional Integration 39 E Forrest Ave *Web:* www.mdiadvantage.com	Shrewsbury	PA	17361	717-227-1800		180
Multi Products Company Inc 7188 SR-39 E *Web:* www.multiproducts.com	Millersburg	OH	44654	330-674-5981		595
Multiband Corp 9449 Science Ctr Dr *NASDAQ: MBND* ■ *TF:* 800-622-0119 ■ *Web:* www.multibandusa.com	New Hope	MN	55428	763-504-3000	504-3060	736
MultiCare Health System 315 Martin Luther King Jr Way PO Box 5299 *Web:* www.multicare.org	Tacoma	WA	98405	253-697-1950	403-1180	353
Multichannel News 28 E 28th St 12th Fl *TF Cust Svc:* 888-343-5563 ■ *Web:* www.multichannel.com	New York	NY	10016	917-281-4700	281-4704	457-9
Multicim Technologies Inc 16 Westminster ave N Ste 306C *Web:* www.multicim.com	Montreal West	QC	H4X1Z1	514-633-6401		180
Multicoat Corp 23331 Antonio Pkwy *TF:* 877-685-8426 ■ *Web:* www.multicoat.com	Rancho Santa Margarita	CA	92688	949-888-7100	888-2555	500
Multi-Color Corp 4053 Clough Woods Dr *NASDAQ: LABL* ■ *Web:* www.multicolorcorp.com	Batavia	OH	45103	513-381-1480	381-2240	413
Multicom Inc 1076 Florida Central Pkwy *TF:* 800-423-2594 ■ *Web:* www.multicominc.com	Longwood	FL	32750	407-331-7779		116
Multicorp Inc 69 W Main St *Web:* www.multicorpfranchising.com	Westminster	MD	21157	410-876-5000		104
Multi-Craft Litho Inc 131 E Sixth St PO Box 72960 *TF:* 800-733-3317 ■ *Web:* www.multi-craft.com	Newport	KY	41072	859-581-2754		627
Multi-Cultural Ctr of Sioux Falls 515 N Main Ave *Web:* www.sfmcc.org	Sioux Falls	SD	57104	605-367-7401	367-7404	50-2
Multicultural Radio Broadcasting 27 William St 11th Fl *Web:* www.mrbi.net	New York	NY	10005	212-966-1059		643
Multidev Technologies Inc 999 de Maisonneuve W Ste 1100 *Web:* chaindrive.com	Montreal	QC	H3A3L4	514-337-6465		180
Multi-Electric Manufacturing Inc 4223 West Lake St *TF:* 800-258-1997 ■ *Web:* www.multielectric.com	Chicago	IL	60624	773-722-1900	722-5694	439
Multi-fab Products LLC N90 W14507 Commerce Dr *TF:* 800-222-2146 ■ *Web:* www.multi-fab.com	Menomonee Falls	WI	53051	262-502-1707		207
Multifeeder Technology Inc 4821 White Bear Pkwy *Web:* www.multifeeder.com	Saint Paul	MN	55110	651-407-3100		757
Multifilm Packaging Corp 1040 N McLean Blvd *Web:* www.multifilm.com	Elgin	IL	60123	847-695-7600		548
Multi-Fineline Electronix Inc (Mflex) 3140 E Coronado St *NASDAQ: MFLX* ■ *Web:* www.mflex.com	Anaheim	CA	92806	714-238-1488		253
Multigon Industries Inc 525 Executive Blvd *TF:* 800-289-6858 ■ *Web:* www.multigon.com	Yonkers	NY	10701	800-289-6858		186
Multi-Level Marketing International Assn (MLMIA) 119 Stanford Ct *Web:* www.mlmia.com	Irvine	CA	92612	949-854-0484		49-18
MultiLing Corp 180 N University Ave 6th Fl *Web:* www.multiling.com	Provo	UT	84601	801-377-2000		196
MultiLingual Solutions Inc 11 N Washington St Ste 300 *Web:* www.mlsolutions.com	Rockville	MD	20850	301-424-7444		194
Multilink Inc 580 Ternes Ln *Web:* www.multi-link.biz	Elyria	OH	44035	440-366-6966		567
Multimatic Products Inc 390 Oser Ave *TF:* 800-767-7633 ■ *Web:* www.multimaticproducts.com	Hauppauge	NY	11788	631-231-1515	231-1625	621
MultiMedia Schools Magazine 143 Old Marlton Pk *TF:* 800-300-9868 ■ *Web:* www.infotoday.com/mmschools	Medford	NJ	08055	609-654-6266	654-4309	457-7
Multi-metal & Manufacturing Company Inc 1500 E I-30 *Web:* www.multi-metal.com	Rockwall	TX	75087	972-771-1376		697
Multi-Pak Corp 180 Atlantic St *Web:* www.multipakcorp.com	Hackensack	NJ	07601	201-342-7474	342-6525	36
Multipet International Inc 265 W Commercial Ave *TF:* 800-900-6738 ■ *Web:* www.multipet.com	Moonachie	NJ	07074	201-438-6600	438-2990	578
Multiplan inc 115 Fifth Ave *TF:* 800-922-4362 ■ *Web:* www.multiplan.com	New York	NY	10003	212-780-2000	780-0420	390
Multi-Plastics Inc 7770 N Central Dr *Web:* www.multi-plastics.com	Lewis Center	OH	43035	740-548-4894	548-5177	603
Multiple Media Inc 465 McGill St Office 1000 *TF:* 866-790-6626 ■ *Web:* www.multiplemedia.com	Montreal	QC	H2Y2H1	514-276-7660		180
Multiple Sclerosis Foundation (MSF) 6520 N Andrews Ave *TF:* 800-225-6495 ■ *Web:* www.msfocus.org	Fort Lauderdale	FL	33309	954-776-6805		48-17
Multiple Ventilation Products Inc 1313 Bigley Ave *Web:* mvphvac.net	Charleston	WV	25302	304-720-8686		189-10
Multiquip Inc 18910 Wilmington Ave *TF:* 800-421-1244 ■ *Web:* www.multiquip.com	Carson	CA	90746	310-537-3700	537-3927	385
Multiseal Inc 4320 Hitch Peters Rd *Web:* www.multiseal-usa.com	Evansville	IN	47711	812-428-3422	428-3432	3
Multiservice Management Co 994 Old Eagle School Rd Ste 1019 *Web:* www.mmco1.com	Wayne	PA	19087	610-971-4850		47

Name / Address	City	State	Zip	Phone	Fax	Class
Multi-shifter Inc 11110 Park Charlotte Blvd *TF:* 800-457-4472 ■ *Web:* www.multi-shifter.com	Charlotte	NC	28278	704-588-9611		358
Multi-Shot LLC 3335 Pollok Dr *TF:* 800-769-5988 ■ *Web:* msenergyservices.com	Conroe	TX	77303	936-442-2500		539
Multisoft Corp 1723 SE 47th Terr *TF:* 888-415-0554 ■ *Web:* www.multisoft.com	Cape Coral	FL	33904	239-945-6433		177
Multisorb Technologies Inc 325 Harlem Rd *TF:* 800-445-9890 ■ *Web:* www.multisorb.com	Buffalo	NY	14224	716-824-8900	824-4128	145
Multistack LLC 1065 Maple Ave *Web:* www.multistack.com	Sparta	WI	54656	608-366-2400		14
Multi-State Lottery Association 4400 NW Urbandale Dr *TF:* 800-955-6886 ■ *Web:* www.musl.com	Urbandale	IA	50322	515-453-1400		452
Multistate Tax Commission 444 N Capitol St NW Ste 425 *Web:* www.mtc.gov	Washington	DC	20001	202-624-8699		734
Multitech Industries Inc 350 Village Dr *Web:* www.multitechind.com	Carol Stream	IL	60188	630-784-9200		729
Multi-Tech Systems 2205 Woodale Dr *TF Cust Svc:* 800-328-9717 ■ *Web:* www.multitech.com	Mounds View	MN	55112	763-785-3500	785-9874	173-3
Multivans Inc 13289 Coleraine Dr *TF:* 800-698-9249 ■ *Web:* www.multivans.com	Bolton	ON	L7E3B6	905-857-3171		478
Multnomah Athletic Club 1849 SW Salmon St *Web:* www.themac.com	Portland	OR	97205	503-223-6251		354
Multnomah Bar Association 620 SW Fifth Ave Ste 1220 *Web:* mbabar.org	Portland	OR	97204	503-222-3275		533
Multnomah County 1221 SW Fourth Ave *Web:* multco.us	Portland	OR	97204	503-823-4000		338
Multnomah County Library 801 SW Tenth Ave *TF:* 800-922-2689 ■ *Web:* www.multcolib.org	Portland	OR	97205	503-988-5123	988-5226	434-3
Multnomah University 8435 NE Glisan St *TF:* 800-275-4672 ■ *Web:* www.multnomah.edu	Portland	OR	97220	503-255-0332	254-1268	167-3
Mulvane Art Museum 1700 SW Jewell Ave *Web:* www.washburn.edu	Topeka	KS	66621	785-670-1124		520
Mulvaney Kahan & Barry 401 W A St Fl 17 *Web:* www.mulvaneybarry.com	San Diego	CA	92101	619-238-1010		445
Mulzer Crushed Stone Inc 534 Mozart St PO Box 249 *TF:* 800-500-2011 ■ *Web:* www.mulzer.com	Tell City	IN	47586	812-547-7921	547-6757	503-5
Mummers Museum 1100 S Second St *Web:* www.mummersmuseum.com	Philadelphia	PA	19147	215-336-3050		520
Muncie Children's Museum 515 S High St *Web:* munciemuseum.com	Muncie	IN	47305	765-286-1660		521
Muncie Power Products Inc 201 E Jackson St *TF:* 800-367-7867 ■ *Web:* www.munciepower.com	Muncie	IN	47305	765-284-7721		770
Muncie Star-Press 345 S High St *TF:* 800-783-7827 ■ *Web:* www.thestarpress.com	Muncie	IN	47305	765-213-5700	213-5850	532-2
Muncie Symphony Orchestra 2000 W University Ave # Ac112 *Web:* www.munciesymphony.org	Muncie	IN	47306	765-285-5531	285-9128	573-3
Muncie Visitors Bureau 3700 S Madison St *TF:* 800-568-6862 ■ *Web:* visitmuncie.org/muncie-sports-plex	Muncie	IN	47302	765-284-2700	284-3002	206
Muncie-Delaware County Chamber of Commerce 401 S High St *TF:* 800-336-1373 ■ *Web:* www.muncie.com	Muncie	IN	47305	765-288-6681	751-9151	139
Munck Wilson Mandala LLP 600 Banner Pl Tower 12770 Coit Rd *TF:* 800-973-1177 ■ *Web:* www.munckwilson.com	Dallas	TX	75251	972-628-3600		428
Mundelein Park & Recreation District 1401 N Midlathian Rd *Web:* mundeleinparks.org	Mundelein	IL	60060	847-566-0650		31
MUNDO Media Inc 120 E Beaver Creek Rd Ste 200 *Web:* www.mundomedia.com	Richmond Hill	ON	L4B4V1	416-342-5646		5
Mundy & Assoc 140 N Eighth St Ste 206 *Web:* www.mundyandassociates.com	Lincoln	NE	68508	402-476-8844		463
Mundy Contract Maintenance Inc 11150 S Wilcrest *Web:* www.mundycos.com	Houston	TX	77099	281-530-8711		260
Munich Reinsurance America Inc 555 College Rd E PO Box 5241 *Web:* www.munichre.com/us	Princeton	NJ	08543	609-243-4200	243-4257	360-4
Municipal Art Gallery 839 N State St	Jackson	MS	39202	601-960-1582		50-2
Municipal Auditorium Arena 1321 Baltimore Ave *TF:* 800-767-7700 ■ *Web:* visitkc.com/convention-center/index.aspx	Kansas City	MO	64105	816-691-3800		720
Municipal Capital Markets Group Inc 5220 Spring Valley Rd Ste 522 *Web:* www.municapital.com	Dallas	TX	75244	972-386-0200		690
Municipal Credit Union PO Box 3205 *TF:* 866-512-6109 ■ *Web:* www.nymcu.org	New York	NY	10007	212-693-4900		219
Municipal Infrastructure Group Ltd, The 8800 Dufferin St Ste 200 *Web:* www.tmig.ca	Vaughan	ON	L4K0C5	905-738-5700		261
Municipal Litigation Reporter 590 Dutch Valley Rd NE *TF:* 800-926-7926 ■ *Web:* www.straffordpub.com	Atlanta	GA	30324	404-881-1141	881-0074	531-7
Municipal Securities Rulemaking Board (MSRB) 1900 Duke St Ste 600 *TF:* 888-475-8376 ■ *Web:* www.msrb.org	Alexandria	VA	22314	703-797-6600	797-6700	49-2
Munilla Construction Management LLC 6201 SW 70th St 2nd Fl *Web:* www.mcm-us.com	Miami	FL	33143	305-541-0000	541-9771	186
MuniMae (MMA Capital Management LLC) 3600 O'Donnell St Ste 600 *OTC:* MMAB ■ *TF:* 855-650-6932 ■ *Web:* www.mmacapitalmanagement.com	Baltimore	MD	21224	443-263-2900		509
Munn Rabot Llc 33 W 17th St Fl 3 *TF:* 800-413-9120 ■ *Web:* www.munnrabot.com	New York	NY	10011	212-727-3900		7
Munot Plastics Inc 2935 W 17th St *Web:* www.munotplastics.com	Erie	PA	16505	814-838-7721		601
Munro & Co Inc 3770 Malvern Rd 71901 PO Box 6048 *TF:* 800-819-1901 ■ *Web:* munroshoes.com	Hot Springs	AR	71902	501-262-6000		301
Munsch Hardt Kopf & Harr PC 500 N Akard St Ste 3800 *Web:* www.munsch.com	Dallas	TX	75201	214-855-7500	855-7584	428
Munson Healthcare 1105 Sixth St *TF:* 800-468-6766 ■ *Web:* www.munsonhealthcare.org	Traverse City	MI	49684	231-935-5000		371
Munson Manor Hospitality House 1220 Medical Campus Dr *Web:* www.munsonhealthcare.org	Traverse City	MI	49684	231-935-2300		372
Munson Medical Ctr 1105 Sixth St *Web:* www.munsonhealthcare.org	Traverse City	MI	49684	231-935-5000		374-3
Munson's Candy Kitchen Inc 174 Hop River Rd *TF:* 888-686-7667 ■ *Web:* www.munsonschocolates.com	Bolton	CT	06043	860-649-4332	649-7209	296-8
Munson-Williams-Proctor Arts Institute 310 Genesee St *Web:* www.mwpai.org	Utica	NY	13502	315-797-0000	797-5608	520
Munters Corp 210 Sixth St PO Box 6428 **Fax:* Cust Svc ■ *TF:* 800-843-5360 ■ *Web:* www.munters.com	Fort Myers	FL	33907	239-936-1555	278-8790*	14
Munters Corp DHI 79 Monroe St *TF Sales:* 800-843-5360 ■ *Web:* www.munters.com	Amesbury	MA	01913	978-241-1100	241-1215	14
Murasaki 23 LaSalle Rd *Web:* murasakijapaneserestaurant.com	West Hartford	CT	06107	860-236-7622		671
Murata Electronics North America Inc 2200 Lake Pk Dr *TF:* 800-704-6079 ■ *Web:* www.murata.com	Smyrna	GA	30080	770-436-1300	436-3030	253
Murata Machinery USA Inc 2120 Queen City Dr **Fax Area Code:* 704 ■ *TF:* 800-428-8469 ■ *Web:* www.muratec-usa.com	Charlotte	NC	28208	800-428-8469	392-6541*	456
Murdoch Marketing 217 E 24th St Ste 220 *TF:* 800-438-7325 ■ *Web:* www.murdochmarketing.com	Holland	MI	49423	616-392-4893		195
Murdock Industrial Supply 1111 E 1st *TF:* 800-876-6867 ■ *Web:* www.mcos.com	Wichita	KS	67214	316-262-4476	263-8100	246
Murdock Webbing Co 27 Foundry St *TF:* 800-375-2052 ■ *Web:* www.murdockwebbing.com	Central Falls	RI	02863	401-724-3000		745-5
Murex Petroleum Corp 363 N Sam Houston Pkwy E Ste 200 *Web:* www.murexpetroleum.com	Houston	TX	77060	281-590-3313		538
Murfee Meadows Inc 120 Office Park Dr Ste 100 *Web:* murfeemeadows.com	Birmingham	AL	35223	205-871-9515		463
Murfie Inc 7 N Pinckney St Ste 300 *Web:* www.murfie.com	Madison	WI	53703	608-515-8180		690
Murfin Drilling Company Inc 250 N Water St Ste 300 *Web:* www.murfininc.com	Wichita	KS	67202	316-267-3241		540
Muriel's 801 Chartres St *Web:* www.muriels.com	New Orleans	LA	70116	504-568-1885	568-9795	671
Murkowski Lisa (Sen R - AK) 522 Hart Bldg *Web:* www.murkowski.senate.gov	Washington	DC	20510	202-224-6665	224-5301	342-2
Murnane Bldg Contractors Inc 104 Sharron Ave *TF:* 800-424-3996 ■ *Web:* www.murnanebuilding.com	Plattsburgh	NY	12901	518-561-4010	561-5926	186
Murnane Paper Corp 345 W Fischer Farm Rd *TF:* 855-632-8191 ■ *Web:* www.murnanepaper.com	Elmhurst	IL	60126	630-530-8222	530-8325	553
Murphy & Grantland PA 4406-B Forest Dr *TF:* 800-445-8629 ■ *Web:* www.murphygrantland.com	Columbia	SC	29260	803-782-4100		428
Murphy & McGonigle 4870 Sadler Rd Ste 301 *Web:* www.mmlawus.com	Glen Allen	VA	23060	804-762-5320		428
Murphy & Miller Inc 600 W Taylor St *Web:* www.murphymiller.com	Chicago	IL	60607	312-427-8900	427-0324	189-10
Murphy & Nolan Inc 340 Peat St PO Box 6689 *TF:* 866-900-6385 ■ *Web:* www.murphynolan.com	Syracuse	NY	13217-6689	315-474-8203	474-8208	492
Murphy & Sons Inc 9148 Corporate Dr *Web:* www.murphyandsons.com	Southaven	MS	38671	662-393-3130	393-8111	186
Murphy Christopher (Sen D - CT) 136 Hart Senate Office Bldg *Web:* www.murphy.senate.gov	Washington	DC	20510	202-224-4041	224-9750	342-2
Murphy Co Mechanical Contractors & Engineers 1233 N Price Rd *Web:* www.murphynet.com	Saint Louis	MO	63132	314-997-6600	997-4536	189-10
Murphy Harpst Children's Centers 338 W Third St SW *TF:* 800-786-2929 ■ *Web:* murphyharpst.org	Rome	GA	30165	706-232-5663		226
Murphy Industries Inc 1650 Cascade Dr *Web:* www.acc-net.com	Marion	OH	43302	740-387-7890		225
Murphy Marine Services Inc 701 Christiana Ave *Web:* www.murphymarine.com	Wilmington	DE	19801	302-571-4700	571-4702	465
Murphy Mckay & Associates Inc 3468 Mt Diablo Blvd Ste B108 *Web:* www.murphymckay.com	Lafayette	CA	94549	925-283-9555		175
Murphy Oil Corp 200 Peach St *TF:* 888-289-9314 ■ *Web:* www.murphyoilcorp.com	El Dorado	AR	71730	870-862-6411	875-7675	580
Murphy Plywood Co 2350 Prairie Rd *TF:* 888-461-4545 ■ *Web:* www.murphyplywood.com	Eugene	OR	97402	541-461-4545	461-4547	613
Murphy Stephanie (Rep D - FL) 1237 Longworth HOB *Web:* stephaniemurphy.house.gov	Washington	DC	20515	202-225-4035		342-2
Murphy Sullivan Kronk 275 College St *Web:* www.mskvt.com	Burlington	VT	05401	802-861-7000		428
Murphy Tim (Rep R - PA) 2332 Rayburn Bldg *Web:* murphy.house.gov	Washington	DC	20515	202-225-2301	225-1844	342-2

Phone | Fax | Class

Murphy Warehouse Co
701 24th Ave SE — Minneapolis MN 55414 — 612-623-1200 — 623-9108 — 803-1
Web: www.murphywarehouse.com

Murphy's Cable Wharf
1751 Lower Water St — Halifax NS B3J3F4 — 902-420-1015 — 423-7942 — 671
Web: www.mtcw.ca

Murphy's Grand Irish Pub
713 King St — Alexandria VA 22314 — 703-548-1717 — 739-4583 — 671
Web: www.murphyspub.com

Murphy, Hesse, Toomey & Lehane LLP
Crown Colony Plaza 300 Crown Colony Dr
Ste 410 — Quincy MA 02169 — 617-479-5000 — 428
Web: www.mhtl.com

MurphyEpson Inc
1650 Watermark Dr Ste 210 — Columbus OH 43215 — 614-221-2885 — 221-2889 — 636
Web: murphyepson.com

Murray & Zuckerman Inc
128 Erie Blvd — Schenectady NY 12305 — 518-382-5483 — 390
Web: mandzinc.com

Murray Area Chamber of Commerce (MACC)
5250 S Commerce Dr Ste 180 — Murray UT 84107 — 801-263-2632 — 263-8262 — 139
Web: www.murraychamber.org

Murray Bank, The 405 S 12th St — Murray KY 42071 — 270-753-5626 — 70
TF: 877-965-1122 ■ *Web:* www.themurraybank.com

Murray Co
1215 Fern Ridge Pkwy Ste 213 — Saint Louis MO 63141 — 314-576-2818 — 434-5780 — 685
TF: 888-323-5560 ■ *Web:* www.murray-company.com

Murray Corp 260 Schilling Cir — Hunt Valley MD 21031 — 410-771-0380 — 771-5576 — 350
Web: www.murraycorp.com

Murray County PO Box 1129 — Chatsworth GA 30705 — 706-695-2413 — 695-8721 — 338
TF: 800-222-1222 ■ *Web:* www.murraycountyga.org

Murray County 2500 28th St — Slayton MN 56172 — 507-836-6148 — 836-8904 — 338
Web: murraycountymn.com

Murray County
10th Wyandotte St PO Box 442 — Sulphur OK 73086 — 580-622-5106 — 338

Murray Devine & Company Inc
1650 Arch St Ste 2700 — Philadelphia PA 19103 — 215-977-8700 — 401
Web: www.murraydevine.com

Murray Guard Inc 58 Murray Guard Dr — Jackson TN 38305 — 731-668-3400 — 664-1343 — 693
TF: 800-238-3830 ■ *Web:* www.murrayguard.com

Murray Kaizer Dental Laboratory
24 Spring Ln Ste 1 — Farmington CT 06032 — 860-677-7700 — 415
TF: 800-349-0900 ■ *Web:* www.murraykaizer.com

Murray Multi-media 2 Cahart Rd — Blairstown NJ 07825 — 908-362-8174 — 7

Murray Patty (Sen D - WA)
154 Russell Bldg — Washington DC 20510 — 202-224-2621 — 224-0238 — 342-2
Web: www.murray.senate.gov

Murray Sheet Metal Co Inc
3112 Seventh St — Parkersburg WV 26104 — 304-422-5431 — 428-4623 — 697
TF: 800-464-8801 ■ *Web:* www.murraysheetmetal.com

Murray State College
1 Murray Campus — Tishomingo OK 73460 — 580-371-2371 — 371-9844* — 162
**Fax:* Admissions ■ *TF:* 800-342-0698 ■ *Web:* www.mscok.edu

Murray State University 102 Curris Ctr — Murray KY 42071 — 270-809-3741 — 809-3780* — 166
**Fax:* Admissions ■ *TF:* 800-272-4678 ■ *Web:* www.murraystate.edu
Hopkinsville
5305 Ft Campbell Blvd — Hopkinsville KY 42240 — 270-707-1525 — 707-1535* — 166
**Fax:* Admissions ■ *TF:* 800-669-7654 ■ *Web:* murraystate.edu

Murray Street Kitchen 110 Murray St — Ottawa ON K1N5M6 — 613-562-7244 — 671
TF: 800-224-3933 ■ *Web:* www.murraystreet.ca

Murray Supply Co (MSC)
102 W Third St — Winston-Salem NC 27101 — 336-546-1780 — 245-0686 — 612
Web: www.murraysupply.com

Murray's 26 S Sixth St — Minneapolis MN 55402 — 612-339-0909 — 671
Web: www.murraysrestaurant.com

Murray, Plumb & Murray 75 Pearl St — Portland ME 04101 — 207-773-5651 — 428
TF: 800-834-1721 ■ *Web:* www.mpmlaw.com

Murray-Calloway County Hospital
803 Poplar St — Murray KY 42071 — 270-762-1100 — 767-3600 — 374-3
TF: 800-275-1268 ■ *Web:* www.murrayhospital.org

Murrays Ford Inc 3007 Blinker Pkwy — Du Bois PA 15801 — 800-371-6601 — 516
TF: 800-371-6601 ■ *Web:* www.murraysford.net

Murrey International Inc
14150 S Figueroa St — Los Angeles CA 90061 — 310-532-6091 — 710
TF: 800-421-1022 ■ *Web:* murreybowling.com

Murrieta Chamber of Commerce
25125 Madison Ave Ste 108 — Murrieta CA 92562 — 951-677-7916 — 677-9976 — 139
Web: www.murrietachamber.org

Murrows Transfer Inc PO Box 4095 — High Point NC 27263 — 336-475-6101 — 475-1240 — 780
TF Cust Svc: 800-669-2928 ■ *Web:* www.murrows.com

Murry's 3107 Green Meadows Way — Columbia MO 65203 — 573-442-4969 — 671
Web: murrysrestaurant.net

Mursix Corp 2401 N Executive Park Dr — Yorktown IN 47396 — 765-282-2221 — 488
Web: mursix.com

Murty Pharmaceuticals Inc
518 Codell Dr — Lexington KY 40509 — 859-266-2446 — 582
TF: 800-626-2930 ■ *Web:* www.mpirx.com

M-USA (Mercy-USA for Aid & Development Inc)
44450 Pinetree Dr Ste 201 — Plymouth MI 48170 — 734-454-0011 — 454-0303 — 48-5
TF: 800-556-3729 ■ *Web:* www.mercyusa.org

Musashi 10110 Johnston Rd — Charlotte NC 28210 — 704-543-5181 — 671
Web: www.musashi-nc.com

Musashi's Japanese Steakhouse
4315 N Western — Oklahoma City OK 73118 — 405-602-5623 — 602-5574 — 671
Web: www.musashis.com

Musashino Sushi Dokoro
3407 Greystone Dr — Austin TX 78731 — 512-795-8593 — 671
Web: www.musashinosushi.com

MUSC (Medical University of South Carolina)
171 Ashley Ave — Charleston SC 29425 — 843-792-1414 — 167-2
Web: academicdepartments.musc.edu
Blood & Marrow Transplant Program
86 Jonathan Lucas St — Charleston SC 29425 — 843-792-9300 — 769
Web: www.muschealth.org/index.html

Muscarelle Museum of Art
PO Box 8795 — Williamsburg VA 23187 — 757-221-2700 — 221-2711 — 520
Web: muscarelle.org

Muscatine Community College
152 Colorado St — Muscatine IA 52761 — 563-288-6001 — 288-6104* — 162
**Fax:* Admissions ■ *TF:* 888-336-3907 ■ *Web:* www.eicc.edu

Muscatine County 401 E Third St — Muscatine IA 52761 — 563-263-5821 — 263-7248 — 338
TF: 800-368-8683 ■ *Web:* www.co.muscatine.ia.us

Muscle & Fitness Hers Magazine
21100 Erwin St — Woodland Hills CA 91367 — 800-340-8954 — 457-13
TF: 800-340-8954 ■ *Web:* www.muscleandfitness.com/muscle-fitness-hers

Muscle Shoals City School District
3200 Wilson Dam Rd — Muscle Shoals AL 35661 — 256-389-2600 — 449
Web: www.mscs.k12.al.us

Musco Sports Lighting LLC
100 First Ave W PO Box 808 — Oskaloosa IA 52577 — 641-673-0411 — 673-4852 — 439
TF: 800-825-6020 ■ *Web:* www.musco.com

Muscular Dystrophy Assn (MDA)
3300 E Sunrise Dr — Tucson AZ 85718 — 520-529-2000 — 48-17
TF: 800-572-1717 ■ *Web:* www.mda.org

Musculoskeletal Transplant Foundation
125 May St Ste 300 — Edison NJ 08837 — 732-661-0202 — 661-2298 — 545
TF: 800-946-9008 ■ *Web:* www.mtf.org

MUSD (Montebello Unified School District)
123 S Montebello Blvd — Montebello CA 90640 — 323-887-7900 — 685
Web: www.montebello.k12.ca.us

Muse Communications Inc
9543 Culver Blvd 2nd Fl — Culver City CA 90232 — 310-945-4100 — 4
Web: www.museusa.com

Muse Concrete Contractors Inc
8599 Commercial Way — Redding CA 96002 — 530-226-5151 — 186
Web: www.museconcrete.com

Muse Entertainment Enterprises Inc
3451 Rue St-Jacques — Montreal QC H4C1H1 — 514-866-6873 — 514
Web: www.muse.ca

Muse, The 130 W 46th St — New York NY 10036 — 212-485-2400 — 485-2789 — 379
TF: 877-692-6873 ■ *Web:* www.themusehotel.com

MuseBox Media LLC 650 Broadway 4th Fl — New York NY 10012 — 646-237-0023 — 809
Web: www.themusebox.net

Musee Conti Historical Wax Museum of New Orleans
917 Rue Conti — New Orleans LA 70112 — 504-525-2605 — 520

Musee de la Civilisation
85 Rue Dalhousie St — Quebec QC G1K8R2 — 418-643-2158 — 520

Musee Des Beaux-Arts De Montreal
1380 Rue Sherbrooke O — Montreal QC H3G1J5 — 514-285-1600 — 520
Web: www.mbam.qc.ca

Museo de las Americas 861 Santa Fe Dr — Denver CO 80204 — 303-571-4401 — 607-9761 — 520
TF: 800-448-3883 ■ *Web:* www.museo.org

Museo del Barrio 1230 Fifth Ave — New York NY 10029 — 212-831-7272 — 520
Web: www.elmuseo.org

Museo Italo-Americano
Fort Mason Ctr Bldg C — San Francisco CA 94123 — 415-673-2200 — 673-2292 — 520
TF: 800-231-4024 ■ *Web:* www.museoitaloamericano.org

Museum & Library of confederate
15 Boyce Ave — Greenville SC 29601 — 864-421-9039 — 520
Web: confederatemuseumandlibrary.org

Museum at Portland Head Light
1000 Shore Rd — Cape Elizabeth ME 04107 — 207-799-2661 — 799-2800 — 520
TF: 800-765-7238 ■ *Web:* www.portlandheadlight.com/museum.html

Museum Facsimiles 117 Fourth St — Pittsfield MA 01201 — 413-499-0020 — 130
TF: 877-499-0020 ■ *Web:* www.museumfacsimiles.com

Museum of African American History
46 Joy St — Boston MA 02114 — 617-725-0022 — 720-5225 — 520
Web: www.afroammuseum.org

Museum of American Financial History
48 Wall St — New York NY 10005 — 212-908-4110 — 908-4601 — 520
Web: www.moaf.org

Museum of American Illustration
128 E 63rd St — New York NY 10065 — 212-838-2560 — 838-2561 — 520
Web: www.societyillustrators.org

Museum of Anthropology
104 Swallow Hall University of Missouri — Columbia MO 65211 — 573-882-3573 — 884-3627 — 520
Web: anthromuseum.missouri.edu

Museum of Anthropology
Wake Forest University Wingate Rd
PO Box 7267 — Winston-Salem NC 27109 — 336-758-5282 — 758-5116 — 520
TF: 888-925-3622 ■ *Web:* www.wfu.edu

Museum of Appalachia
2819 Andersonville Hwy — Clinton TN 37716 — 865-494-7680 — 494-8957 — 520
TF: 800-524-3602 ■ *Web:* museumofappalachia.org

Museum of Art & Archaeology
1 Pickard Hall — Columbia MO 65211 — 573-882-3591 — 884-4039 — 520
TF: 866-447-9821 ■ *Web:* maa.missouri.edu

Museum of Arts & Design
2 Columbus Cir — New York NY 10019 — 212-299-7777 — 520
Web: madmuseum.org

Museum of Arts & Sciences
352 S Nova Rd — Daytona Beach FL 32114 — 386-255-0285 — 520
TF: 866-439-4769 ■ *Web:* www.moas.org

Museum of Arts & Sciences
4182 Forsyth Rd — Macon GA 31210 — 478-477-3232 — 477-3251 — 520
Web: www.masmacon.org

Museum of Aviation PO Box 2469 — Warner Robins GA 31099 — 478-926-2791 — 520
TF: 800-745-3000 ■ *Web:* www.museumofaviation.org

Museum of Boulder 1206 Euclid Ave — Boulder CO 80302 — 303-449-3464 — 938-8322 — 520
Web: www.boulderhistory.org

Museum of Children's Art
1625 Clay Ste 100 — Oakland CA 94612 — 510-465-8770 — 521
Web: www.mocha.org

Museum of Church History & Art
45 NW Temple St — Salt Lake City UT 84150 — 801-240-3310 — 240-5342 — 520
TF: 800-501-2885 ■ *Web:* history.lds.org

Museum of Contemporary Art
220 E Chicago Ave — Chicago IL 60611 — 312-280-2660 — 520
TF: 800-222-7270 ■ *Web:* www.mcachicago.org

Museum of Contemporary Art
250 S Grand Ave — Los Angeles CA 90012 — 213-621-2766 — 620-8674 — 520
Web: www.moca.org

Museum of Contemporary Art Cleveland
11400 Euclid Ave — Cleveland OH 44106 — 216-421-8671 — 421-0737 — 520
Web: www.mocacleveland.org

Phone | Fax | Class

Museum of Contemporary Art Denver
1485 Delgany .... Denver CO 80202 303-298-7554 520
Web: mcadenver.org

Museum of Contemporary Art Inc
770 NE 125th St Joan Lehman Bldg .... North Miami FL 33161 305-893-6211 520
TF: 800-385-4644 ■ *Web:* www.mocanomi.org

Museum of Contemporary Art San Diego
700 Prospect St .... La Jolla CA 92037 858-454-3541 520
Web: www.mcasd.org

Museum of Contemporary Photography
600 S Michigan Ave Columbia College .... Chicago IL 60605 312-663-5554 520
Web: www.mocp.org

Museum of Contemporary Religious Art
221 N Grand Blvd .... Saint Louis MO 63103 314-977-7170 977-2999 520
TF: 800-442-1142 ■ *Web:* www.slu.edu

Museum of Design Atlanta
285 Peachtree Ctr Ave .... Atlanta GA 30303 404-979-6455 520
Web: www.museumofdesign.org

Museum of Discovery
500 President Clinton Ave Ste 150 .... Little Rock AR 72201 501-396-7050 396-7054 520
TF: 800-880-6475 ■ *Web:* museumofdiscovery.org

Museum of Early Southern Decorative Arts (MESDA)
924 S Main St .... Winston-Salem NC 27101 336-721-7360 721-7367 520
Web: www.mesda.org

Museum of Fine Arts
255 Beach Dr NE .... Saint Petersburg FL 33701 727-896-2667 894-4638 520
Web: mfastpete.org

Museum of Fine Arts 1001 Bissonnet St .... Houston TX 77005 713-639-7300 520
Web: www.mfah.org

Museum of Fine Arts Boston
465 Huntington Ave .... Boston MA 02115 617-267-9300 520
Web: www.mfa.org

Museum of Flight
9404 E Marginal Way S .... Seattle WA 98108 206-764-5700 764-5707 520
TF: 800-888-2535 ■ *Web:* www.museumofflight.org

Museum of Florida History
500 S Bronough St RA Gray Bldg .... Tallahassee FL 32399 850-245-6400 245-6433 520
TF: 800-628-2866 ■ *Web:* www.museumoffloridahistory.com

Museum of Geology
South Dakota School of Mines & Technology
501 E St Joseph St .... Rapid City SD 57701 605-394-2467 394-6131 520
TF: 800-544-8162 ■ *Web:* www.sdsmt.edu

Museum of Glass 1801 Dock St .... Tacoma WA 98402 253-284-4750 520
TF General: 866-468-7386 ■ *Web:* www.museumofglass.org

Museum of Health & Medical Science
1515 Hermann Dr .... Houston TX 77004 713-521-1515 526-1434 520
Web: www.thehealthmuseum.org

Museum of History & Art
1100 Orange Ave .... Coronado CA 92118 619-435-7242 435-8504 520
TF: 866-599-7242 ■ *Web:* www.coronadohistory.org

Museum of History & Industry
860 Terry Ave N .... Seattle WA 98109 206-324-1126 324-1346 520
Web: www.mohai.org

Museum of Indian Arts & Culture
710 Camino Lejo PO Box 2087 .... Santa Fe NM 87501 505-476-1250 476-1330 520
Web: www.miaclab.org

Museum of International Folk Art
706 Camino Lejo .... Santa Fe NM 87505 505-476-1200 476-1300 520
TF: 800-475-4182 ■ *Web:* www.internationalfolkart.org

Museum of Jewish Heritage
36 Battery Pl Battery Pk City .... New York NY 10280 646-437-4202 520
Web: www.mjhnyc.org

Museum of Jurassic Technology
9341 Venice Blvd .... Culver City CA 90232 310-836-6131 287-2267 520
Web: www.mjt.org

Museum of Latin American Art
628 Alamitos Ave .... Long Beach CA 90802 562-437-1689 520
TF: 800-448-3883 ■ *Web:* molaa.org

Museum of Life+Science 433 Murray Ave .... Durham NC 27704 919-220-5429 220-5575 520
Web: lifeandscience.org

Museum of Local History 190 Anza St .... Fremont CA 94539 510-623-7907 520
TF: 800-771-8807 ■ *Web:* www.museumoflocalhistory.org

Museum of Making Music
5790 Armada Dr .... Carlsbad CA 92008 760-438-5996 520
TF: 877-551-9976 ■ *Web:* www.museumofmakingmusic.org

Museum of Missouri Military History
2302 Militia Dr .... Jefferson City MO 65101 573-638-9603 638-9676 520
TF: 888-526-6664 ■ *Web:* www.moguard.com

Museum of Modern Art 11 W 53rd St .... New York NY 10019 212-708-9400 520
Web: www.moma.org

Museum of Natural History & Science
1301 Western Ave Cincinnati Museum Ctr .... Cincinnati OH 45203 513-287-7000 520
TF: 800-733-2077 ■ *Web:* www.cincymuseum.org

Museum of Nature & Science
2201 N Field St .... Dallas TX 75201 214-428-5555 520
Web: www.perotmuseum.org

Museum of Nebraska History
15th & P St PO Box 82554 .... Lincoln NE 68508 402-471-4754 471-3314 520
TF: 800-833-6747 ■ *Web:* www.nebraskahistory.org/sites/mnh

Museum of Newport History at the Brick Market
127 Thames St .... Newport RI 02840 401-841-8770 846-1853 520
Web: newporthistory.org

Museum of North Idaho
115 NW Blvd PO Box 812 .... Coeur d'Alene ID 83816 208-664-3448 664-3448 520
TF: 800-344-4867 ■ *Web:* www.museumni.org

Museum of Northern Arizona
3101 N Ft Valley Rd .... Flagstaff AZ 86001 928-774-5211 774-1229 520
Web: www.musnaz.org

Museum of Outdoor Arts
1000 Englewood Pkwy Ste 2-230 .... Englewood CO 80110 303-806-0444 520
Web: www.artcom.com/museums/nv/mr/80111.htm

Museum of Photographic Arts
1649 El Prado .... San Diego CA 92101 619-238-7559 238-8777 520
Web: www.mopa.org

Museum of Russian Art
5500 Stevens Ave S .... Minneapolis MN 55419 612-821-9045 520
Web: www.tmora.org

Museum of San Diego History
1649 El Prado Balboa Pk .... San Diego CA 92101 619-232-6203 232-6297 520
Web: www.sandiegohistory.org

Museum of Science Science Pk .... Boston MA 02114 617-723-2500 589-0454 520
Web: www.mos.org

Museum of Science & History of Jacksonville
1025 Museum Cir .... Jacksonville FL 32207 904-396-6674 520
TF: 800-581-7245 ■ *Web:* www.themosh.org

Museum of Science & Industry
5700 S Lake Shore Dr .... Chicago IL 60637 773-684-1414 520
TF: 800-468-6674 ■ *Web:* www.msichicago.org

Museum of Science & Industry
4801 E Fowler Ave .... Tampa FL 33617 813-987-6000 987-6310 520
TF: 800-995-6674 ■ *Web:* www.mosi.org

Museum of Science & Technology
500 S Franklin St .... Syracuse NY 13202 315-425-9068 520
Web: www.most.org

Museum of Sex 233 Fifth Ave Rm 3b .... New York NY 10016 212-689-6337 520
TF: 800-681-5616 ■ *Web:* museumofsex.com

Museum of South Dakota State Historical Society
900 Governors Dr Cultural Heritage Ctr .... Pierre SD 57501 605-773-3458 773-6041 520
Web: www.history.sd.gov

Museum of Southern History
4304 Herschel St .... Jacksonville FL 32210 904-388-3574 520
TF: 800-347-2688 ■ *Web:* www.scv-kirby-smith.org

Museum of Spanish Colonial Arts
750 Camino Lejo .... Santa Fe NM 87502 505-982-2226 982-4585 520
Web: spanishcolonial.org

Museum of Texas Tech University
3301 Fourth St .... Lubbock TX 79409 806-742-2442 742-1136 520
TF: 800-829-1040 ■ *Web:* www.depts.ttu.edu/museumttu

Museum of The American Quilters Society Inc
215 Jefferson St .... Paducah KY 42001 270-442-8856 520
Web: www.quiltmuseum.org

Museum of the American Railroad
1105 Washington St .... Frisco TX 75034 214-428-0101 426-1937 520
Web: www.museumoftheamericanrailroad.org

Museum of the Americas (MoA)
2500 NW 79th Ave Ste 104 .... Doral FL 33122 305-599-8089 520
Web: www.museumamericas.org

Museum of the City of New York
1220 Fifth Ave .... New York NY 10029 212-534-1672 423-0758 520
TF: 800-258-7359 ■ *Web:* www.mcny.org

Museum of the Everglades
105 W Broadway .... Everglades City FL 34139 239-695-0008 520
Web: colliermuseums.com

Museum of the Grand Prairie
600 N Lombard St PO Box 1040 .... Mahomet IL 61853 217-586-3360 520
Web: www.museumofthegrandprairie.org

Museum of the Mountain Man
700 E Hennick St .... Pinedale WY 82941 307-367-4101 367-6768 520
TF: 877-686-6266 ■ *Web:* www.pinedaleonline.com

Museum of the Moving Image
3601 35th Ave .... Astoria NY 11106 718-777-6800 520

Museum of the National Ctr of Afro-American Artists (NCAAA)
300 Walnut Ave .... Roxbury MA 02119 617-442-8614 520
Web: www.ncaaa.org/museum.html

Museum of the Rockies
600 W Kagy Blvd Montana State University .... Bozeman MT 59717 406-994-1998 994-2682 520
TF: 800-455-3466 ■ *Web:* www.museumoftherockies.org

Museum of the Southern Jewish Experience
PO Box 16528 .... Jackson MS 39236 601-362-6357 366-6293 520
Web: isjl.org

Museum of Tolerance
9786 W Pico Blvd .... Los Angeles CA 90035 310-553-8403 520
TF: 800-900-9036 ■ *Web:* www.wiesenthal.com

Museum of Utah Art & History
825 North 300 West Ste W109 .... Salt Lake City UT 84103 801-364-4080 520
Web: www.muahnet.org

Museum of Vancouver
1100 Chestnut St Vanier Pk .... Vancouver BC V6J3J9 604-736-4431 736-5417 520
Web: www.museumofvancouver.ca

Museum of World Treasures
835 E First St .... Wichita KS 67202 316-263-1311 520
TF: 888-700-1311 ■ *Web:* www.worldtreasures.org

Museum of Yachting
Fort Adams State Pk .... Newport RI 02840 401-848-5777 520
TF: 800-421-3481 ■ *Web:* www.iyrs.edu

Museum Store Products Inc
430 Sandshore Rd Ste 4 5 .... Hackettstown NJ 07840 908-852-2078 522
Web: www.museumstoreproducts.com

Museums at 18th & Vine
1616 E 18th St .... Kansas City MO 64108 816-474-8463 520
Web: americanjazzmuseum.org

Museums of Oglebay Institute
1330 National Rd .... Wheeling WV 26003 304-242-7272 520
TF: 800-624-6988 ■ *Web:* www.oionline.com

Musgrave Pencil Company Inc
701 W Ln St .... Shelbyville TN 37160 931-684-3611 685-1049 571
TF: 800-736-2450 ■ *Web:* pencils.net

Musgrove Mill State Historic Site
398 State Pk Rd .... Clinton SC 29325 864-938-0100 565
Web: www.southcarolinaparks.com

Mushroom Co, The 902 Woods Rd .... Cambridge MD 21613 410-221-8971 221-8952 296-20
Web: www.themushroomcompany.com

Mushroom Rock State Park
200 Horsethief Rd .... Marquette KS 67464 785-546-2565 565
Web: ksoutdoors.com

Music & Arts Centers Inc
4626 Wedgewood Blvd .... Frederick MD 21703 888-731-5396 526
TF: 888-731-5396 ■ *Web:* www.musicarts.com

Music Box Dinner Playhouse
196 Hughes St .... Swoyersville PA 18704 570-283-2195 572
Web: www.musicbox.org

Music Box Theatre
1407 Nicollet Ave .... Minneapolis MN 55403 612-874-1100 572
Web: musicboxtheatre.org

Name / Address	Phone	Fax	Class
Music Celebrations International 1440 S Priest Dr Ste 102 .... Tempe AZ 85281 *TF:* 800-395-2036 ■ *Web:* www.musiccelebrations.com	480-894-3330		772
Music Choice 110 Gibraltar Rd Ste 200 .... Horsham PA 19044 **Fax Area Code:* 215 ■ *TF:* 800-746-4726 ■ *Web:* www.musicchoice.com	646-459-3357	784-5870*	524
Music Ctr of Los Angeles County 135 N Grand Ave........................Los Angeles CA 90012 *Web:* www.musiccenter.org	213-972-7211		572
Music for All 39 W Jackson Pl Ste 150 ....Indianapolis IN 46225 *TF:* 800-848-2263 ■ *Web:* www.musicforall.org	317-636-2263	524-6200	48-11
Music Hall at Fair Park 909 First Ave............ Dallas TX 75210 *TF:* 800-745-3000 ■ *Web:* www.liveatthemusichall.com	214-565-1116	565-0071	572
Music Hall Ctr for the Performing Arts 350 Madison .... Detroit MI 48226 *Web:* www.musichall.org	313-887-8500	887-8502	572
Music Library Assn (MLA) 8551 Research Way Ste 180................. Middleton WI 53562 *TF:* 800-999-8558 ■ *Web:* www.musiclibraryassoc.org	608-836-5825	831-8200	49-11
Music of the Baroque 111 N Wabash Ave Ste 810....................Chicago IL 60602 *TF:* 800-595-4849 ■ *Web:* www.baroque.org	312-551-1414	551-1444	573-3
Music People Inc 154 Woodlawn Rd Ste C ....Berlin CT 06037 **Fax Area Code:* 860 ■ *TF:* 800-289-8889 ■ *Web:* www.musicpeopleinc.com	800-289-8889	828-1353*	246
Music Road Hotel LLC 303 Henderson Chapel Rd ....Pigeon Forge TN 37863 *TF:* 844-993-9644 ■ *Web:* www.musicroadhotel.com	844-993-9644		707
Music Teachers NA (MTNA) 441 Vine St Ste 3100 .... Cincinnati OH 45202 *TF:* 888-512-5278 ■ *Web:* www.mtna.org	513-421-1420	421-2503	49-5
Music Theatre of Wichita 225 W Douglas Ste 202 .... Wichita KS 67202 *TF:* 800-776-7469 ■ *Web:* www.mtwichita.org	316-265-3253	265-8708	573-4
Musical Theatre Southwest (MTS) 6320 Domingo Rd NE Ste B .... Albuquerque NM 87108 *Web:* www.musicaltheatresw.com	505-265-9119		573-2
Musician's Friend Inc PO Box 7479 .... Westlake Village CA 91359 *Web:* www.musiciansfriend.com	801-501-8110		526
Musicians On Call Inc 39 W 32nd St Ste 1103.........................New York NY 10001 *Web:* www.musiciansoncall.org	212-741-2709		720
Musiciansbuy.com Inc 7830 Byron Dr Ste 1...................West Palm Beach FL 33404 *TF:* 877-778-7845 ■ *Web:* www.musiciansbuy.com	561-842-4246	840-9032	526
Musick Peeler & Garrett LLP 1 Wilshire Blvd Ste 2000 ....Los Angeles CA 90017 *Web:* www.musickpeeler.com	213-629-7600		428
Musicorp 2456 Remount Rd............North Charleston SC 29406	843-745-8501		527
Musictoday LLC 5400 Three Notched Rd .... Crozet VA 22932 *TF:* 800-927-7821 ■ *Web:* www.musictoday.com	434-205-7049		225
Musiker Discovery Programs Inc 1326 Old Northern Blvd .... Roslyn NY 11576 *Web:* www.summerdiscovery.com	516-621-3939	625-3438	760
Muska Electric Co 1985 Oakcrest Ave .... Roseville MN 55113 *TF:* 800-694-0884 ■ *Web:* www.muskaelectric.com	651-636-5820		189-4
Muskallonge Lake State Park 30042 County Rd 407.......................Newberry MI 49868 *Web:* www.michigandnr.com	906-658-3338		565
Muskegon Area Chamber of Commerce 380 W Western Ste 202 .... Muskegon MI 49440 *TF:* 800-659-2955 ■ *Web:* www.muskegon.org	231-722-3751	728-7251	139
Muskegon Area District Library 4845 Airline Rd.............................. Muskegon MI 49444 *TF:* 877-569-4801 ■ *Web:* www.madl.org	231-737-6248	737-6307	434-3
Muskegon Community College 221 S Quarterline Rd .... Muskegon MI 49442 **Fax:* Admissions ■ *TF:* 866-711-4622	231-773-9131	777-0471*	162
Muskegon Correctional Facility 2400 S Sheridan Dr .... Muskegon MI 49442 *Web:* www.michigan.gov/corrections	517-335-1426		213
Muskegon County 990 Terrace St............. Muskegon MI 49442 *Web:* www.co.muskegon.mi.us	231-724-6520	724-6673	338
Muskegon County Convention & Visitors Bureau 610 W Western Ave......................... Muskegon MI 49440 *TF:* 800-250-9283 ■ *Web:* www.visitmuskegon.org	231-724-3100	724-1398	206
Muskegon State Park 3560 Memorial Dr .... North Muskegon MI 49445 *Web:* www.michigandnr.com	231-744-3400		565
Muskingum College 163 Stormont St ....New Concord OH 43762 **Fax:* Admissions ■ *TF Admissions:* 800-752-6082 ■ *Web:* www.muskingum.edu	740-826-8211	826-8100*	166
Muskingum County 401 Main St .... Zanesville OH 43701 *Web:* www.muskingumcounty.org	740-455-7104		338
Muskingum County Library System 220 N Fifth St .... Zanesville OH 43701 *Web:* www.muskingumlibrary.org	740-453-0391	455-6357	434-3
Muskingum River State Park 1390 Ellis Dam Rd .... Zanesville OH 43701 *Web:* www.ohiodnr.com	740-453-4377		565
Muskingum Valley Area Chamber of Commerce PO Box 837 ....Beverly OH 45715 *Web:* www.mvacc.com	740-984-8259		139
Muskogee County 229 W Okmulgee Ave .... Muskogee OK 74401 *TF:* 800-444-1187 ■ *Web:* www.cityofmuskogee.com	918-682-6602		338
Muskogee Daily Phoenix 214 Wall St......... Muskogee OK 74401 *TF:* 800-730-3649 ■ *Web:* www.muskogeephoenix.com	918-684-2828	684-2865	532-2
Muslim Community Assn 2301 Plymouth Rd .... Ann Arbor MI 48105 *Web:* www.mca-aa.org	734-665-6772		48-20
Musselman & Hall Contractors LLC 4922 E Blue Banks PO Box 300858 ....Kansas City MO 64130 *TF:* 800-257-4255 ■ *Web:* www.musselmanandhall.com	816-861-1234	861-1237	189-3
Musselman Hotels LLC 2912 Eastpoint Pkwy ....Louisville KY 40223 *Web:* www.musselmanhotels.com	502-426-3006		194
Musselshell County 506 Main St.............. Roundup MT 59072 *Web:* musselshellcounty.org	406-323-1104		338

Name / Address	Phone	Fax	Class
Musser Lumber Company Inc 200 Shoal Ridge Dr .... Rural Retreat VA 24368 *Web:* www.musserlumber.com	276-686-5113	686-5169	191-3
Musser Public Library 304 Iowa Ave.......... Muscatine IA 52761 *Web:* www.musserpubliclibrary.org	563-263-3065		434-3
Musson Rubber Company Inc 1320 E Archwood Ave..........................Akron OH 44306 *TF Cust Svc:* 800-321-2381 ■ *Web:* www.mussonrubber.com	330-773-7651	773-3254	676
Musson Theatrical Inc 890 Walsh Ave .... Santa Clara CA 95050 *TF:* 800-843-2837 ■ *Web:* www.musson.com	408-986-0210	986-9552	722
Mustang Dynamometer 2300 Pinnacle Pkwy .... Twinsburg OH 44087 *TF:* 888-468-7826 ■ *Web:* www.mustangdyne.com	330-963-5400	425-3310	472
Mustang Engineering LP 16001 Pk Ten Pl ....Houston TX 77084 *Web:* www.mustangeng.com	713-215-8000	215-8506	261
Mustang Fuel Corp 9800 N Oklahoma Ave ....Oklahoma City OK 73114 *TF:* 800-332-9400 ■ *Web:* www.mustangfuel.com	405-748-9400		538
Mustang Gas Compression LLC 2500 Woodbine Dr Ste 200 ....Kilgore TX 75663 *Web:* mustangcompression.com	903-218-4459	983-4070	538
Mustang Island State Park 17047 State Hwy 361 .... Port Aransas TX 78373 *Web:* tpwd.texas.gov/state-parks/mustang-island	361-749-5246		565
Mustang Rental Services Inc 15907 E Fwy........................... Channelview TX 77530 *Web:* www.mustangcat.com	281-452-7368		264-3
Mustang Technology Group Lp 6900 K Ave........Plano TX 75074 *Web:* www2.l3t.com/mustangtechnology	972-747-0707		261
Mustang Tractor & Equipment Co 12800 NW Fwy ....Houston TX 77040 *TF:* 800-256-1001 ■ *Web:* www.mustangcat.com	713-460-2000		358
Mustard Seed 4750 N Div.....................Spokane WA 99207 *Web:* www.mustardseedweb.com	509-483-1500		671
Mustel Research Group Ltd 1505 W Second Ave Ste 402 .... Vancouver BC V6H3Y4 *Web:* www.mustelgroup.com	604-733-4213		466
Mutare Software 2325 Hicks Rd.........Rolling Meadows IL 60008 *Web:* www.mutare.com	847-496-9000		177
Mutchler Inc 20 Elm St................. Harrington Park NJ 07640 *Web:* mutchler.net	201-768-1100		146
Muth Electric Inc 1717 N Sanborn PO Box 1400 .... Mitchell SD 57301 *TF:* 800-888-1597 ■ *Web:* www.muthelectric.com	605-996-3983	996-2203	189-4
Mutiny Hotel 2951 S Bayshore Dr................ Miami FL 33133 *TF:* 888-868-8469 ■ *Web:* www.providentresorts.com	305-441-2100	441-2822	379
Mutoh America Inc 2602 S 47th St Ste 102......................... Phoenix AZ 85034 *TF:* 800-996-8864 ■ *Web:* www.mutoh.com	480-968-7772	968-7990	173-6
Muttart Conservatory 9626 96A St........... Edmonton AB T6C4L8 *Web:* www.edmonton.ca	780-496-8755	496-8747	97
Mutual Bank 570 Washington St............... Whitman MA 02382 *Web:* www.mymutualbank.com	781-447-4488		70
Mutual Benefit Group 409 Penn St PO Box 577 .... Huntingdon PA 16652 *TF:* 800-283-3531 ■ *Web:* www.mutualbenefitgroup.com	814-643-3000		528
Mutual Engraving Company Inc 511 Hempstead Ave Ste .... West Hempstead NY 11552 *TF:* 800-433-2996 ■ *Web:* www.mutualengraving.com	516-486-2996		627
Mutual Industries Inc 707 W Grange St ....Philadelphia PA 19120 *TF:* 800-523-0888 ■ *Web:* www.mutualindustries.com	215-927-6000	927-3388	745-3
Mutual Insurance Company of Arizona PO Box 33180 ....Phoenix AZ 85067 *TF:* 800-352-0402 ■ *Web:* www.mica-insurance.com	602-956-5276	468-1710	391-2
Mutual Liquid Gas & Equipment Co Inc 17117 S Broadway St.........................Gardena CA 90248 *TF:* 800-633-3574	800-633-3574		316
Mutual Materials Co 605 119th Ave NE ....Bellevue WA 98005 *TF:* 800-477-3008 ■ *Web:* www.mutualmaterials.com	425-452-2300		150
Mutual Mobile Inc 206 E Ninth St Ste 1400....................... Austin TX 78701 *TF:* 800-208-3563 ■ *Web:* www.mutualmobile.com	800-208-3563		177
Mutual of America Life Insurance Co 320 Pk Ave ....New York NY 10022 *TF:* 800-468-3785 ■ *Web:* www.mutualofamerica.com	212-224-1600		391-2
Mutual of Enumclaw Insurance Co 1460 Wells St.............................. Enumclaw WA 98022 *TF:* 800-366-5551 ■ *Web:* www.mutualofenumclaw.com	360-825-2591	825-6885	391-4
Mutual of Omaha Bank 3333 Farnam St..........Omaha NE 68131 *TF:* 866-351-5646 ■ *Web:* www.mutualofomahabank.com	877-471-7896		70
Mutual of Omaha Co 3300 Mutual of Omaha Plaza ....Omaha NE 68175 *TF:* 800-775-6000 ■ *Web:* www.mutualofomaha.com	402-342-7600		360-4
Mutual of Omaha Insurance Co Mutual of Omaha Plaza.........................Omaha NE 68175 *TF:* 800-775-6000 ■ *Web:* www.mutualofomaha.com	402-342-7600		391-2
Mutual Savings Credit Union Inc 2040 Valleydale Rd.....................Birmingham AL 35244 *Web:* www.mutualsavings.org	205-682-1100		219
Mutual Telecom Services Inc 250 First Ave Ste 301 ....Needham MA 02494 **Fax Area Code:* 781 ■ *TF:* 800-687-2848 ■ *Web:* www.blackbox.com	800-687-2848	449-1996*	189-4
Mutual Trading Company Ltd 431 Crocker St ....Los Angeles CA 90013 *Web:* www.lamtc.com	213-626-9458	626-5130	297-11
Mutual Trust Life Insurance Co 1200 Jorie Blvd .... Oak Brook IL 60522 *TF:* 800-323-7320 ■ *Web:* www.mutualtrust.com	630-990-1000	990-7083	391-2
Mutual Wheel Co Inc 2345 Fourth Ave ....Moline IL 61265 *TF:* 800-798-6926 ■ *Web:* www.mutualwheel.com	309-757-1200	757-1241	61
MutualFirst Financial Inc 110 E Charles St.............................. Muncie IN 47305 *NASDAQ: MFSF* ■ *TF:* 800-382-8031 ■ *Web:* bankwithmutual.com	765-747-2800		360-2
Muza Metal Products Corp 606 E Murdock Ave........................ Oshkosh WI 54901 *TF:* 800-532-2252 ■ *Web:* www.muzametal.com	920-236-3535	236-3520	487

Phone Fax Class

Muzi Motors Inc
557 Highland Ave Needham Heights MA 02494 800-296-9440 57
TF: 800-296-9440 ■ *Web:* www.muzimotors.com

Muzinich & Company Inc 450 Park Ave New York NY 10022 212-888-3413 690
Web: www.muzinich.com

Mv Printing Solutions Inc
23531 Ridge Rt Dr Ste A Laguna Hills CA 92653 949-598-9610 627
Web: mvprintsolutions.com

MV Transportation Inc
5910 N Central Expy Ste 1145 Dallas TX 75206 972-391-4600 468
Web: www.mvtransit.com

MVA Engineering Group Ltd
246 Waterloo St London ON N6B2N4 519-668-4698 256
Web: www.mva.on.ca

MVC (McKechnie Vehicle Components)
27087 Gratiot Ave Fl 2 Roseville MI 48066 586-491-2600 489
Web: www.mvcusa.com

MVC Capital Inc 287 Bowman Ave 2nd Fl Purchase NY 10577 914-510-9400 701-0315 792
NYSE: MVC ■ *TF:* 800-322-2885 ■ *Web:* www.mvccapital.com

MVFF (Mill Valley Film Festival)
1001 Lootens Pl Ste 220 San Rafael CA 94901 415-383-5256 383-8606 282
Web: www.mvff.com

MVM Inc 44620 Guilford Dr Ashburn VA 20147 571-223-4500 223-4474 693
Web: www.mvminc.com

MVM Products LLC
940 Calle Amanecer Ste K San Clemente CA 92673 949-366-1470 591
Web: www.ink-jet.com

MVMA (Maine Veterinary Medical Assn)
97A Exchange St Ste 305 Portland ME 04101 800-448-2772 612-0941* 795
**Fax Area Code: 888* ■ *TF:* 800-448-2772 ■ *Web:* netforum.avectra.com

MVMA (Michigan Veterinary Medical Assn)
2144 Commons Pkwy Okemos MI 48864 517-347-4710 347-4666 795
TF: 800-869-1100 ■ *Web:* www.michvma.org

MVNP
First Hawaiian Ctr 999 Bishop St 24th Fl Honolulu HI 96813 808-536-0881 7
Web: www.mvnp.com

MVP Capital Partners
259 N Radnor-Chester Rd Ste 130 Radnor PA 19087 610-254-2999 402
Web: www.meridian-venture.com

MVP Global Logistics LLC
580 Chelsea St Ste 212 East Boston MA 02128 617-569-6300 311
Web: mvpgloballogistics.com

MVP Health Care 625 State St Schenectady NY 12305 518-370-4793 370-0830* 391-3
**Fax: Hum Res* ■ *TF:* 800-777-4793 ■ *Web:* www.mvphealthcare.com

MVP Laboratories Inc 4805 G St Omaha NE 68117 402-331-5106 331-8776 584
TF: 800-856-4648 ■ *Web:* www.mvplabs.com

MVP Sports Spot 3701 32nd St SE Grand Rapids MI 49512 616-464-1000 717
Web: www.soccerspot.net

MVS Group 1086 Goffle Rd Hawthorne NJ 07506 201-447-1505 387
TF: 800-619-9989 ■ *Web:* www.themvsgroup.com

MVS Inc 3630A Georgia Ave NW Washington DC 20010 202-722-7981 463
Web: www.mvsconsulting.com

MVS Saegertown 1 Crawford St Saegertown PA 16433 814-763-2655 763-2069 454
TF: 800-453-1724 ■ *Web:* www.macleanfoggcs.com

MVSB (Meredith Village Savings Bank)
24 State Rt 25 PO Box 177 Meredith NH 03253 603-279-7986 279-5710 70
TF: 800-922-6872 ■ *Web:* www.mvsb.com

MVSD (Mountain View School District)
3320 Gilman Rd El Monte CA 91732 626-652-4000 685
Web: www.mtviewschools.com

Mw Davis Dumas & Associates Inc
2720 Third Ave S Birmingham AL 35233 205-252-0246 261
Web: www.mwdda.com

Mw Industries Inc 2400 Farrell Houston TX 77073 281-233-0448 567
Web: www.mw-ind.com

MW Mcwong International Inc
1921 Arena Blvd West Sacramento CA 95834 916-371-8080 350

MW Sewall & Co 259 Front St Bath ME 04530 207-442-7994 579

MWA (Mystery Writers of America Inc)
1140 Broadway Ste 1507 New York NY 10001 212-888-8171 888-8107 48-4
Web: www.mysterywriters.org

MWA (Montana Wilderness Assn)
80 South Warren St Helena MT 59601 406-443-7350 443-0750 48-13
Web: www.wildmontana.org

MWA Intelligence Inc
15990 N Greenway Hayden Loop Ste C400 Scottsdale AZ 85260 480-538-5900 177
Web: www.mwaintelligence.com

M-Wave Inc
100 High Grove Blvd Glendale Heights IL 60139 630-318-1900 625
Web: www.mwav.com

MWD 583 San Ysidro Rd Santa Barbara CA 93108 805-969-2271 192
TF: 800-426-4791 ■ *Web:* www.montecitowater.com

MWH Americas Inc
370 Interlocken Blvd Broomfield CO 80021 303-410-4000 261
Web: mwhglobal.com

Mwh Global Inc
380 Interlocken Crescent Ste 200 Broomfield CO 80021 303-533-1900 192
TF: 866-257-5984 ■ *Web:* www.mwhglobal.com

MWI Corp 33 NW Second St Deerfield Beach FL 33441 954-426-1500 426-1582 641
TF: 800-296-7004 ■ *Web:* www.mwicorp.com

Mwi Inc
1269 Brighton Henrietta Townline Rd Rochester NY 14623 585-424-4200 127
Web: www.mwi.com

MWI Veterinary Supply Inc
3041 W Pasadena Dr Boise ID 83705 208-955-8930 584
NASDAQ: MWIV ■ *Web:* www.mwivet.com

Mwl Engineering Corp 6825 SW 81st St Miami FL 33143 305-661-3357 261
Web: mwleng.com

MWM Dexter Inc 107 Washington Ave Aurora MO 65605 417-841-1040 627
Web: www.mwmdexter.com

MWMPC (Michael W Middleton PC)
3330 Longmire Dr College Station TX 77845 979-695-2726 695-2754 787
Web: www.mwmpc.com

MWS Enterprises Inc
5701 Transit Rd East Amherst NY 14051 716-689-0600 297-8
Web: www.arrowmart.com

MWY (Mcgoodwin Williams & Yates Inc)
302 E Millsap Rd Fayetteville AR 72703 479-443-3404 443-4340 261
Web: www.mwyusa.com

MX Consulting Services Inc
544 Paramount Dr Ste 1 Raynham MA 02767 508-821-5855 196
Web: www.mxcsi.com

Mx Group, The 7020 High Grove Blvd Burr Ridge IL 60527 800-827-0170 654-0302* 194
**Fax Area Code: 630* ■ *TF:* 800-827-0170 ■ *Web:* www.themxgroup.com

Mxi Environmental Services Llc
26319 Old Trail Rd Abingdon VA 24210 276-628-6636 196
TF: 800-243-3452 ■ *Web:* www.mxiinc.com

MXL Industries Inc
1764 Rohrerstown Rd Lancaster PA 17601 717-569-8711 569-8716 604
TF: 800-233-0159 ■ *Web:* www.mxl-industries.com

Mxn Corp 1025 Rose Creek Dr Ste 620 Woodstock GA 30189 770-926-1884 196
TF: 800-999-3723 ■ *Web:* mxncorp.com

My Alarm Center LLC
3803 W Chester Pike Ste 100 Newtown Square PA 19073 866-484-4800 693
TF: 866-484-4800 ■ *Web:* www.myalarmcenter.com

My Cleaning Service Inc
2701 Cresmont Ave Baltimore MD 21211 410-889-0505 104
Web: www.mycleaningservice.com

My Eye Media LLC 3515 W Pacific Ave Burbank CA 91505 818-559-7200 514
Web: myeyemedia.com

My Favorite Muffin
500 Lake Cook Rd Ste 475 Deerfield IL 60015 847-948-7520 405-8140 310
TF: 800-251-6101 ■ *Web:* www.babcorp.com

My Jewish Discovery Place Children's Museum
6501 W Sunrise Blvd Plantation FL 33313 954-792-6700 792-4839 520
Web: www.sorefjcc.org

My Museum 425 Washington St Monterey CA 93940 831-649-6444 649-1304 521
Web: www.mymuseum.org

My Old Kentucky Home State Park
501 E Stephen Foster Ave Bardstown KY 40004 502-348-3502 565
Web: www.parks.ky.gov

My Praise ATL 102.5
101 Marietta St 12th Fl Atlanta GA 30303 404-765-9750 688-7686 645-10
Web: mypraiseatl.com

My Receptionist
800 Wisconsin St Ste 410 Eau Claire WI 54703 800-686-0162 737
TF: 800-686-0162 ■ *Web:* www.myreceptionist.com

My Service Depot 8774 Cotter St Lewis Center OH 43035 888-518-0818 764
TF: 888-518-0818 ■ *Web:* www.myservicedepot.com

My Thai 2029 Coultor Dr Amarillo TX 79106 806-355-9541 671
Web: www.mythaiamarillo.com

My Web Times 110 W Jefferson St Ottawa IL 61350 815-433-2000 433-1639 532-2
Web: www.mywebtimes.com

Myakka River State Park 13208 SR 72 Sarasota FL 34241 941-361-6511 361-6501 565
TF: 800-326-3521 ■ *Web:* www.floridastateparks.org

Myanmar Embassy 2300 S St NW Washington DC 20008 202-332-3344 332-4351 257
TF: 800-337-7773 ■ *Web:* www.mewashingtondc.com

Myat Inc 360 Franklin Tpke Mahwah NJ 07430 201-684-0100 645-10
Web: www.myat.com

MyClean Inc 247 W 35th St 9th Fl New York NY 10001 646-912-8473 192
Web: www.myclean.com

Myco Trailers LLC 2703 29th Ave E Bradenton FL 34208 941-748-2397 120
Web: www.mycotrailers.com

MYCOM North America Inc
1080 Holcomb Bridge Rd Bldg 200 Ste 350 Roswell GA 30076 770-776-0000 387

MYCON General Contractors Inc
208 E Louisiana Ste 200 Mckinney TX 75069 972-529-2444 186
Web: www.mycon.com

MyCorporation Business Services Inc
23586 Calabasas Rd Ste 102 Calabasas CA 91302 818-224-7639 387
TF: 800-350-1672 ■ *Web:* www.mycorporation.com

Myelotec Inc
4000 Northfield Way Ste 900 Roswell GA 30076 770-664-4656 476
Web: www.myelotec.com

Myers & Company Architectural Metals
555 Basalt Ave Basalt CO 81621 970-927-4761 492
TF: 800-788-4761 ■ *Web:* www.myersandco.com

Myers Brothers of Kansas City Inc
1210 W 28th St Kansas City MO 64108 816-931-5501 54
TF: 800-264-2404 ■ *Web:* www.myersbrotherskc.com

Myers Container Corp
8435 NE Killingsworth Portland OR 97220 503-501-5830 501-5831 198
TF: 800-406-9377 ■ *Web:* www.myerscontainer.com

Myers Engineering Inc 8376 Salt Lake Ave Bell CA 90201 323-560-4723 771-7789 298
Web: www.myersmixer.com

Myers Industries Inc 1293 S Main St Akron OH 44301 330-253-5592 761-6156* 199
NYSE: MYE ■ **Fax: Acctg* ■ *TF:* 800-468-9716 ■ *Web:* www.myersindustries.com

Myers Power Products Inc
2950 E Philadelphia St Ontario CA 91761 909-923-1800 767
Web: www.myerspowerproducts.com

Myers, Oliver & Price PC
1401 Central Ave NW Ste B Albuquerque NM 87104 505-247-9080 428
Web: moplaw.com

Myers, Widders, Gibson, Jones & Feingold LLP
5425 Everglades St Ventura CA 93003 805-644-7188 428
Web: www.mwgjlaw.com

MyEvent com Inc
221 de la Commune St W Ste 305 Montreal QC H2Y2C9 514-282-7747 396
TF: 888-868-2019 ■ *Web:* www.myevent.com

MyEyeDr Inc 401 Maple Ave W Vienna VA 22180 703-938-5544 544
Web: www.myeyedr.com

myFreightWorld LLC
7133 W 95th St Overland Park KS 66212 877-549-9438 393
TF: 877-549-9438 ■ *Web:* www.myfreightworld.com

MYGOLA INC
4701 Willard Ave Ste 1703 Chevy Chase MD 20815 650-353-7778 377
TF: 800-541-6682 ■ *Web:* www.mygola.com

myITForum.com
6475 Christie Ave Ste 425 Emeryville CA 94608 510-984-6880 387
Web: www.myitforum.com

Mylan 1000 Mylan Blvd Canonsburg PA 15317 724-514-1800 582
TF: 800-527-4278 ■ *Web:* www.mylan.com/en/businesses/rx-products

Name / Address	City	State	Zip	Phone	Fax	Class
Mylan Pharmaceuticals Inc 781 Chestnut Ridge Rd TF: 800-796-9526 ■ Web: mylan.com/products	Morgantown	WV	26505	800-796-9526		582
Mylan Pharmaceuticals ULC 85 Advance Rd TF: 800-575-1379 ■ Web: www.mylan.ca	Etobicoke	ON	M8Z2S6	416-236-2631		583
Myles Standish Monument State Reservation Crescent St Duxbury Web: www.mass.gov	Duxbury	MA	02332	508-747-5360		565
Myles Standish State Forest Cranberry Rd Web: www.mass.gov	South Carver	MA	02366	508-866-2526		565
MyLLC.com Inc 1910 Thomes Ave TF: 888-886-9552 ■ Web: www.myllc.com	Cheyenne	WY	82001	888-886-9552		463
Mynah Technologies 504 Trade Ctr Blvd Web: www.mynah.com	Chesterfield	MO	63005	636-728-2000		177
Mynelle Gardens 4736 Clinton Blvd Web: www.jacksonms.gov	Jackson	MS	39209	601-960-1894	960-1576	97
MyNewPlace.com 343 Sansome St Ste 700 TF: 800-266-0968 ■ Web: www.mynewplace.com	San Francisco	CA	94104	415-348-2009		387
Myoderm Inc 48 E Main St Web: www.myoderm.com	Norristown	PA	19401	610-233-3300		238
MyOpenJobs LLC 203 Main St Ste 100 TF: 800-396-4822 ■ Web: www.myopenjobs.com	Lake Dallas	TX	75065	800-396-4822	446-9634	260
Myotronics-noromed Inc 5870 S 194th St TF: 800-426-0316 ■ Web: www.myotronics.com	Kent	WA	98032	206-243-4214		228
MYR Group 1701 W Golf Rd Twr 3 Ste 1012 TF: 800-360-1321 ■ Web: www.myrgroup.com	Rolling Meadows	IL	60008	847-290-1891	290-1892	189-4
Myra Binstock Legal Search 121 Squire Hill Rd TF: 800-272-4615 ■ Web: www.myrabinstock.com	Upper Montclair	NJ	07043	973-783-6006		260
Myra Museum 2405 Belmont Rd TF: 800-815-1824 ■ Web: www.grandforkshistory.com	Grand Forks	ND	58201	701-775-2216		520
Myre-Big Island State Park 19499 780th Ave TF: 888-646-6367 ■ Web: www.dnr.state.mn.us	Albert Lea	MN	56007	507-379-3403	379-3405	565
Myriad Botanical Gardens/Crystal Bridge Tropical Conservatory 301 W Reno Ave Web: oklahomacitybotanicalgardens.com	Oklahoma City	OK	73102	405-445-7080		97
Myriad Computer Solutions Inc 8040 Bryan Dairy Rd Ste F	Largo	FL	33777	727-541-6000		174
Myriad Genetics Inc 320 Wakara Way NASDAQ: MYGN ■ TF: 800-469-7423 ■ Web: www.myriad.com	Salt Lake City	UT	84108	801-584-3600	584-3640	85
Myriad RBM 3300 Duval Rd TF: 866-726-6277 ■ Web: rbm.myriad.com	Austin	TX	78759	512-835-8026	835-4687	582
Myriad Restaurant Group Inc 249 W Broadway Web: www.myriadrestaurantgroup.com	New York	NY	10013	212-219-9500	219-2380	670
Myrmidon Corp 10555 W Little York Rd TF: 800-880-0771 ■ Web: myrmcorp.com	Houston	TX	77041	713-880-0044	880-4720	697
Myrmo & Sons Inc 3600 Franklin Blvd Web: www.myrmo.com	Eugene	OR	97403	541-747-4565		454
Myron Corp 205 Maywood Ave TF: 877-803-3358 ■ Web: www.myron.com	Maywood	NJ	07607	877-803-3358		9
Myrtle Beach Area Chamber of Commerce 1200 N Oak St TF: 800-356-3016 ■ Web: www.visitmyrtlebeach.com	Myrtle Beach	SC	29577	843-626-7444		139
Myrtle Beach City Hall 937 Broadway St Web: www.cityofmyrtlebeach.com	Myrtle Beach	SC	29577	843-918-1000	918-1028	337
Myrtle Beach Convention Ctr 2101 N Oak St TF: 800-537-1690 ■ Web: www.sheratonmyrtlebeach.com	Myrtle Beach	SC	29577	843-918-5000		205
Myrtle Beach Herald 4761 US 501	Myrtle Beach	SC	29579	843-626-3131		532-4
Myrtle Beach Hotels LLC 2102-B, Cromley Cir Web: www.myrtlebeachhotels.net	Myrtle Beach	SC	29577	843-692-9977		377
Myrtle Beach International Airport 1100 Jetport Rd TF: 800-778-4838 ■ Web: www.flymyrtlebeach.com	Myrtle Beach	SC	29577	843-448-1589	626-9096	27
Myrtle Beach Marriott Resort at Grande Dunes 8400 Costa Verde Dr Web: www.marriott.com	Myrtle Beach	SC	29572	843-449-8880	449-8669	669
Myrtle Beach Reservation Service 1200 N Oak St Web: www.mbhospitality.org	Myrtle Beach	SC	29577	843-626-9668	448-8143	376
Myrtle Beach Resort Vacations 5905 S Kings Hwy PO Box 3936 TF: 888-627-3767 ■ Web: www.myrtle-beach-resort.com	Myrtle Beach	SC	29578	843-238-1559	238-2424	669
Myrtle Beach Speedway 455 Hospitality Ln Web: www.myrtlebeachspeedway.com	Myrtle Beach	SC	29579	843-236-0500		515
Myrtle Beach State Park 4401 S Kings Hwy Web: www.southcarolinaparks.com	Myrtle Beach	SC	29575	843-238-5325		565
Myrtle Waves Water Park 3000 Tenth Ave N Ext TF: 800-960-4573 ■ Web: www.myrtlewaves.com	Myrtle Beach	SC	29577	843-913-9250		32
Mystery Writers of America Inc (MWA) 1140 Broadway Ste 1507 Web: www.mysterywriters.org	New York	NY	10001	212-888-8171	888-8107	48-4
Mystic Aquarium & Institute for Exploration 55 Coogan Blvd TF: 800-733-1830 ■ Web: www.mysticaquarium.org	Mystic	CT	06355	860-572-5955	572-5969	40
Mystic Chamber of Commerce 12 Roosevelt Ave,2nd Fl PO Box 143 TF: 866-572-9578 ■ Web: www.mysticchamber.org	Mystic	CT	06355	860-572-9578	572-9273	139
Mystic Lake Casino Hotel 2400 Mystic Lake Blvd TF: 800-262-7799 ■ Web: www.mysticlake.com	Prior Lake	MN	55372	952-445-9000		133
Mystic Sea Resort 2105 S Ocean Blvd TF: 800-443-7050 ■ Web: www.mysticsea.com	Myrtle Beach	SC	29577	843-448-8446		669
Mystic Seaport -- The Museum of America & the Sea 75 Greenmanville Ave PO Box 6000 TF: 888-973-2767 ■ Web: www.mysticseaport.org	Mystic	CT	06355	860-572-0711	572-5395	520
Mystic Stamp Co 9700 Mill St *Fax Area Code: 800 ■ TF: 866-660-7147 ■ Web: www.mysticstamp.com	Camden	NY	13316	315-245-2690	385-4919*	459
Mystic Valley Wheel Works Inc 480 Trapelo Rd TF: 800-409-4502 ■ Web: www.wheelworks.com	Belmont	MA	02478	617-489-3577		711
Mystikal Solutions LLC 431 Wolf Rd Ste 102	San Antonio	TX	78216	210-979-9300		180
MySuburbanLife.com 1101 W 31st St Ste 100 TF: 800-481-8312 ■ Web: www.mysuburbanlife.com	Downers Grove	IL	60515	630-368-1100	969-0228	532-4
MySupplyChainGroup LLC 1500 First Ave N Ste A111 TF: 888-444-7786 ■ Web: www.mysupplychaingroup.com	Birmingham	AL	35203	205-706-4300		449
My-T Acres Inc 8127 Lewiston Rd	Batavia	NY	14020	585-343-1026		10-11
MYTA Corp 4905 Del Ray Ave, Ste 507 Web: www.myta.com	Bethesda	MD	20814	301-656-6982		196
Mytech Partners Inc 300 Second St NW Web: www.mytech.com	New Brighton	MN	55112	612-659-9800		180
MYTecSoft Inc 989 Knox Abbott Dr Ste 291 Web: www.mytecsoft.com	Cayce	SC	29033	803-244-0255		196
Mythics Inc 1439 N Great Neck Rd Web: www.mythics.com	Virginia Beach	VA	23454	757-412-4362		174
MyTicketIn com 2100 W Loop Ste 205 Web: www.myticketin.com	Houston	TX	77027	713-429-1560		232
Mytina Inc Dba Real Estate Mortgage Exchange 842 Foothill Blvd	La Canada Flintridge	CA	91011	818-507-0077		652
Mytrex Inc 10321 S Beckstead Ln Web: www.rescuealert.com	South Jordan	UT	84095	801-571-4121		476
MyUSACorporation.com Inc 1 Radisson Plaza Ste 800 TF: 877-330-2677 ■ Web: myusacorporation.com	New Rochelle	NY	10801	877-330-2677		317
MZA Associates Corp 2021 Girard Blvd SE Ste 150 Web: www.mza.com	Albuquerque	NM	87106	505-245-9970		544
MZD Advertising 1800 N Meridian St Ste 200 Web: www.zmarketingpartners.com	Indianapolis	IN	46202-1443	317-924-6271		7
Mzinga 10 Burlington Mall Rd Ste 111 *Fax Area Code: 781 ■ TF: 888-694-6428 ■ Web: www.mzinga.com	Burlington	MA	01803	888-694-6428	494-6555*	194
Mzinga Inc 230 Third Ave TF: 888-694-6428 ■ Web: www.mzinga.com	Waltham	MA	02451	781-577-8948	494-6555	178-10

N

Name / Address	City	State	Zip	Phone	Fax	Class
N & b Team Consulting Inc 3625 NW 82nd Ave Ste 207 Web: nbteamconsulting.com	Doral	FL	33166	305-514-2404		196
N & S Supply of Fishkill Inc 205 Old Rt 9 Web: www.nssupply.com	Fishkill	NY	12524	845-896-6291		612
N & S Tractor Co 600 S Hwy 59 Web: www.nstractor.com	Merced	CA	95341	209-383-5888		274
N Barton & Assoc 3629 Old Capital Trail Rd Web: www.nbartoninc.com	Marshallton	DE	19808	302-998-5272		567
N Ccrc 2102 Almaden Rd Ste 125 Web: www.nccrc.org	San Jose	CA	95125	408-445-3000		474
N Cell Systems Inc 1907 E Wayzata Web: ncell.com	Wayzata	MN	55391	952-746-5125		180
N E Florida Educational Consortium 3841 Reid St TF: 800-227-6036 ■ Web: nefec.org	Palatka	FL	32177	386-329-3800		685
N J Coalition of Automotive Retailers 856 River Rd Web: www.njcar.org	Ewing	NJ	08628	609-883-5056		533
N J R Corp 125 Nicholson Ln TF: 800-800-5441 ■ Web: www.njr.com	San Jose	CA	95134	408-321-0200	232-6060	695
N K Bhandari, Consulting Engineers PC 1005 W Fayette St Ste 4A Web: nkbpc.com	Syracuse	NY	13204	315-428-1177		261
N L Fisher Supervision & Engineering Ltd 522 - 11th Ave SW 2nd FL Web: nlfisher.com	Calgary	AB	T2R0C8	403-266-7478		538
N o a Medical Industries Inc 801 Terry Ln TF: 800-633-6068 ■ Web: www.noamedical.com	Washington	MO	63090	636-239-7600		321
N R S I 179 Lafayette Dr TF: 800-331-3117 ■ Web: nrsi.com	Syosset	NY	11791	516-921-5500		242
N Tepperman Ltd 2595 Ouellette Ave TF: 800-265-5062 ■ Web: www.teppermans.com	Windsor	ON	N8X4V8	519-969-9700		321
N W Electric Power Co-op PO Box 565 Web: www.nwepc.com	Cameron	MO	64429	816-632-2121	632-3114	245
N Wasserstrom & Sons Inc 2300 Lockbourne Rd TF: 800-444-4697 ■ Web: www.wasserstrom.com	Columbus	OH	43207	614-228-5550		300
N'digo Profiles 1006 S Michigan Ave Ste 200 Web: ndigo.com	Chicago	IL	60605	312-822-0202		532-3
N'Ware Technologies Inc 2885, 81e Rue Web: www.nwaretech.com	Saint-georges	QC	G6A0C5	418-227-4292		180
N.A. Chaderjian Youth Correctional Facility 7650 S Newcastle Rd PO Box 213014 Web: cdcr.ca.gov	Stockton	CA	95215	209-944-6391		412
N.A.Williams Co 2900 A Paces Ferry Rd TF: 800-241-0551 ■ Web: www.nawilliams.com	Atlanta	GA	30339	770-433-2282		195

Phone | Fax | Class

N.b.c. Truck Equipment Inc
28130 Groesbeck Hwy — Roseville MI 48066 — 586-774-4900 — 772-1280 — 61
TF: 800-778-8207 ■ Web: www.nbctruckequip.com

N.c. Center for Nonprofit Organizations Inc
1110 Navaho Dr Ste 200 — Raleigh NC 27609 — 919-790-1555 — 138
TF: 800-325-3535 ■ Web: www.ncnonprofits.org

N.E.T. Inc 5651 Palmer Way Ste C — Carlsbad CA 92010 — 760-929-5980 — 85
TF: 800-888-4638 ■ Web: www.netmindbody.com

N2it Containers LP 6012 Murphy St — Houston TX 77033 — 713-644-5055 — 311

N9ne Steakhouse 4321 W Flamingo Rd — Las Vegas NV 89103 — 702-933-9900 — 671
Web: www.palms.com

NA Degerstrom Inc 3303 N Sullivan Rd — Spokane WA 99216 — 509-928-3333 — 927-2010 — 502
TF: 800-637-3773 ■ Web: www.nadinc.com

NA for Home Care & Hospice (NAHC)
228 Seventh St SE — Washington DC 20003 — 202-547-7424 — 547-3540 — 49-8
Web: www.nahc.org

NA for Stock Car Auto Racing (NASCAR)
1801 W International Speedway Blvd — Daytona Beach FL 32114 — 704-348-7131 — 48-22
Web: www.nascar.com

NA for the Advancement of Colored People (NAACP)
4805 Mt Hope Dr — Baltimore MD 21215 — 410-580-5777 — 48-8
TF: 877-622-2798 ■ Web: www.naacp.org

NA for Uniformed Services (NAUS)
5535 Hempstead Way — Springfield VA 22151 — 703-750-1342 — 354-4380 — 48-19
TF: 800-842-3451 ■ Web: www.naus.org

Na Go Ya 4921 Brainerd Rd — Chattanooga TN 37411 — 423-899-9252 — 671
Web: www.nagoyatn.com

Na Ho'ola Spa at Hyatt Regency Waikiki Resort
2424 Kalakaua Ave — Honolulu HI 96815 — 808-923-1234 — 926-3415 — 707
TF: 800-233-1234 ■ Web: waikiki.regency.hyatt.com/en/hotel/home.html

NA of Animal Breeders (NAAB)
401 Bernadette Dr — Columbia MO 65203 — 573-445-4406 — 446-2279 — 11-2
Web: www.naab-css.org

NA of Broadcasters (NAB) 1771 N St NW — Washington DC 20036 — 202-429-5300 — 49-14
Web: www.nab.org

NA of Catering And Events (NACE)
9891 Broken Land Pkwy Ste 301 — Columbia MD 21046 — 410-290-5410 — 290-5460 — 49-6
Web: www.nace.net

NA of Chain Drug Stores (NACDS)
413 N Lee St — Alexandria VA 22314 — 703-549-3001 — 836-4869 — 49-18
TF: 800-678-6223 ■ Web: www.nacds.org

NA of Clean Water Agencies (NACWA)
1816 Jefferson Pl NW — Washington DC 20036 — 202-833-2672 — 833-4657 — 49-7
TF: 888-267-9505 ■ Web: www.nacwa.org

NA of College Auxiliary Services (NACAS)
3 Boar's Head Ln Ste B — Charlottesville VA 22903 — 434-245-8425 — 245-8453 — 49-5
Web: www.nacas.org

NA of College Stores (NACS)
500 E Lorain St — Oberlin OH 44074 — 440-775-7777 — 775-4769 — 49-18
TF: 800-622-7498 ■ Web: www.nacs.org

NA of Colleges & Employers (NACE)
62 Highland Ave — Bethlehem PA 18017 — 610-868-1421 — 868-1421 — 49-5
TF: 800-544-5272 ■ Web: www.naceweb.org

NA of Collegiate Directors of Athletics (NACDA)
24651 Detroit Rd — Westlake OH 44145 — 440-892-4000 — 892-4007 — 48-22
TF: 877-887-2261 ■ Web: www.nacda.com

NA of Congregational Christian Churches (NACCC)
8473 S Howell Ave — Oak Creek WI 53154 — 414-764-1620 — 764-0319 — 48-20
TF: 800-262-1620 ■ Web: www.naccc.org

NA of Conservation Districts (NACD)
509 Capitol Ct NE — Washington DC 20002 — 202-547-6223 — 547-6450 — 49-7
TF: 888-695-2433 ■ Web: www.nacdnet.org

NA of Convenience Stores (NACS)
1600 Duke St — Alexandria VA 22314 — 703-684-3600 — 836-4564 — 49-18
TF Cust Svc: 800-966-6227 ■ Web: www.nacsonline.com

NA of Credit Management (NACM)
8840 Columbia 100 Pkwy — Columbia MD 21045 — 410-740-5560 — 740-5574 — 49-2
TF: 800-955-8815 ■ Web: www.nacm.org

NA of Dental Plans (NADP)
12700 Pk Central Dr — Dallas TX 75251 — 972-458-6998 — 458-2258 — 49-9
TF: 800-654-2452 ■ Web: www.nadp.org

NA of Electrical Distributors Inc (NAED)
1181 Corporate Lake Dr — Saint Louis MO 63132 — 314-991-9000 — 991-3060 — 49-18
TF: 888-791-2512 ■ Web: www.naed.org

NA of Elementary School Principals (NAESP)
1615 Duke St — Alexandria VA 22314 — 703-684-3345 — 548-6021 — 49-5
TF: 800-386-2377 ■ Web: www.naesp.org

NA of Federal Credit Unions (NAFCU)
3138 Tenth St N — Arlington VA 22201 — 703-522-4770 — 524-1082 — 49-2
TF: 800-336-4644 ■ Web: www.nafcu.org

NA of Free Will Baptists (NAFWB)
5233 Mt View Rd — Antioch TN 37013 — 615-731-6812 — 731-0771 — 48-20
TF: 877-767-7659 ■ Web: www.nafwb.org

NA of Home Builders PAC
1201 15th St NW — Washington DC 20005 — 202-266-8200 — 266-8400 — 615
TF: 800-368-5242 ■ Web: www.nahb.org

NA of Housing & Redevelopment Officials (NAHRO)
630 'I' St NW — Washington DC 20001 — 202-289-3500 — 289-8181 — 49-7
TF: 877-866-2476 ■ Web: www.nahro.org

NA of Independent Colleges & Universities (NAICU)
1025 Connecticut Ave NW Ste 700 — Washington DC 20036 — 202-785-8866 — 835-0003 — 49-5
TF: 800-574-4243 ■ Web: www.naicu.edu

NA of Insurance & Financial Advisors (NAIFA)
2901 Telestar Ct — Falls Church VA 22042 — 703-770-8100 — 49-9
TF Sales: 877-866-2432 ■ Web: www.naifa.org

NA of Intercollegiate Athletics (NAIA)
1200 Grand Blvd — Kansas City MO 64106 — 816-595-8000 — 595-8200 — 48-22
Web: www.naia.org

NA of Letter Carriers
100 Indiana Ave NW — Washington DC 20001 — 202-393-4695 — 737-1540 — 414
TF: 800-424-5186 ■ Web: www.nalc.org

NA of Neonatal Nurses (NANN)
4700 West Lake Ave — Glenview IL 60025 — 847-375-3660 — 375-6491 — 49-8
TF: 800-451-3795 ■ Web: www.nann.org

NA of Nurse Practitioners in Women's Health
505 C St NE — Washington DC 20002 — 202-543-9693 — 543-9858 — 49-8
Web: www.npwh.org

NA of Parliamentarians (NAP)
213 S Main St — Independence MO 64050 — 816-833-3892 — 833-3893 — 49-12
TF: 888-627-2929 ■ Web: www.parliamentarians.org

NA of Professional Employer Organizations (NAPEO)
707 N St Asaph St — Alexandria VA 22314 — 703-836-0466 — 836-0976 — 49-12
Web: www.napeo.org

NA of Retired Federal Employees
606 N Washington St — Alexandria VA 22314 — 703-838-7760 — 838-7785 — 615
TF: 800-627-3394 ■ Web: www.narfe.org

NA of State Boards of Education (NASBE)
333 John Carlyle St Ste 530 — Alexandria VA 22314 — 703-684-4000 — 49-5
TF: 800-368-5023 ■ Web: www.nasbe.org

NA of State Mental Health Program Directors (NASMHPD)
66 Canal Ctr Plaza Ste 302 — Alexandria VA 22314 — 703-739-9333 — 548-9517 — 49-7
Web: www.nasmhpd.org

NA of Surety Bond Producers (NASBP)
1140 19th St NW Ste 800 — Washington DC 20036 — 202-686-3700 — 686-3656 — 49-9
Web: www.nasbp.org

NA of Television Program Executives (NATPE)
5757 Wilshire Blvd PH-10 — Los Angeles CA 90036 — 310-453-4440 — 453-5258 — 49-14
TF: 800-767-6266 ■ Web: www.natpe.com

NA of Wholesaler-Distributors (NAWD)
1325 G St NW Ste 1000 — Washington DC 20005 — 202-872-0885 — 785-0586 — 49-18
Web: www.naw.org

NA of Women in Construction (NAWIC)
327 S Adams St — Fort Worth TX 76104 — 817-877-5551 — 877-0324 — 49-3
TF: 800-552-3506 ■ Web: www.nawic.org

NAA (Natural Areas Assn) PO Box 1504 — Bend OR 97709 — 541-317-0199 — 48-13
Web: www.naturalareas.org

NAA (National Apartment Assn)
4300 Wilson Blvd Ste 400 — Arlington VA 22203 — 703-518-6141 — 248-9440 — 49-17
TF: 800-632-3007 ■ Web: www.naahq.org

NAA (USA Archery)
1 Olympic Plaza — Colorado Springs CO 80909 — 719-866-4576 — 632-4733 — 48-22
TF: 800-671-1140 ■ Web: www.teamusa.org

NAA (Newspaper Media Alliance)
4401 Wilson Blvd Ste 900 — Arlington VA 22203 — 571-366-1000 — 366-1195 — 49-14
Web: www.naa.org

NAA (National Auctioneers Assn)
8880 Ballentine St — Overland Park KS 66214 — 913-541-8084 — 894-5281 — 49-18
TF: 877-657-1990 ■ Web: www.auctioneers.org

NAAA (National Agricultural Aviation Assn)
1005 E St SE — Washington DC 20003 — 202-546-5722 — 546-5726 — 48-2
Web: www.agaviation.org

NAAA (National Auto Auction Assn)
5320 Spectrum Dr Ste D — Frederick MD 21703 — 301-696-0400 — 631-1359 — 49-18
TF: 800-232-5411 ■ Web: www.naaa.com

NAAB (NA of Animal Breeders)
401 Bernadette Dr — Columbia MO 65203 — 573-445-4406 — 446-2279 — 11-2
Web: www.naab-css.org

NAAB (National Architectural Accrediting Board)
1735 New York Ave NW — Washington DC 20006 — 202-783-2007 — 783-2822 — 48-1
Web: www.naab.org

NAACLS (National Accrediting Agency for Clinical Laboratory Sciences)
8410 W Bryn Mawr Ave Ste 670 — Chicago IL 60631 — 773-714-8880 — 714-8886 — 48-1
Web: www.naacls.org

NAACP (NA for the Advancement of Colored People)
4805 Mt Hope Dr — Baltimore MD 21215 — 410-580-5777 — 48-8
TF: 877-622-2798 ■ Web: www.naacp.org

NAADAC PAC
44 Canal Center Plaza Ste 301 — Alexandria VA 22314 — 703-741-7686 — 741-7698 — 615
TF: 800-377-1136 ■ Web: www.naadac.org

NAAF (National Alopecia Areata Foundation)
14 Mitchell Blvd — San Rafael CA 94903 — 415-472-3780 — 472-5343 — 48-17
TF: 800-723-4238 ■ Web: www.naaf.org

NAAS (Northwest Assn of Accredited Schools)
1510 Robert St Ste 103 — Boise ID 83705 — 208-493-5077 — 48-1
Web: advanc-ed.org

NAB (National Allergy Bureau)
555 E Wells St 11th Fl — Milwaukee WI 53202 — 414-272-6071 — 272-6070 — 48-17
TF: 800-227-2345 ■ Web: aaaai.org/global/nab-pollen-counts.aspx

NAB (NA of Broadcasters) 1771 N St NW — Washington DC 20036 — 202-429-5300 — 49-14
Web: www.nab.org

NAB Construction Corp
112-20 14th Ave — College Point NY 11356 — 718-762-0001 — 961-3789 — 188-4
Web: www.nabconstruction.com

NABC (North American Blueberry Council)
80 Iron Pt Cir Dr — Folsom CA 95630 — 916-983-0111 — 983-9370 — 48-2
Web: www.blueberry.org

NABCA (National Alcohol Beverage Control Assn)
4401 Ford Ave Ste 700 — Alexandria VA 22302 — 703-578-4200 — 820-3551 — 49-7
Web: www.nabca.org

Nabco Entrances Inc
S82W18717 Gemini Dr — Muskego WI 53150 — 877-622-2694 — 480
TF: 888-679-3319 ■ Web: www.nabcoentrances.com

Nabco Inc 1001 Corporate Dr Ste 205 — Canonsburg PA 15317 — 724-746-9617 — 693
Web: www.nabcoinc.com

Nabeel's Cafe 1706 Oxmoor Rd — Homewood AL 35209 — 205-879-9292 — 671
Web: www.nabeels.com

Nabet 700-M Unifor
100 Lombard St Ste 203 — Toronto ON M5C1M3 — 416-536-4827 — 536-0859 — 397
TF: 800-889-9487 ■ Web: nabet700.com

NABET-CWA (NABET-CWA) 501 Third St NW — Washington DC 20001 — 202-434-1254 — 434-1426 — 414
Web: www.nabetcwa.org

Nabholz Construction Corp PO Box 2090 — Conway AR 72033 — 501-505-5800 — 186
Web: www.nabholz.com

Nabors Alaska Drilling Inc
2525 C St Ste 200 — Anchorage AK 99503 — 907-263-6000 — 563-3734 — 540
Web: www.nabors.com

Nabors Drilling International Ltd
515 W Greens Rd Ste 1000 — Houston TX 77067 — 281-874-0035 — 872-5205 — 540
TF: 877-344-7529 ■ Web: nabors.com

Nabors Drilling USA Inc
515 W Greens Rd Ste 1000 — Houston TX 77067 — 281-874-0035 — 872-5205 — 540
TF: 800-422-2066 ■ Web: nabors.com

Nabors Industries Ltd
515 W Greens Rd Ste 1200 — Houston TX 77067 — 281-874-0035 — 872-5205 — 540
NYSE: NBR ■ TF: 800-422-2066 ■ Web: www.nabors.com

Name / Address	City	State	ZIP	Phone	Fax	Class
Nabors Offshore Corp 515 W Greens Rd Ste 500 *Web:* www.nabors.com	Houston	TX	77067	281-874-0406	872-5205	539
Nabtesco Aerospace Inc 17770 NE 78th Pl *Web:* www.nabtescoaero.com	Redmond	WA	98052	425-602-8400		529
NAC (National Automobile Club) 373 Vintage Park Dr Ste E *Web:* www.nacroadservice.com	Foster City	CA	94404	650-294-7000		53
NAC Group Inc 1790 Commerce Ave N *TF:* 866-651-2901 ■ *Web:* nacsemi.com	St Petersburg	FL	33716	727-828-0187	828-0155	246
NACA (National Air Carrier Assn) 1000 Wilson Blvd Ste 1700 *Web:* www.naca.cc	Arlington	VA	22209	703-358-8060	358-8070	49-21
NACAC (North American Council on Adoptable Children) 970 Raymond Ave Ste 106 *TF:* 877-823-2237 ■ *Web:* www.nacac.org	Saint Paul	MN	55114	651-644-3036	644-9848	48-6
Nacarato Volvo Truck 519 New Paul Rd *TF:* 888-392-8486 ■ *Web:* www.nacaratotrucks.com	La Vergne	TN	37086	888-392-8486		516
NACAS (NA of College Auxiliary Services) 3 Boar's Head Ln Ste B *Web:* www.nacas.org	Charlottesville	VA	22903	434-245-8425	245-8453	49-5
NACB (Native American Community Board) PO Box 572 *Web:* www.nativeshop.org	Lake Andes	SD	57356	605-487-7072	487-7964	48-7
NACB Group Inc 10 Starwood Dr *TF:* 800-370-2737 ■ *Web:* www.ncabgroup.com	Hampstead	NH	03841	603-329-4551		246
NACC (Norwegian-American Chamber of Commerce Southwest Chapter) 5219 Pine Arbor Dr *Web:* www.nacchouston.org	Houston	TX	77066	281-537-6879	587-9284	138
NACCAS (National Accrediting Commission of Cosmetology Arts & Sciences) 4401 Ford Ave Ste 1300 *TF:* 877-212-5752 ■ *Web:* www.naccas.org	Alexandria	VA	22302	703-600-7600	379-2200	48-1
NACCC (NA of Congregational Christian Churches) 8473 S Howell Ave *TF:* 800-262-1620 ■ *Web:* www.naccc.org	Oak Creek	WI	53154	414-764-1620	764-0319	48-20
NACCME-PrincetonCME 300 Rike Dr Ste A *Web:* www.naccme.com	Millstone Township	NJ	08535	609-371-1137		242
NACCO Industries Inc 5875 Landerbrook Dr Ste 300 *NYSE:* NC ■ *TF:* 877-756-5118 ■ *Web:* www.nacco.com	Cleveland	OH	44124	440-229-5151		185
NACCO Materials Handling Group Inc 5875 Landerbrook Dr Ste 300 *Web:* www.hyster-yale.com	Cleveland	OH	44124	503-721-6000	721-6001	470
NACD (NA of Conservation Districts) 509 Capitol Ct NE *TF:* 888-695-2433 ■ *Web:* www.nacdnet.org	Washington	DC	20002	202-547-6223	547-6450	49-7
NACDA (NA of Collegiate Directors of Athletics) 24651 Detroit Rd *TF:* 877-887-2261 ■ *Web:* www.nacda.com	Westlake	OH	44145	440-892-4000	892-4007	48-22
NACDS (NA of Chain Drug Stores) 413 N Lee St *TF:* 800-678-6223 ■ *Web:* www.nacds.org	Alexandria	VA	22314	703-549-3001	836-4869	49-18
NACE (NA of Colleges & Employers) 62 Highland Ave *TF:* 800-544-5272 ■ *Web:* www.naceweb.org	Bethlehem	PA	18017	610-868-1421	868-1421	49-5
NACE (NA of Catering And Events) 9891 Broken Land Pkwy Ste 301 *Web:* www.nace.net	Columbia	MD	21046	410-290-5410	290-5460	49-6
NACE International: Corrosion Society 1440 S Creek Dr *TF:* 800-797-6223 ■ *Web:* www.nace.org	Houston	TX	77084	281-228-6200	228-6300	49-13
Nacel Open Door Inc 380 Jackson St Ste 200 *Web:* www.nacelopendoor.org	St. Paul	MN	55101	651-686-0080		148
NACFAM (National Council for Advanced Mfg) 2025 M St NW Ste 800 *TF:* 800-250-3196 ■ *Web:* www.nacfam.org	Washington	DC	20036	202-429-2220	429-2422	49-12
NACHA - Electronic Payments Association 2550 Wasser Terr Ste 400 *TF:* 800-487-9180 ■ *Web:* www.nacha.org	Herndon	VA	20171	703-561-1100	787-0996	49-2
NACHER Corp, The 111 E Angus Dr *Web:* nacher.net	Youngsville	LA	70592	337-856-9144		667
Nachi America Inc 715 Pushville Rd *TF:* 888-340-2747 ■ *Web:* www.nachiamerica.com	Greenwood	IN	46143	317-530-1001	530-1011	75
Nachi Robotic Systems Inc 22285 Roethel Dr *Web:* www.nachirobotics.com	Novi	MI	48375	248-305-6545	305-6542	385
Nachi Technology Inc 713 Pushville Rd/700 N *Web:* www.nachitech.com	Greenwood	IN	46143	317-535-5000		247
Nacho Mama's 2907 O'Donnell St *Web:* www.nachomamascanton.com	Baltimore	MD	21224	410-675-0898		671
Na-Churs/Alpine Solutions 421 Leader St *TF:* 800-622-4877 ■ *Web:* www.nachurs.com	Marion	OH	43302	740-382-5701	383-2615	280
Nacional 27 325 W Huron St *Web:* www.leye.com	Chicago	IL	60654	312-664-2727		671
NACM (NA of Credit Management) 8840 Columbia 100 Pkwy *TF:* 800-955-8815 ■ *Web:* www.nacm.org	Columbia	MD	21045	410-740-5560	740-5574	49-2
Nacm Chicago-midwest 3005 Tollview Dr *Web:* www.nacmchicago.org	Rolling Meadows	IL	60008	847-483-6400		138
NACM South Texas Inc 10887 S Wilcrest Dr *TF:* 866-252-6226 ■ *Web:* www.nacmsouthtexas.org	Houston	TX	77099	281-228-6100		218
NACO Industries Inc 395 W 1400 N *Web:* www.herndon-assoc.com	Logan	UT	84341	435-753-8020		601
Nacogdoches Convention & Visitors Bureau 200 E Main St *TF:* 888-653-3788 ■ *Web:* www.visitnacogdoches.org	Nacogdoches	TX	75961	936-564-7351	462-7688	206
Nacogdoches County 101 W Main St Rm 205 *Web:* co.nacogdoches.tx.us	Nacogdoches	TX	75961	936-560-7733	559-5926	338
Nacogdoches County Chamber of Commerce 2516 N St *Web:* www.nacogdoches.org	Nacogdoches	TX	75965	936-560-5533	560-3920	139
Nacogdoches Medical Ctr 4920 NE Stallings Dr *TF:* 866-898-8446 ■ *Web:* www.nacmedicalcenter.com	Nacogdoches	TX	75965	936-569-9481		374-3
Nacogdoches Memorial Hospital 1204 N Mound St *TF:* 800-427-7240 ■ *Web:* www.nacmem.org	Nacogdoches	TX	75961	936-564-4611	568-8588	374-3
Nacogdoches Public Library 1112 N St *TF:* 800-252-5400 ■ *Web:* ci.nacogdoches.tx.us	Nacogdoches	TX	75961	936-559-2970		434-3
NACS (NA of College Stores) 500 E Lorain St *TF:* 800-622-7498 ■ *Web:* www.nacs.org	Oberlin	OH	44074	440-775-7777	775-4769	49-18
NACS (NA of Convenience Stores) 1600 Duke St *TF Cust Svc:* 800-966-6227 ■ *Web:* www.nacsonline.com	Alexandria	VA	22314	703-684-3600	836-4564	49-18
NACWA (NA of Clean Water Agencies) 1816 Jefferson Pl NW *TF:* 888-267-9505 ■ *Web:* www.nacwa.org	Washington	DC	20036	202-833-2672	833-4657	49-7
NADA (National Automobile Dealers Assn) 8400 Westpark Dr *TF:* 800-252-6232 ■ *Web:* www.nada.org	McLean	VA	22102	703-821-7000	821-7075	49-18
NADAguides.com 3186 K Airway Ave *Web:* www.nadaguides.com	Costa Mesa	CA	92626	714-556-8511		387
NADCA (North American Die Casting Assn) 3250 N Arlington Hts Rd Ste 101 *Web:* www.diecasting.org	Arlington Heights	IL	60004	847-279-0001	279-0002	49-13
Nadel Architects 1990 S Bundy Dr Ste 400 *Web:* www.nadelarc.com	Los Angeles	CA	90025	310-826-2100	826-0182	261
NADF (National Adrenal Diseases Foundation) 505 Northern Blvd *Web:* www.nadf.us	Great Neck	NY	11021	516-487-4992		48-17
Nadine International Inc 2570 Matheson Blvd E Ste 110 *Web:* www.nadineintl.on.ca	Mississauga	ON	L4W4Z3	905-602-1850		261
Nading Mechanical Inc 11673 N County Rd 775 E *Web:* nadingmechanicalinc.com	Hope	IN	47246	812-546-6111		610
Nadler Jerrold (Rep D - NY) 2109 Rayburn HOB *Web:* nadler.house.gov	Washington	DC	20515	202-225-5635		342-2
NADP (NA of Dental Plans) 12700 Pk Central Dr *TF:* 800-654-2452 ■ *Web:* www.nadp.org	Dallas	TX	75251	972-458-6998	458-2258	49-9
Nady Systems Inc 6701 Shellmound St *Web:* www.nady.com	Emeryville	CA	94608	510-652-2411	652-5075	52
NAEA (National Art Education Assn) 1806 Robert Fulton Dr *TF:* 800-299-8321 ■ *Web:* www.arteducators.org	Reston	VA	20191	703-860-8000	860-2960	49-5
NAED (NA of Electrical Distributors Inc) 1181 Corporate Lake Dr *TF:* 888-791-2512 ■ *Web:* www.naed.org	Saint Louis	MO	63132	314-991-9000	991-3060	49-18
NAEDA (Equipment Dealers Assn) 165 N Meramec Ave Ste 430 *Web:* www.equipmentdealer.org	St. Louis	MO	63105	636-349-5000	349-5443	49-18
NAEIR (NAEIR) 560 McClure St *TF:* 800-562-0955 ■ *Web:* www.naeir.org	Galesburg	IL	61401	309-343-0704		48-5
NAESP (NA of Elementary School Principals) 1615 Duke St *TF:* 800-386-2377 ■ *Web:* www.naesp.org	Alexandria	VA	22314	703-684-3345	548-6021	49-5
NAF (National Abortion Federation) 1755 Massachusetts Ave NW *TF:* 800-772-9100 ■ *Web:* www.prochoice.org	Washington	DC	20036	202-667-5881	667-5890	49-8
NAFC (National Acctg & Finance Council) American Trucking Assn 950 N Glebe Rd *TF:* 800-517-7370 ■ *Web:* www.trucking.org	Arlington	VA	22203	703-838-1700		49-1
NAFCU (NA of Federal Credit Unions) 3138 Tenth St N *TF:* 800-336-4644 ■ *Web:* www.nafcu.org	Arlington	VA	22201	703-522-4770	524-1082	49-2
NAFEM (North American Assn of Food Equipment Manufacturers) 161 N Clark St Ste 2020 *TF:* 888-493-5961 ■ *Web:* www.nafem.org	Chicago	IL	60601	312-821-0201	821-0202	49-13
Naffs 3301c State Rt 66 Ste 205 *Web:* naffs.org	Neptune	NJ	07753	732-922-3218		138
NAFSA: Assn of International Educators 1307 New York Ave NW 8th Fl *TF:* 800-435-7352 ■ *Web:* www.nafsa.org	Washington	DC	20005	202-737-3699	737-3657	49-5
NAFWB (NA of Free Will Baptists) 5233 Mt View Rd *TF:* 877-767-7659 ■ *Web:* www.nafwb.org	Antioch	TN	37013	615-731-6812	731-0771	48-20
Nagase America Holdings Inc 546 Fifth Ave 16th Fl *Web:* nagaseamerica.com	New York	NY	10036	212-703-1340		146
Nagel Chase Inc 2323 Delaney Rd *TF:* 800-323-4552 ■ *Web:* www.paysoncasters.com	Gurnee	IL	60031	800-323-4552		350
Nagel Gun & Sports Shop 6201 San Pedro Ave *Web:* nagelsguns.net	San Antonio	TX	78216	210-342-5420		711
Nagelbush Mechanical Inc 1800 NW 49th St Ste 110 *Web:* www.nagelbush.com	Fort Lauderdale	FL	33309	954-736-3000	748-7881	189-10
NAGGL (National Association of Government Guaranteed Lenders) 215 E Ninth Ave *Web:* www.naggl.org	Stillwater	OK	74074	405-377-4022	377-3931	49-2
Nagl Manufacturing Co 3626 Martha St *Web:* www.naglmfg.com	Omaha	NE	68105	402-342-2006		103
Nagle & Associates pa 7780 Brier Creek Pkwy Ste 210 *TF:* 800-411-1583 ■ *Web:* www.naglefirm.com	Raleigh	NC	27617	919-433-0035		428
Nagle Paving Co 39525 W 13 Mile Rd 300 *Web:* www.naglepaving.com	Novi	MI	48377	248-553-0600	553-0669	188-4
Nagle Pumps Inc 1249 Ctr Ave **Fax:* Sales ■ *Web:* www.naglepumps.com	Chicago Heights	IL	60411	708-754-2940	754-2944*	641

Phone | Fax | Class

Nagoya Japanese Restaurant
1155 W Arbrook Blvd . . . . . Arlington TX 76015 817-466-3688 466-3684 671
Web: www.txnagoya.com

Nagoya Sushi 109 Gainsborough Sq . . . . . Chesapeake VA 23320 757-549-7977 671

Nagy & Croniser CPA'S LLP
5564 Woodlawn Ave . . . . . Lowville NY 13367 315-376-6518 2

Naha 500 N Clark St . . . . . Chicago IL 60654 312-321-6242 671
Web: www.naha-chicago.com

Nahan Printing Inc
7000 Saukview Dr PO Box 697 . . . . . Saint Cloud MN 56302 320-251-7611 259-1378 627
Web: www.nahan.com

NAHB Research Ctr
400 Prince Georges Blvd . . . . . Upper Marlboro MD 20774 301-249-4000 430-6180 668
TF: 800-638-8556 ■ *Web:* www.homeinnovation.com

NAHC (NA for Home Care & Hospice)
228 Seventh St SE . . . . . Washington DC 20003 202-547-7424 547-3540 49-8
Web: www.nahc.org

Nahon, Saharovich & Trotz PLC
488 S Menhenhall Rd . . . . . Memphis TN 38117 901-683-7000 428
TF: 800-529-4004 ■ *Web:* www.nstlaw.com

NAHRO (NA of Housing & Redevelopment Officials)
630 'I' St NW . . . . . Washington DC 20001 202-289-3500 289-8181 49-7
TF: 877-866-2476 ■ *Web:* www.nahro.org

Nai Hunneman 303 Congress St . . . . . Boston MA 02210 617-457-3400 652
Web: www.naihunneman.com

NAI solutions
200 104th Ave Ste 324 . . . . . Treasure Island FL 33706 877-624-8311 180
TF: 877-624-8311 ■ *Web:* ldms.com

NAIA (NA of Intercollegiate Athletics)
1200 Grand Blvd . . . . . Kansas City MO 64106 816-595-8000 595-8200 48-22
Web: www.naia.org

NAIC (National Astronomy & Ionosphere Ctr)
Cornell University Space Sciences Bldg . . . . . Ithaca NY 14853 607-255-3735 255-8803 668
TF: 800-824-5419 ■ *Web:* www.naic.edu

NAICS (North American Industry Classification System)
US Census Bureau 4600 Silver Hill Rd . . . . . Washington DC 20233 301-763-4636 340-2
TF: 800-923-8282 ■ *Web:* www.census.gov/eos/www/naics

NAICU (NA of Independent Colleges & Universities)
1025 Connecticut Ave NW Ste 700 . . . . . Washington DC 20036 202-785-8866 835-0003 49-5
TF: 800-574-4243 ■ *Web:* www.naicu.edu

NAIFA (NA of Insurance & Financial Advisors)
2901 Telestar Ct . . . . . Falls Church VA 22042 703-770-8100 49-9
TF Sales: 877-866-2432 ■ *Web:* www.naifa.org

NAIGSO-AA (Native American Indian General Service Office of Alcoholics Anonymous)
PO Box 838 . . . . . Rogersville AL 35652 951-927-2626 48-21
Web: www.naigso-aa.org

NAIHC (National American Indian Housing Council)
122 C S NW Ste 350 . . . . . Washington DC 20001 202-789-1754 789-1758 49-7
TF: 800-284-9165 ■ *Web:* www.naihc.net

Naik Consulting Group p C
200 Metroplex Dr Ste 403 . . . . . Edison NJ 08817 732-777-0030 261
TF: 800-409-1547 ■ *Web:* www.naikgroup.com

NAIL 63 Eddy St . . . . . Providence RI 02903 401-331-6245 7
Web: nail.cc

Nailor Industries Inc 98 Toryork Rd . . . . . Toronto ON M9L1X6 416-744-3300 744-3360 610
Web: www.map-hvac.com

Nailor Industries of Texas Inc
4714 Winfield Rd . . . . . Houston TX 77039 281-590-1172 590-3086 202
Web: www.nailor.com

Nailpro Magazine 7628 Densmore Ave . . . . . Van Nuys CA 91406 818-782-7328 457-21
TF: 800-442-5667 ■ *Web:* www.nailpro.com

Nails Magazine 3520 Challenger St . . . . . Torrance CA 90503 310-533-2400 533-2507 457-21
TF: 888-624-5744 ■ *Web:* www.nailsmag.com

NAIMA (North American Insulation Manufacturers Assn)
44 Canal Ctr Plaza Ste 310 . . . . . Alexandria VA 22314 703-684-0084 684-0427 49-3
Web: insulationinstitute.org

Naimies Beauty Center Inc
12640 Riverside Dr . . . . . Valley Village CA 91607 818-655-9933 77
TF: 800-561-3357 ■ *Web:* www.naimies.com

Naismith Memorial Basketball Hall of Fame
1000 W Columbus Ave . . . . . Springfield MA 01105 413-781-6500 522
TF: 877-446-6752 ■ *Web:* www.hoophall.com

Najafi Cos LLC 2525 E Camelback Rd . . . . . Phoenix AZ 85016 602-476-0600 360-3
Web: najafi.com

Najarian Furniture Company Inc
17560 Rowland St . . . . . City of Industry CA 91748 626-839-8700 320
TF: 888-781-3088 ■ *Web:* www.najarianfurniture.com

Nakama Japanese Steakhouse
1611 E Carson St . . . . . Pittsburgh PA 15203 412-381-6000 381-6643 671
Web: www.eatatnakama.com

Nakanishi Dental Laboratory Inc
2959 Northup Way . . . . . Bellevue WA 98004 425-822-2245 415
TF: 800-735-7231 ■ *Web:* www.nakanishidentallab.com

Nakase Bros Wholesale Nursery
9441 Krepp Dr . . . . . Huntington Beach CA 92646 714-962-6604 292
TF: 800-747-4388 ■ *Web:* www.nakasebros.com

Nakato 1776 Cheshire Bridge Rd NE . . . . . Atlanta GA 30324 404-873-6582 874-7897 671
Web: www.nakatorestaurant.com

Naked Oyster Bistro & Raw Bar
410 Main St . . . . . Hyannis MA 02601 508-778-6500 671
Web: www.nakedoyster.com

Nakina Systems Inc 80 Hines Rd Ste 200 . . . . . Ottawa ON K2K2T8 613-254-7351 254-7352 225
TF: 877-625-4627 ■ *Web:* www.nakinasystems.com

Nakisa Inc 733 Cathcart . . . . . Montreal QC H3B1M6 514-228-2000 177
Web: www.nakisa.com

Naknek Electric Assn Inc 1 School Rd . . . . . Naknek AK 99633 907-246-4261 245

NAL 10416 Investment Cir . . . . . Rancho Cordova CA 95670 916-361-0555 192
TF: 800-774-9555 ■ *Web:* www.nal1.com

Nalco Co 1601 W Diehl Rd . . . . . Naperville IL 60563 630-305-1000 305-2900 145
TF: 800-288-0879 ■ *Web:* www.nalco.com

Nalco Real Estate Corp
24595 Groesbeck Hwy . . . . . Warren MI 48089 586-775-8200 191-3

NALF (North American Limousin Foundation)
7383 S Alton Way Ste 100 . . . . . Englewood CO 80112 303-220-1693 220-1884 48-2
TF: 888-320-8747 ■ *Web:* www.nalf.org

Nalley Lexus Smyrna 2750 Cobb Pkwy SE . . . . . Smyrna GA 30080 877-454-4206 57
TF: 877-454-4206 ■ *Web:* www.nalleylexussmyrna.com

Nalpro Business Solutions LLC
Brier Hill Ct Bldg C . . . . . East Brunswick NJ 08816 732-390-1400 261
TF: 888-868-6360 ■ *Web:* www.nalpro.com

NALS - Assn for Legal Professionals
8159 E 41st St . . . . . Tulsa OK 74145 918-582-5188 582-5907 49-10
Web: www.nals.org

NAMA (National Automatic Merchandising Assn)
20 N Wacker Dr Ste 3500 . . . . . Chicago IL 60606 312-346-0370 704-4140 49-18
Web: www.namanow.org

NAMA (North American Millers Assn)
600 Maryland Ave SW Ste 825-W . . . . . Washington DC 20024 202-484-2200 488-7416 49-6
TF: 800-633-5137 ■ *Web:* www.namamillers.org

NAMA (National Agri-Marketing Assn)
11020 King St Ste 205 . . . . . Overland Park KS 66210 913-491-6500 491-6502 49-18
TF: 800-530-5646 ■ *Web:* www.nama.org

Nama Sushi Bar 506 S Gay St . . . . . Knoxville TN 37902 865-633-8539 739-5819* 671
*Fax Area Code: 615 ■ *Web:* www.namasushibar.com

Namaste Indian Cuisine
6300 NE 117th Ave . . . . . Vancouver WA 98662 360-891-5857 891-5906 671
Web: hstrial-namasteindiac.homestead.com/index.html

NAMCO BANDAI Holdings (USA) Inc
5551 Katella Ave . . . . . Cypress CA 90630 714-816-9500 514
Web: www.namcobandai.com

Name Brands Inc 7215 S Memorial Dr . . . . . Tulsa OK 74133 918-307-0289 157-2
Web: www.halfofhalf.com

Name Maker Inc
4450 Commerce Cir PO Box 43821 . . . . . Atlanta GA 30336 404-691-2237 691-7711 745 5
TF: 800-241-2890 ■ *Web:* www.namemaker.com

Name.com LLC 2500 E Second Ave 2nd Fl . . . . . Denver CO 80206 720-249-2374 399-3167* 396
*Fax Area Code: 303 ■ *Web:* www.name.com

Namecheap Inc
11400 W Olympic Blvd Ste 200 . . . . . Los Angeles CA 90064 310-259-3259 224
Web: www.namecheap.com

Nameplate & Panel Technology
387 Gundersen Dr . . . . . Carol Stream IL 60188 630-690-9360 627
TF: 800-833-8397 ■ *Web:* www.nptec.com

NAMG (North American Membership Group Inc)
12301 Whitewater Dr . . . . . Minnetonka MN 55343 952-936-9333 366
Web: www.namginc.com

Namgis First Nation 49 Atli St . . . . . Alert Bay BC V0N1A0 250-974-5556 138
TF: 888-962-6447 ■ *Web:* www.namgis.bc.ca

NAMI (National Alliance on Mental Illness)
3803 N Fairfax Dr Ste 100 . . . . . Arlington VA 22203 703-524-7600 524-9094 48-17
TF: 800-950-6264 ■ *Web:* www.nami.org

Nami 251 N First Ave Ste 100 . . . . . Minneapolis MN 55401 612-333-1999 333-7449 671

NAMM - International Music Products Assn
5790 Armada Dr . . . . . Carlsbad CA 92008 760-438-8001 438-7327 49-18
TF: 800-767-6266 ■ *Web:* www.namm.org

Nammo Inc 2000 N 14th St Ste 250 . . . . . Arlington VA 22201 703-524-6100 268
Web: www.nammoinc.com

NAMP (North American Meat Processors Assn)
1910 Assn Dr . . . . . Reston VA 20191 703-758-1900 49-6
TF: 800-527-4723 ■ *Web:* meatassociation.com

Nampa Chamber of Commerce
315 11th Ave S . . . . . Nampa ID 83651 208-466-4641 466-4677 139
Web: www.nampa.com

Nampa Public Library (NPL) 215 12th Ave S . . . . . Nampa ID 83651 208-468-5800 434-3

NAMS (North American Menopause Society, The)
5900 Landerbrook Dr Ste 390 . . . . . Mayfield Heights OH 44124 440-442-7550 442-2660 49-8
Web: www.menopause.org

Nan Thai 1350 Spring St NW . . . . . Atlanta GA 30309 404-870-9933 870-9955 671
Web: www.nanfinedining.com

Nan Ya Plastics Corporation America
9 Peach Tree Hill Rd . . . . . Livingston NJ 07039 973-992-2090 601
Web: www.npcam.com

NANA Development Corp
909 W Ninth Ave . . . . . Anchorage AK 99501 907-265-4100 194
Web: www.nana-dev.com

NANA Regional Corporation Inc
1001 E Benson Blvd . . . . . Kotzebue AK 99752 907-442-3301 539
TF: 800-478-3301 ■ *Web:* www.nana.com

Nana Wall Systems Inc
707 Redwood Hwy . . . . . Mill Valley CA 94941 415-383-3148 499
TF: 800-873-5673 ■ *Web:* www.nanawall.com

Nana's 2514 University Dr . . . . . Durham NC 27707 919-493-8545 403-8487 671
TF: 800-246-5262 ■ *Web:* www.nanasdurham.com

Nana's Pasta House
1223 Springbrook Ave . . . . . Moosic PA 18507 570-457-9612 671
Web: www.nanaspastahouse.com

Nanaimo Port Authority
104 Front St PO Box 131 . . . . . Nanaimo BC V9R5H7 250-753-4146 753-4099 618
Web: www.npa.ca

Nanaimo Regional General Hospital
1200 Dufferin Crescent . . . . . Nanaimo BC V9S2B7 250-755-7691 374-2

Nanamed LLC 157 Veterans Dr . . . . . Northvale NJ 07647 201-383-1101 475
Web: www.nanamed.com

Nanavati Consulting Inc
109 Longfellow Dr . . . . . Millersville MD 21108 410-421-5184 396
Web: www.nanavaticonsulting.com

Nance County
209 Esther St PO Box 338 . . . . . Fullerton NE 68638 308-536-2331 536-2742 338
Web: www.co.nance.ne.us

Nance International Inc
2915 Milam St . . . . . Beaumont TX 77701 409-838-6127 664
TF: 877-626-2322 ■ *Web:* nanceinternational.com

Nanco-Nancy Sales Company Inc
22 Willow St . . . . . Chelsea MA 02150 617-884-1700 360-3

Nancy Bailey & Associates Inc
4253 Loch Highland Pkwy NE . . . . . Roswell GA 30075 678-352-1000 195

Nancy Carol Roberts Memorial Library
100 Martin Luther King Junior Pkwy . . . . . Brenham TX 77833 979-337-7201 434-3
Web: cityofbrenham.org

Nancy Chang 372 Chandler St . . . . . Worcester MA 01602 508-752-8899 798-6688 671
Web: www.nancychang.com

Nancy Glass Productions Inc
211 Rock Hill Rd Ste 201 . . . . . Bala Cynwyd PA 19004 610-668-1668 668-1687 514
Web: www.nancyglassproductions.com

Nancy Hoffman Gallery 520 W 27th St . . . . . New York NY 10001 212-966-6676 334-5078 42
Web: www.nancyhoffmangallery.com

Phone | Fax | Class

Nancy Lake State Recreation Area
7278 E Bogard Rd. Wasilla AK 99654 907-745-3975 565
Web: dnr.alaska.gov/parks/units/nancylk/nancylk.htm
Nancy's Pizza 7929 W 171st St. Tinley Park IL 60477 708-614-6100 670
Web: www.nancyspizza.com
Nancy's Specialty Foods
6500 Overlake Pl Newark CA 94560 510-494-1100 123
Web: www.nancys.com
Nanka Seimen Co 3030 Leonis Blvd. Vernon CA 90058 323-585-9967 296-31
NANN (NA of Neonatal Nurses)
4700 West Lake Ave Glenview IL 60025 847-375-3660 375-6491 49-8
TF: 800-451-3795 ■ *Web:* www.nann.org
NanOasis Technologies Inc
4677 Meade St Ste 210 Richmond CA 94804 510-215-0186 612
NanoBio Corp 2311 Green Rd Ste A. Ann Arbor MI 48105 734-302-4000 668
Web: www.nanobio.com
Nanocopoeia Inc
1246 W University Ave Ste 463 St Paul MN 55104 651-209-1184 231
Web: www.nanocopeia.com
Nanohmics Inc 6201 E Oltorf St Austin TX 78741 512-389-9990 261
Web: nanohmics.com
NanoHorizons Inc
270 Rolling Ridge Dr Ste 100 Bellefonte PA 16823 814-355-4700 162
TF: 866-584-6235 ■ *Web:* www.nanohorizons.com
Nanolab Technologies Inc
1708 McCarthy Blvd. Milpitas CA 95035 408-433-3320 743
Web: www.nanolabtechnologies.com
Nanometrics Inc 1550 Buckeye Dr. Milpitas CA 95035 408-545-6000 232-5910 472
NASDAQ: NANO ■ *TF:* 800-553-6546 ■ *Web:* www.nanometrics.com
Nanonation Inc 301 S 13th St Ste 700 Lincoln NE 68508 402-323-6266 177
TF: 866-843-6266 ■ *Web:* www.nanonation.net
Nanophase Technologies Corp
1319 Marquette Dr Romeoville IL 60446 630-771-6700 771-0825 145
OTC: NANX ■ *Web:* www.nanophase.com
NanoScreen
4401 Piggly Wiggly Dr Ste 1000 N Charleston SC 29405 843-881-8841 881-1956 582
Web: www.automatedliquidhandlers.com
Nanotechnology Research & Education Ctr
University of S Florida College of Engineering
4202 E Fowler Ave Tampa FL 33620 813-974-3780 974-3610 743
Web: www.nrec.usf.edu
Nanotechnology Research Ctr
Georgia Institute of Technology
791 Atlantic Dr. Atlanta GA 30332 404-894-5100 894-5028 668
TF: 800-424-9300 ■ *Web:* ien.gatech.edu/nrc-transition-page
Nanovea 6 Morgan Ste 156 Irvine CA 92618 949-461-9292 407
Web: nanovea.com
Nanowave Technologies Inc
425 Horner Ave. Etobicoke ON M8W4W3 416-252-5602 252-7077 647
Web: www.nanowavetech.com
Nansemond Insurance Agency Inc
453 W Washington St. Suffolk VA 23434 757-539-3421 390
Web: nansemondins.com
Nantahala Outdoor Center Inc
13077 Hwy 19 W Bryson City NC 28713 800-232-7238 239
TF: 800-232-7238 ■ *Web:* www.noc.com
Nanticoke Memorial Hospital
801 Middleford Rd Seaford DE 19973 302-629-6611 374-3
TF: 800-222-2189 ■ *Web:* www.nanticoke.org
Nantucket Accommodations
2 Windy Way. Nantucket MA 02554 508-228-9559 901-4032 376
TF: 866-743-3330 ■ *Web:* nantucketaccommodations.com
Nantucket Bank 104 Pleasant St. Nantucket MA 02554 508-228-0580 70
TF: 800-533-9313 ■ *Web:* www.nantucketbank.com
Nantucket County 16 Broad St. Nantucket MA 02554 508-228-7216 325-5313 338
Web: www.nantucket-ma.gov
Nantze Springs Inc 156 W Carroll St Dothan AL 36301 334-794-4218 297-11
Web: www.nantzesprings.com
Nanuet Public Library 149 Church St Nanuet NY 10954 845-623-4281 435
TF: 800-272-3900 ■ *Web:* www.nanuetlibrary.org
Nanz & Kraft Florists Inc
141 Breckenridge Ln. Louisville KY 40207 502-897-6551 897-2082 292
TF: 800-897-6551 ■ *Web:* www.nanzandkraft.com
NAO Inc 1284 E Sedgley Ave. Philadelphia PA 19134 215-743-5300 743-3018 18
TF Cust Svc: 800-523-3495 ■ *Web:* www.nao.com
Naomi Taylor-Kenney Insurance Inc
4322 W El Prado Blvd. Tampa FL 33629 813-902-8300 390
Web: agents.allstate.com
NAP (NA of Parliamentarians)
213 S Main St. Independence MO 64050 816-833-3892 833-3893 49-12
TF: 888-627-2929 ■ *Web:* www.parliamentarians.org
Nap I Inc 2154 W Northwest Hwy Dallas TX 75220 972-401-7488 4
Web: www.napiinc.com
NAP Windows & Doors Ltd
2150 Enterprise Way. Kelowna BC V1Y6H7 250-762-5343 601
TF: 888-762-5311 ■ *Web:* www.napwindows.com
NAPA (National Automotive Parts Assn)
2999 Circle 75 Pkwy. Atlanta GA 30339 770-953-1700 61
TF: 800-538-6272 ■ *Web:* genpt.com
Napa Chamber of Commerce 1556 First St Napa CA 94559 707-226-7455 226-1171 139
TF: 877-807-2249 ■ *Web:* napachamber.com
Napa City-County Library 580 Coombs St Napa CA 94559 707-253-4241 253-4615 434-3
TF: 877-848-7030 ■ *Web:* countyofnapa.org
Napa County 1195 Third St Ste 310. Napa CA 94559 707-253-4421 253-4176 338
TF: 877-279-2976 ■ *Web:* www.countyofnapa.org
Napa Networks Inc
245 Stafford Rd West Ste 202 Ottawa ON K2H9E8 613-248-3417 463
TF: 888-641-1113 ■ *Web:* www.talentmap.com
Napa Printing & Graphics Center Inc
630 Airpark Rd Ste D Napa CA 94558 707-257-6555 627
TF: 800-984-9661 ■ *Web:* www.napaprinting.com
Napa Recycling & Waste Services (NRWS)
820 Levitin Way PO Box 239 Napa CA 94559 707-256-3500 256-3565 804
TF: 800-561-3357 ■ *Web:* www.naparecycling.com
Napa River Inn 500 Main St Napa CA 94559 707-251-8500 251-8504 379
TF: 877-251-8500 ■ *Web:* www.napariverinn.com
Napa State Hospital
2100 Napa-Vallejo Hwy Napa CA 94558 707-253-5000 253-5513 374-5
TF: 866-327-4762 ■ *Web:* www.dsh.ca.gov

Napa Valley College
2277 Napa-Vallejo Hwy Napa CA 94558 707-256-7000 253-3064 162
TF: 800-826-1077 ■ *Web:* www.napavalley.edu
Napa Valley Conference & Visitors Bureau
600 Main St Napa CA 94559 707-251-5895 206
TF: 855-847-6272 ■ *Web:* www.visitnapavalley.com
Napa Valley Register 1615 Second St. Napa CA 94559 707-226-3711 532-2
Web: www.napanews.com
Napaba 1612 K St NW Ste 1400 Washington DC 20006 202-775-9555 533
Web: www.napaba.org
NAPAC Inc 229 Southbridge St. Worcester MA 01608 508-363-4411 609
Web: www.napacinc.com
NAPCO (North American Publishing Co)
1500 Springarden St 12th Fl. Philadelphia PA 19130 215-238-5300 238-5457 637-9
TF: 800-627-2689 ■ *Web:* www.napco.com
NAPCO 2400 Cantrell Rd Ste 116 Little Rock AR 72202 501-374-5884 559
NAPCO Inc 120 Trojan Ave Sparta NC 28675 800-854-8621 86
TF: 800-854-8621 ■ *Web:* www.napcousa.com
NAPCO International Inc
11055 Excelsior Blvd Hopkins MN 55343 952-931-2400 931-2402 807
Web: www.napcointl.com
NAPCO Precast LLC 6949 Low Bid Ln San Antonio TX 78250 210-509-9100 509-9111 183
TF: 800-332-1440 ■ *Web:* www.napcosa.com
NAPCO Security Systems Inc
333 Bayview Ave. Amityville NY 11701 631-842-9400 842-9137 692
NASDAQ: NSSC ■ *TF:* 800-645-9445 ■ *Web:* www.napcosecurity.com
Napco Steel Inc 1800 Arthur Dr West Chicago IL 60185 630-293-1900 293-0881 492
TF: 800-292-8010 ■ *Web:* www.napcosteel.com
NAPEO (NA of Professional Employer Organizations)
707 N St Asaph St Alexandria VA 22314 703-836-0466 836-0976 49-12
Web: www.napeo.org
Naperville Area Chamber of Commerce
55 S Main St Ste 351 Naperville IL 60540 630-355-4141 355-8335 139
TF: 800-455-5600 ■ *Web:* www.naperville.net
Naperville Public Libraries
200 W Jefferson Ave. Naperville IL 60540 630-961-4100 434-3
Web: www.naperville-lib.org
NAPF (Nuclear Age Peace Foundation)
1187 Coast Village Rd Ste 1 PO Box 121 Santa Barbara CA 93108 805-965-3443 568-0466 48-5
NAPH (America's Essential Hospitals)
1301 Pennsylvania Ave NW Ste 950 Washington DC 20004 202-585-0100 585-0101 49-8
Web: essentialhospitals.org
Napili Kai Beach Club
5900 Honoapiilani Rd. Lahaina HI 96761 808-669-6271 669-5740 669
TF: 800-367-5030 ■ *Web:* www.napilikai.com
Naples Bay Resort 1500 Fifth Ave S. Naples FL 34102 239-530-1199 669
TF: 866-605-1199 ■ *Web:* www.naplesbayresort.com
Naples Beach Hotel & Golf Club
851 Gulf Shore Blvd N Naples FL 34102 239-261-2222 261-7380 669
TF: 800-237-7600 ■ *Web:* www.naplesbeachhotel.com
Naples Botanical Garden
4820 Bayshore Dr. Naples FL 34112 239-643-7275 649-7306 97
TF: 877-433-1874 ■ *Web:* www.naplesgarden.org
Naples Daily News 1100 Immokalee Rd Naples FL 34102 239-213-6000 263-4816 532-2
TF: 800-404-7343 ■ *Web:* www.naplesnews.com
Naples Italian Restaurant
5500 Kingston Pk. Knoxville TN 37919 865-584-5033 671
Web: naplesitalianrestaurant.net
Naples Municipal Airport
160 Aviation Dr N Naples FL 34104 239-643-0733 643-4084 27
Web: www.flynaples.com
Naples Museum of Art
5833 Pelican Bay Blvd Naples FL 34108 239-597-1111 520
TF: 800-597-1900 ■ *Web:* artisnaples.org
Naples Ristorante e Pizzeria
1510 Disneyland Dr Anaheim CA 92802 714-776-6200 671
Web: www.patinagroup.com
Naples/Fort Myers Greyhound Track
10601 Bonita Beach Rd Bonita Springs FL 34135 239-992-2411 642
TF: 800-373-3647 ■ *Web:* www.naplesfortmyersdogs.com
Napoleon Spring Works 111 Weires Dr. Archbold OH 43502 419-445-1010 234
TF: 800-338-5399 ■ *Web:* www.lynx-nsw.com
Napoleon/Henry County Chamber of Commerce
611 N Perry St Napoleon OH 43545 419-592-1786 592-4945 139
TF: 800-322-6849 ■ *Web:* henrycountychamber.org
Napoli Italian Restaurant
24960 Redlands Blvd Loma Linda CA 92354 909-796-3770 478-7756 671
Web: napoli-italian.com
Napolitano Grace (Rep D - CA)
1610 Longworth Washington DC 20515 202-225-5256 225-0027 342-2
Web: napolitano.house.gov
Nappi Distributors 615 Main St Gorham ME 04038 207-887-8200 186
Web: www.nappidistributors.com
NAPUS (United Postmasters and Managers of America)
8 Herbert St Alexandria VA 22305 703-683-9027 683-6820 49-7
Web: www.napus.org
NAPWA (National Association of People With AIDS)
8401 Colesville Rd Ste 505 Silver Spring MD 20910 240-247-0880 48-17
TF: 866-846-9366
NARA (National Archives & Records Administration)
8601 Adelphi Rd. College Park MD 20740 866-272-6272 837-0483* 340-20
**Fax Area Code:* 301 ■ *TF:* 866-272-6272 ■ *Web:* www.archives.gov
Nara Sushi
1115 Independence Blvd Ste 104 Virginia Beach VA 23455 757-456-5111 490-0109 671
Web: www.narasushi.com
Narada Productions Inc
4650 N Port Washington Rd Milwaukee WI 53212 414-961-8350 657
NARAL Pro-Choice America
1156 15th St NW Ste 700 Washington DC 20005 202-973-3000 973-3096 48-8
Web: www.prochoiceamerica.org
NARBHA (Northern Arizona Regional Behavioral Health Authority Inc)
1300 S Yale St Flagstaff AZ 86001 928-774-7128 49-15
TF: 877-923-1400 ■ *Web:* www.narbha.org
Narcolepsy Network Inc
46 Union Dr Ste A212 North Kingstown RI 02852 401-667-2523 633-6567 48-17
TF: 888-292-6522 ■ *Web:* www.narcolepsynetwork.org
Narda-MITEQ 100 Davids Dr Hauppauge NY 11788 631-436-7400 436-7430 253
Web: www.miteq.com

Phone Fax Class

Nardin Academy 795 Main St .... Buffalo NY 14203 716-881-6262 148
Web: www.frcdb.org

Nardini Fire Equipment Company Inc
405 County Rd E W .... Saint Paul MN 55126 651-483-6631 483-6945 679
TF: 888-627-3464 ■ *Web:* www.nardinifire.com

Nardone Bros Baking Company Inc
420 New Commerce Blvd .... Wilkes-Barre PA 18706 570-823-0141 823-2581 296-36
TF: 800-822-5320 ■ *Web:* www.nardonebros.com

NAREL (National Air & Radiation Environmental Laboratory)
540 S Morris Ave 540 S Morris Ave .... Montgomery AL 36115 334-270-3400 270-3454 743
Web: www.epa.gov

NARF (Native American Rights Fund)
1506 Broadway .... Boulder CO 80302 303-447-8760 443-7776 49-10
TF: 888-280-0726 ■ *Web:* www.narf.org

NARH (North Adams Regional Hospital)
71 Hospital Ave .... North Adams MA 01247 413-664-5000 374-3
Web: www.nbhealth.org

NARIC (National Rehabilitation Information Ctr)
8400 Corporate Dr Ste 500 .... Landover MD 20785 301-459-5900 459-4263 48-17
TF: 800-346-2742 ■ *Web:* www.naric.com

Narita Trading Company Inc
24 Park Ave .... Clifton NJ 07014 718-628-4382 290
Web: www.naritatrading.com

Naropa University 2130 Arapahoe Ave .... Boulder CO 80302 303-444-0202 546-3536 166
TF: 800-772-6951 ■ *Web:* www.naropa.edu

Narragansett Bay Commission
1 Service Rd .... Providence RI 02905 401-461-8848 539
Web: www.narrabay.com

Narragansett Improvement Co
223 Allens Ave .... Providence RI 02903 401-331-7420 351-6444 653
Web: www.nicori.com

Narricot Industries LP
928 Jaymore Rd Ste C150 .... SouthHampton PA 18966 215-322-3900 745-5

Narrow Fabric Industries Corp
701 Reading Ave .... Reading PA 19611 610-376-2891 745-5
TF: 877-523-6373 ■ *Web:* readingeagle.com

Narrow Gate Foundation
242 Dry Prong Rd .... Williamsport TN 38487 931-583-0633 305
Web: narrowgate.org

NARSA (National Automotive Radiator Service Assn)
3000 Village Run Rd Ste 103 221 .... Wexford PA 15090 724-799-8415 799-8416 49-21
Web: www.narsa.org

Nartron Corp 5000 N US 131 .... Reed City MI 49677 231-832-5525 832-3876 248
Web: www.nartron.com

Narus Inc 570 Maude Ct .... Sunnyvale CA 94085 408-215-4300 178-11

NAS (National Audubon Society)
225 Varick St .... New York NY 10014 212-979-3000 979-3188 48-13
TF: 800-274-4201 ■ *Web:* www.audubon.org

NAS Recruitment Communications
9700 Rockside Rd Ste 170 .... Cleveland OH 44125 866-627-7327 4
TF: 866-627-7327 ■ *Web:* www.nasrecruitment.com

NASA (National Aeronautics & Space Administration)
300 E St SW .... Washington DC 20546 202-358-0001 358-3469 340-20
TF: 800-639-2422 ■ *Web:* www.nasa.gov

NASA TV 300 E St SW .... Washington DC 20546 202-358-0000 358-4338 740
TF: 877-546-1574 ■ *Web:* www.nasa.gov

NASAA (North American Securities Administrators Assn)
750 First St NE Ste 1140 .... Washington DC 20002 202-737-0900 783-3571 49-2
TF: 800-222-1253 ■ *Web:* www.nasaa.org

NASAA (National Assembly of State Arts Agencies)
1029 Vermont Ave NW 2nd Fl .... Washington DC 20005 202-347-6352 737-0526 49-7
Web: www.nasaa-arts.org

NASB (North American Savings Bank)
12520 S 71 Hwy .... Grandview MO 64030 816-765-2200 70
TF: 800-677-6272 ■ *Web:* www.nasb.com

NASB Financial Inc 12520 S 71 Hwy .... Grandview MO 64030 816-765-2200 316-4504 360-2
NASDAQ: NASB ■ *TF:* 800-677-6272 ■ *Web:* www.nasb.com

NASBE (NA of State Boards of Education)
333 John Carlyle St Ste 530 .... Alexandria VA 22314 703-684-4000 49-5
TF: 800-368-5023 ■ *Web:* www.nasbe.org

NASBIC PAC 1100 H St NW Ste 610 .... Washington DC 20005 202-628-5055 628-5080 615
TF: 800-471-6153 ■ *Web:* www.sbia.org

NASBP (NA of Surety Bond Producers)
1140 19th St NW Ste 800 .... Washington DC 20036 202-686-3700 686-3656 49-9
Web: www.nasbp.org

NASCAR (NA for Stock Car Auto Racing)
1801 W International Speedway Blvd .... Daytona Beach FL 32114 704-348-7131 48-22
Web: www.nascar.com

NASCAR Hall of Fame
400 E Martin Luther King Jr Blvd .... Charlotte NC 28202 704-654-4400 522
TF: 800-745-3000 ■ *Web:* www.nascarhall.com

NASCAR SpeedPark 1545 Pkwy .... Sevierville TN 37862 865-908-5500 32
Web: www.nascarspeedpark.com

Nasco Aircraft Brake Inc
13300 Estrella Ave .... Gardena CA 90248 310-532-4430 532-6014 22
Web: www.nascoaircraft.com

NASCO International Inc
901 Janesville Ave .... Fort Atkinson WI 53538 920-563-2446 563-8296 459
TF Orders: 800-558-9595 ■ *Web:* www.enasco.com

NASDAQ OMX Commodities Clearing Co
311 S Wacker Dr Ste 1750 .... Chicago IL 60606 312-568-5900 690

Nasdaq Stock Market Inc 165 Broadway .... New York NY 10006 212-401-8700 691
Web: www.nasdaq.com

NASFAA (National Assn of Student Financial Aid Administrators)
1101 Connecticut Ave Ste 1100 .... Washington DC 20036 202-785-0453 785-1487 49-5
TF: 800-877-8339 ■ *Web:* www.nasfaa.org

Nash Brick Co (A Corp)
532 Nash Brick Rd .... Enfield NC 27823 252-443-4965 751
Web: www.nashbrick.com

Nash Chevrolet Co
630 Scenic Hwy .... Lawrenceville GA 30046 678-317-2797 516
Web: nashchevy.com

Nash Community College
PO Box 7488 .... Rocky Mount NC 27804 252-443-4011 162
Web: www.nashcc.edu

Nash Correctional Institution
2869 US 64 Alt PO Box 600 .... Nashville NC 27856 252-459-4455 459-7728 213
Web: www.ncdps.gov

Phone Fax Class

Nash County
120 W Washington St Ste 3072 .... Nashville NC 27856 252-459-9800 459-9817 338
Web: www.co.nash.nc.us

Nash Entertainment
1438 N Gower St Ste 35 .... Los Angeles CA 90028 323-993-7384 514
Web: www.nashentertainment.com

Nash Finch Co 7600 France Ave S .... Minneapolis MN 55440 952-832-0534 297-8
NASDAQ: NAFC ■ *Web:* spartannash.com

NASH FM 92.3
201 St Charles Ave Ste 201 .... New Orleans LA 70170 504-581-7002 645-110
TF: 800-324-1108 ■ *Web:* www.nashfm923.com

Nash Health Care Systems (NHCS)
2460 Curtis Ellis Dr .... Rocky Mount NC 27804 252-443-8000 374-3
Web: www.nhcs.org

Nash Produce Co
6160 S N Carolina 58 .... Nashville NC 27856 252-443-6011 10-11
TF: 800-334-3032 ■ *Web:* www.nashproduce.com

Nasher Museum of Art at Duke University
2001 Campus Dr Duke University .... Durham NC 27701 919-684-5135 681-8624 520
TF: 800-221-1212 ■ *Web:* www.duke.edu

Nasher Sculpture Ctr 2001 Flora St .... Dallas TX 75201 214-242-5100 242-5155 50-2
Web: www.nashersculpturecenter.org

NASH-FM 97.3 4143 109th St .... Urbandale IA 50322 515-331-9200 645
Web: www.nashfm973.com

Nashoba Regional School District Inc
50 Mechanic St .... Bolton MA 01740 978-779-0539 685
Web: www.nrsd.net

Nashoba Valley Chamber of Commerce
2 Shaker Rd Ste B200 .... Shirley MA 01464 978-772-6976 425-5764 139
Web: www.nvcoc.com

Nashotah House 2777 Mission Rd .... Nashotah WI 53058 262-646-6500 646-6504 167-3
Web: www.nashotah.edu

Nashua Corp 11 Trafalgar Sq 2nd Fl .... Nashua NH 03063 603-880-2323 552-1
TF: 800-430-7488 ■ *Web:* www.nashua.com

Nashua Homes of Idaho Inc PO Box 170008 .... Boise ID 83717 208-345-0222 505
TF: 855-766-0222 ■ *Web:* www.nashuabuilders.com

Nashua Public Library 2 Ct St .... Nashua NH 03060 603-589-4600 594-3457 434-3
TF: 800-424-8580 ■ *Web:* www.nashualibrary.org

Nashville & Davidson County Metropolitan City Hall
100 Metropolitan Courthouse .... Nashville TN 37201 615-862-6000 862-6040 337
Web: www.nashville.gov

Nashville Ballet 3630 Redmon St .... Nashville TN 37209 615-297-2966 297-9972 573-1
TF: 800-410-4216 ■ *Web:* www.nashvilleballet.com

Nashville Business Journal
1800 Church St Ste 300 .... Nashville TN 37203 615-248-2222 248-6246 457-5
Web: www.bizjournals.com

Nashville Chamber of Commerce
211 Commerce St Ste 100 .... Nashville TN 37201 615-743-3000 139
Web: www.nashvillechamber.com

Nashville Convention & Visitors Bureau (NCVB)
150 Fourth Ave N Ste G250 .... Nashville TN 37219 615-259-4730 259-4126 206
TF: 800-657-6910 ■ *Web:* www.visitmusiccity.com

Nashville Convention Ctr
601 Commerce St .... Nashville TN 37203 615-742-2000 205
Web: www.nashvilleconventionctr.com

Nashville Dental Inc
1229 Northgate Business Pkwy .... Madison TN 37115 615-868-3911 475
TF: 800-441-3100 ■ *Web:* www.nashvilledental.com

Nashville Display 306 Hartmann Dr .... Lebanon TN 37087 615-743-2900 233
TF: 800-251-1150 ■ *Web:* www.nashvilledisplay.com

Nashville Film Festival
161 Rains Ave .... Nashville TN 37203 615-742-2500 282
Web: www.nashvillefilmfestival.org

Nashville General Hospital
1818 Albion St .... Nashville TN 37208 615-341-4000 341-4493 374-3
TF: 800-318-2596 ■ *Web:* nashville.gov/hospital-authority.aspx

Nashville Jet 635 Hangar Ln .... Nashville TN 37217 615-933-7894 13
Web: www.nashvillejetcharters.com

Nashville Municipal Auditorium
417 Fourth Ave N .... Nashville TN 37201 615-862-6390 862-6394 572
Web: www.nashville.gov

Nashville National Cemetery
1420 Gallatin Rd S .... Madison TN 37115 615-860-0086 860-8691 136
Web: www.cem.va.gov

Nashville Office Interiors
1621 Church St .... Nashville TN 37203 615-329-1811 321
TF: 877-342-0294 ■ *Web:* www.noifurniture.com

Nashville Predators 501 Broadway .... Nashville TN 37203 615-770-2355 770-2341 716
Web: predators.nhl.com

Nashville Public Library
615 Church St .... Nashville TN 37219 615-862-5800 434-3
Web: www.library.nashville.org

Nashville Ready Mix Inc
605 Cowan St .... Nashville TN 37207 615-256-2071 135
Web: www.nashvillereadymix.net

Nashville Repertory Theatre
161 Rains Ave .... Nashville TN 37203 615-244-4878 349-3222 573-4
Web: nashvillerep.org

Nashville Rescue Mission
639 Lafayette St .... Nashville TN 37203 615-255-2475 48-20
Web: www.nashvillerescuemission.org

Nashville Rubber & Gasket Company Inc
1900 Elm Tree Dr .... Nashville TN 37210 615-883-0030 791
TF: 800-686-5801 ■ *Web:* www.nashvillerubber.com

Nashville Scene
210 12th Ave S Ste 100 .... Nashville TN 37203 615-244-7989 532-5
Web: www.nashvillescene.com

Nashville Shores Holdings LLC
4001 Bell Rd .... Hermitage TN 37076 615-889-7050 360-3
TF: 800-365-5996 ■ *Web:* www.nashvilleshores.com

Nashville State Community College (NSCC)
120 White Bridge Rd .... Nashville TN 37209 615-353-3333 353-3243* 800
**Fax: Admissions* ■ *TF:* 800-272-7363 ■ *Web:* www.nscc.edu

Nashville Steel Co
7211 Centennial Blvd .... Nashville TN 37209 615-350-7933 492
Web: www.nashvillesteel.com/profile.html

Nashville Tempered Glass Corp
1860 Air Ln Dr .... Nashville TN 37210 615-889-6350 330
Web: www.egpglass.com

Name / Address	City	State	Zip	Phone	Fax	Class
Nashville Wire Products Manufacturing Co 199 Polk Ave. *TF:* 800-448-2125 ■ *Web:* www.nashvillewire.com	Nashville	TN	37210	615-743-2500	242-4225	73
Nashville Zoo 3777 Nolensville Rd *TF:* 800-456-6847 ■ *Web:* www.nashvillezoo.org	Nashville	TN	37211	615-833-1534	333-0728	823
Nasiff Associates 841 County Rt 37 *TF:* 866-627-4332 ■ *Web:* nasiff.com	Central Square	NY	13036	315-676-2346		476
Nasland Engineering 4740 Rufner St. *Web:* www.nasland.com	San Diego	CA	92111	858-292-7770		261
NASMHPD (NA of State Mental Health Program Directors) 66 Canal Ctr Plaza Ste 302 *Web:* www.nasmhpd.org	Alexandria	VA	22314	703-739-9333	548-9517	49-7
Nasoft USA Inc 417 E Carmel St *Web:* www.nasoftusa.com	San Marcos	CA	92078	760-410-1210		177
Nason, Yeager, Gerson, White & Lioce PA 3001 PGA Blvd Ste 305 *Web:* nasonyeager.com	Palm Beach Gardens	FL	33410	561-686-3307		428
NASS (National Agricultural Statistics Service) 1400 Independence Ave SW *TF:* 800-727-9540 ■ *Web:* www.nass.usda.gov	Washington	DC	20250	202-720-2707		340-1
NASS (North American Spine Society) 7075 Veterans Blvd. *TF:* 877-774-6337 ■ *Web:* www.spine.org	Burr Ridge	IL	60527	630-230-3600		49-8
Nassal Co, The 415 W Kaley St. *Web:* www.nassal.com	Orlando	FL	32806	407-648-0400	648-0841	106
Nassau Community College 1 Education Dr *Web:* www.ncc.edu	Garden City	NY	11530	516-572-7500	572-9743	162
Nassau County PO Box 870. *TF:* 888-615-4398 ■ *Web:* www.nassauflpa.com	Fernandina Beach	FL	32035	904-491-7300	491-3629	338
Nassau County 240 Old Country Rd *TF:* 800-460-5657 ■ *Web:* www.nassaucountyny.gov	Mineola	NY	11501	516-571-2664	742-4099	338
Nassau County School District 1201 Atlantic Ave *Web:* www.edline.net	Fernandina Beach	FL	32034	904-491-9900		685
Nassau Financial Federal Credit Union 1325 Franklin Ave Ste 500 *TF:* 800-216-2328 ■ *Web:* www.nassaufinancial.org	Garden City	NY	11530	516-742-4900		219
Nassau Inn, The 10 Palmer Sq *Web:* www.nassauinn.com	Princeton	NJ	08542	609-921-7500	921-9385	379
Nassau Library System 900 Jerusalem Ave *Web:* www.nassaulibrary.org	Uniondale	NY	11553	516-292-8920	481-4777	434-3
Nassau Regional Off Track Betting Corp 220 Fulton Ave *Web:* www.nassauotb.com	Hempstead	NY	11550	516-572-2800		452
Nassau Tool Works Inc 34 Lamar St	West Babylon	NY	11704	631-643-5000		454
Nassau University Medical Ctr 2201 Hempstead Tpke *Web:* www.numc.edu	East Meadow	NY	11554	516-572-0123		374-3
Nassau Valley Vineyards 32165 Winery Way *TF:* 800-425-2355 ■ *Web:* www.nassauvalley.com	Lewes	DE	19958	302-645-9463	645-6666	50-7
Nassau Veterans Memorial Coliseum 1255 Hempstead Tpke *TF:* 800-745-3000 ■ *Web:* www.nycblive.com	Uniondale	NY	11553	516-794-9300	794-9389	720
Nasseo Inc 13660 N 94th Dr Ste D-7 *TF:* 866-207-8919 ■ *Web:* nasseo.com	Peoria	AZ	85381	866-207-8919		228
Nastos Construction Inc 1421 Kenilworth Ave NE *Web:* www.nastos.com	Washington	DC	20019	202-398-5500	398-5501	186
Nasuti & Hinkle 8101-A Glenbrook Rd *Web:* nasuti.com	Bethesda	MD	20814	301-222-0010		4
NASW News 750 First St NE Ste 700 *TF:* 800-227-3590 ■ *Web:* www.naswpress.org	Washington	DC	20002	202-408-8600	336-8312	457-16
NATA (National Air Transportation Assn) 4226 King St. *TF:* 800-808-6282 ■ *Web:* www.nata.aero	Alexandria	VA	22302	703-845-9000	845-8176	49-21
NATA (National Athletic Trainers Assn) 2952 N Stemmons Fwy Ste 200 *TF:* 800-879-6282 ■ *Web:* www.nata.org	Dallas	TX	75247	214-637-6282	637-2206	48-22
Natalia's 201 N Macon St. *Web:* natalias.net	Macon	GA	31210	478-741-1380		671
NatAlliance Securities 111 Congress Ave Ste 800 *Web:* www.natalliance.com	Austin	TX	78701	512-609-1700		690
NATCA (National Air Traffic Controllers Assn) 1325 Massachusetts Ave NW *TF:* 800-266-0895 ■ *Web:* www.natca.org	Washington	DC	20005	202-628-5451	628-5767	414
Natchaug State Forest c/o Mashamoquet Brook State Pk RFD 1 Wolf Den Rd. *Web:* www.ct.gov	Pomfret Center	CT	06259	860-928-6121		565
Natchez Convention & Visitors Bureau 640 S Canal St *TF:* 800-647-6724 ■ *Web:* www.visitnatchez.org	Natchez	MS	39120	601-446-6345		206
Natchez Convention Ctr 211 Main St *TF:* 888-475-9144 ■ *Web:* www.natchezconventioncenter.org	Natchez	MS	39120	601-442-5880		205
Natchez National Cemetery 41 Cemetery Rd *Web:* www.cem.va.gov	Natchez	MS	39120	601-445-4981	445-8815	136
Natchez National Historical Park 1 Melrose Montebello Pkwy *Web:* www.nps.gov/natc	Natchez	MS	39120	601-446-5790	442-9516	564
Natchez Newspapers Inc 503 N Canal St	Natchez	MS	39120	601-442-9101	442-7315	637-8
Natchez State Park 230-B Wickcliff Rd *Web:* www.mdwfp.com	Natchez	MS	39120	601-442-2658		565
Natchez Trace National Scenic Trail 2680 Natchez Trace Pkwy *TF:* 800-305-7417 ■ *Web:* www.nps.gov/natt	Tupelo	MS	38804	662-680-4025		564
Natchez Trace State Park 24845 Natchez Trace Rd *Web:* www.state.tn.us	Wildersville	TN	38388	731-968-3742		565
Natchez-Adams County Chamber of Commerce 108 S Commerce St *TF:* 800-647-6724 ■ *Web:* www.natchezchamber.com	Natchez	MS	39120	601-445-4611	445-9361	139
Natchitoches Area Chamber of Commerce 780 Front St Ste 101 *TF:* 877-646-6689 ■ *Web:* www.natchitocheschamber.com	Natchitoches	LA	71457	318-352-6894		139
Natchitoches Parish 200 Church St Ste 210 *Web:* npgov.org	Natchitoches	LA	71457	318-352-2714	352-2715	338
Natchitoches Parish Library 450 Second St *TF:* 800-327-1903 ■ *Web:* www.youseemore.com/natchitoches	Natchitoches	LA	71457	318-357-3280	357-7073	434-3
Natchitoches Regional Medical Center 501 Keyser Ave *TF:* 888-728-8383 ■ *Web:* www.natchitocheshospital.org	Natchitoches	LA	71457	318-214-4200		374-3
Natco 346 W Cerritos Ave *Web:* www.natcoglobal.com	Glendale	CA	91204	818-409-0019		258
Natco Products Corp 155 Brookside Ave	West Warwick	RI	02893	401-828-0300		131
NAT-COM Inc 2622 Audubon Rd *Web:* www.nat-com.com	Eagleville	PA	19403	610-666-7947		188-1
NATE (National Association of Tower Erectors) 8 Second St SE *TF:* 888-882-5865 ■ *Web:* natehome.com	Watertown	SD	57201	605-882-5865	886-5184	49-3
Natel Engineering Co Inc 9340 Owensmouth Ave *TF:* 800-590-5774 ■ *Web:* www.natelems.com	Chatsworth	CA	91311	818-734-6500		625
Natel Telecommunications Lc 907 W Burlington Ave. *Web:* www.natel.net	Fairfield	IA	52556	641-469-6220		225
Nathan Adelson Hospice 4141 Swenson St *Web:* www.nah.org	Las Vegas	NV	89119	702-733-0320		371
Nathan Assoc Inc 2101 Wilson Blvd Ste 1200 *Web:* www.nathaninc.com	Arlington	VA	22201	703-516-7700	351-6162	194
Nathan Bedford Forrest State Park 1825 Pilot Knob Rd *Web:* www.state.tn.us	Eva	TN	38333	731-584-6356		565
Nathan Boone Homestead State Historic Site 7850 N State Hwy V *Web:* www.mostateparks.com	Ash Grove	MO	65604	417-751-3266		565
Nathan Cummings Foundation 475 Tenth Ave 14th Fl. *Web:* www.nathancummings.org	New York	NY	10018	212-787-7300		305
Nathan D. Maier Consulting Engineers Inc 8080 Park Ln Two NorthPark Ste 600 *TF:* 800-527-4135 ■ *Web:* www.ndmce.com	Dallas	TX	75231	214-739-4741		261
Nathan Hale Inn & Conference Ctr 855 Bolton Rd. *Web:* www.nathanhaleinn.com	Storrs	CT	06268	860-427-7888	427-7850	379
Nathan Littauer Hospital & Nursing Home 99 E State St *TF:* 800-962-5660 ■ *Web:* www.nlh.org	Gloversville	NY	12078	518-773-5505		371
Nathan S Kline Institute for Psychiatric Research 140 Old Orangeburg Rd *Web:* www.rfmh.org/nki	Orangeburg	NY	10962	845-398-5500		668
Nathan Sommers Jacobs PC 2800 Post Oak Blvd 61st Fl *Web:* www.nathansommers.com	Houston	TX	77056	713-960-0303		41
Nathan's Famous Inc 1 Jericho Plaza 2nd Fl *NASDAQ: NATH* ■ *Web:* www.nathansfamous.com	Jericho	NY	11753	516-338-8500	338-7220	670
Nathaniel Russell House 51 Meeting St. *Web:* www.historiccharleston.org	Charleston	SC	29401	843-724-8481		50-3
Nathanson & Co 10 Minute Man Hl *Web:* nathansonandcompany.com	Westport	CT	06880	203-227-1816		445
Natick Junior Redmen 15 W St *Web:* www.natickma.gov/184/police-department	Natick	MA	01760	508-653-9900		717
Natick Mall 1245 Worcester St *Web:* www.natickmall.com	Natick	MA	01760	508-655-4800		460
Nation Consulting LLC 5027 W N Ave *Web:* www.nationconsulting.com	Milwaukee	WI	53208	414-344-1733		196
Nation Magazine 33 Irving Pl 8th Fl. *TF Cust Svc:* 800-333-8536 ■ *Web:* www.thenation.com	New York	NY	10003	212-209-5400	982-9000	457-17
Nation of Islam 7351 S Stony Island. *Web:* www.noi.org	Chicago	IL	60649	773-324-6000		48-20
National 4-H Council 7100 Connecticut Ave. *Web:* www.4-h.org	Chevy Chase	MD	20815	301-961-2800		459
National Aamco Dealers Assn 7316 Wisconsin Ave Ste 420	Bethesda	MD	20814	240-497-1500		474
National Able Network Inc 567 West Lake St Ste 1150 *Web:* www.nationalable.org	Chicago	IL	60661	312-994-4200	994-4201	260
National Abortion Federation (NAF) 1755 Massachusetts Ave NW *TF:* 800-772-9100 ■ *Web:* www.prochoice.org	Washington	DC	20036	202-667-5881	667-5890	49-8
National Academies 500 Fifth St NW. *TF:* 800-624-6242 ■ *Web:* www.nas.edu	Washington	DC	20001	202-334-2138	334-2158	49-19
National Academy Museum of Art 1083 Fifth Ave. *Web:* www.nationalacademy.org	New York	NY	10128	212-369-4880		520
National Academy of Education 500 Fifth St NW *Web:* www.naeducation.org	Washington	DC	20001	202-334-1947	334-2350	49-5
National Academy of Engineering 500 Fifth Ave. *Web:* www.nae.edu	Washington	DC	20001	202-334-2431	334-2290	49-19
National Academy of Public Administration 1600 K St Ste 400. *TF:* 800-883-3190 ■ *Web:* www.napawash.org	Washington	DC	20006	202-347-3190	393-0993	49-7
National Academy of Recording Arts & Sciences 3030 Olympic Blvd *TF:* 800-423-2017 ■ *Web:* www.grammy.com	Santa Monica	CA	90404	310-392-3777	392-2306	48-4
National Academy of Television Arts & Sciences 111 W 57th St Ste 600 *Web:* www.emmyonline.org	New York	NY	10019	212-586-8424	246-8129	48-4
National Academy Press 500 Fifth St NW **Fax:* Sales ■ *TF:* 800-624-6242 ■ *Web:* www.nap.edu	Washington	DC	20001	202-334-3313	334-2451*	637-2

Phone | Fax | Class

National Accrediting Agency for Clinical Laboratory Sciences (NAACLS)
8410 W Bryn Mawr Ave Ste 670 .... Chicago IL 60631 773-714-8880 714-8886 48-1
Web: www.naacls.org

National Accrediting Commission of Cosmetology Arts & Sciences (NACCAS)
4401 Ford Ave Ste 1300 .... Alexandria VA 22302 703-600-7600 379-2200 48-1
TF: 877-212-5752 ■ Web: www.naccas.org

National Acctg & Finance Council (NAFC)
American Trucking Assn 950 N Glebe Rd .... Arlington VA 22203 703-838-1700 49-1
TF: 800-517-7370 ■ Web: www.trucking.org

National Acoustics Inc 515 W 36th St .... New York NY 10001 212-695-1252 695-4539 189-9
TF: 800-468-7667 ■ Web: nationalacoustics.com

National Administrators Inc
2003 Jericho Tpke .... New Hyde Park NY 11040 516-348-7186 463
Web: www.fnainsurance.com

National Adoption Ctr
1500 Walnut St Ste 701 .... Philadelphia PA 19102 215-735-9988 735-9410 48-6
Web: www.adopt.org

National Adrenal Diseases Foundation (NADF)
505 Northern Blvd .... Great Neck NY 11021 516-487-4992 48-17
Web: www.nadf.us

National Aeronautic Assn
Hanger 7 1 S Smith Blvd Ste 202 .... Washington DC 20001 703-416-4888 48-22
TF: 800-644-9777 ■ Web: naa.aero

National Aeronautics & Space Administration (NASA)
300 E St SW .... Washington DC 20546 202-358-0001 358-3469 340-20
TF: 800-639-2422 ■ Web: www.nasa.gov

National Afro-American Museum & Cultural Ctr
1350 Brush Row Rd PO Box 578 .... Wilberforce OH 45384 937-376-4944 376-2007 520
TF: 800-752-2603 ■ Web: www.ohiohistory.org

National Agricultural Aviation Assn (NAAA)
1005 E St SE .... Washington DC 20003 202-546-5722 546-5726 48-2
Web: www.agaviation.org

National Agricultural Ctr & Hall of Fame
630 N 126th St .... Bonner Springs KS 66012 913-721-1075 520
TF: 800-800-8000 ■ Web: www.aghalloffame.com

National Agricultural Library
10301 Baltimore Ave Abraham Lincoln Bldg ..... Beltsville MD 20705 301-504-5755 340-1
TF: 800-633-7701 ■ Web: www.nal.usda.gov

National Agricultural Statistics Service (NASS)
1400 Independence Ave SW .... Washington DC 20250 202-720-2707 340-1
TF: 800-727-9540 ■ Web: www.nass.usda.gov

National Agri-Marketing Assn (NAMA)
11020 King St Ste 205 .... Overland Park KS 66210 913-491-6500 491-6502 49-18
TF: 800-530-5646 ■ Web: www.nama.org

National Air & Radiation Environmental Laboratory (NAREL)
540 S Morris Ave 540 S Morris Ave .... Montgomery AL 36115 334-270-3400 270-3454 743
Web: www.epa.gov

National Air & Space Museum (Smithsonian Institution)
Independence Ave & Sixth St SW .... Washington DC 20560 202-633-1000 520
Web: airandspace.si.edu

National Air Carrier Assn (NACA)
1000 Wilson Blvd Ste 1700 .... Arlington VA 22209 703-358-8060 358-8070 49-21
Web: www.naca.cc

National Air Traffic Controllers Assn (NATCA)
1325 Massachusetts Ave NW .... Washington DC 20005 202-628-5451 628-5767 414
TF: 800-266-0895 ■ Web: www.natca.org

National Air Transportation Assn (NATA)
4226 King St .... Alexandria VA 22302 703-845-9000 845-8176 49-21
TF: 800-808-6282 ■ Web: www.nata.aero

National Airline History Museum
201 Lou Holland Dr .... Kansas City MO 64116 816-421-3401 421-3421 520
Web: www.airlinehistory.org

National Alcohol Beverage Control Assn (NABCA)
4401 Ford Ave Ste 700 .... Alexandria VA 22302 703-578-4200 820-3551 49-7
Web: www.nabca.org

National Allergy Bureau (NAB)
555 E Wells St 11th Fl .... Milwaukee WI 53202 414-272-6071 272-6070 48-17
TF: 800-227-2345 ■ Web: aaaai.org/global/nab-pollen-counts.aspx

National Alliance for Caregiving
4720 Montgomery Ln Ste 205 .... Bethesda MD 20814 301-718-8444 652-7711 48-6
Web: caregiving.org

National Alliance for Hispanic Health
1501 16th St NW .... Washington DC 20036 202-387-5000 797-4353 48-17
Web: www.healthyamericas.org

National Alliance for Youth Sports
2050 Vista Pkwy .... West Palm Beach FL 33411 561-684-1141 684-2546 48-22
TF: 800-729-2057 ■ Web: www.nays.org

National Alliance of Media Art
145 Ninth St Ste 250 .... San Francisco CA 94103 415-431-1391 474

National Alliance of Postal & Federal Employees
1628 11th St NW .... Washington DC 20001 202-939-6325 939-6389 414
TF: 800-222-8733 ■ Web: www.napfe.com

National Alliance of Preservation Commissions
1242 1/2 S Lumpkin St University of Georgia .... Athens GA 30602 706-542-8924 48-13
Web: www.uga.edu/sed/pso/programs/napc/napc.htm

National Alliance on Mental Illness (NAMI)
3803 N Fairfax Dr Ste 100 .... Arlington VA 22203 703-524-7600 524-9094 48-17
TF: 800-950-6264 ■ Web: www.nami.org

National Alliance to End Homelessness
1518 K St NW 2nd Fl .... Washington DC 20005 202-638-1526 638-4664 48-5
TF: 800-657-3769 ■ Web: www.endhomelessness.org

National Alopecia Areata Foundation (NAAF)
14 Mitchell Blvd .... San Rafael CA 94903 415-472-3780 472-5343 48-17
TF: 800-723-4238 ■ Web: www.naaf.org

National Alpha Lambda Delta
6800 Pittsford-Palmyra Rd Ste 340 .... Fairport NY 14450 478-744-9595 744-9924 48-16
TF: 800-925-7421 ■ Web: www.nationalald.org

National American Indian Housing Council (NAIHC)
122 C S NW Ste 350 .... Washington DC 20001 202-789-1754 789-1758 49-7
TF: 800-284-9165 ■ Web: www.naihc.net

National American University
321 Kansas City St .... Rapid City SD 57701 605-394-4800 394-4871* 166
*Fax: Admissions ■ TF: 800-843-8892 ■ Web: www.national.edu
Sioux Falls 5801 S Kiwanis Ave .... Sioux Falls SD 57108 605-336-4600 336-4605* 166
*Fax: Admissions ■ TF: 800-388-5430 ■ Web: www.national.edu

National American University Colorado Springs
1915 Jamboree Dr Ste 185 .... Colorado Springs CO 80920 316-448-5400 590-8305* 166
*Fax Area Code: 719 ■ TF: 855-448-2318 ■ Web: www.national.edu

National American University Denver
1325 S Colorado Blvd Ste 100 .... Denver CO 80222 303-876-7100 876-7105* 166
*Fax: Admissions ■ TF: 800-748-2074 ■ Web: www.national.edu

National American University Independence
3620 Arrowhead Ave .... Independence MO 64057 816-412-7700 412-7705 166
TF: 866-628-1288 ■ Web: www.national.edu

National Amputation Foundation
40 Church St .... Malverne NY 11565 516-887-3600 48-17
TF: 800-633-6242 ■ Web: www.nationalamputation.org

National Amusements Inc
846 University Ave .... Norwood MA 02062 781-461-1600 748
Web: www.showcasecinemas.com

National Animal Control Assn
101 N Church St Ste C .... Olathe KS 66061 913-768-1319 768-1378 48-3
TF: 800-324-8503 ■ Web: www.nacanet.org

National Anti-Vivisection Society (NAVS)
53 W Jackson Blvd Ste 1552 .... Chicago IL 60604 312-427-6065 427-6524 48-3
TF: 800-888-6287 ■ Web: www.navs.org

National Apartment Assn (NAA)
4300 Wilson Blvd Ste 400 .... Arlington VA 22203 703-518-6141 248-9440 49-17
TF: 800-632-3007 ■ Web: www.naahq.org

National Aquarium in Baltimore
501 E Pratt St Pier 3 .... Baltimore MD 21202 410-576-3800 576-8641 40
TF: 800-628-9944 ■ Web: www.aqua.org

National Arbitration & Mediation
990 Stewart Ave .... Garden City NY 11530 516-794-8950 794-8518 41
TF: 800-358-2550 ■ Web: www.namadr.com

National Arbor Day Foundation
100 Arbor Ave .... Nebraska City NE 68410 402-474-5655 474-0820 48-13
TF: 888-448-7337 ■ Web: www.arborday.org

National Architectural Accrediting Board (NAAB)
1735 New York Ave NW .... Washington DC 20006 202-783-2007 783-2822 48-1
Web: www.naab.org

National Archives & Records Administration (NARA)
8601 Adelphi Rd .... College Park MD 20740 866-272-6272 837-0483* 340-20
*Fax Area Code: 301 ■ TF: 866-272-6272 ■ Web: www.archives.gov
Archival Research Catalog
8601 Adelphi Rd .... College Park MD 20740 866-272-6272 340-20
TF: 866-272-6272 ■ Web: archives.gov/research/search
Office of Presidential Libraries
8601 Adelphi Rd Rm 2200 .... College Park MD 20740 301-837-3250 837-3199 340-20
Web: www.archives.gov
Office of the Federal Register
800 N Capitol St NW Ste 700-K .... Washington DC 20002 202-741-6000 340-20
TF: 877-684-6448 ■ Web: www.archives.gov/federal-register

National Archives & Records Administration Regional Offices
Central Plains Region
400 W Pershing Rd .... Kansas City MO 64108 816-268-8000 340-20
Web: www.archives.gov
Great Lakes Region 7358 S Pulaski Rd .... Chicago IL 60629 773-940-9001 948-9050 340-20
TF: 800-447-1830 ■ Web: www.archives.gov/great lakes
Mid Atlantic Region
900 Market St .... Philadelphia PA 19107 215-606-0100 606-0116 340-20
Web: www.archives.gov/midatlantic
Northeast Region 380 Trapelo Rd .... Waltham MA 02452 781-663-0130 663-0154 340-20
TF: 866-406-2379 ■ Web: www.archives.gov
Pacific Alaska Region
6125 Sand Pt Way NE .... Seattle WA 98115 206-336-5115 336-5112 340-20
TF: 866-325-7208 ■ Web: www.archives.gov
Pacific Region 1000 Commodore Dr .... San Bruno CA 94066 650-238-3500 238-3507 340-20
TF: 800-234-8861 ■ Web: www.archives.gov
Southeast Region 5780 Jonesboro Rd .... Morrow GA 30260 770-968-2100 968-2547 340-20
TF: 800-447-1830 ■ Web: www.archives.gov/southeast
Southwest Region
501 W Felix St Bldg 1 .... Fort Worth TX 76115 817-551-2051 340-20
Web: www.archives.gov/southwest

National Art Education Assn (NAEA)
1806 Robert Fulton Dr .... Reston VA 20191 703-860-8000 860-2960 49-5
TF: 800-299-8321 ■ Web: www.arteducators.org

National Art Materials Trade Assn
20200 Zion Ave .... Cornelius NC 28031 704-892-6244 892-6247 49-18
TF: 800-349-1039 ■ Web: www.namta.org

National Art Shop
509 S National Ave .... Springfield MO 65802 417-866-3743 866-3748 45
Web: nationalartshop.com

National Artcraft Supply Co
300 Campus Dr .... Aurora OH 44202 330-562-3500 562-3507 43
TF: 888-937-2723 ■ Web: www.nationalartcraft.com

National Assembly of State Arts Agencies (NASAA)
1029 Vermont Ave NW 2nd Fl .... Washington DC 20005 202-347-6352 737-0526 49-7
Web: www.nasaa-arts.org

National Assn of Credit Management
8840 Columbia 100 Pkwy .... Columbia MD 21045 410-740-5560 740-5574 457-5
TF: 800-955-8815 ■ Web: www.nacm.org

National Assn of Student Financial Aid Administrators (NASFAA)
1101 Connecticut Ave Ste 1100 .... Washington DC 20036 202-785-0453 785-1487 49-5
TF: 800-877-8339 ■ Web: www.nasfaa.org

National Assn on Aging
1201 15th St NW Ste 350 .... Washington DC 20005 202-898-2578 49-7
TF: 800-599-8994 ■ Web: www.nasuad.org

National Association of Government Guaranteed Lenders (NAGGL)
215 E Ninth Ave .... Stillwater OK 74074 405-377-4022 377-3931 49-2
Web: www.naggl.org

National Association of Housing and Redevelopment Officials
630 'I' St NW .... Washington DC 20001 202-289-3500 289-8181 457-5
TF: 877-866-2476 ■ Web: www.nahro.org

National Association of Master Appraisers
303 W Cypress St .... San Antonio TX 78212 210-271-0781 49-17

National Association of Nonprofit Accountants & Consultants (NSA)
1801 W End Ave Ste 800 .... Nashville TN 37203 615-373-9880 49-1
TF: 800-231-2524 ■ Web: www.nonprofitcpas.com

National Association of People With AIDS (NAPWA)
8401 Colesville Rd Ste 505 .... Silver Spring MD 20910 240-247-0880 48-17
TF: 866-846-9366

National Association of REALTORS
430 N Michigan Ave .... Chicago IL 60611 800-874-6500 49-17
TF: 800-874-6500 ■ Web: www.realtor.org

	Phone	Fax	Class
National Association of Theatre Owners. (NATO) 1705 N St NW Ste 1130 .... Washington DC 20036 *TF General:* 800-365-5701 ■ *Web:* www.natoonline.org	202-962-0054	962-0370	48-4
National Association of Tower Erectors (NATE) 8 Second St SE .... Watertown SD 57201 *TF:* 888-882-5865 ■ *Web:* natehome.com	605-882-5865	886-5184	49-3
National Association of Town Watch (NATW) 308 E Lancaster Ave Ste 115 .... Wynnewood PA 19096 **Fax Area Code:* 610 ■ *TF:* 800-648-3688 ■ *Web:* www.nationaltownwatch.org	800-648-3688	649-5456*	48-7
National Astronomy & Ionosphere Ctr (NAIC) Cornell University Space Sciences Bldg .... Ithaca NY 14853 *TF:* 800-824-5419 ■ *Web:* www.naic.edu	607-255-3735	255-8803	668
National Athletic Trainers Assn (NATA) 2952 N Stemmons Fwy Ste 200 .... Dallas TX 75247 *TF:* 800-879-6282 ■ *Web:* www.nata.org	214-637-6282	637-2206	48-22
National Auctioneers Assn (NAA) 8880 Ballentine St .... Overland Park KS 66214 *TF:* 877-657-1990 ■ *Web:* www.auctioneers.org	913-541-8084	894-5281	49-18
National Audubon Society (NAS) 225 Varick St .... New York NY 10014 *TF:* 800-274-4201 ■ *Web:* www.audubon.org	212-979-3000	979-3188	48-13
National Australia Bank Americas 245 Pk Ave 28th Fl .... New York NY 10167 *TF:* 866-706-0509 ■ *Web:* www.nab.com.au	212-916-9500		70
National Auto Auction Assn (NAAA) 5320 Spectrum Dr Ste D .... Frederick MD 21703 *TF:* 800-232-5411 ■ *Web:* www.naaa.com	301-696-0400	631-1359	49-18
National Auto Sound Inc 11001 E Hwy 40 .... Independence MO 64055 *Web:* www.nationalautosound.com	816-356-8700		35
National Auto Stores Inc 2512 Quakertown Rd .... Pennsburg PA 18073 *Web:* www.nationalautostores.com	215-679-2300		57
National Automatic Merchandising Assn (NAMA) 20 N Wacker Dr Ste 3500 .... Chicago IL 60606 *Web:* www.namanow.org	312-346-0370	704-4140	49-18
National Automatic Sprinkler Industries 8000 Corporate Dr .... Landover MD 20785 *TF:* 800-638-2603 ■ *Web:* www.nasifund.org	301-577-1700	429-4709	189-13
National Automobile Club (NAC) 373 Vintage Park Dr Ste E .... Foster City CA 94404 *Web:* www.nacroadservice.com	650-294-7000		53
National Automobile Dealers Assn (NADA) 8400 Westpark Dr .... McLean VA 22102 *TF:* 800-252-6232 ■ *Web:* www.nada.org	703-821-7000	821-7075	49-18
National Automobile Museum 10 S Lake St .... Reno NV 89501 *Web:* www.automuseum.org	775-333-9300	333-9309	520
National Automotive Parts Assn (NAPA) 2999 Circle 75 Pkwy .... Atlanta GA 30339 *TF:* 800-538-6272 ■ *Web:* genpt.com	770-953-1700		61
National Automotive Radiator Service Assn (NARSA) 3000 Village Run Rd Ste 103 221 .... Wexford PA 15090 *Web:* www.narsa.org	724-799-8415	799-8416	49-21
National Aviation Academy 150 Hanscom Dr .... Bedford MA 01730 **Fax Area Code:* 781 ■ *TF:* 800-659-2080 ■ *Web:* www.naa.edu	727-535-8727	274-8490*	800
National Ballet 1816 Margaret Ave .... Annapolis MD 21401 *Web:* www.nationalballet.com	301-218-9822	686-7040	573-1
National Ballet of Canada Walter Carsen Centre for the National Ballet of Ca 470 Queens Quay W .... Toronto ON M5V3K4 *Web:* national.ballet.ca	416-345-9686	345-8323	573-1
National Balloon Museum 1601 N Jefferson Way PO Box 149 .... Indianola IA 50125 *Web:* www.nationalballoonmuseum.com	515-961-3714		520
National Bank & Trust Company of Sycamore, The 230 W State St .... Sycamore IL 60178	815-895-2125		70
National Bank of Arizona 335 N Wilmot Rd Ste 100 .... Tucson AZ 85711 *TF:* 800-497-8168 ■ *Web:* www.nbarizona.com	520-571-1500	513-0134	70
National Bank of Blacksburg PO Box 90002 .... Blacksburg VA 24062 *TF:* 800-552-4123 ■ *Web:* www.nbbank.com	540-552-2011	951-6337	70
National Bank, The 852 Middle Rd .... Bettendorf IA 52722 *TF:* 877-321-4347 ■ *Web:* www.bankwithtriumph.com	563-344-3935	823-3350	70
National Bankcard Systems 2600 Via Fortuna Ste 240 .... Austin TX 78746 *Web:* enbs.com	512-494-9200		255
National Bankshares Inc 101 Hubbard St .... Blacksburg VA 24060 *NASDAQ: NKSH* ■ *TF:* 800-552-4123 ■ *Web:* www.nationalbankshares.com	540-951-6300		360-2
National Banner Co 11938 Harry Hines Blvd .... Dallas TX 75234 *TF:* 800-527-0860	972-241-2131		287
National Baptist Convention of America Inc 777 SRL Thornton Fwy .... Dallas TX 75203 *Web:* www.nbcainc.com	214-942-3311		48-20
National Baptist Convention USA Inc 1700 Baptist World Ctr Dr .... Nashville TN 37207 *TF:* 866-531-3054 ■ *Web:* www.nationalbaptist.com	615-228-6292	262-3917	48-20
National Bar Assn (NBA) 1225 11th St NW .... Washington DC 20001 *TF:* 800-327-0200 ■ *Web:* www.nationalbar.org	202-842-3900	289-6170	49-10
National Barn Co 818 N Broadway .... Portland TN 37148 *Web:* www.nationalbarn.com	615-325-2700		106
National Baseball Hall of Fame & Museum 25 Main St .... Cooperstown NY 13326 *TF:* 888-425-5633 ■ *Web:* baseballhall.org	607-547-7200	547-2044	522
National Basketball Assn (NBA) 645 Fifth Ave .... New York NY 10022 *Web:* www.nba.com	212-407-8000	832-3861	714-1
National Basketball Players Assn (NBPA) 1133 Avenue of Americas .... New York NY 10036 *TF:* 800-955-6272 ■ *Web:* www.nbpa.com	212-655-0880	655-0881	48-22
National Bearing Co 1596 Manheim Pk .... Lancaster PA 17604 *Web:* www.nationalbearings.com	717-569-0485	569-1605	75
National Beauty Culturists' League Inc (NBCL) 25 Logan Cir NW .... Washington DC 20005 *Web:* www.nbcl.org	202-332-2695		49-4
National Beef Packing Co LLC 12200 Ambassador Dr Ste 500 PO Box 20046 .... Kansas City MO 64163 *TF:* 800-449-2333 ■ *Web:* www.nationalbeef.com	800-449-2333		473
National Beer Wholesalers Assn (NBWA) 1101 King St Ste 600 .... Alexandria VA 22314 *TF:* 800-300-6417 ■ *Web:* www.nbwa.org	703-683-4300	683-8965	49-6
National Benevolent Assn (NBA) 733 Union Blvd Ste 300 .... St. Louis MO 63108 *TF:* 800-366-3383 ■ *Web:* www.nbacares.org	314-993-9000		48-5
National Bicycle Dealers Assn (NBDA) 777 W 19th St Ste O .... Costa Mesa CA 92627 *Web:* www.nbda.com	949-722-6909		49-4
National Billiard Manufacturing Co 3315 Eugenia Ave .... Covington KY 41015 *TF:* 800-543-0880 ■ *Web:* www.nationalbilliard.com	859-431-4129	431-4179	710
National Biodynamics Laboratory (NBDL) *University of New Orleans College of Engineering* 2000 Lakeshore Dr .... New Orleans LA 70148 **Fax Area Code:* 504 ■ *TF:* 888-514-4275 ■ *Web:* www.uno.edu	888-514-4275	280-7413*	668
National Black MBA Assn (NBMBAA) 180 N Michigan Ave Ste 1400 .... Chicago IL 60601 *Web:* www.nbmbaa.org	312-236-2622		49-12
National Bldg Museum 401 F St NW .... Washington DC 20001 *Web:* www.nbm.org	202-272-2448		520
National Board for Certified Counselors Inc 3 Terrace Way Ste D .... Greensboro NC 27403 *Web:* www.nbcc.org	336-547-0607		21
National Board of Boiler & Pressure Vessel Inspectors 1055 Crupper Ave .... Columbus OH 43229 **Fax:* Cust Svc ■ *TF:* 877-682-8772 ■ *Web:* www.nationalboard.org	614-888-8320	847-1147*	49-7
National Board of Medical Examiners (NBME) 3750 Market St .... Philadelphia PA 19104 *Web:* www.nbme.org	215-590-9500		49-8
National Book Festival Library of Congress 101 Independence Ave SE .... Washington DC 20540 *TF:* 888-714-4696 ■ *Web:* www.loc.gov/bookfest	202-707-2777	707-9199	281
National Book Network Inc 4501 Forbes Blvd Ste 200 .... Lanham MD 20706 *TF:* 800-243-0495 ■ *Web:* www.nbnbooks.com	301-459-3366		95
National Border Patrol Museum 4315 Woodrow Bean TransMtn Rd .... El Paso TX 79924 *TF:* 877-276-8738 ■ *Web:* www.borderpatrolmuseum.com	915-759-6060	759-0992	520
National Braille Press Inc 88 St Stephen St .... Boston MA 02115 *TF:* 888-965-8965 ■ *Web:* www.nbp.org	617-266-6160	437-0456	637-2
National Breast Cancer Coalition (NBCC) 1101 17th St NW Ste 1300 .... Washington DC 20036 *TF:* 800-622-2838 ■ *Web:* www.breastcancerdeadline2020.org	202-296-7477	265-6854	48-17
National Bronze & Metals Inc 2929 W 12th St .... Houston TX 77008 *Web:* www.nbmmetals.com	713-869-9600		492
National Bulk Equipment 12838 Stainless Dr .... Holland MI 49424 *Web:* www.nbe-inc.com	616-399-2220		454
National Bureau of Economic Research 1050 Massachusetts Ave .... Cambridge MA 02138 *TF:* 800-621-8476 ■ *Web:* www.nber.org	617-868-3900	868-2742	668
National Business Assn (NBA) 5151 Beltline Rd Ste 1150 .... Dallas TX 75254 *TF:* 800-456-0440 ■ *Web:* www.nationalbusiness.org	972-458-0900	960-9149	49-12
National Business Aviation Assn (NBAA) 1200 18th St NW Ste 400 .... Washington DC 20036 *TF:* 800-394-6222 ■ *Web:* www.nbaa.org	202-783-9000	331-8364	49-21
National Business Education Assn (NBEA) 1914 Assn Dr .... Reston VA 20191 *TF:* 800-811-1648 ■ *Web:* www.nbea.org	703-860-8300	620-4483	49-5
National Business Furniture Inc 735 N Water St Ste 440 .... Milwaukee WI 53202 *TF Sales:* 800-558-1010 ■ *Web:* www.nationalbusinessfurniture.com	414-276-8511		320
National Business Services 1601 Magoffin Ave .... El Paso TX 79901 *TF Sales:* 800-777-7807 ■ *Web:* www.nbsinc.com	915-544-1271		319-1
National Businesswomen's Leadership Assn PO Box 419107 .... Kansas City MO 64141 *TF:* 800-258-7246 ■ *Web:* www.nationalseminarstraining.com	913-432-7755	432-0824	765
National Cable & Telecommunications Assn (NCTA) 25 Massachusetts Ave NW Ste 100 .... Washington DC 20001 *Web:* www.ncta.com	202-222-2300		49-14
National Cable Television Co-op Inc (NCTC) 11200 Corporate Ave .... Lenexa KS 66219 **Fax Area Code:* 202 ■ *Web:* www.ncta.com	913-599-5900	222-2311*	49-14
National Cancer Institute at Frederick Bldg 427 Rm 1 PO Box B .... Frederick MD 21702 *Web:* ncifrederick.cancer.gov	301-846-1108	846-1494	668
National Cancer Registrars Assn (NCRA) 1340 Braddock Pl Ste 203 .... Alexandria VA 22314 *TF:* 800-621-4111 ■ *Web:* www.ncra-usa.org	703-299-6640	299-6620	48-17
National Capital Planning Commission 401 Ninth St NW N Lobby Ste 500 .... Washington DC 20004 *Web:* www.ncpc.gov	202-482-7200	482-7272	340-20
National Capital Regional Office 1100 Ohio Dr SW .... Washington DC 20242 *Web:* www.nps.gov/ncro	202-619-7000	619-7220	340-13
National Captioning Institute (NCI) 3725 Concorde Pkwy Ste 100 .... Chantilly VA 20151 *TF:* 800-825-6758 ■ *Web:* www.ncicap.org	703-917-7600	917-9853	632
National Car Mart Inc 9255 Brookpark Rd .... Cleveland OH 44129 *Web:* www.nationalcarmart.com	216-505-1750		57
National Cargo Bureau Inc (NCB) 180 Maiden Ln Ste 903 .... New York NY 10038 *Web:* www.natcargo.org	212-785-8300	785-8333	49-21
National Carriers Inc 1501 E Eigth St .... Liberal KS 67901 *TF:* 800-835-9180 ■ *Web:* www.nationalcarriers.com	620-624-1621		780
National CASA Assn (CASA) 100 W Harrison St North Tower Ste 500 .... Seattle WA 98119 *TF:* 800-628-3233 ■ *Web:* www.casaforchildren.org	206-270-0072	270-0078	48-6

Phone | Fax | Class

National Casein Co 601 W 80th St............. Chicago IL 60620 773-846-7300 487-5709 3
TF: 800-424-9300 ■ *Web:* www.nationalcasein.com

National Catastrophe Adjusters Inc
9725 Windermere Blvd....................... Fishers IN 46037 317-915-8888 390
Web: www.ncagroup.com

National Cathedral School
3612 Woodley Rd NW..................... Washington DC 20016 202-537-6300 537-5743 623
Web: www.ncs.cathedral.org

National Catholic Educational Assn (NCEA)
1005 N Glebe Rd Ste 525.................... Arlington VA 22201 571-257-0010 243-0025* 49-5
**Fax Area Code:* 703 ■ *TF:* 800-711-6232 ■ *Web:* www.ncea.org

National Catholic Reporter Publishing Co
115 E Armour Blvd...................... Kansas City MO 64111 816-531-0538 968-2292 637-9
TF: 800-333-7373 ■ *Web:* www.ncronline.org

National Cattlemen's Beef Assn (NCBA)
9110 E Nichols Ave Ste 300................. Centennial CO 80112 303-694-0305 694-2851 48-2
TF: 866-233-3872 ■ *Web:* www.beefusa.org

National Cattlemen's Beef Assn PAC
1301 Pennsylvania Ave NW Ste 300......... Washington DC 20004 202-347-0228 615
Web: beef.org

National Caucus & Ctr on Black Aged Inc (NCBA)
1220 L St NW Ste 800 .... Washington DC 20005 202-637-8400 347-0895 48-6
Web: www.ncba-aged.org

National Cement Company of California Inc
15821 Ventura Blvd Ste 475.................... Encino CA 91436 818-728-5200 182
TF: 800-801-7625 ■ *Web:* www.vicat.com

National Cemetery Administration
810 Vermont Ave NW..................... Washington DC 20420 202-565-4964 340-19
TF: 800-273-8255 ■ *Web:* www.cem.va.gov

National Center for Atmospheric Research (NCAR)
3090 Center Green Dr....................... Boulder CO 80301 303-497-1000 668
Web: www.ncar.ucar.edu

National Center for Drug Free Sport, The
2537 Madison Ave .... Kansas City MO 64108 816-474-8655 415
TF: 800-467-3655 ■ *Web:* www.drugfreesport.com

National Certification Commission for Acupuncture & Oriental Medicine (NCCAOM)
76 S Laura St Ste 1290.................... Jacksonville FL 32202 904-598-1005 598-5001 48-1
Web: www.nccaom.org

National Chemical Laboratories Inc
401 N Tenth St .... Philadelphia PA 19123 215-922-1200 922-5517 151
TF: 800-628-2436 ■ *Web:* www.nclonline.com

National Chemicals Inc
105 Liberty St PO Box 32..................... Winona MN 55987 507-454-5640 858-4141* 151
**Fax Area Code:* 877 ■ *TF Cust Svc:* 800-533-0027 ■ *Web:* www.nationalchemicals.com

National Chicken Council
1152 15th St NW Ste 930.................. Washington DC 20005 202-296-2622 293-4005 48-2
Web: www.eatchicken.com

National Child Care Assn (NCCA)
1325 G St NW Ste 500................... Washington DC 20005 866-536-1945 48-6
TF: 866-536-1945 ■ *Web:* www.nccanet.org

National Child Care Information Center (NCCIC)
9300 Lee Hwy.. Fairfax VA 22031 877-296-2250 340-10
TF: 877-296-2250 ■ *Web:* www.icf.com

National Child Support Enforcement Assn (NCSEA)
1760 Old Meadow Rd Ste 500 .... McLean VA 22102 703-506-2880 506-3266 48-6
Web: www.ncsea.org

National Children's Advocacy Ctr (NCAC)
210 Pratt Ave .... Huntsville AL 35801 256-533-5437 534-6883 48-5
Web: www.nationalcac.org

National Children's Ctr Inc
6200 Second St NW..................... Washington DC 20011 202-722-2300 685
TF: 866-632-9992 ■ *Web:* www.nccinc.org

National Children's Museum
145 Fleet St Ste 202................... National Harbor MD 20745 301-392-2400 520
Web: www.ccm.org

National Christmas Tree Assn (NCTA)
16020 Swingley Ridge Rd Ste 300........... Chesterfield MO 63017 636-449-5070 449-5051 48-2
Web: www.realchristmastrees.org

National Church Residences Inc
2335 N Bank Dr .... Columbus OH 43220 800-388-2151 451-0351* 652
**Fax Area Code:* 614 ■ *TF:* 800-388-2151 ■ *Web:* www.nationalchurchresidences.org

National Church Supply Co, The
PO Box 269 .... Chester WV 26034 304-387-5200 263
TF: 800-627-9900 ■ *Web:* www.ncssolutions.org

National Citizens' Coalition for Nursing Home Reform (NCCNHR)
National Consumer Voice for Quality Long-Term Care
1828 L St NW Ste 801.................. Washington DC 20036 202-332-2275 332-2949 48-17
TF: 866-992-3668 ■ *Web:* www.theconsumervoice.org

National City Chamber of Commerce
901 National City Blvd................... National City CA 91950 619-477-9339 477-5018 139
TF: 800-697-6397 ■ *Web:* www.nationalcitychamber.org

National City Public Library
1401 National City Blvd.................. National City CA 91950 619-470-5800 470-5880 434-3
Web: www.nationalcityca.gov/government/library

National Civic League (NCL) 1889 York St........ Denver CO 80206 303-571-4343 314-6053* 48-7
**Fax Area Code:* 888 ■ *TF:* 800-765-7755 ■ *Web:* www.nationalcivicleague.org

National Civil Rights Museum
450 Mulberry St........................ Memphis TN 38103 901-521-9699 520
Web: www.civilrightsmuseum.org

National Civil War Naval Museum
1002 Victory Dr .... Port Columbus GA 31901 706-327-9798 520
Web: www.portcolumbus.org

National Cleaners Assn 252 W 29th St......... New York NY 10001 212-967-3002 967-2240 49-4
TF General: 800-888-1622 ■ *Web:* www.nca-i.com

National Clearinghouse for Alcohol & Drug Information
11426 Rockville Pk PO Box 2345............. Rockville MD 20847 800-729-6686 340-10
TF: 800-729-6686

National Clothesline Magazine
801 Easton Rd Ste 2....................... Willow Grove PA 19090 215-830-8467 830-8490 457-21
Web: www.natclo.com

National Club Assn (NCA)
1201 15th St NW Ste 450................. Washington DC 20005 202-822-9822 822-9808 48-23
TF: 800-625-6221 ■ *Web:* nationalclub.org

National Coalition Against Censorship (NCAC)
19 Fulton St Ste 407........................ New York NY 10038 212-807-6222 807-6245 48-8
Web: www.ncac.org

National Coalition Against Domestic Violence (NCADV)
1 Broadway Ste B210......................... Denver CO 80203 303-839-1852 831-9251 48-6
TF: 800-799-7233 ■ *Web:* www.ncadv.org

National Coalition for Cancer Survivorship (NCCS)
1010 Wayne Ave Ste 315 .... Silver Spring MD 20910 877-622-7937 48-17
TF: 877-622-7937 ■ *Web:* www.canceradvocacy.org

National Coalition for the Homeless (NCH)
2201 P St NW.............................. Washington DC 20037 202-462-4822 462-4823 48-5
TF: 877-243-1576 ■ *Web:* www.nationalhomeless.org

National Coalition for the Protection of Children & Families (NCPCF)
800 Compton Rd Ste 9224................. Cincinnati OH 45231 513-521-6227 48-6
Web: www.eos.net

National Coalition of Black Meeting Planners (NCBMP)
1800 Diagonal Rd.......................... Alexandria VA 22314 571-366-1779 588-0011* 49-12
**Fax Area Code:* 301 ■ *Web:* www.ncbmp.com

National Coalition of Girls' Schools (NCGS)
50 Leonard St Ste 2C........................ Belmont MA 02478 617-489-0013 489-0024 49-5
Web: www.ncgs.org

National Coalition on Black Civic Participation Inc (NCBCP)
1050 Connecticut Ave NW Ste 700........... Washington DC 20036 202-659-4929 659-5025 48-7
Web: ncbcp.org

National Coalition on Health Care
1120 G St NW Ste 810.................... Washington DC 20005 202-638-7151 48-17
Web: www.nchc.org

National Coalition to Abolish the Death Penalty (NCADP)
1620 L St Ste 250........................ Washington DC 20036 202-331-4090 48-8
Web: www.ncadp.org

National Coatings Inc
3520 Rennie School Rd .... Traverse City MI 49685 231-943-2557 481
TF: 888-947-2557 ■ *Web:* www.nationalcoatings.biz

National Coffee Assn of USA Inc (NCA)
45 Broadway Ste 1140........................ New York NY 10006 212-766-4007 766-5815 49-6
TF: 800-611-6100 ■ *Web:* www.ncausa.org

National Coil Coating Assn (NCCA)
1300 Sumner Ave.......................... Cleveland OH 44115 216-241-7333 241-0105 49-13
Web: www.coilcoating.org

National College
Lexington 2376 Sir Barton Way............... Lexington KY 40509 859-253-0621 800
TF: 877-540-3494 ■ *Web:* national-college.edu

National College of Business & Technology
Charlottesville
3926 Seminole Trl .... Charlottesville VA 22911 434-295-0136 800
Web: national-college.edu
Danville 336 Old Riverside Dr................. Danville VA 24541 434-793-6822 800
TF: 800-666-6221 ■ *Web:* www.national-college.edu
Harrisonburg
1515 Country Club Rd................. Harrisonburg VA 22802 540-432-0943 800
Web: an.edu
Lynchburg 104 Candlewood Ct.............. Lynchburg VA 24502 434-239-3500 800
TF: 800-664-1886 ■ *Web:* national-college.edu
Martinsville 905 N Memorial Blvd........... Martinsville VA 24112 276-632-5621 800
Web: www.national-college.edu
Roanoke Valley 1813 E Main St................. Salem VA 24153 540-986-1800 800
TF: 800-664-1886 ■ *Web:* www.national-college.edu

National College of Business & Technology Bristol
1328 Hwy 11 W .... Bristol TN 37620 423-878-4440 800
TF: 888-956-2732 ■ *Web:* www.national-college.edu

National College of Business & Technology Danville
115 E Lexington Ave........................ Danville KY 40422 859-236-6991 800
Web: national-college.edu

National College of Business & Technology Florence
8095 Connector Dr.......................... Florence KY 41042 859-525-6510 800
TF: 888-956-2732 ■ *Web:* www.national-college.edu

National College of Business & Technology Nashville
1638 Bell Rd................................ Nashville TN 37211 615-333-3344 800
TF: 855-800-1715 ■ *Web:* national-college.edu

National College of Business & Technology Pikeville
50 National College Blvd...................... Pikeville KY 41501 606-478-7200 800
TF: 800-664-1886 ■ *Web:* national-college.edu

National College of Business & Technology Richmond
125 S Killarney Ln .... Richmond KY 40475 859-623-8956 800
Web: national-college.edu

National Collegiate Athletic Assn (NCAA)
700 W Washington St PO Box 6222.......... Indianapolis IN 46206 317-917-6222 917-6888 48-22
Web: www.ncaa.org

National Commerce Bank Services Inc
80 Monroe Ave Ste 250 .... Memphis TN 38103 800-264-2609 690
TF: 800-264-2609 ■ *Web:* www.ncbs.com

National Commission Assn
2501 Exchange Ave Ste 102............. Oklahoma City OK 73108 405-232-3128 446
TF: 800-999-8998 ■ *Web:* www.nationallivestock.com

National Commission on Certification of Physician Assistants
12000 Findley Rd Ste 200 .... Duluth GA 30097 678-417-8100 417-8135 48-1
Web: www.nccpa.net

National Committee for Employer Support of the Guard & Reserve (ESGR)
1555 Wilson Blvd Ste 319 .... Arlington VA 22209 703-696-1386 48-19
TF: 800-336-4590 ■ *Web:* www.esgr.mil

National Committee for Quality Assurance (NCQA)
1100 13th St.............................. Washington DC 20005 202-955-3500 955-3599 48-10
TF: 888-275-7585 ■ *Web:* www.ncqa.org

National Committee for Responsive Philanthropy (NCRP)
2001 S St NW Ste 620 .... Washington DC 20009 202-387-9177 332-5084 48-5
Web: www.ncrp.org

National Committee to Preserve Social Security & Medicare (NCPSSM)
10 G St NE Ste 600....................... Washington DC 20002 202-216-0420 216-0451 48-7
TF: 800-966-1935 ■ *Web:* www.ncpssm.org

National Communication Assn (NCA)
1765 N St NW............................. Washington DC 20036 202-464-4622 464-4600 49-5
Web: www.natcom.org

National Community Action Foundation (NCAF)
PO Box 78214 .... Washington DC 20013 202-842-2092 842-2095 48-7
TF: 800-717-2762 ■ *Web:* ncaf.org

National Community Pharmacists Assn (NCPA)
100 Daingerfield Rd .... Alexandria VA 22314 703-683-8200 683-3619 49-8
TF: 800-544-7447 ■ *Web:* www.ncpanet.org

National Community Renaissance of California
9421 Haven Ave .... Rancho Cucamonga CA 91730 909-483-2444 483-2448 49-3
Web: www.nationalcore.org

National Concrete Masonry Assn
13750 Sunrise Vly Dr....................... Herndon VA 20171 703-713-1900 713-1910 49-3
TF: 877-343-6268 ■ *Web:* www.ncma.org

Phone | Fax | Class

National Concrete Products Co
939 S Mill St Plymouth MI 48170 734-453-8448 183

National Coney Island Inc
27947 Groesbeck Hwy Roseville MI 48066 586-771-7744 670
Web: www.nationalconeyisland.com

National Confectioners Assn (NCA)
1101 30th St NW Ste 200 Washington DC 20007 202-534-1440 337-0637 49-6
Web: www.candyusa.com

National Confectioners Assn PAC (NCA)
1101 30th St NW Ste 200 Washington DC 20007 202-534-1440 337-0637 615
TF: 800-433-1200 ■ *Web:* www.candyusa.com

National Conference of Firemen & Oilers
1212 Bath Ave. Ashland DC 41101 561-227-0626 679-2959* 414
**Fax Area Code:* 253 ■ *Web:* www.ncfo.org

National Conference of State Historic Preservation Officers
444 N Capitol St NW Ste 342 Washington DC 20001 202-624-5465 49-7
Web: www.ncshpo.org

National Conference of State Legislatures
7700 E First Pl Denver CO 80230 303-364-7700 364-7800 49-7
TF: 800-659-2656 ■ *Web:* www.ncsl.org

National Conference on Citizenship (NCOC)
1900 L St NW Ste 800 Washington DC 20036 202-601-7096 48-8
Web: www.ncoc.net

National Congress of American Indians (NCAI)
1516 P St NW Washington DC 20005 202-466-7767 466-7797 48-14
TF: 800-388-2227 ■ *Web:* www.ncai.org

National Congress of Neighborhood Women
249 Manhattan Ave Brooklyn NY 11211 718-388-8915 48-24
Web: neighborhoodwomen.org

National Constitution Ctr
525 Arch St Independence Mall Philadelphia PA 19106 215-409-6600 409-6650 520
Web: www.constitutioncenter.org

National Construction Rentals Inc
15319 Chatsworth St Mission Hills CA 91345 800-352-5675 896-8411 264-3
TF: 800-352-5675 ■ *Web:* www.rentnational.com

National Consumer Law Ctr (NCLC)
7 Winthrop Sq Boston MA 02110 617-542-8010 542-8028 48-8
TF: 800-225-5254 ■ *Web:* www.nclc.org

National Consumers League (NCL)
1701 K St NW Ste 1200 Washington DC 20006 202-835-3323 835-0747 48-10
TF: 800-388-2227 ■ *Web:* www.natlconsumersleague.org

National Contract Management Assn (NCMA)
21740 Beaumeade Cir Ste 125 Ashburn VA 20147 571-382-0082 448-0939* 49-12
**Fax Area Code:* 703 ■ *TF:* 800-344-8096 ■ *Web:* www.ncmahq.org

National Co-op Business Assn (NCBA)
1401 New York Ave NW Ste 1100 Washington DC 20005 202-638-6222 638-1374 49-12
TF: 800-356-9655 ■ *Web:* www.ncba.coop

National Copper & Smelting Company Inc
3333 Stanwood Blvd. Huntsville AL 35811 256-859-4510 492
Web: www.nationaltube.com

National Corn Growers Assn (NCGA)
632 Cepi Dr Chesterfield MO 63005 636-733-9004 733-9005 48-2
TF: 800-222-4734 ■ *Web:* www.ncga.com

National Corporate Housing
365 Herndon Pkwy Ste 111 Herndon VA 20170 866-229-4720 376
TF: 866-229-4720 ■ *Web:* www.nationalcorporatehousing.com

National Corrugated Steel Pipe Assn (NCSPA)
14070 Proton Rd Ste 100 Dallas TX 75244 972-850-1907 490-4219 49-3
Web: www.ncspa.org

National Corvette Museum
350 Corvette Dr Bowling Green KY 42101 270-781-7973 781-5286 520
TF: 800-538-3883 ■ *Web:* www.corvettemuseum.org

National Cotton Council, The
7193 Goodlett Farms Pkwy Cordova TN 38016 901-274-9030 725-0510 49-18
Web: www.cotton.org

National Council for Accreditation of Teacher Education (NCATE)
2010 Massachusetts Ave NW Ste 500 Washington DC 20036 202-466-7496 296-6620 48-1
TF: 800-255-8664 ■ *Web:* www.ncate.org

National Council for Adoption (NCFA)
225 N Washington St Alexandria VA 22314 703-299-6633 299-6004 48-6
TF: 800-366-7773 ■ *Web:* www.adoptioncouncil.org

National Council for Advanced Mfg (NACFAM)
2025 M St NW Ste 800 Washington DC 20036 202-429-2220 429-2422 49-12
TF: 800-250-3196 ■ *Web:* www.nacfam.org

National Council for Air & Stream Improvement Inc (NCASI)
PO Box 13318 Research Triangle Park NC 27709 919-941-6400 941-6401 48-13
TF: 888-448-2473 ■ *Web:* www.ncasi.org

National Council for Prescription Drug Programs (NCPDP)
9240 E Raintree Dr Scottsdale AZ 85260 480-477-1000 767-1042 49-9
TF: 888-665-2600 ■ *Web:* www.ncpdp.org

National Council for the Social Studies (NCSS)
8555 16th St Ste 500 Silver Spring MD 20910 301-588-1800 588-2049 49-5
TF Orders: 800-683-0812 ■ *Web:* socialstudies.org

National Council for the Traditional Arts (NCTA)
8757 Georgia Ave Ste 450 Silver Spring MD 20910 301-565-0654 565-0472 48-4
Web: ncta-usa.org

National Council for Therapeutic Recreation Certification Inc (NCTRC)
7 Elmwood Dr New City NY 10956 845-639-1439 639-1471 49-15
TF: 800-392-0751 ■ *Web:* www.nctrc.org

National Council of Architectural Registration Boards (NCARB)
1801 K St NW Ste 700-K Washington DC 20006 202-783-6500 783-0290 49-7
Web: www.ncarb.org

National Council of Examiners for Engineering & Surveying (NCEES)
280 Seneca Creek Rd Seneca SC 29678 864-654-6824 654-6033 49-3
TF: 800-250-3196 ■ *Web:* www.ncees.org

National Council of Farmer Co-ops (NCFC)
50 F St NW Ste 900 Washington DC 20001 202-626-8700 626-8722 48-2
TF: 800-344-2626 ■ *Web:* www.ncfc.org

National Council of Jewish Women (NCJW)
475 Riverside Dr Ste 1901 New York NY 10115 212-645-4048 645-7466 48-24
TF: 800-829-6259 ■ *Web:* www.ncjw.org

National Council of Juvenile & Family Court Judges (NCJFCJ)
Univ of Nevada PO Box 8970 Reno NV 89507 775-784-6012 784-6628 49-10
TF: 800-527-3223 ■ *Web:* www.ncjfcj.org

National Council of La Raza (NCLR)
1126 16th St NW 6th Fl Washington DC 20036 202-785-1670 776-1792 48-14
Web: www.nclr.org

National Council of Negro Women Inc (NCNW)
633 Pennsylvania Ave NW Washington DC 20004 202-737-0120 737-0476 48-24
Web: www.ncnw.org

National Council of State Boards of Nursing (NCSBN)
111 E Wacker Dr Ste 2900 Chicago IL 60601 312-525-3600 279-1032 49-8
TF: 866-293-9600 ■ *Web:* www.ncsbn.org

National Council of State Housing Agencies (NCSHA)
444 N Capitol St NW Ste 438 Washington DC 20001 202-624-7710 624-5899 49-7
TF: 800-475-2098 ■ *Web:* www.ncsha.org

National Council of Supervisors of Mathematics (NCSM)
6000 E Evans Ave Ste 3-205 Denver CO 80222 303-758-9611 758-9616 49-5
Web: www.mathedleadership.org

National Council of Teachers of English (NCTE)
1111 W Kenyon Rd Urbana IL 61801 217-328-3870 328-0977 49-5
TF: 877-369-6283 ■ *Web:* www.ncte.org

National Council of Teachers of Mathematics (NCTM)
1906 Assn Dr Reston VA 20191 703-620-9840 476-2970 49-5
TF Orders: 800-235-7566 ■ *Web:* www.nctm.org

National Council of Textile Organizations (NCTO)
910 17th St NW Washington DC 20006 202-822-8028 822-8029 49-13
TF: 800-238-7192 ■ *Web:* www.ncto.org

National Council of Women of the US Inc (NCWO)
777 UN Plaza New York NY 10017 212-697-1278 48-7
Web: ncwus.org

National Council on Alcoholism & Drug Dependence Inc (NCADD)
217 Broadway Ste 712 New York NY 10007 212-269-7797 269-7510 48-17
TF: 800-622-2255 ■ *Web:* www.ncadd.org

National Council on Crime & Delinquency (NCCD)
1970 Broadway Ste 500 Oakland CA 94612 510-208-0500 208-0511 48-8
TF: 800-306-6223 ■ *Web:* www.nccdglobal.org

National Council on Disability (NCD)
1331 F St NW Ste 850 Washington DC 20004 202-272-2004 272-2022 340-20
Web: www.ncd.gov

National Council on Economic Education (NCEE)
122 E 42nd St Ste 2600 New York NY 10168 212-730-7007 730-1793 49-5
TF: 800-338-1192 ■ *Web:* www.councilforeconed.org

National Council on Family Relations (NCFR)
1201 W River Pkwy Ste 200 Minneapolis MN 55454 888-781-9331 48-6
TF: 888-781-9331 ■ *Web:* www.ncfr.org

National Council on Problem Gambling Inc
730 11th St NW Ste 601 Washington DC 20001 202-547-9204 547-9206 49-8
TF: 800-522-4700 ■ *Web:* www.ncpgambling.org

National Council on Public History (NCPH)
425 University Blvd 127 Cavanaugh Hall Indianapolis IN 46202-5140 317-274-2716 278-5230 48-7
TF: 800-554-5542 ■ *Web:* www.ncph.org

National Council on Radiation Protection & Measurements (NCRP)
7910 Woodmont Ave Ste 400 Bethesda MD 20814 301-657-2652 907-8768 49-19
TF: 800-462-3683 ■ *Web:* www.ncrponline.org

National Council on the Aging (NCOA)
1901 L St NW 4th Fl Washington DC 20036 202-479-1200 479-0735 48-6
TF: 800-677-1116 ■ *Web:* www.ncoa.org

National Counterintelligence and Security Center, The (ONCIX)
LX/ICC-B Washington DC 20511 703-733-8600 340-20
Web: ncsc.gov

National Court Reporters Assn (NCRA)
8224 Old Courthouse Rd Vienna VA 22182 703-556-6272 556-6291 49-10
TF: 800-272-6272 ■ *Web:* www.ncra.org

National Cowboy & Western Heritage Museum
1700 NE 63rd St Oklahoma City OK 73111 405-478-2250 478-4714 520
TF: 800-886-4222 ■ *Web:* www.nationalcowboymuseum.org

National Cowgirl Museum & Hall of Fame
1720 Gendy St Fort Worth TX 76107 817-336-4475 336-2470 520
TF: 800-476-3263 ■ *Web:* www.cowgirl.net

National CPA Health Care Advisors Assn (HCAA)
1801 W End Ave Ste 800 Nashville TN 37203 615-373-9880 377-7092 49-1
TF: 800-231-2524 ■ *Web:* www.hcaa.com

National Crane Corp 11200 N 148th Waverly NE 68462 402-786-6300 190

National Credit Adjusters LLC
327 W Fourth Ave. Hutchinson KS 67501 877-835-4455 361
TF: 877-835-4455 ■ *Web:* internationalhomescookware.com

National Credit Union Administration
1775 Duke St Alexandria VA 22314 703-518-6300 518-6319 340-20
TF Fraud Hotline: 800-827-9650 ■ *Web:* ncua.gov

National Credit Union Administration Regional Offices
Region 1
9 Washington Sq Washington Ave Ext Albany NY 12205 518-862-7400 862-7420 340-20
TF: 800-755-1030 ■ *Web:* ncua.gov
Region 2 1775 Duke St Ste 4206 Alexandria VA 22314 703-518-6300 519-4620 340-20
Web: www.ncua.gov
Region 3 7000 Central Pkwy Ste 1600 Atlanta GA 30328 678-443-3000 443-3020 340-20
TF: 800-827-9650 ■ *Web:* ncua.gov
Region 4
4807 Spicewood Springs Rd Ste 5200 Austin TX 78759 512-342-5600 342-5620 340-20
Web: ncua.gov
Region 5 1230 W Washington St Ste 301 Tempe AZ 85281 602-302-6000 302-6024 340-20
TF: 800-995-9064 ■ *Web:* ncua.gov

National Crime Prevention Council (NCPC)
2345 Crystal Dr Ste 500 Arlington VA 22202 202-466-6272 296-1356 48-8
TF: 800-627-2911 ■ *Web:* www.ncpc.org

National Criminal Justice Reference Service
PO Box 6000 Rockville MD 20849 202-836-6998 240-5830* 340-14
**Fax Area Code:* 301 ■ *TF:* 800-851-3420 ■ *Web:* www.ncjrs.gov

National Crop Insurance Services (NCIS)
8900 Indian Creek Pkwy Ste 600 Overland Park KS 66210 913-685-2767 685-3080 48-2
TF: 800-951-6247 ■ *Web:* www.ag-risk.org

National Ctr for Agricultural Utilization Research
USDA/ARS 1815 N University St Peoria IL 61604 309-685-4011 681-6686 668
Web: www.ars.usda.gov/Main/docs.htm?docid=3153

National Ctr for Bicycling & Walking (NCBW)
8120 Woodmont Ave Ste 520 Bethesda MD 20814 202-223-3621 656-4225* 48-22
**Fax Area Code:* 301 ■ *TF:* 800-836-6740 ■ *Web:* www.bikewalk.org

National Ctr for Children in Poverty (NCCP)
215 W 125th St 3rd Fl New York NY 10027 646-284-9600 284-9623 48-6
TF: 800-388-7670 ■ *Web:* www.nccp.org

National Ctr for Children's Illustrated Literature Museum
102 Cedar St. Abilene TX 79601 325-673-4586 520
Web: www.nccil.org

	Phone	Fax	Class
National Ctr for Computational Toxicology US Environmental Protection Agency 109 TW Alexander Dr .... Research Triangle Park NC 27709 *Web:* www.epa.gov	919-541-3850		668
National Ctr for Ecological Analysis & Synthesis (NCEAS) 735 State St Ste 300 .... Santa Barbara CA 93101 *Web:* www.nceas.ucsb.edu	805-892-2500	892-2510	668
National Ctr for Education Statistics 1990 K St NW .... Washington DC 20006 *Web:* nces.ed.gov	202-502-7300	502-7466	340-8
National Ctr for Electron Microscopy (NCEM) one cyclotron Rd Bldg 67 .... Berkeley CA 94720 *Web:* foundry.lbl.gov/facilities/ncem	510-486-4000		668
National Ctr for Employee Development (NCED) 2701 E Imhoff Rd .... Norman OK 73071 *TF:* 866-438-6233 ■ *Web:* www.nced.com	405-366-4420		377
National Ctr for Employee Ownership (NCEO) 1736 Franklin St 8th Fl .... Oakland CA 94612 *Web:* www.nceo.org	510-208-1300	272-9510	48-10
National Ctr for Family Literacy (NCFL) 325 W Main St Ste 300 .... Louisville KY 40202 *TF:* 855-937-5668 ■ *Web:* familieslearning.org	502-584-1133	584-0172	48-11
National Ctr for Genetic Resources Preservation (NCGRP) 1111 S Mason St .... Fort Collins CO 80521 *TF:* 800-795-3272 ■ *Web:* www.ars.usda.gov/npa/ftcollins/ncgrp	970-495-3200	221-1427	668
National Ctr for Genome Resources 2935 Rodeo Pk Dr E .... Santa Fe NM 87505 *TF:* 800-450-4854 ■ *Web:* www.ncgr.org	505-982-7840	995-4461	668
National Ctr for Homeopathy (NCH) 1120 Rte 73 Ste 200 .... Mount Laurel NJ 08054 **Fax Area Code:* 856 ■ *Web:* www.homeopathycenter.org	703-548-7790	439-0525*	48-17
National Ctr for Juvenile Justice (NCJJ) 3700 S Water St Ste 200 .... Pittsburgh PA 15203 *TF:* 800-851-3420 ■ *Web:* ncjj.org	412-227-6950	227-6955	48-8
National Ctr for Mfg Sciences (NCMS) 3025 Boardwalk .... Ann Arbor MI 48108 *TF:* 800-222-6267 ■ *Web:* www.ncms.org	734-995-3457	995-1150	668
National Ctr for Missing & Exploited Children (NCMEC) 699 Prince St .... Alexandria VA 22314 *TF:* 800-843-5678 ■ *Web:* www.missingkids.com	703-274-3900	274-2200	48-6
National Ctr for Policy Analysis 12770 Coit Rd Ste 800 .... Dallas TX 75251 *Web:* www.ncpa.org	972-386-6272	386-0924	634
National Ctr for Public Policy Research (NCPPR) 501 Capitol Ct NE Ste 200 .... Washington DC 20002 *Web:* ncppr.org	202-543-4110	543-5975	634
National Ctr for Retirement Benefits Inc 666 Dundee Rd Ste 1200 .... Northbrook IL 60062 **Fax Area Code:* 847 ■ *TF:* 800-666-1000 ■ *Web:* www.ncrb.com	800-666-1000	564-4944*	193
National Ctr for State Courts (NCSC) 300 Newport Ave. .... Williamsburg VA 23185 *TF:* 800-616-6164 ■ *Web:* www.ncsc.org	757-259-1525	220-0449	49-7
National Ctr for Supercomputing Applications University of Illinois Urbana-Champaign 1205 W Clark St Rm 1008 MC-257 .... Urbana IL 61801 *Web:* www.ncsa.illinois.edu	217-244-0072	244-8195	668
National Ctr for Victims of Crime, The 2000 M St NW Ste 480 .... Washington DC 20036 *TF:* 800-394-2255 ■ *Web:* www.victimsofcrime.org	202-467-8700	467-8701	48-8
National Ctr on Institutions & Alternatives 7222 Ambassador Rd .... Baltimore MD 21244 **Fax Area Code:* 410 ■ *TF:* 800-401-4632 ■ *Web:* www.ncianet.org	443-780-1300	597-9656*	634
National Customs Brokers & Forwarders Assn of America Inc (NCBFAA) 1200 18th St NW Ste 901 .... Washington DC 20036 *Web:* www.ncbfaa.org	202-466-0222	466-0226	49-21
National Cutting Horse Assn (NCHA) 260 Bailey Ave .... Fort Worth TX 76107 *TF:* 800-852-1162 ■ *Web:* www.nchacutting.com	817-244-6188	244-2015	48-3
National Cycle Inc 2200 Maywood Dr .... Maywood IL 60153 *TF:* 877-972-7336 ■ *Web:* www.nationalcycle.com	708-343-0400	343-0625	517
National Czech & Slovak Museum & Library 87 16th Ave SW .... Cedar Rapids IA 52404 *Web:* www.ncsml.org	319-362-8500	363-2209	520
National Dairy Council (NDC) 10255 W Higgins Rd Ste 900 .... Rosemont IL 60018 *Web:* www.nationaldairycouncil.org	847-627-3790		48-2
National Dairy Herd Improvement Assn Inc 421 S 9 Mound Rd PO Box 930399 .... Verona WI 53593 *Web:* www.dhia.org	608-848-6455	848-7675	11-2
National Defense Industrial Assn (NDIA) 2111 Wilson Blvd Ste 400 .... Arlington VA 22201 *Web:* www.ndia.org	703-522-1820	522-1885	48-19
National Defense University Fort McNair 300 5th Ave SW .... Washington DC 20319 *Web:* www.ndu.edu	202-685-4700		340-3
National Delivery Systems Inc 8700 Robert Fulton Dr .... Columbia MD 21046 *Web:* www.national-delivery.com	410-312-4770		546
National Development & Research Institutes Inc 71 W 23rd St 4th Fl .... New York NY 10010 **Fax Area Code:* 917 ■ *Web:* www.ndri.org	212-845-4400	438-0894*	668
National Diagnostics Inc 305 Patton Dr .... Atlanta GA 30336 *TF:* 800-526-3867 ■ *Web:* www.nationaldiagnostics.com	404-699-2121	699-2077	231
National Disaster Search Dog Foundation 501 E Ojai Ave .... Ojai CA 93023 *TF:* 888-459-4376 ■ *Web:* www.searchdogfoundation.org	805-646-1015		48-3
National Discount Cruise Co 1401 N Cedar Crest Blvd Ste 110 .... Allentown PA 18104 *TF:* 800-788-8108 ■ *Web:* www.nationaldiscountcruise.com	610-439-4883		771
National Disease Research Interchange (NDRI) 1628 John F Kennedy Blvd 8 Penn Ctr 8th Fl .... Philadelphia PA 19103 *TF:* 800-222-6374 ■ *Web:* www.ndriresource.org	215-557-7361		269
National Distributors Inc 1517 Avco Blvd. .... Sellersburg IN 47172	812-246-6306		449
National Domestic Violence Hotline (NDVH) PO Box 161810 .... Austin TX 78716 *TF:* 800-799-7233 ■ *Web:* www.thehotline.org	512-794-1133		48-6

	Phone	Fax	Class
National Door Industries Inc 6310 Airport Fwy .... Fort Worth TX 76117 *Web:* www.natdoor.com	817-834-7300		596
National Down Syndrome Congress (NDSC) 1370 Ctr Dr Ste 102 .... Atlanta GA 30338 *TF:* 800-232-6372 ■ *Web:* www.ndsccenter.org	770-604-9500	604-9898	48-17
National Down Syndrome Society (NDSS) 666 Broadway 8th Fl. .... New York NY 10012 **Fax Area Code:* 212 ■ *TF:* 800-221-4602 ■ *Web:* www.ndss.org	800-221-4602	979-2873*	48-17
National Drug Intelligence Ctr 319 Washington St 5th Fl .... Johnstown PA 15901 *Web:* www.justice.gov	814-532-4601	532-4690	340-14
National Eating Disorders Assn 200 W 41st St Ste 1203 .... New York NY 10036 *TF:* 800-931-2237 ■ *Web:* www.nationaleatingdisorders.org	212-575-6200	575-1650	48-17
National Economic Council 1600 Pennsylvania Ave NW .... Washington DC 20500 *Web:* www.whitehouse.gov/nec	202-456-1111		340
National Economic Research Assoc Inc 1166 Ave of the Americas 29th Fl .... New York NY 10036 *Web:* www.nera.com	914-448-4000	448-4040	194
National Education Assn (NEA) 1201 16th St NW .... Washington DC 20036 *TF:* 888-552-0624 ■ *Web:* www.nea.org	202-833-4000	822-7974	49-5
National Educational Telecommunications Assn (NETA) 939 S Stadium Rd. .... Columbia SC 29201 *TF:* 866-270-5141 ■ *Web:* www.netaonline.org	803-799-5517	771-4831	632
National Electrical Carbon 251 Forrester Dr .... Greenville SC 29607 **Fax Area Code:* 408 ■ *TF:* 800-471-7842 ■ *Web:* ndt.org	864-284-9728	280-7706*	127
National Electrical Contractors Assn (NECA) 3 Bethesda Metro Ctr Ste 1100 .... Bethesda MD 20814 *TF:* 800-214-0585 ■ *Web:* www.necanet.org	301-657-3110	215-4500	49-3
National Electrical Manufacturers Assn (NEMA) 1300 N 17th St Ste 1752 .... Rosslyn VA 22209 *TF:* 800-699-9277 ■ *Web:* www.nema.org	703-841-3200	841-5900	49-13
National Electrical Manufacturers Representatives Assn (NEMRA) 28 Deer St Ste 302 .... Portsmouth NH 03801 **Fax Area Code:* 603 ■ *TF:* 800-446-3672 ■ *Web:* www.nemra.org	914-524-8650	319-1667*	49-18
National Electronic Alloys Inc 3 Fir Ct .... Oakland NJ 07436 *Web:* www.nealloys.com	201-337-9400	337-9698	492
National Electronic Attachment Inc 3577 Pkwy Ln Ste 250 .... Norcross GA 30092 *TF:* 800-782-5150 ■ *Web:* www.nea-fast.com	800-782-5150		390
National Electronic Distributors Assn (NEDA) 1111 Alderman Dr Ste 400 .... Alpharetta GA 30005 *Web:* www.eciaonline.org	678-393-9990	393-9998	49-18
National Electronics Service Dealers Assn (NESDA) 3608 Pershing Ave .... Fort Worth TX 76107 *TF:* 800-946-0201 ■ *Web:* www.nesda.com	817-921-9061	921-3741	49-18
National Electrostatics Corp 7540 Graber Rd .... Middleton WI 53562 *Web:* www.pelletron.com	608-831-7600		250
National Elevator Industry Inc 1677 County Rd 64 PO Box 838 .... Salem NY 12865 *Web:* www.neii.org	518-854-3100	854-3257	49-3
National Emblem Inc 17036 S Avalon Blvd .... Carson CA 90746 *TF:* 800-877-6185 ■ *Web:* www.nationalemblem.com	310-515-5055	515-5966	258
National Emergency Management Assn (NEMA) PO Box 11910 .... Lexington KY 40578 *Web:* www.nemaweb.org	859-244-8000	244-8239	49-7
National Employee Assistance Services Inc N 17 W 24100 Riverwood Dr Ste 300 .... Waukesha WI 53188 *TF:* 800-634-6433 ■ *Web:* www.empathia.com	262-574-2500		462
National Employment Lawyers Assn (NELA) 417 Montgomery St 4th Fl .... San Francisco CA 94104 *Web:* www.nela.org	415-296-7629	677-9445	49-10
National Endangered Species Act Reform Coalition (NESARC) 1050 Thomas Jefferson St NW 6th Fl .... Washington DC 20007 *Web:* www.nesarc.org	202-333-7481	338-2416	48-2
National Endowment for Democracy (NED) 1025 F St NW Ste 800 .... Washington DC 20004 *Web:* www.ned.org	202-378-9700		48-7
National Endowment for Financial Education (NEFE) 1331 17th St Ste 1200 .... Denver CO 80202 *Web:* www.nefe.org	303-741-6333		48-10
National Endowment for the Arts (NEA) 1100 Pennsylvania Ave NW .... Washington DC 20506 *TF:* 800-634-1121 ■ *Web:* www.arts.gov	202-682-5400		340-20
National Endowment for the Humanities (NEH) 400 Seventh St SW. .... Washington DC 20506 *TF:* 800-634-1121 ■ *Web:* www.neh.gov	202-606-8400	606-8282	340-20
National Energy Research Scientific Computing Ctr (NERSC) Lawrence Berkeley National Laboratory .... Berkeley CA 94720 *TF:* 800-666-3772 ■ *Web:* www.nersc.gov	510-486-5849	486-4300	668
National Energy Technology Laboratory (NETL) 3610 Collins Ferry Rd. .... Morgantown WV 26505 *TF:* 800-432-8330 ■ *Web:* www.netl.doe.gov	304-285-4764		668
National Environmental Balancing Bureau (NEBB) 8575 Grovemont Cir .... Gaithersburg MD 20877 *Web:* www.nebb.org	301-977-3698	977-9589	49-19
National Environmental Health Assn (NEHA) 720 S Colorado Blvd Ste 1000-N .... Denver CO 80246 *TF:* 866-956-2258 ■ *Web:* www.neha.org	303-756-9090	691-9490	49-7
National Environmental Safety & Health Training Assn (NESHTA) 584 Main St .... South Portland ME 04106 *Web:* www.neshta.org	207-771-9020		49-5
National Environmental Satellite Data & Information Service 1335 East-West Hwy. .... Silver Spring MD 20910 *Web:* www.nesdis.noaa.gov	301-713-3578	713-1249	340-2
National Climatic Data Ctr 151 Patton Ave Rm 120 .... Asheville NC 28801 *Web:* www.ncdc.noaa.gov	828-271-4800	271-4876	340-2
National Coastal Data Development Ctr Bldg 1100 Ste 101 .... Stennis Space Center MS 39529 *TF:* 866-732-2382 ■ *Web:* www.ncddc.noaa.gov	228-688-2936	688-2010	340-2

Name / Address	City	State	Zip	Phone	Fax	Class
National Geophysical Data Ctr						
E/GC 325 Broadway	Boulder	CO	80305	303-497-6826	497-6513	340-2
Web: www.ngdc.noaa.gov						
National Oceanographic Data Ctr						
1335 East-West Hwy 8th Fl	Silver Spring	MD	20910	301-713-3277	713-3302	340-2
Web: www.nodc.noaa.gov						
National Enzyme Co Inc						
15366 US Hwy 160	Forsyth	MO	65653	417-546-4796	546-6433	144
TF: 800-825-8545 ■ *Web:* www.nationalenzyme.com						
National Equity Project						
1720 Broadway 4th Fl	Oakland	CA	94612	510-208-0160		242
Web: www.nationalequityproject.org						
National Events Inc 9672 S 700 E Ste 200	Sandy	UT	84070	801-495-9118	495-9128	760
Web: www.nationaleventservices.com						
National Excelsior Co						
1999 N Ruby St	Melrose Park	IL	60160	708-343-4225	681-0041	595
TF: 855-373-9235 ■ *Web:* www.excelsiorhvac.com						
National Exchange Bank & Trust						
130 S Main St PO Box 988	Fond Du Lac	WI	54936	920-921-7700		70
Web: www.nebat.com						
National Exchange Club						
3050 W Central Ave	Toledo	OH	43606	419-535-3232	535-1989	48-15
TF: 800-924-2643 ■ *Web:* www.nationalexchangeclub.org						
National Exposure Research Laboratory						
109 TW Alexander Dr						
Rm D310-G Mail Code: D305-01	Durham	NC	27709	919-541-2106		668
Web: www.epa.gov						
National Eye Institute (BVI)						
Vision Council, The						
225 Reinekers Ln Ste 700	Alexandria	VA	22314	703-548-4560		48-17
TF: 800-372-3937						
National Fabrication Ctr						
9561 Satellite Blvd	Orlando	FL	32837	407-852-6170		477
Web: hanger.com						
National Fabtronix Inc						
28800 Hesperian Blvd	Hayward	CA	94545	510-785-3135	785-1253	697
Web: www.natfab.com						
National Fallen Firefighters Foundation						
PO Box 498	Emmitsburg	MD	21727	301-447-1365		48-19
TF: 888-744-6513 ■ *Web:* www.firehero.org						
National Family Caregivers Assn (NFCA)						
10400 Connecticut Ave Ste 500	Kensington	MD	20895	301-942-6430		48-6
TF: 800-896-3650 ■ *Web:* caregiveraction.org						
National Family Farm Coalition (NFFC)						
110 Maryland Ave NE Ste 307	Washington	DC	20002	202-543-5675	543-0978	48-2
TF: 800-321-3054 ■ *Web:* www.nffc.net						
National Farm Life Insurance Co						
6001 Bridge St	Fort Worth	TX	76112	817-451-9550		390
TF: 800-772-7557 ■ *Web:* www.nflic.com						
National Farm Toy Museum						
1110 16th Ave SE	Dyersville	IA	52040	563-875-2727		520
TF: 877-475-2727 ■ *Web:* www.nationalfarmtoymuseum.com						
National Farmers Organization (NFO)						
528 Billy Sunday Rd Ste 100 PO Box 2508	Ames	IA	50010	515-292-2000	292-7106	48-2
TF: 800-247-2110 ■ *Web:* www.nfo.org						
National Farmers Union News (NFU)						
20 F St NW Ste 300	Washington	DC	20001	202-554-1600	554-1654	531-13
TF: 800-442-8277 ■ *Web:* www.nfu.org						
National Federation of Community Broadcasters (NFCB)						
1970 Broadway Ste 1000	Oakland	CA	94612	510-451-8200		49-14
Web: www.nfcb.org						
National Federation of Community Development Credit Unions (NFCDCU)						
39 Broadway Ste 2140	New York	NY	10006	212-809-1850	809-3274	49-2
TF: 800-437-8711 ■ *Web:* www.cdcu.coop						
National Federation of Democratic Women (NFDW)						
7211 E Lincoln	Wichita	KS	67207	316-612-9709		48-7
Web: www.nfdw.com						
National Federation of Federal Employees						
1225 New York Ave NW Ste 450	Washington	DC	20005	202-216-4420	216-4420	414
Web: www.nffe.org						
National Federation of Paralegal Associations (NFPA)						
23607 Hwy 99 Ste 2-C	Edmonds	WA	98026	425-967-0045	771-9588	49-10
National Federation of Republican Women (NFRW)						
124 N Alfred St	Alexandria	VA	22314	703-548-9688	548-9836	48-7
TF: 800-373-9688 ■ *Web:* www.nfrw.org						
National Federation of State High School Assn (NFHS)						
PO Box 690	Indianapolis	IN	46206	317-972-6900	822-5700	48-22
TF Cust Svc: 800-776-3462 ■ *Web:* www.nfhs.org						
National Federation of the Blind (NFB)						
1800 Johnson St	Baltimore	MD	21230	410-659-9314	685-5653	48-17
TF: 800-392-5671 ■ *Web:* www.nfb.org						
National Fence Systems Inc						
1033 Route One	Avenel	NJ	07001	732-636-5600		186
TF: 800-211-2444 ■ *Web:* www.nationalfencesystems.com						
National FFA Organization						
6060 FFA Dr	Indianapolis	IN	46268	317-802-6060	802-6061	48-2
TF: 800-772-0939 ■ *Web:* www.ffa.org						
National Fiber Technology LLC						
15 Union St	Lawrence	MA	01840	978-686-2964		348
TF Cust Svc: 800-842-2751 ■ *Web:* www.nftech.com						
National Fibromyalgia Partnership Inc (NFP)						
140 Zinn Way	Linden	VA	22642	866-725-4404		48-17
TF: 866-725-4404 ■ *Web:* www.fmpartnership.org						
National Field Service Corp (NFS)						
162 Orange Ave	Suffern	NY	10901	845-368-1600	368-1989	736
Web: nfsco.com						
National Film Board of Canada						
Stn Centre-Ville PO Box 6100	Montreal	QC	H3C3H5	514-283-9000	283-7564	513
TF: 800-267-7710 ■ *Web:* www.nfb.ca						
National Filter Media Corp						
691 North 400 West	Salt Lake City	UT	84103	801-363-6736	531-1293	18
TF: 800-777-4248 ■ *Web:* www.nfm-filter.com						
National Financial Partners Corp (NFP)						
340 Madison Ave 20th Fl	New York	NY	10173	212-301-4000	301-4001	401
NYSE: NFP ■ *Web:* www.nfp.com						
National Fingerprint Inc						
6999 Dolan Rd	Glouster	OH	45732	740-767-3853		692
TF: 888-823-7873 ■ *Web:* www.nationalfingerprint.com						
National Fire & Marine Insurance Co						
3024 Harney St	Omaha	NE	68131	402-536-3000	916-3030	391-4
TF: 866-720-7861 ■ *Web:* www.nationalindemnity.com						
National Fire Protection Assn (NFPA)						
1 Batterymarch Pk	Quincy	MA	02169	617-770-3000	770-0700	48-17
TF: 800-344-3555 ■ *Web:* www.nfpa.org						
National Fire Sprinkler Assn (NFSA)						
40 Jon Barrett Rd	Patterson	NY	12563	845-878-4200	878-4215	49-3
Web: www.nfsa.org						
National Firearms Museum						
11250 Waples Mill Rd	Fairfax	VA	22030	703-267-1600		520
Web: explore.nra.org						
National Fireworks Assn (NFA)						
8224 NW Bradford Ct	Kansas City	MO	64151	816-741-1826		48-10
Web: www.nationalfireworks.org						
National Fish & Wildlife Foundation						
1133 15th St NW Ste 1100	Washington	DC	20005	202-857-0166	857-0162	48-13
Web: www.nfwf.org						
National Fisheries Institute Inc						
7918 Jones Branch Dr Ste 700	McLean	VA	22102	703-752-8880		48-2
TF: 800-424-5156 ■ *Web:* www.aboutseafood.com						
National Fisherman Magazine						
121 Free St	Portland	ME	04101	207-842-5608	842-5603	457-21
TF: 800-959-5073 ■ *Web:* www.nationalfisherman.com						
National Fitness Trade Journal						
PO Box 2490	White City	OR	97503	541-830-0400	830-0410	457-21
TF: 877-867-7835 ■						
Web: msfitness.com/NationalFitness/TradeJournal/nftj.html						
National Flange & Fitting Co						
4420 Creekmont Dr	Houston	TX	77091	713-688-2515		483
National Flavors Inc						
1206 E Crosstown	Kalamazoo	MI	49001	800-525-2431		297-8
TF: 800-525-2431 ■ *Web:* www.nationalflavors.com						
National Floral Supply Inc						
3825 LeonaRdtown Rd Ste 4	Waldorf	MD	20601	301-932-7600		292
TF: 800-932-2772 ■ *Web:* www.flowersonbase.com						
National Fluid Power Assn (NFPA)						
3333 N Mayfair Rd Ste 211	Milwaukee	WI	53222	414-778-3344	778-3361	49-13
Web: www.nfpa.com						
National Food Laboratory Inc						
6363 Clark Ave	Dublin	CA	94568	925-828-1440	833-9239	195
Web: www.nfpa-food.org						
National Football League Players (NFLPA)						
1133 20th St NW	Washington	DC	20036	800-372-2000		48-22
TF: 800-372-2000 ■ *Web:* www.nflpa.com						
National Foreign Trade Council (NFTC)						
1625 K St NW Ste 200	Washington	DC	20006	202-887-0278	452-8160	49-18
Web: www.nftc.org						
National Forest Foundation						
27 Ft Missoula Rd Bldg 27 Ste 3	Missoula	MT	59804	406-542-2805	542-2810	48-13
Web: www.nationalforests.org						
National Forest Recreation Assn (NFRA)						
PO Box 488	Woodlake	CA	93286	559-564-2365	564-2048	48-23
TF: 800-282-2444 ■ *Web:* www.nfra.org						
National Forum for Black Public Administrators (NFBPA)						
777 N Capitol St NE Ste 807	Washington	DC	20002	202-408-9300	408-8558	49-7
TF: 800-488-4845 ■ *Web:* www.nfbpa.org						
National Foundation for Cancer Research (NFCR)						
4600 E W Hwy Ste 525	Bethesda	MD	20814	301-654-1250	654-5824	305
TF: 800-321-2873 ■ *Web:* www.nfcr.org						
National Foundation for Infectious Diseases (NFID)						
4733 Bethesda Ave Ste 750	Bethesda	MD	20814	301-656-0003	907-0878	49-8
TF: 800-708-5478 ■ *Web:* www.nfid.org						
National Frame Builders Assn (NFBA)						
8735 W Higgins Rd Ste 300	Chicago	IL	60631	800-557-6957	375-6495*	49-3
**Fax Area Code:* 847 ■ *TF:* 800-557-6957 ■ *Web:* www.nfba.org						
National Franchise Sales						
1601 Dove St Ste 150	Newport Beach	CA	92660	949-428-0480		317
Web: www.nationalfranchisesales.com						
National Fraternity of Kappa Delta Rho (KDR)						
331 S Main St	Greensburg	PA	15601	724-838-7100	838-7101	48-16
TF: 800-536-5371 ■ *Web:* www.kdr.com						
National Fraud Information Ctr (NFIC)						
1701 K St NW Ste 1200	Washington	DC	20006	202-835-3323		48-10
TF: 800-333-4636 ■ *Web:* www.fraud.org						
National Freedom of Information Coalition						
Univ of Missouri	Columbia	MO	65211	573-882-4856	884-6204	48-8
TF: 866-682-6663 ■ *Web:* www.nfoic.org						
National Fresh Water Fishing Hall of Fame						
10360 Hall of Fame Dr PO Box 690	Hayward	WI	54843	715-634-4440	634-4440	522
Web: www.freshwater-fishing.org						
National Frozen & Refrigerated Foods Assn (NFRA)						
4755 Linglestown Rd Ste 300 Ste 300	Harrisburg	PA	17112	717-657-8601	657-9862	49-6
Web: www.nfraweb.org						
National Frozen Foods Corp						
1600 Fairview Ave E Ste 200	Seattle	WA	98102	206-322-8900	322-4458	296-21
TF: 800-638-8280 ■ *Web:* www.nffc.com						
National Fruit Flavor Company Inc						
935 Edwards Ave	New Orleans	LA	70123	504-733-6757		345
Web: www.nationalfruitflavor.com						
National Fruit Product Co Inc						
701 Fairmont Ave	Winchester	VA	22601	540-662-3401		315-3
TF: 800-655-4022 ■ *Web:* www.whitehousefoods.com						
National Fuel Gas Co						
6363 Main St	Williamsville	NY	14221	716-857-7000	857-7206	360-5
NYSE: NFG ■ *TF Cust Svc:* 800-365-3234 ■ *Web:* nationalfuelgas.com						
National Fuel Gas Supply Corp						
6363 Main St	Williamsville	NY	14221	716-857-7000	857-7206	787
TF Cust Svc: 800-365-3234 ■ *Web:* nationalfuelgas.com						
National Fuel Resources Inc						
165 Lawrence Bell Dr Ste 120	Williamsville	NY	14221	716-630-6778	630-6798	787
TF: 800-839-9993 ■ *Web:* www.nfrinc.com						
National Funeral Directors & Morticians Assn (NFDMA)						
6290 Shannon Pkwy	Union City	GA	30291	770-969-0064	286-6573*	49-4
**Fax Area Code:* 404 ■ *TF:* 800-434-0958 ■ *Web:* www.nfdma.com						
National Funeral Directors Assn (NFDA)						
13625 Bishop's Dr	Brookfield	WI	53005	262-789-1880	789-6977	49-4
TF: 800-228-6332 ■ *Web:* nfda.org						

Name / Address	City	State	Zip	Phone	Fax	Class
National Furniture Liquidators I LLC						
2870 Plant Atkinson Rd SE	Smyrna	GA	30080	404-603-9714		321
Web: www.nflinc.com						
National Futures Assn (NFA)						
300 S Riverside Plaza Ste 1800	Chicago	IL	60606	312-781-1300	781-1467	49-2
TF: 800-621-3570 ■ *Web:* www.nfa.futures.org						
National Gallery of Art						
6th St & Constitution Ave NW	Washington	DC	20565	202-737-4215		520
TF: 800-697-9350 ■ *Web:* www.nga.gov						
National Garden 100 Maryland Ave	Washington	DC	20001	202-225-8333		97
Web: www.usbg.gov						
National Garden Clubs Inc (NGC)						
4401 Magnolia Ave	Saint Louis	MO	63110	314-776-7574	776-5108	48-18
TF: 800-550-6007 ■ *Web:* www.gardenclub.org						
National Gardening Assn (NGA)						
1100 Dorset St	South Burlington	VT	05403	802-863-5251	864-6889	48-18
TF: 800-538-7476 ■ *Web:* www.garden.org						
National Gaucher Foundation (NGF)						
5410 Edson Ln Ste 220	Rockville	MD	20852	770-934-2910		48-17
TF: 800-504-3189 ■ *Web:* www.gaucherdisease.org						
National Gay & Lesbian Task Force (NGLTF)						
1325 Massachusetts Ave NW Ste 600	Washington	DC	20005	202-393-5177	393-2241	48-8
Web: www.thetaskforce.org						
National Genealogical Society (NGS)						
3108 Columbia Pk Ste 300	Arlington	VA	22204	703-525-0050	525-0052	48-18
TF: 800-473-0060 ■ *Web:* www.ngsgenealogy.org						
National Genetics Institute						
2440 S Blvd Ste 235	Los Angeles	CA	90064	310-996-0036		418
TF: 800-352-7788 ■ *Web:* www.ngi.com						
National Geographic Society						
1145 17th St NW	Washington	DC	20036	202-857-7000		49-19
TF: 800-647-5463 ■ *Web:* www.nationalgeographic.com						
National Geographic Society Explorers Hall						
1145 17th St NW	Washington	DC	20036	800-647-5463	429-5709*	520
**Fax Area Code:* 202 ■ *TF:* 800-647-5463 ■ *Web:* www.nationalgeographic.com						
National Geographic Traveler Magazine						
1145 17th St NW	Washington	DC	20036	202-857-7000		457-22
TF: 800-647-5463 ■ *Web:* nationalgeographic.com						
National Glass & Metal Company Inc						
1424 Easton Rd Ste 400	Horsham	PA	19044	215-938-8880	938-7028	189-6
Web: www.ngmco.com						
National Glass Assn (NGA)						
8200 Greensboro Dr Ste 302	McLean	VA	22102	703-442-4890	442-0630	49-13
TF: 866-342-5642 ■ *Web:* www.glass.org						
National Glass Ltd 5744 198th St	Langley	BC	V3A7J2	604-530-2311		361
TF: 800-663-8168 ■ *Web:* www.natglass.com						
National Golf Course Owners Assn (NGCOA)						
291 Seven Farms Dr 2nd Fl	Charleston	SC	29492	843-881-9956	881-9958	48-23
TF: 800-933-4262 ■ *Web:* www.ngcoa.org						
National Golf Foundation (NGF)						
1150 S US Hwy 1 Ste 401	Jupiter	FL	33477	561-744-6006	744-6107	48-22
TF: 800-733-6006 ■ *Web:* www.ngf.org						
National Governors Assn (NGA)						
444 N Capitol St NW Ste 267	Washington	DC	20001	202-624-5300	624-5313	49-7
Web: www.nga.org						
National Graduate School of Quality Management Inc, The						
186 Jones Rd	Falmouth	MA	02540	508-457-1313		166
TF: 800-838-2580 ■ *Web:* www.ngs.edu						
National Grain & Feed Assn (NGFA)						
1250 'I' St NW Ste 1003	Washington	DC	20005	202-289-0873	289-5388	48-2
Web: www.ngfa.org						
National Grange 1616 H St NW	Washington	DC	20006	202-628-3507	347-1091	48-2
TF: 800-447-2643 ■ *Web:* www.nationalgrange.org						
National Grange Mutual Insurance Co						
55 W St	Keene	NH	03431	603-352-4000		391-4
TF: 800-258-5310 ■ *Web:* msagroup.com						
National Grape Co-op Assn Inc						
2 S Portage St	Westfield	NY	14787	716-326-5200		315-5
National Graphics Inc						
248 Branford Rd	North Branford	CT	06471	203-481-2351		627
Web: natgraphics.com						
National Great Blacks in Wax Museum						
1601-03 E N Ave	Baltimore	MD	21213	410-563-3404		520
Web: www.greatblacksinwax.org						
National Greyhound Assn (NGA)						
729 Old US 40	Abilene	KS	67410	785-263-4660	263-4689	48-22
TF: 800-366-1471 ■ *Web:* www.ngagreyhounds.com						
National Grid USA Service Company Inc						
25 Research Dr	Westborough	MA	01582	508-389-2000		360-5
TF: 800-548-8000 ■ *Web:* www.nationalgridus.com						
National Grocers Assn (NGA)						
1005 N Glebe Rd Ste 250	Arlington	VA	22201	703-516-0700	516-0115	49-6
TF: 800-627-6667 ■ *Web:* www.nationalgrocers.org						
National Ground Water Assn (NGWA)						
601 Dempsey Rd	Westerville	OH	43081	614-898-7791	898-7786	48-12
TF: 800-551-7379 ■ *Web:* www.ngwa.org						
National Guard Educational Foundation (NGAUS)						
1 Massachusetts Ave NW	Washington	DC	20001	202-789-0031	682-9358	48-19
TF: 888-226-4287 ■ *Web:* www.ngaus.org						
National Guard Products Inc						
4985 E Raines Rd	Memphis	TN	38118	800-647-7874	255-7874	234
TF: 800-647-7874 ■ *Web:* www.ngp.com						
National Guardian Life Insurance Co (NGL)						
2 E Gilman St	Madison	WI	53703	800-548-2962	257-3940*	391-2
**Fax Area Code:* 608 ■ *TF:* 800-548-2962 ■ *Web:* www.nglic.com						
National Guild of Community Schools of the Arts						
520 Eigth Ave Ste 302	New York	NY	10018	212-268-3337	268-3995	49-5
TF: 800-441-1414 ■ *Web:* www.nationalguild.org						
National Guild of Piano Teachers						
PO Box 1807	Austin	TX	78767	512-478-5775		48-4
Web: pianoguild.com						
National Gypsum Co 2001 Rexford Rd	Charlotte	NC	28211	704-365-7300	329-6421*	347
**Fax Area Code:* 800 ■ *TF:* 800-628-4662 ■ *Web:* nationalgypsum.com						
National Hansen's Disease Program (NHDP)						
1770 Physicians Pk Dr	Baton Rouge	LA	70816	800-221-9393		668
TF: 800-221-9393 ■ *Web:* hrsa.gov						
National Hardwood Lumber Assn (NHLA)						
6830 Raleigh-LaGrange Rd	Memphis	TN	38134	901-377-1818	382-6419	49-3
TF: 800-933-0318 ■ *Web:* www.nhla.com						
National Head Start Assn (NHSA)						
1651 Prince St	Alexandria	VA	22314	703-739-0875	739-0878	48-11
TF: 866-677-8724 ■ *Web:* www.nhsa.org						
National Headache Foundation (NHF)						
820 N Orleans St Ste 217	Chicago	IL	60610	888-643-5552	640-9049*	48-17
**Fax Area Code:* 312 ■ *TF:* 888-643-5552 ■ *Web:* www.headaches.org						
National Health & Environmental Effects Research Laboratory						
109 TW Alexander Dr B305-01	Research Triangle Park	NC	27711	919-541-2281	541-4324	668
Web: www.epa.gov/nheerl						
National Health Council (NHC)						
1730 M St NW Ste 500	Washington	DC	20036	202-785-3910	785-5923	48-17
TF: 800-622-9010 ■ *Web:* www.nationalhealthcouncil.org						
National Health Investors Inc						
222 Robert Rose Dr	Murfreesboro	TN	37129	615-890-9100		654
NYSE: NHI ■ *Web:* nhireit.com						
National Health Management Inc						
4415 Fifth Ave	Pittsburgh	PA	15213	412-578-7800		463
Web: www.independencecourt.com						
National HealthCare Corp						
100 E Vine St PO Box 1398	Murfreesboro	TN	37133	615-890-2020	890-0123	451
NYSE: NHC ■ *TF:* 800-877-1600 ■ *Web:* www.nhccare.com						
National Healthy Mothers Healthy Babies Coalition (HMHB)						
4401 Ford Ave Ste 300	Alexandria	VA	22302	703-837-4792		48-17
Web: www.hmhb.org						
National Hearing Conservation Assn (NHCA)						
3030 W 81st Ave	Westminster	CO	80031	303-224-9022	458-0002	48-17
TF: 866-432-7968 ■ *Web:* www.hearingconservation.org						
National Hemophilia Foundation (NHF)						
7 Penn Plaza Ste 1204	New York	NY	10001	212-328-3700	328-3777	48-17
TF: 800-424-2634 ■ *Web:* www.hemophilia.org						
National Heritage Academies						
3850 Broadmoor Ave SE Ste 201	Grand Rapids	MI	49512	877-223-6402		242
TF General: 877-223-6402 ■ *Web:* www.nhaschools.com						
National High Magnetic Field Laboratory (NHMFL)						
1800 E Paul Dirac Dr	Tallahassee	FL	32310	850-644-0311		668
National Highway Traffic Safety Administration (NHTSA)						
1200 New Jersey Ave SE	Washington	DC	20590	202-366-9550	366-6916	340-17
TF: 888-327-4236 ■ *Web:* www.nhtsa.gov						
National Center for Statistics & Analysis						
1200 New Jersey Ave SE	Washington	DC	20590	202-366-1503	366-7078	340-17
TF: 800-934-8517 ■ *Web:* www.nhtsa.gov						
Vehicle Research & Test Ctr						
10820 SR 347 PO Box B37	East Liberty	OH	43319	937-666-4511	666-3590	340-17
TF: 800-262-8309 ■ *Web:* www.nhtsa.gov						
National Highway Traffic Safety Administration Regional Offices (NHTSA)						
NHTSA Region 1						
1200 New Jersey Ave SE West Bldg	Cambridge	MA	02142	617-494-3427	494-3646	340-17
Web: www.nhtsa.gov						
NHTSA Region 2						
222 Mamaroneck Ave Ste 204	White Plains	NY	10605	914-682-6162	682-6239	340-17
Web: www.nhtsa.gov						
NHTSA Region 3						
1200 New Jersey Ave Ste 6700	Washington	DC	20590	888-327-4236	962-2770*	340-17
**Fax Area Code:* 410 ■ *TF:* 888-327-4236 ■ *Web:* www.nhtsa.gov						
NHTSA Region 4 61 Forsyth St SW	Atlanta	GA	30303	404-562-3739	562-3763	340-17
TF: 800-406-1527 ■ *Web:* www.nhtsa.gov						
NHTSA Region 5						
1200 New Jersey Ave SE	Washington	DC	20590	708-503-8822	503-8991	340-17
TF: 800-406-1527 ■ *Web:* www.nhtsa.gov						
NHTSA Region 6						
819 Taylor St Rm 8A38	Fort Worth	TX	76102	817-978-3653	978-8339	340-17
TF: 800-406-1527 ■ *Web:* www.nhtsa.gov						
NHTSA Region 7						
901 Locust St Rm 466	Kansas City	MO	64106	816-329-3900	329-3910	340-17
TF: 800-406-1527 ■ *Web:* www.nhtsa.gov						
NHTSA Region 8						
12300 W Dakota Ave Ste 140	Lakewood	CO	80228	720-963-3100	963-3124	340-17
TF: 800-406-1527 ■ *Web:* www.nhtsa.gov						
NHTSA Region 9						
201 Mission St Ste 2230	San Francisco	CA	94105	415-744-3089	744-2532	340-17
Web: www.nhtsa.gov						
NHTSA Region 10						
915 Second Ave Ste 3140	Seattle	WA	98174	206-220-7640	220-7651	340-17
TF: 800-406-1527 ■ *Web:* www.nhtsa.gov						
National Hispanic Council on Aging (NHCOA)						
734 15th St NW Ste 1050	Washington	DC	20005	202-347-9733	347-9735	48-6
TF: 800-633-4227 ■ *Web:* www.nhcoa.org						
National Hispanic Cultural Ctr						
1701 Fourth St SW	Albuquerque	NM	87102	505-246-2261	246-2613	50-2
Web: www.nhccnm.org						
National Hispanic Institute (NHI)						
472 FM 1966 Rd	Maxwell	TX	78656	512-357-6137		48-14
National Hispanic University						
14271 Story Rd	San Jose	CA	95127	408-254-6900	254-1369*	166
**Fax:* Admissions ■ *TF:* 877-762-9801 ■ *Web:* www.nhu.edu						
National HME Inc						
7451 Airport Fwy	Richland Hills	TX	76118	817-332-4433		475
Web: www.nationalhme.com						
National Hockey League (NHL)						
1185 Ave of the Americas	New York	NY	10036	212-789-2000	789-2020	716
Web: www.nhl.com						
National Hockey League Players Assn (NHLPA)						
20 Bay St Ste 1700	Toronto	ON	M5J2N8	416-907-9801	313-2301	48-22
Web: www.nhlpa.com						
National Home Furnishings Assn (NHFA)						
500 Giuseppe Ct Ste 6	Roseville	CA	95678	800-422-3778		49-4
TF: 800-422-3778 ■ *Web:* myhfa.org						
National Home Health Care Corp						
700 White Plains Rd Ste 275	Scarsdale	NY	10583	914-722-9000		363
TF: 800-422-4661 ■ *Web:* www.nhhc.net						
National Home Infusion Assn (NHIA)						
100 Daingerfield Rd	Alexandria	VA	22314	703-549-3740	683-1484	49-8
Web: www.nhia.org						
National Homeland Security Research Ctr						
US Environmental Protection Agency						
26 W Martin Luther King Dr	Cincinnati	OH	45268	513-569-7907		668
TF: 888-372-7341 ■ *Web:* www.epa.gov						
National Honor Society (NHS) 1904 Assn Dr	Reston	VA	20191	703-860-0200	476-5432	48-11
TF: 800-253-7746 ■ *Web:* www.nhs.us						

Name / Address	City	State	Zip	Phone	Fax	Class
National Hospice & Palliative Care Organization (NHPCO)						
1700 Diagonal Rd Ste 625	Alexandria	VA	22314	703-837-1500	837-1233	49-8
TF Help Line: 800-658-8898 ■ *Web:* www.nhpco.org						
National Hotel 1677 Collins Ave	Miami Beach	FL	33139	305-532-2311	534-1426	379
TF: 800-327-8370 ■ *Web:* www.nationalhotel.com						
National Housing & Rehabilitation Assn (NH&RA)						
1400 16th St NW Ste 420	Washington	DC	20036	202-939-1750	265-4435	49-17
TF: 800-644-0390 ■ *Web:* www.housingonline.com						
National Housing Conference (NHC)						
1801 K St NW Ste M-100	Washington	DC	20006	202-466-2121	466-2122	49-3
Web: www.nhc.org						
National Humanities Alliance (NHA)						
21 Dupont Cir NW Ste 800	Washington	DC	20036	202-296-4994	872-0884	48-4
Web: www.nhalliance.org						
National HVAC Service Ltd						
100 Bradford Rd Ste 120	Wexford	PA	15090	724-935-9390	935-9533	189-10
Web: www.nationalhvacservice.com						
National Immigration Forum						
50 F St NW Ste 300	Washington	DC	20001	202-347-0040	347-0058	48-8
TF: 800-559-2927 ■ *Web:* www.immigrationforum.org						
National Indemnity Co 3024 Harney St	Omaha	NE	68131	402-536-3000	536-3030	391-4
Web: www.nationalindemnity.com						
National Independent Automobile Dealers Assn (NIADA)						
2521 Brown Blvd	Arlington	TX	76006	817-640-3838	649-5866	49-18
TF: 800-682-3837 ■ *Web:* www.niada.com						
National Independent Flag Dealers Assn (NIFDA)						
7984 S Chicago Ave	Chicago	IL	60617	773-768-8076	768-3138	49-18
TF: 800-356-4085 ■ *Web:* www.nifda.net						
National Indian Gaming Assn (NIGA)						
224 Second St SE	Washington	DC	20003	202-546-7711	546-1755	48-23
TF: 800-937-0010 ■ *Web:* www.indiangaming.org						
National Indian Gaming Commission						
1441 L St NW Ste 9100	Washington	DC	20005	202-632-7003	632-7066	340-20
Web: www.nigc.gov						
National Industrial Lumber Co						
1 Chicago Ave	Elizabeth	PA	15037	800-289-9352	384-3955*	191-3
**Fax Area Code:* 412 ■ *TF:* 800-289-9352 ■ *Web:* www.nilco.net/about-us/locations						
National Industrial Transportation League (NITL)						
7918 Jones Branch Dr Ste 300	McLean	VA	22102	703-524-5011	506-3266	49-21
Web: www.nitl.org						
National Industries for the Blind (NIB)						
1310 Braddock Pl	Alexandria	VA	22314	703-310-0500		48-17
TF Cust Svc: 800-433-2304 ■ *Web:* www.nib.org						
National Infantry Museum						
1775 Legacy Way	Columbus	GA	31903	706-685-5800	545-5158	520
Web: www.nationalinfantrymuseum.org						
National Information Standards Organization (NISO)						
3600 Clipper Mill Rd Ste 302	Baltimore	MD	21211	301-654-2512	685-5278*	49-16
**Fax Area Code:* 410 ■ *TF:* 877-375-2160 ■ *Web:* www.niso.org						
National Inhalant Prevention Coalition (NIPC)						
318 Lindsay St	Chattanooga	TN	37405	423-265-4662	265-4889	48-17
TF: 800-269-4237 ■ *Web:* www.inhalants.org						
National Institute Child Health (CRMC)						
31 Center Dr Bldg 31 Rm 2A32	Bethesda	MD	20892	800-370-2943		668
TF: 800-370-2943						
National Institute for Fitness & Sport Inc, The						
250 University Blvd	Indianapolis	IN	46202	317-274-3432		354
Web: www.nifs.org						
National Institute for Literacy (NIFL)						
1775 'I' St NW Ste 730	Washington	DC	20006	202-233-2025	233-2050	340-8
TF: 800-228-8813 ■ *Web:* www.lincs.ed.gov						
National Institute for Women in Trades Technology & Science (IWITTS)						
1150 Ballena Blvd Ste 102	Alameda	CA	94501	510-749-0200	749-0500	49-19
Web: www.iwitts.org						
National Institute for Work & Learning (NIWL)						
1825 Connecticut Ave NW 7th Fl	Washington	DC	20009	202-884-8186	884-8422	49-12
National Institute of Bldg Sciences (NIBS)						
1090 Vermont Ave NW Ste 700	Washington	DC	20005	202-289-7800	289-1092	49-3
Web: www.nibs.org						
National Institute of Governmental Purchasing Inc (NIGP)						
151 Spring St	Herndon	VA	20170	703-736-8900	736-2818	49-7
TF: 800-367-6447 ■ *Web:* www.nigp.org						
National Institute of Standards & Technology (NIST)						
100 Bureau Dr Sp 1070	Gaithersburg	MD	20899	301-975-6478	926-1630	340-2
TF: 800-877-8339 ■ *Web:* www.nist.gov						
Boulder Laboratories						
325 Broadway MS 104	Boulder	CO	80305	301-975-6478	497-6235*	668
**Fax Area Code:* 303 ■ *Web:* www.nist.gov						
National Institute on Disability & Rehabilitation Research (NIDRR)						
400 Maryland Ave SW	Washington	DC	20202	202-205-8134	245-7323	668
Web: www.ed.gov						
National Institutes of Biomedical Imaging & Bioengineering						
National Institute of Biomedical Imaging & Bioengineering						
6707 Democracy Blvd	Bethesda	MD	20892	301-496-8859	480-0679	340-10
Web: www.nibib.nih.gov						
National Institutes of Health (NIH)						
9000 Rockville Pike	Bethesda	MD	20892	301-496-4000		340-10
TF: 800-411-1222 ■ *Web:* www.nih.gov						
Center for Scientific Review						
6701 Rockledge Dr MSC 7950	Bethesda	MD	20892	301-435-1115		340-10
TF: 800-438-4380 ■ *Web:* www.nih.gov						
Clinical Ctr 10 Ctr Dr	Bethesda	MD	20892	301-496-2563	402-2984	340-10
Web: www.cc.nih.gov						
Library 9000 Rockville Pike Bldg 10	Bethesda	MD	20892	301-496-4000	402-2984	434-1
TF: 800-860-8747 ■ *Web:* www.nih.gov						
National Cancer Institute						
Public Inquiries Office 6116 Executive Blvd						
Rm 3036A	Bethesda	MD	20892	301-435-3848		668
TF: 800-422-6237 ■ *Web:* www.cancer.gov						
National Center for Complementary & Alternative Medicine						
National Institutes of Health						
9000 Rockville Pike	Bethesda	MD	20892	301-594-7103		340-10
TF: 888-644-6226 ■ *Web:* nccih.nih.gov						
National Center on Minority Health & Health Disparities						
6707 Democracy Blvd Ste 800 Ste 800	Bethesda	MD	20892	301-402-1366	480-4049	340-10
Web: www.nimhd.nih.gov						
National Eye Institute						
2020 Vision Pl	Bethesda	MD	20892	301-496-5248		340-10
Web: www.nei.nih.gov						
National Heart Lung & Blood Institute (NHLBI)						
31 Ctr Dr Bldg 31 Rm 5A52 MSC 2486	Bethesda	MD	20892	301-496-5166	402-0818	340-10
Web: www.nhlbi.nih.gov						
National Human Genome Research Institute						
31 Ctr Dr Bldg 31 Rm 4B09	Bethesda	MD	20892	301-402-0911	402-2218	668
Web: www.genome.gov						
National Institute of Arthritis & Musculoskeletal & Skin Diseases						
1 AMS Cir	Bethesda	MD	20892	301-495-4484	718-6366	340-10
TF: 877-226-4267 ■ *Web:* www.niams.nih.gov						
National Institute of Dental & Craniofacial Resear						
9000 Rockville Pike	Bethesda	MD	20892	301-496-3571	402-2185	668
Web: www.nidcr.nih.gov						
National Institute of Diabetes & Digestive & Kidne						
31 Ctr Dr MSC 2560	Bethesda	MD	20892	301-496-3583	480-6741	340-10
Web: www.niddk.nih.gov						
National Institute of Environmental Health Science						
PO Box 12233	Research Triangle Park	NC	27709	919-541-3201	541-2260	340-10
Web: www.niehs.nih.gov						
National Institute of General Medical Sciences						
45 Ctr Dr MSC 6200	Bethesda	MD	20892	301-496-7301		340-10
Web: www.nigms.nih.gov						
National Institute of Mental Health						
6001 Executive Blvd Rm 8184 MSC 9663	Bethesda	MD	20892	301-443-4513	443-4279	340-10
TF: 866-615-6464 ■ *Web:* www.nimh.nih.gov						
National Institute of Neurological Disorders & Stroke						
PO Box 5801	Bethesda	MD	20824	301-496-5751		340-10
TF: 800-352-9424 ■ *Web:* www.ninds.nih.gov						
National Institute of Nursing Research						
31 Ctr Dr Room 5B-13	Bethesda	MD	20892	301-496-8230		668
Web: www.ninr.nih.gov						
National Institute on Aging						
31 Ctr Dr Bldg 31 Rm 5C27 MSC 2292	Bethesda	MD	20892	301-496-1752	496-1072	340-10
Web: www.nia.nih.gov						
National Institute on Alcohol Abuse & Alcoholism						
5635 Fishers Ln MSC 9304	Bethesda	MD	20892	301-443-3885	443-7043	340-10
Web: www.niaaa.nih.gov						
National Institute on Deafness & Other Communication						
31 Ctr Dr MSC 2320	Bethesda	MD	20892	301-496-7243	402-0018	668
TF: 800-241-1044 ■ *Web:* www.nidcd.nih.gov						
National Institute on Drug Abuse						
6001 Executive Blvd Rm 4123	Bethesda	MD	20892	301-443-6480		340-10
Web: www.drugabuse.gov						
National Library of Medicine						
8600 Rockville Pike	Bethesda	MD	20894	301-594-5983	402-1384	340-10
TF: 888-346-3656 ■ *Web:* www.nlm.nih.gov						
Office of Communications & Public Liason						
31 Ctr Dr Bldg 1 Rm 344	Bethesda	MD	20892	301-496-4461	496-0017	340-10
Web: www.nih.gov						
Office of Dietary Supplements						
6100 Executive Blvd Ste 3B01	Bethesda	MD	20892	301-435-2920	480-1845	340-10
Web: www.ods.od.nih.gov						
Office of Rare Diseases						
6701 Democracy Blvd Ste 1001	Bethesda	MD	20892	301-402-4336	480-9655	340-10
TF: 800-942-6825 ■ *Web:* www.rarediseases.info.nih.gov						
National Instrument LLC						
4119 Fordleigh Rd	Baltimore	MD	21215	410-764-0900	764-7719	547
TF: 866-258-1914 ■ *Web:* www.filamatic.com						
National Instruments Corp						
11500 N Mopac Expy	Austin	TX	78759	512-794-0100	683-8411	178-5
NASDAQ: NATI ■ *TF Cust Svc:* 800-433-3488 ■ *Web:* www.ni.com						
National Insulation Assn (NIA)						
99 Canal Ctr Plaza Ste 222	Alexandria	VA	22314	703-683-6422		49-3
TF: 877-968-7642 ■ *Web:* www.insulation.org						
National Insurance Crime Bureau (NICB)						
1111 E Touhy Ave Ste 400	Des Plaines	IL	60018	847-544-7002		49-9
TF: 800-447-6282 ■ *Web:* www.nicb.org						
National Interagency Fire Ctr						
3833 S Development Ave	Boise	ID	83705	208-387-5512		340-13
TF: 877-471-2262 ■ *Web:* www.nifc.gov						
National Interfaith Coalition on Aging (NICA)						
1901 L St NW 4th Fl	Washington	DC	20036	202-479-1200	479-0735	48-6
TF: 800-772-1213 ■ *Web:* www.ncoa.org						
National Interstate Corp 3250 I- Dr	Richfield	OH	44286	330-659-8900	659-8901	391-4
NASDAQ: NATL ■ *TF:* 800-929-1500 ■ *Web:* www.nationalinterstate.com						
National Intramural-Recreational Sports Assn (NIRSA)						
4185 SW Research Way	Corvallis	OR	97333	541-766-8211	766-8284	48-22
Web: www.nirsa.org						
National Inventors Hall of Fame						
3701 Highland Park NW	North Canton	OH	44720	800-968-4332		520
TF: 800-968-4332 ■ *Web:* www.invent.org						
National Investment Co Service Assn (NICSA)						
8400 Westpark Dr 2nd Fl	McLean	VA	22102	508-485-1500	485-1560	49-2
TF: 800-426-1122 ■ *Web:* www.nicsa.org						
National Investor Relations Institute (NIRI)						
8020 Towers Crescent Dr Ste 250	Vienna	VA	22182	703-506-3570	506-3571	49-2
Web: www.niri.org						
National Italian American Sports Hall of Fame						
1431 W Taylor St	Chicago	IL	60607	312-226-5566		522
Web: www.niashf.org						
National Jets						
3495 SW Ninth Ave	Fort Lauderdale	FL	33315	954-359-9900	359-0064	63
TF: 800-327-3710 ■ *Web:* www.nationaljets.com/natjet/jet						
National Jewish Medical & Research Ctr						
1400 Jackson St PO Box 17169	Denver	CO	80206	303-388-4461		374-7
TF: 877-225-5654 ■ *Web:* www.nationaljewish.org						
National Journal						
600 New Hampshire Ave NW	Washington	DC	20037	202-739-8400	833-8069	457-17
TF: 800-613-6701 ■ *Web:* www.nationaljournal.com						
National Jurist Magazine						
7670 Opportunity Rd Ste 105	San Diego	CA	92111	858-300-3200		457-15
Web: www.nationaljurist.com						
National Kappa Kappa Iota Inc						
1875 E 15th St	Tulsa	OK	74104	918-744-0389	744-0578	48-16
TF: 800-678-0389 ■ *Web:* www.nationalkappakappaiota.org						
National Kidney Foundation (NKF)						
30 E 33rd St 8th Fl	New York	NY	10016	212-889-2210		48-17
TF: 800-622-9010 ■ *Web:* www.kidney.org						

	Phone	Fax	Class

National Kitchen & Bath Assn (NKBA)
687 Willow Grove St. . . . . Hackettstown NJ 07840 800-843-6522 852-1695* 49-3
*Fax Area Code: 908 ■ TF: 800-843-6522 ■ Web: www.nkba.org

National Label Company Inc
2025 Joshua Rd . . . . . Lafayette Hill PA 19444 610-825-3250 834-8854 413
Web: www.nationallabel.com

National Labor College
10000 New Hampshire Ave. . . . . Silver Spring MD 20903 301-431-6400 431-5411 800
TF: 888-427-8100 ■ Web: www.nlc.edu

National Labor Relations Board (NLRB)
1099 14th St NW . . . . . Washington DC 20570 202-273-1991 340-20
TF: 866-667-6572 ■ Web: www.nlrb.gov

National Labor Relations Board
Region 1 10 Causeway St 6th Fl . . . . . Boston MA 02222 617-565-6700 565-6725 340-20
TF: 866-667-6572 ■ Web: www.nlrb.gov
Region 2 26 Federal Plaza Rm 3614 . . . . . New York NY 10278 212-264-0300 264-2450 340-20
Web: www.nlrb.gov
Region 3
Niagara Ctr Bldg 130 S Elmwood Ave Ste 630. . . Buffalo NY 14202 716-551-4931 551-4972 340-20
TF: 866-667-6572 ■ Web: www.nlrb.gov
Region 4 615 Chestnut St 7th Fl . . . . . Philadelphia PA 19106 215-597-7601 597-7658 340-20
TF: 800-829-4933 ■ Web: www.nlrb.gov
Region 5 103 S Gay St 8th Fl . . . . . Baltimore MD 21202 410-962-2822 962-2198 340-20
Web: www.nlrb.gov
Region 6 1000 Liberty Ave Rm 904 . . . . . Pittsburgh PA 15222 412-395-4400 395-5986 340-20
Web: www.nlrb.gov
Region 7 477 Michigan Ave Rm 300 . . . . . Detroit MI 48226 313-226-3200 226-2090 340-20
Web: www.nlrb.gov
Region 8 1240 E Ninth St Rm 1695. . . . . Cleveland OH 44199 216-522-3715 522-2418 340-20
TF: 866-667-6572 ■ Web: www.nlrb.gov
Region 9 550 Main St Rm 3003 . . . . . Cincinnati OH 45202 513-684-3686 684-3946 340-20
TF: 866-667-6572 ■ Web: www.nlrb.gov
Region 10 233 Peachtree St NE Ste 1000 . . . . . Atlanta GA 30303 404-331-2896 331-2858 340-20
Web: www.nlrb.gov
Region 11
4035 University Pkwy Ste 200. . . . . Winston-Salem NC 27106 336-631-5201 631-5210 340-20
TF: 866-667-6572 ■ Web: www.nlrb.gov
Region 12 201 E Kennedy Blvd Ste 530 . . . . . Tampa FL 33602 813-228-2641 228-2874 340-20
Web: www.nlrb.gov
Region 13 200 W Adams St. . . . . Chicago IL 60606 312-353-7570 886-1341 340-20
Web: www.nlrb.gov
Region 14 1222 Spruce St Rm 8.302 . . . . . Saint Louis MO 63103 314-539-7770 539-7794 340-20
TF: 866-667-6572 ■ Web: www.nlrb.gov
Region 15 1515 Poydras St Rm 610 . . . . . New Orleans LA 70112 504-589-6361 589-4069 340-20
Web: www.nlrb.gov
Region 16
Federal Bldg 819 Taylor St Rm 8A24 . . . . . Fort Worth TX 76102 817-978-2921 978-2928 340-20
TF: 866-667-6572 ■ Web: www.nlrb.gov
Region 17 8600 Farley St Ste 100. . . . . Overland Park KS 66212 913-967-3000 967-3010 340-20
Web: www.nlrb.gov
Region 18 330 Second Ave S Ste 790. . . . . Minneapolis MN 55401 612-348-1757 348-1785 340-20
TF: 866-667-6572 ■ Web: www.nlrb.gov
Region 19 915 Second Ave # 2948 . . . . . Seattle WA 98174 206-220-6300 220-6305 340-20
TF: 800-547-8367 ■ Web: www.nlrb.gov
Region 20 901 Market St Ste 400 . . . . . San Francisco CA 94103 415-356-5130 356-5156 340-20
TF: 866-667-6572 ■ Web: www.nlrb.gov
Region 21 888 S Figueroa St 9th Fl. . . . . Los Angeles CA 90017 213-894-5200 894-2778 340-20
Web: www.nlrb.gov
Region 22 20 Washington Pl 5th Fl. . . . . Newark NJ 07102 973-645-2100 645-3852 340-20
Web: www.nlrb.gov
Region 24
525 FD Roosevelt Ave Ste 1002. . . . . San Juan PR 00918 787-766-5347 766-5478 340-20
Web: www.nlrb.gov
Region 25
575 N Pennsylvania St Ste 238 . . . . . Indianapolis IN 46204 317-226-7381 226-5103 340-20
TF: 866-667-6572 ■ Web: www.nlrb.gov
Region 26 80 Monroe Ave Ste 350 . . . . . Memphis TN 38103 901-544-0018 544-0008 340-20
TF: 800-669-4000 ■ Web: www.nlrb.gov
Region 27 600 17th St 7th Fl N Tower. . . . . Denver CO 80202 303-844-3551 844-6249 340-20
TF: 800-827-1000 ■ Web: www.nlrb.gov
Region 28 2600 N Central Ave Ste 1800 . . . . . Phoenix AZ 85004 602-640-2160 640-2178 340-20
Web: www.nlrb.gov
Region 29 1 Metrotech Ctr N # A. . . . . Brooklyn NY 11201 718-330-7713 330-7579 340-20
Web: www.nlrb.gov
Region 30
310 W Wisconsin Ave Ste 700. . . . . Milwaukee WI 53203 414-297-3861 297-3880 340-20
TF: 800-827-1000 ■ Web: www.nlrb.gov
Region 31
11150 W Olympic Blvd Ste 700. . . . . Los Angeles CA 90064 310-235-7352 235-7420 340-20
TF: 866-667-6572 ■ Web: www.nlrb.gov
Region 32 1301 Clay St Rm 300N. . . . . Oakland CA 94612 510-637-3300 637-3315 340-20
Web: www.nlrb.gov
Region 34 450 Main St . . . . . Hartford CT 06103 860-240-3522 240-3564 340-20
Web: nlrb.gov

National Ladies Auxiliary Jewish War Veterans of USA Inc
1811 R St NW. . . . . Washington DC 20009 202-667-9061 520
TF: 800-855-2881 ■ Web: www.jwv.org

National Latino Education Institute
2011 W Pershing Rd. . . . . Chicago IL 60609 773-247-0707 533
Web: www.nlei.org

National League for Nursing (NLN)
61 Broadway 33rd Fl. . . . . New York NY 10006 212-363-5555 812-0391 49-8
TF: 800-669-1656 ■ Web: www.nln.org

National League of American Pen Women Inc
1300 17th St NW . . . . . Washington DC 20036 202-785-1997 452-6868 48-4
TF: 800-492-5195 ■ Web: www.nlapw.org

National League of Cities (NLC)
1301 Pennsylvania Ave NW Ste 550. . . . . Washington DC 20004 202-626-3000 626-3043 49-7
TF: 800-892-2757 ■ Web: www.nlc.org

National League of Families of American Prisoners & Missing in Southeast Asia
5673 Columbia Pk Ste 100. . . . . Falls Church VA 22041 703-465-7432 48-19
Web: www.pow-miafamilies.org

National League of Postmasters of the US
1 Beltway Ctr 5904 Richmond Hwy Ste 500 . . . . . Alexandria VA 22303 703-329-4550 329-0466 414
Web: www.unitedpma.org

National Legal Aid & Defender Assn (NLADA)
1140 Connecticut Ave NW Ste 900. . . . . Washington DC 20036 202-452-0620 872-1031 49-10
TF: 800-725-4513 ■ Web: www.nlada.org

National Liberty Museum
321 Chestnut St . . . . . Philadelphia PA 19106 215-925-2800 520
Web: libertymuseum.org

National Library Bindery Co
100 Hembree Pk Dr . . . . . Roswell GA 30076 770-442-5490 92

National Library of Medicine
Lister Hill National Center for Biomedical Communications
8600 Rockville Pike. . . . . Bethesda MD 20894 301-496-4441 480-3035 340-10
Web: www.lhncbc.nlm.nih.gov

National Lift Truck Inc
3333 Mt Prospect Rd . . . . . Franklin Park IL 60131 630-782-1000 111
TF: 800-469-6420 ■ Web: www.nlt.com

National Lighting Company Inc
522 Cortlandt St . . . . . Belleville NJ 07109 973-751-1600 751-4931 439
Web: www.natltg.com

National Little Britches Rodeo Assn (NLBRA)
5050 Edison Ave Ste 105 . . . . . Colorado Springs CO 80915 719-389-0333 578-1367 48-22
TF: 800-763-3694 ■ Web: www.nlbra.org

National Luggage Dealers Assn (NLDA)
1817 Elmdale Ave. . . . . Glenview IL 60026 847-998-6869 998-6884 49-18
TF: 800-411-0705 ■ Web: www.nlda.com

National Lumber 71 Maple St. . . . . Mansfield MA 02048 508-339-8020 339-4518 364
TF: 800-370-9663 ■ Web: www.national-lumber.com

National Lumber & Bldg Material Dealers Assn (NLBMDA)
2025 M St NW . . . . . Washington DC 20036 202-367-1169 367-2169 49-18
Web: www.dealer.org

National Machine 4880 Hudson Dr . . . . . Stow OH 44224 330-688-6494 454
Web: www.nationalmachinegroup.com

National Machinery LLC
161 Greenfield St . . . . . Tiffin OH 44883 419-447-5211 443-2379 456
Web: www.nationalmachinery.com

National Magnetic Sensors Inc
141 Summer St. . . . . Plantsville CT 06479 860-621-6816 250
Web: www.nationalmagnetic.com

National Magnetics Group Inc
1210 Win Dr. . . . . Bethlehem PA 18017 610-867-7600 867-0200 458
Web: www.magneticsgroup.com

National Mail Graphics Corp
300 Old Mill Ln . . . . . Exton PA 19341 610-524-1600 627
Web: www.nmgcorp.com

National Mail Order Assn LLC (NMOA)
2807 Polk St NE. . . . . Minneapolis MN 55418 612-788-1673 788-1147 49-18
TF: 800-992-1377 ■ Web: www.nmoa.org

National Management Assn (NMA)
2210 Arbor Blvd . . . . . Dayton OH 45439 937-294-0421 294-2374 49-12
TF: 800-688-5253 ■ Web: www.nma1.org

National Marfan Foundation (NMF)
22 Manhasset Ave. . . . . Port Washington NY 11050 516-883-8712 883-8040 48-17
TF: 800-862-7326 ■ Web: www.marfan.org

National Marine Electronics Assn (NMEA)
7 Riggs Ave. . . . . Severna Park MD 21146 410-975-9425 975-9450 49-13
TF: 800-808-6632 ■ Web: www.nmea.org

National Marine Fisheries Service Regional Offices
Alaska Regional Office PO Box 21668 . . . . . Juneau AK 99802 907-586-7221 586-7249 340-2
Web: alaskafisheries.noaa.gov
Northeast Section 1 Blackburn Dr . . . . . Gloucester MA 01930 978-281-9300 281-9333 340-2
Web: greateratlantic.fisheries.noaa.gov
Northwest Region 7600 Sand Pt Way NE. . . . . Seattle WA 98115 206-526-6150 526-6426 340-2
Web: www.fisheries.noaa.gov
Southwest Region
501 W Ocean Blvd Ste 4200 . . . . . Long Beach CA 90802 562-980-4000 980-4018 340-2
TF: 800-825-5547 ■ Web: www.nmfs.noaa.gov/ia/permits/contacts.html

National Marine Manufacturers Assn (NMMA)
200 E Randolph Dr Ste 5100 . . . . . Chicago IL 60601 312-946-6200 946-0388 49-21
Web: www.nmma.org

National Marine Representatives Assn (NMRA)
PO Box 360 . . . . . Gurnee IL 60031 847-662-3167 336-7126 49-18
TF: 800-890-3819 ■ Web: www.nmraonline.org

National Marine Sanctuary Foundation
8601 Georgia Ave Ste 501 . . . . . Silver Spring MD 20910 301-608-3040 608-3044 48-13
Web: www.marinesanctuary.org

National Marrow Donor Program (NMDP)
3001 Broadway St NE Ste 100 . . . . . Minneapolis MN 55413 612-627-5800 48-17
TF: 800-526-7809 ■ Web: bethematch.org

National Material LP
1965 Pratt Blvd. . . . . Elk Grove Village IL 60007 847-284-8464 806-4722 492
Web: www.nmlp.com

National Meat Assn (NMA)
1970 Broadway Ste 825 . . . . . Oakland CA 94612 510-763-1533 49-6
TF: 800-248-2862 ■ Web: meatassociation.com

National Medal of Honor Museum of Military History
PO Box 11467 . . . . . Chattanooga TN 37401 423-877-2525 520
TF: 800-854-0675 ■ Web: www.mohm.org

National Media Services Inc
613 N Commerce Ave. . . . . Front Royal VA 22630 540-635-4181 514
Web: www.nationalmediaservices.com

National Mediation Board
1301 K St NW Ste 250E . . . . . Washington DC 20005 202-692-5000 340-20
Web: www.nmb.gov

National Medical Assn (NMA)
8403 Colesville Rd Ste 920 . . . . . Silver Spring MD 20910 202-347-1895 347-0722 49-8
TF: 800-662-0554 ■ Web: www.nmanet.org

National Memorial Cemetery of Arizona
23029 N Cave Creek Rd . . . . . Phoenix AZ 85024 480-513-3600 513-1412 136
Web: www.cem.va.gov

National Mental Health Information Ctr
PO Box 42557 . . . . . Washington DC 20015 800-487-4889 747-5470* 340-10
*Fax Area Code: 240 ■ TF: 800-487-4889 ■ Web: www.samhsa.gov

National Merit Scholarship Corp
1560 Sherman Ave Ste 200 . . . . . Evanston IL 60201 847-866-5100 866-5113 725
Web: www.nationalmerit.org

National Metal Fabricators
2395 Greenleaf Ave. . . . . Elk Grove Village IL 60007 847-439-5321 439-4774 697
TF: 800-323-8849 ■ Web: www.nmfrings.com

National Metalwares Inc
900 N Russell Ave. . . . . Aurora IL 60506 630-892-9000 490
Web: www.nationalmetalwares.com

Name / Address	City	State	ZIP	Phone	Fax	Class
National Meter & Automation 7220 S Fraser St *TF:* 877-212-8340 ■ *Web:* www.nmaai.com	Centennial	CO	80112	303-339-9100	649-1017	610
National Mfg Company Inc 12 River Rd *TF:* 800-362-7231 ■ *Web:* www.natlmfg.com	Chatham	NJ	07928	973-635-8846	635-7810	254
National Middle School Assn (NMSA) 4151 Executive Pkwy Ste 300 *TF:* 800-528-6672 ■ *Web:* www.amle.org	Westerville	OH	43081	614-895-4730	895-4750	49-5
National Milk Producers Federation (NMPF) 2101 Wilson Blvd Ste 400 *Web:* www.nmpf.org	Arlington	VA	22201	703-243-6111	841-9328	49-6
National Milk Producers Federation PAC (NMPF PAC) 2101 Wilson Blvd Ste 400 *Web:* nmpf.org	Arlington	VA	22201	703-243-6111	841-9328	615
National Mining Assn (NMA) 101 Constitution Ave NW Ste 500-E *Web:* www.nma.org	Washington	DC	20001	202-463-2600	463-2666	48-12
National Minority Supplier Development Council (NMSDC) 1359 Broadway 10th Fl *TF:* 800-843-4898 ■ *Web:* www.nmsdc.org	New York	NY	10018	212-944-2430	719-9611	49-18
National Mississippi River Museum & Aquarium 350 E Third St *TF:* 800-226-3369 ■ *Web:* www.mississippirivermuseum.com	Dubuque	IA	52001	563-557-9545		520
National Model Railroad Assn (NMRA) 4121 Cromwell Rd *TF:* 800-654-2256 ■ *Web:* www.nmra.org	Chattanooga	TN	37421	423-892-2846	899-4869	48-18
National Monitoring Center 26800 Aliso Viejo Pkwy Ste 250 *TF:* 800-662-1711 ■ *Web:* www.nmccentral.com	Aliso Viejo	CA	92656	800-662-1711		693
National Motor Club of America Inc (NMC) 130 E John Carpenter Fwy *TF:* 800-523-4582 ■ *Web:* www.nmc.com	Irving	TX	75062	972-999-1099		53
National Motor Freight Traffic Assn (NMFTA) 1001 N Fairfax St Ste 600 *TF:* 866-411-6632 ■ *Web:* www.nmfta.org	Alexandria	VA	22314	703-838-1810	683-6296	49-21
National Motorists Assn (NMA) 402 W Second St *TF:* 800-882-2785 ■ *Web:* www.motorists.org	Waunakee	WI	53597	608-849-6000		49-21
National Multi Housing Council (NMHC) 1850 M St NW Ste 540 *Web:* www.nmhc.org	Washington	DC	20036	202-974-2300	775-0112	49-17
National Multi Housing Council PAC 1850 M St NW Ste 540 *TF:* 866-987-7367 ■ *Web:* www.nmhc.org	Washington	DC	20036	202-974-2300	775-0112	615
National Multiple Sclerosis Society 733 Third Ave 3rd Fl *TF:* 800-344-4867 ■ *Web:* www.nationalmssociety.org	New York	NY	10017	212-986-3240	986-7981	48-17
National Museum of American History (Smithsonian Institution) (NMAH) 12th St & Constitution Ave NW *Web:* americanhistory.si.edu	Washington	DC	20560	202-633-3270	312-1990	520
National Museum of American Illustration 492 Bellevue Ave *TF:* 800-652-6422 ■ *Web:* www.americanillustration.org	Newport	RI	02840	401-851-8949	851-8974	520
National Museum of American Jewish History 101 S Independence Mall E *Web:* www.nmajh.org	Philadelphia	PA	19106	215-923-3811	923-0763	520
National Museum of American Jewish Military History (JWV-NMI) 1811 R St NW *Web:* www.nmajmh.org	Washington	DC	20009	202-265-6280	462-3192	520
National Museum of Dentistry 31 S Greene St *Web:* www.dental.umaryland.edu	Baltimore	MD	21201	410-706-0600	706-8313	520
National Museum of Funeral History 415 Barren Springs Dr *TF:* 800-383-7677 ■ *Web:* www.nmfh.org	Houston	TX	77090	281-876-3063		520
National Museum of Health & Medicine 2500 Linden Ln *Web:* www.medicalmuseum.mil	Silver Spring	MD	20910	202-782-2200		520
National Museum of Mexican Art 1852 W 19th St *Web:* www.nationalmuseumofmexicanart.org	Chicago	IL	60608	312-738-1503	738-9740	520
National Museum of Natural History (Smithsonian Institution) 10th St & Constitution Ave NW *TF:* 866-868-7774 ■ *Web:* naturalhistory.si.edu	Washington	DC	20560	202-633-1000	357-4779	520
National Museum of Naval Aviation 1750 Radford Blvd Ste C *TF General:* 800-247-6289 ■ *Web:* www.navalaviationmuseum.org	Pensacola	FL	32508	850-452-3604	452-3296	520
National Museum of Patriotism 1927 Piedmont Cir *Web:* foundationofpatriotism.org	Atlanta	GA	30324	404-875-0691		520
National Museum of Polo & Hall of Fame 9011 Lake Worth Rd *Web:* www.polomuseum.com	Lake Worth	FL	33467	561-969-3210	964-8299	522
National Museum of Racing & Hall of Fame 191 Union Ave *TF:* 800-562-5394 ■ *Web:* www.racingmuseum.org	Saratoga Springs	NY	12866	518-584-0400	584-4574	522
National Museum of Roller Skating 4730 S St *TF:* 800-423-8212 ■ *Web:* www.rollerskatingmuseum.com	Lincoln	NE	68506	402-483-7551	483-1465	520
National Museum of the American Indian (Smithsonian Institution) 4th St & Independence Ave SW *Web:* www.nmai.si.edu	Washington	DC	20560	202-633-1000		520
National Museum of the American Indian (Smithsonian Institution) 1 Bowling Green *TF:* 800-242-6624 ■ *Web:* www.nmai.si.edu	New York	NY	10004	212-514-3700		520
National Museum of the Marine Corps 18900 Jefferson Davis Hwy *Web:* www.usmcmuseum.org	Triangle	VA	22172	703-221-1581		520
National Museum of the United States Air Force 1100 Spaatz St Wright-Patterson Air Force Base *Web:* www.nationalmuseum.af.mil	Dayton	OH	45433	937-255-3284	255-3286	520
National Museum of Wildlife Art 2820 Rungius Rd PO Box 6825 *TF:* 800-313-9553 ■ *Web:* www.wildlifeart.org	Jackson	WY	83002	307-733-5771	733-5787	520
National Museum of Women in the Arts 1250 New York Ave NW *TF:* 866-875-4627 ■ *Web:* www.nmwa.org	Washington	DC	20005	202-783-5000	393-3234	520

Name / Address	City	State	ZIP	Phone	Fax	Class
National Museum of Woodcarving West US-16	Custer	SD	57730	605-673-4404		520
National Music Museum 414 E Clark St *Web:* orgs.usd.edu	Vermillion	SD	57069	605-677-5306	677-6995	520
National Music Publishers' Assn (NMPA) 975 F St NW Ste 375 *Web:* www.nmpa.org	Washington	DC	20004	202-393-6672		48-4
National Mutual Benefit 6522 Grand Teton Plaza *TF:* 800-779-1936 ■ *Web:* www.nmblife.org	Madison	WI	53719	608-833-1936		391-2
National Nail Corp 2964 Clydon SW *Web:* www.nationalnail.com	Wyoming	MI	49519	616-538-8000		234
National Naval Medical Ctr 8901 Wisconsin Ave	Bethesda	MD	20889	301-295-4000		374-4
National NeedleArts Assn, The (TNNA) 1100-H Brandywine Blvd *TF:* 800-889-8662 ■ *Web:* www.tnna.org	Zanesville	OH	43701	740-455-6773	452-2552	48-18
National Network for Youth, The 741 Eigth St SE *Web:* www.nn4youth.org	Washington	DC	20003	202-783-7949	783-7955	48-6
National Newspaper Assn (NNA) PO Box 7540 *TF:* 800-829-4662 ■ *Web:* nnaweb.org	Columbia	MO	65205	573-777-4980	777-4985	49-14
National Niemann-Pick Disease Foundation Inc (NNPDF) 401 Madison Ave Ste B PO Box 49 *TF:* 877-287-3672 ■ *Web:* www.nnpdf.org	Fort Atkinson	WI	53538	920-563-0930	563-0931	48-17
National Nonwovens PO Box 150 *TF:* 800-333-3469 ■ *Web:* www.nationalnonwovens.com	EastHampton	MA	01027	413-527-3445	527-9570	745-6
National Notary Assn (NNA) 9350 DeSoto Ave *TF:* 800-876-6827 ■ *Web:* www.nationalnotary.org	Chatsworth	CA	91313	818-739-4000		49-12
National Nuclear Security Administration (NNSA) 1000 Independence Ave SW *Web:* www.nnsa.energy.gov	Washington	DC	20585	202-586-5000	586-4892	340-9
National Nursing Staff Development Organization (NNSDO) 330 N Wabash Ave Ste 2000 *TF:* 800-489-1995 ■ *Web:* www.anpd.org	Chicago	IL	60611	312-321-5135	673-6835	49-8
National Ocean Industries Assn (NOIA) 1120 G St NW Ste 900 *TF:* 800-558-9994 ■ *Web:* www.noia.org	Washington	DC	20005	202-347-6900	347-8650	48-12
National Ocean Service 1305 East-West Hwy *Web:* oceanservice.noaa.gov	Silver Spring	MD	20910	301-713-3074	713-4269	340-2
National Oceanic & Atmospheric Administration (NOAA) 1401 Constitution Ave NW *Web:* www.noaa.gov	Washington	DC	20230	202-482-6090	482-3154	340-2
National Odd Shoe Exchange PO Box 1120 *TF:* 800-451-1459 ■ *Web:* www.oddshoe.org	Chandler	AZ	85244	480-892-3484		48-17
National Office Furniture 1205 Kimball Blvd **Fax Area Code: 812 ■ TF:* 800-482-1717 ■ *Web:* www.nationalofficefurniture.com	Jasper	IN	47549	800-482-1717	482-8800*	319-1
National Office Systems Inc 7621 Rickenbacker Dr Ste 400 *Web:* nosinc.com	Gaithersburg	MD	20879	301-840-6264		610
National Oil & Gas Inc 409 N Main St *TF:* 800-322-8454 ■ *Web:* natloil.com	Bluffton	IN	46714	260-824-2220	824-2223	579
National Oilseed Processors Assn 1300 L St NW Ste 1020 *Web:* www.nopa.org	Washington	DC	20005	202-842-0463	842-9126	48-2
National Oilwell Varco (NOV) 7909 Parkwood Cir Dr *NYSE:* NOV ■ *TF:* 888-262-8645 ■ *Web:* www.nov.com	Houston	TX	77036	713-375-3700		183
National Older Worker Career Center 3811 N Fairfax Dr Ste 900 *Web:* www.nowcc.org	Arlington	VA	22203	703-558-4200		260
National Onion Assn (NOA) 822 Seventh St Ste 510 *Web:* www.onions-usa.org	Greeley	CO	80631	970-353-5895	353-5897	48-2
National Optical Astronomy Observatories 950 N Cherry Ave *TF:* 888-809-4012 ■ *Web:* www.noao.edu	Tucson	AZ	85719	520-318-8163	318-8360	668
National Oral Health Information Clearinghouse (NIDCR) 1 NOHIC Way *TF:* 866-232-4528 ■ *Web:* www.nidcr.nih.gov	Bethesda	MD	20892	301-496-4261	480-4098	48-17
National Orange Show Events Ctr 689 SE St *Web:* www.nosevents.com	San Bernardino	CA	92408	909-888-6788		515
National Organization for Albinism & Hypopigmentation (NOAH) PO Box 959 *TF:* 800-648-2310 ■ *Web:* www.albinism.org	East Hampstead	NH	03826	603-887-2310		48-17
National Organization for Rare Disorders (NORD) 55 Kenosia Ave *TF:* 800-999-6673 ■ *Web:* www.rarediseases.org	Danbury	CT	06810	203-744-0100	798-2291	48-17
National Organization for the Reform of Marijuana Laws (NORML) 1600 K St NW Ste 501 *TF:* 888-420-8932 ■ *Web:* www.norml.org	Washington	DC	20006	202-483-5500	483-0057	48-8
National Organization for Victim Assistance (NOVA) 510 King St Ste 424 *TF:* 800-879-6682 ■ *Web:* trynova.org	Alexandria	VA	22314	703-535-6682	535-5500	48-8
National Organization for Women (NOW) 1100 H St NW 3rd Fl *TF:* 855-212-0212 ■ *Web:* www.now.org	Washington	DC	20005	202-628-8669	785-8576	48-24
National Organization of Black Law Enforcement Executives (NOBLE) 4609 Pinecrest Office Pk Dr Ste F *Web:* noblenational.org	Alexandria	VA	22312	703-658-1529	658-9479	49-7
National Organization of Circumcision Information Resource Centers (NOCIRC) PO Box 2512 *TF:* 800-727-8622 ■ *Web:* www.nocirc.org	San Anselmo	CA	94979	415-488-9883	488-9660	48-17
National Organization of Industrial Trade Unions 148-06 Hillside Ave *TF:* 800-510-8003 ■ *Web:* www.noitu.org	Jamaica	NY	11435	718-291-3434		414
National Organization of Life & Health Insurance Guaranty Assn (NOLHGA) 13873 Pk Ctr Rd Ste 329 *Web:* www.nolhga.com	Herndon	VA	20171	703-481-5206	481-5209	49-9

Phone | Fax | Class

National Organization of Mothers of Twins Clubs Inc (NOMOTC)
2000 Mallory Ln Ste 130-600..................Franklin TN 37067-8231 248-231-4480 48-6
Web: www.multiplesofamerica.org

National Organization of Restoring Men (NORM)
3205 Northwood Dr Ste 209..................Concord CA 94520 925-827-4077 827-4119 48-17
Web: www.norm.org

National Organization on Disability (NOD)
77 Water St Ste 204........................New York NY 10005 646-505-1191 48-17
Web: www.nod.org

National Ornamental Metal Museum
374 Metal Museum Dr........................Memphis TN 38106 901-774-6380 520
Web: www.metalmuseum.org

National Osteoporosis Foundation (NOF)
251 18th St S Ste 630......................Arlington VA 22202 202-223-2226 223-2237 48-17
TF: 800-231-4222 ■ Web: www.nof.org

National Outdoor Leadership School
284 Lincoln St.............................Lander WY 82520 307-332-5300 332-1220 685
TF: 800-710-6657 ■ Web: www.nols.edu

National Ovarian Cancer Coalition (NOCC)
2501 Oak Lawn Ave Ste 435..................Dallas TX 75219 888-682-7426 273-4201* 48-17
*Fax Area Code: 214 ■ TF: 888-682-7426 ■ Web: www.ovarian.org

National Paint & Coatings Assn (NPCA)
1500 Rhode Island Ave NW...................Washington DC 20005 202-462-6272 462-8549 49-13
Web: www.paint.org

National Paper & Sanitary Supply
2511 S 156th Cir...........................Omaha NE 68130 402-330-5507 330-4109 559
TF: 800-647-2737 ■ Web: catalog.nationalew.com/catalog

National Park Aquarium
209 Central Ave............................Hot Springs AR 71901 501-624-3474 40
Web: nationalparkaquarium.org

National Park Community College
101 College Dr.............................Hot Springs AR 71913 501-760-4222 760-4236* 162
*Fax: Admissions ■ Web: np.edu

National Park Foundation (NPF)
1201 Eye St NW Ste 550-B...................Washington DC 20005 202-354-6460 371-2066 48-13
Web: www.nationalparks.org

National Park Medical Ctr
1910 Malvern Ave.............Hot Springs National Park AR 71901 501-321-1000 374-3
Web: www.nationalparkmedical.com

National Park Service (NPS)
1849 C St NW Rm 1013.......................Washington DC 20240 202-208-6843 219-0910 340-13
Web: www.nps.gov

Conservation & Outdoor Recreation
1849 C St NW Org Code 2220.................Washington DC 20240 202-354-6900 371-5179 340-13
Web: www.nps.gov/ncrc

National Register of Historic Places
1201 Eye St NW.............................Washington DC 20005 202-354-2201 371-5197 340-13
Web: www.nps.gov/history/index.htm

National Park Service Regional Offices

Alaska Region
240 W Fifth Ave Ste 114....................Anchorage AK 99501 907-644-3510 644-3816 340-13
TF: 800-645-8465 ■ Web: nps.gov

National Park Service Regional Offices Intermountain Region
12795 W Alameda Pkwy.......................Denver CO 80225 303-969-2500 340-13
Web: www.nps.gov

National Park Service Regional Offices NortheastRegion
200 Chestnut St Ste 3......................Philadelphia PA 19106 215-597-7013 597-0815 340-13
Web: www.nps.gov

National Park Service Regional Offices Southeast Region
100 Alabama St SW 1924 Bldg................Atlanta GA 30303 404-507-5600 562-3201 340-13
Web: www.nps.gov

National Park Trust (NPT)
401 E Jefferson St Ste 102.................Rockville MD 20850 301-279-7275 279-7211 48-13
TF: 800-995-7525 ■ Web: www.parktrust.org

National Parking Assn (NPA)
1112 16th St NW Ste 840....................Washington DC 20036 202-296-4336 296-3102 49-3
TF: 800-647-7275 ■ Web: weareparking.org

National Parks Conservation Assn (NPCA)
1300 19th St NW Ste 300....................Washington DC 20036 202-223-6722 48-13
TF: 800-628-7275 ■ Web: www.npca.org

National Parks Magazine
777 Sixth St NW Ste 700....................Washington DC 20001 202-223-6722 454-3333 457-19
TF General: 800-628-7275 ■ Web: npca.org/news/magazine

National Partitions
10300 Goldenfern Ln........................Knoxville TN 37931 865-670-2100 286
TF: 800-996-7266 ■ Web: www.nationalpartitions.com

National Partnership for Women & Families
1875 Connecticut Ave NW Ste 650............Washington DC 20009 202-986-2600 986-2539 48-24
TF: 800-827-5335 ■ Web: www.nationalpartnership.org

National Peace Corps Assn (NPCA)
1900 L St NW Ste 610.......................Washington DC 20036 202-293-7728 293-7554 48-5
TF: 800-336-1616 ■ Web: peacecorpsconnect.org

National Pen Corp (NPC)
12121 Scripps Summit Dr Ste 200............San Diego CA 92131 858-675-3000 9
TF: 800-854-1000 ■ Web: www.pens.com

National Penn Bancshares Inc
645 Hamilton St Ste 1100...................Allentown PA 18101 800-822-3321 360-2
NASDAQ: NPBC ■ TF: 800-822-3321

National Pest Management Assn Inc (NPMA)
10460 N St.................................Fairfax VA 22030 703-352-6762 352-3031 49-4
TF: 800-678-6722 ■ Web: www.pestworld.org

National Pesticide Information Ctr (NPIC)
333 Weniger Hall...........................Corvallis OR 97331 800-858-7378 737-0761* 48-17
*Fax Area Code: 541 ■ TF: 800-858-7378 ■ Web: www.npic.orst.edu

National Petrochemical & Refiners Assn (NPRA)
1667 K St NW Ste 700.......................Washington DC 20006 202-457-0480 457-0486 48-12
Web: www.afpm.org

National Pharmaceutical Council (NPC)
1894 Preston White Dr......................Reston VA 20191 703-620-6390 476-0904 49-8
Web: www.npcnow.org

National Pharmaceutical Services
13660 California St........................Omaha NE 68154 402-965-8800 231
Web: www.pti-nps.com

National Philharmonic
5301 Tuckerman Ln..........................North Bethesda MD 20852 301-493-9283 493-9284 573-3
Web: www.nationalphilharmonic.org

National Pipe & Plastics Inc
3421 Old Vestal Rd.........................Vestal NY 13850 800-836-4350 729-6130* 596
*Fax Area Code: 607 ■ TF: 800-836-4350 ■ Web: www.nationalpipe.com

National Plastek Inc
7050 Dutton Industrial Park Dr.............Dutton MI 49316 616-698-9559 596
Web: www.plastek.com

National Polish-American Sports Hall of Fame
11727 Gallagher St.........................Hamtramck MI 48212 313-407-3300 522
TF: 800-535-2071 ■ Web: www.polishsportshof.com

National Pork Producers Council (NPPC)
122 C St NW Ste 875........................Washington DC 20001 202-347-3600 347-5265 49-6
TF: 800-952-4629 ■ Web: www.nppc.org

National Pork Producers Council PAC
122 C St NW Ste 875........................Washington DC 20001 202-347-3600 347-5265 615
Web: www.nppc.org

National Post 365 Bloor St E 3rd Fl.....Toronto ON M4W3L4 416-383-2300 383-2305 532-1
TF: 800-267-6568 ■ Web: www.nationalpost.com

National Postal Museum (Smithsonian Institution)
2 Massachusetts Ave NE.....................Washington DC 20002 202-633-5555 633-9393 520
Web: www.postalmuseum.si.edu

National Precast Concrete Assn (NPCA)
10333 N Meridian St Ste 272................Indianapolis IN 46290 317-571-9500 571-0041 49-3
TF: 800-366-7731 ■ Web: www.precast.org

National Presidential Wax Museum
609 Hwy 16A................................Keystone SD 57751 605-666-4455 520
Web: www.blackhillsbadlands.com

National Press Club (NPC)
529 14th St NW.............................Washington DC 20045 202-662-7500 662-7569 49-14
Web: www.press.org

National Press Foundation (NPF)
1211 Connecticut Ave NW Ste 310............Washington DC 20036 202-663-7280 49-16
Web: www.nationalpress.org

National Press Photographers Assn (NPPA)
3200 Croasdaile Dr Ste 306.................Durham NC 27705 919-383-7246 383-7261 49-14
TF: 800-786-6277 ■ Web: www.nppa.org

National Presto Industries Inc
3925 N Hastings Way........................Eau Claire WI 54703 715-839-2121 37
NYSE: NPK ■ TF: 800-877-0441 ■ Web: www.gopresto.com

National Printing Converters Inc
18 S Murphy Ave............................Brazil IN 47834 800-877-6724 413
TF: 800-877-6724 ■ Web: www.npclabels.com

National Private Truck Council (NPTC)
950 N Glebe Rd Ste 2300....................Arlington VA 22203 703-683-1300 683-1217 49-21
Web: www.nptc.org

National Product Services Inc
105 Decker Ct Ste 700......................Irving TX 75062 972-373-9484 194

National Propane Gas Assn (NPGA)
1899 L St NW Ste 350.......................Washington DC 20036 202-466-7200 466-7205 48-12
TF: 800-328-1111 ■ Web: www.npga.org

National Property Inspections Inc (NPI)
9375 Burt St Ste 201.......................Omaha NE 68114 402-333-9007 365
TF: 800-333-9807

National Psoriasis Foundation (NPF)
6600 SW 92nd Ave Ste 300...................Portland OR 97223 503-244-7404 245-0626 48-17
TF: 800-723-9166 ■ Web: www.psoriasis.org

National Psychological Assn for Psychoanalysis (NPAP)
40 W 13th St Ste 1.........................New York NY 10011 212-924-7440 989-7543 49-15
TF: 800-365-7006 ■ Web: www.npap.org

National PTA 1250 N Pitt St.............Alexandria VA 22314 703-518-1200 305
TF: 800-307-4782 ■ Web: pta.org

National Public Radio (NPR)
635 Massachusetts Ave NW...................Washington DC 20001 202-513-3232 513-3329 632
TF: 800-989-8255 ■ Web: www.npr.org

National Publisher Services LLC
43 Oak Hills Rd............................Edison NJ 08820 732-548-1667 393
Web: www.nps1.com

National Pump Company LLC
7706 N 71st Ave............................Glendale AZ 85303 623-979-3560 641
TF: 800-966-5240 ■ Web: www.nationalpumpcompany.com

National Quality Assurance - U.S.A. Inc
4 Post Office Sq...........................Acton MA 01720 978-635-9256 463
Web: www.nqa.com/en-us

National Radio Astronomy Observatory (NRAO)
520 Edgemont Rd............................Charlottesville VA 22903 434-296-0211 296-0278 668
Web: www.nrao.edu

National Railroad Museum
2285 S Broadway St.........................Green Bay WI 54304 920-437-7623 437-1291 520
TF: 866-468-7630 ■ Web: www.nationalrrmuseum.org

National Railroad Passenger Corp
60 Massachusetts Ave NE....................Washington DC 20002 202-906-3741 906-3285 649
TF: 800-872-7245 ■ Web: www.amtrak.com

National Railway Equipment Co (NREC)
14400 Robey St.............................Dixmoor IL 60426 708-388-6002 650
TF: 800-253-2905 ■ Web: www.nre.com

National Raisin Co PO Box 219...........Fowler CA 93625 559-834-5981 834-1055 315-5
Web: www.nationalraisin.com

National Ranching Heritage Ctr
3121 Fourth St.............................Lubbock TX 79409 806-742-0498 520
Web: www.depts.ttu.edu

National Ready Mixed Concrete Assn (NRMCA)
900 Spring St..............................Silver Spring MD 20910 301-587-1400 585-4219 49-3
TF: 888-846-7622 ■ Web: www.nrmca.org

National Real Estate Investor Magazine
6151 Powers Ferry Rd NW Ste 200............Atlanta GA 30339 770-955-2500 618-0348 457-5
TF: 800-637-0037 ■ Web: www.nreionline.com

National Realty & Development Corp
3 Manhattanville Rd........................Purchase NY 10577 914-694-4444 655
Web: www.nrdc.com

National Recreation and Park Assn (NSPR)
22377 Belmont Ridge Rd
22377 Belmont Ridge Rd.....................Ashburn VA 20148 703-858-0784 858-0794 48-23
TF: 800-626-6772 ■ Web: www.nrpa.org

National Recreation Reservation Service (NRRS)
PO Box 140.................................Ballston Spa NY 12020 518-885-3639 773
TF: 877-444-6777 ■ Web: www.recreation.gov

National Register Publishing Direct
430 Mountain Ave Ste 403...................New Providence NJ 07974 844-592-4197 637-2
TF: 844-592-4197

Phone Fax Class

National Rehabilitation Assn (NRA)
633 S Washington St .... Alexandria VA 22314 703-836-0850 836-0848 48-17
TF: 888-258-4295 ■ *Web:* www.nationalrehab.org

National Rehabilitation Hospital
102 Irving St NW .... Washington DC 20010 202-877-1000 877-1602 374-6
Web: www.medstarhealth.org

National Rehabilitation Information Ctr (NARIC)
8400 Corporate Dr Ste 500 .... Landover MD 20785 301-459-5900 459-4263 48-17
TF: 800-346-2742 ■ *Web:* www.naric.com

National Reining Horse Assn (NRHA)
3000 NW Tenth St .... Oklahoma City OK 73107 405-946-7400 946-8425 48-3
Web: nrha1.com

National Religious Broadcasters (NRB)
9510 Technology Dr .... Manassas VA 20110 703-330-7000 330-7100 49-14
TF: 800-248-4242 ■ *Web:* www.nrb.org

National Renal Administrators Assn (NRAA)
100 N 20th St .... Philadelphia PA 19103 215-320-4655 564-2175 49-8
TF: 800-638-8299 ■ *Web:* www.nraa.org

National Renderers Assn (NRA)
801 N Fairfax St Ste 205 .... Alexandria VA 22314 703-683-0155 683-2626 48-2
TF: 800-366-2563 ■ *Web:* www.nationalrenderers.org

National Renewable Energy Laboratory (NREL)
1617 Cole Blvd .... Golden CO 80401 303-275-3000 275-4053 668
Web: www.nrel.gov

National Research Corp 1245 Q St .... Lincoln NE 68508 402-475-2525 475-9061 466
NASDAQ: NRCI ■ *TF:* 800-388-4264 ■ *Web:* nrchealth.com

National Research Council (NRC)
500 Fifth St NW .... Washington DC 20001 202-334-2000 48-11
Web: www.nationalacademies.org/nrc

National Research Ctr for Coal & Energy (NRCCE)
West Virginia University
385 Evansdale Dr PO Box 6064 .... Morgantown WV 26506 304-293-2867 293-3749 668
TF: 800-624-8301 ■ *Web:* www.nrcce.wvu.edu

National Research Ctr on English Learning & Achievement (CELA)
School of Education University of Albany B9
1400 Washington Ave .... Albany NY 12222 518-442-5026 442-5933 668
Web: www.albany.edu

National Resource Ctr on Domestic Violence (NRCDV)
6400 Flank Dr Ste 1300 .... Harrisburg PA 17112 800-799-7233 545-9456* 48-6
**Fax Area Code:* 717 ■ *TF:* 800-799-7233 ■ *Web:* www.nrcdv.org

National Resource Ctr on Native American Aging (NRCNAA)
501 N Columbia Rd Rm 4535 .... Grand Forks ND 58202 701-777-6780 777-6779 48-6
TF: 800-896-7628 ■ *Web:* ruralhealth.und.edu

National Resource Ctr on Nutrition Physical Activity & Aging
Florida International Univ
11200 SW Eighth St Bldg OE200 .... Miami FL 33199 305-348-1517 348-1518 48-6
Web: nutrition.fiu.edu

National Restaurant Assn (NRA)
2055 L St NW Ste 700 .... Washington DC 20036 202-331-5900 331-2429 49-6
TF: 800-424-5156 ■ *Web:* www.restaurant.org

National Retail Federation (NRF)
1101 New York Ave NW .... Washington DC 20005 202-783-7971 737-2849 49-18
TF: 800-673-4692 ■ *Web:* www.nrf.com

National Retail Hardware Assn (NRHA)
5822 W 74th St .... Indianapolis IN 46278 317-290-0338 328-4354 49-18
TF Cust Svc: 800-772-4424 ■ *Web:* www.nrha.org

National Review
215 Lexington Ave 11th Fl .... New York NY 10016 212-679-7330 679-6174 457-17
Web: www.nationalreview.com

National Reye's Syndrome Foundation (NRSF)
426 N Lewis St .... Bryan OH 43506 419-924-9000 924-9999 48-17
TF: 800-233-7393 ■ *Web:* www.reyessyndrome.org

National Right to Life Committee Inc (NRLC)
512 Tenth St NW .... Washington DC 20004 202-626-8800 737-9189 48-8
Web: www.nrlc.org

National Right to Work Committee (NRTWC)
8001 Braddock Rd Ste 500 .... Springfield VA 22160 703-321-8510 321-9319 49-12
TF: 800-325-7892 ■ *Web:* nrtw.org

National Risk Management Research Laboratory
US Environmental Protection Agency
26 W Martin Luther King Dr .... Cincinnati OH 45268 513-569-7418 569-7680 668
Web: www.epa.gov/ordntrnt/ord/nrmrl

National Rivet & Manufacturing Co
21 E Jefferson St .... Waupun WI 53963 920-324-5511 324-3388 278
TF: 888-324-5511 ■ *Web:* www.nationalrivet.com

National Roofing Contractors Assn (NRCA)
10255 W Higgins Rd Ste 600 .... Rosemont IL 60018 847-299-9070 299-1183 49-3
TF Cust Svc: 800-323-9545 ■ *Web:* www.nrca.net

National Roofing Contractors Assn PAC (NRCAPAC)
324 Fourth St NE .... Washington DC 20002 202-546-7584 546-9289 615
Web: nrca.net

National Rosacea Society
800 S Northwest Hwy Ste 200 .... Barrington IL 60010 847-382-8971 382-5567 48-17
TF: 888-662-5874 ■ *Web:* www.rosacea.org

National Rubber Technologies Corp
35 Cawthra Ave .... Toronto ON M6N5B3 416-657-1111 656-1231 676
TF: 800-387-8501 ■ *Web:* www.knrubber.com

National Runaway Switchboard (NRS)
3141 N Lincoln Ave .... Chicago IL 60657 773-880-9860 929-5150 48-6
TF: 800-786-2929 ■ *Web:* www.1800runaway.org

National Rural Letter Carriers' Assn
1630 Duke St 4th Fl .... Alexandria VA 22314 703-684-5545 414
Web: www.nrlca.org

National Rural Utilities Co-op Finance Corp
2201 Co-op Way .... Herndon VA 20171 703-709-6700 509
TF: 800-424-2954 ■ *Web:* www.nrucfc.coop

National Rural Water Assn (NRWA)
2915 S 13th St .... Duncan OK 73533 580-252-0629 255-4476 48-12
Web: www.nrwa.org

National Safety Apparel Inc (NSA)
15825 Industrial Pkwy .... Cleveland OH 44135 800-553-0672 941-1130* 576
**Fax Area Code:* 216 ■ *TF:* 800-553-0672 ■ *Web:* www.thinknsa.com

National Safety Council (NSC)
1121 Spring Lake Dr .... Itasca IL 60143 630-285-1121 285-1315 48-17
TF: 800-621-7615 ■ *Web:* www.nsc.org

National Salon Resources Inc
3109 Louisiana Ave N .... Minneapolis MN 55427 763-541-1000 577-2512* 76
**Fax Area Code:* 800 ■ *TF:* 800-622-0003 ■ *Web:* www.nationalsalon.com

Phone Fax Class

National Scholastic Press Assn (NSPA)
2221 University Ave SE Ste 121 .... Minneapolis MN 55414 612-625-8335 626-0720 48-11
Web: www.studentpress.org/nspa

National School Boards Assn (NSBA)
1680 Duke St .... Alexandria VA 22314 703-838-6722 683-7590 49-5
TF: 800-433-9016 ■ *Web:* www.nsba.org

National School District
1500 N Ave .... National City CA 91950 619-336-7500 336-7521 685
Web: www.nsd.us

National School Products
1523 Old Niles Ferry Rd .... Maryville TN 37803 865-984-3960 289-3960* 243
**Fax Area Code:* 800 ■ *TF:* 800-627-9393 ■ *Web:* www.nationalschoolproducts.com

National School Public Relations Assn (NSPRA)
15948 Derwood Rd .... Rockville MD 20855 301-519-0496 519-0494 49-5
Web: www.nspra.org

National School Supply & Equipment Assn (NSSEA)
8380 Colesville Rd Ste 250 .... Silver Spring MD 20910 301-495-0240 495-3330 49-18
TF: 800-395-5550 ■ *Web:* edmarket.org

National Science Foundation (NSF)
4201 Wilson Blvd .... Arlington VA 22230 703-292-5111 292-9232 340-20
TF: 800-877-8339 ■ *Web:* www.nsf.gov

National Science Teachers Assn (NSTA)
1840 Wilson Blvd .... Arlington VA 22201 703-243-7100 243-7177 49-5
TF Sales: 800-722-6782 ■ *Web:* www.nsta.org

National Scouting Museum
1329 W Walnut Hill Ln .... Irving TX 75038 972-580-2100 520
TF: 800-303-3047 ■ *Web:* www.bsamuseum.org

National Sea Grant Program
1315 East-West Hwy .... Silver Spring MD 20910 301-734-1066 713-0799 340-2
Web: www.seagrant.noaa.gov

National Search Assoc
2035 Corte del Nogal Ste 100 .... Carlsbad CA 92011 760-431-1115 683-3044 266
Web: www.nsasearch.com

National Seating Co 200 National Dr .... Vonore TN 37885 423-884-6651 247
Web: www.nsm-seating.com

National Securities Corp
410 Park Ave 14th Fl .... New York NY 10022 212-417-8000 690
TF: 800-742-7730 ■ *Web:* www.nationalsecurities.com

National Security Agency
9800 Savage Rd .... Fort Meade MD 20755 301-688-6524 340-3
Web: www.nsa.gov

National Security Council (NSC)
1600 Pennsylvania Ave NW .... Washington DC 20500 202-456-1414 340
TF: 800-382-9467 ■ *Web:* www.whitehouse.gov/nsc

National Security Technologies LLC
2621 Losee Rd .... Las Vegas NV 89030 702-295-1000 295-2448 261
Web: www.nstec.com

National Sedimentation Laboratory
598 McElroy Dr PO Box 1157 .... Oxford MS 38655 662-232-2924 281-5706 668
Web: www.ars.usda.gov

National Semiconductor Corp
2900 Semiconductor Dr .... Santa Clara CA 95051 408-721-5000 696
Web: www.ti.com

National Seminars Training
6900 Squibb Rd .... Shawnee Mission KS 66202 913-432-7755 432-0824 765
TF: 800-258-7246 ■ *Web:* www.nationalseminarstraining.com

National Senior Golf Assn (NSGA)
200 Perrine Rd Ste 201 .... Old Bridge NJ 08857 800-282-6772 525-9590* 48-22
**Fax Area Code:* 732 ■ *TF:* 800-282-6772 ■ *Web:* www.nationalseniorgolf.com

National Services Group Inc
1682 Langley Ave .... Irvine CA 92614 714-564-7900 189-8
TF: 800-394-6000 ■ *Web:* www.nationalservicesgroup.com

National Severe Storms Laboratory (NSSL)
120 David L Boren Blvd .... Norman OK 73072 405-325-6907 668
Web: www.nssl.noaa.gov

National Sheriffs' Assn (NSA)
1450 Duke St .... Alexandria VA 22314 703-836-7827 683-6541 49-7
TF: 800-424-7827 ■ *Web:* www.sheriffs.org

National Shoe Retailers Assn (NSRA)
7386 N La Cholla Blvd .... Tucson AZ 85741 520-209-1710 49-18
TF: 800-673-8446 ■ *Web:* www.nsra.org

National Shooting Sports Foundation (NSSF)
11 Mile Hill Rd .... Newtown CT 06470 203-426-1320 426-1087 48-22
TF: 866-580-1198 ■ *Web:* www.nssf.org

National Shrine of Our Lady of Lebanon, The
2759 N Lipkey Rd .... North Jackson OH 44451 330-538-3351 538-0455 50-1
Web: www.ourladyoflebanonshrine.com

National Shrine of Our Lady of the Snows
442 S De Mazenod Dr .... Belleville IL 62223 618-397-6700 398-6549 50-1
TF: 800-682-2879 ■ *Web:* www.snows.org

National Sign Corp
1255 Westlake Ave N .... Seattle WA 98109 206-282-0700 285-3091 701
Web: www.nationalsigncorp.com

National Sintered Alloys Inc
Heritage Pk Rt 145 PO Box 332 .... Clinton CT 06413 860-669-8653 669-5428 482
TF: 800-937-2682 ■ *Web:* www.nationalsintered.com

National Ski Areas Assn (NSAA)
133 S Van Gordon St Ste 300 .... Lakewood CO 80228 303-987-1111 986-2345 48-23
Web: www.nsaa.org

National Ski Patrol System Inc (NSP)
133 S Van Gordon St Ste 100 .... Lakewood CO 80228 303-988-1111 49-7
TF: 800-222-5754 ■ *Web:* www.nsp.org

National Sleep Foundation (NSF)
1522 K St NW Ste 500 .... Washington DC 20005 202-347-3471 347-3472 48-17
TF: 800-586-4872 ■ *Web:* www.sleepfoundation.org

National Slovak Society of the USA (NSS)
351 Vly Brook Rd .... McMurray PA 15317 724-731-0094 731-0145 48-14
TF: 800-488-1890 ■ *Web:* www.nsslife.org

National Small Business Assn (NSBA)
1156 15th St NW Ste 1100 .... Washington DC 20005 202-293-8830 872-8543 49-12
TF: 800-345-6728 ■ *Web:* www.nsba.biz

National Soaring Museum
51 Soaring Hill Dr .... Elmira NY 14903 607-734-3128 732-6745 522
Web: www.soaringmuseum.org

National Soccer Coaches Assn of America (NSCAA)
800 Ann Ave .... Kansas City KS 66101 913-362-1747 362-3439 48-22
TF: 800-458-0678 ■ *Web:* www.nscaa.com

Phone | Fax | Class

National Soccer Hall of Fame
1801 S Prairie Ave ... Chicago IL 60616 312-808-1300 808-1301 522
Web: www.ussoccer.com

National Society Daughters of the American Revolution (DAR)
1776 D St NW ... Washington DC 20006 202-628-1776 879-3252 48-19
TF: 800-449-1776 ■ *Web:* www.dar.org

National Society of Accountants (NSA)
1010 N Fairfax St ... Alexandria VA 22314 703-549-6400 549-2984 49-1
TF: 800-966-6679 ■ *Web:* www.nsacct.org

National Society of Black Physicists (NSBP)
1100 N Glebe Rd Ste 1010 ... Arlington VA 22201 703-536-4207 49-19
Web: www.nsbp.org

National Society of Compliance Professionals (NSCP)
22 Kent Rd ... Cornwall Bridge CT 06754 860-672-0843 672-3005 49-12
Web: www.nscp.org

National Society of Genetic Counselors (NSGC)
330 N Wabash Ave Ste 2000 ... Chicago IL 60611 312-321-6834 673-6972 48-17
Web: www.nsgc.org

National Society of Professional Engineers (NSPE)
1420 King St ... Alexandria VA 22314 703-684-2800 836-4875 49-19
TF: 888-285-6773 ■ *Web:* www.nspe.org

National Society of the Sons of the American Revolution (NSSAR)
1000 S Fourth St ... Louisville KY 40203 502-589-1776 589-1671 48-19
Web: www.sar.org

National Softball Hall of Fame & Museum
2801 NE 50th St ... Oklahoma City OK 73111 405-424-5266 424-3855 522
TF: 800-654-8337 ■ *Web:* www.teamusa.org/usa-softball.aspx

National Soil Erosion Research Laboratory
USDA/ARS 275 S Russell St ... West Lafayette IN 47907 765-494-8689 494-5948 668
Web: www.ars.usda.gov

National Speakers Assn (NSA)
1500 S Priest Dr ... Tempe AZ 85281 480-968-2552 968-0911 48-4
Web: www.nsaspeaker.org

National Speakers Bureau
1177 W Broadway Ste 300 ... Vancouver BC V6H1G3 604-734-3663 708
TF: 800-661-4110 ■ *Web:* www.nsb.com

National Speakers Bureau Inc
14047 W Petronalla Dr Ste 102 ... Libertyville IL 60048 847-295-1122 708
TF: 800-323-9442 ■ *Web:* www.nationalspeakers.com

National Specialty Alloys LLC
18250 Keith Harrow Blvd ... Houston TX 77084 281-345-2115 345-1133 492
TF General: 800-847-5653 ■ *Web:* www.nsalloys.com

National Speech and Debate Association's (NFL)
125 Watson St PO Box 38 ... Ripon WI 54971 920-748-6206 748-9478 48-11
Web: www.speechanddebate.org

National Spinal Cord Injury Assn (NSCIA)
75-20 Astoria Blvd Ste 120 ... East Elmhurst NY 11370 718-512-0010 48-17
TF: 800-962-9629 ■ *Web:* www.spinalcord.org

National Spiritual Assembly of the Baha'is of the United States
1233 Central St ... Evanston IL 60201 847-733-3400 48-20
Web: www.bahai.us

National Sporting Goods Assn (NSGA)
1601 Feehanville Dr Ste 300 ... Mount Prospect IL 60056 847-296-6742 391-9827 49-4
TF: 800-815-5422 ■ *Web:* www.nsga.org

National Sports Academy
821 Mirror Lake Dr ... Lake Placid NY 12946 518-523-3460 523-3488 622
Web: www.nationalsportsacademy.com

National Sports Center Foundation, The
1700 105th Ave NE ... Minneapolis MN 55449 763-785-5600 711
TF: 800-333-3333 ■ *Web:* www.nscsports.org

National Sprint Car Hall of Fame & Museum
1 Sprint Capital Pl ... Knoxville IA 50138 641-842-6176 842-6177 522
TF: 800-874-4488 ■ *Web:* www.sprintcarhof.com

National Staff Development Council (NSDC)
504 S Locust St ... Oxford OH 45056 513-523-6029 523-0638 49-5
TF: 800-727-7288 ■ *Web:* www.learningforward.org

National Standard Co Lake St Plant
1631 Lake St ... Niles MI 49120 269-683-8100 182
Web: www.nationalstandard.com

National Standard Parts Assoc Inc
4400 Mobile Hwy ... Pensacola FL 32506 850-456-5771 57
TF: 800-874-6813 ■ *Web:* www.nspa.com

National States Insurance
1830 Craig Park Ct ... St. Louis MO 63146 314-878-0101 390
Web: www.nstates.com

National Steak Processors Inc
301 E Fifth Ave ... Owasso OK 74055 918-274-8787 296-26
Web: www.nationalsteak.com

National Steinbeck Ctr 1 Main St ... Salinas CA 93901 831-796-3833 796-3828 520
TF: 800-643-8899 ■ *Web:* www.steinbeck.org

National Stock Exchange (NSX)
101 Hudson St Ste 1200 ... Jersey City NJ 07302 201-499-3700 691
TF: 800-843-3924 ■ *Web:* www.nsx.com

National Stock Sign Co
1040 El Dorado Ave ... Santa Cruz CA 95062 800-462-7726 476-1734* 701
**Fax Area Code: 831* ■ *TF:* 800-462-7726 ■ *Web:* nationalstocksign.com

National Stone Sand & Gravel Assn (NSSGA)
1605 King St ... Alexandria VA 22314 703-525-8788 525-7782 49-3
TF: 800-342-1415 ■ *Web:* www.nssga.org

National Stores Inc
15001 S Figueroa St ... Gardena CA 90248 310-324-9962 157-2
Web: www.fallasstores.net

National Strand Products Inc
12611 Cain Cir ... Houston TX 77015 713-455-2888 767
Web: www.nationalstrand.com

National Strength & Conditioning Assn (NSCA)
1885 Bob Johnson Dr ... Colorado Springs CO 80906 719-632-6722 632-6367 48-22
TF: 800-815-6826 ■ *Web:* www.nsca.com

National Stroke Assn (NSA)
9707 E Easter Ln ... Centennial CO 80112 800-787-6537 649-1328* 48-17
**Fax Area Code: 303* ■ *TF Cust Svc:* 800-787-6537 ■ *Web:* www.stroke.org

National Student Campaign Against Hunger & Homelessness (NSCAHH)
294 Washington St Ste 500 ... Boston MA 02108 312-544-4436 48-5
Web: www.studentsagainsthunger.org

National Student Nurses Assn (NSNA)
45 Main St Ste 606 ... Brooklyn NY 11201 718-210-0705 210-0710 49-8
Web: www.nsna.org

National Stuttering Assn (NSA)
119 W 40th St 14th Fl ... New York NY 10018 212-944-4050 944-8244 48-17
TF: 800-937-8888 ■ *Web:* www.westutter.org

National Summer Learning Assn
575 S Charles St Ste 310 ... Baltimore MD 21201 410-856-1370 244
Web: www.summerlearning.org

National Sunflower Assn PAC
2401 46th Ave SE Ste 206 ... Mandan ND 58554 701-328-5100 328-5101 615
TF: 888-718-7033 ■ *Web:* www.sunflowernsa.com

National Super Service Company Inc
3115 Frenchman Rd ... Toledo OH 43607 419-531-2121 531-3761 386
TF Cust Svc: 800-677-1663 ■ *Web:* www.nss.com

National Swine Registry
2639 Yeager Rd ... West Lafayette IN 47906 765-463-3594 138
Web: www.nationalswine.com

National Symphony Orchestra
2700 F St NW ... Washington DC 20566 202-416-8000 416-8105 573-3
TF: 800-444-1324 ■ *Web:* www.kennedy-center.org/nso

National System of Garage Ventilation Inc
714 N Church St PO Box 1186 ... Decatur IL 62525 217-423-7314 422-5387 15
TF: 800-728-8368 ■ *Web:* www.nsgv.com

National Tank Truck Carriers Inc
950 N Glebe Rd Ste 520 ... Arlington VA 22203 703-838-1960 49-21
TF: 800-228-9290 ■ *Web:* www.tanktruck.org

National Tax Search LLC
130 S Jefferson St Ste 300 ... Chicago IL 60661 312-233-6440 734
Web: www.nationaltaxsearch.com

National Taxpayers Union (NTU)
108 N Alfred St ... Alexandria VA 22314 703-683-5700 683-5722 48-7
TF: 800-680-7289 ■ *Web:* www.ntu.org

National Tay-Sachs & Allied Diseases Assn (NTSAD)
2001 Beacon St Ste 204 ... Brighton MA 02135 617-277-4463 277-0134 48-17
TF: 800-906-8723 ■ *Web:* www.ntsad.org

National Technical Information Service
5301 Shawnee Rd ... Alexandria VA 22312 703-605-6000 605-6880 197
TF: 800-553-6847

National Technical Information Service (NTIS)
5285 Port Royal Rd ... Springfield VA 22161 703-605-6000 605-6900 668
TF Orders: 800-553-6847 ■ *Web:* www.ntis.gov

National Technical Systems Inc
24007 Ventura Blvd Ste 200 ... Calabasas CA 91302 818-591-0776 591-0899 743
NASDAQ: NTSC ■ *TF:* 800-879-9225 ■ *Web:* www.nts.com

National Technologies Inc
7641 S Tenth St ... Oak Creek WI 53154 414-571-1000 571-1010 621
Web: www.nationaltechnologies.com

National Technology Inc
1101 Carnegie St ... Rolling Meadows IL 60008 847-506-1300 506-1340 625
Web: www.nationaltech.com

National Telecommunications & Information Administration (NTIA)
1401 Constitution Ave NW
HerbertC Hoover Bldg ... Washington DC 20230 202-482-7002 340-2
Web: www.ntia.doc.gov

National Telecommunications Co-op Assn (NTCA)
4121 Wilson Blvd 10th Fl ... Arlington VA 22203 703-351-2000 351-2001 49-20
Web: www.ntca.org

National Textile Assn (NTA)
6 Beacon St Ste 1125 ... Boston MA 02108 617-542-8220 49-13

National Theatre
1321 Pennsylvania Ave NW ... Washington DC 20004 202-628-6161 572
Web: thenationaldc.org

National Theatre of the Deaf (NTD)
139 N Main St ... West Hartford CT 06107 860-236-4193 573-4
Web: www.ntd.org

National Thoroughbred Racing Assn (NTRA)
2525 Harrodsburg Rd Ste 510 ... Lexington KY 40504 800-792-6872 48-22
TF: 800-792-6872 ■ *Web:* www.ntra.com

National Tire & Wheel 5 Garden Ct ... Wheeling WV 26003 800-847-3287 57
TF: 800-847-3287 ■ *Web:* www.ntwonline.com

National Tobacco Company LP
5201 Interchange Way ... Louisville KY 40229 502-778-4421 756
TF Cust Svc: 800-579-0975 ■ *Web:* zigzag.com

National Tool & Mfg Company Inc
100 N 12th St ... Kenilworth NJ 07033 908-276-1600 757

National Tool Warehouse
221 W Fourth St Ste 4 ... Carthage MO 64836 417-358-1919 57
Web: nationaltoolwarehouse.com

National Tooling & Machining Assn (NTMA)
6363 Oak Tree Blvd ... Independence OH 44131 800-248-6862 248-7104* 49-13
**Fax Area Code: 301* ■ *TF:* 800-248-6862 ■ *Web:* www.ntma.org

National Tour Assn (NTA) 546 E Main St ... Lexington KY 40508 859-226-4444 226-4404 48-23
TF: 800-682-8886 ■ *Web:* www.ntaonline.com

National Toxicology Program (NTP)
PO Box 12233 ... Research Triangle Park NC 27709 919-541-0530 541-3687 668
Web: ntp.niehs.nih.gov

National Tractor Pullers Assn (NTPA)
6155-B Huntley Rd ... Columbus OH 43229 614-436-1761 436-0964 48-22
Web: www.ntpapull.com

National Trade Productions Inc
313 S Patrick St ... Alexandria VA 22314 703-683-8500 836-4486 184
TF: 800-687-7469 ■ *Web:* www.ntpshow.com

National Transportation Safety Board (NTSB)
490 L'Enfant Plaza SW ... Washington DC 20594 202-314-6000 314-6293 340-20
Web: www.ntsb.gov

National Travel Systems LP
4314 S Loop 289 Ste 300 ... Lubbock TX 79413 806-794-3336 772
Web: www.nationaltravelsystems.com

National Treasury Employees Union
1750 H St NW ... Washington DC 20006 202-572-5500 572-5643 414
Web: www.nteu.org

National Truck Equipment Assn (NTEA)
37400 Hills Tech Dr ... Farmington Hills MI 48331 248-489-7090 489-8590 49-21
TF: 800-441-6832 ■ *Web:* www.ntea.com

National Truck Leasing System
450 S Summit Ave ... Oakbrook IL 60181 630-953-8878 953-0040 778
TF: 800-729-6857 ■ *Web:* nationalease.com

National Trust for Historic Preservation
1785 Massachusetts Ave NW ... Washington DC 20036 202-588-6000 588-6038 48-13
TF: 800-944-6847 ■ *Web:* savingplaces.org

Name / Address	City	State	Zip	Phone	Fax	Class
National Tube Form Inc 3405 Engle Rd *Web:* www.nationaltubeform.com	Fort Wayne	IN	46809	260-478-2363		595
National Tube Supply Co 925 Central Ave *TF:* 800-229-6872 ■ *Web:* www.nationaltubesupply.com	University Park	IL	60466	708-534-2700		492
National Turkey Federation (NTF) 1225 New York Ave NW Ste 400 *TF:* 866-536-7593 ■ *Web:* www.eatturkey.com	Washington	DC	20005	202-898-0100	898-0203	48-2
National Underground Railroad Freedom Ctr 50 E Freedom Way *TF:* 800-283-8904 ■ *Web:* www.freedomcenter.org	Cincinnati	OH	45202	513-333-7739		520
National Undersea Research Ctr for Hawaii & the Western Pacific University of Hawaii at Manoa 41-305 Kalanianaole Hwy	Waimanalo	HI	96795	808-259-9991		668
National Undersea Research Ctr for the Caribbean *Perry Institute for Marine Science Caribbean Marin* 100 N US Hwy 1 Ste 202 *Web:* www.perryinstitute.org	Jupiter	FL	33477	561-741-0192	741-0193	668
National Undersea Research Ctr for the Mid-Atlantic Bight Rutgers University Institute of Marine & Coastal Sciences 71 Dudley Rd *TF:* 888-776-6537 ■ *Web:* www.marine.rutgers.edu	New Brunswick	NJ	08901	732-932-6555	932-8578	668
National Underwriter Co 4157 Olympic Blvd Ste 225 *TF:* 800-543-0874 ■ *Web:* www.nationalunderwriter.com	Erlanger	KY	41018	800-543-0874	874-1916	637-2
National United PO Box 779 *TF:* 877-628-2265 ■ *Web:* www.natlbank.com	Gatesville	TX	76528	254-865-2211	865-8916	70
National University 11255 N Torrey Pines Rd *TF:* 800-628-8648 ■ *Web:* www.nu.edu	La Jolla	CA	92037	858-642-8000	642-8709	166
National University of Health Sciences 200 E Roosevelt Rd *TF:* 800-826-6285 ■ *Web:* www.nuhs.edu	Lombard	IL	60148	630-629-2000	889-6554	166
National Urban League Inc 120 Wall St *Web:* nul.iamempowered.com	New York	NY	10005	212-558-5300	558-5332	48-8
National Urban Technology Ctr 80 Maiden Ln Ste 606 *TF:* 800-998-3212 ■ *Web:* www.urbantech.org	New York	NY	10038	212-528-7350	528-7355	48-6
National US-Arab Chamber of Commerce 1023 15th St NW Ste 400 *Web:* www.nusacc.org	Washington	DC	20005	202-289-5920	289-5938	138
National US-Arab Chamber of Commerce 1101 17th St, NW Ste 1220 *Web:* www.nusacc.org	Washington	DC	20036	713-963-4620	963-4609	138
National Vaccine Information Ctr (NVIC) 407 Church St Ste H *Web:* www.nvic.org	Vienna	VA	22180	703-938-0342	938-5768	48-17
National Van Lines Inc 2800 W Roosevelt Rd **Fax:* Cust Svc ■ *TF:* 877-590-2810 ■ *Web:* www.nationalvanlines.com	Broadview	IL	60155	708-450-2900	450-9320*	519
National Venture Capital Assn (NVCA) 25 Massachusetts Ave NW Ste 730 *TF:* 800-956-2682 ■ *Web:* www.nvca.org	Washington	DC	20001	703-524-2549	524-3940	615
National Veterinary Associates Inc 29229 Canwood St Ste 100 *TF:* 888-767-7755 ■ *Web:* www.nvaonline.com	Agoura Hills	CA	91301	805-777-7722		794
National Vinyl LLC 7 Coburn St *TF:* 800-424-5300 ■ *Web:* www.nvpwindows.com	Chicopee	MA	01013	413-420-0548		236
National Vision Inc 296 Grayson Hwy *TF Cust Svc:* 800-637-3597 ■ *Web:* www.nationalvision.com	Lawrenceville	GA	30045	770-822-3600		543
National Volunteer Fire Council (NVFC) 7852 Walker Dr Ste 450 *TF:* 888-275-6832 ■ *Web:* www.nvfc.org	Greenbelt	MD	20770	202-887-5700	887-5291	49-4
National Watch & Clock Museum 514 Poplar St *TF:* 800-368-6511 ■ *Web:* www.nawcc.org	Columbia	PA	17512	717-684-8261	684-0878	520
National Water Purifiers Corp 1065 E 14th St	Hialeah	FL	33010	305-887-7065		806
National Water Resources Assn (NWRA) 3800 Fairfax Dr # 4 **Fax Area Code:* 928 ■ *TF:* 800-468-3533 ■ *Web:* www.nwra.org	Arlington	VA	22203	703-524-1544	343-9483*	48-12
National Waterways Conference Inc (NWC) 4650 Washington Blvd Ste 608 *TF:* 866-371-1390 ■ *Web:* www.waterways.org	Arlington	VA	22201	703-243-4090	243-4155	49-21
National Weather Service (NWS) 1325 East-West Hwy *Web:* www.weather.gov	Silver Spring	MD	20910	301-713-0689		340-2
National Hurricane Ctr 11691 SW 17th St *Web:* www.nhc.noaa.gov	Miami	FL	33165	305-229-4470	553-1264	340-2
National Weather Service Regional Offices						
Alaska Region 222 W Seventh Ave Ste 23 Rm 517 *Web:* www.arh.noaa.gov	Anchorage	AK	99513	907-271-5088	271-3711	340-2
Central Region 7220 NW 101st Terr *Web:* www.weather.gov/organization/regional	Kansas City	MO	64153	816-891-7734		340-2
Eastern Region 630 Johnson Ave *Web:* weather.gov/erh	Bohemia	NY	11716	631-244-0100		340-2
Pacific Region 2525 Correa Rd Ste 250 *Web:* www.prh.noaa.gov/pr	Honolulu	HI	96822	808-973-5286		340-2
Southern Region 819 Taylor St Rm 10A06 *Web:* www.srh.noaa.gov	Fort Worth	TX	76102	817-978-1000		340-2
Western Region 125 S State St *Web:* www.wrh.noaa.gov	Salt Lake City	UT	84138	801-524-5133	524-5270	340-2
National Wellness Institute (NWI) 1300 College Ct PO Box 827 *TF:* 877-800-2729 ■ *Web:* www.nationalwellness.org	Stevens Point	WI	54481	715-342-2969	342-2979	48-17
National Western Life Insurance Co 850 E Anderson Ln *NASDAQ: NWLI* ■ **Fax:* Hum Res ■ *TF:* 800-531-5442 ■ *Web:* www.nationalwesternlife.com	Austin	TX	78752	512-836-1010	719-0104*	391-2
National Wetlands Research Ctr 700 Cajundome Blvd *Web:* www.usgs.gov	Lafayette	LA	70506	337-266-8500		668
National Wholesale Company Inc 400 National Blvd **Fax Area Code:* 336 ■ *TF:* 800-480-4673 ■ *Web:* www.shopnational.com	Lexington	NC	27292	800-480-4673	249-9326*	459
National WIC Assn (NWA) 2001 S St NW Ste 580 *TF:* 866-782-6246 ■ *Web:* www.nwica.org	Washington	DC	20009	202-232-5492	387-5281	48-6
National Wild Turkey Federation (NWTF) 770 Augusta Rd PO Box 530 *TF Cust Svc:* 800-843-6983 ■ *Web:* www.nwtf.org	Edgefield	SC	29824	803-637-3106	637-0034	48-3
National Wildlife Federation (NWF) 11100 Wildlife Ctr Dr *TF:* 800-822-9919 ■ *Web:* www.nwf.org	Reston	VA	20190	703-438-6000	438-3570	48-3
National Wildlife Health Ctr 6006 Schroeder Rd *TF:* 800-232-4636 ■ *Web:* www.nwhc.usgs.gov	Madison	WI	53711	608-270-2400	270-2415	668
National Wildlife Magazine 11100 Wildlife Ctr Dr *TF Cust Svc:* 800-822-9919 ■ *Web:* www.nwf.org/nationalwildlife	Reston	VA	20190	703-438-6000		457-19
National Wildlife Refuge Assn (NWRA) 1250 Connecticut Ave NW Ste 600 *Web:* www.refugeassociation.org	Washington	DC	20036	202-292-2402		48-13
National Wildlife Research Ctr 4101 LaPorte Ave *Web:* www.aphis.usda.gov	Fort Collins	CO	80521	970-266-6000	266-6032	668
National Wine & Spirits Inc PO Box 2187 *Web:* www.nwscorp.com	Indianapolis	IN	46206	317-602-6644	602-6720	81-3
National Wire & Cable Corp 136 N San Fernando Rd *Web:* www.nationalwire.com	Los Angeles	CA	90031	323-225-5611	225-4630	814
National Wire Fabric 701 Arkansas St	Star City	AR	71667	870-628-4201	628-3700	688
National Woman's Party 144 Constitution Ave NE *Web:* www.sewallbelmont.org	Washington	DC	20002	202-546-1210	546-3997	48-24
National Women's Hall of Fame 76 Fall St PO Box 335 *Web:* www.womenofthehall.org	Seneca Falls	NY	13148	315-568-8060	568-2976	520
National Women's Health Information Ctr 200 Independence Ave SW *TF:* 800-994-9662 ■ *Web:* www.womenshealth.gov	Washington	DC	20201	800-994-9662		340-10
National Women's Law Ctr (NWLC) 11 Dupont Cir NW Ste 800 *Web:* www.nwlc.org	Washington	DC	20036	202-588-5180	588-5185	48-24
National Women's Political Caucus (NWPC) PO Box 65010 *Web:* www.nwpc.org	Washington	DC	20035	202-785-1100		48-7
National Wood Flooring Assn (NWFA) 111 Chesterfield Industrial Blvd *TF:* 800-422-4556 ■ *Web:* www.woodfloors.org	Chesterfield	MO	63005	636-519-9663		49-3
National Wooden Pallet & Container Assn (NWPCA) 1421 Prince St Ste 340 *Web:* www.palletcentral.com	Alexandria	VA	22314	703-519-6104	519-4720	49-13
National Woodland Owners Assn (NWOA) 374 Maple Ave E Ste 310 *TF:* 800-476-8733 ■ *Web:* www.woodlandowners.org	Vienna	VA	22180	703-255-2700		48-2
National World War I Museum 100 W 26th St *Web:* www.theworldwar.org	Kansas City	MO	64108	816-784-1918		520
National Wrecking Co 2441 N Leavitt St *Web:* www.nationalwrecking.com	Chicago	IL	60647	773-384-2800	384-0403	189-16
National Wrestling Hall of Fame (NWHOF) 405 W Hall of Fame Ave *Web:* nwhof.org	Stillwater	OK	74075	405-377-5243	377-5244	522
National Writers Union (NWU) 256 W 38th St Ste 703 *Web:* www.nwu.org	New York	NY	10018	212-254-0279	254-0673	414
National X-Ray Corp 2310 S Dock Str Ste 110 *Web:* nationalxraycorp.com	Palmetto	Fl	34221?	941-870-3069		743
National Youth Sports Coaches Assn (NYSCA) 2050 Vista Pkwy *TF:* 800-729-2057 ■ *Web:* www.nays.org	West Palm Beach	FL	33411	561-684-1141	684-2546	48-22
National Zoological Park (Smithsonian Institution) 3001 Connecticut Ave NW *Web:* www.nationalzoo.si.edu	Washington	DC	20008	202-633-4888		823
National/AZON 1148 Rochester Rd **Fax Area Code:* 866 ■ *TF:* 800-325-5939 ■ *Web:* www.azon.com	Troy	MI	48083	800-325-5939	318-7323*	552-1
National-Louis University 1000 Capitol Dr **Fax:* Admissions ■ *TF:* 800-443-5522 ■ *Web:* www.nl.edu	Wheeling	IL	60090	847-947-5718	465-5730*	166
Chicago 122 S Michigan Ave **Fax Area Code:* 847 ■ **Fax:* Admissions ■ *TF:* 800-443-5522 ■ *Web:* www.nl.edu	Chicago	IL	60603	888-658-8632	465-5730*	166
NationJob Inc 920 Morgan St Ste T **Fax Area Code:* 515 ■ *TF:* 800-292-7731 ■ *Web:* www.nationjob.com	Des Moines	IA	50309	800-292-7731	243-5384*	260
Nations Financial Group Inc 4000 River Ridge Dr NE PO Box 908 *TF:* 800-351-2471 ■ *Web:* www.nationsfg.com	Cedar Rapids	IA	52406	319-393-9541		691
Nations First Office Repair 1555 E Flamingo Rd Ste 202 *Web:* www.laptoprepairs.com	Las Vegas	NV	89119	702-699-5657		175
Nations Foodservice Inc 11090 San Pablo Ave Ste 200 *Web:* nationsrestaurants.com	El Cerrito	CA	94530	510-237-1952		670
Nationwide Adv Specialty Co 2025 S Cooper St	Arlington	TX	76010	817-461-6161		9
Nationwide Arena 200 W Nationwide Blvd *Web:* www.nationwidearena.com	Columbus	OH	43215	614-246-2000	246-4300	720
Nationwide Biweekly Administration Inc 855 Lower Bellbrook Rd *Web:* www.nbabiweekly.com	Xenia	OH	45385	937-376-5800		5
Nationwide Children's Hospital 700 Children's Dr *TF:* 800-282-5512 ■ *Web:* www.nationwidechildrens.org	Columbus	OH	43205	614-722-2700	722-2716	668
Nationwide Credit Inc (NCI) PO Box 14581 **Fax Area Code:* 770 ■ *TF:* 800-456-4729 ■ *Web:* www.ncirm.com	Des Moines	IA	50306	800-456-4729	612-7335*	160

	Phone	Fax	Class
Nationwide Custom Homes 1100 Rives Rd, Martinsville VA 24115 *Fax Area Code: 276 ■ TF: 800-216-7001 ■ Web: www.nationwide-homes.com	800-216-7001	632-1181*	106
Nationwide Glove Co 925 Bauman Ln, Harrisburg IL 62946	618-252-6303		155-8
Nationwide Graphics Inc 2500 W Loop S Ste 500, Houston TX 77027 Web: www.nwas-llc.com	713-961-4700	961-4701	627
Nationwide Life & Annuity Insurance Co 1 Nationwide Pl, Columbus OH 43215 TF: 800-882-2822 ■ Web: www.nationwide.com	614-249-7111		391-2
Nationwide Lift Trucks Inc 3900 N 28th Terr, Hollywood FL 33020 TF: 800-327-4431 ■ Web: www.toyotanlt.com	954-922-4645	922-8770	57
Nationwide Magazine & Book Distributors Inc 3000 E Grauwyler Rd PO Box 170427, Irving TX 75017 TF General: 800-777-9068 ■ Web: www.nationwidemagazine.com	972-438-7852	721-0613	685
Nationwide Medical Equipment Inc 1510 Stuart Rd Ste 109, Cleveland TN 37312 Web: www.nme.cc	423-478-7433		475
Nationwide Mutual Fire Insurance Co 1 Nationwide Plaza, Columbus OH 43215 TF: 877-669-6877 ■ Web: www.nationwide.com	800-882-2822		391-4
Nationwide Mutual Insurance Co 1 Nationwide Plaza, Columbus OH 43215 TF: 877-669-6877 ■ Web: nationwide.com	877-669-6877		391-2
Nationwide Precision Products Corp 200 Tech Park Dr, Rochester NY 14623 Web: www.hnprecision.com	585-272-7100		454
Nationwide Property & Appraisal Services LLC 10 Foster Ave Ste 3c, Gibbsboro NJ 08026 Web: onestopappraisals.com	856-258-6977		652
Nationwide Title Clearing Inc 2100 Alternate 19 N, Palm Harbor FL 34683 Web: www.nationwidetitleclearing.com	727-771-4000		217
Nationwide Truck Brokers Inc (NTB) 4203 Roger B Chaffee Memorial Blvd SE Ste 2, Grand Rapids MI 49548 TF: 800-446-0682 ■ Web: www.ntbtrk.com	616-878-5554	878-5569	780
Nationwide Uniform Corp 235 Shepherdsville Rd, Hodgenville KY 42748	270-358-4173		155-19
Nationwide Van Lines Inc 1421 NW 65th Ave, Plantation FL 33313 TF: 800-310-0056 ■ Web: www.nationwidevanlines.com	954-585-3945	585-3970	519
Native American Community Board (NACB) PO Box 572, Lake Andes SD 57356 Web: www.nativeshop.org	605-487-7072	487-7964	48-7
Native American Indian General Service Office of Alcoholics Anonymous (NAIGSO-AA) PO Box 838, Rogersville AL 35652 Web: www.naigso-aa.org	951-927-2626		48-21
Native American Rights Fund (NARF) 1506 Broadway, Boulder CO 80302 TF: 888-280-0726 ■ Web: www.narf.org	303-447-8760	443-7776	49-10
Native American Times PO Box 411, Tahlequah OK 74465 TF: 800-367-5390 ■ Web: www.nativetimes.com	918-708-5838		637-8
Native Environmental LLC 3250 S 35th Ave, Phoenix AZ 85009 Web: www.nativeaz.com	602-254-0122		192
Native Eyewear Inc 1114 Neon Forest Cir Unit 5, Longmont CO 80504-7047 TF: 888-776-2848 ■ Web: www.nativeyewear.com	888-776-2848		543
Native Grounds Nursery & Garden Center 1172A S Mt Shasta Blvd, Mount Shasta CA 96067 Web: nativegrounds.org	530-926-0555		511
NATIVE INSTRUMENTS North America Inc 5631 A Hollywood Blvd, Los Angeles CA 90028 Web: www.native-instruments.com	323-467-5260		527
Native Plant Ctr at Westchester Community College 75 Grasslands Rd, Valhalla NY 10595 Web: www.sunywcc.edu	914-606-7870	606-6143	97
Native Pride 11359 Rt 20, Irving NY 14081 TF: 800-619-8618 ■ Web: nativepride.com	716-934-5130		324
Native Seeds-search 3584 E River Rd, Tucson AZ 85718 TF: 866-622-5561 ■ Web: www.nativeseeds.org	520-622-0830		196
NativeX LLC 1900 Medical Arts Ave S, Sartell MN 56377 Web: nativex.com	320-257-7500		736
Natividad Medical Ctr (NMC) 1441 Constitution Blvd, Salinas CA 93906 Web: www.natividad.com	831-755-4111		374-3
Nativo Lodge Hotel 6000 Pan American Fwy NE, Albuquerque NM 87109 TF: 888-628-4861 ■ Web: www.hhandr.com	505-798-4300	798-4305	379
Natixis Securities Americas LLC 1251 Ave of the Americas, New York NY 10020 Web: www.blr.natixis.com	212-891-6100		690
Natl Elevator Industrial Educational Program 11 Larsen Way, Attleboro MA 02763 TF: 800-228-8220 ■ Web: www.neiep.org	508-699-2200		196
NATO (National Association of Theatre Owners.) 1705 N St NW Ste 1130, Washington DC 20036 TF General: 800-365-5701 ■ Web: www.natoonline.org	202-962-0054	962-0370	48-4
NATPE (NA of Television Program Executives) 5757 Wilshire Blvd PH-10, Los Angeles CA 90036 TF: 800-767-6266 ■ Web: www.natpe.com	310-453-4440	453-5258	49-14
Natrol Inc 21411 Prairie St, Chatsworth CA 91311 TF: 800-262-8765 ■ Web: www.natrol.com	818-739-6000		799
Natrona County 200 N Ctr St, Casper WY 82601 Web: www.natronacounty-wy.gov	307-235-9200		338
Natrona County International Airport 8500 Airport Pkwy, Casper WY 82604 TF: 800-634-5012 ■ Web: www.iflycasper.com	307-472-6688	472-1805	27
Natrona County Public Library 307 E Second St, Casper WY 82601 Web: natronacountylibrary.org	307-237-4935	266-3734	434-3
NATSO Inc 1737 King St Ste 200, Alexandria VA 22314 TF: 800-956-9160 ■ Web: www.natso.com	703-549-2100	684-4525	49-21
NATSO PAC 1737 King St Ste 200, Alexandria VA 22314 Web: natso.com	703-549-2100	684-4525	615
Naturade 2030 Main St Ste 630, Irvine CA 92614 *Fax Area Code: 714 ■ TF: 800-421-1830 ■ Web: www.naturade.com	800-421-1830	935 9837*	799
Natural Alternatives International Inc 1185 Linda Vista Dr, San Marcos CA 92078 NASDAQ: NAII ■ TF: 800-848-2646 ■ Web: www.nai-online.com	760-744-7340	744-9589	799
Natural Areas Assn (NAA) PO Box 1504, Bend OR 97709 Web: www.naturalareas.org	541-317-0199		48-13
Natural Bridge Battlefield Historic State Park 7502 Natural Bridge Rd, Tallahassee FL 32305 TF: 800-326-3521 ■ Web: www.floridastateparks.org/naturalbridge	850-922-6007	488-0366	565
Natural Bridge Caverns 26495 Natural Bridge Caverns Rd, Natural Bridge Caverns TX 78266 Web: www.naturalbridgecaverns.com	210-651-6101	651-6144	50-5
Natural Bridge State Park McCauley Rd off Rte 8 PO Box 1757, North Adams MA 01247 Web: www.mass.gov	413-663-6392		565
Natural Bridge State Resort Park 2135 Natural Bridge Rd, Slade KY 40376 TF: 800-325-1710 ■ Web: www.parks.ky.gov	800-325-1710		565
Natural Bridge Wildlife Ranch 26515 Natural Bridge Caverns Rd, San Antonio TX 78266 Web: www.wildliferanchtexas.com	830-438-7400		823
Natural Bridges National Monument HC 60 PO Box 1, Lake Powell UT 84533 TF: 800-645-8465 ■ Web: www.nps.gov/nabr	435-692-1234	692-1111	564
Natural Bridges State Beach 2531 W Cliff Dr, Santa Cruz CA 95060 Web: www.parks.ca.gov/default.asp?page_id=541	831-423-4609		565
Natural Capitalism Solutions Inc 11823 N 75th St, Longmont CO 80503 Web: www.natcapsolutions.org	720-684-6580		804
Natural Casing Co 410 E Railroad St PO Box A, Peshtigo WI 54157 *Fax Area Code: 715 ■ TF: 877-515-0270 ■ Web: www.naturalcasingco.com	877-515-0270	582-3931*	296-26
Natural Factors Nutritional Products Ltd 1550 United Blvd, Coquitlam BC V3K6Y2 *Fax Area Code: 800 ■ TF: 800-663-8900 ■ Web: www.naturalfactors.com	604-777-1757	663-2115*	799
Natural Factors Nutritional Products Ltd 14224 167th Ave SE, Monroe WA 98272 TF: 877-551-2179 ■ Web: www.naturalfactors.com	360-243-3500		799
Natural Gas Services Group Inc (NGSG) 508 W Wall Ste 550, Midland TX 79701 NYSE: NGS ■ Web: www.ngsgi.com	432-262-2700	262-2701	537
Natural Gas Supply Assn (NGSA) 805 15th St NW Ste 510, Washington DC 20005 Web: www.ngsa.org	202-326-9300	326-9330	48-12
Natural Habitat Adventures PO Box 3065, Boulder CO 80307 TF: 800-543-8917 ■ Web: www.nathab.com	303-449-3711	449-3712	760
Natural Hazards Ctr University of Colorado 483 UCB, Boulder CO 80309 Web: www.colorado.edu/hazards	303-492-6818	492-2151	668
Natural Healing College 446 E Vine St, Stockton CA 95202 TF: 800-794-0802 ■ Web: naturalhealingcollege.com	209-390-8076		764
Natural Healthy Concepts 310 N Westhill Blvd, Appleton WI 54914 TF: 866-505-7501 ■ Web: www.naturalhealthyconcepts.com	920-968-2350		345
Natural History Magazine 105 W Hwy 54 Ste 265, Durham NC 27713 *Fax Area Code: 919 ■ Web: www.naturalhistorymag.com	646-356-6500	933-1867*	457-19
Natural History Museum of Los Angeles County 900 Exposition Blvd, Los Angeles CA 90007 TF: 800 959-3131 ■ Web: www.nhm.org	213-763-3466	746-2999	520
Natural Lands Trust Inc 1031 Palmers Mill Rd, Media PA 19063 Web: www.natlands.org	610-353-5587		564
Natural Life Pet Products Inc 205 E 29th St, Pittsburg KS 66762 TF: 800-367-2391 ■ Web: www.nlpp.com	620-230-0888		578
Natural Mktg Institute Inc, The 272 Ruth Rd, Harleysville PA 19438 Web: www.nmisolutions.com	215-513-7300		637-9
Natural Organics Inc 548 Broadhollow Rd, Melville NY 11747 TF: 800-645-9500 ■ Web: www.naturesplus.com	800-645-9500		799
Natural Products Insider Magazine 3300 N Central Ave Ste 3000, Phoenix AZ 85012 TF: 800-454-5760 ■ Web: www.naturalproductsinsider.com	480-990-1101	990-0819	457-21
Natural Resource Ecology Laboratory Colorado State University, Fort Collins CO 80523 Web: www.nrel.colostate.edu	970-491-1982	491-1965	668
Natural Resource Partners LP 1201 Louisiana St Ste 3600, Houston TX 77002 NYSE: NRP ■ TF: 888-334-7102 ■ Web: www.nrplp.com	713-751-7507		501
Natural Resources Conservation Service 1400 Independence Ave SW Rm 5105A, Washington DC 20250 Web: www.nrcs.usda.gov	202-720-7246	720-7690	340-1
Natural Resources Defense Council (NRDC) 40 W 20th St, New York NY 10011 TF: 800-497-2912 ■ Web: www.nrdc.org	212-727-2700	727-1773	48-13
Natural Resources Research Institute (NRRI) *University of Minnesota Duluth* 5013 Miller Trunk Hwy, Duluth MN 55811 TF: 800-234-0054 ■ Web: www.nrri.umn.edu	218-720-4294	720-4219	668
Natural Selection Foodsllc 1721 San Juan Hwy, San Juan Bautista CA 95045 Web: www.ebfarm.com	831-623-7880		123
Natural Springs Water Group 128 LP Auer Rd, Johnson City TN 37604	423-926-7905		805
Natural Standard 1 Davis Sq, Somerville MA 02144 Web: naturalmedicines.therapeuticresearch.com	617-591-3300		479
Natural Structures 2005 Tenth St, Baker City OR 97814 Web: www.naturalstructures.com	541-523-0224		106
Natural Tunnel State Park 1420 Natural Tunnel Pkwy, Duffield VA 24244	276-940-2674		565

	City	State	Zip	Phone	Fax	Class
NaturaLawn of America Inc						
1 E Church St	Frederick	MD	21701	301-694-5440	846-0320	577
TF: 800-989-5444 ■ *Web:* www.naturalawn.com						
Naturally Vitamins 4404 E Elwood St	Phoenix	AZ	85040	480-991-0200	991-0551	799
TF: 800-899-4499 ■ *Web:* www.naturally.com						
NaturalPoint Inc						
33872 SE Eastgate Cir	Corvallis	OR	97333	541-753-6645		173-1
Web: www.naturalpoint.com						
Nature						
National Press Bldg 529 14th St NW						
Ste 968	Washington	DC	20045	202-737-2355	628-1609	457-19
TF: 800-524-0384 ■ *Web:* www.nature.com						
Nature Conservancy						
4245 N Fairfax Dr Ste 100	Arlington	VA	22203	703-841-5300	841-1283	48-13
TF Cust Svc: 800-628-6860 ■ *Web:* www.nature.org						
Nature Conservancy of Canada						
36 Eglinton Ave W Ste 400	Toronto	ON	M4R1A1	416-932-3202	932-3208	48-13
TF: 800-465-8005 ■ *Web:* www.natureconservancy.ca						
Nature's Best 6 Pt Dr Ste 300	Brea	CA	92821	714-255-4600	255-4691	345
TF: 800-800-7799 ■ *Web:* www.naturesbest.net						
Nature's Trees Inc						
550 Bedford Rd	Bedford Hills	NY	10507	914-241-4999		776
TF: 800-341-8733 ■ *Web:* www.savatree.com						
Nature's Value Inc 468 Mill Rd	Coram	NY	11727	631-846-2500		582
Web: www.naturesvalue.com						
Nature's Way Products Inc						
3051 W Maple Loop Dr Ste 125	Lehi	UT	84043	800-962-8873	688-3303	799
TF: 800-962-8873 ■ *Web:* www.naturesway.com						
Naturebridge 28 Geary St Ste 650	San Francisco	CA	94108	415-992-4700		148
Web: www.naturebridge.org						
Natureworks LLC 650 Industrial Park Dr	Blair	NE	68008	402-533-4100		596
Web: www.natureworksllc.com						
Naturex Inc 375 Huyler St	South Hackensack	NJ	07606	201-440-5000		479
Web: www.naturex.com						
Naturipe Berry Growers						
1611 Bunker Hill way	Salinas	CA	93906	831-722-2430		315-1
TF: 800-676-1577 ■ *Web:* www.naturipeberrygrowers.com						
Naturopathica Spa						
74 Montauk Hwy Ste 23	East Hampton	NY	11937	631-329-2525		354
Web: www.naturopathica.com						
Naturwood Home Furnishings Inc						
2711 Mercantile Dr	Rancho Cordova	CA	95742	916-638-2424		361
Web: www.naturwood.com						
Natus Medical Inc						
1501 Industrial Rd	San Carlos	CA	94070	650-802-0400	802-0401	250
NASDAQ: BABY ■ *TF:* 800-255-3901 ■ *Web:* www.natus.com						
Natvar 8720 US Hwy 70 W	Clayton	NC	27520	909-594-3660	553-4156*	600
**Fax Area Code:* 919 ■ *Web:* natvar.tekni-plex.com						
NATW (National Association of Town Watch)						
308 E Lancaster Ave Ste 115	Wynnewood	PA	19096	800-648-3688	649-5456*	48-7
**Fax Area Code:* 610 ■ *TF:* 800-648-3688 ■ *Web:* www.nationaltownwatch.org						
Naugatuck Valley Community College						
750 Chase Pkwy	Waterbury	CT	06708	203-575-8040		162
TF: 800-894-6126 ■ *Web:* www.nv.edu						
Nauman Smith Shissler & Hall LLP						
200 N Third St Fl 18	Harrisburg	PA	17101	717-236-3010		428
TF: 800-631-1274 ■ *Web:* nssh.com						
NAUS (NA for Uniformed Services)						
5535 Hempstead Way	Springfield	VA	22151	703-750-1342	354-4380	48-19
TF: 800-842-3451 ■ *Web:* www.naus.org						
Nauset Beach Club 222 Main St	East Orleans	MA	02653	508-255-8547		671
Web: www.nausetbeachclub.com						
Nautel Ltd						
10089 Peggy'S Cove Rd	Hackett'S Cove	NS	B3Z3J4	902-823-3900		647
TF: 877-662-8835 ■ *Web:* www.nautel.com						
Nautic Partners LLC						
50 Kennedy Plaza 12th Fl	Providence	RI	02903	401-278-6770	278-6387	792
Web: www.nautic.com						
Nautica Retail USA Inc						
40 W 57th St Ste 7	New York	NY	10019	212-541-5757		155-12
Web: www.nautica.com						
Nautical Furnishings Inc						
60 NW 60th St	Fort Lauderdale	FL	33309	954-771-1100		362
Web: www.nauticalfurnishings.com						
Nauticon Imaging Systems Inc						
15878 Gaither Dr	Gaithersburg	MD	20877	301-279-0123		177
TF: 800-670-2855 ■ *Web:* www.nauticon.com						
NAUTICUS the National Maritime Ctr						
1 Waterside Dr	Norfolk	VA	23510	757-664-1000	623-1287	520
TF: 800-664-1080 ■ *Web:* www.nauticus.org						
Nau-Ti-Gal 5360 Westport Rd	Madison	WI	53704	608-246-3130		671
Web: nautigal.com						
Nautilus Entertainment Design Inc						
1010 Pearl St Ste Three	La Jolla	CA	92037	858-456-6395		354
Web: www.n-e-d.com						
Nautilus Group, The 15305 Dallas Pkwy	Addison	TX	75001	972-720-6600		466
TF: 800-695-9695 ■ *Web:* www.thenautilusgroup.com						
Nautilus Inc 17750 SE Sixth Way	Vancouver	WA	98683	360-694-7722	694-7755	267
NYSE: NLS ■ *TF:* 800-628-8458 ■ *Web:* nautilusinc.com						
Nautilus Insurance Group LLC						
7233 E Butherus Dr	Scottsdale	AZ	85260	480-951-0905		391-4
TF: 800-842-8972 ■ *Web:* www.nautilusagents.com						
Nautilus Plus Inc 3550, 1Šre Rue	St-hubert	QC	J3Y8Y5	514-666-5814		706
TF: 800-363-6763 ■ *Web:* www.nautilusplus.com						
Nauvoo State Park PO Box 426	Nauvoo	IL	62354	217-453-2512		565
Web: www.stateparks.com						
NAV CANADA						
77 Metcalfe St PO Box 3411 Stn D	Ottawa	ON	K1P5L6	613-563-5588	563-3426	19
TF: 800-876-4693 ■ *Web:* www.navcanada.ca						
NAV Canada Training & Conference Ctr						
1950 Montreal Rd	Cornwall	ON	K6H6L2	613-936-5800		377
TF: 877-832-6416 ■ *Web:* www.navcentre.ca						
Navajo Agricultural Products Industry						
PO Box 1318	Farmington	NM	87499	505-566-2600		10-11
Web: www.navajopride.com						
Navajo County						
100 E Code Talkers Dr PO Box 668	Holbrook	AZ	86025	928-524-4000	524-4261	338
Web: www.navajocountyaz.gov						
Navajo Express Inc 1400 W 64 Ave	Denver	CO	80221	303-287-3800		780
TF: 800-525-1969 ■ *Web:* www.navajo.com						
Navajo Nation Oil and Gas Company Inc						
50 Narbono Cir W 2nd Fl	St. Michaels	AZ	86511	928-871-4880		536
Web: www.nnogc.net						
Navajo National Monument Highway 564	Tonalea	AZ	86044	928-672-2700	672-2703	564
Web: www.nps.gov						
Navajo State Park PO Box 1697	Arboles	CO	81121	970-883-2208		565
Web: cpw.state.co.us						
Navajo Technical College						
PO Box 849	Crownpoint	NM	87313	505-786-4100	786-5644	165
Web: www.navajotech.edu						
Naval Air Station Fallon						
4755 Pasture Rd	Fallon	NV	89496	775-426-3333		497-4
Naval Air Station Jacksonville						
6801 Roosevelt Blvd	Jacksonville	FL	32212	904-542-2338		497-4
TF: 800-849-6024 ■ *Web:* www.cnic.navy.mil/jacksonville						
Naval Air Station Joint Reserve Base Fort Worth						
1510 Chennault Ave	Fort Worth	TX	76113	817-782-5000		497-4
Web: www.cnic.navy.mil/fortworth						
Naval Air Station Joint Reserve Base New Orleans						
301 Russell Ave	New Orleans	LA	70143	504-678-3254	678-9595	497-4
TF: 800-729-7327 ■ *Web:* www.cnic.navy.mil						
Naval Air Station Key West						
PO Box 9001	Key West	FL	33040	305-293-2425		497-4
Web: www.cnic.navy.mil/keywest						
Naval Air Station Kingsville						
554 Mccain St	Kingsville	TX	78363	361-516-6146	516-6875	497-4
Web: www.cnic.navy.mil/kingsville						
Naval Air Station Lemoore 700 Avenger	Lemoore	CA	93246	559-998-3300		497-4
Web: www.cnic.navy.mil/Lemoore						
Naval Air Station Meridian						
200 Rosenbaum Ave	Meridian	MS	39305	601-679-2211		497-4
Web: cnic.navy.mil						
Naval Air Station North Island						
PO Box 357033	San Diego	CA	92135	619-545-9589	545-6260	497-4
Web: www.cnic.navy.mil						
Naval Air Station Oceana						
1750 Tomcat Blvd	Virginia Beach	VA	23460	757-433-3131		497-4
Web: www.cnic.navy.mil/oceana						
Naval Air Station Patuxent River						
22268 Cedar Point Road Bldg 409	Patuxent River	MD	20670	301-342-3000		497-4
TF: 877-995-5247 ■ *Web:* cnic.navy.mil/patuxent						
Naval Air Station Pensacola Library center						
190 Radford Blvd	Pensacola	FL	32508	800-628-9466		497-4
TF: 800-628-9466 ■ *Web:* navy-lodge.com						
Naval Air Station Whiting Field						
7550 USS Essex St	Milton	FL	32570	850-623-7341		497-4
Web: www.cnic.navy.mil						
Naval Air Station Willow Grove						
PO Box 21	Willow Grove	PA	19090	215-443-1000		497-4
Web: www.cnic.navy.mil						
Naval Air Systems Command						
47123 Buse Rd Bldg 2272, Ste 075	Patuxent River	MD	20670	301-757-1487		340-6
Web: www.navair.navy.mil						
Naval Base Kitsap 120 S Dewey St	Bremerton	WA	98314	360-627-4024		497-4
Web: www.cnic.navy.mil						
Naval Base San Diego 3455 Senn Rd	San Diego	CA	92136	619-556-1011		497-4
TF: 877-995-5247 ■ *Web:* www.cnic.navy.mil/sandiego						
Naval Education & Training Command (NETC)						
250 Dallas St	Pensacola	FL	32508	850-452-4858		340-6
Web: www.netc.navy.mil						
Naval Enlisted Reserve Assn (NERA)						
6703 Farragut Ave	Falls Church	VA	22042	703-534-1329		48-19
TF: 800-776-9020 ■ *Web:* www.nera.org						
Naval Health Research Ctr (NHRC)						
140 Sylvester Rd	San Diego	CA	92152	619-553-8400	553-9389	668
Web: www.med.navy.mil/sites/nhrc						
Naval History and Heritage Command						
805 Kidder Breese St SE						
Washington Navy Yard	Washington	DC	20374-5060	202-433-4882	433-8200	520
Web: www.history.navy.mil						
Naval Hospital 100 Brewster Blvd	Camp Lejeune	NC	28547	910-450-4300	450-4012	374-4
TF: 800-510-7897 ■ *Web:* www.med.navy.mil/sites/nhcl/pages/default.aspx						
Naval Hospital Bremerton 1 Bo1 Rd	Bremerton	WA	98312	360-475-4000		374-4
TF: 800-422-1383 ■ *Web:* www.med.navy.mil						
Naval Hospital Pensacola						
6000 W Hwy 98	Pensacola	FL	32512	850-505-6601	505-6213	374-4
Web: www.med.navy.mil						
Naval Institute for Dental & Biomedical Research (NDRI)						
310-A B St Bldg 1-H	Great Lakes	IL	60088	847-688-1900		668
Web: www.dentalmercury.com						
Naval Institute Press 291 Wood Rd	Annapolis	MD	21402	410-268-6110	295-1049	637-4
TF: 800-233-8764 ■ *Web:* usni.org						
Naval Medical Ctr Portsmouth						
620 John Paul Jones Cir	Portsmouth	VA	23708	757-953-5008		374-4
Naval Medical Ctr San Diego						
34800 Bob Wilson Dr	San Diego	CA	92134	619-532-6400		374-4
Web: www.med.navy.mil						
Naval Research Laboratory (NRL)						
4555 Overlook Ave SW Code 1000	Washington	DC	20375	202-767-3403		668
Web: www.nrl.navy.mil						
Naval Reserve Assn (NRA) 1619 King St	Alexandria	VA	22314	703-548-5800	683-3647*	48-19
**Fax Area Code:* 866 ■ *TF:* 877-628-9411 ■ *Web:* ausn.org						
Naval Sea Systems Command						
1333 Isaac Hull Ave SE						
Washington Navy Yard	Washington	DC	20376	202-781-4123		340-6
TF: 800-356-8464 ■ *Web:* www.navsea.navy.mil						
Naval Special Warfare Command						
2000 Trident Way	San Diego	CA	92155	619-537-1133	537-1986	340-6
Web: www.public.navy.mil						
Naval Station Everett						
2000 W Marine View Dr	Everett	WA	98207	425-304-3366		497-4
Web: www.cnic.navy.mil						
Naval Station Great Lakes						
2601E Paul Jones St	Great Lakes	IL	60088	847-688-3500		497-4
TF: 800-393-0865 ■ *Web:* www.cnic.navy.mil						

	Phone	Fax	Class
Naval Station Mayport PO Box 280032 Mayport FL 32228 TF: 800-872-7245 ■ Web: www.cnic.navy.mil/mayport	904-270-5401	270-5064	497-4
Naval Station Newport 690 Peary St Newport RI 02841	401-841-2232		497-4
Naval Station Pearl Harbor 4827 Bougainville Dr Honolulu HI 96818 Web: www.cnic.navy.mil	808-474-1999		497-4
Naval Submarine Medical Research Laboratory (NSMRL) PO Box 900 Groton CT 06349 *Fax Area Code: 860 ■ Web: www.med.navy.mil/sites/nsmrl/Pages/default.aspx	703-681-9025	694-4809*	668
Naval Support Activity 58 Bennion Rd Annapolis MD 21402 Web: www.usna.edu	410-293-1000	293-3133	497-4
Naval Surface Warfare Ctr (NSWC) 1333 Isaac Hull Ave SE Washington Navy Yard DC 20376 Web: www.navsea.navy.mil/nswc	202-781-4123		668
Carderock Div 9500 MacArthur Blvd West Bethesda MD 20817 *Fax Area Code: 301 ■ Web: www.navsea.navy.mil/nswc/carderock	202-781-0000	227-1968*	668
Dahlgren Div 6149 Welsh Rd Ste 203 Dahlgren VA 22448 TF: 877-845-5656 ■ Web: www.navsea.navy.mil	877-845-5656		668
Naval Undersea Warfare Ctr (NUWC) 1176 Howell St Newport RI 02841 TF: 800-356-8464 ■ Web: www.navsea.navy.mil/nuwc	401-832-7742	832-4390	668
Keyport Div 610 Dowell St Keyport WA 98345 Web: www.navsea.navy.mil/nuwc/keyport/default.aspx	360-396-2699		668
Newport Div 1176 Howell St Newport RI 02841 Web: www.navsea.navy.mil/nuwc/default.aspx	401-832-7742		668
Naval War College Museum 686 Cushing Rd Newport RI 02841 Web: www.usnwc.edu	401-841-4052	841-7074	520
Navarre Beach Realty 8305 Navarre Pkwy Navarre FL 32566 Web: www.navarrebeachrealty.com	850-936-0700		652
Navarro College 3200 W Seventh Ave Corsicana TX 75110 *Fax: Admissions ■ TF: 800-628-2776 ■ Web: www.navarrocollege.edu	903-874-6501	875-7353*	162
Navarro County PO Box 423 Corsicana TX 75151 Web: www.co.navarro.tx.us	903-654-3040	654-3097	338
Navarro County Electric Co-op Inc 3800 Texas 22 PO Box 616 Corsicana TX 75110 TF: 800-771-9095 ■ Web: navarroec.com	903-874-7411		245
Navarro Discount Pharmacies 9400 Miami FL 33178 TF: 866-628-2776 ■ Web: www.navarro.com	866-628-2776		237
Navarro Regional Hospital (NRH) 3201 W Hwy 22 Corsicana TX 75110 Web: www.navarrohospital.com	903-654-6800		374-3
Navarro Research & Engineering Inc 669 Emory Valley Rd Oak Ridge TN 37830 TF: 866-681-5265 ■ Web: www.navarro-inc.com	865-220-9650		192
Navasota Valley Electric Co-op Inc 2281 E US Hwy 79 PO Box 848 Franklin TX 77856 TF: 800-443-9462 ■ Web: www.navasotavalley.com	979-828-3232	828-5563	245
NavCom Defense Electronics Inc 9129 Stellar Ct Corona CA 92883 Web: www.navcom.com	951-268-9230		529
NavCom Technology Inc 20780 Madrona Ave Torrance CA 90503 Web: www.navcomtech.com	310-381-2000		196
Navcor Inc 700 W Georgia St Ste 980 Vancouver BC V7Y1B6 Web: www.navcor.com	604-688-9090		314
Nave Communications Co 8215 Dorsey Run Rd Jessup MD 20794 Web: www.ncctel.com	301-725-6283		246
Navellier Securities Corp 1 E Liberty St Ste 504 Reno NV 89501 TF: 800-887-8671 ■ Web: www.navellier.com	775-785-2300		401
Navhouse Corp 10 Loring Dr Bolton ON L7E1J9 TF: 877-628-6667 ■ Web: www.navhouse.com	905-857-8102	857-8104	21
Naviant Inc 201 Prairie Heights Dr Verona WI 53593 Web: naviant.com	608-848-0924		631
Navicent Health 3351 Northside Dr Macon GA 31210 Web: www.navicenthealth.org	478-633-1000		374-6
Navicent Health 777 Hemlock St Macon GA 31201 Web: www.navicenthealth.org	478-633-1000		374-3
Navigant Consulting Inc 30 S Wacker Dr Ste 3100 Chicago IL 60606 NYSE: NCI ■ *Fax: Mktg ■ TF: 800-621-8390 ■ Web: www.navigant.com	312-583-5700	583-5701*	194
Navigant Cymetrix 2875 Michelle Dr Ste 250 Irvine CA 92606 Web: www.cymetrix.com	714-361-6800		196
Navigate Power LLC 2211 N Elston Ave Ste 309 Chicago IL 60614 TF: 888-601-1789 ■ Web: navigatepower.com	888-601-1709		463
Navigation Solutions LLC 3314 N Central Expy Ste 210 Plano TX 75074 Web: www.navigationsolutions.com	972-633-2301		529
Navigator Development Group Inc 116 S Main St Ste 214 Enterprise AL 36330 Web: www.ndgi.com	334-347-7612		449
Navigator Energy Services LLC 2626 Cole Ave Ste 850 Dallas TX 75204 Web: www.navigatorenergyservices.com	214-880-6000		538
Navigator Management Partners LLC 1400 Goodale Blvd Ste 100 Columbus OH 43212 Web: www.navmp.com	614-796-0090	796-0089	463
Navigators Group Inc 1 Penn Plaza 32nd Fl New York NY 10119 NASDAQ: NAVG ■ TF: 866-408-1922 ■ Web: www.navg.com	212-244-2333	244-4077	360-4
Navigators of Canada 11 St John'S Dr Arva ON N0M1C0 TF: 866-202-6287 ■ Web: www.navigators.ca	519-660-8300		48-20
Navigators, The 3820 N 30th St PO Box 6000 Colorado Springs CO 80934 TF: 866-568-7827 ■ Web: www.navigators.org	719-598-1212	260-0479	48-20
Navigy Inc 4800 Deerwood Campus Pkwy DCC9-1 Jacksonville FL 32246 Web: www.navigy.net	904-363-5490		194
Navii Salon Spa 316 E US Hwy 30 Schererville IN 46375 TF: 800-679-7756 ■ Web: www.navii.com	219-865-6515		77
Navin, Haffty & Associates LLC 200 Cordwainer Dr Ste 100 Norwell MA 02061 Web: www.navinhaffty.com	781-871-6770		463
Navinta LLC 1499 Lower Ferry Rd Ewing NJ 08618 Web: navinta.com	609-883-1135		582
Navis Logistics Network 6551 S Revere Pkwy Ste 250 Centennial CO 80111 *Fax Area Code: 303 ■ TF: 800-344-3528 ■ Web: www.gonavis.com	800-344-3528	741-6653*	549
Navis Pack & Ship Centers 6551 S Revere Pkwy Ste 250 Centennial CO 80111 *Fax Area Code: 303 ■ TF: 800-344-3528 ■ Web: www.gonavis.com	800-344-3528	741-6653*	113
Navitaire Inc 333 S Seventh St Ste 500 Minneapolis MN 55402 TF: 877-216-6787 ■ Web: www.navitaire.com	612-317-7000		194
Navitar Inc 200 Commerce Dr Rochester NY 14623 TF Cust Svc: 800-828-6778 ■ Web: www.navitar.com	585-359-4000	359-4999	591
Navix Diagnostix Inc 100 Myles Standish Blvd Taunton MA 02780 TF: 800-442-1142 ■ Web: www.navixdiagnostix.com	508-977-2807		415
Navmar Applied Sciences Corp 65 W St Rd Bldg C Warminster PA 18974 Web: www.nasc.com	215-675-4900		256
Navopache Electric Co-op Inc 1878 W White Mtn Blvd Lakeside AZ 85929 TF: 800-543-6324 ■ Web: www.navopache.org	928-368-5118	368-6038	245
NavPress 3820 N 30th St Colorado Springs CO 80904 Web: www.navpress.com	719-548-9222		637-3
NAVS (National Anti-Vivisection Society) 53 W Jackson Blvd Ste 1552 Chicago IL 60604 TF: 800-888-6287 ■ Web: www.navs.org	312-427-6065	427-6524	48-3
Navtech Inc 295 Hagey Blvd Ste 200 Waterloo ON N2L6R5 TF: 800-800-6061 ■ Web: www.navtechinc.com	519-747-1170	747-1003	178-10
Navtech Seminars & Gps Supply 5501 Backlick Rd Ste 230 Springfield VA 22151 TF: 800-628-0885 ■ Web: www.navtechgps.com	703-256-8900		403
Navy Exchange Service Command (NEXCOM) 3280 Virginia Beach Blvd Virginia Beach VA 23452 TF: 800-628-3924 ■ Web: www.mynavyexchange.com	757-463-6200		791
Navy League of the US 2300 Wilson Blvd Arlington VA 22201 TF: 800-356-5760 ■ Web: www.navyleague.org	703-528-1775	528-2333	48-19
Navy Personnel Command (NPC) 5720 Integrity Dr Millington TN 38055 TF: 866-827-5672 ■ Web: www.public.navy.mil	901-874-3165	874-2615	340-6
Navy Pier 600 E Grand Ave Chicago IL 60611 TF: 800-595-7437 ■ Web: www.navypier.com	312-595-7437		205
Navy-Marine Corps Relief Society (NMCRS) 875 N Randolph St Ste 225 Arlington VA 22203 TF: 800-654-8364 ■ Web: www.nmcrs.org	703-696-4904	696-0144	48-19
Nawab Indian Cuisine 118A Campbell Ave Roanoke VA 24011 Web: www.nawabonline.com	540-345-5150		671
Nawab Indian Cuisine 204 Monticello Ave Monticello Shopping Ctr Williamsburg VA 23185 TF: 800-219-0976 ■ Web: www.nawabonline.com	757-565-3200		671
Nawab Indian Cuisine 120 S Stratford Rd Winston-Salem NC 27104 Web: www.nawabindiancuisine.com	336-725-3949		671
NAWD (NA of Wholesaler-Distributors) 1325 G St NW Ste 1000 Washington DC 20005 Web: www.naw.org	202-872-0885	785-0586	49-18
NAWIC (NA of Women in Construction) 327 S Adams St Fort Worth TX 76104 TF: 800-552-3506 ■ Web: www.nawic.org	817-877-5551	877-0324	49-3
Naxos of America Inc 1810 Columbia Ave Franklin TN 37064 TF: 877-629-6723 ■ Web: www.naxos.com	615-771-9393	771-6747	657
Naya Restaurant 1057 Second Ave New York NY 10022 Web: www.nayarestaurants.com	212-319-7777		671
Naylor LLC 5950 NW First Pl Gainesville FL 32607 TF: 800-369-6220 ■ Web: www.naylor.com	800-369-6220		7
Naylor Pipe Co 1230 E 92nd St Chicago IL 60619 Web: www.naylorpipe.com	773-721-9400	721-9494	490
Nazarene Theological Seminary 1700 E Meyer Blvd Kansas City MO 64131 TF: 800-831-3011 ■ Web: www.nts.edu	816-268-5400		167-3
Nazareth College of Rochester 4245 E Ave Rochester NY 14618 TF: 800-860-6942 ■ Web: www.naz.edu	585-389-2525		166
Nazareth Hospital 2601 Holme Ave Philadelphia PA 19152 Web: www.mercyhealth.org/nazareth	215-335-6000	335-7740	374-3
Nazcare Inc 599 White Spar Rd Prescott AZ 86303 TF: 877-756-4090 ■ Web: www.nazcare.org	928-442-9205		138
Nazdar 8501 Hedge Ln Terr Shawnee KS 66227 TF: 800-767-9942 ■ Web: www.nazdar.com	913-422-1888	422-2296	388
NB Liebman & Company Inc 4705 Carlisle Pk Mechanicsburg PA 17050 Web: www.nbliebman.com	717-761-4550		321
NBA (National Business Assn) 5151 Beltline Rd Ste 1150 Dallas TX 75254 TF: 800-456-0440 ■ Web: www.nationalbusiness.org	972-458-0900	960-9149	49-12
NBA (Niles Bolton Assoc Inc) 3060 Peachtree Rd NW Ste 600 Atlanta GA 30305 Web: www.nilesbolton.com	404-365-7600		261
NBA (National Basketball Assn) 645 Fifth Ave New York NY 10022 Web: www.nba.com	212-407-8000	832-3861	714-1
NBA (National Benevolent Assn) 733 Union Blvd Ste 300 St. Louis MO 63108 TF: 800-366-3383 ■ Web: www.nbacares.org	314-993-9000		48-5
NBA (National Bar Assn) 1225 11th St NW Washington DC 20001 TF: 800-327-0200 ■ Web: www.nationalbar.org	202-842-3900	289-6170	49-10
NBA Entertainment 450 Harmon Meadow Blvd Secaucus NJ 07094 *Fax: Mail Rm ■ TF: 866-648-4668 ■ Web: nba.com	201-865-1500	865-2626*	514

	Phone	Fax	Class
NBAA (National Business Aviation Assn) 1200 18th St NW Ste 400 .... Washington DC 20036 *TF:* 800-394-6222 ■ *Web:* www.nbaa.org	202-783-9000	331-8364	49-21
NBBJ 223 Yale Ave N .... Seattle WA 98109 *Web:* www.nbbj.com	206-223-5555		261
NBC 26 1391 N Rd .... Green Bay WI 54313 *TF:* 800-800-6619 ■ *Web:* www.nbc26.com	920-494-2626	490-2500	741-55
NBC 33 TV 10000 Perkins Rd .... Baton Rouge LA 70810 *Web:* www.brproud.com	225-766-3233	768-9293	741-13
NBC Universal Inc 30 Rockefeller Plaza .... New York NY 10112 *Web:* www.nbcuniversal.com	212-664-4444		360-3
NBC15 615 Forward Dr .... Madison WI 53711 *Web:* nbc15.com	608-274-1515	271-5194	741-80
NBCC (National Breast Cancer Coalition) 1101 17th St NW Ste 1300 .... Washington DC 20036 *TF:* 800-622-2838 ■ *Web:* www.breastcancerdeadline2020.org	202-296-7477	265-6854	48-17
NBCL (National Beauty Culturists' League Inc) 25 Logan Cir NW .... Washington DC 20005 *Web:* www.nbcl.org	202-332-2695		49-4
Nbcot 12 S Summit Ave Ste 100 .... Gaithersburg MD 20877 *TF:* 800-967-1139 ■ *Web:* www.nbcot.org	301-990-7979		138
NBCVB (North of Boston Convention & Visitors Bureau) I-95 Southbound Exit 60 PO Box 5193 .... Salisbury MA 01952 *TF:* 800-215-9805 ■ *Web:* www.northofboston.org	978-465-6555		206
NBDA (National Bicycle Dealers Assn) 777 W 19th St Ste O .... Costa Mesa CA 92627 *Web:* www.nbda.com	949-722-6909		49-4
NBDL (National Biodynamics Laboratory) *University of New Orleans College of Engineering* 2000 Lakeshore Dr .... New Orleans LA 70148 **Fax Area Code:* 504 ■ *TF:* 888-514-4275 ■ *Web:* www.uno.edu	888-514-4275	280-7413*	668
NBEA (National Business Education Assn) 1914 Assn Dr .... Reston VA 20191 *TF:* 800-811-1648 ■ *Web:* www.nbea.org	703-860-8300	620-4483	49-5
NBFPL (New Bedford Free Public Library) 613 Pleasant St .... New Bedford MA 02740 *Web:* www.newbedford-ma.gov/library	508-991-6275	991-6368	434-3
NBMBAA (National Black MBA Assn) 180 N Michigan Ave Ste 1400 .... Chicago IL 60601 *Web:* www.nbmbaa.org	312-236-2622		49-12
NBMDA (North American Bldg Material Distribution Assn) 330 N Wabash Ave Ste 2000 .... Chicago IL 60611 *TF:* 888-747-7862 ■ *Web:* www.nbmda.org	312-321-6845	644-0310	49-18
NBME (National Board of Medical Examiners) 3750 Market St .... Philadelphia PA 19104 *Web:* www.nbme.org	215-590-9500		49-8
Nbn Infusions 2 Pin Oak Ln Ste 250 .... Cherry Hill NJ 08003 *TF:* 800-253-9111 ■ *Web:* www.nbninfusions.com	856-669-0217	424-8913	475
NBPA (National Basketball Players Assn) 1133 Avenue of Americas .... New York NY 10036 *TF:* 800-955-6272 ■ *Web:* www.nbpa.com	212-655-0880	655-0881	48-22
Nbs Corp 3100 E Slauson Ave .... Vernon CA 90058 *TF:* 800-472-4643 ■ *Web:* www.nbsfasteners.com	323-923-1627		351
NBS Technologies Inc 703 Evans Ave Ste 402 .... Toronto ON M9C5E9 *TF:* 800-595-9149 ■ *Web:* www.nbstech.com	416-621-1911		41
NBT Bancorp Inc 52 S Broad St .... Norwich NY 13815 *NASDAQ: NBTB* ■ *TF:* 800-628-2265 ■ *Web:* www.nbtbancorp.com	607-337-2265		360-2
NBT Bank NA PO Box 351 .... Norwich NY 13815 *TF:* 800-628-2265 ■ *Web:* www.nbtbank.com	607-337-2265		70
Nbt Solutions LLC 188 State St Ste 200 .... Portland ME 04101 *Web:* www.nbtsolutions.com	617-202-3088		180
NBWA (National Beer Wholesalers Assn) 1101 King St Ste 600 .... Alexandria VA 22314 *TF:* 800-300-6417 ■ *Web:* www.nbwa.org	703-683-4300	683-8965	49-6
NC Dynamics Inc (NCDI) 3401 E 69th St .... Long Beach CA 90805 *Web:* www.ncdi.aero	562-634-7392	634-6220	454
NC Machinery Co 17025 W Valley Hwy .... Tukwila WA 98188 *TF:* 800-562-4735 ■ *Web:* www.ncmachinery.com	425-251-9800		385
NCA (National Club Assn) 1201 15th St NW Ste 450 .... Washington DC 20005 *TF:* 800-625-6221 ■ *Web:* nationalclub.org	202-822-9822	822-9808	48-23
NCA (National Confectioners Assn PAC) 1101 30th St NW Ste 200 .... Washington DC 20007 *TF:* 800-433-1200 ■ *Web:* www.candyusa.com	202-534-1440	337-0637	615
NCA (National Coffee Assn of USA Inc) 45 Broadway Ste 1140 .... New York NY 10006 *TF:* 800-611-6100 ■ *Web:* www.ncausa.org	212-766-4007	766-5815	49-6
NCA (National Confectioners Assn) 1101 30th St NW Ste 200 .... Washington DC 20007 *Web:* www.candyusa.com	202-534-1440	337-0637	49-6
NCA (National Communication Assn) 1765 N St NW .... Washington DC 20036 *Web:* www.natcom.org	202-464-4622	464-4600	49-5
NCA Architects PA 1306 Rio Grande Blvd NW .... Albuquerque NM 87104	505-255-6400		261
NCA CASI (North Central Assn Commission on Accreditation & School Improvement) 9115 Westside Pkwy .... Alpharetta GA 30009 *TF:* 888-413-3669 ■ *Web:* advanc-ed.org	888-413-3669		48-1
NCA Partners Inc 1200 Westlake Ave N Ste 600 .... Seattle WA 98109 *Web:* www.nwcap.com	206-689-5615	689-5614	403
NCAA (National Collegiate Athletic Assn) 700 W Washington St PO Box 6222 .... Indianapolis IN 46206 *Web:* www.ncaa.org	317-917-6222	917-6888	48-22
NCAAA (Museum of the National Ctr of Afro-American Artists) 300 Walnut Ave .... Roxbury MA 02119 *Web:* www.ncaaa.org/museum.html	617-442-8614		520
NCAC (National Coalition Against Censorship) 19 Fulton St Ste 407 .... New York NY 10038 *Web:* www.ncac.org	212-807-6222	807-6245	48-8
NCAC (National Children's Advocacy Ctr) 210 Pratt Ave .... Huntsville AL 35801 *Web:* www.nationalcac.org	256-533-5437	534-6883	48-5
NCADD (National Council on Alcoholism & Drug Dependence Inc) 217 Broadway Ste 712 .... New York NY 10007 *TF:* 800-622-2255 ■ *Web:* www.ncadd.org	212-269-7797	269-7510	48-17

	Phone	Fax	Class
NCADD (ACA) 217 Broadway Ste 712 .... New York NY 10007 *TF:* 800-622-2255 ■ *Web:* www.ncadd.org	800-527-5344		48-17
NCADP (National Coalition to Abolish the Death Penalty) 1620 L St Ste 250 .... Washington DC 20036 *Web:* www.ncadp.org	202-331-4090		48-8
NCADV (National Coalition Against Domestic Violence) 1 Broadway Ste B210 .... Denver CO 80203 *TF:* 800-799-7233 ■ *Web:* www.ncadv.org	303-839-1852	831-9251	48-6
NCAE News Bulletin PO Box 27347 .... Raleigh NC 27611 *TF:* 800-662-7924 ■ *Web:* www.ncae.org	919-832-3000	829-1626	457-8
NCAF (National Community Action Foundation) PO Box 78214 .... Washington DC 20013 *TF:* 800-717-2762 ■ *Web:* ncaf.org	202-842-2092	842-2095	48-7
NCAI (National Congress of American Indians) 1516 P St NW .... Washington DC 20005 *TF:* 800-388-2227 ■ *Web:* www.ncai.org	202-466-7767	466-7797	48-14
NCAR (National Center for Atmospheric Research) 3090 Center Green Dr .... Boulder CO 80301 *Web:* www.ncar.ucar.edu	303-497-1000		668
NCARB (National Council of Architectural Registration Boards) 1801 K St NW Ste 700-K .... Washington DC 20006 *Web:* www.ncarb.org	202-783-6500	783-0290	49-7
NCASI (National Council for Air & Stream Improvement Inc) PO Box 13318 .... Research Triangle Park NC 27709 *TF:* 888-448-2473 ■ *Web:* www.ncasi.org	919-941-6400	941-6401	48-13
NCATE (National Council for Accreditation of Teacher Education) 2010 Massachusetts Ave NW Ste 500 .... Washington DC 20036 *TF:* 800-255-8664 ■ *Web:* www.ncate.org	202-466-7496	296-6620	48-1
NCB (National Cargo Bureau Inc) 180 Maiden Ln Ste 903 .... New York NY 10038 *Web:* www.natcargo.org	212-785-8300	785-8333	49-21
NCBA (National Cattlemen's Beef Assn) 9110 E Nichols Ave Ste 300 .... Centennial CO 80112 *TF:* 866-233-3872 ■ *Web:* www.beefusa.org	303-694-0305	694-2851	48-2
NCBA (National Caucus & Ctr on Black Aged Inc) 1220 L St NW Ste 800 .... Washington DC 20005 *Web:* www.ncba-aged.org	202-637-8400	347-0895	48-6
NCBA (National Co-op Business Assn) 1401 New York Ave NW Ste 1100 .... Washington DC 20005 *TF:* 800-356-9655 ■ *Web:* www.ncba.coop	202-638-6222	638-1374	49-12
NCBCP (National Coalition on Black Civic Participation Inc) 1050 Connecticut Ave NW Ste 700 .... Washington DC 20036 *Web:* ncbcp.org	202-659-4929	659-5025	48-7
NCBFAA (National Customs Brokers & Forwarders Assn of America Inc) 1200 18th St NW Ste 901 .... Washington DC 20036 *Web:* www.ncbfaa.org	202-466-0222	466-0226	49-21
NCBMP (National Coalition of Black Meeting Planners) 1800 Diagonal Rd .... Alexandria VA 22314 **Fax Area Code:* 301 ■ *Web:* www.ncbmp.com	571-366-1779	588-0011*	49-12
NCBW (National Ctr for Bicycling & Walking) 8120 Woodmont Ave Ste 520 .... Bethesda MD 20814 **Fax Area Code:* 301 ■ *TF:* 800-836-6740 ■ *Web:* www.bikewalk.org	202-223-3621	656-4225*	48-22
NCC (Newcap Radio) 745 Windmill Rd .... Dartmouth NS B3B1C2 *Web:* www.ncc.ca	902-468-7557		643
NCCA (National Child Care Assn) 1325 G St NW Ste 500 .... Washington DC 20005 *TF:* 866-536-1945 ■ *Web:* www.nccanet.org	866-536-1945		48-6
NCCA (National Coil Coating Assn) 1300 Sumner Ave .... Cleveland OH 44115 *Web:* www.coilcoating.org	216-241-7333	241-0105	49-13
NCCAOM (National Certification Commission for Acupuncture & Oriental Medicine) 76 S Laura St Ste 1290 .... Jacksonville FL 32202 *Web:* www.nccaom.org	904-598-1005	598-5001	48-1
NCCD (National Council on Crime & Delinquency) 1970 Broadway Ste 500 .... Oakland CA 94612 *TF:* 800-306-6223 ■ *Web:* www.nccdglobal.org	510-208-0500	208-0511	48-8
NCCI Holdings Inc 901 Peninsula Corporate Cir .... Boca Raton FL 33487 *TF Cust Svc:* 800-622-4123 ■ *Web:* www.ncci.com	561-893-1000	893-1191	390
NCCIC (National Child Care Information Center) 9300 Lee Hwy .... Fairfax VA 22031 *TF:* 877-296-2250 ■ *Web:* www.icf.com	877-296-2250		340-10
NCCNHR (National Citizens' Coalition for Nursing Home Reform) *National Consumer Voice for Quality Long-Term Care* 1828 L St NW Ste 801 .... Washington DC 20036 *TF:* 866-992-3668 ■ *Web:* www.theconsumervoice.org	202-332-2275	332-2949	48-17
NCCP (National Ctr for Children in Poverty) 215 W 125th St 3rd Fl .... New York NY 10027 *TF:* 800-388-7670 ■ *Web:* www.nccp.org	646-284-9600	284-9623	48-6
NCCS (National Coalition for Cancer Survivorship) 1010 Wayne Ave Ste 315 .... Silver Spring MD 20910 *TF:* 877-622-7937 ■ *Web:* www.canceradvocacy.org	877-622-7937		48-17
NCD (National Council on Disability) 1331 F St NW Ste 850 .... Washington DC 20004 *Web:* www.ncd.gov	202-272-2004	272-2022	340-20
NCD Corp 33801 Curtis Blvd Ste 100 .... Eastlake OH 44095 *Web:* www.ncdcorp.com	440-953-4488		475
NCDA&CS Raleigh Farmers Market 1201 Agriculture St .... Raleigh NC 27603 *Web:* www.ncagr.gov/markets/facilities/markets/raleigh	919-733-7417		460
NCDI (NC Dynamics Inc) 3401 E 69th St .... Long Beach CA 90805 *Web:* www.ncdi.aero	562-634-7392	634-6220	454
NCE Computer Group 1866 Friendship Dr .... El Cajon CA 92020 *Web:* www.ncegroup.com	619-212-3000	596-2881	175
NCEA (National Catholic Educational Assn) 1005 N Glebe Rd Ste 525 .... Arlington VA 22201 **Fax Area Code:* 703 ■ *TF:* 800-711-6232 ■ *Web:* www.ncea.org	571-257-0010	243-0025*	49-5
NCEAS (National Ctr for Ecological Analysis & Synthesis) 735 State St Ste 300 .... Santa Barbara CA 93101 *Web:* www.nceas.ucsb.edu	805-892-2500	892-2510	668
Nceca 4845 Pearl East Cir Ste 101 .... Boulder CO 80301 *Web:* nceca.net	303-828-2811		184
NCED (National Ctr for Employee Development) 2701 E Imhoff Rd .... Norman OK 73071 *TF:* 866-438-6233 ■ *Web:* www.nced.com	405-366-4420		377
NCEE (National Council on Economic Education) 122 E 42nd St Ste 2600 .... New York NY 10168 *TF:* 800-338-1192 ■ *Web:* www.councilforeconed.org	212-730-7007	730-1793	49-5

	Phone	Fax	Class
NCEES (National Council of Examiners for Engineering & Surveying) 280 Seneca Creek Rd .... Seneca SC 29678 *TF:* 800-250-3196 ■ *Web:* www.ncees.org	864-654-6824	654-6033	49-3
NCEM (National Ctr for Electron Microscopy) one cyclotron Rd Bldg 67 .... Berkeley CA 94720 *Web:* foundry.lbl.gov/facilities/ncem	510-486-4000		668
NCEO (National Ctr for Employee Ownership) 1736 Franklin St 8th Fl .... Oakland CA 94612 *Web:* www.nceo.org	510-208-1300	272-9510	48-10
NCFA (National Council for Adoption) 225 N Washington St .... Alexandria VA 22314 *TF:* 800-366-7773 ■ *Web:* www.adoptioncouncil.org	703-299-6633	299-6004	48-6
NCFBMIC (North Carolina Farm Bureau Mutual Insurance Co) PO Box 27427 .... Raleigh NC 27611 *TF:* 800-584-1143 ■ *Web:* www.ncfbins.com	919-782-1705		391-4
NCFC (National Council of Farmer Co-ops) 50 F St NW Ste 900 .... Washington DC 20001 *TF:* 800-344-2626 ■ *Web:* www.ncfc.org	202-626-8700	626-8722	48-2
NCFC Co-op PAC 50 F St NW Ste 900 .... Washington DC 20001 *TF:* 800-344-2626 ■ *Web:* www.ncfc.org	202-626-8700	626-8722	615
NCFL (National Ctr for Family Literacy) 325 W Main St Ste 300 .... Louisville KY 40202 *TF:* 855-937-5668 ■ *Web:* familieslearning.org	502-584-1133	584-0172	48-11
NCFR (National Council on Family Relations) 1201 W River Pkwy Ste 200 .... Minneapolis MN 55454 *TF:* 888-781-9331 ■ *Web:* www.ncfr.org	888-781-9331		48-6
NCGA (National Corn Growers Assn) 632 Cepi Dr .... Chesterfield MO 63005 *TF:* 800-222-4734 ■ *Web:* www.ncga.com	636-733-9004	733-9005	48-2
NCGRP (National Ctr for Genetic Resources Preservation) 1111 S Mason St .... Fort Collins CO 80521 *TF:* 800-795-3272 ■ *Web:* www.ars.usda.gov/npa/ftcollins/ncgrp	970-495-3200	221-1427	668
NCGS (National Coalition of Girls' Schools) 50 Leonard St Ste 2C .... Belmont MA 02478 *Web:* www.ncgs.org	617-489-0013	489-0024	49-5
NCH (National Coalition for the Homeless) 2201 P St NW .... Washington DC 20037 *TF:* 877-243-1576 ■ *Web:* www.nationalhomeless.org	202-462-4822	462-4823	48-5
NCH (National Ctr for Homeopathy) 1120 Rte 73 Ste 200 .... Mount Laurel NJ 08054 **Fax Area Code:* 856 ■ *Web:* www.homeopathycenter.org	703-548-7790	439-0525*	48-17
NCH Corp 2727 Chemsearch Blvd .... Irving TX 75062 *TF:* 800-527-9919 ■ *Web:* www.nch.com	972-438-0211		151
NCH Healthcare System 350 Seventh St N .... Naples FL 34102 *Web:* www.nchmd.org	239-436-5000		374-3
NCH North Naples Hospital 11190 Health Park Blvd .... Naples FL 34110 *Web:* nchmd.org	239-552-7000		374-3
NCHA (National Cutting Horse Assn) 260 Bailey Ave .... Fort Worth TX 76107 *TF:* 800-852-1162 ■ *Web:* www.nchacutting.com	817-244-6188	244-2015	48-3
NCHC (New Castle-Henry County Public Library) 376 S 15th St .... New Castle IN 47362 *Web:* nchcpl.org	765-529-0362		434-3
NCI (Nissan Canada Inc) 5290 Orbitor Dr .... Mississauga ON L4W4Z5 **Fax Area Code:* 905 ■ *TF:* 800-387-0122 ■ *Web:* www.nissan.ca	800-387-0122	629-6553*	59
NCI (Nationwide Credit Inc) PO Box 14581 .... Des Moines IA 50306 **Fax Area Code:* 770 ■ *TF:* 800-456-4729 ■ *Web:* www.ncirm.com	800-456-4729	612-7335*	160
NCI (National Captioning Institute) 3725 Concorde Pkwy Ste 100 .... Chantilly VA 20151 *TF:* 800-825-6758 ■ *Web:* www.ncicap.org	703-917-7600	917-9853	632
NCI Bldg Systems Inc 10943 N Sam Houston PkwyWest .... Houston TX 77064 *NYSE:* NCS ■ *TF:* 888-624-8677 ■ *Web:* www.ncibuildingsystems.com	281-897-7788	477-9674	105
NCI Inc 11730 Plaza America Dr Ste 700 .... Reston VA 20190 *NASDAQ:* NCIT ■ *TF:* 800-274-9694 ■ *Web:* www.nciinc.com	703-707-6900	707-6901	180
NCI Technologies Inc 636 Cure-Boivin Blvd .... Boisbriand QC J7G2A7 *Web:* www.ncitech.ca	450-434-7222		407
NCIC (NCIC Inmate Communications) 607 E Whaley St .... Longview TX 75601 *TF:* 800-382-2887 ■ *Web:* www.ncic.com	903-757-4455	247-2057	736
NCIC Capital Fund 900 Kettering Tower .... Dayton OH 45423 *Web:* www.ncicfund.com	937-222-4422	222-1323	792
NCIC Inmate Communications (NCIC) 607 E Whaley St .... Longview TX 75601 *TF:* 800-382-2887 ■ *Web:* www.ncic.com	903-757-4455	247-2057	736
NCircle Entertainment 12740 Hillcrest Ste 120 .... Dallas TX 75230 *Web:* www.ncircleentertainment.com	214-891-0300		511
nCircle Network Security Inc 101 Second St Ste 400 .... San Francisco CA 94105 *TF:* 866-897-8776 ■ *Web:* www.tripwire.com	503-276-7500	223-0182	177
NCIS (National Crop Insurance Services) 8900 Indian Creek Pkwy Ste 600 .... Overland Park KS 66210 *TF:* 800-951-6247 ■ *Web:* www.ag-risk.org	913-685-2767	685-3080	48-2
NCJFCJ (National Council of Juvenile & Family Court Judges) Univ of Nevada PO Box 8970 .... Reno NV 89507 *TF:* 800-527-3223 ■ *Web:* www.ncjfcj.org	775-784-6012	784-6628	49-10
NCJJ (National Ctr for Juvenile Justice) 3700 S Water St Ste 200 .... Pittsburgh PA 15203 *TF:* 800-851-3420 ■ *Web:* ncjj.org	412-227-6950	227-6955	48-8
NCJW (National Council of Jewish Women) 475 Riverside Dr Ste 1901 .... New York NY 10115 *TF:* 800-829-6259 ■ *Web:* www.ncjw.org	212-645-4048	645-7466	48-24
NCL (National Civic League) 1889 York St .... Denver CO 80206 **Fax Area Code:* 888 ■ *TF:* 800-765-7755 ■ *Web:* www.nationalcivicleague.org	303-571-4343	314-6053*	48-7
NCL (National Consumers League) 1701 K St NW Ste 1200 .... Washington DC 20006 *TF:* 800-388-2227 ■ *Web:* www.natlconsumersleague.org	202-835-3323	835-0747	48-10
NCL Graphic Specialties Inc N29 W 22960 Marjean Ln. .... Waukesha WI 53186 *Web:* nclgs.com	262-832-6100		627
NCLA (North Carolina Library Assn) 1811 Capital Blvd .... Raleigh NC 27604 *TF:* 888-977-3143 ■ *Web:* www.nclaonline.org	919-839-6252	839-6253	435
NCLC (National Consumer Law Ctr) 7 Winthrop Sq .... Boston MA 02110 *TF:* 800-225-5254 ■ *Web:* www.nclc.org	617-542-8010	542-8028	48-8
NCLR (National Council of La Raza) 1126 16th St NW 6th Fl .... Washington DC 20036 *Web:* www.nclr.org	202-785-1670	776-1792	48-14
NCMA (National Contract Management Assn) 21740 Beaumeade Cir Ste 125 .... Ashburn VA 20147 **Fax Area Code:* 703 ■ *TF:* 800-344-8096 ■ *Web:* www.ncmahq.org	571-382-0082	448-0939*	49-12
NCMEC (National Ctr for Missing & Exploited Children) 699 Prince St .... Alexandria VA 22314 *TF:* 800-843-5678 ■ *Web:* www.missingkids.com	703-274-3900	274-2200	48-6
NCMIC Insurance Co 14001 University Ave .... Clive IA 50325 **Fax Area Code:* 800 ■ *TF:* 800-769-2000 ■ *Web:* www.ncmic.com	515-313-4500	996-2642*	391-5
NCMS (National Ctr for Mfg Sciences) 3025 Boardwalk .... Ann Arbor MI 48108 *TF:* 800-222-6267 ■ *Web:* www.ncms.org	734-995-3457	995-1150	668
NCMS Bulletin 222 N Person St .... Raleigh NC 27601 *Web:* www.ncmedsoc.org	919-833-3836	833-2023	457-16
NCNA (North Carolina Nurses Assn) 103 Enterprise St PO Box 12025 .... Raleigh NC 27605 *TF:* 800-626-2153 ■ *Web:* www.ncnurses.org	919-821-4250	829-5807	533
NCNW (National Council of Negro Women Inc) 633 Pennsylvania Ave NW .... Washington DC 20004 *Web:* www.ncnw.org	202-737-0120	737-0476	48-24
NCOA (National Council on the Aging) 1901 L St NW 4th Fl .... Washington DC 20036 *TF:* 800-677-1116 ■ *Web:* www.ncoa.org	202-479-1200	479-0735	48-6
NCOA (Non Commissioned Officers Assn) 9330 Corporate Dr Ste 701 .... Selma TX 78154 *TF:* 800-662-2620 ■ *Web:* www.ncoausa.org	210-653-6161	637-3337	48-19
NCOC (National Conference on Citizenship) 1900 L St NW Ste 800 .... Washington DC 20036 *Web:* www.ncoc.net	202-601-7096		48-8
NCompass International Inc 8223 Santa Monica Blvd. .... West Hollywood CA 90046 *TF:* 800-867-3976 ■ *Web:* www.ncompassonline.com	323-785-1700		195
NCP Solutions 5200 E Lake Blvd .... Birmingham AL 35217 *Web:* www.ncpsolutions.com	205-849-5200		110
NCPA (National Community Pharmacists Assn) 100 Daingerfield Rd .... Alexandria VA 22314 *TF:* 800-544-7447 ■ *Web:* www.ncpanet.org	703-683-8200	683-3619	49-8
NCPC (National Crime Prevention Council) 2345 Crystal Dr Ste 500 .... Arlington VA 22202 *TF:* 800-627-2911 ■ *Web:* www.ncpc.org	202-466-6272	296-1356	48-8
NCPCF (National Coalition for the Protection of Children & Families) 800 Compton Rd Ste 9224 .... Cincinnati OH 45231 *Web:* www.eos.net	513-521-6227		48-6
NCPDP (National Council for Prescription Drug Programs) 9240 E Raintree Dr .... Scottsdale AZ 85260 *TF:* 888-665-2600 ■ *Web:* www.ncpdp.org	480-477-1000	767-1042	49-9
NCPG (Partnership for Philanthropic Planning) 233 McCrea St .... Indianapolis OH 45429 *Web:* pppgd.org	317-269-6274		48-5
NCPH (National Council on Public History) 425 University Blvd 127 Cavanaugh Hall ...... Indianapolis IN 46202-5140 *TF:* 800-554-5542 ■ *Web:* www.ncph.org	317-274-2716	278-5230	48-7
NCPIRG (North Carolina Public Interest Research Group) 112 S Blount St .... Raleigh NC 27601 *Web:* www.ncpirg.org	919-833-2070		633
NCPPR (National Ctr for Public Policy Research) 501 Capitol Ct NE Ste 200 .... Washington DC 20002 *Web:* ncppr.org	202-543-4110	543-5975	634
NCPSSM (National Committee to Preserve Social Security & Medicare) 10 G St NE Ste 600 .... Washington DC 20002 *TF:* 800-966-1935 ■ *Web:* www.ncpssm.org	202-216-0420	216-0451	48-7
NCQA (National Committee for Quality Assurance) 1100 13th St .... Washington DC 20005 *TF:* 888-275-7585 ■ *Web:* www.ncqa.org	202-955-3500	955-3599	48-10
NCRA (National Cancer Registrars Assn) 1340 Braddock Pl Ste 203 .... Alexandria VA 22314 *TF:* 800-621-4111 ■ *Web:* www.ncra-usa.org	703-299-6640	299-6620	48-17
NCRA (National Court Reporters Assn) 8224 Old Courthouse Rd .... Vienna VA 22182 *TF:* 800-272-6272 ■ *Web:* www.ncra.org	703-556-6272	556-6291	49-10
NCRP (National Committee for Responsive Philanthropy) 2001 S St NW Ste 620 .... Washington DC 20009 *Web:* www.ncrp.org	202-387-9177	332-5084	48-5
NCRP (National Council on Radiation Protection & Measurements) 7910 Woodmont Ave Ste 400 .... Bethesda MD 20814 *TF:* 800-462-3683 ■ *Web:* www.ncrponline.org	301-657-2652	907-8768	49-19
NCS (Raytheon Network Centric Systems) 2501 W University Dr .... McKinney TX 75071 *Web:* www.raytheon.com	781-522-3000		529
Ncs Global 32 Innovation Dr. .... Rochester NH 03867 *TF:* 800-711-6010 ■ *Web:* www.newportcomputers.com	603-926-4300		174
NCS Multistage LLC 19450 State Hwy 249 Ste 200 .... Spring TX 77373 *Web:* www.ncsmultistage.com	281-453-2222	652-5846	538
Ncs Subsea Inc 3928 Bluebonnet Dr. .... Stafford TX 77477 *Web:* ncs-subsea.com	281-491-3123		41
NCSBN (National Council of State Boards of Nursing) 111 E Wacker Dr Ste 2900 .... Chicago IL 60601 *TF:* 866-293-9600 ■ *Web:* www.ncsbn.org	312-525-3600	279-1032	49-8
NCSC (National Ctr for State Courts) 300 Newport Ave. .... Williamsburg VA 23185 *TF:* 800-616-6164 ■ *Web:* www.ncsc.org	757-259-1525	220-0449	49-7
NCSD (Nye County School District Inc) PO Box 113 .... Tonopah NV 89049 *TF:* 800-796-6273 ■ *Web:* nyecounty.schoolinsites.com	775-482-6250	402-8573	685
NCSD (Niskayuna Central School District) 1239 Van Antwerp Rd .... Schenectady NY 12309 *TF:* 866-893-6337 ■ *Web:* www.niskyschools.org	518-377-4666	377-4074	685
NCSEA (National Child Support Enforcement Assn) 1760 Old Meadow Rd Ste 500 .... McLean VA 22102 *Web:* www.ncsea.org	703-506-2880	506-3266	48-6

Phone | Fax | Class

NCSEAA (North Carolina State Education Assistance Authority)
PO Box 14103 .... Research Triangle Park NC 27709 919-549-8614 549-8481 725
TF: 800-700-1775 ■ *Web:* www.ncseaa.edu

NCSG Crane & Heavy Haul Services Ltd
11466 Winterburn Rd .... Edmonton AB T5S2Y3 780-455-1075 23
Web: www.ncsg.com

NCSHA (National Council of State Housing Agencies)
444 N Capitol St NW Ste 438 .... Washington DC 20001 202-624-7710 624-5899 49-7
TF: 800-475-2098 ■ *Web:* www.ncsha.org

NCSM (National Council of Supervisors of Mathematics)
6000 E Evans Ave Ste 3-205 .... Denver CO 80222 303-758-9611 758-9616 49-5
Web: www.mathedleadership.org

NCSPA (National Corrugated Steel Pipe Assn)
14070 Proton Rd Ste 100 .... Dallas TX 75244 972-850-1907 490-4219 49-3
Web: www.ncspa.org

NCSS (National Council for the Social Studies)
8555 16th St Ste 500 .... Silver Spring MD 20910 301-588-1800 588-2049 49-5
TF Orders: 800-683-0812 ■ *Web:* socialstudies.org

NCTA (National Council for the Traditional Arts)
8757 Georgia Ave Ste 450 .... Silver Spring MD 20910 301-565-0654 565-0472 48-4
Web: ncta-usa.org

NCTA (National Cable & Telecommunications Assn)
25 Massachusetts Ave NW Ste 100 .... Washington DC 20001 202-222-2300 49-14
Web: www.ncta.com

NCTA (National Christmas Tree Assn)
16020 Swingley Ridge Rd Ste 300 .... Chesterfield MO 63017 636-449-5070 449-5051 48-2
Web: www.realchristmastrees.org

NCTC (National Cable Television Co-op Inc)
11200 Corporate Ave .... Lenexa KS 66219 913-599-5900 222-2311* 49-14
**Fax Area Code:* 202 ■ *Web:* www.ncta.com

NCTD (North County Transit District)
810 Mission Rd .... Oceanside CA 92054 760-966-6500 967-2001 468
TF: 800-827-0829 ■ *Web:* www.gonctd.com

NCTE (National Council of Teachers of English)
1111 W Kenyon Rd .... Urbana IL 61801 217-328-3870 328-0977 49-5
TF: 877-369-6283 ■ *Web:* www.ncte.org

NCTM (National Council of Teachers of Mathematics)
1906 Assn Dr .... Reston VA 20191 703-620-9840 476-2970 49-5
TF Orders: 800-235-7566 ■ *Web:* www.nctm.org

NCTM News Bulletin 1906 Assn Dr .... Reston VA 20191 703-620-9840 476-2970 457-8
TF: 800-235-7566 ■ *Web:* www.nctm.org/news

NCTO (National Council of Textile Organizations)
910 17th St NW .... Washington DC 20006 202-822-8028 822-8029 49-13
TF: 800-238-7192 ■ *Web:* www.ncto.org

NCTRC (National Council for Therapeutic Recreation Certification Inc)
7 Elmwood Dr. .... New City NY 10956 845-639-1439 639-1471 49-15
TF: 800-392-0751 ■ *Web:* www.nctrc.org

NCVB (Nashville Convention & Visitors Bureau)
150 Fourth Ave N Ste G250 .... Nashville TN 37219 615-259-4730 259-4126 206
TF: 800-657-6910 ■ *Web:* www.visitmusiccity.com

NCVMA (North Carolina Veterinary Medical Assn)
1611 Jones Franklin Rd Ste 108 .... Raleigh NC 27606 919-851-5850 851-5859 795
TF: 800-446-2862 ■ *Web:* www.ciclt.net

NCWO (National Council of Women of the US Inc)
777 UN Plaza .... New York NY 10017 212-697-1278 48-7
Web: ncwus.org

NCX Inc
70 E Beaver Creek Rd Unit 2 .... Richmond Hill ON L4B3B2 905-370-7060 179
Web: www.ncxinc.ca

ND Graphic Product Ltd
55 Interchange Way Unit 1 .... Concord ON L4K5W3 416-663-6416 627
TF: 800-811-0194 ■ *Web:* www.ndgraphics.com

Nd Industries Inc 1000 N Crooks Rd .... Clawson MI 48017 248-288-0000 288-0022 481
TF: 800-471-5000 ■ *Web:* www.ndindustries.com

NDA (AMOA-National Dart Assn)
10070 W 190th Pl Ste 200 .... Mokena IL 60448 800-808-9884 226-1310* 48-22
**Fax Area Code:* 708 ■ *TF:* 800-808-9884 ■ *Web:* www.ndadarts.com

NDA Partners LLC 40 Commerce Ln Ste D .... Rochelle VA 22738 540-738-2550 738-2494 463
Web: www.ndapartners.com

NDAA (NDAA) 1400 Crystal D Ste 330 .... Alexandria VA 22314 703-549-9222 836-3195 49-7
Web: www.ndaa.org

NDC (National Dairy Council)
10255 W Higgins Rd Ste 900 .... Rosemont IL 60018 847-627-3790 48-2
Web: www.nationaldairycouncil.org

NDC Infrared Engineering
5314 N Irwindale Ave .... Irwindale CA 91706 626-960-3300 939-3870 201
TF: 800-866-4733 ■ *Web:* www.ndc.com

NDC LLC 6312 S 27th St Ste 202 .... Oak Creek WI 53154 414-761-2040 761-3576 655
Web: www.ndcllc.com

ndd Medical Technologies Inc
300 Brickton Sq Ste 604 .... Andover MA 01810 978-470-0923 475
Web: www.nddmed.com

Ndex Systems Inc
500 Saint-Jacques St Ste 400 .... Montreal QC H2Y1S1 514-288-0908 177
TF: 800-841-5312 ■ *Web:* www.ndexsystems.com

NDH Medical Inc
11001 Roosevelt Blvd N Ste 800 .... St. Petersburg FL 33716 727-570-2293 476
Web: www.ndhmedical.com

NDI Capital Inc
736 Granville St Ste 210 .... Vancouver BC V6Z1G3 604-620-8424 528
Web: ndicapital.com

NDIA (National Defense Industrial Assn)
2111 Wilson Blvd Ste 400 .... Arlington VA 22201 703-522-1820 522-1885 48-19
Web: www.ndia.org

N-Dimension Solutions Inc
9030 Leslie St Unit 300 .... Richmond Hill ON L4B1G2 905-707-8884 225
TF: 866-837-8884 ■ *Web:* www.n-dimension.com

NDMA (North Dakota Medical Assn)
1622 I- Ave. .... Bismarck ND 58503 701-223-9475 223-9476 474
Web: www.ndmed.org

NDPhA (North Dakota Pharmacists Assn)
1641 Capitol Way .... Bismarck ND 58501 701-258-4968 258-9312 585
Web: www.nodakpharmacy.net

NDRI (Naval Institute for Dental & Biomedical Research)
310-A B St Bldg 1-H. .... Great Lakes IL 60088 847-688-1900 668
Web: www.dentalmercury.com

NDRI (National Disease Research Interchange)
1628 John F Kennedy Blvd
8 Penn Ctr 8th Fl .... Philadelphia PA 19103 215-557-7361 269
TF: 800-222-6374 ■ *Web:* www.ndriresource.org

NDS Americas 3500 Highland Ave. .... Costa Mesa CA 92626 714-434-2100 735
TF: 866-398-8749 ■ *Web:* www.cisco.com

NDS Surgical Imaging LLC
5750 Hellyer Ave. .... San Jose CA 95138 408-776-0085 743
TF: 800-342-3757 ■ *Web:* www.ndssi.com

NDS USA LLC 406 E Silver Springs Blvd .... Ocala FL 34470 352-840-9593 809
Web: www.ndsusallc.com

NDSC (National Down Syndrome Congress)
1370 Ctr Dr Ste 102 .... Atlanta GA 30338 770-604-9500 604-9898 48-17
TF: 800-232-6372 ■ *Web:* www.ndsccenter.org

NDSL (North Dakota State Library)
604 E Blvd Ave .... Bismarck ND 58505 701-328-4622 328-2040 434-5
TF: 800-472-2104 ■ *Web:* www.library.nd.gov

NDSS (National Down Syndrome Society)
666 Broadway 8th Fl. .... New York NY 10012 800-221-4602 979-2873* 48-17
**Fax Area Code:* 212 ■ *TF:* 800-221-4602 ■ *Web:* www.ndss.org

NDVH (National Domestic Violence Hotline)
PO Box 161810 .... Austin TX 78716 512-794-1133 48-6
TF: 800-799-7233 ■ *Web:* www.thehotline.org

NE Finch Co 1925 S Darst St .... Peoria IL 61607 309-671-1433 671-1449 780
TF: 800-701-1444 ■ *Web:* nefinch.com

NEA (National Education Assn)
1201 16th St NW .... Washington DC 20036 202-833-4000 822-7974 49-5
TF: 888-552-0624 ■ *Web:* www.nea.org

NEA (National Endowment for the Arts)
1100 Pennsylvania Ave NW .... Washington DC 20506 202-682-5400 340-20
TF: 800-634-1121 ■ *Web:* www.arts.gov

Nea Optical LLC 1426 E Washington .... Jonesboro AR 72401 870-935-2179 543
Web: neaoptical.com

Neace Lukens Inc 2305 River Rd .... Louisville KY 40206 502-894-2100 894-8602 194
TF: 888-499-8092 ■ *Web:* www.neacelukens.com

Neal & Harwell PLC
1201 Demonbreun St Ste 1000 .... Nashville TN 37203 615-244-1713 428
Web: www.nealharwell.com

Neal Advertising LLC
153 Andover St Ste 201 .... Danvers MA 01923 978-774-4444 7
Web: nealadv.com

Neal Analytics LLC
3240 Eastlake Ave E Ste 104 .... Seattle WA 98102 206-286-9200 466
TF: 800-208-2614 ■ *Web:* www.nealanalytics.com

Neal Electri Corp 13250 Kirkham Way .... Poway CA 92064 858-513-2525 513-9488 787
Web: www.nealelectric.com

Neal Mast & Son Inc Greenhouses
1780 4 Mile Rd NW .... Grand Rapids MI 49544 616-784-3323 192
Web: www.nealmastgreenhouses.com

Neal Richard E (Rep D - MA)
341 Cannon HOB .... Washington DC 20515 202-225-5601 225-8112 342-2
Web: neal.house.gov

Neal Systems Inc 122 Terry Dr .... Newtown PA 18940 215-968-7577 138
TF: 800-247-1727 ■ *Web:* www.nealsystems.com

Neal W Farinholt 9939 Hibert St. .... San Diego CA 92131 858-578-6605 390
Web: nealfarinholt.com

Neany Inc 44010 Commerce Ave Ste A .... Hollywood MD 20636 301-373-8700 256
Web: www.neanyinc.com

Neapco Inc 6735 Haggerty Rd .... Belleville MI 48111 734-447-1380 423-1003 60
TF: 800-821-2374 ■ *Web:* www.neapco.com

Near East Foundation
110 Fayette St Ste 710 .... Syracuse NY 13202 315-428-8670 48-5
Web: www.neareast.org

Near North Business Machines
86 W Rd .... Huntsville ON P1H1M1 705-787-0517 321
Web: nearnorthbusiness.com

Near Space Systems Inc
2375 Telstar Dr Ste 115 .... Colorado Springs CO 80920 719-685-8108 21
Web: www.globalnearspace.com

Near-Cal Corp 512 Chaney St .... Lake Elsinore CA 92530 951-245-5400 186
TF: 800-969-3578 ■ *Web:* www.nearcal.com

Nearly Me Technoligies Po Box 21475. .... Waco TX 76702 254-662-1752 477
TF: 800-887-3370 ■ *Web:* www.tgtransforms.com

Nearman Maynard Vallez CPAs & Consultants pa
205 Brandywine Blvd Ste 200 .... Fayetteville GA 30214 770-461-5706 2
TF: 800-288-0293 ■ *Web:* nearman.com

NearSpace
5755 Long Prairie Rd Ste 240 .... Tillamook OR 97141 707-636-5900 177
Web: www.nearspace.com

NEASC (New England Assn of Schools & Colleges)
209 Burlington Rd .... Bedford MA 01730 781-271-0022 541-5400 48-1
Web: www.neasc.org

Nease Lagana Eden & Culley Inc
2100 Riveredge Pkwy .... Atlanta GA 30328 770-956-1800 390
Web: nlec.com

Neat Oh International
790 W Frontage Rd Ste 303 .... Northfield IL 60093 847-441-4290 41
Web: www.neat-oh.com

Neathawk Dubuque & Packett
1 E Cary St .... Richmond VA 23219 804-783-8140 4
Web: ndp.agency

NEBB (National Environmental Balancing Bureau)
8575 Grovemont Cir. .... Gaithersburg MD 20877 301-977-3698 977-9589 49-19
Web: www.nebb.org

NEBCO Inc 1815 Y St PO Box 80268 .... Lincoln NE 68501 402-434-1212 390
Web: www.nebraskaash.com

Nebo Agency Inc
197 East 100 North Ste 100 .... Payson UT 84651 801-465-2535 652

Accountability & Disclosure Commission
State Capitol 11th Fl .... Lincoln NE 68509 402-471-2522 265
Web: nadc.nebraska.gov

Nebraska
Aging Div 301 Centennial Mall S. .... Lincoln NE 68509 402-471-3121 339-28
Web: dhhs.ne.gov
Agriculture Dept
301 Centennial Mall S PO Box 94947 .... Lincoln NE 68509 402-471-2341 471-6876 339-28
Web: www.nda.nebraska.gov
Arts Council 1004 Farnam St. .... Omaha NE 68131 402-595-2122 339-28
TF: 800-341-4067 ■ *Web:* www.nebraskaartscouncil.org

				Phone	Fax	Class
Attorney General 2115 State Capitol TF: 800-727-6432 ■ Web: www.ago.ne.gov	Lincoln	NE	68509	402-471-2683	471-3297	339-28
Banking & Finance Dept (NDBF) 1526 K St Ste 300 Web: www.ndbf.ne.gov	Lincoln	NE	68508	402-471-2171		339-28
Child Support Enforcement Div PO Box 94728 TF: 877-631-9973 ■ Web: dhhs.ne.gov	Lincoln	NE	68509	402-471-3121		339-28
Coordinating Commission for Postsecondary 140 N Eigth St Ste 300 Web: www.ccpe.state.ne.us	Lincoln	NE	68508	402-471-2847	471-2886	725
Correctional Services Dept PO Box 94661 Web: www.corrections.state.ne.us	Lincoln	NE	68509	402-471-2654		339-28
Crime Victim Reparations Programs 301 Centennial Mall S PO Box 94946 Web: www.ncc.state.ne.us	Lincoln	NE	68509	402-471-2194	471-2837	339-28
Economic Development Dept 301 Centennial Mall S TF: 800-426-6505 ■ Web: opportunity.nebraska.gov	Lincoln	NE	68509	402-471-3111	471-3778	339-28
Education Dept 301 Centennial Mall S PO Box 94987 Web: www.education.ne.gov	Lincoln	NE	68509	402-471-2295	471-0117	339-28
Emergency Management Agency 2433 NW 24th St TF: 877-297-2368 ■ Web: www.nema.ne.gov	Lincoln	NE	68524	402-471-7421	471-7433	339-28
Environmental Quality Dept 1200 N St Ste 400 TF: 877-253-2603 ■ Web: www.deq.state.ne.us	Lincoln	NE	68508	402-471-2186	471-2909	339-28
Game & Parks Commission PO Box 30370 Web: outdoornebraska.ne.gov	Lincoln	NE	68503	402-471-0641	471-5528	339-28
Governor PO Box 94848 Web: www.governor.nebraska.gov	Lincoln	NE	68509	402-471-2244	471-6031	339-28
Health & Human Services Dept 301 Centennial Mall S TF: 800-430-3244 ■ Web: dhhs.ne.gov	Lincoln	NE	68508	402-471-3121		339-28
Historical Society 1500 R St TF: 800-833-6747 ■ Web: www.nebraskahistory.org	Lincoln	NE	68501	402-471-3270	471-3100	339-28
Insurance Dept 941 O St Ste 400 TF: 877-564-7323 ■ Web: www.doi.nebraska.gov	Lincoln	NE	68508	402-471-2201		339-28
Investment Finance Authority 1230 'O' St Ste 200 TF: 800-204-6432 ■ Web: www.nifa.org	Lincoln	NE	68508	402-434-3900	434-3921	339-28
Lieutenant Governor PO Box 94863 Web: governor.nebraska.gov	Lincoln	NE	68508	402-471-2256	471-6031	339-28
Motor Vehicles Dept 301 Centennial Mall S Web: www.dmv.nebraska.gov	Lincoln	NE	68509	402-471-3918	471-8694	339-28
Natural Resources Dept 301 Centennial Mall S PO Box 94944 Web: nebraska.gov	Lincoln	NE	68508	402-471-2363	471-6575	339-28
Parks Div 2200 N 33rd St Web: outdoornebraska.ne.gov	Lincoln	NE	68503	402-471-0641		339-28
Parole Board PO Box 94754 Web: www.parole.state.ne.us	Lincoln	NE	68509	402-471-2156		339-28
Power Review Board 301 Centennial Mall S Web: powerreviewboard.nebraska.gov	Lincoln	NE	68508	402-471-2301	471-3715	339-28
Public Accountancy Board 1526 K St Ste 410 TF: 800-564-6111 ■ Web: www.nbpa.ne.gov	Lincoln	NE	68508	402-471-3595	471-4484	339-28
Public Service Commission 1200 N St Ste 300 TF: 800-526-0017 ■ Web: psc.nebraska.gov	Lincoln	NE	68508	402-471-3101	471-0254	339-28
Real Estate Commission 1200 N St Ste 402 PO Box 94667 Web: www.nrec.ne.gov	Lincoln	NE	68509	402-471-2004	471-4492	339-28
Revenue Dept 301 Centennial Mall S PO Box 94818 TF: 800-742-7474 ■ Web: revenue.nebraska.gov	Lincoln	NE	68509	402-471-5729	471-5608	339-28
Secretary of State 1445 K St Ste 2300 Web: sos.ne.gov	Lincoln	NE	68508	402-471-2554	471-3237	339-28
Securities Bureau 1526 K St Ste 300 PO Box 95006 Web: www.ndbf.ne.gov	Lincoln	NE	68508	402-471-3445		339-28
State Court Administrator 1213 State Capitol 1445 K St PO Box 98910 Web: supremecourt.nebraska.gov	Lincoln	NE	68509	402-471-3730	471-2197	339-28
State Electrical Division 521 S 14th St Ste 400 PO Box 95066 Web: www.electrical.nebraska.gov	Lincoln	NE	68508	402-471-3550	471-4297	339-28
State Patrol 1600 Hwy 2 Web: statepatrol.nebraska.gov	Lincoln	NE	68509	402-471-4545		339-28
State Racing Commission 5903 Walker Ave Web: nebraskaracingcommission.com	Lincoln	NE	68507	402-471-4155		712
Supreme Court 1445 K St State Capitol Bldg Web: court.nol.org	Lincoln	NE	68509	402-471-0448	471-3100	339-28
Teacher Certification Office PO Box 94987 Web: www.teaching-certification.com	Lincoln	NE	68509	402-471-2295		339-28
Travel & Tourism Div 301 Centennial Mall S TF: 877-632-7275 ■ Web: www.visitnebraska.com	Lincoln	NE	68509	402-471-3796	471-3026	339-28
Treasurer PO Box 94788 State Capitol Rm 2005 Web: www.treasurer.org/up	Lincoln	NE	68509	402-471-2455	471-4390	339-28
Veterans' Affairs Dept 301 Centennial Mall S Fl 1 PO Box 95083 Web: www.vets.state.ne.us	Lincoln	NE	68509	402-471-2458	471-2491	339-28
Vital Statistics Div 1033 "O" St Ste 130 Web: dhhs.ne.gov	Lincoln	NE	68509	402-471-2871	742-1147	339-28
Vocational Rehabilitation Services Div 3901 N 27th St Ste 6 TF: 800-472-3382	Lincoln	NE	68521	402-471-3231		339-28
Weights & Measures Div 301 Centennial Mall S Web: www.nda.nebraska.gov	Lincoln	NE	68508	402-471-2341		339-28
Workforce Development - Dept of Labor 1111 O St Ste 205 Web: dol.nebraska.gov	Lincoln	NE	68508	402-441-1660	441-6038	259
Nebraska Bankers Association Inc 233 S 13th St Ste 700 TF: 800-593-3881 ■ Web: www.nebankers.org	Lincoln	NE	68508	402-474-1555		138
Nebraska Beef Council 1319 Central Ave TF: 800-421-5326 ■ Web: www.nebeef.org	Kearney	NE	68848	308-236-7551		138
Nebraska Book Co 4700 S 19th St TF: 800-869-0366 ■ Web: www.nebook.com	Lincoln	NE	68512	402-421-7300		96
Nebraska Chamber of Commerce & Industry 1320 Lincoln Mall # 201A TF: 800-221-8185 ■ Web: www.nechamber.net	Lincoln	NE	68508	402-474-4422	474-5681	140
Nebraska Christian College Foundation 12550 S 114th St Web: nechristian.edu	Papillion	NE	68046	402-935-9400		303
Nebraska City Middle School 1700 14th Ave Web: www.nebcitypps.org	Nebraska City	NE	68410	402-873-6033		685
Nebraska College of Technical Agriculture 404 E 7th TF: 800-328-7847 ■ Web: www.ncta.unl.edu	Curtis	NE	69025	308-367-4124	367-5203	800
Nebraska Community Blood Bank 100 N 84th St TF: 877-486-9414 ■ Web: www.ncbb.org	Lincoln	NE	68505	402-486-9414	486-9429	89
Nebraska Correctional Ctr for Women 1107 Recharge Rd TF: 877-634-8463 ■ Web: www.corrections.nebraska.gov	York	NE	68467	402-362-3317	362-3892	213
Nebraska Ctr for Materials & Nanoscience 855 N 16th St N201 NANO Web: www.unl.edu/ncmn	Lincoln	NE	68588	402-472-7886	472-2879	668
Nebraska Dental Assn 7160 S 29th St Ste 1 TF: 888-789-2614 ■ Web: www.nedental.org	Lincoln	NE	68516	402-476-1704	476-2641	227
Nebraska Educational Telecommunications (NET) 1800 N 33rd St TF: 800-868-1868 ■ Web: netdb.unl.edu	Lincoln	NE	68503	800-868-1868		632
Nebraska Farm Bureau Federation 5225 S 16th St TF: 800-742-4016 ■ Web: www.nefb.org	Lincoln	NE	68512	402-421-4400		138
Nebraska Furniture Mart Inc 700 S 72nd St TF: 800-336-9136 ■ Web: www.nfm.com	Omaha	NE	68114	402-397-6100		321
Nebraska House 983285 Nebraska Medical Ctr TF: 800-401-4444 ■ Web: www.nebraskamed.com/transplant	Omaha	NE	68198	402-559-5000	559-3434	372
Nebraska Humane Society Foundation 8929 Ft St TF: 800-545-6244 ■ Web: www.nehumanesociety.org	Omaha	NE	68134	402-444-7800		305
Nebraska Indian Community College PO Box 428 *Fax: Admissions ■ TF: 844-440-6422 ■ Web: www.thenicc.edu	Macy	NE	68039	402-837-5078	837-4183*	165
Nebraska Industries Corp 447 E Walnut St Web: www.nebraskaindustries.com	Wauseon	OH	43567	419-335-6010		489
Nebraska Iowa Supply Company Inc 1160 Lincoln St PO Box 368 Web: www.neiasupply.com	Blair	NJ	68008	402-426-2171		316
Nebraska Jewish Historical Museum 333 S 132nd St	Omaha	NE	68154	402-334-6441		520
Nebraska Lablinc LLC 5440 S St Ste 100 TF: 866-886-5462	Lincoln	NE	68506	402-465-1900	465-1972	418
Nebraska Library Commission 1200 N St Ste 120 TF: 800-307-2665 ■ Web: nlc.nebraska.gov	Lincoln	NE	68508	402-471-2045	471-2083	434-5
Nebraska Lottery 1800 "O" St PO Box 98901 TF: 800-587-5200 ■ Web: www.nelottery.com	Lincoln	NE	68509	402-471-6100	471-6108	452
Nebraska Machinery Co Inc 3501 S Jeffers St TF: 800-494-9560 ■ Web: www.nmc-corp.com	North Platte	NE	69101	308-532-3100		385
Nebraska Medical Assn 233 S 13th St Ste 1200 Web: www.nebmed.org	Lincoln	NE	68508	402-474-4472	474-2198	474
Nebraska Medical Ctr, The 4350 Dewey Ave TF: 800-922-0000 ■ Web: www.nebraskamed.com	Omaha	NE	68105	402-552-2000	552-3267	374-3
Nebraska Methodist Hospital 8303 Dodge St Web: www.bestcare.org	Omaha	NE	68114	402-354-4000		374-3
Nebraska Nurses Assn (NNA) PO Box 3107 TF: 800-582-3014 ■ Web: www.nebraskanurses.org	Kearney	NE	68848	888-885-7025		533
Nebraska Pharmacists Assn 6221 S 58th St Ste A Web: www.npharm.org	Lincoln	NE	68516	402-420-1500	420-1406	585
Nebraska Plastics Inc PO Box 45 TF: 800-445-2887 ■ Web: www.countryestate.com	Cozad	NE	69130	308-784-2500		596
Nebraska Printing Company Inc 4411 W Tampa Bay Blvd	Tampa	FL	33614	813-873-7117		627
Nebraska Public Power District 1414 15th St PO Box 499 TF: 877-275-6773 ■ Web: www.nppd.com	Columbus	NE	68602	402-564-8561		245
Nebraska Realtors Assn 800 S 13th St Ste 200 TF: 800-777-5231 ■ Web: www.nebraskarealtors.com	Lincoln	NE	68508	402-323-6500	323-6501	656
Nebraska Repertory Theatre PO Box 880201 TF: 800-432-3231 ■ Web: www.unl.edu	Lincoln	NE	68588	402-472-2072	472-9055	573-4
Nebraska Republican Party 1610 N St Web: nadc.nebraska.gov	Lincoln	NE	68508	402-475-2122		616-2
Nebraska State Bar Assn 635 S 14th St Ste 200 TF: 800-927-0117 ■ Web: www.nebar.com	Lincoln	NE	68501	402-475-7091	475-7098	72

	City	State	Zip	Phone	Fax	Class
Nebraska State College System 1115 K St Ste 102 *Web:* www.nscs.edu	Lincoln	NE	68508	402-471-2505	471-2669	786
Nebraska State Penitentiary 4201 S 14th St *TF:* 877-634-8463 ■ *Web:* www.corrections.nebraska.gov	Lincoln	NE	68502	402-471-3161		213
Nebraska Statewide Arboretum UNL Keim Hall 102 PO Box 830964 *Web:* plantnebraska.org	Lincoln	NE	68583	402-472-2971	472-8095	97
Nebraska Student Loan Program Inc 1300 O St *Web:* nslp.org	Lincoln	NE	68508	402-475-8686		242
Nebraska Synod Evangelical Lutheran Church in America 4980 S 118th St Ste D *Web:* nebraskasynod.org	Omaha	NE	68137	402-896-5311		48-20
Nebraska Veterinary Medical Assn 2727 W Second St Ste 332 *Web:* www.nvma.org	Hastings	NE	68901	402-463-4704		795
Nebraska Wesleyan University 5000 St Paul Ave *TF:* 800-541-3818 ■ *Web:* www.nebrwesleyan.edu	Lincoln	NE	68504	800-541-3818		166
Nebula Consulting Inc 207 Warwick Way *Web:* www.nebulaconsulting.com	North Wales	PA	19454	215-353-3141		180
NEC (Nueces Electric Co-op) 709 E Main St PO Box 260970 *TF:* 800-632-9288 ■ *Web:* www.nueceselectric.org	Robstown	TX	78380	361-387-2581		245
NEC America Inc 6555 N State Hwy 161 *TF Cust Svc:* 866-632-3226 ■ *Web:* www.necam.com	Irving	TX	75039	214-262-2000		735
NEC Corp of America 10850 Gold Ctr Dr Ste 200 *TF:* 800-632-4636 ■ *Web:* www.necam.com	Rancho Cordova	CA	95670	916-463-7000		173-4
NEC Display Solutions of America Inc 500 Pk Blvd Ste 1100 **Fax:* Sales ■ *TF Cust Svc:* 800-632-4662 ■ *Web:* www.necdisplay.com	Itasca	IL	60143	630-467-3000	467-3010*	173-4
NEC Laboratories America Inc 4 Independence Way *Web:* www.nec-labs.com	Princeton	NJ	08540	609-520-1555		668
NECA (National Electrical Contractors Assn) 3 Bethesda Metro Ctr Ste 1100 *TF:* 800-214-0585 ■ *Web:* www.necanet.org	Bethesda	MD	20814	301-657-3110	215-4500	49-3
Necando Solutions Inc 620 St-Jacques Ste 500 *Web:* necando.com	Montreal	QC	H3C1C7	514-360-4000		196
Necco 178 Private Dr **Fax Area Code:* 740 ■ *TF:* 866-996-3226 ■ *Web:* www.necco.org	South Point	OH	45680	513-771-9600	894-1132*	766
Neci 334 Hecla St *TF:* 888-648-7283 ■ *Web:* www.nitrate.com	Lake Linden	MI	49945	906-296-1000		231
NECN (New England Cable News) 160 Wells Ave *Web:* www.necn.com	Newton	MA	02459	617-630-5000	630-5055	740
Nectar Restaurant 1000 Delta Ave *Web:* www.tastenectar.com	Cincinnati	OH	45208	513-929-0525		671
NED (National Endowment for Democracy) 1025 F St NW Ste 800 *Web:* www.ned.org	Washington	DC	20004	202-378-9700		48-7
NED Corp 31 Town Forest Rd **Fax Area Code:* 508 ■ *TF:* 800-343-6086 ■ *Web:* www.nedkut.com	Oxford	MA	01540	800-343-6086	799-2796*	493
NEDA (National Electronic Distributors Assn) 1111 Alderman Dr Ste 400 *Web:* www.eciaonline.org	Alpharetta	GA	30005	678-393-9990	393-9998	49-18
Nedco Electronics 594 American Way **Fax Area Code:* 800 ■ *TF:* 800-605-2323 ■ *Web:* www.nedcoelectronics.com	Payson	UT	84651	801-465-1790	605-3836*	246
Nedco Supply Inc 4200 W Spring Mtn Rd *TF:* 800-561-3357 ■ *Web:* www.nedco.com	Las Vegas	NV	89102	702-367-0400	362-8365	246
NEDMA 396 Washington St Ste 387 *TF:* 800-831-3134 ■ *Web:* www.nedma.com	Wellesley Hills	MA	02481	781-237-1366		138
NEEBCO Limited Partnership 15 Chenell Dr *Web:* www.neebco.com	Concord	NH	03301	603-228-1133		393
Needham & Co Inc 445 Pk Ave *TF:* 800-903-3268 ■ *Web:* www.needhamco.com	New York	NY	10022	212-371-8300	751-1450	690
Needham Capital Partners 445 Pk Ave *TF:* 800-625-7071 ■ *Web:* www.needhamcapital.com	New York	NY	10022	212-371-8300		792
Needham Public Library 1139 Highland Ave *Web:* www.town.needham.ma.us	Needham	MA	02494	781-455-7559		434-3
NeedleTech Products Inc 452 John L Dietsch Blvd *Web:* www.needletech.com	North Attleboro	MA	02763	508-431-4000		791
Neel-Schaffer Inc 125 S Congress St Ste 1100 *Web:* www.neel-schaffer.com	Jackson	MS	39201	601-948-3178	948-3071	261
Neeltran Inc 71 Pickett District Rd *Web:* www.neeltran.com	New Milford	CT	06776	860-350-5964	350-5024	767
Neenah Foundry Co 2121 Brooks Ave *TF:* 800-558-5075 ■ *Web:* www.nfco.com	Neenah	WI	54956	920-725-7000	729-3661	307
Neenah Paper Inc 3460 Preston Ridge Rd Ste 600 *NYSE: NP* ■ *TF:* 800-561-3357 ■ *Web:* www.neenah.com	Alpharetta	GA	30005	678-566-6500		552-2
Neenah Public Library 240 E Wisconsin Ave PO Box 569 *Web:* www.neenahlibrary.org	Neenah	WI	54957	920-886-6315		434-3
Neenan Co 3325 S Timberline Rd Ste 100 *Web:* neenan.com	Fort Collins	CO	80525	970-493-8747	493-5869	186
Neenan Company LLP, The 2607 Midpoint Dr *Web:* www.neenan.com	Fort Collins	CO	80525	970-493-8747		360-3
Neese Personnel 2709 W I 44 Service Rd *Web:* tneesepersonnel.com	Oklahoma City	OK	73112	405-942-8551		260
NEFE (National Endowment for Financial Education) 1331 17th St Ste 1200 *Web:* www.nefe.org	Denver	CO	80202	303-741-6333		48-10
Neff Engineering Co 7114 Innovation Blvd	Fort Wayne	IN	46818	260-489-6007		261
Neff-Perkins Co 16080 Industrial Pkwy *Web:* www.neffp.com	Middlefield	OH	44062	440-632-1658		677
Neffs Bancorp Inc 5629 Rt 873 PO Box 10 *OTC: NEFB* ■ *Web:* www.neffsnatl.com	Neffs	PA	18065	610-767-3875	767-1890	70
Negative Population Growth (NPG) 2861 Duke St Ste 36 *Web:* www.npg.org	Alexandria	VA	22314	703-370-9510	370-9514	48-13
Negro Leagues Baseball Museum 1616 E 18th St *Web:* www.nlbm.com	Kansas City	MO	64108	816-221-1920	221-8424	522
NEH (National Endowment for the Humanities) 400 Seventh St SW *TF:* 800-634-1121 ■ *Web:* www.neh.gov	Washington	DC	20506	202-606-8400	606-8282	340-20
NEHA (National Environmental Health Assn) 720 S Colorado Blvd Ste 1000-N *TF:* 866-956-2258 ■ *Web:* www.neha.org	Denver	CO	80246	303-756-9090	691-9490	49-7
Nehalem Bay State Park 9500 Sandpiper Ln PO Box 366 *Web:* www.oregonstateparks.org	Nehalem	OR	97131	503-368-5154		565
Nehring Electric Works Inc 1005 E Locust St *TF:* 800-435-4481 ■ *Web:* www.nehringwire.com	DeKalb	IL	60115	815-756-2741	756-7048	814
NEI (Nuclear Energy Institute) 1776 'I' St NW Ste 400 *Web:* www.nei.org	Washington	DC	20006	202-739-8000	785-4019	48-12
NEI (Nesbitt Engineering Inc) 227 N Upper St	Lexington	KY	40507	859-233-3111	259-2717	261
NEI Global Relocation Inc 2707 N 118th St *TF:* 800-533-7353 ■ *Web:* www.neirelo.com	Omaha	NE	68164	402-397-8486		393
NEI Treatment Systems LLC 3530 Wilshire Blvd Ste 1130 *Web:* www.nei-marine.com	Los Angeles	CA	90010	213-383-5855		475
Nei Turner Media Group 91 W Geneva St *TF:* 800-445-9221 ■ *Web:* www.ntmediagroup.com	Williams Bay	WI	53191	262-245-1000		196
Neibart Group 20 Jay St Ste 820 *Web:* www.neibartgroup.com	Brooklyn	NY	11201	718-875-2300		636
Neider & Boucher S C 401 Charmany Dr *Web:* neiderboucher.com	Madison	WI	53705	608-661-4500		445
Neidiger Tucker Bruner Inc 9540 S Maroon Cir Ste 250 *Web:* www.ntbinc.com	Englewood	CO	80112	303-825-1825		690
Neighbor To Family Inc 220 S Ridgewood Ave Ste 260 *Web:* www.neighbortofamily.org	Daytona Beach	FL	32114	386-523-1440		48-15
Neighborcare Health 2101 E Yesler Way *Web:* www.neighborcare.org	Seattle	WA	98122	206-461-7801		237
Neighborhood National Bank 3511 National Ave *Web:* mynnb.com	San Diego	CA	92113	619-239-3360		70
Neighborhood Service Organization Inc 882 Oakman Blvd Ste 1200 *Web:* www.nso-mi.org	Detroit	MI	48238	313-961-4890		48-5
Neighbors Federal Credit Union PO Box 2831 *TF:* 866-819-2178 ■ *Web:* www.neighborsfcu.org	Baton Rouge	LA	70821	225-819-2178	819-8923	219
Neighbors Magazine 1324 Chippenham Dr	Baton Rouge	LA	70808	225-767-8549		457-1
Neighbors Stores Inc 1314 Old Hwy 601 S	Mount Airy	NC	27030	336-789-5561		152
NeighborWorks America 999 N Capitol St NE Ste 900 *TF:* 800-438-5547 ■ *Web:* www.neighborworks.org	Washington	DC	20002	202-760-4000	376-2600	48-10
Neil Enterprises Inc 450 E Bunker Ct *TF:* 800-621-5584 ■ *Web:* www.neilenterprises.com	Vernon Hills	IL	60061	847-549-7627		608
Neil Locke & Associates 550 E Devon Ave Ste 130 *Web:* www.neillocke.com	Itasca	IL	60143	630-285-9085		378
Neil Medical Group Inc 2545 Jetport Rd *TF:* 800-735-9111 ■ *Web:* www.neilmedical.com	Kinston	NC	28504	800-735-9111		238
Neil O. Anderson & Associates Inc 902 Industrial Way *Web:* noanderson.com	Lodi	CA	95240	209-367-3701		261
Neill Aircraft Co 1260 W 15th St *Web:* www.neillaircraft.com	Long Beach	CA	90813	562-432-7981	491-0483	22
Neill-Cochran House Museum 2310 San Gabriel St *Web:* www.nchmuseum.org	Austin	TX	78705	512-478-2335		50-3
Neilson Associates Inc 42 Blue Stone Dr *Web:* www.neilsonassociates.com	Chadds Ford	PA	19317	610-793-0883		463
Neiman Bros Company Inc 3322 W Newport Ave *Web:* www.neimanbrothers.com	Chicago	IL	60618	773-463-3000	463-3181	297-11
Neiman Funds Management LLC 6631 Main St *TF:* 877-385-2720 ■ *Web:* www.neimanfunds.com	Williamsville	NY	14221	877-385-2720		401
Neiman Marcus Group Inc 1618 Main St *Web:* neimanmarcuscareers.com	Dallas	TX	75201	214-743-7600		229
Neko Industries Inc 3017 Douglas Blvd Ste 300 *Web:* www.nekoind.com	Roseville	CA	95661	916-774-7125		196
Nektar Therapeutics 455 Mission Bay Blvd S *NASDAQ: NKTR* ■ *TF:* 800-732-0330 ■ *Web:* www.nektar.com	San Francisco	CA	94158	415-482-5300		85
NELA (National Employment Lawyers Assn) 417 Montgomery St 4th Fl *Web:* www.nela.org	San Francisco	CA	94104	415-296-7629	677-9445	49-10
NELCO Inc 3 Gill St Unit D *TF:* 800-635-2613 ■ *Web:* www.nelcoworldwide.com	Woburn	MA	01801	781-933-1940	933-4763	477
Nelda C and H J Lutcher Stark Foundation The 601 W Green PO Box 909 *TF:* 800-252-9605 ■ *Web:* www.starkfoundation.org	Orange	TX	77631	409-883-3513		303

	Phone	Fax	Class
Nell's 6804 E Green Lake Way N, Seattle WA 98115 *Web:* www.nellsrestaurant.com	206-524-4044		671
Nella's Nursing Home Inc 200 Whiteman Ave, Elkins WV 26241 *Web:* nellasofcrystalsprings.com	304-636-2033		371
Nellie Mae Education Foundation 1250 Hancock St Ste 205N, Quincy MA 02169 *TF:* 877-635-5436 ■ *Web:* www.nmefoundation.org	781-348-4200	348-4299	305
Nellie's Cafe 1226 W Hadley Ave, Las Cruces NM 88005	575-524-9982		671
Nellis Air Force Base 4430 Grissom Ave Ste 107, Nellis AFB NV 89191 *Web:* www.nellis.af.mil	702-652-2750	652-9838	497-1
Nellis Management Corp 2940 104th St, Urbandale IA 50322 *Web:* www.nellismanagement.com	515-252-1742		463
Nello Capital Inc 211 W Washington St Ste 2000, South Bend IN 46601 *TF:* 800-806-3556 ■ *Web:* www.nelloinc.com	574-288-3632		480
Nellson Nutraceutical 5801 Ayala Ave, Irwindale CA 91706 *Web:* www.nellsonllc.com	626-812-6522		123
Nelnet Inc 121 S 13th St Ste 204, Lincoln NE 68508 *NYSE: NNI* ■ *TF:* 888-486-4722 ■ *Web:* www.nelnet.com	402-458-2370		217
Nelrod Co 3109 Lubbock Ave, Fort Worth TX 76109 *TF:* 866-448-0961 ■ *Web:* www.nelrod.com	817-922-9000		196
Nelsen Steel & Wire LP 9400 W Belmont Ave, Franklin Park IL 60131 *Web:* www.nelsensteel.com	847-671-9700		492
NELSON & Associates Interior Design & Space Planning Inc The NELSON Bldg 222-230 Walnut St, Philadelphia PA 19106 *Web:* www.nelsononline.com	215-925-6562		256
Nelson & Co Inc 110 E Broadway, Oviedo FL 32765	407-365-6631		315-2
Nelson & Gilmore 1604 Aviation Blvd, Redondo Beach CA 90278 *Web:* www.nelsongilmore.com	310-376-0296		7
Nelson & Kennard 2180 Harvard St Ste 160 Ste 160, Sacramento CA 95815 *TF:* 866-920-2295 ■ *Web:* nelson-kennard.com	866-920-2295		428
Nelson & Small Inc 212 Canco Rd, Portland ME 04103 **Fax Area Code:* 207 ■ *TF:* 800-341-0780	800-341-0780	221-1125*	38
Nelson A Rockefeller Institute of Government 411 State St, Albany NY 12203 *Web:* www.rockinst.org	518-443-5522	443-5788	634
Nelson Bill (Sen D - FL) 716 Hart Bldg, Washington DC 20510 *Web:* www.billnelson.senate.gov	202-224-5274	228-2183	342-2
Nelson Co 2116 Sparrows Pt Rd, Baltimore MD 21219 *Web:* www.nelsoncompany.com	410-477-3000		551
Nelson County 113 E Steven Foster St, Bardstown KY 40004 *Web:* nelsoncountyclerk.com	502-348-1820	348-1822	338
Nelson County 210 B Ave W Ste 203, Lakota ND 58344 *TF:* 800-472-2286 ■ *Web:* nelsonco.org	701-247-2462		338
Nelson County 84 Courthouse Sq PO Box 336, Lovingston VA 22949 *TF:* 888-662-9400 ■ *Web:* www.nelsoncounty-va.gov	434-263-7000	263-7004	338
Nelson Crab Inc 3088 Kindred Ave, Tokeland WA 98590 *TF:* 800-262-0069 ■ *Web:* seatreats.stores.yahoo.net	800-202-0009		290-13
Nelson Dewey State Park PO Box 658, Cassville WI 53806 *TF:* 888-936-7463 ■ *Web:* dnr.wi.gov/topic/parks/name/nelsondewey	608-725-5374		565
Nelson Electric Supply Co Inc 926 State St, Racine WI 53404 *TF:* 800-806-3576 ■ *Web:* www.nelson-electric.com	262-635-5050	637-2465	246
Nelson Ink 330 Second St N, Middle River MN 56737 *TF:* 800-644-9311 ■ *Web:* nelsonink.com	218-222-3831		195
Nelson Jit Packaging Supplies Inc 4022 W Turney Ave Ste 3, Phoenix AZ 85019 *TF:* 800-939-3647 ■ *Web:* www.nelsonjit.com	623-939-3365		557
Nelson Levine de Luca & Hamilton LLC 518 E Township Line Rd Ste 300, Blue Bell PA 19422 *Web:* www.nldhlaw.com	215-358-5100		445
Nelson Mullins Riley & Scarborough LLP 1320 Main St 17th Fl, Columbia SC 29201 *TF:* 800-237-2000 ■ *Web:* www.nelsonmullins.com	803-799-2000	256-7500	428
Nelson Museum of the West 1714 Carey Ave, Cheyenne WY 82001 *Web:* www.nelsonmuseum.com	307-635-7670		520
Nelson Packaging Company Inc 1801 Reservoir Rd, Lima OH 45804 *TF:* 888-229-3471 ■ *Web:* www.nelsonpackagingco.com	419-229-3471		88
Nelson Public Library 34 Arnold Ln, Bloomfield KY 40004 *Web:* www.nelsoncopublib.org	502-348-3714		435
Nelson Publishing 2500 Tamiami Trl N, Nokomis FL 34275 *TF:* 800-226-6113 ■ *Web:* www.nelsonpub.com	941-966-9521	966-2590	637-9
Nelson Roberts Investment Advisors LLC 1950 University Ave Ste 202, East Palo Alto CA 94303 *TF:* 800-418-7353 ■ *Web:* www.nelsonroberts.com	650-322-4000		401
Nelson Schmidt Inc 600 E Wisconsin Ave, Milwaukee WI 53202 *Web:* nelsonschmidt.com	414-224-0210		7
Nelson Technology Assoc Inc 1051 Hill Meadow Pl, Danville CA 94526 *Web:* nelsontech.com	925-855-3610		177
Nelson Tree Service Inc 3300 Office Pk Dr Ste 205, Dayton OH 45439 *TF:* 800-522-4311 ■ *Web:* www.nelsontree.com	937-294-1313		776
Nelson Westerberg Inc 1500 Arthur Ave, Elk Grove Village IL 60007 *TF:* 800-245-2080 ■ *Web:* www.nelsonwesterberg.com	847-437-2080		519
Nelson White Systems Inc 8725-A Loch Raven Blvd, Baltimore MD 21286 *Web:* www.nelsonwhite.com	410-668-9628		45
Nelson's Plumbing & Electric Inc 25269 US Hwy 12, Tomah WI 54660 *Web:* nelsonsplumbing.net	608-372-5469		610
Nelson, Tietz & Hoye Inc 81 S Ninth St Ste 330, Minneapolis MN 55402 *Web:* www.nth-inc.com	612-344-1500		463
Nelson-Atkins Museum of Art 4525 Oak St, Kansas City MO 64111 *TF:* 800-976-8986 ■ *Web:* www.nelson-atkins.org	816-751-1278		520
Nelson-Jameson Inc 2400 E Fifth St PO Box 647, Marshfield WI 54449 *TF:* 800-826-8302 ■ *Web:* www.nelsonjameson.com	715-387-1151	387-8746	385
Neltner Billing & Consulting Services inc 6463 Taylor Mill Rd, Independence KY 41051 *TF:* 888-635-8637 ■ *Web:* neltnerbilling.com	888-635-8637		196
Nelvana Ltd Corus Quay 25 Dockside Dr, Toronto ON M5A0B5 *Web:* www.nelvana.com	416-479-7000		514
NEMA (National Emergency Management Assn) PO Box 11910, Lexington KY 40578 *Web:* www.nemaweb.org	859-244-8000	244-8239	49-7
NEMA (National Electrical Manufacturers Assn) 1300 N 17th St Ste 1752, Rosslyn VA 22209 *TF:* 800-699-9277 ■ *Web:* www.nema.org	703-841-3200	841-5900	49-13
Nemacolin Woodlands Resort & Spa 1001 Lafayette Dr, Farmington PA 15437 *TF:* 800-422-2736 ■ *Web:* www.nemacolin.com	724-329-8555		669
Nemaha County 1824 N St, Auburn NE 68305 *TF:* 800-368-8683 ■ *Web:* www.nemahacounty.ne.gov	402-274-4213	274-4389	338
Nemaha County 607 Nemaha, Seneca KS 66538 *TF:* 800-259-2829 ■ *Web:* ks-nemaha.manatron.com	785-336-2106	336-6450	338
Nemco Food Equipment Ltd 301 Meuse Argonne, Hicksville OH 43526 *TF:* 800-782-6761 ■ *Web:* www.nemcofoodequip.com	419-542-7751		296
Nemcomed Inc 801 Industrial Dr, Hicksville OH 43526 *Web:* www.nemcomed.com	419-542-7743		477
Nemetschek North America 7150 Riverwood Dr, Columbia MD 21046 *TF:* 888-646-4223 ■ *Web:* www.vectorworks.net	410-290-5114	290-8050	178-8
Nemo 100 Collins Ave, Miami Beach FL 33139 *Web:* www.mylesrestaurantgroup.com	305-532-4550		671
Nemo Tile Co 17702 Jamaica Ave, Jamaica NY 11432 *Web:* www.nemotile.com	718-291-5969		191-1
NEMRA (National Electrical Manufacturers Representatives Assn) 28 Deer St Ste 302, Portsmouth NH 03801 **Fax Area Code:* 603 ■ *TF:* 800-446-3672 ■ *Web:* www.nemra.org	914-524-8650	319-1667*	49-18
Nemschoff Inc 909 N Eigth St, Sheboygan WI 53081 **Fax Area Code:* 920 ■ *TF Cust Svc:* 800-203-8916 ■ *Web:* www.nemschoff.com	800-203-8916	459-1234*	319-3
Nennie & Associates 340 W Exchange St, Sycamore IL 60178 *Web:* www.nenniandassoc.com	815-899-9421		196
Neo Code Software Ltd 425 Carrall St Ste 540, Vancouver BC V6B6E3 *Web:* www.neocodesoftware.com	604-638-0668		396
Neo Corp 289 Silkwood Dr, Canton NC 28716 *TF:* 800-822-1247 ■ *Web:* www.neocorporation.com	800-822-1247		192
Neo Marketing LLC PO Box 8108, Canton OH 44711 **Fax Area Code:* 866 ■ *Web:* www.neomarketingonline.com	330-933-1843	861-5648*	5
Neo Products Corp 99 Record Dr, Henderson TN 38340 *Web:* www.neoproducts.com	731-989-5113		567
Neo-Asia / Neo-China (Weekend Lunch Dim Sum) 6602 Glenwood Ave, Raleigh NC 27612 *Web:* www.neo-china.com	919-703-0303	703-0353	671
Neo-Asia Restaurant 4015 University Dr, Durham NC 27707 *Web:* www.neo-china.com	919-489-2828	489-9898	671
Neocell Wireless 1500 Royal York Rd, Etobicoke ON M9P3B6 *Web:* neocell.wirelessdealer.ca	416-241-6626		736
NeoCom Solutions Inc 10064 Main St, Woodstock GA 30188 *TF:* 800-241-5236 ■ *Web:* www.neocom.biz	678-238-1818		186
Neogard Div Jones-blair Co 2728 Empire Central St, Dallas TX 75235 *TF:* 800-492-9400 ■ *Web:* www.jones-blair.com	214-353-1600		550
Neogen Corp 620 Lesher Pl, Lansing MI 48912 *NASDAQ: NEOG* ■ *TF:* 800-234-5333 ■ *Web:* www.neogen.com	517-372-9200	372-2006	231
NeoGenomics Inc 12701 Commonwealth Dr Ste 9, Fort Myers FL 33913 *Web:* www.neogenomics.com	941-923-1949		418
NeoMed Inc 100 Londonderry Ct Ste 112, Woodstock GA 30188 *Web:* www.neomedinc.com	770-516-2225		475
NeoPhotonics Corp 2911 Zanker Rd, San Jose CA 95134 *TF:* 800-732-0330 ■ *Web:* www.neophotonics.com	408-232-9200		696
Neopost Inc Canada 150 Steelcase Rd W, Markham ON L3R3J9 *TF:* 800-636-7678 ■ *Web:* www.neopost.ca	905-475-3722	475-7699	111
Neoptix Inc 1415 Frank-Carrel Ste 220, Quebec QC G1N4N7 *Web:* www.neoptix.com	418-687-2500		544
Neoris Inc 703 Waterford Way Ste 700, Miami FL 33126 *Web:* www.neoris.com	305-728-6000		177
Neos LLC 20 Church St, Hartford CT 06103 *TF:* 800-808-1902 ■ *Web:* www.neosllc.com	860-519-5601		196
Neos Therapeutics 2940 N Hwy 360 Ste 100, Grand Prairie TX 75050 *TF:* 844-375-8324 ■ *Web:* www.neostx.com	972-408-1300	408-1143	582
neoSaej Corp 77 S Bedford St Ste 450, Burlington MA 01803 *Web:* www.neosaej.com	781-272-1774		174
Neosho Area Chamber of Commerce 216 W Spring St, Neosho MO 64850 *TF:* 800-624-1054 ■ *Web:* www.neoshocc.com	417-451-1925	451-8097	139
Neosho County 100 S Main St Rm 101 PO Box 176, Erie KS 66733 *Web:* www.neoshocountyks.org	620-244-3858	244-3860	338
Neosho County Community College 800 W 14th St, Chanute KS 66720 **Fax:* Admissions ■ *Web:* www.neosho.edu	620-431-2820	431-0082*	162
Ottawa 226 S Beech St, Ottawa KS 66067 **Fax:* Admissions ■ *TF:* 888-466-2588 ■ *Web:* www.neosho.edu	785-242-2067	242-2068*	162
Neosho Trompler Inc 580 S Industrial Dr Stop 1, Hartland WI 53029 *Web:* www.neoshotrompler.com	262-367-5600		454
NeoTech Incubator 6751 Columbia Gateway Dr Ste 500, Columbia MD 21046 *Web:* www.hceda.org	410-313-6550		463
Neotelis Inc 4802 Verdun St Ste 1, Montreal QC H4G1N1 *Web:* www.neotelis.com	514-281-1211		196

	Phone	Fax	Class
NeoTract Inc 4473 Willow Rd Ste 100 .... Pleasanton CA 94588 *Web:* www.neotract.com	925-401-0700		475
Neotropix Inc 351 Phoenixville Pk. .... Malvern PA 19355 *Web:* www.neotropix.com	610-296-8660		743
Neovasc Inc 13700 Mayfield Pl Ste 2135 .... Richmond BC V6V2E4 *TF:* 800-821-3657 ■ *Web:* www.neovasc.com	604-270-4344		476
Neoventa Medical Inc 226 Lowell St. .... Wilmington MA 01887 *Web:* www.neoventa.com	978-657-7750		475
Neovia 801 Garden St Ste 300 .... Santa Barbara CA 93101 *Web:* www.neoviainsurance.com	805-961-3111		41
NEP Electronics Inc 805 Mittel Dr .... Wood Dale IL 60191 *TF:* 800-284-7470 ■ *Web:* www.nepelectronics.com	630-595-8500	595-8706	246
Nepal 820 Second Ave Ste 17B .... New York NY 10017 *Web:* www.un.int/nepal	212-370-3988	953-2038	784
Embassy 2131 Leroy Pl NW .... Washington DC 20008 *Web:* www.nepalembassyusa.org	202-667-4550	667-5534	257
NEPC LLC 255 State St 8th Fl .... Boston MA 02109 *TF:* 800-561-3357 ■ *Web:* www.nepc.com	617-374-1300		401
NephroGenex Inc PO Box 400 .... Jamison PA 18929 *Web:* www.nephrogenex.com	609-986-1780		529
Nephron Pharmaceuticals Corp 4121 SW 34th St .... Orlando FL 32811 *TF:* 800-443-4313 ■ *Web:* www.nephronpharm.com	407-999-2225	872-1733	583
Nephros Inc 41 Grand Ave .... River Edge NJ 07661 *OTC:* NEPH ■ *Web:* www.nephros.com	201-343-5202	343-5207	476
Neposet Valley Chamber of Commerce 190 Vanderbilt Ave .... Norwood MA 02062 *Web:* www.nvcc.com	781-769-1126	769-0808	139
NEPRC (New England Primate Research Ctr) 1 Pine Hill Dr .... Southborough MA 01772 **Fax Area Code:* 508 ■ *Web:* www.hms.harvard.edu	617-432-1000	786-3317*	668
Neptco Inc 30 Hamlet St .... Pawtucket RI 02861 *TF:* 800-354-5445 ■ *Web:* www.neptco.com	401-722-5500	722-6378	732
Neptec Design Group Ltd 302 Legget Dr Ste 202 .... Kanata ON K2K1Y5 *Web:* www.neptec.com	613-599-7602		21
Neptune Chemical Pump Co PO Box 247 .... Lansdale PA 19446 *TF:* 800-255-4017 ■ *Web:* www.psgdover.com	215-699-8700	699-0370	641
Neptune Public Library 25 Neptune Blvd .... Neptune NJ 07753 *TF:* 800-326-3264 ■ *Web:* www.neptunepubliclibrary.org	732-775-8241	774-1132	434-3
Neptune Society 4312 Woodman Ave 3rd Fl .... Sherman Oaks CA 91423 *TF:* 888-637-8863 ■ *Web:* www.neptunesociety.com	888-637-8863		510
Neptune-Benson Inc 6 Jefferson Dr .... Coventry RI 02816 *TF:* 800-832-8002 ■ *Web:* www.neptunebenson.com	401-821-2200		641
NEPW Logistics Inc 55 Logistics Dr .... Auburn ME 04210 *Web:* www.nepw.com	207-333-3345		314
NERA (Naval Enlisted Reserve Assn) 6703 Farragut Ave. .... Falls Church VA 22042 *TF:* 800-776-9020 ■ *Web:* www.nera.org	703-534-1329		48-19
NERAC Inc 1 Technology Dr .... Tolland CT 06084 *Web:* www.nerac.com	860-872-7000	872-6026	387
NERC (North American Electric Reliability Council) 1325 G St NW Ste 600 .... Washington DC 20005 *Web:* www.nerc.com	609-452-8060	452-9550	48-12
Nercon 3972 S US Hwy 45 .... Oshkosh WI 54902 *Web:* www.nerconconveyors.com	920-233-3268	233-3159	207
Nerd Force Inc 97 New Dorp Plaza .... Staten Island NY 10306 *Web:* www.nerdforce.com	718-370-6147	370-6731	180
Nerd Gas Company LLC 441 Landmark Dr P.O. Box 3003 .... Casper WY 82602 **Fax Area Code:* 503 ■ *Web:* www.nerdgas.com	307-234-0583	653-3994*	536
Nerd World Media 8 New England Executive Pk .... Burlington MA 01803	781-272-6599		397
Nerdy Books 135 Main St .... Flemington NJ 08822 *Web:* www.nerdybooks.com	908-788-4676		637-2
Nerel Corp Dba Wheat Ridge Cyclery 7085 W 38th Ave .... Wheat Ridge CO 80033	303-424-3221		711
Nereus Pharmaceuticals Inc 10480 Wateridge Cir. .... San Diego CA 92121 *Web:* www.nereuspharm.com	858-587-4090		668
NERSC (National Energy Research Scientific Computing Ctr) Lawrence Berkeley National Laboratory .... Berkeley CA 94720 *TF:* 800-666-3772 ■ *Web:* www.nersc.gov	510-486-5849	486-4300	668
Nerstrand-Big Woods State Park 9700 170th St E .... Nerstrand MN 55053 *Web:* www.dnr.state.mn.us	507-333-4840		565
NES Associates LLC 6400 Beulah St Ste 300 .... Alexandria VA 22310 *Web:* www.nesassociates.com	703-224-2600		180
NES Healthcare Group Inc 39 Main St PO Box 156 .... Tiburon CA 94920 *Web:* www.neshealth-care.com	631-265-7450		30
NESARC (National Endangered Species Act Reform Coalition) 1050 Thomas Jefferson St NW 6th Fl .... Washington DC 20007 *Web:* www.nesarc.org	202-333-7481	338-2416	48-2
Nesbitt Contracting Company Inc 100 S Price Rd .... Tempe AZ 85281 *Web:* www.nesbitts.com	480-423-7600		188-4
Nesbitt Engineering Inc (NEI) 227 N Upper St .... Lexington KY 40507	859-233-3111	259-2717	261
NESC Staffing Corp 150 Mirona Rd .... Portsmouth NH 03801 *TF:* 800-562-3463 ■ *Web:* www.nesc.com	603-431-9740		721
Nesch LLC 9800 Connecticut Dr .... Crown Point IN 46307 *TF:* 800-405-8576 ■ *Web:* www.neschllc.com	219-644-3505		475
Nesco 2344 S Green St .... Tupelo MS 38801 *Web:* nescoelectric.com	662-840-4750	842-3139	23
NESCO Inc 6140 Parkland Blvd. .... Cleveland OH 44124 *Web:* nescoresource.com	440-461-6000	449-3111	185
Nesco/American Harvest 1700 Monroe St PO Box 237 .... Two Rivers WI 54241 *TF Cust Svc:* 800-288-4545 ■ *Web:* www.nesco.com	920-793-1368	793-1086	37
Nescopeck State Park 1137 Honey Hole Rd .... Drums PA 18222 *Web:* www.dcnr.state.pa.us	570-403-2006		565
NESDA (National Electronics Service Dealers Assn) 3608 Pershing Ave .... Fort Worth TX 76107 *TF:* 800-946-0201 ■ *Web:* www.nesda.com	817-921-9061	921-3741	49-18
Neset Consulting Service Inc 6844 Hwy 40 .... Tioga ND 58852 *Web:* www.nesetconsulting.com	701-664-1492		463
Neshaminy Constructors Inc 1839 Bustleton Pk .... Feasterville PA 19053 *TF:* 800-564-8892 ■ *Web:* www.nci3.com	215-322-2700		194
Neshaminy State Park 3401 State Rd .... Bensalem PA 19020 *Web:* www.dcnr.state.pa.us	215-639-4538		565
Neshoba County 401 Beacon St Ste 201 .... Philadelphia MS 39350 *Web:* www.neshoba.org	601-656-3581		338
NESHTA (National Environmental Safety & Health Training Assn) 584 Main St .... South Portland ME 04106 *Web:* www.neshta.org	207-771-9020		49-5
NESL (New Enterprise Stone & Lime Co Inc) 3912 Brumbaugh Rd. .... New Enterprise PA 16664 *Web:* www.nesl.com	814-766-2211		503-5
NESN (New England Sports Network) 480 Arsenal St Bldg 1 .... Watertown MA 02472 *Web:* www.nesn.com	617-536-9233	536-7814	740
Nespelem Valley Electric Co-op Inc 1009 F St .... Nespelem WA 99155 *TF:* 866-632-9992 ■ *Web:* www.nvec.org	509-634-4571	634-8138	245
NeST Technologies Corp 44901 Falcon Pl Ste 116 .... Sterling VA 20166 *TF:* 800-433-5778 ■ *Web:* www.nesttech.com	703-653-1100		225
NestFamily 1461 S Beltline Rd Ste 500 .... Coppell TX 75019 *TF:* 800-634-4298 ■ *Web:* www.nestlearning.com	972-402-7100		33
Nestle Purina PetCare Co Checkerboard Sq .... Saint Louis MO 63164 *TF:* 800-778-7462 ■ *Web:* www.purina.com	314-982-1000	982-2134	578
Nestle USA Inc 800 N Brand Blvd .... Glendale CA 91203 *Web:* www.nestle.com	818-549-6000		296-8
Nestle Waters North America 105 Pennsylvania Ave. .... Framingham MA 01701 *Web:* www.nestle-watersna.com	508-935-3500		805
NET (Nebraska Educational Telecommunications) 1800 N 33rd St .... Lincoln NE 68503 *TF:* 800-868-1868 ■ *Web:* netdb.unl.edu	800-868-1868		632
Net Access Corp 2300 15th St Ste 300 .... Denver CO 80202 *TF:* 800-638-6336 ■ *Web:* www.cologix.com	973-590-5000	590-5080	736
Net Aspects 1499 Oliver Rd. .... Fairfield CA 94534 *TF:* 800-399-0889 ■ *Web:* netaspects.com	707-399-8060		180
Net Driven 280 Eureka St .... Batesville MS 38606 *Web:* gatewaytire.net	662-563-1143		755
Net Effect Technologies 426 E Duarte Rd .... Monrovia CA 91016 *Web:* neteffecttech.com	626-930-0101		177
Net Element International Inc 1450 S Miami Ave .... Miami FL 33130 *Web:* www.netelement.com	787-993-9650		514
Net Endeavor Inc 982 S Main St. .... Pleasant Grove UT 84062 *Web:* net-endeavor.com	801-796-5582		177
Net Impact LLC, The 16690 Swingley Ridge Rd Ste 165 .... Chesterfield MO 63017 *Web:* www.thenetimpact.com	636-458-7772		195
Net Lease Capital Advisors 10 Tara Blvd .... Nashua NH 03062 *Web:* www.netleasecapital.com	603-598-9500		652
Net Matrix Solutions 10235 W Little York Rd Ste 435 .... Houston TX 77040 *Web:* www.netmatrixsolutions.com	281-598-2600		196
Net (net) Inc Baker Lofts Bldg 217 E 24th St - Ste 010 .... Holland MI 49423 *Web:* www.netnetweb.com	616-546-3100		463
NET Radio 1800 N 33rd St .... Lincoln NE 68503 *TF:* 800-868-1868 ■ *Web:* www.netnebraska.org	800-868-1868		741-74
Net Safety Monitoring Inc 2721 Hopewell Pl NE .... Calgary AB T1Y7J7 *Web:* www.net-safety.com	403-219-0688		477
Net Solutions Technology Center 38 Sams Point Rd Ab .... Beaufort SC 29907	843-525-6469		225
Net Source Inc 8020 Shaffer Pkwy .... Littleton CO 80127 *Web:* www.netsourcestorage.com	303-948-3360		196
Net Talk.Com Inc 1080 NW 163rd Dr. .... Miami FL 33169 *TF:* 800-555-4286 ■ *Web:* www.nettalk.com	305-621-1200		736
Net Theory Inc 64 Fulton St Ste 603 .... New York NY 10038 *Web:* www.nettheory.com	212-868-5950		463
Net World Technology Corp 65 S College St. .... Carlisle PA 17013 *Web:* networldtechnology.com	717-249-7232		196
Net Worth Solutions Inc 1410 Broadway 34th Fl. .... New York NY 10018 *Web:* www.networthsolutionsinc.com	212-278-8200		791
Net2Phone Inc 520 Broad St. .... Newark NJ 07102 *TF:* 800-386-6438 ■ *Web:* www.net2phone.com	973-438-3111		736
Net32 Inc 250 Towne Village Dr .... Cary NC 27513 *TF:* 800-517-1997 ■ *Web:* www.net32.com	919-468-1177		228
NETA (National Educational Telecommunications Assn) 939 S Stadium Rd. .... Columbia SC 29201 *TF:* 866-270-5141 ■ *Web:* www.netaonline.org	803-799-5517	771-4831	632
Neta Scientific Inc 4206 Sylon Blvd .... Hainesport NJ 08036 *TF:* 800-343-6015 ■ *Web:* www.netascientific.com	609-265-8210		475
NetBase Corp 7960 Donegan Dr Ste 225 .... Manassas VA 20109 *Web:* netbasecorp.net	703-396-7909		39
Netblaze Systems Inc 1299 Newell Hill Pl Ste 202 .... Walnut Creek CA 94596 *Web:* www.netblaze.biz	925-932-1765		180
Netbones Inc 2685 Warburton Ave .... Santa Clara CA 95051 *Web:* www.netbones.com	408-249-6091		396
NETC (New England Tropical Conservatory) 413 US Rt 7S PO Box 4715 .... Bennington VT 05201 *Web:* oneworldconservationcenter.org	802-447-7419		97

	Phone	Fax	Class
[illegible] Command) [illegible] Pensacola FL 32508	850-452-4858		340-6
[illegible] 4000 N Cannon Ave Lansdale PA 19446 [illegible] www.netcarrier.com	215-257-4917		681
[N]etcellent System Inc 4030 Valley Blvd Walnut CA 91789 *TF:* 888-595-3818 ■ *Web:* elliott.com	909-598-9019		177
NetCenergy Corp 231 Elm St Warwick RI 02888 *Web:* www.netcenergy.com	401-921-3100		393
Netcetera Consulting Inc 205 - 828 Harbourside Dr North Vancouver BC V7P3R9 *Web:* netcetera.ca	604-980-2700		177
Netchannel Inc 8310 Rio Grande Blvd NW Albuquerque NM 87114 *TF:* 888-843-8282 ■ *Web:* www.netchannel.com	505-843-8282		131
Netchex 1100 N Causeway Blvd Ste 1 Mandeville LA 70471 *Web:* www.netchexonline.com	985-220-1410		260
Netcom Inc 599 S Wheeling Rd Wheeling IL 60090 *Web:* www.netcominc.com	847-537-6300	537-2700	253
Netcom Systems Inc 200 Metroplex Dr Edison NJ 08817 *Web:* www.netcom-sys.com	732-393-6100		225
Netcom Technologies Inc 313 N Berry St Brea CA 92821 *Web:* netcomtechnologies.net	714-256-9229		180
Netcong Elementary School 26 College Rd Netcong NJ 07857 *Web:* www.netcongschool.org	973-347-0020		685
Netcracker Technology Corp 95 Sawyer Rd University Ofc Pk III Waltham MA 02453 *TF:* 800-477-5705 ■ *Web:* www.netcracker.com	781-419-3300	419-3301	463
Netelligent Corp 16401 Swingley Ridge Rd Ste 500 Chesterfield MO 63017 *Web:* www.netelligent.com	314-392-6900		809
Netessentials Inc 705 Eighth St Ste 1000 Wichita Falls TX 76301 *Web:* netess.net	940-767-6387		180
Netfast Communications Inc 989 Ave of the Americas 4th Fl New York NY 10018 *TF:* 888-678-6383 ■ *Web:* www.netfast.com	212-792-5200		224
NetFlix Inc 100 Winchester Cir Los Gatos CA 95032 *NASDAQ: NFLX* ■ *TF:* 866-579-7293 ■ *Web:* netflix.com	408-540-3700		797
NetForecast Inc 955 Emerson Dr Charlottesville VA 22901 **Fax Area Code:* 978 ■ *Web:* www.netforecast.com	434-249-1310	746-7038*	196
Netfronts Web Hosting 459 N 300 W Ste 16 Kaysville UT 84037 *TF:* 800-675-4622 ■ *Web:* netfronts.com	801-497-0878		396
Netgain Information Systems Co 220 Reynolds Ave Bellefontaine OH 43311 *TF:* 855-651-7001 ■ *Web:* www.netgainis.com	937-593-7177		180
NetGain Motors Inc 800 S State St Ste 4 Lockport IL 60441 *Web:* www.go-ev.com	630-243-9100		518
Netgain Networks Inc 8378 Altica Dr Riverside CA 92508 *TF:* 855-667-2364 ■ *Web:* netgainnetworks.com	951-656-0194		179
NetGain Technology Inc 720 W St Germain St Saint Cloud MN 56301 *Web:* www.netgainhosting.com	320-251-4700	251-5030	7
netGuru Inc 1240 N Van Buren St Ste 104 Anaheim CA 92807 *Web:* www.netguru.com	714-638-4878	414-0200	178-10
Nethaway & Clausen PC 6000 W St Joseph Ste 101 Lansing MI 48917	517-321-0019		2
Nethawk Interactive Inc 1255 Park Ave Ste D Emeryville CA 94608 *Web:* www.nethawk.net	510-595-2220		195
Netherland Rubber Co 2931 Exon Ave Cincinnati OH 45241 *TF:* 800-582-1877 ■ *Web:* www.netherlandrubber.com	513-733-0883	733-1096	326
Netherlands			
Consulate General 303 E Wacker Dr Ste 2600 Chicago IL 60601 *Web:* www.the-netherlands.org	312-780-1314		257
Consulate General 666 Third Ave 19th Fl New York NY 10017 *TF:* 877-388-2443 ■ *Web:* www.the-netherlands.org	877-388-2443		257
Embassy 4200 Linnean Ave NW Washington DC 20008 *TF:* 877-388-2443 ■ *Web:* www.the-netherlands.org	877-388-2443		257
Netherlands Board of Tourism & Conventions 215 Park Ave S New York NY 10003 **Fax Area Code:* 212 ■ *Web:* www.holland.com	646-618-0818	370-9507*	775
Netherlands Chamber of Commerce 267 Fifth Ave New York NY 10016	212-265-6460		138
Netimpact Strategies Inc 24917 Castleton Dr Chantilly VA 20152 *Web:* www.netimpactstrategies.com	703-327-7859		809
NetIQ Corp 1233 W Loop S Houston TX 77027 *TF Sales:* 888-323-6768 ■ *Web:* www.netiq.com	713-548-1700	548-1771	178-12
Netivot Hatorah 18 Atkinson Ave Thornhill ON L4J8C8 *TF:* 800-606-0416 ■ *Web:* www.netivot.com	905-771-1234		685
Netkrom Technologies Inc 2134 NW 99th Ave Miami FL 33172 *Web:* www.netkrom.com	305-418-2232		224
NETL (National Energy Technology Laboratory) 3610 Collins Ferry Rd Morgantown WV 26505 *TF:* 800-432-8330 ■ *Web:* www.netl.doe.gov	304-285-4764		668
Netlan Technology Center Inc 39 W 37th St Fl 11 New York NY 10018 *Web:* www.netlan.com	212-730-5900		765
NetLine Corp 750 University Ave Ste 200 Los Gatos CA 95032 *Web:* www.netline.com	408-340-2200		224
Netlink Software Group America Inc 999 Tech Row Madison Heights MI 48071 *TF:* 800-485-4462 ■ *Web:* netlink.com	800-485-4462		196
Netlink Systems Inc 5959 Shallowford Rd PO Box 23054 Chattanooga TN 37421 *Web:* www.netlink-systems.com	423-855-0065		177
Netlist Inc 175 Technology Ste 150 Irvine CA 92618 *Web:* www.netlist.com	949-435-0025	435-0031	696
Netlogix Inc 48 Court St Westfield MA 01085 *Web:* www.netlogix.com	413-568-2777		180
Netmark.com 1930 N Woodruff Ave Idaho Falls ID 83401 *TF:* 800-935-5133 ■ *Web:* www.netmark.com	800-935-5133		195
Netmd Business Inc 38935 Ann Arbor Rd Livonia MI 48150 *Web:* netmdbusiness.com	734-805-0460		363
NetMotion Inc 701 N 34th St Ste 250 Seattle WA 98103 *TF:* 877-818-7626 ■ *Web:* www.netmotionwireless.com	206-691-5500	691-5501	178-1
NetNation Communications Inc 550 Burrard St Ste 200 Vancouver BC V6C2B5 *TF:* 888-277-0000 ■ *Web:* www.netnation.com	604-688-8946	688-8934	808
Neto Sausage Co Inc 288 Brokaw Rd Santa Clara CA 95050 *TF:* 888-362-5242 ■ *Web:* www.netosausage.com	408-296-0818	296-0538	296-26
Netology LLC 1200 Summer St Ste 302 Stamford CT 06905 *Web:* www.netologyllc.com	203-975-9630		177
Netorian 98 S Main St Allentown NJ 08501 *Web:* netorian.com	914-830-0629		180
Netplanner Systems Inc 3145 Northwoods Pkwy Ste 800 Norcross GA 30071 *TF:* 800-795-1975 ■ *Web:* www.netplanner.com	770-662-5482		176
Netpop Research LLC 322 Cortland Ave San Francisco CA 94110 *Web:* netpop.com	415-647-1007		466
NetQuest Corp 523 Fellowship Rd Ste 205 Mt Laurel NJ 08054 *Web:* www.netquestcorp.com	856-866-0505		225
NetRate Systems Inc 3493 Woods Edge Dr Okemos MI 48864 *Web:* www.mcswin.com	517-347-4900		180
Netrition Inc 25 Corporate Cir Ste 118 Albany NY 12203 *TF:* 888-817-2411 ■ *Web:* www.netrition.com	518-464-0765	456-9673	355
Netropole 5630 NE Martin Luther King Jr Portland OR 97211 *Web:* www.portlandmanagedservices.com	503-241-3499		463
NetScout Systems Inc 310 Littleton Rd Westford MA 01886 *NASDAQ: NTCT* ■ *TF:* 800-357-7666 ■ *Web:* www.netscout.com	978-614-4000	614-4004	178-7
Netsertive Inc 2400 Perimeter Park Dr Ste 100 Research Triangle Region NC 27560 *TF:* 800-940-4351 ■ *Web:* www.netsertive.com	800-940-4351		195
NetShape Technologies Inc 31005 Solon Rd Solon OH 44139 *Web:* www.netshapetech.com	440-248-5456	248-5807	485
NETSHARE Inc 359 Bel Marin Keys Ste 24 Novato CA 94949 *Web:* netshare.com	415-883-1700	883-1799	631
Netsmart Technologies Inc 3500 Sunrise Hwy Ste D-122 Great River NY 11739 *TF:* 800-421-7503 ■ *Web:* www.ntst.com	631-968-2000		178-11
Netsoft USA Inc 24 W 25th St 5th Fl New York NY 10010 *Web:* www.epam.com	267-759-9000	759-8989	809
Netsol Technologies Inc 23901 Calabasas Rd Ste 2072 Calabasas CA 91302 *NASDAQ: NTWK* ■ *TF:* 800-732-0330 ■ *Web:* www.netsoltech.com	818-222-9195	222-9197	178-10
Netsource Technology Inc 951 Calle Negocio San Clemente CA 92673 *Web:* www.nstechnology.com	949-713-0800		246
Netspeed Learning Solutions 3016 NE Blakeley St Ste 100 Seattle WA 98105 *TF:* 877-517-5271 ■ *Web:* www.netspeedlearning.com	206-517-5271		194
NetStandard Inc 2000 Merriam Ln Kansas City KS 66106 *Web:* www.netstandard.com	913-262-3888		180
Netsville Inc 72 Cascade Dr Rochester NY 14614 *TF:* 888-638-7845 ■ *Web:* www.netsville.com	585-232-5670	232-4512	189-4
Netswitch 400 Oyster Point Blvd Ste 228 South San Francisco CA 94080 *Web:* www.netswitch.net	415-566-6228		387
Nettech LLC 1851 Hudson Ln Monroe LA 71201 *TF:* 800-627-9393 ■ *Web:* www.nettech.net	318-387-0001		180
NetTel Partners 125 N Eighth St Philadelphia PA 19106 *TF:* 800-519-5257 ■ *Web:* www.nettelpartners.com	267-908-7890		317
Nettempo Inc 130 Battery St Ste 500 San Francisco CA 94111 *Web:* www.nettempo.com	415-992-4900		177
Net-Temps Inc 55 Middlesex St Ste 220 North Chelmsford MA 01863 *TF:* 800-307-0062 ■ *Web:* www.net-temps.com	978-251-7272	251-7250	260
Nettnetts PC SEO LLC 457 State St Ste 1 Binghamton NY 13901 *Web:* www.nettnettspc.com	607-930-3861		175
NettResults LLC 3943 Irvine Blvd Ste 303 Irvine CA 92602 *Web:* www.nettresults.com	949-534-9130		466
Nettwerk 575 W Eighth Ave 5th Fl Vancouver BC V5Z0C4 *Web:* www.nettwerk.com	604-654-2929	654-1993	731
Netuno USA Inc 18501 Pines Blvd Ste 206 Pembroke Pines FL 33029 *Web:* www.netunousa.com	305-513-0904	513-3904	296-14
Netvantage Inc 6510 Hamilton Ave Ste1 Cincinnati OH 45224 *Web:* www.netvantageinc.com	513-729-0207		251
NetVillage.com LLC 342 Main St Laurel MD 20707 *Web:* www.netvillage.com	301-498-7797	498-8110	178-7
NetVoyage Corp 2500 W Executive Pkwy Ste 350 Lehi UT 84043 *Web:* www.netdocuments.com	801-226-6882		180
Netway Solutions Inc 240 Palomino Dr Salisbury NC 28146 *Web:* www.netwaysolutions.com	704-637-6155		180
Netwize Inc 702 Confluence Ave Salt Lake City UT 84123 *TF:* 800-544-8877 ■ *Web:* www.netwize.net	801-747-3200		180
Netwolves Corp 4710 Eisenhower Blvd Ste E-8 Tampa FL 33634 *Web:* www.netwolves.com	813-579-3200	882-0209	736
Netwood Communications 10736 Jefferson Blvd Ste 670 Culver City CA 90230 *TF:* 800-877-7979 ■ *Web:* www.netwood.net	310-442-1530		396
Network 2000 LLC 2100 N Nimitz Hwy Honolulu HI 96819 *TF:* 800-553-2447 ■ *Web:* www.network2000-hi.com	808-848-0000		180

Company / Address	City	State	Zip	Phone	Fax	Class
Network Appliance Inc 495 E Java Dr *NASDAQ: NTAP* ■ *TF Sales:* 800-443-4537 ■ *Web:* www.netapp.com	Sunnyvale	CA	94089	408-822-6000		176
Network Center Communications Inc 2536 W Main Ave *Web:* www.netcentersupply.com	Fargo	ND	58078	701-235-8100		180
Network Company of California 310 Via Vera Cruz *Web:* tncc.com	San Marcos	CA	92078	760-744-0442		175
Network Computing Magazine 600 Community Dr *Web:* www.networkcomputing.com	Manhasset	NY	11030	516-562-5000		457-7
Network Data Security Experts Inc 521 Branchway Rd *Web:* www.ndse.net	North Chesterfield	VA	23236	804-521-7946		177
Network Data Systems Inc 50 E Commerce Dr Ste 120 *Web:* www.network-data.com	Schaumburg	IL	60173	847-385-6700		180
Network Depot LLC 12040 S Lakes Dr Ste 202 *TF:* 800-460-1237 ■ *Web:* www.networkdepot.com	Reston	VA	20191	703-264-7776		179
Network Designs Integration Services Inc 103 Hammond Ave Ste 101 *Web:* www.network-designs.com	Fremont	CA	94539	510-249-9549		196
Network Directions PO Box 511466 *Web:* www.net-directions.com	Milwaukee	WI	53203	414-963-8759		180
Network Dynamics Inc 640 Brooker Creek Blvd Ste 410 *TF:* 877-818-8597 ■ *Web:* www.ndiwebsite.com	Oldsmar	FL	34677	813-818-8597		176
Network Earth Inc 14 Cambridge Ct *TF:* 888-201-5160 ■ *Web:* www.netearth.com	Wappingers Falls	NY	12590	888-201-5160		224
Network Equipment Technologies Inc 6900 Paseo Padre Pkwy *NASDAQ: NWK*	Fremont	CA	94555	510-713-7300		735
Network Experts 260 S Beverly Dr Ste 325 *Web:* www.networkexperts.la	Beverly Hills	CA	90212	310-275-1911		175
Network Frontiers LLC 244 Lafayette Cir *Web:* www.netfrontiers.com	Lafayette	CA	94549	510-962-5192		196
Network Global Logistics (NGL) 320 Interlocken Pkwy Ste 100 *TF:* 866-938-1870 ■ *Web:* www.nglog.com	Broomfield	CO	80021	866-938-1870		546
Network Innovations Inc 4424 Manilla Rd SE *TF:* 888-466-2772 ■ *Web:* www.networkinv.com	Calgary	AB	T2G4B7	403-287-5000		194
Network Insight LLC 10717 Sorrento Valley Rd Ste 100 *Web:* www.centerbeam.com	San Diego	CA	92121	858-450-1180		180
Network Journal, The 39 Broadway Rm 2120 *TF:* 866-259-1465 ■ *Web:* www.tnj.com	New York	NY	10006	212-962-3791		4
Network Magic Unlimited 1723 21st St *TF:* 800-774-0905 ■ *Web:* www.netmagicu.com	Santa Monica	CA	90404	310-449-1411		225
Network Medical Management Inc 1668 S Garfield Ave 2nd Fl *Web:* www.networkmedmgmt.com	Alhambra	CA	91801	626-282-0288		463
Network Multi-Family Security Corp 4221 W John Carpenter Fwy *TF:* 800-541-3138 ■ *Web:* protection1.com	Irving	TX	75063	214-277-7000		693
Network Paper & Packaging Ltd 1391 Kebet Way *Web:* www.netpak.net	Port Coquitlam	BC	V3C6G1	604-941-2999		96
Network Performance Inc 85 Green Mtn Dr *TF:* 800-639-6091 ■ *Web:* www.npi.net	South Burlington	VT	05403	802-859-0808		180
Network Republic 639 Tully Rd	San Jose	CA	95111	408-993-1075		180
Network Services LLC 2065 Kensington Ave *Web:* www.ns-wny.com	Amherst	NY	14226	716-839-5309	839-5301	736
Network Solutions LLC 13861 Sunrise Valley Dr Ste 300 *TF:* 800-361-5712 ■ *Web:* www.networksolutions.com	Herndon	VA	20171	703-668-4600		396
Network Specialty Group Inc 20251 Century Blvd *Web:* www.nsgi-hq.com	Germantown	MD	20874	301-208-9388		180
Network Synergy Corp 126 Monroe Tpke *TF:* 800-955-4441 ■ *Web:* www.netsynergy.com	Trumbull	CT	06611	203-261-2201		180
Network Telephone Services Inc 21135 Erwin St *TF:* 800-742-5687 ■ *Web:* www.nts.net	Woodland Hills	CA	91367	818-992-4300		252
Network Vigilance LLC 10731 Treena St Ste 200 *Web:* www.networkvigilance.com	San Diego	CA	92131	858-695-8676		180
Network World Magazine 492 Old Connecticut Path Ste 200 PO Box 9208 *TF:* 800-622-1108 ■ *Web:* www.networkworld.com	Framingham	MA	01701	800-622-1108		457-7
NetworkElites Services Inc 13657 Jupiter Rd Ste 111 *TF:* 800-331-8923 ■ *Web:* www.networkelites.com	Dallas	TX	75238	972-235-3114		393
Networking Concepts Inc 9881 Broken Land Pkwy Ste 402 *Web:* www.networkingconcepts.com	Columbia	MD	21046	410-381-0100		177
NetworkOmni Multilingual Communications Inc 4353 Park Ter Dr *Web:* www.networkomni.com	Westlake Village	CA	91361	818-706-7890		393
Networks & More Inc 24 Highland Bnd *Web:* andmore.com	Island Heights	NJ	08732	732-929-1485		180
Networks Electronic Co 9750 De Soto Ave *Web:* www.networkselectronic.com	Chatsworth	CA	91311	818-341-0440	718-7133	203
Networks Made Simple Llc 64 Confederate Way *Web:* networksmadesimple.net	Stafford	VA	22554	540-657-5360		175
Networks of Florida 25 W Avery St *TF:* 800-368-2315 ■ *Web:* www.nof.com	Pensacola	FL	32501	850-434-8600	434-8609	180
Networld Inc 300 Lanidex Plaza Ste 1 *TF:* 800-992-3411 ■ *Web:* www.networldinc.com						
Networld Media Group LLC 13100 Eastpoint Park Blvd Ste 100 *TF:* 877-441-7545 ■ *Web:* networldmediagroup.com	Louisv					
NetWorth Services Inc 1661 E Camelback Rd Ste 200 *Web:* www.networthservices.com	Phoenix	AZ				
Netwoven Inc 3837 Stone Pointe Way *Web:* www.netwoven.com	Pleasanton	CA	9458			
Netx Llc 1602 Sibley Ct *Web:* www.netxllc.com	Sheboygan	WI	53081			
Netxar Technologies Inc Ponce St Ste 7 *Web:* www.netxar.com	San Juan	PR	00917	787-765-		
NetXperts Inc 2680 Bishop Dr Ste 102 *TF:* 888-271-9367 ■ *Web:* www.netxperts.com	San Ramon	CA	94583	925-806-0800		
NetXposure Inc 735 SW First Ave 3rd Fl *Web:* netx.net	Portland	OR	97204	503-499-4342		
Netxusa Inc 231 Beverly Rd *TF:* 800-877-1200 ■ *Web:* www.netxusa.com	Greenville	SC	29609	864-271-9868		180
Netzel Grigsby Assoc Inc 9696 Culver Blvd Ste 105 *Web:* www.netzelgrigsby.com	Culver City	CA	90232	310-836-7624	836-9357	317
NetZero Inc 21301 Burbank Blvd *TF:* 800-638-9376 ■ *Web:* www.netzero.net	Woodland Hills	CA	91367	818-287-3000	287-3010	398
Netzsch Inc 119 Pickering Way *TF:* 800-255-2933 ■ *Web:* pumps.netzsch.com/us	Exton	PA	19341	610-363-8010	363-0971	386
Neuber Environmental Services Inc 42 Ridge Rd *TF:* 800-247-1727 ■ *Web:* www.neuberenv.com	Phoenixville	PA	19460	610-933-4332		63
Neuberger Berman Funds PO Box 8403 *TF:* 800-877-9700 ■ *Web:* www.nb.com	Boston	MA	02266	212-476-8800		528
Neuberger Berman LLC 605 Third Ave *TF:* 800-223-6448 ■ *Web:* www.nb.com	New York	NY	10158	800-223-6448		401
Neuberger Museum of Art 735 Anderson Hill Rd Purchase College SUNY *Web:* www.neuberger.org	Purchase	NY	10577	914-251-6100	251-6101	520
Neuberger Quinn Gielen Rubin Gibber PA 1 South St 27th Fl *Web:* www.nqgrg.com	Baltimore	MD	21202	410-332-8550		428
Neubert Millwork Co 1901 Lee Blvd *Web:* www.neubertmillwork.com	North Mankato	MN	56001	507-387-1105		499
NeuCo Inc 12 Post Office Sq 4th Fl *TF:* 800-675-2927 ■ *Web:* www.neuco.net	Boston	MA	02109	617-587-3100		225
Neudesic LLC 8105 Irvine Ctr Dr *TF:* 800-805-1805 ■ *Web:* www.neudesic.com	Irvine	CA	92618	949-754-4500		177
Neuger Communications Group Inc 25 Bridge Sq *Web:* www.neuger.com	Northfield	MN	55057	507-664-0700		449
Neuisys LLC 1500 Pinecroft Rd Ste 212 *TF:* 877-299-9052	Greensboro	NC	27407	877-299-9052	299-9051	743
NeuLion Inc 1600 Old Country Rd *Web:* www.neulion.com	Plainview	NY	11803	516-622-8300		395
Neuma Technology Inc 5450 Canotek Rd Ste 51 *Web:* www.neuma.com	Ottawa	ON	K1J9G3	613-749-9450		179
Neumade Products Corp 30 Pecks Ln Ste 40	Newtown	CT	06470	203-270-1100		591
Neumann Brothers Inc 1435 Ohio St *Web:* www.neumannbros.com	Des Moines	IA	50314	515-243-0156		186
Neumann College 1 Neumann Dr **Fax:* Admissions ■ *TF:* 800-963-8626 ■ *Web:* www.neumann.edu	Aston	PA	19014	610-459-0905	361-5265*	166
Neumayer Equipment Company Inc 5060 Arsenal St *TF:* 800-843-4563 ■ *Web:* www.neumayerequipment.com	Saint Louis	MO	63139	314-772-4501	772-2311	386
Neumedicines Inc 133 N Altadena Dr Ste 310 *Web:* www.neumedicines.com	Pasadena	CA	91107	626-844-3800		668
Neundorfer Inc 4590 Hamann Pkwy *Web:* www.neundorfer.com	Willoughby	OH	44094	440-942-8990		261
Neuralstem Inc 9700 Great Seneca Hwy *Web:* investor.neuralstem.com	Rockville	MD	20850	301-366-4841		85
Neuric Technologies Llc 2929 Buffalo Speedway *Web:* neuric.com	Houston	TX	77098	713-553-1716		809
Neuro Diagnostic Devices Inc 3701 Market St Third Fl **Fax Area Code:* 267	Philadelphia	PA	19104	215-966-6207	499-2001*	743
Neuro Kinetics Inc 128 Gamma Dr *Web:* www.neuro-kinetics.com	Pittsburgh	PA	15238	412-963-6649		475
Neuro Logic Systems Inc 451 Constitution Ave *Web:* www.nlsdisplays.com/index.html	Camarillo	CA	93012	805-389-5435		180
Neurocrine Biosciences Inc 12790 El Camino Rl *NASDAQ: NBIX* ■ *TF:* 800-894-5910 ■ *Web:* www.neurocrine.com	San Diego	CA	92130	858-617-7600	617-7602	85
NeuroGenetic Pharmaceuticals Inc 445 Marine View Ave Ste 101 *Web:* www.neurogeneticpharmaceuticals.com	Del Mar	CA	92014	858-735-5892		231
NeuroMetrix 62 Fourth Ave *NASDAQ: NURO* ■ *TF:* 888-786-7287 ■ *Web:* www.neurometrix.com	Waltham	MA	02451	781-890-9989	890-1556	250
Neuromonics Inc PO Box 351886 *TF:* 866-606-3876 ■ *Web:* www.neuromonics.com	Westminster	CO	80035	866-606-3876		250
Neuronetrix Inc 1044 E Chestnut St *Web:* www.neuronetrix.com	Louisville	KY	40204	502-561-9040		743
NeuroPace Inc 455 N Bernardo Ave *Web:* www.neuropace.com	Mountain View	CA	94043	650-237-2700		475
Neuroptics Inc 2082 Michelson Dr Ste 450 *TF:* 800-208-3343 ■ *Web:* www.neuroptics.com	Irvine	CA	92612	949-250-9792		476

Phone | Fax | Class

Neuros Medical Inc
35010 Chardon Rd Ste 210 .... Willoughby Hills OH 44094 440-951-2565 476
TF: 800-521-9072 ■ *Web:* www.neurosmedical.com

NeuroScience Inc 373 280th St .... Osceola WI 54020 715-294-2144 418
TF: 888-342-7272 ■ *Web:* www.neuroscienceinc.com

Neurosky Inc 125 S Market St Ste 900 .... San Jose CA 95113 408-200-6675 696
Web: www.neurosky.com

NeuroSource Inc
4501 N Winchester Ave Ste .... Chicago IL 60640 773-250-0000 7

Neuro-Tec Inc
975 Cobb Pl Blvd Ste 301 .... Kennesaw GA 30144 800-554-3407 475
TF: 800-554-3407 ■ *Web:* www.neurotec.net

Neurotech Pharmaceuticals Inc
900 Highland Corporate Dr................ Cumberland RI 02864 401-333-3880 668
Web: www.neurotechusa.com

Neurotez Inc 991 Hwy 22 Ste 200 A .... Bridgewater NJ 08807 908-998-1340 668
Web: neurotez.com

NeuroVentures LLC Zero Ct Sq............ Charlottesville VA 22902 434-297-1000 792
Web: www.neuroventures.com

NeuroVigil Inc 7606 Fay Ave.................. La Jolla CA 92037 858-454-5134 743
Web: www.neurovigil.com

Neuse Correctional Institution
701 Stevens Mill Rd..................... Goldsboro NC 27530 919-734-5580 213

NeuStar Inc 21575 Ridgetop Cir .... Sterling VA 20166 571-434-5400 47
TF: 855-638-2677 ■ *Web:* www.neustar.biz

Neutral Posture Inc 3904 N Texas Ave............ Bryan TX 77803 979-778-0502 778-0408 319-1
TF: 800-446-3746 ■ *Web:* neutralposture.com

Neutral Tandem Inc 550 W Adams St Fl 9 .... Chicago IL 60661 312-384-8040 177
Web: www.inteliquent.com

Neutrogena Corp 5760 W 96th St............ Los Angeles CA 90045 310-642-1150 214
TF: 800-582-4048 ■ *Web:* www.neutrogena.com

Neutron Inc 220 Reese Rd............... State College PA 16801 814-237-0902 196
TF: 800-813-4218 ■ *Web:* www.neutronet.com

Neutron Products Inc
22301 Mt Ephraim Rd..................... Dickerson MD 20842 301-349-5001 146
Web: neutronprod.com

Neutronix-Quintel (NXQ)
385 Woodview Ave...................... Morgan Hill CA 95037 408-776-5190 776-1039 695
Web: www.neutronixinc.com

Neuwing Energy Ventures LLC
913 N Market St Ste 1001................. Wilmington DE 19801 302-371-9771 463
Web: www.neuwingenergy.com

Nevada

Accountancy Board
1325 Airmotive Way Ste 220 .... Reno NV 89502 775-786-0231 786-0234 339-29
Web: www.nvaccountancy.com

Administrative Office of the Courts
201 S Carson St Ste 250 .... Carson City NV 89701 775-684-1700 339-29
Web: nevadajudiciary.us

Aging Services Div
1860 E Sahara Ave...................... Las Vegas NV 89104 702-486-3545 486-3572 339-29
Web: adsd.nv.gov

Arts Council 716 N Carson St Ste A .... Carson City NV 89701 775-687-6680 339-29
Web: nac.nevadaculture.org

Attorney General 100 N Carson St........... Carson City NV 89701 775-684-1100 684-1108 339-29
Web: ag.nv.gov

Bill Status 401 S Carson St................ Carson City NV 89701 775-684-6827 433
TF: 800-978-2878 ■ *Web:* www.leg.state.nv.us

Business & Industry Dept
555 E Washington Ave Ste 4900 .... Las Vegas NV 89101 702-486-2750 339-29
Web: www.business.nv.gov

Child & Family Services Div
4126 Technology Way 3rd Fl............ Carson City NV 89706 775-684-4400 684-4455 339-29
Web: www.dcfs.state.nv.us

Child Support Enforcement Office
300 E Second St Ste 1200................... Reno NV 89501 775-448-5150 448-5190 339-29
TF: 800-992-0900 ■ *Web:* dwss.nv.gov

Commission on Ethics
704 W Nye Ln Ste 204.................. Carson City NV 89703 775-687-5469 687-1279 265
Web: www.ethics.nv.gov

Conservation & Natural Resources Dept
901 S Stewart St Ste 1003.............. Carson City NV 89701 775-684-2700 684-2715 339-29
Web: www.dcnr.nv.gov

Corrections Dept
5500 Snyder Ave Bldg 17 .... Carson City NV 89702 775-887-3285 339-29
Web: www.doc.nv.gov

Dept of Employment Training & Rehabilitation
500 E Third St .... Carson City NV 89713 775-684-3911 684-3908 259
Web: www.nvdetr.org

Economic Development Commission
808 W Nye Ln .... Carson City NV 89703 775-687-9900 687-9924 339-29
TF: 800-336-1600 ■ *Web:* www.diversifynevada.com

Education Dept 700 E Fifth St .... Carson City NV 89701 775-687-9200 687-9101 339-29
Web: www.doe.nv.gov

Emergency Management Div
2478 Fairview Dr...................... Carson City NV 89701 775-687-0400 339-29
Web: dem.nv.gov

Environmental Protection Div
901 S Stewart St Ste 4001.............. Carson City NV 89701 775-687-4670 687-5856 339-29
Web: www.ndep.nv.gov

Gaming Commission
1919 College Pkwy PO Box 8003 .... Carson City NV 89706 775-684-7750 687-5817 339-29
Web: gaming.nv.gov

Governor 101 N Carson St Ste 4............. Carson City NV 89701 775-684-5600 684-5781 339-29
Web: nevadatreasurer.gov

Health Div 4150 Technology Way .... Carson City NV 89706 775-684-4200 684-4211 339-29
Web: www.health.nv.gov

Highway Patrol Div 555 Wright Way .... Carson City NV 89711 775-687-5300 339-29
Web: nevadadot.com

Historic Preservation Office
901 S Stewart St Ste 1003.............. Carson City NV 89701 775-684-2700 684-2715 339-29
Web: www.nvshpo.org

Human Resources Dept
4126 Technology Way Rm 100 .... Carson City NV 89706 775-684-4000 339-29
Web: dhhs.nv.gov

Information Technology Dept
100 N Stewart St Ste 100................ Carson City NV 89701 775-684-5800 339-29
Web: it.nv.gov

Insurance Div
1818 E College Pkwy Ste 103 .... Carson City NV 89706 775-687-0700 687-0787 339-29
Web: doi.nv.gov

Legislature 401 S Carson St .... Carson City NV 89701 775-684-6800 339-29
Web: www.leg.state.nv.us

Lieutenant Governor
101 N Carson St Ste 2.................. Carson City NV 89701 775-684-7111 684-7110 339-29
Web: www.ltgov.nv.gov

Medical Examiners Board
1105 Terminal Way Ste 301................... Reno NV 89502 775-688-2559 688-2321 339-29
Web: www.medboard.nv.gov

Motor Vehicles Dept
555 Wright Way....................... Carson City NV 89711 775-684-4368 339-29
TF: 877-368-7828 ■ *Web:* www.dmvnv.com

Parole & Probation Div
1445 Old Hot Springs Rd Ste 104 .... Carson City NV 89706 775-684-2600 339-29
Web: www.dps.nv.gov

Postsecondary Education Commission
8778 S Maryland Pkwy Ste 115............ Las Vegas NV 89123 702-486-7330 486-7340 339-29
Web: www.cpe.state.nv.us

Public Safety Dept 555 Wright Way.......... Carson City NV 89711 775-684-4808 684-4809 339-29
Web: dps.nv.gov

Public Utilities Commission
1150 E William St .... Carson City NV 89701 775-684-6101 684-6110 339-29
Web: puc.nv.gov

Real Estate Div
2501 E Sahara Ave Ste 102 .... Las Vegas NV 89104 702-486-4033 486-4275 339-29
Web: www.red.state.nv.us

Rehabilitation Div
1370 S Curry St....................... Carson City NV 89703 775-684-4040 339-29
Web: detr.state.nv.us

Secretary of State
101 N Carson St Ste 3.................. Carson City NV 89701 775-684-5708 684-5725 339-29
Web: www.nvsos.gov

State Athletic Commission
555 E Washington Ave Ste 3300 .... Las Vegas NV 89101 702-486-2575 486-2577 712
Web: www.boxing.nv.gov

State Parks Div
901 S Stewart St 5th Fl .... Carson City NV 89701 775-684-2770 684-2777 339-29
Web: www.parks.nv.gov

Supreme Court
201 S Carson St Ste 201................ Carson City NV 89701 775-684-1600 684-1601 339-29
Web: www.nevadajudiciary.us

System of Higher Education
2601 Enterprise Rd .... Reno NV 89512 775-784-4901 784-1127 339-29
Web: www.nevada.edu

Taxation Dept
1550 E College Pkwy Ste 115 .... Carson City NV 89706 775-684-2000 684-2020 339-29
Web: tax.nv.gov

Teacher Licensure Office
700 E Fifth St .... Carson City NV 89701 775-607-9200 687-9101 339-29
Web: www.doe.nv.gov

Tourism & Cultural Affairs Dept
716 N Carson St Ste A.................. Carson City NV 89701 775-687-6680 684-6688 339-29
Web: www.nevadaculture.org

Tourism Commission
401 N Carson St .... Carson City NV 89701 800-638-2328 339-29
TF: 800-638-2328 ■ *Web:* www.travelnevada.com

Transportation Dept
1263 S Stewart St .... Carson City NV 89712 775-888-7000 888-7115 339-29
Web: www.nevadadot.com

Treasurer 101 N Carson St Ste 4............ Carson City NV 89701 775-684-5600 684-5781 339-29
Web: nevadatreasurer.gov

Veterans Services Office
5460 Reno Corporate Dr .... Reno NV 89509 775-688-1653 339-29
Web: www.veterans.nv.gov

Vital Statistics Office
4150 Technology Way Ste 104............ Carson City NV 89706 775-684-4242 684-4156 339-29
Web: www.dhhs.nv.gov

Weights & Measures Bureau
2150 Frazier Ave .... Sparks NV 89431 775-353-3782 353-3798 339-29
Web: agri.nv.gov

Welfare Div 2533 N Carson St............. Carson City NV 89706 775-684-0800 684-0844 339-29
Web: www.dwss.nv.gov

Nevada Appeal 580 Mallory Way .... Carson City NV 89701 775-882-2111 423-9696 532-2
TF General: 877-689-3249 ■ *Web:* www.nevadaappeal.com

Nevada Area Vocational School
811 W Hickory St .... Nevada MO 64772 417-448-2090 764
Web: www.nevada.k12.mo.us

Nevada Assn of Realtors
760 Margrave Dr Ste 200 .... Reno NV 89502 775-829-5911 829-5915 656
TF: 800-748-5526 ■ *Web:* www.nvar.org

Nevada Auto Mall Inc
2501 E Austin Blvd.......................... Nevada MO 64772 417-667-3385 57
Web: nevadaautomall.net

Nevada Automotive Test Center
605 Ft Churchill Rd .... Silver Springs NV 89429 775-629-2000 225
TF: 800-785-8989 ■ *Web:* www.natc-ht.com

Nevada Ballet Theatre
1651 Inner Cir .... Las Vegas NV 89134 702-243-2623 804-0365 573-1
TF: 800-326-6868 ■ *Web:* nevadaballet.org

Nevada Contract Carpet
6840 W Patrick Ln .... Las Vegas NV 89118 702-362-3033 362
Web: nevadacontractcarpet.abbeycarpet.com

Nevada County 950 Maidu Ave............. Nevada City CA 95959 530-265-1218 338
Web: www.mynevadacounty.com

Nevada County Depot & Museum
403 W First St S PO Box 592.................. Prescott AR 71857 870-887-5821 338
Web: www.depotmuseum.org

Nevada County Library
980 Helling Way....................... Nevada City CA 95959 530-265-7050 265-9863 434-3
TF: 800-799-7233 ■ *Web:* mynevadacounty.com/nc/library

Nevada Crystal Premium LLC
6185 S Vly View Blvd .... Las Vegas NV 89118 702-892-0535 196
Web: nevadacrystalpremium.com

Nevada Dental Assn
8863 W Flamingo Rd Ste 102............... Las Vegas NV 89147 702-255-4211 255-3302 227
TF: 800-962-6710 ■ *Web:* www.nvda.org

Name / Address	City	State	ZIP	Phone	Fax	Class
Nevada Disability Advocacy & Law Center Inc 2820 W Charleston Blvd Ste 11 *Web:* ndalc.org	Las Vegas	NV	89102	702-257-8150		428
Nevada Donor Network Inc 2055 E Sahara Ave *TF:* 855-683-6667 ■ *Web:* www.nvdonor.org	Las Vegas	NV	89104	702-796-4225	796-4225	545
Nevada Gold & Casinos Inc 133 E Warm Springs Rd Ste 102 *NYSE:* UWN ■ *Web:* www.nevadagold.com	Las Vegas	NV	89119	702-685-1000		132
Nevada Heat Treating Inc 12 Industrial Pkwy Unit C *Web:* www.californiabrazing.com	Carson City	NV	89706	775-246-1040		484
Nevada Irrigation District (NID) 1036 W Main St *TF:* 800-222-4102 ■ *Web:* nidwater.com	Grass Valley	CA	95945	530-273-6185		787
Nevada Magazine 401 N Carson St *TF:* 855-729-7117 ■ *Web:* www.nevadamagazine.com	Carson City	NV	89701	775-687-5416	687-6159	457-22
Nevada Museum of Art 160 W Liberty St *TF:* 800-796-6009 ■ *Web:* www.nevadaart.org	Reno	NV	89501	775-329-3333	329-1541	520
Nevada Power Co 6226 W Sahara Ave *NYSE:* NVE ■ *TF Cust Svc:* 800-331-3103 ■ *Web:* www.nvenergy.com	Las Vegas	NV	89146	702-402-5555		787
Nevada Property 1 LLC 3708 Las Vegas Blvd S *TF:* 800-522-4700 ■ *Web:* www.cosmopolitanlasvegas.com	Las Vegas	NV	89109	702-698-7000		132
Nevada Republican Party 6330 McLeod Dr Ste 1 *Web:* www.nevadagop.org	Las Vegas	NV	89120	702-258-9182	258-9186	616-2
Nevada State Bank PO Box 990 *TF:* 800-727-4743 ■ *Web:* www.nsbank.com	Las Vegas	NV	89125	702-383-0009		70
Nevada State Library & Archives (NSLA) 100 N Stewart St *TF:* 800-922-2880 ■ *Web:* nsla.nv.gov	Carson City	NV	89701	775-684-3360	684-3311	434-5
Nevada State Medical Assn (NSMA) 3700 Barron Way *Web:* nvdoctors.org	Reno	NV	89511	775-825-6788		474
Nevada State Museum 600 N Carson St *Web:* nvculture.org/museums	Carson City	NV	89701	775-687-4810	687-4168	520
Nevada State Railroad Museum 2180 S Carson St *TF:* 800-508-4629 ■ *Web:* www.nsrm-friends.org	Carson City	NV	89701	775-687-6953		520
Nevada System of Higher Education *Henderson* 700 College Dr *Fax: Admissions ■ *Web:* csn.edu	Henderson	NV	89002	702-651-3000	651-3509*	162
Nevada Title Co 2500 N Buffalo Dr Ste 150 *Web:* www.nevadatitle.com	Las Vegas	NV	89128	702-251-5000		390
Nevada Veterinary Medical Assn PO Box 34420 *Web:* www.nevadavma.org	Reno	NV	89533	775-324-5344		795
Nevers Industries Inc 14125 21st Ave N *TF:* 800-258-5591 ■ *Web:* www.nevers.com	Minneapolis	MN	55447	763-210-4206		320
Neville Chemical Co 2800 Neville Rd *TF Cust Svc:* 877-704-4200 ■ *Web:* www.nevchem.com	Pittsburgh	PA	15225	412-331-4200	771-0226	605-2
Neville Public Museum of Brown County 210 Museum Pl *TF:* 800-895-0071 ■ *Web:* www.nevillepublicmuseum.org	Green Bay	WI	54303	920-448-4460	448-4458	520
Nevis Networks Inc 295 Bernardo Ave *Web:* www.nevisnetworks.com	Mountain View	CA	94043	650-254-2500		693
Nevo Technologies Inc 26 Church St *Web:* www.nevo.com	Cambridge	MA	02138	617-354-6386		180
New Accountant Magazine 3525 W Peterson Ave *Web:* www.newaccountantusa.com	Chicago	IL	60659	773-866-9900	866-9881	457-5
New Acton Mobile Industries LLC 809 Gleneagles Ct *TF:* 800-251-1600 ■ *Web:* www.actonmobile.com	Baltimore	MD	21286	800-251-1600		106
New Age Fastening Systems Inc 2 Enterprise Ct *Web:* www.newagestudwelding.com	Sewell	NJ	08080	856-218-8301		480
New Age Industrial Corporation Inc 16788 E Hwy 36 PO Box 520 *TF:* 800-255-0104 ■ *Web:* www.newageindustrial.com	Norton	KS	67654	785-877-5121		317
New Age Metal Fabricating Company Inc 26 Daniel Rd *Web:* www.namf.com	Fairfield	NJ	07004	973-227-9107		697
New Age Protection Inc 6551 Loisdale Cty Ste 801 *Web:* www.new-age-inc.com	Springfield	VA	22150	703-912-3057		463
New Age Technologies Inc 819 W Main St Ste 200 *Web:* www.newat.com	Louisville	KY	40202	502-412-6681		180
New Albany National Cemetery 1943 Ekin Ave *Web:* www.cem.va.gov/cems/nchp/newalbany.asp	New Albany	IN	47150	502-893-3852	893-6612	136
New Albany-Floyd County Public Library 180 W Spring St *Web:* nafclibrary.org	New Albany	IN	47150	812-944-8464		434-3
New Amber Indian Restaurant 3505 Birney Ave *Web:* www.newamberindian.com	Moosic	PA	18507	570-344-7100		671
New America Foundation 1899 L St NW *Web:* www.newamerica.org	Washington	DC	20036	202-986-2700	986-3696	634
New Amsterdam Entertainment Inc 1133 Ave of the Americas Ste 1621 *Web:* www.newamsterdamnyc.com	New York	NY	10036	212-922-1930		513
New Angle Media 535 W Thomas Rd *Web:* www.newanglemedia.com	Phoenix	AZ	85013	602-840-5530		195
New Balance Athletic Shoe Inc 20 Guest St Brighton Landing *TF:* 800-595-9138 ■ *Web:* www.newbalance.com	Brighton	MA	02135	617-783-4000	787-9355	301
New Beacon Hospice Inc 201 Office Park Dr Ste 100 *TF:* 800-626-1101 ■ *Web:* www.newbeacon.org	Birmingham	AL	35223	205-939-8799		793
New Bedford Free Public Library (NBFPL) 613 Pleasant St *Web:* www.newbedford-ma.gov/library	New Bedford	MA	02740	508-991-6275	991-6368	434-3
New Bedford Harbor Development Commission 52 Fisherman S Wharf PO Box 50899 *Web:* www.portofnewbedford.org	New Bedford	MA	02745	508-961-3000	979-1517	618
New Bedford Management Corp 210 E 23rd St 5th Fl *Web:* www.newbedfordmanagement.com	New York	NY	10010	212-674-6123		652
New Bedford Whaling Museum 18 Johnny Cake Hill *TF:* 800-453-5040 ■ *Web:* www.whalingmuseum.org	New Bedford	MA	02740	508-997-0046		520
New Bedford Whaling National Historical Park 33 William St *Web:* www.nps.gov/nebe	New Bedford	MA	02740	508-996-4095	984-1250	564
New Belgium Brewing Co 500 Linden St *Web:* www.newbelgium.com	Fort Collins	CO	80524	970-221-0524		102
New Berlin Plastics Inc 5725 S Westridge Dr *Web:* www.nbplastics.com	New Berlin	WI	53151	262-784-3120		596
New Berlin Public Library 15105 Library Ln *TF:* 800-272-3900 ■ *Web:* www.newberlinlibrary.org	New Berlin	WI	53151	262-785-4980		434-3
New Bern Area Chamber of Commerce 316 S Front St *Web:* www.newbernchamber.com	New Bern	NC	28560	252-637-3111	637-7541	139
New Bern National Cemetery 1711 National Ave *TF:* 800-827-1000 ■ *Web:* www.cem.va.gov	New Bern	NC	28560	252-637-2912	637-7145	136
New Bern-Craven County Public Library 400 Johnson St *Web:* newbern.cpclib.org	New Bern	NC	28560	252-638-7800	638-7817	434-3
New Boston Rtm Inc 19155 Shook Rd *Web:* www.newbostonrtm.com	New Boston	MI	48164	734-753-9956	753-9221	608
New Braunfels Chamber of Commerce 390 S Seguin St *TF:* 800-572-2626 ■ *Web:* innewbraunfels.com	New Braunfels	TX	78130	830-625-2385	625-7918	139
New Braunfels Public Library 700 E Common St *TF:* 800-434-8013 ■ *Web:* www.nbtexas.org	New Braunfels	TX	78130	830-221-4300	608-2151	434-3
New Brighton Area School District 3225 43rd St *Web:* www.nbasd.org	New Brighton	PA	15066	724-843-1795	843-6144	685
New Britain General Campus 100 Grand St *TF:* 800-286-4724 ■ *Web:* thocc.org	New Britain	CT	06050	860-224-5011		374-3
New Britain Herald One Liberty Sq PO BOX 1090 3rd Fl *Web:* www.newbritainherald.com	New Britain	CT	06050	860-225-4601	225-2611	532-2
New Britain Museum of American Art 56 Lexington St *Web:* www.nbmaa.org	New Britain	CT	06052	860-229-0257	229-3445	520
New Britain Rock Cats 230 John Karbonic Way S Main St New Britain Stadiu *Web:* www.milb.com/index.jsp	New Britain	CT	06051	860-224-8383		713
New Brunswick Free Public Library 60 Livingston Ave *Web:* www.lmxac.org	New Brunswick	NJ	08901	732-745-5108		434-3
New Brunswick International Inc 76 Veronica Ave *Web:* www.nbidigi.net	Somerset	NJ	08873	732-828-3633		362
New Brunswick Museum 1 Market Sq *TF:* 888-268-9595 ■ *Web:* www.nbm-mnb.ca	Saint John	NB	E2L4Z6	506-643-2300	643-6081	520
New Brunswick Sports Hall of Fame 503 rue Queen St PO Box 6000 *Web:* nbsportshalloffame.com/sports/default.aspx	Fredericton	NB	E3B5H1	506-453-3747	459-0481	522
New Brunswick Theological Seminary 35 Seminary Pl *TF:* 800-445-6287 ■ *Web:* www.nbts.edu	New Brunswick	NJ	08901	732-247-5241	249-5412	167-3
New Buck Corp 8000 Hwy 226 S PO Box 69 *TF:* 800-561-3357 ■ *Web:* www.buckstove.com	Spruce Pine	NC	28777	828-765-6144	765-0462	357
New Buffalo Corp 1220 N Price Rd *Web:* www.buffalotools.com	St Louis	MO	63132	636-532-9888		361
New Canaan Library 151 Main St *Web:* www.newcanaanlibrary.org	New Canaan	CT	06840	203-594-5000		434-3
New Canaan Nature Ctr 144 Oenoke Ridge *Web:* www.newcanaannature.org	New Canaan	CT	06840	203-966-9577	966-6536	50-5
New Castle Community y 20 W Washington St *TF:* 800-374-9825 ■ *Web:* www.ncymca.org	New Castle	PA	16101	724-658-4766		354
New Castle Correctional Facility 1000 Van Nuys Rd	New Castle	IN	47362	765-593-0111		213
New Castle County Detention Ctr 963 Centre Rd *TF:* 800-969-4357 ■ *Web:* kids.delaware.gov	Wilmington	DE	19805	302-633-3100	995-8393	412
New Castle County Library 750 Library Ave *TF:* 877-225-7351 ■ *Web:* nccde.org	Newark	DE	19711	302-731-7550	731-4019	434-3
New Castle Hotels & Resorts 2 Corporate Dr *TF:* 800-321-2211 ■ *Web:* www.newcastlehotels.com	Shelton	CT	06484	203-925-8370		379
New Castle Industries Inc 1399 Countyline Rd	New Castle	PA	16101	724-656-5600	656-5620	621
New Castle News PO Box 60 *TF:* 800-735-0202 ■ *Web:* www.ncnewsonline.com	New Castle	PA	16103	724-654-6651	654-5976	532-2
New Castle Public Library 424 Delaware St *TF:* 877-225-7351 ■ *Web:* nccde.org/337/New-Castle-Public-Library	New Castle	DE	19720	302-328-1995	328-4412	434-3
New Castle Refractories Co Inc 915 Industrial St *Web:* www.refractoriesinstitute.org	New Castle	PA	16102	724-654-7711	654-6322	663
New Castle-Henry County Public Library (NCHC) 376 S 15th St *Web:* nchcpl.org	New Castle	IN	47362	765-529-0362		434-3

Name / Address	Phone	Fax	Class
New Century Bank 700 W Cumberland St .... Dunn NC 28334 *Web:* www.selectbank.com	910-892-7080		70
New Century Capital Partners Inc 1510 11th St Ste 203 .... Santa Monica CA 90401 *Web:* www.newcenturycap.com	310-451-9073		690
New Century Education Foundation PO Box 43052 .... Upper Montclair NJ 07043 *TF:* 866-326-1133 ■ *Web:* www.newcenturyeducation.org	866-326-1133		178-1
New Century Pharmaceuticals Inc 895 Martin Rd .... Huntsville AL 35824 *Web:* www.newcenturypharm.com	256-461-0024		231
New Century Press Inc 310 First Ave. .... Rock Rapids IA 51246 *TF:* 800-621-0801 ■ *Web:* www.ncppub.com	712-472-2525		532-3
New Channel Direct 2659 Center Rd .... Hinckley OH 44233 *TF:* 800-410-6245 ■ *Web:* www.newchanneldirect.com	330-225-8950		5
New Choices Inc 2501 18th St Ste 201 .... Bettendorf IA 52722 *TF:* 888-355-5502 ■ *Web:* newchoicesinc.com	563-355-5502		363
New City Cafe 4005 SW Gage Ctr Dr. .... Topeka KS 66604	785-271-8646		671
New City Communications 770 N Halsted St Ste 303 .... Chicago IL 60642 *Web:* newcity.com	312-243-8786		532-5
New City Media Inc 301 S Main St Ste 207 .... Blacksburg VA 24060 *Web:* www.insidenewcity.com	540-552-1320		396
New College of Florida 5800 Bay Shore Rd .... Sarasota FL 34243 **Fax:* Admissions ■ *TF:* 800-435-7352 ■ *Web:* www.ncf.edu	941-487-5000	487-5010*	166
New Concept Technology 320 Busser Rd PO Box 0297 .... Emigsville PA 17318 *Web:* www.newconcepttech.com	717-741-0840	741-4301	602
New Conservatory Theatre Centre 25 Van Ness Ave .... San Francisco CA 94102 *Web:* www.nctcsf.org	415-861-4914	861-6988	572
New Constructs LLC 210 Jamestown Pk Ste 201 .... Brentwood TN 37027 *Web:* www.newconstructs.com	615-377-0443		401
NEW Co-op Inc 2626 First Ave S .... Fort Dodge IA 50501 *TF:* 800-362-2233 ■ *Web:* www.newcoop.com	515-955-2040		275
New Country Motor Car Group 358 Broadway Ste 403 .... Saratoga Springs NY 12866 *Web:* www.newcountry.com	518-584-7700		57
New Country Volkswagen of Greenwich 200 W Putnam Ave .... Greenwich CT 06830 *TF:* 866-980-2089 ■ *Web:* newcountry.com	866-584-6747		57
New Covenant Fellowship Church 18901 Waring Stn Rd .... Germantown MD 20874 *Web:* www.fellowshipusa.com	301-444-3100		48-20
New Ctr Community Mental Health Services 2051 W Grand Blvd .... Detroit MI 48208 *Web:* www.newcentercmhs.org	313-961-3200		353
New Dawn Memory Care 2000 S Blackhawk St .... Aurora CO 80014 *Web:* www.newdawnaurora.com	303-952-0791		371
New Day Marketing Ltd 923 Olive St .... Santa Barbara CA 93101 *Web:* www.newdaymarketing.com	805-965-7833		7
New Dimensions Precision Machining Inc 6614 S Union Rd .... Union IL 60180 *Web:* www.newdims.com	815-923-8300		454
New Dimensions Radio Broadcasting Network PO Box 7847 .... Santa Rosa CA 95407 *Web:* www.newdimensions.org	707-468-5215		646
New Dimensions Research Corp 260 Spagnoli Rd .... Melville NY 11747 *TF:* 800-637-8870 ■ *Web:* www.ndrc.com	631-694-1356	694-6097	233
New Directions Behavioral Health LLC PO Box 6729 .... Leawood KS 66206 **Fax Area Code:* 913 ■ *TF:* 800-624-5544 ■ *Web:* www.ndbh.com	800-624-5544	982-8401*	462
New Directions Inc 30800 Chagrin Blvd .... Cleveland OH 44124 *TF:* 800-750-6709 ■ *Web:* newdirections.co	216-591-0324	591-1243	726
New Dominion LLC 1307 S Boulder Ave Ste 400 .... Tulsa OK 74119 *Web:* www.newdominion.net	918-587-6242		536
New Echota State Historic Site 1211 Chatsworth Hwy NE .... Calhoun GA 30701 *Web:* www.gastateparks.org	706-624-1321		565
New Edge Networks 3000 Columbia House Blvd Ste 106 .... Vancouver WA 98661 *TF:* 877-725-3343 ■ *Web:* www.newedgenetworks.com	360-693-9009		398
New England Airlines Inc 56 Airport Rd .... Westerly RI 02891 **Fax Area Code:* 401 ■ *TF:* 800-243-2460 ■ *Web:* www.block-island.com/nea	800-243-2460	596-7366*	25
New England Aquarium 1 Central Wharf .... Boston MA 02110 *Web:* www.neaq.org	617-973-5200		40
New England Art Publishers Inc 10 Railroad St .... Abington MA 02351 *Web:* ww.birchcraft.com	781-878-5151		528
New England Assn of Schools & Colleges (NEASC) 209 Burlington Rd .... Bedford MA 01730 *Web:* www.neasc.org	781-271-0022	541-5400	48-1
New England Baptist Hospital 125 Parker Hill Ave .... Boston MA 02120 *TF:* 855-370-6324 ■ *Web:* www.nebh.org	617-754-5000	734-7804	374-3
New England Bible College & Grace Evangelical Seminary 879 Sawyer St .... South Portland ME 04106 *Web:* www.nebc.edu	207-799-5979		166
New England Cable News (NECN) 160 Wells Ave .... Newton MA 02459 *Web:* www.necn.com	617-630-5000	630-5055	740
New England Capital Partners Inc 1 Gateway Ctr Ste 405 .... Newton MA 02458 *Web:* www.necapitalpartners.com	617-964-7300	964-7301	690
New England Coffee Co 100 Charles St .... Malden MA 02148 *TF:* 800-225-3537 ■ *Web:* www.newenglandcoffee.com	800-225-3537		296-7
New England College 98 Bridge St .... Henniker NH 03242 *TF Admissions:* 800-521-7642 ■ *Web:* www.nec.edu	603-428-2223		166

Name / Address	Phone	Fax	Class
New England College of Business & Finance 10 High St Ste 204 .... Boston MA 02110 *TF:* 888-357-7332 ■ *Web:* www.necb.edu	617-951-2350	951-2533	800
New England Computer Services Inc 322 E Main St 3rd Fl .... Branford CT 06405 **Fax Area Code:* 203 ■ *TF Sales:* 800-766-6327 ■ *Web:* www.necs.com	475-221-8200	208-0889*	178-10
New England Conservatory 290 Huntington Ave .... Boston MA 02115 **Fax:* Admissions ■ *TF:* 800-841-8371 ■ *Web:* necmusic.edu	617-585-1100	585-1115*	166
New England Construction Company Inc 293 Bourne Ave .... Rumford RI 02916 *Web:* www.neconstruction.com	401-434-0112		261
New England Council Inc 98 N Washington St Ste 201 .... Boston MA 02114 *Web:* www.newenglandcouncil.com	617-723-4009	723-3943	140
New England Culinary Institute 56 College St .... Montpelier VT 05602 *TF:* 877-223-6324 ■ *Web:* www.neci.edu	802-223-6324	225-3280	163
New England Development 1 Wells Ave .... Newton MA 02459 *Web:* www.nedevelopment.com	617-965-8700	243-7085	655
New England Federal Credit Union PO Box 527 .... Williston VT 05495 *TF:* 800-400-8790 ■ *Web:* www.nefcu.com	802-879-8790		219
New England Garage Door 15 Campanelli Cir .... Canton MA 02021 *TF:* 800-676-7734 ■ *Web:* www.wayne-dalton.com	781-821-2737		499
New England Historic Genealogical Society 101 Newbury St .... Boston MA 02116 *TF:* 800-625-7738 ■ *Web:* www.historicbostons.com	617-536-5740		434-3
New England Homes 270 Ocean Rd .... Greenland NH 03840 *TF:* 800-800-8831 ■ *Web:* www.newenglandhomes.net	603-436-8830	431-8540	106
New England Industrial Truck Inc 195 Wildwood Ave .... Woburn MA 01801 *Web:* www.neit.com	781-935-9105		385
New England Institute of Art 10 Brookline Pl W .... Brookline MA 02445 *TF:* 800-903-4425 ■ *Web:* www.artinstitutes.edu	617-582-4460		164
New England Institute of Technology 2500 Post Rd .... Warwick RI 02886 *TF:* 800-736-7744 ■ *Web:* www.neit.edu	401-467-7744	738-5122	800
New England Journal of Medicine 10 Shattuck St .... Boston MA 02115 *TF:* 800-843-6356 ■ *Web:* www.nejm.org	617-734-9800	739-9864	457-16
New England Life Flight Inc 1727 Robins St Hangar .... Bedford MA 01730 *TF:* 800-233-8998 ■ *Web:* www.bostonmedflight.org	781-863-2213		13
New England Life Insurance Co 699 Boylston St .... Boston MA 02116 *Web:* metlife.com	617-585-4574		391-2
New England Machinery Inc 2820 62nd Ave E .... Bradenton FL 34203 *Web:* www.neminc.com	941-755-5550	751-6281	547
New England Miniature Ball Corp 163 Greenwood Rd W PO Box 585 .... Norfolk CT 06058 *Web:* www.nemb.com	860-542-5543	542-5058	485
New England Motor Freight Inc 1-71 N Ave E .... Elizabeth NJ 07201	908-965-0100		780
New England Natural Bakers 74 Fairview St E .... Greenfield MA 01301 *TF:* 800-910-2884 ■ *Web:* www.newenglandnaturalbakers.com	413-772-2239	772-2936	296-4
New England Organ Bank 60 First Ave .... Waltham MA 02451 *TF:* 800-446-6362 ■ *Web:* www.neob.org	800-446-6362		545
New England Paper Tube Company Inc 173 Weeden St .... Pawtucket RI 02860	401-725-2610		125
New England Peace Pagoda, The 100 Cave Hill Rd .... Leverett MA 01054 *TF:* 800-228-6483 ■ *Web:* newenglandpeacepagoda.org	413-367-2202		50-1
New England Primate Research Ctr (NEPRC) 1 Pine Hill Dr .... Southborough MA 01772 **Fax Area Code:* 508 ■ *Web:* www.hms.harvard.edu	617-432-1000	786-3317*	668
New England Rehabilitation Hospital of Portland 335 Brighton Ave .... Portland ME 04102	207-775-4000		374-6
New England Revolution Gillette Stadium 1 Patriot Pl .... Foxboro MA 02035 *TF:* 877-438-7387 ■ *Web:* www.revolutionsoccer.net	877-438-7387		717
New England Ropes Inc 848 Airport Rd .... Fall River MA 02720 *TF:* 800-333-6679 ■ *Web:* www.neropes.com	508-678-8200	679-2363	208
New England School of English 36 John F Kennedy St .... Cambridge MA 02138 *Web:* nese.edu	617-864-7170	864-7282	423
New England School of Law 154 Stuart St .... Boston MA 02116 *Web:* www.nesl.edu	617-451-0010		167-1
New England School of Photography 537 Commonwealth Ave .... Boston MA 02215 *TF:* 800-676-3767 ■ *Web:* www.nesop.edu	617-437-1868		590
New England Security Inc 10 Industrial Dr .... Westerly RI 02891 *Web:* newenglandsecurityinc.com	401-596-0660		692
New England Sports Network (NESN) 480 Arsenal St Bldg 1 .... Watertown MA 02472 *Web:* www.nesn.com	617-536-9233	536-7814	740
New England Systems & Software Inc 33 Holly Ln .... Lake George NY 12845 *Web:* www.nessnetworks.com	518-377-4057		177
New England Tropical Conservatory (NETC) 413 US Rt 7S PO Box 4715 .... Bennington VT 05201 *Web:* oneworldconservationcenter.org	802-447-7419		97
New England Typographic Service Inc 206 W Newberry Rd .... Bloomfield CT 06002 *Web:* www.netype.com	860-242-2251		781
New England Wild Flower Society 180 Hemenway Rd .... Framingham MA 01701 *Web:* www.newfs.org	508-877-7630	877-3658	48-13
New England Wood Pellet LLC 141 Old Sharon Rd .... Jaffrey NH 03452 *TF:* 877-981-9663 ■ *Web:* www.pelletheat.com	877-981-9663		819

Phone | Fax | Class

New England Woodcraft Inc
481 North St PO Box 165 Forest Dale VT 05745 802-247-8211 247-8042 319-2
Web: newenglandwoodcraft.com
New England Wooden Ware Corp
205 School St. Gardner MA 01440 978-632-3600 630-1513 100
Web: www.old.newwpkg.com
New Enterprise Rural Electric Co-op Inc
3596 Brumbaugh Rd. New Enterprise PA 16664 814-766-3221 766-3319 245
TF: 800-270-3177 ■ *Web:* www.newenterpriserec.com
New Enterprise Stone & Lime Co Inc (NESL)
3912 Brumbaugh Rd. New Enterprise PA 16664 814-766-2211 503-5
Web: www.nesl.com
New Era Building Systems Inc
451 Southern Ave Strattanville PA 16258 814-764-5581 505
New Era Cap Company Inc
160 Delaware Ave Buffalo NY 14202 716-604-9000 155-9
TF General: 877-632-5950 ■ *Web:* www.neweracap.com
New Era Life Insurance Co PO Box 4884 Houston TX 77210 800-552-7879 391-4
TF: 800-552-7879 ■ *Web:* www.neweralife.com
New Era Ohio LLC 520 W Mulberry St. Bryan OH 43506 419-633-1616 454
TF: 800-488-6903 ■ *Web:* www.neweraohio.com
New Era Optical Co 5575 N Lynch Ave. Chicago IL 60630 773-725-9600 237
TF: 800-548-8125 ■ *Web:* www.neweraopt.com
New Era Petroleum LLC
251 S Thurmond St Sheridan WY 82801 307-673-4812 536
TF: 800-875-7015 ■ *Web:* www.new-era-petroleum.com
New Era Portfolio
2101 E St Elmo Rd Ste 110. Austin TX 78744 512-928-3200 627
Web: www.newerahd.com
New Era Restaurant 10 Massillon Rd Akron OH 44312 330-784-0087 671
New Fairfield Free Public Library
2 Brush Hill Rd New Fairfield CT 06812 203-312-5679 312-5685 434-3
TF: 877-227-7487 ■ *Web:* www.newfairfieldlibrary.org
New Federal Theatre 292 Henry St. New York NY 10002 212-353-1176 748
TF: 800-276-2392 ■ *Web:* www.newfederaltheatre.org
New Generation Mechanical
1133 Empire Central Dr Dallas TX 75247 972-830-9900 830-9993 610
Web: www.newgenm.com
New Generation Research Inc
225 Friend St Ste 801. Boston MA 02114 617-573-9550 573-9554 637-2
TF: 800-468-3810 ■ *Web:* www.turnarounds.com
New Generation Sushi 493 Bloor St W Toronto ON M5S1Y2 416-963-8861 671
Web: newgenerationsushi.com
New Germany State Park
349 Headquarters Ln Grantsville MD 21536 301-895-5453 565
TF: 800-830-3974 ■
Web: dnr.maryland.gov/publiclands/Pages/western/newgermany.aspx
New Glarus Woods State Park (NGWSP)
W5446 County Hwy NN New Glarus WI 53574 608-527-2335 565
Web: dnr.wi.gov
New Gold Inc 666 Burrard St Ste 3110 Vancouver BC V6C2X8 604-696-4100 502
NYSE: NGD ■ *Web:* www.newgold.com
New Hampshire
Accountancy Board
121 S Fruit St Anna Philbrook Bldg. Concord NH 03301 603-271-2219 271-8702 339-30
Web: www.nh.gov
Administrative Office of the Courts
2 Charles Doe Dr. Concord NH 03301 603-271-2521 513-5454 339-30
Web: www.courts.state.nh.us/aoc
Agriculture Markets & Food Dept
PO Box 2042 Concord NH 03302 603-271-3551 271-1109 339-30
Web: agriculture.nh.gov
Arts Council 2 1/2 Beacon St 2nd Fl. Concord NH 03301 603-271-2789 271-3584 339-30
Web: www.nh.gov/nharts
Attorney General 33 Capitol St. Concord NH 03301 603-271-3658 271-2110 339-30
Web: www.nh.gov
Banking Dept 53 Regional Dr Ste 200 Concord NH 03301 603-271-3561 271-1090 339-30
TF: 800-437-5991 ■ *Web:* www.nh.gov
Board of Medicine
121 S Fruit St Ste 301 Concord NH 03301 603-271-1203 271-6702 339-30
TF: 844-711-4357 ■ *Web:* www.oplc.nh.gov/medicine
Bureau of Elderly & Adult Services (BEAS)
129 Pleasant St Concord NH 03301 603-271-9203 271-4643 339-30
Web: www.dhhs.nh.gov
Chief Medical Examiner
246 Pleasant St Ste 218. Concord NH 03301 603-271-1235 271-6308 339-30
Web: doj.nh.gov/medical-examiner
Child Support Services
129 Pleasant St Concord NH 03301 603-271-4427 271-4787 339-30
TF: 800-852-3345 ■ *Web:* www.dhhs.nh.gov/dcss
Children Youth & Families Div
129 Pleasant St 4th Fl Concord NH 03301 603-271-4451 271-4729 339-30
Web: www.dhhs.state.nh.us
Consumer Protection and Antitrust Bureau
33 Capitol St Concord NH 03301 603-271-3643 271-2110 339-30
Web: www.doj.nh.gov
Corrections Dept
105 Pleasant St PO Box 1806 Concord NH 03302 603-271-5600 271-5643 339-30
Web: www.nh.gov
Division of Vital Records Administration
71 S Fruit St. Concord NH 03301 603-271-4650 271-3447 339-30
Web: www.sos.nh.gov/vitalrecords
Education Dept 101 Pleasant St. Concord NH 03301 603-271-3494 271-1953 339-30
Web: www.education.nh.gov
Emergency Management Office
33 Hazen Dr. Concord NH 03305 603-271-2231 223-3609 339-30
TF: 800-735-2964 ■ *Web:* www.nh.gov
Employment Security 32 S Main St. Concord NH 03301 603-224-3311 228-4145 259
TF: 800-852-3400 ■ *Web:* www.nh.gov
Environmental Services Dept
29 Hazen Dr PO Box 95 Concord NH 03301 603-271-3503 339-30
TF: 866-429-9278 ■ *Web:* des.nh.gov
Fish & Game Dept 11 Hazen Dr. Concord NH 03301 603-271-3421 271-5829 339-30
Web: www.wildlife.state.nh.us
General Court 107 N Main St. Concord NH 03301 603-271-2154 339-30
Web: gencourt.state.nh.us
Governor
State House 107 N Main St Rm 208 Concord NH 03301 603-271-2121 271-7680 339-30
TF: 800-852-3456 ■ *Web:* www.nh.gov

Historical Resources Div
19 Pillsbury St 2nd Fl Concord NH 03301 603-271-3483 271-3433 339-30
Web: www.nh.gov/nhdhr
Housing Finance Authority
32 Constitution Dr. Bedford NH 03110 603-472-8623 472-8729 339-30
TF: 800-439-7247 ■ *Web:* www.nhhfa.org
Insurance Dept 21 S Fruit St Ste 14. Concord NH 03301 603-271-2261 271-1406 339-30
Web: www.nh.gov/insurance
Joint Board of Licensure & Certification
121 S Fruit St. Concord NH 03301 603-271-2152 339-30
Web: www.nh.gov
Lottery Commission 14 Integra Dr. Concord NH 03301 603-271-3391 271-1160 452
TF: 800-852-3324 ■ *Web:* www.nhlottery.com
Motor Vehicles Div 23 Hazen Dr Concord NH 03305 603-227-4000 339-30
Web: nh.gov/safety/divisions/dmv
Parks & Recreation Div
172 Pembroke Rd Concord NH 03301 603-271-3556 271-3553 339-30
Web: www.nhstateparks.org
Public Utilities Commission
21 S Fruit St Ste 10 Concord NH 03301 603-271-2431 271-3878 339-30
TF Consumer Assistance: 800-852-3793 ■ *Web:* www.puc.state.nh.us
Real Estate Commission
121 S Fruit St Rm 434 Concord NH 03301 603-271-2152 339-30
Web: www.nh.gov/nhrec
Resources & Economic Development Dept
PO Box 1856 Concord NH 03302 603-271-2411 271-2629 339-30
Web: www.dred.state.nh.us
Revenue Administration Dept
109 Pleasant St Concord NH 03301 603-230-5000 230-5945 339-30
Web: www.revenue.nh.gov
Secretary of State
107 N Main St State House Rm 204 Concord NH 03301 603-271-3242 271-6316 339-30
Web: www.sos.nh.gov
State Government Information 64 S St. Concord NH 03301 603-271-1110 339-30
Web: www.nh.gov
State Office of Veterans Services
275 Chestnut St Rm 517 Manchester NH 03101 603-624-9230 624-9236 339-30
TF: 800-735-2964 ■ *Web:* www.nh.gov
State Police Div 33 Hazen Dr. Concord NH 03305 603-223-8813 339-30
Web: nh.gov/safety/divisions/nhsp
Supreme Court 1 Charles Doe Dr Concord NH 03301 603-271-2646 339-30
Web: www.courts.state.nh.us
Teacher Credentialing Bureau
101 Pleasant St Concord NH 03301 603-271-3494 271-1953 339-30
TF: 866-444-4211 ■ *Web:* www.education.nh.gov
Transportation Dept PO Box 483 Concord NH 03302 603-271-3734 271-3914 339-30
Web: www.nh.gov/dot
Travel & Tourism Development Office
172 Pembroke Rd Concord NH 03302 603-271-2665 271-6870 339-30
Web: www.visitnh.gov
Treasury Dept 25 Capitol St Rm 121 Concord NH 03301 603-271-2621 271-3922 339-30
TF: 800-791-0920 ■ *Web:* www.nh.gov/treasury
Victims' Assistance Commission
33 Capitol St Concord NH 03301 603-271-1284 223-6291 339-30
TF: 800-300-4500 ■ *Web:* www.nh.gov
Vocational Rehabilitation Office
21 S Fruit St Ste 20 Concord NH 03301 603-271-3471 271-7095 339-30
TF: 800-299-1647 ■ *Web:* www.education.nh.gov
Weights & Measures Bureau PO Box 2042 Concord NH 03302 603-271-3685 271-1109 339-30
Web: agriculture.nh.gov
New Hampshire Assn of Realtors
115A Airport Rd Concord NH 03301 603-225-5549 228-0385 656
TF: 800-335-4862 ■ *Web:* nhar.org
New Hampshire Ball Bearings Inc
175 Jaffrey Rd. Peterborough NH 03458 603-924-3311 924-4419* 75
**Fax: Cust Svc* ■ *Web:* www.nhbb.com
New Hampshire Bar Assn
2 Pillsbury St Ste 300. Concord NH 03301 603-224-6942 224-2910 72
TF: 800-541-2195 ■ *Web:* www.nhbar.org
New Hampshire Bill Status
107 N Main St Concord NH 03301 603-271-2121 271-7680 433
Web: www.gencourt.state.nh.us
New Hampshire Catholic Charities Inc
215 Myrtle St Manchester NH 03104 603-669-3030 626-1252 48-20
TF: 800-562-5249 ■ *Web:* www.cc-nh.org
New Hampshire Correctional Industries (NHCI)
105 Pleasant St PO Box 1806. Concord NH 03302 603-271-5600 271-5643 630
Web: www.nh.gov/nhdoc
New Hampshire Democratic Party
105 N State St. Concord NH 03301 603-225-6899 616-1
TF: 800-559-5764 ■ *Web:* nhdp.org
New Hampshire Dental Society
23 S State St. Concord NH 03301 603-225-5961 226-4880 227
TF: 800-244-5961 ■ *Web:* www.nhds.org
New Hampshire Distributors Inc
65 Regional Dr Concord NH 03301 603-224-9991 224-0415 81-1
TF: 800-852-3781 ■ *Web:* nhdist.com
New Hampshire Div of Travel & Tourism Development
172 Pembroke Rd PO Box 1856 Concord NH 03302 603-271-2665 271-6870 206
TF: 800-262-6660 ■ *Web:* www.visitnh.gov
New Hampshire Educator Magazine
9 S Spring St Concord NH 03301 603-224-7751 224-2648 457-8
TF: 866-556-3264 ■ *Web:* www.neanh.org
New Hampshire Electric Co-op
579 Tenney Mtn Hwy Plymouth NH 03264 603-536-1800 536-8682 245
TF: 800-698-2007 ■ *Web:* www.nhec.com
New Hampshire Film Festival
28 Chestnut St Portsmouth NH 03801 603-436-2400 282
Web: www.nhfilmfestival.com
New Hampshire Historical Society
30 Pk St Concord NH 03301 603-228-6688 520
Web: www.nhhistory.org
New Hampshire Hospital 36 Clinton St. Concord NH 03301 603-271-5200 271-5395 374-5
TF: 800-735-2964 ■ *Web:* www.dhhs.nh.gov
New Hampshire Institute of Art
148 Concord St Manchester NH 03104 603-623-0313 647-0658 520
TF: 866-241-4918 ■ *Web:* www.nhia.edu

Name / Address	Phone	Fax	Class
New Hampshire Medical Society			
7 N State St. Concord NH 03301	603-224-1909	226-2432	474
TF: 800-564-1909 ■ *Web:* www.nhms.org			
New Hampshire Music Festival Orchestra			
52 Symphony Ln Center Harbor NH 03226	603-279-3300		573-3
TF: 800-851-8175 ■ *Web:* www.nhmf.org			
New Hampshire Nurses Assn (NHNA)			
210 N State St Ste 1A Concord NH 03301	603-225-3783	228-6672	533
Web: www.nhnurses.org			
New Hampshire Plastics Inc			
1 Bouchard St. Manchester NH 03103	603-669-8523	622-4888	600
TF: 800-258-3036 ■ *Web:* www.nhplastics.com			
New Hampshire Public Interest Research Group (NHPIRG)			
30 S Main St Ste 301-A Concord NH 03301	603-229-1343		633
Web: www.nhpirg.org			
New Hampshire Public Television (NHPTV)			
268 Mast Rd. Durham NH 03824	603-868-1100	868-7552	632
TF: 800-639-8408 ■ *Web:* www.nhptv.org			
New Hampshire Republican State Committee			
10 Water St. Concord NH 03301	603-225-9341	225-7498	616-2
Web: nh.gop			
New Hampshire State Library 20 Pk St Concord NH 03301	603-271-2144	271-2205	434-5
TF: 800-639-5290 ■ *Web:* www.nh.gov			
New Hampshire State Port Authority			
555 Market St. Portsmouth NH 03801	603-436-8500		618
Web: www.portsmouthnh.com			
New Hampshire State Prison			
281 N State St PO Box 14. Concord NH 03302	603-271-1801		213
Web: www.nh.gov/nhdoc/facilities/concord.html			
New Hampshire State Prison for Women			
317 Mast Rd. Goffstown NH 03045	603-668-6137		213
New Hampshire Veterans Home			
139 Winter St Tilton NH 03276	603-527-4400	527-4402	793
TF: 800-735-2964 ■ *Web:* www.nh.gov/veterans			
New Hampton Nursing & Rehabilitation Ctr			
703 S Fourth Ave New Hampton IA 50659	641-394-4153		450
Web: www.nhnrc.com			
New Hampton School 70 Main St New Hampton NH 03256	603-677-3400		622
Web: www.newhampton.org			
New Hanover Correctional Ctr			
330 Division Dr Wilmington NC 28402	910-251-2666	251-2670	213
Web: www.ncdps.gov			
New Hanover County Public Library			
201 Chestnut St Wilmington NC 28401	910-798-6301	798-6312	434-3
Web: www.nhclibrary.org			
New Hanover Regional Medical Ctr			
2131 S 17th St. Wilmington NC 28401	910-343-7000		374-3
TF: 877-228-8135 ■ *Web:* www.nhrmc.org			
New Haven Advocate			
900 Chapel St Ste 1100 New Haven CT 06510	203-789-0010		532-5
Web: www.ct.com			
New Haven Ballet 70 Audubon St. New Haven CT 06510	203-782-9038		573-1
Web: www.newhavenballet.org			
New Haven City Hall 165 Church St. New Haven CT 06510	203-946-8200	946-7683	337
Web: www.cityofnewhaven.com			
New Haven Correctional Ctr			
245 Whalley Ave New Haven CT 06511	203-974-4111		213
New Haven Free Public Library			
133 Elm St New Haven CT 06510	203-946-8130	946-8140	434-3
Web: www.cityofnewhaven.com/library			
New Haven Hotel 229 George St. New Haven CT 06510	203-498-3100	498-0911	379
TF: 800-644-6835 ■ *Web:* www.newhavenhotel.com			
New Haven Legal Assistance Association Inc			
426 State St New Haven CT 06510	203-946-4811		428
TF: 877-829-5500 ■ *Web:* nhlegal.org			
New Haven Premier Suites Hotel			
3 Long Wharf Dr New Haven CT 06511	203-777-5337	777-2808	379
Web: newhavenvillagesuites.com			
New Haven Register 40 Sargent Dr New Haven CT 06511	203-789-5200		532-2
TF: 888-969-0949 ■ *Web:* www.nhregister.com			
New Haven Symphony Orchestra			
4 Hamilton St New Haven CT 06511	203-865-0831	865-0845	573-3
Web: www.newhavensymphony.org			
New Haven Terminal Inc			
100 Waterfront St New Haven CT 06512	203-468-0805	469-6374	465
New Haven Unified School District			
34200 Alvarado Niles Rd Union City CA 94587	510-471-1100		685
Web: www.mynhusd.org			
New Heights Restaurant			
2317 Calvert St NW Washington DC 20008	202-234-4110		671
Web: www.newheightsrestaurant.com			
New High Glass Inc 12713 SW 125th Ave Miami FL 33186	305-232-0840		331
Web: www.newhighglass.net			
New Holland Church Furniture			
313 Prospect St PO Box 217 New Holland PA 17557	800-648-9663	354-2481*	319-3
**Fax Area Code:* 717 ■ *TF:* 800-648 9663 ■ *Web:* www.newhollandwood.com			
New Holland Engineering			
43 E Front St. New Holland OH 43145	740-495-5200		261
TF: 800-734-8155 ■ *Web:* gutterhangers.net			
New Home Trends Inc 4314 148th St SE Bothell WA 98012	425-742-8040		466
Web: www.newhometrends.com			
New Hong Kong Restaurant 2623 E 11th St. Tulsa OK 74104	918-585-5328		671
New Hope Housing Inc			
8407-E Richmond Hwy. Alexandria VA 22309	703-799-2293		48-20
Web: www.newhopehousing.org			
New Horizon Kids Quest Inc			
3405 Annapolis Ln N Ste 100. Plymouth MN 55447	800-941-1007	383-6101*	148
**Fax Area Code:* 763 ■ *TF:* 800-941-1007 ■ *Web:* www.kidsquest.com			
New Horizons Baking Co Inc			
211 Woodlawn Ave. Norwalk OH 44857	419-663-6432		68
Web: www.genesisbaking.com			
New Horizons Computer Learning Centers Inc			
1900 S State College Blvd Ste 450 Anaheim CA 92806	714-940-8000		764
TF: 888-236-3625 ■ *Web:* www.newhorizons.com			
New Horizons Diagnostics Corp			
9110 Red Branch Rd. Columbia MD 21045	410-992-9357	992-0328	231
TF: 800-888-5015 ■ *Web:* www.nhdiag.com			
New Horizons Picture Corp			
11600 San Vicente Blvd Los Angeles CA 90049	310-820-6733		514
New Horizons RV Corp			
2401 Lacy Dr Junction City KS 66441	785-238-7575		120
TF: 800-235-3140 ■ *Web:* www.horizonsrv.com			
New Horizons Worldwide Inc			
1900 S State College Blvd Ste 450. Anaheim CA 92806	888-236-3625		764
TF: 888-236-3625 ■ *Web:* www.newhorizons.com			
New ICM 220 Sam Bishkin El Campo TX 77437	979-578-0543	578-0503	155-4
TF: 800-987-9008 ■ *Web:* www.newicm.com			
New Idea Engineering Inc			
2784 Homestead Rd Ste 173 Santa Clara CA 95051	408-446-3460		5
TF: 866-433-2364 ■ *Web:* www.ideaeng.com			
New Jersey			
Administrative Office of the Cts			
25 Market St PO Box 037 Trenton NJ 08625	609-984-0275	984-6968	339-31
Web: www.judiciary.state.nj.us			
Agriculture Dept PO Box 330. Trenton NJ 08625	609-292-3976	292-3978	339-31
Web: www.state.nj.us/agriculture			
Arts Council 225 W State St PO Box 306 Trenton NJ 08625	609-292-6130	989-1440	339-31
Web: nj.gov			
Attorney General 25 Market St Fl 8 Trenton NJ 08625	609-292-4925	292-3508	339-31
Web: www.state.nj.us			
Banking & Insurance Dept			
20 W State St PO Box 325. Trenton NJ 08625	609-292-7272	984-5273	339-31
TF: 800-446-7467 ■ *Web:* www.state.nj.us/dobi			
Bill Status			
State House Annex PO Box 068. Trenton NJ 08625	609-292-4840	777-2440	433
TF: 800-792-8630 ■ *Web:* www.njleg.state.nj.us			
Board of Public Utilities			
44 S Clinton Ave Newark NJ 07102	800-624-0241	648-4195*	339-31
**Fax Area Code:* 973 ■ *TF:* 800-624-0241 ■ *Web:* www.state.nj.us/bpu			
Child Support Office			
175 S Broad St PO Box 8068. Trenton NJ 08650	877-655-4371		339-31
TF: 877-655-4371 ■ *Web:* www.njchildsupport.org			
Commerce Economic Growth & Tourism Commission			
20 W State St PO Box 820. Trenton NJ 08625	609-777-0885	777-4097	339-31
Web: www.state.nj.us/commerce			
Consumer Affairs Div 124 Halsey St Newark NJ 07102	973-504-6200	273-8035	339-31
TF: 800-242-5846 ■ *Web:* www.njconsumeraffairs.gov			
Economic Development Authority			
PO Box 990 Trenton NJ 08625	609-858-6700		339-31
Web: www.njeda.com			
Education Dept PO Box 500. Trenton NJ 08625	877-900-6960		339-31
TF: 877-900-6960 ■ *Web:* www.state.nj.us/education			
Emergency Management Office			
PO Box 7068 West Trenton NJ 08628	609-882-2000		339-31
Web: www.njsp.org/feedback.html			
Environmental Protection Dept			
401 E State St PO Box 402 Trenton NJ 08625	609-292-2885	292-7695	339-31
Web: www.state.nj.us/dep			
Ethical Standards Commission			
28 W State St Rm 1407 PO Box 082 Trenton NJ 08625	609-292-1892	633-9252	265
TF: 888-223-1355 ■ *Web:* www.state.nj.us/lps/ethics			
Fish Game & Wildlife Div PO Box 400. Trenton NJ 08625	609-292-9410	984-1414	339-31
Web: www.state.nj.us/dep/fgw			
Governor 125 W State St PO Box 001 Trenton NJ 08625	609-292-6000	292-3454	339-31
Web: www.state.nj.us/governor			
Health & Senior Services Dept			
PO Box 360 Trenton NJ 08625	609-292-7837	984-5474	339-31
Web: www.state.nj.us/health			
Higher Education Commission			
20 W State St FL 4 PO Box 542. Trenton NJ 08625	609-292-4310	292-7225	339-31
Web: www.state.nj.us			
Higher Education Student Assistance Authority			
4 Quakerbridge Plaza PO Box 540 Trenton NJ 08625	609-584-4480		725
TF: 800-792-8670 ■ *Web:* www.hesaa.org			
Historical Commission			
225 W State St PO Box 305. Trenton NJ 08625	609-292-6062	633-8168	339-31
Web: www.state.nj.us			
Housing & Mortgage Finance Agency			
637 S Clinton Ave Trenton NJ 08611	609-278-7400		339-31
Web: www.state.nj.us/dca/hmfa			
Human Services Dept			
222 S Warren St PO Box 700. Trenton NJ 08625	609-292-3717	292-3824	339-31
Web: www.state.nj.us/humanservices			
Information Technology Office			
PO Box 212 Trenton NJ 08625	609-633-8975		339-31
Web: www.state.nj.us/it			
Labor & Workforce Development Dept			
1 John Fitch Plaza Third Fl PO Box 110ÿ. Trenton NJ 08625	609-292-2305	695-1174	339-31
Web: lwd.state.nj.us			
Lottery 1333 Brunswick Avenue Cir. Trenton NJ 08648	609-599-5800	599-5935	452
Web: www.state.nj.us			
Mental Health Services Div PO Box 272 Trenton NJ 08625	609-777-0700		339-31
TF: 800-382-6717 ■ *Web:* www.state.nj.us/humanservices/dmhs			
Military & Veterans' Affairs Dept			
101 Eggert Crossing Rd. Lawrenceville NJ 08648	609-530-4600	530-7100	339-31
TF: 800-624-0508 ■ *Web:* www.state.nj.us			
Motor Vehicle Commission			
225 E State St PO Box 160 Trenton NJ 08666	609-292-6500		339-31
Web: www.state.nj.us/mvc			
Parks & Forestry Div PO Box 404 Trenton NJ 08625	609-984-0370		339-31
TF: 800-843-6420 ■ *Web:* www.state.nj.us/dep/parksandforests			
Parole Board PO Box 862 Trenton NJ 08625	609-292-4257	943-4769	339-31
Web: www.state.nj.us/parole			
Secretary of State			
125 W State St PO Box 300 Trenton NJ 08625	609-984-1900	292-7665	339-31
Web: www.state.nj.us			
Securities Bureau			
153 Halsey St Sixth Fl 6th Fl Newark NJ 07102	973-504-3600		339-31
TF: 866-446-8378 ■ *Web:* www.state.nj.us/lps/ca/bos			
State Athletic Control Board			
25 Market St 1st Fl W Wing. Trenton NJ 08625	609-292-0317	292-3756	712
Web: www.state.nj.us/lps/sacb			
State Legislature			
State House Annex PO Box 068. Trenton NJ 08625	609-292-4840		339-31
Web: www.njleg.state.nj.us			
State Medical Examiner PO Box 094 Trenton NJ 08625	609-984-4883		339-31
Web: www.me.nj.gov			

	City	State	ZIP	Phone	Fax	Class
State Police PO Box 7068 Web: www.state.nj.us/lps/njsp	West Trenton	NJ	08628	609-882-2000		339-31
Supreme Court PO Box 970 Web: www.judiciary.state.nj.us/supreme	Trenton	NJ	08625	609-984-7791	396-9056	339-31
Transportation Dept 1035 PkwyAve PO Box 600 Web: www.state.nj.us/transportation	Trenton	NJ	08625	609-530-2000		339-31
Travel & Tourism Div 225 W State St PO Box 460 TF: 800-847-4865 ■ Web: www.visitnj.org	Trenton	NJ	08625	609-599-6540		339-31
Treasurer PO Box 002 Web: www.state.nj.us/treasury	Trenton	NJ	08625	609-292-6748		339-31
Victims of Crime Compensation Board 50 Pk Pl TF: 877-658-2221 ■ Web: www.nj.gov/oag/njvictims	Newark	NJ	07102	973-648-2107	648-3937	339-31
Vital Statistics Bureau 140 E Front St Web: www.state.nj.us	Trenton	NJ	08608	609-586-9316		339-31
Vocational Rehabilitation Services Div (DVRS) 1 John Fitch Way PO Box 110 Web: jobs4jersey.com	Trenton	NJ	08625	609-292-5987	292-8347	339-31
Weights & Measures Office 1261 US Hwy 1 Ste 9 Web: www.njconsumeraffairs.gov/OWM	Avenel	NJ	07001	732-815-4840	382-5298	339-31
Workers' Compensation Div PO Box 381 Web: lwd.dol.state.nj.us/labor/wc/workers/workers_index.html	Trenton	NJ	08625	609-292-2515	633-7783	339-31
Workforce New Jersey 1 John Fitch Plaza Fl 3 Web: lwd.dol.state.nj.us	Trenton	NJ	08611	609-292-2305	695-1174	259
New Jersey Assn of Realtors 295 Pierson Ave Web: www.njrealtor.com	Edison	NJ	08837	732-494-5616	494-4723	656
New Jersey Ballet Co 15 Microlab Rd TF: 800-650-0246 ■ Web: www.njballet.org	Livingston	NJ	07039	973-597-9600	597-9442	573-1
New Jersey Business Forms Manufacturing Co 55 W Sheffield Ave TF: 800-466-6523 ■ Web: www.njbf.com	Englewood	NJ	07631	201-569-4500		110
New Jersey Business Magazine 310 Passaic Ave Web: www.njbmagazine.com	Fairfield	NJ	07004	973-882-5004	882-4648	457-5
New Jersey City University 2039 JFK Blvd TF: 888-441-6528 ■ Web: www.njcu.edu	Jersey City	NJ	07305	201-200-2000	200-2044	166
New Jersey Convention & Exposition Ctr 97 Sunfield Ave TF: 800-367-0070 ■ Web: www.njexpocenter.com	Edison	NJ	08837	732-417-1400		205
New Jersey Democratic State Committee 196 W State St TF: 800-995-3386 ■ Web: www.njdems.org	Trenton	NJ	08608	609-392-3367	396-4778	616-1
New Jersey Dental Assn 1 Dental Plaza PO Box 6020 Web: www.njda.org	North Brunswick	NJ	08902	732-821-9400	821-1082	227
New Jersey Firemen's Home 565 Lathrop Ave TF: 800-852-0137 ■ Web: www.njfh.org	Boonton	NJ	07005	973-334-0024		672
New Jersey Herald 2 Spring St TF: 800-424-3725 ■ Web: www.njherald.com	Newton	NJ	07860	973-383-1500	383-8477	532-2
New Jersey Historical Society Museum 52 Pk Pl TF: 800-637-4636 ■ Web: www.jerseyhistory.org	Newark	NJ	07102	973-596-8500	596-6957	520
New Jersey Institute of Technology University Heights Web: www.njit.edu	Newark	NJ	07102	973-596-3000	596-3461	166
New Jersey Law Journal 238 Mulberry St Web: www.law.com	Newark	NJ	07102	973-642-0075		531-4
New Jersey Legal Copy Inc 501 King Ave TF: 800-426-7965 ■ Web: njlone.com	Cherry Hill	NJ	08002	856-910-0202		113
New Jersey Library Assn (NJLA) PO Box 1534 TF: 800-411-6493 ■ Web: www.njla.org	Trenton	NJ	08607	609-394-8032	394-8164	435
New Jersey Machine Inc 56 Etna Rd TF Sales: 800-432-2990 ■ Web: www.njmpackaging.com	Lebanon	NH	03766	603-448-0300	448-4810	547
New Jersey Manufacturers Insurance Co 301 Sullivan Way TF: 800-232-6600 ■ Web: www.njm.com	West Trenton	NJ	08628	609-883-1300	882-3457	391-4
New Jersey Medical School 185 S Orange Ave Web: njms.rutgers.edu	Newark	NJ	07103	973-972-4631	972-7986	167-2
New Jersey Medical Society 2 Princess Rd TF: 800-706-7893 ■ Web: www.msnj.org	Lawrenceville	NJ	08648	609-896-1766		474
New Jersey Monthly Magazine 55 Pk Pl PO Box 920 TF: 888-419-0419 ■ Web: www.njmonthly.com	Morristown	NJ	07963	973-539-8230	538-2953	457-22
New Jersey Natural Gas Co 1415 Wyckoff Rd TF: 800-221-0051 ■ Web: www.njresources.com	Wall	NJ	07719	732-938-1480	938-3154	538
New Jersey Nets Nets Champion Ctr 390 Murray Hill Pkwy TF: 800-346-6387 ■ Web: www.nba.com	East Rutherford	NJ	07073	201-935-8888		714-1
New Jersey Performing Arts Ctr 1 Ctr St TF: 888-466-5722 ■ Web: www.njpac.org	Newark	NJ	07102	973-642-8989	648-6724	572
New Jersey Pharmacists Assn 760 Alexander Rd PO Box 1 Web: njpharmacists.org	Princeton	NJ	08543	609-275-4246	275-4066	585
New Jersey Principals and Supervisors Assn 12 Centre Dr Web: www.njpsa.org	Monroe Township	NJ	08831	609-860-1200		474
New Jersey Resources Corp 1415 Wyckoff Rd NYSE: NJR ■ TF: 800-221-0051 ■ Web: www.njresources.com	Wall	NJ	07719	732-938-1000		360-5
New Jersey State Bar Assn 1 Constitution Sq New Jersey Law Ctr Web: tcms.njsba.com/PersonifyEbusiness/default.aspx	New Brunswick	NJ	08901	732-249-5000	249-2815	72
New Jersey State Chamber of Commerce 216 W State St Web: www.njchamber.com	Trenton	NJ	08608	609-989-7888	989-9696	140
New Jersey State Museum 205 W State St Web: www.state.nj.us/state/museum	Trenton	NJ	08625	609-292-6300	292-7636	520
New Jersey State Nurses Assn (NJSNA) 1479 Pennington Rd TF: 800-662-0108 ■ Web: www.njsna.org	Trenton	NJ	08618	609-883-5335	883-5343	533
New Jersey State Prison PO Box 861 Web: www.state.nj.us	Trenton	NJ	08625	609-292-9700		213
New Jersey Symphony Orchestra 60 Pk Pl TF: 800-653-8000 ■ Web: www.njsymphony.org	Newark	NJ	07102	973-624-3713	624-2115	573-3
New Jersey Transit Corp 1 Penn Plaza E TF Cust Svc: 800-772-3606 ■ Web: www.njtransit.com	Newark	NJ	07105	973-491-7000		468
New Jersey Veterinary Medical Assn 390 Amwell Rd Ste 402 Web: www.njvma.org	Hillsborough	NJ	08844	908-281-0918	450-1286	795
New Jersey Water Supply Authority Inc 1851 State Rt 31 Web: www.njwsa.org	Clinton	NJ	08809	908-638-6121		539
New Kent County 12001 Courthouse Cir PO Box 98 Web: www.co.new-kent.va.us	New Kent	VA	23124	804-966-9520	966-9528	338
New Landmark, The 5801 Duke St Web: www.landmarkmall.com	Alexandria	VA	22304	703-354-8405		460
New Leaders for New Schools 30 W 26th St 2nd Fl Web: www.newleaders.org	New York	NY	10010	646-792-1070		305
New Leaf Community Markets Inc 1101 Pacific Ave Web: www.newleaf.com	Santa Cruz	CA	95060	831-466-9060		345
New Leaf Paper LLC 510 16th St Ste 520 Web: www.newleafpaper.com	Oakland	CA	94612	415-291-9210		554
New Leaf Publishing Group PO Box 726 TF: 800-999-3777 ■ Web: www.nlpg.com	Green Forest	AR	72638	870-438-5288		637-3
New Lenox Community Park District 1 Manor Dr TF: 800-870-3666 ■ Web: www.newlenoxparks.org	New Lenox	IL	60451	815-485-3584		31
New Lenox School District 122 (NLSD) 102 S Cedar Rd Web: www.nlsd122.org	New Lenox	IL	60451	815-485-2169		685
New Life Camp 701 Mayhew Rd Web: newlifecamp.org	Rose City	MI	48654	989-685-2949		239
New Life Industries Inc 140 Chappells Dairy Rd TF: 800-443-9523 ■ Web: www.newlifeshopper.com	Somerset	KY	42503	606-679-3616		687
New Life Service Co. 39 W Fifth St TF: 800-473-8222 ■ Web: www.nlsco.com	Eureka	CA	95501	707-444-8222		186
New London Nursing & Rehabilitation Ctr 1611 West Lakes Pkwy Web: careinitiatives.org	West Des Moines	IA	50266	319-367-5753		450
New Mather Metals Inc 326 Page Dr Web: www.newmathermetals.com	Franklin	KY	42134	270-598-5900		247
New Mee Fung 350 Booth St Web: newmeefung.com	Ottawa	ON	K1R7K1	613-567-8228		671
New Method Steel Stamps Inc 31313 Kendall Ave TF: 800-582-0199 ■ Web: www.newmethod.org	Fraser	MI	48026	586-293-0200	296-1900	467
New Mexico						
Administrative Office of the Cts 237 Don Gaspar St Web: www.nmcourts.com	Santa Fe	NM	87501	505-827-4800	827-4824	339-32
Adult Parole Board 4337 NM 14 PO Box 27116 Web: www.corrections.state.nm.us	Santa Fe	NM	87502	505-827-8645	827-8533	339-32
Aging Agency 2550 Cerrillos Rd PO Box 27118 TF: 800-432-2080 ■ Web: www.nmaging.state.nm.us	Santa Fe	NM	87505	505-476-4799	476-4836	339-32
Agriculture Dept 3190 S Espina PO Box 30005 Web: www.nmda.nmsu.edu	Las Cruces	NM	88003	575-646-3007	646-8120	339-32
Arts Div 407 Galisteo St Ste 270 TF: 800-879-4278 ■ Web: www.nmarts.org	Santa Fe	NM	87501	505-827-6490	827-6043	339-32
Attorney General 408 Galisteo St Web: www.nmag.gov	Santa Fe	NM	87501	505-490-4060	490-4883	339-32
Child Support Enforcement Div PO Box 25110 TF: 800-288-7207 ■ Web: www.hsd.state.nm.us/csed	Santa Fe	NM	87504	505-476-7207	476-7045	339-32
Children Youth & Families Dept PO Box 5160 TF: 800-610-7610 ■ Web: www.cyfd.org	Santa Fe	NM	87502	800-432-2075		339-32
Consumer Protection Div 408 Galisteo St Villagra Bldg PO Box 1508 TF: 844-255-9210 ■ Web: www.nmag.gov/consumer	Santa Fe	NM	87501	505-827-6000	490-4883	339-32
Corrections Dept (NMCD) 4337 NM 14 PO Box 27116 Web: www.corrections.state.nm.us	Santa Fe	NM	87502	505-827-8645	827-8533	339-32
Crime Victims Reparation Commission 6200 Uptown Blvd Ste 106 TF: 800-306-6262 ■ Web: www.cvrc.state.nm.us	Albuquerque	NM	87110	505-841-9432	841-9437	339-32
Department of Information Technology 715 Alta Vista St PO Box 22550 Web: www.doit.state.nm.us	Santa Fe	NM	87505	505-827-0000		339-32
Department of Veterans Services 5201 Eagle Rock Ave North E Web: www.dvs.state.nm.us	Albuquerque	NM	87113	505-383-2417	383-2413	339-32
Dept of Workforce Solutions 501 Mountain Rd NE PO Box 1928 Web: www.dws.state.nm.us	Albuquerque	NM	87102	505-843-1900	843-1990	339-32
Economic Development Dept PO Box 20003 TF: 800-374-3061 ■ Web: www.gonm.biz	Santa Fe	NM	87504	505-827-0300	827-0328	339-32
Education Dept 300 Don Gaspar St Web: www.sde.state.nm.us	Santa Fe	NM	87501	505-827-5800		339-32
Energy Minerals & Natural Resources Dept 1220 S St Francis Dr	Santa Fe	NM	87505	505-476-3200	476-3220	339-32

	Phone	Fax	Class
Environment Dept 1190 St Francis Dr Ste 4050 ....Santa Fe NM 87502 *TF:* 800-219-6157 ■ *Web:* www.nmenv.state.nm.us	505-827-2855		339-32
Ethics Administration 325 Don Gaspar St Ste 300 ....Santa Fe NM 87501 *TF:* 800-477-3632 ■ *Web:* www.sos.state.nm.us	505-827-3600		265
Finance & Administration Dept 407 Galisteo St ....Santa Fe NM 87501 *Web:* www.nmdfa.state.nm.us	505-827-4985	827-4984	339-32
Financial Institutions Div 2550 Cerrillos Rd 3rd Fl ....Santa Fe NM 87505 *Web:* www.rld.state.nm.us	505-476-4885	476-4670	339-32
Game & Fish Dept 1 Wildlife Way ....Santa Fe NM 87507 *Web:* www.wildlife.state.nm.us	505-476-8000	476-8116	339-32
Governor State Capitol Bldg 490 Santa Fe Trail Rm 400..................Santa Fe NM 87501 *Web:* www.governor.state.nm.us	505-476-2200		339-32
Health Dept 1190 S St Francis Dr Ste N-4100 ....Santa Fe NM 87505 *Web:* nmhealth.org	505-827-2613		339-32
Higher Education Dept 2048 Galisteo St ....Santa Fe NM 87505 *TF:* 800-279-9777 ■ *Web:* www.hed.state.nm.us	505-476-8400		339-32
Highway & Transportation Dept (NMDOT) 1120 Cerrillos Rd PO Box 1149..............Santa Fe NM 87504 *TF General:* 800-432-4269 ■ *Web:* www.dot.state.nm.us	505-827-5100		339-32
Historic Preservation Div Bataan Memorial Bldg 407 Galisteo St Ste 236 ....Santa Fe NM 87501 *Web:* www.nmhistoricpreservation.org	505-827-6320	827-6338	339-32
Human Services Dept (NMHSD) PO Box 2348..............................Santa Fe NM 87504 *TF:* 888-997-2583 ■ *Web:* www.hsd.state.nm.us	505-827-3100	827-3185	339-32
Legislative Council Services 625 Don Gaspar Ave ....Santa Fe NM 87501 *Web:* www.nmlegis.gov	505-986-4600	986-4680	433
Lieutenant Governor 490 Old Santa Fe Trail Rm 417 ....Santa Fe NM 87501 *Web:* www.ltgov.state.nm.us	505-476-2250	476-2257	339-32
Lottery 4511 Osuna Rd NE PO Box 93190........ Albuquerque NM 87199 *TF:* 800-572-1142 ■ *Web:* www.nmlottery.com	505-342-7600	342-7511	452
Medical Board 2055 S Pacheco Bldg 400........Santa Fe NM 87505 *Web:* www.nmmb.state.nm.us	505-476-7220	476-7237	339-32
Mortgage Finance Authority 344 Fourth St SW .... Albuquerque NM 87102 *TF:* 800-444-6880 ■ *Web:* www.housingnm.org	505-843-6880	243-3289	339-32
Professional (Educator) Licensure Unit 300 Don Gaspar St Jerry Apodaca Education Bldg...............Santa Fe NM 87501 *Web:* www.ped.state.nm.us	505-827-6581	827-4148	339-32
Public Accountancy Board 5200 Oakland Ave NE # C .... Albuquerque NM 87109 *Web:* www.rld.state.nm.us	505-222-9850		339-32
Public Regulation Commission 1120 Paseo De Peralta PO Box 1269.........Santa Fe NM 87504 *Web:* www.nmprc.state.nm.us	505-827-4084		339-32
Public Safety Dept 4491 Cerrillos Rd............Santa Fe NM 87507 *Web:* www.dps.state.nm.us	505-827-9000		339-32
Racing Commission 4900 Alameda Blvd NE ....Albuquerque NM 87113 *Web:* www.nmrc.state.nm.us	505-222-0700	222-0713	712
Regulation & Licensing Dept Toney Anaya Bldg 2550 Cerrillos Rd ....Santa Fe NM 87505 *Web:* www.rld.state.nm.us	505-476-4500	476-4511	339-32
Secretary of State 325 Don Gaspar Ste 300 ....Santa Fe NM 87503 *TF:* 800-477-3632 ■ *Web:* www.sos.state.nm.us	505-827-3600	827-8081	339-32
Securities Div 2550 Cerrillos Rd 3rd Fl ....Santa Fe NM 87505 *Web:* www.rld.state.nm.us/Securities	505-476-4580	984-0617	339-32
Standards & Consumers Services Div MSC 3170 PO Box 30005 ....Las Cruces NM 88003 *Web:* www.nmda.nmsu.edu	575-646-1616	646-2361	339-32
State Legislature State Capitol Rm 100.......................Santa Fe NM 87501 *Web:* www.nmlegis.gov	505-986-4751		339-32
State Parks Div 1220 S St Francis Dr ....Santa Fe NM 87505 *TF:* 888-667-2757 ■ *Web:* www.emnrd.state.nm.us/SPD	505-476-3355		339-32
State Police Div 4491 Cerrillos Rd.............Santa Fe NM 87507 *Web:* www.nmsp.dps.state.nm.us	505-827-9000		339-32
Supreme Court 237 Don Gaspar Ave Rm 104.................Santa Fe NM 87501 *Web:* nmsupremecourt.nmcourts.gov	505-827-4860		339-32
Taxation & Revenue Dept 1100 S St Francis Dr.......................Santa Fe NM 87504 *Web:* www.tax.newmexico.gov	505-827-0700		339-32
Tourism Dept 491 Old Santa Fe Trail.........Santa Fe NM 87501 *TF:* 800-545-2070 ■ *Web:* www.newmexico.org	505-827-7400	827-7402	339-32
Treasurer 2055 S Pacheco St Ste 100&200.............Santa Fe NM 87505 *Web:* www.nmsto.gov	505-995-1120		339-32
Vital Records & Health Statistics Bureau 1105 S St Francis Dr.......................Santa Fe NM 87502 *TF:* 866-534-0051 ■ *Web:* nmhealth.org	505-827-0121		339-32
Vocational Rehabilitation Div 435 St Michaels Dr Bldg D ....Santa Fe NM 87505 *TF:* 800-224-7005 ■ *Web:* www.dvrgetsjobs.com	505-954-8500	954-8562	339-32
Workers' Compensation Admin 2410 Ctr Ave SE PO Box 27198.......... Albuquerque NM 87125 *TF:* 800-255-7965 ■ *Web:* www.workerscomp.state.nm.us	505-841-6000		339-32
New Mexico Assn of Commerce & Industry (ACI) 2201 Buena Vista Dr SE Ste 410 Ste 410..... Albuquerque NM 87106 *Web:* www.nmaci.org	505-842-0644	842-0734	140
New Mexico Behavioral Health Institute 3695 Hot Springs Blvd..................... Las Vegas NM 87701 **Fax:* Admissions ■ *TF:* 800-446-5970 ■ *Web:* nmhealth.org/about/ofm/ltcf/nmbhi	505-454-2100	454-5172*	374-5

	Phone	Fax	Class
New Mexico Democratic Party (DPNM) 8214 Second St NW ste A................Albuquerque NM 87114 *Web:* www.dpnm.net	505-830-3650	830-3645	616-1
New Mexico Dental Assn 9201 Montgomery Blvd NE Ste 601.........Albuquerque NM 87111 *TF:* 888-787-1722 ■ *Web:* www.nmdental.org	505-294-1368	294-9958	227
New Mexico Educational Retirement Board 701 Camino de Los Marquez PO Box 26129 ......Santa Fe NM 87502 *TF:* 866-691-2345 ■ *Web:* www.nmerb.org	505-827-8030		528
New Mexico Farm & Ranch Heritage Museum 4100 Dripping Springs Rd ....Las Cruces NM 88011 *TF:* 800-545-9011 ■ *Web:* www.nmfarmandranchmuseum.org	575-522-4100	522-3085	520
New Mexico Highlands University PO Box 9000 .... Las Vegas NM 87701 *TF:* 877-850-9064 ■ *Web:* www.nmhu.edu	505-425-7511	454-3552	166
New Mexico Holocaust & Intolerance Museum & Study Ctr 616 Central Ave SW ....Albuquerque NM 87102 *Web:* www.nmholocaustmuseum.org	505-247-0606		520
New Mexico Institute of Mining & Technology (NMT) 801 Leroy Pl..............................Socorro NM 87801 *TF Admissions:* 800-428-8324 ■ *Web:* www.nmt.edu	505-835-5434		166
New Mexico Junior College 1 Thunderbird Cir............................ Hobbs NM 88240 *TF:* 800-657-6260 ■ *Web:* www.nmjc.edu	505-392-4510		162
New Mexico Legal Aid 301 Gold Ave SW Ste 101 .... Albuquerque NM 87102 *Web:* www.nmlegalaid.org	505-243-7871		445
New Mexico Lions Eye Bank 2501 Yale Blvd SE Ste 100................ Albuquerque NM 87106 *TF:* 888-616-3937 ■ *Web:* www.nmleb.org	505-266-3937		269
New Mexico Magazine PO Box 12002 ....Santa Fe NM 87504 **Fax Area Code:* 505 ■ *TF:* 800-898-6639 ■ *Web:* www.newmexico.org/nmmagazine	800-898-6639	827-6496*	457-22
New Mexico Medical Society (NMMS) 316 Osuna Rd NE Ste 501 .... Albuquerque NM 87107 *TF:* 800-748-1596 ■ *Web:* www.nmms.org	505-828-0237	828-0336	474
New Mexico Museum of Art 107 W Palace Ave...........................Santa Fe NM 87501 *TF:* 877-567-7380 ■ *Web:* www.nmartmuseum.org	505-476-5072	476-5076	520
New Mexico Museum of Natural History & Science 1801 Mtn Rd NW .... Albuquerque NM 87104 *Web:* www.nmnaturalhistory.org	505-841-2800	841-2866	520
New Mexico Museum of Space History Top of Hwy 2001 ....Alamogordo NM 88311 *TF:* 877-333-6589 ■ *Web:* www.nmspacemuseum.org	575-437-2840	434-2245	520
New Mexico Mutual PO Box 27825......... Albuquerque NM 87125 *TF:* 800-788-8851 ■ *Web:* www.nmmcc.com	505-345-7260	345-0656	391-4
New Mexico Newspapers Inc PO Box 450 .... Farmington NM 87499 *Web:* www.daily-times.com	505-325-4545	564-4630	637-8
New Mexico Pharmacists Assn (NMPhA) 2716 San Pedro Dr NE # C.................Albuquerque NM 87110 *Web:* www.nmpharmacy.org	505-265-8729		585
New Mexico Public Interest Research Group (NMPIRG) PO Box 40173 .... Albuquerque NM 87196 *Web:* www.nmpirg.org	505-254-1244		633
New Mexico Republican Party (RPNM) 5150-A San Francisco Rd NE PO Box 94083 .. Albuquerque NM 87109 *Web:* newmexico.gop	505-298-3662		616-2
New Mexico State Fair 300 San Pedro NE .... Albuquerque NM 87108 *TF:* 800-725-2477 ■ *Web:* www.exponm.com	505-222-9700		642
New Mexico State Investment Council 41 Plaza la Prensa ....Santa Fe NM 87507 *TF:* 800-489-8536 ■ *Web:* www.sic.state.nm.us	505-476-9500		401
New Mexico State University (NMSU) MSC-3A PO Box 30001 ....Las Cruces NM 88003 **Fax:* Admissions ■ *TF Admissions:* 800-662-6678 ■ *Web:* www.nmsu.edu	575-646-3121	646-6330*	166
Alamogordo (NMSU-A) 2400 N Scenic Dr.....................Alamogordo NM 88310 *Web:* www.nmsua.edu	575-439-3600	439-3760	162
Carlsbad 1500 University Dr .... Carlsbad NM 88220 *TF:* 888-888-2199 ■ *Web:* carlsbad.nmsu.edu	575-234-9200		162
Grants 1500 Third St.......................... Grants NM 87020 **Fax:* Admissions ■ *Web:* www.grants.nmsu.edu	505-287-6678	287-2329*	162
New Mexico State University Museum Kent Hall PO Box 30001 MSC 3564..........Las Cruces NM 88003 *Web:* univmuseum.nmsu.edu	575-646-5161		520
New Mexico State Veterans Ctr 992 S Broadway St............. Truth or Consequences NM 87901 *TF:* 800-964-3976 ■ *Web:* nmhealth.org/about/ofm/ltcf/nmsvh	575-894-4200	894-4270	793
New Mexico Veterans Memorial 1100 Louisiana Blvd SE .... Albuquerque NM 87108 *Web:* nmvetsmemorial.org	505-256-2042		50-4
New Mexico Veterinary Medical Assn 60 Placitas Trls Rd .... Placitas NM 87043 *Web:* www.nmvma.org	505-867-6373	771-8963	795
New Mexico Women's Correctional Facility 1700 Old US Hwy PO Box 800................. Grants NM 87020 *Web:* cd.nm.gov	505-287-2941	285-6828	213
New Milford Block & Supply 574 Danbury Rd...........................New Milford CT 06776 *TF:* 800-724-1888 ■ *Web:* www.montfortgroup.com	860-355-1101	355-3772	183
New Millenium Directories 1630 S Galena Ave...........................Freeport IL 61032 *Web:* www.bigprintphonebook.com	815-233-5797		4
New Millenium Home Health 6031 Cleveland Ave .... Columbus OH 43231 *Web:* nmilleniumhomehealth.com	614-882-7782		363
New Moon Magazine PO Box 161287 .... Duluth MN 55816 *TF:* 800-381-4743 ■ *Web:* www.newmoon.com	218-878-9673		457-6
NEW MOViN 92.5, The 3650 131st Ave SE Ste 550 ....Bellevue WA 98006	425-653-9462		645
New Museum of Contemporary Art 235 Bowery...............................New York NY 10002 *TF:* 800-737-0702 ■ *Web:* www.newmuseum.org	212-219-1222		520
New Northwest Broadcasters 833 Gambell St..........................Anchorage AK 99501	907-344-4045		645-6
New Objective Inc 2 Constitution Way........... Woburn MA 01801 *TF:* 888-220-2998 ■ *Web:* www.newobjective.com	781-933-9560		419

	Phone	Fax	Class
New Omni Bank NA 1235 S Garfield Ave. Alhambra CA 91801 *Web:* newomnibank.com	626-284-5555		70
New Orange Hills 5017 E Chapman Ave Orange CA 92869 *Web:* www.neworangehills.com	714-997-7090	997-4631	450
New Orleans Baptist Theological Seminary 3939 Gentilly Blvd New Orleans LA 70126 *TF:* 800-662-8701 ■ *Web:* www.nobts.edu	504-282-4455	816-8023	167-3
New Orleans Chamber of Commerce 1515 Poydras St Ste 1010 New Orleans LA 70112 *Web:* www.neworleanschamber.org	504-799-4260	799-4259	139
New Orleans City Business 111 Veterans Memorial Blvd Ste 1440 Metairie LA 70005 *Web:* www.neworleanscitybusiness.com	504-834-9292	832-3550	457-5
New Orleans City Hall 1300 Perdido St New Orleans LA 70112 *TF:* 800-256-2748 ■ *Web:* www.nola.gov	504-658-4000	658-4938	337
New Orleans Cold Storage & Warehouse Company Inc (NOCS) 3411 JouRdan Rd New Orleans LA 70126 *Web:* www.nocs.com	504-944-4400		803-2
New Orleans Film Festival 900 Camp St. New Orleans LA 70130 *Web:* neworleansfilmsociety.org	504-309-6633	309-0923	282
New Orleans Firemens Federal Credit Union PO Box 689 Metairie LA 70004 *TF:* 800-647-1689 ■ *Web:* www.noffcu.org	504-889-9090	889-9082	219
New Orleans Hornets 1450 Poydras St. New Orleans LA 70113 *Web:* www.nba.com	504-593-4700		714-1
New Orleans Jazz National Historical Park 419 Decatur St New Orleans LA 70130 *TF:* 877-520-0677 ■ *Web:* www.nps.gov	504-589-4806	589-3865	564
New Orleans Magazine 110 Veterans Blvd Ste 123 Metairie LA 70005 *TF Edit:* 877-221-3512 ■ *Web:* www.myneworleans.com/new-orleans-magazine	504-828-1380	828-1385	457-22
New Orleans Metropolitan Convention & Visitors Bureau 2020 St Charles Ave New Orleans LA 70130 *TF:* 800-672-6124 ■ *Web:* www.neworleanscvb.com	504-566-5011	566-5046	206
New Orleans Museum of Art 1 Collins Diboll Cir New Orleans LA 70124 *TF:* 800-774-7394 ■ *Web:* www.noma.org	504-658-4100	658-4199	520
New Orleans Pharmacy Museum 514 Chartres St. New Orleans LA 70130 *TF:* 800-568-6968 ■ *Web:* www.pharmacymuseum.org	504-565-8027		520
New Orleans Saints 5800 Airline Dr. Metairie LA 70003 *Web:* www.neworleanssaints.com	504-733-0255	731-1782	715-3
New Orleans Zephyrs, The 6000 Airline Dr. Metairie LA 70003 *Web:* www.milb.com/index.jsp	504-734-5155		354
New Otani Kaimana Beach Hotel 2863 Kalakaua Ave Honolulu HI 96815 *TF:* 800-356-8264 ■ *Web:* www.kaimana.com	808-923-1555	922-9404	379
New Otani North America Reservation Ctr 120 S Los Angeles St Los Angeles CA 90012 *TF Cust Svc:* 800-421-8795 ■ *Web:* newotani.co.jp	213-629-1200	473-1416	376
New Park 1615 Pk St Hartford CT 06106	860-232-1565		671
New Peking 540 Westport Rd. Kansas City MO 64111 *Web:* newpekingkansas.com	816-531-6969	531-9188	671
New Penn Motor Express Inc 625 S Fifth Ave Lebanon PA 17042 *TF Cust Svc:* 800-285-5000 ■ *Web:* www.newpenn.com	717-274-2521	274-5593	780
New Perspective Productions 2949 Smallman St Pittsburgh PA 15201	412-681-1600		514
New Perspective Senior Living 7625 Golden Triangle Dr. Eden Prairie MN 55344 *Web:* www.npseniorliving.com	952-746-3630		793
New Philadelphia City School District (NPCS) 248 Front Ave SW New Philadelphia OH 44663 *Web:* www.npschools.org	330-364-0600	364-9310	186
New Pig Corp 1 Pork Ave. Tipton PA 16684 **Fax Area Code:* 800 ■ *TF:* 800-468-4647 ■ *Web:* www.newpig.com	814-684-0101	621-7447*	151
New Piper Aircraft Inc 2926 Piper Dr Vero Beach FL 32960 *Web:* www.piper.com	772-567-4361		20
NEW Plastics Corp 112 Fourth St. Luxemburg WI 54217 *TF:* 800-666-5207 ■ *Web:* www.newplasticscorp.com	920-845-2326	845-2439	98
New Pond Village 180 Main St. Walpole MA 02081 *Web:* www.norwoodma.brightviewseniorliving.com	508-660-1555	668-8893	672
New Process Steel Corp 1322 N Post Oak Houston TX 77055 *TF:* 800-392-4989 ■ *Web:* www.nps.cc/?pgid=home	713-686-9631	316-1128	492
New Product Insights Inc 433 Ward Pkwy. Kansas City MO 64112 *Web:* www.npinpi.com	816-582-8700		195
New Products Corp 448 N Shore Dr. Benton Harbor MI 49022	269-925-2161		308
New Pros Data Inc 155 Hidden Ravines Dr. Powell OH 43065 *TF:* 800-837-5478 ■ *Web:* www.newpros.com	740-201-0410		387
New Readers Press 104 Marcellus St Syracuse NY 13204 **Fax Area Code:* 866 ■ *TF:* 800-448-8878 ■ *Web:* www.newreaderspress.com	800-448-8878	894-2100*	637-2
New Repertory Theatre 200 Dexter Ave Watertown MA 02472 *TF:* 800-896-7340 ■ *Web:* www.newrep.org	617-923-7060		749
New Republic, The 1620 L St NW Ste 300C Washington DC 20036 *TF:* 800-827-1289 ■ *Web:* www.newrepublic.com	202-508-4444		457-17
New River Community College 5251 College Dr. Dublin VA 24084 **Fax:* Admissions ■ *TF:* 866-462-6722 ■ *Web:* www.nr.edu	540-674-3600	674-3642*	162
New River Electrical Corp PO Box 70 Cloverdale VA 24077 *TF:* 800-525-4628 ■ *Web:* www.newriverelectrical.com	540-966-1650	966-1699	188-10
New River Gorge National River 104 Main St PO Box 246 Glen Jean WV 25846 *Web:* www.nps.gov/neri	304-465-0508	465-0591	564
New River State Park 358 New River State Park Rd Laurel Springs NC 28644 *Web:* www.ncparks.gov/visit/parks/neri/main.php	336-982-2587		565
New River Trail State Park 116 Orphanage Dr Max Meadows VA 24360	276-699-6778		565
New River West Correctional Institution 7819 NW 228th St Raiford FL 32026 *TF:* 800-749-7424 ■ *Web:* dc.state.fl.us	904-368-3000	368-2732	213
New Rivers Restaurant 7 Steeple St Providence RI 02903 *Web:* www.newriversrestaurant.com	401-751-0350		671
New Riverside Ochre Co 75 Old River Rd SE. Cartersville GA 30121 *TF Orders:* 800-248-0176 ■ *Web:* www.nroonline.com	770-382-4568		503-1
New Roc City 19 LeCount Pl New Rochelle NY 10801 *Web:* www.funfuziononline.com	914-637-7575		50-6
New Saigon 630 S Federal Blvd Denver CO 80219 *TF:* 800-275-2420 ■ *Web:* newsaigon.com	303-936-4954		671
New Scale Technologies Inc 121 Victor Heights Pkwy. Victor NY 14564 *Web:* www.newscaletech.com	585-924-4450		544
New Scenic Cafe 5461 N Shore Dr. Duluth MN 55804 *Web:* newsceniccafe.com	218-525-6274		671
New School 66 W 12th St. New York NY 10011 *Web:* www.newschool.edu	212-229-5600		166
New Seabury Resort 20 Red Brook Rd. Mashpee MA 02649 *TF:* 877-687-3228 ■ *Web:* www.newseabury.com	508-539-8200		669
New Seasons Market 7300 SW Beaverton Hwy Portland OR 97225 *Web:* www.newseasonsmarket.com	503-292-6838		327
New Source Energy Partners LP 914 N Broadway Ste 230 Oklahoma City OK 73102 *Web:* www.newsource.com	405-272-3028		536
New South Kitchen & Bar 8140 Providence Rd Ste 300 Charlotte NC 28277 *Web:* www.newsouthkitchen.com	704-541-9990	541-1163	671
New Stage Theatre 1100 Carlisle St Jackson MS 39202 *TF:* 800-446-8979 ■ *Web:* www.newstagetheatre.com	601-948-3531	948-3538	573-4
New Standard Corp 74 Commerce Way York PA 17406 *Web:* www.newstandard.com	717-757-9450	757-2312	488
New Star Lasers Inc 9085 Foothills Blvd Roseville CA 95747 *TF:* 800-328-3881 ■ *Web:* www.newstarlasers.com	916-677-1900		475
New Suncadia LLC 3600 Suncadia Trl Cle Elum WA 98922 *Web:* www.destinationhotels.com/suncadia-resort	509-649-6400		707
New Sweet 98.5, The 5011 Capitol Ave. Omaha NE 68132 *Web:* www.sweet985.com	402-342-2000		645-115
New System Laundry LLC 432 NE Tenth Ave Portland OR 97232 *Web:* www.newsystemlaundry.com	503-232-8181		426
New Target Inc 815 N Royal St Ste 100. Alexandria VA 22314 *TF:* 800-438-7325 ■ *Web:* www.newtarget.com	703-548-3433		180
New Tech Global (NTG) 1030 Regional Pk Dr. Houston TX 77060 *Web:* www.ntglobal.com	281-951-4330	951-8719	261
New Tech Machinery Inc 1300 40th St Ste A Denver CO 80205 *Web:* www.newtechmachinery.com	303-294-0538		190
New Tech Network 1250 Main St Ste 100 Napa CA 94559 *TF:* 800-856-7038 ■ *Web:* www.newtechnetwork.org	707-253-6951		138
New Tech Packaging Inc 2718 Pershing Ave Memphis TN 38112 *Web:* www.newtechpkg.com	901-498-5570		549
New Tech Solutions Inc 4179 Business Ctr Dr Fremont CA 94538 *Web:* www.newtechsolutions.com	510-353-4070		179
New Technologies Inc 4380 Baldwin Rd Holly MI 48442 *Web:* www.newtechnologiesinc.com	810-694-5426	694-1183	180
New Times Broward Palm Beach 16 NE Fourth St Fort Lauderdale FL 33301 *Web:* www.browardpalmbeach.com	954-233-1600	233-1521	532-5
New Trier Township High School District 203 7 Happ Rd. Northfield IL 60093 *Web:* www.newtrier.k12.il.us	847-446-7000	784-7500	685
New Ulm Telecom Inc 27 N Minnesota St New Ulm MN 56073 *OTC:* NULM ■ *TF:* 888-873-6853 ■ *Web:* www.newulmtel.net	507-354-4111	354-1982	736
New Venture Partners LLC (NVP) 430 Mountain Ave Ste 404 Murray Hill NJ 07974 *Web:* www.nvpllc.com	908-464-0900	464-8131	792
New Ventures West PO Box 591525 San Francisco CA 94159 *TF:* 800-332-4618 ■ *Web:* newventureswest.com	800-332-4618		463
New Video Group Inc 902 Broadway 9th Fl. New York NY 10010 *Web:* newvideo.com	212-206-8600		626
New Visions Powerline Communications Inc PO Box 11815 Syracuse NY 13218 *Web:* www.nvplc.com	315-472-6300		387
New Vista Nursing & Rehabilitation Center 8647 Fenwick St. Sunland CA 91040 *TF:* 800-213-0154 ■ *Web:* newvistanursing.com	818-352-1421		793
New Vista Post Acute Care Center 1516 Sawtelle Blvd Los Angeles CA 90025 *TF:* 800-254-9442 ■ *Web:* newvista.com	310-477-5501		793
New Vitality 260 Smith St. Farmingdale NY 11735 *TF:* 888-997-2941 ■ *Web:* www.newvitality.com	888-997-2941		791
New Washington State Bank 402 E Main St PO Box 10 New Washington IN 47162 *TF:* 800-883-0131 ■ *Web:* www.newwashbank.com	812-293-3321	293-3072	70
New Wave Enviro Products Inc 6595 S Dayton St Ste 1000. Englewood CO 80155 *Web:* www.newwaveenviro.com	303-221-3232		612
New Wave Industries Inc 135 Day St Newington CT 06111 *Web:* www.newwaveindustries.com	860-953-9283		180
New Wave Travel 1075 Bay St Toronto ON M5S2B1 *TF:* 800-463-1512 ■ *Web:* www.newwavetravel.net	416-928-3113		772
New Way Air Bearings Inc 50 McDonald Blvd Aston PA 19014 *TF:* 800-394-1046 ■ *Web:* www.newwayairbearings.com	610-494-6700		480
New Ways to Work Inc 103 Morris St Ste A Sebastopol CA 95472 *Web:* www.newwaystowork.org	707-824-4000	824-4410	48-24

Name / Address	City	State	Zip	Phone	Fax	Class
New West Banks of Colorado Inc 55 S Elm Ave *Web:* bankofcolorado.com	Eaton	CO	80615	970-454-1800	454-1802	70
New West Energy Services Inc Ste 500 435 - Fourth Ave SW *Web:* www.newwestenergyservices.com	Calgary	AB	T2P3A8	403-984-9798		539
New West Symphony 2100 E Thousand Oaks Blvd Ste D *Web:* www.newwestsymphony.org	Thousand Oaks	CA	91362	805-497-5800	497-5839	573-3
New West Technologies Inc 4606 SE Division St *Web:* www.newestech.com	Portland	OR	97206	503-235-4656		225
New Westminster Chamber of Commerce 601 Queens Ave *Web:* www.newwestchamber.com	New Westminster	BC	V3M1L1	604-521-7781	521-0057	137
New Windsor Cantonment State Historic Site 374 Temple Hill Rd Rt 300 *Web:* parks.ny.gov/historic-sites/22/details.aspx	Vails Gate	NY	12584	845-561-1765		565
New World Aviation Inc 987 Postal Rd *Web:* www.newworldaviation.com	Allentown	PA	18109	610-231-9555		13
New World Educational Ctr 5818 N Seventh St Ste 200 *Web:* www.nweccharter.com	Phoenix	AZ	85014	602-238-9577		242
New World Group Inc 500 County Ave *TF:* 800-261-1537 ■ *Web:* www.newworldgroup.com	Secaucus	NJ	07094	201-770-1404		627
New World Imports Inc 160 Athens Way *TF:* 800-329-1903 ■ *Web:* www.newworldimports.com	Nashville	TN	37228	615-329-1906		535
New World Library 14 Pamaron Way *TF:* 800-972-6657 ■ *Web:* www.newworldlibrary.com	Novato	CA	94949	415-884-2100	884-2199	637-3
New World Medical Inc 10763 Edison Ct *Web:* www.newworldmedical.com	Rancho Cucamonga	CA	91730	909-466-4304		476
New World Symphony 500 17th St *TF:* 800-597-3331 ■ *Web:* www.nws.edu	Miami Beach	FL	33139	305-673-3330	673-6749	573-3
New World Tortilla 696 Pine St *Web:* www.newworldtortilla.com	Burlington	VT	05401	802-865-1058		671
New Year Tech Inc 12330 Pinecrest Rd Ste 100 *TF:* 800-525-7767 ■ *Web:* www.nyt1.net	Reston	VA	20191	703-564-0290	564-0296	178-12
New York						
Aging Office 2 Empire State Plaza *TF:* 800-342-9871 ■ *Web:* www.aging.ny.gov	Albany	NY	12223	800-342-9871		339-33
Arts Council 300 Park Ave S 10th Fl *Web:* www.nysca.org	New York	NY	10010	212-459-8800		339-33
Athletic Commission 123 William St 20th Fl *TF:* 866-269-3769 ■ *Web:* www.dos.ny.gov	New York	NY	10038	212-417-5700	417-4987	712
Attorney General State Capitol *Web:* www.oag.state.ny.us	Albany	NY	12224	518-474-7330		339-33
Banking Dept 1 State St *TF:* 877-226-5697 ■ *Web:* www.dfs.ny.gov	New York	NY	10004	800-342-3736		339-33
Bill Status 202 Legislative Office Bldg *TF:* 800-342-9860 ■ *Web:* www.assembly.state.ny.us	Albany	NY	12248	518-455-4218		433
Child Support Enforcement Div 40 N Pearl St *TF:* 888-208-4485 ■ *Web:* www.childsupport.ny.gov	Albany	NY	12243	518-474-9081		339-33
Children & Family Services Office 52 Washington St *Web:* ocfs.ny.gov/main	Rensselaer	NY	12144	518-473-7793	486-7550	339-33
Correctional Services Dept 1220 Washington Ave Bldg 2 *Web:* www.doccs.ny.gov	Albany	NY	12226	518-457-8126		339-33
Court of Appeals 20 Eagle St *Web:* www.nycourts.gov	Albany	NY	12207	518-455-7700		339-33
Crime Victims Board 845 Central Ave *Web:* www.ovs.ny.gov	Albany	NY	12206	518-457-8727	457-8658	339-33
Department of Environmental Conservation 625 Broadway Rm 290 *TF:* 800-678-6399 ■ *Web:* www.dec.ny.gov	Albany	NY	12233	518-408-5850		339-33
Division of Consumer Protection 5 Empire State Plaza Ste 2101 *TF:* 800-697-1220 ■ *Web:* www.dos.ny.gov	Albany	NY	12223	518-474-8583	486-3936	339-33
Education Dept 89 Washington Ave *Web:* www.nysed.gov	Albany	NY	12234	518-474-3852		339-33
Emergency Management Office (OEM) 1220 Washington Ave Bldg 22 Ste 101 *Web:* www.dhses.ny.gov/oem	Albany	NY	12226	518-292-2200	322-4990	339-33
Empire State Development 30 S Pearl St 7th Fl *TF:* 800-782-8369 ■ *Web:* www.empire.state.ny.us	Albany	NY	12245	518-292-5100	292-5812	339-33
Environmental Conservation Dept 625 Broadway *Web:* www.dec.ny.gov	Albany	NY	12233	518-891-0235		339-33
Governor State Capitol Executive Chamber *Web:* www.ny.gov	Albany	NY	12224	518-474-8390	474-1513	339-33
Health Dept Empire State Plaza Corning II Tower *TF:* 866-881-2809 ■ *Web:* www.health.ny.gov	Albany	NY	12237	866-881-2809		339-33
Higher Education Services Corp 99 Washington Ave *TF:* 888-697-4372 ■ *Web:* www.hesc.ny.gov	Albany	NY	12255	518-473-1574	474-2839	725
Historic Preservation Div 625 Broadway *TF:* 800-456-2267 ■ *Web:* www.nysparks.com	Albany	NY	12188	518-474-0456		339-33
Housing Finance Agency 641 Lexington Ave *TF:* 866-275-3427 ■ *Web:* www.nyshcr.org	New York	NY	10022	212-688-4000	872-0789	339-33
Insurance Dept 1 Commerce Plaza *Web:* www.dfs.ny.gov	Albany	NY	12260	518-474-6600		339-33
Investor Protection & Securities Bureau 120 Broadway 23rd Fl *Web:* www.ag.ny.gov	New York	NY	10271	212-416-8222	416-8816	339-33
Labor Dept WA Harriman Campus Bldg 12 *TF:* 888-469-7365 ■ *Web:* www.labor.ny.gov	Albany	NY	12240	518-457-9000		259
Lieutenant Governor NYS State Capitol Bldg *Web:* www.governor.ny.gov	Albany	NY	12224	518-474-8390		339-33
Lower Manhattan Development Corp 1 Liberty Plaza 20th Fl *Web:* www.renewnyc.com	New York	NY	10006	212-962-2300	962-2431	339-33
Mental Health Office 44 Holland Ave *TF:* 800-597-8481 ■ *Web:* www.omh.ny.gov	Albany	NY	12229	866-946-9733		339-33
Military & Naval Affairs Div 330 Old Niskayuna Rd *Web:* dmna.ny.gov	Latham	NY	12110	518-786-4786	786-4649	339-33
Motor Vehicles Dept 224-260 S Pearl St *Web:* www.dmv.ny.gov	Albany	NY	12228	518-473-5595		339-33
Office of Court Admin 4 ESP Ste 2001 Empire State Plz *TF:* 800-430-8457 ■ *Web:* www.courts.state.ny.us/admin	Albany	NY	12223	212-428-2100	428-2188	339-33
Office of the Professions 89 Washington Ave 2nd Fl *TF:* 800-442-8106 ■ *Web:* www.op.nysed.gov	Albany	NY	12234	518-474-3817	474-3004	339-33
Parole Div 97 Central Ave *Web:* www.parole.ny.gov	Albany	NY	12206	518-473-9400		339-33
Power Authority 30 S Pearl St 10th Fl *Web:* www.nypa.gov	Albany	NY	12207	518-433-6700		339-33
Public Service Commission 90 Church St *Web:* www.dps.ny.gov	New York	NY	12223	518-474-7080	474-0421	339-33
Secretary of State 99 Washington Ave *Web:* www.dos.ny.gov	Albany	NY	12231	518-473-2492		339-33
State Comptroller 110 State St 15th Fl *Web:* www.osc.state.ny.us	Albany	NY	12236	518-474-4044		339-33
State Education Dept 89 Washington Ave 5N EB *Web:* www.highered.nysed.gov	Albany	NY	12234	518-474-3901		339-33
State Government Information NYS State Capitol Bldg *Web:* www.ny.gov	Albany	NY	12224	518-474-8390		339-33
State Police Div 1220 Washington Ave Bldg 22 *Web:* nytrooper.com	Albany	NY	12226	518-783-3211		339-33
Taxation & Finance Dept WA Harriman Campus Bldg 9 *Web:* www.tax.ny.gov	Albany	NY	12227	518-457-5431		339-33
Technology Office 255 Greenwich Fl 9 *Web:* www.nyc.gov	Albany	NY	10007	212-788-6600		339-33
Temporary & Disability Assistance Office 40 N Pearl St 16th Fl *TF:* 800-342-3009 ■ *Web:* www.otda.ny.gov	Albany	NY	12243	518-473-1090		339-33
Transportation Dept 50 Wolf Rd *Web:* www.dot.ny.gov	Albany	NY	12205	518-457-7082	485-5217	339-33
Veterans' Affairs Div 110 Old Rte 6 Bldg 3 *Web:* www.veterans.ny.gov	Carmel	NY	10512	845-808-1620		339-33
Vital Records Office 800 N Pearl St *TF:* 800-541-2831 ■ *Web:* www.health.ny.gov	Menands	NY	12204	800-541-2831		339-33
Vocational & Educational Services for Individuals 1 Commerce Plaza Rm 1606 *Web:* www.acces.nysed.gov	Albany	NY	12234	518-474-2714	486-4683	339-33
Workers' Compensation Board PO Box 5205 *TF:* 877-632-4996 ■ *Web:* www.wcb.ny.gov	Binghamton	NY	13902	518-402-6070	402-0113	339-33
New York & Co 330 W 34th St *TF:* 800-961-9906 ■ *Web:* www.nyandcompany.com	New York	NY	10001	800-961-9906		157-6
New York Academy of Medicine (NYAM) 1216 Fifth Ave *Web:* www.nyam.org	New York	NY	10029	212-822-7200		49-19
New York Academy of Medicine Library 1216 Fifth Ave *Web:* www.nyam.org/library	New York	NY	10029	212-822-7315	423-0266	434-1
New York Academy of Sciences 250 Greenwich St 40th Fl *TF:* 800-843-6927 ■ *Web:* www.nyas.org	New York	NY	10007	212-298-8600	298-3650	49-19
New York Air Brake Co 748 Starbuck Ave **Fax:* Sales ■ *TF:* 888-836-6922 ■ *Web:* www.nyab.com	Watertown	NY	13601	315-786-5200	786-5675*	650
New York Apple Association Inc 7645 Main St PO Box 350 *TF:* 800-566-4377 ■ *Web:* www.nyapplecountry.com	Fishers	NY	14453	585-924-2171		414
New York Arm Wrestling Assn (NYAWA) PO Box 670952 *Web:* www.nycarms.com	Flushing	NY	11367	718-544-4592	261-8111	48-22
New York Banker 99 Pk Ave 4th Fl **Fax:* PR ■ *TF:* 800-346-3860 ■ *Web:* www.nyba.com	New York	NY	10016	212-297-1600	297-1683*	531-1
New York Barbells 160 Home St *TF:* 800-446-1833 ■ *Web:* www.newyorkbarbells.com	Elmira	NY	14904	607-733-8038	733-1010	267
New York Blood Ctr 310 E 67th St *TF:* 800-688-0900 ■ *Web:* www.nybloodcenter.org	New York	NY	10065	646-456-4281		89
New York Blower Co 7660 Quincy St *TF:* 800-208-7918 ■ *Web:* www.nyb.com	Willowbrook	IL	60527	630-794-5700	794-5776	18
New York Botanical Garden, The 2900 Southern Blvd *TF:* 800-450-1455 ■ *Web:* www.nybg.org	Bronx	NY	10458	718-817-8700		31
New York Business Development Corp (NYBDC) 50 Beaver St Ste 500 *TF:* 800-923-2504 ■ *Web:* www.nybdc.com	Albany	NY	12207	518-463-2268	463-0240	216
New York Career Institute 11 Pk Pl *Web:* www.nyci.edu	New York	NY	10007	212-962-0002	385-7574	800
New York Celebrity Assistants (NYCA) 459 Columbus Ave Ste 216 *Web:* www.nycelebrityassistants.com	New York	NY	10024	212-803-5444		49-12
New York Central Art Supply 62 Third Ave *TF:* 800-950-6111 ■ *Web:* www.nycentralart.com	New York	NY	10003	800-950-6111		45
New York Central Mutual Fire Insurance Co (NYCM) 1899 Central Plaza E **Fax Area Code:* 607 ■ *TF:* 800-234-6926 ■ *Web:* www.nycm.com	Edmeston	NY	13335	800-234-6926	965-2712*	391-4
New York City Ballet Inc 20 Lincoln Ctr David H. Koch Theater *Web:* www.nycballet.com	New York	NY	10023	212-870-5656	870-7791	573-1

Name / Address	Phone	Fax	Class
New York City Children's Ctr-Queens Campus (NYCCC) 74-03 Commonwealth Blvd . . . . . Bellerose NY 11426 *TF:* 800-597-8481 ■ *Web:* www.omh.ny.gov	718-264-4500	740-0968	374-1
New York City College of Technology 300 Jay St. . . . . . Brooklyn NY 11201 **Fax:* Admissions ■ *TF:* 855-492-3633 ■ *Web:* www.citytech.cuny.edu	718-260-5000	260-5504*	166
New York City Ctr 130 W 56th St . . . . . New York NY 10019 *Web:* www.nycitycenter.org	212-247-0430	246-9778	572
New York City Dept of Education 65 Ct St . . . . . Brooklyn NY 11201 *Web:* schools.nyc.gov	718-935-4000		685
New York City Fire Museum 278 Spring St . . . . . New York NY 10013 *Web:* www.nycfiremuseum.org	212-691-1303	352-3117	520
New York City Hall City Hall Pk . . . . . New York NY 10007 *Web:* www.nyc.gov	212-639-9675		337
New York City Health & Hospitals Corp 125 Worth St . . . . . New York NY 10013 *Web:* www.nyc.gov/html/hhc/html/home/home.shtml	212-788-3339		353
New York City Housing Development Corp 110 William St . . . . . New York NY 10038 *Web:* www.nychdc.com	212-227-5500	227-6865	217
New York City Partnership & Chamber of Commerce Inc 1 Battery Pk Plaza 5th Fl . . . . . New York NY 10004 *Web:* www.pfnyc.org	212-493-7400	344-3344	139
New York City Police Museum 100 Old Slip . . . . . New York NY 10005 *Web:* www.nycpm.org/gift-shop	212-480-3100		520
New York Community Bank 615 Merrick Ave . . . . . Westbury NY 11590 *TF:* 877-786-6560 ■ *Web:* www.mynycb.com	877-786-6560		70
New York Community Hospital 2525 Kings Hwy . . . . . Brooklyn NY 11229 *Web:* www.nych.com	718-692-5300		374-3
New York Community Trust 909 Third Ave 22nd Fl . . . . . New York NY 10022 *TF:* 877-829-5500 ■ *Web:* www.nycommunitytrust.org	212-686-0010	532-8528	303
New York Correctional Industries 550 Broadway . . . . . Albany NY 12204 *TF:* 800-436-6321 ■ *Web:* www.corcraft.org	518-436-6321	436-6007	630
New York County Lawyers Association 14 Vesey St . . . . . New York NY 10007 *TF:* 800-255-0569 ■ *Web:* www.nycla.org	212-267-6646		533
New York Cruise Lines Inc Pier 83 W 42nd St at the Hudson River . . . . . New York NY 10036 *Web:* www.circleline42.com	212-630-8120		41
New York Cryo 900 Northern Blvd Ste 230 . . . . . Great Neck NY 11021 *TF:* 877-769-2796 ■ *Web:* www.newyorkcryo.com	516-487-2700	487-2007	545
New York Daily News 450 W 33rd St 3rd Fl . . . . . New York NY 10001 *TF:* 800-692-6397 ■ *Web:* www.nydailynews.com	212-210-2100	643-7831	532-2
New York Downtown Hospital 170 William St . . . . . New York NY 10038 *TF:* 800-804-5447 ■ *Web:* nyp.org	212-312-5000		374-3
New York Education Law Report 360 Hiatt Dr . . . . . Palm Beach FL 33418 **Fax:* Edit ■ *TF:* 800-341-7874 ■ *Web:* www.lrp.com	561-622-6520	622-1375*	531-4
New York Eye & Ear Infirmary 310 E 14th St . . . . . New York NY 10003 *TF:* 800-522-4582 ■ *Web:* www.nyee.edu	212-979-4000	979-4512	374-7
New York Film Festival 70 Lincoln Ctr Plaza . . . . . New York NY 10023 *Web:* www.filmlinc.org	212-875-5610	875-5636	282
New York Fries 199 Four Valley Dr . . . . . Vaughan ON L4K0B8 *Web:* www.newyorkfries.com	416-963-5005		670
New York Giants 1925 Giants Dr . . . . . East Rutherford NJ 07073 *Web:* www.giants.com	201-935-8111		715-3
New York Global Group Inc The Trump Bldg 40 Wall St The Trump Bldg . . . . . New York NY 10005 *Web:* www.nyggroup.com	212-566-0499		401
New York Golf Center 131 W 35th St . . . . . New York NY 10001 *TF:* 800-363-6638 ■ *Web:* www.nygolfcenter.com	212-564-2255		711
New York Graphic Society Ltd 129 Glover Ave . . . . . Norwalk CT 06850 *TF:* 800-221-1032 ■ *Web:* www.nygs.com	203-661-2400		637-10
New York Hall of Science 47-01 111th St . . . . . Queens NY 11368 *TF:* 800-531-0864 ■ *Web:* www.nysci.org	718-699-0005		520
New York Health Care Inc 33 W Hawthorne Ave 3rd Fl . . . . . Valley Stream NY 11580 *OTC:* BBAL ■ *TF:* 888-978-6942 ■ *Web:* www.nyhc.com	718-375-6700		363
New York Historical Society 170 Central Pk W . . . . . New York NY 10024 *Web:* www.nyhistory.org	212-873-3400	874-8706	520
New York Hospital Medical Ctr of Queens 56-45 Main St . . . . . Flushing NY 11355 *Web:* www.nyhq.org	718-670-2000		374-3
New York Hotel Trades 707 Eighth Ave . . . . . New York NY 10036 *Web:* www.hotelworkers.org	212-245-8100		132
New York Imaging Service Inc 5 Jeanne Dr Ste 3 . . . . . Newburgh NY 12550 *Web:* www.nyimagingservice.org	845-561-6947		416
New York Institute of Technology New York Institute of Technology Northern Blvd PO Box 8000 . . . . . Old Westbury NY 11568 *TF:* 800-345-6948 ■ *Web:* www.nyit.edu	516-686-1000		166
Islip PO Box 9029 . . . . . Central Islip NY 11722 *TF:* 800-345-6948 ■ *Web:* www.nyit.edu	516-686-1000		166
Manhattan 1855 Broadway . . . . . New York NY 10023 **Fax:* Admissions ■ *TF:* 800-345-6948 ■ *Web:* www.nyit.edu	212-261-1500	261-1505*	166
New York International Raceway Park 2011 New Rd . . . . . Leicester NY 14481	585-382-3030		515
New York Islanders 1255 Hempstead Tpke . . . . . Uniondale NY 11553 *TF:* 800-843-5678 ■ *Web:* islanders.nhl.com	516-501-6700	501-6762	715-1
New York Islanders 1535 Old Country Rd . . . . . Plainview NY 11803 *TF:* 800-843-5678 ■ *Web:* islanders.nhl.com	516-501-6700		716
New York Jets LLC 1 Jets Dr . . . . . Florham Park NJ 07932 *Web:* www.newyorkjets.com	973-549-4800		713
New York Junior Tennis League Inc 5812 Queens Blvd Ste 1 . . . . . Woodside NY 11377 *Web:* www.nyjtl.org	718-786-7110		354
New York Knicks Madison Sq Garden 2 Pennsylvania Plaza 14th Fl . . . . . New York NY 10121 **Fax:* PR ■ *Web:* www.nba.com/knicks	212-465-6471	465-6498*	714-1
New York Law Journal 120 Broadway 5th Fl . . . . . New York NY 10271 *TF:* 877-256-2472 ■ *Web:* www.newyorklawjournal.com	877-256-2472		457-15
New York Law School 185 W Broadway . . . . . New York NY 10013 *TF:* 877-937-6957 ■ *Web:* www.nyls.edu	212-431-2100	966-1522	167-1
New York Liberty Madison Sq Garden 2 Pennsylvania Plaza . . . . . New York NY 10121 *Web:* www.wnba.com/liberty	212-564-9622	465-6250	714-2
New York Library Assn (NYLA) 6021 State Farm Rd . . . . . Guilderland NY 12084 *TF General:* 800-252-6952 ■ *Web:* www.nyla.org	518-432-6952	427-1697	435
New York Life Foundation 51 Madison Ave . . . . . New York NY 10010 *Web:* www.newyorklife.com	212-576-7341		304
New York Life Insurance & Annuity Corp 51 Madison Ave . . . . . New York NY 10010 *TF:* 800-598-2019 ■ *Web:* nylinvestments.com	212-576-7000		391-2
New York Magazine 75 Varick St . . . . . New York NY 10013 *TF:* 800-678-0900 ■ *Web:* www.nymag.com	212-508-0700		457-22
New York Marriott East Side 525 Lexington Ave . . . . . New York NY 10017 *Web:* marriott.com	212-755-4000		379
New York Medical College 40 Sunshine Cottage Rd . . . . . Valhalla NY 10595 *Web:* www.nymc.edu	914-594-4507		167-2
New York Merchants Protective Company Inc 75 W Merrick Rd . . . . . Freeport NY 11520 *TF:* 888-696-7911 ■ *Web:* www.nympc.com	516-561-5210		693
New York Mets Shea Stadium 123-01 Roosevelt Ave . . . . . Flushing NY 11368 *TF:* 888-652-7467 ■ *Web:* newyork.mets.mlb.com	718-507-6387	507-6395	713
New York Military Academy 78 Academy Ave . . . . . Cornwall On Hudson NY 12520 *TF:* 888-275-6962 ■ *Web:* www.nyma.org	845-534-3710		622
New York Mortgage Trust Inc (NYMT) 52 Vanderbilt Ave Ste 403 . . . . . New York NY 10017 *NASDAQ:* NYMT ■ *TF:* 800-937-5449 ■ *Web:* www.nymtrust.com	212-792-0107		654
New York New York Hotel & Casino 3790 Las Vegas Blvd S . . . . . Las Vegas NV 89109 *TF:* 800-689-1797 ■ *Web:* www.newyorknewyork.com	702-740-6969	740-6700	133
New York News LP 450 W 33rd St 3rd Fl . . . . . New York NY 10001 *Web:* www.nydailynews.com	212-210-2100	643-7831	637-8
New York Observer 915 Broadway 9th Fl . . . . . New York NY 10010 *TF:* 800-542-0420 ■ *Web:* www.observer.com	212-755-2400		532-4
New York Palace Hotel 455 Madison Ave . . . . . New York NY 10022 *TF:* 800-697-2522 ■ *Web:* www.lottenypalace.com	212-888-7000	303-6000	379
New York Philharmonic 10 Lincoln Center Plaza . . . . . New York NY 10023 **Fax:* Mktg ■ *Web:* www.nyphil.org	212-875-5900	875-5717*	573-3
New York Pops 333 W 52nd St Ste 600 . . . . . New York NY 10019 *Web:* www.newyorkpops.org	212-765-7677	315-3199	573-3
New York Post 1211 Ave of the Americas . . . . . New York NY 10036 *TF:* 800-552-7678 ■ *Web:* www.nypost.com	212-930-8000		532-2
New York Power Authority 123 Main St Ste 10-H . . . . . White Plains NY 10601 *Web:* www.nypa.gov	914-681-6200		787
New York Presbyterian Hospital 525 E 68th St . . . . . New York NY 10021 *TF:* 888-694-5700 ■ *Web:* www.nyp.org	212-746-5454	746-4293	374-3
New York Press 28th St and Seventh Ave 20 W Ave . . . . . Chester NY 10001 *Web:* www.nypress.com	212-868-0190		532-5
New York Prime 2350 Executive Ctr Dr NW . . . . . Boca Raton FL 33431 *Web:* www.newyorkprime.com	561-998-3881		671
New York Private Bank & Trust FSB 200 Bellevue Pkwy Ste 150 . . . . . Wilmington DE 19809 *Web:* www.nypbt.com	302-798-2160		70
New York Professional Nurses Union (NYPNU) 241 E 75th St . . . . . New York NY 10021 *Web:* www.nypnu.org	212-988-5565		533
New York Prosecutors Training Institute 107 Columbia St . . . . . Albany NY 12210 *Web:* www.nypti.org	518-432-1100		428
New York Public Library 5th Ave & 42nd St . . . . . New York NY 10018 *Web:* www.nypl.org	917-275-6975		434-3
New York Racing Assn (NYRA) 110-00 Rockaway Blvd PO Box 90 . . . . . Jamaica NY 11420 *TF:* 800-441-4601 ■ *Web:* www.nyra.com	718-641-4700		642
New York Rangers 2 Pennsylvania Plaza . . . . . New York NY 10121 *Web:* rangers.nhl.com	212-465-6553	465-6494	716
New York Red Bulls 600 Cape May St . . . . . Harrison NJ 07029 *TF:* 877-727-6223 ■ *Web:* www.newyorkredbulls.com	877-727-6223		717
New York Replacement Parts Corp 19 School St . . . . . Yonkers NY 10701 *TF:* 800-228-4718 ■ *Web:* www.nyrpcorp.com	914-965-0122		612
New York Republican State Committee 315 State St . . . . . Albany NY 12210 *Web:* newyork.gop	518-462-2601	449-7443	616-2
New York Review of Books 435 Hudson St 3rd Fl . . . . . New York NY 10014 *TF:* 800-354-0050 ■ *Web:* www.nybooks.com	212-757-8070	333-5374	457-11

	Phone	Fax	Class
New York Road Runners Club 9 E 89th St .... New York NY 10128 *Web:* www.nyrr.org	212-860-4455		305
New York School of Interior Design 170 E 70th St .... New York NY 10021 **Fax:* Admissions ■ *TF:* 800-336-9743 ■ *Web:* www.nysid.edu	212-472-1500	472-1867*	166
New York Sports Club 888 Seventh Ave 25th Fl .... New York NY 10106 *Web:* www.mysportsclubs.com	212-246-6700	246-8422	354
New York State Assn of Realtors 130 Washington Ave .... Albany NY 12210 *TF:* 800-462-7585 ■ *Web:* www.nysar.com	518-463-0300	462-5474	656
New York State Bar Assn 1 Elk St .... Albany NY 12207 *TF:* 800-342-3661 ■ *Web:* www.nysba.org	518-463-3200	487-5517	72
New York State Bar News 1 Elk St .... Albany NY 12207 *TF:* 800-442-3863 ■ *Web:* www.nysba.org	518-463-3200	463-4276	457-15
New York State Bridge Authority PO Box 1010 .... Highland NY 12528 *TF:* 800-333-8655 ■ *Web:* www.nysba.state.ny.us	845-691-7245	691-3560	271
New York State Canal Corp 200 Southern Blvd PO Box 189 .... Albany NY 12201 *TF:* 800-422-6254 ■ *Web:* www.canals.ny.gov	518-436-2700		465
New York State Clipping Service 200 Central Pk Ave N .... Hartsdale NY 10530	914-948-2525		624
New York State Dental Assn 20 Corporate Woods Blvd #602 .... Albany NY 12211 *TF:* 800-255-2100 ■ *Web:* www.nysdental.org	518-465-0044	465-3219	227
New York State Electric & Gas Corp 18 Link Dr PO Box 5240 .... Binghamton NY 13904 *TF:* 800-572-1111 ■ *Web:* www.nyseg.com	800-572-1111		787
New York State Library Empire State Plaza .... Albany NY 12230 *Web:* www.nysl.nysed.gov	518-474-5355	474-5786	434-5
New York State Medical Society 865 Merrick Ave PO Box 5404 .... Westbury NY 11590 *TF:* 800-523-4405 ■ *Web:* www.mssny.org	516-488-6100	488-1267	474
New York State Museum 222 Madison Ave .... Albany NY 12230 *Web:* www.nysm.nysed.gov	518-474-5877	486-3696	520
New York State Nurses Assn (NYSNA) 11 Cornell Rd .... Latham NY 12110 *TF:* 800-724-6976 ■ *Web:* www.nysna.org	518-782-9400		533
New York State Veterans Home at Batavia 220 Richmond Ave .... Batavia NY 14020 *Web:* www.nysvets.org	585-345-2000		793
New York State Veterans Home at Oxford 4207 New York 220 .... Oxford NY 13830	607-843-3100		793
New York State Veterans Home at Saint Albans 178-50 Linden Blvd .... Jamaica NY 11434 *Web:* veterans.ny.gov	718-990-0353		793
New York State Veterinary Medical Society 100 Great Oaks Blvd Ste 127 .... Albany NY 12203 *TF:* 800-876-9867 ■ *Web:* www.nysvms.org	518-869-7867	869-7868	795
New York Susquehanna & Western Railway Corp (NYSW) 1 Railroad Ave .... Cooperstown NY 13326 *TF General:* 800-366-6979 ■ *Web:* www.nysw.com	607-547-2555	547-9834	648
New York Teacher Magazine 800 Troy-Schenectady Rd .... Latham NY 12110 *TF:* 800-342-9810 ■ *Web:* www.nysut.org	518-213-6000	213-6415	457-8
New York Theatre Ballet 30 E 31st St .... New York NY 10016 *Web:* www.nytb.org	212-679-0401	679-8171	573-1
New York Theological Seminary 475 Riverside Dr Ste 500 .... New York NY 10115 *Web:* nyts.edu	212-870-1211	870-1236	167-3
New York Times 620 Eigth Ave .... New York NY 10018 *Web:* www.nytco.com	212-556-1234		532-2
New York Times Co Foundation Inc 229 W 43rd St .... New York NY 10036 *Web:* crainsnewyork.com	212-210-0100		304
New York Times News Service Div 620 Eigth Ave .... New York NY 10018 *TF:* 800-698-4637 ■ *Web:* www.nytimes.com	212-556-7652		530
New York Transit Museum Boerum Pl & Schermerhorn St 10th Fl .... Brooklyn NY 11201 *Web:* mta.info/mta/museum	718-694-1600		520
New York University 22 Washington Sq N .... New York NY 10011 **Fax:* Admissions ■ *TF:* 888-243-2358 ■ *Web:* www.nyu.edu	212-998-4500	995-4902*	166
New York University Bobst Library 70 Washington Sq S .... New York NY 10012 *Web:* www.nyu.edu/academics/libraries/elmer-holmes-bobstlibrary.html	212-998-2500	995-4829	434-6
New York University School of Law 110 W Third St .... New York NY 10012 **Fax:* Admissions ■ *TF:* 800-522-0925 ■ *Web:* www.law.nyu.edu	212-998-6100	995-4527*	167-1
New York Women in Film & Television 6 E 39th St Ste 1200 .... New York NY 10016 *Web:* www.nywift.org	212-679-0870		138
New York Yankees Yankee Stadium 161st St & River Ave .... Bronx NY 10451 *Web:* newyork.yankees.mlb.com	718-293-4300	293-8414	713
New York's Hotel Pennsylvania 401 Seventh Ave .... New York NY 10001 *TF:* 800-223-8585 ■ *Web:* www.hotelpenn.com/thehotel.html	212-736-5000	502-8712	379
New Yorker 60 W Market St .... Salt Lake City UT 84101 *Web:* newyorkerslc.com	801-363-0166		671
New Yorker Boiler Company Inc 21 Lincoln Ave .... Lansdale PA 19446 *Web:* www.newyorkerboiler.com	215-855-8055		357
New Yorker Hotel 481 Eigth Ave .... New York NY 10001 *Web:* www.newyorkerhotel.com	212-971-0101		379
New York-New Jersey Trail Conference 156 Ramapo Valley Rd Rt 202 .... Mahwah NJ 07430 *Web:* nynjtc.org	201-512-9348		239
New Zealand			
Consulate General 2425 Olympic Blvd Ste 600-E .... Santa Monica CA 90404 *Web:* www.nzcgla.com	310-566-6555		257
Embassy 37 Observatory Cir NW .... Washington DC 20008 *TF:* 866-639-9325 ■ *Web:* www.mfat.govt.nz/en/embassies	202-328-4800	667-5277	257
New Zealand Tourism Board 501 Santa Monica Blvd Ste 300 .... Santa Monica CA 90401 *Web:* www.newzealand.com/travel	310-395-7480	395-5453	775
NewAge Industries Inc 145 James Way .... SoutHampton PA 18966 *TF:* 800-506-3924 ■ *Web:* www.newageindustries.com	215-526-2300	526-2190	370
Newage Testing Instruments Inc 820 Pennsylvania Blvd .... Feasterville PA 19053 *TF:* 800-806-3924 ■ *Web:* www.hardnesstesters.com	215-355-6900		407
NewAgeSys Inc 231 Clarksville Rd Ste 200 .... Princeton Junction NJ 08550 *TF:* 888-863-9243 ■ *Web:* www.newagesys.com	609-919-9800	919-9830	180
Newalta Corp 211 11 Ave SW .... Calgary AB T2R0C6 *Web:* www.newalta.com	403-806-7000		660
Newark Beth Israel Medical Ctr 201 Lyons Ave .... Newark NJ 07112 *TF:* 800-780-1140 ■ *Web:* www.barnabashealth.org	973-926-7000		374-3
Newark Chamber of Commerce 37101 Newark Blvd .... Newark CA 94560 *TF:* 844-245-8925 ■ *Web:* www.newark-chamber.com	510-744-1000		139
Newark Liberty International Airport 3 Brewster Rd .... Newark NJ 07114 *TF:* 888-397-4636 ■ *Web:* www.panynj.gov/airports/newark-liberty.html	973-961-6000		27
Newark Museum 49 Washington St .... Newark NJ 07102 *TF:* 888-370-6765 ■ *Web:* www.newarkmuseum.org	973-596-6550	642-0459	520
Newark Public Library 5 Washington St .... Newark NJ 07101 *Web:* www.npl.org	973-733-7784		434-3
Newark Public Library 101 W Main St .... Newark OH 43055 *TF:* 800-858-9133 ■ *Web:* www.newarklibrary.info	740-928-3923		434-3
Newark Regional Business Partnership 744 Broad St 26th Fl .... Newark NJ 07102 *TF:* 888-337-3339 ■ *Web:* www.newarkrbp.org	973-522-0099	824-6587	139
Newark School District 100 E Miller St 4th Fl .... Newark NY 14513 *TF:* 877-789-2613 ■ *Web:* www.newarkcsd.org	315-332-3230	332-3517	780
Newark Symphony Hall 1030 Broad St .... Newark NJ 07102 *TF:* 800-745-3000 ■ *Web:* www.newarksymphonyhall.org	973-643-8014		572
Newark Trade Digital Graphics 177 Oakwood Ave .... Orange NJ 07050 *TF:* 800-848-0143 ■ *Web:* www.newarktrade.com	973-674-3727		627
Newark-Wayne Community Hospital 1250 Driving Pk Ave .... Newark NY 14513 *Web:* www.rochestergeneral.org	315-332-2427	332-2371	374-3
Neway Packaging Corp 1973 E Via Arado .... Rancho Dominguez CA 90220 *TF:* 800-456-3929 ■ *Web:* www.newaypackaging.com	310-898-3400		96
Newaygo County 1087 Newell St .... White Cloud MI 49349 *TF:* 800-315-3593 ■ *Web:* www.countyofnewaygo.com	231-689-7200	689-7205	338
Newaygo State Park 2793 Beech St .... Newaygo MI 49337 *Web:* www.michigandnr.com	231-856-4452		565
NewBay Media LLC 28 E 28th St 12th Fl .... New York NY 10016 *Web:* www.newbaymedia.com	212-378-0400	378-0470	457-21
Newberg School District 29 Jt 714 E Sixth St .... Newberg OR 97132 *Web:* www.newberg.k12.or.us	503-554-5000	538-4374	685
Newberry Area Tourism Assn, The PO Box 308 .... Newberry MI 49868 *TF:* 800-832-5216 ■ *Web:* www.newberrytourism.com	906-293-5562		206
Newberry College 2100 College St .... Newberry SC 29108 **Fax:* Admissions ■ *TF:* 800-845-4955 ■ *Web:* www.newberry.edu	803-276-5010	321-5138*	166
Newberry Correctional Facility 13747 E County Rd 428 .... Newberry MI 49868 *Web:* www.michigan.gov/corrections	906-293-6200		213
Newberry County 1226 College St PO Box 156 .... Newberry SC 29108 *Web:* www.newberrycounty.net	803-321-2110	321-2102	338
Newberry County Chamber of Commerce 1209 Caldwell St PO Box 396 .... Newberry SC 29108 *TF:* 800-288-2020 ■ *Web:* newberrycountychamber.com	803-276-4274	276-4373	139
Newberry Electric Co-op Inc 882 Wilson Rd .... Newberry SC 29108 *TF:* 800-479-8838 ■ *Web:* www.nec.coop	803-276-1121		245
Newbn Inc 14240 Proton Rd .... Dallas TX 75244 *TF:* 800-800-8304 ■ *Web:* www.newbenefits.com	972-404-8192		194
Newbold Corp 450 Weaver St .... Rocky Mount VA 24151 *TF:* 800-552-3282 ■ *Web:* www.newboldcorp.com/addressograph	540-489-4400	489-4417	111
newBrandAnalytics Inc 1250 23rd St NW Ste 450 .... Washington DC 20037 *Web:* www.newbrandanalytics.com	202-800-7850		195
Newbridge Securities Corp 1451 W Cypress Creek Rd .... Fort Lauderdale FL 33309 *TF:* 877-447-9625 ■ *Web:* www.newbridgefinancial.com	954-334-3450		690
Newbrook Machines Inc 16 Mechanic St .... Silver Creek NY 14136 *Web:* excelco.net	716-934-2644		482
Newbury College 129 Fisher Ave .... Brookline MA 02445 **Fax:* Admitting ■ *TF:* 800-499-0143 ■ *Web:* www.newbury.edu	617-730-7000	731-9618*	166
Newbury Comics Inc 5 Guest St .... Brighton MA 02135 *Web:* www.newbury.com	617-254-1666	254-1085	525
Newbury Corp 222 Ames St .... Dedham MA 02026 *TF:* 800-688-1825 ■ *Web:* www.ndgroup.com	800-688-1825		390
Newburyport Five Cents Savings Bank Inc, The 63 State St PO Box 350 .... Newburyport MA 01950 *TF:* 877-462-3136 ■ *Web:* www.newburyportbank.com	978-462-3136	462-9672	70
Newby Pridgen Sartip & Masel Llc 4593 Oleander Dr Ste 100 .... Myrtle Beach SC 29577 *Web:* www.newbylaw.com	843-449-9417		445
Newcap Radio (NCC) 745 Windmill Rd .... Dartmouth NS B3B1C2 *Web:* www.ncc.ca	902-468-7557		643
Newcastle Place Inc 12600 N Port Washington Rd .... Mequon WI 53092 *Web:* www.newcastleplacelcs.com	262-387-8800		371
NewClients Inc 3900 Gaskins Rd .... Richmond VA 23233 *Web:* www.newclients.com	804-560-7000		5
NewCloud Networks 160 Inverness Dr W .... Englewood CO 80112 *TF:* 855-255-5001 ■ *Web:* www.newcloudnetworks.com	855-255-5001		387

Phone | Fax | Class

Newcomb & Boyd
303 Peachtree Ctr Ave NE Ste 525 .... Atlanta GA 30303 404-730-8400 730-8401 261
Web: www.newcomb-boyd.com

Newcomb Oil Co LLC
207 E John Rowan Blvd .... Bardstown KY 40004 502-348-3961 348-6346 539
Web: www.newcomboil.com

Newcomb Spring Corp 235 Spring St .... Southington CT 06489 860-621-0111 621-7048 719
TF: 888-579-3051 ■ *Web:* www.newcombspring.com

NewComLink Inc
3900 N Capital Of Texas Hwy Ste 150............ Austin TX 78746 888-988-0603 253
TF: 888-988-0603 ■ *Web:* vyze.com

Newcon Optik 105 Sparks Ave............ North York ON M2H2S5 416-663-6963 529
TF: 877-368-6666 ■ *Web:* www.newcon-optik.com

Newdea Inc
4B Inverness Ct E Ste 1970 .... Englewood CO 80112 720-249-3030 196
Web: www.newdea.com

Newdell Co, The 13750 Hollister Rd............ Houston TX 77086 713-590-1312 789
TF: 877-510-7853 ■ *Web:* www.newdellco.com

Newegg Inc 16839 E Gale Ave........... City of Industry CA 91745 626-271-9700 271-9403 179
TF: 800-390-1119 ■ *Web:* www.newegg.com

Newell Brands 221 River St .... Hoboken NJ 07030 201-610-6600 185
NYSE: NWL ■ *Web:* www.newellbrands.com/pages/index.aspx?redirect=1

Newell Coach Corp 3900 N Main St............. Miami OK 74354 918-542-3344 542-2028 120
TF: 888-363-9355 ■ *Web:* www.newellcoach.com

Newell Paper Co 1212 Grand Ave............ Meridian MS 39301 800-844-8894 483-4900* 553
**Fax Area Code:* 601 ■ *TF:* 800-844-8894 ■ *Web:* www.newellpaper.com

Newell Roadbuilders Inc
13266 US Hwy 31......................... Hope Hull AL 36043 334-288-2702 188-4

Newell Rubbermaid Inc Irwin Tools Div
8935 Northpointe Executive Dr............... Huntersville NC 28078 704-987-4555 758
TF: 800-866-5740 ■ *Web:* www.irwin.com

Newfield Exploration Co
363 N Sam Houston Pkwy E Ste 100 .... Houston TX 77060 281-847-6000 405-4242 536
NYSE: NFX ■ *TF:* 866-902-0562 ■ *Web:* newfield.com

Newfield National Bank 18 SW Blvd............ Newfield NJ 08344 856-692-3440 697-3114 70
Web: www.newfieldbank.com

Newforma Inc 1750 Elm St................. Manchester NH 03104 603-625-6212 177
TF: 800-819-2869 ■ *Web:* www.newforma.com

Newfound Technologies Inc
1050 Kingsmill Pkwy .... Columbus OH 43229 614-318-5000 177
Web: www.nfti.com

Newfoundland Capital Corp Ltd
745 Windmill Rd......................... Dartmouth NS B3B1C2 902-468-7557 643
TSE: NCC.A ■ *Web:* www.ncc.ca

Newgate Mall 36th St & Wall Ave................ Ogden UT 84405 801-621-1161 460
Web: www.newgatemall.com

Newgen Software Inc
1364 Beverly Rd Ste 300 .... Mclean VA 22101 703-749-2855 177
Web: www.newgensoft.com

Newgistics Inc 2700 Via Fortuna Ste 300.......... Austin TX 78746 512-225-6000 225-6001 546
Web: newgistics.com

NewGround Resources Inc
15450 S Outer Forty Dr Ste 300 .... Chesterfield MO 63017 636-898-8100 186
TF: 800-458-8849 ■ *Web:* www.newground.com

Newhall Klein Inc 6109 W Kl Ave............ Kalamazoo MI 49009 269-544-0844 344
TF: 866-639-4255 ■ *Web:* www.newhallklein.com

Newhall Land
25124 Springfield Ct Ste 300.................. Valencia CA 91355 661-255-4000 653
Web: www.valencia.com

Newhouse Dan (Rep R - WA)
1318 Longworth HOB..................... Washington DC 20515 202-225-5816 225-3251 342-2
Web: newhouse.house.gov

Newins Bay Shore Ford Inc
219 W Main St .... Bay Shore NY 11706 631-665-1300 57
Web: www.newinsbayshoreford.com

Newjac Inc 415 S Grant St.................... Lebanon IN 46052 765-483-2190 697
TF: 800-827-3259 ■ *Web:* www.newjac.com

Newland 4790 Eastgate Mall Ste 150........... San Diego CA 92121 858-455-7503 455-5368 652
Web: www.newlandco.com

Newland House Museum
19820 Beach Blvd..................... Huntington Beach CA 92648 714-962-5777 520
TF: 800-777-0133 ■ *Web:* www.hbsurfcity.com/history/newland.htm

Newlands Systems Inc
602-30731 Simpson Rd................... Abbotsford BC V2T6Y7 604-855-4890 80-3
TF: 877-855-4890 ■ *Web:* nsibrew.com

NewlineNoosh Inc
625 Ellis St Ste 300 .... Mountain View CA 94043 650-637-6000 965-1377 178-1
TF: 888-286-6674 ■ *Web:* noosh.com

Nowly Wodc Foodc Inc
4140 W Fullerton Ave........................ Chicago IL 60639 773-489-7000 296-37
TF: 800-621-7521 ■ *Web:* www.newlywedsfoods.com

New-Mac Electric Co-op Inc
12105 E Hwy 86 .... Neosho MO 64850 417-451-1515 245
Web: www.newmac.com

Newman & Company Inc
6101 Tacony St......................... Philadelphia PA 19135 215-333-8700 332-8586 561
TF: 800-523-3256 ■ *Web:* newmanpaperboard.com

Newman Brothers Inc
5609 Ctr Hill Ave .... Cincinnati OH 45216 513-242-0011 205
TF: 800-656-4420 ■ *Web:* www.newmanbrothers.com

Newman Ctr for the Performing Arts
2344 E Iliff Ave .... Denver CO 80208 303-871-7720 871-6507 572
Web: www.newmancenterpresents.com

Newman Grace Inc
6133 Fallbrook Ave.................... Woodland Hills CA 91367 818-713-1678 4
Web: www.newmangrace.com

Newman Regional Health
1201 W 12th Ave .... Emporia KS 66801 620-343-6800 374-3
Web: www.newmanrh.org

Newman Technology Inc 100 Cairns Rd........ Mansfield OH 44903 419-525-1856 247
Web: www.newmantech.com

Newman Theological College (NTC)
10012-84 St............................ Edmonton AB T6A0B2 780-392-2450 462-4013 167-3
TF: 844-392-2450 ■ *Web:* www.newman.edu

Newman University 3100 McCormick Ave........ Wichita KS 67213 316-942-4291 942-4483* 166
**Fax:* Admissions ■ *TF:* 877-639-6268 ■ *Web:* www.newmanu.edu

Newman's Own Inc 246 Post Rd E............. Westport CT 06880 203-222-0136 296-19
Web: www.newmansown.com

Newmans Valve LLC
4655 Wright Rd Ste 250...................... Stafford TX 77477 832-944-5930 944-5929 385

Newmar Corp 355 Delaware St.................. Nappanee IN 46550 574-773-7791 120
TF: 800-731-8300 ■ *Web:* www.newmarcorp.com

Newmar Window Manufacturing Inc
7630 Airport Rd .... Mississauga ON L4T4G6 905-672-1233 601
TF: 800-263-5634 ■ *Web:* www.newmar.com

Newmark Advertising
15821 Ventura Blvd Ste 570.................... Encino CA 91436 818-461-0300 387
Web: www.newmarkad.com

Newmark Grubb Knight Frank
1800 Larimer St .... Denver CO 80202 303-892-1111 652
Web: www.ngkf.com

Newmark Knight Frank 125 Pk Ave............ New York NY 10017 212-372-2000 653
Web: www.ngkf.com

Newmarket Chamber of Commerce
470 Davis Dr............................ Newmarket ON L3Y2P3 905-898-5900 137
Web: www.newmarketchamber.com

NewMarket Corp 330 S Fourth St............. Richmond VA 23219 804-788-5000 788-5688 360-3
NYSE: NEU ■ *TF:* 800-625-5191 ■ *Web:* www.newmarket.com

Newmarket Public Library
438 Park Ave.......................... Newmarket ON L3Y1W1 905-953-5110 42
Web: www.newmarketpl.ca

Newmeyer & Dillion LLP
895 Dove St 5th Fl .... Newport Beach CA 92660 949-854-7000 428
Web: www.newmeyeranddillion.com

Newmont Mining Corp
6363 S Fiddler's Green Cir Ste 800...... Greenwood Village CO 80111 303-863-7414 837-5837 502
NYSE: NEM ■ *Web:* www.newmont.com

Newnan-Coweta Chamber of Commerce
23 Bullsboro Dr .... Newnan GA 30263 770-253-2270 253-2271 139
TF: 800-279-5230 ■ *Web:* www.newnancowetachamber.org

Newpark Mall 2086 Newpark Mall............... Newark CA 94560 510-794-5523 460
TF: 800-345-8082 ■ *Web:* www.newparkmall.com

Newpark Mats & Integrated Services LLC
2700 Research Forest Dr Ste 100......... The Woodlands TX 77381 281-362-6800 539
TF: 877-628-7623 ■ *Web:* www.newpark.com

Newport Aquarium 1 Aquarium Way............ Newport KY 41071 859-261-7444 261-5888 40
TF: 800-406-3474 ■ *Web:* www.newportaquarium.com

Newport Art Museum 76 Bellevue Ave........... Newport RI 02840 401-848-8200 848-8205 520
Web: www.newportartmuseum.org

Newport Asia LLC
601 California St Ste 1168.............. San Francisco CA 94108 415-677-8620 401
Web: www.newportasiallc.com

Newport Avenue Market
1121 NW Newport Ave .... Bend OR 97703 541-382-3940 345
Web: www.newportavemarket.com

Newport Bay Club & Hotel
337 Thames St PO Box 1440 .... Newport RI 02840 401-849-8600 379
Web: www.newportbayclub.com

Newport Beach Chamber of Commerce
1470 Jamboree Rd .... Newport Beach CA 92660 949-729-4400 729-4417 139
TF: 800-772-1213 ■ *Web:* www.newportbeach.com

Newport Beach Conference & Visitors Bureau
1200 Newport Ctr Dr Ste 120............. Newport Beach CA 92660 949-719-6100 206
TF: 800-216-1598 ■ *Web:* www.visitnewportbeach.com

Newport Beach Hotel & Suites
1 Wave Ave.............................. Middletown RI 02842 401-846-0310 847-2621 379
TF: 800-655-1778 ■ *Web:* www.newportbeachhotelandsuites.com

Newport Beachside Hotel & Resort
16701 Collins Ave .... Miami Beach FL 33160 305-949-1300 379
TF: 800-327-5476 ■ *Web:* www.newportbeachsideresort.com

Newport Capital Group LLC
12 Broad St 5th Fl......................... Red Bank NJ 07701 732-741-8400 579
Web: www.newportcapitalgroup.com

Newport CH International LLC
1100 W Town & Country Rd Ste 1388 .... Orange CA 92868 714-572-8881 690
Web: www.newportch.com

Newport City Hall 43 Broadway .... Newport RI 02840 401-846-9600 845-2510 337
TF: 800-556-2484 ■ *Web:* www.cityofnewport.com

Newport Corp 1791 Deere Ave.................. Irvine CA 92606 949-863-3144 253-1680* 544
NASDAQ: NEWP ■ **Fax:* Sales ■ *TF Sales:* 800-222-6440 ■ *Web:* www.newport.com

Newport County 45 Washington Sq .... Newport RI 02840 401-841-8330 846-1673 338
Web: www.courts.ri.gov

Newport County Chamber of Commerce
35 Valley Rd .... Middletown RI 02842 401-847-1600 849-5848 139
TF: 800-976-5122 ■ *Web:* www.newportchamber.com

Newport County Convention & Visitors Bureau
23 America's Cup Ave....................... Newport RI 02840 401-849-8048 206
TF: 800-326-6030 ■ *Web:* discovernewport.org

Newport Creamery LLC
Garden City Ctr 100 Hillside Rd .... Cranston RI 02920 401-944-3397 296-25
Web: www.newportcreamery.com

Newport Creative Communications Inc
33 Railroad Ave.......................... Duxbury MA 02332 781-934-0586 463
Web: www.newportcreative.com

Newport Daily Independent
2408 Hwy 367 N.......................... Newport AR 72112 870-523-5855 532-2
Web: www.newportindependent.com

Newport Daily News 101 Malbone Rd .... Newport RI 02840 401-849-3300 849-3306 532-2
Web: www.newportri.com

Newport Diversified Inc
2301 Dupont Dr Ste 500.......................... Irvine CA 92612 949-851-1355 322
Web: www.nd-inc.com

Newport Electronics Inc
2229 S Yale St .... Santa Ana CA 92704 714-540-4914 546-3022 248
TF Cust Svc: 800-639-7678 ■ *Web:* www.newportinc.com

Newport Grand Jai Alai
150 Admiral Kalbfus Rd .... Newport RI 02840 401-849-5000 133
Web: www.newportgrand.com

Newport Group Securities Inc
300 International Pkwy Ste 270 .... Heathrow FL 32746 407-333-2905 690
Web: felc.com

Newport Harbor Corp 366 Thames St............ Newport RI 02840 401-848-7010 379
Web: www.newportharbor.com

Newport Harbor Hotel & Marina
49 America's Cup Ave....................... Newport RI 02840 401-847-9000 849-6380 379
TF: 800-955-2558 ■ *Web:* www.newporthotel.com

Name / Address	City	State	ZIP	Phone	Fax	Class
[illegible] Society *Web:* [illegible]ewporthistory.org	Newport	RI	02840	401-846-0813	846-1853	520
[illegible]ewport Hospital (NH) 167 Point St. *Web:* www.newporthospital.org	Newport	RI	02903	401-444-3500		374-3
Newport Layton Home Fashions Inc 8515 N Columbia Blvd *Web:* www.newportlayton.com	Portland	OR	97203	503-283-4864	283-4895	746
Newport Leasing Inc 4750 Von Karman Ave *TF Cust Svc:* 800-274-0042 ■ *Web:* www.newportleasing.com	Newport Beach	CA	92660	949-476-0476		264-1
Newport Medical Instruments Inc 1620 Sunflower Ave *TF:* 800-255-6774 ■ *Web:* www.newportnmi.com	Costa Mesa	CA	92626	714-427-5811		250
Newport Mercury 101 Malbone Rd. *Web:* www.newportri.com	Newport	RI	02840	401-380-2371		532-4
Newport News City Hall 2400 Washington Ave. *Web:* www.nnva.gov	Newport News	VA	23607	757-926-8634	926-3503	337
Newport News Inc 711 Third Ave 4th Fl *TF:* 800-324-6458 ■ *Web:* www.spiegel.com	New York	NY	10017	212-986-2585		459
Newport News (Independent City) 2400 Washington Ave. *Web:* www.nnva.gov	Newport News	VA	23607	757-926-8411	926-3503	338
Newport News Public Library System 2400 Washington Ave. *Web:* www.nnva.gov	Newport News	VA	23607	757-926-1350		434-3
Newport News Tourism Development Office 700 Town Ctr Dr Ste 320 *TF:* 888-493-7386 ■ *Web:* www.newport-news.org	Newport News	VA	23606	757-926-1400	926-1441	206
Newport News/Williamsburg International Airport 900 Bland Blvd Ste G *TF:* 800-628-6800 ■ *Web:* flyphf.com	Newport News	VA	23602	757-877-0221		27
Newport on the Levee 1 Levee Way Ste 1113 *Web:* www.newportonthelevee.com	Newport	KY	41071	859-291-0550	291-7020	50-6
Newport Partners LLC 3760 Tanglewood Ln. *TF:* 866-302-0017 ■ *Web:* newportpartnersllc.com	Davidsonville	MD	21035	301-889-0017		743
Newport Private Capital LLC 610 Newport Ctr Dr Ste 600 *Web:* www.privatecapital.com	Newport Beach	CA	92660	949-644-7300		401
Newport Public Library 300 Spring St. *Web:* www.newportlibraryri.org	Newport	RI	02840	401-847-8720	842-0841	434-3
Newport Real Estate Services Inc 3184 Airway Ave Ste H *Web:* www.nres.net	Costa Mesa	CA	92626	714-850-0085		194
Newport Seafood Grill 1717 Freeway Ct *Web:* www.newportbay.com	Salem	OR	97303	503-315-7100		670
Newport Shipyard 1 Washington St *TF:* 800-973-2867 ■ *Web:* www.newportshipyard.com	Newport	RI	02840	401-846-6000	846-6001	098
Newport State Park 475 County Rd NP *TF:* 800-847-9367 ■ *Web:* dnr.wi.gov	Ellison Bay	WI	54210	920-854-2500	854-1914	565
Newport Stationers Inc 17681 Mitchell N *TF:* 800-232-5550 ■ *Web:* www.newportstationers.com	Irvine	CA	92614	949-863-1200	852-8970	535
Newport Strategic Search Inc 175 Calle Magdalena *Web:* www.newportsearch.com	Encinitas	CA	92024	760-274-0100		260
Newport Television LLC 460 Nichols Rd.	Kansas City	MO	64112	816-751-0200		116
Newport This Week 86 Broadway *Web:* www.newportchamber.com	Newport	RI	02840	401-847-7766	846-4974	532-4
Newport Utilities PO Box 519 *TF:* 877-779-8581 ■ *Web:* www.newportutilities.com	Newport	TN	37822	423-625-2800		245
Newport/Cocke County Chamber of Commerce 433-B Prospect Ave *Web:* www.cockecounty.org	Newport	TN	37821	423-623-7201		139
NewRetirement LLC 100 Pine St Ste 590 *TF:* 866-441-0246 ■ *Web:* www.newretirement.com	San Francisco	CA	94111	415-738-2435		530
News & Advance PO Box 10129 *TF:* 800-275-8830 ■ *Web:* www.newsadvance.com	Lynchburg	VA	24506	434-385-5555	385-5538	532-2
News & Observer 215 S McDowell St. *TF:* 800-522-4205 ■ *Web:* www.newsobserver.com	Raleigh	NC	27602	919-829-4500	829-4529	532-2
News & Record 200 E Market St *TF:* 800-553-6880 ■ *Web:* www.greensboro.com	Greensboro	NC	27401	336-373-7000	373-7382	532-2
News America Marketing 1185 Ave of the Americas 27 *TF:* 800-462-0852 ■ *Web:* www.newsamerica.com	New York	NY	10036	212-782-8000	575-5845	5
News Cafe 800 Ocean Dr *Web:* www.newscafe.com	Miami Beach	FL	33139	305-538-6397	538-7817	671
News Corp 1211 Ave of the Americas *NASDAQ: NWSA* ■ *TF:* 800-690-6903 ■ *Web:* www.newscorp.com	New York	NY	10036	212-416-3400		637-9
News Democrat Journal 14522 S Outer 40 Rd *Web:* www.stltoday.com	Chesterfield	MO	63017	636-296-1800		532-4
News Examiner, The 847 Washington St *TF:* 800-847-0465 ■ *Web:* www.news-examiner.net	Montpelier	ID	83254	208-847-0552		532-3
News Gazette 15 Main St *TF:* 800-635-2666 ■ *Web:* www.news-gazette.com	Champaign	IL	61820	217-351-5252	351-5374	532-2
News Gazette Inc, The 48 E Main St. *Web:* www.news-gazette.com	Champaign	IL	61820	217-351-5282		532-3
News Generation Inc 7508 Wisconsin Ave Ste 300 *Web:* newsgeneration.com	Bethesda	MD	20814	301-664-6448		466
News Journal 70 W Fourth St *TF:* 877-424-0216 ■ *Web:* www.mansfieldnewsjournal.com	Mansfield	OH	44903	419-522-3311	521-7415	532-2
News Journal 950 W Basin Rd. *TF:* 800-235-9100 ■ *Web:* www.delawareonline.com	New Castle	DE	19720	302-324-2500	324-5509	532-2
News Journal, The 950 W Basin Rd *Web:* www.delawareonline.com	New Castle	DE	19720	302-324-2650		532-3
News Leader 11 N Central Ave. *TF:* 800-793-2459 ■ *Web:* www.newsleader.com	Staunton	VA	24401	540-885-7281		532-2
News Media Guild 131 W 33rd St 14th Fl *Web:* www.newsmediaguild.org	New York	NY	10001	212-869-9290	840-0687	414

Name / Address	City	State	ZIP	Phone	Fax	Class
News On 6 303 N Boston Ave *Web:* www.newson6.com	Tulsa	OK	74101	918-732-6105	732-6185	741-138
News Publishing Co 1126 Mills St PO Box 286 *Web:* www.newspubinc.com	Black Earth	WI	53515	608-767-3655		637-8
News Radio 1410 WDOV 1575 McKee Rd Ste 206 *Web:* wdov.iheart.com	Dover	DE	19904	302-678-5300		645-176
News Radio 610 70 Foundry St Ste 300 *TF:* 866-999-7200 ■ *Web:* nhnewsnetwork610.iheart.com	Manchester	NH	03102	603-625-6915		645-97
News Radio710 555 Broadcast Dr. *Web:* newsradio710.iheart.com	Mobile	AL	36606	251-450-0100		645-102
News Talk 1490 6555 Carnegie Ave *Web:* www.newstalkcleveland.com	Cleveland	OH	44103	216-579-1111	771-4164	645-38
NEWS TALK 98.7 4711 Old Kingston Pike **Fax:* News Rm ■ *TF:* 800-951-8255 ■ *Web:* www.newstalk987.com	Knoxville	TN	37919	865-588-6511	588-3725*	645-85
News Tribune 1950 S State St *TF:* 800-388-8742 ■ *Web:* www.thenewstribune.com	Tacoma	WA	98405	253-597-8742	597-8274	532-2
Newsbank Inc 5801 Pelican Bay Blvd Ste 600 *TF:* 800-243-7694 ■ *Web:* www.newsbank.com	Naples	FL	34108	239-263-6004	263-3004	387
News-banner Publications Inc 125 N Johnson St. *TF:* 800-579-7476 ■ *Web:* www.news-banner.com	Bluffton	IN	46714	260-824-0224		532-3
Newsday Inc 235 Pinelawn Rd. **Fax:* News Rm ■ *TF:* 888-280-4719 ■ *Web:* www.newsday.com	Melville	NY	11747	631-843-2700	843-5459*	532-2
News-Enterprise 408 W Dixie Ave *TF:* 877-246-2322 ■ *Web:* www.thenewsenterprise.com	Elizabethtown	KY	42701	270-769-1200	769-6965	532-2
Newser LLC 1395 Brickell Ave Ste 800. *Web:* www.newser.com	Miami	FL	33131	305-967-6319		772
Newseum Inc 555 Pennsylvania Ave NW *Web:* www.newseum.org	Washington	DC	20001	202-292-6100		520
News-Herald 501 W 11th St. *Web:* www.newsherald.com	Panama City	FL	32401	850-747-5000		532-2
News-Herald 7085 Mentor Ave **Fax:* News Rm ■ *TF:* 800-947-2737 ■ *Web:* www.news-herald.com	Willoughby	OH	44094	440-951-0000	975-2293*	532-2
News-Herald 1 Heritage Dr Ste 100. *Web:* www.thenewsherald.com	Southgate	MI	48195	734-246-0800	246-2727	532-4
Newslink Group LLC 6910 NW 12th St. *Web:* newslinkgroup.net	Miami	FL	33126	305-594-5754		95
Newsome House Museum & Cultural Ctr 2803 Oak Ave *TF:* 888-493-7386 ■ *Web:* www.newsomehouse.org	Newport News	VA	23607	757-247-2360	926-6754	520
Newsouth Capital Management Inc 999 S Shady Grove Rd Ste 501 *Web:* www.newsouthcapital.com	Memphis	TN	38120	901-761-5561		401
Newspaper Guild-Communications Workers of America, The 501 Third St NW 6th Fl *Web:* www.newsguild.org	Washington	DC	20001	202-434-7177	434-1472	414
Newspaper Media Alliance (NAA) 4401 Wilson Blvd Ste 900 *Web:* www.naa.org	Arlington	VA	22203	571-366-1000	366-1195	49-14
Newspaper Services of America Inc 3025 Highland Pkwy Ste 700 *Web:* nsamedia.com	Downers Grove	IL	60515	630-729-7500		532-3
Newspapers of New England Inc PO Box 1177 *Web:* www.concordmonitor.com	Concord	NH	03302	603-224-5301	224-6949	637-8
NewSpring Capital 555 E Lancaster Ave Ste 444 *Web:* www.newspringcapital.com	Radnor	PA	19087	610-567-2380	567-2388	792
News-Sentinel 600 W Main St	Fort Wayne	IN	46802	260-461-8439	461-8817	532-2
News-Star 411 N Fourth St. *Web:* www.thenewsstar.com	Monroe	LA	71201	318-322-5161		532-2
News-Sun 2227 US 27 S *Web:* www.newssun.com	Sebring	FL	33870	863-385-6155	385-1954	532-4
NewsTalk 95.5 27 N 27th St Crowne Plaza 23rd Fl. *Web:* newstalk955.com	Billings	MT	59101	406-248-7827		645-19
NewStar Fresh Foods LLC 900 Work St. **Fax Area Code:* 831 ■ *TF:* 888-782-7220 ■ *Web:* www.newstarfresh.com	Salinas	CA	93901	805-487-3406	758-7869*	296-19
News-Times 333 Main St. *TF:* 877-542-6057 ■ *Web:* www.newstimes.com	Danbury	CT	06810	203-744-5100	792-8730	532-2
Newstream Enterprises LLC 1925 E Chestnut Expy. *Web:* www.newstreaming.com	Springfield	MO	65802	417-831-3112		61
News-Tribune 426 Second St *TF:* 800-892-6452 ■ *Web:* www.newstrib.com	La Salle	IL	61301	815-223-3200	224-6443	532-2
Newsvine Inc 101 Elliott Ave W Ste 120 *TF:* 800-438-7325 ■ *Web:* www.newsvine.com	Seattle	WA	98119	206-529-4444		532-3
Newsways Distributors Inc 1324 Cypress Ave. *Web:* www.newsways.com	Los Angeles	CA	90065	323-258-6000	256-9999	96
Newsweek Magazine 7 Hanover Sq. *TF Cust Svc:* 800-631-1040 ■ *Web:* www.newsweek.com	New York	NY	10004	800-631-1040		457-17
Newtek Business Services Corp 1981 Marcus Ave Ste 130. *NASDAQ: NEWT* ■ *Web:* www.thesba.com	Lake Success	NY	11042	212-356-9500		792
NewTek Inc 5131 Beckwith Blvd *TF Cust Svc:* 800-862-7837 ■ *Web:* www.newtek.com	San Antonio	TX	78249	210-370-8000	370-8001	178-8
Newtex Industries Inc 8050 Victor Mendon Rd *TF:* 800-836-1001 ■ *Web:* www.newtex.com	Victor	NY	14564	585-924-9135	924-4645	745-3
Newton & Associates Inc 1806 Rocky River Rd *Web:* www.newtonandassociates.com	Charlotte	NC	28213	704-597-4384		194
Newton Convention & Visitor Bureau 300 E 17th St S Ste 400. *TF:* 800-798-0299 ■ *Web:* www.visitnewton.com	Newton	IA	50208	641-792-0299		206
Newton Correctional Facility 307 S 60th Ave W. *Web:* doc.iowa.gov/about-us/about-institutions/newton-correctional-facility	Newton	IA	50208	641-792-7552	791-1683	213
Newton County 1124 Clark St. *Web:* www.co.newton.ga.us	Covington	GA	30014	678-625-1202		338

Name / Address	City	State	Zip	Phone	Fax	Class
Newton County PO Box 68	Decatur	MS	39327	601-635-2368		338
Web: newtoncountyms.net						
Newton County PO Box 312	Jasper	AR	72641	870-446-5124		338
Web: www.newtoncountysheriff.org						
Newton County 201 N Third St	Kentland	IN	47951	219-474-6081	474-5749	338
TF: 888-663-9866 ■ *Web:* www.newtoncounty.in.gov						
Newton County 4117 S 240 W	Morocco	IN	47963	888-663-9866		338
TF: 888-663-9866						
Newton County 115 Ct St PO Box 484	Newton	TX	75966	409-379-5341	379-9049	338
Web: www.co.newton.tx.us						
Newton County Chamber of Commerce						
2101 Clark St	Covington	GA	30014	770-786-7510		139
Web: gocovington.com/chamber						
Newton Distributing Company Inc						
966 Watertown St	Newton	MA	02465	617-969-4002		612
TF: 877-837-7745 ■ *Web:* newtondistributing.com						
Newton Falls Fine Paper Company LLC						
875 County Rt 60	Newton Falls	NY	13666	315-848-3321		557
Newton Free Library						
330 Homer St	Newton Center	MA	02459	617-796-1360	965-8457	434-3
TF: 800-272-3900 ■ *Web:* newtonfreelibrary.net						
Newton Health Care Ctr						
2101 Washington St	Newton	MA	02462	617-969-4660		450
Newton Hills State Park						
28767 482nd Ave	Canton	SD	57013	605-987-2263		565
Web: gfp.sd.gov						
Newton Independent School District						
720 Rusk St	Newton	TX	75966	409-379-8137	379-2189	780
Web: www.newtonisd.net						
Newton Instrument Company Inc						
111 East A St	Butner	NC	27509	919-575-6426		246
Web: www.enewton.com						
Newton Lake State Fish & Wildlife Area						
3490 E 500th Ave	Newton	IL	62448	618-783-3478		565
Web: www.dnr.illinois.gov/Pages/default.aspx						
Newton Manufacturing Co						
854 Angliana Ave Ste 5	Lexington	KY	40508	641-316-0500	402-2341*	9
**Fax Area Code: 859* ■ *TF:* 855-754-8123 ■ *Web:* www.newtonmanufacturing.com						
Newton Media Associates Inc						
824 Greenbrier Pkwy Ste 200	Chesapeake	VA	23320	757-547-5400		6
TF: 800-942-1304 ■ *Web:* www.newtonmedia.com						
Newton Medical Ctr						
5126 Hospital Dr NE	Covington	GA	30014	770-786-7053		374-3
Web: www.piedmont.org						
Newton Memorial Hospital (NMH)						
175 High St	Newton	NJ	07860	973-383-2121		374-3
Web: atlantichealth.org/newton						
Newton One 131 Continental Dr	Newark	DE	19713	302-731-1326		390
Web: newtonone.com						
Newton Public Library (NPL)						
100 N Third Ave W PO Box 746	Newton	IA	50208	641-792-4108	791-0729	434-3
Web: newton.lib.ia.us						
Newton Technology Partners						
550 Bryant St	Palo Alto	CA	94301	650-331-3992		792
Newton Tool & Manufacturing Co						
500 Pedricktown Rd	Swedesboro	NJ	08085	856-241-1500		488
Web: www.newtontool.com						
Newton-Conover City Sch Dist						
605 N Ashe Ave	Newton	NC	28658	828-464-3191		685
Web: www.newton-conover.org						
Newton-Needham Chamber of Commerce						
281 Needham St	Newton	MA	02464	617-244-5300	244-5302	139
TF: 800-832-3747 ■ *Web:* www.nnchamber.com						
Newton-Wellesley Hospital						
2014 Washington St	Newton	MA	02462	617-243-6000		374-3
Web: www.nwh.org						
Newtown Savings Bank Foundation Inc						
39 Main St	Newtown	CT	06470	203-426-2563		70
TF: 800-461-0672 ■ *Web:* www.nsbonline.com						
Newtron Group, The						
8183 W El Cajon Dr	Baton Rouge	LA	70815	225-927-8921		189-4
TF: 800-644-2752 ■ *Web:* www.thenewtrongroup.com						
Newtype Inc 447 Rte 10 E Ste 14	Randolph	NJ	07869	973-361-6000	361-6005	781
Web: www.newtypeinc.com						
NewWave Technologies Inc						
4635 Wedgewood Blvd Ste 107	Frederick	MD	21703	301-624-5300		174
Web: www.newwavetech.com						
NewYork-Presbyterian Hospital						
506 Sixth St	Brooklyn	NY	11215	718-780-3000	965-4324	374-3
Web: www.nym.org						
NewYork-Presbyterian Hospital						
Blood & Marrow Transplant						
3959 Broadway	New York	NY	10032	212-305-5593	305-8428	769
TF: 866-463-2778 ■ *Web:* nyp.org/kids						
Newzones Gallery of Contemporary Art						
730 11th Ave SW	Calgary	AB	T2R0E4	403-266-1972	266-1987	42
TF: 800-419-1298 ■ *Web:* www.newzones.com						
Nex 21 Llc 1400 Urban Ctr Dr Ste 100	Vestavia	AL	35242	205-520-9916		195
TF: 800-375-8181 ■ *Web:* www.nex21.com						
Nex Computing Solutions Inc						
7404 W Detroit St Ste 100	Chandler	AZ	85226	480-838-0287		180
Web: www.nexedge.com						
Nex Transport Inc 13900 SR- 287	East Liberty	OH	43319	937-645-3761		314
Web: nextransportinc.com						
NexAge Technologies USA Inc						
75 Lincoln Hwy Ste 101	Iselin	NJ	08830	732-494-4944		195
TF: 866-866-5800 ■ *Web:* www.nexageusa.com						
Nexant Inc 44 S Broadway Fl 4	White Plains	NY	10601	914-609-0300	609-0399	194
Web: www.nexant.com						
NexBank Securities Inc						
13455 Noel Rd Ste 2240	Dallas	TX	75240	972-308-6700		690
Web: nexbank.com						
Nexcelle LLC						
30 Merchant St Mail Drop W28 Princeton Hill	Cincinnati	OH	45246	513-552-6659		21
Web: www.nexcelle.com						
Nexcess.net LLC 21700 Melrose Ave	Southfield	MI	48075	866-639-2377		225
TF: 866-639-2377 ■ *Web:* www.nexcess.net						
NEXCOM (Navy Exchange Service Command)						
3280 Virginia Beach Blvd	Virginia Beach	V[illegible]				
TF: 800-628-3924 ■ *Web:* www.mynavyexchange.com						
nexDimension Technology Solutions LLC						
10060 Medlock Bridge Rd Ste 100	Johns Creek	GA	3009[illegible]			
Web: www.nexdimension.net						
Nexdine LLC 905B S Main St Ste 203	Mansfield	MA	02048			
Web: www.nexdine.com						
Nexelus 1430 Broadway	New York	NY	10018	646-5[illegible]		
Web: www.nexelus.net						
Nexen Group Inc						
560 Oak Grove Pkwy	Vadnais Heights	MN	55127	651-484-5900	[illegible]	
TF: 800-843-7445 ■ *Web:* www.nexengroup.com						
Nexen Inc 801 Seventh Ave SW	Calgary	AB	T2P3P7	403-699-4000	699-5[illegible]	
NYSE: NXY ■ *TF:* 800-667-7125 ■ *Web:* nexencnoocltd.com						
Nexen Petroleum USA Inc						
945 Bunker Hill Ste 1400	Houston	TX	77024	832-714-5000		53[illegible]
Web: nexencnoocltd.com						
Nexenta Systems Inc						
455 El Camino Real	Santa Clara	CA	95050	408-791-3300		177
TF: 800-441-6683 ■ *Web:* www.nexenta.com						
Nexeo Solutions LLC						
3 Waterway Sq Pl Ste 1000	The Woodlands	TX	77380	281-297-0700		146
Web: nexeosolutions.com						
Nexgen Enterprises Inc						
1099 Greenleaf Ave	Elk Grove Village	IL	60007	847-303-9800		190
Web: gonexgen.com						
Nexgen Pharma Inc						
46 Corporate Pk Ste 100	Irvine	CA	92606	949-863-0340	261-2928	583
Web: www.nexgenpharma.com						
Nexgen Product Design & Development						
3117 Almond Dr	Flower Mound	TX	75028	972-333-3870		463
NexGenix Pharmaceuticals Holdings Inc						
152 W 57th St Ste 11B	New York	NY	10019	212-974-3006		231
Nexio Group Inc, The						
2050 de Bleury St Ste 500	Montreal	QC	H3A2J5	514-798-3707		631
TF: 888-798-3707 ■ *Web:* www.nexio.com						
Nexion 6225 N State Hwy 161 Ste 450	Irving	TX	75038	408-280-6410	271-2039	772
TF: 800-949-6410 ■ *Web:* www.nexion.com						
Nexion Health Inc						
6937 Warfield Ave	Sykesville	MD	21784	410-552-4800		371
Web: www.nexion-health.com						
Nexius Inc 825 Market St Ste 250	Allen	TX	75013	703-650-7777		736
Web: www.nexius.com						
Nexlan 28 W N St	Danville	IL	61832	217-431-7236	477-5731	177
TF: 877-263-9526 ■ *Web:* nexlan.com						
NexLevel Information Technology Inc						
6829 Fair Oaks Blvd Ste 100	Carmichael	CA	95608	916-692-2000		180
Web: www.nexlevelit.com						
Nexonia Inc 2 St Clair Ave E Ste 701	Toronto	ON	M4T2T5	416-480-0688		396
Web: www.nexonia.com						
Nexpay 5121 N Mccoll Rd	Mcallen	TX	78504	956-994-1800		570
Web: www.nexpay.us						
Nexsales Corp						
20660 Stevens Creek Blvd Ste 129	Cupertino	CA	95104	408-831-3800	831-3700	195
Web: www.nexsales.com						
Nexsen Pruet LLC 1230 Main St Ste 700	Columbia	SC	29201	803-771-8900		445
Web: www.nexsenpruet.com						
Next Breath LLC 1450 S Rolling Rd	Baltimore	MD	21227	410-455-5904		743
Web: www.nextbreath.net						
Next Day Flyers						
18711 S Broadwick St	Rancho Dominguez	CA	90220	800-251-9948		5
TF: 800-251-9948 ■ *Web:* www.nextdayflyers.com						
Next Eon Com 40 Meriam St	Wakefield	MA	01880	781-231-3200		180
Web: www.nexteon.com						
NEXT Financial Holdings Inc						
2500 Wilcrest Dr Ste 620	Houston	TX	77042	877-876-6398		690
TF: 877-876-6398 ■ *Web:* www.nextfinancialholdings.com						
Next Generation Energy LLC						
75 Waneka Pkwy	Lafayette	CO	80026	303-665-2000		612
Web: www.ngeus.com						
Next Generation Films Inc						
230 Industrial Dr	Mansfield	OH	44904	419-884-8150		600
Web: www.nextgenfilms.com						
Next IT Corp						
12809 E Mirabeau Pkwy	Spokane Valley	WA	99216	509-242-0767		809
Web: www.nextit.com						
Next Level Games Inc						
208 Robson St 3rd Fl	Vancouver	BC	V6B6A1	604-484-6111	484-6112	761
Web: www.nextlevelgames.com						
Next Level Purchasing						
1315 Coraopolis Heights Rd Ste 2002	Moon Township	PA	15108	412-294-1990		764
Web: www.nextlevelpurchasing.com						
Next Level Security Systems Inc						
6353 Corte Del Abeto Ste 102	Carlsbad	CA	92011	760-444-1410		693
Web: www.nlss.com						
Next Marketing Inc 2820 Peterson Pl	Norcross	GA	30071	770-225-2200		195
Web: www.nextmarketing.com						
Next Model Management						
15 Watts St 6th Fl	New York	NY	10013	212-925-5100	925-5931	506
Web: www.nextmanagement.com						
Next Net Media LLC						
316 California Ave Ste 804	Reno	NV	89509	800-737-5820		387
TF: 800-737-5820 ■ *Web:* nextnetmedia.com						
Next Plumbing Supply						
1839 Old Okeechobee Rd	West Palm Beach	FL	33409	561-689-9060		38
Web: nextps.com						
NEXT Precision Marketing						
10400 Yellow Circle Dr Ste 500	Minnetonka	MN	55343	952-443-6400		4
Web: www.nextcom.com						
Next Step Partners						
1730 Vallejo St Apt 5	San Francisco	CA	94123	415-762-0148		196
Web: www.nextsteppartners.com						
Next Steps Marketing						
1 Polk St Fl 2	San Francisco	CA	94102	415-773-1841		195
TF: 800-447-2334 ■ *Web:* www.nextstepsmarketing.com						
Next Wave Logistics Inc						
28377 Davis Pkwy Ste 607A	Warrenville	IL	60555	630-393-0507		809

Name / Address	City	State	ZIP	Phone	Fax	Class
Next Year's News						
1 S Saint Clair St Ste 1b	Toledo	OH	43604	419-241-3698		532-3
Nextaff LLC						
11225 College Blvd Ste 250	Overland Park	KS	66210	913-562-5620		734
Web: www.nextaff.com						
NexTag.com Inc						
555 Twin Dolphin Dr Ste 370	Redwood City	CA	94065	650-645-4700	341-3779	51
Web: www.nextag.com						
NexTalk Inc						
10757 River Front Pkwy Ste 290	South Jordan	UT	84095	801-274-6001		225
Web: www.nextalk.com						
Nextant Aerospace LLC						
355 Richmond Rd	Cleveland	OH	44143	216-261-9000		21
TF: 800-321-8072 ■ *Web:* www.nextantaerospace.com						
NextEnergy Inc 35 Earl Martin Dr	Elmira	ON	N3B3L4	519-669-1015		610
NextEra Energy Resources LLC						
NextEra Energy Resources LLC						
700 Universe Blvd PO Box 14000	Juno Beach	FL	33408	561-691-7171		787
Web: www.nexteraenergyresources.com						
Nexternal Solutions Inc						
785 Grand Ave Ste 216	Carlsbad	CA	92008	760-730-9015		396
TF: 800-914-6161 ■ *Web:* www.nexternal.com						
Nextest Systems Corp						
875 Embedded Way	San Jose	CA	95138	408-960-2400		472
Web: www.teradyne.com						
NextFuels LLC 86 Third St	Los Altos	CA	94022	650-490-4500		580
NextG Networks Inc 890 Tasman Dr	Milpitas	CA	95035	877-486-9377		614
TF: 877-486-9377 ■ *Web:* www.crowncastle.com						
NextGate Solutions Inc						
3579 E Foothill Blvd Ste 587	Pasadena	CA	91107	626-376-4100		180
Web: www.nextgate.com						
Nextgen Information Services Inc						
906 Olive St Ste 600	Saint Louis	MO	63101	314-588-1212	588-1211	721
Web: www.nextgen-is.com						
Nextgen Networks Inc						
200 Katonah Ave Ste A	Katonah	NY	10536	914-232-8300		261
TF: 866-639-8436 ■ *Web:* www.nninet.com						
NextIO Inc 8303 N MoPac Expy	Austin	TX	78759	512-439-5350		735
Nextiva 8800 E Chaparral Rd Ste 300	Scottsdale	AZ	85250	800-799-0600		387
TF: 800-799-0600 ■ *Web:* www.nextiva.com						
NextMark Inc 33 S Main St 3rd Fl	Hanover	NH	03755	603-643-1307		194
Web: www.nextmark.com						
NextMedia Group Inc						
6312 S Fiddlers Green Cir Ste 205E	Greenwood Village	CO	80111	303-694-9118	694-4940	643
NextPharma Technologies Inc						
5340 Eastgate Mall	San Diego	CA	92121	858-450-3123		582
Web: www.nextpharma.com						
nextPoint Inc 4043 N Ravenswood Ave	Chicago	IL	60613	773-929-4000		177
TF: 888-929-6398 ■ *Web:* www.nextpoint.com						
Nextran Corp 1986 W Beaver St	Jacksonville	FL	32209	904-354-3721		57
TF: 800-347-0225 ■ *Web:* www.nextrancorp.com						
NextRidge Inc 12 Elmwood Rd	Albany	NY	12204	518-292-6505		196
TF: 800-715-2441 ■ *Web:* www.nextridgeinc.com						
Nextrio LLC 4803 E Fifth St	Tucson	AZ	85711	520-545-7100		196
Web: www.nextrio.com						
NextServices Inc 540 Avis Dr Ste H	Ann Arbor	MI	48108	734-677-7700		463
Web: nextservices.net						
Nextware Technologies						
233 Wilshire Blvd Ste 400	Santa Monica	CA	90401	310-955-9919		177
Web: www.nextwaretech.com						
NextWave Wireless Inc						
10350 Science Ctr Dr Ste 210	San Diego	CA	92121	858-731-5300	731-5301	360-3
OTC: WAVE ■ *TF:* 800-461-9330 ■ *Web:* www.nextwave.com						
Nexus Business Solutions						
157 S Kalamazoo Mall Dr Ste 105	Kalamazoo	MI	49007	269-373-1500		226
TF: 800-713-7278 ■ *Web:* www.nexusbusiness.com						
Nexus Corp 10983 Leroy Dr	Northglenn	CO	80233	303-457-9199		106
TF: 800-228-9639 ■ *Web:* www.nexuscorp.com						
Nexus Engineering Inc						
1400 Lone Palm Ave	Modesto	CA	95351	209-572-7399		256
Web: www.nexusengineering.net						
Nexus Inc 50 Sunnyside Ave	Stamford	CT	06902	203-327-7300	324-7623	815
Web: www.nexus.com						
Nexus Office Systems Inc						
898 Featherstone Rd	Rockford	IL	61107	815-227-0170		535
TF: 800-717-2777 ■ *Web:* nexusofficesystems.com						
Nexus Technologies Inc						
11 National Ave	Fletcher	NC	28732	828-681-2844		261
Web: www.nexus-tech.net						
Nexus Valve Inc 9982 E 121st St	Fishers	IN	46037	317-257-6050		612
TF: 800-900-8654 ■ *Web:* www.nexusvalve.com						
Nexus World Services Inc						
7114 W Jefferson Ste 110	Denver	CO	80235	303-988-1243		41
TF: 800-315-0042 ■ *Web:* www.nexusworldservices.com						
nexVortex Inc 510 Spring St Ste 120	Herndon	VA	20170	703-579-0200		387
Web: www.nexvortex.com						
Nexxa Industries Ltd 1-4380 76 Ave SE	Calgary	AB	T2C2J2	403-720-1996		757
Web: www.nexxaindustries.com						
Nexxtworks Inc 30798 US Hwy 19 N	Palm Harbor	FL	34684	888-533-8353		387
TF: 888-533-8353 ■ *Web:* www.nexxtworks.com						
Nexxus Marketing Group LLC, The						
85 Sam Fonzo Dr	Beverly	MA	01915	978-762-3900		225
Web: www.thenexxusgroup.com						
Ney Oil Company Inc 145 S Water St	Ney	OH	43549	419-658-2324	658-2723	324
TF: 800-962-9839 ■ *Web:* www.neyoil.com						
Neyenesch Printers Inc						
2750 Kettner Blvd	San Diego	CA	92101	415-566-1599		627
Web: www.neyenesch.com						
Neyer Properties Inc						
2135 Dana Ave Ste 200	Cincinnati	OH	45207	513-563-7555		652
Web: www.neyer1.com						
Neyra Industries 10700 Evendale Dr	Cincinnati	OH	45241	513-733-1000		46
TF: 800-543-7077 ■ *Web:* www.neyra.com						
Nez Perce County						
1230 Main St PO Box 896	Lewiston	ID	83501	208-799-3020	799-3070	338
Web: www.co.nezperce.id.us						

Name / Address	City	State	ZIP	Phone	Fax	Class
Nez Perce County Historical Society & Museum						
0306 Third St	Lewiston	ID	83501	208-743-2535		520
TF: 800-933-2128 ■ *Web:* npchistsoc.org						
Nez Perce National Historical Park						
39063 US Hwy 95	Spalding	ID	83540	208-843-2261	843-7003	564
TF: 800-537-7962 ■ *Web:* www.nps.gov/nepe						
NF Davis Drier & Elevator Inc						
9421 N Dos Palos Ave	Firebaugh	CA	93622	559-659-3035		275
NFA (National Fireworks Assn)						
8224 NW Bradford Ct	Kansas City	MO	64151	816-741-1826		48-10
Web: www.nationalfireworks.org						
NFA (National Futures Assn)						
300 S Riverside Plaza Ste 1800	Chicago	IL	60606	312-781-1300	781-1467	49-2
TF: 800-621-3570 ■ *Web:* www.nfa.futures.org						
NFA Corp 850 Boylston St Ste 428	Chestnut Hill	MA	02467	617-232-6060		745-5
NFA Group Inc						
2002 A Guadalupe Ave Ste 118	Austin	TX	78705	512-377-1340	692-2824	809
Web: www.buydrm.com						
N-fab Inc						
14925 Stuebner Airline Rd Ste 207	Houston	TX	77069	281-880-6322		697
Web: www.n-fab.com						
NFB (National Federation of the Blind)						
1800 Johnson St	Baltimore	MD	21230	410-659-9314	685-5653	48-17
TF: 800-392-5671 ■ *Web:* www.nfb.org						
NFBA (National Frame Builders Assn)						
8735 W Higgins Rd Ste 300	Chicago	IL	60631	800-557-6957	375-6495*	49-3
**Fax Area Code:* 847 ■ *TF:* 800-557-6957 ■ *Web:* www.nfba.org						
NFBPA (National Forum for Black Public Administrators)						
777 N Capitol St NE Ste 807	Washington	DC	20002	202-408-9300	408-8558	49-7
TF: 800-488-4845 ■ *Web:* www.nfbpa.org						
NFC Global LLC						
240 Gibraltar Rd Ste 150	Horsham	PA	19044	215-657-0800		463
Web: www.nfcglobal.com						
NFCA (National Family Caregivers Assn)						
10400 Connecticut Ave Ste 500	Kensington	MD	20895	301-942-6430		48-6
TF: 800-896-3650 ■ *Web:* caregiveraction.org						
NFCB (National Federation of Community Broadcasters)						
1970 Broadway Ste 1000	Oakland	CA	94612	510-451-8200		49-14
Web: www.nfcb.org						
NFCDCU (National Federation of Community Development Credit Unions)						
39 Broadway Ste 2140	New York	NY	10006	212-809-1850	809-3274	49-2
TF: 800-437-8711 ■ *Web:* www.cdcu.coop						
NFCR (National Foundation for Cancer Research)						
4600 E W Hwy Ste 525	Bethesda	MD	20814	301-654-1250	654-5824	305
TF: 800-321-2873 ■ *Web:* www.nfcr.org						
NFDA (National Funeral Directors Assn)						
13625 Bishop's Dr	Brookfield	WI	53005	262-789-1880	789-6977	49-4
TF: 800-228-6332 ■ *Web:* nfda.org						
NFDMA (National Funeral Directors & Morticians Assn)						
6290 Shannon Pkwy	Union City	GA	30291	770-969-0064	286-6573*	49-4
**Fax Area Code:* 404 ■ *TF:* 800-434-0958 ■ *Web:* www.nfdma.com						
NFDW (National Federation of Democratic Women)						
7211 E Lincoln	Wichita	KS	67207	316-612-9709		48-7
Web: www.nfdw.com						
NFFC (National Family Farm Coalition)						
110 Maryland Ave NE Ste 307	Washington	DC	20002	202-543-5675	543-0978	48-2
TF: 800-321-3054 ■ *Web:* www.nffc.net						
NFHS (National Federation of State High School Assn)						
PO Box 690	Indianapolis	IN	46206	317-972-6900	822-5700	48-22
TF Cust Svc: 800-776-3462 ■ *Web:* www.nfhs.org						
NFI (NFI Industries)						
1515 Burnt Mill Rd	Cherry Hill	NJ	08003	877-634-3777		449
TF: 877-634-3777 ■ *Web:* www.natlfreight.com						
NFI Inc Dba Harrisonburg Honda Mitsubishi Hyundai						
2885 S Main St	Harrisonburg	VA	22801	540-433-1467		57
Web: www.harrisonburghonda.com						
NFI Industries (NFI)						
1515 Burnt Mill Rd	Cherry Hill	NJ	08003	877-634-3777		449
TF: 877-634-3777 ■ *Web:* www.natlfreight.com						
NFIC (National Fraud Information Ctr)						
1701 K St NW Ste 1200	Washington	DC	20006	202-835-3323		48-10
TF: 800-333-4636 ■ *Web:* www.fraud.org						
NFID (National Foundation for Infectious Diseases)						
4733 Bethesda Ave Ste 750	Bethesda	MD	20814	301-656-0003	907-0878	49-8
TF: 800-708-5478 ■ *Web:* www.nfid.org						
NFL (National Speech and Debate Association's)						
125 Watson St PO Box 38	Ripon	WI	54971	920-748-6206	748-9478	48-11
Web: www.speechanddebate.org						
NFL Films Inc 1 Nfl Plaza	Mt Laurel	NJ	08054	856-222-3500		514
Web: www.nflfilms.com						
NFL Network 345 Park Ave	New York	NY	10154	212-450-2000		740
TF: 800-724-3377 ■ *Web:* www.nfl.com/nflnetwork						
NFLPA (National Football League Players)						
1133 20th St NW	Washington	DC	20036	800-372-2000		48-22
TF: 800-372-2000 ■ *Web:* www.nflpa.com						
NFM Welding Engineers						
577 Oberlin Rd SW	Massillon	OH	44647	330-837-3868	837-2230	456
Web: www.nfm.net						
NFO (National Farmers Organization)						
528 Billy Sunday Rd Ste 100 PO Box 2508	Ames	IA	50010	515-292-2000	292-7106	48-2
TF: 800-247-2110 ■ *Web:* www.nfo.org						
Nfocus Consulting Inc						
1594 Hubbard Dr	Lancaster	OH	43130	740-654-5809		196
TF: 800-675-5809 ■ *Web:* www.n-focus.com						
NFP (National Fibromyalgia Partnership Inc)						
140 Zinn Way	Linden	VA	22642	866-725-4404		48-17
TF: 866-725-4404 ■ *Web:* www.fmpartnership.org						
NFP (National Financial Partners Corp)						
340 Madison Ave 20th Fl	New York	NY	10173	212-301-4000	301-4001	401
NYSE: NFP ■ *Web:* www.nfp.com						
NFPA (National Federation of Paralegal Associations)						
23607 Hwy 99 Ste 2-C	Edmonds	WA	98026	425-967-0045	771-9588	49-10
NFPA (National Fire Protection Assn)						
1 Batterymarch Pk	Quincy	MA	02169	617-770-3000	770-0700	48-17
TF: 800-344-3555 ■ *Web:* www.nfpa.org						
NFPA (National Fluid Power Assn)						
3333 N Mayfair Rd Ste 211	Milwaukee	WI	53222	414-778-3344	778-3361	49-13
Web: www.nfpa.com						

Name / Address	City	State	Zip	Phone	Fax	Class
NFR (North Fork Ranch)						
55395 Hwy 285 PO Box B	Shawnee	CO	80475	303-838-9873	838-1549	239
TF: 800-843-7895 ■ *Web:* www.northforkranch.com						
NFRA (National Frozen & Refrigerated Foods Assn)						
4755 Linglestown Rd Ste 300 Ste 300	Harrisburg	PA	17112	717-657-8601	657-9862	49-6
Web: www.nfraweb.org						
NFRA (National Forest Recreation Assn)						
PO Box 488	Woodlake	CA	93286	559-564-2365	564-2048	48-23
TF: 800-282-2444 ■ *Web:* www.nfra.org						
Nfra Inc 77 E Thomas Rd Ste 200	Phoenix	AZ	85012	602-277-0967		261
Web: www.nfrainc.us						
NFRW (National Federation of Republican Women)						
124 N Alfred St	Alexandria	VA	22314	703-548-9688	548-9836	48-7
TF: 800-373-9688 ■ *Web:* www.nfrw.org						
NFS (National Field Service Corp)						
162 Orange Ave	Suffern	NY	10901	845-368-1600	368-1989	736
Web: nfsco.com						
NFSA (National Fire Sprinkler Assn)						
40 Jon Barrett Rd	Patterson	NY	12563	845-878-4200	878-4215	49-3
Web: www.nfsa.org						
NFTC (National Foreign Trade Council)						
1625 K St NW Ste 200	Washington	DC	20006	202-887-0278	452-8160	49-18
Web: www.nftc.org						
NFU (National Farmers Union News)						
20 F St NW Ste 300	Washington	DC	20001	202-554-1600	554-1654	531-13
TF: 800-442-8277 ■ *Web:* www.nfu.org						
Nfusion Design Studio LLC						
400 Fourth Ave S	Nashville	TN	37201	615-850-5530		393
Web: www.nfusiondesignstudio.com						
NG Purvis Farms Inc 2504 Spies Rd	Robbins	NC	27325	910-948-2297		10-6
NGA (National Gardening Assn)						
1100 Dorset St	South Burlington	VT	05403	802-863-5251	864-6889	48-18
TF: 800-538-7476 ■ *Web:* www.garden.org						
NGA (National Glass Assn)						
8200 Greensboro Dr Ste 302	McLean	VA	22102	703-442-4890	442-0630	49-13
TF: 866-342-5642 ■ *Web:* www.glass.org						
NGA (National Governors Assn)						
444 N Capitol St NW Ste 267	Washington	DC	20001	202-624-5300	624-5313	49-7
Web: www.nga.org						
NGA (National Greyhound Assn)						
729 Old US 40	Abilene	KS	67410	785-263-4660	263-4689	48-22
TF: 800-366-1471 ■ *Web:* www.ngagreyhounds.com						
NGA (National Grocers Assn)						
1005 N Glebe Rd Ste 250	Arlington	VA	22201	703-516-0700	516-0115	49-6
TF: 800-627-6667 ■ *Web:* www.nationalgrocers.org						
NGAUS (National Guard Educational Foundation)						
1 Massachusetts Ave NW	Washington	DC	20001	202-789-0031	682-9358	48-19
TF: 888-226-4287 ■ *Web:* www.ngaus.org						
NGC (National Garden Clubs Inc)						
4401 Magnolia Ave	Saint Louis	MO	63110	314-776-7574	776-5108	48-18
TF: 800-550-6007 ■ *Web:* www.gardenclub.org						
Ngci 1420 N Capitol St NW	Washington	DC	20002	202-527-9595		396
TF: 800-601-2944 ■ *Web:* www.ngciglobal.com						
NGCOA (National Golf Course Owners Assn)						
291 Seven Farms Dr 2nd Fl	Charleston	SC	29492	843-881-9956	881-9958	48-23
TF: 800-933-4262 ■ *Web:* www.ngcoa.org						
NGEN Partners LLC						
1114 State St Ste 247	Santa Barbara	CA	93101	805-564-3156		792
Web: www.ngenpartners.com						
NGF (National Gaucher Foundation)						
5410 Edson Ln Ste 220	Rockville	MD	20852	770-934-2910		48-17
TF: 800-504-3189 ■ *Web:* www.gaucherdisease.org						
NGF (National Golf Foundation)						
1150 S US Hwy 1 Ste 401	Jupiter	FL	33477	561-744-6006	744-6107	48-22
TF: 800-733-6006 ■ *Web:* www.ngf.org						
NGFA (National Grain & Feed Assn)						
1250 'I' St NW Ste 1003	Washington	DC	20005	202-289-0873	289-5388	48-2
Web: www.ngfa.org						
NGHS (Northeast Georgia Health System Inc)						
743 Spring St NE	Gainesville	GA	30501	770-535-3553		374-3
Web: www.nghs.com						
NGInstruments Inc 4643 N State Rd 15	Warsaw	IN	46582	574-268-2112		757
TF: 800-255-4576 ■ *Web:* www.nginstruments.com						
NGIRL (North Central Agricultural Research Laboratory)						
2923 Medary Ave	Brookings	SD	57006	605-693-3241	693-5240	668
Web: www.ars.usda.gov/main/docs.htm?docid=2357						
NGK Metals Corp 917 Hwy 11 S	Sweetwater	TN	37874	423-337-5500	645-2328*	308
**Fax Area Code:* 877 ■ *TF:* 800-523-8268 ■ *Web:* www.ngkmetals.com						
NGK Spark Plugs Inc 46929 Magellan	Wixom	MI	48393	248-926-6900		247
TF: 877-473-6767 ■ *Web:* www.ngksparkplugs.com						
Ngk-locke Polymer Insulators Inc						
1609 Diamond Springs Rd	Virginia Beach	VA	23455	757-460-3649	460-3550	816
Web: www.ngk-polymer.com						
NGL (National Guardian Life Insurance Co)						
2 E Gilman St	Madison	WI	53703	800-548-2962	257-3940*	391-2
**Fax Area Code:* 608 ■ *TF:* 800-548-2962 ■ *Web:* www.nglic.com						
NGL (Network Global Logistics)						
320 Interlocken Pkwy Ste 100	Broomfield	CO	80021	866-938-1870		546
TF: 866-938-1870 ■ *Web:* www.nglog.com						
NGLTF (National Gay & Lesbian Task Force)						
1325 Massachusetts Ave NW Ste 600	Washington	DC	20005	202-393-5177	393-2241	48-8
Web: www.thetaskforce.org						
NGM Biopharmaceuticals Inc						
333 Oyster Point Blvd	South San Francisco	CA	94080	650-243-5555		668
Web: www.ngmbio.com						
NGP Energy Capital Management						
5221 N O'Connor Blvd Ste 1100	Irving	TX	75039	972-432-1440		401
TF: 800-850-2903 ■ *Web:* www.ngpenergycapital.com						
nGroup Inc						
1184 Springmaid Ave Ste 104	Fort Mill	SC	29708	704-719-2210		260
Web: www.ngroup.biz/#home						
NGS (National Genealogical Society)						
3108 Columbia Pk Ste 300	Arlington	VA	22204	703-525-0050	525-0052	48-18
TF: 800-473-0060 ■ *Web:* www.ngsgenealogy.org						
NGSA (Natural Gas Supply Assn)						
805 15th St NW Ste 510	Washington	DC	20005	202-326-9300	326-9330	48-12
Web: www.ngsa.org						
NGSG (Natural Gas Services Group Inc)						
508 W Wall Ste 550	Midland	TX	79701	432-262-2700	262-2701	537
NYSE: NGS ■ *Web:* www.ngsgi.com						
Nguoi Viet News 14771 Moran St	Westminster	CA	92683	714-892-9414	894-1381	532-2
Web: www.nguoi-viet.com						
NGWA (National Ground Water Assn)						
601 Dempsey Rd	Westerville	OH	43081	614-898-7791	898-7786	48-12
TF: 800-551-7379 ■ *Web:* www.ngwa.org						
NGWSP (New Glarus Woods State Park)						
W5446 County Hwy NN	New Glarus	WI	53574	608-527-2335		565
Web: dnr.wi.gov						
NH (Newport Hospital) 167 Point St	Newport	RI	02903	401-444-3500		374-3
Web: www.newporthospital.org						
NH Research Inc 16601 Hale Ave	Irvine	CA	92606	949-474-3900	474-7062	248
Web: www.nhresearch.com						
NH Yates & Company Inc						
117 Church Ln # C	Cockeysville	MD	21030	800-878-8181	667-9201*	641
**Fax Area Code:* 888 ■ *TF:* 800-878-8181 ■ *Web:* www.nhyates.com						
NHA (National Humanities Alliance)						
21 Dupont Cir NW Ste 800	Washington	DC	20036	202-296-4994	872-0884	48-4
Web: www.nhalliance.org						
NHC (National Housing Conference)						
1801 K St NW Ste M-100	Washington	DC	20006	202-466-2121	466-2122	49-3
Web: www.nhc.org						
NHC (National Health Council)						
1730 M St NW Ste 500	Washington	DC	20036	202-785-3910	785-5923	48-17
TF: 800-622-9010 ■ *Web:* www.nationalhealthcouncil.org						
NHCA (National Hearing Conservation Assn)						
3030 W 81st Ave	Westminster	CO	80031	303-224-9022	458-0002	48-17
TF: 866-432-7968 ■ *Web:* www.hearingconservation.org						
NHCI (New Hampshire Correctional Industries)						
105 Pleasant St PO Box 1806	Concord	NH	03302	603-271-5600	271-5643	630
Web: www.nh.gov/nhdoc						
NHCOA (National Hispanic Council on Aging)						
734 15th St NW Ste 1050	Washington	DC	20005	202-347-9733	347-9735	48-6
TF: 800-633-4227 ■ *Web:* www.nhcoa.org						
NHCS (Nash Health Care Systems)						
2460 Curtis Ellis Dr	Rocky Mount	NC	27804	252-443-8000		374-3
Web: www.nhcs.org						
NHDP (National Hansen's Disease Program)						
1770 Physicians Pk Dr	Baton Rouge	LA	70816	800-221-9393		668
TF: 800-221-9393 ■ *Web:* hrsa.gov						
Employment Security 32 S Main St	Concord	NH	03301	603-224-3311	228-4145	259
TF: 800-852-3400 ■ *Web:* www.nh.gov						
NHF (National Headache Foundation)						
820 N Orleans St Ste 217	Chicago	IL	60610	888-643-5552	640-9049*	48-17
**Fax Area Code:* 312 ■ *TF:* 888-643-5552 ■ *Web:* www.headaches.org						
NHF (National Hemophilia Foundation)						
7 Penn Plaza Ste 1204	New York	NY	10001	212-328-3700	328-3777	48-17
TF: 800-424-2634 ■ *Web:* www.hemophilia.org						
NHFA (National Home Furnishings Assn)						
500 Giuseppe Ct Ste 6	Roseville	CA	95678	800-422-3778		49-4
TF: 800-422-3778 ■ *Web:* myhfa.org						
NHI (National Hispanic Institute)						
472 FM 1966 Rd	Maxwell	TX	78656	512-357-6137		48-14
NHIA (National Home Infusion Assn)						
100 Daingerfield Rd	Alexandria	VA	22314	703-549-3740	683-1484	49-8
Web: www.nhia.org						
NHK Laboratories Inc						
12230 E Florience Ave	Santa Fe Springs	CA	90670	562-944-5400	944-0266	479
TF: 866-645-5227 ■ *Web:* www.nhklabs.com						
NHL (National Hockey League)						
1185 Ave of the Americas	New York	NY	10036	212-789-2000	789-2020	716
Web: www.nhl.com						
NHLA (National Hardwood Lumber Assn)						
6830 Raleigh-LaGrange Rd	Memphis	TN	38134	901-377-1818	382-6419	49-3
TF: 800-933-0318 ■ *Web:* www.nhla.com						
NHLPA (National Hockey League Players Assn)						
20 Bay St Ste 1700	Toronto	ON	M5J2N8	416-907-9801	313-2301	48-22
Web: www.nhlpa.com						
NHMFL (National High Magnetic Field Laboratory)						
1800 E Paul Dirac Dr	Tallahassee	FL	32310	850-644-0311		668
NHNA (New Hampshire Nurses Assn)						
210 N State St Ste 1A	Concord	NH	03301	603-225-3783	228-6672	533
Web: www.nhnurses.org						
NHPCO (National Hospice & Palliative Care Organization)						
1700 Diagonal Rd Ste 625	Alexandria	VA	22314	703-837-1500	837-1233	49-8
TF Help Line: 800-658-8898 ■ *Web:* www.nhpco.org						
NHPIRG (New Hampshire Public Interest Research Group)						
30 S Main St Ste 301-A	Concord	NH	03301	603-229-1343		633
Web: www.nhpirg.org						
NHPTV (New Hampshire Public Television)						
268 Mast Rd	Durham	NH	03824	603-868-1100	868-7552	632
TF: 800-639-8408 ■ *Web:* www.nhptv.org						
NH&RA (National Housing & Rehabilitation Assn)						
1400 16th St NW Ste 420	Washington	DC	20036	202-939-1750	265-4435	49-17
TF: 800-644-0390 ■ *Web:* www.housingonline.com						
NHRC (Naval Health Research Ctr)						
140 Sylvester Rd	San Diego	CA	92152	619-553-8400	553-9389	668
Web: www.med.navy.mil/sites/nhrc						
NHS (National Honor Society) 1904 Assn Dr	Reston	VA	20191	703-860-0200	476-5432	48-11
TF: 800-253-7746 ■ *Web:* www.nhs.us						
NHSA (National Head Start Assn)						
1651 Prince St	Alexandria	VA	22314	703-739-0875	739-0878	48-11
TF: 866-677-8724 ■ *Web:* www.nhsa.org						
NHT Global Inc						
609 Deep Valley Dr Ste 395	Rolling Hills Estates	CA	90274	972-241-6525		459
Web: www.nhtglobal.com						
NHTI Concord's Community College						
31 College Dr	Concord	NH	03301	603-271-6484	271-7139	162
TF: 800-247-0179 ■ *Web:* www.nhti.edu						
NHTSA (National Highway Traffic Safety Administration)						
1200 New Jersey Ave SE	Washington	DC	20590	202-366-9550	366-6916	340-17
TF: 888-327-4236 ■ *Web:* www.nhtsa.gov						
NHTSA (National Highway Traffic Safety Administration Regional Offices)						
NHTSA Region 1						
1200 New Jersey Ave SE West Bldg	Cambridge	MA	02142	617-494-3427	494-3646	340-17
Web: www.nhtsa.gov						

	Phone	Fax	Class
NIA (National Insulation Assn)			
99 Canal Ctr Plaza Ste 222 .... Alexandria VA 22314	703-683-6422		49-3
TF: 877-968-7642 ■ *Web:* www.insulation.org			
Niacet Corp 400 47th St. .... Niagara Falls NY 14304	716-285-1474	285-1497	144
TF: 800-828-1207 ■ *Web:* www.niacet.com			
NIADA (National Independent Automobile Dealers Assn)			
2521 Brown Blvd .... Arlington TX 76006	817-640-3838	649-5866	49-18
TF: 800-682-3837 ■ *Web:* www.niada.com			
Niagara Blower Co Inc 91 Sawyer Ave. .... Tonawanda NY 14150	716-875-2000	875-1077	14
TF: 800-426-5169 ■ *Web:* www.niagarablower.com			
Niagara College of Applied Arts & Technology			
300 Woodlawn Rd. .... Welland ON L3C7L3	905-641-2252		162
Web: www.niagaracollege.ca			
Niagara Conservation Corp			
45 Horsehill Rd. .... Cedar Knolls NJ 07927	973-829-0800		612
TF: 800-831-8383 ■ *Web:* www.niagaraconservation.com			
Niagara Corp 667 Madison Ave. .... New York NY 10021	212-317-1000	317-1001	723
TF: 877-289-2277 ■ *Web:* www.niagaralasalle.com			
Niagara County PO Box 461 .... Lockport NY 14095	716-439-7022	439-7066	338
TF: 800-460-5657 ■ *Web:* www.niagaracounty.com			
Niagara County Community College			
3111 Saunders Settlement Rd. .... Sanborn NY 14132	716-614-6222	614-6820*	162
**Fax:* Admissions ■ *TF:* 800-875-6269 ■ *Web:* www.niagaracc.suny.edu			
Niagara Cutter Inc 2805 Bellingham Dr. .... Troy MI 48083	248-528-5220		493
TF: 800-832-8326 ■ *Web:* www.niagaracutter.com			
Niagara Duty Free Shop			
5726 Falls Ave .... Niagara Falls ON L2G7T5	905-374-3700		241
TF: 877-642-4337 ■ *Web:* www.niagaradutyfree.com			
Niagara Falls Canada Chamber of Commerce			
4056 Dorchester Rd .... Niagara Falls ON L2E6M9	905-374-3666	374-2972	137
Web: www.niagarafallschamber.com			
Niagara Falls Memorial Medical Ctr			
621 Tenth St .... Niagara Falls NY 14302	716-278-4000		374-3
Web: www.nfmmc.org			
Niagara Falls Public Library			
1425 Main St .... Niagara Falls NY 14305	716-286-4894	286-4885	434-3
TF: 800-462-7652 ■ *Web:* www.niagarafallspubliclib.org			
Niagara Falls Review			
4424 Queen St .... Niagara Falls ON L2R2L3	905-358-5711		532-1
Web: www.niagarafallsreview.ca			
Niagara Falls State Park			
PO Box 1132 .... Niagara Falls NY 14303	716-278-1796		565
Web: www.niagarafallsstatepark.com			
Niagara Fresh Fruit Co			
5796 Wilson Burt Rd .... Burt NY 14028	716-778-7631	778-8768	685
Web: niagarafreshfruit.com			
Niagara Frontier Transportation Authority			
181 Ellicott St. .... Buffalo NY 14203	716-855-7300		468
TF: 800-662-1220 ■ *Web:* www.nfta.com			
Niagara Gazette			
310 Niagara St PO Box 549 .... Niagara Falls NY 14302	716-282-2311	286-3895	532-2
Web: www.niagara-gazette.com			
Niagara Helicopters Ltd			
3731 Victoria Ave .... Niagara Falls ON L2E6V5	905-357-5672		292
TF: 800-281-8034 ■ *Web:* www.niagarahelicopters.com			
Niagara Hospice 4675 Sunset Dr .... Lockport NY 14094	716-439-4417		371
TF: 800-662-1220 ■ *Web:* www.niagarahospice.org			
Niagara Lasalle Corp 110 Hopkins St .... Buffalo NY 14220	716-827-7010		567
Web: www.niagaralasalle.com			
Niagara Parks Botanical Gardens			
7400 Portage Rd PO Box 150 .... Niagara Falls ON L2E6T2	877-642-7275		97
TF: 877-642-7275 ■ *Web:* niagaraparks.com			
Niagara Sheets LLC			
7393 Shawnee Rd. .... North Tonawanda NY 14120	716-799-8310		100
Niagara Tourism & Convention Corp			
10 Rainbow Blvd. .... Niagara Falls NY 14303	716-282-8992	285-0809	206
TF: 877-325-5787 ■ *Web:* www.niagara-usa.com			
Niagara Transformer Corp 1747 Dale Rd .... Buffalo NY 14225	716-896-6500	896-8871	767
TF: 800-817-5652 ■ *Web:* www.niagaratransformer.com			
Niagara University			
5795 Lewiston Rd PO Box 2011 .... Niagara University NY 14109	716-285-1212	286-8710*	166
**Fax:* Admissions ■ *TF:* 800-778-3450 ■ *Web:* www.niagara.edu			
Niagara USA Chamber of Commerce			
6311 Inducon Corporate Dr Ste 2 .... Sanborn NY 14132	716-285-9141	285-0941	139
Web: niagarachamber.org			
NIB (National Industries for the Blind)			
1310 Braddock Pl .... Alexandria VA 22314	703-310-0500		48-17
TF Cust Svc: 800-433-2304 ■ *Web:* www.nib.org			
Nibbi Brothers General Contractors			
1000 Brannan St Ste 102 .... San Francisco CA 94103	415-863-1820	863-1150	186
Web: www.nibbi.com			
NIBCO Inc 1516 Middlebury St. .... Elkhart IN 46515	574-295-3000	295-3307	595
TF: 800-234-0227 ■ *Web:* www.nibco.com			
NIBS (National Institute of Bldg Sciences)			
1090 Vermont Ave NW Ste 700. .... Washington DC 20005	202-289-7800	289-1092	49-3
Web: www.nibs.org			
NIC (North-American Interfraternity Conference)			
3901 W 86th St Ste 390 .... Indianapolis IN 46268	317-872-1112		48-11
Web: www.nicindy.org			
NIC Inc 25501 W Valley Pkwy Ste 300 .... Olathe KS 66061	877-234-3468	498-3472*	178-10
NASDAQ: EGOV ■ **Fax Area Code:* 913 ■ *TF:* 877-234-3468 ■ *Web:* www.egov.com			
NICA (National Interfaith Coalition on Aging)			
1901 L St NW 4th Fl. .... Washington DC 20036	202-479-1200	479-0735	48-6
TF: 800-772-1213 ■ *Web:* www.ncoa.org			
Nicaragua 820 Second Ave Ste 801 .... New York NY 10017	212-490-7997	286-0815	784
Web: www.un.int			
Consulate General 8989 Westheimer St. .... Houston TX 77063	713-789-2762		257
TF: 800-621-0508 ■ *Web:* www.consuladodenicaragua.com			
Consulate General			
820 Second Ave Ste 802 .... New York NY 10017	212-986-6562		257
Embassy 1627 New Hampshire Ave NW ...... Washington DC 20009	202-939-6570		257
TF: 800-333-4636 ■ *Web:* www.consuladodenicaragua.com			
Nicasa 31979 N Fish Lake Rd. .... Round Lake IL 60073	847-546-6450		726
Web: www.nicasa.org			
NICB (National Insurance Crime Bureau)			
1111 E Touhy Ave Ste 400 .... Des Plaines IL 60018	847-544-7002		49-9
TF: 800-447-6282 ■ *Web:* www.nicb.org			

	Phone	Fax	Class
Nice N Easy Grocery Shoppes Inc			
7840 Oxbow Rd .... Canastota NY 13032	315-697-2287		297-8
Web: www.niceneasy.com			
NICE Systems Inc			
301 Rt 17 N 10th Fl .... Rutherford NJ 07070	201-964-2600	964-2610	735
TF: 800-994-4498 ■ *Web:* www.nice.com			
Nice-Pak Products Inc			
Two Nice-Pak Pk. .... Orangeburg NY 10962	845-365-1700	365-1729	558
TF: 800-444-6725 ■ *Web:* www.nicepak.com			
Niceville-Valparaiso Chamber of Commerce			
1055 E John Sims Pkwy .... Niceville FL 32578	850-678-2323	678-2602	139
TF: 800-729-9226 ■ *Web:* www.nicevillechamber.com			
Niche Business Solutions			
2300 Center Ave Ste 4 .... New Bern NC 28562	252-514-4177		226
Niche Directories LLC			
909 N Sepulveda Blvd 11th Fl .... El Segundo CA 90026	877-242-9330		387
TF: 877-242-9330 ■ *Web:* www.nichedirectories.com			
Niche Modern Home 1901 Hwy 190. .... Mandeville LA 70448	985-624-4045		321
TF: 800-914-3538 ■ *Web:* nichemodernhome.biz			
Nichirin Tennessee Inc			
1620 Old Belfast Rd .... Lewisburg TN 37091	931-359-5709		370
Web: www.nichirincanada.com			
Nicholas & Associates			
1001 Feehanville Dr .... Mount Prospect IL 60056	847-394-6200		186
Web: www.nicholasquality.com			
Nicholas County PO Box 227 .... Carlisle KY 40311	859-289-3730		338
TF: 800-642-9066 ■ *Web:* www.carlisle-nicholascounty.org			
Commission 700 Main St Ste 1 .... Summersville WV 26651	304-872-7830	872-7863	338
TF: 800-327-5405 ■ *Web:* www.nicholascountywv.org			
Nicholas Family of Funds			
700 N Water St Ste 1010 .... Milwaukee WI 53202	414-272-6133		528
TF: 800-227-5987 ■ *Web:* www.nicholasfunds.com			
Nicholas Financial Inc			
2454 McMullen Booth Rd Bldg C. .... Clearwater FL 33759	727-726-0763	726-2140	217
NASDAQ: NICK ■ *TF:* 800-237-2721 ■ *Web:* nicholasfinancial.com			
Nicholas Laboratories LLC			
15 Enterprise Ste 550 .... Aliso Viejo CA 92656	949-448-4360		415
Nicholls State University			
906 E First St .... Thibodaux LA 70310	985-446-0561	448-4929*	166
**Fax:* Admissions ■ *TF Admissions:* 877-642-4655 ■ *Web:* www.nicholls.edu			
Nicholls State University Ellender Memorial Library			
906 E First St .... Thibodaux LA 70301	985-448-4646	448-4925	434-6
Web: www.nicholls.edu/library			
Nichols PO Box 291 .... Muskegon MI 49443	231-799-2120		559
TF: 800-442-0213 ■ *Web:* www.enichols.com			
Nichols & Stone			
1 Stickley Dr PO Box 480 .... Manlius NY 13104	315-682-1554		319-2
TF: 800-873-3252 ■ *Web:* www.nichols-stone.com			
Nichols Aboretum			
University of Michigan			
1610 Washington Heights .... Ann Arbor MI 48104	734-647-7600		97
Web: www.lsa.umich.edu			
Nichols Accounting Group PC, The			
230 N Oregon St .... Ontario OR 97914	541-881-1433		2
TF: 800-228-6700 ■ *Web:* www.nicholsaccounting.com			
Nichols Bros Boat Builders Inc			
5400 Cameron Rd. .... Freeland WA 98249	360-331-5500	331-7484	698
Web: www.nicholsboats.com			
Nichols College 124 Ctr Rd. .... Dudley MA 01571	508-213-1560	943-9885	166
TF: 800-470-3379 ■ *Web:* www.nichols.edu			
Nichols House Museum 55 Mt Vernon St .... Boston MA 02108	617-227-6993		520
Web: www.nicholshousemuseum.org			
Nichols Jackson Dillard Hager & Smith LLP			
500 N Akard St 1800 Ross Twr .... Dallas TX 75201	214-965-9900		41
Web: www.njdhs.com			
Nichols Portland 2400 Congress St .... Portland ME 04102	207-774-6121		223
Web: www.gerotor.net			
Nichols Research Inc			
333 W El Camino Real .... Sunnyvale CA 94087	408-773-8200		466
Web: nicholsresearch.com			
Nichols Tillage Tools Inc			
312 Hereford Ave .... Sterling CO 80751	970-522-8676		488
Web: www.nicholstillagetools.com			
Nicholson Construction Co			
2400 Ansys Dr Ste 303. .... Canonsburg PA 15317	412-221-4500		189-5
Web: www.nicholsonconstruction.com			
Nicholson Cos Inc, The			
819 W Little Creek Rd. .... Norfolk VA 23505	757-423-3281		652
Web: thenicholsoncompanies.com			
Nicholson Manufacturing Ltd			
9890 Galaran Rd. .... Sidney BC V8L3S6	250-656-3131		683
Web: www.debarking.com			
Nicholson Memorial Library System			
200 N Fifth St .... Garland TX 75040	972-205-2000		434-3
Web: www.nmls.lib.tx.us			
Nicholson Terminal & Dock Co			
360 E Great Lakes .... Ecorse MI 48229	313-842-4300	843-1091	465
Web: www.nicholson-terminal.com			
Nicholson's Tavern & Pub			
625 Walnut St. .... Cincinnati OH 45202	513-564-9111		671
Web: www.tavernrestaurantgroup.com			
Nick & Sam's Grill 3008 Maple Ave .... Dallas TX 75201	214-871-7444	871-7663	671
Web: www.nick-sams.com			
Nick & Stef's Steakhouse			
330 S Hope St .... Los Angeles CA 90071	213-680-0330		671
Web: www.patinagroup.com			
Nick Alexander Imports Inc			
6333 S Alameda St. .... Los Angeles CA 90001	323-583-1901		57
Web: alexanderbmw.com			
Nick Crivelli Chevrolet Inc			
294 State Ave .... Beaver PA 15009	724-987-5000		57
Web: nickcrivelli.com			
Nick Strimbu Inc 3500 PkwyRd .... Brookfield OH 44403	330-448-4046	448-4106	780
TF: 800-446-8785 ■ *Web:* www.nickstrimbu.com			
Nick's 3496 N Ocean Blvd. .... Fort Lauderdale FL 33308	954-563-6441		671
Web: nicksitalianonline.com			
Nick's English Hut			
423 E Kirkwood Ave .... Bloomington IN 47408	812-332-4040		671
Web: www.nicksenglishhut.com			

				Phone	Fax	Class
Nick's Fishmarket Grill & Bar 222 W Merchandise Mart Plaza #135 *Web:* www.nicks-fishmarket.com	Chicago	IL	60654	312-621-0200		671
Nick's on Broadway 500 Broadway *Web:* nicksonbroadway.com	Providence	RI	02909	401-421-0286		671
Nick's Original House of Ribs 14410 Coastal Hwy *TF:* 800-549-2722 ■ *Web:* www.nickshouseofribs.com	Ocean City	MD	21842	410-250-1984		671
Nickell Moulding Company Inc 3015 Mobile Dr *TF:* 800-838-2151 ■ *Web:* www.nickellmoulding.com	Elkhart	IN	46515	574-264-3129		499
Nickelodeon 1515 Broadway *Web:* www.nick.com	New York	NY	10036	212-258-7500		740
Nickelodeon Suites Resort 14500 Continental Gateway *TF:* 877-642-5111 ■ *Web:* www.nickhotel.com	Orlando	FL	32821	407-387-5437	387-1489	669
Nickers International Ltd PO Box 50066 *TF:* 800-642-5377 ■ *Web:* www.nickersinternational.com	Staten Island	NY	10305	718-448-6283	448-6298	799
Nickerson Business Supplies 876A Lebanon St *TF:* 888-385-9922 ■ *Web:* nickbiz.com	Monroe	OH	45050	513-539-6600		321
Nickerson Corp PO Box 5751 *Web:* www.nickersoncorp.com	Bay Shore	NY	11706	631-666-0200		320
Nickerson State Park 3488 Main St *Web:* mass.gov	Brewster	MA	02631	508-896-3491		565
Nickey Petroleum Company Inc 925 S Lkview Ave *TF:* 800-352-0050 ■ *Web:* nickeypetroleum.com	Placentia	CA	92870	714-547-4123		581
Nicklaus Design 11780 US Hwy 1 Ste 500 *Web:* www.nicklaus.com	North Palm Beach	FL	33408	561-227-0300	227-0548	710
Nicklos Drilling Co 2229 San Felipe Ste 1401 *Web:* www.nicklosdrilling.com	Houston	TX	77019	713-224-5959		540
Nickson Industries Inc 336 Woodford Ave *Web:* www.nickson.com	Plainville	CT	06062	860-747-1671		247
NICL Laboratories 306 Era Dr *Web:* www.nicl.com	Northbrook	IL	60062	847-509-9779		415
Nico Trading LLC 222 W Adams St *Web:* www.citigroup.com	Chicago	IL	60606	312-253-8000		360-2
Nicodemus National Historic Site 510 Washington Ave B1 *Web:* www.nps.gov	Bogue	KS	67625	785-839-4233	839-4325	564
Nicol Scales 7239 Envoy Ct *Web:* www.nicolscales.com	Dallas	TX	75247	214-428-8181	428-8127	639
Nicola Valley Institute of Technology 4355 Mathissi Pl *Web:* www.nvit.bc.ca	Burnaby	BC	V5G4S8	604-602-9555		165
Nicola Wealth Management Ltd 1508 W Broadway 5th Fl *TF:* 800-219-8032 ■ *Web:* www.nicolawealth.com	Vancouver	BC	V6J1W8	604-739-6450		796
Nicola's 1420 Sycamore St *Web:* nicolasotr.com	Cincinnati	OH	45202	513-721-6200	721-1777	671
Nicola-Crosby Real Estate Asset Management Ltd 420-1508 W Broadway *Web:* www.nicolacrosby.com	Vancouver	BC	V6J1W8	778-383-6940		528
Nicolaysen Art Museum 400 E Collins Dr *Web:* www.thenic.org	Casper	WY	82601	307-235-5247		520
Nicolet Plastics Inc 16685 State Rd 32 *Web:* www.nicoletplastics.com	Mountain	WI	54149	715-276-4200		596
Nicolinni's 1912 S Raccoon Rd *Web:* www.nicolinnis.com	Youngstown	OH	44515	330-799-9999		671
Nicolino's Italian Restaurant 2544 Executive Dr	Indianapolis	IN	46241	317-381-6146	381-6170	671
Nicollet County 501 S Minnesota Ave *Web:* www.co.nicollet.mn.us	Saint Peter	MN	56082	507-931-6800	931-9220	338
Nicollet Island Inn 95 Merriam St *Web:* www.nicolletislandinn.com	Minneapolis	MN	55401	612-331-1800	331-6528	671
Nicolson Porter & List 1300 W Higgins Rd Ste 104 *Web:* nplchicago.com	Park Ridge	IL	60068	847-698-7400		652
Nicomm Llc 2235 Gateway Dr *Web:* www.nicomm.net	Sycamore	IL	60178	815-758-0661		196
Nicor Gas 1844 Ferry Rd **Fax Area Code:* 630 ■ *TF:* 888-642-6748	Naperville	IL	60563	888-642-6748	983-6755*	787
Nicros Inc 845 Phalen Blvd *TF:* 800-699-1975 ■ *Web:* www.nicros.com	Saint Paul	MN	55106	651-778-1975		711
NICSA (National Investment Co Service Assn) 8400 Westpark Dr 2nd Fl *TF:* 800-426-1122 ■ *Web:* www.nicsa.org	McLean	VA	22102	508-485-1500	485-1560	49-2
NID (Nevada Irrigation District) 1036 W Main St *TF:* 800-222-4102 ■ *Web:* nidwater.com	Grass Valley	CA	95945	530-273-6185		787
Nida Corp 300 S John Rodes Blvd *TF:* 800-327-6432 ■ *Web:* www.nida.com	Melbourne	FL	32904	321-727-2265	727-2655	703
NIDCR (National Oral Health Information Clearinghouse) 1 NOHIC Way *TF:* 866-232-4528 ■ *Web:* www.nidcr.nih.gov	Bethesda	MD	20892	301-496-4261	480-4098	48-17
Nidec America Corp 50 Braintree Hill Pk Ste 110 *Web:* www.nidec.com	Braintree	MA	02184	781-848-0970	380-3634	518
Nidec Avtron Automation Corp 7555 E Pleasant Valley Rd Bldg 100 *Web:* www.nidec-avtron.com	Independence	OH	44131	216-642-1230		407
Nidec Motor Corp 8050 W Florissant Ave *TF:* 888-637-7333 ■ *Web:* www.usmotors.com	Saint Louis	MO	63136	888-637-7333		518
Nidek Inc 47651 Westinghouse Dr *TF:* 800-223-9044 ■ *Web:* usa.nidek.com	Fremont	CA	94539	510-226-5700		475
NIDRR (National Institute on Disability & Rehabilitation Research) 400 Maryland Ave SW *Web:* www.ed.gov	Washington	DC	20202	202-205-8134	245-7323	668
Niebur Golf Inc 1230 Tenderfoot Hill Rd Ste 100 *Web:* www.nieburdevelopment.com	Colorado Springs	CO	80906	719-527-0313		188-3
Niederauer Inc 1976 W San Carlos St *Web:* westernappliance.com	San Jose	CA	95128	408-297-2440		35
Niedner, Bodeux, Carmichael, Huff, Lenox & Pashos LLP 131 Jefferson St *TF:* 888-572-2192 ■ *Web:* www.niednerlaw.com	Saint Charles	MO	63301	636-949-9300		428
NIEFERT Certified Solutions LLC 5850 Oberlin Dr *Web:* www.niefert.com	San Diego	CA	92121	858-450-9092		809
Nielsen Business Media 770 Broadway *Web:* www.nielsen.com	New York	NY	10003	646-654-4500		637-2
Nielsen Dodge Chrysler Jeep Ram 175 Rt 10 E *Web:* www.nielsendodgechryslerjeepram.com	East Hanover	NJ	07936	973-884-2100		57
Nielsen Media Research Ltd 160 McNabb St *Web:* www.nielsenmedia.ca	Markham	ON	L3R4B8	905-475-9595		195
Nielsen, Merksamer, Parrinello, Gross & Leoni LLP 2350 Kerner Blvd Ste 250 *Web:* www.nmgovlaw.com	San Rafael	CA	94901	415-389-6800		428
Nielsen-Massey Vanillas Inc 1550 S Shields Dr *TF:* 800-525-7873 ■ *Web:* www.nielsenmassey.com	Waukegan	IL	60085	847-578-1550	578-1570	296-15
Nieman Printing Inc 10615 Newkirk St Ste 100 *Web:* niemanprinting.com	Dallas	TX	75220	972-506-7400		627
Niermann Weeks Company Inc 760 Generals Hwy *Web:* www.niermannweeks.com	Millersville	MD	21108	410-923-0123	923-0647	393
Nietzke & Faupel PC 7274 Hartley St *TF:* 855-999-3122 ■ *Web:* nfcpa.com	Pigeon	MI	48755	989-453-3122		2
Nifco America Corp 8015 Dove Pkwy *Web:* www.nifcousa.com	Canal Winchester	OH	43110	614-836-3808		596
NIFDA (National Independent Flag Dealers Assn) 7984 S Chicago Ave *TF:* 800-356-4085 ■ *Web:* www.nifda.net	Chicago	IL	60617	773-768-8076	768-3138	49-18
NIFL (National Institute for Literacy) 1775 'I' St NW Ste 730 *TF:* 800-228-8813 ■ *Web:* www.lincs.ed.gov	Washington	DC	20006	202-233-2025	233-2050	340-8
Nifty After Fifty LLC 1501 E Orangethorpe Ave Ste 180 *Web:* niftyafterfifty.com	Fullerton	CA	92831	714-823-4400		354
NIGA (National Indian Gaming Assn) 224 Second St SE *TF:* 800-937-0010 ■ *Web:* www.indiangaming.org	Washington	DC	20003	202-546-7711	546-1755	48-23
Niger 417 E 50th St *Web:* www.un.int	New York	NY	10022	212-421-3260	753-6931	784
Niger Embassy 2204 R St NW *Web:* www.embassyofniger.org	Washington	DC	20008	202-483-4224	483-3169	257
Nigeria						
Consulate General 828 Second Ave *Web:* www.nigeriahouse.com	New York	NY	10017	212-850-2200	687-1476	257
Embassy 3519 International Ct NW *Web:* www.nigeriaembassyusa.org	Washington	DC	20008	202-986-8400		257
Night Optics USA Inc 15182 Triton Ln Ste 101 *TF:* 800-306-4448 ■ *Web:* www.nightoptics.com	Huntington Beach	CA	92649	714-899-4475		542
Nightforce Optics 336 Hazen Ln *Web:* www.nightforceoptics.com	Orofino	ID	83544	208-476-9814		544
Nightingale-Conant Corp 6245 W Howard St *TF Cust Svc:* 800-557-1660 ■ *Web:* www.nightingale.com	Niles	IL	60714	800-557-1660		513
Nightlinger Colavita & Volpa Pa 991 S Black Horse Pk *Web:* colavita.net	Williamstown	NJ	08094	856-629-3111		2
Nightowl Document Management Services 724 N First St Ste 500 *Web:* nightowldiscovery.com	Minneapolis	MN	55401	612-337-0448		627
NIGP (National Institute of Governmental Purchasing Inc) 151 Spring St *TF:* 800-367-6447 ■ *Web:* www.nigp.org	Herndon	VA	20170	703-736-8900	736-2818	49-7
NIH (National Institutes of Health) 9000 Rockville Pike *TF:* 800-411-1222 ■ *Web:* www.nih.gov	Bethesda	MD	20892	301-496-4000		340-10
NIH Osteoporosis & Related Bone Diseases-National Resource Ctr 2 AMS Cir *TF:* 800-624-2663 ■ *Web:* niams.nih.gov/health_info/bone/default.asp	Bethesda	MD	20892	202-223-0344	293-2356	340-10
NIH Research & Consulting LLC 5645 Coral Ridge Dr Ste 316 *Web:* www.nihresearch.com	Coral Springs	FL	33076	954-753-7747		466
Nihon Kohden America Inc 90 Icon *TF:* 800-325-0283 ■ *Web:* us.nihonkohden.com	Foothill Ranch	CA	92610	949-580-1555	580-1550	475
NII Holdings Inc 1875 Explorer St Ste 1000 *NASDAQ: NIHD* ■ *Web:* www.nii.com	Reston	VA	20190	703-390-5100		736
Nike Ihm Inc 8 Research Park Dr *Web:* www.nikelhm.com	St. Charles	MO	63304	636-939-5300		600
Nike Inc 1 Bowerman Dr *NYSE: NKE* ■ *TF Cust Svc:* 800-344-6453 ■ *Web:* www.nike.com	Beaverton	OR	97005	503-671-6453	646-6926	301
Niki's West 233 Finley Ave W *Web:* nikiswest.com	Birmingham	AL	35204	205-252-5751	252-8163	671
Nikitova LLC 203 N Lasalle Ste 2100	Chicago	IL	60601	773-913-8015	442-0693	514
Nikka Yuko Japanese Garden PO Box 751 *Web:* www.nikkayuko.com	Lethbridge	AB	T1J3Z6	403-328-3511	328-0511	97
Nikkei MC Aluminum America Inc 6875 S Inwood Dr *Web:* www.nmaluminum.net	Columbus	IN	47201	812-342-1141		492
Nikki Beach 1 Ocean Dr S Beach	Miami Beach	FL	33139	305-538-1111		671
Nikkiso Cryo Inc 4661 Eaker St *Web:* nikkisocryo.com	North Las Vegas	NV	89081	702-643-4900		743
Nikkiso Pumps America Inc 3433 N Sam Houston Pkwy W Ste 400 *Web:* www.nikkisopumpsamerica.com	Houston	TX	77086	281-310-6747		641
Nikko 1300 S Blvd *Web:* www.nikkosushibar.net	Charlotte	NC	28203	704-370-0100	370-0123	671

Company / Address	City	State	Zip	Phone	Fax	Class
Niko Resources Ltd 400 Third Ave SW	Calgary	AB	T2P4H2	403-262-1020	263-2686	536
TSE: NKO ■ *Web:* www.nikoresources.com						
Nikolai's Roof 255 Courtland St NE	Atlanta	GA	30303	404-221-6362		671
Nik-O-Lok Co						
3130 N Mitthoeffer Rd	Indianapolis	IN	46235	317-899-6955	899-6977	350
TF: 800-428-4348 ■ *Web:* www.nikolok.com						
Nikon Inc 1300 Walt Whitman Rd	Melville	NY	11747	631-547-4200	547-0299	591
TF Cust Svc: 800-645-6687 ■ *Web:* www.nikonusa.com						
Nikon Precision Inc 1399 Shoreway Rd	Belmont	CA	94002	650-508-4674		696
Web: www.nikon.com						
Niles Audio Corp 1969 Kellog Ave	Carlsbad	CA	92008	760-710-0992		253
TF: 800-289-4434 ■ *Web:* www.nilesaudio.com						
Niles Barton & Wilmer						
111 S Calvert St Ste 1400	Baltimore	MD	21202	410-783-6300	783-6363	428
Web: www.nilesbarton.com						
Niles Bolton Assoc Inc (NBA)						
3060 Peachtree Rd NW Ste 600	Atlanta	GA	30305	404-365-7600		261
Web: www.nilesbolton.com						
Niles Chamber of Commerce						
8060 Oakton St	Niles	IL	60714	847-268-8180	268-8186	139
Web: www.nileschamber.com						
Niles Community School 111 Spruce St	Niles	MI	49120	269-683-0732		685
TF: 888-988-6300 ■ *Web:* nilesschools.schoolwires.net						
Niles Mfg & Finishing Inc 465 Walnut St	Niles	OH	44446	330-544-0402	544-8018	488
Niles Precision Co PO Box 548	Niles	MI	49120	269-683-0585	683-7762	21
Web: www.nilesprecision.com						
Nilfisk-Advance Inc 14600 21st Ave N	Plymouth	MN	55447	454-323-8100	989-6566*	386
**Fax Area Code:* 800 ■ *Web:* www.nilfisk.com/en						
Nill Bros Sports 2814 S 44th St	Kansas City	KS	66106	913-384-4242	384-0107	711
TF: 800-748-7221 ■ *Web:* www.nillbros.com						
Nimbix LLC 2323 Bryan St Ste 1520	Dallas	TX	75201	832-305-6365		809
Web: www.nimbix.net						
Nimble Assessment Systems Inc						
3 Bridge St Ste B101	Newton	MA	02458	617-431-4441		225
Nimbleuser 656 Kreag Rd	Pittsford	NY	14534	585-586-4750		177
TF: 800-647-3863 ■ *Web:* www.nimbleuser.com						
Nimbus Design 2363 Broadway St	Redwood City	CA	94063	650-365-7568		225
Web: www.nimbusdesign.com						
Nimensky Gallinson & Buren PA CPAs						
316 Eisenhower Pkwy	Livingston	NJ	07039	973-533-9200		2
Web: ngbcpa.com						
Nimo's Sushi Bar & Japanese						
921 E Harmony Rd Ste 104	Fort Collins	CO	80525	970-221-1040		671
Web: www.nimossushi.com						
Nims & Assoc						
1445 Technology Ln Ste A8	Petaluma	CA	94954	707-781-6300		177
TF: 877-454-3200 ■ *Web:* www.nimsassociates.com						
Nina's Ristorante 8801 Lead Mine Rd	Raleigh	NC	27615	919-845-1122		671
Web: ninasrestaurant.com						
Nine Dragons Restaurant 4525 17th Ave S	Fargo	ND	58104	701-232-2411		671
Web: www.9dragonsrestaurant.com						
Nine Eagles State Park RR 1	Davis City	IA	50065	641-442-2855	442-2856	565
Web: www.iowadnr.gov						
Nine Energy Service Inc						
16945 Northchase Dr Ste 1600	Houston	TX	77060	281-730-5100		536
Web: nineenergyservice.com						
Nine Health Services Inc						
1139 delaware st	Denver	CO	80204	303-698-4455		636
TF: 800-332-3078 ■ *Web:* www.9healthfair.org						
Nine Quarter Cir Ranch						
5000 Taylor Fork Rd	Gallatin Gateway	MT	59730	406-995-4276	995-4276	239
TF: 800-847-4868 ■ *Web:* www.ninequartercircle.com						
Nine Star Enterprises Inc 730 I St	Anchorage	AK	99501	907-279-7827		260
TF: 800-478-7587 ■ *Web:* www.ninestar.com						
Nine Zero Hotel 90 Tremont St	Boston	MA	02108	617-772-5800	772-5810	379
TF: 866-906-9090 ■ *Web:* www.ninezero.com						
Nines Hotel, The 525 SW Morrison	Portland	OR	97204	877-229-9995		41
TF: 877-229-9995 ■ *Web:* www.thenines.com						
NineSigma Inc						
23611 Chagrin Blvd Ste 320	Cleveland	OH	44122	216-295-4800		466
Web: ninesigma.com						
Ninety Six National Historic Site						
1103 Hwy 248 PO Box 418	Ninety Six	SC	29666	864-543-4068	543-2058	564
Web: www.nps.gov/nisi						
Ninety-Nine Restaurant & Pubs						
291 Mishawum Rd	Woburn	MA	01801	781-935-7210		670
Web: www.99restaurants.com						
Ninety-Nines Inc						
4300 Amelia Earhart Rd	Oklahoma City	OK	73159	405-685-7969	685-7985	48-24
TF: 800-994-1929 ■ *Web:* www.ninety-nines.org						
Ning Inc						
2000 Sierra Point Pkay Ste 1000, 10th Fl	Brisbane	CA	94005	270-514-7000		395
Web: www.ning.com						
Ninilchik State Recreation Area						
PO Box 1247	Soldotna	AK	99669	907-262-5581		565
Web: dnr.alaska.gov/parks/units/nilchik.htm						
Ninja 8433 Oak St	New Orleans	LA	70118	504-866-1119		671
Web: ninjasushineworleans.com						
NinjaTrader LLC 1236 Clarkson St	Denver	CO	80218	312-423-2234		809
Web: www.ninjatrader.com						
Nino Salvaggio International Marketplace						
27900 Harper Ave	St Clair Shores	MI	48081	586-778-3650		345
Web: www.ninosalvaggio.com						
Nino's 1931 Chesire Bridge Rd	Atlanta	GA	30324	404-874-6505		671
Web: www.ninosatlanta.com						
Nino's 3853 Atlantic Ave	Long Beach	CA	90807	562-427-1003		671
TF: 800-876-8063 ■ *Web:* ninoslongbeach.com						
Nino's Vincent's Grappino di Nino						
2817 W Dallas St	Houston	TX	77019	713-522-5120		671
Web: www.ninos-vincents.com						
Nintendo of America Inc						
4820 150th Ave NE	Redmond	WA	98052	425-882-2040	882-3585	762
TF Cust Svc: 800-255-3700 ■ *Web:* www.nintendo.com						
Nintex USA LLC						
10800 NE Eighth St Ste 400	Bellevue	WA	98004	425-324-2400		180
TF: 800-426-4968 ■ *Web:* www.nintex.com						
NinthDecimal Inc						
150 Post St Ste 500	San Francisco	CA	94108	415-821-8600		174
Web: www.ninthdecimal.com						
Ninyo & Moore 5710 Ruffin Rd	San Diego	CA	92123	858-576-1000		261
TF: 800-427-0401 ■ *Web:* www.ninyoandmoore.com						
Niobrara County PO Box 420	Lusk	WY	82225	307-334-2211		338
Web: www.county-clerk.net						
Niobrara National Scenic River						
146 S Hall St PO Box 319	Valentine	NE	69201	402-376-1901	376-1949	564
Web: www.nps.gov/niob						
Niobrara State Park 89261 522 Ave	Niobrara	NE	68760	402-857-3373		565
Web: www.stateparks.com						
Niobrara Valley Electric Membership Corp						
427 N Fourth St	O'Neill	NE	68763	402-336-2803	336-4858	245
Web: www.nvemc.org						
NIOS Restaurant & Wine Bar						
130 W 46th St	New York	NY	10036	212-485-2999		671
Web: www.niosrestaurant.com						
NIPC (National Inhalant Prevention Coalition)						
318 Lindsay St	Chattanooga	TN	37405	423-265-4662	265-4889	48-17
TF: 800-269-4237 ■ *Web:* www.inhalants.org						
NIPCO (Northwest Iowa Power Co-op)						
31002 County Rd C38 PO Box 240	Le Mars	IA	51031	712-546-4141	546-8795	245
Web: www.nipco.coop						
Nipissing University						
100 College Dr PO Box 5002	North Bay	ON	P1B8L7	705-474-3450	495-1772	785
TF: 800-655-5154 ■ *Web:* nipissingu.ca						
Brantford 67 Darling St	Brantford	ON	N3T2K6	519-756-8228	720-9996	785
Web: www.nipissingu.ca						
Nippon Express USA Inc						
590 Madison Ave Ste 2401	New York	NY	10022	212-405-1650		311
Web: www.nipponexpressusa.com						
Nippon Kodo Inc						
2771 Plaza Del Amo Ste 805	Torrance	CA	90503	310-320-8881		787
TF: 888-775-5487 ■ *Web:* www.nipponkodo.com						
Nippon Paper Industries USA Co						
1902 Marine Dr	Port Angeles	WA	98363	360-457-4474		638
TF: 800-331-6314 ■ *Web:* npiusa.com						
Nippon Steel USA Inc						
1251 Ave of the Americas Ste 2320	New York	NY	10020	212-486-7150	593-3049	492
Web: www.nssmc.com						
Nipro Medical Corp 3150 NW 107th Ave	Miami	FL	33172	305-599-7174		475
Web: www.nipro.com						
NIR Roof Care Inc 12191 Regency Pkwy	Huntley	IL	60142	847-669-3444	669-3173	189-12
TF: 800-221-7663 ■ *Web:* www.nir.com						
Nirenstein, Horowitz & Associates PC						
43 Woodland St Ste 520	Hartford	CT	06105	860-548-1000		428
TF: 800-561-3357 ■ *Web:* www.preserveyourestate.net						
NIRI (National Investor Relations Institute)						
8020 Towers Crescent Dr Ste 250	Vienna	VA	22182	703-506-3570	506-3571	49-2
Web: www.niri.org						
Niro Scavone Haller & Niro Ltd						
181 W Madison St Ste 4600	Chicago	IL	60602	312-236-0733		428
Web: www.niroscavone.com						
NIRS (Nuclear Information & Resource Service)						
6930 Carroll Ave Ste 340	Takoma Park	MD	20912	301-270-6477	270-4291	48-8
Web: www.nirs.org						
NIRSA (National Intramural-Recreational Sports Assn)						
4185 SW Research Way	Corvallis	OR	97333	541-766-8211	766-8284	48-22
Web: www.nirsa.org						
Nirvana Systems Inc						
7000 N MoPac Ste 425	Austin	TX	78731	512-345-2545		177
Web: www.omnitrader.com						
NIS Inc 12995 Thomas Creek Rd	Reno	NV	89511	775-852-0640		178-2
Web: nissoftware.net						
Nisbet Oil Co PO Box 35367	Charlotte	NC	28235	704-332-7755	377-1607	579
Web: www.nisbetoil.com						
Nisen & Elliott LLC						
200 W Adams St Ste 2500	Chicago	IL	60606	312-346-7800		428
Web: www.nisen.com						
NISH 8401 Old Courthouse Rd	Vienna	VA	22182	703-560-6800		48-17
Web: www.sourceamerica.org						
Nishiba Industries Corp						
2360 Marconi Ct	San Diego	CA	92154	619-482-9900	482-1585	608
Nishiki Sushi 1501 16th St	Sacramento	CA	95814	916-446-3629		671
Web: nishikisushi.com						
Nishnabotna Valley Rural Electric Co-op						
1317 Chatburn Ave	Harlan	IA	51537	712-755-2166		245
TF: 800-234-5122 ■ *Web:* www.nvrec.com						
Nisivoccia & Company LLP						
200 Valley Rd Ste 300	Mt Arlington	NJ	07856	973-328-1825		2
Web: www.nisivoccia.com						
Niskayuna Central School District (NCSD)						
1239 Van Antwerp Rd	Schenectady	NY	12309	518-377-4666	377-4074	685
TF: 866-893-6337 ■ *Web:* www.niskyschools.org						
NISO (National Information Standards Organization)						
3600 Clipper Mill Rd Ste 302	Baltimore	MD	21211	301-654-2512	685-5278*	49-16
**Fax Area Code:* 410 ■ *TF:* 877-375-2160 ■ *Web:* www.niso.org						
NiSource 1700 MacCorkle Ave SE	Charleston	WV	25314	304-357-2000	357-2000	325
Nisqually Reach Nature Ctr (NRNC)						
4949 D'Milluhr Rd NE	Olympia	WA	98516	360-459-0387		50-5
Web: www.nisquallyestuary.org						
Nissan Canada Inc (NCI)						
5290 Orbitor Dr	Mississauga	ON	L4W4Z5	800-387-0122	629-6553*	59
**Fax Area Code:* 905 ■ *TF:* 800-387-0122 ■ *Web:* www.nissan.ca						
Nissan Motor Corp USA Infiniti Div						
1 Nissan Way	Franklin	TN	37067	800-662-6200		59
TF: 800-662-6200 ■ *Web:* www.infinitiusa.com						
Nissan North America Inc						
25 Vantage way	Nashville	TN	37228	800-647-7261	629-9742*	59
**Fax Area Code:* 905 ■ *TF:* 800-647-7261 ■ *Web:* www.nissanusa.com						
Nissan of Atlantic City						
6021 Black Horse Pike	Egg Harbor Township	NJ	08234	609-383-6100		57
Web: www.admiralnissan.com						
Nissei America Inc 1480 N Hancock St	Anaheim	CA	92807	714-693-3000		111
TF: 800-693-3231 ■ *Web:* www.nisseiamerica.com						
Nissen Chemitec America 350 E High St	London	OH	43140	740-852-3200	852-4547	608
Web: nissenchemitec.com						

Phone | Fax | Class

Nissequogue River State Park
799 St Johnland Rd PO Box 639 ....Kings Park NY 11754 631-269-4927 565
Web: parks.ny.gov/parks/110/details.aspx

Nisshin Steel Co
1701 Golf Rd
Continental Tower 3 Ste 1004..........Rolling Meadows IL 60008 847-290-5100 290-0826 723
Web: www.nisshin-steel.co.jp

Nisshinbo Automotive Corp
42355 Merrill Rd ....Sterling Heights MI 48314 586-997-1000 247
Web: www.nisshinboauto.com/nna.html

Nissho Electronics USA Corp
226 Airport Pkwy ....San Jose CA 95110 408-969-9700 969-9701 178-10
Web: www.nelco.com

Nissin Brake Ohio Inc
1901 Industrial Ave..........................Findlay OH 45840 419-425-6725 247
Web: www.nissinbrake.com

Nissin Foods USA Company Inc
2001 W Rosecrans Ave......................Gardena CA 90249 323-321-6453 515-3751* 296-31
**Fax Area Code:* 310 ■ **Fax:* Sales ■ *Web:* www.nissinfoods.com

Nissin Precision North America Inc
375 Union Rd.......................... Eagle wood OH 45322 937-836-1910 483
Web: nissinoh.com

NIST (National Institute of Standards & Technology)
100 Bureau Dr Sp 1070 .... Gaithersburg MD 20899 301-975-6478 926-1630 340-2
TF: 800-877-8339 ■ *Web:* www.nist.gov

Nistica Inc 745 Rt 202-206 ....Bridgewater NJ 08807 908-707-9500 116
Web: www.nistica.com

Nitek Laser Inc 305 Rt du Port ....Nicolet QC J3T1R7 819-293-4887 757
Web: www.niteklaser.com

Nitel Inc 1101 West Lake St 6th Fl...............Chicago IL 60607 888-450-2100 224
TF: 888-450-2100 ■ *Web:* www.nitelusa.com

Nitelines USA Inc
3065 Peachtree Industrial Blvd Ste 210 ....Duluth GA 30097 877-337-2563 393
TF: 877-337-2563 ■ *Web:* www.nitelinesusa.com

NITL (National Industrial Transportation League)
7918 Jones Branch Dr Ste 300................McLean VA 22102 703-524-5011 506-3266 49-21
Web: www.nitl.org

Nitrex Metal Inc
3474 Poirier Blvd......................Saint-Laurent QC H4R2J5 514-335-7191 335-4160 484
TF: 877-335-7191 ■ *Web:* www.nitrex.com

Nitro Electric Co LLC
4300 First Ave 2nd Fl.......................... Nitro WV 25143 304-204-1500 204-1350* 189-10
**Fax:* Acctg ■ *Web:* www.nitro-electric.com

Nitrous Express Inc
5411 Seymour Hwy .... Wichita Falls TX 76310 940-767-7694 57
TF: 888-463-2781 ■ *Web:* www.nitrousexpress.com

Nitta Casings Inc
141 Southside Ave.......................Bridgewater NJ 08807 908-218-4400 725-2835 298
TF Cust Svc: 800-526-3970 ■ *Web:* www.nittacasings.com

Nitta Corporation of America
7605 Nitta Dr ....Suwanee GA 30024 770-497-0212 385
Web: www.nitta.com

Nitta Gelatin Inc
598 Airport Blvd Ste 900 ....Morrisville NC 27560 919-238-3300 238-3222 296-22
TF: 888-648-8287 ■ *Web:* www.nitta-gelatin.com

Nittany Lion Inn 200 W Pk Ave............State College PA 16803 814-865-8500 865-8501 379
TF: 800-233-7505 ■ *Web:* www.pshs.psu.edu

Nittany Oil Company Inc
1540 Martin St.........................State College PA 16803 814-237-4859 581
Web: www.nittanyoil.com

Nittany Valley Offset
Nittany Vly Offset 1015 Benner Pk ....State College PA 16801 814-238-3071 532-3
Web: www.nittanyvalley.com

Nitterhouse Concrete Products Inc
2655 Molly Pitcher Hwy................Chambersburg PA 17201 717-267-4505 267-4518 183
TF: 800-279-1201 ■ *Web:* www.nitterhouse.com

Nitto Denko Automotive Ohio Inc
1620 S Main St.............................Piqua OH 45356 937-773-4820 54
Web: www.piquatechnologies.com

Nityo Infotech Corporation Inc
2652 Hidden Valley Dr Ste 303.............. Pittsburgh PA 15241 412-226-5546 180
Web: www.nityo.com

Nitze-Stagen & Company Inc
2401 Utah Ave S Ste 305 .... Seattle WA 98134 206-467-0420 467-0423 403
Web: www.nitze-stagen.com

Niven Family Wine Estates
4915 Orcutt Rd...................... San Luis Obispo CA 93401 805-597-8200 315-5
Web: www.baileyana.com

Niven Marketing Group, The
955 Kimberly Dr...................... Carol Stream IL 60188 630-580-6000 195
Web: www.niven.net

Niver Western Wear Inc
PO Box 101224 .... Fort Worth TX 76185 817-924-4299 924-4296 155-20
TF Orders: 800-433-5752

Niveus Medical Inc
849 Independence Ave Ste C ....Mountain View CA 94043 650-336-7922 475
Web: www.niveusmedical.com

NIWL (National Institute for Work & Learning)
1825 Connecticut Ave NW 7th Fl...........Washington DC 20009 202-884-8186 884-8422 49-12

Nix Medical Ctr 414 Navarro St ....San Antonio TX 78205 210-271-1800 374-3
Web: www.nixhealth.com

NIX Neighborhood Lending
1440 Rosecrans Ave................Manhattan Beach CA 90266 310-603-5889 141
Web: nixlending.com

Nixon Gear Inc 1750 Milton Ave .... Syracuse NY 13209 315-488-0100 488-0196 709
Web: gearmotions.com

Nixon-Egli Equipment Company Inc
2044 S Vineyard Ave.........................Ontario CA 91761 909-930-1822 358
Web: www.nixon-egli.com

Niyamit Inc
2201 Cooperative Way Ste 600................Herndon VA 20171 703-788-6590 880-7181 809
Web: www.niyamit.com

Nizhoni Health Systems LLC
5 Middlesex Ave.........................Somerville MA 02145 800-915-3211 363
TF: 800-915-3211 ■ *Web:* nizhonihealth.com

NJ Assn-Osteopathic
1 Distribution Way .... Monmouth Junction NJ 08852 732-940-9000 138
TF: 800-521-3709 ■ *Web:* www.njosteo.com

NJ State Veteran's Memorial Home
132 Evergreen Rd PO Box 3013 ....Edison NJ 08837 732-452-4100 793
Web: nj.gov

NJCAA (NJCAA) 1631 Mesa Ave......... Colorado Springs CO 80906 719-590-9788 590-7324 48-22
Web: www.njcaa.org

NJEA Review 180 W State St...................Trenton NJ 08607 609-599-4561 392-6321 457-8
Web: www.njea.org

NJHCS (East Orange Campus of the VA New Jersey Health Care System)
385 Tremont Ave.......................East Orange NJ 07018 844-872-4681 456-1414* 374-8
**Fax Area Code:* 202 ■ **Fax:* Hum Res ■ *TF General:* 844-872-4681 ■ *Web:* www.usa.gov

NJLA (New Jersey Library Assn)
PO Box 1534 .... Trenton NJ 08607 609-394-8032 394-8164 435
TF: 800-411-6493 ■ *Web:* www.njla.org

NJSNA (New Jersey State Nurses Assn)
1479 Pennington Rd....................... Trenton NJ 08618 609-883-5335 883-5343 533
TF: 800-662-0108 ■ *Web:* www.njsna.org

NJTC Venture Fund
1001 Briggs Rd Ste 280.................Mount Laurel NJ 08054 856-273-6800 792

NJTV 825 Eighth Ave.........................New York NY 10019 609-777-0031 645-166
TF: 800-882-6622 ■ *Web:* www.njtvonline.org

N-K Manufacturing Technologies
1134 Freeman Ave SW..................Grand Rapids MI 49503 616-248-3200 608
Web: www.nkmfgtech.com

Nk Parts Industry Inc Main Facility
777 S Kuther Rd.............................Sidney OH 45365 937-498-4651 88
TF: 800-860-2181 ■ *Web:* www.nkparts.com

N&K Technology Inc 80 Las Colinas Ln......... San Jose CA 95119 408-513-3800 696
Web: www.nandk.com

NKBA (National Kitchen & Bath Assn)
687 Willow Grove St....................Hackettstown NJ 07840 800-843-6522 852-1695* 49-3
**Fax Area Code:* 908 ■ *TF:* 800-843-6522 ■ *Web:* www.nkba.org

NKF (National Kidney Foundation)
30 E 33rd St 8th Fl........................New York NY 10016 212-889-2210 48-17
TF: 800-622-9010 ■ *Web:* www.kidney.org

NKP Medical Marketing Inc
8939 S Sepulveda Blvd Ste 320............Los Angeles CA 90045 866-539-2201 195
TF: 866-539-2201 ■ *Web:* www.nkpmedical.com

NKS Distributors Inc
399 Churchmans Rd......................New Castle DE 19720 302-322-1811 81-3
TF: 800-310-5099 ■ *Web:* www.abwholesaler.com

NKTelco Inc
301 W S St PO Box 219................ New Knoxville OH 45871 419-753-5000 629-1424 224
TF: 888-658-3526 ■ *Web:* www.nktelco.net

NKYCVB (Northern Kentucky Convention & Visitors Bureau)
50 E RiverCenter Blvd Ste 200 .... Covington KY 41011 859-261-4677 261-5135 206
TF: 877-659-8474 ■ *Web:* meetnky.com

NL Industries 16801 Greenspoint Pk Dr...........Houston TX 77060 281-423-3300 143
NYSE: NL ■ *TF:* 800-866-5600 ■ *Web:* www.nl-ind.com

NLADA (National Legal Aid & Defender Assn)
1140 Connecticut Ave NW Ste 900.........Washington DC 20036 202-452-0620 872-1031 49-10
TF: 800-725-4513 ■ *Web:* www.nlada.org

NLBMDA (National Lumber & Bldg Material Dealers Assn)
2025 M St NW ....Washington DC 20036 202-367-1169 367-2169 49-18
Web: www.dealer.org

NLBRA (National Little Britches Rodeo Assn)
5050 Edison Ave Ste 105 .... Colorado Springs CO 80915 719-389-0333 578-1367 48-22
TF: 800-763-3694 ■ *Web:* www.nlbra.org

NLC (National League of Cities)
1301 Pennsylvania Ave NW Ste 550..........Washington DC 20004 202-626-3000 626-3043 49-7
TF: 800-892-2757 ■ *Web:* www.nlc.org

NLC Inc 319 W Main St.......................Jackson MO 63755 573-243-3141 232-3046* 811
**Fax Area Code:* 800 ■ *TF Sales:* 800-594-3958 ■ *Web:* profaxlenco.com

NLC Products Inc
3801 Woodland Heights Rd Ste 100.......... Little Rock AR 72212 501-227-9050 711
Web: www.huntsmart.com

NLDA (National Luggage Dealers Assn)
1817 Elmdale Ave......................... Glenview IL 60026 847-998-6869 998-6884 49-18
TF: 800-411-0705 ■ *Web:* www.nlda.com

NLN (National League for Nursing)
61 Broadway 33rd Fl........................New York NY 10006 212-363-5555 812-0391 49-8
TF: 800-669-1656 ■ *Web:* www.nln.org

NLP Enterprises Inc PO Box 349 .... Owings Mills MD 21117 410-356-7500 356-7525 189-8
Web: www.nlpentinc.com

NLRB (National Labor Relations Board)
1099 14th St NW ....Washington DC 20570 202-273-1991 340-20
TF: 866-667-6572 ■ *Web:* www.nlrb.gov

NLRHC (Northern Lights Regional Health Ctr)
7 Hospital St..........................Fort McMurray AB T9H1P2 780-791-6161 374-2
Web: www.albertahealthservices.ca

NLSD (New Lenox School District 122)
102 S Cedar Rd ....New Lenox IL 60451 815-485-2169 685
Web: www.nlsd122.org

NM Marketing Communications Inc
706 Waukegan Rd.......................... Glenview IL 60025 847-657-6011 636

NMA (National Motorists Assn)
402 W Second St .... Waunakee WI 53597 608-849-6000 49-21
TF: 800-882-2785 ■ *Web:* www.motorists.org

NMA (National Medical Assn)
8403 Colesville Rd Ste 920 .... Silver Spring MD 20910 202-347-1895 347-0722 49-8
TF: 800-662-0554 ■ *Web:* www.nmanet.org

NMA (National Mining Assn)
101 Constitution Ave NW Ste 500-E..........Washington DC 20001 202-463-2600 463-2666 48-12
Web: www.nma.org

NMA (National Management Assn)
2210 Arbor Blvd............................Dayton OH 45439 937-294-0421 294-2374 49-12
TF: 800-688-5253 ■ *Web:* www.nma1.org

NMA (National Meat Assn)
1970 Broadway Ste 825 .... Oakland CA 94612 510-763-1533 49-6
TF: 800-248-2862 ■ *Web:* meatassociation.com

NMAH (National Museum of American History (Smithsonian Institution))
12th St & Constitution Ave NW.............Washington DC 20560 202-633-3270 312-1990 520
Web: americanhistory.si.edu

NMB Technologies Corp
9730 Independence Ave .... Chatsworth CA 91311 818-341-3355 341-8207 173-1
Web: www.nmbtc.com

NMC (National Motor Club of America Inc)
130 E John Carpenter Fwy ....Irving TX 75062 972-999-1099 53
TF: 800-523-4582 ■ *Web:* www.nmc.com

Name / Address	Phone	Fax	Class
NMC (Northside Medical Ctr) 500 Gypsy Ln ... Youngstown OH 44501 *Web:* northsidemedicalcenter.org	330-884-1000		374-3
NMC (Northwest Medical Ctr) 6200 N La Cholla Blvd ... Tucson AZ 85741 *Web:* www.northwestmedicalcenter.com	520-742-9000		374-3
NMC (Natividad Medical Ctr) 1441 Constitution Blvd ... Salinas CA 93906 *Web:* www.natividad.com	831-755-4111		374-3
NMC Resource Corp 1111 Melville St Ste 1100 ... Vancouver BC V6E3V6 *Web:* www.nmcresource.com	604-643-1730		502
NMCC (Northern Maine Community College) 33 Edgemont Dr ... Presque Isle ME 04769 *TF:* 800-535-6682 ■ *Web:* nmcc.edu	207-768-2700	768-2848	800
NMCRS (Navy-Marine Corps Relief Society) 875 N Randolph St Ste 225 ... Arlington VA 22203 *TF:* 800-654-8364 ■ *Web:* www.nmcrs.org	703-696-4904	696-0144	48-19
NMC-Wollard Inc 2021 Truax Blvd ... Eau Claire WI 54703 *TF:* 800-656-6867 ■ *Web:* www.nmc-wollard.com	715-835-3151	835-6625	470
NMDP (National Marrow Donor Program) 3001 Broadway St NE Ste 100 ... Minneapolis MN 55413 *TF:* 800-526-7809 ■ *Web:* bethematch.org	612-627-5800		48-17
NMEA (National Marine Electronics Assn) 7 Riggs Ave. ... Severna Park MD 21146 *TF:* 800-808-6632 ■ *Web:* www.nmea.org	410-975-9425	975-9450	49-13
NMF (National Marfan Foundation) 22 Manhasset Ave. ... Port Washington NY 11050 *TF:* 800-862-7326 ■ *Web:* www.marfan.org	516-883-8712	883-8040	48-17
NMFTA (National Motor Freight Traffic Assn) 1001 N Fairfax St Ste 600 ... Alexandria VA 22314 *TF:* 866-411-6632 ■ *Web:* www.nmfta.org	703-838-1810	683-6296	49-21
NMG Aerospace 4880 Hudson Dr ... Stow OH 44224 *Web:* www.nmgaerospace.com	330-688-6494		22
NMH (Newton Memorial Hospital) 175 High St ... Newton NJ 07860 *Web:* atlantichealth.org/newton	973-383-2121		374-3
NMHC (National Multi Housing Council) 1850 M St NW Ste 540 ... Washington DC 20036 *Web:* www.nmhc.org	202-974-2300	775-0112	49-17
NMI (Northeast-Midwest Institute) 50 F St NW Ste 950 ... Washington DC 20001 *Web:* www.nemw.org	202-544-5200	544-0043	634
NMI Industrial Holdings Inc 8503 Weyand Ave ... Sacramento CA 95828 *TF:* 800-635-7030 ■ *Web:* www.nmiindustrial.com	916-635-7030		492
NMMA (National Marine Manufacturers Assn) 200 E Randolph Dr Ste 5100 ... Chicago IL 60601 *Web:* www.nmma.org	312-946-6200	946-0388	49-21
NMMC (Northern Maine Medical Ctr) 194 E Main St ... Fort Kent ME 04743 *Web:* www.nmmc.org	207-834-3155	834-2949	374-3
NMMS (New Mexico Medical Society) 316 Osuna Rd NE Ste 501 ... Albuquerque NM 87107 *TF:* 800-748-1596 ■ *Web:* www.nmms.org	505-828-0237	828-0336	474
NMOA (National Mail Order Assn LLC) 2807 Polk St NE ... Minneapolis MN 55418 *TF:* 800-992-1377 ■ *Web:* www.nmoa.org	612-788-1673	788-1147	49-18
NMPA (National Music Publishers' Assn) 975 F St NW Ste 375 ... Washington DC 20004 *Web:* www.nmpa.org	202-393-6672		48-4
NMPF (National Milk Producers Federation) 2101 Wilson Blvd Ste 400 ... Arlington VA 22201 *Web:* www.nmpf.org	703-243-6111	841-9328	49-6
NMPF PAC (National Milk Producers Federation PAC) 2101 Wilson Blvd Ste 400 ... Arlington VA 22201 *Web:* nmpf.org	703-243-6111	841-9328	615
NMPhA (New Mexico Pharmacists Assn) 2716 San Pedro Dr NE # C ... Albuquerque NM 87110 *Web:* www.nmpharmacy.org	505-265-8729		585
NMPIRG (New Mexico Public Interest Research Group) PO Box 40173 ... Albuquerque NM 87196 *Web:* www.nmpirg.org	505-254-1244		633
NMRA (National Marine Representatives Assn) PO Box 360 ... Gurnee IL 60031 *TF:* 800-890-3819 ■ *Web:* www.nmraonline.org	847-662-3167	336-7126	49-18
NMRA (National Model Railroad Assn) 4121 Cromwell Rd ... Chattanooga TN 37421 *TF:* 800-654-2256 ■ *Web:* www.nmra.org	423-892-2846	899-4869	48-18
NMS (North Milwaukee State Bank) 5630 W Fond Du Lac Ave ... Milwaukee WI 53216 *TF:* 800-799-5630 ■ *Web:* www.nmsbank.com	414-466-2344	466-6248	70
NMS Capital Group LLC 433 N Camden Dr 4th Fl ... Beverly Hills CA 90210 *TF:* 800-716-2080 ■ *Web:* nmscapital.com	800-716-2080		691
NMS Labs 3701 Welsh Rd ... Willow Grove PA 19090 *TF:* 800-522-6671 ■ *Web:* www.nmslabs.com	215-657-4900	657-2972	418
NMSA (National Middle School Assn) 4151 Executive Pkwy Ste 300 ... Westerville OH 43081 *TF:* 800-528-6672 ■ *Web:* www.amle.org	614-895-4730	895-4750	49-5
NMSDC (National Minority Supplier Development Council) 1359 Broadway 10th Fl ... New York NY 10018 *TF:* 800-843-4898 ■ *Web:* www.nmsdc.org	212-944-2430	719-9611	49-18
NMSU (New Mexico State University) MSC-3A PO Box 30001 ... Las Cruces NM 88003 **Fax:* Admissions ■ *TF Admissions:* 800-662-6678 ■ *Web:* www.nmsu.edu	575-646-3121	646-6330*	166
NMT (New Mexico Institute of Mining & Technology) 801 Leroy Pl ... Socorro NM 87801 *TF Admissions:* 800-428-8324 ■ *Web:* www.nmt.edu	505-835-5434		166
NMV The Marketing Firm Inc 11300 Coloma Rd Ste B-14 ... Gold River CA 95670 *Web:* www.nmvinc.com	916-852-7716		195
NN Inc 2000 Waters Edge Dr ... Johnson City TN 37604 *NASDAQ: NNBR* ■ *TF:* 877-888-0002 ■ *Web:* nninc.com	423-434-8300	743-8870	485
NNA (Nebraska Nurses Assn) PO Box 3107 ... Kearney NE 68848 *TF:* 800-582-3014 ■ *Web:* www.nebraskanurses.org	888-885-7025		533
NNA (National Newspaper Assn) PO Box 7540 ... Columbia MO 65205 *TF:* 800-829-4662 ■ *Web:* nnaweb.org	573-777-4980	777-4985	49-14
NNA (National Notary Assn) 9350 DeSoto Ave ... Chatsworth CA 91313 *TF:* 800-876-6827 ■ *Web:* www.nationalnotary.org	818-739-4000		49-12
NNM Peterson Manufacturing Co 24133 W 143rd St ... Plainfield IL 60544 *TF:* 800-826-9086 ■ *Web:* www.peterson-mfg.com	815-436-9201	436-2863	286
NNPDF (National Niemann-Pick Disease Foundation Inc) 401 Madison Ave Ste B PO Box 49 ... Fort Atkinson WI 53538 *TF:* 877-287-3672 ■ *Web:* www.nnpdf.org	920-563-0930	563-0931	48-17
NNR Global Logistics USA Inc 450 E Devon Ave Ste 260 ... Itasca IL 60143 *TF:* 800-492-7558 ■ *Web:* www.staffingnetwork.com	630-773-1490		449
NNSA (National Nuclear Security Administration) 1000 Independence Ave SW ... Washington DC 20585 *Web:* www.nnsa.energy.gov	202-586-5000	586-4892	340-9
NNSDO (National Nursing Staff Development Organization) 330 N Wabash Ave Ste 2000 ... Chicago IL 60611 *TF:* 800-489-1995 ■ *Web:* www.anpd.org	312-321-5135	673-6835	49-8
NNT Corp 1320 Norwood Ave ... Itasca IL 60143 *TF:* 800-556-9999 ■ *Web:* www.nntcorp.com	630-875-9600		455
No 9 PARK 9 Pk St ... Boston MA 02108 *Web:* www.no9park.com	617-742-9991		671
No Fault Sports Products 2101 Briarglen Dr ... Houston TX 77027 *TF:* 800-462-7766 ■ *Web:* nofaultsports.com	713-683-7101		711
No Fear Plaza Camino Real 2525 El Camino Real Ste 2525 ... Carlsbad CA 92008 *Web:* www.nofear.com	760-720-0189		155-1
No Good Entertainment Inc 9944 Santa Monica Blvd ... Beverly Hills CA 90212 *Web:* www.ngtv.com	310-556-8600		116
No Greater Love 1750 New York Ave NW ... Washington DC 20006	202-445-1500		340-20
No Ordinary Moments Inc 16742 Gothard St Ste 115 ... Huntington Beach CA 92647 *Web:* noordinarymoments.com	714-848-3800		363
No Peace Without Justice (NPWJ) 866 UN Plaza Ste 408 ... New York NY 10017 *Web:* www.npwj.org	212-980-2558	980-1072	48-8
No Starch Press Inc 38 Ringold St ... San Francisco CA 94103 *TF:* 800-420-7240 ■ *Web:* www.nostarch.com	415-863-9900	863-9950	637-2
NOA (National Onion Assn) 822 Seventh St Ste 510 ... Greeley CO 80631 *Web:* www.onions-usa.org	970-353-5895	353-5897	48-2
NOAA (National Oceanic & Atmospheric Administration) 1401 Constitution Ave NW ... Washington DC 20230 *Web:* www.noaa.gov	202-482-6090	482-3154	340-2
Pacific Islands Region 1601 Kapiolani Blvd Rm 1110 ... Honolulu HI 96814 *TF:* 888-674-7411 ■ *Web:* www.fpir.noaa.gov	808-944-2200		340-2
NOAA's Undersea Research Program (NURC) University of N Carolina at Wilmington ... Silver Spring MD 20910 **Fax Area Code:* 301 ■ *Web:* www.nurp.noaa.gov	910-962-2440	713-1967*	668
NOAA's Undersea Research Program *Florida Keys Research Program* 1315 EW Hwy ... Silver Spring MD 20910 *Web:* www.nurp.noaa.gov	301-734-1000	713-1967	668
NOAH (National Organization for Albinism & Hypopigmentation) PO Box 959 ... East Hampstead NH 03826 *TF:* 800-648-2310 ■ *Web:* www.albinism.org	603-887-2310		48-17
Noah Technologies Corp of Texas 1 Noah Pk ... San Antonio TX 78249 *Web:* www.noahtech.com	210-691-2000		143
Noah Webster House 227 S Main St ... West Hartford CT 06107 *Web:* www.noahwebsterhouse.org	860-521-5362	521-4036	520
Noah's Animal Hospitals 5510 Millersville Rd ... Indianapolis IN 46226 *Web:* noahsanimalhospital.com	317-244-7738		794
Noah's Ark Starr Animal Hospital Inc 422 Noth Euclid St ... Fullerton CA 92832 *Web:* www.noahsarkfullerton.com	714-525-2202		794
Noah's Hof Brau 1311 J St ... Modesto CA 95354	209-527-1090		671
Noamex Inc 625 Wortman Ave ... Brooklyn NY 11208 *TF:* 800-640-5917 ■ *Web:* www.noamex.com	718-342-2278	342-2258	156
Noarus Auto Group 6701 Ctr Dr W Ste 925 ... Los Angeles CA 90045 *Web:* www.noarus.com	310-258-0920		57
Noatak National Preserve PO Box 1029 ... Kotzebue AK 99752 *Web:* www.nps.gov/noat	907-442-3890	442-8316	564
Nob Hill 3799 Las Vegas Blvd S MGM Grand Hotel ... Las Vegas NV 89109 *TF Resv:* 800-929-1111 ■ *Web:* www.mgmgrand.com	702-891-1111	891-3036	671
Nob Hill Gazette 5 Third St Ste 222 ... San Francisco CA 94103 *Web:* www.nobhillgazette.com	415-227-0190		457-22
Nobel Automotive Tennessee LLC 190 County Home Rd ... Paris TN 38242 *Web:* nobel-automotive.com/en/site/paris?menu=implantation&site=paris	731-641-8198		370
Nobel Biocare USA Inc 22715 Savi Ranch Pkwy ... Yorba Linda CA 92887 *TF:* 800-993-8100 ■ *Web:* www.nobelbiocare.com	714-282-4800	998-9236	228
Nobel Learning Communities Inc 1615 W Chester Pike Ste 200 ... West Chester PA 19382 *Web:* www.nobellearning.com	484-947-2000		242
Nobel Systems Inc 436 E Vanderbilt Way ... San Bernardino CA 92408 *Web:* www.nobel-systems.com	909-890-5611		180
NobelBiz Inc 5973 Avenida Encinas Ste 202 ... Carlsbad CA 92008 *Web:* www.nobelbiz.com	760-405-0105		387
NobelClad 5405 Spine Rd ... Boulder CO 80301 *NASDAQ: BOOM* ■ *Web:* www.nobelclad.com	303-665-5700	604-1897	482
Nobility Homes Inc 3741 SW Seventh St ... Ocala FL 34474 *OTC: NOBH* ■ *TF:* 800-476-6624 ■ *Web:* www.nobilityhomes.com	352-732-5157	732-4203	505
Nobis Engineering Inc 18 Chenell Dr ... Concord NH 03301 *Web:* nobiseng.com	603-224-4182		261

				Phone	Fax	Class
NOBLE (National Organization of Black Law Enforcement Executives) 4609 Pinecrest Office Pk Dr Ste F *Web:* noblenational.org	Alexandria	VA	22312	703-658-1529	658-9479	49-7
NOBLE 2215 W Chesterfield Blvd *Web:* www.noble.net	Springfield	MO	65807	417-875-5000		7
Noble & Cooley Co 42 Water St *Web:* www.noblecooley.com	Granville	MA	01034	413-357-6321	357-6314	527
Noble & Greenough School 10 Campus Dr	Dedham	MA	02026	781-326-3700		685
Noble Bank & Trust NA 1509 Quintard Ave *Web:* noblebank.com	Anniston	AL	36202	256-741-1800		70
Noble Corp 13135 S Dairy Ashford Rd Ste 800 *NYSE: NE* ■ *TF:* 877-285-4162 ■ *Web:* www.noblecorp.com	Sugar Land	TX	77478	281-276-6100	491-2092	540
Noble Correctional Institution 15708 McConnelsville Rd *Web:* drc.ohio.gov	Caldwell	OH	43724	740-732-5188	732-2651	213
Noble County 101 N Orange St *TF:* 800-840-8757 ■ *Web:* www.nobleco.org	Albion	IN	46701	260-636-2736	636-4000	338
Noble County 15708 McConnelsville Rd *Web:* www.drc.ohio.gov	Caldwell	OH	43724	740-732-5188	732-2651	338
Noble County 300 Courthouse Dr Ste 1 *Web:* www.noblecountyok.com	Perry	OK	73077	580-336-2771	336-4010	338
Noble Energy Inc 100 Glenborough Dr Ste 100 *NYSE: NBL* ■ *TF:* 800-220-5824 ■ *Web:* www.nblenergy.com	Houston	TX	77067	281-872-3100	872-3111	536
Noble Ford Mercury Inc 2406 N Jefferson Way *TF:* 800-496-9984 ■ *Web:* www.nobleford.com	Indianola	IA	50125	515-961-8151		516
Noble Horizons 17 Cobble Rd *TF:* 800-733-2767 ■ *Web:* www.noblehorizons.org	Salisbury	CT	06068	860-435-9851	435-0636	450
Noble House Hotels & Resorts 600 Sixth St S *Web:* www.noblehousehotels.com	Kirkland	WA	98033	425-827-8737	827-6707	379
Noble Investment Group Ltd 2000 Monarch Tower 3424 Peachtree Rd NE *TF:* 800-735-3362 ■ *Web:* www.nobleinvestment.com	Atlanta	GA	30326	404-419-1000		378
Noble Logistic Services Inc 5390 Greens Rd *Web:* www.ndlilogistics.com	Houston	TX	77032	713-690-0200	690-7315	311
Noble Oil Services Inc 5617 Clyde Rhyne Dr *Web:* www.nobleoil.com	Sanford	NC	27330	919-774-8180		541
Noble REMC 300 Weber Rd PO Box 137 *TF:* 800-933-7362 ■ *Web:* www.nobleremc.com	Albion	IN	46701	260-636-2113		245
Noble Roman's Pizza Inc 1 Virginia Ave Ste 300 *Web:* www.nobleromans.com	Indianapolis	IN	46204	317-634-3377		670
Noble Rot 1111 E Burnside 4th Fl *Web:* www.noblerotpdx.com	Portland	OR	97214	503-233-1999		671
Noble Royalties Inc 15601 N Dallas Pkwy Ste 900 *Web:* www.nobleroyalties.com	Addison	TX	75001	972-720-1888		538
Noble Steel Inc 1741 W Lincoln St	Phoenix	AZ	85007	602-257-8822		492
Noble Technologies Corp 2020 Noble Dr *Web:* www.nobletek.com	Wooster	OH	44691	330-287-1500		261
Noble Trade Inc 7171 Jane St *TF:* 800-529-9805 ■ *Web:* www.noble.ca	Concord	ON	L4K1A7	905-760-6800	760-6801	111
Noble Wines Ltd 9860 40th Ave S *Web:* www.thewinebowgroup.com/our-companies/noble-wines	Seattle	WA	98118	206-326-5274		80-3
Nobles Co-op Electric 22636 US Hwy 59 PO Box 788 *TF:* 800-776-0517 ■ *Web:* www.noblesce.coop	Worthington	MN	56187	507-372-7331	372-5148	245
Nobles County 1530 Airport Rd *Web:* www.co.nobles.mn.us	Worthington	MN	56187	507-372-8263		338
Noblesville Chamber of Commerce 601 Conner St *TF:* 800-227-1376 ■ *Web:* www.noblesvillechamber.com	Noblesville	IN	46060	317-773-0086	773-1966	139
NobleWorks Inc 500 Paterson Plank Rd *TF:* 800-346-6253 ■ *Web:* www.nobleworkscards.com	Union City	NJ	07087	201-420-0095		130
Noblis 3150 Fairview Pk Dr S *Web:* www.noblis.org	Falls Church	VA	22042	703-610-2000		668
Nobu 4525 Collins Ave *Web:* www.noburestaurants.com	Miami Beach	FL	33140	212-757-3000		671
Nobu 207 Fifth Ave *Web:* www.noburestaurants.com	San Diego	CA	92101	212-219-0500		671
Nobu 40 W 57th St *Web:* www.noburestaurants.com/los-angeles/experience	New York	NY	10019	212-757-3000	757-6330	671
Nobu's 8643 Olive Blvd *Web:* www.nobusushistl.com	Saint Louis	MO	63132	314-997-2303		671
NOCC (National Ovarian Cancer Coalition) 2501 Oak Lawn Ave Ste 435 **Fax Area Code: 214* ■ *TF:* 888-682-7426 ■ *Web:* www.ovarian.org	Dallas	TX	75219	888-682-7426	273-4201*	48-17
NOCIRC (National Organization of Circumcision Information Resource Centers) PO Box 2512 *TF:* 800-727-8622 ■ *Web:* www.nocirc.org	San Anselmo	CA	94979	415-488-9883	488-9660	48-17
Nockamixon State Park 1542 Mtn View Dr *Web:* www.dcnr.state.pa.us	Quakertown	PA	18951	215-529-7300		565
NOCO Energy Corp 2440 Sheridan Dr *TF:* 800-500-6626 ■ *Web:* www.noco.com	Tonawanda	NY	14150	716-833-6626	832-1312	579
NOCS (New Orleans Cold Storage & Warehouse Company Inc) 3411 JouRdan Rd *Web:* www.nocs.com	New Orleans	LA	70126	504-944-4400		803-2
Noction Inc 1294 Lawrence Sta Rd *Web:* www.noction.com	Sunnyvale	CA	94089	650-618-9823		231
NOD (National Organization on Disability) 77 Water St Ste 204 *Web:* www.nod.org	New York	NY	10005	646-505-1191		48-17
Nodak Electric Co-op Inc 4000 32nd Ave S *TF:* 800-732-4373 ■ *Web:* www.nodakelectric.com	Grand Forks	ND	58201	701-746-4461		245
Nodaway County 403 N Market *Web:* www.nodawaycountymo.us	Maryville	MO	64468	660-582-2251		338
Nodus Technologies Inc 2099 S State College Blvd Ste 250 *Web:* www.nodus.com	Anaheim	CA	92806	909-482-4701		177
Noe Grill Four Riverway *TF:* 888-444-6664	Houston	TX	77056	713-871-8181		671
Noelle Spa-beauty & Wellness 1100 High Ridge Rd *TF:* 800-566-3553 ■ *Web:* www.noelle.com	Stamford	CT	06905	203-322-3445		77
Noel-Smyser Engineering Corp 4005 Industrial Blvd *Web:* www.noel-smyser.com	Indianapolis	IN	46254	317-293-2215		21
Noem Kristi (Rep R - SD) 2457 Rayburn HOB *Web:* noem.house.gov	Washington	DC	20515	202-225-2801	225-5823	342-2
Noerr Programs Corp, The 6632 Fig St *Web:* www.noerrprograms.com	Arvada	CO	80004	303-642-7147		226
Noetix Corp 5010 148th Ave NE Ste 100 *TF:* 866-466-3849 ■ *Web:* www.noetix.com	Redmond	WA	98052	425-372-2699		177
Noevir USA Inc 1095 Main St *TF:* 800-872-8817 ■ *Web:* www.noevirusa.com	Irvine	CA	92614	949-660-1111	660-7168	366
NOF (National Osteoporosis Foundation) 251 18th St S Ste 630 *TF:* 800-231-4222 ■ *Web:* www.nof.org	Arlington	VA	22202	202-223-2226	223-2237	48-17
NOF Metal Coatings NA 275 Industrial Pkwy *Web:* www.metal-coatings.com	Chardon	OH	44024	440-285-2231	285-5009	481
Nofa-ny Certified Organic LLC 840 Upper Front St *TF:* 800-853-2676 ■ *Web:* www.nofany.org	Binghamton	NY	13905	607-724-9851		138
Nogales Chamber of Commerce 123 W Kino Pk *TF:* 800-508-7624 ■ *Web:* thenogaleschamber.com	Nogales	AZ	85621	520-287-3685		139
Nogales City/Santa Cruz County Public Library 518 N Grand Ave *TF:* 800-424-6589 ■ *Web:* nogalesaz.gov	Nogales	AZ	85621	520-287-3343	287-4823	434-3
Nogales Investors Management LLC 9229 W Sunset Blvd Ste 900 *Web:* www.nogalesinvestors.com	Los Angeles	CA	90069	310-276-7439		401
NogginLabs Inc 4621 N Ravenswood Ave Ste 303 *Web:* www.nogginlabs.com	Chicago	IL	60640	773-878-9011		244
Noguska LLC 741 Countyline St *Web:* www.noguska.com	Fostoria	OH	44830	419-435-0404		175
NOHS (North Oaks Health System) PO Box 2668 *Web:* www.northoaks.org	Hammond	LA	70404	985-345-2700		374-3
NOIA (National Ocean Industries Assn) 1120 G St NW Ste 900 *TF:* 800-558-9994 ■ *Web:* www.noia.org	Washington	DC	20005	202-347-6900	347-8650	48-12
Nokham Thai 747 Richmond Rd *Web:* nokhamthai.ca	Ottawa	ON	K2A3Z9	613-724-6135	724-6620	671
Nokia Inc 200 S Mathilda Ave *NYSE: NOK* ■ *Web:* www.nokia.com	Sunnyvale	CA	94086	408-737-0900		735
Nokomis Learning Ctr 5153 Marsh Rd *TF:* 800-562-4957 ■ *Web:* www.nokomis.org	Okemos	MI	48864	517-349-5777		50-2
Nokomis Regional High School 266 Williams Rd *Web:* rsu19.org	Newport	ME	04953	207-368-4354		685
NOLA 534 St Louis St *Web:* www.emerils.com	New Orleans	LA	70130	504-522-6652	524-6178	671
Nolan & Heller LLP 39 N Pearl St 3rd Fl *Web:* www.nolanandheller.com	Albany	NY	12207	518-449-3300		428
Nolan Co 1016 Ninth St SW *TF:* 800-297-1383 ■ *Web:* www.nolancompany.com	Canton	OH	44707	330-453-7922	453-7449	650
Nolan County 100 E Third St Ste 108 *Web:* www.co.nolan.tx.us	Sweetwater	TX	79556	325-235-2462	236-9416	338
Nolan O Luke CPA Pa 830 N Main	Wichita	KS	67203	316-265-0599		2
Nolan Rick (Rep D - MN) 2366 Rayburn HOB *Web:* nolan.house.gov	Washington	DC	20515	202-225-6211	225-0699	342-2
Nolan Ryan Exhibit Ctr 2925 S Bypass 35 *Web:* www.nolanryanfoundation.org	Alvin	TX	77511	281-388-1134		522
Nolde Forest Environmental Education Ctr 2910 New Holland Rd *Web:* www.dcnr.state.pa.us	Reading	PA	19607	610-796-3699		565
Noldus Information Technology Inc 1503 Edwards Ferry Rd NE Ste 201 *TF:* 800-355-9541 ■ *Web:* www.noldus.com	Leesburg	VA	20176	703-771-0440		177
NOLHGA (National Organization of Life & Health Insurance Guaranty Assn) 13873 Pk Ctr Rd Ste 329 *Web:* www.nolhga.com	Herndon	VA	20171	703-481-5206	481-5209	49-9
Nolin Lake State Park 2998 Brier Creek Rd *Web:* www.parks.ky.gov	Mammoth Cave	KY	42259	270-286-4240		565
Nolin Rural Electric Co-op Corp 411 Ring Rd *TF:* 888-637-4247 ■ *Web:* www.nolinrecc.com	Elizabethtown	KY	42701	270-765-6153		245
Noll Manufacturing Co 1320 Performance Dr	Stockton	CA	95206	209-234-1600		697
Nollenberger Capital Partners Inc 101 California St Ste 3100 *Web:* www.nollenbergercapital.com	San Francisco	CA	94111	415-402-6000		690
Nolo.com 950 Parker St *TF:* 800-728-3555 ■ *Web:* www.nolo.com	Berkeley	CA	94710	800-728-3555	645-0895	178-9
Nolte Precise Manufacturing Inc 6850 Colerain Ave *Web:* www.nolteprecise.com	Cincinnati	OH	45239	513-923-3100		757
Nolte State Park 36921 Veazie Cumberland Rd *Web:* www.parks.wa.gov	Enumclaw	WA	98022	360-825-4646		565
Nol-tec Systems Inc 425 Apollo Dr *Web:* www.nol-tec.com	Circle Pines	MN	55014	651-780-8600	780-4400	207
Noltex LLC 3930 Ventura Dr Ste 355 *Web:* www.soarus.com	Arlington Heights	IL	60004	847-255-1211		601
Nomacorc LLC 400 Vintage Park Dr *Web:* www.nomacorc.com	Zebulon	NC	27597	919-460-2200		820
Nomad Technology Group LLC 1315 Read St Unit C *Web:* nomadtechgroup.com	Evansville	IN	47710	812-618-4032		631

Phone | Fax | Class

Nomadic Display Capitol Inc
5617 Industrial Dr. . . . . Springfield VA 22151 703-912-4700 317
TF: 800-336-5019 ■ *Web:* www.nomadicdisplay.com

Nomadix Inc
30851 Agoura Rd Ste 102. . . . . Agoura Hills CA 91301 818-597-1500 177
TF: 800-666-2349 ■ *Web:* www.nomadix.com

Nomanco Inc 501 Nmc Dr . . . . . Zebulon NC 27597 919-269-6500 269-7936 319-1
TF: 800-345-7279 ■ *Web:* www.nomaco.com

NOMC (North Okaloosa Medical Ctr)
151 E Redstone Ave . . . . . Crestview FL 32539 850-689-8100 374-3
Web: www.northokaloosa.com

Nome Convention & Visitors Bureau
301 Front St . . . . . Nome AK 99762 907-443-6555 443-5832 206
Web: www.visitnomealaska.com

Nome Youth Facility 804 E Fourth St. . . . . Nome AK 99762 907-443-5434 443-7295 412
TF: 800-770-5650 ■ *Web:* dhss.alaska.gov

Nomerel LLC 7107 S Yale Ave Ste 306. . . . . Tulsa OK 74136 918-770-4099 261
Web: www.nomerel.com

NoMI 800 N Michigan Ave. . . . . Chicago IL 60611 312-335-1234 239-4000 671
Web: chicago.park.hyatt.com/en/hotel/home.html

Nominum Inc
800 Bridge Pkwy Ste 100. . . . . Redwood City CA 94065 650-381-6000 171
Web: www.nominum.com

NOMOTC (National Organization of Mothers of Twins Clubs Inc)
2000 Mallory Ln Ste 130-600. . . . . Franklin TN 37067-8231 248-231-4480 48-6
Web: www.multiplesofamerica.org

Nomura Securities International Inc
2 World Financial Ctr Bldg B . . . . . New York NY 10281 212-667-9300 690
Web: www.nomura.com

Non Commissioned Officers Assn (NCOA)
9330 Corporate Dr Ste 701. . . . . Selma TX 78154 210-653-6161 637-3337 48-19
TF: 800-662-2620 ■ *Web:* www.ncoausa.org

Nonesuch Records 3300 Warner Blvd . . . . . Burbank CA 91505 818-846-9090 657
Web: www.nonesuch.com

Nonfiction Studios Inc
450, 318 - 11th Ave SE. . . . . Calgary AB T2G0Y2 403-686-8887 224
Web: www.nonfiction.ca

Nonin Medical Inc 13700 First Ave N. . . . . Plymouth MN 55441 763-553-9968 477
Web: www.nonin.com

Non-Intrusive Inspection Technology Inc
23031 Ladbrook Dr. . . . . Dulles VA 20166 703-661-0283 668
Web: www.niitek.com

Noninvasive Medical Technologies Inc
6412 S Arville St. . . . . Las Vegas NV 89118 702-614-3360 463
TF: 888-466-8552 ■ *Web:* www.nmtinc.org

Non-Invasive Monitoring Systems Inc
4400 Biscayne Blvd . . . . . Miami FL 33137 305-575-4200 250
Web: www.nims-inc.com

non-linear creations Inc
987 Wellington St Ste 201 . . . . . Ottawa ON K1Y2Y1 613-241-2067 241-3086 7
TF: 866-915-2997 ■ *Web:* www.nonlinearcreations.com

Nonna's Italian American Cafe
306 S Ave. . . . . Springfield MO 65806 417-831-1222 671
Web: nonnascafe.com

Nonpareil Corp 40 N 400 W . . . . . Blackfoot ID 83221 208-785-5880 785-3656 296-18

Noodles & Co 520 Zang St. . . . . Broomfield CO 80021 720-214-1900 670
Web: www.noodles.com

Nook Industries 4950 E 49th St . . . . . Cleveland OH 44125 216-271-7900 271-7020 620
TF: 800-321-7800 ■ *Web:* www.nookindustries.com

Noon Hour Food Products Inc
215 N Des Plaines . . . . . Chicago IL 60661 312-382-1177 296-13

Noonan Energy Corp 86 Robbins Rd . . . . . Springfield MA 01104 413-734-7396 316
Web: www.noonanenergy.com

Noone & Associates Inc
3 Crossgate Dr . . . . . Mechanicsburg PA 17050 717-458-0482 393
Web: www.nooneappraisals.com

Nooter Construction Co
1500 S Second St. . . . . Saint Louis MO 63104 314-421-7600 186
Web: www.nooterconstruction.com

Nora 2132 Florida Ave NW. . . . . Washington DC 20008 202-462-5143 671
Web: www.noras.com

Nora Lighting Inc 6505 Gayhart St . . . . . Commerce CA 90040 323-767-2600 500-9955* 246
**Fax Area Code:* 800 ■ *TF:* 800-686-6672 ■ *Web:* www.noralighting.com

Norair Engineering Corp
337 Brightseat Rd Ste 200 . . . . . Landover MD 20785 301-499-2202 188
Web: www.norair.com

Noralco Corp 1920 Lincoln Rd. . . . . Pittsburgh PA 15235 412-361-6678 361-6535 189-16
Web: www.noralco.com

NORAM Engineering & Constructors Ltd
200 Granville St Ste 1800. . . . . Vancouver BC V6C1S4 604-681-2030 261
Web: www.noram-eng.com

Noramco Inc 1440 Olympic Dr. . . . . Athens GA 30601 706-353-4400 582
Web: www.noramco.com

Norampac Industries Inc
4001 Packard Rd . . . . . Niagara Falls NY 14303 716-285-3681 561

Noran Instruments Inc 5225 Verona Rd . . . . . Madison WI 53711 608-276-6100 273-5045 419
TF: 800-532-4752 ■ *Web:* www.thermofisher.com/en/home.html

Noranco Inc 1842 Clements Rd. . . . . Pickering ON L1W3R8 905-831-0100 789
Web: www.noranco.com

Noranda Aluminum Inc
801 Crescent Ctr Dr Ste 600. . . . . Franklin TN 37067 615-771-5700 771-5701 485
TF: 800-325-8112

Norandal USA Inc
400 Bill Brooks Dr . . . . . Huntingdon TN 38344 731-986-5011 485

Norandex Bldg Materials Distribution Inc
1 ABC Pkwy Ste 100. . . . . Beloit WA 53511 330-656-8809 191-4
Web: www.norandex.com

Nor-Arc Steel Fabricators
331567 Hwy 11 . . . . . Earlton ON P0J1E0 705-563-2656 757
TF: 800-434-3159 ■ *Web:* www.norarc.com

Norauto Inc 1161 Hwy 111 E. . . . . Amos QC J9T1N2 819-732-6637 57
Web: www.norautonissan.com

Noraxon U.S.A. Inc
15770 N Greenway-Hayden Loop Ste 100 . . . . . Scottsdale AZ 85260 480-443-3413 475
TF: 800-364-8985 ■ *Web:* www.noraxon.com

Norben Import Corp 99 S Newman St. . . . . Hackensack NJ 07601 201-487-0855 293
Web: www.larksilk.com

Norberg-ies 4237 S 74th E Ave . . . . . Tulsa OK 74145 918-665-6888 729
TF: 800-739-9145 ■ *Web:* www.nema7.com

Norbert Cronin & Co
582 Market St . . . . . San Francisco CA 94104 415-981-2222 390

Norbest Inc PO Box 890. . . . . Moroni UT 84646 800-453-5327 597-5416* 297-10
**Fax Area Code:* 888 ■ *TF:* 800-453-5327 ■ *Web:* www.norbest.com

Norbord Inc 1 Toronto St Ste 600. . . . . Toronto ON M5C2W4 416-365-0705 365-3292 613
TSE: NBD ■ *TF:* 888-667-2673 ■ *Web:* www.norbord.com

Nor-Cal Beverage Company Inc
2286 Stone Blvd . . . . . West Sacramento CA 95691 916-372-0600 81-2
TF: 800-331-2059 ■ *Web:* www.ncbev.com

Nor-Cal Controls Inc
1952 Concourse Dr . . . . . San Jose CA 95131 408-435-0400 419
TF: 800-233-2013 ■ *Web:* www.norcal4air.com

Nor-Cal Metal Fabricators
1121 Third St . . . . . Oakland CA 94607 510-833-7157 208-2838 482
Web: www.nc-mf.com

Norcal Mutual Insurance Company Inc
560 Davis St. . . . . San Francisco CA 94111 415-397-9700 835-9817 391-5
TF: 800-652-1051 ■ *Web:* www.norcal-group.com

Nor-Cal Products Inc 1967 S Oregon St . . . . . Yreka CA 96097 530-842-4457 842-9130* 595
**Fax:* Sales ■ *TF:* 800-824-4166 ■ *Web:* www.n-c.com

Norcal Rental Group LLC
318 Stealth Ct. . . . . Livermore CA 94551 925-961-0130 264-3
TF: 800-649-6629 ■ *Web:* www.crescorent.com

Norchem Corp 5649 Alhambra Ave . . . . . Los Angeles CA 90032 323-221-0221 111
Web: norchemcorp.com

Norco Inc 1125 W Amity Rd. . . . . Boise ID 83705 208-336-1643 358
Web: www.norco-inc.com

Norco Products Furniture Mfrs
4985 Blue Mtn Rd. . . . . Missoula MT 59804 406-251-3800 321
TF: 800-662-2300 ■ *Web:* www.norcoproducts.com

Norcon Communications Inc
510 Burnside Ave. . . . . Inwood NY 11096 516-239-0300 52
Web: norconcomm.com

Norcon Corp 5600 Municipal St. . . . . Schofield WI 54476 715-359-5808 186
Web: www.norconcorp.com

Norcon Industries Inc
5412 E Calle Cerrito . . . . . Guadalupe AZ 85283 480-839-2324 321
Web: www.norconindustries.net

Nor-Cote International Inc
506 Lafayette Ave . . . . . Crawfordsville IN 47933 765-362-9180 364-5408 388
TF: 800-488-9180 ■ *Web:* www.norcote.com

Norcraft cabinetry 3020 Denmark Ave. . . . . Eagan MN 55121 651-234-3300 115
Web: www.norcraftcompanies.com

Norcross Corp 255 Newtonville Ave. . . . . Newton MA 02458 617-969-7020 201
Web: www.viscosity.com

Norcross Donald (Rep D - NJ)
1531 Longworth HOB. . . . . Washington DC 20515 202-225-6501 342-2
Web: norcross.house.gov

NORD (National Organization for Rare Disorders)
55 Kenosia Ave. . . . . Danbury CT 06810 203-744-0100 798-2291 48-17
TF: 800-999-6673 ■ *Web:* www.rarediseases.org

NORD Drivesystems 800 Nord Dr. . . . . Waunakee WI 53597 888-314-6673 54
TF: 888-314-6673 ■ *Web:* www.nord.com

Nordaas American Homes Company Inc
10091 State Hwy 22 . . . . . Minnesota Lake MN 56068 507-462-3331 462-3211 187
TF: 800-658-7076 ■ *Web:* nordaashomes.com

NORDAM Group 6911 N Whirlpool Dr . . . . . Tulsa OK 74117 918-878-4000 878-4808* 22
**Fax:* Sales ■ *Web:* www.nordam.com

Nordco Inc 245 W Forest Hill Ave . . . . . Oak Creek WI 53154 414-766-2180 766-2379 190
Web: www.nordco.com

Nordeman Grimm 65 E 55th St 33rd Fl . . . . . New York NY 10022 212-935-1000 266
Web: www.nordemangrimm.com

Nordenia International
14591 State Hwy 177 . . . . . Jackson MO 63755 573-335-4900 335-6172 360-3
Web: www.mondigroup.com

Nordia Inc 3020 Jacques-Bureau 2nd Fl . . . . . Laval QC H7P6G2 514-415-7088 737
TF: 866-858-4367 ■ *Web:* www.nordia.ca

Nordic Heritage Museum
3014 NW 67th St . . . . . Seattle WA 98117 206-789-5707 520
TF: 800-626-8631 ■ *Web:* www.nordicmuseum.com

Nordic Interior Inc 56-01 Maspeth Ave . . . . . Maspeth NY 11378 718-456-7000 200

Nordic Ware 5005 Hwy 7. . . . . Minneapolis MN 55416 952-920-2888 924-8561 486
TF: 877-466-7342 ■ *Web:* www.nordicware.com

Nordica USA Corp 19 Commerce Ave . . . . . West Lebanon NH 03784 603-298-6900 711
Web: www.nordica.com

Nordion 447 March Rd . . . . . Ottawa ON K2K1X8 613-592-2790 592-6937 85
NYSE: NDZ ■ *TF:* 800-465-3666 ■ *Web:* www.nordion.com

Nordis Technologies Inc
4401 NW 124th Ave . . . . . Coral Springs FL 33065 954-323-5500 195
Web: www.nordisdirect.com

Nordisk Systems Inc
13475 SE Johnson Rd . . . . . Milwaukie OR 97222 503-353-7555 196
TF: 800-676-2777 ■ *Web:* nordisksystems.com

Nordmin Engineering Ltd
160 Logan Ave . . . . . Thunder Bay ON P7A6R1 807-683-1730 261
Web: nordmin.com

Nordoff-Robbins Music Therapy Clinic
26 Washington Pl . . . . . New York NY 10003 212-998-5151 726
Web: steinhardt.nyu.edu

Nordon Inc 1 Cabot Blvd E. . . . . Langhorne PA 19047 215-504-4700 111
TF: 800-544-0400 ■ *Web:* www.nordoninc.com

Nordonia Hills School District
9370 Olde 8 Rd. . . . . Northfield OH 44067 330-467-0580 685
Web: www.nordoniaschools.org

Nordson Corp 28601 Clemens Rd . . . . . Westlake OH 44145 440-892-1580 892-9507 386
NASDAQ: NDSN ■ *TF:* 800-321-2881 ■ *Web:* www.nordson.com

Nordson MEDICAL
3325 S Timberline Rd. . . . . Fort Collins CO 80525 970-267-5200 223-0953 608
TF: 888-404-5837 ■ *Web:* www.nordsonmedical.com/default.aspx

Nordstrong Equipment Ltd
5 Chester Ave. . . . . Winnipeg MB R2L1W5 204-667-1553 207
Web: www.nordstrongequipment.com

Norduyn Inc 6200 Henri-Bourassa W. . . . . Montreal QC H4R1C3 514-334-3210 334-2989 57
Web: www.norduyn.com

Nordyne Inc 8000 Phoenix Pkwy . . . . . O'Fallon MO 63368 636-561-7300 14
TF: 800-422-4328 ■ *Web:* www.nortekhvac.com

Name / Address	City	State	Zip	Phone	Fax	Class
Noregon Systems Inc 7009 Albert Pick Rd — *TF:* 800-875-1400 ■ *Web:* www.noregon.com	Greensboro	NC	27409	336-768-4337		809
Nor-Ell Inc 851 Hubbard Ave — *TF:* 877-276-4075 ■ *Web:* www.nor-ell.com	Saint Paul	MN	55104	651-487-1441	488-1626	481
Noren Products Inc 1010 Obrien Dr — *Web:* www.norenproducts.com	Menlo Park	CA	94025	650-322-9500	324-1348	201
Norfolk Academy 1585 Wesleyan Dr — *Web:* www.norfolkacademy.org	Norfolk	VA	23502	757-461-6236		685
Norfolk Botanical Garden 6700 Azalea Garden Rd — *Web:* norfolkbotanicalgarden.org	Norfolk	VA	23518	757-441-5830		97
Norfolk City Hall 810 Union St — *Web:* www.norfolk.gov	Norfolk	VA	23510	757-664-4000		337
Norfolk Collegiate School 7336 Granby St — *Web:* www.norfolkcollegiate.org	Norfolk	VA	23505	757-480-2885		685
Norfolk Convention & Visitors Bureau 232 E Main St — *TF:* 800-368-3097 ■ *Web:* www.visitnorfolktoday.com	Norfolk	VA	23510	757-664-6620	622-3663	206
Norfolk County 614 High St — *Web:* www.norfolkcounty.org	Dedham	MA	02026	781-461-6105	326-6480	338
Norfolk Daily News PO Box 977 — *TF:* 877-371-1020 ■ *Web:* www.norfolkdailynews.com	Norfolk	NE	68702	402-371-1020	371-5802	532-2
Norfolk Dredging Co 110 Centervilless Tpke N — *Web:* www.norfolkdredging.com	Chesapeake	VA	23320	757-547-9391	547-2833	186
Norfolk General Hospital 365 W St — *Web:* www.ngh.on.ca	Simcoe	ON	N3Y1T7	519-426-0750	428-2946	374-2
Norfolk (Independent City) 810 Union St Rm 1101 — *TF:* 800-664-1080 ■ *Web:* www.norfolk.gov	Norfolk	VA	23510	757-664-4242	664-4239	338
Norfolk International Airport 2200 Norview Ave — *Web:* www.norfolkairport.com	Norfolk	VA	23518	757-857-3351	857-3265	27
Norfolk Marriott Waterside 235 E Main St — *TF:* 800-910-5560 ■ *Web:* www.norfolkmarriott.com	Norfolk	VA	23510	757-627-4200		378
Norfolk Public Library 139 Main St — *Web:* library.virtualnorfolk.org	Norfolk	MA	02056	508-528-3380	528-6417	434-3
Norfolk Public Library 235 E Plume St — *Web:* www.norfolkpubliclibrary.org	Norfolk	VA	23510	757-664-7323		434-3
Norfolk Public Schools 800 E City Hall Ave — *TF:* 800-846-4464 ■ *Web:* www.nps.k12.va.us	Norfolk	VA	23510	757-628-3843	628-3820	685
Norfolk Regional Ctr 1700 N Victory Rd PO Box 1209 — *Web:* dhhs.ne.gov	Norfolk	NE	68702	402-370-3400		374-5
Norfolk Scope Arena 201 E Brambleton Ave — *TF:* 800-745-3000 ■ *Web:* www.sevenvenues.com	Norfolk	VA	23510	757-664-6464	664-6990	720
Norfolk Southern Corp 3 Commercial Pl — *NYSE:* NSC ■ **Fax Area Code:* 757 ■ **Fax:* Mktg ■ *TF Cust Svc:* 800-635-5768 ■ *Web:* www.nscorp.com	Norfolk	VA	23510	855-667-3655	629-2361*	468
Norfolk Southern Railway Co 3 Commercial Pl — *TF:* 800-635-5768 ■ *Web:* www.nscorp.com	Norfolk	VA	23510	800-453-2530		648
Norfolk State University 700 Pk Ave — **Fax:* Admissions ■ *TF:* 800-274-1821 ■ *Web:* www.nsu.edu	Norfolk	VA	23504	757-823-8600	823-2078*	166
Norfolk Tides Baseball 150 Park Ave Harbor Pk — *Web:* www.milb.com/index.jsp	Norfolk	VA	23510	757-622-2222		713
Norfolk Veterans Home 600 E Benjamin Ave — *Web:* nebraska.gov	Norfolk	NE	68701	402-370-3330	370-3190	793
Norforge & Machining Inc 195 N Dean St — *TF:* 800-839-3706 ■ *Web:* bushnell.illinois.gov	Bushnell	IL	61422	309-772-3124		483
Norgen Biotek Corp 3430 Schmon Pkwy — *TF:* 866-667-4362 ■ *Web:* www.norgenbiotek.com	Thorold	ON	L2V4Y6	905-227-8848	227-1061	418
Norgenix Pharmaceuticals LLC 101 W Saint John St Ste 307 — *Web:* www.norgenixpharma.com	Spartanburg	SC	29306	864-580-2660		231
Norgren 5400 S Delaware St — **Fax:* Mktg ■ *TF:* 800-514-0129 ■ *Web:* norgren.com/us	Littleton	CO	80120	303-794-5000	795-9487*	790
Noridian Administrative Services LLC 901 40th St S Ste 1 — *Web:* www.noridian.com	Fargo	ND	58103	503-944-8810		390
Noritsu Technical Services 6900 Noritsu Ave — *TF:* 888-435-7448 ■ *Web:* www.noritsuservice.com	Buena Park	CA	90620	714-521-9040		393
Norkfolk 405 Madison Ave — *Web:* www.norfolk.ne.us	Norfolk	NE	68701	402-844-2000		206
Norkol Inc & Converting 11650 W Grand Ave — *Web:* www.norkol.com	Northlake	IL	60164	708-531-1000	531-0030	557
Nor-Lake Inc 727 Second St PO Box 248 — *TF:* 800-388-5253 ■ *Web:* www.norlake.com	Hudson	WI	54016	715-386-2323	386-6149	664
Norlake Mfg Co 39301 Taylor Pkwy — *TF:* 800-225-4876 ■ *Web:* www.norlakemfg.com	Elyria	OH	44035	440-353-3200	353-3232	767
Nor-Lea General Hospital Inc 1600 N Main Ave — *Web:* www.nor-lea.org	Lovington	NM	88260	575-396-6611		374-3
Norlen Inc 900 Grossman Dr — *Web:* www.norlen.com	Schofield	WI	54476	715-359-0506		480
Norlift of Oregon Inc 7373 SE Milwaukie Expy — *TF:* 800-452-0050 ■ *Web:* www.norliftor.com	Portland	OR	97222	503-659-5438		770
NORM (National Organization of Restoring Men) 3205 Northwood Dr Ste 209 — *Web:* www.norm.org	Concord	CA	94520	925-827-4077	827-4119	48-17
Norm Thompson Outfitters Inc 3188 NW Aloclek Dr — **Fax Area Code:* 800 ■ *TF:* 800-547-1160 ■ *Web:* normthompson.blair.com	Hillsboro	OR	97124	877-718-7899	821-1282*	459
Norm's Refrigeration & Ice Equipment Inc 1175 N Knollwood Cir — *TF:* 800-933-4423 ■ *Web:* www.normsrefrigeration.com	Anaheim	CA	92801	714-236-3600		665
Norma Kamali 11 W 56th St — *Web:* www.normakamali.com	New York	NY	10019	212-957-9797		277
Norma's 4200 E Palm Canyon Dr — *Web:* www.starwoodhotels.com/lemeridien	Palm Springs	CA	92264	760-770-5000		671
Normac Inc 93 Industrial Dr PO Box 69 — *Web:* www.normac.com	Hendersonville	NC	28739	828-209-9000	209-9001	455
Normal Public Library 206 W College — *TF:* 800-673-4699 ■ *Web:* www.normalpl.org	Normal	IL	61761	309-452-1757	452-5312	434-3
Norman Bros Produce Inc 7621 SW 87th Ave — *Web:* www.normanbrothers.com	Miami	FL	33173	305-274-9363	596-4541	345
Norman Convention & Visitors Bureau 309 E Main St — *TF:* 800-767-7260 ■ *Web:* www.visitnorman.com	Norman	OK	73069	405-366-8095		206
Norman County 16 Third Ave E — *Web:* www.co.norman.mn.us	Ada	MN	56510	218-784-5473	784-4531	338
Norman Data Defense Systems Inc 9302 Lee Hwy — *Web:* www.norman.com	Fairfax	VA	22031	703-267-6109		178-12
Norman Frede Chevrolet Co 16801 Feather Craft Ln — *TF:* 888-307-1703 ■ *Web:* www.fredechevrolet.com	Houston	TX	77058	281-486-2200		57
Norman Hecht Research Inc 20 Crossways Park Dr N Ste 400 — *Web:* www.normanhechtresearch.com	Woodbury	NY	11791	516-496-8866		466
Norman Howard School 275 Pinnacle Rd — *TF:* 800-933-8779 ■ *Web:* www.normanhoward.org	Rochester	NY	14623	585-334-8010		685
Norman Jones Enlow & Co 226 N Fifth St Ste 500	Columbus	OH	43215	614-228-4000		2
Norman Noble Inc 5507 Avion Park Dr — *Web:* www.normannoble.net	Highland Heights	OH	44143	216-761-5387		583
Norman Ralph (Rep R - SC) 2350 Rayburn HOB — *Web:* norman.house.gov	Washington	DC	20515	202-225-5501		342-2
Norman Regional Hospital 901 N Porter St — *Web:* www.normanregional.com	Norman	OK	73071	405-307-1000		374-3
Norman Scott Company Inc 126 29th St Dr SE — *Web:* www.in-tolerance.com	Cedar Rapids	IA	52403	319-363-8561	363-2106	192
Norman Supply Co 825 SW Fifth St — *Web:* www.morsco.com	Oklahoma City	OK	73109	405-235-9511		609
Norman Technologies LLC 630 Davidson Gateway Dr Ste 250 — *Web:* www.normantech.com	Davidson	NC	28036	704-896-0128		177
Norman Transcript 215 E Comanche St PO Box 1058 — *Web:* www.normantranscript.com	Norman	OK	73069	405-321-1800	366-3516	532-2
Norman W Marcoux CPA Inc 788 University Ave — *Web:* marcouxcpa.com	Sacramento	CA	95825	916-927-7772		2
Norman W Paschall Co Inc 1 Paschall Rd — *TF:* 800-222-3834 ■ *Web:* www.paschall.com	Peachtree City	GA	30269	770-487-7945	487-0840	745-8
Norman Y Mineta San Jose International Airport 1701 Airport Blvd Ste B-1130 — *Web:* www.flysanjose.com	San Jose	CA	95110	408-501-7600	441-4591	27
Norman's Family Restaurant 4949 Stevenson Blvd	Fremont	CA	94538	510-226-7777		671
Norman, Wood, Kendrick & Turner 1130 22nd St S Ridge Park Pl Ste 3000 — *Web:* nwkt.com	Birmingham	AL	35205	205-328-6643		428
Normand's 11639 A Jasper Ave — *TF:* 866-308-4438 ■ *Web:* www.normands.com	Edmonton	AB	T5K2S7	780-482-2600		671
Normandale Community College 9700 France Ave S — *TF:* 866-880-8740 ■ *Web:* www.normandale.edu	Bloomington	MN	55431	952-487-8200		162
Normandeau Assoc Inc 25 Nashua Rd — *Web:* www.normandeau.com	Bedford	NH	03110	603-472-5191	472-7052	192
Normandy Farms Estates 1401 Morris Rd — *TF:* 800-559-2040 ■ *Web:* www.normandyfarm.com	Blue Bell	PA	19422	215-616-8500		672
Normandy Hotel, The 2118 Wyoming Ave NW — *Web:* www.doylecollection.com	Washington	DC	20008	202-483-1350		377
Normandy School District 3855 Lcas Hunt Rd — *Web:* www.normandy.k12.mo.us	Saint Louis	MO	63121	314-493-0400	493-0414	685
NormaTec Industries LP 44 Glen Ave — *Web:* www.normatec.net	Newton Center	MA	02459	617-928-3400		476
NorMed 4310 S 131 Pl Ste 160 — **Fax Area Code:* 206 ■ *TF:* 800-288-8200 ■ *Web:* www.normed.com	Seattle	WA	98168	800-288-8200	242-3315*	477
Norment Security Group Inc 2511 Midpark Dr — *TF:* 800-466-3007 ■ *Web:* cornerstonedetention.com	Montgomery	AL	36109	334-281-8440	286-6421	692
NORML (National Organization for the Reform of Marijuana Laws) 1600 K St NW Ste 501 — *TF:* 888-420-8932 ■ *Web:* www.norml.org	Washington	DC	20006	202-483-5500	483-0057	48-8
Noro-Moseley Partners 3284 Northside Pkwy NW Ste 525 — *Web:* www.noromoseley.com	Atlanta	GA	30327	404-233-1966		792
Norotos Inc 201 E Alton Ave — *Web:* www.norotos.com	Santa Ana	CA	92707	714-662-3113	662-7950	454
NORPAC Foods Inc 930 W Washington St — *TF:* 800-733-9311 ■ *Web:* www.norpac.com	Stayton	OR	97383	503-769-2101		296-21
Norpro Inc 2215 Merrill Creek Pkwy — *Web:* wholesale.norpro.com	Everett	WA	98203	425-261-1000	261-1001	486
Norquay Technology Inc 800 W Front St PO Box 468 — *Web:* www.norquaytech.com	Chester	PA	19013	610-874-4330	874-3575	144
Norquist Salvage Corp 2151 Professional Dr Ste 200 — *Web:* www.thrifttown.com	Roseville	CA	95661	916-787-1070		791
Norred & Associates Inc 1003 Virginia Ave Ste B-100 — *Web:* www.norred.com	Atlanta	GA	30354	404-761-5058		693

Name / Address	Phone	Fax	Class
Norrenberns Foods Inc 205 E Harnett St ..... Mascoutah IL 62258	618-566-7010		345
Norridge Health Care & Rehabilitation Centre 7001 W Cullom Ave ..... Norridge IL 60706	708-457-0700		450
Norris Cylinder Co 4818 W Loop 281 ..... Longview TX 75603 *TF:* 800-527-8418 ■ *Web:* www.norriscylinder.com	903-757-7633	237-7654	223
Norris Dam State Resort Park 125 Village Green Cir ..... Lake City TN 37769 *Web:* www.state.tn.us	865-426-7461		565
Norris Ford 901 Merritt Blvd ..... Baltimore MD 21222 *TF Sales:* 888-205-0310 ■ *Web:* www.norrisford.com	410-285-0200		57
Norris Injury Lawyers Pc 10 Old Montgomery Hwy Ste 250 ..... Birmingham AL 35209 *Web:* www.norrisinjurylawyers.com	205-870-8000		445
Norris Medical Library University of Southern California 2003 Zonal Ave ..... Los Angeles CA 90089 *Web:* www.usc.edu/hsc/nml	323-442-1111	221-1235	434-1
Norris Public Power District 606 Irving St PO Box 399 ..... Beatrice NE 68310 *TF:* 800-858-4707 ■ *Web:* www.norrisppd.com	402-223-4038		245
Norris School District 6940 Calloway Dr ..... Bakersfield CA 93312 *Web:* www.norris.k12.ca.us	661-387-7000	399-9750	188-5
Norris, McLaughlin & Marcus PA 721 Route 202-206 ..... Bridgewater NJ 08807 *Web:* nmmlaw.com	908-722-0700		428
Norris, Perne & French LLP 40 Pearl St N W Ste 300 ..... Grand Rapids MI 49503 *TF:* 800-748-0544 ■ *Web:* www.norrisperne.com	616-459-3421		528
Norriseal 11122 W Little York Rd ..... Houston TX 77041 *Fax: Sales ■ *Web:* norrisealwellmark.com	713-466-3552	896-7386*	537
Norristown Farm Park 2500 Upper Farm Rd ..... Norristown PA 19403 *Web:* www.dcnr.state.pa.us	610-270-0215		565
Norristown State Hospital 1001 Sterigere St ..... Norristown PA 19401	610-313-1000		374-5
Norsan Group Inc 2445 Meadowbrook Pkwy ..... Duluth GA 30096 *Fax Area Code: 770 ■ *Web:* norsan.net	678-242-1640	414-0617*	670
Norsask Farm Equipment Ltd Box 49 ..... North Battleford SK S9A2X6 *TF:* 888-446-8128 ■ *Web:* www.norsaskfarmequipmentltd.com	306-445-8128		111
Norsat International Inc 110-4020 Viking Way ..... Richmond BC V6V2L4 *TSE: NII* ■ *TF:* 800-644-4562 ■ *Web:* www.norsat.com	604-821-2800	821-2801	735
Norsco Inc 1816 Ackley Cir ..... Oakdale CA 95361 *Web:* www.norscoinc.com	209-845-2327		454
Norscot Group Inc 1000 W Donges Bay Rd ..... Mequon WI 53092 *TF:* 800-653-3313 ■ *Web:* www.norscot.com	262-241-3313	241-4904	9
Norshield Corp 3232 Mobile Hwy ..... Montgomery AL 36108 *TF:* 855-659-3716 ■ *Web:* www.norshield.net	334-551-0650		350
Nor-Son Inc 7900 Hastings Rd ..... Baxter MN 56425 *TF:* 800-858-1722 ■ *Web:* www.nor-son.com	218-828-1722	828-0487	186
NorSouth 2000 RiverEdge Pkwy Ste 450 ..... Atlanta GA 30328 *Web:* www.norsouth.com	770-850-8280	850-8230	186
Norstone Financial Corp 130 King St W The Exchange Twr Ste 1800 ..... Toronto ON M5XIE3 *Web:* www.norstonecorp.com	416-357-4107		528
Nortech Systems Inc 7550 Meridian Cir N Ste 150 ..... Maple Grove MN 55369 *NASDAQ: NSYS* ■ *TF:* 800-237-9576 ■ *Web:* www.nortechsys.com	952-345-2244		253
Nortek Air Solutions LLC 13200 Pioneer Trail Ste 150 ..... Eden Prairie MN 55347 *TF:* 800-328-6108 ■ *Web:* www.nortekair.com	952-358-6600		14
Nortek Inc 50 Kennedy Plaza ..... Providence RI 02903 *NASDAQ: NTK* ■ *Web:* www.nortek.com	401-751-1600	751-4610	15
Nortek Security & Control LLC 1950 Camino Vida Roble Ste 150 ..... Carlsbad CA 92008 *TF Cust Svc:* 800-421-1587 ■ *Web:* www.nortekcontrol.com	760-438-7000	931-1340	692
North 44 Degrees 2537 Yonge St ..... Toronto ON M4P2H9 *Web:* north44.mcewangroup.ca	416-487-4897		671
North Adams Common Nursing Home 175 Franklin St ..... North Adams MA 01247 *Web:* www.northadamscommons.org	413-664-4041	664-8447	450
North Adams Home Inc 2259 E 1100th St ..... Mendon IL 62351 *Web:* www.northadamshome.org	217-936-2137	936-2818	450
North Adams Regional Hospital (NARH) 71 Hospital Ave ..... North Adams MA 01247 *Web:* www.nbhealth.org	413-664-5000		374-3
North Africa Journal, The 66 W Flagler St 12th Fl Ste 1204-A ..... Miami FL 33130 *Web:* www.north-africa.com	508-471-3899		387
North Alabama Electric Co-op 41103 US Hwy 72 ..... Stevenson AL 35772 *TF:* 800-572-2900 ■ *Web:* www.naecoop.com	256-437-2281		245
North Alabama Railroad Museum 694 Chase Rd ..... Huntsville AL 35815 *Web:* www.northalabamarailroadmuseum.com	256-851-6276		520
North American Forest Products Inc 27263 May St ..... Edwardsburg MI 49112 *Web:* www.nafpinc.com	269-663-8500		683
North America Cosco Inc 100 Lighting Way Ste 1 ..... Secaucus NJ 07094 *Web:* www.coscoamericas.com	201-422-0500		313
North American Arms Inc 2150 S 950 E ..... Provo UT 84606 *TF:* 800-821-5783 ■ *Web:* www.naaminis.com	801-374-9990		807
North American Assn of Food Equipment Manufacturers (NAFEM) 161 N Clark St Ste 2020 ..... Chicago IL 60601 *TF:* 888-493-5961 ■ *Web:* www.nafem.org	312-821-0201	821-0202	49-13
North American Aviation 7330 N Broadway St ..... Wichita KS 67219 *Web:* www.naavinc.com	316-744-6450		22
North American Bldg Material Distribution Assn (NBMDA) 330 N Wabash Ave Ste 2000 ..... Chicago IL 60611 *TF:* 888-747-7862 ■ *Web:* www.nbmda.org	312-321-6845	644-0310	49-18
North American Blueberry Council (NABC) 80 Iron Pt Cir Dr ..... Folsom CA 95630 *Web:* www.blueberry.org	916-983-0111	983-9370	48-2
North American Cable Equipment Inc 1085 Andrew Dr Ste A ..... West Chester PA 19380 *Web:* www.northamericancable.com	610-429-1821		256
North American Clutch Corp 4360 N Green Bay Ave ..... Milwaukee WI 53209 *Web:* www.noramclutch.com	414-267-4000	267-4024	620
North American Coal Corp 5340 Legacy Dr Bldg I Ste 300 ..... Plano TX 75024 *Web:* www.nacoal.com	972-448-5400		501
North American Container Corp 1811 W Oak Pkwy Ste D ..... Marietta GA 30062 *TF:* 800-929-0610 ■ *Web:* www.nacontainer.com	770-431-4858	431-6957	100
North American Council on Adoptable Children (NACAC) 970 Raymond Ave Ste 106 ..... Saint Paul MN 55114 *TF:* 877-823-2237 ■ *Web:* www.nacac.org	651-644-3036	644-9848	48-6
North American Development Bank 203 S St Mary'S Ste 300 ..... San Antonio TX 78205 *TF:* 800-499-6232 ■ *Web:* www.nadb.org	210-231-8000		70
North American Die Casting Assn (NADCA) 3250 N Arlington Hts Rd Ste 101 ..... Arlington Heights IL 60004 *Web:* www.diecasting.org	847-279-0001	279-0002	49-13
North American Electric Reliability Council (NERC) 1325 G St NW Ste 600 ..... Washington DC 20005 *Web:* www.nerc.com	609-452-8060	452-9550	48-12
North American Enclosures Inc 65 Jetson Ln ..... Central Islip NY 11722 *TF:* 800-645-9209 ■ *Web:* www.naeframes.com	631-234-9500	234-9504	309
North American Equipment Upfitters Inc 6 Sutton Cir ..... Hooksett NH 03106 *Web:* www.naeuinc.com	603-624-6288		190
North American Filter Corp 200 W Shore Blvd ..... Newark NY 14513 *Web:* www.nafcoinc.com	315-331-7000		14
North American Fire Hose 910 E Noble Way ..... Santa Maria CA 93454 *Web:* www.northamericanfirehose.com	805-922-7076	922-0086	678
North American Industries Inc 80 Holton St ..... Woburn MA 01801 *TF:* 800-847-8470 ■ *Web:* www.naicranes.com	781-897-4100	729-3343	470
North American Industry Classification System (NAICS) US Census Bureau 4600 Silver Hill Rd ..... Washington DC 20233 *TF:* 800-923-8282 ■ *Web:* www.census.gov/eos/www/naics	301-763-4636		340-2
North American Insulation Manufacturers Assn (NAIMA) 44 Canal Ctr Plaza Ste 310 ..... Alexandria VA 22314 *Web:* insulationinstitute.org	703-684-0084	684-0427	49-3
North American Lighting Inc 2275 S Main St ..... Paris IL 61944 *Web:* www.nal.com	217-465-6600		438
North American Limousin Foundation (NALF) 7383 S Alton Way Ste 100 ..... Englewood CO 80112 *TF:* 888-320-8747 ■ *Web:* www.nalf.org	303-220-1693	220-1884	48-2
North American Meat Institute (AMIPAC) 1150 Connecticut Ave NW ..... Washington DC 20036 *TF:* 800 611 6100 ■ *Web:* www.meatinstitute.org	202-587-4200	587-4300	615
North American Meat Processors Assn (NAMP) 1910 Assn Dr ..... Reston VA 20191 *TF:* 800-527-4723 ■ *Web:* meatassociation.com	703 758 1900		49 6
North American Medical Corp 1649 Sands Pl SE Ste A ..... Marietta GA 30067 *Web:* www.namcorporation.com	770-541-0012		475
North American Membership Group Inc (NAMG) 12301 Whitewater Dr ..... Minnetonka MN 55343 *Web:* www.namginc.com	952-936-9333		366
North American Menopause Society, The (NAMS) 5900 Landerbrook Dr Ste 390 ..... Mayfield Heights OH 44124 *Web:* www.menopause.org	440-442-7550	442-2660	49-8
North American Mfg Company Ltd 4455 E 71st St ..... Cleveland OH 44105 *Web:* combustion.fivesgroup.com	216-271-6000	641-7852	357
North American Millers Assn (NAMA) 600 Maryland Ave SW Ste 825-W ..... Washington DC 20024 *TF:* 800-633-5137 ■ *Web:* www.namamillers.org	202-484-2200	488-7416	49-6
North American Mission Board SBC 4200 N Pt Pkwy ..... Alpharetta GA 30022 *TF:* 800-634-2462 ■ *Web:* namb.net	770-410-6000		48-5
North American Network Inc 5335 Wisconsin Ave NW ..... Washington DC 20015 *Web:* www.radiospace.com	202-243-0592	243-0594	646
North American Palladium Ltd 1 University Ave Ste 402 ..... Toronto ON M5J2P1 *TSE: PDL* ■ *TF:* 888-360-7590 ■ *Web:* www.napalladium.com	416-360-7590	360-7709	502
North American Pipe Corp 2801 Post Oak Blvd Ste 600 ..... Houston TX 77056 *TF:* 855-624-7473 ■ *Web:* www.northamericanpipe.com	713-840-7473	552-0087	596
North American Plywood Corp 12343 Hawkins St ..... Santa Fe Springs CA 90670 *TF Sales:* 800-421-1372 ■ *Web:* naply.com	562-941-7575		613
North American Products Corp 1180 Wernsing Rd ..... Jasper IN 47546 *Fax Area Code: 800 ■ *TF Cust Svc:* 800-457-7468 ■ *Web:* www.napgladu.com	812-482-2000	457-7458*	455
North American Publishing Co (NAPCO) 1500 Springarden St 12th Fl ..... Philadelphia PA 19130 *TF:* 800-627-2689 ■ *Web:* www.napco.com	215-238-5300	238-5457	637-9
North American Rescue LLC 35 Tedwall Ct ..... Greer SC 29650 *Web:* www.narescue.com	864-675-9800		475
North American Roofing Services Inc 41 Dogwood Rd ..... Asheville NC 28806 *TF:* 800-551-5602 ■ *Web:* www.naroofing.com	828-687-7767	687-1230	189-12
North American Savings Bank (NASB) 12520 S 71 Hwy ..... Grandview MO 64030 *TF:* 800-677-6272 ■ *Web:* www.nasb.com	816-765-2200		70
North American Science Assoc Inc 6750 Wales Rd ..... Northwood OH 43619 *TF:* 866-666-9455 ■ *Web:* www.namsa.com	419-666-9455	662-4386	668
North American Securities Administrators Assn (NASAA) 750 First St NE Ste 1140 ..... Washington DC 20002 *TF:* 800-222-1253 ■ *Web:* www.nasaa.org	202-737-0900	783-3571	49-2

Phone | Fax | Class

North American Specialty Glass
2175 Kumry Rd PO Box 70.............Trumbauersville PA 18970 215-536-0333 536-6872 332
TF: 888-785-5962 ■ *Web:* www.naspecialtyglass.com

North American Specialty Insurance Co
650 Elm St Ste 600.......................Manchester NH 03101 603-644-6600 391-4
TF: 800-542-9200 ■ *Web:* swissre.com

North American Spine Society (NASS)
7075 Veterans Blvd.......................Burr Ridge IL 60527 630-230-3600 49-8
TF: 877-774-6337 ■ *Web:* www.spine.org

North American Stainless Inc
6870 Hwy 42 E..............................Ghent KY 41045 502-347-6000 347-6001 360-3
TF: 800-499-7833 ■ *Web:* www.northamericanstainless.com

North American Steel Co
18300 Miles Ave..........................Cleveland OH 44128 216-475-7300 475-6143 492
TF: 800-321-9310 ■ *Web:* www.northamerican-steel.com

North American Substation Services LLC
190 N Westmonte Dr................Altamonte Springs FL 32714 407-788-3717 788-3767 767
Web: www.nassusa.com

North American Tanning Corp
248 W 35th St Ste 505.....................New York NY 10001 212-643-1702 967-0068 432
TF: 800-278-7344 ■ *Web:* www.natanning.com

North American Title Co
1855 Gateway Blvd Ste 600..................Concord CA 94520 925-935-5599 933-4851 391-6
TF: 800-566-0370 ■ *Web:* www.nat.com/home.aspx

North American Tool Corp
215 Elmwood Ave........................South Beloit IL 61080 815-389-2300 872-3299* 493
**Fax Area Code:* 800 ■ *TF:* 800-872-8277 ■ *Web:* www.natool.com

North American Tungsten Corp Ltd
1188 W Georgia St Ste 1640...............Vancouver BC V6E4A2 604-684-5300 502
Web: www.natungsten.com

North American Van Lines Inc
5001 US Hwy 30 W.....................Fort Wayne IN 46818 260-429-2511 219
TF: 800-348-2111 ■ *Web:* www.northamerican.com

North Arkansas College
1515 Pioneer Dr..........................Harrison AR 72601 870-743-3000 391-3339 162
TF: 800-679-6622 ■ *Web:* www.northark.edu

North Arkansas Electric Co-op Inc
225 S Main St................................Salem AR 72576 870-895-3221 895-6279 245
Web: www.naeci.com

North Arkansas Regional Medical Ctr
620 N Willow St.............................Harrison AR 72601 870-365-2000 374-3
Web: www.narmc.com

North Arkansas Symphony
605 W Dixon St..........................Fayetteville AR 72701 479-521-4166 573-3
TF: 800-410-2535 ■ *Web:* sonamusic.org

North Atlantic 29 Pippy Pl.................St. John's NL A1B3X2 709-463-8811 579-5087 536
TF: 877-635-3645 ■ *Web:* www.northatlantic.ca

North Atlantic Capital
2 City Ctr 5th Fl..............................Portland ME 04101 207-772-4470 772-3257 792
Web: www.northatlanticcapital.com

North Atlantic Corp
1255 Grand Army Hwy......................Somerset MA 02726 508-679-6479 499
Web: www.northatlanticcorp.com

North Atlantic Publishing Systems Inc
66 Commonwealth Ave......................Concord MA 01742 978-371-8989 371-5678 178-1
TF: 800-796-9798 ■ *Web:* www.napsys.com

North Augusta Chamber of Commerce
406 W Ave...........................North Augusta SC 29841 803-279-2323 279-0003 139
TF: 800-922-1262 ■ *Web:* www.northaugustachamber.org

North Baldwin Chamber of Commerce
301 McMeans Ave......................Bay Minette AL 36507 251-937-5665 937-5670 139
TF: 800-634-8104 ■ *Web:* www.northbaldwinchamber.com

North Bay & District Chamber of Commerce
1375 Seymour St..........................North Bay ON P1B8J8 705-472-8480 472-8027 137
TF: 888-249-8998 ■ *Web:* nbdcc.ca

North Bay Bohemian 847 Fifth St............Santa Rosa CA 95404 707-527-1200 527-1288 532-5
TF: 800-478-5080 ■ *Web:* www.bohemian.com

North Bay Nissan Inc
1250 Auto Ctr Dr..........................Petaluma CA 94952 707-769-7700 57
Web: www.northbaynissan.com

North Bay Produce Inc
PO Box 988.............................Traverse City MI 49685 800-678-1941 946-1902* 297-7
**Fax Area Code:* 231 ■ *TF:* 800-678-1941 ■ *Web:* www.northbayproduce.com

North Bay Regional Health Ctr
50 College Dr PO Box 2500.................North Bay ON P1B5A4 705-474-8600 374-2
Web: www.nbrhc.on.ca

North Beach Rt 1A.........................Hampton NH 03842 603-436-1552 565
Web: www.nhstateparks.org

North Beach Bar & Grill
3107 Atlantic Ave....................Virginia Beach VA 23451 757-491-1800 671
TF: 800-292-3297 ■ *Web:* hamptoninnvirginiabeachoceanfront.com

North Beach Pizza Inc
1462 Grant Ave......................San Francisco CA 94133 415-433-2444 670
Web: www.northbeachpizza.com

North Bend State Park 202 N Bend Pk Rd..........Cairo WV 26337 304-643-2931 565
Web: www.northbendsp.com

North Bergen Free Public Library
8411 Bergenline Ave..................North Bergen NJ 07047 201-869-4715 868-0968 434-3
Web: nbpl.org

North Berman & Beebe
1200 New Hampshire Ave NW Ste 725........Washington DC 20036 202-371-1100 371-5527 428
Web: northberman.com

North Bridge Venture Partners
950 Winter St Ste 4600......................Waltham MA 02451 781-290-0004 290-0999 792
Web: www.northbridge.com

North Broward Hospital District
303 SE 17th St.....................Fort Lauderdale FL 33316 954-473-7458 353
Web: www.browardhealth.org

North Broward Medical Ctr
201 E Sample Rd....................Deerfield Beach FL 33064 954-941-8300 374-3
Web: www.browardhealth.org

North Brunswick Library
880 Hermann Rd....................North Brunswick NJ 08902 732-246-3545 434-3
Web: www.northbrunswicklibrary.org

North by Northwest Productions
601 W Broad St..............................Boise ID 83702 208-345-7870 514
Web: www.nxnw.net

North Canton Area Chamber of Commerce
121 S Main St.........................North Canton OH 44720 330-499-5100 499-7181 139
TF: 800-837-3200 ■ *Web:* www.northcantonchamber.org

North Carolina

Administrative Office of the Cts
901 Corporate Center Dr..................Raleigh NC 27607 919-890-1000 339-34
Web: www.nccourts.org

Aging & Adult Service Div
2101 Mail Service Ctr....................Raleigh NC 27699 919-855-3400 339-34
Web: www.ncdhhs.gov

Agriculture Dept
2 W Edenton St 1001 MSC..................Raleigh NC 27601 919-733-7125 733-1141 339-34
TF: 800-735-2962 ■ *Web:* www.ncagr.gov

Arts Council 4632 Mail Service Ctr............Raleigh NC 27699 919-807-6500 807-6532 339-34
Web: www.ncarts.org

Attorney General
9001 Mail Service Ctr....................Raleigh NC 27699 919-716-6400 716-6750 339-34
Web: www.ncdoj.com

Banking Commission 316 W Edenton St.........Raleigh NC 27603 919-733-3016 733-6918 339-34
Web: www.nccob.org

Bill Status 16 W Jones St....................Raleigh NC 27601 919-733-4111 433
Web: www.ncleg.net

Child Support Enforcement Section
PO Box 20800..............................Raleigh NC 27619 252-789-5225 339-34
Web: www.ncdhhs.gov

Commerce Dept 301 N Wilmington St..........Raleigh NC 27699 919-814-4600 339-34
Web: www.nccommerce.com

Community College System
200 W Jones St............................Raleigh NC 27603 919-807-7100 807-7165 339-34
Web: nccommunitycolleges.edu

Consumer Protection Division
9001 Mail Service Ctr....................Raleigh NC 27699 919-716-6000 716-6050 339-34
Web: www.ncdoj.com

Correction Dept
214 W Jones St 4201 MSC..................Raleigh NC 27699 919-716-3700 716-3794 339-34
Web: www.doc.state.nc.us

Cultural Resources Dept
109 E Jones St.............................Raleigh NC 27601 919-807-7385 339-34
Web: www.ncdcr.gov

Department of Public Safety
4201 Mail Service Ctr....................Raleigh NC 27699 919-825-2500 339-34
Web: www.ncem.org

Employment Security Commission
700 Wade Ave PO Box 25903..............Raleigh NC 27605 919-707-1010 733-9420 259
Web: desncc.com/deshome

Ethics Board 424 N Blount St..................Raleigh NC 27601 919-814-3600 715-1644 265
Web: www.ethicscommission.nc.gov

General Assembly 16 W Jones St..............Raleigh NC 27601 919-733-7928 339-34
Web: www.ncleg.net

Governor 116 W Jones St......................Raleigh NC 27603 919-807-4499 339-34
Web: www.governor.state.nc.us

Health & Human Services Dept 2001 MSC.......Raleigh NC 27699 919-855-4800 715-4645 339-34
Web: www.ncdhhs.gov

Housing Finance Agency 3508 Bush St..........Raleigh NC 27609 919-877-5700 877-5701 339-34
TF: 800-393-0988 ■ *Web:* www.nchfa.com

Information Technology Services Office (ITS)
PO Box 17209..............................Raleigh NC 27619 919-754-6000 339-34
Web: www.its.nc.gov

Insurance Dept 1201 MSC......................Raleigh NC 27699 919-807-6075 733-4264 339-34
Web: www.ncdoi.com

Labor Dept 1101 Mail Service Ctr..............Raleigh NC 27699 919-807-2796 339-34
TF: 800-625-2267 ■ *Web:* www.nclabor.com

Lieutenant Governor 310 N Blount St...........Raleigh NC 27601 919-733-7350 733-6595 339-34
Web: ltgov.nc.gov

Marine Fisheries Div
3441 Arendell St....................Morehead City NC 28557 252-726-7021 339-34
TF: 800-682-2632 ■ *Web:* www.ncfisheries.net

Mental Health Developmental Disabilities & Substan
2001 Mail Service Ctr....................Raleigh NC 27699 919-855-4800 339-34
Web: www.ncdhhs.gov/mhddsas

Motor Vehicles Div 1100 New Bern Ave.........Raleigh NC 27699 919-715-7000 339-34
Web: www.ncdot.gov/dmv

Parks & Recreation Div
121 W Jones St NRC Bldg 2nd Fl..........Raleigh NC 27603 919-707-9300 339-34
TF: 877-722-6762 ■ *Web:* www.ncparks.gov

Parole Commission 4222 MSC...................Raleigh NC 27699 919-716-3010 716-3987 339-34
Web: www.ncdps.gov

Public Instruction Dept
301 N Wilmington St.......................Raleigh NC 27601 919-807-3300 807-3445 339-34
Web: www.ncpublicschools.org

Real Estate Commission 1313 Navajo Dr........Raleigh NC 27609 919-875-3700 877-4221 339-34
Web: ncrec.gov

Revenue Dept 4701 Atlantic Ave Ste 118.........Raleigh NC 27604 919-707-0880 850-2954 339-34
Web: www.dor.state.nc.us

Secretary of State 2 S Salisbury St.............Raleigh NC 27601 919-814-5400 807-2010 339-34
Web: www.secstate.state.nc.us

Securities Div PO Box 29622....................Raleigh NC 27626 919-814-5400 807-2183 339-34
TF: 800-688-4507 ■ *Web:* www.secretary.state.nc.us

Social Services Div 2401 MSC..................Raleigh NC 27699 919-733-3055 733-9386 339-34
Web: www.ncdhhs.gov

Standards Div 2 W Edenton St..................Raleigh NC 27699 919-707-3225 715-0524 339-34
Web: www.ncagr.gov

State Highway Patrol
512 N Salisbury St.........................Raleigh NC 27699 919-733-7952 733-1189 339-34
Web: www.ncdps.gov

State Personnel Office
116 W Jones St 3rd Fl Administration Bldg.....Raleigh NC 27603 919-807-4800 733-0653 339-34
Web: www.oshr.nc.gov

State Ports Authority
2202 Burnett Blvd PO Box 9002..........Wilmington NC 28402 910-763-1621 618
TF: 800-334-0682 ■ *Web:* www.ncports.com

State Treasurer 3200 Atlantic Ave..............Raleigh NC 27604 919-814-4000 339-34
Web: www.nctreasurer.com

Supreme Court
2 E Morgan St PO Box 2170..................Raleigh NC 27602 919-831-5700 339-34
Web: www.nccourts.org

Transportation Dept 1 S Wilmington St..........Raleigh NC 27611 877-368-4968 715-7000* 339-34
**Fax Area Code:* 919 ■ *TF:* 877-368-4968 ■ *Web:* www.ncdot.gov

	Phone	Fax	Class
Utilities Commission 4325 Mail Service Ctr Dobbs Bldg .... Raleigh NC 27699 *TF:* 866-380-9816 ■ *Web:* www.ncuc.commerce.state.nc.us	919-733-7320	733-7300	339-34
Veterans Affairs Div 325 N Salisbury St Albemarle Bldg .... Raleigh NC 27603 *Web:* www.doa.nc.gov	919-733-3851	733-2834	339-34
Victims Compensation Services Div 4232 Mail Service Ctr .... Raleigh NC 27699 *TF:* 800-826-6200 ■ *Web:* www.nccrimecontrol.org	919-733-7974		339-34
Vital Records Unit 225 N McDowell St .... Raleigh NC 27603	919-733-3000	733-1511	339-34
Vocational Rehabilitation Services Div 2801 MSC.............................. Raleigh NC 27699 *TF:* 800-689-9090 ■ *Web:* www.ncdhhs.gov	919-855-3500	733-7968	339-34
North Carolina A & T State University 1601 E Market St .... Greensboro NC 27411 **Fax:* Admissions ■ *TF Admissions:* 800-443-8964 ■ *Web:* www.ncat.edu	336-334-7946	334-7478*	166
North Carolina Aquarium at Fort Fisher 900 Loggerhead Rd .... Kure Beach NC 28449 *TF:* 800-832-3474 ■ *Web:* www.ncaquariums.com	910-458-8257	458-6812	40
North Carolina Aquarium on Roanoke Island 374 Airport Rd PO Box 967 .... Manteo NC 27954 *TF:* 800-832-3474 ■ *Web:* www.ncaquariums.com	252-475-2300	473-1980	40
North Carolina Arboretum 100 Frederick Law Olmsted Way.............. Asheville NC 28806 *TF:* 800-228-7275 ■ *Web:* www.ncarboretum.org	828-665-2492	665-2371	97
North Carolina Assn of Pharmacists Brighton Hall 1101 Slater Rd Ste 110............ Durham NC 27703 **Fax Area Code:* 984 ■ *Web:* www.ncpharmacists.org	919-967-2237	439-1649*	585
North Carolina Assn of Realtors Inc 4511 Weybridge Ln.................... Greensboro NC 27407 *TF:* 800-443-9956 ■ *Web:* www.ncrealtors.org	336-294-1415	299-7872	656
North Carolina Auto Racing Hall of Fame 119 Knob Hill Rd Lakeside Pk .... Mooresville NC 28117 *Web:* www.ncarhof.com	704-663-5331		522
North Carolina Botanical Garden *University of North Carolina at Chapel Hill, The* CB 3375 Totten Ctr PO Box 3375........... Chapel Hill NC 27599 *Web:* www.ncbg.unc.edu	919-962-0522	962-3531	97
North Carolina Central University 1801 Fayetteville St .... Durham NC 27707 **Fax:* Admissions ■ *TF Admissions:* 877-667-7533 ■ *Web:* www.nccu.edu	919-530-6100	530-7625*	166
North Carolina Chamber 701 Corporate Ctr Dr Ste 400................. Raleigh NC 27607 *Web:* www.ncchamber.net/mx/hm.asp?id=home	919-836-1400	836-1425	140
North Carolina Correction Enterprises 2020 Yonkers Rd .... Raleigh NC 27604 *Web:* www.doc.state.nc.us	919-716-3600	716-3974	630
North Carolina Correctional Institution for Women 1034 Bragg St............................... Raleigh NC 27610 *Web:* www.ncdps.gov	919-733-4340	733-8031	213
North Carolina Democratic Party 220 Hillsborough St........................ Raleigh NC 27603 *TF:* 800-995-3386 ■ *Web:* www.ncdp.org	919-821-2777	821-4778	616-1
North Carolina Dental Society 1600 Evans Rd .... Cary NC 27513 *TF:* 800-662-8754 ■ *Web:* www.ncdental.org	919-677-1396	677-1397	227
North Carolina Eye Bank Inc 3900 Westpoint Blvd Ste F............. Winston-Salem NC 27103 *TF:* 800-552-9956 ■ *Web:* miraclesinsight.org	336-765-0932		260
North Carolina Farm Bureau Mutual Insurance Co (NCFBMIC) PO Box 27427 .... Raleigh NC 27611 *TF:* 800-584-1143 ■ *Web:* www.ncfbins.com	919-782-1705		391-4
North Carolina Foam Industries Inc 1515 Carter St .... Mount Airy NC 27030 *TF:* 800-346-8229 ■ *Web:* www.ncfi.com	336-789-9161	789-9586	191-4
North Carolina Granite Corp 151 Granite Quarry Trl PO Box 151.......... Mount Airy NC 27030 *TF:* 800-227-6242 ■ *Web:* www.ncgranite.com	336-786-5141	719-2623	724
North Carolina High Country Host 1700 Blowing Rock Rd .... Boone NC 28607 *TF:* 800-438-7500 ■ *Web:* www.highcountryhost.com	828-264-1299	265-0550	206
North Carolina Library Assn (NCLA) 1811 Capital Blvd.......................... Raleigh NC 27604 *TF:* 888-977-3143 ■ *Web:* www.nclaonline.org	919-839-6252	839-6253	435
North Carolina Medical Society 222 N Person St............................ Raleigh NC 27601 *TF:* 800-722-1350 ■ *Web:* www.ncmedsoc.org	919-833-3836	833-2023	474
North Carolina Museum of Art 2110 Blue Ridge Rd .... Raleigh NC 27607 *TF:* 800-222-7270 ■ *Web:* www.ncartmuseum.org	919-839-6262	733-8034	520
North Carolina Museum of History 5 E Edenton St .... Raleigh NC 27601 *TF:* 800-745-3000 ■ *Web:* www.ncdcr.gov	919-807-7900	733-8655	520
North Carolina Museum of Natural Sciences 11 W Jones St .... Raleigh NC 27601 *Web:* www.naturalsciences.org	919-733-7450	733-1573	520
North Carolina Mutual Life Insurance Co 411 W Chapel Hill St .... Durham NC 27701 *TF:* 800-626-1899 ■ *Web:* www.ncmutuallife.com	800-626-1899		391-2
North Carolina Mutual Wholesale Drug Co 816 Ellis Rd .... Durham NC 27703 *TF:* 800-800-8551 ■ *Web:* www.mutualdrugcompany.com/?page_id=26	919-596-2151		238
North Carolina Nurses Assn (NCNA) 103 Enterprise St PO Box 12025 .... Raleigh NC 27605 *TF:* 800-626-2153 ■ *Web:* www.ncnurses.org	919-821-4250	829-5807	533
North Carolina Public Interest Research Group (NCPIRG) 112 S Blount St .... Raleigh NC 27601 *Web:* www.ncpirg.org	919-833-2070		633
North Carolina Railroad Co 2809 Highwoods Blvd Ste 100................. Raleigh NC 27604 *Web:* www.ncrr.com	919-954-7601		711
North Carolina Republican Party PO Box 12905 .... Raleigh NC 27605 *Web:* nc.gop	919-828-6423		616-2
North Carolina School of the Arts 1533 S Main St....................... Winston-Salem NC 27127 *Web:* uncsa.edu	336-770-3399	770-3370	164

	Phone	Fax	Class
North Carolina Sports Hall of Fame 5 E Edenton St NC Museum of History........... Raleigh NC 27601 *TF:* 877-627-6724 ■ *Web:* www.ncdcr.gov	919-807-7900	733-8655	522
North Carolina State Bar 217 E Edenton St PO Box 25996 .... Raleigh NC 27601 *TF:* 800-662-7407 ■ *Web:* ncbar.gov	919-828-4620	821-9168	72
North Carolina State Education Assistance Authority (NCSEAA) PO Box 14103 .... Research Triangle Park NC 27709 *TF:* 800-700-1775 ■ *Web:* www.ncseaa.edu	919-549-8614	549-8481	725
North Carolina State University 2200 Hillsborough St .... Raleigh NC 27695 **Fax:* Admissions ■ *TF:* 800-662-7301 ■ *Web:* www.ncsu.edu	919-515-2011	515-5039*	166
North Carolina State University Libraries CB 7111 .... Raleigh NC 27695 **Fax:* Admin ■ *TF:* 877-601-0590 ■ *Web:* www.lib.ncsu.edu	919-515-2843	515-3628*	434-6
North Carolina Symphony 3700 Glenwood Ave Ste 130.................. Raleigh NC 27612 *Web:* www.ncsymphony.org	919-733-2750	733-9920	573-3
North Carolina Tennis Hall of Fame 2709 Henry St.......................... Greensboro NC 27405 *Web:* www.nctennis.com	336-852-8577	852-7334	522
North Carolina Theatre 1 E S St Memorial Auditorium .... Raleigh NC 27601 *TF:* 800-745-3000 ■ *Web:* www.nctheatre.com	919-831-6941	831-6951	573-4
North Carolina Veterinary Medical Assn (NCVMA) 1611 Jones Franklin Rd Ste 108.............. Raleigh NC 27606 *TF:* 800-446-2862 ■ *Web:* www.ciclt.net	919-851-5850	851-5859	795
North Carolina Wesleyan College 3400 N Wesleyan Blvd .... Rocky Mount NC 27804 **Fax:* Admissions ■ *TF Admissions:* 800-488-6292 ■ *Web:* www.ncwc.edu	252-985-5100	985-5295*	166
North Carolina Zoological Park 4401 Zoo Pkwy............................ Asheboro NC 27205 *TF:* 800-488-0444 ■ *Web:* www.nczoo.org	336-879-7000		823
North Cascades National Park 810 SR 20 .... Sedro Woolley WA 98284 *Web:* www.nps.gov/noca	360-856-5700	856-1934	564
North Central Agricultural Research Laboratory (NGIRL) 2923 Medary Ave .... Brookings SD 57006 *Web:* www.ars.usda.gov/main/docs.htm?docid=2357	605-693-3241	693-5240	668
North Central Assn Commission on Accreditation & School Improvement (NCA CASI) 9115 Westside Pkwy....................... Alpharetta GA 30009 *TF:* 888-413-3669 ■ *Web:* advanc-ed.org	888-413-3669		48-1
North Central Assn Higher Learning Commission 230 S LaSalle St............................ Chicago IL 60604 *TF:* 800-621-7440 ■ *Web:* www.hlcommission.org	312-263-0456	263-7462	49-5
North Central Bronx Hospital 3424 Kossuth Ave............................. Bronx NY 10467 *TF:* 877-207-2134 ■ *Web:* nyc.gov	718-519-5000		374-3
North Central Chamber of Commerce 255 Greenville Ave .... Johnston RI 02919 *Web:* www.nrichamber.com	401-349-4674		139
North Central College 30 N Brainard St .... Naperville IL 60540 **Fax:* Admissions ■ *TF:* 800-411-1861 ■ *Web:* northcentralcollege.edu	630-637-5800	637-5819	166
North Central Correctional Institution 670 Marion-Williamsport Rd PO Box 1812 .... Marion OH 43302 *Web:* drc.ohio.gov/nccc	740-387-7040	387-5575	213
North Central Correctional Institution at Gardner 500 Colony Rd .... Gardner MA 01440	978-630-6000		213
North Central Door Co 900 Carr Lake Rd PO Box 575 .... Bemidji MN 56601 *Web:* www.northcentraldoor.com	218-751-6962		234
North Central Electric Co-op Inc 538 11th St W............................ Bottineau ND 58318 *TF:* 800-247-1197 ■ *Web:* www.nceci.com	701-228-2202	228-2592	245
North Central Electric Co-op Inc 13978 E County Rd 56 .... Attica OH 44807 *TF:* 800-426-3072 ■ *Web:* www.ncelec.org	419-426-3072	426-1245	245
North Central Massachusetts Chamber of Commerce 860 S St .... Fitchburg MA 01420 *TF:* 800-628-8379 ■ *Web:* www.northcentralmass.com	978-353-7600	353-4896	139
North Central Michigan College 1515 Howard St .... Petoskey MI 49770 *TF:* 888-298-6605 ■ *Web:* www.ncmich.edu	231-348-6605		162
North Central Missouri College 1301 Main St .... Trenton MO 64683 **Fax:* Admissions ■ *TF:* 800-880-6180 ■ *Web:* www.ncmissouri.edu	660-359-3948	359-2211*	162
North Central Pennsylvania Regional Planning & Development Commission 651 Montmorenci Rd .... Ridgway PA 15853 *TF:* 800-942-9467 ■ *Web:* www.ncentral.com	814-773-3162	772-7045	194
North Central Public Power District 1409 Main St PO Box 90 .... Creighton NE 68729 *TF:* 800-578-1060 ■ *Web:* www.ncppd.com	402-358-5112	358-5129	245
North Central Regional Library 16 N Columbia St........................ Wenatchee WA 98801 *Web:* www.ncrl.org	509-663-1117		434-3
North Central State College 2441 Kenwood Cir .... Mansfield OH 44906 *TF:* 888-755-4899 ■ *Web:* www.ncstatecollege.edu	419-755-4800	755-4750	800
North Central Telephone Co-op Corp PO Box 70 .... Lafayette TN 37083 *TF:* 800-795-3272 ■ *Web:* www.nctc.com	615-666-2151		736
North Central Texas College 1525 W California St .... Gainesville TX 76240 **Fax:* Admissions ■ *Web:* www.nctc.edu	940-668-7731	665-7075*	162
Bowie 810 S Mill St............................. Bowie TX 76230 *Web:* www.nctc.edu	940-872-4002		162
North Central University 910 Elliot Ave S .... Minneapolis MN 55404 **Fax:* Admissions ■ *TF Admissions:* 800-289-6222 ■ *Web:* www.northcentral.edu	612-343-4460	343-4146*	166
North Ch Area Chamber of Commerce 13301 E Fwy # 100......................... Houston TX 77015 *Web:* www.northchannelarea.com	713-450-3600	450-0700	139
North Channel Capital LLC 5550 S 59th St Ste 22......................... Lincoln NE 68516 *Web:* www.northchannelcapital.wfadv.com	402-421-6500		463
North Charles Street Design Organization 222 W Saratoga St .... Baltimore MD 21201 *Web:* www.ncsdo.com	410-539-4040		4

Phone | Fax | Class

North Charleston Coliseum & Convention Ctr
5001 Coliseum Dr ... North Charleston SC 29418 843-529-5050 529-5010 720
TF: 800-745-3000 ■ Web: www.northcharlestoncoliseumpac.com

North Chicago Public Library
2100 Argonne Dr ... North Chicago IL 60064 847-689-0125 689-9117 434-3
Web: ncplibrary.org

North China 6090 Far Hills Ave ... Dayton OH 45459 937-433-6837 671

North China Garden 2303 Sixth Ave ... Tacoma WA 98403 253-572-5106 671
Web: northchinagardentacoma.com

North Clackamas County Chamber of Commerce
7740 SE Harmony Rd ... Milwaukie OR 97222 503-654-7777 653-9515 139
TF: 800-295-4050 ■ Web: www.yourchamber.com

North Coast Air 4645 W 12th St ... Erie PA 16505 814-836-9220 836-9901 63
Web: www.ncair.com

North Coast Brewing Company Inc
455 N Main St ... Fort Bragg CA 95437 707-964-2739 102
Web: www.northcoastbrewing.com

North Coast Clinical Laboratory Inc
2215 Cleveland Rd ... Sandusky OH 44870 419-626-6012 418
TF: 800-325-5737 ■ Web: www.northcoastlab.com

North Coast Container Corp
8806 Crane Ave ... Cleveland OH 44105 216-441-6214 441-6239 198
Web: www.ncc-corp.com

North Coast Co-op Inc 811 I St ... Arcata CA 95521 707-822-5947 297-8
Web: www.northcoast.coop

North Colorado Medical Ctr
1801 16th St ... Greeley CO 80631 970-352-4121 350-6644 374-3
Web: www.bannerhealth.com

North Country Business Products Inc
1112 S Railroad St SE ... Bemidji MN 56601 218-751-4140 755-6039 320
TF: 800-937-4140 ■ Web: www.ncbpinc.com

North Country Community College
23 Santanoni Ave ... Saranac Lake NY 12983 518-891-2915 891-2915 162
TF: 888-879-6222 ■ Web: www.nccc.edu

North Country Federal Credit Union Inc
69 Swift St Ste 100 ... South Burlington VT 05403 802-657-6847 219
TF: 800-660-3258 ■ Web: www.northcountry.org

North Country Library System
22072 CR 190 ... Watertown NY 13601 315-782-5540 782-6883 434-3
Web: web.ncls.org

North Country School
4382 Cascade Rd ... Lake Placid NY 12946 518-523-9329 622
Web: www.nct.org

North Country Trail Assn 229 E Main St ... Lowell MI 49331 616-897-5987 897-6605 48-23
TF: 866-445-3628 ■ Web: www.northcountrytrail.org

North County Health Services
150 Valpreda Rd ... San Marcos CA 92069 760-736-6767 374-3
Web: www.nchs-health.org

North County Transit District (NCTD)
810 Mission Rd ... Oceanside CA 92054 760-966-6500 967-2001 468
TF: 800-827-0829 ■ Web: www.gonctd.com

North Dade Regional Chamber of Commerce
1300 NW 167th St Ste 2 ... Miami FL 33169 305-690-9123 139
Web: www.thechamber.cc

North Dakota

Accountancy Board
2701 S Columbia Rd Ste D ... Grand Forks ND 58201 701-775-7100 775-7430 339-35
TF: 800-532-5904 ■ Web: www.nd.gov

Aging Services Div
1237 W Divide Ave Ste 6 ... Bismarck ND 58501 701-328-4649 328-8744 339-35
TF: 855-462-5465 ■ Web: www.nd.gov

Agriculture Dept
600 E Blvd Ave Dept 602 ... Bismarck ND 58505 701-328-2231 328-4567 339-35
TF: 800-242-7535 ■ Web: www.nd.gov/ndda

Attorney General
600 E Blvd Ave Dept 125 ... Bismarck ND 58505 701-328-2210 339-35
TF: 800-472-2600 ■ Web: www.ag.nd.gov

Child Support Enforcement Div
1600 E Century Ave Ste 7 ... Bismarck ND 58501 701-328-3582 328-6575 339-35
TF: 800-231-4255 ■ Web: www.nd.gov/dhs/services/childsupport

Children & Family Services Div
600 E Blvd Ave ... Bismarck ND 58505 701-328-2316 328-3538 339-35
Web: www.nd.gov

Consumer Protection Div
1050 E Interstate Ave Ste 200 ... Bismarck ND 58503 701-328-3404 339-35
Web: www.ag.state.nd.us

Corrections & Rehabilitation Dept
3100 Railroad Ave P.O. Box 1898 ... Bismarck ND 58502 701-328-6390 328-6651 339-35
Web: www.nd.gov

Court Administrator Office
600 E Blvd Ave MS180 ... Bismarck ND 58505 701-328-6200 328-2092 339-35
Web: www.ndcourts.gov

Crime Victims Compensation Program
PO Box 5521 ... Bismarck ND 58506 701-328-6195 339-35
TF: 800-445-2322 ■ Web: www.ndcrimevictims.org

Drivers License & Traffic Safety Div
608 E Blvd Ave ... Bismarck ND 58505 701-328-2500 328-2435 339-35
TF: 855-637-6237 ■
Web: www.dot.nd.gov/divisions/safety/trafficsafety.htm

Economic Development & Finance Div
1600 E Century Ave Ste 200-B ... Bismarck ND 58503 701-328-5300 339-35
Web: www.business.nd.gov

Education Standards & Practices Board
2718 Gateway Ave Ste 204 ... Bismarck ND 58503 701-328-9641 328-9647 339-35
Web: www.nd.gov

Emergency Management Div
Fraine Barracks Ln - Bldg 35 ... Bismarck ND 58504 701-328-8100 328-8181 339-35
Web: www.nd.gov/des

Financial Institutions Dept
2000 Schafer St Ste G ... Bismarck ND 58501 701-328-9933 328-0290 339-35
TF: 800-366-6888 ■ Web: www.nd.gov/dfi

Game & Fish Dept 100 N Bismarck Expy ... Bismarck ND 58501 701-328-6300 328-6352 339-35
Web: www.gf.nd.gov

Governor 600 E Blvd Ave Dept 101 ... Bismarck ND 58505 701-328-2200 328-2205 339-35
Web: www.governor.nd.gov

Health Dept 600 E Blvd Ave Dept 301 ... Bismarck ND 58505 701-328-2372 328-4727 339-35
Web: www.ndhealth.gov

Highway Patrol
600 E Blvd Ave Dept 504 ... Bismarck ND 58505 701-328-2455 328-1717 339-35
Web: www.nd.gov

Historical Society 612 E Blvd Ave ... Bismarck ND 58505 701-328-2666 339-35
Web: www.nd.gov

Housing Finance Agency
2624 Vermont Ave PO Box 1535 ... Bismarck ND 58502 701-328-8080 328-8090 339-35
TF: 800-292-8621 ■ Web: www.ndhfa.org

Indian Affairs Commission
600 E Blvd Ave 1st Fl Judicial Wing-Rm 117 ... Bismarck ND 58505 701-328-2428 328-1537 339-35
Web: www.indianaffairs.nd.gov

Information Technology Dept
4201 Normandy St ... Bismarck ND 58505 701-328-3190 339-35
Web: www.nd.gov/itd

Insurance Dept 600 E Blvd Ave ... Bismarck ND 58505 701-328-2440 328-4880 339-35
TF: 800-247-0560 ■ Web: www.nd.gov

Labor and Human Rights Dept
600 E Blvd Ave Dept 406 ... Bismarck ND 58505 701-328-2660 328-2031 339-35
TF: 800-582-8032 ■ Web: www.nd.gov/labor

Legislative Assembly
State Capitol 600 E Blvd Ave 600 E Blvd Ave ... Bismarck ND 58505 701-328-2916 328-3615 339-35
Web: www.legis.nd.gov

Medical Examiners Board
418 E Broadway Ave Ste 12 ... Bismarck ND 58501 701-328-6500 328-6505 339-35
Web: www.ndbomex.org

Office of Governor 600 E Blvd Ave ... Bismarck ND 58505 701-328-2200 328-2205 339-35
Web: governor.nd.gov

Parks & Recreation Dept
1600 E Century Ave Ste 3 PO Box 5594 ... Bismarck ND 58506 701-328-5357 328-5363 339-35
TF: 800-366-6888 ■ Web: www.parkrec.nd.gov

Parole & Probation Div
3100 E Railroad Ave ... Bismarck ND 58501 701-328-6190 328-6651 339-35
Web: www.nd.gov/docr

Public Instruction Dept
600 E Blvd Ave Dept 201 ... Bismarck ND 58505 701-328-2260 328-2461 339-35
Web: www.dpi.state.nd.us

Public Service Commission
600 E Blvd Ave Dept 408 ... Bismarck ND 58505 701-328-2400 328-2410 339-35
Web: www.psc.nd.gov

Racing Commission 500 N Ninth St ... Bismarck ND 58501 701-328-4633 328-4280 712
Web: www.ndracingcommission.com

Real Estate Commission
1110 College Dr Ste 207 Ste 204 ... Bismarck ND 58501 701-328-9749 328-9750 339-35
Web: www.realestatend.org

Secretary of State
600 E Blvd Ave Dept 108 ... Bismarck ND 58505 701-328-2900 328-2992 339-35
TF: 800-352-0867 ■ Web: www.nd.gov/sos

Securities Dept
600 E Blvd Ave State Capitol 5th Fl ... Bismarck ND 58505 701-328-2910 328-2946 339-35
TF: 800-297-5124 ■ Web: www.nd.gov

State Government Information
600 E Blvd Ave Dept 130 4th Fl ... Bismarck ND 58505 701-328-2471 339-35
Web: www.nd.gov

Student Financial Assistance Program
600 E Blvd Ave 10th Fl Dept 215 ... Bismarck ND 58505 701-328-2960 328-2961 725
Web: www.ndus.nodak.edu

Supreme Court 600 E Blvd Ave Dept 180 ... Bismarck ND 58505 701-328-4216 328-2092 339-35
Web: www.ndcourts.gov

Tax Dept 600 E Blvd Ave ... Bismarck ND 58505 701-328-3470 328-3700 339-35
TF: 800-638-2901 ■ Web: www.nd.gov

Testing & Safety Div
600 E Blvd Ave Dept 408 ... Bismarck ND 58505 701-328-2400 328-2410 339-35
TF: 877-245-6685 ■ Web: www.psc.nd.gov

Tourism Div 1600 E Century Ave Ste 2 ... Bismarck ND 58502 701-328-2525 339-35
TF: 800-435-5663 ■ Web: www.ndtourism.com

Transportation Dept 608 E Blvd Ave ... Bismarck ND 58505 701-328-2500 339-35
TF: 855-637-6237 ■ Web: www.dot.nd.gov

Treasurer 600 E Blvd Ave Dept 120 ... Bismarck ND 58505 701-328-2643 328-3002 339-35
Web: www.nd.gov/ndtreas

University System
600 E Blvd Ave Dept 215 ... Bismarck ND 58505 701-328-2960 328-2961 339-35
Web: www.ndus.edu

Veterans Affairs Dept
4201 38th St SW, Ste 104 PO Box 9003 ... Fargo ND 58104 701-239-7165 239-7166 339-35
TF: 866-634-8387 ■ Web: www.nd.gov

Vocational Rehabilitation Div
1237 W Divide Ave Ste 2 ... Bismarck ND 58501 701-328-8800 339-35
TF: 888-862-7342 ■ Web: www.nd.gov

Workers Compensation
1600 E Century Ave Ste 1 ... Bismarck ND 58503 701-328-3800 328-3820 339-35
TF: 800-777-5033 ■ Web: www.workforcesafety.com

North Dakota Assn of Realtors
318 W Apollo Ave ... Bismarck ND 58503 701-355-1010 258-7211 656
TF: 800-279-2361 ■ Web: www.ndrealtors.com

North Dakota Chamber of Commerce
2000 Schafer St PO Box 2639 ... Bismarck ND 58502 701-222-0929 222-1611 140
TF: 800-382-1405 ■ Web: www.ndchamber.com

North Dakota Democratic Party
1902 E Divide Ave ... Bismarck ND 58501 701-255-0460 616 1
Web: www.demnpl.com

North Dakota Dental Assn
1720 Burnt Boat Dr Ste 201 ... Bismarck ND 58503 701-223-8870 892-7068 227
TF: 800-444-1330 ■ Web: www.nddental.com

North Dakota Legislative Council Services
State Capitol Bldg 600 E Blvd Ave ... Bismarck ND 58505 701-328-2916 328-3615 433
TF: 800-366-6888 ■ Web: www.legis.nd.gov

North Dakota Medical Assn (NDMA)
1622 I- Ave ... Bismarck ND 58503 701-223-9475 223-9476 474
Web: www.ndmed.org

North Dakota Mill & Elevator
1823 Mill Rd ... Grand Forks ND 58203 701-795-7000 296-23
TF: 800-538-7721 ■ Web: www.ndmill.com

North Dakota Museum of Art
261Centennial Dr S-7305 ... Grand Forks ND 58202 701-777-4195 777-4425 520
Web: www.ndmoa.com

North Dakota Pharmacists Assn (NDPhA)
1641 Capitol Way ... Bismarck ND 58501 701-258-4968 258-9312 585
Web: www.nodakpharmacy.net

Name / Address	City	State	Zip	Phone	Fax	Class
North Dakota State College of Science						
800 Sixth St N	Wahpeton	ND	58076	701-671-2401	671-2201*	162
*Fax: Admissions ■ TF: 800-342-4325 ■ Web: www.ndscs.edu						
North Dakota State Hospital						
2605 Cir Dr.	Jamestown	ND	58401	701-253-3650	253-3999	374-5
TF: 888-862-7342 ■ Web: www.nd.gov						
North Dakota State Library (NDSL)						
604 E Blvd Ave	Bismarck	ND	58505	701-328-4622	328-2040	434-5
TF: 800-472-2104 ■ Web: www.library.nd.gov						
North Dakota State University						
1301 12th Ave N	Fargo	ND	58105	701-231-8643	231-8802*	166
*Fax: Admissions ■ TF: 800-488-6378 ■ Web: www.ndsu.edu						
North Dakota Veterans Home						
1600 Veterans Dr	Lisbon	ND	58054	701-683-6500	683-6550	793
Web: www.nd.gov						
North Dakota Veterinary Medical Assn						
921 S Ninth St Ste 120	Bismarck	ND	58504	701-221-7740		795
Web: www.ndvma.com						
North Dallas Chamber of Commerce						
10707 Preston Rd	Dallas	TX	75230	214-368-6485	691-5584	139
Web: www.ndcc.org						
North East Mall						
1101 Melbourne St Ste 1000	Hurst	TX	76053	817-284-3427	595-4471	460
TF: 877-746-6642 ■ Web: www.simon.com						
North East MS EPA 10 PR 2050	Oxford	MS	38655	662-234-6331	234-0046	245
TF: 877-234-6331 ■ Web: www.nemepa.org						
North Essex Chamber of Commerce						
26 Park St Ste 2062	Montclair	NJ	07042	973-226-5500	783-4407	139
TF: 800-274-2812 ■ Web: www.northessexchamber.com						
North European Oil Royalty Trust						
43 W Front St Ste 19A	Red Bank	NJ	07701	732-741-4008	741-3140	675
NYSE: NRT ■ TF: 800-368-5948 ■ Web: www.neort.com						
North Face, The						
14450 Doolittle Dr	San Leandro	CA	94577	877-992-0111		710
TF: 855-500-8639 ■ Web: www.thenorthface.com						
North Florida Broadband Authority						
164 NW Madison St	Lake City	FL	32055	386-438-5042		387
Web: www.nfba.net						
North Florida Community College						
325 NW Turner Davis Dr	Madison	FL	32340	850-973-2288		162
TF: 866-937-6322 ■ Web: www.nfcc.edu						
North Florida Lincoln Mercury						
4620 Southside Blvd	Jacksonville	FL	32216	877-941-1435		516
TF: 888-457-1949 ■ Web: northfloridalincoln.com						
North Florida Regional Medical Ctr						
6500 Newberry Rd	Gainesville	FL	32605	352-333-4000		374-3
Web: www.nfrmc.com						
North Fork Radiology PC						
1333 Roanoke Ave Ste 202	Riverhead	NY	11901	631-727-2755		374-3
Web: www.northforkrad.com						
North Fork Ranch (NFR)						
55395 Hwy 285 PO Box B	Shawnee	CO	00475	303-838-9873	838 1540	239
TF: 800 843 7895 ■ Web: www.northforkranch.com						
North Fort Myers Chamber of Commerce						
2787 N Tamiami Trl Unit 10	North Fort Myers	FL	33903	239-997-9111		139
Web: nfmchamber.org						
North Forty Resort LLC						
3765 Mt Hwy 40 W	Columbia Falls	MT	59912	406-862-7740		379
Web: northfortyresort.com						
North Fulton Hospital						
3000 Hospital Blvd	Roswell	GA	30076	770-751-2500	751-2912	374-3
Web: www.wellstar.org						
North Galveston County Chamber of Commerce						
218 FM 517 W	Dickinson	TX	77539	281-534-4380	534-4389	139
Web: www.northgalvestoncountychamber.com						
North Georgia Brick Company Inc						
2405 Oak St W	Cumming	GA	30041	770-886-6555		5
Web: www.northgeorgiabrick.com						
North Georgia Electric Membership Corp						
1850 Cleveland Hwy	Dalton	GA	30721	706 259 9441		245
Web: www.ngemc.com						
North Greenville University						
7801 N Tigerville Rd PO Box 1892	Tigerville	SC	29688	864-977-7000	977-7177*	162
*Fax: Admissions ■ TF: 800-468-6642 ■ Web: www.ngu.edu						
North Growth Management Ltd						
Ste 830 One Bentall Centre 505 Burrard St	Vancouver	BC	V7X1M4	604-688-5440		528
Web: www.northgrowth.com						
North Hampton State Beach						
27 Ocean Blvd	North Hampton	NH	03862	603-227-8722		565
Web: www.nhstateparks.org						
North Harris College						
2700 WW Thorne Rd	Houston	TX	77073	281-618-5400	618-7141*	162
*Fax: Admissions ■ Web: www.lonestar.edu						
North Haven Gardens Inc						
7700 Northaven Rd	Dallas	TX	75230	214-363-5316		323
Web: www.nhg.com						
North Health						
North Shore University Hospital						
300 Community Dr						
9 Tower Large Conference Rm	Manhasset	NY	11030	516-562-8973	734-8836	769
TF: 888-321-3627 ■ Web: www.northwell.edu						
North Hennepin Chamber of Commerce						
229 First Ave NE	Osseo	MN	55369	763-424-6744	424-6927	139
Web: www.nhachamber.com						
North Hennepin Community College						
7411 85th Ave N	Brooklyn Park	MN	55445	763-424-0702	424-0929*	162
*Fax: Admissions ■ TF: 800-818-0395 ■ Web: www.nhcc.edu						
North Hero State Park						
3803 Lakeview Dr	North Hero	VT	05474	802-372-8727		565
Web: www.vtstateparks.com						
North Higgins Lake State Park						
11747 N Higgins Lake Dr	Roscommon	MI	48653	989-821-6125		565
Web: www.michigandnr.com						
North Highland Co, The						
3333 Piedmont Rd NE Ste 1000	Atlanta	GA	30305	404-233-1015	233-4930	721
Web: www.northhighland.com						
North Hill Ventures						
535 Boylston St 6th Fl	Boston	MA	02116	617-600-7050		792
Web: www.northhillventures.com						
North Hunterdon-Voorhees Regional High School District						
1445 SR 31	Annandale	NJ	08801	908-735-2846		685
Web: www.nhvweb.net						
North Idaho College						
1000 W Garden Ave	Coeur d'Alene	ID	83814	208-769-3300	769-3399*	162
*Fax: Library ■ TF: 877-404-4536 ■ Web: www.nic.edu						
North Idaho Correctional Institution						
236 Radar Rd	Cottonwood	ID	83522	208-962-3276		213
Web: www.idoc.idaho.gov						
North Idaho Outlets						
4300 W Riverbend Ave	Post Falls	ID	83854	208-773-4556		460
North Iowa Area Community College						
500 College Dr	Mason City	IA	50401	641-423-1264	422-4385*	162
*Fax: Admissions ■ TF: 888-466-4222 ■ Web: niacc.edu						
North Island College 2300 Ryan Rd	Courtenay	BC	V9N8N6	250-334-5000		166
TF: 800-715-0914 ■ Web: www.nic.bc.ca						
North Island Credit Union						
5898 Copley Dr	San Diego	CA	92111	800-334-8788	769-7956*	219
*Fax Area Code: 858 ■ TF: 800-334-8788 ■ Web: northisland.ccu.com						
North Itasca Electric Co-op Inc						
301 Main Ave PO Box 227	Bigfork	MN	56628	218-743-3131	743-3644	245
TF: 800-762-4048 ■ Web: www.northitascaelectric.com						
North Jersey Regional Chamber of Commerce						
205 Rt 46 W Ste A103	Clifton	NJ	07013	973-470-9300	470-9245	139
TF: 800-552-5880 ■ Web: northjerseychamber.org						
North Kansas City Hospital						
2800 Clay Edwards Dr	North Kansas City	MO	64116	816-691-2000		374-3
Web: www.nkch.org						
North Kingstown Chamber of Commerce						
8045 Post Rd	North Kingstown	RI	02852	401-295-5566	295-5582	139
Web: northkingstownchamberofcommerce.wildapricot.org						
North Lake College						
5001 N MacArthur Blvd	Irving	TX	75038	972-273-3000	273-3112*	162
*Fax: Admissions ■ Web: www.northlakecollege.edu						
North Lake Tahoe Resort Assn						
100 N Lake Blvd	Tahoe City	CA	96145	530-581-6900	581-1686	206
TF: 800-468-2463 ■ Web: www.gotahoenorth.com						
North Lake Tahoe Visitors & Convention Bureau						
PO Box 1757	Tahoe City	CA	96145	530-581-6900	581-1686	206
TF: 800-462-5196 ■ Web: www.gotahoenorth.com						
North Las Vegas Animal Hospital						
2437 E Cheyenne Ave	North Las Vegas	NV	89030	702-642-5353		794
Web: www.huntco.com						
North Las Vegas Chamber of Commerce						
3365 W Craig Rd Ste 25	North Las Vegas	NV	89032	702-642-9595		139
TF: 800-782-4324 ■ Web: www.nlvchamber.org						
North Light Color Inc						
5008 Hillsboro Ave N	Minneapolis	MN	55428	763-531-8222	531-8224	386
Web: www.northlightcolor.com						
North Los Angel County Regional Ctr						
15400 Sherman Way Ste 170	Van Nuys	CA	91406	818-778-1900	756-6140	363
TF: 800-430-4263 ■ Web: www.nlacrc.org						
North Loup State Recreation Area						
7425 S US Hwy 281	Doniphan	NE	68832	308-385-6211		565
Web: outdoornebraska.gov/northloup						
North Love Christian School						
5301 E Riverside Blvd	Rockford	IL	61114	815-877-6021		685
Web: northlove.org						
North Market 59 Spruce St	Columbus	OH	43215	614-463-9664		400
Web: www.northmarket.com						
North Mason School District Inc						
71 E Campus Dr	Belfair	WA	98528	360-277-2300		685
Web: www.nmsd.wednet.edu						
North Memorial Health Care						
3300 Oakdale Ave N	Robbinsdale	MN	55422	763-520-5200		374-3
Web: www.northmemorial.com						
North Memorial Home Health & Hospice						
3500 France Ave N Ste 101	Robbinsdale	MN	55422	763-520-5200		371
Web: northmemorial.com						
North metro Medical Ctr						
1400 Braden St	Jacksonville	AR	72076	501-985-7000		374-3
TF: 800-273-8255 ■ Web: www.northmetromed.com						
North Miami Beach Chamber of Commerce						
16901 NE 19th Ave	North Miami Beach	FL	33162	305-944-8500	944-8191	139
Web: www.nmbchamber.com						
North Miami Beach Public Library						
1601 NE 164th St	North Miami Beach	FL	33162	305-948-2970	787-6007	434-3
Web: nmblib.com						
North Miami Beach/Julius Littman Performing Arts Theater						
17011 NE 19th Ave	North Miami Beach	FL	33162	305-948-2957	787-6040	572
Web: www.littmantheater.com						
North Miami Public Library						
835 NE 132nd St	North Miami	FL	33161	305-891-5535	892-0843	434-3
Web: northmiamifl.gov						
North Milwaukee State Bank (NMS)						
5630 W Fond Du Lac Ave	Milwaukee	WI	53216	414-466-2344	466-6248	70
TF: 800-799-5630 ■ Web: www.nmsbank.com						
North Mississippi Medical Ctr						
830 S Gloster St	Tupelo	MS	38801	662-377-3000		374-3
Web: www.nmhs.net/tupelo						
North Monterey County Unified School District						
8142 Moss Landing Rd	Moss Landing	CA	95039	831-633-3343		685
Web: www.nmcusd.org						
North Museum of Natural History & Science						
400 College Ave	Lancaster	PA	17603	717-291-3941	358-4504	520
TF: 800-732-0999 ■ Web: www.northmuseum.org						
North Oaks Health System (NOHS)						
PO Box 2668	Hammond	LA	70404	985-345-2700		374-3
Web: www.northoaks.org						
North of Boston Convention & Visitors Bureau (NBCVB)						
I-95 Southbound Exit 60 PO Box 5193	Salisbury	MA	01952	978-465-6555		206
TF: 800-215-9805 ■ Web: www.northofboston.org						
North Okaloosa Medical Ctr (NOMC)						
151 E Redstone Ave	Crestview	FL	32539	850-689-8100		374-3
Web: www.northokaloosa.com						
North Oklahoma County Mental Health Center						
4436 NW 50th St	Oklahoma City	OK	73112	405-858-2700		726
TF: 800-522-3511 ■ Web: www.northcare.com						

	Phone	Fax	Class
North Olmsted Chamber of Commerce 28938 Lorain Rd Ste 204 North Olmsted OH 44070 *TF:* 800-954-8742 ■ *Web:* www.nolmstedchamber.org	440-777-3368	777-9361	139
North Olympic Peninsula Visitor & Convention Bureau 618 S Peabody Ste F PO Box 670 Port Angeles WA 98362 *TF:* 800-942-4042 ■ *Web:* www.olympicpeninsula.org	360-452-8552	452-7383	206
North Ontario Library Service 334 Regent St Sudbury ON P3C4E2 *TF:* 800-461-6348 ■ *Web:* olsn.ca	705-675-6467	675-2285	436
North Orange County Escrow Corp 1370 Brea Blvd Ste 110 Fullerton CA 92835 *Web:* www.nocescrow.com/contact	714-526-5400	526-1744	652
North Pacific Corp 5612 Lake Washington Blvd NE Kirkland WA 98033 *Web:* www.npc-usa.com	425-822-1001	822-1004	285
North Pacific Management 1905 SE Tenth Ave Portland OR 97214 *Web:* www.northp.com	503-425-1500		652
North Palm Beach County Chamber of Commerce 800 N US Hwy 1 Jupiter FL 33477 *Web:* www.pbnchamber.com/?npb=1	561-746-7111	745-7519	139
North Park Lincoln 9207 San Pedro St San Antonio TX 78216 *TF:* 888-696-5480 ■ *Web:* nplincoln.com	210-341-8841		57
North Park Theological Seminary 3225 W Foster Ave Chicago IL 60625 *TF:* 800-964-0101 ■ *Web:* www.northpark.edu	773-244-6229	244-6244	167-3
North Park Transportation Co 5150 Columbine St Denver CO 80216 *Web:* www.nopk.com	303-295-0300	295-6244	780
North Park University 3225 W Foster Ave Chicago IL 60625 *TF:* 800-888-6728 ■ *Web:* www.northpark.edu	773-244-5500		166
North Penn Legal Services 507 Linden St Ste 300 Scranton PA 18503 *Web:* northpennlegal.org	570-342-0184		445
North Piedmont Correctional Ctr for Women 1420 Raleigh Rd Lexington NC 27292 *Web:* www.doc.state.nc.us	336-242-1259		213
North Plains Electric Co-op Inc 14585 Hwy 83 N PO Box 1008 Perryton TX 79070 *TF:* 800-272-5482 ■ *Web:* www.npec.org	806-435-5482		245
North Platte Area Chamber & Development 502 S Dewey St North Platte NE 69101 *TF:* 800-781-4415 ■ *Web:* www.nparea.com	308-532-4966	532-4827	139
North Platte Community College *North* 1101 Halligan Dr North Platte NE 69101 **Fax:* Admissions ■ *TF:* 800-658-4308 ■ *Web:* www.mpcc.edu	308-535-3601	534-5767*	162
South 601 W State Farm Rd North Platte NE 69101 **Fax Area Code:* 308 ■ *TF:* 800-658-4348 ■ *Web:* www.mpcc.edu	800-658-4348	535-3794*	162
North Platte Livestock Feeders Inc 3303 W 12th St Hastings NE 68901 *Web:* www.gottschcattlecompany.com	402-463-6215		10-1
North Platte Public Library 120 W Fourth St North Platte NE 69101 *TF:* 800-829-4477 ■ *Web:* ci.north-platte.ne.us	308-535-8036	535-8296	434-3
North Point Recreation Area 38180 297th St Lake Andes SD 57356 *Web:* www.gfp.sd.gov/state-parks/directory/north-point	605-487-7046		565
North Pond 2610 N Cannon Dr Chicago IL 60614 *Web:* www.northpondrestaurant.com	773-477-5845		671
North Quabbin Chamber of Commerce 251 Exchange St Athol MA 01331 *Web:* www.northquabbinchamber.com	978-249-3849		139
North Richland Hills Public Library 9015 Grand Ave North Richland Hills TX 76180 *Web:* www.library.nrhtx.com	817-427-6800	427-6808	434-3
North Ridgeville City School District 5490 Mills Creek Ln North Ridgeville OH 44039 *TF:* 877-644-6457 ■ *Web:* www.nrcs.k12.oh.us	440-327-4444		685
North Ridgeville Visitors Bureau 34845 Lorain Rd North Ridgeville OH 44039 *TF:* 800-334-5910 ■ *Web:* www.nrchamber.com	440-327-3737	327-1474	206
North River Boats Inc 1750 Green Siding Rd Roseburg OR 97471 *TF:* 800-413-6351 ■ *Web:* www.northriverboats.com	541-673-2438		698
North Rose-Wolcott Central School District 11631 Salter Colvin Rd Wolcott NY 14590 *Web:* www.nrwcs.org	315-594-3141	594-2352	685
North Royalton Chamber of Commerce 13737 State Rd North Royalton OH 44133 *TF:* 800-728-6291 ■ *Web:* www.nroyaltonchamber.com	440-237-6180	237-6181	139
North Sails Group LLC 125 Old Gate Ln Milford CT 06460 *Web:* www.northsails.com/us	203-877-7621		733
North Salem Elementary School 140 Zion Hill Rd Salem NH 03079 *Web:* www.sau57.org/northsalem/pages/home.aspx	603-893-7062	893-7062	186
North San Antonio Chamber of Commerce 12930 Country Pkwy San Antonio TX 78216 *TF:* 877-495-5888 ■ *Web:* www.northsachamber.com	210-344-4848	525-8207	139
North Sanpete School District Inc 390 E 700 S Mount Pleasant UT 84647 *Web:* www.nsh.nsanpete.k12.ut.us	435-462-2452	462-3112	685
North Santiam School District 29 J 1155 N Third Ave Stayton OR 97383 *Web:* www.nsantiam.k12.or.us	503-769-6924	769-3578	685
North Santiam State Recreation Area PO Box 549 Detroit OR 97342 *TF:* 800-551-6949 ■ *Web:* www.oregonstateparks.org	800-551-6949		565
North Schuylkill School District 15 Academy Ln Ashland PA 17921 *Web:* www.northschuylkill.net	570-874-0466	874-3334	685
North Seattle Community College 9600 College Way N Seattle WA 98103 *TF:* 866-427-4747 ■ *Web:* www.northseattle.edu	206-527-3600	527-3671	162
North Shore Bank FSB 15700 W Bluemound Rd Brookfield WI 53005 *TF:* 800-236-4672 ■ *Web:* www.northshorebank.com	262-797-3858		70
North Shore Central Illinois Freight Co 5101 S Lawndale Ave Summit IL 60501 *Web:* www.northshorelogistics.net	708-496-8222	496-8449	780
North Shore Chamber of Commerce 5 Cherry Hill Dr Ste 100 Danvers MA 01923 *TF:* 800-339-0080 ■ *Web:* www.northshorechamber.org	978-774-8565	774-3418	139
North Shore Communications Group Inc 85 Eastern Ave Ph Ste 107 Gloucester MA 01930 *Web:* www.northshorecommunications.com	617-967-1227		116
North Shore Community College 1 Ferncroft Rd Danvers MA 01923 **Fax:* Admissions ■ *TF:* 800-841-2900 ■ *Web:* www.northshore.edu	978-762-4000	762-4015*	162
North Shore Country Club 1340 Glenview Rd Glenview IL 60025 *Web:* www.north-shorecc.org	847-729-1200		711
North Shore Country Day School 310 Green Bay Rd Winnetka IL 60093 *Web:* www.nscds.org	847-446-0674	446-0675	623
North Shore Ctr for the Performing Arts in Skokie 9501 N Skokie Blvd Skokie IL 60077 *TF:* 800-745-3000 ■ *Web:* www.northshorecenter.org	847-673-6300	679-3704	572
North Shore Elder Services, Inc 300 Rosewood Dr Ste 200 Danvers MA 01923 *Web:* www.pacenorthshore.org	781-715-6608		48-17
North Shore Gas Co 3001 Grand Ave Waukegan IL 60085 *TF:* 866-556-6004 ■ *Web:* northshoregasdelivery.com	866-556-6004		787
North Shore Medical Ctr 1100 NW 95th St Miami FL 33150 *TF:* 800-984-3434 ■ *Web:* www.northshoremedical.com	305-835-6000		374-3
North Shore Medical Ctr 81 Highland Ave Salem MA 01970 *TF:* 800-262-2463 ■ *Web:* northshorephysicians.org	978-741-1200		374-3
North Shore Recycled Fibers Inc 53 Jefferson Ave Salem MA 01970	978-744-4330		660
North Shore School District 112 (NSSD) 1936 Green Bay Rd Highland Park IL 60035 *Web:* www.nssd112.org	224-765-3000		685
North Shore Skokie Hospital 9600 Gross Pt Rd Skokie IL 60076 *Web:* www.northshore.org	847-677-9600		374-3
North Shore Steel 1566 Miles St Houston TX 77015 *Web:* www.nssco.com	713-453-3533		492
North Shore Trust & Savings 700 S Lewis Ave Waukegan IL 60085 *Web:* www.northshoretrust.com	847-336-4430	336-4438	70
North Shore University Hospital 300 Community Dr Manhasset NY 11030 *TF:* 888-214-4065 ■ *Web:* www.northwell.edu	516-562-0100	562-2352	374-3
North Side Bank & Trust Co, The 4125 Hamilton Ave Cincinnati OH 45223 *Web:* nsbt.net	513-542-7800		70
North Side Chamber of Commerce 809 Middle St Pittsburgh PA 15212 *Web:* www.northsidechamberofcommerce.com	412-231-6500	321-6760	139
North Side Foods Corp 2200 Rivers Edge Dr Arnold PA 15068 *Web:* www.northsidefoods.com	724-335-5800		473
North Sky Capital 33 S Sixth St Ste 4646 Minneapolis MN 55402 *Web:* www.northskycapital.com	612-435-7150		528
North Slope Borough PO Box 69 Barrow AK 99723 *TF:* 800-478-0267 ■ *Web:* www.north-slope.org	907-852-2611	852-0229	338
North South Supply Inc 686 Third Pl Vero Beach FL 32962 *Web:* www.northsouth.net	772-569-3810		610
North Star BlueScope Steel LLC 6767 County Rd Delta OH 43515 **Fax Area Code:* 888 ■ *Web:* www.northstarbluescope.com	419-822-2210	822-2113*	492
North Star Electric Co-op 441 State Hwy 172 NW PO Box 719 Baudette MN 56623 *TF:* 888-634-2202 ■ *Web:* www.northstarelectric.coop	218-634-2202	634-2203	245
North Star Glove Co 2916 S Steele St Tacoma WA 98409 *TF:* 800-423-1616 ■ *Web:* www.northstarglove.com	253-627-7107	627-0597	155-8
North Star Lighting Inc 2150 Parkes Dr Broadview IL 60155 *TF:* 800-229-4330 ■ *Web:* www.northstarlightingsite.com	708-681-4330	681-4006	439
North Star Mall 7400 San Pedro Ave San Antonio TX 78216 *TF:* 800-866-6511 ■ *Web:* www.northstarmall.com	210-342-2325		460
North Star Propellers Inc 2317 Newton Ave San Diego CA 92113	619-239-8309		480
North Star Resource Group Inc 2701 University Ave SE N Star Professional Ctr Minneapolis MN 55414 *TF:* 800-820-4205 ■ *Web:* www.northstarfinancial.com	612-617-6000		390
North Star Terminal & Stevedore Company LLC 790 Ocean Dock Rd Anchorage AK 99501 *TF:* 800-996-8279 ■ *Web:* www.northstarak.com	907-272-7537	272-8927	465
North State Bank Inc 6204 Falls of Neuse Rd Raleigh NC 27609 *TF:* 877-357-2265 ■ *Web:* www.northstatebank.com	919-787-9696		360-2
North State Communications 111 N Main St High Point NC 27261 *Web:* www.northstate.net	336-886-3600		736
North State Steel Inc 1010 W Gum Rd Greenville NC 27834 *TF:* 800-944-0174 ■ *Web:* www.northstatesteel.com	252-830-8884		480
North States Industries Inc 1507 92nd Ln NE Blaine MN 55449 *TF:* 800-848-8421 ■ *Web:* www.northstatesind.com	763-486-1756	486-1763	578
North Sterling State Park 24005 County Rd 330 Sterling CO 80751 *Web:* cpw.state.co.us	970-522-3657		565
North Suburban Chamber of Commerce 76-R Winn St Ste 3D Woburn MA 01801 *TF:* 800-942-9575 ■ *Web:* www.northsuburbanchamber.com	781-933-3499	933-1071	139
North Suburban Medical Ctr (NSMC) 9191 Grant St Thornton CO 80229 *TF:* 877-647-7440 ■ *Web:* www.northsuburban.com	303-451-7800	450-4458	374-3

	Phone	Fax	Class
North Tampa Chamber of Commerce PO Box 82043, Tampa FL 33602 *Web:* northtampachamberofcommerce.wildapricot.org	813-961-2420	961-2903	139
North Texas Health Care Laundry Cooperation Assn 1080 Post Paddock, Grand Prairie TX 75050 *Web:* nthcl.org	469-916-1150		426
North Texas State Hospital 6515 Kemp Blvd, Wichita Falls TX 76308	940-692-1220		374-5
North Toledo Bend State Park 2907 N Toledo Pk Rd, Zwolle LA 71486 *TF:* 888-677-6400 ■ *Web:* www.crt.state.la.us	318-645-4715		565
North Toledo Graphics LLC 5225 Telegraph Rd, Toledo OH 43612 *TF:* 800-535-4296 ■ *Web:* www.northtoledographics.com	419-476-8808		627
North Town Mall 4750 N Div St, Spokane WA 99207 *Web:* www.northtownmall.com	509-482-0209		460
North Valley Regional Chamber of Commerce 9401 Reseda Blvd Ste 100, Northridge CA 91324 *Web:* northridgechamber.org	818-349-5676	349-4343	139
North Vancouver Chamber of Commerce 124 W First St Ste 102, North Vancouver BC V7M3N3 *Web:* www.nvchamber.ca	604-987-4488	987-8272	137
North Vernon Industry 3750 Fourth St, North Vernon IN 47265 *Web:* www.nvic-cwt.com	812-346-8772		596
North Western Electric Co-op Inc 04125 State Rt 576 PO Box 391, Bryan OH 43506 *TF:* 800-647-6932 ■ *Web:* www.nwec.com	419-636-5051	636-0194	245
North Wheeler Recreation Area 29084 N Wheeler Rd, Geddes SD 57342 *Web:* www.gfp.sd.gov	605-487-7046		565
North Wind Inc 1425 Higham St, Idaho Falls ID 83402 *Web:* northwindgrp.com	208-528-8718		192
North Winds Investigations Inc 119 S Second St PO Box 1654, Rogers AR 72756 *TF:* 800-530-4514 ■ *Web:* www.napps.org	479-925-1612	878-5989	400
North York General Hospital (NYGH) 4001 Leslie St, North York ON M2K1E1 *Web:* www.nygh.on.ca	416-756-6000		374-2
North-American Interfraternity Conference (NIC) 3901 W 86th St Ste 390, Indianapolis IN 46268 *Web:* www.nicindy.org	317-872-1112		48-11
Northampton Community College 3835 Green Pond Rd, Bethlehem PA 18020 *Fax: Admissions ■ *TF:* 877-543-0998 ■ *Web:* www.northampton.edu	610-861-5300	861-4560*	162
Monroe 3 Old Mill Rd, Tannersville PA 18372 *TF:* 877-543-0998 ■ *Web:* www.northampton.edu	570-620-9221	620-9317	162
Northampton County 669 Washington St, Easton PA 18042 *Web:* www.northamptoncounty.org	610-559-6700		338
Northampton County PO Box 36, Eastville VA 23347 *Web:* www.co.northampton.va.us	757-678-0465	678-5410	338
Northampton County PO Box 808, Jackson NC 27845 *Web:* www.northamptonnc.com	252-534-2501	534-1166	338
Northampton County School District 701 N Church St PO Box 158, Jackson NC 27845 *Web:* www.northampton.k12.nc.us	252-534-1371	534-4631	685
Northborough Free Library 34 Main St, Northborough MA 01532 *TF:* 800-392-6089 ■ *Web:* northboroughlibrary.org	508-393-5025	393-5027	434-3
Northbridge Financial Corp 105 Adelaide St W Ste 700, Toronto ON M5H1P9 *TF:* 855-620-6262 ■ *Web:* www.nbfc.com	416-350-4400		360-2
Northbridge Group, The 30 Monument Sq Ste 105, Concord MA 01742 *Web:* nbrbridgeinc.com	781-266-2600		463
Northbrook Chamber of Commerce & Industry 2002 Walters Ave, Northbrook IL 60062 *Web:* www.northbrookchamber.org	847-498-5555	498-5510	139
Northbrook Court 1515 Lake Cook Rd, Northbrook IL 60062 *Web:* www.northbrookcourt.com	847-498-8161		460
Northbrook Park District 545 Academy Dr, Northbrook IL 60062 *TF:* 800-334-7661 ■ *Web:* www.nbparks.org	847-291-2960		31
Northbrook Public Library 1201 Cedar Ln, Northbrook IL 60062 *TF:* 800-334-7661 ■ *Web:* northbrook.info	847-272-6224	498-0440	434-3
Northcentral Technical College 1000 W Campus Dr, Wausau WI 54401 *TF:* 888-682-7144 ■ *Web:* www.ntc.edu	715-675-3331	675-9776	800
NorthCoast Asset Management LLC 1 Greenwich Office Pk, Greenwich CT 06831 *TF:* 800-274-5448 ■ *Web:* www.northcoastam.com	203-532-7000		401
Northcoast Behavioral Healthcare System 1756 Sagamore Rd PO Box 305, Northfield OH 44067 *Web:* mha.ohio.gov	330-467-7131	467-2420	374-5
Northcore Technologies Inc 302 E Mall, Etobicoke ON M9B6C7 *NYSE:* NTI	416-640-0400	640-0412	178-7
Northcrest Medical Ctr 100 Northcrest Dr, Springfield TN 37172 *Web:* www.northcrest.com	615-384-2411		374-3
Northeast Air Solutions Inc 3 Lopez Rd, Wilmington MA 01887 *Web:* www.air-eng.com	978-988-2000		492
Northeast Airmotive Inc 1011 Westbrook St, Portland ME 04102 *TF:* 877-354-7881 ■ *Web:* www.northeastair.com	207-774-6318	874-4714	63
Northeast Alabama Community College PO Box 159, Rainsville AL 35986 *TF:* 800-548-2546 ■ *Web:* www.nacc.edu	256-228-6001	228-6861	162
Northeast Alabama Regional Medical Ctr 400 E Tenth St, Anniston AL 36207 *Web:* www.rmccares.org	256-235-5121		374-3
Northeast Bancorp 500 Canal St, Lewiston ME 04240 *NASDAQ:* NBN ■ *TF:* 800-284-5989 ■ *Web:* www.northeastbank.com	207-786-3245		360-2
Northeast Bank 77 Broadway St NE, Minneapolis MN 55413 *Web:* www.northeastbank-mn.com	612-379-8811	362-3262	70
Northeast Baptist Hospital 8811 Village Dr, San Antonio TX 78217 *TF:* 800-201-9353 ■ *Web:* www.baptisthealthsystem.com	210-297-2000	297-0200	374-3
Northeast Battery & Alternator Inc 240 Washington St, Auburn MA 01501 *TF:* 800-441-8824 ■ *Web:* www.northeastbattery.com	508-832-2700	832-2706	61
Northeast Bldg Products Corp 4280 Aramingo Ave, Philadelphia PA 19124 *Web:* www.nbpcorporation.com	215-535-7110	288-9880	234
Northeast Broadcasting Corp 288 S River Rd, Bedford NH 03110	603-668-6400		643
Northeast Capital & Advisory Inc 7 Airport Pk Blvd, Latham NY 12110 *Web:* www.northeastcapital.net	518-426-0100	786-0105	690
Northeast Civil Solutions Inc 381 Payne Rd, Scarborough ME 04074 *TF:* 800-822-2227 ■ *Web:* www.northeastcivilsolutions.com	207-883-1000	883-1001	727
Northeast Community College 801 E Benjamin Ave PO Box 469, Norfolk NE 68702 *Fax: Admissions ■ *TF:* 800-348-9033 ■ *Web:* www.northeast.edu	402-371-2020	844-7396*	162
Northeast Correctional Complex 5249 Hwy 67 W PO Box 5000, Mountain City TN 37683 *Web:* tn.gov	423-727-7387	727-5415	213
Northeast Correctional Ctr 13698 County Rd 46, Bowling Green MO 63334 *Web:* mo.gov	573-324-9975	324-5183	213
Northeast Data Services 1316 College Ave, Elmira NY 14901	607-733-5541		413
Northeast Fisheries Science Ctr 166 Water St, Woods Hole MA 02543 *TF:* 800-315-4000 ■ *Web:* www.nefsc.noaa.gov	508-495-2000	495-2258	668
Northeast Florida Telephone Company Inc 130 N Fourth St, Macclenny FL 32063 *TF:* 800-416-6707 ■ *Web:* www.netcom.net	904-259-2261		387
Northeast Georgia Health System Inc (NGHS) 743 Spring St NE, Gainesville GA 30501 *Web:* www.nghs.com	770-535-3553		374-3
Northeast Guidance Center 2900 Conner Bldg A, Detroit MI 48215 *Web:* www.neguidance.org	313-308-1400		726
Northeast Illinois Regional Commuter Railroad Corp 547 W Jackson Blvd, Chicago IL 60661 *Web:* www.metrarail.com	312-322-6777		468
Northeast Iowa Community College *Calmar* 1625 Hwy 150 S PO Box 400, Calmar IA 52132 *Fax: Admissions ■ *TF:* 800-728-2256 ■ *Web:* www.nicc.edu	563-562-3263	562-4369*	162
Peosta 10250 Sundown Rd, Peosta IA 52068 *Fax: Admissions ■ *TF:* 800-728-7367 ■ *Web:* www.nicc.edu	563-556-5110	557-0347*	162
Northeast Lakeview College 1201 Kitty Hawk Rd, Universal City TX 78148 *Web:* alamo.edu	210-486-5000		165
Northeast Louisiana Power Co-op Inc 1411 Landis St, Winnsboro LA 71295 *Web:* nelpco.coop	318-435-4523	435-3887	245
Northeast Medical Ctr Hospital 18951 Memorial N, Humble TX 77338 *Web:* www.memorialhermann.org	281-540-7700		374-3
Northeast Methodist Hospital 12412 Judson Rd, San Antonio TX 78233 *TF:* 800-333-7333 ■ *Web:* www.sahealth.com	210-757-7000		374-3
Northeast Mississippi Community College 101 Cunningham Blvd, Booneville MS 38829 *Fax: Admissions ■ *TF:* 800-555-2154 ■ *Web:* www.nemcc.edu	662-728-7751	720-7405*	162
Northeast Mississippi Daily Journal 1242 S Green St, Tupelo MS 38804 *TF:* 800-264-6397 ■ *Web:* www.djournal.com	662-842-2611	842-2233	532-2
Northeast Missouri Electric Power Co-op 3705 Business 61 PO Box 191, Palmyra MO 63461 *Web:* www.northeast-power.coop	573-769-2107		245
Northeast Mold & Plastics 137 National Dr, Glastonbury CT 06033 *Web:* www.nemold.com	860-633-7099		596
Northeast Nebraska Public Power District 1410 W Seventh St PO Box 350, Wayne NE 68787 *TF:* 800-750-9277 ■ *Web:* www.nnppd.com	402-375-1360		245
Northeast Ohio Medical University 4209 State Rt 44 PO Box 95, Rootstown OH 44272 *TF:* 800-686-2511 ■ *Web:* neomed.edu	330-325-2511		167-2
Northeast Oklahoma Electric Co-op Inc 443857 E Hwy 60 PO Box 948, Vinita OK 74301 *TF:* 800-256-6405 ■ *Web:* www.neelectric.com	918-256-6405	256-9380	245
Northeast Regional Correctional Facility 1270 W Rt 5, Saint Johnsbury VT 05819	802-748-8151		213
Northeast Rehabilitation Hospital 70 Butler St, Salem NH 03079 *TF:* 800-439-2370 ■ *Web:* www.northeastrehab.com	603-893-2900	893-1628	374-6
Northeast Remsco Construction Inc 1433 Hwy 34 S Bldg B1, Farmingdale NJ 07727 *TF:* 800-879-8204 ■ *Web:* www.northeastconstruction.org	732-557-6100	736-8900	188-7
Northeast State Technical Community College 2425 Hwy 75 PO Box 246, Blountville TN 37617 *TF:* 800-836-7822 ■ *Web:* www.northeaststate.edu	423-323-3191	323-0217	800
Northeast Tarrant Chamber of Commerce 5001 Denton Hwy, Haltom City TX 76117 *Web:* www.netarrant.org	817-281-9376	281-9379	139
Northeast Texas Community College 1735 Chapel Hill Rd, Mount Pleasant TX 75455 *Fax: Admissions ■ *TF:* 800-870-0142 ■ *Web:* www.ntcc.edu	903-572-1911	572-6712*	162
Northeast Times 2512 Metropolitan Dr, Trevose PA 19053 *Web:* www.northeasttimes.com	215-354-3000		532-4
Northeast Towers 199 Brickyard Rd, Farmington CT 06032 *Web:* www.northeasttowers.com	860-677-1999		480
Northeast Valley Health Corp 1172 N Maclay Ave, San Fernando CA 91340 *Web:* www.nevhc.org	818-898-1388		374-3
Northeast Veterans Business Resource Center Po Box 52113, Boston MA 02205 *TF:* 800-542-7232 ■ *Web:* www.nevbrc.org	617-938-3933		463

Name / Address	Phone	Fax	Class
Northeast Wisconsin Technical College PO Box 19042 Green Bay WI 54307 *TF:* 800-422-6982 ■ *Web:* www.nwtc.edu	920-498-5400		800
Northeast Wyoming Board of Cooperative Educational Services Boces 410 N Miller Ave Gillette WY 82716 *Web:* www.newboces.com	307-682-0231		685
Northeastern Connecticut Chamber of Commerce 210 Westcott Rd Danielson CT 06239 *Web:* nectchamber.com	860-774-8001	774-4299	139
Northeastern Illinois University 5500 N St Louis Ave Chicago IL 60625 **Fax:* Admissions ■ *Web:* www.neiu.edu	773-442-4050	442-4020*	166
Northeastern Illinois University Williams Library 5500 N St Louis Ave Chicago IL 60625 *Web:* www.neiu.edu	773-442-4470	442-4531	434-6
Northeastern Junior College 100 College Ave Sterling CO 80751 *TF:* 800-626-4637 ■ *Web:* www.njc.edu	970-521-6600	522-4664	162
Northeastern Log Homes Inc 10 Ames Rd Kenduskeag ME 04450 *TF:* 800-624-2797 ■ *Web:* www.northeasternlog.com	207-884-7000	884-3000	106
Northeastern Nevada Museum 1515 Idaho St Elko NV 89801 *TF:* 800-348-3131 ■ *Web:* www.museumelko.org	775-738-3418		520
Northeastern Oklahoma A&M College 200 I St NE Miami OK 74354 *Web:* neo.edu	918-542-8441		162
Northeastern PA Carton & Finishing Co Inc 4820 Birney Ave US Rt 11 Moosic PA 18507 *Web:* www.nepacartons.com	570-457-7711		554
Northeastern Pennsylvania Philharmonic 4101 Birney Ave Moosic PA 18507 *TF:* 800-762-2222 ■ *Web:* www.nepaphil.org	570-341-1568		573-3
Northeastern REMC 4901 E Pk 30 Dr Columbia City IN 46725 *Web:* www.nremc.com	260-244-6111	625-3407	245
Northeastern Seminary at Roberts Wesleyan College 2265 Westside Dr Rochester NY 14624 *Web:* www.nes.edu	585-594-6800		166
Northeastern State University			
Broken Arrow 3100 E New Orleans Broken Arrow OK 74014 **Fax:* Admissions ■ *Web:* www.nsuba.edu	918-449-6000	449-6190*	166
John Vaughan Library 711 N Grand Ave Tahlequah OK 74464 *Web:* library.nsuok.edu	918-456-5511		434-6
Muskogee 2400 W Shawnee Muskogee OK 74401 *TF:* 800-722-9614 ■ *Web:* www.nsuok.edu	918-683-0040	458-2106	166
Tahlequah 600 N Grand Ave Tahlequah OK 74464 *TF:* 800-722-9614 ■ *Web:* www.nsuok.edu	918-456-5511	458-2342	166
Northeastern Supply Co Inc 8323 Pulaski Hwy Baltimore MD 21237 **Fax:* Sales ■ *TF:* 800-421-8100 ■ *Web:* northeastern.com	410-574-0010	574-3315*	612
Northeastern Technical College 1201 Chesterfield Hwy Cheraw SC 29520 *TF:* 800-921-7399 ■ *Web:* www.netc.edu	843-921-6900	537-6148	162
Northeastern University 360 Huntington Ave Boston MA 02115 **Fax:* Admissions ■ *TF:* 855-476-3391 ■ *Web:* www.northeastern.edu	617-373-2000	373-8780*	166
Northeastern University School of Law 400 Huntington Ave Boston MA 02115 *TF:* 800-732-3400 ■ *Web:* www.northeastern.edu/law	617-373-2395		167-1
Northeastern University Snell Library 360 Huntington Ave Boston MA 02115 *Web:* www.lib.neu.edu	617-373-2350	373-5409	434-6
Northeastern Wisconsin Zoo 4378 Reforestation Rd Green Bay WI 54313 *Web:* www.newzoo.org	920-434-7841		823
Northeast-Midwest Institute (NMI) 50 F St NW Ste 950 Washington DC 20001 *Web:* www.nemw.org	202-544-5200	544-0043	634
Northeern Kentucky Convention Ctr 1 W River Ctr Blvd Covington KY 41011 *Web:* www.nkycc.com	859-261-1500		232
Northern Alberta Institute of Technology 11762 106 St NW Edmonton AB T5G2R1 *TF:* 800-471-8500 ■ *Web:* www.nait.ca	780-471-6248		507
Northern Arizona Regional Behavioral Health Authority Inc (NARBHA) 1300 S Yale St Flagstaff AZ 86001 *TF:* 877-923-1400 ■ *Web:* www.narbha.org	928-774-7128		49-15
Northern Arizona University PO Box 4084 Flagstaff AZ 86011 **Fax:* Admissions ■ *TF Admissions:* 888-628-2968 ■ *Web:* www.nau.edu	928-523-5511	523-6023*	166
Northern Arizona VA Health Care System 500 Hwy 89 N Prescott AZ 86313 *TF:* 800-949-1005 ■ *Web:* www.prescott.va.gov	928-445-4860		374-8
Northern Ballet Theatre 36 Arlington St Nashua NH 03060 *Web:* nbtdc.com	603-889-8408		573-1
Northern Burlington County School District 160 Mansfield Rd E Columbus NJ 08022 *Web:* www.nburlington.com	609-298-3900		685
Northern Business Products Inc PO Box 16127 Duluth MN 55816 *Web:* www.ecinteractiveplus.com/100412/%20	218-726-0167		535
Northern California Community Blood Bank 2524 Harrison Ave Eureka CA 95501 *TF:* 800-427-7623 ■ *Web:* www.nccbb.org	707-443-8004	443-8007	89
Northern California Laborers Apprenticeship Program 1001 Westside Dr San Ramon CA 94583 *Web:* www.norcalaborers.org	925-828-2513		414
Northern California World Trade Ctr 1 Capitol Mall Ste 700 Sacramento CA 95814 *TF:* 855-667-2259 ■ *Web:* www.norcalwtc.org	916-447-9827	443-2672	822
Northern Concrete Pipe Inc 401 Kelton St Bay City MI 48706 *Web:* www.ncp-inc.com	989-892-3545		183
Northern Contours Inc 1355 Mendota Heights Rd Ste 100 Mendota Heights MN 55120 *TF:* 866-344-8132 ■ *Web:* www.northerncontours.com	651-695-1698	695-1714	115
Northern Correctional Institution 287 Bilton Rd Somers CT 06071 *Web:* ct.gov	860-763-8600		213
Northern Data Systems Inc 362 US Route One Falmouth ME 04105 *Web:* www.ndsys.com	207-781-3236		180
Northern Digital 4701 Corporate Ct Bakersfield CA 93311 *Web:* ndi.us	661-322-6044	322-1209	261
Northern Digital Inc 103 Randall Dr Waterloo ON N2V1C5 *TF:* 877-634-6340 ■ *Web:* www.ndigital.com	519-884-5142		407
Northern Eagle Beverage Co 600 16th St Carlstadt NJ 07072 *Web:* www.northerneaglebeverage.com	201-531-7100		297-8
Northern Electric Co-op Inc 39456 133nd St Bath SD 57427 *TF:* 800-529-0310 ■ *Web:* www.northernelectric.coop	605-225-0310		245
Northern Electric Inc 1275 W 124th Ave Westminster CO 80234 *TF:* 877-265-0794 ■ *Web:* www.northernelec.com	303-428-6969	428-6669	787
Northern Engraving Corp 803 S Black River St Sparta WI 54656 *Web:* www.norcorp.com	608-269-6911	366-3725	481
Northern Essex Community College 100 Elliott St Haverhill MA 01830 **Fax:* Admissions ■ *TF:* 800-422-4453 ■ *Web:* www.necc.mass.edu	978-556-3000	556-3729*	162
Northern Exposure Greeting Cards 2301 Circadian Way Ste 300 Santa Rosa CA 95407 *TF:* 800-237-3524 ■ *Web:* www.necards.com	707-546-2153		130
Northern Factory Sales Inc PO Box 660 Willmar MN 56201 *TF:* 800-328-8900 ■ *Web:* www.northernfactory.com	320-235-2288		61
Northern Fruit Co 220 Second St NE East Wenatchee WA 98802 *TF:* 800-828-4106 ■ *Web:* www.northernfruit.com/home	509-884-6651	884-1990	11-1
Northern Gulf Trading Group 164 St Francis St Ste 205 Mobile AL 36602 *Web:* www.ngtg.net	251-432-0757		539
Northern Highland - American Legion State Forest 4125 County Hwy M Boulder Junction WI 54512 *TF:* 800-847-9367 ■ *Web:* dnr.wi.gov	715-385-2727	385-2752	565
Northern Hospital of Surry County 830 Rockford St Mount Airy NC 27030 *Web:* www.northernhospital.com	336-719-7000		374-3
Northern Illinois University 1425 W Lincoln Hwy DeKalb IL 60115 **Fax:* Admissions ■ *TF:* 800-892-3050 ■ *Web:* www.niu.edu	815-753-1000	753-8312*	166
Northern Illinois University College of Law Swen Parson Hall DeKalb IL 60115 *Web:* law.niu.edu/law	815-753-9655	753-4501	167-1
Northern Illinois University University Libraries 1425 W Lincoln Hwy DeKalb IL 60115 *TF:* 800-892-3050 ■ *Web:* www.niu.edu	815-753-1000	753-9803	434-6
Northern Improvement Co 4000 12th Ave NW Fargo ND 58108 *Web:* www.northernimprovement.com	701-277-1225	277-1516	188-4
Northern Indiana Commuter Transportation District 33 E US Hwy 12 Chesterton IN 46304 *TF:* 800-743-3333 ■ *Web:* www.nictd.com	219-926-5744	929-4438	468
Northern Industrial Sales Ltd 3526 Opie Cres Prince George BC V2N2P9 *TF:* 800-668-3317 ■ *Web:* www.northernindustrialsales.ca	250-562-4435		690
Northern Institutional Funds 801 S Canal St C5S Chicago IL 60607 **Fax Area Code:* 312 ■ *TF:* 800-637-1380 ■ *Web:* www.northerntrust.com/asset-management	800-637-1380	557-0411*	528
Northern Inyo Hospital 150 Pioneer Ln Bishop CA 93514 *Web:* www.nih.org	760-873-5811		374-3
Northern Iron & Machine 867 Forest St Saint Paul MN 55106 *Web:* www.northernim.com	651-778-3300	778-1321	307
Northern Jet Management 5500 44th St SE Grand Rapids MI 49512 *TF:* 800-462-7709 ■ *Web:* www.northernjet.net	616-336-4800		23
Northern Kane County Chamber of Commerce 20 S Grove St Ste 101 Carpentersville IL 60110 *Web:* www.nkcchamber.com	847-426-8565		139
Northern Kentucky Chamber of Commerce 300 Buttermilk Pk Ste 330 Fort Mitchell KY 41017 *Web:* www.nkychamber.com	859-578-8800	578-8802	139
Northern Kentucky Convention & Visitors Bureau (NKYCVB) 50 E RiverCenter Blvd Ste 200 Covington KY 41011 *TF:* 877-659-8474 ■ *Web:* meetnky.com	859-261-4677	261-5135	206
Northern Kentucky University Nunn Dr Highland Heights KY 41099 **Fax:* Admissions ■ *TF Admissions:* 800-637-9948 ■ *Web:* www.nku.edu	859-572-5220	572-6665*	166
Northern Kentucky Water District 2835 Crescent Springs Rd Erlanger KY 41018 *TF:* 800-772-4636 ■ *Web:* www.nkywater.org	859-578-9898	578-5456	787
Northern Labs Inc 5800 W Dr PO Box 850 Manitowoc WI 54220 *Web:* www.northernlabs.com	920-684-7137	684-4957	151
Northern Lights College 11401 - Eigth St Dawson Creek BC V1G4G2 *Web:* www.nlc.bc.ca	250-782-5251		166
Northern Lights Enterprises Inc 3474 Andover Rd Wellsville NY 14895 *Web:* www.northernlightscandles.com	585-593-1200		364
Northern Lights Inc 4420 14th Ave NW Seattle WA 98107 *TF:* 800-762-0165 ■ *Web:* www.northern-lights.com	206-789-3880	782-5455	262
Northern Lights Inc 421 Cherry St PO Box 269 Sagle ID 83860 *TF:* 800-326-9594 ■ *Web:* www.nli.coop	208-263-5141		245
Northern Lights Regional Health Ctr (NLRHC) 7 Hospital St Fort McMurray AB T9H1P2 *Web:* www.albertahealthservices.ca	780-791-6161		374-2
Northern Local School District 8700 Sheridan Dr Thornville OH 43076 *Web:* www.nlsd.k12.oh.us	740-743-1303	743-3301	685

Phone | Fax | Class

Northern Louisiana Medical Ctr
401 E Vaughn St .... Ruston LA 71270 318-254-2100 374-3
TF: 800-569-4714 ■ *Web:* www.northernlouisianamedicalcenter.com

Northern Maine Community College (NMCC)
33 Edgemont Dr .... Presque Isle ME 04769 207-768-2700 768-2848 800
TF: 800-535-6682 ■ *Web:* nmcc.edu

Northern Maine Medical Ctr (NMMC)
194 E Main St .... Fort Kent ME 04743 207-834-3155 834-2949 374-3
Web: www.nmmc.org

Northern Management Services Inc
607 Church St .... Sandpoint ID 83864 208-263-1363 194
Web: www.nmsinc.com

Northern Manufacturing Company Inc
132 N Railroad St .... Oak Harbor OH 43449 419-898-2821 697
TF: 800-457-6444 ■ *Web:* www.northernmfg.com

Northern Metal Fab Inc
510 Vandeberg St .... Baldwin WI 54002 715-684-3535 492
Web: www.nmfinc.com

Northern Metal Recycling LLC
2800 Pacific St N .... Minneapolis MN 55411 612-529-9221 686
Web: www.northernmetalrecycling.com

Northern Michigan Review Inc
319 State St .... Petoskey MI 49770 231-347-2544 532-3
Web: www.petoskeynews.com

Northern Michigan University
1401 Presque Isle Ave .... Marquette MI 49855 906-227-2650 227-1747* 166
**Fax:* Admissions ■ *TF:* 800-682-9797 ■ *Web:* www.nmu.edu

Northern Michigan Veneers Inc
710 Rains Dr .... Gladstone MI 49837 906-428-1082 683
Web: www.bessegroup.com/public/.../northern_mi_veneers.php

Northern Natural Gas Co 1111 S 103rd St .... Omaha NE 68124 402-398-7000 398-7006 325
TF: 877-654-0646 ■ *Web:* www.northernnaturalgas.com

Northern Neck Electric Co-op Inc
85 St Johns St PO Box 288 .... Warsaw VA 22572 804-333-3621 245
TF: 800-243-2860 ■ *Web:* www.nnec.coop

Northern Nevada Correctional Ctr
1721 Snyder Dr PO Box 7000 .... Carson City NV 89702 775-887-9297 213
Web: doc.nv.gov

Northern Nevada Medical Ctr
2375 E Prater Way .... Sparks NV 89434 775-331-7000 374-3
Web: www.nnmc.com

Northern New Hampshire Correctional Facility
138 E Milan Rd .... Berlin NH 03570 603-752-2906 752-0405 213
Web: nh.gov

Northern New Mexico College
921 Paseo de Onate .... Espanola NM 87532 505-747-2100 747-5449 162
TF: 800-477-3632 ■ *Web:* www.nnmc.edu

Northern New York Library Network
6721 US Hwy 11 .... Potsdam NY 13676 315-265-1119 434-3
TF: 877-833-1674 ■ *Web:* nnyln.org

Northern News 8 Duncan Ave .... Kirkland Lake ON P2N3L4 705-567-5321 567-5377 532-1
Web: www.northernnews.ca

Northern Oak Capital Management Inc
555 E Wells St Ste 1625 .... Milwaukee WI 53202 414-278-0590 194
TF: 888-283-1884 ■ *Web:* www.northern-oak.com

Northern Ohio Printing Inc
4721 Hinckley Indus Pkwy .... Cleveland OH 44109 216-398-0000 627
TF: 800-407-7284 ■ *Web:* www.nohioprint.com

Northern Oil & Gas Inc
315 Manitoba Ave Ste 200 .... Wayzata MN 55391 952-476-9800 476-9801 538
NYSE: NOG ■ *Web:* www.northernoil.com

Northern Oklahoma College
1220 E Grand St PO Box 310 .... Tonkawa OK 74653 580-628-6200 628-6371* 162
**Fax:* Admissions ■ *TF:* 800-522-0188 ■ *Web:* noc.edu

Northern Pines on Crescent Lake Bed & Breakfast Plus
31 Big Pine Rd .... Raymond ME 04071 207-655-7624 706
Web: www.norpines.com/NorPines.com/Northern_Pines.html

Northern Pipe Products Inc
1302 39th St N .... Fargo ND 58102 701-282-7655 601
Web: www.northernpipe.com

Northern Plains Electric Co-op
1515 W Main St .... Carrington ND 58421 701-652-3156 245
TF: 800-882-2500 ■ *Web:* www.nplains.com

Northern Power Systems Inc 29 Pitman Rd .... Barre VT 05641 802-461-2955 668
TF: 877-906-6784 ■ *Web:* www.northernpower.com

Northern Prairie Wildlife Research Ctr
8711 37th St SE .... Jamestown ND 58401 701-253-5500 253-5553 668
Web: www.npwrc.usgs.gov

Northern Pride Communications Inc
20 Ctr Park Rd .... Topsham ME 04086 207-798-5540 480
Web: www.northernpridecommunications.com

Northern Pulp Nova Scotia Corp
260 Granton Abercrombie Branch Rd .... Abercrombie NS B2H5C6 902-752-8461 638
Web: www.northernpulp.ca

Northern Quest Casino
100 N Hayford Rd .... Airway Heights WA 99001 509-242-7000 133
TF: 877-871-6772 ■ *Web:* www.northernquest.com

Northern Regional Correctional Facility
112 Northern Regional Correctional Dr .... Moundsville WV 26041 304-843-4067 843-4073 213
TF: 866-984-8463 ■ *Web:* www.wvdoc.com

Northern Research Station
11 Campus Blvd Ste 200 .... Newtown Square PA 19073 610-557-4017 557-4095 668
Web: www.nrs.fs.fed.us

Northern Response International Ltd
50 Staples Ave Richmond Hill .... Toronto ON L4B0A7 905-737-6698 195
Web: www.northernresponse.com

Northern Rhode Island Chamber of Commerce
6 Blackstone Vly Pl Ste 402, 2nd Fl .... Lincoln RI 02865 401-334-1000 334-1009 139
Web: www.nrichamber.com

Northern Rio Arriba Electric Co-op
1135 Camino Escondido PO Box 217 .... Chama NM 87520 575-756-2181 756-2200* 245
**Fax Area Code:* 505 ■ *Web:* www.noraelectric.org

Northern Rockies Lodge
Mile 462 Alaska Hwy .... Muncho Lake BC V0C1Z0 250-776-3481 707
TF: 800-663-5269 ■ *Web:* www.northernrockieslodge.com

Northern Screw Machine Company Inc
300 Atwater St .... Saint Paul MN 55117 651-488-2568 621

Northern Security Insurance Co
PO Box 188 .... Montpelier VT 05601 802-223-2341 391-4
TF: 800-451-5000 ■ *Web:* www.vermontmutual.com

Northern Seminary
660 E Butterfield Rd .... Lombard IL 60148 630-620-2180 620-2190 167-3
Web: www.seminary.edu

Northern Stamping Corp
6600 Chapek Pkwy .... Cleveland OH 44125 216-883-8888 488
Web: northernstamping.com

Northern Star Broadcasting LLC
3250 Racquet Club Dr .... Traverse City MI 49684 231-922-4981 643
Web: www.nsbroadcasting.com

Northern State Correctional Facility
2559 Glen Rd .... Newport VT 05855 802-334-3364 334-3367 213
TF: 800-347-0488 ■ *Web:* vermont.gov

Northern State University
1200 S Jay St .... Aberdeen SD 57401 605-626-3011 626-2587* 166
**Fax:* Admissions ■ *TF:* 800-678-5330 ■ *Web:* www.northern.edu

Northern States Financial Corp
1601 N Lewis Ave .... Waukegan IL 60085 847-244-6000 360-2
OTC: NSFC ■ *TF:* 800-339-4432 ■ *Web:* www.norstatesbank.com

Northern States Metals Co
3207 Innovation Pl .... Youngstown OH 44509 330-799-1855 361
Web: extrusions.com

Northern Technologies International Corp (NTIC)
4201 Woodland Rd .... Circle Pines MN 55014 763-225-6600 145
NASDAQ: NTIC ■ *TF:* 800-328-2433 ■ *Web:* natur-tec.com

Northern Tool & Equipment Co
2800 Southcross Dr W .... Burnsville MN 55306 952-894-9510 894-1020 364
TF Cust Svc: 800-222-5381 ■ *Web:* www.northerntool.com

Northern Trailer Ltd
3355 Sugarloaf Rd .... Kamloops BC V2C6C3 250-828-2644 186

Northern Trust PO Box 75986 .... Chicago IL 60675 800-595-9111 557-0411* 528
**Fax Area Code:* 312 ■ *TF:* 800-595-9111 ■ *Web:* www.northerntrust.com/wealth-management

Northern Trust Co 50 S LaSalle St .... Chicago IL 60603 312-630-6000 70
NASDAQ: NTRS ■ *TF:* 888-289-6542 ■ *Web:* www.northerntrust.com

Northern Trust Company of Connecticut
300 Atlantic St Ste 400 .... Stamford CT 06901 312-630-0779 356-9341* 401
**Fax Area Code:* 203 ■ *TF:* 866-876-9944 ■ *Web:* www.ntrs.com

Northern Video Systems Inc
3625 Cincinnati Ave .... Rocklin CA 95765 916-543-4000 246
TF: 800-366-4472 ■ *Web:* www.tri-ed.com

Northern Virginia Community College
Alexandria 3001 N Beauregard St .... Alexandria VA 22311 703-845-6200 845-6046* 162
**Fax:* Admissions ■ *TF:* 855-259-1019 ■ *Web:* www.nvcc.edu
Annandale 8333 Little River Tpke .... Annandale VA 22003 703-323-3000 162
TF: 877-408-2028 ■ *Web:* www.nvcc.edu
Manassas 6901 Sudley Rd .... Manassas VA 20109 703-257-6600 257-6565* 162
**Fax:* Admitting ■ *TF:* 855-259-1019 ■ *Web:* www.nvcc.edu

Northern Virginia Electric Co-op
PO Box 2710 .... Manassas VA 20108 703-335-0500 245
TF: 888-335-0500 ■ *Web:* www.novec.com

Northern Wasco County People's Utility District
2345 River Rd .... The Dalles OR 97058 541-296-2226 245
Web: nwasco.com

Northern Watch
324 Main Ave N .... Thief River Falls MN 56701 218-681-4450 532-4
Web: www.trftimes.com

Northern Waters Library Service
3200 E Lakeshore Dr .... Ashland WI 54806 715-682-2365 685-2704 434-3
TF: 800-228-5684 ■ *Web:* www.nwls.lib.wi.us

Northern Westchester Hospital
400 E Main St .... Mount Kisco NY 10549 914-666-1200 374-3
TF: 877-469-4362 ■ *Web:* www.nwhc.net

Northern Wholesale Supply Inc
6800 Otter Lake Rd .... Lino Lakes MN 55038 651-429-1515 711
TF: 800-333-7777 ■ *Web:* www.northernwholesale.com

Northern X-ray Co
2118 Fourth Ave S .... Minneapolis MN 55404 800-328-5016 475
TF: 800-328-5016 ■ *Web:* www.nxclmaging.com

Northfield an Oldcastle Co
N59 W14909 Bobolink Ave .... Menomonee Falls WI 53051 262-338-5700 183
Web: northfieldblock.com

Northfield Block Co 1 Hunt Ct .... Mundelein IL 60060 847-949-3600 724
Web: northfieldblock.com

Northfield Lines Inc
32611 Northfield Blvd .... Northfield MN 55057 507-645-5267 107
TF: 888-670-8068 ■ *Web:* www.northfieldlines.com

Northfield Mount Hermon School
1 Lamplighter Way .... Gill MA 01354 413-498-3227 498-3152 622
TF: 866-664-4483 ■ *Web:* www.nmhschool.org

Northfield Park Associates LLC
10705 Northfield Rd PO Box 374 .... Northfield OH 44067 330-467-4101 642
Web: www.northfieldpark.com

Northfield Savings Bank (NSB) PO Box 7180 .... Barre VT 05641 800-672-2274 70
TF: 800-672-2274 ■ *Web:* www.nsbvt.com

Northfield Villa & Residency
Villa & Vista, The 2550 21st St .... Gering NE 69341 308-436-3101 436-3493 672
Web: www.northfieldretirement.net

Northfork Electric Co-op
311 E Madden St PO Box 400 .... Sayre OK 73662 580-928-3366 928-3105 245
Web: www.nfecoop.com

Northgate Gonzalez Inc
1201 N Magnolia Ave .... Anaheim CA 92801 714-778-3784 778-3295 345
Web: www.northgatemarkets.com

Northgate Mall 9501 Colerain Ave .... Cincinnati OH 45251 513-385-7065 460
Web: www.mynorthgatemall.com

Northgate Mall
401 NE Northgate Way Ste 210 .... Seattle WA 98125 206-362-4777 361-8760 460
TF: 800-733-3855 ■ *Web:* www.simon.com

Northgate Minerals Corp
181 Bay St Ste 3910 .... Toronto ON M5J2T3 647-260-8880 502
CVE: NXG ■ *Web:* www.auricogold.com

Northlake Engineering Inc
8320 193rd Ave .... Bristol WI 53104 262-857-9600 767
Web: www.northlake-eng.com

Northlan Solutions Inc
2642 Richard Dr .... Saint Paul MN 55110 651-653-4866 180

Name / Address	City	State	ZIP	Phone	Fax	Class
Northland Auto & Truck Accessories 1106 S 29th St W *TF:* 800-736-5302 ■ *Web:* www.northlandautomotive.com	Billings	MT	59102	406-245-0595		54
Northland College 1411 Ellis Ave. *TF:* 800-753-1840 ■ *Web:* www.northland.edu	Ashland	WI	54806	715-682-1224		166
Northland Community & Technical College 1101 US Hwy 1 E **Fax:* Admissions ■ *TF:* 800-959-6282 ■ *Web:* www.northlandcollege.edu	Thief River Falls	MN	56701	218-681-0701	681-0774*	162
East Grand Forks 2022 Central Ave NE *TF:* 800-451-3441 ■ *Web:* www.northlandcollege.edu	East Grand Forks	MN	56721	218-773-3441	793-2842	162
Northland Fishing Tackle LLC 1001 Naylor Dr SE *TF:* 800-786-3474 ■ *Web:* www.northlandtackle.com	Bemidji	MN	56601	218-751-6723		711
Northland Furniture Co 681 SE Glenwood Dr *Web:* www.northlandfurniture.com	Bend	OR	97702	541-389-3600		321
Northland Group Inc 7831 Glenroy Rd Ste 250 *TF:* 800-800-8191 ■ *Web:* www.northlandgroup.com	Edina	MN	55439	952-831-4005		160
Northland Insurance Co 385 Washington St **Fax Area Code:* 651 ■ *TF:* 800-237-9334 ■ *Web:* www.northlandins.com	Saint Paul	MN	55102	800-237-9334	310-4949*	391-4
Northland Machine Inc 35234 US Hwy 2 *Web:* www.northlandmachine.com	Grand Rapids	MN	55744	218-328-6479		757
Northland Pioneer College PO Box 610 **Fax:* Admissions ■ *TF:* 800-266-7845 ■ *Web:* www.npc.edu	Holbrook	AZ	86025	928-532-6111	536-3382*	162
Northland Plastics Inc 1420 S 16th St PO Box 290 **Fax Area Code:* 920 ■ *TF:* 800-776-7163 ■ *Web:* www.northlandplastics.com	Sheboygan	WI	53081	800-776-7163	458-4881*	600
Northland Process Piping Inc 1662 320th Ave. *Web:* www.nppmn.com	Isle	MN	56342	320-679-2119		595
Northland Products Co 1000 Rainbow Dr	Waterloo	IA	50701	319-234-5585		541
Northland Properties Corp 310 1755 W Broadway *Web:* www.northland.ca	Vancouver	BC	V6J4S5	604-730-6610		379
Northland Public Library 300 Cumberland Rd *TF:* 800-964-8888 ■ *Web:* www.northlandlibrary.org	Pittsburgh	PA	15237	412-366-8100		434-3
Northland Regional Chamber of Commerce 634 NW Englewood Rd *Web:* www.northlandchamber.com	Kansas City	MO	64118	816-455-9911		139
Northland Securities Inc 45 S Seventh St Ste 2000 *Web:* www.northlandsecurities.com	Minneapolis	MN	55402	612-851-5900		401
Northland Services Inc 6700 W Marginal Way SW *TF:* 800-426-3113 ■ *Web:* www.northlandservices.com	Seattle	WA	98106	206-763-3000		312
Northland Telecommunications Corp 101 Stewart St Ste 700 *Web:* yournorthland.com	Seattle	WA	98101	206-621-1351		116
Northland Trucking Inc 1515 S 22nd Ave *TF:* 800-214-5564 ■ *Web:* www.northlandtrucking.com	Phoenix	AZ	85009	602-254-0007	254-0455	780
Northleaf Capital Partners 79 Wellington St W PO Box 120 6th Fl **Fax Area Code:* 416 ■ *TF:* 866-964-4141 ■ *Web:* www.northleafcapital.com	Toronto	ON	M5K1N9	866-964-4141	304-0195*	792
Northlich 720 E Pete Rose Way *Web:* www.northlich.com	Cincinnati	OH	45202	513-421-8840		4
Northlight Theatre 9501 Skokie Blvd *Web:* www.northlight.org	Skokie	IL	60077	847-673-6300	679-1879	749
NorthMarq Capital Inc 3500 W American Blvd Ste 500 *Web:* www.northmarq.com	Bloomington	MN	55431	952-356-0100		655
Northmere The Sro Hotel 4943 N Kenmore Ave	Chicago	IL	60640	773-561-4234		132
NorthPark Ctr 8687 N Central Expy *Web:* www.northparkcenter.com	Dallas	TX	75225	214-363-7441		460
Northpoint Mall 1000 N Pt Cir *Web:* www.northpointmall.com	Alpharetta	GA	30022	770-740-9273		460
Northport Medical Ctr 2700 Hospital Dr *TF:* 866-840-0750 ■ *Web:* www.dchsystem.com	Northport	AL	35476	205-333-4500	333-4522	374-3
Northridge Fashion Ctr 9301 Tampa Ave *Web:* www.northridgefashioncenter.com	Northridge	CA	91324	818-885-9700		460
Northridge Hospital Medical Center-Roscoe Blvd Campus 18300 Roscoe Blvd. *Web:* www.northridgehospital.org	Northridge	CA	91328	818-885-8500	885-5321	374-3
Northridge Mall 796 Northridge Mall *Web:* www.shop-northridge-mall.com	Salinas	CA	93906	831-449-7226		460
Northrim BanCorp Inc 3111 C St *NASDAQ: NRIM* ■ *TF:* 800-478-3311 ■ *Web:* www.northrim.com	Anchorage	AK	99503	907-562-0062		70
Northrop Grumman Corp 2980 Fairview Park Dr *NYSE: NOC* ■ *Web:* www.northropgrumman.com	Falls Church	VA	22042	703-280-2900		20
Northrop Grumman Corp Military Aircraft Systems Div 1 Hornet Way *Web:* northropgrumman.com	El Segundo	CA	90245	310-332-1000		20
Northrop Grumman Newport News 13560 Jefferson Ave **Fax:* Hum Res ■ *TF:* 888-493-7386 ■ *Web:* www.newport-news.org	Newport News	VA	23603	757-886-7777	886-7920*	698
Northshire Information Inc 4869 Main St *TF:* 800-437-3700 ■ *Web:* www.northshire.com	Manchester Center	VT	05255	802-362-2200	362-1233	95
Northshore Mall 210 Andover St. *Web:* www.simon.com	Peabody	MA	01960	978-531-3440		460
Northshore Manufacturing Inc 530 Recycle Ctr Dr *Web:* www.builtritehandlers.com	Two Harbors	MN	55616	218-834-5555		295
Northside Health Care 700 Hutchins Ave *Web:* northsidehealthcare.com	Gadsden	AL	35901	256-543-7101		450
Northside Hospital 6000 49th St N *Web:* www.northsidehospital.com	Saint Petersburg	FL	33709	727-521-4411	521-5007	374-3
Northside Hospital 1000 Johnson Ferry Rd NE *Web:* www.northside.com	Atlanta	GA	30342	404-851-8000	851-6010	374-3
Northside Medical Ctr (NMC) 500 Gypsy Ln *Web:* northsidemedicalcenter.org	Youngstown	OH	44501	330-884-1000		374-3
Northside Millwork Inc 301 Millstone Dr. *Web:* www.northsidecabinets.com	Hillsborough	NC	27278	919-732-6100		499
Northside Neighbor & Sandy Springs Neighbor 5290 Roswell Rd NW Ste M *Web:* www.mdjonline.com/neighbor_newspapers	Atlanta	GA	30342	404-256-3100		532-4
Northspan Group Inc, The 221 W First St. *TF:* 800-232-0707 ■ *Web:* www.ardc.org	Duluth	MN	55802	218-722-5545		196
NorthSpring Capital Partners 100 Pinebush Rd *Web:* www.northspringcapitalpartners.com	Cambridge	ON	N1R8J8	519-721-7144		528
Northstar Aerospace Inc 6006 W 73rd St *TSE: NAS* ■ *Web:* www.nsaero.com	Bedford Park	IL	60638	708-728-2000	728-2009	21
Northstar Bank of Texas 400 N Carroll Blvd *Web:* northstarbanks.com	Denton	TX	76201	940-591-1200	384-1947	70
Northstar Battery Co 4000 Continental Way *Web:* www.northstarbattery.com	Springfield	MO	65803	417-575-8200		74
Northstar Broadband LLC 3660 E Covington Ave Ste C *Web:* www.northstarbroadband.net	Post Falls	ID	83854	208-262-9394		681
Northstar Ceramic Trading LLC 14500 East Beltwood Pkwy *TF:* 800-321-0684 ■ *Web:* www.northstarceramics.com	Dallas	TX	75244	972-392-3800	392-3808	761
Northstar Cruises 80 Bloomfield Ave Ste 102 *TF:* 800-249-9360 ■ *Web:* www.northstarcruises.com	Caldwell	NJ	07006	800-249-9360		771
Northstar Financial Services Group LLC 17605 Wright St *Web:* nstar-financial.com	Omaha	NE	68130	402-895-1600		690
Northstar Fire Protection 875 Blue Gentian Rd *Web:* www.northstarfire.com	Eagan	MN	55121	651-456-9111		595
Northstar Global Partners LLC The Prudential Tower 800 Boylston St	Boston	MA	02199	617-375-5800		70
Northstar Industries LLC 126 Merrimack St *Web:* www.northstarind.com	Methuen	MA	01844	978-975-5500		256
Northstar Investment Advisors LLC 700 17th St Ste 2350 *TF:* 800-204-6199 ■ *Web:* www.northstarinvest.com	Denver	CO	80202	303-832-2300		528
Northstar Machine & Tool Company Inc 4212 Enterprise Cir. *Web:* www.northstaraerospace.com	Duluth	MN	55811	218-720-2920		454
NorthStar Management Partners LLC 4 Bellows Rd. *Web:* www.northstarmp.com	Westborough	MA	01581	508-651-0093		463
Northstar Metal Products Inc 591 Mitchell Rd *Web:* www.northstarmetal.com	Glendale Heights	IL	60139	630-446-7800		697
NorthStar Moving Corp 9120 Mason Ave. *TF:* 800-275-7767 ■ *Web:* www.northstarmoving.com	Chatsworth	CA	91311	818-727-0128		519
Northstar Technology Corp 32 Mauchly Ste C *Web:* www.northstar-technology.com	Irvine	CA	92618	949-788-0738		186
Northstar Travel Media LLC 100 Lighting Way *Web:* www.northstartravelgroup.com	Secaucus	NJ	07094	201-902-2000		637-9
Northstar-at-Tahoe PO Box 129 *TF:* 800-466-6784 ■ *Web:* www.northstarcalifornia.com	Truckee	CA	96160	800-466-6784		669
Northtown Automotive Cos Inc 1135 Millersport Hwy *Web:* www.northtownauto.com	Amherst	NY	14226	716-614-7000		57
Northtown Products Inc 5202 Argosy Ave. *TF:* 800-972-7274 ■ *Web:* www.northtowncompany.com	Huntington Beach	CA	92649	714-897-0700		541
Northumberland County PO Box 217 *TF:* 800-296-6393 ■ *Web:* www.co.northumberland.va.us	Heathsville	VA	22473	804-580-3700	580-2261	338
Northumberland County 201 Market St 2nd Fl *TF:* 800-692-4332 ■ *Web:* www.northumberlandco.org	Sunbury	PA	17801	570-988-4167	988-4497	338
Northview Public School 4451 Hunsberger NE *TF:* 866-632-9992 ■ *Web:* www.nvps.net	Grand Rapids	MI	49525	616-363-4857	361-3494	685
Northview Stallion Station 55 Northern Dancer Dr *Web:* www.northviewstallions.com	Chesapeake City	MD	21915	410-885-2855		368
Northville Clock & Watch Shop 132 W Dunlap St *Web:* www.clockone.com	Northville	MI	48167	248-349-4938		410
Northville Downs 301 S Ctr St *TF:* 888-349-7100 ■ *Web:* www.northvilledowns.com	Northville	MI	48167	248-349-1000	348-8955	642
Northville Industries Corp 25 Melville Park Rd	Melville	NY	11747	631-293-4700		579
Northway Communications Inc 105 E Oak St *Web:* www.northwaycom.com	Wausau	WI	54401	715-842-0841		647
Northway Industries Inc 434 Paxtonville Rd PO Box 277 *TF:* 800-838-2151 ■ *Web:* www.northwayind.com	Middleburg	PA	17842	570-837-1564	837-1575	286
Northway Toyota 727 New Loudon Rd *TF:* 877-800-5098 ■ *Web:* www.northwaytoyota.com	Latham	NY	12110	518-783-1951	783-5456	57
Northwest 100 Liberty St PO Box 128 *TF:* 877-672-5678 ■ *Web:* www.northwestsavingsbank.com	Warren	PA	16365	814-726-2140		70
Northwest Administrators Inc 2323 Eastlake Ave E *TF:* 877-304-6702 ■ *Web:* www.nwadmin.com	Seattle	WA	98102	206-329-4900	726-3209	390
Northwest Aerospace Technologies Inc 2210 Hewitt Ave Ste 300	Everett	WA	98201	425-257-2044		743

Name / Address	City	State	Zip	Phone	Fax	Class
Northwest Aluminum Specialties Inc 308 Lakeshore Rd W *TF:* 800-626-2241 ■ *Web:* www.nwaluminum.com	Mississauga	ON	L5H1G8	541-296-6161		492
Northwest Arctic Borough PO Box 1110 *TF:* 800-478-1110 ■ *Web:* www.nwabor.org	Kotzebue	AK	99752	907-442-2500	442-2930	338
Northwest Area Foundation 60 Plato Blvd E Ste 400 *Web:* www.nwaf.org	Saint Paul	MN	55107	651-224-9635	225-7701	303
NorthWest Arkansas Community College 1 College Dr **Fax:* Admissions ■ *TF:* 800-995-6922 ■ *Web:* www.nwacc.edu	Bentonville	AR	72712	479-636-9222	619-2229*	162
Northwest Arkansas Regional Airport 1 Airport Blvd Ste 100 *TF:* 800-433-7300 ■ *Web:* www.flyxna.com	Bentonville	AR	72712	479-205-1000		27
Northwest Arkansas Regional Juvenile Program 36 Johnny Cake Pt Rd *Web:* saysyouth.org	Mansfield	AR	72944	479-928-0166	928-2060	412
Northwest Assn of Accredited Schools (NAAS) 1510 Robert St Ste 103 *Web:* advanc-ed.org	Boise	ID	83705	208-493-5077		48-1
Northwest Bank PO Box 128 *TF:* 800-859-1000 ■ *Web:* www.northwestsavingsbank.com	Warren	PA	16365	814-728-7263		360-2
Northwest Bank & Trust Co 100 E Kimberly Rd *Web:* www.northwestbank.com	Davenport	IA	52806	563-388-2511		690
Northwest Bedding 6102 S Hayford Rd *TF:* 800-456-7686 ■ *Web:* www.nwbedding.com	Spokane	WA	99224	509-244-3000	244-9905	471
Northwest Cabinet Works 453 Ash Rd *Web:* www.nwcabinetworks.com	Kalispell	MT	59901	406-752-8383		115
Northwest Chamber of Commerce 8944 St Charles Rock Rd Ste 300 *Web:* www.northwestchamber.com	St. Louis	MO	63114	314-291-2131	291-2153	139
Northwest Chevrolet 2516 Duss Ave *Web:* www.wrightcars.com	Ambridge	PA	15003	724-266-3380		198
Northwest Christian College 828 E 11th Ave *TF:* 877-463-6622 ■ *Web:* www.nwcu.edu	Eugene	OR	97401	541-343-1641	684-7317	166
Northwest College 231 W Sixth St **Fax:* Admissions ■ *TF:* 800-560-4692 ■ *Web:* nwc.edu	Powell	WY	82435	307-754-6000	754-6249*	162
Northwest Commission on Colleges & Universities (NWCCU) 8060 165th Ave NE Ste 100 *Web:* www.nwccu.org	Redmond	WA	98052	425-558-4224		48-1
Northwest Communications Coop 111 Railroad Ave PO Box 38 *TF:* 800-245-5884 ■ *Web:* www.nccray.com	Ray	ND	58849	701-568-3331		387
Northwest Community Bank 86 Main St *TF:* 800-455-6668 ■ *Web:* www.nwcommunitybank.com	Winsted	CT	06098	860-379-7561		70
Northwest Community Hospital 800 W Central Rd *Web:* www.nch.org	Arlington Heights	IL	60005	847-618-1000		374-3
Northwest Correctional Complex 960 SR 212 *Web:* tn.gov	Tiptonville	TN	38079	731-253-5000	253-5150	213
Northwest Data Service LLC 1169 Hilltop Pkwy Unit 105 *Web:* northwestdata.com	Steamboat Springs	CO	80487	970-879-0734		809
Northwest Data Solutions LLC 2627 C St *TF:* 800-544-0786 ■ *Web:* www.nwds-ak.com	Anchorage	AK	99503	907-227-1676		177
Northwest Designs Ink Inc 13456 SE 27th Pl Ste 200 **Fax Area Code:* 877 ■ *TF:* 800-925-9327 ■ *Web:* nwd.ink	Bellevue	WA	98005	800-925-9327	925-9327*	157-5
Northwest Door Inc 19000 Canyon Rd E *Web:* www.nwdusa.com	Puyallup	WA	98375	253-375-0700		499
Northwest Fisheries Science Ctr 2725 Montlake Blvd E *Web:* www.nwfsc.noaa.gov	Seattle	WA	98112	206-860-3200	860-3217	668
Northwest Florida Ballet 310 Perry Ave SE *Web:* www.nfballet.org	Fort Walton Beach	FL	32548	850-664-7787		573-1
Northwest Florida Blood Ctr 2209 N Ninth Ave *Web:* www.oneblood.org	Pensacola	FL	32503	850-434-2535	432-8941	89
Northwest Florida Daily News PO Box 2949 *Web:* www.nwfdailynews.com	Fort Walton Beach	FL	32549	850-863-1111	863-7834	532-2
Northwest Florida State College 100 College Blvd	Niceville	FL	32578	850-678-5111		162
Northwest Fuel Systems Inc 115 Industry Ct *Web:* nwestco.com	Kalispell	MT	59901	406-755-4343		579
Northwest Georgia Regional Hospital 705 N Div St *Web:* ngoc.com	Rome	GA	30165	706-295-6011		374-5
Northwest Georgia Regional Library 310 Cappes St *Web:* www.ngrl.org	Dalton	GA	30720	706-876-1360		434-3
Northwest Georgia Trade & Convention Ctr 2211 Dug Gap Battle Rd *TF:* 800-824-7469 ■ *Web:* www.visitdaltonga.com	Dalton	GA	30720	706-272-7676		205
Northwest Grain Growers Inc 850 N Fourth Ave *TF:* 800-994-4290 ■ *Web:* www.nwgrgr.com	Walla Walla	WA	99362	509-525-6510	529-6050	275
Northwest Grating Products Inc 9230 Fourth Ave S *Web:* www.network1000.com	Seattle	WA	98108	206-767-3000		492
Northwest Grille 5115 NW 39th Ave	Gainesville	FL	32606	352-376-0500		671
Northwest Herald Inc PO Box 250 *TF:* 800-589-8910 ■ *Web:* www.nwherald.com	Crystal Lake	IL	60039	815-459-4040	459-5640	637-8
Northwest Hospital & Medical Ctr 1550 N 115th St *TF:* 877-694-4677 ■ *Web:* www.nwhospital.org	Seattle	WA	98133	206-364-0500	368-1949	374-3
Northwest Hospital Ctr 5401 Old Ct Rd *TF:* 800-876-1175 ■ *Web:* www.lifebridgehealth.org	Randallstown	MD	21133	410-521-2200		374-3
Northwest Hydraulic Consultants 12787 Gateway Dr S *Web:* nhcweb.com	Seattle	WA	98168	206-241-6000		261
Northwest Indian College 2522 Kwina Rd **Fax:* Admissions ■ *TF:* 866-676-2772 ■ *Web:* www.nwic.edu	Bellingham	WA	98226	360-676-2772	392-4333*	165
Northwest Insurance Network Inc 515 N State St Ste 2100 *Web:* www.northwestinsurance.com	Chicago	IL	60654	312-427-1777		390
Northwest Iowa Community College 603 W Pk St *TF:* 800-352-4907 ■ *Web:* www.nwicc.edu	Sheldon	IA	51201	712-324-5061	324-4136	162
Northwest Iowa Power Co-op (NIPCO) 31002 County Rd C38 PO Box 240 *Web:* www.nipco.coop	Le Mars	IA	51031	712-546-4141	546-8795	245
Northwest La Lions Eye Bank 721 Blvd St	Shreveport	LA	71104	318-222-7999		269
Northwest Labs of Seattle 241 S Holden St *Web:* www.nwlabs1896.com	Seattle	WA	98108	206-763-6252	763-3949	743
Northwest Local School District (NWLSD) 3240 Banning Rd *Web:* www.nwlsd.org	Cincinnati	OH	45239	513-923-1000	923-3644	685
Northwest Manor Health Care Ctr 6440 W 34th St *TF:* 800-293-4930 ■ *Web:* northwesthealthcare.net	Indianapolis	IN	46224	317-293-4930		450
Northwest Medical Ctr 609 W Maple Ave *TF:* 800-734-2024 ■ *Web:* www.northwesthealth.com	Springdale	AR	72764	479-751-5711		374-3
Northwest Medical Ctr (NMC) 6200 N La Cholla Blvd *Web:* www.northwestmedicalcenter.com	Tucson	AZ	85741	520-742-9000		374-3
Northwest Medical Ctr (NWMC) 2801 N SR 7 *Web:* www.northwestmed.com	Margate	FL	33063	954-978-4000		374-3
Northwest Mississippi Community College 4975 Hwy 51 N *Web:* www.northwestms.edu	Senatobia	MS	38668	662-562-3200		162
Northwest Mississippi Regional Medical Ctr 1970 Hospital Dr *TF:* 800-582-2233 ■ *Web:* www.merithealthnorthwestms.com	Clarksdale	MS	38614	662-627-3211		374-3
Northwest Missouri Psychiatric Rehabilitation Ctr 3505 Frederick Ave	Saint Joseph	MO	64506	816-387-2300		374-5
Northwest Missouri State University 800 University Dr **Fax:* Admissions ■ *TF:* 800-633-1175 ■ *Web:* www.nwmissouri.edu	Maryville	MO	64468	660-562-1148	562-1821*	166
Northwest Museum of Arts & Culture 2316 W First Ave *Web:* www.northwestmuseum.org	Spokane	WA	99201	509-456-3931	363-5303	520
Northwest Natural Gas Co 220 NW Second Ave *NYSE:* NWN ■ *TF:* 800-422-4012 ■ *Web:* www.nwnatural.com	Portland	OR	97209	503-226-4211		787
Northwest Nazarene University 623 Holly St **Fax:* Admissions ■ *TF Admissions:* 877-668-4968 ■ *Web:* www.nnu.edu	Nampa	ID	83686	208-467-8000	467-8645*	166
Northwest Outlet 1814 Belknap St *TF:* 800-569-8142 ■ *Web:* www.northwestoutlet.com	Superior	WI	54880	715-392-9838		711
Northwest Pallet Supply Co 3648 Morreim Dr *Web:* www.northwestpallet.com	Belvidere	IL	61008	815-544-6001		200
Northwest Pea & Bean Company Inc 6109 E Desmet Ave *TF:* 800-258-4293 ■ *Web:* co-ag.com	Spokane	WA	99212	509-534-3821	534-4350	296-18
Northwest Pennsylvania's Great Outdoors Visitors Bureau 2801 Maplevale Rd *TF:* 800-348-9393 ■ *Web:* www.visitpago.com	Brookville	PA	15825	814-849-5197	849-1969	206
Northwest Pipe Co 12005 N Burgard *NASDAQ:* NWPX ■ *TF:* 800-989-9631 ■ *Web:* www.nwpipe.com	Portland	OR	97203	503-285-1400		490
Northwest Pipe Fittings Inc 33 S Eigth St W *TF:* 800-937-4737 ■ *Web:* www.northwestpipe.net	Billings	MT	59101	406-252-0142	248-8072	612
Northwest Pipeline LLC 295 Chipeta Way *Web:* www.northwest.williams.com	Salt Lake City	UT	84108	801-583-8800		325
Northwest Precision Fabricators Inc 1765 Red Soils Ct Ste 100 *Web:* www.nwprecision.com	Oregon City	OR	97045	503-557-1951		697
Northwest Print Strategies Inc 8175 SW Nimbus Ave *TF:* 800-648-5156 ■ *Web:* www.nwpsi.com	Beaverton	OR	97008	503-641-5156		589
Northwest Protective Service Inc 801 S Fidalgo 2nd Fl *Web:* www.nwprotective.com	Seattle	WA	98108	206-448-4040	448-2461	693
Northwest R-1 School District 2843 Community Ln *Web:* www.nwr1.k12.mo.us	High Ridge	MO	63049	636-677-3473	677-5480	685
Northwest Regional Library System 898 W 11th St *TF:* 800-622-5437 ■ *Web:* www.nwrls.com	Panama City	FL	32401	850-522-2100	522-2138	434-3
Northwest Rural Public Power District 5613 State Hwy 87 PO Box 249 *TF:* 800-847-0492 ■ *Web:* www.nrppd.com	Hay Springs	NE	69347	308-638-4445	638-4448	245
Northwest School 1415 Summit Ave *Web:* www.northwestschool.org	Seattle	WA	98122	206-682-7309	328-1776	622
Northwest Software Inc 1800 NW 169th Pl Ste B150 *Web:* www.nwsi.com	Beaverton	OR	97006	503-629-5947		260
Northwest Stamping Inc 86365 College View Rd *Web:* www.nwstamping.com	Eugene	OR	97405	541-747-4269		488
Northwest State Community College 22600 SR-34 *TF:* 800-421-3481 ■ *Web:* www.northweststate.edu	Archbold	OH	43502	419-267-5511	267-3688	800
Northwest State Correctional Facility 3649 Lower Newton Rd *Web:* doc.state.vt.us	Swanton	VT	05488	802-524-6771	527-7534	213
Northwest Steel & Pipe Inc 4802 S Proctor St *Web:* www.nwsteel.net	Tacoma	WA	98409	253-473-8888		492
Northwest Swiss-Matic Inc 8400 89th Ave N *TF:* 800-966-0178 ■ *Web:* www.nwswissmatic.com	Minneapolis	MN	55445	763-544-4222	544-6873	621

Phone | Fax | Class

Northwest Technical Institute
950 Blue Gentian Rd Ste 500 .... Eagan MN 55121 952-944-0080 800
TF: 800-813-0383 ■ *Web:* www.globeuniversity.edu/drafting-degree

Northwest Territories Chamber of Commerce
4802 - 50th Ave Unit 13 .... Yellowknife NT X1A1C4 867-920-9505 873-4174 137
Web: www.nwtchamber.com

Northwest Texas Hospital
1501 S Coulter .... Amarillo TX 79106 806-354-1000 374-3
TF: 800-887-1114 ■ *Web:* www.nwths.com

Northwest Trek Wildlife Park
11610 Trek Dr E .... Eatonville WA 98328 360-832-6117 832-6118 823
Web: www.nwtrek.org

Northwest Uav Propulsion Systems
2717 NE Bunn Rd .... Mcminnville OR 97128 503-434-6845 21
Web: www.nwuav.com

Northwest University
5520 108th Ave NE .... Kirkland WA 98033 425-822-8266 889-5224* 166
**Fax:* Admissions ■ *TF Admissions:* 800-669-3781 ■ *Web:* www.northwestu.edu

Northwest Washington Fair Association
1775 Front St .... Lynden WA 98264 360-354-4111 720
TF: 800-578-3048 ■ *Web:* www.nwwafair.com

Northwest Wholesale Inc
1567 N Wenatchee Ave .... Wenatchee WA 98801 509-662-2141 663-4540 276
TF: 800-874-6607 ■ *Web:* www.nwwinc.com

Northwestern Bank
202 N Bridge St PO Box 49 .... Chippewa Falls WI 54729 715-723-4461 723-0586 70
Web: www.northwesternbank.com

Northwestern College
101 Seventh St SW .... Orange City IA 51041 712-707-7000 707-7164* 166
**Fax:* Admissions ■ *TF:* 800-747-4757 ■ *Web:* www.nwciowa.edu

Northwestern College
3003 Snelling Ave N PO Box 130517 .... Saint Paul MN 55113 651-631-5100 631-5680 166
TF: 800-692-4020 ■ *Web:* www.unwsp.edu

Northwestern College Chicago Campus
4829 N Lipps Ave .... Chicago IL 60630 773-777-4220 800
TF: 888-205-2283 ■ *Web:* www.nc.edu

Northwestern Connecticut Community College
Park Pl E .... Winsted CT 06098 860-738-6300 738-6437* 162
**Fax:* Admissions ■ *Web:* www.nwcc.edu

Northwestern Corp PO Box 490 .... Morris IL 60450 815-942-1300 942-4417 55
TF: 800-942-1316 ■ *Web:* www.nwcorp.com

Northwestern Counseling & Support Services Inc
107 Fisher Pond Rd .... Saint Albans VT 05478 802-524-6554 353
TF: 800-834-7793 ■ *Web:* www.ncssinc.org

Northwestern Electric Co-op Inc
2925 William Ave .... Woodward OK 73802 580-256-7425 254-2858 245
TF: 800-375-7423 ■ *Web:* www.nwecok.coop

Northwestern Engineering Co
PO Box 2624 .... Rapid City SD 57709 605-394-3310 341-2558 261
TF: 800-561-3357 ■ *Web:* www.nwemanagement.com

Northwestern Flavors Inc
120 N Aurora St .... West Chicago IL 60185 630-231-0489 296-15

Northwestern Illinois Assn
245 W Exchange St Ste 4 .... Sycamore IL 60178 815-895-9227 895-2971 48-11
Web: www.thenia.org

Northwestern Inc 15054 Oxnard St .... Van Nuys CA 91411 818-786-1581 115

Northwestern Industries Inc
2500 W Jameson St .... Seattle WA 98199 206-285-3140 285-3603 329
TF: 800-426-2771 ■ *Web:* www.nwiglass.com

Northwestern Lehigh Sch Dist
6493 Rt 309 .... New Tripoli PA 18066 610-298-8661 685
Web: www.nwlehighsd.org

Northwestern Meat Inc 2100 NW 23rd St .... Miami FL 33142 305-633-8112 633-6907 297-9
Web: www.numeat.com

Northwestern Medicine Central DuPage Hospital
25 N Winfield Rd .... Winfield IL 60190 630-933-1600 374-3
Web: www.nm.org

Northwestern Memorial Hospital
251 E Huron St .... Chicago IL 60611 312-926-2000 769
Web: www.nmh.org

Northwestern Michigan College
1701 E Front St .... Traverse City MI 49686 231-995-1000 995-1339* 162
**Fax:* Admissions ■ *TF:* 800-748-0566 ■ *Web:* www.nmc.edu

Northwestern Mutual Investment Services LLC
611 E Wisconsin Ave Ste 300 .... Milwaukee WI 53202 866-664-7737 401
TF: 866-664-7737 ■ *Web:* www.northwesternmutual.com

Northwestern Ohio Security Systems Inc
121 E High St .... Lima OH 45801 614-527-7037 693
TF: 800-833-6416 ■ *Web:* www.nwoss.com

Northwestern Oklahoma State University
709 Oklahoma Blvd .... Alva OK 73717 580-327-1700 327-8699 166
Web: nwosu.edu

Northwestern Ontario Sports Hall of Fame
219 May St S .... Thunder Bay ON P7E1B5 807-622-2852 622-2736 522
Web: www.nwosportshalloffame.com

Northwestern Pacific Indemnity Co
15 Mtn View Rd .... Warren NJ 07059 908-903-2000 391-4
TF Claims: 800-252-4670 ■ *Web:* www.chubb.com

Northwestern Polytechnic University
47671 Westinghouse Dr .... Fremont CA 94539 510-592-9688 657-8975 166
TF: 877-878-8883 ■ *Web:* www.npu.edu

Northwestern Products Inc
721 Industrial Pk Rd .... Ashland WI 54806 715-685-9500 328

Northwestern Publishing House
1250 N 113th St .... Milwaukee WI 53226 414-475-6600 637-3
TF Orders: 800-662-6022 ■ *Web:* online.nph.net

Northwestern Rural Electric Co-op Assn Inc
22534 SR Ste 86 .... Cambridge Springs PA 16403 800-472-7910 398-8064* 245
**Fax Area Code:* 814 ■ *TF:* 800-352-0014 ■ *Web:* www.northwesternrec.com

Northwestern State University
175 Sam Sibley Dr .... Natchitoches LA 71497 318-357-4078 357-4660 166
TF: 800-767-8115 ■ *Web:* www.nsula.edu

Northwestern State University Watson Memorial Library
913 University Pkwy .... Natchitoches LA 71497 318-357-4477 357-4470 434-6
TF: 888-540-9657 ■ *Web:* library.nsula.edu

Northwestern Tire Co
1200 Glenwood Ave .... Minneapolis MN 55405 612-377-4900 755
Web: www.northwesterntire.net

Northwestern Tools Inc
3130 Valleywood Dr .... Dayton OH 45429 937-298-9994 298-3715 757
TF: 800-236-3956 ■ *Web:* www.northwesterntools.com

Northwestern University
1801 Hinman Ave .... Evanston IL 60208 847-491-7271 467-2331* 166
**Fax:* Admissions ■ *TF:* 800-227-7368 ■ *Web:* www.northwestern.edu

Northwestern University Feinberg School of Medicine
303 E Chicago Ave .... Chicago IL 60611 312-503-8649 167-2
Web: www.feinberg.northwestern.edu

Northwestern University Library
1970 Campus Dr .... Evanston IL 60208 847-491-7658 491-8306 434-6
Web: www.library.northwestern.edu

Northwestern University School of Law
357 E Chicago Ave .... Chicago IL 60611 312-503-3100 503-0178* 167-1
**Fax:* Admissions ■ *TF:* 800-229-2032 ■ *Web:* www.law.northwestern.edu

Northwest-Shoals Community College
Muscle Shoals
800 George Wallace Blvd .... Muscle Shoals AL 35661 256-331-5200 331-5366* 162
**Fax:* Admissions ■ *TF:* 800-645-8967 ■ *Web:* www.nwscc.edu
Phil Campbell 2080 College Rd .... Phil Campbell AL 35581 256-331-6200 331-6272* 162
**Fax:* Admissions ■ *TF:* 800-645-8967 ■ *Web:* www.nwscc.edu

Northwood Family Office LP
130 King St W Ste 2250 .... Toronto ON M5X1C8 416-502-1245 401
Web: www.northwoodfamilyoffice.com

Northwood Manufacturing Inc
59948 Downs Rd .... La Grande OR 97850 541-962-6274 505
Web: www.northwoodmfg.com

Northwood Meadows State Park
755 First NH Tpke .... Northwood NH 03261 603-485-1031 565
Web: www.nhstateparks.org

Northwood School PO Box 1070 .... Lake Placid NY 12946 518-523-3382 622
Web: www.northwoodschool.com

Northwood University
Texas 1114 W FM 1382 .... Cedar Hill TX 75104 972-291-1541 166
TF: 800-927-9663 ■ *Web:* www.northwood.edu

Northwood University Florida
2600 N Military Trl .... West Palm Beach FL 33409 561-478-5500 166
TF Admissions: 800-458-8325 ■ *Web:* www.northwood.edu

Northwood University Michigan
4000 Whiting Dr .... Midland MI 48640 989-837-4200 837-4490* 166
**Fax:* Admissions ■ *TF:* 800-622-9000 ■ *Web:* www.northwood.edu

Northwood Ventures
485 Underhill Blvd Ste 205 .... Syosset NY 11791 516-364-5544 364-0879 792
Web: www.northwoodventures.com

Northwoods Care Centre
2250 Pearl St .... Belvidere IL 61008 815-544-0358 371
Web: www.northwoodscare.com

Northwoods Mall
2150 Northwoods Blvd .... North Charleston SC 29406 843-797-3062 460
Web: shopnorthwoodsmall.com

Northwoods Paper Converting Inc
230 Corporate Dr .... Beaver Dam WI 53916 920-356-9085 548
Web: www.npc-inc.com

Norton Audubon Hospital
1 Audubon Plaza Dr .... Louisville KY 40217 502-636-7111 374-3
Web: www.nortonhealthcare.com

Norton County 105 S Kansas PO Box 70 .... Norton KS 67654 785-877-5700 338
Web: www.nortoncounty.net

Norton Ditto Company Inc
2425 W Alabama St .... Houston TX 77098 713-688-9800 157-3
Web: www.nortonditto.com

Norton Eleanor Holmes (Rep D - DC)
2136 Rayburn Bldg .... Washington DC 20515 202-225-8050 225-3002 342-2
Web: www.norton.house.gov

Norton Hospital 200 E Chestnut St .... Louisville KY 40202 502-629-8000 374-3
Web: www.nortonhealthcare.com

Norton (Independent City)
618 Virginia Ave PO Box 618 .... Norton VA 24273 276-679-1160 679-3510 338
Web: www.nortonva.org

Norton Industries Inc
20670 Corsair Blvd .... Hayward CA 94545 510-786-3638 350
Web: nortonclamps.com

Norton Museum of Art
1451 S Olive Ave .... West Palm Beach FL 33401 561-832-5196 520
Web: www.norton.org

Norton Outdoor Advertising
5280 Kennedy Ave .... Cincinnati OH 45213 513-631-4864 8
Web: www.norton-outdoor.com

Norton Packaging Inc
20670 Cosair Blvd .... Hayward CA 94545 510-786-3445 198
Web: www.nortonpackaging.com

Norton Sandblasting Equipment
1006 Executive Blvd .... Chesapeake VA 23320 757-548-4842 1
TF: 800-366-4341 ■ *Web:* www.nortonsandblasting.com

Norton Simon Museum
411 W Colorado Blvd .... Pasadena CA 91105 626-449-6840 796-4978 520
Web: nortonsimon.org

Norton Suburban Hospital
4001 Dutchmans Ln .... Louisville KY 40207 502-893-1000 374-3
TF: 800-222-1222 ■ *Web:* www.nortonhealthcare.com

Norton Telegram 215 S Kansas St .... Norton KS 67654 785-877-3361 532-2

Norton's Flowers & Gifts
2900 Washtenaw Ave .... Ypsilanti MI 48197 734-434-2700 292
TF: 800-682-8667 ■ *Web:* www.nortonsflowers.com

Norvanco International Inc
4301 W Vly Hwy Ste 100 .... Sumner WA 98390 253-987-4031 987-4015 311
Web: www.norvanco.com

Norvin Green State Forest
c/o Ringwood State Pk 1304 Sloatsburg Rd .... Ringwood NJ 07456 973-962-7031 565
TF: 800-852-7899 ■ *Web:* www.njparksandforests.org/parks/norvin.html

Norwalk Chamber of Commerce
12040 Foster Rd .... Norwalk CA 90650 562-864-7785 864-8539 139
TF: 800-427-2200 ■ *Web:* norwalkchamber.com

Norwalk Community College
188 Richards Ave .... Norwalk CT 06854 203-857-7000 857-3335* 162
**Fax:* Admissions ■ *Web:* norwalk.edu

Norwalk Compressor Co
1650 Stratford Ave .... Stratford CT 06615 203-386-1234 386-1300 172
TF: 800-556-5001 ■ *Web:* www.norwalkcompressor.com

Name / Address	City	State	Zip	Phone	Fax	Class
Norwalk Concert Hall 125 E Ave *TF:* 800-357-9577 ■ *Web:* www.norwalkct.org	Norwalk	CT	06851	203-854-7900	854-7939	572
Norwalk Concrete Industries Inc 80 Commerce Dr *TF:* 800-733-3624 ■ *Web:* www.nciprecast.com	Norwalk	OH	44857	419-668-8167		183
Norwalk Furniture Corp 100 Furniture Pkwy *Web:* www.norwalkfurniture.com	Norwalk	OH	44857	419-744-3200		319-2
Norwalk Hospital 34 Maple St *TF:* 800-898-4663 ■ *Web:* www.norwalkhospital.org	Norwalk	CT	06856	203-852-2000		374-3
Norwalk Public Library 1 Belden Ave *TF:* 800-382-9463 ■ *Web:* www.norwalklib.org	Norwalk	CT	06850	203-899-2780	866-7982	434-3
Norwalk Transit District (NTD) 275 Wilson Ave *Web:* www.norwalktransit.com	Norwalk	CT	06854	203-852-0000		468
Norwalk-Wilbert Vault Co 425 Harral Ave *TF:* 800-826-9406 ■ *Web:* www.norwalkwilbert.com	Bridgeport	CT	06604	203-366-5678		134
Norway 825 Third Ave 39th Fl *Web:* www.norway-un.org	New York	NY	10022	646-430-7510		784
Consulate General 3410 W Dallas St *Web:* www.norway.org/Embassy	Houston	TX	77019	713-620-4200	620-4290	257
Consulate General 924 E 21st St **Fax Area Code:* 202 ■ *Web:* www.norway.org	Minneapolis	MN	55404	612-332-3338	469-3990*	257
Consulate General 825 Third Ave 38th Fl *Web:* www.norway.org/embassy	New York	NY	10022	646-430-7599		257
Embassy 2720 34th St NW *Web:* www.norway.org	Washington	DC	20008	202-333-6000		257
Norway Savings Bank 261 Main St *Web:* www.norwaysavings.bank	Norway	ME	04268	207-743-7986		70
Norwegian-American Chamber of Commerce Inc, The 655 Third Ave Ste 1810 *Web:* www.naccusa.org	New York	NY	10017	212-885-9737		138
Norwegian-American Chamber of Commerce Southwest Chapter (NACC) 5219 Pine Arbor Dr *Web:* www.nacchouston.org	Houston	TX	77066	281-537-6879	587-9284	138
Norwegian-American Hospital 1044 N Francisco St *TF:* 877-624-9333 ■ *Web:* www.nahospital.org	Chicago	IL	60622	773-292-8200		374-3
Norwell Knoll Nursing Home 329 Washington St	Norwell	MA	02061	781-659-4901		371
Norwell Manufacturing Inc 82 Stevens St *TF:* 800-822-2831 ■ *Web:* www.norwellinc.com	East Taunton	MA	02718	508-823-1751	823-9431	439
Norwesco Inc 4365 Steiner St *Web:* www.norwesco.com	St. Bonifacius	MN	55375	952-446-1945		596
Norwesco Industries (1983) Ltd 6908L - Sixth St SE *Web:* www.norwesco.ab.ca	Calgary	AB	T2H2K4	403-258-3883		111
Norwest Equity Partners 80 S Eighth St Ste 3000 *Web:* www.nep.com	Minneapolis	MN	55402	612-215-1600	215-1601	702
Norwest Venture Partners 525 University Ave Ste 800 *Web:* www.nvp.com	Palo Alto	CA	94301	650-321-8000		792
Norwich Bulletin 66 Franklin St *Web:* www.norwichbulletin.com	Norwich	CT	06360	860-887-9211		532-2
Norwich Clinical Research Associates Ltd 74 E Main St *Web:* www.ncra.com	Norwich	NY	13815	607-334-5850		743
Norwich Partners LLC 10 Morgan Dr Ste 1 *TF:* 800-439-5536 ■ *Web:* www.norwichpartners.com	Lebanon	NH	03766	603-643-2206		378
Norwich Pharma Services 6826 State Hwy 12 *Web:* www.norwichpharma.com	Norwich	NY	13815	607-335-3000		743
Norwich University 158 Harmon Dr *TF:* 800-468-6679 ■ *Web:* www.norwich.edu	Northfield	VT	05663	802-485-2001	485-2032	166
Norwin Chamber of Commerce 321 Main St *TF:* 800-377-3539 ■ *Web:* www.norwinchamber.com	Irwin	PA	15642	724-863-0888	863-5133	139
Norwin School District 281 Mcmahon Dr *Web:* www.norwinsd.org	Irwin	PA	15642	724-861-3000	863-9467	685
Norwin Technologies Corp 10 Prince Pl *Web:* www.norwintechnologies.com	Newburyport	MA	01950	978-462-0909		196
Norwood Builders Inc 250 S NE Hwy Ste 300 *Web:* www.norwoodbuilders.com	Park Ridge	IL	60068	847-655-7700	655-7701	653
Norwood Co 375 Technology Dr *TF:* 800-933-4647 ■ *Web:* www.norwdco.com	Malvern	PA	19355	610-240-4400		186
Norwood Furniture 216 N Gilbert Rd *Web:* www.norwoodfurniture.com	Gilbert	AZ	85234	480-892-0174		321
Norwood Hardware & Supply Company Inc 2906 Glendale Milford Rd *TF:* 800-652-2835 ■ *Web:* www.norwoodhardware.com	Cincinnati	OH	45241	513-733-1175		351
Norwood Hotel 112 Marion St *TF:* 888-888-1878 ■ *Web:* www.norwood-hotel.com	Winnipeg	MB	R2H0T1	204-233-4475	231-1910	379
Norwood Marking Systems 2538 Wisconsin Ave *TF:* 800-626-3464 ■ *Web:* itwnorwood.com	Downers Grove	IL	60515	630-968-0646	968-7672	467
Norwood Promotional Products Inc 14421 Myerlake Cir *TF:* 877-555-2223 ■ *Web:* www.norwood.com	Clearwater	IN	33760	727-538-3527		9
NOS Events Ctr 689 SE St *Web:* www.nosevents.com	San Bernardino	CA	92408	909-888-6788		205
Noshok Inc 1010 W Bagley Rd *Web:* www.noshok.com	Berea	OH	44017	440-243-0888	243-3472	201
Nossack Fine Meats Ltd 7240 Johnstone Dr Ste 100 *Web:* www.nossack.com	Red Deer	AB	T4P3Y6	403-346-5006		296-26
Nossi College of Art 590 Cheron Rd *TF:* 888-986-2787 ■ *Web:* www.nossi.edu	Madison	TN	37115	615-514-2787		166
Not Just Snacks 833 Hope St *Web:* letseat.at	Providence	RI	02906	401-831-1150		671
Not Rocket Science Inc 251 Hwy 21 *TF:* 888-785-8896 ■ *Web:* www.notrs.com	Madisonville	LA	70447	985-845-2334		177

Name / Address	City	State	Zip	Phone	Fax	Class
Notaro & Michalos PC 100 Dutch Hill Rd *TF:* 800-205-9567 ■ *Web:* www.notaromichalos.com	Orangeburg	NY	10962	845-359-7700		428
NotePage Inc 86 Ring Rd *Web:* www.notepage.net	Plympton	MA	02367	781-829-0500		525
Nothing Shocking LLC 513 S Dudley St *Web:* www.mojotone.com	Burgaw	NC	28425	910-259-7291		527
Notions Marketing Corp 1500 Buchanan Ave SW *TF:* 800-748-0250 ■ *Web:* store.notionsmarketing.com	Grand Rapids	MI	49507	616-243-8424	243-8055	195
Notkin Hawaii Inc 738 Kaheka St Ste 301 *Web:* www.notkinhi.com	Honolulu	HI	96814	808-941-6600		261
Noto's Old World Italian 6600 28th St SE *Web:* www.notosoldworld.com	Grand Rapids	MI	49546	616-493-6686		671
Notoco Industries LLC 10380 Airline Hwy *Web:* www.notocoind.com	Baton Rouge	LA	70816	225-292-1303		362
Notre Dame College of Ohio 4545 College Rd *TF:* 800-632-1680 ■ *Web:* www.ndc.edu	South Euclid	OH	44121	216-381-1680		166
Notre Dame de Namur University 1500 Ralston Ave **Fax:* Admissions ■ *TF:* 800-263-0545 ■ *Web:* www.ndnu.edu	Belmont	CA	94002	650-508-3600	508-3426*	166
Notre Dame Law School University of Notre Dame 1329 Biolchini Hall *Web:* www.law.nd.edu	Notre Dame	IN	46556	574-631-6627	631-4197	167-1
Notre Dame of Maryland University 4701 N Charles St **Fax:* Admissions ■ *TF Admissions:* 800-753-3757 ■ *Web:* www.ndm.edu	Baltimore	MD	21210	410-435-0100	532-6287*	166
Notre Dame Radiation Laboratory University of Notre Dame *Web:* www.rad.nd.edu	Notre Dame	IN	46556	574-631-6117		668
Notre Dame Seminary 2901 S Carrollton Ave *Web:* nds.edu	New Orleans	LA	70118	504-866-7426	866-3119	167-3
NOTSOLDSEPARATELY.COM 2 Friends Ave *Web:* www.notsoldseparately.com	Medford	NJ	08055	856-727-8200		180
Nottawaseppi Huron Band of Potawatomi's FireKeepers Development Authority 11177 E Michigan Ave *TF:* 877-353-8777 ■ *Web:* www.firekeeperscasino.com	Battle Creek	MI	49014	877-353-8777		292
Notte Luna 113 N Maryland Ave *Web:* www.notteluna.com	Glendale	CA	91206	818-552-4100	552-3522	671
Nottingham Management Company Inc, The 116 S Franklin St *Web:* www.equityfund.com	Rocky Mount	NC	27804	252-972-9922		401
Nottoway Correctional Ctr 2892 Schutt Rd PO Box 488 *Web:* vadoc.virginia.gov	Burkeville	VA	23922	434-767-5543		213
Nottoway County 344 W Ct House Rd PO Box 92 *Web:* www.nottoway.org	Nottoway	VA	23955	434-645-8696	645-8667	338
Nottoway Plantation 31025 Louisiana Hwy 1 *TF:* 866-527-6884 ■ *Web:* www.nottoway.com	White Castle	LA	70788	225-545-2730	545-8632	520
Notubes 202 Daniel Zenker Dr *Web:* www.notubes.com	Big Flats	NY	14814	607-562-2877		711
Notus Career Management 5 Centerpointe Dr Ste 400 *TF:* 800-431-1990 ■ *Web:* www.getnotus.com	Lake Oswego	OR	97035	800-431-1990		41
Nourtek Services Corp 100 decker ct Ste 191 *Web:* www.nourtek.com	Irving	TX	75062	972-717-2700		225
Nouveau Gallery 2146 Albert St *Web:* www.nouveaugallery.com	Regina	SK	S4P2T9	306-569-9279		42
Nouvelles Images Inc 68 Morgan Ave *TF:* 800-345-1383 ■ *Web:* www.nouvellesimages.com	Danbury	CT	06810	203-730-1004		130
NOV (National Oilwell Varco) 7909 Parkwood Cir Dr *NYSE:* NOV ■ *TF:* 888-262-8645 ■ *Web:* www.nov.com	Houston	TX	77036	713-375-3700		183
NOVA (National Organization for Victim Assistance) 510 King St Ste 424 *TF:* 800-879-6682 ■ *Web:* trynova.org	Alexandria	VA	22314	703-535-6682	535-5500	48-8
Nova 1470 Beachey Pl *TF:* 800-557-6682 ■ *Web:* www.novamedicalproducts.com	Carson	CA	90746	800-557-6682		475
Nova Biologicals Inc 1775 N Loop 336 Ste 4 *TF:* 800-525-0508 ■ *Web:* www.novatx.com	Conroe	TX	77301	936-756-5333		743
Nova Biomedical Corp 200 Prospect St *TF Sales:* 800-458-5813 ■ *Web:* www.novabio.us	Waltham	MA	02454	781-894-0800	894-5915	419
NOVA Chemicals Corp 1000 Seventh Ave SW PO Box 2518 *TF:* 800-561-6682 ■ *Web:* www.novachem.com	Calgary	AB	T2P5C6	403-750-3600	269-7410	605-2
Nova Corp 1445 Sheffler Dr Ste 201 *Web:* www.nova-dine.com	Chambersburg	PA	17201	717-262-9750		196
Nova Corp Inc 74 W Sheffield Ave *Web:* operationnova.com	Englewood	NJ	07631	201-567-4404		317
Nova Creative Group Inc 7812 McEwen Rd Ste 300 *Web:* www.novacreative.com	Dayton	OH	45459	937-434-9200		7
Nova Development Corp 23801 Calabasas Rd Ste 1018 *Web:* www.novadevelopment.com	Calabasas	CA	91302	818-591-9600		177
Nova Electronics Inc 128 S Brent Cir **Fax Area Code:* 860 ■ *Web:* www.code3pse.com	Walnut	CA	91789	909-598-0787	537-0656*	438
Nova Express Millennium Inc 105 - 14271 Knox Way *TF:* 877-566-6839 ■ *Web:* www.novex.ca	Richmond	BC	V6V2Z4	604-278-8044		317
Nova Fisheries 2532 Yale Ave E *TF:* 888-458-6682 ■ *Web:* www.novafish.com	Seattle	WA	98102	206-781-2000	781-9011	285
Nova Fitness Equipment 4511 S 119th Cir *TF:* 800-949-6682 ■ *Web:* www.novafitnessequipment.com	Omaha	NE	68137	402-343-0552		711
Nova Group Inc 185 Devlin Rd *Web:* www.novagrp.com	Napa	CA	94558	707-257-3200		261

				Phone	Fax	Class
Nova Internet Services Inc PO Box 703696 *Web:* www.novaone.net	Dallas	TX	75370	214-904-9600		398
Nova Libra Inc 8609 W Bryn Mawr Ave Ste 208 *TF:* 866-724-1807 ■ *Web:* novalibra.com	Chicago	IL	60631	773-714-1441		177
Nova Lighting Inc 6323 Maywood Ave *TF:* 800-318-9806 ■ *Web:* www.novalamps.com	Huntington Park	CA	90255	323-277-6266		362
Nova Management Inc 659 Abrego St Ste 5 *Web:* www.novamanagement.com	Monterey	CA	93940	831-373-4544		260
Nova Networks Inc 1700 Woodward Dr Ste 100 *TF:* 800-461-2253 ■ *Web:* novanetworks.com	Ottawa	ON	K2C3R8	613-563-6682		525
Nova Partners Inc 201 Moffett Blvd Ste 307 *Web:* www.novapartners.com	Mountain View	CA	94043	650-324-5324		196
Nova Pole International Inc 19433 96th Ave Ste 102 *TF:* 866-874-8889 ■ *Web:* www.novapole.com	Surrey	BC	V4N4C4	604-881-0090		261
Nova Polymers Inc 2650 Eastside Park Rd	Evansville	IN	47715	812-476-0339		599
Nova Power Solutions 23020 Eaglewood Ct Ste 100 *TF:* 800-999-6682 ■ *Web:* www.novapower.com	Sterling	VA	20166	800-999-6682		767
Nova Research Inc 760 McMurray Rd 760 McMurray Rd	Buellton	CA	93427	805-693-9600	693-9668	253
NOVA Scientific Inc 10 Picker Rd *TF:* 800-728-6999 ■ *Web:* www.novascientific.com	Sturbridge	MA	01566	508-347-7679		535
Nova Scotia Dept of Tourism & Culture 1800 Argyle St PO Box 456 *TF:* 800-565-0000 ■ *Web:* www.novascotia.com	Halifax	NS	B3J2R5	902-425-5781	424-2668	774
Nova Scotia Museum of Industry 147 N Foord St *Web:* museumofindustry.novascotia.ca	Stellarton	NS	B0K1S0	902-755-5425	755-7045	520
Nova Scotia Museum of Natural History 1747 Summer St *Web:* naturalhistory.novascotia.ca	Halifax	NS	B3H3A6	902-424-7353	424-0560	520
Nova Scotia Pension Agency Ste 400 Fourth Fl 1949 Upper Water St *Web:* www.novascotiapension.ca	Halifax	NS	B3J3N3	902-424-5070		528
Nova Scotia Power Inc PO Box 910 *TF:* 800-428-6230 ■ *Web:* www.nspower.ca	Halifax	NS	B3J2W5	902-428-6230	428-6108	787
Nova Solutions Inc 421 Industrial Ave **Fax Area Code:* 800 ■ *TF:* 800-730-6682 ■ *Web:* www.novadesk.com	Effingham	IL	62401	217-342-7070	940-6682*	319-1
Nova Southeastern University 3301 College Ave **Fax:* Admissions ■ *TF:* 800-541-6682 ■ *Web:* www.nova.edu	Fort Lauderdale	FL	33314	954-262-8000	262-3811*	166
Nova Southeastern University Shepard Broad Law Ctr 3305 College Ave **Fax:* Admissions ■ *TF:* 800-986-6529 ■ *Web:* www.law.nova.edu	Fort Lauderdale	FL	33314	954-262-6100	262-3844*	167-1
Nova Technology Corp 29 Magnolia Ave *Web:* www.novatechcorp.com	Manchester	MA	01944	978-525-3066		476
Nova Tours & Travel Inc 504 Vine St *TF:* 800-543-6682 ■ *Web:* www.novatours.com	Liverpool	NY	13088	315-451-0260		775
Nova Voice & Data Systems Inc 3909 Oceanic Dr Ste 401 *TF:* 800-558-6744 ■ *Web:* www.enova.us	Oceanside	CA	92056	760-439-5200		179
NovaBone Products LLC 1551 Atlantic Blvd Ste 105 *Web:* www.novabone.com	Jacksonville	FL	32207	904-807-0140		476
Novacap Inc 25111 Anza Dr *Web:* knowlescapacitors.com/novacap	Valencia	CA	91355	661-295-5920	295-5928	253
Novacel 21 Third St *TF:* 877-668-2235 ■ *Web:* www.novacelinc.com	Palmer	MA	01069	413-283-3468	283-3964	548
Novacentrix Corp 200-B Parker Dr Ste 580 *Web:* www.novacentrix.com	Austin	TX	78728	512-491-9500	491-0002	253
Novaces LLC Poydras Ctr 650 Poydras St Ste 2320 *Web:* www.novaces.com	New Orleans	LA	70130	504-544-6888		225
Novacoast Inc 1505 Chapala St *TF:* 800-949-9933 ■ *Web:* www.novacoast.com	Santa Barbara	CA	93101	800-949-9933		180
Novacopy Inc 7251 Appling Farms Pkwy *TF:* 800-264-0637 ■ *Web:* www.novacopy.net	Memphis	TN	38133	901-388-3399	432-2682	535
Novacro Machining Inc 380 Dewitt Rd *TF:* 800-868-1329 ■ *Web:* novacro.com	Stoney Creek	ON	L8E2T2	905-664-2721		454
Novadaq Technologies Inc 5090 Explorer Dr Ste 202 *TSE: NDQ* ■ *Web:* www.novadaq.com	Mississauga	ON	L4W4T9	905-629-3822		382
NovaDel Pharma Inc 1200 Rt 22 E Ste 2000	Bridgewater	NJ	08807	908-203-4640		582
NovaDigm Therapeutics Inc 4201 James Ray Dr Reac 1 Bldg Ste 2200 *Web:* www.novadigm.net	Grand Forks	ND	58202	701-757-5161	335-7121	479
Novaflex Hose Inc 449 Trollingwood Rd	Haw River	NC	27258	336-578-2161		370
NovaFund Advisors 17 Old Kings Hwy S *Web:* www.novafundadvisors.com	Darien	CT	06820	203-831-0111	604-9584	70
Novagard Solutions Inc 5109 Hamilton Ave *TF:* 800-380-0138 ■ *Web:* www.novagard.com	Cleveland	OH	44114	216-881-8111	881-6977	326
NovaGold Resources Inc 789 W Pender St Ste 720 *NYSE: NG* ■ *TF:* 866-669-6277 ■ *Web:* www.novagold.com	Vancouver	BC	V6C1H2	604-669-6227	669-6272	502
Novak Biddle Venture Partners 7501 Wisconsin Ave E Tower Ste 1380 *Web:* www.novakbiddle.com	Bethesda	MD	20814	240-497-1910	223-0255	792
Novalab Group Inc 2350 Power St *TF:* 800-472-4188 ■ *Web:* www.novadent.com	Drummondville	QC	J2C7Z4	819-474-2580		228
NovaLogic Inc 27489 Agoura Rd *TF:* 800-952-5210 ■ *Web:* www.novalogic.com	Agoura Hills	CA	91301	818-880-1997	865-6405	178-6
NovaMed Corp 30 Nutmeg Dr *Web:* www.novamedcorp.com	Trumbull	CT	06611	203-380-6682		45
Novani 900 Kearny St Ste 388 *Web:* www.novani.com	San Francisco	CA	94133	415-731-1111		177
Novanis 3161 W White Oaks Dr Ste 100 *TF:* 800-544-8932 ■ *Web:* www.novanis.com	Springfield	IL	62704	217-698-0999		180
Novant Health Inc 3333 Silas Creek Pkwy *Web:* www.novanthealth.org	Winston-Salem	NC	27103	336-718-5000		353
Novar Controls Corp 6060 Rockside Woods Blvd Ste 400 **Fax Area Code:* 216 ■ *TF:* 800-348-1235 ■ *Web:* www.novar.com	Cleveland	OH	44131	800-348-1235	682-1614*	202
Novarad Corp 752 E 1180 S Ste 200 *Web:* www.novarad.net	American Fork	UT	84003	801-642-1001		174
Novare Capital Management 521 E Morehead St The Morehead Bldg Ste 510 *TF:* 877-334-3698 ■ *Web:* www.novarecapital.com	Charlotte	NC	28202	704-334-3698		528
Novare Surgical Systems Inc 10440 Bubb Rd Ste A *Web:* www.emvllp.com	Cupertino	CA	95014	408-873-3161		476
Novaria Group Inc 6300 Ridglea Pl Ste 916 *Web:* www.novariagroup.com	Fort Worth	TX	76116	817-381-3810		21
Novariant Inc 46610 Landing Pkwy *Web:* www.novariant.com	Fremont	CA	94538	510-933-4800	933-4801	261
Novartis Institutes For Biomedical Research Inc 250 Massachusetts Ave *Web:* www.nibr.com	Cambridge	MA	02139	617-871-8000		583
Novartis Pharmaceuticals Canada Inc 385 boul Bouchard *TF:* 800-465-2244 ■ *Web:* www.novartis.ca	Dorval	QC	H9S1A9	514-631-6775		582
Novartis Pharmaceuticals Co 25 Old Mill Rd **Fax Area Code:* 973 ■ *TF:* 888-669-6682 ■ *Web:* www.us.novartis.com	Suffern	NY	10901	845-368-6000	781-3721*	582
Novartis Vaccines & Diagnostics 350 Massachusetts Ave *NYSE: NVS* ■ *Web:* www.novartis-vaccines.com	Cambridge	MA	02139	862-778-8300		85
Novasel & Schwarte Investments Inc 3170 Hwy 50 Ste 10	South Lake Tahoe	CA	96150	530-577-5050		690
Novaspect Inc 1124 Tower Rd *Web:* www.novaspect.com	Schaumburg	IL	60173	847-956-8020	885-8200	203
Novastar Financial Inc 2114 Central Ste 600 *TF:* 800-591-1137 ■ *Web:* www.novationcompanies.com	Kansas City	MO	64108	816-237-7000		654
Novastar Solutions Com LLC 35200 Plymouth Rd *Web:* www.novastar.net	Livonia	MI	48150	734-453-8003		175
NovaStor Corp 29209 Canwood St **Fax:* Sales ■ *TF:* 800-284-5101 ■ *Web:* www.novastor.com	Agoura Hills	CA	91301	805-579-6700	579-6710*	178-12
Novatec Inc 222 Thomas Ave *TF:* 800-237-8379 ■ *Web:* www.novatec.com	Baltimore	MD	21225	410-789-4811	789-4638	318
Novatech Group Inc 160 Murano St *TF:* 844-986-8001 ■ *Web:* www.groupenovatech.com	Sainte-julie	QC	J3E0C6	844-986-8001		330
Novatek Communications Inc 500 Helendale Rd Ste 280 *Web:* www.novatekcom.com	Rochester	NY	14609	585-482-4070		463
Novato Chamber of Commerce 807 DeLong Ave *TF:* 800-897-1164 ■ *Web:* www.novatochamber.com	Novato	CA	94945	415-897-1164	898-9097	139
NovaTract Surgical Inc 170 Ft Path Rd Ste 13 *Web:* www.novatract.com	Madison	CT	06443	203-533-9710		250
Novatron Corp 401 Loop 59	Atlanta	TX	75551	903-799-6560		472
Novatronics Inc 677 Erie St *TF:* 800-992-1311 ■ *Web:* www.novatronics.com	Stratford	ON	N5A6V6	519-271-3880		504
Novavax Inc 9920 Belward Campus Dr *NASDAQ: NVAX* ■ *TF:* 800-642-1687 ■ *Web:* www.novavax.com	Rockville	MD	20850	240-268-2000	268-2100	85
NovaVision Inc 6401 Congress Ave Ste 140 *Web:* www.novavision.com	Boca Raton	FL	33487	561-558-2000		476
Noveda Technologies Inc 1200 US Hwy 22 E Ste 2000 *Web:* www.noveda.com	Bridgewater	NJ	08807	908-534-8855		536
Novel Iron Works Inc 250 Ocean Rd *Web:* www.noveliron.com	Greenland	NH	03840	603-436-7950		480
Novelaire Technologies LLC 10132 Mammoth Ave *Web:* www.novelaire.com	Baton Rouge	LA	70814	225-924-0427		14
Novelis North America 3560 Lenox Rd Ste 2000 *Web:* www.novelis.com	Atlanta	GA	30326	404-760-4000		485
Novell Design Studio 2100 Felver Ct **Fax Area Code:* 908 ■ *TF:* 888-668-3551 ■ *Web:* www.novelldesignstudio.com	Rahway	NJ	07065	888-668-3551	245-5090*	409
Novelty Inc 351 W Muskegon Dr *Web:* www.noveltyinc.com	Greenfield	IN	46140	317-462-3121		345
November Research Group LLC 2120 University Ave Ste 250 *TF:* 800 713 7278 ■ *Web:* www.novemberresearch.com	Berkeley	CA	94704	415-987-3313		177
Noven Pharmaceuticals Inc 11960 SW 144th St *Web:* www.noven.com	Miami	FL	33186	305-253-5099	251-1887	582
Noventi Ventures 8100 Jarvis Ave Ste 110 *Web:* www.noventivc.com	Newark	CA	94560	650-325-6699	325-7799	792
Noveo Technologies Inc 9655 A Ignace St *TF:* 877-314-2044 ■ *Web:* www.noveo.ca	Brossard	QC	J4Y2P3	450-444-2044		610
Novex Software Developments Inc 8743 Commercial St **Fax Area Code:* 902 ■ *TF:* 888-542-1813 ■ *Web:* novexsoftware.com	New Minas	NS	B4N3C4	888-542-1813	542-1842*	177
Novi Chamber of Commerce, The 41875 W 11 Mile Rd Ste 201 *TF:* 888-440-7325 ■ *Web:* www.novichamber.com	Novi	MI	48375	248-349-3743	349-9719	139
Novi Industries Inc 44000 Grand River	Novi	MI	48375	248-596-0326		811
Novi Precision Products Inc 11777 E Grand River Ave *TF:* 800-691-5792 ■ *Web:* www.noviprecision.com	Brighton	MI	48116	810-227-1024	227-6160	207

Name / Address	City	State	Zip	Phone	Fax	Class
Novi Public Library 45255 W 10 Mile Rd *Web:* www.novilibrary.org	Novi	MI	48375	248-349-0720	349-6520	434-3
NOVIPRO Inc 2055 Peel St Ste 701 *TF:* 866-726-5353 ■ *Web:* www.novipro.com	Montreal	QC	H3A1V4	514-744-5353		180
Novitas Capital 435 Devon Pk Dr Ste 801 *Web:* www.novitascapital.com	Wayne	PA	19087	610-293-4075	254-4240	405
Novix Network Specialists Inc 2000 W Main St Ste J *Web:* www.novixinc.com	Saint Charles	IL	60174	630-443-0036		180
Novo Nordisk of North America Inc 100 College Rd W *TF:* 800-727-6500 ■ *Web:* www.novonordisk-us.com	Princeton	NJ	08540	609-987-5800		582
Novo Nordisk Pharmaceuticals Inc 800 Scudders Mill Rd *TF Cust Svc:* 800-727-6500 ■ *Web:* www.novonordisk-us.com	Princeton	NJ	08536	609-987-5800		582
Novo Solutions Inc 516 S Independence Blvd *TF:* 888-316-4559 ■ *Web:* www.novosolutions.com	Virginia Beach	VA	23452	757-687-6590		180
Novocol Pharmaceutical of Canada Inc 25 Wolseley Ct *Web:* www.septodont.ca	Cambridge	ON	N1R6X3	519-623-4800		231
novoGI Inc PO Box 12363 *TF:* 866-295-7125 ■ *Web:* www.novogi.com	Atlanta	GA	30355	866-295-7125		475
Novogradac & Company LLP 246 First St 5th Fl *Web:* www.novoco.com	San Francisco	CA	94105	415-356-8000	356-8001	2
Novologic Inc 279 W Crogan St *Web:* www.novologic.com	Lawrenceville	GA	30046	770-277-1030		463
Novologix Inc 10400 Viking Dr	Eden Prairie	MN	55344	952-826-2500		225
Novosci 2021 Airport Rd *TF:* 800-854-0567 ■ *Web:* www.novosci.us	Conroe	TX	77301	281-363-4949		476
Novosoft Inc 3803 Mt Bonnel Rd *TF:* 800-598-5532 ■ *Web:* www.novosoft.us	Austin	TX	78731	512-454-1140		177
Novotech Technologies Corp 57 Iber Rd Unit 2 *Web:* www.novotech.com	Ottawa	ON	K2S1E7	613-280-1900		196
Novus Inc 655 Calle Cubitas *TF:* 888-530-4546 ■ *Web:* www.novushoes.com	Guaynabo	PR	00969	787-272-4546	272-4500	301
Novus Law LLC 8770 W Bryn Mawr Ave *Web:* www.novuslaw.com	Chicago	IL	60631	773-632-5900		445
Novus LLC 338 Commerce Dr *Web:* www.novusllc.com	Fairfield	CT	06825	203-331-1112		179
Novus Ventures LP 20111 Stevens Creek Blvd Ste 130	Cupertino	CA	95014	408-252-3900		402
NOVX Systems Inc 9133 Leslie St Ste 110 *TF:* 877-879-6689 ■ *Web:* www.novxsystems.com	Richmond Hill	ON	L4B4N1	905-474-5051		743
NOW (National Organization for Women) 1100 H St NW 3rd Fl *TF:* 855-212-0212 ■ *Web:* www.now.org	Washington	DC	20005	202-628-8669	785-8576	48-24
Now 102.9 14001 N Dallas Pkwy Ste 300 *Web:* www.1029now.com	Dallas	TX	75240	214-866-8000		645-44
Now Courier Inc PO Box 6066 *Fax Area Code: 317 ■ *TF:* 800-543-6066 ■ *Web:* www.nowcourier.com	Indianapolis	IN	46206	800-543-6066	638-5750*	459
NOW Inc 7402 N Eldridge Pkwy *TF:* 800-228-2893 ■ *Web:* www.distributionnow.com	Houston	TX	77041	281-823-4700		530
NOW Magazine 192 Spadina Ave *Web:* www.nowtoronto.com	Toronto	ON	M5T2C2	416-364-1300	364-1166	532-5
NOW Solutions Inc 101 W Renner Rd Ste 300 *Web:* www.nowsolutions.com	Richardson	TX	75082	972-437-3339		177
Nowak Assoc Inc 6075 E Molloy Rd *Web:* www.nowakagency.com	Syracuse	NY	13211	518-452-4200		4
Nowata County 229 N Maple St	Nowata	OK	74048	918-273-0127	273-1936	338
Nowata Printing Co Po Box 472 *TF:* 800-247-6986 ■ *Web:* www.nowataprinting.com	Nowata	OK	74048	918-273-1950		627
Nowcom Corp 4751 Wilshire Blvd Ste 115 *TF:* 800-641-6700 ■ *Web:* www.nowcom.com	Los Angeles	CA	90010	323-692-4040		180
NowDocs International Inc 1985 Lookout Dr *TF:* 888-669-3627 ■ *Web:* www.nowdocs.com	North Mankato	MN	56003	888-669-3627		177
Nowhirecom 21220 Kelly Rd *TF:* 800-724-8546 ■ *Web:* www.nowhire.com	Eastpointe	MI	48021	586-778-8491		260
Nox-Crete Inc 1444 S 20th St *TF:* 800-669-2738 ■ *Web:* www.nox-crete.com	Omaha	NE	68108	402-341-2080	341-9752	145
Noxent Inc 6400 Boul Taschereau Bur 220 *TF:* 800-268-4364 ■ *Web:* www.noxent.com	Brossard	QC	J4W3J2	800-268-4364		196
Noxubee County 198 Washington St PO Box 308 *TF:* 800-487-0165 ■ *Web:* noxubeealliance.com	Macon	MS	39341	662-726-4456		338
Noyce Foundation 419 S San Antonio Rd Ste 213 *Web:* www.noycefdn.org	Los Altos	CA	94022	650-856-2600		305
Noyes Museum of Art 733 Lily Lake Rd *Web:* www.noyesmuseum.org	Oceanville	NJ	08231	609-652-8848		520
NP Dodge Real Estate 8701 W Dodge Rd Ste 300 *TF:* 800-642-5008 ■ *Web:* www.npdodge.com	Omaha	NE	68114	402-397-4900		652
NPA (National Parking Assn) 1112 16th St NW Ste 840 *TF:* 800-647-7275 ■ *Web:* weareparking.org	Washington	DC	20036	202-296-4336	296-3102	49-3
Npa Computers Inc 751 Coates Ave *TF:* 800-873-6724 ■ *Web:* www.npacomputers.com	Holbrook	NY	11741	631-467-2500		175
NPAP (National Psychological Assn for Psychoanalysis) 40 W 13th St Ste 1 *TF:* 800-365-7006 ■ *Web:* www.npap.org	New York	NY	10011	212-924-7440	989-7543	49-15
nParallel LLC 13120 County Rd 6 *Web:* www.nparallel.com	Minneapolis	MN	55441	763-231-4800		195
NPAworldwide 1680 Viewpond Dr SE *TF:* 800-318-4983 ■ *Web:* www.npaworldwide.com	Grand Rapids	MI	49508	616-455-6555		193
NPC (Navy Personnel Command) 5720 Integrity Dr *TF:* 866-827-5672 ■ *Web:* www.public.navy.mil	Millington	TN	38055	901-874-3165	874-2615	340-6
NPC (National Press Club) 529 14th St NW *Web:* www.press.org	Washington	DC	20045	202-662-7500	662 7569	49-14
NPC (National Pharmaceutical Council) 1894 Preston White Dr *Web:* www.npcnow.org	Reston	VA	20191	703-620-6390	476-0904	49-8
NPC (National Pen Corp) 12121 Scripps Summit Dr Ste 200 *TF:* 800-854-1000 ■ *Web:* www.pens.com	San Diego	CA	92131	858-675-3000		9
NPC Inc 13710 Dunnings Hwy *TF:* 800-847-5757 ■ *Web:* www.npcweb.com	Claysburg	PA	16625	814-239-8787		627
NPC International Inc 7300 W 129th St *TF:* 866-299-1148 ■ *Web:* www.npcinternational.com	Overland Park	KS	66213	913-327-5555	327-5850	670
NPCA (National Precast Concrete Assn) 10333 N Meridian St Ste 272 *TF:* 800-366-7731 ■ *Web:* www.precast.org	Indianapolis	IN	46290	317-571-9500	571-0041	49-3
NPCA (National Paint & Coatings Assn) 1500 Rhode Island Ave NW *Web:* www.paint.org	Washington	DC	20005	202-462-6272	462-8549	49-13
NPCA (National Parks Conservation Assn) 1300 19th St NW Ste 300 *TF:* 800-628-7275 ■ *Web:* www.npca.org	Washington	DC	20036	202-223-6722		48-13
NPCA (National Peace Corps Assn) 1900 L St NW Ste 610 *TF:* 800-336-1616 ■ *Web:* peacecorpsconnect.org	Washington	DC	20036	202-293-7728	293-7554	48-5
NPCS (New Philadelphia City School District) 248 Front Ave SW *Web:* www.npschools.org	New Philadelphia	OH	44663	330-364-0600	364-9310	186
NPD Group Inc 900 W Shore Rd *TF:* 866-444-1411 ■ *Web:* www.npd.com	Port Washington	NY	11050	516-625-0700		466
Nperspective LLC 5971 Brick Ct Ste 100-B *Web:* www.nperspective.net	Winter Park	FL	32792	407-679-7600		2
NPES: Assn for Suppliers of Printing Publishing & Converting Technologies 1899 Preston White Dr *TF:* 866-381-9839 ■ *Web:* www.npes.org	Reston	VA	20191	703-264-7200	620-0994	49-16
NPF (National Park Foundation) 1201 Eye St NW Ste 550-B *Web:* www.nationalparks.org	Washington	DC	20005	202-354-6460	371-2066	48-13
NPF (National Psoriasis Foundation) 6600 SW 92nd Ave Ste 300 *TF:* 800-723-9166 ■ *Web:* www.psoriasis.org	Portland	OR	97223	503-244-7404	245-0626	48-17
NPF (National Press Foundation) 1211 Connecticut Ave NW Ste 310 *Web:* www.nationalpress.org	Washington	DC	20036	202-663-7280		49-16
NPG (Negative Population Growth) 2861 Duke St Ste 36 *Web:* www.npg.org	Alexandria	VA	22314	703-370-9510	370-9514	48-13
Npg of Oregon Inc 62990 O B Riley Rd *Web:* www.ktvz.com	Bend	OR	97701	541-383-2121		116
NPGA (National Propane Gas Assn) 1899 L St NW Ste 350 *TF:* 800-328-1111 ■ *Web:* www.npga.org	Washington	DC	20036	202-466-7200	466-7205	48-12
NPI (National Property Inspections Inc) 9375 Burt St Ste 201 *TF:* 800-333-9807	Omaha	NE	68114	402-333-9807		365
NPIC (National Pesticide Information Ctr) 333 Weniger Hall *Fax Area Code: 541 ■ *TF:* 800-858-7378 ■ *Web:* www.npic.orst.edu	Corvallis	OR	97331	800-858-7378	737-0761*	48-17
NPL (Nampa Public Library) 215 12th Ave S	Nampa	ID	83651	208-468-5800		434-3
NPL (Newton Public Library) 100 N Third Ave W PO Box 746 *Web:* newton.lib.ia.us	Newton	IA	50208	641-792-4108	791-0729	434-3
npm Inc 200 Frank H Ogawa Plaza Fifth Fl Ste 500 *Web:* www.npmjs.com	Oakland	CA	94612	619-339-2014		196
NPMA (National Pest Management Assn Inc) 10460 N St *TF:* 800-678-6722 ■ *Web:* www.pestworld.org	Fairfax	VA	22030	703-352-6762	352-3031	49-4
NPower 3 Metrotech Ctr Mezzanine Brooklyn *Web:* www.npower.org	New York	NY	11201	212-564-7010	564-7009	506
NPPA (National Press Photographers Assn) 3200 Croasdaile Dr Ste 306 *TF:* 800-786-6277 ■ *Web:* www.nppa.org	Durham	NC	27705	919-383-7246	383-7261	49-14
NPPC (National Pork Producers Council) 122 C St NW Ste 875 *TF:* 800-952-4629 ■ *Web:* www.nppc.org	Washington	DC	20001	202-347-3600	347-5265	49-6
NPR (National Public Radio) 635 Massachusetts Ave NW *TF:* 800-989-8255 ■ *Web:* www.npr.org	Washington	DC	20001	202-513-3232	513-3329	632
NPR Illinois 91.9 UIS University of Illinois at Springfield 1 University Plz WUIS-130 *TF:* 866-206-9847 ■ *Web:* www.wuis.org	Springfield	IL	62703	217-206-9847		645-155
NPR West 9909 Jefferson Blvd *Web:* www.npr.org	Culver City	CA	90232	310-815-4200		632
NPRA (National Petrochemical & Refiners Assn) 1667 K St NW Ste 700 *Web:* www.afpm.org	Washington	DC	20006	202-457-0480	457-0486	48-12
NPS (National Park Service) 1849 C St NW Rm 1013 *Web:* www.nps.gov	Washington	DC	20240	202-208-6843	219-0910	340-13
NPSS (IEEE Nuclear & Plasma Sciences Society) 3 Park Ave *TF:* 800-678-4333 ■ *Web:* ieee-npss.org	New York	NY	10016	732-981-0060		49-19
NPT (National Park Trust) 401 E Jefferson St Ste 102 *TF:* 800-995-7525 ■ *Web:* www.parktrust.org	Rockville	MD	20850	301-279-7275	279-7211	48-13
NPTA Alliance 330 N Wabash Ave Ste 2000 *TF:* 800-355-6782 ■ *Web:* www.gonpta.com	Chicago	IL	60611	312-321-4092		49-18
NPTC (National Private Truck Council) 950 N Glebe Rd Ste 2300 *Web:* www.nptc.org	Arlington	VA	22203	703-683-1300	683-1217	49-21
NPWJ (No Peace Without Justice) 866 UN Plaza Ste 408 *Web:* www.npwj.org	New York	NY	10017	212-980-2558	980-1072	48-8

Phone | Fax | Class

nQueue Inc 7890 S Hardy Dr Ste 105 .... Tempe AZ 85284 800-299-5933 180
TF: 800-299-5933 ■ *Web:* www.nqueue.com

NRA (National Rehabilitation Assn)
633 S Washington St .... Alexandria VA 22314 703-836-0850 836-0848 48-17
TF: 888-258-4295 ■ *Web:* www.nationalrehab.org

NRA (National Renderers Assn)
801 N Fairfax St Ste 205................... Alexandria VA 22314 703-683-0155 683-2626 48-2
TF: 800-366-2563 ■ *Web:* www.nationalrenderers.org

NRA (National Restaurant Assn)
2055 L St NW Ste 700 .... Washington DC 20036 202-331-5900 331-2429 49-6
TF: 800-424-5156 ■ *Web:* www.restaurant.org

NRA (Naval Reserve Assn) 1619 King St....... Alexandria VA 22314 703-548-5800 683-3647* 48-19
**Fax Area Code:* 866 ■ *TF:* 877-628-9411 ■ *Web:* ausn.org

NRA Group LLC 2491 Paxton St.............. Harrisburg PA 17111 717-540-7636 160
TF: 800-360-9953 ■ *Web:* www.nationalrecovery.com

NRA Institute for Legislative Action
11250 Waples Mill Rd .... Fairfax VA 22030 800-392-8683 267-3918* 615
**Fax Area Code:* 703 ■ *TF:* 800-392-8683 ■ *Web:* www.nraila.org

NRAA (National Renal Administrators Assn)
100 N 20th St.........................Philadelphia PA 19103 215-320-4655 564-2175 49-8
TF: 800-638-8299 ■ *Web:* www.nraa.org

NRAO (National Radio Astronomy Observatory)
520 Edgemont Rd..................... Charlottesville VA 22903 434-296-0211 296-0278 668
Web: www.nrao.edu

NRB (National Religious Broadcasters)
9510 Technology Dr....................... Manassas VA 20110 703-330-7000 330-7100 49-14
TF: 800-248-4242 ■ *Web:* www.nrb.org

NRB Inc 115 S Service Rd W.................Grimsby ON L3M4G3 905-945-9622 186
TF: 800-782-1500 ■ *Web:* www.nrb-inc.com

NRC (National Research Council)
500 Fifth St NW .... Washington DC 20001 202-334-2000 48-11
Web: www.nationalacademies.org/nrc

NRC Realty & Capital Advisors LLC
363 W Erie St Ste 300 E......................Chicago IL 60654 312-278-6800 652
Web: www.nrc.com

NRC Sports Inc 603 Pleasant St................. Paxton MA 01612 800-243-5033 459
TF: 800-243-5033 ■ *Web:* www.nrcsports.com

NRCA (National Roofing Contractors Assn)
10255 W Higgins Rd Ste 600............... Rosemont IL 60018 847-299-9070 299-1183 49-3
TF Cust Svc: 800-323-9545 ■ *Web:* www.nrca.net

NRCAPAC (National Roofing Contractors Assn PAC)
324 Fourth St NE .... Washington DC 20002 202-546-7584 546-9289 615
Web: nrca.net

NRCCE (National Research Ctr for Coal & Energy)
West Virginia University
385 Evansdale Dr PO Box 6064.......... Morgantown WV 26506 304-293-2867 293-3749 668
TF: 800-624-8301 ■ *Web:* www.nrcce.wvu.edu

Nrccua 3651 NE Ralph Powell Rd..........Lees Summit MO 64064 816-525-2201 205
TF: 800-876-1117 ■ *Web:* www.nrccua.org

NRCDV (National Resource Ctr on Domestic Violence)
6400 Flank Dr Ste 1300 .... Harrisburg PA 17112 800-799-7233 545-9456* 48-6
**Fax Area Code:* 717 ■ *TF:* 800-799-7233 ■ *Web:* www.nrcdv.org

NRCNAA (National Resource Ctr on Native American Aging)
501 N Columbia Rd Rm 4535...............Grand Forks ND 58202 701-777-6780 777-6779 48-6
TF: 800-896-7628 ■ *Web:* ruralhealth.und.edu

NRD LLC 2937 Alt Blvd PO Box 310 .... Grand Island NY 14072 716-773-7634 773-7744 201
TF: 800-525-8076 ■ *Web:* www.nrdstaticcontrol.com

NRDC (Natural Resources Defense Council)
40 W 20th St............................New York NY 10011 212-727-2700 727-1773 48-13
TF: 800-497-2912 ■ *Web:* www.nrdc.org

NREC (National Railway Equipment Co)
14400 Robey St ....Dixmoor IL 60426 708-388-6002 650
TF: 800-253-2905 ■ *Web:* www.nre.com

NREC Power Systems 5222 Hwy 311.............Houma LA 70360 985-872-5480 262
TF: 800-851-6732 ■ *Web:* www.nrecps.com

NRECA (Americas electric cooperatives)
4301 Wilson Blvd.......................... Arlington VA 22203 703-907-5939 48-12
Web: www.nreca.coop

NREL (National Renewable Energy Laboratory)
1617 Cole Blvd.............................Golden CO 80401 303-275-3000 275-4053 668
Web: www.nrel.gov

NRF (National Retail Federation)
1101 New York Ave NW .... Washington DC 20005 202-783-7971 737-2849 49-18
TF: 800-673-4692 ■ *Web:* www.nrf.com

NRG Energy Inc 211 Carnegie Ctr ....Princeton NJ 08540 609-524-4500 524-4501 787
NYSE: NRG ■ *Web:* nrg.com

NRG Media 2875 Mt Vernon Rd SE ....Cedar Rapids IA 52403 319-862-0300 643
Web: www.nrgmedia.com

NRH (Navarro Regional Hospital)
3201 W Hwy 22 .... Corsicana TX 75110 903-654-6800 374-3
Web: www.navarrohospital.com

NRHA (National Reining Horse Assn)
3000 NW Tenth St......................Oklahoma City OK 73107 405-946-7400 946-8425 48-3
Web: nrha1.com

NRHA (National Retail Hardware Assn)
5822 W 74th St........................Indianapolis IN 46278 317-290-0338 328-4354 49-18
TF Cust Svc: 800-772-4424 ■ *Web:* www.nrha.org

Nri Electronics Inc 3651 Thurston Ave .... Anoka MN 55303 763-427-9572 625
Web: www.nrielectronics.com

Nrj 98.9 900 Dyouville 1st Fl .... Quebec QC G1R3P7 418-687-9900 687-3106 645-130

NRL (Naval Research Laboratory)
4555 Overlook Ave SW Code 1000...........Washington DC 20375 202-767-3403 668
Web: www.nrl.navy.mil

NRLC (National Right to Life Committee Inc)
512 Tenth St NW.........................Washington DC 20004 202-626-8800 737-9189 48-8
Web: www.nrlc.org

NRMCA (National Ready Mixed Concrete Assn)
900 Spring St............................ Silver Spring MD 20910 301-587-1400 585-4219 49-3
TF: 888-846-7622 ■ *Web:* www.nrmca.org

NRMSC (USGS Northern Rocky Mountain Science Ctr)
2327 University Way Ste 2 .... Bozeman MT 59715 406-994-4293 994-6556 668
Web: www.usgs.gov/centers/norock/connect

NRNC (Nisqually Reach Nature Ctr)
4949 D'Milluhr Rd NE.......................Olympia WA 98516 360-459-0387 50-5
Web: www.nisquallyestuary.org

NRRI (Natural Resources Research Institute)
University of Minnesota Duluth
5013 Miller Trunk Hwy...................... Duluth MN 55811 218-720-4294 720-4219 668
TF: 800-234-0054 ■ *Web:* www.nrri.umn.edu

NRRS (National Recreation Reservation Service)
PO Box 140 .... Ballston Spa NY 12020 518-885-3639 773
TF: 877-444-6777 ■ *Web:* www.recreation.gov

NRS (National Runaway Switchboard)
3141 N Lincoln Ave ....Chicago IL 60657 773-880-9860 929-5150 48-6
TF: 800-786-2929 ■ *Web:* www.1800runaway.org

NRSF (National Reye's Syndrome Foundation)
426 N Lewis St................................Bryan OH 43506 419-924-9000 924-9999 48-17
TF: 800-233-7393 ■ *Web:* www.reyessyndrome.org

NRTA/AARP Bulletin 601 E St NW ....Washington DC 20049 202-434-2277 531-6
TF: 888-867-2277 ■ *Web:* aarp.org/about-aarp/nrta

Nrtoday.com 345 NE Winchester St............Roseburg OR 97470 541-672-3321 673-5994* 532-2
**Fax:* Edit ■ *Web:* www.nrtoday.com

NRTWC (National Right to Work Committee)
8001 Braddock Rd Ste 500..................Springfield VA 22160 703-321-8510 321-9319 49-12
TF: 800-325-7892 ■ *Web:* nrtw.org

NRV Inc N8155 American St......................Ixonia WI 53036 920-261-7000 261-1685 447
TF: 800-558-0002 ■ *Web:* nrvmilk.com

NRWA (National Rural Water Assn)
2915 S 13th St .... Duncan OK 73533 580-252-0629 255-4476 48-12
Web: www.nrwa.org

NRWS (Napa Recycling & Waste Services)
820 Levitin Way PO Box 239 .... Napa CA 94559 707-256-3500 256-3565 804
TF: 800-561-3357 ■ *Web:* www.naparecycling.com

NSA (National Stroke Assn)
9707 E Easter Ln..........................Centennial CO 80112 800-787-6537 649-1328* 48-17
**Fax Area Code:* 303 ■ *TF Cust Svc:* 800-787-6537 ■ *Web:* www.stroke.org

NSA (National Association of Nonprofit Accountants & Consultants)
1801 W End Ave Ste 800 .... Nashville TN 37203 615-373-9880 49-1
TF: 800-231-2524 ■ *Web:* www.nonprofitcpas.com

NSA (National Safety Apparel Inc)
15825 Industrial Pkwy ....Cleveland OH 44135 800-553-0672 941-1130* 576
**Fax Area Code:* 216 ■ *TF:* 800-553-0672 ■ *Web:* www.thinknsa.com

NSA (National Stuttering Assn)
119 W 40th St 14th Fl.......................New York NY 10018 212-944-4050 944-8244 48-17
TF: 800-937-8888 ■ *Web:* www.westutter.org

NSA (National Sheriffs' Assn)
1450 Duke St .... Alexandria VA 22314 703-836-7827 683-6541 49-7
TF: 800-424-7827 ■ *Web:* www.sheriffs.org

NSA (National Society of Accountants)
1010 N Fairfax St .... Alexandria VA 22314 703-549-6400 549-2984 49-1
TF: 800-966-6679 ■ *Web:* www.nsacct.org

NSA (National Speakers Assn)
1500 S Priest Dr .... Tempe AZ 85281 480-968-2552 968-0911 48-4
Web: www.nsaspeaker.org

Nsa Industries LLC
210 Pierce Rd PO Box 54 .... St. Johnsbury VT 05819 802-748-5007 748-0067 697
Web: www.nsaindustries.com

Nsa Nursing Solutions America
2055 State St .... East Petersburg PA 17520 717-560-3863 371
Web: nsinursingsolutions.com

NSAA (National Ski Areas Assn)
133 S Van Gordon St Ste 300................ Lakewood CO 80228 303-987-1111 986-2345 48-23
Web: www.nsaa.org

NSB (Northfield Savings Bank) PO Box 7180....... Barre VT 05641 800-672-2274 70
TF: 800-672-2274 ■ *Web:* www.nsbvt.com

NSBA (National School Boards Assn)
1680 Duke St .... Alexandria VA 22314 703-838-6722 683-7590 49-5
TF: 800-433-9016 ■ *Web:* www.nsba.org

NSBA (National Small Business Assn)
1156 15th St NW Ste 1100.................Washington DC 20005 202-293-8830 872-8543 49-12
TF: 800-345-6728 ■ *Web:* www.nsba.biz

NSBP (National Society of Black Physicists)
1100 N Glebe Rd Ste 1010................... Arlington VA 22201 703-536-4207 49-19
Web: www.nsbp.org

NSC (National Safety Council)
1121 Spring Lake Dr.......................... Itasca IL 60143 630-285-1121 285-1315 48-17
TF: 800-621-7615 ■ *Web:* www.nsc.org

NSC (National Security Council)
1600 Pennsylvania Ave NW ....Washington DC 20500 202-456-1414 340
TF: 800-382-9467 ■ *Web:* www.whitehouse.gov/nsc

NSC Communications
6820 Power Line Dr ....Florence KY 41042 859-727-6640 647
TF: 800-543-1584 ■ *Web:* www.nsccom.com

NSCA (National Strength & Conditioning Assn)
1885 Bob Johnson Dr............... Colorado Springs CO 80906 719-632-6722 632-6367 48-22
TF: 800-815-6826 ■ *Web:* www.nsca.com

NSCAA (National Soccer Coaches Assn of America)
800 Ann Ave..........................Kansas City KS 66101 913-362-1747 362-3439 48-22
TF: 800-458-0678 ■ *Web:* www.nscaa.com

NSCAD University 5163 Duke St................. Halifax NS B3J3J6 902-444-9600 425-2420 785
Web: www.nscad.ca

NSCAHH (National Student Campaign Against Hunger & Homelessness)
294 Washington St Ste 500 ....Boston MA 02108 312-544-4436 48-5
Web: www.studentsagainsthunger.org

NSCC (Nashville State Community College)
120 White Bridge Rd......................... Nashville TN 37209 615-353-3333 353-3243* 800
**Fax:* Admissions ■ *TF:* 800-272-7363 ■ *Web:* www.nscc.edu

NSCIA (National Spinal Cord Injury Assn)
75-20 Astoria Blvd Ste 120.................East Elmhurst NY 11370 718-512-0010 48-17
TF: 800-962-9629 ■ *Web:* www.spinalcord.org

NSCLC (Justice in Aging)
1444 'I' St Ste 1100 ....Washington DC 20005 202-289-6976 49-10
Web: nsclc.org

NSCP (National Society of Compliance Professionals)
22 Kent Rd ....Cornwall Bridge CT 06754 860-672-0843 672-3005 49-12
Web: www.nscp.org

NSDC (National Staff Development Council)
504 S Locust St .... Oxford OH 45056 513-523-6029 523-0638 49-5
TF: 800-727-7288 ■ *Web:* www.learningforward.org

NSEA Voice Magazine
605 S 14th St Ste 200......................... Lincoln NE 68508 402-475-7611 475-2630 457-8
TF: 800-742-0047 ■ *Web:* www.nsea.org

NSF (National Sleep Foundation)
1522 K St NW Ste 500 ....Washington DC 20005 202-347-3471 347-3472 48-17
TF: 800-586-4872 ■ *Web:* www.sleepfoundation.org

NSF (National Science Foundation)
4201 Wilson Blvd........................... Arlington VA 22230 703-292-5111 292-9232 340-20
TF: 800-877-8339 ■ *Web:* www.nsf.gov

	Phone	Fax	Class
NSF-GFTC 88 McGilvray St....Guelph ON N1G2W1 *TF:* 800-673-6275 ■ *Web:* www.gftc.ca	519-821-1246		2
NSGA (National Senior Golf Assn) 200 Perrine Rd Ste 201....Old Bridge NJ 08857 *Fax Area Code: 732 ■ *TF:* 800-282-6772 ■ *Web:* www.nationalseniorgolf.com	800-282-6772	525-9590*	48-22
NSGA (National Sporting Goods Assn) 1601 Feehanville Dr Ste 300....Mount Prospect IL 60056 *TF:* 800-815-5422 ■ *Web:* www.nsga.org	847-296-6742	391-9827	49-4
NSGC (National Society of Genetic Counselors) 330 N Wabash Ave Ste 2000....Chicago IL 60611 *Web:* www.nsgc.org	312-321-6834	673-6972	48-17
Nsight 450 Security Blvd....Green Bay WI 54313 *Web:* www.nsight.com	920-617-7000		387
NSK & Associates Inc 2 Liberty Sq 7th Fl....Boston MA 02109 *Web:* www.nskinc.com	617-303-0480		809
NSK America Corp 1800 Global Pkwy....Hoffman Estates IL 60192 *TF:* 800-585-4675 ■ *Web:* www.nskamericacorp.com	847-843-7664		491
NSK Canada Inc 5585 Mcadam Rd....Mississauga ON L4Z1N4 *Web:* nskamericas.com	905-890-0740		690
NSK Corp 4200 Goss Rd....Ann Arbor MI 48105 *Fax Area Code: 734 ■ *TF:* 888-446-5675 ■ *Web:* www.nskamericas.com	800-675-9930	913-7102*	620
NSK-AKS Precision Ball Co 1100A N First St....Clarinda IA 51632 *Web:* www.aksball-us.com	712-542-6515		75
Nsl Analytical 4450 Cranwood Pkwy....Cleveland OH 44128 *TF:* 877-560-3943 ■ *Web:* www.nslanalytical.com	216-447-1550		743
NSLA (Nevada State Library & Archives) 100 N Stewart St....Carson City NV 89701 *TF:* 800-922-2880 ■ *Web:* nsla.nv.gov	775-684-3360	684-3311	434-5
NSM Insurance Group Inc 555 N Ln Ste 6060....Conshohocken PA 19428 *Web:* www.nsminc.com	610-941-9877		390
NSMA (Nevada State Medical Assn) 3700 Barron Way....Reno NV 89511 *Web:* nvdoctors.org	775-825-6788		474
NSMC (North Suburban Medical Ctr) 9191 Grant St....Thornton CO 80229 *TF:* 877-647-7440 ■ *Web:* www.northsuburban.com	303-451-7800	450-4458	374-3
NSMRL (Naval Submarine Medical Research Laboratory) PO Box 900....Groton CT 06349 *Fax Area Code: 860 ■ *Web:* www.med.navy.mil/sites/nsmrl/Pages/default.aspx	703-681-9025	694-4809*	668
NSNA (National Student Nurses Assn) 45 Main St Ste 606....Brooklyn NY 11201 *Web:* www.nsna.org	718-210-0705	210-0710	49-8
NSO Press Inc 1921 E 68th Ave....Denver CO 80229 *TF:* 800-955-6246 ■ *Web:* www.nsopress.com	303-227-1400		687
NSP (National Ski Patrol System Inc) 133 S Van Gordon St Ste 100....Lakewood CO 80228 *TF:* 800-222-5754 ■ *Web:* www.nsp.org	303-988-1111		49-7
NSPA (National Scholastic Press Assn) 2221 University Ave SE Ste 121....Minneapolis MN 55414 *Web:* www.studentpress.org/nspa	612-625-8335	626-0720	48-11
NSPE (National Society of Professional Engineers) 1420 King St....Alexandria VA 22314 *TF:* 888-285-6773 ■ *Web:* www.nspe.org	703-684-2800	836-4875	49-19
Nspire Health Inc 1830 Lefthand Cir....Longmont CO 80501 *TF:* 800-574-7374 ■ *Web:* www.nspirehealth.com	303-666-5555	666-5588	476
NSPR (National Recreation and Park Assn) 22377 Belmont Ridge Rd 22377 Belmont Ridge Rd....Ashburn VA 20148 *TF:* 800-626-6772 ■ *Web:* www.nrpa.org	703-858-0784	858-0794	48-23
NSPRA (National School Public Relations Assn) 15948 Derwood Rd....Rockville MD 20855 *Web:* www.nspra.org	301-519-0496	519-0494	49-5
NSRA (National Shoe Retailers Assn) 7386 N La Cholla Blvd....Tucson AZ 85741 *TF:* 800-673-8446 ■ *Web:* www.nsra.org	520-209-1710		49-18
NSS (National Slovak Society of the USA) 351 Vly Brook Rd....McMurray PA 15317 *TF:* 800-488-1890 ■ *Web:* www.nsslife.org	724-731-0094	731-0145	48-14
NSS Corp 264 S River Rd Ste 520....Bedford NH 03110	603-296-2900		809
NSSAR (National Society of the Sons of the American Revolution) 1000 S Fourth St....Louisville KY 40203 *Web:* www.sar.org	502-589-1776	589-1671	48-19
NSSD (North Shore School District 112) 1936 Green Bay Rd....Highland Park IL 60035 *Web:* www.nssd112.org	224-765-3000		685
NSSEA (National School Supply & Equipment Assn) 8380 Colesville Rd Ste 250....Silver Spring MD 20910 *TF:* 800-395-5550 ■ *Web:* edmarket.org	301-495-0240	495-3330	49-18
NSSF (National Shooting Sports Foundation) 11 Mile Hill Rd....Newtown CT 06470 *TF:* 866-580-1198 ■ *Web:* www.nssf.org	203-426-1320	426-1087	48-22
NSSGA (National Stone Sand & Gravel Assn) 1605 King St....Alexandria VA 22314 *TF:* 800-342-1415 ■ *Web:* www.nssga.org	703-525-8788	525-7782	49-3
NSSL (National Severe Storms Laboratory) 120 David L Boren Blvd....Norman OK 73072 *Web:* www.nssl.noaa.gov	405-325-6907		668
NSTA (National Science Teachers Assn) 1840 Wilson Blvd....Arlington VA 22201 *TF Sales:* 800-722-6782 ■ *Web:* www.nsta.org	703-243-7100	243-7177	49-5
NSTAR 800 Boylston St....Boston MA 02199 *NYSE:* NST ■ *TF:* 800-662-7764 ■ *Web:* nstar.com	617-424-2000		360-5
NSTAR Global Services Inc 120 Partlo St....Garner NC 27529 *TF:* 877-678-2766 ■ *Web:* www.nstarglobalservices.com	877-678-2766		260
Nstreams Technologies Inc 1914 Junction Ave....San Jose CA 95131	408-734-8889		739
NSWC (Naval Surface Warfare Ctr) 1333 Isaac Hull Ave SE....Washington Navy Yard DC 20376 *Web:* www.navsea.navy.mil/nswc	202-781-4123		668
NSX (National Stock Exchange) 101 Hudson St Ste 1200....Jersey City NJ 07302 *TF:* 800-843-3924 ■ *Web:* www.nsx.com	201-499-3700		691
Nsync Services Inc 850 Greenview Dr....Grand Prairie TX 75050 *TF:* 866-706-7962 ■ *Web:* www.nsyncservices.com	972-641-7426	641-8093	246
NTA (National Textile Assn) 6 Beacon St Ste 1125....Boston MA 02108	617-542-8220		49-13
NTA (National Tour Assn) 546 E Main St....Lexington KY 40508 *TF:* 800-682-8886 ■ *Web:* www.ntaonline.com	859-226-4444	226-4404	48-23
Nta Graphics South Inc 501 Republic Cir....Birmingham AL 35214 *TF:* 888-798-2123 ■ *Web:* www.ntagraphics.com	205-798-2123		627
n-tara Inc 2214 E Fairview Ave....Johnson City TN 37601 *Web:* www.ntara.com	423-926-8272		7
NTB (Nationwide Truck Brokers Inc) 4203 Roger B Chaffee Memorial Blvd SE Ste 2....Grand Rapids MI 49548 *TF:* 800-446-0682 ■ *Web:* www.ntbtrk.com	616-878-5554	878-5569	780
NTB Assoc Inc 525 Louisiana Ave....Shreveport LA 71101 *Web:* ntbainc.com	318-226-9199		261
NTC (Newman Theological College) 10012-84 St....Edmonton AB T6A0B2 *TF:* 844-392-2450 ■ *Web:* www.newman.edu	780-392-2450	462-4013	167-3
NTCA (National Telecommunications Co-op Assn) 4121 Wilson Blvd 10th Fl....Arlington VA 22203 *Web:* www.ntca.org	703-351-2000	351-2001	49-20
NTD (Norwalk Transit District) 275 Wilson Ave....Norwalk CT 06854 *Web:* www.norwalktransit.com	203-852-0000		468
NTD (National Theatre of the Deaf) 139 N Main St....West Hartford CT 06107 *Web:* www.ntd.org	860-236-4193		573-4
NTE Aviation Ltd 1800 Waters Ridge Dr Ste 400....Lewisville TX 75057 *Web:* www.nteaviation.com	972-353-3933	353-3923	770
NTEA (National Truck Equipment Assn) 37400 Hills Tech Dr....Farmington Hills MI 48331 *TF:* 800-441-6832 ■ *Web:* www.ntea.com	248-489-7090	489-8590	49-21
Ntegrity Networks 9652 Canberra Dr....Littleton CO 80130 *Web:* ntegritynetworks.com	303-221-0738		180
Ntelligent Networks Inc 5303 S Florida Ave....Lakeland FL 33813 *Web:* www.ntelligentnetworks.com	863-802-9675		393
NTELOS Holdings Corp 1154 Shenandoah Village Dr....Waynesboro VA 22980 *NASDAQ:* NTLS ■ *TF:* 877-468-3567 ■ *Web:* www.ntelos.com	540-946-3500		736
nternational Propeller Club of the United States 3927 Old Lee Hwy Ste 101-A....Fairfax VA 22030 *Web:* www.propellerclub.us/home	703-691-2777	691-4173	49-21
NTF (National Turkey Federation) 1225 New York Ave NW Ste 400....Washington DC 20005 *TF:* 866-536-7593 ■ *Web:* www.eatturkey.com	202-898-0100	898-0203	48-2
NTG (New Tech Global) 1030 Regional Pk Dr....Houston TX 77060 *Web:* www.ntglobal.com	281-951-4330	951-8719	261
NTG Clarity Networks Inc 2820 Fourteenth Ave Ste 202....Markham ON L3R0S9 *TF:* 800-838-7894 ■ *Web:* www.ntgclarity.com	905-305-1325		224
Nth Consultants Ltd 41700 6 Mile Rd....Northville MI 48168 *Web:* www.nthconsultants.com	248-553-6300		256
Nth Degree Financial Solutions 1500 Noyes St....Evanston IL 60201 *Web:* www.nthdegreefinancial.com	847-328-0907		194
Nth Generation Computing Inc 17055 Camino San Bernardo....San Diego CA 92127 *TF:* 800-467-4448 ■ *Web:* www.nth.com	858-451-2383		180
NTH Power Technologies Inc 555 Mission St Ste 3300....San Francisco CA 94105 *Web:* www.nthpower.com	415-983-9983		792
NthGen Software Inc 4711 Yonge St Ste 506....Toronto ON M2N6K8 *Web:* www.nthgensoftware.com	416-900-0941		224
NTIA (National Telecommunications & Information Administration) 1401 Constitution Ave NW HerbertC Hoover Bldg....Washington DC 20230 *Web:* www.ntia.doc.gov	202-482-7002		340-2
NTIC (Northern Technologies International Corp) 4201 Woodland Rd....Circle Pines MN 55014 *NASDAQ:* NTIC ■ *TF:* 800-328-2433 ■ *Web:* natur-tec.com	763-225-6600		145
N-Tier Solutions Inc 2596 Landmark Dr....Winston-Salem NC 27103 *Web:* www.n-tiersolutions.com	336-765-3500		260
NTIS (National Technical Information Service) 5285 Port Royal Rd....Springfield VA 22161 *TF Orders:* 800-553-6847 ■ *Web:* www.ntis.gov	703-605-6000	605-6900	668
NTL Institute 1901 S Bell St Ste 300....Arlington VA 22202 *Web:* www.ntl.org	202-280-2057		765
NTMA (National Tooling & Machining Assn) 6363 Oak Tree Blvd....Independence OH 44131 *Fax Area Code: 301 ■ *TF:* 800-248-6862 ■ *Web:* www.ntma.org	800-248-6862	248-7104*	49-13
NTN Bearing Corp of America 1600 E Bishop Ct....Mount Prospect IL 60056 *TF:* 800-323-2358 ■ *Web:* www.ntnamericas.com	847-298-7500	699-9744	620
Ntn Bower 2086 Military St S....Hamilton AL 35570 *Web:* ntnbower.com	205-952-9355		75
Ntn Drive Shaft Inc 8251 S International Dr....Columbus IN 47201	812-342-7000		620
Ntn-Bca Corp 401 W Lincoln Ave....Lititz PA 17543	717-627-3623		75
NTN-Bower Corp 707 Bower Rd....Macomb IL 61455 *Web:* www.ntnbower.com	309-837-0440		621
NTP (National Toxicology Program) PO Box 12233....Research Triangle Park NC 27709 *Web:* ntp.niehs.nih.gov	919-541-0530	541-3687	668
NTP Distribution Inc 27150 SW Kinsman Rd....Wilsonville OR 97070 *TF:* 800-242-6987 ■ *Web:* www.ntpdistribution.com	503-570-0171		61
NTP Software 20A NW Blvd Ste 136....Nashua NH 03063 *TF:* 800-226-2755 ■ *Web:* www.ntpsoftware.com	603-622-4400		178-12

Phone | Fax | Class

NTPA (National Tractor Pullers Assn)
6155-B Huntley Rd ... Columbus OH 43229 614-436-1761 436-0964 48-22
Web: www.ntpapull.com

NTRA (National Thoroughbred Racing Assn)
2525 Harrodsburg Rd Ste 510 ... Lexington KY 40504 800-792-6872 48-22
TF: 800-792-6872 ■ *Web:* www.ntra.com

NTS 526 Chestnut St ... Virginia MN 55792 218-741-4290 192
Web: w3.netechnical.com

NTS Communications Inc 1220 Broadway ... Lubbock TX 79401 806-771-0687 186
Web: www.ntscom.com

NTS Development Co
10172 Linn Stn Rd ... Louisville KY 40223 502-426-4800 426-4994 653
Web: www.ntsdevelopment.com

NTS Realty Holdings LP
10172 Linn Station Rd ... Louisville KY 40223 502-426-4800 426-4994 653
NYSE: NLP ■ *Web:* www.ntsdevelopment.com

NTSAD (National Tay-Sachs & Allied Diseases Assn)
2001 Beacon St Ste 204 ... Brighton MA 02135 617-277-4463 277-0134 48-17
TF: 800-906-8723 ■ *Web:* www.ntsad.org

NTSB (National Transportation Safety Board)
490 L'Enfant Plaza SW ... Washington DC 20594 202-314-6000 314-6293 340-20
Web: www.ntsb.gov

NTT DATA, Inc 100 City Sq ... Boston MA 02129 800-745-3263 180
TF: 800-745-3263 ■ *Web:* americas.nttdata.com

NTT DoCoMo USA Inc
757 Third Ave 16th Fl ... New York NY 10017 888-362-6661 736
TF: 888-362-6661 ■ *Web:* www.docomo-usa.com

NTU (National Taxpayers Union)
108 N Alfred St ... Alexandria VA 22314 703-683-5700 683-5722 48-7
TF: 800-680-7289 ■ *Web:* www.ntu.org

NTV International Corp
645 Fifth Ave Ste 303 ... New York NY 10022 212-660-6900 660-6998 514
Web: www.ntvic.com

Nu Horizons Electronics Corp
70 Maxess Rd ... Melville NY 11747 631-396-5000 864-3349* 246
**Fax Area Code:* 256 ■ *TF:* 855-326-4757 ■ *Web:* www.arrow.com

Nu Hotel 85 Smith St ... Brooklyn NY 11201 718-852-8585 378
TF: 800-242-7909 ■ *Web:* www.nuhotelbrooklyn.com

Nu Image Inc 6423 Wilshire Blvd ... Los Angeles CA 90048 310-388-6900 514
Web: www.millenniumfilms.com

Nu Image Marketing 1271 N Tustin Ave ... Anaheim CA 92807 714-575-8947 195
Web: nimarketing.com

Nu Image MedSpa Inc
3753 Howard Hughes Pkwy Ste 200 ... Las Vegas NV 89169 702-784-5922 354

NU Laboratories Inc
312 Old Allerton Rd ... Annandale NJ 08801 908-713-9300 713-9001 743
Web: www.nulabs.com

Nu Promo International
11697 Chesterdale Rd Ste ... Cincinnati OH 45246 513-782-0168 522
Web: 74585.asisupplier.com

Nu Van Technology Inc
2155 Highway 1187 ... Mansfield TX 76063 817-477-1734 779

Nu Way Co-op Inc PO Box Q ... Trimont MN 56176 507-639-2311 276
TF: 800-445-4118 ■ *Web:* www.nuwaycoop.com

Nuance Communications Inc
1 Wayside Rd ... Burlington MA 01803 781-565-5000 178-7
NASDAQ: NUAN ■ *TF:* 800-654-1187 ■ *Web:* www.nuance.com

NuAxis LLC 8603 Westwood Ctr Dr Ste 340 ... Vienna VA 22182 703-481-7400 177
Web: nuaxis.com

NUBE Inc 16238 Ranch Rd Ste F-108 ... Seattle WA 78717 888-400-3133 196
TF: 888-400-3133 ■ *Web:* www.nube.us.com

Nubenco Medical 1 Kalisa Way ... Paramus NJ 07652 201-967-9000 476
TF: 800-633-1322 ■ *Web:* nubenco.com

Nucara Pharmacy 209 E San Marnan Dr ... Waterloo IA 50702 319-236-8891 237
TF: 800-359-2357 ■ *Web:* www.nucara.com

NuCare Pharmaceuticals Inc
622 W Katella Ave ... Orange CA 92867 888-482-9545 583
TF: 888-482-9545 ■ *Web:* www.nucarerx.com

Nu-Cast Inc 29 Grenier Field Rd ... Londonderry NH 03053 603-432-1600 308
Web: www.nu-cast.com

Nucedar Mills Inc 1000 Sheridan St ... Chicopee MA 01022 413-593-8883 596
Web: www.nucedar.com

Nuckolls County PO Box 366 ... Nelson NE 68961 402-225-4361 225-4301 338
Web: www.nuckollscounty.ne.gov

Nuclear Age Peace Foundation (NAPF)
1187 Coast Village Rd Ste 1 PO Box 121 ... Santa Barbara CA 93108 805-965-3443 568-0466 48-5

Nuclear Energy Institute (NEI)
1776 'I' St NW Ste 400 ... Washington DC 20006 202-739-8000 785-4019 48-12
Web: www.nei.org

Nuclear Fuel Services Inc
1205 Banner Hill Rd ... Erwin TN 37650 423-743-9141 143
Web: www.nuclearfuelservices.com

Nuclear Imaging Services LLC
10010 Fairbanks N Houston Rd ... Houston TX 77064 832-467-4404 475
Web: www.nis-mit.com

Nuclear Information & Resource Service (NIRS)
6930 Carroll Ave Ste 340 ... Takoma Park MD 20912 301-270-6477 270-4291 48-8
Web: www.nirs.org
US NRC Region II
61 Forsyth St SW Ste 23T85 ... Atlanta GA 30303 404-562-4400 562-4900 340-20
TF: 800-577-8510 ■ *Web:* www.nrc.gov

Nuclear Regulatory Commission Regional Offices
Region 1
2100 Renaissance Blvd ... King of Prussia PA 19406 610-337-5000 340-20
TF: 800-432-1156 ■ *Web:* www.nrc.gov
Region 3 2443 Warrenville Rd Ste 210 ... Lisle IL 60532 630-829-9500 515-1078 340-20
TF: 800-522-3025 ■ *Web:* www.nrc.gov
Region 4 1600 E Lamar Blvd ... Arlington TX 76011 817-860-8100 340-20
TF: 800-952-9677 ■ *Web:* www.nrc.gov

Nuclear Security Services Corp
701 Willowbrook Centre Pkwy ... Willowbrook IL 60527 630-920-1488 693
TF: 800-275-8319 ■ *Web:* www.g4s.us

Nuclear Waste Technical Review Board (NWTRB)
2300 Clarendon Blvd Ste 1300 ... Arlington VA 22201 703-235-4473 235-4495 340-20
Web: www.nwtrb.gov

NuclearFuel 1200 G St NW Ste 1000 ... Washington DC 20005 202-383-2000 383-2024 531-5
TF: 800-228-9290 ■ *Web:* platts.com/products/nuclear-fuel

Nucleonics Week 2 Penn Plaza 25th Fl ... New York NY 10121 212-904-3070 531-5
TF: 800-752-8878 ■ *Web:* platts.com/products/nucleonics-week

Phone | Fax | Class

Nucleus Software Inc
120 S Wood Ave Ste 10 ... Iselin NJ 08837 732-635-7190 463
Web: www.nucleussoftware.com

NuCo2 Inc 2800 SE Marketplace ... Stuart FL 34997 772-221-1754 781-3500 146
TF: 800-472-2855 ■ *Web:* www.nuco2.com

Nucor Corp 1915 Rexford Rd ... Charlotte NC 28211 704-366-7000 362-4208 480
NYSE: NUE ■ *TF:* 800-294-1322 ■ *Web:* www.nucor.com

Nucor Corp Cold Finish Div
2800 N Governor Williams Hwy ... Darlington SC 29540 704-366-7000 395-8759* 723
**Fax Area Code:* 843 ■ **Fax:* Sales ■ *TF:* 800-333-0590 ■ *Web:* www.nucor.com

Nucor Corp Steel Div 1455 Hagan Ave ... Huger SC 29450 843-336-6000 723
TF: 800-424-9300 ■ *Web:* www.nucorsteel.com

Nucor Corp Vulcraft Div
1501 W Darlington St ... Florence SC 29501 843-662-0381 662-3132 480
Web: www.vulcraft.com

Nucor Steel Marion Inc 912 Cheney Ave ... Marion OH 43302 740-383-4011 492
TF: 800-333-4011 ■ *Web:* www.nucorhighway.com

Nucor-Yamato Steel Co
5929 E State Hwy 18 ... Blytheville AR 72315 870-762-5500 762-1130 723
TF: 800-289-6977 ■ *Web:* www.nucoryamato.com

Nucraft Furniture Co
5151 W River Dr ... Comstock Park MI 49321 616-784-6016 321
TF: 877-682-7238 ■ *Web:* www.nucraft.com

Nucro-Technics
2000 Ellesmere Rd Unit 16 ... Scarborough ON M1H2W4 416-438-6727 438-3463 85
Web: www.nucro-technics.com

NucSafe Inc 601 Oak Ridge Tpke ... Oak Ridge TN 37830 865-220-5050 419
Web: www.nucsafe.com

Nudo Products Inc 1500 Taylor Ave ... Springfield IL 62703 217-528-5636 528-8722 751
TF: 800-826-4132 ■ *Web:* www.nudo.com

Nueces County
901 Leopard St Ste 201 ... Corpus Christi TX 78401 361-888-0111 338
Web: www.nuecesco.com

Nueces Electric Co-op (NEC)
709 E Main St PO Box 260970 ... Robstown TX 78380 361-387-2581 245
TF: 800-632-9288 ■ *Web:* www.nueceselectric.org

Nueces Farm Center Inc
4587 US-77 Business ... Robstown TX 78380 361-289-0066 274
TF: 800-660-8921 ■ *Web:* www.nuecesfarmcenter.net

Nuesoft Technologies Inc
1685 Terrell Mill Rd ... Marietta GA 30067 678-303-1140 177
TF: 800-981-5084 ■ *Web:* www.nuemd.com

Nuevo Laredo 1495 Chattahoochee Ave ... Atlanta GA 30318 404-352-9009 671
Web: www.nuevolaredocantina.com

Nuezra 2620 Augustine Dr Ste 101 ... Santa Clara CA 95054 408-492-9856 261

NuFACTOR Inc
41093 County Ctr Dr Ste B ... Temecula CA 92591 951-296-2516 237
Web: www.nufactor.com

Nugget Markets 157 Main St ... Woodland CA 95695 530-662-5479 668-1246 345
Web: www.nuggetmarket.com

Nugget, The 259 Worthington St W ... North Bay ON P1B3B5 705-472-3200 472-1438 532-1
Web: www.nugget.ca

NuGrowth Solutions
4181 ArlingGate Plaza ... Columbus OH 43228 800-966-3051 388-5811* 195
**Fax Area Code:* 614 ■ *TF:* 800-966-3051 ■ *Web:* nugrowth.com

Nuherbs co 14722 Wicks Blvd ... San Leandro CA 94577 510-534-4372 297-8
TF: 800-233-4307 ■ *Web:* www.nuherbs.com

Nu-Hope Laboratories Inc
12640 Branford St ... Pacoima CA 91331 818-899-7711 477
TF: 800-899-5017 ■ *Web:* www.nu-hope.com

Nujak Development Inc
711 N Kentucky Ave ... Lakeland FL 33801 863-686-1565 186
TF: 888-685-2526 ■ *Web:* www.nujak.com

Nuka Research & Planning Group LLC
1451 N Boone Ln ... Seldovia AK 99663 907-234-7821 192
Web: www.nukaresearch.com

Nulab Inc 2180 Calumet St ... Clearwater FL 33765 727-446-1126 231
Web: www.nulabinc.com

Nulaid Foods Inc 200 W Fifth St ... Ripon CA 95366 209-599-2121 599-5220 297-10
TF: 800-872-3447 ■ *Web:* www.nulaid.com

Nulayer Inc 72 Fraser Ave Ste 201 ... Toronto ON M6K3J7 416-840-4384 463
TF: 800-333-7680 ■ *Web:* www.nulayer.com

Nu-Life Environmental Inc PO Box 1527 ... Easley SC 29641 864-855-5155 385
TF: 800-654-1752 ■ *Web:* www.nulifeenv.com

Nu-Lite Electrical Wholesalers
850 Edwards Ave ... Harahan LA 70123 504-733-3300 736-1617 246
TF: 800-256-1603 ■ *Web:* www.nulite.com

Nulton Diagnostic & Treatment Center PC
214 College Pk ... Johnstown PA 15904 814-262-0025 726
TF: 800-428-2105 ■ *Web:* www.nulton.com

Numara Software Inc
2202 NW Shore Blvd Ste 650 ... Tampa FL 33607 813-227-4500 227-4501 178-12
TF Sales: 855-834-7487 ■ *Web:* www.bmc.com

Numark Brands LLC
105 Fieldcrest Ave Ste 502A ... Edison NJ 08837 800-338-8079 225-0066* 582
**Fax Area Code:* 732 ■ *TF:* 800-338-8079 ■ *Web:* www.numarkbrands.com

Numatic Engineering Inc
7915 Ajay Dr ... Sun Valley CA 91352 818-768-1200 358
Web: www.numaticengineering.com

NumbersOnly Inc
1520 State Hwy 130 N Ste 201 ... North Brunswick NJ 08902 732-940-0033 631
Web: www.numbersonly.com

NuMedics Inc 6950 SW Hampton Rd Ste 221 ... Tigard OR 97223 503-597-3861 174
TF: 800-368-6231 ■ *Web:* www.numedics.com

Numega Solutions LLC
7001 Loisdale Rd ... Springfield VA 22150 703-372-2200 186

Numerex Corp
400 Interstate N Pkwy Ste 1350 ... Atlanta GA 30339 770-693-5950 693-5951 735
NASDAQ: NMRX ■ *TF:* 800-665-5686 ■ *Web:* www.numerex.com

Numeric Computer Systems Inc
275 Oser Ave ... Hauppauge NY 11788 631-486-9000 180
Web: www.ncssuite.com

Numeric Technologies Inc
4200 Cantera Dr ... Warrenville IL 60555 630-955-9060 177
TF: 800-845-8420 ■ *Web:* www.ntsiinc.com

Numerical Control Computer Sciences
2600 Michelson Dr Ste 1700 ... Irvine CA 92612 949-852-3665 553-1911 178-5
Web: www.nccs.com

Company	Phone	Fax	Class
Numerical Precision Inc 2200 Foster Ave ... Wheeling IL 60090 *TF:* 800-252-1272 ■ *Web:* www.numericalprecision.com	847-394-3610	394-3962	454
Numeridex Inc 632 S Wheeling Rd ... Wheeling IL 60090 **Fax Area Code: 847* ■ *TF:* 800-323-7737 ■ *Web:* www.numeridex.com	800-323-7737	541-8392*	112
Numero Uno Web Solutions Inc 7000 Pine Valley Dr Ste 200 ... Vaughan ON L4L4Y8 *Web:* www.numerounoweb.com	905-856-2012		5
Numo Manufacturing Co 1072 E Hwy 175 ... Kaufman TX 75142 *TF:* 800-253-0434 ■ *Web:* www.numomfg.com	972-962-5400		9
Numonics Corp 101 Commerce Dr PO Box 1005 ... Montgomeryville PA 18936 *TF:* 800-523-6716 ■ *Web:* interactivewhiteboards.com	215-362-2766	361-0167	173-1
Numotion 126 Airport Rd ... Scott City MO 63780 *TF:* 877-856-9154 ■ *Web:* www.numotion.com	573-334-0600		475
Nunami Services LLC 410 17th St Ste 570 ... Denver CO 80202 *Web:* www.stockborrow.net	303-914-2819		690
Nunes Devin (Rep R - CA) Longworth HOB Ste 1013 ... Washington DC 20515 *Web:* nunes.house.gov	202-225-2523	225-3404	342-2
Nunhems USA Inc 1200 Anderson Corner Rd ... Parma ID 83660 **Fax: Cust Svc* ■ *TF Cust Svc:* 800-733-9505 ■ *Web:* www.nunhemsusa.com	208-674-4000	674-4090*	694
Nunn-Bush Shoe Co Inc 333 W Estabrook Blvd ... Glendale WI 53212 *Web:* nunnbush.com	414-908-1600		301
Nuo Therapeutics Inc 207A Perry Pkwy Ste 1 ... Gaithersburg MD 20877 *OTC: NUOT* ■ *TF:* 866-298-6633 ■ *Web:* www.nuot.com	866-298-6633		85
NuOrtho Surgical Inc 151 Martine St ... Fall River MA 02723	617-848-8999		477
Nupla Corp 11912 Sheldon St ... Sun Valley CA 91352 *TF:* 800-872-7661 ■ *Web:* www.nuplacorp.com	818-768-6800		610
NURC (NURTEC) University of Connecticut at Avery Pt 1080 Shennecossett Rd ... Groton CT 06340 *Web:* nurtec.uconn.edu	860-405-9121	445-2969	668
NURC (NOAA's Undersea Research Program) University of N Carolina at Wilmington ... Silver Spring MD 20910 **Fax Area Code: 301* ■ *Web:* www.nurp.noaa.gov	910-962-2440	713-1967*	668
Nurol Corp 1531 Marietta Blvd NW ... Atlanta GA 30318 *Web:* nurolpos.com	404-352-3587		88
Nuron Biotech Inc 1 E Uwchlan Ave Ste 302 ... Exton PA 19341	610-968-6700	968-6650	231
Nurse Assist Inc 3400 Northern Cross Blvd ... Fort Worth TX 76137 *TF:* 800-649-6800 ■ *Web:* www.nurseassist.com	817-231-1300		475
Nurse On Call Inc 111 Westwood Pl Ste 400 ... Brentwood TN 37027 *TF:* 855-350-3800 ■ *Web:* www.nurseoncallfl.com	855-350-3800		363
Nurse Staffing LLC 1700 Route 23 N Ste 100 ... Wayne NJ 07470 *Web:* www.nursesapply.com	973-709-1009		193
Nursefinders Inc 12400 High Bluff Dr ... San Diego CA 92130 *TF:* 800-445-0459 ■ *Web:* www.nursefinders.com	877-214-4105		721
Nursery Supplies Inc 1415 Orchard Dr ... Chambersburg PA 17201 *Web:* www.nurserysupplies.com	717-263-7780		596
Nurserymen's Exchange 2651 N Cabrillo Hwy ... Half Moon Bay CA 94019 *TF General:* 800-227-5229 ■ *Web:* www.rocketfarms.com	650-712-4195	712-4290	369
Nurses Unlimited Inc 4100 E Piedras Dr Ste 105 ... San Antonio TX 78228 *Web:* nursesunlimited.com	210-732-4184		363
Nursing Ctr 323 Norristown Rd Ste 200 ... Ambler PA 19002 *TF:* 800-346-7844 ■ *Web:* www.nursingcenter.com	800-787-8985		397
Nursing Ctr 3701 N Martin Luther King Jr Blvd ... Tulsa OK 74106 *TF:* 800-362-1314 ■ *Web:* saintsimeons.org	918-425-3583		793
Nursing Enterprises Inc 5101 Wisconsin Ave NW Ste 250 ... Washington DC 20016	202-526-2400		363
Nursing Personnel Homecare Inc 175 S Ninth St ... Brooklyn NY 11211 *TF:* 800-994-6610 ■ *Web:* www.nursingpersonnelhomecare.com	718-218-8991		371
Nursing Spectrum Greater New York/New Jersey Metro Magazine 1721 Moon Lake Blvd Ste 540 ... Hoffman Estates IL 60169 *TF:* 800-770-0866 ■ *Web:* www.nurse.com	800-770-0866		457-16
NURTEC (NURC) University of Connecticut at Avery Pt 1080 Shennecossett Rd ... Groton CT 06340 *Web:* nurtec.uconn.edu	860-405-9121	445-2969	668
Nushagak Electric & Telephone Co-op Inc 557 Kenny Wren Rd ... Dillingham AK 99576 *TF:* 800-478-5296 ■ *Web:* www.nushtel.com	907-842-5251	842-2799	245
Nussbaum Trucking Inc 19336 N 1425 East Rd ... Normal IL 61748 *TF:* 800-322-7305 ■ *Web:* www.nussbaum.com	309-452-4426		780
Nussbaumer & Clarke Inc 3556 Lake Shore Rd Ste 500 ... Buffalo NY 14219 *TF:* 800-333-2086 ■ *Web:* www.nussclarke.com	716-827-8000		261
Nussle Group, The 828 Slaters Ln Ste 104 ... Alexandria VA 22314	202-540-9045		463
NuStar GP Holdings LLC 19003 I-10 W ... San Antonio TX 78257 *NYSE: NSH* ■ *TF:* 800-866-9060 ■ *Web:* www.nustargpholdings.com	210-918-2000		360-3
Nu-Star Inc 1425 Stagecoach Rd ... Shakopee MN 55379 *TF:* 800-800-9274 ■ *Web:* www.nustarinc.com	952-445-8295		54
NuStar Terminal Canada Partnership 4090 Port Malcolm Rd ... Point Tupper NS B9A1Z5	902-625-1711	625-3098	581
NuStep Inc 5111 Venture Dr Ste 1 ... Ann Arbor MI 48108 *Web:* www.nustep.com	734-769-3939		710
NuTEC Manufacturing 908 Garnet Ct ... New Lenox IL 60451 *Web:* nutecmfg.com	815-722-2800		296
Nu-Tec Tooling Company Inc 13115 State Rt 405 ... Watsontown PA 17777 *TF:* 800-258-9898 ■ *Web:* www.nutectool.com	570-538-2571		249
NuTech Energy Alliance Ltd 7702 FM 1960 E Ste 300 ... Houston TX 77346 *TF:* 800-334-4927 ■ *Web:* www.nutechenergy.com	281-812-4030		727
NuTech Inc 1301 Clinic Dr ... Tyler TX 75701 *Web:* www.nutechrx.com	903-592-8115		231
Nutech Information Systems 1010 Summer St Ste 406 ... Stamford CT 06905 *Web:* www.nutechsoft.com	203-961-8911		180
Nutech Medical Inc 2641 Rocky Ridge Ln ... Birmingham AL 35216 *TF:* 800-824-9194 ■ *Web:* www.nutechmedical.com	205-290-2158		476
Nutechs LLC 6785 Telegraph Rd Ste 350 ... Bloomfield Hills MI 48301 *Web:* www.nutechs.com	248-593-5700		180
Nutfield Technology Inc 1 Wall St Ste 115 ... Hudson NH 03051 *Web:* www.nutfieldtech.com	603-893-6200		407
Nutis Press Inc 3540 E Fulton St ... Columbus OH 43227 *TF:* 800-848-6266 ■ *Web:* nutis.com	614-237-8626		627
Nutley Chamber of Commerce 172 Chestnut St ... Nutley NJ 07110 *TF:* 800-245-1377 ■ *Web:* www.nutleychamber.com	973-667-5300		139
Nutley Free Public Library 93 Booth Dr ... Nutley NJ 07110 *Web:* www.bccls.org	973-667-0405	667-4673	434-3
Nutra Pharma Corp 12502 W Atlantic Blvd ... Coral Springs FL 33071 *TF:* 877-895-5647 ■ *Web:* www.nutrapharma.com	954-509-0911		479
NutraBella Inc 1875 S Grant St Ste 305 ... San Mateo CA 94402 *Web:* www.bellybarproducts.com	650-212-3559		363
Nutra-Blend Inc 3200 Second St ... Neosho MO 64850 *TF:* 800-657-5657 ■ *Web:* www.nutrablend.net	800-657-5657		584
Nutraceutical International Corp 1400 Kearns Blvd ... Park City UT 84060 *NASDAQ: NUTR* ■ *TF:* 800-669-8877 ■ *Web:* www.nutraceutical.com	435-655-6000		799
Nutraceutics Corp 2900 Brannon Ave ... Saint Louis MO 63139 *Web:* www.nutraceutics.com	314-664-6684		231
Nutraceutix Inc 9609 153rd Ave NE ... Redmond WA 98052 *Web:* www.nutraceutix.com	425-883-9518	869-1020	479
Nutramax Laboratories Inc 2208 Lakeside Blvd ... Edgewood MD 21040 *TF:* 800-925-5187 ■ *Web:* www.nutramaxlabs.com	410-776-4000		214
nuTravel Technology Solutions LLC 181 Westchester Ave Ste 302 ... Port Chester NY 10573 *Web:* www.nutravel.com	914-848-4566		180
Nutri Pet Research Inc 227 State Rt 33 ... Manalapan NJ 07726 *Web:* www.nuprosupplements.com	732-786-8822		237
NutriCology Inc 2300 N Loop Rd ... Alameda CA 94502 *Web:* www.nutricology.com	510-263-2000	263-2100	582
NutriCorp International 4025 Rhodes Dr ... Windsor ON N8W5B5 *TF:* 888-446-8874 ■ *Web:* www.nutricorp.com	519-974-8178		743
Nutrifaster Inc 209 S Bennett St ... Seattle WA 98108 *TF:* 800-800-2641 ■ *Web:* www.nutrifaster.com	206-767-5054	762-2209	98
Nutrilawn Inc 25-1040 Martin Grove Rd ... Toronto ON M9W4W4 *Web:* www.nutrilawn.com	416-620-7100		577
Nutrilite Products Inc 5600 Beach Blvd PO Box 5940 ... Buena Park CA 90621 *Web:* www.nutrilite.com	714-562-6200		799
NutriScience Innovations LLC 2450 Reservoir Ave ... Trumbull CT 06611 *Web:* www.nutrisciencеusa.com	203-372-8877	372-9977	479
NutriSystem Inc 600 Office Center Dr Bldg 1 ... Fort Washington PA 19034 *NASDAQ: NTRI* ■ *TF:* 800-585-5483 ■ *Web:* www.nutrisystem.com	215-706-5300		810
Nutrition 21 Inc 1 Manhattanville Rd ... Purchase NY 10577 *Web:* www.nutrition21.com	914-701-4500	696-0860	479
Nutrition Action 1875 Connecticut Way NW Ste 300 ... Washington DC 20009 *Web:* www.cspinet.org	202-332-9110	265-4954	531-8
Nutrition Formulators Inc 10407 N Commerce Pkwy ... Miramar FL 33025 *Web:* www.nutritionformulators.com	954-272-2220		345
Nutrition Management Services Co 2071 Kimberton Rd, Chester Ste ... Kimberton PA 19442 *Web:* www.nmsc.com	610-935-2050		299
Nuts & Volts Magazine 430 Princeland Ct ... Corona CA 92879 *TF Orders:* 800-783-4624 ■ *Web:* www.nutsvolts.com	951-371-8497	371-3052	457-14
Nuttall Gear LLC 2221 Niagra Falls Blvd ... Niagara Falls NY 14304 *TF:* 800-724-6710 ■ *Web:* www.nuttallgear.com	716-298-4100	298-4101	709
Nutting 450 Pheasant Ridge Dr ... Watertown SD 57201 **Fax Area Code: 866* ■ *TF:* 800-533-0337 ■ *Web:* www.accomhs.com	605-882-3000	688-8464*	470
NuVasive Inc 7475 Lusk Blvd ... San Diego CA 92121 *NASDAQ: NUVA* ■ *TF:* 800-475-9131 ■ *Web:* www.nuvasive.com	858-909-1800	909-2000	476
Nuveen Investments Inc 333 W Wacker Dr ... Chicago IL 60606 *TF:* 800-257-8787 ■ *Web:* www.nuveen.com	312-917-7700		690
Nuventive LLC 9800B McKnight Rd Ste 255 ... Pittsburgh PA 15237 *Web:* www.nuventive.com	412-847-0280		179
Nuvera Fuel Cells 129 Concord Rd Bldg 1 ... Billerica MA 01821 *Web:* www.nuvera.com	617-245-7500	245-7511	579
NuView Life Sciences Inc 1389 Center Dr Ste 250 ... Park City UT 84098 *TF:* 888-902-7779 ■ *Web:* www.nuviewinfo.com	888-902-7779		743
NuVision Engineering Inc River Park Commons 2403 Sidney St Ste 700 ... Pittsburgh PA 15203 *TF:* 888-748-8232 ■ *Web:* www.nuvisioneng.com	412-586-1810		256
NuVista Energy Ltd 3500 700 - Second St SW ... Calgary AB T2P2W2 *Web:* www.nuvistaenergy.com	403-538-8500		536
Nuvite Chemical Compounds Corp 213 Freeman St ... Brooklyn NY 11222 *TF:* 800-394-8351 ■ *Web:* www.nuvitechemical.com	718-383-8351	383-0008	151

				Phone	Fax	Class
NUVO Newsweekly 3951 N Meridian St Ste 200	Indianapolis	IN	46208	317-254-2400		532-5
Web: www.nuvo.net						
NuvoMed Inc 2300 E Roy St	Seattle	WA	98112	206-999-9387		475
Nuvue Business Solutions 3061 Berks Way Ste 102	Raleigh	NC	27614	919-562-5599	863-9611*	196
**Fax Area Code:* 888 ■ *TF:* 800-688-8310 ■ *Web:* www.nuvue.com						
NuVue Therapeutics Inc 11135 Sedgefield Rd	Fairfax	VA	22030	703-591-1691		476
TF: 800-368-3529 ■ *Web:* www.nuvuetherapeutics.com						
Nu-Wa Industries Inc 3701 Johnson Rd	Chanute	KS	66720	620-431-2088	431-2513	120
TF: 800-835-0676 ■ *Web:* www.nuwa.com						
NuWare Technology Corp Inc 100 Wood Ave S Ste 122	Iselin	NJ	08830	732-494-0550	494-4586	180
Web: www.nuware.com						
NuWave Technology Partners LLC 5268 Azo Ct	Kalamazoo	MI	49048	269-342-4400		179
TF: 800-557-1238 ■ *Web:* www.nuwavepartners.com						
NuWay Burgers 3441 E Harry	Wichita	KS	67218	316-684-6132		671
Web: www.nuwayburgers.com						
Nu-Way Industries Inc 555 Howard Ave	Des Plaines	IL	60018	847-298-7710	635-8650	697
TF: 888-488-5631 ■ *Web:* www.nuwayindustries.com						
NUWC (Naval Undersea Warfare Ctr) 1176 Howell St	Newport	RI	02841	401-832-7742	832-4396	668
TF: 800-356-8464 ■ *Web:* www.navsea.navy.mil/nuwc						
Nu-Wool Company Inc 2472 Port Sheldon Rd	Jenison	MI	49428	616-669-0100	669-2370	389
TF: 800-748-0128 ■ *Web:* www.nuwool.com						
Nu-Yale Cleaners 6300 Hwy 62	Jeffersonville	IN	47130	812-285-7400	285-7421	426
TF: 888-644-7400 ■ *Web:* www.nuyale.com						
Nuzoo Media Inc 606 W 18th St Apt 3	Chicago	IL	60616	312-421-2129		7
Web: www.nuzoo.com						
Nuzzo & Roberts LLC 1 Town Ctr	Cheshire	CT	06410	203-250-2000		428
TF: 800-973-1177 ■ *Web:* www.nuzzo-roberts.com						
NV Heathorn Co 1155 Beecher St	San Leandro	CA	94577	510-569-9100	569-9106	189-10
Web: www.nvheathorn.com						
NV5 2525 Natomas Pk Dr Ste 300	Sacramento	CA	95833	916-641-9100	641-9222	261
TF: 877-311-4180 ■ *Web:* www.nv5.com						
NVC Logistics Group Inc 1 Pond Rd	Rockleigh	NJ	07647	201-767-0911		311
Web: www.nvclogistics.com						
NVCA (National Venture Capital Assn) 25 Massachusetts Ave NW Ste 730	Washington	DC	20001	703-524-2549	524-3940	615
TF: 800-956-2682 ■ *Web:* www.nvca.org						
NVE Corp 11409 Vly View Rd	Eden Prairie	MN	55344	952-829-9217	996-1600	696
NASDAQ: NVEC ■ *TF:* 800-467-7141 ■ *Web:* www.nve.com						
NVE Pharmaceuticals 15 Whitehall Rd	Andover	NJ	07821	973-786-7862		360-3
TF: 800-526-4387 ■ *Web:* www.stacker2.com						
NVFC (National Volunteer Fire Council) 7852 Walker Dr Ste 450	Greenbelt	MD	20770	202-887-5700	887-5291	49-4
TF: 888-275-6832 ■ *Web:* www.nvfc.org						
NVIC (National Vaccine Information Ctr) 407 Church St Ste H	Vienna	VA	22180	703-938-0342	938-5768	48-17
Web: www.nvic.org						
NVIDIA Corp 2701 San Tomas Expy	Santa Clara	CA	95050	408-486-2000	486-2200	625
NASDAQ: NVDA ■ *Web:* www.nvidia.com						
N-Viro International Corp 2254 Centennial Rd	Toledo	OH	43617	419-535-6374		804
OTC: NVIC ■ *TF:* 800-336-2225 ■ *Web:* www.nviro.com						
Nvision Networking Inc 7450 N Thornydale Rd	Tucson	AZ	85741	520-219-6040		180
TF: 800-553-2447 ■ *Web:* nvisionnet.com						
NVision Solutions Inc 88360 Diamondhead Dr E Ste 301	Diamondhead	MS	39525	228-222-5900		809
Web: www.nvisionsolutions.com						
Nvms Inc 9255 Center St Ste 200	Manassas	VA	20110	703-361-6262		226
TF: 800-804-9496 ■ *Web:* www.nvms.com						
NVP (New Venture Partners LLC) 430 Mountain Ave Ste 404	Murray Hill	NJ	07974	908-464-0900	464-8131	792
Web: www.nvpllc.com						
NVR Inc 11700 Plaza America Dr Ste 500	Reston	VA	20190	703-956-4000		187
NYSE: NVR ■ *Web:* nvrinc.com						
NVT Phybridge 3495 Laird Rd Ste 12	Mississauga	ON	L5L5S5	905-901-3633		610
TF: 888-901-3633 ■ *Web:* www.phybridge.com						
NW Natural 220 NW Second Ave PO Box 6017	Portland	OR	97209	503-226-4211		536
TF: 800-422-4012 ■ *Web:* www.nwnatural.com						
NW Sign Industries Inc 360 Crider Ave	Moorestown	NJ	08057	856-802-1677		701
Web: www.nwsignindustries.com						
NWA (National WIC Assn) 2001 S St NW Ste 580	Washington	DC	20009	202-232-5492	387-5281	48-6
TF: 866-782-6246 ■ *Web:* www.nwica.org						
NWC (National Waterways Conference Inc) 4650 Washington Blvd Ste 608	Arlington	VA	22201	703-243-4090	243-4155	49-21
TF: 866-371-1390 ■ *Web:* www.waterways.org						
NWCCU (Northwest Commission on Colleges & Universities) 8060 165th Ave NE Ste 100	Redmond	WA	98052	425-558-4224		48-1
Web: www.nwccu.org						
NWF (National Wildlife Federation) 11100 Wildlife Ctr Dr	Reston	VA	20190	703-438-6000	438-3570	48-3
TF: 800-822-9919 ■ *Web:* www.nwf.org						
NWFA (National Wood Flooring Assn) 111 Chesterfield Industrial Blvd	Chesterfield	MO	63005	636-519-9663		49-3
TF: 800-422-4556 ■ *Web:* www.woodfloors.org						
NWHOF (National Wrestling Hall of Fame) 405 W Hall of Fame Ave	Stillwater	OK	74075	405-377-5243	377-5244	522
Web: nwhof.org						
NWI (National Wellness Institute) 1300 College Ct PO Box 827	Stevens Point	WI	54481	715-342-2969	342-2979	48-17
TF: 877-800-2729 ■ *Web:* www.nationalwellness.org						
NWL Transformers Inc 312 Rising Sun Rd	Bordentown	NJ	08505	609-298-7300	298-1982	253
TF: 800-742-5695 ■ *Web:* www.nwl.com						
NWLC (National Women's Law Ctr) 11 Dupont Cir NW Ste 800	Washington	DC	20036	202-588-5180	588-5185	48-24
Web: www.nwlc.org						
NWLSD (Northwest Local School District) 3240 Banning Rd	Cincinnati	OH	45239	513-923-1000	923-3644	685
Web: www.nwlsd.org						
NWMC (Northwest Medical Ctr) 2801 N SR 7	Margate	FL	33063	954-978-4000		374-3
Web: www.northwestmed.com						
NWOA (National Woodland Owners Assn) 374 Maple Ave E Ste 310	Vienna	VA	22180	703-255-2700		48-2
TF: 800-476-8733 ■ *Web:* www.woodlandowners.org						
NWPC (National Women's Political Caucus) PO Box 65010	Washington	DC	20035	202-785-1100		48-7
Web: www.nwpc.org						
NWPCA (National Wooden Pallet & Container Assn) 1421 Prince St Ste 340	Alexandria	VA	22314	703-519-6104	519-4720	49-13
Web: www.palletcentral.com						
NWRA (National Water Resources Assn) 3800 Fairfax Dr # 4	Arlington	VA	22203	703-524-1544	343-9483*	48-12
**Fax Area Code:* 928 ■ *TF:* 800-468-3533 ■ *Web:* www.nwra.org						
NWRA (National Wildlife Refuge Assn) 1250 Connecticut Ave NW Ste 600	Washington	DC	20036	202-292-2402		48-13
Web: www.refugeassociation.org						
NWS (National Weather Service) 1325 East-West Hwy	Silver Spring	MD	20910	301-713-0689		340-2
Web: www.weather.gov						
NWT Tourism PO Box 610	Yellowknife	NT	X1A2N5	867-873-7200	873-4059	774
TF: 800-661-0788 ■ *Web:* www.spectacularnwt.com						
NWTF (National Wild Turkey Federation) 770 Augusta Rd PO Box 530	Edgefield	SC	29824	803-637-3106	637-0034	48-3
TF Cust Svc: 800-843-6983 ■ *Web:* www.nwtf.org						
NWTRB (Nuclear Waste Technical Review Board) 2300 Clarendon Blvd Ste 1300	Arlington	VA	22201	703-235-4473	235-4495	340-20
Web: www.nwtrb.gov						
NWU (National Writers Union) 256 W 38th St Ste 703	New York	NY	10018	212-254-0279	254-0673	414
Web: www.nwu.org						
NXQ (Neutronix-Quintel) 385 Woodview Ave	Morgan Hill	CA	95037	408-776-5190	776-1039	695
Web: www.neutronixinc.com						
NxStage Medical Inc 439 S Union St 5th Fl	Lawrence	MA	01843	978-687-4700		476
NASDAQ: NXTM ■ *TF:* 866-697-8243 ■ *Web:* www.nxstage.com						
NXT Energy Solutions Inc 3320 17th Ave SW Ste 302	Calgary	AB	T3E0B4	403-264-7020		537
Web: www.nxtenergy.com						
NY1 75 Ninth Ave	New York	NY	10011	212-379-3311		530
Web: www.ny1.com						
NYACK 350 N Highland Ave	Nyack	NY	10960	845-353-2020		167-3
TF: 800-541-6891 ■ *Web:* nyack.edu						
Nyack Beach State Park 698 N Broadway	Upper Nyack	NY	10960	845-358-1316		565
Web: parks.ny.gov/parks/156/details.aspx						
Nyack College 1 S Blvd	Nyack	NY	10960	845-358-1710	358-3047*	166
**Fax:* Admissions ■ *TF Admissions:* 800-336-9225 ■ *Web:* www.nyack.edu						
Nyack Hospital 160 N Midland Ave	Nyack	NY	10960	845-348-2000	348-2160	374-3
Web: www.nyackhospital.org						
NYAM (New York Academy of Medicine) 1216 Fifth Ave	New York	NY	10029	212-822-7200		49-19
Web: www.nyam.org						
Nyatex Chemical Co 2112 Industrial	Howell	MI	48843	517-546-4046		3
Web: www.nyatex.com						
NYAWA (New York Arm Wrestling Assn) PO Box 670952	Flushing	NY	11367	718-544-4592	261-8111	48-22
Web: www.nycarms.com						
NYBDC (New York Business Development Corp) 50 Beaver St Ste 500	Albany	NY	12207	518-463-2268	463-0240	216
TF: 800-923-2504 ■ *Web:* www.nybdc.com						
NYC & Co 810 Seventh Ave 3rd Fl	New York	NY	10019	212-484-1200		206
NYC Dot 50 21st St	Brooklyn	NY	11232	718-965-3539		350
NYCA (New York Celebrity Assistants) 459 Columbus Ave Ste 216	New York	NY	10024	212-803-5444		49-12
Web: www.nycelebrityassistants.com						
NYCCC (New York City Children's Ctr-Queens Campus) 74-03 Commonwealth Blvd	Bellerose	NY	11426	718-264-4500	740-0968	374-1
TF: 800-597-8481 ■ *Web:* www.omh.ny.gov						
NYCE Corp 400 Plaza Dr	Secaucus	NJ	07094	904-438-6000	330-3374*	69
**Fax Area Code:* 201 ■ *TF:* 888-323-0310 ■ *Web:* www.nyce.net						
NYCM (New York Central Mutual Fire Insurance Co) 1899 Central Plaza E	Edmeston	NY	13335	800-234-6926	965-2712*	391-4
**Fax Area Code:* 607 ■ *TF:* 800-234-6926 ■ *Web:* www.nycm.com						
NYCO Minerals Inc 803 Mtn View Dr	Willsboro	NY	12996	518-963-4262		500
NYDJ Apparel LLC 5401 S Soto St	Vernon	CA	90058	323-581-9040		157-6
TF: 800-407-6001 ■ *Web:* www.nydj.com						
Nye County PO Box 1031	Tonopah	NV	89049	775-482-8127	482-8133	338
Web: www.co.nye.nv.us						
Nye County School District Inc (NCSD) PO Box 113	Tonopah	NV	89049	775-482-6258	482-8573	685
TF: 800-796-6273 ■ *Web:* nyecounty.schoolinsites.com						
Nye Health Services 2230 N Somers Ave	Fremont	NE	68025	402-753-1400		371
Web: nyehealthservices.com						
Nye Lubricants Inc 12 Howland Rd	Fairhaven	MA	02719	508-996-6721	997-5285	541
Web: www.nyelubricants.com						
NYFIX Inc 11 Wall St	New York	NY	10005	212-656-3000		252
TF: 800-633-7646 ■ *Web:* www.nyse.com						
NYGH (North York General Hospital) 4001 Leslie St	North York	ON	M2K1E1	416-756-6000		374-2
Web: www.nygh.on.ca						
Nyhus Communications LLC 720 Third Ave Fl 12	Seattle	WA	98104	206-323-3733		636
Web: www.nyhus.com						
NYLA (New York Library Assn) 6021 State Farm Rd	Guilderland	NY	12084	518-432-6952	427-1697	435
TF General: 800-252-6952 ■ *Web:* www.nyla.org						

	Phone	Fax	Class
NYLIFE Securities Inc 51 Madison Ave Rm 251 .... New York NY 10010 *TF:* 800-695-4785 ■ *Web:* www.newyorklife.com	800-695-4785		690
Nylo Hotels LLC 2178 Broadway Ste 2301 .... New York GA 10024 *Web:* www.nylohotels.com	212-362-1100		378
Nylok Corp 15260 Hallmark Dr................. Macomb MI 48042 *TF:* 800-826-5161 ■ *Web:* www.nylok.com	586-786-0100	786-0598	3
Nylon Corp of America 333 Sundial Ave .... Manchester NH 03103 *TF:* 800-851-2001 ■ *Web:* www.nycoa.net	603-627-5150		605-1
Nylon Magazine 110 Greene St Ste 607 .... New York NY 10012 *Web:* www.nylon.com	212-226-6454		457-11
Nylon Technology 350 Seventh Ave 10th fl .... New York NY 10001 *Web:* www.nylontechnology.com	212-691-1134		177
Nyloncraft Inc 616 W McKinley Ave .... Mishawaka IN 46545 *TF:* 800-704-2888 ■ *Web:* www.nyloncraft.com	574-256-1521	255-3278	604
NYMT (New York Mortgage Trust Inc) 52 Vanderbilt Ave Ste 403.................... New York NY 10017 *NASDAQ: NYMT* ■ *TF:* 800-937-5449 ■ *Web:* www.nymtrust.com	212-792-0107		654
NYP Corp 805 E Grand St .... Elizabeth NJ 07201 *TF:* 800-524-1052 ■ *Web:* www.nyp-corp.com	908-351-6550	351-0108	67
NYPIRG (NYPIRG) 9 Murray St................. New York NY 10007 *TF:* 800-566-5020 ■ *Web:* www.nypirg.org	212-349-6460	349-1366	633
NYPNU (New York Professional Nurses Union) 241 E 75th St .... New York NY 10021 *Web:* www.nypnu.org	212-988-5565		533
Nypro Inc 101 Union St .... Clinton MA 01510 *Web:* www.nypro.com	978-365-9721		596
Nypromold Inc 144 Pleasant St.................. Clinton MA 01510 *Web:* www.nypromold.com	978-365-4547	365-4548	757
NYRA (New York Racing Assn) 110-00 Rockaway Blvd PO Box 90.............. Jamaica NY 11420 *TF:* 800-441-4601 ■ *Web:* www.nyra.com	718-641-4700		642
Nyrstar Clarksville 1800 Zinc Plant Rd........................ Clarksville TN 37041 *Web:* www.nyrstar.com	931-552-4200	552-0471	485
Nysarc Inc 393 Delaware Ave.................... Delmar NY 12054 *TF:* 800-735-8924 ■ *Web:* www.nysarc.org	518-439-8311	439-1893	428
NYSCA (National Youth Sports Coaches Assn) 2050 Vista Pkwy.................... West Palm Beach FL 33411 *TF:* 800-729-2057 ■ *Web:* www.nays.org	561-684-1141	684-2546	48-22
NYSCO Products Inc 2350 Lafayette Ave .... Bronx NY 10473 *Web:* www.nysco.com	718-792-9000	792-7732	125
NYSE Arce 115 Samsone St .... San Francisco CA 94104 *TF:* 877-729-7291 ■ *Web:* www.nyse.com	877-729-7291		691
NYSE Euronext 11 Wall St.................. New York NY 10005 *NYSE: NYX* ■ *TF:* 866-873-7422 ■ *Web:* www.nyse.com	212-656-3000		691
NYSNA (New York State Nurses Assn) 11 Cornell Rd .... Latham NY 12110 *TF:* 800-724-6976 ■ *Web:* www.nysna.org	518-782-9400		533
Nystrom 4719 W 62nd St .... Indianapolis IN 46268	317-612-3901		637-1
Nystrom Inc 9300 73rd Ave N .... Minneapolis MN 55428 **Fax Area Code: 800* ■ *TF:* 800-547-2635 ■ *Web:* www.nystrom.com	763-488-9200	317-8770*	234
NYSW (New York Susquehanna & Western Railway Corp) 1 Railroad Ave.................... Cooperstown NY 13326 *TF General:* 800-366-6979 ■ *Web:* www.nysw.com	607-547-2555	547-9834	648
Nytef Plastics Ltd Inc 6643 42nd Terr N .... West Palm Beach FL 33407 **Fax Area Code: 215* ■ *TF:* 800-646-9833 ■ *Web:* www.nytetplastics.com	561-840-9499	638-7674*	603
NYU Alumni Assn 25 W Fourth St 4th Fl............ New York NY 10012 *Web:* www.alumni.nyu.edu	212-998-6912		305
NYU Langone Medical Ctr 550 First Ave.............................. New York NY 10016 *Web:* www.med.nyu.edu	212-263-7300		374-3
NYU School of Medicine 560 First Ave.......... New York NY 10016 *TF:* 855-698-2220 ■ *Web:* www.med.nyu.edu	212-263-7300	263-0720	167-2
NYX Inc 36111 Schoolcraft Rd .... Livonia MI 48150 *TF:* 800-799-9625 ■ *Web:* www.nyxinc.com	734-462-2385	464-4830	604

O

	Phone	Fax	Class
O & F Machine Products Company Inc 3020 W 20th St PO Box 1363.................. Joplin MO 64802 *Web:* www.ofmachine.com	417-623-7476	623-4736	454
O & G Industries Inc 112 Wall St............. Torrington CT 06790 *Web:* www.ogind.com	860-489-9261	489-9261	186
O & P Edge, The 11154 Huron St Ste 104.................... Northglenn CO 80234 *Web:* www.oandp.com	303-255-0843	255-0844	305
O & S Cattle Co 100 StockyaRds Rd.................. South Saint Paul MN 55075	651-455-5459		446
O & S Trucking Inc 3769 E Evergreen St........................ Springfield MO 65803 *TF:* 855-861-9571 ■ *Web:* www.oandstrucking.com	417-864-4780		780
O Berk Co 3 Milltown Ct........................ Union NJ 07083 *TF:* 800-631-7392 ■ *Web:* www.oberk.com	800-631-7392		385
O Dell Corp 13833 Indian Mound Rd .... Ware Shoals SC 29692 *Web:* www.odellcorp.com	864-861-2222		361
O E C Graphics Inc 555 W Waukau Ave PO Box 2443.............. Oshkosh WI 54902 *TF:* 800-388-7770 ■ *Web:* www.oecgraphics.com	920-235-7770	235-2252	481
O H Anderson Elementary School 666 Warner Ave S........................ Saint Paul MN 55115 *TF:* 800-352-7550 ■ *Web:* www.mahtomedi.k12.mn.us	651-407-2300		685
O Henry Home & Museum 409 E Fifth St.......... Austin TX 78701 *Web:* www.ci.austin.tx.us	512-472-1903		520
O Henry Hotel 624 Green Valley Rd .... Greensboro NC 27408 *TF:* 800-965-8259 ■ *Web:* www.ohenryhotel.com	336-854-2000	854-2223	379
O Hotel 819 S Flower St .... Los Angeles CA 90017 *Web:* ohotelgroup.com	213-623-9904		379
O Keller Tool Engineering Co 12701 Inkster Rd .... Livonia MI 48150	734-425-4504		757
O M Jones Inc PO Box 4375 .... Sonora CA 95370 *Web:* www.micro-tronics.net	209-532-1008	532-1009	253
O M V Medical Inc 6940 Carroll Ave......................... Takoma Park MD 20912 *Web:* www.omvmedical.com	301-270-9212		194
O Neill's Chevrolet & Buick Inc 5 W Main St .... Avon CT 06001 *TF:* 844-315-0960 ■ *Web:* www.oneillschevybuick.com	844-315-0960		57
O P Solutions Inc 350 First Ave Ste MG........................ New York NY 10010 *TF:* 800-659-7659 ■ *Web:* www.pattsy.com	212-979-1000		177
O P T 918 Mission Ave.................... Oceanside CA 92054 *TF:* 800-483-6287 ■ *Web:* www.optcorp.com	760-722-3348		179
O S F Flavors Inc 40 Baker Hollow Rd........... Windsor CT 06095 *TF:* 800-466-6015 ■ *Web:* www.osfflavors.com	860-298-8350	298-8363	297-11
O s u Center for Health Sciences 1111 W 17th St................................ Tulsa OK 74107 *TF:* 800-677-1972 ■ *Web:* www.healthsciences.okstate.edu	918-582-1972		165
O the Oprah Magazine 5700 Wilshire Blvd Ste 120 .... Los Angeles CA 90036 *Web:* www.oprah.com/omagazine	323-602-5500		457-11
O Ya 9 E St Pl................................ Boston MA 02111 *Web:* o-ya.restaurant	617-654-9900		671
O'Bannon Woods State Park 7234 Old Forest Rd SW .... Corydon IN 47112 *Web:* www.in.gov	812-738-8232		565
O'Brien & Company Inc 710 Second Ave Ste 925........................ Seattle WA 98104 *Web:* www.obrienandco.com	206-621-8626		194
O'Brien & Gere Engineers Inc 333 W Washington St....................... Syracuse NY 13202 *Web:* www.obg.com	315-956-6100	463-7554	261
O'Brien County 160 S Hayes Ave............... Primghar IA 51245 *Web:* www.obriencounty.com	712-957-1313	928-3536	338
O'Brien Dental Lab Inc 4311 SW Research Way .... Corvallis OR 97333 *TF:* 800-445-5941 ■ *Web:* www.obriendentallab.com	541-754-1238		415
O'Brien Energy Co 425 Ashley Ridge Blvd Ste 300.............. Shreveport LA 71106 *Web:* www.obrienenergyco.com	318-865-8568		536
O'Brien International 14615 NE 91st St........................... Redmond WA 98052 *TF:* 800-662-7436 ■ *Web:* www.obrien.com	425-202-2100		710
O'Brien Steel Service Co 1700 N E Adams St........................... Peoria IL 61603 *Web:* www.obriensteel.com	309-671-5800		480
O'Brien's Oyster Bar & Restaurant 113 Main St .... Annapolis MD 21401 *Web:* www.obriensoysterbar.com	410-268-6288	267-7767	671
O'Brien, Tanski & Young LLP CityPlace II 185 Asylum St...................... Hartford CT 06103 *TF:* 800-999-1950 ■ *Web:* www.otylaw.com	860-525-2700		428
O'Charley's Inc 3038 Sidco Dr .... Nashville TN 37204 *NASDAQ: CHUX* ■ *Web:* www.ocharleys.com	615-256-8500		670
O'Connell Electric Co 830 Phillips Rd............. Victor NY 14564 *TF:* 800-343-2176 ■ *Web:* www.oconnellelectric.com	585-924-2176	924-4973	189-4
O'Connell Oil Assoc Inc 545 Merrill Rd .... Pittsfield MA 01201 *TF:* 800-464-4894 ■ *Web:* www.oconnelloil.com	413-499-4800	499-6072	324
O'Connell Robertson & Associates Inc 811 Barton Springs Rd Ste 900 .... Austin TX 78704 *Web:* www.oconnellrobertson.com	512-478-7286		261
O'connell, Tivin, Miller & Burns LLC 135 S La Salle St Ste 2300..................... Chicago IL 60603 *Web:* www.otmblaw.com	312-256-8800		428
O'Connor & Drew PC 25 Braintree Hill Office Park Suit .... Braintree MA 02184 *Web:* ocd.com	617-471-1120		2
O'connor Company Inc 16910 W 116th St......... Lenexa KS 66219 *TF:* 888-800-3540 ■ *Web:* www.oconnor-hvac.com	913-894-8788		41
O'Connor Constructors Inc 45 Industrial Dr.............................. Canton MA 02021 **Fax Area Code: 781* ■ *Web:* www.oconnorconst.com	617-364-9000	828-8248*	186
O'Connor Group Inc, The 10 Stearns Rd .... Bedford MA 01730 *Web:* www.theoconnorgroup.com	781-275-2423		463
O'Connor Hospital 2105 Forest Ave .... San Jose CA 95128 *Web:* oconnor.verity.org	408-947-2500		374-3
O'Connor Insurance Agency 12101 Olive Blvd .... St Louis MO 63141 *Web:* oconnor-ins.com	314-434-0038		390
O'Connor Sales Inc 16107 Piuma Ave .... Cerritos CA 90703 *Web:* www.oconnorsales.net	562-403-3848	403-3858	612
O'Connor Woods 3400 Wagner Heights Rd .... Stockton CA 95209 *TF:* 800-957-3308 ■ *Web:* www.oconnorwoods.org	209-956-3400		672
O'Connor's Restaurant & Bar 1160 W Boylston St .... Worcester MA 01606 *Web:* www.oconnorsrestaurant.com	508-853-0789	853-2879	671
O'Currance Teleservices Inc 11747 S Lonepeak Pkwy Ste 100.................... Draper UT 84020 *Web:* www.ocurrance.com	801-736-0500		393
O'Daniel automotive Group 5611 Illinois Rd .... Fort Wayne IN 46804 *TF:* 888-716-3641 ■ *Web:* www.odanielauto.com	888-716-3641		516
O'day Consultants Inc 2710 Loker Ave W Ste 100.................... Carlsbad CA 92010 *TF:* 800-827-4901 ■ *Web:* www.odayconsultants.com	760-931-7700		261
O'Day Equipment Inc 1301 40th St NW............ Fargo ND 58102 *TF:* 800-654-6329 ■ *Web:* www.odayequipment.com	701-282-9260		639
O'Doherty's Irish Grill 525 W Spokane Falls Blvd .... Spokane WA 99201 *Web:* odohertyspub.com	509-747-0322		671
O'donnell Lee Mccowan & Phillips LLC 112 Silver St.................................. Waterville ME 04901 *Web:* www.odonnellandlee.com	207-872-0112		428
O'Fallon Chamber of Commerce 2145 Bryan Vly Commercial Dr .... O'Fallon MO 63366 *TF:* 888-349-1897 ■ *Web:* www.ofallonchamber.org	636-240-1818		139

Name / Address	Phone	Fax	Class
O'Gara Coach Company LLC 8833 W Olympic Blvd. Beverly Hills CA 90211 *TF:* 888-291-5533 ■ *Web:* www.ogaracoach.com	888-291-5533		57
O'Gara Group Inc, The 9113 Le Saint Dr Ste 460 Fairfield OH 45014 *Web:* www.ogaragroup.com	513-338-0660		693
O'hagan Smith & Amundsen 308 W State St Ste 320 Rockford IL 61101 *Web:* salawus.com	815-987-0441		428
O'Halleran Tom (Rep D - AZ) 126 Cannon HOB Washington DC 20515 *Web:* ohalleran.house.gov	202-225-3361		342-2
O'Halloran Adv Inc 270 Saugatuck Ave Westport CT 06880	203-571-1974	341-8681	5
O'halloran International Inc 3311 Adventureland Dr. Altoona IA 50009 *TF:* 800-800-6503 ■ *Web:* www.ohallorans.com	515-967-3300	967-0206	770
O'Hara Gallery 595 Madison Ave. New York NY 10022 *Web:* www.johg.com	212-644-3533		42
O'Hare International Airport *Dept of Aviation* PO Box 66142 Chicago IL 60666 *TF:* 800-832-6352 ■ *Web:* www.flychicago.com	773-686-3700		27
O'Harrow Construction Co 4575 Ann Arbor Rd. Jackson MI 49202 *Web:* www.oharrow.net	517-764-4770	764-5564	186
O'kane Consultants Inc 112 Research Dr. Saskatoon SK S7N3R3 *Web:* www.okc-sk.com	306-955-0702		261
O'Keefe Drilling Co 2000 4 Mile Rd. Butte MT 59701 *TF:* 800-745-5554 ■ *Web:* www.okeefedrilling.com	406-494-3310		656
O'keefe Elevator Company Inc 1402 Jones St. Omaha NE 68102 *TF:* 800-369-6317 ■ *Web:* www.okeefe-elevator.com	402-345-4056		358
O'Keeffe's Inc 325 Newhall St. San Francisco CA 94124 *TF:* 888-653-3333 ■ *Web:* www.okeeffes.com	415-822-4222		234
O'Leary Paint 300 E Oakland Ave Lansing MI 48906 *TF:* 800-477-2066 ■ *Web:* www.olearypaint.com	517-487-2066	487-1680	550
O'Leary's Seafood Restaurant 310 Third St Annapolis MD 21403 *Web:* www.olearysseafood.com	410-263-0884		671
O'Leno State Park 410 SE Oleno Pk Rd High Springs FL 32643 *Web:* www.floridastateparks.org	386-454-1853		565
O'Malley Hansen Communications 180 N Wacker Dr Ste 400 Chicago IL 60606 *Web:* omalleyhansen.com	312-377-0630		636
O'Melveny & Myers LLP 400 S Hope St 10th Fl Los Angeles CA 90071 *Web:* www.omm.com	213-430-6000	430-6407	428
O'More College of Design 423 S Margin St. Franklin TN 37064 *Web:* www.omorecollege.edu	615-794-4254	790-1662	166
O'Neal Construction Inc 525 W William Ann Arbor MI 48103 *Web:* www.onealconstruction.com	734-769-0770		186
O'neal Flat Rolled Metals 1229 S Fulton Ave Brighton CO 80601 *TF:* 800-336-3365 ■ *Web:* www.ofrmetals.com	303-654-0300		492
O'Neal Inc 10 Falcon Crest Dr Greenville SC 29607 *Web:* www.onealinc.com	864-298-2000	298-2200	261
O'Neal Steel Inc 744 41st St N. Birmingham AL 35222 *TF:* 800-861-8272 ■ *Web:* www.onealsteel.com	205-599-8000		492
O'neil & Assoc Inc 495 Byers Rd Miamisburg OH 45342 *Web:* www.oneil.com	937-865-0800	865-5858	637-10
O'neil Data Systems Inc 12655 Beatrice St Los Angeles CA 90066 *Web:* www.oneildata.com	310-448-6400		225
O'Neil Printing Inc 366 N Second Ave Phoenix AZ 85003 *TF:* 800-454-6381 ■ *Web:* www.oneilprint.com	602-258-7789		627
O'Neil Software Inc 11 Cushing Ste 100 Irvine CA 92618 *Web:* oneilsoft.com	949-458-1234		180
O'Neill & Assoc LLC 31 New Chardon St Boston MA 02114 *TF:* 866-989-4321 ■ *Web:* www.oneillandassoc.com	617-646-1000		194
O'Neill Properties Group LP 2701 Renaissance Blvd 4th Fl. King Of Prussia PA 19406 *Web:* www.oneillproperties.com	610-239-6100		652
O'Neill Wetsuits USA 1071 41st Ave PO Box 6300 Santa Cruz CA 95063 *TF:* 800-538-0764 ■ *Web:* www.oneill.com	800-538-0764		710
O'Reilly & Assoc Inc 1005 Gravenstein Hwy N Sebastopol CA 95472 *TF:* 800-998-9938 ■ *Web:* www.oreilly.com	707-829-0515	829-0104	637-11
O'reilly Public Relations 3403 Tenth St Ste 110 Riverside CA 92501 *Web:* www.oreillypr.com	951-781-2240		636
O'Reilly Rancilio PC Sterling Town Ctr 12900 Hall Rd Ste 350 Sterling Heights MI 48313 *TF:* 800-708-3528 ■ *Web:* www.orlaw.com	586-726-1000		428
O'Reilly Talbot & Okun Assoc Inc 293 Bridge St Springfield MA 01103 *Web:* oto-env.com	413-788-6222		261
O'rielly Chevrolet Inc 6100 E Broadway Blvd Tucson AZ 85711 *Web:* www.orielly.com	520-829-4400		57
O'riordan Bethel Law Firm LLP, The 1314 19th St NW Washington DC 20036 *Web:* oriordan-law.com	202-822-1720		428
O'Rorke's Family Eatery 44 Steinwehr Ave Gettysburg PA 17325 *Web:* ororkes.com	717-334-2333		671
O'Rourke Beto (Rep D - TX) 1330 Longworth Bldg Washington DC 20515 *Web:* orourke.house.gov	202-225-4831		342-2
O'Rourke Petroleum Inc 223 McCarty Dr Houston TX 77029 *TF:* 800-729-4275 ■ *Web:* www.orpp.com	713-672-4500		316
O'Rourke Sales Co 3885 Elmore Ave Ste 100 Davenport IA 52807 *Web:* www.orourkesales.com	563-823-1501	823-1534	38
O'Rourke Wrecking Co 660 Lunken Pk Dr. Cincinnati OH 45226 *TF:* 800-354-9850 ■ *Web:* www.orourkewrecking.com	513-871-1400	871-1313	189-16
O'Ryan Group Inc 4010 Pilot Ste 108 Memphis TN 38118 *TF:* 800-253-0750 ■ *Web:* www.oryangroup.com	901-794-4610		701
O'Steen's Restaurant 205 Anastasia Blvd Saint Augustine FL 32080 *Web:* osteensrestaurant.com	904-829-6974		671
O'Sullivan Films Inc 1944 Valley Ave Winchester VA 22601 *TF:* 800-336-9882 ■ *Web:* www.osul.com	540-667-6666		600
O'Neill Hotels & Resorts Ltd 401 W Georgia St Ste 1690 Vancouver BC V6B5A1 *Web:* www.oneillhotels.com	604-684-0444		379
O'Reilly Auto Parts 233 S Patterson Springfield MO 65802 *NASDAQ: ORLY* ■ *TF:* 888-327-7153 ■ *Web:* www.oreillyauto.com	417-862-6708		54
01 Communications Inc 4359 town ctr blvd Ste 217 El Dorado hills CA 95762 *TF:* 888-444-1111 ■ *Web:* www.o1.com	888-444-1111		736
O2Micro International Ltd 3118 Patrick Henry Dr Santa Clara CA 95054 *NASDAQ: OIIM* ■ *Web:* www.o2micro.com	408-987-5920		696
OA (Overeaters Anonymous Inc) PO Box 44020 Rio Rancho NM 87174 *TF:* 866-505-4966 ■ *Web:* www.oa.org	505-891-2664	891-4320	48-21
OA Systems Inc 10783 Edison Ct. Rancho Cucamonga CA 91730 *TF:* 800-477-1357 ■ *Web:* www.oasite.com	909-466-1605		177
OAA (Opticians Assn of America) 3740 Canada Rd. Lakeland TN 38002 *TF:* 800-296-9776 ■ *Web:* www.oaa.org	901-388-2423	388-2348	49-8
OAAA (Outdoor Adv Assn of America Inc) 1850 M St NW Ste 1040 Washington DC 20036 *TF:* 800-325-3694 ■ *Web:* www.oaaa.org	202-833-5566	833-1522	615
OABA-PAC (Outdoor Amusement Business Assn PAC) 1035 S Semoran Blvd Ste 1045A Winter Park FL 32792 *TF:* 800-517-6222 ■ *Web:* www.oaba.org	407-681-9444	681-9445	615
OAG Worldwide 3025 Highland Pkwy Ste 200 Downers Grove IL 60515 *TF:* 800-342-5624 ■ *Web:* www.oag.com	630-515-3230	515-3933	637-10
OAGI (Open Applications Group Inc) PO Box 4897 Marietta GA 30061 **Fax Area Code: 801* ■ *TF:* 800-236-4600 ■ *Web:* www.oagi.org	404-402-1962	740-0100*	49-13
OAH (Organization of American Historians) 112 N Bryan Ave. Bloomington IN 47408 *TF:* 888-737-7006 ■ *Web:* www.oah.org	812-855-7311	855-0696	49-5
Oahe Downstream Recreation Area 20439 Marina Loop Rd. Fort Pierre SD 57532 *Web:* www.gfp.sd.gov	605-223-7722		565
Oahe Electric Co-op Inc 102 S Cranford St PO Box 216 Blunt SD 57522 *TF:* 800-640-6243 ■ *Web:* www.oaheelectric.com	605-962-6243	962-6306	245
Oahu Publications Inc 500 Ala Moana Blvd Ste 7-500 Honolulu HI 96813 *Web:* www.oahupublications.com	808-529-4700		532-3
Oahu Transit Services 811 Middle St Honolulu HI 96819 *Web:* www.thebus.org	808-848-4500	848-4419	468
OAI Corp 4545 W Hillsborough Ave Tampa FL 33614 *Web:* www.oaicorp.com	813-888-8796		344
Oak & More Ltd 4949 SE 25th Ave Portland OR 97202	503-245-4522		286
Oak Assoc Funds PO Box 8233 Denver CO 80201 *TF:* 888-462-5386 ■ *Web:* www.oakfunds.com	888-462-5386		528
Oak Bank 1000 N Rush St Chicago IL 60611 *Web:* www.oakbank.com	312-440-4000		70
Oak Brook Golf Club 1200 Oak Brook Rd. Oak Brook IL 60523 *Web:* www.oak-brook.org	630-990-4233		393
Oak Brook HealthCare & Rehabilitation Centre 2013 Midwest Rd Oak Brook IL 60523 *TF:* 800-213-0154 ■ *Web:* oakbrookcare.com	630-495-0220		793
Oak Brook Hills Marriott Resort 3500 Midwest Rd Oak Brook IL 60523 *TF:* 800-228-9290 ■ *Web:* marriott.com/hotels/propertypage/chimc	630-850-5555		377
Oak Brook Mechanical Services Inc 961 S Rt 83 Elmhurst IL 60126 *Web:* omshvac.com	630-941-3555	941-0294	189-10
Oak Cliff Bible Fellowship 1808 W Camp Wisdom Rd Dallas TX 75232 *Web:* www.ocbfchurch.org	972-228-1281		48-20
Oak Cliff Chamber of Commerce 400 S Zang Blvd Ste 110 Dallas TX 75208 *TF:* 800-833-9106 ■ *Web:* www.oakcliffchamber.org	214-943-4567	943-4582	139
Oak Cliff Office Supply 1876 Lone Star Dr Dallas TX 75212	214-943-7421		535
Oak Creek Energy Systems Inc 500 La Terraza Blvd. Escondido CA 92025 *Web:* www.oces.com	760-975-0910		194
Oak Creek-Franklin Joint School District 7630 S Tenth St Oak Creek WI 53154	414-768-5880		685
Oak Crest DeKalb Area Retirement Ctr 2944 Greenwood Acres Dr DeKalb IL 60115 *Web:* www.oakcrestdekalb.org	815-756-8461		672
Oak Forest - Crestwood Area Chamber of Commerce 15440 S Central Ave. Oak Forest IL 60452 *TF:* 800-334-7661 ■ *Web:* oc-chamber.org	708-687-4600		139
Oak Forest Hospital of Cook County 15900 S Cicero Ave Oak Forest IL 60452	708-687-7200		374-7
Oak Grove School 220 W Lomita Ave Ojai CA 93023 *Web:* oakgroveschool.org	805-646-8236	646-6509	622
Oak Grove Technologies LLC 4140 Parklake Ave Ste 330 Raleigh NC 27612 *TF:* 800-439-5196 ■ *Web:* www.oakgrovetech.com	919-845-1038		463
Oak Hall Inc 6150 Poplar Ave Ste 146 Memphis TN 38119 *TF:* 844-625-4255 ■ *Web:* www.oakhall.com	901-761-3580		157-4
Oak Hall Industries 840 Union St. Salem VA 24153 *TF:* 800-223-0429 ■ *Web:* www.oakhalli.com	540-387-0000	387-2034	155-14

	Phone	Fax	Class
Oak Harbor Chamber of Commerce 32630 SR 20 ... Oak Harbor WA 98277 *Web:* www.oakharborchamber.com	360-675-3755	679-1624	139
Oak Harbor Freight Lines Inc 1339 W Valley Hwy N PO Box 1469 ... Auburn WA 98071 *Web:* www.oakh.com	253-288-8300		314
Oak Hill & Martha Berry Museum 2277 Martha Berry Hwy NW PO Box 490189 .. Mount Berry GA 30149 *Web:* www.berry.edu	706-291-1883		520
Oak Hill Academy 2635 Oak Hill Rd ... Mouth of Wilson VA 24363 *Web:* www.oak-hill.net	276-579-2619		622
Oak Hill Health & Rehabilitation Ctr 544 Pleasant St ... Pawtucket RI 02860 *Web:* kindredhealthcare.com	401-725-8888		450
Oak Hill Technology Inc 12505-A Trl Dr St ... Austin TX 78737 *Web:* www.oakhilltech.com	512-288-0008		180
Oak Hills Christian College 1600 Oak Hills Rd SW ... Bemidji MN 56601 *TF:* 888-751-8670 ■ *Web:* www.oakhills.edu	218-751-8670	751-8825	161
Oak Hollow Mall 921 Eastchester Dr ... High Point NC 27262	336-886-6255		460
Oak Hotels Inc 2424 SR-52 ... Hopewell Junction NY 12533 *TF:* 800-547-0007 ■ *Web:* www.oakhotels.com	845-223-3603		707
Oak Knoll Animal Hospital Ltd 3113 41st St ... Moline IL 61265 *Web:* oakknollanimalhospital.com	309-751-4037		794
Oak Lawn Chamber of Commerce 5120 Museum Dr ... Oak Lawn IL 60453 *Web:* www.oaklawnchamber.com	708-424-8300		139
Oak Lawn Park District 9400 S Kenton Ave ... Oaklawn IL 60453 *TF:* 800-216-1110 ■ *Web:* www.olparks.com	708-857-2222		31
Oak Lawn Public Library 9427 Raymond Ave ... Oak Lawn IL 60453 *Web:* www.olpl.org	708-422-4990	422-5061	434-3
Oak Meadows Elementary School 28600 Poinsettia St ... Murrieta CA 92563	951-246-4210		685
Oak Mountain State Park 200 Terrace Dr PO Box 278 ... Pelham AL 35124 *TF:* 800-252-7275 ■ *Web:* www.alapark.com	205-620-2520	620-2531	565
Oak Orchard State Marine Park c/o Lakeside Beach State Pk Rt 18 ... Carlton NY 14571 *Web:* www.parks.ny.gov	585-682-4888		565
Oak Park Area Convention & Visitors Bureau 1118 Westgate ... Oak Park IL 60301 *TF:* 888-625-7275 ■ *Web:* www.visitoakpark.com	708-524-7800	524-7473	206
Oak Park Mall 11149 W 95th St ... Overland Park KS 66214 *Web:* www.thenewoakparkmall.com	913-888-4400		460
Oak Park Park District 218 Madison St ... Oak Park IL 60302 *Web:* pdop.org	708-383-0002		31
Oak Park Public Library 834 Lake St ... Oak Park IL 60301 *Web:* www.oppl.org	708-383-8200		434-3
Oak Park School District (OPSD) 13900 Granzon ... Oak Park MI 48237 *Web:* www.oakparkschools.org	248-336-7700	336 7738	300-2
Oak Park-River Forest Chamber of Commerce PO Box 4554 ... Oak Park IL 60304 *Web:* www.oprfchambor.org	708-613-0550		139
Oak Plantation Resort & Suites Condominium Assn 4090 Enchanted Oaks Cir ... Kissimmee FL 34741 *TF:* 888-411-4141 ■ *Web:* www.oakplantationresort.com	888-411-4141		378
Oak Products Inc 504 Wade St ... Sturgis MI 49091 *Web:* www.oakpresses.com	269-651-8513	651-8513	456
Oak Ridge Chamber of Commerce 1400 Oak Ridge Tpke ... Oak Ridge TN 37830 *Web:* www.oakridgechamber.org	865-483-1321	483-1678	139
Oak Ridge Financial 701 Xenia Ave S Ste 100 ... Minneapolis MN 55416 *TF:* 800-231-8364 ■ *Web:* www.oakridgefinancial.com	763-923-2200	923-2283	69
Oak Ridge Hotel & Conference Ctr 1 Oak Ridge Dr ... Chaska MN 55318 *Web:* oakridgeminneapolis.com	952-368-3100	368-1488	377
Oak Ridge National Laboratory (ORNL) PO Box 2008 ... Oak Ridge TN 37831 **Fax:* PR ■ *Web:* www.ornl.gov	865-576-2900	574-0595*	668
Oak Ridge Public Library 1401 Oak Ridge Tpke ... Oak Ridge TN 37830 *Web:* www.oakridgetn.gov/department/library/home	865-425-3455		434-3
Oak Ridge Winery 6100 E Victor Rd ... Lodi CA 95240 *TF:* 800-988-6174 ■ *Web:* www.oakridgewinery.com	209-369-4758		50-7
Oak Room 138 St James Ave ... Boston MA 02116 *Web:* oaklongbarkitchen.com	617-585-7222		671
Oak Trace 200 Village Dr ... Downers Grove IL 60516 *Web:* www.lifespacecommunities.com	630-769-6100		371
Oak Tree Systems Inc 694 Frnt St ... Lovingston VA 22949 *Web:* oaktree-systems.com	434-263-6700		809
Oak View Mall 3001 S 144th St ... Omaha NE 68144 *Web:* www.oakviewmall.com	402-330-3332		460
OakBend Medical Ctr 1705 Jackson St ... Richmond TX 77469 *Web:* www.oakbendmedcenter.org	281-341-3000	341-3056	374-3
OakBrook Investments LLC 2300 Cabot Dr Ste 300 ... Lisle IL 60532 *Web:* www.oakbrookinvest.com	630-271-0100		528
Oakbrook Shopping Ctr 100 Oakbrook Ctr ... Oak Brook IL 60523 *Web:* www.oakbrookcenter.com	630-573-0700		460
Oakdale Electric Co-op PO Box 128 ... Oakdale WI 54649 *TF:* 800-241-2468 ■ *Web:* www.oakdalerec.com	608-372-4131		245
Oakdale Precision Inc 7022 Sixth St N ... Oakdale MN 55128 *TF:* 800-661-6029 ■ *Web:* www.oakdaleprecision.com	651-730-7700		757
Oakdale Theatre 95 S Tpke Rd ... Wallingford CT 06492 *Web:* www.oakdale.com	203-269-8721		572
Oakes Motor Sports 1210 S Seventh St ... Oakes ND 58474 *Web:* www.oakesmotorsports.com	701-742-2936		736
Oakgrove Construction Inc 6900 Seneca St ... Elma NY 14059 *TF:* 866-435-1499 ■ *Web:* www.oakgroveconst.com	716-652-2200	655-3919	188-4

	Phone	Fax	Class
Oakhill Correctional Institution 5212 County Hwy M ... Oregon WI 53575 *Web:* doc.wi.gov	608-835-3101	835-6090	213
Oakhill Hospital 11375 Cortez Blvd ... Brooksville FL 34613 *TF:* 877-442-2362 ■ *Web:* www.oakhillhospital.com	352-596-6632	597-6387	374-3
Oakhurst Area Chamber of Commerce 49074 Civic Cir ... Oakhurst CA 93644 *TF:* 800-613-0709 ■ *Web:* www.oakhurstchamber.com	559-683-7766	658-2942	139
Oakhurst Dairy 364 Forest Ave ... Portland ME 04101 *TF:* 800-482-0718 ■ *Web:* www.oakhurstdairy.com	207-772-7468	874-0714	296-27
Oakland Asian Cultural Ctr 388 Ninth St Ste 290 ... Oakland CA 94607 *Web:* www.oacc.cc	510-637-0455	637-0459	50-2
Oakland Athletics 7000 Coliseum Way ... Oakland CA 94621 *Web:* oakland.athletics.mlb.com	510-638-4900		713
Oakland Aviation Museum 8252 Earhart Rd ... Oakland CA 94621 *Web:* www.oaklandaviationmuseum.org	510-638-7100		520
Oakland Ballet Co 2201 Broadway Ste 206 ... Oakland CA 94612 *TF:* 866-711-6037 ■ *Web:* www.oaklandballet.org	510-893-3132		573-1
Oakland Care Center Inc 20 Breakneck Rd ... Oakland NJ 07436 *Web:* oaklandrehabhc.com	201-337-3300		371
Oakland City Hall 1 Frank H Ogawa Plaza ... Oakland CA 94612 *TF:* 800-834-3773 ■ *Web:* www.oaklandnet.com	510-444-2489		337
Oakland City University 138 N Lucretia St ... Oakland City IN 47660 *TF:* 800-737-5125 ■ *Web:* www.oak.edu	812-749-4781	749-1433	166
Oakland Community College 2480 Opdyke Rd ... Bloomfield Hills MI 48304 *TF:* 800-829-1040 ■ *Web:* www.oaklandcc.edu	248-341-2000	341-2199	162
Auburn Hills 2900 Featherstone Rd ... Auburn Hills MI 48326 *Web:* www.oaklandcc.edu	248-232-4100		162
Highland Lakes 7350 Cooley Lake Rd ... Waterford MI 48327 *TF:* 800-829-1040 ■ *Web:* www.oaklandcc.edu	248-942-3100		162
Orchard Ridge 27055 OrchaRd Lake Rd ... Farmington Hills MI 48334 *TF:* 800-877-4253 ■ *Web:* www.oaklandcc.edu	248-522-3400		162
Royal Oak 739 S Washington Ave ... Royal Oak MI 48067 *Web:* www.oaklandcc.edu	248-246-2400		162
Southfield 2480 Opdyke Rd ... Bloomfield Hills MI 48304 **Fax:* Library ■ *TF:* 800-829-1040 ■ *Web:* www.oaklandcc.edu	248-341-2000	233-2828*	162
Oakland Consulting Group Inc 9501 Sheridan St Ste 200 ... Lanham MD 20706 *Web:* www.ocg-inc.com	301-577-4111		180
Oakland Convention & Visitors Bureau 481 Water St ... Oakland CA 94607 *TF:* 800-862-2543 ■ *Web:* www.visitoakland.org	510-839-9000		206
Oakland Convention Ctr 1001 Broadway ... Oakland CA 94607 *TF:* 800-228-9290 ■ *Web:* marriott.com	510-451-4000	835-3466	205
Oakland Elementary School 2415 Brockton Ave ... Royal Oak MI 48067 *Web:* www.royaloakschools.org	248 542-4400		685
Oakland House 7801 Genesta St ... Saint Louis MO 63123 *Web:* www.oaklandhousemuseum.org	314-352-5654		50-3
Oakland Metropolitan Chamber of Commerce 475 14th St Ste 100 ... Oakland CA 94612 *TF:* 800-552-3506 ■ *Web:* www.oaklandchamber.com	510-874-4800	839-8817	139
Oakland Mormon Temple 4770 Lincoln Ave ... Oakland CA 94602 *Web:* www.ldschurchtemples.com	510-531-3200	531-2646	50-1
Oakland Museum of California 1000 Oak St ... Oakland CA 94607 *TF General:* 888-625-6873 ■ *Web:* www.museumca.org	510-238-2200	238-2258	520
Oakland Nursery Inc 1156 Oakland Pk Ave ... Columbus OH 43224 *Web:* www.oaklandnursery.com	614-268-3511		323
Oakland Packaging & Supply 3200 Regatta Blvd Ste F ... Richmond CA 94804 *Web:* www.oakpackaging.com	510-307-4242		557
Oakland Press 48 W Huron St ... Pontiac MI 48342 *TF:* 888-977-3677 ■ *Web:* www.theoaklandpress.com	248-332-8181		637-8
Oakland Public Library 125 14th St ... Oakland CA 94612 *Web:* www.oaklandlibrary.org	510-238-3144	238-2232	434-3
Oakland Raiders 1220 Harbor Bay Pkwy ... Alameda CA 94502 *TF:* 800-724-3377 ■ *Web:* www.raiders.com	510-864-5000	864-5134	715-3
Oakland Schools Foundation 3700 Coolidge Ave ... Oakland CA 94602 *Web:* www.oaklandschoolsfoundation.org	510-842-3461		303
Oakland Schools Inc 2111 Pontiac Lake Rd ... Waterford MI 48328 *Web:* www.oakland.k12.mi.us	248-209-2000	209-2206	685
Oakland Unified School District 1000 Broadway Ste 680 ... Oakland CA 94607 *TF:* 888-604-4636 ■ *Web:* www.ousd.org	510-879-8200		685
Oakland University 2200 Squirrel Rd ... Rochester MI 48309 **Fax:* Admissions ■ *TF Admissions:* 800-625-8648 ■ *Web:* www.oakland.edu	248-370-2100	370-4462*	166
Oakland University Art Gallery Oakland University 208 Wilson Hall ... Rochester MI 48309 *TF:* 800-745-3000 ■ *Web:* www.ouartgallery.org	248-370-3005	370-4208	50-2
Oakland Zoo 9777 Golf Links Rd ... Oakland CA 94605 *Web:* www.oaklandzoo.org	510-632-9525	635-5719	823
Oakland-Alameda County Coliseum 7000 Coliseum Way ... Oakland CA 94621 *Web:* www.coliseum.com	510-569-2121		720
Oaklawn Park 2705 Central Ave ... Hot Springs AR 71901 *TF General:* 800-625-5296 ■ *Web:* www.oaklawn.com	501-623-4411	624-4950	642
Oaklawn Psychiatric Center Inc 330 Lakeview Dr ... Goshen IN 46527 *TF:* 800-282-0809 ■ *Web:* www.oaklawn.org	574-533-1234		726
Oakleaf Waste Management LLC 415 Day Hill Rd ... Windsor CT 06095 *TF:* 800-972-4545 ■ *Web:* wmsbs.wm.com	860-290-1250	290-1251	804
Oakley Inc 1 Icon ... Foothill Ranch CA 92610 *TF Cust Svc:* 800-403-7449 ■ *Web:* www.oakley.com	949-672-6925		542

Name / Address	City	State	Zip	Phone	Fax	Class
Oakley Industries Inc 35166 Automation Dr	Clinton Twp	MI	48035	586-792-1261		489
Web: www.oakley-ind.com						
Oakley Transport Inc 101 ABC Rd	Lake Wales	FL	33859	863-638-1435		449
TF: 800-969-8265 ■ *Web:* oakleytransport.com						
Oakley's Bistro 1464 W 86th St	Indianapolis	IN	46260	317-824-1231	824-0938	671
Web: www.oakleysbistro.com						
Oakley-Lindsay Ctr 300 Civic Ctr Plaza Ste 237	Quincy	IL	62301	217-223-1000	223-1330	205
TF: 800-978-4748 ■ *Web:* www.oakleylindsaycenter.com						
Oakmark Family of Funds 330 W nineth St	Kansas City	MO	64105	617-483-8327		528
TF: 800-625-6275 ■ *Web:* www.oakmark.com						
Oak-Mitsui Inc 80 First St	Hoosick Falls	NY	12090	518-686-4961	686-8080	295
TF: 800-424-8802 ■ *Web:* www.oakmitsui.com						
Oakridge Holdings Inc 1003 400 W ONTARIO St Ste 1003	Chicago	IL	60654	312-505-9267		22
Web: www.oakridgeholdingsinc.com						
Oaks Amusement Park 7805 SE Oaks PkWy	Portland	OR	97202	503-233-5777	236-9143	32
TF: 800-237-5920 ■ *Web:* www.oakspark.com						
Oaks at Denville, The 19 Pocono Rd	Denville	NJ	07834	973-586-6000	586-6030	672
TF: 877-693-7650 ■ *Web:* www.franciscanoaks.com						
Oaks at Ojai 122 E Ojai Ave	Ojai	CA	93023	805-646-5573		706
TF: 800-753-6257 ■ *Web:* www.oaksspa.com						
Oaks Correctional Facility 1500 Caberfae Hwy	Manistee	MI	49660	231-723-8272		213
TF: 800-846-6242 ■ *Web:* www.michigan.gov/corrections						
Oaks, The 350 W Hillcrest Dr	Thousand Oaks	CA	91360	805-495-2032		460
TF: 800-745-3000 ■ *Web:* www.shoptheoaksmall.com						
Oakton Community College 1600 E Golf Rd	Des Plaines	IL	60016	847-635-1600	635-1890*	162
**Fax:* Admissions ■ *TF:* 800-798-8100 ■ *Web:* www.oakton.edu						
Skokie Campus 7701 N Lincoln Ave	Skokie	IL	60077	847-635-1600	635-1497	162
TF: 800-798-8100 ■ *Web:* www.oakton.edu						
Oakton Pavilion Healthcare Facility Inc 1660 Oakton Pl	Des Plaines	IL	60018	847-299-5588		450
Oakview Manor 929 Mixon School Rd	Ozark	AL	36360	334-774-2631		371
TF: 800-566-0294 ■ *Web:* www.oakviewmanor.com						
Oakville Chamber of Commerce 700 Kerr St Ste 200	Oakville	ON	L6K3W5	905-845-6613	845-6475	137
Web: www.oakvillechamber.com						
Oakville-Trafalgar Memorial Hospital 3001 Hospital Gate	Oakville	ON	L6M0L8	905-845-2571	338-4636	374-2
Web: www.haltonhealthcare.on.ca						
Oakwood Capital Management LLC 12121 Wilshire Blvd Ste 1250	Los Angeles	CA	90025	310-772-2600		194
TF: 800-586-0600 ■ *Web:* www.oakwoodcap.com						
Oakwood College 7000 Adventist Blvd	Huntsville	AL	35896	256-726-7356	726-7154*	166
**Fax:* Admissions ■ *TF:* 800-824-5312 ■ *Web:* www.oakwood.edu						
Oakwood Crystal City 400 15th St S	Arlington	VA	22202	703-920-9550		210
TF: 877-902-0832 ■ *Web:* www.oakwood.com						
Oakwood Ctr 197 Westbank Expy	Gretna	LA	70053	504-361-1550		460
Web: www.oakwoodcenter.com						
Oakwood Friends School 22 Spackenkill Rd	Poughkeepsie	NY	12603	845-462-4200		622
Web: www.oakwoodfriends.org						
Oakwood Heritage Hospital 10000 Telegraph Rd	Taylor	MI	48180	313-295-5000	295-5085	374-3
TF: 800-543-9355 ■ *Web:* www.oakwood.org						
Oakwood Laboratories LLC 7670 First Pl Ste A	Oakwood Village	OH	44146	440-359-0000	359-0001	85
Web: www.oakwoodlabs.com						
Oakwood Lakes State Park 46109 202nd St	Bruce	SD	57220	605-627-5441		565
Web: sd.gov						
Oakwood Lanes Inc 234 SR- 31 N	Washington	NJ	07882	908-689-0310		99
Web: www.oakwoodlanes.com						
Oakwood Products Inc 1741 Old Dunbar Rd	West Columbia	SC	29172	803-739-8800	739-6957	144
TF: 800-467-3386 ■ *Web:* www.oakwoodchemical.com						
Oakwood Southshore Medical Ctr 5450 Fort St	Trenton	MI	48183	734-671-3800	671-3564	374-3
TF: 800-543-9355 ■ *Web:* www.oakwood.org						
Oakwood Systems Group Inc 622 Emerson Rd Ste 350	Saint Louis	MO	63141	314-824-3000		180
TF: 800-810-8412 ■ *Web:* www.oakwoodsys.com						
Oakwood Village West 5565 Tancho Dr	Madison	WI	53705	608-230-4000		672
Web: www.oakwoodvillage.net						
Oakwood Worldwide 2222 Corinth Ave	Los Angeles	CA	90064	310-478-1021	444-2210	210
TF: 800-888-0808 ■ *Web:* www.oakwood.com						
Oakworks Inc 923 E Wellspring Rd	New Freedom	PA	17349	717-235-6807	235-6798	475
TF: 800-558-8850 ■ *Web:* www.oakworks.com						
OANDA Corp 140 Broadway 46th Fl	New York	NY	10005	416-593-9436		69
TF: 800-826-8164 ■ *Web:* www.oanda.com						
Oar Net 1224 Kinnear Rd	Columbus	OH	43212	614-292-1956		180
TF: 800-627-6420 ■ *Web:* www.oar.net						
OAS (Organization of American States) 1889 F St NW	Washington	DC	20006	202-458-3000	458-3967	48-7
TF: 888-442-4887 ■ *Web:* www.oas.org						
Oasis Air Conditioning Heating & Sheet Metal Inc 1931 Grimes St	Fallon	NV	89406	775-423-5258		189-10
OASIS Alignment Services Inc 255 Pickering Rd	Rochester	NH	03867	603-332-9641		261
Web: www.oasisalignment.com						
Oasis Cafe 151 South 500 East	Salt Lake City	UT	84102	801-322-0404		671
Web: www.oasiscafeslc.com						
Oasis Carwash LLC 3425 E Flamingo Rd	Las Vegas	NV	89121	702-433-3680		62-1
Web: oasishandcarwash.com						
Oasis Computing Inc 1595 16th Ave	Richmond Hill	ON	L4B3N9	905-709-7456		177
Web: www.oasiscomputing.com						
Oasis Deck & Restaurant 4000 A1A	Saint Augustine	FL	32080	904-471-3424		671
TF: 800-970-3004 ■ *Web:* www.worldfamousoasis.com						
Oasis Foods Inc 2222 Kirkman St	Lake Charles	LA	70601	337-439-5262		345
Oasis Outsourcing 4511 Woodland Corporate Blvd	Tampa	FL	33614	866-709-9401		631
TF: 866-709-9401 ■ *Web:* www.oasisadvantage.com						
Oasis Outsourcing Inc 2054 Vista Pkwy Ste 300	West Palm Beach	FL	33411	888-627-4735		631
TF General: 888-627-4735 ■ *Web:* www.oasisadvantage.com						
Oasis Ranch Management 86235 Ave 52	Coachella	CA	92236	760-398-8850		196
Web: seaviewsales.com						
Oasis Restaurant 2355 Schoenersville Rd	Allentown	PA	18109	610-264-1955		671
Oasis Stage Werks Inc 249 S Rio Grande St	Salt Lake City	UT	84101	801-363-0364		351
TF: 800-952-6865 ■ *Web:* www.oasis-stage.com						
Oasis State Park 1891 Oasis Rd	Portales	NM	88130	575-356-5331		565
Web: www.emnrd.state.nm.us						
Oasis Systems Inc 24 Hartwell Ave	Lexington	MA	02421	781-676-7333		225
Web: www.oasissystems.com						
Oasis Technology Inc 601 E Daily Dr Ste 226	Camarillo	CA	93010	805-445-4833		180
Web: www.oasistechnology.com						
Oasis TV Inc 1875 Century Park E Ste 600	Los Angeles	CA	90067	310-553-4300		740
Oasis, The 6550 Comanche Trl	Austin	TX	78732	512-266-2442		671
Web: www.oasis-austin.com						
Oatey Co 4700 W 160th St	Cleveland	OH	44135	216-267-7100	321-9535*	609
**Fax Area Code:* 800 ■ *TF Cust Svc:* 800-321-9532 ■ *Web:* www.oatey.com						
O-AT-KA Milk Products Co-op Inc 700 Ellicott St	Batavia	NY	14020	585-343-0536	343-4473	296-3
TF: 800-828-8152 ■ *Web:* www.oatkamilk.com						
Oatmeal Studios Inc PO Box 138	Rochester	VT	05767	802-767-3171		627
Web: www.oatmealstudios.com						
OATS Inc 2501 Maguire Blvd Ste 101	Columbia	MO	65201	573-443-4516		314
TF: 800-831-9219 ■ *Web:* www.oatstransit.org						
OB Macaroni Co 3066 S E Loop 820	Fort Worth	TX	76140	817-335-4629		296-31
TF Orders: 800-553-4336 ■ *Web:* www.obmacaroni.com						
OB Sports Golf Management LLC 7025 E Greenway Pkwy Ste 550	Scottsdale	AZ	85254	480-948-1300		463
Web: www.obsports.com						
OBA Financial Services Inc 20300 Seneca Meadows Pkwy	Germantown	MD	20876	301-916-0742		70
NASDAQ: OBAF						
Oba! 555 NW 12th Ave	Portland	OR	97209	503-228-6161	228-2673	671
Web: www.obarestaurant.com						
Obagi Medical Products Inc 3760 Kilroy Airport Way Ste 500	Long Beach	CA	90806	562-628-1007	628-1008	214
TF: 800-636-7546 ■ *Web:* www.obagi.com						
Obc Northwest Inc 1076 SW Berg Pkwy	Canby	OR	97013	503-266-2021		67
Web: www.obcnw.com						
OBCI (Ocean Bio-Chem Inc) 4041 SW 47th Ave	Fort Lauderdale	FL	33314	954-587-6280	587-2813	151
NASDAQ: OBCI ■ *TF:* 800-327-8583 ■ *Web:* www.oceanbiochem.com						
ObdEdge LLC 7117 Florida Blvd	Baton Rouge	LA	70808	225-215-0079	218-0101	809
Web: www.cellcontrol.com						
Obed Wild & Scenic River 208 N Maiden St	Wartburg	TN	37887	423-346-6294	346-3362	564
Web: www.nps.gov						
Obelisk 2029 P St NW	Washington	DC	20036	202-872-1180		671
Ober Gatlinburg Inc 1001 Pkwy Ste 2	Gatlinburg	TN	37738	865-436-5423		31
TF: 800-251-9202 ■ *Web:* obergatlinburg.com						
Oberbeck Grain Co 700 Walnut St	Highland	IL	62249	618-654-2387	654-5862	447
TF: 800-632-2012 ■ *Web:* www.oberbeckgrainco.com						
Oberdorfer LLC 6259 Thompson Rd	Syracuse	NY	13206	315-437-7588		492
Oberfields LLC 1165 Alum Creek Dr	Columbus	OH	43209	614-252-0955		191-4
TF: 800-845-7644 ■ *Web:* www.oberfields.com						
Oberg Industries Inc 2301 Silverville Rd PO Box 368	Freeport	PA	16229	724-295-2121	295-2588	757
Web: www.oberg.com						
Oberlin College and Conservatory 101 N Professor St	Oberlin	OH	44074	440-775-8121	775-6905	166
Web: home.oberlin.edu						
Oberlin College Library 148 W College St	Oberlin	OH	44074	440-775-8285	775-8739	434-6
Web: home.oberlin.edu						
Oberlin Inn 10 E College St	Oberlin	OH	44074	440-775-7001		379
Web: thehotelatoberlin.com						
Obermeyer Wood Investment Counsel, LLLP 501 Rio Grande Pl Ste 107	Aspen	CO	81611	970-925-8747		401
TF: 800-731-3623 ■ *Web:* www.obermeyerwood.com						
Oberon Asset Management LLC 51 Wooster St 4th Fl	New York	NY	10013	917-237-0147		401
Web: www.oberonasset.com						
oberoSPM 7560 Airport Rd Unit 12	Mississauga	ON	L4T4H4	888-815-2996		317
TF: 888-815-2996 ■ *Web:* oberosolutions.com						
Oberto Sausage Co 7060 S 238th St	Kent	WA	98032	253-854-7056		296-26
TF: 877-453-7591 ■ *Web:* www.oberto.com						
Oberweis Securities Inc 3333 Warrenville Rd Ste 500	Lisle	IL	60532	630-577-2300	245-0467	690
Web: www.oberweis.net						
Obetech LLC 800 E Leigh St	Richmond	VA	23219	804-344-5360		416
Web: adv36.com						
OB-GYN Physicians Inc 118 Fairview Dr Ste 100	Franklin	VA	23851	757-562-4156		415
OBI (Ocean Breeze International) 3910 Via Real	Carpinteria	CA	93013	805-684-1747	684-0235	369
Web: www.oceanbreezeintl.com						
OBI (Oklahoma Blood Institute) 1001 N Lincoln Blvd	Oklahoma City	OK	73104	405-278-3100	477-0446*	89
**Fax Area Code:* 918 ■ *TF:* 866-708-4995 ■ *Web:* www.obi.org						
Obi Creative 2920 Farnam St	Omaha	NE	68131	402-493-7999		195
TF: 800-561-3357 ■ *Web:* www.obicreative.com						
Obion County 1604B W Reelfoot Ave	Union City	TN	38261	731-884-2133	884-2719	338
TF: 800-222-8754 ■ *Web:* www.tn.gov						
Obion County Nursing Home 1084 E County Home Rd	Union City	TN	38261	731-885-9065		371
TF: 800-213-0154 ■ *Web:* obioncountynursinghome.com						
Obion County Public Library 1221 E Reelfoot Ave	Union City	TN	38261	731-885-7000		434-3
Web: www.oclibrary.org						

Phone | Fax | Class

Obion River Regional Library Center
542 N Lindell .... Martin TN 38237 731-587-2347 434-3

OBJ (Orlando Business Journal)
255 S Orange Ave Ste 700 .... Orlando FL 32801 407-649-8470 420-1625 457-5
Web: www.bizjournals.com

Object CTalk Inc
1013 W Ninth Ave .... King Of Prussia PA 19406 610-265-1278 41
TF: 800-935-4654 ■ *Web:* www.octalk.com

Object Design Comms Inc
8212 Old Courthouse Rd Ste A .... Vienna VA 22182 703-917-0023 344
Web: www.objectdc.com

Object Edge Inc 315 Lennon Ln .... Walnut Creek CA 94598 925-943-5558 196
Web: www.objectedge.com

Object Management Group (OMG)
140 Kendrick St Ste 300 .... Needham MA 02494 781-444-0404 444-0320 48-9
Web: www.omg.org

Object Research Systems Inc
760 St-Paul W Ste 101 .... Montreal QC H3C1M4 514-843-3861 809
Web: www.theobjects.com

Object Systems Group Inc
8600 Freeport Pkwy Ste 400 .... Irving TX 75063 972-650-2026 196
TF: 800-746-5840 ■ *Web:* www.osgcorp.com

ObjectBuilders Inc
20134 W Vly Forge Cir .... King Of Prussia PA 19406 610-783-7748 177
Web: www.objectbuilders.com

Objectiva Software Solutions Inc
505 Lomas Santa Fe Dr Ste 170 .... Solana Beach CA 92075 760-230-6607 196
TF: 800-878-6975 ■ *Web:* www.objectivasoftware.com

Objective Arts Inc 20 N Wacker Ave .... Chicago IL 60606 312-977-1150 177
Web: objectivearts.com

Objective Interface Systems Inc
220 Spring St Ste 530 .... Herndon VA 20170 703-295-6500 177
Web: www.ois.com

Objective Technologies Inc
712 Heatherglen Dr .... Southlake TX 76092 817-251-6900 177

Objectivity Inc
3099 N First St Ste 200 .... San Jose CA 95134 408-992-7100 992-7171 178-1
TF: 800-767-6259 ■ *Web:* www.objectivity.com

ObjectRiver Inc 21 Pemberton Rd .... Wayland MA 01778 508-651-0767 177
Web: www.objectriver.net

Objectstream Inc
7725 W Reno Ave Ste 307 .... Oklahoma City OK 73127 405-942-4477 225
Web: www.objectstream.com

ObjectVideo Labs
8281 Greensboro Dr Ste 100 .... Tysons VA 22102 571-327-3673 654-9399* 178-7
**Fax Area Code:* 703 ■ *Web:* www.objectvideo.com

Objectwin Technology Inc
14800 St Mary's Ln Ste 100 .... Houston TX 77079 713-782-8200 782-8283 177
Web: www.objectwin.com

Oblate School of Theology
285 Oblate Dr .... San Antonio TX 78216 210-341-1366 167-3
Web: www.ost.edu

Oblong Industries Inc
923 E Third St Ste 111 .... Los Angeles CA 90013 213-683-8863 256
Web: oblong.com

Oboxmedia Inc
4200 St Laurent Blvd Ste 900 .... Montreal QC H2W2R2 514-282-5020 5
Web: oboxmedia.com

Obrien et Al Advertising Inc
3113 Pacific Ave .... Virginia Beach VA 23451 757-422-3231 7
Web: www.obrienetal.com

Obrien Glass Co 4916 W SR- 97 .... Springfield IL 62707 217-522-5660 329

Obs Inc 1324 WTuscarawas St PO Box 6210 .... Canton OH 44706 330-453-3725 580-2429 516
TF: 800-362-9592 ■ *Web:* www.obsinc.net

Observer & Eccentric Newspapers
615 W Lafayette Second Level .... Detroit MI 48226 734-459-2700 459-4224 637-8
TF: 866-887-2737

Observer Dispatch Inc
221 Oriskany Plaza .... Utica NY 13501 315-797-9150 637-8
Web: www.uticaod.com

Observer Newspaper
201 N Federal Hwy Ste 103 .... Deerfield Beach FL 33441 954-428-9045 428-9096 532-4
Web: observernewspaperonline.com

Observer, The 140 S Front St .... Sarnia ON N7T7M8 519-344-3641 332-2951 532-1
TF: 866-541-6757 ■ *Web:* www.theobserver.ca

Observer, The 1594 Sara Rd SE Ste D .... Rio Rancho NM 87124 505-892-8080 892-5719 532-2
Web: www.rrobserver.com

Observera Inc
3856 Dulles S Court Ste I .... Chantilly VA 20151 703-378-3153 225
TF: 800-444-6905 ■ *Web:* www.observera.com

Observer-Reporter 122 S Main St .... Washington PA 15301 724-222-2200 532-2
TF: 800-222-6397 ■ *Web:* www.observer-reporter.com

Obsidian Mortgage Corp
35 Grand Marshall Dr 2nd fl .... Toronto ON M1B5W9 416-283-2377 509
Web: www.obsidianmortgages.com

Obzerv Technologies Inc
400 Jean-Lesage Ste 201 .... Quebec QC G1K8W1 418-524-3522 524-6745 544
Web: www.obzerv.com

OC Jones & Sons Inc 1520 Fourth St .... Berkeley CA 94710 510-526-3424 77
TF: 800-578-8810 ■ *Web:* www.ocjones.com

OC Seacrets Inc 117 49th St .... Ocean City MD 21842 410-524-4900 54
Web: www.seacrets.com

OC Systems Inc
9990 Fairfax Blvd Ste 270 .... Fairfax VA 22030 703-359-8160 177
Web: www.ocsystems.com

OC Tanner Co 1930 S State St .... Salt Lake City UT 84115 800-453-7490 409
TF: 800-453-7490 ■ *Web:* www.octanner.com

OC Weekly 2975 Red Hill Ave Ste 150 .... Costa Mesa CA 92626 714-550-5900 550-5908 532-5
TF: 800-300-4345 ■ *Web:* www.ocweekly.com

OCA (Organization of Chinese Americans)
1322 18th St NW .... Washington DC 20036 202-223-5500 296-0540 48-14
TF: 800-584-7336 ■ *Web:* www.ocanational.org

OCA Ventures 351 W Hubbard St Ste 600 .... Chicago IL 60654 312-327-8400 792
Web: www.ocaventures.com

Ocala Regional Medical Ctr (ORMC)
1431 SW First Ave .... Ocala FL 34478 352-401-1000 374-3
Web: www.ocalahealthsystem.com

Ocala-Marion County Chamber of Commerce
310 SE Third St .... Ocala FL 34471 352-629-8051 629-7651 139
TF: 800-466-5055 ■ *Web:* ocalacep.com

OCB (Old Country Buffet Restaurants)
120 Chula Vista .... Hollywood Park TX 78232 210-403-3725 403-3580 670
Web: www.oldcountrybuffet.com

OCBJ (Orange County Business Journal)
18500 Von Karman Ave Ste 150 .... Irvine CA 92612 949-833-8373 833-8751 457-5
Web: www.ocbj.com

OCC (Optical Cable Corp)
5290 Concourse Dr .... Roanoke VA 24019 540-265-0690 265-0724 814
NASDAQ: OCC ■ *TF:* 800-622-7711 ■ *Web:* www.occfiber.com

OCCC (Orange County Convention Ctr)
9800 International Dr .... Orlando FL 32819 407-685-9800 685-9876 205
TF: 800-345-9845 ■ *Web:* www.occc.net

Occidental Chemical Corp 5005 LBJ Fwy .... Dallas TX 75244 972-404-3800 143
Web: www.oxy.com

Occidental College 1600 Campus Rd .... Los Angeles CA 90041 323-259-2700 341-4875* 166
**Fax:* Admissions ■ *TF Admissions:* 800-825-5262 ■ *Web:* www.oxy.edu

Occidental College Clapp Library
1600 Campus Rd .... Los Angeles CA 90041 323-259-2640 341-4991 434-6
Web: www.oxy.edu

Occidental International Corp
1701 Pennsylvania Ave NW Ste 400 .... Washington DC 20006 202-857-3000 538
Web: www.oxy.com

Occidental Oil & Gas Corp
5 Greenway Plaza Ste 110 .... Houston TX 77046 713-215-7000 536
Web: www.oxy.com

Occk Inc 1710 W Schilling Rd .... Salina KS 67401 785-827-9383 476
TF: 800-526-9731 ■ *Web:* www.occk.com

Occoneechee State Park
1192 Occoneechee Pk Rd .... Clarksville VA 23927 434-374-2210 565
TF: 800-933-7275 ■ *Web:* dcr.virginia.gov

Occupational Care Consultants
3028 Navarre Ave .... Oregon OH 43616 419-697-6850 415
TF: 800-282-7275 ■ *Web:* www.therapyworks.net

Occupational Health Dynamics
197 Cahaba Vly Pkwy .... Pelham AL 35124 205-980-0180 194
TF: 800-553-1911 ■ *Web:* www.ohdusa.com

Occupational Safety & Health Administration (OSHA)
200 Constitution Ave NW .... Washington DC 20210 202-693-1999 693-1659 340-15
TF: 800-321-6742 ■ *Web:* www.osha.gov

Occupational Safety & Health Administration Regional Offices
Region 1 JFK Federal Bldg Rm E-340 .... Boston MA 02203 617-565-9860 565-9827 340-15
TF: 800-321-6742 ■ *Web:* www.osha.gov/oshdir/r01.html
Region 2 201 Varick St Ste 670 .... New York NY 10014 212-337-2378 337-2371 340-15
TF: 800-321-6742 ■ *Web:* www.osha.gov/oshdir/r02.html
Region 3
Curtis Ctr 170 S Independence Mall W
Ste 740W .... Philadelphia PA 19106 215-861-4900 861-4904 340-15
TF: 800-321-6742 ■ *Web:* www.osha.gov
Region 4 61 Forsyth St SW Rm 6T50 .... Atlanta GA 30303 678-237-0400 562-2295* 340-15
**Fax Area Code:* 404 ■ *TF:* 800-321-6742 ■ *Web:* www.osha.gov/oshdir/r04.html
Region 5 230 S Dearborn St Rm 3244 .... Chicago IL 60604 312-353-2220 353-7774 340-15
Web: www.osha.gov/oshdir/r05.html
Region 6 525 Griffin St Ste 602 .... Dallas TX 75202 972-850-4145 850-4149 340-15
Web: www.osha.gov/oshdir/r06.html
Region 7
2300 Main St
Suite 1010 2 Pershing Square Bldg .... Kansas City MO 64108 816-283-8745 283-0547 340-15
Web: www.osha.gov/oshdir/r07.html
Region 8
1244 Speer Blvd
Ste 551 Cesar Chavez Memorial Bldg .... Denver CO 80204 720-264-6550 264-6585 340-15
Web: www.osha.gov/oshdir/r08.html
Region 9 90 Seventh St Ste 18100 .... San Francisco CA 94103 415-625-2547 625-2534 340-15
Web: www.osha.gov/oshdir/r09.html
Region 10 300 Fifth Ave Ste 1280 .... Seattle WA 98104 206-757-6700 757-6705 340-15
TF Help Line: 800-321-6742 ■ *Web:* www.osha.gov/oshdir

Occupational Safety & Health Review Commission
1120 20th St NW 9th Fl .... Washington DC 20036 202-606-5400 606-5050 340-20
Web: www.oshrc.gov

Occupational Safety & Health Review Commission Regional Offices
Atlanta Region
100 Alabama St SW Rm 2R90 .... Atlanta GA 30303 404-562-1640 562-1650 340-20
TF: 800-321-6742 ■ *Web:* www.oshrc.gov

OC&E Woods Line State Trail
46000 Hwy 97 N .... Chiloquin OR 97624 541-883-5558 565
TF: 800-551-6949 ■ *Web:* oregonstateparks.org

Ocean 1218 20th St S .... Birmingham AL 35205 205-933-0999 671
Web: www.oceanbirmingham.com

Ocean Aire PO Box 1245 .... Toms River NJ 08754 732-797-1077 797-1076 63
Web: www.oceanaire.net

Ocean Bank 780 NW 42nd Ave .... Miami FL 33126 305-442-2660 70
TF: 877-688-2265 ■ *Web:* www.oceanbank.com

Ocean Beauty Seafoods Inc
1100 W Ewing St .... Seattle WA 98119 206-285-6800 296-14
TF: 800-365-8950 ■ *Web:* www.oceanbeauty.com

Ocean Bio-Chem Inc (OBCI)
4041 SW 47th Ave .... Fort Lauderdale FL 33314 954-587-6280 587-2813 151
NASDAQ: OBCI ■ *TF:* 800-327-8583 ■ *Web:* www.oceanbiochem.com

Ocean Breeze International (OBI)
3910 Via Real .... Carpinteria CA 93013 805-684-1747 684-0235 369
Web: www.oceanbreezeintl.com

Ocean Breeze Waterpark
849 General Booth Blvd .... Virginia Beach VA 23451 757-422-4444 31
Web: www.oceanbreezewaterpark.com

Ocean Bridge Group
2032 Armacost Ave .... Los Angeles CA 90025 310-392-3200 4
Web: www.oceanbridgemedia.com

Ocean City 340 W Broadway .... Jackson WY 83001 307-734-9768 671
Web: oceancitychinabistro.com

Ocean City Animal Hospital
11843 Ocean Gtwy .... Ocean City MD 21842 410-213-1170 794
TF: 800-283-3846 ■ *Web:* oceancityvet.com

Ocean City City Hall
301 Baltimore Ave .... Ocean City MD 21842 410-289-8931 289-7385 337
TF: 800-626-2326 ■ *Web:* www.oceancitymd.gov

	Phone	Fax	Class
Ocean City Convention & Visitors Bureau			
4001 Coastal Hwy........................Ocean City MD 21842	410-723-8600		206
TF: 800-626-2326 ■ *Web:* www.ococean.com			
Ocean City Hotel-Motel-Restaurant Assn			
PO Box 340..............................Ocean City MD 21843	410-289-6733		376
TF: 800-626-2326 ■ *Web:* www.ocvisitor.com			
Ocean City Life-Saving Station Museum			
813 S Atlantic Ave.......................Ocean City MD 21842	410-289-4991	289-4991	520
TF: 800-235-4045 ■ *Web:* www.ocmuseum.org			
Ocean City Maryland Hotels			
6600 Coastal Hwy........................Ocean City MD 21842	410-524-5252		671
TF: 800-837-3588 ■ *Web:* www.ocmdhotels.com			
Ocean City Public Library			
1735 Simpson Ave Ste 4..................Ocean City NJ 08226	609-399-2434		434-3
Web: oceancitylibrary.org			
Ocean City State Park			
148 State Rt 115..........................Hoquiam WA 98550	360-289-3553		565
Web: www.parks.wa.gov			
Ocean Club Night Club			
10100 Coastal Hwy.......................Ocean City MD 21842	410-703-1970		671
Web: oceancity.com			
Ocean Conservancy			
1300 19th St NW 8th Fl...................Washington DC 20036	202-429-5609	872-0619	48-13
TF: 800-519-1541 ■ *Web:* www.oceanconservancy.org			
Ocean County 118 Washington St............Toms River NJ 08753	732-929-2018	349-4336	338
TF: 800-722-0291 ■ *Web:* www.co.ocean.nj.us			
Ocean County College			
College Dr PO Box 2001...................Toms River NJ 08754	732-255-0400	255-0444	162
Web: www.ocean.edu			
Ocean County Library			
101 Washington St........................Toms River NJ 08753	732-349-6200	473-1356	434-3
Web: theoceancountylibrary.org			
Ocean Ctr 101 N Atlantic Ave.............Daytona Beach FL 32118	386-254-4500	254-4512	205
TF: 800-858-6444 ■ *Web:* www.oceancenter.com			
Ocean Deck 127 S Ocean Ave............Daytona Beach FL 32118	386-253-5224		671
Web: www.oceandeck.com			
Ocean Downs 10218 Racetrack Rd................Berlin MD 21811	410-641-0600		642
Web: www.oceandowns.com			
Ocean Drive Clevelander Inc			
1020 Ocean Dr..........................Miami Beach FL 33139	877-532-4006		707
TF: 877-532-4006 ■ *Web:* www.clevelander.com			
Ocean Edge Resort & Golf Club			
2907 Main St..............................Brewster MA 02631	508-896-9000		669
TF: 800-343-6074 ■ *Web:* www.oceanedge.com			
Ocean Embassy Panama Inc			
6426 Milner Blvd Ste 101....................Orlando FL 32809	407-852-9129		787
Web: www.oceanembassy.com			
Ocean Eyes Optical Inc			
2907 Ocean Ave...........................Brooklyn NY 11235	718-332-1017		237
Web: coolframes.com			
Ocean Five Hotel 436 Ocean Dr...........Miami Beach FL 33139	305-532-7093		379
Web: www.oceanfive.com			
Ocean Flow International LLC			
2100 W Loop S Ste 500.......................Houston TX 77027	713-328-6700		313
Web: www.ocean-flow.com			
Ocean Forest Plaza			
5523 N Ocean Blvd.....................Myrtle Beach SC 29577	800-726-3783	692-5234*	379
**Fax Area Code:* 843 ■ *TF General:* 800-726-3783 ■ *Web:* www.sandsresorts.com			
Ocean Futures Society			
325 Chapala St.......................Santa Barbara CA 93101	805-899-8899	899-8898	48-13
TF: 800-477-7500 ■ *Web:* www.oceanfutures.org			
Ocean House Hotel Partners LLC			
1 Bluff Ave.............................Watch Hill RI 02891	401-584-7000		707
Web: www.oceanhouseri.com			
Ocean Kayak			
125 Gilman Falls Ave Bldg B.................Old Town ME 04468	800-852-9257	827-3647*	710
**Fax Area Code:* 207 ■ *TF:* 800-852-9257 ■ *Web:* www.oceankayak.com			
Ocean Key Resort			
424 Atlantic Ave......................Virginia Beach VA 23451	757-425-2200		379
TF: 800-955-9700 ■ *Web:* www.vsaresorts.com			
Ocean Key Resort & Spa 0 Duval St...........Key West FL 33040	305-296-7701		669
TF: 800-328-9815 ■ *Web:* www.oceankey.com			
Ocean Management Systems Inc			
2021 Goshen Tpke..........................Wallkill NY 12589	619-236-1203		710
TF: 800-325-8439 ■ *Web:* www.omsdive.com			
Ocean Manor Resort			
4040 Galt Ocean Dr..................Fort Lauderdale FL 33308	954-566-7500	564-3075	669
TF: 800-955-0444 ■ *Web:* www.oceanmanor.com			
Ocean Medical Ctr (OMC)			
425 Jack Martin Blvd...........................Brick NJ 08724	732-840-2200		374-3
TF: 800-560-9990 ■ *Web:* www.oceanmedicalcenter.com/omc			
Ocean Mist Farms			
10855 Ocean Mist Pkwy Ste A................Castroville CA 95012	831-633-2144		10-11
TF: 800-654-9300 ■ *Web:* www.oceanmist.com			
Ocean Mist Resort			
97 S Shore Dr.......................South Yarmouth MA 02664	508-398-2633	398-2122	669
TF: 800-655-1972 ■ *Web:* www.oceanmistcapecod.com			
Ocean One Cruise Outlet			
3264 Marilynn St..........................Lancaster CA 93536	661-949-2873		771
Ocean Optics Inc 830 Douglas Ave.............Dunedin FL 34698	727-733-2447	733-3962	544
Web: www.oceanoptics.com			
Ocean Park Hotels Inc			
710 Fiero Ln Ste 14..................San Luis Obispo CA 93401	805-544-0812		379
Ocean Petroleum LLC			
7167 Worcester Hwy Ste.....................Newark MD 21841	410-632-0400		579
Ocean Place Resort & Spa			
1 Ocean Blvd.........................Long Branch NJ 07740	732-571-4000		669
TF: 800-411-6493 ■ *Web:* www.oceanplace.com			
Ocean Pointe Suites at Key Largo			
500 Burton Dr..............................Tavernier FL 33070	305-853-3000	853-3007	379
TF: 800-882-9464 ■ *Web:* www.providentresorts.com/ocean-pointe-suites			
Ocean Products Research Inc 19 Butts Ln........Diggs VA 23045	804-725-3406		208
Web: www.opr-rope.com			
Ocean Properties Hotels Resorts & Affiliates			
1001 E Atlantic Ave Ste 202..............Delray Beach FL 33483	561-279-9900		377
Web: www.oplhotels.com			
Ocean Quest Pools Inc 10208 N Fm 620.........Austin TX 78726	512-258-7379		186
Web: www.oceanquest.com			
Ocean Reef Club			
35 Ocean Reef Dr Ste 200.....................Key Largo FL 33037	305-367-2611		379
TF: 888-422-9944 ■ *Web:* www.oceanreef.com			
Ocean Reef Resort			
7100 N Ocean Blvd.....................Myrtle Beach SC 29572	843-449-4441	497-3041	669
TF: 888-322-6411 ■ *Web:* www.oceanreefmyrtlebeach.com			
Ocean Resort Hotel Waikiki			
3 Waterfront Plaza............................Honolulu HI 96813	808-922-3861	922-3773	379
TF: 877-367-1912 ■ *Web:* www.castleresorts.com			
Ocean Seafood 750 N Hill St................Los Angeles CA 90012	213-687-3088		671
Web: www.oceanseafoodchinatown.com			
Ocean Shipholdings Inc			
16211 Pk Ten Pl...............................Houston TX 77084	281-579-3700	579-0671	698
Web: www.oceanshipholdings.com			
Ocean Shores Convention Ctr			
120 W Chance a La Mer Ave.............Ocean Shores WA 98569	360-289-4411	289-4412	205
TF: 800-874-6737 ■ *Web:* www.oceanshoresconventioncenter.com			
Ocean Sky Hotel & Resort			
4060 Galt Ocean Dr..................Fort Lauderdale FL 33308	954-565-6611	564-7730	379
TF: 800-678-9022 ■ *Web:* www.oceanskyresort.com			
Ocean Spray Cranberries Inc			
1 Ocean Spray Dr..................Lakeville-Middleboro MA 02349	508-946-1000	946-4594	296-20
TF: 800-662-3263 ■ *Web:* www.oceanspray.com			
Ocean State Jobbers Inc			
375 Commerce Pk Rd..................North Kingstown RI 02852	401-295-2672		791
Web: www.oceanstatejoblot.com			
Ocean State Technical Services			
55 Chapman St.............................Providence RI 02905	401-467-8661		794
Web: www.ostservices.com			
Ocean State Tire Company Inc			
51 Worthington Rd...........................Cranston RI 02920	401-946-0880		755
Web: www.oceanstatetire.com			
Ocean State Veterinary Specialists Ltd			
1480 S County Trl.....................East Greenwich RI 02818	401-886-6787		794
Web: www.osvs.net			
Ocean Steel & Construction Ltd			
400 Chesley Dr.............................Saint John NB E2K5L6	506-632-2600		480
Web: www.oceansteel.com			
Ocean Tug & Barge Engineering Corp			
258 E Main St Ste 401.........................Milford MA 01757	508-473-0545		261
Web: www.oceantugbarge.com			
Ocean Walk Resort			
300 N Atlantic.........................Daytona Beach FL 32118	386-323-4800		379
TF: 888-743-2561 ■ *Web:* www.wyndhamoceanwalk.com			
Ocean Walk Shoppes at the Village			
250 N Atlantic Ave Ste 201..............Daytona Beach FL 32118	386-258-9544	238-3864	50-6
Web: www.oceanwalkshoppes.com			
Ocean Waters Spa			
600 N Atlantic Ave.....................Daytona Beach FL 32118	386-267-1660		706
TF: 844-284-2685 ■ *Web:* plazaresortandspa.com			
Ocean's Eleven Casino 121 Brooks St.........Oceanside CA 92054	760-439-6988		452
Web: www.oceans11.com			
Oceana 120 W 49th St.......................New York NY 10020	212-759-5941	759-6076	671
Web: www.oceanarestaurant.com			
Oceana County 100 State St Ste 1..................Hart MI 49420	231-873-4328	873-1391	338
TF: 800-882-5941 ■ *Web:* www.oceana.mi.us			
Oceana Natural Foods Coop			
159 SE Second St.............................Newport OR 97365	541-265-8285		345
Web: www.oceanafoods.org			
Oceana Resorts LLC			
2600 N Ocean Blvd................North Myrtle Beach SC 29577	843-448-3121		378
Web: www.oceanaresorts.com			
OCEANAIR Inc 186A Lee Burbank Hwy............Revere MA 02151	781-286-2700		311
Web: www.oceanair.net			
Oceanaire Seafood Room			
1201 F St NW...........................Washington DC 20004	202-347-2277		671
Web: www.theoceanaire.com			
Oceanaire Seafood Room			
5061 Westheimer Rd Ste 8050..................Houston TX 77056	832-487-8862		671
Web: www.theoceanaire.com			
Oceanaire Seafood Room, The			
50 S Sixth St..........................Minneapolis MN 55402	612-333-2277		671
Web: www.theoceanaire.com			
Oceanaire Seafood Room, The			
30 S Meridian St Ste 100..................Indianapolis IN 46204	317-955-2277		671
Web: www.theoceanaire.com			
Oceancliff Hotel & Resort 65 Ridge Rd.........Newport RI 02840	401-846-6667		379
Web: www.newportexperience.com			
Oceane Marine Shipping Inc			
407 E Maple St..............................Cumming GA 30040	770-888-5941		311
TF: 888-262-3263 ■ *Web:* oceanems.com			
Oceaneering International Inc			
11911 FM 529................................Houston TX 77041	713-329-4500	329-4951	539
NYSE: OII ■ *TF:* 844-381-9324 ■ *Web:* www.oceaneering.com			
Oceanex Income Fund			
630 Rene-Levesque Blvd W Ste 2550..........Montreal QC H3B1S6	514-875-9595		311
TF: 888-875-9595 ■ *Web:* www.oceanex.com			
OceanFirst Bank			
975 Hooper Ave PO Box 2009...............Toms River NJ 08753	732-240-4500	349-5070	70
TF: 888-623-2633 ■ *Web:* www.oceanfirstonline.com			
Oceanfront Lodging Inc			
305 N First St.....................Jacksonville Beach FL 32250	904-249-4949		378
Web: www.bestwesternjacksonvillebeach.com			
OceanGate Inc			
1205 Craftsman Way Ste 112....................Everett WA 98201	425-595-5017		393
Web: www.oceangate.com			
Oceania Cruises Inc			
8300 NW 33rd St Ste 308.........................Miami FL 33122	305-514-2300	514-2222	220
TF: 800-531-5619 ■ *Web:* www.oceaniacruises.com			
Oceanic Companies Inc			
91-462 Komohana St...........................Kapolei HI 96707	808-682-0113		186
Web: www.oceaniccompanies.com			
Oceanic Institute			
41-202 Kalanianaole Hwy...................Waimanalo HI 96795	808-259-7951	259-5971	668
Web: www.oceanicinstitute.org			
Oceanic Medical Products Inc			
8005 Shannon Industrial Park Ln................Atchison KS 66002	913-874-2000		476
Web: www.oceanicmedical.com			

	Phone	Fax	Class
Oceanic USA 2002 Davis St. San Leandro CA 94577 *TF:* 800-435-3483 ■ *Web:* www.oceanicworldwide.com	510-562-0500	569-5404	710
Oceano Hotel & Spa Half Moon Bay Harbor 280 Capistrano Rd Half Moon Bay CA 94019 *TF:* 888-623-2661 ■ *Web:* www.oceanohalfmoonbay.com	650-726-5400		378
Oceanos Inc 892 Plain St. Marshfield MA 02050 *Web:* www.oceanosinc.com	781-804-1010		6
Oceanpro Industries Ltd 1900 Fenwick St NE Washington DC 20002 *Web:* www.profish.com	202-529-3003		297-5
Oceanside Beach State Recreation Site 13000 Whiskey Creek Rd W Tillamook OR 97141 *TF:* 800-551-6949 ■ *Web:* www.oregonstateparks.org	800-551-6949		565
Oceanside Chamber of Commerce 928 N Coast Hwy Oceanside CA 92054 *Web:* www.oceansidechamber.com	760-722-1534	722-8336	139
Oceanside Chamber of Commerce 2721 Harrison Ave Oceanside NY 11572 *Web:* oceansidechamber.org	516-763-9177		139
Oceanside Community Service Television Corp 3038 Industry St. Oceanside CA 92054 *Web:* www.koct.org	760-722-4433		116
Oceanside Museum of Art 704 Pier View Way Oceanside CA 92054 *Web:* www.oma-online.org	760-435-3720		522
Oceanside Public Library 330 N Coast Hwy Oceanside CA 92054 *Web:* www.ci.oceanside.ca.us	760-435-5600		434-3
Oceanside Unified School District (OUSD) 2111 Mission Ave. Oceanside CA 92058 *Web:* www.oside.k12.ca.us	760-966-4000		186
Oceanside Union Free School District 11 145 Merle Ave. Oceanside NY 11572 *Web:* oceansideschools.org	516-678-1200		685
Oceanus Partners 16540 Pointe Village Dr Ste 208 Lutz FL 33558 *TF:* 888-496-1117 ■ *Web:* www.oceanuspartners.com	888-496-1117		196
OceanWorks International Inc 11611 Tanner Rd Ste A Houston TX 77041 *Web:* www.oceanworks.com	281-598-3940		350
Ocenco Inc 10225 82nd Ave Pleasant Prairie WI 53158 *TF:* 800-562-5916 ■ *Web:* www.ocenco.com	262-947-9000	947-9020	678
Oceus Networks Inc 1895 Preston White Dr Ste 300 Reston VA 20191 *TF:* 877-816-2599 ■ *Web:* www.oceusnetworks.com	703-234-9200		387
Oce-USA Inc 5450 N Cumberland Ave Chicago IL 60656 *TF:* 800-877-6232 ■ *Web:* csa.canon.com	773-714-8500		589
OCF (International OCD Foundation) PO Box 961029 Boston MA 02196 *TF:* 800-331-3131 ■ *Web:* iocdf.org	617-973-5801	973-5803	48-17
OCF (Omaha Community Foundation) 302 S 36th St Ste 100 Omaha NE 68131 *TF:* 800-794-3458 ■ *Web:* www.omahafoundation.org	402-342-3458	342-3582	303
OCH Regional Medical Ctr 400 Hospital Rd Starkville MS 39759 *Web:* www.och.org	662-323-4320		374-3
Ochiltree County 511 S Main St. Perryton TX 79070 *Web:* www.co.ochiltree.tx.us	806-435-8039	435-2081	338
Ochlockonee River State Park 429 State Pk Rd Sopchoppy FL 32358 *Web:* www.floridastateparks.org	850-962-2771		565
Ochsner 1514 Jefferson Hwy New Orleans LA 70121 *TF:* 800-343-0269 ■ *Web:* www.ochsner.org	504-842-3000	394-0840	374-3
Ochsner Medical Ctr Baton Rouge 17000 Medical Ctr Dr. Baton Rouge LA 70816 *TF:* 800-231-5257 ■ *Web:* www.ochsner.org	225-752-2470		374-3
Ochsner Medical Ctr West Bank 2500 Belle Chasse Hwy Gretna LA 70056 *TF:* 800-231-5257 ■ *Web:* www.ochsner.org	504-391-5454		374-3
Ockers Co 830 W Chestnut St Brockton MA 02301 *Web:* www.ockers.com	508-586-4642	584-9180	175
OCL (Orangeburg County Library) 510 Louis St. Orangeburg SC 29115 *TF:* 800-922-2594 ■ *Web:* www.orangeburgcounty.org	803-531-4636		434-3
Oclaro Inc 46429 Landing Pkwy. Fremont CA 94538 *NASDAQ: OCLR* ■ *Web:* oclaro.com	510-580-8828		696
OCLC (Online Computer Library Ctr Inc) 6565 Kilgour Pl Dublin OH 43017 **Fax Area Code: 614* ■ *TF:* 800-848-5878 ■ *Web:* www.oclc.org	800-848-5878	764-6096*	49-11
OCM (One Call Medical Inc) 20 Waterview Blvd PO Box 614 Parsippany NJ 07054 *TF:* 800-872-2875 ■ *Web:* www.onecallcm.com	973-257-1000	257-0044	382
OCMC (Ouachita County Medical Ctr) PO Box 797 Camden AR 71711 *TF:* 877-836-2472 ■ *Web:* www.ouachitamedcenter.com	870-836-1000	836-1522	374-3
OCMMC (Orange Coast Memorial Medical Ctr) 9920 Talbert Ave. Fountain Valley CA 92708 *TF:* 877-597-4777 ■ *Web:* www.memorialcare.org	714-378-7000	229-5399	374-3
Ocmulgee Electric Membership Corp 5722 Eastman St. Eastman GA 31023 *TF:* 800-342-5509 ■ *Web:* www.ocmulgeeemc.com	478-374-7001		245
Ocmulgee National Monument 1207 Emery Hwy. Macon GA 31217 *Web:* www.nps.gov/ocmu	478-752-8257	752-8259	564
Oconee County 415 S Pine St. Walhalla SC 29691 *Web:* www.oconeesc.com	864-638-4280	638-4280	338
Oconee County Library 501 W S Broad St. Walhalla SC 29691 *Web:* oconeelibrary.org	864-638-4133		434-3
Oconee County School District PO Box 146 Watkinsville GA 30677 *Web:* www.oconeeschools.org	706-769-5130	769-3500	685
Oconee Electric Membership Corp 3445 US Hwy 80 W Dudley GA 31022 *TF:* 800-522-2930 ■ *Web:* www.oconeeemc.com	478-676-3191		245
Oconee Medical Campus (OMC) 298 Memorial Dr Seneca SC 29672 *Web:* www.ghs.org/locations/oconee-medical-campus	864-882-3351		374-3

	Phone	Fax	Class
Oconee Regional Medical Ctr 821 N Cobb St Milledgeville GA 31061 *TF:* 800-275-5255 ■ *Web:* www.oconeeregional.com	478-454-3505	454-3555	374-3
Oconee State Park 624 State Pk Rd Mountain Rest SC 29664 *TF:* 888-803-0844 ■ *Web:* www.southcarolinaparks.com	864-638-5353		565
Oconee Station State Historic Site 500 Oconee Stn Rd. Walhalla SC 29691 *Web:* www.southcarolinaparks.com	864-638-0079		565
OConnor Engineering 2701 N Ontario St Burbank CA 91504 *Web:* www.ocon.com	818-847-8666	847-1205	591
Oconomowoc Area Chamber of Commerce 175 E Wisconsin Ave Oconomowoc WI 53066 *Web:* www.oconomowoc.org	262-567-2666	567-3477	139
Oconomowoc Convention & Visitors Bureau 174 E Wisconsin Ave Oconomowoc WI 53066 *TF:* 888-936-7463 ■ *Web:* www.oconomowoc-wi.gov	262-569-2186	569-2164	206
Oconomowoc Memorial Hospital 791 Summit Ave Oconomowoc WI 53066 *TF:* 800-242-0313 ■ *Web:* www.prohealthcare.org	262-569-9400	569-0336	374-3
Oconomowoc Residential Programs Inc 1746 Executive Dr. Oconomowoc WI 53066 *TF:* 800-963-0035 ■ *Web:* www.orp.com	262-569-5515		463
Oconto County 301 Washington St Oconto WI 54153 *Web:* www.co.oconto.wi.us	920-834-6800	834-6867	338
Oconto Electric Co-op PO Box 168 PO Box 168 Oconto Falls WI 54154 *TF:* 800-472-8410 ■ *Web:* www.ocontoelectric.com	920-846-2816		245
Ocotillo Wells State Vehicular Recreation Area 5172 Hwy 78 # 10 Borrego Springs CA 92004 *Web:* www.parks.ca.gov	760-767-1302		565
OCP (Oregon Catholic Press) 5536 NE Hassalo St Portland OR 97213 **Fax Area Code: 800* ■ *TF:* 877-596-1653 ■ *Web:* www.ocp.org	503-281-1191	462-7329*	637-3
Ocsea-Afscme Local 390 Worthington Rd Ste A Westerville OH 43082 *TF:* 800-969-4702 ■ *Web:* www.ocsea.org	614-865-4700		414
Octagon Capital Corp 181 University Ave Ste 400 Toronto ON M5H3M7 *Web:* www.octagoncap.com	416-368-3322	368-3811	690
Octal Corp 125 Galway Pl Unit B & C Teaneck NJ 07666 *Web:* www.octalcorporation.com	201-862-1010		360-3
Octane Interlounge 124 N Main St Rockford IL 61101 *Web:* www.octane.net	815-965-4012		671
Octapharma Plasma Inc 10644 Westlake Dr. Charlotte NC 28273 *Web:* octapharmaplasma.com	704-654-4600		743
Octasic Inc 4101 Molson St Ste 300 Montreal QC H1Y3L1 *Web:* www.octasic.com	514-282-8858		201
Octex Corp 901 Sarasota Ctr Blvd Sarasota FL 34240 *Web:* www.octex360.com	941-371-6767		608
OCTG LLP 9200 Sheldon Rd Houston TX 77049 *Web:* www.octg.org	281-456-9057		41
October Company Inc 51 Ferry St EastHampton MA 01027 *TF:* 800-628-9346 ■ *Web:* octobercompany.com	413-527-9380	527-0091	295
October Mountain State Forest 317 Woodland Rd. Lee MA 01238 *Web:* www.mass.gov	413-243-1778		565
OctoClean Franchising Systems 3357 Chicago Ave. Riverside CA 92507 *Web:* www.octoclean.com	951-683-5859		310
Octopus Media LLC 412 Eigth Ave New York NY 10001	212-967-5191		178-8
Ocu-ease Optical Products Inc 920 San Pablo Ave Pinole CA 94564	510-724-0384		237
Ocular Systems Inc Innovation Quarter 101 N Chestnut St Ste 303 Winston-salem NC 27101	336-784-4603		416
Oculis Labs Inc 338 Clubhouse Rd. Hunt Valley MD 21031 *TF:* 800 604 3060 ■ *Web:* www.oculislabs.com	410-891-1701		177
Oculus Technologies Corp 110 Broad St 2nd Fl Boston MA 02110 *Web:* www.oculustech.com	617-426-4277	426-4245	809
Oculus VisionTech Inc 507 837 W Hastings St. Vancouver BC V6C3N6 *Web:* www.ovtz.com	604-685-1017		180
Ocwen Federal Bank FSB 1661 Worthington Rd Ste 100 West Palm Beach FL 33409 *TF:* 800-746-2936 ■ *Web:* www.ocwen.com	561-682-8000		70
Ocwen Financial Corp 1661 Worthington Rd Ste 100 West Palm Beach FL 33409 *NYSE: OCN* ■ *TF:* 800-746-2936 ■ *Web:* www.ocwen.com	561-681-8000		360-2
OCZ Storage Solutions Inc 6373 San Ignacio Ave. San Jose CA 95119 *Web:* ocz.com	408-733-8400		624
ODA 660 York St Ste 101 San Francisco CA 94110	415-970-8400	882-7701	344
Odan Laboratories Ltd 325 Stillview Ave Pointe-Claire QC H9R2Y6 *TF:* 800-387-9342 ■ *Web:* www.odanlab.com	514-428-1628	428-9783	231
Odawa Casino Resort, The 1760 Lears Rd Petoskey MI 49770 *TF:* 877-442-6464 ■ *Web:* www.odawacasino.com	877-442-6464		452
ODC 3153 17th St. San Francisco CA 94110 *Web:* www.odcdance.org	415-863-6606		573-1
Odc Tooling & Molds 119 Roger St Waterloo ON N2J3Z6 *Web:* www.odctooling.com	519-576-8950		757
Odebrecht Construction Inc 201 Alhambra Cir Ste 1400 Coral Gables FL 33134 *Web:* odebrecht.com	305-341-8800	569-1500	186
ODEC (Old Dominion Electric Co-op) 4201 Dominion Blvd. Glen Allen VA 23060 *Web:* odec.com	804-747-0592		245
ODEF (Old Dominion Eye Bank) 9200 Arboretum Pkwy Ste 104 Richmond VA 23236 *TF:* 800-832-0728 ■ *Web:* www.odef.org	804-560-7540	560-4752	269
Odell Associates Inc 212 S Tryon St Ste 980 Charlotte NC 28281 *Web:* www.odell.com	704-414-1000		261

Phone | Fax | Class

Odell Brewing Co
800 E Lincoln Ave ... Fort Collins CO 80524 970-498-9070 102
Web: www.odellbrewing.com

Odell Simms & Lynch Inc
7704 Leesburg Pk ... Falls Church VA 22043 703-903-9797 903-8850 5
Web: www.odellsimms.com

Oden & Associates Inc
119 S Main St Ste 300 ... Memphis TN 38103 901-578-8055 344
TF: 800-371-6233 ■ *Web:* www.oden.com

Oden Industries Inc
301 E Vanderbilt Way Ste 425 ... San Bernardino CA 92408 909-386-0310 177
Web: www.odenindustries.com

Odeon Capital Group LLC
750 Lexington Ave 27th Fl ... New York NY 10022 212-257-6970 690
Web: www.odeoncap.com

Odesia Group Inc
1 Pl Ville-Marie Ste 560 ... Montreal QC H3B0E9 514-876-1155 317
Web: www.odesia.com

Odessa American PO Box 2952 ... Odessa TX 79760 432-337-4661 333-7742 532-2
TF: 800-592-4433 ■ *Web:* www.oaoa.com

Odessa Chamber of Commerce
700 N Grant St Ste 200 ... Odessa TX 79761 432-332-9111 333-7858 139
TF: 800-780-4678 ■ *Web:* www.odessachamber.com

Odessa College 201 W University Blvd ... Odessa TX 79764 432-335-6400 335-6824 162
TF: 866-968-2862 ■ *Web:* www.odessa.edu

Odessa Convention & Visitors Bureau
700 N Grant Ave Ste 200 ... Odessa TX 79761 432-333-7871 333-7858 206
TF: 800-780-4678 ■ *Web:* www.odessacvb.com

Odessa Pumps & Equipment Inc
3209 N County Rd W ... Odessa TX 79764 432-333-2817 641
Web: www.odessapumps.com

Odessa Regional Medical Ctr
520 E Sixth St ... Odessa TX 79761 432-582-8000 374-7
TF: 877-898-6080 ■ *Web:* www.odessaregionalmedicalcenter.com

ODG (Ontario Drive & Gear Ltd)
220 Bergey Ct ... New Hamburg ON N3A2J5 519-662-2840 29
TF: 877-274-6288 ■ *Web:* www.argoatv.com

ODIN Technologies Inc
21631 Red Rum Dr Ste 165 ... Ashburn VA 20147 703-968-0000 180
Web: www.ODINRFID.com

Odiorne Point State Park 570 Ocean Blvd ... Rye NH 03870 603-436-7406 565
Web: www.nhstateparks.org

Odjfs Federal Credit Union
4020 E Fifth Ave ... Columbus OH 43219 614-466-3416 219
TF: 800-221-6327 ■ *Web:* www.odjfscu.com

ODL Inc 215 E Roosevelt Ave ... Zeeland MI 49464 616-772-9111 329
TF: 800-253-3900 ■ *Web:* www.odl.com

Odlum Brown Ltd 250 Howe St Ste 1100 ... Vancouver BC V6C3S9 604-669-1600 844-5342 401
TF: 866-636-8222 ■ *Web:* www.odlumbrown.com

ODM Tool & Manufacturing Co
9550 Joliet Rd ... McCook IL 60525 708-485-6130 485-6540 489
Web: www.odmtool.com

ODNR Oil & Gas Resources Management
2045 Morse Rd Bldg F-3 ... Columbus OH 43229 614-265-6922 265-6910 565
Web: www.oilandgas.ohiodnr.gov

Odom Correctional Institution
PO Box 36 ... Jackson NC 27845 252-534-5611 574-2011 213
Web: www.ncdps.gov

Odon Wagner Gallery 196 Davenport Rd ... Toronto ON M5R1J2 416-962-0438 962-1581 42
TF: 800-551-2465 ■ *Web:* www.odonwagnergallery.com

Odopod Inc 385 Grove St ... San Francisco CA 94102 415-436-9980 344
Web: www.odopod.com

Odor Management Inc
18-6 E Dundee Rd Ste 101 ... Barrington IL 60010 847-304-9111 304-0989 582
TF: 800-662-6367 ■ *Web:* www.odormanagement.com

ODS Cos 601 SW Second Ave ... Portland OR 97204 503-228-6554 521-7898* 391-3
*Fax Area Code: 804 ■ *TF:* 888-221-0802 ■ *Web:* ods-security.com/about-ods

ODW Logistics Inc 1580 Williams Rd ... Columbus OH 43207 614-497-1660 449
TF: 800-743-7062 ■ *Web:* www.odwlogistics.com

Odwalla Inc 1625 N Market Blvd ... Sacramento CA 95834 800-952-5210 296-20
TF: 800-952-5210 ■ *Web:* www.odwalla.com

Odyssey Digital Printing Inc
15 E Fifth St Ste 3700 ... Tulsa OK 74103 918-660-0492 627

Odyssey Fun World 3440 Odyssey Ct ... Naperville IL 60563 630-416-2222 31
Web: www.odysseyfunworld.com

Odyssey HealthCare Inc
717 N Harwood St ... Dallas TX 75201 214-922-9711 451
TF: 855-865-5894 ■ *Web:* gentiva.com

Odyssey Healthcare of Kansas City
4911 S Arrowhead Dr ... Independence MO 64055 816-795-1333 371
TF: 800-944-4357 ■ *Web:* gentiva.com

Odyssey Landscaping Company Inc
5400 W Hwy 12 ... Lodi CA 95242 209-369-6197 776
Web: odysseylandscape.com

Odyssey Logistics & Technology Corp
39 Old Ridgebury Rd - N1 ... Danbury CT 06810 203-448-3900 449
Web: www.odysseylogistics.com

Odyssey Magazine
30 Grove St Ste C ... Peterborough NH 03458 703-885-3400 457-6
TF: 800-821-0115 ■ *Web:* www.cricketmedia.com/blog

Odyssey Marine Exploration Inc
5215 W Laurel St ... Tampa FL 33607 813-876-1776 876-1777 465
NASDAQ: OMEX ■ *TF:* 800-458-4646 ■ *Web:* www.shipwreck.net

Odyssey Medical Technologies LLC
2975 Brother Blvd ... Bartlett TN 38133 901-383-7777 786-6791 475
Web: www.odysseymed.com

Odyssey Re Holdings Corp
300 First Stamford Pl ... Stamford CT 06902 203-977-8000 356-0196 391-4
TF: 866-745-4440 ■ *Web:* www.odysseyre.com

Odyssey Systems Consulting Group Ltd
201 Edgewater Dr Ste 270 ... Wakefield MA 01880 781-245-0111 180
Web: www.odysseyconsult.com

OEA (Ohio Education Assn)
225 E Broad St ... Columbus OH 43215 614-228-4526 228-8771 457-8
TF: 800-282-1500 ■ *Web:* www.ohea.org

OEA (Oregon Education Magazine)
6900 SW Atlanta St Bldg 1 ... Portland OR 97223 503-684-3300 684-8063 457-8
TF: 800-858-5505 ■ *Web:* www.oregoned.org

Phone | Fax | Class

OEC (Otsego Electric Co-op Inc)
3192 County Hwy 11 PO Box 128 ... Hartwick NY 13348 607-293-6622 293-6624 245
Web: www.otsegoec.coop

OEC 104 E I65 Service Rd N ... Mobile AL 36607 251-471-3368 393
Web: www.oecbi.com

OEC Medical Systems Inc
384 Wright Brothers Dr ... Salt Lake City UT 84116 801-328-9300 475
Web: www.gehealthcare.com

Oeco LLC 4607 SE International Way ... Milwaukie OR 97222 503-659-5999 253
Web: www.oeco.com

Oeconnection LLC
4205 Highlander Pkwy ... Richfield OH 44286 330-523-1830 523-1700 177
TF: 888-776-5792 ■ *Web:* www.oeconnection.com

OEM Controls Inc 10 Controls Dr ... Shelton CT 06484 203-929-8431 929-3867 203
Web: www.oemcontrols.com

Oem Fabricators Inc 300 Mcmillan Rd ... Woodville WI 54028 715-698-2111 567
Web: www.oemfab.com

OEM Group Inc 2120 W Guadalupe Rd ... Gilbert AZ 85233 480-558-9200 696
Web: www.oemgroupinc.com

OEM Systems LLC 210 W Oklahoma Ave ... Okarche OK 73762 405-263-7488 263-4765 61
TF: 800-810-7252 ■ *Web:* oemtruckequipment.com

Oesterlen-services for Youth Inc
1918 Mechanicsburg Rd ... Springfield OH 45503 937-399-6101 726
TF: 800-435-7968 ■ *Web:* oesterlen.org

OF Mossberg & Sons Inc
7 Grasso Ave ... North Haven CT 06473 203-230-5300 230-5420* 284
*Fax: Mktg ■ *TF:* 800-363-3555 ■ *Web:* www.mossberg.com

OFA (Orphan Foundation of America)
21351 Gentry Dr Ste 130 ... Sterling VA 20166 571-203-0270 203-0273 48-6
TF: 800-950-4673 ■ *Web:* www.fc2success.org

OFB (Oklahoma Farm Bureau Mutual Insurance Co)
2501 N Stiles Ave ... Oklahoma City OK 73105 405-523-2300 523-2362 391-4
Web: www.okfarmbureau.org

Off Broadway Theatre
272 S Main St ... Salt Lake City UT 84101 801-355-4628 572
Web: www.theobt.org

Off Madison Ave Inc
5555 E Van Buren St Ste 215 ... Phoenix AZ 85008 480-505-4500 4
Web: www.offmadisonave.com

Off the Beaten Path 7 E Beall St ... Bozeman MT 59715 406-586-1311 587-4147 760
TF: 800-445-2995 ■ *Web:* www.offthebeatenpath.com

Off The Wall Company Inc
4814 Bethlehem Pk ... Telford PA 18969 215-453-9400 344
Web: www.offthewall.net

Off Wall Street Consulting Group Inc
22 Hilliard St Ste 3 ... Cambridge MA 02138 617-868-7880 401
Web: www.riverviewpartners.com

Offen Petroleum Inc 5100 E 78th Ave ... Commerce CO 80022 303-297-3835 579
TF: 866-657-3835 ■ *Web:* www.offenpet.com

Office Automation Technologies
11919 W 1-70 Frontage Rd N Ste 123 ... Wheat Ridge CO 80033 303-202-5151 180
TF: 800-522-6452 ■ *Web:* www.oati1.com

Office Beer Bar & Grill
728 Thompson Ave Rt 22 W ... Bridgewater NJ 08805 732-469-0066 670
Web: www.office-beerbar.com

Office Chairs Inc
14815 Radburn Ave ... Santa Fe Springs CA 90670 562-802-0464 319-1
TF: 866-624-4968 ■ *Web:* ocicontract.com

Office Depot Inc
2200 Old Germantown Rd ... Delray Beach FL 33445 561-438-4800 535
NASDAQ: ODP ■ *TF:* 800-937-3600 ■ *Web:* www.officedepot.com

Office Environments
1140 Thomas Busch Memorial Hwy ... Pennsauken NJ 08110 856-773-3000 320
Web: www.oeasheville.com

Office Environments Inc
11407 Granite St ... Charlotte NC 28273 704-714-7200 714-7400 320
TF: 888-861-2525 ■ *Web:* www.office-environments.com

Office Express Supply Inc
8005 W 20th Ave ... Hialeah FL 33014 305-557-1667 321
Web: www.xpressbuy.com

Office Furniture Installers Inc
3167 Spaulding St ... Omaha NE 68111 402-451-8009 321
Web: www.ofi-usa.com

Office Furniture Partnership Inc, The
67 E Park Pl ... Morristown NJ 07960 973-267-6966 321
Web: www.officefurniturepartnership.com

Office Furniture Team
4204 Lindbergh Dr ... Addison TX 75001 972-503-8326 320
Web: www.oftoffice.com

Office Liquidators Inc
11111 W Sixth Ave Unit A ... Denver CO 80215 303-759-3375 317
TF: 800-279-3375 ■ *Web:* m.officeliquidators.com

Office Movers Inc 6500 Kane Way ... Elkridge MD 21075 410-799-7704 468
TF: 800-331-4025 ■ *Web:* www.officemovers.com

Office of Compliance
110 Second St SE Rm LA 200 ... Washington DC 20540 202-724-9250 426-1913 340-20
Web: www.compliance.gov

Office of Disability Employment Policy
200 Constitution Ave NW Ste S1303 ... Washington DC 20210 202-693-7880 693-7888 340-15
TF: 866-633-7365 ■ *Web:* www.dol.gov/odep

Office of General Services
Corning Tower Empire State Plaza
41st Fl Empire State Plz ... Albany NY 12242 518-474-3899 457-3081 205
TF: 877-426-6006 ■ *Web:* ogs.ny.gov

Office of Intergovernmental and External Affairs
Region II 26 Federal Plaza Ste 3835 ... New York NY 10278 212-264-4600 264-1324 340-10
Web: www.hhs.gov/ophs/rha

Office of Justice Programs (OJP)
810 Seventh St NW ... Washington DC 20531 202-307-0703 340-14
Web: ojp.gov
Bureau of Justice Assistance
810 Seventh St NW ... Washington DC 20531 202-616-6500 305-1367 340-14
TF: 888-744-6513 ■ *Web:* www.bja.gov
Community Capacity Development Office
810 Seventh St NW ... Washington DC 20531 202-307-5933 340-14
Web: ojp.gov/ccdo
National Institute of Justice
810 Seventh St NW ... Washington DC 20531 202-307-2942 340-14
Web: www.nij.gov

Name / Address	City	State	ZIP	Phone	Fax	Class
Office for Victims of Crime						
810 Seventh St NW 8th Fl	Washington	DC	20531	202-307-5983	514-6383	340-14
TF: 800-363-0441 ■ *Web:* ojp.gov/ovc						
Office of Juvenile Justice & Delinquency Preventio						
810 Seventh St NW	Washington	DC	20531	202-307-5911	307-2093	340-14
Web: www.ojjdp.gov						
Office of Management & Budget (OMB)						
725 17th St NW	Washington	DC	20503	202-395-3080	395-3888	340
Web: www.whitehouse.gov/omb						
Office of Naval Research (ONR)						
875 N Randolph St Ste 1425	Arlington	VA	22203	703-696-5031	696-5940	668
Web: www.onr.navy.mil						
Office of Personnel Management (OPM)						
1900 E St NW	Washington	DC	20415	202-606-1800		340-20
Web: www.opm.gov						
Office of Population Research						
Princeton University Wallace Hall 2nd Fl	Princeton	NJ	08544	609-258-4870	258-1039	668
Web: www.opr.princeton.edu						
Office of Public Health & Science						
200 Independence Ave SW Rm 716G	Washington	DC	20201	202-690-7694	690-6960	340-10
TF: 877-696-6775 ■ *Web:* www.hhs.gov/ophs						
Region I						
John F Kennedy Federal Bldg Rm 2100	Boston	MA	02203	617-565-1491		340-10
TF: 800-827-1000 ■ *Web:* www.hhs.gov						
Region IX						
90 Seventh St Ste 5-100	San Francisco	CA	94103	415-437-8096	437-8004	340-10
Web: www.hhs.gov						
Region VII						
200 Independence Ave, SW Rm S-1801	Washington	MO	64106	877-696-6775	426-2178*	340-10
**Fax Area Code:* 816 ■ *TF:* 877-696-6775 ■ *Web:* www.hhs.gov						
Office of Public Health & Science Regional Offices						
Region 3						
150 S Independence Mall W Ste 436	Philadelphia	PA	19106	215-861-4639	861-4617	340-10
Web: www.hhs.gov						
Region 4 61 Forsyth St SW Ste 5B95	Atlanta	GA	30303	404-562-7888	562-7899	340-10
Web: www.hhs.gov						
Region 6 1301 Young St Ste 1124	Dallas	TX	75202	214-767-3879	767-3209	340-10
Web: www.hhs.gov						
Office of Science & Technology Policy						
1650 Pennsylvania Ave	Washington	DC	20504	202-456-4444		340
TF: 800-670-6553 ■ *Web:* www.whitehouse.gov						
Office of Special Counsel						
1730 M St NW Ste 218	Washington	DC	20036	202-254-3600	653-5151	340-20
TF: 800-872-9855 ■ *Web:* www.osc.gov						
Office of Special Counsel						
OSC Headquarters						
1730 M St NW Ste 218	Washington	TX	20036	202-254-3600	254-3711	340-20
TF: 800-872-9855 ■ *Web:* www.osc.gov						
Office of Surface Mining Reclamation & Enforcement						
1951 Constitution Ave NW	Washington	DC	20240	202-208-2565		340-13
Web: www.osmre.gov						
Office of the Assistant Secretary for Health						
Region VIII 1961 Stout St Rm 08-148	Denver	CO	80294	303-844-7860	844-2019	340-10
Web: www.hhs.gov						
Office of the Pardon Attorney						
145 N St NE Rm 5E	Washington	DC	20530	202-616-6070	616-6069	340-14
TF: 800-514-0301 ■ *Web:* www.justice.gov						
Office of the President						
1600 Pennsylvania Ave NW	Washington	DC	20500	202-456-1414		340
Web: www.whitehouse.gov						
Office of the US Trade Representative						
600 17th St NW	Washington	DC	20508	202-395-7360		340
Web: www.ustr.gov						
Office of the Vice President						
Eisenhower Executive Office Bldg						
1650 Pennsylvania Ave NW	Washington	DC	20504	202-456-4444		340
Web: whitehouse.gov						
Office of Tribal Justice						
950 Pennsylvania Ave NW	Washington	DC	20530	202-514-2000		340-14
Web: www.justice.gov						
Office on Violence Against Women						
145 N St Ste 10W 121	Washington	DC	20530	202-307-6026	307-2277	340-14
Web: justice.gov/ovw						
Office Pavilion 10030 Bent Oak Dr	Houston	TX	77040	713-803-0000	803-0001	320
Web: www.ophouston.com						
Office Plus of Lake County						
1428 Glen Flora Ave	Waukegan	IL	60085	847-662-5393	662-8761	320
TF: 800-323-6084 ■ *Web:* www.getofficeplus.com						
Office Products Marketing & Advertising Inc						
4211 Division Ave N	Comstock Park	MI	49321	616-785-6061		7
TF: 800-438-7325 ■ *Web:* opma.com						
Office Products Recycling Assoc Inc						
100 W 18th Ave	North Kansas City	MO	64116	816-584-1000		690
Web: www.oprausa.com						
Office Resources Inc 263 Summer St	Boston	MA	02210	617-423-9100	423-5590	535
Web: www.ori.com						
Office Solutions Inc 217 Mt Horeb Rd	Warren	NJ	07059	800-677-1778		179
TF: 800-677-1778 ■ *Web:* www.osi-technology.com						
Office Star Products						
1901 S Archibald PO Box 3520	Ontario	CA	91761	909-930-2000		320
TF: 800-950-7262 ■ *Web:* www.officestar.net						
Office Suppliers Inc						
13621 Crayton Blvd	Hagerstown	MD	21742	301-797-3120		535
Web: www.hyperspacellc.com						
Office Systems of Texas						
104 Lockhaven Dr	Houston	TX	77073	281-443-2996		174
TF: 800-245-2047 ■ *Web:* www.osot.com						
OfficeOps LLC						
619 S Vulcan Ave Ste 106	Encinitas	CA	92024	504-405-0574		177
Officepro Inc 8 Granite Pl Ste 26	Gaithersburg	MD	20878	301-468-3312		177
TF: 800-914-2259 ■ *Web:* www.officeproinc.com						
OfficeVP.com Inc PO Box 401	Spicewood	TX	78669	830-693-1429		366
Web: www.officevp.com						
Official Payments Corp						
3550 Engineering Dr	Norcross	GA	30092	770-325-3100		180
TF: 877-754-4413 ■ *Web:* www.officialpayments.com						
Offinger Management Co						
1100-H Brandywine Blvd	Zanesville	OH	43701	740-452-4541		47
Web: www.offinger.com						

Name / Address	City	State	ZIP	Phone	Fax	Class
Offit Capital Advisors LLC						
485 Lexington Ave 24th Fl	New York	NY	10017	212-588-3276		401
Web: www.offitcapital.com						
Off-Road Magazine						
2400 E Katella Ave 7th fl	Anaheim	CA	92806	714-848-8880	978-6390	457-3
TF: 877-462-6752 ■ *Web:* www.fourwheeler.com						
Offset Impressions Inc						
122 Mtn View Rd	Reading	PA	19607	610-378-1851	378-9107	687
Offset Paperback Manufacturers Inc						
101 Memorial Hwy	Dallas	PA	18612	570-675-5261		626
Web: www.beprintersamerica.com						
Offshore Energy Services Inc						
5900 US Hwy 90 E	Broussard	LA	70518	337-837-1024		539
TF: 800-489-6202 ■ *Web:* www.offshoreenergyservices.com						
Offshore International Inc						
8350 E Old Vail Rd	Tucson	AZ	85747	520-889-0022		803-1
Web: www.offshoregroup.com						
Offshore Process Services Inc						
1206 Park Dr	Mandeville	LA	70471	985-727-2900		261
TF: 800-328-2008 ■ *Web:* www.opsincusa.com						
Offshore Specialty Fabricators LLC						
115 Menard Rd	Houma	LA	70363	985-868-1438		539
TF: 800-256-4695 ■ *Web:* www.osf-llc.com						
Offutt Air Force Base						
906 Sac Blvd Ste 1	Offutt AFB	NE	68113	402-294-1110		497-1
Web: www.offutt.af.mil						
Offwhite 521 Ft St	Marietta	OH	45750	740-373-9010		344
TF: 800-606-1610 ■ *Web:* www.offwhite.com						
OFII (Organization for International Investment)						
1225 19th St NW Ste 501	Washington	DC	20036	202-659-1903	659-2293	49-12
Web: www.ofii.org						
OFIS LP, The 7110 Old Katy Rd	Houston	TX	77024	713-629-5599		321
OFS (OFS Capital Corporation)						
10 S Wacker Dr Ste 2500	Chicago	IL	60606	847-734-2000		69
Web: www.ofscapital.com						
OFS Capital Corporation (OFS)						
10 S Wacker Dr Ste 2500	Chicago	IL	60606	847-734-2000		69
Web: www.ofscapital.com						
OG & E Electric Services						
PO Box 24990	Oklahoma City	OK	73124	405-553-3000		787
TF: 800-272-9741 ■ *Web:* www.oge.com						
Ogb Architectural Millwork						
3711 Paseo Del Norte NE	Albuquerque	NM	87113	505-998-0000		499
Web: www.ogb-am.com						
Ogden City Hall 2549 Washington Blvd	Ogden	UT	84401	801-629-8150	629-8154	337
Web: www.ogdencity.com						
Ogden Cos Inc 606 Green Meadow N	Colleyville	TX	76034	817-656-8570		734
Ogden Eccles Conference Ctr						
2415 Washington Blvd	Ogden	UT	84401	801-689-8600	689-8651	205
TF: 866-472-4627 ■ *Web:* oeccutah.com						
Ogden Eccles Dinosaur Park						
1544 E Pk Blvd	Ogden	UT	84401	801-393-3400		520
TF: 800-501-2885 ■ *Web:* www.dinosaurpark.org						
Ogden House & Gardens						
1520 Bronson Rd	Fairfield	CT	06824	203-259-1598		50-3
Web: www.fairfieldhistoricalsociety.org						
Ogden Mills & Ruth Livingston Mills State Park						
Mills Mansion 1 Rd	Staatsburg	NY	12580	845-889-4646		565
Web: www.nysparks.com/parks/info.asp?parkid=133						
Ogden Museum of Southern Art						
925 Camp St	New Orleans	LA	70130	504-539-9650		520
Web: www.ogdenmuseum.org						
Ogden Nature Ctr 966 W 12th St	Ogden	UT	84404	801-621-7595	621-1867	50-5
Web: www.ogdennaturecenter.org						
Ogden Newspapers Inc 1500 Main St	Wheeling	WV	26003	304-233-0100		637-8
Web: www.owch.com						
Ogden Publications Inc 1503 SW 42nd St	Topeka	KS	66609	785-274-4300		4
TF: 800-678-5779 ■ *Web:* www.ogdenpubs.com						
Ogden Regional Medical Ctr						
5475 Adams Ave Pkwy	Ogden	UT	84405	801-479-2111		374-3
TF: 877-870-3745 ■ *Web:* www.ogdenregional.com						
Ogden Ritnour 33 Sloan St	Roswell	GA	30075	770-597-4703		636
Web: ogdenrit.com						
Ogden Telephone Co						
4726 E Weston Rd	Blissfield	MI	49228	517-443-5595		393
Web: www.ogdentel.com						
Ogden Union Station 2501 Wall Ave	Ogden	UT	84401	801-393-9886		520
Ogden Welding Systems Inc						
372 Div St	Schererville	IN	46375	219-322-5252	865-1825	811
TF: 800-828-9829 ■ *Web:* www.ogdenwelding.com						
Ogden, Gibson, Broocks, Longoria & Hall LLP						
1900 Pennzoil S Twr	Houston	TX	77002	713-844-3000		428
Web: www.ogwbl.com						
Ogden/Weber Convention & Visitors Bureau						
2438 Washington Blvd	Ogden	UT	84401	801-778-6250	399-0783	206
TF: 800-255-8824 ■ *Web:* www.visitogden.com						
Ogden-Hinckley Airport 3909 Airport Rd	Ogden	UT	84405	801-629-8251		27
Web: www.ogdencity.com						
Ogdensburg Bridge & Port Authority						
1 Bridge Plaza	Ogdensburg	NY	13669	315-393-4080	393-7068	618
Web: www.ogdensport.com						
Ogden-Weber Applied Technology College Foundation						
200 N Washington Blvd	Ogden	UT	84404	801-627-8300		305
Web: www.owatc.edu						
OGE Energy Corp 321 N Harvey St	Oklahoma City	OK	73102	405-553-3000		360-5
NYSE: OGE ■ *TF:* 800-272-9741 ■ *Web:* www.oge.com						
Ogemaw County						
806 W Houghton Ave Ste 103	West Branch	MI	48661	989-345-0084		338
Ogihara America Corp						
1480 W McPherson Pk Dr	Howell	MI	48843	517-548-4900	548-6036	489
TF: 800-248-4058 ■ *Web:* www.ogihara.com						
Ogilvy & Mather Worldwide						
636 11th Ave	New York	NY	10036	212-237-4000		4
Web: www.ogilvy.com						
Ogilvy One Worldwide 636 11th Ave	New York	NY	10036	212-237-6000		4
Web: www.ogilvy.com						
Ogilvy Public Relations Worldwide						
636 11th Ave	New York	NY	10036	212-880-5200	370-4636	636
Web: www.ogilvypr.com						

Phone Fax Class

Oglala Lakota College PO Box 629 .... Martin SD 57551 605-455-6000 455-2787 166
Web: www.olc.edu
Ogle County 105 S Fifth St .... Oregon IL 61061 815-732-3201 732-6273 338
TF: 800-242-7642 ■ Web: www.oglecounty.org
Ogle Design 12512 N Gray Rd .... Carmel IN 46033 317-843-1102 344
Web: ogle-design.com
Oglebay Institute's Stifel Fine Arts Ctr
1330 National Rd .... Wheeling WV 26003 304-242-7700 50-2
TF: 800-624-6988 ■ Web: www.oionline.com
Oglebay Institute's Towngate Theatre
2118 Market St .... Wheeling WV 26003 304-233-0820 572
Web: www.oionline.com
Oglebay Resort & Conference Ctr
465 Lodge Dr Oglebay Pk .... Wheeling WV 26003 304-243-4000 669
TF: 800-624-6988 ■ Web: www.oglebay-resort.com
Oglethorpe County 341 W Main St .... Lexington GA 30648 706-743-5270 743-8371 338
Web: onlineoglethorpe.com
Oglethorpe Inc
18302 Highwoods Preserve Pkwy Ste 114 .... Tampa FL 33647 813-978-1933 195
Web: www.oglethorpeinc.com
Oglethorpe Mall 7804 Abercorn Ext .... Savannah GA 31406 912-354-7038 460
Web: www.oglethorpemall.com
Oglethorpe Speedway Park
200 Jesup Rd PO Box 687 .... Pooler GA 31322 912-964-8200 964-9501 515
Web: www.ospracing.net
Oglethorpe University
4484 Peachtree Rd,NE .... Atlanta GA 30319 404-364-8307 364-8491 166
TF: 800-428-4484 ■ Web: www.oglethorpe.edu
Oglethorpe University Museum of Art
4484 Peachtree Rd NE .... Atlanta GA 30319 404-364-8555 520
Web: museum.oglethorpe.edu
Oglevee Ltd 152 Oglevee Ln .... Connellsville PA 15425 724-628-8360 369
Ogmento Inc 134 Spring St .... New York NY 10012 212-226-2736 387
Ogne Alberts & Stuart Pc 1869 E Maple Rd .... Troy MI 48083 248-362-3707 428
Web: oaspc.com
Ogontz Corp 2835 Terwood Rd .... Willow Grove PA 19090 215-657-4770 657-0460 789
TF: 800-523-2478 ■ Web: www.ogontz.com
OGR (International Order of the Golden Rule)
3520 Executive Ctr Dr Ste 300 .... Austin TX 78731 512-334-5504 334-5514 49-4
TF: 800-637-8030 ■ Web: www.ogr.org
OH (Oroville Hospital) 2767 Olive Hwy .... Oroville CA 95966 530-533-8500 374-3
Web: www.orovillehospital.com
O-H Community Partners Ltd
125 S Clark St Ste 1700 .... Chicago IL 60603 312-767-9228 463
Web: ohcommunitypartners.com
Oh Yumm! Bistro
5615 N Illinois St .... Indianapolis IN 46208 317-251-5656 671
Web: www.ohyummbistro.com
Ohana Companies LLC, The
1405 Foulk Rd Foulkstone Plaza Ste 200 ...... Wilmington DE 19803 302-225-5505 195
Web: www.everybodywins.com
OHANA Waikiki Beachcomber Hotel
2300 Kalakaua Ave .... Honolulu HI 96815 866-956-4262 622-4852* 379
*Fax Area Code: 800 ■ TF: 866-956-4262 ■ Web: www.outrigger.com
Ohaus Corp 7 Campus Dr Ste 300 .... Pine Brook NJ 07054 973-377-9000 684
Web: asiapacific.ohaus.com
Ohel Children's Home & Family Services Inc
4510 16th Ave .... Brooklyn NY 11204 718-851-6300 363
TF: 800-603-6435 ■ Web: www.ohelfamily.org
Ohio
Adjutant's General Dept
2825 W Dublin Granville Rd .... Columbus OH 43235 614-336-7000 339-36
Web: www.ong.ohio.gov
Administrative Director of the Supreme Court
65 S Front St 7th Fl .... Columbus OH 43215 614-387-9500 387-9509 339-36
Web: www.supremecourt.ohio.gov
Aging Dept 246 N High St 1st Fl .... Columbus OH 43215 614-466-5500 466-5741 339-36
TF: 800-266-4346 ■ Web: aging.ohio.gov
Agriculture Dept 8995 E Main St .... Reynoldsburg OH 43068 614-728-6201 728-6310 339-36
TF: 800-282-1955 ■ Web: www.agri.ohio.gov
Arts Council 30 E Broad St 33rd Fl .... Columbus OH 43215 614-466-2613 466-4494 339-36
Web: www.oac.ohio.gov
Commerce Dept 77 S High St 23rd Fl .... Columbus OH 43215 614-466-3636 339-36
Web: www.com.state.oh.us
Consumer Protection Section
30 E Broad St 14th Fl .... Columbus OH 43215 614-466-4986 339-36
TF: 800-282-0515 ■ Web: www.ohioattorneygeneral.gov
Department of Veterans Services
77 S High St 7th Fl .... Columbus OH 43215 614-466-9287 387-7317 339-36
Web: dvs.ohio.gov
Dept of Rehabilitation & Correction
770 W Broad St .... Columbus OH 43222 614-752-0800 339-36
Web: www.drc.state.oh.us
Education Dept 25 S Front St .... Columbus OH 43215 877-644-6338 339-36
TF: 877-644-6338 ■ Web: education.ohio.gov
Emergency Management Agency
2855 W Dublin-Granville Rd .... Columbus OH 43235 614-889-7150 889-7183 339-36
Web: www.ema.ohio.gov
Environmental Protection Agency
122 S Front St PO Box 1049 .... Columbus OH 43216 614-644-3020 339-36
Web: www.epa.state.oh.us
Ethics Commission 30 W Spring St L3 .... Columbus OH 43215 614-466-7090 466-8368 265
Web: www.ethics.ohio.gov
Financial Institutions Div
77 S High St 21st Fl .... Columbus OH 43266 614-728-8400 728-0380 339-36
TF: 866-278-0003 ■ Web: com.ohio.gov/fiin
Governor
77 S High St Riffe Center 30th Fl .... Columbus OH 43215 614-466-3555 466-9354 339-36
Web: www.governor.ohio.gov
Health Dept 246 N High St .... Columbus OH 43215 614-466-3543 339-36
Web: www.odh.ohio.gov
Highway Patrol (OSHP)
1970 W Broad St PO Box 182074 .... Columbus OH 43223 614-466-2660 339-36
TF: 877-772-8765 ■ Web: statepatrol.ohio.gov
Historical Society 800 E 17th Ave .... Columbus OH 43211 614-297-2300 339-36
TF: 800-686-6124 ■ Web: www.ohiohistory.org
Housing Finance Agency 57 E Main St .... Columbus OH 43215 614-466-7970 339-36
TF: 888-362-6432 ■ Web: www.ohiohome.org
Information Technology
30 E Broad St Ste 4040 .... Columbus OH 43215 614-466-6930 339-36
Web: das.ohio.gov
Insurance Dept
50 W Town St Third Fl Ste 300 .... Columbus OH 43215 614-644-2658 339-36
TF: 800-686-1526 ■ Web: www.insurance.ohio.gov
Job & Family Services Dept
30 E Broad St 38th Fl .... Columbus OH 43215 614-466-6894 728-7740 339-36
Web: www.jfs.ohio.gov
Legislative Information Office
77 S High St .... Columbus OH 43215 614-728-0711 433
Web: www.lis.state.oh.us
Mental Health Dept
30 E Broad St 36th Fl .... Columbus OH 43215 614-466-2596 752-9453 339-36
TF: 877-275-6364 ■ Web: mha.ohio.gov
Motor Vehicles Bureau
1970 W Broad St .... Columbus OH 43223 614-752-7500 339-36
Web: www.bmv.ohio.gov
Natural Resources Dept 2045 Morse Rd .... Columbus OH 43229 614-265-6565 339-36
Web: www.ohiodnr.com
Office of Governor
77 S High St 30th Fl .... Columbus OH 43215 614-466-3396 339-36
Web: governor.ohio.gov
Parks & Recreation Div
2045 Morse Rd Bldg C-3 .... Columbus OH 43229 614-265-6561 261-8407 339-36
TF: 866-644-6727 ■ Web: www.ohiodnr.com
Parole Board 770 W Broad St .... Columbus OH 43222 614-752-1200 752-1251 339-36
TF: 888-344-1441 ■ Web: www.drc.state.oh.us
Public Utilities Commission
180 E Broad St .... Columbus OH 43215 614-466-3016 752-8351 339-36
TF: 800-686-7826 ■ Web: www.puco.ohio.gov
Racing Commission
77 S High St 18th Fl .... Columbus OH 43215 614-466-2757 466-1900 712
Web: www.racing.ohio.gov
Regents Board 25 S Front St 36th Fl .... Columbus OH 43215 614-466-6000 466-5866 339-36
Web: www.ohiohighered.org
Secretary of State
180 E Broad St 16th Fl .... Columbus OH 43215 614-466-2655 339-36
Web: www.sos.state.oh.us
Securities Div 77 S High St Ste 22 .... Columbus OH 43215 614-644-7381 339-36
Web: www.com.ohio.gov
Supreme Court 65 S Front St .... Columbus OH 43215 614-387-9000 339-36
Web: www.sconet.state.oh.us
Taxation Dept
30 E Broad St 22nd Fl PO Box 530 .... Columbus OH 43215 614-466-2166 466-7979 339-36
TF: 888-405-4089 ■ Web: tax.ohio.gov
Transportation Dept 1980 W Broad St .... Columbus OH 43223 614-466-7170 339-36
Web: dot.state.oh.us
Travel & Tourism Div PO Box 1001 .... Columbus OH 43216 614-466-8844 339-36
TF: 800-282-5393 ■ Web: www.ohio.org
Treasurer 30 E Broad St 9th Fl .... Columbus OH 43215 614-466-2160 339-36
TF: 800-228-1102 ■ Web: www.tos.ohio.gov
Tuition Trust Authority
35 E Chestnut St 8th Fl .... Columbus OH 43215 614-752-9400 725
TF Cust Svc: 800-233-6734 ■ Web: www.collegeadvantage.com
Vital Statistics Unit
246 N High St PO Box 15098 .... Columbus OH 43215 614-466-2531 339-36
Wildlife Div 2045 Morse Rd Bldg G .... Columbus OH 43229 614-265-6300 339-36
TF: 800-945-3543 ■ Web: www.ohiodnr.com/wildlife
Workers' Compensation Bureau
30 W Spring St .... Columbus OH 43215 614-644-6292 339-36
TF: 800-644-6292 ■ Web: www.bwc.ohio.gov
Workforce Developement Office
4020 E Fifth Ave PO Box 1618 .... Columbus OH 43219 888-296-7541 728-8366* 339-36
*Fax Area Code: 614 ■ TF: 888-296-7541 ■ Web: www.jfs.ohio.gov/owd
Youth Services Dept 51 N High St .... Columbus OH 43215 614-466-4314 339-36
TF: 855-577-7714 ■ Web: www.dys.ohio.gov
Ohio a C e p 3510 Snouffer Rd Ste 100 .... Columbus OH 43235 614-792-6506 533
TF: 888-642-2374 ■ Web: www.ohacep.org
Ohio Art Co 1 Toy St .... Bryan OH 43506 419-636-3141 762
OTC: OART ■ TF: 800-800-3141 ■ Web: ohioart.com
Ohio Assn of Realtors 200 E Town St .... Columbus OH 43215 614-228-6675 228-2601 656
TF: 800-868-3225 ■ Web: www.ohiorealtors.org
Ohio Associated Enterprises LLC
97 Corwin Dr .... Painesville OH 44077 440-354-2100 354-5692 815
TF: 888-637-4832 ■ Web: www.meritec.com
Ohio Bag Corp
6044 Rossmoor Lakes Ct .... Boynton Beach FL 33437 561-736-3131 735-0150 349
TF: 800-892-8666 ■ Web: www.ohiobag.com
Ohio Ballet 354 E Market St .... Akron OH 44325 330-972-7900 573-1
Ohio Brass Co 1850 Richland Ave E .... Aiken SC 29801 803-648-8386 642-2959 816
Web: www.hubbellpowersystems.com
Ohio Broach & Machine Co
35264 Topps Industrial Pkwy .... Willoughby OH 44094 440-946-1040 946-0725* 455
*Fax: Sales ■ Web: www.ohiobroach.com
Ohio Business College
5202 Timber Commons Dr .... Sandusky OH 44870 419-627-8345 166
Web: www.ohiobusinesscollege.edu
Ohio Casualty Insurance Co
9450 SewaRd Rd .... Fairfield OH 45014 513-603-2400 867-3840 391-4
TF: 800-843-6446 ■ Web: www.ohiocasualty-ins.com
Ohio Contractors Association
1313 Dublin Rd .... Columbus OH 43215 614-488-0724 138
TF: 800-229-1388 ■ Web: ohiocontractors.org
Ohio Council of Community Schools
3131 Executive Pkwy Ste 306 .... Toledo OH 43606 419-720-5200 685
TF: 800-656-6763 ■ Web: ohioschools.org
Ohio County 413 Main St PO Box 185 .... Rising Sun IN 47040 812-438-2610 438-1215 338
Ohio County 1500 Chapline St .... Wheeling WV 26003 304-234-3656 234-3829 338
Web: www.ohiocounty.wv.gov
Ohio County Board of Education
315 E Union St .... Hartford KY 42347 270-298-3249 685
Web: ohio.k12.ky.us
Ohio County Convention Tourism and Visitors Commission
100 S Walnut St .... Rising Sun IN 47040 812-438-4933 206
TF: 800-634-2650 ■ Web: www.enjoyrisingsun.com
Ohio County Public Library
52 16th St .... Wheeling WV 26003 304-232-0244 232-6848 434-3
Web: ohiocountylibrary.org

Name / Address	City	State	Zip	Phone	Fax	Class
Ohio Craft Museum 1665 W Fifth Ave *TF:* 800-686-1541 ■ *Web:* www.ohiocraft.org	Columbus	OH	43212	614-486-4402	486-7110	520
Ohio Decorative Products Inc 220 S Elizabeth St	Spencerville	OH	45887	419-647-9033	647-4202	308
Ohio Democratic Party 340 E Fulton St *Web:* www.ohiodems.org	Columbus	OH	43215	614-221-6563	221-0721	616-1
Ohio Dental Assn 1370 Dublin Rd *TF:* 800-497-6076 ■ *Web:* www.oda.org	Columbus	OH	43215	614-486-2700	486-0381	227
Ohio Dept of Youth Services 30 W Spring St *Web:* www.dys.ohio.gov	Columbus	OH	43215	614-466-4314		412
Ohio Desk Co 1122 Prospect Ave E *Web:* www.ohiodesk.com	Cleveland	OH	44115	216-623-0600	623-0611	320
Ohio DNR 2045 Morse Rd *Web:* ohiodnr.gov	Columbus	OH	43229	614-265-6565		565
Ohio DNR 4860 E Pk Dr *Web:* parks.ohiodnr.gov/lakehope	London	OH	43140	937-322-5284		565
Ohio Dominican University 1216 Sunbury Rd **Fax:* Admissions ■ *TF:* 800-955-6446 ■ *Web:* www.ohiodominican.edu	Columbus	OH	43219	614-251-4500	251-0156*	166
Ohio Drilling Co 2405 Bostic Blvd SW *TF:* 800-272-1711 ■ *Web:* ohiodrilling.com	Massillon	OH	44647	330-832-1521		189-15
Ohio Edison Co 76 S Main St PO Box 3637 *TF:* 800-736-3402 ■ *Web:* firstenergycorp.com	Akron	OH	44308	330-436-4122		787
Ohio Education Assn (OEA) 225 E Broad St *TF:* 800-282-1500 ■ *Web:* www.ohea.org	Columbus	OH	43215	614-228-4526	228-8771	457-8
Ohio Electric Motors Inc 30 Paint Fork Rd PO Box 168 *Web:* www.ohioelectricmotors.com	Barnardsville	NC	28709	828-626-2901	626-2155	518
Ohio Exterminating Company Inc 1347 N High St *Web:* ohioexterminating.com	Columbus	OH	43201	614-294-6311		577
Ohio Fabricators Co 111 N 14th St *TF:* 800-422-4422 ■ *Web:* www.ohfab.com	Coshocton	OH	43812	740-622-5922	622-3307	454
Ohio Federation of Teachers 1251 E Broad St Frnt *Web:* oh.aft.org	Columbus	OH	43205	614-258-3240		414
Ohio Gas Co PO Box 528 *TF:* 800-331-7396 ■ *Web:* www.ohiogas.com	Bryan	OH	43506	419-636-1117		536
Ohio Gasket & Shim Company Inc 976 Evans Ave **Fax Area Code:* 330 ■ *TF:* 800-321-2438 ■ *Web:* www.ogsindustries.com	Akron	OH	44305	800-321-2438	630-2075*	326
Ohio Grantmakers Forum 37 W Broad St Ste 800 *Web:* www.philanthropyohio.org	Columbus	OH	43215	614-224-1344		533
Ohio Gratings Inc 5299 Southway St SW *Web:* www.ohiogratings.com	Canton	OH	44706	330-477-6707		480
Ohio Health Care Association, The 55 Green Meadows Dr S PO Box 447 *Web:* www.ohca.org	Lewis Center	OH	43035	614-436-4154		138
Ohio Hispanic Coalition 100 East Campus View Blvd Ste 130 *Web:* ohiohispaniccoalition.org	Columbus	OH	43204	614-840-9934		226
Ohio Historical Society 1982 Velma Ave *TF:* 800-686-6124 ■ *Web:* www.ohiohistory.org	Columbus	OH	43211	614-297-2300		520
Ohio House Motel 600 N La Salle Dr *TF:* 866-601-6446 ■ *Web:* www.ohiohousemotel.com	Chicago	IL	60654	312-943-6000		707
Ohio Indemnity Co 250 E Broad St 7th Fl *TF:* 800-628-8581 ■ *Web:* www.ohioindemnity.com	Columbus	OH	43215	614-228-2800	228-5552	391-4
Ohio Legal Assistance Foundation 10 W Broad St Ste 950 *TF:* 800-877-9772 ■ *Web:* www.olaf.org	Columbus	OH	43215	614-715-8560		420
Ohio Light Opera, The 1189 Beall Ave *TF:* 800-362-6474 ■ *Web:* www.ohiolightopera.org	Wooster	OH	44691	330-263-2345	263-2272	573-2
Ohio Lottery Commission 615 W Superior Ave *TF:* 800-686-4208 ■ *Web:* www.ohiolottery.com	Cleveland	OH	44113	216-787-3200	787-3313	452
Ohio Machinery Co 3993 E Royalton Rd *TF:* 800-837-6200 ■ *Web:* www.ohiocat.com	Broadview Heights	OH	44147	440-526-6200	526-9513	358
Ohio Magazine 1422 Euclid Ave Ste 730 *TF:* 800-210-7293 ■ *Web:* www.ohiomagazine.com	Cleveland	OH	44115	216-771-2833	781-6318	457-22
Ohio Magnetics Inc 5400 Dunham Rd *TF:* 800-486-6446 ■ *Web:* www.ohiomagnetics.com	Maple Heights	OH	44137	216-662-8484	662-2911	470
Ohio Manufacturers' Association 33 N High St *TF:* 800-662-4463 ■ *Web:* www.ohiomfg.com	Columbus	OH	43215	614-224-5111		138
Ohio Medical Transportation Inc 2827 W Dblin Granville Rd *TF:* 877-633-3598 ■ *Web:* www.medflight.com	Columbus	OH	43235	614-734-8001		13
Ohio Medicine Magazine 3401 Mill Run Dr *TF:* 800-766-6762 ■ *Web:* osma.org	Hilliard	OH	43026	614-527-6762	527-6763	457-16
Ohio Module Manufacturing Co LLC 3900 Stickney Ave	Toledo	OH	43608	419-729-6700		247
Ohio Motorcycle Dealers Association 655 Metro Pl S Ste 270 *TF:* 800-686-9100 ■ *Web:* oada.com	Dublin	OH	43017	614-766-9100		138
Ohio Municipal Advisory Council 9321 Ravenna Rd Ste K *Web:* www.ohiomac.com	Twinsburg	OH	44087	330-963-7444		401
Ohio Northern University 525 S Main St **Fax:* Admissions ■ *TF Admissions:* 888-408-4668 ■ *Web:* www.onu.edu	Ada	OH	45810	419-772-2000	772-2313*	166
Ohio Northern University Claude W Pettit College of Law 525 S Main St *TF:* 877-452-9668 ■ *Web:* www.law.onu.edu	Ada	OH	45810	419-772-2211	772-3042	167-1
Ohio Northern University Heterick Memorial Library 525 S Main St *TF:* 866-943-5787 ■ *Web:* onu.edu/academics/heterick_memorial_library	Ada	OH	45810	419-772-2181	772-1927	434-6
Ohio Nurses Assn (ONA) 4000 E Main St *TF:* 800-735-0056 ■ *Web:* www.ohnurses.org	Columbus	OH	43213	614-237-5414	237-6074	533
Ohio Nut & Bolt Co 5250 W 164th St **Fax Area Code:* 216 ■ *TF:* 800-437-1689 ■ *Web:* www.buckeyefasteners.com/onb	Brook Park	OH	44142	800-437-1689	267-3228*	278
Ohio Packing Co 1306 Harmon Ave *Web:* www.ohiopacking.com	Columbus	OH	43223	614-239-1600		473
Ohio Paper Tube Co 3422 Navarre Rd SW *Web:* www.ohiopapertube.com	Canton	OH	44706	330-478-5171		125
Ohio Penal Industries (OPI) 1221 McKinley Ave *TF:* 800-237-3454 ■ *Web:* www.opi.state.oh.us	Columbus	OH	43222	614-752-0287	752-0303	630
Ohio Pizza Products Inc 201 Lawton Ave *Web:* www.prestofoods.com	Monroe	OH	45050	937-294-6969		805
Ohio Poultry Association 5930 Sharon Woods Blvd *Web:* www.ohiopoultry.org	Columbus	OH	43229	614-882-6111		533
Ohio Processors Inc 244 E First St *Web:* www.instantwhip.com/home.html	London	OH	43140	740-852-9243		296-10
Ohio Quarter Horse 101 Tawa Rd *TF:* 800-367-1534 ■ *Web:* oqha.com	Richwood	OH	43344	740-943-2346		533
Ohio Reformatory for Women 1479 Collins Ave *Web:* drc.ohio.gov	Marysville	OH	43040	937-642-1065		213
Ohio Republican Party 211 S Fifth St *TF:* 800-282-0515 ■ *Web:* www.ohiogop.org	Columbus	OH	43215	614-228-2481		616-2
Ohio Restaurant Assn 1525 Bethel Rd Ste 201 *TF:* 800-282-9049 ■ *Web:* www.ohiorestaurant.org	Columbus	OH	43220	614-442-3535		242
Ohio River Collieries Co 70245 Bannock Uniontown Rd	Bannock	OH	43972	740-968-3582		501
Ohio River Juvenile Correctional Facility 4696 Gallia Pk *Web:* dys.ohio.gov	Franklin Furnace	OH	45629	740-354-7000		412
Ohio Screw Products Inc 818 Lowell St *Web:* www.ohioscrew.com	Elyria	OH	44035	440-322-6341	322-0750	621
Ohio Stadium 411 Woody Hayes Dr *Web:* www.ohiostatebuckeyes.com	Columbus	OH	43210	614-292-7572	292-0506	720
Ohio Star Forge Co (OSF) 4000 Mahoning Ave NW *Web:* www.ohiostar.com	Warren	OH	44483	330-847-6360	847-6368	483
Ohio State Bar Assn (OSBA) 1700 Lake Shore Dr *TF:* 800-282-6556 ■ *Web:* www.ohiobar.org	Columbus	OH	43204	614-487-2050	487-1008	72
Ohio State Life Insurance Co PO Box 410288 *TF:* 800-752-1387 ■ *Web:* www.ohiostatelife.com	Kansas City	MO	64141	800-752-1387		391-2
Ohio State Medical Assn 3401 Mill Run Dr *TF:* 800-766-6762 ■ *Web:* www.osma.org	Hilliard	OH	43026	614-527-6762	527-6763	474
Ohio State Penitentiary 878 Coitsville HubbaRd Rd *Web:* drc.ohio.gov	Youngstown	OH	44505	330-743-0700		213
Ohio State University 154 W 12th Ave **Fax:* Admissions ■ *TF:* 800-426-5046 ■ *Web:* www.osu.edu	Columbus	OH	43210	614-292-3980	292-4818*	166
Lima 4240 Campus Dr *Web:* www.lima.osu.edu	Lima	OH	45804	419-995-8391	995-8483	166
Mansfield 1760 University Dr *Web:* mansfield.osu.edu	Mansfield	OH	44906	419-755-4011		166
Newark 1179 University Dr **Fax:* Admissions ■ *TF:* 800-963-9275 ■ *Web:* newark.osu.edu	Newark	OH	43055	740-366-3321	364-9645*	166
University Libraries 1858 Neil Ave Mall *TF:* 800-555-1212 ■ *Web:* www.library.osu.edu	Columbus	OH	43210	614-292-6785	292-7859	434-6
Ohio State University College of Medicine & Public Health 370 W Ninth Ave 155 Meiling Hall **Fax:* Admitting ■ *Web:* wexnermedical.osu.edu	Columbus	OH	43210	614-292-2220	247-7959*	167-2
Ohio State University Moritz College of Law 55 W 12th Ave *Web:* www.moritzlaw.osu.edu	Columbus	OH	43210	614-292-2631	292-1492	167-1
Ohio State University Police, The 1680 Madison Ave *TF:* 800-358-4678 ■ *Web:* www.oardc.ohio-state.edu	Wooster	OH	44691	330-287-0111	202-3579	668
Ohio State University Press 1070 Carmack Rd *Web:* ohiostatepress.org	Columbus	OH	43210	614-292-1462	292-2065	637-4
Ohio State University System 190 N Oval Mall 205 Bricker Hall *Web:* www.osu.edu	Columbus	OH	43210	614-292-2424	292-1231	786
Ohio State University Wexner Medical Center, The 410 W Tenth Ave *Web:* wexnermedical.osu.edu	Columbus	OH	43210	614-293-8000		374-3
Ohio State University, The *Health Science Library* 376 W Tenth Ave *Web:* www.hsl.osu.edu	Columbus	OH	43210	614-292-4861	292-1920	434-1
Ohio Steel Industries Inc 2575 Ferris Rd *Web:* www.ohiosteel.com	Columbus	OH	43224	614-471-4800		429
Ohio Steel Sheet & Plate Inc 7845 Chestnut Ridge Rd	Hubbard	OH	44425	330-534-2400		492
Ohio Theatre 55 E State St *TF:* 800-745-3000 ■ *Web:* www.capa.com/venues/ohio-theatre	Columbus	OH	43215	614-469-1045	461-0429	572
Ohio Tool Systems Inc 3863 Congress Pkwy *Web:* www.ohiotool.com	Richfield	OH	44286	330-659-4181		358
Ohio Travel Association 130 E Chestnut St Ste 301 *TF:* 800-896-4682 ■ *Web:* www.ohiotravel.org	Columbus	OH	43215	614-572-1931		772
Ohio Travel Bag Manufacturing Co 6481 Davis Industrial Pkwy *Web:* www.ohiotravelbag.com	Solon	OH	44139	440-498-1955		772
Ohio University 120 Chubb Hall **Fax:* Admissions ■ *TF:* 800-858-6843 ■ *Web:* www.ohio.edu	Athens	OH	45710	740-593-1000	593-0560*	166
Alden Library Park Pl **Fax:* Admin ■ *Web:* www.library.ohiou.edu	Athens	OH	45701	740-593-2699	593-0138*	434-6
Chillicothe 101 University Dr *TF:* 877-462-6824 ■ *Web:* www.ohio.edu/chillicothe	Chillicothe	OH	45601	740-774-7200		166
Eastern 45425 National Rd **Fax:* Admissions ■ *TF:* 800-648-3331 ■ *Web:* www.ohio.edu	Saint Clairsville	OH	43950	740-695-1720	695-7079*	166
Lancaster 1570 Granville Pike **Fax:* Admissions ■ *TF:* 800-444-2910 ■ *Web:* www.ohio.edu	Lancaster	OH	43130	740-654-6711	687-9497*	166

	City	State	Zip	Phone	Fax	Class
Southern 1804 Liberty Ave	Ironton	OH	45638	740-533-4600	533-4632*	166
**Fax:* Admissions ■ *TF:* 800-626-0513 ■ *Web:* ohio.edu/southern						
Zanesville 1425 Newark Rd	Zanesville	OH	43701	740-453-0762	453-6161	166
Web: www.ohio.edu						
Ohio University Press						
19 Cir Dr The Ridges	Athens	OH	45701	740-593-1154	593-4536	637-4
TF Sales: 800-621-2736 ■ *Web:* www.ohioswallow.com						
Ohio Valley Aluminum Company LLC						
1100 Brooks Industrial Rd	Shelbyville	KY	40065	502-633-2783		492
TF: 800-692-4145 ■ *Web:* www.ovaco.com						
Ohio Valley Banc Corp						
420 Third Ave	Gallipolis	OH	45631	740-446-2631		360-2
NASDAQ: OVBC ■ *TF:* 800-468-6682 ■ *Web:* www.ovbc.com						
Ohio Valley Coal Co						
56854 Pleasant Ridge Rd	Alledonia	OH	43902	740-926-1351		501
Ohio Valley Flooring Inc						
5555 Murray Ave	Cincinnati	OH	45227	513-561-3399		361
Web: www.ovf.com						
Ohio Valley General Hospital						
25 Heckel Rd Kennedy Township	McKees Rocks	PA	15136	412-777-6161	777-6363	374-3
TF: 800-826-6762 ■ *Web:* www.ohiovalleyhospital.org						
Ohio Valley Mall						
67800 Mall Rd	Saint Clairsville	OH	43950	740-695-4526	695-4451	460
Web: www.ohiovalleymall.net						
Ohio Valley Manufacturing Inc						
1501 Harrington Memorial Rd	Mansfield	OH	44903	419-522-5818		483
Web: www.ohiovalleymfg.com						
Ohio Valley Medical Ctr 2000 Eoff St	Wheeling	WV	26003	304-234-0123		374-3
Web: ovmc-eorh.com						
Ohio Valley Supply Co						
3512 Spring Grove Ave	Cincinnati	OH	45223	513-681-8300	853-3307	191-3
TF: 800-696-5608 ■ *Web:* www.ovsco.com						
Ohio Valley University						
1 Campus View Dr	Vienna	WV	26105	304-865-6000		166
Ohio Valley Veneer Inc 165 No Name Rd	Piketon	OH	45661	740-289-4979		683
Ohio Veterans Home 3416 Columbus Ave	Sandusky	OH	44870	419-625-2454		793
TF Admissions: 800-572-7934 ■ *Web:* dvs.ohio.gov						
Ohio Veterinary Medical Assn (OVMA)						
3168 Riverside Dr	Columbus	OH	43221	614-486-7253	486-1325	795
TF: 800-662-6862 ■ *Web:* www.ohiovma.org						
Ohio Wesleyan University						
61 S Sandusky St Slocum Hall	Delaware	OH	43015	740-368-2000	368-3314*	166
**Fax:* Admissions ■ *TF:* 800-922-8953 ■ *Web:* www.owu.edu						
OhioHealth Corporate Offices						
1087 Dennison Ave Ste 7	Columbus	OH	43201	614-459-2906		353
Web: www.ohiohealth.com						
OhioHealth Mansfield Hospital						
335 Glessner Ave	Mansfield	OH	44903	419-526-8000		374-3
Web: www.ohiohealth.com/mansfield						
Ohiya Casino 53142 Hwy 12	Niobrara	NE	68760	402-857-3860		452
Web: ohiyacasino.com						
Ohline Corp 1930 W 139th St	Gardena	CA	90249	310-327-4630		499
Ohlinger Industries Inc						
1211 W Melinda Ln	Phoenix	AZ	85027	602-285-0911		757
Web: www.ohlingerind.com						
Ohlone College 43600 Mission Blvd	Fremont	CA	94539	510-659-6000	659-7321*	162
**Fax:* Admissions ■ *Web:* www.ohlone.edu						
Ohly Americas 3388 Bacon St	Rhinelander	WI	54501	320-587-2481	587-8617	296-42
TF: 800-321-2689 ■ *Web:* www.ohly.com						
OHM (Orchard Hiltz & McCliment Inc)						
34000 Plymouth Rd	Livonia	MI	48150	734-522-6711	522-6427	261
TF: 888-522-6711 ■ *Web:* www.ohm-advisors.com						
Ohm Systems Inc 10250 Chester Rd	Cincinnati	OH	45215	513-771-0008	771-0101	463
TF: 800-878-0646 ■ *Web:* www.ohmworld.com						
Ohmart/VEGA Corp 4241 Allendorf Dr	Cincinnati	OH	45209	513-272-0131	272-0133	472
TF: 800-367-5383 ■ *Web:* www.vega.com/home_us						
Ohmite Manufacturing Co						
1600 Golf Rd Ste 850	Rolling Meadows	IL	60008	847-258-0300		253
TF: 866-964-6483 ■ *Web:* www.ohmite.com						
Ohmstede 895 N Main St	Beaumont	TX	77704	409-833-6375	839-4948	91
TF: 800-568-2328 ■ *Web:* www.ohmstede.com						
Ohmx Corp 1801 Maple Ave Ste 6143	Evanston	IL	60201	847-491-8500		231
Web: www.ohmxbio.com						
OHOP Mutual Light Co						
34014 Mountain Hwy E	Eatonville	WA	98328	253-847-4363	847-2877	245
Web: ohop.coop						
Ohr-O'Keefe Museum of Art						
386 Beach Blvd	Biloxi	MS	39530	228-374-5547	436-3641	520
Web: www.georgeohr.org						
OI Corp						
151 Graham Rd PO Box 9010	College Station	TX	77842	979-690-1711	690-0440	419
TF: 800-653-1711 ■ *Web:* www.oico.com						
OIA (Outdoor Industry Assn)						
4909 Pearl E Cir Ste 200	Boulder	CO	80301	303-444-3353	444-3284	49-4
Web: www.outdoorindustry.org						
OIA Global Logistics Inc						
2100 SW River Pkwy	Portland	OR	97201	503-736-5900		311
TF: 800-938-3109 ■ *Web:* oiaglobal.com						
Oic Group Inc 112 State St Ste Llb	Peoria	IL	61602	309-680-5600		180
Web: oicgroup.net						
OIC International						
1875 Connecticut Ave NW Fl 10	Washington	DC	20009	215-842-0220	842-2276	48-5
Web: www.oici.org						
State Ethics Commission						
315 W Ohio St Rm 104	Indianapolis	IN	46202	317-232-3850	232-0707	265
TF: 866-805-8498 ■ *Web:* www.in.gov/ig						
Oil & Gas Asset Clearinghouse L P, The						
500 N Sam Houston Pkwy W Ste 150	Houston	TX	77067	281-873-4600		653
Web: www.ogclearinghouse.com						
Oil & Gas Equipment Corp 8 Rd 350	Flora Vista	NM	87415	505-333-2300	333-2301	386
TF: 800-868-9624 ■ *Web:* www.ogequip.com						
Oil & Gas Journal 1455 W Loop S	Houston	TX	77027	918-831-9423	831-9482	457-21
TF: 800-633-1656 ■ *Web:* www.ogj.com						
Oil Butler International Corp						
1599 US 22	Union	NJ	07083	908-687-3453	687-7617	62-5
Oil Can Henry's 19150 SW 90th Ave	Tualatin	OR	97062	503-783-3888		195
TF: 800-765-6244 ■ *Web:* www.oilcanhenry.com						
Oil Capital Community Credit Union						
4132 E 51st St	Tulsa	OK	74135	918-743-4080		219
TF: 800-725-6622 ■ *Web:* www.oilcapital.com						
Oil Chem Inc 711 W 12th St	Flint	MI	48503	810-235-3040	238-5260	541
Web: www.oilcheminc.com						
Oil Creek District Library Ctr						
2 Central Ave	Oil City	PA	16301	814-678-3054	676-0359	434-3
Web: www.oilcreekdistrictlibrary.org						
Oil Creek Plastics Inc						
45619 State Hwy 27 PO Box 385	Titusville	PA	16354	814-827-3661		596
TF: 800-537-3661 ■ *Web:* oilcreekplastics.com						
Oil Creek State Park 305 State Pk Rd	Oil City	PA	16301	814-676-5915		565
Web: www.dcnr.state.pa.us						
Oil Ctr Research LLC						
106 Montrose Ave	Lafayette	LA	70503	337-993-3559	993-3149	541
TF: 800-256-8977 ■ *Web:* www.oilcenter.com						
Oil Field Development Engineering LLC						
12121 Wickchester Ln	Houston	TX	77079	281-679-9060		261
Web: ofdeng.com						
Oil Mop LLC 131 Keating Dr	Belle Chasse	LA	70037	504-394-6110		192
Web: www.omies.com						
Oil Palace, The 10408 Hwy 64 E	Tyler	TX	75707	903-566-2122	566-4206	205
TF: 800-345-8082 ■ *Web:* www.oilpalace.com						
Oil Price Information Service						
3349 Hwy 138 Bldg D Ste D	Wall	NJ	07719	732-901-8800		531-5
TF Cust Svc: 888-301-2645 ■ *Web:* www.opisnet.com						
Oil Producers Inc of Kansas						
1710 N WaterFrnt Pkwy	Wichita	KS	67206	316-681-0231		536
Web: www.oilprod.com						
Oil States International Inc						
333 Clay St Three Allen Ctr Ste 4620	Houston	TX	77002	713-652-0582	652-0499	539
NYSE: OIS ■ *Web:* www.oilstatesintl.com						
Oil States Skagit SMATCO LLC						
1180 Mulberry Rd	Houma	LA	70363	985-868-0630		539
Web: oilstates.com						
Oil-Dri Corp of America						
410 N Michigan Ave Ste 400	Chicago	IL	60611	312-321-1515	321-1271	500
NYSE: ODC ■ *TF:* 800-645-3747 ■ *Web:* www.oildri.com						
Oiles America Corp						
4510 Enterprise Dr, NW	Concord	NC	28027	704-784-4500		75
Web: www.oiles.com						
Oilgear Co						
2300 S 51st St PO Box 343924	Milwaukee	WI	53219	414-327-1700	327-0532	640
Web: www.oilgear.com						
Oil-Law Records Corp						
8 N W 65th St	Oklahoma City	OK	73116	405-840-1631		224
TF: 888-464-5529 ■ *Web:* www.oil-law.com						
Oilmen's Equipment Corp						
140 Cedar Springs Rd	Spartanburg	SC	29302	864-573-9311		579
Web: www.oilmens.com						
Oilseeds International Ltd						
8 Jackson St	San Francisco	CA	94111	415-956-7251		803-1
Web: www.oilseedssf.com						
Oiltanking Houston LP						
15602 Jacinto Port Blvd	Houston	TX	77015	281-457-7900		581
Web: www.oiltanking.com						
Oishii Boston 1166 Washington St	Boston	MA	02118	617-482-8868		671
Web: www.oishiiboston.com						
Oishii Sushi 277 Bernard Ouest	Montreal	QC	H2V1T5	514-271-8863		671
Web: www.oishii.ca						
Ojai Valley Chamber of Commerce						
201 S Signal St	Ojai	CA	93023	805-646-8126	646-9762	139
Web: www.ojaichamber.org						
Ojai Valley Inn & Spa						
905 Country Club Rd	Ojai	CA	93023	805-640-2068	646-0904	669
TF: 800-422-6524 ■ *Web:* www.ojairesort.com						
Ojai Valley News Inc 408 Bryant Cir # A	Ojai	CA	93023	805-646-1476	646-4281	637-8
Web: www.ojaivalleynews.com						
Ojai Valley School 723 El Paseo Rd	Ojai	CA	93023	805-646-1423	646-0362	622
Web: www.ovs.org						
Ojeda's 2001 Coit Rd Ste 102	Plano	TX	75075	972-599-1300		671
Web: ojedasrestaurant.com						
Oji Bros Farms Inc						
8547 Sawtelle Ave	Yuba City	CA	95991	530-673-0845		10-4
Oji Intertech Inc						
906 W Hanley Rd	North Manchester	IN	46962	260-982-1544		561
Web: www.ojiintertech.com						
Ojo Caliente Mineral Springs Resort						
50 Los Banos Dr PO Box 68	Ojo Caliente	NM	87549	505-583-2233	583-2045	706
TF: 800-222-9162 ■ *Web:* www.ojospa.com						
OJP (Office of Justice Programs)						
810 Seventh St NW	Washington	DC	20531	202-307-0703		340-14
Web: ojp.gov						
OK Corral 326 E Allen St	Tombstone	AZ	85638	520-457-3456		50-3
TF: 800-518-1566 ■ *Web:* www.ok-corral.com						
OK Foods Inc PO Box 1787	Fort Smith	AR	72902	800-635-9441		619
TF: 800-635-9441 ■ *Web:* www.okfoods.com/tenderbird						
OK International						
12151 Monarch St	Garden Grove	CA	92841	714-799-9910	799-9533	253
Web: www.okinternational.com						
Ok Kosher Certification 391 Troy Ave	Brooklyn	NY	11213	718-756-7500		743
TF: 800-368-7699 ■ *Web:* www.ok.org						
OK Tire Stores Inc 19082 21st Ave	Surrey	BC	V3S3M3	604-542-7999		755
Web: www.oktire.com						
OK3 Air 1980 Airport Rd Hngr A	Heber City	UT	84032	435-654-3962		23
Web: www.ok3.aero						
Okaloosa - Walton Security & Surveillancellc						
PO Box 1033	Defuniak Springs	FL	32433	850-892-4550		693
Web: okaloosa-waltonsecurityandsurveillance.com						
Okaloosa Correctional						
3189 Little Silver Rd	Crestview	FL	32539	850-682-0931	689-7803	213
Web: dc.state.fl.us						
Okaloosa County						
101 E James Lee Blvd	Crestview	FL	32536	850-689-5000	689-5818	338
TF: 800-438-8683 ■ *Web:* www.co.okaloosa.fl.us						
Okanagan College 1000 KLO Rd	Kelowna	BC	V1Y4X8	250-762-5445		162
TF: 800-621-3038 ■ *Web:* www.okanagan.bc.ca						

	Phone	Fax	Class
Okanjo Partners Inc 220 E Buffalo St Ste 303 .... Milwaukee WI 53202 *TF:* 800-960-4118 ■ *Web:* www.okanjo.com	414-810-1760		224
Okanogan County 149 N Third Ave PO Box 980 .... Okanogan WA 98840 *Web:* www.okanogancounty.org	509-422-7170	422-7174	338
Okanogan County Electric Co-op 93 W Chewuch Rd .... Winthrop WA 98862 *Web:* okanoganelectriccoop.com	509-996-2228		245
Okaw Truss Inc 368 E St Rt 133 .... Arthur IL 61911 *Web:* www.okawtruss.com	217-543-3371		817
Okay Industries Inc 200 Ellis St .... New Britain CT 06051 *TF:* 800-249-5662 ■ *Web:* www.okayind.com	860-225-8707	225-7047	488
Okee Industries Inc 91 Shield St .... West Hartford CT 06110 *Web:* www.okee.net	860-953-1234		351
Okeechobee Chamber of Commerce 55 S Parrott Ave .... Okeechobee FL 34972 *Web:* www.okeechobeebusiness.com	863-467-6246		139
Okeechobee Correctional Institution 3420 NE 168th St .... Okeechobee FL 34972 *TF:* 800-574-5729 ■ *Web:* dc.state.fl.us	863-462-5400	462-5402	213
Okeechobee County 304 NW Second St .... Okeechobee FL 34972 *Web:* www.co.okeechobee.fl.us	863-763-6441	763-9529	338
Okeechobee Steakhouse 2854 Okeechobee Blvd .... West Palm Beach FL 33409 *Web:* www.okeesteakhouse.com	561-683-5151		671
Okeeffe & Company Marketing Inc 921 King St .... Alexandria VA 22314 *Web:* www.okco.com	703-883-9000		7
Okefenoke Rural Electric Membership Corp (REMC) 14384 Cleveland St PO Box 602 .... Nahunta GA 31553 *TF:* 800-262-5131 ■ *Web:* www.oremc.com	912-462-5131	462-6100	245
Oki Data Americas Inc 2000 Bishops Gate Blvd .... Mount Laurel NJ 08054 *TF Cust Svc:* 800-654-3282 ■ *Web:* www.okidata.com	856-235-2600	222-5320	173-6
OKI Developments Inc 1416 112th Ave NE .... Bellevue WA 98004 *TF:* 877-465-3654 ■ *Web:* www.okigolf.com	425-454-2800	646-6999	360-3
Okiok Data Ltd 655 Promenade du Centropolis Ste 230 .... Laval QC H7T0A3 *Web:* www.okiok.com	450-681-1681		180
OKK Trading Inc 5705 Union Pacific Ave .... Los Angeles CA 90022 *Web:* www.okktoys.com/ecommerce/General/Default.aspx	323-725-8800		241
OKL Can Line Inc 11235 Sebring Dr .... Cincinnati OH 45240 *Web:* www.oklcan.com	513-825-1655		757
Oklahoma			
Administrative Office of the Courts 2100 N Lincoln Blvd Ste 3 .... Oklahoma City OK 73105 *Web:* www.ok.gov	405-556-9300		339-37
Aging Services Div 2401 NW 23rd St Ste 40 .... Oklahoma City OK 73107 *Web:* www.okdhs.org/aging	405-521-2281	521-2086	339-37
Agriculture Food & Forestry Dept 2800 N Lincoln Blvd .... Oklahoma City OK 73106 *Web:* www.oda.state.ok.us	405-521-3864		339-37
Arts Council 2101 N Lincoln Blvd Ste 640 .... Oklahoma City OK 73105 *Web:* arts.ok.gov	405-521-2931	521-6418	339-37
Attorney General 313 NE 21st St .... Oklahoma City OK 73105 *Web:* ok.gov/oag	405-521-3921	521-6246	339-37
Banking Dept 2900 N Lincoln Blvd .... Oklahoma City OK 73105 *Web:* www.ok.gov	405-521-2782	522-2993	339-37
Chief Medical Examiner 901 N Stonewall Ave .... Oklahoma City OK 73117 *Web:* www.state.ok.us	405-239-7141	239-2430	339-37
Commerce Dept 900 N Stiles Ave .... Oklahoma City OK 73104 *TF:* 800-879-6552 ■ *Web:* www.okcommerce.gov	405-815-6552		339-37
Conservation Commission 2800 N Lincoln Blvd Ste 160 .... Oklahoma City OK 73105 *Web:* www.okcc.state.ok.us	405-522-4728		339-37
Consumer Protection Div 3613 NW 56th Ste 240 .... Oklahoma City OK 73112 *Web:* www.ok.gov	405-521-4274		339-37
Corporation Commission (OCC) Jim Thorpe Bldg 2101 N Lincoln PO Box 52000 .... Oklahoma City OK 73152 *Web:* www.occeweb.com	405-521-2211	522-1623	339-37
Corrections Dept 3400 N Martin Luther King Ave .... Oklahoma City OK 73111 *Web:* www.ok.gov	405-425-2500	425-2578	339-37
Development Finance Authority 9220 N Kelley Ave .... Oklahoma City OK 73131 *Web:* www.ok.gov	405-848-9761	848-3314	339-37
Education Dept 2500 N Lincoln Blvd .... Oklahoma City OK 73105 *Web:* www.ok.gov	405-521-3301	521-6205	339-37
Emergency Management Dept 2401 Lincoln Blvd ste C51 .... Oklahoma City OK 73111 *Web:* www.ok.gov	405-521-2481	521-4053	339-37
Employment Security Commission Will Rogers Memorial Office Bldg 2401 N Lincoln Blvd PO Box 52003 PO Box 52003 .... Oklahoma City OK 73152 *Web:* www.ok.gov	405-557-5100		259
Environmental Quality Dept 707 N Robinson .... Oklahoma City OK 73102 *TF:* 800-869-1400 ■ *Web:* www.deq.state.ok.us	405-702-0100	702-1001	339-37
Ethics Commission 2300 N Lincoln Blvd Rm B5 .... Oklahoma City OK 73105 *Web:* www.ok.gov	405-521-3451	521-4905	265
Health Dept 1000 NE Tenth St .... Oklahoma City OK 73117 *Web:* www.health.state.ok.us	405-271-5600		339-37
Historical Society 800 Nahzi Zuhzi Dr .... Oklahoma City OK 73105 *Web:* www.okhistory.org	405-521-2491		339-37
Housing Finance Agency 100 NW 63rd St Ste 200 .... Oklahoma City OK 73116 *TF:* 800-256-1489 ■ *Web:* www.ohfa.org	405-848-1144	879-8822	339-37
Human Services Dept 2400 N Lincoln Blvd Sequoyah Memorial Office Bldg .... Oklahoma City OK 73105 *Web:* www.okdhs.org	405-521-3646	521-6458	339-37
Insurance Dept (OID) 3625 NW 56th Ste 100 .... Oklahoma City OK 73112 *TF:* 800-522-0071 ■ *Web:* www.ok.gov/oid	405-521-2828	521-6635	339-37
Labor Dept 3017 N Stiles Ste 100 .... Oklahoma City OK 73105 *Web:* www.ok.gov	405-521-6100	528-5751	339-37
Legislation Service Bureau 2300 N Lincoln Blvd .... State Capitol Bldg OK 73105 *Web:* www.oklegislature.gov	405-521-4081		433
Lieutenant Governor 2300 N Lincoln Blvd Ste 211 .... Oklahoma City OK 73105 *Web:* www.ok.gov	405-521-2161	522-8694	339-37
Mental Health & Substance Abuse Services Dept 1200 NE 13th St PO Box 53277 .... Oklahoma City OK 73152 *Web:* www.odmhsas.org	405-522-3908	522-3650	339-37
Motor Vehicle Commission 4334 NW Expy Ste 183 .... Oklahoma City OK 73116 *Web:* www.ok.gov	405-607-8227	607-8909	339-37
Pardon & Parole Board 2915 N Classen Blvd Ste 405 .... Oklahoma City OK 73106 *Web:* www.ok.gov/ppb	405-521-6600	602-6437	339-37
Parks Div 900 N Stiles Ave .... Oklahoma City OK 73104 *TF:* 800-652-6552 ■ *Web:* www.travelok.com	800-652-6552		339-37
Personnel Management Office 2101 N Lincoln Blvd Ste G-80 .... Oklahoma City OK 73105 *Web:* www.ok.gov	405-521-2177	524-6942	339-37
Real Estate Commission 1915 N Stiles Ave Ste 200 .... Oklahoma City OK 73105 *TF:* 866-521-3389 ■ *Web:* www.ok.gov	405-521-3387	521-2189	339-37
Rehabilitative Services Dept 3535 NW 58th St Ste 500 .... Oklahoma City OK 73112 *TF:* 800-845-8476 ■ *Web:* www.okrehab.org	405-951-3400	951-3529	339-37
Secretary of State 2300 N Lincoln Blvd Ste 101 .... Oklahoma City OK 73105 *Web:* www.sos.ok.gov	405-521-3912	521-3771	339-37
Securities Dept 204 N Robinson Ave Ste 400 .... Oklahoma City OK 73102 *Web:* www.securities.ok.gov	405-280-7700	280-7742	339-37
State Regents for Higher Education 655 Research Pkwy Ste 200 .... Oklahoma City OK 73104 *Web:* www.okhighered.org	405-225-9100	225-9235	725
Supreme Court 2100 N Lincoln Blvd Ste 3 .... Oklahoma City OK 73105 *Web:* www.ok.gov	405-556-9300		339-37
Tax Commission 2501 N Lincoln Blvd .... Oklahoma City OK 73194 *Web:* www.ok.gov/tax	405-521-3160	521-3826	339-37
Treasurer 2300 N Lincoln Rd Rm 217 .... Oklahoma City OK 73105 *Web:* www.ok.gov	405-521-3191	521-4994	339-37
Veterans Affairs Dept 2311 N Central .... Oklahoma City OK 73105 *Web:* www.ok.gov	405-521-3684	521-6533	339-37
Victim Services Unit 313 NE 21st St .... Oklahoma City OK 73105 *Web:* www.oag.ok.gov/oagweb.nsf/vservices.html	405-521-3921	521-6246	339-37
Vital Records Div 1000 NE Tenth St .... Oklahoma City OK 73117 *TF:* 800-522-0203 ■ *Web:* www.ok.gov	405-271-5600		339-37
Weights & Measures 2800 N Lincoln Blvd Ste 160 .... Oklahoma City OK 73105 *Web:* www.ok.gov	405-521-3864		339-37
Wildlife Conservation Dept (ODWC) PO Box 53465 .... Oklahoma City OK 73111 *Web:* www.wildlifedepartment.com	405-521-3851		339-37
Oklahoma Alliance for Manufacturing Excellence Inc 525 S Main St Ste 210 .... Tulsa OK 74103 *Web:* www.okalliance.com	918-592-0722		138
Oklahoma Aquarium 300 S Aquarium Dr .... Jenks OK 74037 *Web:* www.okaquarium.org	918-296-3474		40
Oklahoma Assn of Realtors 9807 N Broadway .... Oklahoma City OK 73114 *TF:* 800-375-9944 ■ *Web:* okrealtors.com	405-848-9944	848-9947	656
Oklahoma Baptist University 500 W University St .... Shawnee OK 74804 *TF:* 800-654-3285 ■ *Web:* www.okbu.edu	405-275-2850		166
Oklahoma Bar Assn 1901 N Lincoln Blvd PO Box 53036 .... Oklahoma City OK 73105 *TF:* 800-522-8065 ■ *Web:* www.okbar.org	405-416-7000	416-7001	72
Oklahoma Blood Institute (OBI) 1001 N Lincoln Blvd .... Oklahoma City OK 73104 **Fax Area Code:* 918 ■ *TF:* 866-708-4995 ■ *Web:* www.obi.org	405-278-3100	477-0446*	89
Oklahoma Botanical Garden & Arboretum 136 Agricultural Hall Oklahoma State University .... Stillwater OK 74078 *Web:* botanicgarden.okstate.edu	405-744-4531	744-5339	97
Oklahoma Christian University PO Box 11000 .... Oklahoma City OK 73136 **Fax:* Admissions ■ *TF:* 800-877-5010 ■ *Web:* www.oc.edu	405-425-5000	425-5069*	166
Oklahoma City Ballet 7421 N Classen Blvd .... Oklahoma City OK 73116 *Web:* www.okcballet.com	405-843-9898	843-9894	573-1
Oklahoma City City Hall 200 N Walker Ave .... Oklahoma City OK 73102 *Web:* www.okc.gov	405-297-2578	297-3124	337
Oklahoma City Community College 7777 S May Ave .... Oklahoma City OK 73159 **Fax:* Admissions ■ *TF:* 800-621-7440 ■ *Web:* www.occc.edu	405-682-1611	682-7521*	162
Oklahoma City Convention & Visitors Bureau 123 Pk Ave .... Oklahoma City OK 73102 *TF:* 800-225-5652 ■ *Web:* www.visitokc.com	405-297-8912	297-8888	206

	Phone	Fax	Class
Oklahoma City Museum of Art 415 Couch Dr, Oklahoma City OK 73102 *TF:* 800-579-9278 ■ *Web:* www.okcmoa.com	405-236-3100	236-3122	520
Oklahoma City National Memorial & Museum 620 N Harvey Ave, Oklahoma City OK 73102 *TF:* 888-542-4673 ■ *Web:* www.oklahomacitynationalmemorial.org	405-235-3313	235-3315	520
Oklahoma City Philharmonic 424 Colcord Dr Ste B, Oklahoma City OK 73102 *Web:* okcphil.org	405-232-7575	232-4353	573-3
Oklahoma City Public Schools 2500 NE 30th St, Oklahoma City OK 73111 *Web:* www.okcps.org	405-587-0000		685
Oklahoma City University 2501 N Blackwelder Ave, Oklahoma City OK 73106 *Fax: Admissions ■ *TF Admissions:* 800-633-7242 ■ *Web:* www.okcu.edu	405-208-5050	208-5916*	166
Oklahoma City University School of Law 2501 N Blackwelder Ave, Oklahoma City OK 73106 *TF:* 800-230-3012 ■ *Web:* www.okcu.edu	405-208-5000		167-1
Oklahoma City Zoological Park & Botanical Gardens 2101 NE 50th St, Oklahoma City OK 73111 *Web:* www.okczoo.org	405-424-3344	425-0243	823
Oklahoma Correctional Industries 3402 N Martin Luther King Ave, Oklahoma City OK 73111 *TF:* 800-522-3565 ■ *Web:* www.ocisales.com	405-425-7500		630
Oklahoma County 320 Robert S Kerr Ave, Oklahoma City OK 73102 *Web:* www.oklahomacounty.org	405-270-0082		338
Oklahoma Democratic Party 4100 N Lincoln Blvd, Oklahoma City OK 73105 *TF:* 800-547-5600 ■ *Web:* www.okdemocrats.org	405-427-3366		616-1
Oklahoma Dental Assn 317 NE 13th St, Oklahoma City OK 73104 *TF:* 800-876-8890 ■ *Web:* www.okda.org	405-848-8873	848-8875	227
Oklahoma Dept of Libraries 200 NE 18th St, Oklahoma City OK 73105 *TF:* 800-522-8116 ■ *Web:* www.odl.state.ok.us	405-521-2502	525-7804	434-5
Oklahoma Education Association 323 E Madison PO Box 18485, Oklahoma City OK 73154 *TF:* 800-522-8091 ■ *Web:* www.okea.org/about-oea/contact-the-staff	405-528-7785	524-0350	457-8
Oklahoma Electric Co-op 242 24th Ave NW, Norman OK 73069 *TF:* 800-522-6543 ■ *Web:* www.okcoop.org	405-321-2024	217-6900	245
Oklahoma Farm Bureau Mutual Insurance Co (OFB) 2501 N Stiles Ave, Oklahoma City OK 73105 *Web:* www.okfarmbureau.org	405-523-2300	523-2362	391-4
Oklahoma Federal Credit Union 517 NE 36th St, Oklahoma City OK 73105 *TF:* 800-522-8510 ■ *Web:* okfcu.com	405-524-6467	524-1067	219
Oklahoma Flower Market Inc, The 36 N Broadway Cir, Oklahoma City OK 73103	405-232-3143		293
Oklahoma Forensic Ctr 24800 S 4420 Rd, Vinita OK 74301 *TF:* 800-752-9475 ■ *Web:* ok.gov	918-256-7841		374-5
Oklahoma Gazette 3701 N Shartel Ave, Oklahoma City OK 73118 *Web:* okgazette.com	405-528-6000	528-4600	532-5
Oklahoma Jazz Hall of Fame 111 E First St Upper Level, Tulsa OK 74103 *Web:* www.okjazz.org	918-281-8600	948-7737	520
Oklahoma Lions Eye Bank 3840 N Lincoln Blvd, Oklahoma City OK 73105	405-400-7371		269
Oklahoma Medical Research Foundation (OMRF) 825 NE 13th St, Oklahoma City OK 73104 *TF:* 800-522-0211 ■ *Web:* www.omrf.org	405-271-6673		668
Oklahoma Methodist Manor Inc 4134 E 31st St, Tulsa OK 74135 *Web:* www.ommtulsa.org	918-743-2565		48-20
Oklahoma Museum of History 800 Nazih Zuhdi Dr, Oklahoma City OK 73105 *Web:* www.okhistory.org	405-522-5248	522-5402	520
Oklahoma Museum of Natural History 2401 Chautaugua Ave, Norman OK 73072 *Web:* samnoblemuseum.ou.edu	405-325-4712		520
Oklahoma Natural Gas Co 401 N Harvey PO Box 401, Oklahoma City OK 73101 *TF:* 800-664-5463 ■ *Web:* www.oklahomanaturalgas.com	800-664-5463		787
Oklahoma Nurses Assn (ONA) 1111 N Lee Ste 243, Oklahoma City OK 73103 *Web:* www.oklahomanurses.org	405-840-3476	840-3013	533
Oklahoma Panhandle State University 323 Eagle Blvd, Goodwell OK 73939 *Fax: Admitting ■ *TF:* 800-664-6778 ■ *Web:* www.opsu.edu	580-349-2611	349-2302*	166
Oklahoma Pharmacists Assn 45 NE 52nd St, Oklahoma City OK 73105 *Web:* www.opha.com	405-528-3338	528-1417	585
Oklahoma Press Service Inc 3601 N Lincoln Blvd, Oklahoma City OK 73105 *TF:* 888-815-2672 ■ *Web:* www.okpress.com	405-524-4421	524-2201	624
Oklahoma Primary Care Association 4300 N Lincoln Blvd Ste 203, Oklahoma City OK 73105 *Web:* okpca.publishpath.com/default.aspx	405-424-2282		138
Oklahoma Republican State Committee 4031 N Lincoln Blvd, Oklahoma City OK 73105	405-528-3501	521-9531	616-2
Oklahoma Sports Hall of Fame & Jim Thorpe Museum 4040 N Lincoln Blvd, Oklahoma City OK 73105 *Web:* www.oklahomasportshalloffame.org	405-427-1400		522
Oklahoma State Chamber 330 NE Tenth St, Oklahoma City OK 73104 *TF:* 800-788-2464 ■ *Web:* www.okstatechamber.com	405-235-3669	235-3670	140
Oklahoma State Penitentiary Corner of W & Stonewall PO Box 97, McAlester OK 74502 *Web:* www.ok.gov	918-423-4700	423-3862	213
Oklahoma State Reformatory 1700 E First St PO Box 514, Granite OK 73547 *Web:* www.ok.gov	580-480-3700	480-3997	213
Oklahoma State System of Higher Education 655 Research Pkwy Ste 200, Oklahoma City OK 73104 *Web:* www.okhighered.org	405-225-9120	225-9235	786
Oklahoma State University 219 Student Union Bldg, Stillwater OK 74078 *TF:* 800-852-1255 ■ *Web:* www.okstate.edu	405-744-5000	744-7092	166
Oklahoma City 900 N Portland Ave, Oklahoma City OK 73107 *Fax: Admissions ■ *TF:* 800-560-4099 ■ *Web:* www.osuokc.edu	405-947-4421	945-9120*	162
Okmulgee 1801 E Fourth St, Okmulgee OK 74447 *TF:* 800-722-4471 ■ *Web:* go.osuit.edu	918-293-4678	293-4650	800
Tulsa 700 N Greenwood Ave, Tulsa OK 74106 *TF:* 800-522-4002 ■ *Web:* www.osu-tulsa.okstate.edu	918-594-8000	594-8202	166
Oklahoma Telephone & Telegraph Inc 26 N Otis Ave, Dustin OK 74839 *TF:* 800-869-1989 ■ *Web:* www.oklatel.net	800-869-1989		387
Oklahoma Territorial Museum 406 E Oklahoma Ave, Guthrie OK 73044 *TF:* 800-522-8116 ■ *Web:* www.okterritorialmuseum.org	405-282-1889		520
Oklahoma Veterans Ctr Ardmore 1015 S Commerce, Ardmore OK 73401 *TF:* 800-941-2160 ■ *Web:* www.ok.gov	580-223-2266	221-5606	793
Oklahoma Veterans Ctr Claremore PO Box 988, Claremore OK 74018 *TF:* 800-273-8255 ■ *Web:* www.ok.gov	918-342-5432	342-0835	793
Oklahoma Veterans Ctr Clinton PO Box 1209, Clinton OK 73601 *TF:* 800-273-8255 ■ *Web:* www.ok.gov	580-331-2200	323-4834	793
Oklahoma Veterans Ctr Norman 1776 E Robinson St, Norman OK 73071 *TF:* 800-782-5218 ■ *Web:* www.ok.gov	405-360-5600		450
Oklahoma Veterans Ctr Sulphur 200 E Fairlane, Sulphur OK 73086 *Web:* www.ok.gov	580-622-2144		793
Oklahoma Veterans Ctr Talihina 10014 SE 1138th Ave PO Box 1168, Talihina OK 74571 *TF:* 800-941-2160 ■ *Web:* www.ok.gov	918-567-2251	567-2950	793
Oklahoma Veterinary Medical Assn PO Box 14521, Oklahoma City OK 73113 *TF:* 888-491-8833 ■ *Web:* www.okvma.org	405-478-1002	478-7193	795
Oklahoma Waste & Wiping Rag Company Inc 2013 SE 18th St, Oklahoma City OK 73129	405-670-3100		745-8
Oklahoman, The 9000 N Broadway, Oklahoma City OK 73114 *TF:* 800-375-6397 ■ *Web:* www.newsok.com	405-475-3311		532-2
Okland Oil Co 110 N Robinson Ave, Oklahoma City OK 73102 *Web:* www.oklandoil.com	405-236-3046		536
Okmulgee County Hostmonster, Orem UT 84097 *Web:* www.okgenweb.org/~okokmulg	918-756-3042		338
Okmulgee State Park 16830 Dripping Springs Rd, Okmulgee OK 74447 *Web:* www.travelok.com/listings/view.profile/id.5520	918-756-5971	759-9933	565
Okobojo Point Recreation Area 19425 Okobojo Pt Dr, Fort Pierre SD 57532 *Web:* www.gfp.sd.gov	605-223-7722		565
Okonite Co 102 Hilltop Rd, Ramsey NJ 07446 *Web:* www.okonite.com	201-825-0300	825-3524	813
Oktibbeha County 106 Miley Dr, Starkville MS 39759 *Web:* www.gtpdd.com/counties/oktibbeha	662-324-7860		338
Okuma America Corp 11900 W Hall Dr, Charlotte NC 28278 *Web:* www.okuma.com	704-588-7000	588-6503	455
Okuma Fishing Tackle Corp 2310 E Locust Ct, Ontario CA 91761 *TF:* 800-466-5862 ■ *Web:* www.okumafishing.com	909-923-2828		711
Olan Mills Inc 4325 Amnicola Hwy, Chattanooga TN 37406 *Web:* www.olanmills.com	423-622-5141		590
Olana State Historic Site 5720 State Rt 9G, Hudson NY 12534 *Web:* www.olana.org	518-828-0135	828-6742	565
Olathe Chamber of Commerce 18001 W 106th St Ste 160, Olathe KS 66061 *Web:* www.olathe.org	913-764-1050	782-4636	139
Olathe Medical Ctr 20333 W 151st St, Olathe KS 66061 *Web:* www.olathehealth.org	913-791-4200		374-3
Olathe Toyota 685 N Rawhide, Olathe KS 66061 *Web:* www.olathetoyota.com	913-780-9919		516
Olbrich Botanical Gardens 3330 Atwood Ave, Madison WI 53704 *Web:* www.olbrich.org	608-246-4550	246-4719	97
OLCC (Orange Lake Country Club Inc) 8505 W Irlo Bronson Memorial Hwy, Kissimmee FL 34747 *TF:* 800-877-6522 ■ *Web:* www.orangelake.com	407-239-0000	239-5119	669
Old Alabama Town 301 Columbus St, Montgomery AL 36104 *TF:* 888-240-1850 ■ *Web:* www.oldalabamatown.com	334-240-4500		50-3
Old American Insurance Co 3520 Broadway, Kansas City MO 64111 *TF:* 800-733-6242 ■ *Web:* www.oaic.com	816-753-7000		391-2
Old Arsenal Museum 900 State Capitol dr, Baton Rouge LA 70802 *Web:* www.sos.la.gov	225-342-0401		520
Old Barracks Museum 101 Barrack St, Trenton NJ 08608 *TF:* 800-275-4278 ■ *Web:* www.barracks.org	609-396-1776	777-4000	520
Old Bridge Chemicals Inc 554 Waterworks Rd, Old Bridge NJ 08857 *TF:* 800-275-3924 ■ *Web:* www.oldbridgechem.com	732-727-2225	727-2653	143
Old Bridge Public Library 1 Old Bridge Plaza, Old Bridge NJ 08857 *TF:* 800-829-1040 ■ *Web:* www.oldbridgelibrary.org	732-721-5600	607-4816	434-3
Old Bridge Township Raceway Park 230 Pension Rd, Englishtown NJ 07726 *Web:* www.etownraceway.com	732-446-7800	446-1373	515
Old Capitol Museum 100 S State St, Jackson MS 39201 *Web:* www.mdah.state.ms.us	601-576-6920	576-6981	520
Old Chicago 327 Lake Ave S, Duluth MN 55802 *Web:* www.oldchicago.com	218-720-2966		671
Old Chicago Restaurants 100 Superior Plaza Way Ste 100, Superior CO 80027 *Web:* www.oldchicago.com	720-304-2048		670
Old Chickahominy House 1211 Jamestown Rd, Williamsburg VA 23185 *TF:* 800-343-7946 ■ *Web:* oldchickahominy.com	757-229-4689		671

Phone | Fax | Class

Old City Cemetery Museums & Arboretum
401 Taylor St. Lynchburg VA 24501 434-847-1465 856 2004 97
Web: www.gravegarden.org

Old City House Inn
115 Cordova St. Saint Augustine FL 32084 904-826-0113 379
Web: www.oldcityhouse.com

Old Coast Guard Station
2401 Atlantic Ave Virginia Beach VA 23451 757-422-1587 491-8609 520
Web: www.oldcoastguardstation.com

Old Colony Correctional Ctr
1 Admin Rd. Bridgewater MA 02324 508-279-6000 279-6754 213
Web: mass.gov

Old Colony Hospice
1 Credit Union Way. Randolph MA 02368 781-341-4145 297-7345 371
TF: 800-370-1322 ■ *Web:* www.oldcolonyhospice.org

Old Country Buffet Restaurants (OCB)
120 Chula Vista Hollywood Park TX 78232 210-403-3725 403-3580 670
Web: www.oldcountrybuffet.com

Old Country Inn 9906 72nd Ave Edmonton AB T6E0Z3 780-433-3242 671
Web: oldcountryinnedmonton.com

Old Courthouse Museum
200 W Sixth St. Sioux Falls SD 57104 605-367-4210 367-6004 520
Web: siouxlandmuseums.com

Old Cowtown Museum 1865 W Museum Blvd. Wichita KS 67203 316-219-1871 520
Web: www.oldcowtown.org

Old Croton Aqueduct State Historic Park
15 Walnut St. Dobbs Ferry NY 10522 914-693-5259 565
Web: www.parks.ny.gov/parks/96/details.aspx

Old Davidsonville State Park
7953 Hwy 166 S Pocahontas AR 72455 870-892-4708 565
Web: www.arkansasstateparks.com

Old Dillard Museum
1009 NW Fourth St. Fort Lauderdale FL 33311 754-322-8828 520
Web: www.browardschools.com

Old Dominion Brush Co
5118 Glen Alden Dr Richmond VA 23231 800-446-9823 586
TF: 800-446-9823 ■ *Web:* www.odbco.com

Old Dominion Capital Management Inc
815 E Jefferson St. Charlottesville VA 22902 434-977-1550 528
TF: 800-446-2029 ■ *Web:* odcm.com

Old Dominion Electric Co-op (ODEC)
4201 Dominion Blvd. Glen Allen VA 23060 804-747-0592 245
Web: odec.com

Old Dominion Eye Bank (ODEF)
9200 Arboretum Pkwy Ste 104 Richmond VA 23236 804-560-7540 560-4752 269
TF: 800-832-0728 ■ *Web:* www.odef.org

Old Dominion Freight Line Inc
500 Old Dominion Way. Thomasville NC 27360 336-889-5000 780
NASDAQ: ODFL ■ *TF:* 800-432-6335 ■ *Web:* www.odfl.com

Old Dominion Insurance Co
4601 Touchton Rd E Ste 330 Ste 3400 Jacksonville FL 32246 904-642-3000 391-4
TF: 800-226-0875 ■ *Web:* msagroup.com

Old Dominion University Rollins Hall Norfolk VA 23529 757-683-3685 683-3255* 166
**Fax:* Admissions ■ *TF:* 800-348-7926 ■ *Web:* www.odu.edu

Old Dutch Foods Inc
2375 Terminal Rd Roseville MN 55113 651-633-8810 297-3
Web: www.olddutchfoods.com

Old Dutch Mustard Co
98 Cutter Mill Rd Great Neck NY 11021 516-466-0522 466-0762 296-19
Web: pilgrimfoods.net

Old Ebbitt Grill 675 15th St NW Washington DC 20005 202-347-4800 671
Web: www.ebbitt.com

Old Economy Village 270 16th St Ambridge PA 15003 724-266-4500 266-7506 520
TF: 800-732-0999 ■ *Web:* www.oldeconomyvillage.org

Old Edwards Inn & Spa 445 Main St. Highlands NC 28741 866-526-8008 378
TF: 866-526-8008 ■ *Web:* www.oldedwardsinn.com

Old Exchange & Provost Dungeon
122 E Bay St. Charleston SC 29401 843-727-2165 50-3
TF: 888-763-0448 ■ *Web:* oldexchange.org

Old First Reformed Church of Christ
151 N Fourth St Philadelphia PA 19106 215-922-4566 50-1
Web: www.oldfirstucc.org

Old Fishermans Grotto
39 Fishermans Wharf Monterey CA 93940 831-375-4604 375-0391 671
Web: www.oldfishermansgrotto.com

Old Florida Museum
259 San Marco Ave. Saint Augustine FL 32084 904-824-8874 520
TF: 800-813-3208 ■ *Web:* www.oldfloridamuseum.com

Old Fort Harrod State Park
100 S College St. Harrodsburg KY 40330 859-734-3314 565
Web: www.parks.ky.gov

Old Fort Niagara State Historic Site
PO Box 169 Youngstown NY 14174 716-745-7611 745-9141 565
Web: www.oldfortniagara.org

Old Fort Pub
65 Skull Creek Dr. Hilton Head Island SC 29926 843-681-2386 671
Web: oldfortpub.com

Old Fort Western 16 Cony St Augusta ME 04330 207-626-2385 626-2304 520
Web: www.oldfortwestern.org

Old Fourth Street Filling Station, The
871 W Fourth St. Winston-Salem NC 27101 336-724-7600 671
Web: www.theoldfourthstreetfillingstation.com

Old Frankfort Stud
360 Watts Ferry Rd. Frankfort KY 40601 859-233-1717 368

Old Globe, The 1363 Old Globe Way. San Diego CA 92101 619-231-1941 231-5879 573-4
Web: www.oldglobe.org

Old Guard Museum 201 Lee Ave Ft Myer Fort Myer VA 22211 703-696-6670 520
TF: 800-552-3978 ■ *Web:* www.army.mil

Old Harbor Outfit 480 Barnum Ave Bridgeport CT 06608 203-540-5150 711
Web: www.oldharboroutfitters.com

Old Hickory House Restaurant
6538 N Tryon St Charlotte NC 28213 704-596-8014 671

Old Hill Partners
1120 Boston Post Rd 2nd Fl. Darien CT 06820 203-656-3004 401
Web: www.oldhill.com

Old Homestead Steakhouse
56 Ninth Ave. New York NY 10011 212-242-9040 727-1637 671
Web: www.theoldhomesteadsteakhouse.com

Old House 309 W San Francisco St Santa Fe NM 87501 505-988-4455 671
TF: 800-955-4455 ■ *Web:* www.eldoradohotel.com

Old Idaho Penitentiary State Historic Site
2445 Old Penitentiary Rd Boise ID 83712 208-334-2844 334-3225 50-3
Web: history.idaho.gov

Old Las Vegas Mormon Fort State Historic Park
500 E Washington Ave Las Vegas NV 89101 702-486-3511 486-3734 565
Web: www.parks.nv.gov

Old Line Bank 1525 Pointer Ridge Pl. Bowie MD 20716 301-430-2500 430-8723 70
NASDAQ: WSB ■ *TF:* 800-416-6373 ■ *Web:* Www.oldlinebank.com

Old Louisville Historic Preservation District
1340 S Fourth St Louisville KY 40208 502-635-5244 635-5245 50-3
Web: www.oldlouisville.com

Old Mansion Foods
3811 Corporate Rd PO Box 1838 Petersburg VA 23805 804-862-9889 861-8816 296-7
TF: 800-476-1877 ■ *Web:* www.oldmansionfoods.com

Old Master Products Inc
7751 Hayvenhurst Ave Van Nuys CA 91406 818-785-8886 550

Old Mill Antique Mall
310 State St West Columbia SC 29169 803-796-4229 460
Web: oldmillantiquemall.com

Old Mill State Park 33489 240th Ave NW Argyle MN 56713 218-437-8174 565
Web: www.dnr.state.mn.us

Old Mill Toronto 21 Old Mill Rd Toronto ON M8X1G5 416-236-2641 379
TF: 866-653-6455 ■ *Web:* oldmilltoronto.com

Old Mill Winery 403 S Broadway. Geneva OH 44041 800-227-6972 466-4417* 80-3
**Fax Area Code:* 440 ■ *TF:* 800-227-6972 ■ *Web:* www.ohiowines.org

Old Mission San Jose
43148 Mission Blvd Fremont CA 94539 510-657-1797 50-1
TF: 800-471-0991 ■ *Web:* www.saintjosephmsj.org

Old Mission State Park
31732 S Mission Rd. Cataldo ID 83810 208-682-3814 565
Web: parksandrecreation.idaho.gov

Old Mulkey Meetinghouse State Historic Site
38 Old Mulkey Pk Rd Tompkinsville KY 42167 270-487-8481 487-8481 565
Web: www.parks.ky.gov

Old National Bancorp 1 Main St Evansville IN 47708 812-464-1294 70
Web: www.oldnational.com

Old National Bank
1 Main St PO Box 718 Evansville IN 47705 800-731-2265 70
TF: 800-731-2265 ■ *Web:* www.oldnational.com

Old Newbury Crafters 36 Main St Ste 2 Amesbury MA 01913 978-388-4026 388-8430 702
TF: 800-343-1388 ■ *Web:* oldnewburycrafterssilver.com

Old North Church 193 Salem St Boston MA 02113 617-523-6676 50-1
Web: www.oldnorth.com

Old Orchard Ctr 4905 Old Orchard Ctr Skokie IL 60077 847-673-6800 460
Web: www.westfield.com

Old Original Bookbinder's
2306 E Cary St Richmond VA 23223 804-643-6900 671
Web: bookbindersrichmond.com

Old Oyster Factory
101 Marshland Rd Hilton Head Island SC 29926 843-681-6040 671
Web: www.oldoysterfactory.com

Old Pine Street Presbyterian Church
412 Pine St. Philadelphia PA 19106 215-925-8051 50-1
Web: www.oldpine.org

Old Point Financial Corp
1 W Mellen St PO Box 3392 Hampton VA 23663 757-728-1200 360-2
NASDAQ: OPOF ■ *TF:* 800-952-0051 ■ *Web:* www.oldpoint.com

Old Pueblo Archaeology Ctr
2201 W 44th St. Tucson AZ 85713 520-798-1201 798-1966 520
Web: www.oldpueblo.org

Old Republic Insurance Co
133 Oakland Ave. Greensburg PA 15601 724-834-5000 834-4025 391-4
Web: orinsco.com

Old Republic Insured Automotive Services Inc
8282 S Memorial Dr Tulsa OK 74133 918-307-1000 391-5
TF: 800-331-3780 ■ *Web:* www.orias.com

Old Republic International Corp
307 N Michigan Ave Chicago IL 60601 312-346-8100 391-4
Web: oldrepublic.com

Old Republic National Title Insurance Co (ORTIG)
400 Second Ave S. Minneapolis MN 55401 612-371-1111 371-1191 391-6
TF: 800-328-4441 ■ *Web:* www.oldrepublictitle.com

Old Republic Surety
445 S Moorlands Rd Ste 200 Brookfield WI 53005 262-797-2640 797-8353 391-5
TF: 800-217-1792 ■ *Web:* www.orsurety.com

Old Sacramento Business Assn Inc
980 Ninth St Ste 400 Sacramento CA 95814 916-442-8575 442-2053 50-3
Web: www.oldsacramento.com

Old Sacramento Schoolhouse
1200 Front St Sacramento CA 95814 916-483-8818 50-3
Web: www.scoe.net/oldsacschoolhouse

Old Saint Ferdinand's Shrine
1 Rue St Francois Florissant MO 63031 314-837-2110 50-1
Web: oldstferdinandshrine.com

Old Saint Joseph's Church
321 Willings Alley Philadelphia PA 19106 215-923-1733 574-8529 50-1
Web: www.oldstjoseph.org

Old Saint Mary's Church
123 E 13th St Cincinnati OH 45202 513-721-2988 50-1
Web: www.oldstmarys.org

Old Saint Patrick's Church
700 W Adams St. Chicago IL 60661 312-648-1021 50-1
TF: 800-351-6376 ■ *Web:* www.oldstpats.org

Old Salem 600 S Main St Winston-Salem NC 27101 336-721-7300 721-7335 520
TF: 800-441-5305 ■ *Web:* www.oldsalem.org

Old Salty Dog 1601 Ken Thompson Pkwy Sarasota FL 34236 941-388-4311 671

Old San Francisco Steak House
10223 Sahara Dr. San Antonio TX 78216 210-342-2321 340-3135 671
Web: www.theoldsanfrancisco.com

Old Saybrook Chamber of Commerce
1 Main St Old Saybrook CT 06475 860-388-3266 388-9433 139
TF: 800-377-3987 ■ *Web:* www.oldsaybrookchamber.com

Old School Square Cultural Arts Ctr
51 N Swinton Ave Delray Beach FL 33444 561-243-7922 243-7018 572
Web: oldschoolsquare.org

Old Second Bancorp Inc 37 S River St Aurora IL 60506 630-892-0202 892-9630* 360-2
NASDAQ: OSBC ■ **Fax:* Mktg ■ *TF:* 877-866-0202 ■ *Web:* www.oldsecond.com

Phone | Fax | Class

Old Sitka State Historic Site
76 Halibut Point Rd Sitka AK 99835 907-465-4563 565

Old Spaghetti Factory Inc (OSF)
0715 SW Bancroft St Portland OR 97239 503-225-0433 226-6214 670
TF: 800-461-6675 ■ *Web:* www.osf.com

Old State Capitol Museum
300 W Broadway St Frankfort KY 40601 502-564-1792 564-4701 520
Web: history.ky.gov

Old State House 800 Main St Hartford CT 06103 860-522-6766 522-2812 50-3
Web: www.cga.ct.gov/osh

Old State House Museum
300 W Markham St Little Rock AR 72201 501-324-9685 520
Web: www.oldstatehouse.com

Old Stone Fort State Archaeological Park
732 Stone Ft Dr Manchester TN 37355 931-723-5073 565
Web: www.state.tn.us

Old Stone House 3051 M St NW Washington DC 20007 202-426-6851 50-3
Web: www.nps.gov

Old Sturbridge Village
1 Old Sturbridge Village Rd Sturbridge MA 01566 508-347-3362 347-0375 520
Web: www.osv.org

Old Swedes Church & Hendrickson House Museum
606 Church St Wilmington DE 19801 302-652-5629 652-8615 520
Web: www.oldswedes.org

Old Time Pottery Inc
480 River Rock Blvd Murfreesboro TN 37128 615-890-6060 362
Web: oldtimepottery.com

Old Town 522 W Lincoln Ave Milwaukee WI 53207 414-672-0206 671

Old Town Canoe Co
125 Gilman Falls Ave Bldg B Old Town ME 04468 207-827-5513 827-3647 710
TF: 800-343-1555 ■ *Web:* www.oldtowncanoe.com

Old Town Endoscopy Center LLC
5500 Greenville Ave Ste 1100 Dallas TX 75206 214-646-3470 415
Web: www.dhat.com

Old Town Museum 353 Main St Old Town ME 04468 207-827-7256 520
Web: www.old-town.org

Old Town San Diego State Historic Park
4002 Wallace St San Diego CA 92110 619-220-5422 688-3229 565
TF: 800-777-0369 ■ *Web:* www.parks.ca.gov

Old Trail Printing Company Inc, The
100 Fornoff Rd Columbus OH 43207 614-443-4852 627
TF: 800-847-5801 ■ *Web:* www.oldtrailprinting.com

Old Trieste 2335 Morena Blvd San Diego CA 92110 619-276-1841 671
Web: places.singleplatform.com

Old Warsaw, The 2512 Maple Ave Dallas TX 75201 214-528-0032 671
TF: 800-361-4426 ■ *Web:* www.oldwarsaw.com

Old Wisconsin Sausage Co
5030 PlaybiRd Rd Sheboygan WI 53083 877-451-7988 798-1284* 296-26
**Fax Area Code:* 708 ■ *TF:* 877-451-7988 ■ *Web:* www.oldwisconsin.com

Old World Wisconsin
W372 S9727 Hwy 67 PO Box 69 Eagle WI 53119 262-594-6301 594-6342 520
Web: oldworldwisconsin.wisconsinhistory.org

Oldcastle Apg Southinc
108 Buchanan Church Rd Greensboro NC 27405 336-375-5656 183
Web: www.adamsproducts.com

Oldcastle BuildingEnvelope
5005 Lyndon B Johnson Fwy Ste 1050 Dallas TX 75244 866-653-2278 329
TF: 866-653-2278 ■ *Web:* www.obe.com

Oldcastle Materials Inc
900 Ashwood Pkwy Ste 700 Atlanta GA 30338 770-522-5600 522-5608 188-4
Web: www.oldcastlematerials.com

Oldcastle Precast
7921 Southpark Plaza Ste 200 Littleton CO 80120 919-772-6301 772-1209 183
TF: 888-965-3227 ■ *Web:* oldcastleprecast.com

Oldcastle Precast Bldg Systems Div
1401 Trimble Rd Edgewood MD 21040 800-523-9144 612-1214* 189-3
**Fax Area Code:* 410 ■ *TF:* 800-523-9144 ■ *Web:* oldcastleprecast.com

Oldcastle Precast Inc
7921 Southpark Pl Ste 200 Folsom NJ 08037 800-642-3755 183
TF: 800-642-3755 ■ *Web:* www.oldcastleprecast.com

Olde Mill Inn 5835 Dixie Hwy Clarkston MI 48346 248-623-0300 379
Web: oldemillinnofclarkston.com

Olde Pink House 23 Abercorn St Savannah GA 31401 912-232-4286 671
TF: 800-554-1187 ■ *Web:* plantersinnsavannah.com

Olde Ship, The 1120 W 17th St Santa Ana CA 92706 714-550-6700 671
Web: www.theoldeship.com

Olde Tyme Pastries 2225 Geer Rd Turlock CA 95382 209-668-0928 68
Web: www.otpastries.com

Oldenburg Group Inc 1717 W Civic Dr Milwaukee WI 53209 414-977-1717 977-1700 358
Web: www.oldenburggroup.com

Oldfields - Lilly House & Gardens
4000 Michigan Rd Indianapolis IN 46208 317-923-1331 931-1978 97
TF: 800-976-8986 ■ *Web:* www.imamuseum.org

Oldfields School 1500 Glencoe Rd Glencoe MD 21152 410-472-4800 472-6839 622
Web: www.oldfieldsschool.org

Oldham County 100 W Jefferson St LaGrange KY 40031 502-222-1476 222-3210 338
Web: www.oldhamcounty.net

Oldham County PO Box 360 Vega TX 79092 806-267-2667 338
Web: www.co.oldham.tx.us

Oldham County Chamber of Commerce
412 E Main St LaGrange KY 40031 502-222-1635 222-3159 139
TF: 800-264-0521 ■ *Web:* www.oldhamcountychamber.com

Olds College 4500-50 St Olds AB T4H1R6 403-556-8281 162
TF: 800-661-6537 ■ *Web:* www.oldscollege.ca

Olds Products Co
10700 88th Ave Pleasant Prairie WI 53158 262-947-3500 296-19
TF: 800-233-8064 ■ *Web:* www.oldsproducts.com

Olds-olympic Inc PO Box 180 Lynnwood WA 98046 425-778-1000 771-4346 324
Web: www.olds-olympic.com

Ole Bull State Park 31 Valhella VW Cross Fork PA 17729 814-435-5000 565
Web: www.dcnr.state.pa.us

Ole Mexican Foods Inc
6585 Crescent Dr Norcross GA 30071 770-582-9200 296-36
Web: olemex.com

Ole Mole 1030 High Ridge Rd Stamford CT 06905 203-461-9962 671
Web: olemolestamford.com

Ole South Properties Inc
262 Robert Rose Dr Ste 300 Murfreesboro TN 37129 615-896-0019 896-9380 187
Web: www.olesouth.com

Olean General Hospital 515 Main St Olean NY 14760 716-373-2600 374-3
Web: www.ogh.org

Olean Times-Herald 639 Norton Dr Olean NY 14760 716-372-3121 373-6397* 532-2
**Fax:* News Rm ■ *TF:* 800-722-8812 ■ *Web:* www.oleantimesherald.com

Olean Wholesale Grocery Co-op Inc
1587 Haskell Rd PO Box 1070 Olean NY 14760 716-372-2020 297-8
TF: 888-835-3026 ■ *Web:* www.oleanwholesale.com

Oleana Restaurant 134 Hampshire St Cambridge MA 02139 617-661-0505 671
Web: www.oleanarestaurant.com

Oleco Inc 18683 Trimble Ct Spring Lake MI 49456 616-842-6790 814
TF: 800-575-3282 ■ *Web:* globaltec.com

Oleet & Co LLC 452 Fifth Ave New York NY 10018 212-235-2200 194
Web: www.oleet.com

Olentangy Indian Caverns
1779 Home Rd Delaware OH 43015 740-548-7917 50-5
Web: www.olentangyindiancaverns.com

Olesky Associates Inc
865 Washington St Ste 3 Newton MA 02460 781-235-4330 260
TF: 800-486-4330 ■ *Web:* www.olesky.com

Oleson's Foods Inc
3850 N Long Lake Rd Ste A Traverse City MI 49684 231-947-6510 345
Web: www.olesonsfoods.com

Oleta River State Park
3400 NE 163rd St North Miami Beach FL 33160 305-919-1846 919-1845 565
TF: 800-326-3521 ■ *Web:* www.floridastateparks.org

Oley Foundation
214 Hun Memorial MC-28 Albany Medical Ctr Albany NY 12208 518-262-5079 262-5528 48-17
TF: 800-776-6539 ■ *Web:* www.oley.org

Olga Korper Gallery 17 Morrow Ave Toronto ON M6R2H9 416-538-8220 42
Web: www.olgakorpergallery.com

Olga's Kitchen Inc 1940 Northwood Dr Troy MI 48084 248-362-0001 362-2013 670
Web: www.olgas.com

Olgoonik Development LLC
3201 C St Ste 700 Anchorage AK 99503 907-562-8728 562-8751 187
TF: 855-763-2613 ■ *Web:* www.olgoonik.com

Oliff & Berridge PLC
277 S Washington St Ste 500 Alexandria VA 22314 703-836-6400 428
TF: 800-561-3357 ■ *Web:* www.oliff.com

Olin Brass 305 Lewis & Clark Blvd East Alton IL 62024 502-873-3000 485
TF: 800-882-5543 ■ *Web:* www.olinbrass.com

Olin Corp
190 Carondelet Plaza Ste 1530 Clayton MO 63105 314-480-1400 185
NYSE: OLN ■ *Web:* www.olin.com

Olin Corp Olin Chlor Alkali Products Div
490 Stuart Rd NE Cleveland TN 37312 423-336-4850 143
Web: www.olinchloralkali.com/en-us

Olin Corp Winchester Div
427 N Shamrock St East Alton IL 62024 618-258-2000 284
Web: www.winchester.com

Olinde's Furniture
9536 Airline Hwy Baton Rouge LA 70815 225-926-3380 321
TF: 800-420-2337 ■ *Web:* www.olindes.com

Olis Inc 130 Conway Dr Ste A B & C Bogart GA 30622 706-353-6547 353-1972 419
TF: 800-852-3504 ■ *Web:* www.olisweb.com

Oliva Tobacco Co 3104 N Armenia Ave Tampa FL 33607 813-248-4921 756
Web: olivatobacco.com

Olive Branch Chamber of Commerce
9123 Pigeon Roost PO Box 608 Olive Branch MS 38654 662-895-2600 895-2625 139
TF: 800-948-3090 ■ *Web:* www.olivebranchms.com

Olive Garden
1000 Darden Center Dr PO Box 695017 Orlando FL 32869 407-245-4336 670
Web: www.olivegarden.com

Olive Grove Consulting
540 Ralston Ave #2c Belmont CA 94002 650-591-4155 463
Web: theolivegrove.com

Olive Hill Greenhouses Inc
3508 Olive Hill Rd Fallbrook CA 92028 760-728-4596 192
Web: olivehill.net

Olive Real Estate Group
102 N Cascade Ave Ste 250 Colorado Springs CO 80903 719-598-3000 578-0089 652
Web: www.olivereg.com

Olive Tree Restaurant
2201 16th Ave SW Cedar Rapids IA 52404 319-364-0781 671

Olive View Medical Ctr (OVMC)
14445 Olive View Dr Sylmar CA 91342 747-210-3000 374-3
Web: uclaoliveview.org

Olive-Harvey College
10001 S Woodlawn Ave Chicago IL 60628 773-291-6100 291-6185 162
Web: www.ccc.edu

Oliver & Company Inc 1300 S 51st St Richmond CA 94804 510-412-9090 186
Web: www.oliverandco.net

Oliver Capital Partners Inc
102 3016 Fifth Ave NE Calgary AB T2A6K4 403-313-4645 691
Web: www.olcapa.com

Oliver Construction Co
1770 Executive Dr Oconomowoc WI 53066 262-567-6677 780
Web: www.oliverconstruction.com

Oliver County 115 W Main Center ND 58530 701-794-8777 794-3476 338
Web: ndcourts.gov

Oliver Exterminating Corp
658 NW 99th St Miami FL 33150 305-758-1811 577
Web: guaranteepest.com

Oliver Fire Protection & Security
501 Feheley Dr King of Prussia PA 19406 610-277-1331 277-2837 189-13
Web: www.oliverfps.com

Oliver Gear Inc 1120 Niagara St Buffalo NY 14213 716-885-1080 885-1145 709
Web: www.gearmotions.com

Oliver Inlet State Marine Park
400 Willoughby Ave PO Box 111020 Juneau AK 99801 907-465-4563 586-3113 565
TF: 855-277-4491 ■ *Web:* www.dnr.alaska.gov/parks

Oliver Lee Memorial State Park
409 Dog Canyon Rd Alamogordo NM 88310 575-437-8284 439-1290* 565
**Fax Area Code:* 505

Oliver M Dean Inc 125 Brooks St Worcester MA 01606 508-856-9100 429
TF: 800-648-3326 ■ *Web:* www.omdean.com

Oliver Machinery Co 6902 S 194th St Kent WA 98032 253-867-0334 867-0387 821
TF: 800-559-5065 ■ *Web:* www.olivermachinery.net

Phone | Fax | Class

Oliver of Adrian Inc
1111 E Beecher St PO Box 189 .... Adrian MI 49221 517-263-2132 265-8698 455
TF: 877-668-0885 ■ *Web:* www.oliverinstrument.com
Oliver Printing Company Inc
1760 Enterprise Pkwy .... Twinsburg OH 44087 330-425-7890 627
Web: www.oliverprinting.com
Oliver Products Co
445 Sixth St NW .... Grand Rapids MI 49504 616-456-7711 456-5820 298
TF: 800-253-3893 ■ *Web:* www.oliverproducts.com
Oliver Reservoir State Recreation Area
210615 Hwy 71 .... Gering NE 69341 308-436-3777 565
Web: visitnebraska.com
Oliver Russell & Assoc Inc
217 S 11th St .... Boise ID 83702 208-344-1734 636
Web: www.oliverrussell.com
Oliver Staffing Inc
350 Lexington Ave Ste 401 .... New York NY 10016 212-634-1234 260
Web: www.oliverstaffing.com
Oliver Winery 8024 N SR-37 .... Bloomington IN 47404 812-876-5800 50-7
TF: 800-258-2783 ■ *Web:* www.oliverwinery.com
Oliver's 2095 Delaware Ave .... Buffalo NY 14216 716-877-9662 671
TF: 800-821-1881 ■ *Web:* www.oliverscuisine.com
Oliver's 130 S Fifth Ave .... Pocatello ID 83201 208-234-0672 671
Web: www.oliversdining.com
Oliver, Price & Rhodes
1212 S Abington Rd .... Clarks Summit PA 18411 570-585-1200 428
TF: 800-777-9685 ■ *Web:* oprlaw.com
Oliverio's Ristorante on the Wharf
52 Clay St .... Morgantown WV 26505 304-842-7388 671
Web: www.oliverios.sites.morgantowns.com
Olives 3600 Las Vegas Blvd S .... Las Vegas NV 89109 702-693-8181 671
Web: cheftoddenglish.com
Olivet College 320 S Main St .... Olivet MI 49076 269-749-7000 749-6617* 166
**Fax:* Admissions ■ *TF:* 800-456-7189 ■ *Web:* www.olivetcollege.edu
Olivet Nazarene University
1 University Ave .... Bourbonnais IL 60914 815-939-5011 935-4998* 166
**Fax:* Admissions ■ *TF:* 800-648-1463 ■ *Web:* www.olivet.edu
Oliveto Cafe & Restaurant
5655 College Ave .... Oakland CA 94618 510-547-5356 671
Web: www.oliveto.com
Olivia 434 Brannan St .... San Francisco CA 94107 415-962-5700 962-5710 760
TF: 800-631-6277 ■ *Web:* www.olivia.com
Ollie's Bargain Outlet Inc
6295 Allentown Blvd Ste 1 .... Harrisburg PA 17112 717-657-2300 791
TF: 800-219-7052 ■ *Web:* www.ollies.us/home.html
OLM LLC 4 Trefoil Dr .... Trumbull CT 06611 203-445-7700 808
TF: 877-265-6638 ■ *Web:* olm.net
Olmec Systems Inc 85 Bloomfield Ave .... Denville NJ 07834 973-586-6590 180
Web: www.olmec.com
Olmstead Place State Park
921 N Ferguson Rd .... Ellensburg WA 98926 509-925-1943 565
Web: www.parks.wa.gov
Olmstead Properties Inc
575 Eighth Ave Rm 2400 .... New York NY 10018 212-564-6662 652
Web: www.olmsteadinc.com
Olmsted Center for Sight 1170 Main St .... Buffalo NY 14209 716-882-1025 305
TF: 800-829-0500 ■ *Web:* www.olmstedcenter.org
Olmsted Medical Center
210 Ninth St SE .... Rochester MN 55904 507-288-3443 363
Web: www.olmmed.org
Olney Central College 305 NW St .... Olney IL 62450 618-395-7777 392-4816* 162
**Fax:* Admissions ■ *TF:* 866-529-4322
Olney Chamber of Commerce
3460 Olney-Laytonsville Rd Ste 211 .... Olney MD 20832 301-774-7117 774-4944 139
Web: www.olneymd.org
Olney Friends School
61030 Sandy Ridge Rd .... Barnesville OH 43713 740-425-3655 425-3202 622
TF: 800-303-4291 ■ *Web:* www.olneyfriends.org
OLogic 544 E Weddell Dr #7 .... Sunnyvale CA 94089 650-996-1490 387
Web: www.ologicinc.com
Ologie LLC 447 E Main St .... Columbus OH 43215 614-221-1107 463
TF: 800-962-1107 ■ *Web:* ologie.com
Olompali State Historic Park
PO Box 1016 .... Novato CA 94948 415-892-3383 565
Web: www.parks.ca.gov
Olon Industries Inc
42 Armstrong Ave .... Georgetown ON L7G4R9 905-877-7300 877-7383 599
Web: www.olon.ca
Olsen & Thompson Pa
970 Mt Kemble Ave .... Morristown NJ 07960 973-425-3212 2
Web: otcpa.com
Olshan Lumber Co PO Box 1274 .... Houston TX 77251 713-225-5551 220-9400 364
Web: www.olshanlumber.com
Olson 420 N Fifth St .... Minneapolis MN 55401 612-215-9800 4
Web: olson.com
Olson & Company Steel Inc
1941 Davis St .... San Leandro CA 94577 510-567-2200 480
Web: www.olsonsteel.com
Olson Bros Contractors Inc
829 Chambers St .... South Haven MI 49090 269-637-4494 803-3
Olson Engineering Inc
365 W Round Bunch Rd .... Bridge City TX 77611 409-697-3333 261
Web: www.o-engr.com/contactus.php
Olson Pete (Rep R - TX)
2133 Rayburn HOB .... Washington DC 20515 202-225-5951 225-5241 342-2
Web: olson.house.gov
Olson Precast Co (OPC) 2750 Marion Dr .... Las Vegas NV 89115 702-643-4371 643-4510 183
Olson Research Assoc Inc
10290 Old Columbia Rd .... Columbia MD 21046 410-290-6999 290-6726 178-10
TF: 888-657-6680 ■ *Web:* www.olsonresearch.com
Olsson Assoc 1111 Lincoln Mall Ste 111 .... Lincoln NE 68508 402-474-6311 474-5160 261
TF: 877-831-6389 ■ *Web:* olssonassociates.com
Olsson Roofing Company Inc
740 S Lake St .... Aurora IL 60506 630-892-0449 189-12
Web: www.olssonroofing.com
Olsun Electrics Corp
10901 Commercial St .... Richmond IL 60071 800-336-5786 678-4909* 767
**Fax Area Code:* 815 ■ *TF:* 800-336-5786 ■ *Web:* www.olsun.com

Phone | Fax | Class

Oltmans Construction Co
10005 Mission Mill Rd .... Whittier CA 90601 562-948-4242 695-5299 186
Web: www.oltmans.com
Olum's of Binghamton Inc
3701 Vestal Pkwy E .... Vestal NY 13850 607-729-5775 729-6166 321
TF Cust Svc: 855-264-8674 ■ *Web:* www.olums.com
Oly Penn. Inc 245 E Washington St .... Sequim WA 98382 360-683-1456 225
TF: 800-303-8696 ■ *Web:* startpage.olypen.com
Olymel LP
2200 Pratte Ave Pratte .... Saint-Hyacinthe QC J2S4B6 450-771-0400 645-2869 619
TF: 800-361-7990 ■ *Web:* www.olymel.com
Olympia City Hall PO Box 1967 .... Olympia WA 98507 360-753-8447 709-2791 337
TF: 800-451-7985 ■ *Web:* olympiawa.gov
Olympia Entertainment Inc
2211 Woodward Ave .... Detroit MI 48201 313-471-3200 271
Web: www.olympiaentertainment.com
Olympia Financial Group Inc
125 Ninth Ave SE Ste 2300 .... Calgary AB T2G0P6 403-668-8384 261-7512 787
TF: 888-668-8384 ■ *Web:* www.olympiatrust.com
Olympia Group LLC
11411 Southern Highlands Pkwy Ste 300 .... Las Vegas NV 89141 702-220-6565 653
Web: www.olympiagroupcompanies.com
Olympia Lacey Tumwater Visitor & Convention Bureau
103 Sid Snyder Ave SW .... Olympia WA 98501 360-704-7544 704-7533 206
TF: 877-704-7500 ■ *Web:* www.experienceolympia.com
Olympia Medical Ctr
5900 W Olympic Blvd .... Los Angeles CA 90036 310-657-5900 374-3
Web: www.olympiamc.com
Olympia Promotions & Distribution
226 E Jericho Tpke .... Mineola NY 11501 516-775-4500 327
TF: 800-846-7874 ■ *Web:* olympiapromo.com
Olympia Resort & Spa
1350 Royale Mile Rd .... Oconomowoc WI 53066 262-369-4999 369-4998 669
TF: 800-558-9573 ■ *Web:* www.olympiaresort.com
Olympia School District
1113 Legion Way SE .... Olympia WA 98501 360-596-6100 596-6111 685
TF: 855-846-8376 ■ *Web:* www.osd.wednet.edu
Olympia Sports 5 Bradley Dr .... Westbrook ME 04092 207-854-2794 854-4168 711
TF: 800-543-8137 ■ *Web:* www.olympiasports.net
Olympia Theateryyy 174 E Flagler St .... Miami FL 33131 305-374-2444 572
Web: www.gusmancenter.org
Olympia Tile International Inc
1000 Lawrence Ave W .... Toronto ON M6A1C6 416-785-6666 191-4
TF: 800-268-1613 ■ *Web:* www.olympiatile.com
Olympia/Thurston County Chamber of Commerce
809 Legion Way .... Olympia WA 98501 360-357-3362 357-3376 139
TF: 800-798-5143 ■ *Web:* www.thurstonchamber.com
Olympian, The PO Box 407 .... Olympia WA 98507 360-754-5400 357-0202* 532-2
**Fax:* News Rm ■ *TF:* 800-905-0296 ■ *Web:* www.theolympian.com
Olympic Airways 7000 Austin St .... Forest Hills NY 11375 718-269-2200 25
Web: patch.com/foresthills
Olympic College 1600 Chester Ave .... Bremerton WA 98337 360-792-6050 475-7202* 162
**Fax:* Admissions ■ *TF:* 800-259-6718 ■ *Web:* www.olympic.edu
Shelton 937 W Alpine Way .... Shelton WA 98584 360-427-2119 432-5412* 162
**Fax:* Admissions ■ *TF:* 800-259-6718 ■ *Web:* www.olympic.edu
Olympic Corrections Ctr
11235 Hoh Mainline .... Forks WA 98331 360-374-6181 213
Web: doc.wa.gov
Olympic Ctr Arena 2634 Main St .... Lake Placid NY 12946 518-523-1655 523-9275 720
TF: 800-462-6236 ■ *Web:* www.orda.org
Olympic Flight Museum
7637A Old Hwy 99 SE .... Olympia WA 98501 360-705-3925 236-9839 520
Web: www.olympicflightmuseum.com
Olympic Foundry Inc
5200 Airport Way S .... Seattle WA 98108 206-764-6200 492
Web: www.olympicfoundry.com
Olympic Lanes 110 Mason St .... Greeneville TN 37745 423-639-5166 99
Web: www.olympiclanesbowling.com
Olympic Medical Ctr
939 Caroline St .... Port Angeles WA 98362 360-417-7000 374-3
TF: 888-362-6260 ■ *Web:* www.olympicmedical.org
Olympic Metals Inc
5775 Monaco St .... Commerce City CO 80022 303-286-9700 492
Olympic Paint Co
6804 Enterprise Dr .... Louisville KY 40214 502-361-2681 226
Web: www.porterpaints.com
Olympic Products LLC
4100 Pleasant Garden Rd .... Greensboro NC 27406 336-378-9620 601
Web: www.olympic-products.com
Olympic Resource Management
19950 Seventh Ave NE Ste 200 .... Poulsbo WA 98370 360-697-6626 697-1156 752
NASDAQ: POPE ■ *TF:* 800-522-6645 ■ *Web:* www.orminc.com
Olympic Security Services Inc
631 Strander Blvd Ste A .... Tukwila WA 98188 206-575-8531 575-8640 693
Web: www.olympiksecurity.com
Olympic Staffing Services
588 S Grand Ave .... Covina CA 91724 626-447-3558 260
TF: 800-399-5068 ■ *Web:* www.olystaffing.com
Olympic Steel Inc
5096 Richmond Rd .... Bedford Heights OH 44146 216-292-3800 292-3974* 492
NASDAQ: ZEUS ■ **Fax:* Sales ■ *TF:* 800-321-6290 ■ *Web:* www.olysteel.com
Olympic Tavern 2327 N Main St .... Rockford IL 61103 815-962-8758 671
Web: www.theolympictavern.com
Olympic Tool & Machine Company Inc
2100 Bridgewater Rd .... Aston PA 19014 610-494-1600 454
Web: www.olymtool.com
Olympic Venture Partners
116th St 11023 NE .... Kirkland WA 98039 425-889-9192 889-0152 792
Olympic View Publishing LLC
147 W Washington .... Sequim WA 98382 360-683-3311 532-3
Web: olympicviewpublishingcompany.lbu.com
Olympique Expert Building Care
26232 Enterprise Ct .... Lake Forest CA 92630 949-455-0796 463
TF: 866-659-6747 ■ *Web:* www.olympique.net
Olympus Flag & Banner
9000 W Heather Ave .... Milwaukee WI 53224 414-355-2010 355-1931 287
TF: 800-558-9620 ■ *Web:* olympusgrp.com
Olympus Homes Inc PO Box 2999 .... Westerville OH 43086 614-523-2000 187
Web: www.olympushomes.com

Name / Address	City	State	Zip	Phone	Fax	Class
Olympus Partners 1 Stn Pl Ste 1 *TF:* 800-578-7378 ■ *Web:* www.olympuspartners.com	Stamford	CT	06902	203-353-5900		792
Olympus Press Inc 3400 S 150th St *Web:* www.olympuspress.com	Seattle	WA	98188	206-242-2700		627
OM Group Inc 811 Sharon Dr *NYSE: OMG* ■ *TF:* 800-519-0083	Westlake	OH	44145	440-899-2950	808-7114	145
O&M Industries Inc 5901 Ericson Way *Web:* www.omindustries.com	Arcata	CA	95521	707-822-8800		610
OM Records 1890 Bryant St Ste 305 *Web:* www.om records.com	San Francisco	CA	94110	415-904-1800		317
OM Seafood Restaurant 7632 SE Powell Blvd *Web:* omseafood.com	Portland	OR	97206	503-788-3128		671
OMA (Oregon Medical Assn) 11740 SW 68th Pkwy Ste 100 *TF:* 877-605-3229 ■ *Web:* www.theoma.org	Portland	OR	97223	503-619-8000	619-0609	474
Omaha Bedding Co 4011 S 60th St *TF:* 800-279-9018 ■ *Web:* www.omahabeddingco.com	Omaha	NE	68117	402-733-8600		471
Omaha Children's Museum 500 S 20th St *Web:* www.ocm.org	Omaha	NE	68102	402-342-6164	342-6165	521
Omaha Community Foundation (OCF) 302 S 36th St Ste 100 *TF:* 800-794-3458 ■ *Web:* www.omahafoundation.org	Omaha	NE	68131	402-342-3458	342-3582	303
Omaha Community Playhouse 6915 Cass St *TF:* 888-782-4338 ■ *Web:* www.omahaplayhouse.com	Omaha	NE	68132	402-553-0800	553-6288	573-4
Omaha Correctional Ctr 2323 Ave J PO Box 11099 *Web:* www.corrections.nebraska.gov	Omaha	NE	68110	402-522-7014		213
Omaha Downtown Lodging Investors II LLC 1005 Dodge St	Omaha	NE	68102	402-341-4400		379
Omaha Paper Co 6936 L St *TF:* 800-288-7026 ■ *Web:* www.omahapaper.com	Omaha	NE	68117	402-331-3243		638
Omaha Printing Co 4700 F St *Web:* www.omahaprint.com	Omaha	NE	68117	402-734-4400		626
Omaha Public Library 215 S 15th St *Web:* omahalibrary.org	Omaha	NE	68102	402-444-4800	444-4504	434-3
Omaha Public Power District 444 S 16th St Mall *Web:* www.oppd.com	Omaha	NE	68102	402-636-2000		192
Omaha Public Schools 3215 Cuming St *Web:* www.ops.org	Omaha	NE	68131	402-557-2222		685
Omaha Standard Inc 3501 S 11th St Ste 1 *TF:* 800-279-2201 ■ *Web:* www.palfinger.com	Council Bluffs	IA	51501	712-328-7444	328-8383	516
Omaha Steel Castings Co 921 E 12th St *Web:* www.omahasteel.com/contact-us.html	Wahoo	NE	68066	402-558-6000	558-0327	307
Omaha Symphony 1605 Howard St *Web:* www.omahasymphony.org	Omaha	NE	68102	402-342-3836	342-3819	573-3
Omaha Truck Center Inc 10710 I St PO Box 27379 *TF:* 800-866-2204 ■ *Web:* truckcentercompanies.com	Omaha	NE	68127	402-592-2440		126
Omaha Wholesale Hardware Co PO Box 3628 *TF:* 800-238-4566 ■ *Web:* www.omahawh.com	Omaha	NE	68102	402-444-1673	444-1664	351
Omaha World-Herald 1314 Douglas St *TF:* 800-284-6397 ■ *Web:* www.omaha.com	Omaha	NE	68102	402-444-1000		532-2
Oman 305 E 47th St 11th &12th Fl *Web:* www.un.int/wcm/content/site/oman	New York	NY	10017	212-355-3505	644-0070	784
Oman Embassy 2535 Belmont Rd NW *TF:* 800-265-6723 ■ *Web:* www.omani.info	Washington	DC	20008	202-387-1980		257
Oman Systems Inc 3334 Powell Ave *TF:* 800-541-0803 ■ *Web:* www.omanco.com	Nashville	TN	37204	615-385-2500		188
Omar Inc 4601 S Cottage Groove Ste 53452 *Web:* www.omarinc.com	Chicago	IL	60653	708-679-0347	679-0384	475
Omar's Carriage House 313 W Bute St *Web:* omarscarriagehouse.com	Norfolk	VA	23510	757-622-4990		671
OMAX Corp 21409 72nd Ave S *TF:* 800-838-0343 ■ *Web:* www.omax.com	Kent	WA	98032	253-872-2300		697
OMB (Office of Management & Budget) 725 17th St NW *Web:* www.whitehouse.gov/omb	Washington	DC	20503	202-395-3080	395-3888	340
OMB Watch 1742 Connecticut Ave NW *TF:* 866-544-7573 ■ *Web:* www.foreffectivegov.org	Washington	DC	20009	202-234-8494	234-8584	48-7
OMC (Ocean Medical Ctr) 425 Jack Martin Blvd *TF:* 800-560-9990 ■ *Web:* www.oceanmedicalcenter.com/omc	Brick	NJ	08724	732-840-2200		374-3
OMC (Oconee Medical Campus) 298 Memorial Dr *Web:* www.ghs.org/locations/oconee-medical-campus	Seneca	SC	29672	864-882-3351		374-3
OMD Corp 3705 Missouri Blvd *TF:* 866-440-8664 ■ *Web:* www.omdcorp.com	Jefferson City	MO	65109	573-893-8930	893-3487	178-1
OMED of Nevada LLC 800 Stillwell Rd	Reno	NV	89512	775-857-3008		320
Omeda Communications 555 Huehl Rd *Web:* omeda.com	Northbrook	IL	60062	847-564-8900		225
Omedix Inc 7114 E Stetson Dr Ste 360 *TF:* 877-866-3349 ■ *Web:* omedix.com	Scottsdale	AZ	85251	877-866-3349		396
Omega Airline Software 116 N Eighth St *TF:* 800-227-4610 ■ *Web:* www.omegaair.com	Midlothian	TX	76065	972-775-3693		177
Omega Alpha Pharmaceuticals Inc 795 Pharmacy Ave *Web:* omegaalpha.ca	Scarborough	ON	M1L3K2	416-297-6900		297-8
Omega Biologicals Inc 910 Technology Blvd *Web:* omegabiologicals.com	Bozeman	MT	59718	406-586-3790	586-3792	231
Omega Cabinetry Ltd 1205 Peters Dr **Fax:* Cust Svc ■ *Web:* www.omegacabinetry.com	Waterloo	IA	50703	319-235-5700	235-5860*	115
Omega Communications Inc 41 E Washington Ste 110 *Web:* www.omegac.com	Indianapolis	IN	46204	317-264-4000	264-4020	116
Omega Construction Inc 344 Shelleybrook Dr PO Box 250 *Web:* www.omegaconstruction.com	Pilot Mountain	NC	27041	336-368-5156		186
Omega Design Corp 211 Philips Rd *Web:* www.omegadesign.com	Exton	PA	19341	610-363-6555		547
Omega Engineering Inc 1 Omega Dr PO Box 4047 **Fax:* Cust Svc ■ *TF:* 800-826-6342 ■ *Web:* www.omega.com	Stamford	CT	06907	203-359-1660	359-7700*	201
Omega Flex Inc 451 Creamery Way *NASDAQ: OFLX* ■ *TF:* 800-355-1039 ■ *Web:* www.omegaflex.com	Exton	PA	19341	610-524-7272	524-7282	790
Omega Healthcare Investors Inc 200 International Cir Ste 3500 *NYSE: OHI* ■ *TF:* 877-511-2891 ■ *Web:* www.omegahealthcare.com	Hunt Valley	MD	21030	410-427-1700		655
Omega Institute for Holistic Studies 150 Lake Dr *TF:* 800-944-1001 ■ *Web:* www.eomega.org	Rhinebeck	NY	12572	845-266-4444	266-3769	673
Omega International Inc 1937 NE Loop 410 Ste 200 *TF:* 888-558-0701 ■ *Web:* omegaco.com	San Antonio	TX	78217	210-805-8808		360-3
Omega Laboratories Inc 400 N Cleveland Ave *Web:* www.omegalabs.net	Mogadore	OH	44260	330-628-5748		415
Omega Medical Health Systems Inc 1200 E High St Ste 106 *TF:* 866-716-6342 ■ *Web:* www.omegamedicalsystems.com	Pottstown	PA	19464	866-716-6342		475
Omega Metal Treating Inc 1883 Commerce Dr *Web:* www.omegametaltreating.com	De Pere	WI	54115	920-339-8590		484
Omega Moulding Company Ltd 1 Saw Grass Dr *TF:* 800-289-6634 ■ *Web:* www.omegamoulding.com	Bellport	NY	11713	800-289-6634		361
Omega Natchiq Inc 4418 Pesson Rd *Web:* www.asrcenergy.com/services/omega.html	New Iberia	LA	70560	337-560-7600		698
Omega Plastics Inc 24401 Capital Blvd *Web:* www.opinc.com	Clinton Twp	MI	48036	586-954-2100		596
Omega Printing Inc 201-207 Williams St *Web:* omegaprinting.com	Bensenville	IL	60106	630-595-6344		627
Omega Products International 1681 California Ave *TF:* 800-600-6634 ■ *Web:* www.omega-products.com	Corona	CA	92881	951-737-7447	520-2594	191-3
Omega Protein Corp 2105 City W Blvd Ste 500 *TF:* 866-421-0831 ■ *Web:* www.omegaprotein.com	Houston	TX	77042	713-623-0060	940-6122	296-12
Omega Psi Phi Fraternity Inc 3951 Snapfinger Pkwy *TF:* 800-829-4933 ■ *Web:* www.oppf.org	Decatur	GA	30035	404-284-5533	284-0333	48-16
Omega Rail Management 4721 Trousdale Dr Ste 206 *TF:* 800-990-1961 ■ *Web:* www.omegarail.com	Nashville	TN	37220	615-331-1900		649
Omega Security Service Inc 103 Yost Blvd Ste 100A *Web:* www.omega-security.com	Pittsburgh	PA	15221	412-349-0850		693
Omega Shielding Products Inc 1384 Pompton Ave *TF:* 800-828-5784 ■ *Web:* www.omegashielding.com	Cedar Grove	NJ	07009	973-890-7455		326
Omega Sports Inc 130 S Walnut Cir *Web:* www.omegasports.net	Greensboro	NC	27409	336-854-0797		711
Omega Steel Co 3460 Hollenberg Dr *Web:* www.assetcontrols.com	Bridgeton	MO	63044	314-209-0992		492
Omega Tool 308 S Mtn View Ave *TF:* 800-819-4245 ■ *Web:* www.omegatool-usa.com	San Bernardino	CA	92408	909-888-0440	889-8740	254
Omega Waste Management Inc 957 Colusa St *Web:* www.omegawaste.com	Corning	CA	96021	530-824-1890		463
Omega World Travel Inc 3102 Omega Office Pk Dr *TF:* 800-756-6342 ■ *Web:* omegatravel.com	Fairfax	VA	22031	703-359-0200		771
Omegachem Inc 480 rue Perreault *TF:* 800-661-6342 ■ *Web:* www.omegachem.com	St-romuald	QC	G6W7V6	418-837-4444		238
Omegasys It Consulting 229 16th ST Ste 227	San Diego	IL	92101	619-786-0762		463
Omelet 3540 Hayden Ave *Web:* omeletla.com	Culver City	CA	90232	213-427-6400		195
OMG (Object Management Group) 140 Kendrick St Ste 300 *Web:* www.omg.org	Needham	MA	02494	781-444-0404	444-0320	48-9
OMG Inc 153 Bowles Rd *Web:* www.omgroofing.com	Agawam	MA	01001	413-789-0252		350
OMG Midwest Inc 2401 SE Tones Dr Ste 13 *Web:* omgmidwest.com	Ankeny	IA	50021	515-266-9928	263-3878	188-4
Omgeo LLC 55 Thomson Pl *TF:* 866-496-6436 ■ *Web:* www.omgeo.com	Boston	MA	02210	866-496-6436		195
OMHS (Owensboro Health) 811 E Parish Ave PO Box 20007 *TF:* 877-888-6647 ■ *Web:* www.owensborohealth.org	Owensboro	KY	42303	270-688-2000		374-3
Omicron Architecture Engineering Construction Ltd 595 Burrard St Three Bentall Centre Fifth Fl PO Box 49369 *TF:* 877-632-3350 ■ *Web:* www.omicronaec.com	Vancouver	BC	V7X1L4	604-632-3350		256
Omimex Resources Inc 7950 John T White Rd *TF:* 800-570-8024 ■ *Web:* www.omimex.com	Fort Worth	TX	76120	817-460-7777		536
Omitron Inc 7051 Muirkirk Meadows Dr Ste A *Web:* www.omitron.com	Beltsville	MD	20705	301-474-1700		387
Omix-Ada Inc 460 Horizon Dr Ste 400 *Web:* www.omix-ada.com	Suwanee	GA	30024	770-614-6101		54
Omnetics Connector Corp 7260 Commerce Cir E *TF Cust Svc:* 800-343-0025 ■ *Web:* www.omnetics.com	Minneapolis	MN	55432	763-572-0656	572-3925	815
Omnex Engineering and Management Inc 315 E Eisenhower Pkwy Ste 110 *Web:* www.omnex.com	Ann Arbor	MI	48108	734-761-4940		463
Omni Baking Co 2621 Freddy Ln *Web:* www.omnibaking.com	Vineland	NJ	08360	856-691-5642		296-1
Omni Barton Creek Resort & Spa 8212 Barton Club Dr *TF:* 800-336-6158 ■ *Web:* www.omnihotels.com/hotels/austin-barton-creek	Austin	TX	78735	512-329-4000	329-4597	669
Omni Behavioral Health 2904 14th St Apt 3 *Web:* www.omnibehavioralhealth.com	Columbus	NE	68601	402-562-7933		726

Phone | Fax | Class

Omni Cable Corp 2 Hagerty Blvd. . . . . West Chester PA 19382 610-701-0100 701-9870 246
TF: 888-292-6664 ■ Web: www.omnicable.com
Omni Construction Services Inc
533 Airport Blvd Ste 555 . . . . Burlingame CA 94010 650-685-2490 186
Web: www.clearkey.com
Omni Cubed Inc
1390 Broadway Ste B155 . . . . Placerville CA 95667 877-311-1976 226
TF: 877-311-1976 ■ Web: omnicubed.com
Omni Custom Meats Inc
151 Vanderbilt Ct . . . . Bowling Green KY 42103 270-796-6664 296-26
Web: omnimeats.com
Omni Data LLC 11 Research Dr Ste 1. . . . . Woodbridge CT 06525 203-747-7890 180
Web: www.omnianswers.net
Omni Die Casting Inc
1100 Nova Dr SE . . . . Massillon OH 44646 330-830-5500 308
Web: www.omnidiecasting.com
OMNI Engineering Services Inc
370 W Second St Ste 100. Winona MN 55987 507-454-5293 256
Web: omnimn.com
Omni Fitness Club 40 E Norton St . . . . Muskegon MI 49444 231-739-3391 354
Omni Gear 7502 Mesa Rd. . . . . Houston TX 77028 713-635-6331 635-6360 60
Web: www.omnigear.com
Omni Grove Park Inn, The
290 Macon Ave. . . . . Asheville NC 28804 828-252-2711 671
Omni Hotels 4001 Maple Ave. . . . . Dallas TX 75219 402-952-6664 379
TF: 800-843-6664 ■ Web: www.omnihotels.com
Omni Hotels Select Guest Loyalty Program
11819 Miami St 3rd Fl . . . . Omaha NE 68164 800-843-6664 378
TF Cust Svc: 800-843-6664 ■ Web: omnihotels.com/loyalty
Omni Information Systems Inc
1130 Hurricane Shoals Rd Ste 2600. . . . . Lawrenceville GA 30043 678-377-5560 180
TF: 800-598-8549 ■ Web: www.omni-info.com
Omni Interlocken Resort
500 Interlocken Blvd. . . . . Broomfield CO 80021 303-438-6600 669
TF: 800-843-6664 ■ Web: www.omnihotels.com
Omni International Inc
435 12th St SW PO Box 1409. . . . . Vernon AL 35592 205-695-9173 695-6465 319-1
Web: www.omniintlinc.com
Omni Jet Trading Ctr 9415 Jet Ln Ste 3 . . . . Easton MD 21601 410-820-7300 820-5082 770
Web: www.omnijet.com
Omni La Mansion del Rio
112 College St . . . . San Antonio TX 78205 210-518-1000 379
TF: 800-292-7300 ■ Web: www.omnihotels.com
Omni Life Assocates Inc
375 N Broadway Ste 203 . . . . Jericho NY 11753 516-938-2465 390
Web: omniquote.net
Omni Link Corp
1750 Valley View Ln Ste 320 . . . . Dallas TX 75234 972-620-9000 261
Web: www.omnilinkcorp.com
OMNI Management Group LLC
5955 De Soto Ave Ste 100 . . . . Woodland Hills CA 91367 818-906-8300 463
TF: 800-722-9680 ■ Web: www.omnimgt.com
Omni Manufacturing Inc
901 Mckinley Rd. . . . . Saint Marys OH 45885 419-394-7424 403
Web: www.omnimfg.com
Omni Marketing Interactive
847 S Randall Rd Ste 312. . . . . Elgin IL 60123 847-426-4256 426-4257 631
Web: www.search-usability.com
Omni Optical Lab
3255 Executive Blvd Ste 100 . . . . Beaumont TX 77705 409-842-4113 543
Web: www.omnioptical.com
Omni Orlando Resort at Championsgate
1500 Masters Blvd . . . . Champions Gate FL 33896 407-390-6664 669
TF: 800-843-6664 ■ Web: www.omnihotels.com
Omni Plastics Inc 6100 W Ridge Rd. . . . . Erie PA 16506 814-838-6664 596
Web: www.omniplasticserie.com
OMNI Products Inc 3911 Dayton St . . . . Mchenry IL 60050 815-344-3100 677
TF: 800-275-9848 ■ Web: www.omnirail.com
Omni Rancho Las Palmas Resort & Spa
41000 Bob Hope Dr . . . . Rancho Mirage CA 92270 760-568-2727 707
TF: 866-423-1195 ■ Web: www.omnihotels.com
Omni Royal Orleans Hotel
621 St Louis St. . . . . New Orleans LA 70130 504-529-5333 377
Web: www.omnihotels.com/hotels/new-orleans-royal-orleans
Omni Tucson National Golf Resort & Spa
2727 W Club Dr . . . . Tucson AZ 85742 520-297-2271 297-7544 669
Web: www.tucsonnational.com
Omni Valve Company LLC
4520 Chandler Rd. . . . . Muskogee OK 74403 918-687-6100 536
TF: 800-361-6627 ■ Web: www.omnivalve.com
Omni Workspace Co
1300 N Washington Ave Ste 200 . . . . Minneapolis MN 55411 612-627-1700 317
Web: www.omniworkspace.com
Omnia Group Inc, The
1501 W Cleveland St Ste 400. . . . . Tampa FL 33606 813-254-9449 254-8558 196
Web: www.omniagroup.com
Omnia Industries Inc Cedar Grove Plant
5 Cliffside Dr . . . . Cedar Grove NJ 07009 973-239-7272 350
Web: www.omniaindustries.com
Omnicare Inc 201 E Fourth St . . . . Cincinnati OH 45202 800-990-6664 392-3333* 587
NYSE: OCR ■ *Fax Area Code: 859 ■ TF: 800-342-5627 ■ Web: omnicare.com
Omnicell Inc 1201 Charleston Rd . . . . Mountain View CA 94043 650-251-6100 251-6266 420
NASDAQ: OMCL ■ TF: 800-850-6664 ■ Web: www.omnicell.com
Omnicom Group Inc 437 Madison Ave. . . . . New York NY 10022 212-415-3600 415-3530* 360-3
NYSE: OMC ■ *Fax: Hum Res ■ Web: www.omnicomgroup.com
Omnience Inc 1350 Center Dr Ste 100 . . . . Atlanta GA 30338 770-399-3199 399-3170 184
Web: omnienceevents.com
Omnifics Inc
5845 Richmond Hwy Ste 300. . . . . Alexandria VA 22303 703-548-4040 836-8159 393
Web: www.omnifics.com
Omnifilm Entertainment Ltd
111 Water St. . . . . Vancouver BC V6B1A7 604-681-6543 514
TF: 800-507-9077 ■ Web: www.omnifilm.com
Omniglow LLC
865 Memorial Ave. West Springfield MA 01089 413-241-6010 439
Omnigraphics Inc PO Box 31-1640 . . . . Detroit MI 48231 800-234-1340 875-1340 637-2
TF: 800-234-1340 ■ Web: www.omnigraphics.com

Omnikron Systems
20920 Warner Center Ln Ste A . . . . Woodland Hills CA 91367 818-591-7890 196
TF: 800-456-4522 ■ Web: www.omnikron.com
Omnilift Inc
Warwick Commons Industrial Park 1938 Stout Dr
. . . . Warminster PA 18974 215-443-9090 358
Web: www.omnilift.com
Omnilingua Worldwide LLC
306 Sixth Ave SE . . . . Cedar Rapids IA 52401 319-365-8565 317
Web: www.omnilingua.com
Omni-Lite Industries Canada Inc
17210 Edwards Rd . . . . Cerritos CA 90703 562-404-8510 621
TF: 800-577-6664 ■ Web: www.omni-lite.com
Omnilogic Systems Inc 1420 Broad St . . . . Regina SK S4R1Y9 306-586-6116 180
Web: www.omnilogic.net
Omni-Means Ltd
943 Reserve Dr Ste 100 . . . . Roseville CA 95678 916-782-8688 782-8689 261
Web: www.omnimeans.com
Omni-Med.com Inc 160 Pope St . . . . Cookshire QC J0B1M0 819-875-5411 179
TF: 800-567-4808 ■ Web: www.omnimed.com
OmniMetrix LLC 5225 Belle Wood Ct . . . . Buford GA 30518 770-209-0012 407
TF: 800-854-7342 ■ Web: www.omnimetrix.net
OMNIPLEX World Services Corp
14151 Pk Meadow Dr Ste 300 . . . . Chantilly VA 20151 703-652-3100 652-3101 271
TF: 800-356-3406 ■ Web: www.omniplex.com
OmniPoint Inc
3111 W Dr Martin Luther King Jr Blvd Ste 100. . . . . . Tampa FL 33607 813-574-3841 464-7887 196
Omnipress 2600 Anderson St. . . . . Madison WI 53704 608-246-2600 196
Web: omnipress.com
OmniPrint Inc 9700 Philadelphia Ct . . . . Lanham MD 20706 301-731-7000 637-10
Omnipure Filter Company Inc
1904 Industrial Way . . . . Caldwell ID 83605 208-454-2597 45
TF: 800-398-0833 ■ Web: www.omnipure.com
Omnis Network LLC
3655 Torrance Blvd Ste 230 . . . . Torrance CA 90503 310-316-9600 224
Web: www.omnis.com
Omnisource Corp 2205 S Holt Rd. . . . . Indianapolis IN 46241 317-381-5800 686
Web: www.omnisource.com
OmniSource Corp
7575 W Jefferson Blvd . . . . Fort Wayne IN 46804 260-422-5541 423-8500 686
TF: 800-666-4789 ■ Web: www.omnisource.com
OmniSYS-LLC 15950 Dallas Pkwy Ste 350. . . . . Dallas TX 75248 214-459-2574 809
Web: www.omnisys.com
Omnitech Inc 5841 S Corporate Pl . . . . Sioux Falls SD 57108 605-336-0888 177
Web: omnitech-inc.com
Omnitech Labs Inc
215 Boul Du Seminaire S . . . . Saint-jean-sur-richelieu QC J3B8W1 450-359-0891 180
Web: www.omnitechlabs.net
OmniTI Computer Consulting Inc
11830 W Market Pl Ste F . . . . Fulton MD 20759 240-646-0770 631
Web: www.omniti.com
Omnitracs LLC 10290 Campus Point Dr . . . . San Diego CA 92121 800-647-3325 736
TF: 800-348-7227 ■ Web: www.omnitracs.com
Omnitrans Inc 500 Merrick Rd. . . . . Lynbrook NY 11563 516-561-9300 449
Web: www.omnitrans.com
OmniTRAX Inc 252 Clayton St 4th Fl. . . . . Denver CO 80206 303-398-4500 398-4540 651
TF: 800-533-9416 ■ Web: www.omnitrax.com
Omnitronics LLC 6573 Cochran Rd. . . . . Solon OH 44139 440-349-4900 349-4900 52
TF: 800-762-9266 ■ Web: www.cadaudio.com
Omniture Inc 250 Brannan St. . . . . San Francisco CA 94107 408-536-6000 194
Web: www.adobe.com
Omnivex Corp 3300 Hwy 7 Ste 501 . . . . Concord ON L4K4M3 905-761-6640 179
TF: 800-745-8223 ■ Web: www.omnivex.com
Omnivision Entertainment Inc
The Film Ctr 630 Ninth Ave Ste 1012 . . . . New York NY 10036 310-734-6500 582-2199* 738
*Fax Area Code: 212 ■ Web: www.mydamnchannel.com
OmniVision Technologies Inc
4275 Burton Dr. . . . . Santa Clara CA 95054 408-542-3000 542-3001 696
NASDAQ: OVTI ■ Web: www.ovt.com
OmniVue Business Solutions LLC
1355 Windward Concourse Ste 200 . . . . Alpharetta GA 30005 770-587-0095 196
TF: 866-900-6348 ■ Web: www.omnivue.net
Omnni Associates Inc 1 Systems Dr . . . . Appleton WI 54914 920-735-6900 261
TF: 800-571-6677 ■ Web: omnni.com
OMNOVA Solutions Inc 175 Ghent Rd . . . . Fairlawn OH 44333 330-869-4200 745-2
NYSE: OMN ■ TF: 800-475-6701 ■ Web: www.omnova.com
OMNOVA Solutions Inc Performance Chemicals Div
165 S Cleveland Ave. . . . . Mogadore OH 44260 330-628-6536 145
TF: 888-253-5454 ■ Web: www.omnova.com
OMRF (Oklahoma Medical Research Foundation)
825 NE 13th St . . . . Oklahoma City OK 73104 405-271-6673 668
TF: 800-522-0211 ■ Web: www.omrf.org
Omron Corp 55 Commerce Dr . . . . Schaumburg IL 60173 224-520-7650 520-7680 253
Web: www.omron.com
OMRON Corp 1 Commerce Dr. . . . . Schaumburg IL 60173 847-843-7900 843-7787 203
TF: 800-556-6766 ■ Web: www.omron247.com
Omron Healthcare Inc
1925 W Field Ct . . . . Lake Forest IL 60045 847-680-6200 680-6269* 475
*Fax: Cust Svc ■ TF: 877-216-1333 ■ Web: www.omronhealthcare.com
OMRON Scientific Technologies Inc
6550 Dumbarton Cir. . . . . Fremont CA 94555 510-608-3400 744-1442 203
TF: 800-556-6766 ■ Web: www.sti.com
OMT Inc 1-1717 Dublin Ave . . . . Winnipeg MB R3H0H2 204-786-3994 783-5805 395
TF: 888-665-0501 ■ Web: www.omt.net
OMW Corp 21 Pamaron Way Ste G. . . . . Novato CA 94949 415-382-1669 454
TF: 800-272-9102 ■ Web: www.omwcorp.com
OMYA Inc 39 Main St. . . . . Proctor VT 05765 802-459-3311 143
TF: 800-451-4468 ■ Web: www.omya.com/us-en
On 3 Promotional Partners
1543 Sheridan Rd. . . . . Kenosha WI 53140 262-551-8715 317
Web: www.on3promopartners.com
On Assignment Inc
26745 Malibu Hills Rd . . . . Calabasas CA 91301 818-878-7900 721
NYSE: ASGN ■ Web: www.onassignment.com
On Broadway 106 Broadway . . . . Helena MT 59601 406-443-1929 671
Web: onbroadwayinhelena.com

				Phone	Fax	Class
On Campus Marketing LLC 10411 Motor City Dr Ste 650 *Web:* www.ocm.com	Bethesda	MD	20817	301-652-1580		387
On Center Software Inc 8708 Technology Forest Pl Ste 175 *Web:* www.oncenter.com	The Woodlands	TX	77381	281-297-9000		177
On Demand Books 584 Broadway Rm 1100 *Web:* www.ondemandbooks.com	New York	NY	10012	212-966-2222		95
On Line Controls Inc 9 Kane Industrial Dr A. *Web:* onlinecontrols.com	Hudson	MA	01749	978-562-5353	562-8986	476
ON Search Partners LLC 6240 SOM Ctr Rd Ste 230 *Web:* www.onpartners.com	Solon	OH	44139	440-318-1006		260
ON Semiconductor Corp 5005 E McDowell Rd *NASDAQ: ON* ■ *TF:* 800-282-9855 ■ *Web:* www.onsemi.com	Phoenix	AZ	85008	602-244-6600		696
ON Services 6779 Crescent Dr. *TF:* 800-967-2419 ■ *Web:* www.oneventservices.com	Norcross	GA	30071	770-457-0966		738
On Site Gas Systems Inc 35 Budney Rd Budney Industrial Pk *Web:* www.onsitegas.com	Newington	CT	06111	860-667-8888		579
On Site Marketing 1901 Strasburg Rd *Web:* www.onsitemarketing.com	Coatesville	PA	19320	610-486-6900		463
On Target Staffing LLC 398 Comstock St *Web:* www.ontargetstaffingllc.com	New Brunswick	NJ	08901	732-249-8344	249-7341	260
On the Ave Hotel 2178 Broadway 222 W 77th St	New York	NY	10024	212-362-1100	787-9521	377
On the Border Cafe 1350 NW Hwy. *Web:* ontheborder.com	Garland	TX	75041	972-865-7988		671
On The Border mexican grill & cantina 1710 S Power Rd *Web:* www.ontheborder.com	Mesa	AZ	85206	602-247-7510		671
On the Scene 500 N Dearborn St Ste 550 *TF:* 800-588-0445 ■ *Web:* www.onthescene.com	Chicago	IL	60654	312-661-1440		184
On Time Staffing LLC 2 Aquarium Dr Ferry Terminal Bldg Ste 150 *TF:* 866-333-3007 ■ *Web:* www.ontimestaffing.com	Camden	NJ	08103	866-333-3007		260
On Time Transport Inc 135 E Highland Pkwy Ste A *Web:* www.ontimetransport.com	Roselle	NJ	07203	908-298-9500		30
On Tour 201 Cortsen Rd	Pleasant Hill	CA	94523	925-930-9135		760
On Track Marketing Inc 1910 W N Ave. *Web:* www.otmarketing.com	Chicago	IL	60622	773-235-0017		195
ON24 Inc 201 Third St 3rd Fl *Web:* www.on24.com	San Francisco	CA	94103	415-369-8000	369-8388	395
ONA (Ohio Nurses Assn) 4000 E Main St. *TF:* 800-735-0056 ■ *Web:* www.ohnurses.org	Columbus	OH	43213	614-237-5414	237-6074	533
ONA (Oklahoma Nurses Assn) 1111 N Lee Ste 243 *Web:* www.oklahomanurses.org	Oklahoma City	OK	73103	405-840-3476	840-3013	533
ONA (Oregon Nurses Assn) 18765 SW Boones Ferry Rd *TF:* 800-634-3552 ■ *Web:* www.oregonrn.org	Tualatin	OR	97062	503-293-0011	293-0013	533
Ona Beach State Park 5580 S Coast Hwy *TF:* 800-551-6949 ■ *Web:* www.oregonstateparks.org	Newport	OR	97366	800-551-6949		565
Onamac Industries Inc 11504 Airport Rd Bldg G *Web:* www.onamac.com	Everett	WA	98204	425-743-6676	742-2718	454
Onboard Systems International 13915 NW Third Ct. *TF:* 800-275-0883 ■ *Web:* www.onboardsystems.com	Vancouver	WA	98685	360-546-3072		529
On-Call Nursing Agency and Associates of New Orleans 7900 Earhart Blvd *TF:* 800-999-9999 ■ *Web:* www.oncallnursing.com	New Orleans	LA	70125	504-866-0442		793
ONCAP 161 Bay St 49th Fl. *Web:* www.oncap.com	Toronto	ON	M5J2S1	416-214-4300	216-1834	792
OnCard Marketing Inc 276 Fifth Ave Ste 608 *TF:* 866-996-8729 ■ *Web:* www.revtrax.com	New York	NY	10001	866-996-8729		466
OnCell Systems Inc 1160D Pittsford-Victor Rd *Web:* oncell.com	Pittsford	NY	14534	585-419-9844		41
Oncenter Complex 800 S State St. *TF:* 800-776-7548 ■ *Web:* www.oncenter.org	Syracuse	NY	13202	315-435-8000	435-8099	205
ONCIX (The National Counterintelligence and Security Center) LX/ICC-B *Web:* ncsc.gov	Washington	DC	20511	703-733-8600		340-20
Oncogenex Technologies Inc 1001 W Broadway Ste 400 *Web:* oncogenex.com	Vancouver	BC	V6H4B1	604-736-3678		231
Oncologix Tech Inc 1604 W Pinhook Rd Ste 200.	Lafayette	LA	70508	616-977-9933		736
Oncology Nursing Society (ONS) 125 Enterprise Dr **Fax Area Code: 877* ■ *TF:* 866-257-4667 ■ *Web:* www.ons.org	Pittsburgh	PA	15275	412-859-6100	369-5497*	49-8
Oncology Plus Inc 1070 E Brandon Blvd *TF:* 877-410-0779 ■ *Web:* www.oncologyplus.com	Brandon	FL	33511	877-410-0779		237
Oncolytics Biotech Inc 1167 Kensington Crescent NW Ste 210 *TSE: ONC* ■ *TF:* 800-731-5319 ■ *Web:* www.oncolyticsbiotech.com	Calgary	AB	T2N1X7	403-670-7377	283-0858	85
OncoMDx Inc 2458 Embarcadero Way.	Palo Alto	CA	94303	650-532-9500		415
Oncor 1616 Woodall Rodgers Fwy Ste 2M-012 *TF:* 888-313-6862 ■ *Web:* www.oncor.com	Dallas	TX	75202	214-486-2000		787
Oncore Mfg Services LLC 225 Carando Dr	Springfield	MA	01104	413-736-2121		625
OnCorp Direct Inc 1033 Bay St Ste 313 *TF:* 800-461-7772 ■ *Web:* www.oncorp.com	Toronto	ON	M5S3A5	416-964-2677		317
Oncoscope Inc 324 Blackwell St Ste 1120	Durham	NC	27701	919-251-8030		743
OnCure Medical Corp 188 Inverness Dr W Ste 650 *Web:* www.oncure.com	Englewood	CO	80112	303-643-6500	643-6560	374-3
Ondal USA 5140 Commerce Rd *Web:* ondal.com	Richmond	VA	23234	804-279-0320		475
OndaVia Inc 26102 Eden Landing Rd Ste 1 *Web:* www.ondavia.com	Hayward	CA	94545	510-887-3180		407
Onder Shelton O'Leary & Peterson LLC 110 E Lockwood Ave. *Web:* www.onderlaw.com	Saint Louis	MO	63119	314-963-9000		445
Ondine Biomedical Inc 1100 Melville St *Web:* www.ondinebio.com	Vancouver	BC	V6E4A6	604-669-0555	669-0533	231
Onduline North America Inc 4900 Ondura Dr *TF:* 800-777-7663 ■ *Web:* www.ondura.com	Fredericksburg	VA	22407	540-898-7000	898-4991	191-4
One Acadiana 804 E St Mary Blvd. *Web:* www.oneacadiana.org	Lafayette	LA	70503	337-233-2705	234-8671	139
One Call Concepts Inc 7223 Pkwy Dr Ste 210 *Web:* www.occinc.com	Hanover	MD	21076	410-712-0082	712-0838	171
One Call Medical Inc (OCM) 20 Waterview Blvd PO Box 614 *TF:* 800-872-2875 ■ *Web:* www.onecallcm.com	Parsippany	NJ	07054	973-257-1000	257-0044	382
One Consulting Group Inc 977 Ponce De Leon Pl NE Ste 3 *Web:* onecginc.com	Atlanta	GA	30306	404-815-8005		196
One DOT Systems Inc 6566 NW 13th Ct *Web:* www.onedotsystems.net	Plantation	FL	33313	954-327-1490		180
One Earth Oil & Gas Inc 600-6th Ave SW Ste 320	Calgary	AB	T2P0S5	403-984-3151	984-3152	539
One Eighty Consulting Inc 413 N Meridian St *Web:* 180consultinginc.com	Tallahassee	FL	32301	850-412-0300		196
One Fish - Two Fish 2109 W Great Neck Rd *Web:* www.onefish-twofish.com	Virginia Beach	VA	23451	757-496-4350		671
One if by Land Two if by Sea 17 Barrow St. *Web:* www.oneifbyland.com	New York	NY	10014	212-255-8649		671
One Lambda Inc 21001 Kittridge St. *TF:* 800-822-8824 ■ *Web:* www.onelambda.com	Canoga Park	CA	91303	818-702-0042	702-6904	479
One Liberty Properties Inc 60 Cutter Mill Rd Ste 303 *NYSE: OLP* ■ *TF:* 800-937-5449 ■ *Web:* 1liberty.com	Great Neck	NY	11021	516-466-3100	466-3132	655
One Link Wireless 7321 Broadway Ext *TF:* 800-259-2929 ■ *Web:* www.onelinkwireless.com	Oklahoma City	OK	73116	405-840-2345		246
One Market 1 Market St. *TF:* 800-258-3826 ■ *Web:* www.onemarket.com	San Francisco	CA	94105	415-777-5577		671
One Napili Way 5355 Lower Honoapiilani Hwy *Web:* www.onenapiliway.com	Lahaina	HI	96761	808-669-2007		753
One Nation Energy Solutions LLC 401 Studewood St Ste 204 *Web:* www.onenationenergy.com	Houston	TX	77007	713-861-0600		538
One Planet Corp 850 Ridge Ave *Web:* www.one-planet.net	Pittsburgh	PA	15212	412-323-1050		768
One Point Solutions Inc 43422 W Oaks Dr Ste 294 *Web:* www.one-point.com	Novi	MI	48377	248-887-8470		177
One Reverse Mortgage LLC 4445 Eastgate Mall Ste 320 *Web:* www.onereversemortgage.com	San Diego	CA	92121	858-652-5990		509
One Smooth Stone Inc 5222 Main St *Web:* www.onesmoothstone.com	Downers Grove	IL	60515	630-427-4226		463
One Source Industries LLC 185 Technology Dr *TF:* 800-899-4990 ■ *Web:* www.osicreative.com	Irvine	CA	92618	800-899-4990		546
One Source Safety & Health Inc 140 S Village Ave Ste 130 *Web:* 1ssh.com	Exton	PA	19341	610-524-5525		196
One Source Toxicology Laboratory Inc 1213 Genoa Red Bluff Rd *Web:* www.onesourcetox.com	Pasadena	TX	77504	713-920-2559		415
One Southern Indiana 4100 Charlestown Rd *TF:* 800-521-2232 ■ *Web:* www.1si.org	New Albany	IN	47150	812-945-0266	948-4664	139
One Step Logic 17615 Mayall St. *Web:* www.onesteplogic.com	Northridge	CA	91325	818-700-7837		77
One Stop Career Center 359 Bill France Blvd *TF:* 800-476-7574 ■ *Web:* www.careersourcefv.com	Daytona Beach	FL	32114	386-323-7001		260
One Technologies LP 8144 Walnut Hill Ln Ste 600. *TF:* 888-550-8471 ■ *Web:* www.onetechnologies.net	Dallas	TX	75231	888-550-8471		225
One Touch Global Technologies Inc 1401 Dove St Ste 530.	Newport Beach	CA	92660	949-270-0300		174
One Touch Systems Inc 2528 Qume Dr Unit 14 *TF:* 800-227-8862 ■ *Web:* www.onetouchsys.com	San Jose	CA	95131	408-436-4600		178-7
One Trick Pony 136 E Fulton St. *TF:* 800-435-8429 ■ *Web:* www.onetrick.biz	Grand Rapids	MI	49503	616-235-7669		671
One Washington Cir Hotel 1 Washington Cir NW. *TF:* 800-424-9671 ■ *Web:* www.thecirclehotel.com	Washington	DC	20037	202-872-1680		379
One Way Building Services Inc 6811 Washington Ave S *Web:* owbs.net	Minneapolis	MN	55439	952-942-0412		186
One Web Systems Inc 6195 Barfield Rd Ste 170	Atlanta	GA	30328	404-252-5400		177
One World Direct 10 First Ave E *Web:* www.owd.com	Mobridge	SD	57601	605-845-7172		459
One World Theatre 7701 Bee Caves Rd *TF:* 888-616-0522 ■ *Web:* www.oneworldtheatre.org	Austin	TX	78746	512-330-9500	330-9600	572
One Yellow Rabbit Performance Theatre 225 8 Ave SE *Web:* oyr.org	Calgary	AB	T2G0K8	403-264-3224		749
OneAmerica Financial Partners Inc (PML) PO Box 368 *TF:* 800-249-6269 ■ *Web:* www.oneamerica.com	Indianapolis	IN	46206	317-285-1877	285-6462	391-2

Name / Address	City	State	ZIP	Phone	Fax	Class
Onebanc 300 W Capitol Ave *Web:* www.onebanc.com	Little Rock	AR	72201	501-370-4400	370-4505	70
OneBeacon Insurance Group N 605 US-169 Ste 800 *TF:* 800-662-0156 ■ *Web:* onebeacon.com	Plymouth	MN	55441	781-332-7000	332-7904	391-4
OneClass 365 Bloor St E Unit 1902 *TF:* 855-392-6946 ■ *Web:* oneclass.com	Toronto	ON	M4W3L4	855-392-6946		387
OneCoast Network LLC 230 Spring St Ste 1800 *TF:* 866-592-5514 ■ *Web:* www.onecoast.com	Atlanta	GA	30303	866-592-5514	469-9517	361
OneID Inc 580 Howard St Ste 303 *Web:* www.oneid.com	San Francisco	CA	94105	415-590-3712		387
Oneida City School District Inc 565 Sayles St *Web:* www.oneidacsd.org	Oneida	NY	13421	315-363-2550	363-6728	685
Oneida Correctional Facility 6100 School Rd	Rome	NY	13440	315-339-6880		213
Oneida County 10 W Court St *Web:* oneidasheriff.net	Malad City	ID	83252	208-766-2251	766-2891	338
Oneida County 1 S Oneida Ave *Web:* www.co.oneida.wi.gov	Rhinelander	WI	54501	715-369-6144	369-6230	338
Oneida County 800 Pk Ave *Web:* kidsoneida.org	Utica	NY	13501	315-792-9039		338
Oneida County Convention & Visitors Bureau PO Box 551 *TF:* 800-426-3132 ■ *Web:* www.oneidacountytourism.com	Utica	NY	13503	315-724-7221	724-7335	206
Oneida Healthcare Ctr 321 Genesee St *TF:* 800-671-1028 ■ *Web:* www.oneidahealthcare.org	Oneida	NY	13421	315-363-6000	361-2043	374-3
Oneida-Madison Electric Co-op Inc 6630 State Rt 20 *Web:* www.oneida-madison.coop	Bouckville	NY	13310	315-893-1851		245
ONeill & Borges American International Plaza 250 Munoz Rivera Ave Ste 800 *Web:* www.oneillborges.com	San Juan	PR	00918	787-764-8181		428
OneKreate Inc 3850 N 29th Terr *Web:* www.onekreate.com	Hollywood	FL	33020	954-322-7600		5
OneLegacy Transplant Donor Network 221 S Figueroa St Ste 500 *TF:* 800-786-4077 ■ *Web:* www.onelegacy.org	Los Angeles	CA	90012	213-229-5600	229-5601	545
OneMedPlace 219 E 83rd St 4 Fl *Web:* www.onemedplace.com	New York	NY	10028	212-734-1008		466
OneMorePallet.com 9891 Montgomery Rd Ste 122 *TF:* 855-438-1667 ■ *Web:* www.onemorepallet.com	Cincinnati	OH	45242	855-438-1667		387
OneName Corp 18 W Mercer Ste 300 *Web:* onename.com	Seattle	WA	98119	206-812-6000	812-6001	525
Oneonta City School District 31 Ctr St *Web:* www.oneontacsd.org	Oneonta	NY	13820	607-433-8200	433-8290	186
Oneonta Trading Corp 1 Oneonta Way *Web:* www.oneonta.com	Wenatchee	WA	98801	509-663-2191		297-7
Oneplanetweb Inc 322 E Arrollaga St	Santa Barbara	CA	93101	805-963-1056		387
OneRoof Inc 1 Maritime Plaza Ste 1100 *Web:* www.oneroof.com	San Francisco	CA	94111	415-391-0556	391-0559	196
Ones We Love Inc 3901 Westerly Pl Ste 205 *Web:* www.owlus.com	Newport Beach	CA	92660	714-658-1033	464-5383	184
OneSCM 6805 Capital of Texas Hwy Ste 370 *TF:* 800-324-5143 ■ *Web:* onescm.com	Austin	TX	78731	512-231-8191		178-1
Oneshield Inc 62 Forest St *Web:* oneshield.com	Marlborough	MA	01752	774-348-1000		177
Onesmartworld Inc 79 Simcoe St *TF:* 800-387-6278 ■ *Web:* www.onesmartworld.com	Collingwood	ON	L9Y1M3	705-444-1234		193
OneSource Distributors 3951 Oceanic Dr *Web:* www.1sourcedist.com	Oceanside	CA	92056	760-966-4500	966-4599	246
OneSource Inc 1124 Hwy 315 *Web:* www.onesourcehrsolutions.com	Wilkes-barre	PA	18702	570-825-3411		260
OneSource Virtual 5601 N MacArthur Blvd Ste 100 *Web:* www.onesourcevirtual.com	Irving	TX	75038	972-916-9847		631
ONESPRING LLC 980 Birmingham Rd Ste 501-165 *TF:* 888-472-1840 ■ *Web:* www.onespring.net	Alpharetta	GA	30004	888-472-1840		180
OneSubsea LLC 4646 W Sam Houston Pkwy N *TF:* 800-248-8665 ■ *Web:* cameron.slb.com/onesubsea	Houston	TX	77041	713-939-2211		539
Oneta Co 1401 S Padre Island Dr *Web:* www.onetacc.com	Corpus Christi	TX	78416	361-853-0123	853-5327	80-2
OneTouch Direct LLC 4902 W Sligh Ave *TF:* 866-948-4005 ■ *Web:* www.onetouchdirect.com	Tampa	FL	33634	866-948-4005		41
OneUnited Bank 3683 Crenshaw Blvd *TF:* 877-663-8648 ■ *Web:* www.oneunited.com	Los Angeles	CA	90016	323-290-4848	389-0548	70
OneWorkplace 475 Brannan St Ste 210 *Web:* www.oneworkplace.com	San Francisco	CA	94107	415-357-2200		320
Onex Corp 161 Bay St PO Box 700 *Web:* www.onex.com	Toronto	ON	M5J2S1	416-362-7711	362-5765	185
Ongig Inc 708 Montgomery St *Web:* www.ongig.com	San Francisco	CA	94111	415-857-2304		260
ONICON Inc 11451 Belcher Rd S *Web:* www.onicon.com	Largo	FL	33773	727-447-6140		201
Onion River Sports Inc 20 Langdon St *Web:* www.onionriver.com	Montpelier	VT	05602	802-229-9409		711
OnIt Digital LLC 684 S Mountain Rd *Web:* www.onitdigital.com	New York	NY	10956-5274	212-655-9632		195
Onity Inc 4001 Fairview Industrial Dr SE *TF:* 800-424-1433 ■ *Web:* region.onity.com	Salem	OR	97302	800-424-1433		351
Onix Networking Corp 18519 Detroit Ave *TF:* 800-664-9638 ■ *Web:* www.onixnet.com	Lakewood	OH	44107	800-664-9638		174
Online Business Applications Inc 9018 Heritage Pkwy Ste 600 *Web:* www.irmsonline.com	Woodridge	IL	60517	630-243-9810		225
Online Computer Library Ctr Inc (OCLC) 6565 Kilgour Pl *Fax Area Code: 614 ■ *TF:* 800-848-5878 ■ *Web:* www.oclc.org	Dublin	OH	43017	800-848-5878	764-6096*	49-11
Online Copy Corp 48815 Kato Rd *TF:* 800-833-4460 ■ *Web:* onlinecopycorp.com	Fremont	CA	94539	800-833-4460		240
Online Engineering Inc 400 N Cedar St *Web:* www.online-engineering.com	Manistique	MI	49854	906-341-0090		475
Online Marketing Institute 2088 Union St Ste 3 *Web:* www.onlinemarketinginstitute.org	San Francisco	CA	94123	415-450-9524		764
On-Line Strategies Inc 7920 Belt Line Rd Ste 1150 *TF:* 866-237-4900 ■ *Web:* www.olsdallas.com	Dallas	TX	75254	214-466-1000		253
On-line Taxes Inc 724 Jules St *TF:* 800-739-9998 ■ *Web:* olt.com	Saint Joseph	MO	64501	816-232-0095		463
Online Transport System Inc 6311 W Stoner Dr *TF:* 866-543-1235 ■ *Web:* www.onlinetransport.com	Greenfield	IN	46140	317-894-2159		780
On-line Video Design Inc 710 Acacia Ave *Web:* www.onlinevid.com	Melbourne	FL	32904	321-676-5677		514
OnlineMetals.com 1138 W Ewing *TF:* 800-533-6350 ■ *Web:* www.onlinemetals.com	Seattle	WA	98119	800-533-6350		492
Only in San Francisco Pier 39 *Web:* www.pier39.com	San Francisco	CA	94133	415-397-0143	956-8124	327
OnMark Solutions LLC 27780 Berringer Run	Cleveland	OH	44145	440-328-8245		366
OnMedia Communications Company Inc 4400 College Blvd Ste 195 *Web:* www.onmediaadsales.com	Overland Park	KS	66211	913-491-4030		5
Ono Pharma USA Inc 2000 Lenox Dr *Web:* www.ono.co.jp	Trenton	NJ	08648	609-219-1010	219-9229	582
Onondaga Cave State Park 7556 Hwy H *TF:* 877-422-6766 ■ *Web:* www.mostateparks.com	Leasburg	MO	65535	573-245-6576		565
Onondaga Coach Corp PO Box 277 *TF:* 800-451-1570 ■ *Web:* www.onondagacoach.com	Auburn	NY	13021	315-255-2216	255-0925	107
Onondaga Community College 4941 Onondaga Rd *TF:* 800-827-1000 ■ *Web:* www.sunyocc.edu	Syracuse	NY	13215	315-498-2622	498-2107	162
Onondaga County 401 Montgomery St *Web:* www.ongov.net	Syracuse	NY	13202	315-435-2226	435-3455	338
Onondaga County Public Library 447 S Salina St *Web:* www.onlib.org	Syracuse	NY	13202	315-435-1900		434-3
OnPath Business Solutions Inc St Joseph's Bldg 1165 Kenaston St *TF:* 800-299-5608 ■ *Web:* www.onpath.com	Ottawa	ON	K1B3N9	613-564-6565		180
ONPRC (Oregon National Primate Research Ctr) 3181 SW Sam Jackson Pk Rd *Web:* www.ohsu.edu	Portland	OR	97239	503-494-8311		660
Onprocess Technology Inc 200 Homer Ave *Web:* www.onprocess.com	Ashland	MA	01721	508-520-2711		463
onProject Inc 61 S Paramus Rd 3rd Fl *Web:* www.onproject.com	Paramus	NJ	07417	973-971-9970	971-9971	39
On-Q-ity Inc 610 Lincoln St N Bldg 3rd Fl *TF:* 800-777-4643 ■ *Web:* www.On-Q-ity.com	Waltham	MA	02451	781-895-8100		743
ONR (Office of Naval Research) 875 N Randolph St Ste 1425 *Web:* www.onr.navy.mil	Arlington	VA	22203	703-696-5031	696-5940	668
ONRAD Inc 1770 Iowa Ave Ste 280 *Web:* www.onradinc.com	Riverside	CA	92507	951-786-0801		177
Onramp Access LLC 2916 Montopolis Dr Ste 300 *Web:* www.onr.com	Austin	TX	78741	512-322-9200		177
onramp Branding LLC 102 W Third St Ste 700 *Web:* www.thinkonramp.com	Winston-salem	NC	27101	336-397-5394		195
On-Ramp Medical Communications LLC 8770 Purdue Rd	Indianapolis	IN	46268	317-202-3300		393
ONS (Oncology Nursing Society) 125 Enterprise Dr *Fax Area Code: 877 ■ *TF:* 866-257-4667 ■ *Web:* www.ons.org	Pittsburgh	PA	15275	412-859-6100	369-5497*	49-8
Onset Computer Corp PO Box 3450 *TF:* 800-564-4377 ■ *Web:* www.onsetcomp.com	Pocasset	MA	02559	508-759-9500	759-9100	201
Onset Marketing LLC 28525 Beck Rd Ste 125 *Web:* www.onsetmarketing.com	Wixom	MI	48393	248-596-9788		463
Onset Ventures 2400 Sand Hill Rd Ste 150 *Web:* www.onset.com	Menlo Park	CA	94025	650-529-0700	529-0777	792
onShore Networks LLC 1407 W Chicago Ave *Web:* www.onshore.com	Chicago	IL	60642	312-850-5200		225
Onsite Energy Corp 2701 Loker Ave W Ste 107 *TF:* 800-382-6674 ■ *Web:* www.onsitenergy.com	Carlsbad	CA	92010	760-931-2400		192
Onsite Health Diagnostics 1199 S Beltline Rd Ste 120 *TF:* 877-366-7483 ■ *Web:* www.onsitehealthdiagnostics.com	Coppell	TX	75019	877-366-7483		416
Onsite Management Group 4400 Bishop Ln Ste 214 *TF:* 800-207-4807 ■ *Web:* omgservices.com	Louisville	KY	40218	502-583-1664		5
Onsite Occupational Health & Safety Inc 101 N Hart St *TF:* 800-360-3220 ■ *Web:* www.onsiteohs.com	Princeton	IN	47670	812-770-4480		194
Onslow County 4024 Richland Hwy *TF:* 800-932-2144 ■ *Web:* onslowcountync.gov	Jacksonville	NC	28540	910-347-4717	455-7878	338
Onslow County Public Library 58 Doris Ave E *Web:* www.onslowcountync.gov/Library	Jacksonville	NC	28540	910-455-7350	455-1661	434-3

				Phone	Fax	Class
Onslow County Tourism						
1099 Gum Branch Rd	Jacksonville	NC	28540	800-932-2144	347-4705*	206
*Fax Area Code: 910 ■ TF: 800-932-2144 ■ Web: www.onlyinonslow.com						
Onslow Memorial Hospital						
317 Western Blvd	Jacksonville	NC	28541	910-577-2345		374-3
Web: www.onslow.org						
Onsrud Cutter LP 800 Liberty Dr	Libertyville	IL	60048	847-362-1560	362-5028	493
TF: 800-234-1560 ■ Web: www.onsrud.com						
Ontario Area Chamber of Commerce						
251 SW Ninth St	Ontario	OR	97914	541-889-8012	889-8331	206
TF: 866-989-8012 ■ Web: www.ontariochamber.com						
Ontario Association of Archietects						
111 Moatfield Dr	North York	ON	M3B3L6	416-449-5756		138
TF: 800-565-2724 ■ Web: www.oaa.on.ca						
Ontario Centres of Excellence Inc						
156 Front St W Ste 200	Toronto	ON	M5J2L6	416-861-1092		217
TF: 866-759-6014 ■ Web: www.oce-ontario.org						
Ontario Chamber of Commerce						
3200 Inland Empire Blvd Ste 130	Ontario	CA	91764	909-984-2458		139
Web: www.ontario.org						
Ontario Chamber of Commerce						
180 Dundas St W Ste 505	Toronto	ON	M5G1Z8	416-482-5222	482-5879	137
Web: www.occ.ca						
Ontario Christian High School						
931 W Philadelphia St	Ontario	CA	91762	909-984-1756		685
Ontario City Library 215 E C St	Ontario	CA	91764	909-395-2004		434-3
Web: www.ontarioca.gov/library						
Ontario Clean Water Agency						
1 Yonge St Ste 1700	Toronto	ON	M5E1E5	416-775-0500	314-8300	192
TF: 800-667-6292 ■ Web: www.ocwa.com						
Ontario College of Art & Design						
100 McCaul St	Toronto	ON	M5T1W1	416-977-6000	977-6006	785
TF: 800-382-6516 ■ Web: www.ocadu.ca						
Ontario Convention & Visitors Bureau						
2000 E Convention Center Way	Ontario	CA	91764	909-937-3000	937-3080	206
TF: 800-455-5755 ■ Web: www.ontariocc.org						
Ontario Convention Ctr						
2000 E Convention Ctr Way	Ontario	CA	91764	909-937-3000	937-3080	205
TF: 800-455-5755 ■ Web: www.ontariocc.org						
Ontario County 20 Ontario St	Canandaigua	NY	14424	585-396-4200	393-2951	338
TF: 800-247-7273 ■ Web: www.co.ontario.ny.us						
Ontario Dental Nurses & Assistants Association						
869 Dundas St	London	ON	N5W2Z8	519-679-2566		138
TF: 800-461-4348 ■ Web: odaa.org						
Ontario Die Co of America						
1755 Busha Hwy	Marysville	MI	48040	810-987-5060	987-3688	757
Web: www.ontariodie.com						
Ontario Drive & Gear Ltd (ODG)						
220 Bergey Ct	New Hamburg	ON	N3A2J5	519-662-2840		29
TF: 877-274-6288 ■ Web: www.argoatv.com						
Ontario Equestrian Federation						
1 W Pearce St Ste 201	Richmond Hill	ON	L4B3K3	905-709-6545		138
Web: horse.on.ca						
Ontario International Airport						
1923 E Avion St	Ontario	CA	91761	909-937-2700		27
Web: www.lawa.org/welcomeont.aspx						
Ontario Knife Co 26 Empire St	Franklinville	NY	14737	716-676-5527	299-2618*	222
*Fax Area Code: 800 ■ TF: 800-222-5233 ■ Web: www.ontarioknife.com						
Ontario Lottery & Gaming Corp						
70 Foster Dr Ste 800	Sault Sainte Marie	ON	P6A6V2	705-946-6464		642
TF: 800-563-5357 ■ Web: www.olg.ca						
Ontario Medical Supply Ltd						
1100 Algoma Rd	Ottawa	ON	K1B0A3	613-244-8620		363
TF: 800-804-1112 ■ Web: www.oms.ca						
Ontario Minor Hockey Association						
25 Brodie Dr Unit 3	Richmond Hill	ON	L4B3K7	905-780-6642		717
Web: www.omha.net						
Ontario Northland Transportation Commission						
555 Oak St E	North Bay	ON	P1B8L3	705-472-4500		311
TF: 800-363-7512 ■ Web: www.ontarionorthland.ca						
Ontario Nurses Association						
85 Grenville St Ste 400	Toronto	ON	M5S3A2	416-964-8833		414
TF: 800-387-5580 ■ Web: www.ona.org						
Ontario Pc Party 59 Adelaide St E	Toronto	ON	M5H3H1	416-861-9593		615
TF: 800-903-6453 ■ Web: www.ontariopc.com						
Ontario Real Estate Assn						
99 Duncan Mill Rd	Don Mills	ON	M3B1Z2	416-445-9910		652
TF: 866-444-5557 ■ Web: www.orea.com						
Ontario Refrigeration Service						
635 S Mountain Ave	Ontario	CA	91762	909-984-2771		610
Web: www.ontariorefrigeration.com						
Ontario Research and Innovation Optical Network						
360 Bay St 7th Fl	Toronto	ON	M5B1M4	416-507-9860	507-9862	224
Web: www.orano.on.ca						
Ontario Science Ctr 770 Don Mills Rd	Toronto	ON	M3C1T3	416-696-1000	696-3166	520
TF: 888-696-1110 ■ Web: www.ontariosciencecentre.ca						
Ontario Society of Professional Engineers						
4950 Yonge St Ste 2200	North York	ON	M2N6K1	416-223-9961		261
Web: www.ospe.on.ca						
Ontario State Recreation Site						
23751 Old Hwy 30	Huntington	OR	97907	800-551-6949		565
TF: 800-551-6949 ■ Web: www.oregonstateparks.org						
Ontario Systems Corp						
1150 W Kilgore Ave	Muncie	IN	47305	765-751-7000	751-7099	177
Web: www.ontariosystems.com						
Ontario Tourism Marketing Partnership Corp						
10 Dundas St E Ste 900	Toronto	ON	M7A2A1	905-282-1721		774
TF: 800-668-2746 ■ Web: www.ontariotravel.net						
Ontario Universities Application Centre						
170 Research Ln	Guelph	ON	N1G5E2	519-823-1940		165
Web: www.ouac.on.ca						
Ontash & Ermac Inc						
876 Kndrkamak Rd Ste 201	River Edge	NJ	07661	201-265-2189		224
Web: www.ontash.com						
Ontic Engineering & Manufacturing Inc						
4150 N Sam Houston E Pkwy	Houston	TX	77032	818-678-6555		790
Web: www.ontic.com						
Ontility LLC						
3403 N Sam Houston Pkwy Ste 300	Houston	TX	77086	281-854-1400		194
Web: www.ontility.com						
Ontonagon County 725 Greenland Rd	Ontonagon	MI	49953	906-884-4699		338
Web: www.ontonagoncounty.org						
Ontonagon County Rural Assn						
500 James K Paul St	Ontonagon	MI	49953	906-884-4151		245
Web: countrylines.com						
Ontor Ltd 12 Leswyn Rd	Toronto	ON	M6A1K3	416-781-5286		664
TF: 800-567-1631 ■ Web: www.ontor.com						
On-Track Computer Training Corp						
609 Granville St Ste 450 PO Box 10381	Vancouver	BC	V7Y1G6	604-683-0020		764
Web: www.on-track.com						
OnTrack Inc 221 W Main St	Medford	OR	97501	541-772-1777		726
TF: 800-543-9905 ■ Web: www.ontrackrecovery.org						
Onug Communications Inc						
3315 Atlantic Ave	Raleigh	NC	27604	919-876-5455		260
TF: 800-368-1034 ■ Web: onugsolutions.com						
Onyx Computing 10 Avon St	Cambridge	MA	02138	617-876-3876		178-8
Web: www.onyxtree.com						
Onyx EMS LLC 2920 Kelly Ave	Watertown	SD	57201	605-886-2519		253
TF: 800-772-7866 ■ Web: sparton.com						
Onyx Hotel 155 Portland St	Boston	MA	02114	617-557-9955	557-0005	379
TF: 866-660-6699 ■ Web: www.onyxhotel.com						
Onyx Medical Corp						
1800 N Shelby Oaks Dr	Memphis	TN	38134	901-323-6699		475
TF: 800-366-3067 ■ Web: www.onyxmedical.net						
Onyx Meetings & Events Inc						
7200 W 75th St	Overland Park	KS	66204	913-831-7200		463
Web: www.onyxmeetingsandevents.com						
Onyx Specialty Papers Inc						
40 Willow St	South Lee	MA	01260	413-243-1231	243-4602	552-1
Web: onyxpapers.com						
Oohology LLC 1236 S Shelby St	Louisville	KY	40203	502-416-0143		5
Web: www.oohology.com						
OOIDA (Owner-Operator Independent Drivers Assn Inc)						
1 NW OOIDA Dr	Grain Valley	MO	64029	816-229-5791	229-0518	49-21
TF: 800-444-5791 ■ Web: www.ooida.com						
Oostburg State Bank 905 Center Ave	Oostburg	WI	53070	920-564-2336		70
Web: oostburgbank.com						
OP Schuman & Sons Inc						
2001 County Line Rd	Warrington	PA	18976	215-343-1530	343-1633	454
Web: www.opschuman.com						
OPA Restaurant 230 Atwells Ave	Providence	RI	02903	401-351-8282		671
Web: opaprovidence.com						
Opal Financial Group Inc						
10 E 38th St 4th Fl	New York	NY	10016	212-532-9898		196
Web: www.opalgroup.net						
Opal Soft 1288 Kifer Rd # 201	Sunnyvale	CA	94086	408-267-2211		225
TF: 800-632-2022 ■ Web: www.opalsoft.com						
OPB (Oregon Public Broadcasting Inc)						
7140 SW Macadam Ave	Portland	OR	97219	503-244-9900		632
TF: 800-241-8123 ■ Web: www.opb.org						
OPC (Olson Precast Co) 2750 Marion Dr	Las Vegas	NV	89115	702-643-4371	643-4510	183
OPC (Overseas Press Club of America)						
40 W 45th St	New York	NY	10036	212-626-9220		49-14
Web: www.opcofamerica.org						
OPC Farms Inc 22300 Railroad Ave	San Joaquin	CA	93660	559-693-2700		10-4
OPCMIA (Operative Plasterers' & Cement Masons' International Assn of the US & Canada)						
11720 Beltsville Dr Ste 700	Beltsville	MD	20705	301-623-1000	623-1032	49-3
TF: 888-379-1558 ■ Web: www.opcmia.org						
Opco Inc 9710 Portland Ave E	Tacoma	WA	98445	253-531-2229		683
Opechee Construction Corp						
11 Corporate Dr	Belmont	NH	03220	603-527-9090		186
Web: www.opechee.com						
OPEI (Outdoor Power Equipment Institute Inc)						
341 S Patrick St	Alexandria	VA	22314	703-549-7600	549-7604	49-4
TF: 800-558-8767 ■ Web: www.opei.org						
Opelousas-Eunice Public Libraries						
212 E Grolee St	Opelousas	LA	70570	337-948-3693		434-3
Web: opelousaseunicepubliclibrary.org						
Open Air Cinema LLC 1402 W 400 S	Orem	UT	84058	801-796-6800	796-6806	748
TF: 866-319-3280 ■ Web: www.openaircinema.us						
Open Applications Group Inc (OAGI)						
PO Box 4897	Marietta	GA	30061	404-402-1962	740-0100*	49-13
*Fax Area Code: 801 ■ TF: 800-236-4600 ■ Web: www.oagi.org						
Open Arms Hospice						
1836 W Georgia Rd	Simpsonville	SC	29680	864-688-1700	688-1705	371
TF: 866-473-6276 ■ Web: www.openarmshospice.org						
Open Automation Software						
5077 Bear Mtn Dr	Evergreen	CO	80439	303-079-0090		179
TF: 800-533-4994 ■ Web: www.openautomationsoftware.com						
Open Court Publishing Co						
70 E Lake St Ste 800	Chicago	IL	60601	800-815-2280	701-1728*	637-2
*Fax Area Code: 312 ■ TF: 800-815-2280 ■ Web: www.opencourtbooks.com						
Open Dental Software						
Ste 110 3995 Fairview Industrial Dr SE	Salem	OR	97302	503-363-5432		177
TF: 866-239-0469 ■ Web: www.opendental.com						
Open Door Family Medical Ctr Inc						
165 Main St	Ossining	NY	10562	914-941-1263		352
Web: www.opendoormedical.org						
Open Door Mission						
5803 Harrisburg Blvd	Houston	TX	77011	713-923-8743	921-4206	48-20
Web: www.opendoorhouston.org						
Open Door Networks Inc						
110 S Laurel St	Ashland	OR	97520	541-488-4127		178-12
Web: www.opendoor.com						
Open E Cry LLC						
9482 Wedgewood Blvd Ste 150	Powell	OH	43065	614-792-2690		690
Open Geospatial Consortium Inc						
35 Main St Ste 5	Wayland	MA	01778	508-655-5858		138
Web: www.opengeospatial.org						
Open Group						
44 Montgomery St Ste 960	San Francisco	CA	94104	415-374-8280	374-8293	48-9
TF: 800-433-6611 ■ Web: www.opengroup.org						
Open Kitchen Inc 1161 W 21st St	Chicago	IL	60608	312-666-5335		299
TF: 800-339-5334 ■ Web: www.openkitchens.com						
Open Logic Corp 28345 Beck Rd Ste 308	Wixom	MI	48393	248-869-0080		225
Web: www.open-logix.com						

Phone Fax Class

Open Minds 163 York St. . . . . Gettysburg PA 17325 717-334-1329 466
TF: 877-350-6463 ■ *Web:* www.openminds.com

Open Options Corp 1203-20 Erb St W . . . . Waterloo ON N2L1T2 519-884-5898 463
TF: 800-571-0623 ■ *Web:* www.openoptions.com

Open Pantry Food Marts
10505 Corporate Dr Ste 101. . . . . Pleasant Prairie WI 53158 262-857-1156 857-9667 204
TF: 800-242-3358 ■ *Web:* www.openpantry.com

Open Plan Systems Inc
4700 Deepwater Terminal Rd . . . . Richmond VA 23234 804-275-2468 275-2329 319-1
TF: 844-677-6771 ■ *Web:* www.openplan.com

Open Road Entertainment LLC
3003 W Olive Ave Ste 1 . . . . Burbank CA 91505 310-248-3300 7
Web: www.openroadent.com

Open Roads Consulting Inc
103 Watson Rd . . . . Chesapeake VA 23320 757-546-3401 449
Web: www.openroadsconsulting.com

Open Society Institute 400 W 59th St. . . . . New York NY 10019 212-548-0600 548-4679 305
Web: www.opensocietyfoundations.org

Open Space Institute (OSI)
1350 Broadway Ste 201 . . . . New York NY 10018 212-290-8200 244-3441 48-13
Web: www.openspaceinstitute.org

Open Spatial Inc
13575 58th St N Ste 180 . . . . Clearwater FL 33760 800-696-1238 196
TF: 800-696-1238 ■ *Web:* www.openspatial.com

Open Storage Solutions Inc
2 Castleview Dr. . . . . Toronto ON L6T5S9 905-790-0660 174
TF: 800-387-3419 ■ *Web:* www.openstore.com

Open Systems Inc
4301 Dean Lakes Blvd . . . . Shakopee MN 55379 800-328-2276 403-5870* 178-1
**Fax Area Code:* 952 ■ *TF Sales:* 800-328-2276 ■ *Web:* www.osas.com

Open Systems International Inc
3600 Holly Ln N Ste 40 . . . . Minneapolis MN 55447 763-551-0559 809
Web: www.osii.com

Open Systems of Cleveland Inc
22999 Forbes Rd Ste A. . . . . Cleveland OH 44146 440-439-2332 439-3794 174
TF: 888-881-6660 ■ *Web:* www.osinc.com

Open Technology Solutions LLC
8085 S Chester St Ste 100 . . . . Centennial CO 80112 303-708-7140 180
Web: www.open-techs.com

Open Text Corp 275 Frank Tompa Dr. . . . . Waterloo ON N2L0A1 519-888-7111 888-0677 178-7
TSE: OTC ■ *TF General:* 800-499-6544 ■ *Web:* www.opentext.com

Open Text Corp (USA)
100 Tri-State International Pkwy 3rd Fl. . . . . Lincolnshire IL 60069 847-267-9330 267-9332 178-7
TSE: OTC ■ *TF Sales:* 800-499-6544 ■ *Web:* www.opentext.com

Openbay Inc 222 Third St Ste 4000. . . . . Cambridge MA 02142 617-398-8888 387
Web: www.openbay.com

OpenCon Systems Inc 377 Hoes Ln. . . . . Piscataway NJ 08854 732-463-3131 463-3557 178-7
Web: www.opencon.com

OpenConnect Systems Inc
2711 LBJ Fwy Ste 700 . . . . Dallas TX 75234 972-484-5200 484-6100 178-7
TF: 800-551-5881 ■ *Web:* www.openconnect.com

Openet Telecom Inc
1886 Metro Ctr Dr Ste 310. Reston VA 20190 703-400-1820 177
Web: www.openet.com

OpenEye Inc 23221 E Knox Ave. . . . . Liberty Lake WA 99019 509-232-5261 692
Web: www.openeye.net

OpenEye Scientific Software Inc
9 Bisbee Court Ste D . . . . Santa Fe NM 87508 505-473-7385 174
Web: www.eyesopen.com

Openface Inc 3445 Park Ave. . . . . Montreal QC H2X2H6 514-281-8585 225
TF: 800-865-8585 ■ *Web:* www.openface.com

Openfirst LLC 300 N Jefferson St. . . . . Milwaukee WI 53202 414-347-4100 347-4040 809

Openjar Concepts Inc
27710 jefferson ave Ste 302. . . . . Temecula CA 92590 951-296-9222 7
TF: 877-673-6527 ■ *Web:* www.openjar.com

OpenLink Software Inc
10 Burlington Mall Rd Ste 265. . . . . Burlington MA 01803 781-273-0900 229-8030 178-1
Web: www.openlinksw.com

OPENonline 1650 Lake Shore Dr Ste 350. . . . . Columbus OH 43204 614-481-6999 481-6900 635
TF: 888-381-5656 ■ *Web:* www.openonline.com

OpenPeak Inc 1750 Clint Moore Rd . . . . Boca Raton FL 33487 561-893-7800 177
Web: www.openpeak.com

OpenRoad Communications Ltd
12 Water St Ste 210 . . . . Vancouver BC V6B1A5 604-694-0554 809
TF: 800-874-2458 ■ *Web:* www.openroad.ca

OpenRules Inc 53 Riveria Dr . . . . Monroe NJ 08831 732-993-3131 809
Web: openrules.com

OpenSesame Inc
520 NW Davis St Ste 200. . . . . Portland OR 97209 503-808-1268 387
Web: www.opensesame.com

OpenTable Inc
1 Montgomery St Ste 700. . . . . San Francisco CA 94104 415-344-4200 39
Web: www.opentable.com

OpenTV Corp 275 Sacramento St. . . . . San Francisco CA 94111 415-962-5000 962-5300 178-7
Web: www.nagra.com

Openwave Systems Inc
400 Seaport Ct Ste 104. Redwood City CA 94063 650-480-7200 480-8100 178-7
Web: owmobility.com

OpenWorks 4742 N 24th St Ste 450. . . . . Phoenix AZ 85016 602-224-0440 468-3788 310
TF: 800-777-6736 ■ *Web:* www.openworksweb.com

Opera Atelier 157 King St E. . . . . Toronto ON M5C1G9 416-703-3767 749
Web: www.operaatelier.com

Opera Birmingham 3601 Sixth Ave S . . . . Birmingham AL 35222 205-322-6737 322-6206 573-2
Web: www.operabirmingham.org

Opera Carolina
345 N College St Ste 409. . . . . Charlotte NC 28202 704-332-7177 332-6448 573-2
Web: www.operacarolina.org

Opera Colorado
695 S Colorado Blvd Ste 20. . . . . Denver CO 80246 303-778-1500 778-0479 573-2
TF: 800-414-2251 ■ *Web:* www.operacolorado.org

Opera Company of Brooklyn
33 Indian Rd Ste 1G. . . . . New York NY 10034 212-567-3283 573-2
Web: www.operabrooklyn.org

Opera Company of North Carolina
612 Wade Ave Ste 100 . . . . Raleigh NC 27605 919-792-3850 573-2
Web: www.ncopera.org

Opera Company of Philadelphia
1420 Locust St Ste 210 . . . . Philadelphia PA 19102 215-893-3600 893-7801 573-2
Web: www.operaphila.org

Phone Fax Class

Opera Memphis 6745 Wolf River Pkwy . . . . Memphis TN 38120 901-257-3100 573-2
TF: 800-745-3000 ■ *Web:* www.operamemphis.org

Opera News Magazine
70 Lincoln Ctr Plaza 6th Fl. . . . . New York NY 10023 212-769-7080 769-8500 457-9
Web: operanews.com

Opera Omaha 1625 Farnam St Ste 100 . . . . Omaha NE 68102 402-346-4398 346-7323 573-2
TF: 877-346-7372 ■ *Web:* www.operaomaha.org

Opera Orchestra of New York, The
344 E 63rd St Ste B-1. . . . . New York NY 10065 212-906-9137 573-3
Web: www.operaorchestrany.org

Opera Roanoke 541 Luck Ave. Roanoke VA 24016 540-982-2742 573-2
TF: 800-422-8482 ■ *Web:* www.operaroanoke.org

Opera San Jose 2149 Paragon Dr. . . . . San Jose CA 95131 408-437-4450 437-4455 573-2
TF: 877-707-7827 ■ *Web:* operasj.org

Opera Santa Barbara
1330 State St . . . . Santa Barbara CA 93101 805-898-3890 898-3892 573-2
Web: www.operasb.com

Opera Theatre at Wildwood
20919 Denny Rd. . . . . Little Rock AR 72223 501-821-7275 573-2
Web: www.wildwoodpark.org

OperaDelaware 4 S Poplar St . . . . Wilmington DE 19801 302-658-8063 573-2
Web: www.operade.org

Operari Group LLC, The
6800 Park Ten Blvd Ste 170-W. . . . . San Antonio TX 78213 210-298-1291 463
Web: www.operarigroup.com

Operation Technology Inc
17 Goodyear Ste 100 . . . . Irvine CA 92618 949-900-1000 177
Web: etap.com

Operation USA
3617 Hayden Ave Ste A . . . . Culver City CA 90232 310-838-3455 48-5
TF: 800-678-7255 ■ *Web:* www.opusa.org

Operational Security Systems Inc
1231 Collier Rd NW Ste D . . . . Atlanta GA 30318 404-352-0025 189-4
Web: www.ossatl.com

Operational Technologies Corp
4100 NW Loop 410 Ste 230. . . . . San Antonio TX 78229 210-731-0000 731-0008 261
Web: www.otcorp.com

OperationsInc
535 Connecticut Ave 2nd Fl . . . . Norwalk CT 06854 203-322-0538 260
Web: www.operationsinc.com

Operative Plasterers' & Cement Masons' International Assn of the US & Canada (OPCMIA)
11720 Beltsville Dr Ste 700 . . . . Beltsville MD 20705 301-623-1000 623-1032 49-3
TF: 888-379-1558 ■ *Web:* www.opcmia.org

Opex Corp 305 Commerce Dr. . . . . Moorestown NJ 08057 856-727-1100 727-1955 178-10
TF: 800-673-9288 ■ *Web:* www.opex.com

OPGI (Original Parts Group Inc)
1770 Saturn Way . . . . Seal Beach CA 90740 562-594-1000 594-1050 54
TF: 800-243-8355 ■ *Web:* www.opgi.com

Ophelia's on the Bay
9105 Midnight Pass Rd . . . . Siesta Key FL 34242 941-349-2212 671
Web: www.opheliasonthebay.net

Region I
John F Kennedy Federal Bldg Rm 2100. . . . . Boston MA 02203 617-565-1491 340-10
TF: 800-827-1000 ■ *Web:* www.hhs.gov

Ophthalmic Consultants of Boston Inc
50 Staniford St Ste 600. . . . . Boston MA 02114 617-367-4000 543
TF: 800-635-0489 ■ *Web:* www.eyeboston.com

OPI (Ohio Penal Industries)
1221 McKinley Ave. . . . . Columbus OH 43222 614-752-0287 752-0303 630
TF: 800-237-3454 ■ *Web:* www.opi.state.oh.us

OPIC (Overseas Private Investment Corp)
1100 New York Ave NW . . . . Washington DC 20527 202-336-8400 408-9859 340-20
TF: 800-225-5722 ■ *Web:* www.opic.gov

Opici Import Co 25 Deboer Dr. . . . . Glen Rock NJ 07452 201-689-1200 80-3
Web: www.opici.com

Opies Transport Inc 21 Hwy FF PO Box 89 . . . . Eldon MO 65026 573-392-6525 768
Web: www.opiestransport.com

Opinion Access Corp 47-10 32nd Pl . . . . Long Island NY 11101 718-729-2622 225
TF: 888-489-3282 ■ *Web:* www.opinionaccess.com

Opinion Research Corp (ORC)
902 Carnegie Ctr Ste 220. Princeton NJ 08540 800-444-4672 466
TF: 800-444-4672 ■ *Web:* www.orcinternational.com

OPIS
9737 Washingtonian Blvd Ste 200 . . . . Gaithersburg MD 20878 301-287-2645 287-2820 531-5
TF: 888-301-2645 ■ *Web:* www.opisnet.com

Opis Management Resources
10150 Highlands Manor Dr Ste 300. . . . . Tampa FL 33610 813-558-6600 371
Web: www.opismr.com

OPL (Oxnard Public Library)
4300 Saviers Rd . . . . Oxnard CA 93033 805-247-8951 488-1336 434-3
Web: www.oxnard.org/library

Oplink Communications Inc
46335 Landing Pkwy . . . . Fremont CA 94538 510-933-7200 933-7300 735
NASDAQ: OPLK ■ *TF:* 800-732-0330 ■ *Web:* www.oplink.com

OPM (Office of Personnel Management)
1900 E St NW. . . . . Washington DC 20415 202-606-1800 340-20
Web: www.opm.gov

Opmedic Group Inc
1361 Beaumont Ave Ste 301. . . . . Mount-royal QC H3P2W3 514-345-8535 418
TF: 888-776-2732 ■ *Web:* www.groupeopmedic.com

OPNET Technologies Inc
7255 Woodmont Ave . . . . Bethesda MD 20814 240-497-3000 178-12
NASDAQ: OPNT ■ *Web:* riverbed.com

Oporto 2074 Park St . . . . Hartford CT 06106 860-233-3184 671
Web: www.oportohartford.com

Opotek Inc 2233 Faraday Ave Ste E . . . . Carlsbad CA 92008 760-929-0770 544
Web: www.opotek.com

Opp & Seibold General Construction Inc
1220 W Poplar St . . . . Walla Walla WA 99362 509-525-1373 186
TF: 800-468-6444 ■ *Web:* www.oppseibold.com

Oppenheimer & Company Inc
300 Madison Ave . . . . New York NY 10017 212-885-4646 401
Web: www.opco.com

Oppenheimer Cos Inc 877 W Main Ste 700. . . . . Boise ID 83702 208-343-4883 297-8
TF: 800-727-9939 ■ *Web:* www.oppcos.com

Oppenheimer Precision Products
173 Gibraltar Rd . . . . Horsham PA 19044 215-674-9100 253
Web: www.oppiprecision.com

	City	State	Zip	Phone	Fax	Class
OppenheimerFunds Inc 225 Liberty St	New York	NY	10281	800-525-7048		528
TF: 800-525-7048 ■ *Web:* www.oppenheimerfunds.com						
OPPORTUNE 711 Louisiana Ste 3100	Houston	TX	77002	713-622-8955		539
Web: opportune.com						
Opportunity Capital Corp						
2201 Walnut Ave Ste 210	Fremont	CA	94538	510-795-7000		403
Web: www.opportunitycapitalpartners.com						
Opportunity Finance Network						
620 Chestnut St Ste 572	Philadelphia	PA	19106	215-923-4754	923-4755	49-7
Web: ofn.org						
Opposing Views Inc						
371 Dalkeith Ave Ste 901	Los Angeles	CA	90049	310-433-3833		5
Web: www.opposingviews.com						
Oproma Inc 116 Av Gatineau	Gatineau	QC	J8T4J6	819-568-4069		180
TF: 800-584-8819 ■ *Web:* www.oproma.com						
Oprs 1615 Ellis St	Kewaunee	WI	54216	920-388-2788		2
OPSD (Oak Park School District)						
13900 Granzon	Oak Park	MI	48237	248-336-7700	336-7738	360-2
Web: www.oakparkschools.org						
OpSec Security Inc						
1857 Colonial Village Ln	Lancaster	PA	17601	717-293-4110		693
Web: www.aotgroup.com						
Opsol Integrators Inc						
1566 La Pradera Dr	Campbell	CA	95008	408-364-9915		180
Web: www.opsol.com						
OPSWAT Inc 398 Kansas St	San Francisco	CA	94103	415-590-7300		177
TF: 800-652-5601 ■ *Web:* www.opswat.com						
Optek Systems Inc 12 Pilgrim Rd	Greenville	SC	29607	864-272-2640		544
Web: www.opteksystems.com						
Optel Vision Inc						
2680, boul du Parc Technologique	Quebec	QC	G1P4S6	418-688-0334	688-9397	407
Web: www.optelvision.com						
Optelian Inc						
1700 Enterprise Way SE Ste 101	Marietta	GA	30067	770-690-9575		735
Web: www.optelian.com						
Optellios Inc 11 Penns Trl Ste 300	Newtown	PA	18940	215-497-9323		693
Web: www.optellios.com						
Optessa Inc						
5555 Calgary Trl NW Ste 1045	Edmonton	AB	T6H5P9	780-431-8426		179
Web: www.optessa.com						
Optex Inc 13661 Benson Ave Bldg C	Chino	CA	91710	909-993-5770	628-5560	692
TF: 800-966-7839 ■ *Web:* www.optexamerica.com						
Optex Systems Holdings Inc						
1420 Presidential Dr	Richardson	TX	75081	972-644-0722	234-3544	502
OTC: OPXS ■ *Web:* www.optexsys.com						
Opti Care Eye Health Center						
87 Grandview Ave	Waterbury	CT	06708	203-574-2020	596-2230	543
TF: 800-225-5393 ■ *Web:* opticarepc.com						
Opti Staffing Group						
3601 C St Ste 1220	Anchorage	AK	99503	907-677-9675		260
Web: optistaffing.com						
Optibase Inc						
625 Ellis St Ste 102	Mountain View	CA	94043	650-230-2400		180
Optical & Telecommunication Solutions Inc						
16835 Addison Rd Ste 105	Addison	TX	75001	972-931-0360		224
Web: www.optelsol.com						
Optical Cable Corp (OCC)						
5290 Concourse Dr	Roanoke	VA	24019	540-265-0690	265-0724	814
NASDAQ: OCC ■ *TF:* 800-622-7711 ■ *Web:* www.occfiber.com						
Optical Discount Corp						
10415 Slusher Dr Ste 1	Santa Fe Springs	CA	90670	562-946-3050		31
Optical Dynamics Corp						
1966 Production Ct	Louisville	KY	40299	502-671-2020		544
Web: www.opticaldynamics.com						
Optical Filters						
13447 S Mosiertown Rd Ste A	Meadville	PA	16335	814-333-2222		599
Web: www.opticalfiltersusa.com						
Optical Gaging Products Inc						
850 Hudson Ave	Rochester	NY	14621	585-544-0450	544-4998	544
TF: 800-647-4243 ■ *Web:* www.ogpnet.com						
Optical Image Technology Inc						
100 Oakwood Ave Ste 700	State College	PA	16803	814-238-0038		177
Web: www.docfinity.com						
Optical Options						
4620 J C Nichols Pkwy Ste 427	Kansas City	MO	64112	816-561-4907		543
Web: www.cibiseyecare.com						
Optical Physics Co						
26610 Agoura Rd Ste 240	Calabasas	CA	91302	818-880-2907		237
Web: www.opci.com						
Optical Research Assoc						
3280 E Foothill Blvd	Pasadena	CA	91107	626-795-9101	795-9102	178-12
Web: optics.synopsys.com						
Optical Society of America (OSA)						
2010 Massachusetts Ave NW	Washington	DC	20036	202-223-8130	223-1096	49-8
TF: 800-766-4672 ■ *Web:* www.osa.org						
Optical Supply Inc						
1526 Plainfield Ave NE	Grand Rapids	MI	49505	616-361-7177		544
Web: www.optical-supply.com						
OptiCat LLC						
1204 W S Jordan Pkwy ste C2	South Jordan	UT	84095	801-542-0560	952-7901*	393
**Fax Area Code:* 225 ■ *Web:* www.opticat.net						
Opticians Assn of America (OAA)						
3740 Canada Rd	Lakeland	TN	38002	901-388-2423	388-2348	49-8
TF: 800-296-9776 ■ *Web:* www.oaa.org						
Opti-Com Mfg Network Co Inc						
259 Plauche St	New Orleans	LA	70123	504-736-0331	733-9046	816
TF: 800-345-8774 ■ *Web:* opti-com.info						
Opticote Inc 10455 Seymour	Franklin Park	IL	60131	847-678-8900		484
TF: 800-248-6784 ■ *Web:* www.opticote.com						
Opti-Craft Inc 17311 NE Halsey	Portland	OR	97230	503-256-5330		544
Web: www.opticraft-optical.com						
Optim LLC 64 Technology Park Rd	Sturbridge	MA	01566	508-347-5100		544
Web: www.optimnet.com						
Optima Chemical Group LLC						
200 Willacoochee Hwy	Douglas	GA	31535	912-384-5101		146
Web: www.optimachem.com						
Optima Electronic Packaging Systems						
1775 MacLeod Dr	Lawrenceville	GA	30043	770-496-4000	496-4041*	254
**Fax:* Sales ■ *TF:* 800-821-0019 ■ *Web:* optimastantron.com/en/optima-stantron						
Optima Global Solutions Inc						
3131 Princeton Pike Ste 207	Lawrenceville	NJ	08648	609-586-8811		177
TF: 800-520-1816 ■ *Web:* www.optimags.com						
Optima Graphics Inc 1540 Fencorp Ct	Fenton	MO	63026	636-349-3396		344
Web: www.optimagfx.com						
Optima Group Inc 2150 Post Rd	Fairfield	CT	06824	203-255-1066		194
Web: www.optimagroupinc.com						
Optima Health						
4417 Corporation Ln	Virginia Beach	VA	23462	757-552-7174	552-8919	391-3
Web: www.optimahealth.com						
Optima Neuroscience Inc						
13400 Progress Blvd	Alachua	FL	32615	352-371-8281		476
Web: www.optimaneuro.com						
Optima Telecom Inc						
4-20 Cachet Woods Court	Markham	ON	L6C3G1	905-477-0987		180
Web: www.optimatele.com						
Optimae LifeServices Inc						
301 W Burlington Ave	Fairfield	IA	52556	641-472-1684		363
TF: 800-735-2942 ■ *Web:* www.optimaelifeservices.com						
Optimal Care Health Service						
221 W Seventh St Apt 3	Wilmington	DE	19801	302-425-0900		260
Optimal Data Group Inc						
251 Laurier Ave W Ste 900	Ottawa	ON	K1P5J6	613-566-7080		180
Web: www.optimal.ca						
Optimal Electronics Corp						
13915 Burnet Rd Ste 312	Austin	TX	78728	512-372-3415		177
TF: 800-392-8766 ■ *Web:* www.optelco.com						
Optimal Engineering Systems						
6901 Woodley Ave	Van Nuys	CA	91406	818-222-9200		358
TF: 888-777-1826 ■ *Web:* oesincorp.com						
Optimal Hospice Care						
1675 Chester Ave Ste 401	Bakersfield	CA	93301	661-716-4000	716-4004	363
Web: www.optimalcares.com						
Optimal Networks Inc						
15201 Diamondback Dr Ste 220	Rockville	MD	20850	240-499-7900		809
Web: www.optnw.com						
Optimal Outsource 7 Rancho Cir	Lake Forest	CA	92630	949-916-3700		41
TF: 800-561-3357 ■ *Web:* optimaloutsource.com						
Optimal Satcom Inc						
11180 Sunrise Vly Dr Ste 200	Reston	VA	20191	703-657-8800		196
Web: optimalsatcom.com						
Optimal Strategix Group Inc						
Ste 118 140 Terry Dr	Newtown	PA	18940	215-867-1880		196
Web: www.optimalstrategix.com						
Optimetra Inc						
1710 Chapel Hills Dr	Colorado Springs	CO	80920	800-758-9710		225
TF: 800-758-9710 ■ *Web:* www.optimetra.com						
Optimist International						
4494 Lindell Blvd	Saint Louis	MO	63108	314-371-6000	371-6006	48-15
TF: 800-500-8130 ■ *Web:* www.optimist.org						
Optimization Group Inc						
320 S Main St Ste D	Ann Arbor	MI	48104	734-212-2044		7
Web: www.optimizationgroup.com						
Optimized Legal Solutions LLC						
970 W Valley Pkwy Ste 611	Escondido	CA	92025	760-933-9007		463
Optimized Process Designs Inc						
25610 Clay Rd	Katy	TX	77493	281-371-7500		261
Web: www.opd-inc.com						
Optimum Asset Management Inc						
425 De Maisonneuve Blvd W Ste 1620	Montreal	QC	H3A3G5	514-288-7545		528
Web: www.optimumgestion.com						
Optimum Card Solution LLC						
855 S Fiene Dr	Addison	IL	60101	630-458-0077		317
Web: optimumcard.com						
Optimum Computer Solutions Inc						
780 Westridge Rd	The Woodlands	TX	77380	281-364-0539		224
Web: www.ocscorp.com						
Optimum Engineering Solutions Inc						
Country Club View Dr Ste 1	Edwardsville	IL	62025	618-656-8600		256
Web: www.openso.com						
Optimum Health Institute						
6970 Central Ave	Lemon Grove	CA	91945	619-464-3346		706
TF: 800-993-4325 ■ *Web:* www.optimumhealth.org						
Optimum Lead Generation LLC						
12230 Forest Hill Blvd Ste 200	Wellington	FL	33414	561-227-1507		387
Optimum Logistic Solutions						
3540 Seven Bridges Dr Ste 300	Woodridge	IL	60517	630-350-0595	766-3479	631
TF: 800-356-0595 ■ *Web:* www.optimumlogistic.com						
Optimum Outsourcing LLC						
1300 Quail st #202	Newport Beach	CA	92660	949-650-7800		631
Web: www.optimumhr.net						
Optimum Resource Inc						
18 Hunter Rd	Hilton Head Island	SC	29926	843-689-8000	689-8008	178-3
Optimum Solutions Corp 170 Earle Ave	Lynbrook	NY	11563	516-247-5300		177
TF: 800-227-0672 ■ *Web:* www.oscworld.com						
Optimum System Products						
5061 Fwy Dr E	Columbus	OH	43229	614-885-4464		195
TF: 800-869-0632 ■ *Web:* www.optimumcompanies.com						
Optimum Talent Inc 25 York St Ste 1802	Toronto	ON	M5J2V5	416-364-2605		764
TF: 877-364-2605 ■ *Web:* www.optimumtalent.com						
Optimum Technologies Inc						
570 Joe Frank Harris Pkwy PO Box 1537	Cartersville	GA	30120	770-386-3470	382-9047	234
Web: www.otitech.com						
Optimum Window Manufacturing						
28 Canal St	Ellenville	NY	12428	845-647-1900		234
TF: 800-289-6784 ■ *Web:* www.optimumwindow.com						
OPTIMUS | SBR 30 Adelaide St E Ste 600	Toronto	ON	M5C3G8	416-649-6000		463
Web: optimussbr.com						
Optimus Corp 5727 S Lewis Ave Ste 600	Tulsa	OK	74105	918-491-9191		480
Web: www.optimus-tulsa.com						
Optimus Health Care Inc						
982 E Main St	Bridgeport	CT	06608	203-696-3260		353
Web: www.optimushealthcare.org						
Optimus Information Inc						
510-900 Howe St	Vancouver	BC	V6Z2M4	604-736-4600		631
Web: www.optimusinfo.com						
Optimus Solutions LLC						
22 Technology Park S	Norcross	GA	30092	770-447-1951		196
TF: 800-634-8633 ■ *Web:* www.softchoice.com						

Phone | Fax | Class

OptiNose US Inc
1010 Stony Hill Rd Ste 375 .... Yardley PA 19067 267-364-3500 475
Web: www.optinose.com

OPTIO LLC 390 Spaulding Ave SE .... Ada MI 49301 888-981-3282 196
TF: 888-981-3282 ■ *Web:* www.optiodata.com

Option Advisor
5151 Pfeiffer Rd Ste 250 .... Cincinnati OH 45242 513-589-3800 589-3810 531-9
TF: 800-448-2080 ■ *Web:* www.schaeffersresearch.com

Options Group Inc 121 E 18th St .... New York NY 10003 212-982-0900 193
Web: www.optionsgroup.com

OptionsXpress Inc
311 W Monroe Ste 1000 .... Chicago IL 60606 312-630-3300 629-5256 169
TF: 888-280-8020 ■ *Web:* www.optionsxpress.com

Optistreams 2491 Alluvial Ave Ste 68 .... Clovis CA 93611 559-440-6366 396
Web: optistreams.com

Optiwave Systems Inc 7 Capella Ct .... Ottawa ON K2E7X1 613-224-4700 179
TF: 866-576-6784 ■ *Web:* www.optiwave.com

Opto 22 Inc 43044 Business Park Dr .... Temecula CA 92590 951-695-3000 201
Web: www.opto22.com

OptoAtmospherics Inc
1777 Highland Dr Ste B .... Ann Arbor MI 48108 734-975-8777 407
Web: www.optoatmospherics.com

Optometrics Corp
8 Nemco Way Stony Brook Industrial Pk .... Ayer MA 01432 978-772-1700 544
Web: www.dynasil.com/company/optometrics

Optoplex Corp 3374-3390 Gateway Blvd .... Fremont CA 94538 510-490-9930 735
Web: www.optoplex.com

Optoro Inc 5001-A Forbes Blvd .... Lanham MD 20706 301-760-7003 393
Web: www.optoro.com

Optovue Inc 2800 Bayview Dr .... Fremont CA 94538 510-623-8868 543
Web: www.optovue.com

Opts Ideas 1 Gate Six Rd Ste B203 .... Sausalito CA 94965 415-339-2020 339-2025 232
Web: www.optsideas.com

OPT-Sciences Corp 1912 Bannard St .... Cinnaminson NJ 08077 856-829-2800 544
Web: www.optsciences.com

Opus 37 Prince Arthur Ave .... Toronto ON M5R1B2 416-921-3105 671
Web: www.opusrestaurant.com

Opus 21 Management Solutions
680 Commerce Dr Ste 160 .... St Paul MN 55125 651-905-0400 2
Web: www.opus21ms.com

Opus Agency 9000 SW Nimbus Ave .... Beaverton OR 97008 971-223-0777 195
TF: 888-887-8908 ■ *Web:* www.opuseventsagency.com

Opus Bank 19900 MacArthur Blvd 12th Fl .... Irvine CA 92612 949-250-9800 360-2
TF: 855-678-7226 ■ *Web:* www.opusbank.com

Opus Capital Management LLC
221 E Fourth St Ste 2700 .... Cincinnati OH 45202 513-621-6787 401
Web: www.opusinc.com

Opus Framing Ltd 3445 Cornett Rd .... Vancouver BC V5M2H3 604-435-9991 535
TF: 800-663-6953 ■ *Web:* opusartsupplies.com

Opus Group of Cos 10350 Bren Rd W .... Minnetonka MN 55343 952-656-4444 186
Web: www.opus-group.com

Opus Hotel 322 Davie St .... Vancouver BC V6B5Z6 866-642-6787 379
TF: 866-642-6787 ■ *Web:* vancouver.opushotel.com

Opus International Consultants (Canada) Ltd
210-889 Harbourside Dr .... North Vancouver BC V6E4E6 604-990-4800 256
Web: www.opusinternational.ca

Opus One 565 E Larned St .... Detroit MI 48226 313-961-7766 671
Web: www.opus-one.com

Opvantek Inc 28 S State St .... Newtown PA 18940 215-968-7790 463
Web: www.opvantek.com

OPW Engineered Systems 2726 Henkle Dr .... Lebanon OH 45036 513-932-9114 932-9845* 620
**Fax:* Cust Svc ■ *TF Cust Svc:* 800-547-9393 ■ *Web:* www.opwglobal.com/opw-es

OPW Fuel Management Systems
6900 Santa Fe Dr .... Hodgkins IL 60525 708-485-4200 485-4630* 201
**Fax:* Cust Svc ■ *TF:* 800-547-9393 ■ *Web:* www.opwglobal.com

Oquaga Creek State Park
5995 County Rt 20 .... Bainbridge NY 13733 607-467-4160 565
Web: www.parks.ny.gov/parks/27/details.aspx

Oracle Applications Users Group
3525 Piedmont Rd NE Bldg 5 Ste 300 .... Atlanta GA 30305 404-240-0897 177
Web: www.oaug.org

Oracle Capital LLC
1985 E River Rd Ste 111 .... Tucson AZ 85718 520-319-9958 668
Web: www.oraclecapital.com

Oracle Corp 500 Oracle Pkwy .... Redwood Shores CA 94065 650-506-7000 506-7200 178-1
NYSE: ORCL ■ *TF Sales:* 800-392-2999 ■ *Web:* www.oracle.com

Oracle Information Rights Management
500 Oracle Pkwy .... Redwood Shores CA 94065 650-506-7000 178-1
Web: www.oracle.com

Oracle Magazine
500 Oracle Pkwy .... Redwood Shores CA 94065 650-506-7000 633-2424* 457-7
**Fax:* Cust Svc ■ *TF:* 800-392-2999 ■ *Web:* www.oracle.com/oramag/index.html

Oracle Packaging 220 E Polo Rd .... Winston-Salem NC 27105 336-777-5000 777-5440 548
TF: 800-634-3645 ■ *Web:* www.oraclepackaging.com

Oracle Racing Inc 999 Marin St .... San Francisco CA 94124 415-990-7460 713
Web: oracle-team-usa.americascup.com

Oracle State Park 3820 Wildlife Dr .... Oracle AZ 85623 520-896-2425 565
Web: azstateparks.com

Oracular Inc 300 Ohio St .... Oshkosh WI 54902 920-303-0470 180
TF: 800-317-7917 ■ *Web:* www.oracular.com

Oradell Animal Hospital Inc
580 Winters Ave .... Paramus NJ 07652 201-262-0010 794
TF: 800-624-1883 ■ *Web:* www.oradell.com

Oral Arts Dental Laboratory Inc
2700 S Memorial Pkwy .... Huntsville AL 35801 256-533-6670 415
Web: www.oralartsdental.com

Oral BioTech 812 Water Ave NE .... Albany OR 97321 541-928-4445 475
TF: 800-665-3663 ■ *Web:* www.carifree.com

Oral Health America
410 N Michigan Ave Ste 352 .... Chicago IL 60611 312-836-9900 836-9986 48-17
TF: 800-523-3438 ■ *Web:* www.oralhealthamerica.org

Oral Roberts University
7777 S Lewis Ave .... Tulsa OK 74171 918-495-6161 495-6222* 166
**Fax:* Admissions ■ *TF:* 800-678-8876 ■ *Web:* www.oru.edu

Oral Roberts University Library
7777 S Lewis Ave .... Tulsa OK 74171 918-495-6723 434-6
TF: 800-678-8876 ■ *Web:* oru.edu/library

Oral-B Laboratories
600 Clipper Dr Ste 200 .... Belmont CA 94002 800-566-7252 475
TF: 800-566-7252 ■ *Web:* www.oralb.com

OralDNA Labs Inc
7400 Flying Cloud Dr Ste 150 .... Eden Prairie MN 55344 952-400-7772 415
Web: www.oraldna.com

Oran Safety Glass Inc
48 Industrial Pkwy .... Emporia VA 23847 434-336-1620 329

Orange & Rockland Utilities Inc
390 W Rte 59 .... Spring Valley NY 10977 877-434-4100 787
TF Cust Svc: 877-434-4100 ■ *Web:* www.oru.com

Orange Bakery Inc 17751 Cowan Ave .... Irvine CA 92614 949-863-1377 68
Web: www.orangebakery.com

Orange Belt Stages PO Box 949 .... Visalia CA 93279 559-733-4408 733-0538 760
TF: 800-266-7433 ■ *Web:* www.orangebelt.com

Orange Chamber of Commerce
1940 N Tustin St .... Orange CA 92865 714-538-3581 532-1675 139
TF: 888-676-1040 ■ *Web:* www.orangechamber.com

Orange City Area Health System
1000 Lincoln Cir SE .... Orange City IA 51041 712-737-4984 374-3
TF: 800-808-6264 ■ *Web:* www.ochealthsystem.org

Orange Coast Chrysler Jeep Dodge
2929 Harbor Blvd .... Costa Mesa CA 92626 714-549-8023 57
Web: www.ocauto.com

Orange Coast College
2701 Fairview Rd PO Box 5005 .... Costa Mesa CA 92628 714-432-0202 162
TF: 800-352-0050 ■ *Web:* orangecoastcollege.edu

Orange Coast Magazine
3701 Birch St Ste 100 .... Newport Beach CA 92660 949-862-1133 862-0133 457-22
TF: 800-397-8179 ■ *Web:* www.orangecoast.com

Orange Coast Memorial Medical Ctr (OCMMC)
9920 Talbert Ave .... Fountain Valley CA 92708 714-378-7000 229-5399 374-3
TF: 877-597-4777 ■ *Web:* www.memorialcare.org

Orange Coast Title Company Inc
640 N Tustin Ave Ste 106 .... Santa Ana CA 92705 714-558-2836 391-6
Web: www.octitle.com

Orange Correctional Ctr
2110 Clarence Walters Rd .... Hillsborough NC 27278 919-732-9301 213

Orange County 1055 N Main St .... Santa Ana CA 92701 802-685-4610 667-7522* 338
**Fax Area Code:* 714 ■ *Web:* www.vermontjudiciary.org

Orange County 255 Main St .... Goshen NY 10924 845-291-2700 291-2724 338
Web: www.co.orange.ny.us

Orange County
200 S Cameron St PO Box 8181 .... Hillsborough NC 27278 919-732-8181 338
Web: www.co.orange.nc.us

Orange County 801 West Div .... Orange TX 77632 409-882-7055 882-7012 338
Web: www.co.orange.tx.us

Orange County 200 Dailey Dr .... Orange VA 22960 540-661-4550 661-4599 338
TF: 866-803-8641 ■ *Web:* www.ocss-va.org

Orange County
201 S Rosalind Ave 5th Fl .... Orlando FL 32802 407-836-7350 836-5879 338
Web: www.orangecountyfl.net

Orange County 1 Ct St .... Paoli IN 47454 812-723-2411 723-0239 338
Web: www.co.orange.in.us

Orange County 12 Civic Ctr Plaza .... Santa Ana CA 92702 714-834-2500 834-2675 338
Web: ocgov.com

Orange County Business Council
2 Pk Plaza Ste 100 .... Irvine CA 92614 949-476-2242 476-9240 139
Web: www.ocbc.org

Orange County Business Journal (OCBJ)
18500 Von Karman Ave Ste 150 .... Irvine CA 92612 949-833-8373 833-8751 457-5
Web: www.ocbj.com

Orange County Chamber of Commerce
30 Scott's Corners Dr .... Montgomery NY 12549 845-457-9700 457-8799 139
Web: www.orangeny.com

Orange County Community College
115 S St .... Middletown NY 10940 845-344-6222 342-8662 162
TF: 800-233-5744 ■ *Web:* www.sunyorange.edu

Orange County Convention Ctr (OCCC)
9800 International Dr .... Orlando FL 32819 407-685-9800 685-9876 205
TF: 800-345-9845 ■ *Web:* www.occc.net

Orange County Industrial Plastics Inc
4811 E La Palma Ave .... Anaheim CA 92807 800-974-6247 630-6489* 603
**Fax Area Code:* 714 ■ *TF:* 800-974-6247 ■ *Web:* www.ocip.com

Orange County Library System
101 E Central Blvd .... Orlando FL 32801 407-835-7323 434-3

Orange County Museum of Art South Coast Plaza
850 San Clemente Dr 3rd Fl .... Newport Beach CA 92660 949-759-1122 759-5623 520
Web: www.ocma.net

Orange County Public Library
1501 E St Andrew Pl .... Santa Ana CA 92705 714-566-3000 434-3
Web: ocpl.org

Orange County Public Schools
445 W Amelia St .... Orlando FL 32801 407-317-3200 317-3392* 685
**Fax:* Hum Res ■ *TF:* 800-378-9264 ■ *Web:* www.ocps.net

Orange County Regional History Ctr
65 E Central Blvd .... Orlando FL 32801 407-836-8500 520
TF: 800-965-2030 ■ *Web:* www.thehistorycenter.org

Orange County Register
625 N Grand Ave .... Santa Ana CA 92701 714-796-7000 796-5052 532-2
TF: 877-469-7344 ■ *Web:* www.ocregister.com

Orange County Rural Electric Membership Corp
7133 N State Rd 337 PO Box 208 .... Orleans IN 47452 812-865-2229 865-2061 245
TF: 888-337-5900 ■ *Web:* www.myremc.coop

Orange County Transportation Authority
550 S Main St PO Box 14184 .... Orange CA 92863 714-560-6282 468
TF: 800-600-9191 ■ *Web:* www.octa.net

Orange County Zoo 1 Irvine Pk Rd .... Orange CA 92869 714-973-6847 823
Web: www.ocparks.com

Orange County's Credit Union
PO Box 11777 .... Santa Ana CA 92711 714-755-5900 219
TF: 888-354-6228 ■ *Web:* orangecountyscu.org

Orange Door Inc
370 San Bruno Ave W Ste E .... San Bruno CA 94066 650-952-1773 396
TF: 800-322-6962 ■ *Web:* www.orangedoorinc.com

Orange Fence & Supply Company Inc
205 Boston Post Rd .... Orange CT 06477 203-799-2437 200
Web: www.orangefence.com

				Phone	Fax	Class
Orange Julius of America 7505 Metro Blvd *TF:* 866-793-7582 ■ *Web:* www.dairyqueen.com	Minneapolis	MN	55439	952-830-0200		670
Orange Label Art & Advrtg 4000 MacArthur Blvd Ste 520 *Web:* www.orangelabeladvertising.com	Newport Beach	CA	92660	949-631-9900		4
Orange Lake Country Club Inc (OLCC) 8505 W Irlo Bronson Memorial Hwy *TF:* 800-877-6522 ■ *Web:* www.orangelake.com	Kissimmee	FL	34747	407-239-0000	239-5119	669
Orange Line Oil Company Inc 404 E Commercial St *TF:* 800-492-6864 ■ *Web:* www.orangelineoil.com	Pomona	CA	91767	909-623-0533		579
Orange Park Medical Ctr 2001 Kingsley Ave *Web:* www.orangeparkmedical.com	Orange Park	FL	32073	904-276-8500		374-3
Orange Public Library 348 Main St *Web:* www.orangepl.org	Orange	NJ	07050	973-673-0153	673-1847	434-3
Orange Public Library 407 E Chapmen Ave *Web:* www.cityoforange.org/library	Orange	CA	92866	714-288-2400	771-6126	434-3
Orange Regional Juvenile Detention Ctr 2800 S Bumby Ave *Web:* www.djj.state.fl.us	Orlando	FL	32806	407-897-2800	897-2856	412
Orange Regional Medical Ctr 60 Prospect Ave *TF:* 888-321-6762 ■ *Web:* www.ormc.org	Middletown	NY	10940	845-343-2424	333-1560	374-3
Arden Hill Campus 4 Harriman Dr *TF:* 800-633-4227 ■ *Web:* www.ormc.org	Goshen	NY	10924	845-333-1000		374-3
Orange Research Inc 140 Cascade Blvd *TF:* 800-989-5657 ■ *Web:* www.orangeresearch.com	Milford	CT	06460	203-877-5657		201
Orange Shipbuilding Co Inc 710 Market St *Web:* www.conradindustries.com	Orange	TX	77631	409-883-6666		698
Orange Street Food Farm 701 S Orange St *Web:* orangestreetfoodfarm.com	Missoula	MT	59801	406-543-3188		345
Orange Tree Employment Screening 7275 Ohms Ln *TF:* 800-886-4777 ■ *Web:* www.orangetreescreening.com	Minneapolis	MN	55439	952-941-9040	941-9041	635
Orange Tree Golf & Conference Resort 10601 N 56th St *Web:* shellhospitality.com/en/orange-tree-golf-resort	Scottsdale	AZ	85254	480-948-6100		669
Orange Water & Sewer Authority (Inc) 400 Jones Ferry Rd *Web:* www.owasa.org	Carrboro	NC	27510	919-968-4421	968-4464	787
Orangeburg Consolidated School District 5 578 Ellis Ave *Web:* www.ocsd5schools.org	Orangeburg	SC	29115	803-534-5454	533-7953	685
Orangeburg County 1406 Amelia St *Web:* www.orangeburgcounty.org	Orangeburg	SC	29118	803-533-6160	531-7256	338
Orangeburg County Chamber of Commerce 155 Riverside Dr SW PO Box 328 *TF:* 800-545-6153 ■ *Web:* www.orangeburgchamber.com	Orangeburg	SC	29116	803-534-6821	531-9435	139
Orangeburg County Library (OCL) 510 Louis St *TF:* 800-922-2594 ■ *Web:* www.orangeburgcounty.org	Orangeburg	SC	29115	803-531-4636		434-3
Orangeburg Pecan Company Inc 761 Russell St *TF:* 800-845-6970 ■ *Web:* www.uspecans.com	Orangeburg	SC	29115	800-845-6970		276
Orangeburg Public Library 20 Greenbush Rd *Web:* www.orangeburg-library.org	Orangeburg	NY	10962	845-359-2244		435
Orangeburg-Calhoun Technical College 3250 St Matthews Rd *Web:* www.octech.edu	Orangeburg	SC	29118	803-536-0311		162
Orangery, The 5412 Kingston Pk *Web:* www.orangeryknoxville.com	Knoxville	TN	37919	865-588-2964		671
Orangeseed Design Inc 901 N Third St Ste 305 *Web:* www.orangeseed.com	Minneapolis	MN	55401	612-252-9757		4
OrangeSoda Inc 732 E Utah Vly Dr *Web:* www.orangesoda.com	American Fork	UT	84003	801-610-2500		195
Orangevale Chamber of Commerce 9267 Greenback Ln Ste B-91 *TF:* 800-962-1106 ■ *Web:* www.orangevalechamber.com	Orangevale	CA	95662	916-988-0175	988-1049	139
Orasi Software Inc 114 TownPark Dr Ste 400 *Web:* www.orasi.com	Kennesaw	GA	30144	678-819-5300		177
OraSure Technologies Inc 220 E First St *NASDAQ: OSUR* ■ *TF:* 800-869-3538 ■ *Web:* www.orasure.com	Bethlehem	PA	18015	610-882-1820	882-1830	231
ORAU (ORAU) 130 Badger Ave PO Box 117 *Web:* www.orau.org	Oak Ridge	TN	37831	865-576-3146	241-2923	49-5
Orban Inc 8350 E Evans Rd Ste C-4 *Web:* www.orban.com	Scottsdale	AZ	85260	480-403-8300		246
ORBCOMM 22970 Indian Creek Dr Ste 300 *TF Cust Svc:* 800-672-2666 ■ *Web:* www.orbcomm.com	Sterling	VA	20166	703-433-6300	433-6380	681
ORBIS Corp 1055 Corporate Center Dr *TF:* 800-999-8683 ■ *Web:* www.orbiscorporation.com	Oconomowoc	WI	53066	262-560-5000	560-5841	199
Orbis Education Services Inc 11595 N Meridian Ste 400 *Web:* www.orbiseducation.com	Carmel	IN	46032	317-663-0260		242
ORBIS International Inc 520 Eigth Ave 11th Fl *TF:* 800-672-4787 ■ *Web:* www.orbis.org	New York	NY	10018	646-674-5500	674-5599	48-5
Orbit Design 2560 Sheridan Blvd Ste 4 *Web:* www.orbit-design.com	Denver	CO	80214	303-433-1616		195
Orbit International Corp 80 Cabot Ct *NASDAQ: ORBT* ■ *Web:* www.orbitintl.com	Hauppauge	NY	11788	631-435-8300	435-8458	529
Orbit Medical Inc 1701 Quincy Ave Ste 5 *TF:* 800-430-0539 ■ *Web:* www.orbitmedical.com	Naperville	IL	60540	801-713-2020		45
Orbit/FR Inc 506 Prudential Rd *OTC: ORFR* ■ *Web:* www.orbitfr.com	Horsham	PA	19044	215-674-5100	674-5108	647
Orbital Engineering Inc 1344 Fifth Ave *Web:* www.orbitalengr.com	Pittsburgh	PA	15219	412-261-9100	261-2308	261
OrbitCom Inc 1701 N Louise Dr *Web:* www.orbitcom.biz	Sioux Falls	SD	57107	605-977-6900		116
Orbitel Communications LLC 21116 N John Wayne Pkwy Ste B-9 *TF:* 800-998-8084 ■ *Web:* www.orbitelcom.com	Maricopa	AZ	85239	520-568-8890		387
ORC (Opinion Research Corp) 902 Carnegie Ctr Ste 220 *TF:* 800-444-4672 ■ *Web:* www.orcinternational.com	Princeton	NJ	08540	800-444-4672		466
ORC ProTel Inc 17233 Continental Dr *Web:* www.orcprotel.com	Lansing	IL	60438	708-418-0600		41
Orca Bay Seafoods Inc 900 Powell Ave SW *Web:* orcabayseafoods.com	Renton	WA	98057	425-204-9100		296-14
Orca Bay Sports & Entertainment 800 Griffiths Way *Web:* canucks.nhl.com	Vancouver	BC	V6B6G1	604-899-7400	899-7401	360-3
Orca Systems Inc 3990 Old Town Ave Ste C307 *Web:* www.orcasystems.com	San Diego	CA	92110	858-679-9175		668
Orcas International Inc 9 Lenel Rd *Web:* orcasnaturals.com	Landing	NJ	07850	973-448-2801		345
Orcas Island Library District 500 Rose St *TF:* 800-234-5078 ■ *Web:* orcaslibrary.org	East Sound	WA	98245	360-376-4985		435
Orcas Power & Light Co-op 183 Mt Baker Rd *Web:* www.opalco.com	Eastsound	WA	98245	360-376-3500		245
Orchard Beach State Park 2064 N Lakeshore Rd *Web:* www.michigandnr.com	Manistee	MI	49660	231-723-7422		565
Orchard Enterprises Inc 23 E Fourth St 3rd Fl *Web:* www.theorchard.com	New York	NY	10003	212-201-9280	201-9203	523
Orchard Garden Hotel 466 Bush St *TF:* 888-717-2881 ■ *Web:* www.theorchardgardenhotel.com	San Francisco	CA	94108	415-399-9807	393-9917	379
Orchard Hiltz & McCliment Inc (OHM) 34000 Plymouth Rd *TF:* 888-522-6711 ■ *Web:* www.ohm-advisors.com	Livonia	MI	48150	734-522-6711	522-6427	261
Orchard Hotel 665 Bush St *Web:* www.theorchardhotel.com	San Francisco	CA	94108	415-362-8878	362-8088	379
Orchard Machinery Corp 2700 Colusa Hwy *Web:* www.shakermaker.com	Yuba City	CA	95993	530-673-2822	673-0296	273
Orchard Manor Inc 600 Bates Rd *TF:* 800-388-8255 ■ *Web:* orchardmanor.com	Medina	NY	14103	585-798-4100		371
Orchard Park Chamber of Commerce 4211 N Buffalo St Ste 14 *TF:* 800-490-6606 ■ *Web:* orchardparkchamber.org	Orchard Park	NY	14127	716-662-3366	662-5946	139
Orchard Petroleum Inc 3585 Maple St Ste 284 *Web:* www.orchardpetroleum.com	Ventura	CA	93003	805-644-8555		540
Orchard School 615 W 64th St *Web:* www.orchard.org	Indianapolis	IN	46260	317-251-9253		623
Orchard Software Corp 701 Congressional Blvd Ste 360 *TF:* 800-856-1948 ■ *Web:* www.orchardsoft.com	Carmel	IN	46032	317-573-2633	573-2633	177
Orchard Supply Hardware 6450 Via del Oro *TF:* 800-952-5210 ■ *Web:* www.osh.com	San Jose	CA	95119	408-281-3500		364
Orchard View Inc 4055 Skyline Rd *Web:* www.orchardviewfarms.com	The Dalles	OR	97058	541-298-4496	298-1808	315-3
Orchards Hotel, The 222 Adams Rd *Web:* www.orchardshotel.com	Williamstown	MA	01267	413-458-9611	458-3273	379
Orchards Inn of Sedona 254 Hwy N 89 A **Fax Area Code:* 928 ■ *TF:* 888-954-4442 ■ *Web:* www.orchardsinn.com	Sedona	AZ	86336	855-474-7719	282-5710*	379
Orchestra Hall 1111 Nicollet Mall *TF:* 800-292-4141 ■ *Web:* www.minnesotaorchestra.org	Minneapolis	MN	55403	612-371-5600		572
Orchestra Iowa 119 Third Ave SE *Web:* artsiowa.com/orchestra	Cedar Rapids	IA	52401	319-366-8206		573-3
Orchestra New England PO Box 200123 *TF:* 800-595-4849 ■ *Web:* orchestranewengland.org	New Haven	CT	06520	203-777-4690		573-3
Orchestre Metropolitain du Grand Montreal 486 St Catherine St W Ste 401 *Web:* www.orchestremetropolitain.com	Montreal	QC	H3B1A6	514-598-0870		573-3
Orchestre Symphonique de Montreal 260 de Maisonneuve Blvd W 2nd Fl *TF:* 888-842-9951 ■ *Web:* www.osm.ca	Montreal	QC	H2X1Y9	514-842-9951	842-0720	573-3
Orchestro Ste 350 1760 Old Meadow Rd *Web:* orchestro.com	Mclean	VA	22102	703-640-3300		177
Orchid International Group Inc 94 Belinda Pkwy *Web:* www.orchidinternational.com	Mount Juliet	TN	37122	615-754-6600		483
Orchid Stealth Orthopedic Solutions 1489 Cedar St *Web:* www.orchid-orthopedics.com/stealth	Holt	MI	48842	517-694-2300		247
Orchid Suites Inc 1309 Emerson St NW	Washington	DC	20011	202-265-1671		225
Orchids Paper Products Co 4826 Hunt St *NYSE: TIS* ■ *Web:* www.orchidspaper.com	Pryor	OK	74361	918-825-0616		558
Orco Block Co Inc 11100 Beach Blvd *TF:* 800-366-7877 ■ *Web:* www.orco.com	Stanton	CA	90680	714-527-2239	895-4021	183
Orcon Corp 1570 Atlantic St *TF General:* 800-227-0505 ■ *Web:* www.orcon.com	Union City	CA	94587	510-489-8100	489-6436	600
Orcutt Union School District 500 Dyer St *Web:* www.orcutt-schools.net	Orcutt	CA	93455	805-938-8900	938-8919	780
Orcutt/Winslow 3003 N Central Ave *TF:* 800-331-5842 ■ *Web:* www.owp.com	Phoenix	AZ	85012	602-257-1764	257-9029	186
Order Sons of Italy in America (OSIA) 219 E St NE *TF:* 800-552-6742 ■ *Web:* www.osia.org	Washington	DC	20002	202-547-2900	546-8168	48-14
Ordnance Technologies (NA) Inc 7380 Sand Lake Rd Ste 360	Orlando	FL	32819	407-354-3827		21

	City	State	Zip	Phone	Fax	Class
Ordway Ctr for the Performing Arts 345 Washington St	Saint Paul	MN	55102	651-282-3000		572
TF: 800-767-9660 ■ *Web:* www.ordway.org						
Oreck Corp 1400 Salem Rd	Cookeville	TN	38506	800-289-5888		788
TF: 800-289-5888 ■ *Web:* www.oreck.com						
Oregon						
Arts Commission 775 Summer St NE Ste 200	Salem	OR	97301	503-986-0082	986-0260	339-38
Web: www.oregonartscommission.org						
Attorney General 1162 Ct St NE Justice Bldg	Salem	OR	97301	503-378-4400	378-4017	339-38
Web: www.doj.state.or.us						
Child Support Div 1162 Ct St NE Ste 300	Salem	OR	97301	503-947-4388	947-2578	339-38
Web: oregonchildsupport.gov						
Children Adults & Families Div (CAF) 500 Summer St NE E62	Salem	OR	97301	503-945-5600	373-7032	339-38
Web: www.oregon.gov						
Community Colleges & Workforce Development Dept 255 Capitol St NE	Salem	OR	97310	503-378-8648		339-38
Web: www.worksourceoregon.org						
Corrections Dept (DOC) 2575 Ctr St NE	Salem	OR	97301	503-945-9090	373-1173	339-38
Web: www.oregon.gov/DOC						
Crime Victims Service Div 1162 Ct St NE	Salem	OR	97301	503-378-4400	378-5738	339-38
TF: 877-877-9392 ■ *Web:* www.doj.state.or.us/crimev/welcome1.htm						
Dept of Consumer & Business Services 350 Winter St NE PO Box 14480	Salem	OR	97309	503-378-4100	378-6444	339-38
Web: www.oregon.gov						
Dept of Human Services 500 Summer St NE	Salem	OR	97301	503-947-5448	378-2897	339-38
Web: www.oregon.gov/DHS						
Dept of Transportation 355 Capitol St NE Ste 135 Rm 222	Salem	OR	97301	503-986-4000		339-38
TF: 888-275-6368 ■ *Web:* www.oregon.gov/ODOT						
Driver & Motor Vehicle Services Div 1905 Lana Ave NE	Salem	OR	97314	503-945-5000		339-38
Web: www.oregon.gov/ODOT/DMV						
Education Dept 255 Capitol St NE	Salem	OR	97310	503-947-5600	378-5156	339-38
Emergency Management 3225 State St Rm 115	Salem	OR	97301	503-378-2911	373-7933	339-38
Web: www.oregon.gov						
Energy Dept 550 Capitol St NE	Salem	OR	97301	503-378-4040	373-7806	339-38
TF: 800-221-8035 ■ *Web:* oregon.gov						
Environmental Quality Dept 700 NE Multnomah St	Portland	OR	97204	503-229-5696	229-6124	339-38
TF: 800-452-4011 ■ *Web:* www.oregon.gov						
Finance & Corporate Securities Div 350 Winter St NE Rm 410 PO Box 14480	Salem	OR	97309	503-378-4140	947-7862	339-38
TF: 866-814-9710 ■ *Web:* www.oregon.gov						
Financial Fraud/Consumer Protection Section 1162 Ct St NE	Salem	OR	97301	503-378-4400	373-7067	339-38
TF: 877-877-9392 ■ *Web:* www.doj.state.or.us						
Fish & Wildlife Dept (ODFW) 4034 Fairview Industrial Dr SE	Salem	OR	97302	503-947-6000	947-6042	339-38
TF: 800-720-6339 ■ *Web:* www.dfw.state.or.us						
Forestry Dept 2600 State St	Salem	OR	97310	503-945-7200	945-7212	339-38
Web: www.oregon.gov						
Government Standards & Practices Commission 3218 Pringle Rd SE Ste 220	Salem	OR	97302	503-378-5105	373-1456	265
Web: www.oregon.gov						
Governor 900 Ct St NE Ste 160 State Capitol Bldg	Salem	OR	97301	503-378-4582	378-6827	339-30
Web: www.oregon.gov/gov						
Housing & Community Services Dept N Mall Office Bldg 725 Summer St NE Ste B	Salem	OR	97301	503-986-2000	986-2020	339-38
Web: www.oregon.gov/OHCS						
Insurance Div 350 Winter St NE Rm 410 Rm 440	Salem	OR	97309	503-378-4140	947-7862	339-38
TF: 866-814-9710 ■ *Web:* dfr.oregon.gov						
Labor & Industries Bureau 800 NE Oregon St Ste 1045	Portland	OR	97232	971-673-0761	673-0762	339-38
Web: oregon.gov/boli/pages/index.aspx						
Land Conservation & Development Dept 635 Capitol St NE Ste 150	Salem	OR	97301	503-373-0050	378-5518	339-38
TF: 800-735-2900 ■ *Web:* www.oregon.gov						
Legislative Assembly 900 Ct St NE	Salem	OR	97301	503-986-1388		339-38
TF: 800-332-2313 ■ *Web:* www.leg.state.or.us						
Lottery 500 Airport Rd SE	Salem	OR	97301	503-540-1000	540-1001	452
Web: oregonlottery.org						
Measurement Standards Div 635 Capitol St NE Ste 100	Salem	OR	97301	503-986-4670		339-38
Web: www.oregon.gov						
Military Dept 1776 Militia Way SE PO Box 14350	Salem	OR	97309	503-584-3980	584-3987	339-38
TF: 800-452-7500 ■ *Web:* www.oregon.gov						
Oregon Business Development Dept (OBDD) 775 Summer St NE Ste 200	Salem	OR	97301	503-986-0123	581-5115	339-38
TF General: 800-735-2900 ■ *Web:* www.oregon4biz.com						
Parks & Recreation Dept (OPRD) 725 Summer St NE Ste C	Salem	OR	97301	503-986-0707	986-0794	339-38
TF: 800-551-6949 ■ *Web:* www.oregon.gov/OPRD						
Parole & Post-Prison Supervision Board 2575 Ctr St NE Ste 100	Salem	OR	97301	503-945-0900	373-7558	339-38
Web: www.oregon.gov/BOPPPS						
Public Health Div 800 NE Oregon St Ste 465-B	Portland	OR	97232	971-673-1363	673-1309	339-38
Web: public.health.oregon.gov/PHD						
Publication & Distribution Services 900 Ct St NE Rm S 101	Salem	OR	97310	503-986-1243		433
Web: Www.oregonlegislature.gov						
Racing Commission 800 NE Oregon St Ste 310	Portland	OR	97232	971-673-0207	673-0213	339-38
Web: www.oregon.gov						
Revenue Dept 955 Ctr St NE	Salem	OR	97301	503-378-4988	945-8738	339-38
TF: 800-356-4222 ■ *Web:* www.oregon.gov						
Secretary of State 136 State Capitol	Salem	OR	97310	503-986-1523	986-1616	339-38
Web: sos.oregon.gov						
State Court Administrator Office 1163 State St	Salem	OR	97301	503-986-5500	986-5503	339-38
Web: courts.oregon.gov/ojd/osca						
State Police Dept 3565 Trelstad Ave SE	Salem	OR	97317	503-378-3720	378-8282	339-38
Web: www.oregon.gov						
Student Assistance Commission 1500 Valley River Dr Ste 100	Eugene	OR	97401	541-687-7400	687-7414	725
TF: 800-452-8807 ■ *Web:* oregonstudentaid.gov						
Supreme Court 1163 State St	Salem	OR	97301	503-986-5555	986-5730	339-38
Web: courts.oregon.gov						
Treasurer 350 Winter St NE Ste 100	Salem	OR	97301	503-378-4000		339-38
Web: www.oregon.gov						
Veterans' Affairs Dept 700 Summer St NE	Salem	OR	97301	503-373-2000	373-2362	339-38
TF: 800-828-8801 ■ *Web:* www.oregon.gov						
Vital Records Unit 800 NE Oregon St Ste 225 PO Box 14050	Portland	OR	97232	971-673-1190	673-1201	339-38
Web: public.health.oregon.gov						
Vocational Rehabilitation Services Office (OVRS) 700 Summer St NE E-87	Salem	OR	97103	800-692-9666	947-5010*	339-38
*Fax Area Code: 503 ■ TF: 800-692-9666 ■ *Web:* www.oregon.gov						
Workers" Compensation Board 2601 SE 25th St Ste 150	Salem	OR	97302	503-378-3308	373-1684	339-38
Web: www.cbs.state.or.us/wcb						
Oregon Advanced Imaging LLC 881 Ohare Pkwy	Medford	OR	97504	541-608-0350		418
Web: www.oaimaging.com						
Oregon Aero Inc 34020 Skyway Dr	Scappoose	OR	97056	503-543-7399		529
TF: 800-888-6910 ■ *Web:* www.oregonaero.com						
Oregon Air & Space Museum 90377 Boeing Dr	Eugene	OR	97402	541-461-1101	461-1101	520
Web: www.oasmuseum.com						
Oregon Assn of Realtors 2110 Mission St SE	Salem	OR	97308	503-362-3645	362-9615	656
TF: 800-252-9115 ■ *Web:* oregonrealtors.org						
Oregon Ballet Theatre 818 SE Sixth Ave	Portland	OR	97214	503-227-0977	227-4186	573-1
Web: www.obt.org						
Oregon Bankers Assn 777 13th St SE Ste 130	Salem	OR	97301	503-581-3522		138
TF: 800-677-1116 ■ *Web:* oregonbankers.com						
Oregon Canadian Forest Products Inc 31950 Comml St NW	North Plains	OR	97133	503-647-5011		683
Web: www.ocfp.com						
Oregon Catholic Press (OCP) 5536 NE Hassalo St	Portland	OR	97213	503-281-1191	462-7329*	637-3
*Fax Area Code: 800 ■ TF: 877-596-1653 ■ *Web:* www.ocp.org						
Oregon Caves National Monument 19000 Caves Hwy	Cave Junction	OR	97523	541-592-2100	592-3981	564
TF: 877-245-9022 ■ *Web:* www.nps.gov/orca						
Oregon Cherry Growers Inc 1520 Woodrow NE	Salem	OR	97301	503-364-8421		315-3
TF: 800-367-2536 ■ *Web:* oregoncherry.com						
Oregon City Chamber of Commerce 1201 Washington St	Oregon City	OR	97045	503-656-1619	656-2274	139
TF: 800-422-4012 ■ *Web:* www.oregoncity.org						
Oregon City Public Library 606 John Adams	Oregon City	OR	97045	503-657-8269		434-3
Web: orcity.org						
Oregon City School District 62 PO Box 2110	Oregon City	OR	97045	503-785-8000		685
Web: ocsd62.org						
Oregon Coast Aquarium 2820 SE Ferry Slip Rd	Newport	OR	97365	541-867-3474	867-6846	40
TF: 800-452-7888 ■ *Web:* www.aquarium.org						
Oregon Coast Magazine 88906 Highway 101 N Ste 2B	Florence	OR	97439	541-997-8401	997-1124	457-22
TF: 800-348-8401 ■ *Web:* www.oregoncoastmagazine.com						
Oregon College of Art & Craft 8245 SW Barnes Rd	Portland	OR	97225	503-297-5544		166
TF: 800-390-0632 ■ *Web:* www.ocac.edu						
Oregon Community Foundation, The 1221 SW Yamhill St Ste 100	Portland	OR	97205	503-227-6846	274-7771	303
Web: www.oregoncf.org						
Oregon Connection 1125 S First St	Coos Bay	OR	97420	541-267-7804		327
TF: 800-255-5318 ■ *Web:* www.oregonconnection.com						
Oregon Convention Ctr 777 NE Martin Luther King Jr Blvd	Portland	OR	97232	503-235-7575	235-7417	205
TF: 800-791-2250 ■ *Web:* www.oregoncc.org						
Oregon County PO Box 324	Alton	MO	65606	417-778-7475		338
Oregon Democratic Party 232 NE Ninth Ave	Portland	OR	97232	503-224-8200	224-5335	616-1
Web: www.dpo.org						
Oregon Dental Assn PO Box 3710	Wilsonville	OR	97070	503-218-2010	218-2009	227
TF: 800-452-5628 ■ *Web:* www.oregondental.org						
Oregon Education Magazine (OEA) 6900 SW Atlanta St Bldg 1	Portland	OR	97223	503-684-3300	684-8063	457-8
TF: 800-858-5505 ■ *Web:* www.oregoned.org						
Oregon Electric Station 27 E Fifth Ave	Eugene	OR	97401	541-485-4444		671
Web: oesrestaurant.com						
Oregon Employment Dept 875 Union St NE	Salem	OR	97311	503-451-2400	947-1472	259
TF: 877-345-3484 ■ *Web:* www.oregon.gov						
Oregon Environmental Council 222 NW Davis St Ste 309	Portland	OR	97209	503-222-1963		804
TF: 800-332-2313 ■ *Web:* www.oeconline.org						
Oregon Episcopal School 6300 SW Nicol Rd	Portland	OR	97223	503-246-7771		622
Web: www.oes.edu						
Oregon Equipment Service Corp 180 NE Irving Ave	Bend	OR	97701	541-388-2235		189-10
Web: oregonequipmentservice.com						
Oregon Food Bank 7900 NE 33rd Dr	Portland	OR	97211	503-282-0555	282-0922	48-5
TF: 800-777-7427 ■ *Web:* www.oregonfoodbank.org						
Oregon Freeze Dry Inc 525 25th Ave SW	Albany	OR	97322	541-926-6001		296-18
Web: www.ofd.com						
Oregon Garden, The 879 W Main St PO Box 155	Silverton	OR	97381	503-874-8100	339-2996	97
TF: 877-674-2733 ■ *Web:* www.oregongarden.org						
Oregon Health & Science University						
Bone Marrow Transplant Program (OHSU) 3181 SW Sam Jackson Pk Rd	Portland	OR	97239	503-494-1617	494-7086	769
TF: 800-222-1222 ■ *Web:* www.ohsu.edu						
Library 3181 SW Sam Jackson Pk Rd	Portland	OR	97239	503-494-3460	494-3322	434-1
TF: 800-328-2422 ■ *Web:* www.ohsu.edu/xd/education/library						

Name / Address	City	State	ZIP	Phone	Fax	Class
School of Medicine						
3181 SW Sam Jackson Pk Rd L-109	Portland	OR	97239	503-494-7800	494-4629	167-2
TF: 800-775-5460 ■ *Web:* www.ohsu.edu						
Oregon Health & Science University Hospital						
3181 SW Sam Jackson Pk Rd	Portland	OR	97239	503-494-8311	494-3400	166
TF: 800-292-4466 ■ *Web:* www.ohsu.edu						
Oregon Historical Society						
1200 SW Pk Ave	Portland	OR	97205	503-222-1741	221-2035	520
Web: www.ohs.org						
Oregon Institute of Technology						
3201 Campus Dr	Klamath Falls	OR	97601	541-885-1150	885-1024*	166
**Fax:* Admissions ■ *TF:* 800-422-2017 ■ *Web:* www.oit.edu						
Oregon International Port of Coos Bay						
115 Hall Ave	Coos Bay	OR	97420	541-266-7245	266-7244	618
Web: www.portofcoosbay.com						
Oregon Lions Sight & Hearing Foundation						
1010 NW 22nd Ave Ste 144	Portland	OR	97210	503-413-7399		269
TF: 800-635-4667 ■ *Web:* www.olshf.org						
Oregon Maritime Ctr & Museum						
115 SW Ash St Ste 400-C	Portland	OR	97204	503-224-7724		520
Web: www.oregonmaritimemuseum.org						
Oregon Medical Assn (OMA)						
11740 SW 68th Pkwy Ste 100	Portland	OR	97223	503-619-8000	619-0609	474
TF: 877-605-3229 ■ *Web:* www.theoma.org						
Oregon Museum of Science & Industry						
1945 SE Water Ave	Portland	OR	97214	503-797-4000	797-4500	520
TF: 800-955-6674 ■ *Web:* www.omsi.edu						
Oregon Mutual Insurance Co						
PO Box 808	McMinnville	OR	97128	503-472-2141	565-3846	391-4
TF: 800-888-2141 ■ *Web:* www.ormutual.com						
Oregon National Primate Research Ctr (ONPRC)						
3181 SW Sam Jackson Pk Rd	Portland	OR	97239	503-494-8311		668
Web: www.ohsu.edu						
Oregon Nurses Assn (ONA)						
18765 SW Boones Ferry Rd	Tualatin	OR	97062	503-293-0011	293-0013	533
TF: 800-634-3552 ■ *Web:* www.oregonrn.org						
Oregon Potato Co PO Box 3110	Pasco	WA	99302	509-545-4545		296-18
TF: 800-336-6311 ■ *Web:* www.oregonpotato.com						
Oregon Primary Care Association						
310 SW Fourth Ave Ste 200	Portland	OR	97204	503-228-8852		138
TF: 800-735-2900 ■ *Web:* www.orpca.org						
Oregon Public Broadcasting Inc (OPB)						
7140 SW Macadam Ave	Portland	OR	97219	503-244-9900		632
TF: 800-241-8123 ■ *Web:* www.opb.org						
Oregon Recreation Dept 5330 Seaman Rd	Oregon	OH	43616	419-698-7146		706
Web: www.oregonohio.org						
Oregon Scientific Inc						
10778 SW Manhasset Dr	Tualatin	OR	97062	503-783-5100	691-6208	38
Web: global.oregonscientific.com						
Oregon Screw Machine Products Inc						
9291 SE 64th Ave	Portland	OR	97206	503-774-2750		488
Web: www.osmpi.com						
Oregon Shakespeare Festival						
15 S Pioneer St	Ashland	OR	97520	541-482-2111		749
TF: 800-219-8161 ■ *Web:* www.osfashland.org						
Oregon Society of CPAs						
10206 SW Laurel St	Beaverton	OR	97005	503-641-7200		533
TF: 800-255-1470 ■ *Web:* www.orcpa.org						
Oregon State Bar Assn						
16037 SW Upper Boones Ferry Rd	Tigard	OR	97224	503-620-0222	684-1366	72
TF: 800-452-8260 ■ *Web:* www.osbar.org						
Oregon State Bar Bulletin, The						
16037 SW Upper Boones Ferry Rd PO Box 231935	Tigard	OR	97281	503-620-0222	684-1366	457-15
TF: 800-452-8260 ■						
Web: www.osbar.org/publications/bulletin/bulletin.html						
Oregon State Correctional Institution						
3405 Deer Pk Dr SE	Salem	OR	97310	503-373-0101	378-8919	213
Web: www.oregon.gov/doc/ops/prison/pages/osci.aspx						
Oregon State Fair & Expo Ctr						
2330 17th St NE	Salem	OR	97301	503-947-3247	947-3206	205
TF: 800-833-0011 ■ *Web:* oregonstatefair.org						
Oregon State Hospital 2600 Ctr St NE	Salem	OR	97301	503-945-2800	945-2807	374-5
TF: 800-544-7078 ■ *Web:* oregon.gov						
Oregon State Library						
250 Winter NE State Library Bldg	Salem	OR	97301	503-378-4243	588-7119	434-5
Web: www.oregon.gov/osl						
Oregon State Penitentiary 2605 State St	Salem	OR	97301	503-378-2453	378-3897	213
Web: oregon.gov						
Oregon State Pharmacy Assn (OSPA)						
147 SE 102nd Ave	Portland	OR	97216	503-582-9055	253-9172	585
Web: www.oregonpharmacy.org						
Oregon State Public Interest Research Group (OSPIRG)						
1536 SE 11th Ave	Portland	OR	97214	503-231-4181		633
Web: www.ospirg.org						
Oregon State University						
104 Kerr Admin Bldg	Corvallis	OR	97331	541-737-4411	737-2482	166
TF: 800-291-4192 ■ *Web:* www.oregonstate.edu						
Oregon State University Press						
1500 Jefferson St	Corvallis	OR	97331	541-737-3166	737-3170	637-4
TF Orders: 800-426-3797 ■ *Web:* www.oregonstate.edu						
Oregon State University Valley Library						
121 Vly Library	Corvallis	OR	97331	541-737-3331	737-3453*	434-6
**Fax:* Admin ■ *Web:* osulibrary.oregonstate.edu						
Oregon Symphony Orchestra						
921 SW Washington St Ste 200	Portland	OR	97205	503-228-4294	228-4150	573-3
TF: 800-228-7343 ■ *Web:* www.orsymphony.org						
Oregon Trail Electric ConsumersCo-op Inc (OTEC)						
4005 23rd St PO Box 226	Baker City	OR	97814	541-523-3616		245
Web: www.otecc.com						
Oregon Veterans' Home						
700 Veterans Dr	The Dalles	OR	97058	541-296-7190	296-7862	793
TF: 800-846-8460 ■ *Web:* oregon.gov						
Oregon Veterinary Medical Assn						
1880 Lancaster Dr NE Ste 118	Salem	OR	97305	503-399-0311	363-4218	795
TF: 800-235-3502 ■ *Web:* www.oregonvma.org						
Oregon Youth Authority Riverbend (OYA)						
58231 Oregon Hwy 244	La Grande	OR	97850	541-663-8801	663-9181	412
Web: www.oregon.gov						
Oregon Zoo 4001 SW Canyon Rd	Portland	OR	97221	503-226-1561		823
Web: www.oregonzoo.org						
Oregon-California Trails Assn						
524 S Osage St PO Box 1019	Independence	MO	64051	816-252-2276	836-0989	48-23
TF: 888-811-6282 ■ *Web:* www.octa-trails.org						
Oregonian 1320 SW Broadway	Portland	OR	97201	503-221-8100		532-2
TF News Rm: 800-723-3638 ■ *Web:* www.oregonlive.com						
Orelube Corp, The 20 Sawgrass Dr	Bellport	NY	11713	631-205-9700	205-9797	541
TF: 800-645-9124 ■ *Web:* www.orelube.com						
Orem Public Library 58 N State St	Orem	UT	84057	801-229-7050		434-3
Web: lib.orem.org						
Orem Rehabilitation & Nursing Center						
575 E 1400 S	Orem	UT	84097	801-225-4741		371
Web: www.oremrehab.com						
Oren Dunn City Museum						
689 Rutherford Rd PO Box 2674	Tupelo	MS	38801	662-841-6438		520
Web: www.tupeloms.gov/oren-dunn-city-museum						
Oren Elliott Products Inc						
128 W Vine St	Edgerton	OH	43517	419-298-2306	298-3545	253
Web: www.orenelliottproducts.com						
Orenco Systems Inc 814 Airway Ave	Sutherlin	OR	97479	541-459-4449		427
Web: www.orenco.com						
Orfalea Family Foundation						
1283 Coast Village Cir Ste 2	Santa Barbara	CA	93108	805-565-7550		305
Web: www.orfaleafoundation.org						
Orfila Vineyards & Winery						
13455 San Pasqual Rd	Escondido	CA	92025	760-738-6500		50-7
TF: 800-584-8162 ■ *Web:* www.orfila.com						
Orgain Bell & Tucker LLP						
470 Orleans St	Beaumont	TX	77704	409-838-6412		428
Web: www.obt.com						
Orgain Building Supply Co						
65 Commerce St	Clarksville	TN	37040	931-647-1567		191-3
Web: www.orgainbuilding.com						
Organ Recovery Systems Inc						
1 Pierce Pl Ste 475W	Itasca	IL	60143	847-824-2600		475
TF: 800-872-5652 ■ *Web:* www.organ-recovery.com						
Organ Supply Industries Inc						
2320 W 50th St	Erie	PA	16506	814-835-2244	838-0349	527
TF: 800-458-0289 ■ *Web:* www.organsupply.com						
Organ Transport Systems Inc						
6170 Research Rd Ste 103	Frisco	TX	75034	972-987-1312		476
TF: 800-860-2773 ■ *Web:* www.organtransportsystems.com						
Organic Avenue LLC						
149 Fifth Ave 5th FL	New York	NY	10010	212-358-0500	202-7623	345
Web: www.organicavenue.com						
Organic By Nature						
1542 Seabright Ave	Long Beach	CA	90813	562-901-0177		583
Web: www.organicbynatureinc.com						
Organic Inc						
600 California St 8th Fl	San Francisco	CA	94108	415-581-5300		7
Web: www.organic.com						
Organic Milling Co 505 W Allen Ave	San Dimas	CA	91773	909-599-0961	599-5180	296-4
TF: 800-638-8686 ■ *Web:* www.organicmilling.com/contact.html						
Organic Products Trading Compa						
2908 NW 93rd St	Vancouver	WA	98665	360-573-4433		805
Web: www.opitampa.com						
Organic Valley Family of Farms						
1 Organic Way	LaFarge	WI	54639	888-444-6455		297-7
TF: 888-444-6455 ■ *Web:* www.organicvalley.coop						
Organization for International Investment (OFII)						
1225 19th St NW Ste 501	Washington	DC	20036	202-659-1903	659-2293	49-12
Web: www.ofii.org						
Organization for Tropical Studies (OTS)						
410 Swift Ave	Durham	NC	27705	919-684-5774	684-5661	49-5
Web: www.ots.ac.cr						
Organization Management Group						
638 Independence Pkwy Ste 100	Chesapeake	VA	23320	757-473-8701	473-9897	47
Web: www.managegroup.com						
Organization of American Historians (OAH)						
112 N Bryan Ave	Bloomington	IN	47408	812-855-7311	855-0696	49-5
TF: 888-737-7006 ■ *Web:* www.oah.org						
Organization of American States (OAS)						
1889 F St NW	Washington	DC	20006	202-458-3000	458-3967	48-7
TF: 888-442-4887 ■ *Web:* www.oas.org						
Organization of Chinese Americans (OCA)						
1322 18th St NW	Washington	DC	20036	202-223-5500	296-0540	48-14
TF: 800-584-7336 ■ *Web:* www.ocanational.org						
Organizational Dynamics Inc						
790 Boston Rd Ste 201	Billerica	MA	01821	978-671-5454	671-5005	194
TF: 800-634-4636 ■ *Web:* www.orgdynamics.com						
Organo Gold International Inc						
5505 hovander rd	Ferndale	WA	98248	877-674-2661		463
TF: 877-674-2661 ■ *Web:* www.organogold.com						
Organogenesis Inc 150 Dan Rd	Canton	MA	02021	781-575-0775		85
Web: www.organogenesis.com						
Orgill Inc 3742 Tyndale Dr	Memphis	TN	38125	901-754-8850	752-8989	351
TF: 800-347-2860 ■ *Web:* www.orgill.com						
Orgill Singer						
8360 W Sahara Ave Ste 110	Las Vegas	NV	89117	702-796-9100		48-20
TF: 800-745-3065 ■ *Web:* www.orgillsinger.com						
ORI Services Corp						
4565 Ruffner St Ste 201	San Diego	CA	92111	858-576-4422		261
Web: www.oriservices.com						
Oriana House Inc						
885 E Buchtel Ave PO Box 1501	Akron	OH	44305	330-535-8116		726
Web: www.orianahouse.org						
Orica USA Inc 33101 E Quincy Ave	Watkins	CO	80137	303-268-5000	268-5250	268
TF: 800-800-3855 ■ *Web:* www.oricaminingservices.com						
Oricom Internet Inc						
400 Rue Nolin Bureau	Vanier	QC	G1M1E7	418-683-4557		387
Web: www.oricom.ca						
Oriel Stat A Matrix						
1095 Morris Ave Ste 103B	Union	NJ	07083	732-548-0600		463
Web: www.orielstat.com						
Oriel Therapeutics Inc						
630 Davis Dr Ste 120	Morrisville	NC	27560	919-313-1290		231

Phone | Fax | Class

Oriental Institute Museum
1155 E 58th St University of Chicago ... Chicago IL 60637 773-702-9514 702-9853 520
TF: 800-791-9354 ■ *Web:* www.oi.uchicago.edu

Oriental Jade Bangor Mall Blvd. ... Bangor ME 04401 207-947-6969 942-7170 671
TF: 800-522-4700 ■ *Web:* www.orientaljade.com

Oriental Trading Company Inc
5455 S 90th St ... Omaha NE 68127 402-596-1200 459
TF: 800-875-8480 ■ *Web:* www.orientaltrading.com

Oriental Weavers of America
3252 Lower Dug Gap Rd SW ... Dalton GA 30720 706-277-9666 277-9691 131
Web: www.orientalweavers.com

Origen Financial Inc
27777 Franklin Rd Ste 1700 ... Southfield MI 48034 248-746-7000 746-7094 509
OTC: ORGN ■ *Web:* www.origenfinancial.com

Origin LLC 119 E Graham Pl ... Burbank CA 91502 818-848-1648 8
Web: www.originpop.com

Original Appalachian Artworks Inc
1721 Hwy 75 S PO Box 714 ... Cleveland GA 30528 706-865-2171 762
Web: www.cabbagepatchkids.com

Original Artists
9465 Wilshire Blvd Ste 870 ... Beverly Hills CA 90212 310-275-6765 731
Web: www.original-artists.com

Original Benjamin's, The
9593 N Kings Hwy ... Myrtle Beach SC 29572 843-449-0821 671
Web: www.originalbenjamins.com

Original Cake Candle Co, The
102 Sundale Rd ... Norwich OH 43767 740-872-3248 122
TF: 888-444-2253 ■ *Web:* cakecandle.com

Original Fish Market
1001 Liberty Ave. ... Pittsburgh PA 15222 412-227-3657 671
Web: www.originalfishmarket.com

Original Impressions LLC
12900 SW 89th Ct ... Miami FL 33176 305-233-1322 627
TF: 888 853 8644 ■ *Web:* www.originalimpressions.com

Original Joe's 301 S First St ... San Jose CA 95113 408-292-7030 671
Web: www.originaljoes.com

Original Lincoln Logs Ltd
5 Riverside Dr PO Box 135 ... Chestertown NY 12817 800-833-2461 106
TF: 800-833-2461 ■ *Web:* www.lincolnlogs.com

Original Mattress Factory Inc, The
4930 State Rd ... Cleveland OH 44134 216-661-8388 471
Web: originalmattress.com

Original Media LLC
38 E 29th St 5th Fl ... New York NY 10016 212-683-3086 225
Web: www.originalmedia.com

Original Pancake House Franchising Inc
8601 SW 24th Ave ... Portland OR 97219 503-246-9007 670
Web: www.originalpancakehouse.com

Original Parts Group Inc (OPGI)
1770 Saturn Way ... Seal Beach CA 90740 562-594-1000 594-1050 54
TF: 800-243-8355 ■ *Web:* www.opgi.com

Original Productions Inc
308 W Verdugo Ave ... Burbank CA 91502 818-295-6966 514
Web: www.amygdalamusic.com

Original Q Shack, The
2510 University Dr ... Durham NC 27707 919-402-4227 671
Web: theqshackoriginal.com

Original Tandoori Kitchen King
7215 Main St ... Vancouver BC V5X3J3 604-327-8900 671
Web: originaltandoorikitchens.com

OriginClear Inc 5645 W Adams Blvd. ... Los Angeles CA 90016 323-939-6645 536
TF: 877-999-6645 ■ *Web:* www.originclear.com

OriginLab Corp
1 Roundhouse Plaza Ste 303 ... Northampton MA 01060 413-586-2013 177
TF: 800-969-7720 ■ *Web:* www.originlab.com

Origins Natural Resources Inc
767 Fifth Ave. ... New York NY 10153 800-674-4467 214
TF Cust Svc: 800-674-4467 ■ *Web:* www.origins.com

Origo Direct Marketing Communications
20-4480 Chesswood Dr ... Toronto ON M3J2B9 416 398 7678 41
Web: www.origo.ca

Orillia Soldiers' Memorial Hospital (OSMH)
170 Colborne St W ... Orillia ON L3V2Z3 705-325-2201 325-7953* 374-2
**Fax:* Admissions ■ *TF:* 800-387-0073 ■ *Web:* www.osmh.on.ca

Orinda Asset Management LLC
4 Orinda Way Ste 150-A ... Orinda CA 94563 925-253-1300 528
Web: orindamanagement.com

Oriole Park at Camden Yards
333 Camden St ... Baltimore MD 21201 410-547-6100 720
TF: 888-848-2473 ■ *Web:* baltimore.orioles.mlb.com

Orion Advisor Services LLC
17605 Wright St ... Omaha NE 68130 402-496-3513 251
TF: 800-321-6273 ■ *Web:* www.orionadvisor.com

Orion Area Chamber of Commerce
46 W Shadbolt St Ste 112 ... Lake Orion MI 48361 248-693-6300 139
Web: orionlibrary.org

Orion Building Corp
9025 Overlook Blvd Ste 100 ... Brentwood TN 37027 615-321-4499 186
Web: www.orionbldg.com

Orion Communications Inc
7650 Standish Pl Ste 102 ... Rockville MD 20855 301-921-9056 175
Web: www.oricomm.com

Orion Development Group
177 Beach 116th St Ste 4 ... Rockaway Park NY 11694 718-474-4600 194
TF: 800-510-2117 ■ *Web:* www.odgroup.com

Orion Drilling Company LLC
674 Flato Rd ... Corpus Christi TX 78405 361-299-9800 540
Web: www.oriondrilling.com

Orion Enterprises Inc
2850 Fairfax Trafficway ... Kansas City KS 66115 913-342-1653 605-2
Web: www.orionfittings.com

Orion Foods Inc
2930 W Maple St PO Box 85210 ... Sioux Falls SD 57107 800-336-1320 336-1320 393
TF: 800-336-1320 ■ *Web:* orionfoods.com

Orion Futures 1905 W Busch Blvd. ... Tampa FL 33612 813-876-9662 169

Orion Genomics LLC
4041 Forest Park Ave ... Saint Louis MO 63108 314-615-6977 231
Web: www.oriongenomics.com

Orion HealthCorp Inc
1805 Old Alabama Rd Ste 350 ... Roswell GA 30076 678-832-1800 832-1888 352
OTC: ORNH ■ *Web:* www.orionhealthcorp.com

Orion Industries Inc 1 Orion Park Dr ... Ayer MA 01432 978-772-6000 179
Web: www.orionindustries.com

Orion Instruments LLC
2105 Oak Villa Blvd ... Baton Rouge LA 70815 225-906-2343 906-2344 201
TF: 866-556-7466 ■ *Web:* www.orioninstruments.com

Orion Magazine 187 Main St. ... Great Barrington MA 01230 413-528-4422 457-19
TF: 888-909-6568 ■ *Web:* www.orionmagazine.org

Orion Mobility LLC
4 Mountainview Terr Ste 101 ... Danbury CT 06810 203-762-0365 194
TF: 800-476-7787 ■ *Web:* www.orionmobility.com

Orion Registrar Inc 7850 vance dr ... Arvada CO 80003 303-456-6010 463
TF: 800-446-0674 ■ *Web:* www.orion4value.com

Orion Systems Inc
602 Masons Mill Business Pk ... Huntingdon Valley PA 19006 215-659-1207 659-4234 735
TF: 800-935-4654 ■ *Web:* www.orionsystemsinc.net

Orion Systems Integrators Inc
3759 US Hwy 1 S ... Monmouth Junction NJ 08852 877-456-9922 809
TF: 877-456-9922 ■ *Web:* www.orioninc.com

Orion Township Public Library
825 Joslyn Rd ... Lake Orion MI 48362 248-693-3000 693-3009 434-3
Web: www.orionlibrary.org

Orionnet Systems Llc
4141 NW Expy Ste 300 ... Oklahoma City OK 73116 405-286-1674 809
TF: 800-884-8182 ■ *Web:* www.iorion.com

Oriska Insurance Co 1310 Utica St ... Oriskany NY 13424 315-768-2726 390
Web: oriskainsurance.com

Oriskany Battlefield State Historic Site
7801 State Rt 69 ... Oriskany NY 13424 315-768-7224 377-3081 565
Web: parks.ny.gov/historic-sites/21/details.aspx

Oristech Inc Po Box 310069 ... New Braunfels TX 78131 830-620-7422 225
TF: 800-929-9078 ■ *Web:* www.oristech.com

Oritani Financial Corp
370 Pascack Rd PO Box 1329 ... Washington Township NJ 07676 201-664-5400 497-1223 70
NASDAQ: ORIT ■ *TF:* 888-674-8264 ■ *Web:* www.oritani.com

ORIX USA Corp 1717 Main St Ste 900 ... Dallas TX 75201 214-237-2000 216
Web: www.orix.com

Orizon Investment Counsel LLC
16924 Frances St Ste 200 ... Omaha NE 68130 402-330-7008 690
Web: hsmcorizon.com

Orkal Industries LLC
333 Westbury Ave. ... Carle Place NY 11514 516-333-2121 770
Web: www.orkal.com

ORKIN LLC 2170 Piedmont Rd NE ... Atlanta GA 30324 877-250-1652 265-0238* 577
**Fax Area Code:* 510 ■ **Fax:* Cust Svc ■ *TF:* 844-498-4362 ■ *Web:* www.orkin.com

Orland Park Area Chamber of Commerce
8799 W 151 St ... Orland Park IL 60462 708-349-2972 349-7454 139
Web: www.orlandparkchamber.org

Orland Park Public Library
14921 Ravinia Ave ... Orland Park IL 60462 708-428-5100 349-8196 434-3
Web: www.orlandparklibrary.org

Orland Square 288 Orland Sq ... Orland Park IL 60462 708-349-1646 349-8419 460
TF: 877-746-6642 ■ *Web:* www.simon.com/mall/?id=189

Orlandi Inc 131 Executive Blvd. ... Farmingdale NY 11735 631-756-0110 5
Web: www.orlandi-usa.com

Orlando Baking Company Inc
7777 Grand Ave ... Cleveland OH 44104 216 361 1872 391 3469 296-1
TF: 800-362-5504 ■ *Web:* www.orlandobaking.com

Orlando Business Journal (OBJ)
255 S Orange Ave Ste 700 ... Orlando FL 32801 407-649-8470 420-1625 457-5
Web: www.bizjournals.com

Orlando City Hall 400 S Orange Ave ... Orlando FL 32801 407-246-2221 246-2842 337
TF: 800-700-8744 ■ *Web:* www.cityoforlando.net

Orlando Diefenderfer Co
116 S Second St ... Allentown PA 18105 610-434-9595 246
Web: www.diefenderfer.com

Orlando Dodge Chrysler Jeep
4101 W Colonial Dr ... Orlando FL 32808 407-299-1120 57
Web: orlandododge.com

Orlando Endodontic Specialists
610 N Mills Ave Ste 210 ... Orlando FL 32803 407-423-7667 425-8629 360-3
Web: www.midfloridarootcanals.com

Orlando Fashion Square
3201 E Colonial Dr ... Orlando FL 32803 407-896-1132 460

Orlando International Airport
1 Jeff Fuqua Blvd ... Orlando FL 32827 407-825-2001 27
TF: 800-327-1390 ■ *Web:* www.orlandoairports.net

Orlando Magazine
801 N Magnolia Ave Ste 201 ... Orlando FL 32803 407-423-0618 237-6258 457-22
Web: www.orlandomagazine.com

Orlando Magic
8701 Maitland Summit Blvd ... Orlando FL 32810 407-916-2400 714-1
Web: www.nba.com

Orlando Museum of Art
2416 N Mills Ave ... Orlando FL 32803 407-896-4231 896-9920 520
TF: 800-435-7352 ■ *Web:* www.omart.org

Orlando Philharmonic Orchestra
812 E Rollins St Ste 300 ... Orlando FL 32803 407-896-6700 896-5512 573-3
TF: 800-745-3000 ■ *Web:* www.orlandophil.org

Orlando Premium Outlets
8200 Vineland Ave ... Orlando FL 32821 407-238-7787 460
Web: www.premiumoutlets.com

Orlando Regional Chamber of Commerce
75 S Ivanhoe Blvd ... Orlando FL 32804 407-425-1234 835-2500 139
Web: www.orlando.org

Orlando Regional Medical Ctr (ORMC)
1414 Kuhl Ave ... Orlando FL 32806 321-841-5111 374-3
TF: 800-424-6998 ■ *Web:* www.orlandohealth.com

Orlando Regional South Seminole Hospital
555 W State Rd 434 ... Longwood FL 32750 407-767-1200 374-3
Web: www.orlandohealth.com/southseminolehospital

Orlando Repertory Theatre
1001 E Princeton St ... Orlando FL 32803 407-896-7365 897-3284 572
Web: www.orlandorep.com

Orlando Science Ctr
777 E Princeton St ... Orlando FL 32803 407-514-2000 520
Web: www.osc.org

Phone | Fax | Class

Orlando Sentinel 633 N Orange Ave .... Orlando FL 32801 407-420-5000 420-5350 532-2
TF: 800-974-7488 ■ *Web:* www.orlandosentinel.com

Orlando Spring Corp
11131 Winners Cir .... Los Alamitos CA 90720 562-594-8411 492
Web: www.orlandospring.com

Orlando Union Rescue Mission
1525 W Washington St .... Orlando FL 32805 407-423-2131 48-20
Web: www.ourm.org

Orlando Weekly
1505 E Colonial Dr St Ste 200 .... Orlando FL 32803 407-377-0400 377-0420 532-5
TF: 800-474-7576 ■ *Web:* www.orlandoweekly.com

Orlando's 2402 Ave Q .... Lubbock TX 79411 806-747-5998 747-3501 671
Web: www.orlandos.com

Orlando, The 8384 W Third St .... Los Angeles CA 90048 323-658-6600 653-3464 379
Web: www.theorlando.com

Orlando/Orange County Convention & Visitors Bureau Inc
6700 Forum Dr Ste 100 .... Orlando FL 32821 407-363-5872 206
TF: 800-972-3304 ■ *Web:* www.visitorlando.com

Orlans Associates PC
1650 W Big Beaver Rd .... Troy MI 48084 248-502-1400 428
Web: www.orlans.com

Orlantech Inc 230 Lookout Pl .... Maitland FL 32751 407-228-7290 180
Web: www.orlantech.com

Orleans Correctional Facility
3531 Gaines Basin Rd .... Albion NY 14411 585-589-6820 213

Orleans County 3 S Main St Ste 2 .... Albion NY 14411 585-589-5334 589-0181 338
Web: www.orleansny.com

Orleans County 247 Main St .... Newport VT 05855 802-334-3344 334-3385 338
Web: bgs.vermont.gov/facilities/east/orleanscourt

Orleans County Chamber of Commerce
102 N Main St Ste 1 .... Albion NY 14411 585-301-8464 589-7326 139
Web: www.orleanschamber.com

Orleans Grapevine Wine Bar & Bistro
718 - 720 Orleans Ave .... New Orleans LA 70116 504-523-1930 671
Web: www.orleansgrapevine.com

Orleans Homebuilders Inc
3333 St Rd Ste 101 .... Bensalem PA 19020 215-245-7500 653
TF: 800-488-8844 ■ *Web:* orleanshomes.com

Orleans Las Vegas Hotel & Casino
4500 W Tropicana Ave .... Las Vegas NV 89103 702-365-7111 133
TF: 800-675-3267 ■ *Web:* www.orleanscasino.com

Orleans Parish
839 St Charles Ave Ste 305 .... New Orleans LA 70130 504-309-1004 338
TF: 800-368-3749 ■ *Web:* www.neworleans.com

Orleans Parish School Board
3520 General DeGaulle Dr .... New Orleans LA 70114 504-304-3520 685
TF: 800-772-1213 ■ *Web:* opsb.us

Orly International Inc
7710 Haskell Ave .... Los Angeles CA 91406 818-994-1001 214
Web: www.orlybeauty.com

Orman House 177 Fifth St .... Apalachicola FL 32320 850-653-1209 565
Web: www.floridastateparks.org/ormanhouse

Ormat Technologies Inc
6225 Neil Rd Ste 300 .... Reno NV 89511 775-356-9029 356-9039 620
NYSE: ORA ■ *Web:* www.ormat.com

ORMC (Orlando Regional Medical Ctr)
1414 Kuhl Ave .... Orlando FL 32806 321-841-5111 374-3
TF: 800-424-6998 ■ *Web:* www.orlandohealth.com

ORMC (Ocala Regional Medical Ctr)
1431 SW First Ave .... Ocala FL 34478 352-401-1000 374-3
Web: www.ocalahealthsystem.com

ORMCO Corp 1717 W Collins Ave .... Orange CA 92867 714-516-7400 317-6012* 228
**Fax Area Code:* 800 ■ *TF Cust Svc:* 800-854-1741 ■ *Web:* www.ormco.com

Orme School HC 63 PO Box 3040 .... Mayer AZ 86333 928-632-7601 632-7601 622
Web: www.ormeschool.org

Ormec Systems Corp 19 Linden Pk .... Rochester NY 14625 585-385-3520 385-5999 203
TF: 800-656-7632 ■ *Web:* www.ormec.com

Ormond Beach Chamber of Commerce
165 W Granada Blvd .... Ormond Beach FL 32174 386-677-3454 677-4363 139
TF: 800-854-1234 ■ *Web:* www.ormondchamber.com

Ormond Memorial Art Museum & Gardens
78 E Granada Blvd .... Ormond Beach FL 32176 386-676-3347 676-3244 520
Web: www.ormondartmuseum.org

Ormsby Trucking Inc
888 W Railroad St PO Box 67 .... Uniondale IN 46791 260-543-2233 780
Web: www.ormtrk.com

Ornamental Metal Works Inc
2100 N Woodford St .... Decatur IL 62526 217-428-3446 480

Ornamental Mouldingsllc
3804 Comanche Dr .... Archdale NC 27263 336-431-9120 499
Web: www.ornamentalmouldings.com

Orndorff & Spaid Inc
11722 Old Baltimore Pk .... Beltsville MD 20705 301-937-5911 189-12
TF: 800-364-2059 ■ *Web:* www.osroofing.com

Ornim Inc 125 Washington St Ste #7 .... Foxboro MA 02035 866-811-6384 743
TF: 866-811-6384 ■ *Web:* www.ornim.com

ORNL (Oak Ridge National Laboratory)
PO Box 2008 .... Oak Ridge TN 37831 865-576-2900 574-0595* 668
**Fax:* PR ■ *Web:* www.ornl.gov

ORO Restaurant 45 Elm St .... Toronto ON M5G1H1 416-597-0155 671
Web: www.ororestaurant.com

Oro-Cal Mfg Company Inc 1720 Bird St .... Oroville CA 95965 530-533-5065 409
TF: 800-367-6225 ■ *Web:* www.orocal.com

Oronoque Pharmacy Inc 7365 Main St .... Stratford CT 06614 203-378-1111 237

Oroville Area Chamber of Commerce
1789 Montgomery St .... Oroville CA 95965 530-538-2542 538-2546 139
TF: 800-655-4653 ■ *Web:* www.orovillechamber.net

Oroville Hospital (OH) 2767 Olive Hwy .... Oroville CA 95966 530-533-8500 374-3
Web: www.orovillehospital.com

Oroville Union High School District
2211 Washington Ave .... Oroville CA 95966 530-538-2300 685
Web: ouhsd.org

Orphan Foundation of America (OFA)
21351 Gentry Dr Ste 130 .... Sterling VA 20166 571-203-0270 203-0273 48-6
TF: 800-950-4673 ■ *Web:* www.fc2success.org

Orpheum Children's Science Museum
346 N Neil St .... Champaign IL 61820 217-352-5895 521
Web: orpheumkids.net

Orpheum Performing Arts Centre
200 N Broadway .... Wichita KS 67202 316-263-0884 572
Web: www.wichitaorpheum.com

Orpheum Theatre 203 W Adams St .... Phoenix AZ 85003 602-262-6011 572
Web: www.phoenix.gov

Orpheum Theatre 409 S 16th St .... Omaha NE 68102 402-345-0202 345-0222 572
TF: 866-434-8587 ■ *Web:* www.omahaperformingarts.org

Orpheum Theatre 203 S Main St .... Memphis TN 38103 901-525-3000 572
TF: 800-745-3000 ■ *Web:* www.orpheum-memphis.com

Orpheum Theatre 865 Seymour St .... Vancouver BC V6B3L4 604-665-3050 665-2149 572
Web: www.vancouver.ca

Orpheus Chamber Orchestra
490 Riverside Dr 11th Fl .... New York NY 10027 212-896-1700 896-1717 573-3
Web: orpheusnyc.org

Orr & Boss Inc
33900 Harper Ave Ste 103 .... Clinton Township MI 48035 586-416-9090 463
Web: www.orrandboss.com

ORR Associates Inc 2801 M St NW .... Washington DC 20007 202-338-6100 196
Web: www.oai-usa.com

Orr Associates LLC
191 Peachtree St NE Ste 3720 .... Atlanta GA 30303 404-525-3007 2
Web: www.orrcpa.com

Orr Felt Co 750 S Main St .... Piqua OH 45356 937-773-0551 745-6
Web: www.orrfelt.com

Orr Group, The
110 S Stratford Rd Ste 402 .... Winston-salem NC 27104 336-722-7881 194
Web: www.theorrgroup.com

Orr Safety Corp
11601 Interchange Dr .... Louisville KY 40229 502-774-5791 776-8030 679
TF: 800-726-6789 ■ *Web:* www.orrsafety.com

Orrell's Food Service
9827 S NC Hwy 150 .... Linwood NC 27299 336-752-2114 752-2060 297-9
Web: www.orrellsfoodservice.com

Orrick Herrington & Sutcliffe LLP
666 Fifth Ave .... New York NY 10103 212-506-5000 506-5151 428
TF: 866-342-5259 ■ *Web:* www.orrick.com

Orscheln Farm & Home LLC
1800 Overcenter Dr PO Box 698 .... Moberly MO 65270 660-263-4377 269-3500 276
TF: 800-498-5090 ■ *Web:* www.orscheln.com

Orscheln Products LLC
1177 N Morley St .... Moberly MO 65270 660-263-4377 247
Web: www.orschelnproducts.com

ORT American Inc 75 Maiden Ln 10th Fl .... New York NY 10038 212-505-7700 674-3057 48-5
TF: 800-519-2678 ■ *Web:* www.ortamerica.org

Ort Tool & Die Corp 6555 S Dixie Hwy .... Erie MI 48133 419-242-9553 848-4308* 757
**Fax Area Code:* 734 ■ *Web:* www.orttool.com

Ortanique Restaurant
278 Miracle Mile .... Coral Gables FL 33134 305-446-7710 446-9895 671
Web: ortaniquerestaurants.com

Ortec Inc
505 Gentry Memorial Hwy PO Box 1469 .... Easley SC 29641 864-859-1471 859-8580 145
Web: www.ortecinc.com

Orthman Manufacturing Inc
75765 Rd 435 PO Box B .... Lexington NE 68850 308-324-4654 324-5001 273
TF: 800-658-3270 ■ *Web:* www.orthman.com

Ortho Computer Systems Inc
1107 Buckeye Ave .... Ames IA 50010 515-233-1026 177
TF: 800-678-4644 ■ *Web:* www.ortho2.com

Ortho Development Corp
12187 S Business Pk Dr .... Draper UT 84020 801-553-9991 553-9993 477
TF: 800-429-8339 ■ *Web:* www.odev.com

Ortho Kinematics Inc
7004 Bee Cave Rd Bldg III Ste 315 .... Austin TX 78746 512-334-5490 475
Web: www.orthokinematics.com

Ortho Technology Inc
17401 Commerce Park Blvd .... Tampa FL 33647 813-991-5896 476
TF: 800-999-3161 ■ *Web:* www.orthotechnology.com

OrthoAccel Technologies Inc
8275 El Rio St Ste 100 .... Houston TX 77054 832-631-1660 228
Web: www.acceledent.com

Ortho-Clinical Diagnostics Inc
1001 US Rt 202 N .... Raritan NJ 08869 800-828-6316 453-3660* 476
**Fax Area Code:* 585 ■ **Fax:* Cust Svc ■ *TF:* 800-828-6316 ■ *Web:* www.orthoclinical.com

OrthoCor Medical Inc
1251 Red Fox Rd .... Arden Hills MN 55112 952-217-6366 477
Web: www.orthocormedical.com

Orthodent Ltd 311 Viola Ave .... Oshawa ON L1H3A7 905-436-3133 415
TF: 800-267-8463 ■ *Web:* orthodentus.com

Orthodontic Design & Production Inc
1370 Decision St Ste D .... Vista CA 92083 760-734-3995 734-1735 475

Orthodox Union (OU) 11 Broadway .... New York NY 10004 212-563-4000 564-9058 48-20
TF: 855-505-7500 ■ *Web:* www.ou.org

Orthofeet Inc 152A Veterans Dr .... Northvale NJ 07647 201-767-6224 477
Web: orthofeet.com

Orthofix Inc 1720 Bray Central Dr .... McKinney TX 75069 469-742-2500 742-2556 477
TF: 800-527-0404 ■ *Web:* www.orthofix.com

Orthopaedic Hospital
403 W Adams Blvd .... Los Angeles CA 90007 213-742-1000 741-8338 374-7
Web: ortho-institute.org

OrthoPediatrics Corp 2850 Frontier Dr .... Warsaw IN 46582 574-268-6379 477
Web: www.orthopediatrics.com

Orthopedic Designs North America Inc
5912 Breckenridge Pkwy Ste F .... Tampa FL 33610 888-635-8535 475
TF: 888-635-8535 ■ *Web:* www.odi-na.com

OrthoPro LLC
3939 S Wasatch Blvd Ste 19 .... Salt Lake City UT 84124 866-746-0208 746-1057* 477
**Fax Area Code:* 801 ■ *TF:* 866-746-0208 ■ *Web:* www.wright.com

OrthoSensor Inc
1855 Griffin Rd Ste A-310 .... Dania Beach FL 33004 954-577-7770 477
TF: 800-706-5620 ■ *Web:* www.orthosensor.com

Orthotic Prosthetic Center Inc
8330 Professional Hill Dr .... Fairfax VA 22031 703-698-5007 45
TF: 800-328-9077 ■ *Web:* opc1.com

ORTIG (Old Republic National Title Insurance Co)
400 Second Ave S .... Minneapolis MN 55401 612-371-1111 371-1191 391-6
TF: 800-328-4441 ■ *Web:* www.oldrepublictitle.com

Ortiz Enterprises Inc
6 Cushing Way Ste 200 .... Irvine CA 92618 949-753-1414 189-5
Web: www.ortizent.com

Phone | Fax | Class

Ortloff Engineers Ltd
415 W Wall Ave Ste 2000 ... Midland TX 79701 432-685-0277 685-0258 261
Web: www.ortloff.com

Ortman Fluid power
1400 N 30th St Ste 20 ... Quincy IL 62301 217-277-0321 222-1773 223
TF: 844-759-4922 ■ *Web:* www.ortmanfluidpower.com

Ortonville Recreation Area
5779 Hadley Rd ... Ortonville MI 48462 810-797-4439 565
Web: www.michigandnr.com

Orvis International Travel
178 Conservation Way ... Sunderland VT 05250 802-362-8790 362-8795 710
TF: 800-547-4322 ■ *Web:* www.orvis.com

Oryx Insurance Brokerage Inc
2 Ct St ... Binghamton NY 13901 607-724-0173 462-6799* 390
**Fax Area Code:* 888 ■ *Web:* www.oryxinsurance.com

Oryx Midstream Services LLC
4000 N Big Spring Ste 210 ... Midland TX 79705 432-684-4272 536
TF: 800-776-7263 ■ *Web:* www.oryxmidstream.com

OS Kelly Co 318 E N St ... Springfield OH 45503 937-322-4921 527

OSA (Optical Society of America)
2010 Massachusetts Ave NW ... Washington DC 20036 202-223-8130 223-1096 49-8
TF: 800-766-4672 ■ *Web:* www.osa.org

Osage County 205 E Main St ... Linn MO 65051 573-897-2139 338
TF: 800-222-1222 ■ *Web:* www.osagecountyhd.org

Osage County PO Box 226 ... Lyndon KS 66451 785-828-4812 828-4749 338
Web: www.osageco.org

Osage County 900 S St Paul Ave ... Pawhuska OK 74056 918-287-3535 287-6011 338
TF: 800-425-2385 ■ *Web:* ocso.net

Osage Exploration & Development Inc
2445 Fifth Ave Ste 310 ... San Diego CA 92101 619-677-3956 316

Osage Hills State Park
2131 Osage Hills State Pk Rd ... Pawhuska OK 74056 918-336-4141 337-2176 565
TF: 800-622-6317 ■ *Web:* www.travelok.com

Osage LLC 4500 S 129th E Ave Ste 105 ... Tulsa OK 74134 918-582-5633 196
Web: www.osagellc.com

Osage Valley Electric Co-op Assn
1321 N Orange St ... Butler MO 64730 660-679-3131 245
TF: 800-889-6832 ■ *Web:* www.osagevalley.com

Osaka 4205 W Sahara Ave ... Las Vegas NV 89102 702-876-4988 671
TF: 800-351-7400 ■ *Web:* lasvegas-sushi.com

Osaka 244 Adams Ave ... Scranton PA 18503 570-341-9600 671
Web: www.osakacuisine.com

Osaka 8605 Germantown Pk ... Philadelphia PA 19118 215-242-5900 671
Web: www.osakapa.com

Osaka Gas Energy America Corp
1 N Lexington Ave Ste 504 ... White Plains NY 10601 914-253-5500 328-4430 787
Web: www.osakagas.co.jp

Osaka Japanese Restaurant 46 W Ctr St ... Provo UT 84601 801-373-1060 671

Osaka Japanese Restaurant
515 Westheimer Rd ... Houston TX 77006 713-533-9098 671

Osaka Sushi 5012 W Pk Blvd ... Plano TX 75093 972-931-8898 671
Web: osaka-plano.com

OSBA (Ohio State Bar Assn)
1700 Lake Shore Dr ... Columbus OH 43204 614-487-2050 487-1008 72
TF: 800-282-6556 ■ *Web:* www.ohiobar.org

Osbee Industries Inc
99 Calvert St 100 ... Harrison NY 10528 914-777-6611 180
TF: 800-238-2727 ■ *Web:* osbee.com

Osborn & Barr 914 Spruce St ... Saint Louis MO 63102 314-726-5511 4
Web: osbornbarr.com

Osborn Health & Rehabilitation
3333 N Civic Ctr Plaza ... Scottsdale AZ 85251 480-994-1333 450
TF: 800-432-4040 ■ *Web:* osbornhealth.com

Osborn International
5401 Hamilton Ave ... Cleveland OH 44114 216-361-1900 361-1913 103
TF Cust Svc: 800-720-3358 ■ *Web:* www.osborn.com

Osborn Medical Corp 100 W Main St ... Utica MN 55979 507-932-5028 477
TF: 800-254-5438 ■ *Web:* www.osbornmedical.com

Osborn Transportation Inc
1245 W Grand Ave ... Rainbow City AL 35906 256-442-2514 780
TF: 866-215-3659 ■ *Web:* www.osborntransportation.com

Osborne Assn 809 Westchester Ave ... Bronx NY 10455 718-707-2600 48-8
Web: www.osborneny.org

Osborne Bros 201 Eddings Ln ... Nashville TN 37214 615-885-7338 345
Web: osbornefoods.com

Osborne Coinage Co, The
2851 Massachusetts Ave ... Cincinnati OH 45225 513-681-5424 488
Web: www.osbornecoin.com

Osborne Construction Company Inc
10602 NE 38th Pl Ste 100 ... Kirkland WA 98033 425-827-4221 828-4314 186
Web: www.osborne.cc

Osborne County PO Box 160 ... Osborne KS 67473 785-346-2431 346-5252 338
TF: 800-262-8683 ■ *Web:* www.osbornecounty.org

Osborne Industries Inc
120 N Industrial Ave ... Osborne KS 67473 785-346-2192 273
TF: 800-255-0316 ■ *Web:* www.osborneindustries.com

Osborne Partners Capital Management LLC
580 California St Ste 1900 ... San Francisco CA 94104 415-362-5637 401
TF: 800-362-7734 ■ *Web:* www.osbornepartners.com

Osborne Wood Products Inc 4618 Hwy 123 ... Toccoa GA 30577 706-886-1065 321
Web: www.osbornewood.com

Osbornedale State Park 555 Roosevelt Dr ... Derby CT 06418 203-735-4311 565
Web: www.ct.gov

Osbrink Talent Agency Inc
4343 Lankershim Blvd Ste 100 ... Universal city CA 91602 818-760-0991 506
Web: www.osbrinkagency.com

Oscar Anderson House Museum
420 M St PO Box 102205 ... Anchorage AK 99501 907-274-2336 520
Web: www.muni.org

Oscar De La Renta Ltd 11 W 42nd St ... New York NY 10036 212-282-0500 277
Web: www.oscardelarenta.com

Oscar Gruss & Son Inc
55 E 59th st 15th Fl ... New York NY 10022 212-419-4000 317-5907 690
TF: 800-289-9999 ■ *Web:* www.oscargruss.com

Oscar Printing Co
57 Columbia Sq ... San Francisco CA 94103 415-626-8818 687
Web: opportunitymart.com

Phone | Fax | Class

Oscar Scherer State Park
1843 S Tamiami Trail ... Osprey FL 34229 941-483-5956 480-3007 565
TF: 800-326-3521 ■ *Web:* www.floridastateparks.org

Oscar W Larson Co 10100 Dixie Hwy ... Clarkston MI 48348 248-620-0070 579
Web: www.larsonco.com

Oscar Wilson Engines & Parts Inc
826 Lone Star Dr ... O Fallon MO 63366 636-978-1313 873-6720* 386
**Fax Area Code:* 800 ■ *TF:* 800-873-6722 ■ *Web:* www.oscar-wilson.com

Oscar Winski Company Inc
2407 N Ninth St ... Lafayette IN 47904 765-742-1102 492
Web: www.oscarwinski.com

Osceola County 1 Courthouse Sq ... Kissimmee FL 34741 407-742-2000 338
Web: www.osceola.org

Osceola County 301 W Upton Ave ... Reed City MI 49677 231-832-3261 832-6149 338
Web: www.osceola-county.org

Osceola County 300 Seventh St ... Sibley IA 51249 712-754-2523 338
Web: www.osceolacountyia.com

Osceola Electric Co-op Inc
1102 Egret Dr PO Box 127 ... Sibley IA 51249 712-754-2519 245
TF: 888-754-2519 ■ *Web:* www.osceolaelectric.com

Osceola Mental Health Inc
206 Park Pl Blvd ... Kissimmee FL 34741 407-846-0023 720
Web: www.ppbh.org

Osceola Mills Public Library
600 Lingle St ... Osceola Mills PA 16666 814-339-7229 434-3

Osceola News-Gazette 108 Church St ... Kissimmee FL 34741 407-846-7600 402-2946* 532-4
**Fax Area Code:* 321 ■ *Web:* www.aroundosceola.com

Osceola Regional Medical Ctr
700 W Oak St ... Kissimmee FL 34741 407-846-2266 374-3
Web: www.osceolaregional.com

Osco Industries Inc PO Box 1388 ... Portsmouth OH 45662 740-354-3183 307
Web: www.oscoind.com

Oscoda County PO Box 399 ... Mio MI 48647 989-826-1109 826-1136 338
TF: 800-315-3593 ■ *Web:* www.oscodacountymi.com

Oscor Inc 3816 DeSoto Blvd ... Palm Harbor FL 34683 727-937-2511 934-9835* 250
**Fax:* Cust Svc ■ *TF Cust Svc:* 800-726-7267 ■ *Web:* www.oscor.com

Oseberg LLC
12 E California Ave Ste 200 ... Oklahoma City OK 73104 405-618-1647 396
Web: www.oseberg.io

OSF (Ohio Star Forge Co)
4000 Mahoning Ave NW ... Warren OH 44483 330-847-6360 847-6368 483
Web: www.ohiostar.com

OSF (Old Spaghetti Factory Inc)
0715 SW Bancroft St ... Portland OR 97239 503-225-0433 226-6214 670
TF: 800-461-6675 ■ *Web:* www.osf.com

OSF Global Services Inc
6655 Blvd Pierre Bertrand, 204-14 ... Quebec City QC G2K1M1 888-548-4344 631
TF: 888-548-4344 ■ *Web:* www.osf-global.com

OSF Healthcare System
800 NE Glen Oak Ave ... Peoria IL 61603 309-655-2850 655-6869 353
Web: www.osfhealthcare.org

OSF Hospice 2265 W Altorfer Dr ... Peoria IL 61615 800-673-5288 683-7855* 371
**Fax Area Code:* 309 ■ *TF:* 800-673-5288 ■ *Web:* www.osfhealthcare.org/services/home-care

OSF Saint Anthony Medical Ctr
5666 E State St ... Rockford IL 61108 815-226-2000 395-5449 374-3
TF: 800-343-3185 ■ *Web:* www.osfhealthcare.org/saint-anthony

OSF Saint Clare Home
5533 N Galena Rd ... Peoria Heights IL 61616 309-682-5428 450
Web: www.osfhealthcare.org

OSF Saint Francis Medical Ctr
530 NE Glen Oak Ave ... Peoria IL 61637 309-655-2000 374-3
TF: 888-627-5673 ■ *Web:* www.osfhealthcare.org/saint-francis

OSF Saint Joseph Medical Ctr
2200 E Washington St ... Bloomington IL 61701 309-662-3311 374-3
Web: www.osfhealthcare.org/st-joseph

OSF Saint Mary Medical Ctr
3333 N Seminary St ... Galesburg IL 61401 309-344-3161 451-8278 374-3
TF: 877-795-0416 ■ *Web:* www.osfhealthcare.org/st-mary

OSG Tap & Die Inc
676 E Fullerton Ave ... Glendale Heights IL 60139 630-790-1400 790-1477 493
TF: 800-837-2223 ■ *Web:* www.osgtool.com

Osgood Industries Inc 601 Burbank St ... Oldsmar FL 34677 813-855-7337 298
Web: www.osgoodinc.com

Osgood Textile Company Inc
333 Park St ... West Springfield MA 01089 413-737-6488 258
TF: 888-674-6638 ■ *Web:* www.osgoodtextile.com

OSHA (Occupational Safety & Health Administration)
200 Constitution Ave NW ... Washington DC 20210 202-693-1999 693-1659 340-15
TF: 800-321-6742 ■ *Web:* www.osha.gov

OSHA Up-to-Date Newsletter
1121 Spring Lake Dr ... Itasca IL 60143 630-285-1121 285-1315 531-0
TF Cust Svc: 800-621-7615 ■ *Web:* www.nsc.org

Oshawa Harbour Commission
1050 Farewell Ave ... Oshawa ON L1H6N6 905-576-0400 576-5701 618
TF: 800-841-2729 ■ *Web:* portofoshawa.ca

OSHEAN Inc
6946 Post Rd Ste 402 ... North Kingstown RI 02852 401-398-7500 180
Web: www.oshean.org

Oshkosh Chamber of Commerce
120 Jackson St ... Oshkosh WI 54901 920-303-2266 303-2263 139
Web: www.oshkoshchamber.com

Oshkosh Coil Spring Inc
3575 N Main St ... Oshkosh WI 54901 920-235-7620 492
TF: 800-638-8360 ■ *Web:* www.oshkoshcoilspring.com

Oshkosh Convention & Visitors Bureau
2401 W Waukau Ave ... Oshkosh WI 54904 920-303-9200 48-20
TF: 877-303-9200 ■ *Web:* www.visitoshkosh.com

Oshkosh Correctional Institution
1730 W Snell Rd ... Oshkosh WI 54903 920-231-4010 236-2615 213
Web: doc.wi.gov

Oshkosh Door Co 2501 Universal St ... Oshkosh WI 54904 920-233-6161 499
Web: www.oshkoshdoor.com

Oshkosh Northwestern Co 224 State St ... Oshkosh WI 54901 920-235-7700 637-8
TF: 800-924-6168 ■ *Web:* www.thenorthwestern.com

Oshkosh Public Library
106 Washington Ave ... Oshkosh WI 54901 920-236-5200 434-3
TF: 800-236-0850 ■ *Web:* www.oshkoshpubliclibrary.org

Name / Address	City	State	Zip	Phone	Fax	Class
Oshkosh Public Museum 1331 Algoma Blvd *Web:* www.oshkoshmuseum.org	Oshkosh	WI	54901	920-236-5799		520
Oshkosh Specialty Vehicles LLC 12770 44th St N *Web:* www.oshkoshsv.com	Clearwater	FL	33762	727-573-0400		489
Oshkosh Truck Corp 2307 Oregon St *TF:* 800-392-9921 ■ *Web:* www.oshkoshdefense.com	Oshkosh	WI	54903	920-235-9150		516
OSI (Open Space Institute) 1350 Broadway Ste 201 *Web:* www.openspaceinstitute.org	New York	NY	10018	212-290-8200	244-3441	48-13
Osi Consulting Inc 5950 Canoga Ave Ste 300 *Web:* www.osius.com	Woodland Hills	CA	91367	818-992-2700	992-8700	194
Osi Electronics Inc 2385 Pleasant Valley Rd *Web:* www.osielectronics.com	Camarillo	CA	93012	805-499-6877		625
Osi Environmental Inc 3300 E 83rd Pl *Web:* osienv.com	Merrillville	IN	46410	219-942-4886		196
OSI Inc 3950 Birmingham Hwy *Web:* www.osibuildings.com	Montgomery	AL	36108	334-834-3500		186
OSI Industries LLC 1225 Corporate Blvd *Web:* www.osigroup.com	Aurora	IL	60505	630-851-6600		473
OSI Security Devices Inc 1580 Jayken Way *TF:* 800-711-6814 ■ *Web:* www.omnilock.com	Chula Vista	CA	91911	619-628-1000		693
OSI Software Inc 777 Davis St Ste 250 *Web:* www.osisoft.com	San Leandro	CA	94577	510-297-5800	357-8136	178-10
OSI Systems Inc 12525 Chadron Ave *NASDAQ: OSIS* ■ *TF:* 800-579-1639 ■ *Web:* www.osi-systems.com	Hawthorne	CA	90250	310-978-0516		696
OSIA (Order Sons of Italy in America) 219 E St NE *TF:* 800-552-6742 ■ *Web:* www.osia.org	Washington	DC	20002	202-547-2900	546-8168	48-14
Osiris Therapeutics Inc 7015 Albert Einstein Dr *NASDAQ: OSIR* ■ *Web:* www.osiristx.com	Columbia	MD	21046	443-545-1800	545-1701	85
Oski Technology Inc 2513 E Charleston Rd Ste 203 *Web:* www.oskitechnology.com	Mountain View	CA	94043	408-216-7728		225
Osler Hoskin & Harcourt LLP 100 King St W 1 First Canadian Pl Ste 6100 *Web:* www.osler.com	Toronto	ON	M5X1B8	416-362-2111		41
OSMH (Orillia Soldiers' Memorial Hospital) 170 Colborne St W **Fax:* Admissions ■ *TF:* 800-387-0073 ■ *Web:* www.osmh.on.ca	Orillia	ON	L3V2Z3	705-325-2201	325-7953*	374-2
Osmose Inc 980 Ellicott St *TF:* 800-877-7653 ■ *Web:* www.osmose.com	Buffalo	NY	14209	716-882-5905		818
OSO (Ottawa Symphony Orchestra) 2 Daly Ave Ste 250 *Web:* www.ottawasymphony.com	Ottawa	ON	K1N6E2	613-231-7802	231-3610	573-3
OSO BioPharmaceuticals Mfg LLC 4401 Alexander Blvd NE *Web:* www.osobio.com	Albuquerque	NM	87107	505-923-2112		476
Osoyoos Lake State Park 2207 Juniper *Web:* www.oroville-wa.com	Oroville	WA	98844	509-476-2926		565
OSPA (Oregon State Pharmacy Assn) 147 SE 102nd Ave *Web:* www.oregonpharmacy.org	Portland	OR	97216	503-582-9055	253-9172	585
OSPIRG (Oregon State Public Interest Research Group) 1536 SE 11th Ave *Web:* www.ospirg.org	Portland	OR	97214	503-231-4181		633
Osprey Biomedical Corp 1105 N Market St Ste 1300 *Web:* www.ospreybiomedical.com	Wilmington	DE	19801	310-796-5680		476
Osprey Central School 408053 Grey Rd 4 *Web:* www.bwdsb.on.ca	Maxwell	ON	N0C1J0	519-922-2341		685
Osprey Medical Inc 7600 Executive Dr *TF:* 855-860-7584 ■ *Web:* www.ospreymed.com	Eden Prairie	MN	55344	952-955-8230		250
Osprey Software & Systems Inc 13 Osprey Dr	Berkley	MA	02779	508-821-4486		180
Osprey Valley Resorts 18821 Main St *TF:* 800-833-1561 ■ *Web:* www.ospreyvalleygolf.com	Alton	ON	L7K1R1	519-927-9034		707
Osprey Ventures LP 502 Waverley St	Palo Alto	CA	94301	650-473-9250		792
OSRAM Sylvania Inc 100 Endicott St *Web:* www.sylvania.com	Danvers	MA	01923	978-777-1900	750-2152	437
Oss Inc 2000 N Mays Ste 114 *Web:* www.ossjobs.com	Round Rock	TX	78664	512-255-2424		809
OSS.Net Inc PO Box 369 *Web:* www.oss.net	Oakton	VA	22124	703-266-6390		194
Osseon LLC 2330 Circadian Way *TF:* 800-664-8834 ■ *Web:* www.osseon.com	Santa Rosa	CA	95407	707-636-5940		476
Ossian State Bank 102 N Jefferson St *Web:* ossianstatebank.com	Ossian	IN	46777	260-622-4141		70
Ossid Corp 4000 College Rd *TF:* 800-334-8369 ■ *Web:* www.ossid.com	Battleboro	NC	27809	252-446-6177	442-7694	547
Ossining Union Free School District 190 Croton Ave *TF:* 877-769-7447 ■ *Web:* www.ossiningufsd.org	Ossining	NY	10562	914-941-7700	941-7291	685
Ossur 27412 Aliso Viejo Pkwy *TF:* 800-233-6263 ■ *Web:* www.ossur.com	Aliso Viejo	CA	92656	800-233-6263		111
OST Inc 2001 M St NW Ste 3000 *Web:* www.ostglobal.com	Washington	DC	20036	202-466-8099		463
Ostbye & Anderson Inc 10055 51st Ave N **Fax Area Code:* 877 ■ *TF:* 866-553-1515 ■ *Web:* www.ostbye.com	Minneapolis	MN	55442	763-553-1515	553-1515*	409
Osteogenics Biomedical Inc 4620 71st St *Web:* www.cytoplast.com	Lubbock	TX	79424	806-796-1923		476
Osteohealth Co 1 Luitpold Dr *TF:* 800-874-2334 ■ *Web:* www.osteohealth.com	Shirley	NY	11967	631-924-4000		583
Osteomed Corp 3885 Arapaho Rd *TF Cust Svc:* 800-456-7779 ■ *Web:* www.osteomedcorp.com	Addison	TX	75001	972-677-4600		476
Osteotech Inc 710 Medtronic Pkwy *TF:* 800-633-8766 ■ *Web:* www.medtronic.com	Minneapolis	MN	55432	763-514-4000		85
Osterhout Free Library 71 S Franklin St *TF:* 800-925-7737 ■ *Web:* osterhout.info	Wilkes-Barre	PA	18701	570-823-0156		434-3
Osteria 177 177 Main St *Web:* www.osteria177.com	Annapolis	MD	21401	410-267-7700		671
Osteria Del Circo 3600 Las Vegas Blvd S **Fax Area Code:* 702 ■ *TF:* 866-259-7111 ■ *Web:* www.bellagio.com/restaurants/circo.aspx	Las Vegas	NV	89109	888-987-6667	693-8585*	671
Osteria del Mondo 1028 E Juneau Ave *Web:* www.getbianchini.com	Milwaukee	WI	53202	414-291-3770	291-0840	671
Osteria Il Centro 5101 Main St *Web:* osteriailcentro.com	Kansas City	MO	64112	816-561-2369		671
Osteria Panevino 722 Fifth Ave *Web:* www.osteriapanevino.com	San Diego	CA	92101	619-595-7959		671
Osterman & Company Inc 726 S Main St *TF:* 800-914-4437 ■ *Web:* www.osterman-co.com	Cheshire	CT	06410	203-272-2233		605-2
Osterman Jewelers 375 Ghent Rd *TF:* 800-844-7130 ■ *Web:* ostermanjewelers.com	Akron	OH	44333	330-668-5000		410
Ostermancron Inc 10830 Millington Ct *Web:* www.ostermancron.com	Cincinnati	OH	45242	513-771-3377		321
Osterville Free Library 43 Wianno Ave *TF:* 800-783-3837 ■ *Web:* ostervillevillagelibrary.org	Osterville	MA	02655	508-428-5757	428-5557	434-3
Osthoff Resort, The 101 Osthoff Ave PO Box 151 *TF:* 800-876-3399 ■ *Web:* www.osthoff.com	Elkhart Lake	WI	53020	920-876-3366	876-3228	669
Ostler Group Inc, The 7430 S Creek Rd Ste 204 *TF:* 800-261-1537 ■ *Web:* www.ostlergroup.com	Sandy	UT	84093	801-566-6081		7
Ostrom Mushroom Farms 8322 Steilacoom Rd SE *Web:* www.ostrommushrooms.com	Olympia	WA	98513	360-491-1410		10-7
Ostrow Reisin Berk & Abrams Ltd 455 N Cityfront Plaza Dr *Web:* www.orba.com	Chicago	IL	60611	312-670-7444	670-8301	2
OSU Medical Ctr 744 W Ninth St *Web:* www.osumc.net	Tulsa	OK	74127	918-599-1000		374-3
Oswald Company Inc 308 E Eigth St Ste 500 *Web:* www.oswaldco.com	Cincinnati	OH	45202	513-793-8080		610
Oswald Cos 1100 Superior Ave Ste 1500 *TF:* 855-467-9253 ■ *Web:* www.oswaldcompanies.com	Cleveland	OH	44114	216-367-8787		390
Oswego Community Unit School District 308 4175 SR- 71 *Web:* www.sd308.org	Oswego	IL	60543	630-636-3080	636-3688	685
Oswego County 46 E Bridge St *Web:* www.co.oswego.ny.us	Oswego	NY	13126	315-349-8235	349-8237	338
Oswego County Opportunities Inc 239 Oneida St *TF:* 877-342-7618 ■ *Web:* www.oco.org	Fulton	NY	13069	315-598-4717	592-7533	48-15
Oswego Hospital 110 W Sixth St *Web:* oswegohealth.org	Oswego	NY	13126	315-349-5511		374-3
Otani 1625 Golden Gate Plaza *Web:* www.otanicleveland.com	Mayfield Heights	OH	44124	440-442-7098		671
Otani 1532 Laskin Rd *Web:* otanigrill.com	Virginia Beach	VA	23451	757-425-0404		671
Otani Japanese Seafood & Steakhouse 1684 Merriman Rd	Akron	OH	44313	330-836-1500		671
Otb Solutions Group Llc 5727 17Th Ave NE *Web:* www.otbsolutions.com	Seattle	WA	98105	206-528-3757		196
Otc Global Holdings 5151 San Felipe Ste 2200 *TF:* 877-737-8511 ■ *Web:* www.otcgh.com	Houston	TX	77056	713-358-5450		360-3
OTC Markets Group Inc 304 Hudson St 2nd Fl *OTC: OTCM* ■ *Web:* www.otcmarkets.com	New York	NY	10013	212-896-4400	868-3848	252
OTEC (Oregon Trail Electric ConsumersCo-op Inc) 4005 23rd St PO Box 226 *Web:* www.otecc.com	Baker City	OR	97814	541-523-3616		245
Oteco Inc PO Box 1849 *Web:* www.oteco.com	Houston	TX	77251	713-695-3693	695-3520	641
Otelco Inc 505 Third Ave E *NASDAQ: OTT* ■ *Web:* www.otelco.net	Oneonta	AL	35121	205-625-3574		736
Otero County 1000 New York Ave Ste 109 *Web:* www.co.otero.nm.us	Alamogordo	NM	88310	575-434-8849	443-2941	338
Otero County 13 W Third St Rm 210 *TF:* 800-438-3752 ■ *Web:* www.oterogov.com	La Junta	CO	81050	719-383-3020	383-3026	338
Otero County Electric Co-op Inc 202 Burro Ave PO Box 227 *TF:* 800-548-4660 ■ *Web:* www.ocec-inc.com	Cloudcroft	NM	88317	575-682-2521		245
Otero Junior College 1802 Colorado Ave **Fax:* Admissions ■ *TF:* 800-621-7440 ■ *Web:* www.ojc.edu	La Junta	CO	81050	719-384-6831	384-6933*	162
Otesaga, The 60 Lake St *TF:* 800-348-6222 ■ *Web:* www.otesaga.com	Cooperstown	NY	13326	607-547-9931	547-9675	669
Other Firm LLC, The 618 NW Glisan St Ste 201 *Web:* www.theotherfirm.com	Portland	OR	97209	503-336-5359		177
Otherwise Inc 1144 W Randolph St *TF:* 800-438-7325 ■ *Web:* otherwiseinc.com	Chicago	IL	60607	312-226-1144		344
Otics USA Inc 5555 Interstate View Dr *Web:* oticsusa.com	Morristown	TN	37813	423-581-9933		57
Otis College of Art & Design 9045 Lincoln Blvd *TF:* 800-527-6847 ■ *Web:* www.otis.edu	Los Angeles	CA	90045	310-665-6820	665-6821	164
Otis Elevator Co 10 Farm Springs Rd *Web:* www.otisworldwide.com	Farmington	CT	06032	860-676-6000		256
Otis Graphics Inc 290 Grant Ave *Web:* www.otisgraphics.com	Lyndhurst	NJ	07071	201-438-7120		687
Otis McAllister Inc 300 Frank H Ogawa Plaza Ste 400 *Web:* www.otismcallister.com	Oakland	CA	94612	415-421-6010	421-6016	297-11

	Phone	Fax	Class

Otis Technology
6987 Laura St PO Box 582 Lyons Falls NY 13368 315-348-4300 711
TF: 800-743-3323 ■ Web: www.otistec.com

Otis-Magie Insurance Agency Inc
332 W Superior St Ste 700 Duluth MN 55802 218-722-7753 722-7756 390
TF: 800-241-2425 ■ Web: www.otismagie.com

OTO Development LLC
100 Dunbar St Ste 402 Spartanburg SC 29306 864-596-8930 378
Web: www.otodevelopment.com

Otoe County PO Box 726 Nebraska City NE 68410 402-873-9500 338
TF: 800-833-6747 ■ Web: www.co.otoe.ne.us

Otologics LLC 5445 Airport Blvd Boulder CO 80301 303-448-9933 475
Web: www.otologics.com

Otomix Inc 747 Glasgow Ave Inglewood CA 90301 310-215-6100 301
TF: 800-701-7867 ■ Web: www.otomix.com

OTR Wheel Engineering Inc
6 Riverside Industrial Park NE Rome GA 30161 706-235-9781 754
TF: 800-833-6309 ■ Web: www.otrwheel.com

OTS (Ots-Nj LLC) 340 Bismark Rd Jackson NJ 08527 732-833-0600 189-15

OTS (Organization for Tropical Studies)
410 Swift Ave Durham NC 27705 919-684-5774 684-5661 49-5
Web: www.ots.ac.cr

OTS 3924 Clock Pointe Trl Stow OH 44224 877-445-2058 41
TF: 877-445-2058 ■ Web: www.ots.net

OTS Astracon LLC
1812 A Center Park Dr Charlotte NC 28217 704-424-5522 424-5622 311
Web: otsusa.org

OTS International Inc
2615 Industrial Ln Conroe TX 77301 936-539-0099 537
TF: 800-374-2802 ■ Web: otsintl.com

Otsego Club
696 M-32 E Main St PO Box 556 Gaylord MI 49734 989-732-5181 732-0497 669
TF: 800-752-5510 ■ Web: www.otsegoclub.com

Otsego County 197 Main St Cooperstown NY 13326 607-547-4202 547-4260 338
Web: www.otsegocounty.com

Otsego County 225 W Main St Gaylord MI 49735 989-731-7504 338
Web: www.otsegocountymi.gov

Otsego County Chamber
189 Main St Ste 201 Oneonta NY 13820 607-432-4500 432-4506 139
TF: 800-721-1000 ■ Web: otsegocc.com

Otsego Electric Co-op Inc (OEC)
3192 County Hwy 11 PO Box 128 Hartwick NY 13348 607-293-6622 293-6624 245
Web: www.otsegoec.coop

Otsego Lake State Park 7136 Old 27 S Gaylord MI 49735 989-732-5485 565
Web: michigandnr.com

Otsego Mutual Fire Insurance Co
143 Arnold Rd PO Box 40 Burlington Flats NY 13315 607-965-8211 390
Web: otsegomutual.com

Ots-Nj LLC (OTS) 340 Bismark Rd Jackson NJ 08527 732-833-0600 189-15

Otsuka America Inc
1 Embarcadero Ctr Ste 2020 San Francisco CA 94111 415-986-5300 360-3
Web: otsuka-america.com

Otsuka America Pharmaceutical Inc
2440 Research Blvd Rockville MD 20850 301-990-0030 582
TF: 800-562-3974 ■ Web: www.otsuka-us.com

Ott Planetarium 1551 Edvalson St Ogden UT 84408 801-626-6871 598
Web: www.ottplanetarium.org

Ottawa Chamber of Commerce
328 Somerset St W Ottawa ON K2P0J9 613-236-3631 236-7498 137
Web: www.ottawachamber.ca

Ottawa Citizen
1101 Baxter Rd PO Box 5020 Ottawa ON K2C3M4 613-829-9100 726-1198 532-1
TF: 800-267-6100 ■ Web: www.ottawacitizen.com

Ottawa City Hall 110 Laurier Ave W Ottawa ON K1P1J1 613-580-2400 337
TF: 866-261-9799 ■ Web: www.ottawa.ca/city_hall/index_en.html

Ottawa County 414 Washington St Grand Haven MI 49417 616-846-8320 846-8179 338
Web: www.co.ottawa.mi.us

Ottawa County 102 E Central Ave Ste104b Miami OK 74354 918-542-9408 542-8483 338

Ottawa County
307 N Concord St Ste 130 Minneapolis KS 67467 785-392-2279 392-2011 338
Web: www.ottawacounty.org

Ottawa County 315 Madison St Port Clinton OH 43452 419-734-6710 734-6898 338
Web: www.co.ottawa.oh.us

Ottawa Fringe Festival 100-2 Daly Ave Ottawa ON K1N6E2 613-232-6162 747
Web: ottawafringe.com

Ottawa Herald Inc 104 S Cedar St Ottawa KS 66067 785-242-4700 532-3
TF: 800-467-8383 ■ Web: www.ottawaherald.com

Ottawa Macdonald-Cartier International Airport
1000 Airport PkwyPrivate Ste 2500 Ottawa ON K1V9B4 613-248-2000 248-2012 27
TF: 888-901-6222 ■ Web: yow.ca/en

Ottawa Regional Cancer Foundation The
1500 Alta Vista Dr Ottawa ON K1G3Y9 613-247-3527 305
TF: 855-247-3527 ■ Web: www.ottawacancer.ca

Ottawa Senators 1000 Palladium Dr Ottawa ON K2V1A5 613-599-0100 716
TF: 800-444-7367 ■ Web: senators.nhl.com

Ottawa Sun 1101 Baxter Rd Ottawa ON K2C3M4 613-739-7000 739-8041 532-1
TF: 877-624-1463 ■ Web: www.ottawasun.com

Ottawa Symphony Orchestra (OSO)
2 Daly Ave Ste 250 Ottawa ON K1N6E2 613-231-7802 231-3610 573-3
Web: www.ottawasymphony.com

Ottawa Tourism & Convention Authority
150 Elgin St Ste 1405 Ottawa ON K2P1L4 613-237-5150 237-7339 206
TF: 800-363-4465 ■ Web: www.ottawatourism.ca

Ottawa University 1001 S Cedar St Ottawa KS 66067 785-242-5200 166
TF Admissions: 800-755-5200 ■ Web: www.ottawa.edu

Ottawa University Phoenix
10020 N 25th Ave Phoenix AZ 85021 602-371-1188 371-0035 166
TF: 800-235-9586 ■ Web: www.ottawa.edu

Ottawa Visitors Ctr 106 W Lafayette St Ottawa IL 61350 815-434-2737 434-4530 206
TF: 888-688-2924 ■ Web: pickusottawail.com

Ottawa-AM 1200 (Sports) 87 George St Ottawa ON K1N9H7 613-789-2486 645-117
TF: 877-670-1200 ■ Web: www.tsn.ca/radio/ottawa-1200

Otten Johnson Robinson Neff & Ragonetti PC
950 17th St Ste 1600 Denver CO 80202 303-825-8400 825-6525 428
Web: www.ottenjohnson.com

Ottenweller Company Inc
3011 Congressional Pkwy Fort Wayne IN 46808 260-484-3166 484-9798 91
Web: www.ottenweller.com

Otter C. L. "Butch" (R)
700 W Jefferson St Ste 228 PO Box 83720 Boise ID 83720 208-334-2100 334-3454 343
Web: gov.idaho.gov

Otter Creek Management Inc
222 Lakeview Ave Ste 1100 West Palm Beach FL 33401 561-832-4110 401
Web: ottercreekmgt.com

Otter Creek State Park
400 East SR 22 Antimony UT 84712 435-624-3268 565
Web: www.stateparks.utah.gov

Otter Tail Corp
4334 18th Ave SW PO Box 9156 Fargo ND 58106 218-739-8479 360-3
NASDAQ: OTTR ■ TF: 866-410-8780 ■ Web: www.ottertail.com

Otter Tail County 520 Fir Ave W Fergus Falls MN 56537 218-998-8000 998-8438 338
TF: 800-232-9077 ■ Web: www.co.ottertail.mn.us

Otter Tail Power Co
215 S Cascade St Fergus Falls MN 56537 218-739-8200 751-5151 787
TF: 800-257-4044 ■ Web: www.otpco.com

Otter Tail Telcom
230 W Lincoln Ave Fergus Falls MN 56537 218-826-6161 116
TF: 800-247-2706 ■ Web: www.prtel.com

Otterbein College 1 S Grove St Westerville OH 43081 614-823-1500 823-1200* 166
*Fax: Admissions ■ TF Admissions: 800-488-8144 ■ Web: www.otterbein.edu

Otterbein senior lifestyle choices
580 N SR 741 Lebanon OH 45036 513-933-5400 932-1054 672
TF: 888-513-9131 ■ Web: www.otterbein.org

Otterbine Barebo Inc 3840 Main Rd E Emmaus PA 18049 610-965-6018 321
TF: 800-237-8837 ■ Web: www.otterbine.com

Otto Baum Company Inc 866 N Main St Morton IL 61550 309-266-7114 263-1050 189-7
Web: www.ottobaum.com

Otto Bock Healthcare North America Inc
2 Carlson Pkwy N Ste 100 Minneapolis MN 55447 763-553-9464 475
TF: 800-328-4058 ■ Web: www.ottobockus.com

Otto Brehm Inc PO Box 249 Yonkers NY 10710 914-968-6100 968-8926 297-11
TF: 800-272-6886 ■ Web: www.ottobrehm.com

Otto Bremer Foundation
30 E Seventh St Ste 2900 Saint Paul MN 55101 651-227-8036 305
Web: www.ottobremer.org

Otto Candies LLC 17271 US 90 Des Allemands LA 70030 504-469-7700 469-7740 465
Web: www.ottocandies.com

Otto Creative Marketing Inc
1611 Colley Ave Norfolk VA 23517 757-622-4050 636
TF: 800-438-7325 ■ Web: www.thinkotto.com

Otto Dukes Construction Supply Solutions
2556 Agnes St Corpus Christi TX 78405 361-883-0921 350
Web: www.ottodukestools.com

Otto Engineering Inc
2 E Main St Carpentersville IL 60110 847-428-7171 428-1956 729
TF: 888-234-6886 ■ Web: www.ottoexcellence.com

Otto Instrument Service Inc
1441 Valencia Pl Ontario CA 91761 909-930-5800 57
Web: www.ottoinstrument.com

Otto Naumann Ltd 22 E 80th St New York NY 10075 212-734-4443 535-0617 42
Web: www.ottonaumannltd.com

Otto Trucking Inc 4220 E McDowell Ste 108 Mesa AZ 85215 480-641-3500 641-3550 780
Web: www.ottotrucking.com

Otto's Restaurant & Bar
6405 Mineral Pt Rd Madison WI 53705 608-274-4044 274-1358 671
Web: www.ottosrestaurant.com

Ottosen Propeller & Accessories Inc
105 S 28th St Phoenix AZ 85034 602-275-8514 770
TF: 800 528 7551 ■ Web: www.hartzellprop.com

Ottumwa Area Chamber of Commerce
217 E Main St Ottumwa IA 52501 641-682-3465 682-3466 139
TF: 800-255-4268 ■ Web: www.ottumwaiowa.com

Ottumwa Courier 213 E Second St Ottumwa IA 52501 641-684-4611 684-7326* 532-2
*Fax: News Rm ■ TF: 800-532-1504 ■ Web: www.ottumwacourier.com

Ottumwa Public Library
102 W Fourth St Ottumwa IA 52501 641-682-7563 682-4970 434-3
TF: 800-272-3900 ■ Web: ottumwapubliclibrary.org

Ottumwa Regional Health Ctr
1001 Pennsylvania Ave Ottumwa IA 52501 641-684-2300 374-3
TF: 800-933-6742 ■ Web: www.ottumwaregionalhealth.com

O-two Medical Technologies Inc
7575 Kimbel St Mississauga ON L5S1C8 905-677-9410 250
TF: 800-387-3405 ■ Web: www.otwo.com

OTZ Telephone Co-op Inc PO Box 324 Kotzebue AK 99752 907-442-3114 736
TF: 800-478-3111 ■ Web: otz.net

OU (Orthodox Union) 11 Broadway New York NY 10004 212-563-4000 564-9058 48-20
TF: 855-505-7500 ■ Web: www.ou.org

OU Medical Ctr
Bone Marrow Transplant Program
1 S Bryant Edmond OK 73034 405-271-8042 769
Web: www.oumedicine.com

OU Medical Ctr Edmond 1 S Bryant St Edmond OK 73034 405-341-6100 374-3
Web: www.oumedicine.com

Ouabache State Park
4930 E State Rd 201 Bluffton IN 46714 260-824-0926 565
Web: www.in.gov

Ouachita Baptist University
410 Ouachita St Arkadelphia AR 71998 870-245-5000 245-5500* 166
*Fax: Admissions ■ TF Admissions: 800-342-5628 ■ Web: www.obu.edu

Ouachita Citizen 4423 Cypress St West Monroe LA 71291 318-396-0602 532-4
Web: hannapub.com/ouachitacitizen

Ouachita County 109 Goodgame St Camden AR 71701 870-231-5300 231-4329 338
Web: www.ouachitacountysheriff.org

Ouachita County Medical Ctr (OCMC)
PO Box 797 Camden AR 71711 870-836-1000 836-1522 374-3
TF: 877-836-2472 ■ Web: www.ouachitamedcenter.com

Ouachita Electric Co-op Corp
700 Bradley Ferry Rd PO Box 877 Camden AR 71711 870-836-5791 245
TF: 877-252-4538 ■ Web: www.oecc.com

Ouachita Parish 301 S Grand St Ste 104 Monroe LA 71201 318-327-1444 327-1462 338
Web: www.opclerkofcourt.com

Ouachita Parish Public Library
1800 Stubbs Ave Monroe LA 71201 318-327-1490 327-1373 434-3
Web: www.oplib.org

Ouachita Technical College
1 College Cir Malvern AR 72104 501-337-5000 337-9382 162
TF: 800-337-0266 ■ Web: coto.edu

Phone | Fax | Class

Ouellette Plumbing & Heating
36 Dorset Ln. .... Williston VT 05495 802-878-6004 189-10

Ouest 2315 Broadway .... New York NY 10024 212-580-1300 671

Ouisi Bistro 3014 Granville St .... Vancouver BC V6H3J8 604-732-7550 671
Web: www.ouisibistro.com

Ounce of Prevention Fund of Florida Inc, The
111 N Gadsden St Ste 200 .... Tallahassee FL 32301 850-921-4494 317
Web: www.ounce.org

Our Cooperative
525 Old Bellefonte Rd .... Harrison AR 72601 870-743-9100 148
Web: www.oursc.k12.ar.us

Our Lady of Fatima Retreat House
5353 E 56th St .... Indianapolis IN 46226 317-545-7681 545-0095 673
TF: 800-382-9836 ■ *Web:* www.archindy.org

Our Lady of Lourdes Medical Ctr
1600 Haddon Ave .... Camden NJ 08103 856-757-3500 374-3
TF: 888-568-7337 ■ *Web:* www.lourdesnet.org

Our Lady of Lourdes Memorial Hospital
169 Riverside Dr. .... Binghamton NY 13905 607-798-5111 374-3
Web: www.lourdes.com

Our Lady of Lourdes Regional Medical Ctr
4801 Ambassador Caffery Pkwy .... Lafayette LA 70508 337-470-2000 374-3
Web: lourdesrmc.com/pages/home.aspx

Our Lady of the Lake College
7434 Perkins Rd. .... Baton Rouge LA 70808 225-768-1700 768-1726* 166
*Fax: Admissions ■ *TF Admissions:* 877-242-3509 ■ *Web:* www.ololcollege.edu

Our Lady of the Lake Regional Medical Ctr
5000 Hennessy Blvd. .... Baton Rouge LA 70808 225-765-6565 374-3
Web: ololrmc.com/pages/home.aspx

Our Lady of the Lake University
411 SW 24th St .... San Antonio TX 78207 210-434-6711 431-4036* 166
*Fax: Admissions ■ *TF:* 800-436-6558 ■ *Web:* www.ollusa.edu

Our Lady Queen of Peace Catholic School
1600 Hwy 2004 .... Richwood TX 77531 979-265-3909 685
Web: www.olqpschool.org

Our Lady Queen of the Most Holy Rosary Cathedral
2535 Collingwood Blvd .... Toledo OH 43610 419-244-9575 50-1
Web: www.rosarycathedral.org

Our Sunday Visitor Inc
200 Noll Plaza .... Huntington IN 46750 260-356-8400 356-8472 637-8
TF: 800-348-2440 ■ *Web:* www.osv.com

Our Time Ltd 2100 Dorr St. .... Toledo OH 43607 419-537-1666 345
TF: 800-935-9935 ■ *Web:* www.ourtime.com

Our Town 36 Ridge St .... Pearl River NY 10965 845-735-1342 620-9533 532-4
TF: 800-662-1220 ■ *Web:* ourtownnews.com

Ouray County 541 Fourth St PO Box C .... Ouray CO 81427 970-325-4961 325-0452 338
TF: 800-368-8683 ■ *Web:* www.ouraycountyco.gov

OurParents Inc 8521 Leesburg Pk Ste 310 .... Vienna VA 22182 866-531-0695 387
TF: 866-629-1634 ■ *Web:* www.ourparents.com

OUSD (Oceanside Unified School District)
2111 Mission Ave. .... Oceanside CA 92058 760-966-4000 186
Web: www.oside.k12.ca.us

Out of Africa Wildlife Park
4020 N Cherry Rd. .... Camp Verde AZ 86322 928-567-2840 567-2839 823
Web: www.outofafricapark.com

Out There Advertising Inc
22 E Second St .... Duluth MN 55802 218-720-6002 7
TF: 800-438-7325 ■ *Web:* outthereadvertising.com

Outa Knoware International
886 Salem Rd .... Dracut MA 01826 978-688-1388 177
Web: outaknoware.com

Outagamie County 410 S Walnut St .... Appleton WI 54911 920-832-5077 832-2200 338
TF: 800-441-4563 ■ *Web:* www.outagamie.org

Outback Steakhouse Inc
2202 NW Shore Blvd 5th Fl .... Tampa FL 33607 813-282-1225 670
Web: www.outback.com

OutboundEngine
98 San Jacinto Blvd Ste 1300 .... Austin TX 78701 800-562-7315 195
TF: 800-562-7315 ■ *Web:* www.outboundengine.com

OutCast Agency, The
100 Montgomery St Ste 1201 .... San Francisco CA 94104 415-392-8282 636
Web: www.theoutcastagency.com

Outcast Sporting Gear
2021 E Wilson Ln .... Meridian ID 83642 208-955-0476 711
Web: aireindustrial.net

Outdoor Adv Assn of America Inc (OAAA)
1850 M St NW Ste 1040 .... Washington DC 20036 202-833-5566 833-1522 615
TF: 800-325-3694 ■ *Web:* www.oaaa.org

Outdoor Amusement Business Assn PAC (OABA-PAC)
1035 S Semoran Blvd Ste 1045A .... Winter Park FL 32792 407-681-9444 681-9445 615
TF: 800-517-6222 ■ *Web:* www.oaba.org

Outdoor Ch
43445 Business Pk Dr Ste 103 .... Temecula CA 92590 951-699-6991 740
NASDAQ: OUTD ■ *TF:* 800-770-5750 ■ *Web:* www.outdoorchannel.com

Outdoor Connection Inc 424 Neosho .... Burlington KS 66839 620-364-5500 364-5563 771
Web: www.outdoor-connection.com

Outdoor Industry Assn (OIA)
4909 Pearl E Cir Ste 200 .... Boulder CO 80301 303-444-3353 444-3284 49-4
Web: www.outdoorindustry.org

Outdoor Photographer Magazine
25 Braintree Hill Office Pk Ste 404 .... Braintree MA 90025 617-706-9110 536-0102 457-14
TF Cust Svc: 800-283-4410 ■ *Web:* www.outdoorphotographer.com

Outdoor Power Equipment Institute Inc (OPEI)
341 S Patrick St .... Alexandria VA 22314 703-549-7600 549-7604 49-4
TF: 800-558-8767 ■ *Web:* www.opei.org

Outdoor Sports Center 80 Danbury Rd .... Wilton CT 06897 203-762-8797 711
TF: 800-782-2193 ■ *Web:* www.outdoorsports.com

Outdoor Ventures 10579 S Main St .... Hayward WI 54843 715-634-4447 711
TF: 866-710-2846 ■ *Web:* www.outdoorventureshayward.com

Outer Banks Chamber of Commerce
101 Town Hall Dr PO Box 1757 .... Kill Devil Hills NC 27948 252-441-8144 139
Web: www.outerbankschamber.com

Outer Banks Visitors Bureau
1 Visitor Ctr Cir .... Manteo NC 27954 252-473-2138 473-5777 206
TF: 877-629-4386 ■ *Web:* www.outerbanks.org

OuterBox Inc 325 S Main St Fl 3 .... Akron OH 44308 234-542-6503 809
Web: www.outerboxdesign.com

Phone | Fax | Class

Outerlink Corp
187 Ballardvale St Ste A260 .... Wilmington MA 01887 978-284-6070 268-5444 681
TF: 877-688-3770 ■ *Web:* www.outerlink.com

Outermost Inn 81 Lighthouse Rd. .... Aquinnah MA 02535 508-645-3511 671
Web: www.outermostinn.com

Outfest-Los Angeles Gay & Lesbian Film Festival
3470 Wilshire Blvd Ste 935 .... Los Angeles CA 90010 213-480-7088 480-7099 282
TF: 800-726-7147 ■ *Web:* www.outfest.org

Out-fit 25 W Easy St Ste 304 .... Simi Valley CA 93065 310-410-1200 410-1210 711
TF: 800-376-3339 ■ *Web:* www.out-fit.net

OUTFRONT Media Inc 405 Lexington Ave .... New York NY 10174 212-297-6400 8
TF: 800-926-8834 ■ *Web:* www.outfrontmedia.com

Outlet Collection Seattle, The
1101 SuperMall Way .... Auburn WA 98001 253-833-9500 833-9006 460
Web: www.outletcollectionseattle.com

Outlets at Anthem 4250 W Anthem Way .... Phoenix AZ 85086 623-465-9500 460
TF: 888-482-5834 ■ *Web:* www.outletsanthem.com

Outlets at Loveland
5661 McWhinney Blvd .... Loveland CO 80538 970-663-1916 460
Web: www.outletsatloveland.com

Outlook Group Corp 1180 American Dr .... Neenah WI 54956 920-722-2333 627
Web: www.outlookgroup.com

Outokumpu 1101 N Main St. .... Wildwood FL 34785 352-748-1313 416-7473* 490
*Fax Area Code: 800 ■ *TF:* 800-731-7473 ■ *Web:* www.outokumpu.com

Outotec (Canada) Ltd
1551 Corporate Dr .... Burlington ON L7L6M3 905-335-0002 111
TF: 800-654-4567 ■ *Web:* www.outotec.com

Outpatient Imaging Affiliates LLC
4322 Harding Pk Ste 422 .... Nashville TN 37205 615-846-7733 415
TF: 800-899-4489 ■ *Web:* www.oiarad.com

Outpost Lodge 28229 Cow Creek Rd. .... Pierre SD 57501 605-264-5450 671
TF: 800-456-1168 ■ *Web:* www.theoutpostlodge.com

Output Services Inc 6410 O'Dell Pl .... Boulder CO 80301 303-530-3403 627
TF: 800-858-9958 ■ *Web:* www.outputservices.com

Outreach Communications
2801 Glenda St. .... Haltom City TX 76117 817-288-7200 224
TF: 800-982-3760 ■ *Web:* www.outreachcom.com

Outreach Healthcare Inc
269 W Renner Pkwy .... Richardson TX 75080 800-793-0081 363
TF: 800-793-0081 ■ *Web:* www.outreachhealth.com

Outreach International
129 W Lexington PO Box 210 .... Independence MO 64050 816-833-0883 833-0103 48-5
TF: 888-833-1235 ■ *Web:* www.outreach-international.org

Outrigger Energy LLC
1200 Seventeenth St Ste 900 .... Denver CO 80202 720-638-7312 580
Web: outriggerenergy.com

Outrigger Enterprises Group
2375 Kuhio Ave .... Honolulu HI 96815 866-956-4262 622-4852* 379
*Fax Area Code: 800 ■ *TF:* 800-462-6262 ■ *Web:* www.outrigger.com
Outrigger Hotels & Resorts
2375 Kuhio Ave .... Honolulu HI 96815 866-956-4262 622-4852* 379
*Fax Area Code: 800 ■ *Fax: Sales ■ *TF:* 800-688-7444 ■ *Web:* www.outrigger.com

Outrigger Kanaloa at Kona
78-261 Manukai St. .... Kailua-Kona HI 96740 808-322-9625 669
TF: 800-688-7444 ■ *Web:* www.outrigger.com

Outrigger Reef on the Beach
2169 Kalia Rd. .... Honolulu HI 96815 808-923-3111 924-4957 669
TF: 800-688-7444 ■ *Web:* www.outrigger.com

Outrigger Waikiki on the Beach
2335 Kalakaua Ave .... Honolulu HI 96815 808-923-0711 921-9749 379
TF: 800-688-7444 ■ *Web:* www.outrigger.com

Outset Media Corp
106-4226 Commerce Cir .... Victoria BC V8Z6N6 250-592-7374 592-7522 761
Web: www.outsetmedia.com

Outside Magazine 400 Market St .... Santa Fe NM 87501 505-989-7100 457-14
TF General: 888-909-2382 ■ *Web:* www.outsideonline.com

Outside Source Inc
7202 E 71st St .... Indianapolis IN 46256 317-842-4853 344
Web: outsidesource.com

Outside the Lines Inc
529 W Blueridge Ave .... Orange CA 92865 714-637-4747 186
Web: otl-inc.com

Outsource Staffing Inc
2611 Laurel St .... Beaumont TX 77702 409-813-2900 260
Web: outsourcestaffinginc.com

Outsource Testing Inc 1278 Ctr Ct Dr .... Covina CA 91724 909-592-8898 809
TF: 800-201-2274 ■ *Web:* www.outsourcetesting.com

OUTSOURCEIT Inc 6810 Crain Hwy .... La Plata MD 20646 301-539-0200 180
Web: www.outsourceitcorp.com

Outspoken Media Inc
4142 Mariner Blvd Ste 234 .... Spring Hill FL 34609 904-742-6477 631
Web: outspokenmedia.com

Outstart Inc 745 Atlantic Ave 4th Fl .... Boston MA 02111 617-897-6800 897-6801 39
TF: 877-971-9171 ■ *Web:* www.outstart.com

Outten Chevrolet Inc
1701 W Tilghman St .... Allentown PA 18104 610-628-3600 820-5774 57
Web: outtenchevyallentown.com

Outward Bound 910 Jackson St. .... Golden CO 80401 207-510-7533 510-7535 766
TF: 866-467-7651 ■ *Web:* www.outwardbound.org

Ovarian Cancer Research Fund Alliance
1101 14th St NW Ste 850 .... Washington DC 20005 202-331-1332 331-2292 474
TF: 866-399-6262 ■ *Web:* www.ovariancancer.org

Ovation Data Services Inc
14199 Westfair E Dr .... Houston TX 77041 713-464-1300 224
Web: www.ovationdata.com

Ovation Development Corp
6021 S Ft Apache Rd Ste 100 .... Las Vegas NV 89148 702-990-2390 653

Ovation Hair Design
18 Davenport St .... Somerville NJ 08876 908-526-5110 77
Web: ovationhairdesign.com

Ovation Instore 57-13 49th Pl. .... Maspeth NY 11378 718-628-2600 233
TF: 800-553-2202 ■ *Web:* www.ovationinstore.com

Ovation Networks Inc
222 Third Ave SE Ste 276 .... Cedar Rapids IA 52401 319-365-6200 225
TF: 800-561-3357 ■ *Web:* www.ovationnetworks.com

Ovation The Arts Network
2850 Ocean Pk Blvd Ste 225 .... Santa Monica CA 90405 310-430-7575 740
Web: www.ovationtv.com

	Phone	Fax	Class
Ovation Wireless Management Inc 19315 W Catawba Ave Ste 220 Cornelius NC 28031 *Web:* ovationwireless.com	704-714-2111		736
Oven, The 201 N Eigth St Lincoln NE 68508 *Web:* www.theoven-lincoln.com	402-475-6118		671
Over The Mountain Journal 2016 Columbiana Rd Birmingham AL 35216 *Web:* www.otmj.com	205-823-9646	824-1246	532-4
Over The Rainbow Children & Adult Hair Styling Salon 8300 Tampa Ave Ste C Northridge CA 91324 *Web:* www.overtherainbowchildrenssalon.com	818-886-9325		77
Overall Laundry Services Inc 7200 HaRdeson Rd Everett WA 98203	425-347-0123		442
Overbrook Entertainment Inc 10202 W Washington Blvd Culver City CA 90232	310-432-2400	432-2401	514
Overcomers in Christ PO Box 34460 Omaha NE 68134 *TF:* 866-573-0966 ■ *Web:* www.overcomersinchrist.org	866-573-0966		48-21
Overcomers Outreach PO Box 922950 Sylmar CA 91392 *TF:* 800-310-3001 ■ *Web:* www.overcomersoutreach.org	818-833-1803		48-21
OverDrive Inc 1 OverDr Wy Unit C Cleveland OH 44125 *Web:* www.overdrive.com	216-573-6886	573-6888	178-10
Overeaters Anonymous Inc (OA) PO Box 44020 Rio Rancho NM 87174 *TF:* 866-505-4966 ■ *Web:* www.oa.org	505-891-2664	891-4320	48-21
Overfelt Gardens 368 Educational Pk Dr San Jose CA 95133 *Web:* www.sanjoseca.gov	408-251-3323		97
Overhead Conveyor Co 1330 Hilton Rd Ferndale MI 48220 *Web:* www.occ-conveyor.com	248-547-3800	547-8344	207
Overhead Door Company of Sacramento Inc 6756 Franklin Blvd Sacramento CA 95823 *TF:* 800-929-3667 ■ *Web:* www.overheaddoor.com	916-421-3747		189-2
Overhead Door Corp 2501 S State Hwy 121 Bus Ste 200 Lewisville TX 75067 *TF:* 800-275-3290 ■ *Web:* www.overheaddoor.com	469-549-7100	549-7281	234
Overhill Farms Inc 2727 E Vernon Ave Vernon CA 90058 *NYSE: OFI* ■ *TF:* 800-859-6406 ■ *Web:* www.overhillfarms.com	323-582-9977	582-6122	296-36
Overit 435 New Scotland Ave Albany NY 12208 *TF:* 888-978-8147 ■ *Web:* overit.com	518-465-8829		7
Overlake Hospital Medical Ctr 1035 116th Ave NE Bellevue WA 98004 *Web:* www.overlakehospital.org	425-688-5000		374-3
Overland Express Co 5539 Harvey Wilson Dr Houston TX 77020 *Web:* www.overlandexp.com	713-672-6161	672-5040	780
Overland Park Chamber of Commerce 9001 W 110th St Ste 150 Overland Park KS 66210 *Web:* opchamber.org	913-491-3600	491-0393	139
Overland Park Convention & Visitors Bureau 9001 W 110th St Ste 100 Overland Park KS 66210 *TF:* 800-262-7275 ■ *Web:* www.visitoverlandpark.com	913-491-0123	491-0015	206
Overland Park Convention Center Hotel 6100 College Blvd Overland Park KS 66211 *TF:* 800-436-1196 ■ *Web:* www.opconventioncenter.com	913-234-2100		378
Overland Park Regional Medical Ctr 10500 Quivira Rd Overland Park KS 66215 *TF:* 800-849-0829 ■ *Web:* www.oprmc.com	913-541-5000		374-3
Overland Rentals Inc 1901 N State Hwy 360 Ste 340 Grand Prairie TX 75050 *TF:* 800-530-8050 ■ *Web:* www.point-of-rental.com	972-602-9819		177
Overland Sheepskin Company Inc 2096 Nutmeg Ave Fairfield IA 52556 *TF:* 800-683-7526 ■ *Web:* www.overland.com	641-472-8434		157-5
Overland Stockyard Inc 10565 Ninth Ave Hanford CA 93230 *Web:* www.overlandstockyard.com	559-582-0404		446
Overland Storage Inc 4820 Overland Ave San Diego CA 92123 *NASDAQ: OVRL* ■ *TF:* 800-729-8725 ■ *Web:* www.overlandstorage.com	858-571-5555	571-0982	176
Overlay TV Inc 80 Aberdeen St Ste 401 Ottawa ON K1S5R5 *Web:* www.overlay.tv	613-761-6152		4
Overlook Lodge PO Box 351 Bear Mountain NY 10911 *TF:* 800-242-2728 ■ *Web:* www.visitbearmountain.com	845-786-2731	786-2543	379
Overlook Medical Ctr 99 Beauvoir Ave Summit NJ 07902 *TF:* 800-619-4024 ■ *Web:* www.atlantichealth.org	908-522-2000		374-3
Overlook Press 141 Wooster St New York NY 10012 *TF:* 800-527-9703 ■ *Web:* www.overlookpress.com	212-673-2210	673-2296	637-2
Overlook Systems Technologies Inc 1950 Old Gallows Rd Ste 400 Vienna VA 22182 *Web:* www.overlooksys.com	703-893-1411	356-9029	261
Overly Manufacturing Co 574 W Otterman St Greensburg PA 15601 *TF:* 800-979-7300 ■ *Web:* www.overly.com	724-834-7300	830-2871	491
OvernightPrints Inc 1800 E Garry Ave Santa Ana CA 92705 *Web:* www.overnightprints.com	949-231-5632		627
Oversea-Chinese Banking Corp Ltd 1700 Broadway 18th Fl New York NY 10019 *Web:* www.ocbc.com	212-586-6222	586-0636	70
Overseas Adventure Travel 347 Congress St Boston MA 02210 *TF:* 800-221-0814 ■ *Web:* www.oattravel.com	800-221-0814		760
Overseas Development Corp 953 Washington Blvd Stamford CT 06901 *Web:* www.overseasdevelopment.com	203-964-0111		492
Overseas Express Consolidators (Canada) Inc 725 Montee De Liesse Saint Laurent QC H4T1P5 *TF:* 800-501-1790 ■ *Web:* www.oecgroup.ca	514-905-1246		314
Overseas Press Club of America (OPC) 40 W 45th St New York NY 10036 *Web:* www.opcofamerica.org	212-626-9220		49-14
Overseas Private Investment Corp (OPIC) 1100 New York Ave NW Washington DC 20527 *TF:* 800-225-5722 ■ *Web:* www.opic.gov	202-336-8400	408-9859	340-20
Overseas Shipholding Group Inc 666 Third Ave New York NY 10017 *TF:* 800-851-9677 ■ *Web:* www.osg.com	212-953-4100	578-1832	313
Oversee.net 550 S Hope St Ste 200 Los Angeles CA 90071 *Web:* oversee.wpengine.com	213-408-0080		530
Overstock.com Inc 6350 South 3000 East Salt Lake City UT 84121 *NASDAQ: OSTK* ■ *TF Cust Svc:* 800-843-2446 ■ *Web:* www.overstock.com	801-947-3100	944-4629	791
Over-The-Air Wireless Inc 844 NW 49th St Seattle WA 98107 *Web:* www.otawireless.com	206-357-5020		736
Over-the-Rhine Chamber of Commerce 1431 Walnut St Cincinnati OH 45202 *Web:* www.otrchamber.com	513-241-2690		460
Overton Brooks Veterans Affairs Medical Ctr 510 E Stoner Ave Shreveport LA 71101 *TF:* 800-863-7441 ■ *Web:* www.shreveport.va.gov	318-221-8411		374-8
Overton Chicago Gear Inc 530 Westgate Dr Addison IL 60101 *Web:* www.ocgear.com	630-543-9570		709
Overton County 317 E University St Rm 22 Livingston TN 38570 *TF:* 800-876-7393 ■ *Web:* www.overtoncountytn.com	931-823-2631	823-2696	338
Overton County News 415 W Main St Livingston TN 38570 *Web:* www.overtoncountynews.com	931-823-6485		532-3
Overton Hotel & Conference Center 2320 Mac Davis Ln Lubbock TX 79401 *TF:* 800-456-5974 ■ *Web:* www.overtonhotel.com	806-776-7000		132
Overton Power District # 5 615 N Moapa Vly Blvd PO Box 395 Overton NV 89040 *Web:* opd5.com	702-397-2512		245
Overture Ctr for the Arts 201 State St Madison WI 53703 *Web:* www.overture.org	608-258-4141	258-4966	572
Overture Partners LLC 57 Wells Ave # 22 Newton MA 02459 *Web:* www.overturepartners.com	617-614-9600		196
Overture Technologies Inc 9841 Washingtonian Blvd Ste 211 Gaithersburg MD 20878 *Web:* home.overturecorp.com	301-492-2140		225
Overwaitea Food Group 19855 92A Ave Langley BC V1M3B6 *TF:* 800-242-9229 ■ *Web:* www.owfg.com	604-888-1213		345
Overwatch Geospatial Operations 21660 Ridgetop Cir Ste 110 Sterling VA 20166 *TF:* 800-937-6881 ■ *Web:* textronsystems.com/company-overview/rebrand	703-437-7651	437-0039	178-8
Overwraps Packaging LP 3950 La Reunion Pkwy Dallas TX 75212 *Web:* www.overwraps.com	214-634-0427		548
Ovid Technologies Inc 333 Seventh Ave 20th Fl New York NY 10001 *TF:* 800-950-2035 ■ *Web:* www.ovid.com	646-674-6300	674-6301	387
OvisLink Technologies Corp 203 Lemon Creek Dr Ste C Walnut CA 91789 *Web:* www.ovislink.com	909-869-8666		176
OVMA (Ohio Veterinary Medical Assn) 3168 Riverside Dr Columbus OH 43221 *TF:* 800-662-6862 ■ *Web:* www.ohiovma.org	614-486-7253	486-1325	795
OVMC (Olive View Medical Ctr) 14445 Olive View Dr Sylmar CA 91342 *Web:* uclaoliveview.org	747-210-3000		374-3
OW Lee Company Inc 1822 E Francis St Ontario CA 91761 *TF:* 800-776-9533 ■ *Web:* www.owlee.com	909-947-3771	947-6614	319-4
Owasso Chamber of Commerce 315 S Cedar St Owasso OK 74055 *TF:* 800-380-2450 ■ *Web:* www.owassochamber.com	918-272-2141	272-8564	139
Owatonna Area Chamber of Commerce & Tourism 320 Hoffman Dr Owatonna MN 55060 *TF:* 800-423-6466 ■ *Web:* www.owatonna.org	507-451-7970	451-7972	139
Owatonna Peoples Press 135 W Pearl St Owatonna MN 55060 *Web:* www.southernminn.com	507-451-2840	444-2382	637-8
Owatonna Public Library 105 N Elm St Owatonna MN 55060 *TF:* 800-657-3864 ■ *Web:* ci.owatonna.mn.us	507-444-2460	444-2465	434-3
Owatonna Senior High School 333 E School St Owatonna MN 55060 *Web:* www.owatonna.k12.mn.us	507-444-8800		685
Owen Brennan's Restaurant 6150 Poplar Ave Memphis TN 38119 *Web:* www.brennansmemphis.com	901-761-0990	761-9177	671
Owen Community Bank 279 E Morgan St Spencer IN 47460 *TF:* 800-690-2095 ■ *Web:* owencom.com	812-829-2095	829-3069	360-2
Owen County 100 N Thomas St Owenton KY 40359 *Web:* www.owencountyky.us	502-484-3405	484-1004	338
Owen County 60 S Main St Spencer IN 47460 *Web:* www.owencounty.in.gov	812-829-5030		338
Owen Electric Co-op Inc 8205 Hwy 127 N PO Box 400 Owenton KY 40359 *TF:* 800-372-7612 ■ *Web:* www.owenelectric.com	502-484-3471		245
Owen Equipment Co 13101 NE Whitaker Way Portland OR 97230 *TF:* 800-992-3656 ■ *Web:* www.owenequipment.com	503-255-9055		358
Owen Group Inc 220 Technology Dr Ste 100 Irvine CA 92618 *Web:* www.owengroup.com	949-860-4800	860-4810	261
Owen Industries Inc 501 Ave H Carter Lake IA 51510 *TF:* 800-831-9252 ■ *Web:* www.owenind.com	712-347-5500		492
Owen Media Inc 3130 E Madison St Ste 206 Seattle WA 98112 *Web:* www.owenmedia.com	206-322-1167		7
Owen Sound Minor Hockey Group PO Box 13 Owen Sound ON N4K5P1 *Web:* owensoundminorhockey.com	519-371-2467		706
Owen Sound Sun Times 290 Ninth St E Owen Sound ON N4K5P2 *TF:* 800-267-6568 ■ *Web:* www.owensoundsuntimes.com	519-376-2250	376-7190	532-1
Owen Steel Co 727 Mauney Dr Columbia SC 29201 *TF:* 800-261-6270 ■ *Web:* www.owensteel.com	803-251-7680	251-7613	480
Owen-Ames-Kimball Co 300 Ionia Ave NW Grand Rapids MI 49503 *TF:* 800-238-4269 ■ *Web:* www.owen-ames-kimball.com	616-456-1521	458-0770	186
Owens & Assoc Investigations 8765 Aero Dr Ste 306 San Diego CA 92123 **Fax Area Code:* 619 ■ *TF:* 800-297-1343 ■ *Web:* www.owenspi.com	800-297-1343	297-1343*	400

Phone | Fax | Class

Owens & Minor Inc
9120 Lockwood Blvd .... Mechanicsville VA 23116 804-723-7000 723-7100 475
NYSE: OMI ■ *TF:* 800-633-8284 ■ *Web:* www.owens-minor.com

Owens Community College
Findlay 3200 Bright Rd .... Findlay OH 45840 800-466-9367 162
TF: 800-466-9367 ■ *Web:* www.owens.edu
Toledo 30335 Oregon Rd .... Perrysburg OH 43551 419-661-7000 162
TF: 800-466-9367 ■ *Web:* www.owens.edu

Owens Corning 1 Owens Corning Pkwy. .... Toledo OH 43659 419-248-8000 389
NYSE: OC ■ *Web:* www.owenscorning.com

Owens Design Inc 47427 Fremont Blvd .... Fremont CA 94538 510-659-1800 454
Web: www.owensdesign.com

Owens Handle Company Inc
4200 N Frazier St .... Conroe TX 77303 936-856-2981 820

Owens Healthcare 2247 Court St. .... Redding CA 96001 530-246-1075 696-9367* 237
**Fax Area Code:* 800 ■ *Web:* www.owensmedicalsupply.com

Owens Industries Inc
7815 S Sixth St. .... Oak Creek WI 53154 414-764-1212 764-6030 454
Web: www.owensind.com

Owens Liquors Inc
8000 N Kings Hwy .... Myrtle Beach SC 29572 843-449-6833 443
Web: owensliquors.com

Owens Precision Inc
5966 Morgan Mill Rd .... Carson City NV 89701 775-883-4690 757
Web: www.owensprecision.com

Owensboro Community & Technical College
4800 New Hartford Rd .... Owensboro KY 42303 270-686-4400 686-4496 800
TF: 866-755-6282 ■ *Web:* www.octc.kctcs.edu

Owensboro Federal Credit Union
717 Harvard Dr PO Box 1189 .... Owensboro KY 42302 270-683-1054 685-3987 219
TF: 800-264-1054 ■ *Web:* www.ofcuonline.com

Owensboro Grain Co 822 E Second St. .... Owensboro KY 42303 270-926-2032 686-6509 296-29
TF: 800-874-0305 ■ *Web:* www.owensborograin.com

Owensboro Health (OMHS)
811 E Parish Ave PO Box 20007 .... Owensboro KY 42303 270-688-2000 374-3
TF: 877-888-6647 ■ *Web:* www.owensborohealth.org

Owensboro Health Muhlenberg Community Hospital
440 Hopkinsville St .... Greenville KY 42345 270-338-8000 338-8278 374-3
Web: www.mchky.org

Owensboro Symphony Orchestra
211 E Second St. .... Owensboro KY 42303 270-684-0661 573-3
Web: theoso.com

Owensboro-Davies County Tourist Commission
215 E Second St. .... Owensboro KY 42303 270-926-1100 206
TF: 800-489-1131 ■ *Web:* www.visitowensboro.com

Owens-Illinois Inc
1 Michael Owens Way .... Perrysburg OH 43551 567-336-5000 331
NYSE: OI ■ *TF:* 800-766-0600 ■ *Web:* www.o-i.com

Owings Mills 10300 Mill Run Cir. .... Owings Mills MD 21117 410-427-4420 460
Web: www.owingsmillsmall.com

Owl Cos 2465 Campus Dr. .... Irvine CA 92612 949-797-2000 660-4936 360-3
Web: www.owlcompanies.com

Owl Magazine
10 Lower Spadina Ave Ste 400 .... Toronto ON M5V2Z2 416-340-2700 340-9769 457-6
TF: 800-551-6957 ■ *Web:* www.owlkids.com

Owl Wire & Cable Inc
3127 Seneca Tpke .... Canastota NY 13032 315-697-2011 813
TF: 800-765-9473 ■ *Web:* www.owlwire.com

Owlstone Nanotech Inc 761 Main Ave .... Norwalk CT 06851 203-908-4848 692
Web: www.owlstonenanotech.com

Owner-Operator Independent Drivers Assn Inc (OOIDA)
1 NW OOIDA Dr .... Grain Valley MO 64029 816-229-5791 229-0518 49-21
TF: 800-444-5791 ■ *Web:* www.ooida.com

Ownersite Technologies LLC
1425 Market Blvd Ste 330-179 .... Roswell GA 30076 404-402-7117 226
Web: www.ownersite.com

Owosso Public Library 502 W Main St .... Owosso MI 48867 989-725-5134 723-5444 434-3
Web: sdl.lib.mi.us

Owosso Public Schools 645 Alger St .... Owosso MI 48867 989-723-8131 723-7777 685
Web: www.owosso.k12.mi.us

Owsley County PO Box 500 .... Booneville KY 41314 606-593-5735 593-5737 338
Web: elect.ky.gov/contactcountyclerks/pages/n-o.aspx

Owyhee County PO Box 128 .... Murphy ID 83650 208-495-2421 495-1173 338
TF: 800-853-2570 ■ *Web:* www.owyheecounty.net

Owyhee Plaza Hotel 1109 Main St. .... Boise ID 83702 208-343-4611 379
Web: www.owyheeplaza.com

Ox International Inc
13111 NW Fwy 5th Fl .... Houston TX 77040 713-895-6610 895-6691 177
Web: www.oxinternational.com

OX Paper Tube & Core Inc
331 Maple Ave .... Hanover PA 17331 800-414-2476 125
TF: 800-414-2476 ■ *Web:* oxpapertube.com

Oxbo International Corp
7275 Batavia Byron Rd .... Byron NY 14422 585-548-2665 273
Web: www.oxbocorp.com

Oxbow Carbon & Minerals Inc
1601 Forum Pl Ste 1400 .... West Palm Beach FL 33401 561-697-4300 697-1876 536
Web: www.oxbow.com

Oxbow Corp
1601 Forum Pl Ste 1400 .... West Palm Beach FL 33401 561-697-4300 697-1876* 185
**Fax:* Hum Res ■ *Web:* www.oxbow.com

Oxbow Meadows Environmental Learning Ctr
3535 S Lumpkin Rd .... Columbus GA 31903 706-507-8550 507-8549 50-5
TF: 866-264-2035 ■ *Web:* oxbow.columbusstate.edu

Oxbow Park 5731 County Rd 105 NW .... Byron MN 55920 507-775-2451 823

Oxfam America 226 Cswy St 5th Fl. .... Boston MA 02114 617-482-1211 728-2594 48-5
TF: 800-776-9326 ■ *Web:* www.oxfamamerica.org

Oxford Academy 1393 Boston Post Rd .... Westbrook CT 06498 860-399-6247 622
Web: www.oxfordacademy.net

Oxford Academy & Central School
50 S Washington Ave PO Box 192 .... Oxford NY 13830 607-843-2025 843-3241 685
Web: www.oxac.org

Oxford Alloys Inc 2632 Tee Dr .... Baton Rouge LA 70814 225-273-4800 358
TF: 800-562-3355 ■ *Web:* www.oxfordalloys.com

Oxford Bank PO Box 129 .... Addison IL 60101 630-629-5000 628-1575 70
TF: 800-236-2442 ■ *Web:* www.oxford-bank.com

Oxford Biomedical Research Inc
2165 Avon Industrial Dr .... Rochester Hills MI 48309 248-852-8815 852-4466 231
TF: 800-692-4633 ■ *Web:* www.oxfordbiomed.com

Oxford Communications LLC
121 S Alfred St Ste 6 .... Alexandria VA 22314 703-535-6712 393
Web: www.oxfordpromos.com

Oxford Convention & Visitors Bureau
102 Ed Perry Blvd. .... Oxford MS 38655 662-232-2367 206
TF: 800-758-9177 ■ *Web:* visitoxfordms.com

Oxford County
26 Western Ave PO Box 179 .... South Paris ME 04281 207-743-6359 743-1545 338
Web: www.oxfordcounty.org

Oxford County Telephone & Telegraph Company Inc
491 Lisbon St. .... Lewiston ME 04240 207 333 6900 387
Web: oxfordnetworks.com

Oxford Development Co 301 Grant St .... Pittsburgh PA 15219 412-261-1500 642-7543 655
Web: www.oxford-pgh.com

Oxford Financial Group Ltd
11711 N Meridian St Ste 600 .... Carmel IN 46032 317-843-5678 401
TF: 800-722-2289 ■ *Web:* www.ofgltd.com

Oxford Global Resources Inc
100 Cummings Ctr Ste 206L .... Beverly MA 01915 978-236-1182 721
TF: 800-426-9196 ■ *Web:* www.oxfordcorp.com

Oxford Graduate School Inc
500 Oxford Dr. .... Dayton TN 37321 423-775-6596 166
TF: 800-933-6188 ■ *Web:* www.ogs.edu

Oxford Health Plans LLC
48 Monroe Tpke .... Trumbull CT 06611 203-459-9100 459-6464 391-3
TF: 800-444-6222 ■ *Web:* www.oxhp.com

Oxford Health Plans (NJ) Inc
111 Wood Ave S Ste 2 .... Iselin NJ 08830 732-623-1000 391-3
TF: 800-201-6920 ■ *Web:* www.oxhp.com

Oxford Hills Chamber of Commerce
4 Western Ave. .... South Paris ME 04281 207-743-2281 743-0687 139
TF: 800-871-7741 ■ *Web:* www.oxfordhillsmaine.com

Oxford Hotel 1600 17th St. .... Denver CO 80202 303-628-5400 379
TF: 800-228-5838 ■ *Web:* www.theoxfordhotel.com

Oxford Industries Inc
999 Peachtree St NE Ste 688 .... Atlanta GA 30309 404-659-2424 653-1545 155-12
NYSE: OXM ■ *Web:* www.oxfordinc.com

Oxford Instruments Measurement Systems
300 Bake Ave Ste 150. .... Concord MA 01742 800-447-4717 472
TF: 800-447-4717 ■ *Web:* www.oxford-instruments.com

Oxford Life Insurance Co
2721 N Central Ave. .... Phoenix AZ 85004 602-263-6666 277-5901 391-2
TF Cust Svc: 800-308-2318 ■ *Web:* www.oxfordlife.com

Oxford Media Group
70 Wellington St S .... Woodstock ON N4S3H6 519-539-9762 224

Oxford Palace 745 S Oxford Ave. .... Los Angeles CA 90005 213-389-8000 379
Web: www.oxfordhotel.com

Oxford Plains Speedway 877 Main St. .... Oxford ME 04270 207-539-8865 539-8860 515
Web: www.oxfordplains.com

Oxford Properties Group
Royal Bank Plaza North Twr Ste 1100 .... Toronto ON M5J2J2 416-865-8300 655
Web: www.oxfordproperties.com

Oxford Public Library
129 S Franklin Ave .... Oxford WI 53952 608-586-4458 434-3
Web: www.oxfordlibrary.org

Oxford Recreation Dept
6025 Fairfield Rd .... Oxford OH 45056 513-523-6314 564
Web: www.cityofoxford.org

Oxford Suites Boise
1426 S Entertainment Ave. .... Boise ID 83709 208-322-8000 322-8002 379
TF General: 888-322-8001 ■ *Web:* www.oxfordsuitesboise.com

Oxford Suites Spokane Valley
15015 E Indiana Ave. .... Spokane Valley WA 99216 509-847-1000 847-1001 379
TF: 866-668-7848 ■ *Web:* www.oxfordsuitesspokanevalley.com

Oxford Suites Spokane-Downtown
115 W N River Dr .... Spokane WA 99201 509-353-9000 353-9164 379
TF: 800-774-1877 ■ *Web:* www.oxfordsuitesspokane.com

Oxford University Press
198 Madison Ave .... New York NY 10016 212-726-6000 677-1303* 637-2
**Fax Area Code:* 919 ■ *TF Orders:* 800-445-9714

Oxford Valley Mall
225 W Washington St. .... Indianapolis IN 46204 317-636-1600 750-0489* 460
**Fax Area Code:* 215 ■ *TF:* 800-461-3439 ■ *Web:* www.simon.com/mall/oxford-valley-mall

Oxford-Lafayette County Chamber of Commerce
299 W Jackson Ave. .... Oxford MS 38655 662-234-4651 139
TF: 800-880-6967 ■ *Web:* www.oxfordms.com

Oxis International Inc
468 N Camden Dr 2nd Fl .... Beverly Hills CA 90210 310-860-5184 85
OTC: OXIS ■ *Web:* www.oxis.com

Oxley Enterprises Inc
685 Garrisonville Rd Ste 101 .... Stafford VA 22554 540-752-8822 627
Web: www.oxleyenterprises.com

Oxnard Airport 2889 W Fifth St. .... Oxnard CA 93030 805-382-3022 27
Web: iflyoxnard.com

Oxnard Chamber of Commerce
400 E Esplanade Dr Ste 302 .... Oxnard CA 93036 805-983-6118 604-7331 139
TF: 800-695-8171 ■ *Web:* www.oxnardchamber.org

Oxnard City Hall 300 W Third St. .... Oxnard CA 93030 805-385-7803 337
Web: www.oxnard.org

Oxnard College 4000 S Rose Ave .... Oxnard CA 93033 805-986-5800 986-5943* 162
**Fax:* Admissions ■ *Web:* www.oxnardcollege.edu

Oxnard Convention & Visitors Bureau
2775 N Ventura Rd Ste 208 .... Oxnard CA 93036 805-385-7545 385-7571 206
TF: 800-269-6273 ■ *Web:* www.visitoxnard.com

Oxnard Public Library (OPL)
4300 Saviers Rd .... Oxnard CA 93033 805-247-8951 488-1336 434-3
Web: www.oxnard.org/library

	Phone	Fax	Class
Oxus America Inc 2676 Paldan Dr .... Auburn Hills MI 48326 *TF:* 888-475-1568 ■ *Web:* www.oxusamerica.com	248-475-0925	475-0938	476
Oxxford Clothes Inc 1220 W Van Buren St .... Chicago IL 60607 *Web:* www.oxxfordclothes.com	312-829-3600		155-12
Oxy Vinyls Lp 2400 Miller Cut Off Rd .... La Porte TX 77571 *Web:* www.oxy.com/OurBusinesses/Chemicals/Products/Pages/default.aspx	281-476-8000		580
Oxygen Cloud Inc 1600 Seaport Blvd Ste 310 .... Redwood City CA 94063 *Web:* www.oxygencloud.com	650-241-6210		387
Oxygen Ventures 1250 Hampton Hill Ct .... Harrisburg PA 17111 *Web:* oxygenventures.com	717-540-9730		809
OYA (Oregon Youth Authority Riverbend) 58231 Oregon Hwy 244 .... La Grande OR 97850 *Web:* www.oregon.gov	541-663-8801	663-9181	412
Oyster Bar 157 E Levee St .... Brownsville TX 78520	956-542-9786		671
Oyster Consulting LLC 4128 Innslake Dr Ste 150 .... Glen Allen VA 23060 *Web:* www.oysterllc.com	804-965-5400		463
Oyster House 320 Fourth Ave W .... Olympia WA 98501 *Web:* www.oysterhouse.com	360-753-7000		671
Oyster Point Hotel, The 146 Bodman Pl .... Red Bank NJ 07701 *TF:* 800-345-3484 ■ *Web:* www.theoysterpointhotel.com	732-530-8200	747-1875	379
Oyster Pub 555 Seabreeze Blvd .... Daytona Beach FL 32118 *Web:* www.oysterpub.com	386-255-6348		671
OZ Systems Inc 2001 NE Green Oaks Blvd .... Arlington TX 76006 *Web:* www.oz-systems.com	214-631-6161		194
O-Z/Gedney 9377 W Higgins Rd .... Rosemont IL 60018 **Fax Area Code:* 800 ■ *TF:* 800-621-1506 ■ *Web:* www.emerson.com/en-us/commercial-residential/o-zgedney	847-268-6000	356-4714*	816
Ozanne Construction Company Inc 1635 E 25th St .... Cleveland OH 44114 *Web:* www.ozanne.com	216-696-2876	696-8613	186
Ozark Antique 200 S 20th St .... Ozark MO 65721	417-581-5233		460
Ozark Area Chamber of Commerce 294 Painter Ave .... Ozark AL 36360 *TF:* 800-582-8497 ■ *Web:* www.ozarkalchamber.com	334-774-9321	774-8736	139
Ozark Bible Institute & College 906 Summit St PO Box 398 .... Neosho MO 64850 **Fax:* Admissions ■ *Web:* obicollege.com	417-451-2057	451-2059*	166
Ozark Border Electric Co-op 3281 S Westwood .... Poplar Bluff MO 63901 *TF:* 800-392-0567 ■ *Web:* www.ozarkborder.org	573-785-4631		245
Ozark Christian College 1111 N Main St .... Joplin MO 64801 *TF:* 800-299-4622 ■ *Web:* www.occ.edu	417-624-2518	624-0090	161
Ozark Correctional Ctr 929 Honor Camp Ln .... Fordland MO 65652	417-767-4491		213
Ozark County 361 Main St PO Box 605 .... Gainesville MO 65655 *Web:* www.ozarkcounty.net	417-679-4913		338
Ozark Folk Ctr State Park 1032 Pk Ave .... Mountain View AR 72560 *TF:* 800-264-3655 ■ *Web:* www.ozarkfolkcenter.com	870-269-3851		565
Ozark Foothills Region 3019 fair st .... Poplar Bluff MO 63901 *Web:* www.ofrpc.org	573-785-6402	686-5467	338
Ozark Guidance Center Inc 2400 S 48th St .... Springdale AR 72762 *TF:* 800-234-7052 ■ *Web:* www.ozarkguidance.org	479-750-2020		726
Ozark Interests Inc 155 Camp Ozark Dr .... Mount Ida AR 71957 *Web:* www.campozark.com	870-867-4131		239
Ozark Motor Lines Inc 3934 Homewood Rd .... Memphis TN 38118 *TF:* 800-264-4100 ■ *Web:* www.ozark.com	901-251-9711	375-8661	780
Ozark Mountain Poultry 750 W Easy St .... Rogers AR 72756 *Web:* www.ompfoods.com	479-633-8700		619
Ozark National Life Insurance Inc 500 E Ninth St .... Kansas City MO 64106 *Web:* www.ozark-national.com	816-842-6300		391-2
Ozark National Scenic Riverways 404 Watercress Dr PO Box 490 .... Van Buren MO 63965 *TF:* 877-444-6777 ■ *Web:* www.nps.gov/ozar	573-323-4236	323-4140	564
Ozark Ready Mix Company Inc 1115 Bluff Dr .... Osage Beach MO 65065 *TF:* 800-524-6474 ■ *Web:* www.ozarkreadymix.com	573-348-1181		182
Ozark Regional Transit 2423 E Robinson Ave .... Springdale AR 72764 *TF:* 800-865-5901 ■ *Web:* www.ozark.org	479-756-5901		108
Ozark Riverview Manor Inc 1200 W Hall St .... Ozark MO 65721 *Web:* www.ormanor.com	417-581-6025		371
Ozark Steel Fabricators Inc 1 Ozark Steel Dr .... Farmington MO 63640 *Web:* ozarksteel.com	573-756-5741		480
Ozark Trucking Inc 4916 Dudley Blvd .... Mcclellan CA 95652 *Web:* www.ozarktruckinginc.com	916-561-5400		314
Ozarka College 218 College Dr .... Melbourne AR 72556 *TF:* 800-821-4335 ■ *Web:* www.ozarka.edu	870-368-7371	368-2091	162
Ozarks Coca-Cola Dr Pepper Bottling Co 1777 N Packer Rd .... Springfield MO 65803 *TF:* 866-223-4498 ■ *Web:* www.cocacolaozarks.com	417-865-9900	865-7967	98
Ozarks Electric Co-op Corp 3641 W Wedington Dr .... Fayetteville AR 72704 *TF:* 800-521-6144 ■ *Web:* www.ozarksecc.com	479-521-2900		245
Ozarks Medical Ctr 1100 N Kentucky Ave .... West Plains MO 65775 *TF:* 800-356-5395 ■ *Web:* www.ozarksmedicalcenter.com	417-256-9111	257-6770	374-3
Ozarks Technical Community College 1001 E Chestnut Expy .... Springfield MO 65802 *Web:* www.otc.edu	417-447-7500		162
Ozaukee County 121 W Main St PO Box 994 .... Port Washington WI 53074 *Web:* www.co.ozaukee.wi.us	262-284-9411	284-8100	338
Ozeki Sake (USA) Inc 249 Hillcrest Rd .... Hollister CA 95023 *Web:* www.ozekisake.com	831-637-9217		80-3
Ozel Fine Jewelers 4718 Admiralty Way .... Marina Del Rey CA 90292	310-301-9797		410
Ozinga Ready Mix Concrete Inc 400 Blaine St .... Gary IN 46406 *Web:* www.ozinga.com	219-949-9800		135
Ozumo 161 Steuart St .... San Francisco CA 94105 *Web:* www.ozumosanfrancisco.com	415-882-1333		671
OZZ - Event & Fun Ctr 490 N Freedom Blvd .... Provo UT 84601	801-818-9000		671
OZZ Corp 20 Floral Pkwy .... Concord ON L4K4R1 *Web:* www.ozzcorp.com	416-637-7237		610

P

	Phone	Fax	Class
P & C Construction Co 2133 NW York St .... Portland OR 97210 *Web:* www.builtbypandc.com	503-665-0165	667-2565	186
P & D Mechanical Inc 627 Old Hartford Rd .... Colchester CT 06415	860-537-0617		189-10
P & E Distributors Inc 709 Rivergate Pkwy .... Goodlettsville TN 37072 *Web:* www.pedistributors.com	615-851-8060		54
P & F Industries Inc 445 Broadhollow Rd .... Melville NY 11747 *NASDAQ:* PFIN ■ *TF:* 800-327-9403 ■ *Web:* www.pfina.com	631-694-9800	694-9804	759
P & G Steel Products Company Inc 54 Gruner Rd .... Buffalo NY 14227 *Web:* www.pgsteel.com	716-896-7900	896-4129	488
P & H Manufacturing Co 604 S Lodge St .... Shelbyville IL 62565 *Web:* www.phmfg.com	217-774-2123	774-5341	273
P & J Machining Inc 2601 Inter Ave .... Puyallup WA 98372 *Web:* www.pnjmachining.com	253-841-0500		454
P & P Press Inc 6513 N Galena Rd .... Peoria IL 61614 *Web:* pppress.com	309-691-8511		627
P & R Communications Service Inc 700 E First St .... Dayton OH 45402 *Web:* www.pandrcommunications.com	937-512-8100		736
P & R Industries Inc 1524 Clinton Ave N .... Rochester NY 14621 *Web:* pandrindustries.com	585-266-6725		455
P & W Industries LLC 68668 Hwy 59 .... Mandeville LA 70471 *Web:* www.pandwindustries.com	985-892-2461		492
P & W Sales Inc 405 N Hwy 135 .... Kilgore TX 75662 *TF:* 800-813-5207 ■ *Web:* www.p-wsales.com	903-984-2102		358
P A Landers Inc 351 Winter St .... Hanover MA 02339 *TF:* 800-660-6404 ■ *Web:* www.palanders.com	781-826-8818		186
P C Assistance Inc 3200 S Shackleford Rd Ste 9 .... Little Rock AR 72205 *Web:* www.pcassistance.com	501-907-4722		180
P C Whip 4451 Henderson Rd .... Hickory PA 15340 *Web:* www.pcwhip.com	724-356-4070		177
P E La Moreaux & Assoc Inc PO Box 2310 .... Tuscaloosa AL 35403 *Web:* www.pela.com	205-752-5543	752-4043	192
P Flanigan & Sons Inc 2444 Loch Raven Rd .... Baltimore MD 21218 *Web:* www.pflanigan.com	410-467-5900	467-3127	188-4
P Gioioso & Sons Inc 50 Sprague St .... Hyde Park MA 02136 *Web:* www.pgioioso.com	617-364-5800	364-9462	188-10
P i Incentive 220 Duncan Mill Rd Ste 315 .... Toronto ON M3B3J5 *Web:* www.piincentives.com	416-383-0766		196
P J Hoerr Inc 107 Commerce Pl .... Peoria IL 61604 *Web:* www.pjhoerr.com	309-688-9567	688-9556	780
P J Morgan Real Estate Auctioneers 7801 Wakeley Plaza .... Omaha NE 68114 *Web:* www.pjmorgan.com	402-397-7775		652
P J Noyes Company Inc 89 Bridge St .... Lancaster NH 03584 *TF:* 800-522-2469 ■ *Web:* www.pjnoyes.com	800-522-2469		297-8
P J Wine 4898 Broadway .... New York NY 10034 *Web:* www.pjwine.com	212-567-5500		443
P K Electrical 681 Sierra Rose Dr Ste B .... Reno NV 89511 *TF:* 800-677-1997 ■ *Web:* pkelectrical.com	775-826-9010		261
P K W Associates Inc 705 E Ordnance Rd Ste 108 .... Baltimore MD 21226 *TF:* 888-358-3900 ■ *Web:* www.pkwassoc.com	443-773-1000		225
P M C Property Group 3600 W Broad St .... Richmond VA 23230 *Web:* www.pmcpropertygroup.com	215-241-0200		186
P M F Industries Inc 2601 Reach Rd .... Williamsport PA 17701 *Web:* www.pmfind.com	570-323-9944		222
P M Industrial Supply Co 9613 Canoga Ave .... Chatsworth CA 91311 *TF:* 800-382-3684 ■ *Web:* www.pmindustrial.com	818-341-9180		350
P Marshall & Associates LLC 1000 Holcomb Woods Pkwy Ste 210 .... Roswell GA 30076 *Web:* pmass.com	678-280-2325		387
P Murphy & Assoc Inc 2301 W Olive Ave .... Burbank CA 91506 *Web:* www.pmurphy.com	818-841-2002		225
P s i Prime Inc 137 Jackson Ave .... Woodland Park NJ 07424 *TF:* 800-349-4817 ■ *Web:* www.psiprime.com	973-225-9870		809
P T Systems Inc 1980 Olivera Rd Ste A .... Concord CA 94520 *Web:* www.ptsystemsinc.com	925-676-0709		261
P V Rentals Ltd 5810 S Rice Ave .... Houston TX 77081 *TF:* 800-275-7878 ■ *Web:* www.pvrentals.com	713-667-0665		126
P W Feats Inc 3 E Read St .... Baltimore MD 21202 *TF:* 800-403-6447 ■ *Web:* www.featsinc.com	410-727-5575		195
P Wexford's Pub 3313 McHenry Ave .... Modesto CA 95350	209-576-7939		671
P. T. M. Corp 6560 Bethuy Rd .... Fair Haven MI 48023 *TF:* 800-486-2212 ■ *Web:* www.ptmcorporation.com	586-725-2211	725-6753	60

	Phone	Fax	Class
P.E.T. Terra Systems Inc 110 Evans Mill Dr ... Dallas GA 30157 *Web:* www.petsystems.com	770-445-2233		463
P.H. Hagopian Contractor Inc 778 W Town & Country Rd ... Orange CA 92868 *Web:* www.phhagopian.com	714-543-4185		186
P.W. Gillibrand Company Inc 4537 Ish Dr. ... Simi Valley CA 93063 *TF:* 800-424-9300 ■ *Web:* www.pwgillibrand.com	805-526-2195		41
P1 Group Inc 2151 Haskell Ave Bldg 1 ... Lawrence KS 66046 *TF:* 800-376-2911 ■ *Web:* www.p1group.com	785-843-2910		189-10
P2i Inc 1236 Main St ... Hellertown PA 18055 *Web:* www.p2ionline.com	610-814-0550		225
P2S Engineering Inc 5000 E Spring St 8th Fl ... Long Beach CA 90815 *Web:* www.p2seng.com	562-497-2999		261
P3 Inc 213 Highway 35 ... Red Bank NJ 07701 **Fax Area Code:* 978 ■ *TF:* 866-222-5169 ■ *Web:* www.pereless.com	866-222-5169	266-0425*	180
P3 North America Inc 1957 Crooks Rd Ste B ... Troy MI 48084 *Web:* www.p3-group.com	248-792-2277		196
P3I Inc 77 Main St ... Hopkinton MA 01748 *TF:* 800-442-5276 ■ *Web:* www.p3i-inc.com	508-435-7882		463
P4 Performance Management Inc 105 Brooks Ave. ... Raleigh NC 27607 **Fax Area Code:* 919 ■ *TF:* 800-431-0648	800-431-0648	783-1501*	195
PA Inc 6626 Gulf Fwy ... Houston TX 77087 *Web:* www.painc.com	713-570-4900		492
Pa Pellets LLC 958 SR-49 W ... Ulysses PA 16948 *Web:* www.papellets.com	814-848-9970		200
Paasche Airbrush Co 4311 N Normandy ... Chicago IL 60634 *TF Sales:* 800-621-1907 ■ *Web:* www.paascheairbrush.com	773-867-9191	867-9198	43
PABCO Gypsum 37851 Cherry St ... Newark CA 94560 *TF:* 877-449-7786 ■ *Web:* www.pabcogypsum.com	510-792-9555		347
Pabla Indian Cuisine 1516 Second Ave ... Seattle WA 98101 *Web:* pablaindiacuisine.com	206-623-2868		671
Pablo Historical Park 381 Beach Blvd. ... Jacksonville Beach FL 32250 *Web:* www.beachesmuseum.org	904-241-5657		50-3
Pabrai Investment Funds 1220 Roosevelt Ste 200 ... Irvine CA 92620 *Web:* www.pabraifunds.com	949-453-0609		796
Pabst Brewing Co, The 10635 Santa Monica Blvd Ste 350 ... Los Angeles CA 90025 *TF:* 800-947-2278 ■ *Web:* www.pabstbrewingco.com	800-947-2278		102
Pabst Mansion 2000 W Wisconsin Ave. ... Milwaukee WI 53233 *Web:* www.pabstmansion.com	414-931-0808		50-3
Pabst Theater 144 E Wells St ... Milwaukee WI 53202 *Web:* www.pabsttheater.org	414-286-3205		572
PAC (Pocatello Art Ctr) 444 N Main St ... Pocatello ID 83204 *Web:* www.pocatelloartctr.org	208-232-0970		50-2
PAC (Public Affairs Council) 2033 K St NW Ste 700 ... Washington DC 20006 *Web:* www.pac.org	202-872-1790		48-7
PAC Industries Inc 5341 Jaycee Ave ... Harrisburg PA 17112 *Web:* pacindustries.com	717-657-0407		426
Pac Marine Express Inc 19401 S Main St Ste 102 ... Gardena CA 90248 *Web:* www.gopacmarine.com	310-329-2478		311
Pac Tec 12365 Haynes St ... Clinton LA 70722 *TF:* 877-554-2544 ■ *Web:* www.pactecinc.com	877-554-2544		608
Pac Tech USA - Packaging Technologies Inc 328 Martin Ave ... Santa Clara CA 95050 *Web:* www.pactech.com	408-588-1925		557
PACC (Peabody Chamber of Commerce) 24 Main St Ste 28 ... Peabody MA 01960 *Web:* www.peabodychamber.com	978-531-0384	532-7227	139
PACCAR Financial Corp 777 106th Ave NE ... Bellevue WA 98004 *Web:* www.paccarfinancial.com	425-468-7100		216
PACCAR Inc 777 106th Ave NE ... Bellevue WA 98004 *NASDAQ: PCAR* ■ *TF:* 800-286-6467 ■ *Web:* www.paccar.com	425-468-7400	468-8216	516
PACCAR Inc International Div 777 106th Ave NE 12th Fl ... Bellevue WA 98004 *Web:* www.paccar.com	425-468-7400	468-8216	516
PACCAR Leasing Corp 777 106th Ave NE ... Bellevue WA 98004 *TF:* 800-759-2979 ■ *Web:* www.paclease.com	425-468-7877		778
PACCAR Parts 750 Houser Way N ... Renton WA 98057 *Web:* www.paccar.com	425-254-4400		61
Pace & Partners 1223 Turner St Ste 101 ... Lansing MI 48906 *Web:* www.gudmarketing.com	517-267-9800		7
Pace Communications Inc 1301 Carolina St ... Greensboro NC 27401 *Web:* www.paceco.com	336-378-6065		637-9
Pace Computer Solutions Inc 10480 Little Patuxent Pkwy Ste 760 ... Columbia MD 21044 *Web:* www.pace-solutionsinc.com	443-539-0290		177
Pace Dairy Foods Co 2700 Vly High Dr NW ... Rochester MN 55901	507-288-6315		296-5
Pace Engineering Inc 4800 Beidler Rd ... Willoughby OH 44094 *Web:* www.paceparts.net	440-942-1234		190
Pace Gallery, The 32 E 57th St 2th Fl ... New York NY 10022 *Web:* www.pacegallery.com	212-421-3292	421-0835	42
PACE Inc 255 Air Tool Dr ... Southern Pines NC 28387 *Web:* www.paceworldwide.com	910-695-7223		253
Pace Prints 32 E 57th St 3rd Fl ... New York NY 10022 *Web:* www.paceprints.com	212-421-3237	832-5162	42
Pace Products Inc 4510 W 89th St Ste 110 ... Prairie Village KS 66207 **Fax Area Code:* 913 ■ *TF:* 888-389-8203 ■ *Web:* www.paceproducts.com	888-389-8203	469-4067*	46
Pace Resources Inc 445 W Philadelphia St PO Box 15040 ... York PA 17405 *Web:* www.paceresourcesfcu.virtualcu.net	717-852-1390	852-1391	360-3
Pace Staffing Network Inc 14450 NE 29th Pl Ste 200 ... Bellevue WA 98004 *Web:* www.pacestaffing.com	425-454-1075		260
Pace Suburban Bus 550 W Algonquin Rd ... Arlington Heights IL 60005 *Web:* www.pacebus.com	847-364-8130		468
Pace Tech Inc 2040 Calumet St ... Clearwater FL 33765 *TF:* 800-722-3024 ■ *Web:* www.pacetech-med.com	727-442-8118		476
Pace University 1 Pace Plaza ... New York NY 10038 **Fax:* Admissions ■ *TF:* 866-722-3338 ■ *Web:* www.pace.edu	212-346-1200	346-1040*	166
Birnbaum Library 1 Pace Plaza ... New York NY 10038 *TF:* 800-498-2071 ■ *Web:* www.pace.edu/library	212-346-1332	346-1516	434-6
Pleasantville/Briarcliff 861 Bedford Rd ... Pleasantville NY 10570 **Fax:* Admissions ■ *TF:* 866-722-3338 ■ *Web:* www.pace.edu	914-773-3200	773-3851*	166
Pace University School of Law 78 N Broadway ... White Plains NY 10603 **Fax:* Admissions ■ *Web:* www.law.pace.edu	914-422-4210	989-8714*	167-1
Pace's Lodging Corp 4265 45th St S Ste 200 ... Fargo ND 58104 *Web:* propertyresourcesgroup.com	701-281-9500	281-9501	379
Paceco Corp 25503 Whitesell St ... Hayward CA 94545 *Web:* www.pacecocorp.com	510-264-9288	264-9280	470
Pace-Edwards 2400 Commercial Rd ... Centralia WA 98531 *TF:* 800-338-3697 ■ *Web:* www.pace-edwards.com	360-736-9991	736-9992	120
Pacer Corp 14100 Palmetto Frontage Rd Ste 110 ... Miami Lakes FL 33016 *Web:* www.pacerco.com	305-828-7660	828-2551	374-3
Pacer Financial Inc 16 Industrial Blvd ... Paoli PA 19301 *Web:* www.pacerfinancial.com	610-644-8100		401
Pacesetter Claims Service Inc 2871 N Hwy 167 ... Catoosa Ok 74015 *TF:* 888-218-4880 ■ *Web:* www.pacesetterclaims.com	918-665-8887		390
Pacesetter Steel Service Inc 1045 Big Shanty Rd ... Kennesaw GA 30144 *TF:* 800-749-6505 ■ *Web:* www.teampacesetter.com	770-919-8000		492
PaceWorks Inc 16780 Lark Ave ... Los Gatos CA 95032 *Web:* www.paceworks.com	408-354-5711		178-8
Pachaug State Forest Rt 49 PO Box 5 ... Voluntown CT 06384 *Web:* www.ct.gov	860-376-4075		565
Pacheco State Park 38787 Dinosaur Point Rd ... Hollister CA 95023 *Web:* www.parks.ca.gov/default.asp?page_id=560	209-826-6283		565
Pachulski Stang Ziehl Young & Jones Professional Corp 10100 Santa Monica Blvd ... Los Angeles CA 90067 *Web:* pszjlaw.com	310-277-6910		428
Pachyderm Consulting LLC 66 W 38th St Apt 11k Ste 33c ... New York NY 10018 *Web:* pachyderm.net	212-629-7600		180
Paciello Group LLP, The 88 Temple St ... Nashua NH 03060 *Web:* www.paciellogroup.com	603-882-4122		196
Pacific Adhesives Company Inc 8670 23rd Ave ... Sacramento CA 95826 *Web:* www.pacificadhesives.com	916-383-1509		3
Pacific Aerospace & Electronics Inc 434 Olds Stn Rd ... Wenatchee WA 98801 *TF:* 855-285-5200 ■ *Web:* www.pacaero.com	509-667-9600		621
Pacific Agenda 2425 NW Overton St ... Portland OR 97210	503-223-8633		184
Pacific Agri Lands Inc 5206 Hammett Rd ... Modesto CA 95358	209-545-1623		315-5
Pacific Air Cargo 6041 W Imperial Hwy ... Los Angeles CA 90045 *Web:* www.pacificaircargo.com	310-645-2178	645-5290	25
Pacific Alloy Castings Company Inc 5900 E Firestone Blvd ... South Gate CA 90280 *Web:* www.pacificalloy.com	562-928-1387		492
Pacific American Group LLC 104 Caledonia St ... Sausalito CA 94965 *Web:* www.pacamgroup.com	415-331-3838		653
Pacific Asia Museum 46 N Los Robles Ave ... Pasadena CA 91101 *Web:* www.pacificasiamuseum.org	626-449-2742	449-2754	520
Pacific Aviation Museum Pearl Harbor 319 Lexington Blvd ... Honolulu HI 96818 *Web:* www.pacificaviationmuseum.org	808-441-1000		520
Pacific Bag Inc 15300 Woodinville Redmond Rd NE Ste A ... Woodinville WA 98072 *TF:* 800-562-2247 ■ *Web:* www.pacificbag.com	425-455-1128	990-8582	65
Pacific Beach Hotel 2490 Kalakaua Ave ... Honolulu HI 96815 *TF:* 800-367-6060 ■ *Web:* www.pacificbeachhotel.com	808-922-1233	922-0129	379
Pacific Belting Inc 6400 SE 101st Ave Ste 2D ... Portland OR 97266 *Web:* www.pacificbeltinginc.com	503-467-4671		677
Pacific Beverage Co 5305 Ekwill St ... Santa Barbara CA 93111 *Web:* www.pacificbeveragecompany.com	805-964-3574		81-1
Pacific Biometrics Inc 645 Elliott Ave W Ste 300 ... Seattle WA 98119 *TF:* 800-767-9151 ■ *Web:* www.pacbio.com	206-298-0068		231
Pacific Biosciences Inc 1380 Willow Rd ... Menlo Park CA 94025 *TF:* 800-424-9300 ■ *Web:* www.pacb.com	650-521-8000		250
Pacific Bldg Group 9752 Aspen Creek Ct Ste 150 ... San Diego CA 92126 *Web:* www.pacificbuildinggroup.com	858-552-0600	552-0604	685
Pacific Building Maintenance Inc 2646 Palma Dr Ste 320 ... Ventura CA 93003 *TF:* 800-300-4094 ■ *Web:* www.pacificbuildingmaintenance.com	805-642-0214		104
Pacific Building Systems (PBS) 2100 N Pacific Hwy ... Woodburn OR 97071 *TF General:* 800-727-7844 ■ *Web:* www.pbsbuildings.com	503-981-9581	981-9584	105
Pacific Cataract & Laser Institute 2517 NE Kresky Ave ... Chehalis WA 98532 *TF:* 800-888-9903 ■ *Web:* www.pcli.com	360-748-8632	748-3869	798
Pacific Choice Brands Inc 4667 E Date Ave ... Fresno CA 93725	559-237-5583		296-19
Pacific Choice Seafoods Co 16797 SE 130th Ave ... Clackamas OR 97015 *TF:* 800-882-0212 ■ *Web:* www.pacseafood.com	707-442-2981		296-13

Company / Address	City	State	Zip	Phone	Fax	Class
Pacific City Financial Corp 3701 Wilshire Blvd Ste 402 *OTC: PFCF* ■ *Web:* www.paccity.net	Los Angeles	CA	90010	213-210-2000	210-2032	70
Pacific Clay Products Inc 14741 Lake St. *Web:* www.pacificclay.com	Lake Elsinore	CA	92530	951-674-2131		150
Pacific Clinics 800 S Santa Anita Ave. *Web:* www.pacificclinics.org	Arcadia	CA	91006	626-254-5000		374-3
Pacific Coal Resources Ltd 333 Bay St Ste 1100	Toronto	ON	M5H2R2	416-360-8725		501
Pacific Coast Bldg Products Inc 10600 White Rock Rd Bldg B Ste 100. *Web:* www.paccoast.com	Rancho Cordova	CA	95670	916-631-6500		191-4
Pacific Coast Chemical Co 2424 Fourth St *Web:* www.pcchem.com	Berkeley	CA	94710	510-549-3535	549-0890	276
Pacific Coast Container Inc 432 Estudillo Ave *TF:* 800-458-4788 ■ *Web:* www.pcclogistics.com	San Leandro	CA	94577	510-346-6100		650
Pacific Coast Feather Co 1964 Fourth Ave S *TF:* 888-297-1778 ■ *Web:* www.pacificcoast.com	Seattle	WA	98134	206-624-2034		746
Pacific Coast Fruit Co 201 NE Second Ave Ste 100 *TF:* 800-423-4945 ■ *Web:* www.pcfruit.com	Portland	OR	97232	503-234-6411		297-7
Pacific Coast Jet Charter Inc 10600 White Rock Rd *TF:* 800-655-3599 ■ *Web:* www.pacificjet.com	Rancho Cordova	CA	95670	916-631-6507	631-6687	13
Pacific Coast Lighting 20238 Plummer St *TF:* 800-709-9004 ■ *Web:* www.pacificcoastlighting.com	Chatsworth	CA	91311	818-886-9751	886-5751	439
Pacific Coast Manor 1935 Wharf Rd *Web:* covenantcare.com	Capitola	CA	95010	831-476-0770	476-0737	450
Pacific Coast Producers 631 N Cluff Ave *TF:* 877-618-4776 ■ *Web:* canned-fresh.com	Lodi	CA	95240	209-367-8800	367-1084	296-20
Pacific Coast Valuations 740 Corporate Ctr Dr *TF:* 888-623-4001 ■ *Web:* www.pcvmurcor.com	Pomona	CA	91768	888-623-4001		652
Pacific College Oriental Med Inc 7445 Mission Valley Rd Ste 105 *TF:* 800-729-0941 ■ *Web:* www.pacificcollege.edu	San Diego	CA	92108	619-574-6909		166
Pacific Color Graphics 440 Boulder Ct 100d *TF:* 888-551-1482 ■ *Web:* www.pacificcolor.com	Pleasanton	CA	94566	925-600-3006		627
Pacific Combustion Engineering Co 2107 Border Ave *TF:* 800-342-4442 ■ *Web:* www.pacificcombustion.com	Torrance	CA	90501	310-212-6300	212-5333	420
Pacific Communications 18581 Teller Ave *Web:* www.pacificcommunications.com	Irvine	CA	92612	714-427-1900		4
Pacific Concrete Industries 7170 Holz Rd	Lynden	WA	98264	360-734-0910		182
Pacific Consulting Group 643 Bair Is Rd Ste 212 *Web:* www.pcgfirm.com	Redwood	CA	94063	650-327-8108		463
Pacific Continental Corp 111 W Seventh Ave PO Box 10727 *NASDAQ: PCBK* ■ *TF:* 877-231-2265 ■ *Web:* www.therightbank.com	Eugene	OR	97440	541-686-8685		70
Pacific County 300 Memorial Dr. *Web:* www.co.pacific.wa.us	South Bend	WA	98586	360-875-9334		338
Pacific Crest Securities Inc 111 SW Fifth Ave 42nd Fl *TF:* 800-314-9837 ■ *Web:* www.pacific-crest.com	Portland	OR	97204	503-248-0721		690
Pacific Crest Trail Assn (PCTA) 1331 Garden Hwy *Web:* www.pcta.org	Sacramento	CA	95833	916-285-1846	285-1865	48-23
Pacific Data Electric Inc (PDE) 9970 Bell Ranch Dr Ste 109 *Web:* www.pdeinc.com	Santa Fe Springs	CA	90670	562-204-3550		787
Pacific Design Ctr 8687 Melrose Ave. *Web:* www.pacificdesigncenter.com	West Hollywood	CA	90069	310-657-0800	652-8576	320
Pacific Design Engineering (1996) Ltd 8505 Eastlake Dr. *TF:* 800-561-3322 ■ *Web:* www.pde.com	Burnaby	BC	V5A4T7	604-421-1311		393
Pacific Die Casting Corp 6155 S Eastern Ave. *Web:* www.pacdiecast.com	Commerce	CA	90040	323-725-1332	728-1115	308
Pacific Digital Image 333 Broadway *Web:* www.pacdigital.com	San Francisco	CA	94133	415-274-7234		781
Pacific Disaster Ctr 1305 N Holopono St Ste 2 *TF:* 888-808-6688 ■ *Web:* www.pdc.org	Kihei	HI	96753	808-891-0525	891-0526	668
Pacific Echo Inc 23540 Telo Ave *Web:* www.pacificecho.com	Torrance	CA	90505	310-539-1822		360-3
Pacific Edge Hotel 647 S Coast Hwy *Web:* www.pacificedgehotel.com	Laguna Beach	CA	92651	949-494-8566		379
Pacific Empire Radio Corp 403 Capital St. *Web:* pacempire.com	Lewiston	ID	83501	208-743-6564		645-126
Pacific Ethanol Corp 400 Capitol Mall Ste 2060 *NASDAQ: PEIX* ■ *TF:* 866-508-4969 ■ *Web:* www.pacificethanol.net	Sacramento	CA	95814	916-403-2123	446-3937	145
Pacific Event Productions Inc 6989 Corte Santa Fe *Web:* www.pacificevents.com	San Diego	CA	92121	858-458-9908	458-1173	113
Pacific Eyecare 20696 Bond Rd NE *TF:* 800-562-2020 ■ *Web:* www.pacificsurgerycenter.com	Poulsbo	WA	98370	360-779-2020		543
Pacific Fence & Wire Co 13770 SE Ambler Rd *Web:* www.pacificfence.com	Clackamas	OR	97015	503-233-6248		350
Pacific Fibre & Rope Company Inc 903 Flint St. *TF:* 800-825-7673 ■ *Web:* www.pacificfibre.com	Wilmington	CA	90744	310-834-4567		208
Pacific Fibre Products Inc 20 Fibre Way *Web:* www.pacfibre.com	Longview	WA	98632	360-577-7112		683
Pacific Firm The 2501 Ninth St Ste 102 *Web:* www.pacfirm.com	Berkeley	CA	94710	510-647-1000		193
Pacific Fisherman Inc 5351 24th Ave NW *TF:* 877-644-6148 ■ *Web:* pacificfishermen.com	Seattle	WA	98107	206-784-2562	784-1986	698
Pacific Fixture Company Inc 12860 San Fernando Rd Unit B *TF:* 800-272-2349 ■ *Web:* www.pacificfixture.com	Sylmar	CA	91342	818-362-2130	367-8968	286
Pacific Food Importers Inc 18620 80th Ct S Bldg F *TF:* 800-225-4029 ■ *Web:* www.pacificfoodimporters.com	Kent	WA	98134	206-682-2740	622-6259	360-3
Pacific Forge Inc 10641 Etiwanda Ave *Web:* www.pacificforge.com	Fontana	CA	92337	909-390-0701	390-0708	483
Pacific Gas & Electric Co 77 Beale St *TF Cust Svc:* 800-743-5000 ■ *Web:* www.pge.com	San Francisco	CA	94105	415-973-7000		787
Pacific Giant Inc 4625 District Blvd *Web:* www.pacificgiant.com	Vernon	CA	90058	323-587-5000		297-5
Pacific Grain Products International Inc 351 Hanson Way PO Box 2060 *TF Cust Svc:* 800-333-0110 ■ *Web:* www.pgpint.com	Woodland	CA	95776	530-662-5056	662-6074	296-23
Pacific Grinding Wheel Co 13120 State Ave *Web:* www.pgw-co.com	Marysville	WA	98271	360-659-6276		1
Pacific Grove Museum of Natural History 165 Forest Ave *Web:* www.pgmuseum.org	Pacific Grove	CA	93950	831-648-5716		520
Pacific Guardian Life Insurance Company Ltd 1440 Kapiolani Blvd Ste 1700 *TF:* 800-367-5354 ■ *Web:* www.pacificguardian.com	Honolulu	HI	96814	808-955-2236		391-2
Pacific Handy Cutter Inc 17819 Gillette Ave. *TF Cust Svc:* 800-229-2233 ■ *Web:* www.pacifichandycutter.com	Irvine	CA	92614	714-662-1033	662-7595	222
Pacific Health Laboratories Inc 100 Matawan Rd Ste 150 *TF General:* 877-363-8769 ■ *Web:* www.pacifichealthlabs.com	Matawan	NJ	07747	732-739-2900		799
Pacific Horizon Ventures 800 Fifth Ave Ste 4120 *Web:* www.pacifichorizon.com	Seattle	WA	98104	206-682-1181	682-8077	792
Pacific Hospitality Group LLC 2532 Dupont Dr *Web:* www.pacifichospitality.com	Irvine	CA	92612	949-861-4700		707
Pacific Income Advisers Inc 1299 Ocean Ave Second Fl Ste 210 *Web:* www.pacificincome.com	Santa Monica	CA	90401	310-393-1424		401
Pacific Industrial Development Corp 4788 Runway Blvd *Web:* www.pidc.com	Ann Arbor	MI	48108	734-930-9292		492
Pacific Inn 600 Marina Dr *TF:* 866-466-0300 ■ *Web:* thepacificinn.com	Seal Beach	CA	90740	562-493-7501	596-3448	379
Pacific Inn Resort & Conference Centre 1160 King George Hwy *TF:* 800-667-2248 ■ *Web:* www.pacificinn.com	Surrey	BC	V4A4Z2	604-535-1432	531-6979	379
Pacific Instituto 12101 Tukwila Int'l Blvd Ste 330 *TF:* 800-426-3660 ■ *Web:* www.thepacificinstituteretail.com	Seattle	WA	98168	206-628-4800	587-6007	765
Pacific Institute for Research & Evaluation 11720 Beltsville Dr Ste 900 *Web:* www.pire.org	Calverton	MD	20705	301-755-2738	755-2799	668
Pacific Integrated Handling Inc 10215 Portland Ave *Web:* www.pacificintegrated.com	Tacoma	WA	98445	253-535-5888		358
Pacific International Ctr for High Technology Research (PICHTR) 1440 Kapiolani Blvd Ste 1225 *Web:* www.pichtr.org	Honolulu	HI	96814	808-943-9581	943-9582	668
Pacific International Rice Mills Inc 845 Kentucky Ave *TF:* 800-747-4764 ■ *Web:* www.pirmirice.com	Woodland	CA	95695	530-661-6028	661-6028	296-23
Pacific Internet 105 W Clay St *Web:* www.pacific.net	Ukiah	CA	95482	707-468-1005	468-5822	808
Pacific Investment Management Company LLC 840 Newport Ctr Dr. *TF:* 800-387-4626 ■ *Web:* www.pimco.com	Newport Beach	CA	92660	949-720-6000	720-1376	401
Pacific Island Ecosystems Research Ctr (PIERC) 12201 Sunrise Valley Dr Ste 615 *Web:* www.usgs.gov	Reston	VA	20192	703-648-5953		668
Pacific Islands Club Saipan San Antonio St *Web:* www.picresorts.com/saipan	Saipan	MP	96950	670-234-7976		378
Pacific Language Institute 755 Burrard St Ste 300 *Web:* kaplaninternational.ca	Vancouver	BC	V6Z1X6	604-688-8330	688-0638	423
Pacific Legal Foundation 930 G St. *Web:* www.pacificlegal.org	Sacramento	CA	95814	916-419-7111		305
Pacific Life Insurance Co 700 Newport Ctr Dr. *TF:* 800-800-7646 ■ *Web:* www.pacificlife.com	Newport Beach	CA	92660	949-219-3011		391-2
Pacific Lutheran Theological Seminary 2770 Marin Ave **Fax Area Code:* 510 ■ *TF:* 800-235-7587 ■ *Web:* www.plts.edu	Berkeley	CA	94708	800-235-7587	524-2408*	167-3
Pacific Lutheran University 1010 122nd St S. *TF:* 800-274-6758 ■ *Web:* www.plu.edu	Tacoma	WA	98444	253-531-6900		166
Pacific Lutheran University Mortvedt Library 12180 Pk Ave S *Web:* www.plu.edu/~libr	Tacoma	WA	98447	253-535-7500	535-7315	434-6
Pacific Manufacturing Ohioinc 8955 Seward Rd *Web:* www.pacific-ind.co.jp/eng/company/ww/w06	Fairfield	OH	45011	513-642-0055		247
Pacific Marine Credit Union M C X Complex *TF:* 800-736-4500 ■ *Web:* www.pmcu.com	Camp Pendleton	CA	92055	800-736-4500		219
Pacific Marine Environmental Laboratory (PMEL) 7600 Sand Pt Way NE *Web:* www.pmel.noaa.gov	Seattle	WA	98115	206-526-6239	526-6815	668
Pacific Material Handling Solutions Inc 30361 Whipple Rd *Web:* www.pmhsi.com	Hayward	CA	94545	510-429-0303	429-1380	194

Name / Address	City	State	ZIP	Phone	Fax	Class
Pacific Mdf Products Inc 4312 Anthony Ct *Web:* www.pactrim.com	Rocklin	CA	95677	916-660-1882		499
Pacific Mechanical Corp 2501 Annalisa Dr *Web:* www.pmcorporation.com	Concord	CA	94520	925-827-4940	827-0519	189-10
Pacific Medical Inc 1700 N Chrisman Rd *TF:* 800-726-9180 ■ *Web:* www.pacmedical.com	Tracy	CA	95304	800-726-9180	861-5950	477
Pacific Mercantile Bancorp 949 S Coast Dr Ste 105 *NASDAQ: PMBC* ■ *TF General:* 877-450-2265 ■ *Web:* www.pmbank.com	Costa Mesa	CA	92626	714-438-2600	438-1088	360-2
Pacific Meridian Group 222 Juana Ave *Web:* pacificfarms.com	San Leandro	CA	94577	510-618-1600		770
Pacific Metallurgical Inc 925 Fifth Ave S *TF:* 800-428-9436 ■ *Web:* www.pacmet.com	Kent	WA	98032	253-854-4241		484
Pacific Mobile Structures Inc 1554 Bishop Rd *Web:* www.pacificmobile.com	Chehalis	WA	98532	360-748-0121		505
Pacific Modern Homes Inc (PMHI) 9723 Railroad St *TF:* 800-395-1011 ■ *Web:* www.pmhi.com	Elk Grove	CA	95624	916-685-9514		106
Pacific Mutual Holding Co 700 Newport Ctr Dr *TF:* 800-347-7787 ■ *Web:* www.pacificlife.com	Newport Beach	CA	92660	949-219-3011		360-4
Pacific News Service 275 Ninth St *Web:* newamericamedia.org	San Francisco	CA	94103	415-503-4170	503-0970	530
Pacific Northwest Ballet 301 Mercer St *TF:* 800-838-3006 ■ *Web:* www.pnb.org	Seattle	WA	98109	206-441-2424	441-2420	573-1
Pacific Northwest College of Art 1241 NW Johnson St *TF:* 888-390-7499 ■ *Web:* www.pnca.edu	Portland	OR	97209	503-226-4391	821-8978	166
Pacific Northwest Inlander 1227 W Summit Pkwy *TF:* 866-444-3066 ■ *Web:* www.inlander.com	Spokane	WA	99201	509-325-0634	626-5875	532-5
Pacific Northwest National Laboratory (PNNL) 902 Battelle Blvd PO Box 999 **Fax:* Mail Rm ■ *TF:* 888-375-7665 ■ *Web:* www.pnl.gov	Richland	WA	99352	509-375-2121	375-2507*	668
Pacific Northwest Research Station 333 SW First Ave *Web:* www.fs.fed.us/pnw	Portland	OR	97204	503-808-2100	808-2130	668
Pacific Nutritional Inc 6317 NE 131st Ave *Web:* www.pacnut.com	Vancouver	WA	98682	360-253-3197		231
Pacific NW Federal Credit Union (PNWFCU) 12106 NE Marx St *TF:* 866-692-8669 ■ *Web:* www.pnwfcu.org	Portland	OR	97220	503-256-5858	253-5858	219
Pacific Oaks College 5 Westmoreland Pl *TF:* 877-314-2380 ■ *Web:* www.pacificoaks.edu	Pasadena	CA	91103	877-314-2380		166
Pacific Office Interiors 5304 Derry Ave Ste U *Web:* pacificofficeinteriors.com	Agoura Hills	CA	91301	818-735-0333		393
Pacific Packaging Products Inc 24 Industrial Way *TF:* 800-777-0300 ■ *Web:* www.pacificpkg.com	Wilmington	MA	01887	978-657-9100	658-4933	559
Pacific Palisades Post Co 839 Via de la Paz *Web:* palipost.com	Pacific Palisades	CA	90272	310-454-1321	454-1078	637-8
Pacific Palms Conference Resort 1 Industry Hills Pkwy *TF Cust Svc:* 800-524-4557 ■ *Web:* www.pacificpalmsresort.com	City of Industry	CA	91744	626-810-4455	964-9535	669
Pacific Paper Tube Inc 1025 98th Ave *TF:* 888-377-8823 ■ *Web:* www.pacificpapertube.com	Oakland	CA	94603	510-562-8823	562-9002	125
Pacific Paradym Energy Inc 1030 W Georgia St *Web:* www.pacificparadym.com	Vancouver	BC	V6E2Y3	604-689-2646		539
Pacific Pathology Associates Inc 665 Winter St SE *Web:* www.pacificpathologyinc.com	Salem	OR	97301	503-561-5350		418
Pacific Pharmacy Computers Inc 4167 N Golden State Bouelvard Ste 106 *Web:* www.goppc.com	Fresno	CA	93722	559-276-6168		175
Pacific Pines State Park 25904 R St *Web:* www.stateparks.com	Ocean Park	WA	98640	360-902-8844		565
Pacific Piston Ring Co Inc 3620 Eastham Dr *TF:* 800-752-0888 ■ *Web:* www.pacificpistonring.com	Culver City	CA	90232	310-836-3322		128
Pacific Place 600 Pine St *Web:* www.pacificplaceseattle.com	Seattle	WA	98101	206-405-2655		460
Pacific Plaza Hotels Inc 1000 Marina Village Pkwy Ste 100 *TF:* 800-780-7234 ■ *Web:* www.pacificplazahotels.com	Alameda	CA	94501	510-832-6868		378
Pacific Polymers Inc 12271 Monarch St *TF:* 800-888-8340 ■ *Web:* www.pacpoly.com	Garden Grove	CA	92841	714-898-0025		3
Pacific Power & Light 825 NE Multnomah St **Fax Area Code:* 888 ■ **Fax:* Cust Svc ■ *TF Cust Svc:* 888-221-7070 ■ *Web:* www.pacificpower.net	Portland	OR	97232	503-813-6666	800-2851*	787
Pacific Power Group 805 Broadway St Ste 700 *Web:* www.pacificpowergroup.com	Vancouver	WA	98660	360-887-7400		385
Pacific Precision Laboratories Inc 20447 Nordhoff St	Chatsworth	CA	91311	818-700-8977		639
Pacific Premier Bancorp Inc 1600 Sunflower Ave *NASDAQ: PPBI* ■ *TF:* 888-388-5433 ■ *Web:* www.ppbi.com	Costa Mesa	CA	92626	714-431-4000		360-2
Pacific Press 1350 N Kings Rd *TF Cust Svc:* 800-765-6955 ■ *Web:* www.pacificpress.com	Nampa	ID	83687	208-465-2500	465-2531	637-9
Pacific Press Technologies 714 Walnut St *TF:* 800-851-3586 ■ *Web:* www.pacific-press.com	Mount Carmel	IL	62863	618-262-8666	262-7000	456
Pacific Process Systems Inc 5055 California Ave Ste 220 *Web:* www.pps-equipment.com	Bakersfield	CA	93309	661-321-9681		538
Pacific Propeller Inc 5802 S 228th St *Web:* www.pacificpropeller.com	Kent	WA	98032	253-872-7767		22
Pacific Publishing Co 636 Alaska St S PO Box 80156 *Web:* www.pacificpublishingcompany.com	Seattle	WA	98108	206-461-1300		637-8
Pacific Repertory Theater PO Box 222035 *TF:* 866-622-0709 ■ *Web:* www.pacrep.org	Carmel	CA	93922	831-622-0700	622-0703	573-4
Pacific Research Institute for Public Policy (PRI) 1 Embarcadero Ctr *Web:* www.pacificresearch.org	San Francisco	CA	94111	415-989-0833	989-2411	634
Pacific Resources for Education & Learning 900 Ft St Mall Ste 1300 *TF:* 800-377-4773 ■ *Web:* www.prel.org	Honolulu	HI	96813	808-441-1300		242
Pacific Ridge School 6269 El Fuerte St *Web:* www.pacificridge.org	Carlsbad	CA	92009	760-448-9820		685
Pacific Rim 114 W Liberty St *Web:* www.pacificrimbykana.com	Ann Arbor	MI	48104	734-662-9303		671
Pacific Rim 2061 Paramount *Web:* www.pacificrimam.com	Amarillo	TX	79109	806-353-9179		671
Pacific Rim Bistro 303 Peachtree Ctr Ave *Web:* www.pacificrimbistro.com	Atlanta	GA	30303	404-893-0018		671
Pacific Rim Manufacturing Inc 5456 SE International Way *Web:* www.pacificrimmfg.com	Milwaukie	OR	97222	503-654-9543	654-8050	621
Pacific Rim Mechanical 7655 Convoy Ct *TF:* 800-891-4822 ■ *Web:* www.prmech.com	San Diego	CA	92111	858-974-6500	974-6501	14
Pacific Rim Mining Corp 625 Howe St Ste 1050 *OTC: PFRMF* ■ *TF:* 888-775-7097 ■ *Web:* oceanagold.com	Vancouver	BC	V6C2T6	604-689-1976		502
Pacific Rivers (PRC) 317 SW Alder St Ste 900 *Web:* www.pacificrivers.org	Portland	OR	97204	503-228-3555	228-3556	48-13
Pacific Roller Die Co 1321 W Winton Ave *Web:* www.prdcompany.com	Hayward	CA	94545	510-782-7242	887-5639	456
Pacific Salmon Foundation 1682 Seventh Ave W Ste 300 *TF:* 800-663-7090 ■ *Web:* www.psf.ca	Vancouver	BC	V6J4S6	604-664-7664		303
Pacific School of Religion 1798 Scenic Ave *TF:* 800-999-0528 ■ *Web:* www.psr.edu	Berkeley	CA	94709	510-848-0528	845-8948	167-3
Pacific Science Ctr 200 Second Ave N *TF:* 800-664-8775 ■ *Web:* www.pacificsciencecenter.org	Seattle	WA	98109	206-443-2001	443-3631	520
Pacific Scientific Energetic Materials Company Inc 7073 W Willis Dr *Web:* www.psemc.com	Chandler	AZ	85226	480-763-3000		21
Pacific Seacraft PO Box 189 *TF:* 800-561-3357 ■ *Web:* www.pacificseacraft.com	Washington	NC	27889	252-948-1421	948-1422	90
Pacific Security Integrations Inc 99-1285 Halawa Valley Rd *Web:* pacsecinc.com	Aiea	HI	96701	808-484-4000		693
Pacific Service Federal Credit Union PO Box 8191 *TF:* 888-858-6878 ■ *Web:* www.pacificservice.org	Walnut Creek	CA	94596	925-296-6200		219
Pacific Ship Repair 1625 Rigel St *Web:* www.pacship.com	San Diego	CA	92113	619-232-3200		698
Pacific Shipyards International LLC Pier 41 Honolulu Harbor PO Box 31328 *Web:* www.pacificshipyards.com	Honolulu	HI	96817	808-848-6211	848-6279	698
Pacific Shores Inn 4802 Mission Blvd *Web:* www.pacificshoresinn.com	San Diego	CA	92109	858-483-6300	483-9276	379
Pacific Software Publishing Inc 1404 140th Pl NE *TF:* 800-232-3989 ■ *Web:* www.pspinc.com	Bellevue	WA	98007	425-957-0808		180
Pacific Source Inc PO Box 2323 *TF:* 888-343-1515 ■ *Web:* www.pacsource.com	Woodinville	WA	98072	888-343-1515		191-3
Pacific Southwest Railway Museum 4695 Nebo Dr *Web:* www.psrm.org	La Mesa	CA	91941	619-465-7776		520
Pacific Southwest Research Station 800 Buchanan St *Web:* www.fs.fed.us/psw	Albany	CA	94710	510-559-6300	559-6440	668
Pacific Specialty Insurance Co 3601 Haven Ave **Fax Area Code:* 650 ■ *TF:* 800-962-1172 ■ *Web:* www.pacificspecialty.com	Menlo Park	CA	94025	800-962-1172	780-4820*	391-4
Pacific Stainless Products Inc 58500 Mcnulty Way *Web:* www.pacificstainless.com	St Helens	OR	97051	503-397-1277		697
Pacific States Cast Iron Pipe Co 1401 E 2000 S PO Box 1219 *Web:* mcwaneductile.com	Provo	UT	84603	801-373-6910	377-0338	307
Pacific States Felt & Mfg Company Inc 23850 Clawiter Rd *TF:* 800-566-8866 ■ *Web:* www.pacificstatesfelt.net	Hayward	CA	94545	510-783-0277	783-4725	326
Pacific States Marine Fisheries Commissi 205 SE Spokane St Ste 100 *Web:* www.psmfc.org	Portland	OR	97202	503-650-5400		743
Pacific States University 3424 Wilshire Blvd 12th Fl *TF:* 888-200-0383 ■ *Web:* www.psuca.edu	Los Angeles	CA	90010	323-731-2383		166
Pacific Steel & Recycling 1401 Third St NW *TF:* 800-889-6264 ■ *Web:* pacific-steel.com	Great Falls	MT	59404	406-771-7222		492
Pacific Steel Casting Company Inc 1333 Second St *Web:* www.pacificsteel.com	Berkeley	CA	94710	510-525-9200	524-4673	307
Pacific Storage Co PO Box 334 *TF:* 888-823-5467 ■ *Web:* www.pacificstorage.com	Stockton	CA	95201	209-320-6600	465-9533	803-1
Pacific Sun 1200 Fifth Ave Ste 200 *Web:* www.pacificsun.com	San Rafael	CA	94901	415-485-6700	485-6226	532-5
Pacific Sunwear of California Inc 3450 E Miraloma Ave *NASDAQ: PSUN* ■ *Web:* www.pacsun.com	Anaheim	CA	92806	714-414-4000	414-4251	157-4

Company	Address	City	State	ZIP	Phone	Fax	Class	Details
Pacific Supermarket Inc	1420 Southgate Ave	Daly City	CA	94015	650-994-1688		345	
Pacific Surveying & Engineering Services Inc	1812 Cornwall Ave	Bellingham	WA	98225	360-671-7387		261	*TF:* 800-456-2009 ■ *Web:* www.psesurvey.com
Pacific Tech Solutions LLC	15530 Rckfeld Blvd Ste B4	Irvine	CA	92618	949-830-1623		177	*Web:* www.pts1.com
Pacific Terrace Hotel	610 Diamond St	San Diego	CA	92109	858-581-3500	274-2534	379	*TF:* 800-344-3370 ■ *Web:* www.pacificterrace.com
Pacific Theatres Corp	189 The Grove Dr	Los Angeles	CA	90036	323-692-0103		748	*Web:* www.pacifictheatres.com
Pacific Title Archives	10717 Vanowen St	North Hollywood	CA	91605	818-760-4223		514	*TF:* 800-968-9111 ■ *Web:* www.pacifictitlearchives.com
Pacific Tower Properties Inc	2550 Denali St	Anchorage	AK	99503	907-279-0541		104	*Web:* www.pacifictower.com
Pacific Trade International Inc	5515 Security Ln Ste 1100	Rockville	MD	20852	301-816-4200		327	*Web:* chesapeakebaycandle.com
Pacific Transit System	216 N Second St	Raymond	WA	98577	360-875-9418	942-3193	108	*TF:* 800-833-6388 ■ *Web:* www.pacifictransit.org
Pacific Union College	1 Angwin Ave	Angwin	CA	94508	707-965-6336	965-6432*	166	*Fax: Admissions ■ *TF:* 800-862-7080 ■ *Web:* www.puc.edu
Pacific University	2043 College Way	Forest Grove	OR	97116	503-352-2007	352-2975*	166	*Fax: Admissions ■ *TF Admissions:* 800-677-6712 ■ *Web:* www.pacificu.edu
Pacific University Library	2043 College Way	Forest Grove	OR	97116	503-352-1400	352-1416	434-6	*TF:* 800-677-6712 ■ *Web:* pacificu.edu/libraries
Pacific Vista Capital LLC	2211 Encinitas Blvd	Encinitas	CA	92024	760-479-0601		401	*Web:* www.pacvista.com
Pacific Wave Systems Inc	7151 Patterson Dr	Garden Grove	CA	92841	714-893-0152		647	*Web:* www.pacificwavesystems.com
Pacific Western Transportation Ltd	6999 ordan Dr	Mississauga	ON	L5T1K6	905-564-3232		107	*TF:* 800-387-6787 ■ *Web:* www.pacificwesterntoronto.com
Pacific Wings	1 Keolani Pl Ste 30	Kahului	HI	96732	808-873-0877	873-7920	25	*TF:* 888-575-4546
Pacific Wood Laminates Inc	885 Railroad Ave PO Box 820	Brookings	OR	97415	541-469-4177		191-3	*Web:* www.pacificwoodlaminates.com
Pacific Wood Preserving of Oregon Inc	22125 Rock Creek Rd	Sheridan	OR	97378	503-843-2122		818	
Pacific's Edge	120 Highland Dr	Carmel	CA	93923	831-622-5445		671	*Web:* highlandsinn.hyatt.com
Pacifica Chamber of Commerce	225 Rockaway Beach Ave Ste 1	Pacifica	CA	94044	650-355-4122	355-6949	139	*TF:* 800-743-5000 ■ *Web:* pacificachamber.com
Pacifica Graduate Institute	249 Lambert Rd	Carpinteria	CA	93013	805-969-3626		166	*Web:* www.pacifica.edu
Pacifica Hotels	17300 Red Hill Ste 250	Irvine	CA	92614	805-957-0095	486-5970*	652	*Fax Area Code: 949 ■ *TF:* 800-720-0223 ■ *Web:* www.pacificahotels.com
Pacifica Nursing & Rehabilitation Ctr	385 Esplanade Ave	Pacifica	CA	94044	650-993-5576	359-9388	450	*TF:* 800-213-0154 ■ *Web:* pacificarehab.com
Pacifica Radio Foundation	1925 ML King Jr Way	Berkeley	CA	94704	510-849-2590	849-2617	644	*Web:* www.pacifica.org
Pacifica Services Inc	106 S Mentor Ave Ste 200	Pasadena	CA	91106	626-405-0131	405-0059	261	*TF:* 800-655-4148 ■ *Web:* www.pacificaservices.com
Pacifica State Beach	1416 Ninth St	Sacramento	CA	95814	650-738-7381		565	*Web:* www.parks.ca.gov/default.asp?page_id=524
Pacificad Inc	159 S Lincoln St	Spokane	WA	99201	509-326-7789		180	*TF:* 800-722-2621 ■ *Web:* www.pacificad.com
Pacificare of Texas	6200 NW Pkwy	San Antonio	TX	78249	210-474-5000		391-3	*TF:* 800-624-7272 ■ *Web:* uhcwest.com
Pacifico Inc	1190 Coleman Ave Ste 110	San Jose	CA	95110	408-327-8888		7	*Web:* www.pacifico.com
Pacificomm Systems LLC	73-5563 Olowalu St Ste B6	Kailua-Kona	HI	96740	808-329-6440		480	
PacifiCorp	825 NE Multnomah St	Portland	OR	97232	503-813-5000	813-6659*	787	*Fax: Hum Res ■ *TF:* 888-221-7070 ■ *Web:* www.pacificorp.com
Pacira Inc	10450 Science Ctr Dr	San Diego	CA	92121	858-625-2424		85	*Web:* www.pacira.com
Pack Place	2 S Pack Sq	Asheville	NC	28801	828-257-4500		50-2	*Web:* www.packplace.org
Package Concepts & Materials Inc	1023 Thousand Oaks Blvd	Greenville	SC	29607	864-458-7291		600	*Web:* www.packageconcepts.com
Package Development Company Inc	100 Roundhill Dr	Rockaway	NJ	07866	973-983-8500		596	*Web:* www.pkgdev.com
Package Machinery Co	380 Union St Ste 58	West Springfield	MA	01089	413-732-4000	732-1163	547	*Web:* www.packagemachinery.com
Package Pavement Company Inc	PO Box 408	Stormville	NY	12582	845-221-2224	221-0433	46	*TF:* 800-724-8193 ■ *Web:* www.packagepavement.com
Package Right Corp	811 Development Dr	Tipton	IN	46072	765-675-2323		88	*Web:* www.packageright.com
Package Steel Systems, In	15 Harback Rd	Sutton	MA	01590	508-865-5871	865-9130	105	*TF:* 800-225-7242 ■ *Web:* www.packagesteel.com
PackageX Inc	17100 Ventura Blvd Ste 223	Encino	CA	91316	818-789-6910		88	*TF:* 800-780-4707 ■ *Web:* www.packagex.com
Packaging Concepts Inc	9832 Evergreen Indus Dr	Saint Louis	MO	63123	314-329-9700	487-2666	548	*Web:* www.packagingconceptsinc.com
Packaging Corp of America	1955 W Field Ct	Lake Forest	IL	60045	800 456 4725		100	*NYSE: PKG* ■ *TF:* 800-456-4725 ■ *Web:* www.packagingcorp.com
Packaging Distribution Services Inc (PDS)	2308 Sunset Rd	Des Moines	IA	50321	515-243-3156	243-1741	559	*TF:* 800-747-2699 ■ *Web:* www.pdspack.com
Packaging Inc	7200 93rd Ave N Ste 190	Brooklyn Park	MN	55445	952-935-3421	935-0978	492	*TF:* 800-328-6650 ■ *Web:* www.packinc.com
Packaging Innovators Corp	6650 National Dr	Livermore	CA	94550	925-371-2000		596	*Web:* www.packaginginnovators.com
Packaging Machinery Manufacturers Institute (PMMI)	4350 N Fairfax Dr Ste 600	Arlington	VA	22203	703-243-8555	243-8556	49-13	*TF:* 888-275-7664 ■ *Web:* www.pmmi.org
Packaging Material Direct Inc	30405 Solon Rd Ste 9	Solon	OH	44139	440-914-0530		690	*TF:* 800-456-2467 ■ *Web:* www.packagingsuppliesbymail.com
Packaging Personified Inc	246 Kehoe Blvd	Carol Stream	IL	60188	630-793-4288		629	*Web:* www.packagingpersonified.com
Packaging Printing Specialists Inc	3915 Stern Ave	St Charles	IL	60174	630-513-8060		626	*Web:* www.ppsofil.com
Packaging Products Corporation LLC	6820 Squibb Rd	Mission	KS	66202	913-262-3033		627	*Web:* www.packagingproductscorp.com
Packaging Progressions Inc	102 G P Clement Dr	Collegeville	PA	19426	610-489-8601		96	*Web:* www.pacproinc.com
Packaging Services Inc of Tennessee	120 T Elmer Cox Rd	Greeneville	TN	37743	423-787-7711		100	*Web:* www.psipack.com
Packaging Services of Maryland Inc	16461 Elliott Pkwy	Williamsport	MD	21795	301-223-6200	223-8247	549	*TF:* 800-223-6255 ■ *Web:* www.psimd.com
Packaging Solutions Co	PO Box 4321	Bayamon	PR	00958	787-622-7225		601	*Web:* www.flepak.com
Packaging Specialties Inc	300 Lake Rd	Medina	OH	44256	330-723-6000	725-8180	198	*TF:* 800-344-9271 ■ *Web:* www.packspec.com
Packaging Systems International Inc	4990 Acoma St	Denver	CO	80216	303-296-4445	298-1016	547	*TF:* 800-525-6110 ■ *Web:* www.pkgsys.com
Packaging Unlimited LLC	1729 Mccloskey Ave	Louisville	KY	40210	502-515-3900		100	*Web:* www.packagingunlimited.com
Packard Cos, The	9555 Chesapeake Dr Ste 202	San Diego	CA	92123	858-277-4305		652	*Web:* www.packard-1.com
Packard Humanities Institute, The (PHI)	300 Second St	Los Altos	CA	94022	650-948-0150		305	*Web:* www.packhum.org
Packard Industries Inc	1515 N US Hwy 31	Niles	MI	49120	269-684-2550		286	
Packard Transport Inc	24021 S Municipal Dr PO Box 380	Channahon	IL	60410	815-467-9260	467-6939	468	*TF:* 800-467-9260 ■ *Web:* www.packardtransport.com
Packer Engineering Inc	420 N Main St	Montgomery	IL	60538	630-701-7703	701-7732	261	*TF:* 866 264 4126 ■ *Web:* www.packereng.com
Packer Thomas	6601 Westford Pl Ste 101	Canfield	OH	44406	330-533-9777		2	*TF:* 800-943-4278 ■ *Web:* www.packerthomas.com
Packerland Rent-a-mat Inc	12580 W Rohr Ave	Butler	WI	53007	262-781-5321		131	*TF:* 800-472-9339 ■ *Web:* www.packerland.net
Packers Manufacturing Inc	30467 Road 158	Visalia	CA	93292	559-732-4886		547	*Web:* www.thepacker.com
Packers of Indian River Ltd	5700 W Midway Rd	Fort Pierce	FL	34981	772-464-6575		11-1	
Packet Design Inc	2455 Augustine Dr	Santa Clara	CA	95054	408-490-1000	562-0080	178-10	*Web:* www.packetdesign.com
Packing House	900 E Layton Ave	Milwaukee	WI	53207	414-483-5054	483-3481	671	*TF:* 800-727-9477 ■ *Web:* www.foodspot.com/clients/wi/milwaukee
PackLate.com Inc	100 Four Falls Corporate Ctr Ste 104	West Conshohocken	PA	19428	877-472-2552	550-2502*	387	*Fax Area Code: 815 ■ *TF:* 877-472-2552 ■ *Web:* packlate.com
Packless Metal Hose Inc	PO Box 20668	Waco	TX	76702	254-666-7700	666-7893	14	*TF:* 800-347-4859 ■ *Web:* www.packless.com
Packnet Ltd	2950 Lexington Ave Ste 500	Eagan	MN	55121	952-944-9124		683	*Web:* www.packnetltd.com
Packworld USA	539 S Main St	Nazareth	PA	18064	610-746-2765		641	*TF:* 800-523-7752 ■ *Web:* www.packworldusa.com
PacLand	10135 SE Sunnyside Rd Ste 200	Clackamas	OR	97015	503-659-9500	659-2227	463	*Web:* www.pacland.com
PACO Pumps Inc	902 Koomey Rd	Brookshire	TX	77423	281-994-2700		641	*TF:* 800-955-5847 ■ *Web:* www.paco-pumps.com
Paco Steel & Engineering Corp	19818 S Alameda St	Rancho Dominguez	CA	90221	310-537-6375		492	*TF:* 800-421-1473 ■ *Web:* www.pacosteel.com
Paco Winders Manufacturing Inc	2040 Bennett Rd	Philadelphia	PA	19116	215-673-6265	673-2027	556	*Web:* www.pacowinders.com
Pacon Corp	2525 N Casaloma Dr	Appleton	WI	54912	800-333-2545		554	*TF:* 800-333-2545 ■ *Web:* www.pacon.com
Pacon Inc	4249 N Puente Ave	Baldwin Park	CA	91706	626-814-4654		601	*Web:* www.paconinc.com
Pacon Mfg	400 Pierce St	Somerset	NJ	08873	732-764-9070		558	*Web:* www.paconmfg.com
Pacord Inc	240 W 30th St	National City	CA	91950	619-336-2200		698	*Web:* l-3mps.com
Pacotech Inc	1739 Nina Lee Ln	Houston	TX	77018	713-688-0404		196	*Web:* www.pacotech.com
Pac-Paper Inc	6416 NW Whitney Rd	Vancouver	WA	98665	360-695-7771		557	*Web:* www.pacpaperinc.com

Name / Address	City	State	Zip	Phone	Fax	Class
PacPizza LLC 220 Porter Dr Ste 100	San Ramon	CA	94583	925-838-8567	838-5801	670
TF: 800-561-3357 ■ *Web:* pacpizza.com						
Pacrim Engineering 233 W Cerritos Ave	Anaheim	CA	92805	714-683-0470		186
Web: www.pacrimengineering.com						
Pacrim Hospitality Services Inc						
30 Damascus Rd	Bedford	NS	B4A0C1	902-404-7474		194
TF: 877-680-7666 ■ *Web:* www.pacrimhospitality.com						
Pacs Industries Inc 1211 Stewart Ave	Bethpage	NY	11714	516-465-7100	465-7057	729
Web: www.pacsswitchgearllc.com						
Pactiv Corp 1900 W Field Ct	Lake Forest	IL	60045	847-482-2000		561
TF: 888-828-2850 ■ *Web:* www.pactiv.com						
Pact-One Solutions Inc						
8215 S Eastern Ave Ste 101	Las Vegas	NV	89123	866-722-8663		174
TF: 866-722-8663 ■ *Web:* www.pact-one.com						
Pacur LLC 3555 Moser St	Oshkosh	WI	54901	920-236-2888		600
Web: www.pacur.com						
Pad Print Machinery of Vermont Inc						
201 Tennis Way	East Dorset	VT	05253	802-362-0844		628
TF: 800-272-7764 ■ *Web:* www.epsvt.com						
Pad Thai Restaurant 1681 Grand Ave	Saint Paul	MN	55105	651-690-1393		671
Web: padthaiongrand.com						
Padco Inc 2220 Elm St SE	Minneapolis	MN	55414	612-378-7270	378-9388	103
TF: 800-328-5513 ■ *Web:* www.padco.com						
Paddle Tramps Manufacturing Co						
1317 University Ave	Lubbock	TX	79401	806-765-9901		279
TF: 800-548-8552 ■ *Web:* www.paddletramps.com						
Paddock Chevrolet Inc						
3232 Delaware Ave	Kenmore	NY	14217	716-876-0945		57
Web: www.paddockchevrolet.com						
Paddock Laboratories Inc						
3940 Quebec Ave N	Minneapolis	MN	55427	763-546-4676	546-4842	479
Paddock Publications Inc						
155 E Algonquin Rd	Arlington Heights	IL	60005	847-427-4300	427-1301	637-8
TF: 800-464-0729 ■ *Web:* www.dailyherald.com						
Paddock, The 20 Scudder Ave	Hyannis	MA	02601	508-775-7677		671
PADF (Pan American Development Foundation)						
1889 F St NW 2nd Fl	Washington	DC	20006	202-458-3969	458-6316	48-5
TF: 877-572-4484 ■ *Web:* www.padf.org						
Padgett Business Services						
160 Hawthorne Pk	Athens	GA	30606	800-723-4388	543-8537*	2
**Fax Area Code: 706* ■ *TF:* 800-723-4388 ■ *Web:* www.padgettbusinessservices.com						
Padgett Business Services LLC						
140 Mountain Brook Dr	Canton	GA	30115	770-345-6100		610
Web: www.padgettservices.com						
Padgett Inc 901 E Fourth St	New Albany	IN	47150	812-945-2391		480
Web: www.padgett-inc.com						
PADI (Professional Assn of Diving Instructors International)						
30151 Tomas St	Rancho Santa Margarita	CA	92688	949-858-7234	267-1267	48-22
TF Sales: 800-729-7234 ■ *Web:* www.padi.com						
PADI Americas						
30151 Tomas St	Rancho Santa Margarita	CA	92688	949-858-7234	878-4364*	513
**Fax Area Code: 800* ■ *TF:* 800-527-8378 ■ *Web:* kaptest.com						
PADIC Inc 1609 E Broadway	Gainesville	TX	76240	940-665-6130	665-7486	400
Web: www.padic.com						
Padilla Speer Beardsley Inc						
1101 W River Pkwy Ste 400	Minneapolis	MN	55415	612-455-1700		636
Web: www.padillaco.com						
Padre Associates Inc 1861 Knoll Dr	Ventura	CA	93003	805-644-2220		261
Web: www.padreinc.com						
Padre Island National Seashore						
PO Box 181300	Corpus Christi	TX	78480	361-949-8068	949-8023	564
TF: 800-343-2368 ■ *Web:* www.nps.gov/pais						
Padre Pio Foundation of America Inc						
463 Main St	Cromwell	CT	06416	860-635-4996		305
Web: padrepio.com						
Paduano Di Tommaso & Golda						
220 Monmouth Rd	Oakhurst	NJ	07755	732-531-4100		2
Paducah & Louisville Railway Inc						
200 Clark St	Paducah	KY	42003	270-444-4300		648
Web: www.palrr.com						
Paducah Area Chamber of Commerce						
300 S Third St	Paducah	KY	42003	270-443-1746	442-9152	139
Web: www.paducahchamber.org						
Paducah Power System 1500 Broadway	Paducah	KY	42001	270-575-4000		787
Web: www.paducahpower.com						
Paducah Sun 408 Kentucky Ave	Paducah	KY	42003	270-575-8600		532-2
Web: www.paducahsun.com						
Paducah Symphony Orchestra						
760 Broadway	Paducah	KY	42001	270-444-0065	444-0456	573-3
Web: paducahsymphony.org						
Padulo Integrated Inc						
1 St Clair Ave W	Toronto	ON	M4V1K7	416-966-4000		195
Web: www.padulo.ca						
Paesano's 555 E Basse Rd	San Antonio	TX	78209	210-828-5191	828-6329	671
Web: www.prg-sa.com						
Paesano's 508 E 14th St	Plano	TX	75074	972-578-2727		671
Web: www.paesanosrestaurant.net						
Paesano's 3411 Washtenaw Ave	Ann Arbor	MI	48104	734-971-0484	971-0419	671
Web: www.paesanosannarbor.com						
PAFA (Pennsylvania Academy of the Fine Arts Museum)						
118 N Broad St	Philadelphia	PA	19102	215-972-7600	569-0153	520
TF: 800-799-7233 ■ *Web:* www.pafa.org						
PAFCO LLC 201 S Orange Ave Ste 1575	Orlando	FL	32801	407-206-5300		316
Web: www.pafcollc.com						
Page & Assoc Inc						
1979 Lakeside Pkwy Ste 200	Tucker	GA	30084	800-252-5282		796
TF: 800-252-5282 ■ *Web:* www.thelifeline.com						
Page & Jones Inc						
52 N Jackson St 36602 PO Box 2167	Mobile	AL	36652	251-432-1646		311
TF: 800-299-4067 ■ *Web:* www.pageandjones.com						
Page 1 Solutions LLC						
17301 W Colfax Ave Ste 275	Golden	CO	80401	303-233-3886		4
TF: 800-916-3886 ■ *Web:* www.page1solutions.com						
Page County 112 E Main St	Clarinda	IA	51632	712-542-2516	542-6005	338
TF: 800-222-8477 ■ *Web:* www.co.page.ia.us						
Page County 103 S Court St	Luray	VA	22835	540-743-4142		338
Web: www.pagecounty.virginia.gov						
Page Group Inc, The						
8905 Fairview Rd Ste 401	Silver Spring	MD	20910	301-565-4020	565-4024	195
Page Litho Inc 6445 E Vernor Hwy	Detroit	MI	48207	313-921-6880		626
Page One Bookstore						
?5850 Eubank Blvd Ste B-41	Albuquerque	NM	87111	505-294-2026	294-5576	95
Web: www.page1book.com						
Page Public Library 479 Lake Powell Blvd	Page	AZ	86040	928-645-4270		434-3
TF: 800-645-4329 ■ *Web:* www.pagepubliclibrary.org						
Pageau Morel et Associes Inc						
210 Cr,mazie Blvd W Ste 110	Montreal	QC	H2P1C6	819-776-4665		261
Web: www.pageaumorel.com						
Pageplus Cellular 9700 NW 112th Ave	Miami	FL	33178	800-550-2436		387
TF: 800-550-2436 ■ *Web:* www.pagepluscellular.com						
PageSoutherlandPage (PSPAEC)						
1100 Louisiana St Ste 1	Houston	TX	77002	713-871-8484	871-8440	261
Web: pagethink.com						
Page-Walker Arts & History Ctr						
119 Ambassador Loop	Cary	NC	27513	919-460-4963	388-1141	50-2
TF: 800-514-3849 ■ *Web:* www.townofcary.org						
Paging Network of Canada Inc						
1-1685 Tech Ave	Mississauga	ON	L4W0A7	905-614-3100		41
TF: 800-216-0888 ■ *Web:* www.pagenet.ca						
Pagnotti Enterprises Inc						
46 Public Sq Ste 600	Wilkes-Barre	PA	18701	570-825-8700		360-2
Web: www.jeddocoal.com						
Pa-Go Mobile Inc						
150 NE 95th St Ste 307	Seattle	WA	98115	877-425-2196		224
TF: 877-425-2196						
Pagoda Hotel Inc 1525 Rycroft St	Honolulu	HI	96814	808-941-6611		378
Web: www.pagodahotel.com						
PAH (Punxsutawney Area Hospital Inc)						
81 Hillcrest Dr	Punxsutawney	PA	15767	814-938-1800		374-3
Web: www.pah.org						
PAH (Passavant Area Hospital)						
1600 W Walnut St	Jacksonville	IL	62650	217-245-9541		374-3
Web: www.passavanthospital.com						
Pahio Resorts Inc 3970 Wyllie Rd	Princeville	HI	96722	808-826-6549		378
Web: www.pahio.com						
Pahrump Nugget Hotel & Gambling Hall						
681 S Hwy 160	Pahrump	NV	89048	775-751-6500		452
Web: pahrumpnugget.com						
PAI (Population Action International)						
1300 19th St NW Ste 200	Washington	DC	20036	202-557-3400	728-4177	48-5
Web: pai.org						
PAI Management Corp						
5272 River Rd Ste 630	Bethesda	MD	20816	301-656-4224	656-0989	47
Web: www.paimgmt.com						
Paideia School Inc, The						
1509 Ponce De Leon Ave NE	Atlanta	GA	30307	404-377-3491	377-0032	685
Web: www.paideiaschool.org						
Paier College of Art Inc 20 Gorham Ave	Hamden	CT	06514	203-287-3031	287-3021	166
Web: www.paiercollegeofart.edu						
Paige Electric Company LP						
1160 Springfield Rd	Union	NJ	07083	908-687-7810	687-2722	246
TF: 800-327-2443 ■ *Web:* www.paigeelectric.com						
Pain Therapeutics Inc						
7801 N Capital of Texas Hwy Ste 260	Austin	TX	78731	512-501-2444	614-0414	582
NASDAQ: PTIE ■ *Web:* www.paintrials.com						
Paine College 1235 15th St	Augusta	GA	30901	706-821-8200		166
TF: 800-476-7703 ■ *Web:* www.paine.edu						
Paine, Hamblen, Coffin, Brooke & Miller LLP						
717 W Sprague Ave Washington Trust Financial Ctr						
Ste 1200	Spokane	WA	99201	509-455-6000		428
Web: www.painehamblen.com						
Painful Pleasures Inc						
7410 Coca Cola Dr Ste 108	Hanover	MD	21076	410-712-0145		410
Web: www.painfulpleasures.com						
Paint & Decorating Retailers Assn (PDRA)						
1401 Triad Ctr Dr	Saint Peters	MO	63376	636-326-2636		49-18
TF: 800-737-0107 ■ *Web:* www.pdra.org						
Paint Applicator Corp of America						
7 Harbor Park Dr	Port Washington	NY	11050	516-284-3000		690
Web: www.pacoa.com						
Paint Creek State Park						
280 Taylor Rd	Bainbridge	OH	45612	937-981-7061		565
TF: 866-644-6727 ■ *Web:* parks.ohiodnr.gov/paintcreek						
Paint Sundries Solutions Inc						
930 Seventh Ave	Kirkland	WA	98033	425-827-9200		297-8
Web: www.paintsundries.com						
Painted Bride Art Ctr						
230 Vine St	Philadelphia	PA	19106	215-925-9914	925-7402	50-2
TF: 800-745-3000 ■ *Web:* www.paintedbride.org						
Painted Pony Petroleum Ltd						
736 Sixth Ave SW Ste 1800	Calgary	AB	T2P3T7	403-475-0440		539
TF: 866-975-0440 ■ *Web:* www.paintedpony.ca						
Painted Rocks State Park						
3201 Spurgin Rd	Missoula	MT	59804	406-542-5500		565
Web: stateparks.mt.gov						
Painters Supply & Equipment Co						
25195 Brest Rd	Taylor	MI	48180	734-946-8119		550
TF: 800-589-8100 ■ *Web:* www.painters-supply.com						
Painting & Decorating Contractors of America (PDCA)						
2316 Millpark Dr	Maryland Heights	MO	63043	314-514-7322	514-9417	49-3
TF Cust Svc: 800-332-7322 ■ *Web:* www.pdca.org						
Painweek 6 Erie St	Montclair	NJ	07042	973-415-5100		195
Web: www.painweek.org						
Paisan's 4826 Longley Ln	Reno	NV	89502	775-826-9444		671
Web: paisanscatering.com						
Paisano Publications LLC						
28210 Dorothy Dr	Agoura Hills	CA	91301	818-889-8740	889-5214	637-9
TF: 800-323-3484 ■ *Web:* www.paisanopub.com						
Paisano's 4043 SW Tenth St	Topeka	KS	66604	785-273-0100		671
TF: 800-795-8091 ■ *Web:* www.paisanoskansas.com						
Paiute Pipeline Co						
5241 W Spring Mtn Rd	Las Vegas	NV	89146	702-876-7178	873-3820	325
Web: www.paiutepipeline.com						
Pajak Engineering Ltd						
300-707 Seventh Ave SW	Calgary	AB	T2P3H6	403-264-1197		539
Web: www.pajakeng.com						

Name / Address	Phone	Fax	Class
Pajarito Scientific Security Corp			
2532 Camino Entrada .... Santa Fe NM 87507	505-424-6660		639
Web: www.pajaritoscientific.com			
Pajaro Valley Chamber of Commerce			
44 Brennan St PO Box 1748 .... Watsonville CA 95076	831-724-3900		139
Web: www.pajarovalleychamber.com			
Pak Mail Centers of America Inc			
7173 S Havana St Ste 600 .... Centennial CO 80112	303-957-1000		113
TF Cust Svc: 800-778-6665 ■ *Web:* www.pakmail.com			
Pak Rite Industries Inc 4270 High St .... Ecorse MI 48229	313-388-6400		549
Web: www.pakrite.com			
Pak Technologies Inc			
7025 W Marcia Rd .... Milwaukee WI 53223	414-371-3100		463
Web: www.paktech.com			
Pak West Paper & Packaging			
4042 W Garry Ave .... Santa Ana CA 92704	714-557-7420		548
TF: 800-927-7299 ■ *Web:* www.pakwest.com			
Pakarang 303 S Main St .... Providence RI 02903	401-453-3660		671
Web: www.pakarangrestaurant.com			
Pakistan 8 E 65th St .... New York NY 10065	212-879-8600	744-7348	784
Web: www.pakun.org			
Consulate General 12 E 65th St .... New York NY 10065	212 879 5800		257
Web: www.pakistanconsulateny.org			
Consulate General			
10850 Wilshire Blvd Ste 1250 .... Los Angeles CA 90024	310-441-5114	441-9256	257
Web: www.pakconsulatela.org			
Embassy 3517 International Ct NW .... Washington DC 20008	202-243-6500	686-1534	257
Web: www.embassyofpakistanusa.org			
Pakistan International Airlines Corp (PIA)			
1200 New Jersey Ave SE .... Washington DC 20590	800-578-6786		25
TF: 800-578-6786 ■ *Web:* www.piac.com.pk			
Pak-Lite Inc 550 Old Peachtree Rd .... Suwanee GA 30024	770-447-5123		601
Web: www.pliusa.com			
Pak-Rite Ltd 2395 S Burrell St .... Milwaukee WI 53207	414-489-0450		88
Web: www.pak-rite.com			
PakSense Inc 6223 N Discovery Pl .... Boise ID 83713	208-489-9010		201
TF: 877-832-0720 ■ *Web:* www.paksense.com			
Paksys Software LLC			
116 Salem Rd .... North Brunswick NJ 08902	732-297-8908		177
Web: www.paksys.com			
Paktech 1680 Irving Rd .... Eugene OR 97402	541-461-5000		608
Web: www.paktech-opi.com			
PAL General Engineering Inc			
10675 Treena St Ste 103 .... San Diego CA 92121	858-860-5300	860-5556	261
Web: www.palsd.com			
PaLA (Pennsylvania Library Assn)			
220 Cumberland Pkwy Ste 10 .... Mechanicsburg PA 17055	717-766-7663	766-5440	435
TF: 800-622-3308 ■ *Web:* www.palibraries.org			
Pala Casino Resort & Spa			
35008 Pala-Temecula Rd .... Pala CA 92059	760-510-5100	510-5191	669
TF: 877-946-7252 ■ *Web:* www.palacasino.com			
Pala Group 16347 Old Hammond Hwy .... Baton Rouge LA 70816	225-272-5194		188
Web: www.palagroup.com			
Pala Mesa Resort 2001 Old Hwy 395 .... Fallbrook CA 92028	760-728-5881		669
TF: 800-722-4700 ■ *Web:* www.palamesa.com			
Palace Arts Ctr 300 S Main St .... Grapevine TX 76051	817-410-3100		572
Web: www.grapevinetexasusa.com			
Palace Cafe 605 Canal St .... New Orleans LA 70130	504-523-1661		671
Web: www.palacecafe.com			
Palace Cafe, The 139 S Murphy Ave .... Sunnyvale CA 94086	650-622-4171		149
Web: palacecafe.net			
Palace Casino 158 Howard Ave .... Biloxi MS 39530	228-432-8888		132
TF: 800-725-2239 ■ *Web:* www.palacecasinoresort.com			
Palace Casino			
2710 8882-170th St			
Ste 2710, W Edmonton Mall .... Northwest Edmonton AB T5T3J7	780-444-2112	444-1155	133
Web: www.palacecasino.com			
Palace Construction Company Inc			
7 S Galapago St .... Denver CO 80223	303-777-7999		186
Web: www.palaceconst.com			
Palace Hotel			
2 New Montgomery St .... San Francisco CA 94105	415-512-1111	543-0671	379
TF: 866-716-8136 ■ *Web:* www.sfpalace.com			
Palace Kitchen 2030 Fifth Ave .... Seattle WA 98121	206-448-2001		671
Web: www.tomdouglas.com			
Palace of Auburn Hills			
6 Championship Dr .... Auburn Hills MI 48326	248-377-0100		720
TF: 800-745-3000 ■ *Web:* www.palacenet.com			
Palace of Fine Arts Theatre			
3301 Lyon St .... San Francisco CA 94123	415-563-6504		572
Web: www.palaceoffinearts.org			
Palace Printer Inc, The			
5 N Maple Ave .... Greensburg PA 15601	724-836-7777	836-6126	94
TF: 800-247-0108 ■ *Web:* www.palaceprinter.com			
Palace Renaissance & Royale			
11355 SW 84th St .... Miami FL 33173	305-270-7000		672
Web: www.thepalace.org			
Palace Station Hotel & Casino			
2411 W Sahara Ave .... Las Vegas NV 89102	702-367-2411		133
TF Resv: 800-634-3101 ■ *Web:* palacestation.sclv.com			
Palace Theatre 80 Hanover St .... Manchester NH 03101	603-668-5588	668-5804	572
TF: 800-892-6477 ■ *Web:* www.palacetheatre.org			
Palace Theatre 19 Clinton Ave .... Albany NY 12207	518-465-3334		572
TF: 800-745-3000 ■ *Web:* www.palacealbany.com			
Palace Theatre 1564 Broadway .... New York NY 10036	212-730-8200		747
Web: palacetheatreonbroadway.com			
Palace Theatre 34 W Broad St .... Columbus OH 43215	614-469-9850		572
Web: www.capa.com			
Palace, The 601 Vine St .... Cincinnati OH 45202	513-381-6006	651-0256	671
TF: 800-942-9000 ■ *Web:* www.palacecincinnati.com			
Palace, Theatre, The			
1420 Celebrity Cir			
Broadway at the Beach .... Myrtle Beach SC 29577	843-448-9224		572
TF: 888-841-2787 ■ *Web:* www.palacetheatremyrtlebeach.com			
Paladin Associates Inc			
4709 Layfield Dr Ste 100B .... Dunwoody GA 30338	770-395-9156		463
Web: www.paladinassociatesinc.com			
Paladin Data Systems Corp			
19362 Powder Hill Pl NE .... Poulsbo WA 98370	360-779-2400		177
TF: 800-532-8448 ■ *Web:* www.paladindata.com			
Paladin Labs Inc			
100 Blvd Alexis Nihon Ste 600 .... St-Laurent QC H4M2P2	514-340-1112		85
TSE: PLB ■ *TF:* 888-376-7830 ■ *Web:* www.paladin-labs.com			
Paladin Law Group LLP			
1176 Blvd Way .... Walnut Creek CA 94595	925-947-5700		428
Web: www.paladinlaw.com			
Paladin Partners 838 Kirkland Ave .... Kirkland WA 98033	425-260-5354		260
Web: www.paladinpartners.com			
Paladin Registry LLC			
69 Lincoln Blvd Ste A 275 .... Lincoln CA 95648	916-253-3334		260
Web: paladinregistry.com			
Palais de Jade 960 W Moana Ln .... Reno NV 89509	775-827-5233		671
Web: palaisdejadereno.net			
Palama Meat Company Inc			
2029 Lauwiliwili St .... Kapolei HI 96707	808-682-8305	834-8895	296-26
Web: sbcontract.com			
Palamida Inc			
215 Second St 2nd Fl .... San Francisco CA 94105	415-777-9400		174
Web: palamida.com			
Palani Drive 401 Libbie Ave .... Richmond VA 23226	804-285-3200		671
Web: www.palanidrive.com			
Palatin Technologies Inc			
4 B Cedar Brook Dr Cedar Brook Corporate Ctr			
.... Cranbury NJ 08512	609-495-2200		85
NYSE: PTN ■ *Web:* www.palatin.com			
Palatine Area Chamber of Commerce			
579 First Bank Dr #205 .... Palatine IL 60067	847-359-7200	359-7246	139
Web: www.palatinechamber.com			
Palau			
Embassy			
1701 Pennsylvania Ave NW Ste 300 .... Washington DC 20006	202-349-8598		257
Web: palauembassy.com			
Palay Display Industries Inc			
10901 Louisiana Ave S Ste 106 .... Bloomington MN 55438	952-983-2026		791
TF: 800-446-6106 ■ *Web:* www.palaydisplay.com			
Palazzo Steven (Rep R - MS)			
2349 Rayburn HOB .... Washington DC 20515	202-225-5772		342-2
Web: palazzo.house.gov			
Palcam Technologies Ltd			
1300 Ringwell Dr .... Newmarket ON L3Y9C7	905-853-1675	853-1584	454
Web: www.palcam.com			
Palco Marketing Inc			
8555 Revere Ln N .... Maple Grove MN 55369	800-882-4656		711
TF: 800-882-4656 ■ *Web:* www.palcosports.com			
Palena 3529 Connecticut Ave NW .... Washington DC 20008	202-537-9250		671
Palestine Public Library			
2000 S Loop 256 #42 .... Palestine TX 75801	903-729-4121	729-4062	434-3
Web: www1.youseemore.com/palestine			
Palestine Regional Medical Ctr			
2900 S Loop 256 .... Palestine TX 75801	903-731-1000	731-2236	374-3
TF: 800-222-1222 ■ *Web:* www.palestineregional.com			
Paley Ctr for Media, The			
465 N Beverly Dr .... Beverly Hills CA 90210	310-786-1000		520
Web: www.paleycenter.org			
Paley's Place 1204 NW 21st Ave .... Portland OR 97209	503-243-2403		671
TF: 800-289-3031 ■ *Web:* www.paleysplace.net			
PALHACC (President Abraham Lincoln Hotel & Conference Ctr)			
701 E Adams St .... Springfield IL 62701	217-544-8800	544-9607	379
TF: 855-610-8733 ■ *Web:* doubletree3.hilton.com			
Pali Adventures Summer Camp			
30778 Hwy 18 .... Running Springs CA 92382	909-867-5743		239
TF: 800-767-2722 ■ *Web:* www.paliadventures.com			
Palio Communications LLC			
260 Broadway .... Saratoga Springs NY 12866	212-849-9455		7
Web: www.palio.com			
Palisade 2601 W Marina Pl .... Seattle WA 98199	206-285-1000		671
Web: www.palisaderestaurant.com			
Palisade Corp 798 Cascadilla St .... Ithaca NY 14850	607-277-8000	277-8001	178-1
TF: 800-432-7475 ■ *Web:* www.palisade.com			
Palisade State Park			
2200 E Palisade Rd .... Sterling UT 84665	435-835-7275		565
Web: www.stateparks.utah.gov			
Palisades Charter High School			
15777 Bowdoin St .... Pacific Palisades CA 90272	310-230-6623		685
Web: www.palihigh.org			
Palisades Hudson Financial Group LLC			
2 Overhill Rd Ste 100 .... Scarsdale NY 10583	914-723-5000		401
Web: www.palisadeshudson.com			
Palisades Medical Ctr			
7600 River Rd .... North Bergen NJ 07047	201-854-5000		374-3
Web: www.palisadesmedical.org			
Palisades Tennis Club			
1171 Jamboree Rd .... Newport Beach CA 92660	949-644-6900		354
Web: palisadestennis.com/ptc			
Palisades-Kepler State Park			
700 Kepler Dr .... Mount Vernon IA 52314	319-895-6039		565
Web: www.iowadnr.gov			
Palitto Consulting Services Inc			
600 Weber Dr .... Wadsworth OH 44281	330-335-7271		196
Web: www.palittoconsulting.com			
Pall Corp 2200 Northern Blvd .... East Hills NY 11548	516-484-5400	801-9754	386
NYSE: PLL ■ *TF:* 800-645-6532 ■ *Web:* www.pall.com			
Pall Life Sciences 600 S Wagner Rd .... Ann Arbor MI 48103	734-665-0651	913-6495	419
TF: 800-521-1520 ■ *Web:* www.pall.com			
PALLAB (Physician's Automated Laboratory Inc)			
9830 Brimhall Rd .... Bakersfield CA 93312	661-829-2260	829-1317	418
TF: 800-675-2271 ■ *Web:* www.pallab.org			
Palladeo Inc 900 Western Ave .... Glendale CA 91201	818-241-5656	241-7935	393
Palladian Partners Inc			
8484 Georgia Ave Ste 200 .... Silver Spring MD 20910	301-650-8660		463
Web: www.palladianpartners.com			
Palladin Precision Products Inc			
57 Bristol St .... Waterbury CT 06708	203-574-0246	756-9478	621
Web: www.palladin.com			

Name / Address	City	State	Zip	Phone	Fax	Class
Palladium Equity Partners LLC						
1270 Ave of the Americas	New York	NY	10020	212-218-5150		690
Web: www.palladiumequity.com						
Palladium Group Inc						
1331 Pennsylvania Ave NW Ste 600	Washington	DC	20004	202-775-9680		194
Web: www.thepalladiumgroup.com						
Palladium-Item 1175 N a St	Richmond	IN	47374	765-962-1575	973-4570	532-2
Web: www.pal-item.com						
Pallet Consultants Corp						
810 NW 13th Ave	Pompano Beach	FL	33069	954-946-2212		551
TF: 888-782-2909 ■ *Web:* www.palletconsultants.com						
Pallet Factory Inc, The						
3740 Arnold Rd	Memphis	TN	38118	901-795-8300		200
Web: www.thepalletfactory.com						
Pallet Logistics of America LLC						
4100 Platinum Way	Dallas	TX	75237	972-850-5000		820
TF: 800-992-1325 ■ *Web:* www.plofa.com						
Pallet Masters Inc						
655 E Florence Ave	Los Angeles	CA	90001	323-758-6559	758-9600	551
TF: 800-675-2579 ■ *Web:* palletmasters.com						
Pallet Services Inc						
12926 Farm to Market Rd	Mount Vernon	WA	98273	800-769-2245	627-5119*	200
**Fax Area Code:* 253 ■ *TF:* 800-769-2245 ■ *Web:* www.palletservices.com						
PalletOne Inc 1470 US Hwy 17 S	Bartow	FL	33830	863-533-1147	533-3065	551
TF: 800-771-1148 ■ *Web:* www.palletone.com						
Pallett Valo LLP						
77 City Ctr Dr Ste 300	Mississauga	ON	L5B1M5	905-273-3300		428
TF: 800-323-3781 ■ *Web:* www.pallettvalo.com						
Palliative CareCenter & Hospice of Catawba Valley						
3975 Robinson Rd	Newton	NC	28658	828-466-0466	466-8862	371
Web: www.catawbaregionalhospice.org						
Palliser Furniture Upholstery Ltd						
70 Lexington Pk	Winnipeg	MB	R2G4H2	866-444-0777	988-5604*	471
**Fax Area Code:* 204 ■ *TF:* 866-444-0777 ■ *Web:* www.palliser.com						
Palliser Regional Library						
366 Coteau St W	Moose Jaw	SK	S6H5C9	306-693-3669	692-5657	436
Web: www.palliserlibrary.ca						
Pallone Frank Jr (Rep D - NJ)						
237 Cannon Bldg	Washington	DC	20515	202-225-4671	225-9665	342-2
Web: pallone.house.gov						
Palm						
5800 Universal Blvd Hard Rock Hotel	Orlando	FL	32819	407-503-7256	503-2383	671
TF: 866-333-7256 ■ *Web:* www.thepalm.com						
Palm Beach Atlantic University						
PO Box 24708	West Palm Beach	FL	33416	561-803-2000	803-2115*	166
**Fax:* Admissions ■ *TF:* 888-468-6722 ■ *Web:* www.pba.edu						
Palm Beach Chamber of Commerce						
400 Royal Palm Way	Palm Beach	FL	33480	561-655-3282		138
Web: www.palmbeachchamber.com						
Palm Beach Community College						
Belle Glade 1977 College Dr	Belle Glade	FL	33430	561-996-7222		162
Web: www.palmbeachstate.edu						
Boca Raton 3000 St Lucie Ave	Boca Raton	FL	33431	561-862-4340	862-4350	162
Web: palmbeachstate.edu						
Lake Worth 4200 Congress Ave	Lake Worth	FL	33461	561-868-3350	868-3584*	162
**Fax:* Admissions ■ *TF:* 866-576-7222 ■ *Web:* palmbeachstate.edu						
Palm Beach Gardens						
3160 PGA Blvd	Palm Beach Gardens	FL	33410	561-207-5340		162
TF: 866-576-7222 ■ *Web:* www.palmbeachstate.edu						
Palm Beach County Public Library System						
3650 Summit Blvd	West Palm Beach	FL	33406	561-233-2600		434-3
TF: 888-780-4962 ■ *Web:* www.pbclibrary.org						
Palm Beach County School District, The						
3300 Forest Hill Blvd	West Palm Beach	FL	33406	561-434-8000		685
TF: 866-930-8402 ■ *Web:* www.palmbeachschools.org						
Palm Beach Daily Business Review						
324 Datura St Ste 140	West Palm Beach	FL	33401	561-820-2060	820-2077	457-5
TF: 800-777-7300 ■ *Web:* www.dailybusinessreview.com						
Palm Beach Gardens Medical Ctr						
3360 Burns Rd	Palm Beach Gardens	FL	33410	561-622-1411	694-7160	374-3
TF: 800-955-8771 ■ *Web:* www.pbgmc.com						
Palm Beach Illustrated Magazine						
1000 N Dixie Hwy Ste C	West Palm Beach	FL	33401	561-659-6160		457-22
TF: 800-308-7346 ■ *Web:* www.palmbeachillustrated.com						
Palm Beach International Airport						
1000 Turnage Blvd	West Palm Beach	FL	33406	561-471-7420	471-7427	27
Web: www.pbia.org						
Palm Beach Motor Cars Ltd Inc						
915 S Dixie Hwy	West Palm Beach	FL	33401	561-659-6206		57
Web: www.jaguarpalmbeach.com						
Palm Beach Motoring Accessories Inc						
7744 SW Jack James Dr	Stuart	FL	34997	772-286-2701		54
TF: 800-869-3011 ■ *Web:* www.autogeek.net						
Palm Beach Newspapers Inc						
PO Box 24700	West Palm Beach	FL	33416	561-820-4100		637-8
TF: 800-432-7595 ■ *Web:* www.palmbeachpost.com						
Palm Beach North Chamber of Commerce						
5520 PGA Blvd Ste 200	Palm Beach Gardens	FL	33418	561-746-7111	745-7519	139
Web: www.pbnchamber.com/?npb=1						
Palm Beach Opera						
1800 S Australian Ste 301	West Palm Beach	FL	33409	561-833-7888		573-2
TF: 800-435-7352 ■ *Web:* pbopera.org						
Palm Beach Photographic Centre						
415 Clematis St	West Palm Beach	FL	33401	561-253-2600		520
TF: 800-774-2651 ■ *Web:* www.workshop.org						
Palm Beach Post						
2751 S Dixie Hwy	West Palm Beach	FL	33405	561-820-4100		532-2
TF: 800-432-7595 ■ *Web:* www.palmbeachpost.com						
Palm Beach Tan Inc						
633 E State Hwy 121 Ste 500	Coppell	TX	75019	972-966-5300		310
Web: www.palmbeachtan.com						
Palm Beach Zoo at Dreher Park						
1301 Summit Blvd	West Palm Beach	FL	33405	561-533-0887	585-6085	823
Web: www.palmbeachzoo.org						
Palm Canyon Theatre						
538 N Palm Canyon Dr	Palm Springs	CA	92262	760-323-5123		572
Web: www.palmcanyontheatre.org						
Palm Court, The						
7700 E McCormick Pkwy	Scottsdale	AZ	85258	480-991-9000		671
TF: 800-840-0707 ■ *Web:* www.destinationhotels.com/scottsdale resort						
Palm Desert Chamber of Commerce (PDCC)						
72559 Hwy 111	Palm Desert	CA	92260	760-346-6111	346-3263	139
Web: www.pdcc.org						
Palm Garden Hotel						
495 N Ventu Park Rd	Thousand Oaks	CA	91320	805-716-4200		707
TF: 888-816-0002 ■ *Web:* www.palmgardenhotel.com						
Palm Gardens Ctr for Nursing & Rehabilitation						
615 Ave C	Brooklyn	NY	11218	718-633-3300		450
Web: www.palmgardenscenter.com						
Palm Management Corp						
1730 Rhode Island Ave NW Ste 900	Washington	DC	20036	202-775-7256		670
TF: 800-388-7256 ■ *Web:* www.thepalm.com						
Palm Mortuary Inc 1325 N Main St	Las Vegas	NV	89101	702-464-8300		510
Web: www.palmmortuary.com						
Palm Mountain Resort & Spa						
155 S BelaRdo Rd	Palm Springs	CA	92262	760-325-1301	323-8937	669
TF: 800-622-9451 ■ *Web:* www.palmmountainresort.com						
Palm Pictures LLC 110 E 25th St	New York	NY	10010	646-790-1211		225
Web: www.palmpictures.com						
Palm Press Inc						
1442A Walnut St Ste 120	Berkeley	CA	94709	510-486-0502		130
Web: www.palmpressinc.com						
Palm Printing 6001 Business Blvd	Sarasota	FL	34240	941-907-0090		627
TF: 800-367-6790 ■ *Web:* palmprinting.com						
Palm Restaurant 250 W 50th St	New York	NY	10019	212-687-2953		671
TF: 866-333-7256 ■ *Web:* www.thepalm.com						
Palm Restaurant 200 S Broad St	Philadelphia	PA	19102	215-546-7256	546-3088	671
TF: 866-333-7256 ■ *Web:* www.thepalm.com						
Palm Restaurant 6100 Westheimer Rd	Houston	TX	77057	713-977-2544	977-3503	671
TF: 866-333-7256 ■ *Web:* www.thepalm.com						
Palm Restaurant 3391 Peachtree Rd NE	Atlanta	GA	30326	404-814-1955	814-1985	671
Web: www.thepalm.com						
Palm Restaurant						
1730 Rhode Island Ave NW Ste 900	Washington	DC	20036	202-775-7256		670
TF: 800-795-7256 ■ *Web:* www.thepalm.com						
Palm Restaurant, The						
205 Westshore Plaza Dr	Tampa	FL	33609	813-849-7256		671
Web: www.thepalm.com						
Palm Springs Air Museum						
745 N Gene Autry Trl	Palm Springs	CA	92262	760-778-6262		520
Web: palmspringsairmuseum.org						
Palm Springs Art Museum						
101 Museum Dr	Palm Springs	CA	92262	760-322-4800	327-5069	520
Web: www.psmuseum.org						
Palm Springs Chamber of Commerce						
190 W Amado Rd	Palm Springs	CA	92262	760-325-1577		139
TF: 800-852-5711 ■ *Web:* www.pschamber.org						
Palm Springs City Hall						
3200 E Tahquitz Canyon Way	Palm Springs	CA	92262	760-323-8299	322-8332	337
Web: www.ci.palm-springs.ca.us						
Palm Springs Convention Ctr						
277 N Avenida Caballeros	Palm Springs	CA	92262	760-325-6611	778-4102	205
TF: 800-898-7256 ■ *Web:* www.palmspringscc.com						
Palm Springs Desert Resorts Convention & Visitors Authority						
70-100 Hwy 111	Rancho Mirage	CA	92270	760-770-9000		206
TF: 800-967-3767 ■ *Web:* www.visitgreaterpalmsprings.com						
Palm Springs Disposal Services						
4690 E Mesquite Ave	Palm Springs	CA	92264	760-327-1351	323-5132	804
TF: 800-655-4555 ■ *Web:* www.palmspringsdisposal.com						
Palm Springs International Airport						
3200 E Tahquitz Canyon Way	Palm Springs	CA	92262	760-318-3800	318-3815	27
TF: 800-847-4389 ■ *Web:* www.palmspringsca.gov						
Palm Springs Life						
303 N Indian Canyon Dr	Palm Springs	CA	92262	760-325-2333		637-9
TF: 877-704-0564 ■ *Web:* www.palmspringslife.com						
Palm Springs Life Magazine						
303 N Indian Canyon	Palm Springs	CA	92262	760-325-2333	325-7008	457-22
TF: 800-775-7256 ■ *Web:* www.palmspringslife.com						
Palm The Restaurant 701 Ross Ave	Dallas	TX	75202	214-698-0470		671
Web: www.thepalm.com						
Palm, The 140 Fifth Ave S	Nashville	TN	37203	615-742-7256	742-9028	671
Web: www.thepalm.com						
Palm, The 200 Dartmouth St	Boston	MA	02116	617-867-9292	867-0789	671
TF: 866-333-7256 ■ *Web:* www.thepalm.com						
Palm, The 2801 Pacific Ave	Atlantic City	NJ	08401	609-344-7256		671
Web: thepalm.com						
Palma Ceia United Methodist Church						
3723 W Bay To Bay Blvd	Tampa	FL	33629	813-837-1541	837-3600	48-20
Web: palmaceiaumc.org						
Palm-Aire Country Club in Pompano Beach						
2600 N Palm Aire Dr	Pompano Beach	FL	33069	954-975-6225		671
TF: 800-273-5113 ■ *Web:* www.palmairegolf.com						
Palmas Printing Inc 200 East Dr	Melbourne	FL	32904	321-984-4451		627
Web: www.palmasprinting.com						
Palmaz Scientific Inc						
3065 Skyway Ct Ste 1700	Fremont	CA	94539	214-520-9292		194
Web: www.palmazscientific.com						
Palmdale Chamber of Commerce						
817 E Ave Q-9	Palmdale	CA	93550	661-273-3232	273-8508	139
Web: www.palmdalechamber.org						
Palmdale City Library						
700 E Palmdale Blvd	Palmdale	CA	93550	661-267-5600		434-3
TF: 800-788-2782 ■ *Web:* cityofpalmdale.org						
Palmdale Oil Company Inc						
911 N Second St	Fort Pierce	FL	34950	772-461-2300		579
Web: www.palmdaleoil.com						
Palmer & Sicard Inc 140 Epping Rd	Exeter	NH	03833	603-778-1841		189-10
TF: 800-640-5323 ■ *Web:* palmerandsicard.com						
Palmer Advertising						
466 Geary St Ste 301	San Francisco	CA	94102	415-771-2327		7
TF: 800-822-7881 ■ *Web:* palmeradagency.com						
Palmer Asphalt Co						
196 W Fifth St PO Box 58	Bayonne	NJ	07002	201-339-0855	339-8320	46
TF: 800-352-9898 ■ *Web:* www.palmerasphalt.com						

Phone | Fax | Class

Palmer Candy Co
2600 Hwy 75 N PO Box 326 ... Sioux City IA 51102 712-258-5543 258-3224 296-8
TF: 800-483-7253 ■ *Web:* www.palmercandy.com

Palmer College-chiropractic
4705 S Clyde Morris Blvd ... Port Orange FL 32129 386-763-2709 165
Web: palmer.edu

Palmer Correctional Ctr
Correctional Center Rd ... Sutton AK 99674 907-745-5054 746-1574 213
TF: 877-741-0741

Palmer Electric & Showcase Lighting
875 Jackson Ave ... Winter Park FL 32789 407-646-8700 647-8951 189-4
TF: 800-327-8466 ■ *Web:* www.palmer-electric.com

Palmer Events Ctr
900 Barton Springs Rd ... Austin TX 78704 512-404-4500 205
Web: www.austinconventioncenter.com

Palmer Gary (Rep R - AL)
330 Cannon HOB ... Washington DC 20515 202-225-4912 225-2082 342-2
Web: palmer.house.gov

Palmer Gas Company Inc
13 Hall Farm Rd ... Atkinson NH 03811 603-898-7986 316
Web: palmergas.com

Palmer Holland Inc
25000 Country Club Blvd Ste 444 ... North Olmsted OH 44070 800-635-4822 146
TF: 800-635-4822 ■ *Web:* www.palmerholland.com

Palmer House A Hilton Hotel
17 E Monroe St ... Chicago IL 60603 312-726-7500 917-1707 379
Web: www3.hilton.com

Palmer Inn, The 3499 US 1 ... Princeton NJ 08540 609-452-2500 379
TF: 800-688-0500 ■ *Web:* www.palmerinnprinceton.com

Palmer International Inc PO Box 315 ... Skippack PA 19474 610-584-4241 487
Web: palmerint.com

Palmer Investigative Services
624 W Gurley St Ste A ... Prescott AZ 86304 928-778-2951 445-7204 400
TF: [illegible] ■ *Web:* www.palmerinvestigative.com

Palmer Manufacturing
18 N Bechtle Ave ... Springfield OH 45504 937-323-6339 492
TF: 800-457-5456 ■ *Web:* www.palmermfg.com

Palmer Moving & Storage
24660 Dequindre Rd ... Warren MI 48091 586-436-3804 834-3414 519
TF: 800-521-3954 ■ *Web:* www.palmermoving.com

Palmer Paving Corp 25 Blanchard St ... Palmer MA 01069 413-283-8354 289-1939 188-4
TF: 800-244-8354 ■ *Web:* www.palmerpaving.com

Palmer Printing Company Inc
2902 Third St S ... Waite Park MN 56387 320-252-0033 627
TF: 800-882-1844 ■ *Web:* www.palmerprinting.com

Palmer Square 40 Nassau St ... Princeton NJ 08542 609-921-2333 921-3797 460
Web: www.palmersquare.com

Palmer Steel Supplies Inc
4300 Acapulco Ave ... Mcallen TX 78503 956-686-6575 686-7022 190
Web: www.palmersteel.com

Palmer Theological Seminary
588 N Gulph Rd ... King Of Prussia PA 19406 610-896-5000 649-3834 167-3
TF: 800-220-3287 ■ *Web:* www.palmerseminary.edu

Palmer Wahl Instrumentation Group
234 Old Weaverville Rd ... Asheville NC 28804 828-658-3131 201
Web: www.palmerwahl.com

Palmer-christiansen Company Inc
2510 South West Temple ... Salt Lake City UT 84115 801-466-1679 610
Web: palmerchris.com

Palmer-Donavin Manufacturing Co
1200 Steelwood Rd ... Columbus OH 43212 614-486-9657 486-5073 191-3
TF: 800-589-4412 ■ *Web:* www.palmerdonavin.com

Palmerton Area School District
680 Fourth St ... Palmerton PA 18071 610-826-7101 826-4958 685
TF: 800-732-0999 ■ *Web:* www.palmerton.org

Palmetto Brick Co 3501 BrickyaRd Rd ... Wallace SC 29596 843-537-7861 537-4002 150
TF: 800-922-4423 ■ *Web:* www.palmettobrick.com

Palmetto Chevrolet Company Inc
1122 Fourth Ave ... Conway SC 29526 843-248-4283 57
Web: palmettochevy.com

Palmetto Cooperative Services LLC
7440 Broad River Rd ... Irmo SC 29063 803-781-0091 627
TF: 800-234-9603 ■ *Web:* www.palmettocoop.com

Palmetto Dunes Resort
4 Queen Folly Rd ... Hilton Head Island SC 29928 866-380-1778 669
TF: 866-380-1778 ■ *Web:* www.palmettodunes.com

Palmetto GBA LLC
17 Technology Cir AG-905 ... Columbia SC 29203 803-735-1034 177
TF: 800-833-4455 ■ *Web:* www.palmettogba.com

Palmetto Health Baptist Columbia
1333 Taylor St Ste 6F ... Columbia SC 29201 803-296-5010 374-3
Web: www.palmettohealth.org

Palmetto Health Home Care & Hospice
1400 Pickens St ... Columbia SC 29202 803-296-3100 296-3320 371
TF: 800-238-1884 ■ *Web:* www.palmettohealth.org

Palmetto Health Richland
5 Richland Medical Pk ... Columbia SC 29203 803-434-7000 374-3
Web: palmettohealth.org/body.cfm?id=961

Palmetto Industries International Inc
6001 Horizon W Pkwy ... Grovetown GA 30813 706-737-7999 601
TF: 800-243-2451 ■ *Web:* www.palmetto-industries.com

Palmetto Infusion Services LLC
172 Mcswain Dr Ste A ... West Columbia SC 29169 803-771-7740 557
Web: www.palmettoinfusion.com

Palmetto Island State Park
19501 Pleasant Rd ... Abbeville LA 70510 337-893-3930 565
TF: 888-677-3668

Palmetto Lowcountry Behavioral Health LLC
2777 Speissegger Dr ... North Charleston SC 29405 843-747-5830 726
Web: palmettobehavioralhealth.com

Palmetto Pig 530 Devine St ... Columbia SC 29201 803-733-2556 671
Web: palmettopig.com

Palmetto State Bank 601 First St W ... Hampton SC 29924 803-943-2671 70
Web: www.palmettostatebank.com

Palmetto State Park 78 Pk Rd 11 S ... Gonzales TX 78629 830-672-3266 565
Web: tpwd.texas.gov/state-parks/palmetto

Palmetto State Transportation Company Inc
1050 Pk W Blvd ... Greenville SC 29611 864-672-3800 780
TF: 800-269-0175 ■ *Web:* www.palmettostatetrans.com

Palms Casino Resort
4321 W Flamingo Rd ... Las Vegas NV 89103 702-942-7777 133
TF: 866-942-7777 ■ *Web:* palms.com

Palms of Pasadena Hospital
1501 Pasadena Ave S ... Saint Petersburg FL 33707 727-381-1000 374-3
Web: www.palmspasadena.com

Palms Resort 2500 N Ocean Blvd ... Myrtle Beach SC 29577 843-626-8334 669
TF: 800-300-1198 ■ *Web:* www.palmsresort.com

Palms Thai 5900 Hollywood Blvd ... Los Angeles CA 90028 323-462-5073 671
Web: palmsthai.com

Palms West Chamber of Commerce
12794 W Forest Hill Blvd Ste 19 ... Wellington FL 33414 561-790-6200 139
Web: www.cpbchamber.com

Palms West Hospital (PWH)
13001 Southern Blvd ... Loxahatchee FL 33470 561-798-3300 374-3
TF: 877-549-9337 ■ *Web:* www.palmswesthospital.com

Palms, The 3025 Collins Ave ... Miami Beach FL 33140 305-534-0505 534-0515 669
TF: 800-550-0505 ■ *Web:* www.thepalmshotel.com

Palmyra Area School District
1125 Pk Dr ... Palmyra PA 17078 717-838-3144 685
Web: www.palmyraportal.org/website/index.php

Palmyra Bologna Company Inc
230 N College St ... Palmyra PA 17078 717-838-6336 296-26
TF: 800-282-6336 ■ *Web:* www.seltzerslebanon.com

Palmyra Nursing Home Inc
341 N Railroad St ... Palmyra PA 17078 717-838-3011 793
Web: www.pennmed.com

Palo Alto Airport
1925 Embarcadero Rd ... Palo Alto CA 94303 408-918-7700 27
TF: 866-638-2344 ■ *Web:* www.countyairports.org

Palo Alto Chamber of Commerce
355 Alma St ... Palo Alto CA 94301 650-324-3121 324-1215 139
Web: www.paloaltochamber.com

Palo Alto City Library
1213 Newell Rd ... Palo Alto CA 94303 650-329-2436 434-3
Web: cityofpaloalto.org/gov/depts/lib/default.asp

Palo Alto Consulting Group, The
502 Waverley St ... Palo Alto CA 94301 650-796-3064 196
Web: www.paloaltocg.com

Palo Alto Medical Foundation for Health Care Research & Education, The
795 El Camino Real ... Palo Alto CA 94301 650-853-2974 415
TF: 800-478-8837 ■ *Web:* www.pamf.org

Palo Alto Networks Inc
4401 Great America Pkwy ... Santa Clara CA 95054 408-753-4000 196
Web: www.paloaltonetworks.com

Palo Alto Research Ctr Inc (PARC)
3333 Coyote Hill Rd ... Palo Alto CA 94304 650-812-4000 668
Web: www.parc.com

Palo Alto Staffing Services
2471 E Bayshore Rd Ste 525 ... Palo Alto CA 94303 650-493-0223 260
TF: 800-921-2640 ■ *Web:* www.paloaltostaffing.com

Palo Alto Weekly 450 Cambridge Ave ... Palo Alto CA 94306 650-326-8210 326-3928 532-5
Web: www.paloaltoonline.com/weekly

Palo Duro Canyon State Park
11450 Pk Rd 5 ... Canyon TX 79015 806-488-2227 488-2556 565
Web: tpwd.texas.gov/state-parks/palo-duro-canyon

Palo Petroleum Inc
5944 Luther Ln Ste 900 ... Dallas TX 75225 214-691-3676 539
TF: 800-467-8676 ■ *Web:* www.palopetro.com

Palo Pinto County PO Box 219 ... Palo Pinto TX 76484 940-659-1277 338
TF: 844-769-4976 ■ *Web:* www.co.palo-pinto.tx.us

Palo Verde College 1 College Dr ... Blythe CA 92225 760-921-5500 921-3608* 162
*Fax: Admissions ■ *Web:* www.paloverde.edu

Paloma Systems Inc
11250 Waples Mill Rd ... Fairfax VA 22030 703-626-5024 591-0985 809
Web: www.palomasys.com

Palomar College 1140 W Mission Rd ... San Marcos CA 92069 760-744-1150 162
Web: www.palomar.edu

Palomar Mountain State Park
200 Palm Canyon Dr ... Borrego Springs CA 92004 760-742-3462 565
Web: www.parks.ca.gov/default.asp?page_id=637

Palomar Pomerado Health
15615 Pomerado Rd ... Poway CA 92064 858-613-4000 353
TF: 800-628-2880 ■ *Web:* www.palomarhealth.org

Palomar Technologies
2728 Loker Ave W ... Carlsbad CA 92010 760-931-3600 931-5191 811
Web: www.palomartechnologies.com

Palomar Ventures
233 Wilshire Blvd Ste 900 ... Santa Monica CA 90401 310-260-6050 792
Web: www.palomarventures.com

Palomino 49 W Maryland St Ste 189 ... Indianapolis IN 46204 317-974-0400 671
Web: www.palomino.com

Palomino 1420 Fifth Ave ... Seattle WA 98101 206-623-1300 671
Web: www.palomino.com

Palomino Restaurant Rotisseria Bar
1420 Fifth Ave ... Seattle WA 98101 206-623-1300 670
TF: 800-663-1144 ■ *Web:* www.palomino.com

Palomino RV 1200 New Jersey Ave ... Washington MI 20590 269-432-3271 432-2516 120
TF: 888-327-4236 ■ *Web:* www.palominorv.com

Palomino System Innovations Inc
533 College St Ste 404 ... Toronto ON M6G1A8 416-964-7333 179
TF: 866-360-0360 ■ *Web:* www.palominosys.com

Palos Community Hospital
12251 S 80th Ave ... Palos Heights IL 60463 708-923-4000 374-3
Web: www.paloshealth.com

Palos Sports Inc 11711 S Austin Ave ... Alsip IL 60803 708-396-2555 711
TF: 800-233-5484 ■ *Web:* www.palossports.com

Palos Verdes Inn
1700 S Pacific Coast Hwy ... Redondo Beach CA 90277 310-316-4211 379

Palos Verdes Library District
701 Silver Spur Rd ... Rolling Hills Estates CA 90274 310-377-9584 434-3
Web: www.pvld.org

Palos Verdes Peninsula Chamber of Commerce
707 Silver Spur Rd Ste 100 ... Rolling Hills Estates CA 90274 310-377-8111 377-0614 139
Web: www.palosverdeschamber.com

Palos Verdes Peninsula News
609 Deep Valley Dr Ste 200 ... Rolling Hills Estates CA 90274 310-372-0388 532-4
Web: www.pvnews.com

Name / Address	City	State	ZIP	Phone	Fax	Class
Pals International						
900 Wilshire Dr Ste 105	Troy	MI	48084	248-362-2060		768
Web: www.palsintl.com						
Paltech Enterprises Inc						
2560 Bing Miller Ln	Urbana	IA	52345	319-443-2700		499
TF: 800-949-1006 ■ *Web:* www.paltech-entrps.com						
PAM Transportation Services Inc						
297 W Henri De Tonti Blvd	Tontitown	AR	72770	479-361-9111	361-5338	780
NASDAQ: PTSI ■ *TF:* 800-879-7261 ■ *Web:* www.pamtransport.com						
Pamal Broadcasting Ltd 6 Johnson Rd.	Latham	NY	12110	518-786-6600		643
Web: www.pamal.com						
Pamarco 171 E Marquardt Dr	Wheeling	IL	60090	847-459-6000		677
TF Sales: 800-323-7735 ■ *Web:* www.pamarcoglobal.com						
Pamarco Global Graphics						
235 E 11th Ave	Roselle	NJ	07203	908-241-1200	241-4009	629
Web: www.pamarcoglobal.com						
Pambiche 2811 NE Glisan St	Portland	OR	97232	503-233-0511	233-0495	671
Web: www.pambiche.com						
PAMC Ltd 531 W College St	Los Angeles	CA	90012	213-624-8411		374-3
Web: www.pamc.net						
Pamela Ferrari Productions						
1625 Shirley Dr	Pleasant Hill	CA	94523	925-798-1284		232
Web: www.pamelaferrariproductions.com						
Pamlico Capital						
150 N College St Ste 2400	Charlotte	NC	28202	704-414-7150		41
Web: www.pamlicocapital.com						
Pamlico Community College						
PO Box 185	Grantsboro	NC	28529	252-249-1851	249-2377*	162
**Fax:* Library ■ *Web:* www.pamlicocc.edu						
Pamlico County PO Box 776	Bayboro	NC	28515	252-745-3133	745-5514	338
Web: www.pamlicocounty.org						
Pampa Regional Medical Ctr						
1 Medical Plaza	Pampa	TX	79065	806-665-3721		374-3
TF: 800-258-2723 ■ *Web:* www.prmctx.com						
Pampano 209 E 49th St	New York	NY	10017	212-751-4545		671
Web: www.richardsandoval.com						
Pampas Bar & Grill 8690 Aero Dr.	San Diego	CA	92123	858-278-5971		671
Web: www.pampasargentinegrill.com						
Pampered Chef Ltd 1 Pampered Chef Ln	Addison	IL	60101	888-687-2433		366
TF: 888-687-2433 ■ *Web:* www.pamperedchef.com						
Pamplemousse 400 E Sahara Ave	Las Vegas	NV	89104	702-733-2066		671
Web: www.pamplemousserestaurant.com						
Pams Inc 3361 Pomona Blvd	Pomona	CA	91768	909-869-7267		196
TF: 800-621-1662 ■ *Web:* www.pamsinc.com						
Pan Abode Cedar Homes Inc						
1100 Maple Ave SW	Renton	WA	98057	425-255-8260	255-8630	106
TF: 800-782-2633 ■ *Web:* www.panabodehomes.com						
Pan American Development Foundation (PADF)						
1889 F St NW 2nd Fl	Washington	DC	20006	202-458-3969	458-6316	48-5
TF: 877-572-4484 ■ *Web:* www.padf.org						
Pan American Finance LLC						
601 Brickell Key Dr Ste 604	Miami	FL	33131	305-577-9799		401
Web: www.panamfinance.com						
Pan American Screw Inc						
630 Reese Dr SW	Conover	NC	28613	828-466-0060	466-0070	278
TF Cust Svc: 800-951-2222 ■ *Web:* www.panamericanscrew.com						
Pan American Silver Corp						
625 Howe St Ste 1500	Vancouver	BC	V6C2T6	604-684-1175	684-0147	502
TSE: PAA ■ *Web:* www.panamericansilver.com						
Pan American Travel Services						
320 East 900 South	Salt Lake City	UT	84111	801-364-4300		772
TF: 800-364-4359 ■ *Web:* www.panam-tours.com						
Pan Glo 1550 CUSTER AVE Ste	San Francisco	CA	94124	415-648-3325		393
Web: www.pan-glo.com						
Pan Pacific Express Corp						
19481 Harborgate Way	Torrance	CA	90501	310-638-3888		311
Web: www.panpacificusa.com						
Pan Pacific Hotel Vancouver						
999 Canada Pl Ste 300	Vancouver	BC	V6C3B5	604-662-8111		379
TF: 800-937-1515 ■ *Web:* www.panpacific.com						
Pan Pacific Ocean Hotel Inc						
243 Kearny St	San Francisco	CA	94108	415-433-0177		652
Pan Pacific Seattle 2125 Terry Ave	Seattle	WA	98121	206-264-8111		379
TF: 877-324-4856 ■ *Web:* www.panpacific.com						
Pan Pacific Whistler Mountainside						
4320 Sundial Crescent	Whistler	BC	V0N1B4	604-905-2999		669
TF: 888-905-9995 ■ *Web:* www.panpacific.com						
Pan Star Express Corp						
1134 Tower Ln	Bensenville	IL	60106	630-787-1672		311
TF: 800-358-5990 ■ *Web:* www.panstarexpress.com						
Panacea Technologies Inc						
160 Commerce Dr Ste 500	Montgomeryville	PA	18936	267-421-5300		463
TF: 866-800-4271 ■ *Web:* www.panaceatech.com						
Panacore Corp 2015 E Eighth St Ste 242	Odessa	TX	79761	432-580-9933		809
Web: www.panacore.com						
Panalpina						
1776 On-the-Green 67 E Pk Pl	Morristown	NJ	07960	973-683-9000	254-5712	449
TF: 800-843-1687 ■ *Web:* www.panalpina.com						
PANalytical Inc 117 Flanders Rd	Westborough	MA	01581	508-647-1100		419
TF: 800-279-7297 ■ *Web:* www.panalytical.com						
Consulate General						
1100 Poydras St Ste 2615	New Orleans	LA	70163	504-525-3458	524-8960	257
Web: www.consulateofpanama.com						
Consulate General						
2862 McGill Terr NW	Washington	DC	20008	305-447-3700	447-4142	257
Web: embassyofpanama.org						
Embassy 2862 McGill Terr NW	Washington	DC	20008	202-483-1407		257
TF: 800-446-3942 ■ *Web:* embassyofpanama.org						
Panama						
United Nations Mission						
866 UN Plaza Ste 4030	New York	NY	10017	212-421-5420		784
Panama City Beach Convention & Visitors Bureau						
17001 Panama City Beach Pkwy.	Panama City Beach	FL	32413	850-233-5070		206
TF: 800-722-3224 ■ *Web:* www.visitpanamacitybeach.com						
Panama City Beaches Chamber of Commerce						
309 Richard Jackson Blvd	Panama City Beach	FL	32407	850-235-1159	235-2301	139
TF: 800-224-4853 ■ *Web:* www.pcbeach.org						
Panamax Inc 1690 Corporate Cir.	Petaluma	CA	94954	707-283-5900	283-5901	253
TF: 800-472-5555 ■ *Web:* www.panamax.com						
Pan-American Life Insurance Co						
601 Poydras St	New Orleans	LA	70130	877-939-4550		391-2
TF Life Ins: 877-939-4550 ■ *Web:* www.palig.com						
Panaram International						
126 Greylock Ave	Belleville	NJ	07109	973-751-1100		362
TF: 800-872-8695 ■ *Web:* www.usatowl.com						
Panasas Inc 969 W Maude Ave	Sunnyvale	CA	94085	408-215-6800	215-6801	177
TF: 800-726-2727 ■ *Web:* www.panasas.com						
Panasonic 2 Riverfront Plaza	Newark	NJ	07102-5490	201-348-7000	392-6007	52
Web: panasonic.com						
Panasonic Avionics Corp						
26200 Enterprise Way	Lake Forest	CA	92630	949-672-2000	462-7100	52
TF: 877-627-2300 ■ *Web:* panasonic.aero						
Panasonic Corp of North America						
1 Panasonic Way	Secaucus	NJ	07094	877-826-6538	271-3068*	52
**Fax Area Code:* 201 ■ **Fax:* Hum Res ■ *TF Cust Svc:* 800-211-7262 ■ *Web:* www.panasonic.com						
Panasonic Electric Works Corp of America						
629 Central Ave	New Providence	NJ	07974	908-464-3550	464-4128	203
Panavise Products Inc 7540 Colbert Dr	Reno	NV	89511	775-850-2900		697
TF: 800-759-7535 ■ *Web:* www.panavise.com						
Panavision Inc 6219 DeSoto Ave	Woodland Hills	CA	91367	818-316-1000	316-1111	591
TF: 800-260-1846 ■ *Web:* www.panavision.com						
Panchero's Mexican Grill						
2475 Coral Ct Ste B	Coralville	IA	52241	319-545-6565		670
Web: www.pancheros.com						
Pancho Villa 361 Elgin St	Ottawa	ON	K2P1M7	613-234-8872		671
Pancho's Mexican Buffet Inc						
4001 Wheatland Rd	Dallas	TX	75237	972-709-4685		186
Web: panchosmexicanbuffetdfw.com						
Panda Chinese Kitchen 1133 Market St	Wheeling	WV	26003	304-232-7572		671
Panda Express 1717 Walnut Grove Ave.	Rosemead	CA	91770	626-312-5401		670
TF: 800-877-8988 ■ *Web:* www.pandaexpress.com						
Panda Garden 5600 Milgen Rd	Columbus	GA	31907	706-569-8487		671
Panda Garden 123 Franklin St.	Bangor	ME	04401	207-942-2704		671
Panda Inn 506 Horton Plaza	San Diego	CA	92101	619-233-7800		671
Web: pandainn.com						
Panda Inn 111 E Wilson Ave	Glendale	CA	91206	818-502-1234		671
Web: www.pandainn.com						
Panda Kitchen 1986 Hwy 50 E	Carson City	NV	89701	775-882-8128		671
Web: pandakitchencarsoncity.com						
Panda Restaurant Group Inc						
1683 Walnut Grove Ave	Rosemead	CA	91770	626-799-9898		670
TF: 800-877-8988 ■ *Web:* www.pandarg.com						
Panda Travel 1017 Kapahulu Ave Fl 2	Honolulu	HI	96816	808-734-1961		772
TF: 800-303-6702 ■ *Web:* www.pandaonline.com						
Pandel Inc 21 River Dr.	Cartersville	GA	30120	770-382-1034		364
TF: 800-537-3868 ■ *Web:* www.pandel.com						
Pandell Technology Corp						
4838 Richard Rd SW Ste 400	Calgary	AB	T3E6L1	403-271-0701		180
Web: www.pandell.com						
Pandjiris Inc 5151 Northrup Ave	Saint Louis	MO	63110	314-776-6893	776-8763	811
Web: www.pandjiris.com						
Pandol Bros Inc 33150 Pond Rd.	Delano	CA	93215	661-725-3755	725-4741	297-7
Web: www.pandol.com						
Pandora Quaker Bridge Mall						
150 Quaker Bridge Mall	Lawrenceville	NJ	08648	609-799-8177		460
Web: www.pandora.net						
Pandrol Canada Ltd 6910 34th St	Edmonton	AB	T6B2X2	780-413-4281		649
Pandrol USA Lp 501 Sharptown Rd	Bridgeport	NJ	08014	856-467-3227		567
Web: www.pandrolusa.com						
Panduit Corp 17301 Ridgeland Ave	Tinley Park	IL	60477	708-532-1800		815
TF: 888-506-5400 ■ *Web:* www.panduit.com						
Pane E Vino 365 Atwells Ave	Providence	RI	02903	401-223-2230	223-4322	671
Web: www.panevino.net						
Pane E Vino						
8900 E Pinnacle Peak Rd	Scottsdale	AZ	85255	480-473-7900		671
Web: paneevinoaz.com						
Pane e Vino 1715 Union St	San Francisco	CA	94123	415-346-2111		671
Web: www.paneevinotrattoria.com						
Panef Inc 5700 W Douglas Ave	Milwaukee	WI	53218	414-464-7200		579
TF: 800-448-1247 ■ *Web:* www.panef.com						
Panel Processing Inc						
120 N Industrial Hwy	Alpena	MI	49707	989-356-9007	356-9000	819
TF: 800-433-7142 ■ *Web:* www.panel.com						
Panelfold Inc 10700 NW 36th Ave	Miami	FL	33167	305-688-3501	688-0185	286
TF: 800-433-3222 ■ *Web:* www.panelfold.com						
Paneloc Corp 142 Brickyard Rd.	Farmington	CT	06034	860-677-6711	677-8606	350
TF: 800-394-6711 ■ *Web:* www.paneloc.com						
Panera Bread Co 3630 S Geyer Rd	Saint Louis	MO	63127	314-984-1000	909-3300	68
NASDAQ: PNRA ■ *TF:* 800-301-5566 ■ *Web:* www.panerabread.com						
Panetta Institute for Public Policy, The						
California State University Monterey Bay						
100 Campus Ctr Bldg 86E	Seaside	CA	93955	831-582-4200	582-4082	634
Web: www.panettainstitute.org						
Panetta Jimmy (Rep D - CA)						
228 Cannon HOB	Washington	DC	20515	202-225-2861	225-6791	342-2
Web: panetta.house.gov						
Pangaea Global AIDS Foundation						
436 14th St Ste 920	Oakland	CA	94612	510-379-4003		305
Web: pangaeaglobal.org						
Pangaea Information Technologies Ltd						
219 W Chicago Ave	Chicago	IL	60654	312-337-5404		177
TF: 800-746-9554 ■ *Web:* www.pangaeatech.com						
Pangaea Partners Ltd 1210 N Wfield Rd.	Madison	WI	53717	608-347-0192		690
Web: www.pangaeapartners.com						
PanGeo Subsea Inc 277 Water St.	St John's	NL	A1C6L3	709-739-8032		539
TF: 800-309-8935 ■ *Web:* www.pangeosubsea.com						
Pangere Corp 4050 W Fourth Ave	Gary	IN	46406	219-949-1368	944-3028	186
Web: www.pangere.com						
Pango Technology, Inc						
3003 Minnesota Dr Ste 303	Anchorage	AK	99503	907-868-8092		177
Web: pangomedia.com						
Pangolin Laser Systems Inc						
9501 Satellite Blvd Ste 109	Orlando	FL	32837	407-299-2088		177
Web: pangolin.com						

Phone | Fax | Class

Panhandle Co-op Assn
401 S Beltline Hwy W....................Scottsbluff NE 69361 308-632-5301 632-5375 276
TF Cust Svc: 800-732-4546 ■ *Web:* www.panhandlecoop.com

Panhandle Foods Inc
1980 Smith Township SR................Burgettstown PA 15021 724-947-2216 296-36
TF: 800-864-4202 ■ *Web:* panhandlefoodsales.com

Panhandle Northern Railroad
100 E Grand..............................Borger TX 79007 806-273-3513 649
Web: omnitrax.com/our-company/our-railroads/panhandle-northern-railroad-llc

Panhandle Royalty Co
5400 N Grand Blvd
Grand Ctr Bldg Ste 300.................Oklahoma City OK 73112 405-948-1560 948-2038 538
TF: 800-884-4225 ■ *Web:* www.panhandleoilandgas.com

Panhandle Telecommunication Systems Inc (PTSI)
2222 NW Hwy.............................Guymon OK 73942 580-338-2556 736
TF: 800-562-2556 ■ *Web:* www.ptci.net

Panhandle-Plains Higher Education Authority Inc (PPHEA)
1403 23rd St.............................Canyon TX 79015 806-324-4100 48-11

Panhandle-Plains Historical Museum
2503 Fourth Ave..........................Canyon TX 79015 806-651-2244 651-2250 520
TF: 800-655-9809 ■ *Web:* www.panhandleplains.org

Paniagua's Enterprises Development Company LLC
6400 Frankford Ave Ste 30.................Baltimore MD 21206 410-485-9327 387
TF: 800-327-2514 ■ *Web:* www.paniaguas.net

Pankl Aerospace Systems Inc
16615 Edwards Rd.........................Cerritos CA 90703 562-207-6300 21
Web: www.pankl.com

Pannell Kerr Forster Of Texas Pc
5847 San Felipe St.........................Houston TX 77057 713-860-1400 355-3909 2
TF: 800-829-3676 ■ *Web:* www.pkftexas.com

Pannier Corp 207 Sandusky St..............Pittsburgh PA 15212 412-323-4900 323-4962 494
TF: 877-726-6437 ■ *Web:* www.pannier.com

Pannier Graphics 345 Oak Rd................Gibsonia PA 15044 724-265-4900 701
TF: 800-544-8428 ■ *Web:* www.panniergraphics.com

Pan-O-Gold Baking Co
444 E St Germain.......................Saint Cloud MN 56304 320-251-9361 296-1
TF: 800-444-7005 ■ *Web:* www.panogold.com

Panola College 1109 W Panola St............Carthage TX 75633 903-693-2000 693-2031* 162
**Fax:* Admissions ■ *TF:* 800-252-9152 ■ *Web:* www.panola.edu

Panola County 110 Sycamore St Rm 201........Carthage TX 75633 903-693-0302 338
Web: www.co.panola.tx.us

Panola County Chamber of Commerce
300 W Panola St..........................Carthage TX 75633 903-693-6634 693-8578 139
Web: www.carthagetexas.us

Panola Mountain State Park
2600 Georgia 155.........................Stockbridge GA 30281 770-389-7801 565
Web: www.gastateparks.org

Panola Partnership Inc
150-A Public Sq...........................Batesville MS 38606 662-563-3126 563-0704 139
TF: 888-872-6652 ■ *Web:* www.panolacounty.com

Panola-Harrison Electric Co-op
410 E Houston St..........................Marshall TX 75670 903-935-7936 245
TF: 800-972-1093 ■ *Web:* www.phec.us

Panolam Industries International Inc
20 Progress Dr............................Shelton CT 06484 203-925-1556 819
TF: 877-391-4130 ■ *Web:* www.panolam.com

Panoptic Development Inc
131 Wayland Ave.........................Providence RI 02906 401-404-7812 924-9606* 809
**Fax Area Code:* 717 ■ *Web:* www.panopticdev.com

PanOptica Inc
150 Morristown Rd Ste 205...............Bernardsville NJ 07924 908-766-2202 238
Web: panopticapharma.com

Panora Cooperative Telephone Association Inc
114 E Main St.............................Panora IA 50216 641-755-2424 116
TF: 800-205-1110 ■ *Web:* www.panoratelco.com

Panorama Balloon Tours
2683 Via De La Valle 625G...................Del Mar CA 92014 800-455-3592 760
TF: 800-455-3592 ■ *Web:* www.gohotair.com

Panorama City 1751 Cir Ln SE..................Lacey WA 98503 360-456-0111 438-5901 672
TF: 800-999-9807 ■ *Web:* panorama.org

Panorama Consulting Solutions
8200 S Quebec Ste A3-315................Centennial CO 80112 720-515-1377 196
Web: www.panorama-consulting.com

Panorama Helicopters Ltd 360 Airport Rd.........Alma QC G8B5V2 418-668-3046 13
TF: 800-667-9356 ■ *Web:* www.helicopterespanorama.com

Panoramic Corp 4321 Goshen Rd.............Fort Wayne IN 46818 800-654-2027 757
TF: 800-654-2027 ■ *Web:* www.pancorp.com

Panoramic Inc 1500 N Parker Dr..............Janesville WI 53545 608-754-8850 754-5703 101
TF: 800-333-1394 ■ *Web:* www.panoramicinc.com

Panoramic Press Inc 2920 N 35th St...........Phoenix AZ 85018 602-955-2001 627
Web: panoramicpress.com

Panos Greek Taverna
654 SE Marine Dr.........................Vancouver BC V5X2T4 604-322-8824 671
Web: panosgreekvancouver.ca

Panos Restaurant 1504 W 38th St.................Erie PA 16508 814-866-0517 671

Pan-Osten Co 6944 Louisville Rd..........Bowling Green KY 42101 270-783-3900 783-3911 286
TF: 800-472-6678 ■ *Web:* www.panoston.com

Pan-Pacific Plumbing Co
18250 Euclid St.......................Fountain Valley CA 92708 949-474-9170 609
Web: ppmechanical.com

Pantages Hotel 200 Victoria St.................Toronto ON M5B1V8 416-362-1777 379
TF: 855-852-1777 ■ *Web:* www.pantageshotel.com

Pantages Theater 901 Broadway...............Tacoma WA 98402 253-591-5890 591-2013 572
TF: 800-291-7593 ■ *Web:* www.broadwaycenter.org

Pantages Theatre
6233 Hollywood Blvd.....................Los Angeles CA 90028 800-430-8903 572
TF: 800-430-8903 ■ *Web:* www.pantages-theater.com

Pantagraph PO Box 2907.................Bloomington IL 61702 309-829-9000 829-7000 532-2
TF: 800-747-7323 ■ *Web:* www.pantagraph.com

Pantera Energy Co
817 S Polk St Ste 201......................Amarillo TX 79101 806-376-6625 536
Web: www.panteraenergy.com

Panther Creek State Park
2010 Panther Creek Pk Rd.................Morristown TN 37814 423-587-7046 587-7047 565
Web: www.state.tn.us

Panther Racing LLC
5101 Decatur Blvd Ste P..................Indianapolis IN 46241 317-856-9500 642
Web: www.pantherracing.com

Panthera Global Inc
155 N Wacker Dr 42nd Fl.....................Chicago IL 60606 312-214-4660 803-4795 194

Panthera Interactive LLC
2831 St Rose Pkwy Ste 232..................Henderson NV 89052 702-202-4740 7
Web: www.pantherainteractive.com

Pantronix Corp 2710 Lakeview Ct..............Fremont CA 94538 510-656-5898 45
TF: 800-375-8181 ■ *Web:* www.pantronix.com

Pantry Inc 305 Gregson Dr.......................Cary NC 27511 919-774-6700 204
NASDAQ: PTRY

Pants Store, The 8029 Parkway Dr................Leeds AL 35094 205-699-6166 229
Web: www.pantsstore.com

Panurgy Inc 3 Wing Dr Ste 225.............Cedar Knolls NJ 07927 973-625-9686 175
Web: www.panurgy.com

Panzano 909 17th St..........................Denver CO 80202 303-296-3525 671
Web: www.panzano-denver.com

Panzer Dermatology Association
537 Stanton Christiana Rd Ste 107...............Newark DE 19713 302-633-7550 77
Web: www.premierdermde.com

Panzer Nursery Inc
17980 W Baseline Rd......................Beaverton OR 97006 503-645-1185 629-9023 369
TF: 888-212-5327 ■ *Web:* www.panzernursery.com

Paoli Hospital (PH) 255 W Lancaster Ave...........Paoli PA 19301 484-565-1000 374-3
Web: mainlinehealth.org/paoli

Paoli Inc 201 E Martin St.......................Orleans IN 47452 800-472-8669 865-1516* 319-1
**Fax Area Code:* 812 ■ *TF:* 800-472-8669 ■ *Web:* www.paoli.com

Paolo's Restaurant
333 W San Carlos St Ste 150.................San Jose CA 95110 408-294-2558 671
Web: www.paolosrestaurant.com

Paolucci Communication Arts
2516 Via Tejon #114..............Rancho Palos Verdes CA 90274 310-791-2755 4
Web: paoluccicommarts.com

Paonia State Park PO Box 147...............Crawford CO 81415 970-921-5721 565
Web: cpw.state.co.us

PAPA Advertising Inc 1070 W Eighth St............Erie PA 16505 814-454-0236 7
Web: www.papaadvertising.com

Papa Cristos 2771 W Pico Blvd.............Los Angeles CA 90006 323-737-2970 671
Web: papacristos.com

Papa Dio's 5810 N May Ave.............Oklahoma City OK 73120 405-755-2255 671
Web: papadiosokc.com

Papa Gino's Inc 600 Providence Hwy...........Dedham MA 02026 781-326-7552 461-1896 670
TF: 800-727-2446 ■ *Web:* www.papaginos.com

Papa Joe's 1561 Akron Peninsula Rd..............Akron OH 44313 330-923-7999 923-8009 671
Web: papajoes.com

Papa John's International Inc
2002 Papa John's Blvd.....................Louisville KY 40299 502-261-7272 670
NASDAQ: PZZA ■ *TF:* 877-547-7272 ■ *Web:* www.papajohns.com

Papa Murphy's International Inc
8000 NE Pkwy Dr Ste 350...................Vancouver WA 98662 360-260-7272 260-0500 670
TF: 800-727-2478 ■ *Web:* www.papamurphys.com

Papa's Dodge Inc 585 E Main St............New Britain CT 06051 860-225-8751 516
Web: www.papasjeep.com

Papachino's 1212 J St.........................Modesto CA 95354 209-578-5225 671
Web: mypapachinos.com

Papapavlo's Bistro & Bar
501 N Lincoln Ctr..........................Stockton CA 95207 209-477-6133 477-6132 671
Web: www.papapavlos.com

Paparone Corp 702 N White Horse Pk...........Stratford NJ 08084 856-784-0550 650
Web: www.paparonenewhomes.com

Papastavros' Associates Medical Imaging
1701 Augustine Cut Off Bldg 4.............Wilmington DE 19803 302-652-3016 652-2534 57
Web: www.papastavros.com

Papco Inc 4920 Southern Blvd............Virginia Beach VA 23462 757-499-5977 579
TF: 800-899-0747 ■ *Web:* www.papco.com

Pape's Archery Inc 250 Terry Blvd............Louisville KY 40229 502-955-8118 711
Web: www.papesinc.com

Pape-Dawson Engineers Inc
2000 NW Loop 410......................San Antonio TX 78213-2251 210-375-9000 375-9010 261
Web: www.pape-dawson.com

Papen Farms Inc 847 Papen Ln...................Dover DE 19904 302-697-3291 697-2380 10-11

Paper Crafts Magazine
14512 S Ctr Point Way Ste 600..............Bluffdale UT 84065 801-816-8300 457-14
TF: 800-727-2387 ■ *Web:* www.papercraftsmag.com

Paper Cut Inc, The
234 W Northland Ave......................Appleton WI 54911 920-954-6210 561
Web: www.thepapercut.com

Paper Machine Components
11 Old Sugar Hollow Rd.....................Danbury CT 06810 203-792-8686 201
TF: 800-869-5747 ■ *Web:* www.pmc1.com

Paper Machinery Corp
8900 W Bradley Rd PO Box 240100.........Milwaukee WI 53224 414-354-8050 354-8614 556
Web: www.papermc.com

Paper Pak Industries (PPI)
1941 N White Ave..........................La Verne CA 91750 909-392-1750 392-1760 297-9
TF: 888-293-6529 ■ *Web:* www.paperpakindustries.com

Paper Pigeon Inc 14701 SW 94 Ave.............Miami FL 33176 305-235-7887 535
Web: paperpigeonmiami.com

Paper Products Company Inc
760 Commonwealth Dr...................Warrendale PA 15086 412-481-6200 741-9700* 559
**Fax Area Code:* 724 ■ *Web:* www.paperproducts-pgh.com

Paper Shack & Party Store Inc, The
2430 E Texas St.........................Bossier City LA 71111 318-746-4108 566

Paper Source Converting
4800 S Santa Fe Ave.........................Vernon CA 90058 323-583-3800 557
Web: www.papersourcemfg.com

Paper Store Inc 20 Main St......................Acton MA 01720 844-480-7100 566
TF: 844-480-7100 ■ *Web:* www.thepaperstore.com

Paper Systems Inc
185 S Pioneer Blvd......................Springboro OH 45066 937-746-6841 746-1089 554
TF: 888-564-6774 ■ *Web:* www.papersystems.com

Paper Tigers, The
2201 Waukegan Rd Ste 180...............Bannockburn IL 60015 847-919-6500 919-6501 660
TF: 800-621-1774 ■ *Web:* www.papertigers.com

Paper Transport Inc
1250 Mid Valley Dr..........................De Pere WI 54115 800-317-3650 631-1409* 780
**Fax Area Code:* 888 ■ *TF:* 800-317-3650 ■ *Web:* www.papertransport.com

	Phone	Fax	Class
Paperclip Software Inc 1 University Plaza .... Hackensack NJ 07601 *Fax: Hum Res ■ TF: 800-929-3503 ■ Web: www.paperclip.com	201-525-1221	525-1511*	178-1
Papercone Corp 3200 Fern Valley Rd .... Louisville KY 40213 TF: 800-626-5308 ■ Web: papercone.com	502-961-9493	961-9346	263
PaperDirect Inc 1005 E Woodmen Rd .... Colorado Springs CO 80920 *Fax Area Code: 719 ■ TF: 800-272-7377 ■ Web: www.paperdirect.com	800-272-7377	534-1741*	553
Paperdoll Co 4944 Encino Ave .... Encino CA 91316 TF: 866-223-1145 ■ Web: thepaperdollcompany.com	818-906-8411	907-0225	130
Papers Inc 206 S Main St .... Milford IN 46542 TF: 800-733-4111 ■ Web: www.the-papers.com	574-658-4111	658-4701	637-8
PaperThin Inc 300 Congress St Ste 303 .... Quincy MA 02169 Web: www.paperthin.com	617-471-4440		177
PaperWise Inc 3171 E Sunshine .... Springfield MO 65804 TF: 888-828-7505 ■ Web: www.paperwise.com	417-886-7505		177
PaperWorks Industries Inc 5000 Flat Rock Rd .... Philadelphia PA 19127 Web: www.paperworksindustries.com	215-984-7000		561
Papillon Restaurant 37296 Mission Blvd .... Fremont CA 94536 Web: www.papillonrestaurant.com	510-793-6331	793-2789	671
Pappadeaux Seafood Kitchen 1304 E Copeland Rd .... Arlington TX 76011 Web: www.pappadeaux.com	817-543-0545		671
Pappadeaux Seafood Kitchen 76 NE Loop 410 .... San Antonio TX 78216 Web: www.pappadeaux.com	210-340-7143		671
Pappadeaux Seafood Kitchen 3520 Oak Lawn Ave .... Dallas TX 75219 Web: www.pappadeaux.com	214-521-4700		671
Pappajohn Capital Resources 666 Walnut St .... Des Moines IA 50309 Web: www.pappajohn.com	515-244-5746		792
Pappas Macdonnell Inc 135 Rennell Dr .... Southport CT 06890 Web: www.pappasmacdonnell.com	203-254-1944		7
Pappas Restaurants Inc 13939 NW Fwy .... Houston TX 77040 TF: 877-277-2748 ■ Web: www.pappas.com	713-869-0151	869-4932	670
Pappas Seafood House 13939 NW Fwy .... Houston TX 77040 TF: 877-277-2748 ■ Web: www.pappas.com	713-869-0151	869-4932	670
Pappas Telecasting Cos 500 S Chinowth Rd .... Visalia CA 93277	559-733-7800	733-7878	738
Pappasito's Cantina 13070 Hwy 290 .... Houston TX 77040 Web: www.pappasitos.com	713-462-0246		670
Pappasito's Cantina 321 Rd to Six Flags St W .... Arlington TX 76011 Web: www.pappas.com	817-795-3535		671
Pappy's Place 943 N Main Ave .... Springfield MO 65802	417-866-8744		671
Papua New Guinea Embassy 1779 Massachusetts Ave NW Ste 805 .... Washington DC 20036 TF: 800-767-1833 ■ Web: www.pngembassy.org	202-745-3680	745-3679	257
Papyrus Franchise Corp 500 Chadbourne Rd .... Fairfield CA 94533 TF: 800-789-1649 ■ Web: www.papyrusonline.com	800-789-1649		129
Par 4 Plastics Inc 351 Industrial Dr .... Marion KY 42064	270-965-9141		596
PAR Capital Management Inc 200 Clarendon St 48th Fl .... Boston MA 02116 Web: www.parcapital.com	617-526-8990	556-8875	690
PAR Excellence Systems Inc 11500 Northlake Dr .... Cincinnati OH 45249 TF: 800-888-7279 ■ Web: www.parexcellencesystems.com	513-936-9744		177
Par Kut International Inc 40961 Production Dr .... Harrison Twp MI 48045 Web: www.parkut.com	586-468-2947		480
Par Mar Stores 114 A Westview Ave .... Marietta OH 45750 Web: www.parmarstores.com	304-572-3500		297-8
Par Pharmaceutical Cos Inc 6 Ram Ridge Rd .... Chestnut Ridge NY 10977 NYSE: PRX ■ TF: 800-828-9393 ■ Web: www.parpharm.com	800-462-3636		583
Par Plumbing Company Inc 60 N Prospect Ave .... Lynbrook NY 11563 Web: pargroup.com	516-887-4000		189-10
PAR Springer-Miller Systems Inc 782 Mountain Rd .... Stowe VT 05672 Web: www.springermiller.com	802-253-7377		764
Par Systems Inc 707 County Rd E .... Shoreview MN 55126 Web: www.par.com	651-484-7261		207
PAR Technology Corp 8383 Seneca Tpke .... New Hartford NY 13413 NYSE: PAR ■ TF: 800-448-6505 ■ Web: www.partech.com	315-738-0600	738-0562	614
Para Plate 15910 Shoemaker Ave .... Cerritos CA 90703 Web: paraplate.com	562-404-3434		781
Para Systems Inc Minuteman UPS 1455 LeMay Dr .... Carrollton TX 75007 TF: 800-238-7272 ■ Web: www.minutemanups.com	972-446-7363	446-9011	253
Para Usa Inc 10620 Southern Loop Blvd .... Pineville NC 28134 Web: www.para-usa.com	704-930-7600		807
Parabase Genomics Inc 100 Morrissey Blvd University of Massachusetts Ven 3rd Fl .... Boston MA 02125 Web: www.parabasegenomics.com	857-288-0838		743
Paraben Corp 21690 Red Rum Dr Ste 137 .... Ashburn VA 20147 Web: www.paraben.com	801-796-0944		177
Parable Christian Stores 3563 Empleo St .... San Luis Obispo CA 93401 Web: www.parable.com	805-248-7395	201-9026	95
Para-Chem Southern Inc 863 SE Main St PO Box 127 .... Simpsonville SC 29681 TF: 800-763-7272 ■ Web: www.parachem.com	864-967-7691	963-1241	3
Paradata Financial Systems 640 Cepi Dr Ste B .... Chesterfield MO 63005 TF: 800-278-3402 ■ Web: paradatafinancial.com	636-530-4545		180
Parade Publications Inc 711 Third Ave .... New York NY 10017 Web: parade.com	212-450-7000		637-9
Par-A-Dice Hotel 21 Blackjack Blvd .... East Peoria IL 61611 TF: 800-727-2342 ■ Web: www.paradicecasino.com	309-699-7711		379
Paradies Shops 2849 Paces Ferry Rd .... Atlanta GA 30339 Web: paradieslagardere.com	404-344-7905		327
Paradigm 1611 Akron Peninsula Rd Ste A .... Akron OH 44313 TF: 888-249-5727 ■ Web: paradigmequity.com	330-475-1690	475-1695	390
Paradigm Capital Inc 95 Wellington St W Ste 2101 .... Toronto ON M5J2N7 Web: www.paradigmcapinc.com	416-361-9892		401
Paradigm Construction Services Inc 771 Jamacha Rd Ste 526 .... El Cajon CA 92019 Web: www.paradigm-cs.net	858-300-8299		463
Paradigm Design Associates Inc 4 Center Rd Unit 5 .... Old Saybrook CT 06475 TF: 800-495-3295 ■ Web: m.pda4.com	800-495-3295	495-3295	525
Paradigm Financial Advisors LLC 12231 Manchester Rd .... Des Peres MO 63131 Web: www.pfaclient.com	314-966-3400		401
Paradigm Imaging Group 1590 Metro Dr Ste 116 .... Costa Mesa CA 92626 TF: 888-221-7226 ■ Web: www.paradigmimaging.com	714-432-7226		627
Paradigm Learning Inc 2701 N Rocky Pt Dr .... Tampa FL 33607 Web: www.paradigmlearning.com	813-287-9330		194
Paradigm Medical Industries Inc 4273 South 590 West .... Salt Lake City UT 84123 OTC: PDMI	801-977-8970	977-8973	250
Paradigm Metals Inc 15811 Vision Dr .... Pflugerville TX 78660 Web: www.paradigmmetals.com	512-255-2622		697
Paradigm Precision Holdings 404 W Guadalupe Rd .... Tempe AZ 85283	480-839-0501		454
Paradigm Precision Holdings LLC 3651 SE Commerce Ave .... Stuart FL 34997 Web: www.paradigmprecision.com	772-287-7770		21
Paradigm Talent & Literary Agency 360 N Crescent Dr N Bldg .... Beverly Hills CA 90210 Web: paradigmagency.com	310-288-8000	288-2000	731
Paradigm Transportation Solutions Ltd 22 King St S Ste 300 .... Waterloo ON N2J1N8 Web: www.ptsl.com	519-896-3163		463
Paradigms Consulting Group 1200 - 1881 Scarth St .... Regina SK S4P4K9 Web: www.paradigm.sk.ca	306-522-8588		463
Paradime Solutions Inc PO Box 291 .... Clayton GA 30525	770-441-6301		631
Paradise Adv & Mktg Inc 150 Second Ave N Ste 800 .... Saint Petersburg FL 33701 Web: www.paradiseadv.com	727-821-5155		4
Paradise Beverages Inc 94-1450 Moaniani St .... Waipahu HI 96797 *Fax: Sales ■ Web: www.paradisebeverages.com	808-678-4000	677-8280*	81-1
Paradise Chamber of Commerce 5550 Sky Way Ste 1 .... Paradise CA 95969 TF: 800-247-9889 ■ Web: www.paradisechamber.com	530-877-9356	877-1865	139
Paradise Chevrolet 6350 Leland St .... Ventura CA 93003 Web: www.paradisechevrolet.com	805-642-0111		57
Paradise Fx 6711 Valjean Ave Ste A .... Van Nuys CA 91406 TF: 800-794-1407 ■ Web: www.paradisefx.com	818-785-3100		514
Paradise Guest Ranch PO Box 790 .... Buffalo WY 82834 *Fax Area Code: 720 ■ Web: www.paradiseranch.com	307-684-7876	862-2126*	239
Paradise Inc 1200 W MLK Jr Blvd .... Plant City FL 33563 OTC: PARF ■ *Fax Area Code: 813 ■ TF: 800-330-8952 ■ Web: www.paradisefruitco.com	800-330-8952	754-3168*	296-8
Paradise Island Vacations 1000 S Pine Island Rd Ste 800 .... Plantation FL 33324 TF Resv: 888-877-7525 ■ Web: www.atlantis.com	954-809-2000		771
Paradise Plastics 1200 W Dr Martin Luther King Jr Blvd .... Plant City FL 33563 Web: www.paradiseplastics.com	813-752-1155	754-3168	602
Paradise Point Resort & Spa 1404 W Vacation Rd .... San Diego CA 92109 TF: 800-344-2626 ■ Web: www.paradisepoint.com	858-274-4630		669
Paradise Point State Park 33914 NW Paradise Pk Rd .... Ridgefield WA 98642 Web: www.parks.wa.gov	360-263-2350		565
Paradise Point State Recreation Site PO Box 1345 .... Port Orford OR 97465 TF: 800-551-6949 ■ Web: www.oregonstateparks.org	800-551-6949		565
Paradise Post 5399 Clark Rd .... Paradise CA 95969 Web: www.paradisepost.com	530-877-4413		532-4
Paradise Valley Community College 18401 N 32nd St .... Phoenix AZ 85032 *Fax: Admissions ■ Web: paradisevalley.edu	602-787-6500	787-7025*	162
Paradise Valley Hospital 3929 E Bell Rd .... Phoenix AZ 85032 Web: www.abrazohealth.com	602-923-5000		374-3
Paradise Valley Mall 4568 E Cactus Rd .... Phoenix AZ 85032 TF: 800-937-6379 ■ Web: www.theparadisevalleymall.com	602-996-8840		460
Paradise Valley Unified School District 15002 N 32nd St .... Phoenix AZ 85032 Web: www.pvschools.net	602-449-2000		685
Paradise Ventures Inc 2901 Rigsby Ln .... Safety Harbor FL 34695 Web: www.paradisedev.com	727-726-1115		360-2
Paradowski Creative 349 Marshall Ave Ste 200 .... St. Louis MO 63119 Web: paradowski.com	314-241-2150		195
Parady Financial Group Inc 340 Heald Way Ste 226 .... The Villages FL 32163 TF: 855-701-4351 ■ Web: www.paradyfinancial.com	352-751-3016		401
Paraflex Industries 2006 Inc 222 New Rd .... Parsippany NJ 07054 Web: www.paraflex.com	973-340-6040	340-6043	439
Paragon Advising Group LP 3200 SW Fwy Ste 2350 .... Houston TX 77027	713-599-0111		70
Paragon Advisors LLC PO Box 332 .... Madison CT 06443 Web: www.paragonadvisorsllc.com	203-245-9131		463

	Phone	Fax	Class
Paragon Application Systems Inc 326 Raleigh St .... Holly Springs NC 27540 *TF:* 800-444-2947 ■ *Web:* www.paragonedge.com	919-567-9890		177
Paragon Casino Resort 711 Paragon Pl .... Marksville LA 71351 *TF:* 800-946-1946 ■ *Web:* www.paragoncasinoresort.com	800-946-1946		133
Paragon Data Systems Inc 2218 Superior Ave .... Cleveland OH 44114 *Web:* www.paragondatasystems.com	216-621-7571		180
Paragon Development Systems Inc 1823 Executive Dr .... Oconomowoc WI 53066 *TF:* 800-966-6090 ■ *Web:* www.pdsit.net	800-966-6090		174
Paragon Die & Engineering Co 5225 33rd St SE .... Grand Rapids MI 49512 *Web:* www.paragondie.com	616-949-2220	949-2536	757
Paragon Employment Solutions Llc 108 Third St Ste 200 .... Des Moines IA 50309 *TF:* 800-493-2105 ■ *Web:* www.paragonitpros.com	515-288-2128		809
Paragon Engineering Services Inc 2201 S Queen St .... York PA 17402 *Web:* www.peservices.org	717-854-7374	854-5533	261
Paragon Environmental Construction Inc 5664 Mud Mill Rd .... Brewerton NY 13029 *Web:* paragonec.net	315-699-0840		667
Paragon Events 352 NE Third Ave .... Delray Beach FL 33444 *Web:* www.paragon-events.com	561-243-3073		463
Paragon Fabricators Inc 500 Main St .... La Marque TX 77568 *Web:* www.paragontexas.com	409-935-6602		595
Paragon Films Inc 3500 W Tacoma .... Broken Arrow OK 74012 *Web:* www.paragon-films.com	918-250-3456		600
Paragon Furniture Management Inc 2224 E Randol Mill Rd .... Arlington TX 76011 *TF:* 800-451-8546 ■ *Web:* www.paragoninc.com	817-633-3242		320
Paragon Gaming Corp 6650 Via Austi Pkwy Ste 150 .... Las Vegas NV 89119 *Web:* paragongaming.com	702-631-5161		360-3
Paragon Geophysical Services Inc 3500 N Rock Rd Bldg 800 Ste B .... Wichita KS 67226 *Web:* www.paragongeo.com	316-636-5552		538
Paragon Health Pc 2318 Gull Rd Ste B .... Kalamazoo MI 49048 *Web:* www.paragonhealthpc.com	269-341-4554		374-8
Paragon Hotel Corp 5333 N Seventh St Ste A-100 .... Phoenix AZ 85014 *Web:* www.paragonhotels.com	602-248-0811		379
Paragon Industries Inc 2011 S Town E Blvd .... Mesquite TX 75149 *TF:* 800-876-4328 ■ *Web:* www.paragonweb.com	972-288-7557	222-0646	318
Paragon International Inc 2885 N Berkeley Lake Rd Ste 17 .... Duluth GA 30096 *TF:* 800-526-1095 ■ *Web:* www.paragonint.net	678-481-6762		393
Paragon Laboratories 20433 Earl St .... Torrance CA 90503 *TF:* 800-231-3670 ■ *Web:* www.paragonlabsusa.com	310 370 1563		799
Paragon Management Company LLC 4370 La Jolla Village Dr Ste 640 .... San Diego CA 92122 *Web:* www.paragoncompany.com	858-535-9000		652
Paragon Medical Inc 8 Matchett Industrial Park Dr .... Pierceton IN 46562 *TF:* 800-225-6975 ■ *Web:* www.paragonmedical.com	574-594-2140		475
Paragon Mfg Company Inc 2001 N 15th Ave .... Melrose Park IL 60160 *TF:* 800-844-4848 ■ *Web:* www.paragonmanufacturing.com	708-345-1717	345-1721	199
Paragon National Bank 5400 Poplar Ave Ste 350 .... Memphis TN 38119 *Web:* bankparagon.com	901-273-2900		70
Paragon Offshore PLC 3151 Briarpark Dr Ste 700 .... Houston TX 77042 *Web:* www.paragonoffshore.com	832 783 4000		539
Paragon Packaging Inc 7700 Centerville Rd .... Ferndale CA 95536 *Web:* www.paragonpackaging.com	707-786-4004		101
Paragon Packaging Products Inc 625 Beaver Rd .... Girard PA 16417 *Web:* www.parapack.com	814-774-9621		100
Paragon Press Inc 2532 South 3270 West .... Salt Lake City UT 84119 *TF:* 800-748-4894 ■ *Web:* www.paragonpress.com	801-978-3500		627
Paragon Products LLC 4475 Golden Foothill Pkwy .... El Dorado Hills CA 95762 *Web:* www.paragonproducts.net	916-941-9717		641
Paragon Salons Inc 6775 Harrison Ave .... Cincinnati OH 45247 *Web:* paragonsalon.com	513-574-7610		77
Paragon Space Development Corp 3481 E Michigan St .... Tucson AZ 85714 *TF:* 800-767-9054 ■ *Web:* www.paragonsdc.com	520-903-1000		504
Paragon Sporting Goods Corp 867 Broadway 18th St .... New York NY 10003 *TF:* 800-961-3030 ■ *Web:* www.paragonsports.com	212-255-8889		711
Paragon Steel Enterprises LLC 4211 County Rd 61 .... Butler IN 46721 *TF:* 800-411-5677 ■ *Web:* www.pstparagonsteel.com	260-868-1100	868-1101	492
Paragon Supply Co 160 Reaser Ct .... Elyria OH 44035 *TF:* 800-726-8041 ■ *Web:* www.paragon-supply.com	440-365-8040		186
Paragon Systems Inc 13655 Dulles Technology Dr Ste 100 .... Herndon VA 20171 *Web:* www.parasys.com	703-263-7176		692
Paragon Technologies Inc 101 Larry Holmes Dr Ste 500 .... Easton PA 18042 *OTC: PGNT* ■ *Web:* pgntgroup.com	610-252-3205	252-3102	470
Paragould Light Water & Cable (PLWC) 1901 Jones Rd .... Paragould AR 72450 *Web:* www.paragould.com	870-239-7700		116
Paragould Regional Chamber of Commerce 300 W Ct St PO Box 124 .... Paragould AR 72451 *Web:* www.paragould.org	870-236-7684	236-7142	139
Paragraph Book Store Inc 2220 McGill College Ave .... Montreal QC H3A3P9 *TF:* 800-759-0126 ■ *Web:* www.paragraphbooks.com	514-845-5811		95
Paraguay 801 Second Ave Ste 702 .... New York NY 10017	212-687-3490	818-1282	784

	Phone	Fax	Class
Consulate General 25 SE Second Ave Ste 705 .... Miami FL 33131 *Web:* www.consulparmiami.org	305-374-9090	374-5522	257
Embassy 2400 Massachusetts Ave NW .... Washington DC 20008	202-483-6960	234-4508	257
Paragus Strategic I T 112 Russell St .... Hadley MA 01035 *TF:* 800-929-5201 ■ *Web:* paragusit.com	413-587-2666		180
Parallax 2179 W 11th St .... Cleveland OH 44113 *Web:* www.parallaxtremont.com	216-583-9999		671
Parallax Consulting LLC 325 Wood Rd Ste 107 .... Braintree MA 02184 *TF:* 800-762-7702 ■ *Web:* parallax-consulting.com	781-535-6004		196
Parallax Inc 599 Menlo Dr Ste 100 .... Rocklin CA 95765 *TF:* 888-512-1024 ■ *Web:* www.parallax.com	916-624-8333	624-8003	625
Parallax Press 2236 Sixth St .... Berkeley CA 94710 *TF:* 800-863-5290 ■ *Web:* www.parallax.org	510-540-6411		196
Parallel Edge Inc 126 E Beechtree Ln .... Wayne PA 19087 *Web:* www.paralleledge.com	610-293-0101		180
Parallel Partners Inc 1212 S Naper Blvd Ste 119-307 .... Naperville IL 60540 *TF:* 800-869-2008 ■ *Web:* www.parallelpartners.com	630-428-0600		260
Parallels Holding 500 SW 39th St Ste 200 .... Renton WA 98057 *Web:* www.parallels.com	425-282-6400	282-6444	178-11
Parallon Business Solutions LLC 6640 Carothers Pkwy .... Franklin TN 37067 *Web:* parallon.com	615-807-8000		317
Paramedics Plus LLC 352 Glenwood .... Tyler TX 75702 *Web:* www.paramedicsplus.com	903-535-5802		30
Parametric Solutions Inc 831 Jupiter Park Dr .... Jupiter FL 33458 *Web:* www.psnet.com	561-747-6107		256
Parametric Technology Corp (PTC) 140 Kendrick St .... Needham MA 02494 *NASDAQ: PTC* ■ *TF:* 800-613-7535 ■ *Web:* www.ptc.com	781-370-5000	370-6000	178-5
Parametrix Inc 1002 15th St SW .... Auburn WA 98001 *Web:* www.parametrix.com	253-269-1330		261
Paramit Corp 18735 Madrone Pkwy .... Morgan Hill CA 95037 *Web:* www.paramit.com	408-782-5600	782-9991	476
Paramont EO Inc 1000 Davey Rd Ste 100 .... Woodridge IL 60517 *Web:* www.paramont-eo.com	708-345-0000	345-0816	249
Paramount Apparel International Inc 1 Paramount Dr .... Bourbon MO 65441 *TF:* 866-274-4287 ■ *Web:* www.paramountapparel.com	573-732-4411		155-9
Paramount Beauty Distributing Assoc Inc 41 Mercedes Way Ste 34 .... Edgewood NY 11717 *Web:* paramountbeauty.com	631-242-3737		231
Paramount Builders Inc 501 Central Dr .... Virginia Beach VA 23454 *TF:* 888-340-9002 ■ *Web:* www.paramountbuilders.com	757 340 9000		364
Paramount Building Solutions Inc 401 W Baseline Rd Ste 209 .... Tempe AZ 85283 *Web:* www.paramountbldgsol.com	480-348-1177		256
Paramount Canada's Wonderland 9580 Jane St .... Vaughan ON L6A1S6 *TF:* 800-267-2632 ■ *Web:* www.canadaswonderland.com	905-832-8131		32
Paramount Chamber of Commerce 15357 Paramount Blvd .... Paramount CA 90723 *Web:* paramountchamber.com	562-634-3980	634-0891	139
Paramount Chemical Specialties Inc 14750 NE 95th St .... Redmond WA 98052 *TF:* 877-846-7826 ■ *Web:* www.kidsnpetsbrand.com	425-882-2673		151
Paramount Coffee Co 130 N Larch St .... Lansing MI 48912 *Web:* www.paramountcoffee.com	517-372-5500		805
Paramount Components Ltd 2130 Paramount Cres .... Abbotsford BC V2T6A5 *Web:* www.paramount.bc.ca	604-852-2564		480
Paramount Convention Services Inc 5015 Fyler Ave .... Saint Louis MO 63139 *TF:* 800-883-6578 ■ *Web:* www.paramountcs.com	314-621-6677		184
Paramount Cosmetics Inc 93 Entin Rd Ste 4 .... Clifton NJ 07014 *TF:* 800-522-9880 ■ *Web:* www.paramountcosmetics.net	973-472-2323	472-5005	214
Paramount Defenses Inc 620 Newport Ctr Dr Ste 1100 .... Newport Beach CA 92660 *Web:* www.paramountdefenses.com	949-468-5770		387
Paramount Equity Mortgage Inc 8781 Sierra College Blvd .... Roseville CA 95661 *Web:* www.paramountequity.com	916 290 9999		217
Paramount Export Co 175 Filbert St Ste 201 .... Oakland CA 94607 *Web:* www.paramountexport.net	510-839-0150	839-1002	297-7
Paramount Graphics Inc 11000 SW 11th Ste 400 .... Beaverton OR 97005 *Web:* www.paramountgraphics.com	503-641-7771		627
Paramount Group Inc 1633 Broadway Ste 1801 .... New York NY 10019 *Web:* www.paramount-group.com	212-237-3100		653
Paramount Health Care 1901 Indian Wood Cir .... Maumee OH 43537 *TF:* 800-462-3589 ■ *Web:* www.paramounthealthcare.com	419-887-2525		391-3
Paramount Home Entertainment 5555 Melrose Ave .... Los Angeles CA 90038 *Web:* paramount.com	323-956-5000		511
Paramount Hospitality Management LLC 12562 International Dr .... Orlando FL 32821 *Web:* www.paramounthospitality.com	321-329-4054		378
Paramount Hotel 724 Pine St .... Seattle WA 98101 *TF:* 877-821-2011 ■ *Web:* www.paramounthotelseattle.com	206-292-9500	292-8610	379
Paramount Hotel 235 W 46th St .... New York NY 10036 *Web:* www.nycparamount.com	212-764-5500	354-5237	379
Paramount Hotel 808 SW Taylor St .... Portland OR 97205 *TF:* 855-215-0160 ■ *Web:* www.portlandparamount.com	503-223-9900	223-7900	379
Paramount Hotel Group 710 Rt 46 E Ste 206 .... Fairfield NJ 07004 *Web:* www.paramounthotelgroup.com	973-882-0505	882-0043	379
Paramount Industrial Cos Inc 1112 Kingwood Ave .... Norfolk VA 23502 *Web:* www.paramountsleep.com	757-855-3321	855-2029	471

Name / Address	City	State	Zip	Phone	Fax	Class
Paramount Industries Inc 304 N Howard St *TF:* 800-521-5405 ■ *Web:* www.paramountlighting.com/index.php	Croswell	MI	48422	810-679-2551	679-4045	439
Paramount Landscape & Maintenance Inc 402 W Orion St *Web:* www.paramountlandscape.com	Tempe	AZ	85283	480-668-6109		776
Paramount Pallet Inc 1330 Martin Grove Rd *TF:* 800-567-7705 ■ *Web:* www.paramountpallet.com	Toronto	ON	M9W4X3	416-742-6006		820
Paramount Panels Inc 1531 E Cedar *Web:* www.paramountpanels.com	Ontario	CA	91761	909-947-8008	947-8012	22
Paramount Petroleum Corp 14700 Downey Ave *Web:* www.ppcla.com	Paramount	CA	90723	562-531-2060		580
Paramount Pictures Corp 5555 Melrose Ave *Web:* www.paramount.com	Los Angeles	CA	90038	323-956-5000		514
Paramount Precision Products Inc 15255 W Eleven Mile Rd	Oak Park	MI	48237	248-543-2100		697
Paramount Properties 19300 Rinaldi St	Northridge	CA	91327	818-363-4997		685
Paramount Property Management Inc 473 Broadway Ste 500 *Web:* www.paramountassets.com	Bayonne	NJ	07002	201-858-8500		652
Paramount Resources Ltd 4700 Bankers Hall W 888 Third St SW *TF:* 800-372-3930 ■ *Web:* www.paramountres.com	Calgary	AB	T2P5C5	403-290-3600		539
Paramount Sales Company Inc 10140 Gallows Pt Dr	Knoxville	TN	37931	865-470-9977	470-9801	411
Paramount Supply Company Inc 816 SE Ash St *Web:* www.paramountsupply.com	Portland	OR	97214	503-232-4137		612
Paramount Theatre 23 East Galena Blvd *Web:* paramountaurora.com	Aurora	IL	60506	630-896-7676	892-1084	572
Paramount Theatre 352 Cypress St *Web:* www.paramount-abilene.org	Abilene	TX	79601	325-676-9620	676-0642	572
Paramount Theatre 2025 Broadway *TF:* 800-745-3000 ■ *Web:* www.paramounttheatre.com	Oakland	CA	94612	510-465-6400	893-5098	572
Paramount Theatre 123 Third Ave SE *TF:* 800-369-8863 ■ *Web:* www.paramounttheatrecr.com	Cedar Rapids	IA	52401	319-398-5226		572
Paramount WorkPlace 1374 EW Maple Rd *TF:* 800-725-4408 ■ *Web:* paramounttechnologies.com	Walled Lake	MI	48390	248-960-0909	960-1919	39
Paramount, Theatre, The 713 Congress Ave *Web:* www.austintheatre.org	Austin	TX	78701	512-472-5470	472-5824	572
Parasec Inc 2804 Gateway Oaks Dr Ste 200 PO Box 160568 *TF General:* 800-533-7272 ■ *Web:* www.parasec.com	Sacramento	CA	95833	800-533-7272	603-5868	635
Paratech Ambulance Service 9401 W Brown Deer Rd *TF:* 866-525-8888 ■ *Web:* www.paratechambulance.com	Milwaukee	WI	53224	414-358-1111		30
Paratech Incorp 1025 Lambrecht Rd *TF:* 800-435-9358 ■ *Web:* www.paratech-inc.com	Frankfort	IL	60423	800-435-9358		59
Paratek Pharmaceuticals Inc 75 Park Plaza 4th Fl *Web:* paratekpharma.com	Boston	MA	02116	617-275-0040		85
Paratransit Services Inc 4810 Auto Ctr Way Ste Z *Web:* www.paratransit.net	Bremerton	WA	98312	360-377-7176		772
Paravista Inc 1055 Centennial Ave *Web:* www.paravistainc.com	Piscataway	NJ	08854	732-752-1222		627
PARC (Palo Alto Research Ctr Inc) 3333 Coyote Hill Rd *Web:* www.parc.com	Palo Alto	CA	94304	650-812-4000		668
Parc 55 Hotel 55 Cyril Magnin St *Web:* www.parc55hotel.com	San Francisco	CA	94102	415-392-8000		379
Parc Aquarium du Quebec 1675 des Hotels Ave *TF:* 866-659-5264 ■ *Web:* www.sepaq.com	Quebec	QC	G1W4S3	418-659-5264	646-9238	40
Parc Environmental 2706 S Railroad Ave *Web:* parcenvironmental.com	Fresno	CA	93725	559-233-7156		365
Parc Safari 280 Rang Roxham *Web:* www.parcsafari.com	Saint-Bernard-de-Lacolle	QC	J0L1H0	450-247-2727	247-3563	823
Parc Specialty Contractors 1400 Vinci Ave *TF:* 800-511-4809 ■ *Web:* www.parcspecialty.com	Sacramento	CA	95838	916-992-5405		667
Parcel Plus Inc 13121 Louetta Rd *Web:* www.parcelpluscypress.com	Cypress	TX	77429	281-376-0054	376-0056	113
Parcel Pro Inc 1867 Western Way Ste *Web:* www.parcelpro.com	Torrance	CA	90501	310-328-8484		113
Parchem Trading Ltd 415 Huguenot St *TF:* 800-282-3982 ■ *Web:* www.parchem.com	New Rochelle	NY	10801	914-654-6800		231
Parchman Vaughan & Co LLC Symphony Ctr Ste 120 1040 Park Ave *Web:* www.parchmanvaughan.com	Baltimore	MD	21201	410-244-8971		690
Parco Inc 1801 S Archibald Ave *Web:* www.parcoinc.com	Ontario	CA	91761	909-947-2200	923-0288	326
Parco Limited Co 998 Fremont Ave	Dubuque	IA	52003	563-557-1337		670
Pardee Home Museum 672 11th St *TF:* 800-545-2433 ■ *Web:* www.pardeehome.org	Oakland	CA	94607	510-444-2187		520
Pardee-Morris House 325 Lighthouse Rd *Web:* newhavenmuseum.org	New Haven	CT	06512	203-562-4183	562-2002	50-3
Pare Corp 8 Blackstone Valley Pl *Web:* parecorp.com	Lincoln	RI	02865	401-334-4100		261
Parent Co, The PO Box 5036 *Web:* www.theparentco.com	Brentwood	TN	37024	615-221-7000	221-7013	186
Parent Petroleum Inc 37 W 370 Rt 38 *TF:* 800-331-9763 ■ *Web:* www.parentpetroleum.com	Saint Charles	IL	60175	630-584-2505		579
Parental Drug Assn (PDA) 4350 East-West Hwy *Web:* www.pda.org	Bethesda	MD	20814	301-656-5900	986-1093	49-8
Parenti & Raffaelli Ltd 215 Prospect Ave E *Web:* www.parentiwoodwork.com	Mount Prospect	IL	60056	847-253-5550	253-6055	499
Parents Families & Friends of Lesbians & Gays (PFLAG) 1828 L St NW Ste 660 *Web:* www.pflag.org	Washington	DC	20036	202-467-8180	467-8194	48-8
Parents Helping Parents (PHP) 1400 Parkmoor Ave Ste 100 *TF:* 855-727-5775 ■ *Web:* www.php.com	San jose	CA	95126	408-727-5775	286-1116	48-6
Parents of Murdered Children (POMC) 4960 Ridge Ave Ste 2 *TF:* 888-818-7662 ■ *Web:* www.pomc.com	Cincinnati	OH	45209	513-721-5683	345-4489	48-6
Parents Television Council (PTC) 707 Wilshire Blvd Ste 2075 *Web:* w2.parentstv.org	Los Angeles	CA	90017	213-629-9255	629-9254	49-14
Parenty Reitmeier Inc 605 Des Meurons St *TF:* 877-445-3737 ■ *Web:* www.parentyreitmeier.com	Winnipeg	MB	R2H2R1	204-237-3737		317
ParetoLogic Inc 1827 Ft St *Web:* www.paretologic.com	Victoria	BC	V8R1J6	250-370-9229		179
PAREXEL International Corp 195 W St *NASDAQ: PRXL* ■ *Web:* www.parexel.com	Waltham	MA	02451	781-487-9900	487-0525	668
Parfums Givenchy LLC 19 E 57th St *Web:* www.givenchybeauty.com	New York	NY	10022	212-931-2600		574
Parham Santana Inc 7 W 18th St Fl 7 *Web:* www.parhamsantana.com	New York	NY	10011	212-645-7501		506
PARI Respiratory Equipment Inc 2412 PARI Way *Web:* www.pari.com	Midlothian	VA	23112	804-253-7274		476
Paric Corp 77 Westport Plaza Ste 250 *TF:* 800-500-4320 ■ *Web:* www.paric.com	St. Louis	MO	63146	636-561-9500		194
Paris 1624 Knowlton St *Web:* www.paristiaras.com	Cincinnati	OH	45223	513-542-8345		409
Paris Art Label Company Inc 217 River Ave *TF:* 800-326-6206 ■ *Web:* www.parisartlabel.com	Patchogue	NY	11772	631-648-6200		627
Paris Bistro 1500 South 1500 East *Web:* www.theparis.net	Salt Lake City	UT	84105	801-486-5585		671
Paris Business Products 800 Highland Dr *TF Cust Svc:* 800-523-6454 ■ *Web:* www.pariscorp.com	Westampton	NJ	08060	609-265-9200	261-4853	110
Paris Farmers' Union PO Box D *TF:* 800-639-3603 ■ *Web:* www.parisfarmersunion.net	South Paris	ME	04281	207-743-8976	743-8564	276
Paris Foods Corp 3965 Ocean Gateway PO Box 121 *Web:* www.parisfoods.com	Trappe	MD	21673	410-200-9595		297-6
Paris Gibson Square Museum of Art 1400 First Ave N *Web:* www.the-square.org	Great Falls	MT	59401	406-727-8255	727-8256	520
Paris Gourmet of New York Inc 145 Grand St **Fax Area Code:* 201 ■ *TF:* 800-727-8791 ■ *Web:* www.parisgourmet.com	Carlstadt	NJ	07072	800-727-8791	939-5613*	297-8
Paris Junior College 2400 Clarksville St **Fax:* Admissions ■ *TF:* 800-232-5804 ■ *Web:* www.parisjc.edu	Paris	TX	75460	903-785-7661	782-0427*	162
Paris Kitchens 245 W Beaver Creek Rd *Web:* pariskitchens.com	Richmond Hill	ON	L4B1L1	905-886-5751		321
Paris Landing State Park 16055 Hwy 79N *Web:* www.state.tn.us	Buchanan	TN	38222	731-641-4465		565
Paris Las Vegas 3655 Las Vegas Blvd S *TF:* 800-342-7724 ■ *Web:* www.totalrewards.com	Las Vegas	NV	89109	800-522-4700		379
Paris Machining Company Inc 1020 Wes-Lee Dr *Web:* www.lakecityindustriesllc.com/machining.htm	Paris	KY	40361	859-987-6320		350
Paris Miki Usa Inc 2863 152nd Ave NE *Web:* parismikiusa.com	Redmond	WA	98052	425-883-2464		543
Paris Mountain State Park 2401 State Pk Rd *TF:* 866-345-7275 ■ *Web:* www.southcarolinaparks.com	Greenville	SC	29609	864-244-5565		565
Paris National Bank 118 N Main St *Web:* www.tpnbbank.com	Paris	MO	65275	660-327-4181		70
Paris Regional Medical Ctr 820 Clarksville St *TF:* 800-345-8082 ■ *Web:* www.parisregionalmedical.com	Paris	TX	75460	903-785-4521		374-3
Parish International Inc PO Box 468 **Fax Area Code:* 979 ■ *Web:* www.parishforge.com	Hempstead	TX	77445	281-463-9233	826-8224*	483
Parish of Caddo 505 Travis St Ste 800 *Web:* www.caddo.org	Shreveport	LA	71101	318-226-6900	226-6900	338
Paris-Henry County Chamber of Commerce 2508 Eastwood St *TF:* 800-345-1103 ■ *Web:* www.paristnchamber.com	Paris	TN	38242	731-642-3431	642-3454	139
Parisi 4401 Tennyson St *Web:* www.parisidenver.com	Denver	CO	80212	303-561-0234	480-5514	671
Parisi Royal Inc 305 Pheasant Run	Newtown	PA	18940	215-968-6677		319-3
Parisi's Italian Ristorante 1412 S Bend Ave *Web:* www.parisisrestaurant.com	South Bend	IN	46617	574-232-4244		671
Parity Computing Inc 6160 Lusk Blvd Ste C205 *Web:* www.paritycomputing.com	San Diego	CA	92121	858-535-0516		177
Park 'N Fly 2060 Mt Paran Rd Ste 207 **Fax Area Code:* 404 ■ **Fax:* Hum Res ■ *TF Cust Svc:* 800-325-4863 ■ *Web:* www.pnf.com	Atlanta	GA	30327	800-325-4863	264-1115*	562
Park 100 Foods Inc 326 E Adams St *TF:* 800-854-6504 ■ *Web:* www.park100foods.com	Tipton	IN	46072	765-675-3480		296-26
Park 75 75 14th St *Web:* fourseasons.com	Atlanta	GA	30309	404-253-3840		671
Park Anaheim HealthCare Ctr 3435 W Ball Rd	Anaheim	CA	92804	714-827-5880		450
Park Avenue Auto Group 250 W Passaic St *Web:* www.parkavemotors.com	Maywood	NJ	07607	201-843-7900	843-4941	289
Park Avenue Building & Roofing Supplies LLC 2120 Atlantic Ave *Web:* www.parkavebenmoore.com	Brooklyn	NY	11233	718-403-0100	596-5085	191-3

Listing	City	State	Zip	Phone	Fax	Class
Park Bank 7540 W Capitol Dr *Web:* www.parkbankonline.com	Milwaukee	WI	53216	414-466-8000		360-2
Park Cafe 4403 Murphy Rd *Web:* parkcafenashville.com	Nashville	TN	37209	615-383-4409		671
Park Center Inc 909 E State Blvd *Web:* www.parkcenter.org	Fort Wayne	IN	46805	260-481-2700		726
Park Central Hotel 1010 Houston St	Fort Worth	TX	76102	817-336-2011		379
Park Central New York 870 Seventh Ave *Web:* www.parkcentralny.com	New York	NY	10019	212-247-8000		379
Park Central, The 640 Ocean Dr *Web:* www.theparkcentral.com	Miami Beach	FL	33139	305-538-1611	534-7520	379
Park City Chamber of Commerce/Convention & Visitors Bureau 1850 Sidewinder Dr Ste 320 *TF:* 800-453-1360 ■ *Web:* www.visitparkcity.com	Park City	UT	84060	435-649-6100		206
Park City Ctr 142 Pk City Ctr *TF:* 800-408-3477 ■ *Web:* www.parkcitycenter.com	Lancaster	PA	17601	717-393-3851		460
Park City Mountain Resort (PCMR) 1345 Lowell Ave PO Box 39 *TF:* 800-222-7275 ■ *Web:* www.parkcitymountain.com	Park City	UT	84060	435-649-8111	647-5374	669
Park Community Federal Credit Union PO Box 18630 *TF:* 800-626-2870 ■ *Web:* www.parkcommunity.com	Louisville	KY	40261	502-968-3681	964-6704	216
Park Compounding Pharmacy Inc 4333 Park Terrace Dr Ste 160 *Web:* parkcompounding.com	Westlake Village	CA	91361	805-497-8258		238
Park Construction Company Inc 1481 81st Ave NE *Web:* www.parkconstructionco.com	Minneapolis	MN	55432	763-786-9800	786-2952	189-5
Park County 1002 Sheridan Ave *TF:* 800-786-2844 ■ *Web:* www.parkcounty.us	Cody	WY	82414	307-527-8510	527-8515	338
Park County 501 Main St PO Box 1373 *Web:* www.parkco.us	Fairplay	CO	80440	719-836-2771	836-3273	338
Park County 414 E Callender St *Web:* www.parkcounty.org	Livingston	MT	59047	406-222-4110		338
Park County District No 6 919 Cody Ave *Web:* park6.org	Cody	WY	82414	307-587-4283		685
Park County Travel Council (PCTC) 836 Sheridan Ave PO Box 2454 *TF:* 800-393-2639 ■ *Web:* www.yellowstonecountry.org	Cody	WY	82414	307-587-2297	527-6228	206
Park Dietz & Associates Inc 2906 Lafayette Rd *Web:* www.parkdietzassociates.com	Newport Beach	CA	92663	949-723-2211		463
Park Electric Co-op Inc 5706 US Hwy 89 S PO Box 1119 *TF:* 888-298-0657 ■ *Web:* www.parkelectric.coop	Livingston	MT	59047	406-222-3100	222-3418	245
Park Electrochemical Corp 48 S Service Rd Ste 300 *NYSE: PKF* ■ *TF:* 800-522-6645 ■ *Web:* www.parkelectro.com	Melville	NY	11747	631-465-3600	465-3100	625
Park Energy Services LLC 1015 N Broadway Ave Ste 301 *Web:* www.parkenergyservices.com	Oklahoma City	OK	73102	405-896-3169		536
Park Enterprises Inc 226 Jay St *Web:* www.parkent.com	Rochester	NY	14608	585-546-4200		203
Park Expo & Conference Ctr, The 800 Briar Creek Rd *Web:* theparkexpoнc.com	Charlotte	NC	28205	704-333-7709		205
Park Forest Public Library 400 Lakewood Blvd *Web:* www.pfpl.org	Park Forest	IL	60466	708-748-3731	748-8829	434-3
Park Hill Group LLC 280 Park Ave *Web:* www.parkhillgroup.com	New York	NY	10017	212-364-6099		690
Park Hills Leadington Chamber of Commerce (PHLCOC) 12 Municipal Dr *Web:* www.phlcoc.net	Park Hills	MO	63601	573-431-1051	431-2327	139
Park House Eatery 4574 Pk Blvd *Web:* www.parkhouseeatery.com	San Diego	CA	92116	619-295-7275		671
Park House Hotel Corp 1206 48th St *Web:* www.parkhousehotelbrooklyn.com	Brooklyn	NY	11219	718-871-8100		132
Park Hyatt Beaver Creek Resort & Spa 136 E Thomas Pl *Web:* beavercreek.park.hyatt.com/en/hotel/home.html	Avon	CO	81620	970-949-1234	949-4164	669
Park Lane Jewelry 100 E Commerce Dr **Fax Area Code: 847* ■ *TF:* 800-621-0088 ■ *Web:* www.hallenspecialties.com	Schaumburg	IL	60173	800-621-0088	884-7064*	410
Park Lane, The 200 Glenwood Cir *Web:* www.srgseniorliving.com	Monterey	CA	93940	831-250-6159		672
Park Maintenance 20500 Madrona Ave *Web:* www.torrnet.com	Torrance	CA	90503	310-781-6901		564
Park Manor of Quail Valley 2350 Fm 1092 Rd *Web:* parkmanor-quailvalley.com	Missouri City	TX	77459	281-499-9333		371
Park Meadows Retail Resort 8401 Pk Meadows Ctr Dr *TF:* 800-326-3264 ■ *Web:* www.parkmeadows.com	Littleton	CO	80124	303-792-2533		460
Park Meadows Town Ctr 8401 Pk Meadows Ctr Dr *TF:* 800-326-3264 ■ *Web:* www.parkmeadows.com	Lone Tree	CO	80124	303-792-2533		460
Park Nameplate Company Inc 27 Production Dr *Web:* www.parknameplate.com	Dover	NH	03820	603-749-7600		567
Park National Bank 50 N Third St PO Box 3500 *NYSE: PRK* ■ *TF:* 888-791-8633 ■ *Web:* www.parknationalcorp.com	Newark	OH	43058	740-349-8451		360-2
Park Place 5870 E Broadway Blvd *Web:* www.parkplacemall.com	Tucson	AZ	85711	520-747-7575		460
Park Place Assisted Living 2305 Ives Ct *TF:* 800-973-1540 ■ *Web:* www.parkplaceassistedliving.com	Reno	NV	89503	775-746-1188		793
Park Place Corp 6801 Augusta Rd *Web:* www.parkplacecorp.com	Greenville	SC	29605	864-422-8118		471
Park Place Mobile Homes 731 E Arrow Hwy Ste A *TF:* 800-482-7836 ■ *Web:* www.reasons.org	Glendora	CA	91740	626-914-2992		95
Park Place Technologies Inc 5910 Landerbrook Dr *TF:* 877-778-8707 ■ *Web:* www.parkplacetechnologies.com	Cleveland	OH	44124	877-778-8707		177
Park Place Volvo 3515 Inwood Rd *Web:* parkplace.com	Dallas	TX	75209	214-956-5500		57
Park Plaza Hotel Oakland 150 Hegenberger Rd *Web:* www.redlion.com	Oakland	CA	94621	510-635-5300	635-9661	379
Park Plaza Mall 6000 W Markham St *Web:* www.parkplazamall.com	Little Rock	AR	72205	501-664-4956		460
Park Printing Inc 2801 California St NE *TF:* 800-789-3877 ■ *Web:* www.parkprint.com	Minneapolis	MN	55418	612-789-4333		627
Park Record PO Box 3688 *Web:* www.parkrecord.com	Park City	UT	84060	435-649-9014		532-3
Park Regency Care Ctr 1770 W La Habra Blvd **Fax Area Code: 562* ■ *Web:* www.parkregencycare.com	La Habra	CA	90631	714-773-0750	697-8478*	450
Park Regency Real Estate 10146 Balboa Blvd *Web:* parkregency.com	Granada Hills	CA	91344	818-363-6116		652
Park Ridge Child Care Center 1555 Long Pond Rd *Web:* www.rochesterregional.org	Rochester	NY	14626	585-723-7543		374-3
Park Ridge Public Library 20 S Prospect Ave *Web:* www.parkridgelibrary.org	Park Ridge	IL	60068	847-825-3123	825-0001	434-3
Park Ridge Recreation & Park District 2701 Sibley Ave *Web:* prparks.org	Park Ridge	IL	60068	847-692-5127		31
Park Seed Co 1 Parkton Ave *TF Orders:* 800-845-3369 ■ *Web:* www.parkseed.com	Greenwood	SC	29647	800-845-3369		694
Park Shore 1630 43rd Ave E *Web:* www.parkshore.org	Seattle	WA	98112	206-329-0770		672
Park Shore Resort 600 Neapolitan Way *TF:* 855-923-8197 ■ *Web:* www.sunstream.com/naples/park-shore	Naples	FL	34103	855-923-8197		669
Park Shore Waikiki Hotel 2586 Kalakaua Ave *TF:* 866-536-7975 ■ *Web:* www.parkshorewaikiki.com	Honolulu	HI	96815	808-954-7426	923-0311	379
Park South Hotel 124 E 28th St *TF:* 800-315-4642 ■ *Web:* www.parksouthhotel.com	New York	NY	10016	212-448-0888	448-0811	379
Park Summit of Coral Springs 8500 Royal Palm Blvd *Web:* www.fivestarseniorliving.com	Coral Springs	FL	33065	954-752-9500		672
Park To Fly 1900 Jetport Dr Exit 8 off S R 528 (Beachline) *TF:* 888-851-8875 ■ *Web:* www.parktofly.com	Orlando	FL	32809	407-851-8875	851-8011	562
Park Tudor School 7200 N College Ave *Web:* www.parktudor.org	Indianapolis	IN	46240	317-415-2700		685
Park University 8700 NW River Pk Dr *TF:* 800-745-7275 ■ *Web:* www.park.edu	Parkville	MO	64152	816-741-2000	741-9668	166
Park Vista Resort Hotel 705 Cherokee OrchaRd Rd PO Box 30 *TF Sales:* 800-227-5622 ■ *Web:* www.parkvista.com	Gatlinburg	TN	37738	865-436-9211	430-7533	379
Park Water Co 9750 Washburn Rd *TF:* 800-727-5987 ■ *Web:* www.parkwater.com	Downey	CA	90241	562-923-0711	861-5902	787
Park West Asset Management LLC 900 Larkspur Landing Cir Ste 165	Larkspur	CA	94939	415-524-2900		401
Park West Cos Inc 22421 Gilberto Ste A *Web:* www.parkwestlandscape.com	Rancho Santa Margarita	CA	92688	949-546-8300	546-8301	422
Parkallen 7018-109th St *Web:* www.parkallen.com	Edmonton	AB	T6H3C1	587-520-6401		671
Parkdale Mills Inc 531 Cotton Blossom Cir *TF:* 800-331-1843 ■ *Web:* www.parkdalemills.com	Gastonia	NC	28054	704-874-5000	874-5175	745-9
ParkDistributors Inc 347 Railroad Ave *Web:* www.parkdistributors.com	Bridgeport	CT	06604	203-366-7200		350
Parke County 116 W High St Rm 204 *Web:* www.parkecounty-in.gov	Rockville	IN	47872	765-569-5132		338
Parke County Rural Electric Membership Corp 119 W High St *TF:* 800-537-3913 ■ *Web:* www.parkecountyremc.com	Rockville	IN	47872	765-569-3133	569-3360	245
Parke Hotel & Conference Ctr 1413 Leslie Dr *Web:* www.parkehotel.com	Bloomington	IL	61704	309-662-4300		378
Parke-Bell Ltd Inc 709 W 12th St *TF:* 800-457-7456 ■ *Web:* www.touchofclass.com	Huntingburg	IN	47542	812-683-3707	683-5921	114
Parker 3025 W Croft Cir *Web:* www.parker.com	Spartanburg	SC	29302	864-573-7332	583-4299	326
Parker Aerospace Group 14300 Alton Pkwy *Web:* parker.com	Irvine	CA	92618	949-833-3000		22
Parker Ag Services LLC 53036 N Hwy 71 *TF:* 800-794-4408 ■ *Web:* www.parkerag.com	Limon	CO	80828	719-775-9870		463
Parker Boats 2570 N Carolina 101 *Web:* www.parkerboats.net	Beaufort	NC	28516	252-728-5621	728-2770	90
Parker Boiler Co 5930 Bandini Blvd *Web:* www.parkerboiler.com	Los Angeles	CA	90040	323-727-9800	722-2848	357
Parker Chamber of Commerce 19590 E Main St Ste 100 *Web:* www.parkerchamber.com	Parker	CO	80138	303-841-4268	841-8061	139
Parker Compound Bows Inc PO Box 105 *Web:* www.parkerbows.com	Mint Spring	VA	24463	540-337-5426		710
Parker County 1112 Santa Fe Dr *TF:* 800-621-8566 ■ *Web:* parkercountytx.com	Weatherford	TX	76086	817-594-7461		338
Parker Dam State Park 28 Fairview Rd *Web:* www.dcnr.state.pa.us	Penfield	PA	15849	814-765-0630		565
Parker Development Company Inc 4525 Serrano Pkwy *TF:* 800-585-4483 ■ *Web:* www.parkerdevco.com	El Dorado Hills	CA	95762	916-939-4060		261
Parker Drilling Co 1401 Enclave Pkwy Ste 600 *NYSE: PKD* ■ *TF:* 800-468-9716 ■ *Web:* www.parkerdrilling.com	Houston	TX	77077	281-406-2000	406-2001	540
Parker Electronic Systems 300 Marcus Blvd *Web:* www.parker.com	Smithtown	NY	11787	631-231-3737	434-8152	529

Name / Address	City	State	ZIP	Phone	Fax	Class
Parker Fluid Connectors Group 6035 Parkland Blvd *TF General:* 800-272-7537 ■ *Web:* parker.com	Cleveland	OH	44124	216-896-3000	896-4000	370
Parker Furniture 10375 SW Beaverton-Hillsdale Hwy **Fax Area Code:* 971 ■ *TF:* 866-515-9673 ■ *Web:* www.parker-furniture.com	Beaverton	OR	97005	503-644-0155	275-1087*	321
Parker Gas Turbine Fuel Systems Div (GTFSD) 8940 Tyler Blvd *Web:* parker.com	Mentor	OH	44060	440-266-2300	266-2311	21
Parker Hannifin Corp 6035 Parkland Blvd *Web:* parker.com	Cleveland	OH	44124	216-896-3000	514-6738	201
Parker Hannifin Corp Automation Actuator Div 135 Quadral Dr *TF:* 800-272-7537 ■ *Web:* www.parker.com	Wadsworth	OH	44281	330-336-3511	334-3335	223
Parker Hannifin Corp Brass Products Div 6035 Parkland Blvd *TF:* 800-272-7537 ■ *Web:* www.parker.com	Otsego	MI	49078	269-694-9411	694-4614	790
Parker Hannifin Corp Chomerics Div 77 Dragon Ct *Web:* www.parker.com	Woburn	MA	01801	781-935-4850	933-4318	605-2
Parker Hannifin Corp Control System Div 14 Robbins Pond Rd *Web:* parker.com	Devens	MA	01434	978-784-1200		21
Parker Hannifin Corp Cylinder Div 500 S Wolf Rd *TF:* 800-272-7537 ■ *Web:* parker.com	Des Plaines	IL	60016	847-298-2400	294-2655	223
Parker Hannifin Corp Daedal Div 1140 Sandy Hill Rd *TF:* 800-245-6903 ■ *Web:* parker.com	Irwin	PA	15642	724-861-8200		544
Parker Hannifin Corp Electromechanical Automation Div 5500 Business Pk Dr *TF:* 800-358-9068 ■ *Web:* www.parkermotion.com	Rohnert Park	CA	94928	707-584-7558	584-8015	203
Parker Hannifin Corp Finite Filtratio & Separation Div 500 Glaspie St *TF:* 800-521-4357 ■ *Web:* www.parker.com	Oxford	MI	48371	248-628-6400	628-1850	18
Parker Hannifin Corp General Valve Div 26 Clinton Dr Unit 103 *TF:* 800-272-7537 ■ *Web:* www.parker.com	Hollis	NH	03049	800-272-7537		790
Parker Hannifin Corp Hydraulic Pump/Motor Div 2745 Snapps Ferry Rd *Web:* www.parker.com	Greeneville	TN	37745	423-639-8151	787-2418	640
Parker Hannifin Corp Hydraulic Valve Div 520 Ternes Ave **Fax:* Sales ■ *TF:* 800-272-7537 ■ *Web:* www.parker.com	Elyria	OH	44035	440-366-5200	366-5253*	789
Parker Hannifin Corp Instrumentation Pneutronics Div 26 Clinton Dr Ste 103 *Web:* www.parker.com	Hollis	NH	03049	603-595-1500	595-8080	790
Parker Hannifin Corp Instrumentation Products Div 1005 A Cleaner Way *Web:* www.parker.com	Huntsville	AL	35805	256-885-3800	885-3853	595
Parker Hannifin Corp Nichols Portland Div 2400 Congress St *Web:* parker.com	Portland	ME	04102	207-774-6121	774-3601	640
Parker Hannifin Corp Oildyne Div 5520 Hwy 169 N *Web:* parker.com	Minneapolis	MN	55428	763-533-1600	533-0082	223
Parker Hannifin Corp Pneumatic Div 8676 E M 89 *TF:* 877-321-4736 ■ *Web:* www.parker.com	Richland	MI	49083	269-629-5000	629-5385	790
Parker Hannifin Corp Skinner Valve Div 95 Edgewood Ave *TF:* 800-825-8305 ■ *Web:* www.parker.com	New Britain	CT	06051	860-827-2300	827-2384	790
Parker Hannifin Corp Sporlan Div 711 Industrial Ave *Web:* parker.com	Washington	MO	63090	636-239-6524		789
Parker Hannifin Corp Veriflo Div 250 Canal Blvd *TF:* 800-272-7537 ■ *Web:* parker.com	Richmond	CA	94804	510-235-9590	232-7396	201
Parker Industries Inc 1650 Sycamore Ave *Web:* www.parkerind.com	Bohemia	NY	11716	631-567-1000	567-1355	386
Parker Instrumentation Group 6035 Parkland Blvd *TF:* 800-272-7537 ■ *Web:* parker.com	Cleveland	OH	44124	216-896-3000	896-4022	223
Parker Laboratories Inc 286 Eldridge Rd *TF:* 800-631-8888 ■ *Web:* www.parkerlabs.com	Fairfield	NJ	07004	973-276-9500		476
Parker Lumber Co Inc 2192 Eastex Fwy *Web:* www.parkersbuildingsupply.com	Beaumont	TX	77703	409-898-7000		191-3
Parker Lumber Co of Port Arthur Inc 2948 Gulfway Dr *TF:* 855-828-9792 ■ *Web:* www.parkersbuildingsupply.com	Port Arthur	TX	77642	409-983-2745		191-3
Parker Majestic Inc 300 N Pike Rd *TF:* 866-572-7537 ■ *Web:* www.pennunited.com	Sarver	PA	16055	724-352-1551	353-1196	455
Parker McCay PA 9000 Midlantic Dr Ste 300 *TF:* 800-973-1177 ■ *Web:* www.parkermccay.com	Mount Laurel	NJ	08054	856-596-8900		428
Parker McCrory Manufacturing Co 2000 Forest Ave *TF:* 800-662-1038 ■ *Web:* www.parmakusa.com	Kansas City	MO	64108	816-221-2000	221-9879	203
Parker Mktg Research LLC 5405 Dupont Cir *Web:* parkerinsights.com	Milford	OH	45150	513-248-8100		668
Parker Oil Company Inc PO Box 120 *Web:* www.parkeroilcompany.com	South Hill	VA	23970	434-447-3146	447-2646	579
Parker Oil Products Inc 508 California Parker *Web:* www.parkeroilproducts.com	Parker	AZ	85344	928-669-2617		579
Parker Playhouse 707 NE Eigth St **Fax:* Administration ■ *TF:* 800-745-3000 ■ *Web:* www.parkerplayhouse.com	Fort Lauderdale	FL	33304	954-462-0222	524-9952*	572
Parker Poe Adams & Bernstein LLP 3 Wachovia Ctr 401 S Tryon St Ste 3000 *TF:* 866-602-5893 ■ *Web:* www.parkerpoe.com	Charlotte	NC	28202	704-372-9000		428
Parker Powis Inc 775 Heinz Ave *TF:* 800-321-2463 ■ *Web:* www.powis.com	Berkeley	CA	94710	510-848-2463		92
Parker Remick Inc 1106 Harris Ave Ste 201 *TF:* 800-573-7307 ■ *Web:* www.parkerremick.com	Bellingham	WA	98225	360-527-2555		193
Parker Rose Design Inc 10075 Mesa Rim Rd Ste A **Fax Area Code:* 858 ■ *TF:* 800-403-2711 ■ *Web:* parkerrosedesign.com	San Diego	CA	92121	800-403-2711	875-2152*	41
Parker Smith & Feek Inc 2233 112th Ave NE *TF Cust Svc:* 800-457-0220 ■ *Web:* www.psfinc.com	Bellevue	WA	98004	425-709-3600	709-7460	390
Parker Stanbury LLP 444 S Flower St Ste 1900 *Web:* www.parkstan.com	Los Angeles	CA	90071	619-528-1259		428
Parker Steel Co PO Box 2883 *TF:* 800-333-4140 ■ *Web:* www.metricmetal.com	Toledo	OH	43606	419-473-2481	471-2655	492
Parker Swearngin LLP 215 SE Douglas St *Web:* parkerswearngin.biz	Lees Summit	MO	64063	816-434-6770		2
Parker Towing Company Inc PO Box 20908 *TF:* 800-329-1677 ■ *Web:* www.parkertowing.com	Tuscaloosa	AL	35402	205-349-1677	758-0061	465
Parker University 2540 Walnut Hill Ln *TF:* 800-637-8337 ■ *Web:* www.parker.edu	Dallas	TX	75229	972-438-6932		764
Parker's Lighthouse 435 Shoreline Village Dr *Web:* www.parkerslighthouse.com	Long Beach	CA	90802	562-432-6500	436-3551	671
Parker, Kern, Nard & Wenzel 1111 E Herndon Ave Ste 202 *Web:* pknwlaw.com	Fresno	CA	93720	559-449-2558		428
Parker-Hannifin Corp 1160 Ctr Rd *TF:* 800-272-5464 ■ *Web:* parker.com	Avon	OH	44011	440-937-6211	937-5409	770
Parkersburg & Wood County Public Library 3100 Emerson Ave *Web:* parkersburg.lib.wv.us	Parkersburg	WV	26104	304-420-4587	420-4589	434-3
Parkersburg News 519 Juliana St *TF:* 800-642-1997 ■ *Web:* www.newsandsentinel.com	Parkersburg	WV	26101	304-485-1891	485-5122	532-2
Parkersville Landing Historical Park 24 S A St *Web:* portcw.com	Washougal	WA	98671	360-835-2196	835-2197	50-5
ParkerVision Inc 7915 Baymeadows Way *NASDAQ: PRKR* ■ *TF:* 800-532-8034 ■ *Web:* www.parkervision.com	Jacksonville	FL	32256	904-737-1367	731-0958	647
Parkerwhite Inc 230 Birmingham Dr *Web:* www.parkerwhite.com	Cardiff By The Sea	CA	92007	760-783-2020		4
Parkhill Smith & Cooper Inc 4222 85th St *TF:* 800-400-6646 ■ *Web:* www.team-psc.com	Lubbock	TX	79423	806-473-2200		261
Parkhouse Tire Service Inc 5960 Shull St *TF:* 800-831-8473 ■ *Web:* www.parkhousetire.com	Bell Gardens	CA	90201	562-928-0421		54
Parkhurst Manufacturing Co 18999 Hwy Y *TF:* 800-821-7380 ■ *Web:* www.parkhurstmfg.com	Sedalia	MO	65301	660-826-8685		516
Parkin Archeological State Park PO Box 1110 *Web:* www.arkansasstateparks.com	Parkin	AR	72373	870-755-2500		565
Parking Auth City of Rahway 67 Lewis St *Web:* www.rahwayparking.org	Rahway	NJ	07065	732-381-8778		562
Parking Company of America (PCA) 11101 Lakewood Blvd *Web:* www.parkpca.com	Downey	CA	90241	562-862-2118	862-4409	562
Parking Company of America Inc 250 W Court St Ste 200E *Web:* www.parkplaceparking.com	Cincinnati	OH	45202	513-241-0415		562
Parking Concepts Inc 12 Mauchly Bldg I *Web:* parkingconcepts.com	Irvine	CA	92618	949-753-7525		562
Parking Management Inc 1725 Desales St NW Ste 300 *Web:* www.pmi-parking.com	Washington	DC	20036	202-785-9191		562
Parking Panda Corp 3422 Fait Ave *TF:* 800-232-6415 ■ *Web:* www.parkingpanda.com	Baltimore	MD	21224	800-232-6415		562
Parking Solutions Inc 353 W Nationwide Blvd *TF:* 888-469-7690 ■ *Web:* www.parkingsolutionsinc.com	Columbus	OH	43215	614-469-7000		562
Parkinson Construction Company Inc 3905 Perry St *Web:* www.parkinsonconstruction.com	Brentwood	MD	20722	301-985-6080		186
Parkinson's Disease Foundation (PDF) 1359 Broadway *TF:* 800-457-6676 ■ *Web:* www.pdf.org	New York	NY	10018	212-923-4700	923-4778	48-17
Parkit Enterprise Inc Suite 1088 - 999, W Hastings St *TF:* 800-883-2055 ■ *Web:* www.parkitenterprise.com	Vancouver	BC	V6C2W2	604-424-8700		653
Parkland College 2400 W Bradley Ave **Fax:* Admissions ■ *TF:* 888-467-6065 ■ *Web:* www.parkland.edu	Champaign	IL	61821	217-351-2200	353-2640*	162
Parkland College Theatre 2400 W Bradley Ave *TF:* 800-346-8089 ■ *Web:* www.parkland.edu/theatre	Champaign	IL	61821	217-351-2528	373-3899	572
Parkland Community Library 4422 Walbert Ave *Web:* www.parklandlibrary.org	Allentown	PA	18104	610-398-1361		435
Parkland Health & Hospital System 5201 Harry Hines Blvd *Web:* www.parklandhospital.com	Dallas	TX	75235	214-590-8000		374-3
Parkland Health Ctr 1101 W Liberty St *TF:* 800-734-3944 ■ *Web:* www.parklandhealthcenter.org	Farmington	MO	63640	573-756-6451		374-3
Parkland Light & Water Co 12918 Pk Ave *Web:* www.plw.coop	Tacoma	WA	98444	253-531-5666	531-2684	245
Parkland Medical Ctr 1 Parkland Dr *Web:* www.parklandmedicalcenter.com	Derry	NH	03038	603-432-1500		374-3
Parkland Plastics Inc 104 Yoder Dr PO Box 339 *TF:* 800-835-4110 ■ *Web:* www.parklandplastics.com	Middlebury	IN	46540	574-825-4336		661
Parkland School District 1210 Springhouse Rd *Web:* www.parklandsd.org	Allentown	PA	18104	610-351-5503	351-5509	685

Phone Fax Class

Parkline Inc PO Box 65 .... Winfield WV 25213 304-586-2113 586-3842 105
TF: 800-786-4855 ■ *Web:* www.parkline.com

Park-Ohio Holdings Corp (PKOH)
6065 Parkland Blvd .... Cleveland OH 44124 440-947-2000 947-2099 449
NASDAQ: PKOH ■ *TF:* 800-732-0330 ■ *Web:* www.pkoh.com

Parkplace 111 Emerson St. .... Denver CO 80218 844-319-6282 672
TF: 844-319-6282 ■ *Web:* brookdale.com/parkplace-.aspx

Parkridge East Hospital
941 Spring Creek Rd .... Chattanooga TN 37412 423-894-7870 374-3
TF: 800-605-1527 ■ *Web:* www.parkridgeeasthospital.com

Parkridge Medical Ctr
2333 McCallie Ave .... Chattanooga TN 37404 423-698-6061 374-3
Web: www.parkridgemedicalcenter.com

Parks Assoc Inc
15950 N Dallas Pkwy Ste 575 .... Dallas TX 75248 972-490-1113 668
TF: 800-727-5711 ■ *Web:* www.parksassociates.com

Parks at Arlington 3811 S Cooper St. .... Arlington TX 76015 817-467-0200 468-5356 460
TF: 800-780-5733 ■ *Web:* www.theparksmallarlington.com/en.html

Parks at Chehaw 105 Chehaw Pk Rd .... Albany GA 31701 229-430-5275 430-3035 823
Web: www.chehaw.org

Parks Auto Parts Professionals
2320 Savannah Hwy .... Charleston SC 29414 843-556-4703 54
TF: 800-397-2474 ■ *Web:* parksautoparts.com

Parks Bros Farm Inc 6733 Parks Rd .... Van Buren AR 72956 479-474-1125 369
TF: 800-334-5770 ■ *Web:* www.parksbrothers.com

Parks Canada 30 Victoria St .... Gatineau QC J8X0B3 819-420-9486 563
TF: 888-773-8888 ■ *Web:* www.pc.gc.ca/eng/index.aspx

Parks Chamber of Commerce
100 Heart Blvd .... Loves Park IL 61111 815-633-3999 633-4057 139
TF: 800-426-2535 ■ *Web:* www.parkschamber.com

Parks Productions Ltd
2250 Pontiac Rd .... Auburn Hills MI 48326 248-370-9200 195
Web: www.parkspro.com

Parkside Animal Hospital
12962 Publishers Dr. .... Fishers IN 46038 317-849-1440 794
Web: parksidepets.com

Parkside Meadows Retirement Community
2150 W Randolph St. .... Saint Charles MO 63301 636-946-4966 672

Parkside Rotisserie & Bar
76 S Main St. .... Providence RI 02903 401-331-0003 671
TF: 800-745-5555 ■ *Web:* www.parksideprovidence.com

Parksite Inc 1563 Hubbard Ave. .... Batavia IL 60510 800-338-3355 761-6820* 191-3
**Fax Area Code:* 630 ■ *TF:* 800-338-3355 ■ *Web:* www.parksite.com

Parkson Corp
1401 W Cyperess Creek Rd .... Fort Lauderdale FL 33309 888-727-5766 974-6182* 386
**Fax Area Code:* 954 ■ *TF:* 888-727-5766 ■ *Web:* www.parkson.com

Parksville Chamber of Commerce (PDCC)
PO Box 99 .... Parksville BC V9P2G3 250-248-3613 248-5210 137
Web: parksvillechamber.com

Parkview Community Hospital Medical Ctr (PCHMC)
3865 Jackson St. .... Riverside CA 92503 951-688-2211 374-3
Web: www.pchmc.org

Parkview Hospital
2200 Randallia Dr. .... Fort Wayne IN 46805 260-373-4000 374-3
TF: 888-737-9311 ■ *Web:* www.parkview.com

Parkview Medical Ctr 400 W 16th St .... Pueblo CO 81003 719-584-4000 584-7376 374-3
TF: 800-543-4046 ■ *Web:* www.parkviewmc.com

Parkville Insurances Services Inc
15242 E Whittier Blvd PO Box 1275 .... Whittier CA 90603 562-945-2702 945-4297 390
TF: 800-350-2702 ■ *Web:* parkvilleinsurance.com

Parkway Bancorp Inc
4800 N Harlem Ave. .... Harwood Heights IL 60706 708-867-6600 70
Web: www.parkwaybank.com

Parkway Chevrolet Inc
25500 Tomball Pkwy. .... Tomball TX 77375 888-929-4556 516
TF: 888-929-4556 ■ *Web:* www.parkwaychevrolet.com

Parkway Clinical Laboratories Inc
3494 Progress Dr .... Bensalem PA 19020 215-245-5112 418
TF: 800-327-2764 ■ *Web:* www.parkwayclinical.com

Parkway Construction & Assoc LP
1000 Civic Cir .... Lewisville TX 75067 972-221-1979 219-0061 186
Web: www.parkwayconstruction.com

Parkway Corp 150 N Broad St. .... Philadelphia PA 19102 215-575-4000 562
Web: www.parkwaycorp.com

Parkway Electric Inc 11952 James St. .... Holland MI 49424 800-574-9553 392-6880* 787
**Fax Area Code:* 616 ■ *TF:* 800-574-9553 ■ *Web:* www.parkwayelectric.com

Parkway Grill 510 S Arroyo Pkwy .... Pasadena CA 91105 626-795-1001 796-6221 671
Web: www.theparkwaygrill.com

Parkway Inn
125 N Jackson St PO Box 494 .... Jackson WY 83001 800-247-8390 379
TF: 800-247-8390 ■ *Web:* www.parkwayinn.com

Parkway Metal Products Inc
130 Rawls Rd .... Des Plaines IL 60018 847-789-4000 480
Web: www.parkwaymetal.com

Parkway Place Mall
2801 Memorial Pkwy SW .... Huntsville AL 35801 256-533-0700 460
Web: www.parkwayplacemall.com

Parkway Plastics Inc
561 Stelton Rd .... Piscataway NJ 08854 732-752-3636 596
Web: www.parkwayjars.com

Parkway Products Inc 1400 Jamike Ave .... Erlanger KY 41018 859-525-8040 21
Web: www.parkwayproducts.com

Parkway Properties Inc
188 E Capitol St Ste 1000 .... Jackson MS 39201 601-948-4091 949-4077 655
NYSE: PKY ■ *TF:* 800-748-1667 ■ *Web:* www.pky.com

Parkwest Medical Ctr 9352 Pk W Blvd .... Knoxville TN 37923 865-373-1000 374-3
Web: www.treatedwell.com

Parlec Inc 101 Perinton Pkwy .... Fairport NY 14450 585-425-4400 358
TF: 800-866-5872 ■ *Web:* www.parlec.com

Parlee McLaws LLP 421 7 Ave SW .... Calgary AB T2P3Y7 403-294-7000 428
Web: www.parlee.com

Parlin Memorial Library 410 Broadway .... Everett MA 02149 617-394-2300 389-1230 434-3
TF: 800-243-4636 ■ *Web:* www.noblenet.org/everett

Parma Area Chamber of Commerce
7908 Day Dr .... Parma OH 44129 440-886-1700 886-1770 139
TF: 800-248-6862 ■ *Web:* www.parmaareachamber.org

Parmalat Canada Ltd
405 the W Mall 10th Fl .... Toronto ON M9C5J1 800-563-1515 296-27
TF: 800-563-1515 ■ *Web:* www.parmalat.ca

Phone Fax Class

Parman Energy Corp
7101 Cockrill Bend Blvd .... Nashville TN 37209 615-350-7920 316
TF: 800-727-7920 ■ *Web:* www.parmanenergy.com

Parmatech Corp 2221 Pine View Way .... Petaluma CA 94954 707-778-2266 490
Web: atwcompanies.com/parmatech

Parmatown Mall 7899 W Ridgewood Dr .... Parma OH 44129 440-885-5506 460
Web: www.facebook.com

Parmed Pharmaceuticals Inc
4220 Hyde Pk Blvd .... Niagara Falls NY 14305 800-727-6331 727-6330 238
TF: 800-727-6331 ■ *Web:* www.parmed.com

Parmenter Realty Partners
701 Brickell Ave Ste 2020 .... Miami FL 33131 305-379-7500 475
Web: www.parmco.com

Parmer County 401 Third St .... Farwell TX 79325 806-481-3691 338
Web: www.co.parmer.tx.us

Parmly Billings Library
510 N Broadway .... Billings MT 59101 406-657-8258 657-8293 434-3
Web: www.ci.billings.mt.us

Parnassus Investments
1 Market St Steuart Tower Ste 1600 .... San Francisco CA 94105 415-778-0200 690
TF: 800-999-3505 ■ *Web:* www.parnassus.com

Parnell & Crum PA
641 S Lawrence St .... Montgomery AL 36104 334-832-4200 41
TF: 866-629-0912 ■ *Web:* www.parnellcrum.com

Paroscientific Inc 4500 148th Ave NE .... Redmond WA 98052 425-883-8700 407
Web: www.paroscientific.com

Parr Brown Gee & Loveless
101 S 200 E Ste 700 .... Slc UT 84111 801-532-7840 428
Web: www.parrbrown.com

Parr Instrument Co 211 53rd St .... Moline IL 61265 309-762-7716 762-9453 420
TF: 800-872-7720 ■ *Web:* www.parrinst.com

Parr Moto
13120 Westlinks Ter Blvd Unit 4 .... Fort Myers FL 33913 866-772-1381 6
TF: 866-772-1381 ■ *Web:* www.parrmedia.com

Parr Richey Frandsen Patterson Kruse LLP
Capital Ctr N 251 N Illinois St
Ste 1800 .... Indianapolis IN 46204 317-269-2500 269-2514 428
TF: 888-337-7766 ■ *Web:* www.parrlaw.com

Parrett, Porto, Parese & Colwell PC
One Hamden Ctr 2319 Whitney Ave Ste 1-D .... Hamden CT 06518 203-281-2700 281-0700 428
Web: www.pppclaw.com

Parris & Assoc Inc
480 Turnpike St Ste 1 .... South Easton MA 02375 508-230-0255 610
Web: www.parrisandassociates.com

PARRIS Law 43364 Tenth St W .... Lancaster CA 93534 661-429-3399 949-7524 445
Web: rrexparris.com

Parris Printing 211 Whitsett Rd .... Nashville TN 37210 615-832-7170 627
Web: www.parrisprinting.com

Parrish & Heimbecker Ltd (P&H)
201 Portage Ave Ste 1400 .... Winnipeg MB R3B3K6 204-956-2030 943-8233 275
TF: 800-665-8937 ■ *Web:* www.parrishandheimbecker.com

Parrish Medical Ctr
951 N Washington Ave .... Titusville FL 32796 321-268-6111 268-6231 374-3
TF: 800-227-9954 ■ *Web:* www.parrishmed.com

Parrish Tire Company Inc
5130 Indiana Ave .... Winston Salem NC 27106 336-767-0202 744-2716 62-5
TF: 800-849-8473 ■ *Web:* www.parrishtire.com

Parrish-Hare Electrical Supply LP
1211 Regal Row .... Dallas TX 75247 214-905-1001 951-8101 246
Web: www.parrish-hare.com

Pars International Corp
253 W 35th St Fl 7 .... New York NY 10001 212-221-9595 532-3
Web: www.magreprints.com

Parsec Financial Management Inc
6 Wall St .... Asheville NC 28801 828-255-0271 194
TF: 888-877-1012 ■ *Web:* www.parsecfinancial.com

Parsec Inc 1100 Gest St .... Cincinnati OH 45203 513-621-6111 317
Web: www.parsecinc.com

Parseghian Planco LLC
388 second Ave Ste 601 .... New York NY 10010 212-777-7786 731

Parsippany Area Chamber of Commerce
14 N Beverwyck Rd .... Lake Hiawatha NJ 07034 973-402-6400 139
TF: 800-242-4349 ■ *Web:* www.parsippanychamber.org

Parsippany-Troy Hills Public Library
449 Halsey Rd .... Parsippany NJ 07054 973-887-5150 887-5150 434-3
TF: 800-624-4294 ■ *Web:* www.parsippanylibrary.org

Parsley Energy Inc
303 Colorado St Ste 3000 .... Austin TX 78701 432-818-2100 536
TF: 855-214-5200 ■ *Web:* www.parsleyenergy.com

Parsons & Whittemore Inc
4 International Dr .... Rye Brook NY 10573 914-937-9009 638

Parsons Brinckerhoff Inc
1 Penn Plaza 2nd Fl .... New York NY 10119 212-465-5000 465-5096 261

Parsons Buick Co, The 151 E St .... Plainville CT 06062 860-747-1693 747-5734 57
TF: 877-274-2613 ■ *Web:* www.parsonsbuick.com

Parsons Capital Management Inc
10 Weybosset St Ste 1000 .... Providence RI 02903 401-521-2440 401
TF: 888-521-2440 ■ *Web:* www.parsonscapital.com

Parsons Child & Family Ctr
60 Academy Rd .... Albany NY 12208 518-426-2600 447-5234 48-6
TF: 800-342-3009 ■ *Web:* www.parsonscenter.org

Parsons Company Inc 1386 SR- 117 .... Roanoke IL 61561 309-467-9100 454
Web: www.parsonscompany.com

Parsons Corp 100 W Walnut St .... Pasadena CA 91124 626-440-2000 440-2630 261
Web: www.parsons.com

Parsons Dance Co 229 W 42nd St 8th Fl .... New York NY 10036 212-869-9275 944-7417 573-1
Web: www.parsonsdance.org

Parsons Electric LLC
5960 Main St NE .... Minneapolis MN 55432 763-571-8000 571-7210 189-4
TF: 800-403-4832

Parsons Elem. School
899 Hollywood St .... North Brunswick NJ 08902 732-289-3400 685
Web: nbtschools.org

Parsons Infrastructure & Technology
100 W Walnut St .... Pasadena CA 91124 626-440-2000 440-2630 261
Web: www.parsons.com

Parsons New School for Design
65 Fifth Ave .... New York NY 10011 212-229-8989 229-8975* 166
**Fax:* Admissions ■ *TF Admissions:* 800-252-0852 ■ *Web:* www.newschool.edu

Listing	City	State	ZIP	Phone	Fax	Class
Parsons State Hospital & Training Ctr 2601 Gabriel St. *Web:* kdads.ks.gov	Parsons	KS	67357	620-421-6550	421-3623	230
Partec Inc 9301 Belmont Ave. *TF:* 800-345-3851 ■ *Web:* partec-inc.com	Franklin Park	IL	60131	847-678-9520		543
Par-Tech Inc 139 Premier Dr *Web:* www.partechgss.com	Lake Orion	MI	48359	248-276-0213		344
Parter Medical Products Inc 17015 Kingsview Ave *TF:* 800-666-8282 ■ *Web:* www.partermedical.com	Carson	CA	90746	310-327-4417	327-8601	420
Parthenon 56th & Hwy 2 *Web:* www.theparthenon.net	Lincoln	NE	68516	402-423-2222		671
Parthenon Prints Inc PO Box 2505 *Web:* www.parthenonprints.com	Panama City	FL	32402	850-769-8321	769-5374	745-7
Parthenon, The 2600 W End Ave *Web:* nashville.gov/parks-and-recreation/parthenon.aspx	Nashville	TN	37203	615-862-8431	880-2265	520
Participant Media LLC 331 Foothill Rd 3rd Fl. *Web:* www.participantmedia.com	Beverly Hills	CA	90210	310-550-5100		514
Particle Dynamics International LLC 2629 S Hanley Rd *TF:* 800-452-4682 ■ *Web:* pdhllc.com	Saint Louis	MO	63144	314-968-2376	781-3354	582
Particle Measuring Systems Inc 5475 Airport Blvd *TF Cust Svc:* 800-238-1801 ■ *Web:* www.pmeasuring.com	Boulder	CO	80301	303-443-7100	449-6870	419
Partner Assessment Corp 2154 Torrance Blvd Ste 200 *TF:* 800-419-4923 ■ *Web:* www.partneresi.com	Torrance	CA	90501	800-419-4923		192
Partner Reinsurance Co of the US 1 Greenwich Plaza *TF:* 800-831-9146 ■ *Web:* www.partnerre.com	Greenwich	CT	06830	203-485-4200	485-4300	391-2
Partner Software Inc 345 W Hancock Ave. *Web:* www.partnersoft.com	Athens	GA	30601	706-354-1833		809
Partnercomm Inc 2304 I-20 W *Web:* www.partnercomm.net	Arlington	TX	76017	817-465-9277		463
Partners Napier Inc 192 Mill St Ste 600 *TF:* 800-274-4954 ■ *Web:* www.partnersandnapier.com	Rochester	NY	14614	585-454-1010		7
Partners 1St Federal Credit Union 1330 Directors Row *Web:* partners1stcu.org	Fort Wayne	IN	46808	260-471-8336		219
PARTNERS A Tasteful Choice Co 20232 72nd Ave *TF:* 800-632-7477 ■ *Web:* www.partnerscrackers.com	South Kent	WA	98032	253-867-1580		68
Partners Capital Investment Group LLC 50 Rowes Wharf 4th Fl *TF:* 800-782-6620 ■ *Web:* www.partners-cap.com	Boston	MA	02110	617-292-2570		401
Partners HealthCare System Inc 800 Boylston St Ste 1150 *Web:* www.partners.org	Boston	MA	02199	617-278-1000		353
Partners of the Americas 1424 K St NW Ste 700 *TF:* 800-424-8580 ■ *Web:* www.partners.net	Washington	DC	20005	202-628-3300	628-3306	48-5
Partners Riley 1375 Euclid Ave Ste 410 *Web:* www.partnersriley.com	Cleveland	OH	44115	216-241-2141		4
Partners Trust Real Estate Brokerage & Acquisitions 9378 Wilshire Blvd Ste 200 *Web:* www.thepartnerstrust.com	Beverly Hills	CA	90212	310-500-3900		652
Partnership Capital Growth Advisors 1 Embarcadero Ctr PO Box 7 *TF:* 800-832-3775 ■ *Web:* www.pcg-investors.com	Los Gatos	CA	95031	415-705-8008		691
Partnership for a Drug-Free America 405 Lexington Ave Ste 1601 *TF:* 855-378-4373 ■ *Web:* www.drugfree.org	New York	NY	10174	212-922-1560	922-1570	48-17
Partnership for Philanthropic Planning (NCPG) 233 McCrea St *Web:* pppgd.org	Indianapolis	OH	45429	317-269-6274		48-5
Partnerships In Community Living Inc 480 Main St E PO Box 129 *TF:* 800-222-1222 ■ *Web:* www.pclpartnership.org	Monmouth	OR	97361	503-838-2403	838-5815	48-15
Partnersolve Llc 14 Fawn Ridge Rd *Web:* partnersolve.com	Ashland	MA	01721	508-309-3230		260
Parton Lumber Company Inc 251 Parton Rd *TF:* 800-624-1501 ■ *Web:* www.partonlumber.com	Rutherfordton	NC	28139	828-287-4257		683
Partridge Snow & Hahn LLP 180 S Main St *Web:* www.psh.com	Providence	RI	02903	401-861-8200		428
Parts Authority Inc 495 Merrick Rd *Web:* www.partsauthority.com	Rockville Centre	NY	11570	516-678-3900		61
Parts Central Inc 3243 Whitfield St *TF:* 800-226-9396 ■ *Web:* www.partscentral.net	Macon	GA	31204	478-745-0878	746-1177	61
parts com Inc 121 E First St *Web:* www.parts.com	Sanford	FL	32771	407-302-1314		317
PartsBase Inc 905 Clint Moore Rd *TF Cust Svc:* 888-322-6896 ■ *Web:* www.partsbase.com	Boca Raton	FL	33487	561-953-0700	953-0793	770
PartsRiver Inc 3155 Kearney St Ste 210 *TF:* 855-700-7278 ■ *Web:* www.partsriver.com	Fremont	CA	94538	855-700-7278		178-7
Party Cat Inc 2727 Exposition Blvd Ste 119 *Web:* partycat.com	Austin	TX	78703	512-472-8250		627
Party City Corp 25 Green Pond Rd Ste 1 *TF:* 800-727-8924 ■ *Web:* www.partycity.com	Rockaway	NJ	07866	973-453-8600		566
Party Concepts 4691 S Butterfield Dr Palo Verde *Web:* party-concepts.com	Tucson	AZ	85714	520-750-0550		129
Party Fair Inc 4345 US Hwy 9 *TF:* 800-914-3538 ■ *Web:* www.partyfair.com	Freehold	NJ	07728	732-780-1110		566
Party Rental Ltd 275 N St. *Web:* www.partyrentalltd.com	Teterboro	NJ	07608	201-727-4700	727-4701	264-2
Partylite Gifts Inc 59 Armstrong Rd *TF:* 888-999-5706 ■ *Web:* www.partylite.com	Plymouth	MA	02360	508-830-3100	732-5818	366
Parvin State Park 701 Almond Rd *Web:* www.njparksandforests.org	Pittsgrove	NJ	08318	856-358-8616		565
Par-Way Tryson Co 107 Bolte Ln *TF:* 800-844-4554 ■ *Web:* www.parwaytryson.com	Saint Clair	MO	63077	636-629-4545	629-1330	296-30
Parylene Coating Servicesinc 6819 Highway Blvd Ste 510 *Web:* www.paryleneinc.com	Katy	TX	77494	281-391-7665		625
PAS (Percussive Arts Society) 110 W Washington St *Web:* www.pas.org	Indianapolis	IN	46204	317-974-4488	974-4499	48-4
Pas Technologies Inc 10301 N Commerce Pkwy *Web:* www.pas-technologies.com	Miramar	FL	33025	305-624-3173		21
Pasadena Capital Partners LLC PO Box 60786 *Web:* www.pasadenacapitalpartners.com	Pasadena	CA	91116	626-432-7070		528
Pasadena Chamber of Commerce 4334 Fairmont Pkwy *Web:* www.pasadenachamber.org	Pasadena	TX	77504	281-487-7871	487-5530	139
Pasadena Chamber of Commerce & Civic Assn 844 E Green St Ste 208 *Web:* www.pasadena-chamber.org	Pasadena	CA	91101	626-795-3355	795-5603	139
Pasadena City College 1570 E Colorado Blvd **Fax:* Admissions ■ *Web:* www.pasadena.edu	Pasadena	CA	91106	626-585-7123	585-7915*	162
Pasadena Convention & Visitors Bureau 300 E Green St *TF:* 800-307-7977 ■ *Web:* www.visitpasadena.com	Pasadena	CA	91101	626-795-9311	795-9656	206
Pasadena Convention Center 300 E Green St *TF:* 800-307-7977 ■ *Web:* pasadenacenter.visitpasadena.com	Pasadena	CA	91101	626-793-2122		572
Pasadena Heritage 651 S Saint John Ave *Web:* pasadenaheritage.org	Pasadena	CA	91105	626-441-6333		533
Pasadena Playhouse, The 39 S El Molino Ave *Web:* www.pasadenaplayhouse.org	Pasadena	CA	91101	626-356-7529	204-7399	749
Pasadena Public Library 285 E Walnut St *Web:* www.cityofpasadena.net	Pasadena	CA	91101	626-744-4052	585-8396	434-3
Pasadena Public Library 1201 Jeff Ginn Memorial Dr *Web:* www.ci.pasadena.tx.us	Pasadena	TX	77506	713-477-0276	473-9640	434-3
Pasadena Refining Systems Inc 111 Red Bluff Rd *Web:* ww.petrobras.com/en/countries/u-s-a/operations	Pasadena	TX	77506	713-472-2461		580
Pasadena Star-News 911 E Colorado Blvd *Web:* www.pasadenastarnews.com	Pasadena	CA	91106	626-578-6300		532-2
Pasadena Tank Corp 15915 Jacintoport Blvd *Web:* www.ptctanks.com	Houston	TX	77015	281-457-3996		91
Pasadena Weekly 50 S Delacey Ave Ste 200 *TF:* 800-428-1798 ■ *Web:* www.pasadenaweekly.com	Pasadena	CA	91105	626-584-1500	795-0149	532-5
Pasadera Capital LLC 115 W El Prado Ste 1 *Web:* www.pasaderacapital.com	San Antonio	TX	78212	210-804-4240		70
Pasand Indian Cuisine 2600 N Belt Line Rd *Web:* www.pasandrestaurant.com	Irving	TX	75062	972-594-0693	594-8935	671
Pascal's on Ponce 2611 Ponce de Leon Blvd *Web:* www.pascalmiami.com	Coral Gables	FL	33134	305-444-2024	444-9798	671
Pascap Company Inc 4250 Boston Rd *TF:* 800-966-9282 ■ *Web:* pascapco.com	Bronx	NY	10475	718-325-7200	325-7595	686
Pasco 2600 S Hanley Rd Ste 450 *TF:* 800-489-3300 ■ *Web:* pascosystems.com	Saint Louis	MO	63144	314-781-2212		295
Pasco Corp of America 6500 N Marine Dr *Web:* www.pascoamerica.com	Portland	OR	97203	503-289-6500		297-8
Pasco County 7530 Little Rd *TF:* 800-368-2411 ■ *Web:* www.pascocountyfl.net	New Port Richey	FL	34654	727-847-2411	847-8969	338
Pasco County Library System 8012 Library Rd *Web:* www.pascolibraries.org	Hudson	FL	34667	727-861-3020	861-3025	434-3
PASCO Inc 1140 Terex Rd *TF:* 800-842-1820 ■ *Web:* pasco-group.com	Hudson	OH	44236	330-655-7000		225
Pasco Specialty & Manufacturing Inc 11156 Wright Rd *TF:* 800-737-2726 ■ *Web:* www.pascospecialty.com	Lynwood	CA	90262	310-537-7782		612
Pasco-Hernado State College 10230 Ridge Rd **Fax:* Admissions ■ *TF:* 855-669-7472 ■ *Web:* phsc.edu	New Port Richey	FL	34654	727-847-2727	816-3389*	162
North 11415 Ponce de Leon Blvd *TF:* 855-669-7472 ■ *Web:* phsc.edu	Brooksville	FL	34601	352-796-6726	797-5133	162
Pascrell Bill Jr (Rep D - NJ) 2370 Rayburn Bldg *Web:* pascrell.house.gov	Washington	DC	20515	202-225-5751	225-5782	342-2
Pasek Corp 9 W Third St *TF:* 800-628-2822 ■ *Web:* www.pasek.com	South Boston	MA	02127	617-269-7110		693
Paseo 4225 Fremont Ave N *Web:* www.paseorestaurants.com	Seattle	WA	98103	206-545-7440		671
Pasha 919 W International Speedway Blvd *Web:* pashacafedaytona.com	Daytona Beach	FL	32114	386-257-7753		671
Pasha Group Inc 4040 Civic Center Dr Ste 350 *Web:* www.pashagroup.com	San Rafael	CA	94903	415-927-6400	924-5672	313
Paslin Co 25303 Ryan Rd *Web:* www.paslin.com	Warren	MI	48091	586-758-0200		757
Paslode 888 Forest Edge Dr *TF Cust Svc:* 800-682-3428 ■ *Web:* www.paslode.com	Vernon Hills	IL	60061	847-634-1900	634-6602	759
PASNAP (Pennsylvania Assn of Staff Nurses & Allied Professionals) 1 Fayette St Ste 475 *TF:* 800-500-7850 ■ *Web:* www.pennanurses.org	Conshohocken	PA	19428	610-567-2907	567-2915	533
Paso Fino Horse Assn 4047 Iron Works Pkwy Ste 1 *TF:* 800-844-1409 ■ *Web:* www.pfha.org	Lexington	KY	40511	859-825-6000	258-2125	48-3
Paso Robles Inn 1103 Spring St *TF:* 800-676-1713 ■ *Web:* www.pasoroblesinn.com	Paso Robles	CA	93446	805-238-2660	238-4707	379

Name / Address	City	State	Zip	Phone	Fax	Class
Paso Robles Press 829 Tenth St Ste B *TF:* 800-427-2200 ■ *Web:* www.pasoroblespress.com	Paso Robles	CA	93446	805 237 6060	237-6066	532-4
Pason Systems Inc 6130 Third St SE *TSE: PSI* ■ *TF:* 877-255-3158 ■ *Web:* www.pason.com	Calgary	AB	T2H1K4	403-301-3400	301-3499	178-10
Pasquier Panel Products Inc 1510 Puyallup St PO Box 1170 *Web:* www.pasquierpanel.com	Sumner	WA	98390	253-863-6323	891-7993	819
Pasquotank Correctional Institution 527 Commerce Dr *Web:* ncdps.gov	Elizabeth City	NC	27906	252-331-4881	331-4866	213
Pasquotank County PO Box 39 *Web:* www.co.pasquotank.nc.us	Elizabeth City	NC	27907	252-335-0865	335-0866	338
Pass Security LLC 340 Office Court Ste B *TF:* 800-539-9858 ■ *Web:* www.passsecurity.com	Fairview Heights	IL	62208	618-394-1144		693
Passage to India 520 Race St *Web:* www.passagetoindiaharrisburgpa.com	Harrisburg	PA	17104	717-233-1202		671
PassageMaker Magazine 105 Eastern Ave Ste 203 *Web:* www.passagemaker.com	Annapolis	MD	21403	410-990-9086		457-4
Passageways LLC 1551 Win Hentschel Blvd *Web:* www.passageways.com	West Lafayette	IN	47906	765-497-8829		180
Passaic County 401 Grand St *Web:* www.passaiccountynj.org	Paterson	NJ	07505	973-225-3632	754-1920	338
Passaic County Community College 1 College Blvd **Fax:* Admissions ■ *Web:* www.pccc.cc.nj.us	Paterson	NJ	07505	973-684-6800	684-6778*	162
Passaic Engraving Company Inc 41 Brook Ave *Web:* www.passaicengraving.com	Passaic	NJ	07055	973-777-0621		481
Passaic Metal Products Co 5 Central Ave *TF:* 800-247-1727 ■ *Web:* www.pampco.com	Clifton	NJ	07015	973-546-9000		697
Passaic Rubber Co 45 Demarest Dr *Web:* www.passaic.com	Wayne	NJ	07474	973-696-9500		677
Passaic Valley Water Commission 1525 Main Ave *TF:* 877-772-7077 ■ *Web:* www.pvwc.com	Clifton	NJ	07011	973-340-4300	340-5598	787
Passavant Area Hospital (PAH) 1600 W Walnut St *Web:* www.passavanthospital.com	Jacksonville	IL	62650	217-245-9541		374-3
Passavant Retirement Community 401 S Main St *TF:* 888-498-7753 ■ *Web:* www.lutheranseniorlife.org	Zelienople	PA	16063	724-452-5400		672
Passenger Vessel Assn (PVA) 103 Oronoco St Ste 200 *TF:* 800-807-8360 ■ *Web:* www.passengervessel.com	Alexandria	VA	22314	703-518-5005	518-5151	49-21
Passero Assoc 242 W Main St Ste 100 *TF:* 800-836-0365 ■ *Web:* www.passero.com	Rochester	NY	14614	585-325-1000		261
Passionfish 701 Lighthouse Ave *TF:* 800-722-1774 ■ *Web:* www.passionfish.net	Pacific Grove	CA	93950	831-655-3311		671
Passkey Systems 4395 Polaris Ave *Web:* www.passkeysys.com	Las Vegas	NV	89103	702-798-7999		5
Passman & Jones 2500 Renaissance Tower 1201 Elm St *Web:* www.passmanjones.com	Dallas	TX	75270	214-742-2121		428
Passport Corp 16 West St **Fax Area Code:* 845 ■ *TF:* 800-926-6736 ■ *Web:* www.passportcorp.com	Warwick	NY	10990	800-926-6736	986-4160*	178-1
Passport Health Communications Inc 720 Cool Springs Blvd Ste 200 *TF:* 888-661-5657 ■ *Web:* www.passporthealth.com	Franklin	TN	37067	615-661-5657	376-3552	178-10
Passport Online Inc 9786 SW Nimbus Ave *Web:* www.passportonlineinc.com	Beaverton	OR	97008	503-626-7766		225
Passport Program-western 925 Euclid Ave Ste 600 *TF:* 800-626-7277 ■ *Web:* www.psa10a.org	Cleveland	OH	44115	216-621-0303		363
Passport Services Regional Offices						
Boston Agency 10 Cswy St Rm 247 Tip O'Neill Federal Bldg *TF:* 877-487-2778 ■ *Web:* www.travel.state.gov	Boston	MA	02222	877-487-2778		340-16
Connecticut Agency 850 Canal St *TF:* 877-487-2778 ■ *Web:* www.travel.state.gov	Stamford	CT	06902	877-487-2778		340-16
Honolulu Agency 300 Ala Moana Bldg Ste 1-330 *TF:* 877-487-2778 ■ *Web:* www.travel.state.gov	Honolulu	HI	96850	877-487-2778		340-16
Los Angeles Agency 11000 Wilshire Blvd Ste 1000 *TF:* 877-487-2778 ■ *Web:* www.travel.state.gov	Los Angeles	CA	90024	877-487-2778		340-16
New Orleans Agency 365 Canal St Ste 1300 *TF:* 877-487-2778 ■ *Web:* travel.state.gov	New Orleans	LA	70130	877-487-2778		340-16
New York Agency 376 Hudson St 10th Fl *TF:* 877-487-2778 ■ *Web:* www.travel.state.gov	New York	NY	10014	877-487-2778		340-16
Seattle Agency 300 Fifth Ave Ste 600 *Web:* travel.state.gov	Seattle	WA	98104	206-393-0740	393-0739	340-16
Washington (DC) Agency 600 19th St NW 1st Floor Sidewalk Level *TF:* 877-487-2778 ■ *Web:* www.travel.state.gov	Washington	DC	20006	877-487-2778		340-16
Passport Systems Inc 70 Treble Cove Rd 1st Fl *Web:* www.passportsystems.com	Billerica	MA	01862	978-263-9900		743
PASSUR Aerospace Inc 1 Landmark Sq Ste 1900 *TF:* 800-844-9326 ■ *Web:* www.passur.com	Stamford	CT	06901	203-622-4086		177
Passy-Muir Inc 4521 Campus Dr Pmb 273 *TF:* 800-634-5397 ■ *Web:* www.passy-muir.com	Irvine	CA	92612	949-833-8255		477
Pasta House Co 700 New Ballas Rd *Web:* www.pastahouse.com	Saint Louis	MO	63141	314-535-6644	531-2499	670
Pasta Jays 1001 Pearl St *Web:* www.pastajays.com	Boulder	CO	80302	303-444-5800		671
Pastel Journal 4700 E Galbraith Rd *TF:* 800-422-2550 ■ *Web:* www.artistsnetwork.com	Cincinnati	OH	45236	513-531-2222	891-7153	457-2
Pastiche 4260 Herschel St	Jacksonville	FL	32210	904-387-6213		671
Pastiche Modern Eatery 3025 N Campbell Ave *TF:* 800-933-1093 ■ *Web:* www.pasticheme.com	Tucson	AZ	85719	520-325-3333		671
Pastorelli Food Products Inc 162 N Sangamon St *TF:* 800-767-2829 ■ *Web:* www.pastorelli.com	Chicago	IL	60607	312-666-2041	666-2415	296-36
Pastry Star 9445 Washington Blvd N *Web:* www.pastryonline.com	Laurel	MD	20723	301-498-0912		361
Pat Catan's Craft Centers 21160 Drake Rd *TF:* 800-433-3201 ■ *Web:* www.patcatans.com	Strongsville	OH	44149	440-238-7318		45
Pat Hoey Productions 167 Auburn St *Web:* www.thebostonhomeshow.com	Auburn	MA	01501	508-832-3300		184
Pat Milliken Ford Inc 9600 Telegraph Rd *Web:* www.patmillikenford.com	Redford	MI	48239	313-255-3100		57
Pat O'Brien's International Inc 718 St Peter St *TF:* 800-597-4823 ■ *Web:* www.patobriens.com	New Orleans	LA	70116	504-525-4823		670
Pat's Steak House 2437 Brownsboro Rd *Web:* www.patssteakhouselouisville.com	Louisville	KY	40206	502-893-2062	893-2062	671
Patagonia 259 W Santa Clara St *TF Cust Svc:* 800-638-6464 ■ *Web:* www.patagonia.com	Ventura	CA	93001	805-643-8616	648-8020	157-4
Patagonia Lake State Park 400 Patagonia Lake Rd *Web:* azstateparks.com	Patagonia	AZ	85624	520-287-6965		565
Patapsco Valley State Park 8020 Baltimore National Pk *Web:* dnr2.maryland.gov	Ellicott City	MD	21043	410-461-5005		565
Pataula Electric Membership Corp 211 Barkley St	Cuthbert	GA	39840	229-732-3171		245
Patch Plus Consulting Inc 3 Raleigh Cir Ste B *Web:* www.patchplusconsulting.com	Medford	NJ	08055	609-792-6204		765
Patch Rubber Co PO Box H *Web:* www.patchrubber.com	Roanoke Rapids	NC	27870	252-536-2574		676
Patchogue-Medford Library 54-60 E Main St Ste 60 *Web:* www.pmlib.org	Patchogue	NY	11772	631-654-4700		434-3
Pate Dawson Co 402 Commerce Ct *Web:* www.pdco.com	Goldsboro	NC	27534	919-778-3000		123
Pa-Ted Spring Company Inc 137 Vincent P Kelly Rd *Web:* patedspring.com	Bristol	CT	06010	860-582-6368	583-1044	719
Patel & Assoc 266 17th St Ste 200 *Web:* patelcpa.com	Oakland	CA	94612	510-452-5051		2
Patel Burica & Assoc Inc 9283 Research Dr **Fax Area Code:* 714 ■ *Web:* www.pbastructural.com	Irvine	CA	92618	949-943-8080	352-2209*	261
Patel Consultants Corp 1525 Morris Ave *Web:* www.patelcorp.com	Union	NJ	07083	908-964-7575	964-3176	177
Patella Industries Inc 721 Grand Bernier N	Saint-Jean-Sur-Richelieu	QC	J3B8H6	450-359-0040		115
Patene Building Supplies Ltd 641 Speedvale Ave W *TF:* 800-265-8319 ■ *Web:* www.patene.com	Guelph	ON	N1K1E6	519-824-4030		191-1
Patent Calls Inc 2802 Flintrock Trace Ste 202 *Web:* www.patentcalls.com	Austin	TX	78738	512-371-4120	287-5366	387
Patent Trademark & Copyright Law Daily 1801 S Bell St *TF:* 800-372-1033 ■ *Web:* www.bna.com	Arlington	VA	22202	800-372-1033		531-7
Patented Acquisition Corp 2490 CrossPointe Dr *TF:* 800-799-0010 ■ *Web:* thinkpatented.com	Miamisburg	OH	45342	937-353-2299		317
Paternity Testing Corp (PTC) 300 Portland St *TF:* 888-837-8323 ■ *Web:* www.ptclabs.com	Columbia	MO	65201	573-442-9948	442-9870	417
Paterson City Hall 155 Market St *Web:* www.patersonnj.gov	Paterson	NJ	07505	973-321-1500		337
Paterson Free Public Library 250 Broadway *TF:* 800-272-4630 ■ *Web:* www.patersonpl.org	Paterson	NJ	07501	973-321-1223	321-1205	434-3
Paterson Museum 2 Market St *Web:* www.thepatersonmuseum.com	Paterson	NJ	07501	973-321-1260		520
Paterson Pacific Parchment Co 625 Greg St **Fax Area Code:* 800 ■ *TF:* 800-678-8104 ■ *Web:* www.patersonpaper.com	Sparks	NV	89431	775-353-3000	456-8104*	559
Paterson Papers PO Box 2286 *Web:* www.patersonpapers.com	Paterson	NJ	07501	973-278-2410	278-0677	553
PATH (Program for Appropriate Technology in Health) 1455 NW Leary Way *TF:* 800-836-4620 ■ *Web:* www.path.org	Seattle	WA	98107	206-285-3500	285-6619	48-17
Path Logic Inc 950 Riverside Pkwy Ste 90 *TF:* 855-291-4528 ■ *Web:* www.pathlogic.com	West Sacramento	CA	95605	855-291-4528		418
Path Master Inc 1960 Midway Dr *TF:* 855-738-2722 ■ *Web:* www.pathmasterinc.com	Twinsburg	OH	44087	330-425-4994	425-9338	246
Path-2 Ventures LLC 223 E Blvd *TF:* 888-692-1057 ■ *Web:* www.path-2.com	Charlotte	NC	28203	888-692-1057		463
Pathcom Wireless Inc 315 First St E *Web:* www.pathcom.ca	Cochrane	AB	T4C1Z2	403-932-2559	932-2468	246
Patheon 2100 Syntex Ct *Web:* www.patheon.com	Mississauga	ON	L5N7K9	905-821-4001	812-6709	479
Pathfinder Bancorp Inc 214 W First St *NASDAQ: PBHC* ■ *TF:* 800-811-5620 ■ *Web:* www.pathfinderbank.com	Oswego	NY	13126	315-343-0057	342-9403	360-2
Pathfinder Group Park Lane Terr 502 - 5657 Spring Garden Rd PO Box 142 *TF:* 800-200-7284 ■ *Web:* www.pathfinder-group.com	Halifax	NS	B3J3R4	902-425-2445	425-2441	47
Pathfinder International 9 Galen St Ste 217 *Web:* www.pathfinder.org	Watertown	MA	02472	617-924-7200	924-3833	48-5
PathGroup Inc 5301 Virginia Way *TF:* 877-456-6706 ■ *Web:* www.pathgroup.com	Brentwood	TN	37027	615-221-4500		194
Pathlore Software Corp 7965 N High St Ste 300 *Web:* www.sumtotalsystems.com	Columbus	OH	43235	614-781-0036		463
Pathmaker Group LP 635 Fritz Dr Ste 110 *Web:* pathmaker-group.com	Coppell	TX	75019	817-704-3644		174

	Phone	Fax	Class
Pathologists' Regional Laboratory 1225 Highland Ave Clarkston WA 99403 *Web:* pathregional.com	509-758-5576		416
Pathology & Cytology Laboratories Inc 290 Big Run Rd Lexington KY 40503 *TF:* 800-264-0514 ■ *Web:* www.pandclab.com	859-278-9513		415
Pathology Ctr, The 8303 Dodge St Omaha NE 68114 *Web:* thepathologycenter.org	402-354-4540		418
Pathology Group The Mid South 6046 KNIGHT ARNOLD Rd EXT Ste 101 Memphis TN 38115 *Web:* www.trumbulllabs.com	901-542-6800		415
Pathology Inc 19951 Mariner Ave Ste 150 Torrance CA 90503 *Web:* www.pathologyinc.com	310-769-0561		415
Pathology Laboratories Inc 1946 N 13th St Ste 301 Toledo OH 43604 *TF:* 800-281-8804 ■ *Web:* www.pathlabs.org	419-255-4600		415
Path-Tec LLC 1333-A Belfast Ave Columbus GA 31904 *Web:* www.path-tec.com	706-569-6368		476
Pathway Bank 306 S High St Cairo NE 68824 *Web:* pathwaybank.com	308-485-4232		70
Pathway Health Services Inc 2025 Fourth St White Bear Lake MN 55110 *TF:* 800-777-4616 ■ *Web:* www.pathwayhealth.com	651-407-8699		196
Pathway Press 1080 Montgomery Ave NE Cleveland TN 37311 *Web:* www.pathwaypress.org	423-476-4512		637-2
Pathways 200 W Spring St Marquette MI 49855 *TF:* 800-377-6226 ■ *Web:* www.pathwaysup.org	906-225-1181		371
Pathways Home Health Hospice & Private Duty 585 N Mary Ave Sunnyvale CA 94085 *Web:* www.pathwayshealth.org	408-730-5900		363
Pathways to Independence 25 Dundas St W Belleville ON K8P3M7 *TF:* 800-554-1564 ■ *Web:* www.pathwaysind.com	613-962-2541		138
Pathwayz Communications Inc 4176 Canyon Dr Amarillo TX 79109 *Web:* www.pathwayz.com	806-350-9000		506
Patient Advocate Foundation Inc 700 Thimble Shoals Blvd Ste 200 Newport News VA 23606 *TF:* 800-532-5274 ■ *Web:* www.patientadvocate.org	800-532-5274		305
Patient Marketing Group Inc 155 Village Boulavard Ste 200 Princeton NJ 08540 *Web:* www.patientmarketing.com	609-779-6200		7
Patient Recruiting Agency LLC, The 6207 Bee Cave Rd Ste 288 Austin TX 78746 *Web:* tpra.com	512-345-7788		4
PatientKeeper Inc 800 Winter St; , Waltham MA 02451 *TF:* 888-994-2443 ■ *Web:* patientkeeper.com	781-373-6100		476
Patients Rights Council (PRC) PO Box 760 Steubenville OH 43952 *TF:* 800-958-5678 ■ *Web:* www.patientsrightscouncil.org	740-282-3810		48-8
PatientSafe Solutions Inc 5375 Mira Sorrento Pl Ste 500 San Diego CA 92121 *Web:* www.patientsafesolutions.com	858-746-3100		475
Patina 141 S Grand Ave Los Angeles CA 90012 *Web:* www.patinagroup.com	213-972-3331		671
Patina Restaurant Group 141 S Grand Ave Los Angeles CA 90012 *TF:* 866-972-8462 ■ *Web:* www.patinagroup.com	866-972-8462		670
Patioshoppers Inc 41188 Sandalwood Cir Murrieta CA 92562 *TF:* 800-940-6123 ■ *Web:* www.patioshoppers.com	951-696-1700		321
Patoka Lake 3084 N DillaRd Rd Birdseye IN 47513 *Web:* www.in.gov	812-685-2464		565
Patpatia & Associates Inc 1803 Sixth St Ste A Berkeley CA 94710 *Web:* patpatia.com	510-559-7140		195
Patpro Inc 2111 Eisenhower Ave Ste 404 Alexandria VA 22314 *Web:* www.epatpro.com	703-299-8500		41
Patricia Egen Consulting LLC 803 Creek Overlook Chattanooga TN 37415 *Web:* www.egenconsulting.com	423-875-2652		196
Patricia Grand Resort 2710 N Ocean Blvd Myrtle Beach SC 29577 *TF:* 800-255-4763 ■ *Web:* www.oceanaresorts.com	843-448-8453		669
Patricia Lynch Associates Inc 677 Broadway Ste 305 Albany NY 12207 *Web:* www.plynchassociates.com	518-432-9220		463
Patricia Seybold Group 210 Commercial St Boston MA 02109 *TF:* 855-310-0101 ■ *Web:* www.customers.com	617-742-5200	742-1028	463
Patricio Enterprises Inc 125 Wdstream Blvd Stafford VA 22556 *Web:* www.patricioenterprises.com	703-474-4100		463
Patrick & Beatrice Haggerty Museum of Art 13th & Clybourn Sts Marquette University Milwaukee WI 53201 *Web:* www.marquette.edu/haggerty	414-288-7290	288-5415	520
Patrick & Buzarellos LLP 1900 Point W Way Ste 102 Sacramento CA 95815 *Web:* pbpcpas.com	916-920-1604		2
Patrick & Co 560 Market St San Francisco CA 94104 *TF:* 800-323-4329 ■ *Web:* patrickandco.com	415-392-2640	591-0773	535
Patrick Air Force Base 1201 Edward H White Ste C-129 Patrick AFB FL 32925 *Web:* www.patrick.af.mil	321-494-5933		497-1
Patrick County 106 Rucker St PO Box 466 Stuart VA 24171 *Web:* www.co.patrick.va.us	276-694-6094	694-2160	338
Patrick Engineering Inc 4970 Varsity Dr Lisle IL 60532 *TF:* 800-799-7050 ■ *Web:* www.patrickengineering.com	630-795-7200		261
Patrick Henry Community College 645 Patriot Ave Martinsville VA 24112 **Fax:* Admissions ■ *TF:* 855-874-6692 ■ *Web:* www.ph.vccs.edu	276-638-8777	656-0352*	162
Patrick Henry Mall 12300 Jefferson Ave Newport News VA 23602 *Web:* www.shoppatrickhenrymall.com	757-249-4305		460
Patrick Industries Inc 107 W Franklin St PO Box 638 Elkhart IN 46515 *NASDAQ: PATK* ■ *TF:* 800-331-2151 ■ *Web:* www.patrickind.com	574-294-7511	522-5213	115
Patrick Industries Inc Patrick Metals Div 5020 Lincolnway E Mishawaka IN 46544 *TF:* 800-922-9692 ■ *Web:* www.patrickmetals.com	574-255-9692	256-6577	485
Patrick J Kozlowski Accountancy 1127 11th St 225 Sacramento CA 95814	916-448-5191		2
Patrick James Inc 780 W Shaw Ave Fresno CA 93704 *TF:* 888-427-6003 ■ *Web:* www.patrickjames.com	559-224-5500	448-0601	157-3
Patrick Solutions Inc 955 W Third Ave Columbus OH 43212 *Web:* patricksolutions.com	614-255-0300		525
Patrick T Hsu CPA 7927 Garden Grove Blvd Garden Grove CA 92841	714-895-6516		2
Patrick's Hawaiian Cafe 316 SE 123rd Ave Vancouver WA 98683 *Web:* www.hawaiiancafe.com	360-885-0881		671
Patrick's Point State Park 4150 Patrick's Pt Dr Trinidad CA 95570 *Web:* www.parks.ca.gov	707-677-3570		565
Patriot Advertising Inc 1801 E Ave Katy TX 77493 *TF:* 800-793-6543 ■ *Web:* www.patriotadvertising.com	832-239-5775		7
Patriot AM 1150, The 3400 W Olive Ave Ste 550 Burbank CA 91505 *Web:* patriotla.iheart.com	818-559-2252		645
Patriot Buick GMC 4600 E Central Texas Expy Killeen TX 76543 *Web:* patriotcars.com	254-690-7000		516
Patriot Engineering & Environmental Inc 6150 E 75th St Indianapolis IN 46250 *Web:* patrioteng.com	317-576-8058	576-1965	261
Patriot Fire Protection Inc 2707 70th Ave E Fife WA 98424 *Web:* www.patriotfire.com	253-926-2290		610
Patriot Gaming & Electronics Inc 217 N Lindberg St Griffith IN 46319 *Web:* patriotgaming.com	219-922-6400		452
Patriot League 3897 Adler Pl Bethlehem PA 18017 *Web:* www.patriotleague.org	610-691-2414		713
Patriot Ledger 400 Crown Colony Dr PO Box 699159 Quincy MA 02269 *Web:* www.patriotledger.com	617-786-7000	786-7025	532-2
Patriot Machining & Maintenance Services Inc 512 Linden St Franklin OH 45005 *Web:* www.patriotmms.com	937-746-2117		454
Patriot Managed Care Solutions Inc 1800 Augusta Dr Ste 220 Houston TX 77057	713-346-6200	346-6229	177
Patriot National Bancorp Inc 900 Bedford St Stamford CT 06901 *NASDAQ: PNBK* ■ *TF:* 888-728-7468 ■ *Web:* bankpatriot.com	203-251-7200	324-8804	360-2
Patriot Properties Inc 123 Pleasant St Marblehead MA 01945 *TF:* 800-527-9991 ■ *Web:* www.patriotproperties.com	781-586-9670		655
Patriot Rail Company LLC 10060 Skinner Lake Dr Jacksonville FL 32246 *TF:* 855-258-4514 ■ *Web:* www.patriotrail.com	904-423-2540		649
Patriot Security Inc 107 W First St Humble TX 77338 *Web:* www.patriotsecurityinc.com	281-446-3736		693
Patriot Software Inc 2925 E 96th St Ste 100 Indianapolis IN 46240 *Web:* patriotsoftware.net	317-573-5431		179
Patriot Staffing & Services Llc 47 Eggert Ave Metuchen NJ 08840 *TF:* 888-412-6999 ■ *Web:* www.patstaffing.com	888-412-6999		570
Patriot Technologies Inc 5108 Pegasus Ct Ste F Frederick MD 21704 *TF:* 888-417-9899 ■ *Web:* www.patriot-tech.com	301-695-7500	695-4711	177
Patriot Transportation Holding Inc 501 Riverside Ave Ste 500 Jacksonville FL 32202 *NASDAQ: PATI* ■ *TF:* 877-704-1776 ■ *Web:* www.patriottrans.com	877-704-1776		780
Patriot-News 812 Market St Harrisburg PA 17101 *TF:* 800-692-7207 ■ *Web:* www.pennlive.com	717-255-8100		532-2
Patriots Point Naval & Maritime Museum 40 Patriots Pt Rd Mount Pleasant SC 29464 *Web:* www.state.sc.us	803-771-0131		520
Patriots Theater Memorial Dr Trenton NJ 08608 *TF:* 866-847-7682 ■ *Web:* www.state.nj.us	609-984-8484	777-0581	572
Patrizio's Restaurant 1900 Preston Rd Plano TX 75093 *Web:* www.patrizlorestaurant.com	972-964-2200		671
Patrol One 630 S Grand Ave Ste 101 Santa Ana CA 92705 *Web:* www.patrol-one.com	714-541-0999		693
Patrona Corp 1919 S Eads St Ste 202 Arlington VA 22202 *Web:* www.patronacorp.com	571-255-4707		195
Patsy's 72 Seventh Ave Paterson NJ 07524	973-742-9596		671
Patten & Patten Inc 520 Lookout St Chattanooga TN 37403 *TF:* 800-757-3480 ■ *Web:* www.patteninc.com	423-756-3480		194
Patten Industries Inc 635 West Lake St Elmhurst IL 60126 *TF:* 877-688-6812 ■ *Web:* www.pattencat.com	630-279-4400	279-7892	358
Patten Monument Co 3980 W River Dr NE Comstock Park MI 49321 *TF:* 800-627-5371 ■ *Web:* www.pattenmonument.com	616-785-4141		45
Patten University 2433 Coolidge Ave Oakland CA 94601 *TF:* 888-370-7589 ■ *Web:* www.patten.edu	510-261-8500		166
Pattern Insight Inc 465 Fairchild Dr Ste 209 Mountain View CA 94043 *TF:* 866-582-2655 ■ *Web:* patterninsight.com	866-582-2655		177
Patterson Cos Inc 1031 Mendota Heights Rd Saint Paul MN 55120 *NASDAQ: PDCO* ■ *TF:* 800-328-5536 ■ *Web:* www.pattersondental.com	651-686-1600	686-9331	475
Patterson Dental Canada Inc 1205 Henri Bourassa Blvd West Montreal QC H3M3E6 *Web:* www.pattersondental.com/en-ca	514-745-4040		475
Patterson Homestead Historic House Museum Rental Facility 1815 Brown St Dayton OH 45409 *Web:* www.daytonhistory.org	937-222-9724		520

	Phone	Fax	Class
Patterson Office Supplies 3310 N Duncan Rd .... Champaign IL 61822 *TF:* 800-637-1140 ■ *Web:* www.pattersonofficesupplies.com	217-351-5400		110
Patterson Pump Co 2129 Ayersville Rd .... Toccoa GA 30577 *TF:* 800-565-6699 ■ *Web:* www.pattersonpumps.com	706-886-2101	886-0023	641
Patterson State Park c/o Lyman Run State Pk 454 Lyman Run Rd .... Galeton PA 16922 *Web:* www.dcnr.state.pa.us	814-435-5010		565
Patterson-Schwartz & Assoc Inc 7234 Lancaster Pike Ste 100A .... Hockessin DE 19707 *TF:* 877-456-4663 ■ *Web:* www.pattersonschwartz.com	302-234-5270		652
Patterson-UTI Energy Inc 10713 W Sam Houston Pkwy N Ste 800 .... Houston TX 77064 *NASDAQ: PTEN* ■ *TF:* 866-387-1933 ■ *Web:* www.patenergy.com	281-765-7100	765-7175	540
Patti & Sons Inc 8 Berry St .... Brooklyn NY 11249	718-963-1333	388-8671	189-13
Patti Engineering Inc 2110 E Walton Blvd Ste A .... Auburn Hills MI 48326 *TF:* 800-852-0994 ■ *Web:* pattiengineering.com	248-364-3200		261
Pattillo Grounds Management 289 N Price Rd .... Sugar Hill GA 30518	678-288-1010		776
Pattison Sign Group 555 Ellesmere Rd .... Scarborough ON M1R4E8 *TF:* 800-268-6536 ■ *Web:* www.pattisonsign.com	416-759-1111		701
Pattison State Park 6294 S State Rd 35 .... Superior WI 54880 *Web:* dnr.wi.gov/newurl.html	715-399-3111		565
Patton & Patton Software Corp 1796 W Wimbledon Way .... Tucson AZ 85737 *Web:* www.patton-patton.com	520-638-8738		178-8
Patton Electronics Co 7622 Rickenbacker Dr .... Gaithersburg MD 20879 *Web:* www.patton.com	301-975-1000	869-9293	176
Patton Sales Corp 1095 E California St .... Ontario CA 91761 *Web:* www.pattonscorp.com	909-988-0661		320
Patton State Hospital 3102 E Highland Ave .... Patton CA 92369 *Web:* dsh.ca.gov	909-425-7000		374-5
Patton-Kiehl Group Inc 17026 Bull Church Rd .... Woodford VA 22580 *TF:* 888-388-0725 ■ *Web:* www.pattonkiehl.com	804-448-8900		5
Patty Palace Ltd 595 Middlefield Rd .... Scarborough ON M1V3S2 *Web:* pattypalace.net	416-297-0510		297-8
Patuxent Cos 2124 Priest Bridge Dr Ste 18 .... Crofton MD 21114 *TF:* 800-628-4942 ■ *Web:* www.paxcos.com	410-793-0181		189-16
Patuxent River State Park c/o Seneca Creek State Pk 11950 Clopper Rd .... Gaithersburg MD 20878 *Web:* dnr.maryland.gov/publiclands/Pages/central/patuxentriver.aspx	301-924-2127		565
Patuxent Wildlife Research Ctr 12100 Beech Forest Rd .... Laurel MD 20708 *Web:* www.pwrc.usgs.gov	301-497-5500	497-5505	668
Patz & Hall Wine Co 851 Napa Vly Corporate Way Ste A .... Napa CA 94558 *TF:* 877-265-6700 ■ *Web:* www.patzhall.com	707-265-7700		443
Paul Brown Stadium 1 Paul Brown Stadium .... Cincinnati OH 45202 *TF:* 866-621-8383 ■ *Web:* www.bengals.com/stadium/index.html	513-621-3550	621-3570	720
Paul C Buff Inc 2725 Bransford Ave .... Nashville TN 37204 *TF:* 800-443-5542 ■ *Web:* www.paulcbuff.com	615-383-3982	383-0676	439
Paul C Rizzo Assoc Inc 500 Penn Ctr Blvd .... Pittsburgh PA 15235 *Web:* www.rizzoassoc.com	412-856-9700		261
Paul Capital Partners 575 Market St Ste 2500 .... San Francisco CA 94105 *Web:* www.paulcap.com	415-283-4300		792
Paul Casket Co 505 S Green St .... Cambridge City IN 47327	765-478-3991	962-0911	134
Paul Cribbs Insurance Agency Inc 3565 N Crossing Cir .... Valdosta GA 31602 *Web:* paulcribbs.net	229-247-7127		390
Paul D Camp Community College 100 N College Dr PO Box 737 .... Franklin VA 23851 **Fax:* Admissions ■ *TF:* 855-877-3918 ■ *Web:* www.pdc.edu	757-569-6700	569-6795*	162
Hobbs Suffolk 271 Kenyon Rd .... Suffolk VA 23434 **Fax:* Admissions ■ *TF:* 855-877-3918 ■ *Web:* pdc.edu/about/hobbs-suffolk-campus	757-925-6300	925-6370*	162
Paul Davis Systems Canada Ltd 38 Crockford Blvd .... Toronto ON M1R3C2 *TF:* 800-661-5975 ■ *Web:* pauldavis.ca	416-299-8890		192
Paul deLima Co Inc 7546 Morgan Rd .... Liverpool NY 13090 *TF:* 800-962-8864 ■ *Web:* www.delimacoffee.com	315-457-3725	457-3730	296-7
Paul Ecke Ranch Inc 527 Encinitas Ste 104 .... Encinitas CA 92024 *Web:* www.ecke.com	760-753-1134		369
Paul Fredrick Menstyle 223 W Poplar St .... Fleetwood PA 19522 *TF:* 800-247-1417 ■ *Web:* www.paulfredrick.com	610-944-0909	944-6452	157-3
Paul G Allen Family Foundation 505 Fifth Ave S Ste 900 .... Seattle WA 98104 *Web:* www.pgafamilyfoundation.org	206-342-2030		305
Paul Gauguin Cruises Inc 11100 Main St Ste 300 .... Bellevue WA 98004 *Web:* www.pgcruises.com	425-440-6171		31
Paul H Gesswein & Co 255 Hancock Ave .... Bridgeport CT 06605 *TF:* 800-544-2043 ■ *Web:* www.gesswein.com	203-366-5400	366-3953	407
Paul Hanley & Harley Llp 1608 Fourth St Ste 300 .... Berkeley CA 94710 *Web:* www.thepaullawfirm.com	510-559-9980		445
Paul Hastings Janofsky & Walker LLP 515 S Flower St 25th Fl .... Los Angeles CA 90071 *TF:* 800-973-1177 ■ *Web:* www.paulhastings.com	213-683-6000	627-0705	428
Paul Hemmer Construction Co 250 Grandview Dr .... Fort Mitchell KY 41017 *Web:* www.paulhemmer.com	859-341-8300		186
Paul Heuring For 720 N Hobart Rd .... Hobart IN 46342 *Web:* www.paulheuring.com	219-942-3673		57
Paul J Krez Co 7831 N Nagle Ave .... Morton Grove IL 60053 *Web:* www.krezgroup.com	847-581-0017	965-7841	189-9
Paul J Rizzo Conference Ctr *Rizzo Conference Ctr* 150 DuBose House Ln .... Chapel Hill NC 27517 *Web:* www.destinationhotels.com/rizzo-conference-center	919-913-2098	913-2099	377
Paul K Guillow Inc 40 New Salem St PO Box 229 .... Wakefield MA 01880 *TF:* 800-435-9262 ■ *Web:* www.guillow.com	781-245-5255	245-4738	762
Paul Kuhn Gallery 724 11th Ave SW .... Calgary AB T2R0E4 *Web:* www.paulkuhngallery.com	403-263-1162		42
Paul Laurence Dunbar House 219 N Paul Laurence Dunbar St .... Dayton OH 45402 *TF:* 800-860-0148 ■ *Web:* ohiohistory.org	937-224-7061		50-3
Paul M. Grist State Park 1546 Grist Rd .... Selma AL 36701 *TF:* 800-252-7275 ■ *Web:* www.alapark.com	334-872-5846	872-5846	565
Paul May & Associates Inc - Since 1987 17220 Browning Dr .... Orland Park IL 60467 *TF:* 800-201-1206 ■ *Web:* www.paulmayassociates.com	708-479-1111		463
Paul Moak Automotive Inc 740 Larson St .... Jackson MS 39202 *Web:* www.paulmoak.com	601-352-2700		57
Paul Mueller Co 1600 W Phelps St .... Springfield MO 65802 *OTC: MUEL* ■ *TF:* 800-683-5537 ■ *Web:* paulmueller.com	417-831-3000		386
Paul Quinn College 3837 Simpson Stuart Rd .... Dallas TX 75241 *Web:* www.pqc.edu	214-379-5449	379-5448	166
Paul Rand (Sen R - KY) 167 Russell Senate Office Bldg .... Washington DC 20510 *Web:* www.paul.senate.gov	202-224-4343		342-2
Paul Reed Smith Guitars (PRS) 380 Log Canoe Cir .... Stevensville MD 21666 *Web:* www.prsguitars.com	410-643-9970	643-9980	527
Paul Revere's Pizza International Ltd 1570 42nd St NE .... Cedar Rapids IA 52402 *Web:* www.paulreverespizza.com	319-395-9113		670
Paul Risk Assoc Inc 11 W State St .... Quarryville PA 17566 *Web:* www.paulrisk.com	717-786-7308		685
Paul Robeson Theatre *Theatre Alliance of Buffalo* 350 Masten Ave .... Buffalo NY 14209 *TF:* 800-745-3000 ■ *Web:* www.theatrealliancеofbuffalo.com	716-884-2013		572
Paul Sawyier Public Library 319 Wapping St .... Frankfort KY 40601 *Web:* www.pspl.org	502-352-2665	227-2250	434-3
Paul Smith's College 7833 New York 30 PO Box 265 .... Paul Smiths NY 12970 *TF Admissions:* 800-421-2605 ■ *Web:* www.paulsmiths.edu	518-327-6227		166
Paul Stuart Inc Madison Ave & 45th St .... New York NY 10017 *TF Orders:* 800-678-8278 ■ *Web:* www.paulstuart.com	212-682-0320		157-4
Paul T Freund Corp 216 Park Dr .... Palmyra NY 14522 *Web:* www.ptfreund.com	315-597-4873		454
Paul Taylor Dance Co 551 Grand St .... New York NY 10002 *Web:* ptamd.org/ptdc-promo	212-431-5562	966-5673	573-1
Paul W Bryant Museum 300 Paul W Bryant Dr .... Tuscaloosa AL 35487 *TF General:* 866-772-2327 ■ *Web:* bryantmuseum.com	205-348-4668	348-8883	522
Paul Weiss Rifkind Wharton & Garrison LLP 1285 Ave of the Americas .... New York NY 10019 *Web:* www.paulweiss.com	212-373-3000	757-3990	428
Paul Werth Assoc Inc 10 N High St Ste300 .... Columbus OH 43215 *Web:* www.paulwerth.com	614-224-8114		636
Paul Wilmot Communications LLC 581 Sixth Ave .... New York NY 10011 *Web:* www.paulwilmot.com	212-206-7447		636
Paul Wissmach Glass Company Inc 420 Stephen St PO Box 228 .... Paden City WV 26159 *Web:* www.wissmachglass.com	304-337-2253	337-8800	329
Paul's Boutique Inc 99 Rivington St .... New York NY 10002	646-805-0384		157-6
Paul's Fine Italian Dining 3443-B Robinhood Rd .... Winston-Salem NC 27106 *Web:* paulsfineitaliandining.com	336-768-2645		671
Paul's Hauling Ltd 250 Oak Point Hwy .... Winnipeg MB R2R1V1 *TF:* 800-637-5843 ■ *Web:* www.paulshauling.com	204-633-4330		314
Paul's Homewood Cafe 919 W St .... Annapolis MD 21401 *Web:* pauls.publishpath.com	410-267-7891		671
Paula Cooper Gallery 534 W 21st St .... New York NY 10011 *TF:* 800-944-8639 ■ *Web:* www.paulacoopergallery.com	212-255-1105	255-5156	42
Paulaur Corp 105 Melrich Rd .... Cranbury NJ 08512 *Web:* www.paulaur.com	609-395-8844		123
Paulding County 240 Constitution Blvd .... Dallas GA 30132 *TF:* 800-669-8387 ■ *Web:* www.paulding.gov	770-443-7550	443-7537	338
Paulding County 115 N Williams St Ste 101 .... Paulding OH 45879 *Web:* www.pauldingcountyauditor.com	419-399-8205	399-5713	338
Paulding County Carnegie Library 205 S Main St .... Paulding OH 45879 *Web:* www.pauldingcountylibrary.org	419-399-2032		434-3
Paulding County Chamber of Commerce 455 Jimmy Campbell Pkwy .... Dallas GA 30132 *TF:* 800-669-8387 ■ *Web:* www.pauldingchamber.org	770-445-6016	445-3050	139
Paulding-Putman Electric Co-op 910 N Williams St .... Paulding OH 45879 *TF:* 800-686-2357 ■ *Web:* www.ppec.coop	419-399-5015	399-3026	245
Pauler Communications Inc 7271 Engle Rd Ste 309 .... Cleveland OH 44130 *TF:* 800-463-3339 ■ *Web:* townplanner.com	440-243-1229		627
Paulette Wolf Events & Entertainment Inc 1165 N Clark St Ste 613 .... Chicago IL 60610 *Web:* www.pwe-e.com	312-981-2600		184
Pauli Systems Inc 1820 Walters Ct .... Fairfield CA 94533 *TF:* 800-370-1115 ■ *Web:* www.paulisystems.com	707-429-2434		295
Pauline Books & Media 50 St Paul's Ave .... Boston MA 02130 *TF Sales:* 800-876-4463 ■ *Web:* www.pauline.org	617-522-8911	524-8035	637-3
Pauline's 1834 Shelburne Rd .... Burlington VT 05403 *Web:* www.paulinescafe.com	802-862-1081		671

Name / Address	City	State	ZIP	Phone	Fax	Class
Paulo Products Company Inc 5711 W Park Ave *Web:* www.paulo.com	St. Louis	MO	63110	314-647-7500		484
Paulsen Erik (Rep R - MN) 127 Cannon Bldg *Web:* paulsen.house.gov	Washington	DC	20515	202-225-2871	225-6351	342-2
Paulsen Marketing Inc 3510 S First Ave Cir *Web:* www.paulsen.ag	Sioux Falls	SD	57105	605-336-1745		195
Paulson Investment Company Inc 1001 SW Fifth Ave Ste 200 *Web:* www.paulsoninvestment.com	Portland	OR	97204	503-243-6000		690
Paulson Manufacturing Corp 46752 Rainbow Canyon Rd *Web:* www.paulsonmfg.com	Temecula	CA	92592	951-676-2451		596
Paulson Professional Corp 975 Willagillespie Rd	Eugene	OR	97401	541-484-1881		2
Paulus Engineering Inc 2871 E Coronado St *Web:* www.paulusengineering.com	Anaheim	CA	92806	714-632-3975		261
Paulus Sokolowski & Sartor LLC 67 Mountain Blvd Ste B *Web:* www.psands.com	Warren	NJ	07059	732-560-9700		261
Pauwels Canada Inc 101 Rockman St *Web:* www.cgglobal.com	Winnipeg	MB	R3T0L7	204-452-7446		767
PAVAD Medical Inc 40539 Encyclopedia Cir *Web:* www.pavad.com	Fremont	CA	94538	510-226-7300	226-7305	41
Pavco Inc 1935 John Crosland Jr Dr *TF Orders:* 800-321-7735 ■ *Web:* www.pavco.com	Charlotte	NC	28208	704-496-6800	496-6810	145
Pavco Industries Inc PO Box 612 *Web:* www.pavcoind.com	Pascagoula	MS	39568	228-762-3172	762-3170	613
Pavek Museum of Broadcasting 3517 Raleigh Ave *Web:* www.pavekmuseum.org	Saint Louis Park	MN	55416	952-926-8198	929-6105	520
Pavex Inc 4400 Gettysburg Rd *Web:* pavexinc.com	Camp Hill	PA	17011	717-761-1502	761-0329	189-5
Pavilion Financial Corp 1001 Corydon Ave Ste 300 *TF:* 866-954-5101 ■ *Web:* www.pavilioncorp.com	Winnipeg	MB	R3M0B6	204-954-5101		691
Pavliks Com 80 Bell Farm Rd *TF:* 877-728-5457 ■ *Web:* www.pavliks.com	Barrie	ON	L4M5K5	705-726-2966		180
Pavone Inc 1006 Market St *Web:* www.pavone.net	Harrisburg	PA	17101	717-234-8886		4
Pavsner Press Inc 9008 Yellow Brick Rd *TF:* 800-444-7550 ■ *Web:* www.pavsnerpress.com	Baltimore	MD	21237	410-687-7550		627
Pawleys Plantation 70 Tanglewood Dr *TF:* 855-202-4199 ■ *Web:* www.pawleysplantation.com	Pawleys Island	SC	29585	843-237-6000		669
Pawling Central School District 515 Rt 22 *Web:* www.pawlingschools.org	Pawling	NY	12564	845-855-4600		685
Pawling Corp 32 Nelson Hill Rd PO Box 200 **Fax Area Code:* 845 ■ *TF:* 800-431-3456 ■ *Web:* www.pawling.com	Wassaic	NY	12592	800-431-3456	373-9300*	676
Pawnee County 715 Broadway *TF:* 800-950-8742 ■ *Web:* www.pawneecountykansas.com	Larned	KS	67550	620-285-3721	285-2559	338
Pawnee County 500 Harrison St Rm 203 *Web:* www.cityofpawnee.com	Pawnee	OK	74058	918-762-3741		338
Pawnee County 625 Sixth St PO Box 431 *Web:* www.co.pawnee.ne.us	Pawnee City	NE	68420	402-852-2963	852-2963	338
Pawnee State Recreation Area 3900 NW 105th *Web:* outdoornebraska.gov/pawnee	Lincoln	NE	68524	402-796-2362		565
PAWS (Performing Animal Welfare Society) 11435 Simmerhorn Rd *TF:* 800-513-6560 ■ *Web:* www.pawsweb.org	Galt	CA	95632	209-745-2606	745-1809	48-3
Paws Up Outfitters 40060 Paws Up Rd *TF:* 800-473-0687 ■ *Web:* www.pawsup.com	Greenough	MT	59823	406-244-5200		393
Pawtuckaway State Park 128 Mountain Rd *Web:* www.nhstateparks.org	Nottingham	NH	03290	603-895-3031		565
Pawtucket Credit Union 1200 Central Ave *Web:* pcu.org	Pawtucket	RI	02861	401-722-2212		219
Pawtucket Public Library 13 Summer St *TF:* 800-359-3090 ■ *Web:* www.pawtucketlibrary.org	Pawtucket	RI	02860	401-725-3714		434-3
Pax Machine Works Inc PO Box 338 *Web:* www.paxmachine.com	Celina	OH	45822	419-586-2337	586-7123	488
Pax World Fund Family 30 Penhallow St Ste 400 *TF:* 800-767-1729 ■ *Web:* www.paxworld.com	Portsmouth	NH	03801	603-431-8022		528
Paxton & Vierling Steel Co 501 Ave H Carter Lk *TF:* 800-831-9252 ■ *Web:* pvsteelfab.com	Carter Lake	IA	51510	712-347-5500		480
Paxton Co 1111 Ingleside Rd *TF:* 800-234-7290 ■ *Web:* www.paxtonco.com	Norfolk	VA	23502	757-853-6781		770
Paxton Van Lines Inc 5300 Port Royal Rd *TF:* 800-336-4536 ■ *Web:* www.paxton.com	Springfield	VA	22151	703-321-7600		519
Paxton-Mitchell Co 108 S 12th St *Web:* www.paxton-mitchell.com	Blair	NE	68008	402-426-3131	345-6772	307
Pay It Forward House 719 Somonauk St *Web:* www.payitforwardhouse.org	Sycamore	IL	60178	815-762-4882		372
Pay Plus Benefits Inc 1110 N Ctr Pkwy Ste B *TF:* 888-531-5781 ■ *Web:* www.payplusbenefits.com	Kennewick	WA	99336	509-735-1143	735-7668	631
Payce Inc 1220B E Joppa Rd Ste 324 *TF:* 800-729-5910 ■ *Web:* www.paycepayroll.com	Towson	MD	21286	443-279-9000		734
Paychex Inc 911 Panorama Trl S *NASDAQ: PAYX* ■ *TF:* 800-828-4411 ■ *Web:* www.paychex.com	Rochester	NY	14625	585-385-6666		570
Paychex Major Market Services 12647 Alcosta Blvd Ste 200 *TF:* 888-243-9329 ■ *Web:* www.paychex.com	San Ramon	CA	94583	925-242-0700		570
Paycom 7501 W Memorial Rd *TF:* 800-580-4505 ■ *Web:* www.paycomonline.com	Oklahoma City	OK	73142	800-580-4505		734
PayData Payroll Services Inc PO Box 706 *TF:* 800-539-9058 ■ *Web:* www.paydata.com	Essex Junction	VT	05453	802-655-6160		570
Payday Payroll Services 6465 College Park Sq Ste 200 *Web:* www.paydaypayroll.com	Virginia Beach	VA	23464	757-523-0605		570
Payden & Rygel 333 S Grand Ave *TF:* 800-572-9336 ■ *Web:* www.payden.com	Los Angeles	CA	90071	213-625-1900		401
PayEase Inc 2332 Walsh Ave *Web:* www.w-phone.com	Santa Clara	CA	95051	408-567-9300		387
Payette Assoc Inc 290 Congress St 5th Fl *Web:* www.payette.com	Boston	MA	02210	617-895-1000		261
Payette County 1130 Third Ave N Rm 104 *Web:* www.payettecounty.org	Payette	ID	83661	208-642-6000	642-6011	338
PAYjr Inc 4717 Worth St Appartment 2 *Web:* www.payjr.com	Dallas	TX	75246	214-823-5200		226
Payless ShoeSource Inc 3231 SE Sixth Ave *TF:* 877-474-6379 ■ *Web:* www.paylesscorporate.com	Topeka	KS	66607	785-233-5171	368-7519	301
Paylogic 2843 Brownsboro Rd Ste 111 *Web:* www.epaylogic.com	Louisville	KY	40206	502-894-0088		2
Paylogix 1025 Old Country Rd Ste 310 *Web:* paylogix.com	Westbury	NY	11590	516-408-7800		2
Paymaster Technologies Inc 61 Garlisch Dr *TF:* 800-462-4477 ■ *Web:* www.paymastertech.com	Elk Grove Village	IL	60007	847-758-1234		111
Payment America Systems Inc 450 Tenth Cir N *Web:* www.paymentamerica.com	Nashville	TN	37203	615-255-9200		160
Paymetric Inc 1225 Northmeadow Pkwy Ste 110 *TF:* 888-445-4901 ■ *Web:* www.paymetric.com	Roswell	GA	30076	678-242-5281		2
Payne County 315 W Sixth St Ste 202 *Web:* www.paynecounty.org	Stillwater	OK	74074	405-747-8310	747-8304	338
Payne Engineering Co Rt 29 PO Box 70 *TF Orders:* 800-331-1345 ■ *Web:* www.payneng.com	Scott Depot	WV	25560	304-757-7353	757-7305	203
Payne Jr Donald (Rep D - NJ) 132 Cannon HOB *Web:* payne.house.gov	Washington	DC	20515	202-225-3436	225-4160	342-2
Payne Oil Company Inc 962 E Elm St *Web:* payneoil.com	Graham	NC	27253	336-578-0404		316
Payne Printery Inc 3235 Memorial Hwy *TF:* 800-724-3188 ■ *Web:* www.payneinc.net	Dallas	PA	18612	570-675-1147		627
Payne Theological Seminary 1230 Wilberforce Clifton Rd *TF:* 888-816-8933 ■ *Web:* www.payne.edu	Wilberforce	OH	45384	937-376-2946	376-3330	167-3
Payne Trucking Co 10411 Hall Industrial Dr *Web:* www.paynetrucking.com	Fredericksburg	VA	22408	540-898-1346		62-5
Payne, Ross & Associates Advertising Inc 206 E Jefferson St *Web:* www.payneross.com	Charlottesville	VA	22902	434-977-7607		7
PayneCrest Electric & Communications 10411 Baur Blvd *Web:* www.payneelectric.com	Saint Louis	MO	63132	314-996-0400	996-0500	189-4
PayneGroup Inc 1111 Third Ave Ste 2200 *TF:* 888-467-2963 ■ *Web:* www.thepaynegroup.com	Seattle	WA	98101	206-344-8966	344-8268	196
Payne-huber Engineering Inc 8211 E Regal Pl Ste 104 *TF:* 800-545-1148 ■ *Web:* payne-huber.com	Tulsa	OK	74133	918-492-0975		261
Paynes Creek Historic State Park 888 Lake Branch Rd *TF:* 800-326-3521 ■ *Web:* www.floridastateparks.org	Bowling Green	FL	33834	863-375-4717	375-4510	565
Paynes Prairie Preserve State Park 100 Savannah Blvd *Web:* www.floridastateparks.org	Micanopy	FL	32667	352-466-3397		565
Pay-O-Matic Corp 160 Oak Dr *TF:* 888-545-6311 ■ *Web:* www.payomatic.com	Syosset	NY	11791	516-496-4900		141
PayPal Inc PO Box 45950 *Web:* www.paypal.com	Omaha	NE	68145	402-935-2050		251
Paypro Corp 450 Wireless Blvd *TF:* 800-225-5237 ■ *Web:* www.payprocorp.com	Hauppauge	NY	11788	631-777-1100		570
PayReel 211 violet st Ste 100 *Web:* www.payreel.com	Golden	CO	80401	303-526-4900		514
Payright Payroll Service Inc 468 Great Rd (2A) *Web:* www.payrightpayroll.com	Acton	MA	01720	978-263-5004		2
Payroll 1 Inc 34100 Woodward Ave Ste 250 *Web:* www.payroll1.com	Birmingham	MI	48009	248-548-7020		2
Payroll Factory, The 18 E Lancaster Ave *Web:* www.thepayrollfactory.com	Malvern	PA	19355	610-644-4569		570
Payroll Management Inc 348 Miracle Strip Pkwy Ste 39 *Web:* www.pmipeo.com	Fort Walton Beach	FL	32548	850-243-5604		570
Payroll Masters 855 Bordeaux Way *TF:* 800-963-1428 ■ *Web:* www.payrollmasters.com	Napa	CA	94558	707-226-1428		2
Payroll Practitioner's Monthly 3 Bethesda Metro Ctr Ste 250 *TF:* 800-372-1033 ■ *Web:* bna.com/ioma-site-m17179881473	Bethesda	MD	20814	800-372-1033	253-0332	531-2
Payscape Advisors 729 Lambert Dr NE *TF:* 888-351-6565 ■ *Web:* payscape.com/offices/atlanta	Atlanta	GA	30324	888-351-6565		509
Payson Casters Inc 2323 N Delaney Rd *TF:* 800-323-4552 ■ *Web:* www.paysoncasters.com	Gurnee	IL	60031	847-336-6200	782-0158	350
Payson Roundup Newspaper 708 N Beeline Hwy *TF:* 800-253-9405 ■ *Web:* www.paysonroundup.com	Payson	AZ	85541	928-474-5251		532-3
Payspan Inc 7751 Belfort Pkwy Ste 200 *TF:* 877-331-7154 ■ *Web:* www.payspan.com	Jacksonville	FL	32256	877-331-7154		178-1
PayStream Advisors Inc 2923 S Tryon St Ste 240 *Web:* www.paystreamadvisors.com	Charlotte	NC	28203	704-523-7357		195
Payworks Inc 1565 Willson Pl **Fax Area Code:* 204 ■ *TF:* 866-788-3500 ■ *Web:* www.payworks.ca	Winnipeg	MB	R3T4H1	866-788-3500	779-0538*	734

Phone | Fax | Class

Pazazz Printing Inc
5584 Cote-de-Liesse Montreal QC H4P1A9 514-856-3330 627
Web: www.pazazz.com

Pazzaluna 360 St Peter St Saint Paul MN 55102 651-223-7000 671
Web: pazzaluna.com

Pazzo! 853 Fifth Ave S Naples FL 34102 239-434-8494 671
Web: gr8food.net

PB Hoidale Company Inc 3801 W Harry Wichita KS 67213 316-942-1361 791
TF: 800-362-0784 ■ *Web:* www.hoidale.com

PBA (Professional Bowlers Assn)
719 Second Ave Ste 701 Seattle WA 98104 206-332-9688 654-6030 48-22
TF: 800-947-2886 ■ *Web:* www.pba.com

PBA (Professional Beauty Assn)
15825 N 71st St Ste 100 Scottsdale AZ 85254 480-281-0424 905-0708 49-18
TF: 800-468-2274 ■ *Web:* www.probeauty.org

PBA Health 6300 Enterprise Rd Kansas City MO 64120 816-245-5700 231
TF: 800-333-8097 ■ *Web:* pbahealth.com

Pbbs Equipment Corp
N59W16500 Greenway Cir Menomonee Falls WI 53051 262-252-7575 612
TF: 800-236-9620 ■ *Web:* www.pbbs.com

PBCVB (Pine Bluff Convention & Visitors Bureau)
1 Convention Ctr Plaza Pine Bluff AR 71601 870-536-7600 850-2105 206
TF: 800-536-7660 ■ *Web:* www.pinebluffcvb.org

PBE Group, The 1459 Wittens Mill Rd Tazewell VA 24630 276-988-5505 735
Web: pbegrp.com

PBE Warehouse Inc 12171 Pangborn Ave Downey CA 90241 562-803-4691 61
Web: www.pbewarehouse.com

PBEC (Polk-Burnett Electric Co-op)
1001 State Rd 35 Centuria WI 54824 715-646-2191 646-2404 245
TF: 800-421-0283 ■ *Web:* www.polkburnett.com

PBG Builders Inc
1000 NorthChase Dr Ste 307 Goodlettsville TN 37072 615-256-2200 186
TF: 800-925-6085 ■ *Web:* www.pbgbuilders.com

PBHS (Peachford Behavioral Health System)
2151 Peachford Rd Atlanta GA 30338 770-455-3200 374-5
TF: 800-445-1900 ■ *Web:* www.peachford.com

PBI Market Equipment Inc
2667 Gundry Ave Signal Hill CA 90755 562-595-4785 426-2262 300
TF: 800-421-3753 ■ *Web:* www.pbimarketing.com

PBI/Gordon Corp
1217 W 12th St PO Box 014090 Kansas City MO 64101 816-421-4070 474-0462 280
TF: 800-821-7925 ■ *Web:* www.pbigordon.com

PBK Bank Inc 120 Frontier Blvd Stanford KY 40484 606-365-7098 70
TF: 877-230-3711 ■ *Web:* pbkbank.com

PBM Corp 20600 Chagrin Blvd Ste 450 Cleveland OH 44122 216-283-7999 283-7931 39
TF: 800-341-5809 ■ *Web:* www.pbmcorp.com

PBM Graphics Inc 3700 S Miami Blvd Durham NC 27703 919-544-6222 544-6695 627
TF: 800-849-8100 ■ *Web:* www.pbmgraphics.com

PBM Inc 1070 Sandy Hill Rd Irwin PA 15642 724-863-0550 864-9255 790
TF: 800-967-4726 ■ *Web:* www.pbmvalve.com

PBM Plus Inc 300 Techne Ctr Dr Ste B Milford OH 45150 513-248-3071 237
Web: www.pbmplus.com

PBR (Professional Bull Riders Inc)
101 W Riverwalk Pueblo CO 81003 719-242-2800 242-2855 48-15
TF: 800-366-8538 ■ *Web:* www.pbr.com

PBS (Public Broadcasting Service)
2100 Crystal Dr Arlington VA 22202 703-739-5000 739
TF: 866-864-0828 ■ *Web:* www.pbs.org

PBS (Pacific Building Systems)
2100 N Pacific Hwy Woodburn OR 97071 503-981-9581 981-9584 105
TF General: 800-727-7844 ■ *Web:* www.pbsbuildings.com

PBS Engineering & Environmental Inc
4412 SW Corbett Ave Portland OR 97239 503-248-1939 261
Web: pbsenv.com

PBS Supply Company Inc 7013 S 216th St Kent WA 98032 253-395-5550 395-5575 534
TF: 877-727-7515 ■ *Web:* www.pbssupply.com

PBS6
University of Arizona Modern Languages Bldg
1423 E University Blvd Tucson AZ 85719 520-621-5828 741-137
Web: stations.fcc.gov/station-profile/kuat-tv

PBSP (Pelican Bay State Prison)
5905 Lake Earl Dr PO Box 7000 Crescent City CA 95531-7000 707-465-1000 213
TF: 877-256-6877 ■ *Web:* www.cdcr.ca.gov

PC Campana Inc 1374 E 28th St Lorain OH 44055 440-246-6500 492
Web: www.pccampana.com

PC Care Inc 221 Parking Way Lake Jackson TX 77566 979-297-1117 180
TF: 800-460-8070 ■ *Web:* www.pccare-inc.com

PC Connection Inc
730 Milford Rd Rt 101A Merrimack NH 03054 603-683-2000 683-5766 179
NASDAQ: PCCC ■ *TF:* 888-213-0607 ■ *Web:* www.pcconnection.com

PC Connection Inc MacConnection Div
730 Milford Rd Rt 101A Merrimack NH 03054 888-213-0260 179
TF: 888-213-0260 ■ *Web:* www.macconnection.com

PC Doctors LLC 1257 N Eighth St Medford WI 54451 715-748-1911 748-2925 175
Web: pcdrs.com

Pc Focus Computer Co
7500 Mountain Ave Orangevale CA 95662 916-988-0404 177
Web: www.pcfocus.net

PC Godfrey Inc
1816 Rozzells Ferry Rd Charlotte NC 28208 704-334-8604 376-5186 189-10
Web: pcgodfreyservice.com

PC Guardian Anti-Theft Products Inc
2171 E Francisco Blvd Ste G San Rafael CA 94901 415-259-3103 459-1162 180
TF: 800-453-4195 ■ *Web:* www.pcguardian.com

PC Innovations 1555 E Henrietta Rd Rochester NY 14623 585-340-1555 175
TF: 800-337-3808 ■ *Web:* www.pcinnovations.com

PC Jackson Plumbing
3908 Corporation Cir Charlotte NC 28216 704-391-1017 189-10

PC Krause & Associates Inc
3000 Kent Ave West Lafayette IN 47906 765-464-8997 261
Web: pcka.com

Pc Mailing Services Inc
8120 Exchange Dr Ste 100 Austin TX 78754 512-929-7785 5

PC Mall Inc 2555 W 190th St Torrance CA 90504 310-354-5600 179
NASDAQ: PCMI ■ *TF:* 800-555-6255 ■ *Web:* www.pcm.com

PC Professional Inc
1615 Webster St Ste Oakland CA 94612 510-874-5864 175
Web: www.pcprofessional.com

Pc Professor Computer Training & Repair
7056 Beracasa Way Boca Raton FL 33433 561-750-7879 507
TF: 800-973-2022 ■ *Web:* www.pcprofessor.com

PC Richard & Son Inc
150 Price Pkwy Farmingdale NY 11735 631-773-4900 35
TF: 800-696-2000 ■ *Web:* www.pcrichard.com

Pc Treasures Inc 3720 Lapeer Rd Auburn Hills MI 48326 248-969-7800 174
Web: pctreasures.com

Pc Whizdom
297 Daniel Webster Hwy Ste 1 Merrimack NH 03054 603-424-1799 175
Web: www.pcwhizdom.com

PC Works Plus Inc
109 Stadium Dr PO Box 190 Bellwood PA 16617 814-742-9750 180
Web: www.pcworksplus.com

PC World Magazine
501 Second St Ste 600 San Francisco CA 94107 415-243-0505 442-1891 457-7
Web: www.pcworld.com

PC/Nametag 124 Horizon Dr Verona WI 53593 877-626-3824 233-9787* 178-8
**Fax Area Code:* 800 ■ *TF:* 877-626-3824 ■ *Web:* www.pcnametag.com

PCA (Pittsburgh Ctr for the Arts)
6300 Fifth Ave Pittsburgh PA 15232 412-361-0873 361-8338 50-2
Web: center.pfpca.org

PCA (Parking Company of America)
11101 Lakewood Blvd Downey CA 90241 562-862-2118 862-4409 562
Web: www.parkpca.com

PCA (Portland Cement Assn)
5420 Old OrchaRd Rd Skokie IL 60077 847-966-6200 966-9781 49-3
Web: www.cement.org

PCA (Presbyterian Church in America)
1700 N Brown Rd Ste 105 Lawrenceville GA 30043 678-825-1000 825-1001 48-20
Web: www.pcanet.org

PCA Aerospace Inc
17800 Gothard St Huntington Beach CA 92647 714-841-1750 350
Web: www.pcaaerospace.com

PCA Engineering Inc
57 Cannonball Rd PO Box 196 Pompton Lakes NJ 07442 973-616-4501 616-4451 261
TF: 800-666-7221 ■ *Web:* pcaengineering.com/default.asp

PCA Group Inc, The
455 Cayuga Rd Ste 200 Buffalo NY 14225 716-932-7830 177
Web: www.pcatechnologygroup.com

PCA LLC 15 W Aylesbury Rd Timonium MD 21093 410-561-5533 627
Web: www.printpca.com

PCAS-Nanosyn LLC
3331 - B Industrial Dr Santa Rosa CA 95403 707-526-4526 743
Web: nanosyn.com

PCB Group Inc 3425 Walden Ave Depew NY 14043 716-684-0001 684-0987 253
TF: 800-828-8840 ■ *Web:* www.pcb.com

PCBE Inc PO Box 1575 Tacoma WA 98401 253-404-0891 404-0892 457-5
TF: 800-540-8322 ■ *Web:* www.businessexaminer.com

PCC (Pensacola Cultural Ctr)
400 S Jefferson St Pensacola Fl 32502 850-432-2042 572
Web: www.pensacolalittletheatre.com/pcc

PCC Natural Markets Inc
4201 Roosevelt Way NE Seattle WA 98105 206-547-1222 390
TF: 800-903-8823 ■ *Web:* www.pccnaturalmarkets.com

PCC Structurals Inc
4600 SE Harney Dr Portland OR 97206 503-777-3881 306
Web: www.pccstructurals.com

PCCA (Portable Computer & Communications Assn)
PO Box 680 Hood River OR 97031 541-490-5140 410-8447* 48-9
**Fax Area Code:* 413 ■ *Web:* www.pcca.org

PCCI 300 N Lee St Alexandria VA 22314 703-684-2060 256
TF: 800-333-0204 ■ *Web:* www.pccii.com

PCE Pacific Inc 2525 223rd St SE Bothell WA 98021 425-487-9600 358
TF: 800-321-4723 ■ *Web:* www.pcepacific.com

Pce Systems
28530 orchard Lake rd Farmington hills MI 48334 248-932-4888 138
Web: www.pcesystems.com

PCF (Prevent Cancer Foundation)
1600 Duke St Ste 500 Alexandria VA 22314 703-836-4412 836-4413 48-17
TF: 800-227-2732 ■ *Web:* preventcancer.org

PCG (Piedmont Construction Group LLC)
107 Gateway Dr Ste B Macon GA 31210 478-405-8907 405-8908 186
Web: www.piedmontconstructiongroup.com

PCGH (University of Toledo Medical Center, The)
7007 Powers Blvd Parma OH 44129 440-743-3000 743-4386 374-3
TF: 855-292-4292 ■ *Web:* www.uhhospitals.org/parma

PCH Litho Inc 1497 Poinsettia Ave 159 Vista CA 92081 760-798-1190 627
TF: 800-627-5508 ■ *Web:* pchlitho.com

PCHMC (Parkview Community Hospital Medical Ctr)
3865 Jackson St Riverside CA 92503 951-688-2211 374-3
Web: www.pchmc.org

PCI (Pioneer Circuits Inc)
3000 S Shannon St Santa Ana CA 92704 714-641-3132 625
Web: www.pioneercircuits.com

PCI (Peninsula Copper Industries Inc)
220 Calumet St Lake Linden MI 49945 906-296-9918 145
Web: www.pencopper.com

PCI (Protect Controls Inc)
3212 Old Hwy 105 E Conroe TX 77301 713-691-5183 691-0159 105
Web: www.protectcontrols.com

PCI (Phoenix Cable Inc)
145 N Franklin Tpke Ramsey NJ 07446 201-825-9090 116
Web: www.phoenixcable.com

PCI (Precast/Prestressed Concrete Institute)
200 W Adams St Ste 2100 Chicago IL 60606 312-786-0300 786-0353 49-3
Web: www.pci.org

PCI (Project Concern International)
5151 Murphy Canyon Rd Ste 320 San Diego CA 92123 858-279-9690 694-0294 48-5
TF: 877-724-4673 ■ *Web:* www.pciglobal.org

PCI Geomatics Inc
90 Allstate Pkwy Ste 501 Markham ON L3R6H3 905-764-0614 174
Web: www.pcigeomatics.com

PCI Group Inc 11632 Harrisburg Rd Fort Mill SC 29707 803-578-7700 627
TF: 800-589-5651 ■ *Web:* www.pcigroup.com

PCI Group LLC
10801 W Charleston Blvd Ste 650 Las Vegas NV 89135 800-511-1888 260
TF: 800-511-1888 ■ *Web:* www.hillpci.com

	Phone	Fax	Class
PCI Industries Inc 5101 Blue Mound Rd ...... Fort Worth TX 76106 *Web:* www.pottorffcorporate.com	817-509-2300		198
Pci Paper Conversions Inc 6761 Thompson Rd N ...... Syracuse NY 13211	315-437-1641		548
PCI Strategic Management LLC 6811 Benjamin Franklin Dr Ste 200 ...... Columbia MD 21046 *Web:* www.pci-sm.com	410-312-0885		463
PCIO 172 Via Serena ...... Alamo CA 94507 *Web:* www.theportablecio.com	925-552-7953		175
PCiRoads LLC 14123 42nd St NE ...... Saint Michael MN 55376 *Web:* www.pciroads.com	763-497-6100	497-6101	188-4
PCL Construction Enterprises Inc 2000 S Colorado Blvd Ste 2 500 ...... Denver CO 80222 *Web:* www.pcl.com	303-365-6500		186
PCL Construction Group Inc 5410 99th St NW ...... Edmonton AB T6E3P4 *Web:* www.pcl.com	780-733-5000	436-2247	186
PCLD (Pinal County Library District) 92 W Butte Ave ...... Florence AZ 85132 *Web:* www.pinalcountyaz.gov/departments/library	520-866-6457	866-6533	434-3
Pcm Networking 12995 Cleveland Ave Ste 216 ...... Fort Myers FL 33907 *TF:* 800-286-5000 ■ *Web:* www.pcmnetworking.com	239-334-1615		180
PCMA (Pharmaceutical Care Management Assn) 601 Pennsylvania Ave NW ...... Washington DC 20004 *Web:* www.pcmanet.org	202-756-5700		49-8
PCMA (Professional Convention Management Assn) 35 E Wacker Dr Ste 500 ...... Chicago IL 60601 *TF:* 877-827-7262 ■ *Web:* www.pcma.org	312-423-7262	423-7222	49-12
PCMR (Park City Mountain Resort) 1345 Lowell Ave PO Box 39 ...... Park City UT 84060 *TF:* 800-222-7275 ■ *Web:* www.parkcitymountain.com	435-649-8111	647-5374	669
PCMS Datafit Inc 25 Merchant St Executive Centre 3 Ste 400 ..... Cincinnati OH 45246 *Web:* www.pcmsdatafit.com	513-587-3100		177
PCO Services Corp 5840 Falbourne St ...... Mississauga ON L5R4B5 *TF:* 800-800-6754 ■ *Web:* www.orkincanada.ca	905-502-9700		577
PCOM (Philadelphia College of Osteopathic Medicine) 4170 City Ave ...... Philadelphia PA 19131 *TF Admissions:* 800-999-6998 ■ *Web:* www.pcom.edu	215-871-6100		800
PCPS (Pulaski County School District) 202 N Washington Ave ...... Pulaski VA 24301 *Web:* www.pcva.us	540-994-2550		685
PCR (Mid-Atlantic PenFed Realty Berkshire Hathaway HomeServices) 3050 Chain Bridge Rd ...... Fairfax VA 22030 *TF:* 866-225-5778 ■ *Web:* www.penfedrealty.com	703-691-7653	691-7662	655
PCRM (Physicians Committee for Responsible Medicine) 5100 Wisconsin Ave NW Ste 400 ...... Washington DC 20016 *TF:* 866-416-7276 ■ *Web:* www.pcrm.org	202-686-2210	686-2216	49-8
PCS (Portland Ctr Stage) 128 NW Eleventh Ave ...... Portland OR 97209 *TF:* 800-273-1530 ■ *Web:* www.pcs.org	503-445-3700	445-3701	573-4
PCS (Petaluma City Schools) 200 Douglas St ...... Petaluma CA 94952 *Web:* www.petalumacityschools.org	707-778-4813		685
PCS (Precision Computer Services Inc) 175 Constitution Blvd S ...... Shelton CT 06484 *Web:* www.precisiongroup.com	203-929-0000	929-8800	175
PCS Co 34488 Doreka Dr ...... Fraser MI 48026 *TF:* 800-521-0546 ■ *Web:* www.pcs-company.com	586-294-7780		757
PCSB (Putnam County Savings Bank) 2477 Rt 6 PO Box 417 ...... Brewster NY 10509 *Web:* www.pcsb.com	845-279-7101	279-9175	71
PCSC Corp 3541 Challenger St ...... Torrance CA 90503 *Web:* www.pcscsecurity.com	310-303-3600		692
PCSD (Pickens County School District) 1348 Griffin Mill Rd ...... Easley SC 29640 *Web:* www.pickens.k12.sc.us	864-397-1000	855-8159	685
PCT (Power & Composite Technologies LLC) 200 Wallins Corners Rd ...... Amsterdam NY 12010 *Web:* www.pactinc.com	518-843-6825	843-6723	249
PCT Enterprises Inc 145 Middlefield Ct ...... Brentwood CA 94513 *Web:* www.4pct.com	925-634-5552		115
PCTA (Pacific Crest Trail Assn) 1331 Garden Hwy ...... Sacramento CA 95833 *Web:* www.pcta.org	916-285-1846	285-1865	48-23
PCTC (Park County Travel Council) 836 Sheridan Ave PO Box 2454 ...... Cody WY 82414 *TF:* 800-393-2639 ■ *Web:* www.yellowstonecountry.org	307-587-2297	527-6228	206
PCTEL Inc 471 Brighton Dr ...... Bloomingdale IL 60108 *NASDAQ: PCTI* ■ *TF:* 800-323-9122 ■ *Web:* www.pctel.com	630-372-6800	372-8077	178-7
PDA (Presbyterian Disaster Assistance) 100 Witherspoon St ...... Louisville KY 40202 **Fax Area Code:* 502 ■ *TF:* 800-728-7228 ■ *Web:* www.presbyterianmission.org	800-728-7228	569-8039*	48-5
PDA (Property Damage Appraisers Inc) 6100 SW Blvd Ste 200 ...... Fort Worth TX 76109 *TF:* 800-749-7324 ■ *Web:* www.pdacorporation.com	800-749-7324	866-4732	310
PDA (Parental Drug Assn) 4350 East-West Hwy ...... Bethesda MD 20814 *Web:* www.pda.org	301-656-5900	986-1093	49-8
PDC (Porterville Developmental Ctr) 26501 Ave 140 PO Box 2000 ...... Porterville CA 93258 *Web:* www.dds.ca.gov/Porterville/Index.cfm	559-782-2222	784-5630	230
PDC (Petroleum Development Corp) 120 Genesis Blvd PO Box 26 ...... Bridgeport WV 26330 *NASDAQ: PDCE* ■ *TF:* 800-624-3821 ■ *Web:* www.petd.com	303-860-5800		536
PDC Facilities Inc 700 Walnut Ridge Dr ...... Hartland WI 53029 *TF:* 800-545-5998 ■ *Web:* www.pdcbiz.com	262-367-7700	367-7744	186
PDC Machines Inc 1875 Stout Dr ...... Warminster PA 18974 *Web:* www.pdcmachines.com	215-443-9442		454
PDC Productions 3217 N Flood Ave ...... Norman OK 73069 *TF:* 800-277-7491 ■ *Web:* www.pdcproductions.com	405-360-5130		514
PDCA (Painting & Decorating Contractors of America) 2316 Millpark Dr ...... Maryland Heights MO 63043 *TF Cust Svc:* 800-332-7322 ■ *Web:* www.pdca.org	314-514-7322	514-9417	49-3
PDCC (Palm Desert Chamber of Commerce) 72559 Hwy 111 ...... Palm Desert CA 92260 *Web:* www.pdcc.org	760-346-6111	346-3263	139
PDCC (Parksville Chamber of Commerce) PO Box 99 ...... Parksville BC V9P2G3 *Web:* parksvillechamber.com	250-248-3613	248-5210	137
PDE (Pacific Data Electric Inc) 9970 Bell Ranch Dr Ste 109 ...... Santa Fe Springs CA 90670 *Web:* www.pdeinc.com	562-204-3550		787
PDEMC (Pee Dee Electric Membership Corp) 575 US Hwy 52 S ...... Wadesboro NC 28170 *TF:* 800-992-1626 ■ *Web:* www.pdemc.com	704-694-2114	694-9636	245
PDF (Parkinson's Disease Foundation) 1359 Broadway ...... New York NY 10018 *TF:* 800-457-6676 ■ *Web:* www.pdf.org	212-923-4700	923-4778	48-17
PDF Solutions Inc 333 W San Carlos St Ste 700 ...... San Jose CA 95110 *NASDAQ: PDFS* ■ *Web:* www.pdf.com	408-280-7900	280-7915	178-10
PDI 3407 S 31st St ...... Temple TX 76502 *Web:* www.profdata.com	254-771-7100	771-7117	178-1
PDI (Pearlstine Distributors Inc) 1600 Christon Rgonal Pkwy ...... Charleston SC 29492 *TF:* 800-922-1048 ■ *Web:* sc.soeagle.net	843-388-6800	388-6799	443
PDI 4200 Oakleys Ct ...... Richmond VA 23223 *TF:* 800-225-4838 ■ *Web:* smithspower.com/brands/pdi	804-737-9880		729
PDI Financial Group 601 N Lynndale Dr ...... Appleton WI 54914 *TF:* 800-234-7341 ■ *Web:* www.pdifinancial.com	920-739-2303	739-2205	690
PDI Inc 100 American Metro Blvd Ste 201 ...... Hamilton NJ 08619 *NASDAQ: PDII* ■ *TF:* 800-242-7494 ■ *Web:* www.pdi-inc.com	800-242-7494		195
PDK (Phi Delta Kappa International) 408 N Union St ...... Bloomington IN 47407 *TF:* 800-766-1156 ■ *Web:* www.pdkintl.org	812-339-1156	339-0018	48-16
PDM Group LLC 27908 Orchard Lake Rd Ste B ...... Farmington Hills MI 48334 *TF:* 800-683-6457 ■ *Web:* www.thepdmgroup.com	248-626-5500		463
PDM Healthcare 24700 Ctr Ridge Rd Ste 110 ...... Cleveland OH 44145 *Web:* www.pdmhealthcare.com	440-871-1721		194
PDMA (Product Development & Management Assn) 330 N Wabash Ave Ste 2000 ...... Chicago IL 60611 *TF:* 800-232-5241 ■ *Web:* www.pdma.org	312-321-5145		49-12
PdMA Corp 5909-C Hampton Oaks Pkwy ...... Tampa FL 33610 *TF:* 800-476-6463 ■ *Web:* www.pdma.com	813-621-6463		201
PDQ Auto Supply of Manville Inc 240 N First Ave ...... Manville NJ 08835	908-526-0888		57
PDQ Food Stores Inc 2002 Parmenter St ...... Middleton WI 53562 *Web:* www.pdqstores.com	608-831-6600		324
PDQ Legal Services 7890 E McClain Dr Ste 3 ...... Scottsdale AZ 85260	480-556-6660		428
PDQ Manufacturing 2754 Creek Hill Rd ...... Leola PA 17540 *TF:* 800-441-9692 ■ *Web:* www.pdqlocks.com	717-656-4281		350
PDQ Manufacturing Inc 1698 Scheuring Rd ...... De Pere WI 54115 *TF:* 800-227-3373 ■ *Web:* www.pdqinc.com	920-983-8333	983-8330	386
PDQ Print Center Inc 27 Stauffer Industrial Pkÿ ...... Taylor PA 18517 *Web:* www.pdqprint.com	570-343-0414		627
PDQ Printing Inc 3820 S Vly View Blvd ...... Las Vegas NV 89103 *Web:* www.pdqvegas.com	702-876-3235		627
PDR Certified Public Accountants Inc 29750 US Hwy 19 N ...... Clearwater FL 33761 *Web:* pdr-cpa.com	727-785-4447		2
PDRA (Paint & Decorating Retailers Assn) 1401 Triad Ctr Dr ...... Saint Peters MO 63376 *TF:* 800-737-0107 ■ *Web:* www.pdra.org	636-326-2636		49-18
PDS (Personnel Data Systems Inc) 470 Norriftown Rd ...... Blue Bell PA 19422 *TF:* 800-243-8737 ■ *Web:* www.pdssoftware.com	610-238-4600	238-4550	178-1
PDS (Packaging Distribution Services Inc) 2308 Sunset Rd ...... Des Moines IA 50321 *TF:* 800-747-2699 ■ *Web:* www.pdspack.com	515-243-3156	243-1741	559
PDS Development 15190 Marsh Ln ...... Addison TX 75001	972-497-9000		393
PDS Gaming Corp 6280 Annie Oakley Dr ...... Las Vegas NV 89120 *TF:* 800-479-3612 ■ *Web:* www.pdsgaming.com	702-736-0700	740-8692	216
PDX Inc & Affiliates 101 Jim Wright Fwy S ...... Fort Worth TX 76108 *Web:* pdxinc.com	817-246-6760		180
PE Guerin Inc 23 Jane St ...... New York NY 10014 *Web:* www.peguerin.com	212-243-5270	727-2290	350
Pea Ridge National Military Park 15930 Hwy 62 E ...... Garfield AR 72732 *Web:* www.nps.gov	479-451-8122	451-0219	564
Pea River Electric Co-op 1311 W Roy Parker Rd PO Box 969 ...... Ozark AL 36361 *TF:* 800-264-7732 ■ *Web:* www. peariver .com	334-774-2545		245
Peabody & Arnold LLP 600 Atlantic Ave ...... Boston MA 02210 *Web:* www.peabodyarnold.com	617-951-2100	951-2125	428
Peabody Auditorium 600 Auditorium Blvd ...... Daytona Beach FL 32118 *Web:* www.peabodyauditorium.org	386-671-3460	239-6435	572
Peabody Chamber of Commerce (PACC) 24 Main St Ste 28 ...... Peabody MA 01960 *Web:* www.peabodychamber.com	978-531-0384	532-7227	139
Peabody Energy Corp 701 Market St ...... Saint Louis MO 63101 *NYSE: BTU* ■ *Web:* www.peabodyenergy.com	314-342-3400		501
Peabody Energy Corp Peabody Plaza 701 Market St ...... St. Louis MO 63101 *Web:* Www.peabodyenergy.com	314-342-3400		501
Peabody Essex Museum 161 Essex St ...... Salem MA 01970 *TF:* 866-745-1876 ■ *Web:* www.pem.org	978-745-1876	744-6776	520
Peabody Glen Health Care Ctr 199 Andover St ...... Peabody MA 01960 *Web:* ma.care-one.com	978-531-0772		450

Phone | Fax | Class

Peabody Institute Library 82 Main St. .... Peabody MA 01960 978-531-0100 434-3
TF: 800-227-2345 ■ *Web:* www.peabodylibrary.org

Peabody Institute of the Johns Hopkins University
Peabody Conservatory of Music
1 E Mt Vernon Pl .... Baltimore MD 21202 410-659-8110 659-8102 166
TF: 800-368-2521 ■ *Web:* www.peabody.jhu.edu

Peabody Landscape Construction Inc
2253 Dublin Rd .... Columbus OH 43228 614-488-2877 776
Web: www.peabodylandscape.com

Peabody Memphis 149 Union Ave .... Memphis TN 38103 901-529-4000 379
TF: 800-732-2639 ■ *Web:* www.peabodymemphis.com

Peabody Museum of Archaeology & Ethnology
11 Divinity Ave .... Cambridge MA 02138 617-496-1027 495-7535 520
Web: www.peabody.harvard.edu

Peabody Office Furniture Corp
234 Congress St. .... Boston MA 02110 617-542-1902 320
TF: 800-263-2387 ■ *Web:* www.peabodyoffice.com

Peabody Place 100 Peabody Pl Ste 1400 .... Memphis TN 38103 901-260-7348 50-6
Web: www.belz.com

Peabody Properties Inc
536 Granite St. .... Braintree MA 02184 781-794-1000 652
Web: www.ayerlofts.com

Peabody River King State Fish & Wildlife Area
10981 Conservation Rd .... Baldwin IL 62217 618-785-2555 565
Web: www.dnr.state.il.us

Peabody Supply Co Inc PO Box 669 .... Peabody MA 01960 978-532-2200 612
TF: 800-445-5816 ■ *Web:* www.peabodysupply.com

Peace Action 8630 Fenton St .... Silver Spring MD 20910 301-565-4050 565-0850 48-5
TF: 800-228-1220 ■ *Web:* www.peace-action.org

Peace Arch Hospital
15521 Russell Ave .... White Rock BC V4B2R4 604-535-4520 541-5820 374-2
Web: www.pahfoundation.ca

Peace Arch State Park 19 A St .... Blaine WA 98231 360-332-8221 565
Web: www.parks.wa.gov

Peace Bridge Duty Free Inc
1 Peace Bridge Plaza .... Buffalo NY 14213 800-361-1302 241
TF: 800-361-1302 ■ *Web:* www.dutyfree.ca

Peace Corps 1111 20th St NW .... Washington DC 20526 202-692-1040 340-20
TF: 800-424-8580 ■ *Web:* www.peacecorps.gov

Peace Corps Regional Offices
Atlanta Regional Office
1111 20th St NW .... Washington DC 20526 404-562-3456 562-3455 340-20
TF: 855-855-1961 ■ *Web:* www.peacecorps.gov
Chicago Regional Office
230 S Dearborn St Ste 450 .... Chicago IL 60603 312-353-4990 353-4192 340-20
TF: 800-424-8580 ■ *Web:* www.peacecorps.gov
Dallas Regional Office
1100 Commerce St Ste 427 .... Dallas TX 75242 855-855-1961 253-5401* 340-20
**Fax Area Code: 214* ■ *TF:* 855-855-1961 ■ *Web:* www.peacecorps.gov
Denver Regional Office
1999 Broadway Ste 2205 .... Denver CO 80202 855-855-1961 340-20
TF: 855-855-1961 ■ *Web:* www.peacecorps.gov
Los Angeles Regional Office
2361 Rosecrans Ave Ste 155 .... El Segundo CA 90245 310-356-1100 356-1125 340-20
TF: 800-424-8580 ■ *Web:* www.peacecorps.gov
Mid-Atlantic Regional Office
1525 Wilson Blvd Ste 100 .... Arlington VA 22209 202-692-1040 340-20
TF: 800-424-8580 ■ *Web:* www.peacecorps.gov
New York Regional Office
201 Varick St Ste 1025 .... New York NY 10014 212-352-5440 352-5441 340-20
TF: 800-424-8580 ■ *Web:* www.peacecorps.gov
Northwest Regional Office
1601 Fifth Ave Ste 605 .... Seattle WA 98101 206-553-5490 553-2343 340-20
TF: 800-424-8580 ■ *Web:* www.peacecorps.gov
San Francisco Regional Office
1301 Clay St Ste 620-N .... Oakland CA 94612 510-452-8444 452-8441 340-20
TF: 800-424-8580 ■ *Web:* www.peacecorps.gov

Peace Health Medical Group
1162 Willamette St .... Eugene OR 97401 360-734-5400 374-3
Web: peacehealth.org

Peace Operations Training Institute Inc
1309 Jamestown Rd Ste 202 .... Williamsburg VA 23185 757-253-6933 166
Web: peaceopstraining.org

Peace River Chamber of Commerce
10006 96 Ave PO Box 6599 .... Peace River AB T8S1S4 780-624-4166 525-4423* 137
**Fax Area Code: 888* ■ *TF:* 888-525-4423 ■ *Web:* www.peaceriverchamber.com

Peace River Community Health Ctr
10101 68th St. .... Peace River AB T8S1T6 780-624-7500 374-2
Web: www.albertahealthservices.ca

Peace River Electric Cooperative Inc
210 Metheny Rd PO Box 1310 .... Wauchula FL 33873 800-282-3824 201-1814* 245
**Fax Area Code: 866* ■ *TF:* 866-201-1814 ■ *Web:* www.preco.coop

Peace River Regional Medical Ctr
2500 Harbor Blvd .... Port Charlotte FL 33952 941-766-4122 374-3
Web: bayfrontcharlotte.com

Peace Wapiti Public School Division No 76
8611 108 St .... Grande Prairie AB T8V4C5 780-532-8133 685
Web: www.pwsd76.ab.ca

Peaceable Kingdom Press
950 Gilman St Ste 200 .... Berkeley CA 94710 877-444-5195 130
TF: 877-444-5195 ■ *Web:* www.peaceablekingdom.com

Peaceful Valley Ranch
475 Peaceful Valley Rd .... Lyons CO 80540 303-747-2881 747-2167 239
TF: 800-955-6343 ■ *Web:* www.peacefulvalley.com

PeaceHealth
1615 Delaware St PO Box 3002 .... Longview WA 98632 360-414-2000 374-3
TF: 800-438-7562 ■ *Web:* www.peacehealth.org

PeaceHealth Laboratories
123 International Way .... Springfield OR 97477 541-341-8010 415
TF: 800-826-3616 ■ *Web:* www.peacehealthlabs.org

PeaceHealth St Joseph Medical Ctr
2901 Squalicum Pkwy .... Bellingham WA 98225 360-734-5400 374-3
TF: 800-541-7209 ■ *Web:* www.peacehealth.org

Peach County 205 W Church St .... Fort Valley GA 31030 478-825-2535 825-2678 338
Web: www.peachcounty.net

Peach County School District Inc
523 Vineville St .... Fort Valley GA 31030 478-825-5933 825-9970 685
TF: 866-632-9992 ■ *Web:* www.peachschools.org

Phone | Fax | Class

Peach Farm 4 Tyler St .... Boston MA 02111 617-482-1116 671
Web: peachfarmboston.com

Peach State Ambulance Inc
105 Peach State Ct .... Tyrone GA 30290 678-364-0003 30

Peach State Integrated Technologies Inc
3005 Business Pk Dr .... Norcross GA 30071 678-327-2000 327-2030 386
TF: 800-998-6517 ■ *Web:* www.peachstate.com

Peach State Labs Inc (PSL)
180 Burlington Rd PO Box 1087 .... Rome GA 30162 706-291-8743 145
TF: 800-634-1653 ■ *Web:* www.peachstatelabs.com

Peach Trader Inc 6286 Dawson Blvd .... Norcross GA 30093 404-752-6715 791
TF: 888-949-9613 ■ *Web:* www.acitydiscount.com

Peach Tree 6800 Eastwood Tfwy .... Kansas City MO 64129 816-923-0099 671
Web: www.peachtreerestaurants.com

Peachford Behavioral Health System (PBHS)
2151 Peachford Rd .... Atlanta GA 30338 770-455-3200 374-5
TF: 800-445-1900 ■ *Web:* www.peachford.com

Peachin Schwartz & Weingardt Pc
9775 Crosspoint Blvd Ste 100 .... Indianapolis IN 46256 317-574-4280 574-4286 2
Web: www.psw-cpa.com

Peachtree Hotel Group LLC
One Alliance Ctr Ste 430 .... Atlanta GA 30342 404-497-4111 379
Web: www.peachtreehotelgroup.com

Peachtree Packaging Inc
770 Marathon Pkwy .... Lawrenceville GA 30046 770-822-1304 995-8447 8
Web: www.peachtreepackaging.com

Peachtree Planning Corp
5040 Roswell Rd NE .... Atlanta GA 30342 404-260-1600 260-1700 113
TF: 800-366-0839 ■ *Web:* www.peachtreeplanning.com

Peacock Alley 422 E Main St .... Bismarck ND 58501 701-221-2333 671
Web: www.peacock-alley.com

Peacock Cafe 3251 Prospect St NW .... Washington DC 20007 202-625-2740 625-1402 671
Web: www.peacockcafe.com

Peacock Construction Inc
3421 Golden Gate Way .... Lafayette CA 94549 925-283-4550 186
Web: www.peacockconstruction.com

Peacock Suites 1745 S Anaheim Blvd .... Anaheim CA 92805 714-535-8255 379
TF: 800-522-6401 ■ *Web:* www.shellhospitality.com

Peak 10 752 Barret Ave .... Louisville KY 40204 502-315-6015 176
TF: 866-732-5836 ■ *Web:* www.peak10.com

Peak 10 Inc 5150 Mccrimmon Pkwy .... Morrisville NC 27560 704-264-1010 387
Web: www.peak10.com

Peak Completion Technologies Inc
7710 W Hwy 80 .... Midland TX 79706 432-684-4155 539
TF: 800-338-6029 ■ *Web:* peakcompletions.com

Peak Energy Inc PO Box 1110 .... Waynesville NC 28786 828-456-9035 456-9031 324
Web: www.peakenergyonline.com

Peak Environmental Inc
74 Main St 2nd Fl .... Woodbridge NJ 07095 732-326-1010 196
TF: 800-313-2966 ■ *Web:* www.peak-environmental.com

Peak Financial Management Inc
281 Winter St Ste 160 .... Waltham MA 02451 781-487-9500 401
TF: 877-567-9500 ■ *Web:* www.peak-financial.com

Peak International Inc
3432 Greystone Dr Ste 202 .... Austin TX 78731 512-339-4684 124
Web: www.peakf.com

Peak Nutrition Inc
1007 11th Ct PO Box 07 .... Syracuse NE 68446 402-269-2825 799
TF Sales: 800-600-2069 ■ *Web:* www.peaknutrition.com

Peak of the Market
1200 King Edward St .... Winnipeg MB R3H0R5 204-632-7325 297-7
Web: www.peakmarket.com

Peak Oilfield Services Co
2525 C St Ste 201 .... Anchorage AK 99503 907-263-7000 263-7070 539
Web: www.peakalaska.com

Peak Organization Inc, The
25 W 31st St Fl 12 .... New York NY 10001 212-947-6600 463
TF: 800-272-4615 ■ *Web:* www.peakorg.com

Peak Physique Inc 67 Holly Hill Ln .... Greenwich CT 06830 203-625-9595 354

Peak Resorts 17409 Hidden Vly Dr .... Wildwood MO 63025 636-938-7474 549-0064 669
Web: www.peakresorts.com

PEAK Resources Inc 2750 W Fifth Ave .... Denver CO 80204 303-934-1200 180
Web: www.peakresources.com

Peak Sales & Marketing Inc
4751 Lindle Rd Ste 128 .... Harrisburg PA 17111 717-986-0301 195
Web: www.peaksalesmkt.com

Peak Sales Recruiting Inc
64 Beaver St Ste 119 .... New York NY 10004 646-291-8960 41
TF: 800-964-0946 ■ *Web:* www.peaksalesrecruiting.com

Peak Technical Services Inc
583 Epsilon Dr .... Pittsburgh PA 15238 412-696-1080 721
TF: 888-888-7325 ■ *Web:* www.peaktechnical.com

Peak Technologies Inc
10330 Old Columbia Rd .... Columbia MD 21046 800-926-9212 174
TF: 800-926-9212 ■ *Web:* www.peak-ryzex.com

Peak Travel Group 1723 Hamilton Ave .... San Jose CA 95125 800-831-1366 295-5661* 772
**Fax Area Code: 408* ■ *TF:* 800-831-1366 ■ *Web:* www.peaktravelgroup.com

Peak Wellness Center 1263 N 15th St .... Laramie WY 82072 307-745-8915 726
Web: www.peakwellnesscenter.org

Peake DeLancey Printers LLC
2500 Schuster Dr .... Cheverly MD 20781 301-341-4600 627
TF: 800-521-7325 ■ *Web:* www.peakedelancey.com

Peaklogix Inc 14409 Justice Rd .... Midlothian VA 23113 800-849-6332 186
TF: 800-849-6332 ■ *Web:* www.peaklogix.com

Peaks Resort & Golden Door Spa
136 Country Club Dr .... Telluride CO 81435 800-789-2220 669
TF: 800-789-2220 ■ *Web:* www.thepeaksresort.com

Peaks-Kenny State Park
401 State Pk Rd .... Dover-Foxcroft ME 04426 207-564-2003 565
Web: www.maine.gov

Peaksware LLC 2770 Dagny Way Ste 212 .... Lafayette CO 80026 720-406-1839 180
TF: 800-241-4440 ■ *Web:* www.peaksware.com

Peapack-Gladstone Bank
500 Hills Dr Ste 300 PO Box 700 .... Bedminster NJ 07921 908-234-0700 360-2
NASDAQ: PGC ■ *TF:* 800-742-7595 ■ *Web:* www.pgbank.com

Peapod LLC 9933 Woods Dr .... Skokie IL 60077 847-583-9400 583-9494 345
TF: 800-573-2763 ■ *Web:* www.peapod.com

Phone | Fax | Class

Pear Commercial Interiors Inc
1616 Arapahoe St Ste 100 .... Denver CO 80202 303-824-2000 824-2001 320
Web: www.pearcom.com

Pearce & Durick 314 E Thayer Ave .... Bismarck ND 58502 701-223-2890 428
TF: 800-472-2273 ■ *Web:* www.pearce-durick.com

Pearce Bevill Leesburg & Moore Pc
110 Office Pk Dr .... Birmingham AL 35223 205-323-5440 328-8523 2
Web: www.pearcebevill.com

Pearce Steve (Rep R - NM)
2432 Rayburn Bldg .... Washington DC 20515 202-225-2365 342-2
Web: pearce.house.gov

Pearl City High School
100 S Summit St .... Pearl City IL 61062 815-443-2715 685
Web: www.pcwolves.net

Pearl City Nursing Home
919 Lehua Ave .... Pearl City HI 96782 808-453-1919 793
TF: 800-596-0026 ■ *Web:* pcnh.hawaiinursinghomes.com

Pearl Dragon
15229 W Sunset Blvd .... Pacific Palisades CA 90272 310-459-9790 671
Web: www.thepearldragon.com

Pearl Engineering Corp
110 E Grand Ave PO Box 425 .... Wisconsin Rapids WI 54494 715-424-4008 261
Web: www.pearlengineering.com

Pearl Harbor Federal Credit Union (PHFCU)
94-449 Ukee St .... Waipahu HI 96797 800-987-5583 218-6299* 219
**Fax Area Code:* 808 ■ *TF:* 800-987-5583 ■ *Web:* www.phfcu.com

Pearl Hotel, The 1410 Rosecrans St .... San Diego CA 92106 619-226-6100 226-6161 379
Web: www.thepearlsd.com

Pearl Lake State Park PO Box 750 .... Clark CO 80428 970-879-3922 565
Web: cpw.state.co.us

Pearl Law Group
567 Sutter St 3rd Fl .... San Francisco CA 94102 415-771-7500 41
Web: www.immigrationlaw.com

Pearl Meat Packing Company Inc
27 York Ave .... Randolph MA 02368 781-228-5100 228-5123 473
TF: 800-462-3022 ■ *Web:* www.pearlmeat.com

Pearl Oyster Bar 18 Cornelia St .... New York NY 10014 212-691-8211 671
Web: www.pearloysterbar.com

Pearl River Community College
101 Hwy 11 N .... Poplarville MS 39470 601-403-1000 162
TF: 877-772-2338 ■ *Web:* www.prcc.edu

Pearl River County
200 S Main St PO Box 431 .... Poplarville MS 39470 601-403-2300 338
Web: www.pearlrivercounty.net

Pearl River County Library System
900 Goodyear Blvd .... Picayune MS 39466 601-798-5081 798-5082 434-3
Web: www.pearlriver.lib.ms.us

Pearl River Restaurant
4728 99th St NW .... Edmonton AB T6E5H5 780-435-2015 431-2758 671
Web: www.lusoft.ca/pearlriver

Pearl River Valley Electric Power Assn
1422 Hwy 13 N PO Box 1217 .... Columbia MS 39429 601-736-2666 245
TF: 855-277-8372 ■ *Web:* www.prvepa.com

Pearl S Buck Birthplace
8129 Seneca Trl PO Box 126 .... Hillsboro WV 24946 304-653-4430 50-3
Web: www.pearlsbuckbirthplace.com

Pearl Street Grill & Brewery
76 Pearl St .... Buffalo NY 14202 716-856-2337 671
Web: pearlstreetgrill.com

Pearl Therapeutics Inc
200 Saginaw Dr .... Redwood City CA 94063 650-305-2600 231
Web: www.pearltherapeutics.com

Pearl's Oyster Bar
5641 N Classen Blvd .... Oklahoma City OK 73118 405-842-2102 840-0382 671
Web: pearlsokc.com

Pearland Area Chamber of Commerce
6117 Broadway St .... Pearland TX 77581 281-485-3634 485-2420 139
TF: 888-604-5888 ■ *Web:* www.pearlandtexaschamber.us

Pearland Journal 650 FM 1959 .... Houston TX 77034 713-362-7211 922-4499* 532-4
**Fax Area Code:* 281

Pearle Vision Inc 4000 Luxottica Pl .... Mason OH 45040 513-765-4321 543
Web: www.pearlevision.com

Pearlman Industries Inc
6210 S Garfield Ave .... Commerce CA 90040 562-927-5561 295
Web: www.pearlabrasive.com

Pearlridge Ctr 98-1005 Moana Lua Rd .... Aiea HI 96701 808-488-0981 460
Web: www.pearlridgeonline.com

Pearlstine Distributors Inc (PDI)
1600 Charleston Rgonal Pkwy .... Charleston SC 29492 843-388-6800 388-6799 443
TF: 800-922-1048 ■ *Web:* sc.soeagle.net

Pearman Motor Company Ltd 240 N Marcus .... Alto TX 75925 936-858-4188 57
Web: pearmanmotor.com

Pearne & Gordon LLP
1801 E Ninth St Ste 1200 .... Cleveland OH 44114 216-579-1700 428
TF: 800-447-5375 ■ *Web:* www.pearne.com

Pearpoint Inc
72055 Corporate Way .... Thousand Palms CA 92276 760-343-7350 201
TF: 800-688-8094 ■ *Web:* spx.com/en/pearpoint

Pearrygin Lake State Park
561 Bear Creek Rd .... Winthrop WA 98862 509-996-2370 565
Web: www.parks.wa.gov

Pearson & Pipkin Inc
1101 Pennsylvania Ave SE Ste 201 .... Washington DC 20003 202-547-7177 184

Pearson Co 1420 Progress Ave .... High Point NC 27260 336-882-8135 319-2
TF: 800-225-0265 ■ *Web:* www.pearsonco.com

Pearson College
650 Pearson College Dr .... Victoria BC V9C4H7 250-391-2411 166
TF: 800-588-8717 ■ *Web:* www.pearsoncollege.ca

Pearson Dental Supplies Inc
13161 Telfair Ave .... Sylmar CA 91342 818-362-2600 835-3100* 475
**Fax Area Code:* 800 ■ *TF:* 800-535-4535 ■ *Web:* www.pearsondental.com

Pearson Education School Div
1900 E Lake Ave .... Glenview IL 60025 800-348-4474 841-8939* 637-2
**Fax:* Cust Svc ■ *TF:* 800-348-4474 ■ *Web:* www.pearsonschool.com

Pearson Engineering Associates Inc
8825 N 23rd Ave Ste 11 .... Phoenix AZ 85021 602-264-0807 261
TF: 866-747-9754 ■ *Web:* www.peaeng.com

Pearson Foods Corp
1024 Ken O Sha Ind Park Dr SE .... Grand Rapids MI 49508 616-245-50[illegible]
Web: www.pearsonfoods.com

Pearson Group
904 Princess Anne St .... Fredericksburg VA 22401 540-373-4493
Web: pearsonplanners.com

Pearson Inc
1330 Ave of the Americas 7th Fl .... New York NY 10019 212-641-2400 360-3
Web: www.pearson.com

Pearson Packaging Systems
8120 W Sunset Hwy .... Spokane WA 99224 509-838-6226 547
TF: 800-732-7766 ■ *Web:* www.pearsonpkg.com

Pearson Vue 5601 Green Vly Dr .... Bloomington MN 55437 952-681-3000 244
Web: www.pearsonvue.com

Pearson's Candy Co
2140 W Seventh St .... Saint Paul MN 55116 651-698-0356 696-2222 296-8
TF Cust Svc: 800-328-6507 ■ *Web:* pearsonscandy.com

Peasant 194 Elizabeth St .... New York NY 10012 212-965-9511 671
Web: www.peasantnyc.com

Pease & Sons Inc 10601 Waller Rd E .... Tacoma WA 98448 253-531-7700 188
TF: 800-225-6539 ■ *Web:* www.peaseandsons.com

Pease Creek Recreation Area
37270 293rd St .... Geddes SD 57342 605-487-7046 565
Web: www.gfp.sd.gov/state-parks/directory/pease-creek

Pease Industries Inc 7100 Dixie Hwy .... Fairfield OH 45014 513-870-3610 234
Web: www.peasedoors.com

Peavey Electronics Corp
5022 Hartley Peavey Dr .... Meridian MS 39305 601-483-5365 486-1278 52
TF: 877-732-8391 ■ *Web:* www.peavey.com

Peavey Performance Systems
10749 W 84th Terr .... Lenexa KS 66214 913-888-0600 279
Web: www.safetyjackpot.com

Pebble Hill Plantation Hwy 319 .... Thomasville GA 31792 229-226-2344 50-3
TF: 800-628-2866 ■ *Web:* pebblehill.com

Pechanga Resort & Casino
45000 Pechanga Pkwy .... Temecula CA 92592 951-693-1819 695-7410 669
TF: 877-711-2946 ■ *Web:* www.pechanga.com

Pechters Baking 840 Jersey St .... Harrison NJ 07029 973-483-3374 296-1

Peck & Hale LLC 180 Div Ave .... West Sayville NY 11796 631-589-2510 589-2925 678
Web: www.peckhale.com

Peck & Peck CPAs PC 312 S Pacific .... Dillon MT 59725 406-683-4254 2

Peck B G Company Inc 50 Shepard St .... Lawrence MA 01843 978-686-4181 326
TF: 800-832-6405 ■ *Web:* www.bgpeck.com

Peck's Management Partners Ltd
1 Rockefeller Plaza Ste 1427 .... New York NY 10020 212-332-1333 792

Peckham Industries Inc
20 Haarlem Ave .... White Plains NY 10603 914-949-2000 949-2075 46
Web: www.peckham.com

Peco Fasteners Inc 1218 Six Flags Rd .... Austell GA 30168 770-745-1300 350
Web: www.thesefa.com

PECO Foods Inc 3701 Kauloosa Ave .... Tuscaloosa AL 35401 205-345-3955 343-2401 619
TF: 800-624-4493 ■ *Web:* www.pecofoods.com

Peconic Bay Medical Ctr
1300 Roanoke Ave .... Riverhead NY 11901 631-548-6000 548-6048 374-3
Web: www.pbmchealth.org

Pecora Corp 165 Wambold Rd .... Harleysville PA 19438 215-723-6051 799-2518 3
TF: 800-523-6688 ■ *Web:* www.pecora.com

Pecos Benedictine Monastery
Our Lady of Guadalupe Abbey PO Box 1080 .... Pecos NM 87552 505-757-6415 673
Web: www.pecosmonastery.org

Pecos County 103 W Callaghan St .... Fort Stockton TX 79735 432-336-7555 338
Web: www.co.pecos.tx.us

Pecos Enterprise PO Box 2057 .... Pecos TX 79772 432-445-5475 445-4321 532-2
Web: www.pecos.net

Pecos National Historical Park
PO Box 418 .... Pecos NM 87552 505-757-7200 757-7207 564
Web: www.nps.gov/peco

Pedal Valves Inc 13625 River Rd .... Luling LA 70070 985-785-9997 610
TF: 800-431-3668 ■ *Web:* pedalvalve.com

PEDCo E & A Services Inc
11499 Chester Rd Ste 301 .... Cincinnati OH 45246 513-782-4920 261
TF: 800-647-1900 ■ *Web:* www.pedcoea.com

Peddie School 201 S Main St .... Hightstown NJ 08520 609-944-7500 944-7901 622
Web: www.peddie.org

Peddinghaus Corp 300 N Washington Ave .... Bradley IL 60915 815-937-3800 937-4003 455
TF: 800-786-2448 ■ *Web:* www.peddinghaus.com

Pedernales Electric Co-op Inc
PO Box 1 .... Johnson City TX 78636 830-868-7155 868-4767 245
TF: 888-554-4732 ■ *Web:* www.pec.coop

Pedernales Falls State Park
2585 Pk Rd 6026 .... Johnson City TX 78636 830-868-7304 565
Web: tpwd.texas.gov/state-parks/pedernales-falls

Pediatric Home Respiratory Services Inc
2800 Cleveland Ave N .... Roseville MN 55113 651-642-1825 363
TF: 800-225-7477 ■ *Web:* www.pediatrichomeservice.com

Pediatric Services of America Inc
310 Technology Pkwy .... Norcross GA 30092 770-441-1580 363
TF: 800-408-4442 ■ *Web:* www.psahealthcare.com

Pediatric Special Care Inc
17040 W 12 Mile Rd Ste 200 .... Southfield MI 48076 248-557-4800 371
Web: www.pediatricspecialcare.com

Pediatrix Medical Group Inc
1301 Concord Terr .... Sunrise FL 33323 954-384-0175 463
TF: 800-243-3839 ■ *Web:* www.pediatrix.com

Pedigo Products Inc
4000 SE Columbia Way .... Vancouver WA 98661 360-695-3500 567
Web: www.pedigo-usa.com

Pedigree Ski Shop Inc
355 Mamaroneck Ave .... White Plains NY 10605 914-948-2995 711
Web: www.pedigreeskishop.com

Pedigree Technologies
4776 28th Ave S Ste 101 .... Fargo ND 58104 800-470-6581 809
TF: 844-407-9307 ■ *Web:* www.pedigreetechnologies.com

Pedone 49 W 27th St .... New York NY 10001 212-627-3300 627-3966 4
Web: www.pedonepartners.com

Pedorthic Footwear Assn (PFA)
2025 M St NW Ste 800 .... Washington DC 20036 202-367-1145 367-2145 48-17
TF: 800-673-8447 ■ *Web:* www.pedorthics.org

Name / Address	City	State	Zip	Phone	Fax	Class
Pedowitz Group, The 810 Mayfield Rd	Milton	GA	30009	855-738-6584		195
TF: 855-738-6584 ■ *Web:* www.pedowitzgroup.com						
Pedro's 4938 W Glendale Ave	Glendale	AZ	85301	623-937-0807		671
Web: pedrosmexicanfood.com						
Pedro's Mexican Restaurante 3555 E Washington Ave	Madison	WI	53704	608-241-8110	241-8248	671
Web: www.pedrosmadison.com						
Peduzzi Associates Ltd 221 S Alfred St	Alexandria	VA	22314	703-836-7990		196
Web: peduzziassociates.com						
Pee Dee Electric Co-op Inc PO Box 491	Darlington	SC	29540	843-665-4070		245
TF: 866-747-0060 ■ *Web:* pdec.com						
Pee Dee Electric Membership Corp (PDEMC) 575 US Hwy 52 S	Wadesboro	NC	28170	704-694-2114	694-9636	245
TF: 800-992-1626 ■ *Web:* www.pdemc.com						
Peebles Corp, The 2020 Pone de Leon Blvd Ste 907	Coral Gables	FL	33140	305-993-5050		653
Web: www.peeblescorp.com						
Peebles Inc 18910 Park Ave Plaza	Meadville	PA	16335	800-743-8730		229
TF: 800-723-4548 ■ *Web:* www.stage.com/store/?brand=peebles						
Peebles Island State Park 1 Delaware Ave PO Box 295	Waterford	NY	12047	518-237-8643		565
Web: parks.ny.gov/parks/111						
Peeco 7050 W Ridge Rd	Fairview	PA	16415	814-474-5561		454
TF: 800-235-9382 ■ *Web:* www.autodev.com						
Peek 'n Peak Resort 1405 Olde Rd	Clymer	NY	14724	716-355-4141	355-4542	669
TF: 800-772-6906 ■ *Web:* www.pknpk.com						
Peek Properties 258 E Arapaho Rd 160	Richardson	TX	75081	972-783-6040		655
Peel Plastic Products Ltd 49 Rutherford Rd S	Brampton	ON	L6W3J3	905-456-3660		601
Web: www.peelplastics.com						
Peelle Co 373 Nesconset Hwy Ste 311	Hauppauge	NY	11788	905-846-4545	846-2161	234
TF: 800-787-5020 ■ *Web:* www.peelledoor.com						
PeelMaster Packaging Corp 6153 W Mulford St Unit C	Niles	IL	60714	847-966-6161		477
Web: peelmaster.com						
Peer Bearing Co 2200 Norman Dr S	Waukegan	IL	60085	847-578-1000	578-1200*	75
**Fax:* Orders ■ *TF:* 800-433-7337 ■ *Web:* www.peerbearing.com						
PEER Consultants PC 409 12th St SW Ste 603	Washington	DC	20024	202-478-2060	478-2050	192
Web: www.peercpc.com						
Peer Foods Group Inc 1200 W 35th St	Chicago	IL	60609	773-475-2375	927-9859	296-26
TF: 800-365-5644 ■ *Web:* www.peerfoods.com						
PeerDirect Corp 14 Oak Pk	Bedford	MA	01730	781-280-4080		195
Web: www.peerdirect.com						
Peerless Chain Co 1416 E Sanborn St	Winona	MN	55987	507-457-9100	356-1149*	678
**Fax Area Code:* 800 ■ *TF:* 800-533-8056 ■ *Web:* www.peerlesschain.com						
Peerless Cleaners Inc 519 N Monroe St	Decatur	IL	62522	217-423-7703		83
TF: 800-879-7056 ■ *Web:* www.peerlessrestoration.com						
Peerless Concrete Products Co 246 Main St	Butler	NJ	07405	973-838-3060		183
Web: www.peerlessconcrete.com						
Peerless Distributing Co 21700 NW Hwy Ste 1160	Southfield	MI	48075	248-559-1800		579
Peerless Electric Co 1401 W Market St	Warren	OH	44485	330-399-3651		518
TF: 800-676-3651 ■ *Web:* www.peerlesselectric.com						
Peerless Electronics Inc 700 Hicksville Rd	Bethpage	NY	11714	516-594-3500	593-2179	246
TF: 800-285-2121 ■ *Web:* www.peerlesselectronics.com						
Peerless Food Equipment 500 S Vandenmark Rd	Sidney	OH	45365	937-492-4158	492-3688	298
TF: 877-795-7377 ■ *Web:* www.peerlessfood.com						
Peerless Inc 70 Perry St	Buffalo	NY	14203	716-852-4784		111
TF: 800-234-3033 ■ *Web:* www.peerless-inc.com						
Peerless Industrial Group PO Box 949	Clackamas	OR	97015	800-873-1916		678
TF: 800-547-6806 ■ *Web:* www.peerlesschain.com						
Peerless Instrument Company Inc 1966-D Broadhollow Rd	Farmingdale	NY	11735	631-396-6500		203
Web: www.peerless.cwfc.com						
Peerless Insurance Co 62 Maple Ave	Keene	NH	03431	603-352-3221		391-4
TF: 800-542-5385 ■ *Web:* www.peerless-ins.com						
Peerless Lighting Corp 2246 Fifth St	Berkeley	CA	94710	510-845-2760	845-2776	439
Web: www.peerlesslighting.com						
Peerless Maintenance Service Inc PO Box 2772	La Habra	CA	92632	714-871-3380	871-2232	104
Web: www.peerlesssvc.com						
Peerless Manufacturing Co US Hwy 82 E	Shellman	GA	39886	229-679-5353	679-5542	273
TF: 800-225-4617 ■ *Web:* www.peerlessmfg.cc						
Peerless Network Inc 222 S Riverside Plaza Ste 2730	Chicago	IL	60606	312-506-0920		387
TF: 888-380-2721 ■ *Web:* www.peerlessnetwork.com						
Peerless of America Inc 1201 Wabash Ave	Effingham	IL	62401	217-342-0400	342-0412	14
Web: www.peerlessofamerica.com						
Peerless Plastics 510 Willow St	Farmington	MN	55024	651-463-7147		596
Web: www.peerlessplastics.com						
Peerless Pottery Inc 319 S Fifth St	Rockport	IN	47635	800-457-5785	649-6429*	611
**Fax Area Code:* 812 ■ *TF:* 866-457-5785 ■ *Web:* www.peerlesspottery.com						
Peerless Premier Appliance Co 119 S 14th St	Belleville	IL	62222	941-763-3915	235-1771*	36
**Fax Area Code:* 618 ■ *TF:* 800-858-5844 ■ *Web:* www.premierrange.com						
Peerless Products Inc 2403 S Main St	Fort Scott	KS	66701	620-223-4610	224-3107	234
TF: 866-420-4000 ■ *Web:* www.peerless-usa.com						
Peerless Pump Co 2005 Dr Martin Luther King Jr St	Indianapolis	IN	46202	317-925-9661	924-7388	641
TF: 800-879-0182 ■ *Web:* www.peerlesspump.com						
Peerless Saw Co, The 4353 Directors Blvd	Groveport	OH	43125	614-836-5790		273
Web: www.peerlesssaw.com						
Peerless Screw Products Corp 286 Sandbank Rd	Cheshire	CT	06410	203-272-6413		621
Peerless Steak House 2531 N Roan St	Johnson City	TN	37601	423-282-2351	283-0439	671
Web: www.peerlesseatout.com						
Peerless Steel Corp 2450 Austin	Troy	MI	48083	248-528-3200	528-9144	492
TF: 800-482-3947 ■ *Web:* www.peerlesssteel.com						
Peerless Systems Corp 1055 Washington Blvd 8th Fl	Stamford	CT	06901	203-350-0040		178-8
NASDAQ: PRLS ■ *Web:* www.peerless.com						
Peerless Tire Co 5000 Kingston St	Denver	CO	80239	303-371-4300		54
TF: 800-999-7810 ■ *Web:* www.peerlesstyreco.com						
Peerless-Winsmith Inc 172 Eaton St	Springville	NY	14141	716-592-9310		709
Web: www.winsmith.com						
Peery Hotel 110 West 300 South	Salt Lake City	UT	84101	801-521-4300		379
TF: 800-331-0073 ■ *Web:* www.peeryhotel.com						
Peet Frate Line Inc 650 S Eastwood Dr PO Box 1129	Woodstock	IL	60098	815-338-5500	338-1052	780
TF: 800-435-6909 ■ *Web:* www.peetfrateline.com						
Peet's Coffee & Tea Inc 1400 Pk Ave	Emeryville	CA	94608	510-594-2100		159
NASDAQ: GMCR ■ *TF Orders:* 800-999-2132 ■ *Web:* www.peets.com						
Pegasi Energy Resources Corp 218 N Broadway Ave Ste 204	Tyler	TX	75702	903-595-4139		536
Web: www.pegasienergy.com						
Pegasus Engineering Inc 301 W State Rd 434 Ste 309	Winter Springs	FL	32708	407-992-9160		261
Web: www.pegasusengineering.net						
Pegasus Home Health Care 132 N Maryland Ave	Glendale	CA	91206	818-551-1932		363
TF: 800-495-5005 ■ *Web:* www.pegasushomecare.com						
Pegasus International Hotel 501 Southard St	Key West	FL	33040	305-294-9323	294-4741	379
TF: 800-397-8148 ■ *Web:* www.pegasuskeywest.com						
Pegasus Laboratories Inc 8809 Ely Rd	Pensacola	FL	32514	850-478-2770		582
Web: www.pegasuslabs.com						
Pegasus Logistics Group Inc 306 Airline Dr Ste 100	Coppell	TX	75019	469-671-0300	671-0317	449
TF: 800-997-7226 ■ *Web:* www.pegasuslogistics.com						
Pegasus Manufacturing Inc 422 Timber Ridge Rd	Middletown	CT	06457	860-635-8811		697
TF: 800-937-9391 ■ *Web:* www.pegasusmfg.com						
Pegasus Residential LLC 1750 Founders Pkwy Ste 180	Alpharetta	GA	30009	678-347-2802		652
Web: www.pegasusresidential.com						
Pegasus Solutions Co 14000 N Pima Rd Ste 200	Scottsdale	AZ	85260	480-624-6000		335
TF: 800-843-4343 ■ *Web:* www.pegasus.io						
Pegasus Sustainability Solutions Inc 2693 Research Park Dr Ste 201	Fitchburg	WI	53711	888-681-9616		192
TF: 888-681-9616 ■ *Web:* www.pegasus-sustainability.com						
Pegasus Taverna 558 Monroe St	Detroit	MI	48226	313-964-6800	964-0009	671
Web: pegasustavernas.com						
PegasusTSI Inc 5310 Cypress Ctr Dr Ste 200	Tampa	FL	33609	813-876-2424		261
Web: www.pegasustsi.com						
Pegasystems Inc 101 Main St	Cambridge	MA	02142	617-374-9600	374-9620	178-1
NASDAQ: PEGA ■ *Web:* www.pega.com						
Peggy Knight Solutions Inc 1750 Bridgeway	Sausalito	CA	94965	415-289-1777		348
TF: 800-997-7753 ■ *Web:* www.peggyknight.com						
Peggy Lauritsen Design Grp Inc 125 Main St SE Ste 340	Minneapolis	MN	55414	612-623-4200		344
Web: www.pldg.com						
Peggy Notebaert Nature Museum 2430 N Cannon Dr	Chicago	IL	60614	773-755-5100		520
Web: www.naturemuseum.org						
Peg-Perego USA Inc 3625 Independence Dr	Fort Wayne	IN	46808	260-482-8191	484-2940	64
TF Cust Svc: 800-671-1701 ■ *Web:* en.pegperego.com						
Pei Cobb Freed & Partners Architects LLP 88 Pine St	New York	NY	10005	212-751-3122	872-5443	261
Web: www.pcfandp.com						
Pei Wei 7676 E Pinnacle Peak Rd	Scottsdale	AZ	85255	480-888-3000		670
Web: www.peiwei.com						
Pei Wei Asian Diner 7600 N MacArthur Blvd	Irving	TX	75063	972-373-8000		671
Web: peiwei.com						
PEI-Genesis 2180 Hornig Rd	Philadelphia	PA	19116	215-673-0400	552-8022	246
TF: 800-675-1214 ■ *Web:* www.peigenesis.com						
Peirce College 1420 Pine St	Philadelphia	PA	19102	215-545-6400	670-9366*	166
**Fax:* Admissions ■ *TF:* 888-467-3472 ■ *Web:* www.peirce.edu						
Peirce-Phelps Inc 2000 N 59th St	Philadelphia	PA	19131	215-879-7000	879-5141	38
TF: 800-222-2742 ■ *Web:* www.peirce.com						
Peirone Produce Co 9818 W Hallett Rd	Spokane	WA	99224	509-838-3515		297-7
Peirson Patterson LLP 2310 W I-20 Ste 100	Arlington	TX	76017	817-461-5500		428
Web: www.peirsonpatterson.com						
Pekin Area Chamber of Commerce 402 Ct St	Pekin	IL	61554	309-346-2106	346-2104	139
Web: www.pekinchamber.com						
Pekin Daily Times PO Box 430	Pekin	IL	61555	309-346-1111		532-2
TF: 800-888-6397 ■ *Web:* www.pekintimes.com						
Pekin Hospital 600 S 13th St	Pekin	IL	61554	309-347-1151		374-3
Web: www.pekinhospital.org						
Pekin Insurance (FAIA) 2505 Ct St	Pekin	IL	61558	309-346-1161		391-4
TF: 800-322-0160 ■ *Web:* pekininsurance.com						
Pekin Life Insurance Co 2505 Ct St	Pekin	IL	61558	309-346-1161		391-2
OTC: PKIN ■ *TF:* 800-322-0160 ■ *Web:* www.pekininsurance.com						
Pekin Public Library 301 S Fourth St	Pekin	IL	61554	309-347-7111	347-6587	434-3
Web: www.pekinpubliclibrary.org						
Peking 120 Waller Mill Rd	Williamsburg	VA	23185	757-229-2288		671
Web: peking-va.com						
Peking Garden 3306 Ft Blvd	El Paso	TX	79930	915-565-9090		671
Web: pekinggarden2.com						
Peking Garden 1488 University Ave	Saint Paul	MN	55104	651-644-0888	644-1738	671
Web: www.pekinggardenmn.com						
Peking Handicraft Inc 1388 San Mateo Ave	South San Francisco	CA	94080	650-871-3788		361
Web: www.pkhc.com						
Peking House 1125 Van Voorhis Rd	Morgantown	WV	26505	304-598-3333		671
Web: pekinghousewv.com						

Entry	City	State	ZIP	Phone	Fax	Class
Peking Noodle Co Inc 1614 N San Fernando Rd TF: 877-735-4648 ■ Web: www.pekingnoodle.com	Los Angeles	CA	90065	323-223-2023		296-31
Peking Wok 4000 W Dimond Blvd Web: pekingwokak.com	Anchorage	AK	99502	907-248-1648		671
Peko Precision Products Inc 1400 Emerson St TF: 800-669-1535 ■ Web: www.pekoprecision.com	Rochester	NY	14606	585-647-3010	647-1366	454
Pel Hughes Printing Inc 3801 Toulouse St Web: www.pelhughes.com	New Orleans	LA	70119	504-486-8646		627
Pelanchos Mexican Grill 1516 Downtown W Blvd Web: www.pelanchos.com	Knoxville	TN	37919	865-694-9060		671
Pelco 3500 Pelco Way TF: 800-289-9100 ■ Web: www.pelco.com	Clovis	CA	93612	559-292-1981	348-1120	647
Pelco Products Inc 320 W 18th St Web: www.pelcoinc.com	Edmond	OK	73013	405-340-3434		350
Pelco Structural LLC 1501 Industrial Blvd TF: 800-899-7577 ■ Web: www.pelcostructural.com	Claremore	OK	74017	918-283-4004		492
Pelerei Inc 2379 Broad Run Ct Web: www.madelynblair.com	Jefferson	MD	21755	301-371-7100		195
Pelesys Learning Systems Inc Ste 125 - 13500 Maycrest Way Web: www.pelesys.com	Richmond	BC	V6V2N8	604-233-6268		380
Pelham Hotel 444 Common St TF: 888-856-4486 ■ Web: www.thepelhamhotel.com	New Orleans	LA	70130	504-522-4444		379
Pelham Plastics Inc 42 Dick Tracy Dr Web: www.pelhamplastics.com	Pelham	NH	03076	603-886-7226		608
Pelican Aviation 1314 Hangar Dr	New Iberia	LA	70560	337-367-1401		63
Pelican Bay State Prison (PBSP) 5905 Lake Earl Dr PO Box 7000 TF: 877-256-6877 ■ Web: www.cdcr.ca.gov	Crescent City	CA	95531-7000	707-465-1000		213
Pelican Cafe 826 Ocean Dr Web: www.pelicanhotel.com	Miami Beach	FL	33139	305-673-3373		671
Pelican Club 312 Exchange Alley TF: 800-672-6124 ■ Web: www.pelicanclub.com	New Orleans	LA	70130	504-523-1504	522-2331	671
Pelican Grand Beach Resort 2000 N Ocean Blvd TF: 800-525-6232 ■ Web: pelicanbeach.com	Fort Lauderdale	FL	33305	954-568-9431		379
Pelican Ice & Cold Storage Inc 711 Oxley St TF: 800-851-0400 ■ Web: pelicanice.com	Kenner	LA	70062	504-602-0013		380
Pelican Press 5011 Ocean Blvd Ste 206 Web: www.yourobserver.com	Sarasota	FL	34242	941-349-4949		532-4
Pelican Products Inc 147 N Main St TF: 800-542-7344 ■ Web: www.pelican.com	South Deerfield	MA	01373	413-665-2163	665-4801	199
Pelican Rope Works Inc 4001 W Carriage Dr TF: 800-464-7673 ■ Web: www.pelicanrope.com	Santa Ana	CA	92704	714-545-0116	545-7673	208
Pelican's Restaurant 9800 Montgomery Blvd NE Web: pelicansabq.com	Albuquerque	NM	87111	505-298-7678		671
Pelican's Steak & Seafood 130 Shadow Mtn Rd Web: pelicanselpaso.com	El Paso	TX	79912	915-581-1392		671
Pelicans 291 N Air Depot Blvd Web: pelicansok.com	Midwest City	OK	73110	405-732-4392		671
Pelicans Perch Marina & Boatyard 40 Audusson Ave Bayou Chico TF: 800-941-2219 ■ Web: www.pelicansperchmarina.com	Pensacola	FL	32507	850-453-3471	457-1662	465
Pelion Financial Group Inc 369 Lexington Ave Ste 311 Web: www.peliongroup.com	New York	NY	10017	917-639-5450		691
Pelivan Transit 333 S Oak St PO Box B TF: 800-482-4594 ■ Web: www.pelivantransit.org	Big Cabin	OK	74332	918-783-5793		108
Pella Co-op Electric Assn 2615 Washington St TF: 800-619-1040 ■ Web: pella-cea.org	Pella	IA	50219	641-628-1040		245
Pella Corp 102 Main St TF Cust Svc: 877-473-5527 ■ Web: www.pella.com	Pella	IA	50219	641-621-1000		236
Pella Historical Village 507 Franklin St Web: pellahistorical.org	Pella	IA	50219	641-628-4311		520
Pellerin Milnor Corp 700 Jackson St Web: www.milnor.com	Kenner	LA	70062	504-467-9591	469-1849	427
Pellettieri Rabstein & Altman 100 Nassau Pk Blvd TF: 800-432-5297 ■ Web: www.pralaw.com	Princeton	NJ	08540	609-520-0900		428
Pellissippi State Technical Community College 10915 HaRdin Valley Rd *Fax: Admissions ■ Web: www.pstcc.edu	Knoxville	TN	37933	865-694-6400	539-7217*	162
Pelosi Nancy (Rep D - CA) 233 Cannon HOB Web: pelosi.house.gov	Washington	DC	20515	202-225-4965		342-2
Peloton Cycles Inc 1310 E Eisenhower Blvd Web: peloton-cycles.com	Loveland	CO	80537	970-669-5595		711
Peloton Therapeutics Inc 2330 Inwood Rd Ste 226 Web: www.pelotontherapeutics.com	Dallas	TX	75235	972-629-4100		231
Pelvalon Inc 923 Thompson Pl Web: eclipsesystem.com	Sunnyvale	CA	94085	650-276-0130	646-2213	475
Pembina County 301 Dakota St W Ste 1 Web: www.pembinacountynd.gov	Cavalier	ND	58220	701-265-4231	265-4876	338
Pembina Pipeline Corp 585 Eighth Ave SW TSE: PPL ■ TF: 888-428-3222 ■ Web: www.pembina.com	Calgary	AB	T2P1G1	403-231-7500	237-0254	405
Pembina Village Restaurant 333 Pembina Hwy Web: www.pembinavillagerestaurant.com	Winnipeg	MB	R3L2E4	204-477-5439		671
Pembroke Commercial Realty Corp 4460 Corporation Ln Ste 300 Web: www.pembrokerealty.com	Virginia Beach	VA	23462	757-490-3141		652
Pembroke Consulting Inc 1515 Market St Ste 960 Web: www.pembrokeconsulting.com	Philadelphia	PA	19102	215-523-5700	523-5758	463
Pembroke Hill School 400 W 51st St Web: www.pembrokehill.org	Kansas City	MO	64112	816-936-1200		685
Pembroke Hospital 199 Oak St TF: 800-222-2237 ■ Web: arbourhealth.com	Pembroke	MA	02359	781-829-7000		374-5
Pembroke Lakes Mall 11401 Pines Blvd TF: 800-438-7325 ■ Web: www.pembrokelakesmall.com	Pembroke Pines	FL	33026	954-436-3311		460
Pembroke Management Ltd 1002 Sherbrooke St W Ste 1700 TF: 800-667-0716 ■ Web: www.pml.ca	Montreal	QC	H3A3S4	514-848-1991		796
Pembroke Regional Hospital 705 MacKay St TF: 866-996-0991 ■ Web: www.pemreghos.org	Pembroke	ON	K8A1G8	613-732-2811	732-9986	374-2
Pemco Inc 3333 Crocker Ave TF: 888-310-1898 ■ Web: www.pemco-solutions.com	Sheboygan	WI	53082	920-458-2500	458-1265	556
Pemco Ltd 1632 S King St Ste 100 TF: 800-488-3111 ■ Web: www.pemco-limited.com	Honolulu	HI	96826	808-949-0414		463
Pemco World Air Services 4102 N Westshore Blvd Web: www.pemcoair.com	Tampa	FL	33614	813-322-9600		24
PEMCO-Naval Engineering Works Inc 3614 Frederic St Web: www.pemco-inc.com	Pascagoula	MS	39567	228-769-7081		454
Pemcor LLC 2100 State Rd TF: 800-735-1555 ■ Web: www.pemcor.com	Lancaster	PA	17601	717-898-1555		627
Pemex Procurement International Inc 10344 sam houston park dr TF: 888-254-1487 ■ Web: www.pemexprocurement.com	Houston	TX	77064	713-430-3100		536
Pemiscot County 610 Ward Ave Ste 2A Web: www.pemiscotcounty.org	Caruthersville	MO	63830	573-333-4203	333-0440	338
Pemiscot-Dunklin Electric Co-op Hwy 412 W PO Box 509 TF: 800-558-6641 ■ Web: www.pemdunk.com	Hayti	MO	63851	573-757-6641	757-6656	245
Pemko Mfg Company Inc 4226 Transport St TF: 800-283-9988 ■ Web: www.pemko.com	Ventura	CA	93003	805-642-2600	642-4109	326
PEN (Public Education Network) 601 13th St NW Ste 710-S TF: 800-424-9836 ■ Web: www.publiceducation.org	Washington	DC	20005	800-424-9836		48-11
PEN American Ctr 588 Broadway Web: www.pen.org	New York	NY	10012	212-334-1660		48-8
Pen Bay Medical Center 4 Glen Cove Dr # 101 Ste 202 Web: www.penbayhealthcare.org	Rockport	ME	04856	207-596-8000		374-3
PEN Products 2010 E New York St TF: 800-736-2550 ■ Web: www.in.gov	Indianapolis	IN	46201	317-955-6800	234-7635	630
Pen Publishing Interactive Inc 239 s pattie st Web: www.collegefans.com	Wichita	KS	67211	316-651-0551		396
Penacook Place Foundation Inc 150 Water St Web: www.penacookplace.org	Haverhill	MA	01830	978-374-0707		371
Penang Grill 55 Lewis St	Greenwich	CT	06830	203-861-1988		671
Penasco Valley Telecommunications (PVT) 4011 W Main St *Fax Area Code: 575 ■ TF: 800-505-4844 ■ Web: www.pvt.com	Artesia	NM	88210	800-505-4844	746-4142*	736
Pencco Inc 831 Bartlett Rd PO Box 600 TF: 800-864-1742 ■ Web: www.pencco.com	San Felipe	TX	77473	979-885-0005		144
Pence Kelly Construction LLC 2747 Pence Loop SE Web: www.pencekelly.com	Salem	OR	97302	503-587-8129		186
Penco Products Inc 1820 Stonehenge Dr *Fax Area Code: 610 ■ TF: 800-562-1000 ■ Web: www.pencoproducts.com	Oaks	PA	19456	800-562-1000	666-7561*	319-1
Pencom Systems Inc 152 Remsen St Web: www.pencom.com	Brooklyn	NY	11201	718-923-1111	923-6065	631
Pencor Inc 613 Third St Ste 250 Web: www.pencor.com	Palmerton	PA	18071	610-826-2552	826-7626	194
Pencor Services Inc 613 Third St Web: www.pencor.com	Palmerton	PA	18071	610-826-2552		637-2
Pend Oreille County 229 S Garden Ave Web: www.pendoreilleco.org	Newport	WA	99156	509-447-2435		338
Penda Aiken Inc 330 Livingston St TF: 800-570-3118 ■ Web: www.pendaaiken.com	Brooklyn	NY	11217	718-643-4880		260
PendaForm Corp 2344 W Wisconsin St TF: 800-356-7704 ■ Web: pendaform.com/markets_automotive.php	Portage	WI	53901	608-742-5301		60
Pender Correctional Institution 906 Penderlea Hwy Web: www.ncdps.gov	Burgaw	NC	28425	910-259-8735		213
Pender County PO Box 5 Web: www.pendercountync.gov	Burgaw	NC	28425	910-259-1200	259-1402	338
Pender County Public Library 103 S Cowan St PO Box 879 Web: www.pendercountync.gov	Burgaw	NC	28425	910-259-1234		434-3
Pender Memorial Hospital 507 E Fremont St TF: 888-815-5188 ■ Web: www.nhrmc.org	Burgaw	NC	28425	910-259-5451		374-3
Pendle Hill 338 Plush Mill Rd TF: 800-742-3150 ■ Web: www.pendlehill.org	Wallingford	PA	19086	610-566-4507	566-3679	673
Pendleton County 233 Main St Web: pendletoncounty.ky.gov	Falmouth	KY	41040	859-654-4321	654-5047	338
Pendleton County 100 S Main St PO Box 187 Web: www.pendletoncounty.wv.gov	Franklin	WV	26807	304-358-7573	358-2473	338
Pendleton Grain Growers Inc 1000 SW Dorian St PO Box 1248 TF: 800-422-7611 ■ Web: www.pggcountry.com	Pendleton	OR	97801	541-278-5035	276-4839	275
Pendleton Health & Rehabilitation Ctr 44 Maritime Dr TF: 800-515-0839 ■ Web: savaseniorcare.com	Mystic	CT	06355	860-572-1700		450
Pendleton Manor 414 Summit Dr Web: pendletonmanor.com	Greenville	SC	29609	864-271-7562		652

	Phone	Fax	Class
Pendleton Woolen Mills Inc 220 NW Broadway .... Portland OR 97209 *TF:* 800-760-4844 ■ *Web:* www.pendleton-usa.com	503-226-4801	535-5502	155-5
PendoPharm Inc 6111 Royalmount Ave .... Montreal QC H4P2T4 *TF Cust Svc:* 866-926-7653 ■ *Web:* www.pendopharm.com	514-340-5045	733-9684	479
Pendu Manufacturing Inc 718 N Shirk Rd .... New Holland PA 17557 *TF:* 800-233-0471 ■ *Web:* www.pendu.com	717-354-4348	355-2148	821
Penfield Fire Company Inc 1838 Penfield Rd .... Penfield NY 14526 *Web:* www.penfieldfire.org	585-586-2413		186
Penford Corp 7094 S Revere Pkwy .... Centennial CO 80112 *NASDAQ: PENX*	303-649-1900		145
Penfund Bay Adelaide Centre 333 Bay St Ste 610.......... Toronto ON M5H2R2 *Web:* www.penfund.com	416-865-0707		528
Pengate Handling Systems Inc 3 Interchange Pl .... York PA 17406 *Web:* www.pengate.com	717-764-3050		386
Pengo Corp 500 E Hwy 10 .... Laurens IA 50554 *TF Cust Svc:* 800-599-0211 ■ *Web:* www.pengoattachments.com	712-845-2540	845-2497	190
Pengrowth Energy Trust 222 Third Ave SW Ste 2100 .... Calgary AB T2P0B4 *NYSE: PGH* ■ *TF:* 800-223-4122 ■ *Web:* www.pengrowth.com	403-233-0224	265-6251	675
Penguin Air Conditioning Corp 5 Penn Plaza 16th Fl........................ New York NY 10001 *Web:* www.penguinac.com	718-706-6500	706-2536	189-10
Penguin Computing Inc 45800 Northport Loop W .... Fremont CA 94538 *Web:* www.penguincomputing.com	415-954-2800		180
Penguin Group (USA) Inc 375 Hudson St .... New York NY 10014 *TF Sales:* 800-847-5515 ■ *Web:* penguin.com	212-366-2000	366-2933	637-2
Penguin Hotel 1418 Ocean Dr.............. Miami Beach FL 33139 *TF:* 800-235-3296 ■ *Web:* www.penguinsouthbeach.com	305-534-9334		379
Penguin Logistics LLC 4500 Brooktree Rd .... Wexford PA 15090 *Web:* mhfservices.com	724-772-9800		271
Penguin Point Franchise Systems Inc 2691 E US 30 .... Warsaw IN 46580 *TF:* 800-557-5755 ■ *Web:* www.penguinpoint.com	574-267-3107	267-3154	670
Penguin Random House 1745 Broadway........ New York NY 10019 *TF:* 800-733-3000 ■ *Web:* www.penguinrandomhouse.com	212-782-9000	782-5157	637-2
Penguin Random House Inc *Bantam Dell Publishing Group* 1745 Broadway 10th Fl .... New York NY 10019 *TF:* 888-523-9292 ■ *Web:* www.penguinrandomhouse.com	212-782-9000		637-2
Penick Corp 158 Mt Olivet Ave .... Newark NJ 07114 *Web:* www.penickcorp.com	973-621-2800		583
Peniel Solutions LLC 3885 Crestwood Pkwy Ste 275.................. Duluth GA 30096 *TF:* 866-878-2490 ■ *Web:* www.penielsolutions.com	866-878-2490		113
Peninsula Airways Inc 6100 Boeing Ave......................... Anchorage AK 99502 *TF:* 800-448-4226 ■ *Web:* www.penair.com	907-771-2500		25
Peninsula Asset Management Inc 1111 Third Ave W Ste 340 .... Bradenton FL 34205 **Fax Area Code:* 941 ■ *TF:* 800-269-6417 ■ *Web:* www.peninsulaasset.com	000-269-6417	748-2654*	401
Peninsula Ballet Theatre 1880 S Grant St .... San Mateo CA 94402 *Web:* www.peninsulaballet.org	650-342-3262		573-1
Peninsula Beverly Hills 9882 S Santa Monica Blvd .... Beverly Hills CA 90212 *TF:* 800-462-7899 ■ *Web:* www.peninsula.com	310-551-2888	788-2319	379
Peninsula Chamber of Commerce PO Box 6015 .... San Diego CA 92166 *Web:* www.peninsulachamber.com	619-223-1629		139
Peninsula Chicago 108 E Superior St .... Chicago IL 60611 *TF:* 866-288-8889 ■ *Web:* www.peninsula.com	312-337-2888		379
Peninsula Cleaning Service Inc 12610 Patrick Henry Dr Ste A............ Newport News VA 23602 *Web:* www.peninsulacleaning.com	757-833-1603		104
Peninsula College 1502 E Lauridsen Blvd .... Port Angeles WA 98362 *Web:* www.pc.ctc.edu	360-452-9277		162
Peninsula Community Foundation 19101 Peninsula Club Dr.................. Cornelius NC 28031 *Web:* www.thepeninsulacommunityfoundation.org	704-237-0630		303
Peninsula Community Health Services PO Box 960 .... Bremerton WA 98337 *Web:* www.pchsweb.org	360-377-3776	373-2096	374-3
Peninsula Community Theatre 10251 Warwick Blvd PO Box 11056........ Newport News VA 23601 *Web:* www.pctlive.org	757-595-5728		572
Peninsula Copper Industries Inc (PCI) 220 Calumet St........................ Lake Linden MI 49945 *Web:* www.pencopper.com	906-296-9918		145
Peninsula Daily News 305 W First St PO Box 1330............... Port Angeles WA 98362 *TF:* 800-826-7714 ■ *Web:* www.peninsuladailynews.com	360-452-2345	417-3521	532-2
Peninsula Fine Arts Ctr 101 Museum Dr .... Newport News VA 23606 *Web:* www.pfac-va.org	757-596-8175		50-2
Peninsula Gaming Corp 301 Bell St .... Dubuque IA 52001 *Web:* www.diamondjo.com	563-690-4975		133
Peninsula Grill 112 N Market St .... Charleston SC 29401 *TF:* 800-845-7082 ■ *Web:* www.peninsulagrill.com	843-723-0700		671
Peninsula High School 14105 Purdy Dr NW .... Gig Harbor WA 98332 *Web:* www.phs.psd401.net	253-530-4400		685
Peninsula Hospital 1501 Trousdale Dr .... Burlingame CA 94010 *TF:* 800-559-9960 ■ *Web:* www.mills-peninsula.org	650-696-5400		374-3
Peninsula Hospital 2347 Jones Bend Rd....................... Louisville TN 37777 *Web:* www.peninsulabehavioralhealth.org/hospital	865-970-9800		374-5
Peninsula Hospital Ctr (PHC) 51-15 Beach Ch Dr...................... Far Rockaway NY 11691	718-734-2000		374-3
Peninsula Light Co 13315 Goodnough Dr NW .... Gig Harbor WA 98332 *TF:* 888-809-8021 ■ *Web:* www.penlight.org	253-857-5950		245
Peninsula New York 700 Fifth Ave............. New York NY 10019 *TF:* 800-262-9467 ■ *Web:* www.peninsula.com	212-956-2888	903-3949	379
Peninsula Packaging Company LLC 1030 N Anderson Rd .... Exeter CA 93221 *TF:* 800-248-5960 ■ *Web:* peninsulapackaging.com	559-594-6813		601
Peninsula Plastics Co 2800 Auburn Ct .... Auburn Hills MI 48326 *Web:* www.peninsulaplastics.com	248-852-3731		596
Peninsula Regent, The 1 Baldwin Ave .... San Mateo CA 94401 *Web:* www.peninsularegent.com	650-579-5500		672
Peninsula Regional Medical Ctr 100 E Carroll St .... Salisbury MD 21801 *TF:* 800-543-7780 ■ *Web:* www.peninsula.org	410-546-6400	543-7102	374-3
Peninsula State Park 9462 Shore Rd .... Fish Creek WI 54212 *Web:* www.dnr.wi.gov	920-868-3258		565
Peninsula Town Ctr 4410 E Claiborne Sq Ste 212 .... Hampton VA 23666 *Web:* www.peninsulatowncenter.com	757-838-1505		460
Peninsular Cylinder Co 27650 Groesbeck .... Roseville MI 48066 *Web:* www.peninsularcylinders.com	586-775-7211		223
Penland School of Crafts 67 Doras Trl PO Box 37 .... Penland NC 28765 *Web:* www.penland.org	828-765-2359	765-7389	766
Pen-Link Ltd 5944 VanDervoort Dr .... Lincoln NE 68516 *TF:* 800-533-0523 ■ *Web:* www.penlink.com	402-421-8857		177
Penmac Staffing Services Inc 447 South Ave .... Springfield MO 65806 *Web:* www.penmac.com	417-831-9100		260
Penmor Lithographers Inc 8 Lexington St PO Box 2003................. Lewiston ME 04241 *TF:* 800-339-1341 ■ *Web:* penmor.com	207-784-1341		627
Penn Air & Hydraulics Corp 1750 Industrial Hwy .... York PA 17402 *TF:* 888-631-7638 ■ *Web:* www.pennair.com	717-840-8100		641
Penn Aluminum International Inc 1117 N Second St PO Box 490............ Murphysboro IL 62966 *TF All:* 800-445-7366 ■ *Web:* www.pennaluminum.com	618-684-2146		485
Penn Brewery, The 800 Vinial St............ Pittsburgh PA 15212 *Web:* www.pennbrew.com	412-237-9400		671
Penn Color Inc 400 Old Dublin Pk .... Doylestown PA 18901 *TF:* 866-617-7366 ■ *Web:* www.penncolor.com	215-345-6550	345-0270	550
Penn Commercial Inc 242 Oak Spring Rd...................... Washington PA 15301 *TF:* 888-309-7484 ■ *Web:* www.penncommercial.edu	724-222-5330	222-4722	800
Penn Dutch Foods 3201 N State Rd 7........... Margate FL 33063 *TF:* 800-690-8557 ■ *Web:* www.penn-dutch.com	954-974-3900		345
Penn Emblem Co 10909 Dutton Rd............ Philadelphia PA 19154 **Fax Area Code:* 215 ■ *TF:* 800-793-7366 ■ *Web:* www.pennemblem.com	800-793-7366	632-6166*	258
Penn Engineering Components 29045 Ave Penn .... Valencia CA 91355 *Web:* www.pennengineering.com	661-295-2080		295
Penn Fibre Plastics 2434 Bristol Rd .... Bensalem PA 19020 **Fax Area Code:* 215 ■ *TF Cust Svc:* 800-662-7366 ■ *Web:* www.pennfibre.com	800-662-7366	702-9552*	600
Penn Fishing Tackle Manufacturing Co 7 Science Ct .... Columbia PA 29203 *TF:* 800-892-5444 ■ *Web:* pennfishing.com	800-892-5444		710
Penn Foster Career School 925 Oak St .... Scranton PA 18515 *TF:* 800-275-4410 ■ *Web:* pennfoster.edu	570-342-7701		800
Penn Hills Chamber of Commerce 12013 Frankstown Rd...................... Pittsburgh PA 15235 *TF:* 800-559-4880 ■ *Web:* www.pennhillschamber.org	412-795-8741	795-7993	139
Penn Hills School District 260 Aster St .... Pittsburgh PA 15235 *Web:* www.phsd.k12.pa.us	412-793-7000		685
Penn Inc 306 S 45th Ave .... Phoenix AZ 85043 **Fax Area Code:* 888 ■ **Fax:* Cust Svc ■ *TF:* 800-289-7366 ■ *Web:* www.pennracquet.com	800-289-7366	329-7366*	710
Penn Line Service Inc 300 Scottdale Ave.......................... Scottdale PA 15683 *TF All:* 800-448-9110 ■ *Web:* www.pennline.com	724-887-9110	887-0545	188-10
Penn Machine Co 106 Stn St................ Johnstown PA 15905 **Fax Area Code:* 610 ■ *TF:* 800-736-6872 ■ *Web:* www.pennusa.com	814-288-1547	497-3325*	595
Penn Maid Foods Inc 10975 Dutton Rd .... Philadelphia PA 19154 *Web:* www.pennmaid.com	215-824-2800		296-27
Penn Manufacturing Industries Inc 506 Stump Rd...................... Mongtomeryville PA 18936 *Web:* www.pennmfg.com	215-362-1217		757
Penn Mar Castings Inc 500 Broadway .... Hanover PA 17331 *Web:* www.pennmarcastings.com	717-632-4165		492
Penn Metal Fabricators Inc 2103 New Germany Rd.................... Ebensburg PA 15931 *Web:* www.pennmetalfab.com	814-472-6000		198
Penn Mutual 600 Dresher Rd.................. Horsham PA 19044 *TF Cust Svc:* 800-523-0650 ■ *Web:* www.pennmutual.com	215-956-8000	956-7699	391-2
Penn Mutual Life Insurance Co 600 Dresher Rd............................ Horsham PA 19044 *TF Cust Svc:* 800-523-0650 ■ *Web:* www.pennmutual.com	215-956-8000		391-2
Penn National Gaming Inc 825 Berkshire Blvd Ste 200 .... Wyomissing PA 19610 *NASDAQ: PENN* ■ *TF:* 877-565-2112 ■ *Web:* www.hollywoodpnrc.com	877-565-2112		642
Penn National Insurance Co 2 N Second St PO Box 2361................. Harrisburg PA 17101 *TF:* 800-388-4764 ■ *Web:* www.pennnationalinsurance.com	717-234-4941		391-4
Penn Parking Inc 7257 Pkwy Dr Ste 100 .... Hanover MD 21076 *Web:* pennparking.com	410-782-9110		562
Penn Presbyterian Medical Ctr (PPMC) 51 N 39th St........................... Philadelphia PA 19104 *TF:* 800-789-7366 ■ *Web:* pennmedicine.org/penn-presbyterian-medical-center	215-662-8000	662-9212	374-3
Penn Pro Inc 4000 State Rd 60 E PO Box 89................ Mulberry FL 33860 *Web:* www.pennpro.net	863-648-9990		261
Penn Shore Vineyards & Winery 10225 Lake Rd .... North East PA 16428 *TF:* 800-747-0083 ■ *Web:* www.pennshore.com	814-725-8688	725-8689	50-7

Name / Address	City	State	Zip	Phone	Fax	Class
Penn Square Mall 1901 NW Expy	Oklahoma City	OK	73118	405-842-4424		460
Web: www.simon.com						
Penn State College of Medicine						
500 University Dr Rm C1805	Hershey	PA	17033	717-531-6955		167-2
Web: www.pennstatehershey.org						
Penn State Forest						
c/o Bass River State Forest 762 Stage Rd	Tuckerton	NJ	08087	609-296-1114		565
Web: www.njparksandforests.org						
Penn State Health 500 University Dr	Hershey	PA	17033	717-531-6955		769
TF: 800-243-1455 ■ *Web:* www.pennstatehershey.org						
Penn State Milton S Hershey Medical Ctr						
500 University Dr	Hershey	PA	17033	717-531-4196	531-0040	374-3
TF: 800-731-3032 ■ *Web:* hmc.pennstatehealth.org						
Penn State Tool & Die Corp						
260 Westec Dr	Mount Pleasant	PA	15666	724-613-5500		757
TF: 800-442-6908 ■ *Web:* www.pennstatetool.com						
Penn Stater Conference Ctr Hotel						
215 Innovation Blvd	State College	PA	16803	814-863-5000		377
TF: 800-233-7505 ■ *Web:* www.pshs.psu.edu						
Penn Systems Group						
5068 W Chester Pk Ste	Edgemont	PA	19028	610-353-3800		196
TF: 800-650-0035 ■ *Web:* www.pennsys.com						
Penn Treaty Network America Insurance Co						
3440 Lehigh St	Allentown	PA	18103	800-362-0700	967-4616*	391-2
**Fax Area Code:* 610 ■ *TF:* 800-362-0700 ■ *Web:* www.penntreaty.com						
Penn United Technology Inc						
799 N Pike Rd	Cabot	PA	16023	724-352-1507	352-4970	757
TF: 866-572-7537 ■ *Web:* www.pennunited.com						
Penn Veterinary Supply Inc						
53 Industrial Cir	Lancaster	PA	17601	717-656-4121		794
TF: 800-233-0210 ■ *Web:* pennvet.com						
Penn Virginia Corp						
100 Matsonford Rd Ste 200	Radnor	PA	19087	610-687-8900	687-3688	536
NYSE: PVA ■ *TF:* 877-316-5288 ■ *Web:* www.pennvirginia.com						
Penn West Energy Trust						
Penn W Plaza 207 - Ninth Ave SW Ste 200	Calgary	AB	T2P1K3	403-777-2500		675
TF: 866-693-2707 ■ *Web:* www.pennwest.com						
Penn West Petroleum Ltd						
Ninth Ave SW Ste 200	Calgary	AB	T2P1K3	403-777-2500		536
TSE: PWT ■ *TF:* 866-693-2707 ■ *Web:* www.pennwest.com						
Penn's Best Inc PO Box 128	Meshoppen	PA	18630	800-852-3243		780
TF: 800-852-3243 ■ *Web:* www.pennsbest.net						
Penn's Landing						
301 S Columbus Blvd	Philadelphia	PA	19106	215-922-2386	923-2801	50-6
Web: www.delawareriverwaterfront.com						
Penn's View Hotel 14 N Front St	Philadelphia	PA	19106	215-922-7600	922-7642	379
TF: 800-331-7634 ■ *Web:* www.pennsviewhotel.com						
Penn. Manor Senior High School						
100 E Cottage Ave	Millersville	PA	17551	717-872-9520		685
Web: www.pennmanor.net						
Penna State Education Assn Harrisburg						
400 N Third St	Harrisburg	PA	17101	717-255-7000		474
TF: 800-944-7732 ■ *Web:* psea.org						
Pennag Industries Assn						
2215 Forest Hills Dr Ste 39	Harrisburg	PA	17112	717-651-5920		138
Web: pennag.com						
Penn-America Group Inc 420 S York Rd	Hatboro	PA	19040	215-443-3600		360-4
TF: 800-621-5410 ■ *Web:* www.penn-america.com						
Penn-America Insurance Co						
3 Bala Plaza	Bala Cynwyd	PA	19004	215-443-3600	660-8885*	391-4
**Fax Area Code:* 610 ■ *TF:* 800-621-5410 ■ *Web:* www.penn-america.com						
Pennco Tech 3815 Otter St	Bristol	PA	19007	215-785-0111		800
TF General: 844-226-0975 ■ *Web:* www.penncotech.edu						
Penncomp 2050 N Loop West Ste 200	Houston	TX	77018	713-669-0965		196
Web: www.penncomp.com						
Penncorp Servicegroup Inc						
600 N Second St Ste 401	Harrisburg	PA	17101	717-234-2300		635
TF: 800-544-9050 ■ *Web:* www.penncorp.net/default/default.htm						
PennEngineering & Manufacturing Corp						
5190 Old Easton Rd	Danboro	PA	18916	215-766-8853	766-3680	278
TF: 800-237-4736 ■ *Web:* www.pemnet.com						
Pennex Aluminum Company LLC						
50 Community St	Wellsville	PA	17365	717-432-9647		492
Web: www.pennexaluminum.com						
Penney Group Inc						
1309 Topsail Rd Sta A	St. John's	NL	A1B3N4	709-782-3404		360-3
Web: www.penneygroup.ca						
Pennfab Inc 1431 Ford Rd	Bensalem	PA	19020	215-245-1577		492
Web: www.pennfab.com						
Pennfield Corp 2260 Erin Ct	Lancaster	PA	17601	717-299-2561	295-8766	447
Penn-Florida Cos						
1515 N Federal Hwy Ste 306	Boca Raton	FL	33432	561-750-1030		652
Web: www.pennflorida.com						
Pennichuck Corp 25 Manchester St	Merrimack	NH	03054	603-882-5191	913-2362	787
NASDAQ: PNNW ■ *TF:* 800-553-5191 ■ *Web:* www.pennichuck.com						
Pennington County 315 St Joseph St	Rapid City	SD	57701	605-394-2171		338
Web: pennco.org						
Pennington County						
101 Main Ave N PO Box 616	Thief River Falls	MN	56701-0616	218-683-7000	683-7026	338
Web: co.pennington.mn.us						
Pennington School						
112 W Delaware Ave	Pennington	NJ	08534	609-737-1838		622
Web: www.pennington.org						
Pennington Seed Inc 1280 AtlantaHwy	Madison	GA	30650	706-342-1234	342-8071	694
Web: www.pennington.com/lawn-garden/grass-seed						
Pennock Acheson Nielsen Devaney Chartered Accountants						
2201 Toronto Dominion Tower 102 Ave Ste 10088	Edmonton	AB	T5J2Z1	780-496-7774		2
Web: www.pand.ca						
Pennock Co 7135 Colonial Ln	Pennsauken	NJ	08109	215-492-7900		293
Web: www.pennock.com						
PennPIRG (Pennsylvania Public Interest Research Group)						
1420 Walnut St Ste 650	Philadelphia	PA	19102	215-732-3747		633
Web: www.pennpirg.org						
Penn-Plax Inc 35 Marcus Blvd	Hauppauge	NY	11788	631-273-3787		578
Web: www.pennplax.com						
Pennridge Chamber of Commerce						
538 W Market St	Perkasie	PA	18944	215-257-5390	257-6840	139
Web: www.pennridge.com						
Pennridge School District						
1200 N Fifth St	Perkasie	PA	18944	215-257-5011		685
Penn-Roosevelt State Park						
c/o Greenwood Furnace State Pk 15795 Greenwood Rd	Huntingdon	PA	16652	814-667-1800		565
Web: www.dcnr.state.pa.us						
Penns Grove-Carneys Point Regional Board of Education						
100 Iona Ave	Penns Grove	NJ	08069	856-299-4250	299-5226	685
Web: pgcpschools.org						
Pennsauken Free Public Library						
5605 N Crescent Blvd	Pennsauken	NJ	08110	856-665-5959	486-0142	434-3
Web: www.pennsaukenlibrary.org						
PennStuart 208 E Main St	Abingdon	VA	24210	276-628-5151		428
Web: www.pennstuart.com						
PennSuburban Chamber of Commerce						
34 Susquehanna Ave	Lansdale	PA	19446	215-362-9200		139
Web: pennsuburban.org						
Pennswood Village						
1382 Newtown-Langhorne Rd	Newtown	PA	18940	215-968-9110		672
TF: 888-454-1122 ■ *Web:* pennswood.org						
Pennsy Supply Inc 1001 Paxton St	Harrisburg	PA	17104	717-233-4511		182
Web: www.pennsysupply.com						
Pennsylvania						
Administrative Office of the Cts (AOPC) 1515 Market St Ste 1414	Philadelphia	PA	19102	215-560-6300		339-39
Web: www.pacourts.us/judicial-administration						
Aging Dept 555 Walnut St 5th Fl	Harrisburg	PA	17101	717-783-1550	783-6842	339-39
Web: www.aging.state.pa.us						
Agriculture Dept 2301 N Cameron St	Harrisburg	PA	17110	717-787-4737		339-39
Web: www.agriculture.state.pa.us						
Attorney General Strawberry Sq 16th Fl	Harrisburg	PA	17120	717-787-3391	787-8242	339-39
TF: 800-385-1044 ■ *Web:* www.attorneygeneral.gov						
Banking Dept 17 N Second St Ste 1300	Harrisburg	PA	17101	717-783-4721		339-39
TF: 800-722-2657 ■ *Web:* www.dobs.pa.gov						
Child Support Enforcement Bureau PO Box 8018	Harrisburg	PA	17105	717-783-8557		339-39
Web: www.dpw.state.pa.us						
Community & Economic Development Dept 400 N St 4th Fl	Harrisburg	PA	17120	866-466-3972		339-39
TF: 866-466-3972 ■ *Web:* www.newpa.com						
Conservation & Natural Resources Dept 400 Market St 6th Fl	Harrisburg	PA	17101	717-787-2703		339-39
Web: www.dcnr.state.pa.us						
Consumer Advocate 555 Walnut St Fl 5 Forum Pl	Harrisburg	PA	17101	717-783-5048	783-7152	339-39
TF: 800-684-6560 ■ *Web:* www.oca.state.pa.us						
Corrections Dept PO Box 598	Camp Hill	PA	17001	717-728-2573	346-5622	339-39
Web: www.cor.state.pa.us						
Driver & Vehicle Services Bureau 1101 S Front St	Harrisburg	PA	17104	717-787-2977		339-39
TF: 800-932-4600 ■ *Web:* www.dmv.pa.gov						
Education Dept 333 Market St	Harrisburg	PA	17126	717-783-6788		339-39
Web: www.pde.state.pa.us						
Emergency Management Agency 1310 Elmerton Ave	Harrisburg	PA	17110	717-651-2001	651-2021	339-39
Web: pema.pa.gov						
Environmental Protection Dept 400 Market St	Harrisburg	PA	17101	717-783-2300		339-39
Web: www.dep.state.pa.us						
Fish & Boat Commission 1601 Elmerton Ave	Harrisburg	PA	17110	717-705-7800		339-39
Web: www.fish.state.pa.us						
Game Commission 2001 Elmerton Ave	Harrisburg	PA	17110	717-787-4250	772-2411	339-39
Web: www.pgc.state.pa.us						
General Assembly Capitol Bldg	Harrisburg	PA	17120	717-787-5920		339-39
Web: www.legis.state.pa.us						
Governor 508 Main Capitol Bldg	Harrisburg	PA	17120	717-787-2500	772-8284	339-39
Web: www.governor.pa.gov						
Higher Education Assistance Agency 1200 N Seventh St	Harrisburg	PA	17102	800-213-9827	720-3901*	725
**Fax Area Code:* 717 ■ *TF:* 800-213-9827 ■ *Web:* www.pheaa.org						
Historical & Museum Commission 300 N St	Harrisburg	PA	17120	717-787-3362		339-39
Web: www.phmc.state.pa.us						
Homeland Security Office 1800 Elmerton Ave	Harrisburg	PA	17110	717-346-4460		339-39
Web: homelandsecurity.pa.gov						
Housing Finance Agency 211 N Front St	Harrisburg	PA	17101	717-780-3800		339-39
Web: www.phfa.org						
Information Technology Office 209 Finance Bldg	Harrisburg	PA	17120	717-787-5440	787-4523	339-39
Web: www.oit.state.pa.us						
Insurance Dept 1326 Strawberry Sq	Harrisburg	PA	17120	717-787-2317	787-8585	339-39
TF: 877-881-6388 ■ *Web:* www.insurance.pa.gov						
Mental Health & Substance Abuse Office PO Box 2675	Harrisburg	PA	17105	717-787-6443		339-39
Web: www.dhs.pa.gov						
Military & Veterans Affairs Dept Fort Indiantown Gap Bldg 0-47	Annville	PA	17003	717-861-8910	861-8589	339-39
TF: 800-547-2838 ■ *Web:* www.dmva.state.pa.us						
Office of Governor 200 Capitol Bldg 501 N Third St	Harrisburg	PA	17120	717-787-3300		339-39
Web: www.governor.state.pa.us						
Probation & Parole Board 1101 S Front St Ste 5100	Harrisburg	PA	17104	717-787-5699	230-8019	339-39
Web: www.pbpp.state.pa.us						
Public Utility Commission 400 N St Keystone Bldg PO Box 3265	Harrisburg	PA	17120	717-783-1740	787-6641	339-39
TF: 800-692-7380 ■ *Web:* www.puc.state.pa.us						
Public Welfare Dept PO Box 2675	Harrisburg	PA	17105	717-787-2600	772-2062	339-39
Web: Www.dhs.pa.gov						
Revenue Dept Strawberry Sq Rm 1032	Harrisburg	PA	17128	717-787-1382	772-1459	339-39
Web: www.revenue.state.pa.us						

	City	State	ZIP	Phone	Fax	Class
Secretary of the Commonwealth 210 N Office Bldg *Web:* www.dos.state.pa.us	Harrisburg	PA	17120	717-787-5280	787-1734	339-39
Securities Commission 17 N Second St Ste 1300 *Web:* www.dobs.pa.gov	Harrisburg	PA	17101	717-787-2665		339-39
State Ethics Commission PO Box 11470 Rm 309 Finance Bldg *TF:* 800-932-0936 ■ *Web:* www.ethics.state.pa.us	Harrisburg	PA	17108	717-783-1610	787-0806	265
State Parks Bureau 400 Market St Rachel Carson State Office Bldg PO Box 8551 *TF:* 800-637-2757 ■ *Web:* www.dcnr.state.pa.us	Harrisburg	PA	17105	717-787-6640	787-8817	339-39
State Police 1800 Elmerton Ave *Web:* psp.pa.gov	Harrisburg	PA	17110	717-783-5599	705-2185	339-39
State System of Higher Education 2986 N Second St *Web:* www.passhe.edu	Harrisburg	PA	17110	717-720-4000	720-4011	339-39
Supreme Court 468 City Hall *Web:* www.pacourts.us	Philadelphia	PA	19107	215-560-6370		339-39
Transportation Dept 400 N St *TF:* 800-932-4600 ■ *Web:* www.dot.state.pa.us	Harrisburg	PA	17120	717-787-2838		339-39
Treasury Dept 129 Finance Bldg *Web:* www.patreasury.gov	Harrisburg	PA	17120	717-787-2465		339-39
Victims Compensation Assistance Program PO Box 1167 *TF:* 800-233-2339 ■ *Web:* pcv.pccd.pa.gov/Pages/Contact-Directory.aspx	Harrisburg	PA	17108	717-783-5153	787-4306	339-39
Vital Records Div PO Box 1528 PO Box 1528 *TF:* 844-228-3516 ■ *Web:* www.health.pa.gov	New Castle	PA	16103	724-656-3100		339-39
Vocational Rehabilitation Office (OVR) 1521 N Sixth St *TF:* 800-442-6351 ■ *Web:* www.portal.state.pa.us	Harrisburg	PA	17102	717-787-5244		339-39
Workers Compensation Bureau 1171 S Cameron St Rm 324 *TF:* 800-482-2383 ■ *Web:* www.dli.pa.gov/Pages/default.aspx	Harrisburg	PA	17104	717-783-5421		339-39
Workforce Investment Board 901 N Seventh St Ste 103 *Web:* www.paworkforce.state.pa.us	Harrisburg	PA	17120	717-772-4966		259
Pennsylvania AAA Federation 600 N Third St *Web:* www.aaapa.org	Harrisburg	PA	17101	717-238-7192	238-6574	53
Pennsylvania Academy of the Fine Arts *School of Fine Arts* 118 128 N Broad St *TF:* 800-799-7233 ■ *Web:* www.pafa.org	Philadelphia	PA	19102	215-972-7600	569-0153	164
Pennsylvania Academy of the Fine Arts Museum (PAFA) 118 N Broad St *TF:* 800-799-7233 ■ *Web:* www.pafa.org	Philadelphia	PA	19102	215-972-7600	569-0153	520
Pennsylvania Anthracite Heritage Museum McDade Park Bald Mountain Rd Ste 1 *TF:* 800-732-0999 ■ *Web:* anthracitemuseum.org	Scranton	PA	18504	570-963-4804	963-4194	520
Pennsylvania Assn of Realtors 500 N Twelfth St *TF:* 800-555-3390 ■ *Web:* www.parealtor.org	Lemoyne	PA	17043	717-561-1303	561-8796	656
Pennsylvania Assn of Staff Nurses & Allied Professionals (PASNAP) 1 Fayette St Ste 475 *TF:* 800-500-7850 ■ *Web:* www.pennanurses.org	Conshohocken	PA	19428	610-567-2907	567-2915	533
Pennsylvania Avenue National Historic Site 900 Ohio Dr SW 900 Ohio Dr SW *TF:* 800-670-6553 ■ *Web:* www.nps.gov/paav	Washington	DC	20024	202-606-9686		564
Pennsylvania Ballet 1819 John F Kennedy Blvd *TF:* 800-732-0999 ■ *Web:* www.paballet.org	Philadelphia	PA	19103	215-551-7000	551-7224	573-1
Pennsylvania Bar Assn 100 S St *TF:* 800-932-0311 ■ *Web:* www.pabar.org	Harrisburg	PA	17101	717-238-6715	238-1204	72
Pennsylvania Chamber of Business & Industry 417 Walnut St *TF:* 800-225-7224 ■ *Web:* www.pachamber.org	Harrisburg	PA	17101	717-255-3252	255-3298	140
Pennsylvania College of Art & Design 204 N Prince St *TF:* 800-689-0379 ■ *Web:* www.pcad.edu	Lancaster	PA	17603	717-396-7833	396-1339	164
Pennsylvania College of Technology 1 College Ave *TF Admissions:* 800-367-9222 ■ *Web:* www.pct.edu	Williamsport	PA	17701	570-326-3761	321-5551	800
Pennsylvania Convention Ctr 1101 Arch St *TF:* 800-428-9000 ■ *Web:* www.paconvention.com	Philadelphia	PA	19107	215-418-4700		205
Pennsylvania Correctional Industries PO Box 47 *TF General:* 877-673-3724 ■ *Web:* www.cor.pa.gov/pci/pages/default.aspx	Camp Hill	PA	17011	717-425-7292	425-7291	630
Pennsylvania Crusher Corp 600 Abbott Dr *Web:* terrasource.com	Broomall	PA	19008	610-544-7200		190
Pennsylvania Democratic Party 229 State St *Web:* www.padems.com	Harrisburg	PA	17101	717-920-8470	901-7829	616-1
Pennsylvania Dental Assn 3501 N Front St *Web:* www.padental.org	Harrisburg	PA	17110	717-234-5941	232-7169	227
Pennsylvania Dutch Candies 1250 Slate Hill Rd *TF:* 800-233-7082 ■ *Web:* www.padutchcandies.com	Camp Hill	PA	17011	800-233-7082		296-8
Pennsylvania Employees Benefit Trust Fund 150 S 43rd St *Web:* www.pebtf.org	Harrisburg	PA	17111	717-561-4750		41
Pennsylvania Highlands Community College 881 Hills Plaza Dr Ste 450 *TF:* 888-385-7325 ■ *Web:* www.pennhighlands.edu	Ebensburg	PA	15931	814-471-0010	262-6420	162
Pennsylvania Hospital 800 Spruce St *TF:* 800-789-7366 ■ *Web:* www.pennmedicine.org	Philadelphia	PA	19107	215-829-3000		374-3
Pennsylvania Institute of Technology (PIT) 800 Manchester Ave **Fax:* Admissions ■ *TF Admissions:* 800-422-0025 ■ *Web:* www.pit.edu	Media	PA	19063	610-892-1500	892-1533*	800
Pennsylvania Library Assn (PaLA) 220 Cumberland Pkwy Ste 10 *TF:* 800-622-3308 ■ *Web:* www.palibraries.org	Mechanicsburg	PA	17055	717-766-7663	766-5440	435
Pennsylvania Macaroni Co 2010 Penn Ave # 12 *Web:* www.pennmac.com	Pittsburgh	PA	15222	412-471-8330		360-3
Pennsylvania Manufacturers Assn Co 380 Sentry Pkwy *TF:* 800-222-2749 ■ *Web:* pmacompanies.com	Blue Bell	PA	19422	800-222-2749		391-4
Pennsylvania Medical Society 777 E Pk Dr *TF:* 800-228-7823 ■ *Web:* www.pamedsoc.org	Harrisburg	PA	17111	717-558-7750	558-7840	474
Pennsylvania Medical Society Liability Insurance Co (PMSLIC) 777 E Park Dr PO Box 8820 *TF:* 800-228-7823 ■ *Web:* www.pamedsoc.org	Harrisburg	PA	17050	717-558-7750	558-7818	391-5
Pennsylvania Metallurgical Inc 315 Columbia St *TF:* 800-236-8360 ■ *Web:* www.pmiheattreat.com	Bethlehem	PA	18015	610-691-1313		484
Pennsylvania Pharmacists Assn 508 N Third St *Web:* www.papharmacists.com	Harrisburg	PA	17101	717-234-6151		585
Pennsylvania Precision Cast Parts Inc 521 N Third Ave PO Box 1429 *TF:* 800-356-3875 ■ *Web:* www.ppcpinc.com	Lebanon	PA	17042	717-273-3338	273-2662	306
Pennsylvania Public Interest Research Group (PennPIRG) 1420 Walnut St Ste 650 *Web:* www.pennpirg.org	Philadelphia	PA	19102	215-732-3747		633
Pennsylvania Real Estate Investment Trust 200 S Broad St 3rd Fl *NYSE:* PEI ■ *TF:* 866-875-0700 ■ *Web:* www.preit.com	Philadelphia	PA	19102	215-875-0700	546-7311	655
Pennsylvania Renaissance Faire 2775 Lebanon Rd *TF:* 800-377-1277 ■ *Web:* www.parenfaire.com	Manheim	PA	17545	717-665-7021		31
Pennsylvania Republican State Committee 112 State St *TF:* 800-325-3535 ■ *Web:* www.pagop.org	Harrisburg	PA	17101	717-234-4901	231-3828	616-2
Pennsylvania State Athletic Commission 2601 N Third St *Web:* www.dos.pa.gov/pages/default.aspx	Harrisburg	PA	17110	717-787-5720	783-0824	712
Pennsylvania State Employees Credit Union One Innovation Way *TF:* 800-237-7328 ■ *Web:* www.psecu.com	Harrisburg	PA	17110	717-255-1760	772-2272	219
Pennsylvania State University 201 Shields Bldg *TF:* 800-279-8495 ■ *Web:* www.psu.edu	University Park	PA	16802	814-865-4700	863-7590	166
Abington College 1600 Woodland Rd **Fax:* Admissions ■ *Web:* www.abington.psu.edu	Abington	PA	19001	215-881-7300	881-7412*	166
Altoona 3000 Ivyside Pk **Fax:* Admissions ■ *TF:* 800-848-9843 ■ *Web:* www.altoona.psu.edu	Altoona	PA	16601	814-949-5466	949-5564*	166
Beaver 100 University Dr **Fax:* Admissions ■ *TF:* 877-564-6778 ■ *Web:* www.br.psu.edu	Monaca	PA	15061	724-773-3500	773-3578*	162
Berks Tulpehocken Rd PO Box 7009 *Web:* www.bk.psu.edu	Reading	PA	19610	610-396-6000	396-6077	162
Brandywine 25 Yearsley Mill Rd **Fax:* Admissions ■ *TF:* 800-252-3592 ■ *Web:* www.brandywine.psu.edu	Media	PA	19063	610-892-1200	892-1357*	166
DuBois 1 College Pl **Fax:* Admissions ■ *TF:* 800-346-7627 ■ *Web:* www.ds.psu.edu	Du Bois	PA	15801	814-375-4700	375-4784*	162
Fayette 2201 University Dr **Fax:* Admissions ■ *TF:* 877-568-4130 ■ *Web:* www.fe.psu.edu	Lemont Furnace	PA	15456	724-430-4100	430-4175*	162
Harrisburg 777 W Harrisburg Pk **Fax:* Admissions ■ *TF:* 800-222-2056 ■ *Web:* harrisburg.psu.edu	Middletown	PA	17057	717-948-6000	948-6325*	166
Hazleton 76 University Dr *TF:* 800-279-8495 ■ *Web:* www.hn.psu.edu	Hazleton	PA	18202	570-450-3000		162
Libraries 510 Paterno Library *Web:* www.libraries.psu.edu	University Park	PA	16802	814-865-6368	865-3665	434-6
McKeesport 201 Old Main *Web:* www.psu.edu	University Park	PA	16802	412-675-9000		162
Mont Alto 1 Campus Dr **Fax:* Admissions ■ *TF:* 800-392-6173 ■ *Web:* www.ma.psu.edu	Mont Alto	PA	17237	717-749-6000	749-6132*	162
New Kensington 3550 Seventh St Rd Rt 780 *Web:* www.nk.psu.edu	New Kensington	PA	15068	724-334-5466	334-6111	162
Schuylkill 200 University Dr **Fax:* Admissions ■ *Web:* www.sl.psu.edu	Schuylkill Haven	PA	17972	570-385-6000	385-6113*	162
Shenango 147 Shenango Ave **Fax:* Admissions ■ *TF:* 888-275-7009 ■ *Web:* www.shenango.psu.edu	Sharon	PA	16146	724-983-2803	983-2820*	162
Worthington Scranton 120 Ridge View Dr **Fax:* Admissions ■ *TF:* 800-966-6613 ■ *Web:* worthingtonscranton.psu.edu	Dunmore	PA	18512	570-963-2500	963-2524*	162
York 1031 Edgecomb Ave **Fax:* Admissions ■ *TF:* 800-778-6227 ■ *Web:* www.yk.psu.edu	York	PA	17403	717-771-4000	771-4005*	162
Pennsylvania State University at Erie *Behrend College* 4701 College Dr *TF:* 866-374-3378 ■ *Web:* psbehrend.psu.edu	Erie	PA	16563	814-898-6000	898-6044	166
Pennsylvania State University Dickinson Law 150 S College St **Fax:* Admissions ■ *TF:* 800-840-1122 ■ *Web:* law.psu.edu	Carlisle	PA	17013	717-240-5000	241-3503*	167-1
Pennsylvania State University Press 820 N University Dr USB1 Ste C *TF:* 800-326-9180 ■ *Web:* www.psupress.org	University Park	PA	16802	814-865-1327	863-1408	637-4
Pennstate Lehigh Valley 2809 Saucon Valley Rd **Fax:* Admissions ■ *Web:* www.lv.psu.edu	Center Valley	PA	18034	610-285-5000	285-5220*	162
Pennstate Wilkes-Barre Old Rt 115 PO Box PSU **Fax:* Admissions ■ *Web:* www.wb.psu.edu	Lehman	PA	18627	570-675-2171	675-9113*	162
Pennsylvania Steel Company Inc 1717 Woodhaven Dr *Web:* www.pasteel.com	Bensalem	PA	19020	215-633-9600		492
Pennsylvania Tool & Gages Inc PO Box 534 *TF:* 877-827-8285 ■ *Web:* www.patool.com	Meadville	PA	16335	814-336-3136	333-9131	757
Pennsylvania Transformer Technology Inc 30 Curry Ave *Web:* www.patransformer.com	Canonsburg	PA	15317	724-873-2100		767
Pennsylvania Trust Co 5 Radnor Corp Ctr Ste 450 *TF:* 800-975-4316 ■ *Web:* penntrust.com	Radnor	PA	19087	610-975-4300	975-4324	690
Pennsylvania Youth Ballet (PYB) 556 Main St *Web:* www.bglv.org	Bethlehem	PA	18018	610-865-0353		573-1

Name / Address	City	State	ZIP	Phone	Fax	Class
Penntecq Inc 106 Kuder Dr	Greenville	PA	16125	724-646-4250	646-4261	60
Web: www.penntecq.com						
Pennterra Engineering Inc						
3075 Enterprise Dr Ste 100	State College	PA	16801	814-231-8285		261
Web: www.pennterra.com						
Penn-Union Corp 229 Waterford St	Edinboro	PA	16412	814-734-1631	734-4946	815
Web: www.penn-union.com						
Penny Group Inc, The						
1328 Harding Pl	Charlotte	NC	28204	704-372-1400		195
Web: thepennygroup.com						
Penny Laine Papers						
2211 Century Ctr Blvd Ste 110	Irving	TX	75062	972-812-3000	812-3004	130
TF: 800-456-6484 ■ *Web:* pennylainepapers.com						
Penny Ohlmann Neiman Inc						
1605 N Main St	Dayton	OH	45405	937-278-0681		4
Web: ohlmanngroup.com						
Pennyrile Forest State Resort Park						
20781 Pennyrile Lodge Rd	Dawson Springs	KY	42408	800-325-1711		565
TF: 800-325-1711 ■ *Web:* www.parks.ky.gov						
Pennyrile Rural Electric Co-op Corp						
2000 Harrison St PO Box 2900	Hopkinsville	KY	42241	270-886-2555	885-6469	245
TF Cust Svc: 800-297-4710 ■ *Web:* www.precc.com						
Pennzoil - Quaker State Co						
700 Milam St	Houston	TX	77002	713-546-4000		541
Web: www.pennzoil.com						
Penobscot Community Health Center Inc						
103 Maine Ave	Bangor	ME	04401	207-992-9200		237
Web: pchc.com						
Penobscot County 97 Hammond St	Bangor	ME	04401	207-942-8535		338
Web: www.penobscot-county.net						
Penobscot Investment Management Company Inc						
50 Congress St Ste 410	Boston	MA	02109	617-227-3111		401
Web: www.pimboston.com						
Penobscot Marine Museum						
5 Church St PO Box 498	Searsport	ME	04974	207-548-2529	548-2520	520
TF: 800-268-8030 ■ *Web:* www.penobscotmarinemuseum.org						
Penobscot McCrum LLC 28 Pierce St	Belfast	ME	04915	207-338-4360	338-5742	296-21
TF: 800-435-4456 ■ *Web:* www.penobscotmccrum.com						
Penobscot Theatre Co 131 Main St	Bangor	ME	04401	207-942-3333		573-4
TF: 800-756-8326 ■ *Web:* www.penobscottheatre.org						
PenRad Technologies Inc						
114 Commerce Cir	Buffalo	MN	55313	763-475-3388		475
TF: 800-230-7227 ■ *Web:* www.penrad.com						
Penray Cos Inc 440 Denniston Ct	Wheeling	IL	60090	847-459-5000	459-5043	145
TF: 800-373-6729 ■ *Web:* www.penray.com						
Penrod Co						
2809 S Lynnhaven Rd Ste 350	Virginia Beach	VA	23452	757-498-0186	498-1075	191-2
TF: 800-537-3497 ■ *Web:* www.thepenrodcompany.com						
Penrose Hospital						
2222 N Nevada Ave	Colorado Springs	CO	80907	719-776-5000		374-3
TF: 800-398-2045 ■ *Web:* www.penrosestfrancis.org						
Penrose Point State Park						
321 158th KPS	Lakebay	WA	98349	253-884-2514		565
Penrose Room 1 Lake Ave	Colorado Springs	CO	80906	719-634-7711		671
TF: 800-577-9718 ■ *Web:* www.broadmoor.com						
Pensacola Area Chamber of Commerce						
117 W Garden St	Pensacola	FL	32502	850-438-4081	438-6369	139
TF: 800-874-1234 ■ *Web:* www.pensacolachamber.com						
Pensacola Christian College						
250 Brent Ln	Pensacola	FL	32503	850-478-8496	722-3355*	166
**Fax Area Code:* 800 ■ *TF:* 800-722-4636 ■ *Web:* www.pcci.edu						
Pensacola City Hall 222 W Main St	Pensacola	FL	32502	850-435-1626		337
Web: www.cityofpensacola.com						
Pensacola Civic Ctr						
201 E Gregory St	Pensacola	FL	32502	850-432-0800	432-1707	572
TF: 800-745-3000 ■ *Web:* www.pensacolabaycenter.com						
Pensacola Convention & Visitors Bureau						
1401 E Gregory St	Pensacola	FL	32502	850-434-1234		206
TF: 800-874-1234 ■ *Web:* www.visitpensacola.com						
Pensacola Cultural Ctr (PCC)						
400 S Jefferson St	Pensacola	FL	32502	850-432-2042		572
Web: www.pensacolalittletheatre.com/pcc						
Pensacola Greyhound Track						
951 Dog Track Rd	Pensacola	FL	32506	850-455-8595		642
TF: 800-345-3997 ■ *Web:* www.pensacolagreyhoundtrack.com						
Pensacola Gulf Coast Regional Airport						
2430 Airport Blvd Ste 225	Pensacola	FL	32504	850-436-5000	436-5006	27
TF: 800-874-6580 ■ *Web:* www.flypensacola.com						
Pensacola Junior College						
1000 College Blvd	Pensacola	FL	32504	850-484-1000	484-1829*	162
**Fax:* Admissions ■ *TF:* 888-897-3605 ■ *Web:* pensacolastate.edu						
Warrington 5555 W Hwy 98	Pensacola	FL	32507	850-484-2200	484-2375	162
TF: 888-897-3605 ■ *Web:* pensacolastate.edu						
Pensacola Little Theatre (PLT)						
400 S Jefferson St	Pensacola	FL	32502	850-432-2042		573-4
Web: www.pensacolalittletheatre.com						
Pensacola Museum of Art						
407 S Jefferson St	Pensacola	FL	32502	850-432-6247	469-1532	520
Web: www.pensacolamuseum.org						
Pensacola Opera 75 S Tarragona St	Pensacola	FL	32502	850-433-6737		573-2
TF: 800-934-3301 ■ *Web:* www.pensacolaopera.com						
Pensacola Symphony Orchestra						
205 E Zaragossa St PO Box 1752	Pensacola	FL	32502	850-435-2533	444-9910	573-3
Web: www.pensacolasymphony.com						
Pensar Development Inc						
900 E Pine St Ste 201	Seattle	WA	98122	206-284-3134		256
Web: www.pensardevelopment.com						
Penseco Financial Services Corp						
150 N Washington Ave	Scranton	PA	18503	570-346-7741		70
NASDAQ: PFIS ■ *Web:* psbt.com/index.php						
Pension Benefit Guaranty Corp						
1200 K St NW	Washington	DC	20005	202-326-4000		340-20
TF Cust Svc: 800-400-7242 ■ *Web:* www.pbgc.gov						
Pension Consulting Alliance Inc						
514 NW 11th Ave Ste 203	Portland	OR	97209	503-226-1050		194
Web: www.pensionconsulting.com						
Pension Corp						
Stn Prov Govt Po Box 9460	Victoria	BC	V8W9V8	250-387-1002		528
Web: www.pensionsbc.ca						
Pension Real Estate Assn (PREA)						
100 Pearl St 13th Fl	Hartford	CT	06103	860-692-6341	692-6351	49-2
Web: www.prea.org						
Pension Rights Ctr						
1350 Connecticut Ave NW Ste 206	Washington	DC	20036	202-296-3776	833-2472	48-6
TF: 866-735-7737 ■ *Web:* www.pensionrights.org						
Pensionmark Retirement Group						
24 E Cota St	Santa Barbara	CA	93101	805-456-6260		401
TF: 800-201-3187 ■ *Web:* www.pensionmark.com						
Pensions & Investments Magazine						
711 Third Ave	New York	NY	10017	212-210-0100		457-5
Web: www.pionline.com						
Penske Vehicle Services Inc						
1225 E Maple Rd	Troy	MI	48083	248-729-5400		194
TF: 877-210-5290 ■ *Web:* penskevehicleservices.com						
Penski Inc 50 Market St	Potsdam	NY	13676	315-265-8860		260
Web: www.penski.com						
Penso Capital Markets LLC						
68 Carman Ave	Cedarhurst	NY	11516	516-791-3800		690
Web: penso.com						
PENTA Communications Inc						
208 Turnpike Rd Ste 200	Westborough	MA	01581	508-616-9900		463
Web: www.pentamarketing.com						
Penta Engineering PA						
13835 S Lakes Dr	Charlotte	NC	28273	704-588-8877		261
Web: pentaengr.com						
Penta Laboratories						
9740 Cozycroft Ave	Chatsworth	CA	91311	818-882-3872		418
TF: 800-421-4219 ■ *Web:* pentalabs.com						
Pentacle Theater 324 52nd Ave NW	Salem	OR	97304	503-364-7200		572
TF: 800-333-0774 ■ *Web:* www.pentacletheatre.org						
Pentaflex Inc 4981 Gateway Blvd	Springfield	OH	45502	937-325-5551		488
Web: www.pentaflex.com						
Pentagon 2000 Software Inc						
15 W 34th St 5th Fl	New York	NY	10001	212-629-7521	629-7513	178-1
TF: 800-643-1806 ■ *Web:* www.pentagon2000.com						
Pentagon Federal Credit Union						
2930 Eisenhower Ave	Alexandria	VA	22314	800-247-5626	253-6589	219
TF: 800-247-5626 ■ *Web:* www.penfed.org						
Pentagon Optimization Services Inc						
220 7700 - 76 St Close	Red Deer	AB	T4P4G6	403-347-6277		539
Pentair 5500 Wayzata Blvd Ste 600	Minneapolis	MN	55416	763-545-1730	656-5400*	641
**Fax:* Sales ■ *TF Cust Svc:* 800-424-9776 ■ *Web:* www.hypropumps.com						
Pentair 7433 Harwin Dr	Houston	TX	77036	800-545-6258		201
TF: 800-545-6258 ■ *Web:* pentairthermal.com						
Pentair Ltd 1351 Rt 55	Lagrangeville	NY	12450	845-463-7200	463-7291	710
TF: 888-711-7487 ■ *Web:* www.pentaircommercial.com/products/index.php						
Pentair Residential Filtration LLC						
20580 Enterprise Ave	Brookfield	WI	53008	262-784-4490	785-6535	91
TF: 888-784-9065 ■ *Web:* waterpurification.pentair.com/en-us						
Pentair Water Pool & Spa						
1620 Hawkins Ave	Sanford	NC	27330	800-831-7133	284-4151	641
TF: 800-831-7133 ■ *Web:* www.pentairpool.com						
Pentalpha Capital Group LLC						
1 Greenwich Office Park N Bldg	Greenwich	CT	06831	203-660-6100		401
Web: www.pentalphaglobal.com						
Pentastar Aviation 7310 Highland Rd	Waterford	MI	48327	248-666-3630		13
TF: 800-662-9612 ■ *Web:* www.pentastaraviation.com						
Pentax Imaging Co 633 17th St Ste 2600	Denver	CO	80202	303-799-8000		173-6
TF: 800-877-0155 ■ *Web:* www.us.ricoh-imaging.com						
Pentec Health Inc						
4 Creek Pkwy Ste A	Marcus Hook	PA	19061	610-494-8700		363
TF: 800-920-2262 ■ *Web:* www.pentechealth.com						
Pentecostal Assemblies						
2450 Milltower Ct	Mississauga	ON	L7N3J2	905-542-7400	542-7313	48-20
TF: 800-779-7262 ■ *Web:* www.paoc.org						
Pentecostal Theological Seminary						
900 Walker St NE	Cleveland	TN	37311	423-478-1131		167-3
TF: 800-228-9126 ■ *Web:* www.ptseminary.edu						
Pentecostals of Alexandria, The						
2817 Rapides Ave	Alexandria	LA	71301	318-487-8976		95
TF: 800-376-2422 ■ *Web:* www.thepentecostals.org						
Pentek Inc 1 Pk Way	Upper Saddle River	NJ	07458	201-818-5900	818-5692*	625
**Fax:* Acctg ■ *Web:* www.pentek.com						
Pentel of America Ltd						
2715 Columbia St	Torrance	CA	90503	760-200-0547	200-0586	571
TF: 855-528-4101 ■ *Web:* www.pentel.com						
PenTeleData						
540 Delaware Ave PO Box 197	Palmerton	PA	18071	800-281-3564		225
TF: 800-281-3564 ■ *Web:* www.penteledata.net						
Pentera Inc						
8650 Commerce Park Pl Ste G	Indianapolis	IN	46268	317-875-0910		195
Web: www.pentera.com						
Penticton & Wine Country Chamber of Commerce						
553 Railway St	Penticton	BC	V2A8S3	250-492-4103		137
TF: 800-663-5052 ■ *Web:* www.penticton.org						
Penticton Regional Hospital (PRH)						
550 Carmi Ave	Penticton	BC	V2A3G6	250-492-4000	492-9068	374-2
TF: 800-665-1822 ■ *Web:* www.interiorhealth.ca						
Pentland USA Inc						
3333 New Hyde Pk Rd Ste 200	New Hyde Park	NY	11042	516-365-1333		301
Web: www.pentland.com						
Penton Media Inc 1166 Ave 10th Fl	New York	NY	10036	212-204-4200		457-12
TF: 800-525-5003 ■ *Web:* www.penton.com						
Penton Media Inc 1300 E Ninth St	Cleveland	OH	44114	216-696-7000		637-9
Web: www.penton.com						
Pentron Clinical Technologies LLC						
1717 W Collins Ave	Orange	CA	92867	714-516-7557	677-8844*	228
**Fax Area Code:* 877 ■ *TF:* 800-551-0283 ■ *Web:* www.pentron.com						
Pentucket Bank 1 Merrimack St	Haverhill	MA	01830	978-372-7731	372-4499	70
Web: www.pentucketbank.com						
Pentwater Wire Products Inc (PWP)						
474 Carroll St PO Box 947	Pentwater	MI	49449	231-869-6911	869-4020	286
TF: 877-869-6911 ■ *Web:* www.pentwaterwire.com						
Pentz Design Pattern & Foundry						
14823 Main St NE	Duvall	WA	98019	425-788-6490		492
TF: 800-411-6555 ■ *Web:* www.pentzcastsolutions.com						
Penumbra Theatre 270 Kent St	Saint Paul	MN	55102	651-224-3180	288-6789	572
Web: www.penumbratheatre.org						

Name / Address	City	State	ZIP	Phone	Fax	Class
Penwood State Park 560 Simsbury Rd *Web:* www.ct.gov	Bloomfield	CT	06002	860-242-1158		565
Penzeys Spices Inc 12001 W Capitol Dr *Web:* www.penzeys.com	Wauwatosa	WI	53222	414-760-7307		459
People 1271 Sixth Ave Ste 3540 *Web:* www.people.com	New York	NY	10020	212-522-6699		457-6
People Bank 201 N Bardstown Rd *Web:* www.peoplesbankmtw.com	Mount Washington	KY	40047	502-538-7301	538-6606	70
People Care Inc 116 W 32nd St 15th Fl *Web:* www.peoplecare.com	New York	NY	10001	212-631-7300		363
People Creating Success Inc 4474 Market St Ste 1500 *Web:* www.pcs-services.org	Ventura	CA	93003	805-644-9480		672
People First Federal Credit Union 2141 Downyflake Ln *Web:* peoplefirstcu.org	Allentown	PA	18103	610-797-7440		219
People for the American Way (PFAW) 2000 M St NW Ste 400 *TF:* 800-326-7329 ■ *Web:* www.pfaw.org	Washington	DC	20036	202-467-4999	293-2672	48-7
People for the Ethical Treatment of Animals (PETA) 501 Front St *TF:* 800-566-9768 ■ *Web:* www.peta.org	Norfolk	VA	23510	757-622-7382	622-0457	48-3
People Inc 1219 N Forest Rd *TF:* 800-221-5994 ■ *Web:* www.people-inc.org	Williamsville	NY	14231	716-634-8132		672
People Lease Inc 689 Town Ctr Blvd Ste B *TF:* 800-723-3025 ■ *Web:* www.peoplelease.com	Ridgeland	MS	39157	601-987-3025	987-3029	631
People Magazine Time & Life Bldg 1271 Avenue of the Americas 28th Fl *TF:* 800-541-9000 ■ *Web:* www.people.com/people	New York	NY	10020	212-522-3347	522-0883	457-11
People Plus Industrial Inc 1095 Nebo Rd *TF:* 888-825-1500 ■ *Web:* www.peopleplusinc.com	Madisonville	KY	42431	270-825-8939		260
People Productions Video Services Inc 1737 15th St Ste 200 *Web:* www.peopleproductions.com	Boulder	CO	80302	303-449-6086		514
People Skills International 2910 Baily Ave	San Diego	CA	92105	619-262-9951		226
People's Electric Co-op 1600 N Country Club Rd *Web:* www.peoplesec.com	Ada	OK	74820	580-332-3031		245
People's Energy Co-op 1775 Lake Shady Ave S *TF:* 800-214-2694 ■ *Web:* www.peoplesrec.com	Oronoco	MN	55960	507-367-7000	367-7001	245
People's Food Co-op 315 Fifth Ave S *Web:* www.pfc.coop	La Crosse	WI	54601	608-784-5798		345
People's Light & Theatre Co 39 Conestoga Rd *TF:* 800-732-0999 ■ *Web:* www.peopleslight.org	Malvern	PA	19355	610-647-1900	640-9521	749
People's Securities Inc 850 Main St **Fax:* Cust Svc ■ *TF:* 800-894-0300 ■ *Web:* psi.peoples.com	Bridgeport	CT	06601	203-338-7901	338-3087*	690
People's United Bank 850 Main St Bridgeport Ctr *TF:* 800-772-1090 ■ *Web:* www.peoples.com	Bridgeport	CT	06604	203-338-7171		70
People's Weekly World 235 W 23rd St *Web:* www.peoplesworld.org	New York	NY	10011	212-924-2523	229-1713	532-4
Peoplefit Health & Fitness Center 237 Lexington St Ste 110 *TF:* 855-784-4663 ■ *Web:* peoplefit.net	Woburn	MA	01801	781-932-9332		354
Peoplelink Staffing Solutions LLC 431 E Colfax Ave Ste 200 *Web:* www.peoplelinkstaffing.com	South Bend	IN	46617	574-232-5400		260
Peoples 9738 Up River Rd *Web:* www.peoplesrestaurant.com	Corpus Christi	TX	78410	361-241-8087		671
Peoples Bancorp Inc 138 Putnam St *NASDAQ: PEBO* ■ *TF:* 800-374-6123 ■ *Web:* www.peoplesbancorp.com	Marietta	OH	45750	740-373-3155		360-2
Peoples Bancorp of North Carolina Inc 518 W 'C' St *NASDAQ: PEBK* ■ *TF:* 800-948-7195 ■ *Web:* www.peoplesbanknc.com	Newton	NC	28658	828-464-5620		360-2
Peoples Bancshares-Pnt Coupee 805 Hospital Rd PO Box 747 *Web:* www.thefriendlybank.com	New Roads	LA	70760	225-638-3713		780
Peoples Electric Company Inc 277 E Fillmore Ave *TF:* 800-642-9090 ■ *Web:* www.peoplesco.com	Saint Paul	MN	55107	651-227-7711		189-4
Peoples Financial Services Corp 82 Franklin Ave *NASDAQ: PFIS* ■ *TF:* 888-868-3858 ■ *Web:* psbt.com/index.php	Hallstead	PA	18822	570-879-2175		70
Peoples Gas Light & Coke Co 200 E Randolph St *TF Cust Svc:* 866-556-6001 ■ *Web:* northshoregasdelivery.com	Chicago	IL	60601-6302	312-744-7000		787
Peoples Jewellers 1100 Pembroke St E *Web:* www.peoplesjewellers.com	Pembroke	ON	K8A6Y7	613-735-1536		410
Peoples National Bank 5175 N Academy Blvd *TF:* 800-862-6696 ■ *Web:* www.epeoples.com	Colorado Springs	CO	80918	719-528-4000	260-2256	70
Peoples Savings Bank (PSB) 414 N Adams PO Box 248 *TF:* 877-508-2265 ■ *Web:* www.bankpsb.com	Wellsburg	IA	50680	641-869-3721	869-3855	70
Peoples State Bank 445 S Lewis Ave *Web:* peoplesbanktulsa.com	Tulsa	OK	74104	918-583-9800	587-9307	70
PeopleStrategy Inc 5883 Glenridge Dr Ste 200 *TF:* 855-488-4100 ■ *Web:* www.peoplestrategy.com	Atlanta	GA	30328	855-488-4100		178-1
PeopleTec Inc 4901-I Corporate Dr NW *Web:* www.peopletec.com	Huntsville	AL	35805	256-319-3800		261
People-to-People Health Foundation 255 Carter Hall Ln *TF:* 800-544-4673 ■ *Web:* www.projecthope.org	Millwood	VA	22646	540-837-2100	837-1813	48-5
PeopleWorks Inc 224 Main St *TF:* 888-404-3646 ■ *Web:* www.peopleworksinc.com	Alta	IA	51002	712-284-2881		463
Peoria Area Chamber of Commerce 100 SW Water St *TF:* 888-681-6561 ■ *Web:* www.peoriachamber.org	Peoria	IL	61602	309-676-0755	676-7534	139
Peoria Area Convention & Visitors Bureau 456 Fulton St Ste 300 *TF:* 800-747-0302 ■ *Web:* www.peoria.org	Peoria	IL	61602	309-676-0303	676-8470	206
Peoria Ballet 809 W Detweiller Dr *Web:* www.peoriaballet.org	Peoria	IL	61615	309-690-7990	690-7991	573-1
Peoria City Hall 419 Fulton St Ste 401 *Web:* www.peoriagov.org	Peoria	IL	61602	309-494-8565		337
Peoria Civic Ctr 201 SW Jefferson Ave *TF:* 800-745-3000 ■ *Web:* peoriaciviccenter.com	Peoria	IL	61602	309-673-8900	673-9223	572
Peoria County 324 Main St Rm 101 *TF:* 800-843-6154 ■ *Web:* www.co.peoria.il.us	Peoria	IL	61602	309-672-6059	672-6054	338
Peoria Journal Star 1 News Plaza **Fax:* News Rm ■ *TF:* 800-225-5757 ■ *Web:* www.pjstar.com	Peoria	IL	61643	309-686-3000	686-3296*	532-2
Peoria Public Library 8463 W Monroe St *TF:* 800-424-2246 ■ *Web:* www.peoriaaz.gov	Peoria	AZ	85345	623-773-7555		434-3
Peoria Public Library 107 NE Monroe St *Web:* www.peoriapubliclibrary.org	Peoria	IL	61602	309-497-2135		434-3
Peoria Regional Airport 6100 W Everett McKinley Dirksen Pkwy *Web:* www.flypia.com	Peoria	IL	61607	309-697-8272	697-8132	27
Peoria Riverfront Museum 222 SW Washington St *Web:* www.peoriariverfrontmuseum.org	Peoria	IL	61602	309-686-7000		520
Peoria Speedway 3520 W Farmington Rd *TF:* 800-422-3247 ■ *Web:* www.peoriaspeedway.com	Peoria	IL	61604	309-357-3339		515
Peoria Symphony Orchestra 101 State St *TF:* 800-421-4371 ■ *Web:* www.peoriasymphony.org	Peoria	IL	61602	309-671-1096		573-3
PEP Direct Inc 19 Stoney Brook Dr	Wilton	NH	03086	603-654-6141		317
PEP Filters Inc 322 Rolling Hill Rd *TF:* 800-243-4583 ■ *Web:* www.pepfilters.com	Mooresville	NC	28117	704-662-3133	662-3155	806
PEP Wauconda 821 W Algonquin *Web:* www.pepwauconda.com	Algonquin	IL	60102	847-658-4588		488
PEPCO (Professional Electric Products Co) 33210 Lakeland Blvd *TF:* 800-872-7000 ■ *Web:* www.pepconet.com	Eastlake	OH	44095	440-946-3790	942-5883	246
Pepco Energy Services Inc 1300 N 17th St Ste 1600 **Fax Area Code:* 301 ■ *TF:* 800-424-8028 ■ *Web:* www.pepco.com	Arlington	VA	22209	703-253-1800	967-5820*	787
Pepco Holdings Inc 701 Ninth St NW *NYSE: POM* ■ *Web:* www.pepcoholdings.com	Washington	DC	20068	202-872-2000		787
Pepco Sales of Dallas Inc 11310 Gemini Ln *TF:* 877-737-2699 ■ *Web:* www.pepcosales.com	Dallas	TX	75229	972-823-8700		612
Pepe & Chela's 1001 SW Tyler St *Web:* www.pepeandchelas.com	Topeka	KS	66612	785-357-8332		671
Pepe Motors group/Mercedes-Benz of White Plains 50 Bank St *Web:* www.mbwhiteplains.com	White Plains	NY	10606	914-949-4000		57
Pepe's 2429 W Ball Rd *Web:* pepesmexicanfood.com	Anaheim	CA	92804	714-952-9410		671
Pepe's Inc 1325 W 15th St *Web:* www.pepes.com	Chicago	IL	60608	312-733-2500		670
Pepg LLC 9270 S Sandy Pkwy *Web:* pepg.net	Sandy	UT	84070	801-562-2521	562-2551	261
Pepin County Wisconsin 740 Seventh Ave W *Web:* www.co.pepin.wi.us	Durand	WI	54736	715-672-8857	672-8677	338
Pepin Distributing Co 4121 N 50th St *TF:* 800-331-2829 ■ *Web:* www.pepindistributing.com	Tampa	FL	33610	813-626-6176	626-5800	81-1
Pepin Manufacturing Inc 1875 Hwy 61 S *TF:* 800-291-6505 ■ *Web:* www.pepinmfg.com	Lake City	MN	55041	651-345-5655		476
Pepose Vision Institute PC 1815 Clarkson Rd *TF:* 877-862-2020 ■ *Web:* www.peposevision.com	Chesterfield	MO	63017	636-728-0111		476
Pepper Construction 643 N Orleans St *Web:* www.pepperconstruction.com	Chicago	IL	60610	312-266-4700		186
Pepper Group, The 220 N Smith St Ste 406 *Web:* www.peppergroup.com	Palatine	IL	60067	847-963-0333		177
Pepper Hamilton LLP 3000 Two Logan Sq 18th & Arch St *Web:* www.pepperlaw.com	Philadelphia	PA	19103	215-981-4000	981-4750	428
Pepper Sprout 378 Main St *Web:* www.peppersprout.com	Dubuque	IA	52001	563-556-2167		671
Pepper Tree, The 888 W Moreno Ave *Web:* www.peppertreecs.com	Colorado Springs	CO	80905	719-471-4888	471-0997	671
Pepperball Technologies Inc 6540 Lusk Blvd Ste C137 *TF:* 877-887-3773 ■ *Web:* www.pepperball.com	San Diego	CA	92121	858-638-0236		762
Pepperclub 78 Middle St *Web:* pepperclubrestaurant.com	Portland	ME	04101	207-772-0531		671
PepperCom Inc 470 Pk Ave S *Web:* www.peppercomm.com	New York	NY	10016	212-931-6100	931-6159	636
Peppercorn's Grill 357 Main St *Web:* www.peppercornsgrill.com	Hartford	CT	06106	860-547-1714	724-7612	671
Pepperdine University 24255 Pacific Coast Hwy **Fax:* Admissions ■ *TF:* 800-413-0848 ■ *Web:* www.pepperdine.edu	Malibu	CA	90263	310-506-4000	506-4861*	166
Pepperdine University Payson Library 24255 Pacific Coast Hwy *Web:* www.library.pepperdine.edu	Malibu	CA	90263	310-506-4252		434-6
Pepperdine University School of Law 24255 Pacific Coast Hwy **Fax:* Admissions ■ *Web:* www.law.pepperdine.edu	Malibu	CA	90263	310-506-4631	506-7668*	167-1
Pepperell Braiding Company Inc 22 Lowell St *TF:* 800-343-8114 ■ *Web:* www.pepperell.com	Pepperell	MA	01463	800-343-8114		596
Pepperidge Farm Inc 595 Westport Ave *TF PR:* 888-737-7374 ■ *Web:* www.pepperidgefarm.com	Norwalk	CT	06851	203-846-7000		296-1
Pepperl Fuchs Inc 1600 Enterprise Pkwy *Web:* www.pepperl-fuchs.us	Twinsburg	OH	44087	330-425-3555	425-4607	203

Company	City	State	Zip	Phone	Fax	Class
Peppermill Hotel & Casino 2707 S Virginia St *TF:* 800-648-6992 ■ *Web:* www.peppermillreno.com	Reno	NV	89502	775-826-2121		133
Peppermill Restaurant 3524 Severn Ave *TF:* 800-362-1811 ■ *Web:* www.riccobonos.com	Metairie	LA	70002	504-455-2266		671
Peppermint Ridge Inc 825 Magnolia Ave *Web:* peppermintridge.org	Corona	CA	92879	951-273-7320		672
Peppers & Rogers Group 9197 S Peoria St *TF:* 866-986-4414 ■ *Web:* www.peppersandrogersgroup.com	Englewood	CO	80112	303-397-9490	397-9478	195
Peppers Unlimited of Louisiana Inc 602 W Bridge St *Web:* www.peppersunlimitedofla.com	St Martinville	LA	70582	337-394-8035		297-8
Peppler & Associates Inc 22 E Dundee Rd Ste 26 *Web:* peppler.com	Barrington	IL	60010	847-382-6866		177
Pepsi Bottling Ventures LLC 4141 Parklake Ave Ste 600 *TF:* 800-662-8792 ■ *Web:* www.pepsibottlingventures.com	Raleigh	NC	27612	919-865-2300		296-37
PepsiCo Inc 700 Anderson Hill Rd *NYSE: PEP* ■ *TF PR:* 800-433-2652 ■ *Web:* www.pepsico.com	Purchase	NY	10577	914-253-2000		185
Pepsi-Cola Bottling Co of New Haven 101 Hickory St *Web:* www.gopepsi.com	New Haven	MO	63068	573-237-3076		805
Pepsi-Cola Bottling Company of Yuba City Inc 750 Sutter St *Web:* pepsico.com	Yuba City	CA	95991	530-673-9205		80-2
Peptides International Inc 11621 Electron Dr *TF:* 800-777-4779 ■ *Web:* www.pepnet.com	Louisville	KY	40299	502-266-8787	267-1329	231
PER (Public Employees Roundtable) PO Box 75248 *Web:* www.keyinsurancequotes.com	Washington	DC	20013	202-927-4926	927-4920	49-7
Per Mar Security 1910 E Kimberly Rd *TF:* 800-473-7627 ■ *Web:* www.permarsecurity.com	Davenport	IA	52807	563-359-3200	359-6700	692
Perani's Hockey World 1600 Cochran Rd *TF:* 800-240-0178 ■ *Web:* hockeyworld.com	Pittsburgh	PA	15220	412-343-5857		711
Perantinides & Nolan Company LPa 80 S Summit St Ste 300 *TF:* 800-316-0072 ■ *Web:* eyemg.com	Akron	OH	44308	330-434-7873		428
Peraso Technologies Inc 144 Front St W Ste 685 *Web:* www.perasotech.com	Toronto	ON	M5J2L7	416-637-1048		225
PERC Water Corp 959 S Coast Dr ste 315 *Web:* www.percwater.com	Costa Mesa	CA	92626	714-352-7750		192
Percepta LLC 290 Town Ctr Dr FairLn Plaza N Ste 610 *Web:* www.percepta.com	Dearborn	MI	48126	313-390-0157		636
Perceptics Corp 9737 Cogdill Rd Ste 200 **Fax Area Code:* 865 ■ *TF:* 800-448-8544 ■ *Web:* www.perceptics.com	Knoxville	TN	37932	800-448-8544	966-9330*	178-12
PerceptiMed Inc 365 San Antonio Rd *Web:* perceptimed.com	Mountain View	CA	94040	650-941-7000		475
Perception Programs Inc 54 N St *Web:* perceptionprograms.org	Willimantic	CT	06226	860-450-7122		726
Perceptis LLC 325 W McBee Ave Ste 300 *Web:* www.perceptis.com	Greenville	SC	29601	864-214-4360		393
Perceptron Inc 47827 Halyard Dr *NASDAQ: PRCP* ■ *Web:* www.perceptron.com	Plymouth	MI	48170	734-414-6100	414-4700	472
Percival Scientific Inc 505 Research Dr *TF:* 800-695-2743 ■ *Web:* www.percival-scientific.com	Perry	IA	50220	515-465-9363		420
Percussion Software Inc 600 Unicorn Pk Dr *TF:* 800-283-0800 ■ *Web:* www.percussion.com	Woburn	MA	01801	781-438-9900	438-9955	178-1
Percussive Arts Society (PAS) 110 W Washington St *Web:* www.pas.org	Indianapolis	IN	46204	317-974-4488	974-4499	48-4
PercuVision LLC 765 N Hamilton Rd Ste 260A *Web:* www.percuvision.com	Gahanna	OH	43230	614-337-8700		345
Percy Quin State Park 2036 Percy Quin Dr *Web:* www.mdwfp.com/parkview/parks.asp?id=5847	McComb	MS	39648	601-684-3938		565
Perdido Beach Resort 27200 Perdido Beach Blvd *TF:* 800-634-8001 ■ *Web:* www.perdidobeachresort.com	Orange Beach	AL	36561	251-981-9811		669
Perdido Key State Park 15301 Perdido Key Dr *Web:* www.floridastateparks.org/perdidokey	Pensacola	FL	32507	850-492-1595		565
Perdue David (Sen R - GA) 455 Russell Senate Office Bldg *Web:* www.perdue.senate.gov	Washington	DC	20510	202-224-3521	228-1031	342-2
Perdue Farms Inc 31149 Old Ocean City Rd *TF:* 800-473-7383 ■ *Web:* www.perdue.com	Salisbury	MD	21804	410-543-3000		619
Perdue Inc 5 W Forsyth St # 100 *TF:* 800-472-8669 ■ *Web:* www.perdueoffice.com	Jacksonville	FL	32202	904-737-5858		362
Perdue Woodworks Inc 2415 Creek Dr *Web:* www.perduesinc.com	Rapid City	SD	57703	605-341-2101		319-2
Pere Marquette State Park 13112 Visitor Ctr Ln *Web:* www.dnr.illinois.gov/Parks/Pages/PereMarquette.aspx	Grafton	IL	62037	618-786-3323		565
Peregrine Capital Partners LLC 732 Pittsford-Victor Rd *Web:* www.peregrinecapitalpartners.com	Pittsford	NY	14534	585-218-5220		401
Peregrine Pharmaceuticals Inc 14282 Franklin Ave Ste 100 *NASDAQ: PPHM* ■ *TF:* 800-987-8256 ■ *Web:* www.peregrineinc.com	Tustin	CA	92780	714-508-6000	838-5817	85
Peregrine Semiconductor Corp 9380 Carroll Pk Dr *Web:* www.psemi.com	San Diego	CA	92121	858-731-9400	731-9499	696
Peregrine Surgical Ltd 51 Britain Dr *TF:* 877-348-0456 ■ *Web:* www.peregrinesurgical.com	New Britain	PA	18901	215-348-0456		476
Pereira & Azevedo Cpa LLC 52-54 Rome St *Web:* www.njcpas.com	Newark	NJ	07105	973-466-1663		2
Perelson Weiner LLP 1 Dag Hammarskjold Plaza 42nd Fl *Web:* www.pwcpa.com	New York	NY	10017	212-605-3100		2
Perennial Mgmt Ltd 40 Aberdeen Ave *Web:* perennialmanagement.ca	St John'S	NL	A1A5T3	709-754-2057		652
Perennial Public Power District 2122 S Lincoln Ave *TF:* 800-289-0288 ■ *Web:* www.perennialpower.com	York	NE	68467	402-362-3355	362-3623	245
Perey Turnstiles Inc 308 Bishop Ave *Web:* www.turnstile.com	Bridgeport	CT	06610	203-333-9400		693
Perez Art Museum Miami 1103 Biscayne Blvd *Web:* www.pamm.org	Miami	FL	33132	305-375-3000	375-1725	520
Perez Trading Company Inc 3490 NW 125th St *Web:* www.pereztrading.com	Miami	FL	33167	305-769-0761		559
PERF (Police Executive Research Forum) 1120 Connecticut Ave NW Ste 930 *Web:* www.policeforum.org	Washington	DC	20036	202-466-7820	466-7826	49-7
Perfecopy Co 103 W 61st St	Westmont	IL	60559	630-769-9901		628
Perfect 85 Degrees C Inc 2700 Alton Pkwy *Web:* www.85cafe.us	Irvine	CA	92606	949-553-8585		345
Perfect Commerce Inc 1 Compass Way Ste 120 *TF Sales:* 877-871-3788 ■ *Web:* perfect.com	Newport News	VA	23606	757-766-8211		39
Perfect Fit Industries Inc 230 Fifth Ave	New York	NY	10010	212-679-6656		746
Perfect Fit Placement Inc 1263 Berlin Tpke	Berlin	CT	06037	860-828-3127		260
Perfect Game Softball LLC 850 Twixt Town Rd NE *Web:* perfectgame.org	Cedar Rapids	IA	52402	319-298-2923		761
Perfect Home Care Inc 4210 Middlebrook Dr *Web:* www.perfecthomecare.net	Fort Worth	TX	76103	817-534-9600		363
Perfect Image Inc 8505 Crown Crescent Ct *Web:* www.perfectimageprint.com	Charlotte	NC	28227	704-841-2464		627
Perfect North Slopes Inc 19074 Perfect Pl Ln *Web:* perfectnorth.com	Lawrenceburg	IN	47025	812-537-3754		379
Perfect Parties Usa 147 Summit St Unit 6 *Web:* www.perfectpartiesusa.com	Peabody	MA	01960	978-977-0500		366
Perfect Plastic Printing Corp 311 Kautz Rd *Web:* www.perfectplastic.com	Saint Charles	IL	60174	630-584-1600	584-0648	704
Perfect Shutters Inc 12213 Rte 173 *TF:* 800-548-3336 ■ *Web:* www.shuttersinc.com	Hebron	IL	60034	815-648-2401		699
Perfect Sweep Inc 1202 S Expressway Dr *Web:* www.perfectsweep.com	Toledo	OH	43608	419-726-1801		63
Perfect Turf Inc 622 Sandpebble Dr *TF:* 888-796-8873 ■ *Web:* www.perfectturfinc.com	Schaumburg	IL	60193	888-796-8873		601
Perfect World Entertainment Inc 101 Redwood Shores Pkwy Ste 400 *Web:* www.perfectworld.com	Redwood City	CA	94065	650-590-7700		395
PerfectData Corp 1323 Conshohocken Rd *TF:* 800-973-7332 ■ *Web:* www.perfectdata.com	Plymouth Meeting	PA	19462	800-973-7332		534
PerfectForms Inc 2035 Corte Del Nogal Ste 165 *TF:* 866-900-8588 ■ *Web:* www.perfectforms.com	Carlsbad	CA	92011	866-900-8588		174
Perfection Clutch Co 100 Perfection Way *TF:* 800-258-8312 ■ *Web:* www.perfectionclutch.com	Timmonsville	SC	29161	843-326-5544		60
Perfection Gear Inc 9 N Bear Creek Rd *Web:* www.perfectiongear.com	Asheville	NC	28806	828-253-0000	253-2649	709
Perfection Group Inc 2649 Commerce Blvd *Web:* perfectiongroup.com	Cincinnati	OH	45241	513-772-7545		610
Perfection Metal Products Inc 3393 De La Cruz Blvd	Santa Clara	CA	95054	408-496-2950		295
Perfection Spring & Stamping Corp 1449 E Algonquin Rd *TF:* 800-638-2524 ■ *Web:* www.pss-corp.com	Mount Prospect	IL	60056	847-437-3900	437-1322	718
Perfekt Marketing Inc 3015 S 48th St *Web:* www.perfektmarketing.com	Tempe	AZ	85282	602-453-3333		5
Perfekta Inc 480 E 21st St N *Web:* www.perfekta-inc.com	Wichita	KS	67214	316-263-2056	263-0106	454
Perf-O-Log Inc 101 Bolton St **Fax Area Code:* 337 ■ *TF:* 888-892-8276	Lafayette	LA	70508	888-892-8276	235-8972*	536
Perforated Tubes Inc 4850 Fulton St E *TF:* 888-869-5736 ■ *Web:* www.perftubes.com	Ada	MI	49301	616-942-4550	942-2121	492
Perforce Software Inc 2320 Blanding Ave *Web:* perforce.com	Alameda	CA	94501	510-864-7400		177
Perform Better Inc PO Box 8090 *Web:* www.everythingtrackandfield.com	Cranston	RI	02920	401-942-9363		711
Performance Chevrolet Inc 4811 Madison Ave *Web:* www.performancechevy.com	Sacramento	CA	95841	916-331-6777		516
Performance Co, The 1263 US Hwy 59 N *Web:* www.performancetruck.com	Cleveland	TX	77328	281-593-8888		779
Performance Coating International 600 Murray St *Web:* pcoatingsintl.com	Bangor	PA	18013	610-588-7900	588-7901	600
Performance Contracting Group Inc 16400 College Blvd *TF:* 800-255-6886 ■ *Web:* www.pcg.com	Lenexa	KS	66219	913-888-8600	492-8723	189-10
Performance Contractors Inc 9901 Pecu Ln *Web:* www.performance-br.com	Baton Rouge	LA	70810	225-751-4156		188-7

Name / Address	City	State	Zip	Phone	Fax	Class
Performance Designs Inc 1300 E International Speedway Blvd *Web:* www.performancedesigns.com	DeLand	FL	32724	386-738-2224	734-8297	576
Performance Engineering Group Inc 32995 Industrial Rd *TF:* 800-533-0472 ■ *Web:* www.performanceengineering.com	Livonia	MI	48150	734-266-5300		612
Performance Feeders Inc 251 Dunbar *Web:* www.performancefeeders.com	Oldsmar	FL	34677	813-855-2685	855-4296	273
Performance Food Group Co 12500 W Creek Pkwy *TF:* 800-222-5521 ■ *Web:* www.pfgc.com	Richmond	VA	23238	804-484-7700		297-8
Performance Foodservice 12500 W Creek Pkwy *TF:* 800-535-5053 ■ *Web:* performancefoodservice.com	Richmond	VA	23238	804-484-7700		297-8
Performance Funding 11022 N 28th Dr *Web:* www.performancefunding.com	Phoenix	AZ	85029	602-912-0200		272
Performance Inc 1 Performance Way *Fax Area Code: 919 ■ *TF Cust Svc:* 800-727-2453 ■ *Web:* www.performancebike.com	Chapel Hill	NC	27514	800-727-2453	942-5431*	711
Performance Indicator LLC 116 John 1st/South Mill 1st Fl *Web:* www.performanceindicator.com	Lowell	MA	01852	978-459-4500		194
Performance Machining Inc 79 Pennsylvania Ave *Web:* www.performancemachine.com	Irwin	PA	15642	724-864-2499		454
Performance Materials Corp 1150 Calle Suerte *Web:* tencate.com	Camarillo	CA	93012	805-482-1722	482-8776	600
Performance Office Papers 21565 Hamburg Ave *TF:* 800-458-7189 ■ *Web:* www.perfpapers.com	Lakeville	MN	55044	800-458-7189	488-5058	110
Performance Plants Inc 700 Gardiners Rd *Web:* www.performanceplants.com	Kingston	ON	K7M3X9	613-545-0390		292
Performance Polymer Technologies Co 8801 Washington Blvd Ste 109 *Web:* www.pptech.com	Roseville	CA	95678	916-677-1414	677-1474	370
Performance Pulsation Control Inc 3309 Essex Dr Ste 200 *Web:* www.pulsationcontrol.com	Richardson	TX	75082	972-699-8600		610
Performance Software 2095 W Pinnacle Peak Rd Ste 120 *Web:* www.psware.com	Phoenix	AZ	85027	623-780-1517		177
Performance Stamping Company Inc 20 Lake Marian Rd *TF:* 800-935-0393 ■ *Web:* www.performancestamping.com	Carpentersville	IL	60110	847-426-2233		483
Performance Strategies Inc 9350 Castlegate Dr *Web:* www.performancestrategies.com	Indianapolis	IN	46256	317-842-0393	570-4711	304
Performance Support Inc 5775 Carmichael Pkwy *TF:* 800-752-1140 ■ *Web:* www.al-psi.com	Montgomery	AL	36117	334-244-9797		177
Performance Water Products Inc 6902 Aragon Cir *Web:* www.pwqa.org	Buena Park	CA	90620	714-736-0137		610
Performing Animal Welfare Society (PAWS) 11435 Simmerhorn Rd *TF:* 800-513-6560 ■ *Web:* www.pawsweb.org	Galt	CA	95632	209-745-2606	745-1809	48-3
Performing Arts Ctr 735 Anderson Hill Rd *Web:* www.artscenter.org	Purchase	NY	10577	914-251-6200	251-6171	572
Performing Arts Ctr at Rockwell Hall Rockwell Hall Rm 210 1300 Elmwood Ave *Web:* www.buffalostate.edu	Buffalo	NY	14222	716-878-3005	878-4234	572
PerformLine Inc 58 South St *Web:* performline.com	Morristown	NJ	07960	973-590-2305		393
PerformTech Inc 810 King St	Alexandria	VA	22314	703-548-0320		193
Pergo Inc 3128 Highwoods Blvd Ste 100 *TF:* 800-337-3746 ■ *Web:* na.pergo.com	Raleigh	NC	27604	800-337-3746		291
Peri & Sons Farms Inc PO Box 35 *Web:* www.periandsons.com	Yerington	NV	89447	775-463-4444	463-4028	10-11
Peri Formwork Systems Inc 7135 Dorsey Run Rd *Web:* www.peri-usa.com	Elkridge	MD	21075	410-712-7225		190
PERI Software Solutions Inc 570 Broad St *Web:* www.perisoftware.com	Newark	NJ	07102	973-735-9500		177
Pericom Semiconductor Corp 3545 N First St *NASDAQ: PSEM* ■ *TF:* 800-435-2336 ■ *Web:* www.pericom.com	San Jose	CA	95134	408-435-0800	435-1100	696
Periculum Capital Company LLC 4 Ctr Green Ste 200 *Web:* www.periculumcapital.com	Carmel	IN	46032	317-636-1800		70
Peridot Corp 1072 Serpentine Ln *Web:* www.peridotcorp.com	Pleasanton	CA	94566	925-461-8830		492
Peridrome Corp 284 Park Pl *Web:* www.peridrome.com	Brooklyn	NY	11238	917-881-0401		463
Perifitech of Ohio Inc 23108 Felch St *Web:* www.perifitech.com	Cleveland	OH	44128	216-332-0655		173-8
Perillo Tours 577 Chestnut Ridge Rd *TF:* 800-431-1515 ■ *Web:* www.perillotours.com	Woodcliff Lake	NJ	07677	201-307-1234	307-1808	760
Perimeter Church 9500 Medlock Bridge Rd *Web:* www.perimeter.org	Johns Creek	CO	30097	678-405-2000	405-2009	48-20
Perimeter Financial Corp 2 Queen St E Ste 1800 *Web:* www.pfin.ca	Toronto	ON	M5C3G7	416-703-7800		690
Perimeter Mall 4400 Ashford-Dunwoody Rd Ste 1360 *TF:* 800-554-0055 ■ *Web:* www.perimetermall.com	Atlanta	GA	30346	770-394-4270		460
Perimeter Security Solutions Inc 1900 Fannin St *Web:* www.perimetersecuritysolutions.com	Vernon	TX	76384	940-552-2942		693
Perini Management Services Inc 73 Mt Wayte Ave *Web:* www.tutorperini.com	Framingham	MA	01701	508-628-2000	628-2357	655
Perio Sciences LLC 11700 Preston Rd Ste 660 *TF:* 800-915-8110 ■ *Web:* www.periosciences.com	Dallas	TX	75230	800-915-8110		475
Periodical Publishers' Service Bureau 653 W Fallbrook Ave Ste 101 *TF:* 888-206-0350 ■ *Web:* www.ppsb.com	Fresno	CA	93711	888-206-0350		317
Periop Anesthesia Billing 111 Continental Dr Ste 412 *TF:* 800-250-7063 ■ *Web:* periop.com	Newark	DE	19713	800-250-7063		2
Peripheral Dynamics Inc 5150 Campus Dr *TF:* 800-523-0253 ■ *Web:* www.pdiscan.com	Plymouth Meeting	PA	19462	610-825-7090	834-7708	173-7
Peris Cos Inc 282 N Washington St *Web:* www.peris.com	Falls Church	VA	22046	703-533-4700	533-4710	186
Periscope Inc 921 Washington Ave S *Web:* www.periscope.com	Minneapolis	MN	55415	612-399-0500	399-0600	4
Perishable Distributors of Iowa Ltd 2741 SE PDI Pl *Web:* www.contactpdi.com	Ankeny	IA	50021	515-965-6300		297-8
Peritus Partners Inc 703 Briar Ranch Ln *Web:* www.peritusp.com	San Jose	CA	95120	408-228-3724		195
Peritus Public Relations 2829 Second Ave S Ste 335 *Web:* www.perituspr.com	Birmingham	AL	35233	205-267-6673		636
Periyali 35 W 20th St *TF:* 800-685-1447 ■ *Web:* www.periyali.com	New York	NY	10011	212-463-7890		671
PerkinElmer Genetics Inc 90 Emerson Ln *TF:* 800-762-4000 ■ *Web:* www.perkinelmer.com/genetics/index.html	Bridgeville	PA	15017	412-220-2300		418
PerkinElmer Inc 940 Winter St *NYSE: PKI* ■ *TF:* 800-762-4000 ■ *Web:* www.perkinelmer.com	Waltham	MA	02451	203-925-4602	944-4904	253
Perkins & Will 410 N Michigan Ave Ste 1600 *Web:* www.perkinswill.com	Chicago	IL	60611	312-755-0770	755-0775	261
Perkins Capital Management Inc 730 E Lake St *Web:* www.perkinscap.com	Wayzata	MN	55391	952-473-8367		401
Perkins Coie LLP 1201 Third Ave Ste 4800 *TF:* 888-720-8382 ■ *Web:* www.perkinscoie.com	Seattle	WA	98101	206-359-8000	359-9000	428
Perkins County 100 Main St PO Box 426 *Web:* ujs.sd.gov/County_Information/perkins.aspx	Bison	SD	57620	605-244-5626	244-7110	338
Perkins County PO Box 156 *Web:* www.co.perkins.ne.us	Grant	NE	69140	308-352-7560	352-7562	338
Perkins Equipment Div 630 John Hancock Rd *TF:* 800-733-5708 ■ *Web:* www.perkins1.com	Taunton	MA	02780	508-824-2800	821-2670	300
Perkins Group Inc, The 10701 McMullen Creek Pkwy Ste D *Web:* www.perkinsgroup.com	Charlotte	NC	28226	704-543-1111		260
Perkins Investment Management LLC 1 S Wacker Dr *Web:* pwmco.com	Chicago	IL	60606	312-341-9727	341-9737	41
Perkins Oil Company Inc 4707 Pflaum Rd *TF:* 800-631-0037 ■ *Web:* porkincoil.com	Madison	WI	53718	608-221-4736		541
Perkins Restaurant & Bakery 6075 Poplar Ave Ste 800 *TF:* 800-877-7375 ■ *Web:* www.perkinsrestaurants.com	Memphis	TN	38119	901-766-6400		670
Perkins Stone Mansion 550 Copley Rd *TF:* 800-875-4241 ■ *Web:* summithistory.org	Akron	OH	44320	330-535-1120	535-0250	50-3
Perkins Thompson, Attorneys & Counselors at Law 1 Canal Plaza *Web:* perkinsthompson.com	Portland	ME	04101	207-774-2635		428
Perkinson Reprographics Inc 735 E Brill St *TF:* 888-330-8782 ■ *Web:* www.prigraphics.com	Phoenix	AZ	85006	602-393-3131		627
Perkiomen School 200 Seminary St *TF:* 866-966-9998 ■ *Web:* www.perkiomen.org	Pennsburg	PA	18073	215-679-9511	679-1146	622
Perkiomen Valley Chamber of Commerce 351 E Main St *TF:* 800-209-1080 ■ *Web:* perkiomenvalleychamber.org	Collegeville	PA	19426	610-489-6660	454-1270	139
Perko Inc 16490 NW 13th Ave *Web:* www.perko.com	Miami	FL	33169	305-621-7525	620-9978	350
Perlectric 2711 Prosperity Ave *Web:* perlectric.com	Fairfax	VA	22031	703-352-5151	352-5155	189-4
Perley & Rideau Veterans' Health Centre 1750 Russell Rd *Web:* www.perleyrideau.ca	Ottawa	ON	K1G5Z6	613-526-7170		371
Perley-Halladay Assn Inc 1037 Andrew Dr *TF:* 800-248-5800 ■ *Web:* www.perleyhalladay.com	West Chester	PA	19380	610-296-5800	647-1711	803-2
Perlick Corp 8300 W Good Hope Rd *TF:* 800-558-5592 ■ *Web:* www.perlick.com	Milwaukee	WI	53223	414-353-7060	353-7069	664
Perlmart Inc 954 Route 166 *TF:* 800-367-0076 ■ *Web:* shoprite.com	Toms River	NJ	08753	732-341-0700		345
Perlmutter Ed (Rep D - CO) 1410 Longworth Bldg *Web:* perlmutter.house.gov	Washington	DC	20515	202-225-2645	225-5278	342-2
Perma Pom LLC 9611 Hwy 60 S *Web:* www.pepcopoms.com	Lane City	TX	77453	979-532-3106		535
Perma Treat Corp 74 Airline Dr	Durham	CT	06422	860-349-1133		818
Permabit 1 Alewife Ctr Ste 330 *Web:* www.permabit.com	Cambridge	MA	02140	617-252-9600	252-9977	224
Perma-Bound 617 E Vandalia Rd *Fax Area Code: 800 ■ *TF:* 800-637-6581 ■ *Web:* www.perma-bound.com	Jacksonville	IL	62650	217-243-5451	551-1169*	92
Permac Industries Inc 14401 Ewing Ave S *Web:* www.permacindustries.com	Burnsville	MN	55306	952-894-7231		757
PERMAC Securities Inc 285 Grand Ave Bldg No 1 *Web:* www.victorsecurities.com	Englewood	NJ	07631	646-820-8732		690
Permadur Industries Inc 186 Rt 206 S *TF:* 800-392-0146 ■ *Web:* www.permadur.com	Hillsborough	NJ	08844	908-359-9767	359-9773	386

Name / Address	Phone	Fax	Class
Perma-Fix Environmental Services Inc 8302 Dunwoody Pl Ste 250 Atlanta GA 30350 *NASDAQ: PESI* ■ *TF:* 800-365-6066 ■ *Web:* www.perma-fix.com	770-587-9898	587-9937	667
Perma-Fix Northwest Inc 2025 Battelle Blvd Richland WA 99354	509-375-5160		667
Perma-Glaze Inc 1638 Research Loop Rd Ste 160 Tucson AZ 85710 *TF:* 800-332-7397 ■ *Web:* www.permaglaze.com	520-722-9718	296-4393	189-11
Perma-Greetings Inc 2470 Schuetz Rd Maryland Heights MO 63043 *Web:* permagraphics.net	314-567-4606		130
Permal Group, The 900 Third Ave 28th Fl New York NY 10022 *Web:* www.permal.com	212-418-6500		401
Permanent Magnet Company Inc 4437 Bragdon St Lawrence IN 46226	317-547-1336		458
Permanent Mission of Albania 320 E 79th St New York NY 10075 *Web:* www.ambasadat.gov.al	212-249-2059	535-2917	784
Permanent Mission of Cambodia 327 E 58th St New York NY 10022	212-336-0777		784
Permanent Mission of Iraq 14 E 79th St New York NY 10075 *Web:* iraqmission.us	212-737-4433		784
Permanent Mission of Macedonia 866 UN Plaza New York NY 10017 *Web:* www.macedonianembassy.org	212-308-8504		784
Permanent Mission of Mali 111 E 69th St New York NY 10021 *Web:* www.un.int/mali	212-737-4150	472-3778	784
Permanent Mission of Solomon Islands to the United Nations, The 800 Second Ave Ste 400L New York NY 10017 *Web:* www.un.int/solomonislands	212-599-6192	661-8925	784
Permanent Mission of Sweden to the United Nations 885 Second Ave Fl 46 1 Dag Hammarskjold Plz New York NY 10017 *Web:* www.swedenabroad.com	212-583-2500		784
Permanent Mission of the Islamic Republic of Iran to the United Nations 622 Third Ave New York NY 10017 *Web:* www.un.int	212-687-2020	867-7086	784
Permanent Mission of The Kingdom of Bahrain to The United Nations 866 Second Ave 14th & 15th Fls New York NY 10017 *Web:* www.un.int/bahrain	212-223-6200	223-6206	784
Permanent Mission of the Netherlands 666 Third Ave 19th Fl New York NY 10017 *Web:* www.netherlandsmission.org	212-519-9500	370-1954	784
Permanent Mission of the Republic of Cape Verde to the United Nations 27 E 69th St New York NY 10021 *Web:* www.un.int	212-472-0333	794-1398	784
Permanent Mission of the Republic of Serbia to the United Nations - New York 854 Fifth Ave New York NY 10065 *Web:* www.un.int	212-879-8700	879-8705	784
Permanent Mission of the Republic of Seychelles 800 Second Ave Ste 400C New York NY 10017 *Web:* www.un.int/seychelles	212-972-1785	972-1786	784
Permanent Mission of the Republic of the Union of Myanmar 10 E 77th St New York NY 10075 *Web:* mmnewyork.org	212-744-1271		784
Permanent Mission of Ukraine 220 E 51st St New York NY 10022 *Web:* www.ukraineun.org	212-759-7003	355-9455	784
Perma-Pipe Inc 7720 N Lehigh Ave Niles IL 60714 *TF:* 800-392-3299 ■ *Web:* www.permapipe.com	847-966-2235	470-1204	595
Perma-Seal Waterproofing 513 Rogers St Downers Grove IL 60515 *TF:* 800-421-7325 ■ *Web:* www.permaseal.net	630-512-0002		186
Permatech Inc 911 E Elm St Graham NC 27253 *Web:* www.permatech.net	336-578-0701	578-7758	663
Permatile Concrete Products Co 100 Beacon Rd Bristol VA 24203 *TF:* 800-662-5332 ■ *Web:* www.permatile.com	276-669-5332		135
PermaTreat Inc 505 Lafayette Blvd Fredericksburg VA 22401 *TF:* 866-737-6287 ■ *Web:* www.permatreat.com	866-737-6287		192
Permatron Group 2020 Touhy Ave Elk Grove Village IL 60007 *TF:* 800-882-8012 ■ *Web:* www.permatron.com	847-434-1421		17
Perma-Type Company Inc 83 NW Dr Plainville CT 06062 *TF:* 800-243-4234 ■ *Web:* www.perma-type.com	860-747-9999	747-1986	477
Permco Inc 1500 Frost Rd Streetsboro OH 44241 *TF:* 800-626-2801 ■ *Web:* www.permco.com	330-626-2801	626-2805	640
Permedion Inc 350 Worthington Rd Ste H Westerville OH 43082 *TF:* 800-772-2179 ■ *Web:* hmspermedion.com	614-895-9900		194
Permenent Mission of Argentina 1 UN Plaza New York NY 10017	212-688-6300		784
Permenent Mission of Turkey 821 UN Plaza 10th Fl New York NY 10017	212-949-0150		784
Permeon Biologics Inc 1 Kendall Sq Bldg 1400 W Ste 14203 Cambridge MA 02139 *Web:* www.permeonbio.com	617-945-7780		231
Permobil Inc 6961 Eastgate Blvd Lebanon TN 37090 **Fax Area Code: 800* ■ *TF:* 800-736-0925 ■ *Web:* www.permobil.com	615-443-2839	231-3256*	475
Pernod Ricard USA 100 Manhattanville Rd Purchase NY 10577 *Web:* www.pernod-ricard-usa.com	914-848-4800		81-3
Perot Theatre 219 Main St Texarkana TX 75501 *Web:* www.trahc.org	903-792-4992	793-8511	572
Perpetual Energy Inc 605 5 Ave SW Ste 3200 Calgary AB T2P3H5 *TF:* 800-811-5522 ■ *Web:* www.perpetualenergyinc.com	403-269-4400		536
Perquimans County 128 N Church St PO Box 45 Hertford NC 27944 *Web:* www.co.perquimans.nc.us	252-312-5314		338
Perreca Electric Co 520 Broadway Newburgh NY 12550 *TF:* 800-244-1433 ■ *Web:* www.perreca.com	845-562-4080		189-4
Perricone's Marketplace & Cafe 15 SE Tenth St Miami FL 33131 *Web:* www.perricones.com	305-374-9449	371-6647	671
Perrier & Lacoste L L C 365 Canal St Ste 2550 New Orleans LA 70130 *Web:* www.perrierlacoste.com	504-212-8820		445
Perrigo Co 515 Eastern Ave Allegan MI 49010 *NYSE: PRGO* ■ *TF:* 800-719-9260 ■ *Web:* www.perrigo.com	269-673-8451	673-9128	583
Perrin Holden & Davenport Capital Corp 5 Hanover Sq New York NY 10004	212-269-3500		70
Perris Union High School District 155 E Fourth St Perris CA 92570 *Web:* www.puhsd.org	951-943-6369		685
Perritt Laboratories Inc 145 S Main St PO Box 147 Hightstown NJ 08520 *Web:* www.childsafepackaginggroup.com	609-443-4848		743
Perrot State Park W26247 Sullivan Rd Trempealeau WI 54661 *Web:* dnr.wi.gov	608-534-6409		565
Perry & Associates LLC 221 N La Salle St Ste 3100 Chicago IL 60601 *Web:* www.perryllc.com	312-364-9112		261
Perry Anthony Design Group 5331 Limestone Rd Wilmington DE 19808 *Web:* www.perryanthony.com	302-239-6161		77
Perry Area Convention & Visitors Bureau 101 Gen Courtney Hodges Blvd Perry GA 31069 *Web:* www.perryga.com	478-988-8000	988-8005	206
Perry Baromedical Corp 3750 Prospect Ave Riviera Beach FL 33404 *TF:* 800-741-4376 ■ *Web:* www.perrybaromedical.com	561-840-0395		476
Perry Bros Tire Service Inc 610 Wicker St Sanford NC 27330 *Web:* www.perrybros.com	919-775-7225		62-5
Perry Color Card 685 W Ter Dr San Dimas CA 91773 *TF:* 800-662-1800 ■ *Web:* www.perrycolorcard.com	909-599-7954		393
Perry Communications Group Inc 925 L St Ste 1200 Sacramento CA 95814 *Web:* perrycom.com	916-658-0144		636
Perry Construction Group Inc 1440 W 21st St Erie PA 16502 *Web:* www.perryconst.com	814-459-8551	453-5653	186
Perry County 333 Seventh St PO Box 721 Tell City IN 47586 *TF:* 888-343-6262 ■ *Web:* www.pickperry.com	812-547-7933	547-8378	338
Perry County 481 Main St First Fl PO Box 210 Hazard KY 41701 *Web:* www.perrycounty.ky.gov	606-439-1816	439-1686	338
Perry County PO Box 16 Linden TN 37096 *Web:* www.perrycountytennessee.com	931-589-2216	589-2215	338
Perry County 1293 Washington St Marion AL 36756 *TF:* 800-648-5381 ■ *Web:* www.perrycountyalabamachamber.com	334-683-9622		338
Perry County 103 S Main St New Augusta MS 39462 *Web:* chancery10.com	601-964-8398		338
Perry County 25 W Main St PO Box 37 New Bloomfield PA 17068 *TF:* 800-852-2102 ■ *Web:* www.perryco.org	717-582-2131	582-5162	338
Perry County 105 N Main St PO Box 207 New Lexington OH 43764 *TF:* 800-282-6556 ■ *Web:* www.perrycountycourt.com	740-342-3156	342-2188	338
Perry County 310 W Main St Ste 101 Perryville AR 72126 *Web:* perrycoarkansas.org	501-889-5128	889-2574	338
Perry County 3764 State Rts 13-127 Rm 110 PO Box 438 Pinckneyville IL 62274 *Web:* perrycountyclerk.com	618-357-5116	357-3365	338
Perry County District Library 117 S Jackson St New Lexington OH 43764 *TF:* 800-344-5818 ■ *Web:* www.pcdl.org	740-342-4194	342-4204	434-3
Perry County Public Library 289 Black Gold Blvd Hazard KY 41701 *Web:* www.perrycountylibrary.org	606-436-4747		435
Perry Engineering Company Inc 1945 Millwood Pk Winchester VA 22602 *TF:* 800-572-5021 ■ *Web:* www.perryeng.com	540-667-4310	667-7618	189-5
Perry Foam Products 2335 S 30th St Lafayette IN 47909 *Web:* www.perrychemical.com	765-474-3404		596
Perry Green Valley Nursing Home Inc 1103 Birch St Perry OK 73077 *Web:* greenvalleyhealthcare.net	580-336-2285		371
Perry Group International 1 Market Plaza Ste 3600 San Francisco CA 94105 *TF:* 800-580-3950 ■ *Web:* www.perrygroup.com	800-580-3950		378
Perry Homes PO Box 34306 Houston TX 77234 *TF:* 800-247-3779 ■ *Web:* www.perryhomes.com	713-948-7700		187
Perry Insurance 522 Chickering Rd North Andover MA 01845 *Web:* perryins.com	978-685-7690		390
Perry Johnson Registrars Inc 26555 Evergreen Rd Ste 1340 Southfield MI 48076 *TF:* 800-800-7910 ■ *Web:* www.pjr.com	248-358-3388		194
Perry Memorial Library 205 Breckenridge St Henderson NC 27536 *Web:* www.perrylibrary.org	252-438-3316	438-3744	434-3
Perry Products Corp 25 Mt Laurel Rd Hainesport NJ 08036 *Web:* www.perryproducts.com	609-267-1600	267-8724	14
Perry Scott (Rep R - PA) 1207 Longworth HOB Washington DC 20515 *Web:* perry.house.gov	202-225-5836	226-1000	342-2
Perry State Park 5441 Westlake Rd Ozawkie KS 66070 *Web:* ksoutdoors.com/State-Parks/Locations/Perry	785-246-3449		565
Perry Supply Company Inc 2625 Vassar NE Albuquerque NM 87107 *Web:* www.perrysupply.net	505-884-6972		612
Perry Technical Institute 2011 W Washington Ave Yakima WA 98903 *TF:* 888-528-8586 ■ *Web:* www.perrytech.edu	509-453-0374		162
Perry Technology Corp 120 Industrial Park Rd New Hartford CT 06057 *Web:* www.perrygear.com	860-738-2525		22

	Phone	Fax	Class
Perry Veterinary Clinic PLLC			
3180 Rt 246 Perry....New York NY 14530	585-237-5550		794
TF: 800-767-5611 ■ *Web:* www.perryvet.com			
Perry Videx LLC 25 Mt Laurel Rd....Hainesport NJ 08036	609-267-1600	267-4499	386
Web: www.perryvidex.com			
Perry's Ice Cream Company Inc			
1 Ice Cream Plaza....Akron NY 14001	716-542-5492	542-2544	296-25
TF: 800-873-7797 ■ *Web:* www.perrysicecream.com			
Perry's Victory & International Peace Memorial			
93 Delaware Ave PO Box 549....Put-in-Bay OH 43456	419-285-2184	285-2516	564
TF: 800-835-5237 ■ *Web:* www.nps.gov/pevi			
Perryman Financial Advisory Inc			
12221 Merit Dr Ste 1660....Dallas TX 75251	972-770-4800		401
Web: www.billperryman.com			
Perrysburg Area Chamber of Commerce			
105 W Indiana Ave....Perrysburg OH 43551	419-874-9147	872-9347	139
Web: www.perrysburgchamber.com			
Perrywinkles Fine Jewelry			
227 Main St....Burlington VT 05401	802-865-2624		410
TF: 800-983-7174 ■ *Web:* www.perrywinkles.com			
Persante Health Care Inc			
130 Gaither Dr Ste 124....Mt. Laurel NJ 08054	856-234-0770		418
Web: www.persante.com			
Perseverance Theatre 914 Third St....Douglas AK 99824	907-364-2421	364-2603	573-4
Web: www.ptalaska.org			
Pershing County PO Box 736 PO Box 820....Lovelock NV 89419	775-273-2208	273-3015	338
TF: 800-240-7094 ■ *Web:* www.pershingcounty.net			
Pershing Ctr 226 Centennial Mall S....Lincoln NE 68508	402-441-8744		205
Pershing State Park 29277 Hwy 130....Laclede MO 64651	660-963-2299		565
Web: www.mostateparks.com			
Persimmon Group, The			
11 E Fifth St Ste 300....Tulsa OK 74103	918-592-4121		194
Web: www.thepersimmongroup.com			
Persimmon Press PO Box 297....Belmont CA 94002	650-802-8325	910-5095*	130
**Fax Area Code:* 800 ■ *TF:* 800-910-5080 ■ *Web:* www.persimmoncards.com			
Persimmon Technologies Corp			
200 Harvard Mill Sq Ste 110....Wakefield MA 01880	781-587-0677		196
Web: www.persimmontech.com			
Persis Corp 900 Ft St Mall Ste 1725....Honolulu HI 96813	808-599-8000	526-4114	655
Web: www.persis.com			
Person & Covey Inc 616 Allen Ave....Glendale CA 91201	800-423-2341		214
TF: 800-423-2341 ■ *Web:* www.personandcovey.com			
Person Centered Services Inc			
240 N Union St....Stockton CA 95205	209-466-2448		685
Web: www.pcs4dd.com			
Person County 304 S Morgan St Rm 212....Roxboro NC 27573	336-597-1720	599-1609	338
Web: www.personcounty.net			
Person County Public Schools			
304 S Morgan St....Roxboro NC 27573	336-599-2191		685
TF: 866 724-6650 ■ *Web:* www.person.k12.nc.us			
Personal Capital Corp			
726 Main St....Redwood City CA 94063	855-855-8005		401
TF: 855-855-8005 ■ *Web:* www.personalcapital.com			
Personal Care Inc 321 Sycamore St....Decatur GA 30030	404-373-2727		363
Web: personalcare.net			
Personal Eyes Optical Laboratory Co			
2455 Xenium Ln N....Minneapolis MN 55441	763-559-8848		542
Web: www.personaleyesopticallab.com			
Personal Finance Newsletter			
7600A Leesburg Pk W Bldg Ste 300....Falls Church VA 22043	703-394-4931	905-8100	531-9
TF: 800-832-2330 ■ *Web:* www.investingdaily.com			
Personal Genome Diagnostics Inc			
2809 Boston St Ste 503....Baltimore MD 21224	443-602-8833		418
TF: 800-228-8460 ■ *Web:* personalgenome.com			
Personal Products Co			
1 Johnson & Johnson Plaza....New Brunswick NJ 08933	732-524-0400		214
Web: www.jnj.com/our_company/family_of_companies			
PersonalizeDx 2980 Scott St....Vista CA 92081	855-739-5669		415
TF: 855-739-5669 ■ *Web:* www.personalizedxlabs.com/2.html			
Personal-Touch Home Care Inc			
186-18 Hillside Ave....Jamaica NY 11432	718-468-2500	681-2550*	363
**Fax Area Code:* 412 ■ **Fax:* Hum Res ■ *TF:* 888-275-4147 ■ *Web:* www.pthomecare.com			
Personnel Data Systems Inc (PDS)			
470 Norristown Rd....Blue Bell PA 19422	610-238-4600	238-4550	178-1
TF: 800-243-8737 ■ *Web:* www.pdssoftware.com			
Personnel Management Inc			
PO Box 6657....Shreveport LA 71136	318-869-4555	841-4350	631
TF: 800-259-4126 ■ *Web:* www.pmiresource.com			
Personnel Systems Associates Inc			
7551 E Moonridge Ln....Anaheim CA 92808	714-281-8337		196
Web: personnelsystems.com			
Persons Majestic Mfg Co PO Box 370....Huron OH 44839	419-433-9057	433-0182	517
TF: 800-772-2453 ■ *Web:* www.permaco.com			
Perspectiva Architects			
3401 Louisiana St Ste 270....Houston TX 77002	713-520-7580		186
Perspectives Ltd			
20 N Clark St Ste 2650....Chicago IL 60602	800-866-7556	558-1570*	462
**Fax Area Code:* 312 ■ *TF:* 800-866-7556 ■ *Web:* www.perspectivesltd.com			
Perstorp Polyols Inc 600 Matzinger Rd....Toledo OH 43612	419-729-5448	729-3291	144
TF Cust Svc: 800-537-0280 ■ *Web:* www.perstorp.com			
PerSys Medical Co 5310 Elm St....Houston TX 77081	888-737-7978		475
TF: 888-737-7978 ■ *Web:* www.ps-med.com			
Persyst Consulting LLC			
12345 Lake City Way NE Ste 396....Seattle WA 98125	206-396-5825		463
Persystent Technology Corp			
3816 W Linebaugh Ave Ste 305....Tampa FL 33618	813-264-2999	264-2879	809
Perteet Inc			
2707 Colby Ave Ste 900 Ste900....Everett WA 98201	425-252-7700		261
TF: 800-615-9900 ■ *Web:* www.perteet.com			
Perth & District Chamber of Commerce			
34 Herriott St....Perth ON K7H1T2	613-267-3200	267-6797	137
Web: www.perthchamber.com			
Perth Amboy Public Library			
196 Jefferson St....Perth Amboy NJ 08861	732-826-2600		434-3
Web: ci.perthamboy.nj.us			
Perth Amboy Spring Works			
185 Sheridan St....Perth Amboy NJ 08861	732-442-4420		57
Perth-Smiths Falls District Hospital			
60 Cornelia St W....Smiths Falls ON K7A2H9	613-283-2330	283-8990	374-2
TF: 800-267-7946 ■ *Web:* www.psfdh.on.ca			
Pertronix Inc 440 E Arrow Hwy....San Dimas CA 91773	909-599-5955		57
Web: www.pertronix.com			
Peru 820 Second Ave Ste 1600....New York NY 10017	212-687-3336	972-6975	784
Web: www.un.int/peru			
Consulate General			
6795 E Tennessee Ave Ste 550....Denver CO 80224	303-355-8555	355-8555	257
Web: www.consulado.pe/es/Denver/Paginas/Inicio.aspx			
Consulate General			
3450 Wilshire Blvd....Los Angeles CA 90010	213-252-5910	252-8130	257
TF: 855-303-7378 ■ *Web:* www.consulado.pe/paginas/Inicio.aspx			
Consulate General			
444 Brickell Ave Ste M135....Miami FL 33131	877-714-7378	381-6027*	257
**Fax Area Code:* 305 ■ *TF:* 877-714-7378 ■ *Web:* www.consulado.pe/paginas/Inicio.aspx			
Consulate General			
180 N Michigan Ave Ste 1830....Chicago IL 60601	312-782-1599	704-6969	257
Web: www.consulado.pe/paginas/Inicio.aspx			
Peru State College 600 Hoyt St PO Box 10....Peru NE 68421	402-872-3815	872-2296*	166
**Fax:* Admissions ■ *TF:* 800-742-4412 ■ *Web:* www.peru.edu			
Peru State College Library			
600 Hoyt St PO Box 10....Peru NE 68421	402-872-3815	872-2311	434-6
TF: 800-742-4412 ■ *Web:* www.peru.edu			
Pervasive Software Inc			
12365 Riata Trace Pkwy Bldg B....Austin TX 78727	512-231-6000	231-6010	178-12
NASDAQ: PVSW ■ *TF:* 800-287-4383 ■ *Web:* www.pervasive.com			
Pervasive Solutions			
117 Victor Heights Pkwy....Victor NY 14564	585-300-0440		196
Web: www.pervasivesolutions.net			
Peryam & Kroll Research Corp			
6323 N Avondale Ave....Chicago IL 60631	773-774-3100		668
TF: 800-747-5522 ■ *Web:* www.pk-research.com			
PES (IEEE Power Engineering Society)			
IEEE Operations Ctr 445 Hoes Ln....Piscataway NJ 08854	732-562-3883	562-3881	49-19
TF: 800-678-4333 ■ *Web:* www.ieee-pes.org			
Pes Environmental Inc			
7665 Redwood Blvd Ste 100....Novato CA 94947	415-899-1600		261
Web: www.pesenv.com			
PES Payroll Inc 4100 W Burbank Blvd....Burbank CA 91505	818-729-0080		631
TF: 800-301-1992 ■ *Web:* www.pespayroll.com			
PES Structural engineers			
1852 Century Pl NE....Atlanta GA 30345	770-457-5923		261
Web: www.pesengineers.com			
Pescadero State Beach			
1416 Ninth St....Sacramento CA 95814	916-653-6995		565
Web: www.parks.ca.gov/?page_id=522			
Peshtigo River State Forest			
N10008 Paust Ln....Crivitz WI 54114	715-757-3965		565
Web: dnr.wi.gov/newurl.html			
Pest Shield Pest Control Inc			
15329 Tradesman....San Antonio TX 78249	210-525-8823		577
TF: 888-728-8237 ■ *Web:* www.sanantonio-pestcontrol.com			
Pestmaster Services Inc 137 East S St....Bishop CA 93514	760-873-8100		577
Web: www.pestmaster.com			
Pet Adoption Network, The			
4261 Culver Rd....Rochester NY 14622	585-338-9175		794
Web: www.petadoptionnetwork.org			
Pet Dairy 2900 Bristol Hwy....Johnson City TN 37601	423-283-5700		296-25
TF: 800-283-0765 ■ *Web:* www.petdairy.com			
Pet Food Express 500 85th Ave....Oakland CA 94621	510-924-3300		578
Web: www.petfoodexpress.com			
Pet Food Institute (PFI)			
2025 M St NW Ste 800....Washington DC 20036	202-367-1120	367-2120	49-4
Web: www.petfoodinstitute.org			
Pet Health Pharmacy			
12012 N 111th Ave....Youngtown AZ 85363	623-214-2791		237
TF: 800-742-0516 ■ *Web:* www.pethealthpharmacy.com			
Pet Industry Distributors Assn (PIDA)			
2105 Laurel Bush Rd Ste 200....Bel Air MD 21015	443-640-1060		49-18
Web: www.pida.org			
Pet Industry Joint Advisory Council (PIJAC)			
1220 19th St NW Ste 400....Washington DC 20036	202-452-1525	293-4377	49-4
TF: 800-553-7387 ■ *Web:* www.pijac.org			
Pet Network 105 Gordon Baker Rd 8th Fl....Toronto ON M2H3P8	416-756-2404	756-5526	740
Pet Safe International			
10427 Electric Ave....Knoxville TN 37932	865-777-5404		578
TF Cust Svc: 800-732-2677 ■ *Web:* petsafe.net/home			
Pet Sitters International (PSI)			
201 E King St....King NC 27021	336-983-9222		48-3
Web: www.petsit.com			
Pet Supermarket Inc			
1100 International Pkwy....Sunrise FL 33323	954-351-0834	351-0897	578
TF: 866-434-1990 ■ *Web:* www.petsupermarket.com			
Pet Supplies "Plus" Inc			
17197 N Laurel Prk Dre Ste 402....Livonia MI 48152	734-793-6600		578
TF: 800-777-9665 ■ *Web:* www.petsuppliesplus.com			
Pet Supplies Inc 203 N Talbolt St....St Michaels MD 21663	800-738-7877		791
TF: 800-738-7877 ■ *Web:* www.petsupplies.com			
Pet Valu Canada Inc			
225 Royal Crest Crt....Markham ON L3R9X6	905-946-1200		578
TF: 800-845-4759 ■ *Web:* www.petvalu.com			
Pet Vet Animal Hospitals			
4520 Katy Fwy....Houston TX 77007	281-561-0276	629-7737*	794
**Fax Area Code:* 713 ■ *Web:* www.petvethospitals.com			
PETA (People for the Ethical Treatment of Animals)			
501 Front St....Norfolk VA 23510	757-622-7382	622-0457	48-3
TF: 800-566-9768 ■ *Web:* www.peta.org			
Petaluma Adobe State Historic Park			
3325 Old Adobe Rd....Petaluma CA 94954	707-762-4871		565
Web: www.parks.ca.gov			
Petaluma Area Chamber of Commerce			
6 Petaluma Blvd N Ste A-2....Petaluma CA 94952	707-762-2785	762-4721	139
Web: www.petalumachamber.com			
Petaluma City Schools (PCS)			
200 Douglas St....Petaluma CA 94952	707-778-4813		685
Web: www.petalumacityschools.org			

Name / Address	City	State	Zip	Phone	Fax	Class
Petaluma Fairgrounds Speedway 100 Fairgrounds Dr *Web:* www.petaluma-speedway.com	Petaluma	CA	94952	707-763-7223		642
Petaluma Poultry 2700 Lakeville Hwy *Web:* www.petalumapoultry.com	Petaluma	CA	94954	707-763-1904		619
PETCO Animal Supplies Inc 9125 Rehco Rd *TF:* 877-738-6742 ■ *Web:* www.petco.com	San Diego	CA	92121	858-453-7845	784-3489	578
Petco Park 100 Pk Blvd *TF:* 866-800-1275 ■ *Web:* sandiego.padres.mlb.com	San Diego	CA	92101	619-795-5000		720
Pete Baur Buick GMC Inc 14000 Pearl Rd *Web:* petebaur.com	Cleveland	OH	44136	440-580-4256		57
Pete Fowler Construction Services 931 Calle Negocio Ste J *Web:* www.petefowler.com	San Clemente	CA	92673	949-240-9971		196
Pete Lien & Sons Inc 3401 Universal Dr *Web:* www.petelien.com	Rapid City	SD	57709	605-342-7224		503-4
Pete's Road Service Inc 2230 E Orangethorpe Ave *Web:* www.petesrs.com	Fullerton	CA	92831	714-446-1207		754
Pete's Tire Barns Inc 275 E Main St *TF:* 800-239-1833 ■ *Web:* www.petestire.com	Orange	MA	01364	978-544-8811		755
Peter A Sokoloff & Co 550 N Brand Blvd Ste 1650 *TF:* 800-379-6393 ■ *Web:* www.sokoloffco.com	Glendale	CA	91203	818-547-4500		401
Peter A. Mayer Advertising Inc 324 Camp St *Web:* www.peteramayer.com	New Orleans	LA	70130	504-581-7191		7
Peter Baker & Son Co 1349 Rockland Rd *Web:* www.peterbaker.com	Lake Bluff	IL	60044	847-362-3663	362-0707	188-4
Peter Basso Associates Inc 5145 Livernois Ste 100 *Web:* www.peterbassoassociates.com	Troy	MI	48098	248-879-5666		261
Peter Becker Community 800 Maple Ave *Web:* peterbeckercommunity.com	Harleysville	PA	19438	215-256-9501		672
Peter Bell CPA 1735 Dilworth Rd E *Web:* peterbellpllc.com	Charlotte	NC	28203	704-525-9999		2
Peter Dag Portfolio Strategy & Management, The 65 Lake Front Dr *TF:* 800-833-2782 ■ *Web:* www.peterdag.com	Akron	OH	44319	330-644-2782		531-9
Peter Findlay Gallery 16 E 79th St *TF:* 800-894-4548 ■ *Web:* www.findlay.com	New York	NY	10075	212-644-4433	644-1675	42
Peter Glenn Ski & Sports 2901 W Oakland Pk Blvd *TF:* 800-818-0946 ■ *Web:* www.peterglenn.com	Fort Lauderdale	FL	33311	954-484-3606		711
Peter J Bertuglia CPA PC 775 Park Ave *Web:* bertugliacpa.com	Huntington	NY	11743	631-385-7003		2
Peter J McGovern Little League Baseball Museum 539 US Rt 15 Hwy PO Box 3485 *Web:* www.littleleague.org	Williamsport	PA	17701	570-326-1921	326-1074	522
Peter J. Jaensch Immigration 2198 Main St *TF:* 800-870-3676 ■ *Web:* visaamerica.com	Sarasota	FL	34237	941-366-9841		428
Peter King Corp 11040 N 19th Ave *Web:* petekingaz.com	Phoenix	AZ	85029	602-944-4441	943-4876	189-8
Peter Lang Publishing Inc 29 Broadway *TF:* 800-770-5264 ■ *Web:* www.peterlang.com	New York	NY	10006	212-647-7706	647-7707	637-2
Peter Lougheed Ctr 3500 26th Ave NE *TF:* 800-282-9911 ■ *Web:* www.albertahealthservices.ca	Calgary	AB	T1Y6J4	403-943-4555	943-4878	374-2
Peter Luger Steak House 178 Broadway *Web:* www.peterluger.com	Brooklyn	NY	11211	718-387-7400	387-3523	671
Peter Nero & the Philly Pops 1518 Walnut St Ste 1706 *Web:* www.phillypops.com	Philadelphia	PA	19102	215-875-8004		573-3
Peter Pan Bus Lines PO Box 1776 *TF:* 800-343-9999 ■ *Web:* www.peterpanbus.com	Springfield	MA	01102	800-343-9999		107
Peter Pan Seafoods Inc 2200 Sixth Ave Ste 1000 *TF:* 800-331-3522 ■ *Web:* www.ppsf.com	Seattle	WA	98121	206-728-6000	441-9090	296-13
Peter Parts Electronics Inc 6285 Dean Pkwy *Web:* www.peterparts.com	Ontario	NY	14519	585-265-2000		246
Peter Paul Electronics Co Inc 480 John Downey Dr *TF:* 800-825-8377 ■ *Web:* peterpaul.com	New Britain	CT	06051	860-229-4884	223-1734	789
Peter Pepper Products Inc 17929 S Susana Rd *TF:* 800-496-0204 ■ *Web:* www.peterpepper.com	Compton	CA	90221	310-639-0390	639-6013	591
Peter Piper Inc 4745 N Seventh St Ste 350 *TF:* 800-899-3425 ■ *Web:* www.peterpiperpizza.com	Phoenix	AZ	85014	480-609-6400		670
Peter Strain & Assoc 5455 Wilshire Blvd Ste 1812 *Web:* natacharoi.com	Los Angeles	CA	90036	323-525-3391		731
Peter Thomas Roth Labs LLC 460 Pk Ave 22nd Fl *TF:* 800-787-7546 ■ *Web:* www.peterthomasroth.com	New York	NY	10022	212-581-5800	581-5810	214
Peter White Public Library 217 N Front St *TF:* 800-992-9012 ■ *Web:* www.uproc.lib.mi.us	Marquette	MI	49855	906-228-9510	226-1783	434-3
Peter Yegen Jr Yellowstone County Museum 1950 Terminal Cir *TF:* 800-735-2635 ■ *Web:* www.pyjrycm.org	Billings	MT	59105	406-256-6811	254-6031	520
Peter's Choice Nutrition Center 4879 Fountain Ave *TF:* 888-324-9904 ■ *Web:* www.vites.com	Los Angeles	CA	90029	888-324-9904		297-8
Peter's Inn 504 S Ann St *Web:* www.petersinn.com	Baltimore	MD	21231	410-675-7313		671
Peterbilt Motors Co 1700 Woodbrook St **Fax:* Hum Res ■ *Web:* www.peterbilt.com	Denton	TX	76205	940-591-4000	591-4260*	516
Peterborough Regional Health Ctr 1 Hospital Dr *Web:* www.prhc.on.ca	Peterborough	ON	K9J7C6	705-743-2121		374-2
Peters & Company PC 610 S W Alder St 910 *Web:* peterscopc.com	Portland	OR	97205	503-241-8080		2
Peters & Freedman LLP 191 Calle Magdalena Ste 220 *TF:* 800-439-9962 ■ *Web:* www.hoalaw.com	Encinitas	CA	92024	760-436-3441		428
Peters Gary (Sen D - MI) Hart Senate Office Bldg Ste 724 *Web:* www.peters.senate.gov	Washington	DC	20510	202-224-6221		342-2
Peters Main Street Photography 314 N Main St *Web:* www.petersphotography.com	London	OH	43140	740-852-2731		590
Peters Murdaugh Parker Ellzr 123 S Walter St PO Box 1164 *Web:* www.pmped.com	Walterboro	SC	29488	843-549-9544		428
Peters of Nashua 300 Amherst St *Web:* www.petersauto.com	Nashua	NH	03063	603-889-1166		57
Peters Scott (Rep D - CA) 1122 Longworth HOB *Web:* scottpeters.house.gov	Washington	DC	20515	202-225-0508		342-2
Petersburg Chamber of Commerce 325 E Washington St *Web:* www.petersburgvachamber.com	Petersburg	VA	23804	804-733-8131	733-9891	139
Petersburg Fisheries PO Box 1147 *TF:* 877-772-4294 ■ *Web:* www.hookedonfish.com	Petersburg	AK	99833	907-772-4294	772-4472	296-13
Petersburg (Independent City) 135 N Union St Ste 202 *Web:* www.petersburg-va.org	Petersburg	VA	23803	804-733-2301		338
Petersburg National Battlefield 1539 Hickory Hill Rd *Web:* www.nps.gov/pete	Petersburg	VA	23803	804-732-3531	732-0835	564
Petersburg Public Library 201 W Washington St *TF:* 800-543-8911 ■ *Web:* www.ppls.org	Petersburg	VA	23803	804-733-2387	733-7972	434-3
Petersen Aluminum Corp 1005 Tonne Rd **Fax Area Code:* 800 ■ *TF:* 800-323-1960 ■ *Web:* www.pac-clad.com	Elk Grove Village	IL	60007	847-228-7150	722-7150*	697
Petersen Automotive Museum 6060 Wilshire Blvd *Web:* www.petersen.org	Los Angeles	CA	90036	323-930-2277		520
Petersen Health Care Inc 830 W Trlcreek Dr *Web:* www.petersenhealthcare.net	Peoria	IL	61614	309-691-8113		371
Petersen House Museum 1414 W Southern Ave *Web:* www.tempe.gov/museum	Tempe	AZ	85282	480-350-5100	350-5150	520
Petersen Inc 1527 N 2000 W *TF:* 800-410-6789 ■ *Web:* www.peterseninc.com	Ogden	UT	84404	801-732-2000		358
Petersen Industries Inc 4000 SR 60 W *Web:* www.petersenind.com	Lake Wales	FL	33859	863-676-1493		45
PetersenDean Roofing and Solar 39300 Civic Center Dr Ste 300 *TF:* 877-552-4418 ■ *Web:* petersendean.com	Fremont	CA	94538	877-552-4418		46
Peterson & Smith Equine Hospital LLC 4747 SW 60th Ave *Web:* www.petersonsmith.com	Ocala	FL	34474	352-237-6151		794
Peterson Collin C (Rep D - MN) 2204 Rayburn HOB *Web:* collinpeterson.house.gov	Washington	DC	20515	202-225-2165	225-1593	342-2
Peterson Cos, The 12500 Fair Lakes Cir Ste 400 *Web:* www.petersoncos.com	Fairfax	VA	22033	703-227-2000	631-6481	655
Peterson Farms Inc 3104 W Baseline Rd PO Box 115 *Web:* www.petersonfarmsinc.com	Shelby	MI	49455	231-861-7101		296-21
Peterson Industries Inc 616 E Hwy 36 *Web:* www.petersonind.com	Smith Center	KS	66967	785-282-6825		120
Peterson Institute for International Economics 1750 Massachusetts Ave NW *Web:* www.iie.com	Washington	DC	20036	202-328-9000	328-5432	634
Peterson Machine Tool Inc 1100 N Union St **Fax Area Code:* 620 ■ *TF:* 800-835-3528 ■ *Web:* petersonwashandblast.com	Council Grove	KS	66846	800-835-3528	767-6415*	386
Peterson Manufacturing Co 4200 E 135th St *TF:* 800-821-3490 ■ *Web:* www.pmlights.com	Grandview	MO	64030	816-765-2000	761-6693	438
Peterson Milla Hooks 1315 Harmon Pl *Web:* www.pmhadv.com	Minneapolis	MN	55403	612-349-9116		4
Peterson Pacific Corp 29408 Airport Rd *Web:* www.petersoncorp.com	Eugene	OR	97402	541-689-6520		190
Peterson Picture Frame Company Inc 2720 W Belmont Ave *TF:* 800-561-3357 ■ *Web:* www.peterson-picture.com	Chicago	IL	60618	773-463-8888	463-4603	309
Peterson Power Systems Inc 2828 Teagarden St *Web:* www.petersonpower.com	San Leandro	CA	94577	510-895-8400		23
Peterson Products Inc 10 Airpark Vista Blvd *Web:* www.petersonproducts.com	Dayton	NV	89403	775-301-5593		606
Peterson Regional Medical Ctr 551 Hill Country Dr *Web:* www.petersonrmc.com	Kerrville	TX	78028	830-896-4200		374-3
Peterson Spring 21200 Telegraph Rd *Web:* www.pspring.com	Southfield	MI	48033	248-799-5400	357-3176	719
Peterson Steel Corp 61 W Mountain St *TF:* 800-325-3245 ■ *Web:* www.petersonsteel.com	Worcester	MA	01606	508-853-3630		492
Peterson Structural Engineers Inc 9400 SW Barnes Rd Ste 215 *Web:* psengineers.com	Portland	OR	97221	503-292-1635		261
Peterson Tool Company Inc 739 Fesslers Ln PO Box 100830 *Web:* www.petersontool.com	Nashville	TN	37224	615-242-7341	242-7362	454
Peterson Tractor Co 955 Marina Blvd *TF:* 800-590-5945 ■ *Web:* www.petersoncat.com	San Leandro	CA	94577	510-357-6200	352-4570	274

Name / Address	City	State	ZIP	Phone	Fax	Class
Peterson's Nelnet LLC 121 S 13th St Ste 201 *TF:* 877-338-7772 ■ *Web:* www.essayedge.com	Lincoln	NE	68508	609-896-8669		260
PetFoodDirect.com 189 Main St **Fax Area Code: 877* ■ *TF Cust Svc:* 877-738-3663 ■ *Web:* www.petfooddirect.com	Harleysville	PA	19438	215-513-1999	894-5034*	578
Petit Jean Electric Co-op 270 Quality Dr PO Box 37 *TF:* 800-786-7618 ■ *Web:* www.pjecc.com	Clinton	AR	72031	501-745-2493		245
Petit Jean State Park 1285 Petit Jean Mtn Rd *Web:* www.petitjeanstatepark.com	Morrilton	AR	72110	501-727-5441		565
Petit Louis Bistro 4800 Roland Ave *Web:* www.petitlouis.com	Baltimore	MD	21210	410-366-9393		671
Petite Auberge 863 Bush St *Web:* jdvhotels.com/hotels/california	San Francisco	CA	94108	415-928-6000		379
Petitt Barraza LLC 1651 N Glenville Dr Ste 208 *Web:* www.petittbarraza.com	Richardson	TX	75081	214-221-9955		261
Petitti Garden Centers 24964 Broadway Ave *TF:* 800-255-1653 ■ *Web:* www.petittigardencenter.com	Oakwood Village	OH	44146	440-439-6511	439-7736	369
Petland Discounts Inc 355 Crooked Hill Rd *Web:* www.petlanddiscounts.com	Brentwood	NY	11717	631-273-6363		578
Petland Inc 250 Riverside St *TF:* 800-221-5935 ■ *Web:* petland.com	Chillicothe	OH	45601	740-775-2464	775-2575	578
Petlovers Animal Hospital 6425 E Livingston Ave *Web:* petloversah.com	Reynoldsburg	OH	43068	614-866-1912		794
Petmate 2300 E Randol Mill Rd *TF:* 877-738-6283 ■ *Web:* www.petmate.com	Arlington	TX	76011	877-738-6283		578
PetMed Express Inc 1441 SW 29th Ave *NASDAQ: PETS* ■ *TF:* 800-738-6337 ■ *Web:* www.1800petmeds.com	Pompano Beach	FL	33069	954-979-5995	971-0544	578
Peto MacCallum Ltd 165 Cartwright Ave *Web:* www.petomaccallum.com	Toronto	ON	M6A1V5	416-785-5110		261
Petoskey Area Visitors Bureau 401 E Mitchell St *TF:* 800-845-2828 ■ *Web:* www.petoskeyarea.com	Petoskey	MI	49770	231-348-2755	348-1810	206
Petoskey Plastics Inc 1 Petoskey St *Web:* www.petoskeyplastics.com	Petoskey	MI	49770	231-347-2602		600
Petoskey Regional Chamber of Commerce 401 E Mitchell St *Web:* www.petoskeychamber.com	Petoskey	MI	49770	231-347-4150	348-1810	139
Petoskey State Park 2475 M-119 Hwy *Web:* www.michigandnr.com	Petoskey	MI	49712	231-347-2311		565
Petra 3602 West Lake Rd *TF:* 866-906-2931 ■ *Web:* www.petrarestaurant.com	Erie	PA	16505	814-838-7197	833-9543	671
Petra Financial Advisors Inc 2 N Cascade Ave Ste 720 *Web:* www.petrafinancial.com	Colorado Springs	CO	80903	719-636-9000		401
Petra Industries Inc 2101 S Kelly Ave *Web:* www.petra.com	Edmond	OK	73013	405-216-2100		360-3
Petra Manufacturing Co 6600 W Armitage Ave *TF:* 800-888-7387 ■ *Web:* www.petramanufacturing.com	Chicago	IL	60707	773-622-1475		687
Petrella's Italian Cafe 2174 W Nine Mile Rd *Web:* www.petrellasitaliancafe.com	Pensacola	FL	32534	850-471-9444		671
Petrey W L Wholesale Company Inc 10345 Petrey Hwy *Web:* www.petrey.com	Luverne	AL	36049	334-230-5674	335-2422	345
Petricca Industries Inc 550 Cheshire Rd *Web:* unistresscorp.com	Pittsfield	MA	01201	413-442-6926	499-9930	188-4
Petrie Raymond, Professional Chartered Accountants LLP 255 Cremazie Blvd E Ste 1000 *Web:* www.petrieraymond.qc.ca	Montreal	QC	H2M1M2	514-342-4740		463
Petrified Forest National Park PO Box 2217 *TF:* 800-444-7275 ■ *Web:* www.nps.gov	Petrified Forest	AZ	86028	928-524-6228	524-3567	564
Petrini Corp 187 Rosemary St *Web:* www.petrinicorp.com	Needham	MA	02494	781-444-1963		186
Petro Amigos Supply Inc 777 N Eldridge Pkwy Ste 400 *Web:* www.petro-amigos.com	Houston	TX	77079	281-497-0858		755
Petro Lock Inc 45315 N Trevor Ave *Web:* petrolock.com	Lancaster	CA	93534	661-948-6044	948-9524	579
Petro Lucrum Inc 3525 Sage *Web:* www.petrolucrum.com	Houston	TX	77056	832-993-5426		536
Petro Plastics Company Inc 450 S Ave *TF:* 800-486-4738 ■ *Web:* www.petroplastics.com	Garwood	NJ	07027	908-789-1200	789-1381	599
Petro Vista Energy Corp 789 W Pender St Ste 800 *Web:* www.pvecorp.com	Vancouver	BC	V6C1H2	604-638-8067		536
Petrobras 10350 Richmond Ave Ste 1400 *Web:* www.petrobras.com	Houston	TX	77042	713-808-2000		536
PetroCard Systems Inc 730 Central Ave S *TF:* 800-950-3835 ■ *Web:* www.petrocard.com	Kent	WA	98032	253-852-2777		579
Petrocco Farms 14110 Brighton Rd *TF:* 888-876-2207 ■ *Web:* www.petroccofarms.com	Brighton	CO	80601	303-659-6498	659-7645	10-11
Petrochem Recovery Services 635 Maltby Ave *Web:* www.petrochemrecovery.com	Norfolk	VA	23504	757-627-8791		698
Petrodorado Energy Ltd 850 - Second St SW Ste 1500 *Web:* www.petrodorado.com	Calgary	AB	T2P0R8	403-800-9240		536
Petroglyph Beach State Historic Site 400 Willoughby Ave PO Box 111071 *Web:* www.dnr.alaska.gov	Juneau	AK	11071	907-465-4563		565
Petroglyph Energy Inc 960 Broadway Ave Ste 500 *TF:* 800-421-9512 ■ *Web:* www.intermountainindustries.com	Boise	ID	83706	208-685-7600		536
Petrol Adv Inc 443 N Varney St *Web:* petrolad.com	Burbank	CA	91502	323-644-3720		4
Petroleum Analyzer Company LP 8824 Fallbrook Dr *Web:* www.paclp.com	Houston	TX	77064	281-940-1803		419
Petroleum County 302 E Main PO Box 226 *Web:* petroleumcountymt.org	Winnett	MT	59087	406-429-6551	429-6328	338
Petroleum Development Corp (PDC) 120 Genesis Blvd PO Box 26 *NASDAQ: PDCE* ■ *TF:* 800-624-3821 ■ *Web:* www.petd.com	Bridgeport	WV	26330	303-860-5800		536
Petroleum Heat and Power Co Inc 9 W Broad St 3rd Fl *Web:* www.petro.com	Stamford	CT	06902	203-325-5400		316
Petroleum Marketers Assn of America (PMAA) 1901 N Ft Myer Dr Ste 500 *Web:* www.pmaa.org	Arlington	VA	22209	703-351-8000	351-9160	49-18
Petroleum Marketers Assn of America's Small Business Community 1901 N Fort Myer Dr Ste 500 *TF:* 888-372-7341 ■ *Web:* epa.gov	Arlington	VA	22209	703-351-8000	351-9160	615
Petroleum Marketers Inc 3000 Ogden Rd	Roanoke	VA	24018	540-772-4900	772-6900	316
Petroleum Strategies Inc 303 W Wall St *Web:* www.petroleumstrategies.com	Midland	TX	79701	432-682-0292		539
Petroleum Traders Corp 7120 Pointe Inverness Way *TF:* 800-533-0523 ■ *Web:* www.petroleumtraders.com	Fort Wayne	IN	46804	260-432-6622		579
Petroleum Wholesale LP 8550 Technology Forest Pl *Web:* petroleumwholesale.com	The Woodlands	TX	77381	281-681-1000		579
Petrolia Inc 511 Rue Saint-Joseph E 3rd Fl, Rm 304 *Web:* petrolia-inc.com	Quebec	QC	G1K3B7	418-657-1966		536
PetroLiance LLC 739 N State St *TF:* 800-628-7231 ■ *Web:* www.petroliance.com	Elgin	IL	60123	877-738-7699		579
PetroMax Operating Company Inc 603 Main St Ste 201 *Web:* www.petromaxoperating.com	Garland	TX	75040	972-271-0999		539
Petroplex Energy Inc 110 N Marienfeld St Ste 290 *Web:* www.petroplex.net	Midland	TX	79701	432-570-7030		536
PetroQuest Energy Inc 400 E Kaliste Saloom Rd Ste 6000 *NYSE: PQ* ■ *Web:* www.petroquest.com	Lafayette	LA	70508	337-232-7028	232-0044	538
PetroSkills LLC 2930 S Yale Ave *Web:* www.petroskills.com	Tulsa	OK	74114	918-828-2500		539
Petrosouth Inc 234 N Hill St *TF:* 800-564-3132 ■ *Web:* www.petrosouth.com	Griffin	GA	30224	770-227-0804		579
Petrotech Inc 151 Brookhollow Esplanade *Web:* www.petrotechinc.com	New Orleans	LA	70123	504-620-6600		518
Petro-Techna International Ltd 31 Scarsdale Rd *Web:* www.petro-techna.com	Toronto	ON	M3B2R2	416-444-0071	444-0072	539
petroWEB Inc 899 Logan St Ste 511 *Web:* www.petroweb.com	Denver	CO	80203	720-353-4828	524-6785	177
Petruccelli & Osher Attorneys at Law 5100 N Federal Hwy Ste 300 B	Fort Lauderdale	FL	33308	954-771-4118		428
Petry Media Corp 3 East 54 St	New York	NY	10022	212-230-5900		6
Petsky Prunier LLC 60 Broad St 38th Fl *Web:* www.petskyprunier.com	New York	NY	10004	212-842-6020		70
PETsMART Inc 19601 N 27th Ave *NASDAQ: PETM* ■ *TF Cust Svc:* 800-738-1385 ■ *Web:* www.petsmart.com	Phoenix	AZ	85027	623-580-6100		578
Petterino's 150 N Dearborn St *Web:* www.petterinos.com	Chicago	IL	60601	312-422-0150		671
Pettibone Corp 2626 Warrenville Rd *Web:* pettibonellc.com	Downers Grove	IL	60515	630-353-5000	353-5026	190
Pettibone Michigan 1100 Superior Ave *TF:* 800-467-3884 ■ *Web:* www.gopettibone.com	Baraga	MI	49908	906-353-4800	353-6325	470
Pettigrew & Assoc PA 100 E Navajo *Web:* pettigrew.us	Hobbs	NM	88240	575-393-9827		261
Pettigrew & Sons Casket Co 6151 Power Inn Rd *TF:* 800-852-1701 ■ *Web:* www.pettigrewcaskets.com	Sacramento	CA	95824	916-383-0777	383-2445	134
Pettigrew Home & Museum 131 N Duluth Ave *Web:* siouxlandmuseums.com	Sioux Falls	SD	57104	605-367-7097		520
Pettigrew State Park 2252 Lake Shore Rd *Web:* www.ncparks.gov/visit/parks/pett/main.php	Creswell	NC	27928	252-797-4475		565
Pettis County 415 S Ohio *TF:* 800-827-5295 ■ *Web:* www.pettiscomo.com	Sedalia	MO	65301	660-826-5000		338
Pettus Mechanical Services 12647 Hwy 72 *TF:* 800-230-8181 ■ *Web:* www.pettushvac.com	Rogersville	AL	35652	256-389-8181		186
Petty Machine Company Inc 2403 Forbes Rd	Gastonia	NC	28056	704-864-3254	861-1937	744
Petz Enterprises LLC 7575 W Linne Rd *Web:* www.petzent.com	Tracy	CA	95304	209-835-2720		177
PETZL America Inc Freeport Ctr Bldg M-7 Bldg M-7 *Web:* www.petzl.com	Clearfield	UT	84016	801-926-1310	926-1501	711
Peugeot Motors of America Inc 150 Clove Rd Ste 3 *TF:* 800-345-5545 ■ *Web:* www.peugeot.com	Little Falls	NJ	07424	973-812-4444		59
Pevco Sys Intl Inc 1401 Tangier Dr *TF:* 800-296-7382 ■ *Web:* www.pevco.com	Baltimore	MD	21220	410-931-8800		595
Pew Charitable Trust 901 E St NW *Web:* www.pewtrusts.org	Washington	DC	20004	202-887-8800		48-13
Pew Charitable Trusts 2005 Market St 1 Commerce Sq Ste 1700 *TF:* 800-351-6801 ■ *Web:* www.pewtrusts.org	Philadelphia	PA	19103	215-575-9050	575-4939	305
Pexagon Technology Inc 14 Business Park Dr *Web:* www.pexagontech.com	Branford	CT	06405	203-458-3364		173-8
Pexco LLC 2500 Northwinds Pkwy Ste 472 *Web:* www.pexco.com	Alpharetta	GA	30009	404-564-8560	564-8579	600
Peyton's Place 5344 Atlanta Hwy *Web:* peytonsplacelunch.tripod.com	Montgomery	AL	36109	334-396-3630		671
Pez Candy Inc 35 Prindle Hill Rd *Web:* www.pez.com	Orange	CT	06477	203-795-0531		296-8

Phone | Fax | Class

PF Chang's China Bistro
7135 E Camelback Rd. . . . Scottsdale AZ 85251 480-949-2610 671
TF: 800-344-6202 ■ *Web:* pfchangs.com

PF Chang's China Bistro
1805 E River Rd . . . Tucson AZ 85718 520-615-8788 671
Web: www.pfchangs.com

PF Chang's China Bistro
233 Summit Blvd . . . Birmingham AL 35243 205-967-0040 671
Web: www.pfchangs.com

PF Chang's China Bistro
2525 W End Ave . . . Nashville TN 37203 615-329-8901 671
Web: www.pfchangs.com

PF Chang's China Bistro
4325 Glenwood Ave . . . Raleigh NC 27612 919-787-7754 671
Web: www.pfchangs.com

PF Chang's China Bistro
5180 S Kietzke Ln. . . . Reno NV 89511 775-825-9800 671
Web: www.pfchangs.com

PF Chang's China Bistro 1415 15th St . . . Denver CO 80202 303-260-7222 671
Web: www.pfchangs.com

PF Chang's China Bistro
11685 Westheimer Rd. . . . Houston TX 77077 281-920-3553 671
Web: www.pfchangs.com

PF Chang's China Bistro
174 W 300 S. . . . Salt Lake City UT 84101 801-539-0500 671
Web: www.pfchangs.com

PF Chang's China Bistro
1530 J St Ste 100. . . . Sacramento CA 95814 916-288-0970 671
Web: www.pfchangs.com

PF Chang's China Bistro
7077 Friars Rd . . . San Diego CA 92108 619-260-8484 671
Web: www.pfchangs.com

PF Chang's China Bistro
1725 Briargate Pkwy. . . . Colorado Springs CO 80920 719-593-8580 671
Web: www.pfchangs.com

PF Chang's China Bistro
10840 Tamiami Trail N . . . Naples FL 34109 239-596-2174 671
Web: www.pfchangs.com

PF Chang's China Bistro
1401 Waterfront Pkwy. . . . Wichita KS 67206 316-634-2211 671
Web: www.pfchangs.com

PF Chang's China Bistro
2801 N Pacific Ave . . . Atlantic City NJ 08401 609-348-4600 671
Web: www.pfchangs.com

PF Chang's China Bistro
3667 Las Vegas Blvd S. . . . Las Vegas NV 89109 702-836-0955 671
Web: www.pfchangs.com

PF Chang's China Bistro
2633 Edmondson Rd . . . Cincinnati OH 45209 513-531-4567 671
Web: www.pfchangs.com

PF Chang's China Bistro
13700 N Pennsylvania Ave. . . . Oklahoma City OK 73134 405-748-4003 671
Web: www.pfchangs.com

PF Chang's China Bistro 1978 E 21st St. . . . Tulsa OK 74114 918-747-6555 671
Web: www.pfchangs.com

PF Chang's China Bistro
760 Sunland Pk Dr . . . El Paso TX 79912 915-845-0166 671
Web: www.pfchangs.com

PF Chang's China Bistro
255 E Basse Rd. . . . San Antonio TX 78209 210-507-1000 671
Web: www.pfchangs.com

PF Chang's China Bistro
9212 Stony Pt. . . . Richmond VA 23235 804-253-0492 671
Web: pfchangs.com

PF Chang's China Bistro
4551 Virginia Beach Blvd . . . Virginia Beach VA 23462 757-473-9028 671
Web: www.pfchangs.com

PF Chang's China Bistro
400 Pine St Ste 136 . . . Seattle WA 98101 206-393-0070 671
Web: www.pfchangs.com

PF Chang's China Bistro
2418 E Sunrise Blvd. . . . Fort Lauderdale FL 33304 954-565-5877 671
Web: www.pfchangs.com

PF Chang's China Bistro Inc
7676 E Pinnacle Peak Rd . . . Scottsdale AZ 85255 480-888-3000 670
NASDAQ: PFCB ■ *TF:* 866-732-4264 ■ *Web:* www.pfchangs.com

PFA (Pedorthic Footwear Assn)
2025 M St NW Ste 800. . . . Washington DC 20036 202-367-1145 367-2145 48-17
TF: 800-673-8447 ■ *Web:* www.pedorthics.org

Pfaltzgraff Co PO Box 21769 . . . York PA 17402 800-999-2811 730
TF: 800-999-2811 ■ *Web:* www.pfaltzgraff.com

Pfau Industrial Animal Oils
800 Wall St. . . . Jeffersonville IN 47130 812-283-6697 579
Web: pfauoil.com

Pfaudler Inc 1000 W Ave. . . . Rochester NY 14611 585-235-1000 386
Web: www.pfaudler.com

PFAW (People for the American Way)
2000 M St NW Ste 400. . . . Washington DC 20036 202-467-4999 293-2672 48-7
TF: 800-326-7329 ■ *Web:* www.pfaw.org

PFB Corp 100-2886 Sunridge Way NE . . . Calgary AB T1Y7H9 403-569-4300 787
Web: www.pfbcorp.com

PFE Group, The
Cordaville Office Bldg 153 Cordaville Rd
Ste 230. . . . Southborough MA 01772 508-683-1400 683-1401 463
Web: pfegroup.com

Pfeffer Hanniford & Palka CPA's PC
225 E Grand River Ave Ste 104. . . . Brighton MI 48116 810-229-5550 2
Web: phpcpa.com

Pfeiffer Big Sur State Park
c/o Monterey District Office 2211 Garden Rd . . . Monterey CA 93940 831-649-2316 647-6239 565
Web: www.parks.ca.gov/?page_id=570

Pfeiffer University
48380 Hwy 52 N. . . . Misenheimer NC 28109 704-463-1360 463-1363* 166
**Fax:* Admissions ■ *TF:* 800-338-2060 ■ *Web:* www.pfeiffer.edu

Pfeiffer Vacuum Inc 24 Trafalgar Sq . . . Nashua NH 03063 603-578-6500 358
Web: www.pfeiffer-vacuum.com

Pfeiler & Assoc Engineers Inc
22609 La Palma Ave Ste 202 . . . Yorba Linda CA 92887 909-993-5800 993-5801 261
Web: pfeilerassociates.com

Phone | Fax | Class

Pfenex Inc 10790 Roselle St . . . San Diego CA 92121 858-352-4400 668
TF: 844-240-0005 ■ *Web:* www.pfenex.com

PFERD Milwaukee Brush Company Inc
30 Jytek Dr. . . . Leominster MA 01453 978-840-6420 840-6421 103
TF: 800-342-9015 ■ *Web:* www.pferdusa.com

PFF (Progress & Freedom Foundation)
1444 Eye St NW Ste 500. . . . Washington DC 20005 202-289-8928 289-6079 634
Web: www.pff.org

PFI (Pet Food Institute)
2025 M St NW Ste 800. . . . Washington DC 20036 202-367-1120 367-2120 49-4
Web: www.petfoodinstitute.org

PFI Precision Inc
2011 N Dayton Lakeview Rd. . . . New Carlisle OH 45344 937-845-3563 454
Web: www.pfiprecision.com

PFI Tech 5761 Rickenbacker Rd . . . Commerce CA 90040 310-824-1800 196
Web: www.pfitech.com

Pfingsten Partners LLC
300 N LaSalle St Ste 5400 . . . Chicago IL 60654 312-222-8707 222-8708 792
Web: www.pfingsten.com

Pfister Hotel 424 E Wisconsin Ave . . . Milwaukee WI 53202 414-273-8222 273-5025 379
TF: 800-558-8222 ■ *Web:* www.thepfisterhotel.com

Pfister Maintenance Inc
80 E Fifth St . . . Paterson NJ 07524 973-569-9330 191-4
Web: www.pfisterroofing.com

Pfizer Animal Health 5 Giralda Farms . . . Madison NJ 07940 888-963-8471 582
TF: 888-963-8471 ■ *Web:* www.zoetisus.com

Pfizer Canada Inc
17300 TransCanada Hwy . . . Kirkland QC H9J2M5 514-695-0500 582
TF: 800-463-6001 ■ *Web:* www.pfizer.ca

Pfizer Centre Source
7000 Portage Rd. . . . Kalamazoo MI 49001 269-833-2296 231
Web: www.pfizercentreone.com

Pfizer Foundation Inc 235 E 42nd St. . . . New York NY 10017 212-733-2323 304
Web: www.pfizer.com

Pfizer Inc 235 E 42nd St. . . . New York NY 10017 212-733-2323 582
NYSE: PFE ■ *TF:* 800-879-3477 ■ *Web:* www.pfizer.com

Pfizer Inc Animal Health Group
235 E 42nd St. . . . New York NY 10017 212-733-2323 584
TF: 800-879-3477 ■ *Web:* www.pfizer.com

PFLAG (Parents Families & Friends of Lesbians & Gays)
1828 L St NW Ste 660 . . . Washington DC 20036 202-467-8180 467-8194 48-8
Web: www.pflag.org

Pflow Industries
6720 N Teutonia Ave. . . . Milwaukee WI 53209 414-352-9000 207
TF: 800-424-3996 ■ *Web:* www.pflow.com

PFM Capital Inc
1925 Victoria Ave 2nd Fl . . . Regina SK S4P0R3 306-791-4855 528
Web: www.pfm.ca

PFSB (Piedmont FSB)
201 S Stratford Rd . . . Winston-Salem NC 27103 336-770-1000 70
Web: www.piedmontfederal.com

PFSweb Inc 505 Millennium Dr Ste 500 . . . Allen TX 75013 972-881-2900 463
NASDAQ: PFSW ■ *TF:* 888-330-5504 ■ *Web:* www.pfsweb.com

PFT Alexander Inc 3250 E Grant St . . . Signal Hill CA 90755 562-595-1741 246
TF: 800-696-1331 ■ *Web:* www.pft-alexander.com

PFW Systems Corp 850 Medway Park Ct . . . London ON N6G5C6 519-474-3300 177
TF: 800-456-7100 ■ *Web:* www.pfw.com

PG (Procter & Gamble Co)
1 Procter & Gamble Plaza. . . . Cincinnati OH 45202 513-983-1100 185
NYSE: PG ■ *TF:* 800-503-4611 ■ *Web:* www.pg.com

PG & E Corp 77 Beale St 24th Fl . . . San Francisco CA 94105 415-267-7000 973-8719* 360-5
NYSE: PCG ■ **Fax:* Hum Res ■ *TF:* 800-743-5000 ■ *Web:* www.pgecorp.com

PG Exhibits 3510 Himalaya Rd. . . . Aurora CO 80011 303-722-6565 8
Web: www.pgexhibits.com

PG Life Link Inc 167 Gap Way. . . . Erlanger KY 41018 859-283-5900 372-6272 253
TF: 800-287-4123 ■ *Web:* pglifelink.com

PG Publishing Co
34 Blvd of the Allies . . . Pittsburgh PA 15222 412-263-1100 263-1703 637-8
TF Cust Svc: 800-228-6397 ■ *Web:* www.post-gazette.com

PGA National Resort & Spa
400 Ave of the Champions . . . Palm Beach Gardens FL 33418 561-227-2547 625-6204 669
TF: 800-863-2819 ■ *Web:* www.pgaresort.com

PGA of America
100 Ave of the Champions . . . Palm Beach Gardens FL 33418 561-624-8400 48-22
TF: 800-477-6465 ■ *Web:* www.pga.com

PGA Tour Inc
112 PGA Tour Blvd. . . . Ponte Vedra Beach FL 32082 904-285-3700 48-22
Web: www.pgatour.com

PGC (Precision Gasket Co) 5732 Lincoln Dr. . . . Edina MN 55436 952-942-6711 326
Web: www.pgc-solutions.com

PGI (Premiere Global Services Inc)
3280 Peachtree Rd NE Ste 1000. . . . Atlanta GA 30305 719-457-6901 39
NYSE: PGI ■ *TF:* 866-548-3203 ■ *Web:* www.pgi.com

PGM Inc 1215 S 1680 W. . . . Orem UT 84058 801-426-0889 466
Web: www.pgminc.com

PGM Products LLC 1 Commerce Dr . . . Barrington NJ 08007 856-546-0704 499

PGP (Professional Group Plans Inc)
225 Wireless Blvd Ste 200 . . . Hauppauge NY 11788 631-951-9200 951-9623 631
Web: www.pgpbenefits.com

PGR Media 34 Farnsworth St 2nd Fl . . . Boston MA 02210 617-502-8400 6
Web: www.pgrmedia.com

PGT 1070 Technology Dr . . . Nokomis FL 34275 941-480-1600 486-8369 234
TF: 800-282-6019 ■ *Web:* www.pgtindustries.com

PGW (Publishers Group West)
1700 Fourth St. . . . Berkeley CA 94710 510-809-3700 809-3777 96
Web: www.pgw.com

PGW (Philadelphia Gas Works)
800 W Montgomery Ave. . . . Philadelphia PA 19122 215-235-1000 787
TF: 800-242-1776 ■ *Web:* www.pgworks.com

P&H (Parrish & Heimbecker Ltd)
201 Portage Ave Ste 1400 . . . Winnipeg MB R3B3K6 204-956-2030 943-8233 275
TF: 800-665-8937 ■ *Web:* www.parrishandheimbecker.com

PH (Paoli Hospital) 255 W Lancaster Ave. . . . Paoli PA 19301 484-565-1000 374-3
Web: mainlinehealth.org/paoli

PH Hoeft State Park
5001 US Hwy 23 N. . . . Rogers City MI 49779 989-734-2543 565
Web: www.michigandnr.com

Name / Address	City	State	ZIP	Phone	Fax	Class
PH Windsolutions Inc 7562 Chemin de la C"te de Liesse *Web:* phwind.com	Montreal	QC	H4T1E7	514-522-6329		14
Phacil Inc 601 California St *Web:* phacil.com	San Francisco	CA	94108	703-526-1800		180
Phadia US Inc 4169 Commercial Ave *TF:* 800-346-4364 ■ *Web:* www.phadia.com	Portage	MI	49002	269-492-1940		231
Phage Pharmaceuticals Inc 6868 Nancy Ridge Dr Ste 100	San Diego	CA	92121	858-427-9100		231
Phalcon Ltd 505 Main St *Web:* phalconusa.com	Farmington	CT	06032	860-677-9797		787
Phantom Canyon Brewing Co 2 E Pikes Peak Ave *Web:* www.phantomcanyon.com	Colorado Springs	CO	80903	719-635-2800	635-9930	671
Phantom Laboratory Inc, The 2727 SR- 29 *TF:* 800-525-1190 ■ *Web:* www.phantomlab.com	Greenwich	NY	12834	518-692-1190		668
Pharma eMarket LLC 15 E Ridge Pk Ste 225 *Web:* www.monitorforhire.com	Conshohocken	PA	19428	610-862-0909		237
Pharma Tech Industries Inc 1310 Stylemaster Dr *Web:* www.pharma-tech.net	Union	MO	63084	636-583-8664	583-5373	479
PharmaCentra LLC 3000 Northwoods Pkwy *Web:* www.pharmacentra.com	Norcross	GA	30071	770-395-0088		195
Pharmaceutical Advisors LLC 330 Wall St *Web:* www.pharmadvisors.com	Princeton	NJ	08540	609-688-1330		237
Pharmaceutical Assoc Inc 1700 Perimeter Rd *TF:* 888-233-2334 ■ *Web:* www.paipharma.com	Greenville	SC	29605	864-277-7282		231
Pharmaceutical Calibrations & Instrumentation LLC 8100 Brownleigh Dr Ste 100-A *TF:* 877-724-2257 ■ *Web:* www.pci-llc.com	Raleigh	NC	27617	877-724-2257		583
Pharmaceutical Care Management Assn (PCMA) 601 Pennsylvania Ave NW *Web:* www.pcmanet.org	Washington	DC	20004	202-756-5700		49-8
Pharmaceutical Innovations Inc 897 Frelinghuysen Ave *TF:* 800-872-5652 ■ *Web:* www.pharminnovations.com	Newark	NJ	07114	973-242-2900	242-0578	231
Pharmaceutical Law & Industry Report 1801 S Bell St *TF:* 800-372-1033 ■ *Web:* www.bna.com/pharmaceutical-law-industry-p6790	Arlington	VA	22202	800-372-1033		531-7
Pharmaceutical Representative Magazine 641 Lexington Ave 8th Fl *Web:* www.pharmexec.com	New York	NY	10022	212-951-6600	951-6604	457-5
Pharmaceutical Research & Manufacturers of America (PhRMA) 950 F St NW Ste 300 *Web:* www.phrma.org	Washington	DC	20004	202-835-3400	835-3414	49-8
Pharmaceutics International Inc 10819 Gilroy Rd *Web:* www.pharm-int.com	Hunt Valley	MD	21031	410-584-0001		231
Pharmacists Mutual Insurance Co 808 Hwy 18 W PO Box 370 **Fax Area Code:* 515 ■ *TF General:* 800-247-5930 ■ *Web:* www.phmic.com/Default.aspx	Algona	IA	50511	800-247-5930	295-9306*	391-4
Pharmacists Society of the State of New York 210 Washington Ave Ext *TF:* 800-632-8822 ■ *Web:* www.pssny.org	Albany	NY	12203	518-869-6595	464-0618	585
Pharmacogenetics Diagnostic Laboratory LLC 201 E Jefferson St Ste 309 *TF:* 800-626-2930 ■ *Web:* www.pgxlab.com	Louisville	KY	40202	502-569-1584		415
Pharmacommunications Group Inc 100 Renfrew Dr *TF:* 800-267-5409 ■ *Web:* www.pharmacommunications.com	Markham	ON	L3R9R6	905-477-3100		238
Pharmacy Healthcare Solutions Inc 1700 Reisterstown Rd Ste 106 *Web:* www.pharmhs.com	Pikesville	MD	21208	410-653-7305		463
Pharmacy Outcomes Specialists LLC 41 E Main St Ste 200 *Web:* www.pharmout.com	Lake Zurich	IL	60047	847-540-9590		237
Pharmacy Providers of OK 3000 E Memorial Rd	Edmond	OK	73013	405-557-5700		237
Pharmacy Society of Wisconsin 701 Heartland Trl *Web:* www.pswi.org	Madison	WI	53717	608-827-9200	827-9292	585
Pharmacy Systems Inc 5050 Bradenton Ave PO Box 130 *TF:* 800-683-9302 ■ *Web:* www.pharmacysystems.com	Dublin	OH	43017	614-766-0101	766-4448	587
Pharmacy Today Magazine 2215 Constitution Ave NW *TF:* 800-237-2742 ■ *Web:* www.pharmacist.com	Washington	DC	20037	202-628-4410	783-2351	457-16
Pharmacyclics Inc 995 E Arques Ave *NASDAQ: PCYC* ■ *TF:* 877-407-0778 ■ *Web:* www.pharmacyclics.com	Sunnyvale	CA	94085	408-774-0330		85
PharmaForce Inc 960 Crupper Ave *Web:* www.pharmaforceinc.com	Columbus	OH	43229	614-436-2222		238
Pharmagra Labs Inc 158 Mclean Rd *Web:* www.pharmagra.com	Brevard	NC	28712	828-884-8656		415
Pharmakon LLC 475 Martingale Rd Ste 200	Schaumburg	IL	60173	847-995-0509		466
PharmaLogic Inc 1 S Ocean Blvd Ste 206 *Web:* www.pharmalogic.info	Boca Raton	FL	33432	561-416-0085		238
Pharmalucence Inc 29 Dunham Rd *TF:* 800-221-7554 ■ *Web:* www.pharmalucence.com	Billerica	MA	01821	781-275-7120		231
Pharmametrics 220 Commerce Dr Ste 405 *Web:* pharmametricsinc.com	Ft Washington	PA	19034	215-274-1315		231
Pharmanet Development Group Inc 504 Carnegie Ctr *Web:* www.inventivhealthclinical.com	Princeton	NJ	08540	609-951-6800		583
Pharmasave Drugs (National) Ltd 8411 - 200th St Ste 201 *TF:* 800-661-6106 ■ *Web:* www.pharmasave.com	Langley	BC	V2Y0E7	604-455-2400	455-2493	231
Pharmascience Inc 6111 Royalmount Ave Ste 100 *TF:* 866-853-1178 ■ *Web:* www.pharmascience.com	Montreal	QC	H4P2T4	514-340-9800		231
PharmaSeq Inc 11 Deer Park Dr Ste 104 *Web:* www.pharmaseq.com	Monmouth Junction	NJ	08852	732-355-0100	355-0102	194
PharmaSys Inc 216 Towne Village Dr *Web:* www.pharma-sys.com	Cary	NC	27513	919-468-2547		177
Pharmavite LLC 1150 Aviation Pkwy *Web:* www.pharmavite.com	San Fernando	CA	91340	818-837-8000		583
PharmEcology Associates LLC 12229 W N Ave Ste 2 *TF:* 800-213-2654 ■ *Web:* www.pharmecology.com	Wauwatosa	WI	53226	414-292-3959		192
Pharmed Corp 24340 Sperry Dr	Westlake	OH	44145	440-835-0660		475
PharMethod Inc 1170 Wheeler Way *TF:* 800-438-7325 ■ *Web:* www.pharmethod.com	Langhorne	PA	19047	215-354-1212		195
Pharmetics Inc 3695 AutoRt Des Laurentides *TF:* 877-472-4433 ■ *Web:* www.pharmetics.com	Laval	QC	H7L3H7	450-682-8580		231
Pharmgate LLC 161 N Franklin Tpke *Web:* www.pharmgate.com	Ramsey	NJ	07446	201-327-3800		238
Pharmore Ingredients 12569 S 2700 W Ste 201 *Web:* pharmore.com	Riverton	UT	84065	801-446-8188		297-8
Pharmos Corp 99 Wood Ave S Ste 311 *PINK: PARS*	Iselin	NJ	08830	732-452-9556		582
Pharmout Laboratories Inc 1151 Sonora Ct *Web:* www.pharmoutlabs.net	Sunnyvale	CA	94086	408-481-3090		743
Pharos Hospitality LLC 320 S Tryon St Ste 202 *TF:* 800-758-8999 ■ *Web:* www.pharoshospitality.com	Charlotte	NC	28202	704-333-1818		378
Pharr Chamber of Commerce City of Pharr *Web:* www.pharrchamber.com	Pharr	TX	78577	956-787-1481		139
Pharr Memorial Library 118 S Cage blvd *Web:* pharr-tx.gov	Pharr	TX	78577	956-787-3966	787-3345	434-3
Pharr Yarns LLC 100 Main St PO Box 1939 *TF:* 800-374-6754 ■ *Web:* www.pharryarns.com	McAdenville	NC	28101	704-824-3551	824-0072	745-9
Phase 2 Medical Manufacturing Inc 88 Airport Dr *Web:* www.phase2medical.com	Rochester	NH	03867	603-332-8900		415
Phase 3 Marketing & Communications 3560 Atlanta Industrial Dr *Web:* www.phase3mc.com	Atlanta	GA	30331	404-367-9898		344
Phase Matrix Inc 109 Bonaventura Dr *TF:* 877-447-2736 ■ *Web:* www.phasematrix.net	San Jose	CA	95134	408-428-1000	428-1500	248
Phase North 6601 Xylon Ave N *Web:* www.district287.org	Minneapolis	MN	55428	763-533-3821		685
Phase One Inc 200 Broadhollow Rd Ste 312 *TF:* 888-742-7366 ■ *Web:* www.phaseone.com	Melville	NY	11747	631-757-0400	547-9898	591
Phase Technology 6400 Youngerman Cir *TF:* 888-742-7385 ■ *Web:* phasetech.mseaudio.com	Jacksonville	FL	32244	904-777-0700		52
PhaseBio Pharmaceuticals Inc 1 Great Vly Pkwy Ste 30 *Web:* www.phasebio.com	Malvern	PA	19355	610-981-6500		231
Phasetronics Inc 1600 Sunshine Dr *Web:* www.phasetronics.com	Clearwater	FL	33765	727-573-1819		203
PHB Inc 7900 W Ridge Rd *Web:* www.phbcorp.com	Fairview	PA	16415	814-474-5511		308
PHC (Peninsula Hospital Ctr) 51-15 Beach Ch Dr	Far Rockaway	NY	11691	718-734-2000		374-3
PHCC (Plumbing-Heating-Cooling Contractors NA) 180 S Washington St *TF:* 800-533-7694 ■ *Web:* www.phccweb.org	Falls Church	VA	22040	703-237-8100	237-7442	49-3
PHD Inc 9009 Clubridge Dr *TF:* 800-624-8511 ■ *Web:* www.phdinc.com	Fort Wayne	IN	46809	260-747-6151	747-6754	223
PHD Manufacturing Inc 44018 Columbiana-Waterford Rd *Web:* www.phd-mfg.com	Columbiana	OH	44408	330-482-9256		612
PhDx Systems Inc 1001 University Blvd SE Ste 103 *TF:* 888-999-7439 ■ *Web:* www.phdx.com	Albuquerque	NM	87106	505-764-0174	764-0074	39
Pheasant Run Resort & Spa 4051 E Main St *Web:* www.pheasantrun.com	Saint Charles	IL	60174	630-584-6300		669
Phelan & Taylor Produce Co 1860 Front St	Oceano	CA	93445	805-489-2413		11-1
Phelan Hallinan & Schmieg LLP 400 Fellowship Rd Ste 100 *TF:* 800-900-4250 ■ *Web:* www.phelanhallinan.com	Mount Laurel	NJ	08054	856-813-5500		428
Phelps County PO Box 404 *TF:* 800-368-8683 ■ *Web:* www.phelpsgov.org	Holdrege	NE	68949	308-995-4469	995-4368	338
Phelps County 200 N Main St *TF:* 800-522-0938 ■ *Web:* www.phelpscounty.org	Rolla	MO	65401	573-458-6000	458-6119	338
Phelps Dunbar LLP Canal Pl 365 Canal St Ste 2000 *TF:* 800-820-3038 ■ *Web:* www.phelpsdunbar.com	New Orleans	LA	70130	504-566-1311		428
Phelps Fan LLC 10701 I-30 *TF:* 800-561-3449 ■ *Web:* www.phelpsfan.com	Little Rock	AR	72209	501-568-5550	568-3363	14
Phelps Group, The 901 Wilshire Blvd *Web:* phelpsagency.com	Santa Monica	CA	90401	310-752-4400		4
Phelps Memorial Hospital Ctr (PMHC) 701 N Broadway *Web:* www.phelpshospital.org	Sleepy Hollow	NY	10591	914-366-3000		374-3
Phelps School 583 Sugartown Rd *TF:* 800-344-8328 ■ *Web:* www.thephelpsschool.org	Malvern	PA	19355	610-644-1754	644-6679	622
Phelps Sungas Inc 224 Cross Rd *TF:* 800-458-1085 ■ *Web:* sungas.com	Geneva	NY	14456	315-789-3285		316
Phenix City-Russell County Chamber of Commerce 1107 Broad St *Web:* pcrcchamber.com	Phenix City	AL	36867	334-298-3639		139
Phenix Technologies Inc 75 Speicher Dr *Web:* www.phenixtech.com	Accident	MD	21520	301-746-8118	895-5570	248
Phenomenex Inc 411 Madrid Ave *Web:* www.phenomenex.com	Torrance	CA	90501	310-212-0555	328-7768	419

Name / Address	City	State	Zip	Phone	Fax	Class
Phenopath Laboratories PLLC 551 N 34th St Ste 100 *TF:* 888-927-4366 ■ *Web:* www.phenopath.com	Seattle	WA	98103	206-374-9000		415
Phenova Inc 6390 Joyce Dr Ste 100 *Web:* www.phenova.com	Golden	CO	80403	303-940-0033		743
Pherin Pharmaceuticals Inc 4962 El Camino Real Ste 223 *Web:* www.pherin.com	Los Altos	CA	94022	650-961-2703		231
PHF (Phoenix House Foundation Inc) 164 W 74th St 4th Fl *TF:* 888-671-9392 ■ *Web:* www.phoenixhouse.org	New York	NY	10023	888-671-9392		726
PHFCU (Pearl Harbor Federal Credit Union) 94-449 Ukee St **Fax Area Code:* 808 ■ *TF:* 800-987-5583 ■ *Web:* www.phfcu.com	Waipahu	HI	96797	800-987-5583	218-6299*	219
PHH (Port Huron Hospital) 1221 Pine Grove Ave **Fax Area Code:* 877 ■ *TF:* 888-327-0671 ■ *Web:* www.mclaren.org/porthuron/porthuron.aspx	Port Huron	MI	48060	810-987-5000	502-1567*	374-3
PHH Mortgage Corp 3000 Leadenhall Rd *TF:* 800-210-8849 ■ *Web:* www.phhmortgage.com/business	Mount Laurel	NJ	08054	800-210-8849		509
PHI (Packard Humanities Institute, The) 300 Second St *Web:* www.packhum.org	Los Altos	CA	94022	650-948-0150		305
Phi Alpha Theta *National History Honor Society* 4202 E Fowler Ave SOC 107 **Fax Area Code:* 813 ■ *TF:* 800-394-8195 ■ *Web:* www.phialphatheta.org	Tampa	FL	33620	800-394-8195	974-8215*	48-16
Phi Beta Kappa Society 1606 New Hampshire Ave NW *TF:* 800-745-8379 ■ *Web:* www.pbk.org/home	Washington	DC	20009	202-265-3808	986-1601	48-16
Phi Beta Sigma Fraternity Inc 145 Kennedy St NW *TF:* 800-322-4023 ■ *Web:* www.phibetasigma1914.org	Washington	DC	20011	202-726-5434	882-1681	48-16
Phi Chi Theta 1508 E Beltline Rd Ste 104 *Web:* www.phichitheta.org	Carrollton	TX	75006	972-245-7202		48-16
Phi Delta Kappa International (PDK) 408 N Union St *TF:* 800-766-1156 ■ *Web:* www.pdkintl.org	Bloomington	IN	47407	812-339-1156	339-0018	48-16
Phi Delta Phi International Legal Fraternity 1426 21st St NW *TF:* 800-368-5606 ■ *Web:* www.phideltaphi.org	Washington	DC	20036	202-223-6801	223-6808	48-16
Phi Delta Theta 2 S Campus Ave *TF:* 888-373-9855 ■ *Web:* www.phideltatheta.org	Oxford	OH	45056	513-523-6345	523-9200	48-16
PHI Environmental Consulting 4844 Jackson Rd *Web:* www.phiconsulting.com	Ann Arbor	MI	48103	734-332-0800		463
Phi Eta Sigma National Honor Society 1906 College H8s Blvd Ste 11062 *TF:* 800-205-8877 ■ *Web:* www.phietasigma.org	Bowling Green	KY	42101	270-745-6540	745-3893	48-16
PHI Inc 2001 SE Evangeline Thwy PO Box 90808 *NASDAQ:* PHII ■ *TF:* 866-815-7101 ■ *Web:* www.phihelico.com	Lafayette	LA	70508	337-235-2452	235-1357	359
PHI Inc 14955 E Salt Lake Ave *Web:* phihydraulics.com	City of Industry	CA	91746	626-968-9680	333-3610	456
Phi Kappa Phi Foundation 7576 Goodwood Blvd *TF:* 800-804-9880 ■ *Web:* www.phikappaphi.org	Baton Rouge	LA	70806	225-388-4917		305
Phi Kappa Psi 5395 Emerson Way *TF:* 800-486-1852 ■ *Web:* www.phikappapsi.com	Indianapolis	IN	46226	317-632-1852		48-16
Phi Kappa Sigma International Fraternity Inc 2 Timber Dr *TF:* 800-344-7335 ■ *Web:* www.pks.org	Chester Springs	PA	19425	610-469-3282	469-3286	48-16
Phi Kappa Tau 5221 Morning Sun Rd *TF:* 800-758-1906 ■ *Web:* www.phikappatau.org	Oxford	OH	45056	513-523-4193	523-9325	48-16
Phi Kappa Theta National Fraternity 3901 W 86th St Ste 360 *Web:* www.phikaps.org	Indianapolis	IN	46268	317-872-9934	879-1889	48-16
Phi Mu Alpha Sinfonia Fraternity of America Inc 10600 Old State Rd *TF:* 800-473-2649 ■ *Web:* www.sinfonia.org	Evansville	IN	47711	812-867-2433	867-0633	48-16
Phi Mu Fraternity 400 Westpark Dr *TF:* 888-744-6824 ■ *Web:* www.phimu.org	Peachtree City	GA	30269	770-632-2090	632-2136	48-16
Phi Sigma Kappa International 2925 E 96th St *TF:* 888-846-6851 ■ *Web:* www.phisigmakappa.org	Indianapolis	IN	46240	317-573-5420	573-5430	48-16
Phi Sigma Pi National Honor Fraternity Inc 2119 Ambassador Cir *TF:* 800-366-1916 ■ *Web:* www.phisigmapi.org	Lancaster	PA	17603	717-299-4710	390-3054	48-16
Phi Sigma Sigma Fraternity Inc 8178 Lark Brown Rd Ste 202 *TF:* 800-526-1870 ■ *Web:* www.phisigmasigma.org	Elkridge	MD	21075	410-799-1224	799-9186	48-16
Phi Theta Kappa International Honor Society 1625 Eastover Dr *TF:* 800-946-9995 ■ *Web:* www.ptk.org	Jackson	MS	39211	601-984-3504	984-3550	48-16
Phibro Animal Health Corporation 300 Frank W Burr Blvd Ste 21 *TF:* 800-223-0434 ■ *Web:* www.phibrochem.com	Teaneck	NJ	07666	201-329-7300	329-7399	143
Phifer Inc 4400 Kauloosa Ave PO Box 1700 *TF:* 800-633-5955 ■ *Web:* www.phifer.com	Tuscaloosa	AL	35401	205-345-2120	759-4450	413
Phil Long Dealerships 1212 Motor City Dr *TF:* 866-644-1378 ■ *Web:* phillong.com	Colorado Springs	CO	80905	866-644-1378		57
Phil Smart Inc 2025 Airport Way S *TF:* 877-241-4528 ■ *Web:* www.mbseattle.com	Seattle	WA	98122	206-324-5959		57
Phil Smith Automotive Group 4250 N Federal Hwy *Web:* www.philsmithauto.com	Lighthouse Point	FL	33064	954-867-1234		57
Phil Trani's 3490 Long Beach Blvd *Web:* philtrani.com	Long Beach	CA	90807	562-426-3668		671
Phil's BBQ 3750 Sports Arena Blvd *Web:* www.philsbbq.net	San Diego	CA	92110	619-226-6333		671
Philadelphia 76ers 3601 S Broad St *Web:* www.nba.com	Philadelphia	PA	19148	215-339-7600	339-7615	714-1

Name / Address	City	State	Zip	Phone	Fax	Class
Philadelphia Business Journal 400 Market St Ste 1200 *Web:* www.bizjournals.com/philadelphia	Philadelphia	PA	19106	215-238-1450	238-9489	457-5
Philadelphia City Hall 1234 Market St 17th Fl *Web:* ww.phila.gov/pages/default.aspx	Philadelphia	PA	19107	215-563-6417		337
Philadelphia City Paper 123 Chestnut St 3rd Fl *Web:* mycitypaper.com	Philadelphia	PA	19106	215-735-8444		532-5
Philadelphia College of Osteopathic Medicine (PCOM) 4170 City Ave *TF Admissions:* 800-999-6998 ■ *Web:* www.pcom.edu	Philadelphia	PA	19131	215-871-6100		800
Philadelphia Consolidated Holding Corp 231 Saint Asaph's Rd Ste 100 *TF:* 888-647-8639 ■ *Web:* www.phly.com	Bala Cynwyd	PA	19004	610-617-7900	617-7940	391-4
Philadelphia Contributionship Insurance Co 212 S Fourth St **Fax Area Code:* 267 ■ *TF Cust Svc:* 888-627-1752 ■ *Web:* www.contributionship.com	Philadelphia	PA	19106	215-627-1752	765-4611*	391-4
Philadelphia Convention & Visitors Bureau 1700 Market St Ste 3000 *Web:* www.discoverphl.com	Philadelphia	PA	19103	215-636-3300	636-3327	206
Philadelphia County City Hall Broad & Market St *Web:* phila.gov	Philadelphia	PA	19107	215-686-1776	567-7380	338
Philadelphia Daily News PO Box 8263 *Web:* www.philly.com	Philadelphia	PA	19101	215-854-2000		532-2
Philadelphia Dance Co 9 N Preston St Philadanco Way *Web:* www.philadanco.org	Philadelphia	PA	19104	215-387-8200	387-8203	573-1
Philadelphia Eagles NovaCare Complex 1 NovaCare Way *Web:* www.philadelphiaeagles.com	Philadelphia	PA	19145	215-463-2500	339-5464	715-3
Philadelphia Flyers Wachovia Ctr 3601 S Broad St *Web:* flyers.nhl.com	Philadelphia	PA	19148	215-465-4500	389-9476	716
Philadelphia Gas Works (PGW) 800 W Montgomery Ave *TF:* 800-242-1776 ■ *Web:* www.pgworks.com	Philadelphia	PA	19122	215-235-1000		787
Philadelphia Gay News 505 S Fourth St *TF:* 800-292-0429 ■ *Web:* www.epgn.com	Philadelphia	PA	19147	215-625-8501		532-3
Philadelphia Inquirer 801 Market St Ste 300 PO Box 8263 *TF:* 800-341-3413 ■ *Web:* philly.com/subscribe	Philadelphia	PA	19107	215-854-2000		532-2
Philadelphia International Airport 8000 Essington Ave *TF:* 800-514-0301 ■ *Web:* www.phl.org	Philadelphia	PA	19153	215-937-6937	937-6497	27
Philadelphia Macaroni Co 760 S 11th St *Web:* www.philamacaroni.com	Philadelphia	PA	19147	215-923-3141	925-4298	296-31
Philadelphia Magazine 1818 Market St 36th Fl *Web:* www.phillymag.com	Philadelphia	PA	19103	215-564-7700	656-3500	457-22
Philadelphia Mixing Solutions, Ltd 1221 E Main St *Web:* www.philamixers.com	Palmyra	PA	17078	717-832-2800		298
Philadelphia Museum of Art 2600 Benjamin Franklin Pkwy *TF:* 800-732-0999 ■ *Web:* www.philamuseum.org	Philadelphia	PA	19130	215-763-8100	236-4465	520
Philadelphia National Cemetery Haines St & Limekiln Pike *Web:* www.cem.va.gov/cems/nchp/philadelphia.asp	Philadelphia	PA	19138	215-504-5610	504-5611	136
Philadelphia Orchestra 260 S Broad St Ste 1600 *Web:* www.philorch.org	Philadelphia	PA	19102	215-893-1955		573-3
Philadelphia Phillies Citizens Bank Pk 1 Citizens Bank Pk Way *Web:* philadelphia.phillies.mlb.com	Philadelphia	PA	19148	215-463-1000		713
Philadelphia Protestant Home 6500 Tabor Rd *Web:* www.pphfamily.org	Philadelphia	PA	19111	215-697-8000	697-8137	672
Philadelphia Regional Port Authority 3460 N Delaware Ave 2nd Fl *Web:* www.philaport.com	Philadelphia	PA	19134	215-426-2600	426-6800	618
Philadelphia Reserve Supply Co 200 Mack Dr *TF:* 800-347-7726 ■ *Web:* www.prsco.org	Croydon	PA	19021	215-785-3141		191-4
Philadelphia Sign Co 707 W Spring Garden St *Web:* www.philadelphiasign.com	Palmyra	NJ	08065	856-829-1460		701
Philadelphia Sports Clubs 888 Seventh Ave *Web:* www.mysportsclubs.com	New York	NY	10106	212-246-6700	246-8422	354
Philadelphia Sports Hall of Fame Foundation 2701 Grant Ave *Web:* www.phillyhall.org	Philadelphia	PA	19114	215-254-5049		522
Philadelphia Theatre Company 215 S Broad St 10th Fl *Web:* www.philadelphiatheatrecompany.org	Philadelphia	PA	19107	215-985-1400	985-5800	749
Philadelphia Tribune Co 520 S 16th St *Web:* www.phillytrib.com	Philadelphia	PA	19146	215-893-4050	735-3612	637-8
Philadelphia Trust Co, The 1760 Market St 2nd Fl *TF:* 800-541-7774 ■ *Web:* philadelphiatrust.com	Philadelphia	PA	19103	215-979-3434		69
Philadelphia University 4201 Henry Ave **Fax:* Admissions ■ *TF Admissions:* 800-951-7287 ■ *Web:* www.philau.edu	Philadelphia	PA	19144	215-951-2800	951-2907*	166
Philadelphia Vietnam Veterans Memorial 4720 Mercer St *Web:* pvvms646.org	Philadelphia	PA	19137	215-535-0643		50-4
Philadelphia Zoo 3400 W Girard Ave *Web:* www.philadelphiazoo.org	Philadelphia	PA	19104	215-243-1100	243-5385	823
Philander Smith College 900 Daisy Bates Dr **Fax:* Admissions ■ *TF:* 800-446-6772 ■ *Web:* www.philander.edu	Little Rock	AR	72202	501-370-5221	370-5225*	166

Name / Address	City	State	ZIP	Phone	Fax	Class
Philatelic Foundation						
341 W 38th St 5th Fl	New York	NY	10018	212-221-6555	221-6208	48-18
Web: www.philatelicfoundation.org						
Philbrook Museum of Art & Gardens						
2727 S Rockford Rd	Tulsa	OK	74114	918-749-7941		520
TF: 800-324-7941 ■ *Web:* www.philbrook.org						
Philharmonia Baroque Orchestra						
180 Redwood St Ste 200	San Francisco	CA	94102	415-252-1288	252-1488	573-3
Web: www.philharmonia.org						
Philharmonic Ctr for the Arts						
5833 Pelican Bay Blvd	Naples	FL	34108	239-597-1111		572
TF: 800-597-1900 ■ *Web:* artisnaples.org						
Philip Crosby Assoc 306 Dartmouth St	Boston	MA	02116	877-276-7295		194
TF: 877-276-7295 ■ *Web:* www.philipcrosby.com						
Philip Lief Group Inc (PLG)						
130 Wall St	Princeton	NJ	08540	609-430-1000		94
Web: www.philipliefgroup.com						
Philip Morris USA 2325 Bells Rd	Richmond	VA	23234	804-274-2000		756
TF: 800-343-0975 ■ *Web:* www.altria.com						
Philipp Lithographing Co						
1960 Wisconsin Ave PO Box 4	Grafton	WI	53024	262-377-1100		627
Web: www.philipplitho.com						
Philippi-Hagenbuch Inc 7424 W Plank Rd	Peoria	IL	61604	309-697-9200	697-2400	489
TF: 800-447-6464 ■ *Web:* www.philsystems.com						
Philippine Dept of Tourism						
556 Fifth Ave	New York	NY	10036	212-575-7915	302-6759	775
Web: www.tourism.gov.ph						
Philippines 556 Fifth Ave 5th Fl	New York	NY	10036	212-764-1300	840-8602	784
Web: www.un.int						
Consulate General						
447 Sutter St						
6th Fl Philippine Ctr Bldg	San Francisco	CA	94108	415-433-6666	421-2641	257
Web: www.philippinessanfrancisco.org						
Consulate General						
30 N Michigan Ave Ste 2100	Chicago	IL	60602	312-332-6458	332-3657	257
TF: 000 259 7030 ■ *Web:* www.chicagopcg.com						
Consulate General						
3435 Wilshire Blvd Ste 550	Los Angeles	CA	90010	213-639-0980	639-0990	257
Web: www.philippineconsulatela.org						
Consulate General 556 Fifth Ave	New York	NY	10036	212-764-1330	764-6010	257
TF: 866-589-1878 ■ *Web:* www.newyorkpcg.org						
Embassy 1600 Massachusetts Ave NW	Washington	DC	20036	202-467-9300	467-9417	257
TF: 800-527-2820 ■ *Web:* www.philippineembassy-usa.org						
philips 3015 Louis Amos	Lachine	QC	H8T1C4	514-636-0670	636-0460	439
Web: www.lightingproducts.philips.com						
Philips & Cohen LLP						
2000 Massachusetts Ave NW Ste 100	Washington	DC	20036	202-833-4567		428
TF: 800-844-4406 ■ *Web:* www.phillipsandcohen.com						
Philips Advance Light Elctro						
10275 W Higgins Rd	Rosemont	IL	60018	847-390-5000	423-1882*	787
**Fax Area Code:* 888 ■ *TF:* 800-555-0050 ■ *Web:* www.usa.lighting.philips.com						
Philips Arena 1 Philips Dr	Atlanta	GA	30303	404-878-3000		720
TF: 800-745-3000 ■ *Web:* www.philipsarena.com						
Philips Healthcare						
22100 Bothell Everett Hwy	Bothell	WA	98021	800-744-5477		475
TF: 888-744-5477 ■ *Web:* www.dunlee.com						
Philips Healthcare Informatics Inc						
4100 E Third Ave Ste 101	Foster City	CA	94005	650-293-2300	293-2301	382
TF Cust Svc: 877-328-2808 ■ *Web:* www.usa.philips.com						
Philips Lighting Co						
200 Franklin Sq Dr	Somerset	NJ	08873	800-555-0050		437
TF: 800-555-0050 ■ *Web:* www.usa.lighting.philips.com						
Philips Luminaire 776 S Green St	Tupelo	MS	38804	800-234-1890	841-5501*	439
**Fax Area Code:* 662 ■ **Fax:* Hum Res ■ *TF:* 800-234-1890 ■ *Web:* www.lightingproducts.philips.com						
Philips Medical Systems						
3000 Minuteman Rd	Andover	MA	01810	978-659-3000		382
TF: 800-934-7372 ■ *Web:* www.usa.philips.com						
Philips Respironics Georgia Inc						
175 Chastain Meadows Ct	Kennesaw	GA	30144	770-499-1212		250
Web: www.usa.philips.com						
Philipse Manor Hall State Historic Site						
29 Warburton Ave	Yonkers	NY	10701	914-965-4027		565
Web: philipsemanorhall.blogspot.in						
Phillip's Flower Shops Inc						
524 N Cass Ave	Westmont	IL	60559	630-719-5200	719-2292	292
TF: 800-356-7257 ■ *Web:* www.800florals.com						
Phillippi Creek Village Restaurant & Oyster Bar						
5353 S Tamiami Trl	Sarasota	FL	34231	941-925-4444		671
Web: www.creekseafood.com						
Phillips & Assoc PO Box 241040	Los Angeles	CA	90024	310-247-0963	247-0966	317
Web: www.phillipsontheweb.com						
Phillips & Company Securities Inc						
1300 SW Fifth Ave Ste 2100	Portland	OR	97201	503-224-0858		690
TF: 800-572-4765 ■ *Web:* www.phillipsandco.com						
Phillips & Johnston Inc						
21w179 Hill Ave	Glen Ellyn	IL	60137	630-469-8150	469-8048	492
TF: 877-411-8823						
Phillips & Jordan Inc						
10201 Parkside Dr Ste 300	Knoxville	TN	37922	865-688-8342	688-8369	189-5
TF: 800-955-0876 ■ *Web:* www.pandj.com						
Phillips & Temro Industries						
9700 W 74th St	Eden Prairie	MN	55344	952-941-9700	941-2285	60
TF: 800-328-6108 ■ *Web:* www.phillipsandtemro.com						
Phillips & Webster Pllc Attys						
17410 133rd Ave NE ste 301	Woodinville	WA	98072	425-482-1111		428
TF: 800-708-6000 ■ *Web:* www.justiceforyou.com						
Phillips 66 3010 Briarpark Dr	Houston	TX	77042	281-293-6600		787
TF: 800-527-5476 ■ *Web:* www.phillips66.com						
Phillips Academy 180 Main St	Andover	MA	01810	978-749-4000	749-4068	622
TF: 877-445-5477 ■ *Web:* www.andover.edu						
Phillips Automotive Inc						
4949 Virginia Beach Blvd	Virginia Beach	VA	23462	757-499-3771		57
Web: mercedesbenzofvirginiabeach.com						
Phillips Beach Plaza Hotel						
1301 Atlantic Ave	Ocean City	MD	21842	410-289-9121		379
TF: 800-492-5834 ■ *Web:* www.beachplazaoc.com						
Phillips Beth Israel School of Nursing						
776 Ave of the Americas	New York	NY	10001	212-614-6110		800

Name / Address	City	State	ZIP	Phone	Fax	Class
Phillips Brooks School Endowment						
2245 Avy Ave	Menlo Park	CA	94025	650-854-4545		305
Web: www.phillipsbrooks.org						
Phillips Bros Electrical Contractors Inc						
235 Sweet Spring Rd	Glenmoore	PA	19343	610-458-8578	458-8438	189-4
TF: 800-220-5051 ■ *Web:* www.philipsbrothers.com						
Phillips Buick-Pontiac-Gmc Truck Inc						
2160 US Hwy 441	Fruitland Park	FL	34731	352-728-1212		57
TF: 888-664-7454 ■ *Web:* www.phillips-buick.com						
Phillips Collection						
1600 21st St NW	Washington	DC	20009	202-387-2151	387-2436	520
Web: www.phillipscollection.org						
Phillips Community College PO Box 785	Helena	AR	72342	870-338-6474	338-7542	162
TF: 800-582-6953 ■ *Web:* www.pccua.edu						
Phillips Contracting Co PO Box 2069	Columbus	MS	39704	662-328-6250	329-3291	188-4
Web: www.phillipscontracting.com						
Phillips Corp 7390 Coca Cola Dr	Hanover	MD	21076	410-564-2929	564-2949	493
TF: 800-878-4242 ■ *Web:* www.phillipscorp.com						
Phillips County 620 Cherry St Ste 206	Helena	AR	72342	870-338-5505	338-5509	338
Web: phillipscounty.arkansas.gov						
Phillips County PO Box 484	Holyoke	CO	80734	970-854-3616		338
Web: phillipscofair.com						
Phillips County 314 S Second Ave W	Malta	MT	59538	406-654-1776	654-1776	338
Web: www.maltachamber.com						
Phillips County 301 State St	Phillipsburg	KS	67661	785-543-6895		338
Web: phillipscounty.org						
Phillips County Chamber of Commerce						
111 Hickory Hills Dr PO Box 447	Helena	AR	72342	870-338-8327		139
Web: www.phillipscountychamber.org						
Phillips Crab House						
2004 N Philadelphia Ave	Ocean City	MD	21842	410-289-6821		671
Web: www.phillipsseafood.com						
Phillips Distributing Corp						
3010 Nob Hill Rd	Madison	WI	53713	608-222-9177	222-0558	81-3
TF: 800-236-7269 ■ *Web:* www.phillipsdistributing.com						
Phillips Distribution Inc						
3000 E Houston St	San Antonio	TX	78220	210-227-2397		559
TF: 800-580-2397 ■ *Web:* www.phillipsdistribution.com						
Phillips Drugstore Inc 123 E State St	Mauston	WI	53948	608-847-5949		238
Web: www.phillipsrx.com						
Phillips European Restaurant						
26 Corporate Woods	Rochester	NY	14623	585-272-9910		671
Web: www.phillipseuropean.com						
Phillips Exeter Academy 20 Main St	Exeter	NH	03833	603-772-4311		622
TF: 800-245-2525 ■ *Web:* www.exeter.edu						
Phillips Eye Institute						
2215 Pk Ave S	Minneapolis	MN	55404	612-775-8800		374-7
Web: www.allinahealth.org						
Phillips Financial Management LLC						
6920 Pointe Inverness Way Ste 230	Fort Wayne	IN	46804	260-420-7732		194
Web: www.1phillips.com						
Phillips Gold & Company LLP						
1430 Broadway Rm 1200	New York	NY	10018	212-730-1112		2
Web: www.phillipsgold.com						
Phillips Graduate University						
19900 Plummer St	Chatsworth	CA	91311	818-861-6627		166
Web: www.pgu.edu/index.php						
Phillips Group 501 Fulling Mill Rd	Middletown	PA	17057	717-944-0400		535
TF: 800-538-7500 ■ *Web:* www.buyphillips.com						
Phillips Law Group LLC						
1618 Thompson Ave	Atlanta	GA	30344	404-761-6800		428
Web: www.phillipslawatlanta.com						
Phillips Machine Service Inc						
367 George St	Beckley	WV	25801	304-255-0537		386
TF: 800-733-1521 ■ *Web:* www.phillipsmachine.com						
Phillips Manufacturing Co						
4949 S 30th St	Omaha	NE	68107	402-339-3800		234
TF: 800-822-5055 ■ *Web:* www.phillipsmfg.com						
Phillips Murrah PC						
101 N Robinson Ave Corporate Tower						
13th Fl	Oklahoma City	OK	73102	405-235-4100		428
TF: 800-321-6742 ■ *Web:* www.phillipsmurrah.com						
Phillips Mushroom Farms Inc						
1011 Kaolin Rd	Kennett Square	PA	19348	610-925-0520	925-0527	10-7
TF: 800-722-8818 ■ *Web:* www.phillipsmushroomfarms.com						
Phillips Plywood Company Inc						
13599 Desmond St	Pacoima	CA	91331	818-897-7736	897-6571	613
TF Cust Svc: 800-649-6410 ■ *Web:* www.phillipsplywood.com						
Phillips Precision Inc						
7 Paul Kohner Pl	Elmwood Park	NJ	07407	201-797-8820		757
Web: www.phillipsmedicraft.com						
Phillips Property Management						
6106 Macarthur Blvd Ste 102	Bethesda	MD	20816	301-320-0422	229-0937	652
Web: www.phillipspm.com						
Phillips Service Industries Inc						
11878 Hubbard	Livonia	MI	48150	734-853-5000		360-3
Web: www.psi-online.com						
Phillips Sheet Metal Company Inc						
700 Elk St	Buffalo	NY	14210	716-824-3374		697
Web: psmbuffalo.com						
Phillips State Prison						
2989 W Rock Quarry Rd	Buford	GA	30519	770-932-4500	932-4544	213
TF: 800-825-8511 ■ *Web:* dcor.state.ga.us						
Phillips Syrup Corp						
28025 Ranney Pkwy	Westlake	OH	44145	440-835-8001	835-1148	296-15
TF: 800-350-8443 ■ *Web:* www.phillipssyrup.com						
Phillips Theological Seminary						
901 N Mingo Rd	Tulsa	OK	74116	918-610-8303	610-8404	167-3
TF: 800-843-4675 ■ *Web:* www.ptstulsa.edu						
Phillips, Hager & North Investment Management Ltd						
200 Burrard St 20th Fl	Vancouver	BC	V6C3N5	800-661-6141		528
TF: 800-661-6141 ■ *Web:* www.phn.com						
Phillipsburg Board of Education						
445 Marshall St	Phillipsburg	NJ	08865	908-454-3400		685
Web: www.pburgsd.net						
Phillystran Inc						
151 Commerce Dr	Montgomeryville	PA	18936	215-368-6611		208
Web: www.phillystran.com						

Phone | Fax | Class

Philosophy Inc 3809 E Watkins ... Phoenix AZ 85034 | 800-568-3151 | | 214
TF: 800-568-3151 ■ *Web:* www.philosophy.com

Philotechnics Ltd 201 Renovare Blvd ... Oak Ridge TN 37830 | 865-483-1551 | | 271
TF: 888-723-9278 ■ *Web:* www.philotechnics.com

Philpott Rubber Co
1010 Industrial Pkwy ... Brunswick OH 44212 | 330-225-3344 | 225-1999 | 676
Web: www.philpottrubber.com

Philpotts 40 S School St ... Honolulu HI 96813 | 808-533-6771 | | 393
Web: www.philpotts.net

Phin Solutions Inc
14245 St Francis Blvd Ste 105 ... Ramsey MN 55303 | 763-633-7007 | | 180
Web: www.phinsolutions.com

Phinney Bischoff Design House Inc
614 Boylston Ave E ... Seattle WA 98102 | 206-322-3484 | | 344
Web: phinneybischoff.com

Phinney Tool & Die Co
11023 W Center St Ext ... Medina NY 14103 | 585-798-3000 | 798-5612 | 757
TF: 800-665-8089 ■ *Web:* www.phinneytool.com

Phipps Conservatory & Botanical Gardens
1 Schenley Pk ... Pittsburgh PA 15213 | 412-622-6914 | 622-7363 | 97
Web: www.phipps.conservatory.org

Phipps Houses 902 Broadway 13th Fl ... New York NY 10010 | 212-243-9090 | | 186
Web: www.phippsny.org

Phipps Pharmacy Inc
205 B Hospital Dr ... Mckenzie TN 38201 | 731-352-0820 | | 237
Web: phippspharmacy.com

PhishLabs PO Box 20877 ... Charleston SC 29413 | 843-628-3368 | | 196
TF: 877-227-0790 ■ *Web:* www.phishlabs.com

PHLCOC (Park Hills Leadington Chamber of Commerce)
12 Municipal Dr ... Park Hills MO 63601 | 573-431-1051 | 431-2327 | 139
Web: www.phlcoc.net

Phluant Inc 10 E 39th St Ste 1127 ... New York NY 10016 | 646-476-8740 | | 5
Web: www.phluant.com

PHM Hospitality Inc
3300 Oak Lawn Ave Ste 408 ... Dallas TX 75219 | 214-521-0002 | | 463
Web: phmhospitality.com

PHM International Inc
509 Acacia Ave ... Sebastian FL 32958 | 772-388-6496 | | 463
Web: www.phmintl.com

PHMSA (Pipeline & Hazardous Materials Safety Administration)
1200 New Jersey Ave SE E Bldg 2nd Fl ... Washington DC 20590 | 202-366-4433 | 366-3666 | 340-17
Web: www.phmsa.dot.gov

PHMSA (Pipeline & Hazardous Materials Safety Administration Regional Offices)
Central Region (Pipeline)
901 Locust St Rm 462 ... Kansas City MO 64106 | 816-329-3800 | 329-3831 | 340-17
Web: www.phmsa.dot.gov

Phnom Penh 27080 Lorain Ave ... North Olmsted OH 44070 | 216-201-9141 | | 671
Web: ohiorestaurant.com

Pho 777 Vietnamese Restaurant
102 E Second St ... Reno NV 89501 | 775-323-7777 | | 671

Pho 79 9941 W Hazard Ave ... Garden Grove CA 92844 | 714-531-2490 | | 671
Web: pho79.com

Pho Bang New York
1001 St-Laurent Blvd ... Montreal QC H2Z1J4 | 514-954-2032 | | 671

Pho Grand 3195 S Grand Blvd ... Saint Louis MO 63118 | 314-664-7435 | | 671
Web: www.phogrand.com

Pho Saigon 400 Dickinson St ... Springfield MA 01108 | 413-781-4488 | | 671
Web: phosaigonspringfield.com

Pho Tre Bien 6946 Gateway E ... El Paso TX 79915 | 915-598-0166 | | 671
Web: www.photrebien.com

Pho84 354 17th St ... Oakland CA 94612 | 510-832-1338 | | 671
Web: pho84.com

Phoebe Micro Inc 47606 Kato Rd ... Fremont CA 94538 | 510-360-0800 | | 173-3
Web: www.phoebemicro.com

Phoebe Putney Memorial Hospital
417 W Third Ave ... Albany GA 31701 | 229-312-1000 | | 374-3
TF: 866-514-0015 ■ *Web:* www.phoebehealth.com

Phoebe Sumter Medical Ctr
1048 E Forsyth St ... Americus GA 31709 | 229-924-6011 | | 374-3
Web: www.phoebehealth.com

Phoebe's 900 E Genesee St ... Syracuse NY 13210 | 315-475-5154 | | 671
Web: www.phoebessyracuse.com

Phoenecia at Alki 2716 Alki Ave SW ... Seattle WA 98116 | 206-935-6550 | | 671
Web: phoeneciawestseattle.com

Phoenician, The
6000 E Camelback Rd ... Scottsdale AZ 85251 | 480-941-8200 | 947-4311 | 669
TF: 800-888-8234 ■ *Web:* www.thephoenician.com

Phoenix Advertising & Graphics Inc
6101 Adamsville Rd ... Gibsonton FL 33534 | 813-672-1991 | | 7
Web: phoenix4banners.com

Phoenix Aerospace Inc
220 W 80th Terr ... Kansas City MO 64114 | 816-333-3400 | | 21
Web: www.phoenixaerospace.com

Phoenix Air Group Inc
100 Phoenix Air Dr SW ... Cartersville GA 30120 | 770-387-2000 | 387-4545 | 25
Web: www.phoenixair.com

Phoenix AMD International Inc
41 Butler Ct ... Bowmanville ON L1C4P8 | 905-427-7440 | | 361
TF: 800-661-7313 ■ *Web:* www.phoenixamd.com

Phoenix American Inc
2401 Kerner Blvd ... San Rafael CA 94901 | 866-895-5050 | | 216
TF: 866-895-5050 ■ *Web:* www.phxa.com

Phoenix Analysis & Design Inc
7755 S Research Dr Ste 110 ... Tempe AZ 85284 | 480-813-4884 | | 261
Web: padtinc.com

Phoenix Art Museum 1625 N Central Ave ... Phoenix AZ 85004 | 602-257-1222 | 253-8662 | 520
Web: www.phxart.org

Phoenix Baptist Hospital
2000 W Bethany Home Rd ... Phoenix AZ 85015 | 602-249-0212 | | 374-3
Web: www.abrazohealth.com

Phoenix Cable Inc (PCI)
145 N Franklin Tpke ... Ramsey NJ 07446 | 201-825-9090 | | 116
Web: www.phoenixcable.com

Phoenix Cement Co
8800 E Chaparral Rd Ste 155 ... Scottsdale AZ 85250 | 480-850-5757 | 850-5758 | 135
TF: 800-424-9300 ■ *Web:* www.srmaterials.com

Phoenix Children's Hospital
1919 E Thomas Rd ... Phoenix AZ 85016 | 602-546-1000 | 933-0628 | 374-1
TF: 888-908-5437 ■ *Web:* www.phoenixchildrens.org

Phoenix City Hall
200 W Washington St 11th Fl ... Phoenix AZ 85003 | 602-262-7111 | 495-5583 | 337
Web: www.phoenix.gov

Phoenix Closures Inc
1899 High Grove Ln ... Naperville IL 60540 | 630-420-4750 | | 154
Web: www.phoenixclosures.com

Phoenix Co of Chicago Inc
555 Pond Dr ... Wood Dale IL 60191 | 630-595-2300 | | 815
Web: www.phoenixofchicago.com

Phoenix College 1202 W Thomas Rd ... Phoenix AZ 85013 | 602-285-7800 | 285-7700 | 162
TF: 800-266-7845 ■ *Web:* www.phoenixcollege.edu

Phoenix Color 18249 Phoenix Dr ... Hagerstown MD 21742 | 301-733-0018 | | 626
Web: www.phoenixcolor.com

Phoenix Controls 75 Discovery Way ... Acton MA 01720 | 978-795-1285 | 795-1111 | 202
TF: 800-340-0007 ■ *Web:* www.phoenixcontrols.com

Phoenix Convention Ctr 100 N Third St ... Phoenix AZ 85004 | 602-262-6225 | | 205
TF: 800-282-4842 ■ *Web:* www.phoenixconventioncenter.com

Phoenix Converting Co
211 W Booneslick ... Jonesburg MO 63351 | 636-488-3200 | | 548
Web: www.phoenixconvertingco.com

Phoenix Cos Inc, The
1 American Row PO Box 5056 ... Hartford CT 06102 | 860-403-5000 | | 360-4
NYSE: PNX ■ *TF:* 800-628-1936 ■ *Web:* phoenix.nsre.com/index.html

Phoenix Creative Services Inc
611 N Tenth St Ste 700 ... Saint Louis MO 63101 | 314-421-5646 | | 344
Web: www.phoenixcreative.com

Phoenix Ctr for Advanced Legal & Economic Public Policy Studies
5335 Wisconsin Ave NW Ste 440 ... Washington DC 20015 | 202-274-0235 | 244-8257 | 634
Web: www.phoenix-center.org

Phoenix Down Corp 85 US 46 ... Totowa NJ 07512 | 973-812-8100 | 812-9077 | 746
TF: 800-255-3696 ■ *Web:* www.phoenixdown.com

Phoenix Electric Manufacturing Co
3625 N Halsted St ... Chicago IL 60613 | 773-477-8855 | | 518
Web: www.phoenixelectric.com

Phoenix Electronic Enterprises Inc
131 Tillson Ave EXT ... Highland NY 12528 | 845-691-7700 | 691-7759 | 492
Web: www.phoenixmfg.com

Phoenix Elementary School District
1817 N Seventh St ... Phoenix AZ 85006 | 602-257-3755 | | 685
Web: phxschools.org

Phoenix Engineering & Consulting Inc
110 Londonderry Ct Ste 136-C ... Woodstock GA 30188 | 404-216-0140 | | 393
Web: www.phoenix-engineer.com

Phoenix Environmental Laboratories Inc
587 Middle Tpke E ... Manchester CT 06040 | 860-645-3513 | | 743
TF: 800-827-5426 ■ *Web:* www.phoenixlabs.com

Phoenix Fabricators & Erectors Inc
182 S Country Rd 900 E ... Avon IN 46123 | 317-271-7002 | | 480
Web: www.phoenixtank.com

Phoenix Film Festival
7000 E Mayo Blvd Ste 1059 ... Phoenix AZ 85054 | 602-955-6444 | | 282
Web: www.phoenixfilmfestival.com

Phoenix Films Inc PO Box 3816 ... Clearwater FL 33767 | 727-446-0300 | | 600
Web: www.phoenixfilms.com

Phoenix Fire Museum 203 S Claiborne St ... Mobile AL 36602 | 251-208-7569 | | 520
TF: 800-211-7892 ■ *Web:* www.museumofmobile.com

Phoenix Flower Shops
5733 E Thomas Rd Ste 4 ... Scottsdale AZ 85251 | 480-289-4000 | | 292
TF: 888-311-0404 ■ *Web:* www.phoenixflowershops.com

Phoenix Footwear Group Inc
5937 Darwin Ct Ste 109 ... Carlsbad CA 92008 | 760-602-9688 | | 301
OTC: PXFG ■ *TF:* 888-218-7275 ■ *Web:* www.phoenixfootwear.com

Phoenix Forging Company Inc
800 Front St ... Catasauqua PA 18032 | 610-264-2861 | 266-0530 | 483
TF: 800-444-3674 ■ *Web:* www.phoenixforge.com

Phoenix Grand Hotel Salem
201 Liberty St SE ... Salem OR 97301 | 503-540-7800 | | 379
TF: 877-540-7800 ■ *Web:* www.grandhotelsalem.com

Phoenix Greyhound Park
3801 E Washington St ... Phoenix AZ 85034 | 602-273-7181 | | 642
Web: www.phoenixgreyhoundpark.com

Phoenix Group of Virginia Inc
630C Woodlake Dr ... Chesapeake VA 23320 | 757-228-1730 | | 463
Web: www.phoenix-group.com

Phoenix Growth Capital Corp
2401 Kerner Blvd ... San Rafael CA 94901 | 866-895-5050 | | 216
TF: 866-895-5050 ■ *Web:* www.phxa.com

Phoenix Home Care Inc
3033 S Kansas Expy ... Springfield MO 65807 | 417-881-7442 | | 363
TF: 855-881-7442 ■ *Web:* phoenixhomehc.com

Phoenix Hotel 601 Eddy St ... San Francisco CA 94109 | 415-776-1380 | | 379
TF: 800-738-7477 ■ *Web:* jdvhotels.com

Phoenix House Foundation Inc (PHF)
164 W 74th St 4th Fl ... New York NY 10023 | 888-671-9392 | | 726
TF: 888-671-9392 ■ *Web:* www.phoenixhouse.org

Phoenix Housing Network 7050 S G St ... Tacoma WA 98408 | 253-471-5340 | | 656
Web: ccsww.convio.net

Phoenix Innovate Inc 1775 Bellingham ... Troy MI 48083 | 248-457-9000 | | 627
Web: www.phoenixinnovate.com

Phoenix Integration Inc
1275 Drummers Ln One Glenhardie Corporate Ctr
Ste 105 ... Wayne PA 19087 | 540-961-7215 | | 180
Web: www.phoenix-int.com

Phoenix International
812 W Southern Ave ... Orange CA 92865 | 714-283-4800 | 283-1169 | 173-8
Web: www.phenxint.com

Phoenix International Freight Services Ltd
14701 Charlson Rd ... Eden Prairie MN 55347 | 952-937-6761 | 766-6395* | 311
**Fax Area Code:* 630 ■ *TF:* 855-229-6128 ■ *Web:* www.chrobinson.com

Phoenix Leasing Inc
2401 Kerner Blvd ... San Rafael CA 94901 | 866-895-5050 | | 216
TF: 866-895-5050 ■ *Web:* www.phxa.com

Phoenix Lithographing Corp
11631 Caroline Rd ... Philadelphia PA 19154 | 215-698-9000 | | 627
Web: www.phoenixlitho.com

Phoenix Magazine
15169 N Scottsdale Ste 310 ... Scottsdale AZ 85254 | 480-664-3960 | 664-3962 | 457-22
TF: 866-481-6970 ■ *Web:* www.phoenixmag.com

Name / Address	City	State	ZIP	Phone	Fax	Class
Phoenix Manufacturing Inc 3655 E Roeser Rd *TF Cust Svc:* 800-325-6952 ■ *Web:* phoenixmanufacturing.com	Phoenix	AZ	85040	602-437-4833	437-4833	14
Phoenix Manufacturing of GA 34 Industrial Ct E *Web:* www.evapcool.com	Villa Rica	GA	30180	770-459-5255		499
Phoenix Media Communications Group 126 Brookline Ave *TF:* 888-536-7464 ■ *Web:* www.thephoenix.com	Boston	MA	02215	617-536-5390	536-1463	637-8
Phoenix Mercury US Airways Ctr 201 E Jefferson St *Web:* www.wnba.com/mercury	Phoenix	AZ	85004	602-514-8333		714-2
Phoenix Metals Co 4685 Buford Hwy *TF:* 800-241-2290 ■ *Web:* www.phoenixmetals.net	Norcross	GA	30071	770-447-4211		492
Phoenix Modular Inc 5301 W Madison St *Web:* www.phoenixmodular.com	Phoenix	AZ	85043	602-447-6460		186
Phoenix New Times 1201 E Jefferson *Web:* www.phoenixnewtimes.com	Phoenix	AZ	85034	602-271-0040	340-8806	532-5
Phoenix Newspapers Inc 200 E Van Buren St *TF:* 800-331-9303 ■ *Web:* azcentral.com	Phoenix	AZ	85004	602-444-8000	444-8044	637-8
Phoenix Park 'n Swap 3801 E Washington St *TF:* 800-772-0852 ■ *Web:* www.americanparknswap.com	Phoenix	AZ	85034	602-273-1250		271
Phoenix Park Hotel 520 N Capitol St *TF:* 800-824-5419 ■ *Web:* www.phoenixparkhotel.com	Washington	DC	20001	202-638-6900	393-3236	379
Phoenix Pharmaceuticals Inc 330 Beach Rd *TF:* 800-988-1205 ■ *Web:* www.phoenixpeptide.com	Burlingame	CA	94010	650-558-8898		231
Phoenix Pictures Inc 10203 W Washington Blvd Ste 400 *Web:* www.phoenixpictures.com	Los Angeles	CA	90067	424-298-2788	298-2588	514
Phoenix Police Museum 17 S Second Ave Historic City Hall 1st Fl *Web:* phoenixpolicemuseum.org	Phoenix	AZ	85003	602-534-7278		520
Phoenix Precast Products Inc 1856 E Deer Valley Rd *Web:* www.phoenixprecastproducts.com	Phoenix	AZ	85024	602-569-6090		183
Phoenix Process Equipment Co 2402 Watterson Trial *Web:* www.dewater.com	Louisville	KY	40299	502-499-6198	499-1079	386
Phoenix Public Library 1221 N Central Ave *Web:* www.phoenixpubliclibrary.org	Phoenix	AZ	85004	602-261-8847	261-8836	434-3
Phoenix Realty & Trust Co PO Box 87420	Phoenix	AZ	85080	602-494-0202		652
Phoenix Renovation & Restoration Inc 16250 Foster *Web:* www.kcphoenix.com	Overland Park	KS	66085	913-599-0055		186
Phoenix Seminary 4222 E Thomas Rd Ste 400 *TF:* 888-443-1020 ■ *Web:* www.ps.edu	Phoenix	AZ	85018	602-850-8000	850-8080	167-3
Phoenix Sky Harbor International Airport 3400 E Sky Harbor Blvd Ste 3300 *TF:* 800-781-1010 ■ *Web:* skyharbor.com	Phoenix	AZ	85034	602-273-3300		27
Phoenix Society for Burn Survivors Inc 1835 RW Berends Dr SW *TF:* 800-888-2876 ■ *Web:* www.phoenix-society.org	Grand Rapids	MI	49519	616-458-2773	458-2831	48-17
Phoenix Solutions Co 5480 Nathan Ln N Ste 110 *Web:* www.phoenixsolutionsco.com	Plymouth	MN	55442	763-544-2721	546-5617	318
Phoenix Stamping Group LLC 6100 Emmanuel Dr *Web:* www.phoenixstamping.com	Atlanta	GA	30336	404-699-2882		488
Phoenix Suns US Airways Ctr 201 E Jefferson St *TF:* 866-648-4668 ■ *Web:* www.nba.com/suns	Phoenix	AZ	85004	602-379-7900	379-7990	714-1
Phoenix Symphony 1 N First St Ste 200 *TF:* 800-776-9080 ■ *Web:* www.phoenixsymphony.org	Phoenix	AZ	85004	602-495-1117	253-1772	573-3
Phoenix Technologies Ltd 915 Murphy Ranch Rd *TF:* 800-677-7305 ■ *Web:* www.phoenix.com	Milpitas	CA	95035	408-570-1000	570-1001	178-12
Phoenix Transportation Services LLC 335 E Yusen Dr *TF:* 800-860-0889 ■ *Web:* www.phoenix-transportation.net	Georgetown	KY	40324	502-863-0108	863-0029	780
Phoenix Tube Company Inc 1185 Win Dr *TF:* 800-526-2124 ■ *Web:* www.phoenixtube.com	Bethlehem	PA	18017	610-865-5337		492
Phoenix Union High School District (PUHSD) 4502 N Central Ave *TF:* 800-823-4929 ■ *Web:* www.phxhs.k12.az.us	Phoenix	AZ	85012	602-764-1100		685
Phoenix USA Inc 51 E Borden St *Web:* www.phoenixusa.com	Cookeville	TN	38501	931-526-6128		54
Phoenix Zoo 455 N Galvin Pkwy *Web:* www.phoenixzoo.org	Phoenix	AZ	85008	602-273-1341		823
Phoenixville Hospital 140 Nutt Rd *TF:* 800-640-4155 ■ *Web:* www.phoenixvillehospital.com	Phoenixville	PA	19460	610-983-1000		374-3
Phoenixville Regional Chamber of Commerce 171 Bridge St *TF:* 800-432-8322 ■ *Web:* www.phoenixvillechamber.org	Phoenixville	PA	19460	610-933-3070	917-0503	139
Phoinix Group Inc, The 16308 Califonia Ste 100 - 105 *Web:* www.phoinixgroup.com	Tampa	FL	33624	813-962-4000		180
Phone Ware Inc 8902 Activity Rd *TF:* 800-243-8329 ■ *Web:* www.phonewareinc.com	San Diego	CA	92126	858-459-3000		317
PHONE+ Magazine 3300 N Central Ave Ste 300 *Web:* www.channelpartnersonline.com	Phoenix	AZ	85012	480-990-1101	990-0819	457-21
Phone.com Inc 211 Warren St *Web:* www.phone.com	Newark	NJ	07103	973-577-6380		387
Phonic Ear Inc 2080 Lakeville Hwy *TF:* 800-227-0735 ■ *Web:* www.phonicear.com	Petaluma	CA	94954	707-769-1110		477
Phonoscope Ltd 6105 Wline Dr *Web:* www.phonoscope.com	Houston	TX	77036	713-272-4600		116
Phosphate Holdings Inc 100 Web Ste 4 *Web:* www.missphosphates.com	Madison	MS	39110	601-898-9004		360-3
Photo Antiquities-Museum of Photographic History 531 E Ohio St *Web:* www.photoantiquities.org	Pittsburgh	PA	15212	412-231-7881	231-1217	520
Photo Den 315 SE Seventh St *Web:* photoden.com	Grants Pass	OR	97526	541-479-1833	479-8855	225
Photo Diagnostic Systems Inc 85 Swanson Rd *Web:* www.photodiagnostic.com	Boxboro	MA	01719	978-266-0420	266-0425	476
Photo Research Inc 9731 Topanga Canyon Pl *TF:* 877-424-6423 ■ *Web:* www.photoresearch.com	Chatsworth	CA	91311	818-725-9750	725-9770	419
Photo Researchers Inc 307 Fifth Ave 3rd Fl *TF:* 800-833-9033 ■ *Web:* www.sciencesource.com	New York	NY	10016	212-758-3420		593
Photo Resource Hawaii PO Box 1082 *Web:* www.photoresourcehawaii.com	Honoka'a	HI	96727	808-599-7773		593
Photo USA 2140 Colonial Ave *TF:* 888-234-6320 ■ *Web:* www.photousa.com	Roanoke	VA	24015	540-344-0961		588
Photocrazy Inc 509 Raindance St *Web:* www.photocrazy.com	Thousand Oaks	CA	91360	805-492-0562		592
Photodex Corp 11100 Metric Blvd Ste 400 *Web:* www.photodex.com	Austin	TX	78758	512-419-7000		225
Photofabrication Engineering Inc 500 Fortune Dr *Web:* www.photofabrication.com	Milford	MA	01757	508-478-2025		454
PhotoMachining Inc 4 Industrial Dr Unit number 4 *Web:* www.photomachining.com	Pelham	NH	03076	603-882-9944		757
PhotoMedex Inc 40 Ramland Rd S, Second Fl Ste 200 *NASDAQ: PHMD* ■ *TF:* 888-966-1010 ■ *Web:* www.photomedex.com	Orangeburg	NY	10962	215-619-3600		424
Photon Dynamics Inc 5970 Optical Ct	San Jose	CA	95138	408-226-9900		201
Photon Technology International Inc 300 Birmingham Rd PO Box 272 *Web:* www.pti-nj.com	Birmingham	NJ	08011	609-894-4420		544
Photo-scan of Los Angeles 743 Cochran St Ste C *Web:* www.pslasecurity.com	Simi Valley	CA	93065	805-581-4448		693
PhotoSource 5106 Louetta Rd *TF:* 800-786-6277 ■ *Web:* www.photosource.com/cart/pl.php	Spring	TX	77379	281-370-2220		531-13
Photosource International 1910 35th Rd *TF:* 800-786-6277 ■ *Web:* www.photosource.com	Osceola	WI	54020	715-248-3800		637-9
Photronics Inc 15 Secor Rd *NASDAQ: PLAB* ■ *TF:* 800-292-9396 ■ *Web:* www.photronics.com	Brookfield	CT	06804	203-775-9000		696
PHP (Parents Helping Parents) 1400 Parkmoor Ave Ste 100 *TF:* 855-727-5775 ■ *Web:* www.php.com	San jose	CA	95126	408-727-5775	286-1116	48-6
PHR (Physicians for Human Rights) 185 Devonshire St Ste M102 *Web:* physiciansforhumanrights.org	Boston	MA	02110	617-301-4200	301-4250	48-5
PHRI (Public Health Research Institute) International Ctr for Public Health 225 Warren St *Web:* www.phri.org	Newark	NJ	07103	973-854-3100	854-3101	668
PhRMA (Pharmaceutical Research & Manufacturers of America) 950 F St NW Ste 300 *Web:* www.phrma.org	Washington	DC	20004	202-835-3400	835-3414	49-8
Phunware Inc 7800 Shoal Creek Blvd *TF:* 855-521-8485 ■ *Web:* www.phunware.com	Austin	TX	78757	855-521-8485		177
PHX Energy Services Corp 1400-250 2 St SW *TF:* 800-909-9819 ■ *Web:* www.phxtech.com	Calgary	AB	T2P0C1	403-543-4466		536
Phygen LLC 2301 Dupont Ave Ste 110 *TF:* 800-939-7008 ■ *Web:* www.phygenspine.com	Irvine	CA	92612	949-752-7885	752-7886	477
Phyle Inventory Control Specialists Inc 4150 Grange Hall Rd *TF:* 888-303-8482 ■ *Web:* www.picsinv.com	Holly	MI	48442	888-303-8482		393
PhyleTec LLC 4150 Grange Hall Rd *Web:* www.phyletec.com	Holly	MI	48442	248-634-4000		253
Phyllis Kind Gallery 236 W 26th St Ste 503 *Web:* www.phylliskindgallery.com	New York	NY	10001	212-925-1200	941-7841	42
Phylonix Pharmaceuticals Inc 100 Inman St Ste 300 *Web:* www.phylonix.com	Cambridge	MA	02139	617-441-6700		231
Phylway Construction LLC 1074a Hwy 1 *Web:* www.phylway.com	Thibodaux	LA	70301	985-446-9644		188-10
Phyphar Inc 29 Walter Hammond Pl *Web:* www.phyphar.com	Waldwick	NJ	07463	201-444-4648		734
Physcient Inc 112 S Duke St Ste 4A *Web:* www.physcient.com	Durham	NC	27701	919-686-0300		475
Physical Acoustics Corp 195 Clarksville Rd *Web:* www.physicalacoustics.com	Princeton Junction	NJ	08550	609-716-4000		639
Physical Electronics Inc 18725 Lake Dr E *Web:* www.phi.com	Chanhassen	MN	55317	952-828-6100	828-6451	419
Physical Optics Corp 1845 W 205th St *Web:* www.poc.com	Torrance	CA	90501	310-320-3088	320-4667	402
Physical Resource Engineering Inc 4655 N Flowing Wells Rd *TF:* 800-446-4259 ■ *Web:* www.prengr.com	Tucson	AZ	85705	520-690-1669		261
Physical Review Letters 1 Research Rd *Web:* aps.org	Ridge	NY	11961	631-591-4000		531-12
Physician Insurers Assn of America (PIAA) 2275 Research Blvd Ste 250 *TF:* 800-688-2421 ■ *Web:* www.piaa.us	Rockville	MD	20850	301-947-9000	947-9090	49-9
Physician's Automated Laboratory Inc (PALLAB) 9830 Brimhall Rd *TF:* 800-675-2271 ■ *Web:* www.pallab.org	Bakersfield	CA	93312	661-829-2260	829-1317	418
Physicians Committee for Responsible Medicine (PCRM) 5100 Wisconsin Ave NW Ste 400 *TF:* 866-416-7276 ■ *Web:* www.pcrm.org	Washington	DC	20016	202-686-2210	686-2216	49-8
Physicians for Human Rights (PHR) 185 Devonshire St Ste M102 *Web:* physiciansforhumanrights.org	Boston	MA	02110	617-301-4200	301-4250	48-5

Name / Address	City	State	ZIP	Phone	Fax	Class
Physicians for Social Responsibility (PSR) 1875 Connecticut Ave NW Ste 1012 *TF:* 800-459-1887 ■ *Web:* www.psr.org	Washington	DC	20009	202-667-4260	667-4201	49-8
Physicians Laboratory Services Inc 4840 "F" St *TF:* 800-642-1117 ■ *Web:* www.physlab.com	Omaha	NE	68117	402-731-4145		415
Physicians Life Insurance Co 2600 Dodge St *TF:* 800-228-9100 ■ *Web:* physiciansmutual.com	Omaha	NE	68131	402-633-1000		391-2
Physicians Mutual Insurance Co 2600 Dodge St *TF:* 800-228-9100 ■ *Web:* physiciansmutual.com	Omaha	NE	68131	402-633-1000	633-1604	391-2
Physicians Plus Insurance Corp 2650 Novation Pkwy Ste 200 *TF:* 800-545-5015 ■ *Web:* www.pplusic.com	Madison	WI	53713	608-282-8900		391-3
Physicians Regional Medical Center 6101 Pine Ridge Rd *Web:* physiciansregional.com	Naples	FL	34119	239-348-4000		374-3
Physicians Weight Loss Centers of America Inc 395 Springside Dr **Fax Area Code:* 330 ■ *TF:* 800-205-7887 ■ *Web:* www.pwlc.com	Akron	OH	44333	800-205-7887	666-2197*	810
Physick House 321 S Fourth St *Web:* www.philalandmarks.org	Philadelphia	PA	19106	215-925-2251		50-3
Physics Today Magazine 1 Physics Ellipse *TF:* 800-344-6902 ■ *Web:* contact.physicstoday.org	College Park	MD	20740	301-209-3040	209-0842	457-19
Physio-Control Inc 11811 Willows Rd NE **Fax:* Acctg ■ *TF:* 800-442-1142 ■ *Web:* www.physio-control.com	Redmond	WA	98052	425-867-4000	881-2405*	250
Physiotherapy Associates Inc 855 Springdale Dr Ste 200 *Web:* myphysio.com	Exton	PA	19341	610-644-7824		477
Physmark Inc 101 E Pk Blvd Ste 600 *TF:* 800-922-7060 ■ *Web:* www.physmark.com	Plano	TX	75074	972-231-8000		179
Phytron Inc 600 Blair Pk Rd Ste 220 *Web:* www.phytron.com	Williston	VT	05495	802-872-1600	872-0311	518
PI & Information Services LLC PO Box 157 *TF:* 800-477-8211 ■ *Web:* www.pi-info.com	Beaverton	OR	97075	503-643-4274	643-5474	400
Pi Beta Phi Fraternity for Women 1154 Town & Country Commons Dr *Web:* www.pibetaphi.org	Town and Country	MO	63017	636-256-0680	256-8095	48-16
PI Inc 213 Dennis St *Web:* www.pi-inc.com	Athens	TN	37303	423-368-1890		608
Pi Kappa Alpha Fraternity 8347 W Range Cove *Web:* pikes.org	Memphis	TN	38125	901-748-1868	748-3100	48-16
Pi Kappa Phi Fraternity 2015 Ayrsley Town Blvd Ste 200 *Web:* www.pikapp.org	Charlotte	NC	28273	704-504-0888	504-0880	48-16
Pi Lambda Phi Fraternity Inc 60 Newtown Rd Ste 118 *Web:* www.pilambdaphi.org	Danbury	CT	06810	203-740-1044	740-1644	48-16
Pi Sigma Alpha 1527 New Hampshire Ave NW *Web:* office2248.wixsite.com/pi-sigma-alpha	Washington	DC	20036	202-349-9285		48-16
Pi Sigma Epsilon (PSE) 3747 S Howell Ave *TF:* 800-761-9350 ■ *Web:* www.pse.org	Milwaukee	WI	53207	414-328-1952	328-1953	48-16
Pi Tech 522 Shafor Blvd	Dayton	OH	45419	937-272-1813		180
PIA (Pakistan International Airlines Corp) 1200 New Jersey Ave SE *TF:* 800-578-6786 ■ *Web:* www.piac.com.pk	Washington	DC	20590	800-578-6786		25
PIA (Pittsburgh Institute of Aeronautics) 5 Allegheny County Airport *TF:* 800-444-1440 ■ *Web:* www.pia.edu	West Mifflin	PA	15122	412-346-2100	346-2170	800
Pia Group Inc 3520 Ibsen Ave *Web:* www.piagroup.com	Cincinnati	OH	45209	513-351-3300		811
PIA/GATF (Printing Industries of America/Graphic Arts Technical Foundation) 200 Deer Run Rd *TF:* 800-910-4283 ■ *Web:* www.printing.org	Sewickley	PA	15143	412-741-6860	741-2311	49-16
PIAA (Physician Insurers Assn of America) 2275 Research Blvd Ste 250 *TF:* 800-688-2421 ■ *Web:* www.piaa.us	Rockville	MD	20850	301-947-9000	947-9090	49-9
PIAB (President's Foreign Intelligence Advisory Board) White House 1600 Pennsylvania Ave *Web:* www.whitehouse.gov/administration/eop/piab	Washington	DC	20500	202-456-1414		340
Piad Precision Casting Corp 112 Industrial Pk Rd *TF:* 800-441-9858 ■ *Web:* www.piad.com	Greensburg	PA	15601	724-838-5500	838-5520	308
Piano Technicians Guild 4444 Forest Ave *Web:* www.ptg.org	Kansas City	KS	66106	913-432-9975	432-9986	49-4
PianoDisc 4111 N Fwy Blvd *TF:* 800-566-3472 ■ *Web:* www.pianodisc.com	Sacramento	CA	95834	916-567-9999	567-1941	527
Piantedosi Baking Company Inc 240 Commercial St *TF:* 800-339-0080 ■ *Web:* www.piantedosi.com	Malden	MA	02148	781-321-3400	324-5647	296-1
Piasecki Aircraft Corp 519 W Second St *Web:* www.piasecki.com	Essington	PA	19029	610-521-5700		256
Piatt County 101 W Washington St *Web:* www.piattcounty.org	Monticello	IL	61856	217-762-9487	762-7563	338
Piatti 2182 Avenida de la Playa *Web:* piatti.com	La Jolla	CA	92037	858-454-1589		671
Piatti Restaurant Co 835 Fifth Ave *Web:* www.piatti.com	San Rafael	CA	94901	415-380-2525	380-2530	670
Piatti Ristorante & Bar Sacramento 571 Pavilions Ln *Web:* www.piatti.com	Sacramento	CA	95825	916-649-8885	649-8907	671
Piatti Ristorante & Bar San Antonio 255 E Basse Rd Ste 500 *Web:* www.piatti.com	San Antonio	TX	78209	210-832-0300		671
Piatto Ristorante 4925 W Alabama St *Web:* www.piattoristorante.com	Houston	TX	77056	713-871-9722	871-9190	671
Piazza Italia 1129 NW Johnson St *Web:* www.piazzaportland.com	Portland	OR	97209	503-478-0619	227-5199	671
Piazzano's Restaurant 1825 N Grand River Ave *Web:* www.piazzanos.com	Lansing	MI	48906	517-484-9922		671
Pibbs Industries 133-15 32nd Ave *TF:* 800-551-5020 ■ *Web:* www.pibbs.com	Flushing	NY	11354	718-445-8046	461-3910	76
Pibel Lake State Recreation Area 301 Centennial Mall S PO Box 98907 *Web:* visitnebraska.com	Lincoln	NE	68509	308-346-5666		565
PIC Business Systems Inc 5119 Beckwith Blvd Ste 106 *TF:* 800-742-7378 ■ *Web:* www.picbusiness.com	San Antonio	TX	78249	210-690-9106		177
Pic Design Corp 86 Benson Rd PO Box 1004 *TF:* 800-243-6125 ■ *Web:* www.pic-design.com	Middlebury	CT	06762	203-758-8272	758-8271	620
PIC Skate 22 Village Dr *TF:* 800-882-3448 ■ *Web:* www.picskate.com	Riverside	RI	02915	401-490-9334	438-5419	710
PIC USA 100 Bluegrass Commons Blvd Ste 2200 *TF:* 800-325-3398 ■ *Web:* na.pic.com	Hendersonville	TN	37075	615-265-2700		10-6
Picaboo Corp 1160 Chestnut St *Web:* www.picaboo.com	Menlo Park	CA	94025	650-326-3200		177
Picacho Peak State Park PO Box 907 *Web:* azstateparks.com/picacho	Ejoy	AZ	85131	520-466-3183		565
Picacho State Recreation Area 1416 Ninth St *TF:* 800-777-0369 ■ *Web:* www.parks.ca.gov	Sacramento	CA	95814	916-653-6995	654-6374	565
Picante Grill 3810 Broadway *Web:* picantegrill.com	San Antonio	TX	78209	210-822-3797		671
Picante Mexican Restaurant 3235 NW Evangeline Thwy *Web:* www.picantesrestaurant.com	Lafayette	LA	70508	337-896-1200		671
Picarro Inc 480 Oakmead Pkwy *Web:* www.picarro.com	Sunnyvale	CA	94085	408-962-3900		419
Picasso Travel 300 N Continental Blvd Ste 310 *Web:* picassotravel.com	El Segundo	CA	90245	310-645-4400		16
Picasso's 62 W Santa Clara St *Web:* www.picassostapas.com	San Jose	CA	95113	408-298-4400		671
Picasso's Italian Ristorante 4152 W Spring Creek Pkwy *Web:* www.picassosrestaurant.us	Plano	TX	75093	972-618-4143		671
Piccadilly Cafeterias Inc 3332 S Sherwood Forest Blvd **Fax Area Code:* 318 ■ *Web:* www.piccadilly.com	Baton Rouge	LA	70816	225-293-4853	445-4740*	670
Piccadilly Circus Pizza 1007 Okoboji Ave PO Box 188 *TF:* 800-338-4340 ■ *Web:* www.pcpizza.com	Milford	IA	51351	800-338-4340		670
Piccadilly Inn Airport 5115 E McKinley Ave *Web:* www.piccadillyinn.com	Fresno	CA	93727	559-375-7760		379
Piccadilly Inn Express 2305 W Shaw Ave *Web:* www.piccadillyinn.com	Fresno	CA	93711	559-348-5520		379
Piccadilly Printing Co 1000 Valley Ave *Web:* www.picprinting.com	Winchester	VA	22601	540-662-3804		627
Picco Engineering 8611 Jane St Ste 200 *TF:* 888-772-0773 ■ *Web:* www.picco-engineering.com	Concord	ON	L4K2M6	905-760-9688	760-9699	261
Piccola Italia 815 Elm St *Web:* www.piccolaitalianh.com	Manchester	NH	03101	603-606-5100		671
Piccolina Toscana 1412 N DuPont St *Web:* www.piccolinatoscana.com	Wilmington	DE	19806	302-654-8001		671
Piccolo Mondo 829 E Lamar Blvd *Web:* www.piccolomondo.com	Arlington	TX	76011	817-265-9174		671
Picerne Real Estate Group 75 Lambert Lind Hwy *Web:* www.picerne.com	Warwick	RI	02886	401-732-3700	738-6452	653
Picholine 35 W 64th St *TF:* 800-745-3000 ■ *Web:* www.picholinenyc.com	New York	NY	10023	212-724-8585		671
PICHTR (Pacific International Ctr for High Technology Research) 1440 Kapiolani Blvd Ste 1225 *Web:* www.pichtr.org	Honolulu	HI	96814	808-943-9581	943-9582	668
Picis Inc 100 Quannapowitt Pkwy Ste 405 *Web:* picis.com	Wakefield	MA	01880	781-557-3000		178-10
Pick N Save 6950 W State St *Web:* www.picknsave.com	Wauwatosa	WI	53213	414-475-7181		345
Pick Your Part Auto Wrecking Inc 1235 S Beach Blvd *TF:* 800-962-2277 ■ *Web:* www.lkqpickyourpart.com	Anaheim	CA	92804	800-962-2277		54
Pickaway Correctional Institution PO Box 209 *Web:* www.drc.ohio.gov	Orient	OH	43146	614-877-4362	877-4514	213
Pickaway County 139 W Franklin St *Web:* www.pickaway.org	Circleville	OH	43113	740-474-6093	474-8988	338
Pickaway County Chamber of Commerce 114 E Main St *Web:* www.pickaway.com	Circleville	OH	43113	740-474-4923		139
Pickaway County District Public Library 1160 N Court St *TF:* 800-733-2767 ■ *Web:* www.pickawaylib.org	Circleville	OH	43113	740-477-1644	474-2855	434-3
Pickaway County Visitors Bureau 325 W Main St *Web:* www.pickaway.com	Circleville	OH	43113	740-474-3636	420-9181	206
Pickaway-Ross County Joint Vocational School District 895 Crouse Chapel Rd *Web:* pickawayross.com	Chillicothe	OH	45601	740-642-1200		685
Pickens County 1266 E Church St *TF:* 800-801-5437 ■ *Web:* pickenscountyga.gov	Jasper	GA	30143	706-253-8809		338
Pickens County Library 304 Biltmore Rd *Web:* pickens.lib.sc.us	Easley	SC	29640	864-850-7077		434-3
Pickens County School District (PCSD) 1348 Griffin Mill Rd *Web:* www.pickens.k12.sc.us	Easley	SC	29640	864-397-1000	855-8159	685
Pickens Snodgrass Koch & Company PC 3001 Medlin Dr Ste 100 *TF:* 800-424-5790 ■ *Web:* www.pskcpa.com	Arlington	TX	76015	817-664-3000		2
Pickens-Kane Moving Co 410 N Milwaukee Ave *TF:* 888-871-9998 ■ *Web:* www.pickenskane.com	Chicago	IL	60610	312-942-0330		519

Phone | Fax | Class

Pickerel Lake Recreation Area
12980 446th Ave. Grenville SD 57239 605-486-4753 565
Web: gfp.sd.gov

Pickering College 16945 Bayview Ave Newmarket ON L3Y4X2 905-895-1700 895-9076 622
Web: www.pickeringcollege.on.ca

Pickerington Local School District
90 N East St Pickerington OH 43147 614-833-2110 685
Web: www.pickerington.k12.oh.us

Pickett County
1 Courthouse Sq Ste 200 Byrdstown TN 38549 931-864-3798 864-6615 338
TF: 888-406-4704 ■ *Web:* dalehollow.com/info-resources/government

Pickett State Park
4605 Pickett Pk Hwy Jamestown TN 38556 931-879-5821 565
TF: 877-260-0010 ■ *Web:* tnstateparks.com/parks/about/pickett

Pickett's Mill Battlefield State Historic Site
4432 Mt Tabor Church Rd Dallas GA 30157 770-443-7850 565
Web: www.gastateparks.org

PickPoint Corp
4234 Hacienda Dr Ste 101 Pleasanton CA 94588 925-924-1700 475
TF: 800-636-1288 ■ *Web:* www.pickpoint.com

Pickrel Schaeffer & Ebeling
40 N Main St - Kettering Tower Dayton OH 45423 937-223-1130 428
TF: 800-908-4490 ■ *Web:* www.pselaw.com

Pickseed West Disc Inc 33149 Hwy 99 E Tangent OR 97389 541-926-8886 276
Web: www.pickseed.com

PicksPal Inc 1957 Landings Dr Mountain View CA 94043 650-964-1513 396
Web: www.pickspal.com

Pickwick Co 4200 Thomas Dr SW Cedar Rapids IA 52404 800-397-9797 697
TF: 800-397-9797 ■ *Web:* www.pickwick.com

Pickwick Electric Co-op
530 Mulberry Ave Selmer TN 38375 731-645-3411 245
TF: 800-372-8258 ■ *Web:* www.pickwickec.com

Pickwick Landing State Resort Park
PO Box 15 Pickwick Dam TN 38365 731-689-3129 565
Web: tnstateparks.com/parks/about/pickwick-landing

Picnic Time Inc 5131 Maureen Ln Moorpark CA 93021 805-529-7400 200
Web: www.picnictime.com

Pico Envirotec Inc 222 Snidercroft Rd Concord ON L4K2K1 905-760-9512 180
Web: www.picoenvirotec.com

PICO Holdings Inc
7979 Ivanhoe Ave Ste 301 La Jolla CA 92037 858-456-6022 456-6480 360-4
NASDAQ: PICO ■ *TF:* 888-389-3222 ■ *Web:* www.picoholdings.com

Pico Macom Inc 8880 Rehco Rd San Diego CA 92121 858-546-5050 546-5051 647
TF: 800-421-6511 ■ *Web:* www.picomacom.com

Pico Quantitative Trading LLC
120 Wall St 16th Fl New York NY 10005 646-701-6120 690
Web: www.picotrading.com

Pico Rivera Chamber of Commerce
5016 Passons Blvd Pico Rivera CA 90660 562-949-2473 139
TF: 800-901-7211 ■ *Web:* www.picoriverachamber.org

PicoSearch LLC 10 Fawcett St Cambridge MA 02138 617-547-4020 39

Pics Telecom International Corp
1920 Lyell Ave Rochester NY 14606 585-295-2000 295-2020 735
TF: 800-521-7427 ■ *Web:* www.picstelecom.com

Pictorial Offset Corp 111 Amor Ave Carlstadt NJ 07072 201-935-7100 627

Pictou County Chamber of Commerce
980 E River Rd New Glasgow NS B2H3S8 902-755-3463 137
Web: www.pictouchamber.com

Pictsweet Co, The 10 Pictsweet Dr Bells TN 38006 731-663-7600 662-7651* 296-21
**Fax Area Code:* 888 ■ *Web:* www.pictsweetfarms.com

Picture Marketing Inc
1202 Grant Ave Ste D Novato CA 94945 949-623-9889 636
TF: 888-337-8288 ■ *Web:* www.picturemarketing.com

Pictured Rocks National Lakeshore
N8391 Sandpoint Rd PO Box 40 Munising MI 49862 906-387-2607 387-4025 564
Web: www.nps.gov

PIDA (Pet Industry Distributors Assn)
2105 Laurel Bush Rd Ste 200 Bel Air MD 21015 443-640-1060 49-18
Web: www.pida.org

Pidilite USA Inc 100 E Diamong Ave Hazleton PA 18201 570-454-3596 459-1752 146
Web: www.pidilite.com

Pie Consulting & Engineering Inc
6275 Joyce Dr Ste 200 Arvada CO 80403 303-552-0177 261
Web: www.pieglobal.com

Pied Piper Mills Inc 423 E Lake Dr Hamlin TX 79520 325-576-3684 447

Piedmont Airlines Inc
5443 Airport Terminal Rd Salisbury MD 21804 410-742-2996 25
Web: www.piedmont-airlines.com

Piedmont Aviation Component Services LLC
1031 E Mtn St ste 320 Kernersville NC 27284 336-776-6300 20
Web: www.piedmontaviation.com

Piedmont Baptist College
420 S Broad St Winston-Salem NC 27101 336-725-8344 725-5522* 166
**Fax:* Admissions ■ *TF Admissions:* 800-937-5097 ■ *Web:* www.piedmontu.edu

Piedmont College 165 Central Ave Demorest GA 30535 706-776-0103 776-6635* 166
**Fax:* Admissions ■ *TF:* 800-277-7020 ■ *Web:* www.piedmont.edu

Piedmont Community College
1715 College Dr PO Box 1197 Roxboro NC 27573 336-599-1181 597-3817* 162
**Fax:* Admissions ■ *Web:* www.piedmont.cc.nc.us
Caswell County
331 Piedmont Dr PO Box 1150 Yanceyville NC 27379 336-694-5707 694-7086 162
Web: www.piedmont.cc.nc.us

Piedmont Community Health Plan Inc
2512 Langhorne Rd Lynchburg VA 24501 434-947-4463 390
TF: 800-400-7247 ■ *Web:* www.pchp.net

Piedmont Concrete 1318 Jonesville Hwy Union SC 29379 864-427-1756 183
Web: www.piedmontconcrete.net

Piedmont Construction Group LLC (PCG)
107 Gateway Dr Ste B Macon GA 31210 478-405-8907 405-8908 186
Web: www.piedmontconstructiongroup.com

Piedmont Electric Membership Corp
2500 Nc Hwy 86 S Hillsborough NC 27278 919-732-2123 644-1030 245
Web: www.pemc.coop

Piedmont FSB (PFSB)
201 S Stratford Rd Winston-Salem NC 27103 336-770-1000 70
Web: www.piedmontfederal.com

Piedmont Gardens 110 41st St Oakland CA 94611 510-596-2600 672
TF: 800-496-8126 ■ *Web:* www.piedmontgardens.com

Piedmont Geotechnical
3000 Northfield Pl Roswell GA 30076 770-752-9205 256
Web: www.ascomputer.com

Piedmont Geriatric Hospital
PO Box 427 Burkeville VA 23922 434-767-4401 767-2346* 374-7
**Fax Area Code:* 432 ■ *Web:* www.pgh.dbhds.virginia.gov

Piedmont Graphics Inc
6903 International Dr Greensboro NC 27409 336-230-0040 627
Web: www.piedmontgraphics.com

Piedmont Healthcare
1133 Eagle's Landing Pkwy Stockbridge GA 30281 678-604-1000 604-5580 374-3
Web: www.piedmont.org

Piedmont Hospital
1968 Peachtree Rd NW Atlanta GA 30309 404-605-5000 374-3
Web: www.piedmont.org

Piedmont Investment Advisors LLC
2605 Meridian Pkwy Ste 105 Durham NC 27713 919-688-8600 401
Web: www.piedmontinvestment.com

Piedmont Mechanical Inc
116 John Dodd Rd PO Box 4925 Spartanburg SC 29305 864-578-9114 578-5314 189-10
Web: www.piedmontmechanical.com

Piedmont Medical Ctr
222 S Herlong Ave Rock Hill SC 29732 803-329-1234 374-3
TF: 800-222-4218 ■ *Web:* www.piedmontmedicalcenter.com

Piedmont Natural Gas
4720 Piedmont Row Dr PO Box 33068 Charlotte NC 28233 704-364-3120 787
NYSE: PNY ■ *TF:* 800-752-7504 ■ *Web:* www.piedmontng.com

Piedmont Newnan Hospital (PNH)
60 Hospital Rd Newnan GA 30263 770-400-1000 374-3
Web: www.piedmont.org

Piedmont Precision Machine Company Inc
150 Airside Dr Danville VA 24540 434-793-0677 757
Web: www.ppmmach.com

Piedmont Technical College
620 N Emerald Rd Greenwood SC 29646 864-941-8324 800
TF: 800-868-5528 ■ *Web:* www.ptc.edu

Piedmont Triad International Airport
1000 A Ted Johnson Pkwy Greensboro NC 27409 336-665-5600 27
Web: www.flyfrompti.com

Piedmont Truck Tires Inc
PO Box 18228 Greensboro NC 27419 336-668-0091 755
TF: 800-274-8473 ■ *Web:* www.piedmonttrucktires.com

Piedmont Virginia Community College
501 College Dr Charlottesville VA 22902 434-977-3900 961-5425* 162
**Fax:* Admissions ■ *TF:* 800-222-1222 ■ *Web:* www.pvcc.edu

Piehl, Hanson, Beckman PA
700 S Grade Rd SW Hutchinson MN 55350 320-234-4430 2
Web: www.phbcpa.com

Pieper Electric Inc 5070 N 35th St Milwaukee WI 53209 414-462-7700 189-4
TF: 800-424-8802 ■ *Web:* www.pieperpower.com

Pieper O'Brien Herr Architects Ltd
3000 Royal Blvd S Alpharetta GA 30022 770-569-1706 261
Web: www.poharchitects.com

Pier 1 Imports Inc 100 Pier 1 Pl Fort Worth TX 76102 817-252-8000 252-8174 362
NYSE: PIR ■ *TF:* 800-245-4595 ■ *Web:* www.pier1.com

Pier 1 Kids 100 Pier 1 Pl Fort Worth TX 76102 817-252-0000 252-0005 021
TF: 800-433-4035 ■ *Web:* www.pier1.com

Pier 5 Hotel 711 Eastern Ave Baltimore MD 21202 410-539-2000 783-1787 379
TF: 866-583-4162 ■ *Web:* www.harbormagic.com

Pier 99 2822 N Shoreline Blvd Corpus Christi TX 78402 361-887-0764 671
Web: pier99restaurant.com

Pier Foundry & Pattern Shop Inc
51 State St Saint Paul MN 55107 651-222-4461 492
Web: www.pierfoundry.com

Pier House Resort Caribbean Spa
1 Duval St Key West FL 33040 305-296-4600 296-7569 669
TF: 800-723-2791 ■ *Web:* www.pierhouse.com

Pieratt's 110 Mt Tabor Rd Lexington KY 40517 859-268-6000 35
TF: 855-743-7288 ■ *Web:* www.pieratts.com

PIERC (Pacific Island Ecosystems Research Ctr)
12201 Sunrise Valley Dr Ste 615 Reston VA 20192 703-648-5953 668
Web: www.usgs.gov

Pierce & Assoc
1 N Dearborn St Ste 1300 Chicago IL 60602 312-346-9088 428
TF: 800-447-5375 ■ *Web:* www.atty-pierce.com

Pierce & Shearer LLP
730 Polhemus Rd Ste 101 San Mateo CA 94402 650-573-9300 428
Web: www.pierceshearer.com

Pierce Aluminum 34 Forge Pkwy Franklin MA 02038 508-541-7007 541-6077 492
Web: www.piercealuminum.com

Pierce Assoc Inc
4216 Wheeler Ave PO Box 9050 Alexandria VA 22304 703-751-2400 751-2479 189-10
TF: 800-817-4309 ■ *Web:* www.pierceassociates.com

Pierce College 9401 Farwest Dr SW Lakewood WA 98498 253-964-6500 964-6427* 162
**Fax:* Admissions ■ *Web:* www.pierce.ctc.edu
Puyallup 1601 39th Ave SE Puyallup WA 98374 253-840-8400 840-8449* 162
**Fax:* Admissions ■ *TF:* 877-353-6763 ■ *Web:* www.pierce.ctc.edu

Pierce County 312 Nichols St Blackshear GA 31516 912-449-2022 449-2024 338
Web: pc.pcgeorgia.com

Pierce County
414 W Main St PO Box 119 Ellsworth WI 54011 715-273-6851 273-6853 338
Web: www.co.pierce.wi.us

Pierce County 111 W Ct St Rm 1 Pierce NE 68767 402-329-4225 329-6439 338
Web: www.co.pierce.ne.us

Pierce County 240 SE Second St Rugby ND 58368 701-776-6161 776-5707 338
Web: www.piercecountynd.gov

Pierce County 930 Tacoma Ave S Rm 110 Tacoma WA 98402 253-798-7455 798-3428 338
Web: www.co.pierce.wa.us

Pierce County Library System
3005 112th St E Tacoma WA 98446 253-536-6500 537-4600 434-3
TF: 800-346-0995 ■ *Web:* www.piercecountylibrary.org

Pierce County Security Inc
2002 99th St E Tacoma WA 98445 253-535-4433 693
TF: 800-773-4432 ■ *Web:* www.pcswa.com

Pierce Distribution Services Co
PO Box 15600 Loves Park IL 61132 800-466-7397 636-5660* 449
**Fax Area Code:* 815 ■ *TF:* 800-466-7397 ■ *Web:* www.piercedistribution.com

Entry	City	State	ZIP	Phone	Fax	Class
Pierce Mfg Inc 2600 American Dr PO Box 2017 *TF Cust Svc:* 800-974-3723 ■ *Web:* www.piercemfg.com	Appleton	WI	54912	920-832-3000		516
Pierce Pacific Manufacturing Inc 4424 NE 158th PO Box 30509 *TF:* 800-760-3270 ■ *Web:* www.piercepacific.com	Portland	OR	97294	503-808-9110	808-9111	190
Pierce Pepin Co-op Services W7725 US Hwy 10 PO Box 420 *TF:* 800-924-2133 ■ *Web:* www.piercepepin.com	Ellsworth	WI	54011	715-273-4355		245
Pierce Promotions & Event Management Inc 178 Middle St 2nd Fl *Web:* www.piercepromotions.com	Portland	ME	04101	207-523-1700		7
Pierce Pump Company LP 9010 John W Carpenter Fwy *TF:* 800-929-2875 ■ *Web:* www.piercepump.com	Dallas	TX	75247	214-320-3604		358
Pierce Transit 3701 96th St SW PO Box 99070 *TF:* 800-562-8109 ■ *Web:* www.piercetransit.org	Lakewood	WA	98499	253-581-8000	581-8075	468
Pierce-Cote Advertising 683 Main St *Web:* www.pierce-cote.com	Osterville	MA	02655	508-420-5566		7
Pierce-Eislen Inc 9200 E Pima Ctr Pkwy Ste 150 *Web:* www.yardimatrix.com	Scottsdale	AZ	85258	480-663-1149		652
Piercey Automotive Group 16901 Millikan Ave *Web:* www.pierceyautogroup.com	Irvine	CA	92606	949-396-6000		57
Piercon Solutions LLC 63 Beaverbrook Rd Ste 201 *Web:* piercon.net	Lincoln Park	NJ	07035	973-628-9330		261
Piercy Bowler Taylor & Kern 6100 Elton Ave Ste 1000 *Web:* pbtk.com	Las Vegas	NV	89107	702-384-1120		2
Pierpont Inn 550 Sanjon Rd *Web:* www.pierpontinn.com	Ventura	CA	93001	805-643-6144		379
Pierpont Morgan Library 225 Madison Ave *TF:* 800-433-4149 ■ *Web:* www.themorgan.org	New York	NY	10016	212-685-0008	481-3484	520
Pierpont's at Union Station 30 W Pershing Rd Union Station *Web:* www.herefordhouse.com	Kansas City	MO	64108	816-221-5111		671
Pierre Area Chamber of Commerce 800 W Dakota Ave *TF:* 800-962-2034 ■ *Web:* www.pierre.org	Pierre	SD	57501	605-224-7361	224-6485	139
Pierre City Hall 222 E Dakota Ave *Web:* ci.pierre.sd.us	Pierre	SD	57501	605-773-7407	773-7406	337
Pierre Fabre Dermo Cosmetique 8 Campus Dr *Web:* www.pierre-fabre.com	Parsippany	NJ	07054	973-898-1042		231
Pierre Regional Airport 3800 Airport Rd *Web:* cityofpierre.org/154/airport	Pierre	SD	57501	605-773-7447		27
Pierre, The 2 E 61st St *Web:* www.tajhotels.com	New York	NY	10065	212-838-8000	940-8109	379
Pierre-Boucher Hospital 1333 Boul Jacques-Cartier E	Longueuil	QC	J4M2A5	450-468-8111		374-2
Pierson Co 1200 W Harris St *Web:* www.piersoncompany.com	Eureka	CA	95503	707-268-1800	268-1801	186
Pierson Construction Inc 4500 N Route E *Web:* www.piersonconstruction.net	Columbia	MO	65202	573-445-8493		186
Pierson Industries Inc 7 Astro Pl *Web:* www.piersonindustriesinc.com	Rockaway	NJ	07866	973-627-7945		596
Pierson Ranch Recreation Area 31144 Toe Rd *Web:* www.gfp.sd.gov	Yankton	SD	57078	605-668-2985		565
Pietragallo Gordon Alfano Bosick & Raspanti LLP 1 Oxford Centre Fl 38 *TF:* 800-447-5375 ■ *Web:* www.pietragallo.com	Pittsburgh	PA	15219	412-263-2000		428
Pietrantoni Mendez & Alvarez LLP Popular Ctr Bldg 208 Ponce de Leon Ave 19th Fl *Web:* www.pmalaw.com	San Juan	PR	00918	787-274-1212		428
Piezotech LLC 8431 Georgetown Rd Ste 300 *Web:* www.piezotechnologies.com	Indianapolis	IN	46268	317-876-4670		407
Pigeon Brands Inc 179 John St 2nd Fl *Web:* www.pigeonbrands.com	Toronto	ON	M5T1X4	416-532-9950		344
Pigeon Forge Dept of Tourism PO Box 1390 *TF:* 800-251-9100 ■ *Web:* www.mypigeonforge.com	Pigeon Forge	TN	37868	865-453-8574		206
Pigeon Point Light Station State Historic Park 210 Pigeon Pt Rd *Web:* www.parks.ca.gov	Pescadero	CA	94060	650-879-0633		565
Piggly Wiggly 2400 J Terrell Wooten Dr *Web:* www.pwadc.com	Bessemer	AL	35020	205-481-2300		297-8
Piggly Wiggly Carolina Company Inc 176 Croghan Spur Rd Ste 301 *TF:* 800-243-9880 ■ *Web:* thepig.net	Charleston	SC	29407-7555	843-554-9880	202-8200	345
Piggly Wiggly Midwest LLC 2215 Union Ave *TF:* 800-530-7286 ■ *Web:* pigglywiggly.com	Sheboygan	WI	53081	920-457-4433		345
Pignataro Volkswagon 10633 Evergreen Way *Web:* www.pignatarovw.com	Everett	WA	98204	425-348-3141		57
Pigott Inc 3815 Ingersoll Ave *Web:* www.pigottnet.com	Des Moines	IA	50312	515-279-8879	279-7338	320
Pigs Unlimited Inc 23802 Fm 2978 B-3 *Web:* www.pigsunlimited.com	Tomball	TX	77375	281-351-2749		454
PIIRS (Princeton Institute for International & Regional Studies) Princeton University Bendheim Hall *TF:* 888-486-3339 ■ *Web:* www.princeton.edu/piirs	Princeton	NJ	08544	609-258-4852	258-3988	634
PIJAC (Pet Industry Joint Advisory Council) 1220 19th St NW Ste 400 *TF:* 800-553-7387 ■ *Web:* www.pijac.org	Washington	DC	20036	202-452-1525	293-4377	49-4
PIKA Technologies Inc 535 Legget Dr Ste 400 *Web:* www.pikatech.com	Ottawa	ON	K2K3B8	613-591-1555		256
Pike County 115 W Main St	Bowling Green	MO	63334	573-324-2412		338
Pike County PO Box 309 *TF:* 800-433-0567 ■ *Web:* www.co.pike.ms.us	Magnolia	MS	39652	601-783-3362		338
Pike County 506 Broad St *TF:* 866-681-4947 ■ *Web:* www.pikepa.org	Milford	PA	18337	570-296-7613	296-6055	338
Pike County 1 Courthouse Sq	Murfreesboro	AR	71958	870-285-3316		338
Pike County 801 E Main St PO Box 125	Petersburg	IN	47567	812-354-6025		338
Pike County 146 Main St *Web:* www.revenue.ky.gov	Pikeville	KY	41501	606-432-6247	432-6222	338
Pike County 100 E Washington St Courthouse *Web:* www.pikeil.org	Pittsfield	IL	62363	217-285-6812		338
Pike County 120 W Church St PO Box 1147 *Web:* Www.alabama.gov	Troy	AL	36081	334-566-6374		338
Pike County 126 W Second St PO Box 134 *Web:* www.piketravel.com	Waverly	OH	45690	740-947-9650	941-0255	338
Pike County Chamber of Commerce 178 College St *Web:* www.sekchamber.com	Pikeville	KY	41501	606-432-5504	432-7295	139
Pike County Chamber of Commerce 209 E Hartford St *Web:* www.pikechamber.com	Milford	PA	18337	570-296-8700	296-3921	139
Pike County Chamber of Commerce & Economic Development PO Box 5302 *TF:* 800-844-2653 ■ *Web:* www.pikeinfo.com	Summit	MS	39666	601-684-2291	684-4899	139
Pike Distributors Inc 401 E John St PO Box 465 *TF:* 800-542-3474 ■ *Web:* pikedistributors.com	Newberry	MI	49868	906-293-8611		81-1
Pike Electric Corp 100 Pike Way PO Box 868 *NYSE: PIKE* ■ *TF:* 800-424-7453	Mount Airy	NC	27030	336-789-2171		189-4
Pike Industries Inc 3 Eastgate Pk Rd *TF:* 800-283-0803 ■ *Web:* pikeindustries.com	Belmont	NH	03220	603-527-5100	527-5101	188-4
Pike Lake State Park 1847 Pike Lake Rd	Bainbridge	OH	45612	740-493-2212		565
Pike Lumber Company Inc PO Box 247 *TF:* 800-356-4554 ■ *Web:* www.pikelumber.com	Akron	IN	46910	574-893-4511	893-7400	683
Pike National Forest 601 S Weber St *Web:* www.fs.fed.us	Colorado Springs	CO	80903	719-636-1602	477-4233	50-5
Pike Nurseries Holding LLC 3555 Koger Blvd Ste 360 *Web:* www.pikenursery.com	Duluth	GA	30096	770-921-1022		323
Pike Outlets, The 95 S Pine Ave *Web:* www.facebook.com/thepikeoutlets	Long Beach	CA	90802	562-432-8325		50-6
Pike Place Market (PPM PDN) 85 Pike St Rm 500 *Web:* www.pikeplacemarket.org	Seattle	WA	98101	206-682-7453	625-0646	50-6
Pikes Peak Community College						
Centennial 5675 S Academy Blvd *TF:* 800-456-6847 ■ *Web:* www.ppcc.edu	Colorado Springs	CO	80906	719-502-2000		162
Downtown Studio 100 W Pikes Peak Ave *TF:* 800-456-6847 ■ *Web:* www.ppcc.edu	Colorado Springs	CO	80903	719-502-2000		162
Rampart Range 11195 Hwy 83 *TF:* 800-456-6847 ■ *Web:* www.ppcc.edu	Colorado Springs	CO	80921	719-502-2000		162
Pikes Peak Ctr 190 S Cascade Ave *TF:* 866-464-2626 ■ *Web:* www.pikespeakcenter.com	Colorado Springs	CO	80903	719-477-2100	477-2199	572
Pikes Peak Financial Consultants 1544 Shane Cir	Colorado Springs	CO	80907	719-266-8890		690
Pikes Peak Library District PO Box 1579 *Web:* www.ppld.org	Colorado Springs	CO	80901	719-531-6333		434-3
Pikes Peak State Park 15316 Great River Rd *Web:* www.iowadnr.gov	McGregor	IA	52157	563-873-2341		565
Pikes Peak Test Labs Inc 4750 Edison Ave *Web:* www.pptli.com	Colorado Springs	CO	80915	719-596-0802		743
Pikesville Chamber of Commerce 7 Church Ln Ste 14 *Web:* www.pikesvillechamber.org	Pikesville	MD	21208	410-484-2337	484-4151	139
Pikeville College 147 Sycamore St **Fax:* Admissions ■ *TF:* 866-232-7700 ■ *Web:* upike.edu	Pikeville	KY	41501	606-218-5250	218-5255*	166
Pikeville Medical Ctr 911 Bypass Rd *Web:* www.medicalleader.org	Pikeville	KY	41501	606-218-4509		374-3
Pilar Services Inc 13910 Laurel Lakes Ave *Web:* www.pilarservices.net	Laurel	MD	20707	301-362-1569		224
Pilar's Cafe 746 S 'A' St	Oxnard	CA	93030	805-487-1444		671
Pilarski Sinkel & Hankes Ltd 5100 Eden Ave S Ste 304	Edina	MN	55436	952-929-2580		2
Pilat (North America) Inc 460 US Hwy 22 W Ste 408 *Web:* pilat.com	Whitehouse Station	NJ	08889	908-823-9417		196
Pilcher Hamilton Corp 6845 Kingery Hwy *Web:* www.pilcherhamilton.com	Willowbrook	IL	60527	630-655-8100		603
Pilgrim BanCorp 2401 S Jefferson Ave *TF:* 877-303-3111 ■ *Web:* pilgrimbank.com	Mount Pleasant	TX	75455	903-575-2150		70
Pilgrim Hall Museum 75 Ct St *Web:* www.pilgrimhallmuseum.org	Plymouth	MA	02360	508-746-1620		520
Pilgrim Home & Hearth LLC 5600 Imhoff Dr Ste G *Web:* www.pilgrimhearth.com	Concord	CA	94520	925-288-1040		364
Pilgrim Monument & Provincetown Museum 1 High Pole Hill Rd *Web:* www.pilgrim-monument.org	Provincetown	MA	02657	508-487-1310		50-4
Pilgrim Plastic Products Co 1200 W Chestnut St *Web:* www.pilgrimplastics.com	Brockton	MA	02301	508-583-9046		9

Phone | Fax | Class

Pilgrim Psychiatric Ctr
998 Crooked Hill Rd West Brentwood NY 11717 631-761-3500 761-2600 374-5
TF: 800-597-8481 ■ *Web:* www.omh.ny.gov

Pilgrim Quality Solutions
2807 W Busch Blvd Tampa FL 33618 813-915-1663 915-1948 178-1
Web: pilgrimquality.com

Pilgrim Tours & Travel Inc
3071 Main St PO Box 268 Morgantown PA 19543 610-286-0788 286-6262 760
TF: 800-322-0788 ■ *Web:* www.pilgrimtours.com

Pilgrim's Corp 1770 Promontory Cir Greeley CO 80634 800-321-1470 619
NASDAQ: PPC ■ *TF:* 800-321-1470 ■ *Web:* www.pilgrimspride.com

Pilkington Holdings Inc
811 Madison Ave Toledo OH 43697 419-247-3731 247-3821 329
Web: www.pilkington.com

Pillar Financial Advisors LLC
3046 Breckenridge Ln Ste 104 Louisville KY 40220 502-384-3890 401
TF: 800-346-7526 ■ *Web:* www.pillar.net

Pillar Hotels & Resorts LP
6031 Connection Dr Ste 500 Irving TX 75039 972-830-3100 379
Web: pillarhotels.com

Pillar Induction Co
21905 Gateway Rd Brookfield WI 53045 262-317-5300 317-5353 318
TF: 800-558-7733 ■ *Web:* www.pillar.com

Pillar Innovations LLC
92 Corporate Dr Grantsville MD 21536 301-245-4007 407
Web: www.pillarinnovations.com

Pillar of Fire 1302 Sherman St Denver CO 80203 303-839-1500 506
Web: www.pillar.org

Pillar Technologies
475 Industrial Dr Hartland WI 53029 262-367-3060 201
Web: www.pillartech.com

Pillar Technology Group LLC
301 E Liberty St Ste 700 Ann Arbor MI 48104 888-374-5527 809
TF: 888-374-5527 ■ *Web:* www.pillartechnology.com

Pillars Hotel at New River Sound
111 N Birch Rd Fort Lauderdale FL 33304 954-467-9639 763-2845 379
Web: www.pillarshotel.com

Piller Inc 45 Turner Rd Middletown NY 10941 800-597-6937 692-0295* 518
**Fax Area Code:* 845 ■ *TF:* 800-597-6937 ■ *Web:* www.piller.com

Pilling Surgical
2917 Weck Dr Research Triangle Park NC 27709 919-544-8000 361-3914 476
TF Cust Svc: 866-246-6990 ■ *Web:* www.teleflex.com

Pillsbury State Park
100 Pillsbury State Park Rd Washington NH 03280 603-863-2860 565
Web: www.nhstateparks.org

Pillsbury Winthrop Shaw Pittman LLP
50 Fremont St San Francisco CA 94105 415-983-1000 983-1200 428
Web: www.pillsburylaw.com

Pilot Contracting Corp
1452 Donaldson Hwy Erlanger KY 41018 859-525-8585 610
Web: www.pilotbuilds.com

Pilot Knob State Park
2148 340th St Forest City IA 50436 641-581-4835 565
Web: www.iowadnr.gov

Pilot Mountain State Park
1792 Pilot Knob Pk Rd Pinnacle NC 27043 336-325-2355 565
Web: www.ncparks.gov

Pilot Process Systems 306 Keystone Dr Telford PA 18969 215-453-8010 237

Pilot Travel Centers LLC
5508 Lonas Dr Knoxville TN 37939 865-938-1439 324
TF: 800-562-6210 ■ *Web:* www.pilotflyingj.com

Pilot Tribune PO Box 1187 Storm Lake IA 50588 712-732-3130 732-3152 532-2
TF: 800-447-1985 ■ *Web:* www.stormlakepilottribune.com

Pilot, The PO Box 58 Southern Pines NC 28388 910-692-7271 692-9382 532-4
Web: www.thepilot.com

Piltz Williams Larosa & Co
1077 Tommy Munro Dr Biloxi MS 39532 228-374-4141 2
Web: pwlcpa.com

Pilz Automation Safety LP
7150 Commerce Blvd Canton MI 48187 734-354-0272 354-3355 455
Web: www.pilz.com

PIMA (Professional Insurance Marketing Assn)
35 E Wacker Dr Ste 850 Chicago IL 60601 817-569-7462 49-9
Web: www.pima-assn.org

Pima Air & Space Museum
6000 E Valencia Rd Tucson AZ 85706 520-574-0462 574-9238 520
TF: 800-352-0050 ■ *Web:* www.pimaair.org

Pima Community College
401 N Bonita Ave Tucson AZ 85709 520-206-2733 206-4790* 162
**Fax:* Admissions ■ *TF:* 800-860-7462 ■ *Web:* www.pima.edu
Desert Vista 5901 S Calle Santa Cruz Tucson AZ 85709 520-206-5030 206-5050* 162
**Fax:* Admissions ■ *Web:* pima.edu
East 8181 E Irvington Rd Tucson AZ 85709 520-206-7000 206-7875* 162
**Fax:* Admissions ■ *Web:* ecc.pima.edu
West 2202 W Anklam Rd Tucson AZ 85709 520-206-6600 206-6728* 162
**Fax:* Admissions ■ *TF:* 800-860-7462 ■ *Web:* www.pima.edu

Pima County 130 W Congress St Tucson AZ 85701 520-724-9999 740-8171 338
Web: webcms.pima.gov

Pima County Dept of Transportation Transportation Systems Div
201 N Stone Ave 4th Fl Tucson AZ 85701 520-740-6410 740-6341 108
Web: www.dot.pima.gov

Pima County Public Library
101 N Stone Ave Tucson AZ 85701 520-594-5600 594-5621 434-3
TF: 877-705-5437 ■ *Web:* www.library.pima.gov

Pima County School Superintendent
200 N Stone Ave Tucson AZ 85701 520-724-8451 770-4210* 685
**Fax:* Hum Res ■ *Web:* www.schools.pima.gov

Pima Medical Institute
3350 E Grant Rd Ste 200 Tucson AZ 85716 520-326-1600 507
TF: 888-556-7334 ■ *Web:* www.pmi.edu

Pima Valve Inc 6525 W Allison Rd Chandler AZ 85226 520-796-1095 796-4012 790
TF: 800-398-8970 ■ *Web:* www.pimavalve.com

PIMCO Institutional Funds
PO Box 219024 Kansas City MO 64121 800-927-4648 421-2861* 528
**Fax Area Code:* 816 ■ *TF:* 800-927-4648 ■ *Web:* www.pimco.com

Pimlico Race Course
5201 Park Heights Ave Baltimore MD 21215 410-542-9400 133
TF: 800-638-1859 ■ *Web:* pimlico.com

Pin Oak Investment Advisors Inc
510 Bering Dr Ste 100 Houston TX 77057 713-871-8300 401
Web: www.pinoakinc.com

Pin Oak Stud
830 Grassy Spring Rd PO Box 68 Versailles KY 40383 859-873-1420 873-2391 368
Web: www.pinoakstud.com

Pinal County 31 N Pinal St Florence AZ 85232 520-509-3555 866-6512 338
Web: pinalcountyaz.gov

Pinal County Library District (PCLD)
92 W Butte Ave Florence AZ 85132 520-866-6457 866-6533 434-3
Web: www.pinalcountyaz.gov/departments/library

Pinchin Group, The
2470 Milltower Ct Mississauga ON L5N7W5 905-363-0678 192
Web: www.thepinchingroup.com

Pinck & Company Inc 98 Magazine St Boston MA 02119 617-445-3555 188
Web: pinck-co.com

Pinckney Community Schools
2130 E MI 36 Pinckney MI 48169 810-225-3900 685
Web: www.pinckneyschools.org

Pinckney Hugo Group 760 W Genesee St Syracuse NY 13204 315-478-6700 7
Web: www.pinckneyhugo.com

Pinckney Recreation Area
8555 Silver Hill Pinckney MI 48169 734-426-4913 565
Web: michigandnr.com

Pinckneyville Correctional Ctr
5835 SR- 154 Pinckneyville IL 62274 618-357-9722 357-2083 213
Web: illinois.gov

Pincock Allen & Holt A Div of Runge Inc
165 S Union Blvd Ste 950 Lakewood CO 80228 303-986-6950 261
Web: www.rpmglobal.com

Pindler & Pindler Inc
11910 Poindexter Ave Moorpark CA 93021 805-531-9090 194
TF: 800-669-6002 ■ *Web:* www.pindler.com

Pine Bluff Commercial
300 S Beech St Pine Bluff AR 71601 870-534-3400 534-0113 532-2
TF: 800-776-1441 ■ *Web:* www.pbcommercial.com

Pine Bluff Convention & Visitors Bureau (PBCVB)
1 Convention Ctr Plaza Pine Bluff AR 71601 870-536-7600 850-2105 206
TF: 800-536-7660 ■ *Web:* www.pinebluffcvb.org

Pine Bluff Cotton Belt Federal Credit Union
1703 River Pines Blvd Pine Bluff AR 71601 870-535-6365 535-0765 219
TF: 888-249-1904 ■ *Web:* www.pbcottonbeltfcu.coop

Pine Bluff Sand & Gravel Inc
1501 Heart Wood White Hall AR 71602 870-534-7120 182
Web: pbsgc.applicantharbor.com

Pine Butte Guest Ranch 351 S Fork Rd Choteau MT 59422 406-466-2158 239
TF: 877-812-3698 ■ *Web:* www.nature.org

Pine Cliff Energy Ltd
1015 Fourth St SW Ste 850 Calgary AB T2R1J4 403-269-2289 539
Web: www.pinecliffenergy.com

Pine Club, The 1926 Brown St Dayton OH 45409 937-228-7463 228-5371 671
TF: 800-561-3367 ■ *Web:* www.thepineclub.com

Pine Country Bank
412 N Hwy 10 PO Box 25 Royalton MN 56373 320-584-5522 584-8385 70
Web: www.pinecountrybank.com

Pine County 635 Northridge Dr NW Pine City MN 55063 320-591-1400 338
TF: 800-450-7403 ■ *Web:* www.co.pine.mn.us

Pine Crest Inn 85 Pine Crest Ln Tryon NC 28782 828-859-9135 379
TF: 800-633-3001 ■ *Web:* www.pinecrestinn.com

Pine Grove Area School Dist
103 School St Pine Grove PA 17963 570-345-2731 685
Web: www.pgasd.com

Pine Grove Furnace State Park
1100 Pine Grove Rd Gardners PA 17324 717-486-7174 565
TF: 888-727-2757 ■ *Web:* www.dcnr.state.pa.us

Pine Hall Brick Co
2701 Shorefair Dr Winston-Salem NC 27105 800-334-8689 725-3940* 150
**Fax Area Code:* 336 ■ *TF:* 800-334-8689 ■ *Web:* www.pinehallbrick.com

Pine Hills Youth Correctional Facility
4 N Haynes Ave Miles City MT 59301 406-232-1377 232-7432 412
Web: www.cor.mt.gov

Pine Instrument Co
101 Industrial Dr Grove City PA 16127 724-458-6391 458-4648 203
Web: www.pineinstrument.com

Pine Jog Environmental Education Ctr
6301 Summit Blvd West Palm Beach FL 33415 561-686-6600 687-4968 50-5
Web: www.pinejog.fau.edu

Pine Lake State Park
22620 County Hwy S56 Eldora IA 50627 641-858-5832 858-5641 565
Web: www.iowadnr.gov

Pine Manor College 400 Heath St Chestnut Hill MA 02467 617-731-7104 731-7102 166
TF: 800-762-1357 ■ *Web:* www.pmc.edu

Pine Mountain Lake Association
19228 Pine Mtn Dr Groveland CA 95321 209-962-8600 671
TF: 800-280-4388 ■ *Web:* www.pinemountainlake.com

Pine Mountain State Resort Park
1050 State Pk Rd Pineville KY 40977 800-325-1712 565
TF: 800-325-1712 ■ *Web:* www.parks.ky.gov

Pine Needles Lodge & Golf Club
PO Box 88 Southern Pines NC 28388 910-692-7111 692-5349 669
TF: 800-747-7272 ■ *Web:* www.pineneedles-midpines.com

Pine Pointe Hospice & Palliative Care
6261 Peak Rd Macon GA 31210 478-633-5660 633-6247 371
TF: 800-211-1084 ■ *Web:* pinepointehospice.org

Pine Rest Christian Mental Health Services
300 68th St SE PO Box 165 Grand Rapids MI 49501 616-455-5000 831-2608* 374-5
**Fax:* Hum Res ■ *TF:* 800-678-5500 ■ *Web:* www.pinerest.org

Pine Ridge Farms 1800 SE Maury St Des Moines IA 50317 515-266-4100 296-26
TF: 800-523-4559 ■ *Web:* www.pineridgefarmspork.com

Pine Ridge Winery LLC
5901 Silverado Trail Napa CA 94558 800-575-9777 80-3
TF: 800-575-9777 ■ *Web:* www.pineridgevineyards.com

Pine River Capital Management LP
601 Carlson Pkwy Ste 330 Minnetonka MN 55305 612-238-3300 177
TF: 800-642-1687 ■ *Web:* www.pinerivercapital.com

Pine Road Elementary School
3737 Pine Rd Huntingdon Valley PA 19006 215-938-0290 685
Web: www.lmtsd.org

Name / Address	City	State	Zip	Phone	Fax	Class
Pine Run Community 777 Ferry Rd *TF:* 800-992-8992 ■ *Web:* www.pinerun.org	Doylestown	PA	18901	215-345-9000		672
Pine State Trading Co 100 Enterprise Ave *TF:* 800-873-3825 ■ *Web:* www.pinestatetrading.com	Gardiner	ME	04345	207-622-3741		81-1
Pine Telephone System Inc 104 Center St PO Box 706 *Web:* www.pinetel.com	Halfway	OR	97834	541-742-2201		116
Pine Tree Equity Management LP 777 Brickell Ave Ste 1070 *Web:* www.pinetreeequity.com	Miami	FL	33131	305-808-9820		41
Pineapple Hospitality Co 155 108th Ave NE Ste 350 *TF:* 800-733-3855 ■ *Web:* www.staypineapple.com	Bellevue	WA	98004	425-455-5825		707
Pinecrest Gardens 11000 Red Rd *Web:* www.pinecrest-fl.gov	Pinecrest	FL	33156	305-669-6990	669-6944	97
Pinecrest Rehabilitation Hospital 5360 Linton Blvd *Web:* www.delraymedicalctr.com	Delray Beach	FL	33484	561-495-0400		374-6
Pinehurst Resort & Country Club 80 Carolina Vista Dr *TF:* 800-487-4653 ■ *Web:* www.pinehurst.com	Pinehurst	NC	28374	910-295-6811		669
Pineland Telephone Cooperative Inc 30 S Rountree St *TF:* 800-247-1266 ■ *Web:* www.pineland.net	Metter	GA	30439	912-685-2121		387
Pinelands National Reserve 15 Springfield Rd *Web:* www.nps.gov/pine	New Lisbon	NJ	08064	609-894-7300	894-7330	564
Pinelands Regional School District PO Box 248 *Web:* www.prsdnj.org	Tuckerton	NJ	08087	609-296-3106		685
Pinellas County 315 Ct St Rm 601 *TF:* 800-806-5154 ■ *Web:* www.pinellascounty.org	Clearwater	FL	33756	727-464-3485	464-4384	338
Pinellas County Heritage Village 11909 125th St N *Web:* www.pinellascounty.org	Largo	FL	33774	727-582-2123		520
Pinellas Park Mid-County Chamber of Commerce 5851 Pk Blvd *Web:* www.pinellasparkchamber.com	Pinellas Park	FL	33781	727-544-4777	209-0837	139
Pineloch Management Inc 102 W Pineloch Ave Ste 10 *TF:* 800-233-6847 ■ *Web:* www.pineloch.com	Orlando	FL	32806	407-859-3550	650-0303	653
Pineries Bank, The 3601 Main St *Web:* pineries.com	Stevens Point	WI	54481	715-341-5600		70
Pines at Davidson 400 Avinger Ln *TF:* 877-574-8203 ■ *Web:* www.thepinesatdavidson.org	Davidson	NC	28036	704-896-1100		672
Pines Bach 122 W Washington Ave Ste 900 *TF:* 866-443-8661 ■ *Web:* www.cwpb.com	Madison	WI	53703	608-807-0752		428
Pines Lodge 141 Scott Hill Rd *TF Resv:* 855-279-3430 ■ *Web:* pineslodge.rockresorts.com	Beaver Creek	CO	81620	970-429-5043	754-7295	379
Pines of Sarasota Inc 1501 N Orange Ave *Web:* pinesofsarasota.com	Sarasota	FL	34236	941-365-0250		371
Pines Resort, The 103 Shore Rd *TF:* 800-667-4637 ■ *Web:* digbypines.ca	Digby	NS	B0V1A0	902-245-2511		669
Pines Technology 30505 Clemens Rd *TF:* 800-207-2840 ■ *Web:* www.pinestech.com	Westlake	OH	44145	440-835-5553	835-5556	494
Pinestar Technology Inc 400 Apgar Dr Ste 1 *Web:* www.pinestar.com	Somerset	NJ	08873	732-356-0070		809
Pinestone Resort 4252 County Rd Ste 21 *TF:* 800-461-0357 ■ *Web:* www.pinestone-resort.com	Haliburton	ON	K0M1S0	705-457-1800	457-1783	669
Pineville Community Hospital 850 Riverview Ave	Pineville	KY	40977	606-337-3051	337-4284	374-3
Pinewood Preparatory School 1114 Orangeburg Rd *Web:* pinewoodprep.com	Summerville	SC	29483	843-873-1643		685
Piney Creek Ravine State Natural Area 4301 N Lake Dr *Web:* dnr.illinois.gov/Lands/Landmgt/PARKS/R4/pcr.htm	Chester	IL	62233	618-826-2706		565
Piney Woods School 5096 Hwy 49 S PO Box 69 *Web:* www.pineywoods.org	Piney Woods	MS	39148	601-845-2214	845-2604	622
Ping Inc 2201 W Desert Cove Ave PO Box 82000 *TF:* 800-474-6434 ■ *Web:* www.ping.com	Phoenix	AZ	85071	800-474-6434		710
Ping's Cafe 34 Baltimore St *Web:* www.pingscafe.com	Gettysburg	PA	17325	717-334-2234		671
Pinger Inc 97 S Second St Ste 210 *Web:* www.pinger.com	San Jose	CA	95113	408-271-5700		224
Pingree Chellie (Rep D - ME) 2162 Rayburn HOB *Web:* pingree.house.gov	Washington	DC	20515	202-225-6116	225-5590	342-2
Pingree School 537 Highland St *Web:* pingree.org	South Hamilton	MA	01982	978-468-4415		148
Pink Door, The 1919 Post Alley *Web:* www.thepinkdoor.net	Seattle	WA	98101	206-443-3241		671
Pink Jeep Tours Las Vegas Inc 3629 W Hacienda Ave *TF:* 800-873-3662 ■ *Web:* www.pinkjeeptours.com	Las Vegas	NV	89118	702-895-6777		760
Pink Pearl Chinese Seafood 1132 E Hastings St *Web:* www.pinkpearl.com	Vancouver	BC	V6A1S2	604-253-4316	253-4316	671
Pinkard Construction Co 9195 W Sixth Ave *Web:* www.pinkardcc.com	Lakewood	CO	80215	303-986-4555	985-5050	186
Pinkerton & Laws Inc 1165 N Chase Pkwy Ste 100 *Web:* pinkerton-laws.com	Marietta	GA	30067	770-956-9000	618-8688	186
Pinkie's Inc 1426 E Eigth St *Web:* www.pinkiestexas.com	Odessa	TX	79761	432-580-0439	580-0918	443
Pinnacle Advertising and Marketing 1435 N Plum Grove Rd Ste C *Web:* www.pinnacle-advertising.com	Schaumburg	IL	60173	847-255-0000		7
Pinnacle Airlines Corp 40 S Main St 1 Commerce Sq *OTC:* PNCLQ ■ *Web:* www.flypinnacle.com	Memphis	TN	38103	901-348-4100		25
Pinnacle Bancshares Inc 1811 Second Ave *OTC:* PCLB ■ *Web:* www.pinnaclebanc.com/default.aspx	Jasper	AL	35501	205-221-4111	221-8860	360-2
Pinnacle Business Finance Inc 615 Commerce St Ste 101 **Fax Area Code:* 800 ■ *TF:* 800-566-1993 ■ *Web:* www.pinnaclecap.com	Tacoma	WA	98402	253-284-5600	821-5903*	216
Pinnacle Business Systems Inc 3824 S Blvd St Ste 200 *TF:* 800-311-0757 ■ *Web:* www.pbsnow.com	Edmond	OK	73013	800-311-0757	444-3439	225
Pinnacle Communications Corp 19821 Executive Park Cir *TF:* 800-644-9101 ■ *Web:* www.pinnaclecommunications.com	Germantown	MD	20874	301-601-0777		387
PINNACLE Converting Equipment 1720 Toal St *Web:* www.pinnacleconverting.com	Charlotte	NC	28206	704-376-3855		261
Pinnacle Corp, The 201A E Abram St *TF:* 800-325-3535 ■ *Web:* www.pinncorp.com	Arlington	TX	76010	817-795-5555		179
Pinnacle Engineering Inc 7660 Woodway Dr Ste 350 *TF:* 800-381-6164 ■ *Web:* www.pinnacleengr.com	Houston	TX	77063	713-784-1005		261
Pinnacle Entertainment Inc 3980 Howard Hughes Pkwy *NYSE:* PNK ■ *TF:* 877-764-8750 ■ *Web:* www.pnkinc.com	Las Vegas	NV	89169	702-541-7777		132
Pinnacle Exhibits Inc 22400 NW Westmark Dr *Web:* www.pinnacle-exhibits.com	Hillsboro	OR	97124	503-844-4848		7
Pinnacle Films Inc 10701-A S Commerce Blvd *Web:* www.pinnaclefilms.com	Charlotte	NC	28273	704-504-3200		600
Pinnacle Foods Corp 399 Jefferson Rd *TF:* 866-266-7596 ■ *Web:* www.pinnaclefoodscorp.com	Parsippany	NJ	07054	973-541-6620		296-39
Pinnacle Frames & Accents Inc 12303 Technology Blvd Ste 950 *TF:* 888-846-6847 ■ *Web:* nielsenbainbridgegroup.com/pinnacle/home	Austin	TX	78727	888-846-6847		361
Pinnacle Gas Resources Inc 1 E Aalger St	Sheridan	WY	82801	307-673-9710		787
Pinnacle Group International 130 Water St *Web:* www.pinnaclegroup.com	New York	NY	10005	480-994-6173		260
Pinnacle Health Hospital at Community General 4300 Londonderry Rd *TF:* 888-782-5678 ■ *Web:* pinnaclehealth.org	Harrisburg	PA	17109	717-652-3000		374-3
Pinnacle Hotels USA Inc 8369 Vickers St Ste 101 *Web:* www.pinnaclehotelsusa.com	San Diego	CA	92111	858-974-8201		463
Pinnacle Inn Resort 301 Pinnacle Inn Rd *TF:* 800-405-7888 ■ *Web:* www.pinnacleinn.com	Beech Mountain	NC	28604	828-387-2231		669
Pinnacle Management Systems Inc 8500 N Stemmons Fwy Ste 6010 **Fax Area Code:* 888 ■ *TF:* 888-975-1119 ■ *Web:* www.pinnaclemanagement.com	Dallas	TX	75247	703-382-9161	975-9991*	194
Pinnacle Motor Club 510 N Topeka St *TF:* 800-446-1289 ■ *Web:* www.pinnaclemotorclub.com	Wichita	KS	67214	316-261-5430		53
Pinnacle Mountain State Park 11901 Pinnacle Valley Rd *Web:* www.arkansasstateparks.com	Little Rock	AR	72223	501-868-5806	868-5018	565
Pinnacle Performance Improvement Worldwide (PPIW) 101 Main St *TF:* 800-368-3408 ■ *Web:* www.pinnaclecg.com	Pepperell	MA	01463	978-925-9797	925-9798	194
Pinnacle Plastic Products 513 Napoleon Rd *Web:* pinnacleplasticproducts.com	Bowling Green	OH	43402	419-352-8688		608
Pinnacle Precision Sheet Metal Corp 5410 E La Palma Ave *Web:* www.pinnacleprecisionsheetmetal.com	Anaheim	CA	92807	714-777-3129		483
Pinnacle Precision Technologies LLC 2607 Eaton Ln	Racine	WI	53404	262-632-2232		483
Pinnacle Rock State Park 6407 Coal Heritage Rd *Web:* www.pinnaclerockstatepark.com	Bluefield	WV	24701	304-248-8565		565
Pinnacle Sports LLC 313 Medina Rd *Web:* www.pinnaclesports.org	Medina	OH	44256	330-239-0616		713
Pinnacle Staffing Inc PO Box 17589 **Fax Area Code:* 864 ■ *TF:* 888-297-4212 ■ *Web:* pinnaclestaffing.com	Greenville	SC	29606	888-297-4212	987-7351*	721
Pinnacle State Park 1904 Pinnacle Rd *Web:* nysparks.com	Addison	NY	14801	607-359-2767		565
Pinnacle Technical Resources Inc 5501 Lyndon B Johnson Fwy *Web:* pinnacle1.com	Dallas	TX	75240	214-740-2424		180
Pinnacle Trust Partners LLC 540 Hopmeadow St *Web:* www.pinnacletrustpartners.com	Simsbury	CT	06070	860-264-1595		70
Pinnacle West Capital Corp 400 N Fifth St *NYSE:* PNW ■ *TF:* 800-457-2983 ■ *Web:* www.pinnaclewest.com	Phoenix	AZ	85004	602-250-1000		360-5
PinnacleART 1 Pinnacle Way *Web:* www.pinnacleais.com	Pasadena	TX	77504	281-598-1330		256
Pinnacles National Monument 5000 Hwy 146 *TF:* 877-444-6777 ■ *Web:* www.nps.gov/pinn	Paicines	CA	95043	831-389-4485	389-4489	564
Pinnacol Assurance 7501 E Lowry Blvd *TF:* 800-873-7242 ■ *Web:* www.pinnacol.com	Denver	CO	80230	303-361-4000	361-5000	391-4
Pinneast Com Inc 5 Lake Carolina Blvd Ste 230	West Columbia	SC	29229	803-926-9511		174
Pinner Construction Company Inc 1255 S Lewis St *TF:* 800-661-5006 ■ *Web:* www.pinnerconstruction.com	Anaheim	CA	92805	714-490-4000		186
Pinnergy Ltd 111 Congress Ave Ste 2020 *Web:* www.pinnergy.com	Austin	TX	78701	512-343-8880	343-8885	539
Pinney Assoc Inc 4800 Montgomery Ln Ste 400 *Web:* www.pinneyassociates.com	Bethesda	MD	20814	301-718-8440		194
Pino's Salon & Spa 70 Victoria St N *Web:* www.pinosalon.com	Kitchener	ON	N2H5C2	519-578-8898		77
Pinon Family Practice 2300 E 30th St Bldg C2 *Web:* www.pinonfp.com	Farmington	NM	87401	505-324-1000		416

				Phone	Fax	Class
Pinons 105 S Mill St *Web:* www.pinons.net	Aspen	CO	81611	970-920-2021		671
Pinpoint Data 339 Somerset St *Web:* www.couponchek.com	North Plainfield	NJ	07060	908-756-9400		225
Pinpoint Technologies 17802 Irvine Blvd Ste 215 *TF:* 866-603-7770 ■ *Web:* www.pinpoint-tech.com	Tustin	CA	92780	714-505-7600		463
Pinsly Railroad Company Inc 53 Southampton Rd *Web:* www.pinsly.com	Westfield	MA	01085	413-568-6426		649
Pinson Mounds State Archaeological Park 460 Ozier Rd *Web:* www.state.tn.us	Pinson	TN	38366	731-988-5614		565
Pinto Horse Assn of America 7330 NW 23rd St *Web:* www.pinto.org	Bethany	OK	73008	405-491-0111		48-3
Pinto Mucenski Hooper VanHouse & Company Certified Public Accountants PC 42 Market St *Web:* www.pmhvcpa.com	Potsdam	NY	13676	315-265-6080		2
Pintoresco Advisors LLC 466 Foothill Blvd Ste 333 *TF:* 866-217-1140 ■ *Web:* www.pintorescoadvisors.com	La Canada Flintridge	CA	91011	213-223-2070		70
Pinyon Environmental Engineering Resources 9100 W Jewell Ave Ste 200 *TF:* 888-641-7337 ■ *Web:* www.pinyon-env.com	Denver	CO	80232	303-980-5200		463
Piolax Corp 139 Etowah Industrial Ct *Web:* www.piolaxusa.com	Canton	GA	30114	770-479-2227	479-2399	608
Pioneer Air Systems Inc 210 Flatfork Rd *Web:* www.pioneerair.com	Wartburg	TN	37887	423-346-6693		14
Pioneer Arizona Living History Museum 3901 W Pioneer Rd *Web:* www.pioneeraz.org	Phoenix	AZ	85086	623-465-1052		520
Pioneer Bank 21 Second St *TF:* 866-873-9573 ■ *Web:* www.pioneerbanking.com	Troy	NY	12180	518-274-4800		71
Pioneer Broach Co 6434 Telegraph Rd *TF:* 800-621-1945 ■ *Web:* www.pioneerbroach.com	Los Angeles	CA	90040	323-728-1263	722-1699	455
Pioneer Circuits Inc (PCI) 3000 S Shannon St *Web:* www.pioneercircuits.com	Santa Ana	CA	92704	714-641-3132		625
Pioneer Clubs 123 E Elk *TF:* 800-694-2582 ■ *Web:* www.pioneerclubs.org	Carol Stream	IL	60188	800-694-2582		148
Pioneer Construction Company Inc 550 Kirtland St SW *TF:* 800-861-0874 ■ *Web:* www.pioneerinc.com	Grand Rapids	MI	49507	616-247-6966	247-0186	186
Pioneer Contract Services Inc 8090 Kempwood Dr *Web:* www.pioneercontract.com	Houston	TX	77055	713-464-8200	464-7100	186
Pioneer Credit Co 1870 Executive Pk NW *Web:* www.pioneercredit.net	Cleveland	TN	37312	423-476-6511		216
Pioneer Credit Recovery Inc 26 Edward St *TF:* 800-836-2442 ■ *Web:* www.pioneercreditrecovery.com	Arcade	NY	14009	585-492-1234		160
Pioneer Drilling Co 1250 NE Loop 410 Ste 1000 *NASDAQ: PDCE* ■ *Web:* www.pioneeres.com	San Antonio	TX	78209	210-828-7689		540
Pioneer Electric Co-op 300 Herbert St *TF:* 800-239-3092 ■ *Web:* www.pioneerelectric.com	Greenville	AL	36037	334-382-6636		245
Pioneer Electric Co-op 344 W US Rt 36 *TF:* 800-762-0997 ■ *Web:* www.pioneerec.com	Piqua	OH	45356	937-773-2523		245
Pioneer Electric Cooperative Inc 300 Herbert St PO Box 468 *TF:* 800-794-9302 ■ *Web:* www.pioneerelectric.coop	Greenville	AL	36037	620-356-1211		245
Pioneer Electronics (USA) Inc 1925 E Dominguez St *TF:* 800-421-1404 ■ *Web:* www.pioneerelectronics.com	Long Beach	CA	90810	310-952-2000		52
Pioneer Equipment Co 2545 S Sarah St *Web:* www.pioneerequipmentca.com	Fresno	CA	93706	559-486-7580	486-7587	274
Pioneer Exploration LLC 15603 Kuykendahl Ste 200 *Web:* www.pecogas.com	Houston	TX	77090	281-893-9400		536
Pioneer Frozen Foods Inc 627 Big Stone Gap *Web:* www.chguenther.com	Duncanville	TX	75137	972-298-4281		68
Pioneer Golf Inc 609 Castle Ridge Rd Ste 335 *TF:* 800-262-5725 ■ *Web:* www.pioneergolf.com	Austin	TX	78746	512-327-2680	327-8120	760
Pioneer Hi-Bred International Inc PO Box 1000 *TF:* 800-247-6803 ■ *Web:* www.pioneer.com	Johnston	IA	50131	515-535-3200		10-5
Pioneer Inc 5184 Pioneer Rd *Web:* www.pioneerautoind.com	Meridian	MS	39301	601-483-5211		61
Pioneer Industries Inc 111 Kero Rd *Web:* www.pioneerindustries.com	Carlstadt	NJ	07072	201-933-1900	933-9580	234
Pioneer Library System 300 Norman Center Court *Web:* pioneerlibrarysystem.org	Norman	OK	73072	405-801-4500	701-2608	434-3
Pioneer Long Distance Inc PO Box 539 *TF:* 888-782-2667 ■ *Web:* www.pldi.net	Kingfisher	OK	73750	888-782-2667		736
Pioneer Magnetics 1745 Berkeley St *TF:* 800-269-6426 ■ *Web:* www.pioneermagnetics.com	Santa Monica	CA	90404	310-829-6751		393
Pioneer Manufacturing Inc 740 Beechcroft Rd *Web:* www.pioneerleveler.com	Spring Hill	TN	37174	931-486-2296		757
Pioneer Medical Group Inc 17777 Ctr Ct Dr N Ste 400 *Web:* www.pioneermedicalgroup.com	Cerritos	CA	90703	562-229-9452		374-3
Pioneer Memorial Museum 300 N Main St *Web:* www.dupinternational.org	Salt Lake City	UT	84103	801-532-6479	532-4436	520
Pioneer Metal Finishing LLC 486 Globe Ave **Fax Area Code: 920* ■ *TF:* 877-721-1100 ■ *Web:* www.pioneermetal.com	Green Bay	WI	54304	877-721-1100	884-1790*	481
Pioneer Mfg 4529 Industrial Pkwy *TF:* 800-877-1500 ■ *Web:* www.pioneerathletics.com	Cleveland	OH	44135	216-671-5500	671-5502	550
Pioneer Millworks 1180 Commercial Dr *TF:* 800-951-9663 ■ *Web:* www.pioneermillworks.com	Farmington	NY	14425	585-924-9970		752
Pioneer National Latex Co 5000 E 29th St N **Fax Area Code: 800* ■ *TF:* 800-386-4438 ■ *Web:* www.pioneernational.com	Wichita	KS	67220	316-685-2266	329-3864*	762
Pioneer Natural Resources Co 5205 N O'Connor Blvd Ste 200 *NYSE: PXD* ■ *TF:* 888-234-6372 ■ *Web:* www.pxd.com	Irving	TX	75039	972-444-9001		536
Pioneer Newspapers Inc 221 First Ave W Ste 405 *Web:* pioneernewsgroup.com	Seattle	WA	98119	206-284-4424		637-8
Pioneer Oil & Gas Unit B 1206 W S Jordan Pkwy *Web:* www.piol.com	South Jordan	UT	84095	801-566-3000		536
Pioneer Oil LLC 1728 Lampman Dr Ste A *Web:* www.pioneeroil-co.com	Billings	MT	59102	406-254-7071	254-2560	579
Pioneer Pacific College 27501 SW Pkwy Ave *TF:* 800-419-4601 ■ *Web:* pioneerpacific.edu	Wilsonville	OR	97070	503-682-3903		166
Pioneer Paper Stock 155 Irving Ave N *TF:* 800-821-8512 ■ *Web:* www.pioneerintl.com	Minneapolis	MN	55405	612-374-2280	374-5982	660
Pioneer Petrotech Services Inc Ste 1 1431-40 Ave NE *Web:* www.pioneerps.com	Calgary	AB	T2E8N6	403-282-7669		536
Pioneer Photo Albums Inc 9801 Deering Ave *TF:* 800-366-3686 ■ *Web:* www.pioneerphotoalbums.com	Chatsworth	CA	91311	818-882-2161	882-6239	86
Pioneer Pipe Inc 2021 Hanna Rd *Web:* www.pioneerpipeinc.com	Marietta	OH	45750	740-376-2400	373-8964	595
Pioneer Pipe Line Company Inc 245 East 1100 North *Web:* conocophillips.com	North Salt Lake	UT	84054	801-295-2325		597
Pioneer Printing & Stationery Co Inc 514 W 19th St *TF:* 800-876-6564 ■ *Web:* wypioneer.com	Cheyenne	WY	82001	307-635-4114		627
Pioneer Products Inc 1917 S Memorial Dr *Web:* www.pioneerproducts.com	Racine	WI	53403	262-633-6304		454
Pioneer Railcorp 1318 S Johanson Rd *OTC: PRRR* ■ *Web:* www.pioneer-railcorp.com	Peoria	IL	61607	309-697-1400	697-5387	648
Pioneer Square 310 First Ave S *Web:* www.pioneersquare.org	Seattle	WA	98104	206-667-0687		50-6
Pioneer Steel Corp 7447 Intervale St *TF:* 800-999-9440 ■ *Web:* pioneersteel.us	Detroit	MI	48238	313-933-9400	933-1621	492
Pioneer Telephone Assn Inc PO Box 707 *TF:* 800-308-7536 ■ *Web:* www.pioncomm.net	Ulysses	KS	67880	620-356-3211	356-3242	736
Pioneer Telephone Co-op Inc 202 W Broadway Ave PO Box 539 **Fax Area Code: 405* ■ **Fax: Mktg* ■ *TF:* 888-782-2667 ■ *Web:* www.ptci.com	Kingfisher	OK	73750	888-782-2667	699-3053*	736
Pioneer Tool & Forge Inc 101 Sixth St *TF:* 800-359-6408 ■ *Web:* www.breakersteel.com	New Kensington	PA	15068	724-337-4700	337-4707	759
Pioneer Transfer LLC 2034 S St Aubin St PO Box 2567 **Fax Area Code: 712* ■ *TF:* 800-325-4650 ■ *Web:* www.pioneertransfer.com	Sioux City	IA	51106	800-325-4650	274-2946*	311
Pioneer Transportation Corp 2890 Arthur Kill Rd *TF:* 800-550-3214 ■ *Web:* pioneerbus.com	Staten Island	NY	10309	718-984-8077	984-6588	109
Pioneer Wholesale Co 500 W Bagley Rd *TF:* 888-234-5400 ■ *Web:* www.pioneerwholesaleco.com	Berea	OH	44017	440-234-5400	234-5403	44
Pioneer/Eclipse Corp 1 Eclipse Rd *TF Cust Svc:* 800-367-3550 ■ *Web:* pioneereclipse.com	Sparta	NC	28675	336-372-8080	372-2895	386
Pioneerland Library System 410 SW Fifth St *Web:* www.pioneerland.lib.mn.us	Willmar	MN	56201	320-235-6106	214-0187	434-3
Pioneers 10123 William Carey Dr *TF:* 800-755-7284 ■ *Web:* www.pioneers.org	Orlando	FL	32832	407-382-6000	382-1008	48-20
Pioneers Medical Ctr 345 Cleveland St *TF:* 800-332-1168 ■ *Web:* pioneershospital.org	Meeker	CO	81641	970-878-5047		363
Pioneers Memorial Healthcare District (PMHD) 207 W Legion Rd *Web:* www.pmhd.org	Brawley	CA	92227	760-351-3333		374-3
Pioneers Volunteer 1801 California St Ste 225 *TF:* 800-872-5995 ■ *Web:* www.telecompioneers.org	Denver	CO	80202	303-571-1200	572-0520	48-15
Pionite Decorative Surfaces 1 Pionite Rd *Web:* www.pionite.com	Auburn	ME	04210	207-784-9111		291
PIP Printing & Document Services Inc 26722 Plaza Dr Ste 200 *Web:* www.pip.com	Mission Viejo	CA	92691	949-348-5000	348-5066	310
Pipco Cos Ltd, The 1409 W Altorfer Dr	Peoria	IL	61615	309-692-4060		189-10
Pipe & Tube Supply Inc 1407 N Cypress *TF:* 800-770-8823 ■ *Web:* www.pipeandtubesupply.com	North Little Rock	AR	72114	501-372-6556	372-7694	386
Pipe Fabricating & Supply Co 1235 N Kraemer Blvd *Web:* www.pipefab.com	Anaheim	CA	92806	714-630-5200		490
Pipe Products Inc 5122 Rialto Rd *Web:* www.pipeproducts.com	West Chester	OH	45069	513-860-5900		595
Pipe Spring National Monument 406 N Pipe Spring Rd HC 65 PO Box 5 *Web:* www.nps.gov/pisp	Fredonia	AZ	86022	928-643-7105	643-7583	564
Pipe Valves Inc 1200 E Fifth Ave *TF:* 800-321-0466 ■ *Web:* www.pipevalves.com	Columbus	OH	43219	614-294-4971		358
Pipe Welders Inc 2965 W State Rd 84 *Web:* www.pipewelders.com	Fort Lauderdale	FL	33312	954-587-8400		480
Pipeline & Hazardous Materials Safety Administration (PHMSA) 1200 New Jersey Ave SE E Bldg 2nd Fl *Web:* www.phmsa.dot.gov	Washington	DC	20590	202-366-4433	366-3666	340-17
Office of Hazardous Materials Safety 1200 New Jersey Ave SE *TF:* 800-467-4922 ■ *Web:* phmsa.dot.gov	Washington	DC	20590	202-366-4433	366-5713	340-17

	Phone	Fax	Class
Pipeline & Hazardous Materials Safety Administration Regional Offices (PHMSA)			
Central Region (Pipeline) 901 Locust St Rm 462 .... Kansas City MO 64106 *Web:* www.phmsa.dot.gov	816-329-3800	329-3831	340-17
Eastern Region (Pipeline) 820 Bear Tavern Rd Ste 103 .... West Trenton NJ 08628 *Web:* www.phmsa.dot.gov/about/org/eastern-region	609-989-2256	882-1209	340-17
Southern Region 233 Peachtree St NE Ste 602 .... Atlanta GA 30303 *Web:* www.phmsa.dot.gov	404-832-1140	832-1168	340-17
Southwest Region Office 8701 S Gessner Rd Ste 900 .... Houston TX 77074 *Web:* www.phmsa.dot.gov	713-272-2820	272-2821	340-17
Western Region (Pipeline) 12300 W Dakota Ave Ste 110 .... Lakewood CO 80228 *Web:* www.phmsa.dot.gov/about/org/western-region	720-963-3160	963-3161	340-17
Pipeline Development Co, The 870 Canterbury Rd .... Westlake OH 44145 *Web:* plidco.com	440-871-5700		595
Pipeline Group Inc 2850 Red Hill Ave Ste 110 .... Santa Ana CA 92705 *Web:* www.pipelinesoftware.com	949-296-8375		809
Pipeline Industry Benefit Fund 4845 S 83rd E Ave .... Tulsa OK 74145 *Web:* www.pibf.org	918-280-4800		414
Pipeline Interactive Inc 941 Cumberland St. .... Lebanon PA 17042 *TF:* 800-425-8609 ■ *Web:* www.pipelineinteractive.com	717-273-5665		225
Piper Jaffray Cos 800 Nicollet Mall Ste 800 .... Minneapolis MN 55402 *NYSE: PJC* ■ *TF:* 800-333-6000 ■ *Web:* www.piperjaffray.com	612-303-6000		690
Piper Plastics Inc 1840 Enterprise Ct .... Libertyville IL 60048 *Web:* www.piperplastics.com	847-367-0110		454
Piper Products Inc 300 S 84th Ave .... Wausau WI 54401 *TF:* 800-544-3057 ■ *Web:* www.piperonline.net	715-842-2724	842-3125	298
Piper Valve Systems Inc 1020 E Grand Blvd .... Oklahoma City OK 73129 *TF:* 800-481-7311 ■ *Web:* piper-oilfield.com	405-671-2000		539
Piperade 1015 Battery St .... San Francisco CA 94111 *Web:* www.piperade.com	415-391-2555	391-1159	671
Pipestem Resort State Park PO Box 150 .... Pipestem WV 25979 *TF:* 800-225-5982 ■ *Web:* www.pipestemresort.com	304-466-1800		565
Pipestone County 416 S Hiawatha Ave. .... Pipestone MN 56164 *Web:* www.mncounties.org	507-825-1140		338
Pipestone Livestock Auction Market 1500 Seventh St SE .... Pipestone MN 56164 *Web:* www.pipestonelivestock.com	507-825-3306		446
Pipestone Publishing Co PO Box 277 .... Pipestone MN 56164 *TF:* 800-325-6440 ■ *Web:* www.pipestonestar.com	507-825-3333	825-2168	637-8
Pipestone Veterinary Clinic LLC 1300 Hwy 75 S PO Box 188 .... Pipestone MN 56164 *TF:* 800-658-2523 ■ *Web:* www.pipevet.com	507-825-4211		794
Pipette Calibration Services Inc 81 Deborah Rd .... Newton MA 02459 *TF:* 800-356-9526 ■ *Web:* www.pipettecal.com	617-964-0039		743
Piping & Equipment Inc 9100 Canniff St. .... Houston TX 77017 *TF:* 888-889-9683 ■ *Web:* www.pipingequipment.com	713-947-9393		385
Piping Resources Inc 4502 F St .... Omaha NE 68117 *Web:* www.pipingresources.com	402-738-8100		358
Piping Systems Engineering 1905 S Lindsay Rd .... Mesa AZ 85201 *Web:* piping-systems.com	480-345-0052		261
Piping Technology & Products Inc 3701 Holmes Rd PO Box 34506 .... Houston TX 77051 *TF:* 866-746-9172 ■ *Web:* www.pipingtech.com	713-422-2271	731-8640	595
Pipitone Group 3933 Perrysville Ave. .... Pittsburgh PA 15214 *Web:* pipitonegroup.com	412-321-0879		194
Pipkins Inc 14515 N Outer 40 Rd Ste 130 .... Chesterfield MO 63017 *TF:* 800-469-6106 ■ *Web:* www.pipkins.com	314-469-6106	222-2459	177
Pippin Snack Pecan Co 1332 Old Pretoria Rd .... Albany GA 31721 *Web:* georgiapecan.org	229-432-9316		296-28
Piqua Manor 1840 W High St .... Piqua OH 45356 *TF:* 800-321-1245 ■ *Web:* piquamanor.com	937-773-0040		371
Piqua State Bank 1356 Xylan Rd .... Piqua KS 66761 *Web:* piquastatebank.com	620-468-2555		70
Piquniq Management Corp 6613 Brayton Dr .... Anchorage AK 99507	907-522-5234		224
Piraeus Consulting LLC 1408 Fourth Ave, Ste 400 .... Seattle WA 98101 *TF:* 866-747-2387 ■ *Web:* www.piraeusconsulting.com	866-747-2387		396
Piranha 335 W Third St .... Fort Worth TX 76102 *Web:* www.piranhakillersushi.com	817-348-0200		671
Piranha Killer Sushi 7100 Blvd 26 Ste 208 .... Richland Hills TX 76180 *Web:* www.piranhakillersushi.com	682-626-5953		671
Piranha Marketing Inc 4440 S Rural Rd Bldg F .... Tempe AZ 85282 *TF:* 800-275-2643 ■ *Web:* joepolish.com	480-858-0008		195
Pirate's Cove 109 Gainsborough Sq .... Chesapeake VA 23320 *Web:* piratescoveva.com	757-549-7272		671
Pirates Grub & Grog 450 S Victoria Ave. .... Oxnard CA 93030 *Web:* www.piratesgrubngrog.net	805-984-0046		671
Pirates' House 20 E Broad St .... Savannah GA 31401 *TF:* 800-517-9007 ■ *Web:* www.thepirateshouse.com	912-233-5757		671
PIREL Inc 1250 Nobel Ste 190 .... Boucherville QC J4B5H1 *TF:* 800-449-7196 ■ *Web:* www.pirel.com	450-449-5199		180
PIRG (Georgia Public Interest Research Group) 817 W Peachtree St NW Ste 204 .... Atlanta GA 30308 *Web:* www.georgiapirg.org	404-892-3405		633
Pirogue Island State Park PO Box 1630 .... Miles City MT 59301 *Web:* fwp.mt.gov	406-234-0926		565

	Phone	Fax	Class
Piscataquis County 50 Mayo St. .... Dover-Foxcroft ME 04426 *TF:* 800-339-6389 ■ *Web:* www.pcedc.org	207-564-3638		338
Piscataway Park *National Park Service* 13551 Ft Washington Rd .... Fort Washington MD 20616 *Web:* www.nps.gov/pisc	301-763-4600		564
Piscataway/Middlesex/South Plainfield Chamber of Commerce 377 Hoes Ln .... Piscataway NJ 08854	732-394-0220		139
Pisces 1007 Simonton St .... Key West FL 33040 *TF:* 800-848-1317 ■ *Web:* www.pisceskeywest.com	305-294-7100		671
Pisgah Inn PO Box 749 .... Waynesville NC 28786 *Web:* www.pisgahinn.com	828-235-8228		379
Pismo Coast Village Inc 165 S Dolliver St .... Pismo Beach CA 93449 *Web:* www.pismocoastvillage.com	805-773-5649		121
Pistachio Consulting Inc 67 Maple St .... Milton MA 02186 *TF:* 800-747-1941 ■ *Web:* www.pistachioconsulting.com	800-747-1941		196
PIT (Pennsylvania Institute of Technology) 800 Manchester Ave .... Media PA 19063 **Fax:* Admissions ■ *TF Admissions:* 800-422-0025 ■ *Web:* www.pit.edu	610-892-1500	892-1533*	800
Pita Group, The 40 Cold Spring Rd .... Rocky Hill CT 06067 *Web:* www.pitacomm.com	860-293-0157		690
Pita Jungle 4 E University Dr .... Tempe AZ 85281 *Web:* pitajungle.com	480-804-0234		671
Pitango Venture Capital 540 Cowper St Ste 200 .... Palo Alto CA 94301 *Web:* www.pitango.com	650-322-2201	473-1347	792
Pitcairn Properties Inc 165 Township Line Rd .... Jenkintown PA 19046 *Web:* www.pitcairnproperties.com	215-690-3000		653
Pitch 8825 National Blvd. .... Culver City CA 90232 *TF:* 800-908-5395 ■ *Web:* www.thepitchagency.com	424-603-6000		5
Pitch, The 1701 Main St .... Kansas City MO 64108 *TF:* 800-774-4876 ■ *Web:* www.pitch.com	816-561-6061	756-0502	532-5
Pitcher Inn 275 Main St. .... Warren VT 05674 *Web:* www.pitcherinn.com	802-496-6350		379
Pitco Frialator Inc PO Box 501 .... Concord NH 03302 *TF:* 800-258-3708 ■ *Web:* pitco.com	603-225-6684	225-8472	298
Pite Duncan LLP 4375 Jutland Dr Ste 200 .... San Diego CA 92117 *TF:* 800-741-8806 ■ *Web:* www.piteduncan.com	858-750-7600		41
Pitkin County 530 E Main St Ste 101 .... Aspen CO 81611 *Web:* www.pitkincounty.com/249/Clerk-Recorder	970-920-5200		338
Pitmar Tours 7549 140th St Ste 9 .... Surrey BC V3W5J9 *TF:* 877-596-9670 ■ *Web:* www.pitmartours.com	604-596-9670	596-3444	760
Pitney Bowes Group 1 Software 4200 Parliament Pl Ste 600 .... Lanham MD 20706 *TF:* 800-367-6950 ■ *Web:* www.g1.com	301-731-2300		178-1
Pitney Bowes Inc 1 Elmcroft Rd .... Stamford CT 06926 *NYSE: PBI* ■ *TF:* 800-672-6937 ■ *Web:* pitneybowes.com/us	203-356-5000		111
Pitney Bowes Management Services 90 Pk Ave .... New York NY 10016 *TF:* 800-322-8000 ■ *Web:* pitneybowes.com/us	212-808-3800		463
Pitot House Museum 1440 Moss St .... New Orleans LA 70119 *Web:* www.pitothouse.org	504-482-0312		520
Pitt Community College 1986 Pitt Tech Rd PO Box 7007 .... Winterville NC 28590 *Web:* www.pittcc.edu	252-493-7200	321-4401	162
Pitt County 1717 W Fifth St .... Greenville NC 27834 *TF:* 800-395-4357 ■ *Web:* www.pittcountync.gov	252-902-1000	830-6311	338
Pitt County Memorial Hospital 2100 Stantonsburg Rd .... Greenville NC 27835 *Web:* www.vidanthealth.com	252-847-4100		374-3
Pitt Grill Inc 3048 Gertsner Memorial Dr .... Lake Charles LA 70601 *Web:* www.pittgrill.com	337-478-2925		670
Pitt Ohio Express 15 27th St. .... Pittsburgh PA 15222 *TF Cust Svc:* 800-366-7488 ■ *Web:* works.pittohio.com	412-232-3015	232-0944	780
Pitt Plastics Inc 1400 Atkinson Ave .... Pittsburg KS 66762 *TF:* 800-835-0366 ■ *Web:* www.pittplastics.com	800-835-0366	314-8449	66
Pittcon 300 Penn Ctr Blvd Ste 332 .... Pittsburgh PA 15235 *TF:* 800-825-3221 ■ *Web:* www.pittcon.org	412-825-3220		184
Pittenger & Anderson Inc 5533 S 27th St Ste 201 .... Lincoln NE 68512 *TF:* 800-897-1588 ■ *Web:* www.pittand.com	402-328-8800		401
Pittenger Robert (Rep R - NC) 224 Cannon Bldg .... Washington DC 20515 *Web:* pittenger.house.gov	202-225-1976	225-3389	342-2
Pittleman & Assoc 336 E 43rd St. .... New York NY 10017 *Web:* www.pittlemanassociates.com	212-370-9600	370-9608	266
Pittman Dental Laboratory 2355 Centennial Cir .... Gainesville GA 30504 *Web:* www.pittmandental.com	770-534-4457		415
Pitts Enterprises Inc 5734 Hwy 431 PO Box 127 .... Pittsview AL 36871 *Web:* www.pittstrailers.com	334-855-4754		779
Pitts Toyota 210 N Jeffreson St .... Dublin GA 31021 *Web:* www.pittstoyota.com	478-272-3244	272-1534	57
Pittsburg Area Chamber of Commerce 117 W Fourth St .... Pittsburg KS 66762 *TF:* 800-794-4780 ■ *Web:* www.pittsburgareachamber.com	620-231-1000	231-3178	139
Pittsburg Chamber of Commerce 985 Railroad Ave. .... Pittsburg CA 94565 *Web:* pittsburgchamber.org	925-432-7301		139
Pittsburg County 115 E Carl Albert Pkwy .... McAlester OK 74501 *Web:* pittsburg.okcountytreasurers.com	918-423-6895	423-7379	338
Pittsburg State University 1701 S Broadway St .... Pittsburg KS 66762 **Fax:* Admissions ■ *TF:* 800-854-7488 ■ *Web:* www.pittstate.edu	620-235-4251	235-6003*	166
Pittsburg State University Axe Library 1701 S Broadway .... Pittsburg KS 66762 *Web:* axe.pittstate.edu	620-235-4882	235-4090	434-6
Pittsburg Tank & Tower Group 1 Watertank Pl. .... Henderson KY 42420 **Fax:* Sales ■ *Web:* www.watertank.com	270-826-9000	827-4417*	189-14
Pittsburg Wholesale Groceries Inc 727 Kennedy St .... Oakland CA 94606 *TF:* 800-200-4244 ■ *Web:* www.pitcofoods.com	800-200-4244		345

Phone | Fax | Class

Pittsburgh Airport Area Chamber of Commerce
850 Beaver Grade Rd — Moon Township PA 15108 — 412-264-6270 264-1575 139
TF: 800-581-9145 ■ *Web:* www.paacc.com

Pittsburgh Ballet Theatre
2900 Liberty Ave — Pittsburgh PA 15201 — 412-281-0360 281-9901 573-1
TF: 800-441-1414 ■ *Web:* www.pbt.org

Pittsburgh Brewing Co
3340 Liberty Ave — Pittsburgh PA 15201 — 412-682-7400 102
TF: 800-558-4100 ■ *Web:* www.pittsburghbrewing.com

Pittsburgh Business Times
45 S 23th St Ste 200 — Pittsburgh PA 15203 — 412-481-6397 481-9956 457-5
Web: www.bizjournals.com/pittsburgh

Pittsburgh City Hall
414 Grant St City-County Bldg — Pittsburgh PA 15219 — 412-255-2883 255-2821 337
TF: 800-932-0313 ■ *Web:* pittsburghpa.gov

Pittsburgh City Paper
650 Smithfield St Ste 2200 — Pittsburgh PA 15222 — 412-316-3342 316-3388 532-5
TF: 800-848-1880 ■ *Web:* www.pghcitypaper.com

Pittsburgh Civic Light Opera
719 Liberty Ave — Pittsburgh PA 15222 — 412-281-3973 281-5339 573-2
Web: www.pittsburghclo.org

Pittsburgh Corning Corp
800 Presque Isle Dr — Pittsburgh PA 15239 — 724-327-6100 387-3806 389
Web: www.pghcorning.com

Pittsburgh Ctr for the Arts (PCA)
6300 Fifth Ave — Pittsburgh PA 15232 — 412-361-0873 361-8338 50-2
Web: center.pfpca.org

Pittsburgh Design Services Inc
PO Box 469 — Carnegie PA 15106 — 412-276-3000 261
Web: www.pittsdesign.com

Pittsburgh Foundation
5 PPG Pl Ste 250 — Pittsburgh PA 15222 — 412-391-5122 391-7259 303
TF: 800-392-6900 ■ *Web:* www.pittsburghfoundation.org

Pittsburgh Institute of Aeronautics (PIA)
5 Allegheny County Airport — West Mifflin PA 15122 — 412-346-2100 346-2170 800
TF: 800-444-1440 ■ *Web:* www.pia.edu

Pittsburgh Institute of Mortuary Science Inc
5808 Baum Blvd — Pittsburgh PA 15206 — 412-362-8500 362-1684 800
TF: 800-933-5808 ■ *Web:* www.pims.edu

Pittsburgh International Airport
Landside Terminal Fourth Fl Mezz
PO Box 12370 — Pittsburgh PA 15231 — 412-472-3500 472-3636 27
TF: 888-429-5377 ■ *Web:* www.flypittsburgh.com

Pittsburgh Opera 2425 Liberty Ave — Pittsburgh PA 15222 — 412-281-0912 281-4324 573-2
Web: www.pittsburghopera.org

Pittsburgh Penguins 1001 Fifth Ave — Pittsburgh PA 15219 — 412-642-1300 642-1859 716
TF: 800-642-7367 ■ *Web:* penguins.nhl.com

Pittsburgh Pirates
115 Federal St PO Box 7000 — Pittsburgh PA 15212 — 412-321-2827 713
TF: 800-289-2827 ■ *Web:* pittsburgh.pirates.mlb.com

Pittsburgh Plumbing Heating & Industrial (PPHI)
2620 Ridgewood Rd — Akron OH 44313 — 330-762-9621 762-8722 14
Web: www.pphind.com

Pittsburgh Post-Gazette
34 Blvd of the Allies — Pittsburgh PA 15222 — 412-263-1100 391-8452 532-2
Web: www.post-gazette.com

Pittsburgh Public Schools (PPS)
341 S Bellefield Ave — Pittsburgh PA 15213 — 412-622-7920 685
Web: www.pps.k12.pa.us

Pittsburgh Public Theater
621 Penn Ave — Pittsburgh PA 15222 — 412-316-1600 316-8219 573-4
Web: www.ppt.org

Pittsburgh Steak Co
1924 E Carson St — Pittsburgh PA 15203 — 412-381-5505 671
Web: www.pghsteak.com

Pittsburgh Steelers
3400 S Water St — Pittsburgh PA 15203 — 412-432-7800 432-7878 715-3
Web: www.steelers.com

Pittsburgh Supercomputing Ctr
300 S Craig St — Pittsburgh PA 15213 — 412-268-4960 268-5832 668
TF: 800-221-1641 ■ *Web:* www.psc.edu

Pittsburgh Symphony Orchestra
600 Penn Ave
Heinz Hall for the Performing Arts — Pittsburgh PA 15222 — 412-566-7366 392-3311 573-3
TF: 800-743-8560 ■ *Web:* www.pittsburghsymphony.org

Pittsburgh Technical College (PTI)
1111 McKee Rd — Oakdale PA 15071 — 412-809-5100 809-5121* 800
**Fax:* Admissions ■ *TF:* 800-784-9675 ■ *Web:* www.pti.edu

Pittsburgh Theological Seminary
616 N Highland Ave — Pittsburgh PA 15206 — 412-362-5610 363-3260 167-3
TF: 800-451-4194 ■ *Web:* www.pts.edu

Pittsburgh Tribune-Review
503 Martindale St 3rd Fl — Pittsburgh PA 15212 — 412-321-6460 532-2
TF: 800-909-8742 ■ *Web:* triblive.com

Pittsburgh Zoo & PPG Aquarium
1 Wild Pl — Pittsburgh PA 15206 — 412-665-3640 665-3661 823
TF: 800-732-0999 ■ *Web:* www.pittsburghzoo.org

Pittsfield Plastics Engineering Inc
1510 W Housatonic St — Pittsfield MA 01201 — 413-442-0067 596
Web: www.pittsplas.com

Pittsfield State Forest
1041 Cascade St — Pittsfield MA 01201 — 413-442-8992 565
Web: www.mass.gov

Pittsford Federal Cu
1321 Pittsford Mendon Rd — Mendon NY 14506 — 585-624-7474 219
Web: pittsfordfcu.org

Pittsville Homes Inc
5094 Second Ave — Pittsville WI 54466 — 715-884-2511 106

Pittsville Pdq Inc 549 NW Hwy 131 — Holden MO 64040 — 816-850-6915 297-8
Web: shell.com

Pittsylvania County
1 Center St PO Box 426 — Chatham VA 24531 — 434-432-7700 338
Web: pittsylvaniacountyva.gov

Pittsylvania County Public Library
24 Military Dr — Chatham VA 24531 — 434-432-3271 432-1405 434-3
Web: www.pcplib.org

Pittsylvania County Schools
39 Bank St SE PO Box 232 — Chatham VA 24531 — 434-432-2761 432-9560 685
TF: 888-440-6520 ■ *Web:* www.pcs.k12.va.us

Pitzer College 1050 N Mills Ave — Claremont CA 91711 — 909-621-8129 621-8770* 166
**Fax:* Admissions ■ *TF:* 800-748-9371 ■ *Web:* www.pitzer.edu

Piute County 550 N Main — Junction UT 84740 — 435-577-2840 577-2433 338
Web: www.piute.org

Piute State Park PO Box 43 — Antimony UT 84712 — 435-624-3268 565
Web: www.stateparks.utah.gov

Pivot Interiors
3355 Scott Blvd Ste 110 — Santa Clara CA 95054 — 408-432-5600 432-5601 320
Web: www.pivotinteriors.com

Pivot it Inc 3541 Tracy Dr — Santa Clara CA 95051 — 408-836-9314 393
Web: www.pivot-it.com

Pivot Medical Inc
247 Humboldt Courtyard — Sunnyvale CA 94089 — 408-774-1452 475
Web: www.pivotmedical.com

Pivot Point International Inc
1560 Sherman Ave Ste 700 — Evanston IL 60201 — 847-866-0500 514
Web: www.pivot-point.com

Pivot Point Security
1245 Whitehorse Mercerville Rd — Trenton NJ 08619 — 609-581-4600 693
Web: pivotpointsecurity.com

Pivot Systems Inc
2480 N First St Ste 150 — San Jose CA 95131 — 408-435-1000 177
TF: 800-566-4604 ■ *Web:* www.pivotsys.com

Pivotal Health & Fitness LLC
1401 Sam Rittenberg Blvd — Charleston SC 29407 — 843-571-5858 354
Web: www.pivotalfitness.com

PIX 11 220 E 42nd St — New York NY 10017 — 212-949-1100 741-91
Web: pix11.com

Pix System LLC
455 Market St Ste 900 — San Francisco CA 94105 — 415-357-9720 514
Web: www.pixsystem.com

Pixar Animation Studios
1200 Pk Ave — Emeryville CA 94608 — 510-922-3000 33
Web: www.pixar.com

Pixel Systems Inc 47 Greylynne Dr — Princeton NJ 08540 — 609-945-3190 177
TF: 800-331-5114 ■ *Web:* www.pixelsystemsinc.com

Pixel Velocity Inc
3917 Research Park Dr Ste B-1 — Ann Arbor MI 48108 — 734-213-3715 529
Web: www.pixel-velocity.com

Pixeled Business Systems Inc
350 W Ninth Ave Ste 106 — Escondido CA 92025 — 858-566-6060 225
Web: www.pixeled.com

Pixelgate
733 Lakefield Rd Ste A — Westlake Village CA 91361 — 805-446-6254 387
Web: www.pixelgate.net

Pixels & Dots Llc
3181 Linwood Ave Ste 20 — Cincinnati OH 45208 — 513-405-3687 344
TF: 800-589-3660 ■ *Web:* www.pixelsanddots.com

Pixelworks Inc
224 Airport Pkwy Ste 400 — San Jose CA 95110 — 408-200-9200 200-9201 696
NASDAQ: PXLW ■ *TF:* 800-732-0330 ■ *Web:* www.pixelworks.com

Pixia Corp 45615 Willow Pond Plaza — Sterling VA 20164 — 571-203-9665 809
Web: www.pixia.com

Pixstar Inc 1515 Savannah Rd Ste 200 — Lewes DE 19958 — 302-644-8650 177

Pizza Boli's 3 Greenwood Pl Ste 208 — Pikesville MD 21208 — 800-234-2654 544-1505* 670
**Fax Area Code:* 443 ■ *TF:* 800-234-2654 ■ *Web:* www.pizzabolis.com

Pizza Factory Inc 49430 Rd 426 — Oakhurst CA 93644 — 559-683-3377 683-6879 670
TF: 800-654-4840 ■ *Web:* www.pizzafactory.com

Pizza Inn Inc 3551 Plano Pkwy — The Colony TX 75056 — 877-574-9924 670
NASDAQ: RAVE ■ *TF:* 877-574-9924 ■ *Web:* www.pizzainn.com

Pizza King Inc 221 Farabee Dr — Lafayette IN 47905 — 765-447-2172 670
Web: theoriginalpizzaking.com

Pizza Plus Pizza Inc
299 Franklin Dr — Blountville TN 37617 — 423-279-9335 670
Web: www.pizzaplusinc.com

Pizza Pro Inc
2107 N Second St PO Box 1285 — Cabot AR 72023 — 501-605-1175 670
TF: 800-777-7554 ■ *Web:* www.pizzapro.com

Pizza Ranch Inc 204 19th St SE — Orange City IA 51041 — 800-321-3401 670
TF: 800-321-3401 ■ *Web:* www.pizzaranch.com

Pizzagalli Construction Co
193 Tilley Dr — South Burlington VT 05403 — 802-658-4100 186
Web: www.pcconstruction.com

Pizzazz Hair Design at Abacoa Inc
771 Village Blvd Ste 208 — West Palm Beach FL 33409 — 561-689-1177 77
Web: www.pizzazzhair.com/the-salons/village-commons

Pizzeria Bianco 623 E Adams St — Phoenix AZ 85004 — 602-258-8300 671
Web: www.pizzeriabianco.com

Pizzuti Inc 629 N High St Ste 500 — Columbus OH 43215 — 614-280-4000 280-5000 653
Web: www.pizzuti.com

Pj Cook Web Designs Inc
2034 Rainbow Farms Dr — Safety Harbor FL 34695 — 727-712-9493 180
Web: pjcook.com

PJ Hoffmaster State Park
6585 Lake Harbor Rd — Muskegon MI 49441 — 231-798-3711 565
Web: www.michigandnr.com

PJ Keating Co 998 Reservoir Rd — Lunenburg MA 01462 — 978-582-5200 582-7130 188-4
TF: 800-441-4119 ■ *Web:* www.pjkeating.com

PJ Schneiders & Company LLP
152 Himmelein Rd Village Greene E — Medford NJ 08055 — 609-654-8300 2
Web: corrugatedcpa.com

PJA Adv & Mktg 12 Arrow St — Cambridge MA 02138 — 617-492-5899 4
Web: www.agencypja.com

PJS Used Cars & Auto Parts Inc
2708 Caledonia Leroy Rd — Caledonia NY 14423 — 585-538-2391 54
TF: 800-946-5787 ■ *Web:* www.pjs4lkq.com

PK (Promise Keepers) PO Box 11798 — Denver CO 80211 — 866-776-6473 433-1036* 48-20
**Fax Area Code:* 303 ■ *TF:* 866-776-6473 ■ *Web:* promisekeepers.org

PK Network Communications Inc
11 E 47th St — New York NY 10017 — 212-888-4700 463
Web: www.pknetwork.com

PK Partners LLC
3610 River Crossing Pkwy — Indianapolis IN 46240 — 317-817-8888 652
Web: pkpartners.com

PK Safety Supply
1829 Clement Ave Ste 200 — Alameda CA 94501 — 510-337-8880 337-8890 679
TF: 800-829-9580 ■ *Web:* www.pksafety.com

Pk USA Inc 600 W Northridge Dr — Shelbyville IN 46176 — 317-395-5500 395-5501 489
Web: www.pkusa.com

Company	City	State	ZIP	Phone	Fax	Class
PK4 Media 2250 E Maple Ave *TF:* 888-320-6281 ■ *Web:* www.pk4media.com	El Segundo	CA	90245	888-320-6281		387
PKA Marketing 1009 W Glen Oaks Ln Ste 107 *Web:* pkamar.publishpath.com	Mequon	WI	53092	262-241-9414		4
PKC Construction 7802 Barton St	Lenexa	KS	66214	913-782-4646		186
PKC Corp 1 Mill St C13 Ste 355 *TF:* 800-752-5351 ■ *Web:* www.pkc.com	Burlington	VT	05401	802-658-5351	658-3078	178-10
PKF-Mark III Inc 17 Black Smith Rd ste 101 *TF:* 800-364-2059 ■ *Web:* www.pkfmarkiii.com	Newtown	PA	18940	215-968-5031	968-3829	188-4
PKM Electric Co-op Inc 406 N Minnesota St *TF:* 800-552-7366 ■ *Web:* www.pkmcoop.com	Warren	MN	56762	218-745-4711		245
PKM Steel Service Inc 228 E Ave A *Web:* www.pkmsteel.com	Salina	KS	67401	785-827-3638		697
PKMM Inc 265 E Main St Ste B *Web:* pkmminc.com	Oceanport	NJ	07757	732-935-1927		177
PKOH (Park-Ohio Holdings Corp) 6065 Parkland Blvd *NASDAQ: PKOH* ■ *TF:* 800-732-0330 ■ *Web:* www.pkoh.com	Cleveland	OH	44124	440-947-2000	947-2099	449
PKWare Inc 648 N Plankinton Ave Ste 220 *TF:* 800-426-9990 ■ *Web:* pkware.com/about-us	Milwaukee	WI	53203	414-289-9788	289-9789	178-12
PL Communications 417 Victor St *Web:* plcommunications.com	Scotch Plains	NJ	07076	908-889-8888		7
PL Custom Body & Equipment Company Inc 2201 Atlantic Ave *TF:* 800-752-8786 ■ *Web:* www.plcustom.com	Manasquan	NJ	08736	732-223-1411		30
PL Porter Co 3000 Winona Ave *TF:* 888-236-5165 ■ *Web:* www.craneae.com	Burbank	CA	91504	818-526-2600	842-6117	350
PLA (Public Library Assn) 50 E Huron St *TF:* 800-545-2433 ■ *Web:* www.ala.org	Chicago	IL	60611	312-280-5752	280-5029	49-11
Place D'Armes Hotel 625 St Ann St *TF:* 800-366-2743 ■ *Web:* www.placedarmes.com	New Orleans	LA	70116	504-524-4531		379
Place de la Cite 2600 Laurier Blvd *Web:* www.placedelacite.com	Quebec	QC	G1V4T3	418-657-6920	657-6924	460
Place Louis Riel All-Suite Hotel 190 Smith St *TF:* 800-665-0569 ■ *Web:* www.placelouisriel.com	Winnipeg	MB	R3C1J8	204-947-6961	947-3029	379
Place Pigalle 81 Pike St *Web:* www.placepigalle-seattle.com	Seattle	WA	98101	206-624-1756		671
Placecast 184 Rose St *Web:* www.placecast.net	San Francisco	CA	94102	415-501-9759		809
PlaceFull Inc 122 S Jackson St Ste 310 *Web:* placefull.com	Seattle	WA	98104	206-624-0295		387
Placemaking Group 505 14th St 5th fl *TF:* 800-888-4966 ■ *Web:* www.placemakinggroup.com	Oakland	CA	94612	510-835-7900		393
Placemark Investments Inc 16633 Dallas Pkwy *Web:* www.placemark.com	Addison	TX	75001	972-404-8100		401
Placement Strategies Inc 6965 El Camino Real Ste 105-200 *TF:* 866-445-0710 ■ *Web:* www.placementstrategies.com	Carlsbad	CA	92009	909-597-0668		260
Placentia Chamber of Commerce 201 E Yorba Linda Blvd Ste C *TF:* 844-730-0418 ■ *Web:* www.placentiachamber.com	Placentia	CA	92870	714-528-1873	528-1879	139
Placentia-Linda Hospital 1301 N Rose Dr *Web:* www.placentialinda.com	Placentia	CA	92870	714-993-2000	961-5980	374-3
Placentia-Yorba Linda Unified School District (PYLUSD) 1301 E Orangethorpe Ave *Web:* www.pylusd.org	Placentia	CA	92870	714-996-2550		685
Placer County 2954 Richardson Dr *Web:* www.placer.ca.gov	Auburn	CA	95603	530-886-5600	886-5687	338
Placer County Library 350 Nevada St *TF:* 800-488-4308 ■ *Web:* www.placer.ca.gov	Auburn	CA	95603	530-886-4500	886-4555	434-3
Placer County Water Agency 144 Ferguson Rd PO Box 6570 *Web:* www.pcwa.net	Auburn	CA	95604	530-823-4850		787
Placer Title Co 2394 Fair Oaks Blvd *TF:* 800-530-3577 ■ *Web:* www.placertitle.com	Sacramento	CA	95825	916-973-1002	482-3049	391-6
Placer Union High School District 13000 New Airport *Web:* www.puhsd.k12.ca.us	Auburn	CA	95603	530-886-4400		685
Places Real Estate 400 Hibben St Ste 200 *Web:* www.scplaces.com	Mount Pleasant	SC	29464	843-849-3636		652
Placeteco inc 3763 Burrill St *Web:* www.placeteco.com	Shawinigan	QC	G9N6T6	819-539-8808	539-9224	360-2
Placid Lake State Park PO Box 136 *Web:* stateparks.mt.gov	Seeley Lake	MT	59868	406-677-6804		565
Placid Refining Company LLC 1940 Louisiana Hwy 1 N *Web:* www.placidrefining.com	Port Allen	LA	70767	225-387-0278		580
Placitas Realty Inc 03 Homesteads Rd Ste A	Placitas	NM	87043	505-867-8000		652
Placon Corp 6096 McKee Rd *TF:* 800-541-1535 ■ *Web:* www.placon.com	Madison	WI	53719	608-271-5634	271-3162	602
Plaid Enterprises Inc 3225 Westech Dr **Fax:* Mktg ■ *TF:* 800-842-4197 ■ *Web:* www.plaidonline.com	Norcross	GA	30092	678-291-8100	291-8368*	43
Plaid Pantries Inc 10025 SW Allen Blvd *TF:* 800-677-5243 ■ *Web:* www.plaidpantry.com	Beaverton	OR	97005	503-646-4246		204
Plain Dealer 1801 Superior Ave *TF:* 800-362-0727 ■ *Web:* www.cleveland.com	Cleveland	OH	44114	216-999-5000		532-2
Plain Local School District 901 44th St NW *Web:* www.plainlocal.org	Canton	OH	44709	330-492-3500	493-5542	685
Plainfield Asset Management LLC 60 Arch St 2nd Fl *Web:* www.pfam.com	Greenwich	CT	06830	203-302-1700		463
Plainfield Central School District 75 Canterbury Rd *Web:* www.plainfieldschools.org	Plainfield	CT	06374	860-564-6437		685
Plainfield Community Consolidated School District 202 15732 S Howard St *Web:* www.psd202.org/pages/plainfieldsd202	Plainfield	IL	60544	815-577-4000	436-7824	685
Plainfield Correctional Facility 727 Moon Rd *TF:* 800-451-6028 ■ *Web:* in.gov	Plainfield	IN	46168	317-839-2513	837-1875	213
Plainfield Public Library 800 Pk Ave *Web:* www.plainfieldlibrary.info	Plainfield	NJ	07060	908-757-1111	754-0063	434-3
Plainfield Re-Entry Educational Facility 501 W Main St *Web:* in.gov/idoc	Plainfield	IN	46168	317-839-7751	838-7548	412
Plains All American Pipeline LP 333 Clay St Ste 1600 *NYSE: PAA* ■ *TF Mktg:* 800-708-5071 ■ *Web:* www.plainsallamerican.com	Houston	TX	77002	713-646-4100		597
Plains Conservation Ctr 21901 E Hampden Ave *TF:* 800-287-8098 ■ *Web:* www.plainscenter.org	Aurora	CO	80013	303-693-3621		50-5
Plains Cotton Co-op Assn 3301 E 50th St PO Box 2827 *TF:* 800-333-8011 ■ *Web:* www.pcca.com	Lubbock	TX	79408	806-763-8011		275
Plains Dairy Products 300 N Taylor St *TF:* 800-365-5608 ■ *Web:* www.plainsdairy.com	Amarillo	TX	79107	806-374-0385		297-4
Plains Grain & Agronomy LLC 109 Third Ave *TF:* 800-950-2219 ■ *Web:* www.plainsgrain.com	Enderlin	ND	58027	701-437-2400		10-4
Plains Hotel, The 1600 Central Ave *TF:* 800-273-9739 ■ *Web:* www.theplainshotel.com	Cheyenne	WY	82001	307-638-3311		379
Plains Midstream Canada Suite 1400, 607 Eighth Ave SW *Web:* www.plainsmidstream.com	Calgary	AB	T2P0A7	403-298-2100		538
Plains Regional Medical Ctr 2100 N ML King Blvd *TF:* 800-923-6980 ■ *Web:* www.phs.org	Clovis	NM	88101	505-769-2141		374-3
Plains Reporter PO Box 1447 *TF:* 800-950-2165 ■ *Web:* www.willistonherald.com	Williston	ND	58802	701-572-2165	572-9563	532-4
PlainsCapital Corp 2323 Victory Ave Ste 1400 *TF:* 866-762-8392 ■ *Web:* www.plainscapital.com	Dallas	TX	75219	214-252-4100		360-2
Plaintree Systems Inc 110 Decosta St *Web:* www.plaintree.com	Arnprior	ON	K7S0B5	613-623-3434	623-4647	176
Plainview Chamber of Commerce 1906 W Fifth St *Web:* www.plainviewtexaschamber.com	Plainview	TX	79072	806-296-7431	296-0819	139
Plainview Milk Products Co-Op 130 Second St SW *TF:* 800-356-5606 ■ *Web:* www.plainviewmilk.com	Plainview	MN	55964	507-534-3872	534-3992	296-3
Plainview News, The PO Box 9 *Web:* www.theplainviewnews.com	Plainview	NE	68769	402-582-4921	582-4922	532-4
Plainville Farms Inc 304 S Water St PO Box 38 *TF:* 800-962-0445 ■ *Web:* www.plainvillefarms.com	New Oxford	PA	17350	717-624-2191		10-8
Plainwell Community School District 600 School Dr *Web:* www.plainwellschools.org	Plainwell	MI	49080	269-685-5823	685-1108	685
Plan 365 Inc 3201 Glenwood Ave Ste 300 *TF:* 800-642-1186 ■ *Web:* www.plan365inc.com	Raleigh	NC	27612	919-534-2200		463
Plan Administrators Inc 1300 Enterprise Dr *TF:* 800-236-7400 ■ *Web:* www.pai.com	De Pere	WI	54115	800-236-7400		194
Plan b 116 W Illinois St *Web:* www.planbadvertising.com	Chicago	IL	60654	312-222-0303		4
Plan B Technologies Inc 16701 Melford Blvd Ste 300	Annapolis	MD	21401	301-860-1006		177
Plan First Technologies Inc 120 Groton Ave *Web:* www.p1tech.net	Cortland	NY	13045	607-756-9347		196
Plan USA 155 Plan Way *TF:* 800-556-7918 ■ *Web:* www.planusa.org	Warwick	RI	02886	401-738-5600	738-5608	48-6
Planar Systems Inc 1195 NW Compton Dr *NASDAQ: PLNR* ■ *TF:* 866-475-2627 ■ *Web:* www.planar.com	Beaverton	OR	97006	503-748-1100	748-1244	173-4
Planaxis 505 de Maisonneuve Blvd W Ste 200 **Fax Area Code:* 844 ■ *Web:* www.planaxis.com	Montreal	QC	H2Y1L5	514-878-2295	476-0324*	196
Plane State Jail 904 FM 686 *Web:* tdcj.state.tx.us	Dayton	TX	77535	936-258-2476	257-4449	213
Planemasters Ltd 32 W 611 Tower Rd DuPage Airport *TF:* 800-994-6400 ■ *Web:* www.planemasters.com	West Chicago	IL	60185	630-513-2100	377-3283	13
Planes of Fame Air Museum 7000 Merrill Ave #17 *TF:* 800-464-1476 ■ *Web:* www.planesoffame.org	Chino	CA	91710	909-597-3722	597-4755	520
Planesmart! Aviation LLC Addison Airport 15841 Addison Rd *TF:* 888-228-4283 ■ *Web:* www.planesmart.com	Addison	TX	75001	972-380-8004		690
PLANET (Professional Landcare Network) 950 Herndon Pkwy Ste 450 *TF:* 800-395-2522 ■ *Web:* www.landscapeprofessionals.org	Herndon	VA	20170	703-736-9666	736-9668	48-2
Planet 21 8040 Providence Rd Ste 300 *Web:* www.planet21salon.com	Charlotte	NC	28277	704-543-1083		77
Planet Bike 2402 Vondron Rd *TF:* 866-256-8510 ■ *Web:* www.planetbike.com	Madison	WI	53718	608-256-8510		711
Planet Biotechnology Inc 20980 Corsair Blvd *Web:* www.planetbiotechnology.com	Hayward	CA	94545	510-887-1461		668
Planet Consulting LLC 407 N 117th St *Web:* www.planetci.com	Omaha	NE	68154	402-964-1999		463
Planet Forward LLC 800 Hillgrove Ave Ste 200 **Fax Area Code:* 708 ■ *TF:* 888-845-2539 ■ *Web:* theplanetforward.com	Western Springs	IL	60558	888-845-2539	505-4039*	260
Planet Granite 815 Stewart Dr *TF:* 800-726-8106 ■ *Web:* planetgranite.com	Sunnyvale	CA	94085	408-991-9090		148
Planet Hollywood International Inc 4700 Millenia Blvd Ste 400 *TF:* 800-303-5107 ■ *Web:* www.planethollywoodintl.com	Orlando	FL	32839	407-903-5500		670

Name / Address	City	State	ZIP	Phone	Fax	Class
Planet Hollywood Resort & Casino 3667 Las Vegas Blvd S *TF:* 866-919-7472 ■ *Web:* www.caesars.com/planet-hollywood	Las Vegas	NV	89109	702-785-5555		669
Planet Honda 2285 US Hwy 22 W *Web:* www.planethondanj.com	Union	NJ	07083	908-964-1600		57
Planet Paper Box Inc 2841 Langstaff Rd *Web:* www.planetpaper.com	Concord	ON	L4K4W7	416-798-7641		100
Planet Payment Inc 670 Long Beach Blvd *NYSE: PLPM* ■ *Web:* www.planetpayment.com	Long Beach	NY	11561	516-670-3200	670-3520	178-10
Planet Products Corp 4200 Malsbary Rd *Web:* www.planet-products.com	Cincinnati	OH	45242	513-984-5544	984-5580	298
Planet Propaganda 605 Williamson St *Web:* planetpropaganda.com	Madison	WI	53703	608-256-0000		7
Planet Technologies Inc 20400 Observation Dr Ste 107 *Web:* go-planet.com	Germantown	MD	20876	301-721-0100		179
Planet4it 55 Yonge St *Web:* www.planet4it.com	Toronto	ON	M5E1J4	416-363-9888		180
Planetbids Inc 20929 Ventura Blvd *TF:* 800-479-5314 ■ *Web:* home.planetbids.com	Woodland Hills	CA	91364	818-992-1771		175
Planetfone Inc 101 Convention Center Dr *Web:* planetfone.com	Las Vegas	NV	89109	626-792-9978		463
Planetmagpie 2762 Bayview Dr *Web:* www.planetmagpie.com	Fremont	CA	94538	408-341-8770		463
Planetree Inc 130 Division St *TF:* 800-222-2818 ■ *Web:* planetree.org	Derby	CT	06418	203-732-1365		533
Plan-it Interactive 150 W Industrial Way *TF:* 800-660-3735 ■ *Web:* www.interactivegame.com	Benicia	CA	94510	707-752-6010		232
Planit Measuring Co, The 94 Lkshore Rd E Unit C *TF:* 800-933-5136 ■ *Web:* www.planitmeasuring.com	Mississauga	ON	L5G1E3	905-271-7010		317
Planit Solutions Inc 3800 Palisades Dr *TF:* 800-280-6932 ■ *Web:* www.verosoftware.com	Tuscaloosa	AL	35405	205-556-9199		178-5
Plank Enterprises Inc 4404 Anderson Dr *TF:* 800-854-0021 ■ *Web:* www.plankenterprises.com	Eau Claire	WI	54703	715-839-1225		194
PlanMember Financial Corp 6187 Carpinteria Ave *Web:* online.planmember.com	Carpinteria	CA	93013	805-684-1199		401
Planned Administrators Inc PO Box 6927 *TF:* 800-768-4375 ■ *Web:* www.paisc.com	Columbia	SC	29260	803-462-0151		390
Planned Environments Inc 2219 Westlake Dr Ste 100	Austin	TX	78746	512-474-0806	474-5458	256
Planned Furniture Promotions Inc 9 Moody Rd Bldg D Ste 18 *TF:* 800-230-7526 ■ *Web:* www.pfpnow.com	Enfield	CT	06082	860-749-1472		320
Planned Parenthood Action Fund Inc 1110 Vermont Ave NW *TF:* 800-430-4907 ■ *Web:* www.plannedparenthoodaction.org	Washington	DC	20005	202-973-4800	296-3242	615
Planned Parenthood Federation of America 434 W 33rd St *TF:* 800-230-7526 ■ *Web:* www.plannedparenthood.org	New York	NY	10001	212-541-7800	245-1845	48-6
Planned Parenthood of Indiana Inc 200 S Meridian St PO Box 397 **Fax Area Code: 317* ■ *TF:* 800-230-7526	Indianapolis	IN	46206	800-230-7526	637-4337*	353
Planned Systems International Inc 10632 Little Patuxent Pkwy *TF:* 800-275-7749 ■ *Web:* www.plan-sys.com	Columbia	MD	21044	410-964-8000	964-8001	180
Planners Network Inc, The 43418 Business Park Dr *Web:* theplannersnetwork.com	Temecula	CA	92590	703-778-9000		463
Plano Centre 2000 E Springcreek Pkwy *TF:* 800-613-3222 ■ *Web:* plano.gov	Plano	TX	75074	972-422-0296	424-0002	205
Plano Chamber of Commerce 1200 E 15th St *Web:* www.planochamber.org	Plano	TX	75074	972-424-7547	422-5182	139
Plano City Hall 1520 Ave K *TF:* 800-832-5452 ■ *Web:* www.plano.gov	Plano	TX	75074	972-941-7000	423-9587	337
Plano Convention & Visitors Bureau 2000 E Spring Creek Pkwy *TF:* 800-817-5266 ■ *Web:* www.visitplano.com	Plano	TX	75074	972-941-5840	424-0002	206
Plano Molding Co 431 E S St *TF:* 800-226-9868 ■ *Web:* www.planomolding.com	Plano	IL	60545	630-552-3111		199
Plano Public Library System 5024 Custer Rd *TF:* 800-473-5707 ■ *Web:* planolibrary.org	Plano	TX	75023	972-769-4200		434-3
Plano Star Courier 624 Crona Dr Ste 170 *Web:* starlocalmedia.com	Plano	TX	75074	972-398-4200		532-2
Plano Super Bowl Inc 2521 K Ave *Web:* planosuperbowl.com	Plano	TX	75074	972-881-0242		99
Plano Symphony Orchestra 5236 Tennyson Pkwy Ste 200 *Web:* www.planosymphony.org	Plano	TX	75024	972-473-7262	473-4639	573-3
Planogramming Solutions Inc 9080 Golfside Dr *Web:* www.planogrammingsolutions.com	Jacksonville	FL	32256	904-448-0834		195
Plant Affair, The 1931 Blake Ave *TF:* 800-270-0150 ■ *Web:* plantaffair.com	Los Angeles	CA	90039	323-661-4571		393
Plant Delights Nursery Inc 9241 Sauls Rd *TF:* 800-548-0111 ■ *Web:* www.plantdelights.com	Raleigh	NC	27603	919-772-4794	662-0370	323
Plant Engineering Magazine 2000 Clearwater Dr *Web:* www.plantengineering.com	Oak Brook	IL	60523	630-288-8780	288-8781	457-21
Plant Interscapes Inc 6436 Babcock Rd *Web:* www.plantinterscapes.com	San Antonio	TX	78249	281-304-7190		292
Plant Maintenance Service Corp 3000 Fite Rd *Web:* www.pmscmphs.com	Millington	TN	38053	901-353-9880	353-0882	91

Name / Address	City	State	ZIP	Phone	Fax	Class
Plant Process Equipment Inc 280 Reynolds Ave *Web:* www.plant-process.com	League City	TX	77573	281-333-7850	332-6280	537
Plant Reclamation 912 Harbour Way S *TF:* 800-878-4270 ■ *Web:* www.plantreclamation.com	Richmond	CA	94804	510-233-6552	237-6739	189-16
Plant Sciences Inc 342 Green Valley Rd *Web:* www.plantsciences.com	Watsonville	CA	95076	831-728-7771	728-4967	238
Plant Services Magazine 555 W Pierce Rd Ste 301 *TF:* 800-872-9141 ■ *Web:* www.plantservices.com	Itasca	IL	60143	630-467-1300	467-1120	457-21
Plantation Agriculture Museum PO Box 87 *Web:* www.arkansasstateparks.com	Scott	AR	72142	501-961-1409		565
Plantation Inn & Golf Resort 9301 W Fort Island Trail *TF:* 800-632-6262 ■ *Web:* www.plantationoncrystalriver.com	Crystal River	FL	34429	352-795-4211	795-1156	669
Plantation Inn of New England 295 Burnett Rd	Chicopee	MA	01020	413-592-8200	592-9671	379
Plantation Pipe Line Co 1100 Alderman Dr Ste 200 *Web:* www.kindermorgan.com	Alpharetta	GA	30005	770-751-4000	751-4133	597
Plante & Moran PLLC 27400 Northwestern Hwy *TF:* 866-639-9991 ■ *Web:* www.plantemoran.com	Southfield	MI	48034	248-352-2500		2
Planters Cotton Oil Mill Inc 2901 Planters Dr *TF:* 800-264-7070 ■ *Web:* www.plantersoil.com	Pine Bluff	AR	71601	870-534-3631	534-1421	296-29
Planters Electric Membership Corp 1740 Hwy 25 N PO Box 979 *TF:* 888-397-3742 ■ *Web:* www.plantersemc.com	Millen	GA	30442	478-982-4722	982-4798	245
Planters Inn 112 N Market St *TF:* 800-845-7082 ■ *Web:* www.plantersinn.com	Charleston	SC	29401	843-722-2345		379
Planters Inn 29 Abercorn St *TF:* 800-554-1187 ■ *Web:* www.plantersinnsavannah.com	Savannah	GA	31401	912-232-5678	232-8893	379
Planters Oil Inc 217 S Main St	Fitzgerald	GA	31750	229-423-2231		316
PlantForm Corp 1920 Yonge St Ste 200 *Web:* www.plantformcorp.com	Toronto	ON	M4S3E2	416-452-7242		231
PlantIt Wise Inc 215 Industrial Dr *Web:* www.planetwiseinc.com	New Glarus	WI	53574	608-225-6625		192
Plantronics Inc 345 Encinal St *NYSE: PLT* ■ *TF:* 800-544-4660 ■ *Web:* www.plantronics.com	Santa Cruz	CA	95060	831-426-5858	426-6098	735
Plants of the Southwest 3095 Agua Fria Rd *TF:* 800-788-7333 ■ *Web:* www.plantsofthesouthwest.com	Santa Fe	NM	87507	505-438-8888	438-8800	323
Plantscape Inc 3101 Liberty Ave *TF:* 800-303-1380 ■ *Web:* www.plantscape.com	Pittsburgh	PA	15201	412-281-6352		393
Planview Inc 12301 Research BlvdResearch Park Plaza Ste 101 *TF:* 800-856-8600 ■ *Web:* www.planview.com	Austin	TX	78759	512-346-8600	346-9180	178-1
Plaquemine Lock State Historic Site 57730 Main St *TF:* 877-987-7158 ■ *Web:* crt.state.la.us	Plaquemine	LA	70764	225-687-7158		520
Plaquemines Parish 301 Main St *Web:* www.plaqueminesparish.com	Belle Chasse	LA	70037	504-297-5536		338
Plaquemines Parish School Board 557 F Edward Hebert Blvd *TF:* 877-453-2721 ■ *Web:* www.ppsb.org	Belle Chasse	LA	70037	504-595-6400	392-4073	685
PLASA North America 630 Ninth Ave Ste 609 *Web:* www.plasa.org	New York	NY	10036	212-244-1505	244-1502	48-4
Plasco Energy Group Inc 515 Legget D Ste 100 *Web:* www.plascoenergy.com	Kanata	ON	K2K3G4	613-287-3127		196
Plasco Inc 3075 Plainfield Rd *Web:* www.plascoid.com	Dayton	OH	45432	937-254-8444		596
Plascore Inc 615 N Fairview St *TF:* 800-630-9257 ■ *Web:* www.plascore.com	Zeeland	MI	49464	616-772-1220	772-1289	696
Plasencia Group Inc, The 1 N Dale Mabry Hwy Ste 100 *Web:* www.tpghotels.com	Tampa	FL	33609	813-932-1234		463
Plasidyne Engineering & Manufacturing Inc 3230 E 59th St *Web:* www.plasidyne.com	Long Beach	CA	90805	562-531-0510	531-1377	757
Plaskett Stacey (Rep D - VI) 331 Cannon HOB *Web:* plaskett.house.gov	Washington	DC	20515	202-225-1790	225-5517	342-2
Plaskolite Inc 1770 Joyce Ave *TF:* 800-848-9124 ■ *Web:* www.plaskolite.com	Columbus	OH	43219	614-294-3281	297-7287	600
Plasma Protein Therapeutics Assn (PPTA) 147 Old Solomon's Island Rd Ste 100 *Web:* www.pptaglobal.org	Annapolis	MD	21401	202-789-3100		49-8
Plasma Ruggedized Solutions Inc 2284 Ringwood Ave Ste A *TF:* 800-994-7527 ■ *Web:* www.plasmarugged.com	San Jose	CA	95131	408-954-8405		401
Plasma Services Group Inc 1840 County Line Rd Unit 100 *Web:* plasmaservicesgroup.com	Huntingdon Valley	PA	19006	215-355-1288		238
Plasma Technology Inc 1754 Crenshaw Blvd *Web:* www.ptise.com	Torrance	CA	90501	310-320-3373	533-1677	481
PlasmaCare Inc 1128 Main St Ste 300 *Web:* www.plasmacare.com	Cincinnati	OH	45202	513-621-8728		238
PlasmaNet Inc 420 Lexington Ave Ste 2435 *Web:* freelotto.com	New York	NY	10170	212-931-6760	931-6761	225
Plaspack U S A Inc 753 Amron Ave *Web:* www.plaspackusa.com	Antigo	WI	54409	715-623-4449		596
Plaspros Inc 1143 Ridgeview Dr *TF:* 800-752-7776 ■ *Web:* www.plaspros.com	McHenry	IL	60050	815-430-2300	430-2260	604
Plasser American Corp 2001 Myers Rd PO Box 5464 *TF:* 800-388-4825 ■ *Web:* www.plasseramerican.com	Chesapeake	VA	23324	757-543-3526	494-7186	650
Plast O Foam LLC 24601 Capital Blvd *Web:* cignetmolding.net	Clinton Twp	MI	48036	586-307-3790		247
Plas-Tanks Industries Inc 39 Standen Dr *TF:* 800-247-6709 ■ *Web:* www.plastanks.com	Hamilton	OH	45015	513-942-3800	942-3993	199

Company	Phone	Fax	Class
Plastatech Engineering Ltd 725 Morley Dr Saginaw MI 48601 *TF:* 800-892-9358 ■ *Web:* www.plastatech.com	989-754-6500	754-1626	191-4
Plasteak Inc 3563 Copley Rd Copley OH 44321 *TF:* 800-320-1841 ■ *Web:* www.plasteak.com	330-668-2587		186
Plastech Corp 920 S Field Ave Rush City MN 55069 *TF:* 800-259-9007 ■ *Web:* www.plastechcorporation.com	651-407-5700	407-5495	604
Plastek Group 2425 W 23rd St Erie PA 16506 *Web:* www.plastekgroup.com	814-878-4400	878-4529	604
Plaster Fun Time 400 Highland Ave Ste 9 Salem MA 01970 *Web:* www.plasterfuntime.com	978-745-7788		761
Plasterer Equipment Company Inc 2550 E Cumberland St Lebanon PA 17042 *Web:* www.plasterer.com	717-273-2616		358
Plasti Dip International 3920 Pheasant Ridge Dr Blaine MN 55449 *TF:* 800-969-5432 ■ *Web:* www.plastidip.com	800-969-5432		596
Plastic & Steel Supply Company Inc 50 Tannery Rd Readington Industrial Ctr Bldg 3 Branchburg NJ 08876 *TF:* 800-407-3726 ■ *Web:* www.pep-plastic.com	908-534-6111		601
Plastic Card Systems Inc 31 Pierce St Northborough MA 01532 *TF:* 800-742-2273 ■ *Web:* www.plasticard-systems.com	508-351-6210		173-6
Plastic Components Inc N 116 W 18271 Morse Dr Germantown WI 53022 *TF:* 877-253-1496 ■ *Web:* www.plasticcomponents.com	877-253-1496		604
Plastic Composites Co. 8301 Clinton Park Dr Fort Wayne IN 46825 *Web:* pccfiberglass.com	260-484-3139		463
Plastic Container Corp 2508 N Oak St Urbana IL 61802 *TF:* 800-419-6829 ■ *Web:* www.netpcc.com	217-352-2722		601
Plastic Design International Inc 111 Industrial Pk Rd Middletown CT 06457 *Web:* www.plasticdesign.com	860-632-2001	632-1776	604
Plastic Development Co Inc 75 Palmer Industrial Rd PO Box 4007 Williamsport PA 17701 **Fax Area Code:* 570 ■ *TF:* 800-451-1420 ■ *Web:* www.pdcspas.com	800-451-1420	323-8485*	375
Plastic Dress-Up Co 11077 Rush St South El Monte CA 91733 *Web:* www.pdu.com	626-442-7711		777
Plastic Film Corporation of America Inc 1287 Naperville Dr Romeoville IL 60446 *TF:* 800-654-6589 ■ *Web:* www.plasticfilmcorporation.com	630-887-0800		603
Plastic Forming Company Inc 20 S Bradley Rd Woodbridge CT 06525 *TF:* 800-732-2060 ■ *Web:* www.pfccases.com	203-397-1338	389-0420	199
Plastic Ingenuity Inc 1017 Park St Cross Plains WI 53528 *Web:* www.plasticingenuity.com	608-798-3071		596
Plastic Lumberyard LLC 220 E Washington St Norristown PA 19401 *TF:* 800-282-9583 ■ *Web:* www.plasticlumberyard.com	610-277-3900	277-3970	661
Plastic Molded Concepts Inc PO Box 490 Eagle WI 53119 *Web:* www.pmcplastics.com	262-594-5050	594-5075	604
Plastic Moldings Company LLC 9825 Kenwood Rd Ste 302 Cincinnati OH 45242 *TF:* 800-921-5040 ■ *Web:* www.pmcsmartsolutions.com	513-921-5040		604
Plastic Monofil Co Ltd 28 Industrial Dr Milton VT 05468 *Web:* www.plasticmonofil.com	802-893-1543		596
Plastic Package Inc 4600 Beloit Dr Sacramento CA 95838 *TF:* 800-356-6900 ■ *Web:* www.plasticpack.com	916-921-3399		344
Plastic Packaging Inc 1246 Main Ave SE Hickory NC 28602 *Web:* www.ppi-hky.com	828-328-2466		66
Plastic Products Company Inc 30355 Akerson St Lindstrom MN 55045 *Web:* www.plasticproductsco.com	651-257-5980	257-9774	604
Plastic Recycling of Iowa Falls Inc 10252 Hwy 65 Iowa Falls IA 50126 *TF:* 800-338-1438 ■ *Web:* www.plasticrecycling.us	641-648-5073	648-5074	661
Plastic Safety Systems Inc 2444 Baldwin Rd Cleveland OH 44104 **Fax Area Code:* 216 ■ *TF:* 800-662-6338 ■ *Web:* pss-innovations.com	800-662-6338	231-2702*	678
Plastic Technologies Inc 1440 Timberwolf Dr Holland OH 43528 *Web:* www.plastictechnologies.com	419-867-5400		194
Plastic Technology Inc 1115 Farrington St Conover NC 28613 *Web:* www.innofoam.net	828-328-2201		601
Plasticap 177 Crosby Ave Richmond Hill ON L4C2R3 *Web:* plasticap.com	905-883-4343		553
Plasticoid Co 249 W High St Elkton MD 21921 *Web:* www.plasticoid.com	410-398-2800	398-2803	676
Plasticolors Inc 2600 Michigan Ave PO Box 816 Ashtabula OH 44005 *TF:* 888-661-7675 ■ *Web:* www.chromaflo.com	440-997-5137	992-3613	143
Plastic-Plate Inc 5460 Cascade Rd SE Grand Rapids MI 49546 *TF:* 800-704-1078 ■ *Web:* www.lacksenterprises.com	616-949-6570		604
Plasticraft Manufacturing Company Inc 115 Plasticraft Dr Albertville AL 35951 *Web:* www.plasticraftmfg.com	256-878-4105		596
Plasticrest Products Inc 4519 W Harrison St Chicago IL 60624 *TF:* 800-828-2163 ■ *Web:* signaturejewelrypackaging.com	773-826-2163	826-4227	286
Plastics Color & Compounding Inc 14201 Paxton Ave Calumet City IL 60409 *TF:* 800-922-9936 ■ *Web:* www.plasticscolor.com	800-922-9936		605-2
Plastics Design & Mfg 6284 S Nome Ct Centennial CO 80111 *Web:* www.plasticsdesign-mfg.com	303-768-8380		596
Plastics Engineering Company Inc 3518 Lake Shore Rd Sheboygan WI 53083 *Web:* www.plenco.com	920-458-2121	458-1923	605-2
Plastics Group Inc 7409 S Quincy St Willowbrook IL 60527 *Web:* www.theplasticsgroup.net	630-325-1210		604
Plastics International Inc 7600 Anagram Dr Eden Prairie MN 55344 *TF:* 800-776-7769 ■ *Web:* www.plasticsintl.com	952-934-2303		603
Plastics Molding Company Inc 4211 N Broadway Saint Louis MO 63147 *TF:* 800-259-9007 ■ *Web:* plasticsmoldingco.com	314-241-2479	241-3757	604
Plastics One Inc 6591 Merriman Rd Roanoke VA 24018 *Web:* www.plastics1.com	540-772-7950		596
Plastics Plus Technology Inc 1495 Research Dr Redlands CA 92374 *Web:* www.plasticsplus.com	909-747-0555		608
Plastics Research Corp 1400 S Campus Ave Ontario CA 91761 *Web:* www.prccal.com	909-391-2006		199
Plastics Technology Magazine 6915 Valley Ave Cincinnati OH 45244 *Web:* www.ptonline.com	513-527-8800	527-8801	457-21
Plastiflex Company Inc 601-C E Palomar St Ste 424 Chula Vista CA 91911 *Web:* www.plastiflex.com	619-662-8792		370
Plastiform Packaging Inc 114 Beach St Rockaway NJ 07866 *Web:* www.plastiformpkg.com	973-983-8900		557
Plastikon Industries Inc 688 Sandoval Way Hayward CA 94544 *TF:* 800-370-0858 ■ *Web:* www.plastikon.com	510-400-1010	400-1133	608
Plastikos Inc 8165 Hawthorne Dr Erie PA 16509 *Web:* www.plastikoserie.com	814-868-1656		596
Plastimayd LLC 14151 Fir St Oregon City OR 97045 *Web:* www.plastimayd.com	503-654-8502		600
Plastipak Industries Inc 150 Industriel Blvd Boucherville QC J4B2X3 *TF:* 800-387-7452 ■ *Web:* www.plastipak.ca	450-650-2200	650-2201	601
Plastipak Packaging Inc 41605 Ann Arbor Rd Plymouth MI 48170 *Web:* www.plastipak.com	734-455-3600	354-7391	98
Plastiques Milsi Inc Les 2310 Rue de la Province Longueuil QC J4G1G1 *Web:* plastiquesmilsi.com	450-463-4568		608
Plast-O-Matic Valves Inc 1384 Pompton Ave Cedar Grove NJ 07009 *TF:* 800-323-2710 ■ *Web:* www.plastomatic.com	973-256-3000	256-4745	789
Plastomer Corp 37819 Schoolcraft Rd Livonia MI 48150 *TF:* 800-326-6206 ■ *Web:* www.plastomer.com	734-464-0700	464-4792	601
Plastpro Inc 5200 W Century Blvd 9F Los Angeles CA 90045 *TF:* 800-779-0561 ■ *Web:* www.plastproinc.com	310-693-8600	693-8620	608
Plastronics Socket Co Inc 2601 Texas Dr Irving TX 75062 *TF Cust Svc:* 800-582-5822 ■ *Web:* www.plastronics.com	972-258-2580		253
Plastube Inc 590 Simonds S Granby QC J2J1E1 *Web:* www.plastube.com	450-378-2633		601
Plateau Electric Cooperative 16200 Scott Hwy Oneida TN 37841 *Web:* www.plateauelectric.com	423-569-8591		245
Plateau Excavation Inc 375 Lee Industrial Blvd Austell GA 30168 *Web:* plateauexcavation.com	770-948-2600		261
Platfora Inc 1300 S El Camino Real 6th Fl San Mateo CA 94402 *Web:* www.platfora.com	650-918-1100		387
Platform Computing Inc 3760 14th Ave Markham ON L3R3T7 *TF:* 877-528-3676 ■ *Web:* ibm.com	905-948-8448	948-9975	178-1
Plath & Company Inc 1575 Francisco Blvd E San Rafael CA 94901 *TF:* 800-514-4434 ■ *Web:* plathco.com	415-460-1575		186
Platinum Advisors LLC 1215 K St Ste 1150 Sacramento CA 95814 *Web:* www.platinumadvisors.com	916-443-8891		401
Platinum Bank 802 W Lumsden Rd Brandon FL 33511 *Web:* www.platinumbank.com	813-655-1234		509
Platinum Business Corp 14662 Cambridge Cir Laurel MD 20707 **Fax Area Code:* 800 ■ *Web:* www.platinumcorporation.com	301-498-4149	853-7990*	809
Platinum Control Technologies Corp 2822 W Fifth St Fort Worth TX 76107 *TF:* 877-374-1115 ■ *Web:* platinumcontrol.com	817-529-6485		539
Platinum Dragon 814 1/2 W Market St Akron OH 44303	330-434-8108		671
Platinum Equity Holdings *Platinum Equity LLC* 360 N Crescent Dr Beverly Hills CA 90210 *Web:* www.platinumequity.com	310-712-1850		405
Platinum Group of Cos Inc 9121 Oakdale Ave Sute 201 Chatsworth CA 91311 *Web:* www.platinumgroup.org	818-721-3800	721-3811	360-3
Platinum Home Health Care Inc 4903 W 95th St Oak Lawn IL 60453 *Web:* platinumhomehealthcare.com	708-229-9338		363
Platinum Homes LLC 155 County Rd 351 Lynn AL 35575 *Web:* www.platinumhomes-llc.com	205-893-5182		505
Platinum Hotel 211 E Flamingo Rd Las Vegas NV 89169 *TF General:* 877-211-9211 ■ *Web:* www.theplatinumhotel.com	702-365-5000		379
Platinum HR Management LLC 4512 Farragut Rd Brooklyn NY 11203 *Web:* www.platinumhrm.com	718-859-1600		260
Platinum Maintenance Services Corp 120 Broadway 36th Fl New York NY 10271 *Web:* www.platinummaintenance.com	212-535-9700	480-2699	152
Platinum Medical Imaging LLC 1027 SW 30th Ave Deerfield Beach FL 33442	954-596-4945		475
Platinum Personnel 1475 Ellis St Kelowna BC V1Y2A3 *TF:* 800-652-1511 ■ *Web:* www.platinumpersonnel.ca	250-979-7200		260
Platinum Systems Specialists Inc 4715 Yender Ave Lisle IL 60532 *Web:* www.platinum-universe.com	630-375-6800	375-9069	194
Platinum Vault Inc 10554 Norwalk Blvd Santa Fe Springs CA 90670 *TF:* 888-671-2888 ■ *Web:* www.hartleymedical.com	562-903-1494		196

Name / Address	City	State	Zip	Phone	Fax	Class
Plato Woodwork Inc 200 Third St SW	Plato	MN	55370	320-238-2193		115
TF: 800-328-5924 ■ *Web:* www.platowoodwork.com						
Plato's Closet 23021 Outer Dr.	Allen Park	MI	48101	313-278-2300		310
Web: www.platoscloset.com						
Platon Craft & Floral Inc						
1327 N Carolan Ave	Burlingame	CA	94010	650-373-7888		292
Platon Digital Graphics						
136 Oregon St	El Segundo	CA	90245	800-499-0292		627
TF: 800-499-0292 ■ *Web:* platongraphics.com						
Platsky Company Inc 298 Montrose Rd.	Westbury	NY	11590	516-333-9292		612
Web: www.platsky.com						
Platt & Labonia Co						
70 Stoddard Ave	North Haven	CT	06473	203-239-5681	234-7978	697
TF: 800-505-9099 ■ *Web:* www.plattlabonia.com						
Platt Electric Supply						
10605 SW Allen Blvd	Beaverton	OR	97005	503-641-6121	277-7497	246
TF: 800-257-5288 ■ *Web:* www.platt.com						
Platt Luggage Inc 4051 W 51st St	Chicago	IL	60632	773-838-2000	838-2010	453
TF: 800-222-1555 ■ *Web:* www.plattcases.com/default.asp						
Plattco Corp 7 White St.	Plattsburgh	NY	12901	518-563-4640	563-4892	789
TF: 800-352-1731 ■ *Web:* www.plattco.com						
Platte County 2610 14th St.	Columbus	NE	68601	402-563-4902	564-4164	338
Platte County 415 Third St	Platte City	MO	64079	816-858-2232	858-3363	338
Web: www.co.platte.mo.us						
Platte County PO Box 728.	Wheatland	WY	82201	307-322-2315	322-2245	338
Web: www.plattecountywyoming.com						
Platte County Community Center North						
3101 Running Horse Rd	Platte City	MO	64079	816-858-0114		354
Web: www.kansascityymca.org						
Platte Creek Recreation Area						
c/o Snake Creek Recreation Area						
35910 282nd St	Platte	SD	57369	605-337-2587		565
Web: gfp.sd.gov						
Platte River State Park						
14421 346th St.	Louisville	NE	68037	402-234-2217		565
Web: outdoornebraska.gov/platteriver						
Platte Valley Bank of Missouri						
2400 Prairie View Rd PO Box 1250	Platte City	MO	64079	816-858-5400		70
Web: www.plattevalleybank.com						
Platte Valley Youth Services Ctr						
2200 'O' St	Greeley	CO	80631	970-304-6220		412
Platte-Clay Electric Co-op Inc						
1000 W Hwy 92 PO Box 100	Kearney	MO	64060	816-628-3121	628-3141	245
TF: 800-431-2131 ■ *Web:* www.pcec.coop						
Platts 2 Penn Plaza 25th Fl.	New York	NY	10121	212-904-3070		637-9
TF: 800-752-8878 ■ *Web:* www.platts.com						
Plattsburgh North Country Chamber of Commerce						
7061 Rt 9	Plattsburgh	NY	12901	518-563-1000	563-1028	139
TF: 800-347-1992 ■ *Web:* www.northcountrychamber.com						
Plaudit Design						
2470 University Ave W	Saint Paul	MN	55114	651-646-0696		180
Web: www.plauditdesign.com						
Play Advertising Inc						
1455 Lakeshore Rd Ste 208 S.	Burlington	ON	L7S2J1	905-631-8299		7
Web: playadvertising.com						
Playa Azul 415 E William St.	Carson City	NV	89701	775-883-2244		671
Playback Now Inc						
3139 Campus Dr Ste 700	Norcross	GA	30071	770-447-0616		463
TF: 800-241-7785 ■ *Web:* www.playbacknow.com						
Playbill Magazine						
525 Seventh Ave Ste 1801	New York	NY	10018	212-557-5757		457-9
TF: 800-533-4330 ■ *Web:* www.playbill.com						
PlayCore Inc						
401 Chestnut St Ste 410	Chattanooga	TN	37402	877-762-7563	425-3124*	346
**Fax Area Code:* 423 ■ *TF:* 877-762-7563 ■ *Web:* www.playcore.com						
Player's Club Resort						
35 Deallyon Ave	Hilton Head Island	SC	29928	843-785-3355		669
TF: 800-497-7529 ■ *Web:* spinnakerresorts.com						
Playhouse on the Square						
66 S Cooper St	Memphis	TN	38104	901-725-0776	726-5521	572
Web: www.playhouseonthesquare.org						
Playhouse Square						
1501 Euclid Ave Ste 200	Cleveland	OH	44115	216-771-4444	771-0217	572
TF: 866-546-1353 ■ *Web:* www.playhousesquare.org						
Playlore Inc 69 Red Coat Rd	Westport	CT	06880	203-635-4306		631
Web: www.playlore.com						
PlayMakers Repertory Co						
150 Country Club Rd	Chapel Hill	NC	27599	919-962-7529		749
Web: www.playmakersrep.org						
Playmobil USA Inc 26 Commerce Dr	Cranbury	NJ	08512	609-409-1263	395-3015	762
TF: 800-351-8697 ■ *Web:* www.playmobil.com						
PlayMyAd Inc						
7545 Irvine Center Dr Ste 200	Irvine	CA	92618	949-988-2500		5
Web: www.playmyad.com						
Playnation of Wnc						
542 Hendersonville Rd	Asheville	NC	28803	828-776-2731		711
TF: 800-693-6368 ■ *Web:* playnationofwnc.com						
PlayNetwork Inc 8727 148th Ave NE	Redmond	WA	98052	425-497-8100	497-8181	524
Web: www.playnetwork.com						
Playscripts 7 Penn Plaza Ste 904	New York	NY	10001	866-639-7529		791
TF: 866-639-7529 ■ *Web:* www.playscripts.com						
Playspace Designs Inc						
6321 S Heughs Canyon Dr	Salt Lake City	UT	84121	801-274-0212		711
Web: www.playspacedesign.com						
Playwell Group, The						
4743 Iberia Ave Ste C	Dallas	TX	75207	800-726-1816		711
TF: 800-726-1816 ■ *Web:* www.playwellgroup.com						
Playworks Inc 340 Blalock Rd.	Boiling Springs	SC	29316	780-453-6903		711
TF: 800-667-4264 ■ *Web:* www.playworksinc.com						
Playworld Systems Inc						
1000 Buffalo Rd	Lewisburg	PA	17837	570-522-9800	522-3030	346
TF: 800-233-8404 ■ *Web:* playworld.com						
Plaza Art 633 Middleton St.	Nashville	TN	37203	615-254-3368	254-1814	45
TF: 866-668-6714 ■ *Web:* www.plazaart.com						
Plaza Artists Materials of the MidAtlantic Inc						
1990 K Str NW	Washington	DC	20006	202-331-7090	331-3004	45
TF: 866-668-6714 ■ *Web:* www.plazaart.com						
Plaza Azteca 4292 Holland Rd	Virginia Beach	VA	23452	757-431-8135		671
Web: plazaazteca.com						
Plaza College 74-09 37th Ave	Jackson Heights	NY	11372	718-779-1430	779-7423	800
Web: www.plazacollege.edu						
Plaza Fleet Parts Inc						
1520 S Broadway	Saint Louis	MO	63104	314-231-5047	231-5109	61
TF: 800-325-7618 ■ *Web:* plazafleetparts.com						
Plaza Grill 600 E Esplanade Dr.	Oxnard	CA	93036	805-278-5070		671
Plaza Group Inc						
10375 Richmond Ave Ste 1620	Houston	TX	77042	713-266-0707	266-8660	146
TF: 800-876-3738 ■ *Web:* www.theplazagrp.com						
Plaza Home Mortgage Inc						
5090 Shoreham Pl Ste 206	San Diego	CA	92122	858-346-1208	677-6741	509
TF: 866-260-2529 ■ *Web:* www.plazahomemortgage.com						
Plaza Hotel & Casino						
1 Main St PO Box 760	Las Vegas	NV	89101	702-386-2110		379
TF: 800-634-6575 ■ *Web:* www.plazahotelcasino.com						
Plaza Hotel, The						
5th Ave at Central Park S	New York	NY	10019	212-759-3000		378
TF: 888-850-0909 ■ *Web:* www.theplazany.com						
Plaza Inn 900 Medical Arts NE	Albuquerque	NM	87102	505-243-5693		379
Plaza Live, The 425 N Bumby Ave	Orlando	FL	32803	407-228-1220		572
Web: www.plazaliveorlando.com						
Plaza on the River Resort Club Hotel						
121 W St.	Reno	NV	89501	775-786-2200		379
TF: 800-628-5974 ■ *Web:* www.plazaresortclub.com						
Plaza Resort & Spa						
600 N Atlantic Ave	Daytona Beach	FL	32118	844-284-2685		669
TF: 844-284-2685 ■ *Web:* www.plazaresortandspa.com						
Plaza Square Motor Lodge						
2255 Central Blvd	Brownsville	TX	78520	956-546-5104		379
Plaza Suite Hotel Resort						
620 S Peters St	New Orleans	LA	70130	800-770-6721		379
TF: 800-770-6721 ■ *Web:* www.plazaresort.com						
Plaza Suites Silicon Valley						
3100 Lakeside Dr	Santa Clara	CA	95054	408-748-9800		379
TF: 800-345-1554 ■ *Web:* www.theplazasuites.com						
Plaza Tire Service						
2075 Corporate Cr PO Box 2048	Cape Girardeau	MO	63702-2048	800-334-5036	334-0322*	62-5
**Fax Area Code:* 573 ■ *TF:* 800-334-5036 ■ *Web:* plazatireservice.com						
Plaza Travel 16530 Ventura Blvd Ste 106	Encino	CA	91436	818-990-4053		775
TF: 800-347-4447 ■ *Web:* www.plazatravel.com						
Plaza View 245 N Wildwood Dr	Branson	MO	65616	417-335-2798		671
TF: 800-850-6646 ■ *Web:* bransongrandplaza.com						
PLB Sports Inc						
Penn Ctr W Bldg 3 Ste 411	Pittsburgh	PA	15276	412-787-8800		296-8
Web: www.plbsports.com						
PLC Rouse Norton PLLC						
2607 Oberlin Rd #200	Raleigh	NC	27608	919-841-1000		2
Web: www.plccpa.com						
Pleasant Care 508 Westline Dr	Alameda	CA	94501	510-521-5765		793
Web: www.pleasantcare.com						
Pleasant Creek State Recreation Area						
4530 McClintock Rd	Palo	IA	52324	319-436-7716		565
Web: www.iowadnr.gov						
Pleasant Hill Chamber of Commerce						
91 Gregory Ln Ste 11	Pleasant Hill	CA	94523	925-687-0700	676-7422	139
Web: www.pleasanthillchamber.com						
Pleasant Holidays LLC						
2404 Townsgate Rd	Westlake Village	CA	91361	818-991-3390		771
TF: 800-742-9244 ■ *Web:* www.pleasantholidays.com						
Pleasant Nursery Inc						
4234 W Wabash	Springfield	IL	62711	217-522-2222		292
Web: pleasant-nursery.com						
Pleasant River Lumber Co						
432 Milo Rd	Dover-Foxcroft	ME	04426	207-564-8520		683
TF: 800-773-4300 ■ *Web:* www.pleasantriverlumber.com						
Pleasant Trucking Inc						
2250 Industrial Dr PO Box 778	Connellsville	PA	15425	800-245-2402	628-5868*	780
**Fax Area Code:* 724 ■ *TF:* 800-245-2402 ■ *Web:* www.pleasanttrucking.com						
Pleasant Valley Hospital						
2520 Valley Dr	Point Pleasant	WV	25550	304-675-4340		374-3
Web: www.pvalley.org						
Pleasant Valley Nursing Ctr						
8 Peabody Rd	Derry	NH	03038	603-434-1566		450
Pleasant Valley Potato Inc						
275 E Elmore Ave	Aberdeen	ID	83210	208-397-4194		11-1
Web: www.pleasantvalleypotato.com						
Pleasant Valley Sch District						
600 Temple Ave	Camarillo	CA	93010	805-482-2763	987-5511	685
Web: www.pvsd.k12.ca.us						
Pleasant Valley State Prison						
24863 W Jayne Ave PO Box 8500	Coalinga	CA	93210	559-935-4900	386-7461	213
TF: 877-256-6877 ■ *Web:* www.cdcr.ca.gov						
Pleasant View Gardens Inc						
7316 Pleasant St.	Loudon	NH	03307	603-435-8361	435-6849	323
TF: 866-862-2974 ■ *Web:* www.pvg.com						
Pleasanton Chamber of Commerce						
777 Peters Ave	Pleasanton	CA	94566	925-846-5858	846-9697	139
Web: www.pleasanton.org						
Pleasanton Weekly						
5506 Sunol Blvd Ste 100	Pleasanton	CA	94566	925-600-0840		532-3
TF: 800-719-9111 ■ *Web:* www.pleasantonweekly.com						
Pleasants County						
309 Second St PO Box 339	Saint Marys	WV	26170	304-684-1220		338
Pleasantville Union Free School District						
60 Romer Ave	Pleasantville	NY	10570	914-741-1400	741-1499	685
Web: www.pleasantvilleschools.com						
Please Touch Museum						
Memorial Hall Fairmount Pk						
4231 Ave of the Republic	Philadelphia	PA	19131	215-581-3181	581-3183	521
TF: 800-732-0999 ■ *Web:* www.pleasetouchmuseum.org						
Pleasure Bar & Restaurant						
4729 Liberty Ave	Pittsburgh	PA	15224	412-682-9603		671
Web: pleasurebarpittsburgh.com						
Pleiger Plastics Co PO Box 1271	Washington	PA	15301	724-228-2244	228-2253	608
TF: 800-753-4437 ■ *Web:* www.pleiger.com						
Pleora Technologies Inc						
340 Terry Fox Dr Ste 300	Kanata	ON	K2K3A2	613-270-0625	270-1425	668
TF: 888-687-6877 ■ *Web:* www.pleora.com						

Company / Address	City	State	ZIP	Phone	Fax	Class
Pleune Service Co 750 Himes SE *Web:* pleuneservice.com	Grand Rapids	MI	49548	616-243-6374		189-10
Plews Shadley Racher & Braun LLP 1346 N Delaware St *TF:* 800-825-7779 ■ *Web:* www.psrb.com	Indianapolis	IN	46202	317-637-0700		428
Plex Systems Inc 1731 Harmon Rd *Web:* www.plex.com	Auburn Hills	MI	48326	248-391-8001		178-12
Plexipixel Inc 93 Denny Way Ste B *Web:* www.plexipixel.com	Seattle	WA	98109	206-781-1405		344
Plexsys Interface Products Inc 4900 NW Camas Meadows Dr *Web:* www.plexsys.com	Camas	WA	98607	360-838-2500		180
Plextronics Inc 2180 William Pitt Way *Web:* www.plextronics.com	Pittsburgh	PA	15238	412-423-2030		605-2
Plexus Corp 1 Plexus Way PO Box 156 *NASDAQ: PLXS* ■ *TF:* 877-733-7260 ■ *Web:* www.plexus.com	Neenah	WI	54957	920-722-3451	751-5395	625
Plexus Ventures LLC 1701 Waterford Way *Web:* plexusventures.com	Maple Glen	PA	19002	215-542-2727		463
Plexxikon Inc 91 Bolivar Dr *Web:* plexxikon.com	Berkeley	CA	94710	510-647-4000		668
PLF (Public Lands Foundation) PO Box 7226 *TF:* 866-985-9636 ■ *Web:* www.publicland.org	Arlington	VA	22207	703-790-1988		48-13
PLG (Philip Lief Group Inc) 130 Wall St *Web:* www.philipliefgroup.com	Princeton	NJ	08540	609-430-1000		94
PLH Products Inc 6655 Knott Ave *TF:* 800-946-6001 ■ *Web:* www.healthmatesauna.com	Buena Park	CA	90620	714-739-6600		791
PLI (Practising Law Institute) 810 Seventh Ave 26th Fl *TF:* 800-260-4754 ■ *Web:* www.pli.edu	New York	NY	10019	212-824-5700		49-10
Plibrico Co 1010 N Hooker St *TF:* 800-255-8793 ■ *Web:* plibrico.com	Chicago	IL	60622	312-337-9000	337-9003	663
Plimoth Plantation 137 Warren Ave *TF:* 800-262-9356 ■ *Web:* www.plimoth.org	Plymouth	MA	02360	508-746-1622		520
Plitek LLC 69 Rawls Rd *TF:* 800-966-1250 ■ *Web:* www.plitek.com	Des Plaines	IL	60018	800-966-1250		608
Pliteq Inc 1370 Don Mills Rd Unit 300 *TF:* 800-576-2299 ■ *Web:* pliteq.com	Toronto	ON	M3B3N7	416-449-0049		261
PLJ Restaurant 333 Fulton St	San Francisco	CA	94102	415-294-8925		379
PLMA (Private Label Manufacturers Assn) 630 Third Ave *Web:* plma.com	New York	NY	10017	212-972-3131		49-18
Pln & Associates Inc 15400 Jennings Ln Ste 300 *TF:* 800-699-0299 ■ *Web:* www.pln-inc.com	Bowie	MD	20721	301-390-4635		463
Plochman Inc 1333 N Boudreau Rd *Web:* www.plochman.com	Manteno	IL	60950	815-468-3434		296-19
Plote Inc 1100 Brandt Dr *Web:* www.plote.com	Hoffman Estates	IL	60192	847-695-9300		188-4
Plowshare Group Inc 1 Dock St *Web:* www.plowsharegroup.com	Stamford	CT	06902	203-425-3949		4
PLRB (Property Loss Research Bureau) 3025 Highland Pkwy Ste 800 *TF:* 888-711-7572 ■ *Web:* www.plrb.org	Downers Grove	IL	60515	630-724-2200	724-2260	49-9
PLT (Pensacola Little Theatre) 400 S Jefferson St *Web:* www.pensacolalittletheatre.com	Pensacola	FL	32502	850-432-2042		573-4
Plug Power Inc 968 Albany-Shaker Rd *NASDAQ: PLUG* ■ *TF:* 877-474-1993 ■ *Web:* www.plugpower.com	Latham	NY	12110	518-782-7700	782-9060	253
Plum Analytics Inc 808 Firethorn Cir *Web:* www.plumanalytics.com	Dresher	PA	19025	206-331-7297		387
Plum Creek Specialty Hospital 5601 Plum Creek Dr	Amarillo	TX	79124	806-351-1000		450
Plum Grove Inc 2160 Stoningtone Ave *TF:* 866-738-3702 ■ *Web:* www.plumgroveprinters.com	Hoffman Estates	IL	60169	847-882-4020		627
Plum Island Animal Disease Ctr 1400 Independence Ave SW *Web:* www.ars.usda.gov	Washington	DC	20250	631-323-3200	323-3006	668
Plum Market Corp 30777 Northwestern Hwy Ste 301 *TF:* 800-732-5569 ■ *Web:* www.plummarket.com	Farmington Hills	MI	48334	248-706-1600		345
Plumas County 520 Main St Rm 104 *Web:* www.countyofplumas.com	Quincy	CA	95971	530-283-6155	283-6415	338
Plumas County Visitors Bureau 550 Crescent St *TF:* 800-326-2247 ■ *Web:* www.plumascounty.org	Quincy	CA	95971	530-283-6345		206
Plumas-Eureka State Park 310 Johnsville Rd *Web:* www.parks.ca.gov	Blairsden	CA	96103	530-836-2380		565
Plumas-Sierra Rural Electric Co-op 73233 SR 70 *TF:* 800-555-2207 ■ *Web:* www.psrec.coop	Portola	CA	96122	530-832-4261	832-5761	245
Plumb Memorial Library 65 Wooster St *Web:* www.sheltonlibrarysystem.org	Shelton	CT	06484	203-924-1580	924-8422	434-3
Plumb Supply Co 1622 NE 51st Ave *TF:* 800-483-9511 ■ *Web:* www.plumbsupply.com	Des Moines	IA	50313	515-262-9511	262-9790	612
Plumbers Local Union No 68 502 Link Rd	Houston	TX	77009	713-869-3592		414
Plumbers Supply Co 1000 E Main St *TF:* 800-626-5133 ■ *Web:* www.plumbers-supply-co.com	Louisville	KY	40206	502-582-2261	585-5521	612
Plumbing Concepts Inc 2445 Railroad St *Web:* www.plumbingconcepts.com	Corona	CA	92880	951-520-8590		610
Plumbing Distributors Inc 1025 Old Norcross Rd *TF:* 800-262-9231 ■ *Web:* relyonpdi.com	Lawrenceville	GA	30046	770-963-9231		612
Plumbing Industry Board Trade Education Committee 3711 47th Ave *TF:* 800-638-7442 ■ *Web:* www.ualocal1.org	Long Island	NY	11101	718-752-9630		414
Plumbing Manufacturers International (PMI) 1921 Rohlwing Rd Unit G *Web:* www.safeplumbing.org	Rolling Meadows	IL	60008	847-481-5500	481-5501	49-3
Plumbing-Heating-Cooling Contractors NA (PHCC) 180 S Washington St *TF:* 800-533-7694 ■ *Web:* www.phccweb.org	Falls Church	VA	22040	703-237-8100	237-7442	49-3
Plummer Forest Products Inc 401 N Poltatch Rd *Web:* www.plummerforest.com	Post Falls	ID	83854	208-773-7521		683
Plummer House 1091 SW Plummer Ln *Web:* www.rochestermn.gov	Rochester	MN	55902	507-328-2525		50-3
Plump Engineering Inc 914 E Katella Ave *TF:* 800-323-4072 ■ *Web:* www.peica.com	Anaheim	CA	92805	714-385-1835		539
Plump Jack's Squaw Valley Inn 1920 Squaw Valley Rd PO Box 2407 *TF:* 800-323-7666 ■ *Web:* www.plumpjackssquawvalleyinn.com	Olympic Valley	CA	96146	530-583-1576	583-1734	379
Plump's Last Shot 6416 Cornell Ave	Indianapolis	IN	46220	317-257-5867		671
PlumpJack Group 3138 Fillmore St *Web:* www.plumpjack.com	San Francisco	CA	94123	415-346-5712	474-8792	671
Plumrose USA Inc 1901 Butterfield Rd Ste 305 *TF:* 800-526-4909 ■ *Web:* www.plumroseusa.com	Downers Grove	IL	60515	732-624-4040		473
Plums Bank 35 S Lindan Ave *NASDAQ: PLBC* ■ *Web:* www.plumasbank.com	Quincy	CA	95971	530-283-7305		70
Plunkett Research Ltd PO Box 541737 *Web:* www.plunkettresearch.com	Houston	TX	77254	713-932-0000		626
Plunkett's Pest Control 40 NE 52nd Way *TF:* 866-906-1780 ■ *Web:* www.plunketts.net	Fridley	MN	55421	218-723-8464		577
Plures Technologies Inc 5297 Parkside Dr Ste 400	Canandaigua	NY	14424	585-905-0554		529
Plus Group Inc, The (TPG) 7425 Janes Ave Ste 201 *Web:* www.theplusgroup.com	Woodridge	IL	60517	630-515-0500	515-0510	721
PLUS Orthopedics USA Inc 10188 Telesis Ct Ste 300	San Diego	CA	92121	858-550-3800	550-3813	477
PlusOne Solutions Inc 3501 Quadrangle Blvd Ste 120 *TF:* 877-943-0100 ■ *Web:* www.plusonesolutions.net	Orlando	FL	32817	407-359-5929		196
Pluto Corp PO Box 391 *TF:* 800-780-4707 ■ *Web:* www.plutocorp.com	French Lick	IN	47432	812-936-9988	936-2828	98
PLWC (Paragould Light Water & Cable) 1901 Jones Rd *Web:* www.paragould.com	Paragould	AR	72450	870-239-7700		116
PLx Pharma Inc 8285 El Rio Ste 130 *Web:* www.plxpharma.com	Houston	TX	77054	713-842-1249		231
Ply Gem 5020 Weston Pkwy Ste 400 *TF:* 800-786-2726 ■ *Web:* www.plygem.com/wps/portal/home/brands/napco	Cary	NC	27513	888-975-9436	842-3991	697
Ply Gem Holdings Inc 5020 Weston Pkwy Ste 400 *Web:* www.plygem.com	Cary	NC	27513	919-677-4019		608
Ply Gem Windows 615 Carson St	Bryan	TX	77801	979-779-1051		235
Plyler Construction 3505 Texoma Pkwy PO Box 912406 *Web:* www.plylerbuilds.com	Sherman	TX	75091	903-893-6393	892-3523	189-10
PlymKraft Inc 479 Export Cir *TF:* 800-992-0854 ■ *Web:* www.plymkraft.com	Newport News	VA	23601	757-595-0364	595-3993	208
Plymold 615 Centennial Dr *TF:* 800-759-6653 ■ *Web:* www.plymold.com	Kenyon	MN	55946	800-759-6653		319-1
Plymouth Area Chamber of Commerce 134 Court St *Web:* www.plymouthchamber.com	Plymouth	MA	02360	508-830-1620	830-1621	139
Plymouth Community Chamber of Commerce 850 W Ann Arbor Trl *TF:* 800-477-4747 ■ *Web:* www.plymouthchamber.org	Plymouth	MI	48170	734-453-1540		139
Plymouth County 215 Fourth Ave SE **Fax: Acctg* ■ *Web:* www.co.plymouth.ia.us	Le Mars	IA	51031	712-546-6100	546-5784*	338
Plymouth County 134 Ct St *Web:* www.seeplymouth.com	Plymouth	MA	02360	508-747-7533		338
Plymouth Foam Inc 1800 Sunset Dr *Web:* www.plymouthfoam.com	Plymouth	WI	53073	920-893-0535		601
Plymouth Foundry Inc 523 W Harrison St *TF:* 800-847-4766 ■ *Web:* www.plymouthfoundry.com	Plymouth	IN	46563	574-936-2106		492
Plymouth Harbor 700 John Ringling Blvd *Web:* www.plymouthharbor.org	Sarasota	FL	34236	941-365-2600		672
Plymouth Place Inc 315 N LaGrange Rd *Web:* www.plymouthplace.org	La Grange Park	IL	60526	708-354-0340		450
Plymouth Printing Co Inc 450 North Ave E *Web:* www.plymouthprinting.com	Cranford	NJ	07016	908-276-8100		627
Plymouth Public Library 132 S St *TF:* 800-625-7738 ■ *Web:* plymouthpubliclibrary.org	Plymouth	MA	02360	508-830-4250		434-3
Plymouth Rubber Company Inc 275 Tpke St Ste 310 *Web:* www.plymouthrubber.com	Canton	MA	02021	781-828-0220	828-6041	732
Plymouth Spring Company Inc 281 Lake Ave *Web:* www.plymouthspring.com	Bristol	CT	06010	860-584-0594	584-0943	719
Plymouth State University 17 High St **Fax: Admissions* ■ *TF:* 800-842-6900 ■ *Web:* www.plymouth.edu	Plymouth	NH	03264	603-535-2237	535-2714*	166
Plymouth State University Lamson Library 17 High St *Web:* library.plymouth.edu	Plymouth	NH	03264	603-535-2455		434-6
Plymouth Technology Inc 2925 Waterview Dr *TF:* 800-535-5053 ■ *Web:* www.plymouthtechnology.com	Rochester Hills	MI	48309	248-537-0081		612
Plymouth Tube Co 29 W 150 Warrenville Rd *TF Mktg:* 800-323-9506 ■ *Web:* www.plymouth.com	Warrenville	IL	60555	630-393-3550	393-3551	490
Plymouth Village 900 Salem Dr *TF:* 800-391-4552 ■ *Web:* www.plymouthvillage.org	Redlands	CA	92373	909-793-9195		672
Plywood Supply Inc 7036 NE 175th St *TF:* 888-774-9663 ■ *Web:* www.plywoodsupply.com	Kenmore	WA	98028	425-485-8585	485-6195	613
PM Beef Group LLC 2850 Hwy 60 E *TF:* 800-622-5213 ■ *Web:* www.pmbeef.com	Windom	MN	56101	507-831-2761	831-6216	10-1
PM Co 9220 Glades Dr *TF:* 800-327-4359 ■ *Web:* www.pmcompany.com	Fairfield	OH	45011	513-825-7626	825-2877	554

Phone | Fax | Class

PM Construction Co Inc PO Box 728 Saco ME 04072 207-282-7697 186
TF: 800-646-0068 ■ *Web:* www.pmconstruction.com

PM Environmental Inc 3340 Ranger Rd. Lansing MI 48906 517-321-3331 194
Web: www.pmenv.com

Pm Group Inc, The
7550 W I-10 Ste 500 San Antonio TX 78229 210-490-2554 4
Web: thepmgrp.com

PM Parties Inc
701 Matthews Mint Hill Rd Ste C Matthews NC 28105 704-841-1370 327

PM Realty Group 1000 Main St Ste 2400 Houston TX 77002 713-209-5800 209-5702* 655
**Fax:* Hum Res ■ *TF:* 800-222-2162 ■ *Web:* www.pmrg.com

PM Recovery Inc 106 Calvert St. Harrison NY 10528 914-835-1900 411
TF: 800-868-9874 ■ *Web:* www.pmrecovery.com

Pm Resource Group LLC
219 Scott St Ste 165 Beaufort SC 29902 404-247-6968 765
Web: www.pmresourcegroup.com

Pm2 4210 Saltwater Blvd. Tampa FL 33615 813-249-0834 449
Web: www.pm2online.com

PMA (Polish Museum of America)
984 N Milwaukee Ave Chicago IL 60642 773-384-3352 384-3799 520
Web: www.polishmuseumofamerica.org

PMA (Polyurethane Manufacturers Assn)
6737 W Washington St Ste 1420 Milwaukee WI 53214 414-431-3094 49-13
TF: 800-937-8461 ■ *Web:* www.pmahome.org

PMA (Precision Metalforming Assn)
6363 Oak Tree Blvd. Independence OH 44131 216-901-8800 901-9190 49-3
Web: www.pma.org/home

PMA (Produce Marketing Assn)
1500 Casho Mill Rd Newark DE 19711 302-738-7100 731-2409 49-6
Web: www.pma.com

PMA Canada Ltd
231 Oak Park Blvd Ste 400 Oakville ON L6H7S8 905-257-2116 41
TF: 800-667-9463 ■ *Web:* www.pmacanada.com

PMA Capital Corp 380 Sentry Pkwy Blue Bell PA 19422 610-397-5298 360-4
Web: www.pmacompanies.com

Pma Consultants LLC
1 Woodward Ave Ste 1400 Detroit MI 48226 313-963-8863 194
Web: www.pmaconsultants.com

Pma Inc 17128 Edwards Rd Cerritos CA 90703 562-407-9977 627
TF: 800-443-6010 ■ *Web:* www.printmgt.com

PMAA (Petroleum Marketers Assn of America)
1901 N Ft Myer Dr Ste 500 Arlington VA 22209 703-351-8000 351-9160 49-18
Web: www.pmaa.org

Pmalliance Inc
2075 Spencers Way Ste 201 Stone Mountain GA 30087 770-938-4947 463
TF: 866-808-3735 ■ *Web:* www.pm-alliance.com

PMB Helin Donovan LLP
5918 W Courtyard Dr Austin TX 78730 512-258-9670 2
Web: pmbhd.com

PMC Biogenix Inc 1231 Pope St. Memphis TN 38108 901-325-4930 601
Web: www.pmcbiogenix.com

PMC Commercial Trust
17950 Preston Rd Ste 600 Dallas TX 75252 972-349-3200 349-3265 216
NASDAQ: CMCT ■ *TF:* 800-486-3223 ■ *Web:* cimgroup.com/pmc

PMC Global Inc 12243 Branford St Sun Valley CA 91352 818-896-1101 686-2531 145
TF: 800-438-7325 ■ *Web:* www.pmcglobalinc.com

PMC Group Inc
1288 Rt 73 S Pmc Group Bldg Ste 401 Mount Laurel NJ 08054 856-533-1866 608
Web: www.pmc-group.com

PMC Industries 275 Hudson St. Hackensack NJ 07601 201-342-3684 342-3568 547
Web: www.pmc-industries.com

PMC Industries Inc
29100 Lakeland Blvd Wickliffe OH 44092 440-943-3300 944-1974 455
Web: www.pmc-colinet.com/default.asp?id=50

Pmc Mechanical Contractors Inc
15 S Ridge Ave Ambler PA 19002 215-628-3806 610
Web: mcaepa.org

PMC Specialties Group Inc
501 Murray Rd Cincinnati OH 45217 800-543-2466 144
TF: 800-543-2466 ■ *Web:* www.pmcsg.com

PMCS-ICAP 829 W Genesee St. Syracuse NY 13204 315-423-7962 652
TF: 800-245-7627 ■ *Web:* www.pmcs-icap.com

PMD Healthcare 6620 Grant way Allentown PA 18106 484-664-7600 363
Web: www.mypmd.com

Pme Equip Inc 304 Garden Oaks Blvd Houston TX 77018 713-691-3081 358

PMEL (Pacific Marine Environmental Laboratory)
7600 Sand Pt Way NE. Seattle WA 98115 206-526-6239 526-6815 668
Web: www.pmel.noaa.gov

PMG Project Management Group LLC
2723 Houston Ave Houston TX 77009 713-880-2626 186
TF: 800-768-5594 ■ *Web:* www.pmgunited.com

PMHC (Phelps Memorial Hospital Ctr)
701 N Broadway Sleepy Hollow NY 10591 914-366-3000 374-3
Web: www.phelpshospital.org

PMHD (Pioneers Memorial Healthcare District)
207 W Legion Rd Brawley CA 92227 760-351-3333 374-3
Web: www.pmhd.org

PMHI (Pacific Modern Homes Inc)
9723 Railroad St. Elk Grove CA 95624 916-685-9514 106
TF: 800-395-1011 ■ *Web:* www.pmhi.com

PMI (Plumbing Manufacturers International)
1921 Rohlwing Rd Unit G Rolling Meadows IL 60008 847-481-5500 481-5501 49-3
Web: www.safeplumbing.org

PMI (Project Management Institute)
14 Campus Blvd. Newtown Square PA 19073 610-356-4600 356-4647 49-12
TF: 866-276-4764 ■ *Web:* www.pmi.org

PMI Cartoning Inc
850 Pratt Blvd. Elk Grove Village IL 60007 847-437-1427 547
Web: www.pmicartoning.com

PMI Group Inc 3003 Oak Rd Walnut Creek CA 94597 800-288-1970 360-4
OTC: PMI ■ *TF:* 800-288-1970 ■ *Web:* www.pmi-us.com

PMI Mortgage Insurance Co
3003 Oak Rd. Walnut Creek CA 94597 925-658-7878 391-5
Web: www.pmi-us.com

Pmj Solutions Inc 604 Park Pl Rivervale NJ 07675 201-664-8920 317
Web: www.pmjsolutions.com

PML (OneAmerica Financial Partners Inc)
PO Box 368 Indianapolis IN 46206 317-285-1877 285-6462 391-2
TF: 800-249-6269 ■ *Web:* www.oneamerica.com

PML Exploration Services LLC
5208 W Reno Ste 325 Oklahoma City OK 73127 405-606-2701 538
Web: www.pmles.com

PMMC (Pottstown Memorial Medical Ctr)
1600 E High St Pottstown PA 19464 610-327-7000 374-3
Web: www.pottstownmemorial.com

PMMI (Packaging Machinery Manufacturers Institute)
4350 N Fairfax Dr Ste 600 Arlington VA 22203 703-243-8555 243-8556 49-13
TF: 888-275-7664 ■ *Web:* www.pmmi.org

PMOLink LLC 2001 Lakeshore Dr. Mandeville LA 70448 985-674-5968 196
TF: 800-401-5701 ■ *Web:* www.pmolink.com

PMP Corp 25 Security Dr Avon CT 06001 860-677-9656 674-0196 495
TF Cust Svc: 800-243-6628 ■ *Web:* www.pmp-corp.com

PMPA (Precision Machined Products Assn)
6700 W Snowville Rd Brecksville OH 44141 440-526-0300 526-5803 49-13
TF: 800-233-1234 ■ *Web:* www.pmpa.org

PMRS Inc 202 Precision Rd Horsham PA 19044 267-960-3300 743
Web: www.pmrsinc.com

PMS Systems Corp
2800 28th St Ste 109 Santa Monica CA 90405 310-450-2566 450-1311 178-5
TF: 800-755-3968 ■ *Web:* www.assetsmart.com

PMSI (Powerplant Maintenance Specialists Inc)
2900 Bristol St Ste H202 Costa Mesa CA 92626 714-427-6900 427-6906 104

PMSLIC (Pennsylvania Medical Society Liability Insurance Co)
777 E Park Dr PO Box 8820 Harrisburg PA 17050 717-558-7750 558-7818 391-5
TF: 800-228-7823 ■ *Web:* www.pamedsoc.org

PMT Corp 1500 Park Rd. Chanhassen MN 55317 952-470-0866 475
Web: www.pmtcorp.com

PNBC 606 S Main St Princeton IL 61356 309-662-4444 872-0247* 360-2
OTC: PNBC ■ **Fax Area Code:* 815 ■ *TF:* 888-897-2276 ■ *Web:* www.hbtbank.com

PNBC (Progressive National Baptist Convention Inc)
601 50th St NE Washington DC 20019 202-396-0558 398-4998 48-20
TF: 800-876-7622 ■ *Web:* www.pnbc.org

PNC Arena 1400 EdwaRds Mill Rd Raleigh NC 27607 919-861-2300 861-2310 720
TF: 800-745-3000 ■ *Web:* www.thepncarena.com

PNC Bank 1 PNC Plaza 249 Fifth Ave Pittsburgh PA 15222 412-762-2000 762-7829 70
TF: 888-762-2265 ■ *Web:* www.pnc.com

PNC Bank 600 Grant St. Pittsburgh PA 15219 888-762-2265 70
NYSE: PNC-L ■ *TF:* 888-762-2265 ■ *Web:* www.pnc.com

PNC Bank Art Ctr
Exit 116 Garden State Pkwy Holmdel NJ 07733 732-203-2500 572
TF: 800-745-3000 ■ *Web:* livenation.com/venues/16839?from_tm=true

PNC Bank Delaware 300 Delaware Ave Wilmington DE 19899 302-429-1361 70
TF: 888-762-2265 ■ *Web:* www.pnc.com

PNC Bank NA
249 Fifth Ave 1 PNC Plaza Pittsburgh PA 15222 412-762-2000 70
TF: 888-762-2265 ■ *Web:* www.pnc.com

PNC Financial Services Group Inc
The Tower at PNC Plaza
300 Fifth Ave 29th Fl. Pittsburgh PA 15222 412-762-2000 360-2
NYSE: PNC ■ *TF:* 877-762-2000 ■ *Web:* www.pnc.com

PNC Inc 115 E Centre St Nutley NJ 07110 973-284-1600 284-1925 625
Web: www.pnconline.com

PNC Park 115 Federal St. Pittsburgh PA 15212 412-321-2827 720
TF: 866 800 1275 ■ *Web:* pittsburgh.pirates.mlb.com/pit/ballpark

Pneudraulics Inc
8575 Helms Ave Rancho Cucamonga CA 91730 909-980-5366 790
Web: www.pneudraulics.com

Pneumadyne Inc 14425 23rd Ave N Plymouth MN 55447 763-559-0177 789
Web: www.pneumadyne.com

Pneumatic & Hydraulic Systems Company Inc
1338 Petroleum Pkwy. Broussard LA 70518 337-839-1999 358
TF: 877-836-1999 ■ *Web:* pneumaticandhydraulic.com

Pneumatic Diner 501 W First St Reno NV 89503 775-786-8888 671

Pneumatic Scale Angelus 4485 Allen Rd. Stow OH 44224 330-247-1000 928-7077 547
Web: www.psangelus.com

Pneumech Systems Mfg LLC
201 Pneu Mech Dr Statesville NC 28625 704-873-2475 871-2780 18
TF: 800-358-7374 ■ *Web:* www.pneu-mech.com

Pneumercator Inc 120 Finn Ct. Farmingdale NY 11735 631-293-8450 61
Web: www.pneumercator.com

Pneumex Inc 2605 N Boyer Ave. Sandpoint ID 83864 208-265-4105 196
Web: www.pneumex.com

PneumRx Inc 530 Logue Ave. Mountain View CA 94043 650-625-8910 476
TF: 800-226-7625 ■ *Web:* www.pneumrx.com

Pneutek 17 Friars Dr Hudson NH 03051 603-883-1660 882-9165 759
TF: 800-431-8665 ■ *Web:* www.pneutek.com

PNH (Piedmont Newnan Hospital)
60 Hospital Rd Newnan GA 30263 770-400-1000 374-3
Web: www.piedmont.org

PNI Digital Media Inc
425 Carrall St Ste 590 Vancouver BC V6B6E3 604 803 8955 588
TSE: PN ■ *TF:* 800-521-3606 ■ *Web:* www.pnidigitalmedia.com

PNK (River City) LLC
777 River City Casino Blvd. Saint Louis MO 63125 888-578-7289 377
TF: 888-578-7289 ■ *Web:* www.rivercity.com

PNM Resources Inc Alvarado Sq Albuquerque NM 87158 505-241-2700 360-5
NYSE: PNM ■ *TF:* 888-342-5766 ■ *Web:* www.pnmresources.com

PNNL (Pacific Northwest National Laboratory)
902 Battelle Blvd PO Box 999 Richland WA 99352 509-375-2121 375-2507* 668
**Fax:* Mail Rm ■ *TF:* 888-375-7665 ■ *Web:* www.pnl.gov

PNR RailWorks Inc
2595 Deacon St PO Box 2280 Abbotsford BC V2T4X2 604-850-9166 188
Web: www.pnrail.com

PNT Marketing Services Inc
2420 Jackson Ave. Long Island City NY 11101 718-433-4053 195
TF: 800-645-3244 ■ *Web:* www.pntmarketingservices.com

Pnucor Inc
10525 Granite St PO Box 7209 Charlotte NC 28273 704-588-3333 640
Web: www.pnucor.com

PNWFCU (Pacific NW Federal Credit Union)
12106 NE Marx St Portland OR 97220 503-256-5858 253-5858 219
TF: 866-692-8669 ■ *Web:* www.pnwfcu.org

PNY Technologies Inc
100 Jefferson Rd. Parsippany NJ 07054 973-515-9700 560-5590* 288
**Fax:* Sales ■ *TF:* 800-769-0143 ■ *Web:* www3.pny.com

Po 31 Cornelia St. New York NY 10014 212-645-2189 671
Web: www.porestaurant.com

Phone Fax Class

Poblocki Sign Company LLC
922 S 70th St ... West Allis WI 53214 414-453-4010 453-3070 701
TF: 800-776-7064 ■ *Web:* www.poblocki.com

Pocahontas Aluminum Coinc
2001 Industrial Dr. ... Pocahontas AR 72455 870-892-3689 234
Web: www.pocahontasaluminum.com

Pocahontas County PO Box 275 ... Marlinton WV 24954 800-336-7009 338
TF: 800-336-7009 ■ *Web:* www.pocahontascountywv.com

Pocahontas County
99 Ct Sq County Courthouse ... Pocahontas IA 50574 712-335-4208 338
Web: countycriminal.com/court-records

Pocahontas State Park
10301 State Pk Rd ... Chesterfield VA 23832 804-796-4255 796-4004 565
TF: 800-933-7275 ■ *Web:* www.dcr.virginia.gov

Pocan Mark (Rep D - WI)
1421 Longworth Bldg ... Washington DC 20515 202-225-2906 225-6942 342-2
Web: pocan.house.gov

Pocatello Art Ctr (PAC) 444 N Main St ... Pocatello ID 83204 208-232-0970 50-2
Web: www.pocatelloartctr.org

Pocatello City Hall
911 N Seventh Ave ... Pocatello ID 83201 208-234-6163 234-6297 337
Web: www.pocatello.us

Pocatello Downs
10560 N Fairgrounds Rd ... Pocatello ID 83202 208-238-1721 642
Web: theracingjournal.com

Pocatello Regional Airport
1950 Airport Way PO Box 4169 ... Pocatello ID 83205 208-234-6154 233-8418 27
Web: www.pocatello.us

Pocatello Women's Correctional Ctr
1451 Fore Rd ... Pocatello ID 83204 208-236-6360 236-6362 213
Web: idoc.idaho.gov

Pocatello Zoo 2900 S Second Ave ... Pocatello ID 83204 208-234-6264 823

Pochet of America Inc
415 Hamburg Tpke Ste D21 ... Wayne NJ 07470 973-942-4923 124

Pocino Foods Co
14250 Lomitas Ave ... City of Industry CA 91746 626-968-8000 968-0196 296-26
TF: 800-345-0150 ■ *Web:* www.pocinofoods.com

Pocket Opera 469 Bryant St ... San Francisco CA 94107 415-972-8930 573-2
Web: www.pocketopera.org

PocketiNet Communications Inc
45 Terminal Loop Rd Ste 210 ... Walla Walla WA 99362 509-526-5026 224
TF: 800-996-2209 ■ *Web:* www.pocketinet.com

Poclain Hydraulics Inc PO Box 801 ... Sturtevant WI 53177 262-321-0676 385
Web: www.poclain-hydraulics.com

Pocock Racing Shells 615 80Th St SW ... Everett WA 98203 425-438-9048 698
TF: 888-762-6251 ■ *Web:* www.pocock.com

Pocomoke River State Park
3461 Worcester Hwy ... Snow Hill MD 21863 410-632-2566 632-2914 565
TF: 877-620-8367 ■ *Web:* dnr2.maryland.gov

Pocomoke State Forest
580 Taylor Ave ... Annapolis MD 21401 877-620-8367 565
TF: 877-620-8367 ■ *Web:* dnr2.maryland.gov

Pocono Manor Golf Resort & Spa
1 Manor Dr Rt 314 ... Pocono Manor PA 18349 570-839-7111 839-3407 669
TF: 800-233-8150 ■ *Web:* www.poconomanor.com

Pocono Medical Ctr
206 E Brown St ... East Stroudsburg PA 18301 570-421-4000 476-3469 374-3
Web: www.poconohealthsystem.org

Pocono Mountains Vacation Bureau
1004 Main St ... Stroudsburg PA 18360 570-421-5791 421-6927 206
TF: 800-722-9199 ■ *Web:* www.poconomountains.com

Pocono Raceway
Long Pond Rd PO Box 500 ... Long Pond PA 18334 570-646-2300 646-2010 515
TF: 800-722-3929 ■ *Web:* www.poconoraceway.com

Pocono Record 511 Lenox St ... Stroudsburg PA 18360 570-421-3000 421-6284* 532-2
**Fax:* News Rm ■ *TF:* 800-530-6310 ■ *Web:* www.poconorecord.com

Pod Restaurant 3636 Sansom St ... Philadelphia PA 19104 215-387-1803 671
Web: www.podrestaurant.com

Podaddies Inc
1169 Howard St Ste 203 ... San Francisco CA 94103 415-552-9000 5
Web: www.podaddies.com

Podiatry Insurance Company of America
3000 Meridian Blvd Ste 400 ... Franklin TN 37067 615-984-2005 370-9021 391-5
TF: 800-251-5727 ■ *Web:* www.picagroup.com

Poe Paddy State Park c/o Reeds Gap ... Milroy PA 17063 717-667-3622 565
Web: www.dcnr.state.pa.us

Poe Ted (Rep R - TX)
2132 Rayburn Bldg ... Washington DC 20515 202-225-6565 342-2
Web: poe.house.gov

Poepping Stone Bach & Assoc Inc Engr
100 S 54th St PO Box 709 ... Quincy IL 62305 217-223-4605 727
Web: psba.com

Poet 4615 N Lewis Ave ... Sioux Falls SD 57104 605-965-2200 580
Web: poet.com

Poetry Pals Inc
295 SW Brushy Mound Rd ... Burleson TX 76028 817-295-6680 95
TF: 800-424-3950 ■ *Web:* www.poetrypals.com

Poets & Writers Magazine
90 Broad St Ste 2100 ... New York NY 10004 212-226-3586 226-3963 457-10
Web: www.pw.org

Poggemeyer Design Group Inc
1168 N Main St ... Bowling Green OH 43402 419-352-7537 353-0187 261
Web: www.poggemeyer.com

POH Regional Medical Ctr
50 N Perry St ... Pontiac MI 48342 248-338-5000 338-5667 374-3
TF: 888-327-0671 ■ *Web:* www.mclaren.org

Pohanka of Salisbury
2007 N Salisbury Blvd ... Salisbury MD 21801 410-202-3450 516
Web: www.pohankaofsalisbury.com

Pohlman Inc 140 Long Rd ... Chesterfield MO 63005 636-537-1909 537-1930 621
TF: 800-208-6075 ■ *Web:* www.pohlman.com

Pohly Co 867 Boylston St 5th Fl ... Boston MA 02116 617-451-1700 338-7767 637-9
TF: 800-383-0888 ■ *Web:* www.pohlyco.com

Poinsett County 1500 Justice Dr ... Harrisburg AR 72432 870-578-5411 578-4417 338
Web: www.poinsettcountysheriff.org

Poinsett State Park
6660 Poinsett Pk Rd ... Wedgefield SC 29168 803-494-8177 565
Web: www.southcarolinaparks.com

Point 2 Point Global Security Inc
14346 Jarrettsville Pike Ste 200 ... Phoenix MD 21131 410-638-8788 693
Web: www.p2pgsi.net

Point Alliance Inc
20 Adelaide St E Ste 500 ... Toronto ON M5C2T6 416-943-0001 180
TF: 855-947-6468 ■ *Web:* www.pointalliance.com

Point Au Roche State Park
19 Camp Red Cloud Rd ... Plattsburgh NY 12901 518-563-0369 565
Web: parks.ny.gov/parks/30/details.aspx

Point B Communications
600 W Fulton Ste 710 ... Chicago IL 60661 312-867-7750 193
Web: pointbcommunications.com

Point Beach State Forest
9400 County Hwy O ... Two Rivers WI 54241 920-794-7480 565
Web: dnr.wi.gov/newurl.html

Point Defiance Zoo & Aquarium
5400 N Pearl St ... Tacoma WA 98407 253-591-5337 591-5448 823
Web: www.pdza.org

Point Dume State Beach
1925 Las Virgenes Rd ... Calabasas CA 91302 818-880-0363 565
Web: www.parks.ca.gov/default.asp?page_id=623

Point Eight Power Inc
1510 Engineers Rd ... Belle Chasse LA 70037 504-394-6100 729
Web: www.pointeightpower.com

Point Group, The
5949 Sherry Ln Ste 1800 ... Dallas TX 75225 214-378-7970 466
Web: www.thepointgroup.com

Point Lighting Corp
61 W Dudley Town Rd ... Bloomfield CT 06002 860-243-0600 362
Web: www.pointlighting.com

Point Loma Nazarene University
3900 Lomaland Dr ... San Diego CA 92106 619-849-2200 849-2601* 166
**Fax:* Admissions ■ *TF Admissions:* 800-733-7770 ■ *Web:* www.pointloma.edu

Point Lookout State Park
11175 Pt Lookout Rd ... Scotland MD 20687 301-872-5688 872-5084 565
Web: dnr2.maryland.gov

Point Medical Corp
891 E Summit St ... Crown Point IN 46307 219-663-1775 476
Web: pointmedical.com

Point of Sale System Services Inc
2 Shaker Rd Ste F100 ... Shirley MA 01464 978-425-3003 180
Web: mobilety.pssproducts.com/pssmobilestore

Point Park University 201 Wood St ... Pittsburgh PA 15222 412-391-4100 392-3902* 166
**Fax:* Admissions ■ *TF Admissions:* 800-321-0129 ■ *Web:* www.pointpark.edu

Point Pelee National Park of Canada
407 Monarch Ln RR 1 ... Leamington ON N8H3V4 519-322-2365 322-1277 563
TF: 888-773-8888 ■ *Web:* www.pc.gc.ca/pn-np/on/pelee/index.aspx

Point Plaza Suites & Conference Hotel
950 J Clyde Morris Blvd ... Newport News VA 23601 757-599-4460 599-4336 379
TF: 800-841-1112 ■ *Web:* www.pointplazasuites.com

Point Pleasant Beach Chamber of Commerce
517-A Arnold Ave ... Point Pleasant Beach NJ 08742 732-899-2424 139
Web: pointpleasantbeachchamber.com

Point Reyes National Seashore
1 Bear Valley Rd ... Point Reyes Station CA 94956 415-464-5100 663-8132 564
TF: 877-874-2478 ■ *Web:* www.nps.gov

Point Source Power Inc 132 Tharp Dr ... Moraga CA 94556 925-708-7845 696
Web: www.pointsourcepower.com

Point State Park
101 Commonwealth Pl ... Pittsburgh PA 15222 412-471-0235 565
Web: www.dcnr.state.pa.us

Point Sur State Historic Park
Big Sur Stn Ste 1 ... Big Sur CA 93920 831-625-4419 565
Web: www.parks.ca.gov/default.asp?page_id=565

Point to Point Inc
23240 Chagrin Blvd Ste 200 ... Cleveland OH 44122 216-831-4421 4
Web: www.pointtopoint.com

Point, The PO Box 1327 ... Saranac Lake NY 12983 518-891-5674 891-1152 669
TF: 800-255-3530 ■ *Web:* thepointsaranac.com

Point.360 2701 Media Center Dr ... Los Angeles CA 90065 818-565-1400 847-2503 512
NASDAQ: PTSX ■ *Web:* www.point360.com

PointCare Technologies Inc
19 Brigham St Office 9-A ... Marlborough MA 01752 508-537-9769 476
Web: www.pointcare.net

PointCross Life Sciences
1291 E Hillsdale Blvd Ste 304 ... Foster City CA 94404 650-350-1900 463
Web: pointcross.com

Pointe Capital LLC
501 E Kennedy Blvd Ste 1400 ... Tampa FL 33602 813-202-7960 690

Pointe Coupee Electric Membership Corp
2506 False River Dr PO Box 160 ... New Roads LA 70760 225-638-3751 638-8124 245
TF: 800-738-7232 ■ *Web:* www.pcemc.org

Pointe Coupee Parish 201 E Main St ... New Roads LA 70760 225-638-9596 338
Web: laclerksofcourt.org

Pointe General Contractors LLC
1209 Pointe Ctr Dr Ste 105 ... Chattanooga TN 37421 423-755-0844 186
TF: 800-830-9913 ■ *Web:* www.pointecentre.com

Pointe Hilton at Squaw Peak Resort
7677 N 16th St ... Phoenix AZ 85020 602-997-2626 875-1652* 669
**Fax Area Code:* 281 ■ *TF:* 800-685-0550 ■ *Web:* www3.hilton.com

Pointe Hilton Resort at Tapatio Cliffs
11111 N Seventh St ... Phoenix AZ 85020 602-866-7500 875-1652* 669
**Fax Area Code:* 281 ■ *TF:* 800-947-9784 ■ *Web:* www3.hilton.com

Pointe Scientific Inc
5449 Research Dr PO Box 87188 ... Canton MI 48188 734-487-8300 483-1592 231
TF: 800-445-9853 ■ *Web:* www.pointescientific.com

Pointe Technology Group Inc
7272 Pk Cir Dr Ste 200 ... Hanover MD 21076 410-712-9425 180
Web: www.pointetech.com

Pointe-a-Calliere - The Montreal Museum of Archaeology & History
350 Royale Pl Angle Joint ... Old Montreal QC H2Y3Y5 514-872-9150 872-9151 520
Web: www.pacmusee.qc.ca

Pointivity
5355 Mira Sorrento Pl # 600 ... San Diego CA 92121 858-777-6900 39
Web: www.pointivity.com

Pointon Communications 202 South Blvd ... Baraboo WI 53913 608-355-0257 179
Web: www.pointon.com

Name / Address	City	State	ZIP	Phone	Fax	Class
Points International Ltd 171 John St 5th Fl *Web:* www.points.com	Toronto	ON	M5T1X3	416-595-0000		195
Points North Inc 371 Canal Park Dr Ste 210 *Web:* www.points-north.com	Duluth	MN	55802	218-726-1195		179
Points of Light Foundation & Volunteer Ctr National Network 1400 'I' St NW Ste 800 *TF:* 866-545-5307 ■ *Web:* www.pointsoflight.org	Washington	DC	20005	202-729-8000	729-8100	48-5
Pointwise Inc 213 S Jennings Ave *Web:* www.pointwise.com	Fort Worth	TX	76104	817-377-2807		177
Poisoned Pen Bookstore 4014 N Goldwater Blvd *TF:* 888-560-9919 ■ *Web:* www.poisonedpen.com	Scottsdale	AZ	85251	480-947-2974	945-1023	95
Poka Lambro Telephone Cooperative Inc 560 US Hwy 87 *Web:* www.poka.com	Wilson	TX	79381	806-924-7234		225
Pokagon State Park 450 Ln 100 Lake James *Web:* in.gov/ai/errors/dnr_404.html	Angola	IN	46703	260-833-2012		565
Poke 343 E 85th St *Web:* www.pokesushinyc.com	New York	NY	10028	212-249-0569		671
PokerTek Inc 1150 Crews Rd Ste F *NASDAQ: PTEK* ■ *Web:* www.pokertek.com	Matthews	NC	28105	704-849-0860		322
Polack Corp, The 1400 Keystone Ave *TF:* 800-392-8759 ■ *Web:* www.polackcorp.com	Lansing	MI	48911	517-393-3440		535
Poland 750 Third Ave 30th Fl **Fax Area Code:* 212 ■ *Web:* nowyjorkkonz.msz.gov.pl	New York	NY	10017	646-559-7552	517-6771*	784
Embassy 2640 16th St NW *Web:* www.polandembassy.org	Washington	DC	20009	914-909-1800		257
Polar Air Cargo 2000 Westchester Ave *Web:* www.polaraircargo.com	Purchase	NY	10577	914-701-8000	701-8001	12
Polar Beverages Inc 1001 Southbridge St *TF Cust Svc:* 800-701-0000 ■ *Web:* www.polarbev.com	Worcester	MA	01610	508-753-4300		80-2
Polar Communications 110 Fourth St E *Web:* www.polarcomm.com	Park River	ND	58270	701-284-7221		116
Polar Hardware Manufacturing Co 1813 W Montrose Ave *Web:* www.polarmfg.com	Chicago	IL	60613	773-935-8600	935-8749	350
Polar Instruments Inc 18649 SW Farmington Rd *Web:* www.polarinstruments.com	Beaverton	OR	97007	503-356-5270		177
Polar King International Inc 4424 New Haven Ave *TF:* 800-752-7178 ■ *Web:* www.polarking.com	Fort Wayne	IN	46803	260-428-2530		14
Polar Securities Inc 401 Bay St Ste 1900 PO Box 19 *Web:* polaramp.com	Toronto	ON	M5H2Y4	416-367-4364		528
Polar Service Centers 7600 E Sam Houston Pkwy N *TF:* 800-955-8558 ■ *Web:* www.polartank.com	Houston	TX	77049	281-459-6400		779
Polar Tank Trailer Inc 12810 County Rd 17 *TF:* 800-826-6589 ■ *Web:* www.polartank.com	Holdingford	MN	56340	320-746-2255	746-2937	779
Polar Tech Industries Inc 415 E Railroad Ave *Web:* www.polar-tech.com	Genoa	IL	60135	815-784-9000		124
Polar ware 502 Hgwy 67 *TF:* 800-237-3655 ■ *Web:* polarware.com/polarware.htm	Kiel	WI	53402	800-237-3655		489
Polaris Capital Management LLC 121 High St *TF:* 800-241-1151 ■ *Web:* www.polariscapital.com	Boston	MA	02110	617-951-1365		41
Polaris Career Ctr 7285 Old Oak Blvd *Web:* www.polaris.edu	Cleveland	OH	44130	440-891-7600		165
Polaris Consulting Engineers 214 W Main St 208 *TF:* 800-406-3005 ■ *Web:* www.polarisce.com	Moorestown	NJ	08057	856-778-5400		261
Polaris Engineering Inc 212 Pine St *Web:* www.polarisengr.com	Lake Charles	LA	70601	337-497-0652		186
Polaris Fashion Place 1500 Polaris Pkwy *Web:* www.polarisfashionplace.com	Columbus	OH	43240	614-846-1500		460
Polaris Industries Inc 2100 Hwy 55 *NYSE: PII* ■ *Web:* www.polaris.com	Medina	MN	55340	763-542-0500	542-0599	705
Polaris Machining 103 Cedar Ave *Web:* www.polarismachining.com	Marysville	WA	98270	360-653-7676		454
Polaris Pharmaceuticals Inc 9373 Towne Centre Dr Ste 150 *Web:* www.polarispharma.com	San Diego	CA	92121	858-452-6688		231
Polaris Pool Systems Inc 2620 Commerce Way *TF:* 800-822-7933 ■ *Web:* www.polarispool.com	Vista	CA	92081	760-599-9600		806
Polaris Project PO Box 77892 *TF:* 800-551-1300 ■ *Web:* polarisproject.org	Washington	DC	20013	202-745-1001		533
Polarity Inc 11294 Sunrise Park Dr *Web:* www.polarity.net	Rancho Cordova	CA	95742	916-635-3050		261
PolarSat Inc 549 Meloche Ave *Web:* www.polarsat.com	Dorval	QC	H9P2W2	514-635-0040		647
Polestar Capital Inc 180 N Michigan Ave Ste 1905 *Web:* www.polestarvc.com	Chicago	IL	60601	312-984-9090	984-9877	403
Polhemus Savery DaSilva Architects Builders 157 Brewster-Chatham Rd (Rt 137) *Web:* www.psdab.com	East Harwich	MA	02645	508-945-4500	945-9803	186
Poliac Research Corp 12233 Wood Lake Dr *Web:* www.poliac.com	Burnsville	MN	55337	952-882-1772		809
Police & Fire Federal Credit Union 901 Arch St *TF:* 800-228-8801 ■ *Web:* www.pffcu.org	Philadelphia	PA	19107	215-931-0300		219
Police Executive Research Forum (PERF) 1120 Connecticut Ave NW Ste 930 *Web:* www.policeforum.org	Washington	DC	20036	202-466-7820	466-7826	49-7

Name / Address	City	State	ZIP	Phone	Fax	Class
Police Times Magazine 6350 Horizon Dr *Web:* www.aphf.org	Titusville	FL	32780	321-264-0911	264-0033	457-10
Policemen's Annuity & Benefit Fund of Chicago 221 N LaSalle St Ste 1626 *TF:* 800-656-6606 ■ *Web:* www.chipabf.org	Chicago	IL	60601	312-744-3891		390
Policy Research Associates Inc 345 Delaware Ave *TF:* 800-311-4246 ■ *Web:* www.prainc.com	Delmar	NY	12054	518-439-7415		141
Polihale State Park 3060 Eiwa St Ste 306 *Web:* dlnr.hawaii.gov	Lihue	HI	96766	808-274-3444	274-3448	565
Polimaster Inc 2300 Clarendon Blvd Ste 708 *Web:* www.polimaster.us	Arlington	VA	22201	703-525-5075		407
Poling Law Offices 101 Ramey Ct *Web:* www.poling-law.com	Beckley	WV	25801	304-255-0191		445
Polipoli Spring State Recreation Area 54 S High St Rm 101 *Web:* www.hawaii.gov	Wailuku	HI	96793	808-984-8109	984-8111	565
Poliquin Bruce (Rep R - ME) 1208 Longworth HOB *Web:* poliquin.house.gov	Washington	DC	20515	202-225-6306	225-2943	342-2
Polis Jared (Rep D - CO) 1727 Longworth HOB *Web:* polis.house.gov	Washington	DC	20515	202-225-2161	226-7840	342-2
Polish American Congress 5711 N Milwaukee Ave *TF:* 800-621-3723 ■ *Web:* www.pac1944.org	Chicago	IL	60646	773-763-9944		48-14
Polish American Cultural Ctr Museum 308 Walnut St *TF:* 800-422-1275 ■ *Web:* www.polishamericancenter.org	Philadelphia	PA	19106	215-922-1700	922-1518	520
Polish Museum of America (PMA) 984 N Milwaukee Ave *Web:* www.polishmuseumofamerica.org	Chicago	IL	60642	773-384-3352	384-3799	520
Polish National Alliance of the US of North America 6100 N Cicero Ave *Web:* www.pna-znp.org	Chicago	IL	60646	773-286-0500		391-2
Polish National Tourist Office 5 Marina View Plaza Ste 303b *Web:* www.poland.travel	Hoboken	NJ	07030	201-420-9910	584-9153	775
Polisher Research Institute Abramson Ctr for Jewish Life 1425 Horsham Rd *Web:* www.abramsoncenter.org	North Wales	PA	19454	215-371-1895	371-3015	668
Politics & Prose Bookstore 5015 Connecticut Ave NW *TF:* 800-722-0790 ■ *Web:* www.politics-prose.com	Washington	DC	20008	202-364-1919	966-7532	95
Polk Audio Inc 5601 Metro Dr *TF:* 800-377-7655 ■ *Web:* www.polkaudio.com	Baltimore	MD	21215	410-358-3600	764-5266	52
Polk County 100 Polk County Plaza *Web:* www.co.polk.wi.us	Balsam Lake	WI	54810	715-485-9226	485-9104	338
Polk County 330 W Church St PO Box 9005 *Web:* www.polk-county.net	Bartow	FL	33831	863-534-6000	534-7655	338
Polk County 6239 Hwy 411 PO Box 128 *Web:* www.polkgovernment.com	Benton	TN	37307	423-338-4527	338-4558	330
Polk County 102 E Broadway Ste 6 *Web:* www.polkcountycollector.com	Bolivar	MO	65613	417-326-4032	777-8693	330
Polk County 40 Courthouse St PO Box 308 *Web:* www.polknc.org	Columbus	NC	28722	828-894-3301	894-2263	338
Polk County 816 Marion Ave Ste 210 *Web:* www.co.polk.mn.us	Crookston	MN	56716	218-281-5408	281-3808	338
Polk County 850 Main St *Web:* www.co.polk.or.us	Dallas	OR	97338	503-623-8391	831-3015	338
Polk County 111 Ct Ave *TF:* 800-848-0869 ■ *Web:* www.polkcountyiowa.gov	Des Moines	IA	50309	515-286-3000	323-5225	338
Polk County 101 W Church St *Web:* www.co.polk.tx.us	Livingston	TX	77351	936-327-6804	327-6874	338
Polk County 507 Church Ave	Mena	AR	71953	479-394-8123		338
Polk County PO Box 276 *TF:* 800-501-1754 ■ *Web:* polkcounty.nebraska.gov	Osceola	NE	68651	402-747-5431	747-2656	338
Polk County Chamber of Commerce/Development Authority 133 S Marble St *TF:* 800-473-0060 ■ *Web:* www.polkgeorgia.com	Rockmart	GA	30153	770-684-8760		139
Polk County Convention Complex 730 Third St *Web:* www.iowaeventscenter.com	Des Moines	IA	50309	515-564-8001	564-8001	205
Polk County Rural Public Power District 115 W Third St PO Box 465 *TF:* 888-242-5265 ■ *Web:* www.pcrppd.com	Stromsburg	NE	68666	402-764-4381	764-4382	245
Polk County Travel & Tourism 20 E Mills St PO Box 308 *TF:* 800-440-7848 ■ *Web:* www.nc-mountains.org	Columbus	NC	28722	828-894-2324		206
Polk Regional Juvenile Detention Ctr 2155 Bob Phillips Rd	Bartow	FL	33830	863-534-7090		412
Polk State College 999 Ave H NE **Fax:* Admissions ■ *TF:* 800-590-3428 ■ *Web:* www.polk.edu	Winter Haven	FL	33881	863-297-1000	297-1060*	162
Polk-Burnett Electric Co-op (PBEC) 1001 State Rd 35 *TF:* 800-421-0283 ■ *Web:* www.polkburnett.com	Centuria	WI	54824	715-646-2191	646-2404	245
Pollard Friendly Ford Co 3301 S Loop 289 *Web:* pollardfriendlyford.com	Lubbock	TX	79423	806-797-3441		57
Pollard Memorial Library 401 Merrimack St *Web:* www.pollardml.org	Lowell	MA	01852	978-674-4120		434-3
Pollard, The 2 N Broadway *Web:* www.thepollard.com	Red Lodge	MT	59068	406-446-0001		379
Pollock Paper & Packaging 1 Pollock Pl *TF Cust Svc:* 800-843-7320 ■ *Web:* www.pollockpaper.com	Grand Prairie	TX	75050	972-263-2126	262-4737	559
Pollock Planning Assoc Inc 232 Juniper Way *Web:* www.pollockplanning.com	Mountainside	NJ	07092	908-789-4226		194
Pollock Printing Company Inc 928 Sixth Ave S *TF:* 800-349-1205 ■ *Web:* www.pollockprinting.com	Nashville	TN	37203	615-255-0526		627
Pollstar 4697 W Jacquelyn Ave **Fax:* Edit ■ *TF:* 800-344-7383 ■ *Web:* www.pollstar.com	Fresno	CA	93722	559-271-7900	271-7979*	457-9

Company	City	State	Zip	Phone	Fax	Class
Pollution Control Corp 500 W Country Club Rd *TF:* 800-966-1265 ■ *Web:* www.pollutioncontrolcorp.com	Chickasha	OK	73018	800-966-1265		196
Pollution Probe 150 Ferrand Dr Ste 208 *TF:* 877-926-1907 ■ *Web:* www.pollutionprobe.org	Toronto	ON	M3C3E5	416-926-1907	926-1601	48-13
Polly Hill Arboretum 809 State Rd PO Box 561 *Web:* www.pollyhillarboretum.org	West Tisbury	MA	02575	508-693-9426		97
Polly's Pies Restaurant 17198 Norwalk Blvd *Web:* www.pollyspies.com	Cerritos	CA	90703	562-402-2758		671
Polo Grill 2038 Utica Sq *Web:* www.pologrill.com	Tulsa	OK	74114	918-744-4280	749-7082	671
Polpo 554 Old Post Rd *Web:* www.polporestaurant.com	Greenwich	CT	06830	203-629-1999		671
Polsinelli Shalton Flanigan Suelthaus PC 900 W 48th Pl Ste 900 *TF:* 800-422-0893 ■ *Web:* www.polsinelli.com	Kansas City	MO	64112	816-753-1000	753-1536	428
Polsinello Fuels Inc 241 Riverside Ave Drawer 211 *Web:* www.polsinello.com	Rensselaer	NY	12144	518-463-0084		316
POLY (POLY Languages Institute Inc) 5757 Wilshire Blvd Ste 510 *TF:* 877-738-5787 ■ *Web:* www.polylanguages.com	Los Angeles	CA	90036	323-933-9399	686-5384	423
Poly Cast Inc 14140 SW 72nd Ave Ste 100 *Web:* www.poly-cast.com	Tigard	OR	97224	503-620-9850		596
Poly Cycle Inc 5501 Campbells Run Rd *TF:* 800-394-4333 ■ *Web:* www.polycycle.com	Pittsburgh	PA	15205	412-747-1101	747-0749	454
Poly Expert Inc 850 ave Munck *TF:* 877-384-5060 ■ *Web:* www.polyexpert.com	Laval	QC	H7S1B1	514-384-5060		366
POLY Languages Institute Inc (POLY) 5757 Wilshire Blvd Ste 510 *TF:* 877-738-5787 ■ *Web:* www.polylanguages.com	Los Angeles	CA	90036	323-933-9399	686-5384	423
Poly Molding LLC 96 Fourth Ave *TF:* 800-229-7161 ■ *Web:* polymoldingllc.com	Haskell	NJ	07420	973-835-7161	835-2438	601
Poly Plant Project Inc 3099 N Lima St *Web:* www.polyplantproject.com	Burbank	CA	91504	818-848-2111		261
Poly Processing Company Inc 2201 Old Sterlington Rd *Web:* www.polyprocessing.com	Monroe	LA	71203	318-343-7565		596
Poly Systems Inc 3 Industrial Dr *Web:* www.polysystems.com	Steelville	MO	65565	573-775-3300		596
Poly Tech Diamond Co 4 E St PO Box 6 *Web:* www.polytechdiamond.com	North Attleboro	MA	02760	508-695-3561		697
Poly Vinyl Company Inc 320 Range Line Rd *Web:* www.polyvinyl.com	Kohler	WI	53044	920-467-4685		596
Polyad Services Inc 4170 Shoreline Dr	Earth City	MO	63045	314-506-3135		596
Poly-America Inc 2000 W Marshall Dr *TF:* 800-527-3322 ■ *Web:* www.poly-america.com	Grand Prairie	TX	75051	972-337-7100		66
Polycel Structural Foam Inc 68 County Line Rd *Web:* www.polycel.com	Somerville	NJ	08876	908-722-5254	722-7457	601
Polychem Corp 6277 Heisley Rd *Web:* www.polychem.com	Mentor	OH	44060	440-357-1500		596
Poly-Clip System Corp 1000 Tower Rd *Web:* www.polyclip-usa.com	Mundelein	IL	60060	847-949-2800		429
Polycom Inc 4750 Willow Rd *TF:* 800-765-9266 ■ *Web:* www.polycom.com	Pleasanton	CA	94588	800-765-9266		735
PolyConversions Inc 505 Condit Dr *TF:* 888-893-3330 ■ *Web:* www.polyconversions.com	Rantoul	IL	61866	217-893-3330	893-3003	576
Polycor Inc 139 St-Pierre St *Web:* www.polycor.com	Quebec	QC	G1K8B9	418-692-4695		724
Polydeck Screen Corp 1790 Dewberry Rd *Web:* www.polydeckscreen.com	Spartanburg	SC	29307	864-579-4594		596
Polyengineering Inc 1935 Headland Ave *TF:* 888-793-4700 ■ *Web:* www.polyengineering.com	Dothan	AL	36303	334-793-4700		261
Polyethics Industries Inc 301 Forest Ave N *TF:* 800-461-8952 ■ *Web:* polyethics.com	Orillia	ON	L3V6H9	705-329-2266		600
Polyfil 74 Green Pond Rd *TF:* 866-765-9345 ■ *Web:* www.polyfilcorp.com	Rockaway	NJ	07866	973-627-4070		600
Polyflon Co 1 WillaRd Rd *TF:* 800-829-4444 ■ *Web:* www.polyflon.com	Norwalk	CT	06851	203-840-7555	840-7565	253
Polyform Inc 3125 22nd St SE *Web:* www.plasticextrusion.com	Salem	OR	97302	503-585-0163		599
Polyform Products Co 1901 Estes Ave *TF:* 800-222-1222 ■ *Web:* sculpey.com	Elk Grove Village	IL	60007	847-427-0020		791
Polygenesis Corp 4260 US Hwy 1 Ste 5 *Web:* www.polygenesis.com	Monmouth Junction	NJ	08852	732-355-1001		195
Polygon Co 103 Industrial Pk Dr PO Box 176 *TF:* 800-918-9261 ■ *Web:* www.polygoncomposites.com	Walkerton	IN	46574	574-586-3145	586-7336	602
Polygon Network PO Box 4806 *TF:* 800-221-4435 ■ *Web:* www.polygon.net	Dillon	CO	80435	800-221-4435		393
Polyguard Products Inc PO Box 755 *TF:* 800-541-4994 ■ *Web:* www.polyguardproducts.com	Ennis	TX	75120	972-875-8421	875-9425	745-2
PolyJohn Enterprises Corp 2500 Gaspar Ave *Web:* www.polyjohn.com	Whiting	IN	46394	219-659-1152		610
Polymedco Inc 510 Furnace Dock Rd *TF:* 800-431-2123 ■ *Web:* www.polymedco.com	Cortlandt Manor	NY	10567	914-739-5400	739-5890	231
Polymer Concentrates Inc 179 Woodlawn St *Web:* www.polymerconcentrates.com	Clinton	MA	01510	978-365-7335	368-0438	661
Polymer Conversions Inc 5732 Big Tree Rd	Orchard Park	NY	14127	716-662-8550		608
Polymer Corp 180 Pleasant St *Web:* polymercorporation.com	Rockland	MA	02370	781-871-4606	871-5460	604
Polymer Industries LLC 10526 Alabama Hwy 40 PO Box 32 *TF:* 877-489-0039 ■ *Web:* www.polymerindustries.com	Henagar	AL	35978	256-657-5197		601
Polymer Resources Ltd 656 New Britain Ave *TF:* 800-243-5176 ■ *Web:* www.prlresins.com	Farmington	CT	06032	800-243-5176		596
Polymer Solutions Inc 2903-C Commerce St *TF:* 800-762-2478 ■ *Web:* www.polymersolutions.com	Blacksburg	VA	24060	540-961-4300		317
Polymeric Technology Inc 1900 Marina Blvd	San Leandro	CA	94577	510-895-6001		677
Polymet Alloys Inc 1701 Providence Pk Ste 100 *Web:* www.polymetalloys.com	Birmingham	AL	35242	205-981-2200		492
Polymos Inc 3333 Rue F-X-Tessier	Vaudreuil-Dorion	QC	J7V5V5	450-424-5333		608
Polyneer Inc 259-D Samuel Barnet Blvd *Web:* www.polyneer.com	New Bedford	MA	02745	508-998-5225		677
Polynesian Adventure Tours Inc 2880 Kilihau St **Fax:* Resv ■ *TF:* 800-622-3011 ■ *Web:* www.polyadhawaiitours.com	Honolulu	HI	96819	808-833-3000	833-3473*	760
Polynesian Cultural Ctr 55-370 Kamehameha Hwy *TF:* 800-367-7060 ■ *Web:* www.polynesia.com	Laie	HI	96762	808-293-3005		520
Polynesian Resort, The 615 Ocean Shores Blvd NW *TF:* 800-562-4836 ■ *Web:* www.thepolynesian.com	Ocean Shores	WA	98569	360-289-3361		669
PolyOne Corp 33587 Walker Rd *NYSE: POL* ■ *TF:* 866-765-9663 ■ *Web:* www.polyone.com	Avon Lake	OH	44012	440-930-1000	930-3064	605-2
Poly-Pak Industries Inc 125 Spagnoli Rd *TF:* 800-969-1993 ■ *Web:* www.poly-pak.com	Melville	NY	11747	800-969-1993		66
PolyPeptide Laboratories Inc 365 Maple Ave *TF:* 800-338-4965 ■ *Web:* www.polypeptide.com	Torrance	CA	90503	310-782-3569		231
PolyPortables Inc 99 Crafton Dr *Web:* www.polyportables.com	Dahlonega	GA	30533	706-864-3776		350
PolyQuest Inc 1985 Eastwood Rd Ste 206 *Web:* www.polyquest.com	Wilmington	NC	28403	910-342-9554		5
Polysciences Inc 400 Valley Rd *TF Cust Svc:* 800-523-2575 ■ *Web:* www.polysciences.com	Warrington	PA	18976	215-343-6484	343-0214	231
Poly-Seal Corp 1810 Portal St	Baltimore	MD	21224	410-633-1990		596
PolySource LLC 3730 S Elizabeth St Ste B *TF:* 866-558-5300 ■ *Web:* www.polysource.net	Independence	MO	64057	816-540-5300		690
Polyspede Electronics Company Inc 6770 Twin Hills Ave *TF:* 888-476-5944 ■ *Web:* www.polyspede.com	Dallas	TX	75231	214-363-7245	363-7245	518
Poly-Tainer Inc 450 W Los Angeles Ave *Web:* www.polytainer.com	Simi Valley	CA	93065	805-526-3424	526-3430	98
Polytec Products Corp 1190 Obrien Dr *Web:* polytecproducts.com	Menlo Park	CA	94025	650-322-7555		608
Poly-Tech Dental Studio 868 N Garfield Ave *Web:* dentallabspoly-tech.com	Montebello	CA	90640	323-890-9004		415
Polytechnic University *Long Island* 105 Maxess Rd **Fax:* Admissions ■ *TF Admissions:* 877-503-7659 ■ *Web:* engineering.nyu.edu	Melville	NY	11747	631-755-4300	755-4404*	166
Polytex 820 E 140th St *Web:* www.polytexink.com	Bronx	NY	10454	718-402-2000		388
Polytop Corp 110 Graham Dr	Slatersville	RI	02876	401-767-2400		154
Polytron Corp 4400 Wyland Dr *TF:* 888-228-0246 ■ *Web:* www.polytron-corp.com	Elkhart	IN	46516	574-522-0246	522-0457	203
Polytype America Corp 10 Industrial Ave *Web:* www.wifag-polytype.com	Mahwah	NJ	07430	201-995-1000	995-1080	627
Polyurethane Manufacturers Assn (PMA) 6737 W Washington St Ste 1420 *TF:* 800-937-8461 ■ *Web:* www.pmahome.org	Milwaukee	WI	53214	414-431-3094		49-13
Poly-Vac Inc 253 Abby Rd	Manchester	NH	03103	603-647-7822	647-7877	476
Polyvel Inc 100 Ninth St *Web:* www.polyvel.com	Hammonton	NJ	08037	609-567-0080		608
Polyvinyl Films Inc PO Box 753 *TF:* 800-343-6134 ■ *Web:* www.stretchtite.com	Sutton	MA	01590	508-865-3558	865-1562	600
PolyVision Corp 10700 Abbotts Bridge Rd Ste 100 *TF:* 888-325-6351 ■ *Web:* www.polyvision.com	Johns Creek	GA	30097	678-542-3100	542-3200	173-1
Polywest Ltd 110-3240 Idylwyld Dr N *Web:* www.polywest.ca	Saskatoon	SK	S7L5Y7	306-956-7788		770
Polyzen Inc 1041 Classic Rd *Web:* www.polyzen.com	Apex	NC	27539	919-319-9599		476
POM Inc 200 S Elmira Ave PO Box 430 *TF:* 800-331-7275 ■ *Web:* www.pom.com	Russellville	AR	72802	479-968-2880		495
Poma Holding Company Inc 571 W Slover Ave	Bloomington	CA	92316	909-877-2441	877-2006	580
POMC (Parents of Murdered Children) 4960 Ridge Ave Ste 2 *TF:* 888-818-7662 ■ *Web:* www.pomc.com	Cincinnati	OH	45209	513-721-5683	345-4489	48-6
POMCO 2425 James St *TF:* 855-247-0353 ■ *Web:* www.pomco.com	Syracuse	NY	13206	315-432-9171	432-1689	390
Pomerado Hospital 15615 Pomerado Rd *TF:* 800-460-5501 ■ *Web:* www.palomarhealth.org	Poway	CA	92064	858-613-4000		374-3
Pomerantz Marketing 175 Admiral Cochrane Dr Ste 104 *Web:* www.pomagency.com	Annapolis	MD	21401	410-216-9447	216-9320	7
Pomeroy IT Solutions Inc 1020 Petersburg Rd *TF:* 800-846-8727 ■ *Web:* www.pomeroy.com	Hebron	KY	41048	859-586-0600	586-4414	180
Pomfret School 398 Pomfret St PO Box 128 *Web:* www.pomfretschool.org	Pomfret	CT	06258	860-963-6100	963-2042	622
Pomme de Terre State Park Hwy 64B *Web:* www.mostateparks.com	Pittsburg	MO	65724	417-852-4291		565

Name / Address	City	State	Zip	Phone	Fax	Class
Pomona Box Co 301 W Imperial Hwy PO Box 536 *TF:* 800-524-6629 ■ *Web:* www.pomonabox.com	La Habra	CA	90631	714-871-0932		200
Pomona Capital 780 Third Ave 46th Fl *Web:* www.pomonacapital.com	New York	NY	10017	212-593-3639		792
Pomona Chamber of Commerce 101 W Mission Blvd Ste 223 *Web:* www.pomonachamber.org	Pomona	CA	91766	909-622-8484	620-5986	139
Pomona College 333 N College Way *Fax: Admissions ■ *Web:* www.pomona.edu	Claremont	CA	91711	909-621-8134	621-8952*	166
Pomona Public Library 625 S Garey Ave	Pomona	CA	91766	909-620-2043		434-3
Pomona State Park 22900 S Hwy 368 *Web:* ksoutdoors.com/State-Parks/Locations/Pomona	Vassar	KS	66543	785-828-4933		565
Pomona Valley Hospital Medical Ctr 1798 N Garey Ave *Web:* www.pvhmc.org	Pomona	CA	91767	909-865-9500		374-3
Pompaction Inc 119 Blvd Hymus *TF:* 800-461-8870 ■ *Web:* www.pompaction.com	Pointe-claire	QC	H9R1E5	514-697-8600		358
Pompano Beach Amphitheater 1801 NE Sixth St *TF:* 800-745-3000 ■ *Web:* Www.theamppompano.org	Pompano Beach	FL	33060	954-519-5500		572
Pompanoosuc Mills 3184 Rte 5 S *TF:* 800-757-4061 ■ *Web:* www.pompy.com	East Thetford	VT	05043	800-841-6671		361
Pomperaug Woods 80 Heritage Rd *Web:* www.pomperaugwoods.com	Southbury	CT	06488	203-262-6555		672
Pomps Tire Service Inc 1123 Cedar St *TF:* 800-236-8911 ■ *Web:* www.pompstire.com	Green Bay	WI	54301	920-435-8301		755
Ponca City Area Chamber of Commerce 420 E Grand Ave *TF:* 866-763-8092 ■ *Web:* www.poncacitychamber.com	Ponca City	OK	74601	580-765-4400	765-2798	139
Ponca City Library 515 E Grand Ave *Web:* www.poncacityok.gov/index.aspx?nid=155	Ponca City	OK	74601	580-767-0345	767-0374	434-3
Ponca City Publishing Inc 300 N Third St *TF:* 866-765-3311 ■ *Web:* www.poncacity.com	Ponca City	OK	74601	580-765-3311	762-6397	637-8
Ponca City Tourism 420 E Grand Ave PO Box 1109 *TF:* 866-763-8092 ■ *Web:* visitponcacity.com	Ponca City	OK	74602	580-765-4400		206
Ponca State Park 88090 Spur 26 E *Web:* www.outdoornebraska.ne.gov/parks	Ponca	NE	68770	402-755-2284		565
Ponca Tribe 2602 J St *Web:* www.poncatribe-nc.org	Omaha	NE	68107	402-734-5275		418
Ponce Bank 2244 Westchester Ave *Web:* www.poncedeleonbank.com	Bronx	NY	10462	718-931-9000	542-9733	71
Ponce de Leon Springs State Park 2860 Ponce de Leon Springs Rd *Web:* www.floridastateparks.org	Ponce de Leon	FL	32455	850-836-4281		565
Ponce de Leon's Fountain of Youth 11 Magnolia Ave *TF:* 800-350-8222 ■ *Web:* www.fountainofyouthflorida.com	Saint Augustine	FL	32084	904-829-3168		50-3
Pond & Co 3500 Pkwy Ln Ste 600 *Web:* pondco.com	Norcross	GA	30092	678-336-7740		261
Pond House Cafe 1555 Asylum Ave *Web:* www.pondhousecafe.com	West Hartford	CT	06117	860-231-8823	231-8731	671
Ponder Pro Service 202 Moore Rd *Web:* www.ponderproserve.com	Griffin	GA	30223	770-490-2767		809
Pondera County 20 Fourth Ave SW *Web:* www.ponderacountymontana.org	Conrad	MT	59425	406-271-4000	271-4070	338
Ponderosa Motor Inn 1206 Trans Canada Hwy *Web:* www.ponderosamotorinn.bc.ca	Golden	BC	V0A1H0	250-344-2205		378
Ponderosa State Park 1920 N Davis Ave *Web:* parksandrecreation.idaho.gov/parks/ponderosa	McCall	ID	83638	208-634-2164		565
Pong Studios 201 Creditview Rd *Web:* www.pongstudios.com	Woodbridge	ON	L4L9T1	905-264-3555		387
Poniard Pharmaceuticals Inc 750B Attery St Ste 330 *OTC: PARD*	South San Francisco	CA	94111	650-583-3774		85
Pontarelli Limousine Service 2225 W Hubbard St *TF:* 800-322-5466 ■ *Web:* www.pontarellischicago.com	Chicago	IL	60612	312-226-5466	226-1300	441
Pontchartrain 2031 St Charles Ave *TF:* 800-708-6652 ■ *Web:* thepontchartrainhotel.com	New Orleans	LA	70130	800-708-6652		379
Pontchartrain Ctr 4545 Williams Blvd *TF:* 800-745-3000 ■ *Web:* www.pontchartraincenter.com	Kenner	LA	70065	504-465-9985	468-6692	205
Pontchartrain Materials Corp 3819 France Rd *Web:* www.pontchartrain.com	New Orleans	LA	70126	504-949-7571		183
Ponte Vedra Inn & Club 200 Ponte Vedra Blvd *TF:* 800-234-7842 ■ *Web:* www.pontevedra.com	Ponte Vedra Beach	FL	32082	904-285-1111	285-1111	669
Pontiac Coil Inc 5000 Moody Dr *Web:* www.pontiaccoil.com	Clarkston	MI	48348	248-922-1100		567
Pontiac Correctional Ctr 700 W Lincoln St *TF:* 800-275-7877 ■ *Web:* www.illinois.gov	Pontiac	IL	61764	815-842-2816	842-3420	213
Pontiac Lake Recreation Area 7800 Gale Rd *Web:* www.michigandnr.com	Waterford	MI	48327	248-666-1020		565
Pontiac Public Library 60 E Pike St *TF:* 800-894-3592 ■ *Web:* www.pontiac.lib.mi.us	Pontiac	MI	48342	248-758-3942	758-3990	434-3
Pontiac Regional Chamber of Commerce 402 N Telegraph Rd *TF:* 800-477-3172 ■ *Web:* www.pontiacchamber.com	Pontiac	MI	48341	248-335-9600		139
Pontifical College Josephinum 7625 N High St *TF:* 888-252-5812 ■ *Web:* www.pcj.edu	Columbus	OH	43235	614-885-5585	885-2307	167-3
Pontis Research Inc 4195 E Thousand Oaks Blvd Ste 105 *Web:* www.pontisresearch.com	Westlake Village	CA	91362	805-777-7424		693
Pontotoc County 301 S Broadway Ave	Ada	OK	74820	580-332-1425		338
Pontotoc County 34 S Liberty St PO Box 209	Pontotoc	MS	38863	662-489-3900		338
Pontotoc Electric Power Assn 12 S Main St *Web:* www.pepa.com	Pontotoc	MS	38863	662-489-3211	489-5156	245
Ponvia Technology Inc 49-T Sherwood Terr *TF:* 877-217-0875 ■ *Web:* www.ponvia.com	Lake Bluff	IL	60045	877-217-0875		449
PONY Baseball/Softball Inc 1951 Pony Pl PO Box 225 *TF:* 800-853-2414 ■ *Web:* www.pony.org	Washington	PA	15301	724-225-1060	225-9852	48-22
Pony Express National Museum 914 Penn St *TF:* 800-530-5930 ■ *Web:* www.ponyexpress.org	Saint Joseph	MO	64503	816-279-5059	233-9370	520
Poogan's Porch 72 Queen St *Web:* www.poogansporch.com	Charleston	SC	29401	843-577-2337		671
Pool 4 Tool America LLC 34119 W 12 Mile Rd Ste 320 *Web:* www.pool4tool.com	Farmington Hills	MI	48331	248-244-0851		225
Pool Management Group Inc 1210 Warsaw Rd Ste 900 *Web:* www.poolmanagementgroup.com	Roswell	GA	30076	770-993-4665		463
Poole & Kent Corp 4530 Hollins Ferry Rd *TF:* 800-468-0851 ■ *Web:* www.poole-kent.com	Baltimore	MD	21227	410-247-2200	247-2331	189-10
Poolmaster Inc 770 Del Paso Rd *TF:* 800-854-1492 ■ *Web:* www.poolmaster.com	Sacramento	CA	95834	916-567-9800	567-9880	710
Poolpak Technologies Corp 3491 Industrial Dr *Web:* www.poolpak.com	York	PA	17402	717-757-2648		14
Poor Boy's Gourmet 300 Main St *Web:* www.poorboysgourmet.com	Bar Harbor	ME	04609	207-288-4148		671
Poor Boys Steakhouse 739 N Ctr St *Web:* poorboyssteakhouse.com	Casper	WY	82601	307-237-8325		671
POP Displays USA LLC 555 Tuckahoe Rd *Web:* www.diam-int.com	Yonkers	NY	10710	914-771-4200		5
Pop Warner Little Scholars Inc 586 Middletown Blvd Ste C-100 *TF:* 800-257-4268 ■ *Web:* www.popwarner.com	Langhorne	PA	19047	215-752-2691	752-2879	48-22
Popcorn Board 401 N Michigan Ave *TF:* 800-795-3272 ■ *Web:* www.popcorn.org	Chicago	IL	60611	312-644-6610		49-6
Pope County 130 E Minnesota Ave *Web:* www.mncounties.org	Glenwood	MN	56334	320-634-5727		338
Pope County 100 W Main *Web:* popecountyar.com	Russellville	AR	72801	479-968-6064	967-2291	338
Pope County Elementary/Jr. High School 125 State Hwy 146 W *Web:* es.popek12.org	Golconda	IL	62938	618-683-4011	683-6022	338
Pope County Library System 116 E Third St *Web:* popelibrary.org	Russellville	AR	72801	479-968-4368	968-3222	434-3
Pope John Paul Ii High School Office 1901 Jaguar Dr *Web:* pjp.org	Slidell	LA	70461	985-649-0914		685
Pope Scientific Inc 351 N Dekora Woods Blvd *Web:* www.popeinc.com	Saukville	WI	53080	262-268-9300		292
Popejoy Hall UNM Public Events Popejoy Hall UNM Ctr for the Arts MSC 04 2580 *Web:* www.popejoypresents.com	Albuquerque	NM	87131	505-277-3824	277-7353	572
Pope-Leighey House 9000 Richmond Hwy *Web:* www.popeleighey1940.org	Alexandria	VA	22309	703-780-4000		50-3
Popeyes Louisiana Kitchen 5555 Glenridge Connector NE Ste 300 *TF:* 800-322-2885 ■ *Web:* www.popeyes.com	Atlanta	GA	30342	404-459-4450		670
Popham Beach State Park 10 Perkins Farm Ln *Web:* www.maine.gov	Phippsburg	ME	04562	207-389-1335		565
Poplar Bluff Regional Medical Ctr 2620 N Westwood Blvd *TF:* 855-444-7276 ■ *Web:* www.poplarbluffregional.com	Poplar Bluff	MO	63901	573-785-7721		374-3
Poplar Bluff Regional Medical Ctr South Campus 3100 Oak Grove Rd *TF:* 855-444-7276 ■ *Web:* www.poplarbluffregional.com	Poplar Bluff	MO	63901	855-444-7276		374-3
Poplar Forest Capital LLC 70 S Lake Ave Ste 930 *Web:* www.poplarforestllc.com	Pasadena	CA	91101	626-304-6000		528
Poplar Springs Hospital 350 Poplar Dr *Fax: Admitting ■ *TF:* 866-546-2229 ■ *Web:* www.poplarsprings.com	Petersburg	VA	23805	804-733-6874	862-6322*	374-5
Popp Communications 620 Mendelssohn Ave N *Web:* www.popp.com	Golden Valley	MN	55427	763-797-7900		387
Popular Mechanics Magazine 300 W 57th St *Web:* www.popularmechanics.com	New York	NY	10019	212-649-2904		457-14
Popular Woodworking Magazine 4700 E Galbraith Rd *TF Cust Svc:* 877-860-9140 ■ *Web:* www.popularwoodworking.com	Cincinnati	OH	45236	513-531-2690		457-14
Population Action International (PAI) 1300 19th St NW Ste 200 *Web:* pai.org	Washington	DC	20036	202-557-3400	728-4177	48-5
Population Communication 1250 E Walnut St Ste 220 *TF:* 800-515-0839 ■ *Web:* populationcommunication.com	Pasadena	CA	91106	626-793-4750	793-4791	48-5
Population Connection 2120 L St NW Ste 500 *TF:* 800-767-1956 ■ *Web:* www.populationconnection.org	Washington	DC	20037	202-332-2200	332-2302	48-5
Population Council 1 Dag Hammarskjold Plaza 9th Fl *Web:* www.popcouncil.org	New York	NY	10017	212-339-0500	755-6052	668
Population Reference Bureau (PRB) 1875 Connecticut Ave NW Ste 520 *TF:* 800-877-9881 ■ *Web:* www.prb.org	Washington	DC	20009	202-483-1100	328-3937	48-7
Population Research Ctr 123 W Way Fl 2 *Web:* popcenter.uchicago.edu	Chicago	IL	60637	773-256-6315	256-6313	668
Population Research Institute Pennsylvania State University 601 Oswald Tower *Web:* www.pop.psu.edu	University Park	PA	16802	814-865-0486	863-8342	668

				Phone	Fax	Class
Population Resource Ctr (PRC) 1725 K St NW	Washington	DC	20006	202-467-5030		48-5
TF: 800-999-6779 ■ *Web:* prcdc.org						
Population Services International (PSI) 1120 19th St NW Ste 600	Washington	DC	20036	202-785-0072	785-0120	48-17
Web: www.psi.org						
Population-Environment Balance Inc 2000 P St NW Ste 600	Washington	DC	20036	202-955-5700	955-6161	48-7
TF: 800-866-6269 ■ *Web:* www.balance.org						
Populus Group LLC 3001 W Big Beaver Rd Suite 400	Troy	MI	48084	248-712-7900	928-0530	195
Web: www.populusgroup.com						
Poquoson 500 City Hall Ave	Poquoson	VA	23662	757-868-3000	868-3101	338
Web: www.ci.poquoson.va.us						
Por La Mar Nursery Inc 905 S Patterson Ave	Santa Barbara	CA	93160	805-699-4500		323
Web: www.porlamarnursery.com						
Por Mor Construction 2901 S Sante Fe Dr	Englewood	CO	80110	303-789-1551		697
Web: www.pormor.com						
Porcini 2730 Frankfort Ave	Louisville	KY	40206	502-894-8686		671
Web: www.porcinilouisville.com						
Porcupine Mountains Wilderness State Park 33303 Headquarters Rd	Ontonagon	MI	49953	906-885-5275		565
Web: www.michigandnr.com						
Poretta & Orr Inc 450 East St	Doylestown	PA	18901	215-345-1515		7
Web: www.porettaorr.com						
Porex Technologies Corp 500 Bohannon Rd	Fairburn	GA	30213	770-964-1421	969-0954	608
TF Cust Svc: 800-241-0195 ■ *Web:* www.porex.com						
Pork Report 1776 NW 114th St	Des Moines	IA	50325	515-223-2600	223-2646	457-1
TF: 800-456-7675 ■ *Web:* www.pork.org						
Porker's BBQ 1251 Market St	Chattanooga	TN	37402	423-267-2726		671
Porky Products Corp 400 Port Carteret Dr	Carteret	NJ	07008	732-541-0200	969-6110	297-9
TF General: 888-674-6854						
Porsche Cars North America Inc 980 Hammond Dr Ste 1000	Atlanta	GA	30328	770-290-3500	290-3708	59
TF: 800-505-1041 ■ *Web:* www.porsche.com/usa						
Porsche St. Paul 2780 Maplewood Dr	Maplewood	MN	55109	651-691-4810		57
Web: www.porscheofstpaul.com						
Port & Company CPA'S 5730 Commons Park Dr	East Syracuse	NY	13057	315-449-1200		2
Port Alberni Port Authority 2750 Harbour Rd	Port Alberni	BC	V9Y7X2	250-723-5312	723-1114	618
TF: 800-688-6840 ■ *Web:* portalberniportauthority.ca						
Port Angeles Coast Guard Air Station Ediz Hook Rd	Port Angeles	WA	98362	360-417-5840		158
TF: 800-982-8813 ■ *Web:* www.uscg.mil						
Port Arthur 11137 Warwick Blvd	Newport News	VA	23601	757-599-6474		671
Web: www.portarthurva.com						
Port Arthur Convention & Visitors Bureau 3401 Cultural Ctr Dr	Port Arthur	TX	77642	409-985-7822		206
TF: 800-235-7822 ■ *Web:* www.portarthurtexas.com						
Port Arthur News 3501 Turtle Creek Dr # 105	Port Arthur	TX	77642	409-729-6397	724-6840	532-2
TF: 800-661-9036 ■ *Web:* www.panews.com						
Port Arthur Public Library 4615 Ninth Ave	Port Arthur	TX	77642	409-985-8838	985-5969	434-3
Web: www.pap.lib.tx.us						
Port Authority of Allegheny County 345 Sixth Ave 3rd Fl	Pittsburgh	PA	15222	412-566-5500		468
Web: www.portauthority.org						
Port Authority of New York/New Jersey 225 Pk Ave S 15th Fl	New York	NY	10003	212-435-7000		618
Web: www.panynj.gov						
Port Canaveral 445 Challanger Rd	Cape Canaveral	FL	32920	321-783-7831	784-6223	618
TF: 888-767-8226 ■ *Web:* www.portcanaveral.com						
Port City Java Inc 101 Portwatch Way	Wilmington	NC	28412	910-796-6646		296-7
Web: www.portcityjava.com						
Port Colborne-Wainfleet Chamber of Commerce 76 Main St W	Port Colborne	ON	L3K3V2	905-834-9765	834-1542	137
Web: www.pcwchamber.com						
Port Columbus International Airport 4600 International Gateway	Columbus	OH	43219	614-239-4000		27
Web: www.columbusairports.com						
Port Consolidated Inc 3141 SE 14th Ave	Fort Lauderdale	FL	33316	954-522-1182		579
Web: www.portconsolidated.com						
Port Coquitlam Senior Citizens' Housing Society 2111 Hawthorne Ave	Port Coquitlam	BC	V3C1W3	604-941-4051		371
TF: 800-651-1067 ■ *Web:* www.hawthornecare.com						
Port Crescent State Park 1775 Port Austin Rd	Port Austin	MI	48467	989-738-8663		565
Web: www.michigandnr.com						
Port Discovery Children's Museum in Baltimore 35 Market Pl	Baltimore	MD	21202	410-727-8120	727-3042	521
Web: www.portdiscovery.org						
Port Erie Plastics Inc 909 Troupe Rd	Harborcreek	PA	16421	814-899-7602	899-7854	604
Web: www.porterie.com						
Port Everglades 1850 Eller Dr	Fort Lauderdale	FL	33316	954-523-3404	525-1910	618
TF: 800-421-0188 ■ *Web:* www.porteverglades.org						
Port Freeport 1001 N Gulf Blvd	Freeport	TX	77541	979-233-2667	233-5625	618
TF: 800-362-5743 ■ *Web:* www.portfreeport.com						
Port Harbor Marine 1 Spring Point Dr	South Portland	ME	04106	207-767-3254	767-5940	90
Web: www.portharbormarine.com						
Port Health Care 113 Low St	Newburyport	MA	01950	978-462-7373	462-6510	450
Web: whittierhealth.com						
Port Hudson National Cemetery 20978 Port Hickey Rd	Zachary	LA	70791	225-654-3767		136
Web: www.cem.va.gov						
Port Huron Hospital (PHH) 1221 Pine Grove Ave	Port Huron	MI	48060	810-987-5000	502-1567*	374-3
**Fax Area Code:* 877 ■ *TF:* 888-327-0671 ■ *Web:* www.mclaren.org/porthuron/porthuron.aspx						
Port Isabel Lighthouse State Historic Site 421 E Queen Isabella Blvd	Port Isabel	TX	78578	956-943-2262		565
Web: tpwd.texas.gov/state-parks/port-isabel-lighthouse						
Port Jervis City School District 9 Thompson St	Port Jervis	NY	12771	845-858-3100		186
Web: www.pjschools.org						
Port Kashdin & Mcsherry CPAs 111 W Rd	Cortland	NY	13045	607-756-5681		2
Web: pkmcpa.com						
Port Lavaca Wave 107 E Austin St	Port Lavaca	TX	77979	361-552-9788		532-3
Web: www.portlavacawave.com						
Port Ludlow Assoc LLC 70 Breaker Ln	Port Ludlow	WA	98365	360-437-2101		379
Web: portludlowresort.com						
Port Metro Vancouver 999 Canada Pl	Vancouver	BC	V6C3T4	604-665-9000	284-4271*	618
**Fax Area Code:* 866 ■ *TF:* 888-767-8826 ■ *Web:* www.portvancouver.com						
Port of Albany *Albany Port District Commission* 106 Smith Blvd	Albany	NY	12202	518-463-8763	463-8767	618
Web: www.portofalbany.us						
Port of Anacortes 100 Commercial Ave	Anacortes	WA	98221	360-293-3134	293-9608	618
TF: 800-874-4434 ■ *Web:* www.portofanacortes.com						
Port of Anchorage 2000 Anchorage Port Rd	Anchorage	AK	99501	907-343-6200		618
TF: 877-650-8400 ■ *Web:* www.muni.org						
Port of Astoria 422 Gateway Ave	Astoria	OR	97103	503-325-4521	325-4525	618
TF: 800-860-4093 ■ *Web:* www.portofastoria.com						
Port of Baltimore *Maryland Port Administration* 401 E Pratt St	Baltimore	MD	21202	800-638-7519		618
TF General: 800-638-7519 ■ *Web:* www.mpa.maryland.gov						
Port of Beaumont 1225 Main St	Beaumont	TX	77701	409-835-5367	832-9592	618
Web: www.portofbeaumont.com						
Port of Belledune 112 Shannon Dr	Belledune	NB	E8G2W2	506-522-1200		342
Web: www.portofbelledune.ca						
Port of Bellingham 1801 Roeder Ave	Bellingham	WA	98225	360-676-2500	671-6411	618
Web: www.portofbellingham.com						
Port of Brownsville 1000 Foust Rd	Brownsville	TX	78521	956-831-4592	831-5006	618
TF: 800-378-5395 ■ *Web:* www.portofbrownsville.com						
Port of Burns Harbor 6625 S Boundary Dr	Portage	IN	46368	219-787-8636		618
Web: www.portsofindiana.com						
Port of Call 838 Esplanade Ave	New Orleans	LA	70116	504-523-0120		671
Web: portofcallnola.com						
Port of Corpus Christi 222 Power St	Corpus Christi	TX	78401	361-882-5633	882-7110	618
TF: 800-580-7110 ■ *Web:* www.portofcc.com						
Port of Duluth *Duluth Seaway Port Authority* 1200 Port Terminal Dr	Duluth	MN	55802	218-727-8525	727-6888	618
TF: 800-232-0703 ■ *Web:* www.duluthport.com						
Port of Everett 2911 Bond St Ste 202	Everett	WA	98201	425-259-3164	252-7366	618
TF: 800-729-7678 ■ *Web:* www.portofeverett.com						
Port of Galveston 123 25th St	Galveston	TX	77550	409-765-9321	766-6107	618
Web: www.portofgalveston.com						
Port of Grays Harbor 111 S Wooding St	Aberdeen	WA	98520	360-533-9528	533-9505	618
TF: 800-321-1924 ■ *Web:* www.portofgraysharbor.com						
Port of Greater Baton Rouge *Greater Baton Rouge Port Commission* 2425 Ernest Wilson Dr PO Box 380	Port Allen	LA	70767	225-342-1660	342-1666	618
TF: 800-342-8012 ■ *Web:* www.portgbr.com						
Port of Homer 4350 Homer Spit Rd	Homer	AK	99603	907-235-3160	235-3152	618
TF: 800-992-4960 ■ *Web:* www.cityofhomer-ak.gov						
Port of Houston 111 E Loop N	Houston	TX	77029	713-670-2400	671-0359	618
Web: www.portofhouston.com						
Port of Iberia 4611 S Lewis St PO Box 9986	New Iberia	LA	70560	337-364-1065	364-3136	618
Web: www.portofiberia.com						
Port of Jacksonville *Jacksonville Port Authority* 2831 Talleyrand Ave PO Box 3005	Jacksonville	FL	32206	904-357-3000	357-3060	618
TF: 800-874-8050 ■ *Web:* www.jaxport.com						
Port of Lake Charles 150 Marine St	Lake Charles	LA	70601	337-439-3661	493-3523	618
Web: www.portlc.com						
Port of Long Beach 925 Harbor Plaza	Long Beach	CA	90801	562-437-0041	901-1725	618
TF: 800-342-8012 ■ *Web:* www.polb.com						
Port of Longview 10 Port Way	Longview	WA	98632	360-425-3305	425-8650	618
Web: www.portoflongview.com						
Port of Los Angeles 425 S Palos Verdes St	San Pedro	CA	90731	310-732-7678		618
Web: www.portoflosangeles.org						
Port of Miami Dante B Fascell 1015 N America Way	Miami	FL	33132	305-371-7678	347-4843	618
Web: www.miamidade.gov						
Port of Miami Terminal Operating Company LC 1007 N America Way Suite 400	Miami	FL	33132	305-416-7600	374-6724	465
Web: www.pomtoc.com						
Port of Milwaukee 2323 S Lincoln Memorial Dr	Milwaukee	WI	53207	414-286-3511	286-8506	618
TF: 800-367-5690 ■ *Web:* city.milwaukee.gov/port						
Port of Mobile *Alabama State Docks Dept* 250 N Water St	Mobile	AL	36602	251-441-7203	441-7216	618
Web: www.asdd.com						
Port of Monroe *Monroe Port Commission* 2929 E Front St PO Box 585	Monroe	MI	48161	734-241-6480		618
Web: www.portofmonroe.com						
Port of New London *Connecticut Bureau of Aviation & Ports* State Pier	New London	CT	06320	860-443-3856		618
Web: www.ct.gov						
Port of New Orleans 1350 Port of New Orleans Pl	New Orleans	LA	70130	504-522-2551	524-4156	618
TF: 800-776-6652 ■ *Web:* www.portno.com						

Phone Fax Class

Port of Newport 600 SE Bay Blvd .... Newport OR 97365 541-265-7758 265-4235 618
Web: www.portofnewport.com

Port of Nome 307 Belmont St .... Nome AK 99762 907-443-6619 443-5473 618
Web: www.nomealaska.org

Port of Oakland 530 Water St .... Oakland CA 94607 510-627-1100 618
TF: 800-342-5397 ■ *Web:* www.portoakland.com

Port of Olympia 915 Washington St NE .... Olympia WA 98501 360-528-8000 528-8090 618
Web: www.portolympia.com

Port of Orange
Orange County Navigation Port District
1201 Childers Rd. .... Orange TX 77630 409-883-4363 883-5607 618
TF: 800-368-3749 ■ *Web:* www.portoforange.com

Port of Oswego Authority 1 E Second St .... Oswego NY 13126 315-343-4503 343-5498 618
Web: www.portoswego.com

Port of Palm Beach
1 E 11th St Ste 600 .... Riviera Beach FL 33404 561-842-4201 842-4240 618
TF: 877-377-1737 ■ *Web:* www.portofpalmbeach.com

Port of Pascagoula
Jackson County Port Authority
3033 Pascagoula St .... Pascagoula MS 39567 228-762-4041 762-7476 618
Web: www.portofpascagoula.com

Port of Pensacola 700 S Barracks St .... Pensacola FL 32502 850-436-5070 436-5076 618
TF: 800-711-1712 ■ *Web:* www.portofpensacola.com

Port of Pittsburgh
4955 Steubenville Pk Ste 245A .... Pittsburgh PA 15205 412-201-7330 722-1190 618
Web: www.port.pittsburgh.pa.us

Port of Port Angeles
338 W First St PO Box 1350 .... Port Angeles WA 98362 360-457-8527 452-3959 618
Web: www.portofpa.com

Port of Port Arthur
221 Houston Ave .... Port Arthur TX 77640 409-983-2011 983-7572 618
Web: portpa.com

Port of Port Lavaca-Point Comfort
Calhoun Port Authority
PO Box 397 .... Point Comfort TX 77978 361-987-2813 987-2189 618
Web: www.calhounport.com

Port of Portland 7200 NE Airport Way .... Portland OR 97218 503-415-6000 618
TF: 800-547-8411 ■ *Web:* www.portofportland.com

Port of Portland 389 Congress St. .... Portland ME 04101 207-874-8892 874-8473 618
TF: 800-693-3317 ■ *Web:* portlandmaine.gov

Port of Redwood City
675 Seaport Blvd .... Redwood City CA 94063 650-306-4150 369-7636 618
Web: www.redwoodcityport.com

Port of Richmond Commission
900 E Broad St .... Richmond VA 23219 804-646-7000 646-5789 618
TF: 800-467-4943 ■ *Web:* www.richmondgov.com/PortOfRichmond/news.aspx

Port of Sacramento
1110 W Capitol Ave .... West Sacramento CA 95691 916-371-8000 372-4802 618
TF: 800-635-3993 ■ *Web:* www.cityofwestsacramento.org

Port of Saint Helens 100 E St .... Columbia City OR 97018 503-397-2888 397-6924 618
Web: www.portsh.org

Port of San Diego 3165 Pacific Hwy .... San Diego CA 92101 619-686-6200 618
TF: 800-854-2757 ■ *Web:* www.portofsandiego.org

Port of San Francisco
Pier 1 The Embarcadero .... San Francisco CA 94111 415-274-0400 732-0400 618
TF: 800-479-5314 ■ *Web:* www.sfport.com

Port of Seattle 2711 Alaskan Way .... Seattle WA 98111 206-728-3000 728-3280 618
TF: 800-426-7817 ■ *Web:* www.portseattle.org

Port of Sept-Iles
1 Rue Monseigneur Blanche .... Sept-Iles QC G4R5P3 418-968-1231 962-4445 618
Web: www.portsi.com

Port of Seward PO Box 167 .... Seward AK 99664 907-224-3138 224-7187 618
Web: www.cityofseward.net

Port of South Louisiana
171 Belle Terre Blvd PO Box 909 .... LaPlace LA 70068 985-652-9278 618
TF: 866-536-8300 ■ *Web:* www.portsl.com

Port of Stockton
2201 W Washington St. .... Stockton CA 95203 209-946-0246 465-7244 618
TF: 800-344-3213 ■ *Web:* www.portofstockton.com

Port of Tacoma 1 Sitcum Way .... Tacoma WA 98421 253-383-5841 593-4570 618
Web: www.portoftacoma.com

Port of Valdez 412 Ferry Terminal Way .... Valdez AK 99686 907-835-4564 835-4479 618
Web: www.ci.valdez.ak.us

Port of Vancouver
3103 NW Lower River Rd .... Vancouver WA 98660 360-693-3611 735-1565 618
TF: 800-475-8012 ■ *Web:* www.portvanusa.com

Port of Vancouver
100 The Pt 999 Canada Pl .... Vancouver BC V6C3T4 604-665-9000 284-4271* 618
**Fax Area Code:* 866 ■ *Web:* www.portvancouver.com

Port of Wilmington 1 Hausel Rd. .... Wilmington DE 19801 302-472-7678 472-7740 618
Web: www.portofwilmington.com

Port Orange-South Daytona Chamber of Commerce
3431 S Ridgewood Ave. .... Port Orange FL 32129 386-761-1601 788-9165 139
TF: 800-848-3984 ■ *Web:* www.pschamber.com

Port Orchard Chamber of Commerce
1014 Bay St Ste 8 .... Port Orchard WA 98366 360-876-3505 895-1920 139
TF: 800-475-7526 ■ *Web:* www.portorchard.com

Port Panama City 5321 W Hwy 98 .... Panama City FL 32401 850-767-3220 767-3235 618
Web: www.panamacityportauthority.com

Port Plastics Inc
15325 Fairfield Ranch Rd Ste 150 .... Chino Hills CA 91709 480-813-6118 597-0116* 603
**Fax Area Code:* 909 ■ *TF:* 800-800-0039 ■ *Web:* www.portplastics.com

Port Royal State Historic Park
3300 Old Clarksville Hwy .... Adams TN 37010 931-358-9696 565
Web: www.state.tn.us

Port Saint Lucie News
760 NW Enterprise Dr. .... Port Saint Lucie FL 34995 772-287-1550 532-2
Web: www.tcpalm.com

Port Security International LLC
40 Calhoun St Ste 230 .... Charleston SC 29401 843-723-9255 723-9755 693

Port Townsend Marine Science Ctr
532 Battery Way .... Port Townsend WA 98368 360-385-5582 385-7248 520
TF: 800-566-3932 ■ *Web:* www.ptmsc.org

Port Townsend Paper Corp
100 Mill Rd. .... Port Townsend WA 98368 360-385-3170 554
TF: 800-544-0410 ■ *Web:* www.ptpc.com

Port Washington Chamber of Commerce
329 Main St .... Port Washington NY 11050 516-883-6566 139
Web: www.pwguide.com

Porta Bella 425 N Frances St. .... Madison WI 53703 608-256-3186 256-1210 671
Web: www.portabellarest.com

Portabellos 2109 N Pollard St. .... Arlington VA 22207 703-528-1557 671
Web: portabellos.net

Portable Buildings Inc 3235 Bay Rd .... Milford DE 19963 302-335-1300 186
TF: 800-205-5030 ■ *Web:* www.portablebuildingsinc.com

Portable Church Industries Inc
1923 Ring Dr .... Troy MI 48083 248-585-9540 196
TF: 800-939-7722 ■ *Web:* www.portablechurch.com

Portable Computer & Communications Assn (PCCA)
PO Box 680 .... Hood River OR 97031 541-490-5140 410-8447* 48-9
**Fax Area Code:* 413 ■ *Web:* www.pcca.org

Portable Rechargeable Battery Assn (PRBA)
1776 K St 4th Fl .... Washington DC 20006 202-719-4978 49-13
Web: www.prba.org

Portable Technology Solutions LLC
221 David Ct. .... Calverton NY 11933 877-640-4152 177
TF: 877-640-4152 ■ *Web:* www.ptsmobile.com

Porta-Bote International
1074 Independence Ave .... Mountain View CA 94043 650-961-5334 961-3800 90
TF: 800-227-8882 ■ *Web:* www.porta-bote.com

Portaco Inc 1805 Second Ave N .... Moorhead MN 56560 218-236-0223 640
Web: www.portaco.com

Porta-Fab Corp
18080 Chesterfield Airport Rd .... Chesterfield MO 63005 636-537-5555 537-2955 105
TF: 800-325-3781 ■ *Web:* www.portafab.com

Portage & District Chamber of Commerce
56 Royal Rd N. .... Portage la Prairie MB R1N1V1 204-857-7778 856-5001 137
Web: www.portagechamber.com

Portage Community School District
904 De Witt St .... Portage WI 53901 608-742-4867 685
Web: www.portage.k12.wi.us

Portage County
449 S Meridian St 1st Fl. .... Ravenna OH 44266 330-297-9422 297-3696 338
TF: 800-772-3799 ■ *Web:* www.co.portage.oh.us

Portage County 1516 Church St .... Stevens Point WI 54481 715-346-1351 346-1486 338
Web: www.co.portage.wi.us/countyclerk

Portage County Business Council
5501 Vern Holmes Dr .... Stevens Point WI 54481 715-344-1940 344-4473 139
TF: 800-333-6668 ■ *Web:* www.portagecountybiz.com

Portage County District Library
10482 S St .... Garrettsville OH 44231 330-527-4378 527-4370 434-3
TF: 800-500-5179 ■ *Web:* www.portagecounty.lib.oh.us

Portage County Public Library
1001 Main St .... Stevens Point WI 54481 715-346-1544 434-3
TF: 800-264-0766 ■ *Web:* www.uwsp.edu

Portage Cove State Recreation Site
400 Willoughby Ave Third Fl PO Box 111013 ..... Juneau AK 99811 907-465-4563 565
Web: www.dnr.alaska.gov

Portage District Library
300 Library Ln .... Portage MI 49002 269-329-4544 324-9222 434-3
Web: www.portagelibrary.info

Portage Electric Products Inc
7700 Freedom Ave NW .... North Canton OH 44720 330-499-2727 499-1853 202
TF: 888-464-7374 ■ *Web:* www.pepiusa.com

Portage Inc
1075 S Utah Ave Ste 200 .... Idaho Falls ID 83402 208-528-6608 523-8860 192
Web: www.portageinc.com

Portage Lakes Career Ctr
4401 Shriver Rd .... Uniontown OH 44685 330-896-8200 507
TF: 800-917-2081 ■ *Web:* plcc.edu

Portage Lakes State Park
5031 Manchester Rd. .... Akron OH 44319 330-644-2220 565
Web: www.ohiodnr.com

Portage Park Chamber of Commerce
5829 W Irving Pk Rd. .... Chicago IL 60634 773-777-2020 139

Porta-King Building Systems
4133 Shoreline Dr .... Earth City MO 63045 800-284-5346 186
TF: 800-284-5346 ■ *Web:* www.portaking.com

Portal Inc 10 Tracy Dr .... Avon MA 02322 508-588-3030 234
Web: www.portalincorporated.com

Portal Instruments Inc
148 Sidney St. .... Cambridge MA 02139 617-500-4348 475
Web: www.portalinstruments.com

Portec Rail Products Inc
900 Old Freeport Rd .... Pittsburgh PA 15238 412-782-6000 782-1037 650
Web: www.lbfoster-railtechnologies.com

Porten Cos 333 NE Second St .... Delray Beach FL 33483 561-819-1109 653

Porteous, Hainkel & Johnson LLP
704 Carondelet St. .... New Orleans LA 70130 504-581-3838 428
TF: 800-782-2653 ■ *Web:* www.phjlaw.com

Porter & Chester Institute Inc, The
670 Lordship Blvd .... Stratford CT 06615 203-375-4463 148
TF: 800-870-6789 ■ *Web:* www.porterchester.com

Porter & Company PC CPAs
241 Summit Ave Ste 100 .... Greensboro NC 27401 336-370-1000 2
Web: porterandco.com

Porter & Porter PC
1370 Ramar Bay Ste B .... Bullhead City AZ 86442 928-758-4106 2

Porter Adventist Hospital
2525 S Downing St. .... Denver CO 80210 303-778-1955 778-5252 374-3
TF: 800-994-6610 ■ *Web:* www.porterhospital.org

Porter Capital Corp
2112 First Ave N. .... Birmingham AL 35203 205-322-5442 272
TF: 800-737-7344 ■ *Web:* www.portercap.net

Porter Consulting Engineers PC
552 State St .... Meadville PA 16335 814-337-4447 261
TF: 800-541-5941 ■ *Web:* www.pceengineers.com

Porter County 155 Indiana Ave .... Valparaiso IN 46383 219-465-3445 338
Web: porterco.org

Porter Henry & Company Inc
455 E 86th St .... New York NY 10028 212-953-5544 194
Web: www.porterhenry.com

Porter Hills 3600 E Fulton St .... Grand Rapids MI 49546 616-949-4971 954-1795 672
Web: www.porterhills.org

Porter Inc 2200 W Monroe St .... Decatur IN 46733 260-724-9111 90
TF: 800-736-7685 ■ *Web:* www.formulaboats.com

	Phone	Fax	Class
Porter Instrument Company Inc 245 Township Line Rd PO Box 907 .... Hatfield PA 19440 *TF:* 888-723-4001 ■ *Web:* www.porterinstrument.com	215-723-4000	723-2199	201
Porter Khouw Consulting Inc PO Box 4028 .... Crofton MD 21114 *TF:* 800-324-1268 ■ *Web:* www.porterkhouwconsulting.com	410-451-3617		463
Porter Lee Corp 1901 Wright Blvd .... Schaumburg IL 60193 *Web:* www.porterlee.com	847-985-2060		177
Porter Medical Ctr Inc 115 Porter Dr .... Middlebury VT 05753 *TF:* 800-994-6610 ■ *Web:* www.portermedical.org	802-388-4701		463
Porter Novelli International 75 Varick St 6th Fl ....New York NY 10013 *Web:* www.porternovelli.com	212-601-8000	601-8101	636
Porter Pipe & Supply Co 303 S Rohlwing Rd...........................Addison IL 60101 *Web:* www.porterpipe.com	630-543-8145	543-6830	612
Porter Precision Products Inc 2734 Banning Rd .... Cincinnati OH 45239 *TF:* 800-543-7041 ■ *Web:* www.porterpunch.com	513-923-3777	923-1111	757
Porter Rogers Dahlman & Gordon P C 1 Shoreline Plaza 800 N Shoreline Ste 800 S ....Corpus Christi TX 78401 *Web:* www.prdg.com	361-880-5808		445
Porter Truck Sales LP 135 McCarty St ....Houston TX 77029 *TF:* 800-956-2408 ■ *Web:* www.portertrk.com	713-672-2400	672-7343	516
Porter's 200 W First St........................ Duluth MN 55802 *Web:* hiduluth.com	218-727-6746	722-0233	671
Porter's Group LLC 1111 Oates Rd ....Bessemer City NC 28016 *Web:* www.portersfab.com	704-864-1313		490
PorterCorp 4240 136th Ave .... Holland MI 49424 *TF:* 800-354-7721 ■ *Web:* www.portercorp.com	616-399-1963	399-9123	105
Porterville Chamber of Commerce 93 N Main St Ste A....................... Porterville CA 93257 *Web:* www.portervillechamber.org	559-784-7502		139
Porterville College 100 E College Ave........................ Porterville CA 93257 **Fax:* Admissions ■ *TF:* 800-994-6226 ■ *Web:* portervillecollege.edu	559-791-2200	791-2349*	162
Porterville Developmental Ctr (PDC) 26501 Ave 140 PO Box 2000 .... Porterville CA 93258 *Web:* www.dds.ca.gov/Porterville/Index.cfm	559-782-2222	784-5630	230
Porterville Public Library 41 W Thurman Ave....................... Porterville CA 93257 *TF:* 800-984-4636 ■ *Web:* www.ci.porterville.ca.us/depts/library	559-784-0177	781-4396	434-3
Portfolio Defense 7 Mt Lassen Dr Ste D150.................. San Rafael CA 94903 *Web:* portfoliodefense.com	415-492-8262		261
Portfolio Gallery & Educational Ctr 3514 Delmar Blvd........................ Saint Louis MO 63103 *Web:* www.portfoliogallerystl.org	314-533-3323		50-2
Portfolio Recovery Assoc LLC 120 Corporate Blvd Ste 100 Reverside Commerce Ctr...............Norfolk VA 23502 *NASDAQ: PRAA* ■ *TF:* 888-772-7326 ■ *Web:* www.portfoliorecovery.com	888-772-7326		160
Portfolio Strategy Group Inc, The 81 Main St .... White Plains NY 10601 *Web:* www.portfoliostrategygroup.com	914-328-6660		401
Portico Healthnet 2610 University Ave W .... Saint Paul MN 55114 *TF:* 866-489-4899 ■ *Web:* www.porticohealthnet.org	651-603-5100		463
Portland Art Museum 1219 SW Pk Ave..........Portland OR 97205 *Web:* www.portlandartmuseum.org	503-226-2811	226-4842	520
Portland Baroque Orchestra 1020 SW Taylor St Ste 200...................Portland OR 97205 *Web:* www.pbo.org	503-222-6000	226-6635	573-3
Portland Bolt & Manufacturing Company Inc 3441 NW Guam St ....Portland OR 97210 *TF:* 800-547-6758 ■ *Web:* www.portlandbolt.com	503-227-5488		351
Portland Business Alliance 200 SW Market St Ste 150...................Portland OR 97201 *Web:* www.portlandalliance.com	503-224-8684	323-9186	139
Portland Cement Assn (PCA) 5420 Old OrchaRd Rd......................... Skokie IL 60077 *Web:* www.cement.org	847-966-6200	966-9781	49-3
Portland Children's Museum 4015 SW Canyon Rd ....Portland OR 97221 *Web:* www.portlandcm.org	503-223-6500	223-6600	521
Portland City Grill 111 SW Fifth Ave 30th Fl ....Portland OR 97204 *Web:* www.portlandcitygrill.com	503-450-0030		671
Portland Clinic, The 800 SW 13th Ave ....Portland OR 97205 *Web:* www.theportlandclinic.com	503-221-0161		353
Portland Community College *Sylvania* 12000 SW 49th Ave.................Portland OR 97219 **Fax:* Admissions ■ *TF:* 866-922-1010 ■ *Web:* www.pcc.edu	503-244-6111	977-4740*	162
Portland Ctr for the Performing Arts 1111 SW Broadway ....Portland OR 97205 *Web:* www.portland5.com	503-248-4335		572
Portland Ctr Stage (PCS) 128 NW Eleventh Ave.........................Portland OR 97209 *TF:* 800-273-1530 ■ *Web:* www.pcs.org	503-445-3700	445-3701	573-4
Portland Fire Museum 157 Spring St ....Portland ME 04101 *Web:* www.portlandfiremuseum.com	207-772-2040		520
Portland Forge 250 E Lafayette St..............Portland IN 47371 **Fax Area Code:* 219 ■ *Web:* www.atimetals.com	260-726-8121	726-8021*	483
Portland General Electric 121 SW Salmon St............................Portland OR 97204 *NYSE: POR* ■ *TF:* 800-542-8818 ■ *Web:* www.portlandgeneral.com	503-464-8000		787
Portland Global Advisors LLC 217 Commercial St Ste 400 ....Portland ME 04101 *Web:* portlandglobal.com	207-773-2773		401
Portland Harbor Hotel 468 Fore St ....Portland ME 04101 *TF:* 888-798-9090 ■ *Web:* www.portlandharborhotel.com	207-775-9090	775-9990	379
Portland Head Light 1000 Shore Rd ....Cape Elizabeth ME 04107 *TF:* 800-765-7238 ■ *Web:* www.portlandheadlight.com	207-799-2661	799-2800	50-3
Portland Housing Center Inc 3233 NE Sandy Blvd...........................Portland OR 97232 *TF:* 800-325-8098 ■ *Web:* www.portlandhousingcenter.org	503-282-7744		509
Portland Institute for Contemporary Art 415 SW Tenth Ave Ste 300....................Portland OR 97205 *Web:* www.pica.org	503-242-1419	243-1167	50-2
Portland International Airport 7000 NE Airport Way ....Portland OR 97218 *TF:* 800-547-8411 ■ *Web:* www.portofportland.com	503-460-4234		27
Portland International Film Festival 1219 SW Pk Ave..............................Portland OR 97205 *Web:* www.nwfilm.org	503-221-1156	294-0874	282
Portland International Jetport 1001 Westbrook St...........................Portland ME 04102 *Web:* www.portlandjetport.org	207-874-8877	774-7740	27
Portland International Raceway 1940 N Victory Blvd.........................Portland OR 97217 *Web:* www.portlandraceway.com	503-823-7223	823-5896	642
Portland Lobster Co 180 Commercial St............................Portland ME 04112 *Web:* www.portlandlobstercompany.com	207-775-2112		671
Portland (ME) City Hall 389 Congress St.............................Portland ME 04101 *Web:* www.portlandmaine.gov	207-874-8610	874-8612	337
Portland Meadows Horse Track 1001 N Schmeer Rd ....Portland OR 97217 *Web:* www.portlandmeadows.com	503-285-9144	286-9763	642
Portland Metropolitan Exposition Ctr 2060 N Marine Dr.............................Portland OR 97217 *TF:* 800-791-2250 ■ *Web:* www.expocenter.org	503-736-5200	736-5201	205
Portland Museum of Art 7 Congress Sq.........Portland ME 04101 *Web:* www.portlandmuseum.org	207-775-6148	773-7324	520
Portland Observatory 138 Congress St..........Portland ME 04101 *Web:* www.portlandlandmarks.org/observatory.htm	207-774-5561	774-2509	598
Portland Opera 211 SE Caruthers St.............Portland OR 97214 *TF:* 866-739-6737 ■ *Web:* www.portlandopera.org	503-241-1407	241-4212	573-2
Portland (OR) City Hall 1221 SW Fourth Ave Rm 110...................Portland OR 97204 *TF:* 800-444-9247 ■ *Web:* portlandoregon.gov	503-823-4000	823-3588	337
Portland Phoenix 16 York St Ste 102............Portland ME 04101 *Web:* portlandphoenix.me	207-773-8900	773-8905	532-5
Portland Products Inc 271 Morse Dr ....Portland MI 48875 *Web:* www.portlandproducts.com	517-647-4191		492
Portland Public Library 5 Monument Sq ....Portland ME 04101 *TF:* 800-848-5800 ■ *Web:* www.portlandlibrary.com	207-871-1700	871-1703	434-3
Portland Public Schools 501 N Dixon St...............................Portland OR 97227 *TF:* 800-766-8206 ■ *Web:* www.pps.net	503-916-2000	916-3110	685
Portland Regency Hotel 20 Milk St.............Portland ME 04101 *TF:* 800-727-3436 ■ *Web:* www.theregency.com	207-774-4200	775-2150	379
Portland Regional Chamber 443 Congress St..............................Portland ME 04101 *TF:* 800-782-9338 ■ *Web:* www.portlandregion.com	207-772-2811	772-1179	139
Portland Stage Co PO Box 1458 ....Portland ME 04104 *TF:* 800-838-3006 ■ *Web:* www.portlandstage.org	207-774-1043	774-0576	749
Portland State University 1825 SW Broadway PO Box 751................Portland OR 97201 *TF:* 800-547-8887 ■ *Web:* www.pdx.edu	503-725-3000	725-5525	166
Portland State University Millar Library 1875 SW Pk Ave...............................Portland OR 97201 *Web:* library.pdx.edu	503-725-5874		434-6
Portland Symphony Orchestra 50 Monument Sq 2nd Fl........................Portland ME 04101 *Web:* www.portlandsymphony.org	207-773-6128	773-6089	573-3
Portland Teachers Credit Union PO Box 3750 ....Portland OR 97208 *TF:* 800-527-3932 ■ *Web:* www.onpointcu.com	503-228-7077	273-2698	219
Portland Terminal Railroad Co 3500 NW Yeon Ave.............................Portland OR 97210	503-241-9898	241-4494	651
Portland Water District 225 Douglass St PO Box 3553.................Portland ME 04104 *Web:* www.pwd.org	207-761-8310		787
Portland Webworks Inc 5 Milk St..............Portland ME 04101 *Web:* www.portlandwebworks.com	207-773-6600		180
Portlogic Systems Inc First Canadian Pl, 100 King St W Ste 5700 .... Toronto ON M5X1K7 *Web:* www.portlogicsystems.com	647-847-8350		809
Portman Holdings LLC 303 Peachtree St NE Ste 575 ....Atlanta GA 30303 *Web:* www.portmanholdings.com	404-614-5252		655
Portman Rob (Sen R - OH) 448 Russell Bldg ....Washington DC 20510 *Web:* www.portman.senate.gov	202-224-3353	224-9075	342-2
Portneuf Health Partners 777 Hospital Way ....Pocatello ID 83201 *Web:* www.portneuf.org	208-239-1000		374-3
Portnoff Law Associates Ltd 2700 Horizon Dr Ste 100 .... King of Prussia PA 19406 **Fax Area Code:* 484 ■ *TF:* 866-211-9466 ■ *Web:* portnoffonline.com	866-211-9466	690-9301*	428
Portnoy CPA 9283 San Jose Blvd ....Jacksonville FL 32257 *Web:* www.portnoycpa.com	904-731-8005		2
Port-O-Call Hotel 1510 Boardwalk ....Ocean City NJ 08226 *TF:* 800-334-4546 ■ *Web:* www.portocallhotel.com	609-399-8812		379
Portofino 249 E Main St......................Lexington KY 40507 *Web:* www.portofinolexington.com	859-253-9300	258-2488	671
Portofino 3199 Paces Ferry Pl ....Atlanta GA 30305 *Web:* www.portofinobistro.com	404-231-1136		671
Portofino 3124 Eastway Dr.....................Charlotte NC 28205 *Web:* portofinos-us.com	704-568-7933		671
Portofino - The Mirage 3400 Las Vegas Blvd S.....................Las Vegas NV 89109 *Web:* www.mirage.com	702-791-7131	862-1393	671
Portofino Bay Hotel at Universal Orlando - A Loews Hotel 5601 Universal Blvd..........................Orlando FL 32819 *TF:* 800-235-6397 ■ *Web:* www.loewshotels.com	407-503-1000	503-1010	669
Portofino Hotel & Yacht Club 260 Portofino Way ....Redondo Beach CA 90277 *TF:* 800-468-4292 ■ *Web:* www.hotelportofino.com	310-379-8481		379

	Phone	Fax	Class
Portofino Inn & Suites Anaheim 1831 S Harbor Blvd .... Anaheim CA 92802 *TF Resv:* 800-398-3963 ■ *Web:* www.portofinoinnanaheim.com	714-782-7600	782-7619	379
Porto-Fino Restaurant 3124 S Atlantic Ave.................... Daytona Beach FL 32118 *Web:* portofinodaytona.com	386-767-9484		671
Portofino Spa at Portofino Island Resort 10 Portofino Dr........................... Pensacola FL 32561 *TF:* 866-849-0223 ■ *Web:* www.portofinoisland.com	850-916-5000		707
Portola Plaza Hotel 2 Portola Plaza .... Monterey CA 93940 *TF:* 888-222-5851 ■ *Web:* www.portolahotel.com	831-649-4511	649-4511	379
Portola Redwoods State Park 9000 Portola State Park Rd.................. La Honda CA 94020 *Web:* www.parks.ca.gov/default.asp?page_id=539	916-988-0205		565
Portola School 300 Amador Ave .... San Bruno CA 94066 *Web:* sbpsd.k12.ca.us	650-624-3175		685
Portola Systems Inc 7064 Corline Ct Ste B5.................... Sebastopol CA 95472 *Web:* www.portolasystems.net	707-824-8800		180
Portrait Displays Inc 6663 Owens Dr.......................... Pleasanton CA 94588 *Web:* www.portrait.com	925-227-2700		177
Portrait Express 441 N Water St.............. Silverton OR 97381 *TF:* 800-228-3759 ■ *Web:* www.portraitexpress.com	503-873-6365		590
Portrait Innovations Inc 2016 Ayrsley Town Blvd Ste 200.............. Charlotte NC 28273 *Web:* www.portraitinnovations.com	704-499-9359		590
Portraits International 10835 Rockley Rd.......................... Houston TX 77099 *TF:* 888-838-1495 ■ *Web:* www.portraitsinternational.com	281-879-8444		590
Ports America Inc 525 Washington Blvd Ste 1660 .... Jersey City NJ 07310 **Fax Area Code:* 201 ■ *Web:* www.portsamerica.com	732-635-3899	216-9366*	465
Ports O'Call Village Berth 75-79 .... San Pedro CA 90731 *TF:* [illegible] ■ *Web:* www.sanpedro.com/sp_point/portcall.htm	310-548-8076		50-6
Ports Petroleum Company Inc 1337 Blachleyville Rd....................... Wooster OH 44691 *TF:* 800-562-0373 ■ *Web:* www.portspetroleum.com	330-264-1885		324
Portsmouth Abbey School 285 Cory's Ln .... Portsmouth RI 02871 *Web:* www.portsmouthabbey.org	401-683-2000		622
Portsmouth Area Chamber of Commerce 342 Second St PO Box 509 .... Portsmouth OH 45662 *TF:* 800-648-2574 ■ *Web:* www.portsmouth.org	740-353-7647	353-5824	139
Portsmouth Athenaeum 9 Market Sq .... Portsmouth NH 03801 *Web:* www.portsmouthathenaeum.org	603-431-2538		434-4
Portsmouth Daily Times 637 Sixth St .... Portsmouth OH 45662 *TF:* 800-582-7277 ■ *Web:* www.portsmouth-dailytimes.com	740-353-3101		532-2
Portsmouth Public Library 1220 Gallia St.............................. Portsmouth OH 45662	740-354-5688		434-3
Portsmouth Public Library 601 Ct St .... Portsmouth VA 23704	757-393-8501		434-3
Portsmouth Regional Hospital 333 Borthwick Ave .... Portsmouth NH 03801 *TF:* 800-685-8282 ■ *Web:* www.portsmouthhospital.com	603 436 5110		374-3
Portugal-US Chamber of Commerce 590 Fifth Ave 4th Fl .... New York NY 10036 *Web:* www.portugal-us.com	212 354 4627		100
Porzio Bromberg & Newman PC 100 Southgate Pkwy...................... Morristown NJ 07962 *Web:* www.pbnlaw.com	973-538-4006		428
Pos Source 535 Harrison Ave.............. Panama City FL 32401 *TF:* 800-232-1626 ■ *Web:* www.execu-tech.com	850-747-0581		177
Posados Cafe 3421 N Central Expy................ Plano TX 75023 *Web:* posados.com	972-509-4999		671
Posca Bros Dental Laboratory Inc 641 W Willow St......................... Long Beach CA 90806 *TF:* 800-537-6722 ■ *Web:* www.poscabrothers.com	562-427-1811		415
Posen Construction Inc 50500 Design Ln .... Shelby Township MI 48315 *Web:* www.posenconstruction.com	586-731-8442		492
Posey Bill (Rep R - FL) 2150 Rayburn HOB...................... Washington DC 20515 *Web:* posey.house.gov	202-225-3671	225-3516	342-2
Posey Co 5635 Peck Rd........................ Arcadia CA 91006 **Fax Area Code:* 800 ■ *TF:* 800-447-6739 ■ *Web:* www.posey.com	626-443-3143	767-3933*	477
Posey County 126 E Third St Rm 132................. Mount Vernon IN 47620 *TF:* 800-720-0550 ■ *Web:* www.poseycountyin.gov	812-838-1300	838-1344	338
Positech Corp 191 N Rush Lake Rd............. Laurens IA 50554 *TF:* 800-831-6026 ■ *Web:* positech.com	712-841-4548	841-4765	470
Position Marketing Group Inc 215 N DesPlaines St 1st Fl.................. Chicago IL 60661	312-224-8755		5
Positive Education Program Inc 3100 Euclid Ave .... Cleveland OH 44115 *Web:* www.pepcleve.org	216-361-4400	361-8600	685
Positive Technology 8612 Wolftrap Rd .... Vienna VA 22182 *Web:* positek.net	703-242-2362		809
Positron Corp 530 Oakmont Ln............... Westmont IL 60559 *TF:* 866-613-7587 ■ *Web:* www.positron.com	317-576-0183		250
Positron Corp 4614 Wyland Dr .... Elkhart IN 46516 *Web:* www.positroncorp.com	574-295-8777		247
Positron Inc 5101 Buchan St Ste 220 .... Montreal QC H4P2R9 *Web:* www.positronpower.com	514-345-2200	345-2271	668
Positronic Industries Inc 423 N Campbell Ave PO Box 8247........... Springfield MO 65801 *TF:* 800-641-4054 ■ *Web:* www.connectpositronic.com	417-866-2322	866-4115	253
Posner Adv 30 Broad St........................ New York NY 10004 *Web:* www.posnermiller.com	212-867-3900	480-3440	4
Posner Industries Inc 8641 Edgeworth Dr................... Capitol Heights MD 20743 *TF:* 888-767-6377 ■ *Web:* www.posners.com	301-350-1000	350-1050	492
Possum Kingdom State Park PO Box 70 .... Caddo TX 76429 *Web:* tpwd.texas.gov/state-parks/possum-kingdom	940-549-1803		565
Post & Courier 134 Columbus St .... Charleston SC 29403 **Fax:* News Rm ■ *Web:* www.postandcourier.com	843-577-7111	937-5579*	532-2
Post & Courier LLC, The 134 Columbus St .... Charleston SC 29403 *Web:* www.charleston.net	843-577-7111		532-3
Post & Nickel 144 N 14th St................... Lincoln NE 68508 *TF:* 877-667-6107 ■ *Web:* www.postandnickel.com	402-476-3432	476-3454	157-5
Post & Schell PC 4 Penn Ctr 1600 John F Kennedy Blvd........ Philadelphia PA 19103 *Web:* postschell.com	215-587-1000		428
Post Alarm Systems Inc 47 E Saint Joseph St......................... Arcadia CA 91006 *Web:* www.postalarm.com	626-446-7159		693
Post Asylum Inc 5642 Dyer St .... Dallas TX 75206 *Web:* www.postasylum.com	214-363-0162		637-10
Post Bid Ship Inc 7633 E Acoma Dr .... Scottsdale AZ 85260 *Web:* www.postbidship.com	480-327-6652		393
Post Gardens Inc 21189 Huron River Dr...................... Rockwood MI 48173	734-379-9688		369
Post Glover Resistors Inc 1369 Cox Rd.............................. Erlanger KY 41018 *TF Cust Svc:* 800-537-6144 ■ *Web:* www.postglover.com	859-283-0778	283-2978	253
Post Haste Mailing Inc 2962 Cleveland Ave N...................... Roseville MN 55113 *Web:* www.posthastemailing.com	651-639-8359		5
Post Hotel, The 200 Pipestone Rd PO Box 69 .... Lake Louise AB T0L1E0 *TF:* 800-661-1586 ■ *Web:* www.posthotel.com	403-522-3989	522-3966	379
Post Masters 2101 Fillmore St .... Fort Wayne IN 46802 *Web:* postmastersaz.com	260-744-7400		5
Post Modern Co 2734 Walnut St................. Denver CO 80205 *Web:* www.postmodernco.com	303-539-7001		512
Post Modern Group LLC 2941 Alton Pkwy.......... Irvine CA 92606 *Web:* www.postmoderngroup.com	949-608-8700		512
Post Modern Inc 100 Ross St Ste 310 .... Pittsburgh PA 15219 *Web:* www.postmodern-pgh.com	412-391-6635		514
Post No Bills Inc 801 Gervais St............... Columbia SC 29201 *Web:* www.postnobills.com	803-254-4334		4
Post Precision Castings Inc 21 Walnut St.............................. Strausstown PA 19559 *TF:* 800-232-7950 ■ *Web:* www.postprecision.com	610-488-1011	488-6928	306
Post Ranch Inn Hwy 1 PO Box 219.............. Big Sur CA 93920 *TF:* 800-527-2200 ■ *Web:* www.postranchinn.com	831-667-2200		707
Post University 800 Country Club Rd.......... Waterbury CT 06723 **Fax:* Admissions ■ *TF:* 800-345-2562 ■ *Web:* www.post.edu	203-596-4500	756-5810*	166
Postal Connections of America 6136 Frisco Sq Blvd Ste 400 .... Frisco TX 75034 *TF:* 800-707-8257 ■ *Web:* www.postalconnections.com	800-767-8257		310
Postal Presort Inc 820 W Second St N .... Wichita KS 67203 *TF:* 800-235-3033 ■ *Web:* www.postalpresort.com	316-262-3333		5
Postal Regulatory Commission 901 New York Ave NW Ste 200 .... Washington DC 20268 *Web:* www.prc.gov	202-789-6000	789-0891	340-20
PostalAnnex+ Inc 7580 Metropolitan Dr Ste 200 .... San Diego CA 92108 *TF:* 800-456-1525 ■ *Web:* www.postalannex.com	619-563-4800	563-9850	113
PostcardMania 2145 Sunnydale Blvd Bldg 101 .... Clearwater FL 33765 *TF:* 800-628-1804 ■ *Web:* www.postcardmania.com	800-628-1804		366
Postgraduate Center for Mental Health Residence 516 W 50th St............................. New York NY 10019 *Web:* www.pgcmh.org	212-889-5500		726
Post-Journal 15 W Second St .... Jamestown NY 14701 *TF:* 866-756-9600 ■ *Web:* www.post-journal.com	716-487-1111		532-2
Postler & Jaeckle Corp 615 S Ave .... Rochester NY 14620 *TF:* 800-724-4252 ■ *Web:* www.postlerandjaeckle.com	585-546-7450	546-4316	189-10
PostMark Press Inc 16 Spruce St .... Watertown MA 02472 *Web:* www.postmarkpress.com	617-924-3520		130
Postmasters Inc 701 Brazos St Ste 1616 .... Austin TX 78701	512-693-4040		387
Postmedia Network Inc 365 Bloor St E.......... Toronto ON M4W3L4 *TF:* 800-267-6568 ■ *Web:* www.postmedia.com	416-383-2300		530
PostNet International Franchise Corp 1819 Wazee St .... Denver CO 80202 *TF:* 800-841-7171 ■ *Web:* www.postnet.com	303-771-7100	771-7133	113
Postpartum Support International 2200 Pacific Coast Hwy Ste 304A.......... Hermosa Beach CA 90254 *TF:* 800-944-4773 ■ *Web:* www.postpartum.net	800-944-4773		48-17
Post-Register PO Box 1800 .... Idaho Falls ID 83403 *TF:* 800-574-6397 ■ *Web:* www.postregister.com	208-522-1800		532-2
Post-Standard PO Box 4915................... Syracuse NY 13221 *TF:* 866-447-3787 ■ *Web:* www.syracuse.com	315-470-0011		532-2
Post-Star 76 Lawrence St................... Glens Falls NY 12801 *TF:* 800-724-2543 ■ *Web:* www.poststar.com	518-792-3131	761-1255	532-2
Postworks New York 1411 Broadway 11th Fl...................... New York NY 10013 *Web:* postworks.com	212-894-4000	941-0439	512
Posty Cards 1600 Olive St.................. Kansas City MO 64127 **Fax Area Code:* 888 ■ *TF:* 800-821-7968 ■ *Web:* www.postycards.com	816-231-2323	577-3800*	130
Pot Au Feu 44 Custom House St .... Providence RI 02903 *Web:* potaufeu.businesscatalyst.com	401-273-8953	273-8963	671
Pot o Gold Multi-cinema Productions Inc 11555 Central Pkwy Ste 402............... Jacksonville FL 32224 *Web:* www.pogusa.com	904-744-7478		514
Potager 1109 Ogden St .... Denver CO 80218 *Web:* www.potagerrestaurant.com	303-832-5788		671
Potamkin Automotive 6200 NW 167th ...... Miami Lakes FL 33014 *TF:* 855-799-9965 ■ *Web:* www.potamkinautomotive.com	855-799-9965		57
Potash Corp 1101 Skokie Blvd. .... Northbrook IL 60062 *TF:* 800-667-0403 ■ *Web:* www.potashcorp.com	847-849-4200	849-4695	280
Potash Corp of Saskatchewan Inc 122 First Ave S Ste 500 .... Saskatoon SK S7K7G3 *NYSE:* POT ■ *TF:* 800-667-3930 ■ *Web:* www.potashcorp.com	306-933-8500	652-2699	280
Potato Creek State Park 25601 State Rd 4 PO Box 908 .... North Liberty IN 46554 *Web:* www.in.gov	574-656-8186		565
Potatoes USA (USPB) 4949 S Syracuse St Ste 400..................... Denver CO 80237 *Web:* www.uspotatoes.com	303-369-7783	369-7718	48-2

	Phone	Fax	Class
Potawatomi Bingo Casino 1721 W Canal St. Milwaukee WI 53233 *TF:* 800-729-7244 ■ *Web:* www.paysbig.com	414-645-6888		133
Potawatomi Business Development Corp 3215 W State St Ste 300 Milwaukee WI 53208 *TF:* 800-880-1960 ■ *Web:* www.potawatomibdc.com	414-290-9490		393
Potawatomi Inn Pokagan State Pk 6 Ln 100A Lk James Angola IN 46703 *TF:* 877-768-2928 ■ *Web:* www.in.gov/dnr/parklake/inns/potawatomi	260-833-1077	833-4087	669
Potawatomi State Park 3740 County Rd PD Sturgeon Bay WI 54235 *TF:* 800-847-9367 ■ *Web:* www.dnr.wi.gov	920-746-2890	746-2896	565
Potbelly Sandwich Works 222 Merchandise Mart Plaza Ste 2300 Chicago IL 60654 *Web:* www.potbelly.com	312-951-0600		670
Poteau Chamber of Commerce 201 S Broadway Poteau OK 74953 *Web:* poteauchamber.com	918-647-9178	647-4099	139
Poteet Strawberry Festival Association 9199 N State Hwy 16 Poteet TX 78065 *TF:* 888-742-8144 ■ *Web:* www.strawberryfestival.com	830-742-8144		138
Potelco Inc 14103 Stewart Rd Sumner WA 98390 *Web:* www.potelco.net	253-863-0484		256
Poten & Partners Inc 805 Third Ave New York NY 10022 *Web:* www.poten.com	212-230-2000	355-0295	311
Potential Industries Inc 922 E E St. Wilmington CA 90744 *Web:* potentialindustries.com	310-549-5901		660
Potesta & Associates Inc 7012 MacCorkle Ave SE Charleston WV 25304 *Web:* www.potesta.com	304-342-1400		192
Potestivo & Associates PC 811 S Blvd Ste 100 Rochester Hills MI 48307 *TF:* 800-741-8806 ■ *Web:* www.potestivolaw.com	248-853-4400		428
Potholes State Park 6762 Hwy 262 SE Othello WA 99344 *Web:* parks.state.wa.us	509-346-2759		565
Potlatch Corp 601 W First Ave Ste 1600 Spokane WA 99201 *NASDAQ: PCH* ■ *TF:* 800-750-3850 ■ *Web:* www.potlatchcorp.com	509-835-1500		683
Potlatch Corp Wood Products Div 805 Mill Rd PO Box 1388 Lewiston ID 83501 *Web:* www.potlatchcorp.com	509-835-1500		613
Potlatch State Park 21020 N US Hwy 101 Shelton WA 98584 *TF:* 800-833-6388 ■ *Web:* www.parks.wa.gov	360-877-5361		565
Potluck Press 920 S Bayview St Seattle WA 98134 **Fax Area Code:* 206 ■ *TF:* 877-818-5500 ■ *Web:* www.potluckpress.com	877-818-5500	328-4633*	130
Potomac Appalachian Trail Club Inc, The 118 Park St SE Vienna VA 22180 *Web:* patc.net	703-242-0965		148
Potomac Assn, The 540 Water St Jack London Sq. Oakland CA 94607 *TF:* 800-549-8780 ■ *Web:* www.usspotomac.org	510-627-1215	839-4729	50-4
Potomac College 4000 Chesapeake St NW Washington DC 20016 *Web:* potomac.edu	202-686-0876		166
Potomac Communications Group Inc 1133 20th St NW Ste 400 Washington DC 20036 *Web:* www.pcgpr.com	202-466-7391		196
Potomac Conference Corp of Seventh Day Adventists 606 Greenville Ave Staunton VA 24401 *TF:* 800-732-1844 ■ *Web:* www.pcsda.org	540-886-0771	886-5734	48-20
Potomac Electric Corp 1 Westinghouse Plaza Boston MA 02136 *Web:* www.pepco.com	617-364-0400		454
Potomac Healthcare Solutions LLC 1549 Old Bridge Rd Ste 201 Woodbridge VA 22192 *Web:* www.potomachealthcare.com	703-436-9009		196
Potomac Heritage National Scenic Trail PO Box B Harpers Ferry WV 25425 *Web:* www.nps.gov/pohe	304-535-4014		564
Potomac Mills 2700 Potomac Mills Cir Woodbridge VA 22192 *TF:* 877-746-6642 ■ *Web:* www.simon.com	703-496-9301	643-1054	460
Potomac State College 101 Ft Ave Keyser WV 26726 **Fax:* Admissions ■ *TF:* 800-262-7332 ■ *Web:* www.potomacstatecollege.edu	304-788-6800	788-6939*	162
Potomac Supply Corp 1398 Kinsale Rd Kinsale VA 22488 *TF Sales:* 800-365-3900 ■ *Web:* www.potomacsupply.com	804-472-2527	472-5058	551
Potomac Valley Brick & Supply Co 15810 Indianola Dr Ste 100 Rockville MD 20855 *Web:* www.pvbrick.com	301-309-9600	309-0929	150
Potomac-Garrett State Forest 1431 Potomac Camp Rd Oakland MD 21550 *Web:* dnr2.maryland.gov	301-334-2038		565
PotomacWave Consulting 44 Canal Center Plaza Ste 410 Alexandria VA 22314 *Web:* www.potomacwave.com	703-623-5144		196
Potosi Correctional Ctr 11593 State Hwy O Mineral Point MO 63660 *TF:* 800-735-2966 ■ *Web:* mo.gov	573-438-6000	438-6006	213
PotPie 904 Westport Rd Kansas City MO 64111 *Web:* www.kcpotpie.com	816-561-2702		671
Potsdam Specialty Paper Inc 547A Sissonville Rd Potsdam NY 13676 *Web:* www.pspi.us.com	315-265-4000		557
Pottawatomie County 325 N Broadway Shawnee OK 74801 *TF:* 800-799-7233 ■ *Web:* www.pottcoso.com	405-273-1727		338
Pottawatomie County PO Box 187 Westmoreland KS 66549 *Web:* www.pottcounty.org	785-457-3314	457-3507	338
Potter Anderson & Corroon LLP Hercules Plaza 1313 N Market St Wilmington DE 19801 *Web:* www.potteranderson.com	302-984-6000		428
Potter County 900 S Polk St Ste 500 Amarillo TX 79101 *TF:* 800-287-8283 ■ *Web:* www.co.potter.tx.us	806-379-2275	379-2296	338
Potter County 1 N Main St Coudersport PA 16915 *TF:* 800-377-1723 ■ *Web:* www.pottercountypa.net	814-274-8290	274-8284	338
Potter County 201 S Exene PO Box 67 Gettysburg SD 57442 *Web:* ujs.sd.gov/County_Information/potter.aspx	605-765-9472	765-9670	338
Potter Distributing Inc 4037 Roger B Chaffee Blvd Grand Rapids MI 49548 *TF:* 800-748-0568 ■ *Web:* www.potterdistributing.com	616-531-6860	531-9578	38
Potter Electric Signal Company Inc 5757 Phantom Dr Ste 125 Hazelwood MO 63042 *TF:* 800-325-3936 ■ *Web:* www.pottersignal.com	314-878-4321	595-6999	283
Potter Park Zoo 1301 S Pennsylvania Ave Lansing MI 48912 *Web:* www.potterparkzoo.org	517-483-4222	316-3894	823
Potter State Bank of Potter, The 301 Chestnut St Potter NE 69156 *Web:* potterstatebank.com	308-879-4451		70
Potter-Randall Appraisal District 5701 Hollywood Rd (Loop 335) Po Box 7190 Amarillo TX 79114 *Web:* www.prad.org	806-355-8426		393
Potter-Roemer 17451 Hurley St City of Industry CA 91744 *TF:* 800-366-3473 ■ *Web:* www.potterroemer.com	626-855-4890	937-4777	678
Potter-Webster Co 41 NE Walker St Portland OR 97211 *Web:* www.potterwebster.com	503-283-4792		57
Pottstown Memorial Medical Ctr (PMMC) 1600 E High St Pottstown PA 19464 *Web:* www.pottstownmemorial.com	610-327-7000		374-3
Pottsville Free Public Library 215 W Market St Pottsville PA 17901 *Web:* www.pottsvillelibrary.org	570-622-8880	622-2157	434-3
Pottsville Republican 111 Mahantongo St Pottsville PA 17901 *TF:* 800-622-1737 ■ *Web:* www.pottsville.com	570-622-3456		532-2
Potvin & Bouchard Inc 3900 Rue Colbert St-Jean Cp550 Jonquiere QC G7X7W4 *Web:* www.potvinbouchard.qc.ca	418-547-4752		191-1
Poudre River Public Library 201 Peterson St Fort Collins CO 80524 *Web:* www.poudrelibraries.org	970-221-6740		434-3
Poudre School District 2407 LaPorte Ave Fort Collins CO 80521 *Web:* www.psdschools.org	970-482-7420		685
Poudre Valley Hospital 1024 S Lemay Ave Fort Collins CO 80524 *TF:* 800-994-6610 ■ *Web:* www.uchealth.org	970-495-7000		374-3
Poudre Valley Rural Electric Assn Inc 7649 Rea Pkwy Fort Collins CO 80528 *TF:* 800-432-1012 ■ *Web:* www.pvrea.com	970-226-1234		245
Poughkeepsie Journal 85 Civic Ctr Plaza Poughkeepsie NY 12601 *TF:* 800-765-1120 ■ *Web:* www.poughkeepsiejournal.com	845-437-4800	437-4921	532-2
Pounding Mill Quarry Corp 171 St Clair S Crossing Bluefield VA 24605 *TF:* 888-661-7625 ■ *Web:* www.pmqc.com	276-326-1145	322-6805	503-5
Poverty Point National Monument c/o Poverty Point State Pk PO Box 276 Epps LA 71237 *TF:* 888-926-5492 ■ *Web:* www.nps.gov	318-926-5492		564
Poverty Point Reservoir State Park 1500 Poverty Pt Pkwy Delhi LA 71232 *TF:* 800-474-0392 ■ *Web:* www.crt.state.la.us	318-878-7536		565
Poverty Point State Historic Site 6859 Hwy 577 Pioneer LA 71266 *TF:* 888-926-5492 ■ *Web:* www.crt.state.la.us	318-926-5492		565
Poway Chamber of Commerce 14005-B Midland Rd Poway CA 92064 *TF:* 800-829-1040 ■ *Web:* www.poway.com	858-748-0016	748-1710	139
Poway Pilates 14053 Midland Rd Poway CA 92064 *Web:* powaypilates.net	858-748-7864		354
Powder River Correctional Facility 3600 13th St Baker City OR 97814 *Web:* oregon.gov	541-523-6680	523-6678	213
Powder River County PO Box 270 Broadus MT 59317 *TF:* 800-460-5657 ■ *Web:* prco.mt.gov	406-436-2361	436-2151	338
Powder River Energy Corp (PRE) 221 Main St PO Box 930 Sundance WY 82729 **Fax Area Code:* 307 ■ *TF:* 800-442-3630 ■ *Web:* www.precorp.coop	800-442-3630	283-3527*	245
Powder River Transportation 1700 U S 14 Gillette WY 82716 *TF:* 888-970-7233 ■ *Web:* www.coachusa.com	307-682-0960		108
Powder Valley Conservation Nature Ctr 11715 Cragwold Rd Saint Louis MO 63122 *TF:* 800-325-7962 ■ *Web:* mdc.mo.gov	314-301-1500	301-1501	50-5
Powdermet Inc 24112 Rockwell Dr Euclid OH 44117 *Web:* www.powdermetinc.com	216-404-0053		487
POWDR Corp 1794 Olympic Pkwy Ste 210 Park City UT 84098 *Web:* www.powdr.com	435-658-5500		787
Powel House 244 S Third St Philadelphia PA 19106 *TF:* 877-426-8056 ■ *Web:* www.philalandmarks.org	215-627-0364		50-3
Powell County 409 Missouri Ave Deer Lodge MT 59722 *Web:* www.powellcountymontana.com	406-846-3680		338
Powell County PO Box 506 Stanton KY 40380 *Web:* powellcounty.ky.gov/Pages/index.aspx	606-663-2834	663-2905	338
Powell Electronics Inc 200 Commodore Dr Swedesboro NJ 08085 *TF:* 800-235-7880 ■ *Web:* www.powell.com	856-241-8000	241-8630	246
Powell Gardens 1609 NW US Hwy 50 Kingsville MO 64061 *Web:* www.powellgardens.org	816-697-2600	697-2619	97
Powell Industries Inc 8550 Mosely Dr Houston TX 77075 *NASDAQ: POWL* ■ *TF:* 800-480-7273 ■ *Web:* www.powellind.com	713-944-6900	947-4453	729
Powell River General Hospital 5000 Joyce Ave. Powell River BC V8A5R3 *TF:* 800-567-8911 ■ *Web:* www.vch.ca	604-485-3211	485-3243	374-2
Powell River Public Library 4411 Michigan Ave. Powell River BC V8A2S3 *Web:* prpl.ca	604-485-4796		435
Powell Steel Corp 625 Baumgardner Rd Lancaster PA 17603	717-464-2030		480
Powell Systems Inc 162 Churchill-HubbaRd Rd Youngstown OH 44505 *Web:* www.powellsystems.com	330-759-9220	759-9434	470
Powell Technologies 3622 Bristol Hwy Johnson City TN 37601 *TF:* 800-400-7016 ■ *Web:* powell-tech.com	423-282-0111	282-1541	188-7

	City	State	Zip	Phone	Fax	Class
Powell's Books Inc 7 NW Ninth Ave.	Portland	OR	97209	503-228-0540		95
TF: 800-878-7323 ■ *Web:* www.powells.com						
Powell's City of Books						
1005 W Burnside St	Portland	OR	97209	503-228-4651		95
TF: 800-878-7323 ■ *Web:* www.powells.com						
Powell, Trachtman, Logan, Carrle & Lombardo PC						
475 Allendale Rd Ste 200	King Of Prussia	PA	19406	610-354-9700		428
Web: www.powelltrachtman.com						
Power & Composite Technologies LLC (PCT)						
200 Wallins Corners Rd	Amsterdam	NY	12010	518-843-6825	843-6723	249
Web: www.pactinc.com						
Power & Control Engineering Solutions LLC						
12611 East 60th St Ste 200	Tulsa	OK	74146	918-627-7237		261
Web: www.pcescorp.com						
Power & Industrial Air Systems						
5281 Hamilton Blvd	Allentown	PA	18106	610-395-3242		358
TF: 800-468-4285 ■ *Web:* www.pias-usa.com						
Power & Motoryacht Magazine						
260 Madison Ave 4th Fl	New York	NY	10016	860-767-3200		457-4
TF: 800-284-8036 ■ *Web:* www.powerandmotoryacht.com						
Power & Telephone Supply Company Inc						
2673 Yale Ave.	Memphis	TN	38112	901-866-3300		246
TF Cust Svc: 800-238-7514 ■ *Web:* www.ptsupply.com						
Power 105.1 32 Ave of the Americas	New York	NY	10013	212-377-7900		645-111
TF: 800-585-1051 ■ *Web:* www.power1051fm.com						
Power 106 Radio						
2600 W Olive Ave Ste 800	Burbank	CA	91505	818-953-4200		645-10
Web: www.power106.com						
Power 93.9 2120 N Woodlawn St Ste 352	Wichita	KS	67208	316-685-2121		645-175
Web: www.power935.com						
POWER 96 194 NW 187th St.	Miami	FL	33169	305-654-1700	654-1715	645-99
Web: power96.cbslocal.com						
Power Battery Co Inc 25 McLean Blvd	Paterson	NJ	07514	973-523-8630	523-3023	74
Web: powerbatteryco.com						
Power Brake Dies Inc						
263 W 154th St.	South Holland	IL	60473	708-339-5951	339-7737	757
TF: 800-328-2197 ■ *Web:* www.powerbrakedies.com						
Power Buying Dealers Exxonmobil Convenience Stores						
2459 W 208th St Ste 100	Torrance	CA	90501	310-212-9999		297-8
Web: www.vitalife.com						
Power City Electric Inc						
3327 E Olive Ave.	Spokane	WA	99202	509-535-8500	535-4665	189-4
Web: www.powercityelectric.com						
Power Construction Company LLC						
8750 W Bryn Mawr Ave Ste 500	Chicago	IL	60631	312-596-6960		186
Web: www.powerconstruction.net						
Power County 543 Bannock Ave	American Falls	ID	83211	208-226-7610		338
Web: www.co.power.id.us						
Power Creative						
11701 Commonwealth Dr.	Louisville	KY	40299	502-267-0772		4
Web: www.poweragency.com						
Power Depot Inc 3553 NW 78th Ave	Miami	FL	33122	305-592-7100		196
TF: 000 020-4250 ■ *Web:* www.powerdepot.com						
Power Engineering Corp						
PO Box 766	Wilkes-Barre	PA	18703	570-823-8822	823-8143	261
TF: 800-626-0903 ■ *Web:* www.powerengineeringcorp.com						
Power Engineers Inc						
3940 Glenbrook Dr PO Box 1066	Hailey	ID	83333	208-788-3456	788-2082	261
TF: 800-535-8173 ■ *Web:* www.powereng.com						
Power Flame Inc						
2001 S 21st St PO Box 974	Parsons	KS	67357	620-421-0480	421-0948	357
Web: www.powerflame.com						
Power Grid Engineering LLC						
5744 Canton Cove Ste 110	Winter Springs	FL	32708	321-244-0170		188
TF: 877-819-1171 ■ *Web:* www.powergridengineering.com						
Power Gripps Usa Inc 41 Pomola Ave	Sorrento	ME	04677	207-422-2051		711
Web: www.versagripps.com						
Power Integrations 5245 Hellyer Ave.	San Jose	CA	95138	408-414-9200	414-9201	696
NASDAQ: POWI ■ *Web:* www.power.com						
Power Management Concepts LLC						
510 Grumman Rd W Ste 211	Bethpage	NY	11714	516-465-0188		463
Web: www.powermanage.com						
Southeastern Power Administration						
1166 Athens Tech Rd	Elberton	GA	30635	706-213-3800	213-3884	340-9
Web: energy.gov						
Power Motive Corp 5000 Vasquez Blvd	Denver	CO	80216	303-355-5900	388-9328	358
TF: 800-627-0087 ■ *Web:* www.powermotivecorp.com						
Power Organics						
301 S Old Stage Rd	Mount Shasta	CA	96067	530-926-6684		799
TF: 877-769-3795 ■ *Web:* www.klamathbluegreen.com						
Power Partners Inc						
200 Newton Bridge Rd	Athens	GA	30607	706-548-3121		767
Web: abb.com						
Power Piping Co 436 Butler St	Pittsburgh	PA	15223	412-323-6200	323-6334	189-10
TF: 800-229-5205 ■ *Web:* powerpipingcompany.com						
Power Plant Live! 34 Market St	Baltimore	MD	21202	410-727-5483		50-6
Web: www.powerplantlive.com						
Power Plus Sound & Lighting Inc						
2445 Grand Ave	Vista	CA	92081	760-727-1717		38
Web: www.powerpluscorp.com						
Power PR 20521 Earl St	Torrance	CA	90503	310-787-1940	781-1970	636
Web: www.powerpr.com						
Power Process Piping Inc						
45780 Port St.	Plymouth	MI	48170	734-451-0130	451-0763	189-10
TF: 800-839-6446 ■ *Web:* www.ppphq.com						
Power Quality Engineering Inc						
3061 W Whitestone Blvd	Cedar Park	TX	78613	512-267-6656		256
Web: www.pqeinc.com						
Power Repair Service Inc						
314 Mcbride Ln	Corpus Christi	TX	78408	361-289-1471		454
Web: www.powerrepair.net						
Power Service Products Inc						
PO Box 1089	Weatherford	TX	76086	817-599-9486		538
TF: 800-643-9089 ■ *Web:* www.powerservice.com						
Power Station Inc 7360 Reseda Blvd	Reseda	CA	91335	818-344-8148		54
Web: www.mauriss.com						
Power Systems & Controls Inc						
3206 Lanvale Ave	Richmond	VA	23230	804-355-2803		112
TF: 800-962-5893 ■ *Web:* www.pscpower.com						
Power Transmission Distributors Assn (PTDA)						
230 W Monroe St Ste 1410	Chicago	IL	60606	312-516-2100		49-18
Web: www.ptda.org						
Power Vac Services 50 Goebel Ave	Cambridge	ON	N3C1Z1	519-658-4140		104
TF: 800-232-6396 ■ *Web:* www.powervac.ca						
Power Wellness						
2055 W Army Trl Rd Ste 124	Addison	IL	60101	630-570-2600		463
TF: 877-888-2988 ■ *Web:* www.powerwellness.com						
Power Worker's Union, The						
244 Eglinton Ave E	Toronto	ON	M4P1K2	416-481-4491		414
TF: 800-958-8798 ■ *Web:* www.pwu.ca						
Powerain Systems Inc 1 Enterprise Dr	Tower	MN	55790	218-753-5312		427
Web: www.powerain.com						
Powerboss Inc 175 Anderson St.	Aberdeen	NC	28315	910-944-2105		386
Web: powerboss.com						
Powercast Corp 566 Alpha Dr.	Pittsburgh	PA	15238	724-238-3700		261
Web: www.powercastco.com						
PowerChord Inc						
360 Central Ave 5th Fl	St Petersburg	FL	33701	727-823-1530		5
Web: www.powerchord.com						
Powercon Corp PO Box 477	Severn	MD	21144	410-551-6500	551-8451	729
TF: 800-638-5055 ■ *Web:* www.powerconcorp.com						
Powered By Search Inc						
505 Consumers Rd Ste 507	Toronto	ON	M2J4V8	416-840-9044		224
TF: 866-611-5535 ■ *Web:* www.poweredbysearch.com						
Powerex Inc 173 Pavilion Ln.	Youngwood	PA	15697	724-925-7272	925-4393	696
TF: 800-451-1415 ■ *Web:* www.pwrx.com						
Powerfilm Inc 2337 230th St.	Ames	IA	50014	515-292-7606		696
TF: 888-354-7773 ■ *Web:* www.powerfilmsolar.com						
Powerhouse Gym International						
355 S Old Woodward Ste 150.	Birmingham	MI	48009	248-476-2888		354
Web: www.powerhousegym.com						
Powerlink Facilities Management Services						
3031 W Grand Blvd Ste 640	Detroit	MI	48202	313-309-2020		104
TF: 800-465-0772 ■ *Web:* www.powerlinkonline.com						
PowerMed Corp 48 Free St	Portland	ME	04101	207-772-3920		179
Web: www.powermed.com						
PowerMetal Technologies Inc						
2726 Loker Ave W.	Carlsbad	CA	92010	760-607-0404		225
Powernail Co 1300 Rose Rd	Lake Zurich	IL	60047	847-634-3000	634-4943	759
TF: 800-323-1653 ■ *Web:* www.powernail.com						
PowerOneData Inc						
1201 S Alma School Rd Mesa Financial Ctr						
Ste 229	Mesa	AZ	85210	480-668-0700		407
Web: www.p1di.com						
PowerPhone Inc 1321 Boston Post Rd	Madison	CT	06443	203-245-8911		180
Web: www.powerphone.com						
PowerPlan Corp						
2130 Main St Ste 245	Huntington Beach	CA	92648	714-969-5353		809
Web: www.powerplancorp.com						
Powerplant Maintenance Specialists Inc (PMSI)						
2900 Bristol St Ste H202	Costa Mesa	CA	92626	714-427-6900	427-6906	104
Powers & Sons Construction Company Inc						
2030 W 15th Ave	Gary	IN	46404	219-949-3100	949-5906	186
Web: www.powersandsons.com						
Powers & Sons LLC 44700 Helm St	Plymouth	MI	48170	734-354-6575	254-9517	483
TF: 800-444-5427 ■ *Web:* www.powersandsonsllc.com						
Powers & Sons LLC 1013 Mayda Dr	Montpelier	OH	43543	419-485-3151	485-5490	60
Web: www.powersandsonsllc.com						
Powers Agency Inc						
1 W Fourth St 5th Fl	Cincinnati	OH	45202	513-721-5353		7
Web: www.powersagency.com						
Powers David J & Associates Inc						
1871 The Alameda	San Jose	CA	95126	408-248-3500		463
Web: www.davidjpowers.com						
Powers Distributing Company Inc						
3700 Giddings Rd.	Orion	MI	48359	248-393-3700		81-1
Web: powersdistributing.com						
Powers Fasteners Inc 2 Powers Ln	Brewster	NY	10509	914-235-6300	576-6483	493
TF: 800-524-3244 ■ *Web:* www.powers.com						
Powers Manufacturing Co						
1340 Sycamore St PO Box 2157	Waterloo	IA	50704	319-233-6118	234-8048	155-1
Web: www.powersathletic.com						
Powers Products Co 2695 W Third Ave	Denver	CO	80219	307-634-5190		191-2
Web: www.powersproducts.com						
Powers Pyles Sutter & Verville PC						
1501 M St NW 7th Fl	Washington	DC	20005	202-466-6550	785-1756	428
Web: www.powerslaw.com						
Powers Vincent m & Associates						
411 S 13th St Ste 300.	Lincoln	NE	68508	402-474-8000		428
Web: vincepowerslaw.com						
PowerScore Inc 57 Hasell St.	Charleston	SC	29401	800-545-1750		764
TF: 800-545-1750 ■ *Web:* www.powerscore.com						
PowerSecure International Inc						
1609 Heritage Commerce Ct.	Wake Forest	NC	27587	919-556-3056	556-3596	787
NYSE: POWR ■ *Web:* www.powersecure.com						
PowerServe International Inc						
959 Broad St Ste 300	Augusta	GA	30901	706-826-1506		177
Web: www.powerserve.net						
Powersmiths International Corp						
10 Devon Rd.	Brampton	ON	L6T5B5	905-791-1493		767
TF: 800-747-9627 ■ *Web:* www.powersmiths.com						
Powersports Business Magazine						
6420 Sycamore Ln N	Maple Grove	MN	55369	763-383-4400		637-9
Web: www.powersportsbusiness.com						
Powers-Swain Chevrolet Inc						
4709 Bragg Blvd.	Fayetteville	NC	28303	910-864-9500		516
Web: pschevy.com						
Powersteering Software Inc						
401 Congress Ave Ste 1850	Austin	TX	78701	617-492-0707	492-9444	178-7
TF: 866-390-9088 ■ *Web:* www.powersteeringsoftware.com						
Powertex Inc 1 Lincoln Ave.	Rouses Point	NY	12979	518-297-4000		596
Web: www.powertex.com						
Powerton Lake State Fish & Wildlife Area						
7982 S Pk Rd	Manito	IL	61546	309-968-7135		565
Web: www.dnr.state.il.us						
Powertronix Inc 1120 Chess Dr	Foster City	CA	94404	650-345-6800		767
Web: www.powertronix.com						

				Phone	Fax	Class
PowerVision Inc 260 Harbor Blvd. *TF:* 800-392-3808 ■ *Web:* powervisionlens.com	Belmont	CA	94002	650-620-9948		180
Powerwave Technologies Inc 1801 E St Andrew Pl. *NASDAQ: PWAV*	Santa Ana	CA	92705	714-466-1000		647
Powerzone Volleyball Inc 3 Luger Rd. *Web:* www.powerzonevb.com	Denville	NJ	07834	973-983-8208		708
Poweshiek County PO Box 218 *Web:* www.poweshiekcounty.org	Montezuma	IA	50171	641-623-5644		338
Powhatan County 3880 Old Buckingham Rd. *Web:* www.powhatanva.com	Powhatan	VA	23139	804-598-5612	598-5608	338
Powhatan County School District 2320 Skaggs Rd. *Web:* www.powhatan.k12.va.us	Powhatan	VA	23139	804-598-5700		685
Powill Manufacturing & Engineering Inc 21039 N 27th Ave. *Web:* powill.com	Phoenix	AZ	85027	623-780-4100		21
Powin Corp 20550 SW 115th Ave *Web:* powinenergy.com	Tualatin	OR	97062	503-598-6659	598-3941	621
Powrmatic Inc PO Box 439 *TF:* 800-966-9100 ■ *Web:* www.powrmatic.com	Finksburg	MD	21048	410-833-9100	833-7971	357
Powroll Motor Performance 13850 Commercial Lp	Terrebonne	OR	97760	541-923-1290	923-5637	517
Poyner & Spruill LLP 301 Fayetteville St Ste 1900 *TF:* 800-856-4419 ■ *Web:* www.poynerspruill.com	Raleigh	NC	27601	919-783-6400		428
Poynter Institute for Media Studies Inc, The 801 Third St S *Web:* www.poynter.org	St. Petersburg	FL	33701	727-821-9494		507
Pozas Bros Trucking Company Inc 8130 Enterprise Dr *TF:* 800-874-8383 ■ *Web:* pozasbros.com	Newark	CA	94560	510-742-9939	742-9979	780
Pozen Inc 1414 Raleigh Rd Ste 400 *NASDAQ: POZN* ■ *TF:* 800-981-2491 ■ *Web:* www.pozen.com	Chapel Hill	NC	27517	919-913-1030	913-1039	85
Pozzetta Products Inc 3219 S Platte River Dr *Web:* www.pozzetta.com	Englewood	CO	80110	303-783-3172		88
PP Systems International Inc 110 Haverhill Rd Ste 301 *TF:* 866-211-9346 ■ *Web:* www.ppsystems.com	Amesbury	MA	01913	978-834-0505		250
PPA (Professional Photographers of America Inc) 229 Peachtree St NE Ste 2200 *TF:* 800-786-6277 ■ *Web:* www.ppa.com	Atlanta	GA	30303	404-522-8600	614-6400	48-4
PPAI (Promotional Products Assn International) 3125 Skyway Cir N *TF:* 888-426-7724 ■ *Web:* www.ppai.org	Irving	TX	75038	972-252-0404	258-3004	49-18
PPC Industries 3000 E Marshall Ave. *Web:* www.ppcesp.com	Longview	TX	75601	903-758-3395	758-6487	386
Ppc Industries Inc 10101 78th Ave. *Web:* www.ppcind.com	Pleasant Prairie	WI	53158	262-947-0900		596
PPC Mechanical Seals 2769 Mission Dr. *TF:* 800-731-7325 ■ *Web:* www.ppcmechanicalseals.com	Baton Rouge	LA	70805	225-356-4333	355-2126	326
PPD Development Inc 929 N Front St *Web:* www.ppdi.com	Wilmington	NC	28401	910-251-0081		743
PPD Inc 929 N Front St. *NASDAQ: PPDI* ■ *Web:* www.ppdi.com	Wilmington	NC	28401	910-251-0081	762-5820	668
PPG Industries Inc 17451 Von Karman Ave *TF:* 800-544-3338 ■ *Web:* www.ppgaerospace.com	Irvine	CA	92614	949-474-0400	474-7269	550
PPG Industries Inc 1 PPG Pl *NYSE: PPG* ■ *Web:* www.ppg.com	Pittsburgh	PA	15272	412-434-3131		550
PPHEA (Panhandle-Plains Higher Education Authority Inc) 1403 23rd St.	Canyon	TX	79015	806-324-4100		48-11
PPHI (Pittsburgh Plumbing Heating & Industrial) 2620 Ridgewood Rd *Web:* www.pphind.com	Akron	OH	44313	330-762-9621	762-8722	14
PPI (Paper Pak Industries) 1941 N White Ave. *TF:* 888-293-6529 ■ *Web:* www.paperpakindustries.com	La Verne	CA	91750	909-392-1750	392-1760	297-9
PPI (Progressive Policy Institute) 1101 14th St NW Ste 1250 *Web:* progressivepolicy.org	Washington	DC	20005	202-525-3926	525-3941	634
PPI Construction Management Inc 8200 NW 15th Pl Ste B.	Gainesville	FL	32606	352-331-1141	331-9084	194
Ppl Industrial Corp 11649 Pendleton St *Web:* www.ppisupply.com	Sun Valley	CA	91352	818-768-5665		200
PPI Technical Communications Inc 32200 Solon Rd *TF:* 866-364-3370 ■ *Web:* www.ppitechcom.com	Cleveland	OH	44139	440-498-9254		809
PPIW (Pinnacle Performance Improvement Worldwide) 101 Main St *TF:* 800-368-3408 ■ *Web:* www.pinnaclecg.com	Pepperell	MA	01463	978-925-9797	925-9798	194
PPL Corp 2 N Ninth St. *NYSE: PPL* ■ *TF:* 800-342-5775 ■ *Web:* www.pplweb.com	Allentown	PA	18101	610-774-5151		360-5
PPL Electric Utilities Corp 2 N Ninth St *TF Cust Svc:* 800-342-5775 ■ *Web:* www.pplweb.com	Allentown	PA	18101	610-774-5151		787
PPL Global LLC 2 N Ninth St *NYSE: PPL* ■ *TF:* 800-345-3085 ■ *Web:* www.pplweb.com	Allentown	PA	18101	610-774-5151		787
PPLSolutions LLC 2 N Ninth St PL-2. *Web:* www.pplweb.com	Allentown	PA	18101	610-774-2932		396
Ppm America Inc 225 W Wacker Dr Ste 1200. *Web:* www.ppmamerica.com	Chicago	IL	60606	312-634-2500		401
PPM Consultants Inc 1600 Lamy Ln *TF:* 800-761-8675	Monroe	LA	71201	318-323-7270	323-6593	261
PPM PDN (Pike Place Market) 85 Pike St Rm 500 *Web:* www.pikeplacemarket.org	Seattle	WA	98101	206-682-7453	625-0646	50-6
PPMC (Penn Presbyterian Medical Ctr) 51 N 39th St *TF:* 800-789-7366 ■ *Web:* pennmedicine.org/penn-presbyterian-medical-center	Philadelphia	PA	19104	215-662-8000	662-9212	374-3
PPPL (Princeton Plasma Physics Laboratory) James Forrestal Campus Princeton University PO Box 451 *TF:* 800-772-2222 ■ *Web:* www.pppl.gov	Princeton	NJ	08543	609-243-2750	243-2751	668
PPS (Pittsburgh Public Schools) 341 S Bellefield Ave *Web:* www.pps.k12.pa.us	Pittsburgh	PA	15213	412-622-7920		685
PPS Parking Inc 1800 E Garry Ave Ste 107 *Web:* www.occruiser.com	Santa Ana	CA	92705	949-223-8707		562
PPTA (Plasma Protein Therapeutics Assn) 147 Old Solomon's Island Rd Ste 100 *Web:* www.pptaglobal.org	Annapolis	MD	21401	202-789-3100		49-8
PPV Inc 4927 NW Front Ave *Web:* www.ppvnw.com	Portland	OR	97210	503-261-9800		539
P-Q Controls Inc 95 Dolphin Rd *Web:* www.pqcontrols.com	Bristol	CT	06010	860-583-6994		179
PQ Media LLC 2 Stamford Landing Ste 100 *Web:* www.pqmedia.com	Stamford	CT	06902	203-921-0368		466
PQC 4211 Hobson Ct Ste A *Web:* www.pqcworks.com	Fort Wayne	IN	46815	260-420-7374		463
P&R Enterprises Inc 5681 Columbia Pk Ste 101 *Web:* www.p-and-r.com	Falls Church	VA	22041	703-931-1000		256
P-R Farms Inc 2917 E Shepherd Ave *Web:* www.prfarms.com	Clovis	CA	93619	559-299-0201	299-7292	315-3
P&R Fasteners Inc 325 Pierce St *Web:* www.prfasteners.com	Somerset	NJ	08873	732-302-3600		621
Pr Hoffman Machine Products 1517 Commerce Ave. *Web:* www.prhoffman.com	Carlisle	PA	17015	717-243-9900		494
PRA International *PRA* 4130 Parklake Ave Ste 400 *Web:* prahs.com	Raleigh	NC	27612	919-786-8200		85
Prab Inc 5944 E Kilgore Rd. *TF:* 800-968-7722 ■ *Web:* www.prab.com	Kalamazoo	MI	49048	269-382-8200	349-2477	207
Practical Automation Inc 45 Woodmont Rd *Web:* www.practicalautomation.com	Milford	CT	06460	203-882-5640	882-5648	173-6
Practical Horseman Magazine 656 Quince OrchaRd Rd Ste 600 *TF:* 800-877-5396 ■ *Web:* practicalhorsemanmag.com	Gaithersburg	MD	20878	301-977-3900	990-9015	457-14
Practical Imagination Enterprising 18 Losey Rd *TF:* 800-939-4119 ■ *Web:* www.practical-imagination.com	Ringoes	NJ	08551	908-237-2246		195
Practice Concepts 2706 Harbor Blvd. *TF:* 877-778-2020 ■ *Web:* www.practiceconcepts.com	Costa Mesa	CA	92626	714-545-5110		317
Practice Management Consultants Inc 6115 Is Park Ct. *Web:* www.ehrpmc.com	Fort Myers	FL	33908	239-267-5444		196
Practice Technology Inc 1312 E Robinson St *TF:* 866-974-3946 ■ *Web:* prevail.net	Orlando	FL	32801	407-228-4400		177
Practice Velocity LLC 8777 Velocity Dr. *Web:* www.practicevelocity.com	Machesney Park	IL	61115	815-544-7480		180
Practicon Inc 1112 Sugg Pkwy *TF:* 800-959-9505 ■ *Web:* www.practicon.com	Greenville	NC	27834	252-752-5183		228
Practising Law Institute (PLI) 810 Seventh Ave 26th Fl. *TF:* 800-260-4754 ■ *Web:* www.pli.edu	New York	NY	10019	212-824-5700		49-10
Prada 609 W 51st St *Web:* www.prada.com	New York	NY	10019	212-307-9300		277
Prader-Willi Syndrome Assn (USA) 8588 Potter Pk Dr Ste 500 *TF:* 800-926-4797 ■ *Web:* www.pwsausa.org	Sarasota	FL	34238	941-312-0400	312-0142	48-17
Pradip Patel & Co 1701 E Woodfield Rd Ste 817 *Web:* patel-cpa.com	Schaumburg	IL	60173	847-413-0414		2
Prado Group Inc, The 150 Post St Ste 320 *Web:* www.pradogroup.com	San Francisco	CA	94108	415-395-0880		528
Prado Vision & Lasik Ctr 7522 N Himes Ave *TF:* 800-937-3937 ■ *Web:* www.pradovision.com	Tampa	FL	33614	813-931-0500		798
Praemittias Group Inc 8871 Ridgeline Blvd *Web:* www.praemittias.com	Highlands Ranch	CO	80129	720-344-0611		196
Pragati Synergetic Research Inc 801 Moffett Blvd NASA Research Park NASA Ames Rese Ste 1010 *Web:* www.pragati-inc.com	Moffett Field	CA	94035	650-625-0274		466
Pragma Corp, The 116 E Broad St *Web:* www.pragmacorp.com	Falls Church	VA	22046	703-237-9303		195
Pragma Systems Inc 13809 Research Blvd Ste 675 *TF:* 800-224-1675 ■ *Web:* www.pragmasys.com	Austin	TX	78750	512-219-7270	219-7110	178-12
Pragmatek Consulting Group 8500 Normandale Lake Blvd Ste 1060 *TF:* 800-833-3164 ■ *Web:* www.pragmatek.com	Bloomington	MN	55437	612-333-3164		194
Pragmatic Marketing Inc 8910 E Raintree Dr *Web:* www.pragmaticmarketing.com	Scottsdale	AZ	85260	480-515-1411		195
Pragmatics Inc 1761 Business Ctr Dr. *Web:* www.pragmatics.com	Reston	VA	20190	703-761-4033	438-1779	178-10
Prairie Band Casino & Resort 12305 150th Rd *TF:* 888-727-4946 ■ *Web:* www.prairieband.com	Mayetta	KS	66509	785-966-7777		133
Prairie Capital Management LLC 4900 Main St Ste 700 *Web:* www.prairiecapital.com	Kansas City	MO	64112	816-531-1101		401
Prairie Cardiovascular Consultants Ltd 619 E Mason St *Web:* www.prairiecardiovascular.com	Springfield	IL	62701	217-788-0706		194
Prairie City State Vehicular Recreation Area 13300 White Rock Rd *Web:* www.parks.ca.gov	Rancho Cordova	CA	95742	916-985-7378		565

Phone | Fax | Class

Prairie College
330 Fifth Ave NE PO Box 4000 Three Hills AB T0M2N0 403-443-5511 443-5540 785
TF: 800-661-2425 ■ *Web*: www.prairie.edu

Prairie County
200 Ct House Sq Ste 101 Ste 101 Des Arc AR 72040 870-256-4137 338
TF: 800-275-8777 ■ *Web*: prairiecountysheriff.org

Prairie County 217 W Pk St Terry MT 59349 406-635-5575 635-5576 338
Web: visitterrymt.com

Prairie Dog LLC 6155 Oak St Kansas City MO 64113 816-822-3636 7
Web: www.pdog.com

Prairie du Chien Correctional Institution
500 E Parrish St Prairie du Chien WI 53821 608-326-7828 213
Web: doc.wi.gov

Prairie Farms Dairy Inc
1100 N Broadway St Carlinville IL 62626 217-854-2547 854-6426 296-27
TF: 800-654-2547 ■ *Web*: www.prairiefarms.com

Prairie Group Inc 7601 W 79th St Bridgeview IL 60455 708-458-0400 182
TF Sales: 888-988-4400

Prairie Grove Battlefield State Park
506 E Douglas St Prairie Grove AR 72753 479-846-2990 565
Web: www.arkansasstateparks.com

Prairie Hotel 700 Prairie Pk Ln Yelm WA 98597 360-458-8300 458-8301 379
Web: www.prairiehotel.com

Prairie Inc
1260 Iroquois Dr Ste 300 Naperville IL 60563 630-983-6400 180
Web: www.prairieinc.com

Prairie Industries Inc
800 N State Prairie Du Chien WI 53821 608-326-2500 1
Web: www.pind.com

Prairie Knights Casino & Resort
7932 Hwy 24 Fort Yates ND 58538 701-854-7777 854-7786 133
TF: 800-425-8277 ■ *Web*: www.prairieknights.com

Prairie Lakes Area Education Agency
1235 Fifth Ave S Fort Dodge IA 50501 515-574-5500 685
TF: 800-669-2326 ■ *Web*: www.plaea.org

Prairie Lakes Hospital & Care Ctr
401 Ninth Ave NW Watertown SD 57201 605-882-7000 374-3
TF: 877-917-7547 ■ *Web*: www.prairielakes.com

Prairie Land Electric Co-op Inc
14935 US Hwy 36 Norton KS 67654 785-877-3323 245
TF: 800-577-3323 ■ *Web*: www.prairielandelectric.com

Prairie Life Fitness 2275 S 132nd St Omaha NE 68144 402-691-8546 354
Web: www.prairielife.com

Prairie Lights Bookstore
15 S Dubuque St Iowa City IA 52240 319-337-2681 95
TF: 800-295-2665 ■ *Web*: www.prairielights.com

Prairie Management & Development Inc
333 N Michigan Ave Ste 1700 Chicago IL 60601 312-644-1055 644-0686 653

Prairie Meadows 1 Prairie Meadows Dr Altoona IA 50009 515-967-1000 967-1344 133
TF: 800-325-9015 ■ *Web*: www.prairiemeadows.com

Prairie Mission Retirement Village
242 Carroll St Saint Paul KS 66771 620-449-2400 672
TF: 800-404-0421 ■ *Web*: www.pmrv.com

Prairie Pride Co-op 1100 E Main St Marshall MN 56258 507-532-9686 316
Web: www.prairiepridecoop.com

Prairie Public Broadcasting Inc
207 N Fifth St Fargo ND 58102 701-241-6900 239-7650 632
TF: 800-359-6900 ■ *Web*: www.prairiepublic.org

Prairie River Home Care Inc
25 First Ave NE Ste 200 Buffalo MN 55313 507-252-9844 363
Web: www.prhomecare.com

Prairie Rose State Park 680 Rd M47 Harlan IA 51537 712-773-2701 773-2702 565
Web: www.iowadnr.gov

Prairie Schooner Restaurant 445 Pk Blvd Ogden UT 84401 801-392-2712 671
TF: 800-888-8499 ■ *Web*: www.prairieschoonerrestaurant.com

Prairie Spirit Trail 419 S Oak St Garnett KS 66032 785-448-6767 565
Web: bikeprairiespirit.com

Prairie State Bank & Trust
1361 Toronto Rd Springfield IL 62712 217-786-2509 70
Web: www.psbank.net

Prairie State College
202 S Halsted St Chicago Heights IL 60411 708-709-3500 709-3951* 162
**Fax*: Admissions ■ *TF*: 866-255-5437 ■ *Web*: www.prairiestate.edu

Prairie State Park
128 NW 150th Ln Mindenmines MO 64769 417-843-6711 565
Web: www.mostateparks.com

Prairie Valley School Division No 208
Gd Indian Head SK S0G2K0 306-695-3939 623
Web: www.pvsd.ca

Prairie View A & M University
PO Box 519 Prairie View TX 77446 936-857-2626 261-1079* 166
**Fax*: Admissions ■ *TF*: 877-241-1752 ■ *Web*: www.pvamu.edu

Prairie View Sr. High School
13731 Ks Hwy 152 Lacygne KS 66040 913-757-4447 685
TF: 800-231-3056 ■ *Web*: www.pv362.org

Prairie Wetlands Learning Ctr
602 State Hwy 210 E Fergus Falls MN 56537 218-998-4480 50-5
Web: www.fws.gov

Prairie's Edge Casino Resort
5616 Prairies Edge Ln Granite Falls MN 56241 320-564-2121 452
Web: www.prairiesedgecasino.com

PrairieCoast Equipment
15102 101 St Grande Prairie AB T8V0P7 780-532-8402 612
Web: www.prairiecoastequipment.com

Prakat Solutions Inc
6016 Annandale Dr Fort Worth TX 76132 817-846-7541 177
Web: www.prakat.com

Prasco LLC 6125 Commerce Ct Mason OH 45040 513-618-3333 231
TF: 866-525-0688 ■ *Web*: www.prasco.com

Pratt & Whitney 400 Main St East Hartford CT 06108 860-565-4321 21
Web: www.pratt-whitney.com

Pratt & Whitney 17900 Bee Line Hwy Jupiter FL 33478 860-565-4321 504
Web: pw.utc.com

Pratt & Whitney AutoAir Inc
5640 Enterprise Dr Lansing MI 48911 517-393-4040 529
Web: www.autoair.com

Pratt & Whitney Canada Inc
1000 Marie-Victorin Blvd Longueuil QC J4G1A1 450-677-9411 647-3620 21
TF: 800-268-8000 ■ *Web*: www.pwc.ca

Phone | Fax | Class

Pratt Communications 2913 Tech Ctr Santa Ana CA 92705 714-540-6840 707
TF General: 800-980-2323 ■ *Web*: www.prattcommunications.com

Pratt Community College 348 NE SR-61 Pratt KS 67124 620-672-5641 162
TF: 800-794-3091 ■ *Web*: www.prattcc.edu

Pratt County
Pratt County Court House
300 S Ninnescah Pratt KS 67124 620-672-4112 672-9541 338
Web: www.prattcounty.org

Pratt Feeders LLC PO Box 945 Pratt KS 67124 620-672-6448 10-1
Web: www.prattfeeders.com

Pratt Fine Arts Center 1902 S Main St Seattle WA 98144 206-328-2200 720
TF: 800-704-2157 ■ *Web*: www.pratt.org

Pratt Industries Inc
11365 Red Arrow Hwy Bridgman MI 49106 269-465-7676 779
Web: www.prattinc.com

Pratt Industries USA
1800C Sarasota Pkwy Conyers GA 30013 770-918-5678 918-5679 548
TF: 800-835-2088 ■ *Web*: www.prattindustries.com

Pratt Institute 200 Willoughby Ave Brooklyn NY 11205 718-636-3669 636-3670 166
Web: www.pratt.edu

Pratt Paper (La) LLC
10429 Richard Pratt Dv Shreveport LA 71115 318-797-7375 548

Pratt Regional Medical Ctr Corp
200 Commodore St Pratt KS 67124 620-672-7451 374-3
TF: 877-572-2787 ■ *Web*: www.prmc.org

Prattville Machine & Tool Company Inc
240 Jubilee Dr 2nd Fl Peabody MA 01960 978-538-5229 454
Web: www.prattvillemachine.com

Prava Construction Services Inc
2032 Corte Del Nogal Ste 100 Carlsbad CA 92011 760-929-9787 186
Web: www.pravacsi.com

Praxair Inc 39 Old Ridgebury Rd Danbury CT 06810 203-837-2000 143
NYSE: PX ■ *TF*: 800-772-9247 ■ *Web*: www.praxair.com

Praxis Companies LLC, The
435 Industrial Rd Savannah TN 38372 731-925-7656 610

Praxis Consulting Group Inc
9 A/B W Highland Av Philadelphia PA 19118 215-753-0303 463
Web: www.praxiscg.com

Praxis Engineering Technologies Inc
135 National Business Pkwy Annapolis Junction MD 20701 301-490-4299 177
Web: praxiseng.com

Praxis Series Online Educational Testing Service Teaching & Learning Div (ETS)
PO Box 6051 Princeton NJ 08541 609-771-7395 530-0581 244
TF: 800-772-9476 ■ *Web*: www.ets.org

Pray, Walker, Jackman, Williamson, & Marlar
900 Oneok Plaza 100 W Fifth St Tulsa OK 74103 918-581-5500 428
Web: www.praywalker.com

PRB (Population Reference Bureau)
1875 Connecticut Ave NW Ste 520 Washington DC 20009 202-483-1100 328-3937 48-7
TF: 800-877-9881 ■ *Web*: www.prb.org

PRBA (Portable Rechargeable Battery Assn)
1776 K St 4th Fl Washington DC 20006 202-719-4978 49-13
Web: www.prba.org

PRC (Patients Rights Council)
PO Box 760 Steubenville OH 43952 740-282-3810 48-8
TF: 800-958-5678 ■ *Web*: www.patientsrightscouncil.org

PRC (Pacific Rivers)
317 SW Alder St Ste 900 Portland OR 97204 503-228-3555 228-3556 48-13
Web: www.pacificrivers.org

PRC (Population Resource Ctr)
1725 K St NW Washington DC 20006 202-467-5030 48-5
TF: 800-999-6779 ■ *Web*: prcdc.org

PRC Group 40 Monmouth Pk Hwy West Long Branch NJ 07764 732-222-2000 222-6410 655
TF: 800-437-2672 ■ *Web*: www.prcgroup.com

PRCA (Professional Rodeo Cowboys Assn)
101 Pro Rodeo Dr Colorado Springs CO 80919 719-593-8840 48-22
TF: 800-234-7722 ■ *Web*: www.prorodeo.com

PRE (Powder River Energy Corp)
221 Main St PO Box 930 Sundance WY 82729 800-442-3630 283-3527* 245
**Fax Area Code*: 307 ■ *TF*: 800-442-3630 ■ *Web*: www.precorp.coop

PREA (Pension Real Estate Assn)
100 Pearl St 13th Fl Hartford CT 06103 860-692-6341 692-6351 49-2
Web: www.prea.org

Preble County 101 E Main St Eaton OH 45320 937-456-8143 456-8114 338
Web: www.prebco.org

Preble County Chamber of Commerce
122 W Decatur St PO Box 303 Eaton OH 45320 937-456-4949 456-4949 139
Web: www.preblecountyohio.com

Preble Feed & Grain Inc 6035 N 400 W Preble IN 46782 260-547-4452 447
TF: 800-533-2268 ■ *Web*: kentfeeds.com

Preble-Shawnee School District
124 Bloomfield St Camden OH 45311 937-452-1283 685

Precast Specialties Corp
999 Adams St Abington MA 02351 781-878-7220 183
Web: www.precastspecialtiescorp.com

Pre-Cast Specialties Inc
1380 NE 48th St Pompano Beach FL 33064 954-781-4040 183
Web: www.precastspecialties.com

Precast/Prestressed Concrete Institute (PCI)
200 W Adams St Ste 2100 Chicago IL 60606 312-786-0300 786-0353 49-3
Web: www.pci.org

Precept Medical Communications Inc
3 Mtn View Rd Warren NJ 07059 908-647-1272 242

Precept Medical Products Inc
370 Airport Rd Arden NC 28704 828-681-0209 687-3605 576
TF: 800-438-5827 ■ *Web*: www.preceptmed.com

PreCheck Inc
2500 E T C Jester Blvd Ste Houston TX 77008 800-999-9861 363
TF: 800-999-9861 ■ *Web*: www.precheck.com

Precious Chemicals Company Inc
5855 Oberlin Dr San Diego CA 92121 858-455-7900 475
Web: www.captek.com

Precipio Diagnostics LLC
4 Science Pk 3rd Fl New Haven CT 06511 203-787-7888 415
Web: precipiodx.com

Precipitator Services Group Inc
1625 Broad St PO Box 339 Elizabethton TN 37644 423-543-7331 543-8737 18
Web: www.psgtn.net

Company / Address	City	State	Zip	Phone	Fax	Class
Precise Flight Inc 63354 Powell Butte Hwy *TF:* 800-547-2558 ■ *Web:* www.preciseflight.com	Bond	OR	97701	541-382-8684		22
Precise Industries Inc 610 Neptune Ave *TF:* 800-368-3376 ■ *Web:* www.preciseind.com	Brea	CA	92821	714-482-2333		697
Precise Light Surgical Inc 310 W Hamilton Ave Ste 210 *Web:* www.preciselightsurgical.com	Campbell	CA	95008	831-539-3323		475
Precise Machining Mfg 12716 E Pine St *Web:* www.precisemachining.com	Tulsa	OK	74116	918-438-3121		22
Precise Mailing Inc 168 Beacon St *Web:* www.precisemailing.com	South San Francisco	CA	94080	650-589-4000		7
Precise Packaging 300 Riggenbach Rd *Web:* www.precisepackaging.com	Fall River	MA	02720	508-677-2600		596
Precise Printing Equipment 1024 E Arlee Pl	Anaheim	CA	92805	714-991-0427		358
Precise Resource Group Inc 3016 Skyway Cir S *Web:* preciseresourcegroup.com	Irving	TX	75038	972-570-0121		5
Precise Tool & Gage Company Inc 30540 SE 84th St Unit 2 *Web:* www.precisetoolco.com	Preston	WA	98050	425-222-9567		246
Precision Abrasives 3176 Abbott Rd *TF:* 800-722-3967 ■ *Web:* www.wesand.com	Orchard Park	NY	14127	800-722-3967		1
Precision Aerospace Corp 11155 Jersey Blvd Ste A *Web:* www.precision-aerospace.com	Rancho Cucamonga	CA	91730	909-980-8855		22
Precision Aircraft Components Inc 2787 Armstrong Ln	Dayton	OH	45414	937-278-0265		529
Precision Airmotive LLC 14800 40th Ave NE **Fax:* Sales ■ *Web:* www.precisionairmotive.com	Marysville	WA	98271	360-651-8282	651-8080*	24
Precision Assoc Inc 3800 N Washington Ave *TF:* 800-394-6590 ■ *Web:* www.precisionassoc.com	Minneapolis	MN	55412	612-333-7464	342-2417	677
Precision Auto Care Inc 748 Miller Dr SE *OTC:* PACI ■ **Fax Area Code:* 703 ■ *TF:* 866-944-8863 ■ *Web:* www.precisiontune.com	Leesburg	VA	20175	866-944-8863	771-7108*	62-5
Precision Automation Company Inc 1841 Old Cuthbert Rd *Web:* www.precisionautomationinc.com	Cherry Hill	NJ	08034	856-428-7400		194
Precision BioLogic Inc 140 Eileen Stubbs Ave *TF:* 800-267-2796 ■ *Web:* www.precisionbiologic.com	Dartmouth	NS	B3B0A9	902-468-6422		475
Precision Cable Assemblies LLC 16830 Pheasant Dr *Web:* www.pca-llc.com	Brookfield	WI	53005	262-784-7887	784-0681	253
Precision Coating Company Inc 51 Parmenter Rd **Fax Area Code:* 978 ■ *Web:* www.precisioncoating.com	Hudson	MA	01749	781-329-1420	562-9622*	481
Precision Coatings Inc 8120 Goldie St *Web:* www.pcicoatings.com	Commerce Charter Twp	MI	48390	248-363-8361		596
Precision Coil Spring Co 10107 Rose Ave *TF:* 800-242-7214 ■ *Web:* www.pcspring.com	El Monte	CA	91731	626-444-0561	444-3712	719
Precision Component Industries 5325 Southway St SW *Web:* www.precision-component.com	Canton	OH	44706	330-477-6287	477-1052	757
Precision Computer Services Inc (PCS) 175 Constitution Blvd S *Web:* www.precisiongroup.com	Shelton	CT	06484	203-929-0000	929-8800	175
Precision Concepts Group LLC 2701 Boulder Park Ct *Web:* www.precisionconcepts.com	Winston-Salem	NC	27101	336-761-8572		488
Precision Countertops Inc 26200 SW 95th Ave Ste 303 *TF:* 800-548-4445 ■ *Web:* www.precisioncountertops.com	Wilsonville	OR	97070	503-692-6660		115
Precision Custom Components 500 Lincoln St **Fax:* Mktg ■ *Web:* www.pcc-york.com	York	PA	17401	717-848-1126	843-5733*	91
Precision Devices Inc 8840 N Greenview Dr *Web:* www.pdixtal.com	Middleton	WI	53562	608-831-4445		253
Precision Die & Stamping Inc 1704 W Tenth St *Web:* www.precisiondie.com	Tempe	AZ	85281	480-967-2038		483
Precision Drawn Metals Inc 1345 Plainfield Ave *Web:* www.drawnmetals.com	Janesville	WI	53545	608-755-1495		483
Precision Dynamics Corp 13880 Del Sur St *TF:* 800-847-0670 ■ *Web:* www.pdcorp.com	San Fernando	CA	91340	818-897-1111		477
Precision Econowind Inc 8940 N Fork Dr *TF:* 800-269-6301 ■ *Web:* www.precisioneconowind.com	North Fort Myers	FL	33903	239-997-3860		52
Precision Edge Surgical Products Co 415 W 12th Ave *Web:* www.precisionedge.com	Sault Sainte Marie	MI	49783	906-632-4800	632-5619	476
Precision Electronic Glass Inc 1013 Hendee Rd *TF:* 800-982-4734 ■ *Web:* www.pegglass.com	Vineland	NJ	08360	856-691-2234	691-3090	332
Precision Engine Controls Corp 11661 Sorrento Valley Rd *TF:* 800-200-4404 ■ *Web:* www.precisioneng.com	San Diego	CA	92121	858-792-3217		54
Precision Engineered Products LLC 262 Broad St *TF:* 800-722-1357 ■ *Web:* www.polymet.com	North Attleboro	MA	02760	508-695-7700	695-7700	485
Precision Extrusion Inc 12 Glens Falls Technical Pk *Web:* www.precisionextrusion.com	Glens Falls	NY	12801	518-792-1199		596
Precision Fabrics Group Inc 301 N Elm St Ste 600 *TF:* 800-284-8001 ■ *Web:* www.precisionfabrics.com	Greensboro	NC	27401	336-510-8000	510-8004	745-1
Precision Fasteners Tooling Inc 11530 Western Ave *Web:* www.precisionfastenertooling.com	Stanton	CA	90680	714-898-8558	891-4988	757
Precision Filters Inc 240 Cherry St *Web:* www.pfinc.com	Ithaca	NY	14850	607-277-3550		668
Precision Flow Technologies Inc PO Box 149	Saugerties	NY	12477	845-247-0810	247-8764	248
Precision Foods Inc 11457 Olde Cabin Rd Ste 100 *TF:* 800-442-5242 ■ *Web:* www.precisionfoods.com	Saint Louis	MO	63141	314-567-7400		296-37
Precision Gasket Co (PGC) 5732 Lincoln Dr *Web:* www.pgc-solutions.com	Edina	MN	55436	952-942-6711		326
Precision Gears Inc N 13 W 24705 Bluemound Rd *Web:* www.precisiongears.com	Pewaukee	WI	53072	262-542-4261	542-1592	454
Precision Governors Inc 2322 Seventh Ave *Web:* www.pgcontrols.com	Rockford	IL	61104	815-229-5300		203
Precision Graphics Inc 21 County Line Rd *Web:* www.precisiongraphics.us	Somerville	NJ	08876	908-707-8880		481
Precision Grinding & Manufacturing Corp 1305 Emerson St *Web:* www.pgmcorp.com	Rochester	NY	14606	585-458-4300	458-7281	493
Precision H20 Inc 6328 E Utah Ave *TF:* 800-425-2098 ■ *Web:* www.precisionh2o.com	Spokane	WA	99212	509-536-9214	536-9205	1
Precision Heat Treating Corp 2711 Adams Ctr Rd *Web:* www.phtc.net	Fort Wayne	IN	46803	260-749-5125		484
Precision Hose 2200 Centre Park Ct *TF:* 877-850-2662 ■ *Web:* www.precisionhose.com	Stone Mountain	GA	30087	770-413-5680		295
Precision Husky Corp 850 Markeeta Spur Rd *TF:* 800-959-0880 ■ *Web:* www.precisionhusky.com	Moody	AL	35004	205-640-5181	640-1147	190
Precision Hydraulic Cylinders Inc 196 N Hwy 41 *Web:* www.phc-global.com	Beulaville	NC	28518	910-298-0100		358
Precision IBC Inc 8054 Mcgowin Dr *TF:* 800-544-7069 ■ *Web:* www.precisionibc.com	Fairhope	AL	36532	251-990-6789		690
Precision Industries Acquisitions Inc 222 Riggs Ave *Web:* www.pic-design.com	Portland	TN	37148	615-325-4127		489
Precision Kidd Steel Company Inc 1 Quality Way *TF:* 800-945-5003 ■ *Web:* www.precisionkidd.com	Aliquippa	PA	15001	724-378-7670		697
Precision Laboratories Inc 1429 S Shields Dr *TF:* 800-323-6280 ■ *Web:* www.precisionlab.com	Waukegan	IL	60085	847-596-3001	596-3017	145
Precision Machine & Manufacturing Inc 1290 S Bertelsen Rd *TF:* 800-918-3013 ■ *Web:* www.premach.com	Eugene	OR	97402	541-484-9841		454
Precision Machine Works Inc 2024 Puyallup Ave *Web:* www.cadenceaerospace.com	Tacoma	WA	98421	253-272-5119		621
Precision Machined Products Assn (PMPA) 6700 W Snowville Rd *TF:* 800-233-1234 ■ *Web:* www.pmpa.org	Brecksville	OH	44141	440-526-0300	526-5803	49-13
Precision Manufacturing Group LLC 501 Little Falls Rd *TF:* 800-785-0756 ■ *Web:* www.servometer.com	Cedar Grove	NJ	07009	973-785-4630		295
Precision Masking Inc 721 Lavoy Rd *Web:* www.precisionmasking.com	Erie	MI	48133	734-848-4200		480
Precision Metal Inc 1408 SW Eighth St *Web:* www.pmi-inc.net	Pompano Beach	FL	33069	954-942-6303		567
Precision Metal Products Co 353 Garden Ave PO Box 1047 *Web:* www.pmpc1.com	Holland	MI	49422	616-886-1085	298-3524	621
Precision Metal Products Inc 850 W Bradley Ave *Web:* www.pmp-elcajon.com	El Cajon	CA	92020	619-448-2711		483
Precision Metal Products Inc 307 Pepe's Farm Rd *Web:* www.pmpinc.biz	Milford	CT	06460	203-877-4258	878-8353	454
Precision Metal Services Inc 418 Stump Rd *Web:* www.precisionmetalservices.com	Montgomeryville	PA	18936	215-661-0225		492
Precision Metal Works 6901 Preston Hwy *TF:* 877-511-9695 ■ *Web:* www.nth-works.com	Louisville	KY	40219	877-511-9695		757
Precision Metalforming Assn (PMA) 6363 Oak Tree Blvd *Web:* www.pma.org/home	Independence	OH	44131	216-901-8800	901-9190	49-3
Precision Metalsmiths Inc 15583 Brookpark Rd *Web:* avalon-castings.com	Cleveland	OH	44142	216-362-4100		306
Precision Molding Inc 5500 Roberts Matthews Hwy *Web:* www.precision-molding.com	Sparta	TN	38583	931-738-8376	738-8429	602
Precision Multiple Controls Inc 33 Greenwood Ave *Web:* pmcontrols.com	Midland Park	NJ	07432	201-444-0600	445-8575	203
Precision Opinion Inc 101 Convention Center Dr Plaza 124 *Web:* www.precisionopinion.com	Las Vegas	NV	89109	702-483-4000		748
Precision Optics Corp Inc 22 E Broadway *OTC:* PEYE ■ *TF:* 800-447-2812 ■ *Web:* www.poci.com	Gardner	MA	01440	978-630-1800	630-1487	382
Precision Paper Converters LLC 2600 Northridge Dr *Web:* www.cornerstone-business.com	Kaukauna	WI	54130	920-462-0050		558
Precision Paper Tube Company Inc 1033 S Noel Ave *Web:* www.pptube.com	Wheeling	IL	60090	847-537-4250	537-5777	125
Precision Parts & Remanufacturing Co 4411 SW 19th St *TF:* 800-654-3846 ■ *Web:* www.pprok.com	Oklahoma City	OK	73108	405-681-2592	681-2596	247

	Phone	Fax	Class
Precision Pipeline Solutions LLC 617 Little Britain Rd Ste 200................New Windsor NY 12553 *Web:* www.precisionpipelinesolutions.com	845-566-8332		597
Precision Piping & Mechanical Inc 5201 Middle Mt Vernon Rd.................. Evansville IN 47712 *Web:* www.ppmiconstruction.com	812-425-5052	425-5067	189-10
Precision Plastics Inc 900 W Connexion Way..................Columbia City IN 46725 *Web:* www.pplastic.com	260-244-6114		604
Precision Plus Inc 840 Kootman Ln PO Box 168.................. Elkhorn WI 53121 *Web:* www.preplus.com	262-743-1700	743-1701	621
Precision Printer Services Inc 9185 Portage Industrial Dr.................... Portage MI 49024 *Web:* www.precisionprinterservices.com	269-384-5725		589
Precision Products Group Inc 10201 N Illinois St Ste 390.................Indianapolis IN 46290 *TF:* 888-808-4341 ■ *Web:* www.ppgintl.com	317-663-4590		601
Precision Products Inc 316 Limit St............ Lincoln IL 62656 *TF Cust Svc:* 800-225-5891 ■ *Web:* www.precisionprodinc.com	217-735-1590	735-2435	429
Precision Pump & Valve Service Inc 517 Old Goff Mtn Rd..............................Cross Lanes WV 25313 *TF:* 800-339-4513 ■ *Web:* www.ppvs.com	304-776-1710		14
Precision Resource 25 Forest Pkwy............ Shelton CT 06484 *Web:* www.precisionresource.com	203-925-0012		488
Precision Roll Grinders Inc 6356 Chapmans Rd ....Allentown PA 18106 *Web:* www.precisionrollgrinders.com	610-395-6966	481-9130	454
Precision Rubber Plate Company Inc 5620 Elmwood Ave.......................Indianapolis IN 46203 *Web:* www.prpflexo.com	317-783-3226		629
Precision Screw Machine Products Inc 20 Gooch St.............................Biddeford ME 04005 *Web:* www.psmp.com	207-283-0121	283-4824	621
Precision Screw Thread Corp S 82 W 19275 Apollo Dr.................... Muskego WI 53150 *Web:* thopctgroup.com	262-679-9000		454
Precision Sensors Inc 50 Seemans Ln ....Milford CT 06460 *Web:* www.precisionsensors.com	203-877-2795		790
Precision Shooting Equipment Inc 2727 N Fairview Ave..........................Tucson AZ 85705 *TF:* 800-477-7789 ■ *Web:* www.pse-archery.com	520-884-9065		710
Precision Solutions Inc 2525 Tollgate Rd......................... Quakertown PA 18951 *TF:* 800-723-9523 ■ *Web:* www.precisionsolutionsinc.com	215-536-4400		362
Precision Southeast Inc 4900 Hwy 501 PO Box 50610.............Myrtle Beach SC 29579 *Web:* www.precisionsoutheast.com	843-347-4218		608
Precision Specialties Co 1201 East Pecan St......................... Sherman TX 75090 **Fax Area Code:* 903 ■ *TF:* 800-527-3295 ■ *Web:* www.presco.com	800-527-3295	893-2328*	407
Precision Steel Manufacturing Corp 1723 Seibel Dr NE ....Roanoke VA 24012 *Web:* precisionsteelmfg.com	540-985-8963		492
Precision Steel Warehouse Inc 3500 Wolf Rd ....Franklin Park IL 60131 *TF:* 800-323-0740 ■ *Web:* www.precisionsteel.com	847-455-7000	455-1341	492
Precision Strip Inc 86 S Ohio St PO Box 104..................... Minster OH 45865 *Web:* www.precision-strip.com	419-628-2343		494
Precision Tank & Equipment Company Inc 3503 Conover Rd .... Virginia IL 62691 *TF:* 800-258-4197 ■ *Web:* www.precisiontank.com	217-452-7228	452-3956	273
Precision Techniques Inc 1169 E 156 St ....Bronx NY 10474 *Web:* www.precisiontechniques.com	718-991-1440		596
Precision Technologies Inc 14005 Northdale Blvd........................Rogers MN 55374 *Web:* www.circuitboards-pti.com	763-428-2234		454
Precision Technology USA Inc 225 Glade View Dr ....Roanoke VA 24012 *Web:* www.pt-usa.net	540-857-9871		709
Precision Thermoplastic Components Inc PO Box 1296 .... Lima OH 45802 *TF:* 800-860-4505 ■ *Web:* www.ptclima.com	419-227-4500		608
Precision Time Systems Inc 349 McKay Rd ....Bolivia NC 28422 *TF:* 800-849-3429 ■ *Web:* www.precisiontime.com	910-253-9850		407
Precision Tool Technologies Inc 309 13th Ave NW .... Little Falls MN 56345 *Web:* www.precisiontooltech.com	320-632-5320		543
Precision Trading Corp 15800 NW 48th Ave .... Miami Gardens FL 33014 *Web:* www.precisiontrading.com	305-592-4500	593-6169	38
Precision Tube Company Inc 287 Wissahickon Ave......................North Wales PA 19454 *TF:* 800-889-5878 ■ *Web:* www.precisiontube.com	215-699-5801		492
Precision Tube Inc 1025 Fortune Dr .... Richmond KY 40475 *Web:* www.ptube.net	859-623-5595		454
Precision Valve Corp 800 Westchester Ave....................... Rye Brook NY 10573 *TF:* 866-686-8464 ■ *Web:* www.precisionglobal.com	914-969-6500		487
Precision Wall Systems Inc 102 Vander Horck St.......................... Britton SD 57430	605-448-2929		499
Precision Walls Inc 1230 NE MaynaRd Rd ....Cary NC 27513 *TF:* 800-849-9255 ■ *Web:* www.precisionwalls.com	919-832-0380	839-1402	189-9
Precision Wood Products Inc 2456 Aukerman Crk Rd.........................Camden OH 45311 *Web:* www.precisionwoodproducts.com	937-787-3523		551
Precision X-Ray Inc 15 Commerce Dr ....North Branford CT 06471 *Web:* www.pxinc.com	203-484-2011		475
Precisionform Inc 148 W Airport Rd ....Lititz PA 17543 *TF:* 800-233-3821 ■ *Web:* www.precisionform.com	717-560-7610		621
Precitech Precision Inc 44 Blackbrook Rd.............................Keene NH 03431 *TF:* 800-936-8100 ■ *Web:* www.precitech.com	603-357-2511	358-6174	493
Precix Inc 744 Bellville Ave .... New Bedford MA 02745 *TF:* 800-225-8505 ■ *Web:* www.precixinc.com	508-998-4000	998-4100	677
Preclick Corp 140 Ocean Blvd ....Atlantic Highlands NJ 07716 *Web:* www.preclick.com	732-291-7269		180
Preco Electronics Inc 10335 W Emerald St............................Boise ID 83704 *TF:* 866-977-7326 ■ *Web:* www.preco.com	208-323-1000		472
Precoat Metals 1310 Papin St 3rd Fl...................... Saint Louis MO 63103 *Web:* www.precoat.com	317-462-7761		481
Precor Inc 20031 142nd Ave NE ....Woodinville WA 98072 *TF:* 800-786-8404 ■ *Web:* www.precor.com	425-486-9292	486-3856	267
Precorp Inc 2024 N Chappel Dr.............Spanish Fork UT 84660 *Web:* www.precorp.net	801-798-5425		697
Predator Trucking Co 3181 Trumbull Ave .... McDonald OH 44437 *TF:* 800-235-5624 ■ *Web:* www.predatortrucking.com	330-530-0712		780
Predicate Logic Inc 6155 Cornerstone Ct E..................... San Diego CA 92121 *Web:* www.predicate.com	858-715-0100		177
Prediction Sciences LLC 3252 Holiday Ct Ste 209...................... La Jolla CA 92037 *Web:* www.predict.net	858-404-0404		463
Prediction Systems Inc 309 Morris Ave Ste G ....Spring Lake NJ 07762 *Web:* www.predictsys.com	732-449-6800	449-0897	178-8
PredictWallStreet LLC 1840 41st Ave Ste 102-171 ....Capitola CA 95010 *Web:* www.predictwallstreet.com	831-464-0308		466
Preece Inc 26845 Vista Terr................. Lake Forest CA 92630 *Web:* www.preeceinc.com	949-770-9411		21
Pre-employ.com Inc 2301 Balls Ferry Rd ....Anderson CA 96007 *TF:* 800-300-1821 ■ *Web:* www.pre-employ.com	530-378-7680		400
Preference Personnel Inc 2600 Ninth Ave S ....Fargo ND 58103 *Web:* www.preferencepersonnel.com	701-293-6905		260
Preferred Bank Los Angeles 601 S Figueroa St 29th Fl..................Los Angeles CA 90017 *NASDAQ: PFBC* ■ *TF:* 888-673-1808 ■ *Web:* www.preferredbank.com	213-891-1188	622-0369	70
Preferred CommunityChoice PPO 218 W Sixth St .... Tulsa OK 74119 *TF:* 800-884-4776 ■ *Web:* www.ccok.com	918-594-5200		391-3
Preferred Dental Laboratory Inc 37 Woodland Rd...........................Roseland NJ 07068 *Web:* www.preferreddentalgroup.com	973-228-7777		415
Preferred Employers Group Inc 10800 Biscayne Blvd .... Miami FL 33161	305-899-0404		391-4
Preferred Employers Insurance Co PO Box 85478 .... San Diego CA 92186 **Fax Area Code:* 619 ■ *TF Cust Svc:* 888-472-9001 ■ *Web:* www.peiwc.com	866-472-9602	688-3913*	391-4
Preferred Health Systems Inc 8535 E 21st Ct N........................... Wichita KS 67206 *TF:* 800-990-0345 ■ *Web:* chckansas.coventryhealthcare.com	316-609-2345		391-3
Preferred Homecare Infusion LLC 4601 E Hilton Ave Ste 100 ....Phoenix AZ 85034 *TF:* 800-636-2123 ■ *Web:* preferredhomecare.com	480-446-9010		363
Preferred Hotel Group 311 S Wacker Dr Ste 1900 ....Chicago IL 60606 *Web:* preferredhotels.com	312-913-0400	913-5124	379
Preferred Hotels & Resorts Worldwide Inc 311 S Wacker Dr Ste 1900..................Chicago IL 60606 *TF:* 800-650-1281 ■ *Web:* preferredhotels.com	312-913-0400	913-5124	379
Summit Hotels & Resorts 311 S Wacker Dr Ste 1900..................Chicago IL 60606 *TF:* 866-990-9491 ■ *Web:* preferredhotels.com	312-913-0400	913-5124	379
Preferred Meal Systems Inc 5240 St Charles Rd...........................Berkeley IL 60163 **Fax Area Code:* 708 ■ *TF Cust Svc:* 800-886-6325 ■ *Web:* preferredmeals.com	800-886-6325	493-2690*	296-36
Preferred Medical Marketing Corp 15720 Brixham Hill Ave Ste 460............ Charlotte NC 28277 *TF:* 800-543-8176 ■ *Web:* www.pmmconline.com	704-543-8103		177
Preferred Mental Health Management Inc 7309 E 21st St N Ste 110............... Wichita KS 67206 *TF:* 800-819-9571 ■ *Web:* www.pmhm.com	316-262-0444		462
Preferred Mutual Insurance Co 1 Preferred Way ....New Berlin NY 13411 **Fax:* Mail Rm ■ *TF:* 800-333-7642 ■ *Web:* www.preferredmutual.com	607-847-6161	847-8046*	391-4
Preferred Plastics Inc 800 E Bridge St............................ Plainwell MI 49080 *Web:* www.preferredplastics.net	269-685-5873		608
Preferred Popcorn LLC 1132 Ninth Rd ....Chapman NE 68827 *Web:* www.preferredpopcorn.com	308-986-2526		123
Preferred Professional Insurance Company Inc 11605 Miracle Hills Dr Ste 200 ....Omaha NE 68154 *Web:* www.ppicins.com	402-392-1566		390
Preferred Properties of Venice Inc 325 W Venice Ave............................ Venice FL 34285 *Web:* www.venicefIproperties.com	941-485-9602		652
Preferred Rubber Compounding Corp 1020 Lambert St...........................Barberton OH 44203 *Web:* preferredperforms.com	330-798-4790		605-3
Preferred Sands LLC 100 Matsonford Rd One Radnor Corporate Ctr......Radnor PA 19087 *Web:* preferredsands.com	610-834-1969		191-1
Preferred Strategies LLC 2425 Porter St Ste 20......................... Soquel CA 95073 *TF:* 888-232-7337 ■ *Web:* www.preferredstrategies.com	888-232-7337		177
Preferred Systems Solutions Inc 1945 Old Gallows Rd Ste 450.................. Vienna VA 22182 *TF:* 877-422-7149 ■ *Web:* www.pssfed.com	703-663-2777	663-2780	180
Preferred Traveler 4501 Forbes Blvd............ Lanham MD 20706 *TF:* 888-354-6309 ■ *Web:* www.preferredtraveller.com	866-679-8655		531-6
PreferredOne Administrative Services Inc 6105 Golden Hills Dr .... Golden Valley MN 55416 *TF:* 800-451-9597 ■ *Web:* www.preferredone.com	763-847-4000		463
Prefix Corp 1300 W Hamlin Rd .... Rochester Hills MI 48309 *TF:* 800-732-5569 ■ *Web:* www.prefix.com	248-650-1330		261
Preformed Line Products 660 Beta Dr ....Cleveland OH 44143 *NASDAQ: PLPC* ■ *TF:* 800-622-6757 ■ *Web:* www.preformed.com	440-461-5200	442-8816	815

Company / Address	City	State	ZIP	Phone	Fax	Class
Prego 2520 Amherst St	Houston	TX	77005	713-529-2420		671
Web: www.prego-houston.com						
Prein & Newhof Inc						
3355 Evergreen Dr NE	Grand Rapids	MI	49525	616-364-8491	364-6955	261
Web: www.preinnewhof.com						
Preis & Roy PLC						
Versailles Centre 102 Versailles Blvd						
Ste 400	Lafayette	LA	70501	337-237-6062		428
Web: www.pkrlaw.com						
Prejean's Restaurant						
3480 NE Evangeline Trwy	Lafayette	LA	70507	337-896-3247	896-3278	671
Web: www.prejeans.com						
Prelco Inc 94 Blvd Cartier	Rivi Re-Du-Loup	QC	G5R2M9	418-862-2274		329
TF: 800-463-1325 ■ *Web:* www.prelco.ca						
Preload Inc 49 Wireless Blvd STE 200	Hauppauge	NY	11788	631-231-8100	231-8881	183
Web: www.preload.com						
Prelude Systems Inc						
5095 Ritter Rd ste 112	Mechanicsburg	PA	17055	800-579-1047	441-2410*	177
**Fax Area Code:* 717 ■ *TF:* 800-579-1047 ■ *Web:* preludeservices.com						
Premarc Corp 7505 E M 71	Durand	MI	48429	989-288-2661		183
Premco Inc						
55 Research Rd S Shore Industrial Park	Hingham	MA	02043	781-749-0333		454
Web: www.premco.net						
Premcom Corp						
85 Northpointe Pkwy Ste 100	Amherst	NY	14228	716-691-0791		180
Web: www.premcom.com						
Premedia Group LLC						
1185 Revolution Mill Dr Ste 1-16	Greensboro	NC	27405	336-274-2421		344
Web: www.premediagroup.com						
Premera Blue Cross Blue						
7001 220th St SW Bldg 1	Mountlake Terrace	WA	98043	855-629-0987		391-3
TF Cust Svc: 855-629-0987 ■ *Web:* premera.com						
Premier Alaska Tours Inc						
1900 Premier Ct	Anchorage	AK	99502	907-279-0001		760
TF: 888-486-8725 ■ *Web:* www.premieralaskatours.com						
Premier Aluminum LLC						
3633 S Memorial Dr	Racine	WI	53403	262-554-2100		492
TF: 800-254-9261 ■ *Web:* www.premieraluminum.com						
Premier America Credit Union						
19867 Prairie St PO Box 2178	Chatsworth	CA	91313	818-772-4000		219
TF: 800-772-4000 ■ *Web:* www.premieramerica.com						
Premier BPO Inc						
102 Country Ln Ste B	Clarksville	TN	37043	931-551-8888		393
Web: www.premierbpo.com						
Premier Civil Engineering LLC						
1302 Calle Del Norte Ste 2	Laredo	TX	78041	956-717-1199		261
Web: premier-ce.com						
Premier Coach Company Inc 946 Rte 7 S	Milton	VT	05468	802-655-4456	655-4213	107
TF: 800-532-1811 ■ *Web:* www.premiercoach.net						
Premier Colors Inc 100 Industrial Dr	Union	SC	29379	864-427-0338	427-5824	145
TF: 800-245-6944 ■ *Web:* www.premiercolorsinc.com						
Premier Communications						
339 First Ave NE	Sioux Center	IA	51250	712-722-3451		116
Web: www.mtcnet.net						
Premier Community Bankshares Inc						
4095 Valley Pk	Winchester	VA	22602	540-869-6600		360-2
Web: nasdaq.com						
Premier Concrete Products						
5102 Galveston Rd	Houston	TX	77017	713-641-2727	641-1112	183
TF: 800-575-7293 ■ *Web:* www.premier-concrete.com						
Premier Courier Service Inc						
410 Eighth Ave	New York	NY	10001	212-684-0901		317
Web: www.premier-nyc.com						
Premier Dental Products Co						
1710 Romano Dr PO Box 4500	Plymouth Meeting	PA	19462	610-239-6000	239-6171	228
TF: 888-773-6872 ■ *Web:* www.premusa.com						
Premier Die Casting Co 1177 Rahway Ave	Avenel	NJ	07001	732-634-3000	634-0590	308
TF: 800-394-3006 ■ *Web:* www.diecasting.com						
Premier Direct Marketing Inc						
7725 National Tpke Unit 100	Louisville	KY	40214	502-367-6441		195
TF: 800-737-0205 ■ *Web:* premierdm.net						
Premier Electrical Corp						
4401 85th Ave N	Brooklyn Park	MN	55443	763-424-6551	424-5225	189-4
Web: www.premiercorp.net						
Premier Electronics Inc						
465 Rockaway Ave	Valley Stream	NY	11581	516-837-3160		693
Premier Elevator Company Inc						
230 Andrew Dr	Stockbridge	GA	30281	770-389-4951		791
TF: 800-953-3229 ■ *Web:* www.premier-elevator.com						
Premier Equipment Inc						
990 Sunshine Ln	Altamonte Springs	FL	32714	407-786-2000		385
Web: www.premierequipment.com						
Premier Equipment LLC 2025 US Hwy 14 W	Huron	SD	57350	800-627-5469		274
TF: 800-627-5469 ■ *Web:* www.premierequhuron.com						
Premier Eyecare Group Inc						
1524 Cedar Cliff Dr	Camp Hill	PA	17011	717-761-3077		543
TF: 800-731-3937 ■ *Web:* www.premiereyes.com						
Premier Financial Bancorp Inc						
2883 Fifth Ave	Huntington	WV	25702	304-522-1645		360-2
NASDAQ: PFBI						
Premier Gear & Machine Works Inc						
1700 NW Thurman St	Portland	OR	97209	503-227-3514	227-1611	821
TF: 800-766-6705 ■ *Web:* www.premier-gear.com						
Premier Golf 4355 River Green Pkwy	Duluth	GA	30096	770-291-4202	291-5157	771
TF: 866-260-4409 ■ *Web:* www.premiergolf.com						
Premier Graphics LLC						
1248 W Fourth St	Mansfield	OH	44906	419-529-0555		627
TF: 800-511-4881 ■ *Web:* www.premiergraphicsinc.com						
Premier Homecare Inc						
6123 Montrose Rd	Rockville	MD	20852	301-984-1742		363
TF: 800-493-8990 ■ *Web:* www.jssa.org						
Premier Hotel Times Square, The						
133 W 44th St	New York	NY	10036	212-789-7670		379
Web: millenniumhotels.com						
Premier Inc 12255 El Camino Real	San Diego	CA	92130	858-481-2727		353
TF: 877-777-1552 ■ *Web:* www.premierinc.com						
Premier Incentives 6 Admiral Ln	Salem	MA	01970	978-607-0135		384
Web: www.premierincentives.com						
Premier Insurance Corp Inc						
1326 Cape Coral Pkwy E	Cape Coral	FL	33904	239-542-7101		390
Web: premierinsurancecorp.com						
Premier Integrity Solutions Inc						
7 Jamestown St	Russell Springs	KY	42642	270-866-3144		743
Web: www.premierintegrity.com						
Premier Jet Ctr						
3301 NE Cornell Rd Ste A	Hillsboro	OR	97124	503-693-1096		63
Premier Jets 2140 NE 25th Ave	Hillsboro	OR	97124	503-640-2927		13
TF: 800-635-8583 ■ *Web:* www.premierjets.com						
Premier Malt Products Inc						
25760 Groesbeck Hwy Ste 103	Warren	MI	48089	586-443-3355		461
TF Cust Svc: 800-521-1057 ■ *Web:* www.premiermalt.com						
Premier Management Corp						
8894 Stanford Blvd Ste 405	Columbia	MD	21045	443-656-3550		225
TF: 800-564-0483 ■ *Web:* premgtcorp.com						
Premier Manufacturing Corp						
12117 Bennington Ave	Cleveland	OH	44135	216-941-9700	941-9719	389
Premier Medical Group Pc						
1850 Business Pk Dr PO Box 3799	Clarksville	TN	37043	931-245-7000		374-3
Web: www.premiermed.com						
Premier Members Credit Union						
5495 Arapahoe Ave	Boulder	CO	80303	303-657-7000	657-7353	219
TF: 800-468-0634 ■ *Web:* www.pmfcu.org						
Premier Micronutrient Corp						
1801 W End Ave Ste 920	Nashville	TN	37203	615-234-4020		479
Web: www.premiermicronutrient.com						
Premier Network Solutions Inc						
5070 Oaklawn Dr	Cincinnati	OH	45227	513-631-6381		180
Web: prenet.com						
Premier Nursing Services Inc						
444 W Ocean Blvd Ste 1050	Long Beach	CA	90802	562-437-4313		260
Web: www.premiernursing.com						
Premier Pacific Seafoods Inc						
111 W Harrison St	Seattle	WA	98119	206-286-8584	286-8810	297-5
Web: prempac.com						
Premier Paint Roller LLC						
131-11 Atlantic Ave	Richmond Hill	NY	11418	718-441-7700		586
TF: 800-613-0151 ■ *Web:* www.premierpaintroller.com						
Premier Pan Company Inc						
33 Mcgovern Blvd	Crescent	PA	15046	724-457-4220		483
Web: www.prestigehomes.com						
Premier Performance LLC						
278 E Dividend Dr	Rexburg	ID	83440	208-356-0106	359-1414	146
Web: premierwd.com						
Premier Plastics Inc						
5520 Colby Lake Rd	Hoyt Lakes	MN	55750	218-225-3500		596
Web: premierplasticsmn.com						
Premier Pump & Supply Inc						
19 Fruite St	Belmont	NH	03220	603-528-3100		358
Web: www.premierpumponline.com						
Premier Pyrotechnics Inc 25255 Hwy K	Richland	MO	65556	888-647-6863		45
TF: 888-647-6863 ■ *Web:* www.premierpyro.com						
Premier Realty Group						
2 N Sewalls Point Rd	Stuart	FL	34996	772-287-1777		652
TF: 800-915-8517 ■ *Web:* www.premierrealtygroup.com						
Premier Safety & Service Inc						
2 Industrial Pk Dr	Oakdale	PA	15071	724-693-8699	693-8698	386
TF: 800-828-1080 ■ *Web:* www.premiersafety.com						
Premier Staffing Services of New York Inc						
1 N Broadway Ste 801	White Plains	NY	10601	914-428-2233	428-5547	721
Web: www.thepremiergroup.com						
Premier Subaru LLC 150 N Main St	Branford	CT	06405	203-481-0687	481-1861	57
TF: 888-690-6710 ■ *Web:* www.premiersubaru.com						
Premier System Integrators Inc						
140 Weakley Ln	Smyrna	TN	37167	615-355-7200		203
Web: www.premier-system.com						
Premier Tax & Financial Services						
121 W 27th St Ste 1003A	New York	NY	10001	212-807-8201		734
Web: premiertaxandfinancial.com						
Premier Tech Industrial Equipment Group						
1 Premier Ave	Rivere-du-Loup	QC	G5R6C1	418-867-8884	862-6642	684
TF: 866-571-7354 ■ *Web:* www.ptchronos.com						
Premier Tool & Die Cast Corp						
9886 N Tudor Rd	Berrien Springs	MI	49103	269-471-7715	471-3855	308
TF: 800-417-8717 ■ *Web:* www.premierdiecast.com						
Premier Tours 21 S 12th St 9th Fl	Philadelphia	PA	19107	800-545-1910		760
TF: 800-545-1910 ■ *Web:* www.premiertours.com						
Premier Truck Parts Inc						
5800 W Canal Rd	Cleveland	OH	44125	216-642-5000		57
Web: www.premiertruckparts.com						
Premier Valley Bank						
255 E River Pk Cir Ste 180	Fresno	CA	93720	559-438-2002		70
TF: 877-438-2002 ■ *Web:* www.premiervalleybank.com						
PremierComm LLC						
415 N Prince St Ste 200	Lancaster	PA	17603	717-431-7100		196
Web: www.premiercommllc.com						
PremierCo-op Inc 2104 W Pk Ct	Champaign	IL	61821	217-355-1983	355-3478	275
Web: www.premiercooperative.net						
Premiere Concrete Inc						
11332 Red Lion Rd	White Marsh	MD	21162	410-344-1604		186
TF: 800-223-4199 ■ *Web:* premierconcrete.biz						
Premiere Credit of North America LLC						
2002 Wellesley Blvd Ste 100	Indianapolis	IN	46219	866-808-7118		160
TF: 866-808-7118 ■ *Web:* www.premierecredit.com						
Premiere Global Services Inc (PGI)						
3280 Peachtree Rd NE Ste 1000	Atlanta	GA	30305	719-457-6901		39
NYSE: PGI ■ *TF:* 866-548-3203 ■ *Web:* www.pgi.com						
Premiere Hotel						
625 N Ft Lauderdale Beach Blvd	Fort Lauderdale	FL	33304	954-566-7676		379
Premiere Travel Services Inc						
7900 Westpark Dr Ste A60	Mclean	VA	22102	703-893-2288		772
TF: 800-458-8670 ■ *Web:* www.premieretravel.com						
PremierGarage 335 Victory Dr	Herndon	VA	20170	703-707-0009		310
TF: 866-590-9411 ■ *Web:* www.premiergarage.com						
Premins Company Inc, The 1407 Ave M	Brooklyn	NY	11230	718-375-8300		390
Web: preminsco.com						
Premio Foods Inc 50 Utter Ave	Hawthorne	NJ	07506	973-427-1106		296-26
Web: www.premiofoods.com						

Name / Address	City	State	ZIP	Phone	Fax	Class
Premium Color Group LLC						
95-B Industrial	Clifton	NJ	07012	973-472-7007		627
Web: www.premiumcolor.com						
Premium Distributors						
3500 Fort Lincoln Dr NE	Washington	DC	20018	202-526-3900		81-1
TF: 800-926-0055 ■ *Web:* reyesholdings.com						
Premium Distributors of Maryland LLC						
530 Monocacy Blvd	Frederick	MD	21701	301-662-0372		81-1
Web: www.reyesholdings.com						
Premium Distributors of VA LLC						
15001 Northridge Dr	Chantilly	VA	20151	703-227-1200		81-1
Web: reyesholdings.com						
Premium Feeders Inc 705 US Hwy 36	Scandia	KS	66966	785-335-2221		10-1
Premium Plastic Solutions LLC						
59 Bay Hill Dr	Latrobe	PA	15650	724-424-7000		596
Web: www.premiummolding.com						
Premium Retail Services Inc						
618 Spirit Dr	Chesterfield	MO	63005	636-728-0592		193
Web: www.premiumretail.com						
Premium Rx National LLC						
11736 Parklawn Dr	Rockville	MD	20852	301-230-0908		237
Premium Transportation Staffing Inc						
190 Highland Dr	Medina	OH	44256	330-722-7974		734
Web: www.premiumdrivers.com						
Premix Inc						
6151 Wilson Mills Rd Ste 310	Highland Heights	OH	44143	440-224-2181	224-2766	604
Web: www.premix.com						
Premix-Marbletite Manufacturing Co						
1259 NW 21st St	Pompano Beach	FL	33069	954-917-7665		1
TF: 800-432-5097 ■ *Web:* www.premixmarbletite.com						
Prenia Corp						
16625 Redmond Way Ste M-418	Redmond	WA	98052	425-999-4330		177
Web: www.prenia.com						
Prent Corp 2225 Kennedy Rd	Janesville	WI	53546	608-754-0270		002
Web: www.prent.com						
Prentex Alloy Fabricators Inc						
3108 Sylvan Ave	Dallas	TX	75212	214-748-7837	748-7850	295
TF: 877-773-6839 ■ *Web:* www.prentex.com						
Prentice Products						
4236 W Ferguson Rd	Fort Wayne	IN	46809	260-747-3195		627
Web: www.prenticeproducts.com						
Prentice-Hall Inc						
1 Lake St	Upper Saddle River	NJ	07458	800-328-5999		637-2
TF: 800-328-5999 ■ *Web:* www.pearsoned.com						
Prentiss County 1901-B E Chambers	Booneville	MS	38829	662-728-6232		338
Web: www.prentisscounty.org/courts						
Prentiss County Electric Power Assn						
302 W Church St	Booneville	MS	38829	662-728-4433	728-4059	245
Web: www.pcepa.com						
Prentke Romich Co 1022 Heyl Rd	Wooster	OH	44691	330-262-1984	263-4829	202
TF: 800-848-8008 ■ *Web:* www.prentrom.com						
Preparation Canyon State Park						
206 Polk St PO Box 158	Pisgah	IA	51564	712-423-2829		565
Web: www.iowadnr.gov						
Preproduction Plastics Inc						
210 Teller St	Corona	CA	92879	951-340-9680		608
Web: ppiplastics.com						
Presagis						
1301 W George Bush Fwy Ste 120	Richardson	TX	75080	514-341-3874	467-4564*	178-8
**Fax Area Code:* 469 ■ *TF:* 800-361-6424 ■ *Web:* www.presagis.com						
Presby's Inspired Life						
2000 Joshua Rd	Lafayette Hill	PA	19444	610-834-1001		48-20
TF: 877-977-3729 ■ *Web:* www.presbysinspiredlife.org						
Presbyterian Childrens Services Inc						
1220 N Lindbergh Blvd	St. Louis	MO	63132	314-989-9727	427-2682	48-20
TF: 800-383-8147 ■ *Web:* missouri.pchas.org						
Presbyterian Church in America (PCA)						
1700 N Brown Rd Ste 105	Lawrenceville	GA	30043	678-825-1000	825-1001	48-20
Web: www.pcanet.org						
Presbyterian Church (USA)						
100 Witherspoon St	Louisville	KY	40202	502-569-5000		48-20
TF: 888-728-7228 ■ *Web:* www.pcusa.org						
Presbyterian College 503 S Broad St	Clinton	SC	29325	864-833-2820	833-8481*	166
**Fax:* Admissions ■ *TF:* 800-476-7272 ■ *Web:* www.presby.edu						
Presbyterian Communities of South CarolinaEqual Opportunity Housing						
2817 Ashland Rd	Columbia	SC	29210	803-772-5885	772-5872	672
Web: preshomesc.org						
Presbyterian Disaster Assistance (PDA)						
100 Witherspoon St	Louisville	KY	40202	800-728-7228	569-8039*	48-5
**Fax Area Code:* 502 ■ *TF:* 800-728-7228 ■ *Web:* www.presbyterianmission.org						
Presbyterian Espanola Hospital						
1010 Spruce St	Espanola	NM	87532	505-753-7111		374-3
Web: www.phs.org						
Presbyterian Homes Inc, The						
2109 Sandy Ridge Rd	Colfax	NC	27235	336-886-6553		48-15
TF: 800-225-9573 ■ *Web:* www.presbyhomesinc.org						
Presbyterian Hospital						
1100 Central Ave SE	Albuquerque	NM	87106	505-841-1234	462-7756	374-3
TF: 888-977-2333 ■ *Web:* www.phs.org						
Presbyterian Hospital Charlotte						
200 Hawthorne Ln	Charlotte	NC	28204	704-384-4000		374-3
Web: novanthealth.org/presbyterianmedicalcenter.aspx						
Presbyterian Hospital of Dallas						
8200 Walnut Hill Ln	Dallas	TX	75231	214-345-6789		374-3
Web: www.texashealth.org						
Presbyterian Intercommunity Hospital						
12401 Washington Blvd	Whittier	CA	90602	562-698-0811		374-3
Web: pihhealth.org						
Presbyterian Kaseman Hospital						
8300 Constitution Ave NE	Albuquerque	NM	87110	505-291-2000		374-3
TF: 800-356-2219 ■ *Web:* www.phs.org						
Presbyterian Orthopaedic Hospital						
1901 Randolph Rd	Charlotte	NC	28207	704-316-2000		374-7
Web: novanthealth.org/presbyterianmedicalcenter.aspx						
Presbyterian SeniorCare-Southminster Place						
835 S Main St	Washington	PA	15301	724-222-4300		450
Web: www.srcare.org						
Presbyterian SeniorCare-Westminster Place						
1215 Hulton Rd	Oakmont	PA	15139	412-828-5600		450
TF: 877-772-6500 ■ *Web:* www.srcare.org						
Presbyterian Villages Of Michigan						
25300 W Six Mile Rd	Redford	MI	48240	313-541-6000		672
Web: www.pvm.org						
Presbyterians Today Magazine						
100 Witherspoon St	Louisville	KY	40202	800-872-3283	569-8632*	457-18
**Fax Area Code:* 502 ■ *TF:* 800-728-7228 ■ *Web:* www.presbyterianmission.org						
Presbyterian-Saint Luke's Medical Ctr						
1719 E 19th Ave	Denver	CO	80218	303-839-6000		374-3
Web: www.pslmc.com						
Prescient Digital Media Ltd						
80 Sherbourne St Unit 101	Toronto	ON	M5A2R1	416-926-8800		396
Web: www.prescientdigital.com						
Prescient Infotech Inc						
3930 Pender Dr Ste 160	Fairfax	VA	22030	703-218-6233		180
Web: www.prescientinfotech.com						
Presco Inc						
10200 Grogan's Mill Rd Ste 520	The Woodlands	TX	77380	281-292-7792		539
Web: www.prescocorp.com						
Prescolite Inc 701 Millennium Blvd	Greenville	SC	29607	864-678-1000	678-1415	439
TF: 888-777-4832 ■ *Web:* www.prescolite.com						
Prescott Chamber of Commerce						
117 W Goodwin St	Prescott	AZ	86303	928-445-2000	445-0068	139
TF: 800-266-7534 ■ *Web:* www.prescott.org						
Prescott College 220 Grove Ave	Prescott	AZ	86301	877-350-2100	776-5242*	166
**Fax Area Code:* 928 ■ **Fax:* Admissions ■ *TF:* 877-350-2100 ■ *Web:* www.prescott.edu						
Prescott Legal Search Inc						
3900 Essex Ln Ste 1110	Houston	TX	77027	713-439-0911		193
Web: www.prescottlegal.com						
Prescott National Cemetery						
500 Hwy 89 N	Prescott	AZ	86301	928-717-7569	717-7570	136
TF: 800-535-1117						
Prescott Pines Camp						
855 E Schoolhouse Gulch Rd	Prescott	AZ	86303	928-445-5225		239
Web: prescottpines.org						
Prescott Valley Chamber of Commerce						
3001 N Main St Ste 2A	Prescott Valley	AZ	86314	928-772-8857	772-4267	139
TF: 800-355-0843 ■ *Web:* www.pvchamber.org						
Prescreen America Inc						
505 W Abram St Ste 200	Arlington	TX	76010	817-861-6666		260
Prescription Corp of America						
66 Ford Rd Ste 230	Denville	NJ	07834	973-983-6300		391-3
Prescription Solutions						
3515 Harbor Blvd	Costa Mesa	CA	92626	800-788-4863		586
TF: 800-788-4863 ■ *Web:* www.optumrx.com						
Prescription Supply Inc						
2233 Tracy Rd	Northwood	OH	43619	419-661-6600		231
Web: www.prescriptionsupply.com						
Prescriptives Inc 767 Fifth Ave	New York	NY	10153	866-290-6471		214
TF: 866-290-6471 ■ *Web:* www.prescriptives.com						
Presence Saint Joseph Medical Ctr (PSJMC)						
333 N Madison St	Joliet	IL	60435	815-725-7133		374-3
Web: www.presencehealth.org/stjoes						
Presentation College 1500 N Main St	Aberdeen	SD	57401	605-225-1634		166
TF: 800-437-6060 ■ *Web:* www.presentation.edu						
Presentation Concepts Corp						
6517 Basile Rowe	East Syracuse	NY	13057	315-437-1314	437-0110	45
TF: 888-262-7596 ■ *Web:* www.pccav.com						
Presentek Inc						
987 University Ave Ste 11	Los Gatos	CA	95032	408-354-1264		225
Web: www.presentek.com						
Preservation Action						
1307 New Hampshire Ave NW 3rd Fl	Washington	DC	20036	202-637-7873		48-7
Web: www.preservationaction.org						
Preservation Delaware Inc						
1405 Greenhill Ave	Wilmington	DE	19806	302-651-9617	651-9603	50-3
Web: www.preservationde.org						
Preservation Hall 726 St Peter St	New Orleans	LA	70116	504-522-2841		572
TF: 800-264-3655 ■ *Web:* www.preservationhall.com						
Preservation Technologies LP						
111 Thomson Park Dr	Cranberry Township	PA	16066	724-779-2111		321
TF: 800-416-2665 ■ *Web:* www.ptlp.com						
President Abraham Lincoln Hotel & Conference Ctr (PALHACC)						
701 E Adams St	Springfield	IL	62701	217-544-8800	544-9607	379
TF: 855-610-8733 ■ *Web:* doubletree3.hilton.com						
President Benjamin Harrison Home						
1230 N Delaware St	Indianapolis	IN	46202	317-631-1888	632-5488	50-3
Web: www.presidentbenjaminharrison.org						
President Container Inc						
200 W Commercial Ave	Moonachie	NJ	07074	201-933-7500		100
Web: www.presidentcontainergroup.com						
President Global Corp						
6965 Aragon Cir	Buena Park	CA	90620	714-994-2990		296-20
President William Jefferson Clinton Birthplace Home National Historic Site						
117 S Hervey St	Hope	AR	71801	870-777-4455	777-4935	564
Web: www.nps.gov/wicl/index.htm						
President's Council on Fitness Sports & Nutrition						
1101 Wootton Pkwy Ste 560	Rockville	MD	20852	240-276-9567	276-9860	340-10
Web: www.hhs.gov/fitness/index.html						
President's Foreign Intelligence Advisory Board (PIAB)						
White House 1600 Pennsylvania Ave	Washington	DC	20500	202-456-1414		340
Web: www.whitehouse.gov/administration/eop/piab						
Presidential Aviation						
1725 NW 51st Pl Ft Lauderdale Executive Airport	Fort Lauderdale	FL	33309	954-772-8622		13
TF: 888-772-8622 ■ *Web:* presidential-aviation.com						
Presidential Online Bank						
4520 East-West Hwy	Bethesda	MD	20814	301-652-0700	951-3582	70
TF: 800-383-6266 ■ *Web:* www.presidential.com						
Presidio County PO Box 879	Marfa	TX	79843	432-729-4081	729-4920	338
Web: www.txdmv.gov						
Presidio Group Inc, The						
5295 South 300 West Ste 550	Salt Lake City	UT	84107	801-924-1400		194
TF: 800-924-1404 ■ *Web:* www.presidio-group.com						
Presidio Networked Solutions Inc						
7601 Ora Glen Dr Ste 100	Greenbelt	MD	20770	301-313-2000	313-2400	180
TF: 800-452-6926 ■ *Web:* www.presidio.com						

	Phone	Fax	Class
Presidio Trust 103 Montgomery St PO Box 29052 .... San Francisco CA 94129	415-561-5300		340-20
Presima Inc 1000 Jean-Paul-Riopelle Pl Montreal Herald Bldg 4th Fl. .... Montreal QC H2Z2B6 *Web:* www.presima.com	514-673-1375		528
PresiNET Systems Corp 645 Fort St Ste L109. .... Victoria BC V8W1G2 *Web:* www.presinet.com	250-405-5380		387
Presley Tours Inc 16 Presley Pk Dr PO Box 58. .... Makanda IL 62958 *TF:* 800-621-6100 ■ *Web:* www.presleytours.com	618-549-0704		760
Presnell Gage Pllc 1216 Idaho St .... Lewiston ID 83501 *Web:* www.presnellgage.com	208-746-8281	746-5174	2
Presort America Ltd 4227 Williams Rd. .... Groveport OH 43125 *Web:* www.presort.com	614-836-5120		5
Presqu'ile Provincial Park 328 Presqu Pkwy .... Brighton ON K0K1H0 *Web:* ontarioparks.com	613-475-4324		520
Presque Isle County PO Box 110. .... Rogers City MI 49779 *Web:* www.presqueislecounty.org	989-734-3810	734-7635	338
Presque Isle Electric & Gas Co-op PO Box 308 .... Onaway MI 49765 *TF:* 800-423-6634 ■ *Web:* www.pieg.com	989-733-8515	733-2247	245
Presque Isle State Park 301 Peninsula Dr Ste 1. .... Erie PA 16505 *TF:* 888-727-2757 ■ *Web:* www.dcnr.state.pa.us	814-833-7424		565
Presray Corp 32 Nelson Hill Rd PO Box 200 .... Wassaic NY 12592 *TF:* 800-431-3456 ■ *Web:* www.presray.com	845-373-9300	855-8034	326
Presrite Corp 3665 E 78th St. .... Cleveland OH 44105 *Web:* www.presrite.com	216-441-5990	441-2644	483
Press Chemical & Pharmaceutical Laboratories Inc 4231 Donlyn Ct .... Columbus OH 43232	614-863-2802		231
Press Democrat 427 Mendocino Ave .... Santa Rosa CA 95401 *TF:* 800-675-5056 ■ *Web:* www.pressdemocrat.com	707-546-2020	521-5330	532-2
Press Ganey Associates Inc 404 Columbia Pl. .... South Bend IN 46601 *TF:* 800-232-8032 ■ *Web:* www.pressganey.com	800-232-8032		194
Press of Atlantic City 11 Devins Ln .... Pleasantville NJ 08232 *Web:* www.pressofatlanticcity.com	609-272-7000	272-7224	532-2
Press Room Inc, The 100 Youngs Rd. .... Mercerville NJ 08619	609-689-3817		627
Press-A-Print International LLC 1463 Commerce Way .... Idaho Falls ID 83401 *Web:* www.pressaprint.com	208-523-7620		393
Pressco Technology Inc 29200 Aurora Rd .... Cleveland OH 44139 *Web:* www.pressco.com	440-498-2600		639
Presscut Industries Inc 1730 Briercroft Ct. .... Carrollton TX 75006 *TF:* 800-442-4924 ■ *Web:* www.presscut.com	972-389-0615	245-2488	326
Pressed Juicery LLC 1550 17Th St .... Santa Monica CA 90404 *Web:* www.pressedjuicery.com	310-477-7171		345
Pressed4Time Inc 8 Clock Tower Pl Ste 110 .... Maynard MA 01754 *TF:* 800-423-8711 ■ *Web:* www.pressed4time.com	800-423-8711		426
Press-Enterprise 3450 14th St. .... Riverside CA 92501 *Web:* www.pe.com	951-684-1200	368-9023	532-2
Press-Enterprise Inc 3185 Lackawanna Ave. .... Bloomsburg PA 17815 *TF:* 888-484-6345 ■ *Web:* www.pressenterprise.net	570-387-1234		637-8
Press-Enterprise, The 474 W Esplanade Ave .... San Jacinto CA 92583 *Web:* www.pe.com	951-763-3452	763-3450	532-2
Presses Inc 6360 W 73rd St .... Chicago IL 60638 *TF:* 800-927-9393 ■ *Web:* www.theheimgroup.com	708-496-7400	496-7428	456
Pressler & Pressler LLP 7 Entin Rd. .... Parsippany NJ 07054 *Web:* www.pressler-pressler.com	973-753-5100		428
Pressley Ridge 5500 Corporate Dr Ste 400. .... Pittsburgh PA 15237 *TF:* 888-777-0820 ■ *Web:* www.pressleyridge.org	412-872-9400	872-9478	48-6
Pressman Film 312 Arizona Ave .... Santa Monica CA 90401 *Web:* www.pressman.com	310-450-9692	450-9705	514
Pressman Toy Corp 3701 W Plano Pkwy Suite 100 .... Plano TX 75075 *TF Cust Svc:* 800-800-0298 ■ *Web:* www.pressmantoy.com	855-258-8214		762
Pressnet Express Inc 7283 Engineer Rd Ste A/B .... San Diego CA 92111 *TF:* 800-772-7017 ■ *Web:* pressnetexpress.com	858-694-0070		627
Press-Republican 170 Margaret St PO Box 459 .... Plattsburgh NY 12901 *TF:* 800-288-7323 ■ *Web:* www.pressrepublican.com	518-561-2300	561-3362	532-2
Pressroom Restaurant 26-28 W King St. .... Lancaster PA 17603 *Web:* www.pressroomrestaurant.com	717-399-5400		671
Press-Seal Gasket Corp 2424 W State Blvd .... Fort Wayne IN 46808 *TF:* 800-348-7325 ■ *Web:* www.press-seal.com	260-436-0521	436-1908	326
Presstek Inc 55 Executive Dr. .... Hudson NH 03051 *NASDAQ: PRST* ■ *TF:* 800-422-3616 ■ *Web:* www.presstek.com	603-595-7000		781
Press-Telegram 300 Oceangate .... Long Beach CA 90844 *Web:* www.presstelegram.com	562-435-1161	437-7892	532-2
Pressure BioSciences Inc 14 Norfolk Ave .... South Easton MA 02375 *OTC: PBIO* ■ *Web:* pressurebiosciences.com	508-230-1828	230-1829	85
Pressure Product Industries Inc 900 Louis Dr. .... Warminster PA 18974 *Web:* www.pressure-products.com	215-675-1600		172
Pressure Profile Systems Inc 5757 Century Blvd Ste 600. .... Los Angeles CA 90045 *TF:* 888-249-2464 ■ *Web:* www.pressureprofile.com	310-641-8100		201
Pressure Systems Inc 34 Research Dr. .... Hampton VA 23666	757-865-1243		201
Prestage Farms 4651 Taylors Bridge Hwy .... Clinton NC 28329 *Web:* www.prestagefarms.com	910-596-5700		10-6
Presteligence Inc 8328 Cleveland Ave NW .... Canton OH 44720 *TF:* 888-438-6050 ■ *Web:* www.presteligence.com	888-438-6050		180
Prestera Center for Mental Health Services Inc 3375 Us Route 60. .... Huntington WV 25705 *Web:* www.prestera.org	304-525-7851		726
Prestera Trucking 19129 US Rt 52. .... South Point OH 45680 *TF:* 855-761-7943 ■ *Web:* www.prestera.com	740-894-4770		780
Prestige Accommodations International 1231 E Dyer Rd Ste 240 .... Santa Ana CA 92705 *TF:* 800-321-6338 ■ *Web:* www.meetingplanners.com	714-957-9100		184
Prestige Alarm & Specialty Products Inc 7640 Commerce Ln .... Trussville AL 35173 *Web:* www.prestigealarm.com	205-661-4822		693
Prestige Brands International Inc 660 White Plains Rd Ste 250 .... Tarrytown NY 10591 *Web:* www.prestigebrandsinc.com	914-524-6819		214
Prestige Capital Corp 400 Kelby St 14th Fl. .... Fort Lee NJ 07024 *Web:* www.prestigecapital.com	201-944-4455	944-9477	272
Prestige Care Inc 7700 NE Pkwy Dr Ste 300. .... Vancouver WA 98662 *Web:* www.prestigecare.com	360-735-7155		371
Prestige Chrysler Dodge Inc 200 Alpine St .... Longmont CO 80501 *TF:* 866-439-1926 ■ *Web:* www.prestigechryslerdodge.com	303-651-3000		57
Prestige Cleaners Inc 7536 Taggart Ln .... Knoxville TN 37938 *Web:* prestigecleanersinc.net	865-938-7701		426
Prestige Concrete Products 8529 S Pk Cr Ste 320. .... Orlando FL 32819 *Web:* prestigeconcreteproducts.com	407-802-3540	226-0359	182
Prestige Cosmetics Corp 1601 Green Rd .... Pompano Beach FL 33064 *Web:* www.prestigecosmetics.com	954-480-9202	480-9220	214
Prestige Engineering Resources & Technologies Inc 26155 Groesbeck Hwy .... Warren MI 48089 *Web:* www.prestigeeng.com	586-777-1820		393
Prestige Fabricators Inc 2206 Dumont St .... Asheboro NC 27204 *TF:* 800-419-6829 ■ *Web:* www.prestigefab.com	336-672-3383		601
Prestige Financial Services Inc 1420 S 500 W. .... Salt Lake City UT 84115 *TF:* 888-822-7422 ■ *Web:* www.gopfs.com	801-844-2100	844-2600	217
Prestige Graphics Inc 9630 Ridgehaven Ct Ste B .... San Diego CA 92123 *TF:* 800-383-9361 ■ *Web:* www.pgisd.com	858-560-8213		535
Prestige Harbourfront Resort & Convention Centre 251 Harbourfront Dr NE .... Salmon Arm BC V1E2W7 *TF:* 877-737-8443 ■ *Web:* prestigehotelsandresorts.com	250-833-5800		379
Prestige Maintenance USA Ltd 1808 Tenth St Ste 300 .... Plano TX 75074 *TF:* 800-321-4773 ■ *Web:* www.prestigeusa.net	972-578-9801		192
Prestige Medical Corporation International 8600 Wilbur Ave. .... Northridge CA 91324 *TF:* 800-762-3333 ■ *Web:* www.prestigemedical.com	818-993-3030		475
Prestige Properties & Development Company Inc 546 Fifth Ave. .... New York NY 10036	212-944-0444		653
Prestige Resorts & Destinations Ltd 700 E Lake St 2nd Fl. .... Wayzata MN 55391 *Web:* www.prestigeresorts.com	952-473-9559		377
Prestige Security 5721 W Slauson Ave Ste 120 .... Culver City CA 90230 *Web:* www.prestigesecurity.com	310-670-5999		693
Prestige Stamping Inc 23513 Groesbeck Hwy .... Warren MI 48089 *TF:* 800-988-2658 ■ *Web:* www.prestigestamping.com	586-773-2700	773-2700	488
Prestige Technicall Services 7908 Cincinnati Dayton Rd Ste T .... West Chester OH 45069 *Web:* www.prestigetechnical.com	513-779-6800		261
Prestige Travel & Cruises Inc 6175 Spring Mountain Rd .... Las Vegas NV 89146 *TF:* 800-758-5693 ■ *Web:* www.prestigecruises.com	702-251-5552		771
Prestini Musical Instruments Inc 2020 N Aurora Dr .... Nogales AZ 85628 *TF General:* 800-528-6569 ■ *Web:* www.prestiniusa.com	520-287-4931	287-4931	527
Presto Food Stores Inc 1513 James L Redman Pkwy .... Plant City FL 33563	813-754-3511		204
Presto Products Co 670 N Perkins St PO Box 2399. .... Appleton WI 54912 **Fax Area Code:* 920 ■ *TF:* 800-558-3525 ■ *Web:* www.prestoproducts.com	800-558-3525	738-1432*	66
Presto Tape Inc 1626 Bridgewater Rd. .... Bensalem PA 19020 *TF:* 800-331-1373 ■ *Web:* www.prestotape.com	215-245-8555	245-8554	732
Prestolite Electric Holding Inc 46200 Port St. .... Plymouth MI 48170 *Web:* www.prestolite.com	734-582-7200		518
Prestolite Wire Corp 200 Galleria Officentre Ste 212. .... Southfield MI 48034 *TF:* 800-498-3132 ■ *Web:* www.prestolitewire.com	248-355-4422	386-4462	814
Preston Feather Building Ctr PO Box 637 .... Petoskey MI 49770 *Web:* www.prestonfeather.com	231-347-2501		364
Preston Hollow People 750 N St Paul St Ste 2100 .... Dallas TX 75201 *Web:* www.prestonhollowpeople.com	214-739-2244		532-4
Preston Industries Inc 6600 W Touhy Ave .... Niles IL 60714 *TF:* 800-229-7569 ■ *Web:* www.polyscience.com	847-647-0611	647-1155	420
Preston Mobility Inc 13071 Vanier Pl Ste 128. .... Richmond BC V6V2J1 *Web:* www.prestonmobility.com	604-629-8526		736
Preston Partnership 115 Perimeter Ctr Pl Ste 950 .... Atlanta GA 30346 *Web:* www.theprestonpartnership.com	770-396-7248	396-2945	261
Preston Phipps Inc 6400 Vanden Abeele .... Montreal QC H4S1R9 *Web:* prestonphipps.com	514-333-5340		111
Preston Refrigeration Company Inc 3200 Fiberglass Rd. .... Kansas City KS 66115 *TF:* 800-366-2908 ■ *Web:* www.prestonrefrigeration.com	913-621-1813	621-6962	665

Name / Address	City	State	ZIP	Phone	Fax	Class
Preston Wynne Spa Inc 14567 Big Basin Way *TF:* 800-561-3357 ■ *Web:* www.prestonwynne.com	Saratoga	CA	95070	408-741-5525		77
Prestone Printing Company Inc 47-50 30th St *Web:* www.prestoneprinting.com	New York	NY	11101	347-468-7900		627
PrestoTech Solutions 4595 Broadmoor Ave SE Ste 200 *TF:* 800-968-1990 ■ *Web:* www.prestotech.net	Grand Rapids	MI	49512	616-891-4100		387
Presto-X Co 1221 S Saddle Creek Rd Ste 101 *TF:* 800-759-1942 ■ *Web:* www.prestox.com	Omaha	NE	68106	800-759-1942		577
Prestress Engineering Corp 2220 Rt 176 *Web:* www.pre-stress.com	Prairie Grove	IL	60012	815-459-4545	459-6855	183
Prestress Services Inc 7855 NW Winchester Rd *Web:* www.prestressservices.com	Decatur	IN	46733	260-724-7117	724-3349	183
Prestressed Casting Co 1600 S Scenic Ave *Web:* www.prestressedcasting.com	Springfield	MO	65807	417-869-7350		183
Prestressed Systems Inc 4955 Walker Rd Hwy 401 *TF:* 800-238-8226 ■ *Web:* www.theprecaster.com	Windsor	ON	N9A6J3	519-737-1216		135
Prestwood Elementary School 343 E Macarthur St *Web:* www.sonomaschools.org	Sonoma	CA	95476	707-935-6030		685
Pretend City, The Childrens Museum of Orange County 17752 Sky Park Cir Ste 280 *Web:* pretendcity.org	Irvine	CA	92614	949-428-3900		522
PreTesting Group 38 Franklin St *Web:* www.pretesting.com	Tenafly	NJ	07670	201-569-4800		466
Preti, Flaherty, Beliveau, Pachios & Haley LLC 45 Memorial Cir *TF:* 800-497-0282 ■ *Web:* www.preti.com	Augusta	ME	04330	207-623-5300		428
Pretium Packaging LLC 15450 S Outer Forty Dr Ste 120 *Web:* www.pretiumpkg.com	Chesterfield	MO	63017	314-727-8200		601
Pretium Partners Inc 3240 Henderson Rd Ste A *TF:* 800-695-6344 ■ *Web:* www.pretiumpartners.com	Columbus	OH	43220	614-457-1726		196
Prettl Appliance Systems USA Inc 2010 W 15th St	Washington	NC	27889	252-974-5500		596
Prettl Electric Corp 1721 White Horse Rd *Web:* www.prettl.com	Greenville	SC	29605	864-220-1010		247
Pretzelmaker 1346 Oakbrook Dr Ste 170 *TF:* 877-639-2361 ■ *Web:* pretzelmaker.com	Norcross	GA	30093	877-639-2361		670
Pretzels Inc 123 Harvest Rd PO Box 503 *TF:* 800-456-4838 ■ *Web:* www.pretzels-inc.com	Bluffton	IN	46714	260-824-4838	824-0895	296-9
Prevea Health Services Inc 2710 Executive Dr *Web:* www.prevea.com	Green Bay	WI	54304	920-496-4700		363
Prevent Blindness America 211 W Wacker Dr Ste 1700 *TF:* 800-331-2020 ■ *Web:* www.preventblindness.org	Chicago	IL	60606	800-331-2020		48-17
Prevent Cancer Foundation (PCF) 1600 Duke St Ste 500 *TF:* 800-227-2732 ■ *Web:* preventcancer.org	Alexandria	VA	22314	703-836-4412	836-4413	48-17
Prevention Magazine 733 Third Ave *TF:* 800-813-8070 ■ *Web:* www.prevention.com	Emmaus	PA	10017	800-813-8070		457-13
PreventionGenetics LLC 3700 Downwind Dr *Web:* www.preventiongenetics.com	Marshfield	WI	54449	715-387-0484		743
Preventure Inc 2000 Nooseneck Hill Rd **Fax Area Code:* 401 ■ *TF:* 888-321-4326 ■ *Web:* www.preventure.com	Coventry	RI	02816	888-321-4326	385-9320*	706
Preverco Inc 285 Rue De Rotterdam *TF:* 877-667-2725 ■ *Web:* www.preverco.com	Saint-augustin-de-desmaures	QC	G3A2E5	418-878-8930		364
Providence Corp 5685 S 1475 E Ste 2b *Web:* www.previdence.com	Ogden	UT	84403	801-409-0904		463
PreviMed Inc PO Box 10426 *TF:* 800-565-3901 ■ *Web:* www.previmed.com	San Jose	CA	95157	800-565-3901		463
PreViser Corp 20849 Cascade Ridge Dr *Web:* www.previser.com	Mount Vernon	WA	98274	360-941-4715		177
Prevost Car Inc 35 boul Gagnon *TF:* 877-773-8678 ■ *Web:* www.prevostcar.com	Sainte-Claire	QC	G0R2V0	418-883-3391	883-4157	516
Prevue Pet Products Inc 224 N Maplewood Ave *TF:* 800-243-3624 ■ *Web:* prevuepet.com	Chicago	IL	60612	312-243-3624	243-3624	578
Prezacor Inc 170 Cold Soil Rd *TF:* 855-792-3335 ■ *Web:* prezacor.com	Princeton	NJ	08540	855-792-3335		743
Prezza 24 Fleet St *Web:* www.prezza.com	Boston	MA	02113	617-227-1577		671
Prezza Technologies Inc 44 Pleasant St *Web:* www.checkbox.com	Watertown	MA	02472	617-231-8891		396
PRG Nocturne Productions Inc 300 Harvestore Dr *Web:* www.trichromes.com	Dekalb	IL	60115	815-756-9600		514
PRG-Schultz International Inc 600 Galleria Pkwy Ste 100 *TF:* 800-752-5894 ■ *Web:* www.prgx.com	Atlanta	GA	30339	770-779-3900	779-3133	2
PRH (Penticton Regional Hospital) 550 Carmi Ave *TF:* 800-665-1822 ■ *Web:* www.interiorhealth.ca	Penticton	BC	V2A3G6	250-492-4000	492-9068	374-2
PRI (Public Radio International) 401 Second Ave N Ste 500 *Web:* www.pri.org	Minneapolis	MN	55401	612-338-5000	330-9222	644
PRI (Pacific Research Institute for Public Policy) 1 Embarcadero Ctr *Web:* www.pacificresearch.org	San Francisco	CA	94111	415-989-0833	989-2411	634
PRI Group LLC 600 Thomas Dr *TF:* 800-319-8399 ■ *Web:* www.theprigroup.com	Bensenville	IL	60106	708-492-1777		463
Pri Mar Petroleum Inc 1207 Broad St *Web:* www.primarpetro.com	Saint Joseph	MI	49085	269-983-7314		580
Pribuss Engineering Inc 523 Mayfair Ave *Web:* www.pribuss.com	South San Francisco	CA	94080	650-588-0447		261
Pricci 500 Pharr Rd *Web:* www.buckheadrestaurants.com	Atlanta	GA	30305	404-237-2941		671
Price Books & Forms Inc 531 E Sierra Madre Ave **Fax Area Code:* 626 ■ *TF:* 800-423-8961 ■ *Web:* www.autopricebooks.com	Glendora	CA	91741	800-423-8961	768-2162*	637-2
Price Bros Equipment Co 619 S Washington St *Web:* www.pricebroseq.com	Wichita	KS	67211	316-265-9577	265-1062	274
Price Canyon Ranch PO Box 39 *TF:* 800-727-0065 ■ *Web:* www.pricecanyon.com	Rodeo	NM	88056	520-558-2383		239
Price Companies Inc, The 218 Midway Route *TF:* 800-308-3831 ■ *Web:* www.thepricecompanies.com	Monticello	AR	71655	870-367-9751		820
Price County 126 Cherry St *TF:* 800-362-9472 ■ *Web:* www.co.price.wi.us	Phillips	WI	54555	715-339-3325	339-3089	338
Price David (Rep D - NC) 2108 Rayburn Bldg *Web:* price.house.gov	Washington	DC	20515	202-225-1784	225-2014	342-2
Price Edwards & Co 210 Pk Ave Ste 1000 *Web:* www.priceedwards.com	Oklahoma City	OK	73102	405-843-7474	236-1849	655
Price Electric Co-op 508 N Lake Ave PO Box 110 *TF:* 800-884-0881 ■ *Web:* price-electric.com	Phillips	WI	54555	715-339-2155	339-2921	245
Price Ford of Turlock 5200 N Golden State Blvd *Web:* www.pricefordofturlock.com	Turlock	CA	95382	209-669-5200		57
PRICE Futures Group Inc, The 141 W Jackson Blvd Ste 1340A *TF:* 800-769-7021 ■ *Web:* www.pricegroup.com	Chicago	IL	60604	312-264-4300		690
Price Industries Inc 2975 Shawnee Ridge Ct *Web:* www.price-hvac.com	Suwanee	GA	30024	770-623-8050		14
Price Pfister Inc 19701 Da Vinci St *TF:* 800-732-8238 ■ *Web:* www.pfisterfaucets.com	Lake Forest	CA	92610	949-672-4000	672-4000	609
Price Postel & Parma LLP 200 E Carrillo St Fl 4 *Web:* www.melfassett.com	Santa Barbara	CA	93101	805-962-0011		428
Price Pump Co 21775 Eighth St E *Web:* www.pricepump.com	Sonoma	CA	95476	707-938-8441		641
Price Rubber Corp 2733 Gunter Park Dr W *TF:* 800-633-1470 ■ *Web:* www.pricerubber.com	Montgomery	AL	36109	334-277-5470		207
Price Stagner & Company Pllc 501 Darby Creek Rd No 6 *Web:* pricestagner.com	Lexington	KY	40509	859-263-1944		2
Price Steel Ltd 13500 156 St *TF:* 800-661-6789 ■ *Web:* www.pricesteel.com	Edmonton	AB	T5V1L3	780-447-9999		480
Price, Heneveld, Cooper, De Witt & Litton 695 Kenmoor Ave SE *TF:* 800-752-2401 ■ *Web:* www.priceheneveld.com	Grand Rapids	MI	49546	616-949-9610		428
Priced Rite Suites 2327 University Ave *TF:* 800-432-8747 ■ *Web:* www.pricedritesuites.com	Green Bay	WI	54302	920-469-2130		379
Priceline.com LLC 800 Connecticut Ave *NASDAQ:* PCLN ■ *TF:* 800-774-2354 ■ *Web:* www.priceline.com	Norwalk	CT	06854	800-774-2354		51
PriceSmart Inc 9740 Scranton Rd *NASDAQ:* PSMT ■ *Web:* www.pricesmart.com	San Diego	CA	92121	858-404-8800		812
PriceWaiter LLC 426 Market St *TF:* 855-671-9889 ■ *Web:* www.pricewaiter.com	Chattanooga	TN	37421	855-671-9889		387
PricewaterhouseCoopers LLP 300 Madison Ave **Fax Area Code:* 813 ■ *TF:* 800-993-9971 ■ *Web:* www.pwc.com	New York	NY	10017	646-471-4000	286-6000*	2
PriceWeber Marketing Communications Inc 10701 Shelbyville Rd *Web:* www.priceweber.com	Louisville	KY	40243	502-499-9220		7
Pricing Advisor Inc 3535 Roswell Rd Ste 59 *Web:* pricingsociety.com	Marietta	GA	30062	770-509-9933		195
Prickett, Jones & Elliott PA 1310 King St Box 1328 *Web:* prickett.com	Wilmington	DE	19899	302-888-6500		428
Picketts Fort State Park 106 Overtort Ln *Web:* www.pickettsfortstatepark.com	Fairmont	WV	26554	304-363-3030		565
Prickly Pear Southwest Cafe 328 S Main St *TF:* 800-442-1162 ■ *Web:* pricklypearcafe.com	Ann Arbor	MI	48104	734-930-0047		671
Pricon Inc 1831 W Lincoln Ave *TF:* 800-660-1831 ■ *Web:* www.pricon.com	Anaheim	CA	92801	714-758-8832		225
PRIDE (Prison Rehabilitative Industries & Diversified Enterprises Inc) 223 Morrison Rd *Web:* www.prideenterprises.org	Brandon	FL	33511	813-324-8700	689-5390	630
Pride Cleaners Inc 300 E 51st St *Web:* www.pridecleaners.com	Kansas City	MO	64112	816-753-8481		426
Pride Computer Systems 416 S Third St *Web:* www.pridecomputersystems.com	Jacksonville Beach	FL	32250	904-242-9522		175
Pride Engineering Inc 9401 73rd Ave N Ste 200 *Web:* www.pridecan.com	Brookly Park	MN	55428	763-427-6250		454
Pride Hospitality LLC 2129 S Germantown Rd Ste 1 *Web:* www.pridehospitality.com	Germantown	TN	38138	901-751-2212		463
Pride International Inc 5847 San Felipe St Ste 3300 *TF:* 877-736-3772 ■ *Web:* rigzone.com	Houston	TX	77057	713-789-1400	789-1430	539
Pride Manufacturing Co LLC 10 N Main St *Web:* www.pridemfg.com	Burnham	ME	04922	207-487-3322		200

Company / Address	City	State	Zip	Phone	Fax	Class
Pride Mobility Products Corp 182 Susquehanna Ave *TF:* 800-800-8586 ■ *Web:* www.pridemobility.com	Exeter	PA	18643	800-800-8586		477
Pride of Main Street Dairy 214 Main St S	Sauk Centre	MN	56378	320-351-8300		296-27
Pride Products Corp 4333 Veterans Memorial Hwy *TF:* 800-898-5550 ■ *Web:* www.prideproducts.com	Ronkonkoma	NY	11779	631-737-4444		791
Pride Signs Ltd 255 Pinebush Rd *TF:* 800-360-2364 ■ *Web:* www.pridesigns.com	Cambridge	ON	N1T1B9	519-622-4040		261
Pride Solvents & Chemical Co of New York Inc 6 Long Island Ave *TF:* 800-424-8802 ■ *Web:* www.pridesol.com	Holtsville	NY	11742	631-758-0200	758-0290	146
Pride South Florida 4233 NE Sixth Ave *Web:* pridesouthflorida.org	Oakland Park	FL	33334	954-561-2020		474
Pride Transport Inc 5499 W 2455 S *TF:* 800-877-1320 ■ *Web:* pridetransport.com	Salt Lake City	UT	84120	801-972-8890		780
Pridestaff Inc 7535 N Palm Ave Ste 101 *Web:* www.pridestaff.com	Fresno	CA	93711	559-432-7780		193
Pridgeon & Clay Inc 50 Cottage Grove St SW *Web:* www.pridgeonandclay.com	Grand Rapids	MI	49507	616-241-5675	241-1799	489
Priefert Manufacturing Company Inc 2630 S Jefferson Ave PO box 1540 *TF:* 800-527-8616 ■ *Web:* www.priefert.com	Mount Pleasant	TX	75456	903-572-1741		311
Prier Products Inc 4515 E 139th St *TF:* 800-362-1463 ■ *Web:* www.prier.com	Grandview	MO	64030	816-763-4100		610
Priest Lake State Park 314 Indian Creek Pk Rd *TF Resv:* 888-922-6743 ■ *Web:* www.visitidaho.org	Coolin	ID	83821	208-443-2200		565
Priester Aviation 1061 S Wolf Rd *TF:* 888-323-7887 ■ *Web:* www.priesterav.com	Wheeling	IL	60090	847-537-1133	459-0778	24
Priester Pecan Company Inc PO Box 381 *TF:* 800-277-3226 ■ *Web:* www.priesters.com	Fort Deposit	AL	36032	334-227-4301	227-4294	296-28
Prikos & Becker Tool Co 8109 N Lawndale Ave *Web:* prikosandbecker.com	Skokie	IL	60076	847-675-3910		757
Prima 5325 Lyndale Ave S *Web:* primampls.com	Minneapolis	MN	55419	612-827-7376	827-7534	671
PRIMA (Public Risk Management Assn) 700 S Washington St Ste 218 *TF:* 800-228-9290 ■ *Web:* www.primacentral.org	Alexandria	VA	22314	703-528-7701	739-0200	49-7
PRIMA Electro 711 E Main St *Web:* www.prima-na.com	Chicopee	MA	01020	413-598-5200	598-5201	425
Prima Supply Inc 4603 Poplar Level Rd Ste 1 *TF:* 888-810-5043 ■ *Web:* primasupply.com	Louisville	KY	40213	502-966-4578		612
Prima Tech USA 277 Faison McGowan Rd Ste 2 *TF:* 800-458-7454 ■ *Web:* neogen.com/primatech	Kenansville	NC	28349	910-296-6116		475
Primacy 1577 New Britain Ave *Web:* www.theprimacy.com	Farmington	CT	06032	860-679-9332		7
Primal Essence Inc 1351 Maulhardt Ave *Web:* www.primalessence.com	Oxnard	CA	93030	805-981-2409		80-2
Primal Fusion Inc 605-305 King St W *Web:* www.primal.com	Kitchener	ON	N2G1B9	519-741-1243		177
Primal Technologies Inc 3615 Laird Rd Ste 13	Mississauga	ON	L5L5Z8	416-548-3395	548-3396	179
Primanti Bros 46 18th St *TF:* 800-864-8287 ■ *Web:* primantibros.com	Pittsburgh	PA	15222	412-263-2142		671
Primary Automation Systems Inc 13361 Aberdeen St NE *Web:* www.primaryautomation.com	Ham Lake	MN	55304	763-755-3500		596
Primary Children's Medical Ctr 100 N Medical Dr *Web:* www.intermountainhealthcare.org	Salt Lake City	UT	84113	801-662-1000		374-1
Primary Color Inc 9239 Premier Row *TF:* 800-581-9555 ■ *Web:* www.primarycolorinc.com	Dallas	TX	75247	214-630-8800		687
Primary Color Systems Corp 265 Briggs Ave *Web:* www.primarycolor.com	Costa Mesa	CA	92626	949-660-7080		344
Primary Design Inc 90 Washington St 3rd Fl *Web:* primarydesign.com	Haverhill	MA	01832	978-373-1565		344
Primary Flow Signal Inc 800 Wellington Ave *Web:* www.pfsflowproducts.com	Cranston	RI	02910	401-461-6366		358
Primary Freight Services Inc 6545 Caballero Blvd *TF:* 800-635-0013 ■ *Web:* www.primaryfreight.com	Buena Park	CA	90620	310-635-3000		311
Primary Global Research LLC 1975 W El Camino Real Ste 300 *TF:* 888-893-1688 ■ *Web:* www.pg-research.com	Mountain View	CA	94040	888-893-1688		401
Primary Integration LLC 8180 Greensboro Dr Ste 700 *Web:* www.primaryintegration.com	Mclean	VA	22102	703-356-2200		186
Primary Media Outdoor Advertising 2511 Boll St *Web:* primarymedia.com	Dallas	TX	75204	214-880-0440		7
Primary Packaging Inc 10810 Industrial Pkwy NW *Web:* www.primarypackaging.com	Bolivar	OH	44612	330-874-3131	874-3811	88
Primary Staffing Inc 4247 S Kedzie Ave *Web:* www.findingresult.com	Chicago	IL	60632	773-376-0486		631
Primatech Inc 50 Northwoods Blvd *Web:* www.primatech.com	Columbus	OH	43235	614-841-9800		463
Prima-Temp Inc 2820 Wilderness Pl Ste C *TF:* 866-398-1032 ■ *Web:* prima-temp.com	Boulder	CO	80301	866-398-1032		261
Primavista 810 Matson Pl *Web:* www.pvista.com	Cincinnati	OH	45204	513-251-6467		671
Primco Dene Ltd PO Box 2070 *Web:* www.primcodene.com	Cold Lake	AB	T9M1P5	780-594-4034		314
Prime 112 112 Ocean Dr *Web:* www.mylesrestaurantgroup.com	Miami Beach	FL	33139	305-532-8112		671
Prime Adv & Design Inc 7351 Kirkwood Ln N Ste 144 *TF:* 800-275-8777 ■ *Web:* www.primeadvertising.com	Maple Grove	MN	55369	763-424-9406		4
Prime Buchholz & Assoc Inc 273 Corporate Dr Ste 250 *Web:* www.primebuchholz.com	Portsmouth	NH	03801	603-433-1143	433-8661	401
Prime Capital Services Inc 11 Raymond Ave *Web:* www.primefs.com	Poughkeepsie	NY	12603	845-485-3338		690
Prime Care Technologies Inc 6650 Sugarloaf Pkwy Ste 400 *Web:* primecaretech.com	Duluth	GA	30097	770-870-2888		225
Prime Concepts Group Inc 1807 S Eisenhower St *TF:* 800-946-7804 ■ *Web:* www.primeconcepts.com	Wichita	KS	67209	316-942-1111		195
Prime Contractors Inc 17355 Village Green Dr	Houston	TX	77040	281-999-0875	999-0885	186
Prime Controls LP 1725 Lakepointe D *Web:* www.prime-controls.com	Lewisville	TX	75057	972-221-4849	420-4842	177
Prime Cut Restaurant 3219 Tenth Ave S	Great Falls	MT	59405	406-727-2141		671
Prime Engineered Components 1012 Buckingham St PO Box 359 *Web:* www.primeeci.com	Watertown	CT	06795	860-274-6773	274-7939	621
Prime Equipment Group Inc 2000 E Fulton St *Web:* www.primeequipmentgroup.com	Columbus	OH	43205	614-253-8590		296
Prime Financial Credit Union 5656 S Packard Ave *Web:* primefinancialcu.org	Cudahy	WI	53110	414-486-4500		219
Prime Grill, The 550 Madison Ave *Web:* www.theprimegrill.primehospitalityny.com	New York	NY	10022	212-692-9292	697-3652	671
Prime Group Realty Trust 330 N Wabash Ave Ste 2800 *Web:* www.rrpchicago.com	Chicago	IL	60611	312-917-1300	917-1310	655
Prime Inc 2740 N Mayfair PO Box 4208 *TF Cust Svc:* 800-321-4552 ■ *Web:* w3.primeinc.com	Springfield	MO	65803	417-521-3200	521-6878	780
Prime Industries Inc 406 Dividend Dr *Web:* www.primeindustriesusa.com	Peachtree City	GA	30269	770-632-1851		21
Prime Management Services 3416 Primm Ln *TF:* 866-609-1599 ■ *Web:* primemanagement.net	Birmingham	AL	35216	205-823-6106	823-2760	47
Prime Marine Services Inc 312 S Bernard Rd *TF:* 800-644-5963 ■ *Web:* www.primemarineinc.com	Broussard	LA	70518	337-837-6500		539
Prime NDT Services Inc 4345 Independence Dr *Web:* www.primendt.com	Schnecksville	PA	18078	610-262-4954		41
Prime Osborn Convention Ctr 1000 Water St *Web:* www.jaxevents.com/primeosbornconventioncenter	Jacksonville	FL	32204	904-630-4000		205
Prime Products Inc 2755 Remico St SW *Web:* www.primeproductsinc.com	Wyoming	MI	49519	616-531-8970		22
Prime Rate Premium Finance Corp 2141 Enterprise Dr PO Box 100507 *TF Cust Svc:* 800-777-7458 ■ *Web:* www.primeratepfc.com	Florence	SC	29501	843-669-0937	292-1080	217
Prime Resources Corp 1100 Boston Ave *TF:* 877-858-9908 ■ *Web:* www.primeline.com	Bridgeport	CT	06610	203-331-9100	330-0123	9
Prime Rib, The 2020 K St NW *Web:* www.theprimerib.com	Washington	DC	20006	202-466-8811	466-2010	671
Prime Staffing Inc 3806 N Cicero Ave	Chicago	IL	60641	773-685-9399		721
Prime Systems Inc 416 Mission St *TF:* 800-524-0003 ■ *Web:* www.primeuv.com	Carol Stream	IL	60188	630-681-2100		190
Prime Technology LLC 344-352 Twin Lakes Rd PO Box 185 *Web:* www.primetechnology.com	North Branford	CT	06471	203-481-5721	481-8937	248
Prime Therapeutics Inc 1305 Corporate Ctr Dr *TF:* 800-858-0723 ■ *Web:* www.primetherapeutics.com	Eagan	MN	55121	612-777-4000		586
Prime Time International 86-705 Ave 54 Ste A *Web:* www.primetimeproduce.com	Coachella	CA	92236	760-399-4278	399-4281	10-11
Prime Wheel Corp 17705 S Main St *Web:* www.primewheel.com	Gardena	CA	90248	310-516-9126	516-9676	60
PrimeArray Systems Inc 127 Riverneck Rd *TF:* 800-433-5133 ■ *Web:* www.primearray.com	Chelmsford	MA	01824	978-654-6250	654-6249	176
Primebank 37 First Ave NW PO Box 1408 *Web:* primebank.com	Le Mars	IA	51031	712-546-4175		70
PrimeConnections Contact Solutions LLC 301 Brazos St Ste 615 *TF:* 866-976-2747 ■ *Web:* callprimeconnections.com	Austin	TX	78701	866-976-2747		396
PrimeGenesis LLC 200 W Hill Rd *Web:* www.primegenesis.com	Stamford	CT	06902	203-323-8501		463
Prime-Line Products Inc 26950 San Bernardino Ave *Web:* primeline.net	Redlands	CA	92374	909-887-8118		350
Primelite Manufacturing Corp 407 S Main St *Web:* primelite-mfg.com	Freeport	NY	11520	516-868-4411		361
PrimeNet Direct Mktg Solutions LLC 7320 Bryan Dairy Rd *TF:* 800-826-2869 ■ *Web:* www.primenet.com	Largo	FL	33777	727-447-6245		5
Primepak Co 133 Cedar Ln *TF:* 800-786-5613 ■ *Web:* www.primepakcompany.com	Teaneck	NJ	07666	201-836-5060		603
Prime-Pak Foodsinc 2076 Memorial Park Rd	Gainesville	GA	30504	770-536-8708		619
PrimeQ Solutions Inc 26035 Acero Ste 100 *Web:* www.primeq.com	Mission Viejo	CA	92691	949-707-8500		195
Primera Partners LLC 111 Soledad St Ste 1250 *Web:* primerapartners.com	San Antonio	TX	78205	210-444-1400	444-1401	652

Name / Address	City	State	ZIP	Phone	Fax	Class
Primera Plastics Inc 3424 Production Ct *Web:* www.primera-Inc.com	Zeeland	MI	49464	616-748-6248		596
Primera Technology Inc 2 Carlson Pkwy N Ste 375 *TF:* 800-797-2772 ■ *Web:* www.primera.com	Plymouth	MN	55447	763-475-6676	475-6677	173-6
Primerica Financial Services 3120 Breckinridge Blvd *TF:* 800-257-4725 ■ *Web:* www.primerica.com	Duluth	GA	30099	770-381-1000		401
Primeritus Financial Services Inc 440 Metroplex Dr *TF:* 888-833-4238 ■ *Web:* www.primeritus.com	Nashville	TN	37211	888-833-4238		393
Primescape Solutions Inc 510A Herndon Pkwy *Web:* www.primescape.net	Herndon	VA	20170	703-650-1900	650-1901	810
Primesource Staffing LLC 5250 Leetsdale Dr Ste 101 *Web:* www.primesourcestaffing.com	Denver	CO	80246	303-869-2990	869-2997	194
Primestream Corp 15590 NW 15th Ave *Web:* primestream.com	Miami	FL	33169	305-625-4415		809
PriMetrica Inc 5927 Priestly Dr Ste 111 *Web:* www.primetrica.com	Carlsbad	CA	92008	760-651-0030		466
Primevest Capital Corp 400 Burrard St Ste 1730 *Web:* www.primevestcapital.ca	Vancouver	BC	V6C3A6	604-630-7011		528
Primeway Federal Credit Union 12811 Northwest Fwy *Web:* primewayfcu.com	Houston	TX	77040	713-799-6200		219
Primewood Inc 2217 N Ninth St	Wahpeton	ND	58075	701-642-2727		200
Primex Clinical Laboratories Inc 16742 Stagg St Ste 120 *Web:* www.primexlab.com	Van Nuys	CA	91406	818-779-0496		415
Primex Plastics Corp 1235 N 'F' St *TF:* 800-222-5116 ■ *Web:* www.primexplastics.com	Richmond	IN	47374	765-966-7774	935-1083	600
Primitives by Kathy Inc 1817 William Penn Way *TF:* 866-295-2849 ■ *Web:* www.primitivesbykathy.com	Lancaster	PA	17601	866-295-2049		292
Primm Valley Resort & Casino 31900 S Las Vegas Blvd *TF:* 800-926-4455 ■ *Web:* www.primmvalleyresorts.com	Primm	NV	89019	800-926-4455		669
Primmer & Piper P C 100 E State St PO Box 1309 *Web:* www.primmer.com	Montpelier	VT	05601	802-223-2102	223-2628	445
Primo Microphones Inc 1805 Couch Dr *TF:* 800-767-7466 ■ *Web:* www.primomic.com	McKinney	TX	75069	972-548-9807	548-1351	52
Primo's 3309 McKinney Ave *Web:* www.primosdallas.com	Dallas	TX	75204	214-220-0510		671
Primore Inc 2304 W Beecher Rd *Web:* sedco-prv.com	Adrian	MI	49221	517-263-2220	265-6160	789
Primorigen Biosciences Inc 510 Charmany Dr *TF:* 800-372-7442 ■ *Web:* www.primorigen.com	Madison	WI	53719	608-441-8332		05
Primrose Candy Co 4111 W Parker Ave *Web:* www.primrosecandy.com	Chicago	IL	60639	773-276-9522		296-8
Primrose Oil Company Inc 11444 Denton Dr *TF:* 800-275-2772 ■ *Web:* www.primrose.com	Dallas	TX	75229	972-241-1100		541
Primrose School Franchising Co 3660 Cedarcrest Rd *TF:* 800-745-0677 ■ *Web:* www.primroseschools.com	Acworth	GA	30101	770-529-4100	529-1551	148
Primus Builders Inc 8294 Hwy 92 Ste 210 *Web:* www.primusbuilders.com	Woodstock	GA	30189	770-928-7120	928-6548	186
PRIMUS Global Services Inc 1300 W Walnut Hill Ln Ste 160 *Web:* primusglobal.com	Irving	TX	75038	972-753-6500		260
Primus Power Corp 3967 Trust Way *Web:* www.primuspower.com	Hayward	CA	94545	510-342-7600		74
Primus Software Corp 3061 Peachtree Industrial Blvd Ste 110 *Web:* www.primussoft.com	Duluth	GA	30097	770-300-0004		178-2
PRIMUS Sterilizer Company LLC 8719 S 135th St *Web:* www.primus-sterilizer.com	Omaha	NE	68137	402-344-4200		228
Primus Telecommunications (PTGi) 7901 Jones Ranch Dr Ste 900 *NYSE:* PTGI ■ *TF:* 866-385-3360 ■ *Web:* www.ptgi.com	McLean	VA	22102	703-902-2800		736
Primus Venture Partners 5900 Landerbrook Dr Ste 200 *Web:* www.primuscapital.com	Cleveland	OH	44124	440-684-7300		792
Prince & Izant Co 12999 Plaza Dr *Web:* www.princeizant.com	Cleveland	OH	44130	216-362-7000		492
Prince Agri Products Inc 229 Radio Rd *Web:* www.princeagri.com	Quincy	IL	62306	217-222-8854		447
Prince Albert & District Chamber of Commerce 3700 Second Ave W *Web:* www.princealbertchamber.com	Prince Albert	SK	S6W1A2	306-764-6222	922-4727	137
Prince Albert Historical Museum 10 River St E *Web:* www.historypa.com	Prince Albert	SK	S6V8A9	306-764-2992		520
Prince Albert National Park of Canada Northern Prairies Field Unit PO Box 100 *TF Campground Resv:* 877-737-3783 ■ *Web:* www.pc.gc.ca/pn-np/sk/princealbert/index.aspx	Waskesiu Lake	SK	S0J2Y0	306-663-4522		563
Prince Castle Inc 355 E Kehoe Blvd *TF:* 800-722-7853 ■ *Web:* www.princecastle.com	Carol Stream	IL	60188	630-462-8800	462-1460	298
Prince Conti Hotel 830 Conti St *TF:* 800-366-2743 ■ *Web:* www.princecontihotel.com	New Orleans	LA	70112	504-529-4172		379
Prince Contracting LLC 10210 Highland Manor Dr Ste 110 *TF:* 800-321-2424 ■ *Web:* www.princecontracting.com	Tampa	FL	33610	813-699-5900	699-5901	188-4
Prince Corp 8351 County Rd H *TF:* 800-777-2486 ■ *Web:* www.prince-corp.com	Marshfield	WI	54449	715-384-3105	387-6924	578
Prince County Hospital 65 Roy Boapes Ave PO Box 3000 *TF:* 800-465-2425 ■ *Web:* www.pchcare.com	Summerside	PE	C1N2A9	902-438-4200	432-2551	374-2
Prince Edward County 111 S St Second Fl PO Box 304 *Web:* www.co.prince-edward.va.us	Farmville	VA	23901	434-392-5145	392-3913	338
Prince Edward County public School 35 Eagle Dr *Web:* www.pecps.k12.va.us	Farmville	VA	23901	434-315-2100		685
Prince Edward Island Museum & Heritage Foundation 2 Kent St	Charlottetown	PE	C1A1M6	902-368-4000		520
Prince Edward Island National Park of Canada 2 Palmers Ln *TF Campground Resv:* 800-663-7192 ■ *Web:* www.pc.gc.ca	Charlottetown	PE	C1A5V8	902-672-6350	672-6370	563
Prince Edward Island Tourism PO Box 2000 *TF:* 800-463-4734 ■ *Web:* www.gov.pe.ca	Charlottetown	PE	C1A7N8	902-368-4000	368-4438	774
Prince Gallitzin State Park 966 Marina Rd *Web:* www.dcnr.state.pa.us	Patton	PA	16668	814-674-1000		565
Prince George Chamber of Commerce 890 Vancouver St *Web:* www.pgchamber.bc.ca	Prince George	BC	V2L2P5	250-562-2454	562-6510	137
Prince George Citizen 150 Brunswick St *Web:* www.princegeorgecitizen.com	Prince George	BC	V2L2B3	250-562-2441		532-1
Prince George County 6602 Courts Dr PO Box 68 *Web:* www.princegeorgeva.org	Prince George	VA	23875	804-722-8669	732-1967	338
Prince George County Public Schools 6410 Courts Dr *Web:* www.pgs.k12.va.us	Prince George	VA	23875	804-733-2700	733-2737	186
Prince George Electric Co-op 7103 General Mahone Hwy PO Box 168 *Web:* www.pgec.coop	Waverly	VA	23890	804-834-2424		245
Prince George Hotel, The 1725 Market St *TF:* 800-565-1567 ■ *Web:* www.princegeorgehotel.com	Halifax	NS	B3J3N9	902-425-1986		379
Prince George's Chamber of Commerce 4640 Forbes Blvd Ste 130 *Web:* www.pgcoc.org	Lanham	MD	20706	301-731-5000		139
Prince George's Community College 301 Largo Rd **Fax:* Admissions ■ *Web:* www.pgcc.edu	Largo	MD	20774	301-336-6000	322-0119*	162
Prince George's Community Television 9475 Lottsford Rd Ste 125 *Web:* Www.Princegeorgescfcu.Org	Largo	MD	20774	301-386-4085		514
Prince George's County 14741 Governor Oden Bowie Dr *Web:* www.princegeorgescountymd.gov	Upper Marlboro	MD	20772	301-952-3600		338
Prince George's County Conference & Visitors Bureau 622 46th Ave *TF:* 800-579-2294 ■ *Web:* www.amanacolonies.com	Amana	IA	52203	319-622-7622		206
Prince George's County Conference & Visitors Bureau 9200 Basil Ct Ste 101 *Web:* www.visitprincegeorgescounty.com	Largo	MD	20774	301-925-8300	925-2053	206
Prince George's County Memorial Library System 9601 Capital Ln *Web:* pgcmls.info	Largo	MD	20774	301-699-3500		434-3
Prince George's Hospital Ctr 3001 Hospital Dr *TF:* 800-463-6295 ■ *Web:* princegeorgeshospital.org	Cheverly	MD	20785	301-618-2000		374-3
Prince Global Sports LLC 1 Advantage Ct *TF All:* 800-283-6647 ■ *Web:* www.princetennis.com	Bordentown	NJ	08505	609-291-5800	291-5900	710
Prince Lionheart Inc 2421 Westgate Rd *TF:* 800-544-1132 ■ *Web:* www.princelionheart.com	Santa Maria	CA	93455	805-922-2250	922-9442	64
Prince Minerals 21 W 46th St 14th Fl *Web:* www.princecorp.com	New York	NY	10036	646-747-4222		447
Prince Music Theater 1412 Chestnut St *TF:* 800-298-4200 ■ *Web:* www.princetheater.org	Philadelphia	PA	19102	267-239-2941		749
Prince of Peace United Methodist Church of Elk Group 1400 S Arlington Heights Rd *Web:* princeofpeaceumc.org	Elk Grove Village	IL	60007	847-439-0668		48-20
Prince Preferred Guest Program 100 Holomoana St **Fax Area Code:* 808 ■ *TF:* 800-774-6234 ■ *Web:* www.princepreferred.com	Honolulu	HI	96815	800-774-6234	943-4158*	378
Prince Resorts Hawaii 100 Holomoana St *TF:* 888-977-4623 ■ *Web:* www.princeresortshawaii.com	Honolulu	HI	96815	808-956-1111	944-4491	669
Prince Rubber & Plastics Company Inc 137 Arthur St *Web:* www.princerp.com	Buffalo	NY	14207	716-877-7400	877-0743	677
Prince Rupert Port Authority 200-215 Cow Bay Rd *Web:* www.rupertport.com	Prince Rupert	BC	V8J1A2	250-627-8899	627-8980	618
Prince Service & Mfg Inc 7539 Hawkinsville Rd *Web:* www.princeservice.com	Macon	GA	31216	478-788-8162		697
Prince Software Inc 70 Hilltop Rd Ste 2400 *Web:* www.princesoftware.com	Ramsey	NJ	07446	201-934-0022		177
Prince Telecom Inc 551 Mews Dr Ste A *Web:* www.princetelecom.com	New Castle	DE	19720	302-324-1800		187
Prince William County 1 County Complex Ct *Web:* www.pwcgov.org	Woodbridge	VA	22192	703-792-6800		338
Prince William County-Greater Manassas Chamber of Commerce 9720 Capital Ct Ste 203 *TF:* 877-867-3853 ■ *Web:* www.pwchamber.org	Manassas	VA	20110	703-368-6600	368-4733	139
Prince William Forest Park 18100 Pk Headquarters Rd *Web:* www.nps.gov	Triangle	VA	22172	703-221-7181	221-3258	564
Prince William Hospital 8700 Sudly Rd *TF:* 800-526-7101 ■ *Web:* novanthealth.org/princewilliammedicalcenter.aspx	Manassas	VA	20110	703-369-8000	396-5297	374-3

	Phone	Fax	Class
Prince William Regional Chamber of Commerce 9720 Capital Ct Ste 203 .... Manassas VA 20110 *TF:* 877-867-3853 ■ *Web:* pwchamber.org	703-368-6600	368-4733	139
Princess Bayside Beach Hotel & Golf Ctr 4801 Coastal Hwy......................... Ocean City MD 21842 *TF General:* 888-622-9743 ■ *Web:* www.princessbayside.com	410-723-2900		379
Princess Cruises 24844 Rockefeller Ave .... Santa Clarita CA 91355 **Fax:* Sales ■ *TF:* 800-774-6237 ■ *Web:* www.princess.com	661-753-0000	284-4771*	220
Princess House Inc 470 Miles Standish Blvd......................... Taunton MA 02780 *TF Sales:* 800-622-0039 ■ *Web:* www.princesshouse.com	508-823-0711		366
Princess Margaret Hospital 610 University Ave .... Toronto ON M5G2M9 *Web:* www.uhn.ca	416-946-2000		374-7
Princess Pub & Grille 1665 India St .... San Diego CA 92101 *Web:* www.princesspub.com	619-702-3021		671
Princess Royale Oceanfront Hotel & Conference Ctr 9100 Coastal Hwy......................... Ocean City MD 21842 *TF:* 800-476-9253 ■ *Web:* www.princessroyale.com	410-524-7777	524-7787	379
Princeton Battlefield State Park 500 Mercer Rd .... Princeton NJ 08540 *Web:* www.njparksandforests.org	609-921-0074		565
Princeton Capital Management Inc 47 Hulfish St Ste 500 .... Princeton NJ 08542 *Web:* www.pcminvest.com	609-924-6867		194
Princeton Community Hospital 122 12th St............................... Princeton WV 24740 *Web:* www.pchonline.org	304-487-7000	487-2161	374-3
Princeton Excess & Surplus Lines Insurance Co 555 College Rd E .... Princeton NJ 08543 *TF:* 800-544-2378 ■ *Web:* ambest.com	609-243-4200	243-4257	391-4
Princeton Financial Systems LLC 600 College Rd E .... Princeton NJ 08540 *Web:* www.pfs.com	609-987-2400		403
Princeton Forrestal Village 206 Rockingham Row........................ Princeton NJ 08540 *Web:* pfvillage.com	609-799-7400		460
Princeton Gamma-Tech Instruments Inc 303-C College Rd E .... Princeton NJ 08540	609-924-7310		472
Princeton HealthCare System 905 Herrontown Rd.......................... Princeton NJ 08540 *TF:* 866-460-4776 ■ *Web:* www.princetonhcs.org	609-497-3300		363
Princeton Institute for International & Regional Studies (PIIRS) Princeton University Bendheim Hall .... Princeton NJ 08544 *TF:* 888-486-3339 ■ *Web:* www.princeton.edu/piirs	609-258-4852	258-3988	634
Princeton Instruments Inc 3660 Quakerbridge Rd .... Trenton NJ 08619 *Web:* www.princetoninstruments.com	609-587-9797		544
Princeton Insurance Co 746 Alexander Rd PO Box 5322 .... Princeton NJ 08540 *TF:* 800-334-0588 ■ *Web:* www.princetoninsurance.com	609-452-9404	734-8461	391-4
Princeton Packet, The 300 Witherspoon St PO Box 350 .... Princeton NJ 08542 *TF:* 888-747-1122 ■ *Web:* centraljersey.com	609-924-3244	921-2714	637-8
Princeton Partners Inc 205 Rockingham Row........................ Princeton NJ 08540 *Web:* www.princetonpartners.com	609-452-8500		4
Princeton Plasma Physics Laboratory (PPPL) James Forrestal Campus Princeton University PO Box 451 .... Princeton NJ 08543 *TF:* 800-772-2222 ■ *Web:* www.pppl.gov	609-243-2750	243-2751	668
Princeton Public Library 65 Witherspoon St .... Princeton NJ 08542 *Web:* www.princetonlibrary.org	609-924-9529		305
Princeton Radiology Associates P.A. Inc 3674 Route 27 .... Kendall Park NJ 08824 *Web:* www.prapa.com	732-821-5563		418
Princeton Regional Chamber of Commerce 9 Vandeventer Ave .... Princeton NJ 08542 *Web:* www.princetonchamber.org	609-924-1776	924-5776	139
Princeton Regional School District 25 Valley Rd Administration Bldg.............. Princeton NJ 08540 *Web:* www.prs.k12.nj.us	609-806-4200		685
Princeton Review Inc, The 111 Speen St Ste 550.................... Framingham MA 01701 *TF:* 800-273-8439 ■ *Web:* www.princetonreview.com	800-273-8439		242
Princeton Survey Research Assoc 600 Alexander Rd .... Princeton NJ 08540 *Web:* psrai.com	609-924-9204		466
Princeton Theological Seminary 64 Mercer St.............................. Princeton NJ 08540 *TF:* 800-622-6767 ■ *Web:* www.ptsem.edu	609-921-8300	924-2973	167-3
Princeton University 33 Washington Rd .... Princeton NJ 08544 **Fax:* Admissions ■ *TF:* 877-609-2273 ■ *Web:* www.princeton.edu	609-258-3000	258-6743*	166
Princeton University Library 1 Washington Rd .... Princeton NJ 08544 **Fax:* Library ■ *Web:* library.princeton.edu	609-258-4820	258-0441*	434-6
Princeton University Press 41 William St .... Princeton NJ 08540 *TF:* 800-777-4726 ■ *Web:* www.press.princeton.edu	609-258-4900	258-6305	637-4
Princeton University Store 36 University Pl .... Princeton NJ 08540 *Web:* www.pustore.com	609-921-8500		526
Principal Financial Services Inc 711 High St .... Des Moines IA 50392 **Fax Area Code:* 515 ■ *TF:* 800-986-3343 ■ *Web:* www.principal.com/about/giving	502-855-3673	246-5475*	304
Principal Maritime Management LLC 3530 Post Rd Ste 201...................... Southport CT 06890 *Web:* princimar.com	203-292-9580		463
Principal Properties Inc 3295 W 4 Ave .... Hialeah FL 33012 *Web:* principalproperties.com	305-883-7555		652
Principal Technical Services Inc 9960 Research Dr Ste 200 .... Irvine CA 92618 *TF:* 888-787-3711 ■ *Web:* www.ptsstaffing.com	888-787-3711		721
Principia College 13201 Clayton Rd .... St. Louis MO 63131 *TF:* 800-277-4648 ■ *Web:* www.principia.edu	618-374-2131		166

	Phone	Fax	Class
Principia Partners 101 Lindenwood Dr Suite 225 .... Malvern PA 19355 *TF:* 800-378-8330 ■ *Web:* www.principiaconsulting.com	610-363-7815		193
Principle Business Enterprises Inc PO Box 129 .... Dunbridge OH 43414 *TF:* 800-467-3224 ■ *Web:* www.tranquilityproducts.com	419-352-1551		558
Principle Engineering Group Inc 2591 S Ave 2 1/2 E Ste 1 .... Yuma AZ 85365	928-782-5700		261
Princo Instruments Inc 1020 Industrial Hwy .... Southampton PA 18966 *Web:* www.princolevelcontrols.com	215-355-1500		201
Prineville Reservoir State Park 725 Summer St NE Ste C .... Salem OR 97301 *Web:* www.oregonstateparks.org	541-447-4363		565
Prinsco Inc 108 W Hwy 7 PO Box 265........... Prinsburg MN 56281 *TF:* 800-992-1725 ■ *Web:* www.prinsco.com	320-222-6800	978-8602	600
Print Basics Inc 1059 SW 30th Ave .... Deerfield Beach FL 33442 *TF:* 800-800-0052 ■ *Web:* www.printbasics.com	954-354-0700		627
Print Communications Inc 2457 E Washington St .... Indianapolis IN 46201	317-266-8208		626
Print Direction Inc 1600 Indian Brook Way...................... Norcross GA 30093 *TF:* 877-435-1672 ■ *Web:* www.printdirection.com	770-446-6446		627
Print Fulfillment Services LLC 2929 Magazine St........................... Louisville KY 40211	502-776-7704		627
Print House, The 200 Maplewood St .... Malden MA 02148 *TF:* 800-882-1844 ■ *Web:* www.printhouse.com	781-324-4455		627
Print Magazine 10151 Carver Rd Ste 200 .... Blue Ash OH 45242 *TF:* 877-860-9145 ■ *Web:* www.printmag.com	513-531-2690		457-5
Print NW LLC 9914 32nd Ave S .... Tacoma WA 98499 *TF:* 800-826-8260 ■ *Web:* printnw.rocks	253-284-2300		627
Print PAC 2800 Overlook Pkwy................... Atlanta GA 30339 *Web:* www.printpaconline.org	202-730-7970	730-7987	615
Print Papa 1920 Lafayette St Ste L............ Santa Clara CA 95050 *TF:* 800-657-7181 ■ *Web:* www.printpapa.com	408-567-9553		627
Print Resources Inc 1500 E Riverside Dr .... Indianapolis IN 46202 *Web:* www.printindy.com	317-833-7000		41
Print Room 4633 E Broadway Blvd................ Tucson AZ 85711 *Web:* www.theprintroom.com	520-327-5354		344
Print Services & Distribution Assn (PSDA) 330 N Wabash Ave Ste 2000.................. Chicago IL 60611 *TF:* 800-336-4641 ■ *Web:* www.psda.org	800-230-0175		48-9
Print Source Inc, The 404 S Tracy St........... Wichita KS 67209 *TF:* 800-535-9498 ■ *Web:* www.ps-printsource.com	316-945-7052		687
Print Tech LLC 49 Fadem Rd.................. Springfield NJ 07081 *TF:* 800-422-5527 ■ *Web:* www.print-tech.com	908-232-2287		627
Print Time Inc 1105 W 24th Ste 111.......... Kansas City MO 64108 *Web:* www.printtime.com	816-756-3900		627
Print Works 3850 98 St NW................... Edmonton AB T6E3L2 *TF:* 888-452-8921 ■ *Web:* www.printworksprint.com	780-452-8921		627
Printco Graphics Inc 14112 Industrial Rd .... Omaha NE 68144 *TF:* 888-593-1080 ■ *Web:* www.printcographics.com	402-593-1080		225
Printed Circuits Assembly Corp 13221 SE 26th St Ste E..................... Bellevue WA 98005 *Web:* www.pcacorporation.com	425-644-7754	644-6430	625
Printed Image, The 41 S Grant Ave .... Columbus OH 43215 *TF:* 800-464-6087 ■ *Web:* www.printedimage.com	614-221-1412		627
Printed Matter Inc 231 11th Ave .... New York NY 10001 *Web:* www.printedmatter.org	212-925-0325		95
Printed Systems 1265 Gillingham Rd............ Neenah WI 54956 **Fax Area Code:* 888 ■ **Fax:* Sales ■ *TF Sales:* 800-352-2332 ■ *Web:* www.psdtag.com	800-352-2332	321-8247*	413
PrintEdd Products of North America 2641 N Forum Dr .... Grand Prairie TX 75052 *TF:* 800-367-6728 ■ *Web:* www.printedd.com	972-660-3800	641-2564	110
Printek Inc 1517 Townline Rd .... Benton Harbor MI 49022 *TF:* 800-368-4636 ■ *Web:* www.printek.com	269-925-3200	925-8539	173-6
Printer Inc, The 1220 Thomas Beck Rd .... Des Moines IA 50315 *Web:* www.the-printer.com	515-288-7241	288-9234	627
Printers & Stationers Inc 113 N Ct St............................... Florence AL 35630 *TF:* 800-624-5334 ■ *Web:* www.psi-online.net	256-764-8061	764-5024	535
Printfection LLC 3700 Quebec St Unit 100-136 .... Denver CO 80207 *TF:* 866-459-7990 ■ *Web:* www.printfection.com	866-459-7990		195
PrintFleet Inc 275 Ontario St Ste 301 .... Kingston ON K7K2X5 *Web:* www.printfleet.com	613-549-3221		627
Printing Arts Press 8028 Newark Rd.................... Mount Vernon OH 43050 *Web:* www.printingartspress.com	740-397-6106		627
Printing Control Services Inc 1011 Andover Park E .... Tukwila WA 98188 *Web:* printingcontrol.com	206-575-4114		627
Printing House Ltd, The 1403 Bathurst St........................... Toronto ON M5R3H8 *TF:* 800-874-0870 ■ *Web:* www.tph.ca	416-536-6113		344
Printing Images Inc 12266 Wilkins Ave A........................ Rockville MD 20852 *TF:* 866-685-4356 ■ *Web:* www.printingimages.com	301-984-1140		627
Printing Industries of America/Graphic Arts Technical Foundation (PIA/GATF) 200 Deer Run Rd .... Sewickley PA 15143 *TF:* 800-910-4283 ■ *Web:* www.printing.org	412-741-6860	741-2311	49-16
Printing Partners Inc 929 W 16th St........................... Indianapolis IN 46202 *TF:* 800-213-7501 ■ *Web:* www.printingpartners.net	317-635-2282		627
Printing Prep Inc 12 E Tupper St .... Buffalo NY 14203 *TF:* 877-878-7114 ■ *Web:* www.printleader.us	716-852-5011	852-3150	781
Printing Source Inc, The 2373 Ball Dr .... St. Louis MO 63146 *TF:* 800-882-1844 ■ *Web:* www.theprintingsource.com	314-373-7200		627
PrintingForLess.com Inc 100 PFL Way .... Livingston MT 59047 *TF:* 800-930-6040 ■ *Web:* www.printingforless.com	800-930-6040		627
Printmail Systems Inc 23 Friends Ln .... Newtown PA 18940 *TF:* 800-910-4844 ■ *Web:* www.printmailsolutions.com	215-860-4250	860-2204	225

Name / Address	City	State	Zip	Phone	Fax	Class
Print-O-Stat Inc 1011 W Market St *TF:* 800-711-8014 ■ *Web:* www.printostat.com	York	PA	17404	717-854-7821	846-4084	727
Print-O-Tape Inc 755 Tower Rd *TF:* 800-346-6311 ■ *Web:* www.printotape.com	Mundelein	IL	60060	847-362-1476	949-7495	413
Printpack Inc 2800 Overlook Pkwy NE *Web:* www.printpack.com	Atlanta	GA	30339	404-460-7000	460-7165	548
PrintPlace.com 1130 Ave H E *TF:* 877-405-3949 ■ *Web:* www.printplace.com	Arlington	TX	76011	817-701-3555		627
Printpoint Printing Inc 150 S Patterson Blvd *Web:* www.printpointprinting.com	Dayton	OH	45402	937-223-9041		627
Printronix Inc 6440 Oak Canyon Ste 200 *TF:* 800-665-6210 ■ *Web:* www.printronix.com	Irvine	CA	92618	714-368-2300	368-2600	173-6
Printscape Inc 760 Vista Park Dr Ste 7 *Web:* www.myprintscape.com	Pittsburgh	PA	15205	412-788-0640		627
PrintSoft Inc 500 Park Blvd Ste 270 *Web:* www.printsoftamericas.com	Itasca	IL	60143	630-625-5400		809
Printsouth Printing Inc 1114 Silstar Rd *Web:* www.myprintsouth.com	West Columbia	SC	29170	803-796-2619		627
Printswell Inc 135 Cahaba Valley Pkwy *Web:* www.printswell.com	Pelham	Al	35124	205-985-9690		627
Printware LLC 2935 Waters Rd Ste 160 *Web:* www.printwareinc.com	Eagan	MN	55121	651-456-1400		629
Prinzo Group, The 11260 Deerfield Pkwy Ste 100 *Web:* www.prinzogroup.com	Alpharetta	GA	30004	678-496-4615		466
Prior Aviation Service Inc 50 N Airport Dr *Web:* www.prioraviation.com	Buffalo	NY	14225	716-633-1000	633-1432	63
Prior Lake-Savage Area Public School District 719 4540 Tower St SE *TF:* 855-346-1650 ■ *Web:* www.priorlake-savage.k12.mn.us	Prior Lake	MN	55372	952-226-0000	226-0049	685
Priority 1 Consulting 42 Fairview Ln *Web:* www.p1cgroup.com	Plymouth	MA	02360	508-224-5128		445
Priority Business Services Inc 27 Brookline *Web:* www.prioritystaffing.biz	Aliso Viejo	CA	92656	949-222-1122	222-2827	260
Priority Capital Inc 174 Green St *TF:* 800-761-2118 ■ *Web:* prioritycapital.com	Melrose	MA	02176	781-321-8778	321-4108	216
Priority Chevrolet 1495 S Military Hwy **Fax Area Code:* 800 ■ *Web:* www.priorityauto.com	Chesapeake	VA	23320	757-424-1811	236-8951*	57
Priority Designs Inc 100 S Hamilton Rd *Web:* www.prioritydesigns.com	Columbus	OH	43213	614-337-9979	337-9499	261
Priority Distribution Inc 330 Milltown Rd Ste W31 *TF:* 800-576-2378 ■ *Web:* www.pdl3pl.com	East Brunswick	NJ	08816	732-234-1919		311
Priority Express Courier 5 Chelsea Pkwy *TF:* 800-520-4046 ■ *Web:* www.priorityexpress.com	Boothwyn	PA	19061	610-364-3300		540
Priority Health 1231 E Beltline NE *TF:* 800-942-0954 ■ *Web:* www.priorityhealth.com	Grand Rapids	MI	49525	616-942-0954	942-0145	391-3
Priority Management Systems Inc 11160 Silversmith Pl *TF:* 800-437-1032 ■ *Web:* www.prioritymanagement.com	Richmond	BC	V6V2A2	604-214-7772		765
Priority Marketing 8200 College Pkwy Ste 201 *Web:* www.prioritymarketing.com	Fort Myers	FL	33919	239-267-2638		7
Priority Staffing Solutions Inc 42 W 38th St Rm 503 *Web:* www.prioritystaff.com	New York	NY	10018	212-213-2277		260
Priority Wire & Cable Inc PO Box 398 *TF General:* 800-945-5542 ■ *Web:* www.prioritywire.com	North Little Rock	AR	72115	501-372-5444	372-3988	246
Priory Spirituality Ctr 500 College St NE *TF:* 800-880-2777 ■ *Web:* www.stplacid.org	Lacey	WA	98516	360-438-2595	438-9236	673
Priory, The 614 Pressley St *Web:* www.thepriory.com	Pittsburgh	PA	15212	412-231-3338		379
Pri-Pak Inc 2000 Schenley Pl *TF:* 800-274-7632 ■ *Web:* www.pripak.com	Greendale	IN	47025	800-274-7632		88
Prism Assoc Inc 9747 Business Park Ave Ste 217 *Web:* callprism.com	San Diego	CA	92131	858-695-7099		366
Prism Color Corp 31 Twosome Dr *Web:* www.prismcolorcorp.com	Moorestown	NJ	08057	856-234-7515		174
Prism Consulting Inc 1150 Hancock St Ste 400 *Web:* www.prismconsultinginc.com	Quincy	MA	02169	617-328-9896		196
Prism Hotels & Resorts 14800 Landmark Blvd Ste 800 *Web:* www.prismhotels.com	Dallas	TX	75254	214-987-9300		379
Prism Maritime LLC 1416 Kelland Dr Ste B *Web:* prismmaritime.com	Chesapeake	VA	23320	757-460-8800		261
Prism Medical Inc Unit 2 485 Millway Ave *TF:* 877-304-5438 ■ *Web:* www.prismmedicalltd.com	Concord	ON	L4K3V4	416-260-2145		476
PRISM Mktg Services Inc 222 W College Ave Ste 2A *Web:* www.prism-mktg.com	Appleton	WI	54911	920-380-2380		194
Prism Plastics Inc 1544 Hwy 65 *TF:* 877-246-7535 ■ *Web:* www.prismplasticsinc.com	New Richmond	WI	54017	715-246-7535	246-5661	608
Prism Pointe Technologies LLC 1950 Sullivan Rd *TF:* 866-323-4146 ■ *Web:* www.prismpoint.com	College Park	GA	30337	866-323-4146		175
Prism Systems Inc 200 Virginia St *Web:* prismsystems.com	Mobile	AL	36603	251-341-1140		177
Prism Venture Management LLC 117 Kendrick St Ste 200 *Web:* www.prismventure.com	Needham	MA	02494	781-302-4000		792
Prism Visual Software Inc 1 Sagamore Hl Dr Ste 2B *TF:* 800-260-2793 ■ *Web:* www.prismvs.com	Port Washington	NY	11050	516-944-5920		225
Prisma Graphic Corp 2937 E Broadway Rd *TF:* 800-379-5777 ■ *Web:* www.prismagraphic.com	Phoenix	AZ	85040	602-243-5777	268-4804	627
Prismaflex Inc 1645 Queens Way E *TF:* 800-565-3509 ■ *Web:* www.prismaflex.com	Mississauga	ON	L4X3A3	905-279-9793	279-1330	701
Prismatic Development Inc 60 Route 46 *TF:* 800-910-6383 ■ *Web:* www.prisdev.com	Fairfield	NJ	07004	973-882-1133		186
PRISMHR 50 Resnik Rd Ste 200 *TF:* 877-837-4311 ■ *Web:* www.prismhr.com	Plymouth	MA	02360	508-747-7261		225
PrismOne Group Inc 2295 S Hiawassee Rd Ste 418 *Web:* www.prismone.net	Orlando	FL	32835	321-293-1000	292-1001	41
Prison Enterprises PO Box 44314 *Web:* www.doc.louisiana.gov	Baton Rouge	LA	70804	225-342-6633	342-2022	630
Prison Rehabilitative Industries & Diversified Enterprises Inc (PRIDE) 223 Morrison Rd *Web:* www.prideenterprises.org	Brandon	FL	33511	813-324-8700	689-5390	630
Pristech Products Inc 6952 Fairgrounds Pkwy Ste 107 *TF:* 800-432-8722 ■ *Web:* www.pristech.com	San Antonio	TX	78238	210-520-8051	509-7463	172
Pritchard & Jerden Inc 3565 Piedmont Rd Ste2000 *Web:* pjins.com	Atlanta	GA	30305	404-238-9090		390
Pritchard Bieler Gruver & Willison PC 590 Bethlehem Pk *Web:* www.pbgw.com	Colmar	PA	18915	215-997-6700		2
Pritchard Electric Company Inc 2425 Eigth Ave *TF:* 800-873-6176 ■ *Web:* www.pritchardelectric.com	Huntington	WV	25703	304-529-2566	529-2567	189-4
Pritchard Management Associates Inc 517 Wilson Pl Ste 1000 *Web:* www.carlpritchard.com	Frederick	MD	21702	301-662-7877		463
Pritchett Controls Inc 6980 Muirkirk Meadows Dr *TF:* 877-743-2363 ■ *Web:* pritchettcontrols.com	Beltsville	MD	20705	301-470-7300		189-10
Pritchett LLC 8150 N Central Expy Ste 1350 *TF:* 800-992-5922 ■ *Web:* www.pritchettnet.com	Dallas	TX	75206	214-239-9600	239-9650	194
Pritchett Trucking Inc 1050 SE Sixth St PO Box 311 *TF:* 800-486-7504 ■ *Web:* www.pritchetttrucking.com	Lake Butler	FL	32054	386-496-2630	496-2883	780
Pritikin Longevity Ctr & Spa 8755 NW 36th St **Fax:* Resv ■ *TF:* 800-327-4914 ■ *Web:* www.pritikin.com	Doral	FL	33178	305-935-7131	935-7371*	706
Privacy & Data Security Law Resource Ctr 1801 S Bell St *TF:* 800-372-1033	Arlington	VA	22202	703-341-5777		531-7
Privacy Rights Clearinghouse 3100 Fifth Ave Ste B *TF:* 800-269-0271 ■ *Web:* www.privacyrights.org	San Diego	CA	92103	619-298-3396	298-5681	48-10
PrivaSys Inc 1153 Lawrence Dr *Web:* www.privasys.com	Newbury Park	CA	91320	805-498-2310		809
Private Advisors LLC 901 E Byrd St Ste 1400 *Web:* www.privateadvisors.com	Richmond	VA	23219	804-289-6000		401
Private Capital Management 8889 Pelican Bay Blvd Ste 500 *TF:* 800-763-0337 ■ *Web:* www.private-cap.com	Naples	FL	34108	239-254-2500		792
Private Citizen Inc PO Box 233 *Web:* www.private-citizen.com	Naperville	IL	60566	630-393-2370		48-10
Private Client Resources LLC Wilton Corporate Ctr - Riverview 187 Danbury Rd *Web:* www.pcrinsights.com	Wilton	CT	06897	203-762-9006		463
Private Club Associates 2750 Holcomb Bridge Rd Ste 220 *Web:* www.privateclubassociates.com	Alpharetta	GA	30022	678-585-9120		463
Private Export Funding Corp 280 Pk Ave 4th Fl W *Web:* www.pefco.com	New York	NY	10017	212-916-0300	286-0304	216
Private Eyes Inc 190 N Wiget Ln Ste 220 *TF:* 800-767-3263 ■ *Web:* www.privateeyesinc.com	Walnut Creek	CA	94598	925-927-3333		400
Private Label Manufacturers Assn (PLMA) 630 Third Ave *Web:* plma.com	New York	NY	10017	212-972-3131		49-18
Private Lodging Service 1978 Coltman Rd *Web:* privatelodgings.com	Cleveland	OH	44106	216-291-1209		376
Private Party Consignments 11344 I-10 E *TF:* 800-552-6878 ■ *Web:* rvconsignment.com	Baytown	TX	77523	281-303-3000		366
PrivateBancorp Inc 120 S LaSalle St *NASDAQ: PVTB* ■ *TF:* 800-662-7748 ■ *Web:* theprivatebank.com	Chicago	IL	60603	800-662-7748		360-2
Prive Jets LLC 1250 E Hallandale Beach Blvd Ste 505 *Web:* www.privejets.com	Hallandale	FL	33009	305-917-1600		23
Privilege International Inc 2419 Firestone Blvd *Web:* www.privilegeinc.com	South Gate	CA	90280	323-585-0777		321
Priviti Capital Corp 850 444 Fifth Ave S W *TF:* 855-333-9943 ■ *Web:* www.priviticapital.com	Calgary	AB	T2P2T8	403-263-9943		528
Prizm LLC 10 E Stow Rd Ste 100 *Web:* www.prizmllc.com	Marlton	NJ	08053	856-596-5600		463
Prizm Medical Inc 3400 Corporate Way Ste I *Web:* www.prizm-medical.com	Duluth	GA	30096	770-622-0933		476
PRL Aluminum 14760 Don Julian Rd *TF:* 877-775-2586 ■ *Web:* www.prlaluminum.com	City Of Industry	CA	91746	877-775-2586		492
PRL Glass Systems Inc 251 Mason Way *TF:* 800-433-7044 ■ *Web:* www.prlglass.com	City Of Industry	CA	91746	626-961-5890		191-1
Prn Computer Systems Inc 16435 SW Second Dr *Web:* prncomp.com	Pembroke Pines	FL	33027	954-431-5071		809

Company / Address	City	State	ZIP	Phone	Fax	Class
PRN Health Services Inc 4321 W College Ave Ste 200 *TF:* 888-830-8811 ■ *Web:* www.prnhealthservices.com	Appleton	WI	54914	888-830-8811		260
PRN Medical Services LLC 2311 W Utopia Rd *Web:* www.symbiusmedical.com	Phoenix	AZ	85027	623-780-8686		475
Pro Assurance Corp 1250 23rd St NW Ste 250 *TF:* 800-282-6242 ■ *Web:* www.proassurance.com	Washington	DC	20037	202-969-1866	969-1881	391-2
Pro Athlete Inc 10800 N Pomona Ave *TF:* 888-423-2776 ■ *Web:* www.beapro.com	Kansas City	MO	64153	888-423-2776		791
Pro Bono Partnership 237 Mamaroneck Ave Ste 300 *Web:* www.probonopartner.org	White Plains	NY	10605	914-328-0674		428
PRO Building Systems Inc 3678 N Peachtree Rd *TF:* 800-899-8916 ■ *Web:* www.probldgsystems.com	Atlanta	GA	30341	770-455-1791		186
Pro Cat Testing LLC 30844 Century Dr *Web:* www.procat-testing.com	Wixom	MI	48393	248-926-8200		247
Pro Clear Aquatic Systems Inc 2959 Mercury Rd *Web:* www.pro-clear.com	Jacksonville	FL	32207	904-448-6800		520
Pro Company Sound Inc 225 Parsons St **Fax Area Code:* 269 ■ *TF:* 800-253-7360 ■ *Web:* www.procosound.com	Kalamazoo	MI	49007	800-253-7360	388-9681*	492
Pro Computer Service 304 Harper Dr Ste 130 *Web:* www.helpmepcs.com	Moorestown	NJ	08057	856-596-4446		624
Pro Copy 5219 E Fowler Ave *Web:* www.pro-copy.com	Tampa	FL	33617	813-988-5900		627
Pro Fabrication Inc 201 First St *Web:* www.pro-fabrication.com	Madison Lake	MN	56063	507-243-3441		697
Pro Farmer 6612 Chancellor Dr Ste 300 *TF Cust Svc:* 800-772-0023 ■ *Web:* www.agweb.com	Cedar Falls	IA	50613	319-277-1278	277-7982	531-13
Pro Football Hall of Fame 2121 George Halas Dr NW *Web:* www.profootballhof.com	Canton	OH	44708	330-456-8207	456-8175	522
Pro Hockey Life Sporting Goods Inc 4440 Autoroute 440 *Web:* www.prohockeylife.com	Laval	QC	H7P4W6	450-681-8440		711
Pro HR Plus 724 Garland St	Little Rock	AR	72201	501-537-7747		2
Pro Image Sports 233 N 1250 W Ste 200 *Web:* www.proimagesports.com	Centerville	UT	84014	801-296-9999		157-5
Pro It Co 258 W 31st St *Web:* www.proitco.com	Chicago	IL	60616	312-225-6847		180
Pro Lights & Staging News Magazine 6000 S Eastern Ste 14-J *TF General:* 888-667-7438 ■ *Web:* www.plsn.com	Las Vegas	NV	89119	702-932-5585	932-5584	457-21
Pro Logic Consumer Marketing Services 1625 S Congress Ave *TF:* 800-643-3254 ■ *Web:* www.prologicretail.com	Delray Beach	FL	33445	561-454-7600	265-2493	384
Pro Motion Inc 18405 Edison Ave *Web:* www.promotion1.com	Chesterfield	MO	63005	636-449-3162		636
Pro Mujer Inc 253 W 35th St 11th Fl S *TF:* 800-422-7385 ■ *Web:* www.promujer.org	New York	NY	10001	646-626-7000		403
Pro Net Communications Inc 1152 Mainland St Ste 230 *Web:* www.pro.net	Vancouver	BC	V6B5L1	604-606-0660		225
Pro Orthopedic Devices Inc 2884 E Ganley Rd *TF:* 800-523-5611 ■ *Web:* www.proorthopedic.com	Tucson	AZ	85706	520-294-4401		477
Pro Pak California Corp 1070 Samuelson St	Industry	CA	91748	626-810-7694		98
Pro Park America Inc 1 Union Pl *Web:* www.propark.com	Hartford	CT	06103	860-527-2378		192
Pro Pay LLC 7450 W 130th St Ste 220	Overland Park	KS	66213	913-826-6300	492-9171	2
Pro Performance Sports LLC 2081 Faraday Ave *TF:* 877-225-7275 ■ *Web:* www.sklz.com	Carlsbad	CA	92008	877-225-7275		711
Pro Petroleum Inc 4985 N Sloan Ln *TF:* 877-791-4900 ■ *Web:* www.propetroleum.com	Las Vegas	NV	89115	877-791-4900		579
Pro Products LLC 7201 Engle Rd *TF:* 866-357-5063 ■ *Web:* www.proproducts.com	Fort Wayne	IN	46804	260-490-5970	490-9431	806
Pro Security Group 301B S Robinson Dr *TF:* 855-753-7766 ■ *Web:* prosecuritygroup.com	Robinson	TX	76706	254-753-7766		693
Pro Staff Personnel Services 2999 W County Rd 42 Ste 220 *Web:* www.prostaff.com	Burnsville	MN	55306	952-892-3240		721
Pro Staff Sales Inc 6080 Wellington Ave *TF:* 800-482-7324 ■ *Web:* www.prostaffsales.com	Gainesville	GA	30506	678-407-0382		260
Pro Star Aviation LLC 5 Industrial Dr *Web:* www.prostaraviation.com	Londonderry	NH	03053	603-627-7827		261
Pro Star Sports Inc 1133 Winchester Ave *TF:* 800-821-8482 ■ *Web:* www.prostarsports.com	Kansas City	MO	64126	816-241-9737		267
Pro Tapes & Specialties PO Box 53026 *TF:* 800-345-0234 ■ *Web:* www.protapes.com	Newark	NJ	07101	732-346-0900	729-7440	732
Pro Tec Equipment Inc 1298 Lipsey Dr *Web:* www.pro-tecequipment.com	Charlotte	MI	48813	517-541-0303		190
PrO Unlimited Inc 301 Yamato Rd Ste3199 *TF:* 800-291-1099 ■ *Web:* www.prounlimited.com	Boca Raton	FL	33431	800-291-1099		734
Proa Medical Inc 2512 Artesia Blvd Ste 305-C **Fax Area Code:* 888 ■ *TF:* 800-899-3385 ■ *Web:* proamedical.com	Redondo Beach	CA	90278	800-899-3385	395-9288*	475
Proact Marketing Group Inc 2604 NE Industrial Dr Ste 230 *Web:* www.proactmarketing.com	Kansas City	MO	64117	816-472-9898		4
ProAct Services Corp 1140 Conrad Industrial Dr *Web:* www.proact-usa.com	Ludington	MI	49431	231-843-2711		385
Proactive Business Solutions Inc 428 13th St 5th Fl *Web:* www.proactiveok.com	Oakland	CA	94612	510-302-0120		463
Proactive Communications Inc 100 E Whitestone Blvd Ste 148 *Web:* www.proactivecommo.com	Cedar Park	TX	78613	254-699-0067		194
Proactive Diagnostics 2235 Faraday Ave Ste O *Web:* www.plcds.com	Carlsbad	CA	92008	805-405-4620		111
Proactive Management Consulting LLC 2700 Cumberland Pkwy SE *TF:* 877-319-2198 ■ *Web:* www.proactive-management.com	Atlanta	GA	30339	770-319-7468		196
Proactive Networking 229 Marshall Rd *Web:* www.proactivekc.com	Platte City	MO	64079	816-587-7878		180
Proactive Performance Solution 560 Peoples Plaza 139 *Web:* www.proactiveusa.com	Newark	DE	19702	302-375-0451		809
Proactive Sports Inc 1200 SE Second Ave *TF:* 800-369-8642 ■ *Web:* proactivesports.com	Canby	OR	97013	503-263-8583		711
Proair LLC 28731 County Rd 6 *TF:* 800-338-8544 ■ *Web:* www.proairllc.com	Elkhart	IN	46514	574-264-5494	264-2194	14
ProAssurance Corp 100 Brookwood Pl Ste 300 *NYSE: PRA* ■ **Fax:* Cust Svc ■ *TF:* 800-282-6242 ■ *Web:* www.proassurance.com	Birmingham	AL	35209	205-877-4400	802-4799*	360-4
Probaris Technologies Inc 1880 JFK Blvd Ste 1909 *Web:* www.probaris.com	Philadelphia	PA	19103	215-238-0510		809
Procacci Bros Sales Corp 3333 S Front St *Web:* www.procaccibrothers.com	Philadelphia	PA	19148	215-463-8000		297-7
Procaccianti Group, The 1140 Reservoir Ave	Cranston	RI	02920	401-946-4600		379
Pro-cad Software Ltd 12 Elbow River Rd *TF:* 888-477-6223 ■ *Web:* www.procad.com	Calgary	AB	T3Z2V2	403-216-3375		177
ProCamps Inc 4600 McAuley Pl 4th Fl *Web:* www.procamps.com	Cincinnati	OH	45242	513-793-2267		239
Pro-care Home Health Limited 122 W Union St *TF:* 800-579-7967 ■ *Web:* www.christiancarecommunities.org	Hartford	KY	42347	270-298-3112		363
ProCare One Nurses LLC 300 Clayton Rd Ste 1170 *TF:* 800-493-2988 ■ *Web:* www.procareone.com	Concord	CA	94520	800-493-2988		260
ProCare Pharmacy Benefit Manager Inc 1267 Professional Pkwy Ste 100 *TF:* 888-821-5516 ■ *Web:* www.procarerx.com	Gainesville	GA	30507	888-821-5516		809
ProCare Vision Ctr Inc 1955 Newark-Granville Rd *Web:* www.procarevisioncenters.com	Granville	OH	43023	740-587-3937	587-3589	543
Procase Consulting 180 Caster Ave Unit 55 *Web:* www.procaseconsulting.com	Woodbridge	ON	L4L5Y7	905-856-7479		180
Procedyne Corp 11 Industrial Dr *Web:* www.procedyne.com	New Brunswick	NJ	08901	732-249-8347	249-7220	318
Proceedings of the IEEE Magazine 445 Hoes Ln *TF:* 800-678-4333 ■ *Web:* www.ieee.org	Piscataway	NJ	08855	732-562-5478	562-5456	457-21
Procel Temporary Services 2447 Pacific Coast Hwy Ste 207 *TF:* 800-338-9905 ■ *Web:* www.procelnurses.com	Hermosa Beach	CA	90254	310-372-0560		260
Procera Networks Inc 47448 Fremont Blvd *Web:* www.proceranetworks.com	Fremont	CA	94538	510-230-2777		177
ProCertus BioPharm Inc 510 Charmany Dr Ste 175 B	Madison	WI	53719	608-345-4857	277-8041	231
Procesadora Campo Fresco Inc PO Box 755 *Web:* www.campofresco.com	Santa Isabel	PR	00757	787-845-4747	845-3490	80-2
Process Combustion Corp 5460 Curry Rd *Web:* www.pcc-sterling.com	Pittsburgh	PA	15236	412-655-0955	650-5569	318
Process Construction Inc 1421 Queen City Ave *Web:* www.processconstruction.com	Cincinnati	OH	45214	513-251-2211		189-10
Process Control Corp 6875 Mimms Dr *Web:* www.process-control.com	Atlanta	GA	30340	770-449-8810		111
Process Control Technology Inc 4335 Piedras Dr W Ste 175 *Web:* www.gopct.com	San Antonio	TX	78228	210-735-9141	735-9775	178-1
Process Data Control Corp 1803-A W Park Row Dr *TF:* 800-289-6116 ■ *Web:* www.pdccorp.com	Arlington	TX	76013	817-459-4488		180
Process Development & Control Inc 1075 Montour W Industrial Pk *TF:* 888-732-4070 ■ *Web:* www.pdcvalve.com	Coraopolis	PA	15108	724-695-3440		350
Process Displays Co 7108 31st Ave N *Web:* pdinstore.com	Minneapolis	MN	55427	763-546-1133		627
Process Engineering Corp PO Box 279 *Web:* www.pecfrictionfighters.com	Crystal Lake	IL	60039	815-459-1734	459-3676	127
Process Equipment Co 6555 S SR-202 *Web:* www.peco-us.com	Tipp City	OH	45371	937-667-4451	667-9322	454
Process Equipment Inc 2770 Welborn St PO Box 1607 *TF:* 888-663-2028 ■ *Web:* www.processbarron.com	Pelham	AL	35124	205-663-5330	663-6037	18
Process Fab Inc 15644 Clanton Cir *Web:* www.processfab.com	Santa Fe Springs	CA	90670	562-921-1979		454
Process Materials Inc 5625 Brisa St Ste A *Web:* www.processmaterials.com	Livermore	CA	94550	925-245-9626		567
Process Plus LLC 135 Merchant St Ste 300 *Web:* www.processplus.com	Cincinnati	OH	45246	513-742-7590		256

	Phone	Fax	Class
Process Sensors Corp 113 Cedar St .... Milford MA 01757 *Web:* www.processsensors.com	508-473-9901		492
Process Software Corp 959 Concord St .... Framingham MA 01701 *TF:* 800-722-7770 ■ *Web:* www.process.com	508-879-6994	879-0042	178-12
Process Technology 7010 Lindsay Dr .... Mentor OH 44060 *Web:* www.process-technology.com	440-974-1300		14
Processed Metals Innovators LLC 600 21st Ave .... Bloomer WI 54724 *TF:* 888-877-7277 ■ *Web:* www.pmillc.com	715-568-1700		480
ProcessMAP Corp 13450 W Sunrise Blvd Ste 160 .... Sunrise FL 33323 *TF:* 800-229-6655 ■ *Web:* www.processmap.com	954-515-5040		177
Processmodel Inc 10602 S Cvered Bridge Cyn .... Spanish Fork UT 84660 *Web:* www.processmodel.com	801-356-7165		809
ProChon Biotech Ltd 400 Trade St Ste 395 .... Woburn MA 01801	781-305-5035		476
Proco Machinery 1111 Brevik Pl .... Mississauga ON L4W3R7 *TF:* 800-765-9746 ■ *Web:* procomachinery.com	905-602-6066		111
Proco Products Inc PO Box 590 .... Stockton CA 95201 *TF:* 800-344-3246 ■ *Web:* www.procoproducts.com	209-943-6088	943-0242	676
ProCom Inc 28838 US Hwy 69 E PO Box 27 .... Lamoni IA 50140 *Web:* www.procom-inc.com	641-784-8841		737
ProComp Software Consultants Inc 555 Cincinnati-Batavia Pk .... Cincinnati OH 45244 *TF:* 800-783-1668 ■ *Web:* www.procompsoftware.com	513-685-5245		179
Procon Consulting Llc 2300 N Pershing Dr Ste 305 .... Arlington VA 22201 *Web:* www.proconconsulting.com	703-527-7059		196
Procon Products 869 7 Oaks Blvd Ste 120 .... Smyrna TN 37167 *Web:* www.proconpumps.com	615-355-8000	355-8001	641
Proconex Management Group Inc 103 Enterprise Dr .... Hoyerstord PA 19468 *Web:* www.proconexdirect.com	610-495-1835		358
Procopio Cory Hargreaves & Savitch LLP 525 B St Ste 2200 .... San Diego CA 92101 *Web:* www.procopio.com	619-238-1900	235-0398	428
Procor Ltd 2001 Speers Rd .... Oakville ON L6L2X9 *TF:* 888-977-6267 ■ *Web:* www.procor.com	905-827-4111		264-5
Procrane Inc 2440-76 Ave Stn S PO Box 8610 .... Edmonton AB T6E6R2 *Web:* www.sterlingcrane.ca	780-440-4434		23
Procter & Gamble Co (PG) 1 Procter & Gamble Plaza .... Cincinnati OH 45202 *NYSE:* PG ■ *TF:* 800-503-4611 ■ *Web:* www.pg.com	513-983-1100		185
Procter & Gamble Company, The 1 P&G Plaza .... Cincinnati OH 45202 *TF:* 800-683-3738 ■ *Web:* us.pg.com	513-983-1100		582
Proctor Academy 204 Main St PO Box 500 .... Andover NH 03216 *TF:* 800-820-4007 ■ *Web:* www.proctoracademy.org	603-735-6000		622
Proctor Engineering Group Ltd 418 Mission Ave .... San Rafael CA 94901 *TF:* 888-455-5742 ■ *Web:* www.proctoreng.com	415-451-2480		261
Proctor Hospital 5409 N Knoxville Ave .... Peoria IL 61614 *Web:* unitypoint.org/peoria/default.aspx	309-691-1000	683-6190	374-3
Proctor Journal 215 E Fifth St .... Proctor MN 55810 *Web:* www.proctorjournal.com	218-624-3344		532-4
Proctor Sales Inc 20715 50th Ave W .... Lynnwood WA 98036 *TF:* 800-423-4585 ■ *Web:* www.proctorsales.com	425-774-1441		612
Proctor Speedway 800 N Boundary Ave .... Proctor MN 55810 *Web:* www.proctorspeedway.com	218-624-0606		515
Proctor's Theatre 432 State St .... Schenectady NY 12305 *Web:* www.proctors.org	518-382-3884	346-2468	572
Procurity Inc 160 Eagle Dr .... Winnipeg MB R2R1V5	204-632-5506		238
Procurri LLC 5825 Peachtree Corners E Ste A .... Norcross GA 30092 *Web:* www.procurri.com	770-817-9092		196
Pro-data Computer Services Inc 2809 S 160th St Ste 401 .... Omaha NE 68130 *TF:* 800-228-6318 ■ *Web:* www.prodatacomputer.com	402-697-7575		175
Pro-data Control Systems Inc 12405 SW 93rd Ave .... Miami FL 33176 *TF:* 800-638-9450 ■ *Web:* prodatacontrol.com	305-256-5666		396
Prodata Systems Inc 11007 Slater Ave NE .... Kirkland WA 98033 *TF:* 866-582-7485 ■ *Web:* www.prodata.com	425-296-4168	822-3443	39
Prodco International Inc 9408 Boul du Golf .... Montreal QC H1J3A1 *TF:* 888-577-6326 ■ *Web:* www.prodcotech.com	514-324-9796		693
Pro-Dex Inc 2361 McGaw Ave .... Irvine CA 92614 *NASDAQ:* PDEX ■ *TF:* 800-562-6204 ■ *Web:* www.pro-dex.com	800-562-6204		360-3
Prodigy Diabetes Care LLC 2701-A Hutchison McDonald Rd PO Box 481928 . Charlotte NC 28269 *TF:* 800-366-5901 ■ *Web:* www.prodigymeter.com	800-366-5901		476
Prodo Laboratories 27402 Aliso Viejo Pkwy .... Aliso Viejo CA 92656 *Web:* prodolabs.com	949-727-1972		41
Prodo-Pak Corp 77 Commerce St .... Garfield NJ 07026 *Web:* www.prodo-pak.com	973-777-7770	772-0471	547
Produce Marketing Assn (PMA) 1500 Casho Mill Rd .... Newark DE 19711 *Web:* www.pma.com	302-738-7100	731-2409	49-6
Produce Source Partners 13167 Telcourt Rd .... Ashland VA 23005 *TF:* 800-344-4728 ■ *Web:* www.producesourcepartners.com	804-262-8300	264-2313	297-7
Producers Co-op Assoc 300 E Buffalo St .... Girard KS 66743 *TF:* 800-442-2809 ■ *Web:* www.girardcoop.com	620-724-8241		447
Producers Co-op Oil Mill 6 SE Fourth St .... Oklahoma City OK 73129 *Web:* www.producerscoop.net	405-232-7555		296-29
Producers Dairy Foods Inc 250 E Belmont Ave .... Fresno CA 93701 *Web:* www.producersdairy.com	559-264-6583		296-27
Producers Financial 5350 Tomah Dr Ste 3800 .... Colorado Springs CO 80918 *TF:* 800-985-5549 ■ *Web:* www.pfnco.com	719-535-0739		401
Producers Livestock Auction Co 1131 N Bell St .... San Angelo TX 76903 *Web:* www.producersandcargile.com	325-653-3371	653-3370	446
Producers Livestock Marketing Assn 4809 S 114th St .... Omaha NE 68137 *TF:* 800-257-4046 ■ *Web:* producerslivestock.net	402-597-9189	597-9505	446
Producers Management Television Pmtv 681 Moore Rd Ste 100 .... King Of Prussia PA 19406 *Web:* pmtv.com	610-768-1770		514
Producers Peanut Company Inc PO Box 250 .... Suffolk VA 23434 *TF:* 800-847-5491 ■ *Web:* www.producerspeanut.com	757-539-7496	934-7730	296-32
Producers Rice Mill Inc PO Box 1248 .... Stuttgart AR 72160 *TF:* 800-369-7675 ■ *Web:* www.producersrice.com	870-673-4444		296-23
Producers Service Corp 109 Graham St .... Zanesville OH 43701 *Web:* www.producersservicecorp.com	740-454-6253		539
Product Design & Development Magazine 199 E Badger Rd Ste 201 .... Madison WI 53713 *TF:* 800-869-6882 ■ *Web:* www.pddnet.com	973-920-7000		457-21
Product Development & Management Assn (PDMA) 330 N Wabash Ave Ste 2000 .... Chicago IL 60611 *TF:* 800-232-5241 ■ *Web:* www.pdma.org	312-321-5145		49-12
Product Development Corp 20 Ragsdale Dr Ste 100 .... Monterey CA 93940	831-333-1100	333-0110	96
Product Development Technologies Inc 1 Corporate Dr .... Lake Zurich IL 60047 *Web:* www.pdt.com	847-821-3000	821-3020	261
Product Distributors Inc 4200 Beach Dr Ste 2 Ste 2 .... Rapid City SD 57702 *Web:* www.forpd.com	605-341-6500		191-3
Product Evaluation Systems Inc 637 Donohoe Rd .... Latrobe PA 15650 *Web:* www.productevaluationsystems.com	724-834-8848		743
Product Miniature Co 627 Capitol Dr .... Pewaukee WI 53072 *Web:* www.pmplastic.com	262-691-1700		604
Product Mktg Group Inc 978 Douglas Ave .... Altamonte Springs FL 32714 *Web:* eternalmessage.com	407-774-6363		4
Product Quest Mfg LLC 330 Carswell Ave .... Daytona Beach FL 32117 *Web:* www.productquestmfg.com	386-239-8787		231
Product Safety Consulting Inc 605 Country Club Dr Ste I .... Bensenville IL 60106 *TF:* 877-804-3066 ■ *Web:* productsafetyinc.com	630-238-0188		196
Product Support Solutions Inc 7172 Regional St Ste 431 .... Dublin CA 94568 *Web:* www.psshelp.com	925-208-2450		317
Production Automation Co 6200 Bury Dr .... Eden Prairie MN 55346 *Web:* www.gotopac.com	952-903-0333		57
Production Equipment Co 401 Liberty St .... Meriden CT 06450 **Fax Area Code:* 800 ■ *TF:* 800-758-5697 ■ *Web:* www.peco1938.com	203-235-5795	563-4150*	470
Production Management Industries LLC 9761 Hwy 90 E .... Morgan City LA 70380 *TF:* 888-229-3837 ■ *Web:* www.pmi.net	985-631-3837	631-0729	539
Production Masters Inc 204 Fifth Ave .... Pittsburgh PA 15222 *Web:* www.pmi.tv	412-281-8500		514
Production Pattern Co 560 Solon Rd .... Cleveland OH 44146	440-439-3243		567
Production Press Inc 307 E Morgan St .... Jacksonville IL 62650 *TF:* 800-231-3880 ■ *Web:* www.productionpress.com	217-243-3353	245-0400	627
Production Products Co 6176 E Molloy Rd .... East Syracuse NY 13057 *TF:* 800-800-6652 ■ *Web:* www.ppc-online.com	315-431-7200	431-7201	621
Production Resource Group 300 Harvestore Dr .... DeKalb IL 60115 *Web:* www.prg.com	815-756-9600		181
Production Resource Group LLC 539 Temple Hill Rd .... New Windsor NY 12553 *TF:* 800-223-2500 ■ *Web:* www.prg.com	845-567-5700	567-5800	722
Production Tool Supply 8655 E Eight Mile Rd .... Warren MI 48089 **Fax:* Sales ■ *TF:* 800-366-3600 ■ *Web:* www.pts-tools.com	586-755-7770	755-4921*	385
ProductionHUB 1806 Hammerlin Ave .... Winter Park FL 32789 *Web:* www.productionhub.com	407-629-4122		530
Productions USA Inc 1960 N Lincoln Pk W .... Chicago IL 60614 *TF:* 800-594-3250 ■ *Web:* www.productionsusa.com	773-296-6200	296-6333	184
Productive Alternatives Inc 1205 N Tower Rd .... Fergus Falls MN 56537 *TF:* 800-627-3529 ■ *Web:* www.palff.org	218-998-5630	736-2541	230
Productive Plastics Inc 103 W Pk Dr .... Mount Laurel NJ 08054 *Web:* www.productiveplastics.com	856-778-4300	234-3310	602
Productivity Apex Inc 11301 Corporate Blvd Ste 303 .... Orlando FL 32817 *Web:* www.productivityapex.com	407-384-0800		177
Productivity Inc 375 Bridgeport Ave 3rd Fl .... Shelton CT 06484 *TF:* 800-966-5423 ■ *Web:* www.productivityinc.com	203-225-0451	225-0771	765
Productivity Point International Inc 2950 Gateway Ctr Blvd .... Morrisville NC 27560	919-379-5611		764
Products Engineering Corp 2645 Maricopa St .... Torrance CA 90503 *TF:* 800-923-6255 ■ *Web:* www.productsengineering.com	310-787-4500	787-4501	493
Produits Alimentaires Berthelet Inc 1805 Berlier St .... Laval QC H7L3S4 *Web:* www.berthelet.com	514-334-5503	334-3584	296-37
ProEd Communications Inc 25101 Chagrin Blvd Ste 230 .... Beachwood OH 44122 *Web:* www.proedcom.com	216-595-7919		4
Proenergy Services LLC 2001 ProEnergy Blvd .... Sedalia MO 65301 **Fax Area Code:* 660 ■ *TF:* 844-367-4948 ■ *Web:* www.proenergyservices.com	844-367-4948	829-1160*	463

Company	City	State	Zip	Phone	Fax	Class
Professional Aircraft Accessories Inc 7035 Ctr Ln *Web:* www.gopaa.com	Titusville	FL	32780	321-267-1040		529
Professional Ambulance & Oxygen Service Inc 31 Smith Pl. *TF:* 800-653-3640 ■ *Web:* www.proems.com	Cambridge	MA	02138	617-492-2700		30
Professional Assn of Diving Instructors International (PADI) 30151 Tomas St *TF Sales:* 800-729-7234 ■ *Web:* www.padi.com	Rancho Santa Margarita	CA	92688	949-858-7234	267-1267	48-22
Professional Bank Services Inc 6200 Dutchmans Ln Ste 305 *TF:* 800-523-4778 ■ *Web:* www.probank.com	Louisville	KY	40205	502-451-6633	451-6755	194
Professional Beauty Assn (PBA) 15825 N 71st St Ste 100 *TF:* 800-468-2274 ■ *Web:* www.probeauty.org	Scottsdale	AZ	85254	480-281-0424	905-0708	49-18
Professional Bowlers Assn (PBA) 719 Second Ave Ste 701 *TF:* 800-947-2886 ■ *Web:* www.pba.com	Seattle	WA	98104	206-332-9688	654-6030	48-22
Professional Building Systems Inc 72 E Market St *TF:* 800-837-4552 ■ *Web:* www.pbsmodular.com	Middleburg	PA	17842	800-837-4552		106
Professional Bull Riders Inc (PBR) 101 W Riverwalk *TF:* 800-366-8538 ■ *Web:* www.pbr.com	Pueblo	CO	81003	719-242-2800	242-2855	48-15
Professional Coaters Inc 100 Commerce Park Dr *TF:* 800-962-0344 ■ *Web:* www.procoatinc.com	Cabot	AR	72023	501-843-7509		818
Professional Contract Services Inc 718 W FM 1626 *Web:* www.pcsi.org	Austin	TX	78748	512-358-8887	358-8890	152
Professional Convention Management Assn (PCMA) 35 E Wacker Dr Ste 500 *TF:* 877-827-7262 ■ *Web:* www.pcma.org	Chicago	IL	60601	312-423-7262	423-7222	49-12
Professional Cutlery Direct LLC 242 Branford Rd **Fax Area Code:* 800 ■ *TF:* 800-792-6650	North Branford	CT	06471	203-871-1000	296-8039*	222
Professional Electric Products Co (PEPCO) 33210 Lakeland Blvd *TF:* 800-872-7000 ■ *Web:* www.pepconet.com	Eastlake	OH	44095	440-946-3790	942-5883	246
Professional Engineering Consultants PA 303 S Topeka St *Web:* www.pec1.com	Wichita	KS	67202	316-262-2691	262-3003	261
Professional Examination Service 475 Riverside Dr Ste 600 *TF:* 800-347-6647 ■ *Web:* www.proexam.org	New York	NY	10115	212-367-4200	367-4266	244
Professional Graphics Inc 25 Perry Ave *Web:* www.progi.net	Norwalk	CT	06850	203-846-4291		174
Professional Group Plans Inc (PGP) 225 Wireless Blvd Ste 200 *Web:* www.pgpbenefits.com	Hauppauge	NY	11788	631-951-9200	951-9623	631
Professional Instruments Co 7800 Powell Rd *TF:* 800-445-6267 ■ *Web:* www.airbearings.com	Hopkins	MN	55343	952-933-1222	933-3315	75
Professional Insurance Marketing Assn (PIMA) 35 E Wacker Dr Ste 850 *Web:* www.pima-assn.org	Chicago	IL	60601	817-569-7462		49-9
Professional Janitorial Service of Houston Inc 180 New Camellia Blvd *Web:* www.pjs.com	Covington	LA	70433	713-850-0287	963-9420	152
Professional Landcare Network (PLANET) 950 Herndon Pkwy Ste 450 *TF:* 800-395-2522 ■ *Web:* www.landscapeprofessionals.org	Herndon	VA	20170	703-736-9666	736-9668	48-2
Professional Liability Underwriting Society 5353 Wayzata Blvd Ste 600 *TF:* 800-845-0778 ■ *Web:* www.plusweb.org	Minneapolis	MN	55416	952-746-2580	746-2599	49-9
Professional Maintenance Care 4912 Naples St *Web:* www.pmsjanitorial.com	San Diego	CA	92110	619-276-1150		104
Professional Management Assoc LLC 390 Amwell Rd Ste 403 *Web:* www.association-partners.com	Hillsborough	NJ	08844	908-359-1184	359-7619	47
Professional Photographers of America Inc (PPA) 229 Peachtree St NE Ste 2200 *TF:* 800-786-6277 ■ *Web:* www.ppa.com	Atlanta	GA	30303	404-522-8600	614-6400	48-4
Professional Placement Inc 4040 E Camelback Ste 235 *Web:* www.proplacement.com	Phoenix	AZ	85018	602-955-0870	955-0604	721
Professional Plastics Inc 1810 E Valencia Dr *TF:* 800-878-0755 ■ *Web:* www.professionalplastics.com	Fullerton	CA	92831	714-446-6500		601
Professional Power Products Inc 448 W Madison St *Web:* www.professionalpowerproducts.com	Darien	WI	53114	262-882-9000	882-9010	729
Professional Publishing Report 11200 Rockville Pk Ste 504 *Web:* simbainformation.com	Rockville	MD	20852	240-747-3096	747-3004	531-11
Professional Research Consultants Inc 11326 P St *TF:* 800-428-7455 ■ *Web:* www.prccustomresearch.com	Omaha	NE	68137	402-592-5656		194
Professional Risk Solutions LLC 37 Mountain Blvd Ste 3 *Web:* www.prsbrokers.com	Warren	NJ	07059	908-834-8401		390
Professional Rodeo Cowboys Assn (PRCA) 101 Pro Rodeo Dr *TF:* 800-234-7722 ■ *Web:* www.prorodeo.com	Colorado Springs	CO	80919	719-593-8840		48-22
Professional Sales & Service LC 3545 West 1500 South *Web:* pro-sales.com	Salt Lake City	UT	84104	801-977-3961		690
Professional Service Industries Inc (PSI) 1901 S Meyers Rd Ste 400 *TF:* 800-548-7901 ■ *Web:* www.psiusa.com	Oakbrook Terrace	IL	60181	630-691-1490	691-1587	261
Professional Services Council (PSC) 4401 Wilson Blvd Ste 1110 *TF:* 800-353-9118 ■ *Web:* www.pscouncil.org	Arlington	VA	22203	703-875-8059	875-8922	49-12
Professional Shorthand Reporters Inc (PSR) 601 Poydras St Ste 1615 *TF:* 800-536-5255 ■ *Web:* www.psrdepo.com	New Orleans	LA	70130	504-529-5255		445
Professional Software Engineering Inc 780 Lynnhaven Pkwy Ste 350 *TF:* 800-924-1091 ■ *Web:* www.prosoft-eng.com	Virginia Beach	VA	23452	757-431-2400	463-1071	180
Professional Sports Publications 519 Eigth Ave 25th Fl *Web:* www.pspsports.com	New York	NY	10018	212-697-1460		637-9
Professional Staff Management Inc 6801 Lake Plaza Dr Ste D-405 *TF:* 800-967-5515 ■ *Web:* www.psmin.com	Indianapolis	IN	46220	317-816-7007	816-7005	631
Professional Staffing Group 155 Federal St *Web:* www.psgstaffing.com	Boston	MA	02110	617-250-1000		721
Professional Surveyor Magazine 20 W Third St *Web:* xyht.com	Frederick	MD	21701	301-682-6101	682-6105	457-21
Professional Tennis Registry PO Box 4739 *TF:* 800-421-6289 ■ *Web:* www.ptrtennis.org	Hilton Head Island	SC	29938	843-785-7244	686-2033	48-22
Professional Translating Services Inc Douglas Rd *Web:* www.protranslating.com	Coral Gables	FL	33134	305-371-7887		768
Professional Travel Inc 25000 Great Northern Corporate Ctr Ste 170 *TF:* 800-247-0060 ■ *Web:* www.protrav.com	Cleveland	OH	44070	440-734-8800	734-4528	771
Profex Medical Products Inc 2224 E Person Ave *Web:* www.profexmed.com	Memphis	TN	38114	901-452-7485		476
Proffitt & Goodson Inc Old Kingston Pl 4800 Old Kingston Pk Ste 200 *TF:* 866-776-3355 ■ *Web:* www.proffittgoodson.com	Knoxville	TN	37919	865-584-1850		229
Proficient Learning LLC 1508 Military Cutoff Rd Ste 304 *Web:* www.proficientlearning.com	Wilmington	NC	28403	910-509-0104		195
Proficio 1555 Faraday Ave *TF:* 800-779-5042 ■ *Web:* www.proficio.com	Carlsbad	CA	92008	800-779-5042		631
Profile Bank 45 Wakefield St PO Box 1808 *TF:* 800-554-8969 ■ *Web:* www.profilebank.com	Rochester	NH	03866	603-332-2610	332-2519	70
Profile Digital Printing LLC 5449 Marina Dr *Web:* www.profiledpi.com	Dayton	OH	45449	937-866-4241		627
Profile Food Ingredients LLC 1151 Timber Dr *TF:* 877-632-1700 ■ *Web:* profilefoodingredients.com	Elgin	IL	60123	847-622-1700		358
Profile Mktg Research Inc 4020 S 57th Ave Ste 101 *Web:* radius-global.com	Lake Worth	FL	33463	561-965-8300		194
Profiles International Inc 5205 Lake Shore Dr *TF:* 866-751-1644 ■ *Web:* www.profilesinternational.com	Waco	TX	76710	254-751-1644		721
Profiles Placement 20 S Charles St *TF:* 800-906-0044 ■ *Web:* careerprofiles.com	Baltimore	MD	21201	410-244-6400		260
Pro-Financial Asset Management Inc 5090 Oribtor Dr Unit 3	Mississauga	ON	L4W5B5	905-815-6900		528
Profisee Group Inc 2520 Northwinds Pkwy Two Northwinds Ctr *Web:* www.profisee.com	Alpharetta	GA	30009	678-202-8990		387
Profit Point Inc 24 Ayers St *Web:* www.profitpt.com	North Brookfield	MA	01535	435-487-9141		463
Profit Programming Inc 120 Cockysville Rd *TF:* 800-294-2900 ■ *Web:* www.profitprogramming.com	Hunt Valley	MD	21030	410-316-1000		177
Profit Recovery Partners LLC 18231 W McDurmott *Web:* www.prpllc.com	Irvine	CA	92614	949-851-2777		196
Profit Sharing/401(k) Council of America (PSCA) 20 N Wacker Dr Ste 3700 *TF:* 866-614-8407 ■ *Web:* www.psca.org	Chicago	IL	60606	312-419-1863	419-1864	49-12
Profitable Investing 9201 Corporate Blvd *TF:* 800-219-8592 ■ *Web:* www.profitableinvesting.investorplace.com	Rockville	MD	20850	800-211-8566		531-9
Profitsword LLC 9355 Cypress Cove Dr *TF:* 866-930-6543 ■ *Web:* www.profitsword.com	Orlando	FL	32819	407-909-8822		177
Proflowers.com 4840 Eastgate Mall *TF:* 800-580-2913 ■ *Web:* www.proflowers.com	San Diego	CA	92121	800-580-2913		292
ProForma 8800 E Pleasant Valley Rd *TF:* 800-825-1525 ■ *Web:* www.proforma.com	Independence	OH	44131	216-520-8400		627
Pro-Formance Shocks Inc 1715 Lakes Pkwy *Web:* www.proshocks.com	Lawrenceville	GA	30043	770-995-6300		247
Proformative Inc 99 Almaden Blvd Ste 975 *Web:* www.proformative.com	San Jose	CA	95113	408-400-3993		387
Profound Logic Software Inc 396 Congress Park Dr *TF:* 800-540-5532 ■ *Web:* www.profoundlogic.com	Dayton	OH	45459	937-439-7925		525
ProFutures Inc 11719 Bee Cave Rd Ste 200 *Web:* www.profutures.com	Austin	TX	78738	512-263-3800		691
Progenics Pharmaceuticals Inc 777 Old Saw Mill River Rd *NASDAQ:* PGNX ■ *TF:* 866-644-7188 ■ *Web:* www.progenics.com	Tarrytown	NY	10591	914-789-2800	789-2817	85
Progeny Linux Systems Inc 9100 Keystone Crossing Ste 440 *Web:* www.progenylinux.com	Indianapolis	IN	46240	317-833-0313	833-0315	177
Progeny Software LLC 190 Congress Park Dr Ste 140 *Web:* www.progenygenetics.com	Delray Beach	FL	33445	574-968-0822		177
Progeny Systems Corp 9500 Innovation Dr *Web:* progeny.net	Manassas	VA	20110	703-368-6107		180
Progesys Inc 4020 Blvd le Corbusier Ste 201 *TF:* 877-274-8815 ■ *Web:* www.progesys.ca	Laval	QC	H7L5R2	450-667-7646		463
Program for Appropriate Technology in Health (PATH) 1455 NW Leary Way *TF:* 800-836-4620 ■ *Web:* www.path.org	Seattle	WA	98107	206-285-3500	285-6619	48-17

Entry	City	State	ZIP	Phone	Fax	Class
Program Planning Professionals 1340 Eisenhower Pl *TF:* 877-728-2331 ■ *Web:* www.pcubed.com	Ann Arbor	MI	48108	734-741-7770	741-1343	194
Programmer's Paradise Inc 1157 Shrewsbury Ave Ste C *TF:* 800-441-1511 ■ *Web:* www.techxtend.com	Shrewsbury	NJ	07702	732-389-8950	389-0010	174
Pro-Graphics Communications Inc 5664 New Peachtree Rd *Web:* www.prographinc.com	Atlanta	GA	30341	678-597-1050		627
Progress & Freedom Foundation (PFF) 1444 Eye St NW Ste 500 *Web:* www.pff.org	Washington	DC	20005	202-289-8928	289-6079	634
Progress Container Corp 635 Patrick Mill Rd SW *Web:* www.progresscontainer.com	Winder	GA	30680	678-425-2000		100
Progress Energy Inc 410 S Wilmington St *NYSE:* PGN ■ *TF:* 800-452-2777 ■ *Web:* progress-energy.com	Raleigh	NC	27601	919-546-6111		360-5
Progress Group, Inc., The 918 Kennedy Ave *Web:* www.progresspump.com	Schererville	IN	46375	219-322-3700		757
Progress Instruments Inc 807 NW Commerce Dr *TF:* 800-580-9881 ■ *Web:* www.progressthermal.com	Lees Summit	MO	64086	816-524-4442		625
Progress Investment Management Co 33 New Montgomery St 19th Fl *TF:* 800-224-0413 ■ *Web:* www.progressinvestment.com	San Francisco	CA	94105	415-512-3480	512-3475	401
Progress Printing Co 2677 Waterlick Rd **Fax Area Code:* 434 ■ *TF:* 800-572-7804 ■ *Web:* www.progressprintplus.com	Lynchburg	VA	24502	800-572-7804	237-1618*	627
Progress Rail Services 1600 Progress Dr PO Box 1037 *TF:* 800-476-8769 ■ *Web:* www.progressrail.com	Albertville	AL	35950	256-505-6600	593-1249	686
Progress Software Corp 14 Oak Pk *NASDAQ:* PRGS ■ *TF:* 800-477-6473 ■ *Web:* www.progress.com	Bedford	MA	01730	781-280-4000	280-4095	178-1
Progress Unlimited Inc 11431 Cronhill Dr Ste C *Web:* www.progressunlimited.org	Owings Mills	MD	21117	410-363-8550		726
Progress Wire Products Inc 3535 W 140th St *Web:* www.progresswire.com	Cleveland	OH	44111	216-251-2181	251-2699	73
Progress-Index 15 Franklin St *Web:* www.progress-index.com	Petersburg	VA	23803	804-732-3456		532-2
Progressive Bank NA 590 National Rd PO Box 6671 *TF:* 866-235-1923 ■ *Web:* www.progbank.com	Wheeling	WV	26003	304-218-2400		70
Progressive Chevrolet Co 8000 Hills & Dales Rd *Web:* www.progressivechevrolet.com	Massillon	OH	44646	330-833-8564		516
Progressive Communications Corp 18 E Vine St PO Box 791 *TF:* 800-772-5333 ■ *Web:* www.mountvernonnews.com	Mount Vernon	OH	43050	740-397-5333	397-1321	637-8
Progressive Contracting Company Inc 115 Chatham St Ste 301 *Web:* www.progressivecci.com	Sanford	NC	27330	919-718-5454	718-5455	186
Progressive Corporation, The 6300 Wilson Mills Rd Box W33 *TF:* 888-806-9598 ■ *Web:* progressive.com	Mayfield Village	OH	44143	440-461-5000		391-4
Progressive Dynamics Inc 507 Industrial Rd *TF:* 800-848-0558 ■ *Web:* www.progressivedyn.com	Marshall	MI	49068	269-781-4241	781-7802	253
Progressive Employer Services 6407 Parkland Dr *TF:* 888-925-2990 ■ *Web:* www.progressiveemployer.com	Sarasota	FL	34243	941-925-2990	308-1789	631
Progressive Furniture Inc PO Box 308 *Web:* www.progressivefurniture.com	Archbold	OH	43502	828-459-2151	459-9702	319-2
Progressive Hydraulics Inc 350 N Midland Ave *Web:* www.phionline.com	Saddle Brook	NJ	07663	201-791-3400		641
Progressive Impressions 1 Hardman Dr *TF:* 800-664-0444 ■ *Web:* www.whateverittakes.com	Bloomington	IL	61701	309-664-0444	662-2055	637-9
Progressive Information Technologies 315 Busser Rd	Emigsville	PA	17318	717-764-5908		781
Progressive Metal Mfg Co 1300 Channing St *Web:* www.pmmco.com	Ferndale	MI	48220	248-546-2827		489
Progressive Mktg Products Inc 3130 E Miraloma Ave *TF:* 800-368-9700 ■ *Web:* www.mounts.com	Anaheim	CA	92806	714-632-7100		194
Progressive National Baptist Convention Inc (PNBC) 601 50th St NE *TF:* 800-876-7622 ■ *Web:* www.pnbc.org	Washington	DC	20019	202-396-0558	398-4998	48-20
Progressive Plastics Inc 14801 Emery Ave *TF:* 800-252-0053 ■ *Web:* www.progressive-plastics.com	Cleveland	OH	44135	216-252-5595	252-6327	98
Progressive Plumbing Inc 1064 W Hwy 50 *Web:* progressiveplumbing.com	Clermont	FL	34711	352-394-7171		610
Progressive Policy Institute (PPI) 1101 14th St NW Ste 1250 *Web:* progressivepolicy.org	Washington	DC	20005	202-525-3926	525-3941	634
Progressive Produce Co 5790 Peachtree St *TF:* 800-900-0757 ■ *Web:* www.progressiveproduce.com	Los Angeles	CA	90040	323-890-8100		297-7
Progressive Promotions Inc 145 Cedar Ln *Web:* progressivepromotions.com	Englewood	NJ	07631	201-945-0500		701
Progressive Stamping Inc 200 Progressive Dr	Ottoville	OH	45876	419-453-1111		488
Progressive Tool & Manufacturing Co 290 Fifth St NE *Web:* www.ptmmn.com	Pine Island	MN	55963	507-356-8345	356-4557	482
Progressive, The PO Box 952 *Web:* www.theprogressnews.com	Clearfield	PA	16830	814-765-5581	765-5165	637-8
Progrexion Marketing Inc 257 East 200 S Suite 1200 *Web:* www.progrexion.com	Salt Lake City	UT	84111	801-384-4100		393
PROGYMEDIA 1040 Boul Michele-bohec *Web:* www.progi-media.com	Blainville	QC	J7C5E2	514-272-0599		180
Project Access Inc 3900 Birch St Ste 113 *Web:* www.project-access.org	Newport Beach	CA	92660	949-253-6200		41
Project Adventure Inc 719 Cabot St *Web:* www.project-adventure.org	Beverly	MA	01915	978-524-4500		242
Project Concern International (PCI) 5151 Murphy Canyon Rd Ste 320 *TF:* 877-724-4673 ■ *Web:* www.pciglobal.org	San Diego	CA	92123	858-279-9690	694-0294	48-5
Project Connect 1025 W Johnson St 141 Educational Science Bldg *Web:* careers.education.wisc.edu	Madison	WI	53706	608-262-1755	262-9074	260
Project Consulting Services Inc 3300 W Esplanade Ave S Ste 500 *TF:* 855-468-7473 ■ *Web:* www.projectconsulting.com	Metairie	LA	70002	504-833-5321		196
Project Corps 1325 Fourth Ave Ste 1925 *Web:* www.projectcorps.com	Seattle	WA	98101	206-932-7077		463
Project for Public Spaces 419 Lafayette St 7th Fl *Web:* www.pps.org	New York	NY	10003	212-620-5660	620-3821	48-13
Project Inform 273 Ninth St *TF:* 877-435-7443 ■ *Web:* www.projectinform.org	San Francisco	CA	94103	415-558-8669	558-0684	48-17
Project Lifesaver International Headquarters 815 Battlefield Blvd S *TF:* 877-580-5433 ■ *Web:* www.projectlifesaver.org	Chesapeake	VA	23322	757-546-5502		138
Project Management Institute (PMI) 14 Campus Blvd *TF:* 866-276-4764 ■ *Web:* www.pmi.org	Newtown Square	PA	19073	610-356-4600	356-4647	49-12
Project Resources Inc 3760 Convoy St Ste 230 *Web:* www.priworld.com	San Diego	CA	92111	858-505-1000	505-1010	261
Project Safe Neighborhoods *Office of Justice Programs* 810 Seventh St NW *TF:* 888-744-6513 ■ *Web:* www.bja.gov	Washington	DC	20531	202-616-6500	305-1367	197
Project Vote 1350 I St NW Ste 1250 *TF:* 888-546-4173 ■ *Web:* www.projectvote.org	Washington	DC	20005	202-546-4173		48-7
Project X Ltd 4120 Yonge St Ste 215 *Web:* www.pxltd.ca	Toronto	ON	M2P2B8	416-422-8900	422-8901	196
Projectbits Consulting Inc 236 Lead King Dr *Web:* www.projectbits.com	Castle Rock	CO	80108	720-319-8160		809
ProjectDesign Consultants 701 B St Ste 800 *Web:* www.projectdesign.com	San Diego	CA	92101	619-235-6471	234-0349	261
Projection Presentation Technology 5803 Rolling Rd *TF:* 800-377-7650 ■ *Web:* projection.com	Springfield	VA	22152	703-912-1334	912-1350	264-2
Projections Unlimited Inc 15311 Varrenca Pkwy **Fax Area Code:* 949 ■ *TF Cust Svc:* 800-551-4405 ■ *Web:* www.gopui.com	Irvine	CA	92618	714-544-2700	789-0626	246
Projectline Services Inc 506 Second Ave Ste 400 *Web:* www.projectlineservices.com	Seattle	WA	98104	206-382-2025	749-4157	195
Projectools Company Inc 4099 Hwy 36 N *Web:* www.projectools.com	Bellville	TX	77418	713-371-9840		225
Projects Plus Inc 254 W 29th St 5th Fl	New York	NY	10001	212-997-0100		194
Projects Unlimited Inc 6300 Sand Lake Rd *Web:* www.pui.com	Dayton	OH	45414	937-918-2200		625
PROJECTXYZ Inc 1500 Perimeter Pkwy Ste 426 *TF:* 800-849-9472 ■ *Web:* projectxyz.com	Huntsville	AL	35806	256-721-9001		261
ProKarma Inc 8705 SW Nimbus Ave Ste 118 **Fax Area Code:* 503 ■ *Web:* www.prokarma.com	Beaverton	OR	97008	971-317-0700	521-8454*	317
Prolab Nutrition 21411 Prairie St *TF:* 800-776-5221 ■ *Web:* www.prolab.com	Chatsworth	CA	91311	818-739-6000		799
ProLabs Inc 137 Herricks Rd	Garden City Park	NY	11040	516-877-9000		475
Prolamina Corp 840 S Waukegan Rd Ste 208 *TF:* 877-536-2628 ■ *Web:* www.prolamina.com	Lake Forest	IL	60045	877-536-2628		601
ProLender Solutions Inc 6050 Santo Rd Ste 160 *TF:* 800-275-4885 ■ *Web:* www.prolender.com	San Diego	CA	92124	619-258-3595		175
Proliance Surgeons Inc 805 Madison Ste 901 *Web:* www.proliancesurgeons.com	Seattle	WA	98104	206-264-8100		374-3
Pro-Life Action League 6160 N Cicero Ave Ste 600 *Web:* www.prolifeaction.org	Chicago	IL	60646	773-777-2900	777-3061	48-8
Prolifics 5 Hanover Sqr Ste 2001 *TF:* 800-458-3313 ■ *Web:* www.prolifics.com	New York	NY	10004	212-267-7722	608-6753	178-2
Prolifiq Software Inc 8585 SW Watson Ave Ste 200 *TF:* 800-840-7183 ■ *Web:* prolifiq.com	Beaverton	OR	97008	503-684-1415		179
Proline Concrete Tools Inc 2560 Jason Ct *Web:* www.prolinestamps.com	Oceanside	CA	92056	760-758-7240		111
Proline Distributors Inc 1191 S Rogers Cir *Web:* www.prolinedist.com	Boca Raton	FL	33487	561-241-7000		711
Proline Supply Co 6711 Bingle Rd *Web:* www.prolinesupplyco.com	Houston	TX	77092	713-939-9730		45
Pro-line Water Screen Services Inc PO Box 2565 *TF:* 800-882-0795 ■ *Web:* www.intakescreens.com	Pearland	TX	77588	281-992-6730		454
Pro-Link Inc 510 Chapman St *Web:* www.prolinkhq.com	Canton	MA	02021	781-828-9550		77
Prolitec Inc 1235 W Canal St *TF:* 844-247-7599 ■ *Web:* www.prolitec.com	Milwaukee	WI	53233	844-247-7599		261
ProLiteracy Worldwide 1320 Jamesville Ave *TF:* 800-448-8878 ■ *Web:* www.proliteracy.org	Syracuse	NY	13210	315-422-9121	422-6369	48-5

Name / Address	City	State	Zip	Phone	Fax	Class
Prolog Ventures LLC 7701 Forsyth Blvd Ste 1095 *Web:* www.prologventures.com	Saint Louis	MO	63105	314-743-2400		792
ProLogic Inc 1000 Green River Dr Ste 201 *Web:* www.ultra-prologic.com	Fairmont	WV	26554	304-534-3746		809
Prologic Technology Systems Inc 10801-1 N Mopac Expy Ste 120 *Web:* teams.solutions	Austin	TX	78759	512-328-9496		225
ProLogis 4545 Airport Way *NYSE: PLD* ■ *TF:* 800-566-2706 ■ *Web:* www.prologis.com	Denver	CO	80239	303-375-9292	567-5903	655
Prolon Inc 305 Industrial Ave **Fax Area Code:* 888 ■ *TF:* 800-628-7749 ■ *Web:* www.prolon.biz	Port Gibson	MS	39150	601-437-4211	480-9828*	607
Promac Inc 1153 Timber Dr *Web:* www.promac.com	Elgin	IL	60123	847-695-8181		186
Pro-mail Associates Inc 22404 66th Ave S *TF:* 855-867-5081 ■ *Web:* www.pmadm.com	Kent	WA	98032	206-282-2400		195
ProManage LLC 150 N Michigan Ave Ste 2930 *Web:* www.promanageplan.com	Chicago	IL	60603	312-456-0665		194
ProMark Direct Inc 300 N Midland Ave Ste 2 *Web:* www.promarkdirect.com	Saddle Brook	NJ	07663	201-398-9000	398-9212	7
Promark Technology Inc 10900 Pump House Rd Ste B **Fax Area Code:* 301 ■ *TF:* 800-634-0255 ■ *Web:* www.promarktech.com	Annapolis Junction	MD	20701	240-280-8030	725-7869*	174
PRO-MART Industries Inc 17421 Von Karman Ave *Web:* www.deltanovaltd.com	Irvine	CA	92614	949-428-7700		361
Promation Engineering Inc 16138 Flight Path Dr *Web:* promationei.com	Brooksville	FL	34604	352-544-8436		261
PromaxBDA 1522 E Cloverfield Blvd *Web:* www.promaxbda.org	Santa Monica	CA	90404	310-788-7600		138
ProMed Molded Products Inc 15600 Medina Rd *Web:* www.promedmolding.com	Plymouth	MN	55447	763-331-3800		475
Promedia Technology Services 535 Route 46 *TF:* 800-228-8115 ■ *Web:* www.promedianj.com	Little Falls	NJ	07424	973-253-7600		180
ProMedica 2142 N Cove Blvd *TF:* 866-865-4677 ■ *Web:* www.promedica.org	Toledo	OH	43606	419-291-5437		374-3
Promedica Inc 114 Douglas Rd E *TF:* 800-899-5278 ■ *Web:* www.promedica-usa.com	Oldsmar	FL	34677	813-854-1905		476
ProMedical Inc 1 Militia Dr *Web:* promedllc.com	Lexington	MA	02421	781-325-7239		463
Promega Corp 2800 Woods Hollow Rd *TF:* 800-356-9526 ■ *Web:* promega.com	Madison	WI	53711	608-274-4330	277-2516	231
Promenade Rehabilitation & Health Care Ctr 140 Beach 114th St *Web:* www.promenadenh.com	Rockaway Park	NY	11694	718-945-4600	634-8274	450
Promera Health 61 accord park dr *TF:* 888-878-9058 ■ *Web:* www.promerasports.com	Norwell	MA	02061	888-878-9058		363
Promess Inc PO Box 748 *Web:* www.promessinc.com	Brighton	MI	48116	810-229-9334	229-8125	472
Prometheus Laboratories Inc 9410 Carroll Pk Dr **Fax Area Code:* 877 ■ *TF:* 888-892-8391 ■ *Web:* www.prometheuslabs.com	San Diego	CA	92121	888-892-8391	816-4019*	582
Prometric 1501 S Clinton St *TF:* 866-776-6387 ■ *Web:* www.prometric.com	Baltimore	MD	21224	443-455-8000		244
ProMetrics Inc 480 American Ave *TF:* 800-718-9930 ■ *Web:* www.prometrics.com	King Of Prussia	PA	19406	610-265-6344		463
Promex Technologies LLC 3049 Hudson St	Franklin	IN	46131	317-736-0128		475
Promiles Software Development 1900 Texas Ave *TF:* 800-324-8588 ■ *Web:* www.promiles.com	Bridge City	TX	77611	800-324-8588		177
Prominent Fluid Controls Inc 136 Industry Dr *Web:* www.prominent.us	Pittsburgh	PA	15275	412-787-2484	787-0704	248
Promise Hotels Inc 2201 N 77th E Ave *TF:* 866-800-4653 ■ *Web:* www.promisehotels.com	Tulsa	OK	74115	918-858-2779		707
Promise Keepers (PK) PO Box 11798 **Fax Area Code:* 303 ■ *TF:* 866-776-6473 ■ *Web:* promisekeepers.org	Denver	CO	80211	866-776-6473	433-1036*	48-20
Promise Technology Inc 580 Cottonwood Dr *TF Sales:* 800-888-0245 ■ *Web:* www.promise.com	Milpitas	CA	95035	408-228-1400	228-1100	625
Promised Land State Park PO Box 96 *Web:* www.dcnr.state.pa.us	Greentown	PA	18426	570-676-3428		565
Premium LLC 3350 Monte Villa Pkwy Ste 220 *TF:* 877-776-6486 ■ *Web:* www.premium.com	Bothell	WA	98021	425-286-9200		177
Promocentric 5 Forbes Rd *Web:* www.promocentric.net	Newmarket	NH	03857	603-758-6377		226
Promodel Corp 3400 Bath Pike Ste 200 *TF:* 888-900-3090 ■ *Web:* www.promodel.com	Bethlehem	PA	18017	801-223-4600	226-6046	178-10
Promontory Financial Group LLC 1201 Pennsylvania Ave NW Ste 617 *Web:* www.promontory.com	Washington	DC	20004	202-384-1200		194
Promontory Point Capital 322 E Michigan St Ste 500 *Web:* www.promontorypointcapital.com	Milwaukee	WI	53202	414-225-0484		194
Promoshop Inc 5420 McConnell Ave *Web:* www.promoshopinc.com	Los Angeles	CA	90066	310-821-1780		791
ProMost Inc 1616 16th St Ste 350 *TF:* 800-880-4040 ■ *Web:* www.promost.com	San Francisco	CA	94103	415-575-1350		809
Promotion Fulfillment Center 311 21st St *Web:* www.pfcfulfills.com	Camanche	IA	52730	563-259-0105		41
Promotional Media Management 528 Bridge St NW Ste 7 *Web:* promedmgt.com	Grand Rapids	MI	49504	616-456-5555		5
Promotional Products Assn International (PPAI) 3125 Skyway Cir N *TF:* 888-426-7724 ■ *Web:* www.ppai.org	Irving	TX	75038	972-252-0404	258-3004	49-18
Promotions Unlimited 7601 Durand Ave	Sturtevant	WI	53177	262-681-7000	681-7001	5
PROMPT Ambulance Central Inc 9835 Express Dr *TF:* 800-633-3590 ■ *Web:* www.promptambulance.com	Highland	IN	46322	219-934-1010		30
Prompt Mailers Inc 66 Willow Ave *Web:* www.promptmailers.com	Staten Island	NY	10305	718-447-6206		5
Prompton State Park c/o Lackawanna *TF:* 888-727-2757 ■ *Web:* www.dcnr.state.pa.us	North Abington Township	PA	18414	570-945-3239		565
ProMusica Chamber Orchestra 620 E Broad St Ste 300 *Web:* www.promusicacolumbus.org	Columbus	OH	43215	614-464-0066	464-4141	573-3
Pronet Solutions Inc 4313 E Cotton Ctr Blvd Ste 120	Phoenix	AZ	85040	602-650-1100		180
Pronghorn Controls Ltd 101 4919 72 Ave SE *Web:* pronghorn.ca	Calgary	AB	T2C3H3	403-720-2526		358
Pronk Technologies Inc 8933 Lankershim Blvd *TF:* 800-609-9802 ■ *Web:* www.pronktech.com	Sun Valley	CA	91352	818-768-5600		476
Proof Advertising LLC 114 W Seventh St Ste 500 *Web:* www.proof-advertising.com	Austin	TX	78701	512-345-6658		7
ProOrbis LLC 112 Moores Rd Ste 400 *Web:* www.proorbis.com	Malvern	PA	19355	610-240-0200		195
Propaganda Inc 3115 S Grand Blvd Ste 500 *Web:* www.propaganda-inc.com	St. Louis	MO	63118	314-664-8516		7
Pro-Pak Industries Inc 1125 Ford St *Web:* www.pro-pakindustries.com	Maumee	OH	43537	419-729-0751		100
Propak Systems Ltd 440 East Lake Rd NE *TF:* 800-408-4434 ■ *Web:* www.propaksystems.com	Airdrie	AB	T4A2J8	403-912-7000		261
Propane Resources LLC 6950 Squibb Rd Ste 306 *Web:* www.propaneresources.com	Mission	KS	66201	913-262-8345		466
ProPath Laboratory Inc 1355 River Bend Dr *Web:* www.propathlab.com	Dallas	TX	75247	214-638-2000		418
Propel Software Corp 1010 Rincon Cir *Web:* www.propel.com	San Jose	CA	95131	408-571-6300	577-1070	178-7
ProPeople Staffing Services Inc 10369 W Emerald St *Web:* www.propeoplestaffing.com	Boise	ID	83704	208-345-5747		260
Proper Foods Inc 1319 E Pine *Web:* www.properfoods.com	Deming	NM	88030	575-546-4442		123
Proper Mold & Engineering Inc 13870 E 11-Mile Rd *Web:* propertooling.com	Warren	MI	48089	586-779-8787	779-4530	604
Property Casualty Insurers Assn of America 8700 W Bryn Mawr Ave *Web:* www.pciaa.net	Des Plaines	IL	60018	847-297-7800	297-5064	49-9
Property Damage Appraisers Inc (PDA) 6100 SW Blvd Ste 200 *TF:* 800-749-7324 ■ *Web:* www.pdacorporation.com	Fort Worth	TX	76109	800-749-7324	866-4732	310
Property Loss Research Bureau (PLRB) 3025 Highland Pkwy Ste 800 *TF:* 888-711-7572 ■ *Web:* www.plrb.org	Downers Grove	IL	60515	630-724-2200	724-2260	49-9
Property One Inc 4141 Veterans Memorial Blvd Ste 300 *Web:* propertyone.com	Metairie	LA	70002	504-681-3400	681-3438	113
Property Owners Exchange Inc 6630 Baltimore National Pk Ste 208 *TF:* 800-869-3200 ■ *Web:* www.poeknows.com	Catonsville	MD	21228	410-719-0100		635
Property Panorama Inc 9475 Pinecone Dr *TF:* 877-299-6306 ■ *Web:* propertypanorama.com	Mentor	OH	44060	440-290-2200		177
Property Tax Advisors LLC 805 King St *Web:* www.propertytaxadvisors.com	Alexandria	VA	22314	703-518-4425	455-6753	463
Property-Owners Insurance Co PO Box 30660 *TF:* 800-288-8740 ■ *Web:* auto-owners.com	Lansing	MI	48909	517-323-1200	323-8796	391-2
Propet USA Inc 2415 W Valley Hwy N *TF:* 800-877-6738 ■ *Web:* www.propetusa.com	Auburn	WA	98001	253-854-7600	854-7607	301
ProPetro Services Inc 1706 S Midkiff Rd Bldg B PO Box 873 *TF:* 800-221-1037 ■ *Web:* www.propetroservices.com	Midland	TX	79701	432-688-0012		540
ProPhase Labs Inc 621 Shady Retreat Rd *NASDAQ: PRPH* ■ *TF:* 800-505-2653 ■ *Web:* www.prophaselabs.com	Doylestown	PA	18901	215-345-0919		582
Prophet Equity LLC 1460 Main St Ste 200 *Web:* www.prophetequity.com	South Lake	TX	76092	817-898-1500		194
Prophet Systems Innovations 214 N Spruce St *Web:* www.rcsworks.com	Ogallala	NE	69153	308-284-3007	284-4181	180
Propheta Communications 70 E Tenth St Ste 6P *Web:* propheta.com	New York	NY	10003	212-901-6914		636
Prophetline Inc 2120 S Waldron Rd *Web:* www.prophetline.com	Fort Smith	AR	72903	479-452-6526		809
Prophetstown State Recreation Area Riverside Dr PO Box 181 *Web:* dnr.illinois.gov/Lands/Landmgt/PARKS/R1/PROPHET.HTM	Prophetstown	IL	61277	815-537-2926		565
ProPhotonix Inc 32 Hampshire Rd *OTC: STKR* ■ **Fax Area Code:* 781 ■ *TF:* 877-941-8631 ■ *Web:* www.prophotonix.com	Salem	NH	03079	603-893-8778	575-2420*	544
Propipe Technologies Inc 1800 Clayton Ave	Middletown	OH	45042	513-424-5311		595
Proplanner 2321 N Loop Dr Ste 107 *Web:* www.proplanner.com	Ames	IA	50010	515-296-9914		809
Propoco Incentives 8750 W Bryn Mawr Ave Ste 1020 *Web:* www.propco.com	Chicago	IL	60631	773-463-9193		393
Proportion-Air Inc 8250 N 600 W PO Box 218 *Web:* www.proportionair.com	Mccordsville	IN	46055	317-335-2602		201
Propper Mfg Company Inc 36-04 Skillman Ave *TF Cust Svc:* 800-832-4300 ■ *Web:* www.proppermfg.com	Long Island	NY	11101	718-392-6650	482-8909	476

Company	Phone	Fax	Class
Propylon Inc 3429 Derry St .... Harrisburg PA 17111 *Web:* www.propylon.com	717-265-0400		809
Prores Group Inc 16526 W 78th St Ste 310 .... Eden Prairie MN 55346 *Web:* proresgroup.com	952-449-1000		138
ProRodeo Hall of Fame & Museum of the American Cowboy 101 ProRodeo Dr .... Colorado Springs CO 80919 *Web:* www.prorodeo.org	719-528-4703		522
Pros Holdings Inc 3100 Main St Ste 900 .... Houston TX 77002 *NYSE: PRO* ■ *Web:* www.pros.com	713-335-5151	335-8144	178-10
ProScan Imaging LLC 5400 Kennedy Ave .... Cincinnati OH 45213 *Web:* www.proscan.com	513-618-1063		418
Prosci Inc 1367 S Garfield Ave. .... Loveland CO 80537 *TF:* 800-700-2831 ■ *Web:* www.prosci.com	970-203-9332		463
ProSep (USA) Inc 5353 W Sam Houston Pkwy N Ste 150 .... Houston TX 77041 *Web:* prosep.com	281-504-2040		539
Proserv Anchor Crane Group 455 Aldine Bender PO Box 670965 .... Houston TX 77060 *TF:* 800-835-2223 ■ *Web:* www.proservanchor.com	281-405-9048	448-7508	470
Proserv Offshore Inc 13105 Northwest Fwy Ste 250 .... Houston TX 77040	713-462-9990		538
Proshot Concrete Inc 4158 Musgrove Dr .... Florence AL 35630 *TF:* 800-633-3141 ■ *Web:* www.proshotconcrete.com	256-764-5941	764-5946	189-3
Prosite Business Solutions 732 Third St .... New Martinsville WV 26155 *Web:* www.probusinesstools.com	304-455-5900		180
ProSites Inc 27919 Jefferson Ave Ste 103 .... Temecula CA 92590 *Web:* www.prosites.com	951-693-9101		177
Proskauer Rose LLP 1585 Broadway .... New York NY 10036 *TF:* 866-444-3272 ■ *Web:* www.proskauer.com	212-969-3000	969-2900	428
Prosoco Inc 3741 Greenway Cir. .... Lawrence KS 66046 **Fax Area Code: 785* ■ *TF:* 800-255-4255 ■ *Web:* www.prosoco.com	800-255-4255	830-9797*	151
Prosource Fitness Equipment 6503 Hilburn Dr .... Raleigh NC 27613 *TF:* 877-781-8077 ■ *Web:* prosourcefitness.com	919-781-8077		627
ProSource Solutions LLC 4199 Kinross Lakes Pkwy Ste 150 .... Richfield OH 44286 *TF:* 866-549-0279 ■ *Web:* www.prosource-corp.com	866-549-0279		196
Prospec Technologies Inc 3235 Wharton Way .... Mississauga ON L4X2B6 *Web:* prospectech.com	905-629-3100		358
Prospect Airport Services Inc 2130 S Wolf Rd. .... Des Plaines IL 60018 *Web:* www.prospectair.com	847-299-3636		27
Prospect Fastener Corp 1295 Kyle Ct. .... Wauconda IL 60084 *Web:* www.prospectfastener.com	847-526-2950		350
Prospect Foundry LLC 1225 Winter St NE .... Minneapolis MN 55413 *Web:* www.prospectfdry.com	612-331-9282		307
Prospect Medical Holdings Inc 10780 Santa Monica Blvd Ste 400 .... Los Angeles CA 90025 *TF:* 800-708-3230 ■ *Web:* www.prospectmedical.com	310-943-4500		463
Prospect Mold Inc 1100 Main St .... Cuyahoga Falls OH 44221 *Web:* www.prospectmold.com	330-929-3311		757
Prospect Venture Partners 435 Tasso St Ste 200 .... Palo Alto CA 94301 *Web:* www.prospectventures.com	650-327-8800	324-8838	792
Prospection Inc 1750 Av De Vitre. .... Quebec QC G1J1Z6 *Web:* www.prospection.qc.ca	418-521-2248		225
Prospectiv Direct Inc 40 Harvard Mill Sq Ste 1 .... Wakefield MA 01880 *Web:* www.prospectiv.com	781-305-2100		195
Prospector Hotel 375 Whittier St .... Juneau AK 99801 *TF:* 800-478-5866 ■ *Web:* www.prospectorhotel.com	907-586-3737	586-1204	379
Prospectr Marketing 575 SE Ninth St Ste 205 .... Minneapolis MN 55414 *TF:* 800-908-3523 ■ *Web:* www.prospectrmarketing.com	612-200-0874		5
Prospects Influential Inc 1313 E Maple St Ste 548 .... Bellingham WA 98225 *TF:* 800-352-2282 ■ *Web:* www.prospectsinfluential.com	800-352-2282		7
Prosper Advisors Llc 20 Bedford Rd .... Armonk NY 10504	914-730-3500		196
Prospera Financial Services Inc 5429 LBJ Fwy Ste 400 .... Dallas TX 75240 *TF:* 800-289-9999 ■ *Web:* www.prosperafinancial.com	972-581-3000		390
Prosperity Bancshares Inc 1301 N Mechanic .... El Campo TX 77437 *NYSE: PB* ■ *TF:* 800-862-9098 ■ *Web:* www.prosperitybankusa.com	979-543-1426	543-1906	360-2
Prospero Learning Solutions Inc 1075 Bay St Ste 500 .... Toronto ON M5S2B1 *Web:* www.prosperolearning.com	416-360-0606		764
Prosser Wilbert Construction Inc 13730 W 108th St. .... Lenexa KS 66215 *Web:* www.prosserwilbert.com	913-906-0104		186
Prostar Computer Inc 837 Lawson St .... City of Industry CA 91748 *TF:* 888-576-4742 ■ *Web:* www.pro-star.com	626-839-6472		174
Prostate Cancer Foundation 1250 Fourth St .... Santa Monica CA 90401 *Web:* www.pcf.org	310-570-4700		303
ProSteel Security Products Inc 1400 S State St. .... Provo UT 84603 *TF:* 800-333-3288 ■ *Web:* www.prosteel.us	801-373-2385		295
Prosthetic Design Inc 700 Harco Dr .... Clayton OH 45315 *TF:* 800-459-0177 ■ *Web:* prostheticdesign.com	937-836-1464		477
Pro-Stim Services LLC 22503 Katy Fwy. .... Katy TX 77450	281-769-5727		536
Prostrollo Motor Sales Inc 500 Fourth St NE .... Huron SD 57350 **Fax Area Code: 605* ■ *TF:* 866-466-4515 ■ *Web:* www.prostrollo.com	866-466-4515	352-9286*	57
Prosum technology services 2201 Park Pl Ste 102 .... El Segundo CA 90245 *TF:* 888-477-6786 ■ *Web:* www.prosum.com	310-426-0600		39
Prosurg Inc 2195 Trade Zone Blvd. .... San Jose CA 95131 *Web:* prosurg.com	408-945-4044		476
Prosync Technology Group LLC 6021 University Blvd Ste 300 .... Ellicott City MD 21043 *TF:* 800-428-7324 ■ *Web:* www.prosync.com	410-772-7969		177
Prosys Industries Inc 47576 Halyard Dr .... Plymouth MI 48170 *TF:* 800-265-3205 ■ *Web:* prosys-group.com	734-207-3710		358
Pro-system Inc 121 Oakpark Dr .... Mooresville NC 28115 *Web:* www.prosystems.com	704-799-8100		57
Protagon Display Inc 719 Tapscott Rd. .... Toronto ON M1X1A2 *Web:* www.protagon.com	416-293-9500		7
ProtaTek International Inc 2635 University Ave W Ste 140 .... Saint Paul MN 55114 *Web:* www.protatek.com	651-644-5391	644-6831	584
Protean Design Group Inc 100 E Pine St Ste 600 .... Orlando FL 32801 *TF:* 800-782-4414 ■ *Web:* www.proteandg.com	407-246-0044		261
Pro-Tec Fire Services Ltd 2129 S Oneida St .... Green Bay WI 54304 *TF:* 800-242-6352 ■ *Web:* www.protecfire.com	920-494-8851		63
Pro-Tec Refrigeration Inc 3640 N 39th Ave. .... Phoenix AZ 85019 *Web:* protecref.com	602-222-9881		189-10
Protech Armored Products 13386 International Pkwy .... Jacksonville FL 32218 *TF:* 800-654-9943 ■ *Web:* protecharmored.com	904-741-5400		576
Pro-Tech Design & Manufacturing Inc 14561 Marquardt Ave .... Santa Fe Springs CA 90670 *TF:* 800-359-7337 ■ *Web:* www.protechdesign.com/sitepages/protech.aspx	562-207-1680		88
Pro-Tech Energy Solutions LLC 215 Executive Dr. .... Moorestown NJ 08057 *Web:* www.pro-techenergy.com	856-437-6139		466
Pro-tech Security Sales 1313 W Bagley Rd .... Berea OH 44017 *TF:* 800-888-4002 ■ *Web:* www.protechsales.com	440-239-0100		237
Protech Systems Group 3350 Players Club Pkwy. .... Memphis TN 38125 *TF:* 800-459-5100 ■ *Web:* www.psgi.net	901-767-7550		177
Protect Controls Inc (PCI) 3212 Old Hwy 105 E. .... Conroe TX 77301 *Web:* www.protectcontrols.com	713-691-5183	691-0159	105
Protect-All Inc 109 Badger Pkwy .... Darien WI 53114 *TF:* 888-432-8526 ■ *Web:* www.protect-all.com	888-432-8526		554
Protected Investors of America Inc 235 Montgomery St Ste 1050. .... San Francisco CA 94104 *TF:* 800-786-2559 ■ *Web:* www.protectedinvestors.com	800-786-2559		194
Protection Engineering Consultants LLC 14144 Trautwein Rd .... Austin TX 78737 *Web:* www.protection-consultants.com	512-380-1988		261
protection One Alarm Monitoring 1035 N Third St Ste 101 .... Lawrence KS 66044 *TF:* 800-438-4357 ■ *Web:* www.protection1.com	877-776-1911		692
Protection Services Inc 635 Lucknow Rd. .... Harrisburg PA 17110 *TF:* 866-489-1234 ■ *Web:* www.protectionservices.com	717-236-9307	236-1281	701
Protective Armored Systems Inc 100 Valley St. .... Lee MA 01238 *Web:* www.pasarmored.com	413-637-1060		329
Protective Group Inc, The 14100 NW 58th Ct .... Miami Lakes FL 33014 *TF:* 800-727-2440 ■ *Web:* www.protectivegroup.com	305-820-4270		791
Protective Insurance Co 111 Congressional Blvd Ste 500 .... Carmel IN 46032 *TF:* 800-644-5501 ■ *Web:* www.protectiveinsurance.com	800-644-5501		391-5
Protective Life Corp 2801 Hwy 280 S .... Birmingham AL 35223 *NYSE: PL* ■ *TF:* 800-866-9933 ■ *Web:* www.protective.com	205-268-1000		360-4
Protectolite Inc 84 Railside Rd. .... Toronto ON M3A1A3 *Web:* www.protectolite.com	416-444-4484		393
Protectoseal Co 225 W Foster Ave .... Bensenville IL 60106 *TF:* 800-323-2268 ■ *Web:* www.protectoseal.com	630-595-0800	595-8059	124
Protegrity Services Inc 260 Wekiva Springs Rd. .... Longwood FL 32779 **Fax Area Code: 888* ■ *TF:* 800-883-4000	800-883-4000	329-4639*	390
Protegrity USA Inc 5 High Ridge Pk .... Stamford CT 06905 *Web:* www.protegrity.com	203-326-7200		255
Protein Sciences Corp 1000 Research Pkwy. .... Meriden CT 06450 *TF:* 800-488-7099 ■ *Web:* www.proteinsciences.com	203-686-0800	686-0268	85
Protek Cargo 1568 Airport Blvd. .... Napa CA 94558 *TF:* 800-439-1426 ■ *Web:* www.protekcargo.com	707-254-9627		711
Pro-Tek Manufacturing Inc 4849 Southfront Rd .... Livermore CA 94551 *Web:* www.protekmfg.com	925-454-8100		177
Protel Inc 4150 Kidron Rd .... Lakeland FL 33811 *TF:* 800-925-8882 ■ *Web:* www.protelinc.com	863-644-5558	646-5855	735
Protelus 11000 NE 33rd Pl Ste 320 .... Bellevue WA 98004 *TF:* 800-585-0207 ■ *Web:* protelus.com	425-284-2299		466
Protential 6805 Hobson Valley Dr Ste 106 .... Woodridge IL 60517 *Web:* www.protential.com	630-724-0578		195
Proteon Therapeutics Inc 200 W St. .... Waltham MA 02451 *Web:* www.proteontherapeutics.com	781-890-0102		231
Proteos Inc 4717 Campus Dr. .... Kalamazoo MI 49008 *Web:* proteos.business.site	269-372-3480		231
Protestant Episcopal Theological Seminary in Virginia 3737 Seminary Rd .... Alexandria VA 22304 *TF:* 800-941-0083 ■ *Web:* www.vts.edu	703-370-6600		167-3
Proteus Applied Technologies Inc 377 Oyster Point Blvd. .... South San Francisco CA 94080	650-588-7774		476
Proteus Inc 1830 N Dinuba Blvd .... Visalia CA 93291 *TF:* 888-776-9998 ■ *Web:* www.proteusinc.org	559-733-5423		685
Proteus Industries 340 Pioneer Way. .... Mountain View CA 94041 *Web:* www.proteusind.com	650-964-4163		201
Proteus On-Demand Facilities LLC 6727 Oak Ridge Commerce Way SW .... Austell GA 30168 *TF:* 800-633-6966 ■ *Web:* www.proteusondemand.com	770-333-1886		184

Phone | Fax | Class

Proteus Technologies LLC
133 National Business Pkwy. Annapolis Junction MD 20701 443-539-3400 177
Web: proteus-technologies.com

Protide Pharmaceuticals Inc
505 Oakwood Rd Ste 200 Lake Zurich IL 60047 847-726-3100 726-3110 582
TF: 800-552-3569 ■ *Web:* www.protidepharma.com

Protis.com 7212 Mcneil Dr Ste 202 Austin TX 78729 512-258-1282 258-1664 179
Web: protis.com

Proto Corp 10500 47th St N Clearwater FL 33762 727-573-4665 596
Web: www.protocorporation.com

Proto-1 Manufacturing LLC
10 Tower Rd Winneconne WI 54986 920-582-4491 757
TF: 800-372-2123 ■ *Web:* www.proto1mfg.com

Protocall Group, The
1 Mall Dr Ste 100 Cherry Hill NJ 08002 856-667-7500 260
TF: 800-264-1170 ■ *Web:* protocallgroup.com

Protocase Inc
46 Wabana Ct Harbourside Industrial Park Sydney NS B1P0B9 902-567-3335 697
TF: 866-849-3911 ■ *Web:* www.protocase.com

Protochips Inc
3800 Gateway Centre Blvd Ste 306 Morrisville NC 27560 919-341-2612 256
Web: www.protochips.com

Protocol Driven Healthcare Inc
40 Morristown Rd Ste 2D Bernardsville NJ 07924 515-277-1376 463
TF: 888-816-4006 ■ *Web:* www.pdhi.com

Protocol Link Inc
175 E Hawthorn Pkwy Ste 210 Vernon Hills IL 60061 847-549-0390 463
Web: www.protocollink.com

Protocol Networks Inc 15 Shore Dr Johnston RI 02919 877-676-0146 180
TF: 877-676-0146 ■ *Web:* www.protocolnetworks.com

Protogate Inc 12225 World Trade Dr San Diego CA 92128 858-451-0865 225
TF: 877-473-0190 ■ *Web:* www.protogate.com

Protolink Inc
1755 N Collins Blvd Ste 550 Richardson TX 75080 972-644-9763 809
Web: www.protolink.com

Proton Onsite 10 Technology Dr Wallingford CT 06492 203-678-2000 949-8016 253
Web: www.protononsite.com

Proton PRC Ltd 4805 S Colony Blvd The Colony TX 75056 972-931-8200 580
Web: www.protonprc.com

ProtonMedia Inc
1690 Sumneytown Pike Ste 370 Lansdale PA 19446 215-631-1401 463
TF: 800-426-9400 ■ *Web:* www.protonmedia.com

ProtoSource Network
2300 Tulare st Ste 210 Fresno CA 93721 559-486-8638 398
TF: 866-490-8600 ■ *Web:* www.psnw.com

Protostatix Engineering Consultants
10117 Jasper Ave NW Ste 1100 Edmonton AB T5J1W8 780-423-5855 261
Web: protostatix.com

Prototype & Plastic Mold Co
35 Industrial Pk Pl Middletown CT 06457 860-632-2800 632-2249 454
Web: www.proppm.com

Prototype Machine Co
818 Prototype Rd Flatonia TX 78941 361-865-3230 454

Prototypes
1000 N Alameda St Ste 390 Los Angeles CA 90012 213-542-3838 726
Web: www.prototypes.org

ProTrak International Inc
237 W 35th St Ste 507 New York NY 10001 212-265-9833 180
Web: www.protrak.com

Protran Technology LLC 52 Paterson Ave Newton NJ 07860 973-250-4176 693
TF: 800-393-6343 ■ *Web:* www.protrantechnology.com

ProTrans International Inc
8311 N Perimeter Rd Indianapolis IN 46241 317-240-4100 311
Web: www.protrans.com

Protravel International Inc
515 Madison Ave 10th Fl New York NY 10022 212-755-4550 593-4907 771
TF: 800-227-1059 ■ *Web:* www.protravelinc.com

ProTravelGear com
10801 Southern Loop Blvd Pineville NC 28134 704-583-1100 42
Web: www.protravelgear.com

Proulx Mfg 11433 Sixth St Rancho Cucamonga CA 91730 909-980-0662 596
Web: www.proulxmfg.com

ProUroCare Medical Inc
6440 Flying Cloud Dr Ste 101 Eden Prairie MN 55344 952-476-9093 250
Web: www.prourocare.com

Prouty Place State Park 1201 Prouty Rd Austin PA 16922 814-435-5010 565
Web: www.dcnr.state.pa.us

Provade Inc
770 N Jefferson St Ste 230 Milwaukee WI 53202 414-395-8050 180
Web: www.provade.com

Provantage Corp
7249 Whipple Ave NW North Canton OH 44720 330-494-8715 494-5260 174
TF: 800-336-1166 ■ *Web:* www.provantage.com

Provation Medical Inc
800 Washington Ave N Ste 400 Minneapolis MN 55401 612-313-1500 177
Web: www.provationmedical.com

Provco Group
795 E Lancaster Ave Ste 200 Villanova PA 19085 610-520-2010 520-1905 792
Web: provcogroup.com

Provell Inc
855 Village Center Dr Ste 116 North Oaks MN 55127 952-258-2000 258-2100* 463
**Fax:* Hum Res ■ *TF:* 800-624-2946 ■ *Web:* www.provell.com

Provenance Consulting
301 W Sixth St Ste 200 Borger TX 79007 806-273-5100 261
Web: www.provenanceconsulting.com

Provence
1475 Western Ave Stuyvesant Plz Albany NY 12203 518-689-7777 671
Web: provence-restaurant.net

Provender Capital Group
1841 Broadway New York NY 10023 212-271-8888 405

Provest Llc 6155 Rockside Rd Cleveland OH 44131 216-328-0005 445
Web: www.provest.us

Provia Door Inc 2150 SR- 39 Sugarcreek OH 44681 330-852-4711 852-2107 235
TF General: 800-669-4711 ■ *Web:* www.provia.com

Proviatek Inc 80 Broad St Fl 5 New York NY 10004 212-500-6037 525
Web: proviatek.com

ProvibTech Inc
11011 Brooklet Dr Ste 300 Houston TX 77099 713-830-7601 407
Web: www.provibtech.com

Providence Alaska Medical Ctr
3200 Providence Dr Anchorage AK 99508 907-562-2211 374-3
Web: www.providence.org

Providence Athenaeum
251 Benefit St Providence RI 02903 401-421-6970 520
TF: 800-233-1636 ■ *Web:* www.providenceathenaeum.org

Providence Behavioral Health Hospital
1233 Main St Holyoke MA 01040 413-536-5111 726
Web: www.mercycares.com

Providence Biltmore Hotel
11 Dorrance St Providence RI 02903 800-294-7709 379
TF: 800-294-7709 ■ *Web:* www.providencebiltmore.com

Providence Business News
400 Wminster St Ste 600 Providence RI 02903 401-273-2201 274-6580* 457-5
**Fax:* Hum Res ■ *TF:* 800-475-2265 ■ *Web:* www.pbn.com

Providence Casket Co 1 Industrial Cir Lincoln RI 02865 401-726-1700 134

Providence Centralia Hospital
914 S Scheuber Rd Centralia WA 98531 360-736-2803 374-3
TF Help Line: 877-736-2803 ■ *Web:* washington.providence.org

Providence Children's Museum
100 S St Providence RI 02903 401-273-5437 273-1004 521
Web: www.childrenmuseum.org

Providence City Hall
25 Dorrance St Providence RI 02903 401-421-7740 337
Web: providenceri.com

Providence College 1 Cunningham Sq Providence RI 02918 401-865-1000 865-2826* 166
**Fax:* Admissions ■ *TF Admissions:* 800-721-6444 ■ *Web:* www.providence.edu

Providence College & Seminary
10 College Crescent Otterburne MB R0A1G0 204-433-7488 167-3
TF: 800-668-7768 ■ *Web:* www.providenceuc.ca

Providence County 1 Dorrance Plaza Providence RI 02903 401-458-5400 338
TF: 800-745-5555 ■ *Web:* www.courts.ri.gov

Providence Equity Partners LLC
50 Kennedy Plaza 18th Fl Providence RI 02903 401-751-1700 751-1790 792
TF: 800-452-4155 ■ *Web:* www.provequity.com

Providence Everett Medical Ctr
Colby Campus 1321 Colby Ave Everett WA 98201 425-261-4580 261-4583 374-3
Web: www.providence.org

Providence Health & Services (JWCI)
2200 Santa Monica Blvd Santa Monica CA 90404 310-582-7450 315-6148 668
TF: 800-262-6259 ■ *Web:* california.providence.org/saint-johns

Providence Health & Services
9205 SW Barnes Rd Portland OR 97225 503-216-1234 216-4041 374-3
TF: 800-562-8964 ■ *Web:* www.oregon.providence.org

Providence Health & Services
4800 37th Ave SW Seattle WA 98126 206-937-4600 353
Web: www2.providence.org

Providence Healthcare Network
6901 Medical Pkwy Waco TX 76712 254-751-4000 374-3
Web: www.providence.net

Providence Holy Cross Medical Ctr
15031 Rinaldi St Mission Hills CA 91345 818-365-8051 374-3
Web: providence.org

Providence Holy Family Hospital
5633 N Lidgerwood St Spokane WA 99208 509-482-0111 374-3
Web: www2.providence.org

Providence Homes Inc
4901 Belfort Rd Ste 140 Jacksonville FL 32256 904-262-9898 187
TF: 866-836-0981 ■ *Web:* www.providencehomesinc.com

Providence Hospice & Home Care of Snohomish County
2731 Wetmore Ave Everett WA 98201 425-261-4800 371
Web: washington.providence.org

Providence Hospice of Seattle
425 Pontius Ave N Ste 300 Seattle WA 98109 206-320-4000 320-7333 371
TF: 888-782-4445 ■ *Web:* www2.providence.org

Providence Hospital 6801 Airport Blvd Mobile AL 36608 251-633-1000 633-1679* 374-3
**Fax:* Admitting ■ *TF:* 800-561-3357 ■ *Web:* www.providencehospital.org

Providence Hospital
1150 Varnum St NE Washington DC 20017 202-269-7000 374-3
Web: www.provhosp.org

Providence Hospitals 2435 Forest Dr Columbia SC 29204 803-256-5300 256-5935 374-3
TF: 877-508-5433 ■ *Web:* www.yourprovidencehealth.com

Providence Jewelry Museum
1 Spectacle St Cranston RI 02910 401-274-0999 520
Web: providencemuseum.org

Providence Journal 75 Fountain St Providence RI 02902 401-277-7303 532-2
TF: 888-697-7656 ■ *Web:* www.providencejournal.com

Providence Life Services
18601 N Creek Dr Tinley Park IL 60477 708-342-8100 342-8000 672
TF: 800-509-2800 ■ *Web:* www.providencelifeservices.com

Providence Medford Medical Ctr
1111 Crater Lake Ave Medford OR 97504 541-732-5000 374-3
TF: 877-541-0588 ■ *Web:* www.oregon.providence.org

Providence Medical Ctr
8929 Parallel Pkwy Kansas City KS 66112 913-596-4000 596-4801 374-3
TF: 800-281-7777 ■ *Web:* www.providencekc.com

Providence Metallizing Company Inc
51 Fairlawn Ave Pawtucket RI 02860 401-722-5300 724-3410 481
TF: 800-851-9273 ■ *Web:* www.providencemetallizing.com

Providence Mountains State Recreation Area
1416 Ninth St Sacramento CA 95814 800-777-0369 565
TF: 800-777-0369 ■ *Web:* www.parks.ca.gov/default.asp?page_id=615

Providence Mutual Fire Insurance Co
340 E Ave Warwick RI 02886 401-827-1800 822-1872 391-4
TF: 877-763-1800 ■ *Web:* www.providencemutual.com

Providence Oyster Bar
283 Atwells Ave Providence RI 02903 401-272-8866 671
Web: www.providenceoysterbar.com

Providence Performing Arts Ctr
220 Weybosset St Providence RI 02903 401-421-2997 351-7827 572
Web: www.ppacri.org

Providence Playhouse
1256 Providence Rd Scranton PA 18508 570-342-9707 572
Web: actorscircle.org

Providence Portland Medical Ctr
4805 NE Glisan St Portland OR 97213 503-215-1111 374-3
TF: 800-833-8899 ■ *Web:* www.oregon.providence.org

Name / Address	City	State	ZIP	Phone	Fax	Class
Providence Public Library						
150 Empire St	Providence	RI	02903	401-455-8000		434-3
Web: www.provlib.org						
Providence Regional Medical Ctr Everett						
916 Pacific Ave	Everett	WA	98201	425-261-2000	259-8600	374-3
Web: www2.providence.org						
Providence Rest 3304 Waterbury Ave	Bronx	NY	10465	718-931-3000		450
Web: www.providencerest.org						
Providence Sacred Heart Medical Ctr						
101 W Eigth Ave	Spokane	WA	99204	509-474-3170		374-3
TF: 800-442-8534 ■ *Web:* washington.providence.org						
Providence Saint Joseph Medical Ctr						
501 S Buena Vista St	Burbank	CA	91505	818-843-5111		374-3
TF: 800-750-7703 ■ *Web:* california.providence.org						
Providence Saint Peter Hospital (PSPH)						
413 Lilly Rd NE	Olympia	WA	98506	360-491-9480		374-3
TF: 888-492-9480 ■ *Web:* www2.providence.org						
Providence Service Corp 700 Canal St	Stamford	CT	06902	203-307-2800	307-2799	462
NASDAQ: PRSC ■ *Web:* www.prscholdings.com						
Providence Sound Home Care & Hospice						
3432 S Bay Rd NE	Olympia	WA	98506	360-459-8311		371
TF: 800-869-7062 ■ *Web:* www2.providence.org						
Providence St Mary Medical Ctr						
401 W Poplar St PO Box 1477	Walla Walla	WA	99362	509-525-3320		374-3
TF: 877-215-7833 ■ *Web:* www2.providence.org						
Providence Warwick Convention & Visitors Bureau						
10 Memorial Blvd	Providence	RI	02903	401-456-0200	351-2090	206
TF: 800-233-1636 ■ *Web:* www.goprovidence.com						
Provident Advisors LLC						
2800 Niagara Ln N	Plymouth	MN	55447	952-345-5200		401
Provident Bank 3756 Central Ave	Riverside	CA	92506	951-686-6060		360-2
NASDAQ: PROV ■ *TF:* 800-442-5201 ■ *Web:* www.providentbankmortgage.com						
Provident Bank 239 Washington St	Jersey City	NJ	07302	732-590-9200		70
Web: www.snl.com						
Provident Central Credit Union						
303 Twin Dolphin Dr	Redwood City	CA	94065	650-508-0300	508-7202	219
TF: 800-632-4600 ■ *Web:* www.providentcu.org						
Provident Community Bancshares Inc						
2700 Celanese Rd	Rock Hill	SC	29732	803-325-9400		360-2
OTC: PCBS ■ *Web:* www.provcombank.com						
Provident Construction Inc						
12424 E Weaver Pl	Centennial	CO	80111	720-482-0200		186
Web: www.providentconstruction.com						
Provident Savings Bank FSB						
3756 Central Ave	Riverside	CA	92506	951-686-6060	786-4725	70
TF: 800-442-5201 ■ *Web:* www.myprovident.com						
Provident Travel						
11309 Montgomery Rd	Cincinnati	OH	45249	513-247-1100		384
TF: 800-354-8108 ■ *Web:* www.providenttravel.com						
Providge Consulting LLC						
2207 Concord Pike Ste 537	Wilimington	DE	19803	888-927-6583		177
TF: 888-927-6583 ■ *Web:* www.providge.com						
Provigo Inc 400 Ave Suite Croix	Saint-laurent	QC	H4L5P3	514-383-3000		345
Web: www.provigo.ca						
Provimi Foods Inc W2103 County Rd W	Seymour	WI	54165	920-833-6861		10-3
Web: www.provimifoods.com						
Provimi North America Inc						
10 Collective Way PO Box 69	Brookville	OH	45309	800-257-3788	458-2539	447
TF: 888-522-2420 ■ *Web:* www.provimius.com						
Provincetown Public Library						
356 Commercial St	Provincetown	MA	02657	508-487-7094		434-3
Web: provincetownlibrary.org						
Provincial Information & Library Resources Board						
West Newfoundl and-Labrador Div						
4 W St	Corner Brook	NL	A2H0C1	709-634-7333	634-7313	436
Web: www.nlpl.ca						
Provincial Wildlife Park						
149 Creighton Rd	Shubenacadie	NS	B0N2H0	902-758-2040		823
Web: wildlifepark.novascotia.ca						
Provisio Group Ltd, The						
10910 W Sam Houston Pkwy N Ste 500	Houston	TX	77064	281-894-7700		45
Web: www.provisiogroup.com						
Provision Ministry Group PO Box 19700	Irvine	CA	92623	800-597-9931		685
TF: 800-233-3880 ■ *Web:* www.provision.org						
ProVision Partners Coop PO Box 14	Stratford	WI	54484	715-687-4443		276
Web: provisionpartners.coop						
ProVision solar Inc						
69 Railroad Ave Ste A-7	Hilo	HI	96720	808-969-3281	934-7462	357
Web: provisionsolar.com						
Provista Diagnostics Inc						
17301 N Perimeter Dr	Scottsdale	AZ	85255	855-552-7439		743
TF: 855-552-7439 ■ *Web:* www.provistadx.com						
Provista LLC 220 E Las Colinas Blvd	Irving	TX	75039	888-538-4662		317
TF: 888-538-4662 ■ *Web:* www.provistaco.com						
Provo City Hall 351 W Ctr St	Provo	UT	84601	801-852-6100	852-6107	337
Web: provo.org						
Provo City Library 550 N University Ave	Provo	UT	84601	801-852-6650	852-6688	434-3
TF: 800-914-8931 ■ *Web:* provolibrary.com						
Provo School District 280 W 940 N	Provo	UT	84604	801-374-4800	374-4808	685
Web: www.provo.edu						
Provo Towne Ctr 1200 Towne Centre Blvd	Provo	UT	84601	801-852-2400		460
Web: www.provotowncentre.com						
Provo/Orem Chamber of Commerce						
111 S University Ave	Provo	UT	84601	801-851-2555		139
Web: thechamber.org						
Provoast Automation Controls						
12635 Danielson Court Ste 205	Poway	CA	92064	858-748-2237		385
TF: 800-264-7406 ■ *Web:* www.proautocon.com						
Provost-Umphrey Law Firm LLP						
490 Park St	Beaumont	TX	77704	409-835-6000		428
TF: 800-289-0101 ■ *Web:* www.provostumphrey.com						
Proware 7621 E Kemper Rd	Cincinnati	OH	45249	513-489-5477		177
Web: www.proware.com						
Prowess Inc 1844 Clayton Rd	Concord	CA	94520	925-356-0360		177
Web: www.prowess.com						
Pro-west & Associates Inc						
8239 State 371 NW	Walker	MN	56484	218-547-3374		302
Web: www.prowestgis.com						
Proxibid Inc 4411 S 96 St	Omaha	NE	68127	402-505-7770		177
Web: www.proxibid.com						
Proxim Wireless Corp 1561 Buckeye Dr	Milpitas	CA	95035	408-383-7600	383-7680	735
OTC: PRXM ■ *TF:* 800-229-1630 ■ *Web:* www.proxim.com						
Proximex Corp 300 Santana Row Ste 200	San Jose	CA	95128	408-215-9000		177
Web: www.proximex.com						
Proximity Hotel						
704 Green Valley Rd	Greensboro	NC	27408	336-379-8200		132
TF: 800-379-8200 ■ *Web:* www.proximityhotel.com						
Proximo Consulting Services Inc						
2500 Plaza Five	Jersey City	NJ	07311	800-236-9250		177
TF: 800-236-9250 ■ *Web:* www.proximo.com						
Proxy Technologies Inc						
1840 Michael Faraday Dr Ste 220	Reston	VA	20190	301-216-2851		529
Web: www.proxyaviation.com						
Proz com 235 Harrison St	Syracuse	NY	13202	315-463-7323		261
Web: www.proz.com						
Prozyme Inc 3832 Bay Ctr Pl	Hayward	CA	94545	510-638-6900	638-6919	231
TF: 800-457-9444 ■ *Web:* www.prozyme.com						
Prr (PRR) 1501 Fourth Ave Ste 550	Seattle	WA	98101	206-623-0735		636
Web: www.prrbiz.com						
PRS (Paul Reed Smith Guitars)						
380 Log Canoe Cir	Stevensville	MD	21666	410-643-9970	643-9980	527
Web: www.prsguitars.com						
PRS Group Inc, The						
5800 Heritage Landing Dr Ste E	East Syracuse	NY	13057	315-431-0511		637-10
Web: www.prsgroup.com						
PRS Inc 1761 Old Meadow Rd Ste 100	McLean	VA	22102	703-536-9000	448-3723	363
Web: www.prsinc.org						
PRSA (Public Relations Society of America)						
33 Maiden Ln 11th Fl	New York	NY	10038	212-460-1400	995-0757	49-18
TF: 800-350-0111 ■ *Web:* www.prsa.org						
PRTC (PRTC Inc) 201 Anderson Dr	Laurens	SC	29360	864-682-3131		736
Web: www.prtcnet.com						
PRTC Inc (PRTC) 201 Anderson Dr	Laurens	SC	29360	864-682-3131		736
Web: www.prtcnet.com						
Prudential Builders Ctr 3304 E Ferry	Spokane	WA	99202	509-535-2401		38
Web: mystore411.com						
Prudential Financial Inc 751 Broad St	Newark	NJ	07102	973-802-6000		401
NYSE: PRU ■ *TF:* 800-843-7625 ■ *Web:* www.prudential.com						
Prudential Ltd 1737 E 22nd St	Los Angeles	CA	90058	213-746-0360	741-8590	439
Web: www.prulite.com						
Prudential Overall Supply						
PO Box 11210	Santa Ana	CA	92711	949-250-4855	261-1947	442
TF: 800-767-5536 ■ *Web:* www.prudentialuniforms.com						
Prudential Savings Bank						
1834 W Oregon Ave	Philadelphia	PA	19145	215-755-1500		70
TF: 800-554-8969 ■ *Web:* www.prudentialsavingsbank.com						
Pruntytown Correctional Ctr						
PO Box 159	Grafton	WV	26354	304-265-6111	265-6120	213
Web: www.wvdoc.com						
PRWT Services Inc						
1835 Market St 8th Fl	Philadelphia	PA	19103	215-569-8810	569-9893	721
Web: www.prwt.com						
Prx Inc 991 W Hedding St Ste 201	San Jose	CA	95126	408-287-1700		636
TF: 800-438-7325 ■ *Web:* www.prxdigital.com						
Prym-Dritz USA Inc PO Box 5028	Spartanburg	SC	29303	864-576-5050		594
Web: www.dritz.com						
Pryor Products 1819 Peacock Blvd	Oceanside	CA	92056	760-724-8244		476
TF: 800-854-2280 ■ *Web:* www.pryorproducts.com						
PS & Assoc Underwriting Agency Inc						
1776 Legacy Cir Ste 104	Naperville	IL	60563	630-416-0004	416-2246	390
Web: www.psassociate.com						
PS Air Inc 3411 Beech Way SW	Cedar Rapids	IA	52404	319-846-3600		63
TF: 800-742-7894 ■ *Web:* www.psair.com						
PS Business Parks Inc						
701 Western Ave	Glendale	CA	91201	818-244-8080	242-0566	655
NYSE: PSB ■ *TF Cust Svc:* 888-782-6110 ■ *Web:* www.psbusinessparks.com						
PS Energy Group Inc						
4480 N Shallowford Rd Ste 100	Dunwoody	GA	30338	404-321-5711	321-3938	787
TF: 800-334-7548 ■ *Web:* www.psenergy.com						
Ps Graphics & Promotions						
5991 Monticello Dr	Montgomery	AL	36117	334-270-9481		344
Web: psgp.com						
PS International Ltd						
1414 Raleigh Rd Ste 205	Chapel Hill	NC	27517	919-933-7400	933-7441	169
PS Marcato Elevator Co						
4411 11th St	Long Island	NY	11101	718-392-6400		189-1
Web: www.psmarcato.com						
Ps Websolutions Inc						
906 Carriage Path SE Ste 106	Smyrna	GA	30082	877-571-7829		177
TF: 877-571-7829 ■ *Web:* www.pswebsolution.com						
PSA Airlines Inc 3400 Terminal Dr	Vandalia	OH	45377	937-665-2876		25
TF Resv: 800-235-0986 ■ *Web:* www.psaairlines.com						
Psa Constructors Inc						
1516 E Hillcrest St	Orlando	FL	32803	407-898-9119		196
TF: 800-777-6573 ■ *Web:* www.psaonline.com						
PSARA Technologies Inc						
10925 Reed Hartman Hwy Ste 220	Cincinnati	OH	45242	513-791-4418		261
Web: psara.com						
PSB (Peoples Savings Bank)						
414 N Adams PO Box 248	Wellsburg	IA	50680	641-869-3721	869-3855	70
TF: 877-508-2265 ■ *Web:* www.bankpsb.com						
PSB Industries Inc PO Box 1318	Erie	PA	16512	814-453-3651		386
TF: 800-829-1119 ■ *Web:* www.psbindustries.com						
PSC (Professional Services Council)						
4401 Wilson Blvd Ste 1110	Arlington	VA	22203	703-875-8059	875-8922	49-12
TF: 800-353-9118 ■ *Web:* www.pscouncil.org						
PSC 5151 San Felipe Ste 1100	Houston	TX	77056	800-726-1300		192
TF: 800-726-1300 ■ *Web:* www.pscnow.com						
PSC (District of Columbia)						
Aging Office 500 K St NE Ste 900 S	Washington	DC	20002	202-724-5626	724-2008	339-9
Web: www.dcoa.dc.gov						
PSC Electronics						
2307 Calle Del Mundo	Santa Clara	CA	95054	408-737-1333		602
Web: pscelex.com						
PSC Industries 1100 W Market St	Louisville	KY	40203	502-625-7700	625-7837	605-2
Web: pscindustries.com						

Phone | Fax | Class

PSCA (Profit Sharing/401(k) Council of America)
20 N Wacker Dr Ste 3700 .... Chicago IL 60606 312-419-1863 419-1864 49-12
TF: 866-614-8407 ■ *Web:* www.psca.org

PSD Global LLC 505 N Mansfield St .... Alexandria VA 22304 703-531-8773 195
Web: www.psdglobal.com

PSDA (Print Services & Distribution Assn)
330 N Wabash Ave Ste 2000.......... Chicago IL 60611 800-230-0175 48-9
TF: 800-336-4641 ■ *Web:* www.psda.org

PSE (Pi Sigma Epsilon)
3747 S Howell Ave.......... Milwaukee WI 53207 414-328-1952 328-1953 48-16
TF: 800-761-9350 ■ *Web:* www.pse.org

PSEG Power LLC 80 Pk Plaza .... Newark NJ 07101 973-430-7000 787
TF: 800-436-7734 ■ *Web:* www.pseg.com

PSF Industries Inc 65 S Horton St .... Seattle WA 98134 206-622-1252 189-10
TF General: 800-426-1204 ■ *Web:* www.psfindustries.com

PSF Mechanical Inc 9322 14th Ave S .... Seattle WA 98108 206-764-9663 610
Web: www.psfmechanical.com

Psg Consulting Inc Po Box 19212 .... Seattle WA 98119 206-285-2824 463
Web: psgc.com

PSI (Pet Sitters International)
201 E King St.......... King NC 27021 336-983-9222 48-3
Web: www.petsit.com

PSI (Population Services International)
1120 19th St NW Ste 600.......... Washington DC 20036 202-785-0072 785-0120 48-17
Web: www.psi.org

PSI (Professional Service Industries Inc)
1901 S Meyers Rd Ste 400.......... Oakbrook Terrace IL 60181 630-691-1490 691-1587 261
TF: 800-548-7901 ■ *Web:* www.psiusa.com

Psi Chi National Honor Society in Psychology
825 Vine St.......... Chattanooga TN 37403 423-756-2044 48-16
Web: www.psichi.org

Psi Contact Ctr
3160 Haggerty Rd Ste D.......... West Bloomfield MI 48323 248-624-2400 737
TF: 800-560-6226 ■ *Web:* www.psicontactcenter.com

PSI Control Solutions Inc
5808 Long Creek Park Dr.......... Charlotte NC 28269 704-596-5617 729
Web: psicontrolsolutions.com

PSI Health Solutions Inc
1013 Morse Dr.......... Pacific Grove CA 93950 831-373-7712 476
Web: www.psibands.com

PSI International Inc
4000 Legato Rd Ste 850.......... Fairfax VA 22033 703-621-5825 178-10
Web: www.psiint.com

Psi Personnel LLC
252 W Swamp Rd Ste 29.......... Doylestown PA 18901 215-345-6778 260
Web: www.psipersonnel.com

PSI Software Inc 7326 Remcon Cir .... El Paso TX 79912 915-584-4100 179
Web: www.psisoftware.com

PSI Upsilon Fraternity
3003 E 96th St.......... Indianapolis IN 46240 317-571-1833 844-5170 48-16
TF: 800-394-1833 ■ *Web:* www.psiu.org

Psilos Group Managers LLC
140 Broadway 51st Fl.......... New York NY 10005 212-242-8844 792
Web: www.psilos.com

PsiNapse Technology Ltd
5820 Stoneridge Mall Rd Ste 212.......... Pleasanton CA 94588 925-225-0400 260
Web: www.psinapse.com

pSivida Inc 400 Pleasant St.......... Watertown MA 02472 617-926-5000 926-5050 85
NASDAQ: PSDV ■ *Web:* www.psivida.com

PSJMC (Presence Saint Joseph Medical Ctr)
333 N Madison St.......... Joliet IL 60435 815-725-7133 374-3
Web: www.presencehealth.org/stjoes

PSL (Peach State Labs Inc)
180 Burlington Rd PO Box 1087.......... Rome GA 30162 706-291-8743 145
TF: 800-634-1653 ■ *Web:* www.peachstatelabs.com

PSM Industries Inc
14000 Avalon Blvd.......... Los Angeles CA 90061 310-715-9800 295
Web: www.psmindustries.com

Psomas 555 S Flower St Ste 4300.......... Los Angeles CA 90071 213-223-1400 261
Web: www.psomas.com

PSPAEC (PageSoutherlandPage)
1100 Louisiana St Ste 1.......... Houston TX 77002 713-871-8484 871-8440 261
Web: pagethink.com

PSPH (Providence Saint Peter Hospital)
413 Lilly Rd NE.......... Olympia WA 98506 360-491-9480 374-3
TF: 888-492-9480 ■ *Web:* www2.providence.org

PSPrint LLC 2861 Mandela Pkwy.......... Oakland CA 94608 800-511-2009 627
TF: 800-511-2009 ■ *Web:* www.psprint.com

PSR (Physicians for Social Responsibility)
1875 Connecticut Ave NW Ste 1012.......... Washington DC 20009 202-667-4260 667-4201 49-8
TF: 800-459-1887 ■ *Web:* www.psr.org

PSR (Professional Shorthand Reporters Inc)
601 Poydras St Ste 1615.......... New Orleans LA 70130 504-529-5255 445
TF: 800-536-5255 ■ *Web:* www.psrdepo.com

Psr Associates Inc
6629 thornton palms dr.......... Tampa FL 33647 813-412-5246 260
Web: www.psrassociates.com

PSTG Consulting 72 Scollard St.......... Toronto ON M5R1G2 416-593-0000 193
Web: www.pstgconsulting.com

Psyadon Pharmaceuticals Inc
20451 Seneca Meadows Pkwy.......... Germantown MD 20876 301-919-2020 231
Web: www.psyadonrx.com

Psychemedics Corp 125 Nagog Pk Ste 200.......... Acton MA 01720 978-206-8220 264-9236 85
NASDAQ: PMD ■ *TF:* 800-628-8073 ■ *Web:* www.psychemedics.com

Psychiatric Institute of Washington
4228 Wisconsin Ave NW.......... Washington DC 20016 202-885-5600 885-5614 374-5
TF: 800-369-2273 ■ *Web:* www.psychinstitute.com

Psychic Readings by Sylvia
546 Rogers St.......... Lowell MA 01852 978-937-0998 226
Web: www.sylviaspsychicreadings.com

Psychological Services Inc
611 N Brand Blvd Fl 10.......... Glendale CA 91505 818-847-6180 180
Web: corporate.psionline.com

Psychological Software Solutions Inc
4119 Montrose Blvd.......... Houston TX 77006 713-965-6941 177
Web: psiwaresolutions.com

Psychology Software Tools Inc
Sharpsburg Business Park 311 23rd St Ext
Ste 200.......... Sharpsburg PA 15215 412-271-5040 177
Web: www.pstnet.com

Psychology Today Magazine
115 E 23 St 9th Fl.......... New York NY 10010 212-260-7210 260-7445* 457-11
**Fax: Edit* ■ *TF:* 800-931-2237 ■ *Web:* www.psychologytoday.com

Psychopathic Record
32575 Folsom Rd.......... Farmington Hills MI 48336 248-426-0800 657
Web: www.psychopathicrecords.com

Psychotherapy Networker
5135 MacArthur Blvd NW.......... Washington DC 20016 888-851-9498 457-16
TF: 888-851-9498 ■ *Web:* www.psychotherapynetworker.org

Psychsoft PO Box 232.......... Quincy MA 02171 617-471-8733 180
TF: 800-450-6003 ■ *Web:* www.psych-soft.com

PsyMax Solutions LLC
25550 Chagrin Blvd Ste 100.......... Cleveland OH 44122 216-896-9991 194
TF: 866-774-2273 ■ *Web:* www.psymaxsolutions.com

Psyop Inc 45 Howard St 5th Fl.......... New York NY 10013 212-533-9055 344
Web: www.psyop.com

Psytech Solutions
1138 Stone Creek Dr.......... Hummelstown PA 17036 717-583-0349 177
Web: www.psytechsolutions.net

PT Ferro Construction Co
700 Rowell Ave.......... Joliet IL 60433 815-726-6284 726-5614 189-5
Web: www.ptferro.com

PTA Corp 148 Christian St.......... Oxford CT 06478 203-888-0585 888-1757 604
Web: www.ptaplastics.com

PTC (Paternity Testing Corp)
300 Portland St.......... Columbia MO 65201 573-442-9948 442-9870 417
TF: 888-837-8323 ■ *Web:* www.ptclabs.com

PTC (Parents Television Council)
707 Wilshire Blvd Ste 2075.......... Los Angeles CA 90017 213-629-9255 629-9254 49-14
Web: w2.parentstv.org

PTC (Parametric Technology Corp)
140 Kendrick St.......... Needham MA 02494 781-370-5000 370-6000 178-5
NASDAQ: PTC ■ *TF:* 800-613-7535 ■ *Web:* www.ptc.com

PTC Alliance
Copperleaf Corporate Ctr
6051 Wallace Rd Ext Ste 200.......... Wexford PA 15090 412-299-7900 299-2619 490
TF: 800-274-8823 ■ *Web:* www.ptcalliance.com

PTC International Inc
345 N Charles St.......... Baltimore MD 21201 443-682-9127 809
Web: www.ptcintl.com

Ptc Select LLC 2450 N Knoxville Ave.......... Peoria IL 61604 309-685-8400 175
TF: 800-225-2320 ■ *Web:* www.ptcselect.com

PTC Therapeutics Inc
100 Corporate Ct.......... South Plainfield NJ 07080 908-222-7000 231
Web: www.ptcbio.com

PTDA (Power Transmission Distributors Assn)
230 W Monroe St Ste 1410.......... Chicago IL 60606 312-516-2100 49-18
Web: www.ptda.org

PTGi (Primus Telecommunications)
7901 Jones Ranch Dr Ste 900.......... McLean VA 22102 703-902-2800 736
NYSE: PTGI ■ *TF:* 866-385-3360 ■ *Web:* www.ptgi.com

PTI (Pittsburgh Technical College)
1111 McKee Rd.......... Oakdale PA 15071 412-809-5100 809-5121* 800
**Fax: Admissions* ■ *TF:* 800-784-9675 ■ *Web:* www.pti.edu

PTI Engineered Plastics Inc
50900 Corporate Dr.......... Macomb MI 48044 586-263-5100 263-6680 261
Web: www.teampti.com

PTI Technologies Inc
501 Del Norte Blvd.......... Oxnard CA 93030 805-604-3700 604-3701 386
TF: 800-331-2701 ■ *Web:* www.ptitechnologies.com

PTMW Inc 5040 NW US Hwy 24.......... Topeka KS 66618 785-232-7792 697
Web: www.ptmw.com

PTR Baler & Compactor Co
2207 E Ontario St.......... Philadelphia PA 19134 215-533-5100 470
TF: 800-523-3654 ■ *Web:* www.ptrco.com

PTR-Precision Technologies Inc
120 Post Rd.......... Enfield CT 06082 860-741-2281 745-7932 425
TF: 800-329-3537 ■ *Web:* www.ptreb.com

PTS Data Center Solutions Inc
16 Thornton Rd.......... Oakland NJ 07436 201-337-3833 180
Web: www.ptsdcs.com

PTS Laboratories
8100 Secura Way.......... Santa Fe Springs CA 90670 562-347-2500 743
Web: www.ptslabs.com

PTSI (Panhandle Telecommunication Systems Inc)
2222 NW Hwy.......... Guymon OK 73942 580-338-2556 736
TF: 800-562-2556 ■ *Web:* www.ptci.net

Puaa Kaa State Wayside
54 S High St Rm 101.......... Wailuku HI 96793 808-984-8109 984-8111 565
Web: dlnr.hawaii.gov

Pub Cite 191 Rue Theberge.......... Delson QC J5B2J9 450-635-0635 627
Web: pubcite.com

Pub Italia 434 1/2 Preston St.......... Ottawa ON K1S4N4 613-232-2326 671
Web: www.pubitalia.ca

Pub Saint-Alexandre 1087 St Jean St.......... Quebec QC G1R1S3 418-694-0015 694-0178 671
Web: www.pubstalexandre.com

Pub St Patrick 1200 St-Jean St.......... Quebec QC G1R1S8 418-694-0618 671

Pub St-Paul 124 St Paul St E.......... Montreal QC H2Y1G6 514-874-0485 671
Web: www.pubstpaul.com

Pubco Corp 3830 Kelley Ave.......... Cleveland OH 44114 216-881-5300 881-8380 111
TF: 800-878-3399 ■ *Web:* fundinguniverse.com

Public Affairs
1290 Avenue of the Americas 5th Fl.......... New York NY 10104 212-364-1100 637-2
Web: www.publicaffairsbooks.com

Public Affairs Council (PAC)
2033 K St NW Ste 700.......... Washington DC 20006 202-872-1790 48-7
Web: www.pac.org

Public Agenda 6 E 39th St.......... New York NY 10016 212-686-6610 889-3461 634
TF: 800-659-4044 ■ *Web:* www.publicagenda.org

Public Belt Railroad Commission
4822 Tchoupitulas St.......... New Orleans LA 70115 504-896-7410 896-7452 651
TF Cust Svc: 800-524-3421 ■ *Web:* nopb.com

Public Broadcasting Council of Central New York
506 Old Liverpool Rd PO Box 2400.......... Syracuse NY 13220 315-453-2424 451-8824 632
TF: 800-451-9269 ■ *Web:* www.wcny.org

Company	City	State	ZIP	Phone	Fax	Class
Public Broadcasting Northwest Pennsylvania 8425 Peach St *TF:* 800-727-8854 ■ *Web:* www.wqln.org	Erie	PA	16509	814-864-3001	864-4077	632
Public Broadcasting Service (PBS) 2100 Crystal Dr *TF:* 866-864-0828 ■ *Web:* www.pbs.org	Arlington	VA	22202	703-739-5000		739
Public Chicago 1301 N State Pkwy *Web:* www.publichotels.com	Chicago	IL	60610	312-787-3700		671
Public Citizen 1600 20th St NW *Web:* www.citizen.org	Washington	DC	20009	202-588-1000	588-7796	48-7
Public Citizen Health Research Group 1600 20th St NW *Web:* www.citizen.org/hrg	Washington	DC	20009	202-588-1000	588-7796	48-10
Public Company Accounting Oversight Board (PCAOB) 1666 K St NW *Web:* www.pcaobus.org	Washington	DC	20006	202-207-9100		533
Public Consulting Group Inc 148 State St **Fax Area Code:* 617 ■ *TF:* 800-210-6113 ■ *Web:* www.publicconsultinggroup.com	Boston	MA	02109	800-210-6113	426-4632*	194
Public Data Works Inc 2720 Reynolda Rd *Web:* www.publicdataworks.com	Winston-salem	NC	27106	336-725-4456		196
Public Education Network (PEN) 601 13th St NW Ste 710-S *TF:* 800-424-9836 ■ *Web:* www.publiceducation.org	Washington	DC	20005	800-424-9836		48-11
Public Employee Magazine 1625 L St NW *TF:* 800-792-0045 ■ *Web:* www.afscme.org	Washington	DC	20036	202-429-1130	429-1120	457-12
Public Employees Roundtable (PER) PO Box 75248 *Web:* www.keyinsurancequotes.com	Washington	DC	20013	202-927-4926	927-4920	49-7
Public Forum Institute 2300 M St NW	Washington	DC	20037	202-467-2774		48-7
Public Health Institute 555 12th St 10th Fl *TF:* 866-632-9992 ■ *Web:* www.phi.org	Oakland	CA	94607	510-285-5500	285-5501	48-17
Public Health Research Institute (PHRI) International Ctr for Public Health 225 Warren St *Web:* www.phri.org	Newark	NJ	07103	973-854-3100	854-3101	668
Public Health Solutions 220 Church St Fl 5 *Web:* www.healthsolutions.org	New York	NY	10013	646-619-6400		231
Public Impact 504 Dogwood Dr *TF:* 800-352-7550 ■ *Web:* www.publicimpact.com	Carrboro	NC	27510	919-240-7955		195
Public Interest Network 1543 Wazee St Ste 400 *TF:* 800-401-6511 ■ *Web:* www.publicinterestnetwork.org	Denver	CO	80202	303-573-5995		305
Public Lands Foundation (PLF) PO Box 7226 *TF:* 866-985-9636 ■ *Web:* www.publicland.org	Arlington	VA	22207	703 700 1988		48-13
Public Libraries of Saginaw 505 Janes St *Web:* www.saginawlibrary.org	Saginaw	MI	48607	989-755-0904	755-9829	434-3
Public Library Assn (PLA) 50 E Huron St *TF:* 800-545-2433 ■ *Web:* www.ala.org	Chicago	IL	60611	312-280-5752	280-5029	49-11
Public Library of Cincinnati & Hamilton County 800 Vine St *Web:* www.cincinnatilibrary.org	Cincinnati	OH	45202	513-369-6900		434-3
Public Library of Steubenville & Jefferson County 407 S Fourth St *Web:* www.steubenville.lib.oh.us	Steubenville	OH	43952	740-282-9782	282-2919	434-3
Public Library of Youngstown & Mahoning County 305 Wick Ave *Web:* libraryvisit.org	Youngstown	OH	44503	330-744-8636	744-2258	434-3
Public Market of Newington LLC 437 New Britain Ave *Web:* publicmarketnewington.com	Newington	CT	06111	860-667-1454		345
Public Museum of Grand Rapids 272 Pearl St NW Van Andel Museum Ctr *Web:* grpm.org	Grand Rapids	MI	49504	616-456-3977		520
Public Opinion 77 N Third St **Fax:* News Rm ■ *TF:* 800-782-0661 ■ *Web:* www.publicopiniononline.com	Chambersburg	PA	17201	717-264-6161	264-0377*	532-2
Public Opinion Strategies LLC 214 N Fayette St *Web:* www.pos.org	Alexandria	VA	22314	703-836-7655		636
Public Partnerships LLC 40 Broad St 4th Fl *Web:* www.publicpartnerships.com	Boston	MA	02109	617-426-2026		466
Public Policy Institute 1231 Lincoln Dr *Web:* www.siu.edu	Carbondale	IL	62901	618-453-4009		195
Public Radio 89.5 800 Tucker Dr *TF:* 888-594-5947 ■ *Web:* publicradiotulsa.org	Tulsa	OK	74104	918-631-2577	631-3695	645-168
Public Radio International (PRI) 401 Second Ave N Ste 500 *Web:* www.pri.org	Minneapolis	MN	55401	612-338-5000	330-9222	644
Public Relations Society of America (PRSA) 33 Maiden Ln 11th Fl *TF:* 800-350-0111 ■ *Web:* www.prsa.org	New York	NY	10038	212-460-1400	995-0757	49-18
Public Resources Advisory Group Inc 39 Broadway Ste 1210 *Web:* www.pragadvisors.com	New York	NY	10006	212-566-7800		194
Public Risk Management Assn (PRIMA) 700 S Washington St Ste 218 *TF:* 800-228-9290 ■ *Web:* www.primacentral.org	Alexandria	VA	22314	703-528-7701	739-0200	49-7
Public Safety Equipment Inc 10986 N Warson Rd *Web:* code3pse.com	St Louis	MO	63114	314-426-2700		692
Public Sector Consultants Inc 230 N Washington Sq Ste 300 *Web:* www.publicsectorconsultants.com	Lansing	MI	48933	517-484-4954	484-6549	196
Public Service Enterprise Group Inc 80 Pk Plaza *NYSE:* PEG ■ *TF Cust Svc:* 800-436-7734 ■ *Web:* www.pseg.com	Newark	NJ	07102	973-430-7000		360-5
Public Service Research Foundation 320-D Maple Ave E *Web:* www.psrf.org	Vienna	VA	22180	703-242-3575		48-7
Public Storage Inc 701 Western Ave *NYSE:* PSA ■ *TF Cust Svc:* 800-567-0759 ■ *Web:* www.publicstorage.com	Glendale	CA	91201	818-244-8080		803-3
Public Systems Associates Inc 2431 S Acadian Thwy Ste 570 *Web:* publicsystems.org	Baton Rouge	LA	70808	225-346-0618		177
Public Technology Inc 1420 Prince St Ste 200 *TF:* 866-664-6368 ■ *Web:* www.pti.org	Alexandria	VA	22314	202-626-2400		49-7
Public Utility District #1 of Ferry County 686 S Clark Ave PO Box 1039 *Web:* www.fcpud.com	Republic	WA	99166	509-775-3325	775-3326	245
Public Welfare Foundation 1200 U St NW *TF:* 800-275-7934 ■ *Web:* www.publicwelfare.org	Washington	DC	20009	202-965-1800		305
Public Works Commission of The City of Fayetteville North Carolina 955 Old Wilmington Rd PO Box 1089 *TF:* 877-687-7921 ■ *Web:* www.faypwc.com	Fayetteville	NC	28301	910-483-1382		787
Public, Theater, The 425 Lafayette St *Web:* www.publictheater.org	New York	NY	10003	212-539-8500		573-4
Publication Printers Corp 2001 S Platte River Dr *TF:* 888-824-0303 ■ *Web:* www.publicationprinters.com	Denver	CO	80223	303-936-0303	934 6712	627
Publications & Communications Inc 13552 Hwy 183 N Ste A *TF:* 800-678-9724 ■ *Web:* www.pcinews.com	Austin	TX	78750	512-250-9023		637-9
Publications International Ltd 7373 N Cicero Ave *TF General:* 800-777-5582 ■ *Web:* pilbooks.com	Lincolnwood	IL	60712	847 676-3470	676-3671	637-2
Publicis Touchpoint Solutions Inc 1000 Floral Vale Blvd Ste 400 *TF:* 800-672-0676 ■ *Web:* www.touchpointsolutions.com	Yardley	PA	19067	215-525-9800		4
Publicis USA 1675 Broadway *Web:* publicisna.com	New York	NY	10019	212-474-5000		4
Publicitas North America 330 Seventh Ave Fl 5 *Web:* www.publicitas.com	New York	NY	10001	212-330-0720		708
Publick House Historic Resort 277 Main St Rt 131 *TF Cust Svc:* 800-782-5425 ■ *Web:* www.publickhouse.com	Sturbridge	MA	01566	508-347-3313	347-1460	379
Publipage Inc 2055 Rue Peel *TF:* 800-544-8614 ■ *Web:* publipage.com	Montreal	QC	H3A1V4	514-286-1550		7
Publish Or Perish Inc 825 E Roosevelt Rd *Web:* www.publishorperish.com	Lombard	IL	60148	630-627-7227		180
Publishers Group West (PGW) 1700 Fourth St *Web:* www.pgw.com	Berkeley	CA	94710	510-809-3700	809-3777	96
Publishers Press Inc 100 Frank E Simon Ave *TF:* [illegible] 6801 ■ *Web:* www.pubpress.com	Shepherdsville	KY	40165	502-955-6526	543-8808	626
Publishers' Warehouse 150 Industrial Rd *TF:* 800-653-2726 ■ *Web:* www.publisherswarehouse.com	Alabaster	AL	35007	205-980-2820		96
Publishing Group of America Media 341 Cool Springs Blvd Ste 400	Franklin	TN	37067	615-468-6000		637-9
Publix Super Markets Inc 3300 Publix Corporate Pkwy *TF PR:* 800-242-1227 ■ *Web:* www.publix.com	Lakeland	FL	33811	863-688-1188		345
PubMed US National Library of Medicine 8600 Rockville Pike **Fax Area Code:* 301 ■ *TF:* 888-346-3656 ■ *Web:* www.ncbi.nlm.nih.gov	Bethesda	MD	20894	888-346-3656	402-1384*	356
PUC Telecom Inc 765 Queen E *Web:* www.ssmpuc.com	Sault Ste Marie	ON	P6A2A8	705-759-6500		224
Pucci Foods 25447 Industrial Blvd *Web:* puccifoods.wpengine.com	Hayward	CA	94545	510-300-6800		297-9
Puccini & Pinetti 129 Ellis St *Web:* pucciniandpinetti.com	San Francisco	CA	94102	415-392-5500		671
Puccini's 1064 Westside Ave	Jersey City	NJ	07306	201-432-4111		671
Pucel Enterprises Inc 1440 E 36th St *TF:* 800-336-4986 ■ *Web:* www.pucelenterprises.com	Cleveland	OH	44114	216-881-4604	881-6731	470
Pudik Graphics Inc 111 Oakwood Rd *Web:* www.pudik.com	East Peoria	IL	61611	309-694-2900		344
Pueblo Bank & Trust Co 301 W Fifth St *Web:* www.pbandt.com	Pueblo	CO	81003	719-545-1834		70
Pueblo Bonito Golf & Spa Resorts 4350 La Jolla Village Dr *TF:* 800-990-8250 ■ *Web:* www.pueblobonito.com	San Diego	CA	92122	858-642-2050		378
Pueblo Chieftain 825 W Sixth St *TF:* 800-279-6397 ■ *Web:* www.chieftain.com	Pueblo	CO	81003	719-544-3520		532-2
Pueblo Community College 900 W Orman Ave *TF:* 888-642-6017 ■ *Web:* www.pueblocc.edu	Pueblo	CO	81004	719-549-3200		162
Pueblo County 215 W Tenth St *Web:* pueblo.org	Pueblo	CO	81003	719-583-6000	583-4894	338
Pueblo Grande Museum & Archaeological Park 4619 E Washington St *Web:* www.phoenix.gov/recreation/arts/museums/pueblo	Phoenix	AZ	85034	602-495-0901		520
Pueblo Youth Services Ctr 1406 W 17th St	Pueblo	CO	81003	719-546-4902		412
Pueblo Zoo 3455 Nuckolls Ave *Web:* www.pueblozoo.org	Pueblo	CO	81005	719-561-1452		823
Puente Hills Mall 1600 Azusa Ave *TF:* 800-743-3463 ■ *Web:* www.puentehills-mall.com	City of Industry	CA	91748	626-912-8777	913-2719	460
Puerto Rican Chamber of Commerce of South Florida 3550 Biscayne Blvd Ste 306 *Web:* www.puertoricanchamber.com	Miami	FL	33137	305-571-8007	571-8007	138
Puerto Rico Paseo La Princesa *TF:* 800-866-7827 ■ *Web:* topuertorico.org	Old San Juan	PR	00902	787-721-2400	722-1093	775
Puerto Rico Chamber of Commerce PO Box 9024033 *Web:* www.camarapr.org	San Juan	PR	00902	787-721-6060	723-1891	140
Puerto Rico Convention Bureau 100 Calle Guamani *TF:* 800-875-4765 ■ *Web:* www.prconvention.com	San Juan	PR	00907	787-725-2110	725-2133	206

Name / Address	City	State	ZIP	Phone	Fax	Class
Puerto Rico Farm Credit Aca PO Box 363649 *TF:* 000-981-3323 ■ *Web:* prfarmcredit.com	San Juan	PR	00036	787-753-0579		216
Puffin Inn 4400 SpenaRd Rd *TF:* 800-478-3346 ■ *Web:* puffininn.net	Anchorage	AK	99517	907-243-4044	248-6853	379
Puget Energy Inc 10885 NE Fourth St *Web:* www.pugetenergy.com/pages/terms.html	Bellevue	WA	98004	425-454-6363		360-5
Puget Sound Blood Ctr 921 Terry Ave *TF:* 800-366-2831 ■ *Web:* www.psbc.org	Seattle	WA	98104	206-292-6500		89
Puget Sound Educational Service District 800 Oakesdale Ave SW *TF:* 800-664-4549 ■ *Web:* www.psesd.org	Renton	WA	98057	425-917-7600		685
Puget Sound Energy Inc 10885 NE Fourth St *TF:* 888-225-5773 ■ *Web:* www.pse.com	Bellevue	WA	98004	425-452-1234		787
Puget Sound Rope Corp 1012 Second St *TF:* 888-525-8488 ■ *Web:* www.cortlandcompany.com	Anacortes	WA	98221	360-293-8488	293-8480	208
Puget Western Inc 19515 N Creek Pkwy Ste 310 *Web:* pugetwestern.com	Bothell	WA	98011	425-487-6550	487-6565	653
Pugh Capital Management Inc 520 Pk St Ste 2900 *Web:* www.pughcapital.com	Seattle	WA	98101	206-322-4985		401
Pugh Lubricants 701 McDowell Rd PO Box 4006 *Web:* www.pughoil.com	Asheboro	NC	27205	336-629-2061		579
Puglioni's 1137 Van Voorhis Rd *Web:* pugspasta.com	Morgantown	WV	26505	304-599-7521		671
Puglisi Egg Farms Inc 75 Easy St	Howell	NJ	07731	732-938-2373		10-8
Pugster Inc 2835 Sierra Grande St *Web:* pugster.com	Pasadena	CA	91107	626-356-1881		411
PUHSD (Phoenix Union High School District) 4502 N Central Ave *TF:* 800-823-4929 ■ *Web:* www.phxhs.k12.az.us	Phoenix	AZ	85012	602-764-1100		685
Pukaskwa National Park of Canada PO Box 212 *Web:* www.pc.gc.ca	Heron Bay	ON	P0T1R0	807-229-0801	229-2097	563
Puklich Chevrolet Inc 3701 State St *Web:* puklichchevrolet.com	Bismarck	ND	58502	701-223-5800		57
Pulaski County 401 W Markham St Ste 100 *Web:* pulaskicounty.net	Little Rock	AR	72201	501-340-8500		338
Pulaski County 143 Third St NW Ste 1 *TF:* 800-211-5540 ■ *Web:* www.pulaskicounty.org	Pulaski	VA	24301	540-980-7705	980-7717	338
Pulaski County 100 N Main St Ste 202 *TF:* 877-655-7154 ■ *Web:* www.pcgovt.com	Somerset	KY	42501	606-678-4853	679-8642	338
Pulaski County 101 Dublin Park Rd *Web:* www.visitpulaskicounty.org	Dublin	VA	24084	573-774-4701		338
Pulaski County 28 Parkway Dr PO Box 720 *Web:* pulaski.ca.uky.edu	Somerset	KY	42502	606-679-6361		338
Pulaski County Chamber of Commerce 4440 Cleburne Blvd Ste B *TF:* 866-256-8864 ■ *Web:* www.pulaskichamber.info	Dublin	VA	24084	540-674-1991	674-4163	139
Pulaski County Library 60 W Third St *Web:* www.pclibs.org	Pulaski	VA	24301	540-980-7770	980-7775	434-3
Pulaski County Public Library 304 S Main St *Web:* www.pulaskipubliclibrary.org	Somerset	KY	42501	606-679-8401		434-3
Pulaski County School District (PCPS) 202 N Washington Ave *Web:* www.pcva.us	Pulaski	VA	24301	540-994-2550		685
Pulaski Financial Corp 12300 Olive Blvd *NASDAQ: PULB* ■ *TF:* 888-649-3320 ■ *Web:* www.pulaskibank.com	Saint Louis	MO	63141	314-878-2210		360-2
Pulaski State Prison 373 Upper River Rd *Web:* www.dcor.state.ga.us	Hawkinsville	GA	31036	478-783-6000	783-6008	213
Pulaski Technical College 3000 W Scenic Dr *Web:* www.uaptc.edu	North Little Rock	AR	72118	501-812-2200	771-2844	162
Pulau Electronics Corp 12633 Challenger Pkwy *Web:* www.pulau.com	Orlando	FL	32826	407-380-9191	380-9786	311
Pulice Construction Inc 2033 W Mountain View Rd *Web:* www.pulice.com	Phoenix	AZ	85021	602-944-2241		188-4
Pullan Consulting 9360 W Flamingo Rd Ste 110-554 *Web:* www.pullanconsulting.com	Las Vegas	NV	89147	805-558-0361		463
Pulley-Kellam Company Inc 245 Erie St	Huntington	IN	46750	260-356-6326	356-1928	482
Pullman Chamber of Commerce 415 N Grand Ave *TF:* 800-365-6948 ■ *Web:* www.pullmanchamber.com	Pullman	WA	99163	509-334-3565	332-3232	139
Pullman School District 267 240 SE Dexter St *Web:* www.psd267.org	Pullman	WA	99163	509-332-3581		685
Pullman/Holt Corp 10702 N 46th St	Tampa	FL	33617	813-971-2223		386
Pulpo Media Inc 1767 Alcatraz Ave *Web:* www.pulpo.com/en	Berkeley	CA	94703	510-594-2294		387
Pulsafeeder Inc 2883 Brighton-Henrietta Town Line Rd *Web:* www.pulsa.com	Rochester	NY	14623	585-292-8000	424-5619	641
Pulsar It Consulting Inc 9200 Worthington Rd Ste 101 *Web:* gammillgroup.com	Westerville	OH	43082	614-781-3787		196
Pulsar Vascular Inc 4030 Moorpark Ave Ste 110 *Web:* www.pulsarvascular.com	San Jose	CA	95117	408-260-9264		475
PULSE 1301 McKinney St Ste 2500 *TF:* 800-420-2122 ■ *Web:* www.pulsenetwork.com	Houston	TX	77010	713-223-1400		69
Pulse Biomedical Inc 1305 Catfish Ln *Web:* www.qrscard.com	Norristown	PA	19403	610-666-5510		475
Pulse Communications Inc 2900 Towerview Rd **Fax:* Cust Svc ■ *TF Cust Svc:* 800-381-1997 ■ *Web:* www.pulse.com	Herndon	VA	20171	703-471-2900	471-2951*	735

Name / Address	City	State	ZIP	Phone	Fax	Class
Pulse Engineering Inc 12220 World Trade Dr *Web:* www.pulseelectronics.com	San Diego	CA	92128	858-674-8100	674-8262	253
Pulse Home Health Care Inc 2325 Severn Ave Ste 5 *Web:* pulsehomehealthcare.com	Metairie	LA	70001	504-831-7778		363
Pulse Needlefree Systems Inc 8210 Marshall Dr *Web:* www.pulse-nfs.com	Lenexa	KS	66214	913-599-1590		476
Pulse Seismic Inc 421 Seventh Ave SW Ste 2700 *Web:* www.pulseseismic.com	Calgary	AB	T2P4K9	403-237-5559		624
Pulse Technologies Inc 2000 Am Dr *Web:* www.pulsetechinc.com	Quakertown	PA	18951	267-733-0200		454
PulseTech Products Corp 1100 S Kimball Ave *TF:* 800-580-7554 ■ *Web:* www.pulsetech.net	Southlake	TX	76092	817-329-6099		74
Puma 10 Lyberty Way *TF General:* 888-565-7862 ■ *Web:* www.puma.com	Westford	MA	01886	978-698-1000	968-1150	301
Puma Industries Inc 1992 Airways Blvd *TF:* 888-848-1668 ■ *Web:* www.pumaairusa.com	Memphis	TN	38114	901-744-7979		172
Pummills Sporting Goods Inc 2400 W 16th St *Web:* www.pummillsports.com	Sedalia	MO	65301	660-826-0150		711
Pump Audio Inc 5 Pine St *TF:* 800-479-0285 ■ *Web:* www.pumpaudio.com	Tivoli	NY	12583	845-757-5555		393
Pump House, The 796 Chena Pump Rd *Web:* www.pumphouse.com	Fairbanks	AK	99709	907-479-8452	479-8432	671
Pump It Up Party 11411 W 183rd St *TF:* 800-280-2347 ■ *Web:* www.pumpitupparty.com	Orland Park	IL	60467	708-479-2220		138
Pumpco Energy Services Inc 117 Elm Grove Rd *Web:* www.pumpcoservices.com	Valley View	TX	76272	940-726-1800		539
Pumpelly Oil Company LLC 1890 Swisco Rd PO Box 2059 *Web:* www.reladyne.com	Sulphur	LA	70664	337-625-1117		581
Pumper's Premium Stores Inc 4931 Earle Morris Hwy *Web:* www.pumperspremium.com	Easley	SC	29642	864-306-2999		345
Pumping Solutions Inc 1906 S Quaker Ridge Pl *TF:* 800-603-0399 ■ *Web:* www.pump.ws	Ontario	CA	91761	800-603-0399		610
Pumpkin Hollow Farm 1184 Rt 11 *Web:* www.pumpkinhollow.org	Craryville	NY	12521	518-325-3583	325-5633	673
Pun's Toy Shop 839 1/2 Lancaster Ave *Web:* punstoys.com	Bryn Mawr	PA	19010	610-525-9789	527-5514	761
Punahou School 1601 Punahou St *Web:* www.punahou.edu	Honolulu	HI	96822	808-944-5711	944-5779	623
Punch & Associates Inc 3601 W 76th St Ste 225 *TF:* 800-241-5552 ■ *Web:* punchinvest.com	Edina	MN	55435	952-224-4350		528
Punch Media 45 N Third St *Web:* www.punchmedia.biz	Philadelphia	PA	19106	215-592-0120		195
Punch Press Products Inc 2035 E 51st St *Web:* www.punch-press.com	Los Angeles	CA	90058	323-581-7151		567
Punchbowl Inc 50 Speen St Ste 202 *TF:* 877-570-4340 ■ *Web:* punchbowl.com	Framingham	MA	01701	508-589-4486		107
Punchcut LLC 170 Maiden Ln *Web:* punchcut.com	San Francisco	CA	94108	415-445-8855		180
Punchkick Interactive Inc 150 N Michigan Ave Ste 3900 *TF:* 800-549-4104 ■ *Web:* www.punchkick.com	Chicago	IL	60601	800-549-4104		195
Punderson State Park 11755 Kinsman Rd *Web:* parks.ohiodnr.gov/punderson	Newbury	OH	44065	440-564-5465		565
Punxsutawney Area Hospital Inc (PAH) 81 Hillcrest Dr *Web:* www.pah.org	Punxsutawney	PA	15767	814-938-1800		374-3
Puplava Securities Inc 10809 Thornmint Rd 2nd Fl *Web:* www.puplava.com	San Diego	CA	92127	858-487-3939		401
Puppet Labs 308 SW Second Ave 5th Fl *Web:* puppet.com	Portland	OR	97204	503-575-9775		225
Purafil Inc 2654 Weaver Way *TF:* 800-222-6367 ■ *Web:* www.purafil.com	Doraville	GA	30340	770-662-8545	263-6922	18
Puratos Corp 1941 Old Cuthbert Rd *TF All:* 800-654-0036 ■ *Web:* www.puratos.com	Cherry Hill	NJ	08034	856-428-4300	428-2939	296-16
Purcell Construction Inc 277 Dennis St *Web:* www.purcellc.com	Humble	TX	77338	281-548-1000	548-2998	187
Purcell International Group 500 S Kraemer Blvd Ste 102 *Web:* www.purcellintl.com	Brea	CA	92821	714-524-0640		193
Purcell Tire & Rubber Co 301 N Hall St *Web:* www.purcelltire.com	Potosi	MO	63664	573-438-2131		754
Purchase College 735 Anderson Hill Rd **Fax:* Admissions ■ *TF:* 800-553-8118 ■ *Web:* www.purchase.edu	Purchase	NY	10577	914-251-6000	251-6314*	166
Purchase Planners Group Inc 801 S Grand Ave Ste 425 *Web:* www.ppg-la.com	Los Angeles	CA	90017	213-687-4206		4
Purchasing Magazine 225 Wyman St *TF:* 888-393-5000 ■ *Web:* www.buyerzone.com	Waltham	MA	02451	888-393-5000		457-5
Purdue Pharma 575 Granite Ct *TF:* 800-387-5349 ■ *Web:* www.purdue.ca	Pickering	ON	L1W3W8	905-420-6400		231
Purdue University Schleman Hall 475 Stadium Mall Dr **Fax:* Admissions ■ *TF:* 800-743-3333 ■ *Web:* www.purdue.edu	West Lafayette	IN	47907	765-494-1776	494-0544*	166
Calumet 2200 169th St **Fax:* Admissions ■ *TF:* 800-447-8738 ■ *Web:* www.pnw.edu	Hammond	IN	46323	219-989-2400	989-2775*	166
Libraries ADMN 504 W State St **Fax:* Admin ■ *Web:* www.lib.purdue.edu	West Lafayette	IN	47907	765-494-2900	494-0156*	434-6
North Central 1401 S US Hwy 421 **Fax:* Admissions ■ *Web:* www.pnw.edu	Westville	IN	46391	219-785-5200	785-5538*	166
Purdue University Press 504 W State St Stewart Ctr 370 *TF Orders:* 800-247-6553 ■ *Web:* www.thepress.purdue.edu	West Lafayette	IN	47907	765-494-2038	496-2442	637-4

Company	City	State	ZIP	Phone	Fax	Class
Purdy Corp 101 Prospect Ave *TF:* 800-547-0780 ■ *Web:* www.purdy.com	Cleveland	OH	44115	800-547-0780		350
Purdy-McGuire Inc 17300 Dallas Pkwy Ste 3000 *Web:* www.purdy-mcguire.com	Dallas	TX	75248	972-239-5357		261
Pure & Secure LLC 4120 NW 44th St *TF Cust Svc:* 800-875-5915 ■ *Web:* www.mypurewater.com	Lincoln	NE	68524	402-467-9300		806
Pure Auto LLC 164 Market St Ste 250 *TF:* 877-860-7873 ■ *Web:* www.purecars.com	Charleston	SC	29401	877-860-7873		387
Pure Brand Communications LLC 621 Kalamath St *Web:* www.pure-brand.com	Denver	CO	80204	303-625-1085		224
Pure Canadian Gaming Corp 7055 Argyll Rd *Web:* www.purecanadiangaming.com	Edmonton	AB	T6C4A5	780-465-5377		133
Pure Energy Corp 61 S Paramus Rd *Web:* www.pure-energy.com	Paramus	NJ	07652	201-843-8100		579
Pure Energy Services (USA) Inc 9635 Maroon Cir Ste 420 *Web:* www.pure-energy.ca	Englewood	CO	80112	303-708-0200		540
Pure Essence Laboratories Inc 6155 S Sandhill Rd Ste 200 *Web:* www.pureessencelabs.com	Las Vegas	NV	89120	702-990-7400		345
Pure Express Mart 4002 Knight Arnold Rd	Memphis	TN	38118	901-794-3100		297-8
Pure Financial Advisors Inc 3131 Camino del Rio N Ste 1550 *Web:* www.purefinancial.com	San Diego	CA	92108	619-814-4100		401
Pure Humidifier Co 141 Jonathan BlvdN *Web:* www.purehumidifier.com	Chaska	MN	55318	952-368-9335		14
PURE Storage Inc 650 Castro St Ste 400 *TF:* 800-379-7873 ■ *Web:* www.purestorage.com	Mountain View	CA	94041	650-290-6088		173-8
Pure Strategies Inc 47R Englewood Rd *Web:* www.purestrategies.com	Gloucester	MA	01930	970-525-0480		192
Pure Sweet Honey Farm Inc 514 Commerce Pkwy *Web:* puresweethoney.com	Verona	WI	53593	608-845-9601		296-24
Pure Vegetarian 1110 N Old World Third St Ste 600	Milwaukee	WI	53203	414-271-7873		445
Pureflex Inc 4855 Broadmoor Ave *TF:* 800-960-0068 ■ *Web:* www.pureflex.com	Kentwood	MI	49512	616-554-1100	554 3633	326
Pure-Flo Water Co 7737 Mission Gorge Rd *TF Cust Svc:* 800-787-3356 ■ *Web:* www.pureflo.com	Santee	CA	92071	619-448-5120		805
Puregas LLC 226 Commerce St *TF:* 800-521-5351 ■ *Web:* puregas.com	Broomfield	CO	80020	303-427-3700		111
Pure-logic Industries Inc 1730 W Sunrise Blvd Ste A102 *Web:* www.purelogicind.com	Gilbert	AZ	05200	400 802 0306		608
Purematter 350 W Julian St Bldg 3 *Web:* www.purematter.com	San Jose	CA	95110	408-297-7800		4
PurEnergy LLC 4488 Onondaga Blvd *TF:* 800-782-7262 ■ *Web:* www.purenergyllc.com	Syracuse	NY	13219	315-448-2266		463
Purestream Services 2401 Foothill Dr *TF:* 855-778-7342 ■ *Web:* purestreamtechnology.com	Salt Lake City	UT	84109	801-869-4455		538
PureTech Ventures 501 Boylston St Ste 6102 *Web:* puretechhealth.com	Boston	MA	02116	617-482-2333	482-3337	792
Purgatory Chasm State Reservation Purgatory Rd *Web:* www.mass.gov	Sutton	MA	01590	508-234-3733		565
Puritan Backroom Restaurant 245 Hooksett Rd *Web:* www.puritanbackroom.com	North Manchester	NH	03104	603-669-6890		671
Puritan Bakery Inc 1624 E Carson St *Web:* www.puritanbakery.com	Carson	CA	90745	310-830-5451		68
Puritan Manufacturing Inc 1302 Grace St *TF:* 800-331-0487 ■ *Web:* www.purmfg.com	Omaha	NE	68110	402-341-3753		697
Puritan of Cape Cod 408 Main St *TF:* 800-924-0606 ■ *Web:* www.puritancapecod.com	Hyannis	MA	02601	508-775-2400		157-2
PuriTec 4705 S Durango Dr Ste 100-102 **Fax Area Code:* 888 ■ *TF:* 888-491-4100 ■ *Web:* www.puriteam.com	Las Vegas	NV	89147	610-268-5420	759-8905*	17
Purity Cylinder Gases Inc PO Box 9390 *Web:* www.puritygas.com	Grand Rapids	MI	49509	616-532-2375	532-5626	146
Purity Dairies Inc 360 Murfreesboro Rd *Web:* www.puritydairies.com	Nashville	TN	37210	615-244-1970		296-27
Purity Wholesale Grocers Inc 5300 Broken Sound Blvd NW *TF:* 800-323-6838 ■ *Web:* www.pwg-inc.com	Boca Raton	FL	33487	561-994-9360		297-8
Purnell School 51 Pottersville Rd PO Box 500 *TF:* 800-228-9290 ■ *Web:* www.purnell.org	Pottersville	NJ	07979	908-439-2154	439-4088	622
Purolator Inc 5995 Avebury Rd *TF:* 888-744-7123 ■ *Web:* www.purolator.com	Mississauga	ON	L5R3T8	905-712-8101		546
PuroSystems Inc 6001 Hiatus Rd Ste 13 *Web:* www.puroclean.com	Tamarac	FL	33321	954-597-1112		463
Purple Communications Inc 595 Menlo Dr *TF:* 800-900-9478 ■ *Web:* www.purplevrs.com	Rocklin	CA	95765	800-900-9478		387
Purple Cows Inc 3210 N Canyon Rd Ste 307 *Web:* www.purplecows.com	Provo	UT	84604	801-344-8532		194
Purple Forge Corp 900 Greenbank Rd Ste 315 *Web:* www.purpleforge.com	Ottawa	ON	K2J4P6	613-216-2148		224
Purple Heart Service Foundation 7008 Little River Tpke *Web:* www.purpleheartcars.org	Annandale	VA	22003	703-962-1684		303
Purple Parrot Cafe 3810 Hardy St *Web:* www.nsrg.com	Hattiesburg	MS	39402	601-264-0657		671
Purple Sage Motel 1501 E Coliseum Dr *Web:* www.placestostay.com	Snyder	TX	79549	325-573-5491		378
Purple Strategies LLC 815 Slaters Ln *Web:* www.purplestrategies.com	Alexandria	VA	22314	703-548-7877		5
Pursuant 5151 Belt Line Rd Ste 900 *TF:* 800-835-6770 ■ *Web:* www.pursuant.com	Dallas	TX	75254	214-866-7700		317
Pursuit Boats 3901 St Lucie Blvd *TF:* 800-947-8778 ■ *Web:* www.pursuitboats.com	Fort Pierce	FL	34946	772-465-6006	465-6177	90
Pursuit Group, The 31 N Erie St *TF:* 866-478-7783 ■ *Web:* www.thepursuitgroup.com	Toledo	OH	43604	866-478-7783		195
Pursuit of Excellence Inc 10440 N Central Expy Ste 1250 *TF:* 800-356-2025 ■ *Web:* poehr.com	Dallas	TX	75231	214-452-7881		734
Purtis Creek State Park 14225 FM 316 *Web:* tpwd.texas.gov/state-parks/purtis-creek	Eustace	TX	75124	903-425-2332		565
Purves & Assoc Insurance 500 Fourth St *TF:* 800-681-2025 ■ *Web:* purvesinsurance.com	Davis	CA	95616	530-756-5561		390
Purvis Ford Inc 3660 Jefferson Davis Hwy Ste 1 Ste 1 *Web:* purvisford.net	Fredericksburg	VA	22408	540-898-3000		57
Purvis Systems 88 Silva Ln *Web:* www.purvis.com	Middletown	RI	02842	401-849-4750	849-0121	177
PUSH 22 30300 Telegraph Rd *Web:* www.pushtwentytwo.com	Bingham Farms	MI	48025	248-335-9500		5
Push Inc 101 Ernestine St *Web:* www.pushhere.com	Orlando	FL	32801	407-841-2299		7
Push Product Design 2212 Second Ave N *Web:* www.pushpd.com	Birmingham	AL	35203	205-328-3112	328-3115	463
Pushmataha County 302 SW B St *Web:* www.usgennet.org	Antlers	OK	74523	580-298-2512		338
Putman Media Inc 1501 E Woodfield Rd Ste 400N *TF:* 866-666-6033 ■ *Web:* www.putman.net	Schaumburg	IL	60173	630-467-1300		637-9
Putnam Bank 40 Main St PO Box 151 *TF:* 877-275-3342 ■ *Web:* www.putnambank.com	Putnam	CT	06260	860-928-6501		70
Putnam Correctional Institution 128 Yelvington Rd *Web:* www.myflorida.com	East Palatka	FL	32131	386-326-6800	312-2219	213
Putnam County 40 Gleneida Ave Rm 100 *Web:* www.putnamcountyny.com	Carmel	NY	10512	845-225-3641	228-0231	338
Putnam County 121 S Dixie Ave *Web:* www.putnamcountytn.gov	Cookeville	TN	38501	931-526-7106	372-8201	338
Putnam County 117 Putnam Dr Ste A *TF:* 800-253-1077 ■ *Web:* www.putnamcountyga.us	Eatonton	GA	31024	706-485-5826	923-2345	338
Putnam County 1 Courthouse Sq St *Web:* www.co.putnam.in.us	Greencastle	IN	46135	765-653-2648		338
Putnam County 120 N Fourth St Putnam County Courthouse *Web:* www.co.putnam.il.us	Hennepin	IL	61327	815-925-7129	925-7549	338
Putnam County 130 Orie Griffin Blvd *TF:* 800-426-9975 ■ *Web:* putnamsheriff.org/en/home	Palatka	FL	32177	386 329 0808		338
Putnam County 12093 Winfield Rd *Web:* www.putnamcounty.org	Winfield	WV	25213	304-586-0202		338
Putnam County Chamber of Commerce 1100 Reid St *TF:* 800-654-4440 ■ *Web:* www.putnamcountychamber.com	Palatka	FL	32177	386-328-1503	328-7076	139
Putnam County Chamber of Commerce 5664 State Re 34 *Web:* www.putnamchamber.org	Winfield	WV	25213	304-757-6510	757-6562	139
Putnam County Commissioners 245 E Main St Ste 101 *Web:* www.putnamcountyohio.com	Ottawa	OH	45875	419-523-3656		338
Putnam County Convention & Visitors Bureau 971 WV Route 34 Ste 1 *Web:* www.putnamcountycvb.com	Hurricane	WV	25526	304-757-7282		206
Putnam County District Library 136 Putnam Pkwy *Web:* www.mypcdl.org	Ottawa	OH	45875	419-523-3747	523-6477	434-3
Putnam County Library 50 E Broad St *Web:* www.pclibrary.org	Cookeville	TN	38501	931-526-2416	372-8517	434-3
Putnam County Public Library 103 E Poplar St *Web:* pcpl21.org	Greencastle	IN	46135	765-653-2755		434-3
Putnam County Savings Bank (PCSB) 2477 Rt 6 PO Box 417 *Web:* www.pcsb.com	Brewster	NY	10509	845-279-7101	279-9175	71
Putnam Family of Funds PO Box 41203 *TF:* 800-225-1581 ■ *Web:* www.putnam.com	Providence	RI	02940	800-225-1581		528
Putnam Investments 30 Dan Rd PO Box 8383 *TF:* 888-478-8626 ■ *Web:* www.putnam.com	Canton	MA	02021	617-292-1000		401
Putnam Lexus 390 Convention Way *TF:* 888-231-8005 ■ *Web:* www.putnamlexus.com	Redwood City	CA	94063	650-363-8500		57
Putnam Memorial State Park 499 Black Rock Tpke *Web:* www.ct.gov	Redding	CT	06896	203-938-2285		565
Putnam Museum of History & Natural Science 1717 W 12th St *TF:* 800-226-3369 ■ *Web:* putnam.org	Davenport	IA	52804	563-324-1933		522
Putnam Rolling Ladder Inc 32 Howard St *Web:* www.putnamrollingladder.com	New York	NY	10013	212-226-5147	941-1836	421
Putnam Valley School District Inc 146 Peekskill Hollow Rd *TF:* 800-666-5327 ■ *Web:* www.pvcsd.org	Putnam Valley	NY	10579	845-528-8143		685
Putnamville Correctional Facility 1946 W Hwy 40 **Fax:* Warden ■ *Web:* in.gov	Greencastle	IN	46135	765-653-8441	653-7461*	213
Putney Inc 1 Monument Sq Ste 400 *TF:* 866-683-0660 ■ *Web:* www.putneyvet.com	Portland	ME	04101	207-828-0880		238
Putney School 418 Houghton Brook Rd *TF:* 800-999-9080 ■ *Web:* www.putneyschool.org	Putney	VT	05346	802-387-5566	387-6278	622
Putzmeister America 1733 90th St *TF:* 800-553-3414 ■ *Web:* www.putzmeister.com	Sturtevant	WI	53177	800-553-3414		190

	Phone	Fax	Class
Puu o Mahuka Heiau State Monument 1151 Punchbowl St Rm 310 PO Box 621........Honolulu HI 96809 *Web:* www.hawaii.gov	808-587-0300	587-0311	565
Puu Ualakaa State Wayside 2760 Round Top Dr........................Honolulu HI 96809 *Web:* dlnr.hawaii.gov	808-587-0300		565
Puukohola Heiau National Historic Site 62-3601 Kawaihae Rd......................Kawaihae HI 96743 *Web:* www.nps.gov	808-882-7218	882-1215	564
Puyallup Public Library 333 S Meridian..............................Puyallup WA 98371 *TF:* 844-821-8911 ■ *Web:* www.cityofpuyallup.org	253-841-4321	841-5483	434-3
PV Fluid Products 11245 - Vly Ridge Dr NW Suit 322.............Calgary AB T3B5V4 *Web:* www.pvfluid.com	403-640-0331		358
PV Labs Inc 1074 Cooke Blvd................Burlington ON L7T4A8 *Web:* www.pv-labs.com	905-667-7202		692
PVA (Passenger Vessel Assn) 103 Oronoco St Ste 200..................Alexandria VA 22314 *TF:* 800-807-8360 ■ *Web:* www.passengervessel.com	703-518-5005	518-5151	49-21
PVA Consulting Group Inc 20865 Ch de la Cote Nord Ste 200...........Boisbriand QC J7E4H5 *TF:* 877-970-1970 ■ *Web:* www.pva.ca	450-970-1970		463
Pva Inc 2814 Eric Ln.......................Burlington NC 27215 *TF:* 800-274-2538 ■ *Web:* www.pvaglobal.com	336-217-4600		463
PVA Tepla America Inc 251 Corporate Terr..........................Corona CA 92879 *TF Sales:* 800-527-5667 ■ *Web:* pvateplaamerica.com	951-371-2500		203
PVEC 420 Straight Creek Rd PO Box 1528.........New Tazewell TN 37825 *Web:* billing.pve.coop	423-626-5204		245
PVG Asset Management Corp 24918 Genesee Trl Rd.........................Golden CO 80401 *TF:* 800-777-0818 ■ *Web:* www.pvgassetmanagement.com	303-526-0548		401
PVH 200 Madison Ave........................New York NY 10016 *NYSE:* PVH ■ *TF:* 888-203-1112 ■ *Web:* www.pvh.com	212-381-3500		155-12
PVH Neckwear Inc 1735 S Santa Fe Ave.....................Los Angeles CA 90021 *Web:* www.pvh.com	213-688-7970		155-13
PVI Industries LLC 3209 Galvez Ave..........Fort Worth TX 76111 *TF:* 800-784-8326 ■ *Web:* www.pvi.com	817-335-9531	332-6742	91
PVS Chemicals Inc 10900 Harper Ave...........Detroit MI 48213 *TF:* 800-932-8860 ■ *Web:* www.pvschemicals.com	313-921-1200	921-1378	145
PVT (Penasco Valley Telecommunications) 4011 W Main St..............................Artesia NM 88210 *Fax Area Code: 575 ■ *TF:* 800-505-4844 ■ *Web:* www.pvt.com	800-505-4844	746-4142*	736
PV-Tron Inc 8810 Blvd Langelier...........Saint-Leonard QC H1P3H2 *Web:* www.pvtron.com	514-723-2131		196
PW Minor & Son Inc 3 Tread Easy Ave............Batavia NY 14020 *Fax Area Code: 585 ■ *TF:* 800-333-4067 ■ *Web:* www.pwminor.com	800-333-4067	343-1514*	301
PW Stephens Inc 15201 Pipeline Ln Unit B............Huntington Beach CA 92649 *TF:* 800-750-7733 ■ *Web:* www.pwsei.com	714-892-2028	891-9807	667
Pwc Industries Inc 6650 Leopard St......................Corpus Christi TX 78409 *Web:* www.pwcindustries.com	361-289-0557		537
PWH (Palms West Hospital) 13001 Southern Blvd...................Loxahatchee FL 33470 *TF:* 877-549-9337 ■ *Web:* www.palmswesthospital.com	561-798-3300		374-3
PWP (Pentwater Wire Products Inc) 474 Carroll St PO Box 947....................Pentwater MI 49449 *TF:* 877-869-6911 ■ *Web:* www.pentwaterwire.com	231-869-6911	869-4020	286
PW-Philadelphia Weekly 1500 Sansom St 3rd Fl...................Philadelphia PA 19102 *Web:* www.philadelphiaweekly.com	215-563-7400	563-0620	532-5
PWR LLC 6402 Deere Rd.......................Syracuse NY 13206 *TF:* 800-342-0878 ■ *Web:* www.pwrllc.com	315-701-0210	701-0217	767
PXP Inc 2485 Merritt Dr......................Garland TX 75041 *Web:* www.pxpsolutions.com	214-221-7669		627
PYB (Pennsylvania Youth Ballet) 556 Main St............................Bethlehem PA 18018 *Web:* www.bglv.org	610-865-0353		573-1
Pybus Point Lodge PO Box 33497..................Juneau AK 99803 *TF:* 800-947-9287 ■ *Web:* pybuspoint.com	907-790-4866	790-4866	669
Pyco Industries Inc PO Box 841..............Lubbock TX 79404 *TF:* 800-289-7266 ■ *Web:* www.pycoindustriesinc.com	806-747-3434		296-29
PYLUSD (Placentia-Yorba Linda Unified School District) 1301 E Orangethorpe Ave...................Placentia CA 92870 *Web:* www.pylusd.org	714-996-2550		685
Pymatuning State Park PO Box 1000...........Andover OH 44003 *Web:* www.ohiodnr.com	440-293-6030		565
Pymatuning State Park 2660 Williamsfield Rd...................Jamestown PA 16134 *Web:* www.dcnr.state.pa.us	724-932-3141		565
Pyng Medical Corp 210, 13480 Crestwood Pl.................Richmond BC V6V2J9 *TF:* 800-798-1822 ■ *Web:* www.pyng.com	604-303-7964	303-7987	250
Pyramax Bank FSB 7001 W Edgerton Ave....................Greenfield WI 53220	414-421-8200		70
Pyramid Brewing Co 91 S Royal Brougham Way.....................Seattle WA 98134 *TF:* 800-732-0330 ■ *Web:* www.pyramidbrew.com	206-682-8322	682-8420	102
Pyramid Brokerage Co 5786 Widewaters Pkwy.....................Syracuse NY 13214 *Web:* www.pyramidbrokerage.com	315-445-1030		652
Pyramid Checks & Printing Inc 208 Riverside Indus Pkwy.....................Portland ME 04103 *Web:* www.pyramidchecks-printing.com	207-878-9832		627
Pyramid Communications Inc 1932 First Ave Ste 507.......................Seattle WA 98101 *Web:* pyramidcommunications.com	206-374-7788		636
Pyramid Construction Inc 275 N Franklin Tpke.........................Ramsey NJ 07446 *Web:* www.pyramidgroup.biz	201-327-1919	327-0054	187
Pyramid Consulting Inc 11100 Atlantis Pl........................Alpharetta GA 30022 *TF:* 877-248-0024 ■ *Web:* www.pyramidci.com	678-514-3500		225
Pyramid Cos 4 Clinton Sq......................Syracuse NY 13202 *Web:* www.pyramidmg.com	315-422-7000		655
Pyramid Floor Covering Inc 38 Harbor Park Dr....................Port Washington NY 11050 *Web:* www.pyramidfloors.com	516-932-7200		290
Pyramid Grill 1717 N Akard St...................Dallas TX 75201 *TF:* 800-442-1162 ■ *Web:* www.pyramidrestaurant.com	214-720-5249		671
Pyramid Healthcare Solutions Inc 14141 46th St N Ste 1212................Clearwater FL 33762 *Web:* www.pyramidhs.com	727-431-3000		196
Pyramid Hotel Group LLC 1 Post Office Sq Ste 3100.....................Boston MA 02109 *TF:* 800-624-3310 ■ *Web:* www.pyramidadvisors.com	617-412-2800		378
Pyramid Interiors Distributors Inc PO Box 181058..........................Memphis TN 38181 *TF:* 800-456-0592 ■ *Web:* www.pyramidinteriors.com	901-375-4197		191-3
Pyramid Masonry Contractors Inc 2330 Mellon Ct............................Decatur GA 30035 *TF:* 800-536-2225 ■ *Web:* pyramidmasonry.net	770-987-4750	981-7142	189-7
Pyramid Mountain Lumber Inc 379 Boy Scout Rd PO Box 549............Seeley Lake MT 59868 *TF:* 888-800-6135 ■ *Web:* www.pyramidlumber.com	406-677-2201	677-2509	683
Pyramid Peak Design 2950 N Academy Blvd Ste 200.........Colorado Springs CO 80917 *TF:* 800-319-8862 ■ *Web:* pyramidpeak.com	719-598-1186		809
Pyramid Point Post-Acute Rehabilitation Ctr 8530 Township Line Rd..................Indianapolis IN 46260 *TF:* 800-861-0086 ■ *Web:* covenantcare.com/locations	317-876-9955	876-6016	450
Pyramid Precision Machine Inc 6721 Cobra Way.........................San Diego CA 92121 *Web:* www.pyramidprecision.com	858-642-0713		454
Pyramid Software Development Inc 4008 Louetta Rd #404........................Spring TX 77388 *Web:* pyramidsdi.com	281-350-2535		177
Pyramid State Recreation Area 1562 Pyramid Pk Rd.....................Pinckneyville IL 62274 *Web:* www.dnr.illinois.gov/parks/pages/pyramid.aspx	618-357-2574		565
Pyramid Tubular Products LP 2 Northpoint Dr Ste 610.....................Houston TX 77060 *Web:* www.pyramidtubular.com	281-405-8090		539
Pyro-Comm Systems Inc 15531 Container Ln..................Huntington Beach CA 92649 *Web:* www.pyrocomm.com	714-902-8000		693
Pyromation Inc 5211 Industrial Rd..............Fort Wayne IN 46825 *TF:* 800-837-6805 ■ *Web:* www.pyromation.com	260-484-2580	482-6805	201
Pyron Solar Inc 1216 Liberty Way Ste A............Vista CA 92081 *Web:* www.pyronsolar.com	760-599-5100		610
Pyronics Inc 17700 Miles Rd..................Cleveland OH 44128 *TF:* 800-883-9218 ■ *Web:* www.selas.com	216-662-8800	663-8954	318
Pyrotechnic Specialties Inc 1661 Juniper Creek Rd.........................Byron GA 31008 *Web:* www.pyrotechonline.com	478-956-5400		268
Pyrotek Inc 9503 E Montgomery Ave...............Spokane Valley WA 99206 *Web:* www.pyrotek.com	509-926-6212	927-2408	127
Pyrotek Special Effects Inc 7676 Woodbine Ave Ste 7 & 8..................Markham ON L3R2N2 *Web:* www.pyrotekfx.com	905-479-9991		149
Pyure Brands 2277 Trade Ctr Way................Naples FL 34109 *Web:* www.pyuresweet.com	305-509-5096		296-37
Pzena Investment Management Inc 120 W 45th St 20th Fl.....................New York NY 10036 *NYSE:* PZN ■ *Web:* www.pzena.com	212-355-1600		401

Q

	Phone	Fax	Class
Q & D Construction Inc 1050 S 21st St...........Sparks NV 89431 *Web:* www.qdconstruction.com	775-786-2677		186
Q 101.9 6222 NW IH-10......................San Antonio TX 78201 *Web:* q1019.iheart.com	210-736-9700	735-8811	645-143
Q 104.3 32 Ave of the Americas................New York NY 10013 *TF:* 888-872-1043 ■ *Web:* www.q1043.com	212-377-7900		645-111
Q Analysts LLC 4320 Stevens Creek Blvd Ste 130.............San Jose CA 95129 *Web:* www.qanalysts.com	408-907-8500		194
Q Carriers Inc 1415 Maras St.................Shakopee MN 55379 *Web:* www.qcarriers.com	952-445-8718	445-8794	780
Q Center 1405 N Fifth Ave................Saint Charles IL 60174 *TF:* 877-774-4627 ■ *Web:* www.qcenter.com	630-377-3100		31
Q Haute Cuisine 100 LaCaille Pl SW............Calgary AB T2P5E2 *Web:* www.qhautecuisine.com	403-262-5554	237-6108	671
Q Holdings Inc 615 Arapeen Dr Ste 102.................Salt Lake City UT 84108 *Web:* www.qthera.com	801-582-5400		529
Q Interactive Inc 1601 NW 136th Ave...........Sunrise FL 33323	954-653-9000		7
Q Prime Inc 729 Seventh Ave Lbby..............New York NY 10019 *Web:* www.qprime.com	212-302-9790		344
Q. Grady Minor & Associates PA 3800 Via Del Rey.....................Bonita Springs FL 34134 *Web:* www.gradyminor.com	239-947-1144		261
Q.A. Technologies Inc 222 S 15th St Ste 1404.......................Omaha NE 68102 *Web:* www.qat.com	402-391-9200		180
Q102 111 Presidential Blvd Ste 100...........Bala Cynwyd PA 19004 *TF:* 800-521-1021 ■ *Web:* q102.iheart.com	610-784-3333		645
Q104.5- FM (CR) 950 Houston Northcutt Blvd Ste 201......Mount Pleasant SC 29464 *TF:* 844-289-7234 ■ *Web:* q1045.iheart.com	843-884-2534		645
Q105.1 Rocks 2720 Seventh Ave S................Fargo ND 58103 *Web:* www.q1051rocks.com	701-237-4500		645-58
Q93 929 Howard Ave......................New Orleans LA 70113 *Web:* q93.iheart.com	504-679-7300	679-7345	645-110
QA Systems Inc 503 Oakland Ave................Austin TX 78703 *Web:* www.qasystems.com	713-396-0792		180

Name / Address	City	State	ZIP	Phone	Fax	Class
Qa1 Precision Products Inc 21730 Hanover Ave.	Lakeville	MN	55044	952-985-5675		620
Web: www.qa1.net						
QACVB (Quincy Area Convention & Visitors Bureau) 532 Gardner Expy	Quincy	IL	62301	217-214-3700		206
TF: 800-978-4748 ■ *Web:* www.seequincy.com						
QAD Inc 100 Innovation Pl	Santa Barbara	CA	93108	805-566-6100	565-4202	178-1
NASDAQ: QADB ■ *Web:* www.qad.com						
Qal-Tek Associates LLC 3998 Commerce Cir	Idaho Falls	ID	83401	208-523-5557		582
Web: www.qaltek.com						
Qantas Airways Cargo 6555 W Imperial Hwy	Los Angeles	CA	90045	310-665-2280	665-2201	12
TF General: 800-227-0290 ■ *Web:* www.qantas.com/travel/airlines/home/us/en						
Qantas Airways Ltd 6080 Ctr Dr Ste 400	Los Angeles	CA	90045	310-726-1400		25
TF: 800-227-4500 ■ *Web:* www.qantas.com/travel/airlines/home/us/en						
Qatar 809 UN Plaza 4th Fl	New York	NY	10017	212-486-9335	758-4952	784
Web: www.un.org						
Consulate General 1990 Post Oak Blvd Ste 900	Houston	TX	77056	713-355-8221	355 8184	257
Embassy 2555 M St NW	Washington	DC	20037	202-274-1600		257
Qb Corp 1420 Highway 28	Salmon	ID	83467	208-756-4248		817
Web: www.qbcorp.com						
QBE Farmers Union Insurance 5619 DTC Pkwy Ste 300	Greenwood Village	CO	80111	303-337-5500	338-2211	391-4
TF: 800-347-1961 ■ *Web:* www.farmersunioninsurance.com						
QBE Holdings Inc Wall St Plaza 88 Pine St	New York	NY	10005	212-422-1212	422-1313	391-4
TF: 800-362-5448 ■ *Web:* qbena.com						
QBE LLC 14604 Washington St Ste 200	Haymarket	VA	20169	571-766-1022		174
Web: www.qbe.net						
QBE Reinsurance Corp 55 Water St	New York	NY	10041	212-422-1212		391-4
Web: qbena.com						
QC Data International Inc 8000 E Maplewood Ave Ste 300	Greenwood Village	CO	80111	303-783-8888		225
Web: www.qcdata.com						
QC Holdings Inc 9401 Indian Creek Pkwy Ste 1500	Overland Park	KS	66210	866-660-2243		141
NASDAQ: QCCO ■ *TF:* 866-660-2243 ■ *Web:* www.qcholdings.com						
QC Laboratories Inc 10810 Northwest Fwy	Houston	TX	77092	713-695-1133		743
Web: www.qclabs.com						
QCA Systems Ltd #16 7355 72 St	Delta	BC	V4G1L5	604-940-0868		261
Web: www.qcasystems.com						
QCC (Quality Control Corp) 7315 W Wilson Ave	Howard Heights	IL	60706	708-867-5400	887-5009	621
Web: www.qccorp.com						
Qcera Inc 11041 Santa Monica Blvd Ste 818	Los Angeles	CA	90025	310-473-7988		180
Web: www.qcera.com						
Qchc Inc 200 narrows pkwy	Birmingham	AL	35242	205-437-1512		363
Web: www.qchcweb.com						
QCI Asset Management 40A Grove St	Pittsford	NY	14534	585-218-2060	218-2013	401
TF: 800-836-3960 ■ *Web:* www.e-qci.com						
QCP (Quaker City Plating) PO Box 2406	Whittier	CA	90610	562-945-3721		482
Web: www.quakercityplating.com						
QCSS Inc 21925 Field Pkwy Ste 210	Deer Park	IL	60010	847-229-7046		317
TF: 888-229-7046 ■ *Web:* www.qcssinc.com						
Qdigital Corp 6037 S Ft Apache Rd Ste 100	Las Vegas	NV	89148	702-360-9371		180
Web: www.qdigital.com						
Qdoba Restaurant Corp 4865 WaRd Rd Ste 500	Wheat Ridge	CO	80033	720-898-2300	629-2396*	670
**Fax Area Code:* 303 ■ *Web:* www.qdoba.com						
QED Group LLC, The 1820 N Ft Myer Dr Ste 700	Arlington	VA	22209	703-678-4700		463
Web: www.qedgroupllc.com						
QED Inc 1661 W Third Ave	Denver	CO	80223	303-825-5011	893-5019	246
TF: 800-700-5011 ■ *Web:* www.qedelectric.com						
QED Instruments Inc 2920 S Halladay St	Santa Ana	CA	92705	714-546-6010		21
Web: www.qedinstruments.com						
Qed Systems Inc 4646 N Witchduck Rd	Virginia Beach	VA	23455	757-490-5000	490-5027	547
Web: www.qedsysinc.com						
Qeh2 LLC 401 S Wilcox St Ste 202	Castle Rock	CO	80104	303-688-7531		179
Web: www.qeh2.com						
QEP Co Inc 1001 Broken Sound Pkwy NW Ste A	Boca Raton	FL	33487	561-994-5550	241-2830	758
OTC: QEPC ■ *TF Sales:* 800-777-8665 ■ *Web:* www.qep.com						
Q-flex Inc 1301 E Hunter Ave	Santa Ana	CA	92705	714-664-0101		625
Web: qflexinc.com						
QFlow Systems LLC 9317 Manchester Rd	St. Louis	MO	63119	314-968-9906		177
Web: www.qflowsystems.com						
QHR Corp 1620 Dickson Ave Ste 300	Kelowna	BC	V1Y9Y2	250-448-7095		177
TF: 855-550-5004 ■ *Web:* www.qhrtechnologies.com						
Qiva Inc 299 Kansas St	San Francisco	CA	94103	415-762-6000		809
Web: www.qiva.com						
Qivana 5255 Edgewood Dr	Provo	UT	84604	888-874-8262		366
TF: 888-874-8262						
Q-Lab Corp 800 Canterbury Rd	Westlake	OH	44145	440-835-8700		201
Web: www.q-lab.com						
Qlan Corp 23232 Peralta Dr 117	Laguna Hills	CA	92653	949-597-8560		225
TF: 800-353-4679 ■ *Web:* www.griffinoptometric.com						
QlikTech International AB 150 N Radnor Chester Rd Ste E220	Radnor	PA	19087	888-828-9768	975-5987*	178-10
NASDAQ: QLIK ■ **Fax Area Code:* 610 ■ *TF:* 888-828-9768 ■ *Web:* qlik.com						
QLogic Corp 26650 Aliso Viejo Pkwy	Aliso Viejo	CA	92656	949-389-6000	389-6114	696
NASDAQ: QLGC ■ *TF:* 800-662-4471 ■ *Web:* www.qlogic.com						
Qmf Metal & Electronic Solutions Inc 324 Berry Garden Rd	Kernersville	NC	27284	336-996-5570		697
Web: www.qmf-usa.com						
QMI (Quality Mfg Company Inc) PO Box 616	Winchester	KY	40392	859-744-0420		454
TF: 866-460-6459 ■ *Web:* www.qmiky.com						
QNB Corp 15 N Third St PO Box 9005	Quakertown	PA	18951	215-538-5600	538-5765	70
OTC: QNBC ■ *TF:* 800-491-9070 ■ *Web:* qnbbank.com/2690/mirror/redirect.htm						
QOREX LLC 101 Hammer Mill Rd Millbrook Business Ctr	Rocky Hill	CT	06067	860-727-1031		538
Web: www.petrospec.com						
Qosina Corp 2002-Q Orville Dr N	Ronkonkoma	NY	11779	631-242-3000		476
Web: www.qosina.com						
Qosmedix 2002 Orville Dr N	Ronkonkoma	NY	11779	631-242-3270	242-3291	214
TF: 800-421-4772 ■ *Web:* www.qosmedix.com						
QPI Multipress Inc 2222 S Third St	Columbus	OH	43207	614-228-0185	228-2358	456
Web: www.multipress.com						
QPM Aerospace Inc 14341 Fryelands Blvd	Monroe	WA	98272	360-794-9925		697
Web: www.qpm2000.com						
Qrp Inc 2307 Mercantile Dr NE	Leland	NC	28451	910-371-0700		350
Web: www.qrp-inc.com						
QRS Music Technologies 2011 Seward Ave	Naples	FL	34109	239-597-5888		527
Web: www.qrsmusic.com						
QS/Togo Inc 355 Jay St	Coldwater	MI	49036	517-278-2391	279-4680	719
Web: www.qsti.com						
QSA ToolWorks LLC 3100 47th Ave	Long Island	NY	11101	516-935-9151		178-7
TF: 800-784-7018 ■ *Web:* www.qsatoolworks.com						
QSC Audio Products LLC 1675 MacArthur Blvd	Costa Mesa	CA	92626	714-754-6175	754-6174*	52
**Fax:* Mktg ■ *TF:* 800-854-4079 ■ *Web:* www.qsc.com						
QSI (Quality Systems Inc) 18111 Von Karman Ave Ste 600	Irvine	CA	92612	949-255-2600	255-2605	178-10
NASDAQ: QSII ■ *TF Cust Svc:* 800-888-7955 ■ *Web:* www.qsii.com						
QSL Print Communications Inc 3000 Pierce Pkwy	Springfield	OR	97477	541-687-1184		194
Web: www.qslprinting.com						
Qsoft Consulting 38 Baldwin Ln	Glastonbury	CT	06033	860-777-9022		196
TF: 800-648-0686 ■ *Web:* www.qsoftconsultingllc.com						
QSR Automations Inc 2301 Stanley Gault Pkwy	Louisville	KY	40223	502-297-0221		177
Web: www.qsrautomations.com						
QSS Group Inc 4500 Forbes Blvd Ste 200	Lanham	MD	20706	301-577-0700	918-4822	393
Qst Consultations Ltd 11275 Edgewater Dr	Allendale	MI	49401	616-895-5461		231
TF: 866-757-4751 ■ *Web:* qstconsultations.com						
QST Industries Inc 550 W Adams St Ste 200	Chicago	IL	60661	312-930-9400	648-0312	34
Web: www.qst.com						
QST Magazine 225 Main St	Newington	CT	06111	860-594-0200	594-0259	457-14
TF: 888-277-5289 ■ *Web:* arrl.org/members-only/page/16609						
QStar Technologies Inc 8738 Ortega Park Dr	Navarre	FL	32566	850-243-0900		177
Web: www.qstar.com						
QTEC Solutions Inc 110 N Lincoln Ave Ste 201	Corona	CA	92882	951-270-5357		403
Web: www.qtec.us						
Q-tech Corp 10150 Jefferson Blvd	Culver City	CA	90232	310-836-7900	836-2157	253
Web: www.q-tech.com						
QTI (Qual-Tron Inc) 9409 E 55th Pl	Tulsa	OK	74145	918-622-7052	664-8557	253
Web: www.qual-tron.com						
Q-tran Inc 304 Bishop Ave	Bridgeport	CT	06610	203 367-8777		253
Web: www.q-tran.com						
Quabaug Corp 18 School St	North Brookfield	MA	01535	800-842-7267		301
TF: 800-842-7267						
Quabbin Capital Inc 160 Federal St	Boston	MA	02110	617-330-9041		401
Web: www.quabbincapital.com						
Quaboag Hills Chamber of Commerce 3 Converse St	Palmer	MA	01069	413-283-2418	289-1355	139
Web: www.qhma.com						
Quad Cities Chamber 1601 River Dr Ste 310	Moline	IL	61265	309-757-5416		139
Web: www.quadcitieschamber.com						
Quad Cities Convention & Visitors Bureau 1601 River Dr Ste 110	Moline	IL	61265	309-277-0937	764-9443	206
TF: 800-747-7800 ■ *Web:* www.visitquadcities.com						
Quad Cities Realty 1053 Ripon Ave	Lewiston	ID	83501	208-798-7798		652
TF: 877-798-7798 ■ *Web:* qcrhomes.com						
Quad City Bank & Trust 3551 Seventh St	Moline	IL	61265	309-736-3580		360-2
NASDAQ: QCRH ■ *TF:* 866-676-0551 ■ *Web:* www.qcbt.com						
Quad City Botanical Ctr 2525 Fourth Ave	Rock Island	IL	61201	309-794-0991		97
Web: www.qcgardens.com						
Quad City Conservation Alliance Expo Ctr 2621 Fourth Ave	Rock Island	IL	61201	309-788-5912	788-9619	205
TF: 800-273-5436 ■ *Web:* www.qccaexpocenter.com						
Quad Three Group Inc 37 N Washington St	Wilkes-Barre	PA	18701	570-829-4200		261
Web: www.quad3.com						
Quad/Graphics Inc N63 W23075 Main St	Sussex	WI	53089	414-566-6000		627
NYSE: QUAD ■ *Web:* www.qg.com						
Quad656 LLC 656 E Swedesford Rd	Wayne	PA	19087	610-687-6441		260
Web: www.quad656.com						
Quadbase Systems Inc 275 Saratoga Ave Ste 105	Santa Clara	CA	95050	408-982-0835	982-0838	178-7
Web: www.quadbase.com						
Quad-City Peterbilt Inc 8100 N Fairmount St	Davenport	IA	52806	888-774-1618	391-0295*	516
**Fax Area Code:* 563 ■ *TF:* 888-774-1618 ■ *Web:* www.graskpeterbilt.com						
Quad-City Times 500 E Third St	Davenport	IA	52801	563-383-2200	383-2370	532-2
TF: 800-437-4641 ■ *Web:* www.qctimes.com						
Quaddick State Park c/o Mashamoquet Brook State Pk 147 Wolf Den Dr	Pomfret Center	CT	06259	860-928-6121		565
Web: www.ct.gov						
Quadel Consulting 1200 G St NW Ste 700	Washington	DC	20005	202-789-2500	898-0632	194
TF: 866-640-1019 ■ *Web:* www.quadel.com						
Quadel Industries Inc 93759 Troy Ln	Coos Bay	OR	97420	541-269-7351		596
Web: www.quadel.net						
Quadis Technologies Inc 5925 s 56th st.	Lincoln	NE	68516	402-423-4660		138
Web: www.summitgroupsoftware.com						

Company	City	State	Zip	Phone	Fax	Class
Quadlogic Controls Corp 3300 Northern Blvd Fl 2 *TF:* 877-797-6347 ■ *Web:* www.quadlogic.com	Long Island	NY	11101	212-930-9300		196
QuadMed W227 N6103 Sussex Rd *Web:* www.quad-med.com	Sussex	WI	53089	414-566-8100		793
Quadra Chemicals Ltd 3901 Fixtessier *TF:* 800-665-6553 ■ *Web:* www.quadra.ca	Vaudreuil-Dorion	QC	J7V5V5	450-424-0161		146
Quadra Tech Inc 864 E Jenkins Ave *TF:* 800-443-2766 ■ *Web:* www.quadra-techinc.com	Columbus	OH	43207	800-443-2766		198
Quadramed Inc 12110 Sunset Hills Rd Ste 600 *TF:* 800-393-0278 ■ *Web:* www.quadramed.com	Reston	VA	20190	703-709-2300		177
Quadrangle, The 3300 Darby Rd *Web:* www.sunriseseniorliving.com	Haverford	PA	19041	610-642-3000		672
Quadrant 4 System Corp 1501 Woodfield Rd Ste 205 *Web:* www.qfor.com	Rolling Meadows	IL	60173	732-798-3000		180
Quadrant Chemical 200 Industrial Blvd *Web:* www.quadrantchemical.com	Mckinney	TX	75069	972-542-0072		3
Quadrant Corp 14725 SE 36 St *Web:* www.quadranthomes.com	Bellevue	WA	98006	425-455-2900		653
Quadrant Engineering Plastic Products USA 2120 Fairmont Ave PO Box 14235 *TF:* 800-366-0300 ■ *Web:* www.quadrantplastics.com	Reading	PA	19612-4235	610-320-6600	320-6638	602
Quadrants Inc 49132 Wixom Tech Dr	Wixom	MI	48393	248-960-3900	960-9867	186
Quadrants Scientific Inc 10840 Thornmint Rd Ste 110 *Web:* www.quadscience.com	San Diego	CA	92127	858-618-4708		743
Quadratec Inc 1028 Saunders Ln *TF:* 800-745-6037 ■ *Web:* www.quadratec.com	West Chester	PA	19380	800-745-6037		791
Quadravest Capital Management Inc 77 King St W Royal Trust Tower Ste 4500 *Web:* www.quadravest.com	Toronto	ON	M5K1K7	416-304-4440		401
Quadrel Labeling Systems 7670 Jenther Dr *TF:* 800-321-8509 ■ *Web:* www.quadrel.com	Mentor	OH	44060	440-602-4700		547
Quadrex Corp PO Box 3881 *TF Sales:* 800-275-7033 ■ *Web:* www.quadrexcorp.com	Woodbridge	CT	06525	203-393-3112	393-0391	333
Quadris Medical 2030 Lookout Dr *Web:* quadrismedical.com	North Mankato	MN	56003	507-385-2709		231
Quadriscan Inc 6600 Saint-Urbain St Ste 102 *Web:* quadriscan.com	Montreal	QC	H2S3G8	514-277-6022		627
QuadriSpace Corp 705 N Greenville Ave Ste 800 *TF:* 866-337-7223 ■ *Web:* www.quadrispace.com	Allen	TX	75002	972-359-6700		809
Quadros Systems Inc 13850 Gulf Fwy Ste 122 *Web:* quadros.com	Houston	TX	77034	832-351-2830		809
Quadrus Development Inc 640 - Eighth Ave SW Ste 400 *Web:* www.quadrus.com	Calgary	AB	T2P1G7	403-257-0850		180
QuadSystems LLC N61 W23044 Harry's Way *TF:* 866-246-7693	Sussex	WI	53089	866-246-7693		344
QuadW Technologies 600 Enterprise Dr Ste 225 *Web:* www.quadwinc.com	Oak Brook	IL	60523	630-694-4444		5
Quail Creek State Park 472 N 5300 W *Web:* www.stateparks.utah.gov	Hurricane	UT	84737	435-879-2378		565
Quail Hollow Resort 11080 Concord-Hambden Rd *Web:* www.quailhollowresort.com	Painesville	OH	44077	440-497-1100		669
Quail Lodge Resort & Golf Club 8205 Valley Greens Dr *TF:* 866-675-1101 ■ *Web:* www.quaillodge.com	Carmel	CA	93923	831-624-2888		669
Quail Springs Mall 2501 W Memorial Rd *Web:* www.quailspringsmall.com	Oklahoma City	OK	73134	405-755-6530		460
Quail Tools LP 3713 Hwy 14 *Web:* www.quailtools.com	New Iberia	LA	70560	337-364-0407		540
Quaintance-Weaver Inc 324 W Wendover Ave *Web:* www.qwrh.com	Greensboro	NC	27408	336-370-0966	370-0965	379
Quaker BioVentures 2929 Arch St Cira Ctr *Web:* www.quakerbio.com	Philadelphia	PA	19104	215-988-6800	988-6801	792
Quaker Chemical Corp 901 Hector St *NYSE:* KWR ■ *TF:* 800-523-7010 ■ *Web:* quakerchem.com	Conshohocken	PA	19428	610-832-4000	832-8682	145
Quaker City Castings 310 E Euclid Ave *Web:* quakercitycastings.com	Salem	OH	44460	330-332-1566	332-1159	307
Quaker City Plating (QCP) PO Box 2406 *Web:* www.quakercityplating.com	Whittier	CA	90610	562-945-3721		482
Quaker Funds 1180 W Swedesford Rd Ste 150 *TF:* 800-220-8888 ■ *Web:* www.quakerfunds.com	Berwyn	PA	19312	610-455-2200		401
Quaker Gardens 12151 Dale St *Web:* rowntreegardens.org	Stanton	CA	90680	714-530-9100		672
Quaker Heights Nursing Home Inc 514 High St *TF:* 800-319-1317 ■ *Web:* www.quakerheights.org	Waynesville	OH	45068	513-897-6050		371
Quaker Hill Conference Ctr 10 Quaker Hill Dr *Web:* www.qhcc.org/facilities.shtml	Richmond	IN	47374	765-962-5741		673
Quaker Mfg Corp 187 Georgetown Rd *Web:* www.quakermfg.com	Salem	OH	44460	330-332-4631	332-1519	488
Quaker Oats Co 555 W Monroe St *TF:* 800-367-6287 ■ *Web:* www.quakeroats.com	Chicago	IL	60661	312-821-1000		296-36
Quaker Valley School District 203 Graham St *Web:* www.qvsd.org	Sewickley	PA	15143	412-749-3600		685
Quaker Window Products Inc 504 S Hwy 63 PO Box 128 *TF:* 800-347-0438 ■ *Web:* www.quakerwindows.com	Freeburg	MO	65035	800-347-0438		234
Qualaroo Inc 1901 Newport Blvd Ste 175 *TF:* 888-449-3364 ■ *Web:* qualaroo.com	Costa Mesa	CA	92627	888-449-3364		387
Quala-Tel Enterprises 9925 Business Park Ave Ste A *TF:* 800-442-1504 ■ *Web:* www.qualatel.com	San Diego	CA	92131	858-577-2900		195
Qualchoice of Arkansas Inc 12615 Chenal Pkwy Ste 300 *Web:* www.qualchoice.com	Little Rock	AR	72211	501-228-7111		363
Qualcomm Inc 5775 Morehouse Dr *NASDAQ:* QCOM ■ *Web:* www.qualcomm.com	San Diego	CA	92121	858-587-1121	658-2100	735
Qualcomm Stadium 9449 Friars Rd *TF:* 800-400-7115 ■ *Web:* www.sandiego.gov/qualcomm	San Diego	CA	92108	619-641-3100	283-0460	720
QualCorp Inc 27240 Turnberry Ln Ste 200 *TF:* 888-367-6775 ■ *Web:* qualcorp.com	Valencia	CA	91355	661-799-0033		809
Qual-Craft Industries PO Box 559 *TF:* 800-231-5647 ■ *Web:* www.qualcraft.com	Stoughton	MA	02072	781-344-1000		350
Qualex Consulting Services Inc 1111 Kane Concourse Ste 320 *TF:* 877-887-4727 ■ *Web:* www.qlx.com	Bay Harbor Islands	FL	33154	877-887-4727		180
Qual-fab Inc 34250 Mills Rd *Web:* www.qual-fab.net	Avon	OH	44011	440-327-5000		697
Quali Tech Inc 318 Lake Hazeltine Dr *TF:* 800-328-5870 ■ *Web:* www.qualitechco.com	Chaska	MN	55318	952-448-5151	448-3603	447
Qualicaps Inc 6505 Franz Warner Pkwy *TF:* 800-227-7853 ■ *Web:* www.qualicaps.com	Whitsett	NC	27377	336-449-3900	449-3333	582
Qualico Steel Co Inc PO Box 149 *TF:* 866-234-5382 ■ *Web:* www.qualicosteel.com	Webb	AL	36376	334-793-1290	794-0996	480
Qualicom Systems Inc 2100 Electronics Ln *Web:* www.lightningradio.net	Fort Myers	FL	33912	239-481-8700		736
Qualified Remodeler Magazine 1233 Janesville Ave *TF:* 800-547-7377 ■ *Web:* www.forresidentialpros.com	Fort Atkinson	WI	53538	847-920-5996		457-21
Qualified Resources International LLC 78 Kenwood St *Web:* www.qristaffing.com	Cranston	RI	02907	401-946-1002		631
Qualified Staffing Services 5361 Gateway Centre Ste D *Web:* www.q-staffing.com	Flint	MI	48507	810-230-0368		260
Qualigen Inc 2042 Corte Del Nogal *Web:* www.qualigeninc.com	Carlsbad	CA	92011	760-918-9165		419
Qualigence Inc 35200 Schoolcraft Rd *Web:* www.qualigence.com	Livonia	MI	48150	734-432-6300		193
Qualis Corp 689 Discovery Dr NW Ste 400 *Web:* www.qualis-corp.com	Huntsville	AL	35806	256-971-1707		261
Qualis Health PO Box 33400 *TF:* 800-949-7536 ■ *Web:* www.qualishealth.org	Seattle	WA	98133	206-364-9700		374-3
QualiTau Inc 830 Maude Ave *Web:* qualitau.com	Mountain View	CA	94043	408-522-9200		253
Qualitek International Inc 315 Fairbank St *Web:* www.qualitek.com	Addison	IL	60101	630-628-8083	628-6543	145
Qualitek Services Inc 700 N Wickham Rd Ste 101 *TF:* 800-568-4468 ■ *Web:* www.qualitek.biz	Melbourne	FL	32935	321-259-2400		260
Qualitel Corp 11831 Beverly Pk Rd *Web:* qualitel.com	Everett	WA	98204	425-423-8388	423-8398	253
QualiTest Ltd 1139 Post Rd *TF:* 877-882-9540 ■ *Web:* www.qualitestgroup.com	Fairfield	CT	06824	877-882-9540		393
Qualitor Inc 24800 Denso Dr Ste 255 *Web:* www.qualitorinc.com	Southfield	MI	48033	248-204-8600	204-8619	504
Qualitrol Company LLC 1385 Fairport Rd *Web:* www.qualitrolcorp.com	Fairport	NY	14450	585-586-1515	377-0220	201
Quality Administration 14466 N US Hwy 169 *Web:* www.qualityadmin.com	Smithville	MO	64089	816-532-2090		463
Quality Air Heating & Cooling Inc 3395 Kraft Ave SE *Web:* www.qualityaironline.com	Grand Rapids	MI	49512	616-956-6776		697
Quality Aluminum Products Inc 14544 Telegraph Rd	Flat Rock	MI	48134	734-783-0990		697
Quality Asset Recovery 7 Foster Ave Ste 101 *Web:* www.qarcollect.com	Gibbsboro	NJ	08026	856-925-1010		160
Quality Beef Producers 5000 I-40	Wildorado	TX	79098	806-426-3325		10-1
Quality Bending & Fabrication Inc 10005 SW Herman Rd *Web:* qbfinc.com	Tualatin	OR	97062	503-692-0430		454
Quality Beverage Inc 525 Miles Standish Blvd	Taunton	MA	02780	508-822-6200		81-1
Quality Bicycle Products Inc 6400 W 105th St *Web:* peopleforbikes.org	Bloomington	MN	55438	952-941-9391		82
Quality Biological Inc 7581 Lindbergh Dr *TF:* 800-992-2537 ■ *Web:* www.qualitybiological.com	Gaithersburg	MD	20879	301-840-9331		231
Quality Bioresources Inc 1015 N Austin St *TF:* 888-674-7224 ■ *Web:* www.qualbio.com	Seguin	TX	78155	830-372-4797		415
Quality Books Inc 1003 W Pines Rd *TF Cust Svc:* 800-323-4241 ■ *Web:* www.quality-books.com	Oregon	IL	61061	815-732-4450	732-4499	96
Quality Built LLC 401 SE 12th St Ste 200 *TF:* 800-547-5125 ■ *Web:* www.qualitybuilt.com	Fort Lauderdale	FL	33316	954-358-3500		194
Quality Business Solutions Inc 280 Hindman Rd *Web:* qualitybsolutions.net	Travelers Rest	SC	29690	864-834-3985		194
Quality Cable & Electronics 1780 NW 15th Ave Ste 400 *Web:* www.qualitycable.com	Pompano Beach	FL	33069	954-532-0165		116
Quality Castings Co 1200 N Main St *Web:* www.qcfoundry.com	Orrville	OH	44667	330-682-6010	683-3153	307
Quality Circuit Assembly 1709 Junction Ct Ste 380 *Web:* www.qcamfg.com	San Jose	CA	95112	408-441-1001		625

Company	City	State	ZIP	Phone	Fax	Class
Quality Circuits Inc 1102 Progress Dr *Web:* www.qciusa.com	Fergus Falls	MN	56537	218-739-9707	739-9705	625
Quality Control Corp (QCC) 7315 W Wilson Ave *Web:* www.qccorp.com	Howard Heights	IL	60706	708-867-5400	887-5009	621
Quality Control Inspection Inc 40 Tarbell Ave *Web:* qcigroup.com	Cleveland	OH	44146	440-359-1900		365
Quality Craft Ltd 17750-65A Ave Ste 301 *TF:* 800-663-2252 ■ *Web:* www.qualitycraft.com	Surrey	BC	V3S5N4	604-575-5550		290
Quality Custom Cabinetry Inc 125 Peters Rd *Web:* www.qcc.com	New Holland	PA	17557	717-661-6900		115
Quality Customs Broker Inc 4464 S Whitnall Ave *TF:* 888-813-4647 ■ *Web:* www.qualitybrokers.com	Saint Francis	WI	53235	414-482-9447	482-9448	311
Quality Dining Inc 4220 Edison Lakes Pkwy *TF:* 800-589-3820 ■ *Web:* www.qdi.com	Mishawaka	IN	46545	574-271-4600	271-4612	670
Quality Distribution Inc 4041 Pk Oaks Blvd Ste 200 *NASDAQ: QLTY* ■ *TF:* 800-282-2031 ■ *Web:* www.qualitydistribution.com	Tampa	FL	33610	800-282-2031		780
Quality Edge Inc 2712 Walkent Dr NW *TF:* 888-784-0878 ■ *Web:* www.qualityedge.com	Walker	MI	49544	888-784-0878		490
Quality Electrodynamics LLC 700 Beta Dr *Web:* www.qualedyn.com	Mayfield Village	OH	44143	440-638-5106		383
Quality Enclosures Inc 2025 Porter Lake Dr *TF:* 800-881-0051 ■ *Web:* www.qualityenclosures.com	Sarasota	FL	34240	941-378-0051		320
Quality Engineering & Tool Company Inc 380 S Wheatfield St *TF:* 800-637-6809 ■ *Web:* qes1.com	York	PA	17403	203-269-5054		454
Quality Filters Inc 7215 Jackson Rd *Web:* qualityfiltersinc.com	Ann Arbor	MI	48103	734-668-0211		483
Quality Filtration LLC 5215 Linbar Dr Ste 204 *Web:* www.qualityfiltration.com	Nashville	TN	37211	615-833-2400		45
Quality Flow Systems Inc 800 Sixth St NW *Web:* qfsi.net	New Prague	MN	56071	952-758-9445		358
Quality Food Centers 10116 NE 8th *Web:* www.qfconline.com	Bellevue	WA	98004	425-455-0870		345
Quality Forms 4317 W US Rt 36 **Fax Area Code:* 888 ■ *TF:* 866-773-4595 ■ *Web:* www.qualforms.com	Piqua	OH	45356	937-773-4595	550-3937*	110
Quality Frozen Foods Inc 1663 62nd St *Web:* www.qualityfrozenfoods.com	Brooklyn	NY	11204	718-256-9100		297-6
Quality Fuel Networks Inc 15227 herriman blvd *Web:* www.qualityfuel.com	Noblesville	IN	46060	317-774-1076		463
Quality Gold Inc 500 Quality Blvd *TF:* 800-354-9833 ■ *Web:* www.qgold.com	Fairfield	OH	45014	800-354-9833		411
Quality Group Inc, The 5825 Glenridge Dr Ste 3-101 *Web:* opusworks.com	Atlanta	GA	30328	404-843-9525		194
Quality Hill Playhouse 303 W Tenth St *TF:* 800-745-3000 ■ *Web:* www.qualityhillplayhouse.com	Kansas City	MO	64105	816-421-1700		572
Quality Honeycomb LP 624 107th St *Web:* www.qualityhoneycomb.com	Arlington	TX	76011	817-640-1190		21
Quality Hotel-airport 7228 Wminster Hwy *TF:* 877-244-3051 ■ *Web:* qualityhotelvancouverairport.com	Richmond	BC	V6X1A1	604-244-3051		379
Quality Hydraulics & Pneumatics Inc 1415 Wilhelm Rd *Web:* www.qualityhydraulics.com	Mundelein	IL	60060	847-680-8400		358
Quality Incentive Co 3962 Willow Lake Blvd *Web:* www.qualityincentivecompany.com	Memphis	TN	38118	901-367-8200		463
Quality Industries Inc 130 Jones Blvd *TF:* 800-745-8613 ■ *Web:* www.qualityindustries.com	La Vergne	TN	37086	615-793-3000		697
Quality Inn & Suites Naples Golf Resort 4100 Golden Gate Pkwy *TF:* 800-277-0017 ■ *Web:* www.naplesgolfresort.com	Naples	FL	34116	239-455-1010	455-4038	669
Quality Inn Flamingo 1300 N Stone Ave *TF:* 800-792-4885 ■ *Web:* www.flamingohoteltucson.com	Tucson	AZ	85705	520-770-1910	770-0750	379
Quality Inn Halifax Airport 60 Sky Blvd *TF:* 800-667-3333 ■ *Web:* www.airporthotelhalifax.com	Goffs	NS	B2T1K3	902-873-3000		379
Quality IP LLC 145 S River St *Web:* www.qualityip.com	Kent	OH	44240	330-931-4141		562
Quality King Distributors Inc 35 Sawgrass Dr Ste 3 *Web:* www.qkd.com	Bellport	NY	11713	631-737-5555		238
Quality Liquid Feeds Inc PO Box 240 *TF:* 800-236-2345 ■ *Web:* www.qlf.com	Dodgeville	WI	53533	608-935-2345		276
Quality Logistics Systems Inc PO Box 5637 *Web:* www.qualitylogistics.com	Meridian	MS	39302	601-483-0265	483-7928	803-1
Quality Machine & Welding Company Inc PO Box 27345 *Web:* www.qmwkx.com	Knoxville	TN	37927	865-524-2162	524-1830	480
Quality Management Solutions LLC 146 Lowell St Ste 300B *TF:* 800-645-6430 ■ *Web:* www.qmsinc.com	Wakefield	MA	01889	800-645-6430		196
Quality Manufacturing Company Inc 5855 Rockwell Rd *Web:* www.qmiparts.com	Winchester	KY	40391	859-744-0420		454
Quality Manufacturing Corp 4300 NW Urbandale Dr *Web:* qualitymfgcorp.com	Urbandale	IA	50322	515-331-4300		492
Quality Manufacturing Inc 969 Labore Industrial Ct *TF:* 800-243-5473 ■ *Web:* www.qualitymanufacturing.com	Saint Paul	MN	55110	651-483-5473	483-1101	701
Quality Mat Co 6550 Tram Rd *TF:* 800-227-8159 ■ *Web:* www.qmat.com	Beaumont	TX	77713	409-722-4594		131
Quality Meats & Seafoods 700 Center St *TF:* 800-342-4250 ■ *Web:* www.qualitymeats.com	West Fargo	ND	58078	701-282-0202		473
Quality Media Resources Inc 10929 SE 23rd St *TF:* 800-800-5129 ■ *Web:* qmr.com	Bellevue	WA	98004	425-455-0558		463
Quality Medical Reimbursement Services 6695 Highland Rd Ste 106	Waterford	MI	48327	248-666-4266		2
Quality Metal Fabricators Inc 2610 E Fifth Ave *Web:* www.qmf.com	Tampa	FL	33605	813-831-7320		697
Quality Metal Finishing Company Inc 421 N Walnut St *Web:* www.qmfco.com	Byron	IL	61010	815-234-2711		609
Quality Metal Products Inc Orange Rd RR 3 PO Box 273 A *TF:* 888-251-2805 ■ *Web:* www.qualmet.com	Dallas	PA	18612	570-333-4248	333-4967	697
Quality Metalcraft Inc 33355 Glendale St *Web:* www.qualitymetalcraft.com	Livonia	MI	48150	734-261-6700	261-5180	757
Quality Metals Inc 2575 Doswell Ave *Web:* www.qualitymetalsinc.com	St Paul	MN	55108	651-645-5875		492
Quality Mfg Company Inc (QMI) PO Box 616 *TF:* 866-460-6459 ■ *Web:* www.qmiky.com	Winchester	KY	40392	859-744-0420		454
Quality Mold Inc 2200 Massillon Rd *Web:* www.qualitymold.com	Akron	OH	44312	330-645-6653		604
Quality Naturally Foods 18830 E San Jose Ave *Web:* www.qnfoods.com	City of Industry	CA	91748	626-854-6363	965-0978	68
Quality of Life Health Services Inc 1411 Piedmont Cutoff PO Box 97 *TF:* 888-490-0131 ■ *Web:* www.qolhs.org	Gadsden	AL	35902	256-492-0131		374-3
Quality Oil Company LLC 1540 Silas Creek Pkwy *Web:* www.qualityoilnc.com	Winston-Salem	NC	27127	336-722-3441	721-9520	324
Quality Oil Inc 55 N 400 E	Valparaiso	IN	46383	219-462-2951		690
Quality Packaging State Hwy V *Web:* www.qpsima.com	Jackson	MO	63755	573-334-6700		549
Quality Perforating Inc 166 Dundaff St *TF:* 800-872-7373 ■ *Web:* www.qualityperf.com	Carbondale	PA	18407	570-282-4344	282-4627	488
Quality Petroleum Inc 11610 Maybelline Dr *TF:* 800-952-7085 ■ *Web:* www.qualitypetroleuminc.com	North Little Rock	AR	72117	501-955-2166		579
Quality Plywood Specialties Inc 4500 110th Ave N *TF:* 888-722-1181 ■ *Web:* www.qualityplywoodspec.com	Clearwater	FL	33762	727-572-0500	571-3623	191-3
Quality Pork Processors Inc 711 Hormel Century Pkwy *Web:* www.qppinc.net	Austin	MN	55912	507-434-6300		473
Quality Parks International Inc 10404 F Plaza *Web:* www.qpii.com	Omaha	NE	68127	402-339-1911	339-8383	473
Quality Progress *ASQ* 600 N Plankinton Ave PO Box 3005 *TF Cust Svc:* 800-248-1946 ■ *Web:* www.asq.org/pub/qualityprogress	Milwaukee	WI	53201	414-272-8575	272-1734	457-21
Quality Roll LLC 3090 Perkins St *Web:* www.qualityroll.com	Saginaw	MI	48601	810-397-5665		480
Quality Sausage Company Ltd 1925 Lone Star Dr *Web:* www.qualitysausage.com	Dallas	TX	75212	214-634-3400		296-26
Quality Solutions Inc 128 N First St *TF:* 888-328-2454 ■ *Web:* www.qsifacilities.com	Colwich	KS	67030	316-721-3656		261
Quality Sprinkler Company Inc 10301 Old Concord Rd *TF:* 855-880-3998 ■ *Web:* www.qualitysprinkler.com	Charlotte	NC	28213	704-549-8220		610
Quality State Oil Company Inc 2201 Calumet Dr *Web:* www.qualitystateoil.biz	Sheboygan	WI	53083	920-459-5640		579
Quality Synthetic Rubber Inc 1700 Highland Rd *Web:* www.qsr-inc.com	Twinsburg	OH	44087	330-425-8472		677
Quality Systems Inc (QSI) 18111 Von Karman Ave Ste 600 *NASDAQ: QSII* ■ *TF Cust Svc:* 800-888-7955 ■ *Web:* www.qsii.com	Irvine	CA	92612	949-255-2600	255-2605	178-10
Quality Systems Integrated Corp 6720 Cobra Way *Web:* www.qsic.com	San Diego	CA	92121	858-587-9797		625
Quality Systems Solutins Inc 6905 Zachary Dr *Web:* www.qualitysystemssolutions.com	Carpentersville	IL	60110	847-426-9548		809
Quality Tech Services Inc 10525 Hampshire Ave S *Web:* www.qtspackage.com	Bloomington	MN	55438	952-942-8321		476
Quality Technology Services Nj LLC 95 Christopher Columbus Dr *Web:* www.qtitechnology.com	Jersey City	NJ	07302	212-625-7200		387
Quality Texas Foundation 201 Woodland Pk Ste 143 *Web:* www.texas-quality.org	Georgetown	TX	78633	512-656-8946		303
Quality Tool & Stamping Company Inc 541 E Sherman Blvd *Web:* www.qtstamping.com	Muskegon	MI	49444	231-733-2538	733-0983	488
Quality Tool Inc 1220 Energy Park Dr *TF:* 866-997-4647 ■ *Web:* www.qualitytool.com	Saint Paul	MN	55108	651-646-7433		697
Quality Tower Erectors & Service Inc 2280 Tenth St SE *Web:* www.qualitytower.com	Largo	FL	33771	727-585-6176		57
Quality Transformer & Electronics 963 Ames Ave *Web:* www.qte.com	Milpitas	CA	95035	408-263-8444		767
Quality Transportation 36-40 37th St Ste 201 *TF:* 800-677-2838 ■ *Web:* www.qualitytca.com	Long Island	NY	11101	212-308-6333	308-6595	311
Quality Vision International Inc 850 Hudson Ave *Web:* www.qvii.com	Rochester	NY	14621	585-544-0450		544

Name / Address	City	State	ZIP	Phone	Fax	Class
Quality Wholesale Bldg Inc 11701 KinaRd Rd	North Little Rock	AR	72117	501-945-3442		191-3
QualMark Corp 10390 E 48th Ave *Web:* www.qualmark.com	Denver	CO	80238	303-254-8800		407
Qualnetics Corp 2183 Alpine Way *Web:* www.qualnetics.com	Bellingham	WA	98226	360-733-4151		177
Qualortran Inc 236 Carpenter Rd NE *Web:* qualortran.com	Calhoun	GA	30701	706-295-4510		261
Qual-pro Corp 18510 S Figueroa St *Web:* www.qual-pro.com	Gardena	CA	90248	310-329-7535		625
QualPro Inc 3117 Pellissippi Pkwy *TF:* 800-264-0281 ■ *Web:* www.qualproinc.com	Knoxville	TN	37931	865-927-0491		196
Qualstar Corp 3990-B Heritage Oak Ct *NASDAQ: QBAK* ■ *TF:* 800-468-0680 ■ *Web:* www.qualstar.com	Simi Valley	CA	93063	805-583-7744	583-7749	173-8
Qualtech Inc 1880 Leon-Harmel St *TF:* 888-339-3801 ■ *Web:* www.qualtech.ca	Quebec	QC	G1N4K3	418-686-3802		296
Qualtech Laboratories Inc 104 Green Grove Rd *Web:* www.qualtechlabsinc.com	Ocean	NJ	07712	732-918-0207		743
Qualtrics 2250 N University Pkwy Ste 48 C *Web:* www.qualtrics.com	Provo	UT	84604	801-374-6682		466
Qual-Tron Inc (QTI) 9409 E 55th Pl *Web:* www.qual-tron.com	Tulsa	OK	74145	918-622-7052	664-8557	253
QualVu Inc 12039 W Alameda Pkwy Ste Z-2 *Web:* www.qualvu.com	Lakewood	CO	80228	303-984-0218		387
Qualys Inc 1600 Bridge Pkwy *TF:* 866-801-6161 ■ *Web:* www.qualys.com	Redwood Shores	CA	94065	650-801-6100	801-6101	692
Quam-Nichols Company Inc 234 E Marquette Rd *TF:* 800-633-3669 ■ *Web:* www.quamspeakers.com	Chicago	IL	60637	773-488-5800	488-6944	52
Quandel Group Inc 3003 N Front St Ste 203 *TF:* 800-425-4450 ■ *Web:* www.quandel.com	Harrisburg	PA	17110	717-657-0909	652-6282	186
Quanex Building Products 2270 Woodale Dr *TF:* 800-233-4383 ■ *Web:* www.quanex.com	Mounds View	MN	55112	763-231-4000		499
Quanex Building Products Corp 1900 W Loop S Ste 1500 *TF Cust Svc:* 888-475-0633 ■ *Web:* quanex.com	Houston	TX	77027	713-961-4600		235
Quang 2719 Nicollet Ave *Web:* www.quangrestaurant.com	Minneapolis	MN	55408	612-870-4739		671
Quanta Laboratories 3199 De La Cruz Blvd *TF:* 800-552-5546 ■ *Web:* www.quantalabs.com	Santa Clara	CA	95054	408-988-0770		743
Quanta Services Inc 1360 Post Oak Blvd Ste 2100 *NYSE: PWR* ■ *TF:* 800-872-0615 ■ *Web:* www.quantaservices.com	Houston	TX	77056	713-629-7600	629-7676	188-1
Quantcast Corp 201 Third St 2nd Fl *Web:* www.quantcast.com	San Francisco	CA	94103	415-738-4755		387
Quantec Geoscience Ltd 146 Sparks Ave *Web:* quantecgeo.com	Toronto	ON	M2H2S4	416-306-1941		727
Quantech Corp 4528 21st St *TF:* 800-392-3300 ■ *Web:* quantech.net	Long Island City	NY	11101	718-433-1024		809
Quantem Aviation Services Inc 175 Ammon Dr *Web:* qasllc.aero	Manchester	NH	03103	603-647-1717		650
Quantenna Communications Inc 3450 W Warren Ave *TF:* 800-503-4611 ■ *Web:* www.quantenna.com	Fremont	CA	94538	510-743-2260		201
Quantex Laboratories 22 Distribution Blvd *TF:* 800-223-7905 ■ *Web:* www.quantexlabs.com	Edison	NJ	08817	732-248-3335		743
Quantiam Technologies Inc 1651 - 94 St NW *TF:* 877-461-0707 ■ *Web:* www.quantiam.com	Edmonton	AB	T6N1E6	780-462-0707	465-6603	668
Quantico National Cemetery 18424 Joplin Rd *Web:* www.cem.va.gov	Triangle	VA	22172	703-221-2183	221-2185	136
Quantimetrix Corp 2005 Manhattan Beach Blvd *TF:* 800-624-8380 ■ *Web:* quantimetrix.com	Redondo Beach	CA	90278	310-536-0006	536-9977	231
QuantiTech Inc 360A Quality Cir Ste 100 *Web:* www.quantitech.com	Huntsville	AL	35806	256-650-6263		463
Quantlab Financial LLC 3 Greenway Plaza Ste 200 *Web:* www.quantlab.com	Houston	TX	77046	713-333-5440		401
Quantopian Inc 77 Summer St *Web:* www.quantopian.com	Boston	MA	02110	617-752-1454		387
Quantros Inc 691 S Milpitas Blvd Ste 100 *Web:* www.quantros.com	Milpitas	CA	95035	408-957-3300		177
Quantrum Llc 2371 Lkview Dr *Web:* quantrum-llc.com	Beavercreek	OH	45431	937-281-6272		525
Quantum Analytics 3400 East Third Ave *TF:* 800-992-4199 ■ *Web:* www.lqa.com	Foster City	CA	94404	650-312-0900		264-3
Quantum Audio Designs Inc 6408 State Hwy 77 *TF:* 888-545-4404 ■ *Web:* www.quantumaudiodesigns.com	Benton	MO	63736	573-545-4404		526
Quantum Automation Inc 4400 E La Palma Ave *Web:* www.quantumautomation.com	Anaheim	CA	92807	714-854-0800		463
Quantum Aviation Solutions 1720 Epps Bridge Pkwy Ste 108 Number 304 *Web:* www.quantum.aero	Athens	GA	30606	404-348-4839		177
Quantum Capital Management LLC 105 E Mill Rd *TF:* 800-541-7774 ■ *Web:* www.quantumadv.com	Northfield	NJ	08225	609-677-4949		401
Quantum Communications Corp 1266 E Main St Ste 6A	Stamford	CT	06902	203-388-0048	388-0054	643
Quantum Controls Inc 1691 Lake Dr W *Web:* www.quantum-controls.com	Chanhassen	MN	55317	952-361-3694		203
Quantum Corp 224 Airport Pkwy Ste 300 *NYSE: QTM* ■ *TF Tech Supp:* 800-677-6268 ■ *Web:* www.quantum.com	San Jose	CA	95110	408-944-4000		173-8
Quantum Corp 11431 Willows Rd NE **Fax Area Code: 651* ■ *TF:* 800-284-5101 ■ *Web:* www.quantum.com	Redmond	WA	98052	425-881-8004	297-3996*	176
Quantum Corporate Funding Ltd 1140 Ave of the Americas 16th Fl *TF:* 800-352-2535 ■ *Web:* www.quantumfunding.com	New York	NY	10036	212-768-1200	944-8216	272
Quantum Crossings LLC 111 E Wacker Dr Ste 990 *Web:* www.quantumcrossings.com	Chicago	IL	60601	312-467-0065		186
Quantum Dental Technologies Inc 748 Briar Hill Ave *TF:* 866-993-9910 ■ *Web:* www.thecanarysystem.com	Toronto	ON	M6B1L3	866-993-9910		228
Quantum Design Inc 6325 Lusk Blvd *Web:* www.qdusa.com	San Diego	CA	92121	858-481-4400		419
Quantum Devices Inc 112 Orbison St *Web:* www.quantumdev.com	Barneveld	WI	53507	608-924-3000		696
Quantum Dimension Inc 18672 Florida St Ste 302-D *Web:* www.qdimension.com	Huntington Beach	CA	92648	714-893-6004		681
Quantum Foods LLC 750 S Schmidt Rd	Bolingbrook	IL	60440	630-679-2300		296-26
Quantum House 987 45th St *Web:* www.quantumhouse.org	West Palm Beach	FL	33407	561-494-0515	494-0522	372
Quantum Inc PO Box 2791 *TF:* 800-448-1448 ■ *Web:* www.quantumhealth.com	Eugene	OR	97402	541-345-5556		297
Quantum Information Systems Solutions Inc 2805 Pontiac Lake Rd Ste 2C *Web:* www.qinfosys.com	Waterford	MI	48328	248-393-3621		196
Quantum Laboratories Inc 28221 Beck Rd Ste A-11 *Web:* www.quantumlaboratories.com	Wixom	MI	48393	248-348-8378		743
Quantum Management Services Ltd 2000 McGill College Ave Ste 1800 *TF:* 800-978-2688 ■ *Web:* www.quantum.ca	Montreal	QC	H3A3H3	514-842-5555		734
Quantum Marine Engineering of Florida Inc 3790 SW 30th Ave *TF:* 800-807-8360 ■ *Web:* www.quantumhydraulic.com	Fort Lauderdale	FL	33312	954-587-4205		261
Quantum Plastics 21 N Main St *Web:* www.quantumplastics.com	Aberdeen	SD	57401	605-229-7001		596
Quantum Signal LLC 200 N Ann Arbor St *Web:* quantumsignal.com	Saline	MI	48176	734-429-9100		261
Quantum Technology Sciences Inc 1980 N Atlantic Ave Ste 201 *Web:* www.qtsi.com	Cocoa Beach	FL	32931	321-868-0288		261
Quantum Utility Generation LLC 1401 McKinney St Ste 1800 *Web:* www.quantumug.com	Houston	TX	77010	713-485-8600		787
Quantum/ATL 141 Innovation Dr *TF:* 800-677-6268 ■ *Web:* www.quantum.com	Irvine	CA	92617	949-856-7800	856-7799	173-8
Quantum3D Inc 5225 Hellyer Ave Ste 220 *TF:* 888-747-1020 ■ *Web:* www.quantum3d.com	San Jose	CA	95138	408-600-2500		173-2
QuantumDigital Inc 8702 Cross Park Dr Ste 200 *TF:* 800-637-7373 ■ *Web:* quantumdigital.com	Austin	TX	78754	512-837-2300	837-2777	5
Quantus Software 32-62 Scurfield Blvd	Winnipeg	MB	R3Y1M5	204-478-1308		193
Quapaw Quarter Assn 615 E Capitol Ave PO Box 165023 *Web:* www.quapaw.com	Little Rock	AR	72216	501-371-0075		50-3
Quark Inc 1800 Grant St *TF Cust Svc:* 800-676-4575 ■ *Web:* www.quark.com	Denver	CO	80203	800-676-4575		178-8
Quark Pharmaceuticals Inc 6501 Dumbarton Cir *Web:* quarkpharma.com	Fremont	CA	94555	510-402-4020		231
Quarles & Brady LLP 411 E Wisconsin Ave Ste 2400 *Web:* www.quarles.com	Milwaukee	WI	53202	414-277-5000	271-3552	428
Quarles Petroleum Inc 1701 Fall Hill Ave *TF:* 800-201-4328 ■ *Web:* www.quarlesinc.com	Fredericksburg	VA	22401	540-371-2400		581
Quarq Technology Inc 3100 First Ave *TF:* 800-660-6853 ■ *Web:* www.quarq.com	Spearfish	SD	57783	605-642-2226		711
Quarry Hill Nature Ctr 701 Silver Creek Rd NE *TF:* 800-422-0798 ■ *Web:* www.qhnc.org	Rochester	MN	55906	507-328-3950	287-1345	50-5
Quarryhill Botanical Garden 12841 Sonoma Hwy PO Box 232 *Web:* www.quarryhillbg.org	Glen Ellen	CA	95442	707-996-3166	996-3198	97
Quarryville Presbyterian Retirement Community 625 Robert Fulton Hwy *Web:* www.quarryville.com	Quarryville	PA	17566	717-786-7321		672
Quartech Systems Ltd 2160 Springer Ave Ste 200 *Web:* www.quartech.com	Burnaby	BC	V5B3M7	604-291-9686		196
Quarter Master Industries Inc 510 Telser Rd *Web:* www.quartermasterusa.com	Lake Zurich	IL	60047	847-540-8999		247
Quarterpath Inn & Suites 620 York St *Web:* www.quarterpathinnandsuites.com	Williamsburg	VA	23185	757-220-0964		379
Quartier Printing Company Inc 5795 Bridge St E Syracuse *Web:* www.quartierprinting.com	Syracuse	NY	13057	315-449-0900		627
Quartino 626 N State St *Web:* www.quartinochicago.com	Chicago	IL	60610	312-698-5000		671
Quarton Partners LLC 300 Park St Ste 480 *Web:* www.quartoninternational.com	Birmingham	MI	48009	248-594-0400		70
Quartz Lake State Recreation Area c/o Northern Area Office 3700 Airport Way *Web:* www.dnr.alaska.gov	Fairbanks	AK	99709	907-451-2695		565
Quartz Mountain Resort & Conference Ctr 22469 Lodge Rd *TF:* 877-999-5567 ■ *Web:* www.quartzmountainresort.com	Lone Wolf	OK	73655	580-563-2424	563-2422	669
Quartzdyne Inc 4334 W Links Dr *TF:* 800-222-3611 ■ *Web:* www.quartzdyne.com	Salt Lake City	UT	84120	801-266-6958	266-7985	253

Name / Address	City	State	Zip	Phone	Fax	Class
Quasius Investment Corp 4805 Independence Pkwy Ste 100 *Web:* www.gca.net	Tampa	FL	33634	813-249-2514		196
Quast Janke & Co 1010 N Johnson St *Web:* qjc.com	Bay City	MI	48708	989-892-4549		2
Quatech Inc 5675 Hudson Industrial Pkwy *TF:* 800-553-1170 ■ *Web:* bb-elec.com	Hudson	OH	44236	330-655-9000	655-9010	625
Quatred LLC 532 Fourth Range Rd *TF:* 888-395-8534 ■ *Web:* www.quatred.com	Pembroke	NH	03275	888-395-8534		41
Quay County PO Box 1246 *Fax Area Code: 505 ■ *TF:* 800-708-8584 ■ *Web:* www.quaycounty-nm.gov	Tucumcari	NM	88401	575-461-2112	461-6208*	338
Quazar Capital Corp 3535 Plymouth Blvd Ste 210 *TF:* 800-875-8259 ■ *Web:* quazarcapital.com	Minneapolis	MN	55447	763-550-9000		401
Quebe Holdings Inc 1985 Founders Dr *Web:* www.quebe.com	Dayton	OH	45420	937-222-2290		246
Quebec 41 Boul Comtois *Web:* www.csssm.qc.ca	Louiseville	QC	J5V2H8	819-228-2731	228-0425	374-2
Quebec Inn 7175 Blvd Hamel Ouest *TF:* 800-567-5276 ■ *Web:* www.hotelsjaro.com/quebecinn/index-en.aspx	Quebec	QC	G2G1B6	418-872-9831	872-1336	379
Quebec Port Authority 150 Dalhousie St PO Box 80 Stn Haute-Ville *TF:* 800-465-1213 ■ *Web:* www.portquebec.ca	Quebec	QC	G1R4M8	418-648-3640	648-4160	618
Quebecor Media Inc 612 Rue St Jacques *Web:* www.quebecor.com	Montreal	QC	H3C4M8	514-380-1999		637-2
Quechee State Park 1 National Life Dr Davis 2 *Web:* www.vtstateparks.com	Montpelier	VT	05620	802-295-2990		565
Queen Anne Hotel 1590 Sutter St *TF:* 800-227-3970 ■ *Web:* www.queenanne.com	San Francisco	CA	94109	415-441-2828	775-5212	379
Queen Anne's County 107 N Liberty St *Web:* qac.org/410/qactv---website	Centreville	MD	21617	410-758-4098	758-1170	338
Queen Anne's County Chamber of Commerce 1561 Postal Rd *TF:* 800-638-6396 ■ *Web:* www.qacchamber.com	Chester	MD	21619	410-643-8530	643-8477	139
Queen Anne's County Library 121 S Commerce St *Web:* www.quan.lib.md.us	Centreville	MD	21617	410-758-0980	758-0614	434-3
Queen B 51 Means Dr	Platteville	WI	53818	608-349-2000		645
Queen Beach Printers Inc 937 Pine Ave *Web:* www.qbprinters.com	Long Beach	CA	90813	562-436-8201		174
Queen City Grill 2201 First Ave *Web:* www.queencitygrill.com	Seattle	WA	98121	206-441-4311		671
Queen City Printers Inc 701 Pine St *TF:* 800-639-8099 ■ *Web:* www.qcpinc.com	Burlington	VT	05401	802-864-4566		627
Queen City TV & Appliance Company Inc 2430 Queen City Dr *Web:* www.queencityonline.com	Charlotte	NC	28208	704-391-6000	391-6038	35
Queen City Wholesale Inc 1001 E Eighth St *Web:* queencitywholesale.com	Sioux Falls	SD	57103	605-336-3215	336-2423	756
Queen Communications LLC 1215 Anthony Ave *Web:* www.queencommunicationsllc.com	Columbia	SC	29201	803-779-0340		47
Queen Cutlery Co 507 Chestnut St *TF Sales:* 800-222-5233 ■ *Web:* www.queencutlery.com	Titusville	PA	16354	814-827-3673		222
Queen Emma Summer Palace 2913 Pali Hwy *TF:* 800-367-7060 ■ *Web:* daughtersofhawaii.org	Honolulu	HI	96817	808-595-3167	595-4395	50-3
Queen Kapiolani Hotel 150 Kapahulu Ave *TF:* 800-321-2558 ■ *Web:* www.queenkapiolani.com	Honolulu	HI	96815	808-922-1941		379
Queen of Angels Monastery 840 S Main St *Web:* www.benedictine-srs.com	Mount Angel	OR	97362	503-845-6141		50-1
Queen of the Valley Medical Ctr 1000 Trancas St *Web:* www.thequeen.org	Napa	CA	94558	707-252-4411		374-3
Queen Wilhelmina State Park 3877 Arkansas 88 *TF:* 888-287-2757 ■ *Web:* www.arkansasstateparks.com	Mena	AR	71953	479-394-2863		565
Queen's College Faculty of Theology 210 Prince Philip Dr Ste 3000 *TF:* 877-753-0116 ■ *Web:* www.queenscollegemun.ca	Saint John's	NL	A1B3R6	709-753-0116		167-3
Queen's Medical Ctr, The 1301 Punchbowl St *Web:* www.queensmedicalcenter.org	Honolulu	HI	96813	808-691-7171		374-3
Queen's School of Business Goodes Hall 143 Union St Rm 130 *Web:* smith.queensu.ca/index.php	Kingston	ON	K7L3N6	613-533-2301	533-2316	162
Queen's University 99 University Ave *TF:* 800-267-7837 ■ *Web:* www.queensu.ca	Kingston	ON	K7L3N6	613-533-2000	533-2068	785
Queen's University Faculty of Health Sciences 18 Barrie St *Web:* healthsci.queensu.ca	Kingston	ON	K7L3N6	613-533-2544	533-3190	167-2
Queens Borough Public Library 89-11 Merrick Blvd *Web:* www.queenslibrary.org	Jamaica	NY	11432	718-990-0700		434-3
Queens Botanical Garden 43-50 Main St *TF:* 800-433-4149 ■ *Web:* www.queensbotanical.org	Flushing	NY	11355	718-886-3800	463-0263	97
Queens Boulevard Extended Care Facility Corp 61-11 Queens Blvd *Web:* www.qbecf.com	Woodside	NY	11377	718-205-0287		793
Queens Chamber of Commerce 75-20 Astoria Blvd Ste 140 *TF:* 800-931-2297 ■ *Web:* www.queenschamber.org	Jackson Heights	NY	11370	718-898-8500	898-8599	139
Queens College 65-30 Kissena Blvd *TF:* 888-888-0606 ■ *Web:* www.qc.cuny.edu	Flushing	NY	11367	718-997-5000	997-5617	166
Queens County 120-55 Queens Blvd *Web:* www.queensda.org	Kew Gardens	NY	11415	718-286-6000		338
Queens County Farm Museum 73-50 Little Neck Pkwy *Web:* www.queensfarm.org	Floral Park	NY	11004	718-347-3276		520
Queens County Savings Bank 13665 Roosevelt Ave *Web:* www.mynycb.com	Flushing	NY	11354	718-460-4800		70
Queens Courier 38-15 Bell Blvd *TF:* 800-275-8777 ■ *Web:* qns.com	Bayside	NY	11361	718-224-5863	224-5441	532-4
Queens Hospital Ctr 82-68 164th St *TF:* 888-692-6116 ■ *Web:* nyc.gov	Jamaica	NY	11432	718-883-3000		374-3
Queens Museum of Art New York City Bldg *TF:* 866-867-9665 ■ *Web:* www.queensmuseum.org	Queens	NY	11368	718-592-9700	592-5778	520
Queens Tribune 150-50 14th Rd *Web:* www.queenstribune.com	New York	NY	11357	718-357-7400	357-9417	532-4
Queens University of Charlotte 1900 Selwyn Ave *Fax: Admissions ■ *TF:* 800-849-0202 ■ *Web:* www.queens.edu	Charlotte	NC	28274	704-337-2212	337-2403*	166
Queens Zoo 53-51 111th St *Web:* www.wcs.org	Flushing	NY	11368	718-271-1500		823
Queensboro Farm Products Inc 156-02 Liberty Ave Ste 2	Jamaica	NY	11433	718-658-5000		297-4
Queensborough Community College 222-05 56th Ave *Fax: Admissions ■ *TF:* 877-253-7122 ■ *Web:* www.qcc.cuny.edu	Bayside	NY	11364	718-631-6262	281-5189*	162
Queensborough National Bank and Trust Co 113 E Broad St PO Box 467 *TF:* 800-236-2442 ■ *Web:* www.qnbtrust.com	Louisville	GA	30434	478-625-2000	625-2008	780
Queensbury Union Free School 429 Aviation Rd *Web:* www.queensburyschool.org	Queensbury	NY	12804	518-824-5699		685
Queenston Heights National Historic Site 26 Queen St *Web:* www.pc.gc.ca/eng/lhn-nhs/on/queenston/index.aspx	Niagara-On-The-Lake	ON	L0S1J0	905-468-6614	468-4638	563
Queenstown Bank of Maryland 7101 Main St PO Box 120 *TF:* 888-827-4300 ■ *Web:* www.queenstown-bank.com	Queenstown	MD	21658	410-827-8881		70
Queensway-Carleton Hospital 3045 Baseline Rd *Web:* www.qch.on.ca	Ottawa	ON	K2H8P4	613-721-4700	721-2000	374-2
Quehanna Boot Camp 4395 Quehanna Hwy Staff *Web:* www.cor.pa.gov	Karthaus	PA	16845	814-263-4125		213
Quenzel Associates Inc 12801 University Dr *TF:* 800-332-1440 ■ *Web:* www.quenzel.com	Fort Myers	FL	33907	239-226-0040		7
Quest Capital Management Inc 8117 Preston Rd Ste 700 *Web:* www.questadvisor.com	Dallas	TX	75225	214-691-6090		401
Quest Companies Inc 8011 N Point Blvd Ste 201 *TF:* 800-467-9409 ■ *Web:* www.questcompaniesinc.com	Winston-salem	NC	27106	800-467-9409		7
Quest Controls Inc 208 Ninth St Dr W *Web:* www.questcontrols.com	Palmetto	FL	34221	941-729-4799		625
Quest Convergence Systems Inc 43 Metcalf Dr *TF:* 877-933-8776 ■ *Web:* questai.com	Belleville	IL	62223	618-398-3311		261
Quest Corp of America Inc 3837 Northdale Blvd # 242 *Web:* qcausa.com	Tampa	FL	33624	813-926-2942		636
Quest Diagnostics 1311 Calle Batido	San Clemente	CA	92673	949-940-7200		382
Quest Diagnostics at Nichols Institute 33608 Ortega Hwy *TF:* 800-642-4657 ■ *Web:* www.questdiagnostics.com	San Juan Capistrano	CA	92675	949-728-4000		418
Quest Diagnostics Inc 3 Giralda Farms *NYSE: DGX* ■ *TF:* 800-222-0446 ■ *Web:* www.questdiagnostics.com	Madison	NJ	07940	201-393-5000		418
Quest Discovery Services Inc 981 Ridder Park Dr *TF:* 800-477-5335 ■ *Web:* www.questds.com	San Jose	CA	95131	408-441-7000		428
Quest Engineering Inc 2300 Edgewood Ave S *TF:* 800-328-4853 ■ *Web:* www.questenginc.com	Minneapolis	MN	55426	952-546-4441		358
QUEST Integrated Inc 19823 58th Pl S *Web:* www.qi2.com	Kent	WA	98032	253-872-9500		419
Quest Integrated Solutions 31390 Viking Pkwy *Web:* www.dowlinggroup.com	Westlake	OH	44145	440-348-9687		180
Quest Investment Management Inc 1 S W Columbia St Ste 1100 *Web:* www.questinvestment.com	Portland	OR	97258	503-221-0158		401
Quest Partners LLC 126 E 56th St 19th Fl *Web:* www.questpartnersllc.com	New York	NY	10022	212-838-7222		401
Quest Service Group LLC 439 Oak St *Web:* www.questservicegroup.com	Garden City	NY	11530	516-594-7079		393
Quest Software Inc 5 Polaris Way *NASDAQ: QSFT* ■ *TF:* 800-306-9329 ■ *Web:* www.quest.com	Aliso Viejo	CA	92656	949-754-8000	754-8999	178-1
Quest Turnaround Advisors LLC 800 Westchester Ave Ste S-520 *Web:* www.qtadvisors.com	Rye Brook	NY	10573	914-253-8100		194
Questa Engineering Corporation 1220 Brickyard Cove Rd Ste 206	Point Richmond	CA	94801	510-236-6114		535
Questar Assessment Inc 5550 Upper 147th St W *OTC: QUSA* ■ *TF Cust Svc:* 800-800-2598 ■ *Web:* www.questarai.com	Apple Valley	MN	55124	952-997-2700		243
Questar Capital Corp 5701 Golden Hills Dr *TF:* 888-446-5872 ■ *Web:* www.questarcapital.com	Minneapolis	MN	55416	888-446-5872		690
Questar Gas Co PO Box 45841 *TF:* 800-323-5517 ■ *Web:* questargas.com	Salt Lake City	UT	84139	801-324-5111		787
Questar Gas Management Co PO Box 45360 *TF:* 800-323-5517 ■ *Web:* questargas.com	Salt Lake City	UT	84145	801-324-5111		325
Questar InfoComm Inc 180 East 100 South PO Box 45433 *TF:* 800-729-6790 ■ *Web:* www.questarpipeline.com	Salt Lake City	UT	84145	801-324-5856		736
QUESTAR LLC 2905 W Service Rd *Web:* questarweb.com	Eagan	MN	55121	651-688-0089		225

Company / Address	City	State	ZIP	Phone	Fax	Class
Questar Pipeline Co PO Box 45360 *Web:* www.questarpipeline.com	Salt Lake City	UT	84145	801-324-5601		325
Questco 100 Commercial Cir *TF:* 800-256-7823 ■ *Web:* questco.net	Conroe	TX	77304	936-756-1980		734
Questec Constructors Inc 1390 Boone Industrial Dr Ste 260 *Web:* questec.us	Columbia	MO	65202	573-875-0260		189-10
Questech Corp 92 Park St *Web:* www.questech.com	Rutland	VT	05701	802-773-1228		608
Questek Innovations LLC 1820 Ridge Ave *Web:* www.questek.com	Evanston	IL	60201	847-328-5800		177
Questel Orbit 1725 Duke St Ste 625 *TF:* 800-456-7248 ■ *Web:* www.questel.com	Alexandria	VA	22314	703-519-1820	519-1821	635
Questerre Energy Corp 1650 AMEC Place 801 Sixth Ave SW *Web:* www.questerre.com	Calgary	AB	T2P3W2	403-777-1185		536
Questex LLC 275 Grove St Ste 2-130 *TF:* 888-552-4346 ■ *Web:* www.questex.com	Newton	MA	02466	617-219-8300	219-8310	531-13
Questica Inc 980 Fraser Dr Ste 105 *TF:* 877-707-7755 ■ *Web:* www.questica.com	Burlington	ON	L7L5P5	877-707-7755		179
Questionmark Corp 5 Hillandale Ave *TF:* 800-863-3950 ■ *Web:* www.questionmark.com	Stamford	CT	06902	203-358-3950		177
Questmark Information Management Inc 9440 Kirby Dr *TF:* 800-932-4006 ■ *Web:* questmark.net	Houston	TX	77054	713-662-9022		627
Questor 700 E Maple Rd 2nd Fl *Web:* questor.com	Birmingham	MI	48009	248-593-1930	723-3907	194
Questor Technology Inc 1121 940 - Sixth Ave SW *TF:* 844-477-8669 ■ *Web:* www.questortech.com	Calgary	AB	T2P3T1	403-571-1530		539
QuestSoft Corp 23441 S Pointe Dr Ste 270 *TF:* 800-575-4632 ■ *Web:* www.questsoft.com	Laguna Hills	CA	92653	949-837-9506		35
Questus Inc 675 Davis St *Web:* www.questus.com	San Francisco	CA	94111	415-677-5700		7
Quetico LLC 5521 Schaefer Ave *Web:* www.queticollc.com	Chino	CA	91710	909-628-6200		88
Queue Inc 703 Post Rd *TF:* 800-232-2224 ■ *Web:* www.queueinc.com	Fairfield	CT	06824	800-232-2224	775-2729	178-3
Quez Media Marketing 1138 Prospect Ave E *Web:* www.quezmedia.com	Cleveland	OH	44115	216-910-0202		737
Quick Cable Corp 3700 Quick Dr *Web:* www.quickcable.com	Franksville	WI	53126	262-824-3100		116
Quick Color Solutions Inc 829 Knox Rd *TF:* 877-698-0951 ■ *Web:* www.quickcolorsolutions.com	Mc Leansville	NC	27301	336-698-0951		627
Quick Crete Products 731 Parkridge Ave *TF:* 866-703-3434 ■ *Web:* www.quickcrete.com	Norco	CA	92860	866-703-3434		191-1
Quick Eagle Networks Inc 830 Maude Ave	Mountain View	CA	94043	650-962-8282		176
Quick Electronics Inc 10800 76th Ct *Web:* www.quickelectronics.com	Largo	FL	33777	727-546-9299		175
Quick Fuel Fleet Services Inc 11815 W Bradley Rd **Fax Area Code: 414* ■ *TF:* 800-522-6287 ■ *Web:* www.quickfuel.com	Milwaukee	WI	53224	800-522-6287	359-1469*	316
Quick Point Inc 1717 Fenpark Dr *Web:* www.quickpoint.com	Fenton	MO	63026	636-343-9400		9
Quick Search 4155 Buena Vista *Web:* quicksius.com	Dallas	TX	75204	214-358-2880		635
Quick Tab II Inc 241 Heritage Dr *TF:* 800-332-5081 ■ *Web:* www.qt2.com	Tiffin	OH	44883	419-448-6622		627
Quick Tanks Inc PO Box 338 *Web:* www.quicktanks.com	Kendallville	IN	46755	260-347-3850	347-3853	481
Quick Technologies Inc 2508 Highlander Way Ste 200 *Web:* www.qti.com	Carrollton	TX	75006	214-631-6000		177
Quick Way Stampings Inc of Texas 915 Stanley Dr *Web:* sheetmetal-fabricating.com	Euless	TX	76040	817-267-1515		483
QuickCompliance Inc 8A Canal Ct *TF:* 800-752-5478 ■ *Web:* www.quickcompliance.net	Avon	CT	06001	860-676-9400		177
Quickdraft Inc 1525 Perry Dr SW *Web:* www.quickdraft.com	Canton	OH	44710	330-477-4574		358
Quicken Loans Arena 1 Ctr Ct *TF:* 888-894-9424 ■ *Web:* www.theqarena.com	Cleveland	OH	44115	216-420-2000		720
Quickie Manufacturing Corp 1150 Taylor Ln *Web:* www.quickie.com	Riverton	NJ	08077	856-829-7900		103
QuickLogic Corp 1277 Orleans Dr *NASDAQ: QUIK* ■ *Web:* www.quicklogic.com	Sunnyvale	CA	94089	408-990-4000	990-4040	696
Quickmill Inc 760 Rye St *TF:* 800-295-0509 ■ *Web:* www.quickmill.com	Peterborough	ON	K9J6W9	705-745-2961	745-8130	491
QuickPlay Media Inc 901 King St W Ste 200 *Web:* www.quickplay.com	Toronto	ON	M5V3H5	416-916-7529		736
Quicksilver Manufacturing Inc 42214 Sarah Way *Web:* www.quicksilveraircraft.com	Temecula	CA	92590	951-506-0061		20
QuickStart Intelligence Inc 6801 N Capital of Texas Hwy Ste 150 *TF:* 866-991-3924 ■ *Web:* www.quickstart.com	Austin	TX	78731	866-991-3924		177
Quidel Corp 10165 McKellar Ct *NASDAQ: QDEL* ■ *TF:* 800-874-1517 ■ *Web:* www.quidel.com	San Diego	CA	92121	858-552-1100	453-4338	231
Quiel Bros Sign Co 272 S 'I' St *TF:* 800-874-7446 ■ *Web:* www.quielsigns.com	San Bernardino	CA	92410	909-885-4476	888-2239	701
Quiet Light Communications Inc 220 E State St *TF:* 800-433-5778 ■ *Web:* www.quietlightcom.com	Rockford	IL	61104	815-398-6860		7
Quigley Mike (Rep D - IL) 2458 Rayburn HOB *Web:* quigley.house.gov	Washington	DC	20515	202-225-4061	225-5603	342-2
Quigley Tax Service SC 5822 W Fond Du Lac Ave *Web:* quigleytaxserv.com	Milwaukee	WI	53218	414-461-1800		734

Company / Address	City	State	ZIP	Phone	Fax	Class
Quik Stop Markets Inc 4567 Enterprise St *TF:* 800-972-0982 ■ *Web:* quikstop.com	Fremont	CA	94538	510-657-8500		204
Quik Travel Staffing Inc 175 E Olive Ave Ste 101 *TF:* 800-554-7501 ■ *Web:* www.qtstaffing.com	Burbank	CA	91502	818-569-3500		260
Quikbook 381 Pk Ave S 3rd Fl *TF:* 800-789-9887 ■ *Web:* www.quikbook.com	New York	NY	10016	212-779-7666		376
Quikey Manufacturing Co 1500 Industrial Pkwy *Web:* www.quikey.com	Akron	OH	44310	330-633-8106		9
Quikey Manufacturing Co Inc 100 Thorpe Rd *Web:* m.quikey.com	Orlando	FL	32824	407-859-7517		232
QUIKRETE Cos 3490 Piedmont Rd Ste 1300 *TF:* 800-282-5828 ■ *Web:* www.quikrete.com	Atlanta	GA	30305	404-634-9100	842-1424	183
Quiksilver Inc 15202 Graham St *NYSE: ZQK* ■ **Fax Area Code: 714* ■ *TF:* 800-435-9917 ■ *Web:* www.quiksilver.com	Huntington Beach	CA	92649	800-435-9917	889-2325*	155-3
Quikstik Labels 220 Broadway *TF:* 800-225-3496 ■ *Web:* www.qsxlabels.com	Everett	MA	02149	617-389-7570	381-9280	413
Quikteks LLC 373 US 46 *Web:* www.quikteks.com	Fairfield	NJ	07004	973-882-4644		180
Quiktrak Inc 9700 SW Nimbus Ave *TF:* 800-927-8725 ■ *Web:* www.quiktrak.com	Beaverton	OR	97008	800-927-8725		41
QuikTrip Corp 4705 S 129th E Ave *TF:* 800-441-0253 ■ *Web:* www.quiktrip.com	Tulsa	OK	74134	918-615-7700		204
Quiltcraft Industries Inc 1230 E Ledbetter Dr *Web:* quiltcraft.com	Dallas	TX	75216	214-376-1841	376-1852	361
Quilter's Newsletter Magazine 741 Corporate Cir Ste A *TF:* 800-477-6089 ■ *Web:* www.quiltersnewsletter.com	Golden	CO	80401	303-215-5600	215-5601	457-14
Quiltmaker Magazine 741 Corporate Cir Ste A *TF:* 800-388-7023 ■ *Web:* www.quiltmaker.com	Golden	CO	80401	800-881-6634		457-14
Quimby House Inn 109 Cottage St *TF:* 800-344-5811 ■ *Web:* www.quimbyhouse.com	Bar Harbor	ME	04609	207-288-5811		379
Quince 470 Pacific Ave *Web:* www.quincerestaurant.com	San Francisco	CA	94133	415-775-8500	775-8501	671
Quincy & Company Inc 144 Gould St *Web:* quincyinsurance.net	Needham Heights	MA	02494	781-431-9600		390
Quincy Area Chamber of Commerce 300 Civic Ctr Plaza Ste 245 *Web:* www.quincychamber.org	Quincy	IL	62301	217-222-7980	222-3033	139
Quincy Area Convention & Visitors Bureau (QACVB) 532 Gardner Expy *TF:* 800-978-4748 ■ *Web:* www.seequincy.com	Quincy	IL	62301	217-214-3700		206
Quincy College 1250 Hancock St *TF:* 800-698-1700 ■ *Web:* www.quincycollege.edu	Quincy	MA	02169	617-984-1700	984-1794	162
Plymouth 36 Cordage Pk Cir *TF:* 800-698-1700 ■ *Web:* www.quincycollege.edu	Plymouth	MA	02360	508-747-0400		162
Quincy Compressor 3501 Wismann Ln *Web:* www.quincycompressor.com	Quincy	IL	62305	217-222-7700		172
Quincy Correctional Institution 2225 Pat Thomas Pkwy *Web:* dc.state.fl.us	Quincy	FL	32351	850-627-5400	875-3572	213
Quincy Herald-Whig 130 S Fifth St *TF:* 800-373-9444 ■ *Web:* www.whig.com	Quincy	IL	62301	217-223-5100	221-3395	532-2
Quincy Hospitality House 1129 Oak St *Web:* www.blessinghospital.org	Quincy	IL	62301	217-228-3022		372
Quincy Medical Ctr 114 Whitwell St *Web:* steward.org	Quincy	MA	02169	617-773-6100		374-3
Quincy Mutual Fire Insurance Co 57 Washington St *TF:* 800-899-1116 ■ *Web:* www.quincymutual.com	Quincy	MA	02169	800-899-1116	899-7790	391-4
Quincy National Cemetery 36th & Maine St *TF:* 800-827-1000 ■ *Web:* www.cem.va.gov/cems/nchp/quincy.asp	Quincy	IL	62301	309-782-2094	782-2097	136
Quincy Newspapers Inc 130 S Fifth St *TF:* 800-373-9444 ■ *Web:* www.whig.com	Quincy	IL	62301	217-223-5100		637-8
Quincy Public Library 526 Jersey St *TF:* 800-779-4357 ■ *Web:* www.quincylibrary.org	Quincy	IL	62301	217-223-1309		434-3
Quincy Raceways 8000 Broadway St *Web:* www.quincyraceways.com	Quincy	IL	62305	217-224-3843	224-3859	515
Quincy Street Inc 13350 Quincy St *TF:* 800-784-6290 ■ *Web:* www.quincystreetinc.com	Holland	MI	49424	616-399-3330	399-0952	473
Quincy University 1800 College Ave *TF:* 866-703-4004 ■ *Web:* quhawks.com/index.aspx	Quincy	IL	62301	217-222-8020		166
Quine IP Law Group 2033 Clement Ave Ste 200 *Web:* www.quinelaw.com	Alameda	CA	94501	510-337-7871		428
Quinebaug Valley Community College 742 Upper Maple St *Web:* qvcc.edu	Danielson	CT	06239	860-932-4000		162
Quinlan & Company Inc 385 N French Rd Ste 106 *Web:* www.quinlanco.com	Amherst	NY	14228	716-691-6200		7
Quinlan & Fabish Music Co 166 Shore Dr *Web:* www.qandf.com	Burr Ridge	IL	60527	630-654-4111		526
Quinn Communications LC 1155 Main St Ste 109	Jupiter	FL	33458	561-622-7577		631
Quinn Medical Day Spa 6920 W 121st St Ste 102 *Web:* www.quinnplasticsurgery.com	Leawood	KS	66209	913-663-5483		77
Quinn's Lighthouse 1951 Embarcadero Cove *TF:* 800-786-5445 ■ *Web:* www.quinnslighthouse.com	Oakland	CA	94606	510-536-2050	535-1285	671
Quinn, Johnston, Henderson, Pretorius & Cerulo 227 N E Jefferson St *TF:* 800-646-1133 ■ *Web:* www.quinnjohnston.com	Peoria	IL	61602	309-674-1133		428

Phone | Fax | Class

Quinnipiac Chamber of Commerce
50 N Main St .... Wallingford CT 06492 203-269-9891 269-1358 139
Web: www.quinncham.com

Quinnipiac University
275 Mt Carmel Ave .... Hamden CT 06518 203-582-8600 582-8906* 166
**Fax:* Admissions ■ *TF Admissions:* 800-462-1944 ■ *Web:* www.qu.edu

Quinnipiac University School of Law
275 Mt Carmel Ave .... Hamden CT 06518 203-582-3400 167-1
TF: 800-462-1944 ■ *Web:* www.qu.edu

Quinsigamond Community College
670 W Boylston St .... Worcester MA 01606 508-853-2300 854-4357* 162
**Fax:* Admissions ■ *Web:* www.qcc.edu

Quinsigamond State Park
10 Lake Ave N .... Worcester MA 01612 508-755-6880 565
Web: www.mass.gov

QuinStreet Inc 950 Tower Ln 6th Fl .... Foster City CA 94404 650-578-7700 171
Web: www.quinstreet.com

Quintel Management Consulting Inc
5910 S University Ste C18-193 .... Greenwood Village CO 80121 303-781-4771 463
Web: www.quintelmc.com

Quintessence Biosciences Inc
505 S Rosa Rd .... Madison WI 53719 608-441-2950 668

Quintessence Publishing Co
4350 Chandler Dr .... Hanover Park IL 60133 630-736-3600 781
TF: 800-621-0387 ■ *Web:* www.quintpub.com

Quintevents LLC
9300 Harris Corners Pkwy Ste 120 .... Charlotte NC 28269 866-834-8663 195
TF: 866-834-8663 ■ *Web:* www.quintevents.com

Quintiles Transnational Corp
4820 Emperor Blvd .... Durham NC 27703 919-998-2000 582
TF: 866-267-4479 ■ *Web:* www.quintiles.com

QuintilesIMS
100 Alexis-Nihon Ste 800 .... Ville St-Laurent QC H4M2P4 514-855-0888 582
TF General: 866-267-4479 ■ *Web:* www.quintiles.com

Quintron Systems Inc
2105 S Blosser Rd .... Santa Maria CA 93458 805-928-4343 735
Web: www.quintron.com

Quippi Corp 444 S Cedros Ave Ste 410 .... La Jolla CA 92037 888-978-4774 393
TF: 888-978-4774

Quirch Foods Co 7600 NW 82nd Pl .... Miami FL 33166 305-691-3535 593-0272 297-9
TF: 800-458-5252 ■ *Web:* www.quirchfoods.com

Quirks Marketing Rsch Review
4662 Slater Rd .... Saint Paul MN 55122 651-379-6200 7
TF: 800-827-0676 ■ *Web:* www.quirks.com

Quitman County PO Box 582 .... Georgetown GA 39854 229-334-2159 334-2158 338
Web: www.qpublic.net

Quitman County 220 Chestnut St Ste 2 .... Marks MS 38646 662-326-2661 338
Web: www.quitmancountyms.org

Quixote Group Research Marketing
3107 Brassfield Rd Ste 100 .... Greensboro NC 27410 336-605-0363 195
Web: www.quixotegroup.com

Quiznos Corp
7595 Technology Way Ste 200 .... Denver CO 80237 720-359-3300 670
TF: 866-486-2783 ■ *Web:* www.quiznos.com

Quizzle LLC 1042 Woodward Ave .... Detroit MI 48226 800-784-9953 387
TF: 800-784-9953 ■ *Web:* www.quizzle.com

QUMAO 60 York Ct .... Jersey City NJ 07002 [illegible] 170-10
TF Sales: 800-577-1545 ■ *Web:* www.qumas.com

Quoddy Head State Park 973 S Lubec Rd .... Lubec ME 04652 207-733-0911 565
Web: www.maine.gov

Quoizel Inc 6 Corporate Pkwy .... Goose Creek SC 29445 843-553-6700 439
Web: www.quoizel.com

Quorex Construction Ltd
142 Cardinal Crescent .... Saskatoon SK S7L6H6 306-244-3717 186
Web: www.quorex.ca

Quorum Associates LLC
1005 Chapman St .... Yorktown Heights NY 10598 914-320-6251 260
Web: www.quorumassociates.com

Quorum Business Solutions Inc
811 Main St Ste 2000 .... Houston TX 77002 713-430-8601 177
Web: www.qbsol.com

Quorum Consulting Inc
180 Sansome St 10th Fl .... San Francisco CA 94104 415-835-0190 261
Web: quorumconsulting.com

Quorum Health Resources LLC
105 Continental Pl .... Brentwood TN 37027 615-371-7979 194
Web: www.qhr.com

Quorum Hotels & Resorts
5429 Lyndon B Johnson Fwy #625 .... Dallas TX 75240 972-458-7265 991-5647 379
Web: www.quorumhotels.com

Quota International
1420 21st St NW .... Washington DC 20036 202-331-9694 331-4395 48-15
Web: www.quotainternational.org

Quotable Cards Inc
611 Broadway Rm 810 .... New York NY 10012 212-420-7552 420-7558 130
Web: www.quotablecards.com

Quttinirpaaq National Park PO Box 278 .... Iqaluit NU X0A0H0 867-975-4673 975-4674 563
Web: www.pc.gc.ca/pn-np/nu/quttinirpaaq/contact.aspx

QV Investors Inc
222 - Third Ave SW Livingston Pl S Tower
Ste 1008 .... Calgary AB T2P0B4 403-265-7007 528
Web: www.qvinvestors.com

QVC Inc 1200 Wilson Dr .... West Chester PA 19380 484-701-1000 740
TF: 800-367-9444 ■ *Web:* www.qvc.com

Qvidian Corp 175 Cabot St Ste 210 .... Lowell MA 01854 513-631-1155 178-10
TF: 800-272-0047 ■ *Web:* www.qvidian.com

QVL Pharmacy Holdings Inc
4141 Blue Lake Cir Ste 124 .... Dallas TX 75244 972-788-2653 238
Web: www.qvlpharmacy.com

QVS Software Inc 5950 Six Forks Rd .... Raleigh NC 27609 919-676-1991 180
Web: qvssoftware.com

Qwest Investment Management Corp
750 West Pender St Ste 802 .... Vancouver BC V6C2T8 604-601-5804 528
TF: 866-602-1142 ■ *Web:* www.qwestfunds.com

QX 104 177 Lombard Ave 3rd Fl .... Winnipeg MB R3B0W5 204-944-1031 989-5291 645-177
Web: www.qx104fm.com

R

Phone | Fax | Class

R & A Tool & Engineering Co
39127 Ford Rd .... Westland MI 48185 734-981-2000 261
Web: www.randatool.com

R & B Car Company Inc
3811 S Michigan St .... South Bend IN 46614 800-260-1833 516
TF: 800-260-1833 ■ *Web:* www.rbcarcompany.com

R & B Grinding Company Inc
1900 Clark St .... Racine WI 53403 262-634-5538 454
Web: www.rbgrinding.com

R & B Wagner Inc PO Box 423 .... Butler WI 53007 414-214-0444 214-0450 595
TF: 888-243-6914 ■ *Web:* www.wagnercompanies.com

R & B Wholesale Distributors Inc
2350 S Milliken Ave .... Ontario CA 91761 909-230-5400 230-5405 38
TF: 800-627-7539 ■ *Web:* www.rbdist.com

R & D Associates Inc
100 Tenth St .... Catlettsburg KY 41129 606-739-4166 698
Web: www.rdassociates.com

R & D Batteries Inc
3300 Corporate Ctr Dr PO Box 5007 .... Burnsville MN 55306 952-890-0629 890-7912 74
TF: 800-950-1945 ■ *Web:* www.rdbatteries.com

R & D Computers
6767 Peachtree Industrial Blvd Ste B .... Atlanta GA 30092 770-416-0103 589
TF: 800-350-3071 ■ *Web:* www.randdcomp.com

R & d Industries Inc 812 Tenth St .... Milford IA 51351 712-338-2999 180
Web: www.rdi1.com

R & d Machine & Engineering Inc
130 Scarlet Blvd .... Oldsmar FL 34677 813-891-9109 454
Web: www.rdmachine.com

R & D Magazine
100 Enterprise Dr Ste 600 .... Rockaway NJ 07866 973-920-7000 457-19
Web: www.rdmag.com

R & d Professional Services LLC
3000 Keller Springs Rd Ste 200 .... Carrollton TX 75006 214-483-5342 693
Web: www.rndconsult.com

R & D Systems Inc
614 McKinley Pl NE .... Minneapolis MN 55413 612-379-2956 656-4400 231
TF: 800-343-7475 ■ *Web:* www.rndsystems.com

R & D Transportation Services Inc
4036 Adolfo Rd .... Camarillo CA 93012 805-529-7511 311
TF: 800-966-7114 ■ *Web:* rdtsi.com

R & K Building Supplies Inc
25 W Baseline Rd .... Gilbert AZ 85233 480-892-0025 499
Web: www.randkbuildingsupplies.com

R & K Industrial Products Co
1945 Seventh St .... Richmond CA 94801 510-234-7212 234-1923 676
TF: 800-842-7055 ■ *Web:* www.rkwheels.com

R & L Spring Co 1097 Geneva Pkwy .... Lake Geneva WI 53147 262-249-7854 249-7866 719
Web: www.rlspring.com

R & M Energy Systems 301 Premier Rd .... Borger TX 79007 806-274-5293 385
TF Sales: 888-262-8645 ■ *Web:* www.rmenergy.com

R & M Office Furniture
9615 Oates Dr .... Sacramento CA 95827 916-362-1756 362-1086 320
TF: 800-660-1756 ■ *Web:* www.randmoffice.com

R & O Construction Co 933 Wall Ave .... Ogden UT 84404 801-627-1403 186
Web: www.randoco.com

R & R Corrugated Container Inc
360 Minor Rd .... Bristol CT 06010 860-584-1194 100
Web: www.randrcorrugated.com

R & R General Contractors Inc
4666 Faries Pkwy .... Decatur IL 62526 217-428-9591 186
Web: www.randrgc.com

R & R Limousine 4403 Kiln Ct .... Louisville KY 40218 502-458-1862 458-3608 441
TF: 800-582-5576 ■ *Web:* www.rrlimo.com

R & R Marketing LLC
10 Patton Dr .... West Caldwell NJ 07006 973-228-5100 403-8679 81-3
TF: 800-724-3960 ■ *Web:* www.charmer-sunbelt.com

R & R Technologies LLC
7560 E County Line Rd .... Edinburgh IN 46124 812-526-2655 526-9294 604
Web: www.rrtech.com

R & R Trucking Inc
302 Thunder Rd PO Box 545 .... Duenweg MO 64841 417-623-6885 623-6479 780
TF: 800-625-6885 ■ *Web:* www.randrtruck.com

R & S Processing Company Inc
15712 Illinois Ave PO Box 2037 .... Paramount CA 90723 562-531-1403 531-4318 605-3
Web: rsprocessing.com

R & S/Godwin Truck Body Co LLC
5168 S US Hwy 23 PO Box 420 .... Ivel KY 41642 606-874-2151 874-9136 516
TF: 800-826-7413 ■ *Web:* www.rstruckbody.com

R A Burch Construction Company Inc
405 Maple St Bldg B .... Ramona CA 92065 760-788-0800 186
Web: www.raburch.com

R A Zweig Inc 2500 Ravine Way .... Glenview IL 60025 847-832-9001 454
TF: 800-208-6075 ■ *Web:* www.zweig-cnc.com

R B M Co 2700 Texas Ave .... Knoxville TN 37921 865-524-8621 385
TF: 800-521-5656 ■ *Web:* www.rbmcompany.com

R Bistro 888 Massachusetts Ave .... Indianapolis IN 46204 317-423-0312 671
Web: www.rbistro.com

R C Furniture Inc 1111 S Jellick Ave .... Industry CA 91748 626-964-4100 321
Web: www.rcfurniture.com

R C Mc Lean & Assoc Inc
210 N Tustin Ave .... Santa Ana CA 92705 714-347-1000 445
TF: 800-883-7243 ■ *Web:* www.rcmclean.com

R C Romine & Associates Advertising & Marketing
1250 Executive Pl Ste 601 .... Geneva IL 60134 630-208-1020 208-1285 7
Web: www.rcromine.com

R C Willey Home Furnishings
2301 South 300 West .... Salt Lake City UT 84115 801-461-3800 321
Web: www.rcwilley.com

R Cushman & Associates Inc
12623 Newburgh Rd .... Livonia MI 48150 248-477-9900 54

R D A Container Corp 70 Cherry Rd .... Gates NY 14624 585-247-2323 100
TF: 800-937-0028 ■ *Web:* www.rdacontainer.com

	Phone	Fax	Class
R d d Associates LLC 930 Riverview Dr Ste 400, Totowa NJ 07512 — TF: 800-722-7388 ■ Web: www.rddassociates.com	973-812-8070		317
R d Jones & Associates Inc 729 E Pratt St Ste 2000, Baltimore MD 21202 — Web: www.rdjones.com	410-332-4700		393
R d s Delivery Service Company Inc 436 E 11th St Frnt A, New York NY 10009 — Web: www.rdsdelivery.com	212-260-5800		314
R David Thomas Executive Conference Ctr (RDTC) 100 Fuqua Dr PO Box 90120, Durham NC 27708 — Web: www.fuqua.duke.edu	919-660-6400	660-3607	377
R e Dimond & Associates Inc 732 N Capitol Ave, Indianapolis IN 46204 — Web: www.redimond.com	317-634-4672		261
R E I Consultants Inc PO Box 286, Beaver WV 25813 — TF: 800-999-0105 ■ Web: www.reiclabs.com	304-255-2500	255-2572	192
R E Sutton & Assoc 11555 N Meridian St Ste 200, Carmel IN 46032 — *Fax Area Code: 877 ■ Web: www.resutton.com	317-852-1937	470-1968*	260
R e Warner & Associates Inc 25777 Detroit Rd Ste 200, Westlake OH 44145 — Web: www.rewarner.com	440-835-9400		727
R F Monolithics Inc 4441 Sigma Rd, Dallas TX 75244 — Web: www.rfm.com	972-233-2903		246
R F R Metal Fabrication Inc 3204 Knotts Grove Rd, Oxford NC 27565 — TF: 800-229-9950 ■ Web: www.rfr-metalfab.com	919-693-1354		480
R F Stearns Inc 4000 Kruse Way Pl Bldg 3 Ste 100, Lake Oswego OR 97035 — TF: 800-328-2256 ■ Web: www.rfstearns.com	503-601-8700		186
R G Canning Cos 4525 E 59th Pl, Maywood CA 90270 — Web: www.rgcshows.com	323-560-7469		232
R G Engineering Inc 505 London Bridge Rd Unit 101, Virginia Beach VA 23454 — TF: 800-474-6836 ■ Web: www.rgengineering.com	757-463-3045		261
R G S Financial Corp 1700 Jay Ell Dr, Richardson TX 75081 — Web: www.rgsfinancial.com	469-791-4700		317
R H K Hydraulic Cylinder Services Inc 13111 159th St, Edmonton AB T5V1H6 — TF: 800-406-3111 ■ Web: www.rhkhydraulics.com	780-452-2876		393
R J Behar & Company Inc 6861 SW 196th Ave Ste 302, Fort Lauderdale FL 33332 — Web: www.rjbehar.com	954-680-7771		261
R J Julia Booksellers LLC 768 Boston Post Rd, Madison CT 06443 — Web: booksasgifts.com	203-245-3959		95
R J Lanthier Company Inc 485 Corporate Dr, Escondido CA 92029	760-738-9798		610
R J Schinner Company Inc 16950 W Lincoln Ave, New Berlin WI 53151 — TF: 800-234-1460 ■ Web: www.rjschinner.com	262-797-7180	797-7190	791
R J Williams 585 Rugh St, Greensburg PA 15601	724-834-3403		2
R J Wood & Co 652 Arlington Pl, Macon GA 31201	478-741-7044		261
R K Allen Oil Inc 36002 AL Hwy 21, Talladega AL 35161 — TF: 800-445-5823 ■ Web: www.rkallenoil.com	256-362-4261		579
R K Electric Inc 42021 Osgood Rd, Fremont CA 94539 — Web: www.rkelectric.com	510-770-5660	770-5684	189-4
R K Sport Inc 26900 Jefferson Ave, Murrieta CA 92562 — Web: www.stretchformingcorp.com	951-894-7883		711
R Kidd Fuels Corp 1172 Twinney Dr, Newmarket ON L3Y9E2 — TF: 866-274-2315 ■ Web: www.kiddfuels.com	866-274-2315		579
R l Bryan Co, The 301 Greystone Blvd, Columbia SC 29210 — TF: 800-253-5428 ■ Web: www.rlbryan.com	803-779-3560		627
R L f Communications Llc 301 N Elm St Ste 102, Greensboro NC 27401 — Web: rlfcommunications.com	336-553-1800		636
R L Hulett & Company Inc 8000 Maryland Ave Ste 245, St Louis MO 63105 — Web: www.rlhulett.com	314-721-0607		194
R L Turner Corp 1000 W Oak St, Zionsville IN 46077 — Web: www.rlturner.com	317-873-2712	873-1262	187
R L Vallee Inc 280 S Main St, Saint Albans VT 05478 — Web: www.rlvallee.com	802-524-8710		579
R L Zeigler Company Inc 1 Plant St, Selma AL 36703 — Web: www.zmeats.com	334-874-9041		473
R Lazy S Ranch PO Box 308, Teton Village WY 83025 — TF: 800-455-5090 ■ Web: www.rlazys.com	307-733-2655		239
R M Kaul & Associates Inc 10 Bennett Ave, New York NY 10033 — Web: www.rmkaul.com	646-706-1807		195
R M Roach & Sons Inc 333 E John St PO Box 2899, Martinsburg WV 25401 — Web: www.roachenergy.com	304-263-3329		538
R Mcclure Electric 706 Portal St Ste D, Cotati CA 94931 — Web: rmcclure.com	707-792-2101		390
R N Croft Financial Group Inc 218 Steeles Ave E, Thornhill ON L3T1A6 — TF: 877-249-2884 ■ Web: www.croftgroup.com	905-695-7777		401
R O I Media Solutions LLC 11500 W Olympic Blvd Ste 400, Los Angeles CA 90064 — TF: 866-211-2580 ■ Web: www.roims.com	866-211-2580		5
R O Whitesell & Associates Inc 11711 N Pennsylvania St Ste 240, Carmel IN 46032 — Web: www.whitesell.com	317-564-8008	564-8766	246
R R Floody Co 5065 27th Ave, Rockford IL 61109 — TF: 800-678-6639 ■ Web: rrfloody.com	815-399-1931		358
R Seelaus & Company Inc 25 Deforest Ave Ste 304, Summit NJ 07901 — TF: 800-922-0584 ■ Web: www.rseelaus.com	800-922-0584		690
R T Patterson Company Inc 230 Third Ave 2nd Fl, Pittsburgh PA 15222 — Web: www.rtpatterson.com	412-227-6600		261
R Value Inc 2267 N Interstate Ave, Portland OR 97227 — TF: 800-405-2233 ■ Web: www.indowwindows.com	503-284-2260		499
R W Armstrong 300 S Meridian St, Indianapolis IN 46225 — Web: www.rwa.com	317-786-0461		47
R W Collins Co 7225 W 66th St, Chicago IL 60638 — TF: 800-947-8631 ■ Web: www.rwcollins.com	708-458-6868		667
R W Hays Co Inc 1890 S Pacific Hwy, Medford OR 97501 — Web: www.haysoil.com	541-772-2053		579
R W Lyall & Company Inc 2665 Research Dr, Corona CA 92882 — Web: www.rwlyall.com	951-270-1500		201
R W Mercer Co 2322 Brooklyn Rd PO Box 180, Jackson MI 49204 — TF: 877-763-7237 ■ Web: www.rwmercer.com	517-787-2960		186
R W Rog & Company Inc 630 Johnson Ave Ste 103, Bohemia NY 11716 — TF: 877-218-0085 ■ Web: www.rwroge.com	631-218-0077		194
R W Wentworth & Co Inc 217 W 18th St, New York NY 10011 — Web: www.rwwentworth.com	212-627-0467	627-0467	466
R Y Timber Inc 85 Mill Rd, Townsend MT 59644 — Web: www.rytimber.com	406-266-3111		683
R Z Communications 1400 Smith Rd # B101, Austin TX 78721 — Web: www.rzaustin.com	512-386-7336		177
R Zoppo Corp 160 Old Maple St, Stoughton MA 02072 — Web: www.zoppo.com	781-344-8822		186
R. B. Winter State Park 17215 Buffalo Rd, Mifflinburg PA 17844 — Web: www.dcnr.state.pa.us	570-966-1455		565
R. G. Niederhoffer Capital Management Inc 1700 Broadway 39th Fl, New York NY 10019 — Web: www.niederhoffer.com	212-245-0400		528
R. M. Davis Inc 24 City Ctr, Portland ME 04101 — Web: www.rmdavis.com	207-774-0022		401
R. W. Fernstrum & Co 1716 11th Ave PO Box 97, Menominee MI 49858 — Web: www.fernstrum.com	906-863-5553	863-5634	91
R.A. Smith National Inc 16745 W Bluemound Rd Ste 200, Brookfield WI 53005 — Web: www.rasmith.com	262-781-1000	781-8466	189-12
R.C. Brayshaw & Company Inc 45 Waterloo St, Warner NH 03278 — TF: 800-851-7740 ■ Web: www.rcbrayshaw.com	603-456-3101		627
R.C. Dolner LLC 307 Fifth Ave 9th Fl, New York NY 10016 — Web: www.rcdolner.com	212-531-8600	633-1108	449
R.H. Bluestein & Co 260 E Brown St Ste 100, Birmingham MI 48009	248-646-4000		401
R.H. Smith Distributing Co 315 E Wine Country Rd PO Box 6, Grandview WA 98930 — Web: www.rhsmith.com	509-882-3377		581
R.M.Thornton Inc 120 Westhampton Ave, Capitol Heights MD 20743 — Web: www.rmthornton.com	301-350-5000		261
R.O. Anderson Engineering Inc 1603 Esmeralda, Minden NV 89423 — Web: www.roanderson.com	775-782-2322		261
R.O.A. General Inc 1775 N Warm Springs Rd, Salt Lake City UT 84116 — TF: 800-392-2639 ■ Web: reaganoutdoor.com	801-521-1775		8
R.P.C. Contracting Inc 934 W Kitty Hawk Rd, Kitty Hawk NC 27949 — Web: www.rpccontracting.com	252-261-3336		393
R.R. Donnelley Seymour Inc 709 A Ave E, Seymour IN 47274 — Web: www.rrdonnelley.com	812-523-1800		627
R.W. Lynch Company Inc 2333 San Ramon Vly Blvd, San Ramon CA 94583 — TF: 800-594-8940 ■ Web: www.rwlynch.com	925-837-3877		5
R/GA 350 W 39th St, New York NY 10018 — Web: www.rga.com	212-946-4000		7
R2 Unified Technologies 980 N Federal Hwy Ste 410, Boca Raton FL 33432 — TF: 866-464-7381 ■ Web: www.r2ut.com	561-515-6800		196
R2c Group Inc 207 NW Pk Ave, Portland OR 97209 — Web: www.r2cgroup.com	503-222-0025		4
R2t Inc 580 W Crssvlle Rd, Roswell GA 30075 — Web: www.r2tinc.com	770-569-7038		261
R2W Inc 5957 McLeod Dr, Las Vegas NV 89120 — Web: www.r2west.com	702-434-6500		189-4
RA (Ruotolo Assoc Inc) 580 Sylvan Ave Ste M-B, Englewood Cliffs NJ 07632 — TF: 800-786-8656 ■ Web: www.ruotoloassociates.com	201-568-3898	568-8783	317
RA Miller Industries Inc 14500 168th Ave PO Box 858, Grand Haven MI 49417 — TF: 888-845-9450 ■ Web: www.rami.com	616-842-9450		647
RAA (Regional Airline Assn) 2025 M St NW Ste 800, Washington DC 20036 — Web: www.raa.org	202-367-1170	367-2170	49-21
RAAM Global Energy Co 1537 Bull Lea Rd Ste 200, Lexington KY 40511	859-253-1300		536
RAB (Radio Adv Bureau) 125 W 55th St 5th Fl, New York NY 10019 — TF: 800-232-3131 ■ Web: www.rab.com	212-681-7200		49-18
RAB Lighting 170 Ludlow Ave, Northvale NJ 07647 — *Fax Area Code: 888 ■ TF: 888-722-1000 ■ Web: www.rabweb.com	201-784-8600	722-1232*	439
Raba-Kistner Consultants Inc 12821 W Golden Ln, San Antonio TX 78249 — TF: 866-722-2547 ■ Web: www.rkci.com	210-699-9090	699-6426	189-15
Rabbinical Assembly 3080 Broadway, New York NY 10027 — Web: www.rabbinicalassembly.org	212-280-6000		48-20
Rabbit Air 9242 1/2 Hall Rd, Downey CA 90241 — TF: 888-866-8862 ■ Web: www.rabbitair.com	562-861-4688		45
Rabbit Hill Inn 48 Lower Waterford Rd PO Box 55, Lower Waterford VT 05848 — TF: 800-626-3215 ■ Web: www.rabbithillinn.com	802-748-5168	748-8342	379
Rabe Environmental Systems Inc 2300 W 23 St, Erie PA 16506 — Web: www.rabehvac.com	814-456-5374		610
Raben Tire Company Inc 2100 N New York Ave, Evansville IN 47711 — Web: www.rabentire.com	812-465-5565		62-5

Name / Address	City	State	ZIP	Phone	Fax	Class
Rabenhorst Funeral Home Inc 825 Government St. *Web:* www.rabenhorst.com	Baton Rouge	LA	70802	225-383-6831		510
Raber Packing Co 1413 N Raber Rd	Peoria	IL	61604	309-673-0721		473
Rabinovici & Assoc Inc 800 Silks Run Ste 2320 *Web:* www.rabinovicionline.com	Hallandale	FL	33009	305-655-0021		4
Rabinovitz & Associates Pc Attys 721 N Fourth Ave Ste 201 *Web:* uits.arizona.edu	Tucson	AZ	85705	520-624-5526		445
Rable Machine Inc 30 Paragon Pkwy PO Box 1583 *Web:* www.rablemachineinc.com	Mansfield	OH	44901	419-525-2255	525-2371	621
Rabo Bank 1026 E Grand Ave. *TF:* 800-942-6222 ■ *Web:* www.rabobankamerica.com	Arroyo Grande	CA	93420	805-473-7710		70
Rabobank Arena Theater & Convention Ctr 1001 Truxtun Ave *Web:* rabobankarena.com	Bakersfield	CA	93301	661-852-7300	861-9904	205
Rabobank International 245 Pk Ave *Web:* rabobank.com	New York	NY	10167	212-916-7800		360-2
Rabun County 25 Courthouse Sq Ste 201 *Web:* www.gamountains.com	Clayton	GA	30525	706-782-5271		338
Rabun County School District 963 Tiger Connector *Web:* www.rabuncountyschools.org	Tiger	GA	30576	706-212-4350	782-6224	685
Rabun Gap-Nacoochee School 339 Nacoochee Dr *TF:* 800-543-7467 ■ *Web:* www.rabungap.org	Rabun Gap	GA	30568	706-746-7467	746-2594	622
Raccoon Creek State Park 3000 State Rt 18 *Web:* www.dcnr.state.pa.us	Hookstown	PA	15050	724-899-2200		565
Raccoon Mountain Caverns 319 W Hills Dr *TF:* 800-823-2267 ■ *Web:* www.raccoonmountain.com	Chattanooga	TN	37419	423-821-9403		50-5
Raccoon Valley Electric Co-op 28725 Hwy 30 PO Box 486 *TF:* 800-253-6211 ■ *Web:* www.rvec.coop	Glidden	IA	51443	712-659-3649	659-3716	245
Race Face Components Inc 100 Braid St *TF:* 800-527-9244 ■ *Web:* www.raceface.com	New Westminster	BC	V3L3P4	604-527-9996	527-9959	155-1
Racer Parts Wholesale 411 Dorman *Web:* www.racerpartswholesale.com	Indianapolis	IN	46202	317-639-0725		61
RaceTrac Petroleum Inc 3225 Cumberland Blvd Ste 100 *TF:* 800-636-5589 ■ *Web:* www.racetrac.com	Atlanta	GA	30339	770-431-7600		324
Rachlin & Wolfson LLP 390 Bay St Ste 1500 *Web:* www.rachlinlaw.com	Toronto	ON	M5H2Y2	416-367-0202		428
Rachman Group, The 90 Walt Whitman Rd Ste 222 *Web:* www.mrhuntington.com	Huntington Station	NY	11746	631-547-5464		41
Racine Area Mfg & Commerce 300 Fifth St *Web:* www.racinechamber.com	Racine	WI	53403	262-634-1931	634-7422	139
Racine Correctional Institution 2019 Wisconsin St *Web:* doc.wi.gov	Sturtevant	WI	53177	262-886-3214	886-3514	213
Racine County 730 Wisconsin Ave 1st Fl North end *TF:* 800-242-4202 ■ *Web:* www.racinecounty.com	Racine	WI	53403	262-636-3121	636-3491	338
Racine County Convention & Visitors Bureau 14015 Washington Ave *TF:* 800-272-2463 ■ *Web:* realracine.com	Sturtevant	WI	53177	262-884-6400		206
Racine Public Library 75 Seventh St *Web:* www.racinelibrary.info	Racine	WI	53403	262-636-9241	636-9260	434-3
Racine Railroad Products Inc 1955 Norwood Ct *Web:* www.racinerailroad.com	Mount Pleasant	WI	53403	262-637-9681	637-9069	650
Racine Zoo 200 Goold St *Web:* www.racinezoo.org	Racine	WI	53402	262-636-9189	636-9307	823
Rack Attack-car Rack & Hitch Center 745 Worcester Rd *Web:* www.rackattack.com	Framingham	MA	01701	508-879-1444		791
Rack Room Shoes 8310 Technology Dr *Web:* www.rackroomshoes.com	Charlotte	NC	28262	704-501-4674		301
Racking Horse Breeders Assn of America (RHBAA) 67 Horse Ctr Rd *Web:* www.rackinghorse.com	Decatur	AL	35603	256-353-7225		48-3
Racks Inc PO Box 530840 *TF:* 877-920-7225 ■ *Web:* www.racksinc.com	San Diego	CA	92153	619-661-0987		286
Raco General Contractors 1401 Dalon Rd NE *Web:* www.racogc.com	Atlanta	GA	30306	404-873-3567	876-1394	186
RACO Mfg & Engineering Company Inc 1400-62nd St *Web:* www.racoman.com	Emeryville	CA	94608	510-658-6713		201
RACVB (Ridgecrest Area Convention & Visitors Bureau) 643 N China Lake Blvd Ste C *TF:* 800-847-4830 ■ *Web:* racvb.com	Ridgecrest	CA	93555	760-375-8202	375-9850	206
RAD Data Communications Ltd 900 Corporate Dr *TF:* 800-444-7234 ■ *Web:* www.rad.com	Mahwah	NJ	07430	201-529-1100		735
Rad Law Firm 2001 Beach St Ste 600 *TF:* 800-598-1090 ■ *Web:* www.radlawfirm.com	Fort Worth	TX	76103	817-465-8733		428
Rada Manufacturing Co PO Box 838 *TF:* 800-311-9691 ■ *Web:* www.radacutlery.com	Waverly	IA	50677	319-352-5454	352-0770	222
Radakovich Shaw & Blythe LLP 3220 S Higuera St Ste 201 *Web:* radshaw.com	San Luis Obispo	CA	93401	805-544-1557		2
Radar Inc 22214 20TH Ave SE Ste 101 *TF:* 800-282-2524 ■ *Web:* www.radarinc.com	Bothell	WA	98021	800-282-2524		246
Radar Industries Inc 27101 Groesbeck Hwy *TF:* 800-779-0301 ■ *Web:* www.radarind.com	Warren	MI	48089	800-779-0301		489
Radar Media Group Inc 12 Blossom Hill Rd Ste 101a *Web:* www.radarmedia.com	Winchester	MA	01890	781-721-1910		463
Radcliff Hardin County Chamber of Commerce 306 N Wilson Rd *Web:* www.hardinchamber.com	Radcliff	KY	40160	270-351-4450	352-4449	139
Radcliff Wire Inc 97 Ronzo Rd *Web:* www.radcliffwire.com	Bristol	CT	06010	860-583-1305		492
Rad-Comm Systems Corp 7522 Bath Rd *TF:* 800-588-5229 ■ *Web:* www.radcommsystems.com	Mississauga	ON	L4T1L2	905-678-6503		407
Rader Solutions Ltd 537 Cajundome Blvd Ste 209 *TF:* 800-966-4202 ■ *Web:* radersolutions.com	Lafayette	LA	70506	337-205-4652		196
Radewagen Amata (Rep R - AS) 1339 Longworth House Office Bldg *Web:* radewagen.house.gov	Washington	DC	20515	202-225-8577	225-8757	342-2
Radey Thomas Yon & Clark 301 S Bronough St Ste 200 *Web:* www.radeylaw.com	Tallahassee	FL	32301	850-425-6654		428
Radford (Independent City) 619 Second St *Web:* www.courts.state.va.us/courts/combined/radford/home.html	Radford	VA	24141	540-731-3610	731-3692	338
Radford University 801 E Main St **Fax:* Admissions ■ *TF Admissions:* 800-890-4265 ■ *Web:* www.radford.edu	Radford	VA	24142	540-831-5371	831-5038*	166
Radford University McConnell Library 801 E Main St *Web:* library.radford.edu	Radford	VA	24142	540-831-5364	831-6138	434-6
Radgov Inc 6750 N Andrews Ave Ste 200 *Web:* www.radgov.com	Fort Lauderdale	FL	33309	954-938-2800		196
Radiac Abrasives Inc 1015 S College Ave **Fax:* Cust Svc ■ *TF:* 800-851-1095 ■ *Web:* www.radiac.com	Salem	IL	62881	618-548-4200	548-4207*	1
Radial Drilling Services Inc 4921 Spring Cypress *TF:* 800-782-4357 ■ *Web:* radialdrilling.com	Spring	TX	77379	281-374-7507		540
Radian Asset Assurance Inc *Radian Group Inc, The* 335 Madison Ave 25th Fl *TF:* 877-723-4261 ■ *Web:* www.radian.biz	New York	NY	10017	212-983-3100	682-5377	391-5
Radian Group Inc 1601 Market St *NYSE:* RDN ■ *TF:* 800-523-1988 ■ *Web:* www.radian.biz	Philadelphia	PA	19103	215-564-6600		391-5
Radian Research Inc 3852 Fortune Dr *Web:* www.radianresearch.com	Lafayette	IN	47905	765-449-5500		201
Radiance Technologies Inc 350 Wynn Dr *Web:* www.radiancetech.com	Huntsville	AL	35805	256-704-3400		692
Radiancy Inc 40 Ramland Rd S Ste 200 *TF:* 888-661-2220 ■ *Web:* www.radiancy.com	Orangeburg	NY	10962	845-398-1647		475
Radiant Communication Inc 5512 Merrick Rd	Massapequa	NY	11758	516-798-0465		194
Radiant Communications Corp 1600-1050 W Pender St *CVE:* RCN ■ *TF:* 888-219-2111 ■ *Web:* www.radiant.net	Vancouver	BC	V6E4T3	888-219-2111		808
Radiant Electric Co-op Inc PO Box 390 *TF:* 800-821-0956 ■ *Web:* radiantec.coop	Fredonia	KS	66736	620-378-2161		245
Radiant Logic Inc 75 Rowland Way Ste 300 *Web:* www.radiantlogic.com	Novato	CA	94945	415-209-6800		177
Radiant Logistics Inc Third Fl 405 114Th Ave SE *TF:* 800-843-4784 ■ *Web:* www.radiantdelivers.com	Bellevue	WA	98004	425-943-4599		449
Radiant Networks Services Inc 13000 Middletown Industrial Blvd Ste D *Web:* www.radiant-networks.com	Louisville	KY	40223	502-379-4800		180
Radiant Pools Div Trojan Leisure Products LLC 440 N Pearl St *TF:* 866-697-5870 ■ *Web:* www.radiantpools.com	Albany	NY	12207	518-434-4161	432-6554	728
Radiant Research Inc 11500 Northlake Dr Ste 320 *TF:* 855-427-8839 ■ *Web:* www.radiantresearch.com	Cincinnati	OH	45249	513-247-5500		668
Radiant Technologies Inc 2835 Pan American Fwy NE *TF:* 800-289-7176 ■ *Web:* www.ferrodevices.com	Albuquerque	NM	87107	505-842-8007		256
Radiant Vision Systems 22908 NE Alder Crest Dr Ste 100 *Web:* www.radiantvisionsystems.com	Redmond	WA	98053	425-844-0152	844-0153	407
Radianta Inc 320 Goddard Ste 100 *TF:* 866-467-9695 ■ *Web:* www.radianta.com	Irvine	CA	92618	866-467-9695		809
Radiation Monitoring Devices Inc (RMDINC) 44 Hunt St Ste 2 *Web:* www.rmdinc.com	Watertown	MA	02472	617-668-6800		472
Radiation Therapy Services Inc 2270 Colonial Blvd *TF:* 800-437-1619 ■ *Web:* 21co.com	Fort Myers	FL	33907	239-931-7275		352
Radiator Specialty Co 1900 Wilkinson Blvd *TF:* 877-464-4865 ■ *Web:* www.gunk.com	Charlotte	NC	28208	704-688-2405		145
Radiator Specialty Co 600 Radiator Rd *Web:* www.radiatorspecialty.com	Indian Trail	NC	28079	704-821-7643		541
Radical Systems Solutions Inc 360 S Coyote Ln *Web:* www.radicalsys.com	Anaheim	CA	92808	714-280-1619		180
Radicchio 402 Wood St *Web:* www.radicchio-cafe.com	Philadelphia	PA	19106	215-627-6850		671
RadiciSpandex Corp 3145 NW Blvd *Web:* www.radicigroup.com	Gastonia	NC	28052	704-864-5495		605-1
Radient Pharmaceuticals Corp 2492 Walnut Ave Ste 100 *OTC:* RXPC	Tustin	CA	92780	714-505-4461	505-4464	231
RADinfo Systems Inc 43676 Trade Center Pl Ste 100	Dulles	VA	20166	703-713-3313	713-3343	177
Radio Adv Bureau (RAB) 125 W 55th St 5th Fl *TF:* 800-232-3131 ■ *Web:* www.rab.com	New York	NY	10019	212-681-7200		49-18
Radio America 1100 N Glebe Rd Ste 900 *TF:* 800-807-4703 ■ *Web:* www.radioamerica.com	Arlington	VA	22201	703-302-1000		644

	Phone	Fax	Class
Radio City Entertainment LLC 1260 Sixth Ave ... New York NY 10020 *Web:* www.radiocity.com	212-485-7200		181
Radio City Music Hall 1260 Ave of the Americas ... New York NY 10020 *Web:* www.radiocity.com	212-247-4777		572
Radio Communication Service 510 S Pike E ... Sumter SC 29150 *Web:* www.radiocommsc.com	803-773-9743		647
Radio Communications Co 8035 Chapel Hill Rd ... Cary NC 27513 *TF:* 800-508-7580 ■ *Web:* www.rccws.com	919-467-2421		194
Radio Control Boat Modeler 88 Danbury Rd ... Wilton CT 06897 *TF:* 888-235-2021 ■ *Web:* www.airagestore.com	203-431-9000		457-14
Radio Distributing Company Inc 27015 Trolley Industrial Dr ... Taylor MI 48180 *Web:* www.radiodistributing.com	313-295-4500		38
Radio Express Inc 1415 W Magnolia Blvd Ste 201 ... Burbank CA 91506 *Web:* www.radioexpress.com	818-295-5800	295-5801	646
Radio Flyer Inc 6515 W Grand Ave ... Chicago IL 60707 *TF:* 800-621-7613 ■ *Web:* www.radioflyer.com	773-637-7100	637-8874	762
Radio Free Asia 2025 M St NW Ste 300 ... Washington DC 20036 *Web:* www.rfa.org	202-530-4900		644
Radio Free Europe/Radio Liberty (RFE/RL) 1201 Connecticut Ave NW 4th Fl ... Washington DC 20036 *Web:* www.rferl.org	202-457-6900		644
Radio Frequency Company Inc 150 Dover Rd ... Millis MA 02054 *TF:* 800-313-3774 ■ *Web:* www.radiofrequency.com	508-376-9555	376-9944	318
Radio Frequency Systems 200 Pondview Dr ... Meriden CT 06450 *Web:* www.rfsworld.com	203-630-3311	634-2273	647
Radio Guys 2061 Fwy Dr Ste E ... Woodland CA 95776 *Web:* www.theradioguys.com	530-406-0700		179
Radio Holland USA Inc 8943 Gulf Fwy ... Houston TX 77017 *Web:* www.radioholland.com	713-378-2100	378-2101	647
Radio Kansas 815 N Walnut St Ste 300 ... Hutchinson KS 67501 *TF:* 800-723-4657 ■ *Web:* www.radiokansas.org	620-662-6646		645
Radio LOBO 102.9 5100 Commerce Dr ... Bakersfield CA 93309 *Web:* www.radiolobo.com	661-327-9711	327-0797	645-15
Radio Maria 119 N Walnut St ... Champaign IL 61820 *Web:* radiomariarestaurant.com	217-398-7729		671
Radio North 2682 Garfield Rd N Ste 22 ... Traverse City MI 49686 *TF:* 800-274-8255 ■ *Web:* radionorth.com	800-274-8255		647
Radio Research Consortium Inc (RRC) PO Box 1309 ... Olney MD 20830 *TF:* 800-543-7300 ■ *Web:* www.rrconline.org	301-774-6686	774-0976	632
Radio Training Network Inc 5015 S Florida Ave ... Lakeland FL 33813	863-644-3464		643
radio.net 2 Pillsbury St 6th Fl ... Concord NH 03301 *TF:* 800-639-4131 ■ *Web:* www.wevo.radio.net	603-228-8910	224-6052	645
Radiocat 32-A Mellor Ave ... Baltimore MD 21228 *TF:* 800-323-9729 ■ *Web:* www.radiocat.com	800-323-9729		794
Radiodetection Corp 154 Portland Rd ... Bridgton ME 04009 *TF:* 877-247-3797 ■ *Web:* spx.com/en/radiodetection	207-647-9495	647-9496	248
Radiological Imaging Technology Inc 5065 List Dr ... Colorado Springs CO 80919 *Web:* www.radimage.com	719-590-1077		174
Radiological Society of North America (RSNA) 820 Jorie Blvd ... Oak Brook IL 60523 *TF:* 800-381-6660 ■ *Web:* www.rsna.org	630-571-2670	571-7837	49-8
Radiology Business Management Assn (RBMA) 10300 Eaton Pl Ste 460 ... Fairfax VA 22030 *TF:* 888-224-7262 ■ *Web:* www.rbma.org	703-621-3355	621-3356	49-8
Radiology Support Devices Inc 1904 E Dominguez St ... Long Beach CA 90810 *Web:* www.rsdphantoms.com	310-518-0527		476
Radiometrics Midwest Corp 12 E Devonwood ... Romeoville IL 60446 *Web:* www.radiomet.com	815-293-0772	293-0820	743
Radiophone Engineering Inc 534 W Walnut St ... Springfield MO 65806 *TF:* 800-369-2929 ■ *Web:* www.radiophonewireless.com	417-862-6653		246
RadioShack Corp 300 RadioShack Cir ... Fort Worth TX 76102 *NYSE: RSH* ■ *TF:* 800-843-7422 ■ *Web:* www.radioshack.com	817-882-9380		35
Radio-Television News Directors Assn (RTNDA) 1600 K St NW Ste 700 ... Washington DC 20006 *Web:* www.rtdna.org	202-659-6510	223-4007	49-14
RadioU PO Box 1887 ... Westerville OH 43086 *TF:* 877-272-3468 ■ *Web:* www.radiou.com	877-272-3468		645
Radiowirenet Inc 314 Lafayette St ... Jefferson City MO 65101 *TF:* 800-392-8070 ■ *Web:* radiowire.net	573-659-7950		396
Radish Tools 12 Mckendree Ave ... Annapolis MD 21401 *Web:* www.radishtools.com	443-321-2732		317
Radisson 11340 Blondo S Ste 100 ... Omaha NE 68164 *TF:* 888-288-8889 ■ *Web:* www.radisson.com	800-615-7253		669
Radisson Chicago-O'Hare Hotel 1450 E Touhy Ave ... Des Plaines IL 60018 *TF:* 888-201-1718 ■ *Web:* www.radisson.com	847-296-8866		379
Radisson Hotel & Suites 100 W Michigan ... Kalamazoo MI 49007 *Web:* www.radisson.com/austin-hotel-tx-78701/txaustdt	269-343-3333		378
Radisson Hotel & Suites Fort Mc Murray 435 Gregoire Dr ... Fort Mcmurray AB T9H4K7 *Web:* www.radissonfortmcmurray.com	780-743-2400		379
Radisson Hotel Bloomington Mall of America 1700 American Blvd E ... Bloomington MN 55425 *TF Resv:* 800-967-9033 ■ *Web:* www.radisson.com	952-854-8700		379
Radisson Hotel Gateway Seattle-Tacoma Airport 18118 International Blvd ... Seattle WA 98188 *Web:* www.radisson.com	206-244-6666	244-6679	379
Radisson Milwaukee North Shore 7065 N Port Washington Rd ... Milwaukee WI 53217 *TF:* 800-395-7046 ■ *Web:* www.radisson.com	414-351-6960		379
Radisson Resort Parkway 2900 PkwyBlvd ... Kissimmee FL 34747 *TF:* 800-333-3333 ■ *Web:* www.radisson.com	407-396-7000	396-6792	669
RadiSys Corp 5445 NE Dawson Creek Dr ... Hillsboro OR 97124 *NASDAQ: RSYS* ■ *TF:* 800-950-0044 ■ *Web:* www.radisys.com	503-615-1100		625
RADIUS 7700 Wisconsin Ave Ste 400 ... Bethesda MD 20814 *TF:* 800-989-3059 ■ *Web:* www.radiustravel.com	301-718-9500		772
Radius Advertising 10883 Pearl Rd Ste 100 ... Strongsville OH 44136 *Web:* www.radiuscleveland.com	440-638-3800		5
Radius Engineering Inc 1042 West 2780 South ... Salt Lake City UT 84119 *Web:* www.radiuseng.com	801-886-2624		256
Radius Global Solutions LLC 50 W Skippack Pk ... Ambler PA 19002 *Web:* www.radiusgs.com	267-419-1111		160
Radius Partners LLC 360 N Main St Ste 3104 ... Andover MA 01810 *Web:* www.radiuspartnersllc.com	203-557-3845		690
Radius Professional HDD Tools PO Box 3106 ... Weatherford TX 76086 **Fax Area Code:* 817 ■ *TF:* 800-892-9114 ■ *Web:* www.radiushdd.com	800-892-9114	599-3024*	538
Radius Technology Group Inc 804 Pershing Dr Ste 1 ... Silver Spring MD 20910 *Web:* www.radius360.net	301-565-3400		225
Radius Ventures LLC 250 Park Ave Ste 1102 ... New York NY 10017 *Web:* www.radiusventures.com	212-897-7778	397-2656	792
Radixx Solutions International Inc 6310 Hazeltine National Dr ... Orlando FL 32822 *Web:* www.radixx.com	407-856-9009		224
Radley Corp 23077 Greenfield Rd Ste 440 ... Southfield MI 48075 *Web:* www.radley.com	248-559-6858		177
RadNet Inc 1516 Cotner Ave ... Los Angeles CA 90025 *Web:* www.radnet.com	310-445-2800	445-2980	415
Radnor Financial Advisors Inc 485 Devon Park Dr Ste 119 ... Wayne PA 19087 *TF:* 888-271-9922 ■ *Web:* www.radnorfinancial.com	610-975-0280		401
Radnor Lake State Park 1160 Otter Creek Rd ... Nashville TN 37220 *Web:* tnstateparks.com	615-373-3467		565
Radnor Township School Authority 135 S Wayne Ave ... Wayne PA 19087 *Web:* www.rtsd.org	610-688-8100		685
Rado Enterprises 20 Industrial Dr ... Bloomsburg PA 17815 *Web:* www.radoenterprises.com	570-759-0303		595
Radon Control Systems Inc 160 US Route 1 ... Freeport ME 04032 *TF:* 800-698-9655 ■ *Web:* awqinc.com	207-865-9200		35
Radsoft 322 E Sherman Ave ... Coeur D Alene ID 83814 *Web:* www.radsoft.com	208-665-0516		809
Radva Corp 604 17th St PO Box 2900 ... Radford VA 24143 *NYSE: RDVA* ■ *Web:* www.radva.com	540-731-3700		601
RadView Software Inc 991 Hgwy 22 W Ste 200 ... Bridgewater NJ 08807 *TF:* 888-723-8439 ■ *Web:* www.radview.com	908-526-7756		178-12
Radware Inc 575 Corporate Dr Lobby 2 ... Mahwah NJ 07430 *TF:* 888-234-5763 ■ *Web:* www.radware.com	201-512-9771	512-9774	178-11
Radwell International Inc 111 Mt Holly Bypass ... Lumberton NJ 08048 *Web:* www.radwell.com	609-288-9393		190
Rady Children's Hospital (RCH) 3020 Children's Way 3rd Fl ... San Diego CA 92123 **Fax:* Library ■ *TF:* 800-788-9029 ■ *Web:* www.rchsd.org	858-576-1700	966-5859*	374-1
Radyne Corp 211 W Boden St ... Milwaukee WI 53207 *TF:* 800-236-8360 ■ *Web:* www.radyne.com	414-481-8360	481-8303	318
RAE Corp 4615 Prime Pkwy ... McHenry IL 60050 *TF:* 800-323-7049 ■ *Web:* www.raemotors.com	815-385-3500		518
RAE Corp Technical Systems Div 4492 Hunt St PO Box 1206 ... Pryor OK 74361 *Web:* rae-corp.com	918-825-7222	825-0723	14
Rae Engineering & Inspection Ltd 4810 93 St NW ... Edmonton AB T6E5M4 *Web:* www.raeengineering.ca	780-469-2401		261
RAE Systems 3775 N First St ... San Jose CA 95134 *TF:* 877-723-2878 ■ *Web:* www.raesystems.com	408-952-8200	952-8480	201
Raeford-Hoke Chamber of Commerce 101 N Main St ... Raeford NC 28376	910-875-5929		139
Raf Technologies Inc 200 Lexington Ave ... Deland FL 32724 *TF:* 888-876-6424	386-736-1698	736-7338	767
RAF Technology Inc 15400 NE 90th St Ste 300 ... Redmond WA 98052 *TF:* 800-723-8674 ■ *Web:* www.raf.com	425-867-0700		177
Raff Printing Inc PO Box 42365 ... Pittsburgh PA 15203 *Web:* www.raffprinting.com	412-431-4044		627
Raffa Consulting Economists Inc 17 S Osceola Ave Ste 200 ... Orlando FL 32801 *Web:* raffaconsulting.com	407-648-5141		196
Raffa PC 1899 L St NW Ste 900 ... Washington DC 20036 *Web:* www.raffa.com	202-822-5000		2
Raffaello Hotel 201 E Delaware Pl ... Chicago IL 60611 *TF:* 800-898-7198 ■ *Web:* www.chicagoraffaello.com	312-943-5000	924-9158	379
Rafferty's Inc 1750 Scottsville Rd Ste 2 ... Bowling Green KY 42104 *Web:* www.raffertys.com	270-842-0123		670
Raffi's 1100 N BurkehaRdt Rd ... Evansville IN 47715	812-479-9166		671
Raffield Fisheries Inc 1624 Grouper Ave PO Box 309 ... Port Saint Joe FL 32456 *Web:* www.raffieldfisheries.com	850-229-8229	229-8782	285
Raffis Italian Cuisine 1100 N Burkhart Rd ... Evansville IN 47715	812-479-9166		671
Raffles Capital Group Inc 1 Burning Tree Rd ... Greenwich CT 06830 *Web:* www.rafflescapital.com	203-629-5604		401

Name / Address	City	State	Zip	Phone	Fax	Class
Rafn Co 1721 132nd Ave NE *Web:* www.rafn.com	Bellevue	WA	98005	425-702-6600		186
Raft River Rural Electric Co-op Inc 155 N Main St PO Box 617 *TF:* 800-342-7732 ■ *Web:* www.rrelectric.com	Malta	ID	83342	208-645-2211		245
Ragan & Massey Inc 100 Ponchatoula Pkwy *TF:* 800-858-7378 ■ *Web:* raganandmassey.com	Ponchatoula	LA	70454	985-386-6042		237
Ragan & Ragan p C 3100 Rt 138 W *Web:* www.raganlaw.com	Wall Township	NJ	07719	732-280-4100		428
Ragan Communications Inc 316 N Michigan Ave Ste 400 *TF:* 800-878-5331 ■ *Web:* www.ragan.com/main/home.aspx	Chicago	IL	60601	312-960-4100	960-4106	531-2
Ragazzi's 3843 Electric Rd *Web:* www.ragazzis.com	Roanoke	VA	24018	540-989-9022		671
Rage Corp 3949 Lyman Dr *Web:* www.rageplastics.us	Hilliard	OH	43026	614-771-4771		596
RAGE Inc 1313 N Webb Rd Ste 200 *Web:* www.rage-inc.com	Wichita	KS	67206	316-634-1888		196
Rage Unlimited Inc 1/15 Pearl St *Web:* rageunlimited.com	Boulder	CO	80302	303-444-6506		344
Ragin' Shrimp 3624 Central Ave SE *Web:* www.raginshrimp.com	Albuquerque	NM	87108	505-254-1544		671
Raging River Exploration Inc 605 - Fifth Ave SW 17th Fl *Web:* www.rrexploration.com	Calgary	AB	T2P3H5	403-387-2950		536
Raging Waters 2333 S White Rd *Web:* www.rwsplash.com	San Jose	CA	95148	408-238-9900	270-2022	32
Raging Waters Sacramento 1600 Exposition Blvd *Web:* www.rwsac.com	Sacramento	CA	95815	916-924-3747	924-1314	32
Ragland Mills Inc 14079 Hammer Rd *TF:* 800-424-9300 ■ *Web:* www.raglandmills.com	Neosho	MO	64850	417-451-2510		447
Ragnar Benson Construction LLC 250 S NW Hwy *Web:* www.ragnarbenson.com	Park Ridge	IL	60068	847-090-4900	602 9320	186
Rago & Son Inc 1029 51st Ave *Web:* www.rago-son.com	Oakland	CA	94601	510-536-5700		483
Rahmberg Stover & Associates LLC 789 Vinewood Ave *Web:* rahmbergstover.com	Birmingham	MI	48009	248-203-7710		261
Rahway Public Library 2 City Hall Plaza *TF:* 800-952-8392 ■ *Web:* www.rahwaylibrary.org	Rahway	NJ	07065	732-340-1551	340-0393	434-3
Raia & Associates Inc 930 Bunty Station Rd	Delaware	OH	43015	740-369-6882		193
Rail Car Service Co 584 Fairground Rd *TF:* 800-521-2151 ■ *Web:* www.parailcar.com	Mercer	PA	16137	724-662-3660		650
Rail City Casino 2121 Victorian Ave *Web:* www.railcity.com	Sparks	NV	89431	775-359-9440		452
Rail Europe Inc 44 S Broadway 11th Fl *TF:* 800 361 7245 ■ *Web:* www.raileurope.com	White Plains	NY	10601	914-682-2999		775
Rail Exchange Inc 1150 State St *Web:* railexchangeinc.com	Chicago Heights	IL	60411	708-757-3317		770
Rail Transit Consultants Inc 901 S Railroad St *Web:* www.railtransit.com	Penn	PA	15675	724-527-2386		108
RailCrew Xpress LLC 15729 College Blvd *Web:* www.railcrewxpress.com	Lenexa	KS	66219	913-928-5000		108
Railex Corp 89-02 Atlantic Ave *TF:* 800-352-3244 ■ *Web:* www.railexcorp.com	Ozone Park	NY	11416	718-845-5454	738-1020	207
Railhead Corp 12549 S Laramie Ave *TF:* 800-235-1782 ■ *Web:* www.railheadcorp.com	Alsip	IL	60803	700-044-5500		770
Railhead Smokehouse 2900 Montgomery St *Web:* railheadsmokehouse.com	Fort Worth	TX	76107	817-738-9808	732-4059	671
Railinc Corp 7001 Weston Pkwy Ste 200 *Web:* www.railinc.com	Cary	NC	27513	919-651-5193		577
Railplan International Inc 1200 Bernard Dr *TF:* 800-433-3222 ■ *Web:* www.railplan.com	Baltimore	MD	21223	410-947-5900		261
Railroad Bazaar LLC 1207 Eidson St *Web:* www.railroadbazaar.com	Athens	AL	35611	256-232-5800		526
Railroad Construction Co 75-77 Grove St *Web:* www.railnj.com	Paterson	NJ	07503	973-684-0362		186
Railroad Pass Hotel & Casino 2800 S Boulder Hwy *TF:* 800-654-0877 ■ *Web:* www.railroadpass.com	Henderson	NV	89002	702-294-5000	294-0092	133
Railroad Retirement Board 844 N Rush St *TF:* 877-772-5772 ■ *Web:* www.rrb.gov/general/contact_us.asp	Chicago	IL	60611	312-751-4300	751-7136	340-20
Rails Co 101 Newark Way *TF:* 800-217-2457 ■ *Web:* www.railsco.com	Maplewood	NJ	07040	973-763-4320	763-2585	770
Railserve Inc 1691 Phoenix Blvd Ste 110 *TF:* 800-345-7245 ■ *Web:* www.railserveinc.com	Atlanta	GA	30349	770-996-6838		651
Rails-to-Trails Conservancy (RTC) 2121 Ward Ct NW 5th Fl *TF:* 800-944-6847 ■ *Web:* www.railstotrails.org	Washington	DC	20037	202-331-9696	223-9257	48-13
Railtech Ltd 325 Lee Ave *TF:* 877-759-3653 ■ *Web:* www.railtech.ca	Montreal	QC	H9X3S3	514-457-4760	457-7111	770
Railtown 1897 State Historic Park PO Box 1250 *Web:* www.railtown1897.org	Jamestown	CA	95327	209-984-3953		565
Railway Specialties Corp 2979 State Rd *Web:* www.railwayspecialties.com	Croydon	PA	19021	215-788-9242		350
Railway Supply Institute Inc (RSI) 425 Third St Ste 920 *TF:* 800-226-5962 ■ *Web:* www.rsiweb.org	Washington	DC	20024	202-347-4664	347-0047	49-21
RailWorks Comstock 83 Central Ave *Web:* www.railworks.com	East Farmingdale	NY	11735	212-502-7900	502-1865	189-4
RailWorks Corp 5 Penn Plaza *TF:* 800-542-4132 ■ *Web:* www.railworks.com	New York	NY	10001	212-502-7900		188-8

Name / Address	City	State	Zip	Phone	Fax	Class
Raimondo Gina (D) State House *Web:* www.governor.state.ri.us	Providence	RI	02903	401-222-2080	222-8096	343
Raimondo Pettit & Glassman 21515 Hawthorne Blvd Ste 1250 *Web:* www.rpgcpa.com	Torrance	CA	90503	310-540-5990		2
Rain & Hail LLC 9200 Northpark Dr Ste 250 *Web:* www.rainhail.com	Johnston	IA	50131	515-559-1200		390
Rain Creek Baking Co, The 2401 W Almond Ave *Web:* www.raincreekbaking.com	Madera	CA	93637	603-546-2879		297-11
rain Technologies LP, The 11522 W Washington Blvd *Web:* www.thebrain.com	Los Angeles	CA	90066	310-751-5000		174
Rain Trade Corp 19 Skokie Valley Rd *Web:* www.guttersupply.com	Lake Bluff	IL	60044	847-283-0006		697
Rainbo Record Manufacturing Corp 8960 Eton Ave *Web:* www.rainborecords.com	Canoga Park	CA	91304	818-280-1100		797
Rainbow Advertising Lp 3904 W Vickery Blvd *TF:* 800-645-7377 ■ *Web:* www.rainbowadvertising.com	Fort Worth	TX	76107	817-738-3838		7
Rainbow Art Glass Inc 1761 Rt 34 S *TF:* 800-526-2356 ■ *Web:* www.orderrag.com	Farmingdale	NJ	07727	732-681-6003	681-4984	329
Rainbow Chinese 2739 Nicollet Ave S *Web:* www.rainbowrestaurant.com	Minneapolis	MN	55408	612-870-7084		671
Rainbow Computers Corp 6000 NW 97th Ave Ste 21 *Web:* www.rainbowcc.com	Doral	FL	33178	305-592-2611		179
Rainbow Courts Motel & Apartments 915 E Cameron Ave *TF:* 800-772-1213 ■ *Web:* www.rainbowcourts.com	Rockdale	TX	76567	512 446-2361		707
Rainbow Falls State Park 4008 Washington 6 *Web:* www.parks.wa.gov	Chehalis	WA	98532	360-291-3767		565
Rainbow Graphics Inc 933 Tower Rd *Web:* www.rainbowgraphics.com	Mundelein	IL	60060	847-824-9600		627
Rainbow Grocery Co-op Inc 1745 Folsom St *TF:* 877-720-2667 ■ *Web:* rainbow.coop	San Francisco	CA	94103	415-863-0620		345
Rainbow Hospice 1550 Bishop Ct Ste 145 *Web:* www.rainbowhospice.org	Park Ridge	IL	60068	847-685-9900	685-6390	371
Rainbow Inc 1051 Industrial Park Rd *Web:* www.rainbowsvc.com	Clarksville	TN	37040	931-552-7783		454
Rainbow International 1010 N University Park Dr *TF:* 855-724-6269 ■ *Web:* www.rainbowintl.com	Waco	TX	76707	254-756-5463		152
Rainbow Light Nutritional Sys Inc 100 Ave Tea *TF:* 800-635-1233 ■ *Web:* www.rainbowlight.com	Santa Cruz	CA	95060	800-635-1233		479
Rainbow Lodge 2011 Ella Blvd *TF:* 866-861-8666 ■ *Web:* www.rainbow-lodge.com	Houston	TX	77008	713-861-8666		671
Rainbow Manufacturing Co PO Box 70 **Fax:* Cust Svc ■ *Web:* www.rainbowirrigation.com	Fitzgerald	GA	31750	229-423-4341	423-4645*	273
Rainbow Palace 2787 E Oakland Pk Blvd *Web:* www.rainbowpalace.com	Fort Lauderdale	FL	33306	954-565-5652		671
Rainbow Restaurant 212 W Laurel St *Web:* rainbowfortcollins.com	Fort Collins	CO	80521	970-221-2664		671
Rainbow Springs State Park 19158 SW 81st Pl Rd *Web:* www.floridastateparks.org	Dunnellon	FL	34432	352-465-8555		565
Rainbow Treecare Inc 11571 K-Tel Dr *Web:* www.rainbowtreecare.com	Minnetonka	MN	55343	952-922-3810		776
Rainbow Trout Ranch (RTR) 1484 FDR 250 PO Box 458 *TF:* 800-633-3397 ■ *Web:* www.rainbowtroutranch.com	Antonito	CO	81120	719-376-2440		239
Rainbow/PUSH Coalition Inc 930 E 50th St *Web:* www.rainbowpush.org	Chicago	IL	60615	773-373-3366	373-3571	48-5
Rainbows 1007 Church St Ste 408 *Web:* www.rainbows.org	Evanston	IL	60201	847-952-1770		48-6
Raincii 1330 Greengate Dr Ste 300 *Web:* www.raincii.com	Covington	LA	70433	985-635-3400	888-1093	580
Raincity Grill 1193 Denman St	Vancouver	BC	V6G2N1	604-685-7337		671
Raindance Spa at the Lodge at Sonoma Renaissance Resort 1325 Broadway *TF:* 866-263-0758 ■ *Web:* www.marriott.com	Sonoma	CA	95476	707-935-6600		707
Raindancer Steak House 2300 Palm Beach Lakes Blvd *Web:* www.raindancersteakhouse.com	West Palm Beach	FL	33409	561-684-2810		671
Rainforest Action Network (RAN) 221 Pine St 5th Fl *TF:* 800-368-1819 ■ *Web:* www.ran.org	San Francisco	CA	94104	415-398-4404	398-2732	48-13
Rainforest Cafe 12801 W Sunrise Blvd *Web:* www.rainforestcafe.com	Sunrise	FL	33323	954-851-1015		671
Rainforest Cafe 1510 W Loop S *Web:* www.rainforestcafe.com	Houston	TX	77027	713-850-1010		670
Rainforest Cafe 1515 S Disneyland Dr *Web:* www.rainforestcafe.com	Anaheim	CA	92807	714-772-0413		671
Rainier Group Investment Advisory LLC 500 108th Ave N E Ste 2000 *TF:* 800-800-8974 ■ *Web:* rainiergroup.com	Bellevue	WA	98004	425-463-3000		656
Rainier Industries Ltd 18375 Olympic Ave S *TF:* 800-869-7162 ■ *Web:* www.rainier.com	Tukwila	WA	98188	425-251-1800	251-5065	733
Rainier Investment Management Mutual Funds 601 Union St Ste 2801 *TF:* 800-536-4640 ■ *Web:* www.rainierfunds.com	Seattle	WA	98101	800-536-4640		528
Rainier Surgical Inc 1144 29th St NW *Web:* www.rainiersurgical.com	Auburn	WA	98001	253-486-0500	486-0501	475

Phone | Fax | Class

Rainmaker Group Ventures LLC, The
4550 N Point Pkwy Ste 400 Alpharetta GA 30022 678-578-5700 403
TF: 800-669-0871 ■ *Web:* www.letitrain.com

Rainmaker Recording & Creative
1901 E Franklin St Ste 101 Richmond VA 23223 804-771-9300 657
Web: www.rainmakerstudios.com

RainMaker Securities LLC
11390 W Olympic Blvd Ste 380 Los Angeles CA 90064 888-333-1091 691
TF: 888-333-1091 ■ *Web:* www.rainmakersecurities.com

RAINN (Rape Abuse & Incest National Network)
2000 L St NW Ste 406 Washington DC 20036 202-544-1034 544-3556 48-6
TF: 800-656-4673 ■ *Web:* www.rainn.org

Raintree Graphics Inc
5921 Richard St Jacksonville FL 32216 904-396-1653 627
Web: www.raintreegraphics.com

Raintree Resorts Management Company LLC
PO Box 350 Teton Village WY 83025 307-734-9777 378
TF: 866-352-9777 ■ *Web:* www.tetonclub.com

Raintree Systems Inc
27307 Via Industria Temecula CA 92590 951-252-9400 177
Web: www.raintreeinc.com

Raintree, The
102 San Marco Ave. Saint Augustine FL 32084 904-824-7211 671
Web: www.raintreerestaurant.com

Rainwater, Holt & Sexton PA
6315 Ranch Dr Little Rock AR 72223 800-434-4800 428
TF: 800-434-4800 ■ *Web:* www.callrainwater.com

Rainwise Inc 25 Federal St Bar Harbor ME 04609 207-288-5169 407
TF: 800-762-5723 ■ *Web:* www.rainwise.com

Rainy River Community College
1501 Hwy 71 International Falls MN 56649 218-285-7722 285-2239* 162
**Fax:* Admissions ■ *TF:* 800-456-3996 ■ *Web:* www.rainyriver.edu

Raisbeck Engineering Inc
4411 S Ryan Way Seattle WA 98178 206-723-2000 256
Web: www.raisbeck.com

RAJ Manufacturing Inc 2692 Dow Ave Tustin CA 92780 714-838-3110 5
Web: rajswim.com

Raj, The 1734 Jasmine Ave Fairfield IA 52556 641-472-9580 472-2496 706
TF: 800-248-9050 ■ *Web:* www.theraj.com

Raja Rani 400 S Div St. Ann Arbor MI 48104 734-995-1545 671

Rajason Tools Inc 11664 County Rd 42 Tecumseh ON N8N2M1 519-979-1263 358
Web: www.rajasontools.com

Rajdoot 2424 Fourth St SW Calgary AB T2S2T4 403-245-0181 671
Web: www.rajdoot.ca

Rajkowski Hansmeier Ltd
11 Seventh Ave N Saint Cloud MN 56303 320-251-1055 428
TF: 800-445-9617 ■ *Web:* www.rajhan.com

Rajput Indian Cuisine 742 W 21st St. Norfolk VA 23517 757-625-4634 671
Web: www.rajputonline.com

Rak Medical Inc 340 Duquesne Way Sewickley PA 15143 412-741-2880 366
Web: rakmedical.com

Rakuten Marketing
215 Park Ave S 2nd Fl New York NY 10003 646-943-8200 943-8204 7
TF: 888-880-8430 ■ *Web:* rakutenmarketing.com

Rakuten.com Shopping
85 Enterprise St Aliso Viejo CA 92656 949-389-2000 389-2800 791
TF: 800-800-0800 ■ *Web:* www.rakuten.com

Ralco Industries Inc
2720 Auburn Ct Auburn Hills MI 48326 248-853-3200 483
Web: www.ralcoind.com

Ralco Nutrition Inc 1600 Hahn Rd Marshall MN 56258 800-533-5306 447
TF: 800-533-5306 ■ *Web:* www.ralconutrition.com

Raleigh America Inc
6004 S 190th St Ste 101 Kent WA 98032 800-222-5527 872-0257* 82
**Fax Area Code:* 253 ■ *TF:* 800-222-5527 ■ *Web:* www.diamondback.com

Raleigh City Museum
220 Fayetteville St Raleigh NC 27601 919-996-2220 520
TF: 800-315-2621 ■ *Web:* www.cityofraleighmuseum.org

Raleigh Convention Ctr
500 S Salisbury St Raleigh NC 27601 919-996-8500 205
TF: 800-822-6285 ■ *Web:* www.raleighconvention.com

Raleigh Correctional Ctr for Women
1201 S State St. Raleigh NC 27610 919-733-4248 213

Raleigh County 215 Main St. Beckley WV 25801 304-255-9178 338
TF: 800-509-6568 ■ *Web:* raleighcountyassessor.com

Raleigh County Public Library
221 N Kanawha St Beckley WV 25801 304-255-0511 434-3

Raleigh Enterprises
5300 Melrose Ave 4th Fl. Hollywood CA 90038 310-899-8900 899-8910 185
Web: www.raleighenterprises.com

Raleigh General Hospital
1710 Harper Rd Beckley WV 25801 304-256-4100 256-4009 374-3
Web: www.raleighgeneral.com

Raleigh National Cemetery
501 Rock Quarry Rd Raleigh NC 27610 252-637-2912 637-7145 136
TF: 800-827-1000 ■ *Web:* www.cem.va.gov/cems/nchp/raleigh.asp

Raleigh Studios 5300 Melrose Ave Hollywood CA 90038 888-960-3456 514
TF: 888-960-3456 ■ *Web:* www.raleighstudios.com

Raleigh Symphony Orchestra
PO Box 25878 Raleigh NC 27611 919-546-9755 573-3
Web: raleighsymphony.org

Raleigh USA 6004 S 190th St Ste 101 Kent WA 98032 253-395-1100 82
TF: 800-222-5527 ■ *Web:* www.raleighusa.com

Raleigh, The 1775 Collins Ave Miami Beach FL 33139 305-534-6300 707
Web: www.raleighhotel.com

Raleigh-Durham International Airport
PO Box 80001 Raleigh NC 27623 919-840-2123 840-0175 27
TF: 800-252-7522 ■ *Web:* www.rdu.com

Raley's 500 W Capitol Ave Sacramento CA 95605 916-373-3333 373-0881* 345
**Fax:* Cust Svc ■ *TF:* 800-925-9989 ■ *Web:* www.raleys.com

Ra-lin & Associates Bldg Contr
101 Parkwood Cir. Carrollton GA 30117 770-834-4884 186
Web: www.ra-lin.com

Ralls County Courthouse
311 S Main St PO Box 466. New London MO 63459 573-985-5633 985-3446 338
Web: www.rallscountymo.net

Ralls County Electric Co-op
17594 Hwy 19 PO Box 157. New London MO 63459 573-985-8711 245
TF: 877-985-8711 ■ *Web:* www.rallscountyelectric.com

Rally Education LLC 22 Railroad Ave Glen Head NY 11545 516-671-9300 196
Web: www.rallyeducation.com

Rally House & Kansas Sampler
9750 Quivira Rd Lenexa KS 66215 800-645-5394 791
TF: 800-645-5409 ■ *Web:* www.rallyhouse.com

Rally Point Management LLC
630C Anchors St NW Fort Walton Beach FL 32548 850-226-7589 396
Web: www.rallypointmanagement.com

Rallyorg.org
995 Market St 2nd Fl San Francisco CA 94105 888-648-2220 387
TF: 888-648-2220 ■ *Web:* rally.org

Ralm Inc 4620 Mercason Rd. Fayetteville NC 28311 910-486-4491 463

Ralph & Kacoo's
1700 Old Minden Rd Ste 141 Bossier City LA 71111 318-747-6660 671
Web: ralphandkacoos.com

Ralph 'N Rich's 815 Main St. Bridgeport CT 06604 203-366-3597 671
Web: www.ralphnrichs.com

Ralph Andersen & Assoc
5800 Stanford Ranch Rd. Rocklin CA 95765 916-630-4900 463
Web: www.ralphandersen.com

Ralph Brennan's Jazz Kitchen
1590 S Disneyland Dr Downtown Disney Anaheim CA 92802 714-776-5200 999-2123 671
Web: www.rbjazzkitchen.com

Ralph C Mehler Agency Inc
62 E Shenango St. Sharpsville PA 16150 724-962-5757 390
Web: mehlerinsurance.com

Ralph Foster Museum
1 Cultural Ct PO Box 17 Point Lookout MO 65726 417-690-3407 520
Web: www.rfostermuseum.com

Ralph Friedland & Bros
17 Industrial Dr. Keyport NJ 07735 732-290-9800 87
TF: 800-631-2162 ■ *Web:* friedlandshades.com

Ralph H Johnson VA Medical Center
109 Bee St Charleston SC 29401 843-577-5011 374-8
TF: 888-878-6884 ■ *Web:* www.charleston.va.gov

Ralph Marlin & Co 1701 Pearl St Ste 4 Waukesha WI 53186 262-549-5100 155-13

Ralph Moyle Inc (RMI) 55475 N Main St. Mattawan MI 49071 269-668-4531 780
Web: www.ralphmoyle.com

Ralph Pill Electrical Supply Co
50 Von Hillern St Boston MA 02125 617-265-8800 288-1776 246
TF: 800-897-1769 ■ *Web:* www.needco.com

Ralph Rosenberg Court Reporters Inc
1001 Bishop St Ste 2460 Honolulu HI 96813 888-524-5888 445
TF: 888-524-5888 ■ *Web:* www.hawaiicourtreporters.com

Ralph S Inouye Company Ltd
Rm 220E 500 Alakawa St Honolulu HI 96819 808-839-9002 256
Web: www.rsinouye.com

Ralph Stover State Park
6011 State Park Rd Pipersville PA 18947 610-982-5560 565
Web: www.dcnr.state.pa.us

Ralph W. Earl Company Inc
5930 E Molloy Rd. Syracuse NY 13211 315-454-4431 358
Web: www.rwearl.com

Ralph Warner & Sons Inc Plumbing & Heating
161 Berlin St. Southington CT 06489 860-628-6826 189-10

Ralph Wilson Stadium 1 Bills Dr Orchard Park NY 14127 716-648-1800 720
TF: 877-228-4257 ■ *Web:* www.buffalobills.com

Ralphs Grocery Co 1014 Vine St Cincinnati OH 45202 800-576-4377 345
TF Cust Svc: 800-576-4377 ■ *Web:* www.ralphs.com

Ralphs-pugh Company Inc
3931 Oregon St Benicia CA 94510 707-745-6363 207
TF: 800-486-0021 ■ *Web:* www.ralphs-pugh.com

Ralston Discount Liquor
3147 Southmore Blvd. Houston TX 77004 713-524-3045 524-5981 237
Web: www.ralstonliquor.com

Ralston Metal Products Ltd
50 Watson Rd S Guelph ON N1L1E2 800-265-7611 836-9763* 480
**Fax Area Code:* 519 ■ *TF:* 800-265-7611 ■ *Web:* www.ralstonmetal.com

Ralston Middle School 8202 Lakeview St. Omaha NE 68127 402-331-4701 685
Web: ralstonschools.org

Ram Computers Inc
5500 N Western Ave Ste 101c. Oklahoma City OK 73118 405-842-9495 175
Web: www.ramcomputersupply.com

RAM Enterprise Inc 1800 Boulder St. Denver CO 80211 303-433-7094 631
Web: www.rcfdenver.org

Ram Graphics Inc 2408 S Pk Ave. Alexandria IN 46001 800-531-4656 551-6846 687
TF: 800-531-4656

RAM Industrial Services Inc
5460B Pottsville Pk Leesport PA 19533 610-916-8000 203
Web: www.rammotors.com

RAM Industries Inc 13119 Mula Ct Stafford TX 77477 281-495-9056 236
Web: www.ramwindows.com

Ram Manufacturing Co
3172 E Deseret Dr S St George UT 84790 435-673-4603 790
Web: www.ramcompany.com

Ram Precision Industries Inc
11125 Yankee Rd Ste A. Dayton OH 45458 937-885-7700 454
Web: www.ramprecision.com

Ram Restaurant & Brewery
10013 59th Ave SW Lakewood WA 98499 253-588-1788 588-9617 670
Web: www.theram.com

Ram Tool & Supply Co
3620 Eigth Ave S Birmingham AL 35222 205-714-3300 351
Web: www.ram-tool.com

Ram Welding Company Inc 93 Rado Dr Naugatuck CT 06770 203-729-2289 480
TF: 800-927-6485 ■ *Web:* www.ramwelding.com

Ram Winch & Hoist Management LLC
14603 Chrisman Rd Houston TX 77039 281-999-8665 351
Web: www.ramwinch.com

Ram's Horn Restaurant
26200 W 12 Mile Rd. Southfield MI 48034 248-350-3430 670
Web: ramshornrestaurants.com

Rama 327 Fourth Ave San Diego CA 92101 619-501-8424 671

Rama Corp 600 W Esplanade Ave. San Jacinto CA 92583 951-654-7351 654-3748 14
TF: 800-472-5670 ■ *Web:* ramacorporation.com

Ramada Hotel & Suites Lethbridge
2375 Mayor Magrath Dr S Hwy 4 and Mayor Magrath Dr
Lethbridge AB T1K7M1 403-380-5050 707
Web: www.wyndhamhotels.com

Name / Address	City	State	ZIP	Phone	Fax	Class
Ramada Inn Airport 2275 Marina Mile Blvd STATE Rd 84 *TF:* 800-509-9854 ■ *Web:* www.ramadainnairport.com	Fort Lauderdale	FL	33312	954-584-4000		378
Ramada Plaza Beach Resort 1500 Miracle Strip Pkwy SE *TF:* 800-874-8962 ■ *Web:* www.ramadafwb.com	Fort Walton Beach	FL	32548	850-243-9161		378
Ramaker & Assoc Inc 1120 Dallas St *Web:* ramaker.com	Sauk City	WI	53583	608-643-4100		261
Ramallo Bros Printing Inc Carr 1 Km 255 Bo Quebrad	Rio Piedras	PR	00926	787-287-0303	620-8686	627
Ramapo Catskill Library System 619 Rt 17-M *TF:* 800-327-7343 ■ *Web:* www.rcls.org	Middletown	NY	10940	845-343-1131		434-3
Ramapo College of New Jersey 505 Ramapo Valley Rd *Fax: Admissions ■ *Web:* www.ramapo.edu	Mahwah	NJ	07430	201-684-7500	684-7964*	166
Ramapo Mountain State Forest c/o Ringwood State Pk 1304 Sloatsburg Rd *TF:* 800-852-7899 ■ *Web:* www.njparksandforests.org/parks/ramapo.html	Ringwood	NJ	07456	973-962-7031		565
Ramapo Sales & Marketing Inc 4760 Goer Dr Ste F *TF:* 800-866-9173 ■ *Web:* www.ramapoglass.com	North Charleston	SC	29406	800-866-9173		195
Ramapo Wholesalers Inc 54B Kennedy Dr *TF:* 800-458-7329 ■ *Web:* ramapowholesalers.com	Spring Valley	NY	10977	845-425-8400		612
Ramberg & Assoc Pa 1080 SW Wanamaker Rd *Web:* rambergandassociates.com	Topeka	KS	66604	785-273-7276		2
Ramblin Express Transportation 3465 Astrozon Pl *TF:* 800-772-6254 ■ *Web:* www.ramblinexpress.com	Colorado Springs	CO	80910	719-590-8687		108
Ramblin Jack's 520 Fourth Ave E *Web:* www.ramblinjacks.com	Olympia	WA	98501	360-754-8909		671
Ramboll Environ 4350 N Fairfax Dr Ste 300 *Web:* www.ramboll-environ.com	Arlington	VA	22203	703-516-2300	516-2345	192
Rambus Inc 1050 Enterprise Way Ste 700 *NASDAQ: RMBS* ■ *Web:* www.rambus.com	Sunnyvale	CA	94089	408-462-8000	462-8001	696
Rambusch Decorating Co 160 Cornelison Ave *Web:* www.rambusch.com	Jersey City	NJ	07304	201-333-2525	433-3355	329
Ramcel Engineering Co 2926 MacArthur Blvd *Web:* www.ramcel.com	Northbrook	IL	60062	847-272-6980	272-7196	488
Ramco Systems Corp 3150 Brunswick Pk Ste 130 *TF:* 800-472-0201 ■ *Web:* www.ramco.com	Lawrenceville	NJ	08648	609-620-4800		225
Ramco-Gershenson Properties Trust 31500 NW Hwy Ste 300 *NYSE: RPT* ■ *TF:* 800-937-5449 ■ *Web:* rgpt.com	Farmington Hills	MI	48334	248-350-9900	350-9925	655
Ramen-Ya 101 W Fourth St *Web:* www.ramenya.nyc	New York	NY	10014	212-989-5440		671
Ramey Chandler Quinn & Zito 750 Bering Dr Ste 600 *Web:* www.ramey-chandler.com	Houston	TX	77057	713-266-0074		445
Ramey Kemp & Assoc Inc 5808 Faringdon Pl Ste 100 *Web:* rameykemp.com	Raleigh	NC	27609	919-872-5115		261
Ramgen Power Systems LLC 11808 Northup Way Ste W-190 *Web:* www.ramgen.com	Bellevue	WA	98005	425-828-4919		480
Ramius Corp 201-227 Rue Montcalm *Web:* recollective.com	Gatineau	QC	J8Y3B9	613-230-3808		225
Ramona Chamber of Commerce 960 Main St *Web:* www.ramonachamber.com	Ramona	CA	92065	760-789-1311	789-1317	139
Ramos Oil Company Inc 1515 S River Rd *TF Cust Svc:* 800-477-7266 ■ *Web:* www.ramosoil.com	West Sacramento	CA	95691	916-371-2570	371-0635	579
Rampart Brokerage Corp 1983 Marcus Ave Ste C130 *TF:* 800-772-6727 ■ *Web:* www.rampartinsurance.com	New Hyde Park	NY	11042	516-538-7000	390-3555	390
Rampart Investment Management Company LLC 1 International Pl 14th Fl *Web:* www.rampart-im.com	Boston	MA	02110	617-342-6900		401
Rampart Supply Inc 1001 N Union Blvd *TF:* 800-748-1837 ■ *Web:* www.rampartsupply.com	Colorado Springs	CO	80909	719-482-7333		612
RamQuest Software Inc 5801 Tennyson Pkwy Ste 500 *TF:* 800-893-3241 ■ *Web:* www.ramquest.com	Plano	TX	75024	214-291-1600		177
Ramrod Industries LLC 800 S Monroe St *Web:* www.ramrodindustries.com	Spencer	WI	54479	715-659-4996		641
Rams Head Inn 9 W White Horse Pike *Web:* ramsheadinn.com	Galloway	NJ	08205	609-652-1700		671
Ramsbottom Printing Inc 135 Waldron Rd *Web:* www.rpiprinting.net	Fall River	MA	02720	508-730-2220		627
Ramsey Board of Education 266 E Main St *Web:* www.ramsey.k12.nj.us	Ramsey	NJ	07446	201-785-2300	934-6623	685
Ramsey County 524 Fourth Ave NE *Web:* www.co.ramsey.nd.us	Devils Lake	ND	58301	701-662-7001		338
Ramsey County 15 W Kellogg Blvd *TF:* 866-520-7225 ■ *Web:* www.ramseycounty.us	Saint Paul	MN	55102	651-266-8000	266-8039	338
Ramsey County Public Library 4570 N Victoria St *TF:* 888-335-9632 ■ *Web:* www.rclreads.org	Shoreview	MN	55126	651-486-2200	486-2220	434-3
Ramsey House 2614 Thorngrove Pk *Web:* www.ramseyhouse.org	Knoxville	TN	37914	865-546-0745	546-1851	50-3
Ramsey Lake State Recreation Area Ramsey Lake Rd PO Box 97 *Web:* www.dnr.illinois.gov/parks/pages/ramseylake.aspx	Ramsey	IL	62080	618-423-2215		565
Ramsey Land Surveying LLC 8718 SW Pkwy	Austin	TX	78735	512-301-9398		727
Ramsey Popcorn Company Inc 5645 Clover Valley Rd NW *Web:* www.ramseypopcorn.com	Ramsey	IN	47166	812-347-2441		123

Name / Address	City	State	ZIP	Phone	Fax	Class
Ramsey Products Corp 3701 Performance Rd PO Box 668827 *Web:* www.ramseychain.com	Charlotte	NC	28266	704-394-0322	394-9134	620
Ramsey Winch Company Inc 1600 N Garnett Rd *TF:* 800-777-2760 ■ *Web:* www.ramsey.com	Tulsa	OK	74116	918-438-2760	438-6688	190
Ramsey-Shilling Commercial Real Estate Services Inc 6711 Forest Lawn Dr *Web:* www.ramsey-shilling.com	Los Angeles	CA	90068	323-851-6666		652
Ramsoft Systems Inc 29777 Telegraph Rd Ste 2250 *Web:* www.ramsoft.net	Southfield	MI	48034	248-354-0100		177
Ramtech Bldg Systems Inc 1400 Hwy 287 S *Fax Area Code: 817 ■ *TF:* 800-568-9376 ■ *Web:* www.ramtechmodular.com/index.html	Mansfield	TX	76063	800-568-9376	473-3485*	186
Ramtron International Corp 1850 Ramtron Dr *NASDAQ: RMTR* ■ *TF:* 800-541-4736 ■ *Web:* www.cypress.com	Colorado Springs	CO	80921	719-481-7000		696
RAN (Rainforest Action Network) 221 Pine St 5th Fl *TF:* 800-368-1819 ■ *Web:* www.ran.org	San Francisco	CA	94104	415-398-4404	398-2732	48-13
Ran One Inc 7567 Amador Valley Blvd Ste 304 *Fax Area Code: 925 ■ *Web:* global.ranone.com	Dublin	CA	94568	510-535-9730	833-9658*	463
Ranac Computer Corp 4181 E 96th St Ste 280 *TF:* 800-844-0141 ■ *Web:* ranac.com	Indianapolis	IN	46240	317-844-0141		180
Ranal Inc 2851 High Meadow Cir Ste 120	Auburn Hills	MI	48326	248-852-5955		261
Ranbaxy Pharmaceuticals Inc 600 College Rd E Ste 2100	Princeton	NJ	08540	609-720-9200	720-1155	583
Ranch at Steamboat 1800 Ranch Rd *TF:* 888-686-8075 ■ *Web:* www.ranch-steamboat.com	Steamboat Springs	CO	80487	970-879-3000		379
Ranch at Ucross, The 1701 Sheridan Ave *Web:* blairhotels.com	Cody	WY	82414	307-737-2281		206
Ranch Inn 45 E Pearl St *TF:* 800-348-5599 ■ *Web:* www.ranchinn.com	Jackson	WY	83001	307-733-6363	733-0623	379
Ranch Santa Fe Technology 5961 Kearny Villa Rd	San Diego	CA	92123	858-565-7224		177
Ranchers Club of New Mexico 1901 University Blvd NE *Web:* www.theranchersclubofnm.com	Albuquerque	NM	87102	505-889-8071		671
Rancho Alegre Lodge 3600 S Pk Loop Rd PO Box 998 *Web:* www.ranchoalegre.com	Jackson	WY	83001	307-733-7988		379
Rancho Bernardo Inn 17550 Bernardo Oaks Dr *TF:* 800-542-6096 ■ *Web:* www.ranchobernardoinn.com	San Diego	CA	92128	858-675-8500	675-8501	671
Rancho Bldg Materials Co 4701 Wible Rd	Bakersfield	CA	93313	661-831-0831		183
Rancho Chico Family Restaurant 2023 W NW Blvd *Web:* www.mexicanrestaurantspokane.com	Spokane	WA	99205	509-467-0022		671
Rancho Cordova Chamber of Commerce 2729 Prospect Pk Dr Ste 117 *TF:* 800-663-1163 ■ *Web:* www.ranchocordova.org	Rancho Cordova	CA	95670	916-273-5688		139
Rancho Cucamonga Chamber of Commerce 9047 Arrow Route Ste 180 *Web:* www.ranchochamber.org	Rancho Cucamonga	CA	91730	909-987-1012	987-5917	100
Rancho de la Osa Guest Ranch 1 La Osa Ranch Rd *Web:* www.ranchodelaosa.com	Sasabe	AZ	85633	520-339-1086		239
Rancho de los Caballeros 1551 S Vulture Mine Rd *TF:* 800-684-5030 ■ *Web:* www.ranchodeloscaballeros.com	Wickenburg	AZ	85390	928-684-5484		669
Rancho Los Alamitos Historic Ranch & Gardens 6400 E Bixby Hill Rd *Web:* www.rancholosalamitos.com	Long Beach	CA	90815	562-431-3541	430-9694	520
Rancho Los Amigos National Rehabilitation Ctr 7601 E Imperial Hwy *TF:* 877-726-2461 ■ *Web:* dhs.lacounty.gov/wps/portal/dhs/rancho	Downey	CA	90242	562-401-7111		374-6
Rancho Los Cerritos Historic Ranch 4600 Virginia Rd *Web:* www.rancholoscerritos.org	Long Beach	CA	90807	562-570-1755		520
Rancho Pinot Grill 6208 N Scottsdale Rd *Web:* www.ranchopinot.com	Scottsdale	AZ	85253	480-367-8030		671
Rancho Santa Ana Botanic Garden 1500 N College Ave *Web:* www.rsabg.org	Claremont	CA	91711	909-625-8767	626-7670	97
Rancho Santa Fe Protective Services Inc 1991 Vlg Pk Way Ste 100 *TF:* 800-303-8877 ■ *Web:* www.rsfsecurity.com	Encinitas	CA	92024	760-942-0688		693
Rancho Valencia Resort 5921 Valencia Cir PO Box 9126 *TF:* 800-548-3664 ■ *Web:* www.ranchovalencia.com	Rancho Santa Fe	CA	92067	858-756-1123	756-0165	669
Rancho Viejo Resort & Country Club 1 Rancho Viejo Dr *TF:* 800-531-7400	Rancho Viejo	TX	78575	956-350-4000	365-2961	669
ranchogrande 1789 Central Park Ave *Web:* www.ranchograndemex.com	Yonkers	NY	10710	914-337-3056		671
Rancocas Metals Corp 35 Indel Ave *TF:* 800-762-6382 ■ *Web:* www.rancocasmetals.com	Rancocas	NJ	08073	609-267-4120	267-5690	492
Rancocas Nature Ctr 794 Rancocas Rd *Web:* www.njaudubon.org	Westampton	NJ	08060	609-261-2495		544
Rancocas State Park c/o Brendan T Byrne State Forest PO Box 215 *Web:* www.njparksandforests.org/parks/rancocas.html	New Lisbon	NJ	08064	609-726-1191		565
Rand Capital Corp 2200 Rand Bldg *NASDAQ: RAND* ■ *Web:* www.randcapital.com	Buffalo	NY	14203	716-853-0802	854-8480	405
Rand Construction Co 1428 W Ninth St *Web:* www.randsc.com	Kansas City	MO	64101	816-421-4143	421-4144	186
RAND Corp 1776 Main St *TF:* 877-584-8642 ■ *Web:* www.rand.org	Santa Monica	CA	90401	310-393-0411	393-4818	634

Name / Address	City	State	Zip	Phone	Fax	Class
Rand Graphics Inc 500 S Florence St *TF:* 800-435-7263 ■ *Web:* www.randgraphics.com	Wichita	KS	67209	316-942-1218		607
Rand Insurance Inc 1100 E Putnam Ave *Web:* randinsurance.com	Riverside	CT	06878	203-637-1006		390
Rand Logistics Inc 333 Washington St Ste 201 *Web:* www.randlogisticsinc.com	Jersey City	NJ	07302	212-644-3450		313
Rand Machine Products Inc PO Box 72 *Web:* www.randmachine.com	Falconer	NY	14733	716-708-4583		757
Rand McNally 9855 Woods Dr PO Box 7600 *TF:* 800-275-7263 ■ *Web:* www.randmcnally.com	Skokie	IL	60077	800-275-7263		637-1
Randall & Danskin P S 601 W Riverside Ave Ste 1500 *Web:* www.randalldanskin.com	Spokane	WA	99201	509-747-2052		445
Randall Bearings Inc 1046 Greenlawn Ave PO Box 1258 *TF:* 800-626-7071 ■ *Web:* www.randallbearings.com	Lima	OH	45802	419-223-1075	228-0200	483
Randall Bros Inc 665 Marietta St NW *TF Cust Svc:* 800-476-4539 ■ *Web:* www.randallbrothers.com	Atlanta	GA	30313	404-892-6666	875-6102	499
Randall County 501 16th St Ste 305 *Web:* www.randallcounty.org	Canyon	TX	79015	806-468-5505		338
Randall County Feedyard 15000 FM 2219 *Web:* www.frionaindustries.com/locations/randall-county-feedyard	Amarillo	TX	79119	806-499-3701		10-1
Randall Davey Audubon Ctr 1800 Upper Canyon Rd PO Box 9314 *Web:* www.audubon.org/chapter/nm/nm/rdac	Santa Fe	NM	87504	505-983-4609	983-2355	50-5
Randall Foods Inc PO Box 2669 *TF:* 800-427-2632 ■ *Web:* randallfoods.com	Huntington Park	CA	90255	323-261-6565		619
Randall Metals Corp 2483 Greenleaf Ave *Web:* www.randallmetals.com	Elk Grove Village	IL	60007	847-952-9690		492
Randall Mfg LLC 722 Church Rd *TF:* 800-323-7424 ■ *Web:* www.randallmfg.com	Elmhurst	IL	60126	630-782-0001		608
Randall Museum 199 Museum Way *TF:* 866-807-7148 ■ *Web:* www.randallmuseum.org	San Francisco	CA	94114	415-554-9600	554-9609	520
Randall S Miller & Associates PC 43252 Woodward Ave Ste 180 *TF:* 844-322-6558 ■ *Web:* www.millerlaw.biz	Bloomfield Hills	MI	48302	248-335-9200		41
Randall Scott Cycle Company LLC 2897 Mapleton Ave Ste 100 *Web:* www.rscycle.com	Boulder	CO	80301	720-214-0714		711
Randall-Reilly Publishing Co 3200 Rice Mine Rd NE *TF Cust Svc:* 800-633-5953 ■ *Web:* randallreilly.com	Tuscaloosa	AL	35406	800-633-5953		637-9
Rando Machine Corp 1071 Route 31 PO Box 614 *Web:* www.randomachine.com	Macedon	NY	14502	315-986-2761	986-7943	744
Randolph & Son Builders Inc PO Box 410283 *Web:* www.randolphbuilders.com	Charlotte	NC	28241	704-588-7116	588-8280	186
Randolph Area Chamber of Commerce PO Box 391 *TF:* 800-366-3922 ■ *Web:* www.randolphchamber.org	Mount Freedom	NJ	07970	973-361-3462		139
Randolph Austin Company Inc 2119 FM 1626 PO Box 988 *TF:* 800-531-5263 ■ *Web:* www.randolphaustin.com	Manchaca	TX	78652	512-282-1590		641
Randolph College 2500 Rivermont Ave **Fax:* Admissions ■ *TF Admissions:* 800-745-7692 ■ *Web:* www.randolphcollege.edu	Lynchburg	VA	24503	434-947-8000	947-8996*	166
Randolph Community College 629 Industrial Pk Ave *TF:* 800-433-3243 ■ *Web:* www.randolph.edu	Asheboro	NC	27205	336-633-0200	629-4695	162
Randolph Correctional Ctr 2760 US Hwy 220	Asheboro	NC	27205	336-625-2578		213
Randolph County 725 McDowell Rd 2nd Fl *Web:* www.co.randolph.nc.us	Asheboro	NC	27205	336-318-6300	318-6853	338
Randolph County 1 Taylor St *Web:* randolphcountyclerk.com	Chester	IL	62233	618-826-5000		338
Randolph County 1302 N Randolph Ave *TF:* 800-422-3304 ■ *Web:* www.randolphcountywv.com	Elkins	WV	26241	304-636-2780		338
Randolph County 372 Hwy JJ *TF:* 844-277-6555 ■ *Web:* www.randolphcounty-mo.com	Huntsville	MO	65259	844-277-6555		338
Randolph County 3355 US Hwy 431 Ste 11 *Web:* www.randolphcountyal.com	Roanoke	AL	36274	334-863-7280		338
Randolph County 100 S Main St PO Box 230 *Web:* www.randolphcounty.us	Winchester	IN	47394	765-584-7207		338
Randolph County State Recreation Area 4301 S Lake Dr *Web:* www.dnr.illinois.gov/parks/pages/randolphcounty.aspx	Chester	IL	62233	618-826-2706		565
Randolph County Tourism Committee 1 Taylor St Courthouse *Web:* www.randolphco.org	Chester	IL	62233	618-826-5000	826-3750	206
Randolph Electric Membership Corp 879 McDowell Rd PO Box 40 *TF:* 800-672-8212 ■ *Web:* www.randolphemc.com	Asheboro	NC	27204-0040	336-625-5177	626-1551	245
Randolph Health 364 White Oak St PO Box 1048 *Web:* www.randolphhospital.org	Asheboro	NC	27204	336-625-5151	625-4393	374-3
Randolph Packing Co 275 Roma Jean Pkwy *TF:* 800-451-1607 ■ *Web:* www.randolphpacking.com	Streamwood	IL	60107	630-830-3100		296-26
Randolph Public Library 201 Worth St *Web:* www.randolphlibrary.org	Asheboro	NC	27203	336-318-6800	318-6823	434-3
Randolph Savings Bank 129 N Main St *TF:* 877-963-2100 ■ *Web:* www.randolphsavings.com	Randolph	MA	02368	781-963-2100		70
Randolph-Brooks Federal Credit Union PO Box 2097 *TF:* 800-580-3300 ■ *Web:* www.rbfcu.org	Universal City	TX	78148	210-945-3300		219
Randolph-Macon Academy 200 Academy Dr *TF:* 800-272-1172 ■ *Web:* www.rma.edu	Front Royal	VA	22630	540-636-5200	636-5419	622
Randolph-Macon College PO Box 5005 **Fax:* Admissions ■ *TF:* 800-888-1762 ■ *Web:* www.rmc.edu	Ashland	VA	23005	804-752-7200	752-4707*	166
Random Lengths News 1300 S Pacific Ave *Web:* www.randomlengthsnews.com	San Pedro	CA	90731	310-519-1442	832-1000	532-5
Randr Inc 3764 Ninth St *Web:* www.randrinc.com	Riverside	CA	92501	951-369-3427		225
Randsman Artist Management 400 W 43rd St Ste 18E *Web:* www.randsman.com	New York	NY	10036	212-244-5874		731
Randstad Canada Group 810 Boul De Maisonneuve Quest *Web:* www.randstad.ca	Montreal	QC	H3A3E6	514-350-0033		631
Randstad US L P 2015 S Park Pl *TF:* 800-382-7297 ■ *Web:* www.randstadusa.com	Atlanta	GA	30339	800-382-7297		260
Randy'S Jewelry Inc 309 S Main St *Web:* randys-jewelry.com	O Fallon	MO	63366	636-978-1953		410
Randys Environmental Services 4351 US Hwy 12 SE PO Box 169 *Web:* www.randysenvironmentalservices.com	Delano	MN	55328	763-972-3335	972-6042	192
Rane Corp 10802 47th Ave W *TF:* 877-764-0093 ■ *Web:* www.rane.com	Mukilteo	WA	98275	425-355-6000	347-7757	52
R-Anell Custom Homes Inc 235 Anthony Grave Rd *TF Cust Svc:* 800-951-5511 ■ *Web:* www.r-anell.com	Crouse	NC	28033	704-483-5511		505
Ranfac Corp PO Box 635 *Web:* www.ranfac.com	Avon	MA	02322	508-588-4400	584-8588	476
Rangam Consultants Inc 270 Davidson Ave Ste 103 *TF:* 877-388-1858 ■ *Web:* www.rangam.com	Somerset	NJ	08873	908-704-8843	253-6550	225
Rangaswamy & Assoc Inc 304 W Liberty St *Web:* rangaswamy.com	Louisville	KY	40202	502-589-2212		261
Range Inc 1022 Madison St *Web:* www.rangeprinting.com	Brainerd	MN	56401	218-824-1800		627
Range LP Gas 1613 E Camp St *Web:* rangelp.com	Ely	MN	55731	218-365-8888		316
Range Ponds State Park PO Box 475 *Web:* www.maine.gov	Poland Spring	ME	04274	207-998-4104		565
Range Resources Corp 100 Throckmorton St Ste 1200 *NYSE: RRC* ■ *Web:* www.rangeresources.com	Fort Worth	TX	76102	817-870-2601	869-9100	536
Rangeley Lake State Park HC 32 PO Box 5000 *Web:* www.maine.gov	Rangeley	ME	04970	207-864-3858		565
Rangen Inc 115 13th Ave S *TF Cust Svc:* 800-657-6446 ■ *Web:* www.rangen.com	Buhl	ID	83316	208-543-6421	543-6090	447
Ranger American Calle Marginal Lodi 605 Ave 65 Infanteria Villa Ca *Web:* www.rangeramerican.com	San Juan	PR	00924	787-999-6060		693
Ranger College 1100 College Cir **Fax:* Admissions ■ *TF:* 800-772-1213 ■ *Web:* www.rangercollege.edu	Ranger	TX	76470	254-647-3234	647-3739*	162
Ranger Construction Industries Inc 101 Sansbury's Way *TF:* 800-969-9402 ■ *Web:* www.rangerconstruction.com	West Palm Beach	FL	33411	561-793-9400	790-4332	188-4
Ranger Creek Ranch PO Box 47 *Web:* www.rangercreekranch.net	Shell	WY	82441	307-765-4636		239
Ranger Industries Inc 15 Park Rd *Web:* www.rangerink.com	Tinton Falls	NJ	07724	732-389-3535		388
Ranger Steel Supply Corp 1225 N Loop W Ste 650 *Web:* www.rangersteel.com	Houston	TX	77008	713-633-1306		492
Rangers Die Casting Co 10828 S Alameda St *TF:* 877-386-9969 ■ *Web:* www.rangersdiecasting.com	Lynwood	CA	90262	310-764-1800		492
Rangeview Library District 5877 E 120th Ave *TF:* 800-222-3937 ■ *Web:* www.anythinklibraries.org	Thornton	CO	80602	303-288-2001	451-0190	434-3
Ranken Energy Corp 417 W 18th St Ste 101 *Web:* www.ranken-energy.com	Edmond	OK	73013	405-340-2363		536
Rankin County 211 E Government St Ste A *Web:* www.rankinchamber.com	Brandon	MS	39042	601-825-1475	825-9600	338
Rankin County Chamber of Commerce 101 Service Dr *TF:* 800-987-8280 ■ *Web:* www.rankinchamber.com	Brandon	MS	39043	601-825-2268	825-1977	139
Rankin, Hill, Porter & Clark LLP 23755 Lorain Rd Ste 200 *Web:* www.rankinhill.com	North Olmsted	OH	44070	216-566-9700		428
Ranor Inc 1 Bella Dr *Web:* www.ranor.com	Westminster	MA	01473	978-874-0591	874-2748	480
Ran-Pro Farms Inc 2618 County Rd Ste 1149 *Web:* www.ranprofarms.com	Tyler	TX	75704	903-593-7381		192
Ransom & Randolph Co 3535 Briarfield Blvd *TF:* 800-800-7496 ■ *Web:* www.ransom-randolph.com	Maumee	OH	43537	419-865-9497	865-9997	663
Ransom County 204 Fifth Ave W *Web:* www.ag.ndsu.edu/ndsuag	Lisbon	ND	58054	701-683-6128	683-5827	338
Rantec Microwave Systems Inc 24003 Ventura Blvd *Web:* www.rantecantennas.com	Calabasas	CA	91302	818-223-5000	223-5199	647
Rantec Power Systems Inc 1173 Los Olivos Ave *Web:* www.rantec.com	Los Osos	CA	93402	805-596-6000		767
Rapat Corp 919 Odonnel St *TF:* 800-325-6377 ■ *Web:* www.rapat.com	Hawley	MN	56549	218-483-3344	483-3535	207
RAPCO Inc 445 Cardinal Ln *Web:* rapcoinc.com	Hartland	WI	53029	262-367-2292		57
Rape Abuse & Incest National Network (RAINN) 2000 L St NW Ste 406 *TF:* 800-656-4673 ■ *Web:* www.rainn.org	Washington	DC	20036	202-544-1034	544-3556	48-6
Raphael Kansas City 325 Ward Pkwy *TF:* 800-821-5343 ■ *Web:* www.raphaelkc.com	Kansas City	MO	64112	816-756-3800	802-2131	379
Rapid Chevrolet Company Inc 2323 E Mall Dr *TF:* 800-456-2105 ■ *Web:* www.rapidchevrolet.com	Rapid City	SD	57701	605-343-1282		516

Name / Address	City	State	ZIP	Phone	Fax	Class
Rapid City Area Chamber of Commerce 444 Mt Rushmore Rd N *Web:* www.rapidcitychamber.com	Rapid City	SD	57701	605-343-1744	343-6550	139
Rapid City City Hall 300 Sixth St *Web:* www.rcgov.org	Rapid City	SD	57701	605-394-4110	394-6793	337
Rapid City Convention & Visitors Bureau 444 Mt Rushmore Rd N *TF:* 800-487-3223 ■ *Web:* www.visitrapidcity.com	Rapid City	SD	57701	605-718-8484	348-9217	206
Rapid City Journal 507 Main St *TF:* 800-843-2300 ■ *Web:* www.rapidcityjournal.com	Rapid City	SD	57701	605-394-8300	394-8463	532-2
Rapid City Public Library (RCPL) 610 Quincy St *TF:* 800-562-5785 ■ *Web:* www.rcgov.org/library	Rapid City	SD	57701	605-394-4171		434-3
Rapid City Regional Airport 4550 Terminal Rd Ste 102 *TF:* 888-279-2135 ■ *Web:* www.rcgov.org/airport	Rapid City	SD	57703	605-393-9924	394-6190	27
Rapid City Regional Health 353 Fairmont Blvd *Web:* www.regionalhealth.com	Rapid City	SD	57701	605-719-1000		374-3
Rapid Displays 4300 W 47th St *TF:* 800-356-5775 ■ *Web:* www.rapiddisplays.com	Chicago	IL	60632	773-927-1091	927-1091	233
Rapid Engineering Inc 1100 7-Mile Rd NW *TF:* 800-536-3461 ■ *Web:* www.rapidengineering.com	Comstock Park	MI	49321	616-784-0500		318
Rapid Fire Marketing Inc 311 W Third St Ste 1234 *Web:* www.rapid-fire-marketing.com	Carson City	NV	89703	404-261-1196		477
Rapid Focus Security LLC 253 Summer St Ste 303 *TF:* 855-793-1337 ■ *Web:* www.pwnieexpress.com	Boston	MA	02210	855-793-1337		693
Rapid Global Business Solutions Inc 1200 Stephenson Hwy *Web:* www.rgbsi.com	Troy	MI	48083	248-589-1135		261
Rapid Industries 4003 Oaklawn Dr *TF:* 800-727-4381 ■ *Web:* www.rapidindustries.com	Louisville	KY	40219	502-968-3645	968-6331	207
Rapid Insight Inc 53 Technology Ln Ste 112 *TF:* 888-585-6511 ■ *Web:* www.rapidinsightinc.com	Conway	NH	03818	888-585-6511		177
Rapid Line Industries Inc 455 N Ottawa St *TF:* 877-444-9955 ■ *Web:* rapidline.com	Joliet	IL	60432	815-727-4362		111
Rapid Pathogen Screening Inc 7227 Delainey Ct *TF:* 800-876-4766 ■ *Web:* www.rpsdetectors.com	Sarasota	FL	34240	941-556-1850		476
Rapid Press Printing & Copy Center Inc 608 Lake St S *Web:* www.rapidpressprinting.com	Forest Lake	MN	55025	651-464-6200		627
Rapid Printers of Monterey 201 Foam St *Web:* www.rapidprinters.com	Monterey	CA	93940	831-373-1822		627
Rapid Pump & Meter Service Co Inc 285 Straight St PO Box AY *Web:* www.rapidservice.com	Paterson	NJ	07509	973-345-5600	345-0301	627
Rapid Rater Co Po Box 13055 *Web:* www.rapidpress.com	Tallahassee	FL	32317	850-893-7346		627
Rapid Ratings Pty Ltd 86 Chambers St Ste 701 *Web:* www.rapidratings.com	New York	NY	10007	646-233-4600		194
Rapid Response Marketing LLC 7500 West Lake Mead Blvd Ste 9463 *Web:* www.xy7.com	Las Vegas	NV	89128	702-848-3954		193
Rapid Response Monitoring Services Inc 400 W Division St *TF:* 800-558-7767 ■ *Web:* www.rrms.com	Syracuse	NY	13204	800-558-7767		693
Rapid Software Corp 3079 Parr Ln *Web:* www.rapidsw.com	Grapevine	TX	76051	817-251-0615		177
Rapid Transcript Inc 4311 Wilshire Blvd *Web:* www.rapidtranscript.com	Los Angeles	CA	90010	323-964-0400		478
Rapides Parish PO Box 952 *Web:* rapidesclerk.org	Alexandria	LA	71309	318-473-8153	473-4667	338
Rapides Parish Library 411 Washington St *Web:* www.rpl.org	Alexandria	LA	71301	318-445-2411		434-3
Rapides Regional Medical Ctr 211 Fourth St *Web:* www.rapidesregional.com	Alexandria	LA	71301	318-769-3000		374-3
RAPIDS Wholesale Equipment Co 6201 S Gateway Dr *TF:* 800-472-7431 ■ *Web:* rapidswholesale.com	Marion	IA	52302	319-447-1670	447-1680	300
Rapidsoft Systems Inc 7 Diamond Ct *TF:* 800-243-6002 ■ *Web:* www.rapidsoftsystems.com	Princeton Junction	NJ	08550	609-439-4775		631
Rapier Solutions Inc 3095 Senna Dr *Web:* www.rapiersolutions.com	Matthews	NC	28105	704-321-2271		180
Rapit Printing Inc 1415 First Ave NW *Web:* www.rapit.com	New Brighton	MN	55112	651-633-4600		627
Rapp Advertising 30 Commerce St Ste 2 *Web:* www.rappadvertising.com	Springfield	NJ	07081	973-467-5570		7
Rappahannock Community College *Glenns* 12745 College Dr **Fax:* Admissions ■ *TF:* 800-836-9381 ■ *Web:* www.rappahannock.edu	Glenns	VA	23149	804-758-6700	758-6830*	162
Warsaw 52 Campus Dr **Fax:* Admissions ■ *TF:* 800-836-9381 ■ *Web:* www.rappahannock.edu	Warsaw	VA	22572	804-333-6700	333-0106*	162
Rappahannock County 290 Gay St PO Box 519 *Web:* www.rappahannockcountyva.gov	Washington	VA	22747	540-675-5330	675-5331	338
RAPS (Regulatory Affairs Professionals Society) 5635 Fishers Ln Ste 550 *TF:* 800-307-6627 ■ *Web:* www.raps.org	Rockville	MD	20852	301-770-2920	770-2924	49-8
Raptim Humanitarian Travel 6420 Inducon Dr W Ste A *TF:* 800-272-7846 ■ *Web:* www.raptim.org	Sanborn	NY	14132	716-754-9232	754-2881	772
Raptr Inc 701 N Shoreline Blvd *Web:* raptr.com	Mountain View	CA	94043	650-215-1328		225
Raque Food Systems LLC PO Box 99594 *Web:* www.raque.com	Louisville	KY	40269	502-267-9641	267-2352	547
Rare Bird Inc 8555 Cedar Pl Dr Ste 114 *Web:* rarebirdinc.com	Indianapolis	IN	46240	317-251-6744		7
Raritan Bay Medical Ctr 530 New Brunswick Ave *TF:* 800-701-0710 ■ *Web:* www.rbmc.org	Perth Amboy	NJ	08861	732-442-3700		374-3
Raritan Center Travel II 110 Fieldcrest Ave *Web:* www.sairealestate.com	Edison	NJ	08837	732-417-1600		772
Raritan Computer Inc 400 Cottontail Ln *TF:* 800-724-8090 ■ *Web:* www.raritan.com	Somerset	NJ	08873	732-764-8886	764-8887	253
Raritan Pharmaceuticals Inc 8 Joanna Ct *Web:* www.raritanpharm.com	East Brunswick	NJ	08816	732-432-8200		231
Raritan Valley Community College PO Box 3300 **Fax:* Admissions ■ *TF:* 888-326-4058 ■ *Web:* www.raritanval.edu	Somerville	NJ	08876	908-526-1200	704-3442*	162
Ras Kassa's Ethiopian Restaurant 555 30th St *Web:* www.raskassas.com	Boulder	CO	80303	720-421-0778		671
Rasansky Law Firm 2525 McKinnon Ave Ste 625 *OTC:* ATTY ■ *TF:* 800-288-6763 ■ *Web:* www.1800attorney.com	Dallas	TX	75201	800-288-6763		637-6
Rasar State Park 38730 Cape Horn Rd *TF:* 800-863-9358 ■ *Web:* parks.state.wa.us	Concrete	WA	98237	360-826-3942		565
Rash, Chapman, Schreiber, Leaverton & Morrison LLP 2112 Rio Grande St *TF:* 800-989-4992 ■ *Web:* www.rashchapman.com	Austin	TX	78705	512-477-7543		428
Rasi Laboratories Inc 20 Roosevelt Ave *Web:* www.rasilaboratories.com	Somerset	NJ	08873	732-873-8500		231
RASIRC Inc 7815 Silverton Ave *Web:* www.rasirc.com	San Diego	CA	92126	858-259-1220		610
Raskin Jamie (Rep D - MD) 431 Cannon HOB *Web:* raskin.house.gov	Washington	DC	20515	202-225-5341		342-2
Raskob Kambourian Financial Advisors Ltd 4100 N First Ave *Web:* www.rkfin.com	Tucson	AZ	85719	520-690-1999		401
Rasmussen College Inc 4400 W 78th St 6th Fl *TF:* 800-852-0929 ■ *Web:* www.rasmussen.edu	Bloomington	MN	55345	952-545-2000		166
Rasmussen Equipment Co 3333 West 2100 South *TF:* 800 453 8032 ■ *Web:* www.raseq.com	Salt Lake City	UT	84119	801-972-5588		358
Rasmussen Iron Works Inc 12028 E Philadelphia St *Web:* www.rasmussen.biz	Whittier	CA	90601	562-696-8718	698-3510	357
Rasmussen John 730 Sand Lake Rd *Web:* www.rasmussen-usa.com	Orlando	FL	32809	407-859-5255		77
Rason Asphalt Inc 44 Morris Ave	Glen Cove	NY	11542	516-671-1500		46
Rassai 500 Throckmorton St Ste 375	Fort Worth	TX	76102	817-332-0069		225
Rast Iron Works 12895 I-10 E *Web:* www.rastironworks.com	San Antonio	TX	78154	210-659-6704	659-6791	480
Rata Associates LLC 1916 Boothe Cir *Web:* www.rataassociates.com	Longwood	FL	32750	407-831-7282		177
Ratcliffe John (Rep - TX) 325 Cannon HOB *Web:* ratcliffe.house.gov	Washington	DC	20515	202-225-6673	225-3332	342-2
RateHub.ca 411 Richmond St E Ste 208 *TF:* 800-679-9622 ■ *Web:* www.ratehub.ca	Toronto	ON	M5A3S5	800-679-9622		466
RateMyProfessors.com LLC 1515 Broadway *Web:* www.ratemyprofessors.com	New York	NY	10036	212-654-7763		387
Ratespecial LLC 35 N Arroyo Pkwy Ste 250 *TF:* 800-701-0793 ■ *Web:* www.ratespecial.com	Pasadena	CA	91103	626-376-4702		5
Rath & Strong Inc Po Box 170 PO Box 170 *TF:* 800-622-2025 ■ *Web:* www.rathstrong.com	Lexington	MA	02420	781-861-1700	861-1424	194
Rathbun's 112 Krog St Ste R *Web:* www.kevinrathbun.com	Atlanta	GA	30307	404-524-8280	524-8580	671
Rathgeber Goss Associates PC 15871 Crabbs Branch Way *Web:* www.rath-goss.com	Rockville	MD	20855	301-590-0071		261
Rathgeber Hospitality House 1615 12th St *Web:* www.rathgeberhospitalityhouse.org	Wichita Falls	TX	76301	940-764-2400	764-2456	372
Rathskeller Restaurant 401 E Michigan St *Web:* www.rathskeller.com	Indianapolis	IN	46204	317-636-0396	630-4652	671
Rathskeller, The 1132 Auburn St	Rockford	IL	61103	815-963-2922		671
Rational Energies LLC 12200 Middleset Rd Ste 300 *Web:* rationalenergies.com	Eden Prairie	MN	55344	952-807-0080		196
Rationale Technologies Corp 12949 Ridgemist Ln *Web:* rationaleinc.com	Fairfax	VA	22033	703-564-1600		809
Ratner co 1577 Spring Hill Rd Ste 500 *Web:* www.ratnerco.com	Vienna	VA	22182	703-269-5400		77
Ratner Steel Supply Company Inc 2500 W County Rd B *TF:* 800-879-3237 ■ *Web:* www.ratnersteel.com	Roseville	MN	55113	651-631-8515		492
Rattikin Title Co 201 Main St Ste 800 *Web:* rattikintitle.com	Fort Worth	TX	76102	817-332-1171	882-9886	391-6
Rauch Industries Inc 2408 Forbes Rd	Gastonia	NC	28056	704-867-5333		334
Raudenbush Engineering Inc 29 S Union St *Web:* raudeng.com	Middletown	PA	17057	717-944-0883		727
Raulerson Hospital 1796 Hwy 441 N *TF:* 877-549-9337 ■ *Web:* www.raulersonhospital.com	Okeechobee	FL	34972	863-763-2151	824-2991	374-3
Raulli & Sons Inc 213 Teall Ave *Web:* www.raulliandsons.com	Syracuse	NY	13210	315-479-6693		480

Name / Address	City	State	Zip	Phone	Fax	Class
Rauner Bruce (R) 207 Statehouse 207 Statehouse *Web:* www2.illinois.gov/gov/Pages/default.aspx	Springfield	IL	62706	217-782-0244	524-4049	343
Rauxa Direct LLC 275 McCormick Ave A *Web:* www.rauxa.com	Costa Mesa	CA	92626	714-427-1271		5
Ravalli County 215 S Fourth St Ste C *Web:* ravalli.us	Hamilton	MT	59840	406-375-6212	375-6595	338
Ravalli County Electric Co-op Inc 1051 Eastside Hwy *Web:* www.ravallielectric.com	Corvallis	MT	59828	406-961-3001	961-3230	245
Ravalli County Fair 100 Old Corvallis Rd *TF:* 800-225-6779 ■ *Web:* ravalli.us	Hamilton	MT	59840	406-363-3411	375-9152	642
Rave Computer Assn Inc 7171 Sterling Ponds Ct *TF:* 800-966-7283 ■ *Web:* www.rave.com	Sterling Heights	MI	48312	586-939-8230	939-7431	174
Rave Wireless Inc 50 Speen St *TF:* 888-605-7164 ■ *Web:* www.ravemobilesafety.com	Framingham	MA	01701	508-848-2484		177
Rave, The 2401 W Wisconsin Ave *Web:* www.therave.com	Milwaukee	WI	53233	414-342-7283		572
Raven Capital Management LLC 110 Greene St Ste 9G *Web:* ravencm.com	New York	NY	10012	212-966-7926		528
Raven Computers 5952 Odana Rd *TF:* 800-561-3357 ■ *Web:* ravencomputers.com	Madison	WI	53719	608-661-1372		175
Raven Industries Inc 205 E Sixth St *NASDAQ: RAVN* ■ *TF:* 800-243-5435 ■ *Web:* www.ravenind.com	Sioux Falls	SD	57104	605-336-2750	335-0268	600
Raven One to One Marketing 1020 Airport Rd *Web:* raven121.com	Allentown	PA	18109	484-240-6500	240-6505	195
Raven Printing 325 S Union *Web:* www.ravenprinting.com	Lakewood	CO	80228	303-989-9888		627
Raven Rock State Park 3009 Raven Rock Rd *Web:* www.ncparks.gov	Lillington	NC	27546	910-893-4888		565
Raven Software Corp 8496 Greenway Blvd *Web:* www.ravensoftware.com	Middleton	WI	53562	608-833-5791		225
Raven Transport Company Inc 6800 Broadway Ave *Web:* www.idriveraven.com	Jacksonville	FL	32254	904-880-1515		780
Ravensberg Inc 1338 Strassner Dr *Web:* www.ravensberg.com	Saint Louis	MO	63144	314-968-4020		321
Ravensburg State Park 2388 Rauchtown Rd *Web:* www.dcnr.state.pa.us	Jersey Shore	PA	17044	570-966-1455		565
Ravenswood Special Events 1100 W Cermak Rd Unit C411 *TF:* 800-928-2086 ■ *Web:* www.ravenswoodevents.com	Chicago	IL	60608	312-633-2600		366
Ravenswood Studio Inc 6900 N Central Pk Ave *Web:* www.ravenswoodstudio.com	Lincolnwood	IL	60712	847-679-2800	679-2805	393
Ravenswood Winery Inc 18701 Gehricke Rd *TF:* 888-669-4679 ■ *Web:* www.ravenswoodwinery.com	Sonoma	CA	95476	888-669-4679		80-3
Ravi Engineering & Land Surveying PC 2110 S Clinton Ave Ste 1 *Web:* www.ravieng.com	Rochester	NY	14618	585-223-3660		261
Ravine Gardens State Park 1600 Twigg St *TF:* 800-326-3521 ■ *Web:* www.floridastateparks.org	Palatka	FL	32177	386-329-3721	329-3718	565
Raving Consulting Co 475 Hill St # G *Web:* www.ravingconsulting.com	Reno	NV	89501	775-329-7864		463
Ravinia Festival Association 418 Sheridan Rd *Web:* www.ravinia.org	Highland Park	IL	60035	847-266-5000		720
Raw Art Works Inc 37 Central Sq Ste 3 *Web:* www.rawartworks.org	Lynn	MA	01901	781-593-5515		149
Rawah Ranch 11447 N County Rd 103 *TF:* 800-820-3152 ■ *Web:* www.rawahranch.com	Glendevey	CO	82063	800-820-3152		239
Rawhide Chemoil Inc 2650 N Rawhide Dr *Web:* www.rawhidechemoil.com	Fremont	NE	68025	402-721-7601		316
Rawle & Henderson 1339 Chestnut St One S Penn Sq The Widener Bldg 16th Fl *Web:* www.rawle.com	Philadelphia	PA	19107	215-575-4200		428
Rawlins County 607 Main St	Atwood	KS	67730	785-626-3351		338
Rawson Inc 2010 McAllister *TF:* 800-779-1414 ■ *Web:* www.rawsonlp.com	Houston	TX	77092	800-779-1414		246
Raxco Software Inc 6 Montgomery Village Ave Ste 500 *TF Tech Supp:* 800-546-9728 ■ *Web:* www.raxco.com	Gaithersburg	MD	20879	301-527-0803	519-7711	178-12
Raxon Fabrics 261 Fifth Ave *Web:* www.raxon.com	New York	NY	10016	212-532-6816		745-1
Ray Allen Inc 400 W Erie St Ste 400 *Web:* www.rayalleninc.com	Chicago	IL	60654	312-895-0222		225
Ray Angelini Inc 105 Blackwood-Barnsboro Rd *TF:* 800-834-5196 ■ *Web:* www.raiservices.com	Sewell	NJ	08080	856-228-5566		186
Ray Bros & Noble Canning Company Inc 3720 E 150 S PO Box 314 *Web:* www.tiptonguide.com	Hobbs	IN	46047	765-675-7451	675-7400	296-20
Ray Catena Motor Car Corp 910 US Hiwy Rt 1 *Web:* www.raycatena.com	Edison	NJ	08817	732-549-6600		57
Ray County 100 W Main St County Courthouse *Web:* raycountymo.com	Richmond	MO	64085	816-776-3377		338
Ray L Hellwig Plumbing & Heating Inc 1301 Laurelwood Rd *TF:* 800-631-7013 ■ *Web:* www.rlhellwig.com	Santa Clara	CA	95054	408-727-5612		189-10
Ray Norbut State Fish & Wildlife Area 46816 290th Ave *Web:* dnr.illinois.gov/Lands/Landmgt/PARKS/R4/ray.htm	Griggsville	IL	62340	217-833-2811		565
Ray Products Company Inc 1700 Chablis Ave *TF:* 800-423-7859 ■ *Web:* rayplastics.com	Ontario	CA	91761	909-390-9906		602
Ray Quinney & Nebeker 36 S State St Ste 1400 *Web:* www.rqn.com	Salt Lake City	UT	84111	801-532-1500		445
Ray Roberts Lake State Park 100 PW 4137 *Web:* tpwd.texas.gov/state-parks/ray-roberts-lake	Pilot Point	TX	76258	940-686-2148		565
Ray Seraphin Ford Inc 100 Windsor Ave *Web:* rayseraphinfordinc.com	Vernon Rockville	CT	06066	860-875-3369		57
Ray Stone Inc 550 Howe Ave Ste 200 *Web:* www.raystoneinc.com	Sacramento	CA	95825	916-649-7500		652
Ray's Boathouse 6049 Seaview Ave NW *Web:* www.rays.com	Seattle	WA	98107	206-789-3770	781-1960	671
Ray's in the City 240 Peachtree St NW *Web:* www.raysrestaurants.com	Atlanta	GA	30303	404-524-9224		671
Ray's the Steaks 2300 Wilson Blvd *Web:* raysthesteaks.com	Arlington	VA	22201	703-841-7297		671
Raybestos Powertrain LLC 711 Tech Dr *TF:* 800-729-7763 ■ *Web:* www.raybestospowertrain.com	Crawfordsville	IN	47933	800-729-7763		60
Raybourn Group International 9100 PuRdue Rd Ste 200 *TF:* 800-362-2546 ■ *Web:* www.raybourn.com	Indianapolis	IN	46268	317-328-4636	280-8527	47
Rayco Industries Inc 1502 Valley Rd *TF:* 800-505-7111 ■ *Web:* www.raycoindustries.com	Richmond	VA	23222	804-321-7111		492
Raycom Media Inc 201 Monroe St RSA Tower 20th Fl *Web:* www.raycommedia.com	Montgomery	AL	36104	334-206-1400	206-1555	738
Raycom Sports Inc 1900 W Morehead St *Web:* raycomsports.com	Charlotte	NC	28208	704-378-4400		739
Raydon Rentals Ltd 9520 - 51 Ave *Web:* www.catrents.ca	Edmonton	AB	T6E5A6	780-989-1301		23
Rayle Electric Membership Corp 616 Lexington Ave *Web:* www.rayleemc.com	Washington	GA	30673	706-678-2116	678-5381	245
Raymarine Inc 21 Manchester St *TF:* 800-539-5539 ■ *Web:* www.raymarine.com	Merrimack	NH	03054	603-881-5200		529
Raymath Company Inc 2323 W State Rt 55 *TF:* 800-766-0024 ■ *Web:* raymath.com	Troy	OH	45373	937-335-1860		757
Rayment & Collins Ltd 119 Ferrier St *Web:* www.raymentcollins.com	Markham	ON	L3R3K6	905-940-4030		627
Raymon H Mulford Library 3000 Arlington Ave *TF:* 800-321-8383 ■ *Web:* www.utoledo.edu/library/mulford/index.html	Toledo	OH	43614	419-383-4225		434-1
Raymond Bldg Supply Corp 7751 Bayshore Rd *TF:* 877-731-7272 ■ *Web:* www.rbsc.net	North Fort Myers	FL	33917	239-731-8300	731-3299	191-3
Raymond Case Elementary School 8565 Shasta Lily Dr *Web:* blogs.egusd.net/case	Elk Grove	CA	95624	916-681-8820	681-8807	685
Raymond Corp 22 S Canal St *TF General:* 800-235-7200 ■ *Web:* www.raymondcorp.com	Greene	NY	13778	607-656-2311	656-9005	470
Raymond Excavating Co Inc 800 Gratiot Blvd *TF:* 800-837-6770 ■ *Web:* www.raymondexcavating.com	Marysville	MI	48040	810-364-6881		189-5
Raymond Express International (REI) 320 Harbor Way *Web:* www.reiexpress.com	South San Francisco	CA	94080	650-871-8560		311
Raymond F Kravis Ctr for the Performing Arts 701 Okeechobee Blvd **Fax:* Mktg ■ *TF:* 800-572-8471 ■ *Web:* www.kravis.org	West Palm Beach	FL	33401	561-832-7469	833-0691*	572
Raymond Gary State Park Hwy 70 *TF:* 800-622-6317 ■ *Web:* www.travelok.com	Fort Towson	OK	74735	580-873-2307	326-2305	565
Raymond Group Inc, The 8333 Greenway Blvd Ste 200 *Web:* www.raymondteam.com	Middleton	WI	53562	608-833-4100		652
Raymond Handling Concepts Corp 41400 Boyce Rd *TF:* 800-675-2500 ■ *Web:* www.raymondhandling.com	Fremont	CA	94538	510-745-7500	745-7686	264-3
Raymond International 410 High St PO Box 591 *Web:* www.globalrecruiter.com	Santa Cruz	CA	95061	831-429-1234		721
Raymond James Financial Inc 880 Carillon Pkwy *NYSE: RJF* ■ *TF:* 800-248-8863 ■ *Web:* www.raymondjames.com	Saint Petersburg	FL	33716	727-567-1000		690
Raymond James Ltd 2200-925 W Georgia St Cathedral Pl *TF:* 888-545-6624 ■ *Web:* www.raymondjames.ca	Vancouver	BC	V6C3L2	604-659-8000		401
Raymond James Stadium 4201 N Dale Mabry Hwy *TF:* 800-282-0683 ■ *Web:* www.tampasportsauthority.com	Tampa	FL	33607	813-350-6500	673-4308	720
Raymond James (USA) Ltd 2200 - 925 W Georgia St *TF:* 877-570-7558 ■ *Web:* www.rjlu.com	Vancouver	BC	V6C3L2	877-570-7558		691
Raymond L Goodson Jr Inc 5445 La Sierra Ste 300 LB 17 *Web:* rlginc.com	Dallas	TX	75231	214-739-8100	739-6354	261
Raymond L Robinson Law Office 1501 Venera Ave Ste 300	Miami	FL	33146	305-662-7618		445
Raymond M Blasco MD Memorial Library 160 E Front St *TF:* 800-352-0026 ■ *Web:* www.erielibrary.org	Erie	PA	16507	814-451-6900		434-3
Raymond Martin Co 4709 Bluebonnet Blvd Ste A *Web:* www.raymondmartin.com	Baton Rouge	LA	70809	225-291-9300		528
Raymond of New Jersey LLC 1000 Brighton St *Web:* www.raymond-nj.com	Union	NJ	07083	908-624-9570		358
Raymond R Andy Guest Jr Shenandoah River State Park 350 Daughter of Stars Dr *TF:* 800-933-7275 ■ *Web:* www.dcr.virginia.gov	Bentonville	VA	22610	540-622-6840	622-6841	565
Raymond Vineyard 849 Zinfandel Ln *TF:* 800-525-2659 ■ *Web:* www.raymondvineyards.com	Saint Helena	CA	94574	707-963-6941		80-3
Raymour & Flanigan Furniture PO Box 220 *TF:* 800-729-6687 ■ *Web:* www.raymourflanigan.com	Liverpool	NY	13088	315-453-2500		321

Company / Address	City	State	Zip	Phone	Fax	Class
Rayne Plane Inc 9107 Grand Prairie Hwy	Church Point	LA	70525	337-334-2101	634-2813*	273
*Fax Area Code: 713 ■ Web: www.rayneplane.com						
Rayner Covering Systems Inc 665 Schneider Dr	South Elgin	IL	60177	847-695-2264	695-2363	608
TF: 800-648-0757 ■ Web: www.raynercovering.com						
Rayner's Seafood House 7343 Hwy 49	Hattiesburg	MS	39401	601-268-2639		671
Raynor Garage Doors 1101 E River Rd	Dixon	IL	61021	815-288-1431		234
TF: 800-472-9667 ■ Web: www.raynor.com						
Rayonier Inc 225 Water St Ste 1400	Jacksonville	FL	32202	904-357-9100		403
Web: www.rayonier.com						
Rayotek Scientific Inc 11499 Sorrento Valley Rd	San Diego	CA	92121	858-558-3671		696
TF: 800-991-1335 ■ Web: www.rayotek.com						
Raypak Inc 2151 Eastman Ave	Oxnard	CA	93030	805-278-5300	278-5468	357
TF: 800-438-4328 ■ Web: www.raypak.com						
Raytech Industries 475 Smith St	Middletown	CT	06457	860-632-2020	632-1699	1
TF Cust Svc: 800-243-7163 ■ Web: www.raytech-ind.com						
Raytek Inc 1201 Shaffer Rd	Santa Cruz	CA	95061	831-458-3900	425-4561	696
TF: 800-227-8074 ■ Web: www.raytek.com						
Raytex Fabrics Inc 130 Crossways Pk Dr	Woodbury	NY	11797	516-584-1111		594
TF: 800-840-7035 ■ Web: www.raytexindustries.com						
Raytheon Air Traffic Management Systems 870 Winter St	Waltham	MA	02451	781-522-3000	522-5200	529
Web: raytheon.com/capabilities/products/cnsatm						
Raytheon Canada Ltd 360 Albert St Ste 1640	Ottawa	ON	K1R7X7	613-233-4121		529
Web: www.raytheon.com						
Raytheon Co 8170 Maple Lawn Blvd Ste 300	Fulton	MD	20759	240-554-8100	554-8101	178-10
Web: www.solipsys.com						
Raytheon Co 10 Moulton St	Cambridge	MA	02138	617-873-8000	318-5041*	178-10
*Fax Area Code: 703 ■ TF: 866-230-1307 ■ Web: www.raytheon.com/ourcompany/bbn						
Raytheon Computer Products 1001 Boston Post Rd	Marlborough	MA	01752	781-522-3000		176
Web: www.raytheon.com						
Raytheon Integrated Defense Systems 50 Apple Hill Dr	Tewksbury	MA	01876	978-858-5000		529
Web: raytheon.com/ourcompany/businesses						
Raytheon Network Centric Systems (NCS) 2501 W University Dr	McKinney	TX	75071	781-522-3000		529
Web: www.raytheon.com						
Raytheon Professional Services LLC 1200 S Jupiter Rd	Garland	TX	75042	972-205-5100		194
Web: raytheon.com/ourcompany/rps						
Raytheon RF Components (RRFC) 870 Winter St	Waltham	MA	02451	781-522-3000		696
Web: www.raytheon.com						
Raytown Area Chamber of Commerce 5909 Raytown Trafficway	Raytown	MO	64133	816-353-8500	353-8525	139
TF: 800-581-2765 ■ Web: www.raytownchamber.com						
Raytrans Management Inc 1501 Reedsdale St Ste 3001	Pittsburgh	PA	15233	412-321-0100	318-7899	194
Web: www.raytrans.com						
Rayven Inc 431 Griggs St N	Saint Paul	MN	55104	651-642-1112	642-9497	620
TF Cust Svc: 800-878-3776 ■ Web: www.rayven.com						
Razberi Technologies Inc 1628 Valwood Pkwy Ste 148	Carrollton	TX	75006	469-828-3380		693
TF: 800-528-4343 ■ Web: www.razberi.net						
Razoom Inc 545 Bryant St	Palo Alto	CA	94301	650-561-3037	561-3279	246
Web: www.razoom.com						
Razorfish Platforms 7750 Paragon Rd	Dayton	OH	45459	937-723-2300		193
Web: technologyplatforms.razorfish.com						
Razorgator 4216 3/4 Glencoe Ave	Marina Del Rey	CA	90292	310-481-3400		366
Web: www.razorgator.com						
Razorleaf Corp 3766 Fishcreek Rd Ste 291	Stow	OH	44224	330-676-0022		177
Web: www.razorleaf.com						
razr 10590 Wayzata Blvd	Minnetonka	MN	55305	763-404-6100		195
Web: www.razrmarketing.com						
R&B Electronics Inc 1520 Industrial Park Dr Sault	Marie	MI	49783	906-632-1542		22
Web: www.randbelectronics.com						
R-B Financial-mortgages Inc 44028 Mound Rd Ste 3	Sterling Heights	MI	48314	586-254-8435	254-8438	509
Web: www.rbfinancial.com						
RB Milestone Group 125 Park Ave 25th Fl	New York	NY	10168	212-661-0075		401
Web: www.rbmilestone.com						
RB Pamplin Corp 805 SW Broadway Ste 2400	Portland	OR	97205	503-248-1133	248-1175	185
Web: www.pamplin.org						
RB Royal Industries Inc 1350 S Hickory St PO Box 1168	Fond du Lac	WI	54936	920-921-1550	921-4713	621
TF: 800-892-1550 ■ Web: www.rbroyal.com						
Rb Technology Inc 860 Anburn Ct	Fremont	CA	94538	510-770-9922		175
Web: www.rbtech-inc.com						
RBA Group Inc, The 7 Campus Dr Ste 300	Parsippany	NJ	07054	973-946-5600		261
Web: www.rbagroup.com						
RBB Innovations 2-258 Queen St E	Sault Sainte Marie	ON	P6A1Y7	705-942-9053		177
TF: 800-796-7864 ■ Web: rbbinnovations.com						
RBC Bearings Inc 102 Willenbrock Rd PO Box 1953	Oxford	CT	06478	203-267-7001	267-5000	620
TF: 866-722-2376 ■ Web: www.rbcbearings.com						
RBC Capital Markets Royal Bank Plaza 200 Bay St	Toronto	ON	M5J2W7	416-842-7575		690
Web: www.rbcds.com						
RBC Dain Rauscher Inc 60 S Sixth St Ste P10	Minneapolis	MN	55402	800-933-9946		690
TF: 800-933-9946 ■ Web: www.rbcwm-usa.com						
RBC Global Asset Management 225 Franklin St	Boston	MA	02110	617-722-4700		401
RBC Inc 100 N Pitt St Ste 300	Alexandria	VA	22314	703-549-6921	549-6926	261
Web: www.rbcinc.com						
RBC Liberty Insurance PO Box 789	Greenville	SC	29602	864-609-8111		391-2
TF: 800-551-8354 ■ Web: www.rbcinsurance.com						
RBC Royal Bank 1127 Blvd D,carie	Montreal	QC	H4L3M8	800-769-2599	874-3055*	70
*Fax Area Code: 514 ■ TF: 800-769-2599 ■ Web: www.rbcroyalbank.com						
RBC Trust Company (Delaware) Ltd 4550 New Linden Hill Rd Ste 200	Wilmington	DE	19808	302-892-6976		70
TF: 800-441-7698 ■ Web: www.rbctrust.com						
RBCM (Royal British Columbia Museum) 675 Belleville St	Victoria	BC	V8W9W2	250-356-7226		520
TF: 888-447-7977 ■ Web: www.royalbcmuseum.bc.ca						
RBF (Ross Buehler Falk & Company LLP) 1500 Lititz Pk	Lancaster	PA	17601	717-393-2700	393-1743	2
Web: www.rbfco.com						
RBG (Royal Botanical Gardens) 680 Plains Rd W	Burlington	ON	L7T4H4	905-527-1158	577-0375	97
TF: 800-694-4769 ■ Web: www.rbg.ca						
RBI (Riddleberger Bros Inc) 6127 S Valley Pk	Mount Crawford	VA	22841	540-434-1731	432-1691	186
Web: www.rbiva.com						
RBI Corp 10201 Cedar Ridge Dr	Ashland	VA	23005	800-444-7370		358
TF: 800-444-7370 ■ Web: www.rbicorp.com						
RBL Group, The 3507 N University Ave Ste 100	Provo	UT	84604	801-373-4238		765
Web: www.rbl.net						
RBMA (Radiology Business Management Assn) 10300 Eaton Pl Ste 460	Fairfax	VA	22030	703-621-3355	621-3356	49-8
TF: 888-224-7262 ■ Web: www.rbma.org						
RBN Energy LLC 2323 S Shepherd Dr Ste 1010	Houston	TX	77019	888-400-9838		463
TF: 888-400-9838 ■ Web: www.rbnenergy.com						
RBS (Rutgers Business School) 1 Washington Pk 3rd Fl	Newark	NJ	07102	973-353-1821		668
Web: www.business.rutgers.edu/default.aspx?id=645						
RBS Bulk Systems Inc 610 Moraine Rd NE	Calgary	AB	T2A2P3	403-248-1530		314
TF: 800-882-5930 ■ Web: www.rbsbulk.com						
Rbx Inc PO Box 2118	Springfield	MO	65802	800-245-5507		780
TF: 877-450-2200 ■ Web: www.rbxinc.com						
RC Aluminum Industries 2805 NW 75th Ave	Miami	FL	33122	305-592-1515		234
Rc Components Inc 373 Mitch Mcconnell Way	Bowling Green	KY	42101	270-842-6000		82
Web: www.rccomponents.com						
RC Fine Foods PO Box 236	Belle Mead	NJ	08502	908-359-5500	359-6957	296-11
TF: 800-526-3953 ■ Web: www.rcfinefoods.com						
Rc Productions Inc 1756 Lakeshore Dr	Muskegon	MI	49441	231-759-3160		7
Web: www.rcproductions.com						
RC Smith Co 14200 Southcross Dr W	Burnsville	MN	55306	952-854-0711	854-8160	286
TF: 800-747-7648 ■ Web: www.rcsmith.com						
RC Telecom Inc 6250 W Tenth St Ste 1	Greeley	CO	80634	970-356-4572		387
Web: rctelecom.com						
RCA Records 550 Madison Ave	New York	NY	10022	212-930-4000		657
Web: www.rcarecords.com						
RCA Rubber Co 1833 E Market St	Akron	OH	44305	330-784-1291	794-6446	291
TF: 800-321-2340 ■ Web: www.rcarubber.com						
RCEC (Roosevelt County Electric Co-op Inc) 121 N Main St PO Box 389	Portales	NM	88130	575-356-4491		245
Web: www.rcec.org/content/office-location						
RCF Information Systems Inc 4200 Colonel Glenn Hwy Glenn Tech Ctr Ste 100	Beavercreek	OH	45431	937-427-5680		225
Web: rcfinfo.com						
RCG (Rosenthal Collins Group LLC) 216 W Jackson Blvd Ste 400	Chicago	IL	60606	312-460-9200	795-7730*	169
*Fax: Hum Res ■ Web: www.rcgdirect.com						
RCGT Inc 7950 Asheville Hwy	Spartanburg	SC	29303	864-503-0879		401
RCH (Rady Children's Hospital) 3020 Children's Way 3rd Fl	San Diego	CA	92123	858-576-1700	966-5859*	374-1
*Fax: Library ■ TF: 800-788-9029 ■ Web: www.rchsd.org						
RCI (Resort Condominiums International) 9998 N Michigan Rd	Carmel	IN	46032	317-805-8000		753
TF: 800-338-7777 ■ Web: www.rci.com						
RCI (Retail Confectioners International) 2053 S Waverly Ste C	Springfield	MO	65804	417-883-2775	883-1108	49-6
TF: 800-545-5381 ■ Web: www.retailconfectioners.org						
RCI Capital Group Inc 1055 Dunsmuir St Ste 2184	Vancouver	BC	V7X1L3	604-689-0881		690
Web: www.rcicapitalgroup.com						
RCI Consultants Inc 17314 State Hwy 249 Ste 350	Houston	TX	77064	281-970-4221	970-4241	194
Web: www.rcigroup.us						
RCI Custom Products 801 N East St Ste 2A	Frederick	MD	21701	301-620-9130	620-9103	203
TF: 800-546-4724 ■ Web: www.rcicustom.com						
RCI Sound Systems 10721 Hanna St	Beltsville	MD	20705	301-931-9001		246
Web: www.rcisystems.com						
RCI Technologies Inc 1133 Green St	Iselin	NJ	08830	732-382-3000		177
TF: 800-644-0401 ■ Web: www.rci-technologies.com						
RCL (Rusk County Library) 106 E Main St	Henderson	TX	75652	903-657-8557		434-3
Web: www.rclib.org						
RCM Technologies Inc 2500 McClellan Ave Ste 350	Pennsauken	NJ	08109	856-356-4500	356-4600	721
NASDAQ: RCMT ■ TF: 800-322-2885 ■ Web: www.rcmt.com						
RCMA (Religious Conference Management Assn Inc) 7702 Woodland Dr Ste 120	Indianapolis	IN	46278	317-632-1888	632-7909	49-12
TF: 800-221-8235 ■ Web: www.rcmaweb.org						
RCMC (Rush-Copley Medical Ctr) 2000 Ogden Ave	Aurora	IL	60504	630-978-6200		374-3
TF: 866-426-7539 ■ Web: www.rushcopley.com						
RCMP 73 Leikin Dr	Ottawa	ON	K1A0R2	613-993-2999		303
Web: www.rcmp-grc.gc.ca						
RCMP Heritage Ctr 5907 Dewdney Ave	Regina	SK	S4T0P4	306-522-7333		520
TF: 866-567-7267 ■ Web: rcmphc.com						
Rco Engineering Inc 29200 Calahan Rd	Roseville	MI	48066	586-771-8400		247
Web: www.rcoeng.com						
RCO Systems Inc 251 James Jackson Ave	Cary	NC	27513	919-319-3612		180
Web: www.rconet.com						

				Phone	Fax	Class
RCP (Rubbermaid Commercial Products)						
3124 Valley Ave	Winchester	VA	22601	540-667-8700	542-8770	608
TF: 800-347-9800 ■ *Web:* www.rubbermaidcommercial.com						
RCP Block & Brick Inc						
8240 Broadway	Lemon Grove	CA	91945	619-460-7250	460-3926	183
TF: 800-794-4727 ■ *Web:* www.rcpblock.com						
RCPL (Rapid City Public Library)						
610 Quincy St	Rapid City	SD	57701	605-394-4171		434-3
TF: 800-562-5785 ■ *Web:* www.rcgov.org/library						
RCPL (Richland County Public Library)						
1431 Assembly St	Columbia	SC	29201	803-799-9084		434-3
Web: www.richlandlibrary.com						
RCR Plumbing & Mechanical Inc						
12620 Magnolia Ave	Riverside	CA	92503	951-371-5000		610
Web: www.ampam.com						
Rcr Technology Corp						
251 N Illinois St	Indianapolis	IN	46204	317-624-9500		261
Web: www.rcrtechnology.com						
RCS (Retail Construction Services Inc)						
11343 39th St N	Lake Elmo	MN	55042	651-704-9000	704-9100	685
Web: www.retailconstruction.com						
RCS Corp 955 Colony Pkwy	Aiken	SC	29803	803-641-0100		260
Web: www.rcscorporation.com						
RCS Innovations 7075 W Parkland Ct	Milwaukee	WI	53223	414-354-6900		8
TF: 800-373-6873 ■ *Web:* www.rcsinnovations.com						
RCS Services Inc 5506 Mitchelldale St	Houston	TX	77092	713-461-4119	461-2457	463
RCSD (Redwood City School District)						
750 Bradford St	Redwood City	CA	94063	650-423-2200	423-2294	685
Web: www.rcsdk8.net						
RCT (Rural Community Transportation Inc)						
1161 Portland St	Saint Johnsbury	VT	05819	802-748-8170	748-5275	108
Web: sites.google.com/a/rctvt.org/riderct						
RCTV International 4380 NW 128th St	Opa Locka	FL	33054	305-688-7475		742
Web: www.rctvintl.com						
R-Cubed Service & Sales Inc						
11126 Shady Trl	Dallas	TX	75229	972-243-3830		175
TF: 800-672-8233 ■ *Web:* www.rcubed.com						
RCW Energy Services LLC						
4125 Fairway Dr Ste 150	Carrollton	TX	75010	972-394-1000		536
Web: www.rcwenergyservices.com						
RD Data Solutions LLC						
2608 Avalon Dr	Lewisville	TX	75056	214-594-9080		525
TF: 800-690-8401 ■ *Web:* www.rddatasolutions.com						
RD Herbert & Sons Company Inc						
1407 Third Ave N	Nashville	TN	37208	615-242-3501	256-4056	189-12
Web: www.rdherbert.com						
RD Legal Funding LLC 45 Legion Dr	Cresskill	NJ	07626	201-568-9007		403
TF: 800-565-5177 ■ *Web:* www.legalfunding.com						
R&D Logic Inc 1611 Borel Pl Ste 2	San Mateo	CA	94402	650-356-9207	571-1276	177
Web: www.rdlogic.com						
RD Management LLC						
810 Seventh Ave 10th Fl	New York	NY	10019	212-265-6600	459-9133	655
Web: www.rdmanagement.com						
RD Olson Construction						
2955 Main St 3rd Fl	Irvine	CA	92614	949-474-2001	474-1534	186
Web: www.rdolson.com						
RDA Corp						
303 International Cir Ste 340	Hunt Valley	MD	21030	410-308-9300	308-9600	177
TF: 888-441-1278 ■ *Web:* www.rdacorp.com						
RDA Group 450 Enterprise Ct	Bloomfield Hills	MI	48302	248-332-5000	332-4168	466
TF: 800-669-7324 ■ *Web:* www.rdagroup.com						
RDC (Roche Diagnostics Corp)						
9115 Hague Rd PO Box 50457	Indianapolis	IN	46250-0457	800-428-5076	521-6929*	231
**Fax Area Code:* 317 ■ *TF Cust Svc:* 800-428-5076 ■ *Web:* usdiagnostics.roche.com						
Rdk Truck Sales Inc 3214 E Adamo Dr	Tampa	FL	33605	813-241-0711		516
TF: 877-735-4636 ■ *Web:* www.rdk.com						
RDO Equipment Co 700 Seventh St S	Fargo	ND	58103	701-526-9716	526-9717	274
TF: 800-247-4650 ■ *Web:* www.rdoequipment.com						
Rdr Group Inc 48 Tamarack Ln	Pomona	NY	10970	845-354-3897		317
TF: 800-822-6761 ■ *Web:* rdrgroup.com						
RDS Solutions LLC 99 Grayrock Rd	Clinton	NJ	08809	888-473-7435		196
TF: 888-473-7435 ■ *Web:* www.rdssolutions.com						
RDTC (R David Thomas Executive Conference Ctr)						
100 Fuqua Dr PO Box 90120	Durham	NC	27708	919-660-6400	660-3607	377
Web: www.fuqua.duke.edu						
Rdw Group Inc 125 Holden St	Providence	RI	02908	401-521-2700		4
Web: www.rdwgroup.com						
RE Carroll Inc 1570 N Olden Ave	Trenton	NJ	08638	609-695-6211		579
Web: www.recarroll.com						
RE Crawford Construction Inc						
6771 Professional Pkwy W Ste 100	Sarasota	FL	34240	941-907-0010		685
Web: www.recrawford.com						
Re Group Inc						
213 W Liberty St Ste 100	Ann Arbor	MI	48104	734-213-0200		4
Web: www.regroup.us						
RE Lewis Refrigeration Inc						
803 S Lincoln St PO Box 92	Creston	IA	50801	641-782-8183	782-8156	665
TF Cust Svc: 800-264-0767 ■ *Web:* www.relewisinc.com						
RE Olds Transportation Museum						
240 Museum Dr	Lansing	MI	48933	517-372-0529	372-2901	520
Web: www.reoldsmuseum.org						
RE Phelon Company Inc						
2063 University Pkwy	Aiken	SC	29801	803-649-1381		247
Web: fenix-mfg.com						
RE Rawlins Municipal Library						
1000 E Church St	Pierre	SD	57501	605-773-7421		434-3
Web: www.rawlinslibrary.org						
RE Uptegraff Manufacturing Co						
120 Uptegraff Dr PO Box 182	Scottdale	PA	15683	724-887-7700	887-4748	767
Web: www.uptegraff.com						
RE/MAX International Inc						
5075 S Syracuse St	Denver	CO	80237	303-770-5531	796-3599	652
TF Cust Svc: 800-525-7452 ■ *Web:* www.remax.com						
RE/MAX of Western Canada Inc						
7101 Syntex Dr Ste 340	Mississauga	ON	L5N6H5	905-542-2400	542-3340	652
TF: 800-563-3622 ■ *Web:* www.remax.ca						
RE/MAX Ontario-Atlantic						
7101 Syntex Dr	Mississauga	ON	L5N6H5	905-542-2400	542-3340	652
TF: 800-563-3622 ■ *Web:* www.remax.ca						
RE/MAX Quebec Inc 1500 rue Cunard	Laval	QC	H7S2B7	450-668-7743	668-2115	652
TF: 800-361-9325 ■ *Web:* www.remax-quebec.com						
REA 106 Allen Rd	Basking Ridge	NJ	07920	908-484-7200		193
Web: www.r-e-a.com						
REA & Assoc Inc						
419 W High Ave PO Box 1020	New Philadelphia	OH	44663	330-339-6651	308-9506	2
Web: www.reacpa.com						
REA Energy Co-op Inc 75 Airport Rd	Indiana	PA	15701	724-349-4800		245
TF: 800-211-5667 ■ *Web:* www.reaenergy.com						
Rea Magnet Wire Company Inc						
3600 E Pontiac St	Fort Wayne	IN	46803	260-421-7321		813
Web: www.reawire.com						
REACH Air Medical Services						
451 Aviation Blvd	Santa Rosa	CA	95403	707-324-2400	324-2478	26
Web: reachair.com						
Reach Out and Read 29 Mystic Ave	Somerville	MA	02145	617-629-8042		242
Web: www.reachoutandread.org						
Reach Resort 1435 Simonton St	Key West	FL	33040	305-296-5000	296-2830	669
TF: 888-318-4317 ■ *Web:* www.reachresort.com						
Reachable Inc						
855 El Camino Real Ste 260	Palo Alto	CA	94301	650-324-1400		387
Web: www.reachable.com						
ReachForce Inc						
9020-I Capital of Texas Hwy N Ste 270	Austin	TX	78759	512-327-9000		463
Web: www.reachforce.com						
ReachLocal Inc						
21700 Oxnard St Ste 1600	Woodland Hills	CA	91367	818-274-0260		4
NASDAQ: RLOC ■ *Web:* www.reachlocal.com						
Reachsolutions Llc						
7540 Potomac Fall Rd	Mc Lean	VA	22102	703-893-4114		463
Web: www.reachsolutions.com						
REACT Computer Services Inc						
7654 Plaza Ct	Willowbrook	IL	60527	630-323-6200		175
Reaction Audio Visual - Dallas LLC						
9951 Muirlands Blvd	Irvine	CA	92618	949-600-8235		514
Web: reactionav.com						
Reaction Engineering International Inc						
77 West 200 South Ste 210	Salt Lake City	UT	84101	801-364-6925		261
Web: www.reaction-eng.com						
Reactrix Systems Inc PO Box 878	Ramsey	NJ	07446	240-342-6346		637-10
Web: www.reactrix.com						
Read Jones Christoffersen Ltd						
1285 W Broadway Ste 300	Vancouver	BC	V6H3X8	604-738-0048		256
Web: www.rjc.ca						
Readco Kurimoto LLC 460 Grim Ln	York	PA	17406	717-848-2801		494
Web: www.readco.com						
Reader, The 2314 M St PO Box 7360	Omaha	NE	68107	402-341-7323	341-6967	532-5
Web: www.thereader.com						
Readerlink Distribution Services LLC						
1420 Kensington Rd Ste 300	Oak Brook	IL	60523	708-547-4400		96
TF: 800-549-5389 ■ *Web:* www.levybooks.com						
Reading Anthracite Co						
200 Mahantongo St PO Box 1200	Pottsville	PA	17901	570-622-5150		501
Web: www.readinganthracite.com						
Reading Area Community College						
10 S Second St	Reading	PA	19603	610-372-4721	607-6290*	162
**Fax:* Admissions ■ *TF:* 800-626-1665 ■ *Web:* www.racc.edu						
Reading Eagle Co 345 Penn St	Reading	PA	19601	610-371-5000		532-3
Web: readingeagle.com						
Reading Hospital & Medical Ctr						
PO Box 16052	Reading	PA	19612	610-988-8000		374-3
Web: www.readinghealth.org						
Reading International Inc						
6100 Center Dr Ste 900	Los Angeles	CA	90045	213-235-2240	235-2229	748
NASDAQ: RDI ■ *Web:* www.readingrdi.com						
Reading Is Fundamental Inc (RIF)						
1825 Connecticut Ave NW Ste 400	Washington	DC	20009	202-536-3400		48-11
TF: 877-743-7323 ■ *Web:* www.rif.org						
Reading Phillies Baseball Club						
1900 Centre Ave	Reading	PA	19612	610-375-8469		713
Reading Precast Inc						
5494 Pottsville Pike	Leesport	PA	19533	610-926-5000		183
TF: 800-724-4881 ■ *Web:* www.readingprecast.com						
Reading Public Library						
64 Middlesex Ave	Reading	MA	01867	781-944-0840		434-3
Web: www.readingpl.org						
Reading Public Library 100 S Fifth St	Reading	PA	19602	610-655-6355	655-6609	434-3
Web: www.reading.lib.pa.us						
Reading Public Museum & Art Gallery						
500 Museum Rd	Reading	PA	19611	610-371-5850	371-5632	520
Web: readingpublicmuseum.org						
Reading Rock Inc 4600 Devitt Dr	Cincinnati	OH	45246	513-874-2345	874-2520	183
TF: 800-482-6466 ■ *Web:* www.readingrock.com						
Reading Royals Hockey Club						
645 Penn St 3rd Fl	Reading	PA	19601	610-898-7825		717
Web: www.royalshockey.com						
Reading Truck Body Inc						
201 Hancock Blvd	Reading	PA	19611	800-458-2226		516
TF All: 800-458-2226 ■ *Web:* www.readingbody.com						
Reading-muhlenberg Area Vocational-technical School						
2615 Warren Rd	Reading	PA	19604	610-921-7300		764
Web: www.rmctc.org						
Reading-North Reading Chamber of Commerce						
PO Box 771	Reading	MA	01867	978-664-5060		139
Web: www.readingnreadingchamber.org						
Readington Farms Inc						
12 Mill Rd	Whitehouse Station	NJ	08889	908-534-2121	534-5235	296-27
ReadOz LLC 350 W Ontario St Ste 4W	Chicago	IL	60654	312-929-2500		387
Web: www.readoz.com						
Ready At Dawn Studios LLC						
15201 Laguna Canyon Rd Ste 150	Irvine	CA	92618	949-724-1234		809
Web: www.readyatdawn.com						
Ready Auto Transport LLC						
1030 N Colorado St Ste 109	Gilbert	AZ	85233	480-558-3200		311
Web: www.readyautotransport.com						

Name / Address	City	State	ZIP	Phone	Fax	Class
Ready Electric Company Inc 3300 Gilmore Industrial Blvd *Web:* www.readyelec.com	Louisville	KY	40213	502-893-2511	893-2519	189-4
Ready Mixed Concrete Co 4315 Cuming St *TF:* 800-844-5622 ■ *Web:* lymanrichey.com	Omaha	NE	68131	402-556-3600	556-5171	182
Ready Pac Produce Inc 4401 Foxdale Ave *TF:* 800-800-7822 ■ *Web:* www.readypac.com	Irwindale	CA	91706	800-800-7822		296-33
Ready Set Go Services LLC 705 N State St Ste 621 *Web:* rdysetgo.com	Ukiah	CA	95482	707-468-0213		45
Ready Set Work LLC 1487 Dunwoody Dr *Web:* www.readysetwork.com	West Chester	PA	19380	215-689-4323		387
Ready Technologies Inc 101 Capitol Way N Ste 301 *TF:* 877-892-9104 ■ *Web:* www.readyengineering.com	Olympia	WA	98501	360-413-9800		261
Readyforce Inc 1010 Doyle St Ste 200	Menlo Park	CA	94025	650-543-1400		260
ReadyGo Inc 1761 Pilgrim Ave *Web:* www.readygo.com	Mountain View	CA	94040	650-559-8990		177
Ready-to-run Software Inc 212 Cedar Cv *TF:* 800-573-1874 ■ *Web:* www.rtr.com	Lansing	NY	14882	607-533-4002		177
Reagan County 3rd St	Big Lake	TX	76932	325-884-2090		338
Reagan Wireless Corp 720 S Powerline Rd Ste D *TF:* 877-724-3266 ■ *Web:* www.reaganwireless.com	Deerfield Beach	FL	33442	954-596-2355	596-0070	246
Reagent Chemical & Research Inc 115 Rt 202 *TF:* 800-231-1807 ■ *Web:* www.reagentchemical.com	Ringoes	NJ	08551	908-284-2800	284-6090	146
Real 92.3 FM 3400 W Olive Blvd Ste 550 *Web:* real923la.iheart.com	Burbank	CA	91505	818-559-2252		645
Real Asset Management Inc 309 Court Ave Ste 244 *Web:* www.realassetmgt.com	Des Moines	IA	50309	515 699-8564		174
Real Capital Analytics Inc 110 Fifth Ave *Web:* www.rcanalytics.com	New York	NY	10011	212-387-7103		395
Real County PO Box 750 *Web:* www.co.real.tx.us	Leakey	TX	78873	830-232-5202	232-6888	338
Real Don Johnson Motors, The 2101 Central Blvd *Web:* www.realdonjohnson.com	Brownsville	TX	78520	956-546-2288		57
Real Estate Buyer's Agent Council (REBAC) 430 N Michigan Ave **Fax Area Code:* 312 ■ *TF:* 800-648-6224 ■ *Web:* www.rebac.net	Chicago	IL	60611	800-648-6224	329-8632*	49-17
Real Estate Errors & Omissions Insurance Corp 1604 700 W Pender St *Web:* www.reeoic.com	Vancouver	BC	V6C1G8	604-669-0019		390
Real Estate Express 12977 N 40 Dr Ste 108 *TF:* 866 739-7277 ■ *Web:* www.realestateexpress.com	Saint Louis	MO	63141	866-739-7277		652
Real Estate Institute of Bo 1750 - 355 Burrard St *TF:* 800 667-2166 ■ *Web:* www.reibc.org	Vancouver	BC	V6C2G8	604-685-3702		652
Real Estate Institute of Canada 5407 Eglinton Ave W Ste 208 *TF:* 800-542-7342 ■ *Web:* www.reic.ca	Toronto	ON	M9C5K6	416-695-9000		656
Real Estate Law Report 610 Opperman Dr **Fax Area Code:* 612 ■ **Fax:* Sales ■ *TF Cust Svc:* 800-328-4880 ■ *Web:* legalsolutions.thomsonreuters.com	Eagan	MN	55123	651-687-7000	486-4388*	531-7
Real Estate Management Services Group LLC 1100 Fifth Ave S Ste 305 *Web:* www.remsgroup.com	Naples	FL	34102	239-262-3017		401
Real Estate One Inc 25800 NW Hwy Ste 100 *TF:* 800-521-0508 ■ *Web:* www.realestateone.com	Southfield	MI	48075	248-304-6700	263-5966	652
Real Estate Roundtable 801 Pennsylvania Ave NW Ste 720 *Web:* www.rer.org	Washington	DC	20004	202-639-8400	639-8442	49-17
Real Food Company Inc 2140 Polk St *Web:* www.realfoodco.com	San Francisco	CA	94109	415-673-7420		345
Real Foundation Inc 13737 Noel Rd Ste 900 *Web:* www.realfoundations.net	Dallas	TX	75240	214-292-7000		655
Real Goods Solar 833 W S Boulder Rd *NASDAQ:* RSGE ■ *TF:* 888-567-6527 ■ *Web:* rgsenergy.com	Louisville	CO	80027	888-567-6527		620
Real Hip-Hop Network Inc, The 1455 Pennsylvania Ave NW Ste 400 *Web:* rhn.tv	Washington	DC	20004	202-379-3115		116
Real Integrated 40900 woodward ave *Web:* www.realintegrated.com	Bloomfield Hills	MI	48304	248-540-0660		7
Real Intent Inc 990 Almanor Ave Ste 220 *Web:* www.realintent.com	Sunnyvale	CA	94085	408-830-0700		225
Real Interactive LLC 25 Business Park Dr *Web:* www.starpulse.com	Branford	CT	06405	203-488-8447		396
Real Living First Service Realty 13155 SW 42nd St Ste 200 *TF:* 800-899-8477 ■ *Web:* www.realliving.com	Miami	FL	33175	305-551-9400	551-4965	652
Real Living Inc 77 E Nationwide Blvd *Web:* www.realliving.com	Columbus	OH	43215	949 794-7900		310
Real Salt Lake 9256 S State *Web:* www.rsl.com	Sandy	UT	84070	801-727-2700		713
Real Seafood Co 195 Wolf Rd *Web:* www.reelseafoodco.com	Albany	NY	12205	518-458-2068		671
Real Seafood Co 22 Main St *Web:* mainstreetventuresinc.com	Toledo	OH	43605	419-697-4400		671
Real Soft Inc 2540 Route 130 N Ste 118 *Web:* www.realsoftinc.com	Cranbury	NJ	08512	609-409-3636	409-3637	178-11
Real Solutions of Illinois Inc 100 N La Salle St Ste 1400 *Web:* www.realsolutions-us.com	Chicago	IL	60602	312-621-9100		174
Real Story Group, The 3470 Olney-Laytonsville Rd Ste 131 *TF:* 800-325-6190 ■ *Web:* www.realstorygroup.com	Olney	MD	20832	617-340-6464		463
Real Time Consultants Inc 777 Corporate Dr Ste 1 *Web:* www.realtimenet.com	Mahwah	NJ	07430	201-512-1777		174
Real Time Information Services Inc 191 W Shaw Ave Ste 106 *Web:* realtimeca.com	Fresno	CA	93704	559-222-6456		177
Real Time Measurements Inc Bay 18 4750 106th Ave SE *TF:* 800-635-3456 ■ *Web:* www.rty.ca	Calgary	AB	T2C3G5	403-720-3444		539
Real Time Risk Systems Llc 80 Wall St Ste 500 *Web:* realtimerisksystems.com	New York	NY	10005	212-425-3705		226
Real Time Systems Inc 103 Industrial Loop Ste 1100 *Web:* www.real-time-sys.com	Fredericksburg	TX	78624	830-990-2340		246
Real Time Translation Inc 1107 Hazeltine Blvd *Web:* www.rttmobile.com	Chaska	MN	55318	952-479-6180		387
Real Vision Software Inc 3700 Jackson St Ste 203 *TF:* 800-426-9990 ■ *Web:* www.realvisionsoftware.com	Alexandria	LA	71303	318-449-4579		177
Real World Inc 8098 N Via De Negocio *Web:* www.realworldinc.com	Scottsdale	AZ	85258	480-296-0160		7
RealCapitalMarketscom LLC 5780 Fleet St Ste 130 *Web:* www.rcm1.com	Carlsbad	CA	92008	760-602-5080		652
Realdecoy Inc 205 Catherine St *TF:* 800-874-2458 ■ *Web:* www.realdecoy.com	Ottawa	ON	K2P1C3	613-234-9330		177
RealEnergy LLC 1500 Soscol Ferry Rd *Web:* realenergy.com	Napa	CA	94558	707-944-2400		188
Realhome.com Inc 1100 Summer St *Web:* www.alhome.com	Stamford	CT	06905	203-323-7715		226
Realistic Computing Inc 10461 Mill Run Cir *Web:* www.realistic-computing.com	Baltimore	MD	21117	410-744-8144		175
Reality Interactive 386 Main St 6th Fl	Middletown	CT	06457	860-346-2700		652
Reality Technology Inc 2444 Washington St Ste 201 *Web:* www.reality-technology.com	Denver	CO	80205	303-757-1107		225
RealityCheck Inc 2033 N Geyer Rd *TF:* 800-438 7325 ■ *Web:* www.realitycheckinc.com	Saint Louis	MO	63131	314-909-9095		466
Realized Financial Solutions Inc 17 Farmington Ave Ste T4 *Web:* www.realizedfinancialsolutions.com	Plainville	CT	06062	860-747-0002		180
Reallygreatrate Inc 420 S Pacific Coast Hwy Ste 202 *Web:* www.rgrmarketing.com	Redondo Beach	CA	90277	310-540-8900	540-8255	225
RealNetworks Inc 2601 Elliott Ave Ste 1000 *NASDAQ:* RNWK ■ *TF Cust Svc:* 888-484-8256 ■ *Web:* www.realnetworks.com	Seattle	WA	98121	206-674-2700	674-2696	178-8
Realogy Corp 175 Park Ave *Web:* www.realogy.com	Madison	NJ	07940	973-407-2000		652
RealSTEEL 1684 Medina Rd *TF:* 866-965-2688 ■ *Web:* www.wolcottgroup.com	Medina	OH	44256	866-965-2688		180
Realstreet Staffing 2500 Wallington Way Ste 208 *TF:* 877-480-8002 ■ *Web:* www.realstreetstaffing.com	Marriottsville	MD	21104	410-480-8002		463
RealTechNetwork Corp 75A Lake Rd Ste 150 *TF:* 877-276-4904 ■ *Web:* www.realtechnetwork.com	Congers	NY	10920	877-279-4904		5
RealTime Group Inc, The 5217 Tennyson Pkwy Ste 200 *Web:* therealtimegroup.com	Plano	TX	75024	972-985-9100		463
Real-Time Laboratories LLC 990 S Rogers Cir Ste 5 *Web:* www.real-timelabs.com	Boca Raton	FL	33487	561-988-8826		419
Realtime Software Corp 24 Deane Rd *TF:* 800-323-1143 ■ *Web:* www.realtimesw.com	Bernardston	MA	01337	847-803-1100	954-4764	178-1
Realtime Technologies Inc 1523 N Main St *TF:* 800-344-1707 ■ *Web:* www.simcreator.com	Royal Oak	MI	48067	248-548-4876		261
Realtor Magazine 430 N Michigan Ave 9th Fl *TF:* 800-874-6500 ■ *Web:* www.nar.realtor	Chicago	IL	60611	800-874-6500		457-5
Realtors Assn of New Mexico 2201 Bros Rd *TF:* 800-224-2282 ■ *Web:* www.nmrealtor.com	Santa Fe	NM	87505	505-982-2442	983-8809	656
Realty Capital Partners LLC 8333 Douglas Ave *Web:* www.rcpinvestments.com	Dallas	TX	75225	469-533-4000		41
Realty Consulting Services Inc 1628 Colonial Pkwy	Inverness	IL	60067	847-241-2900		2
Realty Executives International Inc 7600 N 16th St Ste 100 *TF:* 800-252-3366 ■ *Web:* www.realtyexecutives.com	Phoenix	AZ	85020	602-957-0747		652
Realty Income Corp 11995 El Camino Real *NYSE:* O ■ *TF:* 877-924-6266 ■ *Web:* www.realtyincome.com	San Diego	CA	92130	858-284-5000		655
Realty Landscaping Corp 2585 Second St Pk *Web:* www.realtylandscaping.com	Newtown	PA	18940	215-598-7334		776
Realty Plus Chicago Inc 453 E 111th St Apt 16	Chicago	IL	60628	773-785-1400		652
RealtyBid International Inc 3225 Rainbow Dr Ste 248 *TF:* 877-518-5600 ■ *Web:* www.realtybid.com	Rainbow City	AL	35906	877-518-5600		393
RealtyShares Inc 637 Natoma St Ste 5 *TF:* 855-880-6050 ■ *Web:* www.realtyshares.com	San Francisco	CA	94103	415-450-6234		387
Ream's Food Stores 160 E Claybourne Ave *Web:* www.reamsfoods.com	Salt Lake City	UT	84115	801-485-8451		355

	Phone	Fax	Class
Reams Asset Management Company LLC 227 Washington St. Columbus IN 47202 *TF:* 800-541-7774 ■ *Web:* www.reamsasset.com	812-372-6606		690
Reardon Associates Inc 450 Washington St Ste LL5 Dedham MA 02026 *Web:* www.reardonassociates.com	781-329-2660		260
Reasio Inc 5214F Diamond Heights Blvd Ste 217 San Francisco CA 94131 *TF:* 888-870-7889 ■ *Web:* www.reesio.com	888-870-7889		387
Reason Magazine 3415 S Sepulveda Blvd Ste 400 Los Angeles CA 90034 *TF Cust Svc:* 888-732-7668 ■ *Web:* www.reason.com	310-391-2245	391-4395	457-17
Reason Public Policy Institute 3415 S Sepulveda Blvd Ste 400 Los Angeles CA 90034 *TF:* 888-732-7668 ■ *Web:* www.reason.org	310-391-2245	391-4395	634
Reata 310 Houston St. Fort Worth TX 76102 *Web:* www.reata.net	817-336-1009		671
Reata Real Estate Services LP 1100 NE Loop 410 Ste 400. San Antonio TX 78209 *Web:* www.reatarealestate.com	210-930-4111		652
Reaveley Engineers & Associates Inc 675 East 500 South Salt Lake City UT 84102 *Web:* www.reaveley.com	801-486-3883		539
Reaxis Inc 941 Robinson Hwy Mcdonald PA 15057 *TF:* 800-426-7273 ■ *Web:* www.reaxis.com	800-426-7273		388
Reb's Web Design & Computer Tech Support LLC 7965 Pipers Path Glen Burnie MD 21061	410-209-0285		180
REBAC (Real Estate Buyer's Agent Council) 430 N Michigan Ave Chicago IL 60611 **Fax Area Code:* 312 ■ *TF:* 800-648-6224 ■ *Web:* www.rebac.net	800-648-6224	329-8632*	49-17
Rebar Engineering Inc 10706 Painter Ave. Santa Fe Springs CA 90670	562-946-2461		189-14
Re-Bath LLC 16879 N 75th Ave Ste 101. Peoria AZ 85382 *TF:* 800-426-4573 ■ *Web:* rebath.com	800-426-4573		189-11
Rebco Inc 1171-1225 Madison Ave. Paterson NJ 07509 *TF:* 800-777-0787 ■ *Web:* www.rebcoinc.com	973-684-0200	684-0118	234
Rebecca Taylor Inc 307 W 36th St 16th Fl. New York NY 10018 *TF:* 888-485-6738 ■ *Web:* www.rebeccataylor.com	888-485-6738		594
Rebel Interactive Inc 1217 S 13th St Omaha NE 68108 *Web:* www.rebelinteractive.com	402-561-0520		809
Rebel State Historic Site 1260 Hwy 1221 Marthaville LA 71450 *TF:* 888-677-3600 ■ *Web:* www.crt.state.la.us	318-472-6255		565
Rebellion Photonics Inc 2327 Commerce St Ste 200 Houston TX 77002 *TF:* 855-677-9999 ■ *Web:* rebellionphotonics.com	713-218-0101		693
Reber Machine & Tool Company Inc 1112 S Liberty Muncie IN 47302 *Web:* rebermachine.com	765-288-0297		757
Rebman Properties Inc 1014 W Fairbanks Ave Winter Park FL 32789 *Web:* www.rebmanproperties.com	407-875-8001	875-8004	652
Reboot Computer Services Inc 7011 Austin St Ste 3a. Forest Hills NY 11375 *Web:* www.rebootcs.com	718-897-7727		175
Reborn Cabinets 2981 E La Palma Ave. Anaheim CA 92806 *TF:* 888-273-2676 ■ *Web:* www.reborncabinets.com	714-630-2220		321
Rebuilders Automotive Supply Company Inc 1650 Flat River Rd Coventry RI 02816 *Web:* www.coresupply.com	401-822-3030		61
Rebuilding Together Inc 1899 L St NW Ste 1000 Washington DC 20036 **Fax Area Code:* 202 ■ *TF:* 800-473-4229 ■ *Web:* rebuildingtogether.org	800-473-4229	483-9081*	48-5
REC (Rural Electric Co-op) 13942 Highway 76 PO Box 609 Lindsay OK 73052 *TF:* 800-259-3504 ■ *Web:* www.recok.coop	405-756-3104	756-8957	245
Rec Consulting Inc 2442 Second Ave San Diego CA 92101 *Web:* rec-consultants.com	619-232-9200		261
Rec Room 512 York Rd. Towson MD 21204 *Web:* torrentnightclub.com	410-337-7178		572
RECARO Aircraft Seating Americas Inc 2275 Eagle Pkwy Fort Worth TX 76177 *Web:* www.recaro-as.com	817-490-9161		22
Receivable Management Inc 107 W Randol Mill Rd Arlington TX 76011 *Web:* receivablemanagement.net	817-261-7534		160
ReceptoPharm Inc 1537 NW 65th Ave. Plantation FL 33313 *Web:* www.receptopharm.com	954-356-1460		238
Reciprocal of America 4200 Innslake Dr Ste 102 Glen Allen VA 23060 *TF:* 800-284-8847 ■ *Web:* www.reciprocalgroup.com	804-747-8600	270-5281	391-5
Reckitt Benckiser Inc 399 Interpace Pkwy PO Box 225. Parsippany NJ 07054 *Web:* www.rb.com	973-404-2600		151
Reco Constructors Inc 710 Hospital St. Richmond VA 23219 *Web:* www.recoconstructors.com	804-644-2611	643-3561	91
Reco Equipment Inc 41245 Reco Rd Belmont OH 41245 *TF:* 800-686-7326 ■ *Web:* www.recoequip.com	740-782-1314	782-1020	190
Recognition Specialties Inc 1710 Harbeck Rd Grants Pass OR 97527 *Web:* nicebadge.com	541-476-3166		701
ReCommunity Recycling 809 W Hill St. Charlotte NC 28208 *Web:* www.recommunity.com	704-697-2000		660
RECON Dynamics LLC 1201 Third Ave Seattle WA 98101 *TF:* 877-480-3551 ■ *Web:* www.recondynamics.com	877-480-3551		693
RECON Environmental Inc 1927 Fifth Ave. San Diego CA 92101 *Web:* www.recon-us.com	619-308-9333		192
Recon Logistics LLC 10205 Queens Way Ste 5 Chagrin Falls OH 44023 *TF:* 866-424-7153 ■ *Web:* reconlogistics.com	440-708-2306		311
Recon Management Services Inc 1907 Ruth St. Sulphur LA 70663 *TF:* 888-301-4662 ■ *Web:* www.recon-group.com	337-583-4662	583-7565	631
Reconditioned Systems Inc (RSI) 2636 S Wilson St Ste 105. Tempe AZ 85282 *TF:* 800-280-5000 ■ *Web:* www.rsisystemsfurniture.com	480-968-1772	894-1907	319-1
Reconnect Mental Health Services 1281 St Clair Ave W Toronto ON M6E1B8 *Web:* www.reconnect.on.ca	416-248-2050		726
Reconstructionist Rabbinical Assn (RRA) 1299 Church Rd Wyncote PA 19095 *Web:* www.therra.org	215-576-5210	576-8051	48-20
Record 4324 Phil Hargett Ct PO Box 3099 Monroe NC 28111 *TF Sales:* 800-438-1937 ■ *Web:* www.record-usa.com	704-289-9212	289-2024	253
Record Center Innovations Inc 3919 W Washington St. Phoenix AZ 85009	602-258-4000		463
Record Exchange, The 1105 W Idaho St. Boise ID 83702 *Web:* www.therecordexchange.com	208-344-8010		525
Record Herald Publishing 30 Walnut St. Waynesboro PA 17268 *Web:* www.therecordherald.com	717-762-2151		532-3
Record Plant Inc 1032 N Sycamore Ave. Hollywood CA 90038 *Web:* www.recordplant.com	323-993-9300	466-8835	657
Record Play Tek Inc 110 E Vistula St. Bristol IN 46507 *TF:* 800-809-5233 ■ *Web:* www.recordplaytek.com	574-848-5233	848-5333	52
Record Search America Inc 1201 N Liberty St Boise ID 83704	208-375-1906		635
Record Searchlight 1101 Twin View Blvd. Redding CA 96003 *TF:* 800-666-1331 ■ *Web:* www.redding.com	530-243-2424		532-2
Record Town Inc 38 Corporate Cir Albany NY 12203 *Web:* www.twec.com	518-452-1242		525
Record, The 501 Broadway Troy NY 12180 *TF:* 800-323-9262 ■ *Web:* www.troyrecord.com	518-270-1200		532-2
Record, The 160 King St E. Kitchener ON N2G4E5 *TF:* 800-265-8261 ■ *Web:* www.therecord.com	519-894-2231	894-3829	532-1
Record, The 1195 Galt St E. Sherbrooke QC J1G1Y7 *Web:* www.sherbrookerecord.com	819-569-9525	821-3179	532-1
Record, The 100 Commons Way Rockaway NJ 07866 *TF:* 888-504-4280 ■ *Web:* www.recordnet.com	888-504-4280		532-3
Record-Courier 1050 W Main St. Kent OH 44240 *TF:* 800-560-9657 ■ *Web:* www.recordpub.com	330-541-9400	296-2698	532-2
Recorder Publishing Co 17 Morristown Rd. Bernardsville NJ 07924	908-766-3900		637-8
Recordflow 1751 e garry ave Santa Ana CA 92705 *TF:* 877-896-7350 ■ *Web:* www.recordflow.com	877-896-7350		463
Record-Gazette 218 N Murray St Banning CA 92220 *Web:* www.recordgazette.net	951-849-4586	849-2437	532-2
Recording for the Blind & Dyslexic (RFB&D) 20 Roszel Rd. Princeton NJ 08540 **Fax Area Code:* 609 ■ *TF:* 800-221-4792 ■ *Web:* www.rfbd.org	800-221-4792	987-8116*	48-17
Recording Industry Assn of America Inc (RIAA) 1025 F St NW 10th Fl. Washington DC 20004 *Web:* www.riaa.com	202-775-0101		48-4
Record-Journal 11 Crown St. Meriden CT 06450 *TF:* 800-228-6915 ■ *Web:* myrecordjournal.com	203-235-1661	639-0210	532-2
Recordnet.com PO Box 900 Stockton CA 95201 *TF:* 800-606-9741 ■ *Web:* www.recordnet.com	209-943-6397	547-8186	532-2
Records Consultants Inc 10826 Gulfdale St. San Antonio TX 78216 *TF:* 877-363-4127 ■ *Web:* www.rcitech.com	877-363-4127		393
RecordSetter LLC 228 Park Ave S Ste 29280 New York NY 10003 *Web:* recordsetter.com	646-912-6611		387
Recordtrak Inc 651 Allendale Rd PO Box 61591. King Of Prussia PA 19406	610-992-5000	354-8946	428
Recourse Communications Inc 112 Intracoastal Pointe Dr Jupiter FL 33477 *Web:* www.rcirecruitmentsolutions.com	561-686-6800		184
Recovered Energy Inc 11455 N Rio Vista Rd Pocatello ID 83202 *Web:* www.recoveredenergy.com	208-637-0645		697
Recovery Partners LLC 4151 N Marshall Way Ste 12 Scottsdale AZ 85251 *Web:* www.recoverypartners.com	480-747-9888		160
Recreation Unlimited 15150 Herriman Blvd Ste B Noblesville IN 46060 *Web:* www.recunlimited.com	317-773-3545	773-2675	711
Recreation Vehicle Dealers Assn (RVDA) 3930 University Dr 3rd Fl Fairfax VA 22030 *TF:* 800-336-0355 ■ *Web:* www.rvda.org	703-591-7130	591-0734	49-18
Recreation Vehicle Industry Assn (RVIA) 1896 Preston White Dr Reston VA 20191 *TF:* 800-336-0154 ■ *Web:* www.rvia.org	703-620-6003	620-5071	49-21
Recreation.gov 1849 C St NW Washington DC 20240 *TF:* 877-444-6777 ■ *Web:* www.recreation.gov	202-208-4743		197
Recreational Equipment Inc (REI) 6750 S 228th St Kent WA 98032 *TF Orders:* 800-426-4840 ■ *Web:* www.rei.com	253-395-3780	891-2523	711
Recreatives Industries Inc 60 Depot St. Buffalo NY 14206 *TF:* 800-255-2511 ■ *Web:* www.maxatvs.com	716-855-2226	855-1094	29
Recruitech International Inc 120 Gibraltar Rd Ste 120 Horsham PA 19044 *TF:* 800-264-1170 ■ *Web:* www.recruitech.com	215-293-1300		193
Recruiters of Minnesota Inc 6110, Blue Circle Dr Ste 110 Minnetonka MN 55343 *Web:* www.recruitersofmn.com	952-767-0089		260
Recruiting Source Inc, The 7487 NW Fourth St. Plantation FL 33317 *Web:* the-recruiting-source-inc.hub.biz	954-585-0266		260
Recruiting Toolbox PO Box 2573. Redmond WA 98073 *TF:* 888-823-2030 ■ *Web:* www.recruitingtoolbox.com	425-557-2100		393
Recruitmilitary LLC 422 W Loveland Ave. Loveland OH 45140 *TF:* 800-226-0841 ■ *Web:* recruitmilitary.com	513-683-5020		260
RecruitWise 704 S Illinois Ave Ste C-202 Oak Ridge TN 37830 *Web:* www.recruitwise.jobs	865-425-0405		260
Recto Molded Products Inc (RMP) 4425 Appleton St Cincinnati OH 45209 *Web:* www.rectomolded.com	513-871-5544		604

Phone Fax Class

Rector Communications Inc
2300 Chestnut St Ste 340a . . . Philadelphia PA 19103 215-963-9661 7
Web: rector.com
Rector-Dunan & Assoc
314 E Highland Mall Blvd . . . Austin TX 78752 512-454-5262 463
Rectory School
528 Pomfret St PO Box 68 . . . Pomfret CT 06258 860-928-7759 928-4961 622
Web: www.rectoryschool.org
Recursion Software Inc
2591 Dallas Pkwy Ste 200 . . . Frisco TX 75034 972-731-8800 731-8881 179
TF: 800-727-8674 ■ *Web:* www.recursionsw.com
Recycle Ann Arbor Inc
2420 S Industrial Hwy . . . Ann Arbor MI 48104 734-662-6288 660
TF: 800-526-3505 ■ *Web:* www.recycleannarbor.org
Recycled Paper Greetings Inc
111 N Canal St Ste 700 . . . Chicago IL 60606 800-777-3331 130
TF: 800-777-3331 ■ *Web:* www.prgreetings.com
Recycled Paperboard Technical Assn
PO Box 5774 . . . Elgin IL 60121 847-622-2544 49-13
Web: www.rpta.org
RecycleMatch LLC
3375 Westpark Dr Ste 321 . . . Houston TX 77005 713-581-0466 387
Recycling Center of Live Oak Inc, The
700 Houston Ave NW . . . Live Oak FL 32064 386-364-5865 660
TF: 800-331-2909 ■ *Web:* www.biggreenball.org
Red Angus Assn of America
4201 N IH-35 . . . Denton TX 76207 940-387-3502 829-6069* 48-2
**Fax Area Code:* 888 ■ *TF:* 800-422-2117 ■ *Web:* www.redangus.org
Red Ball Oxygen Co Inc
609 N Market . . . Shreveport LA 71107 318-425-3211 425-6323 385
TF: 800-551-8150 ■ *Web:* www.redballoxygen.com
Red Barn 455 Riverside Dr . . . Augusta ME 04330 207-623-9485 671
Web: theredbarnmaine.org
Red Barn Investments
5215 Old Orchard Rd Ste 675 . . . Skokie IL 60077 847-920-7100 796
Web: www.redbarnllc.com
Red Barn Theatre 319 Duval St Rear . . . Key West FL 33040 305-296-9911 572
Web: redbarntheatre.com
Red Bell Real Estate LLC
1415 S Main St . . . Salt Lake City UT 84115 801-483-4300 656
Web: www.redbellre.com
Red Blazer, The 72 Manchester St . . . Concord NH 03301 603-224-4101 224-7118 671
Web: www.theredblazer.com
Red Brick Design Inc
150 Westford Rd . . . Tyngsboro MA 01879 978-649-4411 649-4414 395
Red Bud Industries
200 B & E Industrial Dr . . . Red Bud IL 62278 618-282-3801 282-6718 494
TF Cust Svc: 800-851-4612 ■ *Web:* www.redbudindustries.com
Red Butte Garden & Arboretum
300 Wakara Way University of Utah . . . Salt Lake City UT 84108 801-585-0556 97
Web: www.redbuttegarden.org
Red Canoe Credit Union 1418 15th Ave . . . Longview WA 98632 360-425-2130 219
Web: redcanoecu.com
Red Carpet Charters
4820 SW 20th . . . Oklahoma City OK 73128 405-672-5100 107
TF: 888-878-5100 ■ *Web:* www.redcarpetcharters.com
Red Cedar Technology Inc
4572 S Hagadorn Rd Ste 3-A . . . East Lansing MI 48823 517-664-1137 256
Web: www.redcedartech.com
Red Chamber Co 1912 E Vernon Ave . . . Vernon CA 90058 323-234-9000 231-8888 297-5
Web: www.redchamber.com
Red Clay Consolidated School District
1502 Spruce Ave . . . Wilmington DE 19805 302-552-3700 685
Red Clay Interactive
22 Buford Village Way Ste 221 . . . Buford GA 30518 770-297-2430 225
TF: 866-251-2800 ■ *Web:* www.redclayinteractive.com
Red Clay State Historic Park
1140 Red Clay Pk Rd . . . Cleveland TN 37311 423-478-0339 565
Web: www.state.tn.us
Red Cloud Promotions
1600 Sawtelle Blvd Ste 108 . . . Los Angeles CA 90025 310-444-5583 195
Web: redcloudpromotions.com
Red Cross Pharmacy 420 Main St . . . Forest City PA 18421 570-785-5400 237
Web: www.rcrx.com
Red Cross Pharmacy Inc 52 E Arrow St . . . Marshall MO 65340 660-886-5535 237
Web: redcrosspharmacy.com
Red Deer Advocate 2950 Bremner Ave . . . Red Deer AB T4R1M9 403-343-2400 341-6560 532-1
TF: 800-661-0995 ■ *Web:* www.reddeeradvocate.com
Red Deer Chamber of Commerce
3017 Gaetz Ave . . . Red Deer AB T4N5Y6 403-347-4491 343-6188 137
Web: www.reddeerchamber.com
Red Deer Public Library 4818 49 St . . . Red Deer AB T4N1T9 403-346-4576 435
Web: www.rdpl.org
Red Deer Regional Hospital Centre
3942 50th A Ave . . . Red Deer AB T4N4E7 403-343-4422 343-4866 374-2
Web: www.albertahealthservices.ca
Red Devil Inc 1437 S Boulder . . . Tulsa OK 74119 800-423-3845 585-8120* 3
**Fax Area Code:* 918 ■ *TF:* 800-423-3845 ■ *Web:* www.reddevil.com
Red Diamond Inc 400 Park Ave . . . Moody AL 35004 205-577-4000 296-7
TF: 800-292-4651 ■ *Web:* www.reddiamond.com
RED Distribution 345 Hudson St 6th Fl . . . New York NY 10014 917-421-7601 523
Web: www.redmusic.com
Red Dog Saloon 278 S Franklin St . . . Juneau AK 99801 907-463-3658 671
Web: www.reddogsaloon.com
Red Dolly Casino 530 Gregory St . . . Black Hawk CO 80422 303-582-1100 582-1435 133
Web: reddollycasino.net
Red Door By Elizabeth Arden, The
400 E Fairway Ln . . . Galloway NJ 08205 609-404-4100 707
Web: www.reddoorspas.com
Red Door Interactive Inc
350 Tenth Ave Ste 1100 . . . San Diego CA 92101 619-398-2670 7
Web: www.reddoor.biz
Red Dot Corp 1209 W Corsicana St . . . Athens TX 75751 800-657-2234 105
TF Cust Svc: 800-657-2234 ■ *Web:* www.reddotbuildings.com
Red Dot Corp 495 Andover Park E . . . Tukwila WA 98188 206-575-3840 172
Web: www.rdac.com
Red Ewald Inc 2669 US 181 . . . Karnes City TX 78118 830-780-3304 606
TF: 800-242-3524 ■ *Web:* www.redewald.com

Red Feather Marketing Group Inc
332 Main St . . . Madison NJ 07940 973-966-1399 195
Web: www.red-feather.com
Red Fish 8 Archer Rd . . . Hilton Head Island SC 29928 843-686-3388 671
Web: www.redfishofhiltonhead.com
Red Fish Grill 115 Bourbon St . . . New Orleans LA 70130 504-598-1200 671
Web: www.redfishgrill.com
Red Fleet State Park
8750 North Hwy 191 . . . Vernal UT 84078 435-789-4432 565
TF: 800-322-3770 ■ *Web:* stateparks.utah.gov
Red Foundry Inc 1608 S Ashland Ave . . . Chicago IL 60608 888-406-1099 631
TF: 888-406-1099 ■ *Web:* www.redfoundry.com
Red Gold Inc 120 E Oak St . . . Orestes IN 46063 765-754-7527 296-20
TF: 800-772-5726 ■ *Web:* www.redgold.com
Red Hat Inc 1801 Varsity Dr . . . Raleigh NC 27606 919-754-3700 754-3701 178-12
NYSE: RHT ■ *TF:* 888-733-4281 ■ *Web:* www.redhat.com
Red Hat Society Store
431 S Acacia Ave . . . Fullerton CA 92831 714-738-0001 533
TF: 866-386-2850 ■ *Web:* www.redhatsociety.com
Red Haw State Park 24550 US Hwy 34 . . . Chariton IA 50049 641-774-5632 774-8821 565
Web: www.iowadnr.gov
Red Hawk Casino 1 Red Hawk Pkwy . . . Placerville CA 95667 530-677-7000 452
Red Hill Grinding Wheel
335 Dotts St . . . Pennsburg PA 18073 215-679-7964 1
Red Hill Patrick Henry National Memorial
1250 Red Hill Rd . . . Brookneal VA 24528 434-376-2044 564
TF: 800-514-7463 ■ *Web:* www.redhill.org
Red Hill Studios 1017 E St Ste C . . . San Rafael CA 94901 415-457-0440 344
Web: www.redhillstudios.com
Red Hills State Park
RR 2 3571 Ranger Ln . . . Sumner IL 62466 618-936-2469 565
Web: www.dnr.illinois.gov/Parks/Pages/RedHills.aspx
Red Hot & Blue Restaurants Inc
1600 Wilson Blvd . . . Arlington VA 22209 703-276-7427 670
TF: 888-509-7100 ■ *Web:* www.redhotandblue.com
Red Hot & Blue Restaurants Inc
200 Old Mill Bottom Rd S . . . Annapolis MD 21401 410-626-7427 671
TF: 888-509-7100 ■ *Web:* www.redhotandblue.com
Red Hour Films 629 N La Brea Ave . . . Los Angeles CA 90036 323-602-5000 514
Red Iguana 736 W N Temple St . . . Salt Lake City UT 84116 801-322-1489 671
Web: www.rediguana.com
RED Inc Communications
510 Energy Pl . . . Idaho Falls ID 83401 208-528-0051 393
Web: www.redinc.com
Red Inn 15 Commercial St . . . Provincetown MA 02657 508-487-7334 487-5115 671
TF: 866-473-3466 ■ *Web:* www.theredinn.com
Red Jacket Beach Resort
30 Todd Rd . . . South Yarmouth MA 02664 508-398-6941 379
TF: 800-227-3263 ■ *Web:* www.redjacketresorts.com
Red Label Vacations Inc
5450 Explorer Dr Ste 100 . . . Mississauga ON L4W5N1 905-283-6020 772
TF: 866-573-3824 ■ *Web:* www.redtag.ca
Red Lake County
124 Langevin Ave 2nd Fl . . . Red Lake Falls MN 56750 218-253-2590 338
Web: www.co.red-lake.mn.us
Red Lake Electric Co-op Inc
412 International Dr PO Box 430 . . . Red Lake Falls MN 56750 218-253-2168 253-2630 245
TF: 800-245-6068 ■ *Web:* www.redlakeelectric.com
Red Lake Gaming Enterprises Inc
PO Box 543 . . . Red Lake MN 56671 218-679-2111 679-2191 132
TF: 888-679-2501 ■ *Web:* www.sevenclanscasino.com
Red Lambda Inc
400 Colonial Ctr Pkwy Ste 270 . . . Lake Mary FL 32746 407-732-7507 445-5367* 387
**Fax Area Code:* 321 ■ *Web:* www.redlambda.com
Red Level Networks LLC
24371 Catherine Industrial Dr Ste 223 . . . Novi MI 48375 248-412-8200 194
Web: www.redlevelnetworks.com
Red Line Graphics Inc
6430 S Belmont Ave . . . Indianapolis IN 46217 317-784-3777 174
Web: www.redlinegroup.com
Red Lion Christian Academy
1390 Red Lion Rd . . . Bear DE 19701 302-834-2526 685
TF: 800-555-0888 ■ *Web:* www.redlionca.org
Red Lion Controls Inc
20 Willow Springs Cir . . . York PA 17406 717-767-6511 201
Web: www.redlion.net
Red Lion Hotel 621 21St St . . . Lewiston ID 83501 208-799-1000 378
Web: www.redlionlewiston.com
Red Lion Hotels Corp
201 W N River Dr Ste 100 . . . Spokane WA 99201 800-733-5466 325-7324* 379
NYSE: RLH ■ **Fax Area Code:* 509 ■ *TF Resv:* 800-733-5466 ■ *Web:* www.redlion.com
Red Lion Inn 30 Main St PO Box 954 . . . Stockbridge MA 01262 413-298-5545 379
Web: www.redlioninn.com
Red Lion Sacramento Inn
1401 Arden Way . . . Sacramento CA 95815 916-922-0386 378
Web: www.redlionsacramento.com
Red Lion Templin's Hotel on the River
414 E First Ave . . . Post Falls ID 83854 208-773-1611 773-4192 669
TF: 800-733-5466 ■ *Web:* www.redlion.com
Red Lodge Beverages 7 Pepsi Dr . . . Red Lodge MT 59068 406-446-2040 297-8
Red Lodge Mountain Resort
305 Ski Run Rd . . . Red Lodge MT 59068 406-446-2610 226
Web: m.redlodgemountain.com
Red Mesa Restaurant
4912 Fourth St N . . . Saint Petersburg FL 33703 727-527-8728 671
Web: www.redmesarestaurant.com
Red Oak Greenhouses Inc
401 W Coolbaugh St . . . Red Oak IA 51566 712-623-5191 192
Web: redoakgreenhouse.com
Red Onion State Prison
10800 H Jack Rose Hwy PO Box 970 . . . Pound VA 24279 276-796-7510 213
Web: vadoc.virginia.gov
Red Ox Inn 9420 91st St . . . Edmonton AB T6C1Z5 780-465-5727 671
Web: www.theredoxinn.com
Red Parrot, The 348 Thames St . . . Newport RI 02840 401-847-3800 671
TF: 800-442-1162 ■ *Web:* www.redparrotrestaurant.com
Red Path Consulting Group
1011 Washington Ave S Ste 350 . . . Minneapolis MN 55415 612-843-3360 196
Web: redpathcg.com

	Phone	Fax	Class
Red Peacock International Inc 1945 Gardena Ave. Glendale CA 91204 *TF:* 877-774-0037 ■ *Web:* www.redpeacock.com	818-265-7722		246
Red Pepper 1011 University Ave Grand Forks ND 58203 *Web:* www.redpepper.com	701-775-9671		671
Red Pheasant 905 Rte 6A Dennis MA 02638 *Web:* www.redpheasantinn.com	508-385-2133		671
Red Pig Bar-B-Q 2201 Ferguson Rd Johnson City TN 37604	423-282-6585		671
Red Privet LLC 415 Market St Harrisburg PA 17101 *Web:* www.redprivet.com	717-260-5239		466
Red River Broadcasting Co LLC 2001 London Rd Duluth MN 55812 *Web:* www.fox21online.com	218-728-1622		738
Red River Commodities Inc 501 42nd St N Fargo ND 58102 *TF:* 800-437-5539 ■ *Web:* www.redriv.com	701-282-2600	282-5325	694
Red River Computer Company Inc 21 Water St Ste 500 Claremont NH 03743 *TF:* 800-769-3060 ■ *Web:* www.redriver.com	603-448-8880		121
Red River County 200 N Walnut St Clarksville TX 75426 *Web:* www.co.red-river.tx.us	903-427-2401	427-5510	338
Red River Parish Clerk of Court's Office PO Box 485 Coushatta LA 71019 *TF:* 800-256-6660 ■ *Web:* www.redriverclerk.com	318-932-6741	932-3126	338
Red River Sanitors Inc 1522 Corporate Dr Shreveport LA 71107 *TF:* 800-832-7654 ■ *Web:* www.sanitors.com	318-222-6070		192
Red River Specialties Inc 1324 N Hearne Ave Ste 120 Shreveport LA 71107 *TF:* 800-256-3344 ■ *Web:* www.rrsi.com	318-425-5944		276
Red River State Recreation Area 515 Second St NW East Grand Forks MN 56721 *Web:* www.dnr.state.mn.us	218-773-4950		565
Red River Valley Co-op Power Assn 109 Second Ave E Halstad MN 56548 *TF:* 800-788-7784 ■ *Web:* www.rrvcoop.com	218-456-2139		245
Red River Valley School Division 233 Main St N Morris MB R0G1K0 *Web:* www.rrvsd.ca	204-746-2317		685
Red River Zoo 4255 23rd Ave S Fargo ND 58104 *Web:* www.redriverzoo.org	701-277-9240	277-9238	823
Red Robin Gourmet Burgers Inc 6312 S Fiddlers Green Cir Ste 200-N Greenwood Village CO 80111 *NASDAQ: RRGB* ■ *Web:* www.redrobin.com	303-846-6000	846-6013	670
Red Rock Brewing Co 254 South 200 West Salt Lake City UT 84101 *Web:* www.redrockbrewing.com	801-521-7446		671
Red Rock Canyon National Conservation Area 4701 N Torrey Pines Dr Las Vegas NV 89130 *Web:* www.blm.gov	702-515-5350	363-6779	50-5
Red Rock Canyon State Park Hwy 281 S Hinton OK 73047 *Web:* www.travelok.com	405-542-6344		565
Red Rock Distributing Co One NW 50th St Oklahoma City OK 73118 *TF:* 800-323-7109 ■ *Web:* www.redrockdist.com	405-677-3373		449
Red Rock Feeding Co 35415 E Sasco Cir Red Rock AZ 85245	520-682-3448		10-1
Red Rock Ranch, The PO Box 38 Kelly WY 83011 *Web:* www.theredrockranch.com	307-733-6288	733-6287	239
Red Rock Research Ctr 5701 W Charleston Blvd Ste 100 Las Vegas NV 89146 *Web:* www.redrockmedical.com	702-602-6839		743
Red Rock Resort Spa & Casino 11011 W Charleston Blvd Las Vegas NV 89135 *TF:* 866-767-7773 ■ *Web:* redrock.sclv.com	702-797-7777		379
Red Rock State Park 4050 Red Rock Loop Rd Sedona AZ 86336 *Web:* azstateparks.com	928-282-6907		565
Red Rocket Fireworks Company Inc 1166 Porter Rd Rock Hill SC 29730 *Web:* blackcatfireworks.com	803-329-2577		327
Red Rocket Media Group LLC 9351 Eastman Park Dr Ste 218 Windsor CO 80550 *Web:* www.redrocketmg.com	970-674-0079		463
Red Rocks Amphitheater 18300 W Alameda Pkwy Morrison CO 80465 *Web:* www.redrocksonline.com	720-865-2494		572
Red Rocks Community College 13300 W Sixth Ave Lakewood CO 80228 *TF:* 800-361-1728 ■ *Web:* www.rrcc.edu	303-914-6600	914-6666	162
Red Roof Inn 4271 Sidco Dr Nashville TN 37204 *Web:* www.redroof.com	615-832-0093		379
Red Roof Inn Monterey 2227 N Fremont St Monterey CA 93940 *Web:* www.redroofinnmonterey.com	831-372-7586		379
Red Roof Inn Nashville Airport 510 Claridge Dr Nashville TN 37214 *Web:* redroof.com	615-872-0735		379
Red Sky Solutions Llc 3600 Birch St Ste 100 Newport Beach CA 92660 *TF:* 800-527-7397 ■ *Web:* redskysolutions.com	949-273-2639		226
Red Snapper 144 E Ninth St Durango CO 81301 *Web:* www.durangoredsnapper.com	970-259-3417		671
Red Snapper 8430 Ward Pkwy Kansas City MO 64114 *Web:* www.kcredsnapper.com	816-333-8899		671
Red Spot Interactive 1001 jupiter park dr Jupiter FL 33458 *TF:* 800-401-7931 ■ *Web:* www.redspotinteractive.com	800-401-7931		463
Red Spot Paint & Varnish Co Inc 1107 E Louisiana St Evansville IN 47711 *TF:* 877-777-4778 ■ *Web:* www.redspot.com	812-428-9100		550
Red Square Agency Inc 54 Saint Emanuel St Mobile AL 36602 *Web:* redsquaregaming.com	251-476-1283		7
Red Star Oil 802 Purser Dr Raleigh NC 27603 *TF:* 800-774-6033 ■ *Web:* www.redstaroil.com	919-772-1944	779-8871	449
Red Star Tavern & Roast House 503 SW Alder St Portland OR 97204 *TF:* 800-341-8134 ■ *Web:* www.redstartavern.com	503-222-0005	417-3334	671
Red Stone Education Consulting Group 1105 11th St Rapid City SD 57701 *Web:* www.redstoneeducation.org	605-341-3585		244
Red Storm Entertainment Inc 2000 Centregreen Way Ste 300 Cary NC 27513 *Web:* www.redstorm.com	919-460-1776		225
Red Streak Corporation 1627 Main St Kansas City MO 64108 *Web:* www.redstreakcorp.com	816-471-6979		111
Red Tettemer Inc 1 S Broad St 24th Fl Philadelphia PA 19107 *Web:* rtop.com	267-402-1410		4
Red Thread 300 E River Dr East Hartford CT 06108 *TF:* 800-635-4874 ■ *Web:* www.red-thread.com	860-528-9981	528-1843	320
Red Tree inc 820 N 1480 E Orem UT 84097 *Web:* www.redtreeleadership.com	801-655-0200		463
Red Triangle Oil Co 2809 S Chestnut Ave Fresno CA 93725 *Web:* www.redtrianglepropanefresnoca.com	559-485-4320		579
Red Valve Company Inc 600 N Bell Ave Carnegie PA 15106 *Web:* www.redvalve.com	412-279-0044		789
Red Willow County 502 Norris Ave McCook NE 69001 *Web:* www.co.red-willow.ne.us	308-345-1552	345-4460	338
Red Wind Casino 12819 Yelm Hwy Olympia WA 98513 *TF:* 866-946-2444 ■ *Web:* www.redwindcasino.com	360-412-5000		133
Red Wing Shoe Company Inc 314 Main St Red Wing MN 55066 *TF Cust Svc:* 800-733-9464 ■ *Web:* www.redwingshoes.com	651-388-8211		301
Red Wing Software Inc 491 Hwy 19 Red Wing MN 55066 *TF:* 800-732-9464 ■ *Web:* www.redwingsoftware.com	651-388-1106	388-7950	178-1
Red's Old 395 Grill 1055 S Carson St Carson City NV 89701 *Web:* reds395.com	775-887-0395		671
Red7e Inc 637 W Main St Louisville KY 40202 *Web:* www.red7e.com	502-585-3403		7
Redapt Inc 12226 134th CT NE Bldg D Redmond WA 98052 *Web:* www.redapt.com	425-882-0400		196
Redbud E&P Inc 16000 Stuebner Airline Ste 320 Spring TX 77379 *Web:* www.redbudinc.com	832-698-4234		536
RedBuilt LLC 200 E Mallard Dr Boise ID 83706 *Web:* www.redbuilt.com	208-364-1316		817
Redbury Hotel, The 1717 Vine St Los Angeles CA 90028 *TF:* 800-864-8377 ■ *Web:* theredbury.com	323-962-1717		378
REDCAT (Roy & Edna Disney/CALARTS Theater (REDCAT)) 631 W Second St Los Angeles CA 90012 *Web:* www.redcat.org	213-237-2800	237-2811	50-2
Redcliffe Plantation State Historic Site 181 Redcliffe Rd Beech Island SC 29842 *Web:* www.southcarolinaparks.com	803-827-1473		565
Redco Foods Inc 1 Hansen Island Little Falls NY 13365 *TF:* 800-556-6674 ■ *Web:* www.redrosetea.com	315-823-1300		296-40
Redcom Laboratories Inc 1 Redcom Ctr Victor NY 14564 *Web:* www.redcom.com	585-924-7550	924-6572	735
Redd Brown & Williams Real Estate services 201 Bridge St Paintsville KY 41240 *Web:* www.rbandw.com	606-789-8119	789-5414	653
Redd Paper Co 3851 Ctr Loop Orlando FL 32808 *TF:* 800-961-6656 ■ *Web:* www.reddpaper.com	407-299-6656	299-8142	553
Red-D-Arc Inc 667 S Service Rd PO Box 40 Grimsby ON L3M4G1 *TF:* 800-358-8340 ■ *Web:* www.red-d-arc.com	905-643-4212		23
Redding Civic Auditorium 700 Auditorium Dr Redding CA 96001 *Web:* www.reddingcivic.com	530-229-0036	229-0062	572
Reddog Industries Inc 2012 E 33rd St Erie PA 16510 *Web:* www.reddog-erie.com	814-898-4321	899-5671	757
Reddy Ice Holdings Inc 8750 N Central Expy Ste 1800 Dallas TX 75231 *OTC: RDDYQ* ■ *TF:* 800-683-4423 ■ *Web:* www.reddyice.com	214-526-6740		380
Redeemer Catholic Schools 1 McRae St PO Box 1318 Okotoks AB T1S1B3 *Web:* www.redeemer.ab.ca	403-938-2659		623
Redeemer Lutheran Church of Waverly Bremer County Iowa 2001 W Bremer Ave Waverly IA 50677 *Web:* redeemerwaverly.org	319-352-1325		48-20
Redeemer University College 777 Garner Rd E Ancaster ON L9K1J4 *TF:* 877-779-0913 ■ *Web:* www.redeemer.ca	905-648-2131	648-2134	785
Redemptorist Retreat Center 1800 N Timber Trail Ln Oconomowoc WI 53066 *Web:* redemptoristretreat.org	262-567-6900		673
Redemptorist, The 1 Liguori Dr Liguori MO 63057 *TF:* 800-325-9521 ■ *Web:* www.liguori.org	636-464-2500		48-20
Redemtech Inc 4115 Leap Rd Hilliard OH 43026 *TF:* 800-393-7627 ■ *Web:* www.arrowvaluerecovery.com	614-850-3366		178-1
Redex Industries Inc 1176 Salem Pkwy Salem OH 44460 *Web:* www.uddercream.com	330-332-9800		77
Redeye Distribution Inc 449a Trollingwood Rd Haw River NC 27258 *Web:* www.redeyeworldwide.com	336-578-5202		317
Redfin 9890 S Maryland Pkwy Ste 200 Las Vegas NV 89183 *TF:* 800-561-5463 ■ *Web:* www.redfin.com/city/10201/nv/las-vegas	877-973-3346		5
Redford Township Chamber of Commerce 26050 5-Mile Rd Redford MI 48239 *Web:* www.redfordchamber.com	313-535-0960	535-6356	139
RedHawk Energy Corp PO Box 53929 Lafayette LA 70505 *Web:* www.redhawkenergycorp.com	337-269-5933	269-5935	538
Redhawk Network Security LLC 62958 Layton Ave Ste One Bend OR 97701 *Web:* www.redhawksecurity.com	541-382-4360		196
Redhawk Vineyard & Winery 2995 Michigan City Ave NW Salem OR 97304 *TF:* 800-291-6730 ■ *Web:* www.redhawkwine.com	503-362-1596		50-7
Redhills Ventures LLC 908 Trophy Hills Dr Las Vegas NV 89134 *Web:* www.redhillsventures.com	702-233-2160		401

Name / Address	City	State	Zip	Phone	Fax	Class
RedHouse Associates LLC						
802 Lovett Blvd	Houston	TX	77006	713-338-2151		463
Web: www.redhouseassociates.com						
Redi Bag USA 135 Fulton Ave	New Hyde Park	NY	11040	516-746-0600		98
TF: 800-517-2247 ■ *Web:* www.redibagusa.com						
Redi Floors Inc 1791 Williams Dr	Marietta	GA	30066	770-590-7334		362
TF: 800-728-2690 ■ *Web:* www.redi-floors.com						
Redi-Carpet Inc 10225 Mula Rd Ste 120	Stafford	TX	77477	832-310-2000	310-2001	290
Web: www.redicarpet.com						
Redico Inc 1850 S Lee Ct	Buford	GA	30518	800-242-3920	614-1403*	665
**Fax Area Code:* 770 ■ *TF:* 800-242-3920 ■ *Web:* www.redicoinc.com						
Redi-Data Inc 5 Audrey Pl	Fairfield	NJ	07004	973-227-4380		387
TF: 800-433-9016 ■ *Web:* www.redidata.com						
Redi-Direct Marketing Inc						
5 Audrey Pl	Fairfield	NJ	07004	973-808-4500		366
TF: 800-635-5833 ■ *Web:* www.redidirect.com						
Rediker Software Inc 2 Wilbraham Rd	Hampden	MA	01036	413-566-3463		177
TF: 800-213-9860 ■ *Web:* www.rediker.com						
Redi-Mail Direct Mktg						
10 New Maple Ave	Pine Brook	NJ	07058	973-808-4500		5
Web: www.redimail.com						
Redknee Solutions Inc						
2560 Matheson Blvd E Ste 500	Mississauga	ON	L4W4Y9	905-625-2622		736
Web: www.redknee.com						
Redland Brick Inc						
15718 Clear Spring Rd	Williamsport	MD	21795	301-223-7700		150
TF: 800-366-2742 ■ *Web:* redlandbrick.com						
Redlands Bowl 25 Grant St	Redlands	CA	92373	909-793-7316		572
Web: www.redlandsbowl.org						
Redlands Chamber of Commerce						
1 E Redlands Blvd	Redlands	CA	92373	909-793-2546	335-6388	139
TF: 800-966-6428 ■ *Web:* www.redlandschamber.org						
Redlands Community College						
1300 S Country Club Rd	El Reno	OK	73036	405-262-2552	422-1200*	162
**Fax:* Admissions ■ *TF:* 866-415-6367 ■ *Web:* www.redlandscc.edu						
Redlands Community Hospital Foundation						
PO Box 3391	Redlands	CA	92373	909-335-5500		374-3
TF: 888-397-4999 ■ *Web:* www.redlandshospital.org						
Redlands Symphony 1200 E Colton Ave	Redlands	CA	92373	909-748-8018		573-3
Web: www.redlandssymphony.com						
RedLegg 319 1/2 State St Ste A	Geneva	IL	60134	877-811-5040		196
TF: 877-811-5040 ■ *Web:* www.redlegg.com						
Redline Communications Inc						
302 Town Centre Blvd 4th Fl	Markham	ON	L3R0E8	905-479-8344	479-5331	224
Web: rdlcom.com						
Redline Industries Inc 8401 Mosley Rd	Houston	TX	77075	713-946-5355	946-0747	492
Web: www.redlineindustries.com						
Redline Trading Solutions Inc						
18 Commerce Way Ste 6800	Woburn	MA	01801	781-995-3403		174
TF: 888-860-0190 ■ *Web:* www.redlinetrading.com						
Redman Equipment & Mfg Co						
19800 Normandie Ave	Torrance	CA	90502	310-329-1134	324-5656	91
TF: 888-733-2602 ■ *Web:* www.redmaneq.com						
Redman Technologies Inc 10172 108 St	Edmonton	AB	T5J1L3	780 425 6270		180
Web: www.redmantech.com						
RedMane Technology LLC						
8614 W Catalpa Ave Ste 1001	Chicago	IL	60656	773-693-3919		177
TF: 800-625-0327 ■ *Web:* www.redmane.com						
Redmon, Peyton & Braswell LLP						
510 King St Ste 301	Alexandria	VA	22314	703-684-2000		428
Web: www.rpb-law.com						
Redmond Chamber of Commerce						
8383 158th Ave NE Ste 225	Redmond	WA	98052	425-885-4014		139
TF: 800-436-8504 ■ *Web:* www.oneredmond.org						
Redmond Co, The						
W228 N745 Westmound Dr	Waukesha	WI	53186	262-549-9600		194
TF: 800-815-5592 ■ *Web:* www.theredmondco.com						
Redmond Regional Medical Ctr						
501 Redmond Rd	Rome	GA	30165	706-291-0291		374-3
Web: www.redmondregional.com						
Redmond School District						
145 SE Salmon Ave	Redmond	OR	97756	541-923-5437	923-5142	685
Web: www.redmond.k12.or.us						
Redmonk LLC 95 High St Suite 206	Portland	ME	04101	866-733-6665		463
TF: 866-733-6665 ■ *Web:* www.redmonk.com						
Redneck Trailer Supplies						
2100 NW By-Pass	Springfield	MO	65803	417-864-5210	864-7764	779
TF: 877-973-3632 ■ *Web:* www.redneck-trailer.com						
Redner's Markets Inc 3 Quarry Rd	Reading	PA	19605	610-926-3700	926-6327	345
Web: www.rednersmarkets.com						
Redondo Beach Chamber of Commerce & Visitors Bureau						
200 N Pacific Coast Hwy	Redondo Beach	CA	90277	310-376-6911	374-7373	139
Web: www.redondochamber.org						
Redondo Beach Public Library						
303 N Pacific Coast Hwy	Redondo Beach	CA	90277	310-318-0675	318-3809	434-3
Web: redondo.org						
Redondo Systems Inc						
4025 Spencer St Ste 104	Torrance	CA	90503	310-542-6730	542-6771	180
Web: www.redondosystems.com						
RedPeg Marketing						
727 N Washington St	Alexandria	VA	22314	703-519-9000		7
TF: 800-240-1070 ■ *Web:* www.redpegmarketing.com						
Red-Ray Mfg Co Inc						
10-22 County Line Rd	Branchburg	NJ	08876	908-722-0040	722-2535	318
TF: 800-883-9218 ■ *Web:* www.selas.com						
RedRick Technologies Inc						
21624 Adelaide Rd	Mount Brydges	ON	N0L1W0	519-264-2400		475
TF: 800-340-9511 ■ *Web:* www.redricktechnologies.com						
Redrock Canyon Grill						
9221 Lake Hefner Pkwy	Oklahoma City	OK	73120	405-749-1995		671
Web: redrockcanyongrill.com						
RedRock Consultants LLC						
1450 Sutter St No 527	San Francisco	CA	94109	415-246-7625		656
Web: www.redrockconsultants.com						
Redrock Security & Cabling Inc						
6 Morgan Ste 150	Irvine	CA	92618	949-900-3460		693
Web: www.itredrock.com						
REDS Wine Tavern 77 Adelaide St W	Toronto	ON	M5H1P9	416-862-7337		671
Web: www.redswinetavern.com						
Redshift Business Networks Inc						
1020 Railroad Ave Ste A	Novato	CA	94945	415-462-6262		631
Web: www.redshift-networks.com						
RedSky Technologies Inc						
925 W Chicago Ave Ste 300	Chicago	IL	60642	312-432-4300		179
Web: www.redskye911.com						
Redspin Inc						
4690 Carpinteria Ave Ste B	Carpinteria	CA	93013	805-684-6858		177
TF: 800-721-9177 ■ *Web:* www.redspin.com						
Redsson Ltd 104 N Summit St	Toledo	OH	43604	419-244-1111	644-8510*	809
**Fax Area Code:* 866 ■ *Web:* www.redsson.com						
Redstar Media Group LLC						
7685 Williamsport Pk	Falling Waters	WV	25419	304-274-6943		8
Redstone College						
Denver 10851 W 120th Ave	Broomfield	CO	80021	303-466-1714		800
TF: 800-888-3995 ■ *Web:* www.redstone.edu						
Redstone Communications Group Inc						
10031 Maple St	Omaha	NE	68134	402-393-5435		4
Web: www.redstoneweb.com						
Redstone Federal Credit Union						
220 Wynn Dr NW	Huntsville	AL	35893	256-837-6110	722-3655*	219
**Fax:* Cust Svc ■ *TF:* 800-234-1234 ■ *Web:* www.redfcu.org						
Redstone Highlands Health Care Ctr						
6 Garden Ctr Dr	Greensburg	PA	15601	724-832-8400	836-3710	450
TF: 800-732-0999 ■ *Web:* www.redstonehighlands.org						
Redstone Inn 82 Redstone Blvd	Redstone	CO	81623	970-963-2526		379
Web: redstoneinn.thegilmorecollection.com						
Redstone Inn & Suites 504 Bluff St	Dubuque	IA	52001	563-582-1894		379
TF: 800-343-6562 ■ *Web:* www.theredstoneinn.com						
Redstone Properties						
1120 W SR- 89A Ste B2	Sedona	AZ	86336	928-204-2500		652
Web: www.redstoneproperties.com						
RedTail Solutions Inc						
69 Milk St Ste 100	Westborough	MA	01581	508-983-1900		225
TF: 866-764-7601 ■ *Web:* redtailsolutions.com						
Redwater Rustic Grille						
9223 MacLeod Trl S	Calgary	AB	T2J0P6	403-253-4266	253-9045	671
Web: www.redwatergrille.com						
Redwire LLC 1136 Thomasville Rd	Tallahassee	FL	32303	850-219-9473		693
Web: redwireus.com						
Redwood Adventure LLC						
44075 Pipeline Plaza Ste 225	Ashburn	VA	20147	703-858-5676		652
Web: www.c21redwood.com						
Redwood Asset Management Inc						
Richmond Adelaide Centre 120 Adelaide St W						
Ste 2400	Toronto	ON	M5H1T1	416-368-8898		528
TF: 877-313-7011 ■ *Web:* www.redwoodasset.com						
Redwood Capital Group LLC						
1 E Wacker Dr Ste 1600	Chicago	IL	60601	312-995-7300	995-7347	690
Web: www.redwoodcapgroup.com						
Redwood City Public Library						
1044 Middlefield Rd	Redwood City	CA	94063	650-780-7018		434-3
Web: www.redwoodcity.org/library						
Redwood City School District (RCSD)						
750 Bradford St	Redwood City	CA	94063	650-423-2200	423-2294	685
Web: www.rcsdk8.net						
Redwood City-San Mateo County Chamber of Commerce						
1450 Veterans Blvd Ste 125	Redwood City	CA	94063	650-364-1722	364-1729	139
Web: redwoodcitychamber.com						
Redwood Coast Trucking						
2210 Peninsula Dr	Arcata	CA	95521	707-443-0857		780
Redwood County						
403 S Mill St PO Box 130	Redwood Falls	MN	56283	507-637-4016	637-4017	338
Web: www.co.redwood.mn.us						
Redwood Credit Union PO Box 6104	Santa Rosa	CA	95406	707-545-4000		217
TF: 800-479-7928 ■ *Web:* www.redwoodcu.org						
Redwood Day School Parents & Guardians Assn						
3245 Sheffield Ave	Oakland	CA	94602	510 534 0800		685
Web: www.rdschool.org						
Redwood Electric Co-op 60 Pine St	Clements	MN	56224	507-692-2214		245
Web: www.greatrivernergy.com						
Redwood Library & Athenaeum						
50 Bellevue Ave	Newport	RI	02840	401-847-0292	841-5680	434-4
Web: www.redwoodlibrary.org						
Redwood National & State Parks						
1111 Second St	Crescent City	CA	95531	707-465-7335	464-1812	564
Web: www.nps.gov/redw						
Redwood Network Services						
804 N Meadowbrook Dr Ste 135	Olathe	KS	66062	913-254-1005		180
Web: pendello.com						
Redwood Products of Chino Inc						
9301 Remington Ave, Site E	Chino	CA	91710	909-923-5656		499
Web: www.redwoodchino.com						
Redwood Room 300 First Ave NW	Rochester	MN	55901	507-281-2978		671
Redwood Steakhouse 5304 Gateway Ctr Dr	Flint	MI	48507	810-233-8000	233-8833	671
Web: theredwoodlodge.com						
Redwood Toxicology Laboratory Inc						
3650 W Wind Blvd	Santa Rosa	CA	95403	707-577-7959		743
Web: www.redwoodtoxicology.com						
Redwood Trust Inc						
1 Belvedere Pl Ste 300	Mill Valley	CA	94941	415-389-7373		509
NYSE: RWT ■ *TF:* 866-269-4976 ■ *Web:* www.redwoodtrust.com						
RedXDefense LLC 7642 Standish Pl	Rockville	MD	20855	301-279-7970		21
Web: www.redxdefense.com						
Reeb Millwork Corp						
7475 Henry Clay Blvd	Liverpool	NY	13088	315-451-6699		499
TF: 800-862-8622 ■ *Web:* reeb.com						
Reebok International Ltd						
1895 JW Foster Blvd	Canton	MA	02021	781-401-5000		301
TF: 866-870-1743 ■ *Web:* www.reebok.com						
Reebok-CCM Hockey Inc						
3400 Raymond Lasnir	Montreal	QC	H4R3L3	514-461-8000		710
TF: 800-636-5895 ■ *Web:* www.thehockeycompany.com						
Reece & Nichols Realtors						
11601 Granada	Leawood	KS	66211	913-945-3704	491-0930	652
Web: www.reecenichols.com						
Reece-Campbell Inc 320 S Wayne Ave	Cincinnati	OH	45215	513-542-4600	542-4753	360-2
Reed 28 Sword St	Auburn	MA	01501	508-753-6530	753-0127	456
TF: 800-343-6068 ■ *Web:* ptgtools.com						

Phone | Fax | Class

Reed & Brinkman Accounting Inc
208 Sherman St ... Jackson MN 56143 507-847-4222 2
Reed Bingham State Park
542 Reed Bingham Rd ... Adel GA 31620 229-896-3551 565
Web: www.gastateparks.org
Reed Brennan Media Associates Inc
628 Virginia Dr ... Orlando FL 32803 407-894-7300 317
TF: 800-708-7311 ■ *Web:* www.rbma.com
Reed Candle Co 1531 W Poplar St ... San Antonio TX 78207 210-734-4243 734-2342 122
Web: www.reedcandlecompany.com
Reed City Tool & Die Inc
603 E Church St ... Reed City MI 49677 231-832-7500 757
Web: www.reedcitytool.com
Reed College 3203 SE Woodstock Blvd ... Portland OR 97202 503-777-7511 777-7553 166
TF Admissions: 800-547-4750 ■ *Web:* www.reed.edu
Reed College Library
3203 SE Woodstock Blvd ... Portland OR 97202 503-777-7702 777-7786 434-6
Web: library.reed.edu
Reed Gold Mine State Historic Site
9621 Reed Mine Rd ... Midland NC 28107 704-721-4653 721-4657 50-3
TF: 877-628-6386 ■ *Web:* www.nchistoricsites.org
Reed Group Ltd
10155 Westmoor Dr Ste 210 ... Westminster CO 80021 303-247-1860 194
Web: www.reedgroup.com
Reed Jack (Sen D - RI)
728 Hart Bldg ... Washington DC 20510 202-224-4642 224-4680 342-2
Web: www.reed.senate.gov
Reed Lallier Chevrolet Inc
4500 Raeford Rd ... Fayetteville NC 28304 910-426-2000 516
Web: reedlallier.com
REED LLC 13822 Oaks Ave ... Chino CA 91710 909-287-2100 190
Web: www.reedmfg.com
Reed Machinery Inc 10A New Bond St ... Worcester MA 01606 508-595-9090 111
TF: 800-631-4470 ■ *Web:* www.reed-machinery.com
Reed Manufacturing Co 1425 W Eigth St ... Erie PA 16502 814-452-3691 455-1697 758
TF: 800-456-1697 ■ *Web:* www.reedmfgco.com
Reed Mfg Co Inc 1321 S Veterans Blvd ... Tupelo MS 38804 662-842-4472 237-5898* 155-11
**Fax Area Code:* 800 ■ *TF:* 800-466-1154 ■ *Web:* www.reedmanufacturing.com
Reed Motors Inc 3776 W Colonial Dr ... Orlando FL 32808 407-297-7333 57
Web: www.reednissan.com
Reed Oil Co Inc 106 Washington St ... Doniphan MO 63935 573-996-2321 581
TF: 800-290-3056 ■ *Web:* m.reedoil.com
Reed Smith 435 Sixth Ave ... Pittsburgh PA 15219 412-288-3131 288-3063 428
TF: 800-973-1177 ■ *Web:* www.reedsmith.com
Reed Technology & Information Services Inc
7 Walnut Grove Dr ... Horsham PA 19044 215-441-6400 781
Web: www.reedtech.com
Reed Tom (Rep R - NY)
2437 Rayburn HOB ... Washington DC 20515 202-225-3161 226-6599 342-2
Web: reed.house.gov
Reeder & Associates Ltd
1095 Old Roswell Rd Ste F ... Roswell GA 30076 770-649-7523 260
Web: www.reederassoc.com
Reeder Distributors Inc
5450 Wilbarger St ... Fort Worth TX 76119 817-429-5957 429-9052 579
TF: 800-722-3103 ■ *Web:* www.reederdistributors.com
Reed-Lane Inc 359 Newark-Pompton Tpke ... Wayne NJ 07470 973-709-1090 476
TF: 800-575-4224 ■ *Web:* reedlane.com
Reedley College 995 N Reed Ave ... Reedley CA 93654 559-638-3641 638-5040 162
TF: 877-253-7122 ■ *Web:* reedleycollege.edu
Reeds Family Outdoor Outfitters
522 Minnesota Ave NW ... Walker MN 56484 800-346-0019 711
TF: 800-346-0019 ■ *Web:* www.reedssports.com
Reeds Gap State Park
1405 New Lancaster Valley Rd ... Milroy PA 17063 717-667-3622 565
Web: www.dcnr.state.pa.us
Reeds Jewelers Inc PO Box 2229 ... Wilmington NC 28402 910-350-3100 410
TF Orders: 877-406-3266 ■ *Web:* www.reeds.com
Reedsville Co-op Assn Inc
PO Box 460 ... Reedsville WI 54230 920-754-4321 276
TF: 800-236-4047 ■ *Web:* www.countryvisionscoop.com
Reedy Industries Inc
2440 Ravine Way Ste 200 ... Glenview IL 60025 847-729-9450 189-10
Web: www.reedyindustries.com
Reef 105 S Sixth St ... Boise ID 83702 208-287-9200 671
Web: www.reefboise.com
Reef 2600 Travis St ... Houston TX 77006 713-526-8282 671
Web: www.reefhouston.com
Reef Caribbean Restaurants, The
4172 Main St ... Vancouver BC V5V3P7 604-874-5375 671
Web: www.thereefrestaurant.com
Reef Industries Inc
9209 Almeda Genoa Rd ... Houston TX 77075 713-507-4200 507-4295 599
TF: 800-231-6074 ■ *Web:* www.reefindustries.com
Reef Oil & Gas Partners LP
1901 N Central Expy Ste 300 ... Richardson TX 75080 972-437-6792 539
Web: www.reefogc.com
Reef Resort 2101 S Ocean Blvd ... Myrtle Beach SC 29577 843-448-1765 669
TF Cust Svc: 800-845-1212 ■ *Web:* www.reefmyrtlebeach.com
Reef Restaurant, The
880 S Harbor Scenic Dr ... Long Beach CA 90802 562-435-8013 671
Web: www.reefrestaurant.com
Reef, The 4100 Coastal Hwy ... Saint Augustine FL 32084 904-824-8008 671
Web: www.thereefstaugustine.com
Reel FX Inc 301 N Crowdus St ... Dallas TX 75226 214-979-0961 514
Web: www.reelfx.com
Reel Games Inc
1501 NE 13th Ave ... Fort Lauderdale FL 33304 954-563-8253 761
Web: www.reelgamesinc.com
Reel Group Inc
16420 Park Ten Pl Ste 100 ... Houston TX 77084 832-358-2663 260
TF: 800-782-4357 ■ *Web:* www.reelgroup.com
Reelfoot Bank 1491 S First St ... Union City TN 38261 731-885-1010 70
Web: reelfootbank.com
ReelGrobman 96 N Second St ... San Jose CA 95113 408-288-7833 196
Web: www.reelgrobman.com
Reell Precision Manufacturing Corp
1259 Willow Lake Blvd ... Saint Paul MN 55110 651-484-2447 484-3867 620
Web: www.reell.com

Reema Consulting Services Inc
8106 Hallmark Pl ... Gaithersburg MD 20879 301-793-3055 463
Web: reemacsi.com
Reenders Blueberries Farms
14079 168th Ave ... Grand Haven MI 49417 616-842-5238 315-1
Web: www.reendersblueberryfarms.com
Rees Broome PC 1900 Gallows Rd ... Tysons Corner VA 22182 703-790-1911 428
Web: www.reesbroome.com
Rees Scientific Corp
1007 Whitehead Rd Ext ... Trenton NJ 08638 609-530-1055 407
TF: 800-327-3141 ■ *Web:* www.reesscientific.com
Reese Engineering Inc
2021 Pine Hall Rd ... State College PA 16801 814-234-2548 261
Web: www.reeseinc.com
Reese Enterprises Inc
16350 Asher Ave ... Rosemount MN 55068 651-423-1126 423-2662 234
TF: 800-328-0953 ■ *Web:* www.reeseusa.com
Reese Military Sales Inc
2820 Bransford Ave ... Nashville TN 37204 615-298-5774 195
Web: reesemilitarysales.com
Reese Pharmaceutical Co
10617 Frank Ave ... Cleveland OH 44106 800-321-7178 231-6444* 238
**Fax Area Code:* 216 ■ *TF:* 800-321-7178 ■ *Web:* www.reesechemical.com
Reeve Store Equipment Co
9131 Bermudez St ... Pico Rivera CA 90660 562-949-2535 949-3862 286
TF: 800-927-3383 ■ *Web:* www.reeveco.com
Reeves Construction Co Inc
101 Sheraton Ct ... Macon GA 31210 478-474-9092 474-9192 188-4
TF: 800-743-0593 ■ *Web:* www.reevescc.com
Reeves County 100 E Fourth St ... Pecos TX 79772 432-445-5467 445-3997 338
Web: reevescountytexas.net
Reeves Park 600 NW Tenth St ... Miami FL 33136 305-579-6970 564
Web: www.normanok.gov/parks/reaves-park
Reeves-Reed Arboretum 165 Hobart Ave ... Summit NJ 07901 908-273-8787 97
Web: www.reeves-reedarboretum.org
Reeves-Wiedeman Co Inc
14861 W 100th St ... Lenexa KS 66215 913-492-7100 492-6962 612
TF: 800-365-0024 ■ *Web:* rwco.com
Ref-Chem LP
1128 S Grandview PO Box 2588 ... Odessa TX 79761 432-332-8531 188-9
Web: www.ref-chem.com
Refectory Resturant & Bistro
1092 Bethel Rd ... Columbus OH 43220 614-451-9774 671
Web: www.therefectoryrestaurant.com
Reference & User Services Assn (RUSA)
50 E Huron St ... Chicago IL 60611 312-280-4398 944-8085 49-11
TF: 800-545-2433 ■ *Web:* www.ala.org/rusa
Reference Metals Company Inc
1000 Old Pond Rd ... Bridgeville PA 15017 412-221-7008 723
Web: www.cbmm.com.br/en
Referentia Systems Inc
155 Kapalulu Pl Ste 200 ... Honolulu HI 96819 808-840-8500 177
TF: 800-569-6255 ■ *Web:* www.referentia.com
Reflection Riding Arboretum & Botanical Garden
400 Garden Rd ... Chattanooga TN 37419 423-821-1160 97
Web: www.reflectionriding.org
Reflectix Inc 1 School St ... Markleville IN 46056 765-533-4332 548
Web: www.reflectixinc.com
Reflector, The PO Box 2020 ... Battle Ground WA 98604 360-687-5151 687-5162 532-4
Web: www.thereflector.com
Reflex Photonics Inc
1250 Oakmead Pkwy Ste 210 ... Sunnyvale CA 94085 408-501-8886 544
Web: www.reflexphotonics.com
Reflexite Corp 120 Darling Dr ... Avon CT 06001 860-676-7100 676-7199 745-2
TF: 800-654-7570 ■ *Web:* www.orafol.com
Reflexite North America 315 S St ... New Britain CT 06051 860-223-9297 832-9267 678
TF: 800-654-7570 ■ *Web:* www.orafol.com
RefluxMD Inc 10804 Willow Ct Ste B ... San Diego CA 92127 760-668-9904 387
Web: www.refluxmd.com
Reform Judaism Magazine
633 Third Ave ... New York NY 10017 212-650-4240 457-18
Web: reformjudaismmag.org
Reformed Church in America
4500 60th St SE ... Grand Rapids MI 49512 212-870-3071 870-2499 48-20
TF: 800-722-9977 ■ *Web:* www.rca.org
Reformed Episcopal Seminary
826 Second Ave ... Blue Bell PA 19422 610-292-9852 292-9853 167-3
Web: www.reseminary.edu
Reformed Presbyterian Theological Seminary
7418 Penn Ave ... Pittsburgh PA 15208 412-731-6000 731-4834 167-3
Web: www.rpts.edu
Reformed Theological Seminary
5422 Clinton Blvd ... Jackson MS 39209 601-923-1600 923-1654 167-3
TF: 800-543-2703 ■ *Web:* www.rts.edu
Refplus Inc 2777 Grande Allee ... Saint-Hubert QC J4T2R4 450-641-2665 664
Web: www.refplus.com
Refraction Technology Inc
1600 Tenth St Ste A ... Plano TX 75074 214-440-1265 639
Web: www.reftek.com
Refricenter of Miami Inc
7101 NW 43rd St ... Miami FL 33166 305-477-8880 599-9323 665
Web: www.refricenter.net
Refrigerated Food Express Inc
57 Littlefield St ... Avon MA 02322 508-587-4600 588-9655 780
TF: 800-342-8822 ■ *Web:* www.rfxinc.com
Refrigeration Research Inc
525 N Fifth St ... Brighton MI 48116 810-227-1151 227-3700 14
TF: 800-482-0781 ■ *Web:* www.refresearch.com
Refrigeration Sales Corp
9450 Allen Dr Ste A ... Valley View OH 44125 216-881-7800 612
TF: 866-894-8200 ■ *Web:* www.refrigerationsales.net
Refrigeration Service Engineers Society (RSES)
1666 Rand Rd ... Des Plaines IL 60016 847-297-6464 297-5038 49-3
TF: 800-297-5660 ■ *Web:* www.rses.org
Refrigerator Manufacturers Inc
17018 Edwards Rd ... Cerritos CA 90703 562-926-2006 14
TF: 800-847-2557 ■ *Web:* www.rmi-econocold.com
RefrigiWear Inc 54 Breakstone Dr ... Dahlonega GA 30533 706-864-5757 864-5898 155-5
TF Cust Svc: 800-645-3744 ■ *Web:* www.refrigiwear.com

Phone Fax Class

Refugees International (RI)
2001 S St NW Ste 700-K Washington DC 20009 202-828-0110 828-0819 48-5
TF: 800-733-8433 ■ *Web:* www.refugeesinternational.org

Refugio County
808 Commerce St PO Box 704 Refugio TX 78377 361-526-2233 526-1325 338
Web: www.co.refugio.tx.us

RefurbUPS com Inc
379 Spook Rock Rd Bldg J Suffern NY 10901 845-357-6911 180
Web: www.refurbups.com

RefWorks LLC
7200 Wisconsin Ave Ste 601 Bethesda MD 20814 301-961-6700 387
TF: 800-843-7751 ■ *Web:* www.refworks.com

Rega Engineering
1620 S 70th St Ste 103 Lincoln NE 68506 402-484-7342 261
Web: regaengineering.com

Regaalo Inc 75 Congress St Ste L05 Portsmouth NH 03801 603-610-8100 387

Regal Discount Securities Inc
950 Milwaukee Ave Ste 102 Glenview IL 60025 847-375-6024 690
Web: www.eregal.com

Regal Entertainment Group
7132 Regal Ln Knoxville TN 37918 865-922-1123 922-3188 748
NYSE: RGC ■ *TF Cust Svc:* 877-835-5734 ■ *Web:* www.regmovies.com

Regal Marine Industries Inc
2300 Jetport Dr Orlando FL 32809 407-851-4360 857-1256* 90
*Fax: Sales ■ *TF:* 800-877-3425 ■ *Web:* www.regalboats.com

Regal Metal Products Co
3615 Union Ave SE Minerva OH 44657 330-868-6343 295
Web: www.regalmetalproducts.com

Regal Mfg Co Inc 990 Third Ave SE Hickory NC 28602 828-328-5381 745-9

Regal Mold and Die 25208 Leer Dr Elkhart IN 46514 574-262-4110 791
TF: 800-259-9007 ■ *Web:* www.regalmold.com

Regal Plastic Supply Co
111 E Tenth Ave North Kansas City MO 64116 816-421-6290 421-8206 603
TF: 800-627-2102 ■ *Web:* www.regalplastic.com

Regal Press 129 Guild St Norwood MA 02062 781-769-3900 352-3930 627
TF: 800-447-3425 ■ *Web:* www.regalpress.com

Regal Research & Mfg Co Inc
1200 E Plano Pkwy Plano TX 75074 972-494-0359 272-0220 253
Web: www.regalresearch.com

Regal Travel 615 Piikoi St Ste 104 Honolulu HI 96814 808-566-7620 771
TF: 800-799-0865 ■ *Web:* www.regaltravel.com

Regal Ware Inc 1675 Reigle Dr Kewaskum WI 53040 262-626-2121 626-8565 486
TF: 800-800-2850 ■ *Web:* www.regalware.com

Regal-Beloit Corp 200 State St Beloit WI 53511 608-364-8800 364-8818 620
NYSE: RBC ■ *TF:* 800-672-6495 ■ *Web:* www.regalbeloit.com

Regal-Beloit Corp Durst Div PO Box 298 Beloit WI 53512 608-365-2563 365-2182 709
TF: 800-356-0775 ■ *Web:* www.regalpts.com/brands/durst/Pages/durst.aspx

Regali Inc 518 N Interurban St Richardson TX 75081 972-726-8830 45
TF: 800-232-5527 ■ *Web:* www.regaliinc.com

Regalia Manufacturing Co
2018 Fourth Ave Rock Island IL 61201 309-788-7471 788-0788 777
TF: 800-708-7471 ■ *Web:* www.regaliamfg.com

Regalix Inc
1121 San Antonio Rd Ste B200 Palo Alto CA 94303 650-331-1167 195
TF: 888-683-4875 ■ *Web:* www.regalix.com

Regan Communications Group Inc
106 Union Wharf Boston MA 02109 617-488-2800 636
Web: regancomm.com

Regan Group, The 360 W 132nd St Los Angeles CA 90061 310-935-0269 327-7336 4
Web: www.theregangroup.com

Regatta Travel Solutions Inc
325 Winding River Ln Ste 201B Charlottesville VA 22911 800-605-5093 393
TF: 800-605-5093 ■ *Web:* www.regattatravelsolutions.com

Regence Blue Cross Blue Shield of Oregon
PO Box 1071 Portland OR 97207 888-675-6570 391-3
TF: 888-734-3623 ■ *Web:* www.regence.com

Regence BlueCross BlueShield of Utah
2890 E Cottonwood Pkwy Salt Lake City UT 84121 888-367-2119 333-6516* 391-3
*Fax Area Code: 801 ■ *Fax: Hum Res ■ *TF Cust Svc:* 800-624-6519 ■ *Web:* www.regence.com

Regenco LLC 6609R W Washington St Milwaukee WI 53214 414-475-2800 454
Web: www.regencoservices.com

Regency Centers
1 Independent Dr Ste 114 Jacksonville FL 32202 904-598-7000 634-3428 655
NYSE: REG ■ *TF:* 800-950-6333 ■ *Web:* regencycenters.com

Regency Energy Partners LP
2001 Bryan St Ste 3700 Dallas TX 75201 214-750-1771 325
NASDAQ: RGNC ■ *Web:* regencygasservices.com

Regency Enterprises
10201 W Pico Blvd Bldg 12 Los Angeles CA 90035 310-369-8300 514
Web: www.newregency.com

Regency Fairbanks Hotel
95 Tenth Ave Fairbanks AK 99701 907-459-2700 379
TF: 800-478-1320 ■ *Web:* www.regencyfairbankshotel.com

Regency Fire Protection Inc
7651 Densmore Ave Van Nuys CA 91406 818-982-0126 610
Web: www.regencyfire.com

Regency Furniture Inc
7900 Cedarville Rd Brandywine MD 20613 301-782-3800 321
Web: www.regencyfurniture.com

Regency Hotel Management LLC
3211 W Sencore Dr Sioux Falls SD 57107 605-334-2371 194
Web: www.regency-mgmt.com

Regency House Hotel
140 Rt 23 N Pompton Plains NJ 07444 973-696-0900 696-0201 379
TF: 800-392-1316 ■ *Web:* www.regencyhousehotel.com

Regency Infographics Inc (SED)
2867 E Allegheny Ave Philadelphia PA 19134 215-425-8800 425-9715 781
TF: 800-829-0020 ■ *Web:* www.sed.com/desktop-publishing.html

Regency Lighting Co
9261 Jordan Ave Chatsworth CA 91311 800-284-2024 246
TF: 800-284-2024 ■ *Web:* www.regencylighting.com

Regency Limousine International
23-57 83 St East Elmhurst NY 11370 718-507-4000 507-8283 441
TF: 866-754-5466 ■ *Web:* www.regencylimo.com

Regency Mall 5538 Durand Ave Racine WI 53406 262-554-7903 460
Web: www.shopregency-mall.com

Regency Nursing Centre
6631 N Milwaukee Ave Niles IL 60714 847-647-7444 450
Web: www.regencyrehabcenter.com

Regency Outdoor Adv Inc
8820 Sunset Blvd West Hollywood CA 90069 310-657-8883 4
Web: www.regencyoutdoor.com

Regency Plastics Company Ltd
50 Brisbane Rd North York ON M3J2K2 416-661-3000 608
Web: www.regencyplastics.com

Regency Seating Inc 2375 Romig Rd Akron OH 44320 330-848-3700 321
TF: 866-816-9822 ■ *Web:* regencyof.com

Regency Square Mall
9501 Arlington Expy Ste 100 Jacksonville FL 32225 904-725-3830 460
TF: 800-225-6765 ■ *Web:* www.regencysquaremall.com

Regency Suites Calgary
610 Fourth Ave SW Calgary AB T2P0K1 403-231-1000 379
TF: 800-468-4044 ■ *Web:* www.regencycalgary.com

Regency Suites Hotel Midtown Atlanta
975 W Peachtree St Atlanta GA 30309 404-876-5003 817-7511 379
TF: 800-642-3629 ■ *Web:* www.regencysuites.com

Regency Theatres Inc 1440 Eastman Ave Ventura CA 93003 805-658-6544 748
Web: www.regencymovies.com

Regeneron Pharmaceuticals Inc
777 Old Saw Mill River Rd Tarrytown NY 10591 914-847-7000 85
NASDAQ: REGN ■ *Web:* www.regeneron.com

RegeneRx Biopharmaceuticals Inc
15245 Shady Grove Rd Ste 470 Rockville MD 20850 301-208-9191 582
OTC: RGRX ■ *Web:* www.regenerx.com

Regenesis Biomedical Inc
5301 N Pima Rd Scottsdale AZ 85250 480-970-4970 582
Web: www.regenesisbio.com

Regent College 5800 University Blvd Vancouver BC V6T2E4 604-224-3245 224-3097 167-3
TF: 800-663-8664 ■ *Web:* www.regent-college.edu

Regent Energy Group Ltd 3735 - 8 St Nisku AB T9E8J8 780-769-4100 539
Web: www.rglrm.com/combined

Regent Entertainment Partnership LP
8411 Preston Rd Ste 650 Dallas TX 75225 214-373-3434 514
Web: www.regententertainment.com

Regent Products Corp
8999 Palmer St River Grove IL 60171 708-583-1000 301
TF: 800-583-1002 ■ *Web:* www.regentproducts.com

Regent Resources Ltd
1000 605 - Fifth Ave SW Calgary AB T2P3H5 403-264-0018 536
Web: www.regentresources.com

Regent Security Services Inc
2602 Commons Blvd Augusta GA 30909 706-738-8918 693

Regent University
Library
1000 Regent University Dr Virginia Beach VA 23464 757-352-4916 226-4167 434-6
TF: 888-249-1822 ■ *Web:* www.regent.edu/general/library

Regents Bank NA PO Box 9137 La Jolla CA 92038 858-729-7700 454-9052 70
Web: www.regentsbank.com

Regents Point 19191 Harvard Ave Irvine CA 92612 949-988-0849 247-3871* 672
*Fax Area Code: 818 ■ *TF General:* 800-347-3735 ■ *Web:* www.thcbcgroup.org

Regiment Capital Advisors LLC
222 Berkeley St 12th Fl Boston MA 02116 617-488-1600 401

Regina Chamber of Commerce
2145 Albert St Regina SK S4P2V1 306-757-4658 757-4668 137
Web: www.reginachamber.com

Regina Leader Post 1964 Pk St Regina SK S4P3G4 306-781-5211 565-2588 532-1
TF: 800-667-9999 ■ *Web:* www.leaderpost.com

Regina USA Inc 824 Chesapeake Dr Cambridge MD 21613 410-221-2800 350
Web: www.reginausa.com

Regina Villa Associates Inc
51 Franklin St Ste 400 Boston MA 02110 617-357-5772 4
Web: www.reginavilla.com

Reginald F Lewis Museum of Maryland African American History & Culture
830 E Pratt St Baltimore MD 21202 443-263-1800 333-1138* 520
*Fax Area Code: 410 ■ *Web:* www.lewismuseum.org

Reginella's
4000 Virginia Beach Blvd Virginia Beach VA 23452 757-498-9770 671
Web: reginellas.com

Regino's 3816 E Little Creek Rd Norfolk VA 23518 757-588-4300 671
Web: reginosrestaurantofnorfolk.com

Region 4 Education Service Ctr
7145 W Tidwell Rd Houston TX 77092 713-462-7708 764
Web: www.esc4.net

Regional Acceptance Corp
1424 E Fire Tower Rd Greenville NC 27858 252-321-7700 217
TF: 877-722-7299 ■ *Web:* www.regionalacceptance.com

Regional Airline Assn (RAA)
2025 M St NW Ste 800 Washington DC 20036 202-367-1170 367-2170 49-21
Web: www.raa.org

Regional Care Inc 905 W 27th St Scottsbluff NE 69361 308-635-2260 390
Web: www.regionalcare.com

Regional Chamber of Commerce San Gabriel Valley
19720 E Walnut Dr Ste 100A Walnut CA 91789 714-245-5540 139
Web: www.regionalchambersgv.com

Regional Computer Recycling & Recovery LLC
7318 Victor Mendon Rd Victor NY 14564 888-563-1340 179
TF: 888-563-1340 ■ *Web:* www.ewaste.com

Regional Economic Models Inc 433 W St Amherst MA 01002 413-549-1169 549-1038 177
Web: remi.com

Regional Fabricators Inc
1905 Diver Dr New Iberia LA 70560 337-367-3488 723
Web: www.regionalfab.com

Regional Group of Cos Inc, The
1737 Woodward Dr 2nd Fl Ottawa ON K2C0P9 613-230-2100 652
Web: www.regionalgroup.com

Regional Heating & Air Conditioning Inc
2525 Won Rd Colorado Springs CO 80910 719-392-6171 189-10

Regional Hospice of Western Connecticut
30 Milestone Rd Danbury CT 06810 203-702-7400 792-1402 371
Web: regionalhospicect.org

Regional Hospital of Scranton
746 Jefferson Ave Scranton PA 18510 570-348-7100 348-7639 374-3
TF: 800-654-5988 ■ *Web:* commonwealthhealth.net

Regional International Corp
1007 Lehigh Stn Rd Henrietta NY 14467 585-359-2011 61
TF: 800-836-0409 ■ *Web:* www.regionalinternational.com

Regional Jet Ctr 12344 Tower Dr Bentonville AR 72712 479-205-1100 63
Web: www.regionaljetcenter.com

Phone | Fax | Class

Regional Medical Ctr at Memphis
877 Jefferson Ave ... Memphis TN 38103 901-545-7100 374-3
Web: www.regionalonehealth.org

Regional Medical Ctr Bayonet Point
14000 Fivay Rd ... Hudson FL 34667 727-819-2929 374-3
Web: www.rmchealth.com

Regional Medical Ctr of San Jose (RMCSJ)
225 N Jackson Ave ... San Jose CA 95116 408-259-5000 729-2884 374-3
TF: 800-307-7135 ■ *Web:* www.regionalmedicalsanjose.com

Regional Medical Ctr, The
3000 St Matthews Rd ... Orangeburg SC 29118 803-395-2200 374-3
TF: 800-476-3377 ■ *Web:* www.trmchealth.org

Regional Occupational Programs
300 Dana St ... Fort Bragg CA 95437 707-964-9000 507
TF: 800-451-9999 ■ *Web:* mcoe.us

Regional Personnel Services Inc
502 US Hwy 22 Ste 1 ... Lebanon NJ 08833 908-534-8113 260
Web: www.regionalpersonnel.com

Regional Plan Association Inc
4 Irving Pl 7th Fl ... New York NY 10003 212-253-2727 138
TF: 800-755-2453 ■ *Web:* www.rpa.org

Regional Publishing Corp, The
12243 S Harlem Ave ... Palos Heights IL 60463 708-448-4000 532-4
Web: regionalpublishing.com

Regional Research Institute for Human Services (RRI)
Portland State University PO Box 751 ... Portland OR 97207 503-725-4040 725-2140 668
Web: www.rri.pdx.edu

Regional Tissue Bank QEII Health Sciences Centre
5788 University Ave Rm 431 MacKenzie Bldg ... Halifax NS B3H1V7 902-473-4171 473-2170 545
TF: 800-314-6515 ■ *Web:* www.cdha.nshealth.ca/regional-tissue-bank

Regional Transit Authority (RTA)
2817 Canal St ... New Orleans LA 70118 504-827-8300 468
Web: www.norta.com

Regional Transit Service Inc
1372 E Main St ... Rochester NY 14609 585-654-0200 468
Web: www.myrts.com

Regional Transit System (RTS)
Station 5 PO Box 490 ... Gainesville FL 32627 352-334-2600 334-2607 468
Web: www.go-rts.com

Regional Transportation Authority
175 W Jackson Blvd Ste 1550 ... Chicago IL 60604 312-913-3200 468
TF: 800-232-0502 ■ *Web:* www.rtachicago.com

Regional Transportation Commission of Southern Nevada (RTC)
600 S Grand Central Pkwy Ste 350 ... Las Vegas NV 89106 702-676-1500 676-1518 468
TF: 800-228-3911 ■ *Web:* www.rtcsnv.com

Regional Transportation District (RTD)
1600 Blake St ... Denver CO 80202 303-628-9000 468
TF: 800-366-7433 ■ *Web:* www.rtd-denver.com

Regional West Medical Ctr
4021 Ave B ... Scottsbluff NE 69361 308-635-3711 374-3
Web: www.rwhs.org

Regions Bank 1900 Fifth Ave N ... Birmingham AL 35203 800-734-4667 70
TF: 800-734-4667 ■ *Web:* www.regions.com

Regions Financial Corp
1900 Fifth Ave N ... Birmingham AL 35203 866-688-0658 360-2
NYSE: RF ■ *TF:* 866-688-0658 ■ *Web:* www.regions.com

Regions Hospital 640 Jackson St ... Saint Paul MN 55101 651-254-3456 254-9426 374-3
TF: 800-922-2876 ■ *Web:* www.regionshospital.com

Regions Mortgage Inc
215 Forrest St ... Hattiesburg MS 39401 800-986-2462 509
TF: 800-986-2462 ■ *Web:* www.regions.com

Regis College 15 St Mary St ... Toronto ON M4Y2R5 416-922-5474 922-2898 167-3
Web: www.regiscollege.ca

Regis College 235 Wellesley St ... Weston MA 02493 781-768-7000 768-7071 166
TF: 866-438-7344 ■ *Web:* www.regiscollege.edu

Regis Corp 7201 Metro Blvd ... Minneapolis MN 55439 952-947-7777 77
NYSE: RGS ■ *TF:* 888-888-7778 ■ *Web:* www.regiscorp.com

Regis Corp MasterCuts Div
7201 Metro Blvd ... Minneapolis MN 55439 952-947-7777 77
TF: 877-857-2070 ■ *Web:* www.regiscorp.com

Regis Corp Pro-Cuts Div
7201 Metro Blvd ... Minneapolis MN 55439 952-947-7777 77
TF: 877-857-2070 ■ *Web:* www.procuts.com

Regis Corp Regis Hairstylists Div
7201 Metro Blvd ... Minneapolis MN 55439 952-947-7777 77
TF: 877-857-2070 ■ *Web:* www.regissalons.com

Regis Corp SmartStyle Div
7201 Metro Blvd ... Minneapolis MN 55439 952-947-7777 77
TF: 877-857-2070 ■ *Web:* www.smartstyle.com

Regis Group Inc, The PO Box 3323 ... Leesburg VA 20177 703-777-2233 77
Web: www.regisgroup.com

Regis School 7330 Westview Dr ... Houston TX 77055 713-682-8383 685
Web: www.theregisschool.org

Regis Technologies Inc
8210 Austin Ave ... Morton Grove IL 60053 847-967-6000 967-5876 582
TF: 800-323-8144 ■ *Web:* www.registech.com

Regis University 3333 Regis Blvd ... Denver CO 80221 303-458-4100 964-5473 166
TF Admissions: 800-388-2366 ■ *Web:* www.regis.edu
Colorado Springs
7450 Campus Dr Ste 100 ... Colorado Springs CO 80920 800-568-8932 264-7095* 166
*Fax Area Code: 719 ■ *Fax: Admissions ■ *TF:* 800-568-8932 ■ *Web:* www.regis.edu

Register Tapes Unlimited Inc
1445 Langham Creek ... Houston TX 77084 281-206-2500 4
TF: 800-247-4793 ■ *Web:* www.rtui.com

Register.com Inc 575 Eigth Ave 8th Fl ... New York NY 10018 888-734-4783 396
TF: 888-734-4783 ■ *Web:* www.register.com

Registered Representative Magazine
1166 Ave of the Americas 10th Fl ... New York NY 10036 212-204-4200 457-5
TF: 800-525-5003 ■ *Web:* www.penton.com

Register-Guard 3500 Chad Dr ... Eugene OR 97408 541-485-1234 683-7631 532-2
TF: 800-377-7428 ■ *Web:* www.registerguard.com

Register-Herald 801 N Kanawha St ... Beckley WV 25801 304-255-4400 255-4427 532-2
TF: 800-950-0250 ■ *Web:* www.register-herald.com

Register-Star 364 Warren St ... Hudson NY 12534 518-828-1616 532-2
TF: 800-836-4069 ■ *Web:* www.registerstar.com

Registrar Corp 144 Research Dr ... Hampton VA 23666 757-224-0177 463
Web: www.registrarcorp.com

Registry of Interpreters for the Deaf Inc (RID)
333 Commerce St ... Alexandria VA 22314 703-838-0030 838-0454 49-5
TF: 800-356-3035 ■ *Web:* www.rid.org

Regitar USA Inc 2575 Container Dr ... Montgomery AL 36109 334-244-1885 244-1901 351
TF: 877-734-4827 ■ *Web:* www.regitar.com

Regnery Publishing Inc
300 New Jersey Ave NW ... Washington DC 20001 202-216-0600 637-2
Web: www.regnery.com

Rego Mfg Company Inc
1870 E Mansfield St ... Bucyrus OH 44820 419-562-0466 411
Web: www.regoonline.com

Rego-fix Tool Corp
7752 Moller Rd ... Indianapolis IN 46268 317-870-5959 358
TF: 800-999-7346 ■ *Web:* www.rego-fix.com

Regulator Bookshop 720 Ninth St ... Durham NC 27705 919-286-2700 95
Web: regulatorbookshop.com

Regulatory Affairs Professionals Society (RAPS)
5635 Fishers Ln Ste 550 ... Rockville MD 20852 301-770-2920 770-2924 49-8
TF: 800-307-6627 ■ *Web:* www.raps.org

Regulus 238 N Main St ... Woodstock VA 22664 540-459-2142 261
Web: regulus-group.com

Regupol America 33 Keystone Dr ... Lebanon PA 17042 800-537-8737 675-2199* 291
*Fax Area Code: 717 ■ *TF:* 800-537-8737 ■ *Web:* www.regupol.com

Reh Holdings Inc 150 S Sumner St ... York PA 17404 717-843-0021 697

Rehab Plus Therapeutic Products
6104 45th St ... Lubbock TX 79407 806-791-2288 477

Rehababilities Inc
8655 Haven Ave Ste 200 ... Rancho Cucamonga CA 91730 909-989-5699 260
TF: 800-642-5031 ■ *Web:* www.rehababilities.com

Rehabilitation Engineering & Assistive Technology Society of North America (RESNA)
1700 N Moore St Ste 1540 ... Arlington VA 22209 703-524-6686 524-6630 48-17
Web: www.resna.org

Rehabilitation Hospital of Indiana
4141 Shore Dr ... Indianapolis IN 46254 317-329-2000 566-9111 374-6
TF: 866-510-2273 ■ *Web:* www.rhin.com

Rehabilitation Hospital of the Pacific
226 N Kuakini St ... Honolulu HI 96817 808-531-3511 374-6
Web: www.rehabhospital.org

Rehabilitation Institute of Michigan
261 Mack Blvd ... Detroit MI 48201 313-745-1203 374-6
Web: www.rimrehab.org

Rehau Inc 1501 EdwaRds Ferry Rd NE ... Leesburg VA 20176 703-777-5255 777-3053 235
TF: 800-247-9445 ■ *Web:* www.rehau.com

Rehmann Group 5800 Gratiot St Ste 201 ... Saginaw MI 48638 989-799-9580 799-0227 2
TF: 866-799-9580 ■ *Web:* www.rehmann.com

Rehoboth Beach City Hall
229 Rehoboth Ave ... Rehoboth Beach DE 19971 302-227-6181 227-4643 337
Web: www.cityofrehoboth.com

Rehoboth Beach Convention Ctr
229 Rehoboth Ave ... Rehoboth Beach DE 19971 302-227-4641 227-4643 206
TF: 888-743-3628 ■ *Web:* www.cityofrehoboth.com

Rehoboth Beach Public Library
226 Rehoboth Ave ... Rehoboth Beach DE 19971 302-227-8044 227-0597 434-3
TF: 800-404-7080 ■ *Web:* www.rehobothlibrary.org

Rehoboth Beach-Dewey Beach Chamber of Commerce
501 Rehoboth Ave ... Rehoboth Beach DE 19971 302-227-2233 227-8351 139
TF: 800-441-1329 ■ *Web:* www.beach-fun.com

Rehoboth McKinley Christian Hospital
1900 Redrock Dr ... Gallup NM 87301 505-863-7000 374-3
Web: www.rmch.org

Rehrig Pacific Co 4010 E 26th St ... Los Angeles CA 90058 323-262-5145 269-8506 199
TF: 800-421-6244 ■ *Web:* www.rehrigpacific.com

REI 1700 45th St E ... Sumner WA 98352 253-891-2500 891-2523 64
TF: 800-426-4840 ■ *Web:* www.rei.com

REI (Raymond Express International)
320 Harbor Way ... South San Francisco CA 94080 650-871-8560 311
Web: www.reiexpress.com

REI (Recreational Equipment Inc)
6750 S 228th St ... Kent WA 98032 253-395-3780 891-2523 711
TF Orders: 800-426-4840 ■ *Web:* www.rei.com

REI Adventures PO Box 1938 ... Sumner WA 98390 800-622-2236 760
TF: 800-622-2236 ■ *Web:* www.rei.com/adventures

Rei do Gado 939 Fourth Ave ... San Diego CA 92101 619-702-8464 671
Web: www.reidogado.net

REI Systems Inc
45335 Vintage Pk Plaza ... Sterling VA 20166 703-480-9100 689-4680 177
Web: www.reisystems.com

Reichard Buick GMC 161 Salem Ave ... Dayton OH 45406 937-401-2034 57
Web: www.reichardbuick.com

Reichdrill Inc
99 Troy Hawk Run Hwy ... Philipsburg PA 16866 814-342-5500 537
Web: www.reichdrill.com

Reichel Foods Inc
3706 Enterprise Dr SW ... Rochester MN 55902 507-289-7264 123
Web: www.reichelfoods.com

Reichert David G (Rep R - WA)
1127 Longworth HOB ... Washington DC 20515 202-225-7761 225-4282 342-2
Web: reichert.house.gov

Reichert Inc 3362 Walden Ave ... Depew NY 14043 716-686-4500 544
Web: www.reichert.com

Reichhold Inc 2400 Ellis Rd ... Durham NC 27703 919-990-7500 990-7711 605-2
TF: 800-448-3482 ■ *Web:* www.reichhold.com

Reicker, Pfau, Pyle & McRoy LLP
1421 State St Ste B ... Santa Barbara CA 93101 805-966-2440 428
Web: www.reickerpfau.com

Reid Fleming Industrial LLC
7 Industrial Dr ... Saint James MO 65559 573-265-3314 567
Web: www.fleming-mfg.com

Reid Hospital & Health Care Services
1100 Reid Pkwy ... Richmond IN 47374 765-983-3000 374-3
Web: www.reidhosp.com

Reid Hurst Nagy
105-13900 Maycrest Way ... Richmond BC V6V3E2 604-273-9338 2
Web: www.rhncpa.com

Reid Jones McRorie & Williams Inc
2200 Executive St PO Box 669248 ... Charlotte NC 28208 704-537-0012 390
TF: 800-785-2604 ■ *Web:* www.rjmw.com

Phone | Fax | Class

Reid Middleton Inc
728 134th St SW Ste 200 ..... Everett WA 98204 425-741-3800 261
Web: www.reidmiddleton.com

Reid Park Zoo 1100 S Randolph Way ..... Tucson AZ 85716 520-791-3204 823
Web: reidparkzoo.org

Reid State Park 375 Seguinland Rd ..... Georgetown ME 04548 207-371-2303 565
Web: www.maine.gov

Reid Temple African Methodist Episcopal Church
11400 Glenn Dale Blvd ..... Glenn Dale MD 20769 301-352-0320 48-20
Web: reidtemple.org

Reidler Decal Corp
264 Industrial Pk Rd PO Box 8 ..... Saint Clair PA 17970 800-628-7770 429-1528* 413
**Fax Area Code:* 570 ■ *TF:* 800-628-7770 ■ *Web:* www.reidlerdecal.com

Reidsville Recreation Dept
200 N Franklin St ..... Reidsville NC 27320 336-349-1090 564
Web: ci.reidsville.nc.us

Reif Ctr 720 NW Conifer Dr ..... Grand Rapids MN 55744 218-327-5780 572
Web: www.reifcenter.org

Reiff & Nestor Co 50 Reiff St ..... Lykens PA 17048 717-453-7113 453-7555 493
TF: 800-521-3422 ■ *Web:* www.rntap.com

Reigel Plumbing & Heating Inc
1701 S Galvin Ave ..... Marshfield WI 54449 715-387-3411 189-10
Web: reigelplumbing.com

Reigstad & Associates Inc
192 Ninth St W Ste 200 ..... Saint Paul MN 55102 651-292-1123 261
TF: 800-355-8414 ■ *Web:* www.reigstad.com

Reiko Wireless 18 W 27th St ..... New York NY 10001 212-213-1102 736
TF: 888-797-3456 ■ *Web:* www.reikowireless.com

Reilly Construction Co Inc PO Box 99 ..... Ossian IA 52161 563-532-9211 532-9759 188-4
Web: www.reilly-construction.com

Reilly Financial Advisors
7777 Alvarado Rd Ste 116 ..... La Mesa CA 91942 619-698-0794 796
Web: www.rfadvisors.com

Reilly Like & Tenety
179 Little E Neck Rd ..... West Babylon NY 11704 631-669-3000 428

Reilly Penner & Benton LLP
1233 N Mayfair Rd ..... Milwaukee WI 53226 414-271-7800 2
Web: rpb.biz

Reilly Windows & Doors
901 Burman Blvd, Bldg 701 ..... Calverton NY 11933 631-208-0710 499
Web: www.reillywd.com

Reily Foods Co
400 Poydras St 10th FL ..... New Orleans LA 70130 800-535-1961 539-5427* 296-7
**Fax Area Code:* 504 ■ *TF:* 800-535-1961 ■ *Web:* www.frenchmarketcoffee.com

Reimagine Office Furnishings
1212 N 39th St Ste 200 ..... Tampa FL 33605 877-763-4400 321
TF: 877-763-4400 ■ *Web:* www.rofinc.net

Reiman Gardens
Iowa State University
1407 University Blvd ..... Ames IA 50011 515-294-2710 97
Web: www.reimangardens.com

Reimers & Jolivette Inc
2344 NW 24th Ave ..... Portland OR 97210 503-228-7691 228-2721 187
Web: reimersandjolivette.com

Reimers Electra Steam Inc
4407 Martinsburg Pk PO Box 37 ..... Clear Brook VA 22624 540-662-3811 726-4215* 357
**Fax Area Code:* 800 ■ *TF:* 800-872-7562 ■ *Web:* www.reimersinc.com

Reimers-kaufman Concrete Prods
6200 Cornhusker Hwy ..... Lincoln NE 68507 402-434-1855 434-1877 191-1
Web: www.reimerskaufman.com

Reinauer Transportation Companies Inc
1983 Richmond Terr ..... Staten Island NY 10302 718-816-8167 314
Web: www.reinauer.com

Reindl Bindery Company Inc
W194 N11381 McCormick Dr ..... Germantown WI 53022 262-293-1444 293-1445 92
TF: 800-878-1121 ■ *Web:* www.reindlbindery.com

Reindl Printing Inc 1300 Johnson St ..... Merrill WI 54452 715-536-9537 627
TF: 800-236-9637 ■ *Web:* www.reindlprinting.com

Reingold Inc 433 E Monroe Ave ..... Alexandria VA 22301 202-333-0400 463
Web: www.reingold.com

Reinhardt College
7300 Reinhardt College Cir ..... Waleska GA 30183 770-720-5526 720-5899* 166
**Fax:* Admissions ■ *TF:* 877-346-4273 ■ *Web:* www.reinhardt.edu

Reinhardt Corp 3919 State Hwy 23 ..... West Oneonta NY 13861 607-432-6633 316
TF: 800-421-2867 ■ *Web:* www.reinhardthomeheating.com

Reinhart Food Service
7735 Westside Industrial Dr ..... Jacksonville FL 32219 904-781-9888 300
Web: www.rfsdelivers.com

Reinhart Partners Inc
1500 W Market St Ste 100 ..... Mequon WI 53092 262-241-2020 796
Web: www.reinhart-partnersinc.com

Reinhold Industries Inc
12827 E Imperial Hwy ..... Santa Fe Springs CA 90670 562-944-3281 944-7238 504
Web: www.reinhold-ind.com

Reinke Mfg Co Inc 5325 Reinke Rd ..... Deshler NE 68340 402-365-7251 365-4370 273
TF: 866-365-7381 ■ *Web:* www.reinke.com

Reinsel Kuntz Lesher
1330 Broadcasting Rd ..... Wyomissing PA 19610 610-376-1595 463
Web: www.rklcpa.com

Reinstein Public Library
2580 Harlem Rd ..... Cheektowaga NY 14225 716-892-8089 434-3
Web: buffalolib.org

Reinsurance Group of America Inc
1370 Timberlake Manor Pkwy ..... Chesterfield MO 63017 636-736-7000 360-4
NYSE: RGA ■ *TF:* 800-985-4326 ■ *Web:* www.rgare.com

Reis Inc 530 Fifth Ave 5th Fl ..... New York NY 10036 212-921-1122 921-2533 466
NASDAQ: REIS ■ *TF:* 800-366-7347 ■ *Web:* www.reis.com

Reis Nichols Jewelers
789 US Hwy 31 N ..... Greenwood IN 46142 317-883-4467 410
TF: 800-364-4367 ■ *Web:* www.reisnichols.com

Reischling Press Inc
3325 S 116th St Ste 161 ..... Seattle WA 98168 206-905-5999 627
Web: www.rpiprint.com

Reisterstown Lumber Co, The
PO Box 337 ..... Reisterstown MD 21136 410-833-1300 833-6803 364
Web: www.reisterstownlumber.com

Reiter Affiliated Cos 1767 San Juan Rd ..... Aromas CA 93030 805-483-1000 315-1
Web: www.berry.net

Reiter Giuliani Group LLC, The
1 Penn Plaza 36th Fl ..... New York NY 10119 212-786-7626 463
Web: www.reitergiulianigroup.com

Reitmans (Canada) Ltd 250 Sauve St W ..... Montreal QC H3L1Z2 514-384-1140 229
TSE: RET.A ■ *Web:* www.reitmans.com

REITPAC 1875 'I' St NW Ste 600 ..... Washington DC 20006 202-739-9400 739-9401 615
TF: 800-362-7348 ■ *Web:* www.reit.com

Reitz Home Museum 224 SE First St ..... Evansville IN 47706 812-426-1871 426-2179 520
TF: 800-433-3025 ■ *Web:* reitzhome.com

Rejoice Church 13413 E 106th St N ..... Owasso OK 74055 918-272-5291 148
Web: www.rejoicechurch.com

Rejoice Radio PO Box 18000 ..... Pensacola FL 32523 850-479-6570 645-120
TF: 800-726-1191 ■ *Web:* www.rejoice.org

Rejuvenation Inc 2550 NW Nicolai St ..... Portland OR 97210 503-238-1900 526-7329* 439
**Fax Area Code:* 800 ■ *TF:* 888-401-1900 ■ *Web:* www.rejuvenation.com

Rekon Technologies Inc
150 S Los Robles Ave Ste 660 ..... Pasadena CA 91101 626-577-4350 577-4360 809
Web: www.rekon.com

Relais & Chateaux Assn 10 E 53rd St ..... New York NY 10022 212-319-4880 48-23
TF: 800-735-2478 ■ *Web:* relaischateaux.com

Relais International
1690 Woodward Dr Ste 215 ..... Ottawa ON K2C3R8 613-226-5571 226-0998 178-12
TF: 888-294-5244 ■ *Web:* www.relais-intl.com

Relate Corp 900 Avenida Acaso Ste K ..... Camarillo CA 93012 805-482-7381 180
TF: 800-428-3708 ■ *Web:* relate.com

Related Group of Florida
315 S Biscayne Blvd ..... Miami FL 33131 305-460-9900 460-9911 653
Web: www.relatedgroup.com

Related Midwest
350 W Hubbard St Ste 300 ..... Chicago IL 60654 312-595-7400 653
Web: www.relatedmidwest.com

Relationship One Llc
8009 34th Ave S Ste 300 ..... Minneapolis MN 55425 763-355-1025 463
Web: www.relationshipone.com

Relay Specialties Inc 17 Raritan Rd ..... Oakland NJ 07436 201-337-1000 203
TF: 800-526-5376 ■ *Web:* www.relayspec.com

RelayHealth Corp
5995 Windward Pkwy ..... Alpharetta GA 30005 770-237-7164 387
Web: www.relayhealth.com

Relco LLC 2331 Third Ave ..... Willmar MN 56201 320-231-2210 360-3
Web: www.relco.net

Relco Systems Inc
7310 Chestnut Ridge Rd ..... Lockport NY 14094 716-434-8100 434-7229 780
TF: 800-262-1020 ■ *Web:* www.relcosystems.com

ReleaseTEAM Inc
1400 W 122nd Ave Ste 202 ..... Denver CO 80234 720-887-0489 177
Web: www.releaseteam.com

Relevancy Group LLC, The
505 Congress St Ste 602 ..... Boston MA 07762 877-972 6886 466
TF: 877-972-6886 ■ *Web:* www.relevancygroup.com

Relevant Radio
1496 Bellevue St Ste 202 PO Box 10707 ..... Green Bay WI 54311 877-291 0120 644
TF: 877-291-0123 ■ *Web:* www.relevantradio.com

Relevante Inc 1235 Westlakes Dr Ste 280 ..... Berwyn PA 19312 484-403-4100 734
Web: www relevante.com

Reliability Center 501 Westover Ave ..... Hopewell VA 23060 804-458-0645 261
TF: 800-457-0645 ■ *Web:* www.reliability.com

Reliable Carriers Inc
41555 Koppernick Rd ..... Canton MI 48187 734-453-6677 453-8609 468
TF: 800-521-6393 ■ *Web:* www.reliablecarriers.com

Reliable Castings Corp
3530 Spring Grove Ave ..... Cincinnati OH 45223 513-541-2627 541-5696 308
TF: 866-722-2278 ■ *Web:* www.reliablecastings.com

Reliable Chevrolet Inc
800 N Central Expy ..... Richardson TX 75080 972-330-4326 897-6000* 57
**Fax Area Code:* 505 ■ *Web:* www.reliablechevytexas.com

Reliable Container Corp
9206 Santa Fe Springs Rd ..... Santa Fe Springs CA 90670 562 861-6226 100
Web: www.reliablecontainer.com

Reliable Contracting Co Inc
2410 Evergreen Rd Ste 200 ..... Gambrills MD 21054 410-987-0313 188-4
Web: www.reliablecontracting.com

Reliable Energy Services Corp
5069-A Maureen Ln Unit C ..... Moorpark CA 93021 805-517-1717 196
Web: www.reliablelighting.net

Reliable Factory Supply Co
PO Box 340 ..... Thomaston CT 06787 800-288-8464 361
TF: 800-288-8464 ■ *Web:* www.rfsupply.com

Reliable Fire Equipment Co
12845 S Cicero Ave ..... Alsip IL 60803 708-597-4600 389-1150 679
TF: 800-876-3473 ■ *Web:* www.reliablefire.com

Reliable Hardware Co
11319 Vanowen St ..... North Hollywood CA 91605 818-753-8558 350
Web: www.reliablehardware.com

Reliable Life Insurance Co
100 King St W PO Box 557 ..... Hamilton ON L8N3K9 905-523-5587 551-1704* 391-2
**Fax Area Code:* 866 ■ **Fax:* Claims ■ *TF:* 800-465-0661 ■ *Web:* www.reliablelifeinsurance.com

Reliable Machine Co 1327 Tenth Ave ..... Rockford IL 61104 815-968-8803 488
Web: www.reliablemachine.com

Reliable Market 36 Circuit Av ..... Oak Bluffs MA 02557 508-693-1102 345
Web: thereliablemarket.com

Reliable Medical Supply Inc
9401 Winnetka Ave N ..... Brooklyn Park MN 55445 763-255-3800 475
Web: www.reliamed.com

Reliable of Milwaukee Inc
6737 W Washington Ste 3200 ..... Milwaukee WI 53214 414-272-5084 155-18
TF: 800-336-6876 ■ *Web:* www.reliableofmilwaukee.com

Reliable Racing Supply Inc
643 Glen St ..... Queensbury NY 12804 518-793-5677 711
TF: 800-223-4448 ■ *Web:* www.reliableracing.com

Reliable Software Resources Inc
22260 Haggerty Rd Ste 285 ..... Northville MI 48167 248-477-3555 177
Web: www.rsrit.com

Reliable Tire Co
805 N Blackhorse Pk ..... Blackwood NJ 08012 800-342-3426 755
TF All: 800-342-3426 ■ *Web:* www.reliabletire.com

Reliable Transportation Specialists Inc
139 Venturi Dr ..... Chesterton IN 46304 219-926-8850 468
Web: www.reliabletrans.com

Phone | Fax | Class

Reliable Wholesale Lumber Inc
7600 Redondo Cir .... Huntington Beach CA 92648 714-848-8222 847-1605 191-3
TF: 877-795-4638 ■ *Web:* www.rwli.net

Reliance Bancshares Inc
10401 Clayton Rd.... St. Louis MO 63131 314-569-7200 70
OTC: RLBS ■ *Web:* www.reliancebankstl.com

Reliance Connects 61 W Mesquite Blvd .... Mesquite NV 89027 702-346-5211 387
TF: 866-894-4657 ■ *Web:* www.relianceconnects.com

Reliance Controls Corp 2001 Young Ct .... Racine WI 53404 262-634-6155 729
TF: 800-634-6155 ■ *Web:* www.reliancecontrols.com

Reliance Heating & Air Conditioning Inc
1694 Hwy 138 NE.... Conyers GA 30013 770-483-3850 610
Web: www.reliance-hvac.com

Reliance One Inc
1700 Harmon Rd Ste 1 .... Auburn Hills MI 48326 248-922-4500 922-5660 260
Web: www.reliance-one.com

Reliance Pathology Partners LLC
5755 Hoover Blvd.... Tampa FL 33634 813-884-2849 415
Web: www.pims-inc.com

Reliance Power Parts
2535 Business Pkwy.... Minden NV 89423 800-776-3113 791
TF: 800-776-3113 ■ *Web:* www.relianceparts.com

Reliance Protectron Security Services
4209-99 St Ste 102 .... Edmonton AB T6E5V7 780-462-1657 693
Web: www.voxcom.com

Reliance Standard Life Insurance
2001 Market St Ste 1500 .... Philadelphia PA 19103 267-256-3500 391-2
TF: 800-351-7500 ■ *Web:* www.reliancestandard.com

Reliance Steel & Aluminum Co
350 S Grand Ave Ste 5100 .... Los Angeles CA 90071 213-687-7700 687-8792 492
NYSE: RS ■ *TF:* 800-999-2497 ■ *Web:* www.rsac.com

Reliance Tool & Manufacturing Co
900 N State St Ste 101 .... Elgin IL 60123 847-695-1234 695-0931 757
TF: 800-227-8840 ■ *Web:* www.reliancetool.com

Reliance Trading Corporation of America
55 Watermill Ln .... Great Neck NY 11021 516-466-6240 192
Web: beautysilk.com

Reliance Well Service Inc
237 Hwy 79 S.... Magnolia AR 71753 870-234-2700 540

Reliant Energy Retail Services LLC
1201 Fannin St.... Houston TX 77002 866-222-7100 488-4422* 787
**Fax Area Code: 713* ■ *TF:* 866-660-4900 ■ *Web:* www.reliant.com

Reliant Inventory Services Inc
11050 Fancher Rd Lot 110 .... Westerville OH 43082 614-855-2960 317
Web: www.reliant-inv.com

Reliant Transportation Inc
4411 S 86th St Ste 101 PO Box 67009.... Lincoln NE 68526 402-464-7771 464-8124 449
Web: www.reliant-transportation.com

Religence Inc 2090 Green St.... San Francisco CA 94123 415-771-7473 393
Web: www.religence.com

Religion News Service (RNS)
529 14th St NW Ste 425.... Washington DC 20045 202-463-8777 662-7154 530
Web: www.religionnews.com

Religious Conference Management Assn Inc (RCMA)
7702 Woodland Dr Ste 120 .... Indianapolis IN 46278 317-632-1888 632-7909 49-12
TF: 800-221-8235 ■ *Web:* www.rcmaweb.org

Relin, Goldstein & Crane LLP
28 E Main St Ste 1800 .... Rochester NY 14614 585-325-6202 428
TF: 888-984-2351 ■ *Web:* www.rgcattys.net

Relios Inc 6815 Academy Pkwy W NE .... Albuquerque NM 87109 505-345-5304 409
TF: 800-827-6543 ■ *Web:* www.carolynpollack.com

Reliv International Inc
136 Chesterfield Industrial Blvd .... Chesterfield MO 63005 636-537-9715 537-9753 366
NASDAQ: RELV ■ *TF:* 800-735-4887 ■ *Web:* www.reliv.com

Reller Risk Management
6315 Fly Rd .... East Syracuse NY 13057 315-432-8210 390

Relli Technology Inc
1200 S Rogers Cir .... Boca Raton FL 33487 561-886-0200 886-0201 770
Web: www.relli.com

RELO Direct Inc
161 N Clark St Ste 1250.... Chicago IL 60601 312-384-5900 666
TF: 800-621-7356 ■ *Web:* www.relodirect.com

Relocation America International
25800 Northwestern Hwy Ste 210.... Southfield MI 48075 877-500-4466 666
TF: 877-500-4466 ■ *Web:* relocationamericainternational.com

Relton Corp 317 Rolyn Pl.... Arcadia CA 91007 323-681-2551 446-9671* 758
**Fax Area Code: 626* ■ *TF Cust Svc:* 800-423-1505 ■ *Web:* www.relton.com

Rely Services Inc
2354 Hassell Rd Ste B .... Hoffman Estates IL 60169 847-310-8750 195
TF: 866-735-9328 ■ *Web:* relyservices.com

REM Assn Services
2001 Jefferson Davis Hwy Ste 1004.... Arlington VA 22202 703-416-0010 47
Web: www.remservices.biz

Rem Sales Inc 910 Gay Hill Rd .... Windsor CT 06095 860-687-3400 687-3401 385
TF: 877-689-1860 ■ *Web:* www.remsales.com

Rema Dri-Vac Corp 45 Ruby St .... Norwalk CT 06850 203-847-2464 847-3609 427
Web: www.remadrivac.com

Rema Foods Inc
140 Sylvan Ave.... Englewood Cliffs NJ 07632 201-947-1000 360-3
Web: foodimportgroup.com

Remar Inc 6200 E Division St.... Lebanon TN 37090 615-449-0231 88
Web: www.remarinc.com

Remax Villa Realtors
7515 Bergenline Ave.... North Bergen NJ 07047 201-868-3100 868-9440 652
Web: www.remax-villa.com

Rembolt Ludtke LLP
1201 Lincoln Mall Ste 102.... Lincoln NE 68508 402-475-5100 475-5087 445
Web: rembolt lawfirm.com

Rembrandt Commercial Cleaning
20900 Swenson Dr Ste 250 .... Waukesha WI 53186 262-798-1038 104
Web: www.rembrandtcleaning.com

Rembrandt Group LLC, The 2 N Rd Ste 3.... Warren NJ 07059 732-356-1600 180
TF: 800-899-0442 ■ *Web:* www.rembrandtgroup.com

Rembrandt Venture Partners
600 Montgomery St 44th Fl .... San Francisco CA 94111 650-326-7070 528-2901* 792
**Fax Area Code: 415* ■ *Web:* www.rembrandtvc.com

REMC (Okefenoke Rural Electric Membership Corp)
14384 Cleveland St PO Box 602.... Nahunta GA 31553 912-462-5131 462-6100 245
TF: 800-262-5131 ■ *Web:* www.oremc.com

Remco Inc 195 Hempt Rd.... Mechanicsburg PA 17050 717-697-0389 189-10
Web: remcopa.com

Remco Products Corp
4735 W 106th St.... Zionsville IN 46077 317-876-9856 296
TF: 800-585-8619 ■ *Web:* remcoproducts.com

Remcom Inc
315 S Allen St Ste 222 .... State College PA 16801 814-861-1299 174
Web: www.remcom.com

Remcon Plastics Inc 208 Chestnut St.... Reading PA 19602 800-360-3636 599
TF: 800-360-3636 ■ *Web:* www.remcon.com

Remedi Consulting Co
96 Northwoods Blvd Ste A2 .... Columbus OH 43235 614-436-4040 196
TF: 800-490-7143 ■ *Web:* www.remedi.com

Remediation Services Inc
2735 S Tenth St PO Box 587 .... Independence KS 67301 620-331-1200 667
TF: 800-335-1201 ■ *Web:* www.rsi-ks.com

Remedy Temp Inc 3820 State St.... Santa Barbara CA 93105 805-882-2200 898-7111 721
TF: 800-688-6162 ■ *Web:* www.remedystaff.com

Remelt Sources Inc
27151 Tungsten Rd.... Cleveland OH 44132 216-289-4555 289-0939 492
Web: www.remeltsources.com

Remer Inc 205 Marion St.... Seattle WA 98104 206-624-1010 7
Web: www.remerinc.com

Remet Corp 210 Commons Rd.... Utica NY 13502 315-797-8700 306
TF: 877-939-0171 ■ *Web:* www.remet.com

Remi 145 W 53rd St .... New York NY 10019 212-581-4242 671
Web: remi-nyc.com

Reminder Newspaper
2 W Vine St PO Box 1600.... Millville NJ 08332 856-825-8811 825-0011 532-4
Web: reminderusa.net

Reminder Press Inc
130 Old Town Rd PO Box 27 .... Vernon CT 06066 860-875-3366 875-2089 637-8
TF: 888-456-2211 ■ *Web:* courant.com/reminder-news

Reminger & Reminger Company LPa
101 W Prospect Ave .... Cleveland OH 44115 216-687-1311 687-1841 428
TF: 800-486-1311 ■ *Web:* www.reminger.com

Remington & Vernick Engineers Inc
232 Kings Hwy E .... Haddonfield NJ 08033 856-795-9595 261
Web: www.rve.com

Remington Arms Company Inc
870 Remington Dr PO Box 700.... Madison NC 27025 336-548-8700 548-7801 284
TF: 800-243-9700 ■ *Web:* www.remington.com

Remington Club 16925 Hierba Dr.... San Diego CA 92128 858-673-6340 672
Web: www.fivestarseniorliving.com

Remington College
Little Rock
10600 Colonel Glenn Rd Ste 100 .... Little Rock AR 72204 501-312-0007 800
TF: 800-323-8122 ■ *Web:* www.remingtoncollege.edu

Remington College Cleveland
14445 Broadway Ave .... Cleveland OH 44125 216-502-3035 800
Web: www.remingtoncollege.edu

Remington College Dallas
1800 Eastgate Dr .... Garland TX 75041 972-686-7878 800
Web: www.remingtoncollege.edu

Remington College Honolulu
1111 Bishop St Ste 400 .... Honolulu HI 96813 808-772-5978 800
Web: www.remingtoncollege.edu

Remington College Lafayette
303 Rue Louis XIV .... Lafayette LA 70508 337-981-4010 800
Web: www.remingtoncollege.edu

Remington College Largo
6302 E Dr Martin Luther King Jr Blvd Ste 400 .... Tampa FL 33619 800-323-8122 800
TF: 800-323-8122 ■ *Web:* www.remingtoncollege.edu

Remington College Memphis
2710 Nonconnah Blvd .... Memphis TN 38132 901-345-1000 800
Web: www.remingtoncollege.edu

Remington College Tampa
6302 E MLK Blvd Ste 400.... Tampa FL 33619 813-935-5700 800
TF General: 800-323-8122 ■ *Web:* www.remingtoncollege.edu

Remington Hotel Corp
14185 Dallas Pkwy Ste 1150 .... Dallas TX 75254 972-980-2700 379
Web: www.remingtonhotels.com

Remington Park Race Track
1 Remington Pl.... Oklahoma City OK 73111 405-424-1000 642
TF: 866-456-9880 ■ *Web:* www.remingtonpark.com

Remington Seeds
4746 W US Hwy 24 PO Box 9.... Remington IN 47977 219-261-3444 261-2220 10-5
TF: 800-728-7511 ■ *Web:* www.remingtonseeds.com

Remington Suite Hotel
220 Travis St.... Shreveport LA 71101 318-425-5000 379
TF: 800-444-6750 ■ *Web:* www.remingtonsuite.com

Remington's Restaurant
425 Merchants Rd .... Rochester NY 14609 585-482-4434 671

Reminisce Magazine
1610 N Second St Ste 102.... Milwaukee NY 53212 888-859-7838 457-11
TF: 888-859-7838 ■ *Web:* www.reminisce.com

Remke Markets Inc 1299 Cox Ave.... Erlanger KY 41018 859-594-3400 345
Web: www.remkes.com

Remo Inc 28101 Industry Dr.... Valencia CA 91355 661-294-5600 527
TF: 800-525-5134 ■ *Web:* www.remo.com

Remodelers Advantage Inc
14440 Cherry Ln Ct Ste 201.... Laurel MD 20707 301-490-5620 463
Web: www.remodelersadvantage.com

Remote Access Technology Inc
61 Atlantic St .... Dartmouth NS B2Y4P4 902-434-4405 365
TF: 877-356-2728 ■ *Web:* www.rat.ca

Remote Logistics International LLC
6430 Richmond Ave Ste 320 .... Houston TX 77057 713-780-9933 393
Web: www.remotelogisticsinternational.com

Remote Operations Co
200 Pakerland Dr .... Green Bay WI 54303 920-437-4466 180
TF: 888-837-4466 ■ *Web:* www.roccompany.com

Remote Technologies Inc
5775 12th Ave E Ste 180 .... Shakopee MN 55379 952-253-3100 52
Web: www.rticorp.com

RemoteReality Corp
100 Northfield Dr Ste 205.... Windsor CT 06095 508-870-1500 652
Web: www.remotereality.com

	Phone	Fax	Class
REMPREX LLC 7501 S Quincy St Ste 100................ Willowbrook IL 60527 *Web:* www.remprex.com	630-910-0600		631
Remstar International Inc 41 Eisenhower Dr.............................Westbrook ME 04092 **Fax Area Code:* 207 ■ *TF:* 800-639-5805 ■ *Web:* www.kardexremstar.com	800-639-5805	854-1610*	385
Remtec International 1100 Haskins Rd ....Bowling Green OH 43402 *Web:* www.remtec.net	419-867-8990		610
Remuda Ranch Co 1 E Apache St............Wickenburg AZ 85390 *TF:* 800-445-1900 ■ *Web:* www.remudaranch.com	928-684-3913		95
Remy Cointreau USA Inc 1290 Ave of the Americas...................New York NY 10104 *Web:* www.remy-cointreau.com	212-399-4200		81-3
Remy International Inc 600 Corp Dr.......... Pendleton IN 46064 *NYSE:* REMY ■ *TF:* 800-372-3555 ■ *Web:* www.remyinc.com	765-778-6499		60
Rena Ware International Inc 15885 NE 28th St..........................Bellevue WA 98008 *TF:* 800-721-5156 ■ *Web:* www.renaware.com	425-881-6171	882-7500	486
Renacci Jim (Rep R - OH) 328 Cannon HOB ....Washington DC 20515 *Web:* renacci.house.gov	202-225-3876	225-3059	342-2
Renacci Jim (Rep R - OH) 328 Cannon HOB ....Washington DC 20515 *Web:* renacci.house.gov	202-225-3876	225-3059	342-2
Renaissance Computing Institute (RENCI) 100 Europa Dr Ste 540.......................Chapel Hill NC 27517 *Web:* www.renci.org	919-445-9640	445-9669	668
Renaissance Cos, The 8925 E Pima Ctr Pkwy Ste 205............... Scottsdale AZ 85258 *Web:* www.renaissancecos.com	480-967-0880		186
Renaissance Ctr Detroit River.................. Detroit MI 48243 *Web:* marriott.com/hotels/propertypage/dtwdt	313-568-8000		50-6
Renaissance Esmeralda Resort 44-400 Indian Wells Ln ....Indian Wells CA 92210 *TF:* 888-236-2427 ■ *Web:* www.marriott.com	760-773-4444	346-9308	660
Renaissance Group 981 Worcester St ....Wellesley MA 02482 *TF:* 800-514-2667 ■ *Web:* www.renaissanceins.com	800-514-2667		390
Renaissance Learning Inc 2911 Peach St .... Wisconsin Rapids WI 54494 *TF:* 800-338-4204 ■ *Web:* renaissance.com	715-424-3636	424-4242	178-3
Renaissance Macro Research LLC 116 E 16th St 12th Fl ....New York NY 10003 *Web:* www.renmac.com	212-537-8811		401
Renaissance Orlando Resort at SeaWorld 6677 Sea Harbor Dr ....Orlando FL 32821 *TF:* 800-327-6677 ■ *Web:* www.marriott.com/default.mi	407-351-5555	351-9991	669
Renaissance Portsmouth Hotel & Waterfront Conference Ctr 425 Water St...................................Portsmouth VA 23704 *Web:* renaissance-hotels.marriott.com	757-673-3000	673-3030	377
Renaissance Resort at World Golf Village 500 S Legacy Trl......................Saint Augustine FL 32092 *TF:* 888-740-7020 ■ *Web:* www.marriott.com	904-940-8000	940-8008	669
Renaissance Technologies Corp 800 Third Ave..................................New York NY 10022 *Web:* www.rentec.com	212-829-4460		690
Renaissance Theatre Inc 1214 Meridian St .... Huntsville AL 35801 *Web:* www.renaissancetheatre.net	256-536-3117		572
Renaissance Vinoy Resort & Golf Club 501 Fifth Ave NE..................... Saint Petersburg FL 33701 *TF:* 800-468-3571	727-894-1000		669
Renaissance Westchester Hotel 80 W Red Oak Ln .... West Harrison NY 10604	914-694-5400		378
Renal Physicians Assn (RPA) 1700 Rockville Pk Ste 220 .... Rockville MD 20852 *Web:* www.renalmd.org	301-468-3515	468-3511	49-8
Renard Communications Inc 197 Mountain Ave.........................Springfield NJ 07081	973-912-8550		637-9
Renasant Corp 209 Troy St PO Box 709............ Tupelo MS 38802 *NASDAQ:* RNST ■ *TF Cust Svc:* 800-680-1601 ■ *Web:* www.renasantbank.com	662-680-1001		360-2
Renaud Cook Drury Mesaros PA 1 N Central Ste 900 ....Phoenix AZ 85004 *TF:* 800-307-2499 ■ *Web:* www.rcdmlaw.com	602-307-9900		428
Renault Winery Resort 72 N Bremen Ave ....Egg Harbor City NJ 08215 *Web:* www.renaultwinery.com	609-965-2111		80-3
Renbor Sales Solutions Inc 256 Thornway Ave .... Thornhill ON L4J7X8 *TF:* 855-257-2537 ■ *Web:* www.sellbetter.ca	416-671-3555		393
RENCI (Renaissance Computing Institute) 100 Europa Dr Ste 540.......................Chapel Hill NC 27517 *Web:* www.renci.org	919-445-9640	445-9669	668
Renco Corp 116 Third Ave N...................Minneapolis MN 55401 *TF:* 800-359-8181 ■ *Web:* www.rencocorp.com	612-338-6124	333-9026	584
Renco Electronics Inc 595 International Pl .... Rockledge FL 32955 *TF:* 800-645-5828 ■ *Web:* www.rencousa.com	321-637-1000	637-1600	246
Renco Encoders Inc 26 Coromar Dr .... Goleta CA 93117 *TF:* 800-233-0388 ■ *Web:* www.renco.com	847-490-1191		201
Renco Group 1 Rockefeller Plaza # 29...........New York NY 10020 *Web:* www.rencogroup.net	212-541-6000		185
Rencor Controls Inc 21 Sullivan Pkwy .... Fort Edward NY 12828 *TF:* 866-472-7030 ■ *Web:* rencor.com	518-747-4171		358
Rend Lake College 468 N Ken Gray Pkwy ....Ina IL 62846 **Fax:* Admitting ■ *TF:* 800-369-5321 ■ *Web:* rlc.edu	618-437-5321	437-5677*	162
Rend Lake State Fish & Wildlife Area 10885 E Jefferson Rd ....Bonnie IL 62816 *Web:* www.stateparks.com/rendlake.html	618-279-3110		565
Renda Broadcasting Corp 900 Parish St 4th Fl .... Pittsburgh PA 15220 *Web:* www.rendabroadcasting.com	412-875-1800	875-1801	643
Rendersoft Inc 5801 Christie Ave Ste 275 .... Emeryville CA 94608 *TF:* 800-573-1874 ■ *Web:* www.rendersoftinc.com	510-652-3936		180
Rendigs, Fry, Kiely & Dennis LLP 600 Vine St Ste 2650 .... Cincinnati OH 45202 *TF:* 800-274-2330 ■ *Web:* www.rendigs.com	513-381-9200		428
Rendon Group Inc 1875 Conn Ave NW........Washington DC 20009 *Web:* www.rendon.com	202-745-4900		636
Rene Bates Auctioneers Inc 4660 County Rd 1006............................ McKinney TX 75071 *Web:* www.renebates.com	972-548-9636	542-5495	51
Rene Of Paris 9135 Independence Ave .... Chatsworth CA 91311 *TF Sales:* 800-353-7363 ■ *Web:* www.reneofparis.com	800-353-7363		348
Renee's Garden 6060 Graham Hill Rd.............. Felton CA 95018 *TF:* 888-880-7228 ■ *Web:* www.reneesgarden.com	831-335-7228	335-7227	694
Renegade LLC 151 W 25th St 11th Fl ....New York NY 10001 *Web:* www.renegade.com	646-486-7702		7
Renegade Productions Inc 10950 Gilroy Rd Ste J.......................... Hunt Valley MD 21031 *Web:* www.getrenegade.com	410-667-1400		514
Renegade Theatre Co 222 E Superior St.......... Duluth MN 55802 *Web:* www.renegadetheatercompany.org	218-722-6775		572
Renegade/Kibbi LLC 52216 State Rd 15........... Bristol IN 46507 *TF:* 888-522-1126 ■ *Web:* www.renegaderv.com	574-848-1126	848-1127	120
Renesys Corp 1155 Elm St Ste 510........... Manchester NH 03101 *Web:* dyn.com/performance-assurance	603-643-9300		225
ReNew Life Formulas Inc 2076 Sunnydale Blvd .... Clearwater FL 33765 *TF:* 800-830-1800 ■ *Web:* www.renewlife.com	800-830-1800		297-11
Renew Plastics PO Box 480 PO Box 480...... Luxemburg WI 54217 *TF:* 800-666-5207 ■ *Web:* www.renewplastics.com	920-845-2326	845-2335	661
Renewable Choice Energy Inc 4775 Walnut St Ste 230 .... Boulder CO 80301 *Web:* www.renewablechoice.com	303-468-0405		194
Renewable Energy Policy Project (REPP) 1612 K St NW Ste 1200 ....Washington DC 20006	202-293-2898		634
Renewable Fuels Assn (RFA) 425 Third St SW.............................. Washington DC 20024 *Web:* www.ethanolrfa.org	202-289-3835	289-7519	48-12
Renewable Natural Resources Foundation (RNRF) 5430 Grosvenor Ln................................ Bethesda MD 20814 *Web:* www.rnrf.org	301-493-9101	493-6148	48-13
Renewable NRG Systems 110 Riggs Rd .... Hinesburg VT 05461 *Web:* www.nrgsystems.com	802-482-2255		177
Renewal By Andersen Corp 9900 Jamaica Ave S .... Cottage Grove MN 55016 *Web:* www.renewalbyandersen.com	651-769-2210		499
Renfro Corp 661 Linville Rd.......................Mount Airy NC 27030 *TF:* 800-334-9091 ■ *Web:* www.renfro.com	336-719-8000	719-8215	155-10
Renfrow Bros Inc 855 Gossett Rd ....Spartanburg SC 29307 *TF:* 800-260-8412 ■ *Web:* www.renfrowbros.com	864-579-0558		186
Renhill Staffing Services of Texas Inc 102 Rilla Vista Dr ....San Antonio TX 78216 *Web:* www.renhillmgmt.com	210-828-0508		260
Reni Publishing Inc 150 Third St SW........................... Winter Haven FL 33880 *TF:* 800-274-2812 ■ *Web:* www.reni.net	800-274-2812		627
Renier Construction Corp 2164 Citygate Dr........................... Columbus OH 43219 *Web:* www.renier.com	614-866-4580		186
Renishaw Inc 5277 Trillium Blvd .... Hoffman Estates IL 60192 *Web:* www.renishaw.com	847-286-9953	286-9974	385
Renkert Oil 3817 Main St PO Box 246........ Morgantown PA 19543 *TF:* 800-423-6457 ■ *Web:* www.renkertoil.com	610-286-8012		579
Renkim Corp 13333 Allen Rd................. Southgate MI 48195 *Web:* www.renkim.com	734-374-8300		5
Renkus-heinz Inc 19201 Cook St..........Foothill Ranch CA 92610 *TF:* 855-411-2364 ■ *Web:* www.renkus-heinz.com	949-588-9997	588-9514	52
Rennco LLC 300 Elm St .... Homer MI 49245 *TF:* 800-409-5225 ■ *Web:* www.rennco.com	800-409-5225		791
Rennert Bilingual 216 E 45th St..............New York NY 10017 *Web:* www.rennert.com	212-867-8700	867-7666	423
Rennhack Marketing Services Inc 752 Port America Pl .... Grapevine TX 76051	817-481-6516		195
Rennies Advertising Ideas Inc 711 Twinridge Ln .... Richmond VA 23235 *Web:* www.renniesadv.com	804-272-4442		7
Rennoc Corp 645 Pine St.................. Greenville OH 45331 *TF:* 800-372-7100 ■ *Web:* www.rennoc.com	800-372-7100	675-1727	155-5
Renntech Inc 1369 N Killian Dr.................Lake Park FL 33403 *Web:* www.renntechmercedes.com	561-845-7888		57
Reno Chamber Orchestra 925 Riverside Dr Ste 5 .... Reno NV 89503 *Web:* www.renochamberorchestra.org	775-348-9413	348-0643	573-3
Reno City Hall PO Box 1900 .... Reno NV 89505 *Web:* www.reno.gov	775-334-2030	334-2432	337
Reno Contracting Inc 7584 Metropolitan Dr Ste 100 .... San Diego CA 92108 *Web:* renocon.com	619-220-0224	220-0229	186
Reno County 206 W First St................. Hutchinson KS 67501 *Web:* renogov.org	620-694-2934	694-2534	338
Reno Gazette-Journal PO Box 22000 .... Reno NV 89520 *TF:* 800-970-7366 ■ *Web:* www.rgj.com	775-788-6397		532-2
Reno Machine Company Inc 170 Pane Rd.................................Newington CT 06111 *Web:* www.reno-machine.com	860-666-5641		455
Reno News & Review 760 Margrave Dr Ste 100 .... Reno NV 89502 *Web:* www.newsreview.com	775-324-4440	324-2515	532-5
Reno Philharmonic Orchestra 925 Riverside Dr Ste 3 .... Reno NV 89503 *Web:* www.renophil.com	775-323-6393	323-6711	573-3
RENO Refractories Inc 601 Reno Dr .... Morris AL 35116 *TF:* 800-741-7366 ■ *Web:* www.renorefractories.com	205-647-0240		663
RENO Refractories Inc Reftech Div 601 Reno Dr....................................Morris AL 35116 *TF General:* 800-741-7366 ■ *Web:* renorefractories.com	800-741-7366		663
Reno Rodeo Assn 1350 N Wells Ave............... Reno NV 89512 *Web:* www.ci.reno.nv.us	775-329-3877		720
Renodis Inc 476 Robert St N .... Saint Paul MN 55101 *TF:* 866-200-8986 ■ *Web:* www.renodis.com	651-556-1200		449

Name / Address	City	State	Zip	Phone	Fax	Class
Renoir Hotel 45 McAllister St	San Francisco	CA	94102	415-626-5200		707
TF: 800-576-3388 ■ *Web:* www.renoirhotel.com						
Renoir Staffing Services Inc 1301 Marina Vlg Pkwy Ste 350	Alameda	CA	94501	866-672-3709		260
TF: 866-672-3709 ■ *Web:* www.renoirstaffing.com						
Renold Ajax Inc 100 Bourne St	Westfield	NY	14787	716-326-3121	326-6121	620
TF: 800-251-9012 ■ *Web:* www.renold.com						
Renold Jeffrey 2307 Maden Dr	Morristown	TN	37813	423-586-1951	581-2399	207
TF: 800-251-9012 ■ *Web:* www.renoldjeffrey.com						
Reno-Sparks Convention & Visitors Authority PO Box 837	Reno	NV	89504	775-827-7600	827-7678	206
TF: 800-443-1482 ■ *Web:* www.visitrenotahoe.com						
Reno-Sparks Convention Ctr 4590 S Virginia St	Reno	NV	89502	775-827-7600	827-7701	205
TF: 800-367-7366 ■ *Web:* www.visitrenotahoe.com						
Reno-Tahoe International Airport 2001 E Plumb Ln	Reno	NV	89502	775-328-6400	328-6510	27
Web: www.renoairport.com						
Renova Lighting Systems Inc 36 Bellair Ave	Warwick	RI	02886	401-737-6700	737-6750	439
TF: 800-635-6682 ■ *Web:* www.renova.com						
Renovator's Supply Inc Renovators Old ML	Millers Falls	MA	01349	413-423-3300		350
TF: 800-659-2211 ■ *Web:* www.rensup.com						
Renown Regional Medical Ctr 1155 Mill St	Reno	NV	89502	775-982-4100		374-3
Web: www.renown.org						
RenoWorks Software Inc 2816 21 St NE	Calgary	AB	T2E6Z2	403-296-3880		177
TF: 877-980-3880 ■ *Web:* www.renoworks.com						
Renssearch 110 Eigth St	Troy	NY	12180	518-276-6000	276-8559	434-6
Web: library.rpi.edu						
Rensselaer County 1600 Seventh Ave	Troy	NY	12180	518-270-2900	270-2961	338
TF: 800-258-3582 ■ *Web:* www.rensco.com						
Rensselaer County Regional Chamber of Commerce 255 River St	Troy	NY	12180	518-274-7020	272-7729	139
Web: www.renscochamber.com						
Rensselaer Polytechnic Institute 110 Eigth St	Troy	NY	12180	518-276-6216	276-4072*	166
**Fax:* Admissions ■ *TF:* 800-433-4723 ■ *Web:* www.rpi.edu						
Rent A Tire 401 W Division	Arlington	TX	76011	817-795-5771		54
Web: www.rentatire.com						
Rent Rite 1260 E Higgins Rd	Elk Grove Village	IL	60007	847-640-8860	437-4402	264-2
Web: www.rentriteequipment.com						
Rent Rite Inc 7601 N Federal Hwy	Boca Raton	FL	33487	561-995-8832		23
Web: www.rentriterentals.com						
Rent-A-Center Inc 5501 Headquarters Dr	Plano	TX	75024	800-422-8186	943-0113*	264-2
NASDAQ: RCII ■ **Fax Area Code:* 972 ■ **Fax:* Cust Svc ■ *TF:* 800-422-8186 ■ *Web:* www.rentacenter.com/rent-a-center-home						
Rental Research Services Inc 7525 Mitchell Rd Ste 301	Eden Prairie	MN	55344	952-935-5700	935-9212	635
TF: 800-328-0333 ■ *Web:* www.rentalresearch.com						
Rentals Inc 3585 Engineering Dr	Norcross	GA	30092	888-501-7368		387
TF: 888-501-7368 ■ *Web:* www.rentals.com						
Rent-A-PC Inc 265 Oser Ave	Hauppauge	NY	11788	631-273-8888		264-1
TF: 800-888-8686 ■ *Web:* www.smartsourcerentals.com						
Rent-A-Wheel Custom Wheels & Tires in South Gate 2500 Firestone Blvd Ste G	South Gate	CA	90280	323-249-5668		54
Web: mobile.rentawheel.com						
rentbits.com Inc 383 Corona St Ste 301	Denver	CO	80218	303-640-3160		387
TF: 800-782-3452 ■ *Web:* rentbits.com						
Rentech Inc 10877 Wilshire Blvd 10th Fl	Los Angeles	CA	90024	310-571-9800	571-9799	579
NASDAQ: RTK ■ *Web:* www.rentechinc.com						
Rentenbach Constructors Inc 2400 Sutherland Ave	Knoxville	TN	37919	865-546-2440	546-3414	186
TF: 800-583-0148 ■ *Web:* www.rentenbach.com						
Renton Technical College 3000 NE Fourth St	Renton	WA	98056	425-235-2352	235-7832	162
Web: www.rtc.edu						
RentPath, LLC 950 East Paces Ferry Rd NE Ste 2600	Atlanta	GA	30326	678-421-3000		637-9
TF: 800-216-1423 ■ *Web:* rentpath.com						
Rentschler Field 615 Silver Ln	East Hartford	CT	06118	860-610-4700		31
TF: 800-245-8563 ■ *Web:* www.rentschlerfield.com						
Renville County PO Box 68	Mohall	ND	58761	701-756-6398	756-6494	338
Web: www.ndcourts.gov						
Renville County 500 E DePue Ave	Olivia	MN	56277	320-523-3663	523-3692	338
Web: www.renvillecountymn.com						
Renville-Sibley Co-op Power Assn 103 Oak St PO Box 68	Danube	MN	56230	320-826-2593		245
TF: 800-826-2593 ■ *Web:* www.renville-sibley.coop						
RenWeb School Management Software 101 E Renfro St Ste A	Burleson	TX	76028	866-800-6593		623
TF: 866-800-6593 ■ *Web:* www.renweb.com						
Renwick Gallery of the Smithsonian American Art Museum 1661 Pennsylvania Ave NW	Washington	DC	20006	202-633-7970		520
Web: americanart.si.edu/renwick						
Renzios Greek Food 1400 Dell Range Blvd	Cheyenne	WY	82007	307-637-5411		671
Web: renziosgreekfood.com						
Reo Hydraulics & Manufacturing 18475 Sherwood St	Detroit	MI	48234	313-891-2244		295
Web: www.regroup.com						
REO Plastics Inc 11850 93rd Ave N	Maple Grove	MN	55369	763-425-4171	425-0735	604
Web: www.reoplastics.com						
REOTEMP Instrument Corp 10656 Roselle St	San Diego	CA	92121	858-784-0710		201
Web: www.reotemp.com						
Rep Works Marketing LLC 1745 S Alma School Rd Ste 260	Mesa	AZ	85210	602-279-1987	279-1988	61
Web: www.repworksmktg.com						
Repairclinic.com Inc 48600 Michigan Ave	Canton	MI	48188	734-495-3079		351
TF: 800-269-2609 ■ *Web:* www.repairclinic.com						
Repairtech International Inc 16134 Saticoy St	Van Nuys	CA	91406	818-989-2681		359
Web: www.repairtechinternational.com						
Repanich & Clevenger CPA'S 12715 Bel Red Rd Ste 200	Bellevue	WA	98005	425-451-4019		2
Repeat Business Systems Inc 4 Fritz Blvd	Albany	NY	12205	518-869-8116		45
TF: 800-637-4264 ■ *Web:* www.repeatbusinesssystems.com						
Repeated Signal Solutions Inc 7127 Hollister Ave Ste 109	Goleta	CA	93117	805-685-6700		179
Web: www.repeatedsignal.com						
Repertory Dance Theatre 138 West 300 South	Salt Lake City	UT	84101	801-534-1000	534-1110	573-1
Web: www.xmission.com/~rdt						
Repertory Theatre of Saint Louis 130 Edgar Rd	Saint Louis	MO	63119	314-968-7340		573-4
Web: www.repstl.org						
Repete Plastics Inc 2633 Kaneville Ct	Geneva	IL	60134	630-208-4800		596
Repforce Inc 210 Turner Industrial Way	Aston	PA	19014	610-485-7800	364-0530	366
Web: repforce.com						
Replex Mirror Co 11 Mt Vernon Ave	Mount Vernon	OH	43050	740-397-5535		596
Web: www.replex.com						
Repligen Corp 41 Seyon St	Waltham	MA	02453	781-250-0111	250-0115	85
NASDAQ: RGEN ■ *TF Sales:* 800-622-2259 ■ *Web:* www.repligen.com						
Reply Inc 12667 Alcosta Blvd Ste 200	San Ramon	CA	94583	925-983-3400		4
Web: www.reply.eu/en						
Reporter 12247 S Harlem Ave	Palos Heights	IL	60463	708-448-6161	448-4012	532-2
Web: thereporteronline.net						
Reporter, The 916 Cotting Ln	Vacaville	CA	95688	707-448-6401		532-2
Web: www.thereporter.com						
Reporter, The 307 Derstine Ave	Lansdale	PA	19446	215-855-8440		532-2
Web: www.thereporteronline.com						
Reporting Systems Inc 2200 Rimland Dr Ste 305	Bellingham	WA	98226	360-647-6003		177
Web: www.emergencyreporting.com						
Repository 500 Market Ave S	Canton	OH	44702	330-580-8300	454-5745*	532-2
**Fax:* News Rm ■ *Web:* www.cantonrep.com						
REPP (Renewable Energy Policy Project) 1612 K St NW Ste 1200	Washington	DC	20006	202-293-2898		634
Representative of German Industry & Trade 1776 I St NW Ste 1000	Washington	DC	20006	202-659-4777	659-4779	138
Web: www.rgit-usa.com						
Reproduction Enterprises Inc 908 N Prairie Rd	Stillwater	OK	74075	405-377-8037	377-4541	11-2
TF: 866-734-2855 ■ *Web:* www.reproductionenterprises.com						
Reproductive Genetics Institute Inc 2825 N Halsted	Chicago	IL	60657	773-472-4900		415
Web: www.east-westmedical.net						
Repros Therapeutics Inc 2408 Timberloch Pl Ste B-7	The Woodlands	TX	77380	281-719-3400	719-3446	85
NASDAQ: RPRX ■ *TF:* 800-895-6554 ■ *Web:* www.reprosrx.com						
Repsco Inc 2950 Arkins Ct	Denver	CO	80216	303-294-0364		599
Web: www.repsco.com						
Republic Airways Holdings Inc 8909 PuRdue Rd Ste 300	Indianapolis	IN	46268	317-484-6000		360-1
NASDAQ: RJET ■ *Web:* rjet.com						
Republic Bancorp Inc 601 W Market St	Louisville	KY	40202	502-584-3600		360-2
NASDAQ: RBCAA ■ *TF:* 888-540-5363 ■ *Web:* www.republicbank.com						
Republic County 1815 M St Ste 2	Belleville	KS	66935	785-527-7236		338
Web: www.republiccounty.org						
Republic Finance 7031 Commerce Cir	Baton Rouge	LA	70809	225-927-0005		217
TF: 800-317-7662 ■ *Web:* www.republicfinance.com						
Republic Financial Corp 5251 DTC Pkwy Ste 300	Greenwood Village	CO	80111	303-751-3501		216
TF: 800-596-3608 ■ *Web:* www.republic-financial.com						
Republic First Bancorp Inc 50 S 16th St Ste 2400	Philadelphia	PA	19102	215-735-4422		360-2
NASDAQ: FRBK ■ *TF:* 888-875-2265 ■ *Web:* www.myrepublicbank.com						
Republic Foods Inc 1101 Wootton Pkwy Ste 460	Rockville	MD	20852	301-656-6687	656-3934	670
Web: www.republicfoods.com						
Republic Industries 1400 Warren Dri Plant 1	Marshall	TX	75672	903-935-3680		115
Web: www.republicind.com						
Republic Metals Corp 12900 NW 38th Ave	Miami	FL	33054	305-685-8505		410
TF: 888-685-8505 ■ *Web:* republicmetalscorp.com						
Republic Mortgage Insurance Co 101 N Cherry St Ste 101	Winston-Salem	NC	27101	800-999-7642		391-5
TF: 800-999-7642 ■ *Web:* www.rmic.com						
Republic National Distributing Co (RNDC) 6511 Tri County Pkwy	Schertz	TX	78154	210-224-7531		81-3
Web: www.rndc-usa.com						
Embassy of the Republic of Croatia in the United States 2343 Massachusetts Ave NW	Washington	DC	20008	202-588-5899		257
Web: www.croatiaemb.org						
Republic of Texas Bar & Grill 900 N Shoreline Blvd	Corpus Christi	TX	78401	361-887-1600	886-3530	671
Web: omnihotels.com						
Republic Packaging Corp 9160 S Green St	Chicago	IL	60620	773-233-6530	233-6005	601
Web: www.repco.com						
Republic Parking System 633 Chestnut St Ste 2000	Chattanooga	TN	37450	423-756-2771	265-5728	562
Web: www.republicparking.com						
Republic Plastics 355 SCHUMANN Rd	McQueeney	TX	78123	830-557-5574		600
TF: 800-334-4468 ■ *Web:* www.republicplastics.com						
Republic Plumbing Supply Company Inc 890 Providence Hwy	Norwood	MA	02062	800-696-3900	769-7842*	612
**Fax Area Code:* 781 ■ *TF:* 800-696-3900 ■ *Web:* www.republicsupplyco.com						
Republic Powdered Metals Inc 2628 Pearl Rd	Medina	OH	44256	800-382-1218		550
TF: 800-382-1218 ■ *Web:* www.tremcoroofing.com						
Republic Properties Corp 1280 MD Ave SW Ste 280	Washington	DC	20024	202-552-5300		653
Web: www.republicpropertiescorp.com						
Republic Services 1131 N Blue Gum St	Anaheim	CA	92806	714-238-3300	238-3304*	804
**Fax:* Hum Res ■ *TF:* 866-238-2444 ■ *Web:* republicservices.com						
Republic Services Inc 18500 N Allied	Phoenix	AZ	85054	480-627-2700		804
NYSE: RSG ■ *Web:* www.republicservices.com						

Phone | Fax | Class

Republic Services of Southern Nevada
770 E Sahara Ave .... Las Vegas NV 89193 — 702-735-5151 — 804
TF: 800-752-4092 ■ *Web:* www.republicservices.com

Republic Storage Systems LLC
1038 Belden Ave NE........ Canton OH 44705 — 330-438-5800 — 454-7772 — 286
TF Sales: 800-477-1255 ■ *Web:* www.republicstorage.com

Republic Western Insurance Co
2721 N Central Ave........ Phoenix AZ 85004 — 800-528-7134 — 745-6439* — 391-4
**Fax Area Code:* 602 ■ *TF Claims:* 800-528-7134 ■ *Web:* www.repwest.com

Republic, The 333 Second St .... Columbus IN 47201 — 812-372-7811 — 379-5711 — 532-2
TF: 800-876-7811 ■ *Web:* www.therepublic.com

Republica LLC
2153 Coral Way The Republica Bldg........ Miami FL 33145 — 786-347-4700 — 7
Web: republica.net

Republican Co 1860 Main St........ Springfield MA 01103 — 413-788-1000 — 788-1301 — 637-8
TF: 800-828-5597

Republican Governors Assn (RGA)
1747 Pennsylvania Ave NW Ste 250........ Washington DC 20006 — 202-662-4140 — 48-7
Web: www.rga.org

Republican National Committee (RNC)
310 First St SE........ Washington DC 20003 — 202-863-8500 — 616
TF: 800-445-5768 ■ *Web:* www.gop.com

Republican-American Inc
389 Meadow St........ Waterbury CT 06702 — 203-574-3636 — 596-9277 — 637-8
TF: 800-992-3232 ■ *Web:* www.rep-am.com

Republik, The 211 Rigsbee Ave........ Durham NC 27701 — 919-956-9400 — 7
Web: therepublik.net

Reputation Institute Inc
230 Park Ave 4th Fl Ste 453........ New York NY 10169 — 212-495-3855 — 466
Web: reputationinstitute.com

Reputation Rhino LLC
300 Park Ave 12th Fl........ New York NY 10022 — 888-975-3331 — 387
TF: 888-975-3331 ■ *Web:* reputationrhino.com

Request Foods Inc PO Box 2577........ Holland MI 49422 — 616-786-0900 — 786-9180 — 296-36
TF Sales: 800-969-2747 ■ *Web:* www.requestfoods.com

ReQuest Inc
100 Saratoga Village Blvd Ste 45........ Ballston Spa NY 12020 — 518-899-1254 — 899-1251* — 52
**Fax:* Sales ■ *TF Sales:* 800-236-2812 ■ *Web:* www.request.com

Requitest Inc 8614 N Bali Ct........ Ellicott City MD 21043 — 410-465-8637 — 809
Web: requitest.com/index.html

RES Exhibit Services LLC
435 Smith St........ Rochester NY 14608 — 585-546-2040 — 7
TF: 800-482-4049 ■ *Web:* www.res-exhibits.com

RES Mfg Company Inc 7801 N 73rd St........ Milwaukee WI 53223 — 414-354-4530 — 488
TF: 800-334-8044 ■ *Web:* www.resmfg.com

Resoan Environmental Services Ltd
1111 W Hastings St 6th Fl........ Vancouver BC V6E2J3 — 604-689-9460 — 256
Web: www.erm.com/en/locations/canada

Rescar Inc 1101 31st St Ste 250........ Downers Grove IL 60515 — 630-963-1114 — 963-6342 — 651
TF: 800-851-5196 ■ *Web:* www.rescar.com

Resco Plastics Inc 93783 Newport Ln........ Coos Bay OR 97420 — 541-269-5485 — 661
TF: 800-266-5097 ■ *Web:* www.rescoplastics.com

Resco Products Inc
2 Penn Ctr W Ste 430........ Pittsburgh PA 15276 — 412-494-4491 — 494-4571 — 662
TF: 888-283-5505 ■ *Web:* www.rescoproducts.com

Rescraft Plastic Products Inc
9 Woodslee Ave........ Paris ON N3L3V1 — 519-442-4339 — 000
TF: 800-683-4116 ■ *Web:* www.rescraft.com

Rescuecom Corp 2560 Burnet Ave........ Syracuse NY 13206 — 800-737-2837 — 433-5228* — 310
**Fax Area Code:* 315 ■ *TF:* 800-737-2837 ■ *Web:* www.rescuecom.com

Research & Development Solutions Inc
7921 Jones Branch Dr........ Mclean VA 22102 — 703-893-9533 — 261
Web: rdsi.com

Research & Diagnostic Antibodies
2645 W Cheyenne Ave........ North Las Vegas NV 89032 — 702-638-7800 — 638-7801 — 231
TF: 800-858-7322 ■ *Web:* www.rdabs.com

Research & Innovative Technology Administration (RITA)
1200 New Jersey Ave SE........ Washington DC 20590 — 202-366-7582 — 366-3759 — 340-17
TF: 800-853-1351 ■ *Web:* www.rita.dot.gov

Bureau of Transportation Statistics
1200 New Jersey Ave SE........ Washington DC 20590 — 202-366-1270 — 340-17
TF: 800-853-1351 ■ *Web:* www.rita.dot.gov

Office of Research, Development & Technology Programs and Activities
1200 New Jersey Ave SE........ Washington DC 20590 — 800-853-1351 — 366-3759* — 340-17
**Fax Area Code:* 202 ■ *TF:* 800-853-1351 ■ *Web:* www.rita.dot.gov/rdt

Volpe National Transportation Systems Ctr
55 Broadway........ Cambridge MA 02142 — 617-494-2000 — 340-17
Web: www.volpe.dot.gov

Research Assoc Inc 27999 Clemens Rd........ Cleveland OH 44145 — 440-892-9439 — 892-9439 — 400
TF: 800-255-9693 ■ *Web:* www.researchassociatesinc.com

Research Corp
4703 E Camp Lowell Dr Ste 201........ Tucson AZ 85712 — 520-571-1111 — 571-1119 — 305
Web: www.rescorp.org

Research Corp Technologies
101 N Wilmot Rd Ste 600........ Tucson AZ 85711 — 520-748-4400 — 748-0025 — 792
Web: www.rctech.com

Research Data Inc 3900 Carolina Ave........ Richmond VA 23222 — 804-643-3468 — 180
Web: www.researchdata.com

Research Director Inc
914 Bay Ridge Rd Ste 215........ Annapolis MD 21403 — 410-295-6619 — 268-1915 — 466
Web: www.researchdirectorinc.com

Research Electro-optics Inc
5505 Airport Blvd........ Boulder CO 80301 — 303-938-1960 — 245-4396 — 544
Web: www.reoinc.com

Research First Consulting Inc
8 Mockingbird Ln........ Gulfport MS 39507 — 205-995-8866 — 737
Web: www.researchfirst.com

Research for Good Inc
1037 NE 65th St Ste 80212........ Seattle WA 98115 — 425-610-7294 — 466
Web: www.researchforgood.com

Research Foundation of City University of New York, The
230 W 41st St 7th Fl........ New York NY 10036 — 212-417-8300 — 668
Web: www.rfcuny.org

Research Frontiers Inc
240 Crossways Park Dr........ Woodbury NY 11797 — 516-364-1902 — 544
Web: www.smartglass.com

Research Horizons LLC
6423 Montgomery St Ste 12........ Rhinebeck NY 12572 — 845-876-8228 — 4
Web: www.phoenixmi.com

Research Inc 7128 Shady Oak Rd........ Eden Prairie MN 55344 — 952-941-3300 — 941-3628 — 201
Web: pcscontrols.com

Research Institute on Addictions (RIA)
1021 Main St........ Buffalo NY 14203 — 716-887-2566 — 887-2252 — 668
TF: 800-729-6686 ■ *Web:* buffalo.edu/ria.html

Research into Action Inc
3934 NE Mlking Jr Blvd Ste 300........ Portland OR 97212 — 503-287-9136 — 196
TF: 888-492-9100 ■ *Web:* researchintoaction.com

Research Laboratory of Electronics
Massachusetts Institute of Technology
77 Massachusetts Ave........ Cambridge MA 02139 — 617-253-2519 — 253-1301 — 668
Web: www.rle.mit.edu

Research Management Consultants Inc
816 Camarillo Springs Rd Ste J........ Camarillo CA 93012 — 805-987-5538 — 987-2868 — 261
Web: www.rmci.com

Research Medical Ctr
2316 E Meyer Blvd........ Kansas City MO 64132 — 816-276-4000 — 374-3
Web: researchmedicalcenter.com

Research on Demand Inc
2629 State St........ Santa Barbara CA 93105 — 805-963-4095 — 387

Research Products Corp
1015 E Washington Ave........ Madison WI 53703 — 608-257-8801 — 257-4357 — 17
TF: 800-334-6011 ■ *Web:* www.aprilaire.com

Research Psychiatric Ctr
2323 E 63rd St........ Kansas City MO 64130 — 816-444-8161 — 374-5
Web: researchpsychiatriccenter.com

Research Solutions Inc
5435 Balboa Blvd Ste 202........ Encino CA 91316 — 310-477-0354 — 466
Web: www.reprintsdesk.com

Research Technology International Inc
4700 W Chase Ave........ Lincolnwood IL 60712 — 847-677-3000 — 677-1311 — 591
TF Sales: 800-323-7520 ■ *Web:* www.rti-us.com

Research to Prevent Blindness Inc (RPB)
360 Lexington Ave 22nd Fl........ New York NY 10017 — 212-752-4333 — 688-6231 — 48-17
TF: 800-621-0026 ■ *Web:* www.rpbusa.org

Research Triangle Institute
3040 Cornwallis Rd
PO Box 12194........ Research Triangle Park NC 27709 — 919-541-6000 — 541-5985 — 668
TF: 800-334-8571 ■ *Web:* www.rti.org

Research Triangle Park Laboratories
7201 Acc Blvd # 104........ Raleigh NC 27617 — 919-510-0228 — 510-0141 — 85
Web: www.rtp-labs.com

Research Wizard of Tulsa City-County Library
400 Civic Ctr........ Tulsa OK 74103 — 918-596-7991 — 596-2598 — 387
TF: 800-463-3339 ■ *Web:* www.researchwizard.org

Research!America
241 18th St S Ste 501........ Arlington VA 22314 — 703-739-2577 — 739-2372 — 48-5
Web: www.researchamerica.org

Reser's Fine Foods Inc
15570 SW Jenkins Rd........ Beaverton OR 97006 — 503-643-6431 — 296-33
TF: [illegible] ■ *Web:* www.resers.com

Reserve Casino Hotel
321 Gregory St........ Central City CO 80427 — 303-582-0800 — 133
TF: 800-924-6646 ■ *Web:* www.reservecasinohotel.com

Reserve National Insurance Co
601 E Britton Rd........ Oklahoma City OK 73114 — 405-848-7931 — 391-2
Web: www.reservenational.com

Reserve Officers Assn of the US (ROA)
1 Constitution Ave NE........ Washington DC 20002 — 202-479-2200 — 547-1641 — 40 10
TF: 800-809-9448 ■ *Web:* www.roa.org

Reserve Petroleum Co
6801 Broadway Ext Ste 300........ Oklahoma City OK 73116 — 405-848-7551 — 536
TF: 800-690-6903 ■ *Web:* www.reserve-petro.com

Reserve Telephone Company Inc
PO Box T........ Reserve LA 70084 — 985-536-1111 — 536-4815 — 736
TF: 888-611-6111 ■ *Web:* www.rtconline.com

ReserveAmerica Holdings Inc
2480 Meadowvale Blvd Ste 120........ Mississauga ON L5N8M6 — 877-444-6777 — 286-0371* — 773
**Fax Area Code:* 905 ■ *TF:* 877-444-6777 ■ *Web:* www.reserveamerica.com

Reservoir State Park
c/o Niagara Frontier Region
PO Box 1132........ Niagara Falls NY 14303 — 716-284-4691 — 565
Web: parks.ny.gov/parks/75/details.aspx

Reshape Medical
100 Calle Iglesia........ San Clemente CA 92672 — 844-937-7374 — 475
TF: 844-937-7374 ■ *Web:* reshapeready.com

Residence & Conference Centre - Toronto
1760 Finch Ave E........ Toronto ON M2J5G3 — 416-491-8811 — 491-0486 — 379
TF: 877-225-8664 ■ *Web:* www.stayrcc.com

Residence Inn Mystic 40 Whitehall Ave........ Mystic CT 06355 — 860-536-5150 — 707
TF: 800-450-4442 ■ *Web:* www.lakesregion.org

Residences on Georgia
101-1288 W Georgia St........ Vancouver BC V6E4R3 — 604-891-6101 — 891-6103 — 379
Web: www.respal.com

Residential Control Systems
11481 Sunrise Gold Cir Ste 1........ Rancho Cordova CA 95742 — 916-635-6784 — 635-7668 — 202
TF: 888-727-4822 ■ *Web:* www.rcstechnology.com

Residential Mortgage LLC
100 Calais Dr........ Anchorage AK 99503 — 907-222-8800 — 222-8801 — 509
TF: 888-357-2707 ■ *Web:* www.residentialmtg.com

Resilite Sports Products PO Box 764........ Sunbury PA 17801 — 800-843-6287 — 473-8988* — 710
**Fax Area Code:* 570 ■ *TF:* 800-843-6287 ■ *Web:* www.resilite.com

Resilux America LLC
265 John Brooks Rd........ Pendergrass GA 30567 — 706-693-7110 — 601
Web: www.uniqueplastics.com

Resin Systems Corp 62 Rt 101a........ Amherst NH 03031 — 603-673-1234 — 673-4512 — 610
Web: www.resinsystems.com

Resin Technology Group
28 Norfolk Ave........ South Easton MA 02375 — 508-230-8070 — 3
Web: www.resintek.com

Resina West Inc 27455 Bostik Ct........ Temecula CA 92590 — 951-296-6585 — 296-5018 — 298
TF: 800-207-4804 ■ *Web:* www.resina.com

Resinall Corp PO Box 195........ Severn NC 27877 — 800-421-0561 — 605-2
TF: 800-421-0561 ■ *Web:* www.resinall.com

Resinart East Inc 201 Old Airport Rd........ Fletcher NC 28732 — 828-687-0215 — 596
Web: east.resinart.com

Resinoid Engineering Corp
251 O'Neill Dr........ Hebron OH 43025 — 740-928-6115 — 596
Web: www.resinoid.com

	Phone	Fax	Class

ResMed Inc 9001 Spectrum Ctr Blvd.......... San Diego CA 92123 858-836-5000 836-5501 476
NYSE: RMD ■ *TF:* 800-424-0737 ■ *Web:* www.resmed.com

RESNA (Rehabilitation Engineering & Assistive Technology Society of North America)
1700 N Moore St Ste 1540.................. Arlington VA 22209 703-524-6686 524-6630 48-17
Web: www.resna.org

Resnet 1119 Brentfield Dr..................... Mc Lean VA 22101 703-506-0203 506-0205 180
Web: www.resnet.org

Resolute Energy Corp
1700 N Lincoln St Ste 2800.................. Denver CO 80203 303-534-4600 536
Web: www.resoluteenergy.com

RESOLUTE Partners LLC
37 W Center St Ste 301.................. Southington CT 06489 860-628-6800 225
Web: www.resolutepartners.com

Resolute Systems Inc
1550 N Prospect Ave..................... Milwaukee WI 53202 414-276-4774 270-0932 41
TF: 800-776-6060 ■ *Web:* www.resolutesystems.com

Resolute Technology Solutions Inc
433 Main St Ste 600....................... Winnipeg MB R3B1B3 204-927-3520 177
Web: www.resolutets.com

Resolution Digital Studios
2226 W Walnut St.......................... Chicago IL 60612 312-846-4226 514
TF: 800-603-8860 ■ *Web:* www.rdschicago.com

Resolve Inc 1255 23rd St NW Ste 275........ Washington DC 20037 202-944-2300 196
Web: www.resolv.org

RESOLVE Partners LLC
2010 New Garden Rd...................... Greensboro NC 27410 336-346-3095 41
Web: www.resolve-partners.com

Resolve Tech Solutions Inc
15851 N Dallas Pkwy Ste 1103................ Addison TX 75001 214-310-1020 310-1021 463
Web: resolvetech.com

RESOLVE: National Infertility Assn
1760 Old Meadow Rd Ste 500................ McLean VA 22102 703-556-7172 506-3266 48-17
TF: 888-592-4449 ■ *Web:* www.resolve.org

Resort 2 Me 975 Cass St.................. Monterey CA 93940 831-642-6622 376
TF: 800-757-5646 ■ *Web:* www.resort2me.com

Resort at Port Arrowhead, The
3080 Bagnell Dam Blvd PO Box 1930........ Lake Ozark MO 65049 573-365-2334 365-6887 669
TF: 800-532-3575 ■ *Web:* theresortatportarrowhead.com

Resort at Seabrook Island
3772 Seabrook Island Rd.............. Seabrook Island SC 29455 843-768-2500 669
Web: www.discoverseabrook.com

Resort at Squaw Creek
400 Squaw Creek Rd PO Box 3333........ Olympic Valley CA 96146 530-583-6300 581-6632 669
TF: 800-327-3353 ■ *Web:* www.destinationhotels.com/squawcreek

Resort Condominiums International (RCI)
9998 N Michigan Rd......................... Carmel IN 46032 317-805-8000 753
TF: 800-338-7777 ■ *Web:* www.rci.com

Resort Data Processing Inc 211 Eagle Rd......... Avon CO 81620 970-845-1140 177
TF: 877-779-3717 ■ *Web:* www.resortdata.com

Resort Internet
719 Ten Mile Dr PO Box 2718 ste A.............. Frisco CO 80443 970-262-3515 455-3069 387
Web: www.resortinternet.com

Resort Parks International
2901 Cherry Ave......................... Signal Hill CA 90755 562-595-8818 194
TF: 800-635-8498 ■ *Web:* resortparks.com

Resort Semiahmoo 9565 Semiahmoo Pkwy........ Blaine WA 98230 360-318-2000 318-2087 669
TF: 855-917-3767 ■ *Web:* www.semiahmoo.com

Resort Sports Network
Outside Television
33 Riverside Ave 4th Fl................. Westport CT 06880 203-221-9240 740
TF: 888-795-9488 ■ *Web:* www.outsidetelevision.com

Resorts Casino Hotel
1133 Boardwalk......................... Atlantic City NJ 08401 800-334-6378 669
TF: 800-334-6378 ■ *Web:* www.resortsac.com

Resorts of the Canadian Rockies Inc
1505 17th Ave SW.......................... Calgary AB T2T0E2 403-254-7669 378
TF: 800-258-7669 ■ *Web:* www.skircr.com

Resource & Financial Management Systems Inc
3073 Palisades Ct......................... Tuscaloosa AL 35405 800-701-7367 177
TF: 800-701-7367 ■ *Web:* www.rfms.com

Resource Capital Corp
712 Fifth Ave 12th Fl....................... New York NY 10019 212-506-3899 245-6372 654
NYSE: RSO ■ *Web:* www.resourcecapitalcorp.com

Resource Connection Inc
161 S Main St............................. Middleton MA 01949 978-777-9333 777-3360 184
TF: 800-649-5228 ■ *Web:* www.resource-connection.com

Resource Ctr for Assns
10200 W 44th Ave Ste 304............... Wheat Ridge CO 80033 303-422-2615 47

Resource Data Inc
560 E 34th Ave Ste 100................... Anchorage AK 99503 907-563-8100 177
Web: www.resdat.com

Resource Development Corp
280 Daines St Ste 200................... Birmingham MI 48009 248-646-2300 646-0789 39
TF: 800-360-7222 ■ *Web:* www.resourcedev.com

Resource Foundation, The
237 W 35th St Ste 1203.................... New York NY 10001 212-675-6170 268-5325 48-5
Web: www.resourcefnd.org

Resource Inc 1900 Chicago Ave S.......... Minneapolis MN 55404 612-752-8000 752-8001 48-5
Web: www.resource-mn.org

Resource Land Holdings LLC
1530 16th St Ste 300........................ Denver CO 80202 720-723-2850 360-3
Web: www.rlholdings.com

Resource Management Inc
281 Main St Ste 5......................... Fitchburg MA 01420 800-508-0048 631
TF Cust Svc: 800-508-0048 ■ *Web:* www.rmi-solutions.com

Resource Management Service LLC
31 Inverness Ctr Pkwy Ste 360............ Birmingham AL 35242 800-995-9516 991-2807* 302
**Fax Area Code: 205* ■ *TF:* 800-995-9516 ■ *Web:* www.resourcemgt.com

Resource Mfg
7033 Commonwealth Ave Ste 4............ Jacksonville FL 32220 904-693-3686 260
Web: www.resourcemfg.com

Resource Plus 9636 Heckscher Dr........... Jacksonville FL 32226 888-678-8966 345
TF: 888-678-8966 ■ *Web:* www.resourcep.com

Resource Technology Management Inc
251 Maitland Av Ste 215.................... Maitland FL 32701 407-998-8000 225
Web: www.rtm-inc.com

Resources Applications Designs & Controls Inc
3220 E 59th St......................... Long Beach CA 90805 562-272-7231 261

Resources For Living Ltd
4407 Monterey Oaks Blvd..................... Austin TX 78749 512-358-8400 194
Web: www.resourcesforliving.com/login.aspx

Resources for the Future
1616 P St NW........................... Washington DC 20036 202-328-5000 939-3460 634
Web: www.rff.org

Resources Global Professionals
17101 Armstrong Ave.......................... Irvine CA 92614 714-430-6400 721
NASDAQ: RECN ■ *TF:* 800-900-1131 ■ *Web:* www.rgp.com

Resources Unlimited Co
7931 NW 54th Ave.......................... Johnston IA 50131 515-270-0694 193
Web: www.resourcesunlimited.com

Resourcing Edge Inc
1309 Ridge Rd Ste 200...................... Rockwall TX 75087 214-771-4411 734
Web: www.resourcingedge.com

Respec Inc 3824 Jet Dr.................... Rapid City SD 57703 605-394-6400 394-6456 261
Web: www.respec.com

Respira Medical
809 Pinnacle Dr Ste R...................... Linthicum MD 21090 443-200-0055 194
Web: www.respiramedical.com

Respironics Novametrix LLC
5 Technology Dr......................... Wallingford CT 06492 724-387-4000 250
TF: 800-345-6443 ■ *Web:* www.respironics.com

Respondus Inc
8201 164th Ave NE Ste 200 PO Box 3247....... Redmond WA 98052 425-497-0389 225
Web: www.respondus.com

Response Biomedical Corp
1781 75th Ave W.......................... Vancouver BC V6P6P2 604-456-6010 456-6066 419
TSE: RBM ■ *TF:* 888-591-5577 ■ *Web:* www.responsebio.com

Response Design Corp
5541 Simpson Ave....................... Ocean City NJ 08226 888-204-3833 196
TF: 888-204-3833 ■ *Web:* www.responsedesign.com

Response Envelope Inc
1340 S Baker Ave........................... Ontario CA 91761 909-923-5855 923-3639 263
TF: 800-750-0046 ■ *Web:* www.response-envelope.com

Response Staffing Solutions Inc
56 W 45th St 16th Fl....................... New York NY 10036 212-983-8870 260
Web: www.responseco.com

Ressler Motor Co 8474 Huffine Ln........... Bozeman MT 59718 406-587-5501 516
Web: www.resslermotors.com

Rest Haven-York 1050 S George St................ York PA 17403 717-843-9866 846-5894 450
TF: 800-368-1019 ■ *Web:* www.resthavenyork.com

Rest Ministries Inc PO Box 502928........... San Diego CA 92150 858-486-4685 48-21
Web: www.restministries.com

Rest-a-Phone Corp
2801 NW Lower River Rd Ste A.............. Vancouver WA 98660 503-235-6778 608
Web: www.abcplas.com

Restaurant & Stores Equipment Co
230 West 700 South..................... Salt Lake City UT 84101 801-364-1981 300
TF: 800-877-0087 ■ *Web:* rescoslc.com

Restaurant Assoc Inc
132 W 31st St Ste 601...................... New York NY 10001 212-613-5500 670
Web: www.restaurantassociates.com

Restaurant at the Phoenix
812 Race St............................ Cincinnati OH 45202 513-721-8901 671
Web: www.thephx.com/restaurant

Restaurant Aviatic Club
450 de la Gare-du-Palais..................... Quebec QC G1K3X2 418-522-3555 671

Restaurant Beffroi Steak House
775 Honore-Mercier Ave...................... Quebec QC G1R6A5 418-380-2638 671
Web: beffroisteakhouse.com

Restaurant Bouchard 505 Thames St........... Newport RI 02840 401-846-0123 841-8565 671
Web: bouchardnewport.com

Restaurant Bricco 78 LaSalle Rd........... West Hartford CT 06107 860-233-0220 671
Web: www.billygrant.com

Restaurant Chez Rabelais
2 Rue Du Petit-Champlain.................... Quebec QC G1K4H5 418-522-3240 671

Restaurant Developers Corp
7010 Engle Rd Ste 100..................... Cleveland OH 44130 440-625-3080 670
TF: 888-860-5082 ■ *Web:* www.mrhero.com

Restaurant Eve 110 S Pitt St................. Alexandria VA 22314 703-706-0450 671
Web: www.restauranteve.com

Restaurant Gandhi
230 Rue St Paul Oeust....................... Montreal QC H2Y1Z9 514-845-5866 671
Web: www.restaurantgandhi.com

Restaurant Gary Danko
800 N Pt St........................... San Francisco CA 94109 415-749-2060 671
Web: www.garydanko.com

Restaurant Jano Grillades
3883 St-Laurent Blvd....................... Montreal QC H2W1X9 514-849-0646 671

Restaurant L'Initiale 54 St-Pierre St............ Quebec QC G1K4A1 418-694-1818 694-2387 671
Web: restaurantinitiale.com

Restaurant Mysore 4216 St Laurent............ Montreal QC H2W1Z3 514-844-4733 671
Web: www.mysoreindiancuisine.ca

Restaurant Partners Inc
1030 N Orange Ave Ste 200................... Orlando FL 32801 407-839-5070 839-3388 463
Web: www.restaurantpartnersinc.com

Restaurant School at Walnut Hill College
4207 Walnut St......................... Philadelphia PA 19104 215-222-4200 163
TF: 877-925-6884 ■ *Web:* www.walnuthillcollege.edu

Restaurant Solutions Inc
1423 Austell Rd........................... Marietta GA 30008 770-421-1999 45
TF: 800-537-4021 ■ *Web:* www.restaurantsolutionsinc.com

Restaurant Technologies Inc
2250 Pilot Knob Rd Ste 100........... Mendota Heights MN 55120 651-796-1600 379-4082 300
TF: 888-796-4997 ■ *Web:* www.rti-inc.com

Restaurant Zoe 1318 E Union St................. Seattle WA 98122 206-226-2010 671
Web: zoeseattle.com

Restaurants Unlimited Inc
411 First Ave S Ste 200...................... Seattle WA 98104 206-634-0550 670
TF: 877-855-6106 ■ *Web:* www.r-u-i.com

Restek Corp 110 Benner Cir................. Bellefonte PA 16823 814-353-1300 201
Web: www.restek.com

Restless Legs Syndrome Foundation Inc
1610 14th St NW Ste 300................... Rochester MN 55901 507-287-6465 287-6312 48-17
TF: 877-463-6757 ■ *Web:* www.rls.org

Resto Gare 630 Des Meurons St.............. Winnipeg MB R2H2P9 204-237-7072 671
Web: www.restogare.com

Name / Address	City	State	ZIP	Phone	Fax	Class
Reston Hospital Ctr 1850 Town Ctr Pkwy *TF General:* 888-327-8882 ■ *Web:* www.restonhospital.com	Reston	VA	20190	703-689-9000		374-3
Restonic Mattress 201 James E Casey Dr *TF:* 800-898-6075 ■ *Web:* www.restonic.com	Buffalo	NY	14206	716-895-1414		471
Restonic Mattress Corp 737 Main St *TF:* 800-898-6075 ■ *Web:* www.restonic.com	Buffalo	NY	14203	800-898-6075		471
Restoration Hardware Inc 2900 N MacArthur Dr Ste 100 *TF:* 800-910-9836 ■ *Web:* www.restorationhardware.com	Tracy	CA	95376	800-910-9836		362
Result Data Consulting Ltd 110 Polaris Pkwy *Web:* www.resultdata.com	Westerville	OH	43082	614-505-0770	505-0779	809
Resultly LLC 116 W Hubbard St Fl 4 *Web:* www.result.ly	Chicago	IL	60654	312-273-9400		387
RESULTS 750 First St NE Ste 1040 *Web:* www.results.org	Washington	DC	20002	202-783-7100	783-2818	48-5
Results Radio LLC 1355 N Dutton Ave Ste 225	Santa Rosa	CA	95401	707-546-9185		643
Results Telemarketing Inc 100 NE Third Ave Ste 200 *Web:* www.resultstel.com	Fort Lauderdale	FL	33301	954-921-2400	923-8070	737
Results Travel 701 Carlson Pkwy *TF:* 800-456-4000 ■ *Web:* www.carlson.com	Minnetonka	MN	55305	763-212-5000		310
Results:Digital LLC 91 Montvale Ave Ste 104 *Web:* resultsdigital.com	Stoneham	MA	02180	617-250-8580		5
RESUMate Inc 2500 Packard St Ste 200 *TF Cust Svc:* 800-530-9310 ■ *Web:* www.resumate.com	Ann Arbor	MI	48104	734-477-9402		178-10
Resume Solutions 1033 Bay St Ste 317 *TF:* 866-361-1290 ■ *Web:* www.resumesolutions.ca	Toronto	ON	M5S3A5	416-361-1290		41
Resurrection Medical Ctr 7435 W Talcott Ave *Web:* www.presencehealth.org	Chicago	IL	60631	773-774-8000		374-3
Resuscitation International LLC 17797 N Perimeter Dr Ste 105 *Web:* resusintl.com	Scottsdale	AZ	85255	480-240-9495		743
Retail Benefits Inc 9403 Caserta St *TF:* 866-904-6044 ■ *Web:* retailbenefits.com	Lake Worth	FL	33467	866-904-6044		5
Retail Computer Group LLC, The 8194 Traphagen St NW *TF:* 800-944-0917 ■ *Web:* www.trcgllc.com	Massillon	OH	44646	800-944-0917		525
Retail Concepts Inc 10560 Bissonnet St Ste 100 *Web:* www.retailconcepts.cc	Stafford	TX	77099	281-340-5000		711
Retail Confectioners International (RCI) 2053 S Waverly Ste C *TF:* 800-545-5381 ■ *Web:* www.retailconfectioners.org	Springfield	MO	65804	417-883-2775	883-1108	49-6
Retail Construction Services Inc (RCS) 11343 39th St N *Web:* www.retailconstruction.com	Lake Elmo	MN	55042	651-704-9000	704-9100	685
Retail Equation Inc, The 6430 Oak Canyon *TF:* 800-577-7891 ■ *Web:* www.theretailequation.com	Irvine	CA	92618	949-262-5100		396
Retail Industry Leaders Assn (RILA) 1700 N Moore St Ste 2250 *TF:* 800-758-5840 ■ *Web:* www.rila.org	Arlington	VA	22209	703-841-2300	841-1184	49-18
Retail Planning Corp 35 Johnson Ferry Rd *Web:* www.retailplanningcorp.com	Marietta	GA	30068	770-956-8383		652
Retail Pro International LLC 400 Plaza Dr Ste 200 *OTC:* RTPRQ ■ *TF:* 800-738-2457 ■ *Web:* www.retailpro.com	Folsom	CA	95630	916-605-7200		178-10
Retail Resource Group International LLC 226 New Gate Loop *Web:* www.mybevi.com/products	Lake Mary	FL	32746	407-878-6650	732-4565	601
Retail Solutions Providers Assn (RSPA) 10130 Perimeter Pkwy Ste 420 *TF:* 800-782-2693 ■ *Web:* www.gorspa.org	Charlotte	NC	28216	704-357-3124	357-3127	49-18
Retail Systems Research LLC 8725 NE 10 Ct *Web:* www.rsrresearch.com	Miami	FL	33138	305-757-1357		466
Retail Traffic 249 W 17th St *Web:* nreionline.com	New York	NY	10011	212-204-4200		457-21
RetailMLS LLC 12 W 23rd St *Web:* retailmls.com	New York	NY	10010	212-729-1041		387
Retama Park 1 Retama Pkwy *Web:* www.retamapark.com	Selma	TX	78154	210-651-7000		642
RETax Funding PO Box 100350 *TF:* 877-320-5779 ■ *Web:* www.retaxfunding.com	San Antonio	TX	78201	866-206-9310		194
Retech Systems LLC 100 Henry Stn Rd *Web:* www.retechsystemsllc.com	Ukiah	CA	95482	707-462-6522		386
RETEL Services Inc 5871 Glenridge Dr NE Ste 110 *Web:* www.retelservices.com	Atlanta	GA	30328	404-343-2375		256
Rethink Autism Inc 19 W 21st St Ste 403 *Web:* www.rethinkfirst.com	New York	NY	10010	646-257-2919		177
Rethink Innovations 118 Burrs Rd Ste C1 *Web:* www.myrethink.com	Westampton	NJ	08060	609-784-8427		317
Retif Oil & Fuel Inc 527 Destrehan Ave *TF:* 800-349-9000 ■ *Web:* www.retif.com	Harvey	LA	70058	800-349-9000		579
Retina Consultants of Oklahoma 9821 S May Ave Ste C *Web:* retinaconsultantsoklahoma.com	Oklahoma City	OK	73159	405-691-0505		543
Retired & Senior Volunteer Program (RSVP) 1201 New York Ave NW *TF:* 800-833-3722 ■ *Web:* www.nationalservice.gov	Washington	DC	20525	202-606-5000		197
Retired Enlisted Assn (TREA) 15821 E Centre Tech Cir *Web:* www.trea.org	Aurora	CO	80011	303-340-3939	340-4516	48-19
Retirement Advantage Inc, The 47 Park Pl Ste 850 *TF:* 888-872-2364 ■ *Web:* www.tra401k.com	Appleton	WI	54914	888-872-2364		463
Retirement Investment Advisors Inc 3001 United Founders Blvd Ste A *Web:* www.theretirementpath.com	Oklahoma City	OK	73112	405-842-3443	842-3471	401
Retirement Plan Advisors LLC 105 W Adams St Ste 2175 *Web:* www.retirementplanadvisors.com	Chicago	IL	60603	312-701-1100		401
Retirement Research Foundation 8765 W Higgins Rd Ste 430 *TF:* 800-222-2225 ■ *Web:* www.rrf.org	Chicago	IL	60631	773-714-8080	714-8089	305
Retirement System Group Inc 317 Madison Ave 18th Fl	New York	NY	10017	212-503-0100		401
Retlif Inc Testing Laboratories 795 Marconi Ave *TF:* 800-992-4199 ■ *Web:* www.retlif.com	Ronkonkoma	NY	11779	631-737-1500	737-1497	743
Retractable Technologies Inc 511 Lobo Ln *NYSE:* RVP ■ *TF:* 888-806-2626 ■ *Web:* www.vanishpoint.com	Little Elm	TX	75068	972-294-1010	292-3600	477
Retreat Doctors' Hospital 2621 Grove Ave *TF:* 877-330-4290 ■ *Web:* hcavirginia.com	Richmond	VA	23220	804-254-5100		374-3
Retreat Spa & Salon LLC 4246 Washington Rd *Web:* retreatspaandsalon.com	Evans	GA	30809	706-364-8292		77
Retrievex Inc 4 First Ave *Web:* www.retrievex.com	Peabody	MA	01960	978-539-3350		463
Retrocom Energy Strategies Inc 2378 Maritime Dr Ste 110 *TF:* 800-378-2177 ■ *Web:* www.retrostrategies.com	Elk Grove	CA	95758	916-226-6415		261
Rettew Assoc Inc 3020 Columbia Ave *TF:* 800-738-8395 ■ *Web:* www.rettew.com	Lancaster	PA	17603	717-394-3721	394-1063	261
Return Management Services Inc 800 Berkshire Ln N *Web:* www.rmsincorporated.com	Plymouth	MN	55441	952-475-0242		463
Return Path Inc 3 Park Ave 41st Fl *Web:* www.returnpath.com	New York	NY	10016	212-905-5500	905-5501	7
Reuben & Junius LLP 1 Bush St Ste 600 *Web:* www.reubenlaw.com	San Francisco	CA	94104	415-567-9000		428
Reuben H Fleet Science Ctr 1875 El Prado *TF:* 800-310-7106 ■ *Web:* www.rhfleet.org	San Diego	CA	92101	619-238-1233	685-5771	520
Reuben Mc Millan Free Library Association Inc, The 305 Wick Ave *Web:* www.libraryvisit.org	Youngstown	OH	44503	330-744-8636		434-3
Reuland Electric Co 17969 E Railroad St *Web:* www.reuland.com	Industry	CA	91748	626-854-5193		518
Reunion Power LLC 310 Hudson St Ste 2A-B	Hackensack	NJ	07601	201-546-7722		196
Reunion Tower 300 Reunion Blvd E *TF:* 800-880-2336 ■ *Web:* www.reuniontower.com	Dallas	TX	75207	214-651-1234		671
Reuter Organ Co 1220 Timberedge Rd *TF:* 800-827-6710 ■ *Web:* www.reuterorgan.com	Lawrence	KS	66049	785-843-2622	843-3302	527
Reuther Mold & Mfg Co 1225 Munroe Falls Ave *TF:* 800-923-5266 ■ *Web:* www.reuthermold.com	Cuyahoga Falls	OH	44221	330-923-5266	923-9930	757
Rev Rocket, LLC 9000 Executive Pk Dr Bldg D Ste 300 *Web:* foxville43.revrocket.us	Knoxville	TN	37923	865-693-4343	691-6904	741-69
Rev.com Inc 251 Kearny St 8th Fl *TF:* 888-369-0701 ■ *Web:* www.rev.com/translation	San Francisco	CA	94108	888-369-0701		393
REVA Air Ambulance Inc 1745 NW 51 Pl Hngr 73 *Web:* www.flyreva.com	Fort Lauderdale	FL	33309	954-730-9300		30
Reva Capital Markets LLC 45 Broadway 8th Fl *Web:* www.revacap.com	New York	NY	10025	212-464-7363		690
REVA Medical Inc 5751 Copley Dr *Web:* www.revamedical.com	San Diego	CA	92111	858-966-3000		477
Revana Inc 8123 S Hardy Dr *TF:* 800-535-0343 ■ *Web:* www.revana.com	Tempe	AZ	85284	480-902-5900		174
Revcor Inc 251 E Edwards Ave **Fax Area Code:* 847 ■ *TF:* 800-323-8261 ■ *Web:* www.revcor.com	Carpentersville	IL	60110	800-323-8261	426-4630*	18
Reveal Global Intelligence 10800 Sikes Pl Ste 205 *Web:* www.revealglobal.com	Charlotte	NC	28277	704-844-6000		260
Revel Consulting 2226 Third Ave Ste 300 *Web:* www.revelconsulting.com	Seattle	WA	98121	206-407-3173		463
Revelation Software 99 Kinderkamack Rd *TF:* 800-262-4747 ■ *Web:* www.revelation.com	Westwood	NJ	07675	201-594-1422	722-9815	178-2
Revelations Entertainment 1221 Second St 4th Fl *Web:* revelationsent.com	Santa Monica	CA	90401	310-394-3131		514
Revelex Corp 6405 Congress Ave Ste 120 *TF:* 800-992-8064 ■ *Web:* www.revelex.com	Boca Raton	FL	33487	561-988-5588		180
Revels Tractor Company Inc 2217 N Main St *TF:* 800-849-5469 ■ *Web:* www.revelstractor.com	Fuquay Varina	NC	27526	919-552-5697		274
Revenew International LLC 9 Greenway PlZ Ste 1950 *Web:* www.revenew.net	Houston	TX	77046	281-276-4500		734
Revens Revens & St Pierre 946 Centerville Rd *Web:* rrsplaw.com	Warwick	RI	02886	401-822-2900		2
Revent Inc 100 Ethel Rd W *TF:* 800-822-9642 ■ *Web:* www.revent.com	Piscataway	NJ	08854	732-777-9433		296
Revention Inc 1315 W Sam Houston Pkwy North Ste 100 *TF:* 877-738-7444 ■ *Web:* www.revention.com	Houston	TX	77043	877-738-7444		196
RevenueAds Affiliate Network 2304 S Post Rd *Web:* www.leadvisionmedia.com	Midwest City	OK	73130	405-622-5046		5
RevenueWire Inc 3962 Borden St Ste 102 *Web:* www.revenuewire.com	Victoria	BC	V8P3H8	250-590-2273		393
ReVera Inc 3090 Oakmead Village Dr *Web:* www.revera.com	Santa Clara	CA	95051	408-510-7400		407

Name / Address	City	State	Zip	Phone	Fax	Class
Revera Long Term Care Inc 55 Standish Ct	Mississauga	ON	L5R4B2	519-376-3212		371
TF: 800-811-5146 ■ *Web:* www.reveraliving.com						
Reverb Music LLC 3316 N Lincoln Ave.	Chicago	IL	60657	773-525-7773		526
TF: 888-686-7872 ■ *Web:* www.chicagomusicexchange.com						
Revere Control Systems Inc 2240 Rocky Ridge Rd	Birmingham	AL	35216	205-824-0004	824-0439	729
TF: 800-536-2525 ■ *Web:* www.reverecontrol.com						
Revere Copper Products Inc 1 Revere Pk.	Rome	NY	13440	315-338-2022	338-2224*	485
**Fax:* Sales ■ *TF:* 800-448-1776 ■ *Web:* www.reverecopper.com						
Revere Electric Supply Co 2501 W Washington Blvd	Chicago	IL	60612	312-738-3636		249
Web: www.revereelectric.com						
Revere Group, The 325 N LaSalle Ste 325	Chicago	IL	60654	312-873-3400	873-3500	194
TF: 800-745-3263 ■ *Web:* americas.nttdata.com						
Revere Healthcare Ltd 112 Carry St	Cary	IL	60013	847-516-4900		476
TF: 800-828-8225 ■ *Web:* www.reverehc.com						
Revere Hotel Boston Common 200 Stuart St.	Boston	MA	02116	617-482-1800		707
TF: 855-673-8373 ■ *Web:* www.reverehotel.com						
Revere Mills Inc 2860 S River Rd Ste 250	Des Plaines	IL	60018	847-759-6800		361
Web: www.reveremills.com						
Revere Paul House 19 N Sq.	Boston	MA	02113	617-523-2338	523-1775	520
TF: 800-343-1177 ■ *Web:* www.paulreverehouse.org						
Revere Public Library 179 Beach St	Revere	MA	02151	781-286-8380		434-3
TF: 800-925-7737 ■ *Web:* reverepubliclibrary.org						
Reverse Logistics Trends Inc 441 West Main St Ste D	Lehi	UT	84043	801-331-8949		184
Web: www.reverselogisticstrends.com						
Revestor LLC 505 Montgomery St 11th Fl	San Francisco	CA	94111	415-689-4942		387
Web: revestor.com						
Review & Herald Publishing Assn 55 W Oak Ridge Dr.	Hagerstown	MD	21740	301-393-3000	393-3209	637-9
TF: 800-456-3991 ■ *Web:* www.rhpa.org						
ReviewPush 12885 N Hwy 183 Ste 110A	Austin	TX	78750	512-814-8046		387
TF: 800-535-5198 ■ *Web:* www.reviewpush.com						
Revionics Inc 2998 Douglas Blvd Ste 350	Roseville	CA	95661	916-797-6051		253
Web: www.revionics.com						
Revision Military Ltd 7 Corporate Dr	Essex Junction	VT	05452	802-879-7002		543
Web: www.revisionmilitary.com						
Revision Technologies Inc 30 Richard Rd.	Edison	NJ	08820	732-318-6175		180
Web: www.revisiontek.com						
Revision3 Corp 2415 Third St Ste 232	San Francisco	CA	94107	415-734-3500		514
Web: www.revision3.com						
Reviva Inc 5130 Main St NE.	Fridley	MN	55421	763-535-8900		247
Web: www.reviva.com						
Reviva Pharmaceuticals Inc 3900 Freedom Cir Ste 101	Santa Clara	CA	95054	408-960-2209		231
Web: www.revivapharma.com						
Revival Slavic Christian Center of The Assemblies of God 5601 Hemlock St	Sacramento	CA	95841	916-332-2897		48-20
Web: revivalscc.com						
Revive Public Relations LLC 915 Saint Vincent Ave.	Santa Barbara	CA	93101	805-617-2832		636
Web: www.thinkrevivehealth.com						
Revive Spa at the JW Marriott Desert Ridge Resort Phoenix 5350 E Marriott Dr	Phoenix	AZ	85054	480-293-3700		707
TF: 800-845-5279 ■ *Web:* www.marriott.com						
Revivicor Inc 1700 Kraft Dr Ste 2400	Blacksburg	VA	24060	540-961-5559	961-7958	85
Web: www.revivicor.com						
REVL Communications & Systems 650 W 58th Ave Ste J	Anchorage	AK	99518	907-563-8302		647
Web: www.revlinc.net						
Revlon Consumer Products Corp 1501 Williamsboro St.	Oxford	NC	27565	212-527-4000		214
TF: 800-473-8566 ■ *Web:* www.revlon.com						
Revlon Foundation Inc 237 Pk Ave	New York	NY	10017	800-473-8566		304
TF Cust Svc: 800-473-8566 ■ *Web:* www.revlon.com						
Revlon Inc 237 Pk Ave.	New York	NY	10017	212-527-4000		360-3
NYSE: REV ■ *TF:* 800-473-8566 ■ *Web:* www.revlon.com						
Revman International Inc 350 Fifth Ave 70th Fl	New York	NY	10118	212-278-0300		361
Web: www.revman.com						
Revo America Inc 700 Freeport Pkwy Ste 100	Coppell	TX	75019	469-464-2800		692
Web: www.revoamerica.com						
Revolution Agency Inc 1210 E Windsor Ave	Phoenix	AZ	85006	602-956-5465		4
Web: revolutionagency.com						
Revolution Eyewear Inc 2853 Eisenhower St Ste 100	Carrollton	TX	75007	800-986-0010	908-2900*	237
**Fax Area Code:* 866 ■ *TF:* 800-986-0010 ■ *Web:* www.revolutioneyewear.com						
Revolution Studios 225 Santa Monica Blvd 9th FL	Santa Monica	CA	90401	310-255-7000		514
Web: www.revolutionstudios.com						
Revolutionary Engineering Inc 36865 Schoolcraft Rd.	Livonia	MI	48150	734-432-9334		261
Web: www.revoleng.com						
Revolve Clothing Exchange 1620 E Seventh Ave	Tampa	FL	33605	813-242-5970		157-6
Web: revolve.cx						
Revolve Marketing 330 Waymont Ct Ste 100	Lake Mary	FL	32746	407-804-2710	804-2711	195
REVShare Corp 32836 Wolf Store Rd	Temecula	CA	92592	800-819-9945		195
TF: 800-819-9945 ■ *Web:* www.revshare.com						
Revstone Industries LLC 2250 Thunderstick Dr Ste 1203	Lexington	KY	40505	859-294-5590		605-2
Revue & News, The 319 N Main St	Alpharetta	GA	30004	770-442-3278	475-1216	532-4
TF: 800-342-9819 ■ *Web:* www.northfulton.com						
Revzero Inc 2431 Galpin Ct Ste 150	Chanhassen	MN	55317	952-380-9966		454
Web: www.revzeroinc.com						
Rewarder Inc 564 Market St Ste 705	San Francisco	CA	94104	415-217-8855		5
Rewards Network 2 N Riverside Plaza Ste 200	Chicago	IL	60606	866-559-3463		215
TF: 866-844-3753 ■ *Web:* www.rewardsnetwork.com						
Rewind 100.9 420 Western Ave.	South Portland	ME	04106	207-774-4561	774-3788	645
Web: rewind1009.com						
Rewind 92.5 2603 W Bradley Ave	Champaign	IL	61821	217-352-4141		645-30
Web: www.rewind925.com						
Rewind 103.5/104.3 4401 Carriage Hill Ln	Columbus	OH	43220	614-451-2191	451-1831	645-42
Web: rewindcolumbus.com						
Rex Artist Supplies 3160 SW 22 St	Miami	FL	33145	305-445-1413	445-1412	45
TF: 800-739-2782 ■ *Web:* www.rexart.com						
Rex Black Consulting Services Inc 31520 Beck Rd	Bulverde	TX	78163	830-438-4830		180
TF: 866-438-4830 ■ *Web:* www.rbcs-us.com						
Rex Energy Corp 366 Walker Dr	State College	PA	16801	814-278-7267		536
Web: www.rexenergycorp.com						
Rex Engineering Corp 1200 Chaffee Dr	Titusville	FL	32780	321-268-5500		518
Web: www.rex-engineering.com						
Rex Fine Foods Inc 1536 River Oaks Rd W	Harahan	LA	70123	504-602-9487		296-37
Web: www.rexfoods.com						
Rex Healthcare 4420 Lake Boone Trl	Raleigh	NC	27607	919-784-3100		374-3
TF: 800-624-3004 ■ *Web:* www.rexhealth.com						
Rex Heat Treat 951 W Eigth St PO Box 270	Lansdale	PA	19446	215-855-1131	855-2028	484
TF: 800-220-4739 ■ *Web:* www.rexht.com						
Rex Lumber Co 840 Main St	Acton	MA	01720	978-263-0055	263-9806	819
TF: 800-343-0567 ■ *Web:* www.rexlumber.com						
Rex Lumber LLC 5299 Alabama St.	Graceville	FL	32440	850-263-2056		683
Web: www.rex-lumber.com						
Rex Medical LP 1100 E Hector St Ste 245	Conshohocken	PA	19428	610-940-0665		476
Web: www.rexmedical.com						
Rex Moore Electrical Contractors & Engineers 6001 Outfall Cir	Sacramento	CA	95828	916-372-1300	372-4013	189-4
TF: 800-266-1922 ■ *Web:* www.rexmoore.com						
Rex Oil Co Inc 814 & 1000 Lexington Ave	Thomasville	NC	27360	336-472-3368	843-0572*	579
**Fax Area Code:* 800 ■ *TF:* 800-843-0572 ■ *Web:* www.rexoil.com						
Rex Pak Ltd 85 Thornmount Dr	Toronto	ON	M1B5V3	416-755-3324		393
Web: www.rexpak.com						
Rex Pipe & Supply Co 10311 Berea Rd	Cleveland	OH	44102	216-651-1900		610
Web: www.rexpipe.com						
Rex Supply Co 3715 Harrisburg Blvd.	Houston	TX	77003	713-222-2251	225-5739	385
TF: 800-369-0669 ■ *Web:* www.rex-supply.com						
Rex Wine Vinegar Co 828-30 Raymond Blvd	Newark	NJ	07105	973-589-6911		296-41
Rexair Inc 50 W Big Beaver Rd Ste 350	Troy	MI	48084	248-643-7222	643-7676	788
Web: www.rainbowsystem.com						
Rexam Closures & Containers 3245 Kansas Rd	Evansville	IN	47725	812-867-6671		154
Web: www.rexamcatalogue.com						
Rexarc Inc PO Box 7	West Alexandria	OH	45381	937-839-4604	839-5897	790
TF: 877-739-2721 ■ *Web:* www.rexarc.com						
Rexel Canada Inc 5600 Keaton Crescent	Mississauga	ON	L5R3G3	905-712-4004		246
TF: 800-569-6318 ■ *Web:* www.rexel.ca						
Rexel Inc 14951 Dallas Pkwy PO Box 9085	Dallas	TX	75254	972-387-3600		246
TF: 888-739-3577 ■ *Web:* www.rexelusa.com						
Rexel Ryall Electrical Supplies 11775 E 45th Ave	Denver	CO	80239	303-629-7721		246
TF: 888-739-3577 ■ *Web:* www.rexelusa.com						
Rexius Forest By-Products Inc 1275 Bailey Hill Rd	Eugene	OR	97402	541-342-1835	343-4802	293
Web: www.rexius.com						
Rexon Components Inc 24500 Highpoint Rd	Beachwood	OH	44122	216-292-7373		639
Web: www.rexon.com						
Rexton Inc 5010 Cheshire Ln N Ste 2	Minneapolis	MN	55446	763-553-0787		250
Web: www.rexton.com						
Rey's 1130 Buck Jones Rd	Raleigh	NC	27606	919-380-0122		671
Web: www.reysrestaurant.com						
Reyers 40 S Water Ave	Sharon	PA	16146	800-245-1550		301
TF Cust Svc: 800-245-1550 ■ *Web:* www.reyers.com						
Reyes Holdings LLC 6250 N River Rd Ste 9000	Rosemont	IL	60018	847-227-6500		360-3
Web: www.reyesholdings.com						
Reynard Corp 1020 Calle Sombra	San Clemente	CA	92673	949-366-8866		544
Web: www.reynardcorp.com						
Reynolda Gardens of Wake Forest University 100 Reynolda Village	Winston-Salem	NC	27106	336-758-5593		97
Web: www.reynoldagardens.org						
Reynolda House Museum of American Art 2250 Reynolda Rd	Winston-Salem	NC	27106	336-758-5150	758-5704	520
TF: 888-663-1149 ■ *Web:* www.reynoldahouse.org						
Reynolda Village 2201 Reynolda Rd	Winston-Salem	NC	27106	336-758-5584		460
Web: www.reynoldavillage.com						
Reynolds & Reynolds Co 1 Reynolds Way	Dayton	OH	45430	937-485-2000		178-10
TF: 800-767-0080 ■ *Web:* www.reyrey.com						
Reynolds American Inc 401 N Main St PO Box 2990	Winston-Salem	NC	27101	336-741-2000		756
NYSE: LO ■ *Web:* www.reynoldsamerican.com						
Reynolds Co, The 10 Gates St	Greenville	SC	29611	864-232-6791		3
Web: www.reynoldsglue.com						
Reynolds County 2319 Green St	Centerville	MO	63633	573-648-2491		338
Web: reynoldsso.org						
Reynolds De Witt Securities 300 Main St	Cincinnati	OH	45202	513-241-6443		792
Reynolds Hix & Company PA 6729 Academy Rd NE Ste D	Albuquerque	NM	87109	505-828-2900		2
Web: rhcocpa.com						

Name / Address	City	State	ZIP	Phone	Fax	Class
Reynolds Kim (R) State Capitol *Web:* governor.iowa.gov	Des Moines	IA	50319	515-258-1521	281-6611	343
Reynolds Manufacturing Co 501 38th St *Web:* www.reynoldsmfg.com	Rock Island	IL	61201	309-788-7443		757
Reynolds Memorial Hospital (RMH) 800 Wheeling Ave	Glen Dale	WV	26038	304-845-3211		374-3
Reynolds Plantation 100 Linger Longer Rd *TF:* 800-800-5250 ■ *Web:* www.reynoldslakeoconee.com	Greensboro	GA	30642	706-467-0600		669
Reynolds School District 7 Inc 1204 NE 201st Ave *Web:* www.reynolds.k12.or.us	Fairview	OR	97024	503-661-7200	667-6932	685
Reynolds Service Inc 860 Brentwood Dr *Web:* www.rsi.biz	Greenville	PA	16125	724-646-2600		492
Reynolds Smith & Hills Inc 10748 Deerwood Pk Blvd *TF:* 800 741-2014 ■ *Web:* www.rsandh.com	Jacksonville	FL	32256	904-256-2500	256-2501	261
Reynolds Tavern 7 Church Cir *Web:* www.reynoldstavern.org	Annapolis	MD	21401	410-295-9555		671
Reynolds, Mirth, Richards & Farmer LLP Manulife Pl 10180-101 St Ste 3200 *TF:* 800-661-7673 ■ *Web:* www.rmrf.com	Edmonton	AB	T5J3W8	780-425-9510		428
Reynolds-Alberta Museum 6426 40 Ave PO Box 6360 *TF:* 800-661-4726 ■ *Web:* www.history.alberta.ca/reynolds	Wetaskiwin	AB	T9A2G1	780-361-1351	361-1239	520
Reynoldsburg Area Chamber of Commerce 1580 Brice Rd *TF:* 800-314-7003 ■ *Web:* www.reynoldsburgchamber.com	Reynoldsburg	OH	43068	614-866-4753	866-7313	139
Reynoldsburg This Week 7801 N Central Dr *TF:* 888-837-4342 ■ *Web:* www.thisweeknews.com	Lewis Center	OH	43035	740-888-6100	888-6006	532-4
REZ-1 Inc 100 William St Ste 100 *Web:* www.rez1.com	Wellesley	MA	02481	617-928-5000		750
Reznick Group PC 7501 Wisconsin Ave Ste 400 E *Web:* cohnreznick.com	Bethesda	MD	20814	301-652-9100		2
Rf Connect LLC 37735 Enterprise Ct Ste 200 *Web:* www.rfconnect.com	Farmington Hills	MI	48331	248-489-5800		624
RF Cook Manufacturing Co 4585 Allen Rd *TF:* 800-430-7536 ■ *Web:* www.rfcook.com	Stow	OH	44224	330-923-9797	923-8641	455
RF Engineering Inc 13801 Bison Ct *Web:* www.rfe-inc.com	Silver Spring	MD	20906	301-460-8374		177
RF Fisher Electric Co LLC 1707 W 39th Ave *Web:* rffisher.com	Kansas City	KS	66103	913-384-1500		707
RF Inc T/A Frankel Acura 10400 York Rd	Cockeysville	MD	21030	410-666-5300		57
RF Industries 7610 Miramar Rd Bldg 6000 *NASDAQ:* RFIL ■ *TF:* 800-233-1728 ■ *Web:* www.rfindustries.com	San Diego	CA	92126	858-549-6340	549-6345	253
RF Knox Company Inc 4865 Martin Ct SE *Web:* www.rfknox.com	Smyrna	GA	30082	770-434-7401		697
RF Macdonald Co 25920 Eden Landing Rd *Web:* www.rfmacdonald.com	Hayward	CA	94545	510-784-0110		610
RF Murray & Co CPAs PC 3741 Wilder Rd *Web:* rfmurraycpa.com	Bay City	MI	48706	989-686-7740	686-7742	2
RF Ougheltree & Assoc LLC 1050 Wall St W *Web:* rfoins.com	Lyndhurst	NJ	07071	201-964-9881		390
RF Owens Company Inc 1062 Broadway *Web:* www.trucchis.com	Raynham	MA	02767	508-824-7514		345
RF Products Inc 1500 Davis St *Web:* www.rfproducts.com	Camden	NJ	08103	856-365-5500	342-9757	647
RF Binder Partners Inc 950 Third Ave 7th Fl *Web:* www.rfbinder.com	New York	NY	10022	212-994-7600		636
RFA (Renewable Fuels Assn) 425 Third St SW *Web:* www.ethanolrfa.org	Washington	DC	20024	202-289-3835	289-7519	48-12
RFB&D (Recording for the Blind & Dyslexic) 20 Roszel Rd **Fax Area Code:* 609 ■ *TF:* 800-221-4792 ■ *Web:* www.rfbd.org	Princeton	NJ	08540	800-221-4792	987-8116*	48-17
RFC (Roll Forming Corp) 1070 Brooks Industrial Rd *TF:* 800-700-2461 ■ *Web:* www.rfcorp.com	Shelbyville	KY	40065	502-633-4435		697
Rfd & Associates Inc 401 Camp Craft Rd *Web:* www.rfdinc.com	Austin	TX	78746	512-347-9411		177
RFE Investment Partners 36 Grove St *Web:* www.rfeip.com	New Canaan	CT	06840	203-966-2800		402
RFE/RL (Radio Free Europe/Radio Liberty) 1201 Connecticut Ave NW 4th Fl *Web:* www.rferl.org	Washington	DC	20036	202-457-6900		644
RFH (Robert Family Holdings Inc) 12430 Tesson Ferry Rd Ste 313 **Fax Area Code:* 314 ■ *Web:* www.rf-holdings.com	Saint Louis	MO	63128	636-305-2830	965-0309*	548
RFI Communications & Security Systems 360 Turtle Creek Ct *TF:* 800-341-9292 ■ *Web:* www.rfi.com	San Jose	CA	95125	408-298-5400	882-4401	189-4
RFIP Inc 100 W Wilshire Blvd Ste C4 *Web:* rfip.com	Oklahoma City	OK	73116	405-286-0928		736
RFL Electronics Inc 353 Powerville Rd *Web:* www.rflelect.com	Boonton	NJ	07005	973-334-3100	334-3863	735
RG Associates Inc 201 N Charles St Ste 806 *Web:* www.accountingobserver.com	Baltimore	MD	21201	443-977-4370		401
RG Barry Corp 13405 Yarmouth Dr NW *NASDAQ:* DFZ ■ *TF:* 800-848-7560 ■ *Web:* www.rgbarry.com	Pickerington	OH	43147	614-864-6400	866-9787	301
RG Johnson Company Inc 25 S College St *Web:* rgjohnsoninc.com	Washington	PA	15301	724-222-6810	222-6815	501
RG Shakour Inc 254 Tpke Rd *TF:* 800-661-2030 ■ *Web:* interiorsbyrgshakour.com	Westborough	MA	01581	800-661-2030		238
RG Smith Co 1249 Dueber Ave SW *Web:* www.rgscontractors.com	Canton	OH	44706	330-456-3415	456-9638	697
RGA (Republican Governors Assn) 1747 Pennsylvania Ave NW Ste 250 *Web:* www.rga.org	Washington	DC	20006	202-662-4140		48-7
RGA Environmental Inc 1466 66th St *TF:* 800-776-5696 ■ *Web:* www.rgaenv.com	Emeryville	CA	94608	510-547-7771		261
RGB Group Inc 4141 N Miami Ave Ste 210 *Web:* www.rgbgroupinc.com	Miami	FL	33127	305-573-1672		514
RGBS Enterprises 2842 Richmond Terr *Web:* www.rgbse.com	Staten Island	NY	10303	718-981-0734		194
RGC Resources Inc 519 Kimball Ave PO Box 13007 *NASDAQ:* RGCO ■ *TF:* 800-835-7191 ■ *Web:* www.rgcresources.com	Roanoke	VA	24016	540-777-4427		360-5
RGE USA Inc 365 Oliver Cromwell Dr *Web:* www.rgegroup.com	Newport	TN	37821	423-625-4909		608
Rgen Solutions 4156 148th Ave NE Bldg I *TF:* 800-745-0615 ■ *Web:* www.rgensolutions.com	Redmond	WA	98052	425-867-1350		180
RGFCC Corp 627 Cady Dr *TF:* 888-389-1230 ■ *Web:* www.rgfcc.com	Fort Washington	MD	20744	888-389-1230		463
RGH (Riverside General Hospital) *Houston Recovery Ctr* 4514 Lyons Ave *Web:* riversidegeneralhospital.org	Houston	TX	77020	713-331-2501		726
Rgh Enterprises Inc 1810 Summit Commerce Pk *TF:* 800-307-5930 ■ *Web:* www.edgepark.com	Twinsburg	OH	44087	330-963-6998	963-6839	475
RGHS (Rochester Regional Health) 1425 Portland Ave *TF:* 877-922-5465 ■ *Web:* www.rochestergeneral.org	Rochester	NY	14621	585-922-4000		374-3
Rgi Inc 2245 Gilbert Ave Ste 103 *Web:* rgidesign.com	Cincinnati	OH	45206	513-221-2121		344
RGIS LLC 2000 E Taylor Rd *TF:* 800-551-9130 ■ *Web:* www.rgis.com	Auburn Hills	MI	48326	248-651-2511		317
RGL Reservoir Management Inc 700 - Second St SW Ste 610 *Web:* www.rglrm.com/combined	Calgary	AB	T2P2W1	403-269-8088	269-9099	539
Rgm & Assoc 3230 Monument Way *Web:* www.rgmandassociates.com	Concord	CA	94518	925-671-7717		463
RGM Advisors LLC 221 W Sixth St Ste 1600 *Web:* www.rgmadvisors.com	Austin	TX	78701	512-807-5000		401
RGR Pharma Ltd 103 Crystal Harbour Dr *Web:* www.rgrpharma.com	Lasalle	ON	N9J3R6	519-734-6600		231
RGS (Ruffed Grouse Society) 451 McCormick Rd *TF:* 888-564-6747 ■ *Web:* www.ruffedgrousesociety.org	Coraopolis	PA	15108	412-262-4044	262-9207	48-3
RGV Partnership 322 S Missouri St PO Box 1499 *Web:* www.rgvpartnership.com	Weslaco	TX	78596	956-968-3141	968-0210	139
R&h Construction Co 1530 SW Taylor St *Web:* www.rhconst.com	Portland	OR	97205	503-228-7177		186
RH Kyle Furniture Co 1352 Hansford St	Charleston	WV	25301	304-346-0671		320
RH Nicholson & Company Inc 3998 Fair Ridge Dr Ste 200 *Web:* rhnicholson.com	Fairfax	VA	22033	703-261-6100		390
RH Reny Inc 731 Rt 1 *TF:* 800-261-7206 ■ *Web:* www.renys.com	Newcastle	ME	04553	207-563-3177	563-5681	229
RH White Construction Company Inc 41 Central St *TF:* 800-876-3837 ■ *Web:* www.rhwhite.com	Auburn	MA	01501	508-832-3295	832-7084	188-10
RHA Health Services Inc 17 Church St *TF:* 866-742-2428 ■ *Web:* www.rhahealthservices.org	Asheville	NC	28801	828-232-6844		463
RHBAA (Racking Horse Breeders Assn of America) 67 Horse Ctr Rd *Web:* www.rackinghorse.com	Decatur	AL	35603	256-353-7225		48-3
RHCOC (Richmond Hill Chamber of Commerce) 376 Church St S *Web:* www.rhcoc.com	Richmond Hill	ON	L4C9V8	905-884-1961	884-1962	137
Rhea & Kaiser 400 E Diehl Rd *Web:* www.rkconnect.com	Naperville	IL	60563	630-505-1100		4
Rhea County 444 Second Ave *Web:* www.rheacountytn.gov	Dayton	TN	37321	423-775-7832		338
Rhee Bros Inc 7461 Coca Cola Dr *Web:* www.rheebros.com	Hanover	MD	21076	410-381-9000	381-4989	296
Rheem Mfg Company Air Conditioning Div 5600 Old Greenwood Rd *TF:* 800-268-6966 ■ *Web:* www.rheem.com	Fort Smith	AR	72903	479-646-4311		14
Rhein Consulting Laboratories 4475 SW Scholls Ferry Rd Ste 101 *Web:* www.rheinlabs.com	Portland	OR	97225	503-292-1988		196
Rheinland Restaurant 208 N Main St *TF:* 800-299-9617 ■ *Web:* www.rheinlandrestaurant.com	Independence	MO	64050	816-461-5383		671
rhema 1751 Brigantine Dr *Web:* www.rhemahealthproducts.com	Coquitlam	BC	V3K7B4	604-516-0199		345
RheTech Inc 1500 E N Territorial Rd *TF:* 800-869-1230 ■ *Web:* www.rhetech.com	Whitmore Lake	MI	48189	734-769-0585	769-3565	605-2
Rhett House Inn 1009 Craven St *TF:* 888-480-9530 ■ *Web:* www.rhetthouseinn.com	Beaufort	SC	29902	843-524-9030		379
Rhinehart Oil Company Inc 585 E State Rd *Web:* www.rhinehartoil.com	American Fork	UT	84003	801-756-9681		579
Rhinehart's Oyster Bar 3051 Washington Rd *Web:* rhineharts.com	Augusta	GA	30907	706-860-2337		671
Rhinestahl Corp 7687 Innovation Way *Web:* www.rhinestahl.com	Mason	OH	45040	513-229-5300		256
Rhino Foods Inc 79 Industrial Pkwy *TF:* 800-639-3350 ■ *Web:* www.rhinofoods.com	Burlington	VT	05401	802-862-0252	865-4145	296-2
Rhino Gun Safes 607 Garber St *Web:* www.rhinosafe.com	Caldwell	ID	83605	208-454-5545		711

Entry	City	State	ZIP	Phone	Fax	Class
Rhino Linings Corp 9151 Rehco Rd *Web:* www.rhinolatino.com	San Diego	CA	92121	858-450-0441		550
Rhino Medical Staffing 2000 E Lamar Blvd Ste 250 *TF:* 866-267-4466 ■ *Web:* www.rhinomedical.com	Arlington	TX	76006	817-795-2295		507
Rhino Mfg 1820 Bickford Ave *Web:* www.rhinomfginc.com	Snohomish	WA	98290	360-568-0572		697
Rhino Records 3400 W Olive Ave *Fax Area Code: 212 ■ *TF:* 800-546-3670 ■ *Web:* www.rhino.com	Burbank	CA	91505	800-546-3670	956-0529*	657
Rhino Resource Partners LP 424 Lewis Hargett Cir Ste 250 *Web:* www.rhinolp.com	Lexington	KY	40503	859-389-6500		501
RhinoCorps Limited Co 1128 Pennsylvania St NE Ste 100 *Web:* www.rhinocorps.com	Albuquerque	NM	87110	505-323-9836		180
RhinoDox 20 N Upper Wacker Dr Ste 1229 *Web:* www.rhinodoxdocumentstoragechicago.com	Chicago	IL	60606	630-372-8861		196
Rhintek Inc 8835 Columbia 100 Pkwy Ste C *Web:* www.rhintek.com	Columbia	MD	21045	410-730-2575		178-12
Rhiza Inc 5850 Ellsworth Ave Ste 200 *Web:* rhiza.com	Pittsburgh	PA	15232	412-488-0600		224
RHM Fluid Power Inc 375 Manufacturers Dr *TF:* 800-866-3837 ■ *Web:* www.rhmfluidpower.com	Westland	MI	48186	734-326-5400	326-0339	385
Rho Capital Partners Inc 152 W 57th St 23rd Fl *Web:* www.rhoventures.com	New York	NY	10019	212-751-6677	751-3613	792
Rhoades Aviation Inc 4770 Ray Boll Blvd *Web:* www.jlrventures.net/default.asp?sec_id=180007186	Columbus	IN	47203	812-372-1819		12
Rhoades McKee PC 55 Campau Ave NW Ste 300 *Web:* www.rhoadesmckee.com	Grand Rapids	MI	49503	616-235-3500		428
Rhoads & Sinon LLP allfirst Bank Bldg, One S Market Sq 12th Fl *Web:* www.rhoadssinon.com	Harrisburg	PA	17108	717-233-5731		445
Rhode Island						
Agriculture & Resource Marketing Div 235 Promenade St Rm 370 *Web:* www.dem.ri.gov	Providence	RI	02908	401-222-2781	222-6047	339-40
Arts Council 1 Capitol Hill 3rd Fl *Web:* arts.ri.gov	Providence	RI	02908	401-222-3880	222-3018	339-40
Attorney General 150 S Main St *Web:* www.riag.state.ri.us/contact	Providence	RI	02903	401-274-4400		339-40
Board of Governors for Higher Education (RIBGHE) 80 Washington St Ste 524 Shepard Bldg *Web:* www.ribghe.org	Providence	RI	02903	401-456-6000	456-6028	339-40
Child Support Services 77 Dorrance St *TF:* 800-745-5555 ■ *Web:* www.cse.ri.gov	Providence	RI	02903	401-458-4400	458-4465	339-40
Children Youth & Families Dept 101 Friendship St *TF:* 800-742-4453 ■ *Web:* www.dcyf.state.ri.us	Providence	RI	02903	401-528-3502	528-3590	339-40
Consumer Protection Unit 150 S Main St *Web:* www.riag.ri.gov	Providence	RI	02903	401-274-4400	222-5110	339-40
Corrections Dept 40 Howard Ave *Web:* www.doc.state.ri.us	Cranston	RI	02920	401-462-1000		339-40
Court Administrators Office 250 Benefit St *Web:* www.courts.ri.gov	Providence	RI	02903	401-222-3215		339-40
Crime Victim Compensation Program 50 Service Ave *Web:* www.treasury.ri.gov	Warwick	RI	02886	401-462-7650	222-6140	339-40
Economic Development Corp 315 Iron Horse Way Ste 101 *Web:* commerceri.com	Providence	RI	02908	401-278-9100	273-8270	339-40
Elderly Affairs Dept 74 W Rd Hazard Bldg FL 2 *Web:* www.dea.ri.gov	Cranston	RI	02920	401-462-3000		339-40
Elementary & Secondary Education Dept 255 Westminster St *Web:* www.ride.ri.gov	Providence	RI	02903	401-222-4600		339-40
Emergency Management Agency 645 New London Ave *Web:* www.riema.ri.gov	Cranston	RI	02920	401-946-9996	944-1891	339-40
Environmental Management Dept 235 Promenade St *Web:* www.dem.ri.gov	Providence	RI	02908	401-222-6800		339-40
Ethics Commission 40 Fountain St *Web:* www.ethics.ri.gov	Providence	RI	02903	401-222-3790	222-3382	265
General Assembly 82 Smith St *Web:* www.rilin.state.ri.us	Providence	RI	02903	401-222-2466		339-40
Health Dept 3 Capitol Hill *Web:* www.health.ri.gov	Providence	RI	02908	401-222-5960	222-6548	339-40
Higher Education Assistance Authority (RIHEAA) 560 Jefferson Blvd Ste 100 *TF:* 800-922-9855 ■ *Web:* www.riheaa.org	Warwick	RI	02886	401-736-1100	732-3541	725
Historical Preservation & Heritage Commission 150 Benefit St *Web:* eisenhowerhouse.com	Providence	RI	02903	401-222-2678	222-2968	339-40
Housing & Mortgage Finance Corp 44 Washington St *TF:* 800-427-5560 ■ *Web:* www.rhodeislandhousing.org	Providence	RI	02903	401-457-1234		339-40
Human Services Dept 57 Howard Ave Louis Pasteur Bldg *TF:* 855-697-4347 ■ *Web:* www.dhs.ri.gov	Cranston	RI	02920	401-462-5300		339-40
Labor & Training Dept Center General Complex 1511 Pontiac Ave *Web:* www.dlt.ri.us	Cranston	RI	02920	401-462-8000	462-8872	259
Library & Information Services Office 1 Capitol Hil 2nd Fl *Web:* www.olis.ri.gov	Providence	RI	02908	401-574-9300	574-9320	339-40
Lieutenant Governor 82 Smith St Rm 116 *Web:* www.ltgov.ri.gov	Providence	RI	02903	401-222-2371		339-40
Lottery 1425 Pontiac Ave *Web:* www.rilot.com	Cranston	RI	02920	401-463-6500	463-5669	452
Medical Examiner 48 Orms St *Web:* www.health.ri.gov	Providence	RI	02908	401-222-5500	222-5505	339-40
Office of the Governor 82 Smith St *Web:* www.governor.state.ri.us	Providence	RI	02903	401-222-2080	222-8096	339-40
Parks & Recreation Div 1100 Tower Hill Rd *Web:* www.riparks.com	North Kingstown	RI	02852	401-667-6200	667-3970	339-40
Professional Regulation Div 1511 Pontiac Ave *Web:* www.dlt.ri.gov/profregs	Cranston	RI	02920	401-462-8580	462-8528	339-40
Public Utilities Commission 89 Jefferson Blvd *Web:* www.ripuc.org	Warwick	RI	02888	401-941-4500		339-40
Rehabilitation Services Office 40 Fountain St *Web:* www.ors.state.ri.us	Providence	RI	02903	401-421-7005		339-40
State Government Information 40 Fountain St *Web:* www.ri.gov	Providence	RI	02903	401-421-7005		339-40
State Police 311 Danielson Pike *Web:* risp.ri.gov	North Scituate	RI	02857	401-444-1000		339-40
Supreme Court 250 Benefit St *Web:* www.courts.ri.gov	Providence	RI	02903	401-222-3272		339-40
Tourism Div 315 Iron Horse Way Ste 101 *TF:* 800-556-2484 ■ *Web:* www.visitrhodeisland.com	Providence	RI	02908	401-278-9100	273-8270	339-40
Transportation Dept 2 Capitol Hill *Web:* rhodeislandbids.com	Providence	RI	02903	401-222-2495	222-2086	339-40
Treasurer 82 Smith St Rm 102 *Web:* www.treasury.ri.gov	Providence	RI	02903	401-222-2397	222-6140	339-40
Veterans Affairs Div 480 Metacom Ave *Web:* www.vets.ri.gov	Bristol	RI	02809	401-253-8000	254-2320	339-40
Weights & Measures Office 1511 Pontiac Ave *Web:* www.dlt.ri.gov/occusafe/weightsmeasures.htm	Cranston	RI	02920	401-462-8570	462-8576	339-40
Worker's Compensation Div 1511 Pontiac Ave *Web:* www.dlt.ri.gov/wc	Cranston	RI	02920	401-462-8100	462-8105	339-40
Rhode Island Airport Corp 2000 Post Rd Warwick *TF:* 888-268-7222 ■ *Web:* www.pvdairport.com	Warwick	RI	02886	401-691-2000		27
Rhode Island Assn of Realtors 100 Bignall St *TF:* 866-610-8909 ■ *Web:* www.rirealtors.org	Warwick	RI	02888	401-785-9898	941-5360	656
Rhode Island Bar Assn 115 Cedar St *TF:* 877-659-0801 ■ *Web:* www.ribar.com	Providence	RI	02903	401-421-5740	421-2703	72
Rhode Island Blood Ctr 405 Promenade St *TF:* 800-283-8385 ■ *Web:* www.ribc.org	Providence	RI	02908	401-453-8360	453-8557	89
Rhode Island College 600 Mt Pleasant Ave *TF:* 800-669-5760 ■ *Web:* www.ric.edu	Providence	RI	02908	401-456-8000	456-8817	166
Rhode Island Convention Ctr 1 Sabin St *TF:* 800-992-0121 ■ *Web:* www.riconvention.com	Providence	RI	02903	401-458-6000	458-6500	205
Rhode Island Correctional Industries 40 Howard Ave	Cranston	RI	02920	401-462-3700		630
Rhode Island Democratic Party 151 Broadway Ste 310 *Web:* www.ridemocrats.org	Providence	RI	02903	401-272-3367	272-3368	616-1
Rhode Island Foundation 1 Union Stn *TF:* 800-675-2756 ■ *Web:* www.rifoundation.org	Providence	RI	02903	401-274-4564	331-8085	303
Rhode Island Historical Society 110 Benevolent St *Web:* www.rihs.org	Providence	RI	02906	401-331-8575	351-0127	520
Rhode Island Hospital 593 Eddy St *Web:* www.rhodeislandhospital.org	Providence	RI	02903	401-444-4000		374-3
Rhode Island Medical Society 235 Promenade St Ste 500 *TF:* 800-343-7776 ■ *Web:* www.rimed.org	Providence	RI	02908	401-331-3207		474
Rhode Island PBS 50 Pk Ln *TF:* 800-239-5233 ■ *Web:* www.ripbs.org	Providence	RI	02907	401-222-3636	222-3407	632
Rhode Island Philharmonic Orchestra 667 Waterman Ave *Web:* www.ri-philharmonic.org	East Providence	RI	02914	401-248-7070	248-7071	573-3
Rhode Island Public Interest Research Group (RIPIRG) 9 S Angell St Second Fl-A *Web:* www.ripirg.org	Providence	RI	02906	401-608-1201		633
Rhode Island Public Transit Authority 265 Melrose St *TF:* 800-745-5555 ■ *Web:* www.ripta.com	Providence	RI	02907	401-781-9400		468
Rhode Island School of Design 2 College St *TF:* 800-364-7473 ■ *Web:* www.risd.edu	Providence	RI	02903	401-454-6100	454-6309	164
Rhode Island School of Design - Museum of Art 224 Benefit St *Web:* www.risdmuseum.org	Providence	RI	02903	401-454-6502	454-6556	520
Rhode Island State Employees Credit Union 160 Francis St *TF:* 855-322-7428 ■ *Web:* www.ricreditunion.org	Providence	RI	02903	401-751-7440	331-5907	219
Rhode Island State Nurses Assn (RISNA) 150 Washington St Ste 415 *Web:* www.risna.org	Providence	RI	02903	401-331-5644	331-5646	533
Rhode Island Textile Co 211 Columbus Ave *TF:* 800-556-6488 ■ *Web:* www.ritextile.com	Pawtucket	RI	02862	401-722-3700	726-2840	745-5
Rhode Island Veterans' Home 480 Metacom Ave	Bristol	RI	02809	401-253-8000		793
Rhode Island Veterinary Medical Assn 302 Pearl St Ste 108 *Web:* www.rivma.org	Providence	RI	02907	401-751-0944	780-0940	795
Rhodes College 2000 N Pkwy *Fax: Admissions ■ *TF:* 800-844-5969 ■ *Web:* www.rhodes.edu	Memphis	TN	38112	901-843-3700	843-3631*	166

Listing	City	State	ZIP	Phone	Fax	Class
Rhodes College Barret Library 2000 N Pkwy *TF:* 800-844-5969 ■ *Web:* www.rhodes.edu	Memphis	TN	38112	901-843-3000		434-6
Rhodes Computer Services Inc 4324 Washington Rd Ste 103 *Web:* www.rhodesmurphy.com	Evans	GA	30809	706-868-1298		401
Rhodes Holdings LLC 615 Longview Dr **Fax Area Code:* 866 ■ *Web:* rhodesholdings.wordpress.com	Sugar Land	TX	77478	281-435-3917	249-4534*	463
Rhodes International Inc PO Box 25487 *TF Cust Svc:* 800-876-7333 ■ *Web:* www.rhodesbread.com	Salt Lake City	UT	84125	801-972-0122		296-16
Rhodes Manufacturing Inc 7045 Buckeye Valley Rd NE *Web:* www.rhodestanksrus.com	Somerset	OH	43783	740-743-2614		537
Rhodes State College 4240 Campus Dr **Fax:* Admissions ■ *Web:* www.rhodesstate.edu	Lima	OH	45804	419-995-8320	995-8098*	800
Rhodes Technologies Inc 498 Washington St *Web:* www.rhodestec.com	Coventry	RI	02816	401-262-9200		231
Rhodeside Grill 1836 Wilson Blvd *Web:* www.rhodesidegrill.com	Arlington	VA	22201	703-243-0145		671
Rhodes-Joseph & Tobiason Advisors LLC 1177 High Ridge Rd *Web:* www.rjtadvisors.com	Stamford	CT	06905	203-883-8144		463
Rhododendron Species Botanical Garden 2525 S 336th St PO Box 3798 *TF:* 877-242-2528 ■ *Web:* www.rhodygarden.org	Federal Way	WA	98063	253-838-4646	838-4686	97
Rhododendron State Park 424 Rockwood Pond Rd *Web:* www.nhstateparks.org	Fitzwilliam	NH	03447	603-532-8862		565
Rhona Hoffman Gallery 118 N Peoria St *TF:* 800-525-5562 ■ *Web:* www.artnet.com	Chicago	IL	60607	312-455-1990		42
RHP Mechanical Systems Inc 1008 E Fourth St *Web:* www.rhpinc.net	Reno	NV	89512	775-322-9434		261
RHR Adpro Adv LLC 2106 E 16th St PO Box 11854	Russellville	AR	72802	479-280-1990	567-5602	4
RHR International LLP 233 S Wacker Dr 95th Fl *Web:* rhrinternational.com	Chicago	IL	60606	312-924-0800		194
Rhumbline Advisers Corp 265 Franklin St 21st Fl *Web:* www.rhumblineadvisers.com	Boston	MA	02110	617-345-0434		401
Rhythm & Hues Inc 5890 W Jefferson Blvd Ste Q *Web:* www.rhythm.com	Los Angeles	CA	90016	310-448-7500	448-7600	512
Rhythm Band Instruments LLC 1316 E Lancaster Ave *Web:* www.rhythmband.com	Fort Worth	TX	76102	817-335-2561		390
Rhythm Cafe 3800 S Dixie Hwy *Web:* www.rhythmcafe.cc	West Palm Beach	FL	33405	561-833-3406		671
Rhythm City Casino 7077 Elmore Ave *TF:* 844-852-4386 ■ *Web:* rhythmcitycasino.co	Davenport	IA	52807	563-328-8000		133
Rhythm Organism LLC, The 400 N State St Ste 410 *Web:* www.fanfueled.com	Chicago	IL	60654	312-321-0111		387
Rhythm Tech 29 Beechwood Ave *TF:* 800-726-2279 ■ *Web:* rhythmtech.com	New Rochelle	NY	10801	914-636-6900		527
RI (Refugees International) 2001 S St NW Ste 700-K *TF:* 800-733-8433 ■ *Web:* www.refugeesinternational.org	Washington	DC	20009	202-828-0110	828-0819	48-5
RI Lampus Co 816 RI Lampus Ave PO Box 167 **Fax Area Code:* 724 ■ *TF:* 800-872-7310 ■ *Web:* www.lampus.com	Springdale	PA	15144	412-362-3800	274-2181*	183
Ri Ra 123 Church St *Web:* www.rira.com	Burlington	VT	05401	802-860-9401		671
Ri Ra Irish Pub & Restaurant 72 Commercial St *Web:* www.rira.com	Portland	ME	04101	207-761-4446	761-4447	671
RIA (Research Institute on Addictions) 1021 Main St *TF:* 800-729-6686 ■ *Web:* buffalo.edu/ria.html	Buffalo	NY	14203	716-887-2566	887-2252	668
RIA (Robotic Industries Assn) 900 Victors Way Ste 140 *Web:* www.robotics.org	Ann Arbor	MI	48108	734-994-6088	994-3338	49-19
Ria Compliance Consultants Inc 11640 Arbor St Ste 100 *TF:* 877-345-4034 ■ *Web:* www.ria-compliance-consultants.com	Omaha	NE	68144	877-345-4034		196
RIAA (Recording Industry Assn of America Inc) 1025 F St NW 10th Fl *Web:* www.riaa.com	Washington	DC	20004	202-775-0101		40-4
Rialto Center for the Arts 80 Forsyth St NW *Web:* rialto.gsu.edu	Atlanta	GA	30303	404-413-9800	413-9850	572
Rialto Chamber of Commerce 120 N Riverside Ave *TF:* 800-597-4955 ■ *Web:* www.rialtochamber.org	Rialto	CA	92376	909-875-5364	875-6790	139
Rialto Record PO Box 110 *Web:* www.iecn.com	Colton	CA	92324	909-381-9898		532-4
Rialto Theater 310 S Ninth St *TF:* 800-291-7593 ■ *Web:* www.broadwaycenter.org	Tacoma	WA	98402	253-591-5890	591-2013	572
Rialto, The 318 E Congress St *TF:* 800-722-8848 ■ *Web:* www.rialtotheatre.com	Tucson	AZ	85701	520-740-1000		572
Riata Financial Services Inc 245 Landa St *Web:* riatafinancial.com	New Braunfels	TX	78130	830-606-5100		251
Rib Crib Corp 4535 S Harvard Ave *TF:* 800-275-9677 ■ *Web:* www.ribcrib.com	Tulsa	OK	74135	918-712-7427		670
Rib Room 1235 E State Blvd *Web:* www.theribroom.com	Fort Wayne	IN	46805	260-483-9767		671
Riba Foods Inc 3735 Arc St *Web:* www.ribafoods.com	Houston	TX	77063	713-975-7001	975-7036	297-8
Riback Supply Co 2412 Business Loop 70 E PO Box 937 *Web:* www.riback.com	Columbia	MO	65205	573-875-3131	449-8738	350
Ribbeck Engineering Inc 14335 SW 120th St Ste 205 *Web:* ribbeck.co	Miami	FL	33186	305-383-5909		261
Ribbon Technology Corp 825 Taylor Stn Rd *TF:* 800-848-0477 ■ *Web:* www.ribtec.com	Gahanna	OH	43230	614-864-5444	864-5305	813
Ribelin Sales Inc 3857 Miller Pk Dr **Fax Area Code:* 877 ■ *TF:* 800-374-1594 ■ *Web:* www.ribelin.com	Garland	TX	75042	972-272-1594	474-2354*	146
Ribollita 41 Middle St *Web:* ribollitamaine.com	Portland	ME	04101	207-774-2972		671
Ricardo's 5629 E 41st St *Web:* ricardostulsa.com	Tulsa	OK	74135	918-622-2668		671
Ricardo's Restaurant 2112 E Lake Rd *Web:* ricardosrestauranterie.com	Erie	PA	16511	814-455-4947		671
Ricart Automotive Group 4255 S Hamilton Rd *TF:* 888-225-6783 ■ *Web:* www.ricart.com	Columbus	OH	43125	614-836-5321		57
Rice 1608 14th St NW *Web:* www.ricerestaurant.com	Washington	DC	20009	202-234-2400		671
Rice Assoc Inc 10625 Gaskins Way *Web:* ricesurveys.com	Manassas	VA	20109	703-968-3200		727
Rice Cohen International 301 Oxford Valley Rd Ste 1506A *Web:* ricecoheninternational.com	Yardley	PA	19067	215-321-4100		266
Rice County 320 NW Third St *Web:* www.co.rice.mn.us	Faribault	MN	55021	507-332-6101	332-5999	338
Rice County 101 W Commercial St *Web:* www.ricecounty.us	Lyons	KS	67554	620-257-2232	257-3039	338
Rice Energy Inc 400 Woodcliff Dr *Web:* www.riceenergy.com	Canonsburg	PA	15317	724-746-6720		536
Rice Epicurean Markets Inc 5333 Gulfton St *Web:* www.riceepicurean.com	Houston	TX	77081	713-662-7700		345
Rice Financial Products Co 55 Broad St 27th Fl *Web:* www.ricefinancialproducts.com	New York	NY	10004	212-908-9200	908-9299	690
Rice Fruit Co 2760 Carlisle Rd *TF:* 800-627-3359 ■ *Web:* www.ricefruit.com	Gardners	PA	17324	717-677-8131		315-3
Rice Hall James & Assoc LLC 600 W Broadway Ste 1000 *Web:* www.ricehalljames.com	San Diego	CA	92101	619-239-9005		401
Rice Kathleen (Rep D - NY) 1508 Longworth HOB *Web:* kathleenrice.house.gov	Washington	DC	20515	202-225-5516	225-5758	342-2
Rice Lake State Fish & Wildlife Area 19721 N US Hwy 24 *Web:* dnr.illinois.gov/Lands/Landmgt/PARKS/R1/Rice.htm	Canton	IL	61520	309-647-9184		565
Rice Lake Weighing Systems Inc 230 W Coleman St *TF:* 800-472-6703 ■ *Web:* www.ricelake.com/en-us	Rice Lake	WI	54868	800-472-6703		639
Rice Memorial Hospital 301 Becker Ave SW *TF:* 800-642-7709 ■ *Web:* www.ricehospital.com	Willmar	MN	56201	320-235-4543		374-3
Rice Packaging Inc 356 Somers Rd *TF:* 800-367-6725 ■ *Web:* www.ricepackaging.com	Ellington	CT	06029	860-872-8341		101
Rice Tom (Rep R - SC) 223 Cannon HOB *Web:* rice.house.gov	Washington	DC	20515	202-225-9895	225-9690	342-2
Rice Toyota 2630 Battleground Ave *Web:* ricetoyota.com	Greensboro	NC	27408	336-288-1190		198
Rice University 6100 Main St **Fax:* Admissions ■ *TF:* 866-294-4633 ■ *Web:* www.rice.edu	Houston	TX	77005	713-348-0000	348-5323*	166
Riceland Foods Inc PO Box 927 *Web:* www.riceland.com	Stuttgart	AR	72160	870-673-5500		296-23
Ricerca Biosciences LLC 7528 Auburn Rd *TF:* 888-742-3722 ■ *Web:* www.ricerca.com	Concord	OH	44077	440-357-3300	354-6276	668
RiceTec Inc 1925 FM 2917 PO Box 1305 *TF:* 877-580-7423 ■ *Web:* www.ricetec.com	Alvin	TX	77511	281-393-3532	393-3532	296-23
Rich County 20 S Main St *Web:* www.richcountyut.org	Randolph	UT	84064	435-793-2415		338
Rich Gelwarg & Lampf LLP 4 Ethel Rd *Web:* www.rglcpas.com	Edison	NJ	08817	732-287-5565		2
Rich Ltd 3809 Ocean Ranch Blvd Ste 110 *Web:* www.richltd.com	Oceanside	CA	92056	760-722-2300		5
Rich Mountain Community College 1100 College Dr *TF:* 800-612-7440 ■ *Web:* www.rmcc.edu	Mena	AR	71953	479-394-7622		162
Rich Mountain Electric Co-op Inc 515 Janssen PO Box 897 *TF:* 877-828-4074 ■ *Web:* www.rmec.com	Mena	AR	71953	479-394-4140		245
Rich n Ton Calls Inc 2315 Hwy 63 N *Web:* www.rntcalls.com	Stuttgart	AR	72160	870-673-4274		711
Rich Products Corp 1 Robert Rich Way *Web:* www.byronsbbq.com	Buffalo	NY	14213	716-878-8000		578
Rich Ranch 939 Cottonwood Lakes Rd *TF:* 800-532-4350 ■ *Web:* www.richranch.com	Seeley Lake	MT	59868	406-677-2317		239
Rich Worldwide Travel Inc 500 Mamaroneck Ave *TF:* 800-431-1130	Harrison	NY	10528	914-835-7600	835-1666	771
Richard & Karen Carpenter Performing Arts Ctr (CPAC) 6200 Atherton St *Web:* www.carpenterarts.org	Long Beach	CA	90815	562-985-7000	985-7023	572
Richard & Richard Construction Company Inc 234 Venture St Ste 100 *TF:* 800-411-7590 ■ *Web:* www.rrconstruction.com	San Marcos	CA	92078	760-759-2260		186
Richard A Foreman Assoc Inc 330 Emery Dr E *Web:* www.rafamedia.com	Stamford	CT	06902	203-327-2800		116
Richard A Handlon Correctional Facility 1728 Bluewater Hwy *Web:* www.michigan.gov/corrections	Ionia	MI	48846	616-527-3100		213
Richard a Kennedy Law Office 3773 Tibbetts St Ste D *Web:* www.richardakennedy.com	Riverside	CA	92506	951-715-5000		428
Richard A Urbanek Jr DDS Ms PA 5 Eureka Cir Ste B	Wichita Falls	TX	76308	940-696-2002		363
Richard B. Russell State Park 2650 Russell State Pk Rd *Web:* www.gastateparks.org	Elberton	GA	30635	706-213-2045		565

Name / Address	City	State	Zip	Phone	Fax	Class
Richard Bland College 11301 Johnson Rd	Petersburg	VA	23805	804-862-6100	862-6490*	162
*Fax: Admissions ■ Web: www.rbc.edu						
Richard Bong State Recreation Area 26313 Burlington Rd	Kansasville	WI	53139	262-878-5600	878-5615	565
Web: dnr.wi.gov/newurl.html						
Richard Brady & Associates 3710 Ruffin Rd	San Diego	CA	92123	858-496-0500		261
Web: www.richardbrady.com						
Richard Carlton Consulting Inc 1941 Rollingwood Dr	Fairfield	CA	94534	707-422-4053		196
TF: 800-325-2747 ■ Web: www.rcconsulting.com						
Richard Childress Racing Enterprises Inc 425 Industrial Dr	Welcome	NC	27374	336-731-3334	731-5626	713
Web: www.rcrracing.com						
Richard Curtis Assoc Inc 171 E 74th St 2nd Fl	New York	NY	10021	212-772-7363		444
Web: www.curtisagency.com						
Richard E Jacobs Group Inc 25425 Ctr Ridge Rd	Cleveland	OH	44145	440-871-4800	808-6902	655
Web: www.rejacobsgroup.com						
Richard Goettle Inc 12071 Hamilton Ave	Cincinnati	OH	45231	513-825-8100		189-3
Web: www.goettle.com						
Richard Gray Gallery 875 N Michigan Ave 38th Fl	Chicago	IL	60611	312-642-8877	642-8488	42
Web: www.richardgraygallery.com						
Richard Gumz Farms 8905 S Gumz Rd	North Judson	IN	46366	574-896-5441		10-5
Richard H Hutchings Psychiatric Ctr 620 Madison St	Syracuse	NY	13210	315-426-3600		374-5
TF: 800-597-8481						
Richard H Thornton Public Library 210 Main St	Oxford	NC	27565	919-693-1121	693-2244	434-3
Web: www.granville.lib.nc.us						
Richard Harrison Bailey Inc 121 S Niles Ave	South Bend	IN	46617	574-287-8333		4
Web: www.rhb.com						
Richard Heath & Assoc 1320 Harbor Bay Pkwy Ste 140	Alameda	CA	94502	510-748-4330		463
Web: www.rhainc.com						
Richard Hennessy Insurance Agency Inc 6335A SW Capitol Hwy	Portland	OR	97239	503-245-9345		390
Web: statefarm.com						
Richard Henry Group LLC PO Box 45422	Westlake	OH	44145	440-724-2658		41
Web: www.rhgsolutions.com						
Richard J Daley College 226 W Jackson	Chicago	IL	60606	312-553-2500		162
Web: www.ccc.edu						
Richard King Mellon Foundation 500 Grant St Ste 4106	Pittsburgh	PA	15219	412-392-2800		305
TF: 800-424-9836 ■ Web: foundationcenter.org						
Richard L Feigen & Co 34 E 69th St	New York	NY	10021	212-628-0700		42
Web: www.rlfeigen.com						
Richard L. Roudebush VA Medical Ctr 1481 W Tenth St	Indianapolis	IN	46202	317-988-4498		374-8
TF: 888-878-6889 ■ Web: www1.va.gov/directory/guide/facility.asp?id=62						
Richard M Campbell Veterans Home 4605 Belton Hwy	Anderson	SC	29621	864-261-6734		793
Richard N Best Associates Inc 15 Trail Rd	Levittown	PA	19056	215-949-9240		261
Web: rnbest.com						
Richard Nixon Foundation, The 18001 Yorba Linda Blvd	Yorba Linda	CA	92886	714-993-5075	528-0544	434-2
TF: 800-872-8865 ■ Web: www.nixonfoundation.org						
Richard Oil and Fuel LLC 2330 Hwy 70	Donaldsonville	LA	70346	225-473-8389		581
Web: www.popingos.com						
Richard Petty Museum 309 Branson Mill Rd	Randleman	NC	27317	336-495-1143		520
Web: www.richardpettymotorsports.com						
Richard Robitaille Fourrures 329 St Paul St	Quebec	QC	G1K3W8	418-692-9699		520
Richard Rodgers Theatre 226 W 46th St	New York	NY	10036	212-221-1211		747
TF: 866-755-3075 ■ Web: richardrodgerstheatre.com						
Richard Stockton College of New Jersey Jimmie Leeds Rd	Pomona	NJ	08240	609-652-4227	626 6050*	168
*Fax: Admissions ■ Web: intraweb.stockton.edu						
Richard T Kiko Agency Inc 2805 Fulton Dr NW	Canton	OH	44718	330-453-9187	453-1765	466
TF: 800-533-5456 ■ Web: kikoauctions.com						
Richard Wolf Medical Instruments Corp 353 Corporate Woods Pkwy	Vernon Hills	IL	60061	847-913-1113	913-1488	250
TF: 800-323-9653 ■ Web: www.richardwolfusa.com						
Richards & Richards 1741 Elm Hill Pk	Nashville	TN	37210	615-242-9600		608
Web: www.richardsandrichards.com						
Richards Brick Co 234 Springer Ave	Edwardsville	IL	62025	618-656-0230	656-0944	150
Web: www.richardsbrick.com						
Richards Electric Supply Company Inc 4620 Reading Rd	Cincinnati	OH	45229	513-242-8800		246
Web: www.richardselectric.com						
Richards Energy Group 781 S Chiques Rd	Manheim	PA	17545	717-898-6330		463
Web: www.richardsenergy.com						
Richards Graphic Communications Inc 2700 Van Buren St	Bellwood	IL	60104	708-547-6000	547-6044	781
TF: 866-827-3686 ■ Web: www.rgcnet.com						
Richards Group 2801 N Central Expy Ste 100	Dallas	TX	75204	214-891-5700	891-5230	4
Web: www.richards.com						
Richards Industries Inc 3170 Wasson Rd	Cincinnati	OH	45209	513-533-5600	871-0105*	595
*Fax: Sales ■ TF Cust Svc: 800-543-7311 ■ Web: www.richardsind.com						
Richards Layton & Finger PO Box 551	Wilmington	DE	19899	302-651-7700	651-7701	428
Web: www.rlf.com						
Richards Maple Products Inc 545 Water St	Chardon	OH	44024	800-352-4052		296-39
TF: 800-352-4052 ■ Web: www.richardsmapleproducts.com						
Richards Memorial Library 118 N Washington St	North Attleboro	MA	02760	508-699-0122	699-0122	434-3
Web: rmlonline.org						
Richards Packaging Inc 2321 NE Argyle St Ste D	Portland	OR	97211	503-290-0000		601
Web: www.richardspackaging.com						
Richards/Carlberg 1900 W Loop S Ste 1100	Houston	TX	77027	713-965-0764		4
Web: www.richardscarlberg.com						
Richards-Apex Inc 4202-24 Main St	Philadelphia	PA	19127	215-487-1100	487-3090	541
Web: www.richardsapex.com						
Richards-DAR House Museum 256 N Joachim St	Mobile	AL	36603	251-208-7320		520
Web: www.richardsdarhouse.com						
Richardson Bike Mart Inc 1451 W Campbell Rd	Richardson	TX	75080	972-644-1466		711
Web: bikemart.com						
Richardson Chamber of Commerce 411 Belle Grove Dr	Richardson	TX	75080	972-792-2800	792-2825	139
Web: www.richardsonchamber.com						
Richardson Convention & Visitors Bureau 411 W Arapaho Rd Ste 105	Richardson	TX	75080	972-744-4034	744-5834	206
TF: 888-690-7287 ■ Web: www.richardsontexas.org						
Richardson County 1700 Stone St	Falls City	NE	68355	402-245-2911	245-2946	338
Web: www.co.richardson.ne.us						
Richardson Electronics Ltd 40 W 267 Keslinger Rd PO Box 393	LaFox	IL	60147	630-208-2200	208-2550	246
NASDAQ: RELL ■ TF Sales: 800-348-5580 ■ Web: www.rell.com						
Richardson Grove State Park c/o N Coast Redwoods District Office PO Box 2006	Eureka	CA	95502	707-445-6547		565
Web: www.parks.ca.gov/default.asp?page_id=422						
Richardson Manufacturing Co 2209 Old Jacksonville Rd	Springfield	IL	62704	217-546-2249	546-9433	757
TF: 800-428-1133 ■ Web: www.rmc-bigcnc.com						
Richardson Molding Inc 2405 Norcross Dr	Columbus	IN	47201	812-342-0139		596
Web: www.richardsonmolding.com						
Richardson Public Library 900 Civic Ctr Dr	Richardson	TX	75080	972-744-4350	744-5806	434-3
TF: 800-735-2989 ■ Web: www.cor.net						
Richardson Seeds Inc PO Box 60	Vega	TX	79092	806-267-2379	267-2820	276
Web: www.richardsonseeds.com						
Richardson Smith Gardner & Associates 14 N Boylan Ave	Raleigh	NC	27603	919-828-0577		261
TF: 800-922-3795 ■ Web: www.smithgardnerinc.com						
Richards-Wilcox Inc 600 S Lake St	Aurora	IL	60506	800-253-5668	897-6994*	207
*Fax Area Code: 630 ■ TF: 800-253-5668 ■ Web: www.richardswilcox.com						
Richey Joseph Hospice 838 N Eutaw St	Baltimore	MD	21201	410-523-2150		371
Web: www.gilchristhospice.org/josephrichey						
Richey May & Company PC 9605 S Kingston Ct Ste 200	Englewood	CO	80112	303-721-6131		2
Web: www.richeymay.com						
Richey Restoration Inc 9574 Lebanon Rd	Mount Juliet	TN	37122	615-533-3760		83
TF: 800-533-9898 ■ Web: www.richeyrestoration.com						
Richfield Chamber of Commerce 6601 Lyndale Ave S Ste 106	Minneapolis	MN	55423	612-866-5100		139
Web: richfieldmnchamber.org						
Richfield Hospitality Services 7600 E OrchaRd Rd Ste 230-S	Greenwood Village	CO	80111	303-220-2000		379
Web: www.richfield.com						
Richland Area Chamber of Commerce 55 N Mulberry St	Mansfield	OH	44902	419-522-3211	526-6853	139
Web: www.richlandareachamber.com						
Richland Co 2415 Midway Rd Ste 115	Carrollton	TX	75006	214-357-0248		81-1
Richland College 12800 Abrams Rd	Dallas	TX	75243	972-238-6100	238-6346*	162
*Fax: Admissions ■ TF: 800-795-3272 ■ Web: richlandcollege.edu						
Richland Community College 1 College Pk	Decatur	IL	62521	217-875-7200	875-6965*	162
*Fax: Hum Res ■ TF: 800-899-4722 ■ Web: www.richland.edu						
Richland Correctional Institution 1001 Olivesburg Rd	Mansfield	OH	44905	419-526-2100	521-2810	213
TF: 800-686-4208 ■ Web: ohio.gov						
Richland County 2020 Hampton St	Columbia	SC	29204	803-576-2050	576-2137	338
Web: www.richlandonline.com						
Richland County 50 Pk Ave E	Mansfield	OH	44902	419-774-5550	774-5862	338
Web: www.richlandcountyoh.us						
Richland County 103 W Main St Ste 21	Olney	IL	62450	618-392-2151		338
Web: www.richlandclerk.com						
Richland County 181 W Seminary St PO Box 310	Richland Center	WI	53581	608-647-2197	647-6134	338
Web: www.co.richland.wi.us						
Richland County 201 W Main St	Sidney	MT	59270	406-433-1708	433-3731	338
Web: www.richland.org						
Richland County 418 Second Ave N	Wahpeton	ND	58075	701-642-7700	642-7701	338
TF: 800-368-8683 ■ Web: www.co.richland.nd.us						
Richland County Public Library (RCPL) 1431 Assembly St	Columbia	SC	29201	803-799-9084		434-3
Web: www.richlandlibrary.com						
Richland County School District One 1616 Richland St	Columbia	SC	29201	803-231-7000	231-7417*	685
*Fax: Hum Res ■ Web: www.richlandone.org						
Richland Electric Co-op 1027 N Jefferson St	Richland Center	WI	53581	608-647-3173		245
TF: 800-242-8511 ■ Web: rec.coop						
Richland Glass Company Inc 1640 SW Blvd	Vineland	NJ	08360	856-691-1697		332
Web: www.richlandglass.com						
Richland Hospital Inc, The 333 E Second St	Richland Center	WI	53581	608-647-6321		374-3
TF: 888-467-7485 ■ Web: www.richlandhospital.com						

Name / Address	City	State	Zip	Phone	Fax	Class
Richland Investments LLC						
4100 Newport Pl Dr Ste 800	Newport Beach	CA	92660	949-261-7010		401
Web: www.richlandcommunities.com						
Richland LLC 1905 Mines Rd.	Pulaski	TN	38478	931-424-3900		190
Web: www.richlandllc.com						
Richland Mall 3400 Forest Dr	Columbia	SC	29204	803-782-7575		460
Web: www.richlandmallsc.com						
Richland Parish 708 Julia St.	Rayville	LA	71269	318-728-2061	728-7004	338
TF: 800-499-0994 ■ *Web:* lpgov.org						
Richland Public Library						
955 Northgate Dr	Richland	WA	99352	509-942-7454		434-3
Web: www.richland.lib.wa.us						
Richland Ventures 1201 16th Ave S.	Nashville	TN	37212	615-383-8030		792
Richline Group Inc 6701 Nob Hill Rd	Tamarac	FL	33321	954-718-3200	718-3206	360-2
Web: www.richlinegroup.com						
Richloom Fabrics Group 261 Fifth Ave	New York	NY	10016	212-685-5400		594
Web: richloom.com						
Richman Chemical Inc						
768 N Bethlehem Pike Ste 204	Lower Gwynedd	PA	19002	215-628-2946		194
Web: www.richmanchemical.com						
Richman Group of Cos						
340 Pemberwick Rd	Greenwich	CT	06831	203-869-0900		653
Web: www.therichmangroup.com						
Richmar Associates Inc						
283 Brokaw Rd	Santa Clara	CA	95050	408-727-6070		260
Web: www.richmarstaffing.com						
Richmond American Homes Inc						
4350 S Monaco St	Denver	CO	80237	303-773-1100		653
TF: 888-402-4663 ■ *Web:* www.richmondamerican.com						
Richmond Auto Parts Technology Inc						
5000 Corporate Way	Richmond	KY	40475	859-625-1101		247
Web: www.raptech.com						
Richmond Baking Co 520 N Sixth St	Richmond	IN	47374	765-962-8535	962-2253	296-9
Web: www.richmondbaking.com						
Richmond Ballet 407 E Canal St 1st Fl	Richmond	VA	23219	804-344-0906	344-0901	573-1
Web: richmondballet.com						
Richmond Capital Management Inc						
10800 Midlothian Tpke Ste 217	Richmond	VA	23235	804-379-8280		401
Web: www.richmondcap.com						
Richmond Cedric (Rep D - LA)						
420 Cannon HOB	Washington	DC	20515	202-225-6636	225-1988	342-2
Web: richmond.house.gov						
Richmond Chamber of Commerce						
3925 Macdonald Ave	Richmond	CA	94805	510-234-3512	234-3540	139
TF: 866-568-4642 ■ *Web:* www.rcoc.com						
Richmond Chamber of Commerce						
5811 Cooney Rd Ste 101	Richmond	BC	V6X3M1	604-278-2822	278-2972	137
Web: www.richmondchamber.ca						
Richmond City Hall 6911 Rd No 3	Richmond	VA	23219	804-646-7000		337
TF: 800-552-7001 ■ *Web:* www.richmondgov.com						
Richmond Coliseum 601 E Leigh St	Richmond	VA	23219	804-780-4970	780-4606	720
Web: www.richmondcoliseum.net						
Richmond Community College PO Box 1189	Hamlet	NC	28345	910-410-1700	582-7102*	162
**Fax:* Admissions ■ *TF:* 800-908-9946 ■ *Web:* www.richmondcc.edu						
Richmond County 125 S Hancock St	Rockingham	NC	20379	910-997-8211	997-8208	338
Web: richmondnc.com						
Richmond County						
1214 Castleton Ave	Staten Island	NY	10301	718-448-2800	273-8078	338
Web: www.nyc.gov						
Richmond County						
101 Court Cir PO Box 1000	Warsaw	VA	22572	804-333-3781	333-5396	338
Web: www.co.richmond.va.us						
Richmond County Chamber of Commerce						
101 W Broad Ave PO Box 86	Rockingham	NC	28380	910-895-9058	895-9056	139
TF: 800-858-1688 ■ *Web:* www.richmondcountychamber.com						
Richmond County Hospice						
1119 N US Hwy 1	Rockingham	NC	28379	910-997-4464	997-4484	371
Richmond County School System						
864 Broad St	Augusta	GA	30901	706-826-1000		685
Web: www.rcboe.org/home.asp						
Richmond Foundry 126 Collins Rd	Richmond	TX	77469	281-342-5511		307
Web: www.matrixmetalsllc.com						
Richmond Gear PO Box 238	Liberty	SC	29657	864-843-9231	843-1276	709
TF Sales: 800-934-2727 ■ *Web:* www.richmondgear.com						
Richmond Hill Chamber of Commerce (RHCOC)						
376 Church St S	Richmond Hill	ON	L4C9V8	905-884-1961	884-1962	137
Web: www.rhcoc.com						
Richmond Hospital						
7000 Westminster Hwy	Richmond	BC	V6X1A2	604-278-9711		374-2
TF: 800-663-3333 ■ *Web:* www.vch.ca						
Richmond International Airport						
1 Richard E Byrd Terminal D Ste C	Richmond	VA	23250	804-226-3000		27
Web: www.flyrichmond.com						
Richmond International Forest Products Inc						
4050 Innslake Dr Ste 100	Glen Allen	VA	23060	804-747-0111	270-4547	191-3
TF: 800-767-0111 ■ *Web:* www.rifp.com						
Richmond Kickers Soccer Club Inc						
2001 Maywill St Ste 203	Richmond	VA	23230	804-644-5425		717
Web: www.richmondkickers.com						
Richmond Memorial Hospital						
925 Long Dr	Rockingham	NC	28379	910-417-3000		374-3
Web: www.firsthealth.org						
Richmond Metropolitan Convention & Visitors Bureau						
401 N Third St	Richmond	VA	23219	804-782-2777		206
TF: 800-370-9004 ■ *Web:* visitrichmondva.com						
Richmond National Battlefield Park						
3215 E Broad St	Richmond	VA	23223	804-226-1981	771-8522	520
TF: 866-733-7768 ■ *Web:* www.nps.gov						
Richmond North Assoc Inc						
4232 Ridge Lea Rd	Amherst	NY	14226	716-832-5668	832-4236	160
Web: www.rnacollects.com						
Richmond Printing LLC 5825 Schumacher	Houston	TX	77057	713-952-0800		627
TF: 800-839-1154 ■ *Web:* www.richmondprinting.com						
Richmond Public Library						
325 Civic Ctr Plaza	Richmond	CA	94804	510-620-6555	620-6850	434-3
TF: 800-833-2900 ■ *Web:* www.ci.richmond.ca.us						
Richmond Public Library						
101 E Franklin St	Richmond	VA	23219	804-646-7223		434-3
Web: rvalibrary.org						
Richmond Public Relations						
1411 Fourth Ave Ste 610	Seattle	WA	98101	206-682-6979		636
Web: www.richmondpr.com						
Richmond Public Schools						
301 N Ninth St	Richmond	VA	23219	804-780-7700	780-4122	685
Web: web.richmond.k12.va.us						
Richmond State Hospital (RSH)						
498 NW 18th St	Richmond	IN	47374	765-966-0511		374-5
Web: www.in.gov/fssa/dmha/6914.htm						
Richmond Symphony Orchestra						
380 Hubelchison Pkwy PO Box 982	Richmond	IN	47375	765-966-5181	962-8447	573-3
Web: www.richmondsymphony.org						
Richmond Times-Dispatch PO Box 85333	Richmond	VA	23293	804-649-6000	819-1216	637-8
TF: 800-468-3382 ■ *Web:* www.richmond.com						
Richmond Tours 1828 Hylan Blvd	Staten Island	NY	10305	718-979-3111	979-7143	760
Richmond University Medical Ctr						
355 Bard Ave	Staten Island	NY	10310	718-818-1234		374-3
TF: 800-422-8798 ■ *Web:* rumcsi.org						
Richmond, The 1757 Collins Ave	Miami Beach	FL	33139	305-538-2331	531-9021	379
TF: 855-627-3767 ■ *Web:* www.richmondhotel.com						
Richmond/Wayne County Convention & Tourism Bureau						
5701 National Rd E	Richmond	IN	47374	765-935-8687	935-0440	206
TF: 800-828-8414 ■ *Web:* www.visitrichmond.org						
Richmor Aviation Inc						
1142 Rt 9 H Columbia County Airport	Hudson	NY	12534	518-828-9461	828-1303	63
TF: 800-331-6101 ■ *Web:* www.richmor.com						
Richner Communications Inc						
2 Endo Blvd	Garden City	NY	11530	516-569-4000		532-3
Web: www.liherald.com						
Richter & Ratner Contracting Corp						
5505 Flushing Ave	Maspeth	NY	11378	718-497-1600		610
Web: www.richterratner.com						
Richter LLP						
1981 McGill College 11th Fl.	Montreal	QC	H3A0G6	514-934-3400		734
Web: www.richter.ca						
Richter Media Inc						
255 W 23rd St Apt 4ce	New York	NY	10011	212-802-8588		177
Web: www.richtermedia.com						
Richter Studios 1143 W Rundell Pl.	Chicago	IL	60607	312-861-9999		514
Web: www.richterstudios.com						
Richter10.2 Media Group LLC						
600 Cleveland St Bank of America Tower Ste 920	Clearwater	FL	33755	727-447-3600		395
Web: www.richter10point2.com						
Richter7						
280 South 400 West Ste 200	Salt Lake City	UT	84101	801-521-2903		636
Web: www.richter7.com						
Richweb Inc						
4235 Innslake Dr Ste 201	Glen Allen	VA	23060	804-747-8592		225
Web: www.richweb.com						
Richwood Meat Company Inc						
2751 N Santa Fe Ave.	Merced	CA	95348	209-722-8171		296-26
Web: www.richwoodmeat.com						
Rick Engineering Co 5620 Friars Rd	San Diego	CA	92110	619-291-0707		77
Web: www.rickengineering.com						
Rick Husband Amarillo International Airport						
10801 Airport Blvd	Amarillo	TX	79111	806-335-1671	335-1672	27
TF: 800-435-7300 ■ *Web:* airport.amarillo.gov						
Rick Johnson & Assoc of Colorado						
1649 Downing St	Denver	CO	80218	303-296-2200	296-3038	400
TF: 800-530-2300 ■ *Web:* www.denverpi.com						
Rick Steves' Europe Through The Back Door						
130 Fourth Ave N	Edmonds	WA	98020	425-771-8303		772
Web: www.ricksteves.com						
Rick's Cafe Boatyard						
4050 Dandy Trl	Indianapolis	IN	46254	317-290-9300		671
Web: www.rickscafeboatyard.com						
Rickard Circular Folding Co						
325 N Ashland Ave	Chicago	IL	60607	312-243-6300	243-6323	92
TF: 800-747-1389 ■ *Web:* www.rickardbindery.com						
Rickenbacker International Corp						
3895 S Main St.	Santa Ana	CA	92707	714-545-5574		527
Web: www.rickenbacker.com						
Rickenbaugh Cadillac Co 777 Broadway	Denver	CO	80203	303-573-7773		57
Web: rickenbaughvolvo.com						
Ricker Oil Company Inc 30 W 11th St.	Anderson	IN	46016	765-643-3016		297-8
Web: rickersrewards.com						
Ricker Pond State Park						
18 Ricker Pond Camp Ground Rd	Groton	VT	05046	802-584-3821		565
Web: www.vtstateparks.com						
Ricker, Atkinson, Mcbee & Associates Inc						
2105 S Hardy Dr Ste 13	Tempe	AZ	85282	480-921-8100		261
Web: www.rammeng.com						
Ricketts Glen State Park						
695 State Rt 487	Benton	PA	17814	570-477-5675		565
Web: www.dcnr.state.pa.us						
Ricketts Pete (R) PO Box 94848	Lincoln	NE	68509	402-471-2244	471-6031	343
Web: www.governor.nebraska.gov						
Ricks Barbecue 2347 US-43	Leoma	TN	38468	931-852-2324		186
TF: 800-544-5864 ■ *Web:* www.ricksbbq.com						
Rickwood Caverns State Park						
370 Rickwood Pk Rd.	Warrior	AL	35180	205-647-9692	647-9692	565
TF: 800-252-7275 ■ *Web:* www.alapark.com						
Rico Foods Inc 578 E 19th St	Paterson	NJ	07514	973-278-0589		345
Web: www.ricofood.com						
Rico International						
8484 San Fernando Rd	Sun Valley	CA	91352	818-394-2700		527
Web: www.ricoreeds.com						
Ricochet Fuel Distributors Inc						
1201 Royal Pkwy	Euless	TX	76040	817-268-5910		316
TF: 800-721-4147 ■ *Web:* www.ricochetfuel.com						
Ricoh Americas Corp						
5 Dedrick Pl	West Caldwell	NJ	07006	973-882-2000		112
TF: 800-727-1885 ■ *Web:* www.ricoh-usa.com						
Ricoh Electronics Inc						
1100 Valencia Ave	Tustin	CA	92780	714-566-2500		173-7
Web: www.rei.ricoh.com						

Name / Address	City	State	Zip	Phone	Fax	Class
Ricoh Printing Systems America Inc						
2390 Ward Ave Ste A	Simi Valley	CA	93065	805-578-4000	578-4001	173-6
Web: www.rpsa.ricoh.com						
Ricon Corp 7900 Nelson Rd	Panorama City	CA	91402	818-267-3000		256
TF: 800-322-2884 ■ *Web:* www.riconcorp.com						
Ricos Products Company Inc						
830 S Presa St	San Antonio	TX	78210	210-222-1415	226-6453	300
Web: www.ricos.com						
RID (Registry of Interpreters for the Deaf Inc)						
333 Commerce St	Alexandria	VA	22314	703-838-0030	838-0454	49-5
TF: 800-356-3035 ■ *Web:* www.rid.org						
Ridco Casting Co						
6 Beverage Hill Ave	Pawtucket	RI	02860	401-724-0400	724-6320	308
Web: www.ridco.com						
Riddle Memorial Hospital						
1068 W Baltimore Pike	Media	PA	19063	484-227-9400		374-3
TF: 866-225-5654 ■ *Web:* www.mainlinehealth.org						
Riddle Village 1048 W Baltimore Pk	Media	PA	19063	610-891-3700	891-3671	672
Web: www.riddlevillage.com						
Riddleberger Bros Inc (RBI)						
6127 S Valley Pk	Mount Crawford	VA	22841	540-434-1731	432-1691	186
Web: www.rbiva.com						
Ride Inc PO Box 6213	Drayton Valley	AB	T7A1R7	780-621-1570		711
Web: www.rideinc.com						
Rideau Inc 473 Deslauriers	Montreal	QC	H4N1W2	800-363-6464		463
TF: 800-363-6464 ■ *Web:* www.rideau.com						
Rideout Memorial Hospital						
726 Fourth St	Marysville	CA	95901	530-749-4300	751-4226	374-3
TF: 888-923-3800 ■ *Web:* www.frhg.org						
Rider Dickerson Inc						
815 Twenty-Fifth Ave	Bellwood	IL	60104	312-427-2926		627
TF: 800-935-9935 ■ *Web:* www.riderdickerson.com						
Rider University						
2083 Lawrenceville Rd	Lawrenceville	NJ	08648	609-896-5000	895-6645*	166
**Fax:* Admissions ■ *TF:* 800-257-9026 ■ *Web:* www.rider.edu						
Westminster Choir College						
101 Walnut Ln	Princeton	NJ	08540	609-921-7100	921-2538*	166
**Fax:* Admissions ■ *TF:* 800-962-4647 ■ *Web:* www.rider.edu						
Ridewell Corp PO Box 4586	Springfield	MO	65808	417-833-4565		60
TF: 877-434-8088 ■ *Web:* www.ridewellcorp.com						
Ridge Behavioral Health System						
3050 Rio Dosa Dr	Lexington	KY	40509	859-269-2325		374-5
TF: 800-753-4673 ■ *Web:* www.ridgebhs.com						
Ridge Engineering Inc						
3987 Hampstead Mexico Rd	Hampstead	MD	21074	410-239-7716	239-8710	454
Web: www.ridgeeng.com						
Ridge Meadows Hospital						
11666 Laity St	Maple Ridge	BC	V2X7G5	604-463-4111		374-2
TF: 800-935-5669 ■ *Web:* www.fraserhealth.ca						
Ridge Printing Corp						
8900 Yellow Brick Rd	Rosedale	MD	21237	410-668-4780		627
TF: 800-677-1997 ■ *Web:* www.ridgeprinting.com						
Ridge Tahoe						
400 Ridge Club Dr PO Box 5790	Stateline	NV	89449	775-588-3553	588-1551	669
TF: 800-334-1600 ■ *Web:* www.ridgetahoeresort.com						
Ridge Tool Co 400 Clark St	Elyria	OH	44035	440-323-5581		758
Web: www.ridgid.com						
Ridgecrest Area Convention & Visitors Bureau (RACVB)						
643 N China Lake Blvd Ste C	Ridgecrest	CA	93555	760-375-8202	375-9850	206
TF: 800-847-4830 ■ *Web:* racvb.com						
Ridgecrest Chamber of Commerce						
128-B E California Ave Ste B	Ridgecrest	CA	93555	760-375-8331	375-0365	139
TF: 800-829-4933 ■ *Web:* www.ridgecrestchamber.com						
Ridgedale Ctr 12401 Wayzata Blvd	Minnetonka	MN	55305	952-541-4864		460
Web: www.ridgedalecenter.com						
Ridgefield Symphony Orchestra						
77 Danbury Rd	Ridgefield	CT	06877	203-438-3889		573-3
Web: www.ridgefieldsymphony.org						
Ridgeline Consulting Group Inc						
1110 Winchester Trl	Downingtown	PA	19335	610-518-1430		196
Ridgestone Corp						
10880 Wilshire Blvd Ste 910	Los Angeles	CA	90024	310-209-5300		401
Web: www.ridgestonecorp.com						
Ridgetop Group Inc 3580 W Ina Rd	Tuscan	AZ	85741	520-742-3300		261
Web: www.ridgetopgroup.com						
Ridgeview Animal Hospital						
18146 Wright St	Omaha	NE	68130	402-333-3366		794
Web: www.ridgeviewanimalhosp.com						
Ridgeview Institute Inc 3995 S Cobb Dr	Smyrna	GA	30080	770-434-4567		726
Web: www.ridgeviewinstitute.com						
Ridgeview Medical Ctr (RMC)						
500 S Maple St	Waconia	MN	55387	952-442-2191	442-6524	374-3
TF: 800-967-4620 ■ *Web:* www.ridgeviewmedical.org						
RidgeviewTel LLC						
1880 Industrial Cir Ste C	Longmont	CO	80501	303-309-4005		387
Ridgewater College						
Hutchinson 2 Century Ave SE	Hutchinson	MN	55350	320-234-8500		800
TF: 800-722-1151 ■ *Web:* www.ridgewater.edu						
Willmar 2101 15th Ave NW PO Box 1097	Willmar	MN	56201	320-222-5200	222-5216*	800
**Fax:* Admissions ■ *TF:* 800-722-1151 ■ *Web:* www.ridgewater.edu						
Ridgewood High School						
7500 W Montrose Ave	Norridge	IL	60706	708-456-4242	456-0342	449
Web: www.ridgenet.org						
Ridgewood Racquet Club						
249 Ackerman Ave	Ridgewood	NJ	07450	201-652-1991		354
Web: www.ridgewoodracquet.com						
Ridgewood Savings Bank						
71-02 Forest Ave	Ridgewood	NY	11385	718-240-4800		70
TF: 800-250-4832 ■ *Web:* www.ridgewoodbank.com						
Ridgmar Mall 1888 Green Oaks Rd	Fort Worth	TX	76116	817-731-6591	763-5146	460
Web: www.ridgmar.com						
Ridg-U-Rak Inc 120 S Lake St	North East	PA	16428	814-725-8751	725-5659	286
TF: 866-479-7225 ■ *Web:* www.ridgurak.com						
Ridgway State Park 28555 Hwy 550	Ridgway	CO	81432	970-626-5822		565
Web: cpw.state.co.us						
Riding Mountain Park East Gate Registration Complex National Historic Site of Canada						
135 Wasagaming Dr PO Box 299	Onanole	MB	R0J1N0	204-848-7275	848-2596	563
Web: www.pc.gc.ca/eng/lhn-nhs/mb/eastgate/index.aspx						

Name / Address	City	State	Zip	Phone	Fax	Class
Ridley College						
2 Ridley Rd PO Box 3013	Saint Catharines	ON	L2R7C3	905-684-1889	684-8875	622
Web: www.ridley.on.ca						
Ridley Creek State Park						
1023 Sycamore Mills Rd	Media	PA	19063	610-892-3900		565
Web: www.dcnr.state.pa.us						
Ridout Lumber Co 125 Henry Farrar Dr	Searcy	AR	72143	501-268-3929		191-3
Web: www.ridoutlumber.com						
Riechmann Transport Inc						
3328 W Chain of Rocks Rd	Granite City	IL	62040	618-797-6700		780
TF: 800-844-4225 ■ *Web:* www.riechmanntransport.com						
Ried & Agee PLLC 3633 26th St W	Bradenton	FL	34205	941-756-8791		445
Web: www.reidagee.com						
Riedel Marketing Group						
5327 E Pinchot Ave	Phoenix	AZ	85018	602-840-4948		345
Web: 4rmg.com						
Riedell Shoes Inc						
122 Cannon River Ave	Red Wing	MN	55066	651-388-8251	385-5500	710
TF: 800-698-6893 ■ *Web:* www.riedellskates.com						
Rieders, Travis, Humphrey, Waters & Dohrmann						
161 W Third St	Williamsport	PA	17701	570-323-8711		428
TF: 800-326-9259 ■ *Web:* www.riederstravis.com						
Riege Software International u s a						
73 Redding Rd	Georgetown	CT	06829	203-544-9475		311
Web: www.riege.com						
Riegel Consumer Products						
51 Riegel Rd	Johnston	SC	29832	803-275-2541	275-2219	746
TF: 800-845-3251 ■ *Web:* www.riegellinen.com						
Riegel Printing Company Inc						
1 Graphics Dr	Ewing	NJ	08628	609-771-0555		627
TF: 800-882-1844 ■ *Web:* www.riegelprintinginc.com						
Rieke Corp 500 W Seventh St	Auburn	IN	46706	260-925-3700		608
Web: www.riekepackaging.com						
Rieke Office Interiors 2000 Fox Ln	Elgin	IL	60123	847-622-9711		320
Web: www.rieke.com						
Riekes Equipment Co 6703 L St	Omaha	NE	68117	402-593-1181	593-9295	385
TF: 800-856-0931 ■ *Web:* www.riekesequipment.com						
Riel House National Historic Site of Canada						
330 River Rd	Winnipeg	MB	R2M3Z8	519-826-5391	787-6221*	563
**Fax Area Code:* 866 ■ *TF:* 888-773-8888 ■ *Web:* pc.gc.ca/en/agence-agency/courriel-email						
Riemer & Braunstein LLP						
3 Ctr Plaza 6th Fl	Boston	MA	02108	617-523-9000		428
Web: www.riemerlaw.com						
Riephoff Sawmill Inc 763 Rt 524	Allentown	NJ	08501	609-259-7265		683
Web: www.riephoffsawmill.com						
Ries & Ries 2195 River Cliff Dr	Roswell	GA	30076	770-643-0880		195
Web: www.ries.com						
Ries Graphics Ltd 12727 W Custer Ave	Butler	WI	53007	262-781-5720		627
Web: www.riesgraphics.com						
Riesbeck Food Markets Inc						
48661 National Rd	Saint Clairsville	OH	43950	740-695-7050	695-7555	345
Web: www.riesbeckfoods.com						
Riester 3344 E Camelback Rd	Phoenix	AZ	85018	844-602-3344		7
TF: 844-602-3344 ■ *Web:* www.riester.com						
Riesterer & Schnell Inc N2909 Hwy 32	Pulaski	WI	54162	920-822-3077		274
Web: www.rands.com						
RIEtech Global LLC						
3700 Singer Blvd NE Ste A	Albuquerque	NM	87109	505-299-6623		693
Web: www.rietechglobal.com						
Rieter Automotive North America Inc						
38555 Hills Tech Dr	Farmington Hills	MI	48331	248-848-0100	848-0130	60
TF: 800-915-0635 ■ *Web:* www.rieter.com						
Rieth-Riley Construction Company Inc						
3626 Elkhart Rd	Goshen	IN	46526	574-875-5183	875-8405	188-4
Web: rieth-riley.com						
RIF (Reading Is Fundamental Inc)						
1825 Connecticut Ave NW Ste 400	Washington	DC	20009	202-536-3400		48-11
TF: 877-743-7323 ■ *Web:* www.rif.org						
Rife Resources Ltd						
400 144 - Fourth Ave SW	Calgary	AB	T2P3N4	403-221-0800		536
TF: 888-257-1873 ■ *Web:* www.rife.com						
Rifenburg Construction Inc						
159 Brick Church Rd	Troy	NY	12180	518-279-3265	279-4260	188-4
Web: www.rifenburg.com						
Rifle Correctional Ctr						
200 County Rd 219	Rifle	CO	81650	970-625-1700		213
Rifle Falls State Park 5775 Hwy 325	Rifle	CO	81650	970-625-1607		565
Web: cpw.state.co.us						
Rifle Gap State Park 5775 Hwy 325	Rifle	CO	81650	970-625-1607		565
Web: cpw.state.co.us						
Rifle River Recreation Area						
2550 Rose City Rd	Lupton	MI	48635	989-473-2258		565
Web: www.michigandnr.com						
Rigaku Americas Corp						
9009 New Trails Dr	The Woodlands	TX	77381	281-362-2300	364-3628	475
TF: 800-982-1187 ■ *Web:* www.rigaku.com						
Rig-Chem Inc 132 Thompson Rd	Houma	LA	70363	985-873-7208		539
TF: 800-375-7208 ■ *Web:* www.rigchem.com						
Rigel Networks LLC						
1500 Quail St Ste 280	Newport Beach	CA	92660	949-891-2571		196
Web: www.rigelnetworks.com						
Rigel Pharmaceuticals Inc						
1180 Veterans Blvd	South San Francisco	CA	94080	650-624-1100	624-1101	85
NASDAQ: RIGL ■ *TF:* 800-414-3627 ■ *Web:* www.rigel.com						
Rigel Shipping Canada Inc						
3521 Rt 134	Shediac Cape	NB	E4P3G6	506-533-9000		314
Web: www.rigelcanada.com						
Rigg Darlington Group Inc, The						
14 E Welsh Pool Rd	Exton	PA	19341	484-876-2222		390
Rigging International						
1210 Marina Village Pkwy	Alameda	CA	94501	510-865-2400	865-9450	189-1
Web: www.sarens.com						
Riggins Co Lc 410 Rotary St	Hampton	VA	23661	757-826-0525		480
Web: www.rigginscompany.com						
Riggins Inc 3938 S Main Rd	Vineland	NJ	08360	856-825-7600		316
TF: 800-642-9148 ■ *Web:* www.rigginsoil.com						
Riggs Abney Neal Orbison & Lewis Inc						
502 W Sixth St Frisco Bldg	Tulsa	OK	74119	918-587-3161		428
Web: www.riggsabney.com						

	City	State	Zip	Phone	Fax	Class
Riggs Machine & Fabricating Inc 3850 Belford St.	Ashland	KY	41101	606-324-0090		454
Web: www.riggsmachine.com						
Right at Home Inc 6464 Crt St Ste 150	Omaha	NE	68106	402-697-7537	697-0289	310
TF: 877-697-7537 ■ *Web:* www.rightathome.net						
Right at Home Properties PO Box 631154	Irving	TX	75063	972-333-4164		652
Web: www.rightathomeproperties.com						
Right Mfg 7949 Stromesa Ct Ste G	San Diego	CA	92126	858-566-7002	566-7623	482
Web: www.rightmfg.com						
Right Systems Inc 2600 Willamette Dr NE Ste C	Lacey	WA	98516	360-956-0414	956-0336	225
TF: 800-571-1717 ■ *Web:* www.rightsys.com						
Right/Pointe Co 234 Harvestore Dr(PO Box 467)	Dekalb	IL	60115	815-754-5700		3
Web: www.rightpointe.com						
RightAnswer.com Inc 2900 Rodd St	Midland	MI	48641	989-835-5000		387
Web: www.rightanswer.com						
Righteous Babe 341 Delaware Ave PO Box 95	Buffalo	NY	14202	716-852-8020	852-2741	657
TF: 800-664-3769 ■ *Web:* www.righteousbabe.com						
Right-Gard Corp 531 N Fourth St	Denver	PA	17517	717-336-7594		576
RightHand Technologies Inc 6545 N Olmsted Ave	Chicago	IL	60631	773-774-7600		393
TF: 800-561-3357 ■ *Web:* www.righthandtech.com						
Rightside Group Ltd 5808 Lake Washington Blvd NE	Kirkland	WA	98033	425-298-2500		387
TF: 800-732-0330 ■ *Web:* www.rightside.co						
RightStaff Inc 4919 McKinney Ave	Dallas	TX	75205	214-953-0900		260
Web: www.rightstaffinc.com						
RightsTrade LLC 12001 Ventura Pl Ste 500	Studio City	CA	91604	818-762-5811	753-0322	224
Web: www.rightstrade.com						
Rightway Gate Inc 5858 Edison Pl.	Carlsbad	CA	92008	760-736-3700		224
TF: 888-398-4703 ■ *Web:* www.rwgusa.com						
Rigid Hitch Inc 3301 W Burnsville Pkwy	Burnsville	MN	55337	952-895-5001		763
TF Cust Svc: 800-624-7630 ■ *Web:* www.rigidhitch.com						
Rigidized Metals Corp 658 Ohio St.	Buffalo	NY	14203	716-849-4760		492
TF: 800-836-2580 ■ *Web:* www.rigidized.com						
Rigidply Rafters Inc 701 E Linden St.	Richland	PA	17087	717-866-6581		191-3
Web: www.rigidply.com						
RigNet Inc 1880 S Dairy Ashford Rd Ste 300	Houston	TX	77077	281-674-0100		224
TF: 800-638-8844 ■ *Web:* www.rig.net						
Ri-go Lift Truck Ltd 175 Courtland Ave	Concord	ON	L4K4T2	905-738-0094		358
TF: 800-263-7580 ■ *Web:* www.rigolift.com						
Rigsby Food Mart 5602 US Hwy 87 E	San Antonio	TX	78222	210-648-0093		297-8
Web: texaco.com						
Rigsby's Kitchen 698 N High St	Columbus	OH	43215	614-461-7888		671
Web: www.rigsbyskitchen.com						
RIHM Motor Co 2108 University Ave W	Saint Paul	MN	55114	651-646-7833	646-0630	516
Web: www.rihmkenworth.com						
Riiser Energy 709 S 20th Ave	Wausau	WI	54401	715-845-7272		324
TF: 800-570-8024 ■ *Web:* www.riiser.com						
Riker, Danzig, Scherer, Hyland & Perretti LLP 1 Speedwell Ave	Morristown	NJ	07962	973-538-0800		428
TF: 800-284-8663 ■ *Web:* www.riker.com						
RILA (Retail Industry Leaders Assn) 1700 N Moore St Ste 2250	Arlington	VA	22209	703-841-2300	841-1184	49-18
TF: 800-758-5840 ■ *Web:* www.rila.org						
Riley Bennett Egloff LLP 141 E Washington St 4th Fl	Indianapolis	IN	46204	317-636-8000	636-8027	428
Web: www.rbelaw.com						
Riley Construction Company Inc 5301 99th Ave.	Kenosha	WI	53144	262-658-4381		186
TF: 800-393-1826 ■ *Web:* www.rileycon.com						
Riley County 110 Courthouse Plaza	Manhattan	KS	66502	785-537-6300	537-6394	338
Web: rileycountyks.gov						
Riley Gear Corp 1 Precision Dr	St. Augustine	FL	32092	904-829-5652		483
TF: 800-881-3473 ■ *Web:* www.rileygear.com						
Riley Hayes Adv 333 S First St	Minneapolis	MN	55401	612-338-7161		4
Web: www.rileyhayes.com						
Riley Industrial Services Inc 2615 San Juan Blvd PO Box 2014	Farmington	NM	87401	505-327-4947	326-0305	172
Web: www.rileyindustrial.com						
Riley's 312 Pk St.	Syracuse	NY	13203	315-471-7111		671
Rim Country Mechanical Inc 261 N Eighth St	Show Low	AZ	85901	928-537-1803		610
Web: rimcountrymechanical.com						
Rim Country Regional Chamber of Commerce 100 W Main St	Payson	AZ	85547	928-474-4515	474-8812	139
TF: 800-249-2678 ■ *Web:* www.rimcountrychamber.com						
Rim Forest Lumber Company Inc 26491 Pine Ave.	Rimforest	CA	92378	909-337-6262		683
Web: www.rimlumber.com						
RIM Logistics Ltd 200 N Gary Ave	Roselle	IL	60172	630-595-0610	595-0614	449
TF: 888-275-0937 ■ *Web:* www.rimlogistics.com						
Rima Enterprises Inc 5340 Argosy Ave.	Huntington Beach	CA	92649	714-893-4534		628
Web: www.rima-system.com						
Rima Mfg Co 3850 Munson Hwy	Hudson	MI	49247	517-448-8921	448-7142	621
Web: www.rimamfg.com						
Rimage Corp 7725 Washington Ave S	Minneapolis	MN	55439	952-944-8144		173-8
TF: 800-445-8288 ■ *Web:* www.qumu.com						
Rimbey Hospital & Care Ctr 5228 50th Ave PO Box 440	Rimbey	AB	T0C2J0	403-843-2271	843-2506	374-2
Web: albertahealthservices.ca						
Rimex Metals (USA) Inc 2850 Woodbridge Ave	Edison	NJ	08837	732-549-3800	549-6435	481
Web: www.rimexmetals.com						
Rimex Supply Ltd 9726 186th St.	Surrey	BC	V4N3N7	604-888-0025		111
TF: 800-663-9883 ■ *Web:* www.rimex.com						
Rimkus Consulting Group Inc 8 Greenway Plaza Ste 500	Houston	TX	77046	713-621-3550		196
TF: 800-580-3228 ■ *Web:* www.rimkus.com						
Rimrock Corp 1700 Jetway Blvd	Columbus	OH	43219	614-471-5926	471-7388	456
TF: 800-558-7733 ■ *Web:* www.rimrockcorp.com						
Rimrock Dude Ranch 2728 Northfork Rt	Cody	WY	82414	307-587-3970		239
Web: www.rimrockranch.com						
Rimrock Foundation 1231 N 29th St	Billings	MT	59101	406-248-3175	248-3821	726
TF: 800-227-3953 ■ *Web:* www.rimrock.org						
Rimrock Resort Hotel, The 300 Mountain Ave PO Box 1110	Banff	AB	T1L1J2	403-762-3356		669
TF: 888-746-7625 ■ *Web:* www.rimrockresort.com						
RIMS (Risk & Insurance Management Society Inc) 1065 Ave of the Americas 13th Fl	New York	NY	10018	212-286-9292	986-9716	49-9
Web: www.rims.org						
Rimtec Corp 1702 Beverly Rd	Burlington	NJ	08016	609-387-0011	387-1436	605-2
Web: www.rimtec.com						
Rina Group LLC 8180 Corporate Park Dr Ste 140	Cincinnati	OH	45242	513-469-7462		177
Web: www.rinasystems.com						
Rinaldi Printing Co 4514 E Adamo Dr	Tampa	FL	33605	813-247-3921		627
TF: 800-766-3224 ■ *Web:* www.rinaldiprinting.com						
Rinchem Company Inc 6133 Edith Blvd NE	Albuquerque	NM	87107	505-345-3655	998-4378	449
TF: 888-375-2436 ■ *Web:* www.rinchem.com						
Rinck Advertising 2 Great Falls Plaza Unit 8	Auburn	ME	04210	207-755-9470		636
Web: www.rinckadvertising.com						
Rincon Research Corp 101 N Wilmot Rd Ste 101	Tucson	AZ	85711	520-519-4600	519-4747	466
Web: rincon.com						
Rindt-McDuff Associates Inc 334 Cherokee St NE	Marietta	GA	30060	770-427-8123		261
Web: www.rindt-mcduff.com						
Rinehart Oil Inc 2401 N State St	Ukiah	CA	95482	707-462-8811		579
Web: www.rinehartoil.com						
RINET Company LLC 101 Federal St 14th Fl	Boston	MA	02110	617-488-2700		194
Web: www.rinetco.com						
Ring Container Technology 1 Industrial Park Rd	Oakland	TN	38060	800-280-6333	465-1179*	124
*Fax Area Code: 901 ■ *TF:* 800-280-6333 ■ *Web:* www.ringcontainer.com						
Ring Energy Inc 901 W Wall St 3rd Fl.	Midland	TX	79701	432-682-7464		536
Web: ringenergy.com						
Ring of Fire 1099 Chambers St	Eugene	OR	97402	541-343-8488		671
Web: ringoffirerestaurant.wordpress.com						
Ring of Fire Studios LLC 1702 Olympic Blvd Studio A	Santa Monica	CA	90404	310-966-5055		514
TF: 800-598-4008 ■ *Web:* www.ringoffire.com						
Ring's End Inc 181 W Ave	Darien	CT	06820	203-655-2525		752
TF: 800-652-2835 ■ *Web:* www.ringsend.com						
Ringdale Inc 101 Halmar Cove	Georgetown	TX	78628	512-288-9080	288-7210	176
TF: 888-288-9080 ■ *Web:* www.ringdale.com						
Ringfeder Power Transmission USA Corp 165 Carver Ave	Westwood	NJ	07675	201-666-3320		770
Web: www.ringfeder.com						
Ringgold County 109 W Madison St	Mount Ayr	IA	50854	641-464-3239		338
Ringgold Telephone Company Inc 200 Evitt Pkwy PO Box 869	Ringgold	GA	30736	706-965-2345		224
Web: www.rtctel.com						
Ringland-Johnson Construction 1725 Huntwood Dr	Cherry Valley	IL	61016	815-332-8600	332-8411	186
Web: www.ringland.com						
Ringler Assoc Inc 27422 Aliso Creek Rd Ste 200	Aliso Viejo	CA	92656	949-296-9000		509
Web: www.ringlerassociates.com						
Ringling Bros & Barnum & Bailey Circus 8607 Westwood Ctr Dr	Vienna	VA	22182	703-448-4000		149
Web: www.ringling.com						
Ringling College of Art & Design 2700 N Tamiami Trl.	Sarasota	FL	34234	941-351-5100	359-7517	164
TF: 800-255-7695 ■ *Web:* www.ringling.edu						
Ringmaster Jewelers Inc 1990 Healy Dr.	Winston-Salem	NC	27103	336-722-2218		410
Web: ringmasterjewelers.com						
Ringo Drilling I LP 104 Spinks Rd	Tye	TX	79563	325-695-5600		540
Web: www.ringodrilling.com						
Ringold Financial Management Services Inc 850 S Wabash Ave Ste 210	Chicago	IL	60605	312-566-9705		2
Web: www.ringoldfinancial.com						
Ringside SteakHouse, The 2165 W Burnside St	Portland	OR	97210	503-223-1513	223-6908	671
TF: 800-688-4142 ■ *Web:* www.ringsidesteakhouse.com						
Ringwood State Park 1304 Sloatsburg Rd	Ringwood	NJ	07456	973-962-7031		565
TF: 800 852 7899 ■ *Web:* www.njparksandforests.org						
Rink Printing Company Inc 814 S Main St.	South Bend	IN	46601	574-232-7935		627
TF: 800-232-0552 ■ *Web:* www.rinkprinting.com						
Rink Systems Inc 1103 Hershey St.	Albert Lea	MN	56007	507-373-9175	377-1060	14
TF: 800-944-7930 ■ *Web:* www.rinksystems.com						
Rinke Noonan US Bank Plaza 1015 W St Germain St Ste 300	Saint Cloud	MN	56302	320-251-6700		428
TF: 800-318-4473 ■ *Web:* www.rinkenoonan.com						
Rinker Materials Corp Concrete Pipe Div 8311 W Carder Ct.	Littleton	CO	80125	303-791-1600	791-1710	183
TF: 800-909-7763 ■ *Web:* www.rinkerpipe.com						
Rio Bank 1655 N 23rd	Mcallen	TX	78501	956-631-7890	972-1574	70
Web: riobk.com						
Rio Blanco County 555 Main St PO Box 1067	Meeker	CO	81641	970-878-9460	878-3587	338
Web: www.co.rio-blanco.co.us						
RIO Brands 10981 Decatur Rd	Philadelphia	PA	19154	215-632-2800		319-4
Web: riobrands.com						
Rio Bravo Oil Inc 5858 Westheimer Rd Ste 669	Houston	TX	77057	713-787-9060		536
Rio Chama Steakhouse 414 Old Santa Fe Trl	Santa Fe	NM	87501	505-955-0765		671
Web: www.riochamasteakhouse.com						
Rio City Cafe 1110 Front St.	Sacramento	CA	95814	916-442-8226		671
Web: www.riocitycafe.com						

Name / Address	City	State	ZIP	Phone	Fax	Class
Rio Delmar Enterprises 8338 Elliott Rd	Easton	MD	21601	410-822-8866		429
Web: www.stihldcolor.net						
Rio Grande Bible Institute & Language School						
4300 S US Hwy 281	Edinburg	TX	78539	956-380-8100		48-20
Web: www.riogrande.edu						
Rio Grande Cafe						
270 S Rio Grande St	Salt Lake City	UT	84101	801-364-3302		671
Rio Grande Co 201 Santa Fe Dr	Denver	CO	80223	303-825-2211	629-0417	191-1
TF: 800-935-8420 ■ Web: www.riograndeco.com						
Rio Grande County 965 Sixth St	Del Norte	CO	81132	719-657-3334	657-2621	338
TF: 800-214-1240 ■ Web: www.riograndecounty.org						
Rio Grande Electric Co-op Inc						
Hwy 90 & State Hwy 131 PO Box 1509	Brackettville	TX	78832	830-563-2444	563-2450	245
TF: 800-749-1509 ■ Web: www.riogrande.coop						
Rio Grande Mexican Restaurant						
160 Ct St Ste 7	Charleston	WV	25301	304-344-8616		671
Web: www.eatriogrande.com						
Rio Grande Nature Ctr State Park						
2901 Candelaria Rd NW	Albuquerque	NM	87107	505-344-7240	344-4505	565
Web: www.rgnc.org						
Rio Grande Regional Hospital						
101 E Ridge Rd	McAllen	TX	78503	956-632-6000		374-3
Web: www.riohealth.com						
Rio Grande Valley Sugar Growers						
PO Box 459	Santa Rosa	TX	78593	956-636-1411		296-38
Web: www.rgvsugar.com						
Rio Grande Wild & Scenic River						
PO Box 129	Big Bend National Park	TX	79834	432-477-2251	477-1175	564
TF: 800-839-7238 ■ Web: www.nps.gov/rigr						
Rio Grill 101 the Crossroads	Carmel	CA	93923	831-625-5436		671
Web: www.riogrill.com						
Rio Hondo College						
3600 Workman Mill Rd	Whittier	CA	90601	562-692-0921	699-7386	162
TF: 800-785-0585 ■ Web: www.riohondo.edu						
Rio Products International						
5050 S Yellowstone Hwy	Idaho Falls	ID	83402	208-524-7760		208
Web: www.rioproducts.com						
Rio Ranch 9999 Westheimer Rd	Houston	TX	77042	713-952-5000	952-2263	671
Web: www.rioranch.com						
Rio Rancho Chamber of Commerce						
4001 Southern Blvd SE	Rio Rancho	NM	87124	505-892-1533	892-6157	139
Web: rrrcc.org						
Rio Rio Cantina 421 E Commerce St	San Antonio	TX	78205	210-226-8462	226-8443	671
Web: www.rioriorriverwalk.com						
Rio Salado College 2323 W 14Th St	Tempe	AZ	85281	480-517-8000		162
TF: 855-622-2332 ■ Web: www.riosalado.edu						
Rio Technical Services LLC						
4200 S Hulen	Fort Worth	TX	76109	817-735-8264		261
Rio Verde Landscaping						
25609 N Danny Ln	Rio Verde	AZ	85263	480-471-1962	471-0107	187
TF: 800-233-7103 ■ Web: www.theverdes.com						
RioCan Real Estate Investment Trust						
2300 Yonge St Ste 500 PO Box 2386	Toronto	ON	M4P1E4	416-866-3033	866-3020	654
TSE: REI.UN.CA ■ TF: 800-465-2733 ■ Web: www.riocan.com						
RioMar 800 S Peters St	New Orleans	LA	70130	504-525-3474		671
Web: www.riomarseafood.com						
Riordan Lewis & Haden						
10900 Wilshire Blvd Ste 850	Los Angeles	CA	90024	310-405-7200	405-7222	792
Web: www.rlhinvestors.com						
Riordan Mansion State Historic Park						
409 W Riordan Rd	Flagstaff	AZ	86001	928-779-4395		565
Rios Golden Cut Inc 121 N Pk Blvd	San Antonio	TX	78204	210-227-4996		77
Riotel Group 250 Ave du Phare Est	Matane	QC	G4W3N4	418-566-2651		707
TF: 877-566-2651 ■ Web: www.riotel.com						
Riovida Networks 2133 Clinton Ave	Alameda	CA	94501	510-693-0166		195
Rip city radio 620						
13333 SW 68th Pkwy Ste 310	Tigard	OR	97223	503-323-6400		645-128
TF: 844-289-7234 ■ Web: ripcityradio.iheart.com						
Rip Curl Inc 3030 Airway Ave	Costa Mesa	CA	92626	714-422-3642		77
Web: www.ripcurl.com						
Rip Griffin Truck Travel Ctr Inc						
4710 Fourth St	Lubbock	TX	79416	806-795-8785	795-6574	324
TF: 800-333-9330 ■ Web: www.ripgriffin.com						
Ripa Engineering Corp						
9555 Owensmouth Ave Nbr 8	Chatsworth	CA	91311	818-773-8722		261
Web: ripaeng.com						
Ripcho Studio 7630 Lorain Ave	Cleveland	OH	44102	216-631-0664		590
TF: 800-686-7427 ■ Web: www.ripchostudio.com						
Ripcord Llc 3455 Ringsby Ct Ste 103	Denver	CO	80216	303-221-2824		7
Web: ripcordsolutions.com						
Ripe Tomato 5064 N Palm Ave	Fresno	CA	93704	559-225-1850		671
Web: tripadvisor.com						
RIPIRG (Rhode Island Public Interest Research Group)						
9 S Angell St Second Fl-A	Providence	RI	02906	401-608-1201		633
Web: www.ripirg.org						
Ripley Co 46 Nooks Hill Rd	Cromwell	CT	06416	860-635-2200	635-3631	758
TF: 800-528-8665 ■ Web: www.ripley-tools.com						
Ripley County 209 W Highway St	Doniphan	MO	63935	573-996-2212		338
Web: www.ripleycountymissouri.org						
Ripley County 115 N Main St	Versailles	IN	47042	812-689-6115	689-6000	338
Web: www.ripleycounty.com						
Ripley Entertainment Inc						
601 E Palace Pkwy	Grand Prairie	TX	75050	972-263-2391		520
TF: 800-582-7272 ■ Web: www.ripleys.com						
Ripley Entertainment Inc						
7576 Kingspointe Pkwy Ste 188	Orlando	FL	32819	407-345-8010	345-0801	31
TF: 800-713-7278 ■ Web: www.ripleys.com						
Ripley's Aquarium						
1110 Celebrity Cir	Myrtle Beach	SC	29577	843-916-0888		40
TF: 800-734-8888 ■ Web: www.ripleys.com						
Ripley's Believe It or Not! Museum						
1441 Boardwalk	Atlantic City	NJ	08401	609-347-2001		520
Web: ripleys.com						
Ripley's Believe It or Not! Museum						
3326 W Hwy 76	Branson	MO	65616	417-337-5300		520
Web: www.ripleys.com						
Ripley's Believe It or Not! Museum						
901 N Ocean Blvd	Myrtle Beach	SC	29577	843-448-2331		520
TF: 800-905-4228 ■ Web: www.ripleys.com						
Ripley's Believe It or Not! Museum						
4960 Clifton Hill	Niagara Falls	ON	L2G3N4	905-356-2238		520
Web: ripleys.com/niagarafalls						
Ripley's Believe It or Not! Museum						
19 San Marco Ave	Saint Augustine	FL	32084	904-824-1606	829-1790	520
TF: 800-226-6545 ■ Web: www.ripleys.com						
Ripley's Believe It or Not! Museum						
140 N Cache St	Jackson Hole	WY	83001	407-345-8010		520
TF: 800-713-7278 ■ Web: www.ripleys.com						
Ripley's Believe It or Not! Museum						
6780 Hollywood Blvd	Hollywood	CA	90028	323-466-6335		520
Web: www.ripleys.com/hollywood						
Ripley's Believe It or Not! Orlando Odditorium						
8201 International Dr	Orlando	FL	32819	407-345-0501		520
TF: 800-393-1985 ■ Web: www.ripleys.com						
Ripon Chamber of Commerce 114 Scott St	Ripon	WI	54971	920-748-6764	748-6784	139
Web: www.ripon-wi.com						
Ripon College 300 Seward St PO Box 248	Ripon	WI	54971	800-947-4766		166
TF Admissions: 800-947-4766 ■ Web: www.ripon.edu						
Ripon Elementary School 509 W Main St	Ripon	CA	95366	209-599-4225		685
Web: riponusd.net						
Ripon Printers Inc 656 S Douglas St	Ripon	WI	54971	920-748-3136		256
Web: www.riponprinters.com						
Ripon Society 1300 L St NW Ste 900	Washington	DC	20005	202-216-1008		48-7
Web: www.riponsociety.org						
Rippe Keane Mktg Inc						
5950 Seminole Centre Ct Ste 220	Madison	WI	53711	608-277-9097		194
Web: www.rippekeane.com						
Rippey Corp						
5000 Hillsdale Cir	El Dorado Hills	CA	95762	916-939-4332	939-4338	174
Web: www.rippey.com						
Ripple6 Inc 520 Eighth Ave 17th Fl	New York	NY	10018	646-254-6780		5
Rippy Cadillac LLC						
4951 New Centre Dr	Wilmington	NC	28403	910-799-2421		57
Riptide Communications Inc						
2621 Palisade Ave Ste C	Bronx	NY	10463	212-260-5000		636
Web: www.riptidecommunications.com						
Ririe-Woodbury Dance Co						
138 West Broadway	Salt Lake City	UT	84101	801-297-4241	297-4235	573-1
Web: www.ririewoodbury.com						
Ris Corp 5905 Weisbrook Ln Ste 101	Knoxville	TN	37909	865-588-4456		196
TF: 800-433-5778 ■ Web: www.ris-corp.com						
RIS Media Inc 69 E Ave	Norwalk	CT	06851	203-855-1234		652
TF: 800-724-6000 ■ Web: www.rismedia.com						
RISC Networks Inc						
1 Rankin Ave 2nd Fl	Asheville	NC	28801	866-808-1227		196
TF: 866-808-1227 ■ Web: www.riscnetworks.com						
Risch James E (Sen R - ID)						
483 Russell Bldg	Washington	DC	20510	202-224-2752	224-2573	342-2
Web: www.risch.senate.gov						
Riscky's Barbecue 2314 Azle Ave	Fort Worth	TX	76164	817-624-8662	624-3777	670
Web: www.risckys.com						
RISD Store Art Supplies						
30 N Main St	Providence	RI	02903	401-454-6464	454-6453	45
Web: risdstore.com						
Risdall Adv Agency 550 Main St	New Brighton	MN	55112	651-286-6700	631-2561	4
TF: 888-747-3255 ■ Web: www.risdall.com						
Rise Broadband						
61 Inverness Dr E Ste 250	Englewood	CO	80112	303-705-6522		387
Web: risebroadband.com/?ro=r1						
Rise Sushi & Sake Lounge						
3401 N Southport Ave	Chicago	IL	60657	773-525-3535	525-3522	671
Web: www.risesushi.com						
Risetime Inc 130 S Jefferson St	Chicago	IL	60661	312-362-9930		196
Web: www.risetime.com						
Rish Equipment Co PO Box 330	Bluefield	WV	24701	304-327-5124	327-8821	358
Web: www.rish.com						
Rishi Tea LLC 185 S 33rd Ct	Milwaukee	WI	53208	414-747-4001		297-8
TF: 866-747-4483 ■ Web: rishi-tea.com						
Rising Media Inc						
211 E Victoria St Ste E	Santa Barbara	CA	93101	805-965-3184		232
Web: www.risingmedia.com						
Rising Pharmaceuticals Inc						
3 Pearl Ct	Allendale	NJ	07401	201-961-9000		231
Web: www.risingpharma.com						
Rising Results Inc						
201 Edward Curry Ave Ste 202	Staten Island	NY	10314	718-370-8300		401
TF: 800-837-4648 ■ Web: www.risingresults.com						
Rising Star Casino Resort						
777 Rising Star Dr	Rising Sun	IN	47040	812-438-1234		133
TF: 800-472-6311 ■ Web: www.risingstarcasino.com						
Rising Star Services Inc 6106 Cargo Rd	Odessa	TX	79762	432-617-0114		539
Web: www.risingstarservices.com						
Rising Tide Capital Inc						
334 Martin Luther King Dr	Jersey City	NJ	07305	201-432-4316		194
Web: risingtidecapital.org						
Risk & Insurance Management Society Inc (RIMS)						
1065 Ave of the Americas 13th Fl	New York	NY	10018	212-286-9292	986-9716	49-9
Web: www.rims.org						
Risk Integrated LLC 37 Main St	Cold Spring	NY	10516	845-598-1620		261
Web: www.riskintegrated.com						
Risk Management Agency						
1400 Independence Ave SW MS 0801	Washington	DC	20250	202-690-2803	690-2818	340-1
TF: 800-877-8339 ■ Web: www.rma.usda.gov						
Risk Management Assn (RMA)						
1801 Market St Ste 300	Philadelphia	PA	19103	215-446-4000	446-4101	49-2
TF Cust Svc: 800-677-7621 ■ Web: www.rmahq.org						
Risk Management Services Co (RMSC)						
9100 Marksfield Rd	Louisville	KY	40222	502-326-5900	326-5909*	194
*Fax Area Code: 888 ■ Web: www.rmsc.com						
Risk Management Solutions Inc						
7575 Gateway Blvd	Newark	CA	94560	510-505-2500	505-2501	178-10
Web: www.rms.com						
RiskSpan 281 Tresser Blvd Ste 1203	Stamford	CT	06901	203-355-1510		396
Web: www.riskspan.com						

				Phone	Fax	Class
RiskWatch (RWI) 1237 N Gulfstream Ave	Sarasota	FL	34236	800-360-1898		178-10
TF: 800-360-1898 ■ *Web:* riskwatch.com/contact-us						
RISNA (Rhode Island State Nurses Assn)						
150 Washington St Ste 415	Providence	RI	02903	401-331-5644	331-5646	533
Web: www.risna.org						
RISO Inc 800 District Ave Ste 390	Burlington	MA	01803	978-777-7377	777-2517	173-6
TF General: 800-942-7476 ■ *Web:* www.riso.com						
RISQ Inc						
625 Rene-Levesque Blvd W Bureau 300	Montreal	QC	H3B1R2	514-845-7181		387
Web: www.risq.quebec						
Risse Racing Technology Inc						
1240 Redwood Blvd	Redding	CA	96003	530-246-8700		711
Web: www.risseracing.com						
Risser Oil Corp 2865 Executive Dr	Clearwater	FL	33762	727-573-4000	572-9075	579
TF: 800-570-8024 ■ *Web:* www.therissercompanies.com						
Rist-Frost-Shumway Engineering PC						
71 Water St	Laconia	NH	03246	603-524-4647		261
TF: 800-566-0506 ■ *Web:* www.rfsengineering.com						
Ristorante Bacco 737 Diamond St	San Francisco	CA	94114	415-282-4969		671
Web: baccosf.com						
Ristorante Ciao 835 Fourth Ave S	Naples	FL	34102	239-263-3889		671
Web: www.ristoranteciao.com						
Ristorante DaVinci 1180 Bishop St	Montreal	QC	H3G2E3	514-874-2001		671
Web: www.davinci.ca						
Ristorante Murali 1201 S Joyce St	Arlington	VA	22202	703-415-0411		671
Web: www.muraliva.com						
Ristorante SOTTO SOTTO 120 Ave Rd	Toronto	ON	M5R2H4	416-962-0011		671
Web: www.sottosotto.ca						
Ristorante Zebra 32 Lake Ave	Rehoboth Beach	DE	19971	302-226-1160		671
Web: ristorantezebra.us						
RITA (Research & Innovative Technology Administration)						
1200 New Jersey Ave SE	Washington	DC	20590	202-366-7582	366-3759	340-17
TF: 800-853-1351 ■ *Web:* www.rita.dot.gov						
Rita & Joe's 142 Broadway	Jersey City	NJ	07306	201-451-3606		671
Web: www.rita-joes.com						
Rita Hazan Salon 720 Fifth Ave Fl 11	New York	NY	10019	212-586-4343		77
Web: www.ritahazan.com						
Rita's Water Ice Franchise Co LLC						
1401 Bridgetown Pike	Feasterville	PA	19053	215-322-8774		381
Web: www.ritasice.com						
Ritatsu Manufacturing Inc						
700 Old Liberty Church Rd	Beaver Dam	KY	42320	270-730-7010		483
Ritchie Commercial						
34 W Santa Clara St	San Jose	CA	95113	408-971-2700		652
Web: www.ritchiecommercial.com						
Ritchie County 115 E Main St	Harrisville	WV	26362	304-643-2164	643-2906	338
Web: www.ritchiecounty.wv.gov						
Ritchie Engineering Company Inc						
10950 Hampshire Ave S	Bloomington	MN	55438	952-943-1300		14
Web: www.yellowjacket.com						
Ritchie Tractor						
1746 W Lmar Alxander Pkwy	Maryville	TN	37801	865-901-3199		323
TF: 888-319-0282 ■ *Web:* www.ritchietractor.com						
Ritchie, Dillard, Davies & Johnson PC						
606 W Main St Ste 300	Knoxville	TN	37902	865-637-0661		428
Web: www.rddjlaw.com						
Rite Aid Corp 30 Hunter Ln	Camp Hill	PA	17011	717-761-2633		237
NYSE: RAD ■ *TF:* 800-748-3243 ■ *Web:* www.riteaid.com						
Rite Engineering & Manufacturing Corp						
5832 Garfield	Commerce	CA	90040	562-862-2135	861-9821	357
Web: www.riteboiler.com						
Rite Rug Co 3949 Business Park Dr	Columbus	OH	43204	614-261-6060		131
Web: www.riterug.com						
Rite Technology						
1744 Independence Blvd	Sarasota	FL	34234	941-955-2737		708
Web: www.laserrite.com						
Rite Track Inc						
8655 Rite Track Way	West Chester	OH	45069	513-881-7820		454
Web: www.ritetrack.com						
Rite-Hite Corp 8900 N Arbon Dr	Milwaukee	WI	53224	414-355-2600	355-9248	678
TF: 800-456-0600 ■ *Web:* www.ritehite.com						
Ritescreen Company Inc, The						
4314 Route 209	Elizabethville	PA	17023	717-362-7483		234
Web: www.ritescreen.com						
Rite-solutions Inc						
1 Corporate Pl 2nd Fl	Middletown	RI	02842	860-599-1969		317
TF: 800-732-7366 ■ *Web:* www.rite-solutions.com						
Riteway Bus Service Inc Motorcoach Div						
W201 N13900 Fond du Lac Ave	Richfield	WI	53076	262-677-3282	677-3121	107
TF: 800-776-7026 ■ *Web:* goriteway.com						
Ritewood Inc 3643 S 4000 E	Franklin	ID	83237	208-646-2213	646-2217	10-8
Ritrama 800 Kasota Ave SE	Minneapolis	MN	55414	612-378-2277	378-9327	3
TF: 800-328-5071 ■ *Web:* www.ritrama.com						
Ritron Wireless Solutions						
505 W Carmel Dr	Carmel	IN	46032	317-846-1201		647
Web: www.ritron.com						
Ritta & Assoc 568 Grand Ave	Englewood	NJ	07631	201-567-4400		4
Web: www.ritta.com						
Rittal Corp 1 Rittal Pl	Springfield	OH	45504	937-399-0500	390-5599	816
TF: 800-477-4000 ■ *Web:* www.rittal.com/us-en/content/en/start						
Ritt-beyer & Weir Inc						
9900 S Franklin Dr	Franklin	WI	53132	414-421-9505		297-8
Web: www.rbwinc.com						
Rittenhouse Book Distributors Inc						
511 Feheley Dr	King of Prussia	PA	19406	800-345-6425	223-7488*	96
**Fax:* Orders ■ *TF Cust Svc:* 800-345-6425 ■ *Web:* www.rittenhouse.com						
Rittenhouse Hotel						
210 W Rittenhouse Sq	Philadelphia	PA	19103	215-546-9000	732-3364	379
TF: 800-635-1042 ■ *Web:* www.rittenhousehotel.com						
Ritter Technology LLC						
100 Williams Dr	Zelienople	PA	16063	724-452-6000	452-0766	790
Web: www.ritter1.com						
Ritz Barbecue 302 17th St	Allentown	PA	18104	610-432-0952		671
Ritz Camera & Image						
2 Bergen Tpke	Ridgefield Park	NJ	07660	855-622-7489		119
TF Cust Svc: 855-622-7489 ■ *Web:* www.ritzcamera.com						
Ritz Tours & Travel Inc						
233 El Camino Real	Millbrae	CA	94030	650-259-9983		772
TF: 800-345-1688 ■ *Web:* www.ritztours.com						
Ritz, Holman, Butala, Fine LLP						
330 E Kilbourn Ave Two Plaza E Ste 550	Milwaukee	WI	53202	414-271-1451		2
TF: 800-554-1448 ■ *Web:* www.ritzholman.com						
Ritz-Carlton Amelia Island						
4750 Amelia Island Pkwy	Amelia Island	FL	32034	904-277-1100		669
TF: 800-241-3333 ■ *Web:* www.ritzcarlton.com/resorts/amelia_island						
Ritz-Carlton Bachelor Gulch						
0130 Daybreak Ridge	Avon	CO	81620	970-748-6200		669
TF: 800-241-3333 ■ *Web:* www.ritzcarlton.com						
Ritz-Carlton Dallas 2121 McKinney Ave	Dallas	TX	75201	214-922-0200		379
TF Resv: 800-960-7082 ■ *Web:* www.ritzcarlton.com						
Ritz-Carlton Dining Room						
3434 Peachtree Rd	Atlanta	GA	30326	404-237-2700		671
Web: ritzcarlton.com						
Ritz-Carlton Half Moon Bay						
1 Miramontes Pt Rd	Half Moon Bay	CA	94019	650-712-7000		669
TF General: 800-241-3333 ■ *Web:* www.ritzcarlton.com						
Ritz-Carlton Hotel Co LLC, The						
4445 Willard Ave Ste 800	Chevy Chase	MD	20815	301-547-4700	468-4069*	669
**Fax Area Code:* 801 ■ *TF:* 800-241-3333 ■ *Web:* www.ritzcarlton.com						
Ritz-Carlton Hotel Company, The						
4445 Willard Ave Ste 800	Chevy Chase	MD	20815	301-547-4700		707
TF: 800-876-7280 ■ *Web:* www.ritzcarlton.com						
Ritz-Carlton Huntington Hotel & Spa						
4445 Willard Ave Ste 800	Chevy Chase	MD	20815	301-547-4700	468-4069*	669
**Fax Area Code:* 801 ■ *TF:* 800-241-3333 ■ *Web:* www.ritzcarlton.com						
Ritz-Carlton Kapalua						
1 Ritz-Carlton Dr Kapalua	Maui	HI	96761	808-669-6200	669-1566	669
TF Resv: 800-262-8440 ■ *Web:* www.ritzcarlton.com/resorts/kapalua						
Ritz-Carlton Key Biscayne						
455 Grand Bay Dr	Key Biscayne	FL	33149	305-365-4500		669
TF: 800-241-3333 ■ *Web:* www.ritzcarlton.com/resorts/key_biscayne						
Ritz-Carlton Laguna Niguel, The						
1 Ritz Carlton Dr	Dana Point	CA	92629	949-240-2000		669
TF: 800-542-8680 ■ *Web:* www.ritzcarlton.com/resorts/laguna_niguel						
Ritz-Carlton Lodge Reynolds Plantation						
1 Lake Ocle Trl	Greensboro	GA	30642	706-467-0600		669
TF: 877-231-7916 ■ *Web:* www.ritzcarlton.com						
Ritz-Carlton Naples						
280 Vanderbilt Beach Rd	Naples	FL	34108	239-598-3300		669
TF: 800-554-9288 ■ *Web:* www.ritzcarlton.com/resorts/naples						
Ritz-Carlton Naples Golf Resort						
2600 Tiburon Dr	Naples	FL	34109	239-593-2000		669
TF Resv: 877-231-7916 ■ *Web:* www.ritzcarlton.com						
Ritz-Carlton Orlando Grande Lakes						
4012 Central Florida Pkwy	Orlando	FL	32837	407-206-2400		669
TF: 866-922-6882 ■ *Web:* www.ritzcarlton.com						
Ritz-Carlton San Juan, The						
6961 Ave of the Governors Isla Verde	Carolina	PR	00979	787-253-1700	253-1777	669
TF: 800-241-3333 ■ *Web:* www.ritzcarlton.com/en/properties/sanjuan						
Ritz-Carlton Sarasota						
1111 Ritz-Carlton Dr	Sarasota	FL	34236	941-309-2000		669
TF: 800-241-3333 ■ *Web:* www.ritzcarlton.com						
Ritz-Carlton Tysons Corner, The						
1700 Tysons Blvd	McLean	VA	22102	703-506-4300		707
TF: 800-241-3333 ■ *Web:* www.ritzcarlton.com						
Ritz-Craft Corp of Pennsylvania Inc						
15 Industrial Pk Rd	Mifflinburg	PA	17844	570-966-1053		505
TF: 800-326-9836 ■ *Web:* www.ritz-craft.com						
Ritzman Pharmacies Inc						
8614 Hartman Rd	Wadsworth	OH	44281	330-335-2318	335-3222	237
TF: 800-748-3243 ■ *Web:* ritzmanrx.com						
Riu Hotel Florida Beach						
3101 Collins Ave	Miami	FL	33140	305-673-5333	673-9335	379
TF: 888-666-8816 ■ *Web:* www.riu.com						
Riva Yares Gallery 3625 Bishop Ln	Scottsdale	AZ	85251	480-947-3251		42
Web: www.rivayaresgallery.com						
Rival Capital Management Inc						
160 - 99 Scurfield Bvld	Winnipeg	MB	R3Y1Y1	204-992-6210		317
Web: rivalcapital.ca						
RivalHealth LLC						
6601 Hillsborough St Ste 109	Raleigh	NC	27606	919-803-6709		387
TF: 800-716-2455 ■ *Web:* www.rivalhealth.com						
Rivco Products Inc 440 S Pine St	Burlington	WI	53105	262-763-8222	763-8949	517
TF: 888-801-8222 ■ *Web:* www.rivcoproducts.com						
Rivel Research Group Inc						
830 Post Rd E	Westport	CT	06880	203-226-0800		668
Web: www.rivel.com						
river 95.7, The 208 N Thomas Dr	Shreveport	LA	71107	318-222-3122		645-151
Web: www.klkl.fm						
River 97.3 WRVV, The						
600 Corporate Cir	Harrisburg	PA	17110	717-540-8076		645-71
Web: theriver973.iheart.com						
River Bend Business Products						
304 Downtown Plaza	Fairmont	MN	56031	507-235-3800		316
TF: 800-783-3877 ■ *Web:* www.riverbendbusiness.com						
River Bend Industries						
2421 16th Ave S	Moorhead	MN	56560	218-236-1818		199
TF: 800-365-3070 ■ *Web:* www.riverbendind.com						
River Birch Homes Inc						
400 River Birch Dr	Hackleburg	AL	35564	205-935-1997	935-3578	505
Web: www.riverbirchhomes.com						
River Bluff Nursing Home						
4401 N Main St	Rockford	IL	61103	815-877-8061		371
Web: rbnh.org						
River Cafe 1 Water St	Brooklyn	NY	11201	718-522-5200	875-0037	671
Web: www.rivercafe.com						
River Cafe 25 Prince's Island Pk	Calgary	AB	T2P0R1	403-261-7670	261-8795	671
TF: 800-441-1414 ■ *Web:* www.river-cafe.com						
River Center-performing Arts						
Po Box 2425	Columbus	GA	31902	706-256-3607		749
Web: rivercenter.org						
River Cities Capital Funds						
221 E Fourth St Ste 2400	Cincinnati	OH	45202	513-621-9700		402
River City Ale Works 1400 Main St	Wheeling	WV	26003	304-233-4555		671
Web: rivercitybanquets.com						

Name / Address	City	State	ZIP	Phone	Fax	Class
River City Antique Mall & Collector's Market 6363 Hearne Ave.	Shreveport	LA	71108	318-621-1009		460
River City Bank PO Box 15247 *OTC: RCBC* ■ *TF Cust Svc:* 800-564-7144 ■ *Web:* www.rivercitybank.com	Sacramento	CA	95851	916-567-2899		70
River City Brass Band Inc 500 Grant St Ste 2720 *TF:* 800-292-7222 ■ *Web:* www.rivercitybrass.org	Pittsburgh	PA	15219	412-434-7222		573-3
River City Construction LLC 101 Hoffer Ln *TF:* 800-746-9554 ■ *Web:* www.rccllc.com	East Peoria	IL	61611	309-694-3120	694-1332	186
River City Engineering 1011 W County Line Rd *Web:* www.rcetx.com	New Braunfels	TX	78130	830-626-3588	626-3601	77
River City Metal Products Inc 655 Godfrey Ave SW *Web:* www.rcmpinc.com	Grand Rapids	MI	49503	616-235-3746		295
River City Petroleum Inc 840 Delta Ln *Web:* rcpfuel.com	West Sacramento	CA	95691	916-371-4960		780
River Country Co-op 9072 Cahill Ave *Web:* www.rivercountry.coop	Inver Grove Heights	MN	55076	651-451-1151		48-2
River Country Tourism Bureau PO Box 214 *TF:* 800-447-2821 ■ *Web:* www.rivercountry.com	Three Rivers	MI	49093	800-447-2821		206
River East Transcona School Division 589 Roch St *Web:* www.retsd.mb.ca	Winnipeg	MB	R2K2P7	204-667-7130		685
River Falls Journal 2815 Prairie Dr *Web:* www.rivertowns.net	River Falls	WI	54022	715-425-1561		532-3
River Falls Public Library 115 E Elm St *Web:* www.rfcity.org	River Falls	WI	54022	715-425-0908		434-3
River Forest Public Schools 90 7776 Lake St *Web:* www.district90.org	River Forest	IL	60305	708-771-8282	771-8291	780
River Garden Farms Co 41758 County Rd 112	Knights Landing	CA	95645	530-735-6274		10-4
River Garden Hebrew Home for the Aged 11401 Old St Augustine Rd *TF:* 800-468-3571 ■ *Web:* rivergarden.org	Jacksonville	FL	32258	904-260-1818	260-9733	450
River Glen Health Care Ctr 162 S Britain Rd	Southbury	CT	06488	203-264-9600		450
River Heights Chamber of Commerce 5782 Blackshire Path *TF:* 800-625-6079 ■ *Web:* www.riverheights.com	Inver Grove Heights	MN	55076	651-451-2266	451-0846	139
River House Seafood Restaurant 125 W River St *Web:* www.savannahriverhouse.com	Savannah	GA	31401	912-234-1900		671
River Inn 924 25th St NW *Web:* www.theriverinn.com	Washington	DC	20037	202-337-7600	337-6520	379
River Legacy Park 701 NW Green Oaks Blvd *Web:* www.riverlegacy.org	Arlington	TX	76006	817-860-6752	860-1595	520
River Metals Recycling 2045 River Rd *Web:* www.rmrecycling.com	Louisville	KY	40206	502-585-5331	587-8699	686
River Oaks Country Club Inc 1600 River Oaks Blvd *Web:* www.riveroakscc.net	Houston	TX	77019	713-529-4321		354
River Oaks Ctr 96 River Oaks Ctr Dr *TF:* 877-746-6642 ■ *Web:* simon.com/mall?id=190	Calumet City	IL	60409	708-868-0600		460
River Oaks Hospital 1525 River Oaks Rd W *TF:* 800-366-1740 ■ *Web:* www.riveroakshospital.com	New Orleans	LA	70123	504-734-1740	733-3229	374-3
River Parishes Hospital 500 Rue De Sante *TF:* 800-231-5275 ■ *Web:* www.ochsner.org	Laplace	LA	70068	985-652-7000		374-3
River Park Hospital 1230 Sixth Ave *TF:* 800-621-2673 ■ *Web:* www.riverparkhospital.net	Huntington	WV	25701	304-526-9111		374-5
River Recycling Industries Inc 4195 Bradley Rd *TF:* 800-201-0005 ■ *Web:* riverrecyclingind.com	Cleveland	OH	44109	216-459-2100	749-8107	686
River Road Partners LLC 462 S Fourth St Ste 1600 *Web:* www.riverroadllc.com	Louisville	KY	40202	520-298-7875		463
River Rock Casino Resort 8811 River Rd *TF:* 866-748-3718 ■ *Web:* www.riverrock.com	Richmond	BC	V6X3P8	604-247-8900	207-2641	669
River Rock Entertainment Authority 3250 Hwy 128 E *TF:* 877-883-7777 ■ *Web:* www.riverrockcasino.com	Geyserville	CA	95441	707-857-2777		452
River Run Computers Inc 2320 W Camden Rd *Web:* www.river-run.com	Milwaukee	WI	53209	414-228-7474		180
River School 4880 Macarthur Blvd NW *Web:* riverschool.net	Washington	DC	20007	202-337-3554		685
River States Truck & Trailer 3959 N Kinney Coulee Rd *Web:* www.riverstates.com	La Crosse	WI	54601	608-784-1149		57
River Street Inn 124 E Bay St *Web:* www.riverstreetinn.com	Savannah	GA	31401	912-234-6400		379
River Terrace Inn 1600 Soscol Ave *Web:* riverterraceinn.com	Napa	CA	94559	707-320-6910		379
River Trading Company LTD 10900 89th Ave N *Web:* www.rivertradingcompany.com	Maple Grove	MN	55369	763-463-3400		791
River Valley Telecommunications Coop & Cable Tv 1607 Rolling St *Web:* www.ruthventel.com	Ruthven	IA	51358	712-837-5522		116
River View Local School District 26496 SR- 60 *Web:* www.river-view.k12.oh.us	Warsaw	OH	43844	740-824-3521		685
River Walk 110 Broadway Ste 500 *TF:* 800-417-4139 ■ *Web:* www.thesanantonioriverwalk.com	San Antonio	TX	78204	210-227-4262	212-7602	50-6
River West Meeting Associates Inc 3616 N Lincoln Ave *TF:* 888-534-5292 ■ *Web:* www.riverwestmeetings.com	Chicago	IL	60613	773-755-3000		463
River's Edge Hotel & Spa 0455 SW Hamilton Ct *Web:* www.riversedgehotel.com	Portland	OR	97239	503-802-5800		379
River's Edge Resort Cottages 4200 Boat St *TF:* 800-770-3343 ■ *Web:* www.riversedge.net	Fairbanks	AK	99709	907-474-0286	474-3665	379
Riverbank State Park 679 Riverside Dr *Web:* parks.ny.gov/parks/93/details.aspx	New York	NY	10031	212-694-3600		565
Riverbanks Zoo & Botanical Garden 500 Wildlife Pkwy *Web:* www.riverbanks.org	Columbia	SC	29210	803-779-8717	253-6381	823
Riverbay Corp 2049 Bartow Ave *Web:* www.riverbaycorp.com	Bronx	NY	10475	718-320-3300		652
Riverbed Technology Inc 199 Fremont St *NASDAQ: RVBD* ■ *Web:* www.riverbed.com	San Francisco	CA	94105	415-247-8800	247-8801	225
Riverbend Maximum Security Institution 7475 Cockrill Bend Blvd *TF:* 800-770-8277 ■ *Web:* tn.gov	Nashville	TN	37243	615-350-3100	350-3400	213
Riverbend Music Ctr 6295 Kellogg Ave *Web:* www.riverbend.org	Cincinnati	OH	45230	513-232-6220		572
RiverCenter Adler Theatre 136 E Third St *Web:* www.riverctr.com	Davenport	IA	52801	563-326-8500	326-8505	205
Riverchase Galleria 2000 Riverchase Galleria Ste 400 *TF:* 800-980-6467 ■ *Web:* www.riverchasegalleria.com	Hoover	AL	35244	205-985-3020		460
Rivercrest Realty Assoc 8816 Six Forks Rd Ste 201 *Web:* rivercrestrealty.com	Raleigh	NC	27615	919-846-4046		652
Rivercrest Technologies Inc 3811 Creekside Ln *TF:* 800-433-5778 ■ *Web:* www.rcrest.com	Holmen	WI	54636	608-779-2000		180
Riverdale Country School 5250 Fieldston Rd *Web:* www.riverdale.edu	Bronx	NY	10471	718-549-8810	519-2795	685
Riverdale Global 1 Walnut St *Web:* www.riverdalecolor.com	Perth Amboy	NJ	08861	732-376-9300		608
Riverdale Mills Corp 130 Riverdale St *TF:* 800-762-6374 ■ *Web:* www.riverdale.com	Northbridge	MA	01534	508-234-8715	234-9593	279
Riverdale Plating & Heat Treating Inc 680 W 134th St *Web:* www.rpht.com	Riverdale	IL	60827	708-849-2050		484
Riveredge Nature Ctr 4458 W Hawthorne Dr PO Box 26 *TF:* 800-287-8098 ■ *Web:* www.riveredgenaturecenter.org	Newburg	WI	53060	262-375-2715		50-5
Riveredge Resort Hotel 17 Holland St *TF:* 800-365-6987 ■ *Web:* www.riveredge.com	Alexandria Bay	NY	13607	315-482-9917	482-5010	379
River-FM 107.5 (CHR), The 55 Music Sq W *Web:* 1075theriver.iheart.com	Nashville	TN	37203	615-664-2400	664-2434	645-108
Riverfront Barbeque & Grill 300 Water St *Web:* riverfrontbbq.com	Augusta	ME	04330	207-622-8899		671
Riverfront Investment Group LLC 1214 E Cary St *TF:* 866-583-0744 ■ *Web:* www.riverfrontig.com	Richmond	VA	23219	804-549-4800		401
Riverfront Times 6358 Delmar Blvd Ste 200 *Web:* www.riverfronttimes.com	Saint Louis	MO	63130	314-754-5966	754-5955	532-5
Rivergate Mall 1000 Rivergate Pkwy Ste 1 *TF:* 800-447-9778 ■ *Web:* www.rivergate-mall.com	Goodlettsville	TN	37072	615-859-3458		460
Riverhawk Company LP 215 Clinton Rd *Web:* www.riverhawk.com	New Hartford	NY	13413	315-768-4855		295
Riverhead Bldg Supply Corp 1093 Pulaski St *TF:* 800-378-3650 ■ *Web:* www.rbscorp.com	Riverhead	NY	11901	631-727-3650	727-7713	191-3
Riverhead Raceway PO Box 1743 *Web:* www.riverheadraceway.com	Riverhead	NY	11901	631-842-7223		515
Riverland Community College 1900 Eigth Ave NW *TF:* 800-247-5039 ■ *Web:* www.riverland.edu	Austin	MN	55912	507-433-0600	433-0515	162
Riverland Energy Co-op N28988 State Rd 93 PO Box 277 *TF:* 800-411-9115 ■ *Web:* www.riverlandenergy.com	Arcadia	WI	54612	608-323-3381		245
Rivermaid Travelling Co PO Box 350 *Web:* www.rivermaid.com	Lodi	CA	95240	209-369-3586	369-5465	11-1
RiverMead Retirement Community 150 RiverMead Rd *TF:* 800-200-5433 ■ *Web:* rivermead.org	Peterborough	NH	03458	603-924-0062		672
Rivermoor Engineering LLC 146 Front St *Web:* rivermoorengineering.com	Scituate	MA	02066	781-545-2848		261
RiverOne Inc 121 Innovation Dr Ste 150 *Web:* www.riverone.com	Irvine	CA	92617	949-856-1500		525
RiverPoint Group LLC 2200 E Devon Ave Ste 385 *TF:* 800-297-5601 ■ *Web:* www.riverpoint.com	Des Plaines	IL	60018	847-233-9600	233-9602	180
Riverrun International Film Festival 305 W Fourth St Ste 1A *Web:* www.riverrunfilm.com	Winston-Salem	NC	27101	336-724-1502	724-1112	282
Rivers Bridge State Historic Site 325 State Pk Rd *Web:* www.southcarolinaparks.com	Ehrhardt	SC	29081	803-267-3675		565
Rivers Club Inc 301 Grant St *Web:* www.clubcorp.com	Pittsburgh	PA	15219	412-391-5227	391-5016	354
Rivers Metal Products Inc 3100 N 38th St *Web:* www.riversmetal.com	Lincoln	NE	68504	402-466-2329		295

Name / Address	City	State	Zip	Phone	Fax	Class
Rivers Oceans & Mountains Adventures Inc (ROAM) 2622 Front St	Nelson	BC	V1L4B7	888-639-1114		760
TF: 888-639-1114 ■ *Web:* www.iroamtheworld.com						
Riverside Art Museum 3425 Mission Inn Ave	Riverside	CA	92501	951-684-7111		520
Web: www.riversideartmuseum.org						
Riverside Art Shop 1600 Grand Army Hwy	Somerset	MA	02726	508-672-6735		45
TF: 800-354-9899 ■ *Web:* www.riversideart.com						
Riverside Arts Ctr 76 N Huron St	Ypsilanti	MI	48197	734-480-2787		572
TF: 800-398-4297 ■ *Web:* www.riversidearts.org						
Riverside Campus of Ottawa Hospital 1967 Riverside Dr	Ottawa	ON	K1H7W9	613-738-7100	761-5292	374-2
Web: www.ottawahospital.on.ca						
Riverside City Hall 3900 Main St	Riverside	CA	92522	951-826-5312	826-5470	337
Web: www.riversideca.gov						
Riverside City Public Library 3581 Mission Inn Ave	Riverside	CA	92501	951-826-5201	826-5407	434-3
TF: 888-225-7377 ■ *Web:* www.riversideca.gov/library						
Riverside Clay Co Inc 201 Truss Ferry Rd	Pell City	AL	35128	205-338-3366	338-7456	503-2
TF: 800-924-0637 ■ *Web:* riversiderefractories.com						
Riverside Clubhouse 2633 Riverside Blvd	Sacramento	CA	95818	916-448-9988		671
Web: www.riversideclubhouse.com						
Riverside Community College						
Moreno Valley 16130 Lasselle St	Moreno Valley	CA	92551	951-571-6100	571-6188*	162
**Fax:* Admissions ■ *Web:* www.rcc.edu						
Norco 2001 Third St	Norco	CA	92860	951-372-7000		162
Web: www.rcc.edu						
Riverside 4800 Magnolia Ave	Riverside	CA	92506	951-222-8000		162
Web: www.rcc.edu						
Riverside Community Hospital 4445 Magnolia Ave	Riverside	CA	92501	951-788-3000		374-3
Web: riversidecommunityhospital.com						
Riverside Convention & Visitors Bureau 3750 University Ave Ste 175	Riverside	CA	92501	951-222-4700		206
TF: 800-600-7080 ■ *Web:* www.riversidecvb.com						
Riverside Correctional Facility 777 W Riverside Dr	Ionia	MI	48846	616-527-0110		213
Web: www.michigan.gov						
Riverside County Record 4080 Lemon St	Riverside	CA	92501	951-955-1000		532-4
TF: 800-596-1007 ■ *Web:* www.countyofriverside.us						
Riverside County Regional Medical Ctr 26520 Cactus Ave	Moreno Valley	CA	92555	951-486-4000		374-3
TF: 800-994-6610 ■ *Web:* www.rcrmc.org						
Riverside Dental Group 7251 Magnolia Ave	Riverside	CA	92504	951-689-5031		227
Web: www.riversidedentalgroup.com						
Riverside Electronics Ltd 1 Riverside Dr	Lewiston	MN	55952	507-523-3220	523-2031	[illegible]
Web: riversideelectronics.com						
Riverside Farnsley-Moremen Landing 7410 Moorman Rd	Louisville	KY	40272	502-935-6809	935-6821	50-3
Web: riverside-landing.org						
Riverside Foods Inc 2520 Wilson St	Two Rivers	WI	54241	920-793-4511		296-14
TF: 800-678-4511 ■ *Web:* riversidefoods.com						
Riverside Ford [illegible] Ludington St	Escanaba	MI	49829	906-786-1130		57
TF: 877-774-3171 ■ *Web:* www.riversidefordescanaba.com						
Riverside Ford Inc 2089 Riverside Dr	Macon	GA	31204	478-464-2900		57
TF Sales: 800-395-6210 ■ *Web:* www.riversideford.net						
Riverside Forest Products Inc 2912 Professional Pkwy	Augusta	GA	30907	706-855-5500	863-3362	191-3
TF: 888-855-8733 ■ *Web:* www.riversideforest.com						
Riverside Furniture Corp 1400 S Sixth St	Fort Smith	AR	72901	479-785-8100		319-2
Web: www.riverside-furniture.com						
Riverside General Hospital (RGH)						
Houston Recovery Ctr 4514 Lyons Ave	Houston	TX	77020	713-331-2501		726
Web: riversidegeneralhospital.org						
Riverside Group 655 Driving Pk Ave	Rochester	NY	14613	585-458-2090	458-2123	92
TF: 800-777-2463 ■ *Web:* www.riversidegroup.com						
Riverside Health System 701 Town Ctr Dr Ste 1000	Newport News	VA	23606	757-534-7000	534-7087	353
TF: 800-759-1001 ■ *Web:* riversideonline.com						
Riverside Hotel 620 E Las Olas Blvd	Fort Lauderdale	FL	33301	954-467-0671	462-2148	379
Web: www.riversidehotel.com						
Riverside Inn 1 Fountain Ave	Cambridge Springs	PA	16403	814-398-4645		379
Web: www.theriversideinn.com						
Riverside Manufacturing Co 301 Riverside Dr	Moultrie	GA	31768	229-985-5210	890-2932	155-19
TF: 800-841-8677 ■ *Web:* www.riversideuniforms.com						
Riverside Marine Inc 600 Riverside Dr	Essex	MD	21221	410-335-1500		90
TF: 800-448-6872 ■ *Web:* www.riversideboats.com						
Riverside Mattress Co 225 Dunn Rd	Fayetteville	NC	28312	910-483-0461	484-2334	471
TF: 888-288-5195 ■ *Web:* www.riversidemattressinc.com						
Riverside Medical Center Riverside Medical Ctr	Riverside	CA	92507	951-683-6370		186
Web: www.riversidemedicalclinic.com						
Riverside Medical Ctr (RMC) 350 N Wall St	Kankakee	IL	60901	815-933-1671		374-3
Web: www.riversidehealthcare.org						
Riverside Methodist Hospital 3535 Olentangy River Rd	Columbus	OH	43214	614-566-5000		374-3
TF: 800-837-7555 ■ *Web:* www.ohiohealth.com/facilities/riverside						
Riverside Metropolitan Museum 3580 Mission Inn Ave	Riverside	CA	92501	951-826-5273	369-4970	520
Web: www.riversideca.gov/museum						
Riverside Mfg LLC 14510 Lima Rd	Fort Wayne	IN	46818	260-637-4470		203
Web: www.riversidemfg.com						
Riverside Military Academy 2001 Riverside Dr	Gainesville	GA	30501	770-532-6251	291-3364*	622
**Fax Area Code:* 678 ■ *TF:* 800-462-2338 ■ *Web:* www.riversidemilitary.com						
Riverside National Cemetery 22495 Van Buren Blvd	Riverside	CA	92518	951-653-8417	653-5233	136
Web: www.cem.va.gov						
Riverside Refractories Inc 201 Truss Ferry Rd	Pell City	AL	35128	205-338-3366	338-7456	662
TF: 800-924-0637 ■ *Web:* www.riversiderefractories.com						
Riverside Regional Convalescent Ctr 1000 Old Denbigh Blvd	Newport News	VA	23602	757-875-2000	875-2036	450
TF: 800-759-1001 ■ *Web:* riversideonline.com						
Riverside Regional Medical Ctr 500 J Clyde Morris Blvd	Newport News	VA	23601	757-594-2000		374-3
Web: riversideonline.com						
Riverside Scrap Iron 2993 Sixth St	Riverside	CA	92507	951-686-2129	686-8933	686
Web: www.riversidemetalrecycling.com						
Riverside Staffing Services Inc 2322 E Kimberly Rd Paul Revere Sq Ste 20S	Davenport	IA	52807	563-355-5212		260
Web: www.riversidestaffing.com						
Riverside Theatre 116 W Wisconsin Ave	Milwaukee	WI	53203	414-286-3663		572
TF: 800-511-1552 ■ *Web:* www.pabsttheater.org						
Riverside Transit Agency (RTA) 1825 Third St PO Box 59968	Riverside	CA	92517	951-565-5000		468
TF: 800-800-7821 ■ *Web:* www.riversidetransit.com						
Riverside Travel Group Inc 709 NE 102nd Av	Portland	OR	97220	503-255-2950		772
Web: www.riversidetravel.com						
Riverside Unified School District (RUSD) 3380 14th St PO Box 2800	Riverside	CA	92501	951-788-7135	778-5669	685
Web: www.rusdlink.org						
Riverside Youth Correctional Facility 2 Riverside Rd PO Box 88	Boulder	MT	59632	406-225-4500	225-4511	412
Web: mt.gov						
Riverside Zoo 1600 S Beltline Hwy W	Scottsbluff	NE	69361	308-630-6236		823
Riverside-San Bernardino County Indian Health Inc (RSBCIH) 11555 1/2 Potrero Rd	Banning	CA	92220	951-849-4761		353
TF: 800-732-8805 ■ *Web:* www.rsbcihi.org						
Riverstone Billings Inn 880 N 29th St	Billings	MT	59101	406-252-6800	252-6800	379
TF: 800-231-7782 ■ *Web:* www.billingsinn.com						
RiverStone Group Inc 1701 Fifth Ave	Moline	IL	61265	309-757-8250		182
TF: 800-906-2489 ■ *Web:* www.riverstonegrp.com						
Riverstone Holdings LLC 712 Fifth Ave 36th Fl	New York	NY	10019	212-993-0076		360-3
Web: www.riverstonellc.com						
Riverton Elementary School 209 N Seventh St	Riverton	IL	62561	217-629-6001		685
Web: www.rivertonschools.org						
Riverton Memorial Hospital LLC 2100 W Sunset Dr	Riverton	WY	82501	307-856-4161	857-3571	374-3
Web: sagewesthealthcare.com						
RiverTown Crossings 3700 Rivertown Pkwy	Grandville	MI	49418	616-257-5000		460
Web: www.rivertowncrossings.com						
Rivertown Newspaper Group 2760 N Service Dr PO Box 15	Red Wing	MN	55066	651-388-8235	388-3404	637-8
TF: 800-535-1660 ■ *Web:* www.republican-eagle.com						
Rivervalley Behavioral Health Hospital 1100 Walnut St PO Box 1637	Owensboro	KY	42302	270-689-6800		726
TF: 800-737-0696 ■ *Web:* www.rvbh.com						
Riverview Bancorp Inc 900 Washington St Ste 900	Vancouver	WA	98660	360-693-6650	693-6275	360-2
NASDAQ: RVSB ■ *TF:* 800-676-4710 ■ *Web:* www.riverviewbank.com						
Riverview Correctional Facility 1110 Tibbits Dr	Ogdensburg	NY	13669	315-393-8400		213
Riverview Estates 303 Bank Ave	Riverton	NJ	08077	856-829-2274		371
TF: 800-292-2316 ■ *Web:* www.riverviewestates.org						
Riverview Hospital 395 Westfield Rd	Noblesville	IN	46060	317-773-0760		374-3
TF: 800-523-6001 ■ *Web:* riverview.org						
Riverview Intermediate Unit Number 6 Administrative Services 270 Mayfield Rd	Clarion	PA	16214	814-226-7103		685
TF: 800-672-7123 ■ *Web:* www.riu6.org						
Riverview Marina State Recreation Area N Fourth St	Nebraska City	NE	68410	402-873-7222		565
Web: gonebraskacity.com						
Riverview Medical Ctr 1 Riverview Plaza	Red Bank	NJ	07701	732-741-2700		374-3
Web: www.meridianhealth.com/rmc.cfm						
Riverview Plaza Hotel 64 S Water St	Mobile	AL	36602	251-438-4000	415-0123	379
TF: 800-321-2211 ■ *Web:* marriott.com						
Riverview Psychiatric Ctr 250 Arsenal St 11 State House Stn	Augusta	ME	04330	207-624-4600	287-2601	374-5
TF: 888-261-6684 ■ *Web:* maine.gov						
Riverview Regional Medical Ctr 600 S Third St	Gadsden	AL	35901	256-543-5200	543-5888	374-3
Web: www.riverviewregional.com						
Riverwalk Casino Hotel 1046 Warrenton Rd	Vicksburg	MS	39180	601-634-0100		452
TF: 866-615-9125 ■ *Web:* www.riverwalkvicksburg.com						
Riverwalk Marketplace 500 Port Of New Orleans Pl	New Orleans	LA	70130	504-522-1555		460
Web: riverwalkneworleans.com						
Riverwalk Plaza Hotel 100 Villita St	San Antonio	TX	78205	210-225-1234		707
Web: www.riverwalkplaza.com						
Riverwalk Theatre 228 Museum Dr	Lansing	MI	48933	517-482-5700	482-9812	572
Web: www.riverwalktheatre.com						
Riverway Lobster House 1338 Massachusetts 28	South Yarmouth	MA	02664	508-398-2172		671
Web: www.riverwaylobsterhouserestaurant.com						
Riverwood Center 1485 M 139	Benton Harbor	MI	49022	269-925-0585		726
Web: riverwoodcenter.org						
Riverwood Solutions LLC 70 Willow Rd Ste 100	Menlo Park	CA	94025	650-618-7340		463
Web: www.rwsops.com						
Rivet Software Inc 4340 S Monaco St Ste 100	Denver	CO	80237	720-249-2100		177
Web: www.rivetsoftware.com						

Name / Address	City	State	ZIP	Phone	Fax	Class
Riviana Foods Inc PO Box 2636	Houston	TX	77252	713-529-3251		296-23
Web: www.riviana.com						
Rivier College 420 S Main St	Nashua	NH	03060	603-888-1311	891-1799*	166
*Fax: Admissions ■ TF: 800-447-4843 ■ Web: www.rivier.edu						
Riviera Advisors Inc PO Box 41446	Long Beach	CA	90853	800-635-9063		193
TF: 800-635-9063 ■ Web: www.rivieraadvisors.com						
Riviera Beach Public Library						
600 W Blue Heron Blvd	Riviera Beach	FL	33404	561-845-4195	881-7308	434-3
Web: rivierabch.com						
Riviera Cellular & Telecommunicat						
PO Box 997	Riviera	TX	78379	361-296-3232		387
TF: 877-296-3232 ■ Web: www.rivnet.com						
Riviera Finance 220 Ave I	Redondo Beach	CA	90277	800-872-7484	454-8122*	272
*Fax Area Code: 651 ■ TF: 800-872-7484 ■ Web: www.rivierafinance.com						
Riviera Fitness Centers						
3908 Veterans Blvd	Metairie	LA	70002	504-454-5855	454-7717	354
Web: www.rivierafitnesscenters.com						
Riviera Hotel 1431 Robson St	Vancouver	BC	V6G1C1	604-685-1301	685-1335	379
TF: 888-699-5222 ■ Web: rivieravancouver.com						
Rivkin Radler LLP 926 RXR Plaza	Uniondale	NY	11556	516-357-3000		428
TF: 800-973-1177 ■ Web: www.rivkinradler.com						
RIWI Corp, The 459 Bloor St W Ste 200	Toronto	ON	M5S1X9	416-205-9984		224
Web: riwi.com						
RIX Industries Inc						
4900 Industrial Way	Benicia	CA	94510	707-747-5900		172
TF: 800-642-3337 ■ Web: www.rixindustries.com						
Rizzetta & Company Inc						
3434 Colwell Ave Ste 200	Tampa	FL	33614	813-933-5571		463
Web: www.rizzetta.com						
Rizzoli International Publications Inc						
300 Pk Ave S 3rd Fl	New York	NY	10010	212-387-3400	387-3535	637-2
Web: www.rizzoliusa.com						
RJ & Makay LLC						
100 S Ridge St Ste 101	Breckenridge	CO	80424	970-306-0600		138
RJ Burnside & Assoc Ltd						
15 Townline	Orangeville	ON	L9W3R4	519-941-5331		256
Web: www.rjburnside.com						
Rj Computer Networks Inc						
13215 E Penn St Ste 210	Whittier	CA	90602	562-464-3644		180
TF: 800-433-5778 ■ Web: www.rjcomputers.com						
RJ Donovan Correctional Facility at Rock Mountain						
480 Alta Rd	San Diego	CA	92179	619-661-6500	661-6253	213
TF: 877-256-6877 ■ Web: cdcr.ca.gov						
RJ Lee Group Inc 350 Hochberg Rd	Monroeville	PA	15146	724-325-1776	733-1799	417
Web: rjlg.com						
RJ Marshall Co 26776 W 12-Mile Rd	Southfield	MI	48034	248-353-4100	338-7900*	724
*Fax Area Code: 800 ■ TF Cust Svc: 888-514-8600 ■ Web: www.rjmarshall.com						
RJ O'Brien & Assoc						
222 S Riverside Plaza Ste 900	Chicago	IL	60606	312-373-5000	373-5238	169
TF: 866-438-7564 ■ Web: www.rjobrien.com						
RJ Peacock Canning Co 72 Water St	Lubec	ME	04652	207-733-5556	733-0936	296-13
R&J Public Relations LLC						
1140 Route 22 E Ste 200	Bridgewater	NJ	08807	908-722-5757		636
TF: 800-307-6627 ■ Web: www.randjsc.com						
Rj Rebar Inc 1810 S Macedonia	Muncie	IN	47302	765-286-5454		480
RJ Reynolds Tobacco Co						
401 N Main St	Winston-Salem	NC	27102	336-741-5000	741-2998	756
Web: www.rjrt.com						
RJ Rippey Od Pa Dba Vision Vision Source						
1635A S Voss Rd	Houston	TX	77057	713-954-2020		543
RJ Singer International Inc						
4801 W Jefferson Blvd	Los Angeles	CA	90016	323-735-1717		453
Web: www.rjsinger.com						
RJ Thomas Mfg Company Inc PO Box 946	Cherokee	IA	51012	712-225-5115	225-5796	319-4
TF: 800-762-5002 ■ Web: www.pilotrock.com						
Rj Torching Inc 5061 Energy Dr	Flint	MI	48505	810-785-9759		492
Web: www.rjtorching.com						
RJ's Restaurant & Sports Pub						
12743 Jefferson Ave	Newport News	VA	23602	757-874-4246		671
Rjc Designs Inc						
1916 Crain Hwy S Ste 10	Glen Burnie	MD	21061	410-760-7712		196
Web: rjcdesigns.com						
RJE Business Interiors Inc						
623 Broadway St	Cincinnati	OH	45202	513-641-3700		393
TF: 800-236-8232 ■ Web: www.rjecincy.com						
Rjg Inc 3111 Park Dr	Traverse City	MI	49686	231-947-3111		201
Web: www.rjginc.com						
RJH Air Conditioning & Refrige						
12232 Distribution Pl	Beltsville	MD	20705	301-776-7270		189-10
Web: rjhhvacr.com						
RJK Partners LLC 1756 Forest Oaks Dr	Hudson	OH	44236	330-414-8705		196
Web: www.rjkpartners.com						
RJM Sales Inc 454 Park Ave	Scotch Plains	NJ	07076	908-322-7880		358
TF: 800-752-9055 ■ Web: rjmsales.com						
Rjm Wireless Consulting Services Inc						
12300 Perry Hwy Ste 206	Wexford	PA	15090	724-934-1055		196
Web: rjmwireless.com						
RJN Group Inc 200 W Front St	Wheaton	IL	60187	630-682-4700	682-4754	192
TF: 800-227-7838 ■ Web: www.rjn.com						
RJR Fashion Fabrics						
2610 Columbia St Ste B	Torrance	CA	90503	310-222-8782	222-8792	711
TF: 800-422-5426 ■ Web: www.rjrfabrics.com						
Rjr Innovations 1400 St Laurent Blvd	Ottawa	ON	K1K4H4	613-233-1915		193
Web: www.rjrinnovations.com						
RJS & Assoc Inc 1675 Sabre St	Hayward	CA	94545	510-670-9111		135
RJT Compuquest Inc						
222 N Sepulveda Blvd Ste 2250	El Segundo	CA	90245	310-378-6666		180
TF: 800-290-5460 ■ Web: rjtcompuquest.com						
Rk Controls 5901 Corvette St	Commerce	CA	90040	323-887-7066		358
TF: 877-305-8451 ■ Web: www.rkcontrols.com						
RK Engineering Group Inc						
4000 Werly Pl Ste 280	Newport Beach	CA	92660	949-474-0809		261
Web: rkengineer.com						
RK Mechanical Inc 3800 Xanthia St	Denver	CO	80238	303-355-9696	355-8666	189-10
TF: 877-576-9696 ■ Web: www.rkmi.com						
RKA Petroleum Companies Inc						
28340 Wick Rd	Romulus	MI	48174	734-946-2199		579
TF: 866-509-3288 ■ Web: www.rkapetroleum.com						
RKI Inc 2301 Central Pkwy	Houston	TX	77092	713-688-4414	688-8982	470
TF: 800-346-8988 ■ Web: www.rki-us.com						
RK&K 81 Mosher St	Baltimore	MD	21217	410-728-2900		261
Web: www.rkk.com						
RKL eSolutions LLC						
1800 Fruitville Pk	Lancaster	PA	17604	717-735-9109		631
Web: www.rklesolutions.com						
RKO Pictures Inc						
11301 W Olympic Blvd Ste 510	Los Angeles	CA	90064	310-277-0707	566-8940	514
Web: www.rko.com						
RKR Hess Assoc Inc						
112 N Courtland St	East Stroudsburg	PA	18301	570-421-1550		261
Web: rkrhess.com						
RL Adams Plastics Inc						
5955 Crossroads Commerce	Wyoming	MI	49519	616-261-4400		601
TF: 800-968-2241 ■ Web: www.goadams.com						
Rl Deppmann Co 20929 Bridge St	Southfield	MI	48033	248-354-3710		641
TF: 800-589-6120 ■ Web: www.deppmann.com						
RL Drake Co 710 Pleasant Valley Dr	Springboro	OH	45066	937-746-4556	806-1510	647
TF: 800-276-4523 ■ Web: www.rldrake.com						
RL Hudson & Co 2000 W Tacoma	Broken Arrow	OK	74012	918-259-6600		608
Web: www.rlhudson.com						
RL Jordan Oil Co						
1451 Fernwood Glendale Rd	Spartanburg	SC	29307	864-585-2784		297-8
Web: www.hotspotcstore.com						
RL Winston Rod Co						
500 S Main St PO Box 411	Twin Bridges	MT	59754	406-684-5674	684-5533	710
Web: www.web.winstonrods.com						
RLE Technologies Inc						
104 Racquette Dr	Fort Collins	CO	80524	970-484-6510		693
TF: 800-518-1519 ■ Web: rletech.com						
RLI Corp 9025 N Lindbergh Dr	Peoria	IL	61615	309-692-1000	692-1068	360-4
NYSE: RLI ■ TF Cust Svc: 800-331-4929 ■ Web: www.rlicorp.com						
RLI Insurance Co 9025 N Lindbergh Dr	Peoria	IL	61615	309-692-1000	692-1068	391-4
TF: 800-331-4929 ■ Web: www.rlicorp.com						
RLJ Companies LLC, The						
3 Bethesda Metro Ctr Ste 1000	Bethesda	MD	20814	301-280-7700		360-3
Web: www.rljcompanies.com						
Rlj Financial Services Inc						
1788 Mitchell Rd Ste 102	Ceres	CA	95307	209-538-7758		138
TF: 800-240-1050 ■ Web: www.rljfinancial.com						
RLM Communications Inc						
1027 E Manchester Rd	Spring Lake	NC	28390	910-223-1350		179
TF: 877-223-1345 ■ Web: www.rlm-communications.com						
RLM Public Relations Inc						
228 E 45 St 11th Fl	New York	NY	10017	212-741-5106		636
Web: rlmpr.com						
RLR Management Consulting Inc						
77806 Flora Rd Ste D	Palm Desert	CA	92211	760-200-4800	200-4825	193
TF: 888-757-7330 ■ Web: www.rlrmgmt.com						
Rls Logistics 2260 Industrial Way	Vineland	NJ	08360	856-691-2040		196
TF: 800-569-4812 ■ Web: www.rlslogistics.com						
RLTV 5525 Research Park Dr	Baltimore	MD	21228	800-754-8464		116
TF: 800-754-8464 ■ Web: www.rl.tv/about-rltv						
RM Bradley 1 Financial Plaza	Hartford	CT	06103	860-278-2040		652
Web: www.rmbradley.com						
RM Burritt Motors Inc 340 Rt 104 E	Oswego	NY	13126	315-343-8948		690
Web: www.burrittchevy.com						
R&M Consultants Inc						
9101 Vanguard Dr	Anchorage	AK	99507	907-522-1707		727
TF: 800-478-3121 ■ Web: www.rmconsult.com						
Rm Design Studio Ltd						
850 W Bartlett Rd	Bartlett	IL	60103	630-540-1222		396
TF: 800-513-2250 ■ Web: www.rmdesignstudio.com						
RM Educational						
310 Barnstable Rd Ste 101 A&B	Hyannis	MA	02601	508-862-0700	862-0770	242
Web: www.rmeducation.com						
RM Kerner Co 2208 E 33rd St	Erie	PA	16510	814-898-2000		454
Web: www.rmkco.com						
R&M Manufacturing Company LLC						
200 Centennial Dr	Buffalo	MN	55313	763-574-9225		198
Web: www.rmmco.com						
R&M Materials Handling Inc						
4501 Gateway Blvd	Springfield	OH	45502	937-328-5100		358
TF: 800-955-9967 ■ Web: www.rmhoist.com						
RM Mechanical Inc 5998 W Gowen Rd	Boise	ID	83709	208-362-0131		256
Web: www.rmmechanical.net						
RM Palmer Co 77 S Second Ave	West Reading	PA	19611	610-372-8971		296-8
Web: www.rmpalmer.com						
RM Strategic Marketing 800 W End Ave	New York	NY	10025	212-961-1120		194
Web: www.rmstrategicmarketing.com						
RM Towill Corp 2024 N King St Ste 200	Honolulu	HI	96819	808-842-1133	842-1937	261
TF: 800-361-4635 ■ Web: www.rmtowill.com						
RMA (Risk Management Assn)						
1801 Market St Ste 300	Philadelphia	PA	19103	215-446-4000	446-4101	49-2
TF Cust Svc: 800-677-7621 ■ Web: www.rmahq.org						
RMA Group Inc						
12130 Santa Margarita Ct	Rancho Cucamonga	CA	91730	909-989-1751		261
TF: 800-480-4808 ■ Web: www.rmacompanies.com						
RMC (Rockdale Medical Ctr)						
1412 Milstead Ave NE	Conyers	GA	30012	770-918-3000	918-3104	374-3
Web: www.rockdalemedicalcenter.org						
RMC (Riverside Medical Ctr)						
350 N Wall St	Kankakee	IL	60901	815-933-1671		374-3
Web: www.riversidehealthcare.org						
RMC (Ridgeview Medical Ctr)						
500 S Maple St	Waconia	MN	55387	952-442-2191	442-6524	374-3
TF: 800-967-4620 ■ Web: www.ridgeviewmedical.org						
RMC Research Corp						
1000 Market St Bldg 2	Portsmouth	NH	03801	603-422-8888		743
Web: www.rmcresearchcorporation.com						
RMC Water & Environment Inc						
2175 N California Blvd Ste 315	Walnut Creek	CA	94596	925-627-4100		261
Web: www.rmcwater.com						
RMCF (Rocky Mountain Chocolate Factory Inc)						
265 Turner Dr	Durango	CO	81303	970-259-0554		123
NASDAQ: RMCF ■ TF Cust Svc: 888-525-2462 ■ Web: www.rmcf.com						

Name / Address	City	State	ZIP	Phone	Fax	Class
RMCSJ (Regional Medical Ctr of San Jose) 225 N Jackson Ave	San Jose	CA	95116	408-259-5000	729-2884	374-3
TF: 800-307-7135 ■ *Web:* www.regionalmedicalsanjose.com						
RMD Adv 6116 Cleveland Ave	Columbus	OH	43231	614-794-2008		4
Web: www.rmdadvertising.com						
RMD Instruments LLC 44 Hunt St	Watertown	MA	02472	617-668-6900		492
TF: 800-790-4452 ■ *Web:* rmdinc.com						
RMDINC (Radiation Monitoring Devices Inc) 44 Hunt St Ste 2	Watertown	MA	02472	617-668-6800		472
Web: www.rmdinc.com						
RME360 4805 Independence Pkwy Ste 250	Tampa	FL	33634	888-383-8770		5
TF: 888-383-8770 ■ *Web:* www.rme360.com						
RMF Engineering Inc 5520 Research Pk Dr Ste 300	Baltimore	MD	21228	410-576-0505		261
TF: 800-938-5760 ■ *Web:* www.rmf.com						
RMF Printing Technologies Inc 50 Pearl St	Lancaster	NY	14086	716-683-7500		627
TF: 800-828-7999 ■ *Web:* www.rmfprinting.com						
RMF Steel Products Co 4417 E 119th St	Grandview	MO	64030	816-765-4101	765-0067	298
Web: rmfworks.com						
RMG Financial Consulting Inc 813 E Ballard Ave	Colbert	WA	99005	509-468-2956		196
Web: www.rmgfinancial.com						
RMH (Ross Memorial Hospital) 10 Angeline St N	Lindsay	ON	K9V4M8	705-324-6111		374-2
TF: 800-510-7365 ■ *Web:* www.rmh.org						
RMH (Ronald McDonald House) 2524 N State St	Jackson	MS	39216	601-981-5683	981-3613	373
Web: www.rmhcms.org						
RMH (Roxborough Memorial Hospital) 5800 Ridge Ave	Philadelphia	PA	19128	215-483-9900		374-3
Web: www.roxboroughmemorial.com						
RMH (Reynolds Memorial Hospital) 800 Wheeling Ave	Glen Dale	WV	26038	304-845-3211		374-3
RMHC (Ronald McDonald House Charities) 1 Kroc Dr	Oak Brook	IL	60523	630-623-7048	623-7488	48-5
Web: www.rmhc.org						
RMHC (Ronald McDonald House Charities of Kentuckiana) 550 S First St	Louisville	KY	40202	502-581-1416	581-0037	373
Web: www.rmhc-kentuckiana.org						
Little Rock 1009 Wolfe St	Little Rock	AR	72202	501-374-1956		373
Web: rmhclittlerock.org						
RMI (Ralph Moyle Inc) 55475 N Main St	Mattawan	MI	49071	269-668-4531		780
Web: www.ralphmoyle.com						
RMI Direct Marketing Inc 44 Old Ridgebury Rd	Danbury	CT	06810	203-798-0448		195
Web: www.rmidirect.com						
RMLEB (Rocky Mountain Lions Eye Bank) 1675 Aurora Crt Ste El2049 PO Box 6026	Aurora	CO	80045	720-848-3937	848-3938	269
TF: 800-444-7479 ■ *Web:* www.corneas.org						
RMO Inc (Rocky Mountain Orthodontics Inc) 650 W Colfax Ave	Denver	CO	80204	303-592-8200	592-8200*	228
**Fax:* Hum Res ■ *TF:* 800-525-6375 ■ *Web:* www.rmortho.com						
RMP (Recto Molded Products Inc) 4425 Appleton St	Cincinnati	OH	45209	513-871-5544		604
Web: www.rectomolded.com						
RMP Energy Inc 1200-500 4 Ave SW	Calgary	AB	T2P2V6	403-930-6300		536
Web: www.rmpenergyinc.com						
RMPB (Rocky Mountain Public Broadcasting Network) 1089 Bannock St	Denver	CO	80204	303-892-6666	620-5600	632
TF: 800-274-6666 ■ *Web:* www.rmpbs.org						
RMPersonnel Inc 4707 Montana Ave	El Paso	TX	79903	915-565-7674	565-7687	631
TF: 866-333-7176 ■ *Web:* www.rmpersonnel.com						
RMR (Rocky Mountain Recycling) 6510 Brighton Blvd	Commerce	CO	80022	303-288-6868	288-0250	686
Web: www.rmrscrap.com						
RMR Assoc Inc 5870 Hubbard Dr	Rockville	MD	20852	301-230-0045	230-0046	636
TF: 800-261-1537 ■ *Web:* www.rmr.com						
RMRC Services Inc 5870 S Walden Ct	Centennial	CO	80015	303-667-0400		83
Web: www.rockymountainmold.com						
RMS 8227 Northwest Blvd Ste 230	Indianapolis	IN	46278	317-872-8227		463
Web: rms-safety.com						
RMS Telecommunications LLC 5600 Maggie Run Ln	Fuquay Varina	NC	27526	919-567-4620		809
RMS Titanic Inc 3340 Peachtree Rd NE	Atlanta	GA	30326	404-842-2600		465
Web: premierexhibitions.com						
RMSC (Risk Management Services Co) 9100 Marksfield Rd	Louisville	KY	40222	502-326-5900	326-5909*	194
**Fax Area Code:* 888 ■ *Web:* www.rmsc.com						
RMS-Ross Corp 44325 Yale Rd W	Chilliwack	BC	V2R4H2	604-792-5911	792-7148	454
Web: rmsross-public.sharepoint.com						
RMT Woodworth Inc 45755 Five Mile Rd	Plymouth	MI	48170	734-254-0566		484
Web: www.rmtwoodworth.com						
RMW Architecture & Interiors 160 Pine St 4th Fl	San Francisco	CA	94111	415-781-9800		393
Web: www.rmw.com						
Rmx Global Logistics 35715 US Hwy 40 Bldg B	Evergreen	CO	80439	888-824-7365	674-3803*	311
**Fax Area Code:* 303 ■ *TF:* 888-824-7365 ■ *Web:* www.rmxglobal.com						
RMX Holdings Inc 4602 E Thomas Rd	Phoenix	AZ	85018	602-249-5814		182
Web: rmxholdings.com						
RN Fink Mfg Company Inc 1530 Noble Rd PO Box 245	Williamston	MI	48895	517-655-4351	655-5119	98
Web: www.rnfink.com						
RN Johnson Inc (RNJ) 269 Main St PO Box 448	Walpole	NH	03608	603-756-3321	756-3452	274
Web: www.rnjohnsoninc.com						
RNC (Republican National Committee) 310 First St SE	Washington	DC	20003	202-863-8500		616
TF: 800-445-5768 ■ *Web:* www.gop.com						
RNC Genter Capital Management 11601 Wilshire Blvd 25th Fl	Los Angeles	CA	90025	310-477-6543	479-6406	401
TF: 800-877-7624 ■ *Web:* www.rncgenter.com						
RNDC (Republic National Distributing Co) 6511 Tri County Pkwy	Schertz	TX	78154	210-224-7531		81-3
Web: www.rndc-usa.com						
Rndt Inc Nondestructive Testing & Research Services 228 Maple Ave	Johnstown	PA	15901	814-535-5448		743
Web: www.rndt.net						
RNJ (RN Johnson Inc) 269 Main St PO Box 448	Walpole	NH	03608	603-756-3321	756-3452	274
Web: www.rnjohnsoninc.com						
RNL Design 1050 17th St Ste A200	Denver	CO	80265	303-295-1717	292-0845	261
Web: www.rnldesign.com						
Rnr Custom Wheels & Tires 8030 Florida Blvd	Baton Rouge	LA	70806	225-926-7466		57
Web: rnrwheels.com						
RnR RV Ctr 23203 E Knox Ave	Liberty Lake	WA	99019	866-386-4875		57
TF: 866-386-4875 ■ *Web:* www.rnrrv.com						
RNRF (Renewable Natural Resources Foundation) 5430 Grosvenor Ln	Bethesda	MD	20814	301-493-9101	493-6148	48-13
Web: www.rnrf.org						
RNS (Religion News Service) 529 14th St NW Ste 425	Washington	DC	20045	202-463-8777	662-7154	530
Web: www.religionnews.com						
Ro Mai Industries 1605 Enterprise Pkwy	Twinsburg	OH	44087	330-425-9090		608
Web: www.rmihardware.com						
ROA (Reserve Officers Assn of the US) 1 Constitution Ave NE	Washington	DC	20002	202-479-2200	547-1641	48-19
TF: 800-809-9448 ■ *Web:* www.roa.org						
ROACO Logistics Services 500 Country Club Dr	Bensenville	IL	60106	630-595-8631		449
Road & Track Magazine 1499 Monrovia Ave	Newport Beach	CA	92663	949-720-5300		457-3
TF: 800-835-6422 ■ *Web:* www.roadandtrack.com						
Road America N 7390 Hwy 67	Elkhart Lake	WI	53020	920-892-4576	892-4550	515
TF: 800-365-7223 ■ *Web:* www.roadamerica.com						
Road Atlanta Raceway 5300 Winder Hwy	Braselton	GA	30517	770-967-6143		515
TF: 800-849-7223 ■ *Web:* www.roadatlanta.com						
Road Builders Machinery & Supply Company Inc 1001 S Seventh St	Kansas City	KS	66105	913-371-3822	371-3870	385
Web: www.roadbuildersmachinery.com						
Road King Inn Columbia Mall 3300 30th Ave S	Grand Forks	ND	58201	800-707-1391		379
TF: 800-707-1391						
Road Machinery Co 4710 E ElWood St Ste 6	Phoenix	AZ	85040	602-252-7121	253-9690	358
Web: www.roadmachinery.com						
Road Ranger LLC 4930 E State St	Rockford	IL	61108	815-387-1700		345
Web: www.roadrangerusa.com						
Road Sprinkler Fitters Local Union 669 7050 Oakland Mills Rd	Columbia	MD	21046	410-381-4300		414
TF: 800-638-0997 ■ *Web:* www.sprinklerfitters669.org						
Roadrunner Transportation Systems Inc 4900 S Pennsylvania Ave	Cudahy	WI	53110	414-615-1500	615-1513	651
NYSE: RRTS ■ *TF:* 800-831-4394 ■ *Web:* www.rrts.com						
Roadster Factory, The 328 Killen Rd	Armagh	PA	15920	814-446-4444		54
Web: www.the-roadster-factory.com						
Roadtec Inc 800 Manufacturers Rd PO Box 180515	Chattanooga	TN	37405	423-265-0600	267-7104	190
TF: 800-272-7100 ■ *Web:* www.roadtec.com						
Roadtex Transportation Corp 13 Jensen Dr	Somerset	NJ	08873	800-762-3839		780
TF: 800-762-3839 ■ *Web:* www.roadtex.com						
Roadtrip Productions Ltd 1626 Placentia Ave	Costa Mesa	CA	92627	949-764-9121		738
Web: roadtripnation.com						
Roake & Assoc Inc 1684 Quincy Ave	Naperville	IL	60540	630-355-3232		261
Web: roake.com						
ROAM (Rivers Oceans & Mountains Adventures Inc) 2622 Front St	Nelson	BC	V1L4B7	888-639-1114		760
TF: 888-639-1114 ■ *Web:* www.iroamtheworld.com						
Roam Mobility Inc 400 - 311 Water St	Vancouver	BC	V6B1B8	888-762-6487	586-3441	224
TF: 888-762-6487 ■ *Web:* www.roammobility.com						
Roaman's 2300 SE Ave	Indianapolis	IN	46201	800-677-0229	266-3393*	459
**Fax Area Code:* 317 ■ *TF:* 800-677-0229 ■ *Web:* www.roamans.com						
Roan Mountain State Park 1015 Hwy 143	Roan Mountain	TN	37687	423-772-0190		565
Web: tnstateparks.com						
Roane County 1209 N Kentucky St	Kingston	TN	37763	865-376-5556	376-4978	338
TF: 800-386-4686 ■ *Web:* www.roanealliance.org						
Roane County 200 Main St	Spencer	WV	25276	304-927-2860	927-2489	338
Web: roanecounty.wv.gov						
Roane County Chamber of Commerce 1209 N Kentucky St	Kingston	TN	37763	865-376-5572	376-4978	139
Web: www.roanealliance.org						
Roane Medical Ctr 8045 Roane Medical Center Dr	Harriman	TN	37748	865-316-1000		374-3
Web: www.covenanthealth.com						
Roane State Community College 276 Patton Ln	Harriman	TN	37748	865-354-3000	882-4562*	162
**Fax:* Admitting ■ *TF:* 800-343-9104 ■ *Web:* www.roanestate.edu						
Roanoke College 221 College Ln	Salem	VA	24153	540-375-2270	375-2267*	166
**Fax:* Admissions ■ *TF Admissions:* 800-388-2276 ■ *Web:* www.roanoke.edu						
Roanoke County 5204 Bernard Dr	Roanoke	VA	24018	540-772-2004	561-2884	338
Web: roanokecountyva.gov						
Roanoke County Public Library 3131 Electric Rd	Roanoke	VA	24018	540-772-7507	989-3129	434-3
Web: www.roanokecountyva.gov						
Roanoke Electric Co-op 518 NC 561 W	Aulander	NC	27805	252-539-4600	539-4612	245
TF: 800-433-2236 ■ *Web:* www.roanokeelectric.com						
Roanoke Gas Co 519 Kimball Rd	Roanoke	VA	24030	540-777-4427	777-7952	787
TF: 800-552-7945 ■ *Web:* www.roanokegas.com						
Roanoke (Independent City) 210 Reserve Ave SW	Roanoke	VA	24016	540-853-2000	853-1138	338
TF: 800-956-4237 ■ *Web:* www.roanokeva.gov						
Roanoke Regional Airport 5202 Aviation Dr NW	Roanoke	VA	24012	540-362-1999	563-4838	27
TF: 800-433-7300 ■ *Web:* flyroa.com						
Roanoke Regional Chamber of Commerce 210 S Jefferson St	Roanoke	VA	24011	540-983-0700	983-0723	139
TF: 800-924-3543 ■ *Web:* www.roanokechamber.org						

Phone Fax Class

Roanoke Symphony Orchestra
541 Luck Ave Ste 200 Roanoke VA 24016 540-343-6221 343-0065 573-3
Web: www.rso.com

Roanoke Times 201 W Campbell Ave SW Roanoke VA 24011 540-981-3340 981-3346 532-2
TF: 800-346-1234 ■ *Web:* www.roanoke.com

Roanoke Valley Chamber of Commerce
260 Premier Blvd Roanoke Rapids NC 27870 252-537-3513 535-5767 139
TF: 800-280-3999 ■ *Web:* www.rvchamber.com

Roanoke Valley Convention & Visitors Bureau
101 Shenandoah Ave NE Roanoke VA 24016 540-342-6025 342-7119 206
TF: 800-635-5535 ■ *Web:* www.visitroanokeva.com

Roanoke Valley Wine Co 1250 Intervale Salem VA 24153 540-444-4440 375-8877 80-3
Web: rvwc.com

Roanoke-Chowan Community College
109 Community College Rd Ahoskie NC 27910 252-862-1200 862-1355* 162
**Fax:* Admissions ■ *Web:* www.roanokechowan.edu

Roanoke-Chowan Hospital
500 S Academy St Ahoskie NC 27910 252-209-3148 209-3146 374-3
Web: www.vidanthealth.com

Roanwell Corp 2564 Pk Ave Bronx NY 10451 718-401-0288 401-0663 52
Web: www.roanwell.com

Roar Foundation 6867 Soledad Canyon Rd Acton CA 93510 661-268-0380 564
Web: www.shambala.org

Roaring Brook Ranch & Tennis Resort
Rte 9N S Lake George NY 12845 518-668-5767 669
TF: 800-882-7665 ■ *Web:* www.roaringbrookranch.com

Roaring River State Park
12716 Farm Rd 2239 Cassville MO 65625 417-847-2539 565
Web: mostateparks.com

Roaring Run Resort Sales
194 Tannery Rd Champion PA 15622 724-593-7837 377
TF: 800-619-6946 ■ *Web:* roaringrunresort.com

Roaring Spring Blank Book Co
740 Spang St Roaring Spring PA 16673 814-224-5141 86
TF: 800-441-1653 ■ *Web:* www.rspaperproducts.com

Ro-Ark Printing Inc 1600 N 35th St Rogers AR 72756 479-636-1686 627
TF: 800-364-1240 ■ *Web:* www.roarkgroup.com

Roasterie Inc, The 1204 W 27th St Kansas City MO 64108 816-931-4000 345
TF: 800-376-0245 ■ *Web:* www.theroasterie.com

Rob Bailey Communications
310 State Rt 17 Upper Saddle River NJ 07458 201-760-0200 636

Robar Enterprises Inc
17671 Bear Valley Rd Hesperia CA 92345 760-244-5456 244-1819 182
Web: www.robarenterprises.com

Robart Manufacturing Co
625 N 12th St Saint Charles IL 60174 630-584-7616 711
Web: www.robart.com

Robata Grill 3658 The Barnyard Carmel CA 93923 831-624-2643 671
Web: robata-barnyard.com

Robata of Tokyo 39 S Ninth St Allentown PA 18102 610-821-6900 671
Web: www.icloud.com

Robb & Stucky International
13170 S Cleveland Ave Fort Myers FL 33907 239-415-2800 321
Web: robbstuckyintl.com

Robbers Cave State Park Hwy 2 N Wilburton OK 74578 918-465-2565 465-5763 565
TF: 800-654-8240 ■ *Web:* travelok.com

Robberson Ford Lincoln Mercury Mazda
2289 NE Third St Prineville OR 97754 541-447-6820 57
Web: www.robberson.com

Robbie Manufacturing Inc
10810 Mid America Ave Lenexa KS 66219 913-492-3400 492-1543 601
TF: 800-255-6328 ■ *Web:* www.robbieflexibles.com

Robbinex Inc 41 Stuart St Hamilton ON L8L1B5 905-523-7510 317
TF: 888-762-2463 ■ *Web:* www.robbinex.com

Robbins Arroyo LLP 600 B St Ste 1900 San Diego CA 92101 619-525-3990 428
TF: 800-350-6003 ■ *Web:* www.robbinsarroyo.com

Robbins Inc 4777 Eastern Ave Cincinnati OH 45226 513-871-8988 871-7998 683
TF: 800-543-1913 ■ *Web:* www.robbinsfloor.com

Robbins Library
700 Massachusetts Ave Arlington MA 02476 781-316-3200 434-3
Web: robbinslibrary.org

Robbins LLC 3415 Thompson St Muscle Shoals AL 35661 256-383-5441 754
TF: 800-633-3312 ■ *Web:* www.robbinsllc.com

Robbins Lumber Co 53 Ghent Rd Searsmont ME 04973 207-342-5221 683
Web: www.rlco.com

Robbins Mfg Co 13001 N Nebraska Ave Tampa FL 33612 813-971-3030 818
TF: 888-558-8199 ■ *Web:* www.robbinslumber.com

Robbins Parking Service Ltd
1102 Fort St Victoria BC V8V3K8 250-382-4411 562
TF: 800-665-4354 ■ *Web:* www.robbinsparking.com

Robbinsdale Area Schools
4148 Winnetka Ave N New Hope MN 55427 763-504-8000 685
Web: www.rdale.org

Robern Inc 701 N Wilson Ave Bristol PA 19007 215-826-9800 319-2
TF: 800-877-2376 ■ *Web:* www.robern.com

Roberson Motors Inc 3100 Ryan Dr SE Salem OR 97301 503-363-4117 57
TF: 888-281-6220 ■ *Web:* www.robersonmotorschryslerjeep.com

Roberson Museum & Science Ctr
30 Front St Binghamton NY 13905 607-772-0660 771-8905 520
TF: 888-269-5325 ■ *Web:* www.roberson.org

Roberson Wireline Inc
314 SE Ninth Ave Perryton TX 79070 806-435-3087 539
TF: 800-435-3087 ■ *Web:* robersonwireline.com

Robert & Frances Fullerton Art Museum
5500 University Pkwy San Bernardino CA 92407 909-537-7373 537-7068 520
Web: raffma.csusb.edu

Robert A "Bob" Bowers Civic Ctr
3401 Cultural Ctr Dr Port Arthur TX 77642 409-985-8801 205
TF: 800-235-7822 ■ *Web:* www.portarthur.net

Robert A Main & Sons Inc
555 Goffle Rd Wyckoff NJ 07481 201-447-3700 447-0302 621
Web: www.ramsco-inc.com

Robert A Welch Foundation
5555 San Felipe St Ste 1900 Houston TX 77056 713-961-9884 305
Web: www.welch1.org

Robert Abbey Inc 3166 Main Ave SE Hickory NC 28602 828-322-3480 601
Web: www.robertabbey.biz/smart-lighting/default.aspx

Phone Fax Class

Robert Allan Ltd
1639 Second Ave W Ste 230 Vancouver BC V6J1H3 604-736-9466 261
TF: 800-828-9829 ■ *Web:* www.ral.ca

Robert Allen Fabrics Inc
225 Foxboro Blvd Foxboro MA 02035 800-333-3777 332-8256* 594
**Fax:* Sales ■ *TF:* 800-333-3777 ■ *Web:* www.robertallendesign.com

Robert Allen Law
1441 Brickell Ave Ste 1400 Miami FL 33131 305-372-3300 445
TF: 800-208-5801 ■ *Web:* www.robertallenlaw.com

Robert Allerton Park & Conference Ctr
515 Old Timber Rd Monticello IL 61856 217-333-3287 300-3078 97
Web: www.allerton.illinois.edu

Robert B Greenblatt MD Library
Medical College of Georgia
1439 Lny Walker Blvd Augusta GA 30912 706-721-3441 434-1
TF: 800-715-4225 ■ *Web:* www.augusta.edu

Robert Bearden Inc
2601 Industrial Pk Dr PO Box 870 Cairo GA 39828 229-377-6928 780
TF: 888-298-6928 ■ *Web:* www.rbitrucking.com

Robert Bosch LLC
38000 Hills Tech Dr Farmington Hills MI 48331 248-876-1000 52
Web: www.bosch.us

Robert Bosch Tool Corp
1800 W Central Rd Mount Prospect IL 60056 877-267-2499 232-3169* 759
**Fax Area Code:* 224 ■ *TF:* 877-267-2499 ■ *Web:* www.boschtools.com

Robert Bowden Inc
850 White Circle Ct Marietta GA 30060 770-429-9285 499
Web: www.robertbowden.com

Robert Busse & Company Inc
75 Arkay Dr Hauppauge NY 11788 631-435-4711 596
Web: www.busseinc.com

Robert d Niehaus Inc
140 E Carrillo St Santa Barbara CA 93101 805-962-0611 466
Web: www.rdniehaus.com

Robert Dietrick Co Inc PO Box 605 Fishers IN 46038 317-842-1991 842-2698 385
TF: 866-767-1888 ■ *Web:* www.rd-co.com

Robert E Morris Co 910 Gay Hill Rd Windsor CT 06095 860-687-3300 687-3301 385
TF: 800-852-0582 ■ *Web:* www.robertemorris.com

Robert E Nolan Company Inc
92 Hopmeadow St Weatogue CT 06089 860-658-1941 651-3465 194
TF: 800-653-1941 ■ *Web:* www.renolan.com

Robert e Webber Institute for Worship Studies, The
151 Kingsley Ave Orange Park FL 32073 904-264-2172 685
TF: 800-282-2977 ■ *Web:* iws.edu

Robert E. Lee & Associates Inc
1250 Centennial Centre Blvd Hobart WI 54155 920-662-9641 261
TF: 800-986-6388 ■ *Web:* www.releeinc.com

Robert E. Porter Construction Company Inc
1720 W Lincoln St Phoenix AZ 85007 602-253-4911 186
Web: robertporterconstruction.com

Robert F Henry Tile Company Inc
1008 Lagoon Business Loop Montgomery AL 36117 334-269-2518 191-1
Web: www.henrytile.com

Robert F Kennedy Stadium
2400 E Capitol St SE Washington DC 20003 202-608-1100 720
Web: eventsdc.com/venues/rfkstadium/contactinfo.aspx

Robert Family Holdings Inc (RFH)
12430 Tesson Ferry Rd Ste 313 Saint Louis MO 63128 636-305-2830 965-0309* 548
**Fax Area Code:* 314 ■ *Web:* www.rf-holdings.com

Robert Fisher Co 10 E 38th St 6th Fl New York NY 10016 212-532-3253 481-3394 409
TF: 800-526-8052 ■ *Web:* www.rsfisher.com

Robert Frances Group 46 Kent Hills Ln Wilton CT 06897 203-429-8951 196
Web: www.rfgonline.com

Robert Frost Farm Historic Site
122 Rockingham Rd Derry NH 03038 603-432-3091 565
Web: www.nhstateparks.org

Robert Frost Middle School
2206 W 167th St Markham IL 60428 708-210-9929 685

Robert Gibb & Sons Inc 205 SW 40th St Fargo ND 58103 701-282-5900 281-0819 189-10
Web: www.robertgibb.com

Robert Gordon Industries Ltd
1500 Plaza Ave New Hyde Park NY 11040 516-354-8888 361
Web: www.gordonsinclair.com

Robert Group Inc, The
3108 Los Feliz Blvd Los Angeles CA 90039 323-669-9100 194
Web: www.therobertgroup.com

Robert H Peterson Co
14724 Proctor Ave City Of Industry CA 91746 626-369-5085 350
Web: www.rhpeterson.com

Robert H Wager Co 570 Montroyal Rd Rural Hall NC 27045 336-969-6909 969-6375 789
TF: 800-562-7024 ■ *Web:* www.wagerusa.com

Robert H. Meyer Memorial State Beach
1925 Las Virgenes Rd Calabasas CA 91302 818-880-0363 565
Web: www.parks.ca.gov/default.asp?page_id=633

Robert H. Treman State Park
105 Enfield Falls Rd Ithaca NY 14850 607-273-3440 565
Web: parks.ny.gov/parks/135/details.aspx

Robert Hale & Assoc
5405 Morehouse Dr Ste 320 San Diego CA 92121 858-404-0200 466
Web: productsstrategy.com

Robert Half International Inc
2884 Sand Hill Rd Ste 200 Menlo Park CA 94025 650-234-6000 721
NYSE: RHI ■ *Web:* www.roberthalf.com

Robert Half International Inc Accountemps Div
2884 Sand Hill Rd Ste 200 Menlo Park CA 94025 855-396-4598 721
TF: 888-744-9202 ■ *Web:* www.roberthalf.com

Robert Half International Inc OfficeTeam Div
2884 Sand Hill Rd Ste 200 Menlo Park CA 94025 650-234-6000 721
Web: www.roberthalf.com

Robert Heath Trucking Inc
1201 E 40th St Lubbock TX 79404 806-747-1651 747-0339 780
Web: www.robertheath.com

Robert Hull Fleming Museum
61 Colchester Ave University of Vermont Burlington VT 05405 802-656-0750 656-8059 520
TF: 888-382-1222 ■ *Web:* www.uvm.edu

Robert I Goldstein
6507 Wilkins Ave Ste 202 Pittsburgh PA 15217 412-362-9040 2

Phone Fax Class

Robert J Dole Institute of Politics
2350 Petefish Dr . . . Lawrence KS 66045 785-864-4900 864-1414 634
Web: www.doleinstitute.org
Robert J Dole VA Medical Center
5500 E Kellogg St . . . Wichita KS 67218 316-685-2221 651-3666 374-3
TF: 888-878-6881 ■ *Web:* www.wichita.va.gov/index.asp
Robert J Kleberg Public Library
220 N Fourth St . . . Kingsville TX 78363 361-592-6381 434-3
Web: kleberglibrary.com
Robert Jeffrey Hair Studio
3153 N Broadway . . . Chicago IL 60657 773-525-8800 77
Web: robertjeffrey.com
Robert Jones Plumbing Inc 6071 SR- 128 . . . Cleves OH 45002 513-353-2230 353-2247 189-10
Web: robertjonesplumbing.com
Robert K Taylor
2890 N Main St Ste 305 . . . Walnut Creek CA 94597 925-944-7660 2
Robert Kaufman Company Inc
PO Box 59266 . . . Los Angeles CA 90059 310-538-3482 538-9235 594
TF: 800-877-2066 ■ *Web:* www.robertkaufman.com
Robert L. Bayless, Producer LLC
621 17th St Ste 2300 . . . Denver CO 80293 303-296-9900 539
Web: www.rlbayless.com
Robert M Bird Health Sciences Library
1105 N Stonewall Ave . . . Oklahoma City OK 73117 405-271-2285 271-3297 434-1
Web: library.ouhsc.edu
Robert M Degregorio Insurance Agency Inc
34 Woodside Ave . . . Winthrop MA 02152 617-846-3313 390
Robert M Grum Jr CPA
4540 Kearny Villa Rd Ste 108 . . . San Diego CA 92123 858-560-5449 2
Robert Mann Packaging Inc
340 El Camino Real S Bldg 40 . . . Salinas CA 93901 800-345-6766 100
TF: 800-345-6766 ■ *Web:* www.rmp.com
Robert Michael Communications Inc
101 Laurel Rd . . . Voorhees NJ 08043 856-547-4141 7
TF: 800-438-7325 ■ *Web:* www.rmei.com
Robert Miller Gallery 524 W 26th St . . . New York NY 10001 212-366-4774 42
TF: 800-223-9132 ■ *Web:* www.robertmillergallery.com
Robert Mills House & Gardens
1616 Blanding St . . . Columbia SC 29201 803-252-7742 929-7695 50-3
TF: 800-745-3000 ■ *Web:* www.historiccolumbia.org
Robert Mitchell Inc
350 Decarie Blvd via St-Louis and Crevier St
. . . St-laurent QC H4L3K5 514-747-2471 595
Web: www.robertmitchell.com
Robert Mondavi Co 7801 St Helena Hwy . . . Oakville CA 94562 707-226-1395 80-3
TF: 888-766-6328 ■ *Web:* www.robertmondaviwinery.com
Robert Moreno Insurance Services
2260 Savi Ranch Pkwy PO Box 87023 . . . Yorba Linda CA 92887 714-738-1383 921-1106 390
TF: 800-815-7647 ■ *Web:* rmismga.com
Robert Morris College
Chicago 401 S State St . . . Chicago IL 60605 312-935-6800 935-4182 166
TF: 800-762-5960 ■ *Web:* www.robertmorris.edu
DuPage 905 Meridian Lake Dr . . . Aurora IL 60504 630-375-8100 375-8020* 166
**Fax:* Admissions ■ *TF Admissions:* 800-762-5960 ■ *Web:* www.robertmorris.edu
Orland Park 43 Orland Sq Dr . . . Orland Park IL 60462 708-226-3800 226-5350 166
TF: 800-225-1520 ■ *Web:* www.robertmorris.edu
Springfield 3101 Montvale Dr . . . Springfield IL 62704 217-793-2500 793-4210* 166
**Fax:* Admitting ■ *TF:* 800-762-5960 ■ *Web:* www.robertmorris.edu
Robert Morris University
6001 University Blvd . . . Moon Township PA 15108 412-262-8200 397-2425 166
TF: 800-762-0097 ■ *Web:* www.rmu.edu
Robert Morris University Institute of Culinary Arts
401 S State St . . . Chicago IL 60605 312-935-4100 935-4182* 163
**Fax:* Admissions ■ *TF:* 800-762-5960 ■ *Web:* www.robertmorris.edu/culinary
Robert Moses State Park - Long Island
Robert Moses State Pkwy PO Box 247 . . . Babylon NY 11702 631-669-0449 565
Web: parks.ny.gov/parks/7/details.aspx
Robert Moses State Park - Thousand Islands
19 Robinson Bay Rd . . . Massena NY 13662 315-769-8663 565
Web: parks.ny.gov/parks/51/details.aspx
Robert N Karpp Company Inc
480 E First St . . . Boston MA 02127 617-269-5880 269-2387 191-2
TF: 800-244-5886 ■ *Web:* karpp.com
Robert Packer Hospital 1 Guthrie Sq . . . Sayre PA 18840 570-888-6666 374-3
TF: 888-448-8474 ■ *Web:* www.guthrie.org
Robert R McCormick Tribune Foundation
205 N Michigan Ave Ste 4300 . . . Chicago IL 60601 312-445-5000 445-5001 305
TF: 800-435-7352 ■ *Web:* www.mccormickfoundation.org
Robert Rippe & Associates Inc
6117 Blue Cir Dr . . . Minnetonka MN 55343 952-933-0313 196
Web: www.robertrippe.com
Robert Runia 1270 East 8600 Souh Ste 8 . . . Sandy UT 84094 801-566-5111 390
Robert Sharp & Associates Inc
3615 Canyon Lake Dr Ste 1 . . . Rapid City SD 57702 605-341-5226 177
Web: www.robertsharpassociates.com
Robert Sterling Clark Foundation Inc
135 E 64th St . . . New York NY 10065 212-288-8900 303
Web: www.rsclark.org
Robert Talbott Inc
2901 Monterey-Salinas Hwy . . . Monterey CA 93940 831-649-6000 155-13
Web: www.roberttalbott.com
Robert Toombs House State Historic Site
216 E Robert Toombs Ave . . . Washington GA 30673 706-678-2226 565
Web: www.gastateparks.org
Robert Treat Hotel 50 Pk Pl . . . Newark NJ 07102 973-622-1000 622-6410 379
TF: 800-569-2300 ■ *Web:* www.rthotel.com
Robert V. Jensen Inc 4029 S Maple Ave . . . Fresno CA 93725 559-485-8210 579
Web: www.rvjensen.com
Robert W Baird & Company Inc
PO Box 672 . . . Milwaukee WI 53201 414-765-3500 690
TF: 800-792-2473 ■ *Web:* www.rwbaird.com
Robert W Woodruff Foundation Inc
191 Peachtree St NE Ste 3540 . . . Atlanta GA 30303 404-522-6755 522-7026 305
Web: www.woodruff.org
Robert Weed Plywood Corp
705 Maple St PO Box 487 . . . Bristol IN 46507 574-848-4408 848-5679 613
Web: www.robertweedplywood.com

Phone Fax Class

Robert Wood Johnson Foundation
PO Box 2316 . . . Princeton NJ 08543 877-843-7953 305
TF: 877-843-7953 ■ *Web:* www.rwjf.org
Robert Wood Johnson Medical School
675 Hoes Ln . . . Piscataway NJ 08854 732-235-4576 235-5078 167-2
Web: www.rwjms.umdnj.edu
Robert Wood Johnson University Hospital
1 Robert Wood Johnson Pl . . . New Brunswick NJ 08901 732-828-3000 374-3
TF: 888-637-9584 ■ *Web:* www.rwjuh.edu
Robert Wood Johnson University Hospital at Rahway (RWJUHR)
865 Stone St . . . Rahway NJ 07065 732-381-4200 586-7900* 374-3
**Fax Area Code:* 609 ■ *TF:* 800-443-4605 ■ *Web:* www.rwjuhr.com
Robert Wooler Co 1755 Susquehanna Rd . . . Dresher PA 19025 215-542-7600 542-0250 484
Web: www.robertwooler.com
Robertex Associates Inc
207 Boling Industrial Way . . . Calhoun GA 30701 706-602-8080 131
Web: www.robertex.com
Robert-James Sales Inc
2585 Walden Ave . . . Buffalo NY 14225 716-651-6000 492
Web: www.rjsales.com
Roberto Clemente State Park
301 W Tremont Ave . . . Bronx NY 10453 718-299-8750 565
Web: parks.ny.gov/parks/140/details.aspx
Roberto's 908 E Amador Ave . . . Las Cruces NM 88001 575-523-1851 671
Roberto's 603 Crescent Ave . . . Bronx NY 10458 718-733-9503 671
Web: www.usmenuguide.com
Roberts & Allan 2824 Park Ave Ste B . . . Merced CA 95348 209-383-2442 2
Roberts & Holland LLP
825 Eighth Ave 37th Fl . . . New York NY 10019 212-903-8700 428
Web: www.robertsandholland.com
Roberts & Schaefer Co
222 S Riverside Plaza Ste 1800 . . . Chicago IL 60606 312-236-7292 261
Roberts Automatic Products Inc
880 Lake Dr . . . Chanhassen MN 55317 952-949-1000 949-9240 621
TF: 800-879-9837 ■ *Web:* www.robertsautomatic.com
Roberts Co Inc 180 Franklin St . . . Framingham MA 01702 500-075-0077 627
Web: www.firecatalog.com
Roberts Communications Inc
64 Commercial St . . . Rochester NY 14614 585-325-6000 4
Web: www.robertscomm.com
Roberts Communications Network LLC
4175 Cameron St . . . Las Vegas NV 89103 702-227-7500 681
Web: www.robertscomnet.com
Roberts County 122 E Water St PO Box 458 . . . Miami TX 79059 806-868-2341 868-3381 338
Web: www.uccsource.com
Roberts County 411 Second Ave E . . . Sisseton SD 57262 605-698-7336 698-4277* 338
**Fax:* Acctg ■ *Web:* roberts.sdcounties.org
Roberts Dairy Co 2901 Cuming St . . . Omaha NE 68131 402-344-4321 297-4
TF: 800-779-4321 ■ *Web:* hilanddairy.com
Roberts Gallery Ltd 641 Yonge St . . . Toronto ON M4Y1Z9 416-924-8731 42
Web: www.robertsgallery.net
Roberts Hawaii Inc
680 Iwilei Rd Ste 700 . . . Honolulu HI 96817 808-523-7750 522-7872 760
TF: 800-831-5541 ■ *Web:* www.robertshawaii.com
Roberts Home Medical Inc
20465 Seneca Meadows Pkwy . . . Germantown MD 20876 301-353-0300 475
Web: www.robertshomemedical.com
Roberts House Museum
1207 N Carson St . . . Carson City NV 89701 775-887-2174 520
Roberts John G Jr
US Supreme Ct Bldg 1 1st St NE . . . Washington DC 20543 202-479-3000 479-3472 341-4
TF: 800-772-1213 ■ *Web:* www.supremecourt.gov
Roberts Mitani LLC
145 W 57th St 21st Fl . . . New York NY 10019 212-582-9800 690
Roberts Pat (Sen R - KS)
109 Hart Bldg . . . Washington DC 20510 202-224-4774 224-3514 342-2
Web: www.roberts.senate.gov
Roberts PolyPro Inc
5416 Wyoming Ave . . . Charlotte NC 28273 704-588-1794 601
TF: 800-269-7409 ■ *Web:* www.robertspolypro.com
Roberts Printing Co
2049 Calumet St . . . Clearwater FL 33765 727-442-4011 627
TF: 800-704-8693 ■ *Web:* www.robpri.com
Roberts Sinto Corp 3001 W Main St . . . Lansing MI 48917 517-371-2460 371-4930 386
Web: www.robertssinto.com
Roberts Technology Group Inc
120 New Britain Blvd . . . Chalfont PA 18914 215-822-0600 358
Web: rtgpkg.com
Roberts Wesleyan College
2301 Westside Dr . . . Rochester NY 14624 585-594-6000 594-6371* 166
**Fax:* Admissions ■ *TF Admissions:* 800-777-4792 ■ *Web:* www.roberts.edu
RobertsBeauty
9131 Oakdale Ave Ste 110 . . . Chatsworth CA 91311 818-727-1700 361
Web: www.robertscontainer.com
Roberts-Gordon Inc
1250 William St PO Box 44 . . . Buffalo NY 14240 716-852-4400 852-0854 357
TF: 800-828-7450 ■ *Web:* www.rg-inc.com
Roberts-Hamilton
6601 Pkwy Cir Ste A . . . Brooklyn Center MN 55430 763-315-0100 315-0199 612
TF: 800-888-2222 ■ *Web:* www.robertshamilton.com
Robertshaw Industrial Products
1602 Mustang Dr . . . Maryville TN 37801 865-981-3100 981-3168 201
TF: 800-228-7429 ■ *Web:* www.robertshawindustrial.com
Robertson & Assoc CPA'S
1101 N Main St . . . Lakeport CA 95453 707-263-9012 2
Web: robertsoncpa.com
Robertson College
3-265 Notre Dame Ave . . . Winnipeg MB R3B1N9 204-943-5661 165
Web: www.robertsoncollege.com
Robertson County PO Box 1029 . . . Franklin TX 77856 979-828-4130 828-1260 338
Web: www.co.robertson.tx.us
Robertson County PO Box 76 . . . Mount Olivet KY 41064 606-724-5212 724-5022 338
Web: www.robertsoncounty.ky.gov
Robertson County 511 S Brown St . . . Springfield TN 37172 615-384-5895 384-2218 338
TF: 866-355-6134 ■ *Web:* www.robertsoncountytn.org
Robertson County Chamber ofCommerce
503 W Ct Sq . . . Springfield TN 37172 615-384-3800 384-1260 139
Web: robertsonchamber.org

Name / Address	City	State	ZIP	Phone	Fax	Class
Robertson Fuel Systems LLC 800 W Carver Rd Ste 101 *Web:* www.robertsonfuelsystems.com	Tempe	AZ	85284	480-337-7050		21
Robertson Furniture Company Inc 890 Elberton St *TF:* 800-241-0713 ■ *Web:* www.robertson-furniture.com	Toccoa	GA	30577	706-886-1494	886-8998	319-1
Robertson GeoConsultants Inc 580 Hornby St Ste 900 *Web:* www.rgc.ca	Vancouver	BC	V6C3B6	604-684-8072		463
Robertson Heating Supply Co 2155 W Main St *TF:* 800-433-9532 ■ *Web:* www.robertsonheatingsupply.com	Alliance	OH	44601	330-821-9180		612
Robertson Inc 97 Bronte St N *TF:* 800-268-5090 ■ *Web:* www.robertsonscrew.com	Milton	ON	L9T2N8	905-878-2861		278
Robertson Manufacturing Inc 112 Woodland Ave	West Grove	PA	19390	610-869-9600	869-6365	733
Robertson Ryan & Assoc Inc 330 E Kilbourn Ave *Web:* www.robertsonryan.com	Milwaukee	WI	53202	414-271-3575		390
Robertson Supply Inc PO Box 1366 *Web:* www.robertsonsupply.com	Nampa	ID	83653	208-466-8907		612
Robertson Tire Company Inc PO Box 472287 *Web:* www.robertson-tire.com	Tulsa	OK	74147	918-664-2211		54
Robertson Transformer Co 13611 Thornton Rd	Blue Island	IL	60406	708-388-2315	388-2420	190
Robertson's Ready Mix Concrete Inc 200 S Main St Ste 200 *Web:* www.rrmca.com	Corona	CA	92882	951-493-6500		182
Robertsville State Park 900 State Pk Dr *Web:* www.mostateparks.com	Robertsville	MO	63072	636-257-3788		565
Robeson Community College 5160 Fayetteville Rd PO Box 1420 *TF:* 800-359-6971 ■ *Web:* robeson.edu	Lumberton	NC	28360	910-272-3700	272-3328	162
Robeson Correctional Ctr 803 NC Hwy 711 *Web:* www.ncdps.gov	Lumberton	NC	28360	910-618-5535		213
Robeson County 701 N Elm St *Web:* www.co.robeson.nc.us	Lumberton	NC	28358	910-671-3000	671-3010	338
Robesonian, The 2175 N Roberts Ave *Web:* www.robesonian.com	Lumberton	NC	28358	910-739-4322		532-3
Robie & Matthai A Professional Corp Biltmore Tower 500 S Grand Ave 15th Fl *Web:* www.romalaw.com	Los Angeles	CA	90071	213-706-8000		428
Robin America Inc 905 Telser Rd *Web:* subarupower.com	Lake Zurich	IL	60047	847-540-7300		518
Robin Hood Foundation 826 Broadway 9th Fl *Web:* www.robinhood.org	New York	NY	10003	212-227-6601		743
Robin Rug Inc 125 Thames St	Bristol	RI	02809	401-253-8350		131
Robinette Demolition Inc 0 S 560 Hwy 83 *Web:* rdemolition.com	Oakbrook Terrace	IL	60181	630-833-7997	833-8047	189-16
Robins & Morton Group 400 Shades Creek Pkwy Ste 200 *Web:* www.robinsmorton.com	Birmingham	AL	35209	205-870-1000	871-0906	186
Robinson & Geraldo Prof Corp 1316 Pennsylvania Ave *Web:* www.rglaw.net	Washington	DC	20003	202-544-2888		428
Robinson & Maites Inc 35 E Wacker Dr Ste 3500 *Web:* radiant-1.com	Chicago	IL	60601	312-372-9333		194
Robinson & Mcelwee Pllc 700 Virginia St E Ste 400 *Web:* ramlaw.com	Charleston	WV	25301	304-344-5800		428
Robinson & Wood Inc 227 N First St *Web:* www.robinsonwood.com	San Jose	CA	95113	408-298-7120		428
Robinson Aviation 50 Thompson Ave *Web:* www.robinsonaviation.com	East Haven	CT	06512	203-467-9555	467-6346	63
Robinson Ballet 107 Union St *TF:* 800-838-3006 ■ *Web:* www.robinsonballet.org	Bangor	ME	04401	207-990-3140		573-1
Robinson Bradshaw & Hinson Pa 101 N Tryon St Ste 1900 *Web:* www.robinsonbradshaw.com	Charlotte	NC	28246	704-377-2536	378-4000	428
Robinson Correctional Ctr 13423 E 1150th Ave *Web:* www2.illinois.gov	Robinson	IL	62454	618-546-5659	544-2166	213
Robinson Ctr 101 S Spring St PO Box 3232 *TF:* 800-844-4781 ■ *Web:* www.littlerockmeetings.com	Little Rock	AR	72201	501-376-4781	376-7833	572
Robinson Fin Machines Inc 13670 US Hwy 68 *TF:* 800-362-2764 ■ *Web:* www.robfin.com	Kenton	OH	43326	419-674-4152		295
Robinson Helicopter Co 2901 Airport Dr *TF:* 800-905-0655 ■ *Web:* www.robinsonheli.com	Torrance	CA	90505	310-539-0508		20
Robinson Hughes & Christopher Psc 459 W Martin Luther King Blvd *Web:* rhccpas.com	Danville	KY	40422	859-236-6628		2
Robinson Industries Inc 3051 W Curtis Rd *TF:* 877-465-4055 ■ *Web:* www.robinsonind.com	Coleman	MI	48618	989-465-6111	465-1217	548
Robinson Industries Inc 400 Robinson Dr *Web:* www.robinsonfans.com	Zelienople	PA	16063	724-452-6121	452-0388	18
Robinson Jeffers Tor House Foundation 26304 Ocean View Ave *TF:* 844-285-0244 ■ *Web:* www.torhouse.org	Carmel	CA	93923	831-624-1813	624-3696	50-3
Robinson Metal Inc 1740 Eisenhower Dr *TF:* 800-346-2645 ■ *Web:* www.robinsonmetal.com	De Pere	WI	54115	920-494-7411		454
Robinson Mfg Company Inc 798 Market St PO Box 338 *TF:* 800-251-7286 ■ *Web:* www.robinsonmfg.com	Dayton	TN	37321	423-775-2212		155-18
Robinson Pharma Inc 3330 S Harbor Blvd *Web:* www.robinsonpharma.com	Santa Ana	CA	92704	714-241-0235	751-6066	799

Name / Address	City	State	ZIP	Phone	Fax	Class
Robinson Plumbing & Heating Supply Co 195 Broadway *Web:* www.robinsonsupply.com	Fall River	MA	02721	508-675-7433		612
Robinson State Park 428 N St PO Box 42 *Web:* www.mass.gov	Feeding Hills	MA	01030	413-786-2877		565
Robinson Terminal Warehouse Corp 1 Oronoco St *Web:* www.robinsonterminal.com	Alexandria	VA	22314	703-836-8300	836-8307	803-1
Robinson Terrace 28652 New York 23 *Web:* www.robinsonterrace.com	Stamford	NY	12167	607-652-7521	652-3362	450
Robishaw Engineering Inc 10106 Mathewson Ln *TF:* 800-877-1706 ■ *Web:* www.flexifloat.com	Houston	TX	77043	713-468-1706	468-5822	698
Robison Oil Corp 500 Executive Blvd *Web:* www.robisonoil.com	Elmsford	NY	10523	914-345-5700		316
Robocast Inc 89 Fifth Ave *Web:* robocast.com	New York	NY	10003	212-620-0007		177
Robotech C a d Solutions Inc 2 Marine View Plaza Ste 7 *Web:* www.robotechcad.com	Hoboken	NJ	07030	201-792-6300		396
Robotic Industries Assn (RIA) 900 Victors Way Ste 140 *Web:* www.robotics.org	Ann Arbor	MI	48108	734-994-6088	994-3338	49-19
Robotics Institute 5000 Forbes Ave 5000 Forbes Ave *TF:* 800-767-8483 ■ *Web:* www.ri.cmu.edu	Pittsburgh	PA	15213	412-268-3818	268-6436	668
RobotsApps.com Inc 50 California St 15th Fl Ste 1500 *Web:* www.robotappstore.com	San Francisco	CA	94111	415-439-5291		387
RobotWorx Inc 370 W Fairground St *Web:* www.robots.com	Marion	OH	43302	740-251-4312		23
RoboVent Products Group Inc 37900 Mound Rd *Web:* www.robovent.com	Sterling Heights	MI	48310	586-698-1800		610
Robson Communities 9532 E Riggs Rd *TF:* 800-732-9949 ■ *Web:* www.robson.com	Sun Lakes	AZ	85248	800-732-9949		653
Robson Forensic Inc 354 N Prince St *TF:* 800-813-6736 ■ *Web:* www.robsonforensic.com	Lancaster	PA	17603	717-293-9050		194
Robson Technologies Inc 135 E Main Ave *Web:* www.testfixtures.com	Morgan Hill	CA	95037	408-779-8008		261
Robstan Group Inc 400 Admiral Blvd *Web:* www.robstan.com	Kansas City	MO	64106	816-472-8870	472-7765	47
Robstown High School 609 W Hwy 44 *TF:* 800-446-3142 ■ *Web:* www.robstownisd.org	Robstown	TX	78380	361-387-5999		685
Robus Leather Corp 4010 W 86th St Ste C *Web:* www.robus.com	Indianapolis	IN	46268	317-704-7000	702-7001	432
Robustelli Corporate Services 1717 Newfield Ave *Web:* www.rcsltd.com	Stamford	CT	06903	203-322-2790	912-6487	184
Roby Martha (Rep R - AL) 442 Cannon HOB *Web:* roby.house.gov	Washington	DC	20515	202-225-2901	225-8913	342-2
Robyn Inc 7717 W Britton Rd *TF:* 877-211-9711 ■ *Web:* www.robynpromo.com	Oklahoma City	OK	73132	877-211-9711		627
ROC (Rutgers Organics Corp) 201 Struble Rd *TF:* 888-469-2188 ■ *Web:* federalregister.gov	State College	PA	16801	814-238-2424		143
Roc Management & Assoc Inc 1601 Keokuk Ave	Spirit Lake	IA	51360	712-336-3933		670
ROC USA LLC 6 Loudon Rd Suite 501 *Web:* www.rocusa.org	Concord	NH	03301	603-513-2791		138
Roca Mines Inc 490 - 1122 Mainland Ste 490 *Web:* www.rocamines.com	Vancouver	BC	V6B5L1	604-684-2900		502
Rocco Altobelli Inc 14301 Burnsville Pkwy W *Web:* roccoaltobellisalons.com	Burnsville	MN	55306	952-707-1900		77
Rocco's 537 N St Louis Blvd *Web:* roccosoriginalpizza.com	South Bend	IN	46617	574-233-2464		671
Rocco's Capriccio 846 Fawn St *Web:* roccosinlittleitaly.com	Baltimore	MD	21202	410-685-2710		671
Rocco's Grill 12432 Bee Cave Rd Ste A106 *Web:* www.roccosgrill.com	Austin	TX	78738	512-263-8204		671
Rochdale Village Inc 169-65 137th Ave *TF:* 800-275-8777 ■ *Web:* rochdalevillage.com	Jamaica	NY	11434	718-276-5700		655
Roche Bobios 200 Madison St *Web:* www.roche-bobois.com	New York	NY	10016	212-889-0700		321
Roche Bros Supermarkets Inc 70 Hastings St *Web:* rochebros.com	Wellesley Hills	MA	02481	781-235-9400	235-3153	345
Roche Carolina Inc 6173 E Old Marion Hwy	Florence	SC	29506	843-629-4300		582
Roche Constructors Inc 361 71st Ave *TF:* 800-727-5051 ■ *Web:* www.rocheconstructors.com	Greeley	CO	80634	970-356-3611	356-3619	186
Roche Diagnostics Corp (RDC) 9115 Hague Rd PO Box 50457 **Fax Area Code:* 317 ■ *TF Cust Svc:* 800-428-5076 ■ *Web:* usdiagnostics.roche.com	Indianapolis	IN	46250-0457	800-428-5076	521-6929*	231
Roche Molecular Systems Inc 4300 Hacienda Dr *Web:* molecular.roche.com	Pleasanton	CA	94588	925-730-8200		582
Roche Palo Alto LLC 4300 Hacienda Dr *TF:* 888-545-2443 ■ *Web:* www.roche.com	Pleasanton	CA	94588	925-730-8000	730-8388	85
Rocheleau Tool & Die Company Inc 117 Industrial Rd *TF:* 800-315-4379 ■ *Web:* www.rocheleautool.com	Fitchburg	MA	01420	978-345-1723	345-5972	757
Rochelle Foods Inc 1001 S Main St	Rochelle	IL	61068	815-562-4141	562-4149	473
Rochester Aluminum Smelting Canada Ltd 31-35 Freshway Dr *Web:* www.rochesteraluminum.com	Concord	ON	L4K1R9	905-669-1222		492
Rochester Area Chamber of Commerce 220 S Broadway Ste 100 *Web:* www.rochestermnchamber.com	Rochester	MN	55904	507-288-1122	282-8960	139

	Phone	Fax	Class
Rochester Armored Car Company Inc 3937 Leavenworth St .... Omaha NE 68105 *Web:* www.rochesterarmoredcar.com	402-558-9323		693
Rochester Art Ctr 40 Civic Ctr Dr SE .... Rochester MN 55904 *TF:* 800-222-7270 ■ *Web:* www.rochesterartcenter.org	507-282-8629		50-2
Rochester Big & Tall 700 Mission St .... San Francisco CA 94103 *Web:* rochester-big-and-tall.destinationxl.com	415-982-6455		157-3
Rochester Business Journal 45 E Ave Ste 500 .... Rochester NY 14604 *Web:* www.rbj.net	585-546-8303	546-3398	457-5
Rochester City Ballet 1326 University Ave .... Rochester NY 14607 *Web:* www.rochestercityballet.org	585-461-5850	473-8847	573-1
Rochester City School District 131 W Broad St .... Rochester NY 14614 *TF:* 800-743-2110 ■ *Web:* www.rcsdk12.org	585-262-8100		685
Rochester Civic Theatre 20 Civic Ctr Dr SE .... Rochester MN 55904 *TF:* 800-562-1758 ■ *Web:* www.rochestercivictheatre.org	507-282-8481		572
Rochester College 800 W Avon Rd .... Rochester Hills MI 48307 **Fax:* Admissions ■ *TF:* 800-521-6010 ■ *Web:* www.rc.edu	248-218-2011	218-2025*	166
Rochester Colonial Manufacturing Inc 1794 Lyell Ave .... Rochester NY 14606 *TF:* 800-321-8199 ■ *Web:* www.rochestercolonial.com	585-254-8191		234
Rochester Community & Technical College 851 30th Ave SE .... Rochester MN 55904 **Fax:* Admissions ■ *TF:* 800-247-1296 ■ *Web:* www.rctc.edu	507-285-7210	280-3529*	162
Rochester Contemporary Art Ctr 137 E Ave .... Rochester NY 14604 *TF:* 800-745-3000 ■ *Web:* www.rochestercontemporary.org	585-461-2222	461-2223	50-2
Rochester Convention & Visitors Bureau 30 Civic Ctr Dr SE Ste 200 .... Rochester MN 55904 *TF:* 800-634-8277 ■ *Web:* www.rochestercvb.org	507-288-4331	288-9144	206
Rochester Correctional Facility 470 Ford St .... Rochester NY 14608	585-454-2280		213
Rochester Electronics Inc 16 Malcolm Hoyt Dr .... Newburyport MA 01950 *Web:* www.rocelec.com	978-462-9332	462-9512	246
Rochester Gas & Electric Corp 89 E Ave .... Rochester NY 14649 *TF:* 800-743-2110 ■ *Web:* www.rge.com	800-743-2110		787
Rochester Gauges Inc of Texas 11616 Harry Hines Blvd .... Dallas TX 75229 *TF:* 800-821-1829 ■ *Web:* www.rochestergauges.com	972-241-2161	620-1403	201
Rochester Hills Public Library 500 Olde Towne Rd .... Rochester MI 48307 *Web:* www.rhpl.org	248-656-2900		434-3
Rochester Homes Inc 1345 N Lucas St .... Rochester IN 46975 *TF:* 800-860-4554 ■ *Web:* www.rochesterhomesinc.com	800-860-4554		106
Rochester Industrial Control Inc 6400 Furnace Rd .... Ontario NY 14519 *TF:* 800-821-3407 ■ *Web:* www.rochesterindustrial.com	315-524-4555		246
Rochester Institute of Technology 1 Lomb Memorial Dr .... Rochester NY 14623 **Fax:* Admissions ■ *Web:* www.rit.edu	585-475-2411	475-7424*	166
Rochester International Airport (RST) 7600 Helgerson Dr SW .... Rochester MN 55902 *TF:* 800-227-4672 ■ *Web:* flyrst.com	507-282-2328		27
Rochester International Film Festival PO Box 17746 .... Rochester NY 14617 *Web:* www.rochesterfilmfest.org	585-234-7411		282
Rochester Mayor's 201 Fourth St SE .... Rochester MN 55904 *TF:* 800-657-3858 ■ *Web:* rochestermn.gov	507-328-2700	287-7979	337
Rochester Metal Products Corp 616 Indiana Ave PO Box 488 .... Rochester IN 46975 *TF:* 800-422-3372 ■ *Web:* www.rochestermetals.com	574-223-3164		295
Rochester Methodist Hospital 201 W Ctr St .... Rochester MN 55902 *Web:* mayoclinic.org	507-284-2511		374-3
Rochester Midland Corp 333 Hollenbeck St .... Rochester NY 14621 *TF:* 800-836-1627 ■ *Web:* www.rochestermidland.com	585-336-2200	467-4406	145
Rochester Museum & Science Ctr 657 E Ave .... Rochester NY 14607 *Web:* www.rmsc.org	585-271-4320	271-0492	520
Rochester (NY) City Hall 30 Church St .... Rochester NY 14614 *Web:* cityofrochester.gov	585-428-7045	428-6059	337
Rochester Orchestra & Chorale 400 S Broadway .... Rochester MN 55904 *TF:* 800-634-8277 ■ *Web:* www.rochestersymphony.org	507-286-8742		573-3
Rochester Philharmonic Orchestra 108 E Ave .... Rochester NY 14604 *TF:* 800-745-3000 ■ *Web:* www.rpo.org	585-454-7311	325-4905	573-3
Rochester Psychiatric Ctr 1111 Elmwood Ave .... Rochester NY 14620 *TF:* 800-310-1160 ■ *Web:* rochesterhealth.com	585-241-1200		374-5
Rochester Public Library 101 Second St SE .... Rochester MN 55904 *Web:* www.rochesterpubliclibrary.org	507-285-8000		434-3
Rochester Public Library 65 S Main St .... Rochester NH 03867 *Web:* www.rpl.lib.nh.us	603-332-1428	335-7582	434-3
Rochester Regional Chamber of Commerce 71 Walnut Blvd .... Rochester MI 48307	248-651-6700		139
Rochester Regional Health (RGHS) 1425 Portland Ave .... Rochester NY 14621 *TF:* 877-922-5465 ■ *Web:* www.rochestergeneral.org	585-922-4000		374-3
Rochester Repertory Theatre Co 103 Seventh St NE .... Rochester MN 55906 *TF:* 800-456-7651 ■ *Web:* www.rochesterrep.org	507-289-1737		573-4
Rochester Riverside Convention Ctr 123 E Main St .... Rochester NY 14604 *Web:* www.rrcc.com	585-232-7200	232-1510	205
Rochester Shoe Tree Company Inc 1 Cedar Ln .... Ashland NH 03217 *Web:* www.shoekeeper.com	603-968-3301		200
Rochester Yacht Club 5555 Saint Paul Blvd .... Rochester NY 14617 *Web:* www.rochesteryc.com	585-342-5511		713
Rochester-Syracuse Auto Auction 1826 State Rt 414 PO Box 129 .... Waterloo NY 13165 *Web:* www.rsautoauction.com	315-539-5006	539-9508	516
Rochon Corp 3650 Annapolis Ln N Ste 101 .... Plymouth MN 55447 *Web:* www.rochoncorp.com	763-559-9393	559-8101	186
Rock & Gem Magazine 290 Maple Ct Ste 232 .... Ventura CA 93003 *TF:* 866-377-4666 ■ *Web:* www.rockngem.com	805-644-3824		457-14
Rock & Roll Hall of Fame & Museum 1100 Rock & Roll Blvd .... Cleveland OH 44114 *Web:* www.rockhall.com	216-781-7625	515-1283	520
Rock 'N Learn Inc 105 Commercial Cir .... Conroe TX 77304 *TF:* 800-348-8445 ■ *Web:* www.rocknlearn.com	936-539-2731	539-2659	243
Rock 100.5 780 Johnson Ferry Rd NE 5th Fl .... Atlanta GA 30342 *Web:* www.99x.com	404-741-7625		645-10
Rock 103 2650 Thousand Oaks Blvd Ste 4100 .... Memphis TN 38118 *Web:* rock103.iheart.com	901-259-1300		645-98
Rock 106.9 WCCC, The 1039 Asylum Ave .... Hartford CT 06105 *TF:* 800-520-1067 ■ *Web:* www.wccc.com	860-525-1069		645-72
Rock Bottom Brewery 800 LaSalle Plaza .... Minneapolis MN 55402 *Web:* rockbottom.com	612-332-2739		671
Rock Bottom Restaurant & Brewery 4508 University Ave .... West Des Moines IA 50266 *Web:* rockbottom.com	515-267-8900		671
Rock Bridge Memorial State Park 5901 S Hwy 163 .... Columbia MO 65203 *TF:* 800-334-6946 ■ *Web:* www.mostateparks.com	573-449-7402	442-2249	565
Rock Cave IGA Junction of Rt 4 and Rt 20 .... Rock Cave WV 26234 *Web:* www.rockcaveiga.com	304-924-5296		345
Rock City Gardens 1400 Patten Rd .... Lookout Mountain GA 30750 *TF:* 800-854-0675 ■ *Web:* www.seerockcity.com	706-820-2531		50-5
Rock City Mechanical Company LLC 2715 Grandview Ave .... Nashville TN 37211 *Web:* www.rcm-nashville.com	615-251-3045		610
Rock County PO Box 367 .... Bassett NE 68714 *Web:* www.rockcounty.ne.gov	402-684-3933		338
Rock County 51 S Main St .... Janesville WI 53545 *TF:* 800-924-3570 ■ *Web:* www.co.rock.wi.us	608-757-5660	757-5662	338
Rock County 204 E Brown St .... Luverne MN 56156 *TF:* 800-313-2666 ■ *Web:* www.co.rock.mn.us	507-283-5020		338
Rock Creek Lake State Recreation Area 73122 338 Ave .... Enders NE 69027 *Web:* outdoornebraska.gov/rockcreeklake	308-394-5118		565
Rock Creek Outfitters 1530 Riverside Dr .... Chattanooga TN 37406 *TF:* 888-707-6708 ■ *Web:* www.rockcreek.com	423-266-8200		711
Rock Creek Park 5200 Glover Rd NW .... Washington DC 20015 *Web:* www.nps.gov	202-895-6000	895-6015	564
Rock Creek Resort 6380 US Hwy 212 .... Red Lodge MT 59068 *TF:* 800-667-1119 ■ *Web:* www.rockcreekresort.com	406-446-1111		669
Rock Creek State Park 5627 Rock Creek E .... Kellogg IA 50135 *Web:* www.iowadnr.gov	641-236-3722	236-5599	565
Rock Creek Station State Historical Park 57426 710th Rd .... Fairbury NE 68352 *Web:* outdoornebraska.gov/rockcreekstation	402-729-5777		565
Rock Creek Station State Recreation Area 57426 710th Rd .... Fairbury NE 68352 *Web:* www.outdoornebraska.ne.gov/parks	402-729-5777		565
Rock Cut State Park 7318 Harlem Rd .... Loves Park IL 61111 *Web:* www.dnr.illinois.gov/parks/pages/rockcut.aspx	815-885-3311		565
Rock Family Worship Center, The 2300 Memorial Pkwy SW .... Huntsville AL 35801 *Web:* www.therockfwc.org	256-533-9292		48-20
Rock Garden 1951 Bond St .... Green Bay WI 54303 *Web:* comfortsuitesgb.com	920-497-4701	499-5242	671
Rock Hill Mechanical Corp 524 Clark Ave .... Saint Louis MO 63122 *TF:* 800-364-2059 ■ *Web:* www.rhmcorp.com	314-966-0600	966-3679	189-10
Rock Island Argus 1724 Fourth Ave .... Rock Island IL 61201 *TF:* 800-660-2472 ■ *Web:* qconline.com	309-786-6441	786-7639	532-2
Rock Island Capital LLC 1415 W 22nd St Ste 1250 .... Oak Brook IL 60523 *Web:* www.rockislandcapital.com	630-413-9136		360-3
Rock Island County 1504 Third Ave .... Rock Island IL 61201 *TF:* 800-642-5570 ■ *Web:* www.rockislandcounty.org	309-786-4451		338
Rock Island National Cemetery Bldg 118 .... Rock Island IL 61299 *Web:* www.cem.va.gov/cems/nchp/rockisland.asp	309-782-2094	782-2097	136
Rock Island Public Library 401 19th St .... Rock Island IL 61201 *Web:* www.rockislandlibrary.org	309-732-7323		434-3
Rock Island State Park 82 Beach Rd .... Rock Island TN 38581 *TF:* 800-713-6065 ■ *Web:* tnstateparks.com/parks/about/rock-island	931-686-2471		565
Rock Island State Park 1924 Indian Pt Rd .... Washington Island WI 54246 *Web:* dnr.wi.gov/newurl.html	920-847-2235		565
Rock Island Trail State Park 311 E Williams St PO Box 64 .... Wyoming IL 61491 *Web:* www.dnr.illinois.gov	309-695-2228		565
Rock of Ages Corp 560 Graniteville Rd .... Graniteville VT 05654 *TF:* 800-421-0166 ■ *Web:* www.rockofages.com	802-476-3119		724
Rock Point School 1 Rock Pt Rd .... Burlington VT 05408 *Web:* www.rockpointschool.org	802-863-1104	863-6628	622

	Phone	Fax	Class
Rock River Arms Inc 1042 Cleveland Rd .... Colona IL 61241 *TF:* 800-998-7928 ■ *Web:* www.rockriverarms.com	309-792-5780		807
Rock River Lumber & Grain Co 5502 Lyndon Rd PO Box 68 .... Prophetstown IL 61277 *TF:* 800-605-4333 ■ *Web:* www.rockriverag.com	815-537-5131		296-23
Rock River Valley Blood Ctr 3065 N Perryville Rd Ste 105 .... Rockford IL 61114 *TF General:* 877-778-2299 ■ *Web:* www.rrvbc.org	815-965-8751	965-8756	89
Rock Sports Complex LLC, The 7900 W Crystal Ridge Dr .... Franklin WI 53132 *Web:* www.rockcomplex.com	414-529-7676		354
Rock Springs Chamber of Commerce 1897 Dewar Dr .... Rock Springs WY 82901 *TF:* 800-463-8637 ■ *Web:* rockspringschamber.com	307-362-3771	362-3838	139
Rock Springs Guest Ranch 64201 Tyler Rd .... Bend OR 97701 *TF:* 800-225-3833 ■ *Web:* www.rocksprings.com	541-382-1957		239
Rock Springs National Bank 200 Second St PO Box 880 .... Rock Springs WY 82902 *TF:* 800-469-8801 ■ *Web:* www.rsnb.com	307-362-8801	362-9432	69
Rock Springs Run State Reserve 30601 CR 433 .... Sorrento FL 32776 *TF:* 800-326-3521 ■ *Web:* www.floridastateparks.org/rockspringsrun	407-884-2008	884-2039	565
Rock the Vote (RTV) 1001 Connecticut Ave NW Ste 640.......... Washington DC 20036 *Web:* www.rockthevote.com	202-719-9910		48-7
Rock Valley College 3301 N Mulford Rd......................... Rockford IL 61114 **Fax:* Admissions ■ *TF:* 800-973-7821 ■ *Web:* www.rockvalleycollege.edu	815-921-7821	921-4269*	162
Rock Valley Publishing LLC 11512 N Second St.................. Machesney Park IL 61115 *Web:* www.rvpublishing.com	815-877-4044		637-8
Rock Ventures LLC 1074 Woodward Ave .... Detroit MI 48226	313-373-3700		133
Rock View Resort 1049 Parkview Dr .... Hollister MO 65672 *TF:* 800-375-9530 ■ *Web:* www.rockviewresort.com	417-334-4678		379
Rock Wool Manufacturing Co 1400 Seventh Ct PO Box 506 .... Leeds AL 35094 *TF Sales:* 800-874-7625 ■ *Web:* www.deltainsulation.com	205-699-6121	699-3132	389
Rockaway Townsquare Mall 301 Mt Hope Ave .... Rockaway NJ 07866 *Web:* www.simon.com	973-361-4070	361-1561	460
Rockbestos-Surprenant Cable Corp 20 Bradley Pk Rd .... East Granby CT 06026 *TF:* 800-327-7625 ■ *Web:* www.r-scc.com	860-653-8300		814
Rockbridge County 150 S Main St............ Lexington VA 24450 *TF:* 800-420-1663 ■ *Web:* www.co.rockbridge.va.us	540-463-4361	463-5981	338
Rockcastle County 1050 W Main St .... Mount Vernon KY 40456 *Web:* www.rockcastlecountyky.com	606-256-2831	256-8643	338
Rockdale Citizen 969 S Main St NE............ Conyers GA 30012 *Web:* www.rockdalenewtoncitizen.com	770-483-7108	483-5797	532-2
Rockdale County 922 Ct St.................... Conyers GA 30012 *Web:* rockdaleclerk.com	770-278-7900	278-7921	338
Rockdale Grocery Inc 994 Institute St NW....................... Conyers GA 30012 *Web:* www.piggylwiggly-atl.com	770-922-9209		345
Rockdale Medical Ctr (RMC) 1412 Milstead Ave NE...................... Conyers GA 30012 *Web:* www.rockdalemedicalcenter.org	770-918-3000	918-3104	374-3
Rockdale Pipeline Inc PO Box 1157........... Conyers GA 30012 *Web:* www.rockdalepipeline.com	770-922-4123		186
Rockefeller Bros Fund 475 Riverside Dr Ste 900 .... New York NY 10115 *TF:* 800-388-4300 ■ *Web:* www.rbf.org	212-812-4200	812-4299	305
Rockefeller Foundation 420 Fifth Ave .... New York NY 10018 **Fax:* Mail Rm ■ *TF:* 800-233-1138 ■ *Web:* www.rockefellerfoundation.org	212-869-8500	764-3468*	305
Rockefeller Group Technology Solutions Inc 1221 Ave of the Americas................... New York NY 10020 *TF:* 800-699-9199 ■ *Web:* www.rgts.com	212-282-2200		387
Rockefeller State Park Preserve 125 Phelps Way .... Pleasantville NY 10570 *Web:* parks.ny.gov/parks/59/details.aspx	914-631-1470		565
Rockefeller University *Library* 1230 York Ave...................... New York NY 10065 *Web:* rockefeller.edu	212-327-8904		434-6
Rockenwagner *3 Square Cafe + Bakery* 12835 W Washington Blvd .... Los Angeles CA 90066 *Web:* www.rockenwagner.com	310-577-0747		671
Rocker Solenoid Co 1500 W 240th St........................ Harbor City CA 90710 *TF:* 800-352-0050 ■ *Web:* www.rockerindustries.com	310 534 5660		789
Rocket Communications Inc 81 Langton St Unit 12.................. San Francisco CA 94103 *Web:* rocketcom.com	415-863-0101		344
Rocket Direct Communications Inc 532 Central Dr .... Virginia Beach VA 23454 *Web:* www.rocketmediamail.com	757-463-9161		5
Rocket Imaging Inc 12365 Rhea Dr........... Plainfield IL 60585	815-577-6315		627
Rocket Jewelry Packaging & Displays 375 Executive Blvd Ste W-4 .... Elmsford NY 10523 *TF:* 800-762-5521 ■ *Web:* www.rocketbox.com	718-292-5370		199
Rocket Media Inc 3335 E Baseline Rd.......... Gilbert AZ 85234 *TF:* 800-339-7305 ■ *Web:* www.rocketmedia.com	480-699-2579		195
Rocket Supply 404 N Rt 115................... Roberts IL 60962 *TF:* 800-252-6871 ■ *Web:* www.rocketsupply.com	800-252-6871		516
Rocket Whale Inc 3149 Mccully Dr NE .... Atlanta GA 30345 *Web:* rocketwhale.com	404-219-1537		631
RocketCityNow 1309 N Memorial Pkwy .... Huntsville AL 35801 *Web:* www.rocketcitynow.com	256-533-5454	203-8320	741-61
Rocket-Hire LLC 4537 N Robertson St .... New Orleans LA 70117 *Web:* www.rocket-hire.com	504-236-7259		463
Rocketship Inc 110 S 300 W .... Provo UT 84601 *TF:* 800-334-3348 ■ *Web:* www.rocketshipdesign.com	801-373-1922		393
Rockfish Seafood Grill 4701 W Pk Blvd Ste 105....................... Plano TX 75093	972-599-2190		671
Rockfish Seafood Grill 801 E Campbell Rd Ste 300 .... Richardson TX 75081	214-887-9400	821-0138	670

	Phone	Fax	Class
Rockfish Seafood Grill 7400 N MacArthur Blvd .... Irving TX 75063 *Web:* www.rockfish.com	214-574-4111		671
Rockford Acromatic Products Co 611 Beacon St .... Loves Park IL 61111 *Web:* www.rockfordacromatic.com	815-877-7473		454
Rockford Area Chamber of Commerce 598 Byrne Industrial Dr..................... Rockford MI 49341 *TF:* 800-274-2812 ■ *Web:* www.rockfordmichamber.com	616-866-2000	866-2141	139
Rockford Area Convention & Visitors Bureau 102 N Main St .... Rockford IL 61101 *TF:* 800-521-0849 ■ *Web:* www.gorockford.com	815-963-8111	963-4298	206
Rockford Art Museum 711 N Main St........... Rockford IL 61103 *TF:* 800-521-0849 ■ *Web:* www.rockfordartmuseum.org	815-968-2787	316-2179	520
Rockford Career College 1130 s alpine rd .... Rockford IL 61108	815-965-8616		764
Rockford Chamber of Commerce 308 W State St Ste 190...................... Rockford IL 61101 *Web:* www.rockfordchamber.com	815-987-8100	987-8122	139
Rockford City Hall 425 E State St............. Rockford IL 61104 *Web:* www.ci.rockford.il.us	815-987-5590	967-6952	337
Rockford College 5050 E State St............. Rockford IL 61108 **Fax:* Admissions ■ *TF:* 800-892-2984 ■ *Web:* www.rockford.edu	815-226-4000	226-2822*	166
Rockford Corp 600 S Rockford Dr................ Tempe AZ 85281 *OTC:* ROFO ■ *TF:* 800-903-2897 ■ *Web:* www.rockfordcorp.com	480-967-3565	966-3983	52
Rockford Homes Inc 999 Polaris Pkwy Ste 200................... Columbus OH 43240 *Web:* www.rockfordhomes.net	614-785-0015		187
Rockford Institute 928 N Main St .... Rockford IL 61103 *TF:* 800-383-0680 ■ *Web:* chroniclesmagazine.org	815-964-5053		634
Rockford It 6090 Strathmoor Dr................ Rockford IL 61107 *Web:* rockfordit.com	815-316-7575		175
Rockford Manufacturing Co 3901 Little River Rd .... Rockford TN 37853	865-970-3131		208
Rockford Medical & Safety Co 2420 Harrison Ave .... Rockford IL 61108 *TF:* 800-541-2528 ■ *Web:* www.firensafety.com	815-394-0100		477
Rockford Memorial Hospital 2400 N Rockton Ave......................... Rockford IL 61103 *TF:* 800-756-4147 ■ *Web:* www.rockfordhealthsystem.org	815-971-5000		374-3
Rockford Mercantile Agency Inc 2502 S Alpine Rd .... Rockford IL 61108 *TF:* 800-369-6116 ■ *Web:* www.rmacollections.com	815-229-3328		393
Rockford MetroCentre 300 Elm St .... Rockford IL 61101 *TF:* 800-745-3000 ■ *Web:* thebmoharrisbankcenter.com	815-968-5600	968-5451	720
Rockford Process Control Inc 2020 Seventh St .... Rockford IL 61104 *TF:* 800-228-3779 ■ *Web:* rockfordprocess.com	815-966-2000	966-2026	350
Rockford Public Library 215 N Wyman St............................ Rockford IL 61101 *TF:* 800-272-3900 ■ *Web:* www.rockfordpubliclibrary.org	815-965-6731		434-3
Rockford Register Star 99 E State St .... Rockford IL 61104 **Fax:* News Rm ■ *Web:* www.rrstar.com	815-987-1200	987-1365*	532-2
Rockford Spring Co 3801 S Central Ave......................... Rockford IL 61102 *Web:* www.rockfordspring.com	815-968-3000	968-3100	718
Rockford Symphony Orchestra 711 N Main St .... Rockford IL 61103 *TF:* 800-868-7625 ■ *Web:* www.rockfordsymphony.com	815-965-0049	965-0642	573-3
Rockford Systems Inc 4620 Hydraulic Rd .... Rockford IL 61109 **Fax:* Sales ■ *TF Cust Svc:* 800-922-7533 ■ *Web:* www.rockfordsystems.com	815-874-7891	874-6144*	203
Rockford Toolcraft Inc 766 Research Pkwy.......................... Rockford IL 61109 *Web:* www.rockfordtoolcraft.com	815-398-5507		488
Rockhill-York County Convention & Visitors Bureau 452 S Anderson Rd......................... Rock Hill SC 29730 *TF:* 888-702-1320 ■ *Web:* www.visityorkcounty.com	803-329-5200	329-0145	206
Rockhurst University 1100 Rockhurst Rd....................... Kansas City MO 64110 **Fax:* Admissions ■ *TF:* 800-842-6776 ■ *Web:* www.rockhurst.edu	816-501-4000	501-4241*	166
Rockhurst University Continuing Education Ctr Inc PO Box 419107 .... Kansas City MO 64141 *TF:* 800-258-7246 ■ *Web:* www.nationalseminarstraining.com	913-432-7755	432-0824	765
Rocking Horse Ranch Resort 600 Rt 44-55 .... Highland NY 12528 *TF:* 800-647-2624 ■ *Web:* www.rockinghorseranch.com	845-691-2927		669
Rockingham Community College 215 Wrenn Memorial Rd.................... Wentworth NC 27375 *Web:* www.rockinghamcc.edu	336-342-4261	342-1809	162
Rockingham Co-op 1040 S High St .... Harrisonburg VA 22801 *Web:* www.rockinghamcoop.com	540-434-3856	434-6890	275
Rockingham County 10 Rt 125............... Brentwood NH 03833 *Web:* www.nhdeeds.com	603-642-5526	642-5930	338
Rockingham County 20 E Gay St.......... Harrisonburg VA 22802 *TF:* 800-552-7096 ■ *Web:* www.rockinghamcountyva.gov	540-564-3000		338
Rockingham County 371 US Hwy 65 PO Box 101................. Wentworth NC 27375 *Web:* www.co.rockingham.nc.us	336-342-8101	342-8105	338
Rockingham County Public Library 527 Boone Rd................................. Eden NC 27288 *Web:* www.rcpl.org	336-627-1106	623-1258	434-3
Rockingham Dragway 2153 Hwy US 1 N PO Box 70............ Rockingham NC 28379 *Web:* www.rockinghamdragway.com	910-582-3400	582-8667	515
Rockingham New Holland Inc 600 W Market St....................... Harrisonburg VA 22802 *TF:* 800-626-6409 ■ *Web:* rockinghamnh.com	540-434-6791	434-6780	274
Rockingham Park Rockingham Pk Blvd........... Salem NH 03079 *Web:* www.rockinghampark.com	603-898-2311	898-7163	642
Rockingham State Historic Site 84 Laurel Ave .... Kingston NJ 08528 *Web:* www.rockingham.net	609-683-7132		565
Rockingham Steel Inc 2565 John Wayland Hwy .... Harrisonburg VA 22803 *TF:* 800-738-1742 ■ *Web:* www.rockinghamsteel.com	540-433-3000		492
Rock-It Cargo USA Inc 5343 W Imperial Hwy Ste 900 .... Los Angeles CA 90045 *TF:* 800-973-1727 ■ *Web:* www.rockitcargo.com	310-410-0935	410-0628	311

	Phone	Fax	Class
Rockland Aerospace Inc 2111 Baldwin Ave Ste 8 .... Crofton MD 21114 *Web:* www.mhdrockland.com	410-451-0969		20
Rockland Bakery Inc 94 Demarest Mill Rd W........................ Nanuet NY 10954 *Web:* www.rocklandbakery.com	845-623-5800	623-6921	296-1
Rockland Coaches Inc 180 Old Hook Rd ...... Westwood NJ 07675 *Web:* web.coachusa.com/rockland/index.asp	201-263-1254		107
Rockland Community College 145 College Rd.............................. Suffern NY 10901 *TF:* 800-722-7666 ■ *Web:* www.sunyrockland.edu	845-574-4000	574-4433	162
Rockland County 11 New Hempstead Rd .... New City NY 10956 *TF:* 800-662-1220 ■ *Web:* rocklandgov.com	845-638-5100	638-5675	338
Rockland Federal Credit Union 241 Union St .... Rockland MA 02370 *TF:* 800-562-7328 ■ *Web:* www.rfcu.com	781-878-0232	792-3866	219
Rockland Immunochemicals Inc PO Box 326 .... Gilbertsville PA 19525 *TF:* 800-656-7625 ■ *Web:* www.rockland-inc.com	610-369-1008	367-7825	231
Rockland Industries Inc 1601 Edison Hwy .... Baltimore MD 21213 *Web:* www.rocklandflooring.com	410-522-2505		819
Rockland Lake State Park PO Box 217 .... Congers NY 10920 *Web:* parks.ny.gov/parks/81/details.aspx	845-268-3020		565
Rockland Psychiatric Ctr 140 Old Orangeburg Rd .... Orangeburg NY 10962 **Fax:* Admitting ■ *Web:* omh.ny.gov	845-359-1000	680-5580*	374-5
Rockland Trust 435 Market St................ Boston MA 02135 *NASDAQ: PEOP* ■ *Web:* www.rocklandtrust.com	617-254-0813		70
Rocklands 25 S Quaker Ln................... Alexandria VA 22314 *Web:* www.rocklands.com	703-778-8000		671
Rockledge Hook & Ladder Social Hall Rentals 505 Huntingdon Pk....................... Rockledge PA 19046 *Web:* www.rockledgefireco.org	215-379-8373		181
Rocklin Academy, The 6532 Turnstone Way......................... Rocklin CA 95765 *Web:* www.rocklinacademy.com	916-632-6580		685
Rocklin Area Chamber of Commerce 3700 Rocklin Rd............................ Rocklin CA 95677 *TF:* 800-228-3380 ■ *Web:* www.rocklinchamber.com	916-624-2548	624-5743	139
Rocklin Park Hotel 5450 China Garden Rd...................... Rocklin CA 95677 *TF:* 888-630-9400 ■ *Web:* www.rocklinpark.com	916-630-9400	630-9448	379
Rockmount Ranch Wear Manufacturing Co 1626 Wazee St .... Denver CO 80202 *TF:* 800-776-2566 ■ *Web:* www.rockmount.com	303-629-7777	629-5836	155-20
Rockoff Harlan & Rasof Ltd 3818 Oakton St.............................. Skokie Il 60076 *Web:* www.rhrcpa.com	847-675 7777		734
Rockpoint Logistics LLC 901 Bilter Rd .... Aurora IL 60502 *TF:* 800-621 9621 ■ *Web:* www.rockpointlogistics.com	630-801-2900		314
Rockport Capital Partners 160 Federal St 18th Fl .... Boston MA 02110 *Web:* www.rockportcap.com	617-912-1420	912-1449	792
Rockport Company Inc 1895 JW Foster Blvd .... Canton MA 02021 *TF:* 800-828-0545 ■ *Web:* www.rockport.com	781-401-5000		301
Rockport Ctr for the Arts 902 Navigation Cir .... Rockport TX 78382 *Web:* www.rockportartcenter.com	361-729-5519	729-3551	572
Rockport National Bank 16 Main St........... Rockport MA 01966 *Web:* www.institutionforsavings.com	978-546-3411		70
Rockport State Park 51905 WA-20........... Rockport WA 98283 *Web:* www.parks.wa.gov	360-853-8461		565
Rockport Technology Group Inc 5 Industrial Way Ste 2C .... Salem NH 03079 *TF:* 800-399-7053 ■ *Web:* www.rockporttech.com	603-681-0333		180
Rocks State Park 3318 Rocks Chrome Hill Rd .... Jarrettsville MD 21084 *Web:* dnr2.maryland.gov	410-557-7994		565
Rockstar Industries LLP 6012 12th Ave S.............................. Seattle WA 98108	206-297-8330		327
Rock-Tred Corp 405 Oakwood Ave .... Waukegan IL 60085 **Fax:* Cust Svc ■ *Web:* www.rocktred.com	847-673-8200	679-6665*	189-2
Rockview Dairies Inc 7011 Stewart & Gray Rd..................... Downey CA 90241 *TF:* 800-423-2479 ■ *Web:* www.rockviewfarms.com	562-927-5511	928-9866	297-4
Rockville Chamber of Commerce 1 Research Ct # 450........................ Rockville MD 20850 *Web:* www.rockvillechamber.org	301-424-9300	762-7599	139
Rockville Correctional Facility 811 W 50 N .... Rockville IN 47872 *TF:* 800-451-6028 ■ *Web:* in.gov	765-569-3178	569-3178	213
Rockville Fabrics Corp 99 W Hawthorne Ave.................... Valley Stream NY 11580	516-561-9810		594
Rockville Fuel & Feed Company Inc 14901 S Lawn Ln PO Box 1707 .... Rockville MD 20849 *TF:* 800-888-8852 ■ *Web:* rockvilleconcrete.com	301-762-3988	309-3894	182
Rockville General Hospital 31 Union St.......... Vernon CT 06066 *Web:* www.echn.org	860-872-0501		374-3
Rockville School 506 N Beadle St .... Rockville IN 47872 *Web:* www.rockville.k12.in.us	765-569-5686		645-10
Rockwall County Chamber of Commerce 697 E IH- 30.................................. Rockwall TX 75087 *Web:* www.rockwallchamber.org	972-771-5733	772-3642	139
Rockwall County Library 1215 E Yellowjacket Ln..................... Rockwall TX 75087 *Web:* www.rockwallcountytexas.com	972-204-7700		435
Rockwell 1714 N Vermont Ave.............. Los Angeles CA 90027 *Web:* rockwell-la.com	323-661-6163		671
Rockwell Automation Canada Inc 135 Dundas St .... Cambridge ON N1R5N9 *Web:* www.rockwellautomation.com/en_na/overview.page	519-623-1810		690
Rockwell Collins Inc 400 Collins Rd NE .... Cedar Rapids IA 52498 *NYSE: COL* ■ **Fax:* PR ■ *TF:* 888-721-3094 ■ *Web:* www.rockwellcollins.com	319-295-1000	295-1542*	529
Rockwell Farms Inc 332 Rockwell Farms Rd .... Rockwell NC 28138 *TF:* 800-635-6576 ■ *Web:* www.rockwellfarms.com	800-635-6576		369

	Phone	Fax	Class
Rockwell Laser Industries Inc 7754 Camargo Rd Ste 3 .... Cincinnati OH 45243 *TF:* 800-945-2737 ■ *Web:* www.rli.com	513-271-1568		543
Rockwell Medical Inc 30142 Wixom Rd.......... Wixom MI 48393 *NASDAQ: RMTI* ■ *TF:* 800-449-3353 ■ *Web:* www.rockwellmed.com	248-960-9009	960-9119	250
Rockwell's 27 Broadway .... Toledo OH 43604 *Web:* www.mbaybrew.com/rockwells-steakhouse-lounge	419-243-1302		671
Rockwell's Neighborhood Grill 4632 N Rockwell St .... Chicago IL 60625 *Web:* www.rockwellsgrill.com	773-509-1871		671
Rockwood Dry Cleaners 171 Granville St .... Gahanna OH 43230 *Web:* rockwoodcleaners.com	614-471-3700		426
Rockwood Manufacturing Co 300 Main St .... Rockwood PA 15557 *Web:* www.rockwoodmfg.com	814-926-2026		350
Rockwood Retaining Walls Inc 7200 Hwy 63 N.............................. Rochester MN 55906 **Fax Area Code:* 507 ■ *TF:* 800-535-2375 ■ *Web:* www.rockwoodwalls.com	888-288-4045	529-2879*	183
Rockwood Retirement Community 2903 E 25th Ave .... Spokane WA 99223 *TF:* 800-727-6650 ■ *Web:* www.rockwoodretirement.org	509-536-6650	536-6662	672
Rockwood Service Corp 43 Arch St .... Greenwich CT 06830 *Web:* www.rockwoodservice.com	203-869-6734		466
Rocky Fork State Park 9800 N Shore Dr........................... Hillsboro OH 45133 *Web:* www.ohiodnr.com	937-393-4284		565
Rocky Gap State Park 12500 Pleasant Valley Rd.................... Flintstone MD 21530 *Web:* dnr.maryland.gov/publiclands/Pages/western/rockygap.aspx	301-722-1480		565
Rocky Hill Veterans Home & Healthcare Ctr 287 W St................................. Rocky Hill CT 06067 *Web:* www.ct.gov/ctva/cwp/view.asp?a=2005&q=482380	860-721-5891	721-5904	793
Rocky Mount Area Chamber of Commerce 100 Coastline St Ste 200 .... Rocky Mount NC 27804 *Web:* www.rockymountchamber.org	252-446-0323	446-5103	139
Rocky Mount Children's Museum 270 Gay St .... Rocky Mount NC 27804 *Web:* imperialcentre.org	252-972-1167		521
Rocky Mount Cord Co 381 N Grace St........................... Rocky Mount NC 27804 *TF Orders:* 800-342-9130 ■ *Web:* www.rmcord.com	252-977-9130	977-9123	208
Rocky Mount Museum 200 Hyder Hill Rd PO Box 160............... Piney Flats TN 37686 *TF:* 888-538-1791 ■ *Web:* www.rockymountmuseum.com	423-538-7396	538-1086	520
Rocky Mountain Chocolate Factory Inc (RMCF) 265 Turner Dr.............................. Durango CO 81303 *NASDAQ: RMCF* ■ *TF Cust Svc:* 888-525-2462 ■ *Web:* www.rmcf.com	970-259-0554		123
Rocky Mountain College 1511 Poly Dr.......... Billings MT 59102 **Fax:* Admissions ■ *TF:* 800-877-6259 ■ *Web:* www.rocky.edu	406-657-1000	657-1189*	166
Rocky Mountain Escape PO Box 5029........... Hinton AB T7V1X3 *Web:* www.ecolodge.com	780-865-0124		771
Rocky Mountain Fabrication Inc PO Box 16409 .... Salt Lake City UT 84116 *TF:* 800-763-5307 ■ *Web:* www.rmf-slc.com	801-596-2400	322-2702	91
Rocky Mountain Hardware Inc 1020 Airport Way .... Hailey ID 83333 *TF:* 888-788-2013 ■ *Web:* www.rockymountainhardware.com	208-788-2013	788-2577	350
Rocky Mountain Health Plans 2775 Crossroads Blvd PO Box 10600 ..... Grand Junction CO 81502 *TF:* 800-843 0719 ■ *Web:* www.rmhp.org	970-244-7760	244-7880	391-3
Rocky Mountain Lions Eye Bank (RMLEB) 1675 Aurora Crt Ste El2049 PO Box 6026 .... Aurora CO 80045 *TF:* 800-444-7479 ■ *Web:* www.corneas.org	720 848-3937	848-3938	269
Rocky Mountain Log Homes 1883 Hwy 93 S.............................. Hamilton MT 59840 *Web:* www.rockymountainloghomes.com	406-363-5680	363-2109	106
Rocky Mountain Motorcycle Museum & Hall of Fame 5867 N Nevada Ave............. Colorado Springs CO 80918 *Web:* www.themotorcyclemuseum.com	719-487-8005	487-8005	520
Rocky Mountain National Park 1000 Hwy 36 .... Estes Park CO 80517 *Web:* www.nps.gov	970-586-1206	586-1256	564
Rocky Mountain Natural Meats Inc 9757 Alton Way .... Henderson CO 80640 *Web:* www.greatrangebison.com	303-287-7100		473
Rocky Mountain Orthodontics Inc (RMO Inc) 650 W Colfax Ave............................ Denver CO 80204 **Fax:* Hum Res ■ *TF:* 800-525-6375 ■ *Web:* www.rmortho.com	303-592-8200	592-8200*	228
Rocky Mountain Prestress 5801 Pecos St........ Denver CO 80221 *TF:* 800-332-1440 ■ *Web:* www.rmpprestress.com	303-480-1111		364
Rocky Mountain Public Broadcasting Network (RMPB) 1089 Bannock St .... Denver CO 80204 *TF:* 000-274-6666 ■ *Web:* www.rmpbs.org	303-892 6666	620-5600	632
Rocky Mountain Quilt Museum 1213 Washington Ave......................... Golden CO 80401 *Web:* www.rmqm.org	303-277-0377		520
Rocky Mountain Recycling (RMR) 6510 Brighton Blvd......................... Commerce CO 80022 *Web:* www.rmrscrap.com	303-288-6868	288-0250	686
Rocky Mountain Research Station *US Forest Service* 240 W Prospec........... Fort Collins CO 80526 *Web:* www.fs.fed.us/rm	970-498-1100	498-1010	668
Rocky Mountain Tissue Bank 2993 S Peoria St Ste 390 .... Aurora CO 80014 *TF:* 800-424-5169 ■ *Web:* www.rmtb.org	303-337-3330	337-9383	545
Rocky Mountain Transportation Inc 1410 E Edgewood.......................... Whitefish MT 59937 *TF:* 800-543-3105 ■ *Web:* www.rockymountaintrans.com	406-863-1200	863-1213	109
Rocky Mountain Wine Co 133 Big Horn Dr........................... Kalispell MT 59901 *Web:* www.rockymountainwine.com	406-752-9463		443
Rocky Neck State Park PO Box 676............. Niantic CT 06357 *Web:* www.ct.gov	860-739-5471		565
Rocky River Public Library 1600 Hampton Rd.......................... Rocky River OH 44116 *TF:* 800-829-6801 ■ *Web:* www.rrpl.org	440-333-7610		435
Rocky Rococo 105 E Wisconsin Ave......... Oconomowoc WI 53066 *TF:* 800-888-7625 ■ *Web:* www.rockyrococo.com	262-569-5580		670

	Phone	Fax	Class
Rocky Shoes & Boots Inc 39 E Canal St. .... Nelsonville OH 45764 *NASDAQ: RCKY* ■ *TF:* 877-795-2410 ■ *Web:* www.rockyboots.com	740-753-3130		301
Rocky Top Furniture Inc 8957 Lexington Rd .... Lancaster KY 40444 *TF:* 800-332-1143 ■ *Web:* rockytopfurniture.com	859-548-2828		321
Rocky Top Markets LLC 1324 Lawnville Rd .... Kingston TN 37763	865-717-0700		204
Rocky's Italian Restaurant 120 N Sycamore St. .... Branson MO 65616	417-335-4765		671
Rockynet.com Inc 1919 Fourteenth St Ste 617 .... Boulder CO 80302 *Web:* www.rockynet.com	303-444-7052		224
Roco Rescue 7077 Exchequer Dr. .... Baton Rouge LA 70809 *TF:* 800-647-7626 ■ *Web:* www.rocorescue.com	225-755-7626		463
Rocscience 31 Balsam Ave .... Toronto ON M4E3B5 *Web:* www.rocscience.com	416-698-8217		261
Roda Group, The 918 Parker St. .... Berkeley CA 94710 *TF:* 800-462-3277 ■ *Web:* www.rodagroup.com	510-649-1900		41
Rodale Electronics Inc 20 Oser Ave .... Hauppauge NY 11788 *TF:* 800-349-5075 ■ *Web:* www.rodaleelectronics.com	631-231-0044	231-1345	248
Rodale Institute 611 Siegfriedale Rd .... Kutztown PA 19530 *TF:* 800-432-1565 ■ *Web:* www.rodaleinstitute.org	610-683-1400	683-8548	668
Rodbat Security Services 8125 Somerset Blvd .... Paramount CA 90723 *TF:* 877-676-3228 ■ *Web:* www.rmiintl.com	562-806-9098		693
Rodd Hotels & Resorts PO Box 432 .... Charlottetown PE C1A7K7 *Web:* www.roddvacations.com	902-892-7448		377
Rodda Paint Co 6107 N Marine Dr .... Portland OR 97203 *TF:* 800-452-2315 ■ *Web:* www.roddapaint.com	503-521-4300		550
Roddey Engineering Services Inc 10100 Woolworth Rd .... Keithville LA 71047 *Web:* www.themartincompanies.com	318-221-1996		261
Rodeberg & Berryman Inc 119 S First St .... Montevideo MN 56265	320-269-7695		261
Rodefer Moss & Company PLLC 608 Mabry Hood Rd .... Knoxville TN 37932 *Web:* www.rodefermoss.com	865-583-0091		2
Rodeo Plastic Bag & Film Inc 3328 Executive Blvd .... Mesquite TX 75149 *Web:* www.rodeoplasticbag.com	972-216-3331		596
Rodeway Inn 1315 N 27th St. .... Billings MT 59101	406-245-4128		379
Rodey Dickason Sloan Akin & Robb PA 201 Third St NW Ste 2200 .... Albuquerque NM 87102 *TF:* 800-226-2935 ■ *Web:* www.rodey.com	505-765-5900	768-7395	428
Rodgard 92 Msgr Valente Dr. .... Buffalo NY 14206 *Web:* www.rodgard.com	716-823-1411	852-7690	604
Rodgers & Hammerstein Organization, The 229 W 28th St 11th Fl. .... New York NY 10001 *TF:* 800-400-8160 ■ *Web:* www.rnh.com	212-541-6600		514
Rodgers Group Ltd, The 3738 N Tripp Ave .... Chicago IL 60641 *Web:* therodgersgroup.com	773-282-0571		463
Rodgers Instruments LLC 1300 NE 25th Ave. .... Hillsboro OR 97124 *Web:* www.rodgersinstruments.com	503-648-4181	681-0444	527
Rodgers Townsend LLC 1000 Clark Ave. .... Saint Louis MO 63102 *Web:* www.rodgerstownsend.com	314-259-8319		7
Rodheim Mktg Group 125 E Baker St Ste 143 .... Costa Mesa CA 92626	714-557-5100		194
Rodine Communications Inc 214 S Third St .... Sterling CO 80751 *Web:* rodine.com	970-522-5097		396
Rodizio Grill 600 South 700 East .... Salt Lake City UT 84102 *Web:* www.rodiziogrill.com	801-220-0500		671
Rodman Public Library 215 E Broadway St. .... Alliance OH 44601 *Web:* www.rodmanlibrary.com	330-821-2665		434-3
Rodman's Discount Food & Drugs 4301 Randolph Rd .... Silver Spring MD 20906 *Web:* www.rodmans.com	301-946-3100		237
Rodney Babar Inc 4222 Pilot Dr. .... Memphis TN 38118 *Web:* www.baberweb.com	901-794-4445		113
Rodney Hunt Co 46 Mill St .... Orange MA 01364 *TF:* 800-448-8860 ■ *Web:* www.rodneyhunt.com	978-544-2511	544-7204	480
Rodney Strong Vineyards 11455 Old Redwood Hwy .... Healdsburg CA 95448 *TF:* 800-678-4763 ■ *Web:* www.rodneystrong.com	707-431-1533		80-3
Rodney's Oyster House 469 King St W .... Toronto ON M5V1K4 *Web:* www.rodneysoysterhouse.com	416-363-8105	363-6638	671
Rodrigo's Online Store 1320 N Manzanita. .... Orange CA 92867 *Web:* www.rodrigos-shop.com	714-633-7844		299
Rodriguez Chavez Corp 10543 Fisher Rd .... Houston TX 77041 *Web:* www.rchind.com	713-457-0570		393
Roe Dental Laboratory Inc 9565 Midwest Ave .... Garfield Heights OH 44125 *TF:* 800-228-6663 ■ *Web:* www.roedentallab.com	216-663-2233	663-2237	415
Roe Phil (Rep R - TN) 336 Cannon HOB .... Washington DC 20515 *Web:* roe.house.gov	202-225-6356	225-5714	342-2
Roebbelen Construction Inc 1241 Hawks Flight Ct .... El Dorado Hills CA 95762 *TF:* 800-200-9696 ■ *Web:* www.roebbelen.com	916-939-4000	939-4028	186
Roebic Laboratories Inc 25 Connair Rd PO Box 927 .... Orange CT 06477 *TF:* 800-424-9300 ■ *Web:* www.roebic.com	203-795-1283	795-5227	145
Roedel Companies LLC 1134 Gibbons Hwy. .... Wilton NH 03086 *TF:* 800-546-7866 ■ *Web:* www.roedelcompanies.com	603-654-2040		378
Roeder Implement Inc 2550 Rockdale Rd .... Dubuque IA 52003 *TF:* 800-557-1184 ■ *Web:* www.roederimplement.com	563-557-1184	583-1821	274
Roeder Travel Ltd 9805 York Rd. .... Cockeysville MD 21030 *TF:* 800-379-9887 ■ *Web:* www.roedertravel.com	410-667-6090		771
Roehl & Yi Investment Advisors LLC 450 Country Club Rd Ste 160. .... Eugene OR 97401 *TF:* 888-683-4343 ■ *Web:* roehl-yi.com	541-683-2085		690

	Phone	Fax	Class
Roehl Transport Inc 1916 E 29th St PO Box 750 .... Marshfield WI 54449 *TF:* 800-826-8367 ■ *Web:* www.roehl.jobs/corp	715-591-3795		780
Roehlen Engraving 5901 Lewis Rd. .... Sandston VA 23150 *Web:* www.standexengraving.com	804-222-2821		481
Roesch Inc 100 N 24th St .... Belleville IL 62222 **Fax Area Code:* 618 ■ *TF:* 800-423-6243 ■ *Web:* www.roeschinc.com	800-423-6243	233-1186*	481
Roff Enterprises Inc 438 N Frederick Ave .... Gaithersburg MD 20877 *Web:* www.hhcgroup.com	301-963-0762		194
Roffe Container Inc 1802 Second Ave N .... Moorhead MN 56560 *Web:* www.roffecontainer.com	218-233-5145		98
Roffman Miller Assoc Inc 1835 Market St Ste 500 .... Philadelphia PA 19103 *TF:* 800-995-1030 ■ *Web:* www.roffmanmiller.com	215-981-1030	981-0146	401
Rofin-Sinar Inc 40984 Concept Dr .... Plymouth MI 48170 *NASDAQ: RSTI* ■ *Web:* www.rofin.com	734-455-5400		425
Rogan Corp 3455 Woodhead Dr. .... Northbrook IL 60062 *TF:* 800-584-5662 ■ *Web:* www.rogancorp.com	847-498-2300	498-2334	608
Roger a Soape Inc 19450 State Hwy 249 Ste 460. .... Houston TX 77070 *Web:* www.rasoape.com	281-440-6347		690
Roger B Chaffee Planetarium 272 Pearl St NW .... Grand Rapids MI 49504 *Web:* grpm.org/planetarium	616-456-3977		598
Roger Black Studio Inc 107 Third Ave .... St. Pete Beach FL 33706 *Web:* rogerblack.com	212-481-9800		317
Roger D Perry PC 3050 Business Park Cir .... Goodlettsville TN 37072	615-851-6081		2
Roger Dean Chevrolet Inc 2235 Okeechobee Blvd .... West Palm Beach FL 33409 *TF:* 877-827-4705 ■ *Web:* www.rogerdeanchevrolet.com	844-396-5151		57
Roger Dean Stadium 4751 Main St .... Jupiter FL 33458 *Web:* www.rogerdeanstadium.com	561-775-1818	691-6886	720
Roger Grace Associates LLC 109 Greenfield Ct .... Naples FL 34110 *Web:* www.rgrace.com	239-596-8738		193
Roger Mills County 500 E Broadway PO Box 708 .... Cheyenne OK 73628 *Web:* www.rogermills.org	580-497-3350		338
Roger Sherman Inn 195 Oenoke Ridge. .... New Canaan CT 06840 *Web:* www.rogershermaninn.com	203-966-4541	966-0503	379
Roger Sipe CPA Firm LLC 5742 Coventry Ln .... Fort Wayne IN 46804 *TF:* 888-747-3272 ■ *Web:* sipecpa.com	260-432-9996		2
Roger Smith Hotel 501 Lexington Ave .... New York NY 10017 *TF:* 800-445-0277 ■ *Web:* www.rogersmith.com	212-755-1400	758-4061	379
Roger W. Wheeler State Beach 100 Sand Hill Cove Rd .... Narragansett RI 02882 *Web:* www.riparks.com	401-789-3563		565
Roger Ward Inc 17275 Green Mtn Rd .... San Antonio TX 78247 *TF General:* 888-909-3147 ■ *Web:* www.wardnorthamerican.com	210-655-8623	653-0919	780
Roger Williams Medical Ctr 825 Chalkstone Ave .... Providence RI 02908 *Web:* www.rwmc.org	401-456-2000	456-2029	374-3
Roger Williams National Memorial 282 N Main St .... Providence RI 02903 *Web:* www.nps.gov/rowi	401-521-7266	521-7239	564
Roger Williams Park Zoo 1000 Elmwood Ave. .... Providence RI 02907 *TF:* 800-832-3474 ■ *Web:* rwpzoo.org	401-785-3510	941-3988	823
Roger Williams University 1 Old Ferry Rd .... Bristol RI 02809 **Fax:* Admissions ■ *TF:* 800-458-7144 ■ *Web:* www.rwu.edu	401-254-3500	254-3557*	166
Roger Williams University Ralph R Papitto School of Law 10 Metacom Ave. .... Bristol RI 02809 **Fax:* Admissions ■ *TF:* 800-633-2727 ■ *Web:* www.law.rwu.edu	401-254-4500	254-4516*	167-1
Roger's Manufacturing Corp 801 Industrial Pkwy .... West Monroe LA 71291 *Web:* www.rogersmfg.com	318-396-5700		817
Rogers & Brown 2 Cumberland St .... Charleston SC 29401 *Web:* www.rogers-brown.com	843-577-3630	720-8911	311
Rogers & Cowan 1840 Century Park E 18th Fl. .... Los Angeles CA 90067 *Web:* www.rogersandcowan.com	310-854-8100		731
Rogers & Lapan PA 355 Windy Ridge Rd .... Chapel Hill NC 27517 *Web:* rogerslapan.com	919-545-9259		428
Rogers Arena 800 Griffiths Way. .... Vancouver BC V6B6G1 *Web:* rogersarena.com	604-899-7400		720
Rogers Bros Corp 100 Orchard St. .... Albion PA 16401 *TF:* 800-441-9880 ■ *Web:* www.rogerstrailers.com	814-756-4121	756-4830	779
Rogers Centre 1 Blue Jays Way Ste 3000 .... Toronto ON M5V1J1	416-341-3000		720
Rogers Communications Inc 333 Bloor St E 10th Fl .... Toronto ON M4W1G9 *TSE: RCI.B* ■ *TF:* 800-387-0825 ■ *Web:* www.rogers.com	416-935-7777	935-3599	736
Rogers Corp 1 Technology Dr .... Rogers CT 06263 *TF:* 800-237-2267 ■ *Web:* www.rogerscorp.com	860-774-9605	779-5509	605-2
Rogers Corp Durel Div 2225 W Chandler Blvd .... Chandler AZ 85224 *Web:* www.rogerscorp.com	480-917-6000	917-6049	437
Rogers County 219 S Missouri St. .... Claremore OK 74017 *TF:* 800-522-7233 ■ *Web:* www.rogerscounty.org	918-923-4400		338
Rogers Engineering & Manufacturing Inc 112 S Center St .... Cambridge City IN 47327 *Web:* rogersengineering.net	765-478-5444		261
Rogers Foam Corp 20 Vernon St .... Somerville MA 02145 *TF:* 800-951-9276 ■ *Web:* rogersfoam.com	617-623-3010	629-2585	601
Rogers Group Inc 421 Great Cir Rd. .... Nashville TN 37228 *Web:* www.rogersgroupincint.com	615-242-0585		503-4
Rogers Harold (Rep R - KY) 2406 Rayburn Bldg. .... Washington DC 20515 *Web:* halrogers.house.gov	202-225-4601	225-0940	342-2
Rogers Huber & Assoc 973 Lycoming Mall Dr .... Muncy PA 17756 *Web:* rogershuber.com	570-546-2238		2

Name / Address	City	State	Zip	Phone	Fax	Class
Rogers Jewelry Co PO Box 3151 *TF:* 800-877-4221 ■ *Web:* www.thinkrogers.com	Modesto	CA	95353	800-877-4221		410
Rogers Lumber Company Inc 937 Hwy 7 N *Web:* rogerspallet.com	Camden	AR	71701	870-574-0231	574-1206	683
Rogers Machinery Company Inc 14650 SW 72nd Ave PO Box 230429 *TF:* 800-394-6151 ■ *Web:* www.rogers-machinery.com	Portland	OR	97224	503-639-0808		172
Rogers Manufacturing Company Inc 110 Transit Ave *Web:* www.rogersbody.com	Nashville	TN	37210	615-244-9720		190
Rogers Memorial Hospital Inc 34700 Valley Rd *TF:* 800-767-4411 ■ *Web:* rogersbh.org	Oconomowoc	WI	53066	262-646-4411	646-3158	374-5
Rogers Mike (Rep R - AL) 2184 Rayburn HOB *Web:* mikerogers.house.gov	Washington	DC	20515	202-225-3261	226-8485	342-2
Rogers Printing Inc PO Box 215 *TF:* 800-622-5591 ■ *Web:* www.rogersprinting.net	Ravenna	MI	49451	231-853-2244	853-6558	627
Rogers State University 1701 W Will Rogers Blvd **Fax:* Admissions ■ *TF:* 800-256-7511 ■ *Web:* www.rsu.edu	Claremore	OK	74017	918-343-7546	343-7595*	166
Rogers State University Pryor 421 S Elliott St **Fax:* Admissions ■ *TF:* 800-256-7511 ■ *Web:* www.rsu.edu	Pryor	OK	74361	918-825-6117	825-6135*	162
Rogers Stereo Inc 525 Woodruff Rd *TF:* 800-332-1449 ■ *Web:* www.rogersstereo.com	Greenville	SC	29607	864-288-9999		791
Rogers Supply Company Inc PO Box 740 *TF:* 800-252-0406 ■ *Web:* www.rogerssupply.com	Champaign	IL	61824	217-356-0166	356-1768	665
Rogers-Lowell Area Chamber of Commerce 317 W Walnut St *TF:* 800-364-1240 ■ *Web:* www.rogerslowell.com	Rogers	AR	72756	479-636-1240	636-5485	139
Rogers-O'Brien Construction USA 1901 Regal Row *Web:* www.rogers-obrien.com	Dallas	TX	75235	214-962-3000		186
Rogerson Aircraft Corp 2201 Alton Pkwy *Web:* www.rogerson.com	Irvine	CA	92606	949-660-0666		22
Rogerson Kratos Corp 2201 Alton Pkwy *Web:* rogersonaircraft.com/markets-rogerson-kratos	Pasadena	CA	92606	626-449-3090		21
Rogersville/Hawkins County Chamber of Commerce 107 E Main St Ste 100 *Web:* www.rogersvillechamber.us	Rogersville	TN	37857	423-272-2186	272-2186	139
Rogge Capital Management LP 401 Congress Ave Ste 2750	Austin	TX	78701	512-322-0909		401
Rogue Ales Co 2320 OSU Dr *Web:* www.rogue.com	Newport	OR	97365	541-867-3660		102
Rogue Community College 3345 Redwood Hwy **Fax:* Admissions ■ *TF:* 800-411-6508 ■ *Web:* www.roguecc.edu	Grants Pass	OR	97527	541-956-7500	471-3585*	162
Riverside 117 S Central *Web:* www.roguecc.edu	Medford	OR	97501	541-245-7500	245-7648	162
Rogue Credit Union 1370 Center Dr *Web:* www.roguecu.org	Medford	OR	97501	541-858-7328		219
Rogue Valley Manor 1200 Mira Mar Ave *TF:* 800-848-7868 ■ *Web:* www.retirement.org/rvm	Medford	OR	97504	541-857-7214		672
Rogue Valley Youth Correctional Facility 2001 NE 'F' St *TF:* 800-452-2147 ■ *Web:* oregon.gov	Grants Pass	OR	97526	541-471-2862	471-2861	412
Rogue Wave Software Inc 5500 Flatiron Pkwy *TF:* 800-487-3217 ■ *Web:* www.roguewave.com	Boulder	CO	80301	303-473-9118	473-9137	178-2
Rohde & Schwarz Inc 6821 Benjamin Franklin Dr *Web:* www.rohde-schwarz.com	Columbia	MD	21046	410-910-7800		246
Rohde Bros Inc W5745 Woodchuck Ln *Web:* rohdebros.com	Plymouth	WI	53073	920-893-5905		610
Rohde Construction Company Inc 4087 Brockton Dr *Web:* rohdeconstruction.com	Kentwood	MI	49512	616-698-0880		187
ROHL LLC 3 Parker *Web:* www.rohlhome.com	Irvine	CA	92618	714-557-1933		612
Rohn Industries Inc 862 Hersey St *Web:* rohnind.com	St. Paul	MN	55114	651-647-1300		553
ROHN Products LLC 1 Fairholm Ave *Web:* www.rohnnet.com	Peoria	IL	61603	309-566-3000		723
Rohnert Park Chamber of Commerce 101 Golf Course Dr Ste C-7 *Web:* www.rohnertparkchamber.org	Rohnert Park	CA	94928	707-584-1415	584-2945	139
Rohrabacher Dana (Rep R - CA) 2300 Rayburn Bldg *Web:* rohrabacher.house.gov	Washington	DC	20515	202-225-2415	225-0145	342-2
Rohrback Cosasco Systems Inc 11841 E Smith Ave *Web:* cosasco.com	Santa Fe Springs	CA	90670	562-949-0123		350
Rohrer Corp 717 Seville Rd PO Box 1009 *TF:* 800-243-6640 ■ *Web:* www.rohrer.com	Wadsworth	OH	44282	330-335-1541	336-5147	608
Roi Advertising & Communication 5001 Brentwood Stair Rd *Web:* www.roiac.com	Fort Worth	TX	76112	900-464-9564		7
Roi Communications Inc 5274 Scotts Vly Dr *Web:* www.roico.com	Scotts Valley	CA	95066	831-430-0170		196
Roi Consulting Ll Llc 176 Logan St *TF:* 866-465-6470 ■ *Web:* www.roillc.net	Noblesville	IN	46060	866-465-6470		196
ROI4Sales Inc 3355 Quaas Dr *Web:* www.roi4sales.com	West Bend	WI	53095	262-338-1851		463
Roig, Kasperovich, Tutan & Woods PA 1255 S Military Trl Ste 100 *Web:* www.roiglawyers.com	Deerfield Beach	FL	33442	954-834-0330		428
Roka Bioscience Inc 20 Independence Blvd 4th Fl *TF:* 855-765-2246 ■ *Web:* www.rokabio.com	Warren	NJ	07059	908-605-4700		475
Rokeby Museum 4334 Rt 7 *TF:* 800-880-8149 ■ *Web:* www.rokeby.org	Ferrisburgh	VT	05456	802-877-3406	877-3406	520
Rokita Todd (Rep R - IN) 2439 Rayburn HOB *Web:* rokita.house.gov	Washington	DC	20515	202-225-5037	226-0544	342-2
Rol San 323 Spadina Ave	Toronto	ON	M5T2E9	416-977-1128		671
Ro-Lab American Rubber Co Inc 8830 W Linne Rd *TF:* 800-298-2066 ■ *Web:* www.dynatect.com	Tracy	CA	95304	209-836-0965		370
Rolac Contracting Inc 1800 Valley St *Web:* www.rolac-nd.com	Minot	ND	58701	701-839-6525		610
Roland Berger & Partners 177 Huntington Ave 18th Fl **Fax Area Code:* 617 ■ *Web:* www.rolandberger.com	Boston	MA	02115	212-651-9660	310-6601*	194
Roland Berger Strategy Consultants LLC 37000 Woodward Ave Ste 200 *Web:* www.rolandberger.us	Bloomfield Hills	MI	48304	248-729-5000		463
Roland C. Nickerson State Park c/o Nickerson State Pk Rte 6A	Brewster	MA	02631	508-896-3491		565
Roland Cooper State Park 285 Deer Run Dr *TF:* 800-252-7275 ■ *Web:* www.alapark.com	Camden	AL	36726	334-682-4838	682-4050	565
Roland Corp US 5100 S Eastern Ave *Web:* www.roland.com/us	Los Angeles	CA	90040	323-890-3700	890-3701	527
Roland D Kelly Infiniti Inc 155 Andover St Rt 114 *TF:* 855-885-3559 ■ *Web:* www.kellyauto.com	Danvers	MA	01923	855-885-3559		57
Roland DGA Corp 15363 Barranca Pkwy *TF:* 800-542-2307 ■ *Web:* www.rolanddga.com	Irvine	CA	92618	949-727-2100	727-2112	173-6
Roland Machinery Co 816 N Dirksen Pkwy *TF:* 800-252-2926 ■ *Web:* www.rolandmachinery.com	Springfield	IL	62702	217-789-7711	744-7314	358
Roland Park Place 830 W 40th St *Web:* www.rolandparkplace.org	Baltimore	MD	21211	410-243-5700		672
Roland's Electric Inc 307 Suburban Ave *TF:* 800-981-8010 ■ *Web:* www.rolandselectric.com	Deer Park	NY	11729	631-242-8080	242-6392	787
Roland|Criss 2011 E Lamar Blvd Ste 150 *Web:* rolandcriss.com	Arlington	TX	76006	817-861-7963		466
Rolands & Associates Corp 120 Del Rey Gardens Dr *TF:* 800-542-2307 ■ *Web:* www.rolands.com	Del Rey Oaks	CA	93940	831-373-2025		177
Rolenn Mfg 2065 Roberta St *Web:* www.rolenn.com	Riverside	CA	92507	951-682-1185		608
Rolette County PO Box 276 *Web:* www.rolettecounty.com	Rolla	ND	58367	701-477-3816		338
Rolex Watch Usa Inc 2651 N Harwood St Ste 600 *Web:* www.rolex.com	Dallas	TX	75201	214-871-0500		205
Rolf C. Hagen Corp 305 Forbes Blvd *TF Cust Svc:* 800-724-2436 ■ *Web:* www.hagen.com	Mansfield	MA	02048	508-339-9531		578
Rolf Institute of Structural Integration 5055 Chaparral Ct Ste 103 *TF:* 800-530-8875 ■ *Web:* www.rolf.org	Boulder	CO	80301	303-449-5903	449-5978	48-17
Rolf Prima Wheel Systems 940 Wilson St **Fax Area Code:* 888 ■ *TF:* 888-308-7700 ■ *Web:* www.rolfprima.com	Eugene	OR	97402	541-868-1715	851-3748*	517
Rolinc Staffing 333 W Hampden Ave Ste 545 *TF:* 800-211-6633 ■ *Web:* rolinc.com	Englewood	CO	80110	303-781-0055		260
Roll Bond Converting 12855 Vly Branch Ln *Web:* www.rbconverting.com	Dallas	TX	75234	972-866-0880		557
Roll Call 77 K St NE *TF:* 800-432-2250 ■ *Web:* www.rollcall.com	Washington	DC	20002	202-650-6500		531-7
Roll Forming Corp (RFC) 1070 Brooks Industrial Rd *TF:* 800-700-2461 ■ *Web:* www.rfcorp.com	Shelbyville	KY	40065	502-633-4435		697
Roll Master 920 Schriewer *Web:* www.roll-master.com	Seguin	TX	78155	830-386-0991		350
Roll Shutter Systems Inc 21633 N 14th Ave *TF:* 800-551-7655 ■ *Web:* www.rollshuttersystemsusa.com	Phoenix	AZ	85027	623-869-7057		699
Roll'n Oilfield Industries Ltd 305, 5208 - 53 Ave *TF:* 800-662-7139 ■ *Web:* www.rolln.com	Red Deer	AB	T4N5K2	403-343-1710		540
Rolla Area Chamber of Commerce 1311 KingsHwy *TF:* 888-809-3817 ■ *Web:* www.rollachamber.org	Rolla	MO	65401	573-364-3577	364-5222	139
Roll-A-Way Conveyor Inc 2335 N Delaney Rd *TF:* 800-747-9024 ■ *Web:* www.roll-away.com	Gurnee	IL	60031	847-336-5033	336-6542	207
Roll-A-Way Inc 1661 Glenlake Ave **Fax Area Code:* 630 ■ *TF:* 866-749-5424 ■ *Web:* www.roll-a-way.com	Itasca	IL	60143	866-749-5424	980-6364*	699
Rollease Acmeda 200 Harvard Ave *Web:* www.rollease.com	Stamford	CT	06902	203-964-1573	358-5865	620
Rolled Alloys Inc 125 W Sterns Rd *TF:* 800-521-0332 ■ *Web:* www.rolledalloys.com	Temperance	MI	48182	734-847-0561	847-6917	492
Rolled Steel Products Corp 2187 Garfield Ave *TF:* 800-400-7833 ■ *Web:* www.rolledsteel.com	Los Angeles	CA	90040	323-723-8836	888-9866	492
Roller Bearing Company of America 400 Sullivan Way *TF:* 800-390-3300 ■ *Web:* www.rbcbearings.com	West Trenton	NJ	08628	609-882-5050	882-5533	75
Roller Derby Skate Corp PO Box 930 *TF:* 800-835-5767 ■ *Web:* www.rollerderby.com	Litchfield	IL	62056	217-324-3961	324-2213	710
Roller Die & Forming Co of Alabama Inc 107 Industrial Park Dr *Web:* www.rollerdie.com	Eufaula	AL	36027	334-687-4844		455
Roller Skating Assn International (RSAI) 6905 Corporate Dr *TF:* 800-258-8146 ■ *Web:* rollerskating.com	Indianapolis	IN	46278	317-347-2626	347-2636	48-22
Rollex Corp 800 Chasa Ave *TF Cust Svc:* 800-251-3300 ■ *Web:* www.rollex.com	Elk Grove Village	IL	60007	847-437-3000	437-7561	697
Rollin J Lobaugh Inc 240 Ryan Way *Web:* www.rjlobaugh.com	South San Francisco	CA	94080	650-583-9682		621
Rolling Hills Consolidated Library 1904 N Belt Hwy *TF:* 800-466-8664 ■ *Web:* rhcl.org	St Joseph	MO	64506	816-236-2106		434-3
Rolling Hills Electric Co-op Inc 3075B US Hwy 24 *TF:* 800-530-5572 ■ *Web:* www.rollinghills.coop	Beloit	KS	67420	785-378-3151		245

Entry	City	State	Zip	Phone	Fax	Class
Rolling Meadows 3006 McNiel Ave	Wichita Falls	TX	76309	940-691-7511		672
TF: 800-458-9858 ■ *Web:* www.rmeadows.com						
Rolling Meadows Chamber of Commerce 2775 Algonquin Rd Ste 310	Rolling Meadows	IL	60008	847-398-3730	398-3745	139
Web: rmchamber.org						
Rolling Meadows Library 3110 Martin Ln	Rolling Meadows	IL	60008	847-259-6050		435
TF: 800-232-3798 ■ *Web:* www.rmlib.org						
Rolling Mix Management Ltd 7209 Railway St SE	Calgary	AB	T2H2V6	403-253-6426		183
Web: www.rollingmix.com						
Rolling Oaks Mall 6909 N Loop 1604 E	San Antonio	TX	78247	210-651-5601		460
TF: 877-746-6642 ■ *Web:* www.simon.com						
Rolling Oaks Radiology Inc 415 Rolling Oaks Dr	Thousand Oaks	CA	91361	805-778-1513		415
TF: 800-808-5208 ■ *Web:* www.rollingoaksradiology.com						
Rolling Readers USA 2515 Camino del Rio S Ste 330	San Diego	CA	92108	619-516-4095		48-11
Rolling Shield Inc 2500 NW 74th Ave	Miami	FL	33122	800-474-9404	436-5523*	699
**Fax Area Code:* 305 ■ *TF:* 800-474-9404 ■ *Web:* www.rollingshield.com						
Rollins College 1000 Holt Ave	Winter Park	FL	32789	407-646-2000	646-1502*	166
**Fax:* Admissions ■ *TF:* 800-799-2586 ■ *Web:* www.rollins.edu						
Rollins Inc 2170 Piedmont Rd NE	Atlanta	GA	30324	404-888-2000		577
NYSE: ROL ■ *Web:* www.rollins.com						
Rollins Moving & Storage Inc 1900 E Leffel Ln	Springfield	OH	45505	937-325-2484		549
TF: 800-826-8094 ■ *Web:* www.rollins3pl.com						
Rollins State Park 1066 Kearsarge Mountain Rd	Warner	NH	03278	603-456-3808		565
Web: www.nhstateparks.org						
Rollprint Packaging Products Inc 320 S Stewart Ave	Addison	IL	60101	630-628-1700	897-2525*	548
**Fax Area Code:* 260 ■ *Web:* www.rollprint.com						
Rolls Anderson & Rolls 115 Yellowstone Dr	Chico	CA	95973	530-895-1422		261
Web: rarcivil.com						
Rolls-Royce Engine Services Inc 7200 Earhart Rd	Oakland	CA	94621	510-613-1000	635-3221	24
TF: 888-255-4766 ■ *Web:* www.rolls-royce.com						
Rolls-Royce North America 1875 Explorer St Ste 200	Reston	VA	20190	703-834-1700	709-6086	21
TF: 888-269-2377 ■ *Web:* www.rolls-royce.com/northamerica/na						
Rollstock Inc 5720 Brighton Ave	Kansas City	MO	64130	616-570-0430		547
TF: 800-295-2949 ■ *Web:* www.rollstock.com						
Rollx Vans 6591 Hwy 13 W	Savage	MN	55378	952-890-7851	890-1903	62-7
TF: 800-956-6668 ■ *Web:* www.rollxvans.com						
Rolo's Cafe 975 Airport Rd	Huntsville	AL	35802	256-883-7656		671
Rolta Tusc Inc 333 E Butterfield Rd Ste 900	Lombard	IL	60148	630-960-2909		180
TF: 800-755-8872 ■ *Web:* www.rolta.com						
Roma Cafe 3401 Riopelle St	Detroit	MI	48207	313-831-5940		671
Web: www.romacafe.com						
Roma Design Group 1527 Stockton St	San Francisco	CA	94133	415-616-9900		261
Web: roma.com						
Roma Italian Restaurant 3 President Dr	Dover	DE	19901	302-678-1041		671
TF: 800-711-5882 ■ *Web:* www.romadover.com						
Roma Pizzeria Flint G5227 N Saginaw St	Flint	MI	48505	810-787-1061		671
Web: www.romaspizza.com						
Romac Industries Inc 21919 20th Ave SE	Bothell	WA	98021	425-951-6200	951-6201	595
TF: 800-426-9341 ■ *Web:* www.romac.com						
Romac Supply Company Inc 7400 Bandini Blvd	Commerce	CA	90040	800-777-6622		729
TF: 800-777-6622 ■ *Web:* www.romacsupply.com						
Roman Catholic Diocese of Fresno 1550 N Fresno St	Fresno	CA	93703	559-488-7400		685
Web: www.dioceseoffresno.org						
Roman Electric Company Inc 640 S 70th St	Milwaukee	WI	53214	414-771-5400	471-8693	189-4
Web: www.romanelectric.com						
Roman J Claprood Co 242 N Grant Ave	Columbus	OH	43215	614-221-5515		293
TF: 800-543-8862 ■ *Web:* rjclaprood.com						
RoMan Manufacturing Inc 861 47th St SW	Grand Rapids	MI	49509	616-530-8641	530-8953	811
Web: www.romanmfg.com						
Roman Meal Company Inc PO Box 2781	Fargo	ND	58108	253-475-0964		297-8
TF: 800-426-3600 ■ *Web:* www.romanmeal.com						
Romania 573-577 Third Ave	New York	NY	10016	212-682-3273		784
Web: www.un.int						
Consulate General 200 E 38th St	New York	NY	10016	212-682-9123		257
Web: newyork.mae.ro						
Romanian National Tourist Office 600 Third Ave Ste 224	New York	NY	10016	212-545-8484		775
Web: www.romaniatourism.com						
Romano Law Offices & Assoc 5 Irving St	Worcester	MA	01609	508-791-8255		445
TF: 800-409-0771 ■ *Web:* romanoandromano.com						
Romano's Macaroni Grill 4535 Belt Line Rd	Addison	TX	75001	972-386-3831		670
TF: 800-983-4637 ■ *Web:* www.macaronigrill.com						
Romanoff Electric Company LLC 5570 Enterprise Blvd	Toledo	OH	43612	419-726-2627	726-5406	189-4
TF: 800-866-2627 ■ *Web:* quebe.com						
Romanoff Group, The 1288 Research Rd	Gahanna	OH	43230	614-755-4500		116
TF: 800-366-8778 ■ *Web:* www.romanoffgroup.cc						
Romanoff International Supply Corp 9 Deforest St	Amityville	NY	11701	631-842-2400	842-0028	407
TF Cust Svc: 800-221-7448 ■ *Web:* www.romanoff.com						
Romanow Inc 346 University Ave	Westwood	MA	02090	781-320-9200		100
TF: 800-295-1034 ■ *Web:* www.romanowcontainer.com						
Romanza 2707 S Virginia St Peppermill Hotel Casino	Reno	NV	89502	775-826-2121		671
TF: 866-821-9996 ■ *Web:* www.peppermillreno.com						
Romar Cabinet & Top Company Inc 23949 S Northern Illinois Dr	Channahon	IL	60410	815-467-9900		321
TF: 800-600-0134 ■ *Web:* www.romarcabinet.com						
Romar Learning Solutions LLC 28420 Hardy Toll Rd Ste 150	Spring	TX	77373	281-292-5508		194
Web: www.romarlearning.com						
Romar Transportation Systems Inc 3500 S Kedzie Ave	Chicago	IL	60632	773-376-8800		311
TF: 800-621-5416 ■ *Web:* www.romartrans.com						
Rome Area Chamber of Commerce 139 W Dominick St	Rome	NY	13440	315-337-1700	337-1715	139
TF: 800-935-1801 ■ *Web:* www.romechamber.com						
Rome City School District 508 E Second St	Rome	GA	30161	706-236-5050	802-4311	685
Web: www.rcs.rome.ga.us						
Rome Die Casting LLC 29 Westside Industrial Blvd	Rome	GA	30165	706-235-6081		567
Rome Fastener Corp 257 Depot Rd	Milford	CT	06460	203-874-6719	877-0201	594
Web: www.romefast.com						
Rome Group Inc, The 3120 locust	Saint Louis	MO	63103	314-533-0930		195
Web: www.theromegroup.com						
Rome Memorial Hospital 1500 N James St	Rome	NY	13440	315-338-7000	338-7695	374-3
Web: www.romehosp.org						
Rome News-Tribune 305 E Sixth Ave PO Box 1633	Rome	GA	30161	706-290-5252		532-2
Web: northwestgeorgianews.com/rome						
Rome Research Corp 421 Ridge St	Rome	NY	13440	315-339-0491		393
Web: www.pargovernment.com						
Rome Sentinel Co 333 W Dominick St	Rome	NY	13440	315-337-4000	339-6281	637-8
TF: 800-321-0350 ■ *Web:* www.romesentinel.com						
Rome Snowboards Corp 1 Derby Ln Ste 4	Waterbury	VT	05676	802-244-1758		711
Web: www.romesnowboards.com						
Rome Specialty Company Inc Rosco Div 501 W Embargo St	Rome	NY	13440	315-337-8200	339-2523	710
TF: 800-794-8357 ■ *Web:* www.roscoinc.com						
Rome Technologies Inc 412 Headquarters Dr Ste 4	Millersville	MD	21108	410-923-2000		809
Web: rometech.com						
Rome Tool & Die Company Inc 113 Hemlock St	Rome	GA	30161	706-234-6743	234-1242	757
TF: 800-241-3369 ■ *Web:* stemco.com						
Romeo Community School District 316 N Main St	Romeo	MI	48065	586-752-0200	752-0228	685
TF: 888-427-6818 ■ *Web:* www.romeo.k12.mi.us						
Romeo Computer Co 76005 Van Dyke Rd	Bruce Township	MI	48065	586-752-5158		396
TF: 800-734-5202 ■ *Web:* www.romeocomp.com						
Romeo Entertainment Group Inc 5247 N 129th St	Omaha	NE	68164	402-359-1010		317
TF: 800-467-7469 ■ *Web:* www.romeoent.com						
Romeo Rim Inc 74000 Van Dyke Rd	Bruce Township	MI	48065	586-336-5800		596
Web: www.romeorim.com						
Romeo's Euro Cafe 207 N Gilbert Rd Ste 105	Gilbert	AZ	85234	480-962-4224		671
TF: 800-950-0086 ■ *Web:* www.eurocafe.com						
Romeo-Washington Chamber of Commerce 228 N Main St PO Box 175	Romeo	MI	48065	586-752-4436	752-2835	139
Web: www.rwchamber.com						
Romero Mazda 1307 Kettering Dr	Ontario	CA	91761	909-390-8484		57
TF: 888-317-2233 ■ *Web:* www.mazdaofontario.com						
Romeros Food Products Inc 15155 Valley View Ave	Santa Fe Springs	CA	90670	562-802-1858		123
Web: www.romerosfood.com						
Romet Ltd 1080 Matheson Blvd E	Mississauga	ON	L4W2V2	905-624-1591	624-5668	407
TF: 800-387-3201 ■ *Web:* www.rometlimited.com						
Romika USA LLC 3405 Del Webb Ave NE	Salem	OR	97301	503-588-8117		301
TF: 888-777-4174 ■ *Web:* www.romikausa.com						
Romo Incentives Group 1156 Suncast Ln Ste 3	El Dorado Hills	CA	95762	916-941-0350		463
Web: www.romoincentivesgroup.com						
Ron Carter Automotive Group 3205 FM 528	Alvin	TX	77511	281-331-3111		57
Web: www.roncarter.com						
Ron Foth Adv 8100 N High St	Columbus	OH	43235	614-888-7771		4
Web: www.ronfoth.com						
Ron Jon Surf Shop 3850 S Banana River Blvd	Cocoa Beach	FL	32931	321-799-8888	799-8805	711
TF: 888-757-8737 ■ *Web:* www.ronjonsurfshop.com						
Ron Kendall Masonry Inc 101 Benoist Farms Rd	West Palm Beach	FL	33411	561-793-5924	795-2621	189-7
TF: 866-844-1404 ■ *Web:* www.ronkendallmasonry.com						
Ron Sachs Communications Inc 114 S Duval St	Tallahassee	FL	32301	850-222-1996		636
Web: sachsmedia.com						
Ron Tonkin Dealerships 122 NE 122nd Ave	Portland	OR	97230	503-255-4100		57
TF: 855-890-1823 ■ *Web:* tonkinchevrolet.com						
RONA Inc 220 Ch du Tremblay	Boucherville	QC	J4B8H7	514-599-5100		364
TSE: RON ■ *TF:* 866-283-2239 ■ *Web:* www.rona.ca						
Ronald Blue & Company LLC 300 Colonial Ctr Pkwy Ste 300	Roswell	GA	30076	770-280-6000	280-6001	401
TF: 800-841-0362 ■ *Web:* www.ronblue.com						
Ronald C Wornick Jewish Day School 800 Foster City Blvd	Foster City	CA	94404	650-378-2600		685
Web: www.wornickjds.org						
Ronald Feldman Fine Arts Inc 31 Mercer St	New York	NY	10013	212-226-3232	941-1536	42
TF: 800-873-3791 ■ *Web:* www.feldmangallery.com						
Ronald Mark Associates Inc 1227 Central Ave	Hillside	NJ	07205	908-558-0011		41
Web: www.ronaldmark.com						
Ronald McDonald House (RMH) 2524 N State St	Jackson	MS	39216	601-981-5683	981-3613	373
Web: www.rmhcms.org						
Akron 245 Locust St	Akron	OH	44302	330-253-5400		373
TF: 800-262-0333 ■ *Web:* www.akronchildrens.org						
Albany 139 S Lake Ave	Albany	NY	12208	518-438-2655		373
TF: 866-244-8464 ■ *Web:* www.rmhcofalbany.org						
Albuquerque 1011 Yale Ave NE	Albuquerque	NM	87106	505-842-8960	764-0412	373
TF: 877-842-8960 ■ *Web:* www.rmhc-nm.org						

	City	State	ZIP	Phone	Fax	Class
Amarillo 1501 Streit Dr Web: rmhc.org	Amarillo	TX	79106	806-358-8177		373
Ann Arbor 1600 Washington Heights TF: 800-544-8684 ■ Web: www.rmh-annarbor.org	Ann Arbor	MI	48104	734-994-4442	994-4919	373
Atlanta 795 Gatewood Rd NE Web: www.armhc.org	Atlanta	GA	30329	404-315-1133	315-7873	373
Austin 1315 Barbara Jordan Blvd Web: rmhc-ctx.org	Austin	TX	78723	512-472-9844		373
Baltimore 635 W Lexington St Web: www.rmhcbaltimore.org	Baltimore	MD	21201	410-528-1010	727-6177	373
Bangor 654 State St Web: rmhcmaine.org	Bangor	ME	04401	207-942-9003	990-2984	373
Bend 1700 NE Purcell Blvd Web: rmhcofcentraloregon.org	Bend	OR	97701	541-318-4950	318-4994	373
Billings 1144 N 30th St	Billings	MT	59101	406-256-8006		373
Birmingham 1700 Fourth Ave S Web: www.rmhca.org	Birmingham	AL	35233	205-638-7255	638-7256	373
Bismarck 609 N Seventh St Web: rmhcbismarck.org	Bismarck	ND	58501	701-258-8551	258-5076	373
Boise 101 Warm Springs Ave Web: www.rmhcidaho.org	Boise	ID	83712	208-336-5478		373
Boston 229 Kent St	Brookline	MA	02446	617-734-3333		373
Buffalo 780 W Ferry St Web: rmhcwny.org	Buffalo	NY	14222	716-883-1177		373
Burlington 16 S Winooski Ave Web: www.rmhcvt.org	Burlington	VT	05401	802-862-4943	862-2175	373
Camden 550 Mickle Blvd Web: www.ronaldhouse-snj.org	Camden	NJ	08103	856-966-4663		373
Chapel Hill 101 Old Mason Farm Rd Web: www.rmh-chapelhill.org	Chapel Hill	NC	27517	919-913-2040	951-0123	373
Charleston 81 Gadsden St Web: www.rmhcharleston.org	Charleston	SC	29401	843-723-7957	722-2204	373
Charlottesville 300 Ninth St SW Web: www.rmhcharlottesville.org	Charlottesville	VA	22903	434-295-1885	295-7735	373
Chattanooga 200 Central Ave Web: www.rmhchattanooga.com	Chattanooga	TN	37403	423-778-4300	778-4350	373
Chicago 211 E Grand Ave Web: www.rmhccni.org	Chicago	IL	60611	312-888-2500		373
Chicago 1301 W 22nd St Ste 905 Web: www.rmhccni.org	Oak Brook	IL	60523	630-623-5300		373
Chicago Tripp Ave PO Box 7002 Web: www.rmhccni.org	Hines	IL	60141	708-327-2273	327-6000	373
Cleveland 10415 Euclid Ave TF: 800-223-2273 ■ Web: www.rmhcleveland.org	Cleveland	OH	44106	216-229-5758	229-0556	373
Colorado Springs 311 N Logan Ave Web: www.rmhcs.org	Colorado Springs	CO	80909	719-471-1814	471-7147	373
Columbus 1959 Hamilton Rd Web: www.rmhcwga.org	Columbus	GA	31904	706-321-0033	321-0034	373
Corpus Christi 3402 Ft Worth St Web: www.corpuschristirmhc.org	Corpus Christi	TX	78411	361-854-4073	854-9174	373
Dallas 4707 Bengal St Web: www.rmhdallas.org	Dallas	TX	75235	214-631-7354	631-1527	373
Danville 100 N Academy Ave PO Box 300 Web: www.rmhdanville.org	Danville	PA	17821	570-271-6300	271-8182	373
Des Moines 1441 Pleasant St Web: rmhdesmoines.org	Des Moines	IA	50314	515-243-2111	280-3111	373
Detroit 4707 St Antoine St Ste 200 Web: www.rmhc-detroit.org	Detroit	MI	48201	313-745-5909		373
Durham 506 Alexander Ave TF: 866-244-8464 ■ Web: www.rmhdurhamwake.org	Durham	NC	27705	919-286-9305	286-7307	373
Edmonton 7726 107 St NW Web: rmhcna.org	Edmonton	AB	T6E4K3	780-439-5437		373
El Paso 300 E California St Web: www.rmhc.org	El Paso	TX	79902	915-542-1522		373
Falls Church 3312 Gallows Rd TF: 855-227-7435 ■ Web: rmhcdc.org	Falls Church	VA	22042	703-698-7080	698-7745	373
Fargo 1234 Broadway Web: www.rmhcfargo.org	Fargo	ND	58102	701-232-3980		373
Fort Lauderdale 15 SE 15th St Web: rmhcsouthflorida.org	Fort Lauderdale	FL	33316	954-828-1822		373
Fort Myers 16100 Roserush Ct TF: 800-435-7352 ■ Web: www.rmhcswfl.org	Fort Myers	FL	33908	239-437-0202	437-3521	373
Fort Worth 1004 Seventh Ave Web: www.rmhfw.org	Fort Worth	TX	76104	817-870-4942	870-0254	373
Galveston 301 14th St TF: 800-275-2946 ■ Web: www.rmhg.org	Galveston	TX	77550	409-762-8770		373
Grand Rapids 1323 Cedar St NE Web: rmhwesternmichigan.org	Grand Rapids	MI	49503	616-776-1300	776-0368	373
Greater Cincinnati 350 Erkenbrecher Ave Web: www.rmhcincinnati.org	Cincinnati	OH	45229	513-636-7642	636-4887	373
Greenville 529 Moye Blvd Web: www.rmhenc.org	Greenville	NC	27834	252-847-5435		373
Hamilton 1510 Main St W Web: www.rmhcsco.ca	Hamilton	ON	L8S1E3	905-521-9983		373
Hershey 745 W Governor Rd TF: 800-732-0999 ■ Web: www.rmhc-centralpa.org	Hershey	PA	17033	717-533-4001	533-1299	373
Honolulu 1970 Judd Hillside Rd Web: ronaldhousehawaii.org	Honolulu	HI	96822	808-973-5683	955-8794	373
Huntington 1500 17th St Web: rmhchuntington.org	Huntington	WV	25701	304-529-1122		373
Iowa City 730 Hawkins Dr Web: rmhc-easterniowa.org	Iowa City	IA	52246	319-356-3939	353-6873	373
Jacksonville 824 Children's Way Web: rmhcjacksonville.org	Jacksonville	FL	32207	904-807-4663		373
Johnson City 418 N State of Franklin Rd Web: rmhc.org	Johnson City	TN	37604	423-975-5437		373
Joplin 3402 S Jackson Ave PO Box 2688 Web: www.rmhjoplin.org	Joplin	MO	64804	417-624-2273		373
Kansas City 2502 Cherry St Web: www.rmhckc.org	Kansas City	MO	64108	816-842-8321	842-7033	373
Knoxville 1705 W Clinch Ave Web: www.knoxrmhc.org	Knoxville	TN	37916	865-637-7475		373
Lansing 121 S Holmes St	Lansing	MI	48912	517-485-9303		373
Las Vegas 2323 Potosi St TF: 888-248-1561 ■ Web: www.rmhlv.com	Las Vegas	NV	89146	702-252-4663	252-7345	373
Loma Linda 11365 Anderson St Web: rmhcsc.org/lomalinda	Loma Linda	CA	92354	909-558-8300		373
Long Branch 131 Bath Ave Web: www.rmh-cnj.org	Long Branch	NJ	07740	732-222-8755		373
Los Angeles (LARMH) 4560 Fountain Ave Web: rmhcsc.org/losangeles	Los Angeles	CA	90029	323-644-3000	669-0552	373
Macon 1160 Forsyth St Web: www.rmhccga.org	Macon	GA	31201	478-746-4090	746-0580	373
Madera 9161 Randall Way Web: www.rmhccv.org	Madera	CA	93636	559-447-6770		373
Madison 2716 Marshall Ct	Madison	WI	53705	608-232-4660		373
Marshfield 803 W N St Web: www.rmhc-marshfield.org	Marshfield	WI	54449	715-387-5899		373
Memphis 535 Alabama Ave Web: rmhc-memphis.org	Memphis	TN	38105	901-529-4055	523-0315	373
Midtown 1110 N Emporia St Web: www.rmhcwichita.org	Wichita	KS	67214	316-269-4420	269-0665	373
Minneapolis 818 Fulton St SE Web: rmhtwincities.org	Minneapolis	MN	55414	612-331-5752	331-1255	373
Missoula 3003 Fort Missoula Rd Web: www.rmhcwesternmontana.org	Missoula	MT	59804	406-541-7646		373
Montreal 5800 Hudson Rd Web: www.manoirmontreal.qc.ca	Montreal	QC	H3S2G5	514-731-2871	739-8823	373
Morgantown 841 Country Club Dr Web: www.rmhcmorgantown.org	Morgantown	WV	26505	304-598-0050	599-0780	373
New Brunswick 145 Somerset St Web: www.rmh-cnj.org	New Brunswick	NJ	08901	732-249-1222		373
New Haven 501 George St Web: www.rmhc-ctma.org	New Haven	CT	06511	203-777-5683	777-3082	373
New Hyde Park 267-07 76th Ave Web: www.rmhlongisland.org	New Hyde Park	NY	11040	718-343-5683	343-5798	373
New Orleans 4403 Canal St	New Orleans	LA	70119	504-486-6668		373
New York 405 E 73rd St Web: www.rmh-newyork.org	New York	NY	10021	212-639-0100		373
Norfolk 404 Colley Ave Web: www.rmhcnorfolk.org	Norfolk	VA	23507	757-627-5386		373
Northwest Ohio 3883 Monroe St Web: www.rmhctoledo.org	Toledo	OH	43606	419-471-4663	479-6961	373
Oklahoma City 1301 NE 14th St Web: rmhc-okc.org	Oklahoma City	OK	73117	405-424-6873	424-0919	373
Omaha 620 S 38th Ave	Omaha	NE	68105	402-346-9377		373
Orange 383 S Batavia St Web: rmhcsc.org/orangecounty	Orange	CA	92868	714-639-3600	516-3697	373
Orlando 2201 Alden Rd Web: www.rmhccf.org	Orlando	FL	32803	407-898-6127		373
Orlando 1630 Kuhl Ave Web: www.rmhccf.org	Orlando	FL	32806	407-581-1289		373
Ottawa 407 Smyth Rd Web: www.rmhottawa.com	Ottawa	ON	K1H8M8	613-737-5523	737-5524	373
Palo Alto 520 Sand Hill Rd Web: www.ronaldhouse.net	Palo Alto	CA	94304	650-470-6000	470-6010	373
Pasadena 763 S Pasadena Ave Web: rmhcsc.org/pasadena	Pasadena	CA	91105	626-585-1588		373
Pensacola 5200 Bayou Blvd Web: www.rmhc-nwfl.org	Pensacola	FL	32503	850-477-2273		373
Philadelphia 3925 Chestnut St TF: 800-723-0999 ■ Web: www.philarmh.org	Philadelphia	PA	19104	215-387-8406	386-4977	373
Phoenix 501 E Roanoke Ave TF: 877-333-2978 ■ Web: www.rmhcphoenix.com	Phoenix	AZ	85004	602-264-2654		373
Pittsburgh 451 44th St Web: www.rmhcpgh.org	Pittsburgh	PA	15201	412-362-3400	362-8540	373
Portland 2115 SW River Pkwy Web: www.rmhcoregon.org	Portland	OR	97201	971-230-0808		373
Portland 2620 N Commercial Ave Web: www.rmhcoregon.org	Portland	OR	97227	971-230-6700		373
Providence 45 Gay St Web: www.rmhprovidence.org	Providence	RI	02905	401-274-4447	751-3730	373
Richmond 2330 Monument Ave Web: www.rmhc-richmond.org	Richmond	VA	23220	804-355-6517	358-3153	373
Rio Grande Valley, The 1720 Treasure Hills Blvd Web: www.rmhcrgv.org	Harlingen	TX	78550	956-412-7200	412-6300	373
Roanoke 2224 S Jefferson St Web: rmhc-swva.org	Roanoke	VA	24014	540-857-0770	857-9584	373
Rochester 333 Westmoreland Dr Web: www.rmhcrochester.org	Rochester	NY	14620	585-442-5437	442-7330	373
Sacramento 2555 49th St Web: www.rmhcnc.org	Sacramento	CA	95817	916-734-4230		373
Saint Louis 4381 W Pine Blvd Web: www.rmhcstl.com	Saint Louis	MO	63108	314-531-6601	531-6353	373
Saint Louis 3450 Pk Ave Web: www.rmhcstl.com	Saint Louis	MO	63104	314-773-1100	773-2053	373
San Antonio 227 Lewis St Web: ronaldmcdonaldhouse-sa.org	San Antonio	TX	78212	210-223-6014		373
San Antonio 4803 Sid Katz Dr Web: www.rmhcsanantonio.org	San Antonio	TX	78229	210-614-2554		373
San Diego 2929 Children's Way Web: www.rmhcsd.org	San Diego	CA	92123	858-467-4750	467-4757	373
San Francisco 1640 Scott St Web: www.ronaldhouse-sf.org	San Francisco	CA	94115	415-673-0891	673-1335	373
Saskatoon 1011 University Dr Web: www.rmh.sk.ca	Saskatoon	SK	S7N0K4	306-244-5700	244-3099	373
Scranton 332 Wheeler Ave Web: rmhscranton.org	Scranton	PA	18510	570-969-8998		373
Seattle 5130 40th Ave NE TF: 866-987-9330 ■ Web: www.rmhcseattle.org	Seattle	WA	98105	206-838-0600		373
Sleepy Hollow 520 N Rutan Web: www.rmhcwichita.org	Wichita	KS	67208	316-687-2000		373
Spokane 1015 W Fifth Ave Web: rmhcinlandnw.org	Spokane	WA	99204	509-624-0500	624-3267	373
Springfield 34 Chapin Terr Web: www.rmhc-ctma.org	Springfield	MA	01107	413-794-5683		373
Springfield 949 E Primrose St Web: www.rmhcozarks.org	Springfield	MO	65807	417-886-0225		373

	City	State	ZIP	Phone	Fax	Class
Tallahassee 712 E Seventh Ave	Tallahassee	FL	32303	850-222-0056	222-0086	373
Web: www.rmhctallahassee.org						
Tampa 35 Columbia Dr	Tampa	FL	33606	813-254-2398		070
Web: rmhctampabay.org						
Temple 2415 S 47th St	Temple	TX	76504	254-770-0910		373
Web: rmhc-temple.com						
Topeka 825 SW Buchanan St	Topeka	KS	66606	785-235-6852		373
Web: www.rmhcneks.org						
Toronto 240 McCaul St	Toronto	ON	M5T1W5	416-977-0458	977-8807	373
Web: www.rmhctoronto.ca						
Tucson 2155 E Allen Rd	Tucson	AZ	85719	520-326-0060		373
Web: www.rmhctucson.org						
Tulsa 6102 S Hudson Ave	Tulsa	OK	74136	918-496-2727	496-2762	373
Web: www.rmhtulsa.org						
Washington 3727 14th St NE	Washington	DC	20017	202-529-8204	635-3578	373
Web: rmhcdc.org						
Wauwatosa 8948 W Watertown Plank Rd	Wauwatosa	WI	53226	414-475-5333	475-6342	373
Web: rmhcmilwaukee.org						
Wilmington 1901 Rockland Rd	Wilmington	DE	19803	302-656-4847		373
TF: 888-656-4847 ■ *Web:* www.rmhde.org						
Winnipeg 566 Bannatyne Ave	Winnipeg	MB	R3A0G7	204-774-4777	774-2160	373
Web: www.rmhmanitoba.org						
Winston-Salem						
419 S Hawthorne Rd	Winston-Salem	NC	27103	336-723-0228	723-0302	373
TF: 855-227-7435 ■ *Web:* www.rmhws.org						
Ronald McDonald House BC						
4567 Heather St	Vancouver	BC	V5Z0C9	604-736-2957	736-5974	373
Web: www.rmhbc.ca						
Maine 250 Brackett St	Portland	ME	04102	207-780-6282	780-0198	373
Ronald McDonald House Charities (RMHC)						
1 Kroc Dr	Oak Brook	IL	60523	630-623-7048	623-7488	48-5
Web: www.rmhc.org						
Atlanta						
5420 Peachtree Dunwoody Rd	Sandy Springs	GA	30342	404-847-0760		373
Web: www.armhc.org						
Calgary 111 W Campus Pl NW	Calgary	AB	T3B2R6	403-240-3000	240-1277	373
Web: www.ahomeawayfromhome.org						
Dayton 555 Valley St	Dayton	OH	45404	937-224-0047		373
Web: rmhc.org						
Gainesville 1600 SW 14th St	Gainesville	FL	32608	352-374-4404	335-5325	373
TF: 800-435-7352 ■ *Web:* www.rmhcncf.org						
Halifax 1133 Tower Rd	Halifax	NS	B3H2Y7	902-429-4044		373
Web: rmhatlantic.com						
Reno 323 Maine St	Reno	NV	89502	775-322-4663		373
Web: www.rmhc-reno.com						
Sioux City 2500 Nebraska St	Sioux City	IA	51104	712-255-4084	255-4281	373
Web: rmhc-siouxland.org						
Springfield 610 N Seventh St	Springfield	IL	62702	217-528-3314	528-6084	373
Web: www.rmhc-centralillinois.org						
Ronald McDonald House Charities Columbia						
5000 Thurmond Mall Blvd Ste 108	Columbia	SC	29201	803-254-0118	254-8688	373
Web: www.rmhcofcolumbia.org						
Ronald McDonald House Charities of Central Ohio						
711 E Livingston Ave	Columbus	OH	43205	614-227-3700		373
Web: www.rmhc-centralohio.org						
Ronald McDonald House Charities of Denver						
1300 E 21st Ave	Denver	CO	80205	303-832-2667	832-3802	373
Web: www.ronaldhouse.org						
Ronald McDonald House Charities of Kentuckiana (RMHC)						
550 S First St	Louisville	KY	40202	502-581-1416	581-0037	373
Web: www.rmhc-kentuckiana.org						
Ronald McDonald House Charities of Nashville						
Nashville 2144 Fairfax Ave	Nashville	TN	37212	615-343-4000	343-4004	373
Web: www.rmhcnashville.com						
Ronald McDonald House Charities of the Southwest						
3413 Tenth St	Lubbock	TX	79415	806-744-8877	744-3652	373
Web: www.rmhcsouthwest.com						
Ronald McDonald House Charities Southwestern Ontario						
741 Base Line Rd E	London	ON	N6C2R6	519-685-3232		373
Web: www.rmhlondon.ca						
Ronald McDonald House Charities's						
Salt Lake City 935 E Temple	Salt Lake City	UT	84102	801-363-4663	363-0092	373
Web: www.rmhcslc.org/stay-with-us/ronald-mcdonald-house						
Houston 1907 Holcombe Blvd	Houston	TX	77030	713-795-3500		373
Web: www.ronaldmcdonaldhousehouston.org						
Ronald Reagan Bldg & International Trade Ctr						
1300 Pennsylvania Ave NW	Washington	DC	20004	202-312-1300	312-1310	822
TF: 800-984-3775 ■ *Web:* www.itcdc.com						
Ronald Reagan Medical Ctr						
757 Westwood Plaza	Los Angeles	CA	90095	310-825-9111	825-7271	374-3
Web: www.uclahealth.org						
Ronald Reagan Middle School						
620 Division St	Dixon	IL	61021	815-284-7725		685
Web: dixonschools.org						
Ronald Reagan Presidential Library & Museum						
40 Presidential Dr	Simi Valley	CA	93065	805-522-2977	520-9702	434-2
TF: 800-410-8354						
Ronald Reagan Washington National Airport						
1 Aviation Cir	Washington	DC	20001	703-417-8000	417-8371*	27
**Fax:* PR ■ *TF:* 800-435-9294 ■ *Web:* www.mwaa.com						
Ronald T Jepson & Assoc Ps						
222 Grand Ave	Bellingham	WA	98225	360-733-5760		261
Web: jepsonengineering.com						
Ronald T Karpowich CPA 725 Front St	Freeland	PA	18224	570-636-2358		2
Ronan Engineering Co						
21200 Oxnard St	Woodland Hills	CA	91367	800-327-6626	992-6435*	201
**Fax Area Code:* 818 ■ *TF:* 800-327-6626 ■ *Web:* www.ronan.com						
Roncalli High Sch. Sisters						
2000 Mirro Dr	Manitowoc	WI	54220	920-682-8801		685
Web: roncallijets.net						
Roncelli Inc 6471 Metro Pkwy	Sterling Heights	MI	48312	586-264-2060		401
Web: www.roncelli-inc.com						
Roncelli Plastics Inc						
330 W Duarte Rd	Monrovia	CA	91016	626-359-2551		608
Web: www.roncelli.com						
Ronco Communications						
595 Sheridan Dr	Tonawanda	NY	14150	716-873-0760		681
Web: www.ronco.net						
Ronco Consulting Corp						
6710 Oxon Hill Rd Ste 200	Oxon Hill	MD	20745	240-493-3910		692
Rondout Electric Inc						
33 Arlington Ave	Poughkeepsie	NY	12600	845-471-4810		246
Web: rondoutelectric.net						
Ronin Corp 2 Research Way Ste 203	Princeton	NJ	08540	609-452-0060		195
Web: ronin.com						
Ronis Bros 39 Harriet Pl	Lynbrook	NY	11563	516-887-5266	887-5288	464
Web: www.ronis.com						
Ronningen Research & Development Co						
6700 E 'YZ' Ave	Vicksburg	MI	49097	269-649-0520	649-0526	602
Web: www.ronningenresearch.com						
Ronnybrook Farm Dairy Inc						
310 Prospect Hill Rd	Ancramdale	NY	12503	518-398-6455		10-3
Web: www.ronnybrook.com						
Ronpak Inc						
4301 New Brunswick Ave	South Plainfield	NJ	07080	732-968-8000		66
Web: www.ronpak.com						
Ron-Son Foods Inc PO Box 38	Swedesboro	NJ	08085	856-241-7333	241-7338	297-11
Web: www.ronsonfoods.com						
Rood Riddle & Partners PSC						
2150 Georgetown Rd	Lexington	KY	40511	859-233-0371		794
Web: www.roodandriddle.com						
Roof Structures Inc 3333 Yale Way	Fremont	CA	94538	510-226-7171	226-8989	817
Web: www.roofstructures.com						
Roof to deck Decoration Inc						
365 Webster St Ste 6	Saint Paul	MN	55102	651-699-3504		104
TF: 800-841-2805 ■ *Web:* www.rooftodeckdecoration.com						
Roofing & Insulation Supply Inc						
12221 Merit Dr Ste 1015	Dallas	TX	75251	972-239-8309	239-8310	191-4
Web: www.risris.com						
Roofing Products & Bldg Supply Company Inc						
4955 River Rd	Jefferson	LA	70121	504-733-0404		191-4
Web: www.rfgproducts.com						
Roofing Supply Group 8319 N Lamar Blvd	Austin	TX	78753	512-834-4347	834-4352	191-4
Web: rsgroof.com						
Roofing Wholesale Co Inc						
1918 W Grant St	Phoenix	AZ	85009	602-258-3794	256-0932	191-4
Web: www.rwc.org						
Rooftop Media Inc						
188 Spear St Ste 250	San Francisco	CA	94105	800-860-0293		116
TF: 800-860-0293 ■ *Web:* rooftopcomedy.com						
Rook Security						
11350 N Meridian St Ste 600	Carmel	IN	46032	888-712-9531		196
TF: 888-712-9531						
Rooks County 115 N Walnut St	Stockton	KS	67669	785-425-6391	425-6015	338
Web: www.rookscounty.net						
Room & Board Inc						
4600 Olson Memorial Hwy	Golden Valley	MN	55422	763-521-4431	520-0811	319-2
TF: 800-301-9720 ■ *Web:* www.roomandboard.com						
Room 214 Inc 3390 Valmont Rd Ste 214	Boulder	CO	80301	866-624-1851		7
TF: 866-624-1851 ■ *Web:* room214.com						
Roomplace, The 1000-46 Rohlwing Rd	Lombard	IL	60148	630-261-3900		321
TF: 800-318-9806 ■ *Web:* www.theroomplace.com						
Roomstores of Phoenix LLC, The						
3011 E Broadway Rd Ste 100	Phoenix	AZ	85040	602-268-1111		321
Web: arizonaroomstore.com						
Rooney Francis (Rep R - FL)						
120 Cannon HOB	Washington	DC	20515	202-225-2536		342-2
Web: francisrooney.house.gov						
Rooney Tom (Rep R - FL)						
2160 Rayburn HOB	Washington	DC	20515	202-225-5792	225-3132	342-2
Web: rooney.house.gov						
Roose & Ressler Lpa						
111 S Buckeye St Ste 230	Wooster	OH	44691	330-263-5333	263-5033	652
TF: 888-690-5033 ■ *Web:* theohiodisabilitylawyers.com						
Roosevelt & Cross Inc						
1 Exchange Plaza 55 Broadway 22nd Fl	New York	NY	10006	212-344-2500		690
TF: 800-348-3426 ■ *Web:* www.roosevelt-cross.com						
Roosevelt County						
109 W First St Lobby Box 4	Portales	NM	88130	575-356-8562	356-3560	338
Web: www.rooseveltcounty.com						
Roosevelt County 400 Second Ave S	Wolf Point	MT	59201	406-653-6250	653-6289	338
Web: rooseveltcounty.org						
Roosevelt County Electric Co-op Inc (RCEC)						
121 N Main St PO Box 389	Portales	NM	88130	575-356-4491		245
Web: www.rcec.org/content/office-location						
Roosevelt Field Mall						
630 Old Country Rd	Garden City	NY	11530	516-742-8001	742-8004	460
TF: 877-746-6642 ■ *Web:* www.simon.com						
Roosevelt Hotel 45 E 45th St	New York	NY	10017	212-661-9600	885-6168	379
TF: 877-322-8228 ■ *Web:* www.therooseevelthotel.com						
Roosevelt Paper Co						
1 Roosevelt Dr	Mount Laurel	NJ	08054	856-303-4100	642-1949*	553
**Fax:* Sales ■ *TF:* 800-523-3470 ■ *Web:* www.rooseveltpaper.com						
Roosevelt Park Zoo 1219 Burdick Expy	Minot	ND	58701	701-857-4166	857-4169	823
TF: 800-435-5663 ■ *Web:* www.rpzoo.com						
Roosevelt State Park 2149 Hwy 13 S	Morton	MS	39117	601-732-6316		565
Web: www.mdwfp.com						
Roosevelt University						
430 S Michigan Ave	Chicago	IL	60605	312-341-3500		166
TF Admissions: 877-277-5978 ■ *Web:* www.roosevelt.edu						
Albert A Robin						
1400 N Roosevelt Blvd	Schaumburg	IL	60173	847-619-7300	619-8636*	166
**Fax:* Admissions ■ *TF Admissions:* 877-277-5978 ■ *Web:* www.roosevelt.edu						
Roosevelt Warm Springs Institute for Rehabilitation						
6135 Roosevelt Hwy	Warm Springs	GA	31830	706-655-5000		374-6
Roost Home Furnishings						
200 Gate Five Rd Number 116	Sausalito	CA	94965	415-339-9500		321
Web: www.roostco.com						
Rooster Energy Ltd						
16285 Park Ten Pl Ste 120	Houston	TX	77084	832-772-6313		536
Web: www.roosterenergyltd.com						
Rooster Park 901 Thomas St	Seattle	WA	98109	206-801-0189		177
Web: www.roosterpark.com						
Rooster's 253 25th St	Ogden	UT	84401	801-627-6171		671
Web: roostersbrewingco.com						
Root Candles Co 623 W Liberty St	Medina	OH	44256	330-725-6677	725-5624	122
TF: 800-289-7668 ■ *Web:* www.rootcandles.com						

	Phone	Fax	Class
Root Consulting Inc 2018 N Durham Durham Dr .... Houston TX 77008 *Web:* www.rootcon.com	713-523-8976		809
Root Group Inc, The 1790 30th St Ste 140 .... Boulder CO 80301 *Web:* www.rootgroup.com	303-447-8093		180
Root Inc 5470 Main St .... Sylvania OH 43560 *TF:* 800-852-1315 ■ *Web:* www.rootinc.com	800-852-1315		196
Root-Lowell Manufacturing Co 1000 Foreman Rd PO Box 289 .... Lowell MI 49331 *TF:* 800-748-0098 ■ *Web:* www.rlflomaster.com	800-748-0098	968-3555	273
RootsWeb.com 360 W 4800 N .... Provo UT 84604 *TF:* 800-262-3787 ■ *Web:* www.rootsweb.ancestry.com	801-705-7000	705-7001	397
Roper Corp 1507 Broomtown Rd .... La Fayette GA 30728 *Web:* roperappliances.com	706-638-5100		36
Roper Hospital 316 Calhoun St. .... Charleston SC 29401 *Web:* rsfh.com	843-724-2000		374-3
Roper Lake State Park 101 E Roper Lake Rd .... Safford AZ 85546 *Web:* azstateparks.itinio.com	928-428-6760		565
Roper Mobile Technology 7450 S Priest Dr. .... Tempe AZ 85283	480-705-4200		173-2
Roper Mountain Science Ctr 402 Roper Mtn Rd .... Greenville SC 29615 *Web:* www.ropermountain.org	864-355-8900		520
Roper Performing Arts Ctr 340 Granby St. .... Norfolk VA 23510 *Web:* www.tccropercenter.org	757-822-1450		572
Roper Pump Co 3475 Old Maysville Rd. .... Commerce GA 30529 *TF Sales:* 800-944-6769 ■ *Web:* www.roperpumps.com	706-335-5551	335-5490	641
Roper Whitney of Rockford Inc 2833 Huffman Blvd. .... Rockford IL 61103 **Fax:* Sales ■ *TF:* 800-962-3011 ■ *Web:* www.roperwhitney.com	815-962-3011	962-2227*	456
Ropes & Gray LLP 1 International Pl .... Boston MA 02110 *Web:* www.ropesgray.com	617-951-7000	951-7050	428
Ropes Associates Inc 333 N New River Dr 3rd Fl .... Ft. Lauderdale FL 33301 *Web:* www.ropesassociates.com	954-525-6600		196
ROPH (Rush Oak Park Hospital) 520 S Maple Ave. .... Oak Park IL 60304 *TF:* 800-515-0171 ■ *Web:* www.roph.org	708-383-9300		374-3
Rophi Technical Services East 814 S Rosedale Ct .... Grosse Pointe Woods MI 48236 *Web:* www.rophi.com	313-417-2021		180
Roplast Industries Inc 3155 S Fifth Ave .... Oroville CA 95965 *TF:* 800-767-5278 ■ *Web:* www.roplast.com	530-532-9500	532-9576	66
Roppe Corp 1602 N Union St. .... Fostoria OH 44830 *TF:* 800-537-9527 ■ *Web:* www.roppe.com	419-435-8546	435-1056	291
Roque Bluffs State Park 145 Schoppee Pt Rd. .... Roque Bluffs ME 04654 *Web:* www.maine.gov	207-255-3475		565
Roquemore & Roquemore Inc 329 Oaks Trl Ste 212 .... Garland TX 75043 *Web:* www.roquemore.com	972-226-9266		160
Roquette America 1417 Exchange St PO Box 6647 .... Keokuk IA 52632 *Web:* www.roquette.com	319-524-5757	526-2345	296-23
Rorke Data Inc 7626 Golden Triangle Dr. .... Eden Prairie MN 55344 *TF:* 800-328-8147 ■ *Web:* support.rorke.com/legacy	952-829-0300	829-0988	174
Rory Dolan's 890 McLean Ave .... Yonkers NY 10704 *Web:* www.rorydolans.com	914-776-2946	776-6538	671
Ros Technology Services Inc 8500 NW River Park Dr Ste 342 .... Parkville MO 64152 *Web:* www.rosnet.com	816-746-4100		809
Rosa + Wesley Inc 400 S Knoll St Ste B. .... Wheaton IL 60187 *Web:* www.rosawesley.com	630-588-9801	588-9804	94
Rosa's Mexican Grill 328 E University Dr .... Mesa AZ 85201 *Web:* rosasgrill.com	480-964-5451		671
Rosalie's 46 Cottage St .... Bar Harbor ME 04609 *Web:* rosaliespizza.com	207-288-5666		671
Rosalind Franklin University of Medicine & Science Learning Resource Ctr 3333 Green Bay Rd. .... North Chicago IL 60064 *TF:* 800-244-1177 ■ *Web:* www.rosalindfranklin.edu	847-578-3000		434-1
Rosamond Gifford Zoo at Burnet Park 1 Conservation Pl. .... Syracuse NY 13204 *TF:* 800-724-5006 ■ *Web:* rosamondgiffordzoo.org	315-435-8511	435-8517	823
Rosario Resort & Spa 1400 Rosario Rd. .... Eastsound WA 98245 *TF:* 800-562-8820 ■ *Web:* www.rosarioresort.com	360-376-2222	376-2289	669
Rosaryville State Park 7805 W Marlton Ave. .... Upper Marlboro MD 20735 *Web:* dnr.maryland.gov/publiclands/Pages/southern/rosaryville.aspx	301-856-9656		565
Rosati's Pizza 28381 Davis Pkwy Ste 701 .... Warrenville IL 60555 *Web:* rosatispizza.com	630-393-2280	393-2281	670
Rosauers Super Markets Inc 1815 W Garland Ave. .... Spokane WA 99205 *Web:* www.rosauers.com	509-326-8900	328-2483	345
Rosback Co 125 Hawthorne Ave .... Saint Joseph MI 49085 *TF:* 800-542-2420 ■ *Web:* www.rosbackcompany.com	269-983-2582	983-2516	629
Rosboro Lumber Co 2509 Main St .... Springfield OR 97477 *Web:* www.rosboro.com	541-746-8411	726-8919	683
Rosco Laboratories Inc 52 Harbor View Ave .... Stamford CT 06902 *TF:* 800-767-2669 ■ *Web:* www.rosco.com	203-708-8900	708-8919	722
Roscoe & Swanson Accountancy 3848 W Carson St Ste 215 .... Torrance CA 90503 *Web:* rscpa.com	310-540-5300		2
Roscoe Co 3535 W Harrison St .... Chicago IL 60624 *TF Cust Svc:* 888-476-7263 ■ *Web:* www.eroscoe.com	773-722-5000	722-0827	442
Roscoe Medical Inc 21973 Commerce Pkwy .... Strongsville OH 44149 *TF:* 800-376-7263 ■ *Web:* www.roscoemedical.com	440-572-1962		194
Roscoe Moss Co 4360 Worth St. .... Los Angeles CA 90063 *Web:* www.roscoemoss.com	323-263-4111	263-4497	595
Roscoe Steel 1501 S 30th St W. .... Billings MT 59102 *Web:* www.truenorthsteel.com	406-656-2253		480
Roscoe Village 600 N Whitewoman St .... Coshocton OH 43812 *TF:* 800-877-1830 ■ *Web:* www.roscoevillage.com	740-622-7644		520
Roscoe's House of Chicken & Waffles 730 E Broadway .... Long Beach CA 90802 *Web:* www.roscoeschickenandwaffles.com	562-437-8355		671
Roscoe's Root Beer & Ribs 603 Fourth St SE .... Rochester MN 55904 *Web:* roscoesbbq.com	507-285-0501		671
Roscommon County 500 Lake St .... Roscommon MI 48653 *TF:* 800-492-5742 ■ *Web:* www.roscommoncounty.net	989-275-5923	275-8640	338
Rose & Kiernan Inc 99 Troy Rd .... East Greenbush NY 12061 *TF:* 866-488-6582 ■ *Web:* www.rkinsurance.com	518-244-4245	244-4262	391-5
Rose & Sherle Wagner Foundation 224 W 29th St Fl 12 .... New York NY 10001 *TF:* 800-621-4000 ■ *Web:* yayanetwork.org	212-239-0022		305
Rose & Walker Supply Lafayette Inc (RWS) 3565 US Hwy 52 S .... Lafayette IN 47905 *Web:* www.roseandwalkersupply.com	765-471-7070	474-7507	191-2
Rose Aircraft Interiors Inc 132 Flight Ln .... Mena AR 71953 *Web:* www.roseaircraft.com	479-394-2551		63
Rose Assoc Inc 200 Madison Ave. .... New York NY 10016 *TF:* 888-475-8860 ■ *Web:* www.rosenyc.com	212-210-6666		652
Rose Bowl 1001 Rose Bowl Dr. .... Pasadena CA 91103 *TF:* 800-939-1293 ■ *Web:* www.rosebowlstadium.com	626-577-3100	405-0992	720
Rose Bowl Aquatics Ctr 360 N Arroyo Blvd .... Pasadena CA 91103 *Web:* www.rosebowlaquatics.org	626-564-0330		31
Rose Bowl Hall of Fame 391 S Orange Grove Blvd .... Pasadena CA 91184 *Web:* www.tournamentofroses.com	626-449-4100		522
Rose Bros Inc 302 Main St .... Lingle WY 82223 *Web:* rosebrosinc.com	307-837-2261		274
Rose City Rebar & Post Tensioning Co 5512-A NE 105th Ave .... Portland OR 97220 *Web:* www.rosecityrebar.com	503-252-4975		492
Rose Concrete Products Inc 733 Rose Concrete Rd .... Scott City MO 63780 *Web:* www.roseconcrete.com	573-264-2162		183
Rose Displays Ltd 35 Congress St .... Salem MA 01970 *TF:* 800-631-9707 ■ *Web:* www.rosedisplays.com	978-219-8100		194
Rose F. Kennedy Ctr *Albert Einstein College of Medicine* 1410 Pelham Pkwy S. .... Bronx NY 10461 *Web:* www.einstein.yu.edu	718-430-8500	918-7505	668
Rose Financial Services LLC 2 Research Pl Ste 300. .... Rockville MD 20850 *Web:* www.rosefinancial.com	301-527-1130		734
Rose Hill Hospitality House 605 26 1/2 Rd. .... Grand Junction CO 81506 *Web:* www.sclhealth.org	970-243-7068		372
Rose Hill Plantation State Historic Site 2677 SaRdis Rd .... Union SC 29379 *Web:* www.southcarolinaparks.com	864-427-5966		565
Rose Hotel 807 Main St. .... Pleasanton CA 94566 *TF:* 800 843-9540 ■ *Web:* www.rosehotel.net	925-846-8802	846-2272	379
Rose International 16401 Swingley Ridge Rd Ste 300 .... Chesterfield MO 63017 *Web:* www.roseit.com	636-812-4000	812-0076	177
Rose Island Lighthouse Foundation 365 Thames St Second Fl PO Box 1419 .... Newport RI 02840 *Web:* www.roseislandlighthouse.org	401-847-4242	847-7262	50-3
Rose Law Firm A Professional Assn 120 E Fourth St. .... Little Rock AR 72201 *Web:* www.roselawfirm.com	501-375-9131	375-1309	428
Rose Leonard & Sons Inc 212 Decatur St .... Doylestown PA 18901	215-345-9263		610
Rose Medical Ctr 4567 E Ninth Ave .... Denver CO 80220 *TF:* 877-647-7440 ■ *Web:* www.rosemed.com	303-320-2121		374-3
Rose Metal Products Inc 1955 E Div St .... Springfield MO 65803 *Web:* www.rosemetalproducts.com	417-865-1676	865-7673	482
Rose Packing Company Inc 65 S Barrington Rd. .... South Barrington IL 60010 **Fax:* Cust Svc ■ *TF:* 800-323-7363 ■ *Web:* www.rosepacking.com	847-381-5700	381-9436*	473
Rose Plastic USA Lp 525 Technology Dr .... Coal Center PA 15423 *Web:* www.rose-plastic.us	724-938-8530		600
Rose Printing Company Inc 2503 Jackson Bluff Rd .... Tallahassee FL 32304 *TF:* 800-227-3725 ■ *Web:* www.roseprinting.com	850-576-4151		626
Rose Products & Services Inc 545 Stimmel Rd .... Columbus OH 43223 *TF:* 800-264-1568 ■ *Web:* hillyard.com	614-443-7647	443-2771	406
Rose Radiology Boot Ranch 4133 Woodlands Pkwy .... Palm Harbor FL 34685 *TF:* 877-674-7673 ■ *Web:* www.roseradiology.com	727-781-3888		415
Rose Shattuck & Associates LLC 4505 Fair Meadows Ln Ste 205 .... Raleigh NC 27607 *Web:* shattuckconsulting.com	919-256-1675		196
Rose State College 6420 SE 15th St .... Midwest City OK 73110 **Fax:* Admissions ■ *TF:* 866-621-0987 ■ *Web:* www.rose.edu	405-733-7372	736-0309*	162
Rose Tattoo Cafe 1847 Callowhill St .... Philadelphia PA 19130 *Web:* www.rosetattoocafe.com	215-569-8939		671
Rose Thai 5333 Monroe St. .... Toledo OH 43623	419-841-8467		671
Rose Tree Media School District 308 N Olive St .... Media PA 19063 *Web:* www.rtmsd.org	610-627-6000		685
Rose, Snyder & Jacobs LLP 15821 Ventura Blvd Ste 490 .... Encino CA 91436 *Web:* rsjcpa.com	818-461-0600		160
Roseau County 605 Fifth Ave SW .... Roseau MN 56751 *Web:* www.visitnwminnesota.com/Roseau.htm	218-463-2541		338
Roseau Electric Co-op Inc 1107 Third St NE .... Roseau MN 56751 *TF:* 888-847-8840 ■ *Web:* roseauelectric.coop	218-463-1543	463-3713	245

				Phone	Fax	Class
Roseborough Travel Agency Inc 140 E Indiana Ave · *Web:* roseboroughtravel.com	Deland	FL	32724	386-734-7245		775
Rosebud Agency PO Box 170429 · *TF:* 800-937-4451 ■ *Web:* www.rosebudus.com	San Francisco	CA	94117	415-386-3456	386-0599	731
Rosebud Battlefield State Park PO Box 1630 · *Web:* www.stateparks.com	Miles City	MT	59301	406-232-0900		565
Rosebud County 1200 Main St · *Web:* www.rosebudmontana.com	Forsyth	MT	59327	406-346-7322		338
Rosebud Electric Co-op Inc 512 Rosebud Ave PO Box 439 · *TF:* 888-464-9304 ■ *Web:* www.rosebudelectric.com	Gregory	SD	57533	605-835-9624		245
Rosebud Restaurant 1419 W Diversey Pkwy · *TF:* 800-255-2414 ■ *Web:* www.rosebudrestaurants.com	Chicago	IL	60614	773-325-9700		670
Rosebud Wood Products 701 SE 12th St · *TF:* 800-256-4561 ■ *Web:* www.rosebudmfg.com	Madison	SD	57042	605-256-4561	256-3842	115
Roseburg Forest Products Co PO Box 1088 · *TF:* 800-245-1115 ■ *Web:* www.roseburg.com	Roseburg	OR	97470	541-679-3311		683
Roseburg National Cemetery 1770 Harvard Blvd · *TF:* 800-535-1117 ■ *Web:* www.cem.va.gov/cems/nchp/roseburg.asp	Roseburg	OR	97470	541-826-2511		136
Rosecroft Raceway 6336 Rosecroft Dr · *Web:* www.rosecroft.com	Fort Washington	MD	20744	301-567-4500	567-1053	133
Rosedale Barbeque 600 SW Blvd · *Web:* rosedalebarbeque.com	Kansas City	KS	66103	913-262-0343		671
Rosedale Bible College 2270 Rosedale Rd · **Fax Area Code:* 877 ■ *Web:* www.rosedale.edu	Irwin	OH	43029	740-857-1311	857-1312*	161
Rosedale Development Assn 1403 SW Blvd	Kansas City	KS	66103	913-677-5097		50-4
Rosedale on Robson Suite Hotel 838 Hamilton St · *TF:* 800-661-8870 ■ *Web:* www.rosedaleonrobson.com	Vancouver	BC	V6B6A2	604-689-8033	689-4426	379
Rosedale Products Inc 3730 W Liberty Rd PO Box 1085 · *Web:* www.rosedaleproducts.com	Ann Arbor	MI	48106	734-665-8201		520
Rosedale Technical Institute 215 Beecham Dr Ste 2 · *TF:* 800-521-6262 ■ *Web:* www.rosedaletech.org	Pittsburgh	PA	15205	412-521-6200		148
Rosedown Plantation State Historic Site 12501 Hwy 10 · *TF:* 888-376-1867 ■ *Web:* crt.state.la.us	Saint Francisville	LA	70775	225-635-3332		50-3
Rose-Hulman Institute of Technology 5500 Wabash Ave · *TF Admissions:* 800-248-7448 ■ *Web:* www.rose-hulman.edu	Terre Haute	IN	47803	812-877-1511	877-8941	166
Roseland Community Hospital 45 W 111th St · *Web:* roselandhospital.org	Chicago	IL	60628	773-995-3000		374-3
Roselle Savings Bank Inc 235 Chestnut St · *Web:* www.rosellesavings.com	Roselle	NJ	07203	908-245-1885		70
Rosellen Suites at Stanley Park 2030 Barclay St · *TF:* 888-317-6648 ■ *Web:* www.rosellensuites.com	Vancouver	BC	V6G1L5	604-689-4807		379
Rosemarie Arnold Law Offices 1386 Palisade Ave · *Web:* www.rosemariearnold.com	Fort Lee	NJ	07024	201-461-1111		428
Rosemead Chamber of Commerce 3953 Muscatel Ave · *Web:* rosemeadchamber.org	Rosemead	CA	91770	626-288-0811	288-2514	139
Rosemead College of English 8705 E Valley Blvd · *Web:* www.rosemeadcollege.edu	Rosemead	CA	91770	626-285-9668	285-1351	423
Rosemont College 1400 Montgomery Ave · **Fax:* Admissions ■ *TF Admissions:* 888-521-0983 ■ *Web:* www.rosemont.edu	Rosemont	PA	19010	610-527-0200	526-2971*	166
Rosemont Convention Bureau 9301 Bryn Mawr Ave · *TF:* 800-610-6500 ■ *Web:* www.rosemont.com	Rosemont	IL	60018	847-823-2100	696-9700	206
Rosemont Suites 181 W Town St · *Web:* www.whghotels.com	Norwich	CT	06360	860-889-2671		378
Rosemont Theatre 5400 N River Rd · *Web:* rosemont.com/theatre	Rosemont	IL	60018	847-671-5100	671-6405	572
Rosemore Inc One N Charles St 22nd Fl Ste 2300 · *TF:* 800-343-3500 ■ *Web:* www.rosemoreinc.com	Baltimore	MD	21201	410-347-7080		538
Rosen Assoc Management Corp 33 S Service Rd · *Web:* www.rosenmgmt.com	Jericho	NY	11753	516-333-2000		655
Rosen Aviation LLC 1020 Owen Loop S · *Web:* www.rosenaviation.com	Eugene	OR	97402	541-342-3802		57
Rosen Centre Hotel 9840 International Dr · *TF:* 800-204-7234 ■ *Web:* www.rosencentre.com	Orlando	FL	32819	407-996-9840	996-0865	379
Rosen Group LLC, The 44 Wall St Ste 705 · *Web:* rosengrouppr.com	New York	NY	10005	212-255-8455		636
Rosen Hotels & Resorts Inc 9840 International Dr · *TF:* 800-204-7234 ■ *Web:* www.rosenhotels.com	Orlando	FL	32819	407-996-9840	996-0865	379
Rosen Jacky (Rep D - NV) 413 Cannon HOB · *Web:* rosen.house.gov	Washington	DC	20515	202-225-3252		342-2
Rosen Law Firm LLC 18 Broad St Ste 201 · *TF:* 800-237-2000 ■ *Web:* www.rosen-lawfirm.com	Charleston	SC	29401	843-377-1700		428
Rosen Plaza Hotel 9700 International Dr · *TF:* 800-366-9700 ■ *Web:* www.rosenplaza.com	Orlando	FL	32819	407-996-9700	354-5774	379
Rosen Publishing Group Inc, The 29 E 21st St · **Fax Area Code:* 888 ■ *TF:* 800-237-9932 ■ *Web:* www.rosenpublishing.com	New York	NY	10010	800-237-9932	436-4643*	637-2
Rosen Sapperstein & Friedlander Cht 300 Red Brook Blvd · *Web:* rsfchart.com	Owings Mills	MD	21117	410-581-0800		2
Rosen Seymour Shapss Martin & Company LLP 757 Third Ave 6th Fl	New York	NY	10017	212-303-1800	755-5600	2
Rosen Shingle Creek 9939 Universal Blvd · *TF:* 866-996-9939 ■ *Web:* www.rosenshinglecreek.com	Orlando	FL	32819	407-996-9939		379
Rosen's Diversified Inc 1120 Lake Ave PO Box 933 · *TF:* 800-345-0293 ■ *Web:* www.rosensdiversifiedinc.com	Fairmont	MN	56031	507-238-6001		360-3
Rosenbach Museum & Library 2008-2010 Delancey St · *Web:* www.rosenbach.org	Philadelphia	PA	19103	215-732-1600		520
Rosenbaum Family House 30 Family House Dr PO Box 8228 · *TF:* 855-988-2273 ■ *Web:* wvuhealthcare.com/wvuh/404	Morgantown	WV	26506	304-598-6094	598-6412	372
RosenbaumRollins & Olah PC 30230 Orchard Lake Rd Ste 200 · *Web:* www.rrocpas.com	Farmington Hills	MI	48334	248-855-6640		2
Rosenberg Advertising 12613 Detroit Ave · *Web:* rosenbergadv.com	Lakewood	OH	44107	216-529-7910		7
Rosenberg Library 2310 Sealy Ave · *Web:* www.rosenberg-library.org	Galveston	TX	77550	409-763-8854	763-0275	434-3
Rosenberger North America 6970 Central Hwy · *Web:* www.tothtech.com	Pennsauken	NJ	08109	856-662-8700		393
Rosenblatt Securities Inc 40 Wall St 59th Fl · *Web:* rblt.com	New York	NY	10005	212-607-3100		401
Rosenblum & Cohen CPAs 100 Merrick Rd	Rockville Centre	NY	11570	516-763-1212		2
Rosenblum-silverman-sutton Sf Inc 1388 Sutter St Ste 725 · *Web:* www.rssic.com	San Francisco	CA	94109	415-771-4500		401
Rosenboom Machine & Tool Inc 1530 Western Ave · *Web:* www.rosenboom.com	Sheldon	IA	51201	712-324-4854		358
Rosencrantz-Bemis Water Well Co 1105 Hwy 281 Bypass · *TF:* 800-466-2467 ■ *Web:* kansaswaterwelldrilling.com	Great Bend	KS	67530	620-793-5512		189-15
Rosendin Electric Inc 880 N Mabury Rd · *Web:* www.rosendin.com	San Jose	CA	95133	408-286-2800		189-4
Rosenn, Jenkins & Greenwald LLP 15 S Franklin St · *TF:* 800-888-4754 ■ *Web:* www.rjglaw.com	Wilkes-Barre	PA	18711	570-826-5600		428
Rosenstiel School of Marine & Atmospheric Science University of Miami 4600 Rickenbacker Causeway Rosenstiel School · *Web:* www.rsmas.miami.edu	Miami	FL	33149	305-421-4000		166
Rosenthal & Rosenthal Inc 1370 Broadway · *Web:* www.rosenthalinc.com	New York	NY	10018	212-356-1400		272
Rosenthal Appraisal Company Inc 6 W Railroad Ave · *Web:* www.rosappraisal.com	Tenafly	NJ	07670	201-567-4300		41
Rosenthal Automotive Organization 1902 Association Dr · *Web:* www.rosenthalauto.com	Reston	VA	20191	703-553-4300		57
Rosenthal Bros Inc 740 Waukegan Rd Ste 402 · *Web:* www.rosenthalbros.com	Deerfield	IL	60015	847-940-4300		390
Rosenthal Collins Group LLC (RCG) 216 W Jackson Blvd Ste 400 · **Fax:* Hum Res ■ *Web:* www.rcgdirect.com	Chicago	IL	60606	312-460-9200	795-7730*	169
Rosenthal Retirement Planning LP 1412 Main St 6th Fl · *Web:* www.rrp.com	Dallas	TX	75202	214-752-1000		401
Rosenwasser Grossman Consulting 519 8h Ave 20th Fl · *Web:* www.rosenwassergrossman.com	New York	NY	10018	212-564-2424		261
RoseRyan Inc 35473 Dumbarton Ct · *Web:* www.roseryan.com	Newark	CA	94560	510-456-3056		194
Roses Southwest Papers Inc 1701 Second St SW · *Web:* www.rosessouthwestpapers.com	Albuquerque	NM	87102	505-842-0134	242-0342	65
Rosetta Stone Ltd 1919 N Lynn St 7th Fl · *NYSE:* RST ■ **Fax Area Code:* 540 ■ *TF:* 800-788-0822 ■ *Web:* www.rosettastone.com	Arlington	VA	22209	800-788-0822	432-0953*	685
Roseville Chamber of Commerce 650 Douglas Blvd · *Web:* www.rosevillechamber.com	Roseville	CA	95678	916-783-8136		139
Roseville Joint Union High School District Fin Corp 1750 Cirby Way · *Web:* www.rjuhsd.k12.ca.us	Roseville	CA	95661	916-786-2051	786-2681	685
Roseville Medical Ctr 1 Medical Plaza · *TF:* 800-866-7724 ■ *Web:* www.sutterroseville.org	Roseville	CA	95661	916-781-1000	781-1210	374-3
Roseville Public Library 29777 Gratiot Ave · *Web:* www.libcoop.net	Roseville	MI	48066	586-445-5407	445-5499	434-3
Roseville Public Library 225 Taylor St · *TF:* 800-984-4636 ■ *Web:* rosevillelibraryfoundation.org	Roseville	CA	95678	916-774-5221		434-3
Rosewater Supper Club 19 Toronto St · *Web:* www.libertygroup.com	Toronto	ON	M5C2R1	416-214-5888	214-2412	671
Rosewell Toyota 2211 W Second St · *Web:* www.roswelltoyota.com	Roswell	NM	88201	575-622-5860		57
Rosewood Capital 1 Maritime Plaza Ste 1575	San Francisco	CA	94111	415-362-5526	362-1192	792
Rosewood Care Center Holding Co 100 Rosewood Village Dr · *TF:* 800-213-0154 ■ *Web:* www.rosewoodnursing.com	Swansea	IL	62226	618-236-1391		138
Rosewood Hotels & Resorts 500 Crescent Ct Ste 300 · *TF:* 888-767-3966 ■ *Web:* www.rosewoodhotels.com	Dallas	TX	75201	214-880-4200	880-4201	379
Rosewood Hotels and Resorts LLC 2821 Turtle Creek Blvd · *Web:* www.rosewoodhotels.com	Dallas	TX	75219	214-559-2100	528-4187	671
Rosewood Industries Inc 1203 E Central Terr · *TF:* 800-228-3306 ■ *Web:* www.rosewood.net	Stigler	OK	74462	800-228-3306		321

Name / Address	City	State	Zip	Phone	Fax	Class
Rosewood Little Dix Bay PO Box 720 Saint John	Cruz Bay	VI	00831	284-495-5555		377
Web: www.rosewoodhotels.com/en/little-dix-bay-virgin-gorda						
Rosewood Retirement Community 1301 New Stine Rd	Bakersfield	CA	93309	661-834-0620		672
TF: 800-984-4216 ■ *Web:* www.rosewoodretirement.org						
Rosey Baby 4587 N University Dr	Lauderhill	FL	33351	954-749-5627		671
TF: 800-227-0560 ■ *Web:* www.roseybaby.com						
Roshanian & Associates Inc 6404 Wilshire Blvd	Los Angeles	CA	90048	323-933-5252		261
Web: www.roshanian.com						
Roshi Tech Inc 5 Castleton Ct	Merrimack	NH	03054	603-889-2211		177
Web: www.roshitech.com						
Rosicrucian Egyptian Museum & Planetarium 1342 Naglee Ave Rosicrucian Pk	San Jose	CA	95191	408-947-3600		520
TF: 800-882-6672 ■ *Web:* www.rosicrucian.org						
Rosie the Riveter/World War II Home Front National Historical Park 1401 Marina Way S	Richmond	CA	94804	510-232-5050		564
Web: www.nps.gov						
Rosin Eyecare Ctr 6233 W Cermak Rd	Berwyn	IL	60402	708-749-2020		542
TF: 800-499-7674 ■ *Web:* www.rosineyecare.com						
Rosina Food Products Inc 170 French Rd	Buffalo	NY	14227	716-668-0123		296-26
Web: www.rosina.com						
Rosine's 434 Alvarado St	Monterey	CA	93940	831-375-1400	375-2636	671
TF: 800-621-5197 ■ *Web:* www.rosinesmonterey.com						
Rosine's 721 S Weir Canyon Rd	Anaheim	CA	92808	714-283-5141		671
Web: www.rosines.com						
Roskam Peter J (Rep R - IL) 2246 Rayburn HOB	Washington	DC	20515	202-225-4561	225-1166	342-2
Web: roskam.house.gov						
Ros-Lehtinen Ileana (Rep R - FL) 2206 Rayburn Bldg	Washington	DC	20515	202-225-3931	225-5620	342-2
Web: ros-lehtinen.house.gov						
Roslyn Claremont Hotel 1221 Old Northern Blvd	Roslyn	NY	11576	516-625-2700	625-2731	379
TF: 800-626-9005 ■ *Web:* theroslynhotel.com						
Rosner Auto Group 3507 Jefferson Davis Hwy	Fredericksburg	VA	22408	540-898-7900		57
TF Sales: 855-270-6270 ■ *Web:* www.rosnerauto.com						
Ross & Baruzzini 6 S Old Orchard	Saint Louis	MO	63119	314-918-8383		261
Web: www.rossbar.com						
Ross & Matthews PC 3650 Lovell Ave	Fort Worth	TX	76107	817-255-2000		428
TF: 800-458-6982 ■ *Web:* www.rossandmatthews.com						
Ross & Roberts Inc 1299 W Broad St	Stratford	CT	06615	203-378-0363		600
Ross & Wallace Paper Products Inc 204 Old Covington Hwy	Hammond	LA	70403	800-854-2300	345-1370*	65
**Fax Area Code:* 985 ■ *TF:* 800-854-2300 ■ *Web:* www.rossandwallace.com						
Ross Aluminum Castings LLC 815 N Oak Ave	Sidney	OH	45365	937-492-4134		492
TF: 800-633-8629 ■ *Web:* www.rossal.com						
Ross Buehler Falk & Company LLP (RBF) 1500 Lititz Pk	Lancaster	PA	17601	717-393-2700	393-1742	2
Web: www.rbfco.com						
Ross Casting & Innovation LLC 402 S Kuther Rd PO Box 89	Sidney	OH	45365	937-497-4500		492
TF: 800-223-5624 ■ *Web:* www.rciwheels.com						
Ross Controls 1250 Stephenson Hwy	Troy	MI	48083	248-764-1800	764-1850	790
TF: 800-438-7677 ■ *Web:* www.rosscontrols.com						
Ross Correctional Institution 16149 SR 104	Chillicothe	OH	45601	740-774-7050	774-7055	213
Web: drc.ohio.gov						
Ross County 2 N Paint St Ste B	Chillicothe	OH	45601	740-702-3085		338
Web: www.co.ross.oh.us						
Ross Dennis (Rep R - FL) 436 Cannon HOB	Washington	DC	20515	202-225-1252	226-0585	342-2
Web: dennisross.house.gov						
Ross Engineering Inc 32 Westgate Blvd	Savannah	GA	31405	912-238-3300		190
Web: www.storagevessels.com						
Ross Group Inc 2730 Indian Ripple Rd	Dayton	OH	45440	800-734-9304		225
TF: 800-734-9304 ■ *Web:* www.rossgroupinc.com						
Ross Industries Inc 5321 Midland Rd	Midland	VA	22728	540-439-3271	439-2740	298
TF: 800-336-6010 ■ *Web:* www.rossindinc.com						
Ross Island Sand & Gravel Co 4315 SE Mcloughlin Blvd	Portland	OR	97202	503-239-5500		182
Ross Laboratories Inc 3138 Fairview Ave E	Seattle	WA	98102	206-324-3950		529
Web: www.rosslaboratories.com						
Ross Lake National Recreation Area 810 State Rt 20	Sedro Woolley	WA	98284	360-854-7200	856-1934	564
TF: 866-705-5711 ■ *Web:* www.nps.gov/rola						
Ross Marketing Inc 2214 Main St Ste A	Cedar Falls	IA	50613	319-266-5881		195
Web: rossmarketing.net						
Ross Matthews Mills Inc 657 Quarry St	Fall River	MA	02723	508-677-0601		745-5
Ross Memorial Hospital (RMH) 10 Angeline St N	Lindsay	ON	K9V4M8	705-324-6111		374-2
TF: 800-510-7365 ■ *Web:* www.rmh.org						
Ross Metals Corp 54 W 47th St	New York	NY	10036	800-334-7191	768-3018*	485
**Fax Area Code:* 212 ■ *TF:* 800-334-7191 ■ *Web:* www.rossmetals.com						
Ross Neely Systems Inc 1500 Second St	Birmingham	AL	35214	205-798-1137		780
TF: 800-561-3357 ■ *Web:* www.rossneely.com						
Ross Optical Industries Inc 1410 Gail Borden Pl	El Paso	TX	79935	915-595-5417	595-5466	544
TF: 800-880-5417 ■ *Web:* www.rossoptical.com						
Ross Park Mall 1000 Ross Pk Mall Dr	Pittsburgh	PA	15237	412-369-4400		460
TF: 800-642-0788 ■ *Web:* www.simon.com						
Ross Realty Investments Inc 3325 S University Dr Ste 210	Davie	FL	33328	954-452-5000	452-4700	652
TF: 800-370-4202 ■ *Web:* www.ross-realty.com						
Ross Reels 11 Ponderosa Ct	Montrose	CO	81401	970-249-0606		710
Web: www.rossreels.com						
Ross Simons Jewelers Inc 9 Ross Simons Dr	Cranston	RI	02920	800-835-0919		410
TF: 800-835-0919 ■ *Web:* www.ross-simons.com						
Ross Sinclaire & Associates LLC 700 Walnut St Ste 600	Cincinnati	OH	45202	513-381-3939		690
TF: 800-543-1831 ■ *Web:* www.rsanet.com						
Ross Smith Asset Management Inc 407 - Eighth Ave SW Ste 305	Calgary	AB	T2P1E5	403-263-9104		528
Web: www.rsam.ca						
Ross Technology Corp 104 N Maple Ave	Leola	PA	17540	717-656-2200		91
TF: 800-345-8170 ■ *Web:* www.rosstechnology.com						
Ross Valley School District 110 Shaw Dr	San Anselmo	CA	94960	415-454-2162		685
TF: 800-322-6384 ■ *Web:* www.rossvalleyschools.org						
Ross Video Ltd 8 John St	Iroquois	ON	K0E1K0	613-652-4886		797
Web: www.rossvideo.com						
Ross' Grill 237-241 Commercial St Whalers Wharf	Provincetown	MA	02660	508-487-8878		671
Web: www.rossgrille.com						
Ross, Banks, May, Cron & Cavin PC 7700 San Felipe Ste 550	Houston	TX	77063	713-626-1200	623-6014	428
Web: www.rossbanks.com						
Ross, Brittain & Schonberg Company LPA Corporate Plaza II 6480 Rockside Woods Blvd S Ste 350	Cleveland	OH	44131	216-447-1551		428
TF: 800-280-0070 ■ *Web:* www.rbslaw.com						
Rosseau Lake College 1967 Bright St	Rosseau	ON	P0C1J0	705-732-4351	732-6319	622
Web: www.rosseaulakecollege.com						
Rosselló Ricardo La Fortaleza PO Box 9020082	San Juan	PR	00902	787-721-7000	721-5072	343
Web: www.fortaleza.pr.gov						
Rossi Bar & Kitchen 895 N High St	Columbus	OH	43215	614-299-2810		671
Web: rossibarandkitchen.com						
Rossi Building Materials Inc 835 Stewart St	Fort Bragg	CA	95437	707-964-4086		752
Web: www.rossi-ace.com						
Rossi Kimms & Mcdowell LLC 20609 Gordon Park Sq Ste 150	Ashburn	VA	20147	703-726-6020		428
Web: rkmllp.com						
Rossmann Macdonald & Benetti Inc 3838 Watt Ave Ste E500	Sacramento	CA	95821	916-488-8360		2
Web: www.rmb-cpa.com						
Rossmar & Graham Community Assn Management Co 9362 E Raintree Dr	Scottsdale	AZ	85260	480-551-4300	551-6000	655
Web: fsresidential.com						
Rosson House Historic Museum 113 N Sixth St	Phoenix	AZ	85004	602-262-5070		520
Web: heritagesquarephx.org						
Rossum Realty Unlimited 3875 S Jones Blvd Ste 101	Las Vegas	NV	89103	702-368-1850		652
Web: www.rossumrealty.com						
Rostra Precision Controls Inc 2519 Dana Dr	Laurinburg	NC	28352	910-276-4853	276-1354	529
TF Cust Svc: 800-782-3379 ■ *Web:* www.rostra.com						
Roswell Bookbinding Co 2614 N 29th Ave	Phoenix	AZ	85009	602-272-9338	272-9788	92
TF: 888-803-8883 ■ *Web:* www.roswellbookbinding.com						
Roswell Chamber of Commerce 131 W Second St	Roswell	NM	88201	575-623-5695	624-6870	139
TF: 877-849-7679 ■ *Web:* www.roswellnm.org						
Roswell Correctional Ctr 578 W Chickasaw Rd	Hagerman	NM	88232	575-625-3100		213
Web: cd.nm.gov/apd/rcc.html						
Roswell Livestock Auction Sales Inc 900 N Garden PO Box 2041	Roswell	NM	88202	575-622-5580		446
TF: 800-748-1541 ■ *Web:* www.roswelllivestockauction.com						
Roswell Museum & Art Ctr 100 W 11th St	Roswell	NM	88201	575-624-6744		520
Web: roswell-nm.gov/308/Roswell-Museum-Art-Center						
Roswell Park Cancer Institute Elm and Carlton St	Buffalo	NY	14263	716-845-2300		374-7
TF: 877-275-7724 ■ *Web:* www.roswellpark.org						
Roswell Park Cancer Institute Blood & Marrow Transplantation Program Elm & Carlton Sts	Buffalo	NY	14263	716-845-3516		769
TF: 800-685-6825 ■ *Web:* www.roswellpark.org						
Rosy's Fish City 2882 Story Rd	San Jose	CA	95127	408-272-2088		671
RotaDyne 1101 Windham Pkwy	Romeoville	IL	60446	630-769-9700	769-9255	677
Web: www.rotadyne.com						
Rotair Industries Inc 964 Crescent Ave	Bridgeport	CT	06607	203-576-6545		22
Web: www.rotair.com						
Rotary Botanical Gardens 1455 Palmer Dr	Janesville	WI	53545	608-752-3885	752-3853	97
Web: rotarybotanicalgardens.org						
Rotary Drilling Tools USA LP 9022 Vincik Ehlert PO Box 73	Beasley	TX	77417	979-387-3223		190
Rotary Forms Press Inc 835 S High St	Hillsboro	OH	45133	937-393-3426	393-8473	110
TF: 800-654-2876 ■ *Web:* www.rotaryfp.com						
Rotary Foundation, The 1560 Sherman Ave	Evanston	IL	60201	847-866-3000	328-8554	48-5
TF: 800-435-7352 ■ *Web:* www.rotary.org						
Rotary International 1560 Sherman Ave 1 Rotary Ctr	Evanston	IL	60201	847-866-3000	328-8554	48-15
Web: www.rotary.org						
Rotary Lift 2700 Lanier Dr	Madison	IN	47250	812-273-1622		386
TF: 800-445-5438 ■ *Web:* www.rotarylift.com						
Rotary Multiforms Inc 1340 E 11 Mile Rd	Madison Heights	MI	48071	586-558-7960		627
TF: 800-762-5644 ■ *Web:* www.rmi-printing.com						
Rotary Offset Press Inc 6600 S 231st St	Kent	WA	98032	253-813-9900		627
Web: www.rotaryoffsetpress.com						
Rotary Park 2308 Rotary Park Dr	Clarksville	TN	37043	931-648-5732		564
Rotating Machinery Services Inc 2760 Baglyos Cir	Bethlehem	PA	18020	484-821-0702		261
Web: www.rotatingmachinery.com						
Rotating Right Inc 6120 Davies Rd NW	Edmonton	AB	T6E4M9	780-485-2010		518
Rotek Inc 1400 S Chillicothe Rd PO Box 312	Aurora	OH	44202	330-562-4000	562-4620*	75
**Fax:* Sales ■ *TF:* 800-221-8043 ■ *Web:* www.rotek-inc.com						

Name / Address	City	State	Zip	Phone	Fax	Class
Rotella's Italian Bakery Inc 6949 S 108th St *Web:* www.rotellasbakery.com	La Vista	NE	68128	402-592-6600	592-2989	68
Rotenberg Meril Solomon Park 80 W Plaza 1 250 Pehle Ave Ste 101 *Web:* www.rmsbg.com	Saddle Brook	NJ	07663	201-487-8383		2
Roth & Company PC 666 Walnut Ste 1450 *Web:* www.rothcpa.com	Des Moines	IA	50309	515-244-0266		2
Roth Bros Inc 3847 Crum Rd. *TF:* 800-872-7684 ■ *Web:* www.rothbros.com	Youngstown	OH	44515	330-793-5571	793-3930	189-10
Roth Distributing Co 11300 W 47th St *TF:* 800-363-3818 ■ *Web:* www.rothliving.com	Minnetonka	MN	55343	952-933-4428		38
Roth Fabricating Inc 9600 Skyline Dr *Web:* www.rothfabricatinginc.com	Morenci	MI	49256	517-458-7541		480
Roth Farms Inc 27502 CR 880 PO Box 1300 *Web:* www.rothfarms.com	Belle Glade	FL	33430	561-996-2991		10-11
Roth Heating Company Inc 400 W Drexel Ave *Web:* rothheating.com	Oak Creek	WI	53154	414-764-4700		189-10
Roth Observatory International 120 E 79th St Ste 5C *Web:* www.askroth.com	New York	NY	10075	212-861-9420		463
Roth Pump Co PO Box 4330 *TF:* 888-444-7684 ■ *Web:* www.rothpump.com	Rock Island	IL	61204	309-787-1791	787-5142	641
Roth Ready Mix Concrete Co 900 Kieley Pl *TF:* 800-936-4937 ■ *Web:* www.cincinnatireadymix.com	Cincinnati	OH	45217	513-242-8400		182
Roth Staffing Cos LP 450 N State College Blvd Ste 100	Orange	CA	92868	714-939-8600	939-8688	721
Rothberg Logan & Warsco LLP 505 E Washington Blvd. *Web:* www.rlwlawfirm.com	Fort Wayne	IN	46802	260-422-9454		428
Rothbury Farms PO Box 202 *TF:* 877-684-2879 ■ *Web:* rothburyfarms.com	Grand Rapids	MI	49501	877-684-2879		296-1
Rothe Development Inc 4614 Sinclair Rd *TF:* 800-229-5209 ■ *Web:* www.rothe.com	San Antonio	TX	78222	210-648-3131		743
Rothenberger USA 4455 Boeing Dr *TF:* 800-545-7698 ■ *Web:* www.rothenberger-usa.com	Rockford	IL	61109	815-397-7617		455
Rothenbuhler Engineering 524 Rhodes Rd PO Box 708 *Web:* www.rothenbuhlereng.com	Sedro Woolley	WA	98284	360-856-0836	856-2183	700
Rothfus Keith (Rep R - PA) 1205 Longworth HOB *Web:* rothfus.house.gov	Washington	DC	20515	202-225-2065	225-5709	342-2
Rothman Furniture Stores Inc 2101 E Terra Ln *Web:* www.rothmanfurniture.com	O'Fallon	MO	63366	636-978-3500		321
Rothman Goodman Managmnt Corp 27236 Grand Central Pkwy	Queens	NY	11005	718-224-2880		652
Rothman Gordon PC 310 Grant St 3rd Fl Grant Bldg *Web:* www.rothmangordon.com	Pittsburgh	PA	15219	412-338-1100	281-7304	428
Rothmann's Steakhouse & Grill 3 E 54th St *Web:* www.rothmanns54.com	New York	NY	10022	212-319-5500		671
Rothschild North America Inc 1251 Ave of the Americas 51st Fl *Web:* www.rothschild.com	New York	NY	10020	212-403-3500	403-3501	401
Rotier's 2413 Elliston Pl *Web:* rotiersrestaurant.com	Nashville	TN	37203	615-327-9892		671
Rotisserie Italienne 1933 Sainte-Catherine St W *Web:* www.globeater.com	Montreal	QC	H3H1M4	514-935-4436		671
Rotmans Furniture & Carpet 725 Southbridge St *TF:* 800-768-6267 ■ *Web:* www.rotmans.com	Worcester	MA	01610	508-755-5276		321
Roto Rooter Corp 300 Ashworth Rd	West Des Moines	IA	50265	515-223-1343		427
Rotochopper Inc 217 West St PO Box 295 *Web:* www.rotochopper.com	Saint Martin	MN	56367	320-548-3586	548-3372	190
RotoMetrics Group 800 Howerton Ln *TF:* 800-325-3851 ■ *Web:* www.rotometrics.com	Eureka	MO	63025	636-587-3600	587-3701	757
Roton Products Inc 660 E Elliott Ave *Web:* www.roton.com	Saint Louis	MO	63122	314-821-4400		492
Rotonics Manufacturing Inc 6770 Brighton Blvd *TF:* 800-681-4198 ■ *Web:* www.snyderplasticsolutions.com	Commerce	CO	80022	303-227-9300		199
Rotor Clip Company Inc 187 Davidson Ave *TF Cust Svc:* 800-557-6867 ■ *Web:* www.rotorclip.com	Somerset	NJ	08873	732-469-7333	469-7898	326
Rotorcraft Services Group/Rsg Products 3900 Falcon Way W *Web:* www.rotorcraftservices.com	Fort Worth	TX	76106	817-624-6600		22
Roto-Rooter Inc 255 E Fifth St 2500 Chemed Ctr *TF:* 800-768-6911 ■ *Web:* www.rotorooter.com	Cincinnati	OH	45202	513-762-6690		189-10
Rottler Mfg 8029 S 200th St *TF:* 800-452-0534 ■ *Web:* www.rottlermfg.com	Kent	WA	98032	253-872-7050	395-0230	455
Rottler Pest & Lawn Solutions 8625 St Charles Rock Rd *Web:* www.rottler.com	Saint Louis	MO	63114	314-426-6100		577
Rotuba Extruders Inc 1401 S Pk Ave *TF:* 800-282-7933 ■ *Web:* www.rotuba.com	Linden	NJ	07036	908-486-1000	486-0874	599
Rotz Pharmacy Inc 1338 Amherst St *Web:* rotzpharmacy.com	Winchester	VA	22601	540-662-8312		237
Roubini Global Economics LLC 95 Morton St 6th Fl *Web:* roubini.com	New York	NY	10014	212-645-0010		668
Rouge 1240 Eigth Ave SE *Web:* www.rougecalgary.com	Calgary	AB	T2G0M7	403-531-2767	531-2768	671
Rouge Valley Ajax & Pickering 580 Harwood Ave S *TF:* 866-752-6989 ■ *Web:* www.rougevalley.ca	Ajax	ON	L1S2J4	905-683-2320		374-2
Rough Brothers Inc 5513 Vine St *Web:* www.roughbros.com	Cincinnati	OH	45217	513-242-0310		186
Rough Creek Lodge 5165 County Rd 2013 *TF:* 877-907-0754 ■ *Web:* www.roughcreek.com	Glen Rose	TX	76043	254-965-3700		379
Rough Notes Company Inc, The 11690 Technology Dr *TF:* 800-428-4384 ■ *Web:* www.roughnotes.com	Carmel	IN	46032	317-582-1600	816-1000	457-5
Rough Rider Industries 3303 E Main Ave *TF:* 800-732-0557 ■ *Web:* www.roughriderindustries.com	Bismarck	ND	58506	701-328-6161	328-6164	630
Rough River Dam State Resort Park 450 Lodge Rd *TF:* 800-325-1713 ■ *Web:* www.parks.ky.gov	Falls of Rough	KY	40119	270-257-2311		565
Rouis & Company LLP 51 Sullivan St	Wurtsboro	NY	12790	845-888-5656		196
Round Butte Seed Growers Inc 505 C St *TF:* 866-385-7001 ■ *Web:* helenaculver.com	Culver	OR	97734	541-546-5222		323
Round Lake Area Chamber of Commerce & Industry 2007 Civic Ctr Way *TF:* 800-334-7661 ■ *Web:* www.rlchamber.org	Round Lake Beach	IL	60073	847-546-2002	546-2254	139
Round Lake State Park 1880 Dufort Rd *Web:* idahostateparks.reserveamerica.com	Sagle	ID	83860	208-263-3489		565
Round Rock Chamber of Commerce 212 E Main St *Web:* www.roundrockchamber.org	Round Rock	TX	78664	512-255-5805		139
Round Rock ISD 1311 Round Rock Ave *Web:* www.roundrockisd.org	Round Rock	TX	78681	512-464-6000		685
Round Rock Public Library 216 E Main St *Web:* www.roundrocktexas.gov	Round Rock	TX	78664	512-218-7001		434-3
Round Sky Inc 848 N Rainbow Blvd Ste 326 *TF:* 855-826-6284 ■ *Web:* www.roundsky.com	Las Vegas	NV	89107	855-826-6284		317
Round Table Wealth Management 319 Lenox Ave *Web:* roundtablewealth.com	Westfield	NJ	07090	908-789-7310		194
Round Valley Recreation Area 1220 Lebanon-Stanton Rd *Web:* www.njparksandforests.org	Lebanon	NJ	08833	908-236-6355		565
Roundabout Theatre Co 231 W 39th St Ste 1200 *Web:* www.roundabouttheatre.org	New York	NY	10018	212-719-9393	869-8817	747
Roundhouse Marketing Services Inc 560 E Verona Ave *Web:* www.roundhouse-marketing.com	Verona	WI	53593	608-497-2550		463
RoundPegg Inc 1215 Spruce St Ste 201 *Web:* www.roundpegg.com	Boulder	CO	80302	720-663-7344		387
Rounds Mike (Sen R - SD) 502 Hart Senate Office Bldg *Web:* www.rounds.senate.gov	Washington	DC	20510	202-224-5842	224-7482	342-2
Roundtable Investment Partners LLC 280 Park Ave E 23rd Fl *Web:* www.roundtableip.com	New York	NY	10017	212-488-4700		401
Rountree Transport & Rigging Inc 2640 N Ln Ave *TF:* 800-342-5036 ■ *Web:* rountreetransport.com	Jacksonville	FL	32254	904-781-1033	786-6229	780
Rourke & Blumenthal LLP 495 S High St Ste 450 *Web:* www.randbllp.com	Columbus	OH	43215	614-220-9200		428
Rouse Consulting Group Inc 422 16th St *Web:* www.go2rcg.com	Moline	IL	61265	309-762-3589		196
Rouse's Enterprises LLC 1301 Saint Mary St *Web:* www.rouses.com	Thibodaux	LA	70301	985-447-5998		345
Rouse-sirine Associates Ltd 333 Office Sq Ln *TF:* 800-276-2023 ■ *Web:* www.rouse-sirine.com	Virginia Beach	VA	23462	757-490-2300		727
Roush & Yates Racing Engines LLC 297 Rolling Hill, Rd *Web:* www.roushyates.com	Mooresville	NC	28117	704-799-6216		54
Roush Fenway Racing LLC 4600 Roush Pl NW *Web:* www.roushfenway.com	Concord	NC	28027	704-720-4600		713
Roush Manufacturing Inc 12068 Market St *TF:* 800-215-9658 ■ *Web:* www.roush.com	Livonia	MI	48150	734-779-7006		60
Roush Media 84 E Santa Anita Ave *Web:* www.roush-media.com	Burbank	CA	91502	818-559-8648		514
Rousseau Farming Co 9601 W Harrison Ave	Tolleson	AZ	85353	623-936-7100		10-11
Rousseau Metal Inc 105 Ave De Gasp Ouest *TF:* 866-463-4270 ■ *Web:* www.rousseaumetal.com	St Jean-Port-Joli	QC	G0R3G0	418-598-3381		350
Rouster Wire Rope & Rigging Inc 102 Ridge St *Web:* rousterwrr.com	Mabscott	WV	25871	304-252-6031		492
Route 66 21 Cottage St *TF:* 800-347-0950 ■ *Web:* barharborroute66.com	Bar Harbor	ME	04609	207-288-3708		671
Route 66 Casino Hotel 14500 Central Ave *TF:* 866-352-7866 ■ *Web:* www.rt66casino.com	Albuquerque	NM	87121	505-352-7866		133
Route 66 State Park 97 N Outer Rd Ste 1 *Web:* www.mostateparks.com	Eureka	MO	63025	636-938-7198		565
Routeware Inc 16575 SW 72nd Ave *TF:* 800-926-4748 ■ *Web:* www.routeware.com	Portland	OR	97224	503-906-8500		350
Routt County 136 Sixth St PO Box 775227 *Web:* www.co.routt.co.us	Steamboat Springs	CO	80477	970-870-5405	871-8140	338
Roux Assoc Inc 209 Shafter St *TF:* 800-322-7689 ■ *Web:* www.rouxinc.com	Islandia	NY	11749	631-232-2600		193
Rouzer David (Rep R - NC) 424 Cannon HOB *Web:* rouzer.house.gov	Washington	DC	20515	202-225-2731	225-5773	342-2
Rovanco Piping Systems Inc 20535 SE Frontage Rd *Web:* www.rovanco.com	Joliet	IL	60431	815-741-6700	741-4229	595
Rovi Corp 1990 Post Oak Blvd Ste 2300 *TF:* 877-745-6591 ■ *Web:* www.houstonseagle.com	Houston	TX	77056	713-963-1200	622-5457	645-75

Name / Address	City	State	Zip	Phone	Fax	Class
Rovibec Inc 475 Rte du Port	Nicolet	QC	J3T1W3	819-289-5005	289-2203	190
Web: rovibecagrisolutions.com						
ROW2 Technologies Inc						
14 Walsh Dr Suite 200	Parsippany	NJ	07054	973-795-1141	974-4990*	809
**Fax Area Code:* 813 ■ *Web:* www.row2technologies.com						
Rowan Correctional Ctr						
4750 S Main St PO Box 1207	Salisbury	NC	28147	919-838-4000	733-8272	213
Web: www.ncdps.gov						
Rowan Cos 2800 Postoak Blvd Ste 5450	Houston	TX	77056	713-621-7800		185
NYSE: RDC ■ *Web:* www.rowan.com/home/default.aspx						
Rowan County 130 W Innes St	Salisbury	NC	28144	704-216-8170	216-8110	338
Web: www.rowancountync.gov						
Court house 600 W Main St Rm 102	Morehead	KY	40351	606-784-5212	784-2923	338
Web: rowancountyclerk.com						
Rowan County Chamber of Commerce						
204 E Innes St Ste 110	Salisbury	NC	28144	704-633-4221	639-1200	139
Web: www.rowanchamber.com						
Rowan County Convention & Visitors Bureau						
204 E Innes St Ste 120	Salisbury	NC	28144	704-638-3100	642-2011	206
TF: 800-332-2343 ■ *Web:* www.visitsalisburync.com						
Rowan Public Library PO Box 4039	Salisbury	NC	28145	704-216-8243	638-3002	434-3
Web: www.rowancountync.gov						
Rowan Regional Medical Ctr (RRMC)						
612 Mocksville Ave	Salisbury	NC	28144	704-210-5000	210-5562	374-3
TF: 888-844-0080						
Rowan University						
201 Mullica Hill Rd	Glassboro	NJ	08028	856-256-4200	256-4430*	166
**Fax:* Admissions ■ *TF Admissions:* 877-787-6926 ■ *Web:* www.rowan.edu						
Rowan Williams Davies & Irwin Inc						
650 Woodlawn Rd W	Guelph	ON	N1K1B8	519-823-1311		261
TF: 800-241-9149 ■ *Web:* www.rwdi.com						
Rowan-Cabarrus Community College						
North						
1333 Jake Alexander Blvd S PO Box 1595	Salisbury	NC	28146	704-216-7222		162
Web: www.rccc.edu						
South 1531 Trinity Church Rd	Concord	NC	28027	704-216-7222		162
Web: www.rccc.edu						
Rowayton Arts Ctr 145 Rowayton Ave	Rowayton	CT	06853	203-866-2744	866-1123	50-2
Web: rowaytonarts.org						
Rowe Camp & Conference Ctr						
22 Kings Hwy Rd PO Box 273	Rowe	MA	01367	413-339-4954	339-5728	673
TF: 800-909-8333 ■ *Web:* www.rowecenter.org						
Rowe Foundry Inc						
147 W Cumberland St PO Box 130	Martinsville	IL	62442	217-382-4135		492
Web: www.rowefoundry.com						
Rowe Machinery & Automation Inc						
76 Hinckley Rd	Clinton	ME	04927	207-426-2351		494
TF: 800-247-2645 ■ *Web:* www.runwithrowe.com						
Rowell Auctions Inc						
1303 Fourth St SW	Moultrie	GA	31768	229-985-8388		652
Web: rowellauctions.com						
Rowell Chemical Corp						
15 Salt Creek Ln Ste 205	Hinsdale	IL	60521	630-920-8833	920-8994	146
TF: 888-261-7963 ■ *Web:* www.rowellchemical.com						
Rowland Constructors						
14811 N Kierland Blvd Ste 800	Scottsdale	AZ	85254	480-477-8300		610
Web: www.rowlandconstructioncompany.com						
Rowland Institute for Science Inc, The						
100 Edwin H Land Blvd	Cambridge	MA	02142	617-497-4600		522
TF: 800-294-1830 ■ *Web:* www2.rowland.harvard.edu						
Rowland Medical Library						
University of Mississippi 2500 N State St	Jackson	MS	39216	601-984-1231	984-1251	434-1
TF: 800-621-8099 ■ *Web:* www.umc.edu						
Rowland Technologies Inc						
320 Barnes Rd	Wallingford	CT	06492	203-269-9500		600
Web: www.rowlandtechnologies.com						
Rowland Transportation Inc						
40824 Messick Rd	Dade City	FL	33525	352-567-2002		314
TF: 800-338-1146 ■ *Web:* www.rowlandtransportation.com						
Rowlands Sales Company Inc						
Butler Industrial Pk	Hazleton	PA	18201	570-455-5813		358
TF: 800-582-6388 ■ *Web:* www.rowlands.com						
Rowlett Bowl-A-Rama						
5021 Lakeview Pkwy	Rowlett	TX	75088	972-475-7080		99
TF: 800-514-2686 ■ *Web:* www.rowlettbowlarama.com						
Rowlett Chamber of Commerce						
3910 Main St	Rowlett	TX	75088	972-475-3200	463-1699	139
Web: www.rowlettchamber.com						
Rowley Chapman & Barney Ltd						
63 E Main St Ste 501	Mesa	AZ	85201	480-833-1113		428
TF: 888-476-8411 ■ *Web:* www.azlegal.com						
Rowley Properties Inc						
1595 NW Gilman Blvd Ste 1	Issaquah	WA	98027	425-392-6407		652
Web: www.rowleyproperties.com						
Rowley Spring & Stamping Corp						
210 Redstone Hill Rd	Bristol	CT	06010	860-582-8175		719
Web: www.rowleyspring.com						
Rowleys Tires & Automotive Services						
3596 Wilder Rd	Bay City	MI	48706	989-686-1144		57
Web: www.rowleystires.com						
Rowman & Littlefield Publishers Inc						
4501 Forbes Blvd Ste 200	Lanham	MD	20706	301-459-3366	429-5748	637-2
TF: 800-462-6420 ■ *Web:* rowman.com						
Rowmark Inc 2040 Industrial Dr	Findlay	OH	45840	419-425-2407	425-2927	599
TF: 800-243-3339 ■ *Web:* www.rowmark.com						
Rowpar Pharmaceuticals Inc						
16100 N Greenway Hayden Loop Ste 400	Scottsdale	AZ	85260	480-948-6997		583
TF: 800-368-6484 ■ *Web:* www.closys.com						
Roxboro Area Chamber of Commerce						
211 N Main St	Roxboro	NC	27573	336-599-8333	599-8335	139
Web: www.roxboronc.com						
Roxborough Memorial Hospital (RMH)						
5800 Ridge Ave	Philadelphia	PA	19128	215-483-9900		374-3
Web: www.roxboroughmemorial.com						
Roxborough State Park						
4751 Roxborough Dr	Littleton	CO	80125	303-973-3959		565
Web: cpw.state.co.us						
Roxbury Community College						
1234 Columbus Ave	Roxbury Crossing	MA	02120	617-541-5310	427-5316*	162
**Fax:* Admitting ■ *Web:* www.rcc.mass.edu						
Roxbury Correctional Institution						
18701 Roxbury Rd	Hagerstown	MD	21746	240-420-3000		213
Roxbury Latin School						
101 St Theresa Ave	West Roxbury	MA	02132	617-325-4920	325-3585	623
Web: www.roxburylatin.org						
Roxy Trading Inc 389 Humane Way	Pomona	CA	91768	626-610-1388	610-1339	297-11
Web: www.roxytrading.com						
Roy & Associates PC						
433 Frye Farm Rd Ste 7	Greensburg	PA	15601	724-834-3900	834-3390	2
Web: royandassociates.wordpress.com						
Roy & Edna Disney/CALARTS Theater (REDCAT) (REDCAT)						
631 W Second St	Los Angeles	CA	90012	213-237-2800	237-2811	50-2
Web: www.redcat.org						
Roy Anderson Corp 11400 Reichold Rd	Gulfport	MS	39503	228-896-4000		186
TF: 800-688-4003 ■ *Web:* www.rac.com						
Roy Bros Inc 764 Boston Rd	Billerica	MA	01821	978-667-1921	667-5091	780
TF Cust Svc: 800-225-0830 ■ *Web:* www.roybrosinc.com						
Roy E Hanson Jr Mfg						
1600 E Washington Blvd	Los Angeles	CA	90021	213-747-7514	747-7724	91
TF: 800-421-9395 ■ *Web:* www.hansontank.com						
Roy E Whitehead Inc 2245 Via Cerro	Riverside	CA	92509	951-682-1490		115
Web: www.royewhitehead.com						
Roy H Reeve Agency Inc						
13400 Main Rd	Mattituck	NY	11952	631-298-4700		390
Web: www.royreeve.agency						
Roy Houff Co, The 6200 S Oak Pk Ave	Chicago	IL	60638	773-586-8666	586-8790	293
Web: royhouff.com						
Roy J Carver Biotechnology Ctr						
1206 W Gregory	Urbana	IL	61801	217-333-1695	244-0466	668
Web: www.biotech.illinois.edu						
Roy J Carver Charitable Trust						
202 Iowa Ave	Muscatine	IA	52761	563-263-4010	263-1547	305
Web: www.carvertrust.org						
Roy Jorgensen Assoc Inc						
3735 Buckeystown Pk	Buckeystown	MD	21717	301-831-1000		194
Web: www.royjorgensen.com						
Roy Kirby & Sons Inc 1403 Rome Rd	Baltimore	MD	21227	410-536-0808	536-0799	186
Web: www.roykirby.com						
Roy Lake State Park						
11545 Northside Dr	Lake City	SD	57247	605-448-5701		565
Web: gfp.sd.gov						
Roy Miller Freight Lines LLC						
3165 E Coronado St	Anaheim	CA	92806	714-632-5511		314
TF: 800-336-5673 ■ *Web:* www.roymiller.com						
Roy Nichols Motors Ltd						
2728 Courtice Rd	Courtice	ON	L1E2M7	905-436-2222		57
Web: roynicholsmotors.com						
Roy O Martin						
2100 Memorial Dr PO Box 1110	Alexandria	LA	71301	318-448-0405	473-2624	752
Web: www.royomartin.com						
Roy Rogers-Dale Evans Museum						
3950 Green Mtn Dr	Branson	MO	65616	417-339-1900		520
Web: www.royrogers.com						
Roy's 4342 W Boy Scout Blvd	Tampa	FL	33607	813-873-7697		671
Web: www.roysrestaurant.com						
Roy's 620 E Flamingo Rd	Las Vegas	NV	89119	702-691-2053		671
Web: www.roysrestaurant.com						
Roy's 575 Mission St	San Francisco	CA	94105	415-777-0277		671
Web: www.roysrestaurant.com						
Roy's 7151 W Ray Rd	Chandler	AZ	85226	480-705-7697		671
Web: www.roysrestaurant.com						
Roy's 8670 Genesee Ave	San Diego	CA	92122	858-455-1616		671
Web: www.roysrestaurant.com						
Roy's 7760 W Sand Lake Rd	Orlando	FL	32819	407-352-4844		671
Web: www.roysrestaurant.com						
Roy's 26831 S Bay Dr	Bonita Springs	FL	34134	239-498-7697		671
Web: www.roysrestaurant.com						
Roy's 5350 E Marriott Dr	Phoenix	AZ	85054	480-419-7697		671
Web: www.roysrestaurant.com						
Roy's 720 N State St	Chicago	IL	60654	312-787-7599		671
Web: www.roysrestaurant.com						
Roy's Restaurants						
321 W Katella Ave Ste 105	Anaheim	CA	92802	714-776-7697		670
Web: www.roysrestaurant.com						
Roy's Wood Products Inc 329 Thrush Ln	Lugoff	SC	29078	803-438-1590		115
TF: 800-727-1590 ■ *Web:* www.royswoodproducts.com						
Royal & SunAlliance Insurance Co of Canada (RSA)						
18 York St Ste 800	Toronto	ON	M5J2T8	416-366-7511	367-9869	391-4
TF: 800-268-8406 ■ *Web:* www.rsagroup.ca						
Royal Adhesives & Sealants						
2001 W Washington St	South Bend	IN	46628	574-246-5000		3
Web: www.royaladhesives.com						
Royal Alberta Museum						
102nd Ave Ste 12845	Edmonton	AB	T5N0M6	780-453-9100	454-6629	520
Web: www.royalalbertamuseum.ca						
Royal Alexandra Hospital						
10240 Kingsway Ave	Edmonton	AB	T5H3V9	780-735-4111		374-2
TF: 800-332-1414 ■ *Web:* www.albertahealthservices.ca						
Royal Alliance Assoc Inc						
1 World Financial Ctr 14th Fl	New York	NY	10281	800-821-5100		690
TF: 800-821-5100 ■ *Web:* www.royalalliance.com						
Royal Aloha Vacation Club						
1505 Dillingham Blvd Ste 212	Honolulu	HI	96817	808-847-8050	841-5467	753
TF: 800-367-5212 ■ *Web:* www.ravc.com						
Royal Aluminum Company Inc						
620 Market St	Newark	NJ	07105	973-589-8880		234
Web: www.royalaluminum.net						
Royal American Construction Co Inc						
1002 W 23rd St Ste 400	Panama City	FL	32405	850-769-8981		187
Web: royalamericanconstruction.com						
Royal Bank America						
732 Montgomery Ave	Narberth	PA	19072	610-668-4700	668-3670	70
TF: 800-236-2442 ■ *Web:* www.royalbankamerica.com						
Royal Bank of Canada						
200 Bay St 9th Fl S Twr	Toronto	ON	M5J2J5	416-955-7806	974-3535	70
TSE: RY ■ *TF:* 800-769-2599 ■ *Web:* www.rbc.com						

Company / Address	City	State	Zip	Phone	Fax	Class
Royal Baths Manufacturing Co 14635 Chrisman Rd *TF:* 800-826-0074 ■ *Web:* www.royalbaths.com	Houston	TX	77039	281-442-3400	442-1455	375
Royal Bavaria Brewery 3401 S Sooner Rd *Web:* www.royal-bavaria.com	Oklahoma City	OK	73165	405-799-7666		671
Royal Bearing Inc 17719 NE Sandy Blvd *TF:* 800-279-0992 ■ *Web:* www.royalbearing.com	Portland	OR	97230	503-231-0992		385
Royal Beef Feed Yard 11060 N Falcon Rd *Web:* www.irsikanddoll.com	Scott City	KS	67871	620-872-5371	872-3380	10-1
Royal Botanical Gardens (RBG) 680 Plains Rd W *TF:* 800-694-4769 ■ *Web:* www.rbg.ca	Burlington	ON	L7T4H4	905-527-1158	577-0375	97
Royal Brass Inc 2856 Anton Rd *Web:* www.royalbrassandhose.com	Madisonville	KY	42431	270-821-8150		790
Royal British Columbia Museum (RBCM) 675 Belleville St *TF:* 888-447-7977 ■ *Web:* www.royalbcmuseum.bc.ca	Victoria	BC	V8W9W2	250-356-7226		520
Royal Business Forms Inc 3301 Ave E E *TF:* 800-255-9303 ■ *Web:* royalbf.com	Arlington	TX	76011	817-640-5248	633-2164	110
Royal Cabinets 1299 E Phillips Blvd *Web:* www.royalcabinets.com	Pomona	CA	91766	909-629-8565	629-7762	115
Royal Camp Services Ltd 7111 - 67 St *TF:* 877-884-2267 ■ *Web:* www.royalcamp.com	Edmonton	AB	T6B3L7	780-463-8000		779
Royal Canadian Military Institute 426 University Ave *TF:* 800-585-1072 ■ *Web:* www.rcmi.org	Toronto	ON	M5G1S9	416-597-0286	597-6919	520
Royal Canadian Yacht Club, The 141 St George St *Web:* rcyc.ca	Toronto	ON	M5R2L8	416-967-7245		138
Royal Capital Management LLC 623 Fifth Ave 24th Fl	New York	NY	10022	212-920-3400	920-3411	401
Royal Caribbean International 1050 Caribbean Way *TF:* 800-327-6700 ■ *Web:* www.royalcaribbean.com	Miami	FL	33132	305-539-6000		220
Royal Carolina Corp 7305 Old Friendly Rd *Web:* www.royalcarolina.com	Greensboro	NC	27410	336-292-8845	294-2396	745-7
Royal Case Company Inc 419 E Lamar St *Web:* www.royalcase.com	Sherman	TX	75090	903-868-0288	893-7984	453
Royal Chemical Co 1755 Enterprise Pkwy Ste 600	Twinsburg	OH	44087	330-467-1300	405-0975	145
Royal Coach Lines Inc 924 Broadway *Web:* royalcoachlines.com	Thornwood	NY	10594	914-747-9494	747-9497	109
Royal Coach Tours 630 Stockton Ave *TF:* 800-927-6925 ■ *Web:* www.royal-coach.com	San Jose	CA	95126	408-279-4801	286-1410	760
Royal Coachman Worldwide 88 Ford Rd Ste 26 *TF:* 800-472-7433 ■ *Web:* www.royalcoachman.com	Denville	NJ	07834	973-400-3200	675-4365	441
Royal College of Dental Surgeons of Ontario 6 Crescent Rd *TF:* 800-565-4591 ■ *Web:* rcdso.org	Toronto	ON	M4W1T1	416-961-6555		165
Royal Columbian Hospital 330 E Columbia St *TF:* 800-255-4786 ■ *Web:* www.fraserhealth.ca	New Westminster	BC	V3L3W7	604-520-4253	520-4827	374-2
Royal Concrete Pipe Inc 30622 Forest Blvd PO Box 430 *Web:* www.royalenterprises.net	Stacy	MN	55079	651-462-2130		183
Royal Conservatory of Music The 273 Bloor St W *TF:* 800-462-3815 ■ *Web:* www.rcmusic.ca	Toronto	ON	M5S1W2	416-408-2824		627
Royal Consumer Information Products Inc 1160 US 22 **Fax Area Code:* 800 ■ *TF Sales:* 888-261-4555 ■ *Web:* www.royalsupplies.com	Bridgewater	NJ	08807	732-627-9977	232-9769*	111
Royal Contracting Company Ltd 677 Ahua St *TF:* 800-385-6719 ■ *Web:* www.royalcontracting.com	Honolulu	HI	96819	808-839-9006	839-7571	188-4
Royal Crest Dairy Inc 350 S Pearl St *TF:* 888-226-6455 ■ *Web:* www.royalcrestdairy.com	Denver	CO	80209	303-777-2227	744-9173	296-27
Royal Cup Coffee 160 Cleage Dr *TF Cust Svc:* 800-366-5836 ■ *Web:* www.royalcupcoffee.com	Birmingham	AL	35217	800-366-5836		296-7
Royal Cup Coffee and Tea 160 Cleage Dr *TF:* 800-366-5836 ■ *Web:* www.royalcupcoffee.com	Birmingham	AL	35217	800-366-5836		499
Royal Cyber Inc 55 Shuman Blvd Ste 1025 *TF:* 800-426-9990 ■ *Web:* www.royalcyber.com	Naperville	IL	60563	630-355-6292		177
Royal Die & Stamping Co 125 Mercedes Dr *Web:* www.royaldie.com	Carol Stream	IL	60188	630-766-2685		483
Royal Discount Furniture Company Inc 122 S Main St *Web:* www.royalfurniture.com	Memphis	TN	38103	901-527-6407		321
Royal Engineering Inc 34450 Commerce Rd *Web:* royalinc.com	Fraser	MI	48026	586-294-9400		261
Royal Envelope Co 4114 S Peoria St *Web:* royalenv.com	Chicago	IL	60609	773-376-1212	376-0011	263
Royal Expressions Flowers & Gifts 131 S Ln St	Blissfield	MI	49228	517-486-4351		292
Royal Farms Arena 201 W Baltimore St *TF:* 800-780-5733 ■ *Web:* www.royalfarmsarena.com	Baltimore	MD	21201	410-347-2020		720
Royal Food Products LLC 2322 E Minnesota St *Web:* www.royalfp.com	Indianapolis	IN	46203	317-782-2660		296-37
Royal Food Service Company Inc 3720 Zip Industrial Blvd *Web:* www.royalfoodservice.com	Atlanta	GA	30354	404-366-4299		805
Royal Fox Country Club 4405 Royal And Ancient Dr *Web:* www.royalfoxcc.com	Saint Charles	IL	60174	630-584-4000		354
Royal Garden at Waikiki Hotel 440 Olohana St *TF:* 800-428-1932 ■ *Web:* www.extraholidays.com	Honolulu	HI	96815	808-943-0202		379
Royal George Theatre Ctr 1641 N Halsted St *Web:* www.theroyalgeorgetheatre.com	Chicago	IL	60614	312-988-9105		572
Royal Glass Company Inc 3200 De La Cruz Blvd	Santa Clara	CA	95054	408-969-0444		329
Royal Gold Inc 1660 Wynkoop St Ste 1000 *NASDAQ: RGLD* ■ *Web:* www.royalgold.com	Denver	CO	80202	303-573-1660	595-9385	502
Royal Group 1301 S 47th Ave *Web:* royalbox.com	Cicero	IL	60804	708-656-2020		100
Royal Group, The 71 Royal Group Crescent *TF:* 800-263-2353 ■ *Web:* www.royalbuildingproducts.com	Woodbridge	ON	L4H1X9	905-264-0701	850-9184	235
Royal Harvest Foods 55 Avocado St *Web:* www.royalharv.com	Springfield	MA	01104	413-737-8392		619
Royal Hawaiian 2259 Kalakaua Ave *TF:* 800-782-9488 ■ *Web:* royal-hawaiian.com	Honolulu	HI	96815	808-923-7311	931-7098	669
Royal Hilltop 18581 E Hampden Ave *Web:* www.royalhilltop.com	Aurora	CO	80013	303-690-7738		671
Royal Holiday Beach Resort 1988 Beach Blvd *TF Resv:* 800-874-0402 ■ *Web:* www.holidaybeachresort.com	Biloxi	MS	39531	228-388-7553		379
Royal Hotel South Beach 763 Pennsylvania Ave *Web:* www.royalsouthbeach.com	Miami Beach	FL	33139	305-673-9009	673-9244	379
Royal Ice Cream Co 6200 Euclid Ave *Web:* www.pierres.com	Cleveland	OH	44103	216-432-1144		296-25
Royal Industries Inc 225 25th St *TF:* 800-752-9161 ■ *Web:* www.royalindustries.com	Brooklyn	NY	11232	718-369-3046		7
Royal Inland Hospital 311 Columbia St *Web:* rihfoundation.ca	Kamloops	BC	V2C2T1	250-374-5111		374-2
Royal Khyber S Coast Plaza Vlg 1621 W Sunflower Ave *Web:* www.royalkhyber.com	Santa Ana	CA	92704	714-436-1010		671
Royal Lahaina Resort 2780 Kekaa Dr *TF:* 800-222-5642 ■ *Web:* www.hawaiianhotels.com	Lahaina	HI	96761	808-661-3611		669
Royal Machine & Tool Corp 4 Willowbrook Dr PO Box Y *TF:* 800-445-6267 ■ *Web:* www.royalworkholding.com	Berlin	CT	06037	860-828-6555		493
Royal Management Corp 665 W N Ave *TF:* 800-285-9560 ■ *Web:* www.lexingtonhealth.com	Lombard	IL	60148	630-458-4700	748-3701	451
Royal Master Grinders Inc 143 Bauer Dr *Web:* www.royalmaster.com	Oakland	NJ	07436	201-337-8500	337-2324	455
Royal Mausoleum State Monument 2261 Nuuanu Ave *Web:* dlnr.hawaii.gov	Honolulu	HI	96817	808-587-0300		565
Royal Military College of Canada Stn Forces PO Box 17000 *Web:* www.rmcc-cmrc.ca/en	Kingston	ON	K7K7B4	613-541-6000		498
Royal Mouldings Ltd 135 Bearcreek Rd PO Box 610 *TF:* 800-368-3117 ■ *Web:* www.royalbuildingproducts.com	Marion	VA	24354	276-783-8161	782-3285	309
Royal Neighbor Magazine 230 16th St *TF:* 800-627-4762 ■ *Web:* www.royalneighbors.org	Rock Island	IL	61201	309-788-4561		457-10
Royal Oak Foundation, The 35 W 35th St Ste 1200 *TF:* 800-913-6565 ■ *Web:* www.royal-oak.org	New York	NY	10001	212-480-2889	785-7234	48-13
Royal Oak Kitchens & Baths 32790 Woodward Ave *Web:* www.royaloakkitchen.com	Royal Oak	MI	48073	248-549-2944		362
Royal Oak Public Library 222 E Eleven Mile Rd *Web:* www.romi.gov/148/Library	Royal Oak	MI	48067	248-246-3700	545-6220	434-3
Royal Oaks Country Club Club House 7915 Greenville Ave *TF:* 800-752-6632 ■ *Web:* roccdallas.com	Dallas	TX	75231	214-691-6091		711
Royal Ontario Museum 100 Queen's Pk *TF:* 800-263-4433 ■ *Web:* www.rom.on.ca	Toronto	ON	M5S2C6	416-586-8000	586-5504	520
Royal Pacific Resort at Universal Orlando - A Loews Hotel 6300 Hollywood Way *TF:* 800-235-6397 ■ *Web:* www.loewshotels.com	Orlando	FL	32819	407-503-3000	503-3010	669
Royal Pacific Tea Company Inc, The PO Box 6277 *Web:* www.royalpacificintl.com	Scottsdale	AZ	85261	480-951-8251	951-0092	297-11
Royal Palms Resort & Spa 5200 E Camelback Rd *TF:* 800-672-6011 ■ *Web:* www.royalpalmshotel.com	Phoenix	AZ	85018	602-840-3610	840-6927	669
Royal Paper Box Company of California Inc PO Box 458 *TF:* 800-419-6829 ■ *Web:* www.royalpaperbox.com	Montebello	CA	90640	323-728-7041	722-2646	101
Royal Paper Corp 10232 Palm Dr *Web:* www.royal-paper.com	Santa Fe Springs	CA	90670	562-903-9030		194
Royal Park Hotel-brookshire & The Commons 600 E University Dr *TF:* 800-339-2761 ■ *Web:* royalparkhotel.net	Rochester	MI	48307	248-652-2600		379
Royal Park Uniforms Co 14139 Hwy 86 S	Prospect Hill	NC	27314	336-562-3345		155-19
Royal Plastics Inc 9410 Pineneedle Dr *Web:* www.royalplastics.com	Mentor	OH	44060	440-352-1357	352-6681	604
Royal Plaza Hotel 1905 Hotel Plaza Blvd *Web:* www.royalplaza.com	Lake Buena Vista	FL	32830	407-828-2828		378
Royal Processing Co 5710 Old Concord Rd *TF:* 800-532-0434 ■ *Web:* steinfibers.com	Charlotte	NC	28213	704-599-2804	599-2805	745-8
Royal Regency Hotel 165 Tuckahoe Rd *TF:* 800-215-3858 ■ *Web:* www.royalregencyhotelny.com	Yonkers	NY	10710	914-476-6200		379
Royal River Casino & Entertainment Complex 607 S Veterans St *TF:* 800-833-8666 ■ *Web:* www.royalrivercasino.com	Flandreau	SD	57028	605-997-3746		452
Royal Roads University 2005 Sooke Rd *TF:* 800-788-8028 ■ *Web:* www.royalroads.ca	Victoria	BC	V9B5Y2	250-391-2511	391-2500	785
Royal Saskatchewan Museum 2445 Albert St *TF:* 866-984-4964 ■ *Web:* www.royalsaskmuseum.ca	Regina	SK	S4P4W7	306-787-2815	787-2820	520

Entry	City	State	Zip	Phone	Fax	Class
Royal Savings Bank 9226 S Commercial Ave *Web:* www.royalbankweb.com	Chicago	IL	60617	773-768-4800		70
Royal Screw Machine Products Co 409 Lake Ave	Bristol	CT	06010	860-845-8567		621
Royal Sonesta Hotel Boston 40 Edwin H Land Blvd *TF:* 800-766-3782 ■ *Web:* www.sonesta.com/boston	Cambridge	MA	02142	617-806-4200	806-4232	379
Royal Sonesta Hotel New Orleans 800 Iberville St *TF:* 800-766-3782 ■ *Web:* www.sonesta.com	New Orleans	LA	70112	504-586-0300		379
Royal Sonesta Hotel New Orleans 300 Bourbon St *TF:* 800-766-3782 ■ *Web:* sonesta.com/royalneworleans	New Orleans	LA	70130	504-586-0300	586-0335	379
Royal St Charles Hotel LLC 135 Saint Charles Ave. *Web:* www.destinationhotels.com/royal-st-charles	New Orleans	LA	70130	504-587-3700		378
Royal State National Insurance Company Ltd 819 S Beretania St *Web:* www.royalstate.com	Honolulu	HI	96813	808-539-1600		391-2
Royal Suite Lodge 3811 Minnesota Dr	Anchorage	AK	99503	907-563-3114		379
Royal Sun Inn 1700 S Palm Canyon Dr *TF:* 800-619-4786 ■ *Web:* www.royalsuninn.com	Palm Springs	CA	92264	760-327-1564		379
Royal T Management 7419 N Cedar Ave Ste 102 *Web:* royaltmanagement.com	Fresno	CA	93720	559-447-9887		652
Royal Technocrats Inc 7447 Harwin Dr Ste 270 *Web:* royaltechnocrats.com	Houston	TX	77036	713-776-8300		180
Royal Textile Mills Inc 929 Firetower Rd *TF:* 800-334-9361 ■ *Web:* www.dukeathletic-tactical.com	Yanceyville	NC	27379	800-334-9361	934-9360	155-1
Royal Thai 5500 Greenville Ave *Web:* royalthaitexas.com	Dallas	TX	75206	214-691-3555		671
Royal Thai Consulate General *Consulate General* 351 E 52nd St *Web:* www.thaiconsulnewyork.com	New York	NY	10022	212-754-1770		257
Royal Tire Inc 3955 Roosevelt Rd *TF:* 877-454-7070 ■ *Web:* www.royaltire.com	St. Cloud	MN	56301	877-454-7070		755
Royal Tours Inc PO Box 372 PO Box 372 *Web:* www.gowithgaynelle.com	Smithfield	VA	23431	757-569-7616		760
Royal Travel & Tours Inc 122 N First St *Web:* www.royal-travel.com	Dekalb	IL	60115	815-758-8172		772
Royal Trucking Co 1323 Eshman Ave N PO Box 387 **Fax Area Code:* 662 ■ *TF:* 800 321-1293 ■ *Web:* www.royaltruck.com	West Point	MS	39773	800-321-1293	495-1066*	780
Royal Tyrrell Museum Hwy 838 PO Box 7500 *TF:* 888-440-4240 ■ *Web:* www.tyrrellmuseum.com	Drumheller	AB	T0J0Y0	403 823 7707	823-7131	520
Royal University Hospital 103 Hospital Dr *TF:* 800-458-1179 ■ *Web:* saskatoonhealthregion.ca	Saskatoon	SK	S7N0W8	306-655-1000		374-2
Royal Victoria Hospital 201 Georgian Dr *TF:* 800-387-0073 ■ *Web:* www.rvh.on.ca	Barrie	ON	L4M6M2	705-728-9802	728-0982	374-2
Royal Victoria Hospital 687 Pine Ave W *Web:* www.muhc.ca/pfv/rvh	Montreal	QC	H3A1A1	514-934-1934		374-2
Royal Waste Services Inc 18740 Hollis Ave *Web:* royalwaste.com	Hollis	NY	11423	718-526-2623		660
Royal Wine Corp 63 Le Fante Ln *Web:* www.royalwine.com	Bayonne	NJ	07002	201-437-9131		80-3
Royale Energy Inc 3777 WILLOW GLEN Dr *Web:* www.royl.com	El Cajon	CA	92019	619-383-6600		536
Royale Management Services Inc 2319 N Andrews Ave. *TF:* 800-382-1040 ■ *Web:* www.rmsaccounting.com	Fort Lauderdale	FL	33311	954-563-1269		463
Royals Food Town 135 S Main *Web:* royalsfoodtown.com	Loa	UT	84747	435-836-2841		345
Royals Inc 324 SW 16th St. *Web:* royalsfurnitureinc.com	Belle Glade	FL	33430	561-996-7646	996-4480	321
Royalton Hotel 44 W 44th St. *TF:* 800-606-6090 ■ *Web:* www.morganshotelgroup.com	New York	NY	10036	212-869-4400	869-8965	379
Royalty Carpet Mills Inc 17111 Red Hill Ave *TF:* 800-854-8331 ■ *Web:* www.royaltycarpetmills.com	Irvine	CA	92614	949-474-4000	553-8238	131
Royalty Exploration LLC 8309 Southpark Ln Ste B *Web:* royaltyexploration.com	Littleton	CO	80120	303-217-5151		538
Royalty Pharma 110 E 59th St 33rd Fl *Web:* www.royaltypharma.com	New York	NY	10022	212-883-0200		85
Roybal-Allard Lucille (Rep D - CA) 2083 Rayburn HOB *Web:* roybal-allard.house.gov	Washington	DC	20515	202-225-1766	226-0350	342-2
Royce & Assoc LLC 745 Fifth Ave. *TF:* 800-221-4268 ■ *Web:* www.roycefunds.com	New York	NY	10151	800-221-4268		401
Royce Associates A LP 35 Carlton Ave *TF:* 800-424-9300 ■ *Web:* www.royceintl.com	East Rutherford	NJ	07073	201-438-5200		194
Royce Ed (Rep R - CA) 2310 Rayburn HOB *Web:* www.royce.house.gov	Washington	DC	20515	202-225-4111	226-0335	342-2
Royco Inc The World Bldg 8121 Georgia Ave Ste 500	Silver Spring	MD	20910	301-608-2212		652
Royden Construction Co 3423 S 51st Ave *Web:* www.royden.org	Phoenix	AZ	85043	602-484-0028		183
Royer Corp 805 East St. *TF:* 800-457-8997 ■ *Web:* www.royercorp.com	Madison	IN	47250	812-265-3133		711
Royer's Flowers Inc 201 Rohrerstown Rd *Web:* www.royers.com	Lancaster	PA	17603	717-397-0376		292
Roylco Inc 3251 Abbeville Hwy PO Box 13409 *TF:* 800-362-8656 ■ *Web:* www.roylco.com	Anderson	SC	29624	864-296-0043	296-6736	243
Royle Printing Co 745 S Bird St *Web:* www.royle.com	Sun Prairie	WI	53590	608-837-5161		627
Roymal Inc 3 Roymal Ln *TF:* 800-345-9999 ■ *Web:* www.roymalinc.com	Newport	NH	03773	603-863-2410		550
Royse Law Firm PC 1717 Embarcadero Rd *TF:* 800-926-7926 ■ *Web:* www.rroyselaw.com	Palo Alto	CA	94303	650-813-9700		428
Roysons Corp 40 Vanderhoof Ave *TF:* 888-769-7667 ■ *Web:* www.roysons.com	Rockaway	NJ	07866	973-625-7923	625-5917	290
Roytex Inc 16 E 34th St 17th Fl *TF:* 800-221-4268 ■ *Web:* www.roytex.com	New York	NY	10016	212-686-3500	686-4336	155-15
Roytman Info Svc Inc 504 Old Harbor Ct. *Web:* www.roytmanis.com	Dayton	OH	45458	937-885-0821		624
Roywell Services Inc 4545 Bissonnet St Ste 104 *TF:* 800-268-5713 ■ *Web:* roywellservices.com	Bellaire	TX	77401	713-661-4747		538
Rozelle Cosmetics 4260 Loop Rd *TF:* 800-451-4216 ■ *Web:* www.rozelle.com	Westfield	VT	05874	802-744-2270	744-2236	214
Rozovics & Wojcicki PC 1580 N Northwest Hwy Ste 120 *Web:* www.rozcpa.com	Park Ridge	IL	60068	847-699-7600	299-7526	2
RP Design Web Services 17 Meriden Ave Ste 2A *TF:* 800-847-3475 ■ *Web:* www.rpdesign.com	Southington	CT	06489	203-271-7991		177
RP Fedder Corp 740 Driving Pk Ave *TF:* 800-343-4048 ■ *Web:* www.rpfedder.com	Rochester	NY	14613	585-288-1600	288-2481	18
RP Funding Ctr 701 W Lime St *Web:* www.thelakelandcenter.com	Lakeland	FL	33815	863-834-8100	834-8101	205
RP Graphics Group Inc 5990 Falbourne St *Web:* rpgraphics.com	Mississauga	ON	L5R3S7	905-507-8782		627
RP International PO Box 900 *TF:* 877-999-8322 ■ *Web:* www.rpinternational.org	Woodland Hills	CA	91365	818-992-0500	992-3265	48-17
RP Lumber Company Inc 514 E Vandalia St *TF:* 800-377-3111 ■ *Web:* www.rplumber.com	Edwardsville	IL	62025	618-656-1514	656-6785	191-3
RP Machine Enterprises Inc 820 Cochran St. *Web:* www.rpmachine.com	Statesville	NC	28677	704-872-8888	872-5777	455
RPA (Renal Physicians Assn) 1700 Rockville Pk Ste 220 *Web:* www.renalmd.org	Rockville	MD	20852	301-468-3515	468-3511	49-8
RPAC LLC 21490 S Ortigalita Rd *Web:* www.rpacalmonds.com	Los Banos	CA	93635	209-826-0272	826-3882	11-1
RPB (Research to Prevent Blindness Inc) 360 Lexington Ave 22nd Fl *TF:* 800 621-0026 ■ *Web:* www.rpbusa.org	New York	NY	10017	212-752-4333	688-6231	48-17
RPC Inc 2801 Buford Hwy Ste 520 *NYSE: RES* ■ *Web:* www.rpc.net	Atlanta	GA	30324	404-321-2140	321-5483	539
RPC Photonics Inc 330 Clay Rd *Web:* www.rpcphotonics.com	Rochester	NY	14623	585-272-2840		544
RPG Productions 632 S Glenwood Pl *Web:* www.rpgproductions.com	Burbank	CA	91506	818-848-0240	848-2257	512
Rpi Industries Inc 220 Route 70 *Web:* rpiindustries.com	Medford	NJ	08055	609-714-2330		499
RPI Media Inc 265 Racine Dr Ste 201 *TF:* 800-736-0321 ■ *Web:* www.rpimedia.com	Wilmington	NC	28403	910-763-2100		656
Rpl Associates Inc 21650 W 11 Mile Rd. *Web:* www.rplassociates.com	Southfield	MI	48076	248-353-0011		311
Rpl Supplies Inc 141 Lanza Ave Bldg 3A *TF:* 800-524-0914 ■ *Web:* www.rplsupplies.com	Garfield	NJ	07026	973-767-0880	772-6601	174
RPM Direct LLC 24 Arnett Ave Ste 100 *Web:* www.rpmdirectllc.com	Lambertville	NJ	08530	609-566-7150		195
RPM Industries Inc 1444 Lowell St *TF:* 800-669-3676 ■ *Web:* www.rpmindustriesinc.com	Elyria	OH	44035	315-255-1105	252-1167	199
RPM International Inc 2628 Pearl Rd *NYSE: RPM* ■ *TF:* 800-776-4488 ■ *Web:* www.rpminc.com	Medina	OH	44256	330-273-5090	225-8743	550
Rpm Mortgage Inc 3240 Stone Valley Rd W. *Web:* rpm-mtg.com	Alamo	CA	94507	925-295-9300		217
RPM Pizza LLC 15384 Fifth St	Gulfport	MS	39503	228-832-4000		670
RPM Revenue Drivers LLC 140 S Mountain Way Dr	Orem	UT	84058	801-449-0541		463
RPMG Inc 1157 Vly Park Dr Ste 100 *Web:* www.rpmgllc.com	Shakopee	MN	55379	952-465-3220		580
RpmOne Inc 4495 Military Trl Ste 207 *Web:* www.rpmone.com	Jupiter	FL	33458	561-741-4447		390
RPNM (New Mexico Republican Party) 5150-A San Francisco Rd NE PO Box 94083 *Web:* newmexico.gop	Albuquerque	NM	87109	505-298-3662		616-2
RPP Corp 12 Ballard Way *TF:* 800-232-2239 ■ *Web:* www.rppcorp.com	Lawrence	MA	01843	978-689-2800		677
Rpr Graphics Inc 87 Main St. *Web:* www.rprgraphicsinc.com	Peapack	NJ	07977	908-654-8080		781
RPS JD Consulting Inc 404 Camp Craft Rd	Austin	TX	78746	512-347-7588		192
RPS Products Inc 281 Keyes Ave *Web:* www.rpsproducts.com	Hampshire	IL	60140	847-683-3400		18
RR Bowker LLC 630 Central Ave *TF:* 888-269-5372 ■ *Web:* www.bowker.com	New Providence	NJ	07974	908-795-3500		637-2
R&R Contracting Inc 5201 N Washington St *TF:* 800-872-5975 ■ *Web:* www.rrcontracting.net	Grand Forks	ND	58203	701-772-7667		188
RR Donnelley 111 S Wacker Dr **Fax Area Code:* 925 ■ *TF:* 800-742-4455 ■ *Web:* www.rrdonnelley.com	Chicago	IL	60606	800-742-4455	951-1355*	626
RR Donnelley Logistics 1000 Windham Pkwy *TF:* 877-744-3818 ■ *Web:* www.rrdonnelley.com	Bolingbrook	IL	60490	877-744-3818		5
RR Donnelley Response Marketing Services 4101 Winfield Rd *TF:* 800-722-9001 ■ *Web:* www.rrdonnelley.com	Warrenville	IL	60555	630-963-9494		5

Phone | Fax | Class

R&R Partners Inc
900 S Pavillion Ctr Dr ..... Las Vegas NV 89144 702-228-0222 636
Web: www.rrpartners.com

R&R Products Inc 3334 E Milber St ..... Tucson AZ 85714 520-889-3593 386
TF: 800-528-3446 ■ *Web:* www.rrproducts.com

RRA (Reconstructionist Rabbinical Assn)
1299 Church Rd ..... Wyncote PA 19095 215-576-5210 576-8051 48-20
Web: www.therra.org

RRC (Radio Research Consortium Inc)
PO Box 1309 ..... Olney MD 20830 301-774-6686 774-0976 632
TF: 800-543-7300 ■ *Web:* www.rrconline.org

RRC Assoc 4770 Baseline Rd Ste 360 ..... Boulder CO 80303 303-449-6558 449-6587 466
TF: 888-449-4772 ■ *Web:* rrcassoc.com

RRE Ventures LLC
130 E 59th St 17th Fl ..... New York NY 10022 212-418-5100 792
Web: www.rre.com

RRFC (Raytheon RF Components)
870 Winter St ..... Waltham MA 02451 781-522-3000 696
Web: www.raytheon.com

RRI (Regional Research Institute for Human Services)
Portland State University PO Box 751 ..... Portland OR 97207 503-725-4040 725-2140 668
Web: www.rri.pdx.edu

Rrk Assoc
14044 W Petronella Dr Ste 5 ..... Libertyville IL 60048 847-680-0866 196
Web: www.rrkassociates.net

RRMC (Rowan Regional Medical Ctr)
612 Mocksville Ave ..... Salisbury NC 28144 704-210-5000 210-5562 374-3
TF: 888-844-0080

Rrr Development Co
8817 Pleasantwood Ave NW ..... North Canton OH 44720 330-966-8855 454
Web: www.rrrdev.com

RS (IEEE Reliability Society)
IEEE Operations Ctr 445 Hoes Ln ..... Piscataway NJ 08854 732-981-0060 562-6380 49-19
TF: 800-678-4333 ■ *Web:* ieee.org

RS Audley Inc 1113 Route 3A ..... Bow NH 03304 603-224-7724 225-7614 188-4
Web: www.audleyconstruction.com

RS Braswell Company Inc
485 S Cannon Blvd ..... Kannapolis NC 28083 704-933-2269 933-7000 770
TF: 888-628-3550 ■ *Web:* www.rsbraswell.com

RS Consulting USA 39 S LaSalle St ..... Chicago IL 60603 312-368-0800 195
Web: www.rsconsulting-usa.com

RS Corcoran Co 500 N Vine St ..... New Lenox IL 60451 815-485-2156 485-2156 641
TF: 800-637-1067 ■ *Web:* www.corcoranpumps.com

RS Electronics Inc
34443 Schoolcraft Rd ..... Livonia MI 48150 734-525-1155 544-2570* 246
**Fax Area Code:* 800 ■ *TF:* 866-600-6040 ■ *Web:* www.carltonbates.com/content/rs-electronics

RS Harritan & Company Inc
3280 Formex Rd ..... Richmond VA 23224 804-275-7821 610
Web: www.rsharritan.com

RS Hughes Company Inc
1162 Sonora Ct ..... Sunnyvale CA 94086 408-739-3211 385
TF: 877-774-8443 ■ *Web:* www.rshughes.com

Rs Marketing Services LLC
35 Ft Boone Ct ..... Clayton NC 27527 919-585-4556 463
Web: www.rsmsinsights.com

RS Mowery & Sons Inc
1000 Bent Creek Blvd ..... Mechanicsburg PA 17050 717-506-1000 506-1010 187
Web: www.rsmowery.com

RS Owens & Co 5535 N Lynch Ave ..... Chicago IL 60630 773-282-6000 777
TF: 800-282-6200 ■ *Web:* www.rsowens.com

R&S Steel Co 3811 Joliet St ..... Denver CO 80239 303-321-9660 492
Web: www.rssteel.com

RS2 Technologies LLC
400 Fisher St Ste G ..... Munster IN 46321 219-836-9002 692
Web: www.rs2tech.com

RSA (Royal & SunAlliance Insurance Co of Canada)
18 York St Ste 800 ..... Toronto ON M5J2T8 416-366-7511 367-9869 391-4
TF: 800-268-8406 ■ *Web:* www.rsagroup.ca

RSA Engineering Inc
2522 Arctic Blvd Ste 200 ..... Anchorage AK 99503 907-276-0521 261

RSA Security Inc 174 Middlesex Tpke ..... Bedford MA 01730 781-515-5000 178-12
TF: 800-995-5095 ■ *Web:* www.rsa.com

RSAI (Roller Skating Assn International)
6905 Corporate Dr ..... Indianapolis IN 46278 317-347-2626 347-2636 48-22
TF: 800-258-8146 ■ *Web:* rollerskating.com

RSBCIH (Riverside-San Bernardino County Indian Health Inc)
11555 1/2 Potrero Rd ..... Banning CA 92220 951-849-4761 353
TF: 800-732-8805 ■ *Web:* www.rsbcihi.org

RSD Solutions Inc
177 Lincolnshire Dr ..... Fall River NS B2T1P8 902-441-4102 463
Web: www.rsdsolutions.com

RSDC of Michigan LLC 1775 Holloway Dr ..... Holt MI 48842 877-881-7732 480
TF: 877-881-7732 ■ *Web:* www.rsdcmi.com

RSES (Refrigeration Service Engineers Society)
1666 Rand Rd ..... Des Plaines IL 60016 847-297-6464 297-5038 49-3
TF: 800-297-5660 ■ *Web:* www.rses.org

RSF Social Finance
1002A O'Reilly Ave ..... San Francisco CA 94129 415-561-3900 401
Web: www.rsfsocialfinance.org

RSG Forest Products Inc
985 NW Second St ..... Kalama WA 98625 360-673-2825 673-5558 683
Web: www.rsgfp.com

RSH (Richmond State Hospital)
498 NW 18th St ..... Richmond IN 47374 765-966-0511 374-5
Web: www.in.gov/fssa/dmha/6914.htm

RSH Architects
363 Vanadium Rd Ste 200 ..... Pittsburgh PA 15243 412-429-1555 279-7285 186
Web: www.rsharc.com

R-S-H Engineering Inc
909 N 18th St Ste 200 ..... Monroe LA 71201 318-323-4009 261
TF: 888-340-4884 ■ *Web:* www.rsh.com

RSI (Reconditioned Systems Inc)
2636 S Wilson St Ste 105 ..... Tempe AZ 85282 480-968-1772 894-1907 319-1
TF: 800-280-5000 ■ *Web:* www.rsisystemsfurniture.com

RSI (Railway Supply Institute Inc)
425 Third St Ste 920 ..... Washington DC 20024 202-347-4664 347-0047 49-21
TF: 800-226-5962 ■ *Web:* www.rsiweb.org

Rsi Corp 543 Main St ..... Kiowa KS 67070 620-825-4600 196
TF: 888-830-5648 ■ *Web:* www.rsicorp.com

RSI Home Products Inc
400 E Orangethorpe Ave ..... Anaheim CA 92801 714-449-2200 115
Web: www.rsihomeproducts.com

RSI Insurance Brokers Inc
2801 Bristol St Ste 200 ..... Costa Mesa CA 92626 714-546-6616 390
TF: 800-828-5273 ■ *Web:* rsiinsurancebrokers.com

RSI Logistics Inc 2419 Science Pkwy ..... Okemos MI 48864 517-349-7713 194
Web: www.rsilogistics.com

RSM Co 811 Pressley Rd PO Box 31605 ..... Charlotte NC 28231 704-525-6851 525-8368 745-8
Web: www.rsmcompany.com

RSNA (Radiological Society of North America)
820 Jorie Blvd ..... Oak Brook IL 60523 630-571-2670 571-7837 49-8
TF: 800-381-6660 ■ *Web:* www.rsna.org

RSP Architects
1220 Marshall St NE ..... Minneapolis MN 55413 612-677-7100 677-7499 261
Web: www.rsparch.com

RSP Permian Inc 3141 Hood St Ste 500 ..... Dallas TX 75219 214-252-2700 536
Web: www.rsppermian.com

RSPA (Retail Solutions Providers Assn)
10130 Perimeter Pkwy Ste 420 ..... Charlotte NC 28216 704-357-3124 357-3127 49-18
TF: 800-782-2693 ■ *Web:* www.gorspa.org

R-Squared Puckett Inc 2650 Highway 18 ..... Puckett MS 39151 601-825-1171 247
Web: www.r2al.com

RSR Corp 2777 Stemmons Fwy Ste 1800 ..... Dallas TX 75207 214-631-6070 631-6146 485
Web: rsrcorp.com

RSR Group Inc 4405 Metric Dr ..... Winter Park FL 32792 407-677-1000 710
TF: 800-541-4867 ■ *Web:* www.rsrgroup.com

Rsss Lp 711 N Carancahua St ..... Corpus Christi TX 78475 361-993-1790 396
Web: hightouchtechnologies.com

RST (Rochester International Airport)
7600 Helgerson Dr SW ..... Rochester MN 55902 507-282-2328 27
TF: 800-227-4672 ■ *Web:* flyrst.com

Rstn Consulting Llc
1035 Pearl St Lbby 4 ..... Boulder CO 80302 303-447-6878 196
Web: www.rstn.com

RSVP (Retired & Senior Volunteer Program)
1201 New York Ave NW ..... Washington DC 20525 202-606-5000 197
TF: 800-833-3722 ■ *Web:* www.nationalservice.gov

RSVP Direct Inc 550 Northgate Pkwy ..... Wheeling IL 60090 847-215-9054 215-9230 459
TF: 866-507-5182 ■ *Web:* www.rsvpdirect.net

RSVP Publications
6730 W Linebaugh Ave Ste 201 ..... Tampa FL 33625 813-960-7787 310
TF: 800-360-7787 ■ *Web:* www.rsvppublications.com

RSVP Vacations
9200 Sunset Blvd Ste 500 ..... West Hollywood CA 90069 310-432-2300 729-2809* 760
**Fax Area Code:* 612 ■ *TF:* 800-328-7787

RSX Energy Inc
407 Second St SW Ste 1030 ..... Calgary AB T2P2Y3 403-266-0600 538
Web: www.rsxenergy.com

RT Tanaka Engineers Inc
871 Kolu St Ste 201 ..... Wailuku HI 96793 808-242-6861 261

RT Vanderbilt Company Inc
30 Winfield St ..... Norwalk CT 06855 203-853-1400 853-1452 144
TF Cust Svc: 800-243-6064 ■ *Web:* www.rtvanderbilt.com

RT's 3804 Mt Vernon Ave ..... Alexandria VA 22305 703-684-6010 548-0417 671
Web: www.rtsrestaurant.net

RTA (Riverside Transit Agency)
1825 Third St PO Box 59968 ..... Riverside CA 92517 951-565-5000 468
TF: 800-800-7821 ■ *Web:* www.riversidetransit.com

RTA (Greater Cleveland Regional Transit Authority)
1240 W Sixth St ..... Cleveland OH 44113 216-621-9500 468
Web: www.riderta.com

RTA (Regional Transit Authority)
2817 Canal St ..... New Orleans LA 70118 504-827-8300 468
Web: www.norta.com

RTA Furniture Corporation
5500 Linglestown Rd ..... Harrisburg PA 17112 717-540-5500 321
Web: www.justcabinets.com

RTC (Regional Transportation Commission of Southern Nevada)
600 S Grand Central Pkwy Ste 350 ..... Las Vegas NV 89106 702-676-1500 676-1518 468
TF: 800-228-3911 ■ *Web:* www.rtcsnv.com

RTC (Rails-to-Trails Conservancy)
2121 Ward Ct NW 5th Fl ..... Washington DC 20037 202-331-9696 223-9257 48-13
TF: 800-944-6847 ■ *Web:* www.railstotrails.org

RTC
1055 Thomas Jefferson St NW Ste 200 ..... Washington DC 20007 202-625-2111 424-7900 5
Web: www.rtcdirect.com

Rtc Direct Mailing Inc
56 Seip Ln ..... Shoemakersville PA 19555 610-562-5122 5
TF: 800-321-3136 ■ *Web:* rtcdirect.net

RTC Inc 2800 Golf Rd ..... Rolling Meadows IL 60008 847-640-2400 195
Web: www.rtc.com

RTD (Regional Transportation District)
1600 Blake St ..... Denver CO 80202 303-628-9000 468
TF: 800-366-7433 ■ *Web:* www.rtd-denver.com

RTD Financial Advisors Inc
30 S 17th St United Plaza Ste 1620 ..... Philadelphia PA 19103 215-557-3800 194
Web: www.rtdfinancial.com

RTEA (Cloud Peak Energy Inc)
505 S Gillette Ave PO Box 3009 ..... Gillette WY 82717 307-687-6000 262-0604* 501
**Fax Area Code:* 303 ■ *TF:* 866-470-4300 ■ *Web:* www.cloudpeakenergy.com

RTEC (Rural Transit Enterprises Coordinated Inc)
100 E Main St ..... Mount Vernon KY 40456 606-256-9835 108
TF: 800-321-7832 ■ *Web:* www.4rtec.com

RTI Biologics Inc 11621 Research Cir ..... Alachua FL 32615 386-418-8888 418-0342 85
NASDAQ: RTIX ■ *TF:* 877-343-6832 ■ *Web:* www.rtix.com

RTKL Assoc Inc 901 S Bond St ..... Baltimore MD 21231 410-537-6000 276-2136 261
Web: www.rtkl.com

RTL Networks Inc
1391 Speer Blvd Ste 850 ..... Denver CO 80204 303-757-3100 180
Web: www.rtl-networks.com

RTL Robinson Enterprises Ltd
350 Old Airport Rd ..... Yellowknife NT X1A2P4 867-873-6271 311
Web: westcanbulk.ca/rtl

RTM Consulting Inc
4335 Ferguson Dr Ste 210 ..... Cincinnati OH 45245 855-786-2555 786-2329 463
TF: 855-786-2555 ■ *Web:* www.rtmconsulting.net

RTM Productions Inc 130 SE Pkwy Ct ..... Franklin TN 37064 615-503-9700 116
Web: www.horsepowertv.com

Company / Address	City	State	ZIP	Phone	Fax	Class
RTN Federal Credit Union 600 Main St. *TF:* 800-338-0221 ■ *Web:* www.rtn.org	Waltham	MA	02452	781-736-9900	736-9856	219
RTNDA (Radio-Television News Directors Assn) 1600 K St NW Ste 700 *Web:* www.rtdna.org	Washington	DC	20006	202-659-6510	223-4007	49-14
RTP Co 580 E Front St. **Fax:* Hum Res ■ *TF:* 800-433-4787 ■ *Web:* www.rtpcompany.com	Winona	MN	55987	507-454-6900	454-2041*	605-2
RTP Corp 1834 SW Second St *Web:* www.rtpcorp.com	Pompano Beach	FL	33069	954-974-5500	975-9815	201
RTP Technology Corp 95 N Rte 17 *Web:* www.rtptech.com	Paramus	NJ	07652	201-796-2266		196
RTR (Rainbow Trout Ranch) 1484 FDR 250 PO Box 458 *TF:* 800-633-3397 ■ *Web:* www.rainbowtroutranch.com	Antonito	CO	81120	719-376-2440		239
Rtr Financial Services Inc 901 N Broadway Ste 3b *TF:* 800-435-4000 ■ *Web:* rtrfs.com	White Plains	NY	10603	914-644-1701		251
RTS (Regional Transit System) Station 5 PO Box 490 *Web:* www.go-rts.com	Gainesville	FL	32627	352-334-2600	334-2607	468
RTS Financial Service 9300 Metcalf Ste 301 *TF:* 877-242-4390 ■ *Web:* www.rtsfinancial.com	Overland Park	KS	66212	877-242-4390		272
RTS Packaging LLC 504 Thrasher St *TF:* 800-558-6984 ■ *Web:* www.rtspackaging.com	Norcross	GA	30071	800-558-6984		101
RTV (Rock the Vote) 1001 Connecticut Ave NW Ste 640 *Web:* www.rockthevote.com	Washington	DC	20036	202-719-9910		48-7
RTW Inc 8500 Normandale Lake Blvd Ste 1400 PO Box 390327 *TF Sales:* 800-789-2242 ■ *Web:* www.rtwi.com	Bloomington	MN	55437	952-893-0403	893-3700	391-4
RTY Installations Inc 13903 Ballantyne Meadows Dr	Charlotte	NC	28277	704-544-0726		131
Rtz Associates Inc 150 Grand Ave Ste 200 *Web:* rtzsystems.com	Oakland	CA	94612	510-986-6700		177
Ru San's 505 12th Ave S *Web:* rusansjapanese.com	Nashville	TN	37203	615-252-8787		671
RUAN Transportation Management Systems 666 Grand Ave 3200 Ruan Ctr *TF:* 866-782-6669 ■ *Web:* www.ruan.com	Des Moines	IA	50309	866-782-6669		289
Ruane Cunniff & Goldfarb Inc 9 W 57th St Ste 5000 *TF:* 800-686-6884 ■ *Web:* www.sequoiafund.com	New York	NY	10019	212-832-5280	832-5298	401
Rubatino Refuse Removal Inc 2812 Hoyt Ave *TF:* 800-584-3578 ■ *Web:* www.rubatino.com	Everett	WA	98201	425-259-0044	339-4196	804
RubbAir Door Div Eckel Industries Inc 100 Groton Shirley Rd *TF:* 800-966-7822 ■ *Web:* www.rubbair.com	Ayer	MA	01432	978-772-0480	772-7114	235
Rubber & Plastics Inc 7401 NE 47th Ave *Web:* www.conveyorbelt.com	Vancouver	WA	98661	360-567-4280		370
Rubber & Plastics News 1725 Merriman Rd *Web:* www.rubbernews.com	Akron	OH	44313	330-836-9180		532-3
Rubber Enterprises Inc 2083 Reek Rd *Web:* www.rubberenterprises.com	Imlay City	MI	48444	810-724-2400		370
Rubber Industries Inc 200 Cavanaugh Dr *Web:* www.rubberindustries.com	Shakopee	MN	55379	952-445-1320	445-7934	676
Rubbercraft Corp of California 3701 Conant St *Web:* www.rubbercraft.com	Long Beach	CA	90808	310-328-5402	618-1832	326
Rubberlite Inc 2501 Guyan Ave *Web:* www.rubberlite.com	Huntington	WV	25703	304-525-3116	523-4316	601
Rubbermaid Commercial Products (RCP) 3124 Valley Ave *TF:* 800-347-9800 ■ *Web:* www.rubbermaidcommercial.com	Winchester	VA	22601	540-667-8700	542-8770	608
Rubberset Co 101 W Prospect Ave *TF:* 800-345-4939 ■ *Web:* www.rubberset.com	Cleveland	OH	44115	800-345-4939		103
Ruben Cos 600 Madison Ave *Web:* www.rubenco.com	New York	NY	10022	212-293-9400		652
Rubenstein & Ziff Inc 11516 K-Tel Dr *Web:* www.quiltworksonline.com	Minnetonka	MN	55343	952-854-1460		711
Rubenstein Bros Inc 102 St Charles Ave *TF:* 800-725-7823 ■ *Web:* rubensteinsneworleans.com	New Orleans	LA	70130	504-581-6666		157-3
Rubicon Group Ltd, The 125 Windsor Dr Ste 118 *Web:* www.rubgrp.com	Oak Brook	IL	60523	630-574-7766		177
Rubicon Inc 9156 Hwy 75 PO Box 517 *Web:* www.huntsman.com	Geismar	LA	70734	225-673-6141	673-6442	605-2
Rubicon Marketing Inc 10925 Estate Ln Ste 208 *Web:* rubiconmarketing.com	Dallas	TX	75238	214-478-3929	432-1112	463
Rubicon Minerals Corp 121 King St W Ste 830 *NYSE: RBY* ■ *TF:* 844-818-1776 ■ *Web:* www.rubiconminerals.com	Toronto	ON	M5H3T9	416-766-2804	792-4601	502
Rubicon Programs 2500 Bissell Ave *TF:* 800-390-2699 ■ *Web:* www.rubiconprograms.org	Richmond	CA	94804	510-235-1516		260
Rubin & Levin PC 500 Marott Ctr 342 Massachusetts Ave *Web:* www.rubin-levin.com	Indianapolis	IN	46204	317-634-0300		428
Rubin Bros Inc 2241 S Halsted St *TF:* 800-283-9490 ■ *Web:* www.rubinbrothers.com	Chicago	IL	60608	312-942-1111		155-19
Rubin Communications Group Inc 4542 Bonney Rd Ste B *Web:* rubincommunications.com	Virginia Beach	VA	23462	757-456-5212		636
Rubin Licatesi PC 600 Old Cntry Rd Ste 440 *Web:* www.lawyerintl.com	Garden City	NY	11530	718-712-6864		445
Rubin Museum, The 150 W 17th St *TF:* 800-745-3000 ■ *Web:* www.rubinmuseum.org	New York	NY	10011	212-620-5000		522
Rubin Postaer & Assoc 2525 Colorado Ave *Web:* www.rpa.com	Santa Monica	CA	90404	310-394-4000		4
RubinBrown LLP 1 N Brentwood Blvd Ste 1100 *Web:* www.rubinbrown.com	Saint Louis	MO	63105	314-290-3300	290-3400	2
Rubino & McGeehin Consulting Group Inc 6903 Rockledge Dr Ste 1200 *Web:* www.rubino.com	Bethesda	MD	20817	301-564-3636		734
Rubio Marco (Sen R - FL) 284 Russell Bldg *Web:* www.rubio.senate.gov	Washington	DC	20510	202-224-3041		342-2
Rubio's Restaurants Inc 1902 Wright Pl Ste 300 *TF:* 800-354-4199 ■ *Web:* www.rubios.com	Carlsbad	CA	92008	760-929-8226	929-8203	670
Ruby Falls 1720 S Scenic Hwy *TF:* 800-755-7105 ■ *Web:* www.rubyfalls.com	Chattanooga	TN	37409	423-821-2544	821-6705	50-5
Ruby Hill Golf Shop 3400 W Ruby Hill Dr *Web:* rubyhill.com	Pleasanton	CA	94566	925-417-5850		711
Ruby River Steak House 4286 Riverdale Rd *Web:* www.rubyriver.com	Ogden	UT	84405	801-622-2320		671
Ruby River Steakhouse 1454 S University Ave *Web:* www.rubyriver.com	Provo	UT	84601	801-371-0648		671
Ruby Room 155 Portland St *Web:* www.onyxhotel.com/ruby-room/index.html	Boston	MA	02114	617-557-9950	557-0005	671
Ruby Stein Wagner 300 Rue Leo-pariseau Ste 1900 *TF:* 866-842-3911 ■ *Web:* rsw.ca	Montreal	QC	H2X4B5	514-842-3911		2
Ruby Tequila's 2001 S Georgia *TF:* 800-514-1489 ■ *Web:* www.rubytequilas.com	Amarillo	TX	79109	806-358-7829		671
Ruby Tuesday Inc 150 W Church Ave *NYSE: RT* ■ *Web:* www.rubytuesday.com	Maryville	TN	37801	865-379-5700		670
Ruby's Diner 1 Main St *Web:* www.rubys.com	Huntington Beach	CA	92648	714-969-7829		671
Ruchi 11168 Antioch Rd *Web:* www.ruchicuisine.com	Overland Park	KS	66210	913-661-9088		671
Rucker & Associates Inc 7009 N Ridge Dr Ste 300 *Web:* www.ruckerassociates.com	Raleigh	NC	27615	919-873-1268	873-1769	463
Ruckus Wireless Inc 350 W JAVA Dr *Web:* www.ruckuswireless.com	Sunnyvale	CA	94089	650-265-4200		647
Rudd Container Corp 4600 S Kolin *Web:* www.ruddcontainer.com	Chicago	IL	60632	773-847-7600		100
Rudd Equipment Co 4344 Poplar Level Rd *TF:* 800-527-2282 ■ *Web:* www.ruddequipment.com	Louisville	KY	40213	502-456-4050	459-8695	358
Ruder Finn 425 E 53rd St *Web:* www.ruderfinn.com	New York	NY	10022	212-593-6400	593-6397	636
Rudolf Steiner College 9200 Fair Oaks Blvd *Web:* www.steinercollege.edu	Fair Oaks	CA	95628	916-963-4000		166
Rudolph & Sletten Inc 1600 Seaport Blvd Ste 350 *Web:* www.rsconstruction.com	Redwood City	CA	94063	650-216-3600	599-9112	186
Rudolph Brothers 6550 Oley Speaks Way *TF:* 800-600-9508 ■ *Web:* www.rudolphbros.com	Canal Winchester	OH	43110	614-833-0707		711
Rudolph Foods Company Inc 6575 Bellefontaine Rd *TF:* 800-241-7675 ■ *Web:* www.rudolphfoods.com	Lima	OH	45804	419-648-3611	648-4087	296-9
Rudolph Technologies Inc 16 Jonspin Rd *NASDAQ: RTEC* ■ *TF:* 877-467-8365 ■ *Web:* www.rudolphtech.com	Wilmington	MA	01887	973-691-1300		472
Rudy's Country Store & Bar BQ 4930 S Loop 289 *Web:* www.rudysbbq.com	Lubbock	TX	79414	806-797-1777		671
Rue & Associates Inc 7264 Hanover Green Dr *Web:* www.rueassociates.com	Mechanicsville	VA	23111	804-730-7455		196
Rue Franklin 341 Franklin St *TF:* 800-897-8766 ■ *Web:* www.ruefranklin.com	Buffalo	NY	14202	716-852-4416		671
rue21 Inc 800 Commonwealth Dr Ste 100 *NASDAQ: RUE* ■ *Web:* www.rue21.com	Warrendale	PA	15086	724-776-9780	741-9020	157-6
Ruehlen Supply Company Inc 491 Corban Ave SE *TF:* 800-225-3410 ■ *Web:* www.ruehlensupply.com	Concord	NC	28025	704-788-2180		612
Ruekert & Mielke Inc W233 N2080 Ridgeview Pkwy *Web:* www.ruekertmielke.com/#infrastructure-strategies	Waukesha	WI	53188	262-542-5733	542-5631	261
Ruf Strategic Solutions 1533 E Spruce St *TF:* 800-829-8544 ■ *Web:* www.ruf.com	Olathe	KS	66061	800-829-8544		466
Ruffed Grouse Society (RGS) 451 McCormick Rd *TF:* 888-564-6747 ■ *Web:* www.ruffedgrousesociety.org	Coraopolis	PA	15108	412-262-4044	262-9207	48-3
Ruffin & Payne Inc 4000 Vawter Ave *Web:* www.ruffin-payne.com	Richmond	VA	23222	804-329-2691	321-4940	499
Ruffin Bldg Systems Inc 6914 Hwy 2	Oak Grove	LA	71263	318-428-2305	428-2231	105
Ruffin Cos 1522 S Florence St *Web:* www.ruffinco.com	Wichita	KS	67209	316-942-7940		655
Ruffin Hotels LP 4700 Airport Plaza Dr	Long Beach	CA	90815	562-425-5210		379
Rug Doctor LP 4701 Old Shepard Pl *TF:* 800-784-3628 ■ *Web:* www.rugdoctor.com	Plano	TX	75093	800-784-3628		264-2
Rug Hooking Magazine 3400 Dundee Rd Ste 220 *TF:* 866-375-8626 ■ *Web:* www.rughookingmagazine.com	Northbrook	IL	60062	717-796-0411		457-14
Rugg Mfg Company Inc 554 Willard St **Fax Area Code:* 978 ■ *TF:* 800-633-8772 ■ *Web:* www.rugg.com	Leominster	MA	01453	413-773-5471	401-2188*	429
Rugged Systems Inc 13000 Danielson St Q *TF:* 888-584-2673 ■ *Web:* www.coresystemsusa.com	Poway	CA	92064	858-391-1006		225
Ruggeri-Jensen-Azar & Assoc 4690 Chabot Dr *Web:* rja-gps.com	Pleasanton	CA	94588	925-227-9100		57
Ruggie Wealth Management 2100 Lake Eustis Dr *TF:* 888-343-2711 ■ *Web:* www.ruggiewealth.com	Tavares	FL	32778	352-343-2700		463

Company	City	State	Zip	Phone	Fax	Class
Ruggles Service Corp 2209 Dickens Rd *Web:* www.societyhq.com	Richmond	VA	23230	804-282-0062		47
Ruhle Cos Inc 99 Wall St *Web:* www.ruhle.com	Valhalla	NY	10595	914-761-2600	761-0405	253
Ruhlin Company Inc PO Box 190 *Web:* www.ruhlin.com	Sharon Center	OH	44274	330-239-2800	239-1828	186
Ruhof Corp, The 393 Sagamore Ave *Web:* www.ruhof.com	Mineola	NY	11501	516-294-5888		194
Ruhrpumpen Inc 4501 S 86th E Ave *Web:* www.ruhrpumpen.com	Tulsa	OK	74145	918-627-8400		537
Ruiz Foods Inc PO Box 37 *TF:* 800-477-6474 ■ *Web:* www.elmonterey.com	Dinuba	CA	93618	559-591-5510	591-1593	296-36
Ruiz Raul (Rep D - CA) 1319 Longworth Bldg *Web:* ruiz.house.gov	Washington	DC	20515	202-225-5330	225-1238	342-2
Rukert Terminals Corp 2021 S Clinton St *Web:* www.rukert.com	Baltimore	MD	21224	410-276-1013		465
RuleSphere International Inc 327 Still River Rd RT 110 PO Box 152 *Web:* www.rulesphere.com	Still River	MA	01467	978-456-8253		396
Rulesware LLC 10 N Martingale Rd Ste 400 *Web:* www.rulesware.com	Schaumburg	IL	60173	312-224-8501		196
Rulmeca Corp 6508 Windmill Way Ste B *Web:* www.rulmecacorp.com	Wilmington	NC	28405	910-794-9294		636
Rulon Co 2000 Ring Way Rd *Web:* www.rulonco.com	St Augustine	FL	32092	904-584-1400		200
RuMar Manufacturing Corp 925 S St *Web:* www.rumar.com	Mayville	WI	53050	920-387-2104	387-2367	697
Rumbi Island Grill 358 South 700 East *Web:* rumbi.com	Salt Lake City	UT	84102	801-530-1000		671
Rumble Tuff Inc 865 N 1430 W *TF:* 855-228-8388 ■ *Web:* www.rumbletuff.com	Orem	UT	84057	801-609-8168	796-2688	319-2
Rumpf Corp, The 701 Jefferson Ave *TF:* 800-579-7967 ■ *Web:* www.job1usa.com	Toledo	OH	43604	419-255-5005		260
Rumpke 10795 Hughes Rd *TF:* 800-582-3107 ■ *Web:* www.rumpke.com	Cincinnati	OH	45251	800-582-3107		804
Rumsey Electric Co 15 Colwell Ln *TF:* 800-462-2402 ■ *Web:* www.rumsey.com	Conshohocken	PA	19428	610-832-9000	941-8181	246
Rumsey Hall School 201 Romford Rd *Web:* www.rumseyhall.org	Washington Depot	CT	06794	860-868-0535	868-7907	622
Run Consultants LLC 925 N Point Pkwy Ste 160 *TF:* 866-457-2193 ■ *Web:* www.runconsultants.com	Alpharetta	GA	30005	866-457-2193		260
Run Energy LP 5009 S Danville Dr *Web:* www.runenergy.com	Abilene	TX	79602	325-795-1550		393
Rundle-Spence Manufacturing Co PO Box 510008 *TF:* 800-783-6060 ■ *Web:* www.rundle-spence.com	New Berlin	WI	53151	262-782-3000		612
Runge Conservation Nature Ctr 2901 W Truman Blvd *TF:* 800-392-1111 ■ *Web:* www.mdc.mo.gov	Jefferson City	MO	65109	573-751-4115	751-4467	50-5
Runnells Specialized Hospital of Union County 40 Watchung Way *Web:* www.ucnj.org	Berkeley Heights	NJ	07922	908-771-5700		374-7
Runnels County 613 Hutchings Ave Rm 303 *Web:* www.co.runnels.tx.us	Ballinger	TX	76821	325-365-2137	365-4823	338
Runner Technologies Inc 6530 W Rogers Cir Ste 31 *Web:* runnertech.com	Boca Raton	FL	33487	561-395-9322		177
Runner's Edge Inc, The 3195 N Federal Hwy *TF:* 888-361-1950 ■ *Web:* runnersedgeboca.com	Boca Raton	FL	33431	561-361-1950		711
Runners Forum of Carmel Inc 620 Station Dr *Web:* www.runnersforum.com	Carmel	IN	46032	317-844-1558		711
Running Foxes Petroleum Inc 6855 S Havana St Ste 400 *Web:* www.runningfoxes.com	Centennial	CO	80112	303-617-7242		579
Runtime Design Automation 2560 Mission College Blvd Ste 130 *Web:* runtimeinc.com	Santa Clara	CA	95054	408-492-0940		261
Runway Tire Service Inc 4115 19th Ave *TF:* 800-843-4665 ■ *Web:* www.runwaytireservice.com	Astoria	NY	11105	718-545-5200		54
Runyon's 9810 W Sample Rd *Web:* www.runyonsofcoralsprings.com	Coral Springs	FL	33065	954-752-2333		671
Runza National Inc 5931 S 58th St *Web:* runza.com	Lincoln	NE	68516	402-423-2394		670
Runzheimer International 1 Runzheimer Pk *TF:* 800-558-1702 ■ *Web:* www.runzheimer.com	Waterford	WI	53185	262-971-2200	971-2254	193
Ruotolo Assoc Inc (RA) 580 Sylvan Ave Ste M-B *TF:* 800-786-8656 ■ *Web:* www.ruotoloassociates.com	Englewood Cliffs	NJ	07632	201-568-3898	568-8783	317
Rupe's Hydraulics Sales & Service 725 N Twin Oaks Valley Rd *TF:* 800-354-7873 ■ *Web:* rupeshydraulics.com	San Marcos	CA	92069	760-744-9350		790
Rupp Arena 430 W Vine St *TF:* 800-745-3000 ■ *Web:* www.rupparena.com	Lexington	KY	40507	859-233-4567	253-2718	720
Ruppersberger C A Dutch (Rep D - MD) 2416 Rayburn Bldg *Web:* ruppersberger.house.gov	Washington	DC	20515	202-225-3061	225-3094	342-2
Ruprecht Co 1301 Allanson Rd *Web:* www.ruprechtcompany.com	Mundelein	IL	60060	312-829-4100		296-26
Rupununi Bar & Grill 119 Main St *TF:* 800-248-8454 ■ *Web:* www.rupununi.com	Bar Harbor	ME	04609	207-288-2886		671
Rural Coalition 1029 Vermont Ave NW Ste 601 *Web:* www.ruralco.org	Washington	DC	20005	202-628-7160	393-1816	48-2
Rural Community Transportation Inc (RCT) 1161 Portland St *Web:* sites.google.com/a/rctvt.org/riderct	Saint Johnsbury	VT	05819	802-748-8170	748-5275	108
Rural Development 1400 Independence Ave SW *TF:* 800-414-1226 ■ *Web:* www.rd.usda.gov	Washington	DC	20250	202-720-9540	720-1725	340-1
Rural Electric Convenience Co-op Co 3973 W SR 104 PO Box 19 *TF:* 800-245-7322 ■ *Web:* www.recc.coop	Auburn	IL	62615	217-438-6197	438-3212	245
Rural Electric Co-op (REC) 13942 Highway 76 PO Box 609 *TF:* 800-259-3504 ■ *Web:* www.recok.coop	Lindsay	OK	73052	405-756-3104	756-8957	245
Rural Health Resource Ctr 525 S Lake Ave Ste 320 *TF:* 800-997-6685 ■ *Web:* ruralcenter.org	Duluth	MN	55802	218-727-9390		449
Rural Mutual Insurance Company Inc 1241 John Q Hammons Dr *TF:* 800-362-7881 ■ *Web:* www.ruralins.com	Madison	WI	53717	608-836-5525		391-4
Rural Resources Community Action 956 S Main St *TF:* 800-538-7659 ■ *Web:* www.ruralresources.org	Colville	WA	99114	509-684-8421	684-4740	148
Rural Telephone Service Company Inc PO Box 158 *TF:* 877-625-7872 ■ *Web:* www.nex-tech.com	Lenora	KS	67645	785-567-4281	567-4401	736
Rural Transit Enterprises Coordinated Inc (RTEC) 100 E Main St *TF:* 800-321-7832 ■ *Web:* www.4rtec.com	Mount Vernon	KY	40456	606-256-9835		108
Rural Utilities Service 1400 Independence Ave SW *Web:* www.rd.usda.gov	Washington	DC	20250	202-720-9545		340-1
Rural/Metro Corp 9221 E Via de Ventura *TF:* 800-352-2309 ■ *Web:* www.ruralmetro.com	Scottsdale	AZ	85258	800-352-2309		30
Rural-Urban Record 24487 Squire Rd	Columbia Station	OH	44028	440-236-8982		532-4
Rurbanc Data Services Inc 7622 N SR- 66 *Web:* www.rdsiweb.com	Defiance	OH	43512	419-783-8800		225
Ruritan National 5451 Lyons Rd PO Box 487 *TF:* 877-787-8727 ■ *Web:* www.ruritan.org	Dublin	VA	24084	540-674-5431	674-2304	48-15
RUSA (Reference & User Services Assn) 50 E Huron St *TF:* 800-545-2433 ■ *Web:* www.ala.org/rusa	Chicago	IL	60611	312-280-4398	944-8085	49-11
Rusch Inc 2917 Weck Dr PO Box 12600 *TF:* 866-246-6990 ■ *Web:* teleflex.com/en/usa/notfound.html	Research Triangle Park	NC	27709	919-544-8000	361-3914	477
Ruscilli Construction Co Inc 5000 Arlington Ctr Blvd Ste 300 *Web:* www.ruscilli.com	Columbus	OH	43220	614-876-9484	876-0253	186
Rusco Inc 450 Gravers Rd Ste 220	Plymouth Meeting	PA	19462	610-313-9955		809
RUSD (Riverside Unified School District) 3380 14th St PO Box 2800 *Web:* www.rusdlink.org	Riverside	CA	92501	951-788-7135	778-5669	685
Rush Bobby L (Rep D - IL) 2188 Rayburn HOB *Web:* rush.house.gov	Washington	DC	20515	202-225-4372	226-0333	342-2
Rush County 101 E Second St County Courthouse **Fax:* Acctg ■ *Web:* www.rushcounty.in.gov	Rushville	IN	46173	765-932-2077	938-1163*	338
Rush Enterprises Inc 555 IH 35 S Ste 500 *NASDAQ: RUSHA* ■ *TF:* 800-973-7874 ■ *Web:* www.rushenterprises.com	New Braunfels	TX	78130	830-626-5200	626-5310	264-3
Rush Foundation Hospital 1314 19th Ave *Web:* www.rushhealthsystems.org	Meridian	MS	39301	601-483-0011	703-4427	374-3
Rush Gears Inc 550 Virginia Dr *TF:* 800-523-2576 ■ *Web:* www.rushgears.com	Fort Washington	PA	19034	800-523-2576	635-6273	709
Rush Industries Inc 118 N Wrenn St *TF:* 800-524-0258 ■ *Web:* www.rushfurniture.com	High Point	NC	27260	336-886-7700	886-2227	319-2
Rush Moore LLP 737 BISHOP St Ste 2400 *Web:* www.rmhawaii.com	Honolulu	HI	96813	808-521-0400	521-0497	428
Rush Oak Park Hospital (ROPH) 520 S Maple Ave *TF:* 800-515-0171 ■ *Web:* www.roph.org	Oak Park	IL	60304	708-383-9300		374-3
Rush Shelby Energy Inc 2777 S 840 W PO Box 55 *TF General:* 800-706-7362 ■ *Web:* www.rse.coop	Manilla	IN	46150	765-544-2600		245
Rush System for Health 1653 W Congress Pkwy *Web:* www.rush.edu	Chicago	IL	60612	312-942-5000	942-5831	353
Rush Truck Ctr - Lubbock 4515 Ave A *TF:* 888-987-2458 ■ *Web:* rushtruckcenters.com	Lubbock	TX	79404	806-747-2579	747-4171	510
Rush Truck Ctr - Whittier 2450 Kella Ave *TF:* 877-605-7623 ■ *Web:* rushtruckcenters.com	Whittier	CA	90601	562-551-5000		57
Rush University 600 S Paulina St *Web:* www.rushu.rush.edu	Chicago	IL	60612	312-942-7100		166
Rush University Medical Ctr 1653 W Congress Pkwy *Web:* www.rush.edu	Chicago	IL	60612	312-942-5000		374-3
Rush Wisconsin West 2500 Hauser St *Web:* www.crusa-soccer.com	La Crosse	WI	54601	608-785-2250		713
Rush-Copley Medical Ctr (RCMC) 2000 Ogden Ave *TF:* 866-426-7539 ■ *Web:* www.rushcopley.com	Aurora	IL	60504	630-978-6200		374-3
Rusher Loscavio & LoPresto 369 Pine St Ste 221 *Web:* www.rll.com	San Francisco	CA	94104	415-765-6583		266
Rush-Henrietta Central School District 2034 Lehigh Stn Rd *Web:* www.rhnet.org	Henrietta	NY	14467	585-359-5000	359-5045	685
Rushmore Cave 13622 Hwy 40 *TF:* 800-344-8826 ■ *Web:* www.rushmorecave.com	Keystone	SD	57751	605-255-4384		50-5
Rushmore Forest Products 23848 Hwy 385 PO Box 619 *TF:* 866-466-5254 ■ *Web:* neimanenterprises.com	Hill City	SD	57745	605-574-2512		683
Rushmore Plaza Civic Ctr 444 Mt Rushmore Rd *Web:* www.gotmine.com	Rapid City	SD	57701	605-394-4115	394-4119	205

Name / Address	City	State	ZIP	Phone	Fax	Class
Rushmore View Inn 610 Hwy 16A	Keystone	SD	57751	605-666-4466		379
Rushworks 800 Parker Sq Ste 200	Flower Mound	TX	75028	469-293-1024		179
Web: www.rushworks.tv						
Rusk County 115 N Main St Ste 206	Henderson	TX	75652	903-657-0330		338
Web: www.co.rusk.tx.us						
Rusk County 311 Miner Ave E	Ladysmith	WI	54848	715-532-2100	532-2237	338
Web: www.ruskcounty.org						
Rusk County ElectricCo-op Inc						
3162 State Hwy 43 E	Henderson	TX	75652	903-657-4571		245
Web: www.rcelectric.org						
Rusk County Library (RCL)						
106 E Main St	Henderson	TX	75652	903-657-8557		434-3
Web: www.rclib.org						
Rusk High School 203 E Seventh St	Rusk	TX	75785	903-683-5592		685
TF: 800-877-8339 ■ *Web:* www.ruskisd.net						
Rusk State Hospital 805 N Dickinson Dr	Rusk	TX	75785	903-683-3421	683-7400	374-5
Web: www.dshs.texas.gov/mhhospitals/RuskSH						
Rusken Packaging Inc PO Box 2100	Cullman	AL	35056	256-734-0092	734-3008	101
TF: 800-232-8108 ■ *Web:* www.rusken.com						
Ruskin Manufacturing Co						
3900 Doctor Greaves Rd	Grandview	MO	64030	816-761-7476	765-8955	607
Web: www.ruskin.com						
Ruskin Moscou Faltischek PC						
East Tower 15th Fl 1425 RXR Plaza	Uniondale	NY	11556	516-663-6600		428
Web: www.rmfpc.com						
Ruskin Rooftop Systems						
1625 Diplomat Dr	Carrollton	TX	75006	972-247-7447		14
Web: www.ruskinrooftopsystems.com						
Russ Bassett Co 8189 Byron Rd	Whittier	CA	90606	562-945-2445	698-8972	286
TF: 800-350-2445 ■ *Web:* www.russbassett.com						
Russ Blakely & Assoc						
620 Lindsay St Ste 201	Chattanooga	TN	37403	423-266-8306		41
Web: www.rbabenefits.com						
Russ Darrow Group Inc						
W133 N8569 Executive Pkwy	Menomonee Falls	WI	53051	262-250-9600		57
Web: russdarrow.com						
Russ Lyon Sotheby's International Realty						
21040 N Pima Rd	Scottsdale	AZ	85255	480-502-3500		652
Web: www.russlyon.com						
Russ Reid Company Inc						
2 N Lake Ave Ste 600	Pasadena	CA	91101	626-449-6100		5
Web: www.russreid.com						
Russ' Restaurants Inc 390 E Eigth St	Holland	MI	49423	616-396-6571	396-6755	670
TF: 800-521-1778 ■ *Web:* www.russrestaurants.com						
Russel Metals Inc						
6600 Financial Dr	Mississauga	ON	L5N7J6	905-819-7777	819-7409	492
TSE: RUS ■ *TF:* 800-268-0750 ■ *Web:* www.russelmetals.com						
Russelectric Inc 99 Industrial Pk Rd	Hingham	MA	02043	781-749-6000		729
TF: 800-225-5250 ■ *Web:* www.russelectric.com						
Russell C Davis Planetarium						
201 E Pascagoula St	Jackson	MS	39201	601-960-1552		598
Web: www.jacksonms.gov/index.aspx?nId=142						
Russell Cave National Monument						
3729 County Rd 98	Bridgeport	AL	35740	256-495-2672	495-9220	564
TF: 866-705-5711 ■ *Web:* www.nps.gov/ruca						
Russell Cellular Inc						
5624 S Hwy FF	Battlefield	MO	65619	417-886-7542		736
Web: www.russellcellular.com						
Russell Construction Company Inc						
4600 E 53rd St	Davenport	IA	52807	563-459-4600		187
Web: www.russellco.com						
Russell Corp 755 Lee St	Alexander City	AL	35010	256-500-4000		155-1
Russell County						
410 Monument Sq PO Box 397	Jamestown	KY	42629	270-343-2112	343-2134	338
Web: www.rcfcky.com						
Russell County 137 Highland Dr	Lebanon	VA	24266	276-889-8000	889-8011	338
Web: www.russellcountyva.us						
Russell County 1000 Broad St	Phenix City	AL	36867	334-298-7979	298-7979	338
Web: russellcountyprobate.us						
Russell County						
401 N Main St PO Box 113	Russell	KS	67665	785-483-4641	483-5725	338
Web: ks-russellco.manatron.com						
Russell County News 958 Wichita Ave	Russell	KS	67665	785-483-2116		532-2
Russell County Public Library						
248 W Main St	Lebanon	VA	24266	276-889-8044	889-8045	434-3
Web: www.russell.lib.va.us						
Russell Florist Inc						
5001 Gravois Ave	Saint Louis	MO	63116	314-351-4676		292
Web: russellfloriststlouis.net						
Russell Food Equipment Ltd						
1255 Venables St	Vancouver	BC	V6A3X6	604-253-6611		14
TF: 800-663-0707 ■ *Web:* www.russellfood.ca						
Russell Forest Products Inc						
719 Railroad St SW	Hartselle	AL	35640	256-773-1607		111
Web: www.russellforest.com						
Russell Herder						
275 Market St Ste 319	Minneapolis	MN	55405	612-455-2360		7
Web: www.russellherder.com						
Russell Investment Group						
1301 Second Ave Ste 18	Seattle	WA	98101	800-787-7354		401
TF: 800-787-7354 ■ *Web:* russellinvestments.com/us						
Russell Investments						
1301 Second Ave 18th Fl	Seattle	WA	98101	206-505-7877		401
TF: 800-426-7969 ■ *Web:* russellinvestments.com/us						
Russell Johns Associates LLC						
5020 W Linebaugh Ave Ste 210	Tampa	FL	33624	727-443-7667		5
Web: russelljohns.com						
Russell Karting Specialties Inc						
PO Box 1220	Raymore	MO	64083	816-322-3330	322-2860	57
TF: 800-821-3359 ■ *Web:* russellkarting.com						
Russell Phillips & Associates LLC						
500 Cross Keys Office Pk	Fairport	NY	14450	585-223-1130		463
Web: www.phillipsllc.com						
Russell Reynolds Assoc Inc						
200 Pk Ave 23rd Fl	New York	NY	10166	212-351-2000		266
TF: 800-259-0470 ■ *Web:* www.russellreynolds.com						
Russell Sage College 45 Ferry St	Troy	NY	12180	518-244-2217	244-6880*	166
**Fax:* Admissions ■ *TF Admissions:* 888-837-9724 ■ *Web:* www.sage.edu						

Name / Address	City	State	ZIP	Phone	Fax	Class
Russell Sage Foundation						
112 E 64th St	New York	NY	10065	212-750-6000	371-4761	668
Web: www.russellsage.org						
Russell Standard Corp						
285 Kappa Dr Ste 300	Pittsburgh	PA	15238	800-323-3053		46
TF General: 800-323-3053 ■ *Web:* www.russellstandard.com						
Russell Stephens LLC						
445 S Figueroa St Ste 2600	Los Angeles	CA	90071	213-612-7711		463
Web: www.russellstephens.com						
Russell Steve (Rep R - OK)						
128 Cannon HOB	Washington	DC	20515	202-225-2132	226-1463	342-2
Web: russell.house.gov						
Russell Stover Candies Inc						
4900 Oak St	Kansas City	MO	64112	816-842-9240		296-8
TF: 800-477-8683 ■ *Web:* www.russellstover.com						
Russell's 1918 Ash St	Scranton	PA	18510	570-961-8949		671
Russellville Area Chamber of Commerce						
708 W Main St	Russellville	AR	72801	479-968-2530	968-5894	139
Web: www.russellvillechamber.org						
Russellville Steel Company Inc						
PO Box 1538	Russellville	AR	72811	479-968-2211	968-3486	492
Web: www.rsvlsteel.com						
Russia 136 E 67th St	New York	NY	10065	212-861-4900	628-0252	784
Web: russiaun.ru						
Consulate General						
600 University St Ste 2510	Seattle	WA	98121	206-728-0232		257
Web: seattle.mid.ru/web/seattle-en/main						
Consulate General 2790 Green St	San Francisco	CA	94123	415-928-6878	929-0306	257
Web: www.consulrussia.org						
Consulate General 9 E 91st St	New York	NY	10128	212-534-3782		257
Web: newyork.mid.ru						
Embassy 2650 Wisconsin Ave NW	Washington	DC	20007	202-298-5700	298-5735	257
Web: www.russianembassy.org						
Russian Fort Elizabeth State Historical Park						
3060 Eiwa St Ste 306	Lihue	HI	96766	808-274-3444	274-3448	565
Web: dlnr.hawaii.gov						
Russian National Tourist Office						
224 W 30th St Ste 701	New York	NY	10001	646-473-2233	473-2205	775
TF: 877-221-7120 ■ *Web:* www.russia-travel.com						
Russin Lumber Corp 21 Leonards Dr	Montgomery	NY	12549	845-457-4000	457-4010	191-3
TF: 800-724-0010 ■ *Web:* www.russinlumber.com						
Russ-Knits Inc 520 E Main St	Candor	NC	27229	910-974-4114	974-4023	745-4
Web: www.russknits.com						
Russo & Steele LLC 5230 S 39th St	Phoenix	AZ	85040	602-252-2697		57
Web: russoandsteele.com						
Russo Corp 1421 Mims Ave SW	Birmingham	AL	35211	205-923-4434		186
Web: www.russocorp.com						
Russo Farms Inc 1962 SE Ave	Vineland	NJ	08360	856-692-5942		10-11
Web: russofarms.com						
Russo Partners LLC						
12 W 27th St 4th Fl	New York	NY	10001	212-845-4200	845-4260	636
Web: www.russopartnersllc.com						
Russtech Inc 1338 Vickers Rd	Tallahassee	FL	32303	850-562-9811		768
TF: 800-682-8242 ■ *Web:* www.russtechinc.com						
Rust College 150 Rust Ave	Holly Springs	MS	38635	662-252-8000	252-2258*	166
**Fax:* Admissions ■ *TF:* 888-886-8492 ■ *Web:* www.rustcollege.edu						
Rust Constructors Inc						
2 Perimeter Pk S Ste 300 W	Birmingham	AL	35243	205-995-7171		187
Web: rustconstructors.azurewebsites.net						
Rust Orling Architecture Inc						
1215 Cameron St	Alexandria	VA	22314	703-836-3205		186
TF: 800-424-3996 ■ *Web:* www.rustorling.com						
Rusted Moon Outfitters Inc						
6410 Cornell Ave	Indianapolis	IN	46220	317-253-4453		711
Web: www.rustedmoonoutfitters.com						
Rustic Canyon Partners						
100 Wilshire Blvd Ste 200	Santa Monica	CA	90401	310-998-8000		792
Web: rusticcanyon.com						
Rustler Lodge						
10380 East Hwy 210 PO Box 8030	Alta	UT	84092	801-742-2200	742-3832	669
TF: 888-532-2582 ■ *Web:* www.rustlerlodge.com						
Rust-Oleum Corp						
11 E Hawthorn Pkwy	Vernon Hills	IL	60061	847-367-7700		550
TF: 800-323-3584 ■ *Web:* www.rustoleum.com						
Ruston/Lincoln Chamber of Commerce						
2111 N Trenton St	Ruston	LA	71270	318-255-2031	255-3481	139
TF: 800-392-9032 ■ *Web:* www.rustonlincoln.org						
Rusty Hardin & Associates LLP						
5 Houston Ctr 1401 McKinney Ste 2250	Houston	TX	77010	713-652-9000		428
TF: 800-404-3970 ■ *Web:* rustyhardin.com						
Rusty Parrot Lodge & Spa PO Box 1657	Jackson	WY	83001	307-733-2000	733-5566	669
TF: 800-458-2004 ■ *Web:* www.rustyparrot.com						
Rusty Pelican 2425 N Rocky Pt Dr	Tampa	FL	33607	813-281-1943		671
Web: www.therustypelican.com						
Rusty Rudder Restaurant						
113 Dickinson St	Dewey Beach	DE	19971	302-227-3888		671
Web: rustyrudderdewey.com						
Rusty's Pizza Parlors Inc						
228 W Carrillo St Ste F	Santa Barbara	CA	93101	805-963-9127	962-5054	670
Web: www.rustyspizza.com						
Rutan Poly Industries Inc 39 Siding Pl	Mahwah	NJ	07430	201-529-1474		297-8
TF: 800-872-1474 ■ *Web:* www.rutanpoly.com						
Rutberg & Company LLC						
351 California St Ste 1100	San Francisco	CA	94104	415-371-1186		690
Web: www.rutbergco.com						
Rutgers Business School (RBS)						
1 Washington Pk 3rd Fl	Newark	NJ	07102	973-353-1821		668
Web: www.business.rutgers.edu/default.aspx?id=645						
Rutgers Gardens						
112 Ryders Ln						
Cook College/Rutgers University	New Brunswick	NJ	08901	732-932-8451	932-7060	97
Web: www.rutgersgardens.rutgers.edu						
Rutgers Organics Corp (ROC)						
201 Struble Rd	State College	PA	16801	814-238-2424		143
TF: 888-469-2188 ■ *Web:* federalregister.gov						
Rutgers The State University of New Jersey						
Camden 406 Penn St	Camden	NJ	08102	856-225-6104	225-6498*	166
**Fax:* Admissions ■ *Web:* www.camden.rutgers.edu						

	City	State	ZIP	Phone	Fax	Class
Libraries 169 College Ave	New Brunswick	NJ	08901	732-932-7505	932-1101	434-6
Web: www.libraries.rutgers.edu						
Newark 249 University Ave Rm 100	Newark	NJ	07102	973-353-5205	353-1440*	166
**Fax:* Admissions ■ *Web:* www.newark.rutgers.edu						
School of Law Camden 217 N Fifth St	Camden	NJ	08102	856-225-6375		167-1
TF: 800-466-7561 ■ *Web:* www.camlaw.rutgers.edu						
University Libraries 165 Bevier Rd	Piscataway	NJ	08854	732-445-3854	445-5703	434-1
Web: www.libraries.rutgers.edu						
Rutgers University Foundation						
7 College Ave Winants Hall	New Brunswick	NJ	08901	732-932-7777		166
TF: 800-641-7940 ■ *Web:* www.rutgers.edu						
Rutgers University Press						
106 Somerset St 3rd Fl	New Brunswick	NJ	08901	848-445-7762	745-4935*	637-4
**Fax Area Code:* 732 ■ *TF:* 800-848-6224 ■ *Web:* www.rutgersuniversitypress.org						
Rutgers, The State University of New Jersey						
Rutgers Biomedical and Health Sciences						
Stanley S Bergen Bldg 65 Bergen Street	Newark	NJ	07103	973-972-4400		167-2
Web: rbhs.rutgers.edu						
Ruth Bancroft Garden						
1552 Bancroft Rd	Walnut Creek	CA	94598	925-210-9663	256-1889	97
Web: www.ruthbancroftgarden.org						
Ruth Eckerd Hall						
1111 McMullen Booth Rd	Clearwater	FL	33759	727-791-7060		572
TF: 800-875-8682 ■ *Web:* www.rutheckerdhall.com						
Ruth Enlow Library 6 N Second St	Oakland	MD	21550	301-334-3996	334-4152	434-3
TF: 800-656-4673 ■ *Web:* www.relib.net						
Ruth Lilly Medical Library						
975 W Walnut St IB 100	Indianapolis	IN	46202	317-274-7182		434-1
TF: 877-952-1988 ■ *Web:* www.library.medicine.iu.edu						
Ruth's Chris Steak House						
7720 Jones-Maltsberger Rd	San Antonio	TX	78216	210-821-5051		671
Web: www.ruthschris.com						
Ruth's Chris Steak House						
500 Ala Moana Blvd Restaurant Row	Honolulu	HI	96813	808-599-3860		671
TF: 800-442-1162 ■ *Web:* www.ruthschris.com						
Ruth's Chris Steak House						
7001 N Scottsdale Rd Ste 290	Scottsdale	AZ	85253	480-991-5988		671
Web: www.ruthschris.com						
Ruth's Chris Steak House						
2513 Berlin Tpke	Newington	CT	06111	860-666-2202		671
Web: www.ruthschris.com						
Ruth's Chris Steak House						
2300 Woodcrest Pl	Birmingham	AL	35209	205-879-9995		671
Web: www.ruthschris.com						
Ruth's Chris Steak House						
2320 Salzedo St	Coral Gables	FL	33134	305-461-8360		671
Web: www.ruthschris.com						
Ruth's Chris Steak House						
661 N Federal Hwy 1	North Palm Beach	FL	33408	561-863-0660		671
Web: www.ruthschris.com						
Ruth's Chris Steak House						
224 S Beverly Dr	Beverly Hills	CA	90212	310-859-8744		671
Web: www.ruthschris.com						
Ruth's Chris Steak House						
2058 Airport Blvd	Mobile	AL	36606	251-476-0516		671
Web: www.ruthschris.com						
Ruth's Chris Steak House 6 PPG Pl	Pittsburgh	PA	15222	412-391-4800		671
Web: www.ruthschris.com						
Ruth's Chris Steak House						
301 Severn Ave	Annapolis	MD	21403	410-990-0033		671
Web: www.ruthschris.com						
Ruth's Chris Steak House						
600 Water St	Baltimore	MD	21202	410-783-0033		671
Web: www.ruthschris.com						
Ruth's Chris Steak House						
7550 High Cross Blvd	Columbus	OH	43235	614-885-2910		671
Web: www.ruthschris.com						
Ruth's Chris Steak House						
3633 Veterans Memorial Blvd	Metairie	LA	70002	504-888-3600		671
Web: www.ruthschris.com						
Ruth's Chris Steak House						
920 Second Ave S	Minneapolis	MN	55402	612-672-9000		671
Web: www.ruthschris.com						
Ruth's Chris Steak House						
1601 Van Ness Ave	San Francisco	CA	94109	415-673-0557		671
Web: www.ruthschris.com						
Ruth's Chris Steak House 727 Pine St	Seattle	WA	98101	206-624-8524		671
Web: www.ruthschris.com						
Ruth's Chris Steak House						
145 Richmond St W Hilton Toronto Hotel	Toronto	ON	M5H2L2	416-955-1455		671
Web: www.ruthschris.com						
Ruth's Chris Steak House						
1030 W Canton Ave Ste 100	Winter Park	FL	32789	407-622-2444		671
Web: www.ruthschris.com						
Ruth's Chris Steak House						
1201 Riverplace Blvd	Jacksonville	FL	32207	904-396-6200		671
Web: www.ruthschris.com						
Ruth's Chris Steak House						
7501 W Sand Lake Rd	Orlando	FL	32819	407-226-3900		671
Web: www.ruthschris.com						
Ruth's Chris Steak House						
267 Marietta St	Atlanta	GA	30313	404-223-6500		671
Web: ruthschris.net						
Ruth's Chris Steak House						
6100 Dutchman's Ln 16th Fl	Louisville	KY	40205	502-479-0026		671
Web: www.ruthschris.com						
Ruth's Chris Steak House						
107 W Sixth St	Austin	TX	78701	512-477-7884		671
Web: ruthschris.com						
Ruth's Chris Steak House						
2231 Crystal Dr 11th Fl	Arlington	VA	22202	703-979-7275		671
Web: www.ruthschris.com						
Ruth's Chris Steak House						
2201 E Camelback Rd	Phoenix	AZ	85016	602-957-9600		671
Web: www.ruthschris.com						
Ruth's Chris Steak House						
17840 Dallas Pkwy	Dallas	TX	75287	972-250-2244		671
Web: www.ruthschris.com						
Ruth's Chris Steak House						
2100 W End Ave	Nashville	TN	37203	615-320-0163		671
Web: www.ruthschris.com						
Ruth's Chris Steakhouse						
2010 Renaissance Pk Pl	Cary	NC	27513	919-677-0033		671
Web: www.ruthschris.com						
Ruth's Chris Steakhouse						
1355 N Harbor Dr	San Diego	CA	92101	619-233-1422		671
Web: www.ruthschris.com						
Ruth's Hospitality Group Inc						
1030 W Canton Ave Ste 100`	Winter Park	FL	32789	407-333-7440	833-9625	670
NASDAQ: RUTH ■ *Web:* www.ruthschris.com						
Rutheford & Chekene						
375 Beale St Ste 310	San Francisco	CA	94105	415-568-4400		256
TF: 800-786-4452 ■ *Web:* www.ruthchek.com						
Rutherford B Hayes Presidential Ctr						
Spiegel Grove	Fremont	OH	43420	419-332-2081	332-4952	434-2
TF: 800-998-7737 ■ *Web:* www.rbhayes.org						
Rutherford Controls Int'l Corp						
210 Shearson Crescent	Cambridge	ON	N1T1J6	519-621-7651		350
TF: 800-265-6630 ■ *Web:* www.rutherfordcontrols.com						
Rutherford Correctional Ctr						
549 Ledbetter Rd	Spindale	NC	28160	828-286-4121	286-9285	213
Web: www.doc.state.nc.us						
Rutherford County						
319 N Maple St Ste 121	Murfreesboro	TN	37130	615-898-7800	898-7830	338
Web: rutherfordcountytn.gov						
Rutherford County 289 N Main St	Rutherfordton	NC	28139	828-287-6060	287-6210	338
Web: www.rutherfordcountync.gov						
Rutherford County Chamber of Commerce						
501 Memorial Blvd	Murfreesboro	TN	37129	615-893-6565	890-7600	139
TF: 800-716-7560 ■ *Web:* www.rutherfordchamber.org						
Rutherford County Chamber of Commerce						
162 N Main St	Rutherfordton	NC	28139	828-287-3090	287-0799	139
TF: 866-478-4646 ■ *Web:* www.rutherfordcoc.org						
Rutherford Electric Membership Corp						
186 Hudlow Rd PO Box 1569	Forest City	NC	28043	828-245-1621	248-2319	245
TF: 800-521-0920 ■ *Web:* www.remc.com						
Rutherford Institute						
PO Box 7482	Charlottesville	VA	22906	434-978-3888	978-1789	48-8
TF: 800-225-1791 ■ *Web:* www.rutherford.org						
Rutherford John (Rep R - FL)						
230 Cannon HOB	Washington	DC	20515	202-225-2501		342-2
Web: rutherford.house.gov						
Rutherford Regional Health System						
288 S Ridgecrest Ave	Rutherfordton	NC	28139	828-286-5000		374-3
TF: 800-542-4225 ■ *Web:* www.myrutherfordregional.com						
Rutland Herald PO Box 668	Rutland	VT	05702	800-498-4296		532-2
TF: 800-498-4296 ■ *Web:* www.rutlandherald.com						
Rutland Mental Health Services Inc						
78 S Main St	Rutland	VT	05701	802-775-2381		726
TF: 800-775-1000 ■ *Web:* www.rmhsccn.org						
Rutland Plastic Technologies						
10021 Rodney St	Pineville	NC	28134	704-553-0046	552-6589	605-2
TF: 800-438-5134 ■ *Web:* www.rutlandinc.com						
Rutland Plywood Corp 1 Ripley Rd	Rutland	VT	05701	802-747-4000		683
Web: www.rutply.com						
Rutland Region Chamber of Commerce						
50 Merchants Row	Rutland	VT	05701	802-773-2747		338
TF: 800-756-8880 ■ *Web:* www.rutlandvermont.com						
Rutland Regional Medical Ctr						
160 Allen St	Rutland	VT	05701	802-775-7111	747-1620	374-3
Web: www.rrmc.org						
Rutland State Park 2 Crawford Rd	Rutland	MA	01543	508-886-6333		565
Web: www.mass.gov						
Rutledge State Prison 7175 Manor Rd	Columbus	GA	31907	706-568-2340		213
Rutt HandCrafted Cabinetry						
215 Diller Ave	New Holland	PA	17557	717-351-1700		115
Web: ruttcabinetry.com						
Rutter Dairy Inc 2100 N George St	York	PA	17404	717-848-9827		296-27
Web: www.rutters.com						
Ruttger's Bay Lake Lodge						
25039 Tame Fish Lake Rd PO Box 400	Deerwood	MN	56444	218-678-2885	678-2864	669
TF: 800-450-4545 ■ *Web:* www.ruttgers.com						
Ruttura & Sons Construction Co Inc						
200 Cabot St	West Babylon	NY	11704	631-454-0291	454-8804	189-5
Web: www.ruttura.com						
R-V Industries Inc 584 Poplar Rd	Honey Brook	PA	19344	610-273-2457	273-3361*	386
**Fax:* Sales ■ *Web:* www.rvii.com						
RV World Inc of Nokomis						
2110 Tamiami Trl N	Nokomis	FL	34275	941-966-2182		57
TF: 800-262-2182 ■ *Web:* www.rvworldinc.com						
RVDA (Recreation Vehicle Dealers Assn)						
3930 University Dr 3rd Fl	Fairfax	VA	22030	703-591-7130	591-0734	49-18
TF: 800-336-0355 ■ *Web:* www.rvda.org						
RVIA (Recreation Vehicle Industry Assn)						
1896 Preston White Dr	Reston	VA	20191	703-620-6003	620-5071	49-21
TF: 800-336-0154 ■ *Web:* www.rvia.org						
RVing Women (RVW)						
879 N Plaza Dr Ste B103	Apache Junction	AZ	85120	480-671-6226	671-6230	48-23
TF: 888-557-8464 ■ *Web:* rvingwomen.org						
RVision Inc 2445 Fifth Ave Ste 450	San Diego	CA	92101	619-233-1403		628
Web: www.rvisionusa.com						
RVM Inc 40 Rector St 17th Fl	New York	NY	10006	800-525-7915		396
TF: 800-525-7915 ■ *Web:* www.rvminc.com						
RVW (RVing Women)						
879 N Plaza Dr Ste B103	Apache Junction	AZ	85120	480-671-6226	671-6230	48-23
TF: 888-557-8464 ■ *Web:* rvingwomen.org						
RW Advertising Inc 313 Canal St	Lemont	IL	60439	630-257-1179		7
RW Allen LLC 1015 Broad St	Augusta	GA	30901	706-733-2800	733-3879	186
Web: www.rwallen.com						
RW Beckett Corp PO Box 1289	Elyria	OH	44036	440-327-1060	327-1064	357
TF: 800-645-2876 ■ *Web:* www.beckettcorp.com						
RW Engineering & Surveying Inc						
6225 N 89th Cir	Omaha	NE	68134	402-573-2205		261
Web: rwomaha.com						
RW Norton Art Gallery						
4747 Creswell Ave	Shreveport	LA	71106	318-865-4201	869-0435	520
TF: 800-551-8682 ■ *Web:* www.rwnaf.org						

Name / Address	City	State	ZIP	Phone	Fax	Class
RW Pressprich & Company Inc Research Div 452 Fifth Ave 12th Fl *Web:* www.pressprich.com	New York	NY	10018	212-832-6200		401
RW Sauder Inc 570 Furnace Hills Pk *TF:* 800-233-0413 ■ *Web:* www.saudereggs.com	Lititz	PA	17543	717-626-2074	626-0493	297-10
RW Screw Products Inc 999 Oberlin Rd SW *TF:* 866-797-2739 ■ *Web:* rwscrew.com	Massillon	OH	44647	330-837-9211	837-9223	621
RW Setterlin Bldg Co 560 Harmon Ave *Web:* www.setterlin.com	Columbus	OH	43223	614-459-7077		186
RW Summers Railroad Contractor Inc 3693 E Gandy Rd *TF:* 800-736-4255 ■ *Web:* www.rwsummers.net	Bartow	FL	33830	863-533-8107	533-8100	188-8
RW Warner Inc 217 Monroe Ave *Web:* www.rwwarner.com	Frederick	MD	21701	301-662-5387	698-0451	189-10
Rwanda 124 E 39th St	New York	NY	10016	212-679-9010		784
Rwanda Embassy 1875 Connecticut Ave N W *Web:* www.rwandaembassy.org	Washington	DC	20009	202-232-2882	232-4544	257
RWC Inc 2105 S Euclid Ave *TF:* 800-443-9353 ■ *Web:* www.rwcinc.com	Bay City	MI	48706	989-684-4030	684-3960	811
RWDSU 30 E 29th St *TF:* 866-781-4430 ■ *Web:* rwdsu.info	New York	NY	10016	212-684-5300	779-2809	414
RWH Trucking Inc 2970 Old Oakwood Rd *TF:* 800-256-8119 ■ *Web:* www.rwhtrucking.com	Oakwood	GA	30566	800-256-8119		780
RWI (RiskWatch) 1237 N Gulfstream Ave *TF:* 800-360-1898 ■ *Web:* riskwatch.com/contact-us	Sarasota	Fl	34236	800-360-1898		178-10
RWI Ventures 545 Middlefield Rd Ste 220 *Web:* www.rwigroup.com	Menlo Park	CA	94025	650-543-3300		401
RWJ University Hospital at Hamilton 1 Hamilton Health Pl *Web:* www.rwjhamilton.org	Hamilton	NJ	08690	609-586-7900		374-3
RWJUHR (Robert Wood Johnson University Hospital at Rahway) 865 Stone St **Fax Area Code:* 609 ■ *TF:* 800-443-4605 ■ *Web:* www.rwjuhr.com	Rahway	NJ	07065	732-381-4200	586-7900*	374-3
RWM Casters Co PO Box 668 **Fax Area Code:* 704 ■ *TF:* 800-634-7704 ■ *Web:* www.rwmcasters.com	Gastonia	NC	28053	800-634-7704	868-4205*	350
RWS (Rose & Walker Supply Lafayette Inc) 3565 US Hwy 52 S *Web:* www.roseandwalkersupply.com	Lafayette	IN	47905	765-471-7070	474-7507	191-2
Rx Advantage Inc 7101 Hwy 90 Ste 300 *Web:* www.rxadvantage-inc.com	Daphne	AL	36526	251-625-6100		237
Rx Inc Dba Lo Cost Pharmacy 612 E 69th St	Savannah	GA	31405	912-352-0375		237
Rx Optical 1700 S Pk St *TF:* 800-792-2737 ■ *Web:* www.rxoptical.com	Kalamazoo	MI	49001	269-342-0003		543
Rx Scan 2478 Lackey Old State Rd *TF:* 800-572-2648 ■ *Web:* rxscan.com	Delaware	OH	43015	740-548-1725		238
Rx Systems Inc 121 Point West Blvd *TF:* 800-922-9142 ■ *Web:* www.rxsystems.com	St. Charles	MO	63301	800-922-9142		548
RX Worldwide Meetings Inc 3060 Communications Pkwy Ste 200 *TF:* 800-562-1713 ■ *Web:* www.rx-worldwide.net	Plano	TX	75093	214-291-2920	291-2930	184
Rx.com 101 Jim Wright Fwy S Ste 200 *TF:* 800-433-5719 ■ *Web:* www.rx.com	Fort Worth	TX	76108-2202	817-246-6760		237
RXD Pharmacies Inc 724 Haddon Ave	Collingswood	NJ	08108	856-858-9292		237
RxMosaic Healthcare 711 Third Ave Fl 19 *Web:* rxmosaichealth.com	New York	NY	10017	212-336-7500		231
RXR REALTY 625 Rex Plaza *Web:* www.rxrrealty.com	Uniondale	NY	11556	516-506-6000	506-6800	655
RxResults LLC 320 Executive Court Ste 301 *Web:* rxresults.com	Little Rock	AR	72205	501-367-8402		463
Rxusa Inc 81 Seaview Blvd *TF:* 800-764-3648 ■ *Web:* www.rxusa.com	Port Washington	NY	11050	516-467-2500	467-2539	237
Ryad Consulting Inc 4876 Township Trce *Web:* ryadconsulting.com	Marietta	GA	30066	770-650-8468		196
Ryan & Coscia PC 256 Essex St *Web:* ryancoscia.com	Salem	MA	01970	978-744-1760		2
Ryan Alternative Staffing Inc 6936 Market St *Web:* www.ryanstaffing.com	Boardman	OH	44512	330-781-1172		260
Ryan Automotive LLC 200 Carter Dr	Edison	NJ	08817	732-650-1550		57
Ryan Cos US Inc 50 S Tenth St Ste 300 *Web:* www.ryancompanies.com	Minneapolis	MN	55403	612-492-4000		186
Ryan FireProtection Inc 9740 E 148th St *TF:* 800-409-7606 ■ *Web:* www.indianasubcontractors.org	Noblesville	IN	46060	800-409-7606		610
Ryan Group Inc, The 14110 Dallas Pkwy *Web:* www.ryangroupinc.com	Dallas	TX	75254	972-385-7781		194
Ryan Herco Products Corp 3010 N San Fernando Blvd *TF:* 800-848-1141 ■ *Web:* www.rhfs.com	Burbank	CA	91504	818-841-1141	973-2600	603
Ryan Inc Central 2700 E Racine St *TF:* 800-424-8964 ■ *Web:* www.ryancentral.com	Janesville	WI	53545	608-754-2291	754-3290	189-5
Ryan International Airlines Inc 4949 Harrison Ave	Rockford	IL	61108	815-316-5420		12
Ryan Iron Works Inc 1830 Broadway *Web:* www.ryanironworks.net	Raynham	MA	02767	508-822-8001		189-14
Ryan Lawn & Tree Inc 9120 Barton St *Web:* ryanlawn.com	Overland Park	KS	66214	913-381-1505		274
Ryan Manufacturing Inc 6606 Machmueller St *TF:* 800-532-2252 ■ *Web:* ryanmfg.com	Schofield	WI	54476	715-359-2565		757
Ryan Miller & Assoc 9700 Reseda Blvd Ste 200 *Web:* rmasearch.com	Northridge	CA	91324	818-638-5080		260
Ryan Paul (Rep R - WI) 1233 Longworth Bldg *Web:* paulryan.house.gov	Washington	DC	20515	202-225-3031	225-3393	342-2
Ryan Public Safety Solutions Inc 12119 US Hwy 431 *TF:* 800-241-2467 ■ *Web:* www.rpss911.com	Guntersville	AL	35976	256-279-0082		196
Ryan Smith & Carbine Ltd Mead Bldg 98 Merchants Row *Web:* www.rsclaw.com	Rutland	VT	05702	802-786-1000		428
Ryan Tim (Rep D - OH) 1126 Longworth Bldg *Web:* timryan.house.gov	Washington	DC	20515	202-225-5261	225-3719	342-2
Ryan Trading Corp 2500 Westchester Ave Ste 102 *Web:* www.ryantrading.com	Purchase	NY	10577	914-253-6767		296-20
Ryan's 719 Coliseum Dr *Web:* www.ryansrestaurant.com	Winston-Salem	NC	27106	336-724-6132	724-5761	671
Ryan's Family Steak House 1004 W Anthony Dr *Web:* www.ryans.com	Champaign	IL	61821	217-352-7403		671
Ryan's Grill at Ward Ctr 1200 Ala Moana Blvd *Web:* www.ryansgrill.com	Honolulu	HI	96814	808-591-9132		671
Ryan-Biggs Assoc PC 257 Ushers Rd *Web:* ryanbiggs.com	Clifton Park	NY	12065	518-406-5506		261
Ryansharkey LLP 12700 Sunrise Vly Dr *Web:* ryansharkey.com	Reston	VA	20191	703-652-1124		2
Ryantech Inc 1794 Olympic Pkwy Ste 250 *TF:* 800-323-5771 ■ *Web:* www.ryantechinc.com	Park City	UT	84098	435-647-0118		225
Rybar Group Inc, The 3150 Owen Rd *Web:* therybargroup.com	Fenton	MI	48430	810-750-6822		196
Rybovich Spencer Group 4200 N Flagler Dr *Web:* www.rybovich.com	West Palm Beach	FL	33407	561-844-1800		90
Rycan Technologies Inc 349 W Main St Ste 4 *Web:* www.rycan.com	Marshall	MN	56258	507-532-3324		396
Rycon Construction Inc 2525 Liberty Ave *TF:* 800-883-1901 ■ *Web:* www.ryconinc.com	Pittsburgh	PA	15222	412-392-2525	392-2526	186
Rydal Park 1515 The Fairway *Web:* www.rydalpark.org	Rydal	PA	19046	215-885-6800		672
Rydalch Electric Inc 250 Plymouth Ave *Web:* www.rydalchelectric.com	Salt Lake City	UT	84115	801-205-1813		189-4
Rydell Chevrolet Inc 18600 Devonshire St *TF:* 866-697-5167 ■ *Web:* chevynorthridge.com	Northridge	CA	91324	866-697-5167		516
Ryder CRSA Logistics 1275 Kingsway Ave *Web:* www.crsalog.com	Port Coquitlam	BC	V3C1S2	604-941-8228	941-4600	311
Ryder Material Handling 210 Annagem Blvd *TF:* 800-268-2125 ■ *Web:* rydermaterialhandling.com	Mississauga	ON	L5T2V5	905-565-2100		358
Ryder System Inc 11690 NW 105th St *NYSE:* R ■ *TF:* 800-297-9337 ■ *Web:* www.ryder.com	Miami	FL	33178	305-500-3726		778
Rydex Funds 805 King Farm Blvd Ste 600 *TF Cust Svc:* 800-820-0888 ■ *Web:* guggenheiminvestments.com	Rockville	MD	20850	301-296-5100		528
Rye Ford Inc 1151 Boston Post Rd *Web:* ryeford.com	Rye	NY	10580	914-967-6300		57
Rye Harbor State Park 1730 Ocean Blvd *Web:* www.nhstateparks.org	Rye	NH	03870	603-227-8722		565
Rye Patch State Recreation Area 2505 Rye Patch Reservoir Rd *Web:* www.parks.nv.gov	Lovelock	NV	89419	775-538-7321		565
Ryerson Inc 227 W Monroe St *TF:* 800-733-6120 ■ *Web:* www.ryerson.com	Chicago	IL	60606	312-292-5000		492
Ryerson Station State Park 361 Bristoria Rd *Web:* www.dcnr.state.pa.us	Wind Ridge	PA	15380	724-428-4254		565
Ryerson University 350 Victoria St *TF:* 866-592-8882 ■ *Web:* www.ryerson.ca	Toronto	ON	M5B2K3	416-979-5000	979-5170	785
Ryko Solutions Inc 1500 SE 37th St *Web:* www.ryko.com	Grimes	IA	50111	515-986-3700		427
Rylander Clay & Opitz LLP 3200 Riverfront Dr Ste 200 *Web:* www.rylander-cpa.com	Fort Worth	TX	76107	817-332-2301		734
Ryley Carlock & Applewhite Pa 1 N Central Ave Ste 1200 *Web:* www.rcalaw.com	Phoenix	AZ	85004	602-258-7701	257-9582	428
Ryman Auditorium 116 Fifth Ave N *TF:* 800-733-6779 ■ *Web:* www.ryman.com	Nashville	TN	37219	615-458-8700	458-8701	572
Rymax Corp 19 Chapin Rd Bldg B *Web:* www.rymaxinc.com	Pine Brook	NJ	07058	973-808-4066		195
Rynel Inc 11 Twin Rivers Dr *Web:* www.rynel.com	Wiscasset	ME	04578	207-882-0200		601

	City	State	ZIP	Phone	Fax	Class
Ryness Company Inc, The 801 San Ramon Valley Blvd *Web:* www.ryness.com	Danville	CA	94526	925-820-8100		656
Rynone Mfg Corp PO Box 128 *TF:* 800-839-1654 ■ *Web:* www.rynone.com	Sayre	PA	18840	570-888-5272	888-1175	115
Ryobi Die Casting Inc 800 W Mausoleum Rd *Web:* www.ryobidiecasting.com	Shelbyville	IN	46176	317-398-3398		60
Ryobi Technologies Inc 1428 Pearman Dairy Rd *TF:* 800-525-2579 ■ *Web:* www.ryobitools.com	Anderson	SC	29625	800-525-2579		351
Ryokan College 11965 Venice Blvd Ste 304 **Fax:* Admissions ■ *TF:* 866-796-5261 ■ *Web:* www.ryokan.edu	Los Angeles	CA	90066	310-390-7560	391-9756*	166
Ryson International Inc 300 Newsome Dr *Web:* www.ryson.com	Yorktown	VA	23692	757-898-1530	898-1580	207
Ryte Byte Inc s4125a rocky point rd *Web:* www.rytebyteinc.com	Baraboo	WI	53913	608-356-6822		225
Rytec Corp 1 Cedar Pkwy *TF:* 800-628-1909 ■ *Web:* www.rytecdoors.com	Jackson	WI	53037	262-677-9046		234
Rywant Alvarez Jones Russo & Guyton pa 407 Courthouse Sq *Web:* rywantalvarez.com	Inverness	FL	34450	352-341-4441		428
RZ & Company Inc 6602 Odana Rd *Web:* rzco.com	Madison	WI	53719	608-827-7979		77

S

	City	State	ZIP	Phone	Fax	Class
S (Stanton Territorial Health Authority) 550 Byrne Rd PO Box 10 *Web:* www.stha.hss.gov.nt.ca	Yellowknife	NT	X1A2N1	867-669-4111	669-4128	374-2
S & A Custom Built Homes 2121 Old Gatesburg Rd Ste 200 *Web:* www.sahomebuilder.com	State College	PA	16803	814-231-4780		653
S & B Engineers & Constructors Ltd 7825 Pk Pl Blvd *Web:* www.sbec.com	Houston	TX	77087	713-645-4141		261
S & C Electric Co 6601 N Ridge Blvd *TF:* 800-621-5546 ■ *Web:* www.sandc.com	Chicago	IL	60626	773-338-1000		729
S & D Coffee Inc 300 Concord Pkwy *TF Cust Svc:* 800-933-2210 ■ *Web:* www.sdcoffeetea.com	Concord	NC	28027	800-933-2210	950-4378	296-7
S & D Oyster Co 2701 McKinney Ave *Web:* sdoyster.com	Dallas	TX	75204	214-880-0111		671
S & E Specialty Polymers LLC 140 Leominster-Shirley Rd *Web:* sespoly.com	Lunenburg	MA	01462	978-537-8261	537-5310	605-2
S & G Concrete Co 2110 Philadelphia Rd *Web:* vulcanmaterials.com	Edgewood	MD	21040	410-679-0500		182
S & H Express Inc 400 Mulberry St *TF:* 800-637-9782 ■ *Web:* www.sandhexpress.com	York	PA	17403	717-848-5015	852-8722	449
S & K Electronics Inc 56301 US Hwy 93 *Web:* www.skecorp.com	Ronan	MT	59864	406-883-6241	883-6228	253
S & L International 150 E Colorado Blvd Ste 203 *Web:* www.slinternational.com	Pasadena	CA	91105	626-405-0999		196
S & M Machine Service Inc 109 E Highland Dr *TF:* 800-323-1579 ■ *Web:* www.snmmachine.com	Oconto Falls	WI	54154	920-846-8130	846-4803	455
S & M Moving Systems Inc 12128 Burke St *TF:* 800-528-4561 ■ *Web:* www.smmoving.com	Santa Fe Springs	CA	90670	562-567-2100		519
S & ME Inc 3201 Spring Forest Rd *TF Cust Svc:* 800-849-2517 ■ *Web:* www.smeinc.com	Raleigh	NC	27616	919-872-2660	876-3958	192
S & P Communications 6712 Randolph Blvd *TF:* 800-741-5073 ■ *Web:* www.spcomm.com	San Antonio	TX	78233	210-656-5073		736
S & p Tax Solutions Ltd 95 Revere Dr Ste A *TF:* 800-447-4930 ■ *Web:* www.sandptax.com	Northbrook	IL	60062	847-480-4400		2
S & S Concrete & Materials LLC 3000 Pass Canyon Rd	Bullhead City	AZ	86442	928-754-1999		190
S & S Cycle Inc 14025 County Hwy G *Web:* www.sscycle.com	Viola	WI	54664	608-627-1497		82
S & s Industrial Equipment & Supply Company Inc 7 Chelten Way *TF:* 800-282-3506 ■ *Web:* www.sandsindustrial.com	Trenton	NJ	08638	609-695-3800		358
S & S Industries Inc 5 Odell Plaza *Web:* www.sandsindustries.com	Yonkers	NY	10701	914-885-1500		813
S & S Industries Inc 115 Clemmons Rd	Mount Juliet	TN	37122	615-754-8000	754-8011	389
S & S Management Services Inc 1 Regency Dr *Web:* www.ssmgt.com	Bloomfield	CT	06002	860-243-3977	286-0787	47
S & S Mills Inc 414 C N Pk Dr *TF:* 800-241-4013 ■ *Web:* www.ssmillsinc.com	Dalton	GA	30720	706-277-3677		131
S & S Steel Services Inc 444 E 29th St	Anderson	IN	46016	765-622-4545	622-4556	492
S & S Steel Warehouse Inc 2521 State St	Chicago Heights	IL	60411	708-757-9400		492
S & S Technology 10625 Telge Rd *TF:* 800-231-1747 ■ *Web:* www.ssxray.com	Houston	TX	77095	281-815-1300	815-1444	382
S & S Tire & Auto Service Center 1475 Jingle Bell Ln *TF:* 800-685-6794 ■ *Web:* www.sstire.com	Lexington	KY	40509	800-685-6794		54
S & S Transport Inc PO Box 12579 *TF:* 800-726-8022 ■ *Web:* www.sstransport.com	Grand Forks	ND	58208	800-726-8022		780
S & S Worldwide Inc 75 Mill St *TF Orders:* 800-243-9232 ■ *Web:* www.ssww.com	Colchester	CT	06415	860-537-3451	537-2563	459
S & S X-Ray Products Inc 10625 Telge Rd *TF:* 800-231-1747 ■ *Web:* www.ss-technology.com	Houston	TX	77095	281-815-1300		697
S & W Ready Mix Concrete Co 1300 Highway 17 N *Web:* www.snwreadymix.com	New Bern	NC	28560	252-633-2115		190
S Abraham & Sons Inc PO Box 1768 *TF General:* 866-248-3163 ■ *Web:* www.sasinc.com	Grand Rapids	MI	49501	616-453-6358	453-9259	297-8
S B Foot Tanning Co 805 Bench St *Web:* www.sbfoot.com	Red Wing	MN	55066	651-388-4731		432
S Brewer Enterprises 2151 Jamieson Ave Ste 1607	Alexandria	VA	22314	703-567-1284		667
S C & A Construction Inc 3411 Silverside Rd Shipley Bldg Ste 200 *Web:* www.scaconstructs.com	Wilmington	DE	19810	302-478-6030		186
S D Deacon Corp 17681 Mitchell N Ste 100 *Web:* www.deacon.com	Irvine	CA	92614	949-222-9060	222-0596	186
S f Association Management Services 655 Beach St Fl 1 *Web:* sf-ams.org	San Francisco	CA	94109	415-561-8523		463
S Himmelstein & Co 2490 Pembroke Ave *Web:* www.himmelstein.com	Hoffman Estates	IL	60169	847-843-3300		407
S Howes Company Inc 25 Howard St *TF:* 888-255-2611 ■ *Web:* www.showes.com	Silver Creek	NY	14136	716-934-2611		298
S I Systems Ltd 335 Eighth Ave SW Ste 1210 *Web:* www.sisystems.com	Calgary	AB	T2P1C9	403-450-5174		260
S Jet 1251 W Blee Rd *Web:* www.spectrajetinc.com	Springfield	OH	45502	937-323-5804	323-8168	13
S K C Communication Products Inc 8320 Hedge Ln Terr **Fax Area Code:* 800 ■ *TF:* 800-882-7779 ■ *Web:* www.skccom.com	Shawnee Mission	KS	66227	913-422-4222	454-4752*	246
S Klahr Inc 45 Randolph Dr	Dix Hills	NY	11746	631-462-9630		366
S L Nusbaum Insurance Agency Inc 500 W 21st St Ste 300 *Web:* nusbauminsurance.com	Norfolk	VA	23517	757-622-4653		390
S Lichtenberg & Co Inc 295 Fifth Ave Rm 918 *TF Cust Svc:* 800-422-5842 ■ *Web:* www.lichtenberg.com	New York	NY	10016	212-689-4510		746
S Parker Hardware Manufacturing Corp PO Box 9882 *TF:* 800-772-7537 ■ *Web:* www.sparker.com	Englewood	NJ	07631	201-569-1600	569-1082	350
S R C Corp PO Box 30676 *TF:* 800-888-4545 ■ *Web:* www.steveregan.com	Salt Lake City	UT	84130	801-268-4500	268-4596	276
S R C Refrigeration 6615 19 Mile Rd *TF:* 800-521-0398 ■ *Web:* www.srcrefrigeration.com	Sterling Heights	MI	48314	586-254-0610	254-0485	610
S R Snodgrass AC 2100 Corporate Dr *TF:* 800-580-7738 ■ *Web:* www.srsnodgrass.com	Wexford	PA	15090	724-934-0344		2
S Rose Inc 1213 Prospect Ave E	Cleveland	OH	44115	216-781-8200		321
S s White Burs Inc 1145 Towbin Ave *Web:* www.sswhitedental.com	Lakewood	NJ	08701	732-905-1100		228
S Schwab Co Inc 12101 Upper Potomac Industrial Pk St *Web:* times-news.com	Cumberland	MD	21502	301-729-4488	722-4870	155-4
S Systems Corp 5777 W Century Blvd Ste 520 *Web:* www.s-sc.com	Los Angeles	CA	90045	310-215-0248	642-3738	261
S t & p Communications Inc 320 Springside Dr Ste 150 *TF:* 800-609-0609 ■ *Web:* www.stpinc.com	Fairlawn	OH	44333	330-668-1932		224
S T Bunn Construction 1904 University Blvd	Tuscaloosa	AL	35401	205-752-8195	349-4288	780
S T Specialty Foods Inc 8700 Xylon Ave N *Web:* www.stspecialtyfoods.com	Brooklyn Park	MN	55445	763-493-9600		123
S V Microwave Inc 2400 Centre Pk W Dr *Web:* www.svmicrowave.com	West Palm Beach	FL	33409	561-840-1800	842-6277	253
S W Cole Engineering Inc 37 Liberty Dr *Web:* www.swcole.com	Bangor	ME	04401	207-848-5714		256
S. B. Elliott State Park c/o Parker Dam State Pk 28 Fairview Rd *Web:* www.dcnr.state.pa.us	Penfield	PA	15849	814-765-0630		565
S. Emerson Group Inc 407 E Lancaster Ave *TF:* 800-223-3273 ■ *Web:* www.emersongroup.com	Wayne	PA	19087	610-971-9600		195
S. Freedman & Sons Inc 3322 Pennsy Dr *TF:* 800-545-7277 ■ *Web:* www.sfreedman.com	Landover	MD	20785	301-322-5000	772-7563	559
S. J. Smith Company Inc 3707 W River Dr *Web:* www.sjsmith.com	Davenport	IA	52802	563-263-1829		385
S.A. White Oil Company Inc 590 Atlanta St SE *TF:* 800-524-0604 ■ *Web:* www.sawhite.com	Marietta	GA	30060	770-427-1387		579
S.A.F.E. Management LLC Arizona 1 Cardinals Dr *Web:* www.safemanagement.net	Glendale	AZ	85305	623-433-7300		184
FAMU Libraries 1500 S Martin Luther King Blvd *TF:* 800-540-6754 ■ *Web:* www.famu.edu/library	Tallahassee	FL	32307	850-599-3370	561-2293	434-6
S.H. Hirth & Associates Inc 36 W 44th St Ste 610 *Web:* www.shhirthandassociates.com	New York	NY	10036	212-997-1187		195
S.l.c. Meter Service Inc 10375 Dixie Hwy *TF:* 800-433-4332 ■ *Web:* www.slcmeter.com	Davisburg	MI	48350	248-625-0667	625-8650	385
S.Rothschild 1407 Broadway 10th Fl *Web:* www.srothschild.com	New York	NY	10018	212-354-8550		155-3
S.S. Mechanical Corp 17631 Metzler Ln *TF:* 800-876-4045 ■ *Web:* www.ssmechanical.biz	Huntington Beach	CA	92647	714-847-1317		261
S.S. Papadopulos & Associates Inc 7944 Wisconsin Ave *Web:* www.sspa.com	Bethesda	MD	20814	301-718-8900		539
S/L/A/M Collaborative 80 Glastonbury Blvd *Web:* www.slamcoll.com	Glastonbury	CT	06033	860-657-8077		261

Name	Address	City	State	Zip	Phone	Fax	Class
S/n Precision Enterprises Inc	145 Jordan Rd *Web:* www.pacamor.com	Troy	NY	12180	518-283-8002	283-8032	75
S2L Inc	531 Versailles Dr Ste 202 *Web:* s2li.com	Maitland	FL	32751	407-475-9163		261
S2Tech	720 Spirit 40 Park Dr *Web:* www.s2tech.com	Chesterfield	MO	63005	636-530-9286		177
S2Verify LLC	Box 2597 *Web:* www.s2verify.com	Roswell	GA	30077	770-649-8282		260
S3 Ventures	6300 Bridgepoint Pkwy Bldg One Ste 405 *Web:* www.s3vc.com	Austin	TX	78730	512-258-1759		177
S4 NetQuest	580 N Fourth St Ste 600 *Web:* www.s4netquest.com	Columbus	OH	43215	614-220-5700		463
SA (Sexaholics Anonymous)	PO Box 3565 *TF:* 866-424-8777 ■ *Web:* www.sa.org	Brentwood	TN	37024	615-370-6062	370-0882	48-21
SA (Salem Academy)	942 Lancaster Dr NE *Web:* www.salemacademy.org	Salem	OR	97301	503-378-1219		622
Sa Bai Thong	6802 ODANA Rd *Web:* www.sabaithong.com	Madison	WI	53719	608-238-3100		671
SA Comunale Company Inc	2900 Newpark Dr *TF:* 800-776-7181 ■ *Web:* www.sacomunale.com	Barberton	OH	44203	330-706-3040	861-0060	189-13
SA Day Mfg Co Inc	1489 Niagara St *TF:* 800-747-0030 ■ *Web:* www.saday.com	Buffalo	NY	14213	716-881-3030	881-4353	145
SA Healy Co	901 N Green Valley Pkwy Ste 260 *TF:* 800-431-2584 ■ *Web:* www.sahealy.com	Henderson	NV	89074	702-754-6400	754-6450	261
SA Recycling LLC	2411 N Glassell St *TF:* 800-468-7272 ■ *Web:* www.sarecycling.com	Orange	CA	92865	714-632-2000	630-5836	686
SA Scientific Ltd	4919 Golden Quail *Web:* www.ntextechnologies.com	San Antonio	TX	78240	210-699-8800		231
SAA (Society of American Archivists)	17 N State St Ste 1425 *TF:* 866-722-7858 ■ *Web:* www2.archivists.org	Chicago	IL	60602	312-606-0722		48-4
SAA (Sex Addicts Anonymous)	PO Box 70949 *TF:* 800-477-8191 ■ *Web:* www.saa-recovery.org	Houston	TX	77270	713-869-4902	692-0105	48-21
SAA (Society for American Archaeology)	900 Second St NE Ste 12 *TF:* 800-759-5219 ■ *Web:* www.saa.org	Washington	DC	20002	202-789-8200	789-0284	49-5
Saab Barracuda LLC	608 E Mcneill St *Web:* www.saabgroup.com	Lillington	NC	27546	910-893-2094		21
Saad Enterprises Inc	1515 S University Blvd *Web:* www.saadhealthcare.com	Mobile	AL	36609	251-380-3800		475
Saags Products Inc	1799 Factor Ave *Web:* www.saags.com	San Leandro	CA	94577	510-352-8000		296-26
Saalfeld Griggs PC	Park Pl 250 Church St SE Ste 200 *Web:* www.sglaw.com	Salem	OR	97301	503-399-1070		428
Saanich Peninsula Chamber of Commerce	10382 Pat Bay Hwy *Web:* www.peninsulachamber.ca	North Saanich	BC	V8L5S8	250-656-3616	656-7111	137
Saar's Inc	32199 State Rt 20 *TF:* 800-743-0437 ■ *Web:* www.saarsmarketplacefoods.com	Oak Harbor	WA	98277	360-675-3000		237
Saatchi & Saatchi	375 Hudson St *Web:* www.saatchiny.com	New York	NY	10014	[illegible]	[illegible]	4
Saba Software Inc	2400 Bridge Pkwy *OTC:* SABA ■ *TF:* 877-722-2101 ■ *Web:* www.saba.com	Redwood Shores	CA	94065	650-581-2500	696-1773	178-3
Sabatino's	901 Fawn St *Web:* www.sabatinos.com	Baltimore	MD	21202	410-727-9414	837-6540	671
Sabatino's	4441 W Irving Pk Rd *Web:* www.sabatinoschicago.com	Chicago	IL	60641	773-283-8331		671
Sabel Steel Industries Inc	749 N Ct St *Web:* www.sabelsteel.com	Montgomery	AL	36104	334-265-6771	264-3692	492
Saber Plumbing Co	325 Market Pl *Web:* saberplumbing.com	Escondido	CA	92029	760-480-5716		189-10
Sabert Corp	2288 Main St Ext *Fax Area Code: 732 ■ *TF:* 800-722-3781 ■ *Web:* www.sabert.com	Sayreville	NJ	08872	800-722-3781	721-0622*	548
Sabert Corp	879 Main St *Web:* sabert.com	Sayreville	NJ	08872	732-721-5546		596
Sabertooth Technologies	5944 Coral Ridge Dr # 215 Ste 215 *Web:* sabertoothweb.com	Coral Springs	FL	33076	954-635-5545		196
Sabey Corp	12201 Tukwila International Blvd 4th Fl *Web:* www.sabey.com	Seattle	WA	98168	206-281-8700	282-9951	655
SABIA Inc	10911 Technology Pl *Web:* www.sabiainc.com	San Diego	CA	92127	858-217-2200		501
Sabian Ltd	219 Main St *TF:* 800-817-2242 ■ *Web:* www.sabian.com	Meductic	NB	E6H2L5	506-272-2019	272-2040	527
Sabin Corp	3800 Constitution Ave PO Box 788 *Fax Area Code: 800 ■ *TF:* 800-457-4500 ■ *Web:* www.cookgroup.com	Bloomington	IN	47403	812-339-2235	554-8335*	599
Sabin Robbins Paper Co	9365 Allen Rd	West Chester	OH	45069	513-874-5270		557
Sabina Motors & Controls Inc	1440 N Burton Pl *Web:* www.sabinadrives.com	Anaheim	CA	92806	714-956-0480	956-0486	201
Sabine County	1555 Worth St PO Box 717 *TF:* 800-986-5336 ■ *Web:* www.sabinecountytexas.com	Hemphill	TX	75948	409-787-2732	787-2158	338
Sabine Parish	400 S Capital Rm 102 PO Box 419 *Web:* www.sabineparishclerk.com	Many	LA	71449	318-256-6223		338
Sabine Pass Battleground State Park & Historic Site	6100 Dowling Rd *Web:* tpwd.texas.gov/spdest/parkinfo/former_tpwd_parks	Port Arthur	TX	77640	512-463-7948		565
Sabine River Authority of Texas	12777 State Hwy 87 *Web:* www.sra.dst.tx.us	Orange	TX	77631	409-746-2192	746-3780	202
Sabine Universal Products Inc	945 Houston Ave *Web:* supus.com	Port Arthur	TX	77640	409-982-9446		770
Sabinsa Corp	20 Lake Dr *Web:* www.sabinsa.com	East Windsor	NJ	08520	732-777-1111	777-1443	479
Sabio Information Technologies Inc	7715 NW 48th St Ste 350-360 *Web:* www.sabioit.com	Doral	FL	33166	305-676-8290		196
Sablan Gregorio (Rep D - MP)	2411 Rayburn HOB *TF:* 877-446-3465 ■ *Web:* sablan.house.gov	Washington	DC	20515	202-225-2646	226-4249	342-2
Sable Networks Inc	3171 Jay St	Santa Clara	CA	95054	408-727-5514		225
Sable Systems International Inc	3840 N Commerce St Ste 1 *Fax Area Code: 702 ■ *TF:* 800-330-0465 ■ *Web:* www.sablesys.com	North Las Vegas	NV	89032	800-330-0465	269-4445*	201
Sabor Latino	211 N Main St *Web:* annarborsabor.com	Ann Arbor	MI	48104	734-214-7775		671
Sabor Latino Restaurant	112 Green Springs Hwy *Web:* www.misaborlatino.webs.com	Homewood	AL	35209	205-942-9480	942-9428	671
Sabor!	5712 Bellaire Blvd	Houston	TX	77081	713-667-6001		671
Sabra Dipping Co LLC	2420 49th St *TF:* 888-957-2272 ■ *Web:* www.sabra.com	Astoria	NY	11103	888-957-2272		296-37
Sabra Dipping Co LLC	535 Smith St *Web:* sabra.com	Farmingdale	NY	11735	516-249-0151		123
Sabre Companies LLC, The	1891 New Scotland Rd *TF:* 800-349-2799 ■ *Web:* www.thesabrecompanies.com	Slingerlands	NY	12159	518-514-1572		192
Sabre Corp	PO Box 134 *Web:* www.sabreyachts.com	South Casco	ME	04077	207-655-3831	655-5050	90
Sabre Holdings Corp	3150 Sabre Dr *Web:* www.sabre.com	Southlake	TX	76092	682-605-1000		360-3
Sabre Inc	3150 Sabre Dr *Web:* www.sabre.com	Southlake	TX	76092	682-605-1000		335
Sabre Industries Inc	8653 E Hwy 67 *TF:* 866-254-3707 ■ *Web:* www.sabreindustriesinc.com	Alvarado	TX	76009	817-852-1700	852-1703	261
Sabre Solution, The	200 East 31st St *TF:* 888-494-7200 ■ *Web:* thesabresolution.com	Savannah	OK	31401	912-355-7200		180
SABRE Strategic Partners	5025 Orbitor Dr Bldg 3 Ste 300 *TF:* 800-314-3346 ■ *Web:* sabrelife.com	Mississauga	ON	L4W4Y5	905-206-0900	206-1600	391-2
Sabre Travel Network	3150 Sabre Dr *Web:* www.sabretravelnetwork.com/home	Southlake	TX	76092	682-605-1000		772
Sabreliner Corp	1390 Hwy H *Web:* www.sabrelineraviation.com	Perryville	MO	63775	573-543-2212		20
Sabretech Consulting LLC	154 Lewis St *TF:* 800-267-1715 ■ *Web:* www.sabretechllc.com	Hillsdale	MI	49242	517-437-7150		196
Sabrient Systems LLC	115 S La Cumbre Ln Ste 100 *TF:* 888-502-3605 ■ *Web:* www.sabrient.com	Santa Barbara	CA	93105	805-730-7777		668
SAC (Smith Affiliated Capital)	800 Third Ave 12th Fl *TF:* [illegible] ■ *Web:* www.smithcapital.com	New York	NY	10022	212-644-9440	644-1979	403
Sac & Fox Casino	1322 US Hwy 75 *Web:* www.sacandfoxcasino.com	Powhattan	KS	66527	785-467-8000		133
Sac County	100 NW State St *Web:* www.saccounty.org	Sac City	IA	50583	712-662-4492	662-7358	338
SAC Federal Credit Union (SAFCU)	11515 S 39th St *TF:* 800-228-0392 ■ *Web:* www.sacfcu.com	Bellevue	NE	[illegible]	402-292-8000		219
Sac n Pac	1405 United Dr *Web:* www.sacnpac.com	San Marcos	TX	78666	512-392-6484		297-8
Sac Osage Electric Co-op Inc	4815 E Hwy 54 PO Box 111 *TF:* 800-876-2701 ■ *Web:* www.sacosage.com	El Dorado Springs	MO	64744	417-876-2721	876-5368	245
Sacajawea State Park	2503 Sacajawea Pk Rd *Web:* www.parks.wa.gov	Pasco	WA	99301	509-545-2361		565
SACAM (Sousa Archives & Ctr for American Music)	1103 S Sixth St 236 Harding Band Bldg *Web:* www.library.illinois.edu	Champaign	IL	61820	217-244-9309	244-8695	520
SACAMA (Shemer Arts Ctr & Museum Assn Inc)	5005 E Camelback Rd *Web:* www.shemerartcenter.org	Phoenix	AZ	85018	602-262-4727		520
SACC (Swedish-American Chamber of Commerce Atlanta Inc)	4775 Peachtree Industrial Blvd Bldg 300 Ste 300 *Web:* www.sacc-georgia.org	Norcross	GA	30092	770-670-2480		138
Saccani Distributing Co	2600 Fifth St PO Box 1764 *Web:* www.saccanidist.com	Sacramento	CA	95818	916-441-0213		81-1
Saccucci Honda	1350 W Main Rd *Web:* www.saccuccihonda.com	Middletown	RI	02842	401-847-4737		57
Sachem Central School District At Holbrook	245 Union Ave *Web:* www.sachem.edu	Holbrook	NY	11741	631-471-1300		685
Sachem Inc	821 Woodward St *Web:* www.sacheminc.com	Austin	TX	78704	512-444-3626	445-5066	144
Sachs Waldman Pc	1000 Farmer St *TF:* 800-638-6722 ■ *Web:* www.sachswaldman.com	Detroit	MI	48226	313-965-3464		428
Sachse Real Estate Company Inc	315 S Beverly Dr Ste 415 *Web:* www.sachsere.com	Beverly Hills	CA	90212	310-284-7100		652
Sackett & Assoc	1055 Lincoln Ave *TF:* 800-913-3000 ■ *Web:* www.sackettlaw.com	San Jose	CA	95125	408-295-7755		428
Sackett Ranch Inc	2939 Neff Rd NE	Stanton	MI	48888	989-762-5049		10-11
Sackrider & Company Inc	1925 Wabash Ave *Web:* sackrider.com	Terre Haute	IN	47807	812-232-9492		2
Sacks Cafe	328 G St *Web:* www.sackscafe.com	Anchorage	AK	99501	907-274-4022		671
Sacks Tierney PA	4250 N Drinkwater Blvd 4th Fl *TF:* 800-973-1177 ■ *Web:* www.sackstierney.com	Scottsdale	AZ	85251	480-425-2600		428
Saco Industries Inc	17151 Morse St *Web:* www.sacoindustries.com	Lowell	IN	46356	219-696-2800		115
Sacor Financial Inc	1911 Douglas Blvd 85-126 *TF:* 866-556-0231 ■ *Web:* www.sacor.net	Roseville	CA	95661	866-556-0231		393

	Phone	Fax	Class
Sacramento Bag Manufacturing Co 440 N Pioneer Ave Ste 300.................. Woodland CA 95776 *TF:* 800-287-2247 ■ *Web:* www.sacbag.com	530-662-6130	662-6381	67
Sacramento Ballet 1631 K St............... Sacramento CA 95814 *TF:* 800-925-9989 ■ *Web:* sacballet.org	916-552-5800	552-5815	573-1
Sacramento Bee PO Box 15779............ Sacramento CA 95852 *TF Cust Svc:* 800-284-3233 ■ *Web:* www.sacbee.com	916-321-1000	321-1109	532-2
Sacramento Business Journal 1400 X St................................ Sacramento CA 95818 *Web:* www.bizjournals.com/sacramento	916-447-7661		457-5
Sacramento City College 3835 Freeport Blvd........................ Sacramento CA 95822 **Fax:* Admissions ■ *TF:* 800-700-4144 ■ *Web:* www.scc.losrios.edu	916-558-2351	558-2190*	162
Sacramento City Hall 915 'I' St............ Sacramento CA 95814 *Web:* www.cityofsacramento.org	916-808-7200	808-7672	337
Sacramento City Unified School District 5735 47th Ave.............................. Sacramento CA 95824 *TF:* 800-766-1822 ■ *Web:* www.scusd.edu	916-643-7400	643-9440	685
Sacramento Coast Guard Air Station 6037 Price Ave............................ McClellan CA 95652 *Web:* www.uscg.mil	916-643-7659		158
Sacramento Computer Power Inc 829 W Stadium Ln......................... Sacramento CA 95834 *Web:* www.sacpower.com	916-923-2772		518
Sacramento Container Corp 4841 Urbani Ave............................Mcclellan CA 95652 *Web:* www.saccontainer.biz	916-614-0580		100
Sacramento Convention & Visitors Bureau 1608 'I' St.................................. Sacramento CA 95814 *TF:* 800-292-2334 ■ *Web:* visitsacramento.com	916-808-7777	808-7788	206
Sacramento Convention Ctr 1400 J St.................................. Sacramento CA 95814 *TF:* 800-337-9285 ■ *Web:* www.sacramentoconventioncenter.com	916-808-5291	808-7687	205
Sacramento County 700 H St Rm 7650....... Sacramento CA 95814 *TF:* 800-807-6755 ■ *Web:* www.saccounty.net	916-874-5833	874-5885	338
Sacramento Employment & Training Agency 925 Del Paso Blvd........................ Sacramento CA 95815 *Web:* www.seta.net	916-263-3800		721
Sacramento History Museum 101 'I' St.................................. Sacramento CA 95814 *TF:* 800-448-3883 ■ *Web:* www.historicoldsac.org/museum/default.asp	916-808-7059		521
Sacramento International Airport 6900 Airport Blvd.......................... Sacramento CA 95837 *TF:* 800-872-7245 ■ *Web:* www.sacairports.org	916-929-5411		27
Sacramento Kings ARCO Arena 1 Sports Pkwy .... Sacramento CA 95834 *TF:* 800-231-8750 ■ *Web:* www.nba.com/kings	916-928-0000	928-0727	714-1
Sacramento Metro Chamber of Commerce 1 Capital Mall Ste 300 .... Sacramento CA 95814 *Web:* www.metrochamber.org	916-552-6800	443-2672	139
Sacramento Natural Foods Cooperative Inc 1900 Alhambra Blvd......................... Sacramento CA 95816 *TF:* 800-796-6009 ■ *Web:* sacfood.coop	916-455-2667		345
Sacramento News & Review 1124 Del Paso Blvd .... Sacramento CA 95815 *TF:* 800-831-2345 ■ *Web:* www.newsreview.com	916-498-1234	498-7920	532-5
Sacramento Public Library 828 'I' St.................................. Sacramento CA 95814 *TF:* 800-561-4636 ■ *Web:* www.saclibrary.org	916-264-2770		434-3
Sacramento Regional Transit District 1400 29th St............................... Sacramento CA 95816 *Web:* www.sacrt.com	916-321-2800	444-2156	468
Sacramento Stucco Co 1550 PkwyBlvd...........................West Sacramento CA 95691 *Web:* www.westernblended.com	916-372-7442	372-4836	500
Sacramento Theatre Co 1419 H St.......... Sacramento CA 95814 *Web:* www.sactheatre.org	916-443-6722	446-4066	573-4
Sacramento Zoo 3930 W Land Pk Dr .... Sacramento CA 95822 *TF:* 866-570-7318 ■ *Web:* www.saczoo.org	916-808-5888		823
Sacred Heart HealthCare System 421 Chew St..............................Allentown PA 18102 *TF:* 800-994-6610 ■ *Web:* www.shh.org	610-776-4500		374-3
Sacred Heart Home 359 Summer St......... New Bedford MA 02740 *TF:* 800-272-3900 ■ *Web:* www.dhfo.org	508-996-6751	996-5189	450
Sacred Heart Hospital 900 W Clairemont Ave .... Eau Claire WI 54701 *TF:* 888-445-4554 ■ *Web:* www.sacredhearteauclaire.org	715-717-4121		374-3
Sacred Heart Hospital of Pensacola 5151 N Ninth Ave.......................... Pensacola FL 32504 *TF:* 800-874-1026 ■ *Web:* www.sacred-heart.org	850-416-7000	416-7337	374-3
Sacred Heart Medical Ctr 1255 Hilyard St...............................Eugene OR 97401 *TF:* 800-288-7444 ■ *Web:* www.peacehealth.org	541-686-7300		374-3
Sacred Heart Rehabilitation Institute 2323 N Lake Dr............................Milwaukee WI 53211 *Web:* www.columbia-stmarys.org	414-298-6750		374-6
Sacred Heart School of Theology 7335 S Hwy 100..............................Franklin WI 53132 *Web:* shsst.edu	414-425-8300	529-6999	167-3
Sacred Heart University 5151 Pk Ave........... Fairfield CT 06825 *Web:* www.sacredheart.edu	203-371-7999	365-7609	166
Sacred Heart University Edgerton Ctr for Performing Arts 5151 Pk Ave.................................Fairfield CT 06825 *Web:* www.edgertoncenter.org	203-371-7908	365-4858	572
Sadat Associates Inc 1545 Lamberton Rd .... Trenton NJ 08611 *Web:* www.sadat.com	609-826-9600		261
SADD (Students Against Destructive Decisions) 255 Main St .... Marlborough MA 01752 *TF:* 877-723-3462 ■ *Web:* www.sadd.org	508-481-3568	481-5759	48-6
Saddle Butte Pipeline LLC 858 Main Ave Ste 301 ....Durango CO 81301 *Web:* www.sbpipeline.com	970-375-3150		539
Saddle Creek Corp 3010 Saddle Creek Rd .... Lakeland FL 33801 *Web:* www.sclogistics.com	863-665-0966		449
Saddleback College 28000 Marguerite Pkwy .... Mission Viejo CA 92692 **Fax:* Admissions ■ *Web:* www.saddleback.edu	949-582-4500	347-8315*	162
Saddleback Educational Publishing Inc 3 Watson.................................Costa Mesa CA 92626 *Web:* www.sdlback.com	949-860-2500		96
Saddleback Memorial Medical Ctr 24451 Health Ctr Dr .... Laguna Hills CA 92653 *TF:* 800-553-6537 ■ *Web:* www.memorialcare.org	949-837-4500		374-3
Sadie's 6230 Fourth St NW.............. Albuquerque NM 87107 *Web:* www.sadiessalsa.com	505-345-5339		671
Sadler's Smokehouse Ltd PO Box 1088.......Henderson TX 75653 *TF:* 800-777-5581 ■ *Web:* www.sadlerssmokehouse.com	903-655-7265		296-26
Sadlers Creek State Park 940 Sadlers Creek Rd........................Anderson SC 29626 *Web:* www.southcarolinaparks.com	864-226-8950		565
Sadoff & Rudoy Industries LLP 240 W Arndt St..............................Fond du Lac WI 54936 *TF General:* 877-972-3633 ■ *Web:* www.sadoff.com	920-921-2070	921-1283	686
SAE (Sigma Alpha Epsilon Fraternity) 1856 Sheridan Rd.............................. Evanston IL 60201 *TF:* 800-233-1856 ■ *Web:* www.sae.net	847-475-1856	475-2250	48-16
SAE (Society of Automotive Engineers Inc) 400 Commonwealth Dr..................... Warrendale PA 15096 *TF:* 877-606-7323 ■ *Web:* www.sae.org	724-776-4841	776-0790	49-21
SAE Circuits Colorado Inc 4820 N 63rd St.................................. Boulder CO 80301 *TF:* 800-234-9001 ■ *Web:* www.saecircuits.com	303-530-1900	530-0210	625
SAE Power Inc 130 Knowles Dr Ste 118 .... Los Gatos CA 95032 *Web:* www.saepower.com	408-369-2200	369-4911	253
Saebo Inc 2709 Water Ridge Pkwy Ste 100 Six LakePointe Plz................... Charlotte NC 28217 **Fax Area Code:* 855 ■ *TF:* 888-284-5433 ■ *Web:* www.saebo.com	888-284-5433	414-0037*	475
SAEC (South Alabama Electric Co-op) PO Box 449 ....Troy AL 36081 *TF:* 800-556-2060 ■ *Web:* www.southaec.com	334-566-2060	566-8949	245
Saelens Corp 100 Veterans Dr.............Johnson Creek WI 53038 *Web:* www.diamondprecision.com	920-699-8880		350
SAEM (Society for Academic Emergency Medicine) 2340 S River Rd Ste 200................. Des Plaines IL 60018 *TF:* 800-829-1040 ■ *Web:* www.saem.org	847-813-9823	813-5450	49-8
Saenger Theatre 118 S Palafox Pl .... Pensacola FL 32502 *Web:* www.pensacolasaenger.com	850-595-3880	595-3886	572
Saenger Theatre 6 S Joachim St ....Mobile AL 36602 *TF:* 800-745-3000 ■ *Web:* www.mobilesaenger.com	251-208-5600		572
SAES Pure Gas Inc 4175 Santa Fe Rd .... San Luis Obispo CA 93401 *TF:* 800-934-3628 ■ *Web:* www.saespuregas.com	805-541-9299	541-9399	386
SAF (Santa Fe Municipal Airport) 121 Aviation Dr PO Box 909....................Santa Fe NM 87504 *TF:* 866-773-2587 ■ *Web:* santafenm.gov/airport	505-955-2900	955-2905	27
SAF (Society of American Florists) 1601 Duke St..............................Alexandria VA 22314 *TF:* 800-336-4743 ■ *Web:* www.safnow.org	703-836-8700	836-8705	49-4
SAF (Society of American Foresters) 10100 Laureate way .... Bethesda MD 20814 *TF:* 866-897-8720 ■ *Web:* www.eforester.org	301-897-8720	897-3690	48-2
Safari Books Online LLC 1003 Gravenstein Hwy N ....Sebastopol CA 95472 *TF:* 800-521-0600 ■ *Web:* my.safaribooksonline.com	707-827-4100		95
Safari Circuits Inc 411 Washington St............Otsego MI 49078 *TF:* 888-694-7230 ■ *Web:* www.safaricircuits.com	269-694-9471	692-2651	176
Safari Micro Inc 2185 W Pecos Rd............ Chandler AZ 85224 *TF:* 888-446-4770 ■ *Web:* www.safarimicro.com	888-446-4770		196
Safari West Wildlife Preserve & Tent Camp 3115 Porter Creek Rd ....Santa Rosa CA 95404 *TF:* 800-616-2695 ■ *Web:* www.safariwest.com	707-579-2551	579-8777	823
Safariland LLC 13386 International Pkwy ....Jacksonville FL 32218 *TF:* 800-347-1200 ■ *Web:* www.safariland.com/our-brands/aba	904-741-5400		576
Safas Corp 2 Ackerman Ave .... Clifton NJ 07011 *TF:* 800-472-6854 ■ *Web:* www.safascorp.com	973-772-5252		601
Safco Products Co 9300 W Research Ctr Rd.................. New Hope MN 55428 *TF Cust Svc:* 800-328-3020 ■ *Web:* www.safcoproducts.com	763-536-6700	536-6784	319-1
SAFCU (SAC Federal Credit Union) 11515 S 39th St ....Bellevue NE 68123 *TF:* 800-228-0392 ■ *Web:* www.sacfcu.com	402-292-8000		219
SAFE (Secure America's Future Economy) 214 N Spring Valley Rd.................... Wilmington DE 19807 *Web:* www.s-a-f-e.org	302-478-0676		48-7
Safe & Civil Schools 2451 Willamette St ....Eugene OR 97405 *TF:* 800-323-8819 ■ *Web:* www.safeandcivilschools.com	541-345-1442		242
Safe 1 Credit Union PO Box 2203 ....Bakersfield CA 93303 *TF:* 800-322-4529 ■ *Web:* www.safe1.org	661-327-3818		219
Safe Auto Insurance Co 4 Easton Oval PO Box 182109 .... Columbus OH 43219 *TF:* 800-723-3288 ■ *Web:* www.safeauto.com	614-231-0200		391-4
Safe Banking Systems LLC 114 Old Country Rd Ste 320...................Mineola NY 11501 *TF:* 800-869-0751 ■ *Web:* www.safe-banking.com	631-547-5400		177
SAFE Credit Union 3720 Madison Ave .... North Highlands CA 95660 *TF:* 800-733-7233 ■ *Web:* www.safecu.org	916-979-7233		219
Safe Federal Credit Union 201 N 12th St...................... West Columbia SC 29169 *Web:* www.safefed.org	803-796-7782		219
Safe Flight Instrument Corp 20 New King St.......................... White Plains NY 10604 *Web:* www.safeflight.com	914-946-9500	946-7882	529
Safe Harbor Access Systems LLC 211 N Koppers Rd ....Florence SC 29506 *Web:* www.safe-harbor.com	843-679-6888		480
Safe Home Security Inc 55 Sebethe Dr.........Cromwell CT 06416 *Web:* www.safehomesecurityinc.com	860-262-4000		693
Safe House 779 N Front St.................. Milwaukee WI 53202 *Web:* safe-house.com	414-271-2007		671
Safe Kids Worldwide 1301 Pennsylvania Ave NW Ste 1000.........Washington DC 20004 *Web:* www.safekids.org	202-662-0600	393-2072	48-6

Name / Address	City	State	Zip	Phone	Fax	Class
Safe Passage International Inc 333 Metro Pk *Web:* www.safe-passage.com	Rochester	NY	14623	585-292-4910		177
Safe Security PO Box 3888 Ste A *Web:* safesecurity.us	Silverdale	WA	98383	360-698-9800		693
Safe Systems Inc 11395 Old Roswell Rd *Web:* www.safesystems.com	Alpharetta	GA	30009	770-752-0550		225
Safeamerica Credit Union 6001 Gibraltar Dr *TF:* 800-972-0999 ■ *Web:* www.safeamerica.com	Pleasanton	CA	94588	925-734-4111		219
Safeco Field 1250 First Ave S *Web:* seattle.mariners.mlb.com	Seattle	WA	98134	206-346-4000	346-4050	720
Safeco Insurance Co of America 1001 Fourth Ave *Web:* www.safeco.com	Seattle	WA	98154	206-545-5000		391-4
SafeData LLC 250A Ctrville Rd	Warwick	RI	02886	401-734-5866	737-2099	809
Safegate Airport Systems 7101 Northland Cir N Ste 110 *Web:* www.safegate.com	Minneapolis	MN	55428	763-535-9299		63
Safeguard Business Systems Inc 8585 N Stemmons Fwy Ste 600 N **Fax Area Code:* 800 ■ *TF:* 800-523-2422 ■ *Web:* www.gosafeguard.com	Dallas	TX	75247	855-778-3124	439-3423*	142
Safeguard Chemical Corp 411 Wales Ave *TF:* 800-536-3170 ■ *Web:* www.safeguardchemical.com	Bronx	NY	10454	718-585-3170	585-3657	280
SafeGuard Health Enterprises Inc 95 Enterprise Ste 100 *TF:* 800-880-1800 ■ *Web:* www.metlife.com	Aliso Viejo	CA	92656	949-425-4300	425-4586	391-3
Safeguard Products Inc 2710 Division Hwy *TF:* 800-433-1819 ■ *Web:* www.safeguardproducts.com	New Holland	PA	17557	717-354-4586		237
Safeguard Properties Inc 7887 Safeguard Cir *TF:* 800-852-8306 ■ *Web:* www.safeguardproperties.com	Valley View	OH	44125	216-739-2900		509
Safeguard Scientifics Inc 170 N Radnor-Chester Rd Ste 200 *NYSE:* SFE ■ *Web:* www.safeguard.com	Radnor	PA	19087	610-293-0600	293-0601	792
Safeguard Security & Communications Inc 8454 N 90th St *TF:* 800-426-6060 ■ *Web:* safeguardsecurity.com	Scottsdale	AZ	85258	480-609-6200		693
Safeguards Technology LLC 75 Atlantic St *Web:* www.safeguards.com	Hackensack	NJ	07601	201-488-1022		692
Safelite Group Inc 2400 Farmers Dr *TF:* 877-664-8931 ■ *Web:* www.safelite.com	Columbus	OH	43235	877-664-8931		62-2
Safemark Systems LP 2101 Park Ctr Dr Ste 125 *Web:* www.safemark.com	Orlando	FL	32835	407-299-0044		350
SafeNet Consulting Inc 5810 Baker Rd *TF:* 800-472-3272 ■ *Web:* www.safenetconsulting.com	Minnetonka	MN	55345	952-930-3636		177
SafePlug 260 Pkwy Dr Ste 150 *Web:* www.safeplug.com	Lincolnshire	IL	60069	847-543-0980		253
Safer Foundation 571 W Jackson Blvd *Web:* www.saferfoundation.org	Chicago	IL	60661	312-922-2200	922-0839	48-6
Safer Healthcare Partners LLC 7000 E Arapahoe Rd Ste 204	Centennial	CO	80112	303-298-8083		41
SAFER Systems LLC 5284 Adolfo Rd Ste 100 *Web:* www.safersystemv10.com	Camarillo	CA	93012	805-383-9711	383-6344	177
Saferack Manufacturing 219 Safety Ave *Web:* www.saferack.com	Andrews	SC	29510	843-264-8096		697
Safetec of America Inc 887 Kensington Ave *TF:* 800-456-7077 ■ *Web:* www.safetec.com	Buffalo	NY	14215	716-895-1822	895-2969	151
Safe-T-Gard Corp 4975 Miller St Ste B *TF Cust Svc:* 800-356-9026 ■ *Web:* www.safetgard.com	Wheat Ridge	CO	80033	303-763-8900	763-8071	576
Safetran Traffic Systems Inc 1485 Garden of the Gods Rd *TF:* 800-372-9253 ■ *Web:* www.safetran-traffic.com	Colorado Springs	CO	80907	719-599-5600	599-3853	700
Safety & Ecology Corp 2800 Solway Rd SEC Business Ctr *Web:* www.sec-tn.com	Knoxville	TN	37931	865-690-0501		667
Safety Analysis & Forensic Engineering 5665 Hollister Ave *TF:* 800-426-7866 ■ *Web:* www.saferesearch.com	Goleta	CA	93117	805-964-0676	964-7669	668
Safety Center Inc 3909 Bradshaw Rd *Web:* www.safetycenter.org	Sacramento	CA	95827	916-366-7233		196
Safety Components International Inc 40 Emery St *TF:* 800-896-6926 ■ *Web:* www.safetycomponents.com	Greenville	SC	29605	864-240-2692		678
Safety Council of The Ozarks 1111 S Glenstone Ave Ste 1-103 *Web:* nscozarks.org	Springfield	MO	65804	417-869-2121		726
Safety First Systems LLC 65 Route 4 E *Web:* www.safetyfirst.com	River Edge	NJ	07661	201-267-8900		41
Safety Harbor Resort & Spa 105 N Bayshore Dr *TF:* 888-237-8772 ■ *Web:* www.safetyharborspa.com	Safety Harbor	FL	34695	727-726-1161		669
Safety Insurance Group Inc 20 Custom House St *NASDAQ:* SAFT ■ *Web:* safetyinsurance.com	Boston	MA	02110	617-951-0600		391-4
Safety Management Systems Inc 2916 N University Ave *Web:* www.safetyms.com	Lafayette	LA	70507	337-521-3400		41
Safety Products Inc 3517 Craftsman Blvd **Fax Area Code:* 800 ■ *TF:* 800-248-6860 ■ *Web:* www.spisafety.com	Lakeland	FL	33803	863-665-3601	330-0395*	679
Safety Sam Inc 2626 S Roosevelt St Ste 2 *TF:* 866-478-6980 ■ *Web:* www.safetyservicescompany.com	Tempe	AZ	85282	866-478-6980		765
Safety Seal 8100 Belvedere Rd	West Palm Beach	FL	33411	561-790-5801		191-1
Safety Seal Piston Ring Co 4000 Airport Rd **Fax:* Sales ■ *TF Sales:* 800-962-3631 ■ *Web:* www.sswesco.com	Marshall	TX	75672	903-938-9241	938-9317*	128
Safety Service Systems Inc 4036 N Nashville Ave *Web:* www.safetyservicesystems.com	Chicago	IL	60634	773-282-4900		693
Safety Shoe Distributors of Oki 10156 Reading Rd *Web:* safetyshoedistributors.com	Cincinnati	OH	45241	513-563-4220		301
Safety Speed Cut Mfg Co Inc 13943 Lincoln St NE *TF:* 800-772-2327 ■ *Web:* www.safetyspeed.com	Ham Lake	MN	55304	763-755-1600	755-6080	821
Safety Supply South Inc 100 Centrum Dr *TF Cust Svc:* 800-522-8344 ■ *Web:* www.safetysupplysouth.com	Irmo	SC	29063	800-522-8344		679
Safety Syringes Inc 2875 Loker Ave E	Carlsbad	CA	92010	760-918-9908	918-0565	476
Safety Technology International Inc 2306 Airport Rd *TF:* 800-888-4784 ■ *Web:* www.sti-usa.com	Waterford	MI	48327	248-673-9898		608
Safety Training Seminars 598 Vermont St *TF:* 800-470-9026 ■ *Web:* www.cprcpr.com	San Francisco	CA	94107	415-437-1600		138
Safety-Kleen Corp 2600 N Central Expwy Ste 400 *TF:* 800-669-5740 ■ *Web:* www.safety-kleen.com	Richardson	TX	75080	800-323-5040		667
Safeware Inc 3200 HubbaRd Rd *TF Cust Svc:* 800-331-6707 ■ *Web:* www.safewareinc.com	Landover	MD	20785	301-683-1234	683-1200	679
Safe-Way Bus Co 6030 Carmen Ave	Inver Grove Heights	MN	55076	651-451-1375		109
Safeway Foods Inc MS 10501 PO Box 29093 *Web:* safeway.com	Phoenix	AZ	85038	317-547-8528		297-8
Safeway Inc 5918 Stoneridge Mall Rd *NYSE:* SWY ■ *Web:* www.safeway.com	Pleasanton	CA	94588	925-467-3000	467-3323	345
Safeway Industrial Services LLC 308 E Air Depot Rd *Web:* www.safewayind.com	Glencoe	AL	35905	256-492-3704		196
Safeway Insurance Group 790 Pasquinelli Dr *TF:* 800-273-0300 ■ *Web:* www.safewayinsurance.com	Westmont	IL	60559	630-887-8300		391-4
Safeway Sign Co 9875 Yucca Rd **Fax Area Code:* 760 ■ *TF:* 800-637-7233 ■ *Web:* www.safewaysign.com	Adelanto	CA	92301	800-637-7233	246-5512*	701
Safford City - Graham County Library 808 Seventh Ave *Web:* www.cityofsafford.us	Safford	AZ	85546	928-432-4165	348-3209	434-3
Safford Unified School District 1 734 W 11th St *Web:* www.saffordusd.k12.az.us	Safford	AZ	85546	928-348-7000		685
Saffron Patch 20600 Chagrin Blvd Twr E Bldg *Web:* www.thesaffronpatch.com	Shaker Heights	OH	44122	216-295-0400		671
Saffron Technology Inc 1000 CentreGreen Way Ste 160 *Web:* saffrontech.com	Cary	NC	27513	919-468-8201		179
SAFH (Sutter Auburn Faith Community Hospital) 11815 Education St *TF:* 800-478-8837 ■ *Web:* www.sutterauburnfaith.org	Auburn	CA	95602	530-888-4500	888-0011	374-3
SAF-Holland USA 1950 Industrial Blvd *Web:* corporate.safholland.com	Muskegon	MI	49442	231-773-3271		60
Safra National Bank of New York 546 Fifth Ave *Web:* www.safra.com	New York	NY	10036	212-704-5500	704-9397	70
Safran USA Inc 2000 Clarendon Blvd *Web:* www.safran-usa.com	Arlington	VA	22201	703-351-9898		815
Safstrom & Company PS 1325 Fourth Ave Ste 1120 *Web:* safstrom.com	Seattle	WA	98101	206-622-6456		734
Saft America Inc 313 Crescent St NE *Web:* www.saftbatteries.com	Valdese	NC	28690	828-874-4111		74
Saf-T-Cab Inc PO Box 2587 *TF:* 800-344-7491 ■ *Web:* www.saftcab.com	Fresno	CA	93745	559-268-5541	268-5822	516
Saf-t-co Supply 1300 E Normandy Pl *Web:* www.saftco.com	Santa Ana	CA	92705	714-547-9975		191-1
Saf-T-Gard International Inc 205 Huehl Rd *TF:* 800-548-4273 ■ *Web:* www.saftgard.com	Northbrook	IL	60062	847-291-1600	291-1610	679
Safway Services Inc N 19 W 24200 Riverwood Dr *TF:* 800-558-4772 ■ *Web:* www.safway.com	Waukesha	WI	53188	262-523-6500		264-3
SAG (Screen Actors Guild) 5757 Wilshire Blvd *TF:* 800-724-0767 ■ *Web:* www.sagaftra.org	Los Angeles	CA	90036	323-954-1600	549-6775	414
Sag Harbor Industries Inc 1668 Sag Harbor Tpke *TF:* 800-724-5952 ■ *Web:* www.sagharborind.com	Sag Harbor	NY	11963	631-725-0440	725-4234	518
Saga Communications Inc 73 Kercheval Ave *NYSE:* SGA ■ *Web:* sagacom.com	Grosse Pointe Farms	MI	48236	313-886-7070	886-7150	643
Saga Japanese Steak House 8383 S Tamiami Trl *Web:* sagasteakhouse.com	Sarasota	FL	34238	941-924-2800		671
Saga Musical Instruments Inc 137 Utah Ave *Web:* www.sagamusic.com	South San Francisco	CA	94080	650-588-5558		526
Sagadahoc County 752 High St *Web:* www.sagcounty.com	Bath	ME	04530	207-443-8200	443-8213	338
Sagamore Health Network 11555 N Meridian St Ste 400 *TF:* 800-364-3469 ■ *Web:* www.sagamorehn.com	Carmel	IN	46032	317-573-2886		391-3
Sagamore Hill National Historic Site 20 Sagamore Hill Rd *Web:* www.nps.gov/sahi	Oyster Bay	NY	11771	516-922-4788	922-4792	564
Sagamore Insurance Co 111 Congressional Blvd Ste 500 *TF:* 800-317-9402 ■ *Web:* www.sagamoreinsurance.com	Carmel	IN	46032	800-317-9402		391-4
Sagamore, The 110 Sagamore Rd *TF:* 866-384-1944 ■ *Web:* www.thesagamore.com	Bolton Landing	NY	12814	518-644-9400	743-6036	669
Sagarsoft Inc 78 Eastern Blvd *Web:* www.sagarsoft.com	Glastonbury	CT	06033	860-633-2025		177
Sage 2378 N Federal Hwy *Web:* www.sagecafe.net	Fort Lauderdale	FL	33305	954-565-2299		671
Sage 271 17th St NW *TF:* 800-368-2405 ■ *Web:* www.sage.com	Atlanta	GA	30363	866-996-7243		178-1

Phone | Fax | Class

Sage Advantage
9414 E San Salvador Dr Ste 250 ... Scottsdale AZ 85258 480-941-0094 737
TF: 800-724-7749 ■ Web: www.sageadvantage.com

Sage Advisory Services Ltd Co
5900 SW Pkwy Bldg 1 Ste 100 ... Austin TX 78735 512-327-5530 401
TF: 800-541-7774 ■ Web: www.sageadvisory.com

Sage Centers
1410 Monument Blvd Ste 100 ... Concord CA 94520 925-627-7243 794
Web: sagecenters.com

Sage College 12125 Day St Ste L ... Moreno Valley CA 92557 951-781-2727 166
TF: 800-222-1231 ■ Web: www.sagecollege.edu

Sage College of Albany
140 New Scotland Ave ... Albany NY 12208 518-292-1730 292-1912* 166
*Fax: Admissions ■ TF Admissions: 888-837-9724 ■ Web: www.sage.edu

Sage Computing Inc
11491 Sunset Hills Rd Ste 350 ... Reston VA 20190 703-742-7881 177
Web: sagecomputing.com

Sage Consulting Group
1623 Blake St Ste 400 ... Denver CO 80202 303-571-0237 261
Web: www.sageconsulting.com

Sage Data Security LLC
2275 Congress St ... Portland ME 04102 207-879-7243 177
Web: www.sagedatasecurity.com

Sage Direct Inc
3400 Raleigh Dr SE ... Grand Rapids MI 49512 616-940-8311 5
Web: www.sagedirect.com

Sage Environmental Consulting LP
4611 Bee Caves Rd Ste 100 ... Austin TX 78746 512-327-0288 192
Web: www.sageenvironmental.com

Sage Financial Group
300 Barr Harbor Dr Five Tower Bridge
Ste 200 ... West Conshohocken PA 19428 484-342-4400 194
TF: 800-613-1327 ■ Web: www.sagefinancial.com

Sage Group LLC, The
11111 Santa Monica Blvd Ste 2200 ... Los Angeles CA 90025 310-478-7899 401
Web: www.sagellc.com

Sage Hospitality Resources LLC
1575 Welton St Ste 300 ... Denver CO 80202 303-595-7200 379
Web: www.sagehospitality.com

Sage Microsystems Inc 18 N Village Ave ... Exton PA 19341 610-524-1300 177
TF: 800-724-7400 ■ Web: www.sagemicrosystems.com

Sage Petroleum 2148 S Jefferson St ... Casper WY 82601 307-265-6992 536
Web: sagepetroleum.com

Sage Publications Inc
2455 Teller Rd ... Thousand Oaks CA 91320 805-499-9774 499-0871 637-2
TF: 800-818-7243 ■ Web: www.sagepub.com

Sage Room 81 Pope Ave ... Hilton Head Island SC 29928 843-785-5352 671
Web: www.thesageroom.com

Sage Rutty & Company Inc
100 Corporate Woods Ste 300 ... Rochester NY 14623 585-232-3760 401
Web: www.sagerutty.com

Sage Telecom Inc
3300 E Renner Rd Ste 350 Bldg 2 ... Richardson TX 75082 214-495-4700 736

Sage V Foods LLC
12100 Wilshire Blvd Ste 605 ... Los Angeles CA 90025 310-820-4496 345
Web: www.sagevfoods.com

Sage YMCA of Metro Chicago
701 Manor Rd ... Crystal Lake IL 60014 815-459-4455 31
Web: www.ymcachicago.org

Sage's Cafe 368 E 100 S, ... Salt Lake City UT 84101 801-322-3790 671
Web: www.sagescafe.com

Sagebrush Steakhouse 129 Fast Ln ... Mooresville NC 28117 704-660-5939 799-6199 670
TF: 877-704-5939 ■ Web: www.sagebrushsteakhouse.com

SageLogix Inc
9100 E Panorama Dr Ste 100 ... Englewood CO 80112 303-925-0100 177
Web: www.sagelogix.com

Sagent Pharmaceuticals Inc
1901 N Roselle Rd ... Schaumburg IL 60195 847-908-1600 908-1601 582
NASDAQ: SGNT ■ Web: www.sagentpharma.com

SagePoint Financial Inc
2800 N Central Ave Ste 2100 ... Phoenix AZ 85004 800-552-3319 690
TF: 800-552-3319 ■ Web: www.sagepointfinancial.com

Sager Electronics Inc 19 Lorena Dr ... Middleboro MA 02346 508-947-8888 947-0869 246
TF: 800-724-3780 ■ Web: www.sager.com

Sager Metal Strip Company LLC
100 Boone Dr ... Michigan City IN 46360 219-874-3609 492
Web: www.sagermetal.com

Sager's Seafood Plus Inc
4802 Bridal Wreath Dr ... Richmond TX 77406 281-342-8833 297-5
TF: 800-929-3474 ■ Web: sagersseafoodplus.com

SageRider Inc
3330 F County Rd 56 Ste 160 ... Stafford TX 77477 281-271-7095 539
Web: www.sageriderinc.com

Sagerock.com 15 Broad St ... Akron OH 44305 330-379-9000 225
Web: www.sagerock.com

SAGES (Society of American Gastrointestinal & Endoscopic Surgeons)
11300 W Olympic Blvd Ste 600 ... Los Angeles CA 90064 310-437-0544 437-0585 49-8
Web: www.sages.org

Sagestone Spa & Salon
Red Mountain Resort
1275 East Red Mtn Cir ... Ivins UT 84738 435-673-4905 706
TF: 877-246-4453 ■ Web: www.redmountainresort.com

SageView Advisory Group LLC
1920 Main St Ste 800 ... Irvine CA 92614 949-955-1395 194
Web: www.sageviewadvisory.com

Sageworks Inc 5565 Centerview Dr ... Raleigh NC 27606 919-851-7474 317
Web: www.sageworks.com

Sagient Research Systems Inc
3655 Nobel Dr Ste 540 ... San Diego CA 92122 858-623-1600 401
Web: www.sagientresearch.com

Saginaw Chippewa Tribal College
2274 Enterprise Dr ... Mount Pleasant MI 48858 989-775-4123 775-4528 165
TF: 800-225-8172 ■ Web: www.sagchip.org

Saginaw Control & Engineering Inc
95 Midland Rd ... Saginaw MI 48638 989-799-6871 799-4524 816
TF: 800-234-6871 ■ Web: www.saginawcontrol.com

Saginaw Correctional Facility
9625 Pierce Rd ... Freeland MI 48623 989-695-9880 213
Web: www.michigan.gov

Saginaw County 111 S Michigan Ave ... Saginaw MI 48602 989-790-5200 338
Web: www.saginawcounty.com

Saginaw County Chamber of Commerce
515 N Washington Ave 2nd Fl ... Saginaw MI 48607 989-752-7161 752-9055 139
TF: 866-657-9357 ■ Web: www.saginawchamber.org

Saginaw Machine Systems (SMS)
800 N Hamilton St ... Saginaw MI 48602 989-753-8465 455
Web: www.saginawmachine.com

Saginaw News 203 S Washington Ave ... Saginaw MI 48607 989-752-7171 532-2
TF: 877-611-6397 ■ Web: www.mlive.com

Saginaw Pipe Company Inc
1980 Hwy 31 S PO Box 8 ... Saginaw AL 35137 205-664-3670 838-8069* 492
*Fax Area Code: 717 ■ TF: 800-433-1374 ■ Web: www.saginawpipe.com

Saginaw Valley State University
7400 Bay Rd ... University Center MI 48710 989-964-4200 790-0180 166
TF: 800-968-9500 ■ Web: www.svsu.edu

Saginaw Valley State University Zahnow Library
7400 Bay Rd ... University Center MI 48710 989-964-4240 964-4383 434-6
TF: 800-968-9500 ■ Web: www.svsu.edu/library

Sagitec Solutions LLC
422 County Rd D E ... Little Canada MN 55117 612-284-7130 180
Web: sagitec.com

Sagittarius Hair Designs Ltd
1136 Conrad Ct ... Hagerstown MD 21740 301-797-8008 77
Web: www.sagittariussalon.com

Sagon Phior 2107 Sawtelle Blvd ... Los Angeles CA 90025 310-575-4441 4
Web: sagonphior.com

Saguache County
501 Fourth St PO Box 176 ... Saguache CO 81149 719-655-2512 655-2730 338
Web: www.saguachecounty.net

Saguaro Lake Ranch 13020 Bush Hwy ... Mesa AZ 85215 480-984-2194 669
TF: 800-868-5617 ■ Web: www.saguarolakeranch.com

Saguaro National Park
3693 S Old Spanish Trl ... Tucson AZ 85730 520-733-5100 733-5183 564
Web: www.nps.gov

Saguaro Resources Ltd
3000 500 - Fourth Ave SW ... Calgary AB T2P2V6 403-453-3040 536
TF: 855-835-4434 ■ Web: saguaroresources.com

Saguenay Port Authority
6600 Quai-Marcel-Dionne Rd ... La Baie QC G7B3N9 418-697-0250 697-0243 618
Web: www.portsaguenay.ca

Saguenay-Lac-Saint-Jean Integrated Health and Social Services Ctr
930 Jacques-Cartier St E ... Chicoutimi QC G7H7K9 418-545-4980 545-8791 374-2
TF: 800-370-4980 ■ Web: santesaglac.com

Saguenay-Saint Lawrence Marine Park
182 Rue de l'Eglise ... Tadoussac QC G0T2A0 418-235-4703 235-4686 563
Web: pc.gc.ca/amnc%2dnmca/qc/saguenay

SAH (Society of Architectural Historians)
1365 N Astor St ... Chicago IL 60610 312-573-1365 573-1141 48-13
Web: www.sah.org

Sahadi Fine Foods Inc 4215 First Ave ... Brooklyn NY 11232 718-369-0100 297-8
Web: www.sahadifinefoods.com

Sahara Energy Ltd 700 4 Ave SW Ste 610 ... Calgary AB T2P3J4 403-232-1359 232-1307 539
Web: www.saharaenergyltd.com

Sahara Restaurant 143 Highland St ... Worcester MA 01609 508-798-2181 671
Web: eatsahara.com

Sahlen Packing Company Inc
318 Howard St ... Buffalo NY 14206 716-852-8677 296-26
TF: 800-466-8165 ■ Web: www.sahlen.com

Sahlman Seafoods Inc
1601 Sahlman Dr PO Box 5009 ... Tampa FL 33605 813-248-5726 247-5787 285
Web: www.sahlmanseafood.com

Sahouri Insurance & Associates Inc
8200 Grnsburg Dr Ste 1550 ... Mclean VA 22102 703-883-0500 390
TF: 855-242-6660 ■ Web: sahouri.com

SAI (Sigma Alpha Iota) 1 Tunnel Rd ... Asheville NC 28805 828-251-0606 251-0644 48-16
Web: www.sai-national.org

Sai Ann International Inc
28428 Golf Pointe Blvd ... Farmington Hills MI 48331 248-324-1604 809
TF: 800-265-0099 ■ Web: www.saiann-inc.com

Sai Cafe 2010 N Sheffield Ave ... Chicago IL 60614 773-472-8080 472-0699 671
Web: www.saicafe.com

SAI Consulting Engineers Inc
1350 Penn Ave Ste 300 ... Pittsburgh PA 15222 412-392-8750 392-8785 261
Web: www.saiengr.com

SAI Engineering Inc
13662 Office Pl Ste 101 ... Woodbridge VA 22192 703-590-8200 256
Web: www.saimep.com

Sai Gai Japanese Steakhouse
7521 Granby St ... Norfolk VA 23505 757-423-1000 671

SAI Systems International Inc
12 Progress Dr ... Shelton CT 06484 203-929-0790 180
Web: www.saisystems.com

SAIC Inc (Science Application International Corp Inc)
1710 SAIC Dr ... McLean VA 22102 703-676-4300 178-5
TF: 866-400-7242 ■ Web: www.saic.com

Saigon 4205 High Pt Rd ... Greensboro NC 27407 336-294-9286 671
Web: www.saigonrestaurant.net

Saigon 221 E N St ... Rapid City SD 57701 605-348-8523 671
Web: saigonrestaurantrc.com

Saigon 85 Clarence St ... Ottawa ON K1N7B5 613-789-7934 671

Saigon 1904 Pacific Ave ... Stockton CA 95204 209-463-2274 671

Saigon Cafe 440 W 300 S ... Provo UT 84601 801-812-1173 671
Web: saigoncafeprovo.biz

Saigon Le 51 N Cleveland St ... Memphis TN 38104 901-276-5326 671

Saigon on Fifth 3900 Fifth Ave ... San Diego CA 92103 619-220-8828 671
Web: saigononfifth.menutoeat.com

Saigon Rendez-vous 117 Fifth Ave SW ... Olympia WA 98501 360-352-1989 671
Web: saigonrendezvous.com

SAIL Magazine 10 Bokum Rd ... Essex CT 06426 860-767-3200 767-1048 457-4
TF: 800-745-7245 ■ Web: www.sailmagazine.com

Sail Venture Partners LP
3161 Michelson Dr Ste 750 ... Irvine CA 92612 949-398-5100 398-5101 792
Web: www.sailcapital.com

Sailfish Club of Florida Inc, The
1338 N Lake Way ... Palm Beach FL 33480 561-844-0206 354
Web: www.sailfishclub.com

Phone | Fax | Class

Sailing World Magazine
55 Hammarlund Way ..... Middletown RI 02842 401-845-5100 845-5180 457-4
TF Cust Svc: 866-436-2460 ■ *Web:* www.sailingworld.com

Sailor's Creek Battlefield State Park
6541 Saylers Creek Rd ..... Rice VA 23966 804-561-7510 565
Web: www.dcr.virginia.gov

Sain Construction Co
713 Vincent St ..... Manchester TN 37355 931-728-7644 186
Web: www.sainconstruction.com

Sainergy Inc
1999 S Bascom Ave Ste 700 ..... Campbell CA 95008 408-532-9800 624
Web: www.sainergy.net

Saint Agnes HealthCare
900 S Caton Ave ..... Baltimore MD 21229 410-368-6000 374-3
TF: 800-875-8750 ■ *Web:* www.stagnes.org

Saint Agnes Medical Ctr
1303 E Herndon Ave ..... Fresno CA 93720 559-450-3000 374-3
Web: www.samc.com

Saint Albans School Mount St Alban ..... Washington DC 20016 202-537-6435 537-6434 623
Web: www.stalbansschool.org

Saint Albert Chamber of Commerce
71 St Albert Rd ..... Saint Albert AB T8N6L5 780-458-2833 458-6515 137
TF: 800-207-9410 ■ *Web:* www.stalbertchamber.com

Saint Alexius Hospital
Broadway Campus 3933 S Broadway ..... Saint Louis MO 63118 314-865-7000 865-7983 374-3
TF: 800-245-1431 ■ *Web:* www.stalexiushospital.com

Saint Alexius Medical Ctr
1555 Barrington Rd ..... Hoffman Estates IL 60169 847-843-2000 490-2570 374-3
TF: 800-432-5005 ■ *Web:* www.alexianbrothershealth.org

Saint Alphonsus Regional Medical Ctr
1055 N Curtis Rd ..... Boise ID 83706 208-367-2121 374-3
TF: 877-401-3627 ■ *Web:* www.saintalphonsus.org

Saint Ambrose University
518 W Locust St ..... Davenport IA 52803 563-333-6000 333-6243* 166
**Fax:* Admissions ■ *TF Admissions:* 800-383-2627 ■ *Web:* www.sau.edu

Saint Andrew's Abbey
31001 N Valyermo Rd ..... Valyermo CA 93563 661-944-2178 673
Web: www.valyermo.com

Saint Andrew's College 15800 Yonge St ..... Aurora ON L4G3H7 905-727-3178 727-9032 622
TF: 877-378-1899 ■ *Web:* www.sac.on.ca

Saint Andrew's School 3900 Jog Rd ..... Boca Raton FL 33434 561-210-2000 622

Saint Andrew's School
63 Federal Rd ..... Barrington RI 02806 401-246-1230 246-0510 622
Web: www.standrews-ri.org

Saint Andrew's-Sewanee School
290 QuintaRd Rd ..... Sewanee TN 37375 931-598-5651 622
Web: www.sasweb.org

Saint Andrews Estates
375 Morris Rd ..... West Point PA 19446 561-487-4728 672
TF Mktg: 866-897-3490 ■ *Web:* www.actsretirement.org

Saint Andrews Presbyterian College
1700 Dogwood Mile ..... Laurinburg NC 28352 910-277-5555 277-5020* 166
**Fax:* Admissions ■ *TF:* 800-763-0198 ■ *Web:* www.sa.edu

Saint Andrews State Park
4607 State Pk Ln ..... Panama City FL 32408 850-233-5140 565
Web: www.floridastateparks.org

Saint Anne's Hospital
795 Middle St ..... Fall River MA 02721 508-674-5600 374-3
TF: 800-488-5959 ■ *Web:* stcward.org

Saint Anne's-Belfield School
2132 Ivy Rd ..... Charlottesville VA 22903 434-296-5106 622
Web: www.stab.org

Saint Anselm College
100 St Anselm Dr ..... Manchester NH 03102 603-641-7500 641-7550 166
TF: 888-426-7356 ■ *Web:* www.anselm.edu

Saint Anthony Central Hospital
11600 W Second Pl ..... Lakewood CO 80228 720-321-0000 374-3
Web: www.stanthonyhosp.org

Saint Anthony College of Nursing
5658 E State St ..... Rockford IL 61108 815-395-5091 166
TF: 800-977-8449 ■ *Web:* sacn.edu

Saint Anthony Hospital
1000 N Lee St ..... Oklahoma City OK 73101 405-272-7000 374-3
TF: 800-227-6964 ■ *Web:* www.saintsok.com

Saint Anthony Retreat Ctr
300 E Fourth St ..... Marathon WI 54448 715-443-2236 443-2235 673
Web: www.sarcenter.com

Saint Anthony the - A Wyndham Historic Hotel
300 E Travis St ..... San Antonio TX 78205 210-227-4392 379

Saint Anthony's Catholic High School
3200 McCullough Ave ..... San Antonio TX 78212 210-832-5600 832-5633 622
Web: www.sachs.org

Saint Anthony's Hospice
2410 S Green St ..... Henderson KY 42420 270-826-2326 831-2169 371
TF: 866-380-2326 ■ *Web:* www.stanthonyshospice.org

Saint Anthony's Hospital
1200 Seventh Ave N ..... Saint Petersburg FL 33705 727-825-1100 374-3
Web: baycare.org/sah

Saint Anthony's Medical Ctr
10010 Kennerly Rd ..... Saint Louis MO 63128 314-525-1000 374-3
TF: 800-554-9550 ■ *Web:* www.stanthonysmedcenter.com

Saint Anthony's Memorial Hospital
503 N Maple St ..... Effingham IL 62401 217-342-2121 374-3
Web: www.stanthonyshospital.org

Saint Augustine Alligator Farm
999 Anastasia Blvd ..... Saint Augustine FL 32080 904-824-3337 823
Web: www.alligatorfarm.com

Saint Augustine City Hall
PO Box 210 ..... Saint Augustine FL 32085 904-825-1040 209-4286 337
Web: www.staugustinegovernment.com

Saint Augustine College
1345 W Argyle St ..... Chicago IL 60640 773-878-8756 878-0937* 162
**Fax:* Admissions ■ *TF:* 800-621-7440 ■ *Web:* www.staugustine.edu

Saint Augustine Lighthouse & Museum
81 Lighthouse Ave ..... Saint Augustine FL 32080 904-829-0745 808-1248 520
Web: www.staugustinelighthouse.com

Saint Augustine National Cemetery
104 Marine St ..... Saint Augustine FL 32084 352-793-7740 793-9560 136
TF: 800-273-8255 ■ *Web:* www.cem.va.gov/cems/nchp/staugustine.asp

Phone | Fax | Class

Saint Augustine's College
1315 Oakwood Ave ..... Raleigh NC 27610 919-516-4000 516-5805* 166
**Fax:* Admissions ■ *TF Admissions:* 800-948-1126 ■ *Web:* www.st-aug.edu

Saint Barnabas Hospice & Palliative Care Ctr
95 Old Short Hills Rd ..... West Orange NJ 07052 973-322-4800 322-4795 371
Web: www.barnabashealth.org

Saint Barnabas Medical Ctr
94 Old Short Hills Rd ..... West Orange NJ 07052 973-322-5000 374-3
TF: 888-724-7123 ■ *Web:* www.barnabashealth.org

Saint Bernard Parish Library
2600 Palmisano Blvd ..... Chalmette LA 70043 504-279-0448 434-3
Web: www.stbernard.lib.la.us

Saint Bernard Preparatory School
1600 St Bernard Dr SE ..... Cullman AL 35055 256-739-6682 734-2925 622
Web: www.stbernardprep.com

Saint Bernard State Park
501 St Bernard Pkwy ..... Braithwaite LA 70040 504-682-2101 565
TF: 888-677-7823 ■ *Web:* www.crt.state.la.us

Saint Bernard's Medical Ctr
225 E Jackson ..... Jonesboro AR 72401 870-207-7300 374-3
Web: www.stbernards.info

Saint Bernard's School of Theology & Ministry
120 French Rd ..... Rochester NY 14618 585-271-3657 167-3
Web: www.stbernards.edu

Saint Bernardine Medical Ctr
2101 N Waterman Ave ..... San Bernardino CA 92404 909-883-8711 881-4546 374-3
Web: www.stbernardinemedicalcenter.org

Saint Brides Correctional Ctr
701 Sanderson Rd ..... Chesapeake VA 23322 757-421-6600 213

Saint Catharine College
2735 BaRdstown Rd ..... Saint Catharine KY 40061 859-336-5082 162
Web: sccky.accountsupport.com

Saint Catherine Hospital
4321 Fir St ..... East Chicago IN 46312 219-392-1700 374-3
TF: 800-859-5553 ■ *Web:* www.comhs.org

Saint Catherine Hospital (SCH)
401 E Spruce St ..... Garden City KS 67846 620-272-2222 374-3
Web: stcatherinehosp.org

Saint Catherine of Siena Medical Ctr
50 Rt 25 A ..... Smithtown NY 11787 631-862-3000 862-3105 374-3
Web: www.stcatherines.chsli.org

Saint Catherine's School
6001 Grove Ave ..... Richmond VA 23226 804-288-2804 285-8169 622
Web: www.st.catherines.org

Saint Charles Borromeo Seminary
100 E Wynnewood Rd ..... Wynnewood PA 19096 610-667-3394 167-3
Web: www.scs.edu

Saint Charles Chamber of Commerce
2201 First Capitol Dr ..... Saint Charles MO 63301 636-946-0633 139
Web: www.gstccc.com

Saint Charles City County Library District
77 Boone Hill Dr ..... Saint Peters MO 63376 636-441-2300 434-3

Saint Charles County
201 N Second St ..... St. Charles MO 63301 636-949-7900 338
Web: www.sccmo.org

Saint Charles Parish
15045 River Rd PO Box 302 ..... Hahnville LA 70057 985-783-5000 783-2067 338
Web: www.stcharlesgov.net

Saint Charles Vision
8040 St Charles Ave ..... New Orleans LA 70118 504-866-6311 543
Web: www.stcharlesvision.com

Saint Clair Correctional Facility
1000 St Clair Rd ..... Springville AL 35146 205-467-6111 213

Saint Clair County
165 Fifth Ave Ste 100 ..... Ashville AL 35953 205-594-2100 594-2110 338
Web: www.stclairco.com

Saint Clair County 10 Public Sq ..... Belleville IL 62220 618-277-6600 338
Web: www.co.st-clair.il.us

Saint Clair County
201 McMorran Blvd Rm 2900 ..... Port Huron MI 48060 810-985-2200 985-4796 338
Web: www.stclaircounty.org

Saint Clair County Library System
210 McMorran Blvd ..... Port Huron MI 48060 810-987-7323 987-7874 434-3
TF: 877-987-7323 ■ *Web:* www.sccl.lib.mi.us

Saint Clair Square
134 St Clair Sq ..... Fairview Heights IL 62208 618-632-7567 460
Web: www.stclairsquare.com

Saint Claire Regional Medical Ctr
222 Medical Cir ..... Morehead KY 40351 606-783-6500 374-3
Web: www.st-claire.org

Saint Clare's Hospital 25 Pocono Rd ..... Denville NJ 07834 973-625-6000 374-3
Web: www.saintclares.com

Saint Cloud Area Convention & Visitors Bureau
525 Hwy 10 S Ste 1 ..... Saint Cloud MN 56304 320-251-4170 656-0401 206
TF: 800-264-2940 ■ *Web:* www.granitecountry.com

Saint Cloud Hospital
1406 Sixth Ave ..... Saint Cloud MN 56303 320-251-2700 255-5711 374-3
TF: 800-835-6652 ■ *Web:* www.centracare.com

Saint Cloud Technical & Community College
1540 Northway Dr ..... Saint Cloud MN 56303 320-308-5089 308-5981 800
TF: 800-222-1009 ■ *Web:* www.sctcc.edu

Saint Cloud Times
3000 Seventh St N PO Box 768 ..... Saint Cloud MN 56303 320-255-8700 532-2
TF: 877-424-4921 ■ *Web:* www.sctimes.com

Saint Cloud/Greater Osceola Chamber of Commerce
1200 New York Ave ..... Saint Cloud FL 34769 407-892-3671 892-5289 139
TF: 800-000-0000 ■ *Web:* www.stcloudflchamber.com

Saint Croix County 1101 Carmichael Rd ..... Hudson WI 54016 715-386-4600 381-4400 338
Web: www.co.saint-croix.wi.us

Saint Croix Electric Co-op
1925 Ridgeway St ..... Hammond WI 54015 715-796-7000 796-7070 245
TF: 800-924-3407 ■ *Web:* www.scecnet.net

Saint Croix Forge Inc
5195 Scandia Trl ..... Forest Lake MN 55025 866-668-7642 483
TF: 866-668-7642 ■ *Web:* www.stcroixforge.com

Saint Croix Island International Historic Site
PO Box 247 ..... Calais ME 04619 207-454-3871 288-8813 564
Web: www.nps.gov/sacr

Phone Fax Class

Saint Croix National Scenic Riverway
401 N Hamilton St Saint Croix Falls WI 54024 715-483-3284 483-3288 564
Web: www.nps.gov

Saint Croix Press Inc
1185 S Knowles Ave New Richmond WI 54017 715-246-5811 246-2486 637-9
TF: 800-826-6622 ■ *Web:* www.stcroixpress.com

Saint Croix State Park
30065 St Croix Pk Rd Hinckley MN 55037 320-384-6591 565
TF: 888-646-6367 ■ *Web:* www.dnr.state.mn.us

Saint Croix Valley Chamber of Commerce
39 Union St Calais ME 04619 207-454-2308 139
Web: visitstcroixvalley.com

Saint David's Medical Ctr
919 E 32nd St Austin TX 78705 512-476-7111 374-3
Web: www.stdavids.com

Saint Dominic-Jackson Memorial Hospital
969 Lakeland Dr Jackson MS 39216 601-200-2000 374-3
Web: www.stdom.com

Saint Edward State Park
14445 Juanita Dr NE Kenmore WA 98028 425-823-2992 565
Web: www.parks.wa.gov

Saint Elizabeth Home
1 Saint Elizabeth Way East Greenwich RI 02818 401-471-6060 471-6072 450
TF: 800-213-7193 ■ *Web:* www.stelizabethcommunity.org

Saint Elizabeth Hospital
1506 S Oneida St Appleton WI 54915 920-738-2000 374-3
TF: 800-223-7332 ■ *Web:* www.affinityhealth.org

Saint Elizabeth Medical Ctr
2209 Genesee St Utica NY 13501 315-798-8100 798-8344 374-3
Web: www.stemc.org

Saint Elizabeth Regional Medical Ctr
555 S 70th St Lincoln NE 68510 402-219-8000 374-3
Web: www.chihealthstelizabeth.com

Saint Elizabeth's Medical Ctr
2209 Genesee St Utica NY 13501 315-801-8100 374-3
Web: www.stemc.org

Saint Elizabeths Hospital
1100 Alabama Ave SE Washington DC 20032 202-299-5100 374-5
Web: www.stelizabethseast.com

Saint Elmo Steak House
127 S Illinois St Indianapolis IN 46225 317-635-0636 671
Web: www.stelmos.com

Saint Emilion 3617 W Seventh St Fort Worth TX 76107 817-737-2781 671
Web: www.saint-emilionrestaurant.com

Saint Francis Care 114 Woodland St Hartford CT 06105 860-714-4000 353
Web: www.stfranciscare.org

Saint Francis College
180 Remsen St Brooklyn Heights NY 11201 718-522-2300 166
Web: www.sfc.edu

Saint Francis County
313 S Izard St Forrest City AR 72335 870-261-1700 338
Web: stfranciscountyar.org

Saint Francis Health Ctr
1700 SW Seventh St Topeka KS 66606 785-295-8000 374-3
TF: 855-578-3726 ■ *Web:* www.stfrancistopeka.org

Saint Francis Hospital
2122 Manchester Expy Columbus GA 31904 706-596-4000 374-3
Web: www.mystfrancis.com

Saint Francis Hospital 5959 Pk Ave Memphis TN 38119 901-765-1000 374-3
TF: 800-994-6610 ■
Web: www.saintfrancishosp.com/en-us/pages/default.aspx

Saint Francis Hospital 6161 S Yale Ave Tulsa OK 74136 918-494-2200 374-3
TF: 800-362-4992 ■ *Web:* www.saintfrancis.com

Saint Francis Hospital
7th N Clayton St Wilmington DE 19805 302-421-4100 374-3
Web: www.stfrancishealthcare.org

Saint Francis Hospital
333 Laidley St Charleston WV 25301 304-347-6500 374-3
TF: 800-321-1245 ■ *Web:* www.stfrancishospital.com

Saint Francis Hospital & Medical Ctr
114 Woodland St Hartford CT 06105 860-714-4000 374-3
TF: 800-993-4312 ■ *Web:* www.stfranciscare.org

Saint Francis Hospital Muskogee
300 Rockefeller Dr Muskogee OK 74401 918-682-5501 374-3
Web: www.eastarhealth.com

Saint Francis Medical Ctr
3630 E Imperial Hwy Lynwood CA 90262 310-900-8900 900-4505* 374-3
**Fax:* Admitting ■ *Web:* stfrancis.verity.org

Saint Francis Medical Ctr
211 St Francis Dr Cape Girardeau MO 63703 573-331-3000 331-5009 374-3
Web: sfmc.net

Saint Francis Medical Ctr
601 Hamilton Ave Trenton NJ 08629 609-599-5000 374-3
TF: 888-216-3293 ■ *Web:* www.sfmc.net

Saint Francis Memorial Hospital
900 Hyde St San Francisco CA 94109 415-353-6000 353-6631* 374-3
**Fax:* Admitting ■ *Web:* www.saintfrancismemorial.org

Saint Francis Retreat Ctr
549 Mission VineyaRd Rd San Juan Bautista CA 95045 831-623-4234 623-9046 673
Web: www.stfrancisretreat.com

Saint Francis University
117 Evergreen Dr Loretto PA 15940 814-472-3000 166
Web: www.francis.edu

Saint Francis Xavier University
PO Box 5000 Antigonish NS B2G2W5 902-863-3300 867-2329* 785
**Fax:* Admissions ■ *TF Admissions:* 877-867-7839 ■ *Web:* www.stfx.ca

Saint Francois County
1 W Liberty St Farmington MO 63640 573-756-3623 431-6967 338
Web: www.sfcgov.org

Saint Francois State Park
8920 US Hwy 67 N Bonne Terre MO 63628 573-358-2173 565
Web: www.mostateparks.com

Saint George Library Ctr
5 Central Ave Staten Island NY 10301 718-442-8560 312-4781* 434-3
**Fax Area Code:* 646 ■ *TF:* 800-342-3688

Saint George's Anglican Church
227 Wharncliffe Rd N London ON N6H2B6 519-438-2994 438-2995 50-1
Web: www.stgeorgeslondon.ca

Saint George's Church
2222 Brunswick St Halifax NS B3K2Z3 902-423-1059 423-0897 50-1
Web: www.roundchurch.ca

Saint Gobain Abrasives
2600 Tenth Ave Watervliet NY 12189 518-266-2200 1
Web: www.saint-gobain-abrasives.com

Saint Gregory Luxury Hotel & Suites
2033 M St NW Washington DC 20036 202-530-3600 379
Web: www.capitalhotelswdc.com

Saint Gregory's University
1900 W MacArthur St Shawnee OK 74804 405-878-5100 878-5198 166
TF Admissions: 888-784-7347 ■ *Web:* www.stgregorys.edu

Saint Helena Hospital
10 Woodland Rd Saint Helena CA 94574 707-963-3611 374-3
Web: www.adventisthealth.org

Saint Innocent Winery 5657 Zena Rd NW Salem OR 97304 503-378-1526 50-7
TF: 800-831-4916 ■ *Web:* www.stinnocentwine.com

Saint James Bay State Marine Park
400 Willoughby Ave Ste 500 Juneau AK 99811 907-465-4563 586-3113 565
Web: dnr.alaska.gov

Saint James Healthcare 400 S Clark St Butte MT 59701 406-723-2500 374-3
Web: www.sclhealth.org/locations/st-james-healthcare

Saint James Hotel 330 Magazine St New Orleans LA 70130 504-304-4000 379
Web: www.saintjameshotel.com

Saint James Mercy Hospital
411 Canisteo St Hornell NY 14843 607-324-8000 324-8115 374-3
TF: 800-346-2211 ■ *Web:* www.stjamesmercy.org

Saint James Parish
5800 Hwy 44 PO Box 106 Convent LA 70723 225-562-2286 562-2279 338
Web: www.stjamesla.com

Saint James School
17641 College Rd Saint James MD 21740 301-733-9330 739-1310 622
Web: www.stjames.edu

Saint Jerome's University
290 Westmount Rd N Waterloo ON N2L3G3 519-884-8110 785
Web: www.sju.ca

Saint Joe State Park
2800 Pimville Rd Park Hills MO 63601 573-431-1069 565
Web: www.mostateparks.com

Saint John Board of Trade (SJBT)
34 Harvey Rd Saint John NL A1C2G1 506-634-8111 632-2008 137
Web: www.sjboardoftrade.com

Saint John Hospital Inc of Kansas
3500 S Fourth St Leavenworth KS 66048 913-680-6000 374-3
Web: www.providencekc.com

Saint John Macomb-Oakland Hospital
Oakland Ctr
27351 Dequindre Rd Madison Heights MI 48071 248-967-7000 374-3
Web: www.stjohnprovidence.org/oakland

Saint John Port Authority
111 Water St Saint John NB E2L0B1 506-636-4869 636-4443 618
Web: www.sjport.com

Saint John Regional Hospital
400 University Ave PO Box 2100 Saint John NB E2L4L2 506-648-7121 648-7765 374-2
Web: horizonnb.ca

Saint John Regional Library
1 Market Sq Saint John NB E2L4Z6 506-643-7220 643-7225 436
Web: saintjohnlibrary.com

Saint John the Baptist Parish
1801 W Airline Hwy LaPlace LA 70068 985-652-9569 652-4131 338
Web: www.sjbparish.com

Saint John Vianney Theological Seminary
1300 S Steele St Denver CO 80210 303-282-3427 167-3
Web: www.sjvdenver.org

Saint John's Hospital
800 E Carpenter St Springfield IL 62769 217-544-6464 374-3
TF: 855-228-4438 ■ *Web:* www.st-johns.org

Saint John's Hospital & Health Ctr
2121 Santa Monica Blvd Santa Monica CA 90404 310-829-5511 374-3
Web: california.providence.org/saint-johns

Saint John's Northwestern Military Academy
1101 N Genesee St Delafield WI 53018 262-646-7115 622
TF: 800-752-2338 ■ *Web:* www.sjnma.org

Saint John's On the Lake
1840 N Prospect Ave Milwaukee WI 53202 414-831-7300 672
Web: www.saintjohnsmilw.org

Saint John's Preparatory School
1857 Watertower Rd PO Box 4000 Collegeville MN 56321 320-363-3321 363-3322 622
TF: 800-525 7737 ■ *Web:* www sjprep.net

Saint John's Restaurant
1278 Market St Chattanooga TN 37402 423-266-4400 671
Web: www.stjohnsrestaurant.com

Saint John's Riverside Hospital
ParkCare Pavilion 2 Pk Ave Yonkers NY 10703 914-964-7300 374-3
Web: www.riversidehealth.org

Saint John's Seminary 127 Lake St Brighton MA 02135 617-254-2610 167-3
Web: www.sjs.edu

Saint John's Seminary
5012 Seminary Rd Camarillo CA 93012 805-482-2755 167-3
TF: 800-711-6232 ■ *Web:* www.stjohnsem.edu

Saint John's University
8000 Utopia Pkwy Queens NY 11439 718-990-2000 990-2096* 166
**Fax:* Admissions ■ *TF:* 888-978-5646 ■ *Web:* www.stjohns.edu
Staten Island 300 Howard Ave Staten Island NY 10301 718-390-4500 390-4298* 166
**Fax:* Admissions ■ *Web:* www.stjohns.edu

Saint John's University Alcuin Library
2835 Abbey Plaza Collegeville MN 56321 320-363-2122 363-2126 434-6
TF: 800-544-1489 ■ *Web:* csbsju.edu/libraries

Saint John's-Ravenscourt School
400 S Dr Winnipeg MB R3T3K5 204-477-2400 477-2429 622
TF: 800-437-0040 ■ *Web:* www.sjr.mb.ca

Saint Johns County
4010 Lewis Speedway Saint Augustine FL 32084 904-819-3600 819-3661 338
Web: www.co.st-johns.fl.us

Saint Johns County Chamber of Commerce
1 News Pl Saint Augustine FL 32084 904-829-5681 139
Web: www.stjohnscountychamber.com

Phone | Fax | Class

Saint Johns River Community College
5001 St Johns Ave .... Palatka FL 32177 386-312-4200 162
TF: 888-757-2293 ■ *Web:* www.sjrstate.edu
St.Augustine 2990 College Dr .... Saint Augustine FL 32084 904-808-7400 162
Web: sjrstate.edu

Saint Joseph Area Chamber of Commerce
3003 Frederick Ave .... Saint Joseph MO 64506 816-232-4461 364-4873 139
TF: 800-748-7856 ■ *Web:* www.saintjoseph.com

Saint Joseph Cathedral
521 N Duluth Ave .... Sioux Falls SD 57104 605-336-7390 50-1
Web: stjosephcathedral.net

Saint Joseph Convention & Visitors Bureau
109 S Fourth St .... Saint Joseph MO 64501 816-233-6688 233-9120 206
TF: 800-785-0360 ■ *Web:* www.stjomo.com

Saint Joseph County
125 W Main St PO Box 189 .... Centreville MI 49032 269-467-5500 467-5628 338
Web: www.stjosephcountymi.org

Saint Joseph County 101 S Main St .... South Bend IN 46601 574-235-9635 235-9838 338
Web: www.stjosephcountyindiana.com

Saint Joseph County Public Library
304 S Main St .... South Bend IN 46601 574-282-4630 434-3
Web: www.sjcpl.lib.in.us

Saint Joseph Hospital
1375 East 19th Ave .... Denver CO 80218 303-812-2000 467-8966 374-3
Web: sclhealthsystem.org

Saint Joseph Hospital
1 St Joseph Dr .... Lexington KY 40504 859-313-1000 374-3
Web: kentuckyonehealth.org

Saint Joseph Hospital 172 Kinsley St .... Nashua NH 03061 603-882-3000 374-3
TF: 800-222-1222 ■ *Web:* www.stjosephhospital.com

Saint Joseph Hospital
1100 W Stewart Dr .... Orange CA 92868 714-633-9111 374-3
Web: www.sjo.org

Saint Joseph Hospital 700 Broadway .... Fort Wayne IN 46802 260-425-3000 374-3
TF: 800-258-0974 ■ *Web:* www.lutheranhealth.net

Saint Joseph Hospital East
150 N Eagle Creek Dr .... Lexington KY 40509 859-967-5000 374-3
Web: kentuckyonehealth.org

Saint Joseph Medical Ctr (SJMC)
7601 Osler Dr .... Towson MD 21204 410-337-1000 374-3
Web: www.stjosephtowson.com

Saint Joseph Medical Ctr
1401 St Joseph Pkwy .... Houston TX 77002 713-757-1000 657-7123 374-3
Web: www.sjmctx.com

Saint Joseph Medical Ctr
2500 Bernville Rd .... Reading PA 19605 610-378-2000 374-3
TF: 800-678-2332 ■ *Web:* www.thefutureofhealthcare.org

Saint Joseph Mercy Ann Arbor
5301 McAuley Dr .... Ypsilanti MI 48197 734-712-3456 712-3855 374-3
TF: 866-522-8268 ■ *Web:* www.stjoeshealth.org

Saint Joseph Mercy Hospital Port Huron
2001 Electric Ave .... Port Huron MI 48060 810-985-1500 374-3

Saint Joseph Mercy Oakland
44405 Woodward Ave .... Pontiac MI 48341 248-858-3000 858-3155 374-3
TF: 800-396-1313 ■ *Web:* www.stjoesoakland.org

Saint Joseph Regional Medical Ctr
415 Sixth St .... Lewiston ID 83501 208-743-2511 374-3
TF: 800-678-2511 ■ *Web:* www.sjrmc.org

Saint Joseph Regional Medical Ctr Mishawaka
5215 Holy Cross Pkwy .... Mishawaka IN 46545 574-335-5000 374-3
TF: 800-274-1314 ■ *Web:* www.sjmed.com

Saint Joseph's College
Brooklyn 245 Clinton Ave .... Brooklyn NY 11205 718-940-5300 636-8303* 166
**Fax:* Admissions ■ *Web:* www.sjcny.edu

Saint Joseph's College NY
Suffolk 155 W Roe Blvd .... Patchogue NY 11772 631-687-5100 166
Web: www.sjcny.edu

Saint Joseph's College of Maine
278 Whites Bridge Rd .... Standish ME 04084 207-893-7746 893-7862* 166
**Fax:* Admissions ■ *TF Admissions:* 800-338-7057 ■ *Web:* www.sjcme.edu

Saint Joseph's General Hospital
2137 Comox Ave .... Comox BC V9M1P2 250-339-2242 339-1432 374-2
TF: 800-663-9203 ■ *Web:* www.sjghcomox.ca
London
268 Grosvenor St PO Box 5777 Station B .... London ON N6A4V2 519-646-6100 374-2
Web: www.sjhc.london.on.ca

Saint Joseph's Health Ctr
Guelph 100 Westmount Rd .... Guelph ON N1H5H8 519-824-6000 374-2
Web: www.sjhcg.ca
Toronto 30 The Queensway .... Toronto ON M6R1B5 416-530-6000 374-2
Web: www.stjoestoronto.ca

Saint Joseph's Healthcare Hamilton
50 Charlton Ave E .... Hamilton ON L8N4A6 905-522-1155 521-6140 374-2
TF: 800-461-2156 ■ *Web:* stjoes.ca

Saint Joseph's Hospital
3001 W Dr Martin Luther King Jr Blvd .... Tampa FL 33607 813-870-4000 870-4132 374-3
TF: 800-229-2273

Saint Joseph's Hospital
555 E Market St .... Elmira NY 14901 607-737-4499 737-7837 374-3
TF: 800-952-2662 ■ *Web:* www.arnothealth.org

Saint Joseph's Hospital
2661 County Hwy I .... Chippewa Falls WI 54729 715-723-1811 374-3
TF: 877-723-1811 ■ *Web:* www.stjoeschipfalls.com

Saint Joseph's Hospital Health Ctr
301 Prospect Ave .... Syracuse NY 13203 315-448-5111 374-3
TF: 888-785-6371 ■ *Web:* www.sjhsyr.org

Saint Joseph's Hospital of Atlanta
5665 Peachtree Dunwoody Rd NE .... Atlanta GA 30342 404-851-7001 374-3
Web: www.emoryhealthcare.org

Saint Joseph's Lifecare Ctr
99 Wayne Gretzky Pkwy .... Brantford ON N3S6T6 519-751-7096 753-7996 374-2
TF: 888-699-7817 ■ *Web:* www.sjlc.ca

Saint Joseph's Medical Ctr
1800 N California St .... Stockton CA 95204 209-943-2000 374-3
Web: www.stjosephscares.org

Saint Joseph's Medical Ctr (SJMC)
127 S Broadway .... Yonkers NY 10701 914-378-7000 374-3
TF: 800-804-5447 ■ *Web:* saintjosephs.org

Phone | Fax | Class

Saint Joseph's Regional Medical Ctr
703 Main St .... Paterson NJ 07503 973-754-2000 754-2208 374-3
TF: 800-446-5400 ■ *Web:* www.stjosephshealth.org

Saint Joseph's Seminary
201 Seminary Ave .... Yonkers NY 10704 914-968-6200 167-3
Web: www.archny.org

Saint Joseph's University
5600 City Ave .... Philadelphia PA 19131 610-660-1000 660-1314* 166
**Fax:* Admissions ■ *TF:* 877-648-3758 ■ *Web:* www.sju.edu

Saint Jude Children's Research Hospital Stem Cell Transplantation Div
262 Danny Thomas Pl .... Memphis TN 38105 901-595-3300 769
TF: 800-822-6344 ■ *Web:* www.stjude.org

Saint Jude Medical
St Jude Medical Inc .... St Paul MN 55117 651-756-2000 756-3301 476
NYSE: STJ ■ *TF:* 800-328-9634 ■ *Web:* www.sjm.com

Saint Jude Medical Ctr
101 E Valencia Mesa Dr .... Fullerton CA 92835 714-871-3280 374-3
TF: 800-378-4189 ■ *Web:* www.stjudemedicalcenter.org

Saint Jude The Apostle School
7171 Glenridge Dr NE .... Atlanta GA 30328 770-394-2880 804-9248 685
Web: saintjude.net

Saint Kitts & Nevis
414 E 75th St 5th Fl .... New York NY 10021 212-535-1234 535-6854 784
TF: 800-582-6208 ■ *Web:* www.stkittsnevis.org

Saint Kitts & Nevis Embassy
414 E 75th St 5th Fl .... New York NY 10021 202-686-2636 686-5740 257
Web: www.stkittsnevis.org

Saint Landry Parish
118 S Ct St Ste 207 .... Opelousas LA 70570 337-942-5606 338
Web: www.stlandry.org

Saint Lawrence County 48 Ct St .... Canton NY 13617 315-379-2237 379-2302 338
Web: www.co.st-lawrence.ny.us

Saint Lawrence Rehabilitation Ctr
2381 Lawrenceville Rd .... Lawrenceville NJ 08648 609-896-9500 374-6
Web: www.slrc.org

Saint Lawrence Seaway Development Corp
1200 New Jersey Ave SE .... Washington DC 20590 202-366-0091 366-7147 340-17
TF: 800-785-2779 ■ *Web:* www.seaway.dot.gov

Saint Lawrence State Park Golf Course
4955 State Hwy 37 .... Ogdensburg NY 13669 315-393-2286 565
Web: parks.ny.gov/parks/70/details.aspx

Saint Lawrence University 23 Romoda Dr .... Canton NY 13617 315-229-5261 229-5818* 166
**Fax:* Admissions ■ *TF Admissions:* 800-285-1856 ■ *Web:* www.stlawu.edu

Saint Leo University
33701 State Rd 52 .... Saint Leo FL 33574 352-588-8200 588-8257* 166
**Fax:* Admissions ■ *TF:* 800-334-5532 ■ *Web:* www.saintleo.edu
Palatka Ctr
33701 State Rd 52 PO Box 6665 .... Saint Leo FL 33574 352-588-8200 166
TF: 800-334-5532 ■ *Web:* www.saintleo.edu

Saint Louis Art Museum
1 Fine Arts Dr .... Saint Louis MO 63110 314-721-0072 721-6172 520
TF: 800-775-2000 ■ *Web:* www.slam.org

Saint Louis Bride Magazine
1006 Olive St Ste 202 .... Saint Louis MO 63101 314 588-8313 457-22
Web: bridestl.com

Saint Louis Cathedral
615 Pere Antoine Alley .... New Orleans LA 70116 504-525-9585 525-9583 50-1
Web: www.stlouiscathedral.org

Saint Louis Children's Hospital
1 Children's Pl .... Saint Louis MO 63110 314-454-6000 374-1
TF: 800-427-4626 ■ *Web:* www.stlouischildrens.org

Saint Louis Christian College
1360 Grandview Dr .... Florissant MO 63033 314-837-6777 837-8291 161
TF Admissions: 800-887-7522 ■ *Web:* stlchristian.edu

Saint Louis City Hall
1200 Market St .... Saint Louis MO 63103 314-622-3201 622-4061 337
Web: stlouis-mo.gov

Saint Louis College of Pharmacy
4588 Parkview Pl .... Saint Louis MO 63110 314-367-8700 446-8304* 166
**Fax:* Admissions ■ *TF:* 800-278-5267 ■ *Web:* www.stlcop.edu

Saint Louis Community College (STLCC)
300 S Broadway .... Saint Louis MO 63102 314-539-5000 539-5170* 162
**Fax:* Admissions ■ *Web:* www.stlcc.edu
Forest Park 5600 Oakland Ave .... Saint Louis MO 63110 314-644-9100 644-9375* 162
**Fax:* Admissions ■ *Web:* www.stlcc.edu/fp

Saint Louis Correctional Facility
8585 N Croswell Rd .... Saint Louis MI 48880 989-681-6444 213
Web: www.michigan.gov

Saint Louis County 41 S Central Ave .... Clayton MO 63105 314-615-5000 615-7890 338
Web: www.stlouisco.com

Saint Louis County Library (SLCL)
1640 S Lindbergh Blvd .... Saint Louis MO 63131 314-994-3300 434-3
TF: 800-473-0060 ■ *Web:* www.slcl.org

Saint Louis Embroidery
1759 Scherer Pkwy .... Saint Charles MO 63303 636-724-2200 258
TF: 800-457-6676 ■ *Web:* patch.com/stcharles

Saint Louis Executive Conference Ctr
701 Convention Plaza .... Saint Louis MO 63101 314-342-5050 205
TF: 800-325-7962 ■ *Web:* www.explorestlouis.com

Saint Louis Music Inc
1400 Ferguson Ave .... Saint Louis MO 63133 314-727-4512 527
TF: 800-727-4512 ■ *Web:* www.stlouismusic.com

Saint Louis Paper & Box Co
3843 Garfield Ave .... Saint Louis MO 63113 314-531-7900 531-0968 559
TF: 800-779-7901 ■ *Web:* www.stlpaper.com

Saint Louis Public Library (SLPL)
1301 Olive St .... Saint Louis MO 63103 314-241-2288 539-0393 434-3
TF: 800-916-8938 ■ *Web:* www.slpl.org

Saint Louis Public Schools
801 N 11th St .... Saint Louis MO 63101 314-231-3720 345-2650* 685
**Fax:* Hum Res ■ *TF:* 800-755-3901 ■ *Web:* www.slps.org

Saint Louis Science Ctr
5050 Oakland Ave .... Saint Louis MO 63110 314-289-4400 535-0104 520
TF: 800-456-7572 ■ *Web:* www.slsc.org

Saint Louis Symphony Orchestra
718 N Grand Blvd .... Saint Louis MO 63103 314-533-2500 286-4111 573-3
TF: 800-232-1880 ■ *Web:* www.stlsymphony.org

Phone | Fax | Class

Saint Louis University
221 N Grand Blvd, Saint Louis MO 63103 — 314-977-7288 — 977-7136* — 166
*Fax: Admissions ■ TF: 800-758-3678 ■ Web: www.slu.edu
Parks College of Engineering Aviation & Technology
3450 Lindell Blvd, Saint Louis MO 63103 — 314-977-8203 — 977-8403 — 166
Web: parks.slu.edu

Saint Louis University Hospital
3635 Vista Ave, Saint Louis MO 63110 — 314-577-8000 — 577-8003 — 374-3
Web: www.ssmhealth.com/sluhospital

Saint Louis University Museum of Art
3663 Lindell Blvd, Saint Louis MO 63108 — 314-977-3399 — 520
Web: sluma.slu.edu

Saint Louis University School of Law
3700 Lindell Blvd, Saint Louis MO 63108 — 314-977-2766 — 167-1
TF: 800-758-3678 ■ Web: www.slu.edu

Saint Louis University School of Medicine
1 N Grand, Saint Louis MO 63103 — 800-758-3678 — 977-9825* — 167-2
*Fax Area Code: 314 ■ TF: 800-758-3678 ■ Web: www.slu.edu/colleges/med

Saint Louis Zoological Park
1 Government Dr, Saint Louis MO 63110 — 314-781-0900 — 823
TF: 800-966-8877 ■ Web: www.stlzoo.org

Saint Lucia 800 Second Ave Fl 5, New York NY 10017 — 212-697-9360 — 697-4993 — 784
Web: saintluciamissionun.org
Consulate General
800 Second Ave 5th Fl, New York NY 10017 — 212-697-9360 — 697-4993 — 257
Web: saintluciaconsulateny.org
Embassy 3216 New Mexico Ave NW, Washington DC 20016 — 202-364-6792 — 257
TF: 800-456-3984 ■ Web: www.state.gov/r/pa/ei/bgn/2344.htm

Saint Lucia Tourist Board
800 Second Ave Ste 910, New York NY 10017 — 212-867-2950 — 775
TF: 800-456-3984 ■ Web: www.stlucia.org/?src=orgredirection

Saint Lucie County Library System
2300 Virginia Ave, Fort Pierce FL 34982 — 772-462-1100 — 434-3
Web: www.stlucieco.gov

Saint Lucie Medical Ctr
1800 SE Tiffany Ave, Port Saint Lucie FL 34952 — 772-335-4000 — 398-3608 — 374-3
TF: 800-382-3522 ■ Web: www.stluciemed.com

Saint Lucie Regional Juvenile Detention Ctr
1301 Bell Ave, Fort Pierce FL 34982 — 772-468-3940 — 412

Saint Luke Baptist Church
476 Glen Iris Dr NE, Atlanta GA 30308 — 404-688-0528 — 48-20

Saint Luke Institute Foundation Inc
8901 New Hampshire Ave, Silver Spring MD 20903 — 301-445-7970 — 305
TF: 800-463-6295 ■ Web: sli.org

Saint Luke's Cornwall Hospital
Cornwall Campus 19 Laurel Ave, Cornwall NY 12518 — 845-534-7711 — 374-3

Saint Luke's Home Care & Hospice
3100 Broadway St Ste 1000, Kansas City MO 64111 — 816-756-1160 — 756-0838 — 371
TF: 888-303-7576 ■ Web: saintlukeshealthsystem.org

Saint Luke's Hospital (SLH)
1026 A Ave NE, Cedar Rapids IA 52406 — 319-369-7211 — 369-8105 — 374-3
Web: unitypoint.org/cedarrapids/default.aspx

Saint Luke's Hospital
232 S Woods Mill Rd, Chesterfield MO 63017 — 314-434-1500 — 374-3
TF: 800-735-2966 ■ Web: www.stlukes-stl.com

Saint Luke's Hospital
4401 Wornall Rd, Kansas City MO 64111 — 816-932-2000 — 932-5990 — 374-3
Web: www.saintlukeshealthsystem.org

Saint Luke's Hospital & Regional Trauma Ctr
915 E First St, Duluth MN 55805 — 218-249-5555 — 932-6871* — 374-3
*Fax Area Code: 816 ■ TF: 866-261-5915 ■ Web: www.saintlukeshealthsystem.org/services

Saint Luke's Hospital of New Bedford
101 Page St, New Bedford MA 02740 — 508-997-1515 — 374-3
TF: 800-497-1727 ■ Web: www.southcoast.org/stlukes

Saint Luke's Medical Ctr
1800 E Van Buren St, Phoenix AZ 85006 — 602-251-8100 — 251-8207 — 374-3
TF: 800-446-2279 ■ Web: www.stlukesmedcenter.com

Saint Luke's Regional Medical Ctr
2720 Stone Park Blvd, Sioux City IA 51104 — 712-279-3500 — 279-7958 — 374-3
TF: 800-352-4660 ■ Web: www.unitypoint.org

Saint Luke's Rehabilitation Institute
711 S Cowley St, Spokane WA 99202 — 509-473-6000 — 473-6978 — 374-6
Web: www.st-lukes.org

Saint Mark Village
2655 Nebraska Ave, Palm Harbor FL 34684 — 727-785-2580 — 672
TF: 800-706-4513 ■ Web: www.stmarkvillage.com

Saint Mark's Hospital
1200 East 3900 South, Salt Lake City UT 84124 — 801-268-7111 — 374-3
TF: 800-370-1983 ■ Web: www.stmarkshospital.com

Saint Mark's School
25 Marlborough Rd, Southborough MA 01772 — 508-786-6000 — 786-6120 — 622
Web: www.stmarksschool.org

Saint Martin Parish Library
201 Porter St, Saint Martinville LA 70582 — 337-394-2207 — 394-2248 — 434-3
Web: stmartinparishlibrary.org/site.php

Saint Martin's University
5300 Pacific Ave SE, Lacey WA 98503 — 360-438-4311 — 412-6189* — 166
*Fax: Admissions ■ TF Admissions: 800-368-8803 ■ Web: www.stmartin.edu

Saint Martin's Wine Bistro
3020 Greenville Ave, Dallas TX 75206 — 214-826-0940 — 826-1229 — 671
Web: www.stmartinswinebistro.com

Saint Mary Medical Ctr
1500 S Lake Pk Ave, Hobart IN 46342 — 219-942-0551 — 374-3
Web: www.comhs.org/stmary

Saint Mary Medical Ctr
1050 Linden Ave, Long Beach CA 90813 — 562-491-9000 — 374-3
Web: www.stmarymedicalcenter.org

Saint Mary Mercy Hospital
36475 Five-Mile Rd, Livonia MI 48154 — 734-655-4800 — 374-3
TF: 800-464-7492 ■ Web: www.stmarymercy.org

Saint Mary of Nazareth Hospital Ctr
2233 W Div St, Chicago IL 60622 — 312-770-2000 — 374-3
Web: www.presencehealth.org

Saint Mary Seminary & Graduate School of Theology
28700 Euclid Ave, Wickliffe OH 44092 — 440-943-7600 — 167-3
Web: www.stmarysem.edu

Saint Mary's Cathedral 203 E Tenth St, Austin TX 78701 — 512-476-6182 — 476-8799 — 50-1
Web: www.smcaustin.org

Saint Mary's Catholic Church
155 Market St, Memphis TN 38105 — 901-522-9420 — 50-1

Saint Mary's College Le Mans Hall, Notre Dame IN 46556 — 574-284-4587 — 284-4841* — 166
*Fax: Admissions ■ TF Admissions: 800-551-7621 ■ Web: www.saintmarys.edu

Saint Mary's College of California
1928 St Mary's Rd, Moraga CA 94556 — 925-631-4000 — 376-7193* — 166
*Fax: Admissions ■ TF Admissions: 800-800-4762 ■ Web: www.stmarys-ca.edu

Saint Mary's College of Maryland
47645 College Dr, Saint Marys City MD 20686 — 240-895-2000 — 166
TF Admissions: 800-492-7181 ■ Web: www.smcm.edu

Saint Mary's Correctional Ctr
2880 N Pleasants Hwy, Saint Marys WV 26170 — 304-684-5500 — 684-5506 — 213
Web: www.wvdoc.com

Saint Mary's County
41770 Baldridge St PO Box 653, Leonardtown MD 20650 — 301-475-4200 — 475-4935 — 338
Web: www.co.saint-marys.md.us

Saint Mary's General Hospital
911 Queen's Blvd, Kitchener ON N2M1B2 — 519-744-3311 — 749-6426 — 374-2
TF: 800-749-7560 ■ Web: www.smgh.ca

Saint Mary's Health Care
200 Jefferson St SE, Grand Rapids MI 49503 — 616-685-5000 — 374-3
Web: www.mercyhealthsaintmarys.com

Saint Mary's Health Care System
1230 Baxter St, Athens GA 30606 — 706-389-3000 — 374-3
TF: 800-233-7864 ■ Web: www.stmarysathens.org

Saint Mary's Health Ctr
6420 Clayton Rd, Richmond Heights MO 63117 — 314-768-8000 — 768-8011 — 374-3
Web: www.ssmhealth.com

Saint Mary's Hospice of Northern Nevada
690 Sierra Rose Dr, Reno NV 89511 — 775-770-3081 — 371

Saint Mary's Hospital
1800 E Lake Shore Dr, Decatur IL 62521 — 217-464-2966 — 374-3
Web: www.stmarysdecatur.com

Saint Mary's Hospital
56 Franklin St, Waterbury CT 06706 — 203-709-6000 — 374-3
Web: www.stmh.org

Saint Mary's Hospital
427 Guy Pk Ave, Amsterdam NY 12010 — 518-842-1900 — 374-3
Web: www.smha.org

Saint Mary's Hospital
1300 Massachusetts Ave, Troy NY 12180 — 518-268-5000 — 374-3
Web: www.stmarysmadison.com

Saint Mary's Hospital
1216 Second St SW, Rochester MN 55902 — 507-255-5123 — 374-3
Web: mayoclinic.org

Saint Mary's Hospital
2251 N Shore Dr, Rhinelander WI 54501 — 715-361-2000 — 374-3
TF Cust Svc: 800-578-0840 ■ Web: www.ministryhealth.org

Saint Mary's Hospital Ctr
3830 Lacombe Ave, Montreal QC H3T1M5 — 514-345-3511 — 374-2
Web: www.smhc.qc.ca

Saint Mary's Hospital for Children Inc
29-01 216th St, Bayside NY 11360 — 718-281-8800 — 450
Web: www.stmaryskids.org

Saint Mary's Hospital Medical Ctr
1726 Shawano Ave, Green Bay WI 54303 — 920-498-4200 — 374-3
TF: 800-666-5606 ■ Web: www.stmgb.org

Saint Mary's Medical Ctr
450 Stanyan St, San Francisco CA 94117 — 415-668-1000 — 374-3
Web: www.stmarysmedicalcenter.org

Saint Mary's Medical Ctr
2635 N Seventh St, Grand Junction CO 81501 — 800-458-3888 — 374-3
TF: 800-458-3888 ■ Web: stmarygj.org

Saint Mary's Medical Ctr
201 NW Rd Mize Rd, Blue Springs MO 64014 — 816-228-5900 — 655-5408 — 374-3
TF: 800-311-2039 ■ Web: www.stmaryskc.com

Saint Mary's Medical Ctr of Evansville
3700 Washington Ave, Evansville IN 47750 — 812-485-4000 — 374-3
Web: www.stmarys.org/smlocation

Saint Mary's Regional Medical Ctr
1808 W Main St, Russellville AR 72801 — 479-968-2841 — 374-3
Web: www.saintmarysregional.com

Saint Mary's Regional Medical Ctr
93 Campus Ave, Lewiston ME 04240 — 207-777-8100 — 374-3
Web: www.stmarysmaine.com

Saint Mary's Regional Medical Ctr
305 S Fifth St, Enid OK 73701 — 580-233-6100 — 374-3
Web: www.stmarysregional.com

Saint Mary's Regional Medical Ctr
235 W Sixth St, Reno NV 89503 — 775-770-3000 — 770-7474 — 374-3
Web: www.saintmarysreno.com

Saint Mary's River State Park
c/o Pt Lookout State Pk 11175 Pt Lookout Rd, Scotland MD 20687 — 301-872-5688 — 565
TF: 800-830-3974 ■
Web: dnr.maryland.gov/publiclands/Pages/southern/stmarysriver.aspx

Saint Mary's School
900 Hillsborough St, Raleigh NC 27603 — 919-424-4000 — 424-4122 — 622
TF: 800-948-2557 ■ Web: www.sms.edu

Saint Mary's Seminary & University
5400 Roland Ave, Baltimore MD 21210 — 410-864-4000 — 167-3
Web: www.stmarys.edu

Saint Mary's University 923 Robie St, Halifax NS B3H3C3 — 902-420-5756 — 420-5141 — 785
Web: www.smu.ca

Saint Mary's University
1 Camino Santa Maria, San Antonio TX 78228 — 210-436-3126 — 166
TF Admissions: 800-367-7868 ■ Web: www.stmarytx.edu

Saint Mary's University of Minnesota
700 Terr Heights, Winona MN 55987 — 507-452-4430 — 166
TF: 800-635-5987 ■ Web: www.smumn.edu

Saint Mary-Corwin Medical Ctr
1008 Minnequa Ave, Pueblo CO 81004 — 719-557-4000 — 374-3
TF: 800-228-4039 ■ Web: www.stmarycorwin.org

Saint Mary-of-the-Woods College
3301 St Mary Rd, Saint Mary Of The Woods IN 47876 — 812-535-5106 — 535-5010* — 166
*Fax: Admissions ■ TF: 800-926-7692 ■ Web: www.smwc.edu

Saint Marys Carbon Co
259 Eberl St, Saint Marys PA 15857 — 814-781-7333 — 834-9201 — 127
Web: www.stmaryscarbon.com

Name / Address	City	State	Zip	Phone	Fax	Class
Saint Meinrad Archabbey 200 Hill Dr *TF:* 800-682-0988 ■ *Web:* www.saintmeinrad.edu	Saint Meinrad	IN	47577	812-357-6585	357-6325	673
Saint Meinrad School of Theology 200 Hill Dr *Web:* www.saintmeinrad.edu	Saint Meinrad	IN	47577	812-357-6611		167-3
Saint Michael's College 1 Winooski Pk *TF:* 800-762-8000 ■ *Web:* www.smcvt.edu	Colchester	VT	05439	802-654-2000	654-2906	166
Saint Michael's Hospital 30 Bond St *TF:* 866-797-0000 ■ *Web:* www.stmichaelshospital.com	Toronto	ON	M5B1W8	416-360-4000	864-5870	374-2
Saint Michael's Hospital 900 Illinois Ave *TF:* 800-420-2622 ■ *Web:* www.ministryhealth.org	Stevens Point	WI	54481	715-346-5000		374-3
Saint Michael's Medical Ctr 111 Central Ave *TF:* 800-633-4227 ■ *Web:* www.smmcnj.org	Newark	NJ	07102	973-877-5000		374-3
Saint Michael's University School 3400 Richmond Rd *TF:* 800-661-5199 ■ *Web:* www.smus.ca	Victoria	BC	V8P4P5	250-592-2411	592-2812	622
Saint Michaels Harbour Inn & Marina 101 N Harbor Rd *TF:* 800-955-9001 ■ *Web:* www.harbourinn.com	Saint Michaels	MD	21663	410-745-9001		379
Saint Norbert Arts & Cultural Centre (SNAC) 100 Rue des Ruines du Monastere *Web:* www.snac.mb.ca	Winnipeg	MB	R3V1B9	204-269-0564	261-1927	50-2
Saint Norbert College 100 Grant St **Fax:* Admissions ■ *TF Admissions:* 800-236-4878 ■ *Web:* www.snc.edu	De Pere	WI	54115	920-403-3005	403-4072*	166
Saint Patrick Hospital 500 W Broadway St *Web:* montana.providence.org/hospitals/st-patrick	Missoula	MT	59802	406-543-7271		374-3
Saint Patrick School 9040 Hutchins St *Web:* stpatrickwhitelake.org	White Lake	MI	48386	248-698-3240		685
Saint Patrick's Seminary & University 320 Middlefield Rd *Web:* www.stpsu.edu	Menlo Park	CA	94025	650-325-5621		167-3
Saint Paul Area Chamber of Commerce 401 N Robert St Ste 150 *Web:* www.saintpaulchamber.com	Saint Paul	MN	55101	651-223-5000	223-5119	139
Saint Paul Chamber Orchestra 408 St Peter St 3rd Fl *TF:* 800-982-2787 ■ *Web:* www.thespco.org	Saint Paul	MN	55102	651-291-1144	292-3281	573-3
Saint Paul City Hall 15 W Kellogg Blvd 390 City Hall *TF:* 800-895-1999 ■ *Web:* www.stpaul.gov	Saint Paul	MN	55102	651-266-8510	266-8521	337
Saint Paul College 235 Marshall Ave *TF:* 800-227-6029 ■ *Web:* www.saintpaul.edu	Saint Paul	MN	55102	651-846-1600	846-1703	800
Saint Paul Foundation, The 101 Fifth St E Ste 2400 *TF:* 800-875-6167 ■ *Web:* www.saintpaulfoundation.org	Saint Paul	MN	55101	651-224-5463	224-8123	303
Saint Paul Hotel 350 Market St *TF:* 800-292-9292 ■ *Web:* www.saintpaulhotel.com	Saint Paul	MN	55102	651-292-9292		379
Saint Paul Linoleum & Carpet Co 2956 Ctr Ct *Web:* www.stpaullinocpt.com	Eagan	MN	55121	651-686-7770		290
Saint Paul Public Library 90 W Fourth St *TF:* 888-335-9632 ■ *Web:* www.sppl.org	Saint Paul	MN	55102	651-266-7000	266-7060	434-3
Saint Paul RiverCentre 175 W Kellogg Blvd *Web:* www.rivercentre.org	Saint Paul	MN	55102	651-265-4800	265-4899	205
Saint Paul RiverCentre Convention & Visitors Authority 175 W Kellogg Blvd *Web:* www.rivercentre.org	Saint Paul	MN	55102	651-265-4800		206
Saint Paul School of Theology 4370 W 109th St Ste 300 *TF:* 800-825-0378 ■ *Web:* www.spst.edu	Overland Park	KS	66211	800-825-0378		167-3
Saint Paul Stamp Works Inc 87 Empire Dr *TF:* 800-671-5164 ■ *Web:* www.stpaulstamp.com	Saint Paul	MN	55103	651-222-2100	228-1314	467
Saint Paul University 223 Main St *TF:* 800-637-6859 ■ *Web:* www.ustpaul.ca	Ottawa	ON	K1S1C4	613-236-1393	782-3014	785
Saint Paul's Church National Historic Site 897 S Columbus Ave *TF:* 866-705-5711 ■ *Web:* www.nps.gov	Mount Vernon	NY	10550	914-667-4116	667-3024	564
Saint Paul's College 115 College Dr	Lawrenceville	VA	23868	646-961-4954		166
Saint Paul's Episcopal Church 1430 J St *Web:* www.stpaulssacramento.org	Sacramento	CA	95814	916-446-2620		50-1
Saint Paul's Hospital 1702 20th St W	Saskatoon	SK	S7M0Z9	306-655-5000		374-2
Saint Paul's School 325 Pleasant St *Web:* www.sps.edu	Concord	NH	03301	603-229-4600		622
Saint Peter's Health Care Services 315 S Manning Blvd *TF:* 800-432-7876 ■ *Web:* www.sphcs.org	Albany	NY	12208	518-525-1550		374-3
Saint Peter's Seminary 1040 Waterloo St N *TF:* 888-548-9649 ■ *Web:* www.stpetersseminary.ca	London	ON	N6A3Y1	519-432-1824	432-0964	167-3
Saint Peter's University Hospital 254 Easton Ave *Web:* www.saintpetershcs.com	New Brunswick	NJ	08901	732-745-8600		374-3
Seminole 9200 113th St N *Web:* www.spcollege.edu/se/campus	Seminole	FL	33772	727-394-6000	394-6132	162
Saint Petersburg Museum of History (SPMOH) 335 Second Ave NE	Saint Petersburg	FL	33701	727-894-1052		520
Saint Petersburg Public Library 3745 Ninth Ave N *Web:* www.splibraries.org	Saint Petersburg	FL	33713	727-893-7724		434-3
Saint Photios Greek Orthodox National Shrine 41 St George St *Web:* www.stphotios.org	Saint Augustine	FL	32085	904-829-8205	829-8707	50-1
Saint Regis Aspen 315 E Dean St *TF General:* 888-627-7198 ■ *Web:* www.stregisaspen.com	Aspen	CO	81611	970-920-3300		707
Saint Regis Culvert Inc 202 Morrell St *TF:* 800-527-4604 ■ *Web:* www.stregisculvert.com	Charlotte	MI	48813	517-543-3430	543-2313	697
Saint Regis Hotel 602 Dunsmuir St *TF:* 800-770-7929 ■ *Web:* www.stregishotel.com	Vancouver	BC	V6B1Y6	604-681-1135	683-1126	379
Saint Regis Hotel Winnipeg 285 Smith St *TF:* 800-663-7344 ■ *Web:* www.stregishotel.net	Winnipeg	MB	R3C1K9	204-942-0171	943-3077	379
Saint Regis Resort Aspen 315 E Dean St *TF:* 888-627-7198 ■ *Web:* www.stregisaspen.com	Aspen	CO	81611	970-920-3300		669
Saint Rita's Medical Ctr (SRMC) 730 W Market St	Lima	OH	45801	419-227-3361		374-3
Saint Rose Dominican Hospital *Rose de Lima Campus* 102 E Lake Mead Blvd *Web:* www.strosehospitals.org	Henderson	NV	89015	702-564-2622		374-3
Saint Rose Hospital 27200 Calaroga Ave *Web:* www.strosehospital.org	Hayward	CA	94545	510-264-4000	887-7421	374-3
Saint Stanislaus College 304 S Beach Blvd *Web:* www.ststan.com	Bay Saint Louis	MS	39520	228-467-9057		622
Saint Stephen's & Saint Agnes School 1000 St Stephen's Rd *Web:* www.sssas.org	Alexandria	VA	22304	703-751-2700	683-5930	623
Saint Stephen's Episcopal School 6500 St Stephen's Dr *Web:* www.sstx.org	Austin	TX	78746	512-327-1213		622
Saint Tammany Parish Hospital 1202 S Tyler St *TF:* 800-749-6273 ■ *Web:* www.stph.org	Covington	LA	70433	985-898-4000	898-4394	374-3
Saint Tammany Parish Library 310 W 21st Ave *Web:* www.sttammany.lib.la.us	Covington	LA	70433	985-893-6280	871-1271	434-3
Saint Tammany Parish Tourist & Convention Commission (KOSCVB) 111 Capital Dr *TF:* 800-800-6090 ■ *Web:* visitkosciuskocounty.org	Warsaw	IN	46582	574-269-6090	269-2405	206
Saint Tammany Parish Tourist & Convention Commission 68099 Hwy 59 *TF:* 800-634-9443 ■ *Web:* www.louisiananorthshore.com	Mandeville	LA	70471	985-892-0520	892-1441	206
Saint Tammany West Chamber of Commerce 610 Hollycrest Blvd *Web:* www.sttammanychamber.org	Covington	LA	70433	985-892-3216	893-4244	139
Saint Thomas Aquinas College 125 Rt 340 *TF:* 800-262-3257 ■ *Web:* www.stac.edu	Sparkill	NY	10976	845-398-4000	398-4114	166
Saint Thomas Choir School 202 W 58th St *Web:* www.choirschool.org	New York	NY	10019	212-247-3311		622
Saint Thomas Hospital 4220 HaRding Rd *TF:* 800-400-5800 ■ *Web:* www.sthealth.com	Nashville	TN	37205	615-222-2111		374-3
Saint Thomas Hospital 444 N Main St *TF:* 800-237-8662 ■ *Web:* www.summahealth.org	Akron	OH	44310	330-375-3000		374-3
Saint Thomas University 51 Dineen Dr *TF:* 877-788-4443 ■ *Web:* w3.stu.ca/stu	Fredericton	NB	E3B5G3	506-452-0640		785
Saint Thomas University 16401 NW 37th Ave *TF:* 800-367-9010 ■ *Web:* www.stu.edu	Miami Gardens	FL	33054	305-628-6546	628-6591	166
Saint Thomas University School of Law 16401 NW 37th Ave **Fax:* Admissions ■ *TF:* 800-245-4569 ■ *Web:* stu.edu/law	Miami Gardens	FL	33054	305-623-2310	623-2357*	167-1
Saint Thomas-Elgin General Hospital 189 Elm St *TF:* 800-310-1122 ■ *Web:* www.stegh.on.ca	Saint Thomas	ON	N5R5C4	519-631-2020	631-1825	374-2
Saint Tikhon's Orthodox Theological Seminary St Tikhon's Rd PO Box 130 *Web:* www.stots.edu	South Canaan	PA	18459	570-561-1818		167-3
Saint Timothy's School 8400 Greenspring Ave *Web:* www.stt.org	Stevenson	MD	21153	410-486-7400		622
Saint Vincent & the Grenadines *Consulate General* 801 Second Ave	New York	NY	10017	212-687-4490		257
Saint Vincent Charity Hospital (SVCH) 2351 E 22nd St *TF:* 800-750-0750 ■ *Web:* www.stvincentcharity.com	Cleveland	OH	44115	216-861-6200		374-3
Saint Vincent College 300 Fraser Purchase Rd **Fax:* Admissions ■ *TF:* 800-782-5549 ■ *Web:* www.stvincent.edu	Latrobe	PA	15650	724-532-6600	805-2953*	166
Saint Vincent de Paul Regional Seminary 10701 S Military Trail *Web:* www.svdp.edu	Boynton Beach	FL	33436	561-732-4424	737-2205	167-3
Saint Vincent Health Ctr 232 W 25th St *Web:* ahn.org/locations/saint-vincent-hospital	Erie	PA	16544	814-452-5000		374-3
Saint Vincent Hospital 835 S Van Buren St *TF:* 800-211-2209 ■ *Web:* www.stvincenthospital.org	Green Bay	WI	54301	800-211-2209		374-3
Saint Vincent Hospital-Worcester Medical Ctr 123 Summer St *TF:* 877-633-2368 ■ *Web:* www.stvincenthospital.com	Worcester	MA	01608	508-363-5000		374-3
Saint Vincent Medical Ctr 2131 W Third St *Web:* stvincent.verity.org	Los Angeles	CA	90057	213-484-7111		374-3
Saint Vincent Rehabilitation Hospital 2201 Wildwood Ave *Web:* stvincentrehabhospital.com	Sherwood	AR	72120	501-834-1800		374-6
Saint Vincent Seminary 300 Fraser Purchase Rd *Web:* www.saintvincentseminary.edu	Latrobe	PA	15650	724-532-6600	532-5052	167-3
Saint Vincent Women's Hospital 8111 Township Line Rd *TF:* 800-582-8258 ■ *Web:* www.stvincent.org	Indianapolis	IN	46260	317-415-8111		374-7
Saint Vincent's Hospital 810 St Vincent's Dr *TF:* 800-965-7231 ■ *Web:* www.stvhs.com	Birmingham	AL	35205	205-939-7000		374-3
Saint Vincent's Medical Ctr 2800 Main St *TF:* 877-255-7847 ■ *Web:* www.stvincents.org	Bridgeport	CT	06606	203-576-6000		374-3

Phone | Fax | Class

Saint Vrain State Park
3525 State Hwy 119 Firestone CO 80504 303-678-9402 565
Web: cpw.state.co.us

Saint Xavier University
3700 W 103rd St Chicago IL 60655 773-298-3000 298-3076* 166
**Fax:* Admissions ■ *TF:* 800-462-9288 ■ *Web:* www.sxu.edu

Sainte Genevieve County
5 Basler Dr Sainte Genevieve MO 63670 573-883-5820 883-5312 338

Sainte Marie among the Iroquois Museum
6680 Onondaga Lake Pkwy Liverpool NY 13088 315-453-6768 520
Web: ongov.net

Saint-Gaudens National Historic Site
139 St Gaudens Rd Cornish NH 03745 603-675-2175 675-2701 564
Web: www.nps.gov/saga

Saint-Gobain Advanced Ceramics Latrobe
4702 Route 982 Latrobe PA 15650 724-539-6000 539-6070 249
TF: 800-438-7237

Saint-Gobain Ceramics & Plastics Inc
1 New Bond St Worcester MA 01615 508-795-5000 751
Web: www.refractories.saint-gobain.com

Saint-Gobain Corp 20 Moores Rd Malvern PA 19355 610-893-6000 639-6629* 329
**Fax Area Code:* 855 ■ *Web:* www.saint-gobain-northamerica.com

Saint-Jacques
6112 Falls of the Neuse Rd Raleigh NC 27609 919-862-2770 862-2771 671
Web: saintjacquesfrenchcuisine.com

Saints Mary & Elizabeth Hospital
1850 Bluegrass Ave Louisville KY 40215 502-361-6000 217-1050 374-3
Web: www.kentuckyonehealth.org

Saints Ventures LLC
2020 Union St San Francisco CA 94123 415-773-2080 792
Web: www.saintscapital.com

SAISD (San Antonio Independent School District)
141 Lavaca St San Antonio TX 78210 210-554-2200 299-5600* 685
**Fax:* Hum Res ■ *TF:* 866-632-9992 ■ *Web:* www.saisd.net

Sajar Plastics Inc
15285 S State Ave PO Box 37 Middlefield OH 44062 440-632-5203 632-1848 604
Web: www.sajarplastics.com

SAJE Technology LLC
765 Dixon Ct Hoffman Estates IL 60192 847-756-7603 496-4515 735
Web: www.saje-tech.com

Saji-Ya 695 Grand Ave Saint Paul MN 55105 651-292-0444 671
Web: www.sajiya.com

SAK Management Services LLC
1 Northfield Plaza Ste 210 Northfield IL 60093 847-446-8400 194
Web: www.sakmgmt.com

Sakana 2026 P St NW Washington DC 20036 202-887-0900 671

Sakana Grill 116 Second Ave SW Calgary AB T2P3J9 403-290-1118 290-1120 671
Web: sakanagrill.ca

Sakata Farms Inc E Bromley Ln Brighton CO 80601 303-659-1559 10-11

Sakata Seed America Inc
18095 Serene Dr Morgan Hill CA 95037 408-778-7758 778-7768 694
Web: www.sakata.com

Sakatah Lake State Park
50499 Sakatah Lake State Pk Rd Waterville MN 56096 507-362-4438 565
TF: 888-646-6367 ■ *Web:* www.dnr.state.mn.us

Sake Cafe 2830 Magazine St New Orleans LA 70115 504-894-0033 671
Web: www.sakecafeonmagazine.com

Saker Aviation Services Inc
20 South St New York NY 10004 212-776-4046 363-6792 63
Web: www.sakeraviation.com

Sakki Computers Inc
22B Hempstead Tpke Farmingdale NY 11735 516-293-1609 180
TF: 800-267-1772 ■ *Web:* www.sakki.com

Sakonnet Vineyards
162 W Main Rd Little Compton RI 02837 401-635-8486 50-7
TF: 800-919-4637 ■ *Web:* www.sakonnetwine.com

Sakrete 8201 Arrowridge Blvd Charlotte NC 28273 704-525-1621 529-5261 183
TF: 800-424-9300 ■ *Web:* www.bonsalamerican.com/html/contact.html

Saks Inc 12 E 49th St New York NY 10017 212-940-5305 215
TF: 800-736-3402 ■ *Web:* www.saksincorporated.com

Saks Jandel 5510 Wisconsin Ave Chevy Chase MD 20815 301-652-2250 157-6
Web: thebridalsalonatsaksjandel.com

Sakura 7201 N Keystone Ave Indianapolis IN 46240 317-259-4171 253-7846 671
Web: www.indysakura.com

Sakura 5828 W Jefferson Blvd Fort Wayne IN 46804 260-459-2022 671

Sakura 6194 Hwy 49 Hattiesburg MS 39401 601-545-9393 671
Web: facebook.com

Sakura Bana 4800 I-55 N Jackson MS 39211 601-982-3035 671

Sakura Finetek USA Inc
1750 W 214th St Torrance CA 90501 310-972-7800 972-7888 419
TF: 800-725-8723 ■ *Web:* www.sakura-americas.com

Sakura Japanese Restaurant
350 St Peter St Saint Paul MN 55102 651-224-0185 671
Web: www.sakurastpaul.com

Sakura Restaurant 1175 W Rt 66 Flagstaff AZ 86001 928-773-8880 671
Web: www.radisson.com

Sakurabana 57 Broad St Boston MA 02109 617-542-4311 671
Web: sakurabanaboston.com

Sal Deforte's 1400 PkwyAve Serenity Plz Ewing NJ 08628 609-406-0123 671
Web: www.saldefortesristorante.com

Sal's 1242 Richmond Rd Williamsburg VA 23185 757-220-2641 671
TF: 800-889-5002 ■ *Web:* www.salsbyvictor.com

Saladax Biomedical Inc
116 Research Dr Bethlehem PA 18015 610-419-6731 231
Web: www.saladax.com

Saladino's Inc 3325 W Figarden Dr Fresno CA 93711 559-271-3700 297
Web: www.saladinos.com

Saladmaster Inc
230 Westway Pl Ste 101 Arlington TX 76018 817-633-3555 633-5544 486
TF: 800-765-5795 ■ *Web:* www.saladmaster.com

Salamonie Lake 9214 Lost Bridge Rd W Andrews IN 46702 260-468-2125 565
Web: www.in.gov

Salazar Service & Trucking Corp
1360 S US 385 Andrews TX 79714 432-699-3900 539
Web: www.salazarservice.com

Salcha River State Recreation Site
c/o Northern Area Office 3700 Airport Way Fairbanks AK 99709 907-451-2695 565
Web: www.dnr.alaska.gov/parks/units/salcha.htm

Salco Products Inc 1385 101st St Ste A Lemont IL 60439 630-783-2570 783-2590 650
Web: www.salcoproducts.com

Saleem Fish Supreme 2198 Pio Nono Ave Macon GA 31206 478-788-8600 671

Saleen Automotive Inc 2735 Wardlow Rd Corona CA 92882 800-888-8945 59
TF: 800-888-8945 ■ *Web:* www.saleen.com

Salem Academy (SA) 942 Lancaster Dr NE Salem OR 97301 503-378-1219 622
Web: www.salemacademy.org

Salem Area Chamber of Commerce
1110 Commercial St NE Salem OR 97301 503-581-1466 581-0972 139
Web: www.salemchamber.org

Salem Area Chamber of Commerce
713 E State St Salem OH 44460 330-337-3473 337-3474 139
TF: 800-644-6292 ■ *Web:* www.salemohiochamber.org

Salem Associates Inc
7074 Peachtree Indus Blvd Norcross GA 30071 770-729-8089 196
Web: www.salemassociates.com

Salem Athenaeum, The 337 Essex St Salem MA 01970 978-744-2540 744-7536 434-4
Web: www.salemathenaeum.net

Salem Center 401 Center St NE Salem OR 97301 503-399-9676 460
Web: www.salemcenter.com

Salem Chamber of Commerce 265 Essex St Salem MA 01970 978-744-0004 745-3855 139
TF: 800-392-6100 ■ *Web:* www.salem-chamber.org

Salem City Hall 555 Liberty St SE Rm 220 Salem OR 97301 503-588-6255 588-6354 337
Web: www.cityofsalem.net

Salem College 601 S Church St Winston-Salem NC 27101 336-721-2600 917-5572* 166
**Fax:* Admissions ■ *TF Admissions:* 800-327-2536 ■ *Web:* www.salem.edu

Salem Community College
460 Hollywood Ave Carneys Point NJ 08069 856-299-2100 351-2763* 162
**Fax:* Admissions ■ *TF:* 800-433-3243 ■ *Web:* www.salemcc.edu

Salem Conference Ctr
200 Commercial St SE Salem OR 97301 503-589-1700 205
TF Sales: 877-589-1700 ■ *Web:* salemconventioncenter.org

Salem Convention & Visitors Assn
181 High St NE Salem OR 97301 503-581-4325 581-4540 206
TF: 800-874-7012 ■ *Web:* www.travelsalem.com

Salem County 94 Market St Salem NJ 08079 856-935-7510 935-6725 338
Web: www.salemcountynj.gov/cmssite

Salem Electric 633 Seventh St NW Salem OR 97304 503-362-3601 371-2956 245
Web: www.salemelectric.com

Salem Electric Company Inc
3933 Westpoint Blvd PO Box 26784 Winston-Salem NC 27114 336-765-0221 765-7286 189-4
Web: www.salemelectriccoinc.com

Salem Five & Savings Bank 210 Essex St Salem MA 01970 978-745-5555 745-1073 70
TF Cust Svc: 800-850-5000 ■ *Web:* www.salemfive.com

Salem Group, The
2 TransAm Plaza Dr Ste 170 Oakbrook Terrace IL 60181 630-932-7000 721
Web: www.saleminc.com

Salem Hospital 665 Winter St SE Salem OR 97301 800-876-1718 374-3
TF: 800-876-1718 ■ *Web:* www.salemhealth.org

Salem (Independent City)
114 N Broad St PO Box 869 Salem VA 24153 540-375-3000 338
Web: salemva.gov

Salem International University
223 W Main St Salem WV 26426 304-326-1109 166
TF: 800-283-4562 ■ *Web:* www.salemu.edu

Salem Maritime National Historic Site
160 Derby St Salem MA 01970 978-740-1650 740-1654 564
Web: www.nps.gov/sama

Salem Metal Fabricators Inc
21 Lonergan Rd Middleton MA 01949 978-774-2100 697
Web: www.salemmetal.com

Salem Museum 801 E Main St Salem VA 24153 540-389-6760 389-6760 520
TF: 800-346-3334 ■ *Web:* www.salemmuseum.org

Salem Public Library 370 Essex St Salem MA 01970 978-744-0860 434-3
TF: 800-660-2868 ■ *Web:* www.noblenet.org/salem

Salem Public Library 555 Liberty St SE Salem OR 97301 503-588-6071 588-6055 434-3
Web: www.cityofsalem.net/departments/library

Salem Radio Network
6400 N Beltline Rd Ste 210 Irving TX 75063 972-831-1920 831-8626 646
Web: www.srnonline.com

Salem Ready Mix Concrete Inc
2250 Salem Industrial Dr Salem VA 24153 540-387-1171 182
Web: salemreadymix.com

Salem State College 352 Lafayette St Salem MA 01970 978-542-6000 542-6893 166
Web: www.salemstate.edu

Salem Tools Inc 1602 Midland Rd Salem VA 24153 800-390-4348 375-3807* 386
**Fax Area Code:* 540 ■ *TF:* 800-390-4348 ■ *Web:* www.salemtools.com

Salem Tube Inc 951 Fourth St Greenville PA 16125 724-646-4301 646-4311 490
Web: www.salemtube.com

Salem Veterans Affairs Medical Ctr
1970 Roanoke Blvd Salem VA 24153 540-982-2463 374-8
TF: 888-982-2463 ■ *Web:* va.gov

Salem Witch Museum
19 1/2 Washington Sq N Salem MA 01970 978-744-1692 520
TF: 800-392-6100 ■ *Web:* www.salemwitchmuseum.com

Salem/Roanoke County Chamber of Commerce
611 E Main St Salem VA 24153 540-387-0267 387-4110 139
Web: www.s-rcchamber.org

Salem-Keizer Public Schools
2450 Lancaster Dr NE Salem OR 97305 503-399-3000 375-7802* 685
**Fax:* Hum Res ■ *TF:* 877-293-1090 ■ *Web:* www.salkeiz.k12.or.us

Salem-Republic Rubber Co
475 W California Ave Sebring OH 44672 330-938-9801 938-9809 370
TF: 800-686-4199 ■ *Web:* www.salem-republic.com

Salena's Mexican Restaurant
302 N Goodman St At the Vlg Gate Rochester NY 14607 585-256-5980 671
Web: www.salenas.com

SalePoint Inc
9909 Huennekens St Ste 205 San Diego CA 92121 858-546-9400 225
Web: www.salepoint.com

Sales & Marketing Management Magazine
27020 Noble Rd Excelsior MN 55331 651-292-0165 401-7899* 457-5
**Fax Area Code:* 952 ■ *Web:* www.salesandmarketing.com

Sales Automation Support Inc
N28 W23000 Roundy Dr Ste 105 Perwaukee WI 53151 262-754-8712 54
Web: www.salesautomationsupport.com

Sales Benchmark Index
2021 McKinney Ave Ste 550 Dallas TX 75201 888-556-7338 5
TF: 888-556-7338 ■ *Web:* www.salesbenchmarkindex.com

Phone | Fax | Class

Sales Concepts Inc 610 Hembree Pkwy.......... Roswell GA 30076 678-624-9229 463
TF: 800-229-2328 ■ *Web:* www.salesconcepts.com

Sales Effectiveness Inc
570 W Crssvlle Rd .... Roswell GA 30075 770-552-6612 463
Web: www.saleseffectiveness.com

Sales Evolution LLC 2837 Dogwood Ln......... Broomall PA 19008 610-353-8686 195
Web: www.salesevolution.com

Sales Gauge 1186 Old Marlborough Rd...........Concord MA 01742 781-910-0077 393
Web: www.sales-gauge.com

Sales Leader 2222 Sedwick Dr .... Durham NC 27713 800-223-8720 508-2592 531-10
TF: 800-223-8720 ■ *Web:* www.dartnellcorp.com

Sales Performance International Inc
6201 Fairview Rd Ste 400.................... Charlotte NC 28210 704-227-6500 242
Web: www.spisales.com

Sales Readiness Group Inc
8015 SE 28th St Ste 206..................Mercer Island WA 98040 800-490-0715 195
TF: 800-490-0715 ■ *Web:* www.salesreadinessgroup.com

Sales Simplicity Software
325 E Elliot Rd .... Chandler AZ 85225 480-892-2500 177
Web: www.salessimplicity.net

Sales Tax Resource Group
16882 Bolsa Chica St Ste 206 .... Huntington Beach CA 92649 714-377-2600 2
Web: www.salestaxresource.com

Salesconx Inc 701 Seventh Ave Ste 9E..........New York NY 10036 212-453-9880 387
Web: www.salesconx.com

Salesforce.Com Foundation
The Landmark @ One Market Ste 300 .... San Francisco CA 94105 800-667-6389 305
TF: 800-667-6389 ■ *Web:* www.salesforce.org

Salesian High School
2851 Salesian Ave .... Richmond CA 94804 510-234-4433 685

Salesnet 6340 Sugarloaf Pkwy Ste 200 .... Duluth GA 30097 866-732-8632 39
TF: 866-732-8632 ■ *Web:* www.salesnet.com

Salford Systems Inc
9685 Via Excelencia Ste 208................. San Diego CA 92126 619-543-8880 177
TF: 800-972-1430 ■ *Web:* www.salford-systems.com

Salice America Inc
2123 Crown Centre Dr .... Charlotte NC 28227 704-841-7810 350
TF: 800-222-9652 ■ *Web:* www.saliceamerica.com

Salida Union School District
4801 Sisk Rd .... Salida CA 95368 209-545-0339 780
Web: stancoe.org/scoe/districts/salida

Salient Corp 203 Colonial Dr................ Horseheads NY 14845 607-739-4511 466
Web: www.salient.com

Salin Bank 8455 Keystone Xing..............Indianapolis IN 46240 317-452-8000 685
TF: 800-320-7536 ■ *Web:* www.salin.com

Salina Area Chamber of Commerce
120 W Ash St .... Salina KS 67401 785-827-9301 827-9758 139
TF: 877-725-4625 ■ *Web:* www.salinakansas.org

Salina Concrete Products Inc
1100 W Ash .... Salina KS 67401 785-827-7281 182
Web: www.salinaconcreteproducts.com

Salina Journal PO Box 740..................... Salina KS 67402 785-823-6363 827-6363 532-2
TF: 800-827-6363 ■ *Web:* www.salina.com

Salina Public Library 301 W Elm St.............. Salina KS 67401 785-825-4624 823-0706 434-3
TF: 800-362-2642 ■ *Web:* www.salinapubliclibrary.org

Salina Regional Health Ctr
400 S Santa Fe Ave.......................... Salina KS 67401 785-452-7000 374-3
Web: www.srhc.com

Salina Vortex Corp 1725 Vortex Ave.............. Salina KS 67401 785-825-7177 789
Web: www.vortexglobal.com

Salinas Valley Chamber of Commerce
119 E Alisal St ....Salinas CA 93901 831-751-7725 424-8639 139
TF: 888-678-2871 ■ *Web:* www.salinaschamber.com

Salinas Valley Memorial Hospital (SVMH)
450 E Romie Ln ....Salinas CA 93901 831-757-4333 374-3
TF: 800-813-4673 ■ *Web:* www.svmh.com

Salinas Valley State Prison
31625 Hwy 101 N............................Soledad CA 93960 831-678-5500 678-5503 213
Web: cdcr.ca.gov

Saline Area Schools
7265 Saline Ann Arbor Rd .... Saline MI 48176 734-429-8000 685
Web: www.salineschools.org

Saline County 200 N Main St Ste 117.............Benton AR 72015 501-303-5630 338
TF: 800-438-6233 ■ *Web:* www.salinecounty.org

Saline County 10 E Poplar St Ste 17........... Harrisburg IL 62946 618-253-5096 338

Saline County 19 E Arrow St.................. Marshall MO 65340 660-886-7777 886-2603 338
TF: 800-735-2966 ■ *Web:* www.salinecountymo.org

Saline County 300 W Ash Rm 215 .... Salina KS 67402 785-309-5820 309-5826 338
TF: 800-262-8683 ■ *Web:* www.saline.org

Saline County 215 S Ct St..................... Wilber NE 68465 402-821-2374 821-3381 338
Web: www.co.saline.ne.us

Saline County Public Library
1800 Smithers ....Benton AR 72015 501-778-4766 434-3
TF: 800-476-4466 ■ *Web:* www.salinecountylibrary.org

Saline County State Fish & Wildlife Area
85 Glen O Jones Rd .... Equality IL 62934 618-276-4405 565
Web: dnr.illinois.gov/Lands/Landmgt/PARKS/R5/SALINE.HTM

Saline Memorial Hospital
1 Medical Pk Dr.............................Benton AR 72015 501-776-6000 776-6019 374-3
TF: 800-284-0311 ■ *Web:* www.salinememorial.org

Salisbury Area Chamber of Commerce
144 E Main St.............................Salisbury MD 21801 410-749-0144 860-9925 139
Web: www.salisburyarea.com

Salisbury Bancorp Inc
5 Bissell St PO Box 1868 .... Lakeville CT 06039 860-435-9801 435-0631 360-2
NASDAQ: SAL ■ *TF:* 800-222-9801 ■ *Web:* www.salisburybank.com

Salisbury Beach State Reservation
Beach Rd Rt 1A............................Salisbury MA 01952 978-462-4481 565

Salisbury Hotel 123 W 57th St .... New York NY 10019 212-246-1300 977-7752 379
TF: 888-692-5757 ■ *Web:* www.nycsalisbury.com

Salisbury Inc 29085 Airpark Dr.................. Easton MD 21601 410-770-4901 702
TF: 855-255-5309 ■ *Web:* salisburyinc.net

Salisbury Management Inc
120 Shrewsbury St........................... Boylston MA 01505 508-869-0764 652

Salisbury Mansion 40 Highland St.............Worcester MA 01609 508-753-8278 753-9070 50-3
Web: www.worcesterhistory.org

Phone | Fax | Class

Salisbury Motor Company Inc
700 W Innes St.............................Salisbury NC 28144 704-636-1341 57
Web: www.salisburymotorcompany.com

Salisbury National Cemetery
501 Statesville Blvd ....Salisbury NC 28144 704-636-2661 636-1115 136
Web: www.cem.va.gov/cems/nchp/salisbury.asp

Salisbury Ocean City-Wicomico County Regional Airport
5485 Airport Terminal Rd ....Salisbury MD 21804 410-548-4827 27
TF: 800-720-5387 ■ *Web:* flysbyairport.com

Salisbury Post 131 W Innes St ....Salisbury NC 28144 704-797-7678 639-0003 637-8
TF: 800-546-5664

Salisbury School 251 Canaan Rd ....Salisbury CT 06068 860-435-5732 435-5750 622
Web: www.salisburyschool.org

Salisbury University
1200 Camden Ave............................Salisbury MD 21801 410-543-6000 546-6016* 166
**Fax:* Admissions ■ *TF:* 888-543-0148 ■ *Web:* www.salisbury.edu

Salisbury University Blackwell Library
1101 Camden Ave............................Salisbury MD 21801 410-543-6130 543-6203 434-6
TF: 888-543-0148 ■ *Web:* www.salisbury.edu/library

Salisbury Zoological Park
755 S Pk Dr ....Salisbury MD 21804 410-548-3188 860-0919 823
Web: www.salisburyzoo.org

Salish Kootenai College PO Box 70 ....Pablo MT 59855 406-275-4800 275-4801* 165
**Fax:* Admissions ■ *TF:* 877-752-6553 ■ *Web:* www.skc.edu

Salish Lodge & Spa
6501 Railroad Ave DE.......................Snoqualmie WA 98065 425-888-2556 888-9634 669
TF: 800-272-5474 ■ *Web:* www.salishlodge.com

Salishan Lodge & Golf Resort
PO Box 118 ....Gleneden Beach OR 97388 800-452-2300 764-3681* 669
**Fax Area Code:* 541 ■ *TF:* 800-452-2300 ■ *Web:* www.salishan.com

Salit Steel Ltd
7771 Stanley Ave .... Niagara Falls ON L2E6V6 905-354-5691 492
TF: 800-263-7110 ■ *Web:* www.salitsteel.com

Salix Pharmaceuticals Inc
8510 Colonnade Ctr Dr......................... Raleigh NC 27615 919-862-1000 862-1095 582
NASDAQ: SLXP ■ *TF:* 800-508-0024 ■ *Web:* www.salix.com

Salk Institute for Biological Studies
PO Box 85800 .... San Diego CA 92186 858-453-4100 552-8285 668
TF: 866-358-4354 ■ *Web:* www.salk.edu

Sallie Mae 12061 Bluemont Way................. Reston VA 20190 703-810-3000 848-1949* 217
**Fax Area Code:* 800 ■ *TF Cust Svc:* 888-272-5543 ■ *Web:* www.salliemae.com

Sallisaw Chamber of Commerce
301 E Cherokee Ave .... Sallisaw OK 74955 918-775-2558 775-4021 139
Web: sallisawchamber.com

Sally Beauty Company Inc
3001 Colorado Blvd ....Denton TX 76210 940-898-7500 76
TF: 800-777-5706 ■ *Web:* www.sallybeauty.com

Sally Silver Cos PO Box 1265............... Marblehead MA 10945 781-890-7272 260
Web: www.sallysilver.com

Salman Partners Inc
1095 W Pender St 17th Fl.................... Vancouver BC V6E2M6 604-685-2450 685-2471 690

Salmon Lake State Park PO Box 136 .... Seeley Lake MT 59868 406-677-6804 565
Web: stateparks.mt.gov

Salmon River Electric Co-op Inc
1130 Main St PO Box 384 ....Challis ID 83226 208-879-2283 879-2596 245
TF: 877-806-2283 ■ *Web:* www.srec.org

Salmon River State Forest
c/o Eastern District HQ 209 Hebron Rd ..... Marlborough CT 00447 860-295-9523 565
Web: www.ct.gov

Salmonier Nature Park PO Box 190 .... Holyrood NL A0A2R0 709-229-7888 229-7078 823
Web: www.env.gov.nl.ca

Salon Marrow Dyckman Newman & Broudy LLP
292 Madison Ave ....New York NY 10017 888-317-8676 445
TF: 888-317-8676 ■ *Web:* www.salonmarrow.com

Salon Service Group Inc
1520 E Evergreen ....Springfield MO 65803 417-761-7309 77
TF: 800-933-5733 ■ *Web:* www.salonservicegroup.com

Salon Services & Supplies Inc
740 SW 34th St .... Renton WA 98057 425-251-8840 77
TF: 800-251-4247 ■ *Web:* www.salonservicesnw.com

Salon.com 101 Spear St Ste 203........... San Francisco CA 94105 415-645-9200 171
Web: www.salon.com

Saloon 750 S Seventh St...................Philadelphia PA 19147 215-627-1811 671
Web: www.saloonrestaurant.net

Salpicon 1252 N Wells St......................Chicago IL 60610 312-988-7811 671
Web: www.salpicon.com

Salsa 6 Patton Ave.......................... Asheville NC 28801 828 252-9005 252-9805 671
Web: salsasnc.com

Salsa a la Salsa
1420 Nicollet Ave ....Minneapolis MN 55403 612-813-1970 671
Web: www.salsaalasalsa.com

Salsbury Industries Inc
1010 E 62nd St...........................Los Angeles CA 90001 323-846-6700 846-6800 286
TF: 800-624-5299 ■ *Web:* www.mailboxes.com

Salt & Pepper 6515 Bowness Rd NW .... Calgary AB T3B0E8 403-247-4402 671
Web: www.saltnpepper.ca

Salt Branding LLC
1620 Montgomery St Ste 120............ San Francisco CA 94111 415-616-1500 195
Web: saltbranding.com

Salt Cellar 550 N Hayden Rd .... Scottsdale AZ 85257 480-947-1963 941-0929 671
Web: www.saltcellarrestaurant.com

Salt Fork State Park 14755 Cadiz Rd .... Lore City OH 43755 740-439-3521 565
Web: www.ohiodnr.com

SALT Group, The
1845 Sidney Baker St........................Kerrville TX 78028 830-257-1290 734
TF: 888-257-1266 ■ *Web:* thesaltgroup.com

Salt Institute
700 N Fairfax St Ste 600.................... Alexandria VA 22314 703-549-4648 49-6
Web: www.saltinstitute.org

Salt Lake Cable & Harness Inc
421 W 900 N .... North Salt Lake UT 84054 801-292-4999 463
TF: 800-958-4578 ■ *Web:* www.saltlakecable.com

Salt Lake City Chamber of Commerce
175 East University Blvd 400 S
Ste 600..............................Salt Lake City UT 84111 801-364-3631 328-5098 139
Web: www.slchamber.com

Salt Lake City City Hall
451 S State St.......................Salt Lake City UT 84111 801-535-7704 535-6331 337
Web: www.slcgov.com

Name / Address	City	State	ZIP	Phone	Fax	Class
Salt Lake City International Airport						
776 N Terminal Dr PO Box 145550	Salt Lake City	UT	84116	801-575-2400	575-2645	27
TF: 800-595-2442 ■ *Web:* www.slcairport.com						
Salt Lake City Public Library						
210 East 400 South	Salt Lake City	UT	84111	801-524-8200	322-8196	434-3
Web: www.slcpl.org						
Salt Lake City Weekly						
248 S Main St	Salt Lake City	UT	84101	801-575-7003	575-6106	532-5
Web: cityweekly.net						
Salt Lake Community College						
Redwood 4600 S Redwood Rd	Salt Lake City	UT	84130	801-957-4111	957-4444	162
Web: www.slcc.edu						
South City 1575 S State St	Salt Lake City	UT	84115	801-957-4111		162
Web: www.slcc.edu						
Salt Lake Community College Grand Theatre						
1575 S State St	Salt Lake City	UT	84115	801-957-3322		572
TF: 800-524-9400 ■ *Web:* www.slcc.edu/the-grand						
Salt Lake County						
2001 S State St Ste S2200	Salt Lake City	UT	84190	801-468-3000	468-3440	338
Web: slco.org						
Salt Lake County Library System						
2197 E Ft Union Blvd	Salt Lake City	UT	84121	801-943-4636	942-6323	434-3
Web: www.slcolibrary.org						
Salt Lake Mailing & Printing Inc						
1841 S Pioneer Rd	Salt Lake City	UT	84104	801-923-4800		627
Web: www.saltlakemailing.com						
Salt Lake Regional Medical Ctr						
1050 East South Temple	Salt Lake City	UT	84102	801-350-4111	350-4522	374-3
Web: www.saltlakeregional.com						
Salt Lake School District						
440 East 100 South	Salt Lake City	UT	84111	801-578-8599	578-8689	685
Web: slcschools.org						
Salt Lake Temple						
50 W N Temple St	Salt Lake City	UT	84150	801-240-2640	240-1550	50-1
TF: 800-453-3860 ■ *Web:* www.lds.org						
Salt Lake Tribune						
90 South 400 West Ste 700	Salt Lake City	UT	84101	801-257-8742	257-8525	532-2
Web: www.sltrib.com						
Salt Lick 18300 FM 1826	Driftwood	TX	78619	512-858-4959		671
Web: www.saltlickbbq.com						
Salt Palace Convention Ctr						
100 W Temple	Salt Lake City	UT	84101	385-468-2222		205
Web: www.visitsaltlake.com						
Salt Point State Park 25050 Hwy 1	Jenner	CA	95450	707-847-3221		565
Web: www.parks.ca.gov/default.asp?page_id=453						
Salt River Bay National Historical Park & Ecological Preserve						
2100 Church St Ste 100	Christiansted	VI	00820	340-773-1460	773-5995	564
TF: 866-705-5711 ■ *Web:* www.nps.gov/sari						
Salt River Electric Co-op Corp						
111 W Brashear Ave	Bardstown	KY	40004	502-348-3931		245
TF: 800-221-7465 ■ *Web:* www.srelectric.com						
Salt River Project (SRP) 1521 N Project Dr	Tempe	AZ	85281	602-236-5900	236-2442	787
TF: 800-258-4777 ■ *Web:* www.srpnet.com						
Salt Springs State Park						
c/o Lackawanna	North Abington Township	PA	18414	570-945-3239		565
TF: 888-727-2757 ■ *Web:* www.dcnr.state.pa.us						
Salt Water Cowboy's						
299 Dondanville Rd	Saint Augustine	FL	32084	904-471-2332		671
TF: 800-342-4007 ■ *Web:* www.saltwatercowboys.com						
Salt Water Sportsman Magazine						
460 N Orlando Ave Ste 200	Winter Park	FL	32789	407-628-4802		457-20
TF: 800-759-2127 ■ *Web:* www.saltwatersportsman.com						
Saltech Systems Inc 137 Lynn Ave Ste 200	Ames	IA	50014	515-598-4347		177
TF: 800-247-3900 ■ *Web:* www.saltechsystems.com						
Salter Bus Lines Inc 212 Hudson Ave	Jonesboro	LA	71251	318-259-2522	259-2522	107
TF: 800-223-8056 ■ *Web:* www.salter.us						
Salter Labs 100 Sycamore Rd	Arvin	CA	93203	661-854-3166	854-3850	476
TF: 800-421-0024 ■ *Web:* www.salterlabs.com						
Salter Mitchell Inc						
117 S Gadsden St	Tallahassee	FL	32301	850-681-3200		636
Web: www.saltermitchell.com						
Saltgrass Steak House						
520 Meyerland Plaza Mall	Houston	TX	77096	713-665-2226		671
Web: www.saltgrass.com						
Salton Sea State Recreation Area						
100-225 State Pk Rd	North Shore	CA	92254	760-393-3052		565
Web: www.parks.ca.gov/?page_id=639						
Saltwater State Park						
25205 Eigth Pl S	Des Moines	WA	90190	253 661-4956		565
Web: www.parks.wa.gov						
Salty Dog Cafe, The						
232 S Sea Pines Dr	Hilton Head Island	SC	29928	843-671-5199		671
TF: 877-725-8936 ■ *Web:* www.saltydog.com						
Salty's on Alki Beach						
1936 Harbor Ave SW	Seattle	WA	98126	206-937-1600	937-1430	671
Web: www.saltys.com						
Saluda's 751 Saluda Ave	Columbia	SC	29205	803-799-9500		671
Web: www.saludas.com						
Salus Group Benefits Inc						
37525 Mound Rd	Sterling Heights	MI	48310	866-991-9907		260
TF: 866-991-9907 ■ *Web:* thesalusgroup.com						
Salva O'renick 1810 Cherry St	Kansas City	MO	64108	816-842-6996		4
Salvagnini America Inc						
27 Bicentennial Ct	Hamilton	OH	45015	513-874-8284	874-2229	386
Web: www.salvagnini.com						
Salvation Cafe 140 Broadway	Newport	RI	02840	401-847-2620		671
Web: www.salvationcafe.com						
Salvatore's 1333 Boston Rd	Springfield	MA	01119	413-782-9968	796-7601	671
Web: www.salvatoresrestaurant.net						
Salvatore's Hospitality						
6461 Transit Rd	Buffalo	NY	14043	716-683-7990		379
TF: 877-456-4097 ■ *Web:* www.salvatores.net/garden_place/index.html						
Salve Regina University						
100 Ochre Pt Ave	Newport	RI	02840	401-847-6650	848-2823*	166
*Fax: Admissions ■ *Web:* www.salve.edu						
Salve Regina University McKillop Library						
100 Ochre Pt Ave	Newport	RI	02840	401-341-2291	341-2951	434-6
TF: 800-388-6139 ■ *Web:* library.salve.edu						

Name / Address	City	State	ZIP	Phone	Fax	Class
Salvi & Schostok Pc						
218 N Martin Luther King Jr Ave	Waukegan	IL	60085	847-249-1227		428
TF: 800-900-4250 ■ *Web:* www.salvilaw.com						
Salvona Technologies LLC						
65 Stults Rd Bldg 1	Dayton	NJ	08810	609-655-0173		479
Web: www.salvona.com						
Salzgitter Mannesmann International (USA) Inc						
1770 St James Pl Ste 500	Houston	TX	77056	713-386-7900		492
TF: 800-848-0867 ■ *Web:* www.salzgitter-usa.com						
Sam A. Baker State Park						
Rt 1 PO Box 18150	Patterson	MO	63956	573-856-4411		565
Web: www.mostateparks.com						
Sam Bell Maxey House State Historic Site						
812 S Church St	Paris	TX	75460	903-785-5716		565
Web: www.thc.texas.gov						
Sam Clar Office Furniture Inc						
1221 Diamond Way	Concord	CA	94520	925-602-3900		321
TF: 800-726-2527 ■ *Web:* www.samclar.com						
Sam Diego's 950 Iyanough Rd Rt 132	Hyannis	MA	02601	508-771-8816	771-0174	671
Web: www.samdiegos.com						
Sam Hatfield Realty Inc						
4470 Mansford Rd	Winchester	TN	37398	931-968-0500		652
TF: 866-959-7474 ■ *Web:* samhatfield.com						
Sam Hausman Meat Packer Inc						
4261 Beacon	Corpus Christi	TX	78403	361-883-5521	883-1003	473
TF: 800-364-5521 ■ *Web:* www.hausmanfoods.com						
Sam Hawk 660 N Freedom Blvd	Provo	UT	84601	801-377-7766		671
Sam Houston Electric Co-op Inc						
1157 E Church St	Livingston	TX	77351	936-327-5711	328-1244	245
TF: 800-458-0381 ■ *Web:* www.samhouston.net						
Sam Houston Jones State Park						
107 Sutherland Rd	Lake Charles	LA	70611	337-855-2665		565
TF: 888-677-7264 ■ *Web:* www.crt.state.la.us						
Sam Houston Race Park						
7575 N Sam Houston Pkwy W	Houston	TX	77064	281-807-8700	807-8777	642
Web: www.shrp.com						
Sam Houston State University						
1903 University Ave	Huntsville	TX	77340	936-294-1111	294-3758*	166
*Fax: Admissions ■ *TF:* 866-232-7528 ■ *Web:* www.shsu.edu						
Sam Levitz Furniture 3430 E 36th St	Tucson	AZ	85713	520-389-6452		321
Web: www.samlevitz.com						
Sam Miller's Restaurant						
1210 E Cary St	Richmond	VA	23219	804-644-5465		671
Web: www.sammillers.com						
Sam Moore Furniture Industries						
1556 Dawn Dr	Bedford	VA	24523	540-586-8253	586-8497	319-2
Web: www.sammoore.com						
Sam Parr State Fish & Wildlife Area						
13225 E State Hwy 33	Newton	IL	62448	618-783-2661		565
Web: dnr.illinois.gov/Lands/Landmgt/PARKS/R5/SAMPARR.HTM						
Sam S Accursio Farms & Well						
1225 NW Second St	Homestead	FL	33030	305-246-3455		10-11
Sam S Sloven CPA Inc						
3025 S Parker Rd Ste 733	Aurora	CO	80014	303-750-0050		734
Sam Taylor's Barbeque						
435 S Cherry St	Glendale	CO	80246	303-388-9300	388-2276	671
Web: samtaylorsbbq.com						
Sam Zax Assoc 14 Wood Rd	Braintree	MA	02184	781-303-1700		261
Sam's Appliance & Television Rental Inc						
5050 E Belknap St	Fort Worth	TX	76117	817-665-5050		321
Web: www.samsfurniture.com						
Sam's No 3 2580 S Havana St	Aurora	CO	80014	303-751-0347		671
Web: www.samsno3.com						
Sam's on the Waterfront						
2020 Chesapeake Harbour Dr E	Annapolis	MD	21403	410-263-3600		671
Web: www.samsonthewaterfront.com						
Sam's Steakhouse 10205 Gravois Rd	Saint Louis	MO	63123	314-849-3033		671
Web: www.samssteakhouse.com						
Sam's Town Hotel & Casino Shreveport						
315 Clyde Fant Pkwy	Shreveport	LA	71101	877-770-7867		133
TF: 877-770-7867 ■ *Web:* www.samstownshreveport.com						
Sam's Town Hotel & Gambling Hall						
5111 Boulder Hwy	Las Vegas	NV	89122	702-456-7777		133
TF: 800-897-8696 ■ *Web:* www.samstownlv.com						
Sama Eye Wear						
8460 Santa Monica Blvd	West Hollywood	CA	90069	323-822-3955		237
TF: 800-645-1300 ■ *Web:* www.samaeyewear.net						
Samaritan Albany General Hospital						
1046 Sixth Ave SW	Albany	OR	97321	541-812-4000		374-3
Web: www.samhealth.org						
Samaritan Hospice 5 Eves Dr Ste 300	Marlton	NJ	08053	856-596-1600	596-7881	371
TF: 800-229-8183 ■ *Web:* www.samaritannj.org						
Samaritan Hospital 2215 Burdett Ave	Troy	NY	12180	518-271-3300		374-3
Web: www.nehealth.com						
Samaritan Medical Ctr						
830 Washington St	Watertown	NY	13601	315-785-4000		374-3
TF: 877-888-6138 ■ *Web:* www.samaritanhealth.com						
Samaritan Pharmaceuticals Inc						
101 Convention Ctr Dr Ste 310	Las Vegas	NV	89109	702-735-7001	737-7016	85
OTC: SPHC						
Samaritan Village						
138-02 Queens Blvd	Briarwood	NY	11435	718-206-2000	206-2399	726
TF: 800-532-4357 ■ *Web:* samaritanvillage.org						
Samarkand, The 2550 Treasure Dr	Santa Barbara	CA	93105	805-687-0701	687-3386	672
TF: 800-510-2020 ■ *Web:* thesamarkand.org						
Sambatek Inc						
12800 Whitewater Dr Ste 300	Minnetonka	MN	55343	763-476-6010		194
Web: www.sambatek.com						
Sambazon Inc						
209 Avenida Fabricante Suite 200	San Clemente	CA	92673	877-726-2296		297-7
TF: 877-726-2296 ■ *Web:* www.sambazon.com						
Sambe Construction Company Inc						
1650 Hylton Rd	Pennsauken	NJ	08110	856-663-7751		186
Sambo's Tavern 283 Front St	Leipsic	DE	19901	302-674-9724		671
Samco Capital Markets						
4617 Montrose Blvd Ste C202	Houston	TX	77006	512-794-9100		401
Web: www.samcocap.com						

Phone | Fax | Class

SAME (Society of American Military Engineers)
607 Prince St ... Alexandria VA 22314 703-549-3800 684-0231 48-19
TF: 800-336-3097 ■ *Web:* www.same.org

SameDay Security Inc
506 S Main St Ste 1000 10th Fl ... Las Cruces NM 88001 575-522-4046 475
TF: 866-572-3274 ■ *Web:* www.lifesupportmedical.com

Samet Corp
309 Gallimore Dairy Rd Ste 102
PO Box 8050 ... Greensboro NC 27409 336-544-2600 544-2638 186
Web: www.sametcorp.com

Sametz Blackstone Assoc
40 W Newton St Blackstone Sq ... Boston MA 02118 617-266-8577 344
Web: www.sametz.com

Samford University
800 Lakeshore Dr ... Birmingham AL 35229 205-726-3673 726-2171* 166
**Fax:* Admissions ■ *TF Admissions:* 800-888-7218 ■ *Web:* www.samford.edu

Samford University Cumberland School of Law
800 Lakeshore Dr ... Birmingham AL 35229 205-726-2011 167-1
Web: cumberland.samford.edu

SAMHSA (Substance Abuse & Mental Health Services Administration)
1 Choke Cherry Rd ... Rockville MD 20857 240-276-2000 276-2010 340-10
TF: 877-726-4727 ■ *Web:* www.samhsa.gov

Samick Music Corp 1329 Gateway Dr ... Gallatin TN 37066 615-206-0077 527
Web: www.smcmusic.com

Sammons Ctr for the Arts
3630 Harry Hines Blvd ... Dallas TX 75219 214-520-7789 522-9174 572
Web: www.sammonsartcenter.org

Sammons Enterprises Inc
5949 Sherry Ln Ste 1900 ... Dallas TX 75225 214-210-5000 185
Web: www.sammonsenterprises.com

Sammons Trucking 3665 W Broadway ... Missoula MT 59808 406-728-2600 549-4989 780
TF: 800-548-9276 ■ *Web:* www.sammonstrucking.com

Sammy G's 265 S Palm Canyon Dr ... Palm Springs CA 92262 760-320-8041 671
Web: sammygsrestaurant.com

Sammy's Barbeque 2126 Leonard St ... Dallas TX 75201 214-880-9064 671
Web: sammystexasbbq.com

Samon's Tiger Stores Inc
2511 Monroe NE ... Albuquerque NM 87110 505-884-4615 612
TF: 800-123-4567 ■ *Web:* www.samons.biz

Samos 600 Oldham St ... Baltimore MD 21224 410-675-5292 671
Web: www.samosrestaurant.com

Samoset Resort 220 Warrenton St ... Rockport ME 04856 207-594-2511 594-0722 669
TF: 800-341-1650 ■ *Web:* www.samosetresort.com

Sampan 675 East 2100 South ... Salt Lake City UT 84106 801-467-3663 671
Web: www.esampan.com

Sampan Chinese Restaurant
985 Peters Creek Pkwy ... Winston-Salem NC 27103 336-777-8266 671

Sampco Inc
651 W Washington Blvd Ste 300 ... Chicago IL 60661 312-346-1506 346-8302 297-9
TF: 800-767-0689 ■ *Web:* www.sampcoinc.com

SAMPE (Society for the Advancement of Material & Process Engineering)
21680 Gateway Center Dr Ste 300 ... Diamond Bar CA 91765 626-331-0616 262-1431* 49-19
**Fax Area Code:* 801 ■ *TF:* 800-562-7360 ■ *Web:* www.sampe.org

Sampers Financial Inc
79 Midland Ave ... Montclair NJ 07042 973-744-1014 401
TF: 800-627-9667 ■ *Web:* www.sampersfinancial.com

Sampo Inc 119 Remsen Rd ... Barneveld NY 13304 315-896-2606 896-6575 710
Web: guns-slashriku.wixsite.com/sampo

Sampson Community College PO Box 318 ... Clinton NC 28329 910-592-8081 592-8048* 162
**Fax:* Admissions ■ *TF:* 800-334-1203 ■ *Web:* sampsoncc.edu

Sampson Correctional Institution
700 NW Blvd Hwy 421N ... Clinton NC 28328 910-592-2151 592-2543 213
TF: 800-368-1985 ■ *Web:* www.ncdps.gov

Sampson County 435 Rowan Rd ... Clinton NC 28328 910-592-6308 592-1945 338
Web: www.sampsonnc.com

Sampson County Schools 437 Rowan Rd ... Clinton NC 28328 910-592-1401 590-2445 685
Web: www.sampson.k12.nc.us

Sampson Regional Medical Ctr
607 Beaman St ... Clinton NC 28328 910-592-8511 590-2321 374-3
TF: 800-827-5312 ■ *Web:* www.sampsonrmc.org

Sampson State Park 6096 Rt 96A ... Romulus NY 14541 315-585-6392 565
Web: www.nysparks.com/parks/info.asp?parkid=100

Sampson-Bladen Oil Co Inc
510 Commerce St PO Box 469 ... Clinton NC 28329 910-592-4177 324
TF: 800-849-4177 ■ *Web:* www.sboil.com

Samrat 2529 Apalachee Pkwy ... Tallahassee FL 32301 850-942-1993 942-8091 671
TF: 800-628-2866 ■ *Web:* samratindianrestaurantfl.com

SAMS (Society of Accredited Marine Surveyors Inc)
7855 Argyle Forest Blvd Ste 203 ... Jacksonville FL 32244 904-384-1494 388-3958 48-1
TF: 800-344-9077 ■ *Web:* www.marinesurvey.org

Sams Discount Food Mart
5703 Timuquana Rd ... Jacksonville FL 32210 904-573-8899 297-8

Sams Technical Publishing
9850 E 30th St ... Indianapolis IN 46229 800-428-7267 552-3910 637-2
TF Cust Svc: 800-428-7267 ■ *Web:* www.samswebsite.com

SAMSA Inc 5560 Gratiot Ste D ... Saginaw MI 48638 989-790-0507 177
Web: www.samsa.com

Samsill Corp 5740 Hartman Rd ... Fort Worth TX 76119 817-536-1906 535-6900 86
TF: 800-255-1100 ■ *Web:* www.samsill.com

Samson Manufacturing Co
231 E 13th St ... Waynesboro GA 30830 706-554-2129 746

Samson Oil and Gas USA Inc
1726 Cole Blvd Ste 210 ... Lakewood CO 80401 303-295-0344 536
Web: www.samsonoilandgas.com

Samson Resources Corp
15 E Fifth St Ste 1000 ... Tulsa OK 74103 918-591-1791 591-1796 539
Web: www.samson.com

Samson Rope Technologies Inc
2090 Thornton Rd ... Ferndale WA 98248 360-384-4669 299-9246* 208
**Fax Area Code:* 800 ■ *TF Cust Svc:* 800-227-7673 ■ *Web:* www.samsonrope.com

Samson Technologies Inc
45 Gilpin Ave ... Hauppauge NY 11788 631-784-2200 514
TF: 800-372-6766 ■ *Web:* www.samsontech.com

Samsung Austin Semiconductor LLC
12100 Sam Sung Blvd ... Austin TX 78754 512-672-1000 186
Web: www.cleanairforce.org

Samsung Semiconductors Inc
3655 N First St ... San Jose CA 95134 408-544-4000 544-4980 696
TF General: 800-726-7864 ■ *Web:* www.usa.samsungsemi.com

Samsung Telecommunications America LLP
1301 E Lookout Dr ... Richardson TX 75082 972-761-7000 761-7001 735
TF: 800-726-7864 ■ *Web:* www.samsung.com

Samtan Engineering Corp 127 Wyllis Ave ... Malden MA 02148 781-322-7880 454
Web: www.samtanengineering.com

Samtec Inc 520 Parkeast Blvd ... New Albany IN 47150 812-944-6733 948-5047 253
TF: 800-726-8329 ■ *Web:* www.samtec.com

Samuel A Ramirez & Co Inc
61 Broadway Ste 2924 ... New York NY 10006 800-888-4086 690
TF: 800-888-4086 ■ *Web:* www.ramirezco.com

Samuel Aaron International/ The Aaron Group
31-00 47th Ave ... Lic NY 11101 718-392-5454 409
Web: www.the-aaron-group.com/SAI/html/SAIindex

Samuel Cabot Inc 100 Hale St ... Newburyport MA 01950 978-465-1900 550
TF: 800-877-8246 ■ *Web:* www.cabotstain.com

Samuel Engineering Inc
8450 E Crescent Pkwy ... Greenwood Village CO 80111 303-714-4840 261
Web: www.samuelengineering.com

Samuel French Inc 45 W 25th St ... New York NY 10010 212-206-8990 95
TF: 866-598-8449 ■ *Web:* www.samuelfrench.com

Samuel Goldwyn Films
9570 W Pico Blvd Ste 400 ... Los Angeles CA 90035 310-860-3100 872-5077 514
Web: www.samuelgoldwynfilms.com

Samuel Mahelona Memorial Hospital
4800 Kawaihau Rd ... Kapaa HI 96746 808-822-4961 823-4100 374-7
Web: www.smmh.hhsc.org

Samuel Merritt College
370 Hawthorne Ave ... Oakland CA 94609 510-869-6576 869-6525* 166
**Fax:* Admissions ■ *TF Admissions:* 800-607-6377 ■ *Web:* www.samuelmerritt.edu

Samuel P. Taylor State Park
PO Box 251 ... Lagunitas CA 94938 415-488-9897 565
Web: www.parks.ca.gov

Samuel S. Lewis State Park
6000 Mt Pisgah Rd ... York PA 17406 717-432-5011 565
Web: www.dcnr.state.pa.us

Samuel Shapiro & Company Inc
100 N Charles St One Charles Ctr Ste 1200 ... Baltimore MD 21201 410-539-0540 311
Web: www.shapiro.com

Samuel Steel Pickling Co
1400 Enterprise Pkwy ... Twinsburg OH 44087 330-963-3777 963-0770 307
Web: www.samuelsteel.com

Samuel t Wood Co 2704 Cedar Dr ... Riva MD 21140 410-798-7440 610

Samuel Whitehorne House 416 Thames St ... Newport RI 02840 401-849-7300 50-3
Web: www.newportrestoration.org

Samuels Diamonds
9607 Research Blvd Ste 100 Bldg F ... Austin TX 78759 512-343-6363 410
TF: 877-388-1836 ■ *Web:* www.samuelsjewelers.com

Samuels Group Inc
311 Financial Way St 300 ... Wausau WI 54401 715-842-2222 186
TF: 800-369-6220 ■ *Web:* www.samuelsgroup.net

Samuels Public Library
330 E Criser Rd ... Front Royal VA 22630 540-635-3153 434-3
TF: 800-431-4712 ■ *Web:* www.samuelslibrary.net

Samuels, Miller, Schroeder, Jackson & Sly LLP
225 N Water St Ste 301 ... Decatur IL 62523 217-429-4325 428
Web: www.samuelsmiller.com

Samurai Grill & Sushi Bar
9500 Montgomery Blvd NE ... Albuquerque NM 87111 505-275-6601 671
Web: www.abqsamurai.com

Samy's Camera Inc
431 S Fairfax Ave ... Los Angeles CA 90036 323-938-2420 692-0750 119
TF: 800-321-4726 ■ *Web:* www.samys.com

San Angelo Chamber of Commerce
418 W Ave B ... San Angelo TX 76903 325-655-4136 658-1110 206
TF: 800-252-1381 ■ *Web:* www.sanangelo.org

San Angelo Community Medical Ctr
3501 Knickerbocker Rd ... San Angelo TX 76904 325-949-9511 947-6550 374-3
Web: www.sacmc.com

San Angelo Convention Ctr Coliseum & Auditorium
500 Rio Concho Dr ... San Angelo TX 76903 325-653-9577 205
Web: cosatx.us

San Angelo Standard Times Inc
34 W Harris ... San Angelo TX 76901 325-659-8100 659-8173 637-8
TF: 800-588-1884 ■ *Web:* www.gosanangelo.com

San Antonio Botanical Garden & Lucile Halsell Conservatory
555 Funston Pl ... San Antonio TX 78209 210-207-3250 207-3274 97
Web: www.sabot.org

San Antonio Business Journal
8200 IH 10 W Ste 820 ... San Antonio TX 78230 210-341-3202 457-5
Web: www.bizjournals.com/sanantonio

San Antonio Children's Museum
2800 Broadway ... San Antonio TX 78209 210-212-4453 521
Web: www.sakids.org

San Antonio City Hall
PO Box 839966 ... San Antonio TX 78283 210-207-7040 207-7027 337
Web: www.sanantonio.gov

San Antonio Community Hospital
999 San BernaRdino Rd ... Upland CA 91786 909-985-2811 374-3
Web: www.sarh.org

San Antonio Convention & Visitors Bureau
203 S St Marys St Ste 200 ... San Antonio TX 78205 210-207-6700 207-6768 206
TF: 800-447-3372 ■ *Web:* www.visitsanantonio.com

San Antonio Current 915 Dallas St ... San Antonio TX 78215 210-227-0044 227-6611 532-5
Web: sacurrent.com

San Antonio Express-News
Ave E & Third St ... San Antonio TX 78205 210-250-3000 250-3105 532-2
TF: 800-555-1551 ■ *Web:* www.mysanantonio.com

San Antonio Eye Bank
9150 Huebner Rd Ste 105 ... San Antonio TX 78240 210-614-1209 269
Web: www.saeyebank.org

San Antonio Independent School District (SAISD)
141 Lavaca St ... San Antonio TX 78210 210-554-2200 299-5600* 685
**Fax:* Hum Res ■ *TF:* 866-632-9992 ■ *Web:* www.saisd.net

San Antonio International Airport (SAT)
9800 Airport Blvd Rm 2041 ... San Antonio TX 78216 210-207-3411 207-3500* 27
**Fax:* PR ■ *TF:* 800-237-6639 ■ *Web:* www.sanantonio.gov/aviation

San Antonio Lighthouse for The Blind
2305 Roosevelt Ave ... San Antonio TX 78210 210-533-5195 586
Web: www.idworld.net

Name / Address	City	State	Zip	Phone	Fax	Class
San Antonio Livestock Exposition Inc PO Box 200230 *Web:* www.sarodeo.com	San Antonio	TX	78220	210-225-0575		446
San Antonio Missions National Historical Park 2202 Roosevelt Ave *TF:* 866-945-7920 ■ *Web:* www.nps.gov/saan	San Antonio	TX	78210	210-534-8833	534-1106	564
San Antonio Municipal Auditorium 200 E Market St PO Box 1809 *TF:* 877-504-8895 ■ *Web:* www.sahbgcc.com	San Antonio	TX	78205	210-207-8500	223-1495	572
San Antonio Museum of Art 200 W Jones Ave *Web:* samuseum.org	San Antonio	TX	78215	210-978-8100	978-8134	520
San Antonio Public Library 600 Soledad St *Web:* www.sanantonio.gov/library	San Antonio	TX	78205	210-207-2500		434-3
San Antonio Sam's Club 5565 Dezavala Rd *Web:* www.sanantoniosams.com	San Antonio	TX	78249	210-641-4810		671
San Antonio Silver Stars 1 AT & T Ctr *Web:* wnba.com/stars	San Antonio	TX	78219	210-444-5090		714-2
San Antonio Spurs 1 AT & T Ctr *Web:* www.nba.com/spurs	San Antonio	TX	78219	210-444-5000	444-5003	714-1
San Antonio State Hospital 6711 S Braunfels Ave *Web:* www.dshs.texas.gov/mhhospitals/SanAntonioSH/default.shtm	San Antonio	TX	78223	210-532-8811	531-7780	374-5
San Antonio Symphony 711 Navarro St Ste235 *TF:* 800-417-4139 ■ *Web:* sasymphony.org	San Antonio	TX	78205	210-554-1000	554-1008	573-3
San Antonio Zoological Gardens & Aquarium 3903 N St Mary's St *Web:* www.sazoo-aq.org	San Antonio	TX	78212	210-734-7184	734-7291	823
San Augustine County 223 N Harrison *Web:* www.co.san-augustine.tx.us	San Augustine	TX	75972	936-275-2452	275-2263	338
San Benito County 440 Fifth St Rm 206 *TF:* 800-503-9230 ■ *Web:* www.cosb.us	Hollister	CA	95023	831-636-4029	636-2939	338
San Benito Public Library 101 W Rose St *TF:* 800-444-1187 ■ *Web:* www.cityofsanbenito.com	San Benito	TX	78586	956-361-3860	361-3867	434-3
San Bernard Electric Co-op Inc 309 W Main St *TF:* 800-364-3171 ■ *Web:* www.sbec.org	Bellville	TX	77418	979-865-3171	865-9706	245
San Bernardino Area Chamber of Commerce PO Box 658 *TF:* 800-928-5091 ■ *Web:* www.sbachamber.org	San Bernardino	CA	92402	909-885-7515	384-9979	139
San Bernardino City Hall 300 N 'D' St *Web:* www.ci.san-bernardino.ca.us	San Bernardino	CA	92418	909-384-5211	384-5158	337
San Bernardino Convention & Visitors Bureau 1955 Hunts Ln *TF:* 800-867-8366 ■ *Web:* www.san-bernardino.org	San Bernardino	CA	92408	909-891-1151		206
San Bernardino County 385 N Arrowhead Ave *TF:* 888-818-8988 ■ *Web:* sbcounty.gov	San Bernardino	CA	92415	909-387-8306		338
San Bernardino Valley College 701 S Mt Vernon Ave *Web:* www.valleycollege.edu	San Bernardino	CA	92410	909-384-4400		162
San Bruno Chamber of Commerce 618 San Mateo Ave *Web:* www.sanbrunochamber.com	San Bruno	CA	94066	650-588-0180		139
San Bruno Public Library 701 Angus Ave W *TF:* 800-866-5153 ■ *Web:* www.sanbruno.ca.gov	San Bruno	CA	94066	650-616-7078	876-0848	434-3
San Carlos Chamber of Commerce 610 Elm St Ste 206 *Web:* www.sancarloschamber.org	San Carlos	CA	94070	650-593-1068	593-9108	139
San Carlos Hotel 150 E 50th St *TF:* 800-722-2012 ■ *Web:* www.sancarloshotel.com	New York	NY	10022	212-755-1800	688-9778	379
San Chez 38 Fulton St W *Web:* www.sanchezbistro.com	Grand Rapids	MI	49503	616-774-8272		671
San Clemente Chamber of Commerce 1100 N El Camino Real *TF:* 877-411-3662 ■ *Web:* www.scchamber.com	San Clemente	CA	92672	949-492-1131	492-3764	139
San Clemente State Beach c/o Orange Coast District Office 3030 Avenida del Presidente *Web:* www.parks.ca.gov/default.asp?page_id=646	San Clemente	CA	92672	949-492-3156		565
San Damiano Retreat Ctr 710 Highland Dr PO Box 767 *Web:* www.sandamiano.org	Danville	CA	94526	925-837-9141	837-0522	673
San Diego Air & Space Museum 2001 Pan American Plaza Balboa Pk *Web:* sandiegoairandspace.org	San Diego	CA	92101	619-234-8291	233-4526	520
San Diego Aircraft Carrier Museum 910 N Harbor Dr Navy Pier *TF:* 800-447-2637 ■ *Web:* www.midway.org	San Diego	CA	92101	619-544-9600	544-9188	520
San Diego Archaeological Ctr 16666 San Pasqual Valley Rd *Web:* www.sandiegoarchaeology.org	Escondido	CA	92027	760-291-0370	291-0371	520
San Diego Assn of Governments-sandag 401 B St Ste 800 *Web:* www.sandag.org	San Diego	CA	92101	619-699-1900		463
San Diego Automotive Museum 2080 Pan American Plaza Balboa Pk *Web:* www.sdautomuseum.org	San Diego	CA	92101	619-231-2886	231-9869	520
San Diego Ballet 2650 Truxtun Rd *Web:* sandiegoballet.org	San Diego	CA	92106	619-294-7378		573-1
San Diego Botanic Garden 230 Quail Gardens Dr PO Box 230005 *Web:* www.sdbgarden.org	Encinitas	CA	92023	760-436-3036	632-0917	97
San Diego Business Journal 4909 Murphy Canyon Rd Ste 200 *Web:* www.sdbj.com	San Diego	CA	92123	858-277-6359		457-5
San Diego Chargers 4020 Murphy Canyon Rd *TF:* 877-242-7437 ■ *Web:* www.chargers.com	San Diego	CA	92123	858-874-4500	292-2760	715-3
San Diego Christian College 2100 Greenfield Dr *TF:* 800-676-2242 ■ *Web:* www.sdcc.edu	El Cajon	CA	92019	619-441-2200		166
San Diego City College 1313 Pk Blvd *Fax: Admissions ■ *Web:* www.sdcity.edu	San Diego	CA	92101	619-388-3400	388-3241*	162
San Diego City Hall 202 C St *TF:* 866-470-1308 ■ *Web:* www.sandiego.gov	San Diego	CA	92101	619-533-4000	533-4045	337
San Diego Coastal Chamber of Commerce 1104 Camino Del Mar Ste 1 *Web:* www.delmarchamber.org	Del Mar	CA	92014	858-755-4844	793-5293	139
San Diego Community Newspaper 4645 Cass St Fl 2 *TF:* 800-952-5953 ■ *Web:* www.sdnews.com	San Diego	CA	92109	858-270-3103		532-3
San Diego Concierge 4379 30th St Ste 4 *TF:* 800-979-9091 ■ *Web:* www.sandiegoconcierge.com	San Diego	CA	92104	619-280-4121		376
San Diego Convention & Visitors Bureau 2215 India St *Web:* www.sandiego.org	San Diego	CA	92101	619-232-3101	696-9371	206
San Diego Convention Ctr 111 W Harbor Dr *TF:* 866-257-3772 ■ *Web:* visitsandiego.com	San Diego	CA	92101	619-525-5000	525-5005	205
San Diego County 1600 Pacific Hwy Rm 166 *Web:* www.sandiegocounty.gov	San Diego	CA	92101	619-531-5413	531-5219	338
San Diego County Credit Union 6545 Sequence Dr *Fax Area Code: 858 ■ *TF:* 877-732-2848 ■ *Web:* www.sdccu.com	San Diego	CA	92121	877-732-2848	597-6509*	219
San Diego County Library System 5560 Overland Ave Ste 110 *TF:* 800-952-5666 ■ *Web:* www.sdcl.org	San Diego	CA	92123	858-694-2415		434-3
San Diego County Psychiatric Hospital 3853 Rosecrans St *Web:* www.sandiegocounty.gov	San Diego	CA	92110	619-692-8200		374-5
San Diego Culinary Institute (SDCI) 8024 La Mesa Blvd *Web:* sandiegoculinary.edu	La Mesa	CA	91941	619-644-2100	644-2106	163
San Diego Daily Transcript 2131 Third Ave *Fax: Edit ■ *TF:* 800-697-6397 ■ *Web:* www.sddt.com	San Diego	CA	92101	619-232-4381	236-8126*	532-2
San Diego East County Chamber of Commerce 201 S Magnolia Ave *TF:* 800-402-8765 ■ *Web:* eastcountychamber.org	El Cajon	CA	92020	619-440-6161	440-6164	139
San Diego Eye Bank (SDEB) 9246 Lightwave Ave Ste 120 *TF:* 800-393-2265 ■ *Web:* www.sdeb.org	San Diego	CA	92123	858-694-0400	565-7368	269
San Diego Film Festival 2683 Via de la Valle Ste G210 *Web:* www.sdfilmfest.com	Del Mar	CA	92014	619-818-2221		282
San Diego Foundation, The 2508 Historic Decatur Rd Ste 200 *Web:* www.sdfoundation.org	San Diego	CA	92106	619-235-2300	239-1710	303
San Diego Futures Foundation 4283 El Cajon Blvd Ste 220 *TF:* 800-464-4000 ■ *Web:* www.sdfutures.org	San Diego	CA	92105	619-269-1684		303
San Diego Gas & Electric Co 101 Ash St *Fax Area Code: 858 ■ *Fax: Cust Svc ■ *TF:* 800-411-7343 ■ *Web:* www.sdge.com	San Diego	CA	92101	619-696-2000	654-1755*	787
San Diego Hall of Champions Sports Museum 2131 Pan American Plaza *Web:* www.sdhoc.com	San Diego	CA	92101	619-699-2302	234-4543	520
San Diego International Airport - Lindbergh Field 3225 N Harbor Dr San Diego County Regl Airport Authority 3rd Fl *Web:* www.san.org	San Diego	CA	92101	619-400-2404		27
San Diego Jewish Academy 11860 Carmel Creek Rd *Web:* www.sdja.com	San Diego	CA	92130	858-704-3700		685
San Diego Marriott Hotel & Marina 333 W Harbor Dr *Web:* www.marriott.com/hotels/travel/sandt-san-diego-marriott-hotel-and-marina	San Diego	CA	92101	619-234-1500		378
San Diego Mesa College 7250 Mesa College Dr *TF:* 800-875-7117 ■ *Web:* sdmesa.edu	San Diego	CA	92111	619-388-2600	388-2960	162
San Diego Miramar College 10440 Black Mountain Rd *Web:* www.sdmiramar.edu	San Diego	CA	92126	619-388-7844		162
San Diego Model Management 438 Camino del Rio S Ste 116 *Web:* www.sdmodel.com	San Diego	CA	92108	619-296-1018		506
San Diego Model Railroad Museum 1649 El Prado *Web:* sdmrm.org	San Diego	CA	92101	619-696-0199		520
San Diego Museum of Art 1450 El Prado Balboa Pk PO Box 122107 *TF:* 800-442-7847 ■ *Web:* www.sdmart.org	San Diego	CA	92101	619-232-7931	232-9367	520
San Diego Museum of Man 1350 El Prado Balboa Pk *TF:* 800-626-6579 ■ *Web:* www.museumofman.org	San Diego	CA	92101	619-239-2001	239-2749	520
San Diego Natural History Museum 1788 El Prado PO Box 121390 *TF:* 877-946-7797 ■ *Web:* www.sdnhm.org	San Diego	CA	92101	619-232-3821	232-0248	520
San Diego Opera 233 A St Ste 500 *TF:* 800-988-4253 ■ *Web:* www.sdopera.org	San Diego	CA	92101	619-232-7636	231-6915	573-2
San Diego Plastics Inc 2220 Mckinley Ave *TF:* 800-925-4855 ■ *Web:* www.sdplastics.com	National City	CA	91950	619-477-4855		603
San Diego Printers 9190 Camino Santa Fe *Web:* www.sdprinters.com	San Diego	CA	92121	858-684-5200		627
San Diego Public Library 820 E St *TF:* 866-470-1308 ■ *Web:* www.sandiego.gov/public-library	San Diego	CA	92101	619-236-5800	236-5878	434-3
San Diego Regional Chamber of Commerce 402 W Broadway Ste 1000 *Web:* www.sdchamber.org	San Diego	CA	92101	619-544-1300		139
San Diego Repertory Theatre 79 Horton Plaza *Web:* www.sdrep.org	San Diego	CA	92101	619-231-3586		573-4

Phone | Fax | Class

San Diego State University
5500 Campanile Dr. San Diego CA 92182 619-594-5200 166
Web: www.sdsu.edu
Imperial Valley 720 Heber Ave. Calexico CA 92231 760-768-5500 166
Web: www.ivcampus.sdsu.edu

San Diego Supercomputer Ctr (SDSC)
9500 Gilman Dr La Jolla CA 92093 858-534-5000 534-5056 668
TF: 800-451-4515 ■ *Web:* www.sdsc.edu

San Diego Symphony Orchestra
1245 Seventh Ave. San Diego CA 92101 619-235-0804 573-3
Web: www.sandiegosymphony.org

San Diego Transit Corp 100 16th St San Diego CA 92101 619-238-0100 468

San Diego Trolley Inc
1255 Imperial Ave. San Diego CA 92101 619-595-4949 649

San Diego Unified School District
4100 Normal St San Diego CA 92103 619-725-8000 685
Web: www.sandiegounified.org

San Diego Union-Tribune
350 Camino De La Reina San Diego CA 92108 619-299-3131 293-1896 532-2
TF: 800-244-6397 ■ *Web:* www.sandiegouniontribune.com

San Diego World Trade Ctr
2980 Pacific Hwy San Diego CA 92101 619-615-0868 822
Web: www.wtca.org

San Diego Yacht Club Sailing Foundation
1011 Anchorage Ln San Diego CA 92106 619-221-8400 305
Web: sdycsf.org

San Diego Zoo 2920 Zoo Dr. San Diego CA 92101 619-231-1515 823
Web: www.sandiegozoo.org

San Diego Zoo Safari Park
15500 San Pasqual Valley Rd. Escondido CA 92027 760-747-8702 823
TF Cust Svc: 877-363-6237 ■ *Web:* www.sdzsafaripark.org

San Dieguito Printers
1880 Diamond St San Marcos CA 92078 760-744-0910 637-10
Web: www.sd-print.com

San Dimas Chamber of Commerce
246 E Bonita Ave. San Dimas CA 91773 909-592-3818 592-0178 139
TF: 800-371-5465 ■ *Web:* www.sandimaschamber.com

San Dimas Community Hospital
1350 W Covina Blvd. San Dimas CA 91773 909-599-6811 374-3
Web: www.sandimashospital.com

San Domenico School
1500 Butterfield Rd. San Anselmo CA 94960 415-258-1905 622
Web: www.sandomenico.org

San Felasco Hammock Preserve State Park
12720 NW 109 Ln Alachua FL 32615 386-462-7905 565
Web: www.floridastateparks.org

San Felipe's Casino Hollywood
25 Hagon Rd. Algodones NM 87001 505-867-6700 452
TF: 877-529-2946 ■ *Web:* sanfelipecasino.com

San Francisco 49ers
4949 Centennial Blvd Santa Clara CA 95054 408-562-4949 727-4937 716-3
Web: www.49ers.com

San Francisco Art Institute
800 Chestnut St San Francisco CA 94133 415-771-7020 164
TF: 800-345-7324 ■ *Web:* www.sfai.edu

San Francisco Ballet
455 Franklin St. San Francisco CA 94102 415-865-2000 861-2684 573-1
Web: www.sfballet.org

San Francisco Bay Guardian
135 Mississippi St San Francisco CA 94107 415-255-3100 532-5
TF: 800-870-6397 ■ *Web:* www.sfbg.com

San Francisco Botanical Garden
9th Ave & Lincoln Way San Francisco CA 94122 415-661-1316 331-1316 97
Web: www.sfbotanicalgarden.org

San Francisco Chamber of Commerce
235 Montgomery St 12th Fl San Francisco CA 94104 415-392-4520 392-0485 139
TF: 855-808-2387 ■ *Web:* www.sfchamber.com

San Francisco Chronicle
901 Mission St. San Francisco CA 94103 415-777-1111 896-1107 532-2
TF: 866-732-4766 ■ *Web:* www.sfgate.com

San Francisco City & County
1 Dr Carlton B Goodlett Pl
City Hall Rm 362 San Francisco CA 94102 415-554-4851 554-4849 338
Web: sfgsa.org

San Francisco Conservatory of Music
50 Oak St San Francisco CA 94102 415-864-7326 503-6299 166
TF: 800-999-8219 ■ *Web:* www.sfcm.edu

San Francisco Design Ctr
2 Henry Adams St Ste 450 San Francisco CA 94103 415-490-5800 490-5885 321
Web: www.sfdesigncenter.com

San Francisco Examiner
835 Market St Ste 550 San Francisco CA 94103 415-359-2860 359-2766 532-2
Web: www.sfexaminer.com

San Francisco Federal Credit Union
770 Golden Gate Ave San Francisco CA 94102 415-775-5377 775-5340 219
TF: 800-852-7598 ■ *Web:* www.sanfranciscofcu.com

San Francisco Film Society
39 Mesa St Ste 110 San Francisco CA 94129 415-561-5000 440-1760 282
Web: www.sffilm.org

San Francisco Fire Dept Museum
655 Presidio Ave. San Francisco CA 94115 415-563-4630 520
TF: 800-545-2433 ■ *Web:* guardiansofthecity.org

San Francisco Food Co
14054 Catalina St. San Leandro CA 94577 510-357-7343 123
Web: www.sffoodbank.org

San Francisco Foundation
1 Embarcadero Ctr Ste 1400. San Francisco CA 94111 415-733-8500 477-2783 303
Web: www.sff.org

San Francisco General Hospital Medical Ctr
500 Parnassus Ave. San Francisco CA 94143 415-476-9000 206-8942 374-3
TF: 800-723-7140 ■ *Web:* psych.ucsf.edu/sfgh

San Francisco Giants
AT & T Pk 24 Willie Mays Plz. San Francisco CA 94107 415-972-2000 713
Web: sanfrancisco.giants.mlb.com

San Francisco Herb & Natural Food Co
47444 Kato Rd Fremont CA 94538 510-770-1215 123
Web: www.herbspicetea.com

San Francisco International Airport
PO Box 8097 San Francisco CA 94128 650-821-8211 821-5005 27
TF: 800-435-9736 ■ *Web:* www.flysfo.com

San Francisco Magazine
243 Vallejo St. San Francisco CA 94111 415-398-2800 398-6777 457-22
TF: 866-736-2499 ■ *Web:* www.modernluxury.com

San Francisco Maritime National Historical Park
2 Marina Blvd Bldg E San Francisco CA 94123 415-561-7000 556-1624 564
Web: www.nps.gov/safr

San Francisco Museum of Modern Art
151 Third St San Francisco CA 94103 415-357-4000 357-4037 520
TF: 800-637-5196 ■ *Web:* www.sfmoma.org

San Francisco Music Box Co
5370 W 95th St. Prairie Village KS 66207 800-227-2190 327
TF: 800-227-2190 ■ *Web:* www.sanfranciscomusicbox.com

San Francisco National Cemetery
Presidio of San Francisco
1 Lincoln Blvd San Francisco CA 94129 650-589-7737 873-6578 136
TF: 800-827-1000 ■ *Web:* www.cem.va.gov/cems/nchp/sanfrancisco.asp

San Francisco Opera
301 Van Ness Ave. San Francisco CA 94102 415-861-4008 573-2
TF: 800-308-2898 ■ *Web:* www.sfopera.com

San Francisco Public Library
100 Larkin St San Francisco CA 94102 415-557-4400 557-4239 434-3
Web: www.sfpl.org

San Francisco Reservations
360 22nd St Ste 300. Oakland CA 94612 510-628-4450 376

San Francisco State University
1600 Holloway Ave. San Francisco CA 94132 415-338-1111 338-7196* 166
**Fax:* Admissions ■ *Web:* www.sfsu.edu

San Francisco Symphony
201 Van Ness Ave. San Francisco CA 94102 415-864-6000 573-3
Web: www.sfsymphony.org

San Francisco Theological Seminary
105 Seminary Rd San Anselmo CA 94960 415-451-2800 451-2851 167-3
TF: 800-447-0020 ■ *Web:* www.sfts.edu

San Francisco Travel Assn
201 Third St Ste 900. San Francisco CA 94103 415-974-6900 227-2602 206
TF: 855-847-6272 ■ *Web:* www.sanfrancisco.travel

San Francisco Unified School District
555 Franklin St. San Francisco CA 94102 415-241-6000 685
Web: www.sfusd.edu

San Francisco VA Medical Ctr
4150 Clement St. San Francisco CA 94121 415-221-4810 374-8
TF: 877-487-2838 ■ *Web:* www.sanfrancisco.va.gov

San Francisco War Memorial & Performing Arts Ctr (SFWMPAC)
401 Van Ness Ave Rm 110 San Francisco CA 94102 415-621-6600 621-5091 572
Web: www.sfwmpac.org

San Francisco Zoo 1 Zoo Rd San Francisco CA 94132 415-753-7080 823
TF: 800-226-3369 ■ *Web:* www.sfzoo.org

San Gabriel Chamber of Commerce
620 W Santa Anita St San Gabriel CA 91776 626-576-2525 289-2901 139
TF: 800-229-2343 ■ *Web:* sangabrielchamber.org

San Gabriel Mission
428 S Mission Dr San Gabriel CA 91776 626-457-3035 282-5308 50-1
Web: www.sangabrielmissionchurch.org

San Gabriel Nursery & Florist
632 S San Gabriel Blvd. San Gabriel CA 91776 626-286-3782 323
Web: www.sgnurserynews.com/site

San Gabriel Valley Medical Ctr
438 W Las Tunas Dr San Gabriel CA 91776 626-289-5454 374-3
TF: 888-214-3874 ■ *Web:* www.sgvmc.com

San Gabriel Valley Newspaper Group
1210 N Azusa Canyon Rd. West Covina CA 91790 626-962-8811 637-8
Web: www.sgvn.com

San Isabel Electric
893 E Enterprise Dr. Pueblo West CO 81007 719-547-2160 547-2229 245
TF: 800-279-7432 ■ *Web:* www.siea.com

San Jacinto Battleground State Historic Site
3523 Battleground Rd. La Porte TX 77571 281-479-2431 479-5618 565
Web: tpwd.texas.gov

San Jacinto College
Central 8060 Spencer Hwy Pasadena TX 77505 281-476-1501 162
TF: 800-725-6465 ■ *Web:* www.sanjac.edu
North 5800 Uvalde Rd. Houston TX 77049 281-458-4050 459-7688* 162
**Fax:* Admissions ■ *TF:* 800-877-8339 ■ *Web:* www.sanjac.edu
South 13735 Beamer Rd Houston TX 77089 281-998-6150 922-3485 162
Web: www.sanjac.edu

San Jacinto County
1 State Hwy 150 Rm 2 Coldspring TX 77331 936-653-2324 653-5604 338
Web: www.co.san-jacinto.tx.us

San Jacinto Mall
1496 San Jacinto Mall Baytown TX 77521 281-421-3908 421-7377 460
Web: www.sanjacintomall.com

San Jacinto Methodist Hospital (SJMH)
4401 Garth Rd Baytown TX 77521 281-420-8600 374-3
Web: www.houstonmethodist.org

San Jacinto Museum of History
1 Monument Cir. La Porte TX 77571 281-479-2421 520
Web: www.sanjacinto-museum.org

San Jacinto River Authority
1577 Dam Site Rd. Conroe TX 77304 936-588-1111 787
Web: www.sjra.net

San Jacinto Valley Academy Inc
480 N San Jacinto Ave San Jacinto CA 92583 951-654-6113 685
Web: www.sjva.net

San Jamar Inc 555 Koopman Ln. Elkhorn WI 53121 262-723-6133 14
TF: 800-248-9826 ■ *Web:* www.sanjamar.com

San Joaquin College of Law
901 Fifth St. Clovis CA 93612 559-323-2100 166
Web: www.sjcl.edu

San Joaquin Community Hospital
2615 Eye St Bakersfield CA 93301 661-395-3000 374-3
Web: www.adventisthealth.org/sjch/pages/default.aspx

San Joaquin County
222 E Weber Ave Second Fl Rm 202 PO Box 990. Stockton CA 95201 209-468-2400 468-0371 338
Web: www.sjgov.org

Phone | Fax | Class

San Joaquin County Fairgrounds
1658 S Airport Way ... Stockton CA 95206 209-466-5041 466-5739 642
Web: sanjoaquinfairgrounds.com

San Joaquin County Historical Society & Museum
11793 N Micke Grove Rd ... Lodi CA 95240 209-331-2055 331-2057 520
Web: www.sanjoaquinhistory.org

San Joaquin Delta College
5151 Pacific Ave ... Stockton CA 95207 209-954-5151 954-5769* 162
**Fax:* Admissions ■ *TF:* 800-835-4611 ■ *Web:* www.deltacollege.edu

San Joaquin Gardens 5555 N Fresno St ... Fresno CA 93710 559-435-1999 672
TF: 800-333-3333 ■ *Web:* theterracesatsanjoaquin.com

San Joaquin General Hospital (SJGH)
500 W Hospital Rd ... French Camp CA 95231 209-468-6000 374-3

San Joaquin Helicopters
1407 S Lexington ... Delano CA 93215 661-725-1898 725-5401 359
TF: 800-661-8041 ■ *Web:* www.sjhelicopters.com

San Joaquin Hotel 1309 W Shaw Ave ... Fresno CA 93711 559-225-1309 379
Web: www.sjhotel.com

San Joaquin Refining Company Inc
3129 Standard St ... Bakersfield CA 93308 661-327-4257 327-3236 580
Web: www.sjr.com

San Joaquin Valley National Cemetery
32053 W McCabe Rd ... Santa Nella CA 95322 209-854-1040 854-3944 136
Web: www.cem.va.gov/cems/nchp/sanjoaquinvalley.asp

San Joaquin Valley Rehabilitation Hospital
7173 N Sharon Ave ... Fresno CA 93720 559-436-3600 374-6
Web: www.sanjoaquinrehab.com

San Jose Boiler Works Inc
1585 Schallenberger Rd ... San Jose CA 95131 408-295-5235 612
Web: www.sanjoseboiler.com

San Jose City College
2100 Moorpark Ave ... San Jose CA 95128 408-298-2181 298-1935* 162
**Fax:* Admissions ■ *TF:* 888-397-4339 ■ *Web:* www.sjcc.edu

San Jose City Hall
200 Santa Clara St ... San Jose CA 95113 408-535-3500 292-6731 337
Web: www.sanjoseca.gov

San Jose Convention & Visitors Bureau
408 Almaden Blvd ... San Jose CA 95110 408-295-9600 277-3535 206
TF: 800-726-5673 ■ *Web:* www.sanjose.org

San Jose Convention Ctr (SJC)
150 W San Carlos St ... San Jose CA 95110 408-792-4194 277-3535 205
TF: 800-726-5673 ■ *Web:* www.sanjose.org

San Jose Ctr for the Performing Arts
255 Almaden Blvd ... San Jose CA 95113 408-792-4111 277-3535 572
TF: 800-726-5673 ■ *Web:* www.sanjose.org

San Jose Delta Assoc Inc
482 Sapena Ct ... Santa Clara CA 95054 408-727-1448 727-6019 500
TF: 800-290-2796 ■ *Web:* www.sanjosedelta.com

San Jose Downtown Association
28 N First St Ste 1000 ... San Jose CA 95113 408-279-1775 533
Web: www.sjdowntown.com

San Jose Film Festival - CineQuest
PO Box 720040 ... San Jose CA 95172 408-995-5033 282
Web: www.cinequest.org

San Jose Heritage Rose Garden (SJHRG)
438 Coleman Ave ... San Jose CA 95110 408-298-7657 97
Web: www.grpg.org

San Jose Mailing & Printing
1445 Monterey Hwy ... San Jose CA 95110 408-971-1911 5
TF: 800-560-0400 ■ *Web:* sanjosemailing.com

San Jose Mercury News
750 Ridder Pk Dr ... San Jose CA 95190 408-920-5000 288-8060 532-2
Web: www.mercurynews.com

San Jose Municipal Stadium
588 E Alma Ave ... San Jose CA 95112 408-297-1435 297-1453 720
Web: www.milb.com

San Jose Museum of Art
110 S Market St ... San Jose CA 95113 408-271-6840 294-2977 520
TF: 800-258-3826 ■ *Web:* www.sjmusart.org

San Jose Museum of Quilts & Textiles
520 S First St ... San Jose CA 95113 408-971-0323 520
Web: www.sjquiltmuseum.org

San Jose Public Library
150 E San Fernando St ... San Jose CA 95113 408-808-2000 434-3
TF: 800-735-2929 ■ *Web:* www.sjpl.org

San Jose Redevelopment Agency
200 E Santa Clara St 14th Fl ... San Jose CA 95113 408-535-8500 261
Web: www.sjredevelopment.org

San Jose Silicon Valley Chamber of Commerce (SJSVCC)
101 W Santa Clara St ... San Jose CA 95113 408-291-5250 286-5019 139
Web: www.sjchamber.com

San Jose Stage Co 490 S First St ... San Jose CA 95113 408-283-7142 573-4
Web: www.sanjose-stage.com

San Jose State University
1 Washington Sq ... San Jose CA 95192 408-924-1000 924-2050 166
TF: 800-273-8255 ■ *Web:* www.sjsu.edu

San Jose Unified School District
855 Lenzen Ave ... San Jose CA 95126 408-535-6000 535-2377* 685
**Fax:* Hum Res ■ *TF:* 800-433-3243 ■ *Web:* www.sjusd.org

San Juan Airlines Co
4000 Airport Rd Ste A ... Anacortes WA 98221 360-293-4691 13
TF: 800-874-4434 ■ *Web:* www.sanjuanairlines.com

San Juan Capistrano Chamber of Commerce
31421 La Matanza St ... San Juan Capistrano CA 92675 949-493-4700 489-2695 139
Web: www.sanjuanchamber.com

San Juan College 4601 College Blvd ... Farmington NM 87402 505-326-3311 566-3500* 162
**Fax:* Admissions ■ *TF:* 866-426-1233 ■ *Web:* www.sanjuancollege.edu

San Juan County 100 S Oliver Dr ... Aztec NM 87410 505-334-9481 334-3168 338
Web: www.sjcounty.net

San Juan County
350 Ct St Number 5 ... Friday Harbor WA 98250 360-378-2163 378-3967 338
TF: 800-762-3716 ■ *Web:* www.sanjuanco.com

San Juan County PO Box 338 ... Monticello UT 84535 435-587-3223 587-2425 338
Web: www.sanjuancounty.org

San Juan County 1557 Greene St ... Silverton CO 81433 970-387-5671 338
TF: 800-251-5866 ■ *Web:* sanjuancountycolorado.us

San Juan Golf & Country Club Golf Shop
806 Golf Course Rd ... Friday Harbor WA 98250 360-378-2254 711
TF: 800-451-8910 ■ *Web:* www.sjgolfclub.com

San Juan Island National Historical Park
4668 Cattle Point Rd PO Box 429 ... Friday Harbor WA 98250 360-378-2240 378-2615 564
Web: www.nps.gov/sajh

San Juan National Historic Site
501 Norzagaray St ... San Juan PR 00901 787-729-6960 289-7972 564
Web: www.nps.gov/saju

San Juan Regional Medical Ctr
801 W Maple St ... Farmington NM 87401 505-609-2000 374-3
TF: 800-642-7828 ■ *Web:* www.sanjuanregional.com

San Leandro Adult School
2255 Bancroft Ave ... San Leandro CA 94577 510-618-4420 685
Web: www.sanleandro.k12.ca.us

San Leandro Chamber of Commerce
120 Estudillo Ave ... San Leandro CA 94577 510-317-1400 139
Web: www.sanleandrochamber.com

San Lorenzo Unified School District (SLZUSD)
15510 Usher St ... San Lorenzo CA 94580 510-317-4600 685
Web: www.slzusd.org

San Luis Butane Distributors Inc
PO Box 3068 ... Paso Robles CA 93447 805-239-0616 579
Web: www.deltaliquidenergy.com

San Luis Garbage Co
4388 Old Santa Fe Rd ... San Luis Obispo CA 93401 805-543-0875 804
Web: wasteconnections.com

San Luis Obispo Botanical Garden
3450 Dairy Creek Rd ... San Luis Obispo CA 93405 805-541-1400 541-1466 97
Web: www.slobg.org

San Luis Obispo Chamber of Commerce
1039 Chorro St ... San Luis Obispo CA 93401 805-781-2777 543-1255 139
TF: 800-634-1414 ■ *Web:* www.slochamber.org

San Luis Obispo City-County Library
995 Palm St ... San Luis Obispo CA 93401 805-781-5991 434-3
Web: www.slolibrary.org

San Luis Obispo County
1055 Monterey St ... San Luis Obispo CA 93408 805-781-5000 834-4636* 338
**Fax Area Code:* 800 ■ *TF:* 800-834-4636 ■ *Web:* www.slocounty.ca.gov

San Luis Obispo High School
1499 San Luis Dr ... San Luis Obispo CA 93401 805-596-4040 685
Web: www.slcusd.org

San Luis Obispo New Times
505 Higuera St ... San Luis Obispo CA 93401 805-546-8208 546-8641 532-5
TF: 800-546-4219 ■ *Web:* www.newtimesslo.com

San Luis Resort Spa & Conference Ctr
5222 Seawall Blvd ... Galveston Island TX 77551 409-744-1500 744-8452 669
TF Cust Svc: 800-445-0090 ■ *Web:* www.sanluisresort.com

San Luis Rey Downs
5772 Camino Del Rey ... Bonsall CA 92003 760-724-1098 642

San Luis State Park & Wildlife Area
PO Box 150 ... Mosca CO 81146 719-378-2020 565
Web: cpw.state.co.us

San Luis Tallow Co
445 Prado Rd ... San Luis Obispo CA 93401 805-543-8660 296-12

San Luis Valley Regional Medical Ctr
106 Blanca Ave ... Alamosa CO 81101 719-589-2511 374-3
Web: www.sanluisvalleyhealth.org

San Luis Valley Rural Electric Co-op
3625 US Hwy 160 W ... Monte Vista CO 81144 719-852-3538 245
TF: 800-332-7634 ■ *Web:* www.slvrec.com

San Manuel Amphitheater
2575 Glen Helen Pkwy ... San Bernardino CA 92407 909-880-6500 572
Web: www.livenation.com

San Manuel Indian Bingo & Casino
777 San Manuel Blvd ... Highland CA 92346 800-359-2464 133
TF: 800-359-2464 ■ *Web:* www.sanmanuel.com

San Marcos Academy
2801 Ranch to Market 12 ... San Marcos TX 78666 512-353-2400 753-8031 622
TF Admissions: 800-428-5120 ■ *Web:* www.smabears.org

San Marcos Area Chamber of Commerce
202 N CM Allen Pkwy ... San Marcos TX 78666 512-393-5900 393-5912 139
Web: www.sanmarcostexas.com

San Marcos Chamber of Commerce
904 W San Marcos Blvd ... San Marcos CA 92078 760-744-1270 744-5230 139
TF: 800-814-7241 ■ *Web:* www.sanmarcoschamber.com

San Marcos de Apalache Historic State Park
148 Old Ft Rd ... Saint Marks FL 32327 850-925-6216 565
Web: www.floridastateparks.org

San Marcos Public Library
625 E Hopkins St ... San Marcos TX 78666 512-393-8200 754-8131 434-3
Web: www.ci.san-marcos.tx.us

San Marino Ristorante 66 Charlton St ... New York NY 10014 212-206-3766 206-8147 784
Web: www.sanmarinosoho.com

San Mateo Area Chamber of Commerce
1700 S El Camino Real Ste 108 ... San Mateo CA 94402 650-401-2440 139
TF: 800-799-1737 ■ *Web:* www.sanmateoca.org

San Mateo County
455 County Ctr 4th Fl ... Redwood City CA 94063 650-599-1388 338
Web: www.smcgov.org

San Mateo County Convention & Visitors Bureau
111 Anza Blvd Ste 410 ... Burlingame CA 94010 650-348-7600 348-7687 206
TF: 800-288-4748 ■ *Web:* www.smccvb.com

San Mateo County Times
477 Ninth Ave Ste 110 ... San Mateo CA 94402 408-920-5000 348-4446* 532-2
**Fax Area Code:* 650 ■ *TF:* 800-870-6397 ■ *Web:* www.mercurynews.com/san-mateo-county

San Mateo County Transit District
1250 San Carlos Ave PO Box 3006 ... San Carlos CA 94070 650-508-6200 468
TF: 800-660-4287 ■ *Web:* www.smctd.com

San Mateo Marriott
1770 S Amphlett Blvd ... San Mateo CA 94402 650-653-6000 379
Web: www.sanmateomarriott.com

San Miguel County
500 W National St Ste 200 ... Las Vegas NM 87701 505-425-9333 425-7019 338
Web: www.smcounty.net

San Miguel County PO Box 548 ... Telluride CO 81435 970-728-3954 728-4808 338
Web: www.sanmiguelcounty.org

San Miguel Joint Un School Dst.
1601 L St ... San Miguel CA 93451 805-467-3216 685
Web: www.sanmiguelschools.org

San Miguel Mission
401 Old Santa Fe Trl ... Santa Fe NM 87501 505-983-3974 50-1

Phone | Fax | Class

San Miguel Power Assn Inc
170 W Tenth Ave ... Nucla CO 81424 970-864-7311 864-7257 245
TF: 800-864-7256 ■ *Web:* www.smpa.com

San Miguel Produce Inc
4444 Naval Air Rd ... Oxnard CA 93033 805-488-0981 10-11
Web: www.cutnclean.com

San Pablo Chamber of Commerce
13925 San Pablo Ave ... San Pablo CA 94806 510-234-2067 234-0604 139
Web: ci.san-pablo.ca.us

San Pasqual Battlefield State Historic Park
15808 San Pasqual Valley Rd ... Escondido CA 92027 760-737-2201 565
Web: www.parks.ca.gov

San Pasqual Fiduciary Trust Co
550 S Hope St Ste 550 ... Los Angeles CA 90071 213-452-8500 41
Web: www.spftc.com

San Patricio Electric Co-op Inc
402 E Sinton St ... Sinton TX 78387 361-364-2220 364-3467 245
TF: 888-740-2220 ■ *Web:* www.sanpatricioelectric.org

San Pedro Peninsula Chamber of Commerce
390 W Seventh St ... San Pedro CA 90731 310-832-7272 832-0685 139
Web: www.sanpedrochamber.com

San Pedro Playhouse
800 W Ashby Pl PO Box 12356 ... San Antonio TX 78212 210-733-7258 734-2651 572
Web: www.theplayhousesa.org

San Pedro Underwater Archaeological Preserve State Park
US 1 ... Islamorada FL 33036 305-664-2540 565
Web: www.floridastateparks.org/sanpedro

San Rafael Chamber of Commerce
817 Mission Ave ... San Rafael CA 94901 415-454-4163 454-7039 139
Web: srchamber.com

San Rafael Public Library
1400 Fifth Ave ... San Rafael CA 94901 415-485-3323 434-3
Web: www.cityofsanrafael.org

San Rafael Ranch State Park
2036 Duquesne Rd ... Patagonia AZ 85624 520-394-2447 565
Web: azstateparks.com

San Ramon Chamber of Commerce
2410 Camino Ramon #125 ... San Ramon CA 94583 925-242-0600 242-0603 139
TF: 800-786-1000 ■ *Web:* www.sanramon.org

San Ramon Valley Conference Ctr
3301 Crow Canyon Rd ... San Ramon CA 94583 925-866-7500 377
Web: www.sanramonvalleyconferencecenter.com

San Saba County 500 E Wallace Ste 202 ... San Saba TX 76877 325-372-3614 372-6484 338
Web: www.co.san-saba.tx.us

San Sebastian Winery
157 King St ... Saint Augustine FL 32084 904-826-1594 826-1595 50-7
TF: 888-352-9463 ■ *Web:* www.sansebastianwinery.com

San Vicente Inn & Golf Course
24157 San Vicente Rd ... Ramona CA 92065 760-789-3788 788-6115 669
TF: 800-776-1289 ■ *Web:* www.sdcea.net

San Xavier Del Bac Mission
1950 W San Xavier Rd ... Tucson AZ 85746 520-294-2624 50-1
Web: www.sanxaviermission.org

San Ysidro Chamber of Commerce
663 E San Ysidro Blvd ... San Ysidro CA 92173 619-428-1281 139
Web: www.sanysidrochamber.org

San Ysidro Ranch
900 San Ysidro Ln ... Santa Barbara CA 93108 805-565-1700 565-1995 669
Web: www.sanysidroranch.com

San Ysidro School District
4350 Otay Mesa Rd ... San Ysidro CA 92173 619-428-4476 428-9355 685
Web: www.sysd.k12.ca.us

Sanaa's 401 E Eigth St ... Sioux Falls SD 57103 605-275-2516 671
Web: sanaacooks.com

SanBio Inc 231 S Whisman Rd ... Mountain View CA 94041 650-625-8965 668
Web: www.san-bio.com

SANBlaze Technology Inc
1 Monarch Dr Ste 204 ... Littleton MA 01460 978-679-1400 173-8
Web: www.sanblaze.com

Sanborn Chevrolet Inc 1210 S Cherokee Ln ... Lodi CA 95240 209-642-4954 516
Web: www.sanbornchevrolet.com

Sanborn County PO Box 56 ... Woonsocket SD 57385 605-796-4515 338
Web: ujs.sd.gov

Sanborn Head & Assoc Inc
20 Foundry St ... Concord NH 03301 603-229-1900 261
Web: sanbornhead.com

Sancap Abrasives 16123 Armour St NE ... Alliance OH 44601 330-821-3510 821-3516 1
TF: 800-433-6663

Sancap Liner Technology Inc
16125 Armour St NE ... Alliance OH 44601 330-821-1166 600
Web: www.sancapliner.com

Sanchez Linda (Rep D - CA)
2329 Rayburn HOB ... Washington DC 20515 202-225-6676 226-1012 342-2
Web: lindasanchez.house.gov

Sanctuary at Bellbrook
873 W Avon Rd ... Rochester Hills MI 48307 248-656-6300 450
Web: www.trinityhealthseniorcommunities.org/bellbrook-rochester-hills

Sanctuary Beach Resort Monterey Bay
3295 Dunes Rd ... Marina CA 93933 831-883-9478 707
TF: 855-693-6583 ■ *Web:* www.thesanctuarybeachresort.com

Sanctuary for Families Po Box 1406 ... New York NY 10268 212-349-6009 428
Web: www.sanctuaryforfamilies.org

Sanctuary Marketing Group Inc
219 E Maple St Ste 125 ... North Canton OH 44720 330-266-1188 5
TF: 800-438-7325 ■ *Web:* www.sanctuarymg.com

Sanctuary on Camelback Mountain
5700 E McDonald Dr ... Paradise Valley AZ 85253 480-948-2100 669
TF: 800-245-2051 ■ *Web:* www.sanctuaryoncamelback.com

Sand Assoc 3560 Green St ... Harrisburg PA 17110 717-238-5558 238-4626 184
Web: www.sandassociates.com

Sand Bar State Park 1215 US Rt 2 ... Milton VT 05468 802-893-2825 565
Web: www.vtstateparks.com

Sand Bridge State Park
c/o R B Winter State Pk 17215 Buffalo Rd ... Mifflinburg PA 17844 570-966-1455 565
Web: www.dcnr.state.pa.us

Sand Cherry Associates Inc
8 Sand Cherry ... Littleton CO 80127 303-933-9494 463
Web: www.sandcherryassociates.com

Sand Creek Massacre National Historic Site
910 Wansted ... Eads CO 81036 719-438-5916 564
Web: www.nps.gov/sand

Sand Creek Post & Beam 116 W First St ... Wayne NE 68787 402-833-5600 106
TF: 800-561-3357 ■ *Web:* www.sandcreekpostandbeam.com

Sand Dunes Resort Hotel
201 74th Ave N ... Myrtle Beach SC 29572 800-726-3783 669
TF: 800-726-3783 ■ *Web:* www.sandsresorts.com

Sand Hollow State Park
4405 W 3600 S ... Hurricane UT 84737 435-680-0715 565
Web: www.stateparks.utah.gov

Sand Island State Recreation Area
PO Box 621 ... Honolulu HI 96809 808-832-3781 565
Web: dlnr.hawaii.gov

Sand Lake Imaging 9350 Turkey Lake Rd ... Orlando FL 32819 407-363-2772 415
Web: www.sandlakeimaging.com

Sand Mountain Electric Co-op
402 Main St W ... Rainsville AL 35986 256-638-2153 245
TF: 877-843-2512 ■ *Web:* www.smec.coop

Sand Mountain Reporter
1603 Progress Dr ... Albertville AL 35950 256-840-2987 532-3
Web: www.sandmountainreporter.com

Sand Pearl Resort LLC
500 Mandalay Ave ... Clearwater Beach FL 33767 727-441-2425 378
TF: 800-456-7263 ■ *Web:* www.sandpearl.com

Sand Ridge State Forest
PO Box 111 ... Forest City IL 61532 309-597-2212 565
Web: www.dnr.illinois.gov/Parks/Pages/SandRidge.aspx

Sand Seed Service Inc 4765 Hwy 143 ... Marcus IA 51035 712-376-4135 376-4140 694
TF: 800-352-2228 ■ *Web:* www.sandsofiowa.com

Sand Steel Bldg Co 101 Browell St ... Emerado ND 58228 701-594-4435 594-4438 189-1
Web: www.sandsteelbuilding.com

Sand Technology Inc 8 Ave SW Ste 920 ... Calgary AB T2P3S8 403-218-2010 178-1
NYSE: SNDTF ■ *TF:* 877-468-2538 ■ *Web:* www.sand.com

Sandals Resorts International
4950 SW 72nd Ave ... Miami FL 33155 305-284-1300 669
TF: 888-726-3257 ■ *Web:* www.sandals.com

Sandalwood Securities Inc
101 Eisenhower Pkwy ... Roseland NJ 07068 973-228-5466 796
Web: www.sandalwoodsecurities.com

Sandata Technologies Inc
26 Harbor Pk Dr ... Port Washington NY 11050 516-484-4400 484-6084 178-11
TF Sales: 800-544-7263 ■ *Web:* www.sandata.com

Sandbar Waterfront Restaurant
100 Spring Ave ... Anna Maria FL 34216 941-778-0444 778-3997 671
Web: sandbar.groupersandwich.com

Sandbox Industries Inc
1000 W Fulton Market Ste 213 ... Chicago IL 60607 312-243-4100 295
Web: www.sandboxindustries.com

Sandcastle Water Park
1000 Sandcastle Dr ... Pittsburgh PA 15120 412-462-6666 462-0827 32
Web: www.sandcastlewaterpark.com

Sandel Avionics Inc 2401 Dogwood Way ... Vista CA 92081 760-727-4900 21
TF: 877-726-3357 ■ *Web:* www.sandel.com

Sandella's LLC 263 Farmington Ave ... Farmington CT 06030 203-544-9984 544-9981 670
Web: www.sandellas.com

Sandelman & Assoc Inc
257 La Paloma Ste 1 ... San Clemente CA 92672 949-388-5600 668
TF: 888-897-7881 ■ *Web:* www.sandelman.com

Sanden International (USA) Inc
601 S Sanden Blvd ... Wylie TX 75098 972-442-8400 172
Web: www.sanden.com

Sanderling
400 S El Camino Real Ste 1200 ... San Mateo CA 94402 650-401-2000 792
Web: www.sanderling.com

Sanderling Resort & Spa 1461 Duck Rd ... Duck NC 27949 252-261-4111 669
TF: 800-701-4111 ■ *Web:* www.sanderling-resort.com

Sanders 1907 22 S Third St ... Grand Forks ND 58201 701-746-8970 671

Sanders Bernard (Sen I - VT)
332 Dirksen Bldg ... Washington DC 20510 202-224-5141 228-0776 342-2
Web: www.sanders.senate.gov

Sanders Bros Inc 1709 Old Georgia Hwy ... Gaffney SC 29341 864-489-1144 480
Web: www.sandersbros.com

Sanders County
111 Main St PO Box 519 ... Thompson Falls MT 59873 406-827-6942 827-4388 338
Web: co.sanders.mt.us

Sanders Ford Inc
1135 Lejeune Blvd ... Jacksonville NC 28540 910-455-1911 516
TF General: 888-897-8527 ■ *Web:* sandersfordsales.com

Sanders Software Consulting Inc
3008 W 30th St ... Lawrence KS 66047 785-865-5111 175
Web: www.sanderssoftware.com

Sanders/Wingo Adv Inc
221 N Kansas Ste 900 ... El Paso TX 79901 915-533-9583 4
Web: www.sanderswingo.com

Sanderson Industries Inc
3550 Atlanta Industrial Pkwy ... Atlanta GA 30331 404-699-2022 489

Sanderson-MacLeod Inc
1199 S Main St PO Box 50 ... Palmer MA 01069 413-283-3481 289-1919 103
TF: 866-522-3481 ■ *Web:* www.sandersonmacleod.com

Sandestin Golf & Beach Resort
9300 Emerald Coast Pkwy W ... Sandestin FL 32550 850-267-8000 669
TF: 800-277-0800 ■ *Web:* www.sandestin.com

Sandhill Regional Library System
412 E Franklin St ... Rockingham NC 28379 910-997-3388 434-3
Web: www.ncmail.net

Sandhill TelephoneCo-op Inc
PO Box 519 ... Jefferson SC 29718 843-658-3434 658-7700 736
Web: www.shtc.net

Sandhills Bank 300 King St E ... Bethune SC 29009 843-334-2265 70
Web: www.sandhillsbank.com

Sandhills Community College
3395 Airport Rd ... Pinehurst NC 28374 910-692-6185 695-3981* 162
**Fax:* Admissions ■ *TF:* 800-338-3944 ■ *Web:* www.sandhills.edu

Sandhills Horticultural Gardens
3395 Airport Rd ... Pinehurst NC 28374 910-695-3882 97
Web: sandhillshorticulturalgardens.com

Sandhills Publishing 120 W Harvest Dr ... Lincoln NE 68521 402-479-2181 479-2195 637-9
TF: 800-331-1978 ■ *Web:* www.sandhills.com

Phone | Fax | Class

Sandia National Laboratories - California (SNL)
7011 E Ave PO Box 969 .... Livermore CA 94551 925-294-3000 668
Web: www.sandia.gov

Sandia National Laboratories - New Mexico (SNL)
1515 Eubank SE PO Box 5800 .... Albuquerque NM 87123 505-845-0011 668
TF: 800-356-4872 ■ *Web:* www.sandia.gov

Sandia Resort & Casino
30 Rainbow Rd NE .... Albuquerque NM 87113 505-796-7500 133
TF: 800-526-9366 ■ *Web:* www.sandiacasino.com

Sandiago's Grill at the Tram
40 Tramway Rd NE .... Albuquerque NM 87122 505-856-6692 856-6692 671
Web: www.sandiapeakrestaurants.com

SanDisk Corp 601 McCarthy Blvd .... Milpitas CA 95035 408-801-1000 801-8657 288
NASDAQ: SNDK ■ *TF:* 866-726-3475 ■ *Web:* www.sandisk.com

Sandler O'Neill + Partners LP
1251 Avenue of the Americas 6th Fl ....New York NY 10020 212-466-7800 690
TF: 800-635-6851 ■ *Web:* www.sandleroneill.com

Sandler Partners
1200 Artesia Blvd Ste 305 .... Hermosa Beach CA 90254 310-796-1393 224
TF: 800-825-1055 ■ *Web:* www.sandlerpartners.com

Sandler Sales Institute
10411 Stevenson Rd...................... Stevenson MD 21153 410-653-1993 358-7858 765
Web: www.sandler.com

Sandman Hotels Inns & Suites
1755 W Broadway Ste 310 .... Vancouver BC V6J4S5 604-730-6600 730-4645 379
Web: www.sandmanhotels.ca

Sandmeyer Steel Co
1 Sandmeyer Ln .... Philadelphia PA 19116 215-464-7100 677-1430 723
TF: 800-523-3663 ■ *Web:* www.sandmeyersteel.com

Sandor Development Co
5725 N Scottsdale Rd Ste C-195 .... Scottsdale AZ 85250 480-949-9011 652
Web: sandordev.com

Sandoval Brian (R) Capitol Bldg............ Carson City NV 89701 775-684-5670 684-5683 343
Web: gov.nv.gov

Sandoval County
1500 Idalia Rd Bldg D...................... Bernalillo NM 87004 505-867-7500 338
Web: www.sandovalcountynm.gov

SandPoint Consulting Inc
2716 Colonial Way.................... Bloomfield Hills MI 48304-1625 248-481-2072 196
Web: www.sandpointc.com

Sandra Feinstein-Gamm Theatre
172 Exchange St.......................... Pawtucket RI 02860 401-723-4266 573-4
Web: www.gammtheatre.org

Sandridge Energy Inc
123 Robert S Kerr Ave.................. Oklahoma City OK 73102 405-429-5500 536
Web: www.sandridgeenergy.com

Sandridge Food Corp (SFC) 133 Commerce Dr.... Medina OH 44256 330-725-2348 722-3998 296-33
TF: 800-627-2523 ■ *Web:* www.sandridge.com

Sands Brothers Asset Management
15 Valley Dr .... Greenwich CT 06831 203-661-7500 690
Web: www.sandsbros.com

Sands Casino Resort Bethlehem
77 Sands Blvd .... Bethlehem PA 18015 877-726-3777 379
TF: 877-726-3777 ■ *Web:* www.pasands.com

Sands Central Inn
1525 Central Ave .... Hot Springs AR 71901 501-624-1258 379

Sands Expo & Convention Ctr
201 Sands Ave .... Las Vegas NV 89169 702-733-5556 733-5568 205
TF: 800-265-2235 ■ *Web:* www.sandsexpo.com

Sands Ocean Club Resort
9550 Shore Dr .... Myrtle Beach SC 29572 888-999-8485 379
TF General: 888-999-8485 ■ *Web:* www.sandsresorts.com

Sands Regency Casino Hotel
345 N Arlington Ave .... Reno NV 89501 775-348-2200 379
TF Resv: 800-233-4939 ■ *Web:* www.sandsregency.com

Sandstone Asset Management Inc
115 101 - Sixth St SW .... Calgary AB T2P5K7 403-218-6125 528
TF: 866-318-6140 ■ *Web:* www.sandstoneam.com

Sandstone Group Inc
223 N Water St Ste 500 .... Milwaukee WI 53202 414-902-6700 360-3
Web: www.diachemix.com

Sandstrom Trade & Technology Inc
610 Niagara St .... Welland ON L3B5Y5 905-732-1307 476

Sandt Products Inc 1275 Loop Rd............ Lancaster PA 17601 717-299-4900 548
Web: www.sandtproducts.com

Sandusky County 622 Croghan St .... Fremont OH 43420 419-334-6100 334-6104 338
Web: www.sandusky-county.com

Sandusky Electric Inc
1513 Sycamore Line......................... Sandusky OH 44870 419-625-4015 625-9438 246
TF: 800-356-1243 ■ *Web:* www.sanduskyelectric.com

Sandusky International Inc
615 W Market St............................ Sandusky OH 44870 419-626-5340 556

Sandusky Lee Corp
16125 Widmere Rd PO Box 517...................... Arvin CA 93203 661-854-5551 854-2003 286
TF Cust Svc: 800-886-8688 ■ *Web:* www.sanduskycabinets.com

Sandusky Packaging Corp
2016 George St............................. Sandusky OH 44870 419-626-8520 557
Web: www.sanduskypackaging.com

Sandusky Register 314 W Market St .... Sandusky OH 44870 419-625-5500 532-2
TF: 800-466-1243 ■ *Web:* www.sanduskyregister.com

Sandusky Speedway 614 W Perkins Ave .... Sandusky OH 44870 419-625-4084 515
Web: www.sanduskyspeedway.com

Sandusky-Chicago Abrasive Wheel Co
532 W Fourth St...................... Michigan City IN 46360 219-879-6601 1
TF: 800-843-4980 ■ *Web:* www.sanduskychicago.com

Sandvik Inc 1702 Nevins Rd .... Fair Lawn NJ 07410 201-794-5000 794-5165 360-3

Sandvik Mining & Construction USA LLC
13500 NW CR 235 .... Alachua FL 32615 386-462-4100 537
Web: www.miningandconstruction.sandvik.com

Sandvik Process Systems LLC
21 Campus Rd .... Totowa NJ 07512 973-790-1600 492
TF: 800-359-2358 ■ *Web:* www.processsystems.sandvik.com

Sandvik Special Metals LLC
235407 E SR 397 .... Kennewick WA 99337 509-586-4131 485
Web: www.smt.sandvik.com

Sandwich Glass Museum
129 Main St PO Box 103 .... Sandwich MA 02563 508-888-0251 888-4941 520
Web: www.sandwichglassmuseum.org

Sandwich Isle Pest Solutions Inc
96-1368 Waihona St......................... Pearl City HI 96782 808-456-7716 577
TF: 800-325-1671 ■ *Web:* www.sandwichisle.com

Sandwich Lodge & Resort
54 Rt 6A - Old King's Hwy.................... Sandwich MA 02563 508-888-2275 888-8102 379
TF: 800-282-5353 ■ *Web:* sandwichlodge.com

Sandy Alexander Inc 200 Entin Rd.............. Clifton NJ 07014 973-470-8100 627
Web: www.sandyinc.com

Sandy Area Chamber of Commerce
35 East 9270.................................. Sandy UT 84070 801-566-0344 566-0346 139
Web: www.sandychamber.com

Sandy Creek Covered Bridge State Historic Site
c/o Mastodon State Historic Site
1050 Museum Dr .... Imperial MO 63052 636-464-2976 565
Web: www.mostateparks.com

Sandy Farms 34500 SE Hwy 211................. Boring OR 97009 503-668-4525 315-1

Sandy Point State Park
1100 E College Pkwy .... Annapolis MD 21409 410-974-2149 565
TF: 877-620-8367 ■ *Web:* dnr2.maryland.gov

Sandy River Co
217 Commercial St PO Box 110................ Portland ME 04112 207-558-6053 652
Web: sandyrivercompany.com

Sandy Sansing Chevrolet
6200 N Pensacola Blvd...................... Pensacola FL 32505 850-476-2480 57
TF Sales: 888-885-1844 ■ *Web:* www.sandysansingchevrolet.com

Sandy Spring Bancorp Inc
17801 Georgia Ave............................ Olney MD 20832 301-774-6400 360-2
NASDAQ: SASR ■ *TF:* 800-399-5919 ■ *Web:* www.sandyspringbank.com

Sandy Spring Friends School
16923 Norwood Rd...................... Sandy Spring MD 20860 301-774-7455 924-1115 622
Web: www.ssfs.org

Sandy Valley Fasteners LLC
528 Broadway St.......................... Paintsville KY 41240 606-788-0222 350
Web: www.sandyvalleyfasteners.com

Sanese Services Inc 6465 Busch Blvd......... Columbus OH 43229 614-436-1234 299
TF: 800-589-3410 ■ *Web:* avifoodsystems.com

Sanexen Environmental Services Inc
9801 Rue la MartiniŠre........................ Varennes QC H1C1Z3 450-652-9990 192
Web: www.sanexen.com

Sanford & Company PA 812 Dequeen .... Mena AR 71953 479-394-5414 2
Web: sanford-cpa.com

Sanford Aircraft Services Inc
701 Rod Sullivan Rd.......................... Sanford NC 27330 919-708-5549 63
TF: 800-237-6902 ■ *Web:* www.sanford-aircraft.com

Sanford Area Chamber of Commerce
115 Chatham St Ste 4 PO Box 519............. Sanford NC 27330 919-775-7341 884-2547* 139
**Fax Area Code: 855* ■ *Web:* growsanfordnc.com/chamber

Sanford Chamber of Commerce
400 E First St .... Sanford FL 32771 407-322-2212 322-8160 139
Web: www.sanfordchamber.com

Sanford Consortium For Regenerative Medicine
2880 torrey pines scenic dr .... La jolla CA 92037 858-246-1071 743
TF: 800-222-1222 ■ *Web:* www.sanfordconsortium.org

Sanford Correctional Ctr
417 Prison Camp Rd .... Sanford NC 27330 919-776-4325 774-1866 213
Web: www.ncdps.gov

Sanford Health 1300 Anne St NW.............. Bemidji MN 56601 218-751-5430 374-3
TF: 800-833-8979 ■ *Web:* www.nchs.com

Sanford Herald, The 217 E First St .... Sanford FL 32771 407-322-2611 323-9408 532-2
TF: 800-955-8770 ■ *Web:* www.mysanfordherald.com

Sanford J Greenburger Assoc Inc
55 Fifth Ave................................ New York NY 10003 212-206-5600 463-8718 444
Web: www.greenburger.com

Sanford Mark R (Rep R - SC)
2211 Rayburn HOB........................ Washington DC 20515 202-225-3176 342-2
Web: sanford.house.gov

Sanford Museum & Planetarium
117 E Willow St .... Cherokee IA 51012 712-225-3922 598
Web: www.sanfordmuseum.org

Sanford Organization Inc, The (TSO)
1000 N Rand Rd Ste 214 .... Wauconda IL 60084 847-526-2010 526-3993 47
TF: 800-353-6878 ■ *Web:* www.tso.net

Sanford Restaurant
1547 N Jackson St .... Milwaukee WI 53202 414-276-9608 278-8509 671
Web: www.sanfordrestaurant.com

Sanford Rose Associates International Inc
6860 Dallas Pkwy Ste 302 .... Plano TX 75287 972-616-7870 260
Web: sanfordrose.net

Sanford USD Medical Ctr
1305 W 18th St........................... Sioux Falls SD 57117 605-333-1000 374-3
Web: www.sanfordhealth.org

Sanford's Grub & Pub LLC
61 SE Wyoming Blvd .... Casper WY 82609 307-315-6040 671
Web: thegrubandpub.com

Sanford-Brown
1345 Mendota Heights Rd .... Mendota Heights MN 55120 651-905-3400 800
TF: 888-247-4238 ■ *Web:* www.browncollege.edu

Sanford-Brown College
Boston 126 Newbury St.......................... Boston MA 02116 617-578-7100 800
TF: 877-809-2444 ■ *Web:* www.sanfordbrown.edu

Sanford-Springvale Chamber of Commerce
917 Main St Ste B............................ Sanford ME 04073 207-324-4280 139
Web: sanfordspringvalechamberofcommerce.wildapricot.org

Sangamo BioSciences Inc
501 Canal Blvd Ste A100 .... Richmond CA 94804 510-970-6000 236-8951 85
NASDAQ: SGMO ■ *Web:* www.sangamo.com

Sangamon Antique Mall
3050 E Sangamon Ave...................... Springfield IL 62702 217-522-7740 460

Sangamon County
200 S Ninth St Rm 204...................... Springfield IL 62701 217-753-6700 338
Web: www.co.sangamon.il.us

Sanganois State Fish & Wildlife Area
3594 County Rd 200 N.................... Chandlerville IL 62627 309-546-2628 565
Web: www.dnr.illinois.gov/hunting/factsheets/pages/sanganois.aspx

Sangchris Lake State Park
9898 Cascade Rd .... Rochester IL 62563 217-498-9208 565
Web: www.dnr.illinois.gov/Parks/Pages/SangchrisLake.aspx

Phone | Fax | Class

Sanger & Eby Design LLC
501 Chestnut St .... Cincinnati OH 45203 513 784-9046 344
Web: www.sangereby.com

Sangre de Cristo Arts & Conference Ctr
210 N Santa Fe Ave .... Pueblo CO 81003 719-295-7200 295-7230 572
TF: 800-247-2336 ■ *Web:* www.sdc-arts.org

Sangre de Cristo Electric Assn
29780 US Hwy 24 .... Buena Vista CO 81211 719-395-2412 395-8742 245
TF: 800-933-3823 ■ *Web:* www.myelectric.coop

Sangre de Cristo Hospice
1207 Pueblo Blvd Way .... Pueblo CO 81005 719-542-0032 371
Web: socohospice.org

Sanibel & Captiva Islands Chamber of Commerce
1159 Cswy Rd .... Sanibel FL 33957 239-472-1080 472-1070 139
TF: 800-851-5088 ■ *Web:* www.sanibel-captiva.org

Sanibel Harbour Marriott Resort & Spa
17260 Harbour Pt Dr .... Fort Myers FL 33908 239-466-4000 466-2266 669
TF: 800-767-7777 ■ *Web:* www.marriott.com

Sanibel Inn 937 E Gulf Dr .... Sanibel FL 33957 239-472-3181 379
TF: 866-565-5480 ■ *Web:* www.theinnsofsanibel.com

Sani-Clean Distributors
57 Industrial Way .... Portland ME 04103 207-797-8240 406

Sanilac County
60 W Sanilac Ave Rm 203 .... Sandusky MI 48471 810-648-3212 648-5466 338
Web: www.sanilaccounty.net

SaniServ Inc 451 E County Line Rd .... Mooresville IN 46158 317-831-7030 831-7036 298
TF: 800-733-8073 ■ *Web:* www.saniserv.com

Sanitary Services Co Inc
21 Bellwether Way Ste 404 .... Bellingham WA 98225 360-734-3490 671-0239 804
TF: 888-333-9882 ■ *Web:* www.ssc-inc.com

Sanitation District 1 of Northern Kentucky
1045 Eaton Dr .... Fort Wright KY 41017 859-578-7450 804
Web: www.sd1.org

Sanky Perlowin Assoc Inc
Sanky Communications Inc
599 11th Ave 6th Fl .... New York NY 10036 212-868-4300 317
Web: www.sankyinc.com

Sanli Pastore & Hill Inc
Sanli Pastore & Hill 1990 S Bundy Dr
Ste 800 .... Los Angeles CA 90025 310-571-3400 194
Web: www.sphvalue.com

San-Mar Laboratories Inc
4 Warehouse Ln .... Elmsford NY 10523 914-592-3130 231
Web: processtechnologies.com

Sanmina Corp 2700 N First St .... San Jose CA 95134 408-964-3500 964-3440 625
NASDAQ: SANM ■ *Web:* www.sanmina-sci.com

Sanofi Pasteur Inc Discovery Dr .... Swiftwater PA 18370 570-839-7187 839-7187* 85
**Fax:* Hum Res ■ *TF Orders:* 800-822-2463 ■ *Web:* www.sanofipasteur.us

Sanofi-Aventis Canada
2150 St Elzear Blvd W .... Laval QC H7L4A8 514 331 9220 85
TF: 800-363-6364 ■ *Web:* sanofi-aventis.ca/index.html

Sanofi-Aventis US LLC
55 Corporate Dr .... Bridgewater NJ 08807 908-981-5000 231
Web: sanofi.us

S-Anon International Family Groups Inc
PO Box 111242 .... Nashville TN 37222 615-833-3152 48-21
TF: 800-210-8141 ■ *Web:* www.sanon.org

Sanrio Inc 570 Eccles Ave .... South San Francisco CA 94080 650-952-2880 872-1077 328
TF: 800-759-6454 ■ *Web:* www.sanrio.com

Sans Inc 10 White Wood Ln .... North Branford CT 06471 203-488-0046 180
Web: www.sansinc.com

Sans Souci 24 Public Sq .... Cleveland OH 44113 216-902-4095 671
Web: www.marriott.com

Sansei Seafood Restaurant & Sushi Bar
Waikiki Beach Marriot Resort & Spa
2552 Kalakauna Ave .... Honolulu HI 96815 808-931-6286 671
Web: www.sanseihawaii.com

Sansiveri Kimball & Company LLP
55 Dorrance St .... Providence RI 02903 401-331-0500 2
Web: sansiveri.com

Sansom Street Oyster House
1516 Sansom St .... Philadelphia PA 19102 215-567-7683 671
Web: www.oysterhousephilly.com

Santa Ana Chamber of Commerce
1631 W Sunflower Ave Ste C35 .... Santa Ana CA 92704 714-541-5353 541-2238 139
TF: 800-587-4230 ■ *Web:* www.santaanachamber.com

Santa Ana City Hall
20 Civic Ctr Plaza .... Santa Ana CA 92701 714-647-6900 647-6954 337
Web: www.ci.santa-ana.ca.us

Santa Ana College 1530 W 17th St .... Santa Ana CA 92706 714-564-6000 564-6455* 162
**Fax:* Admissions ■ *Web:* www.sac.edu

Santa Ana Public Library
26 Civic Ctr Dr .... Santa Ana CA 92701 714-647-5250 434-3
Web: www.ci.santa-ana.ca.us/library

Santa Ana Star Casino
54 Jemez Dam Rd .... Bernalillo NM 87004 505-867-0000 452
Web: www.santaanastar.com

Santa Ana Zoo 1801 E Chestnut Ave .... Santa Ana CA 92701 714-835-7484 550-0346 823
Web: www.santaanazoo.org

Santa Anita Park 285 W Huntington Dr .... Arcadia CA 91007 626-574-7223 642
Web: www.santaanita.com

Santa Barbara Botanic Garden
1212 Mission Canyon Rd .... Santa Barbara CA 93105 805-682-4726 97
Web: www.sbbg.org

Santa Barbara City College
721 Cliff Dr .... Santa Barbara CA 93109 805-965-0581 963-7222* 162
**Fax:* Admissions ■ *TF:* 877-232-3919 ■ *Web:* www.sbcc.edu

Santa Barbara Control Systems
5375 Overpass Rd .... Santa Barbara CA 93111 805-683-8833 407
TF: 800-621-2279 ■ *Web:* www.sbcontrol.com

Santa Barbara Cottage Hospital
PO Box 689 .... Santa Barbara CA 93102 805-682-7111 374-3
TF: 800-273-8255 ■ *Web:* www.cottagehealth.org

Santa Barbara County PO Box 159 .... Santa Barbara CA 93102 805-568-2550 568-3247 338
Web: www.countyofsb.org

Santa Barbara Independent
122 W Figueroa St .... Santa Barbara CA 93101 805-965-5205 965-5518 532-5
Web: www.independent.com

Santa Barbara Infrared Inc
30 S Calle Cesar Chavez Ste D .... Santa Barbara CA 93103 805-965-3669 201
Web: www.sbir.com

Santa Barbara Inn
901 E Cabrillo Blvd .... Santa Barbara CA 93103 805-966-2285 379
TF: 800-231-0431 ■ *Web:* www.santabarbarainn.com

Santa Barbara International Film Festival
1528 Chapala St Ste 203 .... Santa Barbara CA 93101 805-963-0023 282
Web: sbiff.org

Santa Barbara Metropolitan Transit District
550 Olive St .... Santa Barbara CA 93101 805-963-3364 468
Web: www.sbmtd.gov

Santa Barbara Museum of Art
1130 State St .... Santa Barbara CA 93101 805-963-4364 966-6840 520
TF: 800-549-9869 ■ *Web:* www.sbma.net

Santa Barbara Museum of Natural History
2559 Puesta Del Sol Rd .... Santa Barbara CA 93105 805-682-4711 569-3170 520
Web: www.sbnature.org

Santa Barbara News-Press Publishing Co
715 Anacapa St .... Santa Barbara CA 93101 805-564-5200 966-6258 637-8
TF: 800-654-3292 ■ *Web:* www.newspress.com

Santa Barbara Public Library
40 E Anapamu St .... Santa Barbara CA 93101 805-962-7653 564-5660 434-3
TF: 800-354-9660 ■ *Web:* santabarbaraca.gov

Santa Barbara Region Chamber of Commerce
924 Anacapa St Ste 1 .... Santa Barbara CA 93101 805-965-3023 966-5954 139
TF: 800-204-3131 ■ *Web:* www.sbchamber.org

Santa Barbara Speakers Bureau LLC (SBSB)
PO Box 30768 .... Santa Barbara CA 93130 805-682-7474 708
Web: santabarbaraca.com/businesses/santa-barbara-speakers-bureau

Santa Barbara Symphony
1330 State St Ste 102 .... Santa Barbara CA 93101 805-898-9386 573-3
Web: www.thesymphony.org

Santa Barbara Unified School District
720 Santa Barbara St .... Santa Barbara CA 93101 805-963-4338 685
Web: www.sbunified.org

Santa Barbara Visitors Bureau & Film Commission
1601 Anacapa St .... Santa Barbara CA 93101 805-966-9222 966-1728 206
TF: 800-676-1266 ■ *Web:* www.santabarbaraca.com

Santa Barbara Zoological Gardens
500 Ninos Dr .... Santa Barbara CA 93103 805-962-5339 962-1673 823
Web: www.sbzoo.org

Santa Cabrini Hospital
6887 rue Chtelain .... Montreal QC H1T1P7 514-252-1535 374-2
Web: ciusss-estmtl.gouv.qc.ca

Santa Catalina Ranger District
5700 N Sabino Canyon Rd .... Tucson AZ 85750 520-749-8700 50-5
Web: www.fs.fed.us

Santa Catalina School
1500 Mark Thomas Dr .... Monterey CA 93940 831-655-9300 655-7535 622
Web: www.santacatalina.org

Santa Clara Chamber of Commerce
1850 Warburton Ave .... Santa Clara CA 95050 408-244-8244 244-7830 139
Web: www.santaclarachamber.com

Santa Clara City Library
2635 Homestead Rd .... Santa Clara CA 95051 408-615-2900 434-3
TF: 800-945-2288 ■
Web: santaclaraca.gov/government/departments/library

Santa Clara Convention Ctr
5001 Great America Pkwy .... Santa Clara CA 95054 408-748-7000 205
TF: 800-272-6822 ■ *Web:* www.santaclara.org

Santa Clara Convention/Visitors Bureau
1850 Warburton Ave .... Santa Clara CA 95050 408-244-9660 244-9202 206
TF: 800-272-6822 ■ *Web:* www.santaclara.org

Santa Clara County
70 W Hedding St 11th Fl E Wing .... San Jose CA 95110 408-299-5105 295-2192 338
Web: www.sccgov.org

Santa Clara County Library
14600 Winchester Blvd .... Los Gatos CA 95032 408-293-2326 364-0161 434-3
TF: 800-286-1991 ■ *Web:* www.sccl.org

Santa Clara University
500 El Camino Real .... Santa Clara CA 95053 408-554-4000 554-5255 166
Web: www.scu.edu

Santa Clara University School of Law
500 El Camino Real .... Santa Clara CA 95053 408-554-4361 167-1
Web: www.scu.edu

Santa Clara Valley Medical Ctr
751 S Bascom Ave .... San Jose CA 95128 408-885-5000 374-3
TF: 800-814-4351 ■ *Web:* www.scvmc.org

Santa Clara Valley Transportation Authority (VTA)
3331 N First St .... San Jose CA 95134 408-321-5555 468
TF: 800-894-9908 ■ *Web:* www.vta.org

Santa Clarita Valley Chamber of Commerce
27451 Tourney Rd Ste 160 .... Santa Clarita CA 91355 661-702-6977 702-6980 139
TF: 800-952-5225 ■ *Web:* www.scvchamber.com

Santa Cruz Beach Boardwalk
400 Beach St .... Santa Cruz CA 95060 831-423-5590 32
Web: www.beachboardwalk.com

Santa Cruz Chamber of Commerce
611 Ocean St Ste 1 .... Santa Cruz CA 95060 831-457-3713 423-1847 139
TF: 866-282-5900 ■ *Web:* www.santacruzchamber.org

Santa Cruz Civic Auditorium
307 Church St .... Santa Cruz CA 95060 831-420-5240 420-5261 572
Web: www.cityofsantacruz.com

Santa Cruz County 2150 N Congress Dr .... Nogales AZ 85621 520-761-7800 338
TF: 800-275-8777 ■ *Web:* www.co.santa-cruz.az.us

Santa Cruz County
701 Ocean St Rm 230 .... Santa Cruz CA 95060 831-454-2800 338
TF: 800-815-2666 ■ *Web:* www.co.santa-cruz.ca.us

Santa Cruz County Conference & Visitors Council
303 Water St Ste 100 .... Santa Cruz CA 95060 831-425-1234 425-1260 206
TF: 800-833-3494 ■ *Web:* www.santacruz.org

Santa Cruz County Fair & Rodeo
3142 Arizona 83 PO Box 85 .... Sonoita AZ 85637 520-455-5553 455-5330 642
TF: 800-490-1715 ■ *Web:* sonoitafairgrounds.com

Santa Cruz Mission State Historic Park
303 Big Trees Park Rd .... Felton CA 95018 831-335-6318 429-2870 565
Web: www.parks.ca.gov/default.asp?page_id=548

Phone | Fax | Class

Santa Cruz Nutritionals
2200 Delaware Ave .... Santa Cruz CA 95060 831-457-3200 296-8
Web: www.santacruznutritionals.com

Santa Cruz Seaside Co 400 Beach St .... Santa Cruz CA 95060 831-423-5590 31
TF: 800-421-1180 ■ *Web:* www.beachboardwalk.com

Santa Cruz Sentinel Inc
207 Church St .... Santa Cruz CA 95060 831-423-4242 532-3
TF: 800-952-2335 ■ *Web:* www.santacruzsentinel.com

Santa Cruz Symphony 307 Church St .... Santa Cruz CA 95060 831-462-0553 426-1193 573-3
Web: www.santacruzsymphony.org

Santa Fe Air Ctr Inc
121 Aviation Dr Bldg 3005 .... Santa Fe NM 87507 505-471-2525 63
Web: www.santafejet.biz

Santa Fe Cafe
807 William Hilton Pkwy .... Hilton Head Island SC 29928 843-785-3838 671
Web: www.santafehhi.com

Santa Fe Chamber of Commerce
1644 St Michael's Dr .... Santa Fe NM 87507 505-988-3279 984-2205 139
Web: www.santafechamber.com

Santa Fe Children's Museum
1050 Old Pecos Trl .... Santa Fe NM 87505 505-989-8359 989-7506 521
Web: www.santafechildrensmuseum.org

Santa Fe City Hall 200 Lincoln Ave .... Santa Fe NM 87501 505-955-6520 337
Web: www.santafenm.gov

Santa Fe Community College
6401 Richards Ave .... Santa Fe NM 87508 505-428-1000 162
TF: 800-345-1807 ■ *Web:* www.sfcc.edu

Santa Fe Community College Teaching Zoo
3000 NW 83rd St .... Gainesville FL 32606 352-395-5604 823
Web: www.sfcollege.edu/zoo

Santa Fe Convention Ctr
201 W Marcy St .... Santa Fe NM 87501 505-955-6200 955-6222 206
TF: 800-777-2489 ■ *Web:* www.santafe.org

Santa Fe County 102 Grant Ave .... Santa Fe NM 87501 505-986-6200 995-2740 338
Web: www.co.santa-fe.nm.us

Santa Fe Extruders & Printing
15315 Marquardt Ave .... Santa Fe Springs CA 90670 562-921-8991 596
Web: www.sfext.com

Santa Fe Independent School District
PO Box 370 .... Santa Fe TX 77510 409-925-3526 685
Web: www.sfisd.org

Santa Fe Municipal Airport (SAF)
121 Aviation Dr PO Box 909 .... Santa Fe NM 87504 505-955-2900 955-2905 27
TF: 866-773-2587 ■ *Web:* santafenm.gov/airport

Santa Fe National Cemetery
501 N Guadalupe St .... Santa Fe NM 87501 505-988-6400 988-6497 136
Web: www.cem.va.gov

Santa Fe New Mexican, The
202 E Marcy St PO Box 2048 .... Santa Fe NM 87504 505-983-3303 532-2
TF: 800-203-1347 ■ *Web:* www.santafenewmexican.com

Santa Fe Opera, The 301 Opera Dr .... Santa Fe NM 87506 505-986-5900 573-2
TF: 800-280-4654 ■ *Web:* www.santafeopera.org

Santa Fe Partners LLC
1512 Pacheco St Ste D202 .... Santa Fe NM 87505 505-989-8180 989-8185 45

Santa Fe Performing Arts
1050 Old Pecos Trail .... Santa Fe NM 87502 505-982-7992 572
Web: www.sfperformingarts.org

Santa Fe Playhouse 142 E DeVargas St .... Santa Fe NM 87501 505-988-4262 572
TF: 800-777-2489 ■ *Web:* www.santafeplayhouse.org

Santa Fe Preparatory School
1101 Camino De Cruz Blanca .... Santa Fe NM 87505 505-982-1829 685
Web: www.sfprep.org

Santa Fe Professional Duplicating Inc
1248 San Felipe Ave .... Santa Fe NM 87505 505-983-3101 627
Web: www.ptig.com

Santa Fe Public Library
145 Washington Ave .... Santa Fe NM 87501 505-955-6780 434-3
TF: 800-825-6639 ■ *Web:* www.santafelibrary.org

Santa Fe Reporter 132 E Marcy St .... Santa Fe NM 87501 505-988-5541 988-5348 532-5
TF: 800-908-8126 ■ *Web:* sfreporter.com

Santa Fe Rubber Products Inc
12306 E Washington Blvd .... Whittier CA 90606 562-693-2776 693-4936 326
Web: www.santaferubber.com

Santa Fe Station 4949 N Rancho Dr .... Las Vegas NV 89130 702-658-4900 133
TF Resv: 888-786-7389 ■ *Web:* santafestation.sclv.com

Santa Fe Symphony Orchestra & Chorus Inc
551 W Cordova Rd Ste D Ste D .... Santa Fe NM 87505 505-983-3530 982-3888 573-3
Web: www.santafesymphony.org

Santa Fe Trail Ctr 1349 K-156 Hwy .... Larned KS 67550 620-285-2054 285-7401 520
Web: www.santafetrailcenter.org

Santa Fe University of Art & Design
1600 St Michaels Dr .... Santa Fe NM 87505 800-456-2673 473-6011* 166
**Fax Area Code:* 505 ■ **Fax:* Admissions ■ *TF:* 800-456-2673 ■ *Web:* www.santafeuniversity.edu

Santa Gertrudis Breeders International
PO Box 1257 .... Kingsville TX 78364 361-592-9357 592-8572 48-2
Web: www.santagertrudis.com

Santa Margarita Catholic High School
22062 antonio pkwy .... Rancho Santa Margarita CA 92688 949-766-6000 685
Web: www.eaglesfootball.com

Santa Maria Ford Lincoln
1035 E Battles Rd .... Santa Maria CA 93454 805-925-2445 57
Web: santamariaford.com

Santa Maria Inn 801 S Broadway .... Santa Maria CA 93454 805-928-7777 928-5690 379
TF: 800-462-4276 ■ *Web:* www.santamariainn.com

Santa Maria Museum of Flight Inc
3015 Airpark Dr .... Santa Maria CA 93455 805-922-8758 522
Web: www.smmof.org

Santa Maria Public Library
420 S Broadway .... Santa Maria CA 93454 805-925-0994 928-7432 434-3
Web: www.cityofsantamaria.org

Santa Maria Times PO Box 400 .... Santa Maria CA 93456 805-925-2691 928-5657 532-2
TF: 800-788-1200 ■ *Web:* www.santamariatimes.com

Santa Maria Tire Inc
249 Montgomery Ave .... Oxnard CA 93036 805-642-0174 57
Web: www.smtire.com

Santa Maria Valley Chamber of Commerce
614 S Broadway .... Santa Maria CA 93454 805-925-2403 139
TF: 800-331-3779 ■ *Web:* www.santamaria.com

Santa Maria-Bonita School Dist
708 S Miller St .... Santa Maria CA 93454 805-928-1783 685
Web: www.smbsd.org

Santa Monica Amusements LLC
380 Santa Monica Pier .... Santa Monica CA 90401 310-260-8744 32
Web: www.pacpark.com

Santa Monica Chamber of Commerce
1234 Sixth St Ste 100 .... Santa Monica CA 90401 310-393-9825 394-1868 139
Web: www.smchamber.com

Santa Monica Civic Auditorium
1855 Main St .... Santa Monica CA 90401 310-458-8551 205
TF: 866-728-3229 ■ *Web:* smgov.net/departments/ccs/civicauditorium

Santa Monica College
1900 Pico Blvd .... Santa Monica CA 90405 310-434-4000 434-3645* 162
**Fax:* Admissions ■ *TF:* 800-624-1200 ■ *Web:* www.smc.edu

Santa Monica Convention & Visitors Bureau
1920 Main St Ste B .... Santa Monica CA 90405 310-319-6263 319-6273 206
TF: 800-544-5319 ■ *Web:* www.santamonica.com

Santa Monica Mountains National Recreation Area
401 W Hillcrest Dr .... Thousand Oaks CA 91360 805-370-2300 370-1851 564
TF: 888-275-8747 ■ *Web:* www.nps.gov/samo

Santa Monica Museum of Art
2525 Michigan Ave Ste G1 .... Santa Monica CA 90404 310-586-6488 520
Web: www.smmoa.org

Santa Monica Partners
1865 Palmer Ave Ste 108 .... Larchmont NY 10538 914-833-0958 2
Web: www.smplp.com

Santa Monica Public Library
1343 Sixth St .... Santa Monica CA 90401 310-458-8608 434-3
Web: www.smpl.org

Santa Monica State Beach
c/o Angeles District Office
1925 Las Virgenes Rd .... Calabasas CA 91302 818-880-0363 565
Web: www.parks.ca.gov/default.asp?page_id=624

Santa Monica UCLA Medical Ctr
1250 16th St .... Santa Monica CA 90404 310-319-4000 374-3
Web: www.uclahealth.org/homepage_sanmon.cfm?id=265

Santa Paula Chamber of Commerce
200 N Tenth St .... Santa Paula CA 93060 805-525-5561 139
Web: santapaulachamber.net

Santa Rosa Chamber of Commerce
637 First St .... Santa Rosa CA 95404 707-545-1414 545-6914 139
Web: www.santarosachamber.com

Santa Rosa Correctional Institution
5850 E Milton Rd .... Milton FL 32583 850-983-5800 983-5907 213
Web: dc.state.fl.us

Santa Rosa County
6495 Caroline St Ste F .... Milton FL 32570 850-983-1900 338
TF: 800-488-0800 ■ *Web:* www.santarosa.fl.gov

Santa Rosa County Chamber of Commerce
5247 Stewart St .... Milton FL 32570 850-623-2339 623-4413 139
TF: 800-239-8732 ■ *Web:* www.srcchamber.com

Santa Rosa Junior College
1501 Mendocino Ave .... Santa Rosa CA 95401 707-527-4011 527-4798 162
Web: www.santarosa.edu

Santa Rosa Memorial Hospital (SRMH)
1165 Montgomery Dr .... Santa Rosa CA 95405 707-546-3210 374-3
TF: 800-627-8106 ■ *Web:* stjosephhealth.org/about-us

Santa Rosa Press Democrat Inc, The
427 Mendocino Ave PO Box 569 .... Santa Rosa CA 95402 707-526-8570 532-3
Web: www.pressdemocrat.com

Santa Rosa Symphony (SRS)
50 Santa Rosa Ave Ste 410 .... Santa Rosa CA 95404 707-546-8742 573-3
Web: srsymphony.org

Santa Susana Pass State Historic Park
1925 Las Virgenes Rd .... Calabasas CA 91302 818-880-0363 565
Web: www.parks.ca.gov/default.asp?page_id=611

Santacafe 231 Washington Ave .... Santa Fe NM 87501 505-984-1788 671
Web: www.santacafe.com

Santana Row 3055 Olin Ave Ste 2100 .... San Jose CA 95128 408-551-4611 50-6
Web: www.santanarow.com

Santasiero's 1329 Niagara St .... Buffalo NY 14213 716-886-9197 671

Santec Inc 3501 Challenger St .... Torrance CA 90503 310-542-0063 361
TF: 800-284-4050 ■ *Web:* www.santecfaucet.com

Santee Chamber of Commerce
10315 Mission Gorge Rd .... Santee CA 92071 619-449-6572 139
Web: santeechamber.com

Santee Electric Co-op Inc
424 Sumter Hwy .... Kingstree SC 29556 843-355-6187 245
TF: 800-922-1604 ■ *Web:* www.santee.org

Santee School District
9625 Cuyamaca St .... Santee CA 92071 619-258-2300 685
Web: www.santeesd.net

Santee State Park 251 State Pk Rd .... Santee SC 29142 803-854-2408 854-4834 565
Web: www.southcarolinaparks.com

Santek Components LLC
1060 Holland Ave Ste A .... Clovis CA 93612 559-294-6015 246
TF: 800-553-2447 ■ *Web:* www.santekcomp.com

Santen Inc 6401 Hollis St Ste 125 .... Emeryville CA 94608 415-268-9100 231
Web: www.santeninc.com

Santeon Group Inc
12110 Sunset Hills Rd Ste 630 .... Reston VA 20190 703-970-9200 395
Web: www.santeon.com

Santiago Canyon College
8045 E Chapman Ave .... Orange CA 92869 714-628-4900 628-4723* 162
**Fax:* Admissions ■ *Web:* www.sccollege.edu

Santie Oil Co 126 Larcel Dr .... Sikeston MO 63801 314-436-3569 138
TF: 800-748-7788 ■ *Web:* www.santiemidwest.com

Santillana USA Publishing Co
2023 NW 84th Ave .... Doral FL 33122 305-591-9522 248-9518* 637-2
**Fax Area Code:* 888 ■ *TF:* 800-245-8584 ■ *Web:* www.santillanausa.com

Santinelli International Inc
325 Oser Ave .... Hauppauge NY 11788 800-644-3343 454
TF: 800-644-3343 ■ *Web:* www.santinelli.com

Santini Foods Inc
16505 Worthley Dr .... San Lorenzo CA 94580 510-317-8888 297-8
Web: www.santinifoods.com

Phone | Fax | Class

Santo Insurance & Financial Services Inc
224 Main St ... Salem NH 03079 603-890-6439 390
Web: santoinsurance.com

Santora CPA Group
220 Continental Dr
Ste 112 Christiana Executive Campus ... Newark DE 19713 302-737-6200 2
TF: 800-347-0116 ■ *Web:* www.santoracpagroup.com

Santorini Greek Taverna
1502 Centre St N ... Calgary AB T2E2R9 403-276-8363 671
Web: www.santorinirestaurant.com

Santoro Oil Company Inc
101 Corliss St. ... Providence RI 02904 401-942-5000 316
TF: 800-225-0808 ■ *Web:* www.santorooil.com

Santos Enterprises 5400 Alameda Ave. ... El Paso TX 79905 915-779-3641 345
Web: www.foodcityep.com

SANUWAVE Health Inc
11475 Great Oaks Way Ste 150 ... Alpharetta GA 30022 678-581-6843 476
Web: www.sanuwave.com

Sanyo Denki America Inc
468 Amapola Ave ... Torrance CA 90501 310-783-5400 174
Web: www.sanyo-denki.com

Sanyo Fisher Co 21605 Plummer St ... Chatsworth CA 91311 818-998-7322 717-2759 52

SAP 100 Consilium Pl ... Scarborough ON M1H3E3 416-791-7100 791-7101 178-1
TF: 888-777-1727 ■ *Web:* www.sap.com

SAP America Inc
3999 W Chester Pk ... Newtown Square PA 19073 610-661-1000 178-1
TF: 800-872-1727 ■ *Web:* www.sap.com

SAP USA Truck & Auto Parts Inc
5301 NW 74 Ave Ste 200 ... Miami FL 33166 305-594-2844 54
Web: www.sapcorp.net

Sapa Inc 7933 NE 21st Ave. ... Portland OR 97211 503-802-3000 481
TF: 800-547-0790 ■ *Web:* www.sapagroup.com

Sapers & Wallack Inc
275 Washington St Ste 205 ... Newton MA 02458 617-225-2600 401
TF: 800-463-3273 ■ *Web:* www.sapers-wallack.com

SAPIEN Technologies Inc
841 Latour Court Ste D ... Napa CA 94558 707-252-8700 177
Web: www.sapien.com

Sapiens International Corp
4000 CentreGreen Way Ste 150 ... Cary NC 27513 919-405-1500 405-1700 178-10
NASDAQ: SPNS ■ *TF:* 888-281-1167 ■ *Web:* www.sapiens.com

Sapient Capital Management LLC
4020 Lake Creek Dr PO Box 1590 ... Wilson WY 83014 307-733-3806 792
Web: www.sapientcapital.com

Sapient Corp 131 Dartmouth St 3rd Fl. ... Boston MA 02116 617-621-0200 621-1300 809
NASDAQ: SAPE ■ *TF:* 866-796-6860 ■ *Web:* www.sapient.com

Sapona Mfg Company Inc
2478 Cedar Falls Rd ... Cedar Falls NC 27230 336-625-2727 626-0876 745-9
TF: 800-280-0474 ■ *Web:* www.saponamfg.com

Sapor Cafe & Bar
428 Washington Ave N ... Minneapolis MN 55401 612-375-1971 671
Web: www.saporcafe.com

Sapp Bros Truck Stops Inc
9915 S 148th St ... Omaha NE 68138 402-895-7038 895-1057 324
TF: 800-233-4059 ■ *Web:* sappbros.net/travel-centers

Sapp Bros. Petroleum Inc
9915 S 148th St ... Omaha NE 68138 402-895-2202 579
TF: 800-233-4059 ■ *Web:* www.sappbros.net

Sapphire Grill 110 W Congress St. ... Savannah GA 31401 912-443-9962 443-9964 671
Web: www.sapphiregrill.com

Sapphire Infotech Inc
200 Brown Rd Ste 200 ... Fremont CA 94539 510-360-0990 809
Web: www.sapphireinfotech.com

Sapphire International Inc
101 Merritt Blvd ... Trumbull CT 06611 203-375-8668 178-1

Sapphire Scientific Inc
2604 Liberator ... Prescott AZ 86301 928-445-3030 427
Web: www.sapphirescientific.com

Sapphire Technologies Inc
6660 Taylor Dr Ste 105 ... Red Deer AB T4P1Y3 412-798-8990 466
Web: www.sapphiretech.org

Sappi Pulp Americas LP
925 Westchester Ave Ste 115 ... West Harrison MA 10604 914-253-8660 423-5494* 552-1
**Fax Area Code:* 617 ■ **Fax:* Mail Rm ■ *Web:* www.na.sappi.com

Sappington House Museum
1015 S Sappington Rd ... Crestwood MO 63126 314-822-8171 520
Web: sappingtonhouse.org

Sapporo Fantasy Japanese Steak
2939 C Battleground Ave ... Greensboro NC 27408 336-282-5345 671

Sapporo Restaurant 230 Commercial St ... Portland ME 04101 207-772-1233 671
Web: www.sappororestaurant.com

Sapta Global Inc
267 Amboy Ave Ste 125 ... Woodbridge NJ 07095 732-602-0240 809
Web: www.saptanet.com

Saputo Inc
6869 boul Metropolitain ... Saint-Leonard QC H1P1X8 514-328-6662 296-5
NYSE: SAP ■ *Web:* www.saputo.com

Sara E Cooley CPA
2240 Shelter Island Dr ... San Diego CA 92106 619-758-9743 2

Sara Hightower Regional Library
205 Riverside Pkwy NE ... Rome GA 30161 706-236-4600 434-3
Web: rome.shrls.org

Sara's 724 Dublin St ... New Orleans LA 70118 504-861-0565 671

Saracen Energy Partners LP
3033 W Alabama ... Houston TX 77098 713-285-2900 579
Web: www.saracenenergy.com

Sarafinchin Associates Ltd
238 Galaxy Blvd ... Toronto ON M9W5R8 416-674-1770 261
Web: www.sarafinchin.com

Sarah Bush Lincoln Health Ctr (SBLHC)
1000 Health Ctr Dr PO Box 372 ... Mattoon IL 61938 217-258-2525 258-4117 374-3
TF: 800-345-3191 ■ *Web:* www.sarahbush.org

Sarah House Inc 100 Roberts Ave ... Syracuse NY 13207 315-475-1747 372
Web: sarahsguesthouse.org

Sarah Lawrence College 1 Meadway ... Bronxville NY 10708 800-888-2858 395-2515* 166
**Fax Area Code:* 914 ■ **Fax:* Admissions ■ *TF:* 800-888-2858 ■ *Web:* www.sarahlawrence.edu

Sarah P Duke Gardens 420 Anderson St ... Durham NC 27708 919-684-3698 668-3610 97
TF: 800-234-3368 ■ *Web:* gardens.duke.edu

Sarakem Corp 15 Buell St ... Hanover NH 03755 603-643-5720 271
Web: sarakem.com

Saranac Glove Co 999 LOmbardi Ave ... Green Bay WI 54304 920-435-3737 435-7618 155-8
TF: 800-727-2622 ■ *Web:* www.saranacglove.com

Saraphino's
3074 E Layton Ave St Francis ... Saint Franci WI 53235 414-744-0303 671
Web: saraphinossaintfranciswi.com

Sarasota Ballet of Florida
5555 N Tamiami Trail ... Sarasota FL 34243 941-359-0099 573-1
Web: www.sarasotaballet.org

Sarasota Film Festival
332 Cocoanut Ave. ... Sarasota FL 34236 941-364-9514 364-8411 282
TF: 800-435-7352 ■ *Web:* www.sarasotafilmfestival.com

Sarasota Herald-Tribune 1741 Main St ... Sarasota FL 34236 941-953-7755 361-4800 532-2
TF: 866-284-7102 ■ *Web:* www.heraldtribune.com

Sarasota Jungle Gardens
3701 Bay Shore Rd ... Sarasota FL 34234 941-355-5305 823
TF: 877-681-6547 ■ *Web:* www.sarasotajunglegardens.com

Sarasota Kennel Club Inc
5400 Bradenton Rd ... Sarasota FL 34234 941-355-7744 642
TF: 800-729-7244 ■ *Web:* www.sarasotakennelclub.com

Sarasota Memorial Hospital
1700 S Tamiami Trl ... Sarasota FL 34239 941-917-9000 374-3
TF: 800-764-8255 ■ *Web:* www.smh.com

Sarasota Opera 61 N Pineapple Ave ... Sarasota FL 34236 941-366-8450 955-5571 573-2
TF: 866-951-0111 ■ *Web:* www.sarasotaopera.org

Sarasota Orchestra 709 N Tamiami Trl ... Sarasota FL 34236 941-953-4252 953-3059 573-3
TF: 866-508-0611 ■ *Web:* www.sarasotaorchestra.org

Sarasota-Bradenton International Airport
6000 Airport Cir ... Sarasota FL 34243 941-359-5200 359-5054 27
TF: 800-711-1712 ■ *Web:* www.srq-airport.com

Sarasota-Manatee Jewish Housing Council Inc
1951 N Honore Ave. ... Sarasota FL 34235 941-379-3553 672
Web: avivaseniorlife.org

Saratoga Chamber of Commerce
14485 Big Basin Way ... Saratoga CA 95070 408-867-0753 867-5213 139
Web: www.saratogachamber.org

Saratoga Convention & Tourism Bureau
60 Railroad Pl Ste 301 ... Saratoga Springs NY 12866 518-584-1531 584-2969 206
TF: 855-424-6073 ■ *Web:* www.discoversaratoga.org

Saratoga County 40 McMaster St ... Ballston Spa NY 12020 518-885-5381 884-4726 338
Web: www.saratogacountyny.gov

Saratoga County Chamber of Commerce
28 Clinton St ... Saratoga Springs NY 12866 518-584-3255 798-0163 139
TF: 855-765-7873 ■ *Web:* www.saratoga.org

Saratoga Eagle Sales & Service Inc
45 Duplainville Rd ... Saratoga Springs NY 12866 518-581-7377 581-7777 81-1
TF: 800-310-5099 ■ *Web:* www.abwholesaler.com

Saratoga Gaming & Raceway
342 Jefferson St PO Box 356 ... Saratoga Springs NY 12866 518-584-2110 642
TF: 800-727-2990 ■ *Web:* www.saratogacasino.com

Saratoga Hilton 534 Broadway ... Saratoga Springs NY 12866 518-584-4000 584-7430 379
TF: 800-445-8667 ■ *Web:* www.hilton.com

Saratoga Honda 3402 Rt 9 ... Saratoga Springs NY 12866 888-658-2303 57
TF: 888-658-2303 ■ *Web:* www.saratogahonda.com

Saratoga Hospital
211 Church St ... Saratoga Springs NY 12866 518-587-3222 580-4122 374-3
Web: www.saratogahospital.org

Saratoga Liquor Company Inc
3215 James Day Ave. ... Superior WI 54880 715-394-4487 443
TF: 800-472-6923 ■ *Web:* www.saratogaliquor.com

Saratoga National Historical Park
648 Rt 32 ... Stillwater NY 12170 518-664-9821 564
TF: 800-562-5394 ■ *Web:* www.nps.gov/sara

Saratoga Performing Arts Ctr (SPAC)
108 Ave of the Pines ... Saratoga Springs NY 12866 518-584-9330 584-0809 572
TF: 800-838-3006 ■ *Web:* www.spac.org

Saratoga Race Course
267 Union Ave ... Saratoga Springs NY 12866 718-641-4700 642
TF: 800-814-7846 ■ *Web:* www.saratogaracetrack.com

Saratoga Spa State Park
19 Roosevelt Dr ... Saratoga Springs NY 12866 518-584-2535 565
Web: parks.ny.gov/parks/saratogaspa

Saratoga Springs City Ctr
522 Broadway ... Saratoga Springs NY 12866 518-584-0027 584-0117 205
TF: 800-447-5224 ■ *Web:* saratogacitycenter.org

Sarbanes John P (Rep D - MD)
2444 Rayburn Bldg ... Washington DC 20515 202-225-4016 225-9219 342-2
Web: sarbanes.house.gov

SARCOM Inc AEP Colloids Div 6299 Rt 9N ... Hadley NY 12835 518-696-9900 696-9997 146
TF: 800-848-0658 ■ *Web:* www.aepcolloids.com

Sarcoma Foundation of America Inc, The
9899 Main St Ste 204 ... Damascus MD 20872 301-253-8687 305
TF: 800-333-6513 ■ *Web:* www.curesarcoma.org

Sardee Industries Inc
5100 Academy Dr Ste 400 ... Lisle IL 60532 630-824-4200 358
Web: www.sardee.com

Sardella's Restaurant
30 Memorial Blvd W ... Newport RI 02840 401-849-6312 671
Web: www.sardellas.com

Sardine Factory, The 701 Wave St ... Monterey CA 93940 831-373-3775 671
TF: 800-232-4141 ■ *Web:* www.sardinefactory.com

Sarducci's 3 Main St ... Montpelier VT 05602 802-223-0229 671
Web: www.sarduccis.com

Sare Plastics 14600 Commerce St NE ... Alliance OH 44601 330-821-4299 608
Web: www.sareplastics.com

Sares-Regis Group 18802 Bardeen Ave ... Irvine CA 92612 949-756-5959 756-5955 655
Web: www.sares-regis.com

Sarfino & Rhoades LLP
11921 Rockville Pk Ste 501 ... North Bethesda MD 20852 301-770-5500 2
Web: www.sarfinoandrhoades.com

Sargent & Greenleaf Inc
1 Security Dr ... Nicholasville KY 40356 859-885-9411 885-3063 350
TF: 800-826-7652 ■ *Web:* www.sargentandgreenleaf.com

Sargent & Lundy LLC 55 E Monroe St ... Chicago IL 60603 312-269-2000 261
Web: www.sargentlundy.com

Sargent Art Inc 100 E Diamond Ave ... Hazleton PA 18201 570-454-3596 459-1752 43
TF: 800-424-3596 ■ *Web:* www.sargentart.com

Name / Address	City	State	ZIP	Phone	Fax	Class
Sargent Controls & Aerospace 5675 W Burlingame Rd *TF:* 800-230-0359 ■ *Web:* www.sargentaerospace.com	Tucson	AZ	85743	520-744-1000	744-9494	223
Sargent Corp 378 Bennoch Rd *Web:* www.sargent-corp.com	Stillwater	ME	04489	207-827-4435	827-6150	188-4
Sargent County 355 Main St *TF:* 866-634-8387 ■ *Web:* sargentnd.com	Forman	ND	58032	701-724-6241	724-6244	338
Sargent Manufacturing Co 100 Sargent Dr *TF:* 800-727-5477 ■ *Web:* www.sargentlock.com	New Haven	CT	06511	800-727-5477		350
Sargento Foods Inc 1 Persnickety Pl *TF:* 800-243-3737 ■ *Web:* www.sargento.com	Plymouth	WI	53073	920-893-8484		296-5
Sarkes Tarzian Inc 205 N College Ave Ste 800	Bloomington	IN	47404	812-332-7251		738
Sarnoff Corp 201 Washington Rd PO Box 5300 *Web:* sri.com/engage/products-solutions	Princeton	NJ	08543	609-734-2000		668
Sarpy County 1210 Golden Gate Dr Ste 1118 *Web:* www.co.sarpy.ne.us	Papillion	NE	68046	402-593-2100	593-4360	338
Sarpy County Chamber of Commerce 7775 Olson Dr Ste 207 *Web:* www.sarpychamber.org	Papillion	NE	68046	402-339-3050		139
Sarreid Ltd 3905 Airport Dr NW *Web:* www.sarreid.com	Wilson	NC	27896	252-291-1414	237-1592	320
Sarstedt Inc 1025 St James Church Rd	Newton	NC	28658	828-465-4000		596
Sartomer Co 502 Thomas Jones Way *TF:* 800-345-8247 ■ *Web:* www.sartomer.com	Exton	PA	19341	610-363-4100	363-4140	605-2
Sartori 107 Pleasant View Rd *TF Cust Svc:* 800-558-5888 ■ *Web:* www.sartoricheese.com	Plymouth	WI	53073	800-558-5888		296-5
SAS (Scandinavian Airlines System) 301 Route 17 N Ste 500 **Fax Area Code:* 201 ■ *TF:* 800-221-2350 ■ *Web:* www.flysas.com	Rutherford	NJ	07070	800-437-5807	896-3735*	25
SAS Institute Inc 100 SAS Campus Dr *TF:* 800-727-0025 ■ *Web:* www.sas.com	Cary	NC	27513	919-677-8000	677-4444	178-1
Sas Safety Corp 3031 Gardenia Ave **Fax Area Code:* 800 ■ *TF:* 800-262-0200 ■ *Web:* www.sassafety.com	Long Beach	CA	90807	562-427-2775	244-1938*	477
SAS Shoemakers 1717 SAS Dr *TF:* 877-782-7463 ■ *Web:* www.sasshoes.com	San Antonio	TX	78224	877-782-7463		301
Sasaki Assoc Inc 64 Pleasant St *Web:* www.sasaki.com	Watertown	MA	02472	617-926-3300	924-2748	261
Sascha's 527 N Charles St *Web:* www.saschas.com	Baltimore	MD	21201	410-539-8880		671
Sasco Capital Inc 10 Sasco Hill Rd *Web:* www.sascocap.com	Fairfield	CT	06430	203-254-6800		401
SASCO Electric 2750 Moore Ave *TF:* 800-477-4422 ■ *Web:* www.sasco.com	Fullerton	CA	92833	714-870-0217	738-3571	189-4
Sashco Inc 720 S Rochester Ave Ste D *TF:* 800-600-3232 ■ *Web:* www.sashcoinc.com	Ontario	CA	91761	909-937-8222	937-8223	189-6
Saskatchewan Health Research Foundation 324-111 Research Dr *TF:* 800-975-1699 ■ *Web:* www.shrf.ca	Saskatoon	SK	S7N3R2	306-975-1680	975-1688	231
Saskatchewan Indian Gaming Authority 250 - 103 C Packham Ave *TF:* 800-306-6789 ■ *Web:* www.siga.sk.ca	Saskatoon	SK	S7N4K4	306-477-7777		133
Saskatchewan Roughrider Football Club 1910 Piffles Taylor Way PO Box 1966 *TF:* 888-474-3377 ■ *Web:* www.riderville.com	Regina	SK	S4P3E1	306-569-2323	566-4280	715-2
Saskatchewan Sports Hall of Fame & Museum 2205 Victoria Ave *Web:* www.sshfm.com	Regina	SK	S4P0S4	306-780-9232		522
Saskatoon 477 Haywood Rd *Web:* saskatoonrestaurant.com	Greenville	SC	29607	864-297-7244		671
Saskatoon Business College Ltd 221 Third Ave N *TF:* 800-679-7711 ■ *Web:* www.sbccollege.ca	Saskatoon	SK	S7K2H7	306-244-6333		162
Saskatoon City Hospital 701 Queen St *TF:* 855-655-7612 ■ *Web:* www.saskatoonhealthregion.ca	Saskatoon	SK	S7K0M7	306-655-8000		374-2
Saskatoon Inn Hotel & Conference Centre 2002 Airport Dr *Web:* www.saskatooninn.com	Saskatoon	SK	S7L6M4	306-242-1440		378
Sasnak Management Corp 1877 N Rock Rd	Wichita	KS	67206	316-683-2611		670
SA-SO Co 525 N Great SW Pkwy *Web:* www.sa-so.com	Arlington	TX	76011	972-641-4911	660-3684	701
Sasol North America Inc 900 Threadneedle St Ste 100 *Web:* www.sasolnorthamerica.com	Houston	TX	77079	281-588-3000		144
Sasol Wax North America Corp 21325-B Cabot Blvd *Web:* www.sasolwax.com	Hayward	CA	94545	510-783-9295		146
Sassafras Natural Resources Management Area 13070 Crouse Mill Rd *Web:* www.dnr.state.md.us	Queen Anne	MD	21657	410-820-1668		565
Sassafraz 100 Cumberland St *Web:* www.sassafraz.ca	Toronto	ON	M5R1A6	416-964-2222	964-2402	671
Sasse Ben (Sen R - NE) 136 Russell Senate Office Bldg *Web:* www.sasse.senate.gov	Washington	DC	20510	202-224-4224		342-2
Sassi Ristorante 10455 E Pinnacle Peak Pkwy *Web:* www.sassi.biz	Scottsdale	AZ	85255	480-502-9095		671
Sassoon Salons 399 Boylston St *Web:* www.sassoon.com	Boston	MA	02116	617-236-7697		77
Sassy Inc 2305 Breton Industrial Pk Dr *TF:* 800-323-6336 ■ *Web:* www.sassybaby.com	Kentwood	MI	49508	616-243-0767	243-1042	64
SAT (San Antonio International Airport) 9800 Airport Blvd Rm 2041 **Fax:* PR ■ *TF:* 800-237-6639 ■ *Web:* www.sanantonio.gov/aviation	San Antonio	TX	78216	210-207-3411	207-3500*	27
Satair USA Inc 3993 Trade Port Blvd Ste 100 *Web:* www.satair.com	Atlanta	GA	30354	404-675-6333	675-6311	770
Satake USA Inc 10905 Cash Rd *Web:* www.satake-usa.com	Stafford	TX	77477	281-276-3600	494-1427	547
Satay 3202 W Anderson Ln *Web:* www.satayusa.com	Austin	TX	78757	512-467-6731		671
Satay Sarinah 512A S Van Dorn St *Web:* www.sataysarinah.com	Alexandria	VA	22304	703-370-4313	370-9672	671
Satchidananda Ashram Yogaville (SAYVA) 108 Yogaville Way *TF Resv:* 800-858-9642 ■ *Web:* yogaville.org	Buckingham	VA	23921	434-969-3121		673
Satcom Direct Inc 1901 Hwy A1A *TF:* 800-601-3099 ■ *Web:* www.satcomdirect.com	Satellite Beach	FL	32937	321-777-3000		177
Satcom Resources LLC 101 Eagle Rd Ste 7 PO Box 1639 *Web:* www.satcomresources.com	Avon	CO	81620	970-748-3094		177
Satcom Scientific Inc 5644 Commerce Dr *Web:* www.satcomscientific.com	Orlando	FL	32839	407-856-1050	855-7640	647
Satellite Broadcasting & Communications Assn (SBCA) 1730 M St NW Ste 600 *TF:* 800-541-5981 ■ *Web:* www.sbca.com	Washington	DC	20036	202-349-3620	349-3621	49-14
Satellite Hotel 411 Lakewood Cir *TF:* 800-423-8409 ■ *Web:* www.satellitehotel.net	Colorado Springs	CO	80910	719-596-6800		379
Satellite Industries Inc 2530 Xenium Ln N *TF:* 800-328-3332 ■ *Web:* www.satelliteindustries.com	Minneapolis	MN	55441	800-328-3332	328-3334	505
Satellite Logistics Group Inc 12621 Featherwood Ste 390 *TF:* 877-795-7540 ■ *Web:* www.slg.com	Houston	TX	77034	281-902-5500	902-5501	311
Satellite Management Services Inc 4529 E Bwy Rd *TF:* 800-788-8388 ■ *Web:* www.smstv.com	Phoenix	AZ	85040	602-386-4444		224
Satellite Receivers Ltd/Cash Depot 1740 Cofrin Dr Ste 2 *TF:* 800-776-8834 ■ *Web:* www.cashdepotplus.com	Green Bay	WI	54302	800-776-8834		116
Satellite Shelters Inc 2530 Xenium Ln N *TF:* 800-328-3332 ■ *Web:* www.satelliteco.com	Plymouth	MN	55441	763-553-1900		106
Satellite Store 7412 Preston Hwy *Web:* www.thesatellitestore.com	Louisville	KY	40219	502-966-0045		188-10
Satellite Systems Corp 101 Malibu Dr *Web:* www.satsyscorp.com	Virginia Beach	VA	23452	757-463-3553	463-3891	647
Sather Financial Group Inc 120 E Constitution St *TF:* 800-234-1040 ■ *Web:* www.satherfinancial.com	Victoria	TX	77901	361-570-1800		251
Sathre Bergquist Inc 150 Broadway Ave S *Web:* sathre.com	Wayzata	MN	55391	952-476-6000		261
Saticoy Lemon Assn 7560 E Bristol Rd *TF:* 800-859-9262 ■ *Web:* www.saticoylemon.com	Ventura	CA	93003	805-654-6500		315-2
Satin Fine Foods Inc 32 Leone Ln Ste 1 *Web:* satinice.com	Chester	NY	10918	845-469-1034		297-8
Satisfaction Restaurant 905 W Main St Ste 37 *Web:* www.satisfactionrestaurant.com	Durham	NC	27701	919-682-7397		671
SatisfYd 47 E Chicago Ave Ste 360 *TF:* 800-562-9557 ■ *Web:* satisfyd.com	Naperville	IL	60540	800-562-9557		196
Satlantic Inc Richmond Terminal Pier 9 3481 N Marginal Rd *Web:* www.satlantic.com	Halifax	NS	B3K5X8	902-492-4780		407
Satmetrix Systems Inc 1100 Pk Pl Ste 210 *TF:* 866-697-2103 ■ *Web:* www.satmetrix.com	San Mateo	CA	94403	866-943-3760		177
Sato America Inc 10350A Nations Ford Rd *TF:* 888-871-8741 ■ *Web:* www.satoamerica.com	Charlotte	NC	28273	704-644-1650	644-1662	173-6
Satori Software Inc 1301 Fifth Ave Ste 2200 *TF:* 800-553-6477 ■ *Web:* www.satorisoftware.com	Seattle	WA	98101	206-357-2900	357-2901	178-1
Satov Consultants Inc 250 The Esplanade Ste 200 *Web:* www.satovconsultants.com	Toronto	ON	M5A1J2	416-777-9000		463
Sattell Johnson Appel & Co Sc 111 Heritage Reserve Ste 100 *Web:* sattell.com	Menomonee Falls	WI	53051	414-273-0500		2
Satterfield & Pontikes Construction Inc 11000 Equity Dr Ste 100 *Web:* www.satpon.com	Houston	TX	77041	713-996-1300	996-1400	186
Satterlund Supply Company Inc 26277 Sherwood *Web:* www.satterlund.com	Warren	MI	48091	586-755-9700		492
Satuit Technologies Inc 100 Grossman Dr *Web:* satuit.com	Braintree	MA	02184	781-871-7788		177
Saturday Evening Post, The 1100 Waterway Blvd *TF:* 800-829-5576 ■ *Web:* www.saturdayeveningpost.com	Indianapolis	IN	46202	317-634-1100	637-0126	457-11
Saturday Knight Ltd 4330 Winton Rd *Web:* www.skldirect.com	Cincinnati	OH	45232	513-641-1400	242-2805	746
Saturn Electronics & Engineering Inc 2120 Austin Ave *Web:* www.elmanalytics.com	Rochester Hills	MI	48309	248-853-5724	299-8514	625
Saturn Electronics Corp 28450 Northline Rd *Web:* www.saturnelectronics.com	Romulus	MI	48174	734-941-8100	941-3707	625
Saturn Fasteners Inc 425 S Varney St *TF:* 800-947-9414 ■ *Web:* www.saturnfasteners.com	Burbank	CA	91502	818-846-7145		350
Saturn Freight Systems Inc PO Box 680308 *Web:* www.saturnfreight.com	Marietta	GA	30068	770-952-3490	693-5749	311
Saturn Industries Inc 157 Union Tpke *TF:* 800-775-1651 ■ *Web:* www.saturnedm.com	Hudson	NY	12534	518-828-9956	828-9868	127
Saturn Infotech Inc 1120 Welsh Rd Ste 110 *Web:* saturninfotech.com	North Wales	PA	19454	267-337-6779		196
Saturn Production Inc 305 E 86th St *Web:* www.iperceptions.com	New York	NY	10028	212-348-7300		434-3
Saturn Systems Inc 314 W Superior St Ste 1015 *TF:* 888-638-4335 ■ *Web:* www.saturnsys.com	Duluth	MN	55802	218-623-7200		177

Phone | Fax | Class

Saturna Capital Corp
1300 N State St . . . . . Bellingham WA 98225 360-734-9900 401
TF: 888-732-6262 ■ *Web:* www.saturna.com
Saturno Design 421 SW Hall St. . . . . Portland OR 97201 503-478-1830 180
Web: www.saturnodesign.com
Satya Jewelry Inc 330 Bleecker St. . . . . New York NY 10014 212-243-7313 410
Web: www.satyajewelry.com
Sauber Manufacturing Co 10 N Sauber Rd. . . . . Virgil IL 60151 630-365-6600 190
TF: 800-323-9147 ■ *Web:* www.saubermfg.com
Saucebox 214 SW Broadway . . . . . Portland OR 97205 503-241-3393 671
Web: www.saucebox.com
Saucon Technologies Inc
2455 Baglyos Cir . . . . . Bethlehem PA 18020 484-241-2500 180
TF: 800-287-3114 ■ *Web:* www.saucontds.com
Saucony Inc 191 Spring St . . . . . Lexington MA 02420 800-282-6575 301
TF: 800-282-6575 ■ *Web:* www.saucony.com
Saucy-Q Bar B Que 1111 Government St . . . . . Mobile AL 36604 251-433-7427 671
Web: www.saucyqbarbque.com
Sauder School of Business
2053 Main Mall . . . . . Vancouver BC V6T1Z2 604-822-8399 685
Web: www.sauder.ubc.ca
Sauder Village 22611 SR 2. . . . . Archbold OH 43502 419-446-2541 445-5251 520
TF: 800-590-9755 ■ *Web:* www.saudervillage.org
Sauder Woodworking Co 502 Middle St. . . . . Archbold OH 43502 419-446-2711 319-2
TF Cust Svc: 800-523-3987 ■ *Web:* www.sauder.com
Saudi Arabia
Consulate General
5718 Westheimer Rd Ste 1500. . . . . Houston TX 77057 713-785-5577 273-6937 257
Web: www.saudiembassy.net
Consulate General
866 Second Ave 5th Fl. . . . . New York NY 10017 212-752-2740 257
Web: www.saudiembassy.net
Embassy 601 New Hampshire Ave NW . . . . . Washington DC 20037 202-342-3800 944-5983 257
Web: www.saudiembassy.net
Sauer Compressors USA Inc
64 Log Canoe Cir. . . . . Stevensville MD 21666 410-604-3142 172
Web: www.sauerusa.com
Sauer Holdings Inc 30 51st St . . . . . Pittsburgh PA 15201 412-687-4100 256
TF: 800-767-3263 ■ *Web:* sauerholdings.com
Sauer Inc
11223 Phillips Pkwy Dr E. . . . . Jacksonville FL 32256 904-262-6444 189-10
Web: www.sauer-inc.com
Sauers Group Inc, The
1585 Roadhaven Dr . . . . . Stone Mountain GA 30083 770-621-8888 627
Web: www.sauersgroup.com
Saugatuck Capital Co 187 Danbury Rd. . . . . Wilton CT 06897 203-348-6669 324-6995 792
Web: www.saugatuckcapital.com
Saugus Free Public Library
295 Central St. . . . . Saugus MA 01906 781-231-4168 434-3
Web: www.noblenet.org
Saugus High School
21900 Centurion Way . . . . . Santa Clarita CA 91350 661-297-3900 685
Web: www.hartdistrict.org
Saugus Iron Works National Historic Site
244 Central St. . . . . Saugus MA 01906 781-233-0050 231-7345 564
Web: www.nps.gov
Saugus Speedway
22500 Soledad Canyon Rd . . . . . Saugus CA 91350 661-259-3886 259-8534 515
Web: www.saugusspeedway.com
Saugus Union School, The
24930 Ave Stanford . . . . . Santa Clarita MA 91355 661-294-5300 186
Web: www.saugususd.org
Sauk County 505 S Broadway St . . . . . Baraboo WI 53913 608-355-3286 355-3522 338
Web: www.co.sauk.wi.us
Sauk Rapids Recreation Program
901 First St S . . . . . Sauk Rapids MN 56379 320-253-6631 564
Web: www.isd47.org
Sauk Technologies
300 N Dekora Woods Blvd . . . . . Saukville WI 53080 262-268-3800 279
Sauk Valley Community College
173 Illinois Rt 2 . . . . . Dixon IL 61021 815-288-5511 288-3190* 162
**Fax:* Admissions ■ *Web:* www.svcc.edu
Saul 200 Eastern Pkwy. . . . . Brooklyn NY 11238 718-935-9842 671
Web: www.saulrestaurant.com
Saul Centers Inc
7501 Wisconsin Ave Ste 1500E . . . . . Bethesda MD 20814 301-986-6200 986-6079 655
NYSE: BFS ■ *Web:* www.saulcenters.com
Saul Ewing LLP
Centre Sq W 1500 Market St 38th Fl . . . . . Philadelphia PA 19102 215-972-7777 428
TF: 800-447-5375 ■ *Web:* www.saul.com
Sault Area Chamber of Commerce
2581 I-75 Business Spur . . . . . Sault Sainte Marie MI 49783 906-632-3301 632-2331 139
TF: 800-647-2858 ■ *Web:* www.saultstemarie.org
Sault College of Applied Arts & Technology, The
443 Northern Ave . . . . . Sault Sainte Marie ON P6A5L3 705-759-6700 162
TF: 800-461-2260 ■ *Web:* www.saultcollege.ca
Sault Sainte Marie Convention & Visitors Bureau
225 E Portage Ave. . . . . Sault Sainte Marie MI 49783 906-632-3366 206
TF: 800-647-2858 ■ *Web:* www.saultstemarie.com
Sault Star, The
145 Old Garden River Rd . . . . . Sault Sainte Marie ON P6A5M5 705-759-3030 532-1
TF: 800-465-4149 ■ *Web:* www.saultstar.com
Sault Ste Marie Canal National Historic Site of Canada
1 Canal Dr . . . . . Sault Sainte Marie ON P6A6W4 705-941-6262 941-6206 563
Web: www.pc.gc.ca/eng/lhn-nhs/on/ssmarie/index.aspx
Saunders & Associates LLC
2520 E Rose Garden Ln . . . . . Phoenix AZ 85050 602-971-9977 407
Web: www.saunders-assoc.com
Saunders Archery Co
1874 14th Ave PO Box 1707. . . . . Columbus NE 68601 402-564-7176 564-3260 710
TF Cust Svc: 800-228-1408 ■ *Web:* www.sausa.com
Saunders Bros LLC 256 Main St. . . . . Locke Mills ME 04255 207-875-2853 875-2857 820
TF: 800-632-3379 ■ *Web:* www.saundersbros.com
Saunders Construction Inc
1705 17th St Ste 350 . . . . . Denver CO 80202 303-699-9000 186
Web: www.saundersinc.com
Saunders County PO Box 61. . . . . Wahoo NE 68066 402-443-8101 443-8174 338
Web: www.saunderscounty.ne.gov

Saunders Electronics
192 Gannett Dr . . . . . South Portland ME 04106 207-228-1888 767
Web: saunderselectronics.com
Saunders Hotel Group Ltd
240 Newbury St . . . . . Boston MA 02116 617-861-9000 379
Web: www.saundershotelgroup.net
Saunders Manufacturing Co
65 Nickerson Hill Rd. . . . . Readfield ME 04355 207-685-9860 488
TF: 800-341-4674 ■ *Web:* www.saunders-usa.com
Sauper Associates Inc
1317 Rt 73 Ste 205. . . . . Mount Laurel NJ 08054 856-778-3800 809
Web: sauper.com
Sause Bros 3710 NW Front Ave. . . . . Portland OR 97210 503-222-1811 222-2010 465
TF: 800-488-4167 ■ *Web:* www.sause.com
Savage & Assoc Inc 4427 Talmadge Rd. . . . . Toledo OH 43623 419-475-8665 194
Web: www.savageandassociates.com
Savage Arms Inc 100 Springdale Rd. . . . . Westfield MA 01085 413-568-7001 378-4688* 284
**Fax Area Code:* 714 ■ *TF:* 800-243-3220 ■ *Web:* www.savagearms.com
Savage Design Group Inc
4203 Yoakum Blvd 4th Fl . . . . . Houston TX 77006 713-522-1555 344
Web: www.savagebrands.com
Savage IO Inc 8 S Lyon St. . . . . Batavia NY 14020 585-250-4216 173-8
Web: www.savageio.com
Savage Saws
31 Commerce St E Haven Industrial Pk . . . . . East Haven CT 06512 609-267-8501 267-1366 455
Web: www.savagesaws.com
Savanna Pallets Co
41496 State Hwy 65 . . . . . McGregor MN 55760 218-768-2077 551
TF: 800-326-0247 ■ *Web:* www.savannapallets.com
Savanna Portage State Park
55626 Lake Pl. . . . . McGregor MN 55760 218-426-3271 426-4437 565
TF: 888-646-6367 ■ *Web:* www.dnr.state.mn.us
Savannah Area Convention & Visitors Bureau
101 E Bay St. . . . . Savannah GA 31401 912-661-2662 644-6499 206
TF: 800-517-9007 ■ *Web:* www.visitsavannah.com
Savannah City Hall PO Box 1027. . . . . Savannah GA 31402 912-651-6441 651-4260 337
Web: savannahga.gov
Savannah Civic Ctr
301 W Oglethorp Ave . . . . . Savannah GA 31401 912-651-6550 651-6552 572
TF: 800-337-1101 ■ *Web:* www.savannahga.gov
Atlanta 1600 Peachtree St PO Box 77300 . . . . . Atlanta GA 30357 404-253-2700 253-3466 164
TF: 877-722-3285 ■ *Web:* www.scad.edu
Savannah College of Art and Design
342 Bull St . . . . . Savannah GA 31402 912-525-5100 525-5986 164
TF: 800-869-7223 ■ *Web:* www.scad.edu
Savannah Distributing Co Inc
2425 W Gwinnett St . . . . . Savannah GA 31415 912-233-1167 233-1557 81-1
TF General: 800-551-0777 ■ *Web:* www.savdist.com
Savannah ePASS 7000 LaRoche Ave. . . . . Savannah GA 31406 912-352-8221 671
TF: 800-989-5585 ■ *Web:* savannahepass.com
Savannah History Museum
303 ML King Jr Blvd. . . . . Savannah GA 31401 912-651-6840 520
Web: www.chsgeorgia.org
Savannah International Trade & Convention Ctr
1 International Dr . . . . . Savannah GA 31421 912-447-4000 447-4722* 205
**Fax:* Sales ■ *Web:* www.savtcc.com
Savannah Magazine PO Box 1088. . . . . Savannah GA 31402 912-652-0423 457-22
Web: www.savannahmagazine.com
Savannah Mall 14045 Abercorn St . . . . . Savannah GA 31419 912-927-7467 460
Web: www.savannahmall.com
Savannah Morning News
1375 Chatham Pkwy. . . . . Savannah GA 31405 912-236-9511 525-0795 532-2
TF: 800-533-1150 ■ *Web:* savannahnow.com
Savannah River National Laboratory
Savannah River Site . . . . . Aiken SC 29808 803-646-0485 668
Web: srnl.doe.gov
Savannah Suites 3421 Wrightsboro Rd . . . . . Augusta GA 30909 706-849-3100 132
Web: www.savannahsuites.com
Savannah Technical College
5717 White Bluff Rd . . . . . Savannah GA 31405 912-443-5700 443-5705 800
Web: www.savannahtech.edu
Savannah/Hilton Head International Airport
400 Airways Ave. . . . . Savannah GA 31408 912-964-0514 964-0877 27
Web: www.savannahairport.com
Savant Capital LLC 190 Buckley Dr . . . . . Rockford IL 61107 815-227-0300 194
Web: www.savantcapital.com
Savant Investment Group LLC
461 Second St Ste 925. . . . . San Francisco CA 94107 415-926-7200 401
Web: www.savantig.com
Savant Manufacturing Inc
2930 Hwy 383 PO Box 520. . . . . Kinder LA 70648 337-738-5896 738-3215 350
TF: 800-326-6880 ■ *Web:* www.savantmfg.com
Savant Technology Group Inc
2682 Bishop Dr Ste 210. . . . . San Ramon CA 94583 925-461-4510 387
Web: www.savant-us.com
SAVE - Suicide Awareness Voices of Education
8120 Penn Ave S Ste 470. . . . . Bloomington MN 55431 952-946-7998 829-0841 49-15
TF: 888-511-7283 ■ *Web:* www.save.org
Save America's Forests
4 Library Ct SE. . . . . Washington DC 20003 202-544-9219 544-7462 48-13
TF: 800-729-1363 ■ *Web:* www.saveamericasforests.org
Save Mart Supermarkets Inc
PO Box 4278 . . . . . Modesto CA 95352 209-577-1600 345
Web: www.savemart.com
Save the Manatee Club (SMC)
500 N Maitland Ave Ste 210. . . . . Maitland FL 32751 407-539-0990 539-0871 48-3
TF: 800-432-5646 ■ *Web:* www.savethemanatee.org
Save-A-Lot Ltd
100 Corporate Office Dr . . . . . Earth City MO 63045 314-592-9100 345
Web: www.save-a-lot.com
SaveDaily.com Inc
3020 Old Ranch Pkwy Ste 140. . . . . Seal Beach CA 90740 562-795-7500 787
Web: www.savedailyinc.com
Savelli's Italian restaurant
3055 Sutherland Ave. . . . . Knoxville TN 37919 865-521-9085 671
Web: www.savellisknoxville.com
SaveMart Pharmacy
241 W Roseville Rd . . . . . Lancaster PA 17601 717-569-7384 238
Web: www.savemartpa.com

	City	St	Zip	Phone	Fax	Class
SaveOnResorts.com 5962 La Place Ct Ste 100	Carlsbad	CA	92008	858-625-0630		775
Web: www.saveonresorts.com						
Saver Systems Inc PO Box 1058	Campbellsville	KY	42719	270-465-8675		297-8
Web: www.savergroup.com						
Savers Property & Casualty Insurance Company 11880 College Blvd Ste 500	Overland Park	KS	66210	913-339-5000	451-2382	391-4
SaveUp Inc 480 Second St Ste 202	San Francisco	CA	94107	415-578-9949		387
Web: www.saveup.com						
Saveur Magazine 15 E 32nd St 12th Fl	New York	NY	10016	212-219-7400		457-11
Web: www.saveur.com						
Savills Studley Inc 399 Pk Ave 11th Fl	New York	NY	10022	212-326-1000	326-1034	652
Web: www.studley.com						
Savin Engineers PC 3 Campus Dr	Pleasantville	NY	10570	914-769-3200	747-6686	261
Web: www.savinengineers.com						
Savings Bank Life Insurance Co of Massachusetts, The (SBLI) 1 Linscott Rd	Woburn	MA	01801	781-938-3500		391-2
Web: www.sbli.com						
Savino Del Bene USA Inc 1905 S Mt Prospect Rd Ste D	Des Plaines	IL	60018	847-390-3600		194
Web: www.savinodelbene.com						
Savio's 516 S Van Dorn St	Alexandria	VA	22304	703-212-9651		671
Web: www.saviosrestaurant.com						
Savis Inc 9 N Wabash Ave Ste 102	Chicago	IL	60602	847-797-8857		196
Web: www.savis-inc.com						
Savitz Research Solutions 13747 Montfort Dr Ste 211	Dallas	TX	75240	972-386-4050	661-3198	466
Web: www.savitzresearch.com						
Sav-Mart Co 1729 N Wenatchee Ave	Wenatchee	WA	98801	509-663-1671		229
Web: www.savmart.net						
Sav-Mor Drug Stores 43155 W Nine-Mile Rd	Novi	MI	48376	248-348-1570		237
Web: www.sav-mor.com						
Savoir-Faire 40 Leveroni Ct	Novato	CA	94949	415-884-8090		45
TF: 800-994-5993 ■ Web: www.savoirfaire.com						
Savon Plating & Powder Coating Inc 17 W Watkins Rd	Phoenix	AZ	85003	602-252-4311		481
Web: sav-onplating.com						
Savoy Medical Ctr 801 Poinciana Ave	Mamou	LA	70554	337-457-3135		374-3
Web: www.savoymedical.com						
Savoy Mountain State Forest 260 Central Shaft Rd	Florida	MA	01247	413-663-8469		565
Web: www.mass.gov						
Savoy Restaurant & Martini Bar 641 Merrimon Ave	Asheville	NC	28804	828-253-1077		671
Web: www.savoyasheville.com						
Savveo Inc 2108 S Blvd Ste 104	Charlotte	NC	28203	704-295-0100		5
Web: savveo.com						
Saw Mill River Audubon Inc 275 Millwood Rd	Chappaqua	NY	10514	914-666-6503	666-7430	50-5
Web: www.sawmillriveraudubon.org/pruyn.html						
Saw Service & Supply Inc 11925 Zelis Rd	Cleveland	OH	44135	216-252-5600		273
Web: www.sawservicesupply.com						
Sawaddee Thai Restaurant 93 Hope St	Providence	RI	02906	401-831-1122	831-1121	671
Web: www.sawaddeerestaurant.com						
Sawasdee Thai 4250 Main St	Vancouver	BC	V5V3P9	604-876-4030		671
Web: www.sawasdeethairestaurant.com						
Sawatdee 555 Osborne St	Winnipeg	MB	R3L2B3	204-284-8424		671
Sawatdee 607 Washington Ave S	Minneapolis	MN	55415	612-338-6451	338-6498	671
Web: www.sawatdee.com						
Sawatdee Thai Cuisine 10938 N 56th St	Tampa	FL	33617	813-985-2071		671
Web: sawatdeethaioftampa.com						
Sawbridge Studios 1015 Tower Ct	Winnetka	IL	60093	847-441-2441		321
Web: sawbridge.com						
Sawbrook Steel Castings Co 425 Shepherd Ave	Cincinnati	OH	45215	513-554-1700	554-0092	307
TF: 800-827-4020 ■ Web: www.sawbrooksteel.com						
Sawgrass Marriott Resort & Beach Club 1000 PGA Tour Blvd	Ponte Vedra Beach	FL	32082	904-285-7777	285-0906	669
TF: 800-228-9290 ■ Web: www.marriott.com						
Sawgrass Mills 12801 W Sunrise Blvd	Sunrise	FL	33323	954-846-2300	846-2312	460
Web: www.simon.com						
Sawmill Creek Resort 400 Sawmill Creek Dr	Huron	OH	44839	419-433-3800		669
TF: 800-729-6455 ■ Web: www.sawmillcreekresort.com						
Sawnee Electric Membership Corp 543 Atlantic Hwy	Cumming	GA	30028	770-887-2363		245
TF: 800-635-9131 ■ Web: www.sawnee.com						
Sawtooth Botanical Garden (SBG) 11 Gimlet Rd PO Box 928	Ketchum	ID	83340	208-726-9358		97
Web: www.sbgarden.org						
Sawtooth Group 141 W Front St	Red Bank	NJ	07701	732-945-1004		4
Web: www.sawtoothgroup.com						
Sawtooth Software Inc 1457 East 840 North	Orem	UT	84097	360-681-2300		809
Web: www.sawtoothsoftware.com						
Sawyer County 10610 Main St Ste 10	Hayward	WI	54843	715-634-4866	634-3666	338
TF: 877-699-4110 ■ Web: www.sawyercountygov.org						
Sawyer Free Library 2 Dale Ave	Gloucester	MA	01930	978-281-9763		434-3
TF: 800-392-6089 ■ Web: www.sawyerfreelibrary.org						
Sawyer Nursery Inc 5401 Port Sheldon St	Hudsonville	MI	49426	616-669-9094		292
TF: 888-378-7800 ■ Web: www.sawyernursery.com						
Sawyer Products Inc 605 Seventh Ave N	Safety Harbor	FL	34695	727-725-1177		791
Web: www.sawyer.com						
Saxco International LLC 200 Gibraltar Rd Ste 101	Horsham	PA	19044	215-443-8100		360-3
Web: www.saxco.com						
Saxe Doernberger & Vita PC 1952 Whitney Ave	Hamden	CT	06517	203-287-2100		428
TF: 800-973-1177 ■ Web: www.sdvlaw.com						
Saxe Real Estate Management Service 1999 Van Ness Ave	San Francisco	CA	94109	415-474-3171	447-8652	655
Web: www.saxerealestate.com						
Saxon Group Inc, The 790 Brogdon Rd	Suwanee	GA	30024	770-271-2174		186
Saxon Shoes 11800 W Broad St Ste 2750	Richmond	VA	23233	804-285-3473	285-8526	301
TF General: 800-686-5616 ■ Web: shop.saxonshoes.com						
Saxton Inc Design Group 600 Third St SE Ste 300	Cedar Rapids	IA	52401	319-365-6967		320
Web: www.saxtoninc.com						
Saybrook Capital LLC 11400 W Olympic Blvd	Los Angeles	CA	90064	310-899-9200		401
Web: www.saybrook.net						
Saybrook Point Inn & Spa 2 Bridge St	Old Saybrook	CT	06475	860-395-2000		669
TF: 800-243-0212 ■ Web: www.saybrook.com						
Sayer Energy Advisors 1620 540 - Fifth Ave SW	Calgary	AB	T2P0M2	403-266-6133		528
Web: www.sayeradvisors.com						
Sayers Group LLC 825 Corporate Woods Pkwy	Vernon Hills	IL	60061	800-323-5357		180
TF: 800-323-5357 ■ Web: www.sayers.com						
Sayle Oil Company Inc 410 W Main	Charleston	MS	38921	662-647-5802		324
Web: www.sayleoil.com						
Saylent Technologies Inc 122 Grove St Ste 300	Franklin	MA	02038	508-570-2161		177
TF: 800-241-6631 ■ Web: www.saylent.com						
Saylor Beall Mfg Company Inc 400 N Kibbee St	Saint Johns	MI	48879	989-224-2371	224-8788	172
TF: 800-248-9001 ■ Web: www.saylor-beall.com						
Sayreville Free Public Library 1050 Washington Rd	Parlin	NJ	08859	732-727-0212		434-3
Web: www.lmxac.org						
SAYVA (Satchidananda Ashram Yogaville) 108 Yogaville Way	Buckingham	VA	23921	434-969-3121		673
TF Resv: 800-858-9642 ■ Web: yogaville.org						
Saz's 5539 W State St	Milwaukee	WI	53208	414-453-2410		671
Web: www.sazs.com						
SB Ballard Construction Co 2828 Shipps Corner Rd	Virginia Beach	VA	23453	757-440-5555	451-2873	189-3
TF: 800-296-0209 ■ Web: www.sbballard.com						
S&B Industrial Minerals North America Inc 920 Cassatt Rd Ste 205	Berwyn	PA	19312	610-647-1123		501
SB International Inc 3626 N Hall St Ste 910	Dallas	TX	75219	214-526-4423	526-1503	492
Web: sbisteel.com						
SB Whistler & Sons Inc PO Box 270	Medina	NY	14103	585-318-4630	798-5612	757
TF: 800-828-1010 ■ Web: www.sbwhistler.com						
SBA (Small Business Administration) 409 Third St SW	Washington	DC	20416	202-205-6600	205-6802	340-20
TF: 800-827-5722 ■ Web: www.sba.gov						
SBA (Small Business Administration Regional Offices) Region 1 10 Cswy St Ste 265A	Boston	MA	02222	617-565-8416	565-8420	340-20
Web: www.sba.gov/about-offices-list/3						
SBA Communications Corp 5900 Broken Sound Pkwy NW	Boca Raton	FL	33487	561-995-7670		170
NASDAQ: SBAC ■ TF: 800-487-7483 ■ Web: www.sbasite.com						
SBA Materials Inc 9430-H San Mateo Blvd NE	Albuquerque	NM	87113	505-924-2807		601
Web: www.sbamaterials.com						
SBAA (Spina Bifida Assn) 1600 Wilson Blvd Ste 250	Washington	DC	20007	202-944-3285		48-17
TF: 877-686-6444 ■ Web: www.spinabifidaassociation.org						
Sbar's Inc 14 Sbar Blvd	Moorestown	NJ	08057	856-234-8220	234-9159	44
TF: 800-989-7227 ■ Web: www.sbarsonline.com						
SBBI Inc 3282 State Hwy 82 PO Box 770	Sonoita	AZ	85637	520-455-5983		186
Web: www.sbbiaz.com						
SBC (Countryside Bank) 6734 Joliet Rd	Countryside	IL	60525	708-485-3100	485-3106	70
Web: www.bankcountryside.com						
SBC (Southern Baptist Convention) 901 Commerce St	Nashville	TN	37203	615-244-2355		48-20
TF: 866-722-5433 ■ Web: www.sbc.net						
SBC Adv Ltd 333 W Nationwide Blvd	Columbus	OH	43215	614-255-2333		4
Web: www.sbcadvertising.com						
SBC Foundation 130 E Travis St Ste 350	San Antonio	TX	78205	800-591-9663		304
TF: 800-591-9663 ■ Web: www.att.com						
SBCA (Satellite Broadcasting & Communications Assn) 1730 M St NW Ste 600	Washington	DC	20036	202-349-3620	349-3621	49-14
TF: 800-541-5981 ■ Web: www.sbca.com						
SBCC (South Baldwin Chamber of Commerce) 112 W Laurel Ave PO Box 1117	Foley	AL	36535	251-943-3291	943-6810	139
TF: 877-461-3712 ■ Web: www.southbaldwinchamber.com						
SBCC Inc 1711 Dell Ave	Campbell	CA	95008	408-379-5500		106
Web: www.sbci.com						
SBE (Society of Broadcast Engineers Inc) 9102 N Meridian St Ste 150	Indianapolis	IN	46260	317-846-9000	846-9120	49-14
TF: 800-237-1776 ■ Web: www.sbe.org						
Sbeeg Holdings LLC 8000 Beverly Blvd	Los Angeles	CA	90048	323-655-8000		360-3
Web: sbe.com						
SBG (Sawtooth Botanical Garden) 11 Gimlet Rd PO Box 928	Ketchum	ID	83340	208-726-9358		97
Web: www.sbgarden.org						
SBGH (St-Boniface Hospital) 409 Tache Ave	Winnipeg	MB	R2H2A6	204-233-8563	231-0041*	374-2
*Fax: Hum Res ■ Web: www.saintboniface.ca						
SBL (Society of Biblical Literature) The Luce Ctr 825 Houston Mill Rd	Atlanta	GA	30329	404-727-3100	727-3101	48-20
TF: 866-727-9955 ■ Web: www.sbl-site.org						
SBL (Silas Bronson Library) 267 Grand St	Waterbury	CT	06702	203-574-8222	574-8055	434-3
Web: www.bronsonlibrary.org						
SBLC (Small Business Legislative Council) 4800 Hampden Ln 6th Fl	Bethesda	MD	20814	202-639-8500		49-12
Web: www.sblc.org						
SBLHC (Sarah Bush Lincoln Health Ctr) 1000 Health Ctr Dr PO Box 372	Mattoon	IL	61938	217-258-2525	258-4117	374-3
TF: 800-345-3191 ■ Web: www.sarahbush.org						
SBLI (Savings Bank Life Insurance Co of Massachusetts, The) 1 Linscott Rd	Woburn	MA	01801	781-938-3500		391-2
Web: www.sbli.com						

Phone Fax Class

SBM (South Bend Museum of Art)
120 S St Joseph St ... South Bend IN 46601 574-235-9102 235-5782 520
TF: 800-301-4961 ■ *Web:* www.southbendart.org

SBM (Society of Behavioral Medicine)
555 E Wells St Ste 1100 ... Milwaukee WI 53202 414-918-3156 276-3349 49-15
Web: www.sbm.org

SBP Consulting 4900 38th Ave Ste 5 ... Moline IL 61265 732-631-0002 196
Web: www.sbpcorp.com

SBS (Storage Battery Systems Inc)
N56 W16665 Ridgewood Dr ... Menomonee Falls WI 53051 262-703-5800 703-3073 246
TF: 800-554-2243 ■ *Web:* www.sbsbattery.com

SBS (Spanish Broadcasting System Inc)
2601 S Bayshore Dr PH 2 ... Coconut Grove FL 33133 305-441-6901 446-5148 643
NASDAQ: SBSA ■ *TF:* 800-579-1639 ■ *Web:* www.spanishbroadcasting.com

SBS Studios LLC
8400 Baymeadows Way Ste 4 ... Jacksonville FL 32256 904-352-2401 809
TF: 800-434-8301 ■ *Web:* www.sbsstudios.com

SBS Transit Inc
3747 Colorado Ave ... Sheffield Village OH 44054 440-949-8121 107
Web: loraincounty.com

SBSB (Santa Barbara Speakers Bureau LLC)
PO Box 30768 ... Santa Barbara CA 93130 805-682-7474 708
Web: santabarbaraca.com/businesses/santa-barbara-speakers-bureau

SBSO (South Bend Symphony Orchestra)
127 N Michigan St ... South Bend IN 46601 574-232-6343 232-6627 573-3
TF: 800-537-6415 ■ *Web:* www.southbendsymphony.com

SBUH (Stony Brook University Hospital)
101 Nicolls Rd ... Stony Brook NY 11794 631-444-4000 374-3
Web: www.stonybrookmedicine.edu

SBV Venture Partners
454 Ruthven Ave ... Palo Alto CA 94301 650-522-0085 401

SBW Consulting Inc
2820 Northup Way Ste 230 ... Bellevue WA 98004 425-827-0330 194
Web: www.sbwconsulting.com

SC Anderson Inc PO Box 81747 ... Bakersfield CA 93308 661-392-7000 391-9999 186
Web: www.scanderson.com

Sc Builders Inc 910 Thompson Pl ... Sunnyvale CA 94085 408-328-0688 186
Web: www.scbuildersinc.com

SC Engineers Inc
17075 Via Del Campo 1st Fl ... San Diego CA 92127 858-946-0333 261
Web: scengineers.net

SC Johnson & Son Inc 1525 Howe St ... Racine WI 53403 262-260-2154 260-6004 151
Web: www.scjohnson.com

SCA (Society of Cardiovascular Anesthesiologists)
2209 Dickens Rd ... Richmond VA 23230 804-282-0084 282-0090 49-8
TF: 800-283-6296 ■ *Web:* www.scahq.org

SCA (Shipbuilders Council of America)
20 F St NW Ste 500 ... Washington DC 20001 202-347-5462 49-21
Web: www.shipbuilders.org

SCA (Student Conservation Assn)
689 River Rd PO Box 550 ... Charlestown NH 03603 603-543-1700 543-1828 48-13
TF: 888-722-9675 ■ *Web:* www.thesca.org

SCA Americas
2929 Arch St Ste 2600 ... Philadelphia PA 19104 610-499-3700 499-3391 558
Web: www.sca.com

SCA Direct
11200 Waples Mill Rd Ste 150 ... Fairfax VA 22030 703-293-6339 7
Web: www.scadirect.com

SC&A Inc 1608 Spring Hill Rd Ste 400 ... Vienna VA 22182 703-893-6600 821-8236 668
Web: www.scainc.com

SCAA (Specialty Coffee Assn of America)
117 W Fourth St Ste 300 ... Santa Ana CA 92701 562-624-4100 624-4101 49-6
TF: 800-995-9019 ■ *Web:* www.scaa.org

Scadaware Inc 1602 Rhodes Ln ... Bloomington IL 61704 309-665-0135 177
Web: www.scadaware.com

Scaffs Inc 134 SE Colburn Ave ... Lake City FL 32025 386-752-7344 204
Web: scaffs.com

Scafidi Cranston & Assoc LLC
42 S Main St ... Medford Lakes NJ 08055 609-953-8699 2
Web: scafidicranston.com

Scala Inc 350 Eagleview Blvd Ste 350 ... Exton PA 19341 610-363-3350 177
Web: www.scala.com

Scala's Bistro 432 Powell St ... San Francisco CA 94102 415-395-8555 671
Web: www.scalasbistro.com

Scalability Experts Inc
1203 Crestside Dr ... Coppell TX 75019 469-635-6200 177
Web: www.scalabilityexperts.com

Scalable Display Technologies Inc
585 Massachusetts Ave 4th Fl ... Cambridge MA 02139 617-864-9300 194
Web: www.scalabledisplay.com

Scalamandre Silks Inc
350 Wireless Blvd ... Hauppauge NY 11788 631-467-8800 467-9448 745-1
TF: 800-932-4361 ■ *Web:* scalamandre.com

Scalar Decisions Inc
1 Toronto St 3rd Fl ... Toronto ON M5C2V6 416-202-0020 257-0174* 177
**Fax Area Code:* 866 ■ *TF:* 866-364-5588 ■ *Web:* www.scalar.ca

Scale Auto Magazine
21027 Crossroads Cir ... Waukesha WI 53186 262-796-8776 457-14
TF Cust Svc: 800-533-6644 ■ *Web:* www.scaleautomag.com

Scale Models Unlimited 400 S Front St ... Memphis TN 38103 901-577-5155 261
Web: www.smu.com

Scale Venture Partners
950 Tower Ln Ste 700 ... Foster City CA 94404 650-378-6000 378-6040 792
Web: www.scalevp.com

Scaled Composites Inc
1624 Flight Line Rd ... Mojave CA 93501 661-824-4541 824-4174 20
Web: www.scaled.com

ScaleGrid 4205 148th Ave NE Ste 100 ... Bellevue WA 98007 425-460-4917 396
Web: www.scalegrid.net

Scalehouse, The 974 Rd E ... Schuyler NE 68661 402-352-3686 361

ScaleMatrix Inc
5775 Kearny Villa Rd ... San Diego CA 92123 858-633-4300 631
Web: www.scalematrix.com

ScaleMP Inc 2175 Lemoine Ave Ste 401 ... Fort Lee NJ 07024 201-429-9740 177
Web: www.scalemp.com

Scales & Shells Restaurant & Raw Bar
527 Thames St ... Newport RI 02840 401-846-3474 671
Web: www.scalesandshells.com

Phone Fax Class

Scales Air Compressor Corp
110 Voice Rd ... Carle Place NY 11514 516-248-9096 248-9639 172
TF: 877-798-0454 ■ *Web:* www.scalesair.com

Scalia Antonin
US Supreme Ct Bldg 1 1st St NE ... Washington DC 20543 202-479-3000 479-3472 341-4
TF: 800-772-1213 ■ *Web:* www.supremecourt.gov

Scalini Fedeli 165 Duane St ... New York NY 10013 212-528-0400 671
Web: www.scalinifedeli.com

Scalise Steve (Rep R - LA)
2338 Rayburn Bldg ... Washington DC 20515 202-225-3015 342-2
Web: scalise.house.gov

Scalo Northern Italian Grill
3500 Central Ave SE ... Albuquerque NM 87106 505-255-8781 265-7850 671
Web: www.scalonobhill.com

SCAN (Sports Cardiovascular & Wellness Nutritionists)
230 Washington Ave Extn Ste 101 ... Albany NY 12203 518-254-6730 463-8656 49-8
TF General: 800-249-2875 ■ *Web:* www.scandpg.org

SCAN Health Plan
3800 Kilroy Airport Way Ste 100 ... Long Beach CA 90806 562-989-5100 352
TF: 800-247-5091 ■ *Web:* www.scanhealthplan.com

SCANA Corp 220 Operation Way ... Cayce SC 29033 803-217-9000 360-5
NYSE: SCG ■ *TF:* 800-251-7234 ■ *Web:* www.scana.com

SCANA Energy Marketing
220 Operation Way ... Cayce SC 29033 803-217-9000 787
TF: 800-472-1051 ■ *Web:* www.scana.com

ScanAps 6133 Bristol Pkwy Ste 301 ... Culver City CA 90230 310-670-1700 387
Web: www.scanaps.com

Scanbuy Inc 10 E 39th St Tenth Fl ... New York NY 10016 212-278-0178 180
Web: www.scanlife.com

Scandent Group Inc
340 Interstate N Pkwy Ste 340 ... Atlanta GA 30339 770-303-4448 396
Web: www.scandent.com

Scandia Packaging Machinery Co
15 Industrial Rd ... Fairfield NJ 07004 973-473-6100 473-7226 547
Web: www.scandiapack.com

Scandic Spring Inc
700 Montague St ... San Leandro CA 94577 510-352-3700 492
TF: 800-344-4539 ■ *Web:* www.scandic.com

Scandinave Spa Mont-Tremblant
4280 Montee Ryan ... Mont Tremblant QC J8E1S4 819-425-9595 354
Web: www.scandinave.com

Scandinavian Airlines System (SAS)
301 Route 17 N Ste 500 ... Rutherford NJ 07070 800-437-5807 896-3735* 25
**Fax Area Code:* 201 ■ *TF:* 800-221-2350 ■ *Web:* www.flysas.com

Scandinavian Tourist Boards
655 Third Ave ... New York NY 10017 212-885-9700 775
Web: www.goscandinavia.com

Scandrill Inc 11777 Katy Fwy Ste 470 ... Houston TX 77079 281-496-5571 540
Web: www.scandrill.com

Scania USA Inc
121 Interpark Blvd Ste 601 ... San Antonio TX 78216 210-403-0007 616
TF: 800-272-2642 ■ *Web:* www.scania.com

Scanics 723 S Neil St Ste 101 ... Champaign IL 61825 217-403-4000 175
Web: scanics.com

Scanline Vfx La Inc
12950 Culver Blvd ... Los Angeles CA 90066 310-827-1555 514
Web: scanlinevfx.com

Scanner Applications Inc
400 Milford Pkwy ... Milford OH 45150 513-248-5588 466
Web: www.scanapps.com

Scannicchio 2500 S Broad St ... Philadelphia PA 19145 215-468-3900 468-3900 671
Web: www.scannicchio.com

Scanning America Inc 1440 N Third St ... Lawrence KS 66044 785-749-7471 317
Web: www.scanningamerica.com

Scan-Optics Inc 169 Progress Dr ... Manchester CT 06042 860-645-7878 645-7995 178-8
TF: 800-543-8681 ■ *Web:* www.scanoptics.com

ScanSource Inc 6 Logue Ct ... Greenville SC 29615 864-288-2432 174
NASDAQ: SCSC ■ *TF:* 800-944-2432 ■ *Web:* www.scansource.com

Scantek Infomanagement Solutions Inc
1100 Easton Rd ... Willow Grove PA 19090 215-882-5000 396
Web: www.scantek.info

Scantibodies Laboratory Inc
9336 Abraham Way ... Santee CA 92071 619-258-9300 258-9366 231
TF: 800-279-9181 ■ *Web:* www.scantibodies.com

Scantron Corp 34 Parker ... Irvine CA 92618 949-639-7500 639-7710 173-7
TF: 800-722-6876 ■ *Web:* www.scantron.com

Scanwell Logistics (NYC) Inc
1995 Linden Blvd ... Elmont NY 11003 516-285-8100 314
Web: www.scanwell.com

Scap Auto Group 421 Tunxis Hill Rd ... Fairfield CT 06825 203-384-9300 57
Web: www.scapauto.com

Scarab Behavioral Health Services LLC
3203 Brick Church Pk ... Nashville TN 37207 615-262-7822 363
Web: scarabhealth.com

Scaramouche Restaurant 1 Benvenuto Pl ... Toronto ON M4V2L1 416-961-8011 671
TF: 800-826-4180 ■ *Web:* www.scaramoucherestaurant.com

Scarantino's 1524 E Colorado St ... Glendale CA 91205 818-247-9777 671
Web: www.scarantinos.com

Scarborough Downs 90 Payne Rd ... Scarborough ME 04070 207-883-4331 883-2020 642
TF: 800-711-5882 ■ *Web:* www.scarboroughdowns.com

Scarborough Historical Museum
1007 Brimley Rd ... Toronto ON M1P3E8 416-338-8807 520
Web: toronto.ca

Scarborough Hospital Birchmount campus
3030 Birchmount Rd ... Scarborough ON M1W3W3 416-495-2400 495-2562 374-2
Web: www.tsh.to

Scarborough Hospital General Div
3050 Lawrence Ave E ... Scarborough ON M1P2V5 416-438-2911 431-8204 374-2
Web: www.tsh.to

Scarbrough International Ltd
10841 Ambassador Dr ... Kansas City MO 64153 816-891-2400 311
Web: www.scarbrough-intl.com

Scarritt Group Inc
7636 N Oracle Rd Ste 100 ... Tucson AZ 85704 520-529-0000 463
Web: www.scarrittgroup.com

Scarsdale Public Schools
2 Brewster Rd ... Scarsdale NY 10583 914-721-2410 685
TF: 888-837-6437 ■ *Web:* www.scarsdaleschools.k12.ny.us

Phone | Fax | Class

Scarsdale Security Systems Inc
132 Montgomery Ave ... Scarsdale NY 10583 914-722-2200 693
Web: scarsdalesecurity.com/index.html

Scarsin Corp 2 Brock St W Ste 201 ... Uxbridge ON L9P1P2 905-852-0086 195
Web: www.scarsin.com

Scat Enterprises Inc
1400 Kingsdale Ave ... Redondo Beach CA 90278 310-370-5501 57
Web: www.procarbyscat.com

Scattergood Friends School
1951 Delta Ave ... West Branch IA 52358 319-519-1860 643-7485 622
Web: www.scattergood.org

SCB (Shipowners Claims Bureau)
1 Battery Pk Plaza 31st Fl ... New York NY 10004 212-847-4500 847-4599 49-21
TF: 800-774-8724 ■ *Web:* www.american-club.com

SCB Bancorp Inc 1501 E Eldorado St ... Decatur IL 62521 217-428-7781 70
TF: 888-769-2265 ■ *Web:* www.soybank.com

SCB Distributors 15608 New Century Dr ... Gardena CA 90248 310-532-9400 96
TF: 800-729-6423 ■ *Web:* scbdistributors.com

SCB Marketing 5131 Industry Dr ... Melbourne FL 32940 321-622-5986 530
Web: scbmarketing.com

SCBT Financial Corp
950 John C Calhoun Dr ... Orangeburg SC 29115 803-534-2175 360-2
NASDAQ: SCBT ■ *TF:* 800-277-2175 ■ *Web:* www.southstatebank.com

SCC (Society of Cosmetic Chemists)
120 Wall St Ste 2400 ... New York NY 10005 212-668-1500 668-1504 49-19
Web: www.scconline.org

SCC (Superior Crane Corp)
208 Wilmont Dr PO Box 1464 ... Waukesha WI 53189 262-542-0099 542-7767 386
Web: www.superiorcrane.com

SCC Soft Computer Inc
5400 Tech Data Dr ... Clearwater FL 33760 727-789-0100 789-0124 180
TF: 800-763-8352 ■ *Web:* www.softcomputer.com

SCCA (Sports Car Club of America)
6700 SW Topeka Blvd Ste 300 ... Topeka KS 66619 785-357-7222 232-7228 48-18
TF: 800-770-2055 ■ *Web:* www.scca.com

SCCM (Society of Critical Care Medicine)
500 Midway Dr Ste 200 ... Mount Prospect IL 60056 847-827-6869 827-6886 49-8
Web: www.sccm.org

SCDAA (Sickle Cell Disease Assn of America)
3700 Koppers St Ste 570 ... Baltimore MD 21202 410-528-1555 528-1495 48-17
TF: 800-421-8453 ■ *Web:* www.sicklecelldisease.org

SCE (Soil Consultant Engineering)
9303 Ctr St ... Manassas VA 20110 703-366-3000 366-3400 261
Web: www.soilconsultants.net

Scelzi Equipment Inc
1030 W Gladstone St ... Azusa CA 91702 626-334-0573 516
TF: 800-858-2883 ■ *Web:* www.seinc.com

Scenarios Usa 80 Hanson Pl Ste 305 ... Brooklyn NY 11217 718-230-4381 242
Web: scenariosusa.org

Scene Weaver 649 Rosewood Dr Ste B ... Columbia SC 29201 803-252-0662 361
Web: www.sceneweaver.com

Scenic Airlines Inc
1265 Airport Rd ... Boulder City NV 89005 702-638-3300 639-3275 760
TF: 800-634-6801 ■ *Web:* www.scenic.com

Scenic Beach State Park
9565 Scenic Beach Rd NW ... Seabeck WA 98380 360-830-5079 565
TF: 888-226-7688 ■ *Web:* www.parks.wa.gov

Scenic Prints Landscape Photos
536 Sweetwater St ... Lander WY 82520 307-332-1532 592
Web: www.scenicprints.com

Scenic Rivers Energy Co-op
231 N Sheridan St ... Lancaster WI 53813 608-723-2121 245
TF: 800-236-2141 ■ *Web:* www.sre.coop

Scenic Solutions 16135 New Ave ... Lemont IL 60439 630-243-1804 499
TF: 800-328-5858 ■ *Web:* www.scenicsolutions.com

Scenic State Park 56956 Scenic Hwy 7 ... Bigfork MN 56628 218-743-3362 565
Web: www.dnr.state.mn.us

Scentisphere LLC 97 Old Rt 6 ... Carmel NY 10512 845-225-3600 77
TF: 800-258-7783 ■ *Web:* www.oscom.net

ScentSational Technologies LLC
425 York Rd ... Jenkintown PA 19046 215-886-7777 393
Web: www.scentsationaltechnologies.com

SCF Partners 600 Travis Ste 6600 ... Houston TX 77002 713-227-7888 227-7850 41
Web: www.scfpartners.com

SCF Securities Inc
155 E Shaw Ave Ste 102 ... Fresno CA 93710 559-456-6100 390
TF: 800-289-9999 ■ *Web:* www.scfsecurities.com

SCFM Compressor Systems
3701 S Maybelle Ave ... Tulsa OK 74107 918-663-1309 172
TF: 800-874-7719 ■ *Web:* www.scfm.com

SCFTA (Segerstrom Center for the Arts)
600 Town Ctr Dr ... Costa Mesa CA 92626 714-556-2121 556-8984 572
Web: www.scfta.org/home/default.aspx

SCG (Southern Connecticut Gas)
60 Marsh Hill Rd ... Orange CT 06477 866-268-2887 787
TF: 866-268-2887 ■ *Web:* www.soconngas.com

SCG Governmental Affairs LLC
201 S Monroe St Ste 301 ... Tallahassee FL 32301 850-513-0004 636
Web: www.scggov.com

SCH (Saint Catherine Hospital)
401 E Spruce St ... Garden City KS 67846 620-272-2222 374-3
Web: stcatherinehosp.org

SCH (Sunbury Community Hospital)
350 N 11th St ... Sunbury PA 17801 570-286-3333 374-3
Web: www.sunburyhospital.com

SCH (Southside Community Hospital)
800 Oak St ... Farmville VA 23901 434-392-8811 374-3
Web: sch.centrahealth.com

SC&H Group LLC 910 Ridgebrook Rd ... Sparks MD 21152 410-403-1500 403-1570 2
TF: 800-832-3008 ■ *Web:* www.scandh.com

Schadegg Mechanical Inc
225 Bridgepoint Dr S ... St. Paul MN 55075 651-292-9933 697
Web: www.schadegg-mech.com

Schaefer Ambulance Service Inc
4627 Beverly Blvd ... Los Angeles CA 90004 323-468-1600 30
TF: 800-328-0118 ■ *Web:* www.schaeferamb.com

Schaefer Brush Manufacturing Company Inc
1101 S Prairie Ave ... Waukesha WI 53186 262-547-3500 586
TF: 800-347-3501 ■ *Web:* schaeferbrush.com

Schaefer Marine Inc
158 Duchaine Blvd ... New Bedford MA 02745 508-995-9511 360-3
Web: schaefermarine.com

Schaefer Pyrotechnics Inc
376 Hartman Bridge Rd ... Ronks PA 17572 717-687-0647 268

Schaefer Systems International Inc
10021 Westlake Dr ... Charlotte NC 28241 704-944-4500 588-1862 199
TF: 800-876-6000 ■ *Web:* ssi-schaefer.us

Schaefer The Law Firm of John f
380 N Old Woodward Ave Ste 320 ... Birmingham MI 48009 248-642-6655 428
TF: 800-227-9553 ■ *Web:* lfjfs.com

Schaeffer & Associates Ltd
6 Ronrose Dr ... Concord ON L4K4R3 905-738-6100 261
Web: www.schaeffers.com

Schaeffer Mfg Company Inc
102 Barton St ... Saint Louis MO 63104 314-865-4100 865-4107 541
TF Cust Svc: 800-325-9962 ■ *Web:* www.schaefferoil.com

Schaeffer Nassar Schneidegg Consulting Engineers LLC
1425 Cantillon Blvd ... Mays Landing NJ 08330 609-625-7400 261
Web: www.snsce.com

Schaeffer's Investment Research Inc
5151 Pfeiffer Rd Ste 250 ... Cincinnati OH 45242 513-589-3800 589-3810 637-9
TF: 800-448-2080 ■ *Web:* www.schaeffersresearch.com

Schaeffler Group USA Inc
308 Springhill Farm Rd ... Fort Mill SC 29715 803-548-8500 548-8599 75
TF: 800-361-5841 ■ *Web:* www.schaeffler.us

SCHAERER MEDICAL USA Inc
675 Wilmer Ave ... Cincinnati OH 45226 513-561-2241 475
Web: www.schaerermayfieldusa.com

Schafer Condon Carter Inc
1029 W Madison ... Chicago IL 60607 312-464-1666 344
Web: www.sccadv.com

Schafer Corp 321 Billerica Rd ... Chelmsford MA 01824 703-516-6000 261
TF: 800-499-6456 ■ *Web:* www.schafercorp.com

Schafer Gear Works Inc
4701 Nimtz Pkwy ... South Bend IN 46628 574-234-4116 234-4115 709
Web: schaferindustries.com

Schafer State Park W 1365 Schafer Pk Rd ... Elma WA 98541 360-482-3852 565
Web: parks.state.wa.us

Schafer Veterinary Consultants LLC
800 Helena Ct ... Fort Collins CO 80524 970-224-5103 794
Web: schaferveterinary.com

Schaff Piano Supply Co
451 Oakwood Rd ... Lake Zurich IL 60047 847-438-4556 438-4615 527
TF: 800-747-4266 ■ *Web:* www.schaffpiano.com

Schaffer Consulting 707 Summer St ... Stamford CT 06901 203-322-1604 194
Web: www.schafferresults.com

Schaffer Grinding Co
848 S Maple Ave ... Montebello CA 90640 323-724-4476 724-2635 454
Web: www.schaffergrinding.com

Schaffer Library of the Health Sciences
Albany Medical College 47 New Scotland Ave ... Albany NY 12208 518-262-5586 434-1
Web: www.amc.edu/academic/schaffer

Schaffer Specialty Welding Inc
109 Industrial Ave ... Milltown WI 54858 715-825-2424 757
TF: 800-532-2252 ■ *Web:* www.schafferwelding.com

Schaffner Mfg Company Inc
21 Herron Ave Schaffner Ctr ... Pittsburgh PA 15202 412-761-9902 761-8998 1
Web: www.schaffnermfg.com

Schahet Hotels Inc
9333 N Meridian St ... Indianapolis IN 46260 317-848-9000 194
Web: www.schahethotels.com

Schakowsky Jan (Rep D - IL)
2367 Rayburn Bldg ... Washington DC 20515 202-225-2111 226-6890 342-2
Web: schakowsky.house.gov

Schaller & Weber Inc 22-35 46th St ... Astoria NY 11105 718-721-5480 956-9157 296-26
TF Orders: 800-847-4115 ■ *Web:* www.schallerweber.com

Schaller Telephone Co
111 w Second st ... Schaller IA 51053 712-275-4211 387
Web: www.schallertel.net

Schalmont Central School District
4 Sabre Dr ... Schenectady NY 12306 518-355-9200 355-9203 685
Web: www.schalmont.org

Schambach Plumbing & Heating Inc
40W899 Russell Rd ... Elgin IL 60124 847-464-5373 189-10

Scharer Insurance Inc 454 E Ctr St ... Marion OH 43302 740-387-4311 390
Web: scharerinsurance.com

Scharf Investments LLC
5619 Scotts Vly Dr Ste 140 ... Scotts Valley CA 95066 831-429-6513 401
TF: 800-422-6172 ■ *Web:* www.scharfinvestments.com

Scharf's Schiller Park Restaurant
2683 Clinton St ... West Seneca NY 14224 716-895-7249 671
Web: www.scharfsrest.com

Scharine Group, The
4213 N Scharine Rd ... Whitewater WI 53190 608-883-2880 186
TF: 800-472-2880 ■ *Web:* www.thescharinegroup.com

Schatten Properties Management Company Inc
1514 S St ... Nashville TN 37212 615-329-3011 327-2343 653
TF: 800-892-1315 ■ *Web:* www.schattenproperties.com

Schatz Bearing Corp
10 Fairview Ave ... Poughkeepsie NY 12601 845-452-6000 452-1660 75
TF: 800-554-1406 ■ *Web:* www.schatzbearing.com

Schatz Brian (Sen D - HI)
722 Hart Bldg ... Washington DC 20510 202-224-3934 228-1153 342-2
Web: www.schatz.senate.gov

Schaumburg Park District
235 E Beech Dr ... Schaumburg IL 60193 847-985-2115 31
Web: www.parkfun.com

Schaumburg Specialties Co
550 Albion Ave Unit 30 ... Schaumburg IL 60193 800-834-8125 111
TF: 800-834-8125 ■ *Web:* www.shopcraftracks.com

Schaumburg Township District Library (STDL)
130 S Roselle Rd ... Schaumburg IL 60193 847-985-4000 434-3
Web: www.schaumburglibrary.org

Schawbel Corp 26 Crosby Dr ... Bedford MA 01730 781-541-6900 37
TF: 866-753-3837 ■ *Web:* www.thermacell.com/mosquito-repellent

Schawk Inc 1695 S River Rd ... Des Plaines IL 60018 847-827-9494 627
NYSE: SGK ■ *Web:* www.schawk.com

	City	State	Zip	Phone	Fax	Class
Schechter Dokken Kanter CPA'S 100 Washington Ave S Ste 1600 *TF:* 800-241-8768 ■ *Web:* www.sdkcpa.com	Minneapolis	MN	55401	612-332-5500		734
Schechter Wealth Strategies 251 Pierce St *Web:* www.schechterwealth.com	Birmingham	MI	48009	248-731-9500		401
Schecter Guitar Research Inc 10953 Pendleton St *TF:* 800-660-6621 ■ *Web:* www.schecterguitars.com	Sun Valley	CA	91352	800-660-6621		527
Schedel Arboretum & Gardens 19255 W Portage River S Rd *Web:* www.schedel-gardens.org	Elmore	OH	43416	419-862-3182		97
Schedulicity Inc 424 E Main Ste 201 *Web:* www.schedulicity.com	Bozeman	MT	59715	406-582-0494		177
Scheef & Stone LLP 500 N Akard St Ste 2700 *TF:* 800-447-5375 ■ *Web:* www.solidcounsel.com	Dallas	TX	75201	214-706-4200		428
Scheeser Buckley Mayfield Inc 1540 Corporate Woods Pkwy *TF:* 800-451-0221 ■ *Web:* www.sbmce.com	Uniontown	OH	44685	330-896-4664		261
Scheibel Halaska 735 N Water St Ste 200 *Web:* www.trefoilgroup.com	Milwaukee	WI	53202	414-272-6898		463
Scheid Vineyards Inc 305 Hilltown Rd *Web:* www.scheidvineyards.com	Salinas	CA	93908	831-455-9990	455-9998	315-5
Scheig Assoc PO Box 2628 **Fax Area Code: 800* ■ *Web:* www.scheig.com	Gig Harbor	WA	98335	253-858-3534	766-3533*	196
Scheinkman & ScheinkmanPA 18 NE Second Ave	Dania Beach	FL	33004	954-920-6173		2
Scheirer Machine Company Inc 3200 Industrial Blvd *TF:* 800-448-4590 ■ *Web:* www.scheirer.com	Bethel Park	PA	15102	412-833-6500	833-8110	454
Schemmer Assoc Inc, The 1044 N 115th St	Omaha	NE	68154	402-493-4800		261
Schenck AccuRate Inc 746 E Milwaukee St PO Box 208 *TF:* 800-558-0184 ■ *Web:* www.accuratefeeders.com	Whitewater	WI	53190	262-473-2441		407
Schenck Business Solutions 200 E Washington St *TF:* 800-236-2246 ■ *Web:* www.schenckso.com	Appleton	WI	54911	920-731-8111	731-8037	2
Schenck Trebel Corp 535 Acorn St *TF:* 800-873-2357 ■ *Web:* www.schenck-usa.com	Deer Park	NY	11729	631-242-4010	242-5077	684
Schendel Pest Services 1035 SE Quincy St *TF:* 800-591-7378 ■ *Web:* www.schendelpest.com	Topeka	KS	66612	785-232-9357		577
Schenectady County 620 State St *TF:* 800-950-3228 ■ *Web:* www.schenectadycounty.com	Schenectady	NY	12305	518-285-8435	388-4224	338
Schenectady County Community College 78 Washington Ave *Web:* www.sunysccc.edu	Schenectady	NY	12305	518-381-1200		162
Schenectady County Public Library System 99 Clinton St *Web:* www.scpl.org	Schenectady	NY	12305	518-388-4500	386-2241	434-3
Schenectady Hardware & Electric Company Inc PO Box 338 *Web:* www.sheinc.com	Schenectady	NY	12301	518-346-2369	372-7549	189-4
Schenectady Museum & Suits-Bueche Planetarium 15 Nott Terr Heights *Web:* www.schenectadymuseum.org	Schenectady	NY	12308	518-382-7890	382-7893	520
Schenectady Steel Company Inc 18 Mariaville Rd *Web:* www.schenectadysteel.com	Schenectady	NY	12306	518-355-3220		480
Schenk Packing Co Inc 8204 288th St NW *Web:* www.schenkpacking.com	Stanwood	WA	98292	360-629-6290		473
Schenkel's All-Star Dairy LLC 1019 Flax Mill Rd	Huntington	IN	46750	260 356 4225		297-4
SchenkelShultz Architects 200 E Robinson St Ste 300 *Web:* www.schenkelshultz.com	Orlando	FL	32801	407-872-3322	872-3303	261
Schenker Inc 150 Albany Ave *TF:* 800-843-1687 ■ *Web:* www.dbschenkerusa.com	Freeport	NY	11520	516-377-3000		311
Schenker of Canada Ltd 5935 Airport Rd 10th Fl *TF:* 800-461-3686 ■ *Web:* www.dbschenker.ca	Mississauga	ON	L4V1W5	905-676-0676		311
Scher Fabrics Inc 450 Fashion Ave	New York	NY	10123	212-382-2266		594
Schererville Chamber of Commerce 122 E Joliet St *Web:* schererivillechamber.org	Schererville	IN	46375	219-322-5412		139
Schetky Northwest Sales Inc 8430 NE Killingsworth St *TF:* 800-255-8341 ■ *Web:* www.schetkynw.com	Portland	OR	97220	503-287-4141		516
Scheurer Hospital Inc 170 N Caseville Rd *TF:* 800-690-9972 ■ *Web:* www.scheurer.org	Pigeon	MI	48755	989-453-3223	856-2209	374-3
Schewel Furniture Company Inc 1031 Main St *Web:* schewels.com	Lynchburg	VA	24504	434-522-0200		321
Schiavone Construction Company Inc 150 Meadowlands Pkwy 3rd Fl *Web:* www.schiavoneconstruction.com	Secaucus	NJ	07094	201-867-5070		188-4
Schick Shadel Hospital 12101 Ambaum Blvd SW *TF:* 800-500-6395 ■ *Web:* schickshadel.com	Seattle	WA	98146	800-500-6395		726
Schiefelbusch Institute for Life Span Studies *Univ of Kansas Robert Dole Human Development Ctr* 1000 Sunnyside Ave Rm 1052 *Web:* www.lsi.ku.edu/lsi	Lawrence	KS	66045	785-864-4295	864-5323	668
Schiele Museum of Natural History & James H Lynn Planetarium 1500 E Garrison Blvd *Web:* www.schielemuseum.org/planetarium.php	Gastonia	NC	28054	704-866-6908	866-6041	520
Schiff Adam (Rep D - CA) 2372 Rayburn HOB *Web:* schiff.house.gov	Washington	DC	20515	202-225-4176	225-5828	342-2
Schiff Hardin LLP 233 S Wacker Dr 6600 Sears Tower *TF:* 800-561-3357 ■ *Web:* www.schiffhardin.com	Chicago	IL	60606	312-258-5500	258-5600	428
Schiff's Restaurant Service Inc 3410 N Main Ave *Web:* www.myschiffs.com	Scranton	PA	18508	570-343-1294		297-8
Schiffer Mason Contractors Inc 2190 Delhi St NE PO Box 250 *Web:* www.schiffermasonry.com	Holt	MI	48842	517-694-2566		189-7
Schiffman Sheridan & Brown PC 2080 Linglestown Rd Ste 201 *Web:* ssbc-law.com	Harrisburg	PA	17110	717-540-9170		428
Schildberg Construction Co PO Box 358 *TF:* 800-233-4327 ■ *Web:* schildberg.com	Greenfield	IA	50849	641-743-2131		440
Schiller & Knapp LLP 950 New Loudon Rd Ste 109 *Web:* www.schillerknapp.com	Latham	NY	12110	518-786-9069		428
Schiller Ducanto & Fleck 225 E Deerpath Ste 270 *Web:* www.sdflaw.com	Lake Forest	IL	60045	847-615-8300		41
Schiller Grounds Care Inc 1028 St Rd *Web:* www.littlewonder.com	Southampton	PA	18966	215-357-5110		429
Schilli Transportation Services Inc 6358 W US Hwy 24 *Web:* www.schilli.com	Remington	IN	47977	219-261-2101		780
Schilling Bros Inc 5400 US Hwy 45 *Web:* www.schillingbros.com	Mattoon	IL	61938	217-234-6478		274
Schilling Wildlife Management Area 17614 Schilling Refuge Rd *Web:* calendar.outdoornebraska.gov	Plattsmouth	NE	68048	402-296-0041		50-5
Schimenti Construction Co 650 Danbury Rd *Web:* www.schimenti.com	Ridgefield	CT	06877	914-244-9100	244-9103	186
Schindler Cohen & Hochman LLP 100 Wall St 15th Fl *Web:* www.schlaw.com	New York	NY	10005	212-277-6300		428
Schindler Elevator Corp 20 Whippany Rd **Fax: Mail Rm* ■ *TF:* 800-225-3123 ■ *Web:* www.schindler.com	Morristown	NJ	07960	973-397-6500	397-3619*	256
Schlachman, Belsky & Weiner PA 300 E Lombard St Ste 1100 *TF:* 800-547-4529 ■ *Web:* www.sbwlaw.com	Baltimore	MD	21202	410-685-2022		428
Schlage Lock Co 3899 Hancock Expy *Web:* consumer.schlage.com	Colorado Springs	CO	80911	719-896-3000		350
Schlagel Inc 491 N Emerson *TF:* 800-328-8002 ■ *Web:* www.schlagel.com	Cambridge	MN	55008	763-689-5991		273
Schlager Group Inc 325 N Saint Paul Ste 3425 **Fax Area Code: 214* ■ *TF:* 888-416-5727 ■ *Web:* www.schlagergroup.com	Dallas	TX	75201	888-416-5727	347-9469*	94
Schlegel Systems Inc 1555 Jefferson Rd *TF:* 888-924-7694 ■ *Web:* www.amesbury.com	Rochester	NY	14623	585-427-7200		326
Schlegel Villages Inc 325 Max Becker Dr Ste 201 *Web:* schlegelvillages.com	Kitchener	ON	N2E4H5	519-571-1873		371
Schleicher County 164 US 190	Eldorado	TX	76936	325-853-2132		338
Schlenner Wenner & Co 630 Roosevelt Rd *TF:* 877-616-0286 ■ *Web:* www.swcocpas.com	Saint Cloud	MN	56301	320-251-0286		2
Schlesinger's Chop House 1106 William Styron Sq S *Web:* www.schlesingerssteaks.com	Newport News	VA	23606	757-599-4700		671
Schlessman Seed Co 11513 US Rt 250 *TF:* 888-534-7333 ■ *Web:* www.schlessman-seed.com	Milan	OH	44846	419-499-2572	499-2574	694
Schleuniger Inc 87 Colin Dr *TF Tech Supp:* 877-902-1470 ■ *Web:* www.schleuniger.com	Manchester	NH	03103	603-668-8117	668-8119	456
Schley County 49 Pecan St	Ellaville	GA	31806	229-937-2609		338
Schlichter, Bogard & Denton 100 S Fourth St Ste 900 *TF:* 800-873-5297 ■ *Web:* uselaws.com	St. Louis	MO	63102	314-621-6115		428
Schlitterbahn Beach Waterpark 33261 State Pk Rd Hwy 100 *Web:* www.schlitterbahn.com	South Padre Island	TX	78597	956-772-7873	761-3960	32
Schlitterbahn Waterpark Resort 381 E Austin St *Web:* www.schlitterbahn.com	New Braunfels	TX	78130	830-625-2351		32
Schlitz Audubon Nature Ctr 1111 E Brown Deer Rd *TF:* 800-897-4161 ■ *Web:* www.schlitzaudubon.org	Bayside	WI	53217	414-352-2880	352-6091	50-5
Schlueter Co 320 N Main St *TF:* 800-359-1700 ■ *Web:* www.schlueterco.com	Janesville	WI	53545	608-755-5444	755-5440	298
Schlumberger Ltd 5599 San Felipe Ste 100 *NYSE: SLB* ■ *Web:* www.slb.com	Houston	TX	77056	713-513-2000	513-2006	538
Schlumberger Wireline & Testing 210 Schlumberger Dr *TF:* 800-272-7328 ■ *Web:* www.slb.com	Sugar Land	TX	77478	281-285-4551		539
Schmeiser Olsen & Watts LLP 18 E University Dr Ste 101 *Web:* iplawusa.com	Mesa	AZ	85201	480-655-0073		445
Schmidt Assoc PC 2530 S Grand Ave *Web:* schmidt-cpapc.com	Carthage	MO	64836	417-358-6090		2
Schmidt Baking Company Inc 7801 Fitch Ln *Web:* www.schmidtbaking.com	Baltimore	MD	21236	410-668-8200		296-1
Schmidt Bros. Inc 420 N Hallett Ave *TF:* 800-200-7318 ■ *Web:* www.schmidtbrosinc.com	Swanton	OH	43558	419-826-3671		186
Schmidt Consulting Services Inc 405 McKnight Park Dr *Web:* www.schmidtcs.com	Pittsburgh	PA	15237	412-367-1226		195
Schmidt Custom Floors Inc N8W22590 Johnson Dr *Web:* www.schmidtflooring.com	Waukesha	WI	53186	262-547-8763		131
Schmidt Electric Coy L P 9701 FM 1625 *Web:* www.schmidt-electric.com	Austin	TX	78747	512-243-1450		189-4
Schmidt Machine Co 7013 Ohio 199 *TF:* 866-368-3814 ■ *Web:* www.schmidtmachine.com	Upper Sandusky	OH	43351	419-294-3814	294-2607	274
Schmidt Printing Inc 1101 Frontage Rd NW *Web:* www.schmidt.com	Byron	MN	55920	507-775-6400	775-6655	627

Phone | Fax | Class

Schmidt Westergard & Company PLLC
77 W University Dr Mesa AZ 85201 480-834-6030 2
Web: sw-cpa.com

Schmidt's Auto Inc 1621 Beld St Madison WI 53715 608-257-0505 62-5
Web: www.schmidtsauto.com

Schmidt's Sausage Haus
240 E Kossuth St Columbus OH 43206 614-444-6808 445-3072 671
Web: www.schmidthaus.com

Schmidt-Goodman Office Products
1920 N Broadway Rochester MN 55906 507-282-3870 321
TF: 800-247-0663 ■ *Web:* www.schmidtgoodman.com

Schmiede Corp
1865 Riley Creek Rd PO Box 1630 Tullahoma TN 37388 931-455-4801 454
TF: 800-535-1851 ■ *Web:* www.schmiedecorp.com

Schmitt Industries Inc
2765 NW Nicolai St Portland OR 97210 503-227-7908 223-1258 472
NASDAQ: SMIT ■ *Web:* www.schmittindustries.com

Schmitt Music Co
2400 Fwy Blvd Brooklyn Center MN 55430 763-566-4560 526
TF: 800-220-5252 ■ *Web:* www.schmittmusic.com

Schmitz Ready Mix Inc
5400 N 124th St Milwaukee WI 53225 414-831-2400 182
Web: www.schmitzmix.com

Schmuckal Oil Co 1516 Barlow St Traverse City MI 49686 231-946-2800 941-7435 324
Web: www.schmuckaloil.com

Schnabel Engineering Inc
9800 JEB Stuart Pkwy Ste 200 Glen Allen VA 23059 804-264-3222 261
Web: www.schnabel-eng.com

Schnadig International Corp
4200 Tudor Ln Greensboro NC 27410 800-468-8730 319-2
TF: 800-468-8730 ■ *Web:* www.schnadig.com

Schnake Turnbo Frank Inc
20 E Fifth St Ste 1500 Tulsa OK 74103 918-582-9151 7
Web: www.schnake.com

Schneck Medical Ctr 411 W Tipton St Seymour IN 47274 812-522-2349 374-3
TF: 800-234-9222 ■ *Web:* www.schneckmed.org

Schneeberger Inc 11 Deangelo Dr Bedford MA 01730 781-271-0140 275-4749 472
Web: www.schneeberger.com

Schneider Bradley (Rep D - IL)
1432 Longworth HOB Washington DC 20515 202-225-4835 342-2
Web: schneider.house.gov

Schneider Capital Management Corp
460 E Swedesford Rd Ste 2000 Wayne PA 19087 610-687-8080 401
TF: 800-275-2382 ■ *Web:* schneidercap.com

Schneider Corp 8901 Otis Ave Indianapolis IN 46216 317-826-7100 826-7200 261
TF: 866-973-7100 ■ *Web:* schneidercorp.com

Schneider Downs & Company Inc
1133 Penn Ave Pittsburgh PA 15222 412-261-3644 261-4876 2
TF: 800-846-7587 ■ *Web:* www.schneiderdowns.com

Schneider Electric Buildings LLC
1354 Clifford Ave Loves Park IL 61111 888-444-1311 186
TF: 888-444-1311 ■ *Web:* www.schneider-electric.com

Schneider Group 5400 Bosque Blvd Ste 680 Waco TX 76710 254-776-3550 776-3767 184
Web: www.sgmeet.com

Schneider Homes Inc
6510 Southcenter Blvd Tukwila WA 98188 206-248-2471 187
Web: www.schneiderhomes.com

Schneider Institute for Health Policy
Brandeis University 415 S St Waltham MA 02454 781-736-3964 634
Web: sihp.brandeis.edu

Schneider Laboratories Inc
2512 W Cary St Richmond VA 23220 804-353-6778 743
TF: 800-785-5227 ■ *Web:* slabinc.com

Schneider National Inc
3101 S Packerland Dr PO Box 2545 Green Bay WI 54306 920-592-2000 449
TF: 800-558-6767 ■ *Web:* www.schneider.com

Schneider Optics Century Div
7701 Haskell Ave Van Nuys CA 91406 818-766-3715 505-9865 591
TF: 800-228-1254 ■ *Web:* www.schneideroptics.com

Schneider Packaging Equipment Company Inc
5370 Guy Young Rd Brewerton NY 13029 315-676-3035 676-2875 547
TF: 800-829-9266 ■ *Web:* www.schneiderpackaging.com

Schneider's Dairy Inc 726 Frank St Pittsburgh PA 15227 412-881-3525 881-7722 296-27
TF: 800-243-3730 ■ *Web:* www.schneidersdairypgh.com

Schneiderman & Sherman
23938 Research Dr Ste 300 Farmington Hills MI 48335 248-539-7400 428
TF: 866-867-7688 ■ *Web:* sspclegal.com

Schneller Inc 6019 Powdermille Rd Kent OH 44240 330-673-1400 599
Web: www.schneller.com

Schnitzer Steel Industries Inc
6241 SE 111th Ave Portland OR 97266 503-224-9900 723
NASDAQ: SCHN ■ *Web:* www.schnitzersteel.com

Schnuck Markets Inc
11420 Lackland Rd Saint Louis MO 63146 314-994-4400 345
TF: 800-264-4400 ■ *Web:* www.schnucks.com

Schodack Island State Park
1 Schodack Way PO Box 7 Schodack Landing NY 12156 518-732-0187 565
Web: newyorkstateparks.reserveamerica.com

Schoeller-Bleckmann Energy Services LLC
712 Saint Etienne Rd Broussard LA 70518 337-837-2030 539
Web: www.sbesllc.com

Schoeneck Containers Inc
2160 S 170th St New Berlin WI 53151 262-786-9360 98
Web: www.schoeneck.com

Schoeneckers Inc
7630 Bush Lake Rd Minneapolis MN 55439 952-835-4800 113
Web: www.biworldwide.com

Schoeneman's Building Materials Center
4000 S Western Ave Sioux Falls SD 57105 605-339-0745 191-3
Web: www.schoenemans.com

Schoenmann Produce Company Inc
6950 Neuhaus St Houston TX 77061 713-923-2728 923-5897 461
Web: www.schoenmannproduce.com

Schoepfle Garden 12882 Diagonal Rd La Grange OH 44050 440-458-5121 458-8924 97
TF: 800-526-7275 ■ *Web:* www.metroparks.cc

Schofield Brothers of New England Inc
1071 Worcester Rd Framingham MA 01701 508-879-0030 261
TF: 800-696-2874 ■ *Web:* www.schofieldbros.com

Phone | Fax | Class

Schoharie County
284 Main St PO Box 429 Schoharie NY 12157 518-295-8347 295-8482 338
TF: 800-227-3552 ■ *Web:* www.schohariecounty-ny.gov

Schoharie County Chamber of Commerce
143 Caverns Rd Howes Cave NY 12092 518-296-8820 296-8825 139
TF: 800-432-7447 ■ *Web:* www.schohariechamber.com

Schoharie Crossing State Historic Site
129 Schoharie St PO Box 140 Fort Hunter NY 12069 518-829-7516 565
TF: 800-456-2267 ■ *Web:* parks.ny.gov/historic-sites/27/details.aspx

Schoitz Engineering Inc
4901 Sergeant Rd Hwy 63 S Waterloo IA 50704 319-234-6615 757
Web: www.schoitz.com

Scholarcraft Inc PO Box 170748 Birmingham AL 35217 205-841-1922 319-3
Web: www.scholarcraft.com

Scholars Inn Gourmet Cafe
717 N College Ave Bloomington IN 47404 812-332-1892 671
TF: 800-765-3466 ■ *Web:* www.scholarsinn.com

Scholarship America
1 Scholarship Way PO Box 297 Saint Peter MN 56082 507-931-1682 48-11
TF: 800-537-4180 ■ *Web:* www.scholarshipamerica.org

Scholarship Foundation of Santa Barbara
2253 Las Positas Rd Santa Barbara CA 93105 805-687-6065 305
Web: www.sbscholarship.org

Scholastic Book Fairs Inc
1080 Greenwood Blvd Lake Mary FL 32746 573-632-1687 96
TF: 800-874-4809 ■ *Web:* www.scholastic.com/bookfairs

Scholastic Coach & Athletic Director Magazine
557 Broadway New York NY 10012 212-343-6100 457-8
TF General: 800-724-6527 ■ *Web:* www.scholastic.com/coach

Schold Machine Corp 7201 W 64th Pl Chicago IL 60638 708-458-3788 111
TF: 800-464-9377 ■ *Web:* www.schold.com

Scholle Packaging Corporation
200 W N Ave Northlake IL 60164 708-562-7290 562-6569 548
Web: www.scholleipn.com

Scholtz & Company LLC
107 Elm St 4 Stamford Plaza 5th Fl Norwalk CT 06902 203-714-9900 528
Web: www.scholtzandco.com

Schomburg Ctr for Research in Black Culture
515 Malcolm X Blvd New York NY 10037 212-491-2200 434-4
Web: nypl.org

School Annual Publishing Co
2568 Park Ctr Blvd State College PA 16801 800-436-6030 637-2
TF: 800-436-6030 ■ *Web:* www.schoolannual.com

School Board of Highlands County Florida
PO Box 9300 Sebring FL 33871 863-471-5555 471-5600 685
TF: 877-357-7456 ■ *Web:* www.highlands.k12.fl.us

School District of Cheltenham Township
2000 Ashbourne Rd Elkins Park PA 19027 215-886-9500 685
Web: www.cheltenham.org

School District of Hartford
675 E Rossman St Hartford WI 53027 262-673-3155 673-3548 685
Web: www.hartfordjt1.k12.wi.us

School District of Philadelphia
440 N Broad St Philadelphia PA 19130 215-400-4000 685
Web: www.phila.k12.pa.us

School District of The Chathams
58 Meyersville Rd Chatham NJ 07928 973-457-2500 685
TF: 800-225-5425 ■ *Web:* www.chatham-nj.org

School Employees Retirement System of Ohio
300 E Broad St Ste 100 Columbus OH 43215 614-222-5853 528
TF: 800-878-5853 ■ *Web:* www.ohsers.org

School for International Training
1 Kipling Rd Brattleboro VT 05302 802-257-7751 166
Web: www.sit.edu

School Innovations & Advocacy Inc
5200 Golden Foothill Pkwy El Dorado Hills CA 95762 877-954-4357 487-6441* 463
*Fax Area Code: 888 ■ *TF:* 877-954-4357 ■ *Web:* www.sia-us.com

School Law News
360 Hiatt Dr Palm Beach Gardens FL 33418 800-341-7874 622-2423* 531-4
*Fax Area Code: 561 ■ *TF:* 800-341-7874 ■ *Web:* www.lrp.com

School Loop Inc 49 Powell St San Francisco CA 94102 650-351-5060 196
Web: www.schoolloop.com

School Nurse Supply Co
1690 Wright Blvd Schaumburg IL 60193 800-485-2737 685
TF: 800-485-2737 ■ *Web:* www.schoolnursesupplyinc.com

School Nutrition Assn (SNA)
700 S Washington St Ste 300 Alexandria VA 22314 703-739-3900 739-3915 49-6
TF: 800-877-8822 ■ *Web:* www.schoolnutrition.org

School of Advertising Art Inc
1725 E David Rd Dayton OH 45440 937-294-0592 7
TF: 800-421-3481 ■ *Web:* www.saa.edu

School of the Art Institute of Chicago
36 S Wabash Ave Chicago IL 60603 312-629-6100 166
TF Admissions: 800-232-7242 ■ *Web:* www.artic.edu

School of the Museum of Fine Arts
230 The Fenway Boston MA 02115 617-369-3626 369-4264* 166
*Fax: Admissions ■ *TF Admissions:* 800-643-6078 ■ *Web:* www.smfa.edu

School of Visual Arts 209 E 23rd St New York NY 10010 212-592-2000 592-2116 164
TF: 800-436-4204 ■ *Web:* www.sva.edu

School Photo Marketing
35 Vanderburg Rd Marlboro NJ 07746 732-431-0440 195
TF: 877-543-9745 ■ *Web:* www.schoolphotoonline.com

School Specialty Inc PO Box 1579 Appleton WI 54912 419-589-1600 882-5603* 243
NASDAQ: SCHS ■ *Fax Area Code: 920 ■ *TF:* 888-388-3224 ■ *Web:* www.schoolspecialty.com

School Webmasters 2846 E Nora St Mesa AZ 85213 602-750-4556 177
TF: 888-750-4556 ■ *Web:* www.schoolwebmasters.com

SchoolCity Inc
2900 Lakeside Dr Ste 270 Santa Clara CA 95054 800-343-6572 963-3384* 177
*Fax Area Code: 650 ■ *TF:* 800-343-6572 ■ *Web:* www.schoolcity.com

Schoolcraft College 18600 Haggerty Rd Livonia MI 48152 734-462-4400 462-4553* 162
*Fax: Admissions ■ *TF:* 800-433-7747 ■ *Web:* www.schoolcraft.edu

Schoolcraft County
300 Walnut St Rm 169 Manistique MI 49854 906-341-3630 338
Web: www.schoolcraftcounty.net

SchoolDocs LLC 5944 Luther Ln Ste 600 Dallas TX 75225 866-311-2293 387
TF: 866-311-2293 ■ *Web:* www.schooldocs.com

Schools Financial Credit Union
1485 Response Rd Ste 126 Sacramento CA 95815 916-569-5400 219
TF: 800-962-0990 ■ *Web:* www.schools.org

Name / Address	City	State	ZIP	Phone	Fax	Class
Schools Wstrn Area Career & Technology Ctr 688 Western Ave *TF:* 800-575-9399 ■ *Web:* www.wactc.net	Canonsburg	PA	15317	724-746-2890		685
School-Tech Inc 745 State Cir *TF:* 800-521-2832 ■ *Web:* www.school-tech.com	Ann Arbor	MI	48108	800-521-2832	654-4321	346
Schoolwires Inc 330 Innovation Blvd Ste 301 *TF:* 877-427-9413 ■ *Web:* www.schoolwires.com	State College	PA	16803	877-427-9413		242
Schooner Ernestina New Bedford State Pier *Web:* ernestina.org	New Bedford	MA	02741	508-992-4900		565
Schooner Surprise PO Box 272 *TF:* 866-732-2473 ■ *Web:* www.wanderbirdcruises.com	Belfast	ME	04915	207-236-4687		220
Schoppe Company Inc 352 Van Buren Ave *Web:* schoppe.net	Salt Lake City	UT	84115	801-467-5466		189-10
Schostak Bros & Company Inc 17800 Laurel Pk Dr N Ste 200C *Web:* www.schostak.com	Livonia	MI	48152	248-262-1000	262-1814	653
Schott Corp 1401 Air Wing Rd	San Diego	CA	92154	507-223-5572	223-5055	253
Schott International Inc 2850 Gilchrist Rd *TF:* 877-661-2121 ■ *Web:* www.schotttextiles.com	Akron	OH	44305	330-794-2121	794-2122	594
Schott Management Group Llc 441 Carlisle Dr Ste D *Web:* www.schottmanagement.net	Herndon	VA	20170	703-437-9500		474
SCHOTT North America, Inc. 615 Hwy 68 *Web:* www.us.schott.com/flatglass/english	Sweetwater	TN	37874	423-337-3522	337-7979	329
Schrader Kurt (Rep D - OR) 2431 Rayburn HOB *Web:* schrader.house.gov	Washington	DC	20515	202-225-5711	225-5699	342-2
Schramm Inc 800 E Virginia Ave *TF:* 888-737-9438 ■ *Web:* www.schramminc.com	West Chester	PA	19380	610-696-2500	696-6950	537
Schramm Park State Recreation Area 15810 Hwy 50 *Web:* www.outdoornebraska.ne.gov/parks	Louisville	NE	68037	402-332-3901		565
Schreiber Corp 29945 Beck Rd *Web:* www.schreiberroofing.com	Wixom	MI	48393	248-926-1500	926-1788	189-12
Schreiber Foods Inc PO Box 19010 *Web:* www.schreiberfoods.com	Green Bay	WI	54307	920-437-7601		296-5
Schreiber Foods International Inc 600 E Crescent Ave Ste 103 *TF:* 800-631-7070 ■ *Web:* www.ambrosia-foods.com	Upper Saddle River	NJ	07458	201-327-3535	327-2812	297-11
Schreiber LLC 100 Schreiber Dr *Web:* www.schreiberwater.com	Trussville	AL	35173	205-655-7466	655-7669	806
Schreiber Translations Inc 51 Monroe St Ste 101 *TF:* 800-822-3213 ■ *Web:* www.schreibernet.com	Rockville	MD	20850	301-424-7737		768
Schreiner Capital Management Inc 111 Summit Dr	Exton	PA	19341	610-524-7310		401
Schreiner University 2100 Memorial Blvd **Fax:* Admissions ■ *TF:* 800-343-4919 ■ *Web:* www.schreiner.edu	Kerrville	TX	78028	830-792-7217	792-7226*	166
Schreiner's Iris Gardens 3625 Quinaby Rd NE *TF:* 800-525-2367 ■ *Web:* www.schreinersgardens.com	Salem	OR	97303	503-393-3232	393-5590	97
Schrickel Rollins & Assoc Inc 1161 Corporate Dr W Ste 200 *TF:* 800-523-0056 ■ *Web:* www.sradesign.com	Arlington	TX	76006	817-649-3216	649-7645	422
Schroder 875 Third Ave *Web:* www.schroders.com/en/us	New York	NY	10022	212-641-3830		690
Schroder Investment Management North America Inc (SIMNA) 7 Bryant Pk *TF:* 800-730-2932 ■ *Web:* www.schroders.com/us	New York	NY	10018	212-641-3800	632-2954	690
Schroeder & Bogardus Die Company Inc 1130 Red Gum St	Anaheim	CA	92806	714-630-2270	630-1739	757
Schroeder America 5620 Business Pk *TF:* 877-404-2488 ■ *Web:* schroederamerica.com	San Antonio	TX	78218	210-662-8200		665
Schroeder Industries LLC 580 W Pk Rd *TF:* 800-722-4810 ■ *Web:* www.schroederindustries.com	Leetsdale	PA	15056	724-318-1100	318-1200	207
Schroeder Measurement Technologies Inc 25400 Hgwy 19 Ste 285 *Web:* www.smttest.com	Clearwater	FL	33763	727-738-8727	734-9578	463
Schroeder's Cafe 240 Front St *Web:* www.schroederssf.com	San Francisco	CA	94111	415-421-4770		671
Schroeder's Flowerland Inc 1530 S Webster Ave *TF:* 800-236-4769 ■ *Web:* www.schroederflowers.com	Green Bay	WI	54301	920-436-6363		292
Schroer & Assoc PC 42 N Second St *Web:* schroer-cpa.com	Council Bluffs	IA	51503	712-322-8734		2
Schroer Manufacturing Co 511 Osage Ave *TF:* 800-444-1579 ■ *Web:* www.shor-line.com	Kansas City	KS	66105	913-281-1500		419
Schroeter Goldmark & Bender Ps 810 Third Ave *TF:* 800-809-2234 ■ *Web:* sgb-law.com	Seattle	WA	98104	206-622-8000		445
Schrudder Performance Group Inc 7681 Tylers Place Blvd Ste 141 *Web:* schrudderperformance.com	West Chester	OH	45069	513-666-4578		463
Schubert Club Museum, The 75 W Fifth St 302 Landmark Ctr *TF:* 800-767-9660 ■ *Web:* www.schubert.org	Saint Paul	MN	55102	651-292-3267	292-4317	520
Schubert Communications Inc 112 Schubert Dr *Web:* www.schubertb2b.com	Downingtown	PA	19335	610-269-2100		7
Schubert Nursery Inc 7715 Gorman Dr	Browns Summit	NC	27214	336-656-1981		292
Schuette Mfg & Steel Sales Inc 5028 Hwy 42 *TF:* 800-626-6409 ■ *Web:* www.schuettemfg.com	Manitowoc	WI	54220	920-758-2491	758-2599	273
Schuette Stores Inc 17919 Saint Rose Rd *Web:* www.schuettesmarket.com	Breese	IL	62230	618-526-7203		297-8
Schuff International Inc 420 S 19th Ave *OTC:* SHFK ■ *Web:* www.schuff.com	Phoenix	AZ	85009	602-252-7787		360-3
Schuff Steel Co 420 S 19th Ave *Web:* www.schuff.com	Phoenix	AZ	85009	602-252-7787		189-14
Schuff Steel Inc 1920 Ledo Rd *TF:* 866-252-4628 ■ *Web:* www.schuff.com	Albany	GA	31707	678-821-7061		480
Schukei Chevrolet Inc 721 S Monroe *TF:* 866-918-6497 ■ *Web:* www.schukeichevy.com	Mason City	IA	50401	641-423-5402		57
Schuler & Shook 750 N Orleans St Ste 400 *Web:* www.schulershook.com	Chicago	IL	60654	312-944-8230		722
Schuler Books & Music Inc 2660 28th St SE *Web:* www.schulerbooks.com	Grand Rapids	MI	49512	616-942-2561		95
Schulich School of Medicine & Dentistry Western University *Web:* www.schulich.uwo.ca	London	ON	N6A5C1	519-661-3459	661-3797	167-2
Schulman Ronca & Bucuvalas Inc 275 Seventh Ave Ste 2700 *Web:* www.srbi.com	New York	NY	10001	646-486-8400		466
Schulmerich Carillons Inc Carillon Hill *TF:* 800-772-3557 ■ *Web:* www.schulmerichbells.com	Sellersville	PA	18960	215-257-2771	257-1910	527
Schulte Building Systems Inc 17600 Badtke Rd *TF:* 877-257-2534 ■ *Web:* www.sbslp.com	Hockley	TX	77447	281-304-6111		106
Schulte Roth & Zabel LLP 919 Third Ave *Web:* www.srz.com	New York	NY	10022	212-756-2000	593-5955	428
Schultz Collins Lawson Chambers Inc 455 Market St Ste 1250 *TF:* 877-291-2205 ■ *Web:* www.schultzcollins.com	San Francisco	CA	94105	415-291-3000		401
Schultz Lubricants Inc 164 Shrewsbury St *TF:* 800-262-3962 ■ *Web:* www.schultzlubricants.com	West Boylston	MA	01583	508-835-4446		541
Schultze Asset Management LP 800 Westchester Ave S-632 *Web:* www.samco.net	Rye Brook	NY	10573	914-701-5260		401
Schulz & Urbanski PC 6 Forest Park Dr	Farmington	CT	06032	860-678-9042		2
Schulz Electric Co 30 Gando Dr *Web:* schulzelectric.com	New Haven	CT	06513	203-562-5811		45
Schulze & Burch Biscuit Co 1133 W 35th St *Web:* www.schulzeburch.com	Chicago	IL	60609	773-927-6622		68
Schumacher & Seiler Inc 10 W Aylesbury Rd *TF:* 800-992-9356 ■ *Web:* www.schumacherseiler.com	Timonium	MD	21093	410-465-7000		612
Schumacher Companies Inc, The 392 Pleasant St *Web:* www.dschumacher.com	West Bridgewater	MA	02379	508-427-7707		422
Schumacher Electric Corp 801 E Business Ctr Dr *TF:* 800-621-5485 ■ *Web:* www.batterychargers.com	Mount Prospect	IL	60056	800-621-5485		253
Schumacher Elevator Co 1 Schumacher Way PO Box 393 *TF:* 800-779-5430 ■ *Web:* www.schumacherelevator.com	Denver	IA	50622	319-984-5676	984-6316	256
Schumacher European Ltd 18530 N Scottsdale Rd *Web:* mbofnorthscottsdale.com	Phoenix	AZ	85054	480-991-1155		57
Schumacher Group 200 Corporate Blvd Ste 201 *TF:* 800-893-9698 ■ *Web:* www.schumacherclinical.com	Lafayette	LA	70508	800-893-9698		353
Schumann Printers Inc 701 S Main St *Web:* www.spiweb.com	Fall River	WI	53932	920-484-3348		627
Schumer Charles E (Sen D - NY) 322 Hart Bldg *Web:* www.schumer.senate.gov	Washington	DC	20510	202-224-6542	228-3027	342-2
Schundler Co 150 Whitman Ave *TF:* 800-628-9990 ■ *Web:* www.schundler.com	Edison	NJ	08817	732-287-2244	287-4185	500
Schunk Graphite Technology W146 N9300 Held Dr *Web:* www.schunkgraphite.com	Menomonee Falls	WI	53051	262-253-8720		127
SCHUNKÿGmbHÿ&ÿCo.ÿKG 211 Kitty Hawk Dr *Web:* schunk.com/de_en/homepage	Morrisville	NC	27560	919-572-2705		127
Schupp Company Inc 418 N Mosley Rd	St. Louis	MO	63141	314-421-5200		7
Schurman Fine Papers 500 Chadbourne Rd *TF Sales:* 800-789-1649 ■ *Web:* www.papyrusonline.com	Fairfield	CA	94533	800-789-1649		552-2
Schurz Communications Inc 1301 E Douglas Rd *Web:* www.schurz.com	Mishawaka	IN	46545	574-247-7237		532-3
Schust Engineering Inc 701 North St *TF:* 800-686-9297 ■ *Web:* www.schustengineering.com	Auburn	IN	46706	800-686-9297		189-12
Schuster Electronics Inc 11320 Grooms Rd *TF:* 800-521-1358 ■ *Web:* www.schusterusa.com	Cincinnati	OH	45242	800-521-1358		246
Schutt Industries Inc 185 Industrial Ave *TF:* 800-488-2022 ■ *Web:* www.schuttindustries.com	Clintonville	WI	54929	715-823-8025		779
Schutte & Koerting LLC 2510 Metropolitan *Web:* www.s-k.com	Trevose	PA	19053	215-639-0900	639-1597	386
Schutte Lumber Co 3001 SW Blvd *Web:* www.schuttelumber.com	Kansas City	MO	64108	816-753-6262		821
Schuur Solutions 2500 E Imperial Hwy Ste 201 *Web:* schuur.com	Brea	CA	92821	714-986-9990		180
Schuyler County Hwy 136 E *Web:* www.courts.mo.gov	Lancaster	MO	63548	660-457-3784	457-3016	338
Schuyler County PO Box 200 *Web:* www.schuylercountyillinois.com	Rushville	IL	62681	217-322-4734	322-6164	338
Schuyler County 105 Ninth St *Web:* www.schuylercounty.us	Watkins Glen	NY	14891	607-535-8133	535-8130	338

Name / Address	Phone	Fax	Class
Schuyler Mansion State Historic Site 32 Catherine St. Albany NY 12202 *TF:* 800-456-2267 ■ *Web:* parks.ny.gov/historic-sites/33/details.aspx	518-434-0834		565
Schuylerville Central School District 14-18 Spring St. Schuylerville NY 12871 *Web:* www.schuylervilleschools.org	518-695-3255		610
Schuylkill Chamber of Commerce 91 S Progress Ave. Pottsville PA 17901 *TF:* 800-755-1942 ■ *Web:* www.schuylkillchamber.com	570-622-1942	622-1638	139
Schuylkill County 401 N Second St. Pottsville PA 17901 *Web:* www.co.schuylkill.pa.us	570-622-5570		338
Schuylkill Haven Area School Authority 120 Haven St. Schuylkill Haven PA 17972 *Web:* www.haven.k12.pa.us	570-385-6705		685
Schuylkill Medical Center 420 S Jackson St. Pottsville PA 17901	570-621-5000		374-3
Schuylkill Valley School District 929 Lakeshore Dr. Leesport PA 19533 *Web:* www.schuylkillvalley.org	610-926-1706		685
Schwaab Inc 11415 W Burleigh St. Milwaukee WI 53222 **Fax Area Code:* 800 ■ *TF:* 800-935-9877 ■ *Web:* www.schwaab.com	414-771-4150	935-9866*	467
Schwabe & Assoc Inc 8525 SW 92nd St Ste B6. Miami FL 33156	305-270-1990		690
Schwabe Williamson & Wyatt Pacwest Ctr 1211 SW Fifth Ave Stes 1600-1900 Ste. Portland OR 97204 *Web:* www.schwabe.com	503-222-9981		445
Schwan's Co 115 W College Dr. Marshall MN 56258 *TF:* 800-533-5290 ■ *Web:* www.theschwanfoodcompany.com	507-532-3274		296-36
Schwank Inc 2 Schwank Way at Hwy 56N. Waynesboro GA 30830 *TF:* 877-446-3727 ■ *Web:* www.schwankgroup.com	877-446-3727		357
Schwartz Brothers Restaurants 325 118th Ave SE Ste 106. Bellevue WA 98005 *Web:* www.schwartzbros.com	425-455-3948	451-3573	670
Schwartz Ctr for the Arts 226 S State St. Dover DE 19901 *Web:* www.schwartzcenter.com	302-678-5152	678-1267	572
Schwartz Farms Inc 32296 190th St. Sleepy Eye MN 56085 *Web:* www.schwartzfarms.com	507-794-5779		10-6
Schwartz Hannum PC 11 Chestnut St. Andover MA 01810 *Web:* shpclaw.com	978-623-0900		428
Schwartz Heslin Group Inc (SHG) 8 Airport Park Blvd. Latham NY 12110 *TF:* 800-700-3536 ■ *Web:* www.shggroup.com	518-786-7733		463
Schwartz Industries Inc 6909 E 11-Mile Rd. Warren MI 48092 *Web:* sharedvision.net	586-759-1777	759-0808	454
Schwartz Investment Counsel Inc 801 W Ann Arbor Trl Ste 244. Plymouth MI 48170 *Web:* www.schwartzinvest.com	734-455-7777		528
Schwartz Lasson Harris Ltd 2 Walnut Grove Dr. Horsham PA 19044 *Web:* slhcpas.com	215-956-9700		2
Schwartz Levitsky Feldman Ch A 2300 Yonge St Ste 1500 PO Box 2434. Toronto ON M4P1E4 *Web:* www.slf.ca	416-785-5353		445
Schwartz Ruth & Co 6 W 18th St Ste 6r. New York NY 10011 *Web:* www.rcspr.com	212-463-0684		636
Schwartz Semerdjian Ballard & Cauley LLP 101 W Broadway Ste 810. San Diego CA 92101 *Web:* www.schwartzsemerdjian.com	619-236-8821		428
Schwartz Steel Service Inc 525 N Broad St. Gastonia NC 28054 *Web:* www.schwartzsteel.com	704-865-9576		492
Schwarz 8338 Austin Ave. Morton Grove IL 60053 **Fax Area Code:* 847 ■ *TF:* 800-323-4903 ■ *Web:* www.schwarz.com	800-323-4903	966-1271*	559
Schwarz Gallery 1806 Chestnut St. Philadelphia PA 19103 *Web:* www.schwarzgallery.com	215-563-4887	561-5621	42
Schwebel Baking Co PO Box 6018. Youngstown OH 44501 *TF:* 800-860-2867 ■ *Web:* www.schwebels.com	330-783-2860	782-1774	296-1
Schweikert David (Rep R - AZ) 2059 Rayburn HOB. Washington DC 20515 *Web:* schweikert.house.gov	202-225-2190	225-0096	342-2
Schweitzer E O Mfg Company Inc 450 Enterprise Pkwy. Lake Zurich IL 60047 **Fax Area Code:* 509 ■ *Web:* selinc.com	847-362-8304	332-7990*	248
Schweitzer Engineering Lab Inc 2350 NE Hopkins Ct Production Bldg. Pullman WA 99163 *Web:* www.selinc.com	509-332-1890		203
Schweitzer-Mauduit International Inc 100 N Pt Ctr E Ste 600. Alpharetta GA 30022 *NYSE:* SWM ■ *TF:* 800-514-0186 ■ *Web:* www.swmintl.com	770-569-4271		557
Schweizer Dipple Inc 7227 Div St. Oakwood Village OH 44146 *TF:* 800-776-7181 ■ *Web:* www.schweizer-dipple.com	440-786-8090	786-8099	189-10
Schweizer Emblem Co 1022 Busse Hwy. Park Ridge IL 60068 *TF Cust Svc:* 800-942-5215 ■ *Web:* www.schweizer-emblem.com	847-292-1022	292-1028	258
Schwend Inc 28945 Johnston Rd. Dade City FL 33523 *TF:* 800-243-7757 ■ *Web:* www.schwendinc.com	352-588-2220	588-2221	779
Schwendiman Sutton & Simmons Pllc / Psp Inc 39 Professional Plaza. Rexburg ID 83440 *Web:* www.suttonsimmons.com	208-356-3452		2
Schwerdtle Stamp Co 166 Elm St. Bridgeport CT 06604 *TF:* 800-535-0004 ■ *Web:* www.schwerdtle.com	203-330-2750	330-2760	467
Schwing America Inc 5900 Centerville Rd. St Paul MN 55127 *Web:* www.schwing.com	651-429-0999		190
Schwing Bioset Inc 350 SMC Dr. Somerset WI 54025 *Web:* www.schwingbioset.com	715-247-3433		791
SCI (Sister Cities International) 1301 Pennsylvania Ave NW Ste 850. Washington DC 20004 *Web:* www.sister-cities.org	202-347-8630	393-6524	48-7
SCI (Smart Card Integrators Inc) 2424 N Ontario St. Burbank CA 91504 *Web:* www.sci-s.com	818-847-1022		178-12
SCI 180 Attwell Dr Ste 600. Toronto ON M9W6A9 *TF:* 866-773-7735 ■ *Web:* www.scilogistics.com	416-401-3011		314
SCI Global Structural Contours Inc PO Box 4970. Greenwich CT 06830 *Web:* www.sciglobal.com	203-531-4400	531-4403	189-1
SCI Infrastructure LLC 2825 S 154th St. SeaTac WA 98188 *Web:* www.sciinfrastructure.com	206-242-0633		610
Sciaky Inc 4915 W 67th St. Chicago IL 60638 *TF:* 800-654-6543 ■ *Web:* www.sciaky.com	708-594-3800	594-9213	811
SciCan Ltd 701 Technology Dr. Canonsburg PA 15317 *TF:* 800-572-1211 ■ *Web:* www.scican.com	724-820-1600	820-1479	475
SciClone Pharmaceuticals Inc 950 Tower Ln Ste 900. Foster City CA 94404 *NASDAQ:* SCLN ■ *TF:* 800-724-2566 ■ *Web:* www.sciclone.com	650-358-3456	358-3469	582
SCI-Coal Township 1 Kelley Dr. Coal Township PA 17866 *Web:* www.cor.pa.gov/Facilities/StatePrisons/Pages/Coal-Twp.aspx	570-644-7890		213
Scicom Data Services Ltd 10101 Bren Rd E. Minnetonka MN 55343	952-933-4200	936-4132	225
Scicom Infrastructure Services Inc 2250 N Druid Hills Rd NE Ste 238. Atlanta GA 30329 *Web:* www.scicominfra.com	404-636-9882		177
Scicon Technologies Corp 27525 Newhall Ranch Rd. Valencia CA 91355 *Web:* www.scicontech.com	661-295-8630		454
SCI-Dallas 1000 Follies Rd. Dallas PA 18612 *Web:* www.cor.pa.gov	570-675-1101		213
Sciemetric Instruments Inc 359 Terry Fox Dr Ste 100. Ottawa ON K2K2E7 *TF:* 877-931-9200 ■ *Web:* www.sciemetric.com	613-254-7054		246
Science & Engineering Services (SESI) 6992 Columbia Gateway Dr. Columbia MD 21046 *Web:* www.sesi-md.com	443-539-0139		544
Science & Environmental Policy Project 1600 S Eads St Ste 712-S. Arlington VA 22202 *Web:* www.sepp.org	212-664-4555		634
Science Application International Corp Inc (SAIC Inc) 1710 SAIC Dr. McLean VA 22102 *TF:* 866-400-7242 ■ *Web:* www.saic.com	703-676-4300		178-5
Science Applications International Corp 10260 Campus Pt Dr. San Diego CA 92121 *TF:* 800-760-4332 ■ *Web:* www.saic.com	703-676-4300		668
Science Central 1950 N Clinton St. Fort Wayne IN 46805 *TF:* 888-240-7268 ■ *Web:* www.sciencecentral.org	260-424-2400	422-2899	520
Science Club for Girls Inc 136 Magazine St. Cambridge MA 02139 *Web:* scienceclubforgirls.org	617-391-0361		148
Science Ctr of Iowa 401 W Martin Luther King Jr Pkwy. Des Moines IA 50309 *Web:* www.sciowa.org	515-274-6868	274-3404	520
Science Factory Children's Museum & Planetarium 2300 Leo Harris Pkwy. Eugene OR 97401 *Web:* www.sciencefactory.org	541-682-7888	484-9027	521
Science Magazine 1200 New York Ave NW. Washington DC 20005 *TF:* 866-434-2227 ■ *Web:* www.sciencemag.org	202-326-6500	842-1065	457-19
Science Museum of Minnesota 120 W Kellogg Blvd. Saint Paul MN 55102 *TF:* 800-221-9444 ■ *Web:* www.smm.org	651-221-9444	221-4777	520
Science Museum of Viriginia 2500 W Broad St. Richmond VA 23220 *TF:* 800-659-1727 ■ *Web:* www.smv.org	804-864-1400		598
Science Museum of Western Virginia 1 Market Sq. Roanoke VA 24011 *Web:* www.smwv.org	540-342-5710	224-1240	520
Science Museum Oklahoma 2100 NE 52nd St. Oklahoma City OK 73111 *TF:* 800-532-7652 ■ *Web:* sciencemuseumok.org	405-602-6664		520
Science News 1719 N St NW. Washington DC 20036 *TF Cust Svc:* 800-552-4412 ■ *Web:* www.sciencenews.org	202-785-2255		457-19
Science Place, The 2201 N Field St. Dallas TX 75201 *Web:* www.perotmuseum.org	214-428-5555	756-5916	521
Science Source, The 299 Atlantic Hwy. Waldoboro ME 04572 *Web:* www.thesciencesource.com	207-832-6344		200
Science Spectrum-Omni Theater 2579 S Loop 289. Lubbock TX 79423 *Web:* sciencespectrum.org	806-745-2525		520
ScienceCare Inc 21410 N 19th Ave Ste 126. Phoenix AZ 85027 **Fax Area Code:* 602 ■ *TF:* 800-417-3747 ■ *Web:* www.sciencecare.com	800-417-3747	331-4344*	545
ScienceMedia Inc 6450 Lusk Blvd Ste E206. San Diego CA 92121 *Web:* sciencemedia.com	858-625-9261	625-9262	344
Scienscope Inc 5751 Schaefer Ave. Chino CA 91710 *Web:* www.scienscope.com	909-590-7273		201
Scientech Inc 5649 Arapahoe Ave. Boulder CO 80303 *TF:* 800-525-0522 ■ *Web:* www.scientech-inc.com	303-444-1361	444-9229	684
Scientia Global Inc 2210 Front St Ste 204. Melbourne FL 32901 *TF:* 800-543-8968 ■ *Web:* www.scientiaglobal.com	321-733-1971		195
Scientific Drilling Controls Inc 16701 Greenspoint Pk Dr Ste 200. Houston TX 77060 *TF:* 800-514-8949 ■ *Web:* www.scientificdrilling.com	281-443-3300		540
Scientific Equipment & Furniture Assn (SEFA) 65 Hilton Ave. Garden City NY 11530 *TF:* 877-294-5424 ■ *Web:* www.sefalabs.com	516-294-5424	294-2758	49-19
Scientific Games Corp 750 Lexington Ave 25th Fl. New York NY 10022 *NASDAQ:* SGMS ■ *TF:* 800-827-2946 ■ *Web:* www.scientificgames.com	212-754-2233		322
Scientific Games Holdings Corp 1500 Bluegrass Lakes Pkwy. Alpharetta GA 30004	770-664-3700		52
Scientific Industries Inc 70 Orville Dr. Bohemia NY 11716 *TF:* 888-850-6208 ■ *Web:* www.scientificindustries.com	631-567-4700		419
Scientific Learning Corp 300 Frank H Ogawa Plaza Ste 600. Oakland CA 94612 *OTC:* SCIL ■ *TF:* 888-665-9707 ■ *Web:* www.scilearn.com	510-444-3500	444-3580	178-3
Scientific Molding Corp Ltd 330 SMC Dr. Somerset WI 54025 *Web:* www.smcltd.com	715-247-3500	247-3611	418

Name / Address	City	State	Zip	Phone	Fax	Class
Scientific Plastics Company Inc 550 Elizabeth St *Web:* scientificplasticscorp.com	Waukesha	WI	53106	262-548-1120		596
Scientific Polymer Products Inc 6265 Dean Pkwy *Web:* www.scientificpolymer.com	Ontario	NY	14519	585-265-0413	265-1390	605-2
Scientific Protein Laboratories Inc 700 E Main St PO Box 158 *TF:* 800-334-4775 ■ *Web:* www.spl-pharma.com	Waunakee	WI	53597	608-849-5944		479
Scientific Systems Company Inc 500 W Cummings Pk Ste 3000 *Web:* www.ssci.com	Woburn	MA	01801	781-933-5355		256
Scientific Technologies Corp 4400 E Broadway Blvd Ste 705 *Web:* www.stchome.com	Tucson	AZ	85711	520-202-3333		356
Scientist, The 478 Bay St Ste A213 *TF:* 888-781-0328 ■ *Web:* www.the-scientist.com	Midland	ON	L4R1K9	705-528-6888		457-19
Sciforma Corp 985 University Ave Ste 5 *TF Sales:* 800-533-9876 ■ *Web:* www.sciforma.com	Los Gatos	CA	95032	408-354-0144		178-1
SCI-Graterford PO Box 246 **Fax Area Code:* 484 ■ *Web:* www.cor.pa.gov/Facilities/StatePrisons/Pages/Graterford.aspx	Graterford	PA	19426	610-489-4151	961-7907*	213
SCI-Greene 169 Progress Dr Staff *Web:* www.cor.pa.gov/Facilities/StatePrisons/Pages/Greene.aspx#.WXoifYjyuM8	Waynesburg	PA	15370	724-852-2902		213
SCI-Greensburg 165 SCI Ln	Greensburg	PA	15601	724-837-4397		213
SCI-Houtzdale PO Box 1000 *Web:* www.cor.pa.gov/Facilities/StatePrisons/Pages/Houtzdale.aspx	Houtzdale	PA	16698	814-378-1000		213
SCI-Huntingdon 1100 Pike St *Web:* www.cor.pa.gov	Huntingdon	PA	16654	814-643-2400		213
SciImage Inc 4916 El Camino Real *Web:* www.scimage.com	Los Altos	CA	94022	650-694-4858		809
SCI-Mahanoy 301 Morea Rd	Frackville	PA	17932	570-773-2158		213
SCIMEDX Corp 100 Ford Rd *TF:* 800-221-5598 ■ *Web:* www.scimedx.com	Denville	NJ	07834	973-625-8822	625-8796	231
SCI-Muncy PO Box 180	Muncy	PA	17756	570-546-3171		213
Scio Mutual Telephone Assn 38770 N Main St PO Box 1100 *Web:* www.smt-net.com	Scio	OR	97374	503-394-2995		116
Scion Aviation LLC 3693 E County Rd 30 *Web:* www.scionaviation.com	Fort Collins	CO	80528	970-207-1721		127
Scion Medical Technologies LLC 90 Oak St *TF:* 888-582-6211 ■ *Web:* www.scionmedtech.com	Newton	MA	02464	888-582-6211	963-9112	743
Scion Steel Inc 21555 Mullin Ave *TF:* 800-288-2127 ■ *Web:* www.scionsteel.com	Warren	MI	48089	586-755-4000	757-5210	723
Scioto County 602 Seventh St Rm 103 *Web:* www.sciotocountydirectory.net	Portsmouth	OH	45662	740-355-8313	353-7358	338
Scioto Downs Inc 6000 S High St *TF:* 800-514-3049 ■ *Web:* www.sciotodowns.com	Columbus	OH	43207	614-295-4700		642
Scioto Sign Company Inc 6047 US Rt 68 N *TF:* 800-572-4686 ■ *Web:* www.sciotosigns.com	Kenton	OH	43326	419-673-1261	675-3298	701
Scioto Trail State Park 144 Lake Rd *TF:* 866-644-6727 ■ *Web:* parks.ohiodnr.gov	Chillicothe	OH	45601	866-644-6727		565
SCIP (Strategic and Competitive Intelligence Professional) 7550 IH 10 W Ste 400 *Web:* www.scip.org	San Antonio	TX	78229	703-739-0696	739-2524	49-12
SCI-Pittsburgh 3001 Beaver Rd *Web:* www.cor.pa.gov	Pittsburgh	PA	15233	412-761-1955	766-8225	213
Sci-Port Discovery Ctr 820 Clyde Fant Pkwy *TF:* 877-724-7678 ■ *Web:* www.sciport.org	Shreveport	LA	71101	318-424-3466	222-5592	520
Scireg Inc 12733 Directors Loop *TF:* 800-222-1222 ■ *Web:* www.scireg.com	Woodbridge	VA	22192	703-494-6500		196
SCI-Retreat 660 SR 11 *Web:* www.cor.pa.gov/Facilities/StatePrisons/Pages/Retreat.aspx	Hunlock Creek	PA	18621	570-735-8754	733-1041	213
SCI-Rockview 1 Rockview Pl PO Box A *Web:* www.cor.pa.gov/Pages/default.aspx	Bellefonte	PA	16823	814-355-4874	355-6026	213
SCI-Smithfield 1120 Pike St PO Box 999 *Web:* www.cor.pa.gov/Facilities/StatePrisons/Pages/Smithfield.aspx	Huntingdon	PA	16652	814-643-6520		213
SCI-Somerset 1590 Walters Mill Rd *Web:* www.cor.pa.gov	Somerset	PA	15510	814-443-8100	443-8137	213
SciTech Publishing Inc 911 Paverstone Dr Ste B *Web:* www.theiet.org/resources/books/scitech	Raleigh	NC	27615	919-847-2434		95
Scivantage Inc 499 Washington Blvd 11th Fl *TF:* 866-724-0260 ■ *Web:* www.scivantage.com	Jersey City	NJ	07310	646-452-0050	452-0049	174
Scivolutions Inc 2260 Raeford Ct	Gastonia	NC	28052	704-853-0100		231
SCI-Waymart PO Box 256 Ste 6 *Web:* www.cor.pa.gov/Facilities/StatePrisons/Pages/Waymart.aspx	Waymart	PA	18472	570-488-5811		213
SciWorks Science Ctr & Environmental Park of Forsyth County 400 Hanes-Mill Rd *Web:* www.sciworks.org	Winston-Salem	NC	27105	336-767-6730	661-1777	520
SCL (Sumitomo Canada Ltd) 150 King St W Ste 2304 *Web:* www.sumitomocanada.com	Toronto	ON	M5H1J9	416-860-3800	365-3141	360-3
SCLA (South Carolina Library Assn) PO Box 1763 *Web:* www.scla.org	Columbia	SC	29202	803-252-1087	252-0589	435
Sclafani's Cooking School Inc 107 Gennaro Pl *Web:* www.sclafanicookingschool.com	Metairie	LA	70005	504-833-7861		163
Scleroderma Foundation 300 Rosewood Dr Ste 105 *TF:* 800-722-4673 ■ *Web:* www.scleroderma.org	Danvers	MA	01923	978-463-5843	463-5809	48-17
SCNA (South Carolina Nurses Assn) 1821 Gadsden St *Web:* www.scnurses.org	Columbia	SC	29201	803-252-4781	779-3870	533
SCOLA 21557 270th St *TF:* 800-860-6762 ■ *Web:* www.scola.org	McClelland	IA	51548	712-566-2202	566-2502	740
Scolari's Food & Drug Co 950 Holman Way *Web:* www.scolaristores.com	Sparks	NV	89431	775-575-1381		345
Scolaro, Shulman, Cohen, Fetter & Burstein PC Franklin Sq 507 Plum St Ste 300 *Web:* www.scolaro.com	Syracuse	NY	13204	315-471-8111		428
Scolding Locks Corp 1520 W Rogers Ave	Appleton	WI	54914	920-733-5561		214
Scoliosis Assn Inc 2500 N Military Trail	Boca Raton	FL	33431	561-994-4435		48-17
Scoliosis Research Society 555 E Wells St Ste 1100 *Web:* www.srs.org	Milwaukee	WI	53202	414-289-9107		138
Scomi Oiltools Inc 6818 N Sam Houston Pkwy W *Web:* www.scomigroup.com.my	Houston	TX	77064	281-260-6016		190
Sconyer's Bar-B-Que 2250 Sconyers Way *Web:* sconyersbar-b-que.com	Augusta	GA	30906	706-790-5411	790-1505	671
Sconza 1 Sconza Candy Ln *Web:* www.sconzacandy.com	Oakdale	CA	95361	209-845-3700	845-3737	296-8
Scoot & Doodle Inc 2625 Middlefield Rd Ste 223 *TF:* 888-563-9224	Palo Alto	CA	94306	888-563-9224		387
Scope Seven Inc 2201 Park Pl Ste 100 *Web:* zoodigital.com	El Segundo	CA	90245	310-220-3939		514
Scopelitis , Garvin , Light , Hanson & Feary PLC 600 Republic Centre 633 Chestnut St *TF:* 800-973-1177 ■ *Web:* www.scopelitis.com	Chattanooga	TN	37450	423-266-2769		428
Score 726 E Anaheim St *TF:* 800-626-7774 ■ *Web:* www.scoresports.com	Wilmington	CA	90744	800-626-7774		155-19
Score a Goal in The Classroom 819 Penn St *Web:* scoreagoal.org	Fort Worth	TX	76102	817-429-4024		196
SCORE Assn 1175 Herndon Pkwy Ste 900 **Fax Area Code:* 703 ■ *TF:* 800-634-0245 ■ *Web:* www.score.org	Herndon	VA	20170	800-634-0245	487-3066*	49-12
Score Technologies Inc 13 Bow Cir Ste 147 *Web:* scoretechnologies.com	Hilton Head	SC	29928	843-384-9855		396
Score, The 500 King St W 4th Fl *Web:* thescore.com	Toronto	ON	M5V1L9	416-479-8812	361-2045	740
Scorelogix LLC 100 Lake Dr Ste 205 *Web:* www.scorelogix.com	Newark	DE	19702	302-294-6532	380-4202	194
Scorpion Design Inc 28480 Ave Stanford Ste 100 *TF:* 866-622-5648 ■ *Web:* www.scorpion.co	Valencia	CA	91355	866-622-5648		180
Scorr Marketing 2201 Central Ave Ste A *Web:* www.scorrmarketing.com	Kearney	NE	68847	308-237-5567		636
Scosche Industries Inc PO Box 2901 *TF:* 800-363-4490 ■ *Web:* www.scosche.com	Oxnard	CA	93034	805-486-4450	486-9996	253
Scot Forge Co 8001 Winn Rd PO Box 8 *TF:* 800-435-6621 ■ *Web:* www.scotforge.com	Spring Grove	IL	60081	847-587-1000	587-2000	483
Scot Pump 6437 Pioneer Rd PO Box 286 *Web:* www.scotpump.com	Cedarburg	WI	53012	262-377-7000	377-7330	641
Scotch & Sirloin 3999 Maple Rd *Web:* scotchnsirloinrestaurant.net	Amherst	NY	14226	716-837-4900		671
Scotch Gulf Lumber 1850 Conception St Rd *TF:* 800-496-3307 ■ *Web:* www.gulflumber.com	Mobile	AL	36610	251-457-6872	452-7110	683
Scotch Lumber Co 119 W Main St PO Box 38 *Web:* scotchplywood.com	Fulton	AL	36446	334-636-4424		683
Scotch Malt Whiskey Society 10210 NW 50th St *Web:* www.smwsa.com	Sunrise	FL	33351	954-749-2440		354
Scotch Plains-Fanwood Board of Education 2280 Evergreen Ave *Web:* www.spfk12.org	Scotch Plains	NJ	07076	908-889-5331		685
Scotchman Industries Inc 180 E Hwy 14 *TF:* 800-843-8844 ■ *Web:* www.scotchman.com	Philip	SD	57567	605-859-2542	859-2499	493
Scotia Capital Markets 1 Liberty Plaza *TF:* 877-294-3435 ■ *Web:* www.gbm.scotiabank.com	New York	NY	10006	212-225-5000	225-5090	690
Scotland County PO Box 489 *TF:* 800-913-6109 ■ *Web:* www.scotlandcounty.org	Laurinburg	NC	28353	910-277-2406	277-2411	338
Scotland County 117 S Market St	Memphis	MO	63555	660-465-8605		338
Scotland Manufacturing Inc 22261 Skyway Church Rd *Web:* www.scotlandmanufacturing.com	Laurinburg	NC	28353	910-844-3956		488
Scotland Memorial Hospital 500 Lauchwood Dr *TF:* 800-557-9249 ■ *Web:* www.scotlandhealth.org	Laurinburg	NC	28352	910-291-7000		374-3
Scotsman Ice Systems 775 Corporate Woods Pkwy *TF Cust Svc:* 800-726-8762 ■ *Web:* www.scotsman-ice.com	Vernon Hills	IL	60061	847-215-4500	913-9844	664
Scotsman Inn West 5922 W Kellogg St *TF:* 800-950-7268 ■ *Web:* www.scotsmaninnwichita.com	Wichita	KS	67209	316-943-3800	943-3800	379
Scott & White Health Plan 2401 S 31st St *TF:* 800-321-7947 ■ *Web:* www.sw.org	Temple	TX	76508	254-298-3000		391-3
Scott & White Memorial Hospital 2401 S 31st St *TF:* 800-792-3710 ■ *Web:* www.sw.org	Temple	TX	76508	254-724-2111	724-2786	374-3
Scott Advertising & Publishing 30595 8 Mile Rd *Web:* www.scottpublications.com	Livonia	MI	48152	248-477-6650		627
Scott Air Force Base 101 Heritage Dr *Web:* www.scott.af.mil	Scott AFB	IL	62225	618-256-1110		497-1
Scott Arboretum of Swarthmore College 500 College Ave *Web:* www.scottarboretum.org	Swarthmore	PA	19081	610-328-8025		97
Scott Austin (Rep R - GA) 2417 Rayburn HOB *Web:* austinscott.house.gov	Washington	DC	20515	202-225-6531	225-3013	342-2
Scott Brown Media Group 645 Pressley Rd Ste D *Web:* sbmg.com	Charlotte	NC	28217	704-525-9775		7
Scott Builders Inc 8105 - 49 Ave Close *TF:* 800-970-0308 ■ *Web:* www.scottbuilders.com	Red Deer	AB	T4P2V5	403-343-7270	346-4310	186

				Phone	Fax	Class
Scott Community College 500 Belmont Rd	Bettendorf	IA	52722	563-441-4001	441-4131*	162
*Fax: Admissions ■ TF: 888-336-3907 ■ Web: www.eicc.edu						
Scott Construction Inc 560 Munroe Ave	Lake Delton	WI	53940	608-254-2555	254-2249	188-4
TF: 800-843-1556 ■ Web: www.scottconstruct.com						
Scott County 131 S Winchester St PO Box 188	Benton	MO	63736	573-545-3549	545-3540	338
Web: www.scottcountymo.com						
Scott County 416 W Fourth St	Davenport	IA	52801	563-326-8647	326-8298	338
Web: www.scottcountyiowa.com						
Scott County 151 Erle Johnston Dr	Forest	MS	39074	601-469-2928		338
Web: cityofforest.com						
Scott County 336 Water St	Gate City	VA	24251	276-386-6521	386-9198	338
Web: www.scottcountyva.com						
Scott County 101 E Main St	Georgetown	KY	40324	502-863-7850	863-7852	338
Web: www.scottky.com						
Scott County 282 Ct St	Huntsville	TN	37756	423-663-2588		338
Web: www.scottcounty.com						
Scott County 210 W	Scott City	KS	67871	620-872-2640		338
Web: ks-scott.manatron.com						
Scott County 200 Fourth Ave W	Shakopee	MN	55379	952-445-7750		338
Web: www.co.scott.mn.us						
Scott County 190 W First St	Waldron	AR	72958	479-637-2642	637-0124	338
Scott County 35 E Market St	Winchester	IL	62694	217-742-5217	742-5853	338
Web: www.illinoiscourts.gov						
Scott County Library System 1615 Weston Ct	Shakopee	MN	55379	952-707-1770		434-3
TF: 877-772-8346 ■ Web: www.scottlib.org						
Scott County Library System 200 N Sixth Ave	Eldridge	IA	52748	563-285-4794	285-4743	434-3
Web: scottcountylibrary.org						
Scott Danahy Naylon Company Inc (SDN) 300 Spindrift Dr	Williamsville	NY	14221	716-633-3400	633-4306	390
TF: 800-728-6362 ■ Web: www.sdnins.com						
Scott David (Rep D - GA) 225 Cannon Bldg	Washington	DC	20515	202-225-2939	225-4628	342-2
Web: davidscott.house.gov						
Scott Electric 1000 S Main St PO Box S	Greensburg	PA	15601	724-834-4321	426-9598*	246
*Fax Area Code: 800 ■ TF: 800-442-8045 ■ Web: www.scottelectricusa.com						
Scott Enterprises Inc 2225 Downs Dr 6th Fl Exce Stes	Erie	PA	16509	814-868-9500		387
TF: 877-866-3445 ■ Web: www.visitscott.com						
Scott Equipment Co 605 Fourth Ave NW	New Prague	MN	56071	952-758-2591		298
Web: www.scottequipment.com						
Scott Family of Dealerships 3333 Lehigh St	Allentown	PA	18103	610-421-4514	967-6227	57
TF: 800-301-0876 ■ Web: www.scottcars.com						
Scott Fetzer Co 28800 Clemens Rd	Westlake	OH	44145	440-892-3000	892-3033	386
TF: 800-275-8777 ■ Web: scottfetzer.com						
Scott Fetzer Company Scot Laboratories Div 16841 Pk Cir Dr	Chagrin Falls	OH	44023	440-543-3033		151
TF: 800-486-7268 ■ Web: scotstuffdirect.com						
Scott Fly Rod Co 2355 Air Pk Way	Montrose	CO	81401	800-728-7208	249-4172*	710
*Fax Area Code: 970 ■ TF: 800-728-7208 ■ Web: www.scottflyrod.com						
Scott Health & Safety 4320 Goldmine Rd PO Box 569	Monroe	NC	28110	704-291-8300	291-8340	576
TF: 800-247-7257 ■ Web: www.scottsafety.com						
Scott Howell & Company Inc 3900 Willow St Ste 200	Dallas	TX	75226	214-951-9494	688-0555	4
Web: www.scotthowell.com						
Scott Industrial Systems Inc 4433 Interpoint Blvd	Dayton	OH	45424	937-233-8146	416-6023*	470
*Fax Area Code: 800 ■ TF: 800-416-6023 ■ Web: www.scottindustrialsystems.com						
Scott Industries Inc 1573 Hwy 136 W PO Box 7	Henderson	KY	42419	270-831-2037	831-2039	389
TF: 800-951-9276 ■ Web: www.scott-mfg.com						
Scott Joplin House State Historic Site 2658 Delmar Blvd	Saint Louis	MO	63103	314-340-5790		565
Web: www.mostateparks.com						
Scott Logistics Corp PO Box 391	Rome	GA	30162	706-234-1184	234-1184	311
TF: 800-893-6689 ■ Web: www.scottlogistics.com						
Scott Madden & Assoc Inc 2626 Glenwood Ave Ste 480	Raleigh	NC	27608	919-781-4191		194
Web: www.scottmadden.com						
Scott Marcus & Assoc 121 Johnson Rd Ste 1	Blackwood	NJ	08012	856-227-0800		445
Web: www.marcuslaw.net						
Scott Memorial Library 1020 Walnut St	Philadelphia	PA	19107	215-503-6994	923-3203	434-1
Scott N Schumaker 217 E Maple Rd	Troy	MI	48083	248-457-0800		390
Web: statefarm.com						
Scott Petroleum Corporation Inc 102 Main St	Itta Bena	MS	38941	662-254-9024		581
TF: 800-647-9397 ■ Web: www.scottpetroleuminc.com						
Scott Phil (R) 109 State St Pavilion Office Bldg	Montpelier	VT	05609	802-828-3333	828-3339	343
Web: governor.vermont.gov						
Scott Powers Stuidos Inc 381 Powers Ave S Ste 809	New York	NY	10016	212-242-4700		514
Web: www.scottpowers.com						
Scott Public Relations 21201 Victory Blvd Ste 270	Canoga Park	CA	91303	818-610-0270		636
Web: scottpublicrelations.com						
Scott Resort & Spa, The 4925 N Scottsdale Rd	Scottsdale	AZ	85251	480-945-7666	946-4056	707
TF: 800-528-7867						
Scott Rice Office Works 14720 W 105th St	Lenexa	KS	66215	913-888-7600		321
Web: www.scottrice.com						
Scott Rick (R) PL 05 The Capitol 400 S Monroe St	Tallahassee	FL	32399	850-488-7146		343
Web: www.flgov.com						
Scott Safety Supply Services Inc 5012 Caxton St W PO Box 1983	Whitecourt	AB	T7S1P7	780-778-3389		538
Web: www.scottsafety.ca						
Scott Sheldon LLC 3985 Medina Rd Ste 220	Medina	OH	44256	330-952-1671		463
TF: 877-467-7552 ■ Web: www.scott-sheldon.com						
Scott Swimming Pools Inc 75 Washington Rd	Woodbury	CT	06798	203-263-2108		186
TF: 800-947-8631 ■ Web: www.scottpools.com						
Scott Tim (Sen R - SC) 717 Hart Senate Office Bldg	Washington	DC	20510	202-224-6121	228-5143	342-2
TF: 855-425-6324 ■ Web: www.scott.senate.gov						
Scott Turbon Mixer Inc 9351 Industrial Way	Adelanto	CA	92301	760-246-3430		298
Web: www.scottmixer.com						
Scott USA Inc PO Box 2030	Sun Valley	ID	83353	208-622-1000	622-1005	710
TF: 800-292-5874 ■ Web: www.scott-sports.com						
Scott Yaw Associates LLC 1074 Park Ave	Wycombe	PA	18980	215-598-9977		195
Web: www.scottyaw.com						
Scott's Liquid Gold Inc 4880 Havana St	Denver	CO	80239	303-373-4860		151
OTC: SLGD ■ TF: 800-447-1919 ■ Web: www.scottsliquidgold.com						
Scott's Seafood Grill & Bar 4800 Riverside Blvd	Sacramento	CA	95822	916-379-5959	489-2447	671
Web: www.scottsseafood.net						
Jack London Square 2 Broadway	Oakland	CA	94607	510-444-3456		671
Web: www.scottsjls.com						
Scottdale Bank & Trust 125 S Arch St	Connellsville	PA	15425	724-628-3200		70
Web: sbtbank.com						
Scottdel Inc 400 Church St	Swanton	OH	43558	419-825-2341	825-1523	131
TF: 800-446-2341 ■ Web: www.scottdel.com						
Scott-Gross Company Inc 664 Magnolia Ave	Lexington	KY	40505	800-967-6874	737-5452*	324
*Fax Area Code: 859 ■ TF: 800-967-6874						
Scottish Heritage USA 315 Page Rd Ste 10	Pinehurst	NC	28374	910-295-4448	295-3147	48-14
TF: 800-451-0694 ■ Web: www.scottishheritageusa.org						
Scottish Re Inc 14120 Ballantyne Corporate Pl Ste 300	Charlotte	NC	28277	704-542-9192	542-5744	360-4
Web: www.scottishre.com						
Scottish Rite Cathedral 160 S Scott Ave	Tucson	AZ	85701	520-622-8364		50-1
Web: tucsonscottishrite.org						
Scott-Mc Rae Advertising 701 Riverside Pk Pl	Jacksonville	FL	32204	904-354-4000		57
Web: scottmcraejobs.com						
Scottrade Ctr 1401 Clark Ave	Saint Louis	MO	63103	314-622-5400	622-5410	720
Web: www.scottradecenter.com						
Scotts Bluff County 1825 Tenth St	Gering	NE	69341	308-436-6600	436-3178	338
Web: www.scottsbluffcounty.org						
Scotts Miracle Gro Products Inc 14111 Scottslawn Rd	Marysville	OH	43041	937-644-0011		280
TF: 888-270-3714 ■ Web: www.scotts.com/smg						
Scotts Miracle-Gro Co 14111 Scottslawn Rd	Marysville	OH	43041	937-644-0011		280
NYSE: SMG ■ TF Cust Svc: 800-543-8873 ■ Web: www.scotts.com						
Scotts Valley Unified School District Inc 4444 Scotts Valley Dr Ste 5b	Scotts Valley	CA	95066	831-438-1820	438-2314	685
Web: www.svusd.santacruz.k12.ca.us						
Scottsdale Area Chamber of Commerce 7501 E McCormick Pkwy Ste 202-N	Scottsdale	AZ	85258	480-355-2700	355-2710	139
TF: 800-916-1515 ■ Web: www.scottsdalechamber.com						
Scottsdale Camelback Resort 6302 E Camelback Rd	Scottsdale	AZ	85251	480-947-3300		669
TF: 800-891-8585 ■ Web: www.scottsdalecamelback.com						
Scottsdale City Hall 7447 E Indian School Rd	Scottsdale	AZ	85251	480-312-3111	312-2888	337
Web: www.scottsdaleaz.gov						
Scottsdale Community College 9000 E Chaparral Rd	Scottsdale	AZ	85256	480-423-6000	423-6200*	162
*Fax: Admissions ■ TF: 800-784-2433 ■ Web: www.scottsdalecc.edu						
Scottsdale Convention & Visitors Bureau 4343 N Scottsdale Rd Ste 170	Scottsdale	AZ	85251	480-421-1004	421-9733	206
TF: 800-782-1117 ■ Web: www.experiencescottsdale.com						
Scottsdale Ctr for the Performing Arts 7380 E Second St	Scottsdale	AZ	85251	480-994-2787	874-4699	572
Web: www.scottsdaleperformingarts.org						
Scottsdale Culinary Institute 8100 E Camelback Rd Ste 1001	Scottsdale	AZ	85251	480-990-3773	990-0351	163
TF: 888-557-4222 ■ Web: www.chefs.edu						
Scottsdale Gun Club 14860 N Northsight Blvd	Scottsdale	AZ	85260	480-348-1111		711
TF: 800-987-7719 ■ Web: www.scottsdalegunclub.com						
Scottsdale Historical Museum 7333 E Scottsdale Mall	Scottsdale	AZ	85251	480-945-4499		520
TF: 800-307-3610 ■ Web: www.scottsdalemuseum.com						
Scottsdale Museum of Contemporary Art (SMOCA) 7374 E Second St	Scottsdale	AZ	85251	480-874-4666		520
TF: 800-745-3000 ■ Web: www.smoca.org						
Scottsdale Osborn Medical Center 7400 E Osborn Rd	Scottsdale	AZ	85251	480-882-4000		374-3
TF: 800-984-8015 ■ Web: www.honorhealth.com						
Scottsdale Plaza Resort 7200 N Scottsdale Rd	Scottsdale	AZ	85253	480-948-5000	998-5971	669
TF: 800-832-2025 ■ Web: www.scottsdaleplaza.com						
Scottsdale Shea Medical Center 9003 E Shea Blvd	Scottsdale	AZ	85260	480-323-3000		374-3
Web: www.honorhealth.com						
Scottsdale Stadium 7408 E Osborn Rd	Scottsdale	AZ	85251	480-312-2586	312-7729	720
TF: 877-229-5042 ■ Web: www.scottsdaleaz.gov/stadium						
Scottsdale Symphony Orchestra 3127 N 81st Pl	Scottsdale	AZ	85251	480-945-8071		573-3
Scottsdale Tribune 6991 Camelback Rd	Scottsdale	AZ	85251	480-970-2330	970-2360	532-2
Web: www.eastvalleytribune.com						
Scotttrade 8205 E Regal Ct	Tulsa	OK	74133	918-369-4333		690
TF: 800-619-7283 ■ Web: www.scottrade.com						
Scotty's Fashions Inc 636 Pen Argyl St	Pen Argyl	PA	18072	610-863-6454		155-21
TF: 800-528-7909 ■ Web: www.scottysfashions.com						

	Phone	Fax	Class
Scoular Co 2027 Dodge St. . . . . Omaha NE 68102 *TF:* 800-488-3500 ■ *Web:* www.scoular.com	402-342-3500		275
Scout Boats Inc 2531 US 78. . . . . Summerville SC 29483 *Web:* www.scoutboats.com	843-821-0068	821-4786	90
Scout Stuff PO Box 7143. . . . . Charlotte NC 28241 *TF:* 800-323-0736 ■ *Web:* www.scoutstuff.org	800-323-0736		791
Scouting Magazine 1325 W Walnut Hill Ln PO Box 152079 . . . . Irving TX 75015 *TF:* 800-323-0732 ■ *Web:* www.scoutingmagazine.org	972-580-2000	580-2079	457-10
Scouts Canada 1345 Baseline Rd . . . . Ottawa ON K2C0A7 *TF:* 800-449-6367 ■ *Web:* www.scouts.ca	613-225-2770		711
Scovill Fasteners Inc 1802 Scovill Dr. . . . . Clarkesville GA 30523 **Fax:* Cust Svc ■ *TF Cust Svc:* 888-726-8455 ■ *Web:* www.scovill.com	706-754-1000	754-4000*	594
Scovill Zoo 71 S Country Club Rd . . . . Decatur IL 62521 *Web:* www.decatur-parks.org	217-421-7435		823
SCP (Standard Concrete Products Inc) PO Box 1360 . . . . Columbus GA 31902 *Web:* www.standardconcrete.net	706-322-3274		188-4
SCP Construction LLC 5340 W Luke Ave . . . . Glendale AZ 85301 *Web:* www.scpaz.com	623-931-9131		194
SCP Private Equity Partners 1200 Liberty Ridge Dr. Chesterbrook PA 19087 *Web:* www.scppartners.com	610-995-2900	975-9546	405
SCPPA (Southern California Public Power Authority) 225 S Lake Ave Ste 1250 . . . . Pasadena CA 91101 *Web:* www.scppa.org	626-793-9364	793-9461	787
SCPPD (South Central Public Power District) 275 S Main St PO Box 406. Nelson NE 68961 *TF:* 800-557-5254 ■ *Web:* www.southcentralppd.com	402-225-2351		245
SCR Construction Company Inc 5420 FM 2218 Rd. . . . . Richmond TX 77469 *Web:* www.scrconstruction.net	281-344-0700	344-0099	186
SC&RA (Specialized Carriers & Rigging Assn) 5870 Trinity Pkwy Ste 200 . . . . Centreville VA 20120 *Web:* www.scranet.org	703-698-0291	698-0297	49-21
Scranton City Hall 340 N Washington Ave. . . . . Scranton PA 18503 *Web:* www.scrantonpa.gov	570-348-4100	348-4207	337
Scranton Counseling Ctr Inc 326 Adams Ave. . . . . Scranton PA 18503 *Web:* www.scrantonscc.org	570-348-6100		353
Scranton Cultural Ctr 420 N Washington Ave . . . . Scranton PA 18503 *Web:* www.scrantonculturalcenter.org	570-346-7369	346-7365	572
Scranton Mfg Company Inc 101 State St PO Box 336 . . . . Scranton IA 51462 *TF:* 800-831-1858 ■ *Web:* www.scrantonmfg.com	712-652-3396	652-3399	273
Scranton Motors Inc 777 Talcottville Rd . . . . Vernon CT 06066 *Web:* scrantonmotors.com	860-872-9145		57
Scranton Products Inc 801 E Corey St Scranton PA 18505 *Web:* www.scrantonproducts.com	[illegible]		[illegible]
Scranton Public Library 500 Vine St. . . . . Scranton PA 18509 *Web:* www.albright.org	570-348-3000		434-3
Scranton School District 425 N Washington Ave . . . . Scranton PA 18503 *TF:* 800-214-5264 ■ *Web:* www.scrsd.org	570-348-3474	348-3563	685
Scranton Times-Tribune 149 Penn Ave. . . . . Scranton PA 18503 *TF:* 800-228-4637 ■ *Web:* thetimes-tribune.com	570-348-9100	348-9135	532-2
Scrapbook Factory Inc 2004 W Hwy 50 Ste D. . . . . Ofallon IL 62269 *Web:* www.scrapbookfactorystore.com	618-628-8877		270
Scream Agency LLC 1501 Wazee St Ste 1b . . . . Denver CO 80202 *Web:* www.screamagency.com	303-893-8608		7
Screamer Design LLC 107 Leland St Ste 3. . . . . Austin TX 78704 *Web:* screamerco.com	512-691-7894		7
SCREC (Sullivan County Rural Electric Co-op Inc) 5675 Rt 87 PO Box 65 . . . . Forksville PA 18616 *TF:* 800-570-5081 ■ *Web:* www.screc.com	570-924-3381		245
Screen Actors Guild (SAG) 5757 Wilshire Blvd. . . . . Los Angeles CA 90036 *TF:* 800-724-0767 ■ *Web:* www.sagaftra.org	323-954-1600	549-6775	414
Screen Graphics of Florida Inc 1801 N Andrews Ave. Pompano Beach FL 33069 *TF:* 800-346-4420 ■ *Web:* www.screen-graphics.com	800-346-4420		687
Screen Industry Art Inc 214 Industrial Park Dr. Soddy Daisy TN 37379	423-332-6190		687
Screen Machine Inc 3855 Wabash Ave . . . . San Diego CA 92104	619-281-3355		687
Screen Tech Inc 470 Needles Dr. . . . . San Jose CA 95112 *Web:* www.screentechinc.com	408-885-8750		295
Screen Works 2201 W Fulton St . . . . Chicago IL 60612 *TF Cust Svc:* 800-294-8111 ■ *Web:* www.thescreenworks.com	312-243-8265		722
Screen Works Inc 3970 Image Dr. . . . . Dayton OH 45414 *TF:* 800-536-9111 ■ *Web:* screenworksinc.com	937-264-9111		344
Screenco Enterprises 9 Bell Rd. . . . . Selma AL 36701 *Web:* www.screenco.biz	334-872-0051		627
Screeningone Inc 2233 W 190th St . . . . Torrance CA 90504 *TF:* 888-327-6511 ■ *Web:* www.screeningone.com	888-327-6511		218
Screenmobile 72-050A Corporate Way. . . . . Thousand Palms CA 92276 *Web:* www.screenmobile.com	760-343-3500		310
ScreenPlay Inc 3411 Thorndyke Ave W . . . . Seattle WA 98119 *Web:* www.screenplayinc.com	206-625-9901		5
ScreenScape Networks Inc 133 Queen St 3rd Fl. . . . . Charlottetown PE C1A7K4 *TF:* 800-225-5627 ■ *Web:* www.screenscape.com	902-368-1975		7
Screenz 5212 N Clark St. . . . . Chicago IL 60640 *Web:* screenz.com	773-912-1565		225
Screven County 101 S Main St. . . . . Sylvania GA 30467 *Web:* www.screvencounty.com	912-564-7878		338
Screw Conveyor Corp 700 Hoffman St. . . . . Hammond IN 46327 *Web:* www.screwconveyor.com	219-931-1450	931-0209	207
SCRI International Inc 2023 N Atlantic Ave Ste 310. . . . . Cocoa Beach FL 32931 *Web:* www.scri.com	321-868-8273		466
Scribe Inc 842 S Second St . . . . Philadelphia PA 19147 *Web:* scribenet.com	215-336-5094		196
Scribendi Inc 405 Riverview Dr Ste 304 . . . . Chatham ON N7M0N3 *Web:* www.scribendi.com	519-351-1626		393
Scribner Associates Inc 150 E Connecticut Ave . . . . Southern Pines NC 28387 *Web:* www.scribner.com	910-695-8884		757
Scribner Cohen & Company SC 400 E Mason St Ste 300. Milwaukee WI 53202 *TF:* 888-730-0045 ■ *Web:* scribnercohen.com	414-271-1700		2
Scripps College 1030 Columbia Ave. . . . . Claremont CA 91711 **Fax:* Admissions ■ *TF:* 800-770-1333 ■ *Web:* scrippscollege.edu	909-621-8149	607-7508*	166
Scripps Green Hospital 10666 N Torrey Pines Rd . . . . La Jolla CA 92037 *TF:* 800-727-4777 ■ *Web:* www.scripps.org	858-455-9100		374-3
Scripps Green Hospital Blood & Marrow Transplant Ctr 10666 N Torrey Pines Rd . . . . La Jolla CA 92037 *Web:* scripps.org	858-554-8597		769
Scripps Health 4275 Campus Pt Ct. . . . . San Diego CA 92121 *TF:* 800-727-4777 ■ *Web:* www.scripps.org	800-727-4777		353
Scripps Howard Foundation 312 Walnut St Ste 2800 . . . . Cincinnati OH 45201 *TF:* 800-888-3000 ■ *Web:* www.scripps.com/foundation	513-977-3035	977-3800	304
Scripps Howard Inc PO Box 5380 . . . . Cincinnati OH 45202 *TF:* 800-888-3000 ■ *Web:* www.scripps.com	513-977-3000		637-8
Scripps Howard News Service (SHNS) 1090 Vermont Ave NW Ste 1000. . . . . Washington DC 20005 *Web:* www.shns.com	202-408-1484	408-2062	530
Scripps Institution of Oceanography (SIO) 8622 Kennel Way . . . . La Jolla CA 92037 *Web:* scripps.ucsd.edu	858-534-3624		668
Scripps Laboratories Inc 6838 Flanders Dr . . . . San Diego CA 92121 *Web:* www.scrippslabs.com	858-546-5800	546-5812	231
Scripps Memorial Hospital-Encinitas 354 Santa Fe Dr . . . . Encinitas CA 92024 *Web:* www.scripps.org	760-633-6501		374-3
Scripps Memorial Hospital-La Jolla 9888 Genesee Ave . . . . La Jolla CA 92037 *TF:* 800-727-4777 ■ *Web:* www.scripps.org	800-727-4777		374-3
Scripps Mercy Hospital 4077 Fifth Ave. . . . . San Diego CA 92103 *TF:* 800-906-9762 ■ *Web:* www.scripps.org	619-294-8111		374-3
Scripps Networks LLC 9721 Sherrill Blvd. . . . . Knoxville TN 37932 *Web:* www.diynetwork.com	865-694-2700		740
Scripps Ranch Swim & Racquet Club 9875 Aviary Dr . . . . San Diego CA 92131 *Web:* srsrc.com	858-271-6222		354
Scripps Research Institute 10550 N Torrey Pines Rd . . . . La Jolla CA 92037 **Fax:* Hum Res ■ *Web:* www.scripps.edu	858-784-1000	784-9004*	668
Script Care Inc 6380 Folsom Dr . . . . Beaumont TX 77706 *TF:* [illegible] ■ *Web:* www.scriptcare.com	800-880-9988		586
Script to Screen Productions 200 N Tustin Ave Ste 200 . . . . Santa Ana CA 92705 *TF:* 800-453-0003 ■ *Web:* www.scripttoscreen.com	714-558-3971		514
ScriptLogic Corp 6000 Broken Sound Pkwy NW . . . . Boca Raton FL 33487 *TF:* 800-306-9329 ■ *Web:* www.quest.com	561-886-2400	886-2499	178-12
ScriptSave 4911 E Broadway Blvd Ste 200 . . . . Tucson AZ 85711 *TF:* 800-347-5985 ■ *Web:* www.scriptsave.com	800-347-5985		586
SCRMC (South Central Regional Medical Ctr) 1220 Jefferson St . . . . Laurel MS 39440 *Web:* www.scrmc.com	601-426-4000		374-3
ScrubaDub Auto Wash Centers Inc 172 Worcester Rd . . . . Natick MA 01760 *Web:* www.scrubadub.com	508-650-1155	655-9261	62-1
Scrugg's Barbeque 7529 Moores Mill Rd . . . . Huntsville AL 35811 *Web:* www.scruggsbbq.com	256-859-6800		671
Scruggs Company Inc PO Box 2065 . . . . Valdosta GA 31604 *TF:* 800-230-7263 ■ *Web:* scruggscompany.com	229-242-2388	242-7109	188-4
SCS (Structural Component Systems Inc) 1255 Front St . . . . Fremont NE 68026 *TF:* 800-844-5622 ■ *Web:* www.scstruss.com	402-721-5622		187
SCS (Society for Modeling & Simulation International) 11315 Rancho Bernardo Rd Ste 139. . . . . San Diego CA 92127 *Web:* www.scs.org	858-277-3888	277-3930	48-9
SCS Engineers 3900 Kilroy Airport Way Ste 100 . . . . Long Beach CA 90806 *TF:* 800-326-9544 ■ *Web:* www.scsengineers.com	562-426-9544	427-0805	261
SCSD (Sweetwater County School District 1) 3550 Foothill Blvd . . . . Rock Springs WY 82901 **Fax Area Code:* 888 ■ *Web:* www.swcotwater1.org	307-352-3400	503-7562*	780
SCT (Stockton Civic Theatre) 2312 Rose Marie Ln . . . . Stockton CA 95207 *Web:* www.sctlivetheatre.com	209-473-2400	473-1502	573-4
SCTE (Society of Cable Telecommunications Engineers) 140 Philips Rd . . . . Exton PA 19341 *TF:* 800-542-5040 ■ *Web:* www.scte.org	610-363-6888	363-5898	49-19
Scuba Com Inc 1752 Langley Ave. . . . . Irvine CA 92614 *TF:* 800-347-2822 ■ *Web:* www.scuba.com	949-221-9300		711
Scully Capital Services Inc 1730 M St NW Ste 204. Washington DC 20036 *Web:* www.scullycapital.com	202-775-3434		251
Scully Jones Seibert Corp 1901 S Rockwell St. . . . . Chicago IL 60608	773-247-5900		493
Scully Oil Company Inc 150 E Flint St PO Box 398 . . . . Lyndon Station WI 53944 *Web:* www.scullyoil.com	608-666-2662	666-2239	449
Scully Signal Co 70 Industrial Way. . . . . Wilmington MA 01887 *TF:* 800-272-8559 ■ *Web:* www.scully.com	617-692-8600	692-8620	201
SCUP (Society for College & University Planning) 339 E Liberty St Ste 300. Ann Arbor MI 48104 *TF:* 800-228-5424 ■ *Web:* www.scup.org	734-669-3270	998-6532	49-5
Scurlock Industries of Springfield Inc 3401 W Commercial St. Springfield MO 65803 *Web:* www.scurlockindustries.com	417-862-5088		183
Scurry County 1806 25th St Ste 300. . . . . Snyder TX 79549 *Web:* www.co.scurry.tx.us	325-573-5332	573-7396	338

Name / Address	City	State	ZIP	Phone	Fax	Class
Scusset Beach State Reservation 20 Scusset Beach Rd *Web:* www.mass.gov	Sandwich	MA	02563	508-888-0859		565
SD Ireland Co 193 Industrial Ave *TF:* 800-339-4565 ■ *Web:* www.sdireland.com	Williston	VT	05495	802-863-6222		183
SD Richman Sons Inc 2435 Wheatsheaf Ln *Web:* www.sdrichmansons.com	Philadelphia	PA	19137	215-535-5100	288-1043	686
Sda Consulting Inc 3011 183rd St # 377 *TF:* 800-823-2990 ■ *Web:* www.sdaci.com	Homewood	IL	60430	800-823-2990		180
SDB Inc 810 W First St *Web:* www.sdb.com	Tempe	AZ	85281	480-967-5810	967-5841	186
SDB Trade International LP 817 Southmore Ave Ste 301 *Web:* thesdbgroup.com	Houston	TX	77502	713-475-0048		791
SDCC (Selkirk & District Chamber of Commerce) 200 Eaton Ave *Web:* www.selkirkanddistrictchamber.ca	Selkirk	MB	R1A0W6	204-482-7176	482-5448	137
SDCI (San Diego Culinary Institute) 8024 La Mesa Blvd *Web:* sandiegoculinary.edu	La Mesa	CA	91941	619-644-2100	644-2106	163
SDEB (San Diego Eye Bank) 9246 Lightwave Ave Ste 120 *TF:* 800-393-2265 ■ *Web:* www.sdeb.org	San Diego	CA	92123	858-694-0400	565-7368	269
SDG Corp 55 N Water St *Web:* www.sdgc.com	Norwalk	CT	06854	203-866-8886		317
SDG Systems LLC 330 Perry Hwy Ste 200 *Web:* www.sdgsystems.com	Harmony	PA	16037	724-452-9366		179
SDG, Inc 200 N Broadway St *Web:* www.sharpeclothing.com	Checotah	OK	74426	918-473-2233		157-2
SDI (System Development Integration Inc) 33 W Monroe St Ste 400 *Web:* www.sdipresence.com	Chicago	IL	60603	312-580-7500	580-7600	180
SDI (System Dynamics International Inc) 560 Discovery Dr NW *Web:* www.sdi-inc.com	Huntsville	AL	35806	256-895-9000		261
SDI 330 N Wabash Ave Ste 200 *Web:* www.sditravel.com	Chicago	IL	60611	312-587-8200	587-7111	772
SDI Presence LLC 33 W Monroe St Ste 400 *TF:* 888-968-7734 ■ *Web:* www.sdisolutions.com	Chicago	IL	60603	312-580-7500	580-7600	693
SDI Technologies Inc 1299 Main St *TF:* 800-333-3092 ■ *Web:* www.sditechnologies.com	Rahway	NJ	07065	800-333-3092		52
SDK Laboratories 1000 Corey Rd *Web:* www.sdklabs.com	Hutchinson	KS	67501	620-665-5661		743
SDK Software Inc 11320 86th Ave N *Web:* www.sdksoft.com	Maple Grove	MN	55369	763-657-1189		177
SDL Capital LP 480 San Antonio Rd Ste 200 *Web:* www.sdlventures.com	Mountain View	CA	94040	650-559-9355		401
SDL International 2550 N First St Ste 301 *Web:* www.sdl.com	San Jose	CA	95131	408-743-3600		178-1
SDLC Partners LP 2790 Mosside Blvd Ste 705 *Web:* www.sdlcpartners.com	Monroeville	PA	15146	412-373-1950		196
SDMS (Society of Diagnostic Medical Sonography) 2745 Dallas Pkwy *TF:* 800-229-9506 ■ *Web:* www.sdms.org	Plano	TX	75093	214-473-8057	473-8563	49-8
SDN (Scott Danahy Naylon Company Inc) 300 Spindrift Dr *TF:* 800-728-6362 ■ *Web:* www.sdnins.com	Williamsville	NY	14221	716-633-3400	633-4306	390
SDN Global Inc 11702 Blalock Forest *Web:* sdn.global	Houston	TX	77024	630-730-1667		177
SDNA (South Dakota Nurses Assn) PO Box 1015 **Fax Area Code: 888* ■ *TF:* 888-425-3032 ■ *Web:* www.sdnursesassociation.org	Pierre	SD	57501	605-945-4265	425-3032*	533
SDPB (South Dakota Public Broadcasting) 555 N Dakota St PO Box 5000 *TF:* 800-456-0766 ■ *Web:* www.sdpb.org	Vermillion	SD	57069	605-677-5861	677-5010	632
SDR Ventures Inc 5613 DTC Pkwy Ste 830 *TF:* 800-289-9999 ■ *Web:* sdrventures.com	Greenwood Village	CO	80111	720-221-9220		796
Sds Consulting Corp 3115 12 St NE Ste 310 *TF:* 888-533-4544 ■ *Web:* www.sdsconsulting.ca	Calgary	AB	T2E7J2	403-221-8077		449
SDS Lumber Co PO Box 266 *TF:* 800-386-2555 ■ *Web:* sdslumber.com	Bingen	WA	98605	509-493-2155	493-2535	613
SDSC (San Diego Supercomputer Ctr) 9500 Gilman Dr *TF:* 800-451-4515 ■ *Web:* www.sdsc.edu	La Jolla	CA	92093	858-534-5000	534-5056	668
SDSMA (South Dakota State Medical Assn) 2600 W 49th St Ste 200 PO Box 7406 *Web:* sdsma.org	Sioux Falls	SD	57117	605-336-1965	274-3274	457-16
SDT North America Inc PO Box 682 *TF:* 800-667-5325 ■ *Web:* www.sdtnorthamerica.com	Cobourg	ON	K9A4R5	905-377-1313		358
SDV Construction Inc 6436 Edith Blvd NE *TF:* 800-280-0536 ■ *Web:* www.sdvconstruction.com	Albuquerque	NM	87107	505-883-3176		186
SDV Solutions Inc 133 Waller Mill Rd Ste 100 *TF:* 800-800-7056 ■ *Web:* www.sdvsolutions.us	Williamsburg	VA	23185	757-903-2068		174
SE Technologies LLC 98 Vanadium Rd Bldg D *Web:* www.se-env.com	Bridgeville	PA	15017	412-221-1100	257-6103	261
SEA (Software Engineering of America Inc) 1230 Hempstead Tpke *TF:* 800-272-7322 ■ *Web:* www.seasoft.com	Franklin Square	NY	11010	516-328-7000	354-4015	178-12
Sea Blue 503 Hwy 17 N *Web:* www.seabluewinebar.com	North Myrtle Beach	SC	29582	843-249-8800		671
Sea Blue 1 Borgata Way *TF Cust Svc:* 877-786-9900 ■ *Web:* www.theborgata.com	Atlantic City	NJ	08401	609-317-1000	317-1039	671
SEA BOX Inc 1 Sea Box Dr *Web:* www.seabox.com	Cinnaminson	NJ	08077	856-303-1101		770
Sea Breeze Inc 441 Route 202 *TF:* 800-732-2733 ■ *Web:* www.seabreezesyrups.com	Towaco	NJ	07082	973-334-7777	334-2617	296-15
Sea Breeze Ocean View Motel, The 323 State Hwy 3 *Web:* www.seabreeze.us	Bar Harbor	ME	04609	207-288-3565		378
Sea Captain's House 3002 N Ocean Blvd *Web:* www.seacaptains.com	Myrtle Beach	SC	29577	843-448-8082		671
Sea Cat Boats Inc 1005 Marina Rd *Web:* www.seacatboats.com	Titusville	FL	32796	321-268-2628		90
Sea Catch 1054 31st St NW *Web:* www.seacatchrestaurant.com	Washington	DC	20007	202-337-8855		671
Sea Chambers Motel 67 Shore Rd *Web:* www.seachambers.com	Ogunquit	ME	03907	207-646-9311		379
Sea Cloud Cruises Inc 282 Grand Ave Ste 3 *TF:* 888-732-2568 ■ *Web:* www.seacloud.com	Englewood	NJ	07631	201-227-9404	227-9424	220
SEA Com Corp 7030 220th St SW *Web:* www.seacomcorp.com	Mountlake Terrace	WA	98043	425-771-2182	771-2650	647
Sea Crest Resort & Conference Ctr 350 Quaker Rd *TF:* 800-225-3110 ■ *Web:* www.seacrestbeachhotel.com	North Falmouth	MA	02556	508-540-9400	548-0556	669
Sea Eagle Boats Inc 19 N Columbia St Ste 1 *TF:* 800-748-8066 ■ *Web:* www.seaeagle.com	Port Jefferson	NY	11777	631-791-1799	473-7398	710
Sea Engineering Inc 863 N Nimitz *Web:* seaengineering.com	Honolulu	HI	96817	808-536-3603		261
Sea Fare Group Inc 2360 W Commodore Way Ste 210 *Web:* seafaregroup.com	Seattle	WA	98199	206-789-5741	789-0504	466
Sea Fox Boat Company Inc 2550 Hwy 52 *Web:* www.seafoxboats.com	Moncks Corner	SC	29461	843-761-6090	761-6139	90
Sea Fresh USA Inc 45 All American Way *Web:* seafreshusa.com	North Kingstown	RI	02852	401-583-0200		296-14
Sea Galley Restaurant 4101 Credit Union Dr *Web:* seagalleyanchorage.com	Anchorage	AK	99503	907-563-3520	563-6382	671
Sea Gardens Beach & Tennis Resort 615 N Ocean Blvd *Web:* www.seagardens.com	Pompano Beach	FL	33062	954-943-6200		669
Sea Grant Assn (SGA) 5784 York Complex P.O. Box 1950 *Web:* www.sga.seagrant.org	Ocean Springs	MS	39566	207-581-1435	581-1426	48-13
Sea Grill Restaurant 19 W 49th St *Web:* www.patinagroup.com	New York	NY	10020	212-332-7610		671
Sea Gull Lighting Products LLC A Generations Brands Co 301 W Washington St *TF:* 800-347-5483 ■ *Web:* www.seagulllighting.com	Riverside	NJ	08075	856-764-0500		439
Sea Gull Motel on the Beach 2613 Atlantic Ave *TF:* 800-426-4855 ■ *Web:* www.seagullinn.net	Virginia Beach	VA	23451	757-425-5711		379
Sea Harvest Packing Co PO Box 818 *TF:* 800-627-4300 ■ *Web:* www.seaharvest.com	Brunswick	GA	31521	912-264-3212	264-2749	296-14
Sea Island Co 100 Cloister Dr *TF:* 800-732-4752 ■ *Web:* seaisland.com	Sea Island	GA	31561	912-638-3611		655
Sea Island Software Inc 330 Bampfield Dr *Web:* www.hurrevac.com	Mount Pleasant	SC	29464	843-881-0593		809
Sea Launch Company LLC 2700 Nimitz Rd *Web:* www.sea-launch.com	Long Beach	CA	90802	562-951-7000		504
Sea Life Park 41-202 Kalanianaole Hwy *Web:* www.sealifeparkhawaii.com	Waimanalo	HI	96795	808-259-2500		40
Sea Lion Caves 91560 Hwy 101 *TF:* 800-230-5350 ■ *Web:* www.sealioncaves.com	Florence	OR	97439	541-547-3111	547-3545	50-5
SEA Ltd 7349 Worthington-Galena Rd *TF:* 800-782-6851 ■ *Web:* www.sealimited.com	Columbus	OH	43085	800-782-6851		463
Sea Magazine 17782 Cowan St Ste C *TF:* 800-873-7327 ■ *Web:* www.seamagazine.com	Irvine	CA	92614	949-660-6150	660-6172	457-4
Sea Mar Community Health Ctr 1040 S Henderson St *TF:* 855-289-4503 ■ *Web:* www.seamar.org	Seattle	WA	98108	206-763-5277	788-3204	353
Sea Mist Farms 10855 Ocean Mist Pkwy *Web:* www.oceanmist.com	Castroville	CA	95012	831-633-2144		10-11
Sea Mist Resort 1200 S Ocean Blvd *TF:* 800-793-6507 ■ *Web:* www.myrtlebeachseamist.com	Myrtle Beach	SC	29577	843-448-1551		669
Sea of Diamonds.com 606 S Olive St Ste 1026 *Web:* www.steindiamonds.com	Los Angeles	CA	90014	213-226-0150		410
Sea Palms Golf & Tennis Resort 5445 Frederica Rd *TF:* 800-841-6268 ■ *Web:* www.seapalms.com	Saint Simons Island	GA	31522	912-638-3351	634-8029	669
Sea Pearl Seafood Company Inc 14120 Shell Belt Rd *TF:* 800-872-8804 ■ *Web:* sea-pearl.com	Bayou La Batre	AL	36509	251-824-2129		393
Sea Pines Resort, The 32 Greenwood Dr *TF:* 866-561-8802 ■ *Web:* www.seapines.com	Hilton Head Island	SC	29928	843-785-3333		653
Sea Ranch Lodge 60 Sea Walk Dr PO Box 44 *TF:* 800-732-7262 ■ *Web:* www.searanchlodge.com	The Sea Ranch	CA	95497	707-785-2371		379
Sea Research Foundation Inc 55 Coogan Blvd *Web:* blog.searesearch.org	Mystic	CT	06355	860-572-5955		31
Sea Rim State Park PO Box 356 *Web:* tpwd.texas.gov/state-parks/sea-rim	Sabine Pass	TX	77655	409-971-2559		565
Sea Shepherd Conservation Society 1225 Wold Rd *Web:* www.seashepherd.org	Friday Harbor	WA	98250	360-370-5650		196
Sea Siam Restaurant 16103 Bolsa Chica St	Huntington Beach	CA	92649	714-846-8986		671
Sea Spa at Loews Coronado Bay Resort 4000 Loews Coronado Bay Rd *TF:* 800-235-6397 ■ *Web:* www.loewshotels.com	Coronado	CA	92118	619-424-4000	424-4000	707
Sea Tow Services International Inc 1560 Youngs Ave PO Box 1178 *TF:* 800-473-2869 ■ *Web:* www.seatow.com	Southold	NY	11971	631-765-3660		465

Name / Address	City	State	Zip	Phone	Fax	Class
Sea Trail Corp 75A Clubhouse Rd *TF:* 888-321-9048 ■ *Web:* www.seatrail.com	Sunset Beach	NC	28468	910-287-1100		653
Sea Venture Resort 100 Ocean View Ave *TF:* 800-443-7778 ■ *Web:* www.seaventure.com	Pismo Beach	CA	93449	805-773-4994	773-0924	669
Sea View Hotel 9909 Collins Ave *TF:* 800-447-1010 ■ *Web:* www.seaview-hotel.com	Bal Harbour	FL	33154	305-866-4441	866-1898	379
Sea Watch International Ltd 8978 Glebe Pk Dr *Web:* www.seawatch.com	Easton	MD	21601	410-822-7500	822-1266	296-14
Sea Watch Restaurant 6002 N Ocean Blvd *Web:* www.seawatchontheocean.com	Fort Lauderdale	FL	33308	954-781-2200		671
Seabee Corp 712 First St NW *TF:* 800-738-2854 ■ *Web:* www.seabeecylinders.com	Hampton	IA	50441	641-456-4871	456-2387	223
Seabee Museum 99 23rd Ave *Web:* www.seabeehf.org	Port Hueneme	CA	93043	805-982-5167		520
Seaberg Industries Inc 8301 42nd St W *Web:* www.seaberginc.com	Rock Island	IL	61201	309-787-9494		454
SeaBird Exploration Americas Inc 1155 N Dairy Ashford Ste 206 *Web:* www.sbexp.com	Houston	TX	77079	281-556-1666		536
Seaboard Asphalt Products Co 3601 Fairfield Rd *TF:* 800-536-0332 ■ *Web:* www.seaboardasphalt.com	Baltimore	MD	21226	410-355-0330	355-5864	46
Seaboard Corp 9000 W 67th St *NYSE: SEB* ■ *TF:* 866-676-8886 ■ *Web:* www.seaboardcorp.com	Shawnee Mission	KS	66202	913-676-8800	676-8872	185
Seaboard Folding Box Co Inc 35 Daniels St *TF:* 800-225-6313 ■ *Web:* www.seaboardbox.com	Fitchburg	MA	01420	978-342-8921	342-1105	101
Seaboard Foods 9000 W 67th St Ste 200 *TF:* 800-262-7907 ■ *Web:* www.seaboardfoods.com	Shawnee Mission	KS	66202	913-261-2600		10-6
Seaboard International Forest Products LLC 22F Cotton Rd *TF:* 800-669-6800 ■ *Web:* www.sifp.com	Nashua	NH	03063	603-881-3700		191-3
Seaboard Marine 8001 NW 79th Ave *TF:* 866-676-8886 ■ *Web:* www.seaboardmarine.com	Miami	FL	33166	305-863-4444	863-4400	313
Seaborn Health Care PO Box 41158 *TF:* 800-335-6176 ■ *Web:* www.seabornhc.com	Saint Petersburg	FL	33743	727-398-1710		393
Seabridge Gold Inc 106 Front St E Ste 400 *TSE: SEA* ■ *Web:* www.seabridgegold.net	Toronto	ON	M5A1E1	416-367-9292	367-2711	502
Seabrook Bros & Sons Inc 85 Finley Rd *Web:* www.seabrookfarms.com	Bridgeton	NJ	08302	856-455-8080	455-9282	296-21
Seabrook International LLC 15 Woodworkers Way *Web:* www.seabrookinternational.com	Seabrook	NH	03874	603-474-1919		476
Seabury Venture Partners PO Box 2249 *Web:* seaburypartners.com	Redwood City	CA	94064	650-373-1030		528
SeaChange International Inc 50 Nagog Pk *NASDAQ: SEAC* ■ *Web:* www.schange.com	Acton	MA	01720	978-897-0100	897-0132	647
Seacoast Banking Corp of Florida PO Box 9012 PO Box 9012 *NASDAQ: SBCF* ■ *TF Alt:* 800-706-9991 ■ *Web:* www.seacoastbanking.com	Stuart	FL	34995	772-287-4000	[illegible]	[illegible]
Seacoast Capital Partners 55 Ferncroft Rd *Web:* www.seacoastcapital.com	Danvers	MA	01923	978-750-1300		402
Seacoast Laboratory Data Systems Inc 195 New Hampshire Ave Ste 140 *Web:* www.sldsi.com	Portsmouth	NH	03801	603-431-4114		177
Seacoast Media Group 111 New Hampshire Ave *Web:* www.seacoastonline.com	Portsmouth	NH	03801	603-436-1800		532-3
Seacoast Science Center Inc 570 Ocean Blvd *TF:* 800-964-5545 ■ *Web:* www.seacoastsciencecenter.org	Rye	NH	03870	603-436-8043		520
Seacoast Suites Hotel 5101 Collins Ave *Web:* www.seacoastsuites.com	Miami Beach	FL	33140	305-865-5152		379
Seacomm Erectors Inc 32527 SR 2 PO Box 1740 *TF:* 800-292-7181 ■ *Web:* www.seacomm.com	Sultan	WA	98294	360-793-6564	793-4402	188-1
Seacon Engineering Associates Inc 716B Lakeside Dr W *Web:* www.seaconeng.com	Mobile	AL	36693	251-662-0300		261
SEACOR Holdings Inc 2200 Eller Dr PO Box 13038 *NYSE: CKH* ■ *TF:* 800-516-6203 ■ *Web:* www.seacorholdings.com	Fort Lauderdale	FL	33316	954-523-2200	524-9185	667
Seacrest Oceanfront Resort on the South Beach 803 S Ocean Blvd *TF:* 888-889-8113 ■ *Web:* www.myrtlebeach-resorts.com	Myrtle Beach	SC	29577	888-889-8113		669
Seacrest Village Inc 1001 Ctr St *Web:* seacrestvillagenj.com	Little Egg Harbor Twp	NJ	08087	609-296-9292		793
Sea-Dog Corp 3402 Smith Ave *Web:* www.sea-dog.com	Everett	WA	98201	425-259-0194		770
SeaDream Yacht Club 601 Brickell Key Dr Ste 1050 *TF:* 800-707-4911 ■ *Web:* www.seadream.com	Miami	FL	33131	305-631-6110	631-6110	220
Seadrill Americas Inc 11210 Equity Dr Ste 150 *Web:* www.seadrill.com	Houston	TX	77041	713-329-1150		540
Seafare of Williamsburg 1632 Richmond Rd *TF:* 800-219-0976 ■ *Web:* www.seafareofwilliamsburg.com/contact.php	Williamsburg	VA	23185	757-229-0099		671
Seafarer Motel 2079 Main St *TF:* 800-786-2772 ■ *Web:* www.chathamseafarer.com	Chatham	MA	02633	508-432-1739		379
Seafarers International Union 5201 Auth Way *TF:* 800-252-4674 ■ *Web:* www.seafarers.org	Camp Springs	MD	20746	301-899-0675	899-7355	414
Seafood Cove 8547 Westminster Blvd	Garden Grove	CA	92844	714-895-7964		671
Seafood Producers Co-op 2875 Roeder Ave *Web:* www.spcsales.com	Bellingham	WA	98225	360-733-0120	733-0513	296-14
SeaGate Convention Centre 401 Jefferson Ave *Web:* www.toledo-seagate.com	Toledo	OH	43604	419-255-3300	255-7731	205
Seagate Technology LLC 10200 S De Anza Blvd *Web:* www.seagate.com	Cupertino	CA	95014	831-438-6550		173-8
Seagrave Fire Apparatus LLC 105 E 12th St *Web:* www.seagrave.com	Clintonville	WI	54929	715-823-2141	823-5768	516
Seagull Book & Tape Inc 1720 S Redwood Rd *TF:* 800-999-6257 ■ *Web:* www.seagullbook.com	Salt Lake City	UT	84104	800-999-6257		95
Seagull Printing Services Inc 6969 High Tech Dr *TF:* 800-584-6989 ■ *Web:* seagullprinting.com	Midvale	UT	84047	801-565-1393		627
Seagull Scientific Inc 1616 148th Ave SE *Web:* seagullscientific.com	Bellevue	WA	98007	425-641-1408		225
Seahorse Fitness Inc 69 Columbia St *Web:* www.seahorseswimclub.com	New York	NY	10002	212-254-3651		354
Seal Beach Chamber & Business Assn 201 Eigth St Ste 110 *Web:* www.sealbeachchamber.org	Seal Beach	CA	90740	562-799-0179	795-5637	139
Seal Methods Inc 11915 Shoemaker Ave *TF:* 800-423-4777 ■ *Web:* www.sealmethodsinc.com	Santa Fe Springs	CA	90670	562-944-0291	946-9439	326
Seal Systems Inc 17505 N 79th Ave Ste 201 *Web:* www.sealsystems.com	Glendale	AZ	85308	865-380-0005		809
Sea-Land Chemical Co 821 Wpoint Pkwy *Web:* sealandchem.com	Westlake	OH	44145	440-871-7887		261
Sealant Equipment & Engineering Inc 45677 Helm St PO Box 701460 *Web:* www.sealantequipment.com	Plymouth	MI	48170	734-459-8600		780
Sealaska Corp 1 Sealaska Plaza Ste 400 *Web:* www.sealaska.com	Juneau	AK	99801	907-586-1512	586-2304	448
Sealco Commercial Vehicle Products Inc 215 E Watkins St **Fax Area Code:* 800 ■ *Web:* www.sealcocvp.com	Phoenix	AZ	85004	602-253-1007	222-2334*	60
Sealco Data Center Services Ltd 1761 International Pkwy Ste 127 *TF:* 800-283-5567 ■ *Web:* www.sealco.net	Richardson	TX	75081	972-234-5567		104
Sea-Lect Plastic Corp 3420 Smith Ave *Web:* sealectplastics.com	Everett	WA	98201	425-339-0288		757
Sealed Air Corp 200 Riverfront Blvd *NYSE: SEE* ■ *Web:* www.sealedair.com	Elmwood Park	NJ	07407	201-791-7600		88
Sealed Air Corp Packaging Products Div 301 Mayhill St *TF:* 800-648-9093 ■ *Web:* sealedair.com	Saddle Brook	NJ	07663	201-712-7000	712-7070	548
Sealed Unit Parts Company Inc 2230 Landmark Pl *TF:* 800-333-9125 ■ *Web:* www.supco.com	Allenwood	NJ	08720	732-223-6644	223-1617	14
Sealift Inc 68 W Main St *Web:* www.sealiftinc.com	Oyster Bay	NY	11771	516-922-1101		313
Sealing Devices Inc 4400 Walden Ave *TF Cust Svc:* 800-727-3257 ■ *Web:* www.sealingdevices.com	Lancaster	NY	14086	716-684-7600	684-0760	326
Sealing Equipment Products Co Inc 123 Airpark Industrial Rd *TF:* 800-633-4770 ■ *Web:* www.sepco.com	Alabaster	AL	35007	800-633-4770		326
Seals-Eastern Inc 134 Pearl St *Web:* www.sealseastern.com	Red Bank	NJ	07701	732-747-9200		326
Seaman Corp 1000 Venture Blvd *TF:* 800-927-8578 ■ *Web:* www.seamancorp.com	Wooster	OH	44691	330-262-1111	263-6950	745-2
Seaman Paper Co of Massachusetts 51 Main St *TF:* 800-784-7783 ■ *Web:* www.seamanpaper.com	Otter River	MA	01436	978-632-1513	632-6319	557
Seaman Unified School District 345 901 NW Lyman Rd *Web:* www.seamanschools.org	Topeka	KS	66608	785-575-8600		685
Seamans Capital Management LLC 500 Boylston St Ste 420 *Web:* www.seamanscapital.com	Boston	MA	02116	781-890-5225		401
Seamar Holdings LLC 13715 N Promenade Blvd *Web:* www.seamardivers.com/about.php	Stafford	TX	77477	281-208-2522		536
SEAMARK Asset Management Ltd 1801 Hollis St Ste 810 *TF:* 888-303-5055 ■ *Web:* www.seamark.ca	Halifax	NS	B3J3N4	902-423-9367		528
SeaMates International Inc 316 Main St PO Box 436 *TF:* 800-541-4538 ■ *Web:* www.seamates.com	East Rutherford	NJ	07073	201-896-8899		194
Seamen's Bank 221 Commercial St PO Box 659 *TF:* 855-227-5347 ■ *Web:* www.seamensbank.com	Provincetown	MA	02657	508-487-0035	487-8421	70
Seamless Technologies Inc 35 Airport Rd *TF:* 800-340-0505 ■ *Web:* www.seamlessti.com	Morristown	NJ	07960	973-326-8900		111
SeamlessWeb Professional Solutions LLC 232 Madison Ave Ste 1409 *TF:* 800-905-9322	New York	NY	10016	800-905-9322		299
Sean Wong - State Farm Insurance Agent 7035 Hwy 6 N *Web:* statefarm.com	Houston	TX	77095	281-550-0555		390
Seaport Group LLC Research Division, The 360 Madison Ave 22nd Fl *TF:* 800-289-9999 ■ *Web:* seaportglobal.com	New York	NY	10017	212-616-7700		401
Seaport Hotel & World Trade Ctr 1 Seaport Ln *TF:* 877-732-7678 ■ *Web:* www.seaportboston.com	Boston	MA	02210	617-385-4000	385-4001	379
Seaport Marina Hotel 6400 E Pacific Coast Hwy *Web:* www.seaportmarinahotel.com	Long Beach	CA	90803	562-434-8451	598-6028	379
Seaport Village 849 W Harbor Dr Ste D *Web:* www.seaportvillage.com	San Diego	CA	92101	619-235-4014	696-0025	50-6

Name	Address	City	State	ZIP	Phone	Fax	Class	Other
Seaport World Trade Ctr Boston	200 Seaport Blvd	Boston	MA	02210	617-385-4212	385-5090*	822	*Fax: Sales ■ TF: 800-440-3318 ■ Web: www.seaportboston.com
Seaquest State Park	3030 Spirit Lake Hwy	Castle Rock	WA	98611	360-274-8633		565	Web: www.parks.wa.gov
SEARAC (Southeast Asia Resource Action Ctr)	1628 16th St NW 3rd Fl	Washington	DC	20009	202-667-4690	667-6449	48-5	TF: 888-907-1485 ■ Web: www.searac.org
Search Company International	1535 Grant St Ste 140	Denver	CO	80203	303-863-1800	863-7767	635	TF: 800-727-2120 ■ Web: www.searchcompanyintl.com
Search Guru Inc, The	21887 Lorain Rd Ste 71	Cleveland	OH	44126	440-306-2418		260	Web: www.thesearchguru.com
Search Network Ltd	1503 42nd St Ste 210	West Des Moines	IA	50266	515-223-1153		635	TF: 800-383-5050 ■ Web: www.searchnetworkltd.com
Search Wizards Inc	15 Paradise Plaza Ste 261	Sarasota	FL	34239	404-846-9500		260	Web: www.searchwizards.net
SearchDex	17330 Preston Rd Ste 240B	Dallas	TX	75252	214-999-0889		463	Web: www.searchdex.com
Searcher: The Magazine for Database Professionals	143 Old Marlton Pk	Medford	NJ	08055	609-654-6266	654-4309	457-7	TF: 800-300-9868 ■ Web: www.infotoday.com/searcher
Searchlight Group Inc	1 W St Apt 3602	New York	NY	10004	212-425-4800		260	Web: www.searchlightjobs.com
Searchlogix Group, The	2950 Cherokee St NW Ste 1000	Kennesaw	GA	30144	770-517-2660		193	Web: searchlogixgroup.com
Searchpros Staffing	6363 Auburn Blvd	Citrus Heights	CA	95621	916-721-6000		260	Web: spstaffing.com
SearchTec Inc	314 N 12th St Ste 100	Philadelphia	PA	19107	215-963-0888	851-8775	635	Web: www.searchtec.com
Searchwide Inc	320 Myrtle St W	Stillwater	MN	55082	651-275-1370		193	TF: 888-386-6390 ■ Web: searchwide.com
Searchwright Inc	101 Second St Ste 2200	San Francisco	CA	94105	415-538-1500		260	Web: searchwright.com
Searcy County	PO Box 1385	Marshall	AR	72650	870-448-2557		338	TF: 800-257-8690 ■ Web: www.searcycountyarkansas.org
Searcy Denney Scarola Barnhart	Po Box 3626	West Palm Beach	FL	33402	561-686-6300		428	TF: 800-780-8607 ■ Web: www.searcylaw.com
Searing Industries Inc	8901 Arrow Route	Rancho Cucamonga	CA	91730	909-948-3030		492	TF: 800-874-4412 ■ Web: www.searingindustries.com
Searles Valley Minerals	9401 Indian Creek Pkwy Ste 1000	Overland Park	KS	66210	913-344-9500		503-1	TF: 800-637-2775 ■ Web: www.svminerals.com
Sears Canada Inc	290 Yonge St Ste 700	Toronto	ON	M5B2C3	416-362-1711		229	TSE: SCC ■ TF: 877-987-3277 ■ Web: www.sears.ca
Sears Holdings Corp	3333 Beverly Rd	Hoffman Estates	IL	60179	847-286-2500		360-3	NASDAQ: SHLD ■ TF: 800-549-4505 ■ Web: www.searsholdings.com
Sears Imported Autos Inc	13500 Wayzata Blvd	Minnetonka	MN	55305	952-546-5301	546-2899	57	Web: www.searsimports.com
Sears Manufacturing Co	1718 S Concord St PO Box 3667	Davenport	IA	52808	563-383-2800		689	TF Cust Svc: 800-553-3013 ■ Web: www.searsseating.com
Sears Roebuck & Co	3333 Beverly Rd	Hoffman Estates	IL	60179	847-286-2500		229	TF: 800-349-4358 ■ Web: www.sears.com
Sears Tower	233 S Wacker Dr	Chicago	IL	60606	312-875-9447	906-8193	50-3	TF: 877-759-3325 ■ Web: www.theskydeck.com
SEAS Education	971 Coley Dr	Mountain Home	AR	72653	870-425-6933		525	Web: seaseducation.com
Seashore Food Distributors Inc	1 Satt Blvd PO Box 235	Rio Grande	NJ	08242	609-886-3100		345	Web: www.seashorefood.com
Seaside Civic & Convention Ctr	415 First Ave	Seaside	OR	97138	503-738-8585	738-0198	205	TF: 800-394-3303 ■ Web: www.seasideconvention.com
Seaside Golf Vacations	218 Main St	North Myrtle Beach	SC	29582	877-732-6999		771	TF: 877-732-6999 ■ Web: www.seasidegolf.com
Seaside Inn	541 E Gulf Dr	Sanibel Island	FL	33957	239-472-1400		379	TF: 866-565-5092 ■ Web: www.theinnsofsanibel.com
Seasongood & Mayer LLC	414 Walnut St Ste 300	Cincinnati	OH	45202	513-621-0580		690	Web: www.rbccm.com
Seasons 52	7700 Sand Lake Rd	Orlando	FL	32819	407-354-5212		671	Web: www.seasons52.com
Seasons at Rose Creek	1500 Rose Creek Pkwy E	Fargo	ND	58104	701-235-5000		671	
Seasons Hospice & Palliative Care	750 The City Dr S Ste 120	Orange	CA	92868	714-980-0900		371	TF: 877-508-0644 ■ Web: www.seasons.org
Seasons Restaurant at Highland Lake Inn	86 Lilly Pad Ln	Flat Rock	NC	28731	828-696-9094		707	TF: 800-635-5101 ■ Web: hlinn.com
Seasons Rotisserie & Grill	2031 Mountain Rd NW	Albuquerque	NM	87104	505-766-5100	766-5252	671	Web: www.seasonsabq.com
Seasons' Enterprises Ltd	1790 W Cortland Ct Ste B PO Box 965	Addison	IL	60101	630-628-0211		296-11	
Seasons-4 Inc	4500 Industrial Access Rd	Douglasville	GA	30134	770-489-0716	489-2938	14	TF: 800-888-9900 ■ Web: www.seasons4.net
SeaSpace Corp	13000 Gregg St	Poway	CA	92064	858-746-1100		647	Web: www.seaspace.com
Seastrom Mfg Company Inc	456 Seastrom St	Twin Falls	ID	83301	208-737-4300		350	TF: 800-634-2356 ■ Web: www.seastrom-mfg.com
Seat of the Soul Foundation	PO Box 3310	Ashland	OR	97520	541-482-1515	482-9417	48-20	TF: 877-733-4279 ■ Web: www.seatofthesoul.com
SEA-TAC (Seattle-Tacoma International Airport)	17801 International Blvd PO Box 68727	Seattle	WA	98158	206-787-5388		27	TF: 800-544-1965 ■ Web: portseattle.org/sea-tac
Seaton Companies, The	860 W Evergreen Ave	Chicago	IL	60642	312-915-0700		193	Web: www.seatoncorp.com
Seats Inc	1515 Industrial St	Reedsburg	WI	53959	608-524-8261		689	TF: 800-443-0615 ■ Web: www.seatsinc.com
Seattle Aquarium	1483 Alaskan Way Pier 59	Seattle	WA	98101	206-386-4300	386-4328	40	TF: 800-853-1964 ■ Web: www.seattleaquarium.org
Seattle Art Museum	1300 First Ave	Seattle	WA	98101	206-654-3100		520	TF: 800-937-9582 ■ Web: www.seattleartmuseum.org
Seattle Asian Art Museum	1400 E Prospect St Volunteer Pk	Seattle	WA	98112	206-654-3210		520	Web: www.seattleartmuseum.org
Seattle Athletic Club	2020 Western Ave	Seattle	WA	98121	206-443-1111		354	Web: www.sacdt.com
Seattle Cancer Care Alliance	825 Eastlake Ave E PO Box 19023	Seattle	WA	98109	206-288-1024		769	TF: 800-804-8824 ■ Web: www.seattlecca.org
Seattle Children's Hospital	4800 Sand Pt Way NE	Seattle	WA	98105	206-987-2000	987-5060*	374-1	*Fax: Admitting ■ TF: 866-987-2000 ■ Web: www.seattlechildrens.org
Seattle City Hall	600 Fourth Ave 2nd Fl	Seattle	WA	98104	206-684-8888	684-8587	337	Web: www.seattle.gov
Seattle Ctr	305 Harrison St	Seattle	WA	98109	206-684-7200		572	Web: www.seattlecenter.com
Seattle Daily Journal of Commerce	PO Box 11050	Seattle	WA	98111	206-622-8272	622-8416	532-2	Web: www.djc.com
Seattle Foundation	1200 Fifth Ave Ste 1300	Seattle	WA	98101	206-622-2294	622-7673	303	Web: www.seattlefoundation.org
Seattle Genetics Inc	21823 30th Dr SE	Bothell	WA	98021	425-527-4000	527-4001	85	NASDAQ: SGEN ■ Web: www.seattlegenetics.com
Seattle Golf Club Pro Shop LLC	210 NW 145th St	Shoreline	WA	98177	206-363-8811		711	Web: www.seattlegolfclub.com
Seattle Hospitality Group	16 W Harrison St	Seattle	WA	98119	206-674-3021	623-2540	184	Web: www.shworldwide.com
Seattle International Film Festival	305 Harrison St	Seattle	WA	98109	206-464-5830	264-7919	282	Web: www.siff.net
Seattle Lab Inc	11730 118th Ave NE Ste 400	Kirkland	WA	98034	425-825-7000		809	Web: www.seattlelab.com
Seattle Lighting Fixture Co	222 Second Ave Ext S	Seattle	WA	98104	206-622-4736		362	TF Cust Svc: 800-689-1000 ■ Web: www.seattlelighting.com
Seattle Mailing Bureau Inc	700 SW 34th St	Renton	WA	98057	206-431-5700		5	TF: 800-463-3339 ■ Web: seattlemailing.com
Seattle Manufacturing Corp	6930 Salashan Pkwy	Ferndale	WA	98248	360-366-5534	366-5723	576	TF: 800-426-6251 ■ Web: smcgear.com
Seattle Mariners	Safeco Field 1250 First Ave S	Seattle	WA	98134	206-346-4000	346-4050	713	TF: 800-255-7932 ■ Web: seattle.mariners.mlb.com
Seattle Marriott Waterfront Hotel	2100 Alaskan Way	Seattle	WA	98121	206-443-5000		378	Web: www.gowestmarriott.com
Seattle Medical & Rehabilitation Ctr	555 16th Ave	Seattle	WA	98122	206-324-8200		450	TF: 800-752-6096 ■ Web: seattlemedicalpostacute.com
Seattle Musical Theatre	7400 Sand Pt Way NE Ste 101-N	Seattle	WA	98103	206-363-2809		573-2	Web: www.seattlemusicaltheatre.org
Seattle Opera	1020 John St	Seattle	WA	98109	206-389-7600	389-7651	573-2	TF Sales: 800-426-1619 ■ Web: www.seattleopera.org
Seattle Pacific University	3307 Third Ave W	Seattle	WA	98119	206-281-2000	281-2544*	166	*Fax: Admissions ■ TF: 800-366-3344 ■ Web: www.spu.edu
Seattle Post-Intelligencer	101 Elliott Ave W 2nd Fl	Seattle	WA	98119	206-448-8000	448-8166	532-2	TF: 800-542-0820 ■ Web: www.seattlepi.com
Seattle Premium Outlets	10600 Quil Ceda Blvd	Tulalip	WA	98271	360-654-3000		460	Web: www.premiumoutlets.com
Seattle Public Library	1000 Fourth Ave	Seattle	WA	98104	206-386-4636	386-4119	434-3	TF: 800-829-3676 ■ Web: www.spl.org
Seattle Public Schools	PO Box 34165	Seattle	WA	98124	206-252-0000		685	Web: www.seattleschools.org
Seattle Repertory Theatre (SRT)	155 Mercer St PO Box 900923	Seattle	WA	98109	206-443-2210	443-2379	573-4	TF: 877-900-9285 ■ Web: www.seattlerep.org
Seattle Seahawks	12 Seahawks Way	Renton	WA	98056	888-635-4295		715-3	TF: 888-635-4295 ■ Web: www.seahawks.com
Seattle Service Bureau Inc	18820 Aurora Ave Ste 205	Seattle	WA	98133	206-533-0877	542-8994	160	Web: www.nsbi.net
Seattle Snohomish Mill Co Inc	9525 Airport Way	Snohomish	WA	98296	360-568-2171		683	
Seattle Sport Sciences Inc	24066 NE 53rd Pl	Redmond	WA	98053	425-939-0015		526	Web: www.seattlesportsciences.com
Seattle SuperSonics	1201 Third Ave Ste 1000	Seattle	WA	98101	206-281-5800	281-5839	714-1	TF: 800-743-7021 ■ Web: www.nba.com
Seattle Symphony	200 University St	Seattle	WA	98101	206-215-4700	215-4701	573-3	TF: 866-833-4747 ■ Web: www.seattlesymphony.org

Name / Address	City	State	Zip	Phone	Fax	Class
Seattle Tennis Club 922 Mcgilvra Blvd E *TF:* 800-205-6940 ■ *Web:* seattletennisclub.org	Seattle	WA	98112	206-324-3200		354
Seattle Theatre Group 911 Pine St *TF:* 877-784-4849 ■ *Web:* www.stgpresents.org	Seattle	WA	98101	206-467-5510		720
Seattle Times 1120 John St *Web:* seattletimes.com	Seattle	WA	98109	206-464-2111	464-2261	532-2
Seattle University 901 12th Ave. **Fax:* Admissions ■ *TF:* 800-426-7123 ■ *Web:* www.seattleu.edu	Seattle	WA	98122	206-296-6000	296-5656*	166
Seattle University Lemieux Library 901 12th Ave. *TF:* 800-426-7123 ■ *Web:* www.seattleu.edu/lemlib	Seattle	WA	98122	206-296-6210	296-2572	434-6
Seattle University School of Law 901 12th Ave PO Box 222000 **Fax:* Admissions ■ *Web:* www.law.seattleu.edu	Seattle	WA	98122	206-398-4200	398-4058*	167-1
Seattle Weekly 307 Third Ave S Ste 2 *Web:* www.seattleweekly.com	Seattle	WA	98104	206-623-0500	467-4338	532-5
Seattle's Convention & Visitors Bureau 701 Pike St Ste 800 *TF:* 866-732-2695 ■ *Web:* www.visitseattle.org	Seattle	WA	98101	206-461-5800	461-5855	206
Seattle's Best Coffee LLC PO Box 3717 *TF:* 800-611-7793 ■ *Web:* seattlesbest.com	Seattle	WA	98124	800-611-7793		159
Seattle-Tacoma International Airport (SEA-TAC) 17801 International Blvd PO Box 68727 *TF:* 800-544-1965 ■ *Web:* portseattle.org/sea-tac	Seattle	WA	98158	206-787-5388		27
Seaway Bank & Trust Co 645 E 87th St *Web:* www.seawaybank.us	Chicago	IL	60619	773-487-4800		70
Seaway Manufacturing Corp 2250 E 33rd St *TF:* 800-458-2244 ■ *Web:* www.seawaymfg.com	Erie	PA	16510	814-898-2255		234
Seaway Printing Company Inc 1609 Western Ave Ste *TF:* 800-622-3255 ■ *Web:* www.seawayprinting.com	Green Bay	WI	54303	920-468-1500		627
SeaWorld Orlando 7007 Sea World Dr *Web:* seaworldparks.com	Orlando	FL	32821	407-351-3600		32
SeaWorld San Diego 500 SeaWorld Dr *TF:* 800-257-4268 ■ *Web:* www.seaworld.com	San Diego	CA	92109	619-226-3901		32
Seay Oil Company Inc 700 W 15th St *Web:* www.seayoil.com	Hopkinsville	KY	42240	270-885-5488		579
Sebacia Inc 2905 Premiere Pkwy Ste 150 *TF:* 888-935-4411 ■ *Web:* www.sebacia.com	Duluth	GA	30097	888-935-4411		475
Sebago Inc 9341 Courtland Dr *TF:* 866-699-7367 ■ *Web:* www.sebago.com	Rockford	MI	49351	616-866-5500	866-5625	301
Sebago Lake State Park 11 Pk Access Rd *Web:* www.maine.gov	Casco	ME	04055	207-693-6613		565
Sebago Technics Inc 75 John Roberts Rd Ste 1A *Web:* sebago-technics.com	South Portland	ME	04106	207-200-2100		261
Sebaly Shillito & Dyer 1900 Kettering Tower 40 N Main St *Web:* ssdlaw.com	Dayton	OH	45423	937-222-2500		428
Sebasco Harbor Resort 20 Kenyon Rd *TF:* 800-225-3819 ■ *Web:* www.sebasco.com	Phippsburg	ME	04562	207-389-1161	389-2004	669
Sebastian County 35 S Sixth St Rm 105 *TF:* 800-637-9314 ■ *Web:* sebastiancountyar.gov	Fort Smith	AR	72901	479-782-5065	784-1567	338
Sebastian Inlet State Park 9700 S A1A *Web:* www.floridastateparks.org	Melbourne Beach	FL	32951	321-984-4852		565
Sebastian River Area Chamber of Commerce 700 Main St *Web:* www.sebastianchamber.com	Sebastian	FL	32958	772-589-5969	589-5993	139
Sebastian River Medical Ctr 13695 US Hwy 1 *Web:* sebastianrivermedical.org	Sebastian	FL	32958	772-589-3186		374-3
Sebastiani Vineyards Inc 389 Fourth St E *TF:* 855-232-2338 ■ *Web:* www.sebastiani.com	Sonoma	CA	95476	707-933-3230		80-3
Sebastopol Area Chamber of Commerce 265 S Main St *Web:* www.sebastopol.org	Sebastopol	CA	95472	707-823-3032	823-8439	139
Sebastopol State Historic Site PO Box 900 *Web:* www.seguintexas.gov	Seguin	TX	78156	830-379-4833		565
Sebesta Blomberg & Assoc Inc 1450 Energy Park Dr Ste 300 *TF:* 877-706-6858 ■ *Web:* www.sebesta.com	St Paul	MN	55108	651-634-0775		261
Sebewaing Tool & Engineering Co 415 Union St *TF:* 800-453-2207 ■ *Web:* sebewaingtool.com	Sebewaing	MI	48759	989-883-2000		350
Sebis Direct Inc 6516 W 74th St *TF:* 800-275-8777 ■ *Web:* www.sebis.com	Bedford	IL	60638	312-243-9300		5
Sebring International Raceway 113 Midway Dr *TF:* 800-626-7223 ■ *Web:* www.sebringraceway.com	Sebring	FL	33870	863-655-1442	655-1777	515
Sebring Software Inc 1400 Cattlemen Rd Ste A *Web:* www.sebringsoft.com	Sarasota	FL	34232	941-377-0715		195
SEC (Shelby Electric Co-op) 1355 IL-128 state PO Box 560 *TF:* 800-677-2612 ■ *Web:* www.shelbyelectric.coop	Shelbyville	IL	62565	217-774-3986		245
SEC (Securities & Exchange Commission) 100 F St NE *TF:* 800-732-0330 ■ *Web:* www.sec.gov	Washington	DC	20549	202-942-8088	772-9295	340-20
SEC Energy Products & Services LP 9523 Fairbanks N *Web:* www.sec-ep.com	Houston	TX	77064	281-890-9977		539
Sechrist Industries Inc 4225 E La Palma Ave *TF:* 800-732-4747 ■ *Web:* www.sechristusa.com	Anaheim	CA	92807	714-579-8400	579-0814	476
Sechrist-Hall Co 102 Omaha	Corpus Christi	TX	78408	361-884-5264		189-12
SECNAP Network Security Corp 3651 FAU Blvd Ste 400 *Web:* www.secnap.com	Boca Raton	FL	33431	561-999-5000		809
SECO (Southeast Electric Co-op Inc) 110 S Main St *TF:* 888-485-8762 ■ *Web:* www.seecoop.com	Ekalaka	MT	59324	406-775-8762		245

Name / Address	City	State	Zip	Phone	Fax	Class
SECO Manufacturing Company Inc 4155 Oasis Rd *Web:* www.surveying.com	Redding	CA	96003	530-225-8155		407
Seco Tools 2805 Bellingham Dr **Fax:* Cust Svc ■ *TF:* 800-832-8326 ■ *Web:* www.secotools.com	Troy	MI	48083	248-528-5200	528-5600*	493
SECO/Warwick Corp 180 Mercer St *Web:* www.secowarwick.com	Meadville	PA	16335	814-332-8400	724-1407	318
Seco-Larm USA Inc 16842 Millikan Ave *TF:* 800-662-0800 ■ *Web:* www.seco-larm.com	Irvine	CA	92606	949-261-2999	261-7326	692
Secom International 9610 Bellanca Ave *Web:* www.secomintl.com	Los Angeles	CA	90045	310-641-1290		693
Secon Rubber & Plastics Inc 240 Kaskaskia Dr *Web:* www.seconrubber.com	Red Bud	IL	62278	618-282-7700		326
Second Amendment Foundation 12500 NE Tenth Pl *TF:* 800-426-4302 ■ *Web:* www.saf.org	Bellevue	WA	98005	425-454-7012	451-3959	48-8
Second City Chicago 1608 N Wells St *TF:* 800-775-2000 ■ *Web:* www.secondcity.com	Chicago	IL	60614	312-664-4032	664-9837	573-4
Second Cup Ltd 6303 Airport Rd *TF:* 877-212-1818 ■ *Web:* www.secondcup.com	Mississauga	ON	L4V1R8	877-212-1818		159
Second Empire 330 Hillsborough St *Web:* www.second-empire.com	Raleigh	NC	27603	919-829-3663		671
Second Harvest Food Bank of Central Florida 411 Mercy Dr	Orlando	FL	32805	407-295-1066		48-5
Second Street Grill 200 E Fremont St *TF:* 800-634-6460 ■ *Web:* fremontcasino.com	Las Vegas	NV	89101	702-385-3232		671
Second Street Restaurant & Tavern 140 Second St *TF:* 800-889-5002 ■ *Web:* www.secondst.com	Williamsburg	VA	23185	757-220-2286		671
SECOS Inc 18301 Von Karman Ave Ste 460 *Web:* www.secos.com	Irvine	CA	92612	949-794-0021		387
Secova Inc 5000 Birch St W Tower Ste 1400 *TF:* 800-257-0011 ■ *Web:* www.secova.com	Newport Beach	CA	92660	714-384-0530		194
SECPA (Southeast Colorado Power Assn) 901 W 3rd *TF:* 800-332-8634 ■ *Web:* www.secpa.com	La Junta	CO	81050	719-384-2551	384-7320	245
Secrest Arboretum 1680 Madison Ave *Web:* secrest.osu.edu	Wooster	OH	44691	330-464-2148		97
Secrest Wardle Lynch Hampton Po Box 3040 *Web:* www.secrestwardle.com	Farmington Hills	MI	48333	248-851-9500		428
Secret Garden Spa at the Prince of Wales Hotel 6 Picton St *TF:* 888-669-5566 ■ *Web:* www.vintage-hotels.com	Niagara on-the-Lake	ON	L0S1J0	905-468-3246	468-5521	707
Secret Ingredient Marketing 217 Knight Dr *Web:* www.secretingredientmarketing.com	San Rafael	CA	94901	415-963-4000		466
Secret Location Inc 134 Peter St Unit 102 *Web:* secretlocation.com	Toronto	ON	M5V2H2	416-646-2400		5
Secret Weapon Marketing 5870 W Jefferson Blvd *Web:* www.secretweapon.net	Los Angeles	CA	90016	310-656-5999		7
Secretariat PO Box 3509 *Web:* [illegible]	Wilmington	DE	19807	302-654-4479	654-4117	184
Secretary of Agriculture 1400 Independence Ave SW Rm 200A *TF:* 800-832-1355 ■ *Web:* www.usda.gov	Washington	DC	20250	202-720-3631	720-2166	340-1
Secretary of Commerce 1401 Constitution Ave NW *Web:* www.commerce.gov	Washington	DC	20230	202-482-2000		340-2
Secretary of Education 400 Maryland Ave SW *TF:* 800-872-5327 ■ *Web:* www.ed.gov/news/staff/bios/spellings.html	Washington	DC	20202	202-401-3000		340-8
Secretary of Energy 1000 Independence Ave SW *Web:* energy.gov/about-us	Washington	DC	20585	202-586-6210	586-4403	340-9
Secretary of Health & Human Services 200 Independence Ave SW *Web:* www.hhs.gov/about	Washington	DC	20201	202-690-7000	690-7755	340-10
Secretary of Homeland Security Naval Security Stn *Web:* www.dhs.gov/dhspublic	Washington	DC	20528	202-282-8000		340-11
Secretary of Labor 200 Constitution Ave NW Rm S2018 *TF:* 866-487-2365 ■ *Web:* www.dol.gov	Washington	DC	20210	202-693-6000		340-15
Secretary of State 2201 C St NW *TF:* 800-877-8339 ■ *Web:* www.state.gov	Washington	DC	20520	202-647-4000		340-16
Bureau of Intelligence & Research 2201 C St NW *Web:* www.state.gov/s/inr	Washington	DC	20520	202-895-3500		340-16
Office of the Chief of Protocol 2201 C St NW *Web:* www.state.gov/s/cpr	Washington	DC	20520	202-647-1735		340-16
Office of the Coordinator for Counterterrorism 2201 C St NW Rm 2206 *Web:* www.state.gov/s/ct	Washington	DC	20520	202-895-3500		340-16
Secretary of the Interior 1849 C St NW *TF:* 800-200-4853 ■ *Web:* www.doi.gov	Washington	DC	20240	202-208-3100		340-13
Secretary of the Treasury 1500 Pennsylvania Ave NW *TF:* 800-829-1040 ■ *Web:* www.treasury.gov	Washington	DC	20220	202-622-2000	622-6415	340-18
Secretary of Transportation 1200 New Jersey Ave SE *TF:* 855-368-4200 ■ *Web:* www.transportation.gov	Washington	DC	20590	855-368-4200		340-17
Secretary of Veterans Affairs 810 Vermont Ave NW *TF:* 844-698-2311 ■ *Web:* www1.va.gov/opa/bios	Washington	DC	20420	844-698-2311		340-19
Board of Veterans' Appeals 810 Vermont Ave NW **Fax Area Code:* 202 ■ *TF:* 800-923-8387 ■ *Web:* www.bva.va.gov	Washington	DC	20420	800-923-8387	495-6803*	340-19
Center for Minority Veterans 810 Vermont Ave *TF:* 800-273-8255 ■ *Web:* www.va.gov	Washington	DC	20420	202-461-6191		340-19

Name / Address	City	State	Zip	Phone	Fax	Class
Center for Women Veterans 810 Vermont Ave NW *Fax Area Code: 202 ■ TF: 800-273-8255 ■ Web: www1.va.gov/womenvet	Washington	DC	20420	800-827-1000	273-7092*	340-19
Sector Micro Computers Inc 399 Hoover Ave Ste 2 TF: 800-631-2894 ■ Web: sectormicro.com	Bloomfield	NJ	07003	973-429-1113		179
Sector3 Appraisals Inc 8802 69th Rd Web: www.sector3appraisals.com	Forest Hills	NY	11375	718-268-4376		41
SECU (State Employees' Credit Union) PO Box 29606 TF: 888-732-8562 ■ Web: www.ncsecu.org	Raleigh	NC	27626	919-857-2150	857-2000	219
SecuGen Corp 2065 Martin Ave Ste 108 Web: www.secugen.com	Santa Clara	CA	95050	408-727-7787	834-7762	84
Secular Organizations for Sobriety (SOS) 4773 Hollywood Blvd Web: www.cfiwest.org/sos	Hollywood	CA	90027	323-666-4295		48-21
Secura Insurance Cos PO Box 819 TF: 800-558-3405 ■ Web: www.secura.net	Appleton	WI	54912	920-739-3161		391-4
Securance LLC 6922 W Linebaugh Ave Ste 101 TF: 877-578-0215 ■ Web: www.securanceconsulting.com	Tampa	FL	33625	877-578-0215		180
Securboration Inc 1050 W Nasa Blvd Ste 156 TF: 800-433-5778 ■ Web: www.securboration.com	Melbourne	FL	32901	321-409-5252		809
Secure America's Future Economy (SAFE) 214 N Spring Valley Rd Web: www.s-a-f-e.org	Wilmington	DE	19807	302-478-0676		48-7
Secure Communication Systems Inc 1740 E Wilshire Ave Web: www.securecomm.com	Santa Ana	CA	92705	714-547-1174	547-1343	647
Secure Mentem Inc 1910 Towne Centre Blvd Ste 250 Web: www.securementem.com	Annapolis	MD	21401	443-603-0200		693
Secure Network Systems LLC 4282 York St Web: www.securenetworksystems.com	Dacono	CO	80514	303-637-7617		41
Secure Passage 8400 W 110th St Ste 400 Web: www.firemon.com	Shawnee Mission	KS	66210	913-948-9575		809
Secure Resolutions Inc 1921 S Alma School Rd Ste 201 Web: www.secureresolutions.com	Mesa	AZ	85210	480-491-7016		226
Secured Digital Applications Inc 230 Pk Ave 10th Fl	New York	NY	10169	212-551-1747	808-3020	246
SecureOne Data Solutions LLC 2801 N 33rd Ave Ste 1 Web: www.datacenteraz.com	Phoenix	AZ	85009	602-415-1111		225
SecureUSA Inc 4250 Keith Bridge Rd Ste 160 Web: www.secureusa.net	Cumming	GA	30041	770-205-0789		692
Securian Financial Group Inc 400 and 401 Robert St N Web: www.securian.com	Saint Paul	MN	55101	651-665-3500	665-4488	360-4
Securiguard Inc 6858 Old Dominion Dr Ste 307 Web: www.securiguardinc.com	Mclean	VA	22101	703-821-6777		693
Securisyn Medical LLC 9150 Commerce Ctr Cir Ste 135 Web: www.securisyn.com	Highlands Ranch	CO	80129	303-952-4551		475
Securitas Security Services USA Inc 2 Campus Dr TF: 800-555-0906 ■ Web: www.securitas.com	Parsippany	NJ	07054	973-267-5300		692
Securitech Inc 8230 E Broadway Blvd TF: 888-792-4473 ■ Web: www.hiresafe.com	Tucson	AZ	85710	520-721-0305		635
Securities & Exchange Commission (SEC) 100 F St NE TF: 800-732-0330 ■ Web: www.sec.gov	Washington	DC	20549	202-942-8088	772-9295	340-20
Office of Investor Education & Advocacy 100 F St NE Web: sec.gov/servlet/sec/investor	Washington	DC	20549	202-942-8088	772-9295	340-20
Securities & Exchange Commission Regional Offices						
Atlanta Regional Office 3475 Lenox Rd NE Ste 1000 Web: www.sec.gov	Atlanta	GA	30326	404-842-7600		340-20
Boston Regional Office 33 Arch St 23rd Fl Web: www.sec.gov/contact/addresses.htm	Boston	MA	02110	617-573-8900		340-20
Chicago Regional Office 175 W Jackson Blvd Ste 900 Web: www.sec.gov	Chicago	IL	60604	312-353-7390	353-7398	340-20
Denver Regional Office 1801 California St Ste 1500 Web: www.sec.gov	Denver	CO	80202	303-844-1000	844-1010	340-20
Fort Worth Regional Office Burnett Plaza Ste 1900 801 Cherry St, Unit 18 Web: sec.gov	Fort Worth	TX	76102	817-978-3821		340-20
Los Angeles Regional Office 5670 Wilshire Blvd 11th Fl TF: 800-732-0330 ■ Web: www.sec.gov	Los Angeles	CA	90036	323-965-3998	965-3815	340-20
Miami Regional Office 801 Brickell Ave Ste 1800 TF: 800-222-1253 ■ Web: www.sec.gov	Miami	FL	33131	305-982-6300		340-20
New York Regional Office 3 World Financial Ctr Ste 400 Web: www.sec.gov	New York	NY	10281	212-336-1100		340-20
Philadelphia Regional Office Mellon Independence Ctr 701 Market St Web: www.sec.gov	Philadelphia	PA	19106	215-597-3100		340-20
Salt Lake Regional Office 15 W S Temple St Ste 1800 Web: sec.gov	Salt Lake City	UT	84101	801-524-5796		340-20
San Francisco Regional Office 44 Montgomery St Ste 2600 Web: sec.gov	San Francisco	CA	94104	415-705-2500		340-20
Securities Center Inc, The 245 E St TF: 800-244-1718 ■ Web: www.securitiescenter.com	Chula Vista	CA	91910	619-426-3550		690
Securities Industry & Financial Markets Assn (SIFMAA) 120 Broadway 35th Fl TF: 888-367-7966 ■ Web: www.sifma.org	New York	NY	10271	212-313-1200	313-1301	49-2
Securities Investors Protection Corp 805 15th St NW Ste 800 Web: www.sipc.org	Washington	DC	20005	202-371-8300		391-5
Securities Law Daily 1801 S Bell St TF: 800-372-1033 ■ Web: www.bna.com/securities-law-daily-p5944	Arlington	VA	22202	800-372-1033		531-7
Securities Service Network Inc 9729 Cogdill Rd Ste 301 TF: 866-843-4635 ■ Web: www.ssnetwork.com	Knoxville	TN	37932	866-843-4635		690
Securitron Magnalock Corp 10027 S 51st St Ste 102 *Fax Area Code: 866 ■ TF Sales: 800-624-5625 ■ Web: www.securitron.com	Phoenix	AZ	85044	623-582-4626	582-4641*	350
Security & Access Systems 3811 Rutledge Rd NE Web: www.securityandaccess.com	Albuquerque	NM	87109	505-823-1561		693
Security & Data Technologies Inc 101 Pheasant Run	Newtown	PA	18940	215-550-6110		693
Security 101 LLC 2465 Mercer Ave Ste 101 TF: 888-909-4101 ■ Web: www.security101.com	West Palm Beach	FL	33401	888-909-4101		693
Security America Inc 3412 Chesterfield Ave Ste TF: 888-832-6732 ■ Web: www.securityamerica.com	Charleston	WV	25304	304-925-4747		693
Security Bank & Trust Co 735 11th St E Web: www.security-banks.com	Glencoe	MN	55336	320-864-3171	864-5133	685
Security Bank of Pulaski County 110 Lynn St PO Box S Web: www.sbpc.com	Waynesville	MO	65583	573-774-6417	774-6465	70
Security Benefit Group of Cos 1 Security Benefit Pl *Fax: Cust Svc ■ TF: 800-888-2461 ■ Web: www.securitybenefit.com	Topeka	KS	66636	785-438-3000	368-1772*	360-4
Security Check LLC 2612 Jackson Ave W	Oxford	MS	38655	662-234-0440		111
Security Corp 22325 Roethel Dr TF: 877-374-5700 ■ Web: www.securitycorp.com	Novi	MI	48375	877-374-5700		692
Security Credit Services LLC 2653 W Oxford Loop Ste 108 TF: 866-699-7889 ■ Web: www.securitycreditservicesllc.com	Oxford	MS	38655	662-281-7220		403
Security Defense Systems Corp 160 Pk Ave *Fax Area Code: 973 ■ TF: 800-325-6339 ■ Web: www.securitydefense.com	Nutley	NJ	07110	800-325-6339	235-0132*	692
Security Door Controls Inc 801 Avenida Acaso TF: 800-413-8783 ■ Web: www.sdcsecurity.com	Camarillo	CA	93012	805-494-0622		350
Security Engineered Machinery Company Inc 5 Walkup Dr PO Box 1045 TF Sales: 800-225-9293 ■ Web: www.semshred.com	Westborough	MA	01581	508-366-1488	836-4154	111
Security Equipment Inc 13505 C St Web: www.sei-security.com	Omaha	NE	68144	402-333-3233		693
Security Escrow & Title Insurance Agency 337 S Main Ste 110 TF: 855-319-9820 ■ Web: securityescrowutah.com	Cedar City	UT	84720	435-867-0402		390
Security Federal Bank (SFB) 238 Richland Ave W TF: 866-851-3000 ■ Web: www.securityfederalbank.com	Aiken	SC	29801	803-641-3000		71
Security Finance Corp PO Box 3146 TF All: 800-395-8195 ■ Web: www.security-finance.com	Spartanburg	SC	29304	864-582-8193		217
Security Fire Protection Co Inc 4495 Mendenhall Rd S TF: 888-274-8595 ■ Web: www.securityfire.com	Memphis	TN	38141	901-362-6250	366-7869	189-13
Security First Corp 29811 Santa Margarita Pkwy Ste 600 TF: 888-884-7152 ■ Web: securityfirstcorp.com	Rancho Santa Margarita	CA	92688	949-858-7525		84
Security Funds 1 Security Benefit Pl TF: 800-888-2461 ■ Web: www.securitybenefit.com	Topeka	KS	66636	785-438-3000	438-5177	528
Security Horizon Inc 5350 Tomah Dr Ste 3200 Web: www.securityhorizon.com	Colorado Springs	CO	80918	719-488-4500		693
Security Industry Assn (SIA) 8405 Colesville Rd Ste 500 TF: 866-817-8888 ■ Web: www.securityindustry.org	Silver Spring	MD	20910	703-683-2075	683-2469	49-4
Security Information Systems Inc 6314 Kingspointe Pkwy Ste 3 Web: www.securitysoftware.com	Orlando	FL	32819	407-345-1550		693
Security Instrument Corp of Delaware 309 W Newport Pk Web: www.securityinstrument.com	Wilmington	DE	19804	302-633-5621		693
Security Letter 166 E 96th St	New York	NY	10128	212-348-1553		531-1
Security Life Insurance Co of America 10901 Red Cir Dr TF: 800-328-4667 ■ Web: www.securitylife.com	Minnetonka	MN	55343	952-544-2121	945-3419	391-2
Security Management Systems Inc 225 Community Dr Ste 150 Web: www.securitymgt.com	Great Neck	NY	11021	516-450-3120		693
Security Metal Products Corp 5700 Hannum Ave Ste 250 Web: www.secmet.com	Culver City	CA	90230	310-641-6690		480
Security Mutual Insurance Co 2417 N Triphammer Rd PO Box 4620 Web: www.securitymutual.com	Ithaca	NY	14852	607-257-5000		391-6
Security Mutual Life Insurance Co of New York 100 Court St PO Box 1625 *Fax: Cust Svc ■ TF: 800-927-8846 ■ Web: www.smlny.com	Binghamton	NY	13901	607-723-3551	723-8665*	391-2
Security National Bank 40 S Limestone St Web: www.securitynationalbank.com	Springfield	OH	45502	937-324-6800		70
Security National Bank of Enid 201 W Maine Ave Web: www.snbenid.com	Enid	OK	73701	580-234-5151		70
Security National Bank of Omaha (Inc) 1120 S 101st St PO Box 31400 Web: www.snbconnect.com	Omaha	NE	68124	402-344-7300		70

Phone | Fax | Class

Security National Bank of Sioux City Iowa
601 Pierce St — Sioux City IA 51101 — 712-277-6500 — 70
Web: www.snbonline.com

Security National Financial Corp (SNFC)
5300 South 360 West Ste 250
PO Box 57250 — Salt Lake City UT 84123 — 801-264-1060 — 391-2
NASDAQ: SNFCA ■ *TF:* 800-574-7117 ■ *Web:* www.securitynational.com

Security Resource Group Inc
300-1914 Hamilton St — Regina SK S4P3N6 — 306-522-0135 — 693
Web: www.securityresourcegroup.com

Security Risk Solutions Inc
698 Fishermans Bnd — Mount Pleasant SC 29464 — 843-647-1556 — 463
Web: www.securityrisksolutions.com

Security Service Federal Credit Union
16211 La Cantera Pkwy — San Antonio TX 78256 — 210-476-4000 — 444-3000 — 219
TF: 800-527-7328 ■ *Web:* www.ssfcu.org

Security Signal Devices Inc
1740 N Lemon St — Anaheim CA 92801 — 800-888-0444 — 692
TF: 800-888-0444 ■ *Web:* www.ssdalarm.com

Security Square Mall
6901 Security Blvd — Baltimore MD 21244 — 410-265-6000 — 281-1473 — 460
TF: 800-977-2769 ■ *Web:* www.securitysquare.com

Security State Bank & Trust (Inc)
201 W Main St PO Box 471 — Fredericksburg TX 78624 — 830-997-7575 — 997-7994 — 70
Web: www.ssbtexas.com

Security Supply Corp 196 Maple Ave — Selkirk NY 12158 — 518-767-2226 — 767-2065 — 612
TF: 800-333-2226 ■ *Web:* www.secsupply.com

Security Traders Assn 1115 Broadway — New York NY 10010 — 646-699-5996 — 659-5249* — 49-2
**Fax Area Code:* 202 ■ *Web:* www.securitytraders.org

Security Van Lines LLC
100 W Airline Dr — Kenner LA 70062 — 800-794-5961 — 780
TF: 800-218-6915 ■ *Web:* securitymayflower.com

SecurLinx Holding Corp
150 Clay St Ste 440 — Morgantown WV 26501 — 304-284-5020 — 809
Web: www.securlinx.com

SecurTek Monitoring Solutions Inc
70-1st Ave N — Yorkton SK S3N1J6 — 306-786-4330 — 693
Web: www.securtek.com

Securus Technologies Inc
14651 Dallas Pkwy — Dallas TX 75254 — 972-277-0300 — 277-0301 — 736
TF: 800-844-6591 ■ *Web:* www.securustech.net

SED (Regency Infographics Inc)
2867 E Allegheny Ave — Philadelphia PA 19134 — 215-425-8800 — 425-9715 — 781
TF: 800-829-0020 ■ *Web:* www.sed.com/desktop-publishing.html

SED International Inc
3505 Newpoint Pl Ste 450 — Lawrenceville GA 30043 — 770-243-1200 — 174

SED Systems 18 Innovation Blvd — Saskatoon SK S7N3R1 — 306-931-3425 — 933-1486 — 246
Web: www.sedsystems.ca

SEDA Construction Co
2120 Corporate Sq Blvd Ste 3 — Jacksonville FL 32216 — 904-724-7800 — 727-9500 — 653
Web: www.sedaconstruction.com

Seda France Inc
10200 McKalla Pl Ste 400 — Austin TX 78758 — 512-206-0105 — 96
TF: 800-474-0854 ■ *Web:* www.sedafrance.com

SEDALCO Construction Services
4100 Fossil Creek Blvd — Fort Worth TX 76137 — 817-831-2245 — 831-2248 — 186
Web: www.sedalco.com

Sedalia Area Chamber of Commerce
600 E Third St — Sedalia MO 65301 — [illegible] — [illegible] — 139
TF: 800-422-3247 ■ *Web:* www.sedaliachamber.com

Sedan Floral Inc
406 S School St PO Box 339 — Sedan KS 67361 — 620-725-3111 — 725-5257 — 369
Web: www.sedanfloral.com

Sedano's Supermarkets 3140 W 76 St — Hialeah FL 33018 — 305-364-2303 — 556-6981 — 345
Web: www.sedanos.com

Sedco 2304 W Beecher Rd PO Box 624 — Adrian MI 49221 — 517-263-2220 — 265-6160 — 790
Web: www.sedco-prv.com

Seder & Chandler
339 Main St Burnside Bldg — Worcester MA 01608 — 508-757-7721 — 428
Web: www.sederlaw.com

Sedgewick Industries
667 W Ward Ave — High Point NC 27260 — 336-885-9300 — 885-9174 — 319-1
Web: www.sedgewick.com

Sedgwick County 315 Cedar St Ste 200 — Julesburg CO 80737 — 970-474-2531 — 474-3507 — 338
Web: sedgwickcountygov.net

Sedgwick County 525 N Main St Rm 211 — Wichita KS 67203 — 316-660-9222 — 383-7961 — 338
TF: 800-527-0709 ■ *Web:* sedgwickcounty.org

Sedgwick County Electric Co-op
1355 S 383rd St W — Cheney KS 67025 — 316-542-3131 — 245
Web: www.sedgwickcountyelectric.coop

Sedgwick County Zoo 5555 W Zoo Blvd — Wichita KS 67212 — 316-660-9453 — 942-3781 — 823
Web: www.scz.org

SEDL 4700 Mueller Blvd — Austin TX 78723 — 512-476-6861 — 476-2286 — 668
TF: 800-476-6861 ■ *Web:* www.sedl.org

Sedlak Interiors Inc 34300 Solon Rd — Solon OH 44139 — 440-248-2424 — 321
TF: 800-260-2949 ■ *Web:* www.sedlakinteriors.com

Sedlak Management Consultants Inc
Metropolitan Plaza 22901 Millcreek Blvd
Ste 600 — Highland Hills OH 44122 — 216-206-4700 — 206-4840 — 194
Web: www.jasedlak.com

Sedo.com LLC 161 First St 4th Fl — Cambridge MA 02142 — 617-499-7200 — 387
Web: www.sedo.com

SEDONA Corp
1003 W Ninth Ave 2nd Fl — King Of Prussia PA 19406 — 610-337-8400 — 177
TF: 800-815-3307 ■ *Web:* www.sedonacorp.com

Sedona Rouge Hotel & Spa
2250 W SR- 89A — Sedona AZ 86336 — 928-203-4111 — 379
TF: 866-312-4111 ■ *Web:* www.sedonarouge.com

Sedona Staffing
7380 Clairemont Mesa Blvd Ste 209 — San Diego CA 92111 — 858-268-9844 — 41
Web: www.sedonastaffing.com

SEE Science Ctr 200 Bedford St — Manchester NH 03101 — 603-669-0400 — 669-0400 — 520
Web: www.see-sciencecenter.org

See Water Inc 121 N Dillon St — San Jacinto CA 92583 — 951-487-8073 — 487-0557 — 201
TF: 888-733-9283 ■ *Web:* www.seewaterinc.com

See World Satellites Inc
1321 Wayne Ave — Indiana PA 15701 — 724-463-3200 — 116
TF: 800-435-2808 ■ *Web:* www.seeworld.biz

See's Candies Inc
210 El Camino Real — South San Francisco CA 94080 — 650-761-2490 — 296-8
TF Cust Svc: 800-877-7337 ■ *Web:* www.sees.com

SeeClickFix Inc
746 Chapel St Ste 207 — New Haven CT 06510 — 203-752-0777 — 387
Web: www.seeclickfix.com

Seed Hawk Inc Hwy 9 PO Box 123 — Langbank SK S0G2X0 — 306-538-2221 — 273
TF: 800-667-4295 ■ *Web:* www.seedhawk.com

Seed Mackall & Cole LLP
1332 Anacapa St Ste 200 — Santa Barbara CA 93101 — 805-963-0669 — 428
Web: seedmackall.com

Seedorff Masonry Inc
408 W Mission St — Strawberry Point IA 52076 — 563-933-2296 — 933-4114 — 189-7
TF: 800-642-5904 ■ *Web:* www.seedorff.com

Seeds of Peace 183 Powhatan Rd — Otisfield ME 04270 — 212-573-8040 — 239
Web: www.seedsofpeace.org

Seedway LLC 1734 Railroad Pl — Hall NY 14463 — 585-526-6391 — 526-6832 — 694
TF: 800-836-3710 ■ *Web:* www.seedway.com

SEEK Careers/Staffing Inc
1160 Opportunity Dr — Grafton WI 53024 — 262-377-8888 — 375-6677 — 721
Web: www.seekcareers.com

Seeker Rod Co 700 N Batavia Unit B — Orange CA 92868 — 714-769-1700 — 710
Web: seekerrods.com

Seekins Ford Lincoln Inc
1625 Seekins Ford Dr — Fairbanks AK 99701 — 907-459-4000 — 57
Web: seekins.com

Seelbach Hilton Louisville
500 S Fourth St — Louisville KY 40202 — 502-585-3200 — 585-9239 — 379
TF: 800-333-3399 ■ *Web:* www.seelbachhilton.com

Seelye Craftsmen Co
2220 Fernbrook Ln — Minneapolis MN 55447 — 763-577-0700 — 697
Web: www.seelyecraft.com

Seelye Plastics Inc
9700 Newton Ave S — Bloomington MN 55431 — 800-328-2728 — 881-3503* — 603
**Fax Area Code:* 952 ■ **Fax:* Sales ■ *TF:* 800-328-2728 ■ *Web:* seelyeplastics.com

SeeMore Putter Co, The
277 Mallory Sta Ste 119 — Franklin TN 37067 — 615-435-8015 — 711
TF: 800-985-8170 ■ *Web:* www.seemore.com

seepex Inc 511 Speedway Dr — Enon OH 45323 — 937-864-7150 — 864-7157 — 641
TF: 800-695-3659 ■ *Web:* www.seepex.com

SeePoint Technology LLC
2619 Manhattan Beach Blvd — Redondo Beach CA 90278 — 310-725-9660 — 535-9234 — 614
TF: 888-587-1777 ■ *Web:* www.seepoint.com

Seer Capital Management LP
1177 Ave of the Americas 34th Fl — New York NY 10036 — 212-850-9000 — 690
Web: seercap.com

SEER Technology Inc
2681 Parleys Way Ste 201 — Salt Lake City UT 84109 — 801-746-7888 — 419
TF: 877-505-7337 ■ *Web:* www.seertechnology.com

Seevibes 3414 Park Ave Ste 300 — Montreal QC H2X2H5 — 514-439-6909 — 195
Web: seevibes.com

SEFA (Scientific Equipment & Furniture Assn)
65 Hilton Ave — Garden City NY 11530 — 516-294-5424 — 294-2758 — 49-19
TF: 877-294-5424 ■ *Web:* www.sefalabs.com

Sefar Printing Solutions Inc
111 Calumet St — Depew NY 14043 — 716-683-4050 — 685-9469 — 745-3
TF: 800-995-0531 ■ *Web:* www.sefar.com

Sefcor Inc 1150 [illegible] Rd — Griffin GA 30224 — 770-227-8297 — 567
Web: www.sefcor.com

Sefton Resources Inc
2050 S Oneida St Ste 102 — Denver CO 80224 — 303-759-2700 — 536
TF: 800-829-2002 ■ *Web:* www.seftonresources.com

SEG (Society of Exploration Geophysicists)
8801 S Yale Ave Ste 500 PO Box 702740 — Tulsa OK 74137 — 918-497-5500 — 497-5557 — 48-12
Web: www.seg.org

SEGA of America Inc
350 Rhode Island St Ste 400 — San Francisco CA 94103 — 415-701-6000 — 701-6001 — 762
TF: 800-872-7342 ■ *Web:* www.sega.com

Segal Co 333 W 34th St — New York NY 10001 — 212-251-5000 — 193
Web: www.segalco.com

Segall Bryant & Hamill
540 W Madison St Ste 1900 — Chicago IL 60661 — 312-474-1222 — 401
TF: 800-836-4265 ■ *Web:* www.sbhic.com

Segerstrom Center for the Arts (SCFTA)
600 Town Ctr Dr — Costa Mesa CA 92626 — 714-556-2121 — 556-8984 — 572
Web: www.scfta.org/home/default.aspx

Segmedica Inc
935 Sheridan Dr Ste 120 — Tonawanda NY 14150 — 716-754-8744 — 466
Web: segmedica.com

Seguin Area Chamber of Commerce
116 N Camp St — Seguin TX 78155 — 830-379-6382 — 379-6971 — 139
TF: 877-330-3331 ■ *Web:* www.seguinchamber.com

Seguin Independent School District
1221 E Kingsbury St — Seguin TX 78155 — 830-372-5771 — 379-0392 — 685
TF: 866-632-9992 ■ *Web:* www.seguin.k12.tx.us

Seguin Moreau Napa Cooperage Inc
151 Camino Dorado — Napa CA 94558 — 707-252-3408 — 200
Web: seguinmoreaunapa.com

Segway Inc 14 Technology Dr — Bedford NH 03110 — 603-222-6000 — 222-6001 — 516
TF: 866-473-4929 ■ *Web:* www.segway.com

SEI 1 Freedom Vly Dr — Oaks PA 19456 — 610-676-1000 — 528
NASDAQ: SEIC ■ *TF:* 800-342-5734 ■ *Web:* www.seic.com

SEI (Software Engineering Institute)
4500 Fifth Ave — Pittsburgh PA 15213 — 412-268-5800 — 268-6257* — 668
**Fax:* Cust Svc ■ *TF:* 888-201-4479 ■ *Web:* www.sei.cmu.edu

SEI (Stephenson Equipment Inc)
7201 Paxton St — Harrisburg PA 17111 — 717-564-3434 — 264-3
TF: 800-325-6455 ■ *Web:* www.stephensonequipment.com

SEI (System Engineering International Inc)
5115 Pegasus Ct Ste Q — Frederick MD 21704 — 301-694-9601 — 694-9608 — 787
TF: 800-765-4734 ■ *Web:* www.seipower.com

SEI (Steel Edge Inc)
716 W Mesquite Ave — Las Vegas NV 89106 — 702-386-0023 — 492
Web: www.steeledgeinc.com

SEI Group Inc
689 Discovery Dr Ste 310 — Huntsville AL 35806 — 256-533-0500 — 261
Web: www.seigroupinc.com

Name / Address	City	State	Zip	Phone	Fax	Class
Sei/Aarons Inc 3108 Piedmont Rd NE Ste 160 *Web:* seiaarons.com	Atlanta	GA	30305	404-495-9707		321
SEIA (Solar Energy Industries Assn) 600 14th St NW Ste 800 *Web:* www.seia.org	Washington	DC	20004	202-682-0556	682-0559	48-12
Seibels House & Garden 1616 Blanding St *Web:* www.historiccolumbia.org	Columbia	SC	29201	803-252-1770	929-7695	50-3
Seico Security Systems 132 Court St *TF:* 800-272-0316 ■ *Web:* seicosecurity.com	Pekin	IL	61554	309-347-3200		693
Seidcon Inc 1911 Riviera Dr *Web:* www.seidcon.com	Vista	CA	92084	760-510-9800	510-9806	809
Seidel Schroeder & Co 304 E Blue Bell Rd *Web:* www.ssccpa.com	Brenham	TX	77833	979-836-6131	830-8131	2
Seidel Tanning Corp 1306 E Meinecke Ave *TF:* 800-826-6379 ■ *Web:* www.seideltanning.com	Milwaukee	WI	53212	414-562-4030		432
Seiden Group 112 Madison Ave *Web:* www.seidenadvertising.com	New York	NY	10016	212-223-8700		4
Seigle's 1331 Davis Rd *Web:* www.seigles.com	Elgin	IL	60123	847-742-2000		364
Seiko Corp of America 1111 MacArthur Blvd *TF Cust Svc:* 800-545-2783 ■ *Web:* www.seikousa.com	Mahwah	NJ	07430	201-529-5730		153
Seiko Instruments USA Inc 21221 S Western Ave Ste 250 *TF Sales:* 800-688-0817 ■ *Web:* www.seikoinstruments.com	Torrance	CA	90501	310-517-7700	517-7709	153
Seiko Instruments USA Inc Business & Home Office Products Div (SII) 21221 S Western Ave Ste 250 *TF:* 800-688-0817 ■ *Web:* labelprinters.sii-thermalprinters.com	Torrance	CA	90501	310-517-7700	517-7779	173-6
Seiko Optical Products of America Inc 575 Corporate Dr *Web:* www.seikoeyewear.com	Mahwah	NJ	07430	201-529-9099		544
Seiler Instrument & Mfg Company Inc 3433 Tree Court Industrial Blvd *TF:* 800-489-2282 ■ *Web:* www.seilerinst.com	Saint Louis	MO	63122	314-968-2282		544
Seiler LLP 3 Lagoon Dr Ste 400 *Web:* www.seiler.com	Redwood City	CA	94065	650-365-4646	368-4055	2
Seilevel Inc 3410 Far W Blvd *Web:* www.seilevel.com	Austin	TX	78731	512-527-9952		177
SEIMAX Technologies LP 4805 Westway Park Bouvelard Ste 100 *Web:* www.seismicventures.com	Houston	TX	77041	281-240-1234		536
Seismic Energy Products LP (SEP) 518 Progress Way	Athens	TX	75751	903-675-8571		676
Seismic LLC 7550 Teague Rd Ste 404 **Fax Area Code:* 866 ■ *Web:* www.seismicllc.com	Hanover	MD	21076	410-799-7700	338-6405*	261
Seismic Productions Llc 7010 Santa Monica Blvd *TF:* 800-279-0041 ■ *Web:* www.seismicproductions.com	Los Angeles	CA	90038	323-957-3350		7
Seismic Source Co 9425 E Tower Rd *Web:* seismicsource.com	Ponca City	OK	74604	580-362-3402		539
Seitel Inc 10811 S Westview Cir Dr Bldg C Ste 100 *Web:* www.seitel.com	Houston	TX	77043	713-881-8900		538
Seitel Systems LLC 1200 Western Ave Ste 100 *Web:* seitelsystems.com	Seattle	WA	98101	206-832-2875		180
Seitz LLC 212 Industrial Ln *TF:* 800-261-2011 ■ *Web:* www.seitzllc.com	Torrington	CT	06790	860-489-0476		604
Seitz Technical Products Inc 729 Newark Rd *Web:* www.seitz.com	Avondale	PA	19311	610-268-0371		567
Seiu Local 503 488 E 11th Ave Ste B100 *TF:* 800-452-2146 ■ *Web:* www.seiu503.org	Eugene	OR	97401	541-342-1055		414
Seize The Deal LLC 1851 N Greenville Ave Ste 100 *TF:* 866-210-0881 ■ *Web:* www.seizethedeal.com	Richardson	TX	75081	866-210-0881		387
SEJ (Society of Environmental Journalists) 1629 K St NW Ste 300 **Fax Area Code:* 215 ■ *Web:* www.sej.org	Washington	DC	20006	202-558-2300	884-8175*	49-14
SEK Genetics 9525 70th Rd **Fax Area Code:* 620 ■ *TF:* 800-443-6389 ■ *Web:* www.sekgenetics.com	Galesburg	KS	66740	800-443-6389	763-2231*	11-2
SEKAI Electronics Inc 14600 Industry Cir *Web:* www.sekai-electronics.com	La Mirada	CA	90638	714-736-4180		647
Sekas International Ltd 345 Seventh Ave 9th Fl *Web:* www.sekasinternational.com	New York	NY	10001	212-629-6095	629-6097	155-7
Sekisui 25 S Belvedere Blvd *Web:* www.sekisuiusa.com	Memphis	TN	38104	901-725-0005		671
Sekisui America Corp 333 Meadowlands Pkwy *Web:* www.sekisui-corp.com	Secaucus	NJ	07094	201-423-7960	423-7979	603
Sekisui Diagnostics LLC 4 Hartwell Pl *Web:* www.sekisuidiagnostics.com	Lexington	MA	02421	781-652-7800		476
Sekisui Japanese Restaurant 4724 Poplar Ave *Web:* www.sekisuiusa.com	Memphis	TN	38117	901-767-7770		671
Sekisui of Chattanooga 1120 Houston St *Web:* www.sekisuichattanooga.com	Chattanooga	TN	37402	423-267-4600		671
Sekisui Voltek LLC 100 Shepard St *TF:* 800-225-0668 ■ *Web:* www.sekisuivoltek.com	Lawrence	MA	01843	978-685-2557	685-9861	601
Seko Worldwide Inc 1100 Arlington Heights Rd Ste 600 **Fax Area Code:* 518 ■ *TF:* 800-228-2711 ■ *Web:* www.sekologistics.com	Itasca	IL	60143	630-919-4800	785-4594*	449
Sekuworks LLC 9487 Dry Fork Rd	Harrison	OH	45030	513-202-1210		627
Selamat Designs 231 S Maple Ave *Web:* www.selamatdesigns.com	South San Francisco	CA	94080	650-243-4840		96
Selas Heat Technology Company LLC 130 Keystone Dr *TF:* 800-523-6500 ■ *Web:* www.selas.com	Montgomeryville	PA	18936	215-646-6600	646-3536	318
Selbert Perkins Design 432 Culver Blvd *Web:* www.selbertperkins.com	Playa Del Rey	CA	90293	310-822-5223		344
Selby Furniture Hardware Company Inc 321 Rider Ave *TF:* 800-334-3512 ■ *Web:* www.selbyhardware.com	Bronx	NY	10451	718-993-3700	993-3143	350
Selby Public Library 1331 First St *Web:* www.selbylibraryfriends.org	Sarasota	FL	34236	941-365-5228		434-3
Selby Venture Partners PO Box Q *Web:* selbyventures.com	Menlo Park	CA	94026	650-300-5882		792
Selbysoft Inc 8326 Woodland Ave E *TF:* 800-454-4434 ■ *Web:* www.selbysoft.com	Puyallup	WA	98371	253-770-2993		177
Selco Community Credit Union 299 E 11th Ave *TF:* 800-445-4483 ■ *Web:* www.selco.org	Eugene	OR	97401	541-686-8000		219
Selden Fox Ltd 619 Enterprise Dr *Web:* www.seldenfox.com	Oak Brook	IL	60523	630-954-1400		2
Selden Neck State Park c/o Gillette Castle State Pk 67 River Rd *Web:* www.ct.gov	East Haddam	CT	06423	860-526-2336		565
Selden's Home Furnishings 1802 62nd Ave E *Web:* seldens.com	Tacoma	WA	98424	253-922-5700		321
Seldovia Native Association Inc 101 W Benson Blvd Ste 302 *Web:* www.snai.com	Anchorage	AK	99515	907-868-8006		378
Select Computing Inc 3001 Broadway St NE Ste 655 *TF:* 800-433-5778 ■ *Web:* www.selectcomputing.com	Minneapolis	MN	55413	612-331-5535		180
Select Design Ltd 208 Flynn Ave Ste 1A *TF:* 800-880-4780 ■ *Web:* www.selectdesign.com	Burlington	VT	05401	802-864-9075		687
Select Engineered Systems 7991 W 26th Ave *TF:* 800-342-5737 ■ *Web:* www.selectses.com	Hialeah	FL	33016	305-823-5410		693
Select Group LLC, The 5520 Capital Ctr Dr *Web:* www.selectgroup.com	Raleigh	NC	27606	919-459-1400		260
Select Group Real Estate Inc 409 Century Park Dr *Web:* selectgroupre.com	Yuba City	CA	95991	530-237-1800		652
Select Medical Corp 4714 Gettysburg Rd *TF:* 888-735-6332 ■ *Web:* www.selectmedical.com	Mechanicsburg	PA	17055	717-972-1100		463
Select Portfolio Management Inc 120 Vantis *TF:* 800-445-9822 ■ *Web:* www.selectportfolio.com	Aliso Viejo	CA	92656	949-975-7900		401
Select Portfolio Servicing Inc PO Box 65250 *TF:* 800-258-8602 ■ *Web:* www.spservicing.com	Salt Lake City	UT	84165	800-258-8602		217
Select Publishing Inc 6417 Normandy Ln *TF:* 800-278-5670 ■ *Web:* www.selectpub.com	Madison	WI	53719	608-277-5787		366
Select Restaurants Inc 2000 Auburn Dr 1 Chagrin Highlands *Web:* www.selectrestaurants.com	Cleveland	OH	44122	216-464-6606	464-8565	670
Select Rx 11414 E 51st St *Web:* www.selectrx.com	Tulsa	OK	74146	918-461-8103		237
Select Sales & Mktg Inc 549 Mercury Ln	Brea	CA	92821	714-990-3755		466
Select Sires Inc 11740 US Hwy 42 N *Web:* www.selectsires.com	Plain City	OH	43064	614-873-4683	873-5751	11-2
Select Staffing 3820 State St *TF:* 844-864-0634 ■ *Web:* www.select.com	Santa Barbara	CA	93105	805-882-2200	898-7111	721
Select Stainless LLC 11145 Monroe Rd *Web:* www.selectstainless.com	Matthews	NC	28105	704-841-1090		697
Select Technical Staffing Inc 1025 S 108th St Ste 205 *Web:* selecttechnicalstaffing.com	Milwaukee	WI	53214	414-476-9331		260
Selectable Media Inc 168 Fifth Ave Ste 302 *Web:* selectablemedia.com	New York	NY	10010	212-796-6214		5
Select-A-Ticket Inc 25 Rt 23 S *TF:* 800-735-3288 ■ *Web:* www.selectaticket.com	Riverdale	NJ	07457	973-839-6100	839-0870	750
Selected Funds PO Box 8243 *TF:* 800-243-1575 ■ *Web:* www.selectedfunds.com	Boston	MA	02266	800-243-1575		528
Selected Funeral & Life Insurance Co 119 Convention Blvd *Web:* sflic.net	Hot Springs National Park	AR	71902	501-624-2172		391-2
Selected Independent Funeral Homes 500 Lake Cook Rd Ste 205 *TF:* 800-323-4219 ■ *Web:* www.selectedfuneralhomes.org	Deerfield	IL	60015	847-236-9401	236-9968	49-4
Selection Management Systems Inc 155 Tri County Pkwy Ste 150 *Web:* www.selection.com	Cincinnati	OH	45246	513-522-8764		193
Selection Resource Inc 10940 Wilshire Blvd Ste 925 *Web:* www.selectresources.com	Los Angeles	CA	90024	310-824-8999		196
Selective Enterprises Inc 10701 Texland Blvd *TF:* 800-334-1207 ■ *Web:* www.unitedsupplyco.com	Charlotte	NC	28273	704-588-3310		361
Selective First Realty 4110 Main St *Web:* selectivefirstrealty.com	Flushing	NY	11355	718-461-2510		652
Selective Insurance Group Inc 40 Wantage Ave *NASDAQ: SIGI* ■ *TF:* 800-777-9656 ■ *Web:* www.selective.com	Branchville	NJ	07890	973-948-3000		360-4
Selective Service System 1515 Wilson Blvd *TF:* 888-655-1825 ■ *Web:* www.sss.gov	Arlington	VA	22209	847-688-6888		340-20
Selective Service System Regional Offices						
Region 1 PO Box 94638 *TF:* 888-655-1825 ■ *Web:* www.sss.gov	Palatine	IL	60094	847-688-6888		340-20
Region 2 PO Box 94638 *TF:* 888-655-1825 ■ *Web:* www.sss.gov	Palatine	IL	60094	847-688-6888		340-20
Select-O-Hits Inc 1981 Fletcher Creek Dr *TF:* 800-346-0723 ■ *Web:* www.selectohits.com	Memphis	TN	38133	901-388-1190		523
Selectpath Benefits & Financial Inc 310-700 Richmond St *TF:* 888-327-5777 ■ *Web:* www.selectpath.ca	London	ON	N6A5C7	519-675-1177		390

	City	State	Zip	Phone	Fax	Class
SelectPath Inc 10820 Central Ave SE. *Web:* www.selectpath.com	Albuquerque	NM	87123	505-275-4001		387
Selectquote Insurance Services 595 Market St 10th Fl. **Fax Area Code: 800* ■ *TF:* 800-670-3213 ■ *Web:* www.selectquote.com	San Francisco	CA	94105	415-543-7338	436-7000*	390
SelecTransportation Resources LLC 9550 N Loop E. *TF:* 800-299-4200 ■ *Web:* www.selectransportation.com	Houston	TX	77029	713-672-4115		791
Selectron Technologies Inc 12323 SW 66th Ave. *Web:* www.selectrontechnologies.com	Portland	OR	97223	503-443-1400		179
Selectus Consulting LLC 17875 Kandel Rd. *TF:* 800-426-4256 ■ *Web:* selectusconsulting.com	Marysville	OH	43040	937-644-8562		196
Selectx Pharmaceuticals Inc 1 Innovation Dr. *Web:* www.selectxpharm.com	Worcester	MA	01605	508-798-0216		583
Selee Corp 700 Shepherd St. *TF:* 800-842-3818 ■ *Web:* www.selee.com	Hendersonville	NC	28792	828-697-2411	693-1868	144
Selerity Technologies Inc 1950 South 900 West Ste S3. *Web:* www.selerity.com	Salt Lake City	UT	84104	801-978-2295		743
Selerix Systems Inc 2851 Craig Dr Ste 300. *Web:* www.selerix.com	Mckinney	TX	75070	469-452-7076		194
SELEX Inc 11300 W 89th St. *TF:* 800-765-0861 ■ *Web:* us.selex-es.com	Overland Park	KS	66214	913-495-2600	492-0870	529
Self Funding Administrators Corp 339 Busch'S Frontage Rd.	Annapolis	MD	21401	410-757-4200		390
Self Industries Inc 3491 Mary Taylor Rd. *Web:* selfindustries.com	Birmingham	AL	35235	205-655-3284	655-3288	198
Self Magazine 4 Times Sq. *TF:* 800-274-6111 ■ *Web:* www.self.com	New York	NY	10036	212-286-2860		457-11
Self Maples & Copeland Pc 1601 Second Ave E. *Web:* cpasmc.com	Oneonta	AL	35121	205-625-3472		2
Self Opportunity Inc 808 Office Park Cir. *TF:* 800-594-7036 ■ *Web:* www.selfopportunity.com	Lewisville	TX	75057	214-222-1500		194
Self Regional Hospital 1325 Spring St. *Web:* www.selfregional.org	Greenwood	SC	29646	864-725-4111		374-3
Self Storage Assn (SSA) 1900 N Beauregard St Ste 450. *TF:* 888-735-3784 ■ *Web:* www.selfstorage.org	Alexandria	VA	22311	703-575-8000	575-8901	49-21
Self-Employed America Magazine PO Box 241. *TF:* 800-649-6273 ■ *Web:* www.nase.org	Annapolis Junction	MD	20701	800-649-6273		457-5
Selfhelp Community Services Inc 520 Eigth Ave 5th Fl. *TF:* 866-735-1234 ■ *Web:* www.selfhelp.net	New York	NY	10018	866-735-1234		000
Selflock Screw Products Co Inc 461 E Brighton Ave. *Web:* sspmfg.com	Syracuse	NY	13210	315-541-4464	475-1093	621
Self-Seal Container Corp 401 E Fourth St. *TF:* 800-334-1438 ■ *Web:* www.selfsealtubes.com	Bridgeport	PA	19405	610-275-2300		125
Selig Enterprises Inc 1100 Spring St NW Ste 550. *Web:* www.seligenterprises.com	Atlanta	GA	30309	404-876-5511	875-2629	655
Selig Group Inc 342 E Wabash Ave. *Web:* www.seligsealing.com	Forrest	IL	61741	815-785-2100		295
Seligman & Assoc 1 Town Sq Ste 1913. *Web:* www.seligmangroup.com	Southfield	MI	48076	248-862-8000		655
Selkirk & District Chamber of Commerce (SDCC) 200 Eaton Ave. *Web:* www.selkirkanddistrictchamber.ca	Selkirk	MB	R1A0W6	204-482-7176	482-5448	137
Selkirk Canada Corp 375 Green Rd. *TF:* 800-263-9308 ■ *Web:* www.selkirkcorp.com	Stoney Creek	ON	L8E4A5	905-662-6600		183
Selkirk College 301 Frank Beinder Way. *TF:* 888-953-1133 ■ *Web:* www.selkirk.ca	Castlegar	BC	V1N4L3	250-365-7292	365-6568	166
Selkirk Shores State Park 7101 State Rt 3. *Web:* parks.ny.gov/historic-sites/33/details.aspx	Pulaski	NY	13142	315-298-5737		565
Sell My Timeshare Now LLC 383 Central Ave Ste 260. *TF:* 877-815-4227 ■ *Web:* www.sellmytimesharenow.com	Dover	NH	03820	603-516-0200		387
Selland Arena 700 M St. *TF:* 800-745-3000 ■ *Web:* www.fresnoconventioncenter.com	Fresno	CA	93721	559-445-8100	445-8110	720
Selland Auto Transport Inc 615 S 96th St. *Web:* www.sellandauto.com	Seattle	WA	98108	206-767-5960	767-0604	780
Sellars 6565 N 60th St. *TF:* 800-237-8454 ■ *Web:* sellarscompany.com	Milwaukee	WI	53223	414-353-5650	353-5707	745-6
Sellen Construction Co Inc 227 Westlake Ave N. *TF:* 800-767-3263 ■ *Web:* www.sellen.com	Seattle	WA	98109	206-682-7770	623-5206	186
Sellers Equipment Inc 400 N Chicago St. *Web:* www.sellersequipment.com	Salina	KS	67401	785-823-6378	823-8083	358
Sellex International Corp 88 E Broad St Ste 1220. *Web:* www.sellexinternational.com	Columbus	OH	43215	614-463-1986		463
Selling Power Magazine 1140 International Pkwy. *TF:* 800-752-7355 ■ *Web:* www.sellingpower.com	Fredericksburg	VA	22406	540-752-7000	752-7001	457-5
Selling Simplified Inc 7400 E Orchard Rd Ste 350S. *Web:* sellingsimplified.com	Greenwood Village	CO	80111	720-638-8500		195
Selling Source LLC 325 E Warm Springs Rd Ste 200. *TF:* 800-251-6147 ■ *Web:* sellingsource.com	Las Vegas	NV	89119	702-407-0707	407-0711	194
Sellmark Corp 2201 Heritage Pkwy. *Web:* www.sellmark.net	Mansfield	TX	76063	817-225-0310		544
Sellmore Industries Inc 815 Smith St. *Web:* www.sellmoreind.com	Buffalo	NY	14206	716-854-1600		234
Sellstrom Manufacturing Co 2050 Hammond Dr. *TF:* 800-323-7402 ■ *Web:* www.sellstrom.com	Schaumburg	IL	60173	847-358-2000		576
Selltis LLC 3500 Hwy 190 Ste 200. *Web:* www.selltis.com	Mandeville	LA	70471	985-727-3455		177
Selma University 1501 Lapsley St. *TF:* 800-860-8800 ■ *Web:* selmauniversity.org	Selma	AL	36701	334-872-2533		166
Selma-Dallas County Chamber of Commerce 912 Selma Ave. *TF:* 800-457-3562 ■ *Web:* www.selmaalabama.com	Selma	AL	36701	334-875-7241	875-7142	139
Selman Breitman LLP 11766 Wilshire Blvd. *Web:* www.selmanlaw.com	Los Angeles	CA	90025	310-445-0800	473-2525	428
Selmer Co 2200 Woodale Ave. *Web:* theboldtcompany.com	Green Bay	WI	54313	920-434-0230		187
Selmet Inc 33992 SE 7 Mile Ln PO Box 689. *Web:* www.selmetinc.com	Albany	OR	97322	541-926-7731		308
Selrico Services Inc 717 W Ashby Pl. *Web:* selricoservices.com	San Antonio	TX	78212	210-737-8220	737-7994	670
Selsoft Inc 303 S Jupiter Ste 110. *TF:* 800-986-1775 ■ *Web:* www.selsoftinc.com	Allen	TX	75002	217-721-3186		177
Seltzer Caplan Mcmahon Vitek 2100 Symphony Towers 750 B St. *TF:* 800-726-3339 ■ *Web:* www.scmv.com	San Diego	CA	92101	619-685-3003		428
Selva Grill 1345 Main St. *Web:* www.selvagrill.com	Sarasota	FL	34236	941-362-4427		671
Selway Corp PO Box 287. *Web:* www.selwaycorp.com	Stevensville	MT	59870	406-777-5471	777-5473	821
SEM (Society for Experimental Mechanics Inc) 7 School St. *TF:* 800-627-8258 ■ *Web:* www.sem.org	Bethel	CT	06801	203-790-6373	790-4472	49-19
SEM (Society for Ethnomusicology) Indiana University 1165 E 3rd St Morrison Hall 005. *TF:* 800-933-9330 ■ *Web:* www.ethnomusicology.org	Bloomington	IN	47405	812-855-6672	855-6673	48-4
SEMA (Specialty Equipment Market Assn) 1575 S Vly Vista Dr. *Web:* www.sema.org	Diamond Bar	CA	91765	909-396-0289	860-0184	49-21
SEMA Equipment Inc 11555 Hwy 60 Blvd. *TF:* 800-569-1377 ■ *Web:* www.semaequip.com	Wanamingo	MN	55983	507-824-2256	824-2668	274
Se-Ma-No Electric Co-op 601 N Business 60. *Web:* semano.com	Mansfield	MO	65704	417-924-3243		245
Semantic Research Inc 4922 N Harbor Dr. *Web:* www.semanticresearch.com	San Diego	CA	92106	619-222-4050		637-10
Semasys Inc 702 Ashland St. *TF Cust Svc:* 800-231-1425 ■ *Web:* www.semasys.com	Houston	TX	77007	713-869-8331	869-5077	286
SEMATECH 2706 Montopolis Dr. *Web:* www.sematech.org	Austin	TX	78741	512-356-3500		668
SemCAMS 521 Third Ave SW Ste 1200. *Web:* www.semgroupcorp.com/businessunits/semcams.aspx	Calgary	AB	T2P3T3	403-536-3000		707
Semcasting Inc 41 High St. *Web:* semcasting.com	North Andover	MA	01845	978-684-7580		5
SEMCO ENERGY Gas Co 1411 Third St Ste A. *TF:* 800-624-2019 ■ *Web:* www.semcoenergygas.com	Port Huron	MI	48060	800-624-2019		580
Semco Manufacturing Co 705 E Business 83. *TF:* 800-910-1003 ■ *Web:* semcoice.com	Pharr	TX	78577	956-683-1411		664
Semco Plastic Co 5301 Old Baumgartner Rd. *Web:* www.semcoplastics.com	Saint Louis	MO	63129	314-487-4557		608
SemGroup LP 6120 S Yale Ave Ste 700. *Web:* www.semgroupcorp.com	Tulsa	OK	74136	918-524-8100		325
Semi Dice Inc PO Box 3002. *Web:* www.semidice.com	Los Alamitos	CA	90720	562-594-4631	430-5942	246
Semicon Associates 695 Laco Dr.	Lexington	KY	40510	859-255-3664	255-6829	253
Semiconductor Circuits Inc 49 Range Rd. *Web:* www.dcdc.com	Windham	NH	03087	603-893-2330	893-6280	253
Semiconductor Environmental Safety & Health Assn (SESHA) 1313 Dolley Madison Blvd Ste 402. *TF:* 800-883-0698 ■ *Web:* www.seshaonline.org	McLean	VA	22101	703-790-1745	790-2672	49-19
Semiconductor Equipment & Materials International 3081 Zenker Rd. *TF:* 877-746-7788 ■ *Web:* www.semi.org	San Jose	CA	95134	408-943-6900	428-9600	49-19
Semiconductor Process Equipment Corp 27963 Franklin Pkwy. *Web:* www.team-spec.com	Valencia	CA	91355	661-257-0934		696
Semifab Inc 150 Great Oaks Blvd. *Web:* www.semifab.com	San Jose	CA	95119	408-414-5928		696
Semi-Kinetics Inc 20191 Windrow Dr Ste A. *Web:* www.semi-kinetics.com	Lake Forest	CA	92630	949-830-7364	830-7385	695
Semikron Inc 11 Executive Dr. *Web:* semikron.com	Hudson	NH	03051	603-883-8102		696
Seminary Co-op Bookstore 5757 S University Ave. *Web:* www.semcoop.com	Chicago	IL	60637	773-752-4381	752-8507	95
Seminary of the Immaculate Conception 440 W Neck Rd. *Web:* icseminary.edu	Huntington	NY	11743	631-423-0483		167-3
Seminary of the southwest (SSW) 501 E 32nd PO Box 2247. *TF:* 800-252-5400 ■ *Web:* www.ssw.edu	Austin	TX	78705	512-472-4133	472-3098	167-3
Seminoe State Park Seminoe Dam Rt. *Web:* wyoparks.state.wy.us	Sinclair	WY	82334	307-320-3013		565
Seminole Canyon State Park & Historic Site PO Box 820. *Web:* tpwd.texas.gov/state-parks/seminole-canyon	Comstock	TX	78837	432-292-4464		565
Seminole Casino Hollywood 4150 N State Rd 7. *Web:* www.seminolehollywoodcasino.com	Hollywood	FL	33021	954-961-3220		133

Name / Address	City	State	ZIP	Phone	Fax	Class
Seminole Casino Immokalee						
506 S First St	Immokalee	FL	34142	800-218-0007		133
TF: 800-218-0007 ■ *Web:* www.seminoleimmokaleecasino.com						
Seminole Coconut Creek Casino						
5550 NW 40th St	Coconut Creek	FL	33073	954-977-6700		133
Web: www.seminolecoconutcreekcasino.com						
Seminole Community College						
100 Weldon Blvd	Sanford	FL	32773	407-708-4722		162
TF: 800-590-3428 ■ *Web:* seminolestate.edu						
Oviedo 2505 Lockwood Blvd	Oviedo	FL	32765	407-971-5000	971-5012	162
Web: seminolestate.edu						
Seminole County 200 S Knox Ave	Donalsonville	GA	39845	229-524-2878		338
TF: 800-436-7442 ■ *Web:* www.seminolecountyga.com						
Seminole County 1101 E First St	Sanford	FL	32771	407-665-7945	665-7939*	338
**Fax:* Hum Res ■ *Web:* www.seminolecountyfl.gov						
Seminole County						
126 S Wewoka Ave PO Box 779	Wewoka	OK	74884	405-257-3371	257-6465	338
Web: seminole.oklahoma.usassessor.com						
Seminole County Convention & Visitors Bureau						
1515 International Pkwy Ste 1013	Lake Mary	FL	32746	407-665-2900	665-2920	206
TF: 800-800-7832 ■ *Web:* www.visitseminole.com						
Seminole County Public Library						
215 N Oxford Rd	Casselberry	FL	32707	407-665-0000		434-3
Web: www.seminolecountyfl.gov/lls/library						
Seminole County Public Library - North Branch						
150 N Palmetto Ave	Sanford	FL	32771	407-665-1620	330-3120	434-3
Web: www.seminolecountyfl.gov/lls/library						
Seminole Energy Services LLC						
1323 E 71st St Ste 300	Tulsa	OK	74136	918-492-2840	492-3075	325
Web: www.seminoleenergy.com						
Seminole Feed						
335 NE Watula Ave PO Box 940	Ocala	FL	34470	352-732-4143		447
TF: 800-683-1881 ■ *Web:* www.seminolefeed.com						
Seminole Hard Rock Hotel & Casino Hollywood						
1 Seminole Way	Hollywood	FL	33314	866-502-7529		669
TF: 866-502-7529 ■ *Web:* www.theseminolecasinos.com						
Seminole Hard Rock Hotel & Casino Tampa (SHRH & C)						
5223 N Orient Rd	Tampa	FL	33610	813-627-7625	983-0242*	133
**Fax Area Code:* 954 ■ *TF General:* 866-388-4263 ■ *Web:* www.seminolehardrocktampa.com						
Seminole Marine						
2501 Milestone Industrial Pk	Cairo	GA	39828	229-377-2125	377-1855	90
Web: www.sailfishboats.com						
Seminole Precast Manufacturing Inc						
331 Benson Junction Rd	Debary	FL	32713	386-668-7323		183
Web: www.seminoleprecast.com						
Seminole State College						
2701 Boren Blvd PO Box 351	Seminole	OK	74868	405-382-9950		162
TF: 877-738-6365 ■ *Web:* sscok.edu						
Seminole State Park						
7870 State Pk Dr	Donalsonville	GA	39845	229-861-3137		565
Web: www.gastateparks.org						
Seminole Towne Ctr 200 Towne Ctr Cir	Sanford	FL	32771	407-323-2262		460
TF: 877-746-6642 ■ *Web:* www.simon.com						
Seminole Valley Farm						
1400 Seminole Valley Rd NE	Cedar Rapids	IA	52411	319-378-9240		50-3
Web: seminolevalleyfarmmuseum.net						
SemiProbe Inc 276 E Allen St	Winooski	VT	05404	802-860-7000		246
TF: 800-604-9822 ■ *Web:* www.semiprobe.com						
SemiTorr Inc 10655 Manhasset Dr	Tualatin	OR	97062	503-682-7052		196
TF: 800-222-2903 ■ *Web:* www.semitorrinc.com						
Semling-Menke Company Inc PO Box 378	Merrill	WI	54452	715-536-9411	536-3067	236
TF: 800-333-2206 ■ *Web:* www.semcowindows.com						
Semonin Realtors						
600 N Hurstbourne Pkwy Ste 200	Louisville	KY	40222	502-425-4760		652
TF: 800-548-1650 ■ *Web:* www.semonin.com						
Semple Brown 1160 Santa Fe Dr	Denver	CO	80204	303-571-4137		708
Web: www.sbdesign-pc.com						
Sempra Energy Corp 101 Ash St	San Diego	CA	92101	619-696-2000		360-5
NYSE: SRE ■ *TF:* 800-411-7343 ■ *Web:* www.sempra.com						
Semtech Corp 200 Flynn Rd	Camarillo	CA	93012	805-498-2111	498-3804	696
NASDAQ: SMTC ■ *Web:* www.semtech.com						
SemWare Corp 730 Elk Cove Ct	Kennesaw	GA	30152	678-355-9810	355-9812	178-2
Web: www.semware.com						
Sen Plex Corp 938 Kohou St	Honolulu	HI	96817	808-848-0111		655
Web: www.senplex.com						
Sen. George J Mitchell Scholarship Resea						
75 Washington Ave Ste 2E	Portland	ME	04101	207-773-7700		305
TF: 888-220-7209 ■ *Web:* mitchellinstitute.org						
SenaReider Inc 299 Cannery Row Ste E	Monterey	CA	93940	831-372-4961		7
Web: www.senareider.com						
Senate House State Historic Site						
296 Fair St	Kingston	NY	12401	845-338-2786		565
TF: 800-456-2267 ■ *Web:* parks.ny.gov/historic-sites/18/details.aspx						
Senate Luxury Suites 900 SW Tyler St	Topeka	KS	66612	785-233-5050		379
TF: 800-488-3188 ■ *Web:* www.senatesuites.com						
Senator Frank S Farley State Marina						
600 Huron Ave	Atlantic City	NJ	08401	609-441-8482		565
Web: www.njparksandforests.org						
Senator Inn & Spa of Augusta						
284 Western Ave	Augusta	ME	04330	207-622-8800		707
TF: 877-772-2224 ■ *Web:* www.senatorinn.com						
Senator International Inc						
1630 Holland Rd	Maumee	OH	43537	419-887-5805		321
Web: www.thesenatorgroup.com/americas/allermuir						
Senator John Heinz Pittsburgh Regional History Ctr						
1212 Smallman St	Pittsburgh	PA	15222	412-454-6000		520
TF: 800-359-0758 ■ *Web:* www.heinzhistorycenter.org						
SENCO 4270 Ivy Pointe Blvd	Cincinnati	OH	45245	800-543-4596	388-3100*	759
**Fax Area Code:* 513 ■ *TF Tech Supp:* 800-543-4596 ■ *Web:* www.sencobrands.com						
Sencore Inc 3200 W Sencore Dr	Sioux Falls	SD	57107	605-339-0100	335-6379	248
TF: 800-736-2673 ■ *Web:* www.sencore.com						
Sendec Corp 72 Perinton Pkwy	Fairport	NY	14450	585-425-3390	425-3392	203
TF: 800-295-8000 ■ *Web:* apitech.com						
Senderex Cargo Inc						
17022 Montanero Ave Ste 6	Carson	CA	90746	310-342-2900		311
Web: www.senderex.com						
Sendio Inc 4911 Birch St Ste 150	Newport Beach	CA	92660	949-274-4375		180
Web: www.sendio.com						

Name / Address	City	State	ZIP	Phone	Fax	Class
Sendmail Inc						
6475 Christie Ave Ste 350	Emeryville	CA	94608	510-594-5400	594-5429	178-7
Sen-Dure Products Inc						
6785 NW 17th Ave	Fort Lauderdale	FL	33309	954-973-1260		91
TF: 800-394-5112 ■ *Web:* www.sen-dure.com						
Seneca College 1750 Finch Ave E	Toronto	ON	M2J2X5	416-491-5050		165
Web: www.senecacollege.ca						
Seneca Consulting Group Inc						
111 Smithtown Byp Ste 112	Hauppauge	NY	11788	631-577-4092		466
TF: 866-487-4157 ■ *Web:* www.senecaconsulting.com						
Seneca County 111 Madison St	Tiffin	OH	44883	419-447-4550		338
TF: 800-775-9767 ■ *Web:* www.seneca-county.com						
Seneca County 1 DiPronio Dr	Waterloo	NY	13165	315-539-1945	539-3789	338
Web: www.co.seneca.ny.us						
Seneca County Chamber of Commerce						
2020 Rt 5 & 20 W	Seneca Falls	NY	13148	315-568-2906	568-1730	139
TF: 800-732-1848 ■ *Web:* fingerlakesgateway.com						
Seneca Creek State Park						
11950 Clopper Rd	Gaithersburg	MD	20878	301-924-2127		565
Web: dnr2.maryland.gov						
Seneca Falls School District						
98 Clinton St	Seneca Falls	NY	13148	315-568-5818		685
Web: www.sfcs.k12.ny.us						
Seneca Falls Technology Group						
314 Fall St	Seneca Falls	NY	13148	315-568-5804	568-5800	455
Web: www.sftg.com						
Seneca Flight Operations						
2262 Airport Dr	Penn Yan	NY	14527	315-536-4471	536-4558	13
Web: www.senecaflight.com						
Seneca Foods Corp 3736 S Main St	Marion	NY	14505	315-926-8100	926-8300	296-20
NASDAQ: SENEA ■ *TF:* 800-622-6757 ■ *Web:* www.senecafoods.com						
Seneca Foundry Inc						
240 Mackinlay Kantor Dr	Webster City	IA	50595	515-832-1722		492
TF: 800-247-1039 ■ *Web:* www.senecafoundry.com						
Seneca Fouts Memorial State Natural Area						
Wygant Trail	Hood River	OR	97031	800-551-6949		565
TF: 800-551-6949 ■ *Web:* www.oregonstateparks.org						
Seneca Lake State Park 1 Lakefront Dr	Geneva	NY	14456	315-789-2331		565
Seneca Niagara Casino						
310 Fourth St	Niagara Falls	NY	14303	716-299-1100		133
TF: 877-873-6322 ■ *Web:* www.senecaniagaracasino.com						
Seneca Park Zoo 2222 St Paul St	Rochester	NY	14621	585-336-7200	342-1477	823
TF: 800-745-3000 ■ *Web:* www.senecaparkzoo.org						
Seneca Partners Inc						
300 Park St Ste 400	Birmingham	MI	48009	248-723-6650		194
Web: www.senecapartners.com						
Seneca Resources Corp						
1201 Louisiana St Ste 400	Houston	TX	77002	713-654-2600		536
TF: 800-365-3234 ■ *Web:* natfuel.com						
Seneca Sawmill Co 90201 Hwy 99	Eugene	OR	97440	541-689-1011		683
TF: 800-851-9484 ■ *Web:* www.senecasawmill.com						
Seneca State Forest						
10135 Browns Creek Rd	Dunmore	WV	24934	304-799-6213	799-6213	565
Web: www.senecastateforest.com						
Seneca Tank Inc 5585 NE 16th St	Des Moines	IA	50313	515-262-5900		57
TF: 800-362-2910 ■ *Web:* www.senecatank.com						
Seneca Wire & Manufacturing Co						
319 S Vine St	Fostoria	OH	44830	419-435-9261		813
Senegal 747 Third Ave 21st Fl	New York	NY	10017	212-517-9030	517-3032	784
Web: www.un.int						
Senergy Petroleum LLC 622 S 56th Ave	Phoenix	AZ	85043	602-272-6795		579
TF: 800-964-0076 ■ *Web:* www.brownevans.com						
Senes Oak Ridge Center for Risk Analysis Inc						
102 Donner Dr	Oak Ridge	TN	37830	865-483-6111		196
Web: senes.com						
Senesco Marine LLC						
10 Macnaught St	North Kingstown	RI	02852	401-295-0373		698
Web: www.senescomarine.com						
Senet Inc 94 River Rd Ste 101	Hudson	NH	03051	603-880-8484		407
TF: 800-636-7832 ■ *Web:* www.enertrac.com						
Senex Explosives Inc 710 Millers Run Rd	Cuddy	PA	15031	412-221-3218		268
Senga Engineering 1525 E Warner Ave	Santa Ana	CA	92705	714-549-8011		261
TF: 877-978-8159 ■ *Web:* senga-eng.com						
Sengen Inc						
9001 Highland Woods Blvd Ste 203	Bonita Springs	FL	34134	239-908-6700		809
Web: www.sengen.com						
Senior Aerospace Jet Products						
9106 Balboa Ave	San Diego	CA	92123	858-430-2203	278-8768	621
Web: www.seniorplc.com/aerospace/company.cfm/9						
Senior Aerospace Ketema Div						
790 Greenfield Dr	El Cajon	CA	92021	619-442-3451	440-1456	21
Web: www.sfketema.com						
Senior Alternatives For Living						
26211 Central Park Blvd	Southfield	MI	48076	800-350-0770		5
TF: 800-350-0770 ■ *Web:* www.alternativesforseniors.com						
Senior Care Pharmacy						
4455 Morris Park Dr	Mint Hill	NC	28227	704-545-8641		237
Web: www.seniorcarepharmacy-al.com						
Senior Corps 1201 New York Ave NW	Washington	DC	20525	202-606-5000		197
TF: 800-833-3722 ■ *Web:* www.nationalservice.gov						
Senior Flexonics Inc 300 E Devon Ave	Bartlett	IL	60103	630-837-1811		480
Web: seniorflexonics.com						
Senior Flexonics Inc Metal Bellows Div						
1075 Providence Hwy	Sharon	MA	02067	781-784-1400	784-1405	386
Web: www.metalbellows.com						
Senior Flexonics Pathway Division						
2400 Longhorn Industrial Dr	New Braunfels	TX	78130	830-629-8080		480
Web: www.pathwayb.com						
Senior Housing Management Inc						
208 35th St Dr SE Ste 500	Cedar Rapids	IA	52403	319-363-6094		193
Web: www.seniorhousingcompanies.com						
Senior Housing Properties Trust						
255 Washington St	Newton	MA	02458	617-796-8350	796-8349	655
NYSE: SNH ■ *TF:* 866-511-5038 ■ *Web:* www.snhreit.com						
Senior Lifestyle Corp						
303 E Upper Wacker Dr Ste 2400	Chicago	IL	60601	312-673-4333		672
TF: 800-277-5889 ■ *Web:* www.seniorlifestyle.com						

Phone | Fax | Class

Senior Market Sales Inc (SMS)
8420 W Dodge Rd Ste 510 .... Omaha NE 68114 402-397-3311 397-0455 390
TF: 800-786-5566 ■ *Web:* www.seniormarketsales.com

Senior Marketing Specialist
801 Gray Oak Dr .... Columbia MO 65201 800-689-2800 195
TF: 800-689-2800 ■ *Web:* www.smsteam.net

Senior Resource Group
500 Stevens Ave Ste 100 .... Solana Beach CA 92075 858-792-9300 656
Web: www.srgseniorliving.com

Senior Settlements LLC
1000 S Lenola Rd Bldg 1 Ste 202 .... Maple Shade NJ 08052 856-235-2133 235-1294 796
TF: 800-834-0628 ■ *Web:* www.seniorsettlementsllc.com

Senior Softball USA
2701 K St Ste 101A .... Sacramento CA 95816 916-326-5303 326-5304 48-22
TF: 888-244-9499 ■ *Web:* www.seniorsoftball.com

Senior Whole Health LLC (SWH)
58 Charles St .... Cambridge MA 02141 617-494-5353 494-5599 353
TF: 888-794-7268 ■ *Web:* www.seniorwholehealth.com

Senior World 6501 N Sheridan Rd .... Peoria IL 61614 309-495-4530 726
TF: 800-421-4371 ■ *Web:* ipmr.org

Seniority Benefit Group
6365 Riverside Dr .... Dublin OH 43017 614-799-1403 390
TF: 800-589-7326 ■ *Web:* www.senioritybenefitgroup.com

Seniors First Foundation Inc
5395 L B Mcleod Rd .... Orlando FL 32811 407-292-0177 305
Web: www.seniorsfirstinc.org

Seniorsplus 8 Falcon Rd .... Lewiston ME 04243 207-795-4010 795-4009 672
TF: 800-427-1241 ■ *Web:* www.seniorsplus.org

Sennett Security Products
4212A Technology Ct .... Chantilly VA 20151 703-803-8880 627
Web: banknote.com

Sennheiser Electronics Corp
1 Enterprise Dr .... Old Lyme CT 06371 860-434-9190 434-1759 246
TF: 877-736-6434 ■ *Web:* en-us.sennheiser.com

Seno Jewelry LLC
259 W 30th St 10th Fl .... New York NY 10001 212-868-3808 411
TF: 888-468-0888 ■ *Web:* www.ippolita.com

Seno Medical Instruments Inc
5253 Prue Rd Ste 315 .... San Antonio TX 78240 210-615-6501 475
Web: www.senomedical.com

Senomyx Inc 4767 Nexus Centre Dr .... San Diego CA 92121 858-646-8300 404-0752 145
NASDAQ: SNMX ■ *Web:* www.senomyx.com

Senor Fish 9530 Viscount Blvd Ste 1A .... El Paso TX 79925 915-598-3630 671

Senor Frogs
1304 Celebrity Cir R-8 .... Myrtle Beach SC 29577 843-444-5506 671
Web: www.senorfrogs.com

Senor Ric's 13200 E Mississippi Ave .... Aurora CO 80012 303-750-9000 671
Web: www.senorrics.net

Senova Systems Inc 1230 Bordeaux Dr .... Sunnyvale CA 94089 415-324-8505 419
Web: www.senovasystems.com

SenovvA Inc 1401 E Third St .... Los Angeles CA 90033 213-689-6900 689-6911 23
Web: www.senovva.com

Sensato Investors LLC
1 Sansome St Ste 3430 .... San Francisco CA 94104 415-391-4600 528
Web: www.sensatoinvestors.com

Senscio Systems Inc
1740 Massachusetts Ave .... Boxborough MA 01719 978-635-9090 177
TF: 800-638-8376 ■ *Web:* www.sensciosystems.com

Sense Corp
2731 Sutton Blvd Ste 200 .... Saint Louis MO 63143 314-266-3700 180
Web: www.sensecorp.com

Sensenbrenner F James (Rep R - WI)
2449 Rayburn Bldg .... Washington DC 20515 202-225-5101 225-3190 342-2
Web: sensenbrenner.house.gov

Sensible Vision Inc
40376 Blue Star Hwy Ste 11 .... Covert MI 49043 269-932-4548 809
Web: www.sensiblevision.com

Sensical Inc Decals 31115 Aurora Rd .... Solon OH 44139 216-641-1141 687
Web: sensical.com

Sensidyne Inc 16333 Bay Vista Dr .... Clearwater FL 33760 727-530-3602 539-0550 201
TF: 800-451-9444 ■ *Web:* www.sensidyne.com

Sensient Technologies Corp
777 E Wisconsin Ave .... Milwaukee WI 53202 414-271-6755 347-3785 296-15
NYSE: SXT ■ *TF:* 800-558-9892 ■ *Web:* www.sensient.com

Sensitech Inc
800 Cummings Ctr Ste 258x .... Beverly MA 01915 978-927-7033 171
TF: 800-843-8367 ■ *Web:* www.sensitech.com

Sensitile Systems LLC
1735 Holmes Rd .... Ypsilanti MI 48197 313-872-6314 499
TF: 800-784-7129 ■ *Web:* www.sensitile.com

Sensitron Semiconductor
221 W Industry Ct .... Deer Park NY 11729 631-586-7600 695
Web: www.sensitron.com

Senske Services 400 N Quay St .... Kennewick WA 99336 877-944-4007 577
TF: 877-944-4007 ■ *Web:* www.senske.com

Sensor Dynamics Inc
4568 Enterprise St .... Fremont CA 94538 510-623-1459 354
Web: sensordynamics.com

Sensor Geophysical Ltd
736-6 Ave SW Ste 1300 .... Calgary AB T2P3T7 403-237-7711 41
Web: sensorgeo.com

Sensor Systems Inc
8929 Fullbright Ave .... Chatsworth CA 91311 818-341-5366 341-9059 647
Web: www.sensorantennas.com

Sensor Systems LLC
2800 Anvil St N .... Saint Petersburg FL 33710 727-347-2181 347-7520 472
TF: 800-688-2181 ■ *Web:* www.sensorsllc.com

Sensorlink Corp 1360 Stonegate Way .... Ferndale WA 98248 360-595-1000 246
TF: 800-732-6762 ■ *Web:* www.sensorlink.com

Sensormatic Electronics Corp
6600 Congress Ave .... Boca Raton FL 33487 561-912-6000 912-6097 692
TF: 800-327-1765 ■ *Web:* www.sensormatic.com

SensorMedics Corp
22745 Savi Ranch Pkwy .... Yorba Linda CA 92887 714-283-2228 250
TF: 800-231-2466 ■ *Web:* www.carefusion.com

Sensorwise Inc 2908 Rogerdale Rd .... Houston TX 77042 713-952-3350 261
Web: www.sensorwise.com

Phone | Fax | Class

SensoryEffects Flavor Co
231 Rock Industrial Park Dr .... Bridgeton MO 63044 314-291-5444 296-37
TF: 800-422-5444 ■ *Web:* www.sensoryeffects.com

Senspex Inc
9798 Coors Blvd NW Bldg B .... Albuquerque NM 87114 505-891-0034 696
TF: 800-952-3386 ■ *Web:* www.senspex.com

Senstar Corp 119 John Cavanaugh Dr .... Ottawa ON K0A1L0 613-839-5572 693
Web: senstar.com

Sensus USA Inc
8601 Six Forks Rd Stes 300 & 700 .... Raleigh NC 27615 919-845-4000 201
TF: 800-638-3748 ■ *Web:* www.sensus.com

Sentara Careplex Hospital
3000 Colliseum Dr .... Hampton VA 23666 757-736-1000 374-3
TF: 800-736-8272 ■ *Web:* www.sentara.com

Sentara Healthcare
6015 Poplar Hall Dr .... Norfolk VA 23502 757-455-7000 353
Web: www.sentara.com

Sentara Leigh Hospital
830 Kempsville Rd .... Norfolk VA 23502 757-261-6000 374-3
TF: 800-237-4822 ■ *Web:* www.sentara.com/hospitals

Sentara Martha Jefferson Hospital (MJH)
500 Martha Jefferson Dr .... Charlottesville VA 22911 434-654-7000 374-3
TF: 888-652-6663 ■ *Web:* www.sentara.com

Sentara Norfolk General Hospital
600 Gresham Dr .... Norfolk VA 23507 434-517-3100 374-3
Web: www.sentara.com/hospitals

Sentara Obici Hospital
2800 Godwin Blvd .... Suffolk VA 23434 757-934-4000 374-3
TF: 800-736-8272 ■ *Web:* www.sentara.com

Sentara Virginia Beach General Hospital
1060 First Colonial Rd .... Virginia Beach VA 23454 757-395-8000 374-3
TF: 800-736-8272 ■ *Web:* www.sentara.com/hospitals

Sentara Williamsburg Regional Medical Ctr
100 Sentara Cir .... Williamsburg VA 23188 757-984-6000 374-3
Web: www.sentara.com

Sentari Technologies Inc
16775 Addison Rd Ste 600 .... Addison TX 75001 972-716-0893 180
Web: www.sentari.com

SENTEL Corp
2800 Eisenhower Ave Ste 300 .... Alexandria VA 22314 571-481-2000 481-2046 261
Web: www.sentel.com

Sentencing Project
1705 DeSales St NW 8th Fl .... Washington DC 20036 202-628-0871 628-1091 48-8
Web: sentencingproject.org

Sentient Energy Inc 880 Mitten Rd .... Burlingame CA 94010 650-523-6680 407
Web: www.sentient-energy.com

Sentient Jet 100 Grossman Dr 4th Fl .... Braintree MA 02184 781-763-0200 871-8002 13
TF: 866-602-0044 ■ *Web:* www.sentient.com

Sentinel & Enterprise PO Box 730 .... Fitchburg MA 01420 978-343-6911 342-1158 532-2
TF: 800-221-2078 ■ *Web:* www.sentinelandenterprise.com

Sentinel Bldg Systems Inc
237 S Fourth St PO Box 348 .... Albion NE 68620 402-395-5076 395-6369 307
TF: 800-327-0790 ■ *Web:* www.sentinelbuildings.com

Sentinel Brokers Company Inc
20 Broadway .... Massapequa NY 11758 516-541-9100 690

Sentinel Development Solutions Inc
4015 Beltline Rd Ste 100 .... Addison TX 75001 515-564-0585 692-8415* 809
**Fax Area Code: 972* ■ *TF:* 877-395-8976 ■ *Web:* www.sentinelds.com

Sentinel Fence LLC 1527 NC Hwy 711 .... Lumberton NC 28360 910-735-1351 567
Web: www.sent-fence.com

Sentinel Hotel 614 SW 11th Ave .... Portland OR 97205 503-224-3400 241-2122 379
TF: 888-246-5631 ■ *Web:* www.sentinelhotel.com

Sentinel Integrity Solutions Inc
6606 Miller Rd 2 .... Houston TX 77049 281-457-2225 743
Web: sentinelintegrity.com

Sentinel Offender Services LLC
201 Technology Dr .... Irvine CA 92618 949-453-1550 693
Web: www.sentineladvantage.com

Sentinel Power Services Inc
7517 E Pine St .... Tulsa OK 74115 918-359-0350 532-3
TF: 800-831-9550 ■ *Web:* www.sentinelpowerservices.com

Sentinel Process Systems Inc
3265 Sunset Ln .... Hatboro PA 19040 919-462-7108 329-9669* 330
**Fax Area Code: 888* ■ *TF:* 800-345-3569 ■ *Web:* www.sentinelprocess.com

Sentinel Real Estate Corp
1251 Ave of the Americas .... New York NY 10020 212-408-5000 603-8253 655
Web: www.sentinelcorp.com

Sentinel Structures Inc
477 S Peck Ave .... Peshtigo WI 54157 715-582-4544 582-4932 817
Web: www.sentinelstructures.com

Sentinel Systems Corp
1620 Kipling St .... Lakewood CO 80215 303-242-2000 532-3
TF: 800-456-9955 ■ *Web:* www.sentinelsystems.com

Sentinel Technologies Inc
2550 Warrenville Rd .... Downers Grove IL 60515 630-769-4300 175
TF: 800-769-4343 ■ *Web:* www.sentinel.com

Sentinel Transportation LLC
3521 Silverside Rd Ste 2A .... Wilmington DE 19810 302-477-1640 532-3
Web: www.sentineltrans.com

Sentinel Wealth Management Inc
11710 Plaza America Dr Ste 130 .... Reston VA 20190 703-787-5770 401
TF: 800-767-3263 ■ *Web:* www.sentinelwealth.com

Sentinel, The 457 E N St .... Carlisle PA 17013 717-243-2611 243-3121 532-2
TF: 800-829-5570 ■ *Web:* www.cumberlink.com

Sentinel, The 300 W Sixth St .... Hanford CA 93230 559-582-0471 532-2
TF: 888-606-0605 ■ *Web:* hanfordsentinel.com

Sentinel-Record
300 Spring St .... Hot Springs National Park AR 71902 501-623-7711 532-2
TF: 800-552-1055 ■ *Web:* www.hotsr.com

Senton Printing & Packaging Inc
1669 Oxford St E .... London ON N5V2Z5 519-455-5500 627
TF: 800-445-9808 ■ *Web:* www.senton.com

Sentran LLC 4355 E Lowell St Ste F .... Ontario CA 91761 909-605-1544 362
TF: 888-545-8988 ■ *Web:* www.sentranllc.com

Sentry 360 Security Inc
23807 W Andrew Rd Ste B .... Plainfield IL 60585 630-355-3440 693
Web: sentry360.com

Name / Address	City	State	ZIP	Phone	Fax	Class
Sentry Alarm Systems of America Inc						
8 Thomas Owens Way	Monterey	CA	93940	831-375-2727		693
TF: 800-424-7773 ■ *Web:* sentryalarm.com						
Sentry BioPharma Services Inc						
4605 Decatur Blvd Ameriplex Pk	Indianapolis	IN	46241	317-856-5889		583
TF: 866-757-7400 ■ *Web:* www.sentrybps.com						
Sentry Electric 185 Buffalo Ave	Freeport	NY	11520	516-379-4660	378-0624	439
Web: www.sentrylighting.com						
Sentry Equipment & Erectors Inc						
13150 E Lynchburg Salem Tpke	Forest	VA	24551	434-525-0769	525-1701	386
Web: www.sentryequipment.com						
Sentry Equipment Corp						
966 Blue Ribbon Cir N	Oconomowoc	WI	53066	262-567-7256	567-4523	419
Web: www.sentry-equip.com						
Sentry Group 900 Linden Ave	Rochester	NY	14625	585-381-4900	381-2940*	692
**Fax:* Cust Svc ■ *TF Cust Svc:* 800-828-1438 ■ *Web:* www.sentrysafe.com						
Sentry Hospitality Ltd						
136 E 57th St Ste 1003	New York	NY	10022	212-753-5347		463
Web: www.sentryhospitality.com						
Sentry Insurance A Mutual Co						
1800 N Point Dr	Stevens Point	WI	54481	715-346-6000		391-4
TF: 800-456-4642 ■ *Web:* www.sentry.com						
Sentry Insurance Co						
2 Technology Park Dr	Westford	MA	01886	800-373-6879	999-4642	391-4
TF: 800-373-6879 ■ *Web:* Www.sentry.com						
Sentry Investments Inc						
Commerce Court W 199 Bay St Ste 2700						
PO Box 108	Toronto	ON	M5L1E2	416-861-8729		528
TF: 888-246-6656 ■ *Web:* www.sentry.ca						
Sentry Life Insurance Co						
1800 N Pt Dr	Stevens Point	WI	54481	715-346-6000		391-2
TF: 800-373-6879 ■ *Web:* www.sentry.com						
Sentry Security LLC 339 Egidi Dr	Wheeling	IL	60090	847-353-7200		693
TF: 888-272-7080 ■ *Web:* www.sentrysecurity.com						
Sentry Technology Corp						
1881 Lakeland Ave	Ronkonkoma	NY	11779	800-645-4224	739-2124*	692
OTC: SKVY ■ **Fax Area Code:* 631 ■ *TF:* 800-645-4224 ■ *Web:* www.sentrytechnology.com						
Sentry Watch Inc 1705 Holbrook St	Greensboro	NC	27403	336-292-6468		693
TF: 800-632-4961 ■ *Web:* www.sentrywatch.com						
Senture LLC 460 Industrial Blvd	London	KY	40741	606-877-6670		624
Web: www.senture.com						
Senvoy LLC 115 SE Yamhill St	Portland	OR	97214	503-234-7722		311
TF: 866-373-6869 ■ *Web:* www.senvoy.com						
SEO com LLC						
14870 S Pony Express Rd Ste 100	Bluffdale	UT	84065	800-351-9081		7
TF: 800-351-9081 ■ *Web:* www.seo.com						
Seong's Sushi Bar 740 W Ninth St	Juneau	AK	99801	907-586-4778		671
Web: seongssushibar.com						
SEOP Inc 1621 Alton Pkwy Ste 105	Irvine	CA	92606	877-231-1557		7
TF: 877-231-1557 ■ *Web:* www.seop.com						
SEP (Seismic Energy Products LP)						
518 Progress Way	Athens	TX	75751	903-675-8571		676
SEP Communications LLC						
1100 Holland Dr	Boca Raton	FL	33487	561-998-0870		627
Web: sepcommunications.com						
sephora.com Inc						
525 Market St 1st Market Twr 32nd Fl	San Francisco	CA	94105	415-284-3300		214
TF Cust Svc: 877-737-4672 ■ *Web:* www.sephora.com						
SEPLSO (Southeastern Public Library System of Oklahoma)						
401 N Second St	McAlester	OK	74501	918-426-0456	569-8188*	434-3
**Fax Area Code:* 866 ■ *TF:* 800-562-9520 ■ *Web:* oklibrary.net						
SEPM (Society for Sedimentary Geology)						
4111 S Darlington Ste 100	Tulsa	OK	74135	918-610-3361	621-1685	49-19
TF: 800-865-9765 ■ *Web:* www.sepm.org						
Sepp Leaf Products Inc						
381 Pk Ave S Ste 1301	New York	NY	10016	212-683-2840	725-0308	44
TF: 800-971-7377 ■ *Web:* www.seppleaf.com						
SepSensor Inc						
257 Simarano Dr Annex II	Marlborough	MA	01752	508-229-2291		407
SEPTA (Southeastern Pennsylvania Transportation Authority)						
1234 Market St	Philadelphia	PA	19107	215-580-7800		468
Web: www.septa.org						
Septagon Construction 113 E Third St	Sedalia	MO	65301	660-827-2115		186
TF: 800-733-5999 ■ *Web:* www.septagon.com						
Sept-Iles Chamber of Commerce						
700 boul Laure Bureau 237	Sept-Iles	QC	G4R1Y1	418-968-3488	968-3432	137
Web: www.ccseptiles.com						
Sequa Corp Precoat Metals Div						
1310 Papin St 3rd Fl	Saint Louis	MO	63103	314-436-7010	436-7050	481
Web: www.precoatmetals.com						
Sequachee Valley Electric Co-op						
512 Cedar Ave PO Box 31	South Pittsburg	TN	37380	423-837-8605	837-9836	245
TF: 800-923-2203 ■ *Web:* www.svalleyec.com						
Sequatchie Concrete Service Inc						
406 Cedar Ave	South Pittsburg	TN	37380	423-837-7913		183
TF: 800-824-0824 ■ *Web:* www.seqconcrete.com						
Sequatchie County						
22 Cherry St PO Box 595	Dunlap	TN	37327	423-949-3479		338
Sequel Data Systems Inc						
11824 Jollyville Rd Ste 400	Austin	TX	78759	512-918-8841		196
TF: 800-818-7229 ■ *Web:* www.sequeldata.com						
Sequel Energy LLC						
8101 E Prentice Ave Ste 1175	Greenwood Village	CO	80111	303-468-2106		536
Web: www.sequelenergy.com						
Sequel Studio LLC 12 W 27th St	New York	NY	10001	212-994-4320		344
Web: sequelstudio.com						
Sequel Venture Partners						
4430 Arapahoe Ave Ste 220	Boulder	CO	80303	303-546-0400	546-9728	792
Web: www.sequelvc.com						
Sequence Controls Inc						
150 Rosamond St	Carleton	ON	K7C1V2	613-257-7356		203
TF: 800-663-1833 ■ *Web:* www.sequencecontrols.com						
Sequenom						
301 Michigan St NE Ste 580	Grand Rapids	MI	49503	877-821-7266	202-9108*	416
**Fax Area Code:* 858 ■ *TF:* 877-821-7266 ■ *Web:* www.sequenomcmm.com						
Sequenom Inc 3595 John Hopkins Ct	San Diego	CA	92121	858-202-9000	202-9001	85
NASDAQ: SQNM ■ *TF:* 877-821-7266 ■ *Web:* www.sequenom.com						
Sequent Energy Management LP						
1200 Smith St Ste 900	Houston	TX	77002	832-397-1700		194
Web: www.sequentenergy.com						
Sequim Bay State Park 269035 Hwy 101	Sequim	WA	98382	360-683-4235		565
Web: www.parks.wa.gov						
Sequins International Inc						
60-01 31st Ave	Woodside	NY	11377	718-204-0002	204-0999	745-5
TF: 800-221-5801 ■ *Web:* www.sequinsdirect.com						
Sequoia 1777 Botelho Dr Ste 300	Walnut Creek	CA	94596	925-945-0900		405
Web: www.experiencesequoia.com						
Sequoia & Kings Canyon National Parks						
47050 Generals Hwy	Three Rivers	CA	93271	559-565-3341	565-3730	564
Web: www.nps.gov/seki						
Sequoia Brewing Co 777 E Olive St	Fresno	CA	93728	559-264-5521		671
Web: sequoiabrewing.com						
Sequoia Capital						
2800 Sand Hill Rd Ste 101	Menlo Park	CA	94025	650-854-3927		792
TF: 800-321-1111 ■ *Web:* www.sequoiacap.com						
Sequoia Company of Restaurants						
1583 Coal Harbour Quay	Vancouver	BC	V6G3E7	604-687-5684		671
TF: 800-201-8596 ■ *Web:* www.vancouverdine.com						
Sequoia Equipment Company Inc						
PO Box 2747	Fresno	CA	93745	559-441-1122	441-0454	358
Web: www.sequoiaequipment.com						
Sequoia Fund Inc						
767 Fifth Ave Ste 4701	New York	NY	10153	212-832-5280	832-5298	528
TF: 800-686-6884 ■ *Web:* www.sequoiafund.com						
Sequoia Hospital 170 Alameda Ave	Redwood City	CA	94062	650-369-5811		374-3
Web: www.sequoiahospital.org						
Sequoia Insurance Co						
31 Upper Ragsdale Dr	Monterey	CA	93940	831-657-9459		391-2
Sequoia Park Zoo 3414 W St	Eureka	CA	95503	707-441-4263		823
Web: www.sequoiaparkzoo.net						
Sequoia Vacuum Systems Inc						
164 Jefferson Dr	Menlo Park	CA	94025	650-322-7281		788
Sequoias Portola Valley, The						
Northern California Presbyterian Homes & Services						
501 Portola Rd	Portola Valley	CA	94028	650-851-1501	851-5007	672
Web: www.ncphs.org						
Sequoias San Francisco						
1400 Geary Blvd	San Francisco	CA	94109	415-922-9700	567-2576	672
Web: www.ncphs.org						
Sequoyah Bay State Park						
6237 E 100th St N	Wagoner	OK	74467	918-683-0878	687-6797	565
TF: 800-622-6317 ■ *Web:* www.travelok.com						
Sequoyah County 120 E Chickasaw Ave	Sallisaw	OK	74955	918-775-4516		338
Web: sequoyah.oklahoma.usassessor.com						
Sequoyah State Park & Western Hills Guest Ranch						
17131 Pk 10	Hulbert	OK	74441	918-772-2046	772-3042	565
Web: www.travelok.com						
Sequoyah Technologies LLC						
6666 S Sheridan Ste 210	Tulsa	OK	74133	918-493-7200		809
Web: www.seqtek.com						
Seraaj Family Homes Inc						
400 Cotton Gin Rd	Montgomery	AL	36117	334-271-2402		260
Web: www.seraajfh.com						
Sera-Brynn LLC						
5806 Harbour View Blvd Ste 204	Suffolk	VA	23435	757-243-1257		196
Web: sera-brynn.com						
SeraCare Life Sciences Inc						
37 Birch St	Milford	MA	01757	508-244-6400	634-3394	89
NASDAQ: SRLS ■ *TF:* 800-676-1881 ■ *Web:* www.seracare.com						
Seracon Consulting 595 Rosebud Ct	Saline	MI	48176	734-944-1065		463
Serafina 2043 Eastlake Ave E	Seattle	WA	98102	206-323-0807		671
Web: www.serafinaseattle.com						
Serapid Inc 34100 Mound Rd	Sterling Heights	MI	48310	586-274-0774		757
TF: 800-663-4514 ■ *Web:* www.serapid.com						
Consulate General						
201 E Ohio St Ste 200	Chicago	IL	60611	312-670-6707		257
Web: www.scgchicago.org						
Embassy 2134 Kalorama Rd NW	Washington	DC	20008	202-332-0333	332-3933	257
Web: www.serbiaembusa.org						
Sercel Inc 17200 Pk Row	Houston	TX	77084	281-492-6688	579-6555	472
Web: www.sercel.com						
Serco Group Inc						
1818 Library St Ste 1000	Reston	VA	20190	703-939-6000	939-6001	271
Web: www.serco.com						
Serco Inc 1818 Library St Ste 1000	Reston	VA	20190	703-939-6000	939-6000	24
TF: 866-628-6458 ■ *Web:* www.serco-na.com						
Serendipity Interactive LLC						
181 N Main St	Mooresville	NC	28115	704-230-2352		195
Web: www.serendipityinteractive.com						
Serendipity Systems Inc PO Box 10477	Sedona	AZ	86339	928-282-6831	282-4383	178-10
Web: www.serendipsys.com						
Serengeti Eyewear Inc						
9200 Cody St	Overland Park	KS	66214	913-752-3400	752-3550	542
TF Cust Svc: 800-423-3537 ■ *Web:* www.serengeti-eyewear.com						
Serengeti Systems Inc						
1108 Lavaca St Ste 110 PMB 431	Austin	TX	78701	512-345-2211	345-2211	178-12
TF: 800-634-3122 ■ *Web:* www.serengeti.com						
Serenity Lane 1 Serenity Ln PO Box 8549	Coburg	OR	97408	541-687-1110	683-9061	726
TF: 800-543-9905 ■ *Web:* www.serenitylane.org						
Serenity Packaging Corp						
1601 E Main St Ste 2E	Saint Charles	IL	60174	630-762-9870		385
Web: www.serenitypkg.com						
Sereno Group Real Estate						
369 S San Antonio Rd	Los Altos	CA	94022	650-947-2900		652
Web: www.serenogroup.com						
Sererra Consulting Group LLC						
4590 MacArthur Blvd Ste 500	Newport Beach	CA	92660	877-276-3774	266-9032*	196
**Fax Area Code:* 949 ■ *TF:* 877-276-3774 ■ *Web:* www.sererra.com						
Seretta Construction Inc 2604 Clark St	Apopka	FL	32703	407-290-9440	290-9372	189-3
Web: www.seretta.com						
Serfco Termite & Pest Control Inc						
1701 S Walton Blvd	Bentonville	AR	72712	479-273-2220		577
Serfilco Ltd 2900 MacArthur Blvd	Northbrook	IL	60062	847-559-1777	559-1141	641
TF: 800-323-5431 ■ *Web:* www.serfilco.com						

Company / Address	City	State	Zip	Phone	Fax	Class
Sergeant Alvin C. York State Historic Park 2609 N York Hwy *Web:* tnstateparks.com/parks/about/sgt-alvin-c-york	Pall Mall	TN	38577	931-879-6456		565
Sergenian's Residential Flooring 2805 W Beltline Hwy *Web:* sergenians.com	Madison	WI	53713	608-271-1111		290
SERI (Society for Ecological Restoration International) 1017 O St NW *Fax Area Code: 270 ■ *TF:* 866-895-4735 ■ *Web:* ser.org	Washington	DC	20001	202-299-9518	626-5485*	48-13
Serigraph Inc 3801 E Decorah Rd *TF:* 800-279-6060 ■ *Web:* www.serigraph.com	West Bend	WI	53095	262-335-7200	335-7699	687
Serino Coyne Inc 1515 Broadway 36th Fl *Web:* www.serinocoyne.com	New York	NY	10036	212-626-2700		4
Serna & Co PC 6031 W Ih-20 Ste 251 *Web:* serna.com	Arlington	TX	76017	817-483-3884		2
Seroka & Assoc 200 S Executive Dr *TF:* 800-236-3699 ■ *Web:* www.seroka.com	Waukesha	WI	53005	262-523-3740		195
SERPs Inc 1410 NW Johnson St *Web:* serps.com	Portland	OR	97209	503-683-3470		387
Serra Automotive 3118 E Hill Rd *Web:* serrausa.com	Grand Blanc	MI	48439	810-694-1720		57
Serra Corp 3590 Snell Ave *Web:* www.serracorp.com	San Jose	CA	95133	510-651-7333	657-5860	697
Serra International Inc 75 Montgomery St Ste 300 *Web:* www.serraintl.com	Jersey City	NJ	07302	201-860-9600		311
Serra Retreat Ctr 3401 Serra Rd *Web:* www.serraretreat.com	Malibu	CA	90265	310-456-6631	456-9417	673
Serrano Hotel 405 Taylor St *TF:* 866-575-9941 ■ *Web:* www.serranohotel.com	San Francisco	CA	94102	415-885-2500	474-4879	379
Serrano Jose E (Rep D - NY) 2354 Rayburn HOB *Web:* serrano.house.gov	Washington	DC	20515	202-225-4361	225-6001	342-2
Serta Mattress/AW Inc 3 Golf Ctr Ste 392 *TF:* 888-557-3782 ■ *Web:* www.serta.com	Hoffman Estates	IL	60169	888-708-1466		471
Sertapak Packaging Corp 1039 Dundas St *TF:* 800-265-1162 ■ *Web:* www.sertapak.com	Woodstock	ON	N4S0B1	519-539-3330		601
Serti Informatique Inc 7555 Beclard St *TF:* 800-361-6615 ■ *Web:* www.serti.com	Montreal	QC	H1J2S5	514-493-1909		196
Sertoma International 1912 E Meyer Blvd *TF:* 800-593-5646 ■ *Web:* www.sertoma.org	Kansas City	MO	64132	816-333-8300	333-4320	48-5
Serva Group LLC 1045 Keystone Ave *Web:* www.servagroup.com	Catoosa	OK	74015	918 266 0700		538
Serv-a-lite Products Inc 3451 Morton Dr *TF:* 800-800-4900 ■ *Web:* www.hillmangroup.com	East Moline	IL	61244	800-800-4900		351
Servall Co 6761 E Ten Mile Rd *TF:* 800-856-9874 ■ *Web:* 1stsourceservall.com	Center Line	MI	48015	586 754 0006		00
Servant Systems Inc 13770 Is Lake Rd *TF:* 800-598-9460 ■ *Web:* servantsystems.com	Chelsea	MI	48118	734-475-1619		809
Servco Pacific Inc 2850 Pukoloa Ste 300 *Web:* www.servco.com	Honolulu	HI	96819	808-564-1300	523-3937	57
SERVE 5900 Summit Ave Ste 201 *TF:* 800-755-3277 ■ *Web:* www.serve.org	Browns Summit	NC	27214	336-315-7400	315-7457	668
Serve You Custom Prescription Management 10201 Innovation Dr Ste 600 *TF:* 888-243-6890 ■ *Web:* www.serve-you-rx.com	Milwaukee	WI	53226	414-410-8100	410-8181	586
Server Products Inc 3601 Pleasant Hill Rd PO Box 98 *TF:* 800-558-8722 ■ *Web:* www.server-products.com	Richfield	WI	53076	262-628-5600	628-5110	298
Server Room Furniture 4775 Paris St *TF:* 800-468-6888 ■ *Web:* www.periphman.com	Denver	CO	80239	303-371-8651	371-8643	658
Server Technology Inc 1040 Sandhill Dr *TF:* 800-835-1515 ■ *Web:* www.servertech.com	Reno	NV	89521	775-284-2000	284-2065	176
ServerLift Corp 17453 N 25th Ave *Web:* www.serverlift.com	Phoenix	AZ	85023	602-254-1557		196
ServerLogic Corp 2800 Northup Way Ste 120 *Web:* www.serverlogic.com	Bellevue	WA	98004	425-803-0378		177
Service 800 Inc 2190 W Wayzata Blvd *Web:* www.service800inc.com	Minneapolis	MN	55356	952-475-3747		466
Service by Air Inc 222 Crossways Pk Dr *TF:* 800-243-5545 ■ *Web:* www.sbaglobal.com	Woodbury	NY	11797	800-243-5545		12
Service Champ Inc 180 New Britain Blvd *Web:* www.servicechamp.com	Chalfont	PA	18914	215-822-8500		61
Service Communications Inc 15223 NE 90th St Ste 100 *TF:* 800-488-0468 ■ *Web:* www.servicecommunications.com	Redmond	WA	98052	800-488-0468		179
Service Companies Inc, The 14750 NW 77th Court Ste 100 *TF:* 800-385-8800 ■ *Web:* www.theservicecompanies.com	Miami Lakes	FL	33016	305-681-8800		393
Service Construction Supply Inc PO Box 13405 *TF:* 866-729-4968 ■ *Web:* www.serviceconstructionsupply.com	Birmingham	AL	35202	205-252-3158	252-5720	191-3
Service Corp International 1929 Allen Pkwy *NYSE: SCI* ■ *TF:* 800-758-5804 ■ *Web:* www.sci-corp.com	Houston	TX	77019	713-522-5141		510
Service Electric Cable TV & Communications 2260 Ave A *TF:* 800-232-9100 ■ *Web:* www.sectv.com	Bethlehem	PA	18017	610-865-9100	865-7888	116
Service Electric Supply Inc 15424 Oakwood Dr *TF:* 800-426-7575 ■ *Web:* www.servelectric.com	Romulus	MI	48174	734-229-9100	229-9101	246
Service Elements Inc 15029 N Thompson Peak Pkwy Ste B111-444 *Web:* www.serviceelements.com	Scottsdale	AZ	85260	480-538-0123		256
Service Employees International Union 1800 Massachusetts Ave NW *TF:* 800-424-8592 ■ *Web:* www.seiu.org	Washington	DC	20036	202-730-7000		414
Service Express Inc 3854 Broadmoor Ave SE *Web:* www.serviceexpress.com	Grand Rapids	MI	49512	616-698-2221		175
Service General Corp 13 E Laurel St *TF:* 800-659-2273 ■ *Web:* www.servicegeneral.net	Georgetown	DE	19947	302-856-3500		141
Service Graphics LLC 8350 Allison Ave *TF:* 800-884-9876 ■ *Web:* www.mysgi.com	Indianapolis	IN	46268	317-471-8246		687
Service Guide Inc 3605 Warren Meadville Rd *Web:* www.serviceguideinc.com	Cortland	OH	44410	330-637-6060		454
Service Ideas Inc 2354 Ventura Dr *TF:* 800-328-4493 ■ *Web:* www.serviceideas.com	Woodbury	MN	55125	651-730-8800	730-8880	300
Service Industry Assn (SIA) 2164 Histroic Decatur Rd Villa 19 *Web:* www.servicenetwork.org	San Diego	CA	92106	619-221-9200		49-12
Service King Collision Repair Centers 808 S Central Expy *TF:* 866-730-5464 ■ *Web:* www.serviceking.com	Richardson	TX	75080	972-960-7595	980-4266	62-4
Service Linen Supply Inc 903 S Fourth St *Web:* www.servicelinen.com	Henton	WA	98057	425-255-8686		442
Service Litho-Print Inc 50 W Fernau Ave *Web:* www.service-litho.com	Oshkosh	WI	54901	920-231-3060		627
Service Management Systems 7135 Charlotte Pike Ste 100 *Web:* www.smsclean.com	Nashville	TN	37209	615-399-1839		152
Service Master By Guthrie 405 N Jefferson Ave *Web:* www.smbymccann.com	Canonsburg	PA	15317	724-746-5700		104
Service Motor Co W9614 State Hwy 96 *Web:* www.servicemotor.com	Dale	WI	54931	920-779-4311		385
Service Objects Inc 133 E de la Guerra St Ste 10 *Web:* www.serviceobjects.com	Santa Barbara	CA	93101	805-963-1700		177
Service Oil Inc 1718 E Main Ave *Web:* www.stamart.com	West Fargo	ND	58078	701-277-1050	277-1723	324
Service Paper Co 4501 W Vly Hwy E Ste A *Web:* bunzldistribution.com	Sumner	WA	98390	253-321-3300		96
Service Performance Insight 6260 Winter Hazel Dr Four Bridges *Web:* www.spiresearch.com	Liberty Township	OH	45044	513-759-5443		466
Service Products Inc 5900 W 51st St *Fax Area Code: 708 ■ *TF:* 800-567-1877 ■ *Web:* www.serviceproductsinc.com	Chicago	IL	60638	773-767-2360	496-1818*	233
Service Roundtable 131 W Main St *Web:* www.serviceroundtable.com	Lewisville	TX	75057	817-416-0978		610
Service Spring Corp 4370 Moline Martin Rd *TF:* 800-752-8522 ■ *Web:* www.sscorp.com	Millbury	OH	43447	419-838-0081	838-6071	718
Service Steel Aerospace Corp 4609 70th St E *TF:* 800-426-9794 ■ *Web:* www.ssa-corp.com	Fife	WA	98424	253-627-2910		492
Service Steel Inc 4200 E Schrimsher Lane SW Ste 2B7	Huntsville	AL	35805	503-224-9500	243-6697	492
Service Systems Assoc Inc 4699 Marion St *Web:* www.kmssa.com	Denver	CO	80216	303-322-3031		328
Service Technologies Inc 1284 Logan Cir NW *Web:* servicetechnologies.net	Atlanta	GA	30318	404-355-6262		196
ServiceMaster Clean 3839 Forrest Hill Irene Rd *TF General:* 844-319-5401 ■ *Web:* www.servicemasterclean.com/about-us/contact us	Memphis	TN	38125	800-245-4622		152
Servigistics Sns Inc 2300 Windy Ridge Pkwy 450 N Tower	Atlanta	GA	30339	770-565-2340		180
Serviko Inc 2670 Rue Duchesne *Web:* www.serviko.com	Saint-laurent	QC	H4R1J3	514-332-2600		260
ServIT Inc 3721 Cherokee St *TF:* 800-752-4542 ■ *Web:* www.servit.net	Kennesaw	GA	30144	770-499-6300		196
Servo Corp of America 123 Frost St *Web:* www.servo.com	Westbury	NY	11590	516-938-9700	938-9644	544
Servo Products Co 34940 Lakeland Blvd *TF:* 800-521-7359 ■ *Web:* www.servoproductsco.com	Eastlake	OH	44095	440-942-9999	942-9100	455
Servotronics Inc 1110 Maple St PO Box 300 *NYSE: SVT* ■ *Web:* www.servotronics.com	Elma	NY	14059	716-655-5990	655-6012	789
Servpro Industries Inc 801 Industrial Blvd *TF:* 800-826-9586 ■ *Web:* www.servpro.com	Gallatin	TN	37066	615-451-0600	451-0291	152
Serv-U-Clean 207 Edgeley Blvd *Web:* www.servuclean.com	Concord	ON	L4K4B5	416-667-0696		152
SERVUS 4201 Mannheim Rd Ste A *Web:* www.greatservus.com	Jasper	IN	47546	812-482-3212		670
SES Advisors Inc 10 Shurs Ln Ste 102 *TF:* 800-935-9935 ■ *Web:* www.sesadvisors.com	Philadelphia	PA	19127	215-508-1600		194
SES World Skies 4 Research Way *Fax: Mktg ■ *Web:* www.ses.com	Princeton	NJ	08540	609-987-4000	987-4517*	681
SESAC Inc 55 Music Sq E *TF:* 800-826-9996 ■ *Web:* www.sesac.com	Nashville	TN	37203	615-320-0055	321-6290	48-4
Sesame Inn 715 Washington Rd *Web:* sesameinn.com	Pittsburgh	PA	15228	412-341-2555		671
Sesame Place 100 Sesame Rd *Web:* www.sesameplace.com	Langhorne	PA	19047	215-752-7070	741-5307	32
Sesame Software Inc 5201 Great America Pkwy Ste 320 *TF:* 866-474-7575 ■ *Web:* www.sesamesoftware.com	Santa Clara	CA	94160	408-550-7999		260
Sesame Workshop 1 Lincoln Plaza *Web:* www.sesameworkshop.org	New York	NY	10023	212-595-3456		514
Sesco Lighting Inc 1133 W Morse Blvd Ste 100 *Web:* www.sescolighting.com	Winter Park	FL	32789	407-629-6100	629-6168	439
SESHA (Semiconductor Environmental Safety & Health Assn) 1313 Dolley Madison Blvd Ste 402 *TF:* 800-883-0698 ■ *Web:* www.seshaonline.org	McLean	VA	22101	703-790-1745	790-2672	49-19

Phone | Fax | Class

SESI (Science & Engineering Services)
6992 Columbia Gateway Dr, Columbia MD 21046 — 443-539-0139 — 544
Web: www.sesi-md.com

Sesquicentennial State Park
9564 Two Notch Rd, Columbia SC 29223 — 803-788-2706 — 788-4414 — 565
TF: 888-245-9300 ■ *Web:* www.southcarolinaparks.com

SESRC (Social & Economic Sciences Research Ctr)
Washington State University
Wilson Hall Rm 133 PO Box 644014, Pullman WA 99164 — 509-335-1511 — 335-0116 — 668
TF: 800-932-5393 ■ *Web:* www.sesrc.wsu.edu

Sessions Pete (Rep R - TX)
2233 Rayburn HOB, Washington DC 20515 — 202-225-2231 — 225-5878 — 342-2
Web: sessions.house.gov

Sessions Specialty Co
5090 Styers Ferry Rd, Lewisville NC 27023 — 336-766-2880 — 723-0055* — 146
**Fax Area Code:* 800 ■ *TF:* 800-763-0077 ■ *Web:* www.sessionsusa.com

Set & Service Resources LLC
8303 Six Forks Rd Ste 207, Raleigh NC 27615 — 919-787-5571 — 260
TF: 800-561-3357 ■ *Web:* www.sasrlink.com

SET Consulting Inc
5821 Windermere Ln, Fairfield OH 45014 — 240-296-0800 — 463
Web: www.setconsulting.com

Set Solutions Inc
1800 W Loop S Ste 700, Houston TX 77027 — 713-956-6600 — 956-9678 — 174
TF: 888-353-0574 ■ *Web:* www.setsolutions.com

SETA (Southeast Tissue Alliance)
6241 NW 23rd St Ste 400, Gainesville FL 32653 — 352-248-2114 — 545
TF: 866-432-1164 ■ *Web:* www.donorcare.org

Seta Corp 6400 E Rogers Cir, Boca Raton FL 33499 — 561-994-2660 — 459
Web: www.setacorporation.com

SETAC (Society of Environmental Toxicology & Chemistry)
1010 N 12th Ave, Pensacola FL 32501 — 850-469-1500 — 469-9778 — 49-19
Web: www.setac.org

Setai, The 2001 Collins Ave, Miami Beach FL 33139 — 305-520-6000 — 379
TF: 888-625-7500 ■ *Web:* www.thesetaihotel.com

Setco Sales Co 5880 Hillside Ave, Cincinnati OH 45233 — 513-941-5110 — 941-6913 — 455
TF: 800-543-0470 ■ *Web:* www.setco.com

Setcom Corp
3019 Alvin DeVane Blvd Ste 560, Austin TX 78741 — 650-965-8020 — 647
TF: 800-645-1285 ■ *Web:* www.setcomcorp.com

Setel 1165 s Sixth st, Macclenny FL 32063 — 904-259-1300 — 387
TF: 800-662-0716 ■ *Web:* setel.net

SETEL UC
720 Cool Springs Blvd Ste 520, Franklin TN 37067 — 615-874-6000 — 787
TF: 800-743-1340 ■ *Web:* seteluc.com

SetFocus LLC 4 Century Dr, Parsippany NJ 07054 — 973-889-0211 — 260
Web: www.setfocus.com

Sethness Products Co
3422 W Touhy Ave, Lincolnwood IL 60712 — 847-329-2080 — 329-2090 — 296-15
TF: 888-772-1880 ■ *Web:* www.sethness.com

Setina Manufacturing Company Inc
2926 Yelm Hwy SE, Olympia WA 98501 — 800-426-2627 — 393
TF: 800-426-2627 ■ *Web:* www.setina.com

Seton Hall University
400 S Orange Ave, South Orange NJ 07079 — 973-761-9332 — 275-2321* — 166
**Fax:* Admissions ■ *TF:* 800-992-4723 ■ *Web:* www.shu.edu

Seton Hall University Immaculate Conception Seminary
400 S Orange Ave, South Orange NJ 07079 — 973-761-9575 — 167-3
TF: 800-843-4255 ■ *Web:* www.shu.edu

Seton Hill University
1 Seton Hill Dr, Greensburg PA 15601 — 724-838-4255 — 830-1294* — 166
**Fax:* Admissions ■ *TF:* 800-826-6234 ■ *Web:* www.setonhill.edu

Seton Home Study School
1350 Progress Dr, Front Royal VA 22630 — 540-636-9990 — 685
TF: 800-542-1066 ■ *Web:* www.setonhome.org

Seton Hotel 144 E 40th St, New York NY 10016 — 212-889-5301 — 463
TF: 866-697-3866 ■ *Web:* www.setonhotelny.com

Seton Imaging 2950 Elmwood Ave, Buffalo NY 14217 — 716-447-6856 — 592
Web: www.setonimaging.com

Seton League House 3207 Medical Pkwy, Austin TX 78705 — 512-324-1999 — 372
Web: www.seton.net

Seton Medical Ctr 1201 W 38th St, Austin TX 78705 — 512-324-1000 — 374-3
Web: www.seton.net

Seton Medical Ctr 1900 Sullivan Ave, Daly City CA 94015 — 650-992-4000 — 374-3
TF: 800-371-2176 ■ *Web:* seton.verity.org

Seton Medical Ctr Coastside
600 Marine Blvd, Moss Beach CA 94038 — 650-563-7100 — 450
Web: verity.org

Seton Shoal Creek Hospital
3501 Mills Ave, Austin TX 78731 — 512-324-2000 — 374-5
TF: 800-749-6160 ■ *Web:* www.seton.net

Setpoint Systems Inc 2835 Commerce Way, Ogden UT 84401 — 801-621-4117 — 194
Web: www.setpointusa.com

Setra Systems Inc 159 Swanson Rd, Boxborough MA 01719 — 978-263-1400 — 264-0292 — 472
TF: 800-257-3872 ■ *Web:* www.setra.com

Settle & Pou PC 3333 Lee Pkwy 8th Fl, Dallas TX 75219 — 214-520-3300 — 428
TF: 800-538-4661 ■ *Web:* www.settlepou.com

Settlers Life Insurance Co
1969 Lee Hwy, Bristol VA 24201 — 276-645-4300 — 645-4399 — 391-2
TF: 800-523-2650

Setton Pistachio of Terra Bella Inc
9370 Rd 234 PO Box 11089, Terra Bella CA 93270 — 559-535-6050 — 535-6089 — 297-11
Web: www.settonfarms.com

Setu Inc 388 B Great Rd Ste 20, Acton MA 01720 — 978-263-0262 — 809
Web: www.setu.com

Setzer Pharmacy Inc 1685 Rice St, St Paul MN 55113 — 651-488-0251 — 237
Web: setzerrx.com

Seubert Excavators Inc 604 King St, Cottonwood ID 83522 — 208-962-3501 — 189-5

Seva Foundation 1786 Fifth St, Berkeley CA 94710 — 510-845-7382 — 305
TF: 877-764-7382 ■ *Web:* www.seva.org

Seva Technologies LLC
1618 Mahan Ctr Blvd, Tallahassee FL 32308 — 850-391-4832 — 226
TF: 800-486-1571 ■ *Web:* www.sevatechnologies.com

Sevatec Inc
3112 Fairview Park Dr, Falls Church VA 22042 — 571-766-1300 — 196
Web: www.sevatec.com

Sevcon 155 Northboro Rd, Southborough MA 01772 — 508-281-5500 — 203
NASDAQ: SEV ■ *Web:* www.sevcon.com

Seven Arrows Elementary School Inc
15240 La Cruz Dr, Pacific Palisades CA 90272 — 310-230-0257 — 685
Web: www.sevenarrows.com

Seven Bros Grill 846 Market St, Paterson NJ 07513 — 973-684-2579 — 671

Seven Crown Resorts Inc PO Box 16247, Irvine CA 92623 — 949-588-7400 — 378
Web: www.sevencrown.com

Seven Days
255 S Champlain St Ste 5 PO Box 1164, Burlington VT 05401 — 802-864-5684 — 532-5
Web: www.7dvt.com

Seven Degrees
891 Laguna Canyon Rd, Laguna Beach CA 92651 — 949-376-1555 — 196
TF: 800-478-9702 ■ *Web:* www.seven-degrees.com

Seven Dials Media 2449 Wendover Dr, Naperville IL 60565 — 630-355-6199 — 4

Seven Gables Inn 26 N Meramec Ave, Saint Louis MO 63105 — 314-863-8400 — 863-8846 — 379
TF: 800-433-6590 ■ *Web:* sevengablesinn.com

Seven Glaciers Restaurant
1000 Arlberg Ave, Girdwood AK 99587 — 907-754-2237 — 671

Seven Hills 1550 Hyde St, San Francisco CA 94109 — 415-775-1550 — 671
Web: sevenhillssf.com

Seven Lakes State Park
14390 Fish Lake Rd, Holly MI 48442 — 248-634-7271 — 565
Web: www.michigandnr.com

Seven Lazy P Guest Ranch PO Box 178, Choteau MT 59422 — 406-466-2044 — 239
Web: www.sevenlazyp.com

Seven Oaks Capital Assoc LLC
7854 Anselmo Ln PO Box 82360, Baton Rouge LA 70810 — 225-757-1919 — 757-1916 — 272
TF: 800-511-4588 ■ *Web:* www.sevenoakscapital.com

Seven Oaks General Hospital
2300 McPhillips St, Winnipeg MB R2V3M3 — 204-632-7133 — 697-2106 — 374-2
Web: sogh.ca

Seven Peaks Water Park
1330 East 300 North, Provo UT 84606 — 801-373-8777 — 32
Web: www.sevenpeaks.com

Seven Pines National Cemetery
400 E Williamsburg Rd, Sandston VA 23150 — 804-795-2031 — 795-1064 — 136
TF: 800-535-1117 ■ *Web:* www.cem.va.gov/cems/nchp/sevenpines.asp

Seven R Transportation Inc
2818 Queen City Dr Ste G, Charlotte NC 28266 — 704-391-0694 — 311
Web: www.sevenr.com

Seven Rivers Regional Medical Ctr (SRRMC)
6201 N Suncoast Blvd, Crystal River FL 34428 — 352-795-6560 — 795-8369 — 374-3
TF: 800-339-1811 ■ *Web:* www.sevenriversregional.com

Seven Seventeen Credit Union Inc
3181 Larchmont Ave NE, Warren OH 44483 — 330-372-8100 — 219
Web: www.sscu.net

Seven Springs Mountain Resort
777 Waterwheel Dr, Champion PA 15622 — 814-352-7777 — 669
TF: 800-452-2223 ■ *Web:* www.7springs.com

Seven Step RPO 3 Ctr Plaza, Boston MA 02108 — 212-334-9750 — 260
Web: www.sevensteprpo.com

Seven-Eleven Hawaii Inc
1755 Nuuanu Ave, Honolulu HI 96817 — 808-526-1711 — 204

Sevenrooms Inc 127 W 24th St 5th Fl, New York NY 10011 — 212-242-5607 — 393
Web: www.sevenrooms.com

Sevenson Environmental Services Inc
2749 Lockport Rd, Niagara Falls NY 14305 — 716-284-0431 — 284-7645 — 667
Web: www.sevenson.com

Seventh Generation Inc 60 Lake St, Burlington VT 05401 — 802-658-3773 — 658-1771 — 151
TF: 800-456-1191 ■ *Web:* www.seventhgeneration.com

Seventh Mountain Resort
18575 SW Century Dr, Bend OR 97702 — 541-382-8711 — 669
TF: 800-428-1932 ■ *Web:* www.seventhmountain.com

Seventh-day Adventist World Church
12501 Old Columbia Pike, Silver Spring MD 20904 — 301-680-6000 — 680-6090 — 48-20
TF: 800-226-1119 ■ *Web:* www.adventist.org

Seventrees Corp 2181 M-139 S, Benton Harbor MI 49022 — 269-925-8111 — 400
TF: 800-839-7574 ■ *Web:* www.7trees.com

SevenTwenty Strategies
1220 19th St NW Ste 300, Washington DC 20036 — 202-962-3955 — 225
TF: 800-296-2747 ■ *Web:* www.720strategies.com

Seventy Seven Energy Inc
777 NW 63rd St, Oklahoma City OK 73116 — 405-608-7777 — 540
Web: www.77nrg.com

Severance Hall 11001 Euclid Ave, Cleveland OH 44106 — 216-231-7300 — 572
TF: 800-686-1141 ■ *Web:* www.clevelandorchestra.com

Severn Bancorp Inc
200 Westgate Cir Ste 200, Annapolis MD 21401 — 410-260-2000 — 841-6296 — 70
NASDAQ: SVBI ■ *TF:* 800-752-5854 ■ *Web:* www.severnbank.com

Severn Trent Services
580 Virginia Dr Ste 300, Fort Washington PA 19034 — 215-646-9201 — 806
TF: 800-637-8873 ■ *Web:* www.severntrentservices.com

Severson Dells Nature Ctr
8786 Montague Rd, Rockford IL 61102 — 815-335-2915 — 335-2471 — 50-5
Web: www.seversondells.com

Sevier County 115 N Third St Ste 102, De Queen AR 71832 — 870-642-2852 — 642-3896 — 338
TF: 800-501-1754 ■ *Web:* www.seviercountyar.com

Sevier County 125 Ct Ave Ste 108 W, Sevierville TN 37862 — 865-453-4654 — 453-8763 — 338
Web: www.seviercountytn.org

Sevier County Public Library
408 High St, Sevierville TN 37862 — 865-453-3532 — 365-1667 — 434-3
TF: 800-945-6500 ■ *Web:* www.sevierlibrary.org

Sevilla Riverside
3252 Mission Inn Ave, Riverside CA 92507 — 951-778-0611 — 671
Web: www.cafesevilla.com

Seville Flexpack Corp
9905 S Ridgeview Dr, Oak Creek WI 53154 — 414-761-2751 — 761-3140 — 608
Web: sevilleflexpack.com

Sevin Rosen Funds
13455 Noel Rd Ste 1670, Dallas TX 75240 — 972-702-1100 — 702-1103 — 792
TF: 800-694-4460 ■ *Web:* www.srfunds.com

Seviroli Foods 601 Brook St, Garden City NY 11530 — 516-222-6220 — 222-0534 — 296-36
Web: www.seviroli.com

Sevy's Grill 8201 Preston Rd Ste 100, Dallas TX 75225 — 214-265-7389 — 671
Web: www.sevys.com

Sew Biz Industries 174 Cross St, Central Falls RI 02863 — 401-724-8410 — 155-6

Seward & Kissel 1 Battery Park Plaza, New York NY 10004 — 212-574-1200 — 480-8421 — 428
Web: www.sewkis.com

Name / Address	City	State	Zip	Phone	Fax	Class
Seward & Monde 296 State St *Web:* sewardmonde.com	North Haven	CT	06473	203-248-9341		2
Seward Convention & Visitors Bureau 2001 Seward Hwy *TF:* 800-257-7760 ■ *Web:* seward.com	Seward	AK	99664	907-224-8051	224-5353	206
Seward County 515 N Washington *Web:* www.sewardcountyks.org	Liberal	KS	67901	620-626-3212		338
Seward County PO Box 190 *Web:* www.connectseward.org	Seward	NE	68434	402-643-2883		338
Seward County Community College 1801 N Campus Ave PO Box 1137 *TF:* 800-373-9951 ■ *Web:* www.sccc.edu	Liberal	KS	67905	620-624-1951	629-2725	162
Seward County Rural Public Power District 3111 Progressive Rd PO Box 69 *Web:* www.sewardppd.com	Seward	NE	68434	402-643-2951	646-4695	245
Seward Motor Freight Inc PO Box 126 *TF:* 800-786-4468 ■ *Web:* www.sewardmotor.com	Seward	NE	68434	402-643-4503	643-3199	780
Sewell C Biggs Museum of American Art 406 Federal St *TF:* 800-225-8331 ■ *Web:* www.biggsmuseum.org	Dover	DE	19901	302-674-2111	674-5133	520
Sewell Printing Service Inc 2697 Apple Valley Rd NE *Web:* www.sewellprinting.com	Atlanta	GA	30319	404 237 2553		627
Sewell Terri A (Rep D - AL) 2201 Rayburn HOB *Web:* sewell.house.gov	Washington	DC	20515	202-225-2665	226-9567	342-2
Sewerage & Water Board of New Orleans 625 Saint Joseph St Rm 140 *TF:* 800-981-6652 ■ *Web:* www.swbno.org	New Orleans	LA	70165	504-529-2837		804
SEW-Eurodrive Inc 1295 Old Spartanburg Hwy *TF:* 800-428-9347 ■ *Web:* www.seweurodrive.com	Lyman	SC	29365	864-439-7537	439-0566	709
Sewickley Valley Hospital 720 Blackburn Rd *TF:* 800-400-6180 ■ *Web:* www.heritagevalley.org	Sewickley	PA	15143	412-741-6600		374-3
Sewn Products Equipment Suppliers Assn (SPESA) 9650 Strickland Rd Ste 103-324 *Web:* www.spesa.org	Raleigh	NC	27615	919-872-8909	872-1915	49-13
Sewon America Inc 1000 Sewon Blvd *Web:* www.se-won.com/company/com05.html	La Grange	GA	30240	706-298-5800		186
Sex & Love Addicts Anonymous (SLAA) 1550 NE Loop 410 Ste 118 *Web:* www.slaafws.org	San Antonio	TX	78209	210-828-7900	828-7922	48-21
Sex Addicts Anonymous (SAA) PO Box 70949 *TF:* 800-477-8191 ■ *Web:* www.saa-recovery.org	Houston	TX	77270	713-869-4902	692 0105	48-21
Sexaholics Anonymous (SA) PO Box 3565 *TF:* 866-424-8777 ■ *Web:* www.sa.org	Brentwood	TN	37024	615-370-6062	370-0882	48-21
Sexauer Ltd 3-6990 Creditview Rd	Mississauga	ON	L5N8R9	905-821-8292		612
Sexton Printing Inc 250 Lothenbach Ave *Web:* www.sextonprinting.com	St. Paul	MN	55118	651-457-9255		627
Seybold John & Company Ltd 800 Busse Hwy Ste 200 *Web:* www.johnseybold.com	Park Ridge	IL	60068	847-696-1060		2
Seyer Industries Inc 66 Patmos Ct *Web:* www.seyerind.com	St. Peters	MO	63376	636-928-1190		697
Seyfarth Shaw LLP 131 S Dearborn St Ste 2400 *Web:* www.seyfarth.com	Chicago	IL	60603	312-460-5000	460-7000	428
Seyferth & Associates Inc 40 Monroe Ctr NW *TF:* 800-435-9539 ■ *Web:* www.seyferthpr.com	Grand Rapids	MI	49503	616-776-3511		636
Seymour Duncan Inc 5427 Hollister Ave *TF:* 800-738-6226 ■ *Web:* www.seymourduncan.com	Santa Barbara	CA	93111	805-964-9610		526
Seymour Johnson Air Force Base 1510 Wright Bros Ave *TF:* 800-525-0102 ■ *Web:* www.seymourjohnson.af.mil	Seymour Johnson AFB	NC	27531	919-722-0027	722-0007	497-1
Seymour Mfg Co Inc PO Box 248 *Web:* www.seymourmidwest.com	Seymour	IN	47274	812-522-2900		758
Seymour of Sycamore Inc 917 Crosby Ave *TF:* 800-435-4482 ■ *Web:* www.seymourpaint.com	Sycamore	IL	60178	815-895-9101	895-8475	550
Seyon Lodge State Park 1 National Life Dr *TF:* 888-409-7579 ■ *Web:* www.vtstateparks.com/htm/seyon.htm	Vermont	VT	05620	802-584-3829		565
SF Weekly 185 Berry St Ste 3800 *Web:* www.sfweekly.com	San Francisco	CA	94107	415-536-8100	777-1839	532-5
SFAA (Surety & Fidelity Assn of America) 1101 Connecticut Ave NW Ste 800 *Web:* www.surety.org	Washington	DC	20036	202-463-0600	463-0606	49-9
SFASU (Stephen F Austin State University Steen Library) 1936 N St *TF:* 800 765-1534 ■ *Web:* www.sfasu.edu	Nacogdoches	TX	75962	936-468-3401		434-6
SFB (Security Federal Bank) 238 Richland Ave W *TF:* 866-851-3000 ■ *Web:* www.securityfederalbank.com	Aiken	SC	29801	803-641-3000		71
SFC (Sandridge Food Corp) 133 Commerce Dr *TF:* 800-627-2523 ■ *Web:* www.sandridge.com	Medina	OH	44256	330-725-2348	722-3998	296-33
SFC Graphics 110 E Woodruff Ave *TF:* 800-537-1130 ■ *Web:* www.sfcgraphics.com	Toledo	OH	43604	419-255-1283		701
Sfcc Inc 2410 Squire Pl Ste B *Web:* www.sfccinc.net	Dallas	TX	75234	972-484-2480		186
SFE Investment Counsel Inc 801 S Figueroa St Ste 2100 *TF:* 800-445-6320 ■ *Web:* www.sfeic.com	Los Angeles	CA	90017	213-612-0220		690
SFFC (South Fork Forest Camp) 48300 Wilson River Hwy *Web:* www.oregon.gov	Tillamook	OR	97141	503-842-2811	842-7943	213
SFHCC (Elmwood Healthcare Ctr & Specialty Hospital) 401 N Broadway *Web:* elmwoodcommunities.com	Green Springs	OH	44836	419-639-2626		374-7
SFI Electronics Inc 400A Clanton Rd *Web:* www.sfi-electronics.com	Charlotte	NC	28217	704-522-0800		693
SFI of Tennessee LLC 4768 Hungerford Rd *Web:* www.sfifab.com	Memphis	TN	38118	901-363-1571		803-1
SFI-Gray Steel Ltd 3511 W 12th St *Web:* www.sfigray.com	Houston	TX	77008	713-864-6450		480
SFN (Society for Neuroscience) 1121 14th St NW Ste 1010 *Web:* www.sfn.org	Washington	DC	20005	202-962-4000	962-4941	49-8
SFPA (Southern Forest Products Assn) 6660 Riverside Dr Ste 212 *TF:* 866-574-4155 ■ *Web:* www.sfpa.org	Metairie	LA	70003	504-443-4464		48-2
SFRi LLC 242 California St *Web:* www.sfrillc.com	San Francisco	CA	94111	415-394-3900		693
SFS intec Inc Spring St & Van Reed Rd *TF:* 800-234-4533 ■ *Web:* www.sfsintecusa.com	Wyomissing	PA	19610	610-376-5751		621
SFSA (Steel Founders' Society of America) 780 McArdle Dr Ste G *Web:* www.sfsa.org	Crystal Lake	IL	60014	815-455-8240	455-8241	49-13
SFSP (Society of Financial Service Professionals) 19 Campus Blvd Ste 100 *TF:* 800-392-6900 ■ *Web:* www.financialpro.org	Newtown Square	PA	19073	610-526-2500	527-4010	49-9
SFU (Simon Fraser University) *Burnaby* 8888 University Dr MBC 1150 *Web:* www.sfu.ca	Burnaby	BC	V5A1S6	778-782-2667	782-5496	785
SFWMPAC (San Francisco War Memorial & Performing Arts Ctr) 401 Van Ness Ave Rm 110 *Web:* www.sfwmpac.org	San Francisco	CA	94102	415-621-6600	621-5091	572
SG Footwear Inc 3 University Plaza Ste 400 *Web:* www.sgfootwear.com	Hackensack	NJ	07601	201-342-1200		301
S&G Manufacturing Group LLC 4830 Northwest Pkwy *Web:* www.sgmgroup.com	Hilliard	OH	43026	614-334-3600		427
SG Wholesale Roofing Supplies Inc 1101 E Sixth St *TF Cust Svc:* 800-464-2461 ■ *Web:* www.sgroof.com	Santa Ana	CA	92701	714-568-1906	568-1915	191-4
SG360 Inc 1351 S Wheeling Rd *Web:* www.sggerdahl.com	Wheeling	IL	60090	847-541-1080		627
SGA (Sea Grant Assn) 5784 York Complex P.O. Box 1950 *Web:* www.sga.seagrant.org	Ocean Springs	MS	39566	207-581-1435	581-1426	48-13
SGB Enterprises Inc 24844 Anza Dr Ste A *Web:* www.sgbent.com	Valencia	CA	91355	661-294-8306		21
SGCD (Society of Glass & Ceramic Decorators) PO Box 2489 *TF:* 800-444-2742 ■ *Web:* www.sgcd.org	Zanesville	OH	43702	740-588-9882	588-0245	48-4
SGH (Sharp Grossmont Hospital) 5555 Grossmont Ctr Dr *TF:* 800-827-4277 ■ *Web:* www.sharp.com/grossmont	La Mesa	CA	91942	619-740-6000		374-3
SGH (Southwest General Hospital) 7400 Barlite Blvd *TF:* 877-898-6080 ■ *Web:* www.swgeneralhospital.com	San Antonio	TX	78224	210-921-2000		374-3
SGH Golf Inc 6805 Mt Vernon Ave *TF:* 800-284-8884 ■ *Web:* www.sghgolf.com	Cincinnati	OH	45227	513-984-0414	984-9648	771
SGI (Silicon Graphics Inc) 900 N McCarthy Blvd *TF:* 800-800-7441 ■ *Web:* www.sgi.com	Milpitas	CA	95035	669-900-8000		176
SGI Delivery Solutions 250 A Lyon Ln *Web:* www.sgi-solutions.com	Birmingham	AL	35211	205 941 2575		317
SGIA (Specialty Graphic Imaging Assn) 10015 Main St *TF:* 888-385-3588 ■ *Web:* www.sgia.org	Fairfax	VA	22031	703-385-1335	273-0456	49-16
SGL Carbon LLC 307 Jamestown Rd *TF:* 800 828-6601 ■ *Web:* www.sglgroup.com	Morganton	NC	28655	828-437-3221	432-5885	127
SGNA (Society of Gastroenterology Nurses & Assoc Inc) 401 N Michigan Ave *TF:* 800 245 7462 ■ *Web:* www.sgna.org	Chicago	IL	60611	312-321-5165	673-6694	49-8
SGS 291 Fairfield Ave *Web:* www.sgsgroup.us.com	Fairfield	NJ	07004	973-575-5252	575-7175	743
SGS Architects Engineers Inc 1 Tyler Ct *Web:* www.sgsarchitects.com	Carlisle	PA	17015	717-249-4569		261
SGS Canada Inc 6490 Vipond Dr *TF General:* 877-747-7658 ■ *Web:* www.sgs.ca	Mississauga	ON	L5T1W8	905-364-3757	364-0344	743
SGS North America Inc 201 State Rt 17 N *TF:* 800-645-5227 ■ *Web:* www.sgsgroup.us.com	Rutherford	NJ	07070	201-508-3000	508-3183	360-3
Sgs Technologie LLC 6817 Southpoint Pkwy Ste 2104 *Web:* www.sgstechnologies.net	Jacksonville	FL	32216	904-332-4534		180
SGT Inc 7701 Greenbelt Rd Ste 400 *Web:* www.sgt-inc.com	Greenbelt	MD	20770	301-614-8600	614-8601	24
Sgv International LLC 6500 Katy Fwy Ste 200 *Web:* www.sgvinternational.com	Houston	TX	77024	713-647-7555		463
SGW Integrated Marketing Communications Inc 219 Changebridge Rd *Web:* www.sgw.com	Montville	NJ	07045	973-299-8000		7
SH (Sherrill House Inc) 135 S Huntington Ave *TF:* 800-539-9767 ■ *Web:* www.sherrillhouse.org	Jamaica Plain	MA	02130	617-731-2400	731-8671	450
SH (Shive-Hattery Inc) 316 Second St SE Ste 500 PO Box 1599 *TF:* 800-798-0227 ■ *Web:* www.shive-hattery.com	Cedar Rapids	IA	52406	319-362-0313	362-2883	261
SH Enterprises Inc 4000 Central Dr *Web:* www.shenter.com	Wausau	WI	54401	715-848-1200		492
SH Leggitt Co 1000 Civic Center Loop	San Marcos	TX	78666	512-396-2257		790
Shaadi Karoge Inc 108 W 13th St *Web:* www.shaadikaroge.com	Wilmington	DE	19801	510-402-4486		387
ShabaShabu 3080 Wake Forest Rd *Web:* shabashabu.net	Raleigh	NC	27609	919-501-7755	501-7479	671
Shabbona Lake State Park 4201 Shabbona Grove Rd *Web:* shabbonalake.com	Shabbona	IL	60550	815-824-2106		565
Shabu Shabu House 127 Japanese Village Plaza Mall	Los Angeles	CA	90012	213-680-3890		671
Shackelford County 225 S Main St *Web:* shackelfordcounty.org	Albany	TX	76430	325-762-2232		338

Name / Address	City	State	ZIP	Phone	Fax	Class
Shackford Head State Park 106 Hogan Ave — *TF:* 800-400-6856 ■ *Web:* www.maine.gov	Bangor	ME	04401	207-941-4014		565
Shackleton Group Inc 1410 Vance St Ste 205 — *Web:* shkgrp.com	Lakewood	CO	80214	303-482-2370		94
Shade Inc 5049 Russell Cir — *Web:* www.shadeinc.com	Lincoln	NE	68507	402-466-3393		463
Shade Systems Inc 4150 SW 19th St — *TF:* 800-609-6066 ■ *Web:* www.shadesystemsinc.com	Ocala	FL	34474	352-237-0135		295
Shade Tree Service Company Inc 520 S Hwy Dr — *Web:* www.stsco.net	Fenton	MO	63026	636-343-1212	343-5660	776
Shader Bros Corp 6325 Edgewater Dr — *Web:* www.personalministorage.com	Orlando	FL	32810	407-297-3683		803-3
Shades of Green on Walt Disney World Resort 1950 W Magnolia Palm Dr — *TF:* 888-593-2242 ■ *Web:* www.shadesofgreen.org	Lake Buena Vista	FL	32830	407-824-3400	824-3665	379
Shades Restaurant 21100 Pacific Coast Hwy — *Web:* www.waterfrontresort.com/dining/shades	Huntington Beach	CA	92648	714-845-8000	845-8424	671
Shadin LP 6831 Oxford St — *TF:* 800-328-0584 ■ *Web:* www.shadin.com	St Louis Park	MN	55426	952-927-6500		529
Shadmoor State Park 900 Montauk Hwy — *Web:* parks.ny.gov/parks/16	Montauk	NY	11954	631-668-3781		565
Shadow Beverages & Snacks LLC 4650 E Cotton Ctr Blvd Ste 240 — *Web:* www.shadowbev.com	Phoenix	AZ	85040	480-371-1100		406
Shadow Financial Systems Inc 1551 S Washington Ave — *Web:* www.shadowfinancial.com	Piscataway	NJ	08854	732-225-6800		180
Shadow Mountain Resort & Club 45-750 San Luis Rey — *TF:* 800-472-3713 ■ *Web:* www.shadowmountainresort.com	Palm Desert	CA	92260	760-346-6123		669
Shadow-soft LLC 185 Wentworth Terr — *Web:* www.shadow-soft.com	Alpharetta	GA	30022	770-740-8030		177
Shady Maple Farm Market Inc 1324 Main St — *Web:* www.shady-maple.com	East Earl	PA	17519	717-354-4981		345
Shady Side Academy 423 Fox Chapel Rd — *Web:* www.shadysideacademy.org	Pittsburgh	PA	15238	412-968-3000	968-3213	622
Shadyside Nursing & Rehabilitation Ctr 5609 Fifth Ave — *TF:* 800-366-1232 ■ *Web:* manorcare.com	Pittsburgh	PA	15232	412-362-3500	362-1951	374-6
Shafer Commercial Seating 4101 E 48th Ave — *Web:* www.shafer.com	Denver	CO	80216	303-322-7792	393-1836	319-1
Shafer Vineyards 6154 Silverado Trl — *TF:* 800-366-6516 ■ *Web:* www.shafervineyards.com	Napa	CA	94558	707-944-2877		443
Shafer's Tour & Charter 500 N St — *TF:* 800-287-8986 ■ *Web:* www.shaferbus.com	Endicott	NY	13760	607-797-2006		107
Shaffer Trucking Inc 49 E Main St PO Box 418 — **Fax Area Code:* 800 ■ *TF Cust Svc:* 800-669-0322 ■ *Web:* cretecarrier.com	New Kingstown	PA	17072	402-475-9521	669-2181*	780
Shaffstall Corp 8531 Bash St — *TF:* 800-357-6250 ■ *Web:* www.shaffstall.com	Indianapolis	IN	46250	317-842-2077		173-8
Shaftesbury Films Inc 18 Logan Ave Ste 100 — *Web:* www.shaftesbury.ca	Toronto	ON	M4M2M8	416-363-1411	363-1428	514
Shah & Associates Inc 416 N Frederick Ave — *Web:* www.shahpe.com	Gaithersburg	MD	20877	301-926-2797		261
Shah Smith & Assoc Inc 2825 Wilcrest Ste 350 — *Web:* www.shahsmith.com/page.cfm?page=home	Houston	TX	77042	713-780-7563		261
Shah's Mongolian Grill 9148 Taylorsville Rd — *Web:* www.shahsmongoliangrill.com	Louisville	KY	40299	502-493-0234		671
Shaheen Bros Inc PO Box 897 — *Web:* www.shaheenbros.com	Amesbury	MA	01913	978-388-6776	388-6617	297-8
Shaheen Carpet Mills Inc 3742 US Hwy 41 NW PO Box 167 — *Web:* temp.shaheencarpet.com	Resaca	GA	30735	706-629-9544	625-5341	361
Shaheen Jeanne (Sen D - NH) 506 Hart Senate Office Bldg — *Web:* www.shaheen.senate.gov	Washington	DC	20510	202-224-2841	228-3194	342-2
Shahrazad 2847 N Oakland Ave — *Web:* www.shahrazadrestaurant.com	Milwaukee	WI	53211	414-964-5475	964-5471	671
Shajani LLP 5212 48 St — *Web:* shajani.ca	Red Deer	AB	T4N7C3	403-347-1384		2
Shakamak State Park 6265 W State Rd 48 — *Web:* www.in.gov	Jasonville	IN	47438	812-665-2158		565
Shaker Consulting Group Inc 3201 Entp Pkwy Ste 360 — *TF:* 888-485-7633 ■ *Web:* shakercg.com	Cleveland	OH	44122	888-485-7633		463
Shaker Group Inc, The 862 Albany Shaker Rd — *TF:* 800-267-0314 ■ *Web:* www.theshakergroup.com	Latham	NY	12110	518-786-9286		449
Shaker Heights Public Library 16500 Van Aken Blvd — *TF:* 800-954-8742 ■ *Web:* www.shakerlibrary.org	Cleveland	OH	44120	216-991-2030		434-3
Shaker Recruitment Adv & Communications 1100 Lake St 3rd Fl — *TF:* 800-323-5170 ■ *Web:* www.shaker.com	Oak Park	IL	60301	708-383-5320		4
Shaker Village of Pleasant Hill 3501 Lexington Rd — *TF:* 800-734-5611 ■ *Web:* www.shakervillageky.org	Harrodsburg	KY	40330	859-734-5411	734-5411	520
Shakespeare & Company Inc 70 Kemble St — *Web:* www.shakespeare.org	Lenox	MA	01240	413-637-1199		749
Shakespeare Fishing Tackle Co 7 Science Ct — *TF Cust Svc:* 800-466-5643 ■ *Web:* www.shakespeare-fishing.com	Columbia	SC	29203	803-754-7000		710
Shakespeare Monofilaments & Specialty Polymers 6111 Shakespeare Rd — *TF:* 800-845-2110 ■ *Web:* www.shakespearemonofilaments.com	Columbia	SC	29223	803-754-7011	786-2568	608
Shakespeare Theatre 516 Eigth St SE — *TF:* 877-487-8849 ■ *Web:* www.shakespearetheatre.org	Washington	DC	20003	202-547-3230	547-0226	573-4
Shakey's USA 2200 W Valley Blvd — *TF:* 800-979-4722 ■ *Web:* www.shakeys.com	Alhambra	CA	91803	626-576-0616		670
Shaklee Corp 4747 Willow Rd — *TF:* 800-742-5533 ■ *Web:* www.shaklee.com	Pleasanton	CA	94588	925-924-2000		366
Shales McNutt Construction 425 Renner Dr — *TF:* 800-527-8569 ■ *Web:* www.shalesmcnutt.com	Elgin	IL	60123	847-622-1214		186
Shalimar 307 S Main St — *Web:* www.shalimarrestaurant.com	Ann Arbor	MI	48104	734-663-1500	929-9129	671
Shalimar 3711 Hillsboro Pk — *Web:* shalimarfinedining.com	Nashville	TN	37215	615-269-8577	292-0330	671
Shallbetter Inc 3110 Progress Dr — *Web:* www.shallbetter.com	Oshkosh	WI	54901	920-232-8888		767
Shallco Inc 308 Components Dr — *Web:* www.shallco.com	Smithfield	NC	27577	919-934-3135		246
Shalon Ventures 155 Island Dr — *Web:* www.shalon.com	Palo Alto	CA	94301	650-566-8200		111
Shamaley Buick GMC 955 Crockett Way — *Web:* www.shamaleybuickgmc.com	El Paso	TX	79922	915-317-5958		57
Shambaugh & Son LP 7614 Opportunity Dr — *TF:* 866-890-7794 ■ *Web:* www.shambaugh.com	Fort Wayne	IN	46825	260-487-7777	487-7701	189-10
Shambhala Mountain Ctr 151 Shambhala Wy — *TF:* 888-788-7221 ■ *Web:* www.shambhalamountain.org	Red Feather Lakes	CO	80545	970-881-2184	881-2909	673
Shamin Hotels Inc 2000 Ware Bottom Spring Rd — *Web:* www.shaminhotels.com	Chester	VA	23836	804-777-9000		378
Shamokin Filler Company Inc PO Box 568 — *TF:* 800-577-8008 ■ *Web:* www.shamokinfiller.com	Shamokin	PA	17872	570-644-0437		190
Shamokin Valley Railroad Co 356 Priestley Ave — *Web:* www.nshr.com	Northumberland	PA	17857	570-473-7949		649
Shamrock Acquisition Corp 10901 Danka Cir N Ste B — *Web:* www.shamrockclean.com	Saint Petersburg	FL	33716	727-585-6007	446-1800	104
Shamrock Cabinet & Fixture Corp 10201 E 65th St — *TF:* 800-821-5410 ■ *Web:* www.shamrockcabinet.com	Raytown	MO	64133	816-737-2300	356-7835	115
Shamrock Communications Inc 149 Penn Ave — *TF:* 800-228-4637 ■ *Web:* www.thetimes-tribune.com	Scranton	PA	18503	570-348-9100		643
Shamrock Cos Inc, The 24090 Detroit Rd — *Web:* www.shamrockcompanies.net	Westlake	OH	44145	440-899-9510	250-2180	360-3
Shamrock Farms Co 40034 W Clayton Rd — *Web:* www.shamrockfarms.net	Stanfield	AZ	85172	602-477-2462		10-3
Shamrock Foods 3900 E Camelback Rd Ste 300 — *TF:* 800-289-3663 ■ *Web:* www.shamrockfoods.com	Phoenix	AZ	85018	602-477-2500		296-27
Shamrock High School 100 S Illinois St	Shamrock	TX	79079	806-256-3227		685
Shamrock Holdings Inc 3500 W Olive Ave — *TF:* 800-355-2116 ■ *Web:* www.shamrock.com	Burbank	CA	91505	818-845-4444		360-3
Shamrock Office Solutions Inc 6908 Sierra Ct Ste A — *Web:* www.shamrockoffice.com	Dublin	CA	94568	925-875-0480		179
Shamrock Scientific Specialty Systems Inc 34 Davis Dr — **Fax Area Code:* 800 ■ *TF:* 800-323-0249 ■ *Web:* www.shamrocklabels.com	Bellwood	IL	60104	708-547-9005	248-1907*	413
Shamrock Steel Sales Inc 238 W County Rd S — *TF:* 800-299-2317 ■ *Web:* www.shamrocksteelsales.com	Odessa	TX	79763	432-337-2317	337-5049	492
Shamrock Structures LLC 1440 Davey Rd — *Web:* www.shamrockstructures.com	Woodridge	IL	60517	630-739-3215		668
Shamrock Technologies Inc Foot Of Pacific St — *TF:* 800-349-1822 ■ *Web:* www.shamrocktechnologies.com	Newark	NJ	07114	973-242-2999		146
ShaNah Spa at the Bishop's Lodge 1297 Bishop — *Web:* www.bishopslodge.com	Santa Fe	NM	87506	505-983-6377		707
Shanahan's Limited Partnership 13139 80th Ave — *TF:* 888-591-5999 ■ *Web:* www.shanahans.com	Surrey	BC	V3W3B1	604-591-5111	591-3171	499
Shanaman Sports Museum of Tacoma 2727 E 'D' St — *Web:* www.tacomasportsmuseum.com	Tacoma	WA	98421	206-627-5857		522
Shandon Baptist Church 5250 Forest Dr — *Web:* www.shandon.org	Columbia	SC	29206	803-782-1300		48-20
Shands Hospital at the University of Florida 1600 SW Archer Rd — *TF:* 855-483-7546 ■ *Web:* ufhealth.org	Gainesville	FL	32608	352-265-0111	627-4173	374-3
Shane Co 9790 E Arapahoe Rd — *TF:* 866-467-4263 ■ *Web:* www.shaneco.com	Greenwood Village	CO	80112	303-799-4700		410
Shane Homes Ltd 5661 Seventh St NE — *Web:* www.shanehomes.com	Calgary	AB	T2E8V3	403-536-2200		364
Shane's Rib Shack 9404 W Westgate Blvd #C101 — *Web:* www.shanesribshack.com	Glendale	AZ	85305	623-877-7427		378
Shaner Hotel Group 1965 Waddle Rd — **Fax:* Hum Res ■ *TF:* 800-546-7866 ■ *Web:* www.shanercorp.com	State College	PA	16803	814-234-4460	278-7295*	379
Shang Hai 3051 25th St SW — *Web:* fargoshanghai.com	Fargo	ND	58103	701-280-5818		671
Shanghai Inn 1937 N Glenstone Ave	Springfield	MO	65803	417-865-5111		671
Shanghai Mama's 216 E Sixth St — *Web:* www.shanghaimamas.com	Cincinnati	OH	45202	513-241-7777		671
Shanghai Restaurant 3433 Hillsborough Rd — *Web:* www.shanghai.ypguides.net	Durham	NC	27705	919-383-7581		671
Shanghai Restaurant 651 Somerset St W	Ottawa	ON	K1R5K3	613-233-4001		671

Name / Address	City	State	Zip	Phone	Fax	Class
Shanghai Terrace 108 E Superior St *Web:* chicago.peninsula.com	Chicago	IL	60611	312-573-6744		671
Shangri La Botanical Gardens & Nature Ctr 2111 W Pk Ave *Web:* starkculturalvenues.org	Orange	TX	77630	409-670-9113	670-9341	97
Shangri La Chinese Gourmet 4248 Buena Vista Rd *Web:* www.shangrilacolumbus.com	Columbus	GA	31907	706-568-7554		671
Shangri-La Hotel Toronto 188 University Ave *Web:* www.shangri-la.com	Toronto	ON	M5H0A3	647-788-8888		379
Shank Constructors Inc 3501 85Th Ave N *Web:* www.shankconstructors.com	Brooklyn Park	MN	55443	763-424-8300		610
Shank Public Relations Counselors Inc 5310 Hallwood Ct Ste 101 *Web:* shankpr.com	Indianapolis	IN	46254	317-293-5590	293-5706	636
Shank Wealth Management LLC 2627 Chestnut Ridge Dr Ste 110 *TF:* 888-359-3133 ■ *Web:* shankwm.com	Kingwood	TX	77339	281-359-3133		690
Shanks Extracts Inc 350 Richardson Dr *TF:* 800-346-3135 ■ *Web:* www.shanks.com	Lancaster	PA	17603	717-393-4441		297-8
Shanley Pump & Equipment Inc 2525 S Clearbrook Dr *Web:* www.shanleypump.com	Arlington Heights	IL	60005	847-439-9200		641
Shannahan Crane & Hoist Inc 11695 Wakeside Crossing Ct *TF:* 800-291-4872 ■ *Web:* www.shannahancrane.com	Saint Louis	MO	63146	314-965-2800		358
Shannon & Assoc LLP 1851 Central Pl S Ste 225 *Web:* www.shannon-cpas.com	Kent	WA	98030	253-852-8500		2
Shannon Airport 3380 Shannon Airport Cir	Fredericksburg	VA	22408	540-373-4431		63
Shannon County 18529 Main St PO Box 187 *Web:* www.shannon-county.com	Eminence	MO	65466	573-226-3414	226-5325	338
Shannon Diversified Inc 1360 E Locust St *TF:* 800-794-2345 ■ *Web:* sdiquality.com	Ontario	CA	91761	909-560-0801		104
Shannon Medical Ctr (SMC) 120 E Harris Ave *TF:* 800-368-1019 ■ *Web:* www.shannonhealth.com	San Angelo	TX	76903	325-653-6741	658-8295	374-3
Shannon Precision Fastener LLC 31600 Stephenson Hwy *Web:* www.shannonpf.com	Madison Heights	MI	48071	248-589-9670		492
Shannon Systems LLC 173 Spark St *Web:* www.b2bgateway.net	Brockton	MA	02302	508-894-2150		636
Shanor Electric Supply Inc 1276 Military Rd *Web:* www.shanorelectric.com	Kenmore	NY	14217	716-876-0711	876-7375	246
Shan-Rod Inc 7308 Orr Rd *Web:* shanrodinc.com	Berlin Heights	OH	44814	419-588-2066		789
Shanti Bithi Nursery Inc 71 Trinity Pass	Stamford	CT	06903	203-329-0768		323
Shanty Creek Resort 5780 Shanty Creek Rd *TF:* 800-678-4111 ■ *Web:* www.shantycreek.com	Bellaire	MI	49615	231-533-8621		669
Shapard Research LLC 820 NE 63rd St Uppr E *TF:* 800-569-3311 ■ *Web:* www.shapard.com	Oklahoma City	OK	73105	405-607-4664		466
Shapco Inc 1666 20th St Ste 100	Santa Monica	CA	90404	310-264-1666		352
Shape Corp 1900 Hayes St *TF:* 800-275-8777 ■ *Web:* www.shapecorp.com	Grand Haven	MI	49417	616-846-8700	846-3464	480
Shape LLC 2105 Corporate Dr *TF:* 800-367-5811 ■ *Web:* www.shapellc.com	Addison	IL	60101	630-620-8394	620-0784	767
Shape Magazine 4 New York Pl *Web:* www.shape.com	New York	NY	10004	212-545-4800		457-13
Shaped Wire Inc 30000 Solon Rd *Web:* www.shapedwire.com	Solon	OH	44139	440-248-7600	248-5491	813
Shapemasters Inc PO Box 11128 *TF:* 800-207-6457 ■ *Web:* www.shapemasters.com	Southport	NC	28461	910-278-1434	278-1944	188-3
Shapeways BV 419 Park Ave S *Web:* www.shapeways.com	New York	NY	10016	718-974-8010		387
Shapiro/West & Assoc 141 El Camino Dr Ste 205	Beverly Hills	CA	90212	310-278-8896		731
Share Corp 7821 N Faulkner Rd *TF:* 800-776-7192 ■ *Web:* www.sharecorp.com	Milwaukee	WI	53224	414-355-4000	355-0516	151
SHARE El Salvador 2425 College Ave *Web:* www.share-elsalvador.org	Berkeley	CA	94704	510-848-8487		48-5
Share Our Strength 1730 M St NW Ste 700 *TF:* 800-969-4767 ■ *Web:* www.nokidhungry.org	Washington	DC	20036	202-393-2925	347-5868	48-5
SHARE Pregnancy & Infant Loss Support Inc 402 Jackson St *TF:* 800-821-6819 ■ *Web:* www.nationalshare.org	Saint Charles	MO	63301	636-947-6164	947-7486	48-21
ShareASale.com Inc 15 W Hubbard St Ste 500 *Web:* www.shareasale.com	Chicago	IL	60654	312-321-0487		393
Shared Imaging LLC 801 Phoenix Lake Ave *Web:* www.sharedimaging.com	Streamwood	IL	60107	630-483-3980		475
shared logic group inc, The 6904 Spring Vly Dr Ste 305 *TF:* 877-865-0083 ■ *Web:* www.sharedlogic.com	Holland	OH	43528	419-865-0083		177
Shared Service Systems Inc 1725 S 20th St *TF:* 800-228-9976 ■ *Web:* www.sharedomaha.com	Omaha	NE	68108	402-536-5300		475
SharedReviews com Inc 1938 Bloor St W *Web:* sharedreviews.com	Toronto	ON	M6P4J2	416-619-0992		224
Sharefax Credit Union Inc 1147 Old SR- 74 *Web:* sharefax.org	Batavia	OH	45103	513-753-2440		219
Shareintel 151 Rowayton Ave *Web:* www.shareintel.com	Rowayton	CT	06853	203-838-5471		317
Sharenet Inc 5600 Explorer Dr *Web:* www.sharenetinc.com	Mississauga	ON	L4W4Y2	905-206-0884	206-9783	401
ShareSquared Inc 2155 Verdugo Blvd Ste 33 *TF:* 800-445-1279 ■ *Web:* www.sharesquared.com	Montrose	CA	91020	800-445-1279		180
Sharetracker LLC 1300 Clay St Ste 600 *TF:* 888-628-3088 ■ *Web:* www.sharetracker.net	Oakland	CA	94612	888-628-3088		466
Sharf Woodward & Associates Inc 5900 Sepulveda Blvd *TF:* 877-482-6687 ■ *Web:* www.swjobs.com	Van Nuys	CA	91411	818-989-2200		260
Shari's Restaurant & Pies 9400 SW Gemini Dr *TF:* 800-433-5334 ■ *Web:* www.sharis.com	Beaverton	OR	97008	503-605-4299	605-4260	670
Sharian Inc 368 W Ponce de Leon Ave *TF:* 800-561-3357 ■ *Web:* sharian.com	Decatur	GA	30030	404-373-2274		152
Sharif Designs Ltd 34-12 36th Ave	Long Island	NY	11106	718-472-1100		430
Shark Industries Ltd 6700 Bleck Dr *TF:* 800-537-4275 ■ *Web:* www.sharkind.com	Rockford	MN	55373	763-565-1900		1
Sharkey County PO Box 218 *Web:* sharkey.msghn.org/addresses.html	Rolling Fork	MS	39159	662-873-2755		338
Sharkey Howes & Javer Inc 720 S Colorado Blvd Ste 600 S Twr *TF:* 800-557-9380 ■ *Web:* www.shwj.com	Denver	CO	80246	303-639-5100		194
Sharks Success Marketing Ent 1532 Pickwood Ave *Web:* www.sharkssuccess.com	Fern Park	FL	32730	407-260-9780		195
Sharon Coating LLC 277 Sharpsville Ave *Web:* nlmk.com/en/about/map-of-assets/sharon-coating	Sharon	PA	16146	724-981-3545	981-3009	307
Sharon Health Care Ctr 27 Hospital Hill Rd *TF:* 800-547-3443 ■ *Web:* athenahealthcare.com	Sharon	CT	06069	860-364-1002	364-0237	450
Sharon Public Library 11 N Main St *TF:* 800-825-3260 ■ *Web:* www.townofsharon.net	Sharon	MA	02067	781-784-1578		434-3
Sharon Regional Health System 740 E State St *Web:* sharonregionalhealth.org	Sharon	PA	16146	724-983-3911	983-3842	374-3
Sharon Towers 5100 Sharon Rd *TF:* 800-720-7434 ■ *Web:* www.sharontowers.org	Charlotte	NC	28210	704-553-1670		672
Sharonville Convention Ctr 11355 Chester Rd *TF:* 800-294-3179 ■ *Web:* www.sharonvilleconventioncenter.com	Sharonville	OH	45246	513-771-7744	772-5745	205
Sharp & Cobos PC 4705 Spicewood Springs Rd Ste 100 *TF:* 800-447-5375 ■ *Web:* sharpcobos.com	Austin	TX	78759	512-473-2265		428
Sharp Bros Seed Co 1005 S Sycamore *TF:* 800-462-8483 ■ *Web:* www.sharpseed.com	Healy	KS	67850	620-398-2231	398-2220	694
Sharp Bus Lines Ltd 567 Oak Park Rd *Web:* www.sharpbus.com	Brantford	ON	N3T5L8	519-751-3434		107
Sharp Chula Vista Medical Ctr 751 Medical Ctr Ct *Web:* www.sharp.com/hospital	Chula Vista	CA	91911	619-482-5800		374-3
Sharp County 718 Ash Flat Dr *Web:* www.ark.org/propertytax/sharp/index.php	Ash Flat	AR	72513	870-994-7334		338
Sharp Decisions Inc 1040 Ave of the A *TF:* 800 742 7792 ■ *Web:* www.sharpdecisions.com	New York	NY	10018	212-481-5533	481-8751	113
Sharp Electronics Corp 1 Sharp Plaza *TF:* 800-237-4277 ■ *Web:* www.sharpusa.com	Mahwah	NJ	07430	201-529-8200		52
Sharp Energy Inc 648 Ocean Hwy *TF:* 888-742-7740 ■ *Web:* www.sharpenergy.com	Pocomoke City	MD	21851	888-742-7740		316
Sharp Grossmont Hospital (SGH) 5555 Grossmont Ctr Dr *TF:* 800-827-4277 ■ *Web:* www.sharp.com/grossmont	La Mesa	CA	91942	619-740-6000		374-3
Sharp Health Plan 4305 University Ave Ste 200 *TF:* 800-359-2002 ■ *Web:* www.sharphealthplan.com	San Diego	CA	92105	619-228-2300		391-3
Sharp Healthcare 8695 Spectrum Ctr Blvd *TF:* 800-827-4277 ■ *Web:* www.sharp.com	San Diego	CA	92123	858-499-4000	499-5237	353
Sharp Innovations Inc 117 SW End Ave *TF:* 888-575-8977 ■ *Web:* www.sharpinnovations.com	Lancaster	PA	17603	717-290-6760		809
Sharp Laboratories Of America Inc 5750 NW Pacific Rim Blvd *Web:* www.sharplabs.com	Camas	WA	98607	360-817-8400		668
Sharp Memorial Hospital 7901 Frost St *Web:* sharp.com	San Diego	CA	92123	858-939-3400		374-3
Sharp Microelectronics of the Americas 5700 NW Pacific Rim Blvd *Web:* www.sharpsma.com	Camas	WA	98607	360-834-2500		253
Sharp Shooter Spectrum Ventures LLC 11901 W 48th Ave	Wheat Ridge	CO	80033	303-962-2345		592
Sharp Shopper 2475 S Main St Ste A *TF:* 800-438-7325 ■ *Web:* www.sharpshopper.net	Harrisonburg	VA	22801	540-434-8848		345
Sharp Shopper Inc 1100 Sharp Ave *Web:* sharpshopper.net	Ephrata	PA	17522	717-733-9555		345
Sharp Sky Partners 520 Baker Bldg 706 Second Ave S *Web:* www.sharpsky.com	Minneapolis	MN	55402	612-339-3444		193
Sharp Water Culligan 129 Columbia Rd *Web:* sharpwater.com	Salisbury	MD	21801	410-742-3333		806
Sharpe Consulting LLC 16913 Macduff Ave *Web:* www.sharpeconsulting.biz	Olney	MD	20832	301-570-5127		463
Sharpe Kawam Carmosino & Company LLC 1 Mars Ct Ste 1 *Web:* skcandco.com	Boonton	NJ	07005	973-335-1112		2
Sharpe Planetarium 3050 Central Ave *TF:* 800-250-8611 ■ *Web:* www.memphismuseums.org	Memphis	TN	38111	901-636-2362	320-6391	598
Sharpe Resources Corp 3258 Mob Neck Rd *Web:* www.sharperesourcescorporation.com	Heathsville	VA	22473	804-580-8107		501
Sharphat Inc 333 Sylvan Ave Ste 324 *Web:* sharphat.com	Englewood Cliffs	NJ	07632	201-503-0020		180
Sharp-Mesa Vista Hospital 7850 Vista Hill Ave *TF:* 800-827-4277 ■ *Web:* www.sharp.com	San Diego	CA	92123	858-278-4110		374-5

Name	Address	City	State	ZIP	Phone	Fax	Class
Sharprint Silkscreen & Graphics Inc	4200 W Wrightwood Ave *TF:* 888-800-5646 ■ *Web:* www.sharprint.com	Chicago	IL	60639	773-862-9300		627
Sharpsville Container Corp	600 Main St *Web:* sharpsvillecontainer.com	Sharpsville	PA	16150	724-962-1100		100
Sharrard McGee & Company PA	1321 Long St *Web:* www.sharrardmcgee.com	High Point	NC	27262	336-884-0410		2
Shartsis Friese & Ginsburg LLP	1 Maritime Plaza 18th Fl *Web:* www.sflaw.com	San Francisco	CA	94111	415-421-6500	421-2922	428
Sharut Furniture Inc	220 Passaic St	Passaic	NJ	07055	973-473-1000		820
Shasta Beverages Inc	26901 Industrial Blvd *TF:* 800-834-9980 ■ *Web:* www.shastapop.com	Hayward	CA	94545	510-783-3200		80-2
Shasta College	11555 Old Oregon Trl PO Box 496006 *Web:* www.shastacollege.edu	Redding	CA	96049	530-242-7500		800
Shasta County	1643 Market St *TF:* 800-735-2922 ■ *Web:* www.co.shasta.ca.us	Redding	CA	96099	530-225-5730	225-5454	338
Shasta Inc	300 Steel St *Web:* shastainc.com	Aliquippa	PA	15001	724-378-8280		723
Shasta Public Library	1100 Parkview Ave *TF:* 800-735-2922 ■ *Web:* www.shastalibraries.org	Redding	CA	96001	530-245-7250		434-3
Shasta Qa	1538 Market St *TF:* 800-555-5211 ■ *Web:* www.shastaqa.com	Redding	CA	96001	530-242-5799		177
Shasta Regional Medical Ctr (SRMC)	1100 Butte St *Web:* www.shastaregional.com	Redding	CA	96001	530-244-5400		374-3
Shasta State Historic Park	c/o Northern Buttes District Office 400 Glen Dr *Web:* www.parks.ca.gov/default.asp?page_id=456	Oroville	CA	95966	530-243-8194		565
Shasta Ventures	2440 Sand Hill Rd Ste 300 *Web:* www.shastaventures.com	Menlo Park	CA	94025	650-543-1700		792
Shattuck-Saint Mary's School	1000 Shumway Ave PO Box 218 *TF:* 800-421-2724 ■ *Web:* www.s-sm.org	Faribault	MN	55021	507-333-1616	333-1661	622
Shatz Norman C Company Inc	3570 St Rd *TF:* 800-743-9406 ■ *Web:* www.shatzusa.com	Bensalem	PA	19020	215-245-5511		711
Shavel Assoc	13 Roszel Rd *Web:* www.shavel.com	Princeton	NJ	08540	609-452-1800		361
Shaver Properties Inc	6010 Old Dixie Hwy Ste K *Web:* www.shavermillwork.com	Vero Beach	FL	32967	772-569-3466		499
Shaw & Sullivan P C	1221 Cameron St *Web:* shawcpa.com	Alexandria	VA	22314	703-548-2776		2
Shaw Air Force Base	517 Lance Ave Ste 106 *TF:* 800-235-7776 ■ *Web:* www.shaw.af.mil	Shaw AFB	SC	29152	803-895-2019		497-1
Shaw Communications Inc	630 Third Ave SW *TSE: SJR/B* ■ **Fax:* Mktg ■ *TF:* 888-472-2222 ■ *Web:* www.shaw.ca	Calgary	AB	T2P4L4	403-750-4500	750-4501*	116
Shaw Construction Company LLC	300 Kalamath St *TF:* 800-964-3444 ■ *Web:* www.shawconstruction.net	Denver	CO	80223	303-825-4740	825-6403	187
Shaw Electric Co	22100 Telegraph Rd *TF:* 800-968-0177 ■ *Web:* www.shawelectric.com	Southfield	MI	48033	248-228-2000	228-2080	189-4
Shaw Glass Company Inc	55 Bristol Dr *Web:* www.solarseal.com	South Easton	MA	02375	508-238-0112		330
Shaw Industries Inc	616 E Walnut Ave *TF:* 800-441-7429 ■ *Web:* www.shawfloors.com	Dalton	GA	30722	800-441-7429		131
Shaw Pipeline Services Inc	4250 N Sam Houston Pkwy E Ste 180 *TF:* 866-912-5314 ■ *Web:* www.shawpipeline.com	Houston	TX	77032	832-601-0850		539
Shaw Satellite Services Inc	2055 Flavelle Blvd *Web:* www.shawdirect.ca/english	Mississauga	ON	L5K1Z8	905-403-2020		681
Shaw Systems Assoc Inc	6200 Savoy Dr Ste 600 *Web:* www.shawsystems.com	Houston	TX	77036	713-782-7730		177
Shaw University	118 E S St **Fax:* Admissions ■ *TF Admissions:* 800-214-6683 ■ *Web:* www.shawu.edu	Raleigh	NC	27601	919-546-8275	546-8271*	166
Shaw's Crab House Chicago	21 E Hubbard St *Web:* www.shawscrabhouse.com	Chicago	IL	60611	312-527-2722		671
Shaw/Stewart Lumber Co	645 Johnson St NE *TF:* 800-233-0101 ■ *Web:* www.shawstewartlumberco.com	Minneapolis	MN	55413	612-378-1520		499
Shawano Country Chamber of Commerce	1263 S Main St *TF:* 800-235-8528 ■ *Web:* www.shawanocountry.com	Shawano	WI	54166	715-524-2139	524-3127	139
Shawano County	311 N Main St *Web:* www.co.shawano.wi.us	Shawano	WI	54166	715-526-9150	524-5157	338
ShawCor Ltd	25 Bethridge Rd *TSE: SCL/A* ■ *TF:* 855-744-5789 ■ *Web:* www.shawcor.com	Toronto	ON	M9W1M7	416-743-7111	743-7199	537
Shawe & Rosenthal LLP	1 S St Ste 1800 *Web:* www.shawe.com	Baltimore	MD	21202	410-752-1040		445
Shawmut Design & Construction	560 Harrison Ave *Web:* www.shawmut.com	Boston	MA	02118	617-622-7000		186
Shawmut Mills	2770 Dove St *Web:* www.shawmutcorporation.com	Port Huron	MI	48060	810-987-2222		113
Shawnee Chamber of Commerce	15100 W 67th St Ste 202 *Web:* www.shawneekschamber.com	Shawnee	KS	66217	913-631-6545	631-9628	139
Shawnee Chemical Company Inc	136 Main St Ste 300 *Web:* www.shawchem.com	Princeton	NJ	08540	609-799-3930		601
Shawnee Community College	8364 Shawnee College Rd **Fax:* Admitting ■ *TF:* 800-481-2242 ■ *Web:* www.shawneecc.edu	Ullin	IL	62992	618-634-3200	634-3300*	162
Shawnee Correctional Ctr	6665 SR-146 E *Web:* www.illinois.gov	Vienna	IL	62995	618-658-8331		213
Shawnee County	200 SE Seventh St *TF:* 800-383-1183 ■ *Web:* www.snco.us	Topeka	KS	66603	785-233-8200	291-4912	338
Shawnee Milling Company Inc	201 S Broadway PO Box 1567 *TF:* 800-654-2600 ■ *Web:* www.shawneemilling.com	Shawnee	OK	74802	405-273-7000	273-7333	296-23
Shawnee Mission Medical Ctr	9100 W 74th St *Web:* www.shawneemission.org	Shawnee Mission	KS	66204	913-676-2000		374-3
Shawnee State Park	4404 SR- 125 *Web:* www.ohiodnr.com	West Portsmouth	OH	45663	740-858-6652		565
Shawnee State Park	132 State Pk Rd *Web:* www.dcnr.state.pa.us	Schellsburg	PA	15559	814-733-4218		565
Shawnee State University	940 Second St *TF:* 800-959-2778 ■ *Web:* www.shawnee.edu	Portsmouth	OH	45662	740-351-3221	351-3111	166
Shawnee State University Clark Memorial Library	940 Second St *Web:* shawnee.edu	Portsmouth	OH	45662	740-351-4778		434-6
Shawnee Steel & Welding Inc	6124 Merriam Dr *Web:* www.shawnee-steel.com	Merriam	KS	66203	913-432-8046		567
Shawnee Systems Inc	3616 Church St *Web:* www.shawneesystems.com	Cincinnati	OH	45244	513-561-4803		627
Shawnee Telephone Co	PO Box 69 *TF:* 800-461-3956 ■ *Web:* myshawnee.net	Equality	IL	62934	618-276-4211		736
Shawnigan Lake School (SLS)	1975 Renfrew Rd *Web:* www.shawnigan.ca	Shawnigan Lake	BC	V0R2W1	250-743-5516		622
Shaws Menswear Inc	1061 Village Park Dr Ste 204	Greensboro	GA	30642	706-454-5041		157-3
Shawsheen Rubber Company Inc	PO Box 4296 *Web:* www.shawsheencc.com	Andover	MA	01810	978-475-1710	475-8603	552-1
Shawver & Associates LLC	5959 S Staples Ste 102 *Web:* www.stxpi.com	Corpus Christi	TX	78413	361-880-8968	880-8971	400
Shawver & Son Inc	144 NE 44th St *Web:* www.shawver.net	Oklahoma City	OK	73105	405-525-9451	525-6136	189-4
Shaw-Winkler Inc	4910 Dawn Ave *Web:* shawwinkler.com	East Lansing	MI	48823	517-351-5720		189-10
SHAZAM Inc	6700 Pioneer Pkwy *Web:* www.shazam.net	Johnston	IA	50131	515-288-2828		225
SHC International Inc	1031 Aldridge Rd Ste I *Web:* www.shc-intl.com	Vacaville	CA	95688	707-448-6076		360-3
SHDR (Stanley Hunt DuPree & Rhine)	7701 Airport Ctr Dr **Fax Area Code:* 252 ■ *TF:* 800-930-2441 ■ *Web:* www.shdr.com	Greensboro	NC	27409	800-768-4873	293-9048*	193
Shea Brothers Inc	65 Innerbelt Rd *Web:* www.sheabrothers.com	Somerville	MA	02143	617-623-2001		627
Shea Concrete Products Inc	87 Haverhill Rd *TF:* 800-696-7432 ■ *Web:* www.sheaconcrete.com	Amesbury	MA	01913	978-388-1509		770
Shea Homes Inc	8800 N Gainey Ctr Dr Ste 370 *Web:* m.sheahomes.com	Scottsdale	AZ	85258	480-367-3701		653
Shea's Performing Arts Ctr	646 Main St *TF:* 866-341-5945 ■ *Web:* www.sheas.org	Buffalo	NY	14202	716-847-1410	847-1644	572
Sheaff Brock Investment Advisors LLC	10401 N Meridian St Ste 100 *TF:* 866-575-5700 ■ *Web:* www.sheaffbrock.com	Indianapolis	IN	46290	317-705-5700		401
Shealy Electrical Wholesalers Inc	422 Fairforest Way *TF:* 800-868-5980 ■ *Web:* www.shealyelectrical.com	Greenville	SC	29607	864-242-6880	235-6097	246
Shealy's Truck Ctr Inc	1340 Bluff Rd *TF:* 800-951-8580 ■ *Web:* www.shealytruck.com	Columbia	SC	29201	803-771-0176	771-4879	516
Shea-Porter Carol (Rep D - NH)	1530 Longworth HOB *Web:* shea-porter.house.gov	Washington	DC	20515	202-225-5456		342-2
Shearer & Associates Inc	4960 Corporate Dr Ste 100 *TF:* 800-998-4697 ■ *Web:* shearerassociates.us	Huntsville	AL	35805	256-830-1031		196
Shearer Equipment	7762 Cleveland Rd *Web:* www.shearerequipment.com	Wooster	OH	44691	330-345-9023		246
Shearman & Sterling LLP	599 Lexington Ave *TF:* 800-973-1177 ■ *Web:* www.shearman.com	New York	NY	10022	212-848-4000	848-7179	428
Sheboygan County	615 N Sixth St *Web:* www.sheboygancounty.com	Sheboygan	WI	53081	920-459-3068	459-3921	338
Sheboygan County Chamber of Commerce	621 S Eigth St *Web:* www.sheboygan.org	Sheboygan	WI	53081	920-457-9491	457-6269	139
Sheboygan Paint Company Inc	1439 N 25th St PO Box 417 *TF:* 800-773-7801 ■ *Web:* www.shebpaint.com	Sheboygan	WI	53082	920-458-2157	458-5620	550
Sheboygan Paper Box Co	716 Clara Ave PO Box 326 *Web:* www.spbox.com	Sheboygan	WI	53082	920-458-8373	458-2901	101
Sheboygan Press	632 Center Ave PO Box 358 *TF:* 800-686-3900 ■ *Web:* www.sheboyganpress.com	Sheboygan	WI	53081	920-457-7711		532-2
Shed, The	113 1/2 E Palace Ave *Web:* www.sfshed.com	Santa Fe	NM	87501	505-982-9030		671
Shee Atika Inc	315 Lincoln St Ste 300 *TF:* 800-478-3534 ■ *Web:* www.sheeatika.com	Sitka	AK	99835	907-747-3534	747-5727	113
Sheedy Drayage Company Inc	1215 Michigan St *Web:* sheedydrayage.com	San Francisco	CA	94107	415-648-7171	648-1535	780

Name / Address	City	State	Zip	Phone	Fax	Class
Sheehan Pipe Line Construction Co						
2431 E 61st St Ste 700	Tulsa	OK	74136	918-747-3471	747-9888	188-10
TF: 800-259-8210 ■ *Web:* www.sheehanpipeline.com						
Sheehy & Assoc 2297 Lexington Rd	Louisville	KY	40206	502-456-9007		4
Web: www.sheehy1.com						
Sheehy Auto Stores						
12701 Fair Lakes Cir	Fairfax	VA	22033	703-802-3480		57
Web: www.sheehy.com						
Sheely's Furniture & Appliance Company Inc						
11450 S Ave	North Lima	OH	44452	330-549-3901		321
TF: 877-549-9144 ■ *Web:* www.sheelys.com						
SheerVision Inc(NDA)						
4030 Palos Verdes Dr N Ste 104	Rolling Hills Estates	CA	90274	310-265-8918		544
TF: 877-678-4274 ■ *Web:* www.sheervision.com						
Sheet Metal & Air Conditioning Contractors' NA (SMACNA)						
4201 Lafayette Ctr Dr	Chantilly	VA	20151	703-803-2980	803-3732	49-3
Web: www.smacna.org						
Sheet Metal Connectors Inc						
5850 Main St NE	Minneapolis	MN	55432	763-572-0000		697
Web: www.smcduct.com						
Sheet Metal Engineers Inc						
303 Tower Rd	Augusta	GA	30907	706-863-6575		697
Sheetz Inc 5700 Sixth Ave	Altoona	PA	16602	814-941-5106	941-5105	204
TF: 800-487-5444 ■ *Web:* www.sheetz.com						
Sheffer Corp 6990 Cornell Rd	Cincinnati	OH	45242	513-489-9770	489-3034*	223
**Fax:* Sales ■ *Web:* www.sheffercorp.com						
Sheffield Manufacturing Inc						
9131 Glenoaks Blvd	Sun Valley	CA	91352	818-767-4948		21
Web: www.sheffield-mfg.com						
Sheffield Metals International Inc						
5467 Evergreen Pkwy	Sheffield Village	OH	44054	440-934-8500		492
TF: 800-283-5262 ■ *Web:* www.sheffieldmetals.com						
Sheffield Resource Network						
2239 N Hayden Rd	Scottsdale	AZ	85257	480-968-6199		463
Web: www.sheffieldnet.com						
Shefield Group 2265 W Railway St	Abbotsford	BC	V2S2E3	604-859-1014	859-1711	159
Web: www.shefield.com						
Sheila Greco Associates LLC						
174 State Hwy 67	Amsterdam	NY	12010	518-843-4611		393
TF: 888-400-8049 ■ *Web:* www.sheilagreco.com						
Sheiness, Glover & Grossman LLP						
4544 Post Oak Pl Dr Ste 270	Houston	TX	77027	713-374-7000		466
Web: www.sgglawyers.com						
Sheladia Assoc Inc						
15825 Shady Grove Rd Ste 100	Rockville	MD	20850	301-590-3939		261
Web: www.sheladia.com						
Shelba D. Johnson Trucking Inc						
PO Box 7287	High Point	NC	27264	336-476-2000	476-0187	780
Web: www.sdjtrucking.com						
Shelborne Wyndham Grand South Beach						
1801 Collins Ave	Miami Beach	FL	33139	305-531-1271	531-2206	379
Web: www.shelbornewyndhamgrand.com						
Shelburne Farms 1611 Harbor Rd.	Shelburne	VT	05482	802-985-8686	985-8123	48-13
TF: 800-286-6022 ■ *Web:* www.shelburnefarms.org						
Shelburne Murray Hill						
303 Lexington Ave	New York	NY	10016	212-689-5200	779-7068	379
TF: 866-233-4642 ■ *Web:* www.affinia.com						
Shelburne Museum 5555 Shelburne Rd	Shelburne	VT	05482	802-985-3346	985-2331	520
TF: 800-205-8033 ■ *Web:* www.shelburnemuseum.org						
Shelby County 100 Hurst St.	Center	TX	75935	936-598-5600	598-3701	338
Web: www.co.shelby.tx.us						
Shelby County Main St	Columbiana	AL	35051	205-669-3760		338
TF: 800-272-4263 ■ *Web:* www.shelbyal.com						
Shelby County 612 Ct St	Harlan	IA	51537	712-755-3831	755-3200	338
TF: 800-735-3942 ■ *Web:* www.shco.org						
Shelby County 315 1/2 E Main St	Shelbyville	IL	62565	217-774-1499		338
Shelby County 25 W Polk St	Shelbyville	IN	46176	317-392-6330	392-6393	338
Web: www.co.shelby.in.us						
Shelby County 1000 Detention Rd	Shelbyville	KY	40065	502-633-2343	647-1457	338
Web: shelbycounty.ky.gov/pages/default.aspx						
Shelby County 129 E Ct St Ste 100	Sidney	OH	45365	937-498-7226	498-1293	338
TF: 800-688-4820 ■ *Web:* www.co.shelby.oh.us						
Shelby County Chamber of Commerce						
501 N Harrison St.	Shelbyville	IN	46176	317-398-6647	392-3901	139
TF: 800-318-4083 ■ *Web:* www.shelbychamber.net						
Shelby County Chamber of Commerce						
316 Main St	Shelbyville	KY	40065	502-633-1636	633-7501	139
TF: 800-880-1420 ■ *Web:* www.shelbycountykychamber.com						
Shelby County Missouri						
204-B N Ctr						
Inside Lillard's Insurance Agency	Shelbina	MO	63468	573-822-9651		338
Web: shelbycountymo.com						
Shelby County Office of Tourism						
315 E Main St.	Shelbyville	IL	62565	217-774-2244		206
TF: 800-874-3529 ■ *Web:* www.lakeshelbyville.com						
Shelby County Reporter						
115 N Main St	Columbiana	AL	35051	205-669-3131	669-4217	532-4
TF: 800-761-2393 ■ *Web:* www.shelbycountyreporter.com						
Shelby Electric Co-op (SEC)						
1355 IL-128 state PO Box 560	Shelbyville	IL	62565	217-774-3986		245
TF: 800-677-2612 ■ *Web:* www.shelbyelectric.coop						
Shelby Energy Co-op Inc						
620 Old Finchville Rd	Shelbyville	KY	40065	502-633-4420		245
TF: 800-292-6585 ■ *Web:* www.shelbyenergy.com						
Shelby Engineering Ltd						
9632 54 Ave NW	Edmonton	AB	T6E5V1	780-438-2540		261
Web: www.shelbyengineering.ca						
Shelby Industries Inc						
175 McDaniels Rd	Shelbyville	KY	40065	502-633-2040		190
Web: www.shelbyindustries.com						
Shelby Materials						
157 E Rampart St PO Box 242	Shelbyville	IN	46176	800-548-9516		182
TF: 800-548-9516 ■ *Web:* www.shelbymaterials.com						
Shelby Richard C (Sen R - AL)						
304 Russell Bldg	Washington	DC	20510	202-224-5744	224-3416	342-2
Web: www.shelby.senate.gov						
Shelby State Bank 242 N Michigan Ave.	Shelby	MI	49455	231-861-2123		70
Web: shelbybank.com						
Shelby Systems Inc						
7345 Goodlett Farms Pkwy	Cordova	TN	38016	901-757-2372		177
TF: 800-877-0222 ■ *Web:* www.shelbysystems.com						
Shelby Township Library						
51680 Van Dyke Hwy	Shelby Township	MI	48316	586-739-7414	726-0535	434-3
Web: www.shelbytwplib.org						
Shelby Williams Industries Inc						
810 W Hwy 25/70	Newport	TN	37821	423-623-0031	319-9371*	319-3
**Fax Area Code:* 866 ■ *TF General:* 800-873-3252 ■ *Web:* shelbywilliams.com						
Shelbyville Daily Union						
100 W Main St	Shelbyville	IL	62565	217-774-2161	774-5732	532-2
TF: 800-772-1213 ■ *Web:* www.shelbyvilledailyunion.com						
Shelbyville State Fish & Wildlife Area						
562 State Hwy 121 PO Box 42A	Bethany	IL	61914	217-665-3112		565
Web: www.dnr.illinois.gov/parks/pages/shelbyville.aspx						
Shelbyville-Bedford County Chamber of Commerce						
100 N Cannon Blvd	Shelbyville	TN	37160	931-684-3482	684-3483	139
Web: www.shelbyvilletn.com						
Shelbyville-Shelby County Public Library						
57 W Broadway	Shelbyville	IN	46176	317-398-7121	421-2758	434-3
Web: www.myshelbylibrary.org						
Sheldahl Inc 1150 Sheldahl Rd	Northfield	MN	55057	507-663-8000		696
TF: 800-927-3580 ■ *Web:* www.sheldahl.com						
Sheldon Gross Realty Inc						
80 Main St	West Orange	NJ	07052	973-325-6200		652
Web: www.sheldongrossrealty.com						
Sheldon Jackson Museum 104 College Dr.	Sitka	AK	99835	907-747-8981	747-3004	520
Web: museums.alaska.gov						
Sheldon Laboratory Systems Inc						
102 Kirk St PO Box 836	Crystal Springs	MS	39059	601-892-2731		419
TF: 800-531-7604 ■ *Web:* www.sheldonlabs.com						
Sheldon Lake State Park & Environmental Learning Ctr						
15315 Beaumont Hwy at Pk Rd 138	Houston	TX	77049	281-456-2800		565
Web: tpwd.texas.gov/state-parks/sheldon-lake						
Sheldon Manufacturing Corp						
300 N 26th Ave	Cornelius	OR	97113	503-640-3000		697
Web: www.shellab.com						
Sheldon Museum of Art PO Box 880300	Lincoln	NE	68588	402-472-2461		520
TF: 800-833-6747 ■ *Web:* www.sheldonartmuseum.org						
Sheldon's Express Pharmacy Inc						
843 Fairview Ave	Bowling Green	KY	42101	270-842-4515		238
Web: sheldonsrx.com						
Sheldons' Inc 626 Ctr St	Antigo	WI	54409	715-623-2382	623-3001	710
Web: www.mepps.com						
Shelko Consulting Llc						
545 N Maple Ave	Ridgewood	NJ	07450	201-444-2089		196
Web: www.shelko.com						
Shell Canada Ltd 400 Fourth Ave SW	Calgary	AB	T2P0J4	403-691-3111		536
TF: 877-656-3111 ■ *Web:* www.shell.ca						
Shell Chemical Co 910 Louisiana St	Houston	TX	77002	713-241-6161		144
TF: 800-331-3703 ■ *Web:* www.shell.com						
Shell Chemical Lp - Mobile						
400 Industrial Pkwy Ext E	Saraland	AL	36571	251-675-7040		580
Web: www.shell.com/business-customers/chemicals.html						
Shell Energy North America						
1000 Main 12th Fl	Houston	TX	77002	713-767-5300		787
Web: www.shell.us						
Shell House Restaurant, The						
8 Gateway Blvd	Savannah	GA	31419	912-927-3280		671
Web: shellhouseseafoodsavannah.com						
Shell Island Ocean Front Suites						
2700 N Lumina Ave	Wrightsville Beach	NC	28480	910-256-8696		707
TF: 800-689-6765 ■ *Web:* www.shellisland.com						
Shell Lubricants 1000 Main 12th Fl	Houston	TX	77002	713-767-5300		541
TF Cust Svc: 866-818-5501 ■ *Web:* www.shell.us						
Shell Lumber & Hardware Co						
2733 SW 27th Ave	Miami	FL	33133	305-856-6401		752
Web: www.shelllumber.com						
Shell Machine Works Inc						
5317 Agnes St	Corpus Christi	TX	78405	361-883-7073		567
Web: www.shellmachineworks.com						
Shell Oil Co 910 Louisanna St	Houston	TX	77002	713-241-6161		536
TF: 888-467-4355 ■ *Web:* www.shell.us						
Shell Point Village						
15101 Shell Pt Blvd	Fort Myers	FL	33908	239-466-1131		672
TF Mktg: 800-780-1131 ■ *Web:* www.shellpoint.org						
Shell Vacations Club						
40 Skokie Blvd Ste 350	Northbrook	IL	60062	847-564-4600		753
Web: www.shellvacationsclub.com						
Shelley Electric Inc 3619 W 29th St S	Wichita	KS	67217	316-945-8311		189-4
Web: www.shelleyelectric.com						
Shelly Assoc Inc 17171 Murphy Ave	Irvine	CA	92614	949-417-8070	417-8075	253
Web: www.shellyinc.com						
Shelly Automotive Group						
Irvine BMW 9881 Research Dr	Irvine	CA	92618	888-853-7429		57
TF: 888-853-7429 ■ *Web:* www.shellygroup.com						
Shelly Co 80 Pk Dr	Thornville	OH	43076	740-246-6315		188-4
Web: www.shellyco.com						
Shelly Enterprises 3120 Old State Rd.	Telford	PA	18969	215-723-5108		499
Web: www.shellyslumber.com						
SheltAir Aviation Services Fort Lauderdale						
4860 NE 12th Ave	Fort Lauderdale	FL	33334	954-771-2210	771-3745	63
TF: 800-700-2210 ■ *Web:* www.sheltairaviation.com						
Shelter Canadian Properties Ltd						
2600 Seven Evergreen Pl	Winnipeg	MB	R3L2T3	204-475-9090		652
Web: www.scpl.com						
Shelter Enterprises 8 Saratoga St	Cohoes	NY	12047	518-237-4100		234
Web: www.shelter-ent.com						
Shelter Group, The						
218 N Charles St Ste 220	Baltimore	MD	21201	410-962-0595	347-0587	653
Web: www.theSheltergroup.com						
Shelter Island State Marine Park						
PO Box 111071	Juneau	AK	99811	907-465-4563		565
Web: dnr.alaska.gov/parks/cabins/south.htm						
Shelter Mortgage Company LLC						
4000 W Brown Deer Rd	Milwaukee	WI	53209	414-716-2800		77
Web: www.sheltermortgage.com						
ShelterLogic Corp 150 Callendar Rd	Watertown	CT	06795	860-945-6442		105
TF: 800-932-9344 ■ *Web:* www.shelterlogic.com						

	Phone	Fax	Class

Shelton City School District
382 Long Hill Ave.... Shelton CT 06484 | 203-924-1023 | | 685
Web: www.sheltonpublicschools.org

Shelton Group 12400 Coit Rd Ste 650.... Dallas TX 75251 | 972-239-5119 | | 636
Web: www.sheltongroup.com

Shelton State Community College
9500 Old Greensboro Rd.... Tuscaloosa AL 35405 | 205-391-2211 | 391-3910* | 162
**Fax:* Admissions ■ *TF:* 877-211-7722 ■ *Web:* www.sheltonstate.edu

Shelton-Mason County Chamber of Commerce
215 W Railroad Ave PO Box 2389.... Shelton WA 98584 | 360-426-2021 | 426-8678 | 139
TF: 800-576-2021 ■ *Web:* www.sheltonchamber.org

Shelton-McMurphey-Johnson House
303 Willamette St.... Eugene OR 97401 | 541-484-0808 | | 50-3
Web: www.smjhouse.org

Shelton-Turnbull Printers Inc
3403 W Seventh Ave.... Eugene OR 97402 | 541-687-1214 | | 627
Web: www.stprint.com

Shelving Inc 32 S Squirrel Rd.... Auburn Hills MI 48326 | 248-852-8600 | | 361
TF: 800-637-9508 ■ *Web:* www.shelving.com

Shemer Arts Ctr & Museum Assn Inc (SACAMA)
5005 E Camelback Rd.... Phoenix AZ 85018 | 602-262-4727 | | 520
Web: www.shemerartcenter.org

Shenandoah at the Arbor
10631 Los Alamitos Blvd.... Los Alamitos CA 90720 | 562-431-1990 | | 671
Web: eatatthearbor.com

Shenandoah County
600 N Main St Ste 102.... Woodstock VA 22664 | 540-459-6167 | 459-6192 | 338
Web: shenandoahcountyva.us

Shenandoah Electronic Intelligence Inc
220 University Blvd.... Harrisonburg VA 22801 | 540-434-7075 | | 256

Shenandoah Furniture Inc
225 Beaver Creek Dr.... Martinsville VA 24112 | 276-632-0502 | | 321

Shenandoah Life Insurance Co
2301 Brambleton Ave.... Roanoke VA 24015 | 540-985-4400 | 985-4444 | 391-2
TF: 800-848-5433 ■ *Web:* www.shenlife.com

Shenandoah National Park
3655 US Hwy 211E.... Luray VA 22835 | 540-999-3500 | 999-3601 | 564
TF: 800-732-0911 ■ *Web:* www.nps.gov/shen

Shenandoah Telecommunications Co
500 Shentel Way.... Edinburg VA 22824 | 540-984-5224 | 984-3438 | 360-3
NASDAQ: SHEN ■ *TF:* 800-743-6835 ■ *Web:* www.shentel.com

Shenandoah University
1460 University Dr.... Winchester VA 22601 | 540-665-4581 | | 166
TF: 800-432-2266 ■ *Web:* www.su.edu

Shenandoah Valley Westminster-Canterbury
300 Westminster-Canterbury Dr.... Winchester VA 22603 | 540-665-5914 | | 672
TF: 800-492-9463 ■ *Web:* www.svwc.org

Shenandoah Wood Preserving Inc
301 E 16th St.... Scotland Neck NC 27874 | 252-826-4151 | | 818

Shenango Advanced Ceramics LLC
606 McCleary Ave.... New Castle PA 16101 | 724-652-6668 | | 662
Web: rescoproducts.com

Shenango Valley Chamber of Commerce
41 Chestnut Ave.... Sharon PA 16146 | 724-981-5880 | 981-5480 | 139
Web: www.svchamber.com

Shen-Heights TV Assoc Inc
380 Maple Wood Dr.... Hazle Township PA 18202 | 570-462-1911 | | 116
Web: www.shenhgts.net

Shenipsit State Forest
166 Chestnut Hill Rd Rt 190.... Stafford Springs CT 06076 | 860-684-3430 | 684-4130 | 565
Web: www.ct.gov/dep/cwp/view.asp?a=2716&q=332506

Shenkman Capital Management Inc
461 Fifth Ave 22nd Fl.... New York NY 10017 | 212-867-9090 | | 194
TF: 800-541-7774 ■ *Web:* www.shenkmancapital.com

Shenvalee Golf Resort
9660 Fairway Dr.... New Market VA 22844 | 540-740-3181 | | 669
TF: 888-339-3181 ■ *Web:* www.shenvalee.com

Shepard Exposition Services
1531 Carroll Dr NW.... Atlanta GA 30318 | 404-720-8600 | 720-8750 | 184
Web: www.shepardes.com

Shepard State Park 1034 Graveline Rd.... Gautier MS 39553 | 228-497-2244 | | 565
Web: www.mdwfp.com

Shepard Steel Company Inc
110 Meadow St.... Hartford CT 06114 | 860-525-4446 | | 480
TF: 800-225-1111 ■ *Web:* www.shepardsteel.com

Shepeard Community Blood Ctr
1533 Wrightsboro Rd.... Augusta GA 30904 | 706-737-4551 | | 89
Web: www.shepeardblood.org

Shephard's Beach Resort
619 S Gulfview Blvd.... Clearwater Beach FL 33767 | 727-441-6875 | | 379
TF: 800-237-8477 ■ *Web:* www.shephards.com

Shepherd Caster Corp
203 Kerth St.... Saint Joseph MI 49085 | 269-983-7351 | | 350
TF: 800-253-0868 ■ *Web:* www.shepherdcasters.com

Shepherd CE Company Inc
2221 Canada Dry St.... Houston TX 77023 | 713-924-4300 | 928-2324 | 600
TF: 800-324-6733 ■ *Web:* www.ceshepherd.com

Shepherd Chemical Co 4900 Beech St.... Cincinnati OH 45212 | 513-731-1110 | | 143
Web: www.shepchem.com

Shepherd Ctr 2020 Peachtree Rd NE.... Atlanta GA 30309 | 404-352-2020 | 350-7341 | 374-6
Web: www.shepherd.org

Shepherd Electric Supply
7401 Pulaski Hwy.... Baltimore MD 21237 | 410-866-6000 | 866-6001 | 246
TF Sales: 800-253-1777 ■ *Web:* www.shepherdelec.com

Shepherd Express
207 E Buffalo St Ste 410.... Milwaukee WI 53202 | 414-276-2222 | 276-3312 | 532-5
TF: 800-554-1448 ■ *Web:* shepherdexpress.com

Shepherd of the Hills Homestead & Outdoor Theatre
5586 W Hwy 76.... Branson MO 65616 | 417-334-4191 | | 572
TF: 800-653-6288 ■ *Web:* theshepherdofthehills.com

Shepherd Oil Company LP 1831 S Main.... Blackwell OK 74631 | 580-363-4280 | | 324
TF: 800-256-1712 ■ *Web:* www.shepherdoil.com

Shepherd University
301 N King St.... Shepherdstown WV 25443 | 304-876-5000 | 876-5165* | 166
**Fax:* Admissions ■ *TF:* 800-344-5231 ■ *Web:* www.shepherd.edu

Shepherd Valley Waldorf School
6500 Dry Creek Pkwy.... Niwot CO 80503 | 303-652-0130 | | 685
Web: shepherdvalley.org

Shepherd Ventures
11526 Sorrento Valley Rd Ste F.... San Diego CA 92121 | 858-509-4744 | 509-3662 | 792
Web: www.shepherdventures.com

Shepherd's Home Hardware Ltd
3525 Mill St.... Armstrong BC V0E1B0 | 250-546-3002 | | 350
TF: 800-667-4321 ■ *Web:* www.shepherdshardware.com

Shepherd, Finkelman, Miller & Shah LLP
65 Main St.... Chester CT 06412 | 860-526-1100 | | 428
Web: www.sfmslaw.com

Shepherdsville-Bullitt County Tourist & Convention Commission
395 Paroquet Springs Dr.... Shepherdsville KY 40165 | 502-543-8687 | 543-4889 | 206
TF: 800-526-2068 ■ *Web:* www.travelbullitt.org

Sheplers Inc 6501 W Kellogg Dr.... Wichita KS 67209 | 888-835-4004 | | 157-5
TF: 888-835-4004 ■ *Web:* www.sheplers.com

Shepley Bulfinch 2 Seaport Ln.... Boston MA 02210 | 617-423-1700 | 451-2420 | 261
TF: 800-934-9691 ■ *Web:* shepleybulfinch.com

Sheppard Air Force Base
419 G Ave Ste 3.... Sheppard AFB TX 76311 | 940-676-2511 | 676-4245 | 497-1
TF: 877-676-1847 ■ *Web:* www.sheppard.af.mil

Sheppard Motors 2300 W Seventh Ave.... Eugene OR 97402 | 541-343-8811 | | 57
TF Sales: 877-362-1865 ■ *Web:* www.sheppardmotors.com

Sheppard Mullin Richter & Hampton LLP
333 S Hope St 48th Fl.... Los Angeles CA 90071 | 213-620-1780 | 620-1398 | 428
Web: www.sheppardmullin.com

Sheppard Pratt Health System (SPHS)
6501 N Charles St.... Baltimore MD 21285 | 410-938-3000 | | 374-5
TF: 800-627-0330 ■ *Web:* www.sheppardpratt.org

Sheppard T Powell Assoc LLC
1915 Aliceanna St.... Baltimore MD 21231 | 410-327-3500 | | 256
Web: www.stpa.com

Sheraton Agoura Hills Hotel
30100 Agoura Rd.... Agoura Hills CA 91301 | 818-707-1220 | | 707
TF: 866-716-8134 ■ *Web:* www.sheratonagourahills.com

Sheraton Atlanta 165 Courtland St NE.... Atlanta GA 30303 | 404-659-6500 | | 378
TF: 800-325-3535 ■ *Web:* www.sheratonatlantahotel.com

Sheraton Colonial Hotel & Golf Club Boston North
1 Audubon Rd.... Wakefield MA 01880 | 781-245-9300 | 245-9300 | 379
TF: 866-716-8133 ■ *Web:* www.starwoodhotels.com

Sheraton Columbia Hotel
10207 Wincopin Cir.... Columbia MD 21044 | 410-730-3900 | | 378
TF: 888-627-8318 ■ *Web:* www.sheratoncolumbia.com

Sheraton Crescent Hotel
2620 W Dunlap Ave.... Phoenix AZ 85021 | 602-943-8200 | | 378
TF: 800-434-7894 ■ *Web:* www.sheratoncrescent.com

Sheraton Denver Tech Center Hotel
7007 S Clinton St.... Greenwood Village CO 80112 | 303-799-6200 | | 707
TF: 800-525-3177 ■ *Web:* www.sheratondenvertech.com

Sheraton Fishermans Wharf (San Francisco, CA)
2500 Mason St.... San Francisco CA 94133 | 415-362-5500 | | 707
TF: 866-716-8134 ■ *Web:* www.sheratonatthewharf.com

Sheraton Gateway Hotel Los Angeles
6101 W Century Blvd.... Los Angeles CA 90045 | 310-642-1111 | | 379
TF: 888-627-7104 ■ *Web:* www.sheratonlax.com

Sheraton Gunter Hotel
205 E Houston St.... San Antonio TX 78205 | 210-227-3241 | | 707
TF: 866-716-8134 ■ *Web:* www.sheratongunter.com

Sheraton Iowa City Hotel
210 S Dubuque St.... Iowa City IA 52240 | 319-337-4058 | | 378
Web: www.sheratoniowacity.com

Sheraton Kauai Resort 2440 Hoonani Rd.... Koloa HI 96756 | 808-742-1661 | | 669
TF Resv: 800-325-3535 ■ *Web:* sheraton-kauai.com

Sheraton Maui Resort
2605 Kaanapali Pkwy.... Lahaina HI 96761 | 808-661-0031 | 661-0458 | 669
Web: sheraton-maui.com

Sheraton Music City Hotel (Nashville Tenn)
777 McGavock Pk.... Nashville TN 37214 | 615-885-2200 | | 378
Web: www.starwoodhotels.com

Sheraton Nashville Downtown Hotel
623 Union St.... Nashville TN 37219 | 615-259-2000 | | 378
TF: 800-325-3535 ■ *Web:* www.sheratonnashvilledowntown.com

Sheraton New York Hotel & Towers
811 Seventh Ave.... New York NY 10019 | 212-581-1000 | | 377
Web: www.sheratonnewyork.com

Sheraton Oklahoma City Hotel
1 N Broadway.... Oklahoma City OK 73102 | 405-235-2780 | | 378
TF: 888-627-8416 ■ *Web:* www.sheratonokc.com

Sheraton Old San Juan Hotel
100 Calle Brumbaugh.... San Juan PR 00901 | 787-289-1914 | | 377
TF: 888-627-8185 ■ *Web:* www.sheratonoldsanjuan.com

Sheraton Phoenix Downtown Hotel
340 N Third St.... Phoenix AZ 85004 | 602-262-2500 | | 707
TF: 866-716-8134 ■ *Web:* www.sheratonphoenixdowntown.com

Sheraton Premiere at Tysons Corner
8661 Leesburg Pk.... Tysons VA 22182 | 703-448-1234 | | 378
TF: 800-572-7666 ■ *Web:* www.sheratontysonscorner.com

Sheraton Raleigh Hotel
421 S Salisbury St.... Raleigh NC 27601 | 919-834-9900 | | 707
TF: 888-627-8319 ■ *Web:* www.sheratonraleigh.com

Sheraton Safari Hotel & Suites
12205 S Apopka Vineland Rd.... Orlando FL 32836 | 407-239-0444 | | 707
TF: 800-325-3535 ■ *Web:* www.sheratonlakebuenavistaresort.com

Sheraton Sand Key Resort
1160 Gulf Blvd.... Clearwater Beach FL 33767 | 727-595-1611 | | 669
TF: 800-456-7263 ■ *Web:* www.sheratonsandkey.com

Sheraton Suites Calgary Eau Claire
255 Barclay Parade SW.... Calgary AB T2P5C2 | 403-266-7200 | | 379
TF: 866-716-8134 ■ *Web:* sheratonsuites.com

Sheraton Universal Hotel
333 Universal Hollywood Dr.... Universal City CA 91608 | 818-980-1212 | | 378
Web: www.sheratonuniversal.com

Sheraton Waikiki 2255 Kalakaua Ave.... Honolulu HI 96815 | 808-922-4422 | | 669
TF: 800-325-3535 ■ *Web:* sheraton-waikiki.com

Sheraton Washington North Hotel
4095 Powder Mill Rd.... Beltsville MD 20705 | 301-937-4422 | | 707
TF: 866-716-8134 ■ *Web:* www.sheratoncollegeparknorth.com

Sheraton Wild Horse Pass Resort & Spa
5594 W Wild Horse Pass Blvd.... Chandler AZ 85226 | 602-225-0100 | 225-0300 | 669
TF: 800-325-3535 ■ *Web:* www.wildhorsepassresort.com

Name / Address	City	State	Zip	Phone	Fax	Class
Shercon Inc 6262 Katella Ave	Cypress	CA	90630	714-548-3999		676
TF: 888-227-5847 ■ *Web:* www.caplugs.com						
Sheridan College						
3059 Coffeen Ave PO Box 1500	Sheridan	WY	82801	307-674-6446	674-7205	162
TF: 800-913-9139 ■ *Web:* www.sheridan.edu						
Gillette 300 W Sinclair St	Gillette	WY	82718	307-686-0254		162
TF: 800-913-9139 ■ *Web:* www.sheridan.edu						
Sheridan County 100 W Laurel Ave	Plentywood	MT	59254	406-765-1660	765-2609	338
Web: www.co.sheridan.mt.us						
Sheridan County PO Box 39 PO Box 39	Rushville	NE	69360	308-327-5650		338
Web: sheridancountyne.com						
Sheridan County 224 S Main St Ste B-2	Sheridan	WY	82801	307-674-2500		338
TF: 800-565-4502 ■ *Web:* www.sheridancounty.com						
Sheridan County						
North Dakota 215 E Second St	McClusky	ND	58463	701-363-2207		338
Web: www.co.sheridan.nd.us						
Sheridan County Chamber of Commerce						
1517 E Fifth St	Sheridan	WY	82801	307-672-2485	672-7321	139
TF: 800-453-3650 ■ *Web:* www.sheridanwyomingchamber.org						
Sheridan Electric Co-op Inc						
PO Box 227	Medicine Lake	MT	59247	406-789-2231		245
TF: 888-472-1533 ■ *Web:* www.sheridanelectric.coop						
Sheridan Group						
11311 McCormick Rd Ste 260	Hunt Valley	MD	21031	410-785-7277	785-7217	626
TF: 800-352-2210 ■ *Web:* www.sheridan.com						
Sheridan Group Inc, The						
2045 Pontius Ave	Los Angeles	CA	90025	310-575-0664		321
Web: www.sheridaninc.com						
Sheridan Healthcare Inc						
1613 NW 136th Ave Ste 200	Sunrise	FL	33323	800-437-2672		463
TF: 800-437-2672 ■ *Web:* www.sheridanhealthcare.com						
Sheridan Legacy Group						
400 N Michigan Ave Ste 900	Chicago	IL	60611	312-548-7064		528
Web: sheridancp.com						
Sheridan Livestock Auction Company Inc						
Sale Barn Rd	Rushville	NE	69360	308-327-2406		446
TF: 800-672-3492 ■ *Web:* sheridanlivestock.com						
Sheridan Memorial Hospital						
1401 W Fifth St	Sheridan	WY	82801	307-672-1000		374-3
TF: 800-994-6610 ■ *Web:* www.sheridanhospital.org						
Sheridan Pond 8130 S Lakewood Pl	Tulsa	OK	74137	918-901-9449		379
Web: www.sheridanpondapartmentstulsa.com						
Shermag Inc 3035 Boul Industriel	Sherbrooke	QC	J1L2T9	819-566-1515	566-7323	319-2
TF: 800-567-3419 ■ *Web:* www.shermag.com						
Sherman & Armbruster LLP						
609 Treybourne Dr	Greenwood	IN	46142	317-881-6670		2
Web: shermanandarmbruster.com						
Sherman & Assoc 333 Harmon Ave NW	Warren	OH	44483	330-399-4500	399-6747	5
Web: www.shermanexperience.com						
Sherman & Reilly Inc						
400 W 33rd St	Chattanooga	TN	37410	423-756-5300	756-2948	470
TF Sales: 800-251-7780 ■ *Web:* www.sherman-reilly.com						
Sherman Brad (Rep D - CA)						
2242 Rayburn Bldg	Washington	DC	20515	202-225-5911	225-5879	342-2
Web: sherman.house.gov						
Sherman Bros Trucking						
32921 Diamond Hill Dr PO Box 706	Harrisburg	OR	97446	541-995-7751		780
TF: 800-547-8980 ■ *Web:* www.shermantrucking.com						
Sherman Capital Markets LLC						
200 Meeting St Ste 206	Charleston	SC	29401	843-266-1717		401
Sherman Clay & Company Inc						
1111 Bayhill Dr Ste 450	San Bruno	CA	94066	650-952-2300		526
TF: 800-448-4904 ■ *Web:* www.shermanclay.com						
Sherman County 813 Broadway Ste 302	Goodland	KS	67735	785-890-4800		338
Sherman County PO Box 456	Loup City	NE	68853	308-745-1513	745-0297	338
Web: www.co.sherman.ne.us						
Sherman County PO Box 270	Stratford	TX	79084	806-366-2371	366-5670	338
Web: www.co.sherman.tx.us						
Sherman Financial Group LLC						
335 Madison Ave	New York	NY	10017	212-922-1616		69
Web: sfg.com						
Sherman Hill National Historic District						
1620 Pleasant Ste 204	Des Moines	IA	50314	515-284-5717		50-3
Web: www.historicshermanhill.com						
Sherman International Corp						
367 Mansfield Ave	Pittsburgh	PA	15220	412-928-2880		194
TF: 800-745-6008 ■ *Web:* www.shermaninternational.com						
Sherman Library & Gardens						
2647 E Coast Hwy	Corona del Mar	CA	92625	949-673-2261	675-5458	97
Web: www.slgardens.org						
Sherman Mechanical Inc 1075 Alexander Ct	Cary	IL	60013	847-462-1020		35
Web: www.shermanmech.com						
Sherman Oaks Hospital & Health Ctr						
4929 Van Nuys Blvd	Sherman Oaks	CA	91403	818-981-7111		374-3
TF: 800-288-2020 ■ *Web:* www.shermanoakshospital.org						
Sherman Public Library						
421 N Travis St	Sherman	TX	75090	903-892-7240		434-3
Web: www.barr.org						
Sherman Reservoir State Recreation Area						
79025 Sherman Dam Rd Ste 1	Loup City	NE	68853	308-745-0230		565
Web: outdoornebraska.gov						
Sherman West Court 1950 Larkin Ave	Elgin	IL	60123	847-742-7070		450
Web: shermanwestcourt.com						
Shermco Industries Inc						
2425 E Pioneer Dr	Irving	TX	75061	972-793-5523		261
TF: 800-589-6343 ■ *Web:* www.shermco.com						
Shermeta, Adams & Von Allmen PC						
901 Tower Dr Ste 400	Troy	MI	48098	248-519-1700		428
TF: 800-451-7992 ■ *Web:* www.shermeta.com						
Shernoff Bidart Darras & Echeverria LLP						
600 S Indian Hill Blvd	Claremont	CA	91711	909-621-4935		428
TF: 800-458-3386 ■ *Web:* shernoff.com						
Sherpa Adventure Gear Inc						
7857 S 180th St	Kent	WA	98032	425-251-0760		157-6
TF: 877-724-8735 ■ *Web:* www.sherpaadventuregear.com						
Sherpa Digital Media Inc						
509 Seaport Ct	Redwood City	CA	94063	877-989-7794		5
TF: 866-989-7794 ■ *Web:* www.sherpadigitalmedia.com						
Sherpa Marketing 8448 Maourer Rd	Lenexa	KS	66219	646-567-8305		195
Web: www.sherpamarketing.net						
Sherpalo PO Box 2627	Saratoga	CA	02627	650-319-2220		463
Web: www.sherpalo.com						
Sherrard Kuzz LLP 155 University Ave	Toronto	ON	M5H3B7	416-603-0700		428
TF: 800-411-2900 ■ *Web:* www.sherrardkuzz.com						
Sherrard Roe Voigt & Harbison PLC						
150 Third Ave S Ste 1100	Nashville	TN	37201	615-742-4200		445
Web: sherrardroe.com						
Sherrick Aerospace 307 Emery Dr	Nashville	TN	37214	615-872-1050		186
Web: www.sherrickco.com						
Sherrill Furniture Co						
2405 Highland Ave NE	Hickory	NC	28601	828-322-2640		319-2
Web: www.sherrillfurniture.com						
Sherrill House Inc (SH)						
135 S Huntington Ave	Jamaica Plain	MA	02130	617-731-2400	731-8671	450
TF: 800-539-9767 ■ *Web:* www.sherrillhouse.org						
Sherrill-Lubinski Corp						
240 Tamal Vista Blvd	Corte Madera	CA	94925	415-927-8400		177
TF: 800-548-6881 ■ *Web:* www.sl.com						
Sherritt International Corp						
1133 Yonge St	Toronto	ON	M4T2Y7	416-924-4551	924-5015	502
TSE: S ■ *TF:* 800-704-6698 ■ *Web:* www.sherritt.com						
Sherrod Vans Inc						
3151 Industrial Blvd	Waycross	GA	31503	800-824-6333		62-7
TF: 800-824-6333 ■ *Web:* www.sherrodvans.com						
Sherry Matthews Inc 200 S Congress Ave	Austin	TX	78704	512-478-4397		4
TF: 877-478-4397 ■ *Web:* www.sherrymatthews.com						
Sherry Mfg 3287 NW 65th St	Miami	FL	33147	305-693-7000	691-6132	155-3
TF: 800-741-4750 ■ *Web:* www.sherrymfg.com						
Sherry-Lehmann Wine & Spirits						
505 Pk Ave	New York	NY	10022	212-838-7500	838-9285	443
Web: www.sherry-lehmann.com						
Sherry-Netherland Hotel						
781 Fifth Ave	New York	NY	10022	212-355-2800	319-4306	379
TF: 877-743-7710 ■ *Web:* www.sherrynetherland.com						
Sherwin Manor Nursing Ctr						
7350 N Sheridan Rd	Chicago	IL	60626	773-274-1000		450
TF: 800-213-0154 ■ *Web:* www.sherwinmanor.com						
Sherwin Miller Museum of Jewish Art						
2021 E 71st St	Tulsa	OK	74136	918-492-1818	492-1888	520
Web: www.jewishmuseum.net						
Sherwin-Williams Automotive Finishes						
4440 Warrensville Ctr Rd	Warrensville Heights	OH	44128	216-332-8330		550
TF: 800-798-5872 ■ *Web:* sherwin-automotive.com						
Sherwood 2200 N Main St	Washington	PA	15301	724-225-8000	225-6188	789
TF: 888-508-2583 ■ *Web:* www.sherwoodvalve.com						
Sherwood America						
6120 Valley View Buena Pk	Buena Park	CA	90620	714-739-2000	739-2009	52
Web: www.sherwoodamerica.com						
Sherwood Construction Company Inc						
3219 W May St	Wichita	KS	67213	316-943-0211	943-3772	188-4
Web: www.sherwoodcompanies.com						
Sherwood Design Engineers						
58 Maiden Ln 3rd Fl	San Francisco	CA	94108	415-677-7300		261
Web: www.sherwoodengineers.com						
Sherwood Food Distributors						
12499 Evergreen	Detroit	MI	48228	313-659-7300		805
Web: www.sherwoodfoods.com						
Sherwood Forest Plantation						
14501 John Tyler Memorial Hwy	Charles City	VA	23030	804-829-5377		520
TF: 800-422-8011 ■ *Web:* www.sherwoodforest.org						
Sherwood Fox Arboretum						
University of Western Ontario						
1151 Richmond St	London	ON	N6A5B7	519-850-2542	661-3935	97
Web: uwo.ca						
Sherwood Island State Park						
PO Box 188	Greens Farms	CT	06838	203-226-6983		565
Web: www.ct.gov						
Sherwood Mall 5308 Pacific Ave	Stockton	CA	95207	209-952-6277		460
Web: www.sherwoodmall.com						
Sherwood Oaks						
100 Norman Dr	Cranberry Township	PA	16066	724-776-8100	776-8468	672
TF: 800-642-2217 ■ *Web:* www.sherwood-oaks.com						
Sherwood Windows Ltd 37 Iron St	Toronto	ON	M9W5E3	416-675-3262		350
TF: 800-770-5256 ■ *Web:* www.sherwoodwindows.com						
Sherwood-Logan & Assoc Inc						
2140 Renard Ct	Annapolis	MD	21401	410-841-6810		261
Web: sherwoodlogan.com						
Sherzer & Assoc Insurance Inc						
110 Stony Point Rd Ste 120	Santa Rosa	CA	95401	707-573-1010		390
Web: www.sherzer.com						
Shetler Moving & Storage Inc						
1253 E Diamond Ave	Evansville	IN	47711	812-421-7750	421-7759	780
TF: 800-321-5069 ■ *Web:* www.shetlermoving.com						
Sheyenne Tooling & Mfg						
701 Lenham Ave SW	Cooperstown	ND	58425	701-797-2700		454
Web: www.sheyennemfg.com						
SHI (Software House International)						
290 Davidson Ave	Somerset	NJ	08873	888-764-8888		174
TF: 888-764-8888 ■ *Web:* www.shi.com						
SHI Corp 35W Broadway Ste 104	Salt Lake City	UT	84101	888-764-8888		174
TF: 888-764-8888 ■ *Web:* www.shi-corp.com						
Shiao Lan Kung 930 Race St	Philadelphia	PA	19107	215-928-0282		671
Shiawassee County 208 N Shiawassee St	Corunna	MI	48817	989-743-2242	743-2241	338
TF: 800-342-2455 ■ *Web:* www.shiawassee.net						
Shibata Floral Company Supplies						
620 Brannan St	San Francisco	CA	94107	415-495-8611		292
TF: 800-676-1212 ■ *Web:* www.shibatafc.com						
Shibuya Hoppmann Corp						
13129 Airpark Dr Ste 120	Elkwood	VA	22718	540-829-2564	829-1726	547
TF Cust Svc: 800-368-3582 ■ *Web:* www.shibuyahoppmann.com						
Shick Tube Veyor Corp						
4346 Clary Blvd	Kansas City	MO	64130	816-861-7224	921-1901	207
TF: 877-744-2587 ■ *Web:* www.shickusa.com						
Shiel Medical Laboratory Inc						
Brooklyn Navy Yard Bldg 292 63 Flushing Ave	Brooklyn	NY	11205	718-552-1000		415
TF: 800-553-0873 ■ *Web:* www.shiel.com						

	Phone	Fax	Class
Shiel Sexton Company Inc 902 N Capitol Ave Indianapolis IN 46204 *Web:* www.shielsexton.com	317-423-6000	423-6300	186
Shield Air Solutions Inc 3708 Greenhouse Rd Houston TX 77084 *TF:* 800-237-2095 ■ *Web:* shieldair.com	281-944-4300		14
Shield Engineering Inc 4301 Taggart Creek Rd Charlotte NC 28208 *TF:* 800-395-5220 ■ *Web:* www.shieldengineering.com	704-394-6913		261
Shields & Company Inc 890 Winter St Ste 160 Waltham MA 02451 *Web:* www.shieldsco.com	781-890-7033		401
Shields Bag & Printing Co 1009 Rock Ave Yakima WA 98902 *TF:* 800-541-8630 ■ *Web:* shieldsbag.com	509-248-7500	248-6304	66
SHIELDS Electronics Supply Inc 4722 Middlebrook Pk Knoxville TN 37921 *TF:* 800-583-0148 ■ *Web:* shieldselectronics.com	865-588-2421		179
Shields Inc 2625 Hope Church Rd Winston-Salem NC 27103 *TF:* 800-294-3462 ■ *Web:* www.shieldsinc.com	336-765-9040	765-3715	189-9
Shifamed LLC 745 Camden Ave Ste A Campbell CA 95008 *Web:* www.shifamed.com	408-560-2500	903-4095	475
Shiffler Equipment Sales Inc 745 S St Chardon OH 44024 *Web:* www.chairglides.com	440-285-9175		362
SHIFT Communications LLC 275 Washington St Ste 410 Newton MA 02458 *Web:* www.shiftcomm.com	617-779-1800	779-1899	636
SHIFT Energy Inc 75 Prince William St Saint John NB E2L2B2 *Web:* www.shiftenergy.com	506-642-9422		192
ShiftCentral Inc 210 John St Ste 100 Moncton NB E1C0B8 *TF:* 866-551-5533 ■ *Web:* www.shiftcentral.com	866-551-5533		5
ShiftWise Inc 200 SW Market St Ste 700 Portland OR 97201 *TF:* 866-399-2220 ■ *Web:* www.shiftwise.net	866-399-2220		809
Shige Japanese Cuisine 100 N Eigth St Ste 215 Boise ID 83702 *Web:* www.shigescuisine.com	208-338-8423		671
Shikatani Lacroix Design Inc 387 Richmond E Toronto ON M5A1P6 *TF:* 800-992-4978 ■ *Web:* www.sld.com	416-367-1999		5
Shikellamy School District 200 Island Blvd Sunbury PA 17801 *Web:* www.shikbraves.org	570-286-3721		685
Shikellamy State Park Bridge Ave Sunbury PA 17801 *Web:* www.dcnr.state.pa.us	570-988-5557		565
Shiki Hana 222 Post Rd Fairfield CT 06824 *Web:* shikihanafairfield.com	203-259-5950	259-5428	671
Shiki Sushi 207 N Carolina 54 Durham NC 27713 *Web:* shikitasu.com	919-484-4108		671
Shiley-Marcos Alzheimer's Disease Research Ctr 8950 Villa La Jolla Dr Ste C129 La Jolla CA 92037 *Web:* www.adrc.ucsd.edu	858-622-5800	622-1012	668
Shilo Inn Hotel Salt Lake City 206 SW Temple Salt Lake City UT 84101 *TF:* 800-222-2244 ■ *Web:* www.shiloinns.com	800-222-2244		379
Shilo Inn Suites Hotel Portland Airport 117707 NE Airport Way Portland OR 97220 *TF:* 800-222-2244 ■ *Web:* www.shiloinns.com	503-252-7500	254-0794	379
Shilo Inn Suites Salem 3304 Market St Salem OR 97301 *TF:* 800-222-2244 ■ *Web:* www.shiloinns.com	503-581-4001	399-9385	379
Shilo Inns Suites Hotels 11600 SW Shilo Ln Portland OR 97225 *TF:* 800-222-2244 ■ *Web:* www.shiloinns.com	503-641-6565		379
Shiloh Industries Corp 880 Steel Dr Valley City OH 44280 *TF:* 800-414-3627 ■ *Web:* www.shiloh.com	330-558-2600		489
Shiloh National Military Park 1055 Pittsburg Landing Rd Shiloh TN 38376 *TF:* 800-426-8366 ■ *Web:* www.nps.gov/shil	731-689-5696	689-5450	564
Shiloh Service Inc 85 Mtn View Pl North Huntingdon PA 15642 *Web:* shilohservice.com	724-863-0190		175
Shimadzu Medical Systems 20101 S Vermont Ave Torrance CA 90502 *TF General:* 800-477-1227 ■ *Web:* www.shimadzu.com	310-217-8855	217-0661	382
Shimadzu Precision Instruments inc 3645 N Lakewood Blvd Long Beach CA 90808 *Web:* www.shimadzu.com	310-517-9910	517-9180	22
Shimadzu Scientific Instruments Inc 7102 Riverwood Dr Columbia MD 21046 *TF:* 800-477-1227 ■ *Web:* www.ssi.shimadzu.com	410-381-1227	381-1222	419
Shimano American Corp 1 Holland Dr Irvine CA 92618 *Web:* www.shimano.com	949-951-5003	768-0920	82
Shimek State Forest 33653 Rt J56 Farmington IA 52626 *Web:* www.iowadnr.gov	319-878-3811		565
Shimento 1350 Hayes St Benicia CA 94510 *TF:* 877-211-8708 ■ *Web:* www.shimento.com	877-211-8708		721
Shimer College 3424 S State St Chicago IL 60616 *TF:* 800-215-7173 ■ *Web:* www.shimer.edu	312-235-3506		166
Shimkus John (Rep R - IL) 2217 Rayburn HOB Washington DC 20515 *Web:* shimkus.house.gov	202-225-5271	225-5880	342-2
Shimokaji & Associates Pc 8911 Research Dr Irvine CA 92618 *TF:* 800-973-1177 ■ *Web:* www.shimokaji.com	949-788-9961		445
Shimpo 1701 Glenlake Ave Itasca IL 60143 *TF:* 800-842-1479 ■ *Web:* www.nidec-shimpo.com	630-924-7138		190
Shinano Kenshi Corp 6065 Bristol Pkwy Culver City CA 90230 *TF:* 800-755-0752 ■ *Web:* www.shinano.com	310-693-7600	693-7599	518
Shindler, Anderson, Goplerud & Weese P.C 5015 Grand Ridge Dr Ste 100 West Des Moines IA 50265	515-223-4567		428
Shine Advertising 612 W Main St Ste 105 Madison WI 53703 *Web:* shineunited.com	608-442-7373		7
Shine Investment Advisory Services Inc 9892 Rosemont Ave Ste 100 Lone Tree CO 80124 *TF:* 800-996-3426 ■ *Web:* www.shineinvestments.com	303-740-8600		401
SHINE Medical Technologies Inc 2555 Industrial Dr Ste 140 Monona WI 53713 *Web:* shinemed.com	608-210-1060		743
SHINE Systems & Technologies 1 Morton Dr Ste 100 Charlottesville VA 22903 *Web:* shinesystems.com	434-422-4220		180
Shine Tidelands State Park 202 NE Pk St Poulsbo WA 98370 *Web:* parks.state.wa.us	360-902-8844		565
Shin-Etsu Handotai America Inc 4111 NE 112th Ave Vancouver WA 98682-6776 *Web:* www.sehamerica.com	360-883-7053	883-7074	696
Shin-etsu Magnetics Inc 2372 Qume Dr Ste B San Jose CA 95131 *Web:* www.shinetsu.co.jp	408-383-9240	383-9245	458
Shin-Etsu Microsi Inc 10028 S 51st St Phoenix AZ 85044 *Web:* www.microsi.com	480-893-8898	893-8637	695
Shin-Etsu Silicones of America 1150 Damar Dr Akron OH 44305 *TF:* 800-544-1745 ■ *Web:* www.shinetsusilicones.com	330-630-9860	630-9855	144
Shingobee Builders Inc PO Box 8 Loretto MN 55357 *Web:* www.shingobee.com	763-479-1300	479-3267	186
Shinsei Corp 1001 Southpark Dr Peachtree City GA 30269 *Web:* www.shinseiusa.com	770-487-2294		596
Shintech Inc 3 Greenway Plaza Ste 1150 Houston TX 77046 *Web:* www.shintechinc.com	713-965-0713	965-0629	605-2
Shioi Construction Inc 98-724 Kuaho Pl Pearl City HI 96782 *Web:* shioihawaii.com	808-487-2441		186
Ship & Shore Environmental Inc 2474 N Palm Dr Signal Hill CA 90755 *Web:* www.shipandshore.com	562-997-0233		697
Shipbuilders Council of America (SCA) 20 F St NW Ste 500 Washington DC 20001 *Web:* www.shipbuilders.org	202-347-5462		49-21
Shipcom Wireless Inc 11200 Richmond Ave Ste 552 Houston TX 77082 *Web:* www.shipcomwireless.com	281-558-5252		225
Shipley Associates Inc 532 N 900 W Kaysville UT 84037 *Web:* www.shipleywins.com	801-544-9787		463
Shipley Energy 415 Norway St York PA 17403 **Fax Area Code:* 800 ■ *TF:* 800-839-1849 ■ *Web:* www.shipleyenergy.com	717-848-4100	839-1849*	316
Shipowners Claims Bureau (SCB) 1 Battery Pk Plaza 31st Fl New York NY 10004 *TF:* 800-774-8724 ■ *Web:* www.american-club.com	212-847-4500	847-4599	49-21
Shippensburg Area Chamber of Commerce 53 W King St Shippensburg PA 17257 *Web:* www.shippensburg.org	717-532-5509	532-7501	139
Shippensburg Pump Company Inc PO Box 279 Shippensburg PA 17257 *TF:* 800-849-1130 ■ *Web:* www.shipcopumps.com	717-532-7321		641
Shippensburg University 1871 Old Main Dr Shippensburg PA 17257 **Fax:* Admissions ■ *TF:* 800-822-8028 ■ *Web:* www.ship.edu	717-477-1231	477-4016*	166
Shippers Express Co 1651 Kerr Dr Jackson MS 39204 *TF:* 800-647-2480	601-948-4251	948-5232	780
Shippers Group, The 8901 Forney Rd Dallas TX 75227 *Web:* www.shipperswarehouse.com	214-381-5050		803-1
Ship-Right Solutions LLC 165 Pleasant Ave South Portland ME 04106 *Web:* www.shiprightsolutions.com	207-321-3500		317
Ships of the Sea Maritime Museum 41 Martin Luther King Junior Blvd Savannah GA 31401 *TF:* 800-496-7938 ■ *Web:* www.shipsofthesea.org	912-232-1511		520
Shipshewana/LaGrange County Convention & Visitors Bureau 350 S Van Buren St Ste H Shipshewana IN 46565 *TF:* 800-254-8090 ■ *Web:* visitshipshewana.org	260-768-4008		206
Shipside Crating Co Lp 16400 Jacinto Port Blvd Houston TX 77015 *Web:* www.shipsidecrating.com	281-457-2647		549
Shira Accessories Ltd 28 W 36th St New York NY 10018	212-594-4455		408
Shiraz Specialty Pharmacy 205 E Casino Rd Ste B17 Everett WA 98208 *Web:* www.shirazpharmacy.com	425-356-3276		237
Shirl K Floral Designs 2701 Pontoon Rd Granite City IL 62040 *Web:* www.shirlkfloral.com	618-797-6210		292
Shirley Contracting Corp 8435 Backlick Rd Lorton VA 22079 *Web:* www.shirleycontracting.com	703-550-8100	550-7897	188-4
Shirley Plantation 501 Shirley Plantation Rd Charles City VA 23030 *Web:* www.shirleyplantation.com	804-829-5121		50-3
Shiro's Sushi Restaurant 2401 Second Ave Seattle WA 98121 *Web:* www.shiros.com	206-443-9844		671
Shiroki North America Inc 1111 W Broad St Smithville TN 37166 *Web:* www.shiroki-na.com	615-597-8870		567
Shirtcliff Oil Co PO Box 6003 Myrtle Creek OR 97457 *TF:* 800-422-0536 ■ *Web:* www.shirtcliffoil.com	541-863-5268	863-5144	324
Shiva 2514 Times Blvd Houston TX 77005 *Web:* www.shivarestaurant.com	713-523-4753	523-4754	671
Shive-Hattery Inc (SH) 316 Second St SE Ste 500 PO Box 1599 Cedar Rapids IA 52406 *TF:* 800-798-0227 ■ *Web:* www.shive-hattery.com	319-362-0313	362-2883	261
Shively Bros Inc 2919 S Grand Travers St PO Box 1520 Flint MI 48501 *TF:* 800-530-9352 ■ *Web:* www.shivelybros.com	810-232-7401	232-3219	385
Shively Labs 188 Harrison Rd PO Box 389 Bridgton ME 04009 *TF:* 888-744-8359 ■ *Web:* www.shively.com	207-647-3327	647-8273	647
Shivvers Inc 614 W English St Corydon IA 50060 *TF:* 800-245-9093 ■ *Web:* www.shivvers.com	641-872-1005	872-1593	273
SHLP (Simpson Housing LLLP) 8110 E Union Ave Ste 200 Denver CO 80237 *Web:* www.simpsonhousing.com	303-283-4100		653

Phone | Fax | Class

SHN Consulting Engineers & Geologists Inc
812 W Wabash .... Eureka CA 95501 707-441-8855 261
Web: www.shn-engr.com

SHNS (Scripps Howard News Service)
1090 Vermont Ave NW Ste 1000 .... Washington DC 20005 202-408-1484 408-2062 530
Web: www.shns.com

Sho Mi 419 Lincoln Ctr .... Stockton CA 95207 209-951-3525 671
Web: shomirestaurant.com

Sho-Air International
5401 Argosy Ave .... Huntington Beach CA 92649 949-476-9111 476-9991 311
TF: 800-227-9111 ■ *Web:* www.shoair.com

Shoal Creek Living History Museum
7000 NE Barry Rd Hodge Pk .... Kansas City MO 64156 816-792-2655 520
TF: 800-634-3942 ■ *Web:* www.shoalcreeklivinghistorymuseum.com

Shoal Point Energy Ltd
1060-1090 Georgia St W .... Vancouver BC V6E3V7 416-637-2181 536
Web: www.shoalpointenergy.com

Shoals Chamber of Commerce
20 Hightower Pl PO Box 1331 .... Florence AL 35630 256-764-4661 766-9017 139

Shoalwater Bay Casino
4112 State Hwy 105 .... Tokeland WA 98590 360-267-2048 132
TF: 866-992-3675 ■ *Web:* www.swbcasino.com

Shock Tech Inc 360 Rt 59 .... Airmont NY 10952 845-368-8600 57
Web: www.shocktech.com

Shock Trauma Air Rescue Society (STARS)
1441 Aviation Pk NE .... Calgary AB T2E8M7 403-295-1811 275-4891 30
Web: www.stars.ca

Shockoe Commerce Group LLC
11 S 12th St 4th Fl .... Richmond VA 23219 804-343-3441 354
TF: 866-570-0498 ■ *Web:* www.shockoecommerce.com

Shoco Oil Inc 5135 E 74th Ave .... Commerce CO 80037 303-289-1677 579
TF: 800-854-5553 ■ *Web:* www.shocooil.com

Shodeen Inc 17 N First St .... Geneva IL 60134 630-232-0300 653
Web: shodeen.com

Shoe Carnival Inc
7500 E Columbia St .... Evansville IN 47715 812-867-6471 301
NASDAQ: SCVL ■ *TF Cust Svc:* 800-430-7463 ■ *Web:* www.shoecarnival.com

Shoe Sensation Inc
253 America Pl .... Jeffersonville IN 47130 812-288-7659 288-7747 301
TF: 800-347-9511 ■ *Web:* www.shoesensation.com

Shoe Service Institute of America (SSIA)
18 School St .... North Brookfield MA 01535 508-867-7731 569-8333* 49-4
**Fax Area Code:* 410 ■ *TF:* 800-354-6378 ■ *Web:* www.ssia.info

Shoe Show of Rocky Mountain Inc
2201 Trinity Church Rd .... Concord NC 28027 704-782-4143 301
TF Cust Svc: 888-557-4637 ■ *Web:* www.shoeshow.com

Shoei Foods (USA) Inc
1900 Feather River Blvd .... Olivehurst CA 95961 530-742-7866 805

Shoemaker Construction Co
100 Front St Ste 365 .... West Conshohocken PA 19428 610-941-5500 941-5525 186
Web: www.shoemakerco.com

Shofer'S Furniture Company LLC
930 S Charles St .... Baltimore MD 21230 410-752-4212 321
Web: shofers.com

Shoffner Mechanical Industrial & Service Co Inc
3600 Papermill Dr .... Knoxville TN 37909 865-523-1129 610
Web: skmes.com

Shofu Dental Corp 1225 Stone Dr .... San Marcos CA 92078 760-736-3277 476
TF: 800-837-4630 ■ *Web:* www.shofu.com

Shogun 821 E Third Ave .... Spokane WA 99202 509-534-7777 671
Web: shogunspokane.com

Shogun 3700 S Ninth St .... Lincoln NE 68502 402-421-7100 671

Shogun Japanese Steak House
2815 Cantrell Rd .... Little Rock AR 72202 501-666-7070 671
Web: www.shogunlr.com

Shogyo International Corp
6851 Jericho Tpke .... Syosset NY 11791 516-921-9111 921-3777 253
Web: www.shogyo.com

Shoku 1312 Grandview Ave .... Columbus OH 43212 614-485-9490 671
Web: shokugrandview.com

Shoney's Restaurants Inc
1717 Elm Hill Pk Ste B1 .... Nashville TN 37210 800-708-3558 670
TF: 800-708-3558 ■ *Web:* www.shoneys.com

Shook & Fletcher Insulation Co
4625 Valleydale Rd .... Birmingham AL 35242 205-991-7606 991-7745 191-4
TF: 888-829-2575 ■ *Web:* www.shookandfletcher.com

Shook & Fletcher Mechanical Contractors Inc
2915 Richard Arrington Jr Blvd N .... Birmingham AL 35203 205-252-9400 252-9407 189-10
Web: shook-fletcher.com

Shook & Stone Attorneys at Law
710 S Fourth St .... Las Vegas NV 89101 702-385-2220 428
TF: 888-662-2013 ■ *Web:* www.shookandstone.com

Shook Builder Supply Co
1400 16th St NE .... Hickory NC 28601 828-328-2051 328-2425 817
TF: 800-968-0758 ■ *Web:* shookbuildersupply.com

Shook Construction 4977 Northcutt Pl .... Dayton OH 45414 937-276-6666 276-6676 188-7
Web: www.shookconstruction.com

Shook Hardy & Bacon LLP
2555 Grand Blvd .... Kansas City MO 64108 816-474-6550 421-5547 428
TF: 855-380-7584 ■ *Web:* www.shb.com

Shoosmith Bros Inc 11800 Lewis Rd .... Chester VA 23831 804-748-5823 748-8482 189-5
Web: www.shoosmith.com

Shoot The Hoop Inc
30911 First Ave S .... Federal Way WA 98003 253-835-5049 222-1100* 5
**Fax Area Code:* 707

Shooter McGees 5239 Duke St .... Alexandria VA 22304 703-751-9266 671
Web: www.shootermcgees.com

Shooters International Inc
63 Berkeley St .... Toronto ON M5A2W5 416-862-1959 514
TF: 800-572-6592 ■ *Web:* www.shootersfilm.com

Shooting Star Casino Hotel & Event Ctr
777 SE Casino Rd .... Mahnomen MN 56557 218-935-2711 452
TF: 800-453-7827 ■ *Web:* www.starcasino.com

Shop 'n Save 10461 Manchester Rd .... Kirkwood MO 63122 314-984-0322 345
TF: 800-428-6974 ■ *Web:* www.shopnsave.com

Shop 'N Save Liquors
20 Independence Ave .... Quincy MA 02169 617-773-2060 786-9797 443
Web: shopnsaveliquors.com

Shop at North Bridge, The
520 N Michigan Ave .... Chicago IL 60611 312-327-2300 460
Web: www.theshopsatnorthbridge.com

Shop Floor Automations Inc
5360 Jackson Dr .... La Mesa CA 91942 619-461-4000 225
TF: 877-611-5825 ■ *Web:* www.shopfloorautomations.com

Shopko LLC 700 Pilgrim Way .... Green Bay WI 54304 920-429-2211 229
TF: 800-791-7333 ■ *Web:* www.shopko.com

Shoplet.com 39 Broadway Ste 2030 .... New York NY 10006 212-619-3353 617-3389 791
TF: 800-757-3015 ■ *Web:* www.shoplet.com

Shoppa's Material Handling Ltd
15217 Grand River Rd .... Fort Worth TX 76155 817-359-1100 112
TF: 800-303-6582 ■ *Web:* www.shoppas.com

Shopper Local 2327 Englert Dr .... Durham NC 27713 877-251-4592 414
TF: 877-251-4592 ■ *Web:* www.shopperlocal.com

Shoppers Drug Mart Inc
243 Consumers Rd .... Toronto ON M2J4W8 800-746-7737 237
TSE: SC ■ *TF:* 800-746-7737 ■ *Web:* www1.shoppersdrugmart.ca

Shoppers Food & Pharmacy
10501 Martin Luther King Jr Hwy .... Bowie MD 20720 240-544-0180 544-0187 345
Web: www.shoppersfood.com

Shopping Centers Today
1221 Ave of the Americas .... New York NY 10020 646-728-3800 589-5555* 531-13
**Fax Area Code:* 212 ■ *TF:* 888-427-2885 ■ *Web:* www.icsc.org

Shopping Ch, The
Credit Card Dept 59 Ambassador Dr .... Mississauga ON L5T2P9 888-202-0888 740
TF: 888-202-0888 ■ *Web:* www.theshoppingchannel.com

Shopping Channel Direct, The
59 Ambassador Dr .... Mississauga ON L5T2P9 888-202-0888 195
TF: 888-202-0888 ■ *Web:* theshoppingchanneldirect.com

Shopping.com Inc
8000 Marina Blvd 5th Fl .... Brisbane CA 94005 650-616-6500 114
Web: www.shopping.com

ShoppingSpot 1840 Oak Ave .... Evanston IL 60201 847-866-1830 866-1880 397
TF: 866-800-0366 ■ *Web:* www.shoppingspot.com

ShoppingTown Mall 3649 Erie Blvd E .... Dewitt NY 13214 315-446-9159 460
Web: www.shoppingtownmall.com

ShopRite PO Box 7812 .... Edison NJ 08818 800-746-7748 251-9519* 345
**Fax Area Code:* 732 ■ *TF:* 800-746-7748 ■ *Web:* www.shoprite.com

ShopRite Supermarkets Inc
600 York St .... Elizabeth NJ 07207 908-527-3300 345
TF: 800-746-7748 ■ *Web:* www.shoprite.com

Shops at Briargate
1885 Briargate Pkwy .... Colorado Springs CO 80920 719-265-6264 460
Web: thepromenadeshopsatbriargate.com

Shops at Carolina Furniture of Williamsburg
5425 Richmond Rd .... Williamsburg VA 23188 757-565-3000 565-4476 321
Web: www.carolina-furniture.com

Shops at Columbus Circle, The
10 Columbus Cir .... New York NY 10019 212-823-6300 50-6
Web: www.theshopsatcolumbuscircle.com

Shops at Hilltop North East & West
Laskin Rd .... Virginia Beach VA 23451 757-428-2224 460
Web: www.hilltopshops.com

Shops at Houston Center
1200 Mckinney Ste 545 .... Houston TX 77010 713-759-1442 460
Web: www.shopsathc.com

Shops at La Cantera
15900 La Cantera Pkwy Ste 6698 .... San Antonio TX 78256 210-582-6255 460
Web: www.theshopsatlacantera.com

Shops at Liberty Place
1625 Chestnut St .... Philadelphia PA 19103 215-851-9055 460
Web: www.shopsatliberty.com

Shops at Riverwoods
4801 N University Ave .... Provo UT 84604 801-802-8430 460
Web: www.shopsatriverwoods.com

Shops at Tanforan, The
1150 El Camino Real .... San Bruno CA 94066 650-873-2000 873-4210 460
TF: 800-786-1000 ■ *Web:* www.theshopsattanforan.com

Shops at Willow Bend
6121 W Pk Blvd Ste 1000 .... Plano TX 75093 972-202-4900 460
Web: www.shopwillowbend.com

Shops at Woodlake 725 Woodlake Rd .... Kohler WI 53044 920-459-1713 460
TF: 855-444-2838 ■ *Web:* www.americanclubresort.com

Shopsmith Inc 6530 Poe Ave .... Dayton OH 45414 937-898-6070 722-3965* 759
OTC: SSMH ■ **Fax Area Code:* 800 ■ *TF Cust Svc:* 800-543-7586 ■ *Web:* www.shopsmith.com

Shoptology Inc
7800 N Dallas Pkwy Ste 160 .... Plano TX 75024 469-287-1200 195
Web: www.goshoptology.com

Shop-Vac Corp
2323 Reach Rd PO Box 3307 .... Williamsport PA 17701 570-326-0502 326-7185 386
TF: 844-807-7711 ■ *Web:* www.shopvac.com

Shorcan Brokers Ltd
20 Adelaide St E Ste 1000 .... Toronto ON M5C2T6 416-360-2500 690
Web: www.shorcan.com

Shore Acres State Park
89039 Cape Arago Hwy .... Coos Bay OR 97420 541-888-3732 565
Web: www.oregonstateparks.org

Shore Bancshares Inc 18 E Dover St .... Easton MD 21601 410-822-1400 360-2
NASDAQ: SHBI ■ *Web:* www.shorebancshares.com

Shore Capital Partners LLC
1 E Wacker Dr Ste 400 .... Chicago IL 60601 312-348-7580 528
Web: www.shorecp.com

Shore Crest Vacation Villas
4709 S Ocean Blvd .... North Myrtle Beach SC 29582 843-361-3600 669
Web: www.bluegreenrentals.com

Shore Distributors Inc 807 Brown St .... Salisbury MD 21804 410-749-3121 612
TF: 800-561-3357 ■ *Web:* www.shoredist.com

Shore Drugs Inc 30 E Main St .... Bay Shore NY 11706 631-665-3000 237

Shore Line Trolley Museum
17 River St .... East Haven CT 06512 203-467-6927 467-7635 520
Web: www.bera.org

Shore Memorial Hospital
1 E New York Ave .... Somers Point NJ 08244 609-653-3500 374-3
Web: shoremedicalcenter.org

Shore Memorial Hospital
20480 Market St PO Box 430 .... Onancock VA 23417 757-302-2100 414-8633 374-3
TF: 800-834-7035 ■ *Web:* www.riversideonline.com/shore

Name / Address	City	State	Zip	Phone	Fax	Class
Shore Morgan Young 300 W Wilson Bridge Rd TF: 800-288-2117 ■ Web: shoremorganyoung.com	Worthington	OH	43085	614-888-2117		690
Shorebird Beach Broiler 2169 Kalia Rd Outrigger Reef Hotel Web: www.shorebirdwaikiki.com	Honolulu	HI	96815	808-922-2887		671
Shoreland Inc 933 N Mayfair Rd Ste 208 Web: www.shoreland.com	Milwaukee	WI	53226	414-290-1900		177
Shoreline Amphitheatre 1 Amphitheatre Pkwy Web: www.mountainviewamphitheater.com	Mountain View	CA	94043	650-967-4040		572
Shoreline Chamber of Commerce 18560 First Ave NE Web: shorelinechamber.org	Shoreline	WA	98155	206-361-2260		139
Shoreline Chamber Of Commerceÿ 764 E Main St Web: shorelinechamberct.com	Branford	CT	06405	203-488-5500		139
Shoreline Community College 16101 Greenwood Ave N TF: 866-427-4747 ■ Web: www.shoreline.edu	Shoreline	WA	98133	206-546-4101	546-5835	162
Shoreline Container Inc 4450 N 136th Ave PO Box 1993 TF: 800-968-2088 ■ Web: www.shorelinecontainer.com	Holland	MI	49422	616-399-2088	399-7240	100
Shoreline Grill 98 San Jacinto Blvd Web: www.shorelinegrill.com	Austin	TX	78701	512-477-3300		671
Shoreline Partners LLC 6310 Greenwich Dr Ste 120 Web: www.shoreline.com	San Diego	CA	92122	858-587-9800		194
Shoreline Publishing Group 125 Santa Rosa Pl *Fax Area Code: 800 ■ Web: www.shorelinepublishing.com	Santa Barbara	CA	93109	805-564-1004	840-6713*	94
Shoreline Village 429 Shoreline Village Dr # 100 Web: www.shorelinevillage.com	Long Beach	CA	90802	562-435-2668		50-6
Shores Resort & Spa, The 2637 S Atlantic Ave Web: www.shoresresort.com	Daytona Beach Shores	FL	32118	386-767-7350	760-3651	379
Shorewest Realtors Inc 17450 W N Ave TF: 800-434-7350 ■ Web: www.shorewest.com	Brookfield	WI	53008	262-827-4200		652
Shorewood-Troy Public Library District 650 Deerwood Dr TF: 800-359-2163 ■ Web: www.shorewoodtroylibrary.org	Shorewood	IL	60404	815-725-1715	725-1722	434-3
Shorr Packaging Inc 800 N Commerce St TF: 888-885-0055 ■ Web: www.shorr.com	Aurora	IL	60504	630-978-1000		559
Short Freight Lines Inc 459 S River Rd PO Box 357 TF: 800-248-0625 ■ Web: www.shortfreightlines.com	Bay City	MI	48707	989-893-3505	893-3151	780
Short Hills Tours 46 Chatham Rd Ste 1 TF: 800-348-6871 ■ Web: www.shorthillstours.com	Short Hills	NJ	07078	973-467-2113	467-3353	760
Short Order Lp 12521 Amherst Dr Web: www.shortorder.com	Austin	TX	78727	512-610-3600		45
Short-Elliott-Hendrickson Inc 3535 Vadnais Ctr Dr TF: 800-325-2055 ■ Web: www.sehinc.com	Saint Paul	MN	55110	651-490-2000	490-2150	261
Shorter College 604 N Locust St	North Little Rock	AR	72114	501-374-6305		162
Shorter University 315 Shorter Ave *Fax: Admissions ■ TF: 800-868-6980 ■ Web: www.shorter.edu	Rome	GA	30165	706-233-7319	233-7224*	166
Shorty Small's Great American Restaurant 11100 N Rodney Parham Rd Web: www.shortysmalls.com	Little Rock	AR	72212	501-224-3344		671
Shorty's 1050 Bicentennial Dr Web: shortysmex.com	Manchester	NH	03104	603-625-1730		671
Shorty's Bar-B-Cue 5111 Monroe St Web: www.mancys.com	Toledo	OH	43623	419-841-9505		671
Shorty's Bar-B-Q 5989 S University Dr Web: www.shortys.com	Davie	FL	33328	954-680-9900		671
Shoshone County 700 Bank St TF: 800-325-7940 ■ Web: www.shoshonecounty.org	Wallace	ID	83873	208-752-3331	752-4304	338
Shot Tower Historical State Park 176 Orphanage Dr Web: www.dcr.virginia.gov	Foster Falls	VA	24360	276-699-6778		565
Show Management Services Inc 1963 University Ln Web: www.rocexhibitions.com	Lisle	IL	60532	630-271-8210		317
Show Me Ctr 1333 N Sprigg St Web: www.showmecenter.biz	Cape Girardeau	MO	63701	573-651-2297	651-5054	720
Show Media 4775 W Teco Ave Ste 115 Web: www.showmedia.com	Las Vegas	NV	89118	702-778-5313		396
Show Pros Entertainment Services Inc PO Box 12599 Web: www.showprostaff.com	Charlotte	NC	28220	704-525-3784	525-3785	721
Showa Aluminum Corp of America 10500 O'Day-Harrison Rd	Mt. Sterling	OH	43143	740-869-3333		247
Showa Best Glove Inc 579 Edison St TF: 800-241-0323 ■ Web: www.showagroup.com/global	Menlo	GA	30731	800-241-0323		432
Showa Denko America 420 Lexington Ave Ste 2850 Web: www.showadenko.us	New York	NY	10170	212-370-0033	370-4566	696
Showalter Flying Service 600 Herndon Ave TF: 800-759-4295 ■ Web: www.showalter.com	Orlando	FL	32803	407-326-6062		63
Showbest Fixture Corp 4112 Sarellen Rd Web: www.showbest.com	Henrico	VA	23231	804-222-5535	222-7220	286
Showcase Honda 1333 E Camelback Rd Web: www.showcasehonda.com	Phoenix	AZ	85014	602-464-7145		57
Show-me Publishing Inc 2049 Wyandotte St Web: ingrams.com	Kansas City	MO	64108	816-842-9994		532-3
Showplace Wood Products Inc 1 Enterprise St TF: 877-512-2500 ■ Web: www.showplacewood.com	Harrisburg	SD	57032	605-743-2200		115
Showtime Concession Supply Inc 200 SE 19th St Web: www.showplacemarket.com/showtimeconcessionsupply	Moore	OK	73160	405-895-9902		297-3
Showtime Networks Inc 1633 Broadway Web: www.sho.com	New York	NY	10019	212-708-1600	708-1390	740
Showtime Pictures LLC 281 S Vineyard Rd Ste 108 Web: www.showtimepictures.com	Orem	UT	84058	954-449-8844	449-8858	592
SHPTV (Smoky Hills Public Television) 604 Elm St TF: 800-337-4788 ■ Web: www.shptv.org	Bunker Hill	KS	67626	785-483-6990	483-4605	632
Shred Works Inc 1601 Bayshore Hwy Ste 211 Web: www.shredworks.com	Burlingame	CA	94010	510-729-7110		317
Shredder Company LLC, The 7380 Doniphan Dr	Canutillo	TX	79835	915-877-3814		358
Shreve Crump & Low Inc 39 Newbury St TF: 800-328-4326 ■ Web: www.shrevecrumpandlow.com	Boston	MA	02116	617-267-9100		410
Shreve Land Company Inc 624 Travis St Ste 100 Web: www.shreveland.com	Shreveport	LA	71101	318-226-0056	226-0064	187
Shreve Memorial Library 424 Texas St Web: www.shreve-lib.org	Shreveport	LA	71101	318-226-5897	226-4780	434-3
Shreveport City Hall PO Box 31109 Web: www.shreveportla.gov	Shreveport	LA	71130	318-673-5370	673-5099	337
Shreveport Convention Ctr 400 Caddo St Web: shreveportcenter.com	Shreveport	LA	71101	318-841-4000		184
Shreveport Opera 212 Texas St Ste 101 Web: www.shreveportopera.org	Shreveport	LA	71101	318-227-9503	227-9518	573-2
Shreveport Regional Airport 5103 Hollywood Ave Web: www.shreveportla.gov	Shreveport	LA	71109	318-673-5370		27
Shreveport Symphony Orchestra 619 Louisiana Ave Web: www.shreveportsymphony.com	Shreveport	LA	71101	318-222-7496	222-7490	573-3
Shreveport-Bossier Convention & Tourist Bureau 629 Spring St TF: 800-551-8682 ■ Web: www.shreveport-bossier.org	Shreveport	LA	71101	318-222-9391	222-0056	206
SHRH & C (Seminole Hard Rock Hotel & Casino Tampa) 5223 N Orient Rd *Fax Area Code: 954 ■ TF General: 866-388-4263 ■ Web: www.seminolehardrocktampa.com	Tampa	FL	33610	813-627-7625	983-0242*	133
Shrine Auditorium & Exposition Ctr 665 W Jefferson Blvd Web: www.shrineauditorium.com	Los Angeles	CA	90007	213-748-5116		205
Shrine of Saint John Neumann 1019 N Fifth St Web: www.stjohnneumann.org	Philadelphia	PA	19123	215-627-3080	627-3296	50-1
Shriners Hospitals for Children 2900 N Rocky Pt Dr TF: 800-237-5055 ■ Web: www.shrinershospitalsforchildren.org	Tampa	FL	33607	813-281-0300		353
Shriners Hospitals for Children Boston 51 Blossom St TF: 800-255-1916 ■ Web: www.shrinershospitalsforchildren.org	Boston	MA	02114	617-722-3000	523-1684	374-1
Shriners Hospitals for Children Canada 1529 Cedar Ave TF: 800-361-7256 ■ Web: shrinershospitalsforchildren.org	Montreal	QC	H3G1A6	514-842-4464		374-1
Shriners Hospitals for Children Chicago 2211 N Oak Pk Ave Web: www.shrinershq.org	Chicago	IL	60707	773-622-5400		374-1
Shriners Hospitals for Children Cincinnati 3229 Burnet Ave TF: 800-875-8580 ■ Web: shrinershospitalcincinnati.org	Cincinnati	OH	45229	513-872-6000	872-6999	374-1
Shriners Hospitals for Children Erie 1645 W Eigth St TF: 800-873-5437 ■ Web: shrinershospitalsforchildren.org	Erie	PA	16505	814-875-8700	875-8756	374-1
Shriners Hospitals for Children Galveston 2900 Rocky Pt Dr TF: 844-739-0849 ■ Web: shrinershospitalsforchildren.org	Tampa	Fl	33607	813-281-0300		374-1
Shriners Hospitals for Children Greenville 950 W Faris Rd TF: 800-361-7256 ■ Web: www.shrinershospitalsforchildren.org	Greenville	SC	29605	864-271-3444		374-1
Shriners Hospitals for Children Honolulu 1310 Punahou St Web: www.shrinershq.org	Honolulu	HI	96826	808-941-4466		374-1
Shriners Hospitals for Children Houston 6977 Main St Web: www.shrinershq.org	Houston	TX	77030	713-797-1616		374-1
Shriners Hospitals for Children Lexington 1900 Richmond Rd TF: 800-668-4634 ■ Web: shrinershospitalsforchildren.org	Lexington	KY	40502	859-266-2101	268-5636	374-1
Shriners Hospitals for Children Los Angeles 3160 Geneva St *Fax Area Code: 213 ■ *Fax: Admitting ■ TF: 888-486-5437 ■ Web: www.shrinershospitalsforchildren.org/Locations/losangeles	Los Angeles	CA	90020	864-240-8155	387-7528*	374-1
Shriners Hospitals for Children Northern California 2425 Stockton Blvd Web: www.shrinershq.org	Sacramento	CA	95817	916-453-2000		374-1
Shriners Hospitals for Children Philadelphia 3551 N Broad St TF: 800-281-4050 ■ Web: www.shrinershospitalsforchildren.org	Philadelphia	PA	19140	215-430-4000	430-4079	374-1
Shriners Hospitals for Children Portland 3101 SW Sam Jackson Pk Rd Web: www.shrinershospitalsforchildren.org	Portland	OR	97239	503-241-5090		374-1
Shriners Hospitals for Children Salt Lake City Fairfax Rd & Virginia St TF: 800-313-3745 ■ Web: www.shrinershospitalsforchildren.org	Salt Lake City	UT	84103	801-536-3500		374-1
Shriners Hospitals for Children Shreveport 3100 Samford Ave Web: www.shrinershospitalsforchildren.org	Shreveport	LA	71103	318-222-5704	424-7610	374-1
Shriners Hospitals for Children Spokane 911 W Fifth Ave Web: www.shrinershq.org	Spokane	WA	99204	509-455-7844		374-1
Shriners Hospitals for Children Tampa 12502 N Pine Dr *Fax Area Code: 864 ■ *Fax: Admitting ■ TF: 800-237-5055 ■ Web: shrinershospitalsforchildren.org	Tampa	FL	33612	813-972-2250	240-3113*	374-1
Shriners Hospitals for Children Twin Cities 2025 E River Pkwy Web: www.shrinershq.org	Minneapolis	MN	55414	612-596-6100		374-1

Listing	City	State	Zip	Phone	Fax	Class
Shriver House Museum 309 Baltimore St *Web:* www.shriverhouse.org	Gettysburg	PA	17325	717-337-2800		520
SHRM (Society for Human Resource Management) 1800 Duke St *TF:* 800-283-7476 ■ *Web:* www.shrm.org	Alexandria	VA	22314	703-548-3440	836-0367	49-12
SHRM Global Forum 1800 Duke St *TF:* 800-283-7476 ■ *Web:* www.shrm.org/global	Alexandria	VA	22314	703-548-3440	535-6490	171
SHSMD (Society for Healthcare Strategy & Market Development) 155 N Wacker Dr Ste 400 *TF:* 800-242-2626 ■ *Web:* www.shsmd.org	Chicago	IL	60606	312-422-3888	278-0883	49-8
Shtofman Co 1905 W Gentry Pkwy	Tyler	TX	75702	903-592-0861		301
Shubert Foundation Inc, The 234 W 44th St *Web:* www.shubertfoundation.org	New York	NY	10036	212-944-3777		305
Shubert Theater 247 College St *TF:* 800-745-3000 ■ *Web:* www.shubert.com	New Haven	CT	06510	203-624-1825	789-2286	572
Shubert Theatre 225 W 44th St *Web:* www.telecharge.com	New York	NY	10036	212-239-6200		747
Shuert Industries Inc 6600 Dobry Rd *Web:* www.shuert.com	Sterling Heights	MI	48314	586-254-4590		711
Shugart Enterprises LLC 221 Jonestown Rd *Web:* www.shugartenterprises.com	Winston-Salem	NC	27104	336-765-9661	765-1295	187
Shugart Studios Inc 812 College Ave	Levelland	TX	79336	806-897-1754		590
Shuhei Inc 23360 Chagrin Blvd *Web:* shuheirestaurant.com	Beachwood	OH	44122	216-464-1720		670
Shui Spa at Crowne Pointe Historic Inn 82 Bradford St *TF:* 877-276-9631 ■ *Web:* www.crownepointe.com	Provincetown	MA	02657	508-487-6767		707
Shula's Steak 2 6842 Main St *Web:* www.donshula.com	Miami Lakes	FL	33014	305-820-8047		671
Shula's Steak House 4860 W Kennedy Blvd *TF:* 800-888-7012 ■ *Web:* www.donshula.com	Tampa	FL	33609	813-286-4366		671
Shula's Steak House 6843 Main St *Web:* www.donshula.com	Miami Lakes	FL	33014	305-817-4072	817-4002	671
Shula's Steak House 5111 Tamiami Trl N *Web:* www.donshula.com	Naples	FL	34103	239-430-4999		671
Shula's Steak House 1000 Riverchase Galleria *Web:* www.donshula.com	Birmingham	AL	35244	205-444-5750		671
Shular Hospitality 9475 Hwy 49 *Web:* www.shularhospitality.com	Gulfport	MS	39503	228-868-1888	867-2983	656
Shults Management Group Inc 181 E Fairmount Ave	Lakewood	NY	14750	716-763-1551		57
Shultz Steel Company Inc 5321 Firestone Blvd *TF:* 800-451-6956 ■ *Web:* www.shultzsteel.com	South Gate	CA	90280	323-564-3281		492
Shumaker Consulting Engineer PC 143 Court St *TF:* 800-995-1384 ■ *Web:* www.shumakerengineering.com	Binghamton	NY	13901	607-798-9091		261
Shuman Plastics Inc 35 Neoga St *TF:* 800-803-6242 ■ *Web:* www.shuman-plastics.com	Depew	NY	14043	716-685-2121	685-3236	605-2
Shumsky Enterprises Inc 811 E Fourth St *TF:* 800-223-2203 ■ *Web:* www.shumsky.com	Dayton	OH	45402	937-223-2203		4
Shun Fat Supermarket Inc 421 N Atlantic Blvd *TF:* 800-495-7222 ■ *Web:* www.shunfatsupermarket.com	Monterey Park	CA	91754	626-308-3998		345
Shun Lee Palace 155 E 55th St *Web:* www.shunleepalace.com	New York	NY	10022	212-371-8844		671
Shur-Co Inc 2309 Shur-Lok St PO Box 713 *TF:* 800-474-8756 ■ *Web:* www.shurco.com	Yankton	SD	57078	605-665-6000	665-0501	733
Shure Inc 5800 W Touhy Ave *TF:* 800-257-4873 ■ *Web:* www.shure.com	Niles	IL	60714	847-866-2200	600-1212	52
Shure Manufacturing Corp 1901 W Main St *TF:* 800-227-4873 ■ *Web:* www.shureusa.com	Washington	MO	63090	636-390-7100	390-7171	319-1
Shure-line Construction Inc PO Box 249 *Web:* www.shure-line.com	Kenton	DE	19955	302-653-4610		480
SHURflo Pump Mfg Company Inc 5900 Katella Ave *TF:* 800-854-3218 ■ *Web:* www.shurflo.com	Cypress	CA	90630	562-795-5200	795-7554	641
Shur-Lok Corp 2541 White Rd *Web:* www.shur-lok.com	Irvine	CA	92614	949-474-6000		21
Shurtape Technologies LLC 1712 Eigth St Dr SE **Fax Area Code: 800* ■ *TF:* 888-442-8273 ■ *Web:* www.shurtape.com	Hickory	NC	28602	828-322-2700	335-7651*	732
ShurTech Brands 32150 Just Imagine Dr *TF:* 800-321-0253 ■ *Web:* shurtech.com	Avon	OH	44011	440-937-7000		535
Shurtleff & Andrews Corp 1875 West 500 South *Web:* www.shurtleff-slc.com	Salt Lake City	UT	84104	801-973-9096		189-14
Shuster Bill (Rep R - PA) 2079 Rayburn HOB *Web:* shuster.house.gov	Washington	DC	20515	202-225-2431	225-2486	342-2
Shuster Corp 55 Samuel Barnet Blvd *Web:* www.shustercorp.com	New Bedford	MA	02745	508-999-3261	990-2157	370
Shuster's Bldg Components 2920 Clay Pk **Fax Area Code: 800* ■ *TF:* 800-676-0640 ■ *Web:* www.shusters.com	Irwin	PA	15642	724-446-7000	676-0640*	499
Shuster's Transportation Inc 750 E Valley St	Willits	CA	95490	707-459-4131		780
Shutler Consulting Engineers Inc 12503 Bel Red Rd *Web:* shutler.com	Bellevue	WA	98005	425-450-4075		261
Shutter Mill Inc 8517 S Perkins Rd *TF:* 800-416-6455 ■ *Web:* www.kirtz.com	Stillwater	OK	74074	405-377-6455	377-1010	699
Shutterbug Magazine 1419 Chaffee Dr Ste 1 *TF:* 800-829-3340 ■ *Web:* www.shutterbug.com	Titusville	FL	32780	321-269-3212		457-14
Shutterfly.com 2800 Bridge Pkwy Ste 101 *TF:* 800-732-0330 ■ *Web:* www.shutterfly.com	Redwood City	CA	94065	650-610-5200	654-1299	588
Shutters on the Beach 1 Pico Blvd *Web:* www.shuttersonthebeach.com	Santa Monica	CA	90405	310-458-0030		379
Shutterstock Inc 350 Fifth Ave Fl 21 *Web:* www.shutterstock.com	New York	NY	10118	646-419-4452		592
Shuttleworth Inc 10 Commercial Rd *TF:* 800-444-7412 ■ *Web:* www.shuttleworth.com	Huntington	IN	46750	260-356-8500	359-7810	207
Shwiff Levy & Polo LLP 433 California St Ste 1000 *Web:* www.slpconsults.com	San Francisco	CA	94104	415-291-8600		734
SI Group Inc 2750 Balltown Rd *Web:* www.siigroup.com	Schenectady	NY	12301	518-347-4200	346-6908	605-2
SI Holdings 3267 Bee Caves Rd Ste 107 *TF:* 866-551-4646 ■ *Web:* sysinformation.com	Austin	TX	78746	866-551-4646		396
SI Jacobson Mfg Co 1414 Jacobson Dr *Web:* www.sij.com	Waukegan	IL	60085	847-623-1414		548
SI Organization Inc, The 15052 Conference Ctr Dr *TF:* 800-220-1500 ■ *Web:* www.vencore.com	Chantilly	VA	20151	571-313-6000		261
Si Senor Restaurant 1551 E Amador Ave *Web:* www.sisenor.com	Las Cruces	NM	88001	575-527-0817		671
SIA (Service Industry Assn) 2164 Histroic Decatur Rd Villa 19 *Web:* www.servicenetwork.org	San Diego	CA	92106	619-221-9200		49-12
SIA (Survivors of Incest Anonymous) PO Box 190 *Web:* www.siawso.org	Benson	MD	21018	410-893-3322		48-21
SIA (SnowSports Industries America) 8377 Greensboro Dr Ste B *TF:* 800-213-7193 ■ *Web:* www.snowsports.org	McLean	VA	22102	703-556-9020	821-8276	49-4
SIA (Security Industry Assn) 8405 Colesville Rd Ste 500 *TF:* 866-817-8888 ■ *Web:* www.securityindustry.org	Silver Spring	MD	20910	703-683-2075	683-2469	49-4
SIAG Aerisyn LLC 959 Windtower Dr *Web:* www.siag.de	Chattanooga	TN	37402	423-648-3884		518
SIAM (Society for Industrial & Applied Mathematics) 3600 Market St 6th Fl *TF:* 800-447-7426 ■ *Web:* www.siam.org	Philadelphia	PA	19104	215-382-9800	386-7999	49-19
Siam Cafe 3951 St Clair Ave	Cleveland	OH	44114	216-361-2323		671
Siam Cafe 316 McCall St	Nashville	TN	37211	615-834-3181		671
Siam Garden Thai Restaurant 3125 MLK St N *Web:* www.siamgardenthai1.com	Saint Petersburg	FL	33704	727-822-0613		671
Siam Orchid 12 N Main St *Web:* www.siamorchid.net	Concord	NH	03301	603-228-1529		671
Siamab Therapeutics Inc 90 Bridge St ste 100 *Web:* www.siamab.com	Newton	CA	92081	858-623-0276		743
Siano Appliance Distributors Inc 5372 Pleasant View Rd *TF:* 800-742-6699 ■ *Web:* www.sianoappliance.com	Memphis	TN	38134	901-382-5833	372-7621	38
SIB Development & Consulting Inc 796 Meeting St *TF:* 800-204-5757 ■ *Web:* www.aboutsib.com	Charleston	SC	29403	843-576-3606		463
Sibble Computer Consulting 1720 Venables St *Web:* pdscc.com	Vancouver	BC	V5L2H4	604-739-3709		177
Sibel Ayse Halac Iron Works Inc 21675 Ashgrove Ct *TF:* 800-467-7862 ■ *Web:* www.sahalac.com	Sterling	VA	20166	703-406-4766		492
Siben & Siben LLP 90 E Mn St *TF:* 800-576-1707 ■ *Web:* www.sibensiben.com	Bay Shore	NY	11706	631-665-3400		428
Sibley County 400 Court St PO Box H *Web:* www.co.sibley.mn.us	Gaylord	MN	55334	507-647-5377	237-4062	338
Sibley State Park 800 Sibley Pk Rd *TF:* 888-646-6367 ■ *Web:* www.dnr.state.mn.us	New London	MN	56273	320-354-2055		565
Siboney Corp 325 N Kirkwood Rd	Saint Louis	MO	63122	314-822-3163		178-3
SIC Biometrics Inc 555 Larocque Rd *Web:* www.sic.ca	Valleyfield	QC	J6T4C8	450-424-2772		693
Sica Consultants Inc 883 Briarwoods Rd *Web:* www.sicafletcher.com	Franklin Lakes	NJ	07417	201-805-1561		390
Sica Hollow State Park 44950 Park Rd 44950 Park Rd *Web:* gfp.sd.gov	Sisseton	SD	57262	605-448-5701		565
SICB (Society for Integrative & Comparative Biology) 1313 Dolley Madison Blvd Ste 402 *TF:* 800-955-1236 ■ *Web:* www.sicb.org	McLean	VA	22101	703-790-1745	790-2672	49-19
Siciliano Inc 3601 Winchester Rd *Web:* www.sicilianoinc.com	Springfield	IL	62707	217-585-1200	585-1211	188-10
Sickle Cell Disease Assn of America (SCDAA) 3700 Koppers St Ste 570 *TF:* 800-421-8453 ■ *Web:* www.sicklecelldisease.org	Baltimore	MD	21202	410-528-1555	528-1495	48-17
Sico North America Inc 7525 Cahill Rd *TF:* 800-328-6138 ■ *Web:* www.sicoinc.com	Minneapolis	MN	55439	952-941-1700	941-6737	319-3
Sicpa Securink Corp 8000 Research Way *Web:* www.sicpa.com/22/931.asp	Springfield	VA	22153	703-455-8050		388
SID (Society for Information Display) 1475 S Bascom Ave Ste 114 *TF:* 800-350-0111 ■ *Web:* www.sid.org	Campbell	CA	95008	408-879-3901	879-3833	48-9
SID (Society for Investigative Dermatology Inc) 526 Superior Ave E Ste 540 *Web:* www.sidnet.org	Cleveland	OH	44114	216-579-9300	579-9333	49-8
Sid Factor 7 Inc 1827 Pearl St Ste 1 *Web:* sidfactor.com	Boulder	CO	80302	303-449-5323		195
Sid Goldstien - Civil Engineer Inc 650 Alamo Pintado Rd Ste 302 *Web:* sjgce.com	Solvang	CA	93463	805-688-1526		261
Sid Harvey Industries Inc 605 Locust St *Web:* www.sidharvey.com	Garden City	NY	11530	516-745-9200	222-9027	612
Sid Lee Inc 75 Rue Queen Bureau 1400 *Web:* www.sidlee.com	Montreal	QC	H3C2N6	514-282-2200		195

	Phone	Fax	Class
Sid Richardson Carbon & Energy Cos 201 Main St, Fort Worth TX 76102 *Web:* www.sidrich.com	817-390-8600		145
Sidbury House 1609 N Chaparral St, Corpus Christi TX 78401	361-883-9352		50-3
Side Effects Software Inc 123 Front St W Ste 1401, Toronto ON M5J2M2 *TF:* 888-504-9876 ■ *Web:* www.sidefx.com	416-504-9876		179
Side Street Inn 1225 Hopaka St, Honolulu HI 96814 *Web:* www.sidestreetinn.com	808-591-0253	732-7333	671
Sidel Inc 5600 Sun Ct, Norcross GA 30092 **Fax Area Code:* 770 ■ *Web:* www.sidel.com	678-221-3000	447-0084*	547
Sidel Systems Usa Inc 12500 El Camino Real, Atascadero CA 93422 *TF:* 800-668-5003 ■ *Web:* www.sidelsystems.com	805-462-1250		358
SIDES & Assoc Inc 222 Jefferson St Ste B, Lafayette LA 70501 *Web:* www.sides.com	337-233-6473		4
Sideshow Media 611 Broadway Ste 734, New York NY 10012 *Web:* www.sideshowbooks.com	212-674-5335		94
Sidewalk Moving Picture Festival 310 18th St N, Birmingham AL 35203 *Web:* www.sidewalkfest.com	205-324-0888		282
Sidewinder Conversions 44658 Yale Rd W, Chilliwack BC V2R0G5 *TF:* 888-266-2299 ■ *Web:* www.sidewinder-conversions.com	604-792-2082	792-8920	62-7
Sidley Austin LLP 787 Seventh Ave, New York NY 10019 *TF:* 800-306-5230 ■ *Web:* www.sidley.com	312-853-7000	853-7036	428
Sidney Kimmel Comprehensive Cancer Ctr at Johns Hopkins 401 N Broadway The Harry & Jeanette Weinberg Bldg Ste 1100, Baltimore MD 21231 *Web:* www.hopkinsmedicine.org	410-955-5222	955-6787	668
Sidney Lanier Cottage 935 High St, Macon GA 31201 *Web:* historicmacon.org	478-743-3851		50-3
Sidney Street Cafe 2000 Sidney St, Saint Louis MO 63104 *Web:* www.sidneystreetcafestl.com	314-771-5777		671
Sidney Tax Service Inc 115 Second St NE, Sidney MT 59270	406-433-3131		734
Sidney Transportation Services 777 W Russell Rd PO Box 946, Sidney OH 45365 *TF:* 800-743-6391 ■ *Web:* www.sidneytransportationservices.com	937-498-2323		685
Sidney-Shelby County Chamber of Commerce 101 S Ohio Ave 2nd Fl, Sidney OH 45365 *Web:* www.sidneyshelbychamber.com	937-492-9122	498-2472	139
Sidran Inc 1050 Venture Ct Ste 100, Carrollton TX 75006 *TF:* 800-969-5015 ■ *Web:* www.sidraninc.com	214-352-7979	352-0439	155-20
Sidus Investment Management LLC 767 Third Ave 15th Fl, New York NY 10017 *Web:* www.sidusfunds.com	212-751-6644		401
Sidwell Co Inc 675 Sidwell Ct, Saint Charles IL 60174 *TF:* 877-743-9355 ■ *Web:* www.sidwellco.com	630-549-1000	549-1111	727
Sidwell Friends School 3825 Wisconsin Ave NW, Washington DC 20016 *Web:* www.sidwell.edu	202-537-8100	537-8138	623
SIE Computing Solutions Inc 10 Mupac Dr, Brockton MA 02301 *TF:* 800-926-8722 ■ *Web:* www.atrenne.com/acs	508-588-6110		407
Sieben Polk PA 1640 S Frontage Rd Ste 200, Hastings MN 55033 *TF:* 800-620-1829 ■ *Web:* www.siebenpolklaw.com	651-437-3148		428
Siebenthaler Co 3001 Catalpa Dr, Dayton OH 45405 *TF:* 800-243-6550 ■ *Web:* www.siebenthaler.com	937-274-1154		323
Siebert Cisneros Shank & Co LLC 100 Wall St 18th Fl, New York NY 10005 *TF:* 800-334-6800 ■ *Web:* www.sbsco.com	646-775-4850		690
Siebert Financial Corp 885 Third Ave, New York NY 10022 *NASDAQ: SIEB* ■ *TF:* 877-327-8379 ■ *Web:* www.siebertnet.com	212-644-2400	486-2784	360-3
Sieck 311 E Chase St, Baltimore MD 21202 *TF:* 800-624-7134	410-685-4660	685-1547	293
Siegel & Gale 625 Ave of the Americas 4th Fl, New York NY 10011 *Web:* siegelgale.com	212-453-0400		7
Siegel & Stockman USA 126 W 25th St, New York NY 10001 *Web:* www.siegel-stockman.com	212-633-0138		464
Siegel Display Products 300 Sixth Ave N, Minneapolis MN 55401 **Fax Area Code:* 800 ■ *TF:* 800-626-0322 ■ *Web:* www.siegeldisplay.com	612-340-1493	230-5598*	232
Siegel Suites Tropicana 3890 Graphic Center Dr, Las Vegas NV 89118	702-507-9999		378
Siegers Seed Co 13031 Reflections Dr, Holland MI 49424 *TF:* 800-962-4999 ■ *Web:* www.siegers.com	616-786-4999	994-0333	276
Siegfried Group LLP, The 1201 Market St, Wilmington DE 19801 *Web:* siegfriedgroup.com	302-984-1800		2
Siegfried USA LLC 33 Industrial Pk Rd, Pennsville NJ 08070 *TF Cust Svc:* 877-763-8630 ■ *Web:* www.siegfried.ch	856-678-3601	678-8201	479
Siegwerk USA Co 3535 SW 56th St, Des Moines IA 50321 *TF:* 800-728-8200 ■ *Web:* www.siegwerk.com	515-471-2100	471-2200	388
Sielc Technologies 804 Seton Ct Ste 221, Prospect Heights IL 60070 *Web:* www.sielc.com	847-229-2629		358
Sielox LLC 170 E Ninth Ave, Runnemede NJ 08078 *TF:* 800-424-2126 ■ *Web:* www.sielox.com	856-939-9300		692
Siemens Bldg Technologies Inc 1000 Deerfield Pkwy, Buffalo Grove IL 60089 *Web:* www.buildingtechnologies.siemens.com	847-215-1000	215-1093	202
Siemens Bldg Technologies Inc Fire Safety Div 8 Fernwood Rd, Florham Park NJ 07932 *TF:* 888-303-3353 ■ *Web:* usa.siemens.com/infrastructure-cities/us/en	973-593-2600	593-6670	283
Siemens Canada Ltd 1550 Appleby Line, Burlington ON L7L6X7 *TF:* 800-236-2967 ■ *Web:* www.siemens.com	905-319-3600		735
Siemens Corp 300 New Jersey Ave Ste 1000, Washington DC 20001 **Fax Area Code:* 678 ■ **Fax:* Mktg ■ *TF:* 800-743-6367 ■ *Web:* www.usa.siemens.com	212-258-4000	867-7450*	185
Siemens Financial Services Inc 170 Wood Ave S, Iselin NJ 08830 *TF:* 800-327-4443 ■ *Web:* finance.siemens.com	732-590-6500		216
Siemens Mfg Company Inc 410 W Washington St, Freeburg IL 62243 *Web:* www.siemensmfg.com	618-539-3000		625
Siemens Milltronics Process Instruments Inc 1954 Technology Dr, Peterborough ON K9J6X7 *Web:* w3.siemens.com	705-745-2431		201
Siemens Mobility 7464 French Rd, Sacramento CA 95828 *Web:* usa.siemens.com/infrastructure-cities/us/en	916-681-3000		650
Siemens Molecular Imaging Inc 810 Innovation Dr, Knoxville TN 37932 *Web:* healthcare.siemens.com	865-218-2000		382
Siemens Power Generation 4400 N Alafaya Trl, Orlando FL 32826 **Fax Area Code:* 918 ■ **Fax:* Hum Res ■ *Web:* www.energy.siemens.com	407-736-4197	831-9161*	518
Siemens Power Transmission & Distribution Inc 7000 Siemens Rd, Wendell NC 27591 *TF:* 800-347-6659 ■ *Web:* siemens.com	919-365-2200		620
Siemens Product Lifecycle Management Software Inc 5800 Granite Pkwy Ste 600, Plano TX 75024 *TF:* 800-498-5351 ■ *Web:* www.plm.automation.siemens.com	972-987-3000	987-3397	178-10
Siemens Water Technologies Corp 181 Thorn Hill Rd, Warrendale PA 15086	724-772-0044	772-1360	806
Siemer Milling Co 111 W Main St, Teutopolis IL 62467 *TF:* 800-826-1065 ■ *Web:* www.siemermilling.com	217-857-3131	857-3092	296-23
Siemer, Austin, Resch, Fuhr & Totten 307 N Third St, Effingham IL 62401 *Web:* siemeraustin.com	217-342-9291		428
Siemon Co 101 Siemon Co Dr, Watertown CT 06795 *TF:* 866-548-5814 ■ *Web:* www.siemon.com	860-945-4200	945-4225	814
Siena College 515 Loudon Rd, Loudonville NY 12211 **Fax:* Admissions ■ *TF Admissions:* 888-287-4362 ■ *Web:* www.siena.edu	518-783-2300	783-2436*	166
Siena Ctr 5635 Erie St, Racine WI 53402 *TF:* 800-769-9373 ■ *Web:* racinedominicans.org	262-639-4100		673
Siena Engineering Group Inc 50 Mall Rd Ste 203, Burlington MA 01803 *Web:* sienaengineeringgroup.com	781-221-8400		226
Siena Heights University 1247 E Siena Heights Dr, Adrian MI 49221 *TF:* 800-521-0009 ■ *Web:* www.sienaheights.edu	517-263-0731	264-7745	166
Siena Hotel 1505 E Franklin St, Chapel Hill NC 27514 *TF:* 800-223-7379 ■ *Web:* www.sienahotel.com	919-929-4000	968-8527	379
Siepert & Company LLP Cpa 1920 W Hart Rd, Beloit WI 53511 *Web:* www.siepert.com	608-365-2266		2
Sierra Aluminum Co 2345 Fleetwood Dr, Riverside CA 92509 *Web:* www.sierraaluminum.com	951-781-7800		492
Sierra Bancorp 86 N Main St PO Box 1930, Porterville CA 93257 *NASDAQ: BSRR* ■ *TF:* 888-454-2265 ■ *Web:* bankofthesierra.com	559-782-4900		360-2
Sierra Bullets LLC 1400 W Henry St, Sedalia MO 65301 *Web:* www.sierrabullets.com	660-827-6300		711
Sierra Business Council 10183 Truckee Airport Rd Ste 202, Truckee CA 96161 *Web:* sierrabusiness.org	530-582-4800	582-1230	196
Sierra Club 85 Second St 2nd Fl, San Francisco CA 94105 *Web:* www.sierraclub.org	415-977-5500	977-5799	48-13
Sierra Club Canada 412-1 Nicholas St, Ottawa ON K1N7B7 *TF:* 888-810-4204 ■ *Web:* www.sierraclub.ca	613-241-4611	241-2292	48-13
Sierra Club of Canada Bc Chapter 301 - 2994 Douglas St, Victoria BC V8T4N4 *Web:* www.sierraclub.bc.ca	250-386-5255		138
Sierra Coastal Partners Inc 2000 -1177 W Hasting St, Vancouver BC V6E2K3 *Web:* www.sierracoastal.com	604-442-2425		463
Sierra College *Nevada County* 250 Sierra College Dr, Grass Valley CA 95945 **Fax:* Admissions ■ *TF:* 800-242-4004 ■ *Web:* www.sierracollege.edu	530-274-5300	274-5324*	162
Sierra Community College 5100 Sierra College Blvd, Rocklin CA 95677 *TF:* 800-242-4004 ■ *Web:* www.sierracollege.edu	916-624-3333		162
Sierra Converting Corp 1400 Kleppe Ln, Sparks NV 89431 *Web:* www.sierraconverting.com	775-331-8221		557
Sierra County 100 Courthouse Sq Ste 11 PO Box D, Downieville CA 95936 *Web:* www.sierracounty.ca.gov	530-289-3295	289-2830	338
Sierra Creative Systems Inc 7283 Bellaire Ave Ste 2, North Hollywood CA 91605 *TF:* 800-961-4877 ■ *Web:* www.theaddressers.com	818-503-0691		809
Sierra Donor Services 1760 Creekside Oak Dr Ste 220, Sacramento CA 95833 *TF:* 877-401-2546 ■ *Web:* sierradonor.org	916-567-1600		545
Sierra Electric Co-op Inc 610 Hwy 195 PO Box 290, Elephant Butte NM 87935 *Web:* www.sierraelectric.org	575-744-5231		245
Sierra Electronics 690 E Glendale Ave Ste 9B, Sparks NV 89432 *TF:* 800-874-7515 ■ *Web:* www.sierraelectronics.com	775-359-1121		246
Sierra Energy 1020 Winding Creek Rd Ste 100, Roseville CA 95678 *TF:* 800-576-2264 ■ *Web:* www.sierraenergyexpress.com	916-218-1600		579
Sierra Forest Products 9000 Rd 234, Terra Bella CA 93270 *Web:* www.sierrafp.com	559-535-4893		683
Sierra Group, The 588 N Gulph Rd # 110, King Of Prussia PA 19406 *TF:* 800-973-7687 ■ *Web:* www.thesierragroup.com	610-992-0288		194
Sierra Health Foundation 1321 Garden Hwy, Sacramento CA 95833 *TF:* 800-475-0175 ■ *Web:* www.sierrahealth.org	916-922-4755		305
Sierra Hr Partners Inc 7112 N Fresno St Ste 450, Fresno CA 93720 *Web:* sierrahr.com	559-431-8090		193
Sierra Infosys Inc 6001 Savoy Dr Ste 210, Houston TX 77036 *Web:* www.sierratec.com	713-747-9693		463

	Phone	Fax	Class
Sierra Instruments Inc 5 Harris Ct Bldg L........................ Monterey CA 93940 *TF:* 800-866-0200 ■ *Web:* www.sierrainstruments.com	831-373-0200	373-4402	201
Sierra Land Group Inc 801 N Brand Blvd Ste 1010 .... Glendale CA 91203	818-247-3681		379
Sierra Leone 245 E 49th St .... New York NY 10017 *Web:* www.un.int/sierraleone	212-688-1656	688-4924	784
Sierra Magazine 85 Second St 2nd Fl.................... San Francisco CA 94105 *TF:* 866-338-1015 ■ *Web:* www.sierraclub.org/sierra	415-977-5500	977-5794	457-19
Sierra Military Health Services Inc 111 Market Pl Ste 410 .... Baltimore MD 21202	410-547-9040		391-3
Sierra Monitor Corp 1991 Tarob Ct .... Milpitas CA 95035 *OTC: SRMC* ■ *TF:* 888-509-1970 ■ *Web:* www.sierramonitor.com	408-262-6611	262-9042	472
Sierra Nevada Brewing Co 1075 E 20th St .... Chico CA 95928 *Web:* www.sierranevada.com	530-893-3520		102
Sierra Nevada College 999 Tahoe Blvd............................ Incline Village NV 89451 *TF:* 866-412-4636 ■ *Web:* www.sierranevada.edu	775-831-1314		166
Sierra Nevada Corp (SNC) 444 Salomon Cir .... Sparks NV 89434 *Web:* www.sncorp.com	775-331-0222	331-0370	253
Sierra Nevada Memorial Hospital 155 Glasson Way .... Grass Valley CA 95945 *Web:* www.snmh.org	530-274-6000		374-3
Sierra NV Healthcare Systems (VA Medical Ctr) 975 Kirman Ave .... Reno NV 89502 *TF:* 888-838-6256 ■ *Web:* www.reno.va.gov	775-786-7200		374-8
Sierra Pacific Industries 19794 Riverside Ave....................... Anderson CA 96007 *Web:* spi-ind.com	530-378-8000	378-8109	683
Sierra Pacific West 2125 La Mirada Dr .... Vista CA 92081 *TF:* 800-479-5314 ■ *Web:* sierrapacificwest.com	760-599-0755		261
Sierra Pacific Windows 11400 Reading Rd .... Red Bluff CA 96080 *Web:* www.sierrapacificwindows.com	530-529-5108		499
Sierra Ready Mix LLC 4150 Smiley Rd .... North Las Vegas NV 89081 *Web:* www.sierrareadymix.com	702-644-8700		182
Sierra Receivables Management Inc 2500 Goodwater Ave........................ Redding CA 96002 *TF:* 800-237-3205 ■ *Web:* www.sierrareceivables.com	530-224-1360		160
Sierra Safari Zoo 10200 N Virginia St............. Reno NV 89506 *TF:* 800-238-2463 ■ *Web:* www.sierrasafarizoo.com	775-677-1101		823
Sierra Select Distributors 4320 Roseville Rd................... North Highlands CA 95660 *Web:* www.sierraselect.com	916-483-9295		4
Sierra Trading Post Inc 5025 Campstool Rd .... Cheyenne WY 82007 *Web:* www.sierratradingpost.com	307-775-8050		229
Sierra Tucson Inc 39580 S Lago Del Oro Pkwy .... Tucson AZ 85739 *TF:* 800-842-4487 ■ *Web:* www.sierratucson.com/?nocookies=true	520-624-4000		720
Sierra Ventures 1400 Fashion Island Blvd Ste 1010 .... San Mateo CA 94404 *Web:* www.sierraventures.com	650-854-1000		792
Sierra Video Systems Inc 104 New Mohawk Rd .... Nevada City CA 95959 *Web:* www.sierravideo.com	530-478-1000		647
Sierra View District Hospital (SVDH) 465 W Putnam Ave........................ Porterville CA 93257 *Web:* www.sierra-view.com	559-784-1110		374-3
Sierra Vista Mall 1050 Shaw Ave................ Clovis CA 93612 *Web:* www.sierravistamall.com	559-299-5070		460
Sierra Vista Regional Medical Ctr (SVRMC) 1010 Murray Ave .... San Luis Obispo CA 93405 *TF:* 866-904-6871 ■ *Web:* www.sierravistaregional.com	805-546-7600		374-3
Sierra Volkswagen Inc 510 E Norris Dr........... Ottawa IL 61350 *TF:* 877-854-2771 ■ *Web:* www.sierravw.com	866-374-5828		57
Sierra West Express Inc 850 Bergin Way .... Sparks NV 89431	775-355-9595		449
Sierra Wireless Inc 13811 Wireless Way.......................... Richmond BC V6V3A4 *TF:* 800-251-5866 ■ *Web:* www.sierrawireless.com	604-231-1100	231-1109	173-3
Sierrita Mining & Ranching Company Inc 9333 White Hills Loop .... Sahuarita AZ 85629	520-625-1204		189-5
Siewert Cabinet & Fixture Manufacturing Inc 2640 Minnehaha Ave .... Minneapolis MN 55406 *Web:* www.siewertcabinet.com	612-721-4456		499
Sifco Custom Machining 2430 Winnetka Ave...................... Minneapolis MN 55427 *Web:* www.sifco.com/minneapolis	763-544-3511		21
Sifco Industries Inc 970 E 64th St............. Cleveland OH 44103 *NYSE: SIF* ■ *Web:* www.sifco.com	216-881-8600	432-6281	24
SIFMAA (Securities Industry & Financial Markets Assn) 120 Broadway 35th Fl........................ New York NY 10271 *TF:* 888-367-7966 ■ *Web:* www.sifma.org	212-313-1200	313-1301	49-2
Sift Media (US), Inc 120 E 23rd St 4th Fl .... New York NY 10010 *TF:* 855-253-8392 ■ *Web:* www.accountingweb.com	855-253-8392		530
SIG Mfg Company Inc 401 S Front St.......... Montezuma IA 50171 *TF Sales:* 800-247-5008 ■ *Web:* www.sigmfg.com	641-623-5154	623-3922	762
SIG SAUER Inc 18 Industrial Dr .... Exeter NH 03833 *TF:* 866-345-6744 ■ *Web:* www.sigsauer.com	603-772-2302	772-9082	284
Sigal Construction Corp 2231 Crystal Dr Ste 200......................... Arlington VA 22202 *Web:* www.sigal.com	703-302-1500	302-1520	186
Sigel's Beverages LP 2960 Anode Ln .... Dallas TX 75220 *Web:* www.sigels.com	214-350-1271	357-3490	443
Sight Society of Northeastern New York Inc *Lions Eye Bank at Albany* 6 Executive Pk Dr.............................. Albany NY 12203 *Web:* www.lionseyebankalbany.org	518-489-7606	489-7607	269
SightLife 221 Yale Ave N Ste 450.............. Seattle WA 98109 *TF:* 800-847-5786 ■ *Web:* www.sightlife.org	206-682-8500	682-4666	269
SightLine Systems Corp 4035 Ridge Top Rd Ste 510 .... Fairfax VA 22030 *Web:* sightline.com	703-563-3000		624
Sightly Enterprises Inc 910 Camino Del Mar Ste F...................... Del Mar CA 92014 *Web:* www.sightly.com	951-225-7000		393
SightSound Technologies Inc 311 S Craig St Ste 205..................... Pittsburgh PA 15213 *Web:* www.sightsound.com	412-621-6100		525
SightWorks Inc 2505 SE 11th Ave Ste 250 .... Portland OR 97202 *Web:* www.sightworks.com	503-223-4184		5
Sigit Automation Inc 840 Seventh Ave SW Ste 1710................. Calgary AB T2P3G2 *Web:* www.sigit.com	403-723-4256		261
Sigler Companies Inc 3100 S Riverside Dr PO Box 887 .... Ames IA 50010 *TF:* 800-750-6997 ■ *Web:* www.sigler.com	515-232-6997		627
SIGMA (Society of Independent Gasoline Marketers of America) 3930 Pender Dr Ste 340........................ Fairfax VA 22030 *TF:* 800-922-0972 ■ *Web:* www.sigma.org	703-709-7000	709-7007	49-18
Sigma Alpha Epsilon Fraternity (SAE) 1856 Sheridan Rd.......................... Evanston IL 60201 *TF:* 800-233-1856 ■ *Web:* www.sae.net	847-475-1856	475-2250	48-16
Sigma Alpha Iota (SAI) 1 Tunnel Rd........... Asheville NC 28805 *Web:* www.sai-national.org	828-251-0606	251-0644	48-16
Sigma Analysis & Management Ltd 101 College St Ste 345...................... Toronto ON M5G1L7 *Web:* www.sigmaanalysis.com	416-260-6291		401
Sigma Associates Inc 1900 St Antoine St Ste 500.................... Detroit MI 48226 *Web:* www.sigmaassociates.com	313-963-9700		186
Sigma Breakthrough Technologies Inc 123 N Edward Gary 2nd Fl .... San Marcos TX 78666 *TF:* 888-752-7070 ■ *Web:* www.sbtionline.com	512-353-7489		463
Sigma Business Solutions Inc 55 York St.................................. Toronto ON M5J1R7 *TF:* 855-594-1991 ■ *Web:* www.sigma-sbs.com	855-594-1991		809
Sigma Chi Fraternity 1714 Hinman Ave......... Evanston IL 60201 *TF:* 877-829-5500 ■ *Web:* www.sigmachi.org	847-869-3655	869-4906	48-16
Sigma Corp of America 15 Fleetwood Ct .... Ronkonkoma NY 11779 *TF:* 800-896-6858 ■ *Web:* www.sigmaphoto.com	631-585-1144		542
Sigma Delta Tau 714 Adams St................... Carmel IN 46032 *TF:* 800-526-1870 ■ *Web:* sigmadeltatau.org	317-846-7747	575-5562	48-16
Sigma Design 5521 Jackson St .... Alexandria LA 71303 *TF Sales:* 888-990-0900 ■ *Web:* www.arriscad.com	318-449-9900		178-8
Sigma Designs Inc 1778 Mcarthy Blvd........... Milpitas CA 95035 *NASDAQ: SIGM* ■ *Web:* www.sigmadesigns.com	408-262-9003		696
Sigma Electronics Inc 1027 Commercial Ave................. East Petersburg PA 17520 *TF:* 866-569-2681 ■ *Web:* www.sigmatechsys.com	717-569-2926	569-4056	253
Sigma Environmental Services Inc 1300 W Canal St........................... Milwaukee WI 53233 *TF:* 800-413-7225 ■ *Web:* www.thesigmagroup.com	414-643-4200	643-4210	667
Sigma Financial Corp 300 Parkland Plaza .... Ann Arbor MI 48103 *TF:* 800-289-9999 ■ *Web:* www.sigmafinancial.com	734-663-1611		690
Sigma Gamma Rho Sorority Inc 1000 Southhill Dr Ste 200 .... Cary NC 27513 *TF:* 888-747-1922 ■ *Web:* www.sgrho1922.org	919-678-9720	678-9721	48-16
Sigma Kappa Sorority 8733 Founders Rd .... Indianapolis IN 46268 *Web:* www.sigmakappa.org	317-872-3275	872-0716	48-16
Sigma Nu Fraternity Inc 9 N Lewis St PO Box 1869.................. Lexington VA 24450 *Web:* www.sigmanu.org	540-463-1869	463-1669	48-16
Sigma Partners 156 Diablo Rd Ste 320.......... Danville CA 94526 *TF:* 800-358-8228 ■ *Web:* www.sigmapartners.com	650-853-1700	853-1717	792
Sigma Phi Epsilon Fraternity 310 S Blvd .... Richmond VA 23220 *TF:* 800-767-1901 ■ *Web:* www.sigep.org	804-353-1901	359-8160	48-16
Sigma Pi Fraternity 106 N Castle Heights Ave......................... Lebanon TN 37087 *TF:* 800-332-1897 ■ *Web:* www.sigmapi.org	615-373-5728	373-8949	48-16
Sigma Plastics Group Page & Schuyler Aves Bldg 5 .... Lyndhurst NJ 07071 *Web:* www.sigmaplasticsgroup.com	201-933-6000	933-6429	600
Sigma Resources LLC 7950 Saltsburg Rd .... Pittsburgh PA 15239 *Web:* www.sigma-resources.com	412-712-1070		196
Sigma Sigma Sigma Foundation 225 N Muhlenberg St..................... Woodstock VA 22664 *Web:* trisigma.org	540-459-4212		379
Sigma Solutions Inc 607 E Sonterra Blvd Ste 250.............. San Antonio TX 78258 *TF:* 800-567-5964 ■ *Web:* www.sigmasolinc.com	210-348-9876	348-9124	225
Sigma Space Corp 4600 Forbes Blvd .... Lanham MD 20706 *Web:* www.optotraffic.com	301-552-6000		256
Sigma Stretch Film Corp Page & Schuyler Aves Bldg 8................ Lyndhurst NJ 07071 *TF:* 800-672-9727 ■ *Web:* www.sigmastretchtools.com	201-507-9100		601
Sigma Systems Canada Inc 55 York St Ste 1100 .... Toronto ON M5J1R7 *TF:* 888-782-6468 ■ *Web:* www.sigma-systems.com	416-943-9696		177
Sigma Systems Inc 201 Boston Post Rd Ste 201.............. Marlborough MA 01752 *Web:* www.sigmainc.com	508-925-3200		721
Sigma Tau Gamma 101 Ming St PO Box 54 .... Warrensburg MO 64093 *Web:* websites.omegafi.com/omegaws/sigmataugamma	660-747-2222		48-16
Sigma Tek Inc 1001 Industrial Rd .... Augusta KS 67010 *Web:* www.sigmatek.com	316-775-6373		22
Sigma Test Labs 1480 W 178th St .... Gardena CA 90248 *Web:* www.sigmatestlabs.com	310-324-9465	532-6216	743
Sigma Theta Tau International 550 W N St.............................. Indianapolis IN 46202 *TF:* 888-634-7575 ■ *Web:* www.nursingsociety.org	317-634-8171	634-8188	48-16
Sigma Xi Scientific Research Society 3106 E NC Hwy 54 PO Box 13975 .. Research Triangle Park NC 27709 *TF:* 800-243-6534 ■ *Web:* www.sigmaxi.org	919-549-4691	549-0090	48-16
Sigma-Aldrich Corp 3050 Spruce St.......... Saint Louis MO 63103 *NASDAQ: SIAL* ■ **Fax Area Code:* 800 ■ *TF:* 800-325-3010 ■ *Web:* www.sigmaaldrich.com	314-771-5765	325-5052*	145
SigmaBleyzer 123 N Post Oak Ln Ste 410......... Houston TX 77024 *Web:* www.sigmableyzer.com	713-621-3111		194

	Phone	Fax	Class
Sigman Heating & Air Conditioning 6200 Old Saint Louis Rd. . . . . Belleville IL 62223 *Web:* sigmanhvacr.com	618-234-4343		189-10
Sigman Janssen Stack Sewall & Pitz 303 S Memorial Dr. . . . . Appleton WI 54911 *TF:* 800-775-1441 ■ *Web:* www.sigmanlegal.com	920-731-5201		428
Sigma-Netics Inc 2 N Corporate Dr . . . . . . Riverdale NJ 07457 *Web:* www.sigmanetics.com	973-227-6372		729
Sigmatech Inc 4901-C Corporate Dr. . . . . . Huntsville AL 35805 *Web:* www.sigmatech.com	256-382-1188		242
SigmaTEK Systems LLC 1445 Kemper Meadow Dr . . . . Cincinnati OH 45240 *Web:* www.sigmanest.com	513-674-0005		174
SigmaTron International Inc 2201 Landmeier Rd . . . . Elk Grove Village IL 60007 *NASDAQ: SGMA* ■ *TF:* 800-700-9095 ■ *Web:* www.sigmatronintl.com	847-956-8000		625
Sigmetrix 2240 Bush Dr Ste 200 . . . . Mckinney TX 75070 *Web:* www.sigmetrix.com	972-542-7517		809
Sign Biz Inc 24681 La Plaza Ste 270 . . . . . . Dana Point CA 92629 *TF:* 800-633-5580 ■ *Web:* www.signbiz.com	949-234-0408		196
Sign Builders Inc 4800 Jefferson Ave PO Box 28380 . . . . . . Birmingham AL 35228 **Fax Area Code:* 205 ■ *TF:* 800-222-7330 ■ *Web:* www.signbuilders.com	800-222-7330	923-2124*	701
Sign Designs Inc 204 Campus Way . . . . . . Modesto CA 95352 *TF:* 800-421-7446 ■ *Web:* www.signdesigns.com	209-524-4484	521-0272	701
Sign Resource Inc 6135 District Blvd. . . . . . Maywood CA 90270 *TF:* 800-423-4283 ■ *Web:* www.signresource.net	323-771-2098		701
Signa Engineering Corp 2 Northpoint Dr Ste 700 . . . . Houston TX 77060 *TF:* 800-987-3331 ■ *Web:* www.signaengineering.com	281-774-1000		261
Signal Hill Equity Partners 2 Carlton St Ste 1700 . . . . Toronto ON M5B1J3 *Web:* www.signalhillequity.com	416-847-1502		528
Signal Industrial Products Corp 1601 Cowart St. . . . . Chattanooga TN 37408 *TF:* 800-728-1326 ■ *Web:* www.signalproducts.com	423-756-4980		351
Signal Magazine 4400 Fair Lakes Ct. . . . . . . Fairfax VA 22033 *TF:* 800-336-4583 ■ *Web:* www.afcea.org/signal	703-631-6100	631-6188	457-5
Signal Mountain Lodge PO Box 50. . . . . Moran WY 83013 *TF:* 800-543-2847 ■ *Web:* www.signalmountainlodge.com	307-543-2831	543-2569	669
Signal Peak 2755 E Cottonwood Pkwy Ste 520 . . . . . . Salt Lake City UT 84121 *Web:* www.spv.com	801-942-8999	942-1636	792
Signal Point Systems Inc 1270 Shiloh Rd Ste 100 . . . . Kennesaw GA 30144 *TF:* 800-814-6502 ■ *Web:* sigpoint.com	770-499-0439		186
Signal Securities Inc 700 Throckmorton St . . . . Fort Worth TX 76102 *TF:* 800-957-4256 ■ *Web:* www.signalsecurities.com	817-877-4256		196
Signal Transformer Company Inc 500 Bayview Ave. . . . . Inwood NY 11096 *TF:* 866-239-5777 ■ *Web:* belfuse.com/signal	516-239-5777	239-7208	253
Signal Travel & Tours Inc 219 E Main St . . . . . . Niles MI 49120 *TF:* 800-811-1522 ■ *Web:* www.signaltravel.com	269-684-2880		772
Signalert Corp 150 Great Neck Rd Ste 301. . . . . Great Neck NY 11021 *TF:* 800-829-6229 ■ *Web:* www.systemsandforecasts.com	516-829-6444		401
Signalfire Wireless Telemetry Inc 43 Broad St. . . . . Hudson MA 01749 *TF:* 800-772-0878 ■ *Web:* www.signal-fire.com	978-212-2868		645-10
Signalisation Ver-Mac Inc 1781 Bresse. . . . . . Quebec QC G2G2V2 *TF:* 888-488-7446 ■ *Web:* www.ver-mac.com	418-654-1303	654-0517	407
SignalPoint Communications Corp 433 Hackensack Ave Continental Plz 6th Fl . . . . Hackensack NJ 07601 *TF:* 877-928-3292 ■ *Web:* www.signalpointcommunications.com	201-968-9797	968-1886	736
Signal-Tech 4985 Pittsburgh Ave. . . . . Erie PA 16509 *TF:* 877-547-9900 ■ *Web:* www.signal-tech.com	814-835-3000		196
Sign-A-Rama 2121 Vista Pkwy. . . . . West Palm Beach FL 33411 *TF All:* 800-776-8105 ■ *Web:* www.signarama.com	561-640-5570	640-5580	701
Signator Investors Inc 197 Clarendon St C-8. . . . . Boston MA 02116 *TF:* 800-543-6611 ■ *Web:* www.signatorinvestors.com	800-543-6611		401
Signature Bank 565 Fifth Ave 12th Fl . . . . . . New York NY 10017 *NASDAQ: SBNY* ■ *TF:* 866-744-5463 ■ *Web:* www.signatureny.com	646-822-1500		70
Signature Breads Inc 100 Justin Dr. . . . . Chelsea MA 02150 *TF:* 888-602-6533 ■ *Web:* www.signaturebreads.com	888-602-6533		296-1
Signature Capital LLC 100 Commercial St. . . . . Portland ME 04101 *Web:* www.signaturecapital.com	207-773-8123		792
Signature Control Systems Inc 738 E Main St. . . . . Ravenna OH 44266 *Web:* www.signaturecontrol.com	720-641-1131		201
Signature Custom Cabinetry Inc 434 Springville Rd . . . . Ephrata PA 17522 *Web:* www.signaturecab.com	717-738-4884		115
Signature Estate & Investment Advisors LLC 2121 Ave Of The Stars Ste 1600. . . . . Los Angeles CA 90067 *TF:* 800-472-1066 ■ *Web:* www.seia.com	310-712-2323		401
Signature Eyewear Inc 498 N Oak St . . . . . . Inglewood CA 90302 *OTC: SEYE* ■ *TF:* 800-765-3937 ■ *Web:* www.signatureeyewear.com	310-330-2700		542
Signature Flight Support 201 S Orange Ave Ste 1100-S . . . . Orlando FL 32801 *Web:* www.signatureflight.com	407-648-7200		63
Signature Graphics Inc 1000 Signature Dr . . . . Porter IN 46304 *TF:* 800-356-3235 ■ *Web:* www.signaturegraphicsinc.com	219-926-4994	926-7231	344
Signature Hardware 2700 Crescent Springs Pike . . . . Erlanger KY 41017 *TF:* 866-855-2284 ■ *Web:* www.signaturehardware.com	859-647-7564	431-4012	350
Signature Health Care LLC 12201 Bluegrass Pkwy . . . . Louisville KY 40299 *Web:* ltcrevolution.com	502-568-7800		450
Signature Homes Inc 4670 Willow Rd Ste 200. . . . . Pleasanton CA 94588 *Web:* www.sigprop.com	925-463-1122		656
Signature Inc 5115 Parkcenter Ave . . . . Dublin OH 43017 *TF:* 800-398-0518 ■ *Web:* signatureworldwide.com	614-766-5101		194
Signature Printing Inc 5 Almeida Ave. . . . . East Providence RI 02914 *TF:* 800-882-1844 ■ *Web:* www.signatureprinters.com	401-438-1200		627
Signature Services Corp 2705 Hawes Ave . . . . . . Dallas TX 75235 *TF:* 800-929-5519 ■ *Web:* www.signatureservices.com	214-353-2661		299
Signature Theatre 4200 Campbell Ave. . . . . Arlington VA 22206 *TF:* 800-491-6126 ■ *Web:* www.sigtheatre.org	703-820-9771	820-7790	573-4
Signatures 220 Bloor St W. . . . . Toronto ON M5S1T8	416-324-5885		671
Signcraft Screenprint Inc 100 A J Harle Dr. . . . . Galena IL 61036 *TF:* 800-733-5150 ■ *Web:* www.signcraftinc.com	815-777-3030		687
Signe's Bakery & Cafe 93 Arrow Rd . . . . Hilton Head Island SC 29928 *TF:* 866-807-4463 ■ *Web:* www.signesbakery.com	843-785-9118	785-6144	671
Signet Armorlite 1001 Armorlite Dr . . . . San Marcos CA 92069 *Web:* www.signetarmorlite.com	760-744-4000		542
Signet Inc 1801 Shelby Oaks Dr N Ste 12. . . . . Memphis TN 38134 *TF:* 800-654-3889 ■ *Web:* www.gosignet.com	901-387-5555		195
Signet Marking Devices 3121 Red Hill Ave. . . . . Costa Mesa CA 92626 *TF:* 800-421-5150 ■ *Web:* www.signetmarking.com	714-549-0341		467
Signia Capital Management LLC 108 N Washington St Ste 305. . . . . Spokane WA 99201 *Web:* www.signiacapital.com	509-789-8970		401
Signiant Inc 152 Middlesex Tpke. . . . . Burlington MA 01803 *Web:* www.signiant.com	781-221-4000		177
Signifi Solutions Inc 2100 Matheson Blvd E Ste 100. . . . . Mississauga ON L4W5E1 *TF:* 877-744-6434 ■ *Web:* www.signifi.com	905-602-7707		177
Signix Inc 1110 Market St Ste 402. . . . . Chattanooga TN 37402 *TF:* 877-890-5350 ■ *Web:* www.signix.net	877-890-5350		525
Signs by Tomorrow USA Inc 8681 Robert Fulton Dr . . . . Columbia MD 21046 *TF:* 800-765-7446 ■ *Web:* www.signsbytomorrow.com	410-312-3600	312-3520	701
Signs Now 5368 Dixie Hwy Ste 1 . . . . Waterford MI 48329 *TF:* 800-356-3373 ■ *Web:* www.signsnow.com	248-596-8600	596-8601	701
Signs Now 8681 Robert Fulton Dr. . . . . Columbia FL 21046 *TF:* 877-336-7331 ■ *Web:* www.signsnow.com	410-312-3600	312-3520	5
Signtech Electrical Adv Inc 4444 Federal Blvd. . . . . San Diego CA 92102 **Fax Area Code:* 866 ■ *TF:* 877-885-1135 ■ *Web:* www.signtech.com	619-527-6100	275-6115*	701
Signtronix 1445 W Sepulveda Blvd . . . . Torrance CA 90501 **Fax Area Code:* 310 ■ **Fax:* Sales ■ *TF:* 800-729-4853 ■ *Web:* www.signtronix.com	800-729-4853	539-3554*	701
Signum Group LLC 1900 The Exchange SE Bldg 200 . . . . Atlanta GA 30339 *TF:* 800-383-6970 ■ *Web:* www.signumgroup.com	770-514-8111		463
Sign-ups & Banners Corp 2764 W T C Jester Blvd . . . . Houston TX 77018 *TF:* 877-682-7979 ■ *Web:* www.signupsandbanners.com	713-682-7979		627
Signus Medical LLC 18888 Lake Dr E . . . . . . Chanhassen MN 55317 *Web:* www.signusmedical.com	952-294-8700		475
Siguler Guff & Co LLC 825 Third Ave 10th Fl . . . . New York NY 10022 *Web:* www.sigulerguff.com	212-332-5100	332-5120	792
SIHI (Strategic Investments & Holdings Inc) 4445 N A1A Ste 247. . . . . Vero Beach FL 32963 *Web:* www.sihi.net	716-857-6000	857-6490	792
SIHI Pumps Inc 303 Industrial Blvd . . . . Grand Island NY 14072 *Web:* www.sihi-pumps.com	716-773-6450	773-2330	641
SII (Seiko Instruments USA Inc Business & Home Office Products Div) 21221 S Western Ave Ste 250. . . . . Torrance CA 90501 *TF:* 800-688-0817 ■ *Web:* labelprinters.sii-thermalprinters.com	310-517-7700	517-7779	173-6
SII Investments Inc 5555 W Grande Market Dr . . . . Appleton WI 54913 *TF:* 800-426-5975 ■ *Web:* www.siionline.com	920-996-2600		690
SIIA (Software & Information Industry Assn) 1090 Vermont Ave NW 6th Fl. . . . . Washington DC 20005 *Web:* www.siia.net	202-289-7442	289-7097	48-9
SIIG Inc 6078 Stewart Ave. . . . . Fremont CA 94538 *Web:* www.siig.com	510-657-8688		625
Sika Corp 201 Polito Ave . . . . Lyndhurst NJ 07071 *TF:* 800-933-7452 ■ *Web:* www.usa.sika.com	201-933-8800		145
Sika Sarnafil Inc 100 Dan Rd . . . . Canton MA 02021 *TF:* 800-451-2504 ■ *Web:* usa.sarnafil.sika.com	781-828-5400	828-5365	46
Sikich LLP 1415 W Diehl Rd Ste 400 . . . . Naperville IL 60563 *TF:* 877-279-1900 ■ *Web:* www.sikich.com/sg	630-566-8400	566-8401	2
Sikkema Jenkins & Co 530 W 22nd St . . . . New York NY 10011 *Web:* www.sikkemajenkinsco.com	212-929-2262	929-2340	42
Sikorsky Aircraft Corp 6900 Main St PO Box 9729 . . . . Stratford CT 06615 *Web:* www.lockheedmartin.com/us/what-we-do/aerospace-defense/sikorsky.html	203-386-4000		20
Silanis Technology Inc 8200 Decarie Blvd Ste 300 . . . . Montreal QC H4P2P5 *Web:* www.esignlive.com	514-337-5255		177
Silas Bronson Library (SBL) 267 Grand St . . . . Waterbury CT 06702 *Web:* www.bronsonlibrary.org	203-574-8222	574-8055	434-3
Silberline Mfg Company Inc 130 Lincoln Dr PO Box B . . . . Tamaqua PA 18252 *TF:* 800-348-4824 ■ *Web:* www.silberline.com	570-668-6050	668-0197	143
Silberman Langner Assoc 6050 Santo Rd . . . . San Diego CA 92124 *Web:* silbermanlangner.com	858-268-3330		2
Silbrico Corp 6300 River Rd . . . . Hodgkins IL 60525 *TF:* 800-323-4287 ■ *Web:* www.silbrico.com	708-354-3350	354-6698	500
Silco Oil Company Inc 181 E 56th Ave Ste 600 . . . . Denver CO 80216	303-292-0500		579
Silego Technology Inc 1715 Wyatt Dr. . . . . Santa Clara CA 95054 *Web:* www.silego.com	408-327-8800		246
Silencerco LLC 5511 S 6055 W. . . . . West Valley City UT 84118 *Web:* www.silencerco.com	801-417-5384		807
Silent Knight 7550 Meridian Cir Ste 100. . . . . Maple Grove MN 55369 *TF:* 800-328-0103 ■ *Web:* www.silentknight.com	763-493-6400	493-6475	283
Silent Solutions Inc 8704 Lee Hwy . . . . Fairfax VA 22031 *Web:* www.silentsolutions.com	703-849-8246		809

				Phone	Fax	Class
Silestone 2245 Texas Dr Ste 600 .... Sugar Land	TX	77479		281-494-7277		607
Web: www.silestoneusa.com						
Silex Technology America Inc						
167 W 7065 S Ste 330 .... Midvale	UT	84047		801-747-0656		396
Web: www.silexamerica.com						
Silgan Containers Corp						
21800 Oxnard St Ste 600 .... Woodland Hills	CA	91367		818-348-3700		124
Web: www.silgancontainers.com						
Silgan Holdings Inc						
4 Landmark Sq Ste 400 .... Stamford	CT	06901		203-975-7110	975-7902	124
NASDAQ: SLGN ■ TF: 800-732-0330 ■ Web: www.silganholdings.com						
Silgan Plastics Corp						
14515 N Outer Forty Ste 210 .... Chesterfield	MO	63017		800-274-5426	469-5387*	98
*Fax Area Code: 314 ■ TF: 800-274-5426 ■ Web: www.silganplastics.com						
Silicomm Corp PO Box 751024 .... Dayton	OH	45475		937-610-0535	604-4082*	809
*Fax Area Code: 630 ■ Web: www.silicomm.com						
Silicon Alley Group 1 Austin Ave 2nd Fl. .... Iselin	NJ	08830		732-326-1600		195
Silicon Engines Ltd						
3550 W Salt Creek Ln .... Arlington Heights	IL	60005		847-637-1180		196
Silicon Graphics Inc (SGI)						
900 N McCarthy Blvd .... Milpitas	CA	95035		669-900-8000		176
TF: 800-800-7441 ■ Web: www.sgi.com						
Silicon Laboratories Inc						
400 W Cesar Chavez .... Austin	TX	78701		512-416-8500	416-9669	696
NASDAQ: SLAB ■ TF: 877-444-3032 ■ Web: www.silabs.com						
Silicon Microstructures Inc						
1701 Mccarthy Blvd .... Milpitas	CA	95035		408-577-0100		696
Web: www.si-micro.com						
Silicon Valley Assn of Realtors						
19400 Stevens Creek Blvd Ste 100 .... Cupertino	CA	95014		408-200-0100	200-0101	652
TF: 877-699-6787 ■ Web: www.silvar.org						
Silicon Valley Bank (SVB)						
3003 Tasman Dr .... Santa Clara	CA	95054		408-654-7400		70
TF: 800-579-1639 ■ Web: www.svb.com						
Silicon Valley Business Journal						
125 S Market St 11th Fl .... San Jose	CA	95113		408-295-3800	295-5028	457-5
Web: www.bizjournals.com						
Silicon Valley Staffing						
2336 Harrison St .... Oakland	CA	94612		510-923-9898	923-9313	721
TF: 877-660-6000 ■ Web: www.svsjobs.com						
Silicon Valley University						
2160 Lundy Ave Ste 110 .... San Jose	CA	95131		408-435-8989		166
TF: 800-561-3357 ■ Web: www.svuca.edu						
Silicone Specialties Inc						
430 S Rockford Ave .... Tulsa	OK	74120		918-587-5567		351
TF: 888-243-0672 ■ Web: www.ssicm.com						
Siliconix Inc 2201 Laurelwood Rd .... Santa Clara	CA	95054		408-988-8000	567-8950	696
Web: www.vishay.com						
Silipos Inc 7049 Williams Rd .... Niagara Falls	NY	14304		716-283-0700		582
TF: 800-229-4404 ■ Web: www.silipos.com						
Silk Software Corp						
15440 Laguna Canyon Rd Ste 210 .... Irvine	CA	92618		949-748-3700		177
Web: www.silksoftware.com						
Silke Communications Inc 680 Tyler St .... Eugene	OR	97402		541-687-1611		179
Web: www.silkecom.com						
Silks 222 Sansome St .... San Francisco	CA	94104		415-986-2020		671
TF: 800-526-6566 ■ Web: www.mandarinoriental.com						
Silkscreening by Classic Graphix						
12152 Woodruff Ave .... Downey	CA	90241		562-940-0806		258
Web: www.classicgraphix.com						
Silktown Roofing Inc						
27 Pleasant St .... Manchester	CT	06040		860-647-0198		189-12
Web: www.silktownroofing.com						
Silkworm Inc 102 S Sezmore Dr .... Murphysboro	IL	62966		618-687-4077		687
TF: 800-826-0577 ■ Web: www.silkworminK.com						
Silky O'Sullivan's 183 Beale St .... Memphis	TN	38103		901-522-9596	522-8462	671
Web: www.silkyosullivans.com						
Sill Associates 21 Edgewood Dr .... Mechanicsburg	PA	17055		717-691-6730		260
Web: www.sillandassociates.com						
Sillies Greeting Card Co						
14762 Oak Run Ln .... Burnsville	MN	55306		952-892-5666		130
Silliman Associates Inc Thomas						
425 N Lee St .... Alexandria	VA	22314		703-548-4100		463
TF: 800-454-5554 ■ Web: www.tsilliman.com						
Sills Cummis & Gross PC						
1 Riverfront Plaza The Legal Ctr .... Newark	NJ	07102		973-643-7000		428
Web: www.sillscummis.com						
Silo 1133 Austin Hwy .... San Antonio	TX	78209		210-824-8686		671
TF: 800-504-2374 ■ Web: www.siloelevatedcuisine.com						
Siloam Biosciences LLC						
413 Northland Blvd .... Cincinnati	OH	45240		513-429-2976		415
Web: www.siloambio.com						
Siloam Springs State Park						
938 E 3003rd Ln .... Clayton	IL	62324		217-894-6205		565
Web: www.dnr.illinois.gov/Parks/Pages/SiloamSprings.aspx						
Siltronic Corp 7200 NW Front Ave .... Portland	OR	97210		503-243-2020	564-3219*	696
*Fax Area Code: 898 ■ *Fax: Sales ■ TF: 800-724-7378 ■ Web: www.siltronic.com						
Siluria Technologies Inc						
409 Illinois St Ste 100 .... San Francisco	CA	94158		415-978-2170		580
Web: siluria.com						
Silva International Inc 523 N Ash St .... Momence	IL	60954		815-472-3535		345
Web: silva-intl.com						
SILVACO Inc						
4701 Patrick Henry Dr Bldg 2 .... Santa Clara	CA	95054		408-567-1000		225
Web: www.silvaco.com						
Silvan Ridge/Hinman Vineyards						
27012 Briggs Hill Rd .... Eugene	OR	97405		541-345-1945		50-7
TF: 800-264-2519 ■ Web: www.silvanridge.com						
Silvanus Products						
40 Merchant St .... Sainte Genevieve	MO	63670		800-822-2788		596
TF: 800-822-2788 ■ Web: www.silvanusproducts.com						
Silvas Oil Company Inc						
3217 E Lorena Ave .... Fresno	CA	93725		559-233-5171		579
Web: www.silvasoil.com						
Silver & Archibald LLP						
997 S Milledge Ave .... Athens	GA	30605		706-548-8122		428
TF: 877-526-6281 ■ Web: silverandarchibald.com						

				Phone	Fax	Class
Silver Airways Corp						
1100 Lee Wagener Blvd Ste 201 .... Fort Lauderdale	FL	33315		954-985-1500		25
TF: 844-674-5837 ■ Web: www.silverairways.com						
Silver Bullet Technology Inc						
25 W Cedar St Ste 440 .... Pensacola	FL	32502		850-437-5880		179
Web: www.sbullet.com						
Silver City-Grant County Chamber of Commerce						
201 N Hudson St .... Silver City	NM	88061		575-538-3785		139
TF: 800-548-9378 ■ Web: www.silvercity.org						
Silver Cloud Hotel Seattle Broadway						
1100 Broadway .... Seattle	WA	98122		206-325-1400	324-1995	379
TF: 800-590-1801 ■ Web: www.silvercloud.com						
Silver Cloud Inn Seattle-Lake Union						
1150 Fairview Ave N .... Seattle	WA	98109		206-447-9500	812-4900	379
TF General: 800-330-5812 ■ Web: www.silvercloud.com						
Silver Cloud Inn University District						
5036 25th Ave NE .... Seattle	WA	98105		206-526-5200	522-1450	379
TF: 800-205-6940 ■ Web: www.silvercloud.com						
Silver Companies 1001 E Telecom Dr .... Boca Raton	FL	33431		561-981-5252		528
Web: www.silvercompanies.com						
Silver Creative Group Llc						
50 N Main St .... Norwalk	CT	06854		203-855-7705		7
TF: 800-780-8710 ■ Web: silvercreativegroup.com						
Silver Creek Financial ServicesInc						
175 Hwy 82 .... Lostine	OR	97857		541-569-2272		734
TF: 866-569-0020 ■ Web: silvercreekteam.com						
Silver Diner Inc 12276 Rockville Pk .... Rockville	MD	20852		301-770-0333	770-2832	670
TF: 866-561-0518 ■ Web: www.silverdiner.com						
Silver Dragon Restaurant						
106 Third Ave SE .... Calgary	AB	T2G0B6		403-264-5326		671
Silver Eagle Distributors LP						
7777 Washington Ave .... Houston	TX	77007		713-869-4361	867-8112	81-1
TF: 855-332-2110 ■ Web: silvereagle.com						
Silver Eagle Manufacturing Company Inc						
5825 NE Skyport Way .... Portland	OR	97218		503-281-0727		247
Web: www.silvereaglemfg.com						
Silver Edge Co-op 39999 Hilton Rd .... Edgewood	IA	52042		563-928-6419		276
TF: 800-632-5953 ■ Web: www.silveredgecoop.com						
Silver Engineering Inc						
255 East Dr Ste A .... Melbourne	FL	32904		321-676-7596		261
Web: silvereng.com						
Silver Eye Ctr for Photography						
1015 E Carson St .... Pittsburgh	PA	15203		412-431-1810	431-5777	50-2
Web: www.silvereye.org						
Silver Falls State Park						
20024 Silver Falls Hwy SE .... Sublimity	OR	97385		503-873-8681		565
Web: www.oregonstateparks.org						
Silver Fox Restaurant & Lounge						
3422 S Energy Ln .... Casper	WY	82604		307-235-3000		671
Web: www.silverfoxcasper.com						
Silver Fox Steakhouse						
1651 S University Dr .... Fort Worth	TX	76107		817-332-9060		671
Web: www.silverfoxcafe.com						
Silver Fox Tours & Motorcoaches						
3 Silver Fox Dr .... Millbury	MA	01527		508-865-6000	865-4660	760
TF: 800-342-5998 ■ Web: www.silverfoxcoach.com						
Silver Freedman Taff & Tiernan LLP						
3299 K St NW Ste 100 .... Washington	DC	20007		202-295-4500		734
Web: www.sftlaw.com						
Silver Golub & Teitell LLP						
184 Atlantic St .... Stamford	CT	06904		203-325-4491		428
Web: www.sgtlaw.com						
Silver Heights Capital Management Inc						
90 Adelaide St W Ste 400 .... Toronto	ON	M5H3V9		416-342-5626		528
Web: www.silverheights.com						
Silver Institute, The						
1400 I St NW Ste 550 .... Washington	DC	20005		202-835-0185	835-0155	49-4
Web: www.silverinstitute.org						
Silver King Hotel 1485 Empire Ave .... Park City	UT	84060		435-649-5500		379
TF: 888-667-2775 ■ Web: www.allseasonsresortlodging.com						
Silver King Refrigeration Inc						
1600 Xenium Ln N .... Minneapolis	MN	55441		763-923-2441		664
TF: 800-328-3329 ■ Web: www.silverking.com						
Silver Lake College						
2406 S Alverno Rd .... Manitowoc	WI	54220		920-686-6175	684-7082*	166
*Fax: Admissions ■ TF: 800-236-4752 ■ Web: www.sl.edu						
Silver Lake Resort Owners Association Inc						
7751 Black Lake Rd .... Kissimmee	FL	34747		407-397-2828		378
Web: www.takeme2orlando.com						
Silver Lake State Park						
9679 W State Pk Rd .... Mears	MI	49436		231-873-3083		565
Web: michigandnr.com						
Silver Lake State Park						
138 Silver Lake Rd .... Hollis	NH	03049		603-465-2342		565
Web: www.nhstateparks.org						
Silver Lake Technology Management LLC						
2775 Sand Hill Rd Ste 100 .... Menlo Park	CA	94025		650-233-8120	233-8125	401
Web: www.silverlake.com						
Silver Legacy Capital Corp						
407 N Virginia St .... Reno	NV	89501		800-687-8733		690
TF: 800-687-8733						
Silver Legacy Resort & Casino						
407 N Virginia St .... Reno	NV	89501		775-325-7401	325-7474	133
TF: 800-687-8733 ■ Web: www.silverlegacyreno.com						
Silver Lerner Schwartz Fertel						
8707 Skokie Blvd Ste 400 .... Skokie	IL	60077		847-676-2000		734
TF: 800-436-0316 ■ Web: www.slsf.com						
Silver Oaks Communications 824 17th St .... Moline	IL	61265		309-797-9898		344
TF: 800-842-0824 ■ Web: www.silveroaks.com						
Silver Oven Studios Inc						
953 Islington St Ste 22 .... Portsmouth	NH	03801		603-570-7300		177
Web: www.silveroven.com						
Silver Palate 211 Knickerbocker Rd .... Dumont	NJ	07628		201-568-0110		296-41
Web: silverpalate.com						
Silver Reef Casino 4876 Haxton Way .... Ferndale	WA	98248		360-383-0777		132
TF: 866-383-0777 ■ Web: silverreefcasino.com						
Silver Research Consortium (SRC)						
2525 Meridian Pkwy Ste 100 .... Durham	NC	27713		919-361-4647	361-1957	49-19
TF: 800-247-6265 ■ Web: www.ilzro.org						

	Phone	Fax	Class
Silver River State Park 1425 NE 58th Ave. Ocala FL 34470 *Web:* www.floridastateparks.org	352-236-7148		565
Silver Saddle Ranch & Club Inc 20751 Aristotle Dr California City CA 93505 *TF:* 888-430-8728 ■ *Web:* www.silversaddle.com	760-373-8617		653
Silver Sands State Park c/o Osbornedale State Pk 555 Roosevelt Dr Derby CT 06418 *Web:* www.ct.gov/dep/cwp/view.asp?a=2716&q=325262	203-735-4311		565
Silver Shield Security Inc 2107 N First St Ste 100 San Jose CA 95131	408-435-1111		693
Silver Smith Hotel & Suites 10 S Wabash Ave Chicago IL 60603 *TF:* 800-979-0084 ■ *Web:* www.silversmithchicagohotel.com	312-372-7696	372-7320	379
Silver Springs Bottled Water Company Inc PO Box 926 Silver Springs FL 34489 *TF:* 800-556-0334 ■ *Web:* www.ssbwc.com	800-556-0334		297-11
Silver Springs Citrus Inc 25411 N Mare Ave Howey in the Hills FL 34737 *Web:* silverspringscitrus.com	352-324-2101	324-2033	315-2
Silver Springs Farminc 640 Meetinghouse Rd. Harleysville PA 19438	215-256-4321		473
Silver Springs State Fish & Wildlife Area 13608 Fox Rd. Yorkville IL 60560 *Web:* www.dnr.illinois.gov/Parks/Pages/SilverSprings.aspx	630-553-6297		565
Silver Springs State Park 5656 E Silver Springs Blvd. Silver Springs FL 34488 *Web:* www.floridastateparks.org	352-236-7148		32
Silver Springs-Martin Luther School 512 W Township Line Rd Plymouth Meeting PA 19462 *TF:* 800-774-5516 ■ *Web:* www.silver-springs.org	610-825-4440		685
Silver Spur Corp 16010 Shoemaker Ave Cerritos CA 90703 *Web:* www.silverspurcorp.com	562-921-6880		238
Silver Standard Resources Inc 999 W Hastings St Ste 1180 Vancouver BC V6C2W2 *TSE:* SSO ■ *TF:* 888-338-0046 ■ *Web:* www.silverstandard.com	604-689-3846	689-3847	502
Silver Star Automotive Group 3601 Auto Mall Dr Thousand Oaks CA 91362 *TF:* 877-813-1334 ■ *Web:* www.silverstarcadillac.com	800-472-5450		57
Silver Star Meats Inc 1720 Middletown Rd PO Box 393 McKees Rocks PA 15136 *TF:* 800-548-1321 ■ *Web:* www.silverstarmeats.com	412-771-5539		296-26
Silver State Gaming Inc 6145 S Rainbow Ste 100 Las Vegas NV 89118 *Web:* www.silverstategaminginc.com	702-255-1777		196
Silver State Industries 1721 Snyder Ave. Carson NV 89702 *Web:* www.ssi.nv.gov	702-682-3147	486-9908	630
Silver State Materials LLC 4005 Dean Martin Dr Las Vegas NV 89103	702-650-5000		183
Silver Strand State Beach 5000 Highway 75 Coronado CA 92118 *Web:* www.parks.ca.gov/default.asp?page_id=654	619-435-5184		565
Silver Strike Lanes LLC 1281 Kimmerling Rd #8 Gardnerville NV 89460 *Web:* www.silverstrikelanes.com	775-265-5454		99
Silver Strong & Associates 227 First St. Ho Ho Kus NJ 07423 *Web:* www.thoughtfulclassroom.com	201-612-6605		244
Silver Terrace Nurseries Inc 501 N St Pescadero CA 94060	650-879-2110		369
Silver Towne LP 120 E Union City Pike PO Box 424 Winchester IN 47394 *TF:* 800-788-7481 ■ *Web:* www.silvertowne.com	765-584-7481	584-1246	327
Silverado Cable Co 1840 W First Ave. Mesa AZ 85202 *Web:* www.silveradocable.com	480-655-8751		116
Silverado Resort & Spa 1600 Atlas Peak Rd. Napa CA 94558 *TF:* 800-532-0500 ■ *Web:* www.silveradoresort.com	707-257-0200		669
Silverado Stages Inc 241 Prado Rd San Luis Obispo CA 93401 *TF:* 888-383-8109 ■ *Web:* www.silveradostages.com	805-545-8400		760
Silverberg Jewelry Co 6730 22nd Ave N St Petersburg FL 33710 *Web:* www.silverbergjewelry.com	727-381-2666		410
SilverBirch Hotels & Resorts 1600 - 1030 W Georgia St Vancouver BC V6E2Y3 *TF:* 800-431-0070 ■ *Web:* www.silverbirchhotels.com	604-646-2447	646-2404	379
Silvercrest Asset Management Group LLC 1330 Ave of the Americas 38th Fl New York NY 10019 *Web:* www.silvercrestgroup.com	212-649-0600		401
Silvercup Studios 3402 Starr Ave Long Island NY 11101 *Web:* www.silvercupstudios.com	718-906-3000		657
Silverdale Beach Hotel 3073 NW Bucklin Hill Rd Silverdale WA 98383 *TF:* 800-544-9799 ■ *Web:* www.silverdalebeachhotel.com	360-698-1000	692-0932	379
Silvergate Bank 4275 Executive Sq Ste 800 La Jolla CA 92037 *TF:* 800-595-5856 ■ *Web:* www.silvergatebank.com	858-362-6300	362-6333	70
Silverhawk Aviation Inc 1751 W Kearney Ave. Lincoln NE 68524 *TF:* 800-479-5851 ■ *Web:* www.silverhawkaviation.com	402-475-8600		63
Silverleaf Resorts Inc 1221 Riverbend Dr Ste 120 Dallas TX 75247 *TF:* 800-544-8468 ■ *Web:* www.silverleafresorts.com/contact-us	214-631-1166	689-8671	753
Silver-Line Plastics 900 Riverside Dr. Asheville NC 28804 *Web:* www.slpipe.com	828-252-8755		596
Silverman & Light Inc 1201 Park Ave Ste 100 Emeryville CA 94608 *Web:* www.silvermanlight.com	510-655-1200		261
Silverman McGovern Staffing & Recruiting 284 W Exchange St. Providence RI 02903 *Web:* www.silvermanmcgovern.com	401-632-0580		260
Silvermine Arts Ctr 1037 Silvermine Rd New Canaan CT 06840 *TF:* 800-424-0160 ■ *Web:* www.silvermineart.org	203-966-9700	966-2763	50-2
SilverRail Technologies Inc 300 Trade Ctr Ste 5500 Woburn MA 01801 *Web:* www.silverrailtech.com	617-934-6786		387
SilverStone Group 11516 Miracle Hills Dr Ste 100 Omaha NE 68154 *TF:* 800-288-5501 ■ *Web:* www.silverstonegroup.com	402-964-5400	964-5454	390
SilverSun Technologies Inc 5 Regent St Ste 520 Livingston NJ 07039 *Web:* www.silversuntech.co	973-758-6108		787
SilverTech Inc 196 Bridge St. Manchester NH 03104 *TF:* 800-603-9936 ■ *Web:* www.silvertech.com	603-669-6600		195
Silvertip Inc 600 St Mary St Lewisburg PA 17837 *Web:* silvertip-inc.com	570-523-1206		189-10
Silverton Hotel & Casino 3333 Blue Diamond Rd. Las Vegas NV 89139 *TF:* 866-722-4608 ■ *Web:* www.silvertoncasino.com	702-263-7777		133
Silverton Marine Corp 301 Riverside Dr. Millville NJ 08332 *Web:* www.eggharborgroup.com	609-965-2300		90
Silverwood Partners LLC Silverwood Farm Pl 32 Pleasant St. Sherborn MA 01770 *Web:* www.silverwoodpartners.com	508-651-2194		690
Silvestri Studio Inc 8125 Beach St Los Angeles CA 90001 *TF:* 800-647-8874 ■ *Web:* www.silvestricalifornia.com	323-277-4420		464
Silvi Concrete Products Inc 355 Newbold Rd. Fairless Hills PA 19030 *TF:* 800-426-6273 ■ *Web:* www.silvi.com	215-295-0777		182
Silvon Software Inc 900 Oakmont Ln Ste 400 Westmont IL 60559 *TF:* 800-874-5866 ■ *Web:* www.silvon.com	630-655-3313	655-3377	178-1
Silynx Communications Inc 9901 Belward Campus Dr Ste 150 Rockville MD 20850 *Web:* www.silynxcom.com	301-217-9223		647
SIM (Society for Information Management) 15000 Commerce Pkwy Ste C Mount Laurel NJ 08054 *TF:* 800-387-9746 ■ *Web:* www.simnet.org	312-527-6734		48-9
Sim USA Inc PO Box 7900 Charlotte NC 28241 *TF:* 800-521-6449 ■ *Web:* www.simusa.org	800-521-6449		48-20
Sima Products 125 Commerce Dr. Hauppauge NY 11788 *Web:* simaproducts.com	631-435-0200		52
Simacor LLC 10700 Hwy 55 Ste 170 Plymouth MN 55441 *TF:* 888-284-4415 ■ *Web:* www.simacor.com	763-544-4415		180
Simage LLC 300 N Elizabeth St Ste 100C Chicago IL 60607 *TF:* 888-729-7796	888-729-7796		5
Simantel Group 321 SW Water St Peoria IL 61602 *Web:* www.simantel.com	309-674-7747		7
Simard 1212 32nd ave Lachine QC H8T3K7 *TF:* 800-388-7947 ■ *Web:* www.simard.ca	905-670-2005		393
Simark Controls Ltd 10509-46 St S E Ste 10509 Calgary AB T2C5C2 *TF:* 800-565-7431 ■ *Web:* www.simarkcontrols.com	403-236-0580		358
Simba Information 11200 Rockville Pk Ste 504 Rockville MD 20852 *TF:* 888-297-4622 ■ *Web:* simbainformation.com	240-747-3096	747-3004	637-9
Simba Technologies Inc 938 W Eigth Ave Vancouver BC V5Z1E5 *TF:* 800-286-8000 ■ *Web:* www.simba.com	604-633-0008		177
Simbex LLC 10 Water St Ste 410 Lebanon NH 03766 *Web:* www.simbex.com	603-448-2367		261
Simbionix USA Corp 7100 Euclid Ave Baker Electric Bldg Ste 180 Cleveland OH 44103 *Web:* www.simbionix.com	216-229-2040		475
Simco Drilling Equipment Inc PO Box 448 Osceola IA 50213 *TF:* 800-338-9925 ■ *Web:* www.simcodrill.com	641-342-2166	342-6764	190
Simco Electronics 3131 Jay St. Santa Clara CA 95054 *TF:* 866-299-6029 ■ *Web:* www.simco.com	408-734-9750	734-9780	743
Simco Leather Corp 99 Pleasant Ave Johnstown NY 12095	518-762-7100		432
Simco Sales Service of Pennsylvania Inc 101 Commerce Dr Moorestown NJ 08057 *Web:* www.jackjillicecream.com	856-813-2300		297-4
Simcoe & District Chamber of Commerce 95 Queensway W Simcoe ON N3Y2M8 *Web:* www.simcoechamber.on.ca	519-426-5867	428-7718	137
Simcoe Parts Service Inc 6795 Industrial Pkwy Alliston ON L9R1W1 *Web:* www.simcoeparts.com	705-435-7814		311
Simcrest Inc 700 Central Expy Ste 310 Allen TX 75013 *Web:* www.simcrest.com	214-644-4000		177
Simek's Inc 940 Hastings Ave Saint Paul Park MN 55071 *Web:* www.simeks.com	651-459-5578		345
Simeri's Old Town Tap 1505 W Indiana Ave South Bend IN 46613 *Web:* simerisoldtowntap.weebly.com	574-289-1361		671
Simflo Pumps Inc 754 E Maley St PO Box 849 Willcox AZ 85644 *Web:* www.simflo.com	520-384-2273	384-4042	641
Simi Valley Chamber of Commerce 40 W Cochran St Ste 100 Simi Valley CA 93065 *Web:* www.simivalleychamber.org	805-526-3900	526-6234	139
Simi Valley Hospital (SVH) 2975 N Sycamore Dr Simi Valley CA 93065 *Web:* www.adventisthealth.org	805-955-6000		374-3
Simione Healthcare Consultants LLC 4130 Whitney Ave. Hamden CT 06518 *Web:* www.simioneconsultants.com	203-287-9288		463
SIMKAR Corp 700 Ramona Ave Philadelphia PA 19120 **Fax:* Cust Svc ■ *TF:* 800-523-3602 ■ *Web:* www.simkar.com	215-831-7700	831-7703*	439
Simkiss Cos 2 Paoli Office Pk PO Box 1787 Paoli PA 19301 *Web:* www.simkiss.com	610-727-5300	727-5414	390
Simlab.net 579 Pompton Ave Cedar Grove NJ 07009 *Web:* www.simlab.net	973-571-0055		772
Simmons & Company International 700 Louisiana Ste 1900 Houston TX 77002 *Web:* www.simmonspjc.com	713-236-9999		401

Name / Address	City	State	ZIP	Phone	Fax	Class
Simmons Co 1 Concourse Pkwy Ste 800 *Web:* www.simmons.com	Atlanta	GA	30328	770-512-7700		471
Simmons College 300 The Fenway **Fax:* Admissions ■ *TF:* 800-345-8468 ■ *Web:* www.simmons.edu	Boston	MA	02115	617-521-2000	521-3190*	166
Simmons College Beatley Library 300 The Fenway *TF:* 800-831-4284 ■ *Web:* www.simmons.edu	Boston	MA	02115	617-521-2780	521-3093	434-6
Simmons Engineering Corp 400 Regency Dr *TF:* 800-252-3381 ■ *Web:* simcut.com	Glendale Heights	IL	60139	630-912-2880		261
Simmons Farm Raised Catfish Inc 2628 Erickson Rd *Web:* www.simmonscatfish.com	Yazoo City	MS	39194	662-746-5687	746-8625	296-14
Simmons Firm LLC, The 230 W Monroe Ste 2221 *TF:* 844-955-2774 ■ *Web:* www.simmonsfirm.com	Chicago	IL	60606	844-955-2774		445
Simmons First National Corp 501 Main St *NASDAQ: SFNC* ■ *TF:* 877-245-1234	Pine Bluff	AR	71601	866-246-2400		360-2
Simmons Foods Inc 601 N Hico St *Web:* simmonsfoods.com	Siloam Springs	AR	72761	479-524-8151		619
Simmons Investigative & Security Agency Inc 76 S Winter Park Dr *Web:* www.simmonssecurity.com	Casselberry	FL	32707	407-699-5308		693
Simmons Machine Tool Corp 1700 N Broadway *Web:* smtgroup.com	Albany	NY	12204	518-462-5431	462-0371	455
Simmons Perrine Moyer Bergman PLC 115 Third St SE Ste 1200 *Web:* www.spmblaw.com	Cedar Rapids	IA	52401	319-366-7641		428
Simmons Pet Foods Inc 316 N Hico *Web:* simmonspetfood.com	Siloam Springs	AR	72761	479-524-8151		578
Simmons-Boardman Publishing Corp 55 Broad St 26th fl 26th Fl *TF:* 800-257-5091 ■ *Web:* www.simmonsboardman.com	New York	NY	10004	212-620-7200	633-1165	637-9
Simmons-rockwell Inc 784 County Rd 64 *TF:* 888-520-2213 ■ *Web:* www.simmons-rockwell.com	Elmira	NY	14903	607-796-5555		57
Simms Fishing Products Corp 101 Evergreen Dr *TF:* 800-217-4667 ■ *Web:* www.simmsfishing.com	Bozeman	MT	59715	406-585-3557	585-3562	710
SIMNA (Schroder Investment Management North America Inc) 7 Bryant Pk *TF:* 800-730-2932 ■ *Web:* www.schroders.com/us	New York	NY	10018	212-641-3800	632-2954	690
Simon & Arrington Inc 6215 Brookshire Terr *Web:* www.s-a.us	Fort Myers	FL	33912	305-718-0630		525
Simon & Assoc Inc 3200 Commerce St *TF:* 800-763-4234 ■ *Web:* simonassoc.com	Blacksburg	VA	24060	540-951-4234		261
Simon & Geherin PLLC 1310 S Main St Ste 11 *Web:* www.simongeherin.com	Ann Arbor	MI	48104	734-997-0870		428
Simon & Schuster Interactive 1230 Ave of the Americas *TF:* 800-223-2336 ■ *Web:* www.simonandschuster.biz	New York	NY	10020	212-698-7000	632-8099	637 1
Simon & Seafort's Saloon & Grill 420 L St *Web:* www.simonandseaforts.com	Anchorage	AK	99501	907-274-3502		671
Simon Consulting LLC 3200 N Central Ave Ste 2460 *Web:* www.simonconsulting.net	Phoenix	AZ	85012	602-279-7500		196
Simon Foundation for Incontinence PO Box 815 *Web:* www.simonfoundation.org	Wilmette	IL	60091	847-864-3913	864-9758	48-17
Simon Fraser University (SFU) *Burnaby* 8888 University Dr MBC 1150 *Web:* www.sfu.ca	Burnaby	BC	V5A1S6	778-782-2667	782-5496	785
Harbour Centre 515 W Hastings St *Web:* www.sfu.ca	Vancouver	BC	V6B5K3	778-782-5000	782-5219	785
Surrey 250 - 13450 102 Ave *Web:* www.sfu.ca/campuses/surrey.html	Surrey	BC	V3T0A3	778-782-7400	782-7403	785
Simon G Jewelry Inc 528 State St *TF:* 800-627-2661 ■ *Web:* www.simongjewelry.com	Glendale	CA	91203	818-500-9697		410
Simon Golub & Sons Inc 5506 Sixth Ave S *Web:* www.simongolub.com	Seattle	WA	98108	206-762-4800		360-3
Simon Group Inc, The 1506 Old Bethlehem Pk *Web:* www.simongroup.com	Sellersville	PA	18960	215-453-8700		4
Simon Lever & Co 444 Murry Hill Cir *TF:* 800-784-8566 ■ *Web:* www.simonlever.com	Lancaster	PA	17601	717-569-7081		2
Simon Metals LLC 2202 E River St *TF:* 800-562-8464 ■ *Web:* www.simonmetals.com	Tacoma	WA	98421	253-272-9364		686
Simon Property Group Inc 225 W Washington St *NYSE: SPG* ■ *Web:* www.simon.com	Indianapolis	IN	46204	317-636-1600		655
Simon Roofing & Sheet Metal Corp 70 Karago Ave *TF:* 800-523-7714 ■ *Web:* www.simonroofing.com	Youngstown	OH	44512	330-629-7663	629-7399	46
Simon Wiesenthal Ctr 1399 Roxbury Dr Ste 100 *TF:* 800-900-9036 ■ *Web:* www.wiesenthal.com	Los Angeles	CA	90035	310-553-9036		48-8
Simon's Rock College of Bard 84 Alford Rd *Web:* www.simons-rock.edu	Great Barrington	MA	01230	413-644-4400		166
Simoncomputing Inc 5350 Shawnee Rd Ste 200 *Web:* simoncomputing.com	Alexandria	VA	22312	703-914-5454		177
Simonds International 135 Intervale Rd *TF:* 800-343-1616 ■ *Web:* www.simondsint.com	Fitchburg	MA	01420	800-343-1616	541-6224	682
Simonian Fruit Co 511 N Seventh St PO Box 340 *Web:* www.simonianfruit.com	Fowler	CA	93625	559-834-5921		297-7
Simoniz Car Wash 435 Eastern Ave *TF:* 800-339-3949 ■ *Web:* www.washdepot.com	Malden	MA	02148	781-321-1900		62-1
Simoniz USA 201 Boston Tpke **Fax Area Code:* 860 ■ *TF:* 800-227-5536 ■ *Web:* www.simoniz.com	Bolton	CT	06043	800-227-5536	645-6070*	151
Simonmed Imaging 6900 E Camelback Rd Ste 700 *Web:* www.simonmed.com	Scottsdale	AZ	85251	480-614-8555		415
Simons Bitzer & Assoc PC 8350 S Emerson Ave Ste 100 *TF:* 866-702-5090 ■ *Web:* www.simonsbitzer.com	Indianapolis	IN	46237	317-782-3070		2
Simons Trucking Inc 920 Simon Dr PO Box 8 *TF:* 800-373-2580 ■ *Web:* www.simonstrucking.com	Farley	IA	52046	563-744-3304	744-3726	780
Simonsen Industries Inc 500 Iowa 31 *TF:* 800-831-4860 ■ *Web:* www.simonsen-industries.com	Quimby	IA	51049	712-445-2211	445-2626	273
Simonsen Laboratories Inc 1180-C Day Rd *TF:* 800-424-7755 ■ *Web:* www.simlab.com	Gilroy	CA	95020	408-847-2002	847-4176	11-2
Simonson Properties Co 535 First St NE *TF:* 888-843-8789 ■ *Web:* www.simonson-lumber.com	Saint Cloud	MN	56304	320-252-9385		364
Simonton Court Historic Inn & Cottages 320 Simonton St *TF:* 800-944-2687 ■ *Web:* www.simontoncourt.com	Key West	FL	33040	800-944-2687		379
Simonton Windows Inc 5300 Briscoe Rd PO Box 1646 *Web:* www.simonton.com	Parkersburg	WV	26102	304-428-8261		608
SimPak International LLC 2107 Production Dr *Web:* www.simpakinternational.com	Louisville	KY	40299	502-671-8250		601
SimPhonics Inc 3226 N Falkenburg Rd *Web:* www.simphonics.com	Tampa	FL	33619	813-623-9917		261
Simple Computer Repair 1000 N Green Valley Pkwy *Web:* www.simplecomputerrepair.com	Henderson	NV	89074	702-483-5464		196
Simple Pc 101 Grace St	Greenwood	SC	29649	864-223-3344		175
Simple Verity Inc 1218 Third Ave Ste 169 **Fax Area Code:* 206 ■ *TF:* 855-583-7489 ■ *Web:* www.simpleverity.com	Seattle	WA	98101	617-905-7467	512-3480*	393
Simplegrid Technology Inc 40 Baldwin Rd *TF:* 800-282-6242 ■ *Web:* www.simplegrid.com	Parsippany	NJ	07054	973-265-2838		393
SimpleSignal Inc 34232 Pacific Coast Hwy *Web:* www.simplesignal.com	Dana Point	CA	92629	949-487-3333		224
Simplesoft Inc 257 Castro St Ste 220 *Web:* www.smplsft.com	Mountain View	CA	94041	650-965-4515		177
SimpleSolve Inc 1 Airport Pl Ste 3 *TF:* 800-999-5368 ■ *Web:* www.simplesolve.com	Princeton	NJ	08540	609-452-2323		809
SimpleTuition Inc 268 Summer St Ste 502 *TF:* 800-448-4904 ■ *Web:* simpletuition.com	Boston	MA	02210	617-630-6100		387
Simplex Equipment Rental 9740 Boul de l'Acadie *Web:* www.simplex.ca	Montreal	QC	H4N1L8	514-331-7777		23
Simplex Homes 1 Simplex Dr *Web:* www.simplexind.com	Scranton	PA	18504	570-346-5113		106
Simplex Inc 5300 Rising Moon Rd *TF:* 800-637-8603 ■ *Web:* www.simplexdirect.com	Springfield	IL	62711	217-483-1600	483 1616	253
Simplex Manufacturing Co 13340 NE Whitaker Way *Web:* simplex.aero	Portland	OR	97230	503-257-3511		57
Simplicity Consulting Inc 6710 108th Ave NE Ste 203 *TF:* 888-252-0385 ■ *Web:* www.simplicityci.com	Kirkland	WA	98033	888-252-0385		196
Simplicity Manufacturing Inc PO Box 702 *TF:* 800-837-6836 ■ *Web:* www.simplicitymfg.com	Milwaukee	WI	53201	800-837-6836		429
Simplifile LC 4844 N 300 W Ste 202 *TF:* 800 460-5657 ■ *Web:* simplifile.com	Provo	UT	84604	801-373-0151		225
Simplion Technologies Inc 1525 McCarthy Blvd Ste 228 *TF:* 800-566-4604 ■ *Web:* www.simplion.com	Milpitas	CA	95035	408-935-8686		196
Simply Fondue 2108 Greenville Ave *Web:* www.simplyfondue.com	Dallas	TX	75206	214-827-8878		671
Simply Fresh Foods Inc 6535 Caballero Blvd Bldg C *Web:* www.ffci.us	Buena Park	CA	90620	714-562-5000	562-5002	297-8
Simply Healthcare Plans Inc 1701 Ponce De Leon Blvd Ste 300 *TF:* 877-577-9042 ■ *Web:* www.simplyhealthcareplans.com	Coral Gables	FL	33134	305-408-5890		194
Simply Ideas LLC 5348 SW 34th Way *Web:* www.simplyideas.com	Hollywood	FL	33312	954-391-7123		195
Simply Orange Juice Co 2659 Orange Ave *TF:* 800-871-2653 ■ *Web:* www.simplyorangejuice.com	Apopka	FL	32703	800-871-2653		296-20
Simply Whispers 50 Perry Ave **Fax Area Code:* 774 ■ *TF:* 800-451-5700 ■ *Web:* www.romanresearch.com	Attleboro	MA	02703	508-455-0864	203-3974*	415
Simpson College 701 N 'C' St **Fax:* Admissions ■ *TF:* 800-362-2454 ■ *Web:* www.simpson.edu	Indianola	IA	50125	515-961-6251	961-1870*	166
Simpson County PO Box 459 *Web:* www.simpsontax.com	Mendenhall	MS	39114	601-847-1744	847-2119	338
Simpson County Development Foundation 176 W Court St PO Box 127 *Web:* www.simpsoncounty.biz	Mendenhall	MS	39114	601-847-2375	847-2380	187
Simpson Door Co 400 Simpson Ave *TF:* 800-746-7766 ■ *Web:* www.simpsondoor.com	Mccleary	WA	98557	800-746-7766		683
Simpson Electric Co 520 Simpson Ave *Web:* www.simpsonelectric.com	Lac Du Flambeau	WI	54538	715-588-3311	588-1248	248
Simpson Gumpertz & Heger Inc 41 Seyon St Bldg 1 Ste 500 *TF:* 800-729-7429 ■ *Web:* www.sgh.com	Waltham	MA	02453	781-907-9000	907-9009	261
Simpson House 2101 Belmont Ave *TF:* 800-222-2476 ■ *Web:* www.simpsonhouse.org	Philadelphia	PA	19131	215-878-3600		672
Simpson Housing LLLP (SHLP) 8110 E Union Ave Ste 200 *Web:* www.simpsonhousing.com	Denver	CO	80237	303-283-4100		653
Simpson Investment Co 917 E 11th St *Web:* simpson.com	Tacoma	WA	98421	253-779-6400		360-3
Simpson Mfg Company Inc 5956 W Las Positas Blvd *NYSE: SSD* ■ *TF:* 800-925-5099 ■ *Web:* www.simpsonmfg.com	Pleasanton	CA	94588	925-560-9000		15

Name / Address	City	State	ZIP	Phone	Fax	Class
Simpson Mike (Rep R - ID) 2084 Rayburn HOB *Web:* simpson.house.gov	Washington	DC	20515	202-225-5531	225-8216	342-2
Simpson Norton Corp 4144 S Bullard Ave *TF:* 877-859-8676 ■ *Web:* www.simpsonnorton.com	Goodyear	AZ	85338	623-932-5116	932-5299	274
Simpson Performance Products Inc 328 FM 306 *TF:* 800-997-7333 ■ *Web:* www.simpsonraceproducts.com	New Braunfels	TX	78130	830-625-1774		60
Simpson Strong-Tie Company Inc 5956 W Las Positas Blvd *TF:* 800-925-5099 ■ *Web:* www.strongtie.com	Pleasanton	CA	94588	925-560-9000	847-1597	350
Simpson Thacher & Bartlett LLP 425 Lexington Ave *Web:* www.stblaw.com	New York	NY	10017	212-455-2000	455-2502	428
Simpson Timber Co 917 E 11th St *Web:* www.simpson.com	Tacoma	WA	98421	253-779-6400		683
Simpson University 2211 College View Dr **Fax:* Admissions ■ *TF:* 888-974-6776 ■ *Web:* www.simpsonu.edu	Redding	CA	96003	530-226-4606	226-4861*	166
Simpson's Eggs Inc 5015 Hwy 218 E *TF:* 800-726-1330 ■ *Web:* www.simpsonseggs.com	Monroe	NC	28110	704-753-1478	753-4762	10-8
Simpsons on The Spot Auto Detailing 2953 Pleasant Grove Rd	Lansing	MI	48910	517-393-7910		57
Simrex Corp 5490 Broadway St *Web:* www.simrex.com	Lancaster	NY	14086	480-926-6069		647
Sims & Steele Consulting PO Box 8305 Ste 3a *Web:* simsandsteele.com	Asheville	NC	28801	828-254-9004		196
Sims Bark Company Inc 1765 Spring Valley Rd *TF:* 800-346-3216 ■ *Web:* www.simsbark.com	Tuscumbia	AL	35674	256-381-8323		683
Sims Brothers Recycling 1011 S Prospect St PO Box 1170 *TF:* 800-536-7465 ■ *Web:* www.simsbros.com	Marion	OH	43302	740-387-9041		686
Sims Cab Depot 200 Moulinette Rd *TF:* 800-225-7290 ■ *Web:* www.cabdepot.com	Long Sault	ON	K0C1P0	613-534-2289		480
Sims Recycling Solutions Holdings Inc 1600 Harvester Rd *TF:* 800-270-8220 ■ *Web:* www.simsrecycling.com	West Chicago	IL	60185	630-231-6060		787
Simsbury Public Library 725 Hopmeadow St *Web:* www.simsburylibrary.info	Simsbury	CT	06070	860-658-7663	658-6732	434-3
Simtech Inc 66A Floydville Rd *TF:* 800-255-3503 ■ *Web:* www.simtech-inc.com	East Granby	CT	06026	860-653-2408		770
Sim-Tex LP 20880 FM 362 Rd *TF:* 866-829-8939 ■ *Web:* www.sim-tex.com	Waller	TX	77484	713-450-3940		492
Simtrol Inc 520 Guthridge Ct Ste 250	Norcross	GA	30092	678-365-2315		178-12
Simulaids 16 Simulaids Dr PO Box 1289 *Web:* www.simulaids.com	Saugerties	NY	12477	845-679-2475	679-8996	678
Simulations Plus Inc 42505 Tenth St W *NASDAQ: SLP* ■ *TF:* 888-266-9294 ■ *Web:* www.simulations-plus.com	Lancaster	CA	93534	661-723-7723	723-5524	178-10
Simulent Inc 203 College St Ste 302 *Web:* www.simulent.com	Toronto	ON	M5T1P9	416-979-5544		261
Simulis LLC 6450 Louetta Rd Ste 140	Spring	TX	77379	713-956-9000	956-9898	538
SimulTrans LLC 455 N Whisman Rd Ste 400 *TF:* 800-726-9891 ■ *Web:* www.simultrans.com	Mountain View	CA	94043	650-605-1300		768
Simunition Ltd 65 Sandscreen Rd *TF:* 800-465-8255 ■ *Web:* simunition.com	Avon	CT	06001	860-404-0162		463
Simutek Inc 3136 E Ft Lowell Rd *TF:* 800-549-4505 ■ *Web:* www.simutek.com	Tucson	AZ	85716	520-321-9077		35
Sinai Hospital of Baltimore 2401 W Belvedere Ave *TF:* 800-876-1175 ■ *Web:* www.sinai-balt.com	Baltimore	MD	21215	410-601-9000		374-3
Sinapis Pharma Inc 3610 Holly Grove Ave *Web:* www.sinapispharma.com	Jacksonville	FL	32217	904-619-0043		231
Sincera Consulting Llc 3735 Dohm Dr *Web:* www.sincera.net	Charlevoix	MI	49720	231-547-0478		809
Sinclair & Rush Inc 123 Manufacturers Dr *TF:* 800-526-6273 ■ *Web:* www.sinclair-rush.com	Arnold	MO	63010	636-282-6800	282-6888	600
Sinclair Broadcast Group Inc 10706 Beaver Dam Rd *NASDAQ: SBGI* ■ *Web:* www.sbgi.net	Hunt Valley	MD	21030	410-568-1500	568-1533	738
Sinclair Community College 444 W Third St *TF:* 800-315-3000 ■ *Web:* www.sinclair.edu	Dayton	OH	45402	937-512-3000		162
Sinclair Dental Company Ltd 900 Harbourside Dr *TF:* 800-241-3743 ■ *Web:* www.sinclairdental.com	North Vancouver	BC	V7P3T8	604-986-1544		475
Sinclair Manufacturing Company Inc 12 S Worcester St *Web:* www.sinclairmfg.com	Norton	MA	02766	508-222-7440		567
Sinclair Oil Corp PO Box 30825 *Web:* www.sinclairoil.com	Salt Lake City	UT	84130	801-524-2700	524-2880	580
Sinclair Pratt Cameron PC 1630 Donna Dr Ste 103 *Web:* spc-eng.com	Virginia Beach	VA	23451	757-417-0565		261
Sinclair Printing Co 4005 Whiteside St *Web:* www.sinclairprinting.com	Los Angeles	CA	90063	323-264-4000		627
Sindel, Sindel & Noble PC 8008 Carondelet Ave Ste 301 *TF:* 866-489-5504 ■ *Web:* www.sindellaw.com	Saint Louis	MO	63105	314-721-6040		428
Sine Irish Pub & Restaurant 1327 E Cary St *Web:* www.sineirishpub.com/cms_richmond	Richmond	VA	23218	804-649-7767	649-0661	671
Sinema Krysten (Rep D - AZ) 1725 Longworth HOB *Web:* sinema.house.gov	Washington	DC	20515	202-225-9888	225-9731	342-2
Sing Sing Correctional Facility 354 Hunter St *Web:* www.doccs.ny.gov	Ossining	NY	10562	914-941-0108		213
Sing Tao Newspapers San Francisco Ltd 5000 Marina Blvd Ste 300 *Web:* www.stgloballink.com	Brisbane	CA	94005	650-808-8800	808-8801	627
Singapore 318 E 48th St *Web:* www.mfa.gov.sg/newyork	New York	NY	10017	212-223-3331	826-5028	784
Consulate General 595 Market St Ste 2450 *Web:* www.mfa.gov.sg	San Francisco	CA	94105	415-543-4775	543-4788	257
Embassy 3501 International Pl NW *Web:* www.mfa.gov.sg	Washington	DC	20008	202-537-3100	537-0876	257
Singapore Airlines KrisFlyer 380 World Way Ste 336B *TF:* 800-742-3333 ■ *Web:* www.singaporeair.com	Los Angeles	CA	90045	310-647-6144		26
Singapore Airlines Ltd 222 N Sepulveda Blvd Ste 1600 *TF:* 800-742-3333 ■ *Web:* www.singaporeair.com	El Segundo	CA	90245	310-647-1922		25
Singapore Press Holdings 529 14th St NW National Press Bldg Ste 916 *Web:* www.sph.com.sg	Washington	DC	20045	202-662-8726	662-8729	637-8
Singapore Sam's 555 11th Ave SW Ste 101 *TF:* 800-944-8778 ■ *Web:* www.singaporesams.com	Calgary	AB	T2R1P6	403-234-8088	266-6883	671
Singer & Levick Pc 16200 Addison Rd Ste 140 *Web:* www.singerlevick.com	Addison	TX	75001	972-380-5533		428
Singer Group Inc, The 12915 Dover Rd *Web:* www.singergrp.com	Reisterstown	MD	21136	410-561-7561		186
Singer Lewak Greenbaum & Goldstein LLP 10960 Wilshire Blvd 7th Fl *TF:* 877-754-4557 ■ *Web:* www.singerlewak.com	Los Angeles	CA	90024	310-477-3924	478-6070	2
Singer Sewing Co 1224 Hill Quaker Blvd PO Box 7017 *TF:* 877-738-9869 ■ *Web:* www.singerco.com	La Vergne	TN	37086	615-213-0880	213-0994	37
Singer Specs 211 W Lincoln Hwy *Web:* singerspecs.net	Exton	PA	19341	610-524-8886		543
Singh Homes Inc 7125 OrchaRd Lake Rd Ste 200 *TF:* 800-209-9992 ■ *Web:* www.singhweb.com	West Bloomfield	MI	48322	248-865-1600	865-1630	653
Singha Thai 2237 S 108th St *Web:* www.singhathaimilwaukee.com	Milwaukee	WI	53227	414-541-1234		671
Singing Machine Company Inc, The 6601 Lyons Rd Bldg A-7 *OTC: SMDM* ■ *TF:* 866-670-6888 ■ *Web:* www.singingmachine.com	Coconut Creek	FL	33073	954-596-1000	596-2000	246
Singing River Electric Power Assn Inc 11187 Old Hwy 63 PO Box 767 *TF:* 800-371-5417 ■ *Web:* www.singingriver.com	Lucedale	MS	39452	601-947-4211	947-6548	245
Singing River Hospital 2809 Denny Ave *Web:* www.singingriverhealthsystem.com	Pascagoula	MS	39581	228-809-5000		374-3
Single Digits Inc 4 Bedford Farms Dr Ste 210 *Web:* www.singledigits.com	Bedford	NH	03110	603-580-1539		224
Single Mothers by Choice Inc (SMC) PO Box 1642 *Web:* www.singlemothersbychoice.org	New York	NY	10028	212-988-0993		48-21
Single Pebble 133 Bank St *Web:* www.asinglepebble.com	Burlington	VT	05401	802-865-5200		671
Single Source Technologies Inc 2600 Superior Ct *TF:* 800-336-7283 ■ *Web:* www.singlesourcetech.com	Auburn Hills	MI	48326	248-232-6232		358
SinglePoint Solutions Inc 9710 Park Plaza Ave Ste 201 *Web:* www.sptsolutions.com	Louisville	KY	40241	502-212-4017		196
Singletary Lake State Park 6707 NC 53 Hwy E *Web:* www.ncparks.gov	Kelly	NC	28448	910-669-2928		565
Singlewire Software LLC 2601 W Beltline Hwy Ste 510 *TF:* 800-561-3357 ■ *Web:* www.singlewire.com	Madison	WI	53713	608-661-1140		41
SinJu 1022 NW Johnson St *Web:* www.sinjurestaurant.com	Portland	OR	97209	503-223-6535		671
Sinkyone Wilderness State Park PO Box 245 *Web:* www.parks.ca.gov	Whitethorn	CA	95489	707-986-7711		565
Sinnemahoning State Park 8288 First Fork Rd *Web:* www.dcnr.state.pa.us	Austin	PA	16720	814-647-8401		565
Sinopec Daylight Energy Ltd 112-4th Ave SW Sun Life Plaza E Tower Ste 2700 *TF:* 877-266-6901 ■ *Web:* www.sinopecdaylight.com	Calgary	AB	T2P0H3	403-266-6900		536
Sinte Gleska University 101 Antelope Lake Cir Dr PO Box 105 *TF:* 800-786-7673 ■ *Web:* www.sintegleska.edu	Mission	SD	57555	605-856-8100	856-4194	165
Sintel Inc 18437 171st Ave *TF:* 800-394-8276 ■ *Web:* www.sintelinc.com	Spring Lake	MI	49456	616-842-6960		454
Sinton Dairy Foods Co LLC 3801 Sinton Rd	Colorado Springs	CO	80907	719-633-3821	667-7470	296-10
Sintz & Assoc Inc 57 S Park Blvd	Greenwood	IN	46143	317-889-3000		390
SinuSys Corp 4030 Fabian Way *TF:* 855-474-6879 ■ *Web:* sinusys.com	Palo Alto	CA	94303	650-213-9988		475
SIO (Scripps Institution of Oceanography) 8622 Kennel Way *Web:* scripps.ucsd.edu	La Jolla	CA	92037	858-534-3624		668
SIOR (Society of Industrial & Office Realtors) 1201 New York Ave NW Ste 350 *Web:* www.sior.com	Washington	DC	20005	202-449-8200	216-9325	49-17
Sioux Automation Ctr Inc 877 First Ave NW *TF:* 866-722-1488 ■ *Web:* www.siouxautomation.com	Sioux Center	IA	51250	712-722-1488		274
Sioux Chief Manufacturing Company Inc 24110 S Peculiar Dr *Web:* www.siouxchief.com	Peculiar	MO	64078	816-779-6104		612
Sioux City Art Ctr 225 Nebraska St *TF:* 800-222-7270 ■ *Web:* siouxcityartcenter.org	Sioux City	IA	51101	712-279-6272	255-2921	520

Phone | Fax | Class

Sioux City Brick & Tile Co
310 S Floyd Blvd .... Sioux City IA 51101 712-258-6571 252-3215 150
TF: 800-665-8483 ■ *Web:* www.siouxcitybrick.com

Sioux City Convention Ctr
801 Fourth St .... Sioux City IA 51101 712-279-4800 279-4900 205
TF: 800-593-2228 ■ *Web:* www.visitsiouxcity.org/convention-center

Sioux City Foundry Co 801 Div St .... Sioux City IA 51102 712-252-4181 252-4197 307
TF: 800-831-0874 ■ *Web:* www.siouxcityfoundry.com

Sioux City Journal 515 Pavonia St .... Sioux City IA 51101 712-293-4300 279-5059 532-2
TF: 800-397-3530 ■ *Web:* www.siouxcityjournal.com

Sioux City Public Library
529 Pierce St .... Sioux City IA 51101 712-255-2933 434-3
TF: 800-662-3303 ■ *Web:* www.siouxcitylibrary.org

Sioux City Public Museum
2901 Jackson St .... Sioux City IA 51104 712-279-6174 520
Web: www.sioux-city.org

Sioux City Symphony Orchestra
518 Pierce St .... Sioux City IA 51101 712-277-2111 252-0224 573-3
Web: www.siouxcitysymphony.org

Sioux County PO Box 158 .... Harrison NE 69346 308-668-2443 668-2443 338
Web: www.co.sioux.ne.us

Sioux Empire Medical Museum
1305 W 18th St .... Sioux Falls SD 57105 605-333-6397 520
Web: www.sdmuseums.org

Sioux Falls Area Chamber of Commerce
200 N Phillips Ave Ste 102 .... Sioux Falls SD 57104 605-336-1620 139
TF: 800-693-3644 ■ *Web:* www.siouxfalls.com

Sioux Falls Arena 1201 NW Ave .... Sioux Falls SD 57104 605-367-7288 338-1463 720
TF: 800-338-3177 ■ *Web:* www.sfarena.com

Sioux Falls City Hall
224 W Ninth St .... Sioux Falls SD 57104 605-367-8000 367-7801 337
Web: siouxfalls.org

Sioux Falls Construction Company Inc
800 S Seventh Ave .... Sioux Falls SD 57101 605-332-5968 334-9342 188-4
Web: journeyconstruction.com

Sioux Falls Convention & Visitors Bureau
200 N Phillips Ave Ste 102 .... Sioux Falls SD 57104 605-336-1620 336-6499 206
TF: 800-333-2072 ■ *Web:* visitsiouxfalls.com

Sioux Falls Regional Airport
2801 Jaycee Ln .... Sioux Falls SD 57104 605-336-0762 367-7374 27
Web: www.sfairport.com

Sioux Falls School District
201 E 38th St .... Sioux Falls SD 57105 605-367-7900 367-4637* 685
**Fax:* Hum Res ■ *Web:* www.sf.k12.sd.us

Sioux Falls Seminary
2100 S Summit .... Sioux Falls SD 57105 605-336-6588 335-9090 167-3
TF: 800-440-6227 ■ *Web:* www.sfseminary.edu

Sioux Honey Assn Co-op
301 Lewis Blvd .... Sioux City IA 51101 712-258-0638 296-24
Web: www.suebee.com

Sioux Steel Co 196 1/2 E Sixth St .... Sioux Falls SD 57104 605-336-1750 336-2528 273
TF: 800-557-4609 ■ *Web:* www.siouxsteel.com

Sioux Tools Inc 250 Snap-on Dr .... Murphy NC 28906 828-835-9765 835-9685 759
TF Orders: 800-722-7290 ■ *Web:* www.siouxtools.com

Sioux Valley-Southwestern Electric Co-op Inc
47092 SD Hwy 34 PO Box 216 .... Colman SD 57017 605-534-3535 245
TF: 800-234-1960 ■ *Web:* www.siouxvalleyenergy.com

Siouxland Chamber of Commerce
101 Pierce St .... Sioux City IA 51101 712-255-7903 258-7578 139
TF: 800-228-7903 ■ *Web:* www.siouxlandchamber.com

Sioux-Preme Packing Co
4241 US 75th Ave .... Sioux Center IA 51250 800-735-7675 473
TF General: 800-735-7675 ■ *Web:* www.siouxpreme.com

SIPA (Specialized Information Publishers Assn)
8229 Boone Blvd Ste 260 .... Vienna VA 22182 703-992-9339 992-7512 49-14
TF: 800-356-9302 ■ *Web:* www.siia.net

Sipi Metals Corp 1720 N Elston Ave .... Chicago IL 60642 773-276-0070 485
Web: www.sipimetals.com

SiPix Imaging Inc 47485 Seabridge Dr .... Fremont CA 94538 510-743-2849 173-6
Web: www.eink.com

Siquis Ltd 1340 Smith Ave Ste 300 .... Baltimore MD 21209 410-323-4800 7
Web: www.siquis.com

SIR (Society of Interventional Radiology)
3975 Fair Ridge Dr Ste 400 N .... Fairfax VA 22033 703-691-1805 691-1855 49-8
TF: 800-488-7284 ■ *Web:* www.sirweb.org

Sir Benedict's Tavern
805 E Superior St .... Duluth MN 55802 218-728-1192 728-9878 671
Web: www.sirbens.com

Sir Francis Drake Hotel
450 Powell St .... San Francisco CA 94102 415-392-7755 391-8719 379
TF: 800-795-7129 ■ *Web:* www.sirfrancisdrake.com

Sir Mortimer B Davis Jewish General Hospital
3755 Cote Sainte-Catherine .... Montreal QC H3T1E2 514-340-8222 374-2
Web: www.jgh.ca

Sir Speedy Inc 26722 Plaza Dr .... Mission Viejo CA 92691 949-348-5000 348-5066 627
TF: 800-854-8297 ■ *Web:* www.sirspeedy.com

Sir Winston's Restaurant & Lounge
1126 Queens Hwy .... Long Beach CA 90802 562-435-3511 671
TF: 877-342-0738 ■ *Web:* www.queenmary.com

SIRCHIE Finger Print Laboratories Inc
100 Hunter Pl .... Youngsville NC 27596 919-554-2244 554-2266 84
TF: 800-356-7311 ■ *Web:* www.sirchie.com

Siren Telephone Company Inc
7723 W Main St .... Siren WI 54872 715-349-2224 224
TF: 800-924-3405 ■ *Web:* sirentel.com

Sires Albio (Rep D - NJ)
2342 Rayburn Bldg .... Washington DC 20515 202-225-7919 226-0792 342-2
Web: sires.house.gov

Sirius Canada Inc 135 Liberty St .... Toronto ON M6K1A7 888-539-7474 736
TF: 888-539-7474 ■ *Web:* www.siriusxm.ca

Sirius Solution LLC 1233 W Loop S .... Houston TX 77027 713-888-0488 194
Web: www.sirsol.com

Sirius Technical Services Inc
6215 Rangeline Rd Ste 102 .... Theodore AL 36582 251-443-1166 260
Web: www.siriustechnical.com

SiriusDecisions Inc 187 Danbury Rd .... Wilton CT 06897 203-665-4000 194
Web: www.siriusdecisions.com

Sirmilik National Park PO Box 300 .... Pond Inlet NU X0A0S0 867-899-8092 899-8104 563
Web: www.pc.gc.ca

Sirois Tool Company Inc
169 White Oak Dr .... Berlin CT 06037 860-828-5327 757
Web: www.siroistool.com

Sirona Dental Systems LLC
4835 Sirona Dr Ste 100 .... Charlotte NC 28273 704-587-0453 228
TF: 800-659-5977 ■ *Web:* cereconline.com

Sirote & Permutt Pc
2311 Highland Ave S .... Birmingham AL 35205 205-930-5100 930-5101 428
Web: www.sirote.com

Sirsi Corp 3300 N Ashton Blvd Ste 500 .... Lehi UT 84043 800-288-8020 177
TF: 800-288-8020 ■ *Web:* www.sirsidynix.com

Sirtrack Ltd 845 Pheasant Ln .... North Liberty IA 52317 905-836-6680 647
Web: www.sirtrack.co.nz

SIRVA Inc 1 Parkview Plaza .... Terrace IL 60181 630-570-3050 666
TF: 800-341-5648 ■ *Web:* www.sirva.com

SIS (Software Information Systems Inc)
165 Barr St .... Lexington KY 40507 859-977-4747 977-4750 180
TF: 800-337-6914 ■ *Web:* www.thinksis.com

SIS International Research Inc
11 E 22nd St 2nd Fl .... New York NY 10010 212-505-6805 668
Web: www.sisinternational.com

Sisbarro Dealerships
425 W Boutz Rd .... Las Cruces NM 88005 575-524-7707 57
TF: 800-215-8021 ■ *Web:* www.sisbarro-buickgmc.com

Sise Inn, The 40 Ct St .... Portsmouth NH 03801 603-433-1200 379
Web: thehotelportsmouth.com

Sisk Kathy Enterprises 1874 Polson Ave .... Clovis CA 93611 559-323-1472 737
TF: 800-477-1278 ■ *Web:* kathysiskenterprises.com

Siskin Hospital for Physical Rehabilitation
1 Siskin Plaza .... Chattanooga TN 37403 423-634-1200 792-5636* 374-6
**Fax Area Code:* 630 ■ *TF:* 800-852-7157 ■ *Web:* www.siskinrehab.org

Siskin Steel & Supply Co Inc
1901 Riverfront Pkwy .... Chattanooga TN 37408 423-756-3671 756-3671 492
TF: 800-756-3671 ■ *Web:* www.siskin.com

Siskinds LLP
680 Waterloo St PO Box 2520 .... London ON N6A3V8 519-672-2121 428
TF: 877-672-2121 ■ *Web:* www.siskinds.com

Siskiyou Corp 110 SW Booth St .... Grants Pass OR 97526 541-479-8697 419
TF: 877-313-6418 ■ *Web:* www.siskiyou.com

Siskiyou County 201 Fourth St .... Yreka CA 96097 530-842-8005 842-8013 338
Web: www.co.siskiyou.ca.us

Siskiyou County Library 719 Fourth St .... Yreka CA 96097 530-841-4175 434-3

Sisseton Wahpeton College
12572 BIA Hwy 700 .... Sisseton SD 57262 605-698-3966 742-0394 165
TF: 800-478-7337 ■ *Web:* www.swc.tc

Sister Cities International (SCI)
1301 Pennsylvania Ave NW Ste 850 .... Washington DC 20004 202-347-8630 393-6524 48-7
Web: www.sister-cities.org

Sister Sam LLC 2150 E Tenth St .... Los Angeles CA 90021 213-228-1930 157-6
Web: www.bailey44.com

Sisters Network Inc 2922 Rosedale St .... Houston TX 77004 713-781-0255 780-8998 48-21
TF: 866-781-1808 ■ *Web:* www.sistersnetworkinc.org

Sisters of Charity Hospital of Buffalo
2157 Main St .... Buffalo NY 14214 716-862-1000 374-3
TF: 800-698-4543 ■ *Web:* www.chsbuffalo.org/facilities/hospitals/soch

Sisters of Charity Hospital, St Joseph Campus
2605 Harlem Rd .... Cheektowaga NY 14225 716-891-2400 862-2006 374-3
TF: 800-698-4543 ■ *Web:* www.chsbuffalo.org

Sisters of Charity of Saint Augustine Health System
2475 E 22nd St .... Cleveland OH 44115 216-696-5560 696-2204 353
TF: 800-245-1150 ■ *Web:* www.sistersofcharityhealth.org

Sisters of Mary of the Presentation Health System
1202 Page Dr SW PO Box 10007 .... Fargo ND 58106 701-237-9290 235-0906 353
Web: www.smphs.org

Sisters of Mercy Health System
14528 S Outer Forty Ste 100 .... Chesterfield MO 63017 314-628-3656 353
Web: www.mercy.net

Sisters of Mercy of The Americas Northeast Community
55 E Cedar St .... Newington CT 06111 860-594-8619 48-20

Sisters of Saint Francis
1545 S Layton Blvd .... Milwaukee WI 53215 414-383-9038 48-20
Web: www.lbwn.org

Sisters of st Francis of Assisi of
3221 S Lake Dr .... Saint Francis WI 53235 414-744-1160 48-20
Web: lakeosfs.org

Sisters of the Holy Family of Nazareth Sacred Heart Province
310 N River Rd .... Des Plaines IL 60016 847-298-6760 353

Sisters of The Presentation
281 Masonic Ave .... San Francisco CA 94118 415-422-5001 48-20
Web: www.presentationsisterssf.org

SISU Inc 7635 N Fraser Way Ste 102 .... Burnaby BC V5J0B8 604-420-6610 582
TF: 800-663-4163 ■ *Web:* www.sisu.com

Sit 'n Sleep 14300 S Main St .... Gardena CA 90248 310-604-8903 604-8903 321
TF: 877-262-4006 ■ *Web:* www.sitnsleep.com

Sit Investment Assoc Inc
80 S Eigth St 3300 IDS Ctr .... Minneapolis MN 55402 612-332-3223 332-1911 401
TF: 800-847-4836 ■ *Web:* www.sitinvest.com

Sita World Travel Inc
16250 Ventura Blvd .... Encino CA 91436 818-990-9530 771
TF: 800-421-5643 ■ *Web:* www.sitatours.com

Sitar Indian Cuisine
6004 Kingston Pk .... Knoxville TN 37919 865-588-1828 671
Web: sitarknoxville.com

Sitar Indian Cuisine 116 21st Ave N .... Nashville TN 37203 615-321-8889 321-2688 671
Web: www.sitarnashville.com

Sitar of India 702 Lee St E .... Charleston WV 25311 304-346-3745 720-6260 671
Web: sitarofindia.org

SITE 120 Pembina Rd Ste 170 .... Sherwood Park AB T8H0M2 780-400-7483 540
Web: www.siteenergy.com

SITE (Society of Incentive & Travel Executives)
401 N Michigan Ave .... Chicago IL 60611 312-321-5148 48-23
Web: www.siteglobal.com

Site Design Concepts Inc
127 W Market St Ste 200 .... York PA 17401 717-757-9414 261
Web: sitedc.com

SITE Santa Fe 1606 Paseo de Peralta .... Santa Fe NM 87501 505-989-1199 989-1188 48-4
Web: www.sitesantafe.org

	Phone	Fax	Class
Site Tech Systems 541 Atlantic Ave .... Murrells Inlet SC 29576 *TF:* 800-470-2895 ■ *Web:* sitetechsystems.com	843-357-4400		463
Sitegoal LLC 2417 Ashdale Dr Ste B .... Austin TX 78757 *Web:* www.sitegoals.com	512-474-2025		180
SITEL Corp 3102 W End Ave Two American ctr Ste 900 .... Nashville TN 37203 *Web:* www.sitel.com	615-301-7100		737
SiteLogic 111 Second St NW Ste 506 .... Canton OH 44702 *Web:* www.sitelogicmarketing.com	330-445-2890		466
Siteman Cancer Ctr 4921 Parkview Pl .... Saint Louis MO 63110 *TF:* 800-600-3606 ■ *Web:* www.siteman.wustl.edu	314-362-5196		668
SiteMaster Inc 6914 S Yorktown Ave Ste 210 .... Tulsa OK 74136 *TF:* 800-422-4133 ■ *Web:* www.sitemaster.com	918-663-2232		480
SiteStuff Inc 12401 Research Blvd Bldg 1 Ste 250 .... Austin TX 78759 *Web:* www.sitestuff.com	512-514-7800		809
SiteTuners com Inc 4420 Hotel Circle Ct Ste 330 .... San Diego CA 92108 *TF:* 800-521-6056 ■ *Web:* www.sitetuners.com	619-223-8020	255-1540	196
Sitex Corp 1300 Commonwealth Dr .... Henderson KY 42420 *TF:* 800-278-3537 ■ *Web:* www.sitex-corp.com	270-827-3537		442
SiTime Corp 990 Almanor Ave .... Sunnyvale CA 94085 *Web:* www.sitime.com	408-328-4400		177
Sitka City & Borough 100 Lincoln St .... Sitka AK 99835 *TF:* 800-532-0908 ■ *Web:* www.cityofsitka.com	907-747-3294	747-7403	338
Sitka Convention & Visitors Bureau 303 Lincoln St Ste 4 .... Sitka AK 99835 *TF:* 800-557-4852 ■ *Web:* www.sitka.org	907-747-5940		206
Sitka Harbor 617 Katlian St .... Sitka AK 99835 *TF:* 866-948-8683 ■ *Web:* cityofsitka.com	907-747-3439	747-6278	618
Sitka National Cemetery 803 Sawmill Creek Rd .... Sitka AK 99835 *TF:* 800-273-8255 ■ *Web:* www.cem.va.gov	907-384-7075	384-7111	136
Sitka National Historical Park 106 Metlakatla St .... Sitka AK 99835 *Web:* www.nps.gov	907-747-6281	747-5938	564
Sitkins Group Inc 6700 Winkler Rd Ste 4 .... Fort Myers FL 33919 *Web:* www.sitkins.com	239-337-2555		195
Sitonit Seating 6415 Katella Ave .... Cypress CA 90630 *Web:* www.sitonit.net	714-995-4800		321
Sitrick And Company 11999 San Vicente Blvd PH .... Los Angeles CA 90049 *TF:* 800-288-8809 ■ *Web:* www.sitrick.com	310-788-2850	788-2855	636
Sitters & More Inc 125 A Stonebridge Blvd .... Jackson TN 38305 *Web:* sittersandmore.com	731-660-0001		363
Sitting Bull College 9299 Hwy 24 .... Fort Yates ND 58538 **Fax:* Admissions ■ *Web:* www.sittingbull.edu	701-854-8000	854-3403*	165
Sitting Bull Crystal Caverns 13745 S Hwy 16 .... Rapid City SD 57702	605-342-2777		50-5
Sitton Buick GMC 2640 Laurens Rd .... Greenville SC 29607 *TF:* 888-484-8009 ■ *Web:* www.sittongm.com	864-990-4569		57
Situation Management Systems Inc 98 Spit Brook Rd Ste 201 .... Nashua NH 03062 *TF:* 800-515-8498 ■ *Web:* situationmanagementsystems.com	603-897-1200		765
Situs Inc 4665 SW Fwy .... Houston TX 77027 *Web:* www.situs.com	713-328-4403		652
SIU (Southern Illinois University School of Medicine Medical Library) 801 N Rutledge St .... Springfield IL 62702 *Web:* www.siumed.edu/lib	217-545-2122	545-0988	434-1
SIU School of Medicine 520 N Fourth St PO Box 19670 .... Springfield IL 62794 *TF:* 800-342-5748 ■ *Web:* www.siumed.edu	217-545-8000		167-2
SIU University Museum 1000 Faner Dr Faner Hall Door 12 Mail Code 4508 .... Carbondale IL 62901 *Web:* www.museum.siu.edu	618-453-5388	453-7409	520
SIU's Advanced Coal and Energy Research Ctr 405 W Grand Ave .... Carbondale IL 62901 *Web:* acerc.siu.edu	618-536-5521	453-7346	668
Siuslaw School District 97j 2111 Oak St .... Florence OR 97439 *Web:* www.greatschools.org	541-997-2651		685
Sivaco Wire Group 800 Rue Ouellette .... Marieville QC J3M1P5 *TF:* 800-876-9473 ■ *Web:* www.sivaco.com	450-658-8741	460-2744	813
Sivad Business Solutions LLC 6400 Head Rd .... Wilmington NC 28409 *Web:* www.sivadsolutions.com	202-499-1700		196
Sivalls Inc 2200 E Second St .... Odessa TX 79761 *Web:* www.sivalls.com	432-337-3571	337-2624	91
Sivananda Yoga Vedanta Center 1185 Vicente St .... San Francisco CA 94116 *Web:* www.sivananda.org	415-681-2731		148
Siver Insurance Consultants 805 Executive Center Dr W Ste 110 .... St. Petersburg FL 33702 *Web:* www.siver.com	727-577-2780		466
Sivyer Steel Corp 225 S 33rd St .... Bettendorf IA 52722 *Web:* www.sivyersteel.com	563-355-1811		307
Siwel Consulting Inc 71 W 23rd St Ste 1907 .... New York NY 10010 *Web:* www.siwel.com	212-691-9326	929-6815	178-1
Six Degrees LLC 8040 E Gelding Dr .... Scottsdale AZ 85260 *Web:* www.six-degrees.com	480-627-9850		708
SIX Financial Information USA Inc 1 Omega Dr River Bend Centre Bldg 3 .... Stamford CT 06907 *Web:* www.six-group.com	203-353-8100		624
Six Flags America 13710 Central Ave .... Mitchellville MD 20721 *Web:* www.sixflags.com/parks/america	301-249-1500		32
Six Flags Discovery Kingdom 1001 Fairgrounds Dr .... Vallejo CA 94589 *Web:* www.sixflags.com	707-644-4000		32
Six Flags Fiesta Texas 17000 IH-10 W .... San Antonio TX 78257 *TF:* 800-370-7488 ■ *Web:* www.sixflags.com	210-697-5000		32
Six Flags Great Adventure 1 Six Flags Blvd .... Jackson NJ 08527 *TF:* 800-772-2287 ■ *Web:* www.sixflags.com/parks/greatadventure	732-928-1821		32
Six Flags Great America 542 N Rt 21 .... Gurnee IL 60031 *Web:* www.sixflags.com	847-249-2133		32
Six Flags Hurricane Harbor Dallas 1800 E Lamar Blvd .... Arlington TX 76006 *Web:* www.sixflags.com/parks/hurricaneharbordallas	817-265-3356		32
Six Flags Hurricane Harbor Los Angeles 26101 Magic Mtn Pkwy .... Valencia CA 91355 *TF:* 800-326-3264 ■ *Web:* www.sixflags.com/parks/hurricaneharborla	661-255-4527		32
Six Flags Magic Mountain 26101 Magic Mountain Pkwy .... Valencia CA 91355 *Web:* www.sixflags.com	661-255-4100		32
Six Flags New England 1623 Main St .... Agawam MA 01001 **Fax:* Mktg ■ *TF:* 800-370-7488 ■ *Web:* www.sixflags.com	413-786-9300	821-2402*	32
Six Flags Over Georgia 275 Riverside Pkwy SW .... Austell GA 30168 *TF:* 800-327-0700 ■ *Web:* www.sixflags.com	770-948-9290		32
Six Flags Over Texas 2201 Rd to Six Flags .... Arlington TX 76011 *TF:* 800-342-4305 ■ *Web:* www.sixflags.com/parks/overtexas	817-640-8900	607-6148	32
Six Flags Saint Louis 4900 Six Flags Rd PO Box 60 .... Eureka MO 63025 *Web:* www.sixflags.com/parks/stlouis	636-938-5300		32
Six Flags White Water Park 250 Cobb Pkwy N Ste 100 .... Marietta GA 30062 **Fax Area Code:* 636 ■ *Web:* www.sixflags.com	770-948-9290	587-2753*	32
Six Flags Wild Safari 1 Six Flags Blvd .... Jackson NJ 08527 *TF:* 800-772-2287 ■ *Web:* www.sixflags.com/parks/wildsafari	732-928-1821		32
Six Pence Pub 245 Bull St .... Savannah GA 31401 *Web:* www.sixpencepub.com	912-233-3151		671
Six Red Marbles LLC 10 City Sq 3rd Fl Charlestown .... Boston MA 02129 *Web:* www.sixredmarbles.com	857-588-9000		225
Six Robblees' Inc 11010 Tukwila International Blvd .... Tukwila WA 98168 *TF:* 800-275-7499 ■ *Web:* www.sixrobblees.com	206-767-7970	763-7416	61
SIX Safety Systems Inc 250031 Mountain View Trail Ste 1 .... Calgary AB T3Z3S3 *Web:* www.sixsafetysystems.com	403-932-7955		407
Six States Distributors Inc 247 West 1700 South .... Salt Lake City UT 84115 *TF Cust Svc:* 800-453-5703 ■ *Web:* www.sixstates.com	801-488-4666	488-4676	61
Sixteenth Street Baptist Church 1530 Sixth Ave N .... Birmingham AL 35203	205-251-9402		50-1
Sixth & i Historic Synagogue 600 I St NW .... Washington DC 20001 *Web:* sixthandi.org	202-408-3100		48-20
Sixth Floor Museum 411 Elm St .... Dallas TX 75202 *TF:* 888-485-4854 ■ *Web:* www.jfk.org	214-747-6660		520
Sixth Sense Media 4220 NC Hwy 55 Ste 340 .... Durham NC 27713 *TF:* 800-573-1874 ■ *Web:* www.sixthsensemedia.com	919-484-2442		195
Sixth Star Entertainment & Marketing Inc 21 NW Fifth St .... Fort Lauderdale FL 33301 *Web:* www.sixthstar.com	954-462-6760		195
Sixth Street Grill 55 W Sixth Ave .... Eugene OR 97401 *Web:* www.sixthstreetgrill.com	541-485-2961		671
Sixthman LTD 437 Memorial Dr SE Ste A10 .... Atlanta GA 30312 *TF:* 877-749-8462 ■ *Web:* www.sixthman.net	404-525-0222		760
Sixty Hotels 206 Spring St 4th FL .... New York NY 10012 *TF:* 877-431-0400 ■ *Web:* sixtyhotels.com	877-431-0400		707
Sizemore Inc 2116 Walton Way .... Augusta GA 30904 *TF:* 800-445-1748 ■ *Web:* www.sizemoreinc.com	706-736-1456		692
Sizerville State Park 199 E Cowley Run Rd .... Emporium PA 15834 *Web:* www.dcnr.state.pa.us	814-486-5605		565
Sizzler Restaurants 25910 Acero Rd Ste 350 .... Mission Viejo CA 92691 *Web:* www.sizzler.com	949-273-4497		670
Sizzling Wok International Inc 2560 Shell Rd .... Richmond BC V6X0B8	604-207-8871		670
SJ Amoroso Construction Co Inc 390 Bridge Pkwy .... Redwood Shores CA 94065 *Web:* www.sjamoroso.com	650-654-1900	654-9002	188-7
SJ Grillo 420 Jericho Tpke .... Jericho NY 11753	516-681-3433		2
S-j Transportation Co Inc PO Box 169 .... Woodstown NJ 08098 *TF:* 800-524-2552 ■ *Web:* www.sjtransportation.com	856-769-2741	769-9811	780
SJB Group Inc 5745 Essen Ln Ste 200 .... Baton Rouge LA 70810 *TF:* 800-421-1919 ■ *Web:* www.sjbgroup.com	225-769-3400	769-3596	261
SJBT (Saint John Board of Trade) 34 Harvey Rd .... Saint John NL A1C2G1 *Web:* www.sjboardoftrade.com	506-634-8111	632-2008	137
SJC (San Jose Convention Ctr) 150 W San Carlos St .... San Jose CA 95110 *TF:* 800-726-5673 ■ *Web:* www.sanjose.org	408-792-4194	277-3535	205
SJE-Rhombus 22650 County Hwy 6 PO Box 1708 .... Detroit Lakes MN 56502 *TF:* 800-746-6287 ■ *Web:* www.sjerhombus.com	218-847-1317	847-4617	201
SJF Material Handling Equipment 211 Baker Ave .... Winsted MN 55395 *TF:* 800-598-5532 ■ *Web:* www.sjf.com	320-485-2824	485-2832	386
SJGH (San Joaquin General Hospital) 500 W Hospital Rd .... French Camp CA 95231	209-468-6000		374-3
SJH Elmer Hospital 501 W Front St .... Elmer NJ 08318 *Web:* www.inspirahealthnetwork.org	856-363-1000		374-3
SJH Regional Medical Ctr (SJHRMC) 1505 W Sheman Ave .... Vineland NJ 08360 *TF:* 800-770-7547 ■ *Web:* www.inspirahealthnetwork.org	856-641-8000		374-3

Phone Fax Class

SJHRG (San Jose Heritage Rose Garden)
438 Coleman Ave ... San Jose CA 95110 408-298 7657 97
Web: www.grpg.org

SJHRMC (SJH Regional Medical Ctr)
1505 W Sheman Ave ... Vineland NJ 08360 856-641-8000 374-3
TF: 800-770-7547 ■ *Web:* www.inspirahealthnetwork.org

SJI (State Justice Institute)
11951 Freedom Dr Ste 1020 ... Reston VA 20190 571-313-8843 313-1173 340-20
Web: www.sji.gov

SJMC (Saint Joseph Medical Ctr)
7601 Osler Dr ... Towson MD 21204 410-337-1000 374-3
Web: www.stjosephtowson.com

SJMC (Saint Joseph's Medical Ctr)
127 S Broadway ... Yonkers NY 10701 914-378-7000 374-3
TF: 800-804-5447 ■ *Web:* saintjosephs.org

SJMH (San Jacinto Methodist Hospital)
4401 Garth Rd ... Baytown TX 77521 281-420-8600 374-3
Web: www.houstonmethodist.org

SJMH (Stonewall Jackson Memorial Hospital)
230 Hospital Plaza ... Weston WV 26452 304-269-8000 269-8090 374-3
TF: 866-637-0471 ■ *Web:* www.stonewalljacksonhospital.com

Sjostrom & Sons Inc PO Box 5766 ... Rockford IL 61125 815 226 0330 226-8060 186
Web: www.sjostromconstruction.com

SJSVCC (San Jose Silicon Valley Chamber of Commerce)
101 W Santa Clara St ... San Jose CA 95113 408-291-5250 286-5019 139
Web: www.sjchamber.com

SJW Corp 110 W Taylor St ... San Jose CA 95110 408-279-7900 279-7917 360-5
NYSE: SJW ■ *TF:* 800-743-5000 ■ *Web:* www.sjwater.com

S&K /Air Power 317 Dewitt Ave E ... Mattoon IL 61938 217-258-8500 385
Web: www.skairpower.com

SK Food Group Inc 4600 37th Ave SW ... Seattle WA 98126 206-935-8100 366
TF: 800-722-6290 ■ *Web:* skfoodgroup.com

SK Food International Inc
4666 Amber Vly Pkwy ... Fargo ND 58104 701-356-4106 356-4102 297-11
Web: www.skfood.com

SK Textile Inc 2938 E 54th St ... Vernon CA 90058 323-581-8986 258
TF: 800-323-0628 ■ *Web:* www.sktextile.com

SKA Consulting Engineers Inc
300 Pomona Dr ... Greensboro NC 27407 336-855-0993 261
Web: skaeng.com

Skadden Arps Slate Meagher & Flom LLP
4 Times Sq ... New York NY 10036 212-735-3000 735-2000 428
TF: 800-973-1177 ■ *Web:* www.skadden.com

Skaggs Family Records
PO Box 2478 ... Hendersonville TN 37077 615-264-8877 264-8899 657
Web: www.skaggsfamilyrecords.com

Skagit County
205 W Kincaid St Rm 103 ... Mount Vernon WA 98273 360-336-9440 338
TF: 800-562-6000 ■ *Web:* www.skagitcounty.net

Skagit Farmers Supply
1833 Pk Ln PO Box 266 ... Burlington WA 98233 360-757-6053 757-4143 48-2
Web: www.skagitfarmers.com

Skagit Valley Casino Resort
5984 N Darrk Ln ... Bow WA 98232 360 724 7777 133
TF: 877-275-2448 ■ *Web:* www.theskagit.com

Skagit Valley College
2405 E College Way ... Mount Vernon WA 98273 360-416-7600 416-7890* 162
**Fax:* Admissions ■ *TF:* 877-385-5360 ■ *Web:* www.skagit.edu

Skagit Valley Herald
1000 E College Way PO Box 578 ... Mount Vernon WA 98273 360-424-3251 424-5300* 532-2
**Fax:* News Rm ■ *TF:* 800-683-3300 ■ *Web:* www.goskagit.com

Skagit Valley Hospital
300 Hospital Pkwy ... Mount Vernon WA 98273 360-424-4111 374-3
Web: www.skagitvalleyhospital.org

Skagway Visitor Information
245 Broadway PO Box 1029 ... Skagway AK 99840 907-983-2854 983-3854 206
TF: 888-762-1898 ■ *Web:* www.skagway.com

Skamania County
240 Vancouver Ave PO Box 790 ... Stevenson WA 98648 509-427-3770 427-3777 338
TF: 800-375-5283 ■ *Web:* www.skamaniacounty.org

Skamania Lodge
1131 SW Skamania Lodge Way PO Box 189 ... Stevenson WA 98648 509-427-7700 427-2547 377
TF: 800-221-7117 ■ *Web:* www.destinationhotels.com/skamania

Skanska USA Bldg Inc
389 Interpace Pkwy 5th Fl ... Parsippany NJ 07054 973-753-3500 188-7
Web: www.usa.skanska.com

Skanska USA Inc 350 Fifth Ave ... New York NY 10118 718-767-2600 643-0646* 186
**Fax Area Code:* 503 ■ *Web:* www.skanska.com

Skanska USA Inc 295 Bendix Rd ... Virginia Beach VA 23452 757-420-4140 188-5
Web: skanska.com

Skate One 30 S La Patera Ln ... Santa Barbara CA 93117 805-964-1330 964 0511 710
TF: 800-288-7528 ■ *Web:* www.skateone.com

Skaug Truck Body Works Inc
1404 First St ... San Fernando CA 91340 818-365-9123 516

SKB Corp 434 W Levers Pl ... Orange CA 92867 714-637-1252 637-0491 453
TF Sales: 800-410-2024 ■ *Web:* www.skbcases.com

SKBA Capital Management
44 Montgomery St Ste 3500 ... San Francisco CA 94104 415-989-7852 989-2114 401
Web: www.skba.com

SKC Inc 863 Vly View Rd ... Eighty Four PA 15330 724-941-9701 941-1369 420
Web: www.skcinc.com

Skechers USA Inc
228 Manhattan Beach Blvd ... Manhattan Beach CA 90266 310-318-3100 301
NYSE: SKX ■ *TF Cust Svc:* 800-746-3411 ■ *Web:* www.skechers.com

Skee-Ball Amusement Games
121 Liberty Ln ... Chalfont PA 18914 215-997-8900 322
Web: www.skeeball.com

Skeeter Products Inc 1 Skeeter Rd ... Kilgore TX 75662 903-984-0541 90
Web: www.skeeterboats.com

Skeleton Key
3260 Hampton Ave Ste 200 ... Saint Louis MO 63139 314-353-4300 180
Web: www.skeletonkey.com

Skelmier Llc 55 Davis Sq ... Somerville MA 02144 617-625-1551 809
Web: www.roaster.org

Skelton, Brumwell & Associates Inc
93 Bell Farm Rd Ste 107 ... Barrie ON L4M5G1 705-726-1141 261
TF: 877-726-1141 ■ *Web:* www.skeltonbrumwell.ca

SKF USA Inc Roller Bearing Div
20 Industrial Dr ... Hanover PA 17331 717-637-8981 75
Web: skf.com

Ski Bromont 150 Champlain ... Bromont QC J2L1A2 450-534-2200 379
TF: 866-276-6668 ■ *Web:* www.skibromont.com

Ski Magazine 5720 Flatiron Pkwy ... Boulder CO 80301 303-253-6300 457-20
TF: 888-444-8151 ■ *Web:* www.skinet.com

SKI Pro 1924 W Eigth St ... Mesa AZ 85201 480-962-6910 711
Web: www.skipro.com

Ski Shawnee Inc
339 Hollow Rd ... Shawnee On Delaware PA 18356 570-421-7231 31
TF: 800-233-4218 ■ *Web:* www.shawneemt.com

Ski Stop 197 S Service Rd ... Plainview NY 11803 516-249-7980 711
TF: 800-282-6665 ■ *Web:* www.sunandski.com

Skidata Inc 1 Harvard Way Ste 5 ... Hillsborough NJ 08844 908-243-0000 196
Web: www.skidata.com

Skidaway Island State Park
52 Diamond Cswy ... Savannah GA 31411 912-598-2300 598-2365 565
Web: www.gastateparks.org/info/skidaway

Skidmore College
815 N Broadway ... Saratoga Springs NY 12866 518-580-5000 580-5584* 166
**Fax:* Admissions ■ *TF:* 800-867-6007 ■ *Web:* www.skidmore.edu

Skidmore Owings & Merrill
224 S Michigan Ave Ste 1000 ... Chicago IL 60604 312-554-9090 360-4545 261
TF: 800-561-3357 ■ *Web:* www.som.com

Skidmore Studio 1555 Broadway ... Detroit MI 48226 313-446-8200 344
Web: www.skidmorestudio.com

Skier's Choice Inc
1717 Henry G Ln St ... Maryville TN 37801 865-983-9924 983-9950 90
TF: 800-320-2779 ■ *Web:* www.supraboats.com

Skilcraft LLC 5184 Limaburg Rd ... Burlington KY 41005 859-371-0799 697
Web: skilcraft.com

Skill Creations Inc
2101 Royall Ave PO Box 10628 ... Goldsboro NC 27532 919-734-7338 735-5004 48-15
Web: www.skillcreations.com

Skilled Care Pharmacy Inc
6175 Hi Tek Ct ... Mason OH 45040 513-459-7455 583
TF: 800-334-1624 ■ *Web:* www.skilledcare.com

Skillforce Inc
405 Williams Court Ste 106 ... Baltimore MD 21220 866-581-8989 260
TF: 866-581-8989 ■ *Web:* www.skillforce.com

Skilligalee 5416 Glenside Dr ... Richmond VA 23228 804-672-6200 671

Skillman Corp, The
3834 S Emerson Ave Bldg A ... Indianapolis IN 46203 317-783-6151 194
Web: www.skillman.com

Skillpath Seminars 6900 Squibb Rd ... Mission KS 66201 913-362-3900 195
TF: 800-873-7545 ■ *Web:* www.skillpath.com

Skillpoint Alliance
201 E Second St Ste B ... Austin TX 78701 512-323-6773 765
Web: www.skillpointalliance.org

Skills International LLC
11 Falcon Lks Dr ... South Barrington IL 60010 647-725-3360 260
Web: www.skillsinternational.com

SkillSoft PLC 107 NE Blvd ... Nashua NH 03062 603-324-3000 765
TF: 877-545-5763 ■ *Web:* www.skillsoft.com

SkillStorm Commercial Services LLC
6414 NW Fifth Way ... Ft Lauderdale FL 33309 954-566-4647 260
Web: www.skillstorm.com

SkillsUSA 14001 James Monroe Hwy ... Leesburg VA 20176 703-777-8810 777-8999 48-11
TF: 800-321-8422 ■ *Web:* www.skillsusa.org

Skin Cancer Foundation
149 Madison Ave Ste 901 ... New York NY 10016 212-725-5176 725-5751 48-17
Web: www.skincancer.org

SkinMedica Inc 5770 Armada Dr ... Carlsbad CA 92008 760-448-3600 214

Skinner & Kennedy Co
9451 Natural Bridge Rd ... Saint Louis MO 63134 314-426-2800 627
TF: 800-426-3094 ■ *Web:* www.skinnerkennedy.com

Skinner Transfer Corp PO Box 438 ... Reedsburg WI 53959 608-524-2326 524-9660 780
TF: 800-356-9350 ■ *Web:* www.skinnertransfer.com

Skippers Seafood & Chowder House
2987 Santiam Hwy SE ... Albany OR 97322 541-926-8623 671
Web: www.skipperseafoodandchowder.com

Skipping Stone Inc
83 Pine St Ste 101 ... West Peabody PA 01960 978-717-6100 196
Web: www.skippingstone.com

Skirball Cultural Ctr
2701 N Sepulveda Blvd ... Los Angeles CA 90049 310-440-4500 50-2
Web: www.skirball.org

SKIRITAI Capital LLC
1 Ferry Bldg Ste 255 ... San Francisco CA 94111 415-677-5460 401
Web: www.skiritai.com

Skitter Inc
3230 Peachtree Corners Cir Ste 200 ... Norcross GA 30092 678-894-8808 647
Web: www.skitter.tv

SKL Company Inc 545 Island Rd ... Ramsey NJ 07446 201-825-6633 411

Sklar Exploration Company LLC
401 Edwards St Ste 1601 ... Shreveport LA 71101 318-227-8668 539
Web: www.sklarexploration.com

Skoah Metrotown Inc
4800 Kingsway Ste 103 ... Burnaby BC V5H4J2 604-433-0200 354
Web: skoah.com

Skoda Minotti 6685 Beta Dr ... Cleveland OH 44143 440-449-6800 734
Web: www.skodaminotti.com

Skoflo Industries Inc
14241 NE 200th # A ... Woodinville WA 98072 425-485-7816 789
Web: www.skoflo.com

Skogman Construction Company Inc
411 First Ave ... Cedar Rapids IA 52401 319-363-8285 366-7257 187
Web: www.skogman.com

Skokie Chamber of Commerce
5002 Oakton St PO Box 106 ... Skokie IL 60077 847-673-0240 673-0249 139
TF: 800-526-8441 ■ *Web:* www.skokiechamber.org

Skokie Public Library 5215 Oakton St ... Skokie IL 60077 847-673-7774 673-7797 434-3
Web: www.skokielibrary.info

Skokie Valley Beverage Co
199 Shepard Ave ... Wheeling IL 60090 847-541-1500 541-2059 81-1
Web: www.svbco.com

Phone | Fax | Class

Skol Manufacturing Co
4444 N Ravenswood Ave .... Chicago IL 60640 773-878-5959 492
Web: skolmfg.com

Skoler, Abbott & Presser PC
1 Monarch Pl Ste 2000.................... Springfield MA 01144 413-737-4753 428
TF: 800-274-6774 ■ *Web:* skoler-abbott.com

Skolnik Industries Inc
4900 S Kilbourn Ave........................ Chicago IL 60632 773-735-0700 198
TF: 800-441-8780 ■ *Web:* www.skolnik.com

SKS Bottle & Packaging Inc
2600 Seventh Ave Bldg 60 W.................. Watervliet NY 12189 518-880-6980 385
TF: 800-880-6990 ■ *Web:* www.sks-bottle.com

Skunk Studios LLC 463 Bryant St.......... San Francisco CA 94107 415-777-0900 809
Web: www.skunkstudios.com

Skurka Aerospace Inc
4600 Calle Bolero PO Box 2869.............. Camarillo CA 93011 805-484-8884 482-7771 518
Web: www.skurka-aero.com

Skuttle Manufacturing Co
101 Margaret St .... Marietta OH 45750 740-373-9169 373-9565 14
TF: 800-848-9786 ■ *Web:* www.skuttle.com

Sky & Telescope Magazine
90 Sherman St .... Cambridge MA 02140 617-864-7360 864-6117 457-19
TF: 800-253-0245 ■ *Web:* www.skyandtelescope.com

Sky Adv Inc 14 E 33rd St APT 7s............. New York NY 10016 212-677-2500 4
Web: www.skyad.com

Sky Bird Travel & Tours Inc
24701 Swanson .... Southfield MI 48033 248-372-4800 16
TF: 888-759-2473 ■ *Web:* www.skybirdtravel.com

Sky Bright 65 Aviation Dr...................... Gilford NH 03249 603-528-6818 63
TF: 800-639-6012 ■ *Web:* www.skybright.com

Sky Climber Wind Solutions LLC
1800 Pittsburgh Dr........................ Delaware OH 43015 740-203-3900 393
Web: www.skyclimberwindsolutions.com

Sky Cylinder Testing
2220 Lexington Rd .... Evansville IN 47720 812-423-1759 743
Web: www.skycylinder.com

Sky Dragon Buffet 34 17th Ave NW .... Rochester MN 55901 507-281-1813 671

Sky High Entertainment
777 Blvd Lebourgneuf Ste 160................. Quebec QC G2J1C3 418-682-1443 514
Web: www.shemovie.com

Sky High Marketing 3550 E Post Rd .... Las Vegas NV 89120 702-436-0867 436-0905 195
TF: 800-246-7447 ■ *Web:* www.skyhighmarketing.com

Sky Hospitality LLC
5999 Central Ave Ste 102............. Saint Petersburg FL 33710 727-576-5167 377
Web: www.skyhospitality.com

Sky Hotel 709 E Durant Ave .... Aspen CO 81611 970-925-6760 925-6778 379
TF: 800-882-2582 ■ *Web:* www.theskyhotel.com

Sky I T Group LLC 330 Seventh Ave .... New York NY 10001 212-868-7800 196
TF: 866-641-6017 ■ *Web:* www.skyitgroup.com

Sky Lakes Medical Ctr
2865 Daggett Ave...................... Klamath Falls OR 97601 541-882-6311 374-3
Web: www.skylakes.org

Sky Mart Sales Corp
9475 NW 13th St PO Box 522007 .... Miami FL 33172 305-592-0263 592-8359 57
Web: www.skymartsales.com

Sky Meadows State Park
11012 Edmonds Ln .... Delaplane VA 20144 540-592-3556 565

Sky Publishing Corp 90 Sherman St .... Cambridge MA 02140 617-864-7360 864-6117 637-9
TF: 800-253-0245 ■ *Web:* skyandtelescope.com

Sky Radio Network Inc
5320 Laurel Canyon Blvd................ Valley Village CA 91607 818-762-6800 116

Sky Ranch 24657 CR 448.............................. Van TX 75790 903-266-3300 148
TF: 800-962-2267 ■ *Web:* www.skyranch.org

Sky Room 40 S Locust Ave.................. Long Beach CA 90802 562-983-2703 671
Web: theskyroom.com

Sky Sox Stadium
4385 Tutt Blvd
Security Service Field............ Colorado Springs CO 80922 719-597-1449 597-2491 720
TF: 866-698-4253 ■ *Web:* www.milb.com

Sky Ute Casino 14324 US Hwy 172 N............. Ignacio CO 81137 970-563-7777 133
TF: 888-842-4180 ■ *Web:* www.skyutecasino.com

Sky Valley Golf Club
568 Sky Vly Way........................... Sky Valley GA 30537 706-746-5302 669
Web: skyvalleycountryclub.com

Skybank Financial Services Corp
1444 Biscayne Blvd Ste 309...................... Miami FL 33132 800-617-9980 225
TF: 800-617-9980 ■ *Web:* www.skybankfinancial.com

Skybooks Inc 1310 Tradeport Dr............. Jacksonville FL 32218 904-741-8700 57
TF: 866-929-8700 ■ *Web:* www.skybooks.com

Skybox Security Inc
2099 Gateway Pl Ste 450 .... San Jose CA 95110 408-441-8060 177
TF: 800-628-8686 ■ *Web:* www.skyboxsecurity.com

Skybridge Global Inc
Northridge Center II 375 Northridge Rd
Ste 400...................................... Atlanta GA 30350 770-373-2300 178-1
Web: www.skybridgeglobal.com

Skycasters LLC
1520 S Arlington St # 100 .... Akron OH 44306 330-785-2100 224
Web: www.skycasters.com

SkyCity Restaurant 400 Broad St................. Seattle WA 98109 206-905-2100 671
TF: 800-937-9582 ■ *Web:* www.spaceneedle.com

Skycom Avionics Inc 2441 Aviation Rd .... Waukesha WI 53188 262-521-8180 57
TF: 800-443-4490 ■ *Web:* www.skycomavionics.com

Skycraft Parts & Surplus Inc
2245 W Fairbanks Ave .... Winter Park FL 32789 407-628-5634 791
Web: www.skycraftsurplus.com

Skyemed Pharmacy
1332 N Federal Hwy.................... Pompano Beach FL 33062 866-778-8255 237
TF: 866-778-8255 ■ *Web:* www.skyemed.com

SkyFuel Inc 18300 W Hwy 72 .... Arvada CO 80007 303-330-0276 696
Web: www.skyfuel.com

Skygone Inc 1000 New York St Ste 107.......... Redlands CA 92374 888-759-4471 363-4076* 196
**Fax Area Code: 909* ■ *TF:* 888-759-4471

Skyhawks Sports Academy Inc
6311 E Mt Spokane Park Dr Ste B .... Mead WA 99021 509-466-6590 239
Web: www.skyhawks.com

Skyjack Inc 55 Campbell Rd........................ Guelph ON N1H1B9 519-837-0888 111
Web: www.skyjack.com

Skyland Travel Inc
445 Sixth Ave W Ste 100 .... Vancouver BC V5Y1L3 604-685-6885 775
Web: www.escapes.ca

Skylands PO Box 302.......................... Ringwood NJ 07456 973-962-9534 97
Web: www.njbg.org

Skylight Books 1818 N Vermont Ave.......... Los Angeles CA 90027 323-660-1175 660-0232 95
Web: www.skylightbooks.com

Skylight Opera Theatre
158 N Broadway .... Milwaukee WI 53202 414-291-7811 291-7815 573-2
Web: www.skylightmusictheatre.org

Skylight Studios Video Prodctns
109 Squirrel Ln.............................. Levittown NY 11756 516-579-0245 514

Skyline Asset Management LP
120 S Lasalle St Ste 1320..................... Chicago IL 60603 312-913-0900 528
Web: www.skylinelp.com

Skyline Assisted and Independent Living
7300 Graceland Dr # 120B .... Omaha NE 68134 402-572-5750 672
Web: skylinerc.com

Skyline Chili Inc
4180 Thunderbird Ln .... Fairfield OH 45014 513-874-1188 670
Web: www.skylinechili.com

Skyline College 3300 College Dr .... San Bruno CA 94066 650-738-4100 162
Web: www.skylinecollege.edu

Skyline Construction
505 Sansome St 7th Fl................... San Francisco CA 94111 415-908-1020 186
Web: www.skylineconstruction.build

Skyline Corp 2520 By-Pass Rd .... Elkhart IN 46514 574-294-6521 120
NYSE: SKY ■ *TF:* 800-348-7469 ■ *Web:* www.skylinecorp.com

Skyline Displays Bay Area Inc
44111 Fremont Blvd.......................... Fremont CA 94538 510-490-9900 8
TF: 800-328-2725 ■ *Web:* www.skyline.com

Skyline Hotel 725 Tenth Ave .... New York NY 10019 212-586-3400 379
Web: www.skylinehotelny.com

Skyline Industries Inc
1201 Forum Way S......................... Fort Worth TX 76140 817-551-1967 22
Web: www.skyline-usa.com

Skyline Madison Campus
500 Hospital Dr .... Madison TN 37115 615-769-5000 374-3
TF: 800-277-9715 ■ *Web:* tristarskylinemadison.com

Skyline Medical Ctr
3441 Dickerson Pike.......................... Nashville TN 37207 615-769-2000 374-3
TF: 800-242-5662 ■ *Web:* tristarskyline.com

Skyline Medical Inc
2915 Commers Dr Ste 900........................ Eagan MN 55121 651-389-4800 476
Web: www.skylinemedical.com

Skyline Network Engineering LLC
6956-F Aviation Blvd .... Glen Burnie MD 21061 410-795-2700 176
Web: www.skylinenet.net

Skyline New York
740 Old Willets Path Ste 5 .... Hauppauge NY 11788 631-586-9400 8
Web: www.skyline.com

Skyline North 1604 Wayneport Rd............. Macedon NY 14502 315-986-4600 393
TF: 800-783-4377 ■ *Web:* www.skyline.com

Skyline Pest Solutions Inc
1745 Pennsylvania Ave.................... Mcdonough GA 30253 678-432-5464 577
TF: 800-264-4611 ■ *Web:* www.skylinepest.com

Skyline Products
2903 Delta Dr .... Colorado Springs CO 80910 800-759-9046 697
TF: 800-759-9046 ■ *Web:* www.skylineproducts.com

Skyline Properties South Inc
50 116th Ave SE Ste 120 .... Bellevue WA 98004 425-455-2065 652
TF: 800-753-6156 ■ *Web:* www.skylineproperties.com

Skyline Steel LLC
8 Woodhollow Rd Ste 102 .... Parsippany NJ 07054 866-875-9546 492
TF: 866-875-9546 ■ *Web:* www.skylinesteel.com

Skyline Technologies Inc
1400 Lombardi Ave............................ Green Bay WI 54304 920-437-1360 177
Web: skylinetechnologies.com

Skyline Telephone Membership Corp
PO Box 759 .... West Jefferson NC 28694 336-877-3111 736
TF: 877-475-9546 ■ *Web:* www.skyline.org

Skyline Ultd Inc
16333 S Great Ste 121 .... Round Rock TX 78681 703-373-2330 180
Web: www.skyline-ultd.com

Skylink Travel
980 Ave of the Americas...................... New York NY 10018 212-573-8980 573-8878 16
TF: 800-247-6659 ■ *Web:* www.skylinkus.com

Skymicro Inc
2060 E Avenida De Los Arboles Ste D344 .. Thousand Oaks CA 91362 805-491-8995 52
Web: www.skymicro.com

Skyservice Airlines Inc 9785 Ryan Ave........... Dorval QC H9P1A2 514-636-3300 636-4855 13
TF: 888-985-1402 ■ *Web:* skyservice.com

Skystone Ryan
Skystone Partners LLC
635 W Seventh St Ste 107................ Cincinnati OH 45203 513-241-6778 317
TF: 800-883-0801 ■ *Web:* www.skystonepartners.com

SkyTech Inc 550 Airport Rd .... Rock Hill SC 29732 803-366-5108 366-1519 63
TF: 888-386-3596 ■ *Web:* www.skytechinc.com

SkyTech Inc
701 Wilson Pt Rd Ste 3 PO Box 4942............ Baltimore MD 21220 410-574-4144 770
TF: 800-394-1334 ■ *Web:* www.skytechinc.com

SkyTel Corp PO Box 2469 .... Jackson MS 39225 800-759-8737 736
TF Cust Svc: 800-759-8737 ■ *Web:* www.skytel.com

Skytop Lodge 1 Skytop .... Skytop PA 18357 570-595-7401 669
TF: 800-345-7759 ■ *Web:* www.skytop.com

Skyview Memorial Lawn
200 Rollingwood Dr .... Vallejo CA 94591 707-644-7474 510
TF: 800-574-2530 ■ *Web:* www.skyviewmemorial.com

Skywalker Communications Inc
9390 Veterans Memorial Pkwy .... O'Fallon MO 63366 636-272-8025 272-8214 246
TF: 800-844-9555 ■ *Web:* www.skywalker.com

Skyward Inc 5233 Coye Dr .... Stevens Point WI 54481 715-341-9406 178-12
TF: 800-236-0001 ■ *Web:* www.skyward.com

Skyway Precision Inc
41225 Plymouth Rd .... Plymouth MI 48170 734-454-3550 621
Web: www.skywayprecision.com

Skyway Towers LLC
20525 Amberfield Dr Ste 102............... Land O Lakes FL 34638 813-960-6200 246
Web: www.skywaytowers.com

Name / Address	City	State	ZIP	Phone	Fax	Class
Skyway West 555 W Hastings St	Vancouver	BC	V0N2W2	604-482-1225		224
Web: www.skywaywest.com						
SkyWeaver Inc 1501 Broadway 25th Fl	New York	NY	10036	646-571-8596		387
Web: www.skyweaver.com						
Skyweb Networks 2710 State St	Saginaw	MI	48602	989-792-8681		180
TF: 866-575-9932 ■ *Web:* skywebonline.com						
SkyWest Airlines 444 S River Rd	Saint George	UT	84790	435-634-3000	634-3105	25
TF: 800-255-2877 ■ *Web:* www.skywest.com						
Skyworks LLC 100 Thielman Dr	Buffalo	NY	14206	716-822-5438		264-3
TF: 877-601-5438 ■ *Web:* www.skyworksllc.com						
Skyworks Solutions Inc 20 Sylvan Rd	Woburn	MA	01801	781-376-3000		696
NASDAQ: SWKS ■ *Web:* www.skyworksinc.com						
Skyy Consulting Inc						
1335 Fourth St Ste 200	Santa Monica	CA	90401	213-221-2289		224
Web: www.callfire.com						
SL Green Realty Corp						
420 Lexington Ave	New York	NY	10170	212-594-2700	216-1790	655
NYSE: SLG ■ *Web:* www.slgreen.com						
SL Power Electronics Inc						
6050 King Dr Bldg A	Ventura	CA	93003	805-486-4565	712-2040*	253
**Fax Area Code:* 858 ■ *TF:* 800-235-5929 ■ *Web:* www.slpower.com						
S&L Travel Partners Inc						
210 Aspen Airport Business Ctr Ste AA	Aspen	CO	81611	970-925-9500		772
Web: www.ski.com						
SLA (Special Libraries Assn)						
331 S Patrick St	Alexandria	VA	22314	703-647-4900	647-4901	49-11
TF: 866-446-6069 ■ *Web:* www.sla.org						
SLAA (Sex & Love Addicts Anonymous)						
1550 NE Loop 410 Ste 118	San Antonio	TX	78209	210-828-7900	828-7922	48-21
Web: www.slaafws.org						
SLAC (Stanford Linear Accelerator Ctr)						
2575 Sand Hill Rd	Menlo Park	CA	94025	650-926-3300	926-4999	668
Web: www.slac.stanford.edu						
Slack & Company Inc						
233 N Michigan Ave Ste 3050	Chicago	IL	60601	312-970-5800	970-5850	9
Web: www.slackandcompany.com						
Slack & Davis LLP						
2705 Bee Caves Rd Ste 220	Austin	TX	78746	512-795-8686		428
TF: 800-455-8686 ■ *Web:* www.slackdavis.com						
Slack Auto Parts 404 Main St SW	Gainesville	GA	30501	770-535-6000		791
TF: 800-364-4314 ■ *Web:* www.slackautoparts.com						
Slack Inc 6900 Grove Rd	Thorofare	NJ	08086	856-848-1000	848-6091	637-9
TF: 800-257-8290 ■ *Web:* www.slackinc.com						
Slade Gorton Company Inc						
225 Southampton St	Boston	MA	02118	617-442-5800	442-9090	297-5
TF: 800-225-1573 ■ *Web:* www.sladegorton.com						
Slade Quilty & Assoc CPA'S LLP						
26619 Carmel Ctr Pl Ste 102	Carmel	CA	93923	831-625-8740		2
Slam Dunk Networks Inc						
2600 S El Camino Real	San Mateo	CA	94403	650-525-3902		174
Slane Hosiery Mills Inc						
313 S Centennial St	High Point	NC	27261	336-883-4136		155-10
Web: www.slanehosiery.com						
Slant Fin Corp 100 Forest Dr	Greenvale	NY	11548	516-484-2600	484-2600	14
TF: 800-875-2389 ■ *Web:* www.slantfin.com						
Slanted Door 1 Ferry Bldg Ste 3	San Francisco	CA	94111	415-861-8032		671
Web: www.slanteddoor.com						
Slash Pine Electric Membership Corp						
794 W Dame Ave	Homerville	GA	31634	912-487-5201	487-2948	245
Web: slashpineemc.com						
Slate Magazine 1707 L St NW Ste 800	Washington	DC	20036	212-445-5330		457-17
Web: www.slate.com						
Slate Professional Resources Inc						
800 W Main St Ste 204	Freehold	NJ	07728	732-303-6329		631
Web: www.slateprofessional.com						
Slate Properties Inc						
200 Front St W Ste 2400	Toronto	ON	M5V3K2	416-644-4264	947-9366	528
Slate Springs Glove Co						
148 Vance St	Calhoun City	MS	38916	662-637-2222		155-8
Slater Memorial Museum						
108 Crescent St	Norwich	CT	06360	860-887-2506		520
Web: slatermuseum.org						
Slater Partners LLC 204 Galway Dr	Chapel Hill	NC	27517	919-933-6883	636-5192*	463
**Fax Area Code:* 443 ■ *Web:* www.slaterpartners.com						
Slater Technology Fund						
3 Davol Sq Ste A340	Providence	RI	02903	401-831-6633		415
Web: www.slaterfund.com						
Slaton Independent School District						
140 E Panhandle St	Slaton	TX	79364	806-828-6591		685
Web: www.slatonisd.net						
Slaughter Louise (Rep D - NY)						
2469 Rayburn Bldg	Washington	DC	20515	202-225-3615	225-7822	342-2
Web: www.louise.house.gov						
Slave Haven Underground Railroad Museum						
826 N Second St	Memphis	TN	38173	901-527-3427		520
TF: 800-979-3370 ■ *Web:* www.slavehavenundergroundrailroadmuseum.org						
Slawson Cos Inc 727 N Waco St Ste 400	Wichita	KS	67203	316-263-3201		536
Web: www.slawsoncompanies.com						
Slay Industries Inc						
1441 Hampton Ave	Saint Louis	MO	63139	314-647-7529	647-5240	449
TF: 800-852-7529 ■ *Web:* www.slay.com						
Slayton Arboretum of Hilsdale College						
33 E College St	Hillsdale	MI	49242	517-607-2241		97
Web: hillsdale.edu/home						
SLB (South Louisiana Bank)						
1362 W Tunnel Blvd PO Box 1718	Houma	LA	70361	985-851-3434	879-3095	70
Web: ayeee.com						
SLC Recycling Industries Inc						
8701 E 8 Mile Rd	Warren	MI	48089	586-759-6600	759-6518	686
Web: fptscrap.com						
SLCL (Saint Louis County Library)						
1640 S Lindbergh Blvd	Saint Louis	MO	63131	314-994-3300		434-3
TF: 800-473-0060 ■ *Web:* www.slcl.org						
Sleep America Inc						
1202 N 54th Ave Ste 111	Phoenix	AZ	85043	602-269-7000		321
Sleep Country Canada LP						
140 Wendell Ave	North York	ON	M9N3R2	416-242-4774		364
Web: www.sleepcountry.ca						
Sleep Design 5808 Berry Brook Dr	Houston	TX	77017	713-227-0121		471
TF: 800-603-3375 ■ *Web:* sleep-designs.com						
Sleep Innovations Inc						
187 Rt 36 Ste 101	West Long Branch	NJ	07764	732-263-0800		471
Sleep Train Inc 2205 Plaza Dr	Rocklin	CA	95765	800-919-2337		471
TF: 800-919-2337 ■ *Web:* www.sleeptrain.com						
Sleep Train Pavilion at Concord						
2000 Kirker Pass Rd	Concord	CA	94521	925-676-8742		572
Web: www.livenation.com						
Sleeping Bear Dunes National Lakeshore						
9922 Front St	Empire	MI	49630	231-326-5134	326-5382	564
Web: www.nps.gov/slbe						
Sleeping Giant State Park						
200 Mt Carmel Ave	Hamden	CT	06518	203-287-5658		565
Web: www.ct.gov						
Sleepy Hollow Cemetery						
540 N Broadway	Sleepy Hollow	NY	10591	914-631-0081		50-3
Web: www.sleepyhollowcemetery.org						
Sleepy Hollow State Park						
7835 E Price Rd	Laingsburg	MI	48848	517-651-6217		565
Web: www.michigandnr.com						
Sletten Construction Company Inc						
1000 25th St N	Great Falls	MT	59401	406-761-7920	761-0923	186
TF: 800-483-2557 ■ *Web:* www.slettencompanies.com						
Slevin & Hart PC						
1625 Massachusetts Ave NW Ste 450	Washington	DC	20036	202-797-8700		428
TF: 800-926-7926 ■ *Web:* www.slevinhart.com						
SLH (Solheim Senior Community)						
2236 Merton Ave	Los Angeles	CA	90041	323-257-7518		672
Web: www.solheimlutheran.org						
SLH (Saint Luke's Hospital)						
1026 A Ave NE	Cedar Rapids	IA	52406	319-369-7211	369-8105	374-3
Web: unitypoint.org/cedarrapids/default.aspx						
SlickData 252 Nassau St 2nd Fl	Princeton	NJ	08542	609-736-0036		196
Web: www.slickdata.com						
SlickEdit Inc						
3000 Aerial Ctr Pkwy Ste 120	Morrisville	NC	27560	919-473-0070	473-0080	178-2
TF: 800-934-3348 ■ *Web:* www.slickedit.com						
Slide Inn, The 2348 SE Ankeny	Portland	OR	97214	503-236-4997		671
Web: www.slideinnpdx.com						
Slide Rock State Park 6871 N Hwy 89A	Sedona	AZ	86336	928-282-3034		565
Web: azpra.org						
Slidell Memorial Hospital (SMH)						
1001 Gause Blvd	Slidell	LA	70458	985-643-2200		374-3
TF: 800-256-9822 ■ *Web:* slidellmemorial.org						
Slidematic Products Co						
4520 W Addison St	Chicago	IL	60641	773-545-4213	545-0797	488
Web: www.slidematicproducts.com						
Slifer Designs 216 Main St Ste C-100	Edwards	CO	81632	970-926-8200		393
Web: www.sliferdesigns.com						
Sligh Cabinets Inc						
103 Calle Propano	Paso Robles	CA	93446	805-239-2550		115
Web: www.slighcabinets.com						
Slight Edge Solutions Inc						
28 Dominic Dr	Monroe	NJ	08831	646-342-9407		809
Slightly North of Broad						
192 E Bay St	Charleston	SC	29401	843-723-3424	724-3811	671
TF: 800-874-9600 ■ *Web:* snobcharleston.com						
Slinger Manufacturing Company Inc						
760 Hilldale Rd	Slinger	WI	53086	262-644-5256		454
Web: www.slingermfg.com						
SlingShot Communications Inc						
8723 E Via de Commercio	Scottsdale	AZ	85258	480-626-8625		387
Web: www.slingshot.com						
Slingshot LLC 208 N Market St Ste 500	Dallas	TX	75202	214-634-4411	634-5511	4
Web: www.slingshot.com						
Slippery Rock University						
1 Morrow Way	Slippery Rock	PA	16057	724-738-9000	738-2913*	166
**Fax:* Admissions ■ *TF:* 800-929-4778 ■ *Web:* www.sru.edu						
Sliters Lumber & Building Supply						
55 Somers Rd	Somers	MT	59932	406-857-3306		364
Web: www.sliters.com						
Slk Global Bpo Services 4032 Aladdin Dr	Plano	TX	75093	972-758-5497		624
Web: www.slkglobalbpo.com						
SLM Corp 12061 Bluemont Way	Reston	VA	20190	703-810-3000		217
NASDAQ: SLM ■ *TF Cust Svc:* 888-272-5543 ■ *Web:* www.salliemae.com						
SLM Manufacturing Corp						
215 Davidson Ave	Somerset	NJ	08873	732-469-7500	469-5546	600
TF: 800-526-3708 ■ *Web:* www.slmcorp.com						
SL-Montevideo Technology Inc						
2002 Black Oak Ave	Montevideo	MN	56265	320-269-6562	269-7662	518
Web: www.slmti.com						
SLMP LLC 407 Interchange St	Mckinney	TX	75071	972-436-1010		475
TF: 800-442-3573 ■ *Web:* www.statlab.com						
Sloan Accoustics Inc						
49 Bloomfield Ave Ste 101	Mountain Lakes	NJ	07046	973-227-3555	227-8731	393
Web: www.sloanandcompany.com						
Sloan Construction Co Inc						
250 Plemmons Rd	Duncan	SC	29334	864-968-2250	968-2255	188-4
TF: 800-431-2584 ■ *Web:* www.sloan-construction.com						
Sloan Implement Co						
120 N Business 51	Assumption	IL	62510	217-226-4411	226-3351	274
TF: 800-745-4020 ■ *Web:* www.sloans.com						
Sloan Management Review						
77 Massachusetts Ave E60-100	Cambridge	MA	02139	617-253-7170	258-9739	457-5
TF: 800-876-5764 ■ *Web:* www.sloanreview.mit.edu						
Sloan Museum 1221 E Kearsley St	Flint	MI	48503	810-237-3450	237-3451	520
Web: www.sloanlongway.org						
Sloan Valve Co						
10500 Seymour Ave	Franklin Park	IL	60131	847-671-4300	671-6944	609
TF: 800-982-5839 ■ *Web:* www.sloan.com						
Sloan's Dry Cleaning Inc						
3001 N Main St	Los Angeles	CA	90031	323-225-1303		426
Sloane & Co 7 Times Sq 17th Fl	New York	NY	10036	212-486-9500		636
Web: www.sloanepr.com						
Sloat Garden Ctr Inc 420 Coloma St	Sausalito	CA	94965	415-332-0657		323
Web: www.sloatgardens.com						

Name / Address	City	State	Zip	Phone	Fax	Class
Slocum Adhesives Corp 2500 Carroll Ave. *TF:* 800-476-8569 ■ *Web:* www.slocumadhesives.com	Lynchburg	VA	24501	434-847-5671		711
Slomin's Inc 125 Lauman Ln *TF:* 800-252-7663 ■ *Web:* www.slomins.com	Hicksville	NY	11801	516-932-7000		692
Slope County 206 S Main St	Amidon	ND	58620	701-879-6275	879-6278	338
Slope Drugs & Surgical Supply Inc 406 Fifth Ave.	Brooklyn	NY	11215	718-788-8899		237
Slope Electric Co-op Inc 116 E 12th St PO Box 338 *TF:* 800-559-4191 ■ *Web:* www.slopeelectric.coop	New England	ND	58647	701-579-4191		245
Sloss Furnaces National Historic Landmark 20 32nd St N *Web:* www.slossfurnaces.com	Birmingham	AL	35222	205-324-1911		520
Slovakia 801 Second Ave 12th Fl *Web:* www.mzv.sk/nyc	New York	NY	10017	212-286-8434	286-8439	784
Slovakia Embassy 3523 International Ct NW *Web:* www.mzv.sk/washington	Washington	DC	20008	202-237-1054	237-6438	257
Slovene National Benefit Society 247 W Allegheny Rd *TF:* 800-843-7675 ■ *Web:* www.snpj.org	Imperial	PA	15126	724-695-1100		391-2
Slovenia						
Consulate General 120 E 56th St Ste 320 *Web:* www.culture.si	New York	NY	10022	212-370-3581		257
Embassy 2410 California St NW *Web:* washington.embassy.si	Washington	DC	20008	202-386-6601	386-6633	257
Slover & Loftus LLP 1224 17th St NW *Web:* www.sloverandloftus.com	Washington	DC	20036	202-347-7170		428
SLPL (Saint Louis Public Library) 1301 Olive St *TF:* 800-916-8938 ■ *Web:* www.slpl.org	Saint Louis	MO	63103	314-241-2288	539-0393	434-3
SLR Contracting & Service Company Inc 260 Michigan Ave. *Web:* www.slrcontracting.com	Buffalo	NY	14203	716-896-8148		186
SLS (Society of Laparoendoscopic Surgeons) 7330 SW 62nd Pl Ste 410 *Web:* www.sls.org	Miami	FL	33143	305-665-9959	667-4123	49-8
SLS (Shawnigan Lake School) 1975 Renfrew Rd *Web:* www.shawnigan.ca	Shawnigan Lake	BC	V0R2W1	250-743-5516		622
SLS Hotel South Beach 1701 Collins Ave *Web:* slshotels.com	Miami Beach	FL	33139	305-674-1701		707
SLT (Spirit Lake Tribe) PO Box 359 *Web:* www.spiritlakenation.com	Fort Totten	ND	58335	701-766-4221	766-4126	804
Sluice Boxes State Park 4600 Giant Springs Rd *Web:* www.fwp.mt.gov	Great Falls	MT	59405	406-454-5840		565
Slumberland Inc 3060 Centerville Rd *TF:* 888-957-5862 ■ *Web:* www.slumberland.com	Little Canada	MN	55117	888-957-5862		321
Slutzky Wolfe & Bailey LLP 2255 Cumberland Pkwy SE Ste 1300 *Web:* swbatl.com	Atlanta	GA	30339	770-438-8000		428
Sly Inc 8300 Dow Cir *TF:* 800-334-2957 ■ *Web:* www.slyinc.com	Strongsville	OH	44136	440-891-3200	891-3210	18
SLZUSD (San Lorenzo Unified School District) 15510 Usher St. *Web:* www.slzusd.org	San Lorenzo	CA	94580	510-317-4600		685
SM & A 18400 Von Karman Ave Ste 500 *Web:* www.smawins.com	Irvine	CA	92612	949-975-1550	975-1624	178-10
SM Arnold Inc 7901 Michigan Ave *TF Cust Svc:* 800-325-7865 ■ *Web:* www.smarnold.com	Saint Louis	MO	63111	314-544-4103	544-3159	103
SM Engineering Co 9 Ninth Ave N *Web:* www.smeng.com	Hopkins	MN	55343	952-938-7407		261
SMA (SMA Services Inc) 35 West Lakeshore Dr.	Birmingham	AL	35209	205-945-1840		49-8
SMA (Steel Manufacturers Assn) 1150 Connecticut Ave NW Ste 715 *Web:* www.steelnet.org	Washington	DC	20036	202-296-1515	296-2506	49-13
SMA Services Inc (SMA) 35 West Lakeshore Dr.	Birmingham	AL	35209	205-945-1840		49-8
SMACNA (Sheet Metal & Air Conditioning Contractors' NA) 4201 Lafayette Ctr Dr *Web:* www.smacna.org	Chantilly	VA	20151	703-803-2980	803-3732	49-3
Small Business & Entrepreneurship Council 301 Maple Ave W Ste 690 *Web:* www.sbecouncil.org	Vienna	VA	22180	703-242-5840		49-12
Small Business Administration (SBA) 409 Third St SW *TF:* 800-827-5722 ■ *Web:* www.sba.gov	Washington	DC	20416	202-205-6600	205-6802	340-20
National Women's Business Council 409 Third St SW Ste 210 *Web:* www.nwbc.gov	Washington	DC	20024	202-205-3850	205-6825	340-20
Small Business Administration Regional Offices (SBA)						
Region 1 10 Cswy St Ste 265A *Web:* www.sba.gov/about-offices-list/3	Boston	MA	02222	617-565-8416	565-8420	340-20
Region 3 1150 First Ave Ste 1001 *Web:* www.sba.gov/about-offices-list/3	King Of Prussia	PA	19406	610-382-3092		340-20
Region 4 233 Peachtree St NE Ste 1800 *Web:* www.sba.gov/about-offices-list/3	Atlanta	GA	30303	404-331-4999	331-2354	340-20
Region 5 500 W Madison St Ste 1150 *Web:* www.sba.gov/about-offices-list/3	Chicago	IL	60661	312-353-0357	353-3426	340-20
Region 6 4300 Amon Carter Blvd Ste 108 *TF:* 800-274-2812 ■ *Web:* www.sba.gov	Fort Worth	TX	76155	817-684-5581	684-5588	340-20
Region 6 1301 Young St *TF:* 800-772-1213 ■ *Web:* www.ssa.gov/dallas	Dallas	TX	75202	214-767-9401	767-8986	340-20
Region 7 100 Walnut Ste 530 *TF:* 800-827-5722 ■ *Web:* www.sba.gov	Kansas City	MO	64106	816-426-4840	426-4848	340-20
Region 8 721 19th St Ste 426 **Fax Area Code:* 202 ■ *Web:* sba.gov	Denver	CO	80202	303-844-2607	292-3582*	340-20
Region 9 330 N Brand Blvd Ste 1200 **Fax Area Code:* 202 ■ *TF:* 800-877-8339 ■ *Web:* www.sba.gov	Glendale	CA	91203	818-552-3437	481-0344*	340-20
Region 10 2401 Fourth Ave Ste 400 *Web:* www.sba.gov	Seattle	WA	98121	206-553-5676	553-4155	340-20
Region 10 701 Fifth Ave Ste 2900 *TF:* 800-772-1213 ■ *Web:* www.ssa.gov	Seattle	WA	98104	206-615-2236		340-20
Small Business Legislative Council (SBLC) 4800 Hampden Ln 6th Fl *Web:* www.sblc.org	Bethesda	MD	20814	202-639-8500		49-12
Small Business Times 126 N Jefferson St Ste 403 *Web:* biztimes.com	Milwaukee	WI	53202	414-277-8181		532-3
Small Mine Development LLC 967 E Parkcenter Blvd. *Web:* www.undergroundmining.com	Boise	ID	83706	208-338-8880	338-8881	186
Small Parts Inc 600 Humphrey St. *Web:* www.smallpartsinc.com	Logansport	IN	46947	574-753-6323	753-6660	488
Small Planet Foods Inc 106 Woodworth St *TF:* 800-624-4123 ■ *Web:* www.smallplanetfoods.com	Sedro Woolley	WA	98284	360-855-0100		296-18
Small Plates 1521 Broadway St. *Web:* www.smallplates.com	Detroit	MI	48226	313-963-0702		671
Small Precision Tools Inc 1330 Clegg St. *Web:* www.smallprecisiontools.com	Petaluma	CA	94954	707-765-4545	778-2271	695
Small Tube Products Company Inc PO Box 1017 *TF:* 800-226-3553 ■ *Web:* www.smalltubeproducts.com	Duncansville	PA	16635	814-695-4491	695-4304	490
Smallwood & Stewart Inc 5 E 20th St. *Web:* www.smallwoodandstewart.com	New York	NY	10003	212-505-3268		94
Smallwood Reynolds Stewart Stewart & Assoc Inc (SRSSA) 1 Piedmont Ctr 3565 Piedmont Rd Ste 303 *Web:* www.srssa.com	Atlanta	GA	30305	404-233-5453		261
Smallwood State Park 2750 Sweden Pt Rd *Web:* dnr2.maryland.gov/pages/default.aspx	Marbury	MD	20658	301-743-7613		565
SMAR International Corp 6001 Stonington St Ste 100 *Web:* www.smar.com	Houston	TX	77040	713-849-2021		246
Smardan-Hatcher Company Inc 810 East Mason St *TF:* 800-427-0696 ■ *Web:* www.smardan.com	Santa Barbara	CA	93103	805-963-8991		612
Smardt Chiller Group Inc 1800 Trans Canada Hwy *Web:* www.smardt.com	Dorval	QC	H9P1H7	514-426-8989		480
SMART (Special Military Active Retired Travel Club) 600 University Office Blvd Ste 1A *TF:* 800-354-7681 ■ *Web:* www.smartrving.org	Pensacola	FL	32504	850-478-1986		48-23
SMART (Suburban Mobility Authority for Regional Transportation) 535 Griswold St Ste 600 *TF:* 866-962-5515 ■ *Web:* www.smartbus.org	Detroit	MI	48226	313-223-2100		468
Smart & Final Inc 600 Citadel Dr *TF:* 800-894-0511 ■ *Web:* www.smartandfinal.com	Commerce	CA	90040	323-869-7500		345
Smart Alabama LLC 121 Shin Young Dr. *Web:* www.smart-alabama.com	Luverne	AL	36049	334-335-5800		247
Smart Apparel US Inc 525 Seventh Ave Ste 1901 *Web:* smartapparelus.com	New York	NY	10018	212-329-3400		155-12
Smart Business Network Inc 835 Sharon Dr Ste 200 *TF:* 800-988-4726 ■ *Web:* www.sbnonline.com	Cleveland	OH	44145	440-250-7000		532-3
Smart Cabling Solutions Inc 1250 N Winchester St. *TF:* 877-390-9501 ■ *Web:* www.thinkscs.com	Olathe	KS	66061	913-390-9501		224
Smart Card Alliance Inc 191 Clarkville Rd *TF:* 800-556-6828 ■ *Web:* www.smartcardalliance.org	Princeton Junction	NJ	08550	609-799-5654	799-7032	49-2
Smart Card Integrators Inc (SCI) 2424 N Ontario St. *Web:* www.sci-s.com	Burbank	CA	91504	818-847-1022		178-12
Smart Choice Communications LLC 16 W 45Th St *TF:* 800-217-3096 ■ *Web:* www.smartchoiceus.com	New York	NY	10036	212-660-7300		387
Smart City Networks 5795 W Badura Ave Ste 110 *TF:* 888-446-6911 ■ *Web:* www.smartcity.com	Las Vegas	NV	89118	702-943-6000	943-6001	736
Smart Creations Inc 1799 St Johns Ave	Highland Park	IL	60035	847-433-3451		410
Smart Dolphins It Solutions Inc 3995 Quadra St Ste 303 *Web:* smartdolphins.com	Victoria	BC	V8X1J8	250-721-2499		175
Smart Electronics & Assembly Inc 2000 W Corporate Way *Web:* www.smartelec.com	Anaheim	CA	92801	714-991-6500		253
Smart Eye Care Ctr 255 Western Ave *TF:* 800-459-5800 ■ *Web:* www.smarteyecare.com	Augusta	ME	04330	207-622-5800		237
Smart Furniture Inc 430 Market St. *TF:* 888-467-6278 ■ *Web:* www.smartfurniture.com	Chattanooga	TN	37402	423-267-7007		321
Smart Imaging Technologies Inc 1770 Saint James Pl Ste 414 *TF:* 877-280-1100 ■ *Web:* www.smartimtech.com	Houston	TX	77056	713-589-3500		419
Smart Inc 400 Poydras St Ste 2305 *Web:* www.smartinc1.com	New Orleans	LA	70130	504-566-0900		463
Smart Industries Corp 1626 Delaware Ave *TF:* 800-553-2442 ■ *Web:* www.smartind.com	Des Moines	IA	50317	515-265-9900	265-3148	322
SMART IT Services Inc 34715 Van Dyke Ave. *Web:* www.smartservices.com	Sterling Heights	MI	48312	586-258-0650		387
Smart Levels Media Inc 16 Hammond *Web:* www.smartlevels.com	Irvine	CA	92618	949-540-0500		179
Smart LLC Smart TuitionOne Woodbridge Ctr Ste 800 *TF:* 866-395-2986 ■ *Web:* www.smarttuition.com	Woodbridge	NJ	07095	866-395-2986		393
Smart Machine Technologies Inc 650 Frith Dr *Web:* www.smartmachine.com	Ridgeway	VA	24148	276-632-9853		295
SMART Modular Technologies Inc 39870 Eureka Dr. *NASDAQ: SMOD* ■ *TF:* 800-956-7627 ■ *Web:* www.smartm.com	Newark	CA	94560	510-623-1231	623-1434	173-1

	City	State	ZIP	Phone	Fax	Class
Smart MultiMedia Inc						
1113 Vine St Ste 239	Houston	TX	77002	713-574-6690		738
Web: www.smartgeometrics.com						
Smart Papers LLC 601 N B St	Hamilton	OH	45013	513-869-5000		548
Smart Pipe Company Inc						
1319 W Sam Houston Pkwy Ste 100	Houston	TX	77043	281-945-5700		595
Web: www.smart-pipe.com						
Smart Power Systems Inc						
1760 Stebbins Dr	Houston	TX	77043	713-464-8000		253
TF: 800-882-8285 ■ *Web:* www.smartpowersystems.com						
SMART Recovery 7304 Mentor Ave Ste F	Mentor	OH	44060	440-951-5357	951-5358	48-21
TF: 866-951-5357 ■ *Web:* www.smartrecovery.org						
Smart Safety Group						
2535 Camino Del Rio S Ste 125	San Diego	CA	92108	619-491-3099		196
TF: 877-345-7627 ■ *Web:* www.smartsafetygroup.com						
Smart Staffing Service Inc						
132 Central St Ste 210	Foxboro	MA	02035	508-698-9988		260
Web: www.smart-tek.net						
Smart System Technology & Commercialization Ctr						
5450 Campus Dr	Canandaigua	NY	14424	585-919-3000		393
TF: 800-460-8720 ■ *Web:* www.stcmems.com						
SMART Technologies Inc						
3636 Research Rd NW	Calgary	AB	T2L1Y1	403-245-0333		173-1
TSE: SMA ■ *TF:* 888-427-6278 ■ *Web:* www.smarttech.com						
Smart Transaction Systems Inc						
1803 S Foothills Hwy Ste 205	Boulder	CO	80303	303-494-9760		5
Web: www.smart-transactions.com						
Smart Union (SMWIA)						
1750 New York Ave NW 6th Fl	Washington	DC	20006	202-662-0800	662-0894	49-3
TF: 800-457-7694 ■ *Web:* www.smwia.org						
Smart Warehousing LLC						
18905 Kill Creek Rd	Edgerton	KS	66021	913-888-3222		803-1
Web: www.smartwarehousing.com						
Smart Web Concepts Inc						
701 Riverside Ave Ste 3	Roseville	CA	95678	916-782-2288		225
Web: boostlogics.com						
Smart Work Network Inc						
135 S Main St Ste 402	Greenville	SC	29601	864-233-3007		463
Web: www.smartworknetwork.com						
SmartAction Company LLC						
390 N Sepulveda Blvd Ste 2150	El Segundo	CA	90245	310-776-9200		387
TF: 800-671-6898 ■ *Web:* www.smartaction.com						
SmartBargains Inc 40 Broad St Ste 205	Boston	MA	02109	877-222-6660		229
TF: 877-222-6660 ■ *Web:* www.smartbargains.com						
Smartech Systems Inc						
500 E Brighton Ave	Syracuse	NY	13210	315-701-2316		180
TF: 800-486-8850 ■ *Web:* www.s2ieng.com						
SmarTek21 LLC						
12910 Totem Lake Blvd NE Ste 200	Kirkland	WA	98034	425-242-3786		196
Web: www.smartek21.com						
SmarterTools Inc						
1903 W Parkside Ln Ste 106	Phoenix	AZ	85027	623-434-8050		177
Web: www.smartertools.com						
Smarterville Productions LLC						
934 Plaza Dr Ste 150	Montoursville	PA	17754	800-532-3607		45
TF: 800-532-3607						
Smartguys Advertising & Design Inc						
4322 Scotia Dr	Fort Wayne	IN	46814	260-625-6427		7
Web: www.smartguys.biz						
Smarties Candy Co 1091 Lousons Rd	Union	NJ	07083	908-964-0660		296-8
Web: www.smarties.com						
SmarTire Systems Inc						
6900 Graybar Rd Ste 2110	Richmond	BC	V3W0A5	440-329-9000	329-9203	60
TF: 800 247-2725 ■ *Web:* www.smartire.com						
SmartIT Staffing Inc						
6500 Technology Ctr Dr Ste 300	Indianapolis	IN	46278	317-634-0211		260
TF: 800-336-4466 ■ *Web:* gotsmartit.com						
Smartleaf Inc 210 Broadway 4th Fl	Cambridge	MA	02139	617-453-0714	491-5556	809
Web: www.smartleaf.com						
SmartLink Internet Strategies Inc						
8895 N Military Trl Ste B202	Palm Beach Gardens	FL	33410	561 688-8155		631
Web: thinksmartlink.com						
SMARTLogix Inc 10306 Barberville Rd	Ft. Mill	SC	29707	803-547-8265		317
Web: www.smartlogixinc.com						
Smartorg Inc 855 oak grove ave	Menlo Park	CA	94025	650-328-1612		225
Web: www.smartorg.com						
Smartpak Equine LLC						
40 Grissom Rd Ste 500	Plymouth	MA	02360	774-773-1000		366
TF: 888-752-5171 ■ *Web:* www.smartpakequine.com						
SmartProcure LLC						
700 W Hillsboro Blvd Ste 4-100	Deerfield Beach	FL	33441	954-420-9900		387
TF: 800-561-3357 ■ *Web:* smartprocure.us						
SmartPros Ltd. 12 Skyline Dr	Hawthorne	NY	10532	732-741-1600		765
Web: sp.smartpros.com/pages/index.aspx						
SmartRevenue Inc						
263 Tresser Blvd 9th Fl	Stamford	CT	06901	203-733-9156		466
Web: smartrevenue.com						
Smartronix Inc 44150 Smartronix Way	Hollywood	MD	20636	301-373-6000	373-7171	177
TF: 866-442-7767 ■ *Web:* www.smartronix.com						
SmarTrunk Systems Inc						
867 Bowsprit Rd	Chula Vista	CA	91914	619-426-3781	426-3788	735
Web: www.smartrunk.com						
Smartsat Inc 8222 118th Ave Ste 600	Largo	FL	33773	727-535-6880		387
TF: 800-445-1139 ■ *Web:* smartsat.com						
SmartScrubs LLC 3400 E Mcdowell Rd	Phoenix	AZ	85008	800-800-5788		475
TF: 800-800-5788 ■ *Web:* www.smartscrubs.com						
Smartsearch Marketing						
4450 Arapahoe Ave Ste 100	Boulder	CO	80303	303-444-3134		195
Web: smartsearchmarketing.com						
Smarttech Enterprises 1300 Chisolm Trl	Dayton	OH	45458	937-885-7144		317
Web: www.smarttechreport.com						
Smartware Computer Services						
2821 S Bay St Ste B	Eustis	FL	32726	352-483-4350		175
TF: 800-796-5000 ■ *Web:* scs3.com						
Smarty Ants Inc 1400 Rollins Rd	Burlingame	CA	94010	800-952-5210		387
TF: 800-952-5210 ■ *Web:* www.smartyants.com						
Smashing Ideas Inc						
2211 Elliott Ave Ste 110	Seattle	WA	98121	206-378-0100		33
Web: smashingideas.com						
SMBC (Sumitomo Mitsui Banking Corp)						
277 Pk Ave	New York	NY	10172	212-224-4000	593-9522	70
Web: www.smbcgroup.com						
SMC (Single Mothers by Choice Inc)						
PO Box 1642	New York	NY	10028	212-988-0993		48-21
Web: www.singlemothersbychoice.org						
SMC (Somerset Medical Ctr)						
110 Rehill Ave	Somerville	NJ	08876	908-685-2200		374-3
TF: 888-637-9584 ■ *Web:* rwjuh.edu						
SMC (Southwestern Michigan College)						
58900 Cherry Grove Rd	Dowagiac	MI	49047	269-782-1000	782-1331	162
TF: 800-456-8675 ■ *Web:* www.swmich.edu						
SMC (Shannon Medical Ctr)						
120 E Harris Ave	San Angelo	TX	76903	325-653-6741	658-8295	374-3
TF: 800-368-1019 ■ *Web:* www.shannonhealth.com						
SMC (Save the Manatee Club)						
500 N Maitland Ave Ste 210	Maitland	FL	32751	407-539-0990	539-0871	48-3
TF: 800-432-5646 ■ *Web:* www.savethemanatee.org						
SMC Business Councils						
600 Cranberry Woods Dr Ste 190	Cranberry Township	PA	16066	412-371-1500		138
TF: 800-553-3260 ■ *Web:* www.smc.org						
Smc Corp of America						
10100 SMC Blvd	Noblesville	IN	46060	317-899-4440		223
Web: www.smcusa.com						
Smc Electrical Products Inc						
6072 Ohio River Rd	Huntington	WV	25702	304-522-7697		729
Web: www.smcelectrical.com						
SMC Metal Fabricators Inc						
2100 S Oakwood Rd	Oshkosh	WI	54904	920-426-6080		492
Web: www.smcmetal.com						
SMCC (Southern Maine Community College)						
2 Ft Rd	South Portland	ME	04106	207-741-5500	741-5760	800
TF: 877-282-2182 ■ *Web:* www.smccme.edu						
SMCI (Supermicro Computer Inc)						
980 Rock Ave	San Jose	CA	95131	408-503-8000	503-8008	625
NASDAQ: SMCI ■ *Web:* www.supermicro.com/index.cfm						
SMD (Surface Mount Distribution Inc)						
1 Oldfield	Irvine	CA	92618	949-470-7700	470-7777	246
TF: 800-820-7634 ■ *Web:* www.smdinc.com						
SME (Society of Mfg Engineers) 1 SME Dr	Dearborn	MI	48128	313-425-3000	425-3400	49-13
TF Cust Svc: 800-733-4763 ■ *Web:* www.sme.org						
SME (Society for Mining Metallurgy & Exploration Inc)						
8307 Shaffer Pkwy	Littleton	CO	80127	303-973-9550	973-3845	49-13
TF: 800 763-3132 ■ *Web:* www.smenet.org						
S&ME Inc 6190 Enterprise Ct	Dublin	OH	43016	614-793-2226		256
Smeal Fire Apparatus Co						
610 W Fourth St PO Box 8	Snyder	NE	68664	402-568-2224		283
Web: www.smeal.com						
SMEPA (South Mississippi Electric Power Assn)						
7037 US Hwy 49	Hattiesburg	MS	39402	601-268-2083		245
Web: www.smepa.coop						
SMF Inc 1550 Industrial Pk	Minonk	IL	61760	309-432-2586	432-2390	454
TF: 800-548-2930 ■ *Web:* www.smf-inc.com						
SMH (Slidell Memorial Hospital)						
1001 Gause Blvd	Slidell	LA	70458	985-643-2200		374-3
TF: 800-256-9822 ■ *Web:* slidellmemorial.org						
SMH (Southeast Missouri Hospital)						
1701 Lacey St	Cape Girardeau	MO	63701	573-334-4822		374-3
TF: 800-800-5123 ■ *Web:* www.sehealth.org						
SMI (Speedway Motorsports Inc)						
5555 Concord Pkwy S	Concord	NC	28027	704-455-3239		181
NYSE: TRK ■ *TF:* 800-732-0330 ■ *Web:* www.speedwaymotorsports.com						
SMI (Spring Manufacturers Institute)						
2001 Midwest Rd Ste 106	Oak Brook	IL	60523	630-495-8588	495-8595	49-13
TF: 866-482-5569 ■ *Web:* www.smihq.org						
SMI Companies Inc 1456 Hwy 317 S	Franklin	LA	70538	337-836-9894		317
TF: 800-264-9894 ■ *Web:* www.smicompanies.com						
SMI Manufacturing Inc						
13312 E Hardy Toll Rd	Houston	TX	77039	281-449-0345		757
Web: www.ameriforgegroup.com						
SMI properties 5239 zMax Blvd	Harrisburg	NC	28075	704-455-9499		656
Web: www.smiproperties.com						
Smi Travel Inc 1170 Nikki View Dr	Brandon	FL	33511	813-315-9840		226
Web: smitrav.com						
Smile Train Inc 41 Madison Ave Ste 28	New York	NY	10010	212-689-9199	689-9299	48-5
TF: 877-543-7645 ■ *Web:* www.smiletrain.org						
Smilebox Inc 15809 Bear Creek Pkwy	Redmond	WA	98052	360-797-5269		225
TF: 800-561-3357 ■ *Web:* www.smilebox.com						
Smith 5306 Hollister Rd	Houston	TX	77040	713-430-3000	430-3099	246
TF: 800-468-7866 ■ *Web:* globalpurchasing.com						
Smith & Butterfield Co Inc						
2800 Lynch Rd	Evansville	IN	47711	812-422-3261	429-0532	535
TF: 800-321-6543 ■ *Web:* www.smithbutterfield.com						
Smith & DeShields Inc						
165 NW 20th St	Boca Raton	FL	33431	561-395-0808		234
TF: 800-741-0808 ■ *Web:* www.smithanddeshields.com						
Smith & Greene Co 19015 66th Ave S	Kent	WA	98032	425-656-8000		300
TF: 800-232-8050 ■ *Web:* www.smithandgreene.com						
Smith & Howard PC						
271 17th St NW Ste 1600	Atlanta	GA	30363	404-874-6244	874-1658	2
Web: www.smith-howard.com						
Smith & Keene Electric Service Inc						
833 Live Oak Dr	Chesapeake	VA	23320	757-420-1231		189-4
Web: www.smithandkeene.com						
Smith & Loveless Inc						
14040 Santa Fe Trail Dr	Lenexa	KS	66215	913-888-5201		427
Web: www.smithandloveless.com						
Smith & Nephew Inc 1450 E Brooks Rd	Memphis	TN	38116	901-396-2121		477
TF Cust Svc: 800-238-7538 ■ *Web:* www.smith-nephew.com						
Smith & Nephew Inc						
970 Lake Carillon Dr 310	Saint Petersburg	FL	33716	727-392-1261	392-6914	477
TF Cust Svc: 800-876-1261 ■ *Web:* smith-nephew.com						
Smith & Nephew Inc Endoscopy Div						
150 Minuteman Rd	Andover	MA	01810	978-749-1000	749-1599	476
TF: 800-343-5717 ■ *Web:* www.smith-nephew.com						
Smith & Oby Co						
7676 Northfield Rd	Walton Hills	OH	44146	440-735-5333	735-5334	189-10
TF: 800-776-7181 ■ *Web:* www.smithandoby.com						

Name / Address	City	State	Zip	Phone	Fax	Class
Smith & Richardson Manufacturing Co PO Box 589	Geneva	IL	60134	630-232-2581	232-2610	621
TF: 800-426-0876 ■ *Web:* www.smithandrichardson.com						
Smith & Smith CPAs PC 2423 US Hwy 2 E	Kalispell	MT	59901	406-755-4567		2
Smith & Wesson Academy 299 Page Blvd	Springfield	MA	01104	413-846-6461	736-0776	766
TF: 800-331-0852 ■ *Web:* www.smith-wesson.com						
Smith & Wesson Corp 2100 Roosevelt Ave	Springfield	MA	01104	413-781-8300	747-3317	284
TF Cust Svc: 800-331-0852 ■ *Web:* www.smith-wesson.com						
Smith & Wesson Holding Corp 2100 Roosevelt Ave	Springfield	MA	01104	413-781-8300	747-3317	284
NASDAQ: SWHC ■ *TF:* 800-372-6454 ■ *Web:* www.smith-wesson.com						
Smith & Wollensky 4145 the Strand W Easton Town Ctr	Columbus	OH	43219	614-416-2400		671
Web: www.smithandwollensky.com						
Smith & Wollensky 3767 Las Vegas Blvd S	Las Vegas	NV	89109	702-862-4100		671
Web: www.smithandwollensky.com						
Smith & Wollensky 101 Station Landing Ste 100	Medford	MA	02155	617-600-3500		671
Web: www.smithandwollensky.com						
Smith & Wollensky Restaurant Group Inc 318 N State St	Chicago	IL	60654	312-670-9900		670
Web: www.smithandwollensky.com						
Smith Adam (Rep D - WA) 2264 Rayburn HOB	Washington	DC	20515	202-225-8901	225-5893	342-2
Web: adamsmith.house.gov						
Smith Adrian (Rep R - NE) 320 Cannon HOB	Washington	DC	20515	202-225-6435	225-0207	342-2
Web: adriansmith.house.gov						
Smith Affiliated Capital (SAC) 800 Third Ave 12th Fl	New York	NY	10022	212-644-9440	644-1979	403
TF: 888-387-3298 ■ *Web:* www.smithcapital.com						
Smith Anglin Financial LLC 16000 Dallas Pkwy Ste 850	Dallas	TX	75248	972-267-1244		2
Web: www.smithanglin.com						
Smith Bovill Pc 200 Saint Andrews Rd	Saginaw	MI	48638	989-792-9641		428
TF: 800-799-2234 ■ *Web:* www.smithbovill.com						
Smith Brooks Bolshoun & CoLLP 2680 18th St Ste 200	Denver	CO	80211	303-480-1200		2
Web: sbbllp.com						
Smith Bros Construction 444 S Cedros Ave	Solana Beach	CA	92075	858-350-1445		187
Web: www.smithbrothersconstruction.com						
Smith Brothers Restaurant Corporation 100 E Corson St Ste 320	Pasadena	CA	91103	626-577-2400	577-8330	670
Web: www.smithbrothersrestaurants.com						
Smith Cast Iron Boilers 260 N Elm St	Westfield	MA	01085	413-562-9631	562-3799	357
Web: www.westcastboilers.com						
Smith Chapel Free Will Baptist Church 519 Boundary Ln	Fayetteville	NC	28301	910-483-4437		48-20
Smith Chris (Rep R - NJ) 2373 Rayburn Bldg	Washington	DC	20515	202-225-3765	225-7768	342-2
Web: chrissmith.house.gov						
Smith College 7 College Ln	NorthHampton	MA	01063	413-584-2700	585-2527	166
TF: 800-383-3232 ■ *Web:* www.smith.edu						
Smith County 122 Turner High Cir	Carthage	TN	37030	615-735-9833		338
Web: www.smithcountychamber.org						
Smith County PO Box 517	Raleigh	MS	39153	601-782-4751		338
Smith County 218 S Grant St	Smith Center	KS	66967	785-282-5110	686-4014	338
Web: www.smithcoks.com						
Smith Crossing 10501 Emilie Ln Ofc	Orland Park	IL	60467	708-326-2300		371
Web: smithcrossing.org						
Smith Dairy 1381 Dairy Ln	Orrville	OH	44667	330-683-8710		296-27
Web: www.smithsbrand.com						
Smith Dray Line 320 Frontage Rd	Greenville	SC	29611	866-642-6389		519
TF: 866-642-6389 ■ *Web:* www.smithdray.com						
Smith Engineering Co 2201 San Pedro Dr NE 4-200	Albuquerque	NM	87110	505-884-0700		261
TF: 800-819-9893 ■ *Web:* www.smithengineering.pro						
Smith Equipment Mfg Co 2601 Lockheed Ave	Watertown	SD	57201	605-882-3200		811
TF Cust Svc: 866-931-9730 ■ *Web:* www.smithequipment.com						
Smith Falls State Park 90165 Smith Falls Rd	Valentine	NE	69201	402-376-1306		565
Web: outdoornebraska.gov						
Smith Fastener Co 3613 Florence Ave	Bell	CA	90201	323-587-0382		350
Web: smithfast.com						
Smith Flooring Inc 1501 W Hwy 60 PO Box 99	Mountain View	MO	65548	417-934-2291	934-2295	683
Web: www.smithflooring.com						
Smith Fork Ranch 45362 Needle Rock Rd	Crawford	CO	81415	970-921-3454	921-3475	239
TF: 855-539-1492 ■ *Web:* www.smithforkranch.com						
Smith Foundry Co 1855 E 28th St	Minneapolis	MN	55407	612-729-9395	729-2519	307
Web: www.smithfoundry.com						
Smith Frozen Foods Inc 101 Depot St	Weston	OR	97886	541-566-3515		296-21
Web: www.smithfrozenfoods.com						
Smith Gambrell & Russell LLP 1230 Peachtree St NE Promenade II Ste 3100	Atlanta	GA	30309	404-815-3500		41
Web: www.sgrlaw.com						
Smith Gardens Inc 4164 Meridian St Ste 400	Bellingham	WA	98226	360-733-4671		369
TF: 800-755-6256 ■ *Web:* www.smithgardens.com						
Smith Goolsby Artis & Reams Psc 1330 Carter Ave	Ashland	KY	41101	606-329-1171		2
Smith Graham & Co 600 Travis St Ste 6900	Houston	TX	77002	713-227-1100		401
TF: 800-739-4470 ■ *Web:* smithgraham.com						
Smith Growth Partners Mill Centre PH 3000 Chestnut Ave	Baltimore	MD	21211	410-235-7004		636
TF: 800-438-7325 ■ *Web:* www.smithgrowthpartners.com						
Smith Hartvigsen PLLC The Walker Ctr 175 South Main St Ste 300	Salt Lake City	UT	84111	801-413-1600		428
TF: 877-825-2064 ■ *Web:* www.smithhartvigsen.com						
SMITH HAYES Financial Services Corp 1225 L St Ste 200	Lincoln	NE	68508	402-476-3000		690
Smith Hulsey & Busey 225 Water St Ste 1800	Jacksonville	FL	32202	904-359-7700	359-7708	428
Web: www.smithhulsey.com						
Smith Industries Inc 2781 Gunter Park Dr E	Montgomery	AL	36109	334-277-8520		198
Web: www.jrsmith.com						
Smith Jason (Rep R - MO) 1118 Longworth HOB	Washington	DC	20515	202-225-4404	226-0326	342-2
Web: jasonsmith.house.gov						
Smith Jewelers C W 603 Wisconsin Ave	North Fond Du Lac	WI	54937	920-922-6259		410
Web: www.cwsmithjewelers.com						
Smith Keller Miner & O'shea 69 Delaware Ave Rm 1212	Buffalo	NY	14202	716-855-3611		428
Web: www.smithminerlaw.com						
Smith Koelling Dykstra & Ohm PC 1605 N Convent	Bourbonnais	IL	60914	815-937-1997		2
Web: skdocpa.com						
Smith Lamar (Rep R - TX) 2409 Rayburn HOB	Washington	DC	20515	202-225-4236	225-8628	342-2
Web: lamarsmith.house.gov						
Smith Linden & Basso 5120 Birch St Ste 200	Newport Beach	CA	92660	949-752-0660		2
Web: www.slb-cpa.com						
Smith Management Group 1860b Williamson Ct	Louisville	KY	40223	502-587-6482		196
Web: www.smithmanage.com						
Smith Mazure Director Wilkins Young & Yagerman PC 111 John St 20th Fl	New York	NY	10038	212-964-7400		428
Web: www.smithmazure.com						
Smith McDonald Corp 1270 Niagara St	Buffalo	NY	14213	800-753-8548		608
TF: 800-753-8548 ■ *Web:* www.smithmcdonald.com						
Smith McDowell House Museum 283 Victoria Rd	Asheville	NC	28801	828-253-9231		520
Web: www.wnchistory.org						
SMITH Mfg Company Inc 1610 S Dixie Hwy	Pompano Beach	FL	33060	954-941-9744	545-0348	82
TF: 800-653-9311 ■ *Web:* www.smithmfg.com						
Smith Micro Software Inc 51 Columbia St Ste 200	Aliso Viejo	CA	92656	949-362-5800	362-2300	178-7
NASDAQ: SMSI ■ *Web:* www.smithmicro.com						
Smith Motors Inc of Hammond 6405 Indianapolis Blvd	Hammond	IN	46320	219-845-4000		57
TF: 877-392-2689 ■ *Web:* www.smithchevyusa.com						
Smith Mountain Industries Inc 1000 Dillard Dr	Forest	VA	24551	434-385-1305		96
Smith Nadenbousch Insurance Inc 132 S Queen St	Martinsburg	WV	25401	304-263-3388		390
Web: smnains.com						
Smith Packing Company Inc 105-125 Washington St	Utica	NY	13503	315-732-5125	732-5129	296-26
Web: www.smithpacking.com						
Smith Peterson Law Office 133 W Broadway PO Box 249	Council Bluffs	IA	51503	712-328-1833		428
Web: www.smithpeterson.com						
Smith Plantation Home 935 Alpharetta St	Roswell	GA	30075	770-641-3978	641-3974	50-3
TF: 800-776-7935 ■ *Web:* www.roswellgov.com						
Smith Power Products Inc 3065 W California Ave	Salt Lake City	UT	84104	801-415-5000	415-5700	385
TF: 800-658-5352 ■ *Web:* www.smithpowerproducts.com						
Smith Protective Services Inc 1801 Royal Ln Ste 250	Dallas	TX	75229	214-631-4444		693
TF: 800-631-1384 ■ *Web:* www.smithprotective.com						
Smith Pump Co Inc 301 M B Industrial	Woodway	TX	76712	254-776-0377	776-0023	641
Web: www.smithpump.com						
Smith Ranch Homes 400 Deer Valley Rd Ste L	San Rafael	CA	94903	415-491-4918	491-0254	672
TF: 800-772-6264 ■ *Web:* www.smithranchhomes.com						
Smith Ready Mix Inc 251 W Lincolnway	Valparaiso	IN	46383	219-462-3191	465-4025	182
Web: www.smithreadymix.com						
Smith Research Inc 710 Estate Dr	Deerfield	IL	60015	847-948-0440		463
Web: www.smithresearch.com						
Smith Reynolds Airport 3801 N Liberty St	Winston-Salem	NC	27105	336-767-6361	767-8556	27
Web: www.smithreynolds.org						
Smith Richardson Foundation Inc 60 Jesup Rd	Westport	CT	06880	203-222-6222		305
Web: www.srf.org						
Smith River State Park 4600 Giant Springs Rd	Great Falls	MT	59405	406-454-5840		565
Web: www.fwp.mt.gov						
Smith Robertson Museum & Cultural Ctr 528 Bloom St	Jackson	MS	39202	601-960-1457		520
Smith Rock State Park 9241 NE Crooked River Dr	Terrebonne	OR	97760	541-548-7501		565
Web: www.oregonstateparks.org						
Smith Schafer & Assoc Ltd 220 S Broadway Ste 102	Rochester	MN	55904	507-288-3277		2
Web: www.smithschafer.com						
Smith Seckman Reid Inc 2995 Sidco Dr	Nashville	TN	37204	615-383-1113		261
Web: ssr-inc.com						
Smith Southwestern Inc 1850 N Rosemont	Mesa	AZ	85205	480-854-9545		292
TF: 800-783-3909 ■ *Web:* www.smith-southwestern.com						
Smith State Prison 9676 Hwy 301 N	Glennville	GA	30427	912-654-5000	654-5131	213
Web: www.dcor.state.ga.us						
Smith System Driver Improvement Institute Inc 2301 E Lamar Blvd Ste 250	Arlington	TX	76006	817-652-6969		162
TF: 800-777-7648 ■ *Web:* www.drivedifferent.com						

Phone | Fax | Class

Smith Systems Transportation Inc
417 Ninth Ave ... Scottsbluff NE 69361 800-897-5571 311
TF: 800-897-5571 ■ *Web:* smithsystemsus.weebly.com

Smith Tank & Steel Inc 42422 Hwy 30 ... Gonzales LA 70737 225-644-8747 186
Web: www.smith-tank.net

Smith Travel Research Inc
735 E Main St ... Hendersonville TN 37075 615-824-8664 466
Web: www.str.com

Smith Village Home Furnishings
34 N Main St ... Jacobus PA 17407 717-428-1921 321
TF: 800-242-1921 ■ *Web:* smithvillage.com

Smith Whiley & Co
141 Weston St PO Box 480 ... Hartford CT 06103 860-548-2513 548-2518 405
Web: www.smithwhiley.com

Smith, Anderson, Blount, Dorsett, Mitchell & Jernigan, LLP
2500 First Union Capitol Ctr ... Raleigh NC 27602 919-821-1220 428
TF: 800-973-1177 ■ *Web:* www.smithlaw.com

Smith, Kaplan, Allen & Reynolds Advertising Agency Inc
111 S 108th Ave ... Omaha NE 68154 402-330-0110 7
Web: skar.com

Smith, Katzenstein & Jenkins LLP
1000 W St Ste 1501 PO Box 410 ... Wilmington DE 19899 302-652-8400 652-8405 428
Web: www.skjlaw.com

Smith, Sovik, Kendrick & Sugnet PC
250 S Clinton St Ste 600 ... Syracuse NY 13202 315-474-2911 428
TF: 800-675-0011 ■ *Web:* www.smithsovik.com

Smithahn Company Inc 836 E N St ... Bethlehem PA 18017 610-866-4461 492
Web: smithahn.com

Smith-Cairns Ford 900 Central Pk Ave ... Yonkers NY 10704 914-377-8100 377-8118 516
Web: www.smith-cairns.com

Smithco Engineering Inc
6312 S 39th W Ave ... Tulsa OK 74132 918-446-4406 445-2857 91
Web: www.smithco-eng.com

Smithco Inc 34 W Ave ... Wayne PA 19087 610-688-4009 688-6069 429
TF: 877-833-7648 ■ *Web:* www.smithco.com

Smith-Cooper International
2867 Vail Ave ... Commerce CA 90040 323-890-4455 890-4456 492
Web: www.smithcooper.com

Smith-Edwards-Dunlap Co
2867 E Allegheny Ave ... Philadelphia PA 19134 215-425-8800 626
TF: 800-829-0020 ■ *Web:* www.sed.com

Smithereen Pest Management Services
7400 N Melvina Ave ... Niles IL 60714 847-647-0010 647-0606 577
TF: 800-336-3500 ■ *Web:* smithereen.com

Smithers Group Inc, The 425 W Market St ... Akron OH 44303 330-762-7441 743
Web: smithers.com

Smithfield Foods Inc
200 Commerce St ... Smithfield VA 23430 757-365-3000 473
NYSE: SFD ■ *Web:* www.smithfieldfoods.com

Smithfield Manufacturing Inc
237 Kraft St ... Clarksville TN 37040 931-552-4327 648-4460 621

Smithgall Woods Conservation Area & Lodge
61 Tsalaki Trl ... Helen GA 30545 706-878-3087 565
TF: 800-864-7275 ■ *Web:* www.gastateparks.org/info/smithgall

Smithgeiger LLC
31365 Oak Crest Dr Ste 150 ... Westlake Village CA 91361 818-874-2000 195
TF: 800-977-4130 ■ *Web:* smithgeiger.com

SmithGifford Inc
106 W Jefferson St ... Falls Church VA 22046 703-532-5992 5
Web: www.smithgifford.com

Smithgroup Communications Inc
267 SE 33rd Ave ... Portland OR 97214 503-239-4215 514
Web: smithgrp.com

SmithGroup Inc
500 Griswold St Ste 1700 ... Detroit MI 48226 313-983-3600 983-3636 261
Web: www.smithgroupjjr.com

Smith-Kettlewell Eye Research Institute
2318 Fillmore St ... San Francisco CA 94115 415-345-2000 345-8455 668
Web: www.ski.org

Smithlain Enterprises Inc
1300 Meridian St Ste 15 ... Huntsville AL 35801 256-704-7880 196
Web: www.smithlain.com

Smith-Midland Corp
5119 Catlett Rd PO Box 300 ... Midland VA 22728 540-439-3266 439-1232 183
OTC: SMID ■ *TF:* 800-724-4881 ■ *Web:* www.smithmidland.com

Smiths Detection 2202 Lakeside Blvd ... Edgewood MD 21040 410-510-9100 472
TF: 800-297-0955 ■ *Web:* www.smithsdetection.com

Smiths Interconnect Microwave Components Inc
8851 SW Old Kansas Ave ... Stuart FL 34997 772-286-9300 767
Web: www.rflabs.com

Smiths Medical ASD Inc
160 Weymouth St ... Rockland MA 02370 781-878-8011 878-8201 477
TF: 800-258-5361 ■ *Web:* www.smiths-medical.com

Smiths Medical MD Inc
1265 Grey Fox Rd ... Saint Paul MN 55112 651-633-2556 628-7459 477
TF: 800-258-5361 ■ *Web:* www.smiths-medical.com

Smiths Medical Respiratory Support Products
5200 Upper Metro Pl Ste 200 ... Dublin OH 43017 214-618-0218 734-0254* 477
**Fax Area Code:* 614 ■ *TF:* 800-258-5361 ■ *Web:* www.smiths-medical.com

Smithsonian Air & Space Magazine
PO Box 37012 ... Washington DC 20013 202-633-6070 633-6085 457-19
TF Cust Svc: 800-766-2149 ■ *Web:* www.airspacemag.com

Smithsonian Environmental Research Ctr
647 Contees Wharf Rd ... Edgewater MD 21037 443-482-2200 482-2380 668
Web: www.serc.si.edu

Smithsonian Folkways Recordings
600 Maryland Ave SW Ste 200 ... Washington DC 20024 202-633-6450 633-6477 657
TF: 800-410-9815 ■ *Web:* www.folkways.si.edu

Smithsonian Institution
SI Bldg Rm 153 MRC 010 PO Box 37012 ... Washington DC 20013 202-633-1000 520
Web: www.si.edu

Smithsonian Institution Business Ventures Div
600 Maryland Ave SW Ste 6000 ... Washington DC 20024 202-633-6080 637-9
TF: 800-521-5330 ■ *Web:* www.si.edu

Smithsonian Institution Cullman Library
1000 Constitution Ave NW
Natural History Bldg ... Washington DC 20560 202-633-2240 633-0219 434-4
Web: library.si.edu

Smithsonian Institution Dibner Library of the History of Science & Technology
Smithsonian Institution NMAH 1041 MRC 672
PO Box 37012 ... Washington DC 20013 202-633-3872 633-9102 434-4
Web: library.si.edu

Smithsonian Magazine
600 Maryland Ave Ste 6001 ... Washington DC 20024 202-633-6090 457-11
TF: 800-766-2149 ■ *Web:* www.smithsonianmag.com

Smithsonian National Museum of African Art
950 Independence Ave SW ... Washington DC 20560 202-633-4600 357-4879 520
Web: africa.si.edu

Smithsonian National Zoological Park
3001 Connecticut Ave NW ... Washington DC 20008 202-633-4888 823
Web: nationalzoo.si.edu

Smithsonian Tropical Research Institute (STRI)
9100 Panama City PL ... Washington DC 20521 703-487-3770 786-2557* 668
**Fax Area Code:* 202 ■ *Web:* www.stri.si.edu

Smithtown Chamber of Commerce
79 E Main St Ste E ... Smithtown NY 11787 631-979-8069 979-2206 139
TF: 800-548-4337 ■ *Web:* www.smithtownchamber.org

Smithville Communications Inc
1600 W Temperance St ... Ellettsville IN 47429 812-876-2211 736
Web: www.smithville.com

Smitty's Canada Ltd
501 18th Ave SW Ste 600 ... Calgary AB T2S0C7 403-229-3838 229-3899 670
TF: 800-563-7853 ■ *Web:* www.smittys.ca

Smitty's Supply Inc
63399 Hwy 51 N PO Box 530 ... Roseland LA 70456 985-748-9687 748-3004 541
TF: 800-256-7575 ■ *Web:* www.smittysinc.net

SMK Electronics Corp USA
1055 Tierra Del Rey ... Chula Vista CA 91910 619-216-6400 216-6498 253
Web: www.smk.co.jp

SMMA (Symmes Maini & McKee Assoc)
1000 Massachusetts Ave ... Cambridge MA 02138 617-547-5400 648-4920* 261
**Fax Area Code:* 800 ■ *Web:* www.smma.com

SMMC (Southern Maine Medical Ctr)
1 Medical Ctr Dr PO Box 626 ... Biddeford ME 04005 207-283-7000 283-7020 374-3
Web: mainehealth.org/southern-maine-health-care

SMO (Southern Maryland Oil Co Inc)
109 N Maple Ave ... La Plata MD 20646 888-222-3720 579
TF: 888-222-3720 ■ *Web:* www.smoenergy.com

Smoak Davis & Nixon LLP
5011 Gate Pkwy Bldg 100 Ste 300 ... Jacksonville FL 32256 904-396-5831 2
Web: www.sdnllp.com

SMOCA (Scottsdale Museum of Contemporary Art)
7374 E Second St ... Scottsdale AZ 85251 480-874-4666 520
TF: 800-745-3000 ■ *Web:* www.smoca.org

Smock Fansler Corp
2910 W Minnesota St ... Indianapolis IN 46241 317-248-8371 244-4507 189-3
Web: www.smockfansler.com

Smoke Magazine 26 Broadway ... New York NY 10004 212-391-2060 827-0945 457-14
TF: 800-766-2633 ■ *Web:* www.smokemag.com

Smokehouse, The
34 Palmetto Bay Rd ... Hilton Head Island SC 29928 843-842-4227 671
Web: www.smokehousehhi.com

Smoker Craft PO Box 65 ... New Paris IN 46553 866-719-7873 90
TF: 866-719-7873 ■ *Web:* www.smokercraft.com

Smoker Smith & Associates Pc
339 W Governor Rd Ste 202 ... Hershey PA 17033 717-533-5154 2
TF: 888-277-1040 ■ *Web:* www.smokersmith.com

Smokey Bones BBQ 2074 Interchange Rd ... Erie PA 16565 814-868-3388 671
Web: www.smokeybones.com

Smokey Bones BBQ & Grill
1405 Greenbrier Pkwy ... Chesapeake VA 23320 757-361-6843 671
Web: www.smokeybones.com

Smokin Joes Cigars LLC
2293 Saunders Settlement Rd ... Sanborn NY 14132 716-261-9327 156
Web: www.smokinjoes.com

Smokin' Guns BBQ 1218 Swift Ave ... Kansas City MO 64116 816-221-2535 221-2606 671
Web: www.smokingunsbbq.com

Smoky Hills Public Television (SHPTV)
604 Elm St ... Bunker Hill KS 67626 785-483-6990 483-4605 632
TF: 800-337-4788 ■ *Web:* www.shptv.org

Smoky Mountain Knife Works Inc
2320 Winfield Dunn Pkwy PO Box 4430 ... Sevierville TN 37876 865-453-5871 362
Web: www.smkw.com

Smoky Mountain Pizzeria Grill
408 E 41st St ... Boise ID 83714 208-433-9596 671
Web: www.smokymountainpizza.com

Smoky Mountain Truck Ctr LLC
841 Eastern Star Rd ... Kingsport TN 37663 800-451-1508 349-0431* 57
**Fax Area Code:* 423 ■ *TF:* 800-451-1508 ■ *Web:* www.smtruckcenter.com

Smoky Mountain Visitors Bureau
7906 E Lamar Alexander Pkwy ... Townsend TN 37882 865-448-6134 206
TF: 800-525-6834 ■ *Web:* www.smokymountains.org

Smoky Shadows Motel & Conference Ctr
4215 Pkwy ... Pigeon Forge TN 37863 865-453-7155 379
Web: www.smokyshadows.com

Smoky's Club 3005 University Ave ... Madison WI 53705 608-233-2120 671
Web: www.smokysclub.com

Smolin, Lupin & Company PA
165 Passaic Ave 4th Fl ... Fairfield NJ 07004 973-439-7200 2
Web: www.smolin.com

Smoll & Banning CPAs LLC
2410 Central Ave ... Dodge City KS 67801 620-225-6100 2
TF: 800-499-8881 ■ *Web:* smollbanning.com

Smoot Construction Co
1907 Leonard Ave ... Columbus OH 43219 614-253-9000 186
Web: www.smootconstruction.com

Smooth Fusion Inc 5502 58th St Ste 500 ... Lubbock TX 79414 806-771-3873 177
Web: www.smoothfusion.com

Smooth Solutions Inc 300-2 Route 17 S ... Lodi NJ 07644 973-249-6666 180
Web: smoothsolutions.com

Smooth-On Inc 2000 St John St ... Easton PA 18042 610-252-5800 252-6200 43
TF: 800-762-0744 ■ *Web:* www.smooth-on.com

Smp Communications Corp
7626 E Greenway Rd Ste 100 ... Scottsdale AZ 85260 480-905-4100 514
TF: 888-796-3342 ■ *Web:* smpcom.com

Listing	Phone	Fax	Class
SMPS (Society for Marketing Professional Services) 99 Canal Ctr Plaza .... Alexandria VA 22314 *TF:* 800-292-7677 ■ *Web:* www.smps.org	703-549-6117	549-2498	49-18
SMPTE (Society of Motion Picture & Television Engineers) 3 Barker Ave .... White Plains NY 10601 *Web:* www.smpte.org	914-761-1100	761-3115	48-4
SMR Technologies Inc 93 Nettie Fenwick Rd .... Fenwick WV 26202 *TF:* 800-767-6899 ■ *Web:* www.smrtech.com	304-846-6636		676
SMS (Systems Maintenance Services Inc) 10420 Harris Oaks Blvd Ste C .... Charlotte NC 28269 *TF:* 877-405-0330 ■ *Web:* www.sysmaint.com	877-405-0330		175
SMS (Senior Market Sales Inc) 8420 W Dodge Rd Ste 510 .... Omaha NE 68114 *TF:* 800-786-5566 ■ *Web:* www.seniormarketsales.com	402-397-3311	397-0455	390
SMS (Saginaw Machine Systems) 800 N Hamilton St .... Saginaw MI 48602 *Web:* www.saginawmachine.com	989-753-8465		455
SMS Concast America Inc 100 Sandusky St .... Pittsburgh PA 15212 *Web:* www.sms-concast.ch	412-237-8950	237-8951	261
SMS Data Products Group Inc 1751 Pinnacle Dr 12th Fl .... McLean VA 22102 **Fax Area Code: 703* ■ *TF:* 800-331-1767 ■ *Web:* www.sms.com	800-331-1767	356-4831*	180
SMS Demag Inc 100 Sandusky St .... Pittsburgh PA 15212 *Web:* sms-millcraft.us	412-231-1200	231-3995	261
Sms Direct Inc 7540 Mason King Ct .... Manassas VA 20109 *Web:* www.smsdirect.com	703-392-0123		195
SMS Financial LLC 6829 N 12th St .... Phoenix AZ 85014 *Web:* smsfinancial.net	602-944-0624		401
SMS Marketing Services Inc 777 Terrace Ave Ste 401 .... Hasbrouck Heights NJ 07604 *Web:* www.sms-inc.com	201-865-5800		5
SMS Productions Inc 10555 Guilford Rd Ste 114 .... Jessup MD 20794 *TF:* 800-289-7671 ■ *Web:* www.smsproductions.com	301-953-0011		627
SMS proTECH 1089 Fairington Dr .... Sidney OH 45365 *TF:* 800-870-4340 ■ *Web:* perryprotech.com	937-498-7080		624
SMT Farms 8420 US 95 .... Yuma AZ 85365	928-341-9616		10-11
SMT Inc 7300 ACC Blvd .... Raleigh NC 27617 *TF:* 888-214-4804 ■ *Web:* www.smtcoinc.com	919-782-4804	781-1498	697
SMTBUSA (Sumitomo Mitsui Trust Bank (USA)) 111 River St .... Hoboken NJ 07030 *Web:* logon.sumitomotrustusa.com	201-420-9470		70
SMTC Corp 635 Hood Rd .... Markham ON L3R4N6 *NASDAQ: SMTX* ■ *Web:* www.smtc.com	905-479-1810	479-1877	253
Smucker Lloyd (Rep R - PA) 516 Cannon HOB .... Washington DC 20515 *Web:* smucker.house.gov	202-225-2411	225-2013	342-2
Smuggler's Inn 6920 MacLeod Trl S .... Calgary AB T2H0L3 *Web:* www.smugglers.ca	403-253-5355		671
Smugglers Notch State Park 6443 Mountain Rd .... Stowe VT 05672 *Web:* www.vtstateparks.com	802-253-4014		565
Smugglers' Notch Resort 4323 Vermont Rt 108 S .... Jeffersonville VT 05464 *TF:* 800-451-8752 ■ *Web:* www.smuggs.com	802-644-8851	644-1230	669
SMW Autoblok Corp 285 Egidi Dr .... Wheeling IL 60090 *Web:* www.smwautoblok.com	847-215-0591		358
SMWIA (Smart Union) 1750 New York Ave NW 6th Fl .... Washington DC 20006 *TF:* 800-457-7694 ■ *Web:* www.smwia.org	202-662-0800	662-0894	49-3
Smyth Cos Inc 1085 Snelling Ave N .... Saint Paul MN 55108 *TF:* 800-473-3464 ■ *Web:* www.smythco.com	651-646-4544		413
Smyth County 109 W Main St Rm 144 .... Marion VA 24354 *Web:* www.smythcounty.org	276-782-4044	782-4045	338
Smyth County Community Hospital 565 Radio Hill Rd .... Marion VA 24354 *Web:* www.mountainstateshealth.com/scch	276-378-1000		374-3
Smythe 700 - 355 Burrard St .... Vancouver BC V6C2G8 *Web:* www.smythecpa.com	604-687-1231		2
Smythe Volvo Inc 40 River Rd .... Summit NJ 07901 *Web:* smythevolvo.com	908-273-4200		57
SNA (School Nutrition Assn) 700 S Washington St Ste 300 .... Alexandria VA 22314 *TF:* 800-877-8822 ■ *Web:* www.schoolnutrition.org	703-739-3900	739-3915	49-6
SNAC (Saint Norbert Arts & Cultural Centre) 100 Rue des Ruines du Monastere .... Winnipeg MB R3V1B9 *Web:* www.snac.mb.ca	204-269-0564	261-1927	50-2
SNAC international 1600 Wilson Blvd Ste 650 .... Arlington VA 22209 *TF:* 800-628-1334 ■ *Web:* www.sfa.org	703-836-4500		49-6
Snack Factory LLC 11 Tamarack Cir .... Skillman NJ 08558 *Web:* www.snackfactory.com	609-683-5400		96
Snacks Unlimited 1 General Mills Blvd .... Minneapolis MN 55426 *TF:* 800-248-7310 ■ *Web:* www.generalmills.com	763-764-7600		296-35
Snake Creek Recreation Area 35316 SD Hwy 44 .... Platte SD 57369 *Web:* gfp.sd.gov	605-337-2587		565
Snake Den State Park 2321 Hartford Ave .... Johnston RI 02919 *Web:* www.riparks.com	401-222-2632		565
Snake River Brewing Co 265 S Millward St .... Jackson WY 83001 *Web:* www.snakeriverbrewing.com	307-739-2337		671
Snake River Correctional Institution 777 Stanton Blvd .... Ontario OR 97914 *TF:* 800-454-1207 ■ *Web:* www.oregon.gov	541-881-5000	881-5009	213
Snake River Grill 84 E Broadway .... Jackson WY 83001 *Web:* www.snakerivergrill.com	307-733-0557		671
Snake River Lodge & Spa 7710 Granite Loop Rd .... Teton Village WY 83025 *Web:* www.snakeriverlodge.rockresorts.com	307-732-6000		378
SNAME (Society of Naval Architects & Marine Engineers) 601 Pavonia Ave Ste 400 .... Jersey City NJ 07306 *TF:* 800-798-2188 ■ *Web:* www.sname.org	201-798-4800	798-4975	49-21
SNAP (Survivors Network of Those Abused by Priests) PO Box 6416 .... Chicago IL 60680 *TF:* 877-762-7432 ■ *Web:* www.snapnetwork.org	312-455-1499		48-21
Snap Inc 4080 Lafayette Ctr Dr Ste 340 .... Chantilly VA 20151 *TF:* 866-234-7627 ■ *Web:* www.snapinc.net	703-393-6400		180
Snap Surveys Ltd 210 Commerce Way Ste 200 .... Portsmouth NH 03801 *Web:* www.snapsurveys.com	603-610-8700		809
Snapdragon Associates Llc 8 Commerce Dr Ste 102A .... Bedford NH 03110 *TF:* 800-667-1264 ■ *Web:* www.snapdragonassociates.com	603-621-9037		260
Snapfinger 3025 Windward Plaza Ste 150 .... Alpharetta GA 30005 *Web:* www.snapfinger.com	678-739-4650		387
SnapGoods Inc 155 Water St .... Brooklyn NY 11201 *Web:* www.snapgoods.com	347-651-0845		387
Snap-on Credit LLC 950 Technology Way Ste 301 .... Libertyville IL 60048 *TF:* 877-777-8455 ■ *Web:* www.snaponcredit.com	877-777-8455	777-9375	216
Snap-on Diagnostics 420 Barclay Blvd .... Lincolnshire IL 60069 *TF:* 800-424-7226 ■ *Web:* www1.snapon.com	847-478-0700		248
Snap-on Inc 2801 80th St .... Kenosha WI 53143 *NYSE: SNA* ■ *TF:* 877-762-7664 ■ *Web:* www.snapon.com	262-656-5200	656-5577	758
SnapOne Inc 3490 Route 1 Bldg 16 .... Princeton NJ 08540	609-720-1900		736
Snapping Shoals Electric Membership Corp 14750 Brown Bridge Rd .... Covington GA 30016 *TF:* 888-999-1416 ■ *Web:* ssemc.com	770-786-3484		245
Snappy Tomato Pizza Co 6111 A Burgundy Hill Dr .... Burlington KY 41005 *TF:* 888-463-7627 ■ *Web:* www.snappytomato.com	859-525-4680	525-4686	670
Snap-Tite Autoclave Engineers Div 8325 Hessinger Dr .... Erie PA 16509 *TF:* 800-458-0409 ■ *Web:* snap-tite.com	814-838-5700		91
Snap-Tite Inc 8325 Hessinger Dr .... Erie PA 16509 *Web:* www.snap-tite.com	814-838-5700		595
Snaptron Inc 960 Diamond Valley Dr .... Windsor CO 80550 *Web:* www.snaptron.com	970-686-5682		203
Snavely Associates Ltd 112 W Foster Ave Ste 401 .... State College PA 16804 *TF:* 800-599-4582 ■ *Web:* www.snavelyassociates.com	814-234-3672		344
SNBC (Sun Bancorp Inc) 350 Fellowship Rd Ste 101 .... Mount Laurel NJ 08054 *NASDAQ: SNBC* ■ *TF:* 800-786-9066 ■ *Web:* www.sunnationalbank.com	800-760-4786		360-2
SNBL USA Ltd 6605 Merrill Creek Pkwy .... Everett WA 98203 *Web:* snbl.com	425-407-0121		668
SNC (Sierra Nevada Corp) 444 Salomon Cir .... Sparks NV 89434 *Web:* www.sncorp.com	775-331-0222	331-0370	253
SNC Lavalin Group Inc 455 Rene-Levesque Blvd W .... Montreal QC H2Z1Z3 *TSE: SNC* ■ *Web:* www.snclavalin.com	514-393-1000	866-0795	261
SNC Mfg Company Inc 101 W Waukau Ave .... Oshkosh WI 54902 *TF:* 800-558-3325 ■ *Web:* www.sncmfg.com	920-231-7370	231-1090	253
SNC-Lavalin 455 Ren,-L,vesque Blvd W .... Montreal QC H2Z1Z3 *Web:* www.snclavalin.com/en	514-393-1000		192
SNC-Lavalin 19015 N Creek Pkwy Ste 300 .... Bothell WA 98011 *Web:* www.slthermal.com	425-489-8000		579
SND (Society for News Design) 424 E Central Blvd Ste 406 .... Orlando FL 32801 *Web:* www.snd.org	407-420-7748	420-7697	49-14
SNE Enterprises Inc 880 Southview Dr .... Mosinee WI 54455 *TF:* 800-826-5509 ■ *Web:* crestlinewindows.com	715-693-7000		236
Snead State Community College 220 N Walnut St PO Box 734 .... Boaz AL 35957 **Fax: Admissions* ■ *Web:* www.snead.edu	256-593-5120	593-7180*	162
Sneades Ace Home Center Inc 1750 Prosper Ln .... Owings MD 20736 *Web:* acehardware.com	410-257-2963		364
Sneakers Sports Bar & Grill 207 W Superior St .... Duluth MN 55802	218-727-7494		671
Sneed Elementary School 9855 Pagewood Ln .... Houston TX 77042 *Web:* sneed.aliefisd.net	713-789-6979		685
Snell & Wilmer LLP 1 Arizona Ctr 400 E Van Buren St Ste 1900 .... Phoenix AZ 85004 *TF:* 800-322-0430 ■ *Web:* www.swlaw.com	602-382-6000	382-6070	428
Snell Acoustics 300 Jubilee Dr .... Peabody MA 01960 *Web:* www.snellacoustics.com	978-538-6262		52
Snell House 21 Atlantic Ave .... Bar Harbor ME 04609 *TF:* 866-763-5524 ■ *Web:* www.snellhouse.com	207-288-8004		379
Snell MotorsInc 1900 Madison Ave .... Mankato MN 56001 *Web:* snellmotors.com	507-345-4626		57
Snellings Walters Insurance Agency 1117 Perimeter Ctr W W101 .... Atlanta GA 30338 *Web:* www.snellingswalters.com	770-396-9600		390
Snelson Company Inc 601 W State St .... Sedro Woolley WA 98284 *TF:* 800-624-6536 ■ *Web:* www.snelsonco.com	360-856-6511	856-5816	188-10
Snethkamp Chrysler Dodge Jeep Ram 11600 Telegraph Rd .... Redford MI 48239 *TF:* 888-455-6146 ■ *Web:* www.snethkampchryslerjeep.net	313-255-2700		516
SNFC (Security National Financial Corp) 5300 South 360 West Ste 250 PO Box 57250 .... Salt Lake City UT 84123 *NASDAQ: SNFCA* ■ *TF:* 800-574-7117 ■ *Web:* www.securitynational.com	801-264-1060		391-2
SNI (Southern Newspapers Inc) 5701 Woodway Dr .... Houston TX 77057 *Web:* sninews.com	713-266-5481	266-1847	637-8
Snider Industries Llp 3311 Sue Belle Lake Rd .... Marshall TX 75670 *Web:* www.sniderindustries.com	903-938-9221		683
Snipp Interactive Inc 6708 Tulip Hill Terr .... Bethesda MD 20816 *Web:* www.snipp.com	604-718-5454		195
Snite Museum of Art University of Notre Dame .... Notre Dame IN 46556 *Web:* sniteartmuseum.nd.edu	574-631-5466	631-8501	520

Phone | Fax | Class

SNK America Inc
1150 Feehanville Dr .... Mount Prospect IL 60056 847-364-0801 364-4363 455
Web: www.snkamerica.com

SNL (Sandia National Laboratories - California)
7011 E Ave PO Box 969 .... Livermore CA 94551 925-294-3000 668
Web: www.sandia.gov

SNL (Sandia National Laboratories - New Mexico)
1515 Eubank SE PO Box 5800 .... Albuquerque NM 87123 505-845-0011 668
TF: 800-356-4872 ■ *Web:* www.sandia.gov

SNM (Society of Nuclear Medicine)
1850 Samuel Morse Dr .... Reston VA 20190 703-708-9000 708-9015 49-8
TF: 888-633-5343 ■ *Web:* snmmi.org

SNMP Research International Inc
3001 Kimberlin Heights Rd .... Knoxville TN 37920 865-579-3311 579-6565 178-12
TF: 877-644-5866 ■ *Web:* www.snmp.com

Snodgrass & Son's Construction Company Inc
2700 S George Washington Bldg .... Wichita KS 67210 316-687-3110 687-5853 685
Web: snodgrassconstruction.com

Snohomish County 3000 Rockefeller Ave .... Everett WA 98201 425-388-3411 338
TF: 800-584-3578 ■ *Web:* snohomishcountywa.gov

Snohomish Flying Service Inc
9900 Airport Way .... Snohomish WA 98296 360-568-1541 568-6034 63
TF: 800-827-1000 ■ *Web:* www.snohomishflying.com

Snoopy's Pier
13313 S Padre Island Dr .... Corpus Christi TX 78418 361-949-8815 671
Web: snoopyspier.com

Snooth Inc 240 E Roemer Way .... Santa Maria CA 10016 646-723-4328 387
Web: www.snooth.com

Snoqualmie Entertainment Authority
37500 SE N Bend Way .... Snoqualmie WA 98065 425-888-1234 133
Web: www.snocasino.com

Snorkel 2009 Roseport Rd .... Elwood KS 66024 785-989-3000 989-3070 470
TF: 800-255-0317 ■ *Web:* www.snorkellifts.com

Snow Canyon State Park
1002 Snow Canyon Dr .... Ivins UT 84738 435-628-2255 565
Web: www.stateparks.utah.gov

Snow Christensen & Martineau
10 Exchange Pl .... Salt Lake City UT 84111 801-521-9000 428
Web: www.scmlaw.com

Snow College
150 College Ave PO Box 1037 .... Ephraim UT 84627 435-283-7000 283-7157* 162
**Fax:* Admissions ■ *TF:* 800-848-3399 ■ *Web:* www.snow.edu

Snow Goer Magazine
10405 Sixth Ave N Ste 210 .... Plymouth MN 55441 800-710-5249 457-20
TF: 800-710-5249 ■ *Web:* www.snowgoer.com

Snow Hill Chamber of Commerce
5485 Airport Terminal Rd .... Salisbury MD 21804 410-632-2080 139
TF: 800-852-0335 ■ *Web:* www.snowhillmd.com

Snow Jr & King Inc 2415 Church St .... Norfolk VA 23504 757-627-8621 189-7
Web: www.snowjrandking.com

Snow King Resort
400 E Snow King Ave Jackson Hole .... Jackson WY 83001 307-733-5200 733-4086 669
TF: 800-522-5464 ■ *Web:* www.snowking.com

Snow Valley Mountain Resort
35100 State Hwy 18 PO Box 2337 .... Running Springs CA 92382 909-867-2751 867-7687 669
TF: 800-680-7669 ■ *Web:* www.snow-valley.com

Snow's/Doxsee Inc 994 Ocean Dr .... Cape May NJ 08204 609-884-0440 296-13

Snowbasin Ski Resort
3925 E Snowbasin Rd .... Huntsville UT 84317 801-620-1100 669
TF: 888-437-5488 ■ *Web:* www.snowbasin.com

SnowBear Ltd 155 Dawson Rd .... Guelph ON N1H1C1 519-767-1115 480
TF: 800-767-1115 ■ *Web:* www.snowbear.com

Snowbird Mountain Lodge
4633 Santeetlah Rd .... Robbinsville NC 28771 828-479-3433 479-3473 379
TF: 800-941-9290 ■ *Web:* www.snowbirdlodge.com

Snowbird Ski & Summer Resort
Hwy 210 PO Box 929000 .... Snowbird UT 84092 801-742-2222 947-8227 669
TF: 800-453-3000 ■ *Web:* www.snowbird.com

Snowbound Software
309 Waverley Oaks Rd Ste 401 .... Waltham MA 02452 617-607-2000 607-2002 178-10
Web: www.snowbound.com

Snowdale State Park 501 S 439 .... Salina OK 74361 918-434-2651 435-2101 565
TF: 800-622-6317 ■ *Web:* www.travelok.com

Snowfire 100 Us Rt 2 .... Waterbury VT 05676 802-244-5606 57
TF: 800-287-5606 ■ *Web:* snowfireauto.com

Snowline Engineering
4261 Business Dr .... Cameron Park CA 95682 530-677-2675 261
TF: 800-361-6083 ■ *Web:* www.snowlineengineering.com

Snowmass Club PO Box G-2 .... Snowmass Village CO 81615 970-923-5600 923-6944 669
Web: www.snowmassclub.com

Snowshoe Mountain Resort
10 Snowshoe Dr .... Snowshoe WV 26209 304-572-1000 669
TF: 877-441-4386 ■ *Web:* www.snowshoemtn.com

SnowSports Industries America (SIA)
8377 Greensboro Dr Ste B .... McLean VA 22102 703-556-9020 821-8276 49-4
TF: 800-213-7193 ■ *Web:* www.snowsports.org

Snowy Owl Inn 41 Village Rd .... Waterville Valley NH 03215 603-236-8383 379
TF: 800-766-9969 ■ *Web:* www.snowyowlinn.com

SNPRC (Southwest National Primate Research Ctr)
Texas Biomedical Research Institute
PO Box 760549 .... San Antonio TX 78245 210-258-9400 668
Web: www.snprc.org

SNtial Technologies Inc
150 N Michigan Ave Ste 2800 .... Chicago IL 60601 630-452-4735 317
Web: www.sntialtech.com

Snug Harbor Cultural Ctr
1000 Richmond Terr .... Staten Island NY 10301 718-448-2500 572
Web: www.snug-harbor.org

Snuggle Bugz 3245 Fairview St .... Burlington ON L7N3L1 905-631-0005 321
Web: snugglebugz.ca

SNUPI Technologies Inc
4512 University Way NE .... Seattle WA 98105 206-673-2707 693
Web: www.wallyhome.com

Snyder & Assoc Inc PO Box 1159 .... Ankeny IA 50023 515-964-2020 964-7938 261
TF General: 888-964-2020 ■ *Web:* www.snyder-associates.com

Snyder Brothers Inc
1 Glade Park Dr .... Kittanning PA 16201 724-548-8101 536
Web: www.snyderbrothersinc.com

Snyder Capital Corp 5110 Pk Ln .... Dallas TX 75220 214-754-0500 14

Snyder Chevrolet 524 N Perry St .... Napoleon OH 43545 567-341-4132 57
TF: 800-569-3957 ■ *Web:* www.snyderchevrolet.com

Snyder County 9 W Market St .... Middleburg PA 17842 570-837-4207 837-4282 338
Web: www.snydercounty.org

Snyder Industries Inc 4700 Fremont St .... Lincoln NE 68504 402-467-5221 465-1220 199
Web: www.snydernet.com

Snyder Langston Inc 17962 Cowan St .... Irvine CA 92614 949-863-9200 863-1087 186
Web: www.snyderlangston.com

Snyder Manufacturing Corp
1541 W Cowles St .... Long Beach CA 90813 562-432-2038 151
TF: 800-395-6478 ■ *Web:* www.snydermanufacturing.com

Snyder of Berlin 1313 Stadium Dr .... Berlin PA 15530 814-267-4641 296-35
TF: 888-257-8042 ■ *Web:* www.snyderofberlin.com

Snyder Paper Corp
250 26th St Dr SE PO Box 758 .... Hickory NC 28603 828-328-2501 222-8562* 559
**Fax Area Code:* 800 ■ *TF:* 800-222-8562 ■ *Web:* www.snydersolutions.com

Snyder Rick (R) PO Box 30013 .... Lansing MI 48909 517-373-3400 343
Web: www.michigan.gov/gov

Snyder Roofing & Sheet Metal Inc
12650 SW Hall Blvd .... Tigard OR 97223 503-620-5252 684-3310 189-12
Web: snyder-builds.com

Snyder Tire 401 Cadiz Rd .... Steubenville OH 43953 740-264-5543 755
TF: 800-967-8473 ■ *Web:* www.snydertire.com

Snyder's of Hanover
1250 York St PO Box 6917 .... Hanover PA 17331 717-632-4477 632-7207 296-9
TF: 800-233-7125 ■ *Web:* snyderslance.com

So Low Environmental Equipment Company Inc
10310 Spartan Dr .... Cincinnati OH 45215 513-772-9410 14
Web: www.so-low.com

So Ya Japenese Restaurant
12715 Warwick Blvd
Corner Shoppes Center .... Newport News VA 23606 757-930-0156 671

So. Cal. Sandbags Inc 12620 Bosley Ln .... Corona CA 92883 951-277-3404 385
TF: 800-834-8682 ■ *Web:* www.socalsandbags.com

SOA (Society of Actuaries)
475 N Martingale Rd Ste 600 .... Schaumburg IL 60173 847-706-3500 706-3599 49-9
Web: www.soa.org

SOAP Group, The PO Box 7828 .... Portland ME 04112 207-772-0066 195
Web: www.thesoapgroup.com

Soap Plant 4633 Hollywood Blvd .... Los Angeles CA 90027 323-663-0122 327
Web: www.soapplant.com

SoapNet LLC 500 S Buena Vista St .... Burbank CA 91521 818-560-1000 740

SOAProjects Inc
495 N Whisman Rd Ste 100 .... Mountain View CA 94043 650-960-9900 196
Web: soaprojects.com

Soapy Smith's Pioneer Restaurant
543 Second Ave .... Fairbanks AK 99701 907-451-8380 671

SOAR (Soar Corp)
5200 Constitution Ave NE .... Albuquerque NM 87110 505-268-6110 464-0445* 657
**Fax Area Code:* 215 ■ *TF:* 866-616-4450

Soar Corp (SOAR)
5200 Constitution Ave NE .... Albuquerque NM 87110 505-268-6110 464-0445* 657
**Fax Area Code:* 215 ■ *TF:* 866-616-4450

Soaring Eagle Casino & Resort
6800 E Soaring Eagle Blvd .... Mount Pleasant MI 48858 888-732-4537 133
TF: 888-732-4537 ■ *Web:* www.soaringeaglecasino.com

Soaring Society of America
Jack Gomez Blvd .... Hobbs NM 00240 575-392-1177 533
Web: www.ssa.org

Soave Enterprises LLC
3400 E Lafayette St .... Detroit MI 48207 313-567-7000 567-0966 686
Web: www.soave.com

Soba 5847 Ellsworth Ave .... Pittsburgh PA 15232 412-362-5656 671
Web: www.bigburrito.com

SoBe Seafood Co 3100 Clarendon Blvd .... Arlington VA 22201 703-527-1283 671

Sobel & Company LLC
293 Eisenhower Pkwy Ste 290 .... Livingston NJ 07039 973-994-9494 2
TF: 800-471-2468 ■ *Web:* www.sobel-cpa.com

Sobel Westex Inc 2670 Western Ave .... Las Vegas NV 89109 888-887-6235 361
TF: 888-887-6235 ■ *Web:* www.sobelwestex.com

Sobeys Inc 115 King St .... Stellarton NS B0K1S0 902-752-8371 345
TF: 800-723-3929 ■ *Web:* www.sobeys.com

Sobik's Subs
620 Crown Oak Ctr Dr Ste 104 .... Longwood FL 32750 407-671-2600 670
Web: www.sobiks.com

Soboba Casino 23333 Soboba Rd .... San Jacinto CA 92583 951-665-1000 452
TF: 866-476-2622 ■ *Web:* www.soboba.com

Soby's 207 S Main St .... Greenville SC 29601 864-232-7007 671
Web: www.sobys.com

SOCAN 41 Valleybrook Dr .... Toronto ON M3B2S6 416-445-8700 138
TF: 800-557-6226 ■ *Web:* www.socan.ca

SOCAP International
625 N Washington St Ste 304 .... Alexandria VA 22314 703-519-3700 549-4886 48-10
TF: 800-477-7845 ■ *Web:* www.socap.org

Soccer 4 All
1306 Fm 1092 Rd Ste 101 .... Missouri City TX 77459 281-499-6665 711
Web: www.soccer4all.com

Soccer City LLC 5770 Springdale Rd .... Cincinnati OH 45247 513-741-8480 720
Web: indoorsoccercity.com

Social & Economic Sciences Research Ctr (SESRC)
Washington State University
Wilson Hall Rm 133 PO Box 644014 .... Pullman WA 99164 509-335-1511 335-0116 668
TF: 800-932-5393 ■ *Web:* www.sesrc.wsu.edu

Social & Scientific Systems Inc
8757 Georgia Ave 12th Fl .... Silver Spring MD 20910 301-628-3000 628-3001 180
TF: 800-984-3775 ■ *Web:* www.s-3.com

Social Annex Inc
5301 Beethoven St Ste 260 .... Los Angeles CA 90066 866-802-8806 387
TF: 866-802-8806 ■ *Web:* www.socialannex.com

Social Communications Co
650 Castro St Ste 100 .... Mountain View CA 94041 650-425-7801 194
Web: www.sococo.com

Social Compact 113 S W St .... Alexandria VA 22314 202-547-2581 652
Web: www.socialcompact.org

Social Science Research Council (SSRC)
810 Seventh Ave .... New York NY 10019 212-377-2700 377-2727 634
Web: www.ssrc.org

Name / Address	Phone	Fax	Class
Social Security Administration (SSA) 6401 Security Blvd........................Baltimore MD 21235 *TF:* 800-772-1213 ■ *Web:* www.ssa.gov	410-965-8904		340-20
Social Security Administration Regional Offices			
Region 1 JFK Federal Bldg Rm 1900............Boston MA 02203 *TF:* 800-451-9800 ■ *Web:* www.ssa.gov/boston	617-565-2870	565-2143	340-20
Region 2 26 Federal Plaza Rm 40-102.........New York NY 10278 *TF:* 800-772-1213 ■ *Web:* www.ssa.gov/ny	212-264-4036		340-20
Region 4 61 Forsyth St SW Ste 23T30...........Atlanta GA 30303 *TF:* 800-772-1213 ■ *Web:* www.ssa.gov/atlanta	800-772-1213		340-20
Region 5 600 W Madison St PO Box 8280.......Chicago IL 60680 *TF:* 800-772-1213 ■ *Web:* www.ssa.gov	312-575-4050		340-20
Social Security Advisory Board 400 Virginia Ave SW Ste 625..............Washington DC 20024 *Web:* www.ssab.gov	202-475-7700	475-7715	340-20
Social Strategy1 5000 Sawgrass Village Cir Ste 30.....Ponte Vedra Beach FL 32082 *TF:* 877-771-3366 ■ *Web:* www.socialstrategy1.com	877-771-3366		387
Social Studies School Service 10200 Jefferson Blvd......................Culver City CA 90232 **Fax Area Code:* 800 ■ *TF:* 800-421-4246 ■ *Web:* www.socialstudies.com	310-839-2436	944-5432*	95
Social Work Magazine 750 First St NE Ste 700.....................Washington DC 20002 *TF:* 800-227-3590 ■ *Web:* www.naswpress.org	202-408-8600	336-8312	457-16
Social Work p.r.n. Inc 10680 Barkley Ste 100..................Overland Park KS 66212 *TF:* 800-595-9648 ■ *Web:* www.socialworkprn.com	913-648-2984		260
SocialChorus 703 Market St Ste 470..................San Francisco CA 94103 *Web:* www.socialchorus.com	415-655-2700		387
SocialCode LLC 151 W 26th St Fl 9...........New York NY 10001 *TF:* 844-608-4610 ■ *Web:* www.socialcode.com	844-608-4610		5
Sociale 3665 Sacramento St..............San Francisco CA 94118 *Web:* sfsociale.com	415-921-3200		671
SocialFlow Inc 52 Vanderbilt Ave 12th Fl....................New York NY 10017 *Web:* www.socialflow.com	212-883-9844		387
Socialist Labor Party of America PO Box 218..........................Mountain View CA 94042 *TF:* 800-283-8647 ■ *Web:* www.slp.org	408-280-7266	280-6964	616
Societe Des Traversiers Du Quebec 250 Rue Saint-Paul.........................Quebec QC G1K9K9 *Web:* www.traversiers.com	418-643-2019		342
Societe Generale USA 245 Park Ave...........New York NY 10167 *Web:* cib.societegenerale.com/en	212-278-6000		70
Societe Grics 5100 Rue Sherbrooke E...........Montreal QC H1V3R9 *Web:* grics.ca	514-251-3700		225
Society Consulting LLC 901 104th Ave NE..........................Bellevue WA 98004 *Web:* societyconsulting.com	206-420-3500		180
Society for Academic Emergency Medicine (SAEM) 2340 S River Rd Ste 200...................Des Plaines IL 60018 *TF:* 800-829-1040 ■ *Web:* www.saem.org	847-813-9823	813-5450	49-8
Society for American Archaeology (SAA) 900 Second St NE Ste 12...................Washington DC 20002 *TF:* 800-759-5219 ■ *Web:* www.saa.org	202-789-8200	789-0284	49-5
Society for Biomaterials 1120 Rte 73 Ste 200....................Mount Laurel NJ 08054 *Web:* www.biomaterials.org	856-439-0826	439-0525	49-19
Society for College & University Planning (SCUP) 339 E Liberty St Ste 300....................Ann Arbor MI 48104 *TF:* 800-228-5424 ■ *Web:* www.scup.org	734-669-3270	998-6532	49-5
Society for Ecological Restoration International (SERI) 1017 O St NW.............................Washington DC 20001 **Fax Area Code:* 270 ■ *TF:* 866-895-4735 ■ *Web:* ser.org	202-299-9518	626-5485*	48-13
Society for Ethnomusicology (SEM) Indiana University 1165 E 3rd St Morrison Hall 005...........Bloomington IN 47405 *TF:* 800-933-9330 ■ *Web:* www.ethnomusicology.org	812-855-6672	855-6673	48-4
Society for Experimental Mechanics Inc (SEM) 7 School St...................................Bethel CT 06801 *TF:* 800-627-8258 ■ *Web:* www.sem.org	203-790-6373	790-4472	49-19
Society for Healthcare Epidemiology of America 1300 Wilson Blvd Ste 300...................Arlington VA 22209 *TF:* 800-358-9295 ■ *Web:* www.shea-online.org	703-684-1006	684-1009	49-8
Society for Healthcare Strategy & Market Development (SHSMD) 155 N Wacker Dr Ste 400......................Chicago IL 60606 *TF:* 800-242-2626 ■ *Web:* www.shsmd.org	312-422-3888	278-0883	49-8
Society for Human Resource Management (SHRM) 1800 Duke St...........................Alexandria VA 22314 *TF:* 800-283-7476 ■ *Web:* www.shrm.org	703-548-3440	836-0367	49-12
Society for Imaging Science & Technology (IS&T) 7003 Kilworth Ln........................Springfield VA 22151 *TF:* 800-654-2240 ■ *Web:* www.imaging.org	703-642-9090	642-9094	49-16
Society for Industrial & Applied Mathematics (SIAM) 3600 Market St 6th Fl..................Philadelphia PA 19104 *TF:* 800-447-7426 ■ *Web:* www.siam.org	215-382-9800	386-7999	49-19
Society for Information Display (SID) 1475 S Bascom Ave Ste 114.................Campbell CA 95008 *TF:* 800-350-0111 ■ *Web:* www.sid.org	408-879-3901	879-3833	48-9
Society for Information Management (SIM) 15000 Commerce Pkwy Ste C..............Mount Laurel NJ 08054 *TF:* 800-387-9746 ■ *Web:* www.simnet.org	312-527-6734		48-9
Society for Integrative & Comparative Biology (SICB) 1313 Dolley Madison Blvd Ste 402.............McLean VA 22101 *TF:* 800-955-1236 ■ *Web:* www.sicb.org	703-790-1745	790-2672	49-19
Society for Investigative Dermatology Inc (SID) 526 Superior Ave E Ste 540..................Cleveland OH 44114 *Web:* www.sidnet.org	216-579-9300	579-9333	49-8
Society for Marketing Professional Services (SMPS) 99 Canal Ctr Plaza.......................Alexandria VA 22314 *TF:* 800-292-7677 ■ *Web:* www.smps.org	703-549-6117	549-2498	49-18
Society for Medical Decision Making 390 Amwell Rd Ste 402................Hillsborough NJ 08844 *Web:* www.smdm.org	908-359-1184	450-1119	49-8
Society for Mining Metallurgy & Exploration Inc (SME) 8307 Shaffer Pkwy...........................Littleton CO 80127 *TF:* 800-763-3132 ■ *Web:* www.smenet.org	303-973-9550	973-3845	49-13
Society for Modeling & Simulation International (SCS) 11315 Rancho Bernardo Rd Ste 139...........San Diego CA 92127 *Web:* www.scs.org	858-277-3888	277-3930	48-9
Society for Neuroscience (SFN) 1121 14th St NW Ste 1010................Washington DC 20005 *Web:* www.sfn.org	202-962-4000	962-4941	49-8
Society for News Design (SND) 424 E Central Blvd Ste 406...................Orlando FL 32801 *Web:* www.snd.org	407-420-7748	420-7697	49-14
Society for Protective Coatings (SSPC) 40 24th St 6th Fl.........................Pittsburgh PA 15222 *TF:* 877-281-7772 ■ *Web:* www.sspc.org	412-281-2331	281-9995	49-13
Society for Research in Child Development (SRCD) 2950 S State St Ste 401...................Ann Arbor MI 48104 *Web:* www.srcd.org	734-926-0600	926-0601	49-5
Society for Risk Analysis (SRA) 1313 Dolley Madison Blvd Ste 402...........McLean VA 22101 *Web:* www.sra.org	703-790-1745	790-2672	49-19
Society for Scholarly Publishing (SSP) 10200 W 44th Ave Ste 304...............Wheat Ridge CO 80033 *Web:* www.sspnet.org	303-422-3914		49-16
Society for Sedimentary Geology (SEPM) 4111 S Darlington Ste 100.......................Tulsa OK 74135 *TF:* 800-865-9765 ■ *Web:* www.sepm.org	918-610-3361	621-1685	49-19
Society for Social Work Leadership in Health Care 100 N 20th St 4th Fl......................Philadelphia PA 19103 *TF:* 866-237-9542 ■ *Web:* www.sswlhc.org	215-599-6134	564-2175	49-15
Society for Surgery of the Alimentary Tract (SSAT) 900 Cummings Ctr Ste 221-U...................Beverly MA 01915 *TF:* 866-849-5866 ■ *Web:* www.ssat.com	978-927-8330	524-8890	49-8
Society for Technical Communication (STC) 9401 Lee Hwy Ste 300.........................Fairfax VA 22031 *Web:* www.stc.org	703-522-4114	522-2075	49-14
Society for the Advancement of Material & Process Engineering (SAMPE) 21680 Gateway Center Dr Ste 300..........Diamond Bar CA 91765 **Fax Area Code:* 801 ■ *TF:* 800-562-7360 ■ *Web:* www.sampe.org	626-331-0616	262-1431*	49-19
Society for Vascular Surgery (SVS) 633 N St Clair St 22nd Fl......................Chicago IL 60611 *TF:* 800-258-7188 ■ *Web:* vascular.org	312-334-2300	334-2320	49-8
Society Hill Playhouse 507 S Eigth St..........................Philadelphia PA 19147 *Web:* www.societyhillplayhouse.org	215-923-0210		572
Society of Accredited Marine Surveyors Inc (SAMS) 7855 Argyle Forest Blvd Ste 203...........Jacksonville FL 32244 *TF:* 800-344-9077 ■ *Web:* www.marinesurvey.org	904-384-1494	388-3958	48-1
Society of Actuaries (SOA) 475 N Martingale Rd Ste 600.............Schaumburg IL 60173 *Web:* www.soa.org	847-706-3500	706-3599	49-9
Society of American Archivists (SAA) 17 N State St Ste 1425.......................Chicago IL 60602 *TF:* 866-722-7858 ■ *Web:* www2.archivists.org	312-606-0722		48-4
Society of American Florists (SAF) 1601 Duke St............................Alexandria VA 22314 *TF:* 800-336-4743 ■ *Web:* www.safnow.org	703-836-8700	836-8705	49-4
Society of American Foresters (SAF) 10100 Laureate way.......................Bethesda MD 20814 *TF:* 866-897-8720 ■ *Web:* www.eforester.org	301-897-8720	897-3690	48-2
Society of American Gastrointestinal & Endoscopic Surgeons (SAGES) 11300 W Olympic Blvd Ste 600............Los Angeles CA 90064 *Web:* www.sages.org	310-437-0544	437-0585	49-8
Society of American Military Engineers (SAME) 607 Prince St.............................Alexandria VA 22314 *TF:* 800-336-3097 ■ *Web:* www.same.org	703-549-3800	684-0231	48-19
Society of Animal Artists Inc 5451 Sedona Hills Dr.......................Berthoud CO 80513 *Web:* www.societyofanimalartists.com	970-532-3127	532-2537	48-4
Society of Architectural Historians (SAH) 1365 N Astor St...............................Chicago IL 60610 *Web:* www.sah.org	312-573-1365	573-1141	48-13
Society of Automotive Engineers Inc (SAE) 400 Commonwealth Dr...................Warrendale PA 15096 *TF:* 877-606-7323 ■ *Web:* www.sae.org	724-776-4841	776-0790	49-21
Society of Behavioral Medicine (SBM) 555 E Wells St Ste 1100....................Milwaukee WI 53202 *Web:* www.sbm.org	414-918-3156	276-3349	49-15
Society of Biblical Literature (SBL) The Luce Ctr 825 Houston Mill Rd..............Atlanta GA 30329 *TF:* 866-727-9955 ■ *Web:* www.sbl-site.org	404-727-3100	727-3101	48-20
Society of Broadcast Engineers Inc (SBE) 9102 N Meridian St Ste 150...............Indianapolis IN 46260 *TF:* 800-237-1776 ■ *Web:* www.sbe.org	317-846-9000	846-9120	49-14
Society of Cable Telecommunications Engineers (SCTE) 140 Philips Rd.................................Exton PA 19341 *TF:* 800-542-5040 ■ *Web:* www.scte.org	610-363-6888	363-5898	49-19
Society of California Pioneers Society of California Pioneers 300 Fourth St.........................San Francisco CA 94107 *Web:* www.californiapioneers.org	415-957-1849	957-9858	520
Society of Cardiovascular Anesthesiologists (SCA) 2209 Dickens Rd.........................Richmond VA 23230 *TF:* 800-283-6296 ■ *Web:* www.scahq.org	804-282-0084	282-0090	49-8
Society of Corporate Secretaries and Governance Professionals 240 W 35th St Ste 400.....................New York NY 10001 *Web:* main.societycorpgov.org/home	212-681-2000	681-2005	49-12
Society of Cosmetic Chemists (SCC) 120 Wall St Ste 2400.......................New York NY 10005 *Web:* www.scconline.org	212-668-1500	668-1504	49-19
Society of Critical Care Medicine (SCCM) 500 Midway Dr Ste 200...............Mount Prospect IL 60056 *Web:* www.sccm.org	847-827-6869	827-6886	49-8
Society of Decorative Painters 393 N McLean Blvd...........................Wichita KS 67203 *Web:* www.decorativepainters.org	316-269-9300	269-9191	48-18
Society of Diagnostic Medical Sonography (SDMS) 2745 Dallas Pkwy.............................Plano TX 75093 *TF:* 800-229-9506 ■ *Web:* www.sdms.org	214-473-8057	473-8563	49-8
Society of Environmental Journalists (SEJ) 1629 K St NW Ste 300...................Washington DC 20006 **Fax Area Code:* 215 ■ *Web:* www.sej.org	202-558-2300	884-8175*	49-14

Name / Address	Phone	Fax	Class
Society of Environmental Toxicology & Chemistry (SETAC) 1010 N 12th Ave.......... Pensacola FL 32501 *Web:* www.setac.org	850-469-1500	469-9778	49-19
Society of Exploration Geophysicists (SEG) 8801 S Yale Ave Ste 500 PO Box 702740.......... Tulsa OK 74137 *Web:* www.seg.org	918-497-5500	497-5557	48-12
Society of Financial Service Professionals (SFSP) 19 Campus Blvd Ste 100.......... Newtown Square PA 19073 *TF:* 800-392-6900 ■ *Web:* www.financialpro.org	610-526-2500	527-4010	49-9
Society of Gastroenterology Nurses & Assoc Inc (SGNA) 401 N Michigan Ave.......... Chicago IL 60611 *TF:* 800-245-7462 ■ *Web:* www.sgna.org	312-321-5165	673-6694	49-8
Society of Glass & Ceramic Decorators (SGCD) PO Box 2489.......... Zanesville OH 43702 *TF:* 800-444-2742 ■ *Web:* www.sgcd.org	740-588-9882	588-0245	48-4
Society of Incentive & Travel Executives (SITE) 401 N Michigan Ave.......... Chicago IL 60611 *Web:* www.siteglobal.com	312-321-5148		48-23
Society of Independent Gasoline Marketers of America (SIGMA) 3930 Pender Dr Ste 340.......... Fairfax VA 22030 *TF:* 800-922-0972 ■ *Web:* www.sigma.org	703-709-7000	709-7007	49-18
Society of Industrial & Office Realtors (SIOR) 1201 New York Ave NW Ste 350.......... Washington DC 20005 *Web:* www.sior.com	202-449-8200	216-9325	49-17
Society of Interventional Radiology (SIR) 3975 Fair Rdige Dr Ste 400 N.......... Fairfax VA 22033 *TF:* 800-488-7284 ■ *Web:* www.sirweb.org	703-691-1805	691-1855	49-8
Society of Laparoendoscopic Surgeons (SLS) 7330 SW 62nd Pl Ste 410.......... Miami FL 33143 *Web:* www.sls.org	305-665-9959	667-4123	49-8
Society of Mfg Engineers (SME) 1 SME Dr.......... Dearborn MI 48128 *TF Cust Svc:* 800-733-4763 ■ *Web:* www.sme.org	313-425-3000	425-3400	49-13
Society of Motion Picture & Television Engineers (SMPTE) 3 Barker Ave.......... White Plains NY 10601 *Web:* www.smpte.org	914-761-1100	761-3115	48-4
Society of Naval Architects & Marine Engineers (SNAME) 601 Pavonia Ave Ste 400.......... Jersey City NJ 07306 *TF:* 800-798-2188 ■ *Web:* www.sname.org	201-798-4800	798-4975	49-21
Society of Nuclear Medicine (SNM) 1850 Samuel Morse Dr.......... Reston VA 20190 *TF:* 888-633-5343 ■ *Web:* snmmi.org	703-708-9000	708-9015	49-8
Society of Petroleum Engineers (SPE) 222 Palisades Creek Dr.......... Richardson TX 75080 *TF:* 800-456-6863 ■ *Web:* www.spe.org	972-952-9393	952-9435	48-12
Society of Petrophysicists & Well Log Analysts (SPWLA) 8866 Gulf Fwy Ste 320.......... Houston TX 77017 *Web:* www.spwla.org	713-947-8727	947-7181	48-12
Society of Plastics Engineers (SPE) 13 Church Hill Rd.......... Newtown CT 06470 *Web:* www.4spe.org	203-775-0471	775-8490	49-13
Society of Professional Benefit Administrators (SPBA) 2 Wisconsin Cir Ste 670.......... Chevy Chase MD 20815 *Web:* www.spbatpa.org	301-718-7722	718-9440	49-12
Society of Professional Journalists (SPJ) 3909 N Meridian St.......... Indianapolis IN 46208 *TF:* 800-331-1212 ■ *Web:* www.spj.org	317-927-8000	920-4789	49-14
Society of Saint Andrew (SoSA) 3383 Sweet Hollow Rd.......... Big Island VA 24526 *TF:* 800-333-4597 ■ *Web:* www.endhunger.org	434-299-5956	299-5949	48-5
Society of Teachers of Family Medicine (STFM) 11400 Tomahawk Creek Pkwy Ste 540.......... Leawood KS 66211 *TF:* 800-274-7928 ■ *Web:* www.stfm.org	913-906-6000	906-6096	49-8
Society of Telecommunications Consultants (STC) 13275 California 89.......... Old Station CA 96071 *TF:* 800-782-7670 ■ *Web:* sctcconsultants.org	530-335-7313		49-20
Society of Thoracic Surgeons (STS) 633 N St Clair St Ste 2320.......... Chicago IL 60611 *TF:* 877-865-5321 ■ *Web:* www.sts.org	312-202-5800	202-5801	49-8
Society of Toxicology (SOT) 1821 Michael Faraday Dr Ste 300.......... Reston VA 20190 *TF:* 800-826-6762 ■ *Web:* www.toxicology.org	703-438-3115	438-3113	49-8
Society of Tribologists & Lubrication Engineers (STLE) 840 Busse Hwy.......... Park Ridge IL 60068 *TF:* 800-537-7683 ■ *Web:* www.stle.org	847-825-5536	825-1456	49-13
Society of Vacuum Coaters (SVC) 71 Pinon Hill Pl NE.......... Albuquerque NM 87122 *TF:* 800-443-8817 ■ *Web:* www.svc.org	505-856-7188	856-6716	49-13
Society of Women Engineers (SWE) 130 E Randolph St Ste 3500.......... Chicago IL 60601 *TF:* 877-793-4636 ■ *Web:* societyofwomenengineers.swe.org	312-596-5223	596-5252	49-19
Society'S Assets Inc 5200 Washington Ave Ste 225.......... Racine WI 53406 *TF:* 800-378-9128 ■ *Web:* societysassets.org	262-637-9128		363
Sockwell Partners Inc 800 E Blvd Ste 200.......... Charlotte NC 28203 *Web:* www.sockwell.com	704-372-1865		260
SOCMA (Synthetic Organic Chemical Manufacturers Assn) 1850 M St NW Ste 700.......... Washington DC 20036 *Web:* www.socma.com	202-721-4100	296-8120	49-19
SoCo Group Inc, The 5962 Priestly Dr.......... Carlsbad CA 92008 *Web:* www.thesocogroup.com	760-804-8460		579
Socorro County 101 Plaza St.......... Socorro NM 87801 *Web:* www.socorrochamber.org	575-835-0424		338
Socorro Electric Co-op Inc 215 Manzanares Ave PO Box H.......... Socorro NM 87801 *TF:* 800-351-7575 ■ *Web:* www.socorroelectric.com	575-835-0560		245
Socrates Academy 3909 Weddington Rd.......... Matthews NC 28105 *TF:* 800-382-6010 ■ *Web:* socratesacademy.us	704-321-1711		685
Socratic Technologies Inc 2505 Mariposa St.......... San Francisco CA 94110 *TF:* 800-576-2728 ■ *Web:* www.sotech.com	415-430-2200		668
Soderberg Mfg Company Inc 20821 Currier Rd.......... Walnut CA 91789 *TF:* 800-544-2570 ■ *Web:* www.soderberg.aero	909-595-1291		438
Soderholm Wholesale Foods 1100 Wilburn Rd.......... Sun Prairie WI 53590	608-834-9850		297-8
Sodexho 9801 Washingtonian Blvd.......... Gaithersburg MD 20878 *TF:* 888-763-3967 ■ *Web:* sodexousa.com/usen/default.aspx	301-987-4000		299
Sodexo Canada Ltd 5420 N Service Rd Ste 501.......... Burlington ON L7L6C7 *Web:* ca.sodexo.com	905-632-8592		671
Soex West USA LLC 3294 E 26th St.......... Vernon CA 90058 *Web:* www.soexgroup.de	323-264-8300		156
Sof Tec Solutions Inc 384 Inverness Pkwy # 211 Ste 211.......... Englewood CO 80112 *Web:* www.softecinc.com	303-662-1010	662-1060	225
Sofec Inc 14741 Yorktown Plaza.......... Houston TX 77040 *Web:* www.sofec.com	713-510-6600	510-6601	261
Soffront Software Inc 45437 Warm Springs Blvd.......... Fremont CA 94539 *TF:* 800-763-3766 ■ *Web:* www.soffront.com	510-413-9000	413-9027	178-1
Sofia Hotel 150 W Broadway.......... San Diego CA 92101 *TF:* 800-826-0009 ■ *Web:* www.thesofiahotel.com	619-234-9200	544-9879	379
Sofinnova Ventures Inc 3000 Sand Hill Rd Bldg 4 Ste 250.......... Menlo Park CA 94025 *Web:* www.sofinnova.com	650-681-8420	322-2037	792
Sofitel Philadelphia Hotel 120 S 17th St.......... Philadelphia PA 19103 *TF:* 800-743-0053 ■ *Web:* www.sofitel.com	215-569-8300		707
Sofradir EC Inc 373 Route 46W.......... Fairfield NJ 07004 *Web:* www.sofradir-ec.com	973-882-0211	882-0997	692
Soft Science 3921 Oceanic Dr Ste 801.......... Oceanside CA 92056 *Web:* www.softsciencetech.com	281-861-0832		177
Soft Surroundings 2280 Schuetz Rd Ste 100.......... Maryland Heights MO 63146 *Web:* www.softsurroundings.com/FAQ/?faqId=133	314-262-4949		157-6
Soft Tex Manufacturing Co 100 N Mohawk St.......... Cohoes NY 12047 *Web:* www.bedpillows.com	518-235-3645		362
Softassist Inc 700 American Ave.......... King Of Prussia PA 19406 *Web:* www.softassist.com	610-265-8484		180
Softchalk LLC 22 S Auburn Ave.......... Richmond VA 23221 *TF:* 877-638-2425 ■ *Web:* softchalk.com	877-638-2425		177
Softcom Technology Consulting Inc 10 Bay St.......... Toronto ON M5J2R8 *TF:* 800-333-7680 ■ *Web:* softcom.com	416-957-7400		225
Soft-Con Enterprises Inc 6505 Belcrest Rd Ste 120.......... Hyattsville MD 20782 *TF:* 800-613-7456 ■ *Web:* www.softcon1.com	301-429-0075		180
Softdocs Inc 920 Hemlock Dr.......... Columbia SC 29201 *Web:* www.softdocs.com	803-695-6044		177
Softech & Associates Inc 1570 Corporate Dr Ste B.......... Costa Mesa CA 92626 *TF:* 877-638-3241 ■ *Web:* www.softechis.com	714-427-1122		180
Softech Inc 28104 Orchard Lake Rd Ste 100.......... Farmington Hills MI 48334 *Web:* dentech.com	248-855-6130		177
Softechnologies Inc 1504 W Northwest Blvd Ste C.......... Spokane WA 99205 *Web:* www.softechnologies.com	509-327-4624		179
Softek International Inc 242 Old New Brunswick Rd Ste 320.......... Piscataway NJ 08854 *TF:* 800-677-1997 ■ *Web:* www.softekintl.com	732-287-3337		180
Softek Service Inc 1101 14th St NW Ste 850.......... Washington DC 20005 *TF:* 800-561-3357 ■ *Web:* www.softekdc.com	202-747-5000		177
Softek Solutions Inc 4500 W 89th St Ste 100.......... Prairie Village KS 66207 *Web:* www.softek-solutions.com	913-649-1024		525
Softential Inc 607 Herndon Pkwy Ste 202.......... Herndon VA 20170 *Web:* www.softential.com	703-650-0001		180
Softeq Development Corp 14027 Memorial Dr Ste 302.......... Houston TX 77079 *Web:* www.softeq.com	713-827-2228		177
Softerware Inc 132 Welsh Rd Ste 140.......... Horsham PA 19044 *TF:* 800-220-8111 ■ *Web:* www.softerware.com	215-628-0400	628-0585	177
Softex Inc 9300 Jollyville Rd Ste 201.......... Austin TX 78759 *TF:* 800-677-7305 ■ *Web:* www.softexinc.com	512-452-8836		809
Softgate Systems 185 Hudson St Harborside Plaza 5 - Suite 1710.......... Jersey City NJ 07302 **Fax Area Code:* 973 ■ *TF:* 888-477-7297 ■ *Web:* softgate.tionetworks.com	888-477-7297	830-1576*	509
Softlayer Technologies Inc 4849 Alpha Rd.......... Dallas TX 75244 *TF Sales:* 866-398-7638 ■ *Web:* www.softlayer.com	214-442-0600	442-0601	225
SoftLEAD Technology Partners Inc 100 S Citrus Ave Ste: 201 Ste.......... Covina CA 91723 *Web:* www.softlead.com	626-915-0001		809
Soft-Lite LLC 10250 Philipp Pkwy.......... Streetsboro OH 44241 *TF:* 800-551-1953 ■ *Web:* www.soft-lite.com	330-528-3400	528-3501	235
Softman Products LLC 13470 Washington Blvd.......... Marina Del Rey CA 90292 *Web:* www.buycheapsoftware.com	310-305-3644		177
Softmart Inc 450 Acorn Ln.......... Downingtown PA 19335 *TF Cust Svc:* 800-328-1319 ■ *Web:* www.softmart.com	610-518-4000	518-3000	174
SoftNice Inc 5050 Tilghman St Ste 115.......... Allentown PA 18104 *Web:* www.softnice.com	610-871-0400		196
Softomate LLC 901 N Pitt St Ste 325.......... Alexandria VA 22314 *TF:* 877-243-8735 ■ *Web:* www.softomate.com	877-243-8735		530
Softplan Systems Inc 8118 Isabella Ln.......... Brentwood TN 37027 *TF:* 800-248-0164 ■ *Web:* www.softplan.com	615-370-1121		177
Softplc Corp 25603 Red Brangus Rd.......... Spicewood TX 78669 *Web:* www.softplc.com	512-264-8390		177
SoftPress Systems Inc 3020 Bridgeway Ste 408.......... Sausalito CA 94965 *TF:* 800-853-6454 ■ *Web:* www.softpress.com	415-331-4820	331-4824	178-8
Softresources LLC 11411 NE 124th St Ste 270.......... Kirkland WA 98034 *TF:* 800-268-3340 ■ *Web:* www.softresources.com	425-216-4030		195
Softrim Corp 9210 Estero Park Commons Blvd Ste 5.......... Estero FL 33928 *TF:* 800-757-1773 ■ *Web:* www.softrim.com	239-449-4444		180

Name / Address	City	State	Zip	Phone	Fax	Class
Softrisc Communication Solutions Inc 575 N Pastoria Ave — *Web:* www.softrisc.com	Sunnyvale	CA	94085	408-333-9775		177
Softrock-FM 98.9 (AC) 83 E Shaw Ave Ste 150 — *TF:* 800-423-5870 ■ *Web:* softrock989.iheart.com	Fresno	CA	93710	559-230-4300	243-4301	645-64
SoftSol Resources Inc 46755 Fremont Blvd — *Web:* www.softsol.com	Fremont	CA	94538	510-824-2000		177
Softsolutions Inc 325 Mtn Ave SW — *Web:* www.softsolutionsit.com	Roanoke	VA	24016	540-345-1045		180
SoftThinks USA Inc 11940 Jollyville Rd Ste 225-S — *TF:* 800-305-1754 ■ *Web:* www.softthinks.com	Austin	CA	78759	800-305-1754		809
SoftVu LLC 2029 Wyandotte St Ste 100 — *Web:* www.SoftVu.com	Kansas City	MO	64108	816-895-8828		809
Software & Information Industry Assn (SIIA) 1090 Vermont Ave NW 6th Fl — *Web:* www.siia.net	Washington	DC	20005	202-289-7442	289-7097	48-9
Software & Services of Louisiana LLC 1120 S Pointe Pkwy — *Web:* softwareservices.net	Shreveport	LA	71105	318-865-1505		177
Software AG USA 11700 Plaza America Dr Ste 700 — *TF:* 877-724-4965 ■ *Web:* www.softwareag.com	Reston	VA	20190	703-860-5050	391-6975	178-1
Software Answers Inc 6770 W Snowville Rd Ste 200 — *Web:* www.software-answers.com	Brecksville	OH	44141	440-526-0095		764
Software Business Systems Inc 7401 Metro Blvd Ste 550 — *Web:* sbsweb.com	Minneapolis	MN	55439	952-835-0100		525
Software Consulting Services LLC 630 Selvaggio Dr Ste 420 — *Web:* www.newspapersystems.com	Nazareth	PA	18064	610-746-7700	746-7900	178-10
Software Engineering Institute (SEI) 4500 Fifth Ave — **Fax:* Cust Svc ■ *TF:* 888-201-4479 ■ *Web:* www.sei.cmu.edu	Pittsburgh	PA	15213	412-268-5800	268-6257*	668
Software Engineering of America Inc (SEA) 1230 Hempstead Tpke — *TF:* 800-272-7322 ■ *Web:* www.seasoft.com	Franklin Square	NY	11010	516-328-7000	354-4015	178-12
Software Engineering Services Corp 1311 Ft Crook Rd S — *TF:* 800-244-1278 ■ *Web:* www.sessolutions.com	Bellevue	NE	68005	402-292-8660		668
Software Enterprises Inc 5380 Twin Hickory Rd — *Web:* www.softent.com	Glen Allen	VA	23059	804-747-6436		179
Software Folks Inc 212 Carnegie Ctr Suite 206 — **Fax Area Code:* 561 ■ *Web:* www.softwarefolks.com	Princeton	NJ	08540	609-919-6327	743-4644*	809
Software House International (SHI) 290 Davidson Ave — *TF:* 888-764-8888 ■ *Web:* www.shi.com	Somerset	NJ	08873	888-764-8888		174
Software Information Systems Inc (SIS) 165 Barr St — *TF:* 800-337-6914 ■ *Web:* www.thinksis.com	Lexington	KY	40507	859-977-4747	977-4750	180
Software Methods Inc 770 E Market St — *Web:* www.software-methods.com	West Chester	PA	19382	610-430-8956		177
Software Partners Inc 447 Old Boston Rd Rt 1 — *Web:* www.softwarepartners.com	Topsfield	MA	01983	978-887-6409		88
Software Professionals Inc 1029 Long Prairie Rd Ste A — *Web:* www.spius.net	Flower Mound	TX	75022	972-518-0198		177
Software Pursuits Inc 1900 S Norfolk St — *TF:* 800-367-4823 ■ *Web:* www.softwarepursuits.com	San Mateo	CA	94403	650-372-0900	372-2912	178-12
Software Solutions Unlimited Inc 9595 SW Gemini Dr — *Web:* www.ssui.com	Beaverton	OR	97008	971-249-5400		2
Software Synergy Inc 151 Hwy 33 E — *Web:* ssi-corp.com	Manalapan	NJ	07726	732-617-9300		261
Software Technology Group 555 S 300 E — *TF:* 888-595-1001 ■ *Web:* stgconsulting.com	Salt Lake City	UT	84111	801-595-1000	595-1080	180
Software Toolbox 148A E Charles St — *Web:* www.softwaretoolbox.com	Matthews	NC	28105	704-849-2773		177
Software Unlimited Inc 1314 Bedford Ave Ste 201 — *Web:* medicalmastermind.com	Baltimore	MD	21208	410-602-9250		179
Softworld Inc 281 Winter St Ste 301 — *TF:* 877-899-1166 ■ *Web:* www.softworldinc.com	Waltham	MA	02451	781-466-8882		721
Softwyre Inc 14916 Wade Blvd — *TF:* 800-506-4309 ■ *Web:* www.softwyre.com	Maumelle	AR	72113	501-734-0017		809
SOG Specialty Knives & Tools LLC 6521 212th St SW — *TF:* 888-405-6433 ■ *Web:* www.sogknives.com	Lynnwood	WA	98036	425-771-6230		361
Sogetel Inc 111, rue du 12-Novembre — *TF:* 866-764-3835 ■ *Web:* www.sogetel.com	Nicolet	QC	J3T1S3	866-764-3835		387
Sohar Inc 5601 W Slauson Ave Ste 257 — *Web:* www.sohar.com	Culver City	CA	90230	310-338-0990		809
Sohn Manufacturing Inc 544 Sohn Dr — *TF:* 800-229-3346 ■ *Web:* www.sohnmanufacturing.com	Elkhart Lake	WI	53020	920-876-3361	876-2952	413
SoHo Grand Hotel 310 W Broadway — *TF:* 800-965-3000 ■ *Web:* www.sohogrand.com	New York	NY	10013	212-965-3000	965-3200	379
Soho House Beach House LLC 4385 collins ave — *Web:* www.sohobeachhouse.com	Miami Beach	FL	33140	786-507-7900		707
SoHo Metropolitan Hotel 318 Wellington St W — *TF:* 866-764-6638 ■ *Web:* www.metropolitan.com/soho	Toronto	ON	M5V3T4	416-599-8800	599-8801	379
SOHOware Inc 1250 Oakmead Pkwy Ste 210 — *Web:* www.sohoware.com	Sunnyvale	CA	94085	408-565-9888	565-9889	176
Sohum Inc 1055 Minnesota Ave Ste 6 — *Web:* www.sohum.biz	San Jose	CA	95125	408-265-2391		177
Soi Four Bangkok Eatery 5421 College Ave — *Web:* soifour.com	Oakland	CA	94618	510-655-0889		671
Soil & Materials Engineers Inc 43980 Plymouth Oaks Blvd — *Web:* www.sme-usa.com	Plymouth	MI	48170	734-454-9900	454-0629	261
Soil & Water Conservation Society (SWCS) 945 SW Ankeny Rd — *TF:* 800-843-7645 ■ *Web:* www.swcs.org	Ankeny	IA	50023	515-289-2331	289-1227	48-13
Soil Consultant Engineering (SCE) 9303 Ctr St — *Web:* www.soilconsultants.net	Manassas	VA	20110	703-366-3000	366-3400	261
Soil Engineering Construction Inc 927 Arguello St — *Web:* soilengineeringconstruction.com	Redwood City	CA	94063	650-367-9595	367-8139	189-5
Soil Science Society of America (SSSA) 677 S Segoe Rd — *TF:* 800-272-7737 ■ *Web:* www.soils.org	Madison	WI	53711	608-273-8080	273-2021	48-2
Soilmoisture Equipment Corp 801 S Kellogg Ave — *TF:* 888-964-0040 ■ *Web:* www.soilmoisture.com	Goleta	CA	93117	805-964-3525		419
Sojam LLC Dba Martin J Braun Co 6325 Erdman Ave	Baltimore	MD	21205	410-488-3990		189-10
Sojourner-Douglass College 500 N Caroline St	Baltimore	MD	21205	410-276-1844		166
Sokol & Co 5315 Dansher Rd — *TF Cust Svc:* 800-328-7656 ■ *Web:* www.solofoods.com	Countryside	IL	60525	708-482-8250		296-1
Sol Azteca 1459 Montgomery Hwy	Vestavia Hills	AL	35216	205-979-4902		671
Sol Jewelry Designs Inc 550 S Hill St Ste 1020 — *TF:* 888-323-7772 ■ *Web:* soljewelry.com	Los Angeles	CA	90013	213-622-7772		410
Sol Schwartz & Assoc 7550 W I-10 Ste 1200 — *Web:* www.ssacpa.com	San Antonio	TX	78229	210-384-8000	384-8011	2
Sol Y Luna 2811 Seventh Ave S — *Web:* www.birminghammenus.com	Birmingham	AL	35233	205-322-1186		671
Solacom Technologies Inc 84 Jean-Proulx — *Web:* www.solacom.com	Gatineau	QC	J8Z1W1	613-693-0641		529
Solage Calistoga 755 Silverado Trl — *TF:* 866-942-7442 ■ *Web:* solage.aubergeresorts.com	Calistoga	CA	94515	866-942-7442		707
Solai & Cameron Inc 3410 W Van Buren — *Web:* www.solcam.com	Chicago	IL	60624	773-506-2720		177
Solanco School District 121 S Hess St — *Web:* www.solanco.k12.pa.us	Quarryville	PA	17566	717-786-8401	786-8245	685
Solano Coalition for Bett 744 Empire St Ste 210 — *TF:* 800-978-7547 ■ *Web:* www.solanocoalition.org	Fairfield	CA	94585	800-978-7547		363
Solano Community College 4000 Suisun Valley Rd — **Fax:* Admissions ■ *Web:* www.solano.edu	Fairfield	CA	94534	707-864-7171	864-7175*	162
Solano County 675 Texas St Ste 2700	Fairfield	CA	94533	707-784-6200	784-6209	338
Solano County Fair 900 Fairgrounds Dr — *TF:* 800-700-2482 ■ *Web:* www.scfair.com	Vallejo	CA	94589	707-551-2000	642-7947	642
Solano County Library 1150 Kentucky St — *TF:* 866-572-7587 ■ *Web:* www.solanocounty.com	Fairfield	CA	94533	866-572-7587		435
Solar Atmospheres Inc 1969 Clearview Rd — *TF:* 800-347-3236 ■ *Web:* www.solaratm.com	Souderton	PA	18964	215-721-1502		484
Solar Bat Enterprises Inc 3628 E County Rd 600 N — *Web:* www.solarbat.com	Brazil	IN	47834	812-986-3551		543
Solar Communications Inc 1120 Frontenac Rd — *Web:* www.solarcommunications.com	Naperville	IL	60563	630-983-1400		627
Solar Compounds Corp 1201 W Blancke St — *Web:* www.solarcompounds.com	Linden	NJ	07036	908-862-2813	862-8061	3
Solar Electric Systems 742 Hampshire Rd Ste A — *Web:* www.solarelectricalsystems.com	Westlake Village	CA	91361	805-497-9808		610
Solar Energy Industries Assn (SEIA) 600 14th St NW Ste 800 — *Web:* www.seia.org	Washington	DC	20004	202-682-0556	682-0559	48-12
Solar Energy Systems LLC 1205 Manhattan Ave Ste 1210 — *TF:* 800-374-4494 ■ *Web:* www.solaresystems.com	Brooklyn	NY	11222	718-389-1545		612
Solar Industries Inc PO Box 27337 — *TF:* 800-449-2323 ■ *Web:* www.solarindustriesinc.com	Tucson	AZ	85726	520-519-8258		191-3
Solar Light Co Inc 100 E Glenside Ave — *Web:* www.solarlight.com	Glenside	PA	19038	215-517-8700		610
Solar Plastics Inc 860 Johnson Dr — *Web:* www.solarplastics.com	Delano	MN	55328	763-972-5600		596
Solar Power Industry 440 Jonathan Willey Rd — *Web:* www.solarpowerindustries.com	Belle Vernon	PA	15012	724-379-5180		696
Solar Solutions & Distribution LLC 2500 W Fifth Ave — *TF:* 855-765-3478 ■ *Web:* www.soldist.com	Denver	CO	80204	303-948-6300		696
Solar Store LLC, The 2833 N Country Club Rd — *TF:* 855-743-1603 ■ *Web:* www.solarstore.com	Tucson	AZ	85716	520-322-5180		610
Solar Technologies Inc 26180 Enterprise Way Bldg 100	Lake Forest	CA	92630	949-458-1080		180
Solar Tours 1629 K St NW Ste 604 — *TF:* 800-388-7652 ■ *Web:* www.solartours.com	Washington	DC	20006	202-861-5864		16
Solar Turbines Inc 2200 Pacific Hwy — **Fax:* Sales ■ *Web:* mysolar.cat.com	San Diego	CA	92101	619-544-5000	544-5825*	262
Solarbos Inc 310 Stealth Ct — *Web:* www.solarbos.com	Livermore	CA	94551	925-456-7744		153
Solari Enterprises Inc 1572 N Main St — *Web:* www.solari-ent.com	Orange	CA	92867	714-282-2520		652
Solaria Corp 6200 Paseo Padre Pkwy — *Web:* www.solaria.com	Fremont	CA	94555	510-270-2500		620
Solaris Paper Inc 13415 Carmenita Rd — *Web:* www.solarispaper.com	Santa Fe Springs	CA	90670	562-653-1680		558

				Phone	Fax	Class
Solarity Credit Union 110 N Fifth Ave *Web:* solaritycu.org	Yakima	WA	98902	509-248-1720		219
Solarus 440 E Grand Ave. *TF:* 800-421-9282 ■ *Web:* www.solarus.net	Wisconsin Rapids	WI	54494	715-421-8111	421-6081	736
Solatech Inc 1560 N Main St Ste 102 *Web:* www.solatech.com	High Point	NC	27262	336-889-2455		525
Solatube International Inc 2210 Oak Ridge Way *TF:* 888-765-2882 ■ *Web:* www.solatube.com	Vista	CA	92081	760-477-1120		696
Solazyme Inc 225 Gateway Blvd *NASDAQ: SZYM* ■ *TF:* 877-917-9075 ■ *Web:* solazymeindustrials.com	South San Francisco	CA	94080	650-780-4777	989-6700	470
Solco Plumbing Supply Inc 413 Liberty Ave. *Web:* www.solco.com	Brooklyn	NY	11207	718-345-1900		612
Soldier Field 1410 S Museum Campus Dr *Web:* www.soldierfield.net	Chicago	IL	60605	312-235-7000	235-7030	720
Soldier of Fortune Magazine 2135 11th St. *Web:* www.sofmag.com	Boulder	CO	80302	303-449-3750		457-12
Soldier's National Museum 777 Baltimore St. *Web:* gettysburgbattlefieldtours.com	Gettysburg	PA	17325	717-334-4890		520
Soldiers & Sailors Memorial Auditorium 399 McCallie Ave *Web:* www.chattanooga.gov	Chattanooga	TN	37402	423-757-5580		572
Soldiers & Sailors National Military Museum & Memorial 4141 Fifth Ave. *Web:* www.soldiersandsailorshall.org	Pittsburgh	PA	15213	412-621-4253	683-9339	520
Soldiers Delight Natural Environment Area 5100 Deer Park Rd *TF:* 800-830-3974 ■ *Web:* dnr.maryland.gov/publiclands/Pages/central/soldiersdelight.aspx	Owings Mills	MD	21117	410-461-5005		565
Soldiers Memorial Military Museum 1315 Chestnut St *Web:* mohistory.org/soldiersmemorial	Saint Louis	MO	63103	314-622-4550		520
Soldream Inc 203 Hartford Tpke *Web:* www.soldream.com	Tolland	CT	06084	860-871-6883		697
Sole East LLC 90 Second House Rd. *Web:* www.soleeast.com	Montauk	NY	11954	631-668-2105		707
Sole Proprietor, The 118 Highland St *Web:* www.thesole.com	Worcester	MA	01609	508-798-3474	753-4889	671
Solebury School 6832 Phillips Mill Rd *TF:* 800-675-6900 ■ *Web:* www.solebury.org	New Hope	PA	18938	215-862-5261	862-3366	622
Solectek Corp 6370 Nancy Ridge Dr Ste 109 *Web:* www.solectek.com	San Diego	CA	92121	858-450-1220	457-2681	176
Solekai Systems Corp 3398 Carmel Mtn Rd *Web:* www.solekai.com	San Diego	CA	92121	858-436-2040	436-2041	261
Solem, Mack & Steinhoff PC 3333 S Bannock St Ste 900 *Web:* solemlaw.com	Englewood	CO	80110	303-761-4900		428
Soleno Inc 1100 Rt 133 CP 837 *Web:* www.soleno.com	Saint-jean-sur-richelieu	QC	J2X4J5	450-347-7855		492
Solenture Inc 2 Gateway Ctr Ste 1600 *Web:* www.solenture.com	Pittsburgh	PA	15222	412-281-5472		193
Soleo Communications Inc 209 High Point Dr Ste 300 *Web:* www.soleo.com	Victor	NY	14564	585-641-4300		224
Solera 5410 E Colfax Ave *Web:* www.solerarestaurant.com	Denver	CO	80220	303-388-8429		671
Soleratec LLC 2430 Auto Park Way Ste 205 *TF:* 800-720-7378 ■ *Web:* www.soleratec.com	Escondido	CA	92029	760-743-7200		177
Solers Inc 950 N Glebe Rd Ste 1100 *Web:* www.solers.com	Arlington	VA	22203	703-526-0001	908-9353	177
Solex Academy Inc 350 E Dundee Rd Ste 200 *TF:* 866-797-6539 ■ *Web:* www.solex.edu	Wheeling	IL	60090	847-229-9595		685
Solheim Senior Community (SLH) 2236 Merton Ave *Web:* www.solheimlutheran.org	Los Angeles	CA	90041	323-257-7518		672
Soliant Consulting Inc 14 N Peoria St 2H *TF:* 800-582-0170 ■ *Web:* www.soliantconsulting.com	Chicago	IL	60607	312-850-3830		177
Soliant LLC 1872 Hwy 9 Bypass *TF:* 800-288-9401 ■ *Web:* www.paintfilm.com	Lancaster	SC	29720	803-285-9401	313-8227	600
Solid Border Inc 1806 Turnmill St. *TF:* 800-213-8175 ■ *Web:* www.solidborder.com	San Antonio	TX	78248	800-213-8175	887-9974	180
Solid Concepts Inc 28309 Ave Crocker *TF:* 888-311-1017 ■ *Web:* www.stratasysdirect.com	Valencia	CA	91355	661-295-4400		454
Solid Earth Inc 228 Holmes Ave NE 12th Fl *Web:* www.solidearth.com	Huntsville	AL	35801	256-536-0606		652
Solid Light Inc 438 S Third St *Web:* www.solidlight-inc.com	Louisville	KY	40202	502-562-0060		344
Solid State Devices Inc 14701 Firestone Blvd *Web:* www.ssdi-power.com	La Mirada	CA	90638	562-404-4474		696
Solid State Scientific Corp 27-2 Wright Rd. *Web:* www.solidstatescientific.com	Hollis	NH	03049	603-465-5686		256
Solid Waste Assn of North America (SWANA) 1100 Wayne Ave Ste 700 *TF:* 800-467-9262 ■ *Web:* swana.org	Silver Spring	MD	20910	301-585-2898	589-7068	531-5
SolidBoss Worldwide Inc 200 Veterans Blvd. *TF:* 888-258-7252 ■ *Web:* www.solidboss.com	South Haven	MI	49090	269-637-6356	637-6356	754
Solidia Technologies Inc 11 Colonial Dr *Web:* www.solidiatech.com	Piscataway	NJ	08854	908-315-5901		724
Solidiform Inc 3928 Lawnwood St. *TF:* 800-784-3313 ■ *Web:* www.solidiform.com	Fort Worth	TX	76111	817-831-2626	831-8258	492
Solidscape Inc 316 Daniel Webster Hwy *Web:* www.solid-scape.com	Merrimack	NH	03054	603-429-9700		494
Solidus Technical Solutions Inc 17 Forsythia Rd *Web:* www.solidus-ts.com	Leominster	MA	01453	978-534-8363		809
SolidWorks Corp 300 Baker Ave *TF:* 800-693-9000 ■ *Web:* www.solidworks.com	Concord	MA	01742	978-371-5011		178-10
Solien Technology Inc 1411 Fifth St Ste 406 *TF:* 800-822-9111 ■ *Web:* www.solien.com	Santa Monica	CA	90401	310-576-2727		180
Soligenix Inc 29 Emmons Dr Ste C-10 *OTC: SNGX* ■ *TF:* 800-678-9147 ■ *Web:* soligenix.com	Princeton	NJ	08540	609-538-8200	452-6467	85
Solis Capital Partners LLC 23 Corporate Plaza Ste 215 *Web:* www.soliscapital.com	Newport Beach	CA	92660	949-296-2440		360-3
Solisco Inc 120 10e Rue *TF:* 800-463-4188 ■ *Web:* www.solisco.com	Scott	QC	G0S3G0	418-387-8908		627
Solitron Devices Inc 3301 Electronics Way *OTC: SODI* ■ **Fax:* Mktg ■ *Web:* www.solitrondevices.com	West Palm Beach	FL	33407	561-848-4311	863-5946*	696
Solitude Ski Resort 12000 Big Cottonwood Canyon *TF:* 800-748-4754 ■ *Web:* www.skisolitude.com	Solitude	UT	84121	801-534-1400	517-7705	669
Solix Inc 30 Lanidex Plaza W PO Box 685 *TF:* 800-200-0818 ■ *Web:* www.solixinc.com	Parsippany	NJ	07054	973-581-6700		708
Solix Technologies Inc 4701 Patrick Henry Dr Bldg 20 *Web:* www.solix.com	Santa Clara	CA	95054	408-654-6400		177
Solmax International Inc 2801 Marie-Victorin Blvd *TF:* 800-571-3904 ■ *Web:* www.solmax.com	Varennes	QC	J3X1P7	450-929-1234		146
Solmetric Corp 117 Morris St Ste 100 *Web:* www.solmetric.com	Sebastopol	CA	95472	707-823-4600		407
Solo Printing Inc 7860 NW 66th St. *TF:* 800-325-0118 ■ *Web:* www.soloprinting.com	Miami	FL	33166	305-594-8699	599-5245	627
Soloflex Inc 1281 NE 25th Ave Ste I *TF:* 800-547-8802 ■ *Web:* www.soloflex.com	Hillsboro	OR	97124	800-547-8802		267
Soloflight Design 126 Sloan St. *Web:* www.soloflightdesign.com	Roswell	GA	30075	770-925-1115		5
SOLOMO Technology Inc 222 W Washington Ave Ste 705 *Web:* solomotechnology.com	Madison	WI	53703	608-220-1900		387
Solomon Consulting Group LLC 6836 W 121st St Ste 2B	Overland Park	KS	66209	913-971-0082		180
Solomon Corp 103 W Main *TF:* 800-234-2867 ■ *Web:* www.solomoncorp.com	Solomon	KS	67480	785-655-2191		620
Solomon Group 825 Girod St. *TF:* 800-657-1887 ■ *Web:* www.solomongroup.com	New Orleans	LA	70113	504-252-4500		226
Solomon Hardwick & Associates LLC 1160 Folly Rd *TF:* 800-201-3187 ■ *Web:* www.solomonhardwick.com	Charleston	SC	29412	843-406-6680		463
Solomon Pond Mall 601 Donald Lynch Blvd. *TF:* 877-746-6642 ■ *Web:* simon.com/mall?id=339	Marlborough	MA	01752	508-303-6255	303-0206	460
Solomon R Guggenheim Museum 1071 Fifth Ave. *TF:* 800-329-6109 ■ *Web:* www.guggenheim.org	New York	NY	10128	212-423-3500		520
Solon Manufacturing Co 425 Center St *TF:* 800-323-9717 ■ *Web:* www.solonmfg.com	Chardon	OH	44024	440-286-7149		492
Solowave Investments Ltd 103 Bauer Pl Ste 5	Waterloo	ON	N2L6B5	519-725-5379		528
Solstice Capital 81 Washington St Ste 303 *Web:* www.solcap.com	Salem	MA	01970	617-523-7733		792
Solta Medical Inc 25881 Industrial Blvd *TF:* 877-782-2286 ■ *Web:* www.thermage.com	Hayward	CA	94545	877-782-2286		250
Soltrix Technology Solutions Inc 16 Thomas Newton Dr *Web:* www.soltrixsolutions.com	Westborough	MA	01581	774-293-1293		809
Solusia Inc PO Box 11805 *Web:* www.solusia.com	Atlanta	GA	30355	404-601-1100		256
Solutek Corp 94 Shirley St. *TF:* 800-403-0770 ■ *Web:* www.solutekcorporation.com	Boston	MA	02119	617-445-5335	445-9623	145
Solutia Consulting Inc 1241 Amundson Cir *Web:* www.solutiaconsulting.com	Stillwater	MN	55082	651-351-0123		180
Solution Beacon LLC 14419 Greenwood Ave N Ste 332 *Web:* www.solutionbeacon.com	Seattle	WA	98133	206-366-6606		180
Solution Design Group Inc 7500 Olson Memorial Hwy Ste 300 *Web:* solutiondesign.com	Minnetonka	MN	55305	952-278-2500		809
Solution Partners Inc 1770 N Park St Ste 100 *Web:* www.solpart.com	Naperville	IL	60563	630-416-1335		180
Solution Systems Inc 3201 Tollview Dr. *Web:* www.solsyst.com	Rolling Meadows	IL	60008	847-590-3000		174
Solutioninc Technologies Ltd 5692 Bloomfield St. *TF:* 888-496-2221 ■ *Web:* www.solutioninc.com	Halifax	NS	B3K1T2	902-420-0077		364
Solutions 21 152 Wabash St *TF:* 866-765-2121 ■ *Web:* solutions21.com	Pittsburgh	PA	15220	866-765-2121		463
Solutions AE Inc 236 Auburn Ave *TF:* 888-562-4441 ■ *Web:* www.solutionsae.org	Atlanta	GA	30303	888-562-4441		463
Solutions Development Corp 12220 Charles St *Web:* www.sdc-world.com	La Plata	MD	20646	301-638-3040		177
Solutions for Assns Inc 140 N Bloomingdale Rd *Web:* www.sfainc.biz	Bloomingdale	IL	60108	630-351-8669		47
Solutions Plus 35583 Atlantic Ave. *Web:* www.splus.net	Millville	DE	19967	302-539-6421		196

	Phone	Fax	Class
SolutionsIQ Inc 6801 185th Ave NE Ste 200 .... Redmond WA 98052 *TF:* 800-235-4091 ■ *Web:* www.solutionsiq.com	425-451-2727		180
SolutionStream 249 N 1200 E .... Lehi UT 84043 *TF:* 800-314-3451 ■ *Web:* www.solutionstream.com	801-492-7700		396
Solv Staffing LLC 333 W Hampden Ave Ste 830 .... Englewood CO 80110 *Web:* www.solvnetwork.com	303-590-1640		260
Solvate com Inc 405 Greenwich St Ste 2A .... New York NY 10013 *Web:* www.solvate.com	646-720-7110		260
Solvay America Inc 3333 Richmond Ave .... Houston TX 77098 *TF General:* 800-365-6565 ■ *Web:* www.solvay.com	713-525-6000	525-7887	582
Solvay Bank 1537 Milton Ave .... Solvay NY 13209 *Web:* www.solvaybank.com	315-468-1661		70
Solvay Chemicals Inc 3333 Richmond Ave .... Houston TX 77098 *TF:* 800-765-8292	713-525-6000	525-2435	503-1
Solvay Draka Inc 6900 Elm St .... Commerce CA 90040 *Web:* www.solvaydraka.com	323-725-0050		596
Solvents & Chemicals Inc 1904 Mykawa Rd .... Pearland TX 77581 *TF:* 800-622-3990 ■ *Web:* www.solvchem.com	281-485-5377		146
Solvera Solutions Inc 201 - 1853 Hamilton St .... Regina SK S4P2C1 *TF:* 800-727-5835 ■ *Web:* www.solvera.ca	306-757-3510		196
Solvere LLC 69 Mcadenville Rd .... Belmont NC 28012 *TF:* 800-561-3357 ■ *Web:* www.solvere.net	704-829-1015		180
Solving International 1755 The Exchange Ste 380 .... Atlanta GA 30339	770-988-2600		194
SOMA Medical Assessments Ltd 7368 Yonge St Ste 206 .... Thornhill ON L4J8H9 *Web:* www.somamedical.com	905-881-8855		41
Somach Simmons & Dunn 500 Capitol Mall Ste 1000 .... Sacramento CA 95814 *Web:* www.somachlaw.com	916-446-7979		428
Somagen Diagnostics Inc 9220 25th Ave. .... Edmonton AB T6N1E1 *TF:* 800-661-9993 ■ *Web:* www.somagen.com	780-702-9500	438-6595	475
Somalia 425 E 61st St Ste 702 .... New York NY 10065 *Web:* www.un.int/somalia	212-688-9410		784
Somat Engineering Inc 660 Woodward Ave Ste 2430 .... Detroit MI 48226 *Web:* www.somateng.com	313-963-2721		261
SOMC (Southern Ohio Medical Ctr) 1805 27th St. .... Portsmouth OH 45662 *Web:* www.somc.org	740-356-5000		374-3
Somers Cove Marina 715 Broadway .... Crisfield MD 21817 *TF:* 800-967-3474 ■ *Web:* somerscovemarina.com	410-968-0925		565
Somers Mansion State Historic Site 1000 Shore Rd .... Somers Point NJ 08244 *Web:* www.njparksandforests.org	609-927-2212		565
Somerset Capital Group Ltd 612 Wheelers Farms Rd .... Milford CT 06461 *TF:* 877-282-9922 ■ *Web:* www.somersetcapital.com	203-701-5100	301-3253	264-2
Somerset Community College 808 Monticello St. .... Somerset KY 42501 *TF:* 877-629-9722 ■ *Web:* www.somerset.kctcs.edu	606-679-8501	676-9065	162
Somerset Consulting Group Inc PO Box 180344 Ste 120 .... Austin TX 78718 *Web:* www.somersetcg.com	512-327-0090		196
Somerset County 11440 Ocean Hwy PO Box 243 .... Princess Anne MD 21853 *TF:* 800-521-9189 ■ *Web:* www.visitsomerset.com	410-651-2968		338
Somerset County 41 Ct St. .... Skowhegan ME 04976 *Web:* www.somersetcounty-me.org	207-474-9861	474-7405	338
Somerset County 300 N Center Ave .... Somerset PA 15501 *Web:* www.co.somerset.pa.us	814-445-1400	445-1447	338
Somerset County 20 Grove St. .... Somerville NJ 08876 *TF:* 800-701-0710 ■ *Web:* www.co.somerset.nj.us	908-231-7006	253-8853	338
Somerset County Business Partnership 360 Grove St. .... Bridgewater NJ 08807 *TF:* 800-848-6368 ■ *Web:* www.scbp.org	908-218-4300	722-7823	139
Somerset County Chamber of Commerce 601 N Ctr Ave .... Somerset PA 15501 *Web:* www.somersetcountychamber.com	814-445-6431	443-4313	139
Somerset County Library 1 Vogt Dr .... Bridgewater NJ 08807 *Web:* www.somerset.lib.nj.us	908-526-4016	526-5221	434-3
Somerset CPAs PC 3925 River Crossing Pkwy Ste 300 .... Indianapolis IN 46240 *Web:* somersetcpas.com	317-472-2200		2
Somerset Door & Column Co 174 Sagamore St .... Somerset PA 15501 *TF:* 800-242-7916 ■ *Web:* doorandcolumn.com	814-444-9427	443-1658	499
Somerset Fine Arts PO Box 869 .... Fulshear TX 77441 **Fax Area Code: 713* ■ *TF Sales:* 800-444-2540 ■ *Web:* www.somersetfineart.com	800-444-2540	932-7861*	637-10
Somerset Hills Hotel (SSH) 200 Liberty Corner Rd .... Warren NJ 07059 *TF:* 800-688-0700 ■ *Web:* www.thesomersethillshotel.com	908-647-6700	647-8053	379
Somerset Hospital 225 S Ctr Ave .... Somerset PA 15501 *Web:* www.somersethospital.com	814-443-5000		374-3
Somerset Inn 2601 W Big Beaver Rd .... Troy MI 48084 *TF:* 800-228-8769 ■ *Web:* www.somersetinn.com	248-643-7800	643-2296	379
Somerset Management Group LLC 1215 Livingston Ave Ste 306 .... New Jersey NJ 08902 **Fax Area Code: 757* ■ *Web:* somersetmgmt.com	732-228-8200	366-0022*	195
Somerset Medical Ctr (SMC) 110 Rehill Ave. .... Somerville NJ 08876 *TF:* 888-637-9584 ■ *Web:* rwjuh.edu	908-685-2200		374-3
Somerset Patriots Baseball Club 1 Patriots Pk .... Bridgewater NJ 08807 *Web:* somersetpatriots.com	908-252-0700		354
Somerset Pharmaceuticals Inc 2202 NW Shore Blvd Ste 450 .... Tampa FL 33607 *Web:* www.somersetpharm.com	813-288-0040		582
Somerset Rural Electric Co-op 223 Industrial Pk Rd .... Somerset PA 15501 *TF:* 800-443-4255 ■ *Web:* www.somersetrec.com	814-445-4106		245
Somerset Trust Co 151 W Main St PO Box 777 .... Somerset PA 15501 *TF:* 800-972-1651 ■ *Web:* www.somersettrust.com	814-443-9200		70
Somerset Valley Rehab Ctr 1621 Rt 22 W .... Bound Brook NJ 08805 *TF:* 800-321-1245 ■ *Web:* care-one.com	732-469-2000		450
Somerset Valley Ymca 2 Green St .... Somerville NJ 08876 *Web:* www.somersetcountyymca.org	908-722-4567		354
Somerset Welding & Steel Inc 10558 Somerset Pk .... Somerset PA 15501 *TF:* 800-777-2671 ■ *Web:* www.jjbodies.com	814-444-3400	443-2621	516
Somerset-Pulaski County Chamber of Commerce 445 S Hwy 27 Ste 101 .... Somerset KY 42501 *TF:* 877-629-9722 ■ *Web:* somersetpulaskichamber.com	606-679-7323	679-1744	139
Somerville Chamber of Commerce 2 Alpine St PO Box 44034 .... Somerville MA 02144 *Web:* www.somervillechamber.org	617-776-4100		139
Somerville Public Library (SPL) 79 Highland Ave .... Somerville MA 02143 *Web:* www.somervillepubliclibrary.org	617-623-5000		434-3
Somete Group LLC 1316 NEW HAMPSHIRE AVE NW APT 607 .... Washington DC 20036	202-223-4920	223-4921	463
Somethingcool.com LLC 121a E High St. .... Potosi MO 63664 *Web:* somethingcool.com	573-436-2665		180
Somma Tool Company Inc 109 Scott Rd .... Waterbury CT 06705 *Web:* www.sommatool.com	203-753-2114	756-5489	493
Sommer Electric Corp 818 Third St NE .... Canton OH 44704 *TF:* 800-766-6373 ■ *Web:* www.sommerelectric.com	330-455-9454		246
Sommer Metalcraft Corp 315 Poston Dr .... Crawfordsville IN 47933 **Fax Area Code: 765* ■ *TF:* 888-876-6637 ■ *Web:* www.sommermetalcraft.com	888-876-6637	359-4201*	482
Sommer's Automotive 7211 W Meq .... Mequon WI 53092 *TF:* 888-494-4193 ■ *Web:* www.sommerscars.com	262-242-0100		57
Sommermaid Creamery Inc PO Box 350 .... Doylestown PA 18901 *Web:* www.sommermaid.com	215-345-6160	345-4945	296-3
Somnus Therapeutics Inc 135 US Hwy 202/206 Ste 9 .... Bedminster NJ 07921 *Web:* www.softekinfo.com	908-901-0300		668
SOMO (South Mountains State Park) 3001 S Mtns State Pk Ave. .... Connelly Springs NC 28612 *Web:* www.ncparks.gov	828-433-4772		565
Sompo America Insurance Services LLC 777 Third Ave 24th Fl .... New York NY 10017 *TF:* 800-208-3614 ■ *Web:* www.sompous.com	212-416-1200	416-1205	391-4
Sonalysts Inc 215 Waterford Pkwy N. .... Waterford CT 06385 *TF:* 800-526-8091 ■ *Web:* www.sonalysts.com	860-442-4355	447-8883	261
Sonar Entertainment 2121 Ave of the Stars Ste 2150 .... Los Angeles CA 90067 *Web:* sonarent.com	424-230-7140		514
Sonar Products Inc 609 Industrial Rd .... Carlstadt NJ 07072 *Web:* sonarproductsinc.com	201-729-1116		111
SonarMed Inc 12220 N Meridian St Ste 150 .... Carmel IN 46032 *TF:* 866-853-3684 ■ *Web:* www.sonarmed.com	317-489-3161		250
Sonas Consulting 17905 Apricot Way .... Castro Valley CA 94546 *Web:* www.sonasconsulting.com	650-619-4853		196
Sonata Capital Group Inc 2001 Sixth Ave Ste 3410 .... Seattle WA 98121 *Web:* www.sonatacap.com	206-256-4400		401
Sonatech Inc 879 Ward Dr .... Santa Barbara CA 93111 *Web:* channeltechgroup.com	805-683-1431	690-5388	529
Sonatype Inc 12501 Prosperity Dr Ste 350 .... Silver Spring MD 20904 *Web:* www.sonatype.com	301-684-8080		177
Sonavation Inc 3970 RCA Blvd Ste 7003 .... Palm Beach Gardens FL 33410 *Web:* sonavation.com	561-209-1201		693
Sonawane Webdynamics Inc 44031 Pipeline Plaza Ste 305 .... Ashburn VA 20147 *Web:* www.sonawane.com	703-723-9191		195
Sonepar USA 510 Walnut St Ste 400 .... Philadelphia PA 19106 *Web:* www.sonepar-us.com	215-399-5900		246
Sonesta Hotel & Suites Coconut Grove 2889 McFarlane Rd .... Miami FL 33133 *TF:* 800-766-3782 ■ *Web:* sonesta.com/coconutgrove	305-529-2828	529-2008	379
Sonetics Corp 7340 SW Durham Rd .... Portland OR 97224 *TF:* 800-833-4558 ■ *Web:* www.firecom.com	800-833-4558		647
Sonetronics Inc PO Box L .... West Belmar NJ 07719 *Web:* www.sonetronics.com	732-681-5016	681-5216	735
Sonfarrel Inc 3000-3010 E La Jolla St. .... Anaheim CA 92806 *Web:* www.sonfarrel.com	714-630-7280		454
Song of the Morning Yoga Retreat Ctr 9607 Sturgeon Valley Rd .... Vanderbilt MI 49795 *Web:* www.songofthemorning.org	989-983-4107		673
Songkran Thai Restaurant 2309 S Ridgewood Ave. .... South Daytona FL 32119	386-760-0300		671
Songwriters Guild of America 5120 Virginia Way C22 Ste 321 .... Brentwood TN 37027 *TF:* 800-524-6742 ■ *Web:* Www.sgacap.com	615-742-9945		48-4
Soniat House 1133 Chartres St .... New Orleans LA 70116 *TF:* 800-544-8808 ■ *Web:* www.soniathouse.com	504-522-0570		379
Sonic Air Systems Inc 1050 Beacon St .... Brea CA 92821 *TF:* 800-827-6642 ■ *Web:* www.sonicairsystems.com	714-255-0124	255-8366	18
Sonic Automotive Inc 4401 Colwick Rd .... Charlotte NC 28211 *NYSE: SAH* ■ *Web:* www.sonicautomotive.com	704-566-2400		57
Sonic Corp 300 Johnny Bench Dr. .... Oklahoma City OK 73104 *NASDAQ: SONC* ■ *TF:* 877-828-7868 ■ *Web:* sonicdrivein.com	405-225-5000		670
Sonic Corp 1 Research Dr. .... Stratford CT 06615 *TF:* 866-493-1378 ■ *Web:* www.sonicmixing.com	203-375-0063	378-4079	298
Sonic Drive-in Restaurants 300 Johnny Bench Dr. .... Oklahoma City OK 73104 *TF:* 877-828-7868 ■ *Web:* www.sonicdrivein.com	405-225-5000		670
Sonic Healthcare USA Inc 9737 Great Hills Trl Ste 100 .... Austin TX 78759 *Web:* www.sonichealthcareusa.com	512-439-1600		415

	Phone	Fax	Class
Sonic Innovations Inc 2501 Cottontail Ln .... Somerset NJ 08873 *TF:* 888-678-4327 ■ *Web:* www.sonici.us	888-423-7834		477
Sonic Manufacturing Corp 950 Lee St .... Elk Grove Village IL 60007 *Web:* www.sonicmfg.com	847-228-0015		454
Sonic power boats 309 Angle Rd .... Fort Pierce FL 34947 *Web:* www.sonicboats.net	772-429-8888		90
Sonic Sales & Service 2101 W Kansas St .... Liberty MO 64068	816-407-9183		260
Sonicor Inc 82 Otis St .... West Babylon NY 11704 *TF:* 800-864-5022 ■ *Web:* www.sonicor.com	631-920-6555	920-6080	782
SonicPool Post Production 6860 Lexington Ave .... Los Angeles CA 90038 *Web:* www.sonicpool.com	323-460-4649		514
Sonics & Materials Inc 53 Church Hill Rd .... Newtown CT 06470 *OTC: SIMA* ■ *TF:* 800-745-1105 ■ *Web:* www.sonics.com	203-270-4600	270-4610	782
SonicWALL Inc 2001 Logic Dr .... San Jose CA 95124 *TF:* 888-557-6642 ■ *Web:* www.sonicwall.com	408-745-9600	745-9300	176
Sonit Systems LLC 130 W Field Dr .... Archbold OH 43502 *TF:* 800-296-0018 ■ *Web:* www.sonit.com	419-446-2151		180
Sonivate Medical Inc 8305 SW Creekside Pl Ste C .... Beaverton OR 97008 *Web:* sonivate.com	503-616-4357		743
Soniya Technology International 3130 De La Cruz Blvd Ste 98 .... Santa Clara CA 95054 *Web:* www.soniyatechnology.com	408-493-0310		177
Sonjara Inc 207 Park Ave .... Falls Church VA 22046 *Web:* www.sonjara.com	571-297-6383		344
Sonnabend & Shu CPAS Inc 5832 Melvin Ave .... Tarzana CA 91356	818-776-0060		2
Sonnenalp Resort of Vail 20 Vail Rd .... Vail CO 81657 *TF:* 800-654-8312 ■ *Web:* www.sonnenalp.com	970-476-5656	476-1639	669
Sonnenberg Gardens 151 Charlotte St .... Canandaigua NY 14424 *Web:* www.sonnenberg.org	585-394-4922	394-2192	97
Sonnhalter 1320 Sumner Ave Ste 4 .... Berea OH 44017 *Web:* www.sonnhalter.com	440-234-1812		7
Sonny Bryan's Smoke House 4030 N MacArthur Blvd Ste 222 .... Irving TX 75038 **Fax Area Code:* 214 ■ *Web:* www.sonnybryans.com	972-650-9564	596-1081*	671
Sonny Bryan's Smokehouse 12720 Hilcrest Rd Ste 910 .... Dallas TX 75230 *Web:* www.sonnybryans.com	214-350-1800	350-3738	670
Sonny Williams' Steak Room 500 President Clinton Ave .... Little Rock AR 72201 *Web:* www.sonnywilliamssteakroom.com	501-324-2999		671
Sonny's Franchise Co 2605 Maitland Ctr Pkwy Ste C .... Maitland FL 32751 *Web:* www.sonnysbbq.com	407-660-8888		310
Sonobana Japanese Restaurant & Grocery 10 White Bridge Rd .... Nashville TN 37205 *Web:* www.sonobananashville.com	615-356-6600		671
Sonobi 444 W New England Ave Ste 215 .... Winter Park FL 32789 *TF:* 800-223-0088 ■ *Web:* sonobi.com	386-320-5400		5
Sonobond Ultrasonics Inc 1191 McDermott Dr .... West Chester PA 19380 *TF:* 800-323-1269 ■ *Web:* sonobondultrasonics.com	610-696-4710	692-0674	811
Sonoco 1 N Second St .... Hartsville SC 29550 *NYSE: SON* ■ *TF:* 800-377-2692 ■ *Web:* www.sonoco.com	800-377-2692		601
Sonoma County 575 Admin Dr Ste 104A .... Santa Rosa CA 95403 *Web:* sonomacounty.ca.gov	707-565-2431	565-3778	338
Sonoma County Fairgrounds 1350 Bennett Valley Rd .... Santa Rosa CA 95404 *Web:* www.sonomacountyfair.com	707-545-4200	573-9342	642
Sonoma County Library Third & E Sts .... Santa Rosa CA 95404 *TF:* 800-984-4636 ■ *Web:* sonomalibrary.org	707-545-0831		434-3
Sonoma County Transit 355 W Robles Ave .... Santa Rosa CA 95407 *TF:* 800-345-7433 ■ *Web:* www.sctransit.com	707-585-7516		468
Sonoma Developmental Ctr 15000 Arnold Dr .... Eldridge CA 95431 **Fax:* Admitting ■ *TF:* 800-862-0007 ■ *Web:* www.dds.ca.gov	707-938-6000	938-3605*	230
Sonoma Graphic Products Inc 961 Stockton Ave .... San Jose CA 95110 *TF:* 800-250-4252 ■ *Web:* www.sgpweb.com	408-294-2072		601
Sonoma Index-Tribune PO Box C .... Sonoma CA 95476 *Web:* www.sonomanews.com	707-938-2111	938-1600	532-4
Sonoma Index-Tribune Inc 117 W Napa St .... Sonoma CA 95476 *Web:* www.sonomanews.com	707-938-2111	938-1600	637-8
Sonoma Outfitters 2412 Magowan Dr .... Santa Rosa CA 95405 *TF:* 800-290-1920 ■ *Web:* www.sonomaoutfitters.com	707-528-1920		711
Sonoma Raceway Hwy S 37 & 121 .... Sonoma CA 95476 *TF:* 800-870-7223 ■ *Web:* www.sonomaraceway.com	707-938-8448	938-8430	515
Sonoma State Historic Park c/o Diablo Vista District Office 845 Casa Grande Rd .... Petaluma CA 94954 *Web:* www.parks.ca.gov	707-769-5652		565
Sonoma State University 1801 E Cotati Ave .... Rohnert Park CA 94928 **Fax:* Admissions ■ *Web:* www.sonoma.edu	707-664-2880	664-2060*	166
Sonoma State University University Library 1801 E Cotati Ave .... Rohnert Park CA 94928 *Web:* library.sonoma.edu	707-664-2397	664-2090	434-6
Sonoma Technical Support Services 505-8840 210th St Ste 342 .... Langley BC V1M2Y2 *TF:* 866-898-3123 ■ *Web:* www.sonomaservices.com	866-898-3123		196
Sonoma Valley Chamber of Commerce 651A Broadway .... Sonoma CA 95476 *TF:* 800-222-1222 ■ *Web:* www.sonomachamber.org	707-996-1033	996-9402	139
Sonoma Valley Film Festival 103A E Napa St .... Sonoma CA 95476 *Web:* www.sonomafilmfest.org	707-933-2600	933-2602	282
Sonoma Valley Unified School District (SVUSD) 17850 Railroad Ave .... Sonoma CA 95476 *Web:* www.svusdca.org	707-935-6000		685
Sonoma Wire Works 101 First St Ste 587 .... Los Altos CA 94022 *TF:* 800-787-1013 ■ *Web:* www.sonomawireworks.com	650-948-2003		177
SonomaWest Holdings Inc 2064 Hwy 116 .... Sebastopol CA 95472 *TF:* 800-906-6060 ■ *Web:* sonomawestholdings.com	707-824-2534	829-4630	655
Sonometrics Corp 500 Nottinghill Rd .... London ON N6K3P1 *Web:* www.sonometrics.com	519-474-6464		261
SonoPlot Inc 3030 Laura Ln Ste 120 .... Middleton WI 53562 *Web:* www.sonoplot.com	608-824-9311		419
Sonora Regional Medical Ctr (SRMC) 1000 Greenly Rd .... Sonora CA 95370 *TF Compliance:* 877-336-3566 ■ *Web:* www.adventisthealth.org	209-536-5000		374-3
Sonoran Science Academy 5741 E Ironwood St .... Tucson AZ 85708 *Web:* www.sonoranschools.org	520-300-5699		685
Sonos Inc 614 Chapala St .... Santa Barbara CA 93101 *TF:* 800-680-2345	800-680-2345		180
Sonoscan Inc 2149 Pratt Blvd .... Elk Grove Village IL 60007 *Web:* www.sonoscan.com	847-437-6400	437-1550	743
SonoSite Inc 21919 30th Dr SE .... Bothell WA 98021 *NASDAQ: SONO* ■ *TF:* 888-482-9449 ■ *Web:* www.sonosite.com	425-951-1200	951-1201	382
Sonoted Llc 1 Trotting Horse Ct .... Catonsville MD 21228 *Web:* www.sonoted.com	410-744-3950		396
Sons of Norway 1455 West Lake St .... Minneapolis MN 55408 *TF:* 800-945-8851 ■ *Web:* www.sofn.com	612-827-3611	827-0658	48-14
Sons Tool Inc 460 Thompson Rd .... Woodville WI 54028 *Web:* www.sonstool.com	715-698-2471	698-2335	488
Sonsie 327 Newbury St .... Boston MA 02115 *TF:* 800-235-6426 ■ *Web:* www.sonsieboston.com	617-351-2500		671
Sonsray Machinery LLC 1475 Pioneer Way .... El Cajon CA 92020 *Web:* www.sonsraymachinery.com	619-873-0123		23
Sonstegard Foods Co 5005 S Bur Oak Pl Ste 102 .... Sioux Falls SD 57108 *TF:* 800-533-3184 ■ *Web:* www.sonstegard.com	800-533-3184		619
Sony Computer Entertainment America Inc 919 E Hillsdale Blvd .... Foster City CA 94404 *Web:* playstation.com/en-us/home	650-655-8000		762
Sony Corp of America 550 Madison Ave .... New York NY 10022 *TF:* 800-282-2848 ■ *Web:* www.sony.com	212-833-6800		52
Sony Creative Software 1617 Sherman Ave .... Madison WI 53704 *TF:* 800-577-6642 ■ *Web:* www.sonycreativesoftware.com	608-256-3133	250-1745	178-9
Sony DADC US INC 1800 N Fruitridge Ave .... Terre Haute IN 47804 *Web:* www.sonydadc.com	812-462-8100		658
Sony Electronics Inc 1 Sony Dr .... Park Ridge NJ 07656 *TF Cust Svc:* 800-222-7669 ■ *Web:* www.sony.com	201-930-1000		52
Sony Music Entertainment 550 Madison Ave .... New York NY 10022 **Fax:* Sales ■ *Web:* www.sonymusic.com	212-833-8000	833-[illegible]*	637
Sony Music Nashville 1400 18th Ave S .... Nashville TN 37212 *Web:* www.sonymusicnashville.com	615-301-4300		657
Sony of Canada Ltd 115 Gordon Baker Rd .... Toronto ON M2H3R6 *TF:* 800-961-7669 ■ *Web:* www.sony.com/all-electronics	416-499-1414	497-1774	52
Sony Pictures Animation 9050 W Washington Blvd .... Culver City CA 90232 *Web:* sonypicturesanimation.com	310-840-8000		33
Sony Pictures Classics 550 Madison Ave 8th Fl .... New York NY 10022 *Web:* sonypictures.com	212-833-8833		511
Sony Pictures Entertainment Inc 10202 W Washington Blvd .... Culver City CA 90232 *Web:* www.sonypictures.com	310-244-4000		514
Sony/ATV Music Publishing LLC 25 Madison Ave 24th Fl .... New York NY 10010 *Web:* www.sonyatv.com/cookiepolicy.php?re=lw==	212-833-7730		637-7
Sooner Pipe LLC 1331 Lamar St Ste 970 4 Houston Ctr .... Houston TX 77010 *TF:* 800-888-9161 ■ *Web:* www.soonerpipe.com	713-759-1200	759-0442	385
Sooner Southwest Bankshares Inc 1751 E 71st St .... Tulsa OK 74136	918-496-4242		70
SOPAKCO Inc 118 S Cypress St .... Mullins SC 29574 *Web:* www.sopakco.com	843-464-7851		803-1
Sopark Corp 3300 S Pk Ave .... Buffalo NY 14218 *TF:* 866-576-7275 ■ *Web:* www.sopark.com	716-822-0434	822-5062	625
Sopheon Corp 3001 Metro Dr .... Bloomington MN 55425 *TF:* 800-856-8600 ■ *Web:* www.sopheon.com	952-851-7500	851-7599	387
Sophia Spirituality Ctr 751 S Eigth St .... Atchison KS 66002 *Web:* www.mountosb.org	913-360-6173		673
Sophie Station Suites 1717 University Ave .... Fairbanks AK 99709 **Fax Area Code:* 907 ■ *TF:* 800-528-4916 ■ *Web:* www.fountainheadhotels.com	800-528-4916	479-7951*	379
Sophisticated Business Systems Inc 6600 LBJ Fwy Ste 210 .... Dallas TX 75240 *TF:* 800-801-9005 ■ *Web:* www.ateras.com	972-664-9005		177
SophLogic Global LLC 8374 Market St Ste 133 .... Bradenton FL 34202 *Web:* www.sophlogic.com	941-932-8570		260
Sophono Inc 5744 Central Ave Ste 100 .... Boulder CO 80301 *Web:* sophono.com	720-407-5160		477
Sophos Inc 3 Van de Graaff Dr 2nd Fl .... Burlington MA 01803 **Fax Area Code:* 781 ■ *TF:* 866-866-2802 ■ *Web:* www.sophos.com	866-866-2802	494-5801*	178-1
Soquelec Ltd 5757 Cavendish Blvd Ste 540 .... Montreal QC H4W2W8 *Web:* www.soquelec.com	514-482-6427	482-1929	419
SOR Inc 14685 W 105th St .... Lenexa KS 66215 *TF:* 800-676-6794 ■ *Web:* sorinc.com	913-888-2630	888-0767	201
Sorabol *Sorabol Korean Restaurant* 805 Keeaumoku St .... Honolulu HI 96814 *Web:* www.sorabolhawaii.com	808-947-3113		671

Phone | Fax | Class

Sorbee International Ltd
9990 Global Rd. Philadelphia PA 19115 215-677-5200 677-7736 296-8
Web: www.sorbee.com
Sorbothane Inc 2144 State Rt 59. Kent OH 44240 330-678-9444 326
TF: 800-838-3906 ■ *Web:* www.sorbothane.com
Sordoni Construction Co
1 Pluckemin Way 2nd Fl. Bedminster NJ 07921 908-879-1130 879-1147 186
Web: www.sordoniconstruction.com
Sordoni Construction Services Inc
45 Owen St. Forty Fort PA 18704 570-287-3161 186
Web: www.sordoni.com
Sorensen Craig F Construction Inc
918 S 2000 W. Syracuse UT 84075 801-773-4390 540
Web: www.gosci.com
Sorensen Vance & Company PC
3115 East Lion Ln Ste 220 Salt Lake City UT 84121 801-733-5055 2
Web: sorensenvance.com
Sorenson Bioscience 6507 S 400 W Murray UT 84107 801-266-9334 596
Web: www.sorbio.com
Sorenson Communications Inc
4192 Riverboat Rd Ste 100 Salt Lake City UT 84123 801-287-9400 287-9401 253
Web: www.sorenson.com
Sorenson Engineering Inc
32032 Dunlap Blvd. Yucaipa CA 92399 909-795-2434 795-7190 621
TF: 800-486-1329 ■ *Web:* www.sorensoneng.com
Sorenson Media Inc
13961 Minuteman Dr Ste 100. Draper UT 84020 801-501-8650 544
TF: 888-767-3676 ■ *Web:* www.sorensonmedia.com
Sorin Group USA Inc 14401 W 65th Way Arvada CO 80004 303-424-0129 467-6584 476
TF: 800-289-5759 ■ *Web:* www.sorin.com
Sorling Northrup
1 N Old State Capitol Plaza Ste 200
PO Box 5131 Springfield IL 62705 217-544-1144 428
Web: www.sorlinglaw.com
Sorna Corp 2020 Silver Bell Rd Ste 17 Eagan MN 55122 651-406-9900 476
TF: 800-275-4524 ■ *Web:* www.sorna.com
Soroc Products Inc Plastics Div
4349 S Dort Hwy Burton MI 48529 810-743-2660 743-5922 602
TF: 800-326-6206 ■ *Web:* www.sorocproducts.com
Soroc Technology Inc
607 Chrislea Rd Woodbridge ON L4L8A3 905-265-8000 174
Web: www.soroc.com
Soroptimist International of the Americas
1709 Spruce St. Philadelphia PA 19103 215-893-9000 893-5200 48-5
TF: 800-435-7352 ■ *Web:* www.soroptimist.org
Sorrento Assoc Inc
2211 Encinitas Blvd Ste 200 San Diego CA 92130 858-792-2700 792-5070 402
Sorrento Electronics Inc
4949 Greencraig Ln San Diego CA 92123 858-522-8300 522-8300 472
TF: 800-252-1180 ■ *Web:* ga.com
Sorrento Hotel 900 Madison St. Seattle WA 98104 206-622-6400 671
TF: 800-426-1265 ■ *Web:* www.hotelsorrento.com
Sorteo Games Inc
6725 Mesa Ridge Rd Ste 102 San Diego CA 92121 858-554-0297 225
sortimat Technology
2242 N Palmer Dr. Schaumburg IL 60173 847-925-1234 393
Web: www.sortimat.com
Sorvive Technologies Inc
2090 Buford Hwy Ste 1b. Buford GA 30518 770-614-3122 387
Web: www.sorvive.com
SOS (Store Opening Solutions)
800 Middle Tennessee Blvd Murfreesboro TN 37129 877-388-9262 449
TF: 877-388-9262 ■ *Web:* www.store-solutions.com
SOS (Secular Organizations for Sobriety)
4773 Hollywood Blvd Hollywood CA 90027 323-666-4295 48-21
Web: www.cfiwest.org/sos
SOS Children's Villages-USA
1001 Connecticut Ave NW Ste 1250. Washington DC 20036 202-347-7920 48-6
TF General: 888-767-4543 ■ *Web:* www.sos-usa.org
Sos Global Express Inc 2803 Trent Rd. New Bern NC 28562 252-635-1400 311
Web: sosglobal.com
SOS Printing Inc 8135 Ronson Rd San Diego CA 92111 858-292-1800 627
SoSA (Society of Saint Andrew)
3383 Sweet Hollow Rd Big Island VA 24526 434-299-5956 299-5949 48-5
TF: 800-333-4597 ■ *Web:* www.endhunger.org
SOT (Society of Toxicology)
1821 Michael Faraday Dr Ste 300. Reston VA 20190 703-438-3115 438-3113 49-8
TF: 800-826-6762 ■ *Web:* www.toxicology.org
Sotax Corp 2400 Computer Dr Westborough MA 01581 508-417-1112 407
Web: www.sotax.com
Sotech Inc
12011 Guilford Rd Annapolis Junction MD 20701 301-470-7015 177
Sotech Nitram Inc 1695 Boul Laval Laval QC H7S2M2 450-975-2100 311
TF: 877-664-8726 ■ *Web:* www.sotechnitram.com
Sotheby's Inc 1334 York Ave. New York NY 10021 212-606-7000 51
Web: www.sothebys.com
Sotheby's International Realty
38 E 61st St New York NY 10065 212-606-7660 652
TF: 866-899-4747 ■ *Web:* www.sothebysrealty.com
Sothys USA Inc 1500 NW 94th Ave. Miami FL 33172 305-594-4222 592-5785 238
TF: 800-325-0503 ■ *Web:* www.sothys-usa.com
Soto Darren (Rep D - FL)
1429 Longworth HOB Washington DC 20515 202-225-9889 225-9742 342-2
Web: soto.house.gov
Sotto Sopra 405 N Charles St Baltimore MD 21201 410-625-0534 671
Web: sottosoprainc.com
Sotto Sotto Cucina Italiana
313 N Highland Ave Atlanta GA 30307 404-523-6678 671
Web: www.sottosottorestaurant.com
Soucy Holding Inc
5450 Saint-Roch St Drummondville QC J2B6W3 819-474-9008 60
TF: 844-474-4740 ■ *Web:* www.soucy-group.com
Soudan Underground Mine State Park
1302 McKinley Park Rd Soudan MN 55782 218-753-2245 753-2246 565
TF: 888-646-6367 ■ *Web:* www.dnr.state.mn.us
Souderton Area School District
760 Lower Rd Souderton PA 18964 215-723-6061 723-8897 685
Web: www.soudertonsd.org

Phone | Fax | Class

Souhegan Valley Chamber of Commerce
69 New Hampshire 101A Amherst NH 03031 603-673-4360 139
Web: www.souhegan.net
Soukup Bush & Assoc CPAs PC
2032 Caribou Dr Ste 200 Fort Collins CO 80525 970-223-2727 2
Web: soukupbush.com
Soulard's Restaurant
1731 S Seventh St Saint Louis MO 63104 314-241-7956 241-7956 671
Web: www.soulards.com
Soulman's Barbeque 3410 Broadway Blvd. Garland TX 75043 972-271-6885 671
Web: soulmans.com
Sound & Cellular Inc
824 W Yellowstone Hwy Casper WY 82601 307-234-7256 539
TF: 800-689-7256 ■ *Web:* www.soundandcellular.com
Sound Around Inc 1600 63rd St Brooklyn NY 11204 718-535-1800 246
Web: www.soundaroundusa.com
Sound Brokerage International LLC
3600 Port Of Tacoma Rd Ste 301 Tacoma WA 98424 253-922-7718 311
Web: www.soundbrokerage.com
Sound Casket Co
20350 71st Ave NE Ste G Arlington WA 98223 360-403-3132 134
Sound Com Corp 227 Depot St Berea OH 44017 440-234-2604 234-2614 52
TF: 800-628-8739 ■ *Web:* www.soundcom.net
Sound Glass Sales Inc 5501 75th St W Tacoma WA 98499 253-473-7477 189-6
TF: 800-468-9949 ■ *Web:* www.soundglass.com
Sound Hospitality Management LLC
3850 Bird Rd Ste 302 Miami FL 33146 305-448-2898 448-2958 463
Web: www.soundhospitality.com
Sound Image 2415 W Vineyard Ave. Escondido CA 92029 760-737-3900 23
TF: 800-962-9422 ■ *Web:* www.sound-image.com
Sound Imagingŷlnc 7580 Trade St San Diego CA 92121 866-530-7850 476
TF: 866-530-7850 ■ *Web:* www.soundimaging.com
Sound Inc 1550 Shore Rd. Naperville IL 60563 630-369-2900 246
Web: www.soundinc.com
Sound Propeller Services Inc
7916 Eighth Ave S Seattle WA 98108 206-788-4202 454
Web: www.soundprop.com
Sound Publishing Inc
11323 Commando Rd W Unit Main Everett WA 98204 360-394-5800 394-5829 637-8
Web: www.soundpublishing.com
Sound Shore Fund 3 Canal Plaza Portland ME 04101 800-754-8758 528
TF: 800-754-8758 ■ *Web:* www.soundshorefund.com
Sound Shore Management Inc
8 Sound Shore Dr Ste 180 Greenwich CT 06830 203-629-1980 401
TF: 800-551-1980 ■ *Web:* www.soundshore.com
Sound Sleep Products
14901 Puyallup St E Sumner WA 98390 253-891-1293 321
Web: www.soundsleep.com
Sound Vision 432 Boston Post Rd Wayland MA 01778 508-358-9000 261
Web: www.soundvisioninc.com
Soundair Inc 1826 Bickford Ave. Snohomish WA 98290 360-453-2300 22
Web: www.soundair.com
SoundBite Communications Inc
22 Crosby Dr Bedford MA 01730 650-466-1100 466-1260 736
NASDAQ: SDBT ■ *TF:* 888-436-3797 ■ *Web:* genesys.com/soundbite
Soundcoat Co 1 Burt Dr. Deer Park NY 11729 631-242-2200 242-2246 389
TF: 800-394-8913 ■ *Web:* www.soundcoat.com
Soundearth 2811 Fairview Ave E Seattle WA 98102 206-306-1900 196
Web: www.soundearthinc.com
Soundview Executive Book Summaries
511 School House Rd Ste 300 Kennett Square PA 19348 484-730-1270 453-5062* 196
**Fax Area Code: 800* ■ *TF:* 800-786-6279 ■ *Web:* www.summary.com
Soundview Preparatory School
370 Underhill Ave. Yorktown Heights NY 10598 914-962-2780 685
TF: 800-682-9857 ■ *Web:* www.soundviewprep.org
Soundwich Inc 881 Wayside Rd Cleveland OH 44110 216-486-2666 247
Web: www.soundwich.com
Soup2Nuts Inc 311 Arsenal St. Watertown MA 02472 617-600-2222 116
Souplantation
15822 Bernardo Ctr Dr Ste A San Diego CA 92127 858-675-1600 670
TF: 800-242-5353 ■ *Web:* www.souplantation.com
Source Audio LLC 120 Cummings Pk. Woburn MA 01801 781-932-8080 527
Web: www.sourceaudio.net
Source Communications Inc
433 Hackensack Ave. Hackensack NJ 07601 201-343-5222 343-5710 4
Web: www.sourcead.com
Source Data Products Inc
18350 Mt Langley St Fountain Valley CA 92708 714-593-0387 196
TF: 800 333 2669 ■ *Web:* www.source-data.com
Source Group Inc, The
3478 Buskirk Ave Ste 100. Pleasant Hill CA 94523 925-944-2856 193
Web: www.thesourcegroup.net
Source Intelligence LLC
1921 Palomar Oaks Way Ste 205 Carlsbad CA 92008 877-916-6337 192
TF: 877-916-6337 ■ *Web:* www.sourceintelligence.com
Source Interlink Cos Inc
27500 Riverview Ctr Blvd Bonita Springs FL 34134 239-949-4450 96
Source Marketing LLC 761 Main Ave Norwalk CT 06851 203-291-4000 7
Web: www.sourcecxm.com
Source Media Inc
1 State St Plaza 27th Fl. New York NY 10004 212-803-8200 637-9
TF: 800-221-1809 ■ *Web:* www.sourcemedia.com
Source North America Corp
510 S Westgate. Addison IL 60101 847-364-9000 580
TF: 800-621-5524 ■ *Web:* www.sourcena.com
Source One Distribution Services
1220 Morse Ave Royal Oak MI 48067 248-399-5060 5
Web: www.sourceone-dist.com
Source One Personnel Inc
2 Carnegie Rd. Lawrenceville NJ 08648 609-895-9700 260
TF: 800-364-0727 ■ *Web:* www.source1-financial.com
Source One Technical Solutions LLC
1952 Route 22 E Bound Brook NJ 08805 732-748-8643 196
Web: www.source1tek.com
Source Photonics Inc
8521 Fallbrook Ave Ste 200 West Hills CA 91304 818-773-9044 773-0261 177
Web: www.sourcephotonics.com

	City	State	ZIP	Phone	Fax	Class
Source Production & Equipment Company Inc						
113 Teal St	Saint Rose	LA	70087	504-464-9471		407
Web: www.spec150.com						
Source Technologies						
2910 Whitehall Pk Dr	Charlotte	NC	28273	704-969-7500	969-7595	178-1
TF: 800-922-8501 ■ *Web:* www.sourcetech.com						
Source2 1245 W Fairbanks Ave	Winter Park	FL	32789	407-893-3711		260
TF: 800-557-6704 ■ *Web:* www.source2.com						
Source4 3944 S Morgan	Chicago	IL	60609	773-247-4141	247-1313	110
Web: www.source4.com						
Sourcebooks Inc						
1935 Brookdale Rd Ste 139	Naperville	IL	60563	630-961-3900	961-2168	637-2
TF: 800-432-7444 ■ *Web:* www.sourcebooks.com						
SourceGear LLC 115 N Neil St Ste 408	Champaign	IL	61820	217-356-0105		631
Web: www.sourcegear.com						
SourceLink Inc 500 Pk Blvd Ste 415	Itasca	IL	60143	866-947-6872		5
TF: 866-947-6872 ■ *Web:* www.sourcelink.com						
SourceMedical Solutions Inc						
100 Grandview Pl Ste 400	Birmingham	AL	35243	866-245-8093		225
TF: 866-245-8093 ■ *Web:* www.sourcemed.net						
SourceN Inc						
4848 San Filipe Rd #150 116	San Jose	CA	95135	831 297-2838		196
Web: sourcen.com						
Sourcentra Inc 150 Speen St	Framingham	MA	01701	508-405-2605		88
TF: 800-482-4440 ■ *Web:* www.sourcentra.com						
SourcePoint Staffing LLC						
12745 W Capitol Dr	Brookfield	WI	53005	414-755-8600		260
TF: 800-447-0515 ■ *Web:* www.sourcepointstaffing.com						
Sourcery, The						
450 Mission St Ste 406	San Francisco	CA	94105	415-418-7156		260
Web: www.thesourcery.com						
Sourcing Interests Group (SIG)						
221 N Hogan St #389	Jacksonville	FL	32202	904-310-9560		721
Web: www.sig.org						
Sousa Archives & Ctr for American Music (SACAM)						
1103 S Sixth St 236 Harding Band Bldg	Champaign	IL	61820	217-244-9309	244-8695	520
Web: www.library.illinois.edu						
Sousa Court Reporters						
1013 Garces Ave	Las Vegas	NV	89101	702-765-7100		196
Web: www.sousa.com						
Sousley Sound & Communications						
1005 Tieton Dr	Yakima	WA	98902	509-248-4848		246
Web: www.sousley.com						
Soutex Inc 357 Rue Jackson	Quebec	QC	G1N4C4	418 871 2455		261
TF: 800-463-2839 ■ *Web:* www.soutex.ca						
South Africa 333 E 38th St 9th Fl	New York	NY	10016	212-213-5583	692-2498	784
Web: www.southafrica-newyork.net						
Consulate General						
200 S Michigan Ave Ste 600	Chicago	IL	60604	312-939-7929	939-2588	257
Web: www.sachicago.pwpsystems.com						
Consulate General						
333 E 38th St 9th Fl	New York	NY	10016	212-213-4880	213-0102	257
Web: www.southafrica-newyork.net						
Embassy 3051 Massachusetts Ave NW	Washington	DC	20008	202-232-4400	265-1607	257
Web: www.saembassy.org						
South African Airways						
1200 S Pine Island Rd Ste 650	Plantation	FL	33324	954-769-5000	769-5079*	25
**Fax:* Sales ■ *TF:* 800-722-9675 ■ *Web:* www.flysaa.com						
South African Consulate-General						
6300 Wilshire Blvd Ste 600	Los Angeles	CA	90048	323-651-0902		257
Web: www.dirco.gov.za						
South Alabama Electric Co-op (SAEC)						
PO Box 449	Troy	AL	36081	334-566-2060	566 8940	245
TF: 800-556-2060 ■ *Web:* www.southaec.com						
South Alabama Regional Planning Commission						
110 Beauregard St	Mobile	AL	36633	251-433-6541		196
Web: www.sarpc.org						
South Arkansas Arboretum						
PO Box 7010	El Dorado	AR	71731	888-287-2757		565
TF: 888-287-2757 ■						
Web: www.arkansasstateparks.com/southarkansasarboretum						
South Arkansas Community College						
PO Box 7010	El Dorado	AR	71731	870-862-8131		162
TF: 800-955-2289 ■ *Web:* www.southark.edu						
South Atlantic Capital Inc 614 W Bay St	Tampa	FL	33606	813-253-2500		792
Web: www.southatlantic.com						
South Atlantic Packaging Corp						
3932 Westpoint Blvd	Winston-Salem	NC	27103	336-774-3122		317
Web: southatlanticpackaging.com						
South Baldwin Chamber of Commerce (SBCC)						
112 W Laurel Ave PO Box 1117	Foley	AL	36535	251-943-3291	943-6810	139
TF: 877-461-3712 ■ *Web:* www.southbaldwinchamber.com						
South Bay Correctional Facility						
600 US Hwy 27 S	South Bay	FL	33493	561-992-9505	992-9551	213
TF: 800-574-5729 ■ *Web:* dc.state.fl.us						
South Bay Expressway LP						
1129 La Media Rd	San Diego	CA	92154	619-661-7070		415
TF: 888-889-1515 ■ *Web:* www.southbayexpressway.com						
South Bay Galleria						
1815 Hawthorne Blvd Ste 201	Redondo Beach	CA	90278	310-371-7546		460
TF: 800-876-4766 ■ *Web:* www.southbaygalleria.com						
South Bay Hospital						
4016 Sun City Ctr Blvd	Sun City Center	FL	33573	813-634-3301		374-3
TF: 888-499-1293 ■ *Web:* www.southbayhospital.com						
South Bay Union School District						
601 Elm Ave	Imperial Beach	CA	91932	619-628-1600		685
Web: www.sbusd.org						
South Baylo University						
1126 N Brookhurst St	Anaheim	CA	92801	714-533-1495	533-6040	166
TF: 888-642-2956 ■ *Web:* www.southbaylo.edu						
South Beach Grill						
45 Cubbedge Rd	Saint Augustine	FL	32080	904-471-8700		671
Web: www.southbeachgrill.net						
South Beach Marina Inn & Vacation Rentals						
232 S Sea Pines Dr	Hilton Head Island	SC	29928	843-671-6498	671-7495	379
TF: 800-367-3909 ■ *Web:* www.sbinn.com						
South Beach Psychiatric Ctr						
777 Seaview Ave	Staten Island	NY	10305	718-667-2300		374-5
Web: omh.ny.gov						
South Beach State Park						
5580 S Coast Hwy	Newport	OR	97366	541-867-4715		565
TF: 800-452-5687 ■ *Web:* oregonstateparks.org						
South Belt-Ellington Chamber of Commerce						
10500 Scarsdale Blvd	Houston	TX	77089	281-481-5516		139
Web: www.southbeltchamber.com						
South Bend City Hall						
227 W Jefferson Blvd Ste 1300 S	South Bend	IN	46601	574-235-9221	235-9173	337
Web: www.southbendin.gov						
South Bend Medical Foundation						
530 N Lafayette Blvd	South Bend	IN	46601	574-234-4176	234-1561	418
TF: 800-544-0925 ■ *Web:* www.sbmflab.org						
South Bend Museum of Art (SBM)						
120 S St Joseph St	South Bend	IN	46601	574-235-9102	235-5782	520
TF: 800-301-4961 ■ *Web:* www.southbendart.org						
South Bend Regional Airport						
4477 Progress Dr	South Bend	IN	46628	574-282-4590		27
Web: www.flysbn.com						
South Bend Symphony Orchestra (SBSO)						
127 N Michigan St	South Bend	IN	46601	574-232-6343	232-6627	573-3
TF: 800-537-6415 ■ *Web:* www.southbendsymphony.com						
South Bend Tribune						
225 W Colfax Ave	South Bend	IN	46626	574-235-6464		532-2
TF: 800-220-7378 ■ *Web:* www.southbendtribune.com						
South Bend/Mishawaka Convention & Visitors Bureau						
401 E Colfax Ave Ste 310	South Bend	IN	46617	800-519-0577		206
TF: 800-519-0577 ■ *Web:* www.visitsouthbend.com						
South Boston Speedway						
1188 James D Hagood Hwy PO Box 1066	South Boston	VA	24592	434-572-4947	575-8992	515
TF: 877-440-1540 ■ *Web:* www.southbostonspeedway.com						
South Broadway Cultural Ctr						
1025 Broadway Blvd SE	Albuquerque	NM	87102	505-848-1320	848-1329	50-2
TF: 866-441-6075 ■ *Web:* cabq.gov						
South Brunswick Public Library						
110 Kingston Ln	Monmouth Junction	NJ	08852	732-329-4000		434-3
Web: www.lmxac.org						
South Brunswick Public Schools						
231 Black Horse Ln PO Box 181	Monmouth Junction	NJ	08852	732-297-7800		186
Web: www.sbschools.org						
South by Southwest Film Festival						
500 E Cesar Chavez St	Austin	TX	78701	512-467-7979	451-0754	282
Web: www.sxsw.com						
South Cape Beach State Park						
Great Oak Rd	Mashpee	MA	02649	508-457-0495		565
Web: www.mass.gov						
South Carolina						
Adoption Services Div PO Box 1520	Columbia	SC	29202	803-898-7561		339-41
Web: dss.sc.gov						
Agriculture Dept						
1200 Senate St 5th Fl Wade Hampton Bldg	Columbia	SC	29201	803-734-2210	734-2192	339-41
Web: agriculture.sc.gov						
Arts Commission 1000 Gervais St	Columbia	SC	29201	803-734-8696	734-8526	339-41
Web: www.state.sc.us						
Attorney General						
1000 Assembly St Rm 519	Columbia	SC	29201	803-734-3970	253-6283	339-41
Business Carolina Inc (BCI)						
1523 Huger St Ste A	Columbia	SC	29201	803-461-3801	461-3819	339-41
Web: www.bcilending.com						
Child Support Enforcement Office						
3150 Harden St Ext PO Box 1469	Columbia	SC	29203	803-898-9210		339-41
TF: 800-768-5858 ■ *Web:* www.state.sc.us/dss/csed						
Commerce Dept 1201 Main St Ste 1600	Columbia	SC	29201	803-737-0400	737-0418	339-41
TF: 800-868-7232 ■ *Web:* www.sccommerce.com						
Commission on Higher Education						
1122 Lady St Ste 300	Columbia	SC	29201	803-737-2260	737-2297	339-41
Web: www.che.sc.gov						
Corrections Dept 4444 Broad River Rd	Columbia	SC	29210	803-896-8500		339-41
Web: www.doc.sc.gov						
Education Lottery PO Box 11949 4th Fl	Columbia	SC	29211	803-737-2002	737-2005	452
Web: www.sceducationlottery.com						
Emergency Management Div (SCEMD)						
2779 Fish Hatchery Rd	West Columbia	SC	29172	803-737-8500	737-8570	339-41
Web: scemd.org						
Ethics Commission						
5000 Thurmond Mall Ste 250	Columbia	SC	29201	803-253-4192	253-7539	265
Web: ethics.sc.gov						
Health & Environmental Control Dept						
2600 Bull St	Columbia	SC	29201	803-898-4123		339-41
Web: www.scdhec.gov						
Health & Human Services Dept						
1801 Main St	Columbia	SC	29201	803-898-2500		339-41
Higher Education Tuition Grants Commission						
115 Atrium Wy Ste 102	Columbia	SC	29203	803-896-1120	896-1126	725
Web: www.sctuitiongrants.com						
Highway Patrol						
5400 Broad River Rd Bldg 12	Columbia	SC	29212	803-896-9689	896-9685	339-41
Web: www.scdps.gov						
Historic Preservation Office						
8301 Parklane Rd	Columbia	SC	29223	803-896-6196		339-41
Web: scdah.sc.gov						
Insurance Dept (SCDOI)						
1201 Main St Ste 1000 PO Box 100105	Columbia	SC	29201	803-737-6160	737-6231	339-41
Web: www.doi.sc.gov						
Labor Licensing & Regulation Dept						
110 Centerview Dr	Columbia	SC	29210	803-896-4300	896-4393	339-41
Web: www.llr.state.sc.us						
Law Enforcement Div						
4400 Broad River Rd PO Box 21398	Columbia	SC	29210	803-896-7001		339-41
Web: www.sled.sc.gov						
Legislature						
1105 Pendleton St 223 Blatt Bldg	Columbia	SC	29201	803-212-6200		339-41
Web: www.scstatehouse.gov						
Medical Examiners Board						
PO Box 11289 Ste 202	Columbia	SC	29211	803-896-4500	896-4515	339-41
Web: www.llr.state.sc.us						
Mental Health Dept						
2414 Bull St PO Box 485	Columbia	SC	29202	803-898-8581		339-41
TF: 800-273-8255 ■ *Web:* www.state.sc.us/dmh						

				Phone	Fax	Class
Motor Vehicles Div PO Box 1498 *Web:* www.scdps.gov	Blythewood	SC	29016	803-896-3870	896-2698	339-41
Natural Resources Dept 1000 Assembly St *Web:* www.dnr.sc.gov	Columbia	SC	29201	803-734-4007	734-4300	339-41
Office of Governor 1100 Gervais St The Honorable Henry McMaster State House *Web:* governor.sc.gov	Columbia	SC	29201	803-734-2100	734-5167	339-41
Parks Recreation & Tourism Dept 1205 Pendleton St *Web:* www.southcarolinaparks.com	Columbia	SC	29201	803-734-1700		339-41
Probation Parole & Pardon Services Dept 2221 Devine St Ste 600 PO Box 50666 *Web:* www.dppps.sc.gov	Columbia	SC	29250	803-734-9220	734-5664	339-41
Professional & Occupational Licensing Boards 110 Centerview Dr Kingstree Bldg *Web:* www.llr.state.sc.us/pol.asp	Columbia	SC	29210	803-896-4300	896-4310	339-41
Secretary of State 1205 Pendleton St Ste 525 *Web:* www.scsos.com	Columbia	SC	29201	803-734-2170		339-41
Securities Div 1000 Assembly St PO Box 11549 *Web:* www.scag.gov/scsecurities	Columbia	SC	29211	803-734-9916		339-41
Social Services Dept 1535 Confederate Ave *TF:* 800-616-1309 ■ *Web:* dss.sc.gov	Columbia	SC	29202	803-898-7601		339-41
State Government Information 1301 Gervais St Ste 710 *TF:* 866-340-7105 ■ *Web:* sc.gov	Columbia	SC	29201	803-771-0131	771-7660	339-41
State Housing Finance & Development Authority 300 Outlet Pointe Blvd Ste C *TF:* 800-476-0412 ■ *Web:* www.sha.state.sc.us	Columbia	SC	29210	803-896-9001		339-41
State Ports Authority 176 Concord St *TF:* 800-845-7106 ■ *Web:* www.scspa.com	Charleston	SC	29401	843-723-8651	577-8710	618
Supreme Court 1231 Gervais St Supreme Court Bldg *Web:* dss.sc.gov	Columbia	SC	29201	803-734-1080	734-1499	339-41
Transportation Dept 955 Pk St PO Box 191 *Web:* www.scdot.org	Columbia	SC	29202	803-737-1302	737-2038	339-41
Treasurer 116 Wade Hampton Bldg Capitol Complex *Web:* www.state.sc.us/treas	Columbia	SC	29211	803-734-2101	734-2690	339-41
Veterans Affairs Div 1205 Pendleton St Ste 463 *TF:* 800-827-1000 ■ *Web:* va.sc.gov	Columbia	SC	29201	803-734-0200	734-4014	339-41
Victim Assistance Div 1205 Pendleton St *Web:* www.sova.sc.gov	Columbia	SC	29201	803-734-1900	734-1708	339-41
Vocational Rehabilitation Dept 1410 Boston Ave PO Box 15 *TF:* 800-832-7526 ■ *Web:* www.scvrd.net	West Columbia	SC	29171	803-896-6500		339-41
Wildlife & Freshwater Fisheries Div 1000 Assembly St PO Box 167 *Web:* www.dnr.sc.gov/divisions/wildlife.html	Columbia	SC	29202	803-734-3886	734-6020	339-41
South Carolina Aquarium 100 Aquarium Wharf **Fax Area Code: 866* ■ *TF:* 800-722-6455 ■ *Web:* www.scaquarium.org	Charleston	SC	29401	843-577-3474	210-1059*	40
South Carolina Assn of Realtors 3780 Fernandina Rd *TF:* 800-233-6381 ■ *Web:* www.screaltors.org	Columbia	SC	29210	803-772-5206	798-6650	656
South Carolina Assn of Veterinarians PO Box 11766 *TF:* 800-441-7228 ■ *Web:* www.scav.org	Columbia	SC	29211	803-254-1027	254-3773	795
South Carolina Bar 950 Taylor St *TF:* 877-797-2227 ■ *Web:* www.scbar.org	Columbia	SC	29201	803-799-6653	799-4118	72
South Carolina Bill Status PO Box 142 *Web:* www.scstatehouse.gov	Columbia	SC	29201	803-212-6200		433
South Carolina Book Festival PO Box 5287 *Web:* www.schumanities.org	Columbia	SC	29250	803-771-2477	771-2487	281
South Carolina Botanical Garden 150 Discovery Ln Clemson University *Web:* www.clemson.edu/public/scbg	Clemson	SC	29634	864-656-3405	656-6230	97
South Carolina Chamber of Commerce 1301 Gervais St Ste1100 *TF:* 800-799-4601 ■ *Web:* www.scchamber.net	Columbia	SC	29201	803-799-4601	779-6043	140
South Carolina Children's Theatre 153 Augusta St *TF:* 800-774-5986 ■ *Web:* www.scchildrenstheatre.org	Greenville	SC	29601	864-235-2885	235-0208	573-4
South Carolina Civil War Museum 4857 Hwy 17 Bypass S *Web:* mbisr.com	Myrtle Beach	SC	29577	843-293-3377		520
South Carolina Democratic Party 915 Lady St Ste 111 *TF:* 800-841-1817 ■ *Web:* www.scdp.org	Columbia	SC	29201	803-799-7798	765-1692	616-1
South Carolina Dental Assn 120 Stonemark Ln *TF:* 800-327-2598 ■ *Web:* www.scda.org	Columbia	SC	29210	803-750-2277	750-1644	227
South Carolina Education Association, The 421 Zimalcrest Dr *TF:* 800-422-7232 ■ *Web:* www.thescea.org	Columbia	SC	29210	803-772-6553		533
South Carolina Educational Television Commission (ETV) 1101 George Rogers Blvd *TF:* 800-922-5437 ■ *Web:* www.scetv.org	Columbia	SC	29201	803-737-3200		632
South Carolina Elastic Co 201 S Carolina Elastic Rd *TF:* 800-845-6700 ■ *Web:* www.ritextile.com	Landrum	SC	29356	864-457-3388		745-5
South Carolina ETV Commission 1041 George Rogers Blvd *Web:* www.scetv.org	Columbia	SC	29201	803-737-3200		741
South Carolina Federal Credit Union PO Box 190012 *TF:* 800-845-0432 ■ *Web:* www.scfederal.org	North Charleston	SC	29419	843-797-8300		219
South Carolina Library Assn (SCLA) PO Box 1763 *Web:* www.scla.org	Columbia	SC	29202	803-252-1087	252-0589	435
South Carolina Medical Assn 132 W Pk Blvd *TF:* 800-327-1021 ■ *Web:* www.scmedical.org	Columbia	SC	29210	803-798-6207	772-6783	474
South Carolina Nurses Assn (SCNA) 1821 Gadsden St *Web:* www.scnurses.org	Columbia	SC	29201	803-252-4781	779-3870	533
South Carolina Pharmacy Assn 1350 Browning Rd *Web:* www.scrx.org	Columbia	SC	29210	803-354-9977	354-9207	585
South Carolina Philharmonic 721 Lady St *Web:* www.scphilharmonic.com	Columbia	SC	29201	803-771-7937	771-0268	573-3
South Carolina Press Assn 106 Outlet Pointe Blvd PO Box 11429 *TF:* 888-727-7377 ■ *Web:* www.scpress.org	Columbia	SC	29210	803-750-9561	551-0903	624
South Carolina Prison Industries 4444 Broad River Rd **Fax:* Cust Svc ■ *Web:* www.doc.sc.gov	Columbia	SC	29210	803-896-8516	896-2173*	630
South Carolina Republican Party, The 1913 Marion St *Web:* www.sc.gop	Columbia	SC	29201	803-988-8440	988-8444	616-2
South Carolina State Library 1430 Senate St *Web:* www.state.sc.us	Columbia	SC	29201	803-734-8666	734-8676	434-5
South Carolina State Museum 301 Gervais St *Web:* www.scmuseum.org	Columbia	SC	29201	803-898-4921	898-4969	520
South Carolina State University 300 College St NE *TF Admissions:* 800-260-5956 ■ *Web:* www.scsu.edu	Orangeburg	SC	29117	803-536-7000	536-8990	166
South Central Arkansas Electric Co-op 4818 Highway 8 W PO Box 476 *TF:* 800-814-2931 ■ *Web:* www.scaec.com	Arkadelphia	AR	71923	870-246-6701		245
South Central College *Faribault* 1225 Third St *TF:* 800-422-0391 ■ *Web:* www.southcentral.edu	Faribault	MN	55021	507-332-5800	332-5888	162
Mankato 1920 Lee Blvd *TF:* 800-722-9359 ■ *Web:* www.southcentral.edu	North Mankato	MN	56003	507-389-7200	388-9951	162
South Central Correctional Facility 555 Forest Ave PO Box 279 *Web:* www.tn.gov	Clifton	TN	38425	931-676-5372	676-5104	213
South Central Electric Assn 71176 Tiell Dr PO Box 150 *TF:* 888-805-7232 ■ *Web:* www.southcentralelectric.com	Saint James	MN	56081	507-375-3164	375-3166	245
South Central Indiana Rural Electric Membership Corp 300 Morton Ave *TF:* 800-264-7362 ■ *Web:* www.sciremc.com	Martinsville	IN	46151	765-342-3344		245
South Central Library System 4610 S Biltmore Ln *TF:* 855-516-7257 ■ *Web:* www.scls.info	Madison	WI	53718	608-246-7970		434-3
South Central Oil Company Inc 2121 W Main St *Web:* www.southcentraloil.com	Albemarle	NC	28001	704-982-2173		579
South Central Power Company Inc 2780 Coon Path Rd *TF:* 800-282-5064 ■ *Web:* www.southcentralpower.com	Lancaster	OH	43130	740-653-4422	681-4488	245
South Central Public Power District (SCPPD) 275 S Main St PO Box 406 *TF:* 800-557-5254 ■ *Web:* www.southcentralppd.com	Nelson	NE	68961	402-225-2351		245
South Central Regional Medical Ctr (SCRMC) 1220 Jefferson St *Web:* www.scrmc.com	Laurel	MS	39440	601-426-4000		374-3
South Charlotte Nissan 9215 S Blvd *TF:* 888-411-1423 ■ *Web:* www.scottclarknissan.com	Charlotte	NC	28273	704-552-9191		57
South China 4613 S Mason St Unit D1 *Web:* www.mingsouthchina.com	Fort Collins	CO	80525	970-225-6886		671
South China 548 Courthouse Rd	Gulfport	MS	39507	228-896-9832		671
South City Kitchen 1144 Crescent Ave *Web:* fifthgroup.com	Atlanta	GA	30309	404-873-7358		671
South Coast Botanic Garden 26300 Crenshaw Blvd *TF:* 800-228-9290 ■ *Web:* www.southcoastbotanicgarden.org	Palos Verdes Peninsula	CA	90274	310-544-6815		97
South Coast Construction Services Inc 3235 Fuqua St *Web:* www.sccsi.net	Houston	TX	77047	713-222-2308		186
South Coast Lumber Co 885 Railroad Ave PO Box 670 *Web:* www.socomi.com	Brookings	OR	97415	541-469-2136	469-3487	613
South Coast Plaza 3333 Bristol St *TF:* 800-782-8888 ■ *Web:* www.southcoastplaza.com	Costa Mesa	CA	92626	800-782-8888		460
South Coast Repertory 655 Town Ctr Dr *Web:* www.scr.org	Costa Mesa	CA	92626	714-708-5500	708-5576	749
South Coast Terminals Inc 7401 Wallisville Rd *Web:* www.scterm.com	Houston	TX	77020	713-672-2401		541
South Coast Water District 31592 W St *Web:* www.scwd.org	Laguna Niguel	CA	92651	949-499-4555		787
South College 3904 Lonas Dr *TF:* 877-557-2575 ■ *Web:* www.southcollegetn.edu	Knoxville	TN	37909	865-251-1800		800
South College-Asheville 140 Sweeten Creek Rd *TF:* 800-207-7847 ■ *Web:* www.southcollegenc.edu	Asheville	NC	28803	828-398-2500		800
South County Chamber of Commerce 4179 Crescent Dr Ste A *TF:* 800-927-7294 ■ *Web:* southcountychamber.org	Saint Louis	MO	63129	314-894-6800		139
South County Ctr 18 S County Centerway *Web:* www.shopsouthcountycenter.com	Saint Louis	MO	63129	314-892-8954		460
South County Hospital 100 Kenyon Ave *Web:* www.southcountyhealth.org	Wakefield	RI	02879	401-782-8000	783-6330	374-3

Name / Address	City	State	Zip	Phone	Fax	Class
South Cumberland Recreation Area						
11745 US 41	Monteagle	TN	37356	931-924-2956		565
Web: www.state.tn.us						
South Dade Electrical Supply						
13100 SW 87th Ave	Miami	FL	33176	305-238-7131	251-5254	246
Web: www.south-dade.com						
South Dakota						
Adult Services & Aging Office						
700 Governors Dr	Pierre	SD	57501	605-773-3656	773-6834	339-42
Web: dhs.sd.gov/LTSS/default.aspx						
Agriculture Dept 523 E Capitol Ave	Pierre	SD	57501	605-773-3594		339-42
Web: ci.pierre.sd.us						
Arts Council 711 E Wells Ave	Pierre	SD	57501	605-773-3131	952-3625*	339-42
**Fax Area Code:* 800 ■ *Web:* www.artscouncil.sd.gov						
Attorney General 1302 E Hwy 14 Ste 1	Pierre	SD	57501	605-773-3215	773-4106	339-42
Web: sd.gov						
Banking Div 1601 N Harrison Ave Ste 1	Pierre	SD	57501	605-773-3421	773-6184	339-42
Web: dlr.sd.gov/banking/default.aspx						
Career Ctr Div 116 W Missouri Ave	Pierre	SD	57501	605-773-3372	773-6680	259
Web: dlr.sd.gov/localoffices/pierre						
Child Protection Services						
700 Governors Dr	Pierre	SD	57501	605-773-3227	773-6834	339-42
Web: dss.sd.gov						
Child Support Div 700 Governors Dr	Pierre	SD	57501	605-773-3641	773-7295	339-42
TF: 800-286-9145 ■ *Web:* dss.sd.gov/childsupport						
Consumer Protection Div						
1302 E Hwy 14 Ste 3	Pierre	SD	57501	605-773-4400	773-7163	339-42
TF: 800-300-1986 ■ *Web:* sd.gov						
Corrections Dept 500 E Capital Ave	Pierre	SD	57501	605-773-3478	773-3194	339-42
Web: doc.sd.gov						
Crime Victims' Compensation Program						
700 Governors Dr	Pierre	SD	57501	605-773-5884	773-4085	339-42
Web: dss.sd.gov						
Department of Health						
Robert Hayes Bldg 600 E Capitol Ave	Pierre	SD	57501	605-773-3361	773-5683	339-42
TF: 800-738-2301 ■ *Web:* sd.gov						
Department of Tribal Relations						
302 E Dakota	Pierre	SD	57501	605-773-3415	773-6592	339-42
Web: www.sdtribalrelations.com						
Education Dept 800 Governors Dr	Pierre	SD	57501	605-773-3134		339-42
Web: www.doe.sd.gov						
Emergency Management Office						
118 W Capitol Ave	Pierre	SD	57501	605-773-3231		339-42
Web: dps.sd.gov						
Environment & Natural Resources Dept						
523 E Capitol Ave	Pierre	SD	57501	605-773-3151	773-6035	339-42
Web: denr.sd.gov						
Finance & Management Bureau						
500 E Capitol Ave	Pierre	SD	57501	605-773-3411	773-4711	339-42
Web: bfm.sd.gov						
Gaming Commission						
445 E Capitol Ave Ste 101	Pierre	SD	57501	605-773-6050	773-6053	712
Web: sd.gov						
Governor 500 E Capitol Ave	Pierre	SD	57501	605-773-3212		339-42
Web: sd.gov						
Highway Patrol Div 118 W Capitol Ave	Pierre	SD	57501	605-773-3105	773-6046	339-42
Web: dps.sd.gov						
Housing Development Authority						
PO Box 1237	Pierre	SD	57501	605-773-3181	773-5154	339-42
Web: www.sdhda.org						
Insurance Div 124 S Euclid Ave 2nd Fl	Pierre	SD	57501	605-773-3563	773-5369	339-42
Web: dlr.sd.gov						
Labor Dept 123 W Missouri Ave	Pierre	SD	57730	605-773-3101	773-6184	339-42
Web: www.sdjobs.org						
Legislature						
Capitol Bldg 500 E Capitol Ave 3rd Fl	Pierre	SD	57501	605-773-3251	773-4576	339-42
Web: legis.sd.gov						
Lieutenant Governor 500 E Capitol Ave	Pierre	SD	57501	605-773-3661	773-4711	339-42
Web: sd.gov						
Military & Veterans Affairs Dept						
2823 W Main St	Rapid City	SD	57702	605-737-6721		339-42
Web: bhr.sd.gov						
Motor Vehicle Div 445 E Capital Ave	Pierre	SD	57501	605-773-3541	773-2550	339-42
Web: dor.sd.gov						
Pardons & Parole Board						
1600 N Dr PO Box 5911	Sioux Falls	SD	57117	605-367-5040		339-42
Web: doc.sd.gov						
Parks & Recreation Div						
523 E Capitol Ave	Pierre	SD	57501	605-223-7660	773-6245	339-42
Web: gfp.sd.gov						
Personnel Bureau 500 E Capitol Ave	Pierre	SD	57501	605-773-3148	773-4344	339-42
TF: 877-573-7347 ■ *Web:* bhr.sd.gov						
Public Utilities Commission						
500 E Capitol Ave	Pierre	SD	57501	605-773-3201		339-42
Web: sd.gov						
Real Estate Commission						
221 W Capitol Ave Ste 101	Pierre	SD	57501	605-773-3600	773-7175	339-42
Web: sd.gov						
Regents Board 306 E Capitol Ave Ste 200	Pierre	SD	57501	605-773-3455		339-42
Web: www.sdbor.edu						
Rehabilitation Services Div						
500 E Capitol Ave	Pierre	SD	57501	605-773-3318		339-42
TF: 877-873-8500 ■ *Web:* sd.gov						
Revenue 445 E Capitol Ave	Pierre	SD	57501	605-773-3311		339-42
Web: dor.sd.gov						
Secretary of State						
500 E Capitol Ave Ste 204	Pierre	SD	57501	605-773-3537	773-6580	339-42
Web: www.sdsos.gov						
Securities Div 445 E Capitol Ave FL 2	Pierre	SD	57501	605-773-3563	773-5953	339-42
Web: sd.gov						
Social Services Dept 700 Governors Dr	Pierre	SD	57501	605-773-3165	773-4855	339-42
TF: 800-597-1603 ■ *Web:* dss.sd.gov						
State Court Administrator						
500 E Capitol Ave	Pierre	SD	57501	605-773-3474	773-8437	339-42
Web: ujs.sd.gov						
State Government Information						
500 E Capitol Ave	Pierre	SD	57501	605-773-3212		339-42
Web: www.sd.gov						
State Historical Society						
900 Governors Dr	Pierre	SD	57501	605-773-3458	773-6041	339-42
Web: www.history.sd.gov						
Supreme Court 500 E Capitol Ave	Pierre	SD	57501	605-773-3474	773-8437	339-42
Web: ujs.sd.gov						
Tourism Office 711 E Wells Ave	Pierre	SD	57501	605-773-3301		339-42
TF: 800-732-5682 ■ *Web:* www.travelsd.com						
Treasurer 500 E Capitol Ave Ste 212	Pierre	SD	57501	605-773-3379	773-3115	339-42
Web: sdtreasurer.gov						
Weights & Measures Office						
118 W Capitol Ave	Pierre	SD	57501	605-773-3697	773-6631	339-42
Web: dps.sd.gov						
South Dakota Assn of Realtors						
204 N Euclid Ave	Pierre	SD	57501	605-224-0554	224-8975	656
TF: 800-227-5877 ■ *Web:* www.sdrealtor.org						
South Dakota Chamber of Commerce & Industry						
108 N Euclid Ave	Pierre	SD	57501	605-224-6161	224-7198	140
TF: 800-742-8112 ■ *Web:* www.sdchamber.biz						
South Dakota Democratic Party						
335 N Main Ave Ste 200	Sioux Falls	SD	57104	605-271-5405		616-1
Web: www.sddp.org						
South Dakota Dental Assn						
804 N Euclid Ave Ste 103	Pierre	SD	57501	605-224-9133	224-9168	227
TF: 866-551-8023 ■ *Web:* www.sddental.org						
South Dakota Discovery Ctr & Aquarium						
805 W Sioux Ave	Pierre	SD	57501	605-224-8295		520
Web: sd-discovery.org						
South Dakota Lions Eye Bank						
4501 W 61st St N	Sioux Falls	SD	57107	605-373-1008		269
TF: 800-245-7846 ■ *Web:* www.dakotasight.org						
South Dakota National Guard Museum						
425 E Capitol Ave	Pierre	SD	57501	605-773-3269		520
TF: 800-827-1000 ■ *Web:* military.sd.gov/default.html						
South Dakota Newspaper Services						
1125 32nd Ave	Brookings	SD	57006	605-692-4300		624
TF: 800-658-3697 ■ *Web:* www.sdna.com						
South Dakota Nurses Assn (SDNA)						
PO Box 1015	Pierre	SD	57501	605-945-4265	425-3032*	533
**Fax Area Code:* 888 ■ *TF:* 888-425-3032 ■ *Web:* www.sdnursesassociation.org						
South Dakota Pharmacists Assn						
PO Box 518	Pierre	SD	57501	605-224-2338	224-1280	585
Web: www.sdpha.org						
South Dakota Public Broadcasting (SDPB)						
555 N Dakota St PO Box 5000	Vermillion	SD	57069	605-677-5861	677-5010	632
TF: 800-456-0766 ■ *Web:* www.sdpb.org						
South Dakota Republican State Central Committee						
PO Box 1099	Pierre	SD	57501	605-224-7347		616-2
Web: www.southdakotagop.com						
South Dakota School of Mines & Technology						
501 E St Joseph St	Rapid City	SD	57701	605-394-2414	394-1268	166
TF: 800-544-8162 ■ *Web:* www.sdsmt.edu						
South Dakota State Library						
800 Governors Dr	Pierre	SD	57501	605-773-3131	773-4950	434-5
TF: 800-423-6665 ■ *Web:* www.library.sd.gov						
South Dakota State Medical Assn (SDSMA)						
2600 W 49th St Ste 200 PO Box 7406	Sioux Falls	SD	57117	605-336-1965	274-3274	457-16
Web: sdsma.org						
South Dakota State Penitentiary						
1600 N Dr PO Box 5911	Sioux Falls	SD	57117	605-367-5051	367-5038	213
Web: doc.sd.gov						
South Dakota State University						
PO Box 2201	Brookings	SD	57007	605-688-4121	688-6891	166
TF: 800-952-3541 ■ *Web:* www.sdstate.edu						
South Dakota State University Briggs Library						
1300 N Campus Dr Ste 119	Brookings	SD	57007	605-688-5106	688-6133	434-6
TF: 800-786-2038 ■ *Web:* www.sdstate.edu						
South Dakota Symphony Orchestra						
301 S Main Ave	Sioux Falls	SD	57104	605-335-7933		573-3
Web: www.sdsymphony.org						
South Dakota Wheat Growers Assn						
908 Lamont St SE	Aberdeen	SD	57401	605-225-5500	225-0859	275
TF: 888-429-4902 ■ *Web:* www.wheatgrowers.com						
South Davis Community Hospital						
401 S 400 E	Bountiful	UT	84010	801-295-2361		450
Web: www.sdch.com						
South East Health Integration Network						
71 Adam St	Belleville	ON	K8N5K3	613-967-0196		474
Web: www.southeastlhin.on.ca						
South Florida Business Journal						
6400 N Andrews Ave Ste 200	Fort Lauderdale	FL	33309	954-949-7600		457-5
Web: www.bizjournals.com						
South Florida Community College						
600 W College Dr	Avon Park	FL	33825	863-453-6661	453-2365*	162
**Fax:* Admissions ■ *TF:* 800-590-3428 ■ *Web:* www.southflorida.edu						
South Florida Museum 201 Tenth St W	Bradenton	FL	34205	941-746-4131	747-2556	520
Web: www.southfloridamuseum.org						
South Florida Science Museum						
4801 Dreher Trail N	West Palm Beach	FL	33405	561-832-1988	833-0551	520
Web: www.sfsciencecenter.org						
South Florida Sun-Sentinel						
200 E Las Olas Blvd	Fort Lauderdale	FL	33301	954-356-4000		532-2
TF Cust Svc: 800-548-6397 ■ *Web:* www.sun-sentinel.com						
South Fork Forest Camp (SFFC)						
48300 Wilson River Hwy	Tillamook	OR	97141	503-842-2811	842-7943	213
Web: www.oregon.gov						
South Fork State Recreation Area						
353 Lower S Fork Unit 8	Spring Creek	NV	89815	775-744-4346		565
Web: www.parks.nv.gov						
South Gate Chamber of Commerce						
3350 Tweedy Blvd	South Gate	CA	90280	323-567-1203		139
Web: sgchamber.org						
South Georgia Medical Ctr						
2501 N Patterson St	Valdosta	GA	31602	229-333-1000		374-3
TF: 800-476-7378 ■ *Web:* www.sgmc.org						
South Georgia Pecan Co 309 S Lee St	Valdosta	GA	31601	229-244-1321	247-6361	296-28
Web: georgiapecan.com						
South Georgia Regional Library						
300 Woodrow Wilson Dr	Valdosta	GA	31602	229-333-0086	333-7669	434-3
TF: 800-735-4271 ■ *Web:* www.sgrl.org						

Name / Address	Phone	Fax	Class
South Haven Public Schools Inc 554 Green St. South Haven MI 49090 *Web:* www.shps.org	269-637-0520		685
South Higgins Lake State Park 106 State Pk Dr. Roscommon MI 48653 *Web:* www.michigandnr.com	989-821-6374		565
South Hills Chamber of Commerce 1910 Cochran Rd Ste 140. Pittsburgh PA 15220 *TF:* 800-539-2968 ■ *Web:* www.shchamber.org	412-306-8090	306-8093	139
South Hills Country Club Golf Shop 2655 S Citrus St. West Covina CA 91791 *TF:* 800-242-1996 ■ *Web:* www.southhillscountryclub.org	626-339-1231		711
South Hills School of Business & Technology 480 Waupelani Dr. State College PA 16801 *Web:* www.southhills.edu	814-234-7755		166
South Holland Public Library 16250 Wausau South Holland IL 60473 *Web:* shlibrary.org	708-331-5262		435
South Jersey Healthcare HospiceCare 2848 S Delsea Dr Bldg 1 Vineland NJ 08360 *TF:* 800-770-7547 ■ *Web:* www.inspirahealthnetwork.org	800-770-7547		371
South Jersey Port Corp 101 Joseph A Balzano Blvd Camden NJ 08103 *Web:* www.southjerseyport.com	856-757-4969	757-4903	618
South Jersey Radiology Associates PA 100 Carnie Blvd Voorhees NJ 08043 *Web:* www.sjra.com	856-751-5522		415
South Kansas City Chamber of Commerce 406 E Bannister Rd Ste F Kansas City MO 64131 *Web:* southkcchamber.com	816-761-7660	761-7340	139
South Kent School 40 Bulls Bridge Rd South Kent CT 06785 **Fax Area Code:* 888 ■ *Web:* www.southkentschool.org	860-927-3539	803-0040*	622
South Kentucky Rural Electrical Co-op 925 N Main St PO Box 910. Somerset KY 42502 *TF:* 800-264-5112 ■ *Web:* www.skrecc.com	606-678-4121	679-8279	245
South Kitsap School District 1962 Hoover Ave SE. Port Orchard WA 98366 *Web:* www.skitsap.wednet.edu	360-874-7000	874-7068	685
South Llano River State Park 1927 Park Rd 73. Junction TX 76849 *Web:* tpwd.texas.gov	325-446-3994		565
South Louisiana Bank (SLB) 1362 W Tunnel Blvd PO Box 1718 Houma LA 70361 *Web:* ayeee.com	985-851-3434	879-3095	70
South Mall 3300 Lehigh St. Allentown PA 18103 *Web:* www.shopsouthmall.com	610-791-0606		460
South Metro Denver Chamber of Commerce 2154 E Commons Ave Centennial CO 80122 *Web:* www.bestchamber.com	303-795-0142	795-7520	139
South Metro Regional Chamber of Commerce 683 Miamisburg Centerville Rd Ste 210. Dayton OH 45459 *TF:* 800-824-5124 ■ *Web:* www.smrcoc.org	937-433-2032	433-6881	139
South Miami Hospital 6200 SW 73rd St Miami FL 33143 *TF:* 800-228-6557 ■ *Web:* www.baptisthealth.net	786-662-4000		374-3
South Mississippi Correctional Institution 22689 Hwy 63 N PO Box 1419. Leakesville MS 39451 *Web:* www.mdoc.ms.gov/Pages/default.aspx	601-394-5600	394-4451	213
South Mississippi Electric Power Assn (SMEPA) 7037 US Hwy 49. Hattiesburg MS 39402 *Web:* www.smepa.coop	601-268-2083		245
South Montgomery County Woodlands Chamber of Commerce 1400 Woodloch Forest Dr Ste 300 The Woodlands TX 77380 *Web:* www.woodlandschamber.org	281-367-5777	292-1655	139
South Motors Infiniti 16915 S Dixie Hwy Miami FL 33157 *Web:* www.southinfiniti.com	305-256-2000		57
South Mountain Community College 7050 S 24th St Phoenix AZ 85042 **Fax:* Admissions ■ *TF:* 855-622-2332 ■ *Web:* www.southmountaincc.edu	602-243-8000	243-8199*	162
South Mountain Restoration Ctr 10058 S Mountain Rd. South Mountain PA 17261 *Web:* www.dhs.pa.gov	717-749-3121		450
South Mountain Secure Treatment Unit 10056 S Mtn Rd South Mountain PA 17261	717-749-7904		412
South Mountain State Park c/o S Mtn Recreation Area 21843 National Pk Boonsboro MD 21713 *Web:* dnr.maryland.gov/publiclands/Pages/western/southmountain.aspx	301-791-4767		565
South Mountains State Park (SOMO) 3001 S Mtns State Pk Ave. Connelly Springs NC 28612 *Web:* www.ncparks.gov	828-433-4772		565
South Nassau Communities Hospital One Healthy Way. Oceanside NY 11572 *TF:* 877-768-8462	516-632-3000	377-5385	374-3
South Oaks Hospital 400 Sunrise Hwy Amityville NY 11701 *Web:* south-oaks.org	631-608-5610	264-5259	374-5
South of the Border Tours 7937 E Coronado Rd Tucson AZ 85750	520-760-4000		760
South Oklahoma City Chamber of Commerce 701 SW 74 St. Oklahoma City OK 73139 *Web:* www.southokc.com	405-634-1436	634-1462	139
South Orangetown School District (Inc), The 160 Van Wyck Rd Blauvelt NY 10913 *Web:* socsd.org	845-680-1000		685
South Padre Island Convention & Visitors Bureau 7355 Padre Blvd. South Padre Island TX 78597 *TF:* 800-767-2373 ■ *Web:* www.sopadre.com	956-761-6433		206
South Padre Island Convention Centre 7355 Padre Blvd. South Padre Island TX 78597 *TF:* 800-657-2373 ■ *Web:* www.sopadre.com	956-761-3000	761-3024	205
South Park Cafe 108 S Pk St San Francisco CA 94107 *Web:* www.southparkcafe.com	415-495-7275		671
South Park Mall 2310 SW Military Dr. San Antonio TX 78224 *Web:* www.visitsouthpark.com	210-921-0534	921-0628	460
South Penn Eye Care (SPECS) 250 E Walnut St Hanover PA 17331 *TF:* 800-367-7629 ■ *Web:* www.southpenneyecare.com	717-632-6063		798
South Piedmont Community College 680 Hwy 74 Polkton NC 28135 **Fax:* Admissions ■ *Web:* www.spcc.edu	704-272-5300	272-5303*	162
South Pier Inn on the Canal 701 Lake Ave S. Duluth MN 55802 *TF:* 800-430-7437 ■ *Web:* www.southpierinn.com	218-786-9007		379
South Plains Academy 4008 Ave R Lubbock TX 79412	806-744-0330		685
South Plains College 1401 S College Ave Levelland TX 79336 **Fax:* Admissions ■ *Web:* www.southplainscollege.edu	806-894-9611	897-3167*	162
South Plains Electric Co-op Inc PO Box 1830 Lubbock TX 79408 *TF:* 800-658-2655 ■ *Web:* www.spec.coop	806-775-7766	775-7796	245
South Plains Mall 6002 Slide Rd Lubbock TX 79414 *TF:* 800-283-9490 ■ *Web:* www.southplainsmall.com	806-792-4653		460
South Point Hotel & Casino 9777 Las Vegas Blvd S. Las Vegas NV 89183 *TF:* 866-796-7111 ■ *Web:* www.southpointcasino.com	702-796-7111		379
South Point Systems Inc 1019 US Hwy 431 Boaz AL 35957 *TF:* 800-426-9990 ■ *Web:* www.southpoint.net	256-593-1337		225
South Pole 222 Bridge Plaza S. Fort Lee NJ 07024 *Web:* www.southpole-usa.com	201-242-5900		157-4
South Puget Sound Community College 2011 Mottman Rd SW Olympia WA 98512 **Fax:* Admissions ■ *TF:* 800-986-9585 ■ *Web:* spscc.edu	360-754-7711	596-5709*	162
South River Electric Membership Corp 17494 US 421 S PO Box 931 Dunn NC 28335 *TF:* 800-338-5530 ■ *Web:* www.sremc.com	910-892-8071	230-2981	245
South River Technologies Inc 1910 Towne Centre Blvd Ste 250 Annapolis MD 21401 *Web:* www.southrivertech.com	410-266-0667		177
South Salt Lake Chamber of Commerce 220 E Morris Ave Ste 150. South Salt lake City UT 84115 *Web:* www.sslchamber.com	801-466-3377		139
South San Antonio Chamber of Commerce 3315 Sidney Brooks Dr Ste 200 San Antonio TX 78235 *Web:* www.southsachamber.org	210-533-1600	314-2769	139
South San Antonio Independent School District 5622 Ray Ellison Dr San Antonio TX 78242 *Web:* www.southsanisd.net	210-977-7000		685
South San Francisco Chamber of Commerce 213 Linden Ave. South San Francisco CA 94080 *Web:* www.ssfchamber.com	650-588-1911	588-2534	139
South San Francisco Public Library 840 W Orange Ave South San Francisco CA 94080 *TF:* 800-735-2929 ■ *Web:* www.ssf.net	650-829-3860	829-3866	434-3
South San Francisco Unified School District 398 B St South San Francisco CA 94080 *Web:* www.ssfusd.org	650-877-8700		685
South Seas Island Resort 5400 Plantation Rd Captiva FL 33924 *TF:* 866-565-5089 ■ *Web:* www.southseas.com	239-472-5111	472-7541	669
South Seattle Community College 6000 16th Ave SW Seattle WA 98106 *Web:* www.southseattle.edu	206-764-5300	764-7947	162
South Shore Chamber of Commerce 1050 Hingham St Rockland MA 02370 **Fax Area Code:* 617 ■ *TF:* 800-519-5992 ■ *Web:* www.southshorechamber.org	781-421-3900	479-9274*	139
South Shore Cultural Ctr 7059 S Shore Dr. Chicago IL 60649 *Web:* www.chicagoparkdistrict.com	773-256-0149		50-2
South Shore Educational Collaborative 75 Abington St Hingham MA 02043 *Web:* www.ssec.org	781-749-7518		166
South Shore Harbor Development Ltd 2525 S Shore Blvd Ste 207. League City TX 77573	281-334-7501		653
South Shore Harbour Resort & Conference Ctr 2500 S Shore Blvd League City TX 77573 *TF Resv:* 800-442-5005 ■ *Web:* www.sshr.com	281-334-1000	334-1157	669
South Shore Hospital 55 Fogg Rd. South Weymouth MA 02190 *TF:* 800-439-2370 ■ *Web:* www.southshorehospital.org	781-340-8000	337-3768	374-3
South Shore Hospital (SSH) 8012 S Crandon Ave. Chicago IL 60617 *Web:* www.southshorehospital.com	773-356-5000		374-3
South Shore Music Circus 130 Sohier St Cohasset MA 02025 *TF:* 800-514-3849 ■ *Web:* www.themusiccircus.org	781-383-9850	383-9804	572
South Shore Plaza 250 Granite St. Braintree MA 02184 *TF:* 877-746-6642 ■ *Web:* www.simon.com	781-843-8200	843-4708	460
South Shore State Park c/o Eldon Hazlet State Recreation Area 20100 Hazlet Pk Rd Carlyle IL 62231 *Web:* www.dnr.state.il.us	618-594-3015		565
South Shore Transportation Inc 4010 Columbus Ave Sandusky OH 44870 *TF:* 888-428-0879 ■ *Web:* www.sshoretrans.com	419-626-6267	626-9640	780
South Side Chamber of Commerce 1100 E Carson St Pittsburgh PA 15203 *Web:* www.southsidechamber.org	412-431-3360		139
South Side Machine Works Inc 3761 Eiler St. Saint Louis MO 63116 *Web:* www.southsidemachine.net	314-481-7171	481-9271	454
South Sioux City Convention & Visitors Bureau 4401 Dakota Ave. South Sioux City NE 68776 *TF:* 866-494-1307 ■ *Web:* visitsouthsiouxcity.com	402-494-1307		206
South Sound Speedway 3730 183rd Ave SW Rochester WA 98579 *TF:* 800-543-6238 ■ *Web:* www.southsoundspeedway.com	360-858-1464		515
South st Paul Steel Supply Company Inc 200 Hardman Ave N South Saint Paul MN 55075 *TF:* 800-456-7777 ■ *Web:* www.sspss.com	651-451-6666		492
South State Inc 202 Reeves Rd. Bridgeton NJ 08302 *TF:* 800-247-1727 ■ *Web:* southstateinc.com	856-451-5300	455-3461	46
South Street Financial Corp 103 N Second St. Albemarle NC 28001 *OTC:* SSFC ■ *Web:* bankofnc.com	704-982-9184	983-1308	360-2
South Street Seaport 19 Fulton St. New York NY 10038 *Web:* www.southstreetseaport.com	212-732-8257	964-8056	50-6

Phone | Fax | Class

South Street Seaport Museum
12 Fulton St .... New York NY 10038 212-748-8600 520
Web: www.southstreetseaportmuseum.org

South Street Securities LLC
825 Third Ave 35th Fl .... New York NY 10022 212-824-0738 690
Web: www.southstreetsecurities.com

South Suburban College
15800 S State St .... South Holland IL 60473 708-596-2000 225-5806* 162
**Fax:* Admissions ■ *TF:* 800-609-8056 ■ *Web:* ssc.edu

South Summit School District
375 E 300 S .... Kamas UT 84036 435-783-4301 685
Web: www.ssummit.k12.ut.us

South Tacoma Honda 7802 S Tacoma Way .... Tacoma WA 98409 253-472-2300 57
TF: 888-497-2416 ■ *Web:* www.southtacomahonda.com

South Tahoe Refuse Co
2140 Ruth Ave .... South Lake Tahoe CA 96150 530-541-5105 544-2608 804
Web: www.southtahoerefuse.com

South Texas Blood & Tissue Ctr
6211 IH-10 W .... San Antonio TX 78201 210-731-5555 731-5501 89
TF: 800-292-5534 ■ *Web:* southtexasblood.org

South Texas Botanical Gardens & Nature Ctr
8545 S Staples St .... Corpus Christi TX 78413 361-852-2100 852-7875 97
TF: 800-848-0078 ■ *Web:* www.stxbot.org

South Texas College of Law
1303 San Jacinto St .... Houston TX 77002 713-659-8040 167-1
Web: www.stcl.edu

South Texas Institute for the Arts
1902 N Shoreline Blvd .... Corpus Christi TX 78401 361-825-3500 825-3520 520
Web: www.artmuseumofsouthtexas.org

South Texas Money Management Ltd
700 N Saint Mary's Ste 100 .... San Antonio TX 78205 210-824-8916 401
TF: 800-805-1385 ■ *Web:* stmmltd.com

South Texas Veterans Health Care System
7400 Merton Minter St .... San Antonio TX 78229 210-617-5300 374-8
TF: 800-209-7377 ■ *Web:* www.southtexas.va.gov

South Toledo Bend State Park
120 Bald Eagle Rd .... Anacoco LA 71403 337-286-9075 565
TF: 888-398-4770 ■ *Web:* www.crt.state.la.us

South University
Montgomery 5355 Vaughn Rd .... Montgomery AL 36116 334-395-8800 166
TF: 866-629-2962 ■ *Web:* www.southuniversity.edu

South University Columbia
9 Science Ct .... Columbia SC 29203 803-799-9082 166
TF: 800-688-0932 ■ *Web:* www.southuniversity.edu

South University Savannah
709 Mall Blvd .... Savannah GA 31406 912-201-8000 166
TF: 800-688-0932 ■ *Web:* www.southuniversity.edu

South University West Palm Beach
9801 Belvedere Rd University Ctr .... West Palm Beach FL 33411 561-273-6500 166
TF: 800-688-0932 ■ *Web:* www.southuniversity.edu

South Valley Drywall Inc
12362 Dumont Way .... Littleton CO 80125 303-791-7212 470-0116 189-9
Web: www.southvalleydrywall.com

South Valley Specialties 547 W 9320 S .... Sandy UT 84070 801-566-3977 677
Web: www.svsco.com

South Water Kitchen 225 N Wabash Ave .... Chicago IL 60601 312-236-9300 671
Web: www.southwaterkitchen.com

South Western Communications Inc
1071 Rosebud Ln .... Newburgh IN 47630 812-477-6495 246
TF: 800-903-8432 ■ *Web:* www.swc.net

South Whidbey Island State Park
4128 Smugglers Cove Rd .... Freeland WA 98249 360-331-4559 565
Web: parks.state.wa.us

South Whidbey School Dist 206
5520 Maxwelton Rd .... Langley WA 98260 360-221-6100 221-3835 685
Web: www.sw.wednet.edu

South Woods State Prison
215 Burlington Rd S .... Bridgeton NJ 08302 856-459-7000 459-7140 213
Web: state.nj.us

South Yuba River State Park
17660 Pleasant Valley Rd .... Penn Valley CA 95946 530-432-2546 565
Web: www.parks.ca.gov

South/Shore Controls Inc
4485 N Ridge Rd .... Perry OH 44081 440-259-2500 259-2500 203
TF: 800-962-0688 ■ *Web:* www.southshorecontrols.com

Southampton Chamber of Commerce
76 Main St .... SoutHampton NY 11968 631-283-0402 283-8707 139
Web: www.southamptonchamber.com

Southampton County 22350 Main St .... Courtland VA 23837 757-653-2200 653-2547 338
Web: www.southamptoncounty.org

Southampton Hospital
240 Meeting House Ln .... SoutHampton NY 11968 631-726-8200 283-5730 374-3
Web: www.southamptonhospital.org

Southampton Inn 91 Hill St .... SoutHampton NY 11968 631-283-6500 283-6559 379
TF: 800-832-6500 ■ *Web:* www.southamptoninn.com

Southampton Memorial Hospital
100 Fairview Dr .... Franklin VA 23851 757-569-6100 374-3
Web: www.smhfranklin.com

Southard Communications Inc
111 John St Ste 630 .... New York NY 10038 212-777-2220 636
TF: 800-745-3000 ■ *Web:* www.southardinc.com

Southaven Chamber of Commerce
500 Main St .... Southaven MS 38671 662-342-6114 342-6365 139
Web: www.southavenchamber.com

Southbend Inc
1100 Old Honeycutt Rd .... Fuquay Varina NC 27526 919-762-1000 762-1121 298
TF: 800-755-4777 ■ *Web:* www.southbendnc.com

Southboro Medical Group Inc
24 Newton St .... Southborough MA 01772 508-481-5500 460-3221 374-3
Web: reliantmedicalgroup.org/?sb

Southbridge Sheet Metal Works Inc
441 Main St .... Sturbridge MA 01566 508-347-7800 347-9118 697
Web: ssmwusa.com

Southco 210 N Brinton Lake Rd .... Concordville PA 19331 610-459-4000 459-4012 350
TF: 877-821-0666 ■ *Web:* www.southco.com

Southco Distributing Co
2201 S John St .... Goldsboro NC 27530 919-735-8012 297-8
TF: 800-969-3172 ■ *Web:* www.southcodistributing.com

Phone | Fax | Class

Southco Inc of North Carolina
3125 N Kerr Ave .... Wilmington NC 28405 910-763-3451 492
Web: www.southcoinc.com

Southcoast Cabinet Co 755 Pinefall Ave .... Walnut CA 91789 909-594-3089 115
Web: www.southcoastcabinet.com

SouthCrest Hospital 8801 S 101st E Ave .... Tulsa OK 74133 918-294-4000 374-3
Web: hillcrestsouth.com

Southdale Ctr 10 Southdale Ctr .... Edina MN 55435 952-925-7874 925-7856 460
TF: 877-746-6642 ■ *Web:* simon.com/mall?id=1249

Southdata Inc 201 Technology Ln .... Mt Airy NC 27030 800-549-4722 177
TF: 800-549-4722 ■ *Web:* www.southdata.com

Southeast Alabama Medical Ctr
1108 Ross Clark Cir .... Dothan AL 36301 334-793-8111 677-4901 374-3
Web: www.samc.org

Southeast Arkansas College
1900 Hazel St .... Pine Bluff AR 71603 870-543-5900 162
TF: 888-732-7582

Southeast Asia Resource Action Ctr (SEARAC)
1628 16th St NW 3rd Fl .... Washington DC 20009 202-667-4690 667-6449 48-5
TF: 888-907-1485 ■ *Web:* www.searac.org

Southeast Colorado Power Assn (SECPA)
901 W 3rd .... La Junta CO 81050 719-384-2551 384-7320 245
TF: 800-332-8634 ■ *Web:* www.secpa.com

Southeast Community College
Beatrice 4771 W Scott Rd .... Beatrice NE 68310 402-228-3468 228-2218* 162
**Fax:* Admissions ■ *TF:* 800-233-5027 ■ *Web:* www.southeast.edu
Lincoln 8800 'O' St .... Lincoln NE 68520 402-471-3333 437-2404* 162
**Fax:* Admissions ■ *TF:* 800-642-4075 ■ *Web:* www.southeast.edu
Milford 600 State St .... Milford NE 68405 402-761-2131 761-2324 800
TF: 800-933-7223 ■ *Web:* www.southeast.edu

Southeast Computer Solutions Inc
15165 NW 77th Ave Ste 2009 .... Miami FL 33014 305-556-4697 177
TF: 888-773-2161 ■ *Web:* www.southeastcomputers.com

Southeast Connections LLC
2720 Dogwood Dr SE .... Conyers GA 30013 404-659-1422 186
TF: 800-280-6570 ■ *Web:* www.seconnections.com

Southeast Culvert Inc
1094 Bankhead Hwy .... Winder GA 30680 770-963-5041 595
Web: www.southeastculvert.com

Southeast Dallas Chamber of Commerce
802 S Buckner Blvd .... Dallas TX 75217 214-398-9590 139
Web: www.sedallaschamber.org

Southeast Delco School District
1560 Delmar Dr .... Folcroft PA 19032 610-522-4300 449
Web: www.sedelco.org

Southeast Electric Co-op Inc (SECO)
110 S Main St .... Ekalaka MT 59324 406-775-8762 245
TF: 888-485-8762 ■ *Web:* www.seecoop.com

Southeast Fabricators Inc
7301 University Blvd E .... Cottondale AL 35453 205-556-3227 480
TF: 800-932-3227 ■ *Web:* www.sefab.com

Southeast Fisheries Science Ctr
75 Virginia Beach Dr .... Miami FL 33149 305-361-4200 361-4219 668
Web: www.sefsc.noaa.gov

Southeast Fuels Inc
620 Green Valley Rd Ste 303 .... Greensboro NC 27408 336-854-1106 316
Web: www.southeastfuels.com

Southeast Georgia Health System Brunswick Campus
2415 Parkwood Dr .... Brunswick GA 31520 912-466-7000 466-7013 374-3
Web: www.sghs.org

Southeast Industrial Equipment Inc
12200 Steele Creek Rd .... Charlotte NC 28273 704-399-9700 393-1714 470
TF: 866-696-9125 ■ *Web:* www.sielift.com

Southeast Kentucky Community & Technical College
Cumberland 700 College Rd .... Cumberland KY 40823 606-589-2145 589-3175* 162
**Fax:* Admissions ■ *TF:* 888-274-7322 ■ *Web:* southeast.kctcs.edu
Middlesboro Campus
1300 Chichester Ave .... Middlesboro KY 40965 606-242-2145 248-3233 162
TF: 888-274-7322 ■ *Web:* southeast.kctcs.edu
Whitesburg 2 Long Ave .... Whitesburg KY 41858 606-633-0279 589-3377 162
TF: 888-274-7322 ■ *Web:* southeast.kctcs.edu

Southeast Milk Inc
1950 SE Hwy 484 PO Box 3790 .... Belleview FL 34420 800-598-7866 245-9434* 296-27
**Fax Area Code:* 352 ■ *TF:* 800-598-7866 ■ *Web:* www.southeastmilk.org

Southeast Missouri Hospital (SMH)
1701 Lacey St .... Cape Girardeau MO 63701 573-334-4822 374-3
TF: 800-800-5123 ■ *Web:* www.sehealth.org

Southeast Missouri Mental Health Ctr
1010 W Columbia St .... Farmington MO 63640 573-218-6792 374-5
Web: dmh.mo.gov

Southeast Missouri State University
1 University Plaza .... Cape Girardeau MO 63701 573-651-2000 651-5936* 166
**Fax:* Admissions ■ *TF:* 866-562-6801 ■ *Web:* www.semo.edu

Southeast Missourian
301 Broadway St .... Cape Girardeau MO 63701 573-335-6611 334-7288 532-2
TF: 800-879-1210 ■ *Web:* www.semissourian.com

Southeast Modular Mfg
2500 Industrial St .... Leesburg FL 34748 352-728-2930 106
Web: www.southeastmodular.net

Southeast Museum of Photography
1200 W International Speedway Blvd Bldg 100
Daytona Beach Community College .... Daytona Beach FL 32114 386-506-4475 520
TF: 800-354-8332 ■ *Web:* www.smponline.org

Southeast Regional Library
49 Bison Ave .... Weyburn SK S4H0H9 306-848-3100 842-2665 436
Web: southeastlibrary.ca

Southeast Regional Library
775 N Greenfield Rd .... Gilbert AZ 85234 602-652-3000 434-3
TF: 800-275-8777 ■ *Web:* mcldaz.org

Southeast State Correctional Facility
546 State Farm Rd .... Windsor VT 05089 802-674-6717 674-2249 213
Web: www.doc.state.vt.us

Southeast Technical Institute
2320 N Career Ave .... Sioux Falls SD 57107 605-367-8355 367-4372* 800
**Fax:* Hum Res ■ *TF:* 800-247-0789 ■ *Web:* www.southeasttech.edu

Southeast Tissue Alliance (SETA)
6241 NW 23rd St Ste 400 .... Gainesville FL 32653 352-248-2114 545
TF: 866-432-1164 ■ *Web:* www.donorcare.org

Name / Address	City	State	ZIP	Phone	Fax	Class
Southeast Valley Regional Association of Realtors 1363 S Vineyard *Web:* www.sevrar.com	Mesa	AZ	85210	480-833-7510		533
Southeast Volusia Chamber of Commerce 115 Canal St *Web:* www.sevchamber.com	New Smyrna Beach	FL	32168	386-428-2449	423-3512	139
Southeastern Aluminum Products Inc 4925 Bulls Bay Hwy *TF Sales:* 800-243-8200 ■ *Web:* www.southeasternaluminum.com	Jacksonville	FL	32254	904-781-8200	224-8068	234
Southeastern Asset Management Inc 6410 Poplar Ave Ste 900 *TF:* 800-445-9469 ■ *Web:* www.southeasternasset.com	Memphis	TN	38119	901-761-2474		401
Southeastern Baptist College 4229 Hwy 15 N *Web:* www.southeasternbaptist.edu	Laurel	MS	39440	601-426-6346	426-6347	161
Southeastern Baptist Theological Seminary 120 S Wingate St *TF:* 800-284-6317 ■ *Web:* www.sebts.edu	Wake Forest	NC	27587	919-556-3101		167-3
Southeastern Community College 1500 W Agency Rd **Fax:* Admissions ■ *TF:* 866-722-4692	West Burlington	IA	52655	319-752-2731	752-4957*	162
Southeastern Community College PO Box 151 **Fax:* Admissions ■ *Web:* www.sccnc.edu	Whiteville	NC	28472	910-642-7141	642-1267*	162
Southeastern Community College South 335 Messenger Rd **Fax:* Admissions ■ *TF:* 866-722-4692 ■ *Web:* scciowa.edu	Keokuk	IA	52632	319-524-3221	524-8621*	162
Southeastern Computer Consultants Inc 5166 Potomac Dr Ste 400 *Web:* www.teamscci.com	King George	VA	22485	301-695-5311	695-6101	180
Southeastern Construction & Maintenance Co Inc 1150 Pebbledale Rd PO Box 1055 *Web:* www.southeasternconst.com	Mulberry	FL	33860	863-428-1511	428-1110	189-14
Southeastern Correctional Institution 5900 B I S Rd *TF:* 800-237-3454 ■ *Web:* ohio.gov	Lancaster	OH	43130	740-653-4324	653-0779	213
Southeastern Ctr for Contemporary Art 750 Marguerite Dr *Web:* www.secca.org	Winston-Salem	NC	27106	336-725-1904	722-6059	50-2
Southeastern Electric Co-op Inc 1514 E Hwy 70 PO Box 1370 *TF:* 866-924-1315 ■ *Web:* www.se-coop.com	Durant	OK	74702	580-924-2170		245
Southeastern Equipment Company Inc 10874 E Pike Rd *TF:* 800-798-5438 ■ *Web:* www.southeasternequip.com	Cambridge	OH	43725	740-432-6303	432-3303	358
Southeastern Freight Lines Inc 420 Davega Rd **Fax:* Cust Svc ■ *TF:* 800-637-7335 ■ *Web:* www.sefl.com	Lexington	SC	29073	803-794-7300	939-3462*	780
Southeastern Illinois College 3575 College Rd **Fax:* Admissions ■ *TF:* 866-338-2742 ■ *Web:* www.sic.edu	Harrisburg	IL	62946	618-252-5400	252-3062*	162
SouthEastern Illinois Electric Co-op 585 Hwy 142 S PO Box 251 *TF:* 800-833-2611 ■ *Web:* www.seiec.com	Eldorado	IL	62930	618-273-2611	273-3886	245
Southeastern Indiana Rural Electric Membership Corp 712 S Buckeye St *TF:* 800-737-4111 ■ *Web:* www.seiremc.com	Osgood	IN	47037	812-689-4111	689-6987	245
Southeastern Louisiana University 500 Western Ave **Fax:* Admissions ■ *TF:* 800-222-7358 ■ *Web:* www.southeastern.edu	Hammond	LA	70402	985-549-2062	549-5632*	166
Southeastern Louisiana University Sims Memorial Library SLU 10896 *Web:* www.southeastern.edu	Hammond	LA	70402	985-549-3860	549-3995	434-6
Southeastern Metal Products LLC 1420 Metals Dr *Web:* www.sempllc.com	Charlotte	NC	28206	704-596-4017		697
Southeastern Metals Mfg Company Inc 11801 Industry Dr *TF:* 800-874-0335 ■ *Web:* www.semetals.com	Jacksonville	FL	32218	904-757-4200		234
Southeastern Ohio Regional Medical Ctr 1341 Clark St *Web:* www.seormc.org	Cambridge	OH	43725	740-439-8000		374-3
Southeastern Oklahoma State University 1405 N Fourth St **Fax:* Admissions ■ *TF:* 800-435-1327 ■ *Web:* www.se.edu	Durant	OK	74701	580-745-2000	745-7502*	166
Southeastern Paperboard Inc 100 S Harris Rd *TF:* 800-229-7372 ■ *Web:* www.southeasternpaperboard.com	Piedmont	SC	29673	864-277-7353		554
Southeastern Pennsylvania Transportation Authority (SEPTA) 1234 Market St *Web:* www.septa.org	Philadelphia	PA	19107	215-580-7800		468
Southeastern Plastics Corp 15 Home News Row *Web:* www.seplasticsurgery.com	New Brunswick	NJ	08901	732-846-8500		596
Southeastern Printing Company Inc 3601 SE Dixie Hwy *Web:* www.seprint.com	Stuart	FL	34997	772-287-2141		781
Southeastern Public Library System of Oklahoma (SEPLSO) 401 N Second St **Fax Area Code:* 866 ■ *TF:* 800-562-9520 ■ *Web:* oklibrary.net	McAlester	OK	74501	918-426-0456	569-8188*	434-3
Southeastern Regional Medical Ctr 300 W 27th St *Web:* www.srmc.org	Lumberton	NC	28358	910-671-5000	671-5200	374-3
Southeastern Stages Inc 260 University Ave SW *TF:* 800-231-2222 ■ *Web:* www.southeasternstages.com	Atlanta	GA	30315	404-591-2780	591-2745	108
Southeastern Technology Inc 905 Industrial Dr *Web:* www.southeasterntech.com	Murfreesboro	TN	37129	615-890-1700		567
Southeastern University 1000 Longfellow Blvd *TF:* 800-500-8760 ■ *Web:* seu.edu	Lakeland	FL	33801	863-667-5000	667-5200	166
Southeastern Wholesale Tire Co 4721 Trademark Dr *TF General:* 800-849-9215 ■ *Web:* www.southeasterntireonline.com	Raleigh	NC	27610	919-832-3900	861-4357	755
Southerland Inc 1973 Southerland Dr *TF Cust Svc:* 800-443-1183 ■ *Web:* www.southerlandsleep.com	Nashville	TN	37207	615-226-9650		471
Southern Accent 595 Markham St *Web:* www.southernaccent.com	Toronto	ON	M6G2L7	416-536-3211		671
Southern Accents Magazine 2100 Lakeshore Dr *TF:* 877-262-5866 ■ *Web:* www.southernliving.com	Birmingham	AL	35209	205-445-6000		457-22
Southern Adirondack Library System 22 Whitney Pl *Web:* www.sals.edu	Saratoga Springs	NY	12866	518-584-7300		434-3
Southern Adventist University 4881 Taylor Cir *TF:* 800-768-8437 ■ *Web:* www.southern.edu	Collegedale	TN	37315	423-236-2000	236-1000	166
Southern Air Inc 2655 Lakeside Dr *TF:* 800-743-1214 ■ *Web:* www.southern-air.com	Lynchburg	VA	24501	434-385-6200	385-9081	189-10
Southern Arizona Veterans Healthcare System 3601 S Sixth Ave *TF:* 800-470-8262 ■ *Web:* tucson.va.gov	Tucson	AZ	85723	520-792-1450		374-8
Southern Arkansas University 100 E University St **Fax:* Admissions ■ *TF:* 800-332-7286 ■ *Web:* web.saumag.edu	Magnolia	AR	71753	870-235-4000	235-5005*	166
Southern Assn of Colleges & Schools 1866 Southern Ln *TF:* 888-413-3669 ■ *Web:* www.sacs.org	Decatur	GA	30033	404-679-4500	679-4558	49-5
Southern Audio Services 14763 Florida Blvd *TF Cust Svc:* 800-843-8823 ■ *Web:* www.bazooka.com	Baton Rouge	LA	70819	225-272-7135	272-9844	52
Southern Banc Company Inc 221 S Sixth St *OTC:* SRNN ■ *Web:* www.sobanco.com	Gadsden	AL	35901	256-543-3860		360-2
Southern Baptist Convention (SBC) 901 Commerce St *TF:* 866-722-5433 ■ *Web:* www.sbc.net	Nashville	TN	37203	615-244-2355		48-20
Southern Baptist Theological Seminary 2825 Lexington Rd **Fax:* Admitting ■ *TF:* 800-626-5525 ■ *Web:* www.sbts.edu	Louisville	KY	40280	502-897-4011	897-4723*	167-3
Southern Biotechnology Assoc Inc 160A Oxmoor Blvd *TF:* 800-722-2255 ■ *Web:* www.southernbiotech.com	Birmingham	AL	35209	205-945-1774	945-8768	231
Southern Bleacher Company Inc 801 Fifth St *TF:* 800-433-0912 ■ *Web:* www.southernbleacher.com	Graham	TX	76450	940-549-0733		106
Southern Bowl 1010 US Hwy 31 S *TF:* 800-463-3339 ■ *Web:* www.royalpin.com	Greenwood	IN	46143	317-881-8686		99
Southern Cable Communications 2101 S Fraser St *Web:* www.sccc.tv	Georgetown	SC	29440	843-546-2200		116
Southern California Aviation Inc 18438 Readiness St *Web:* comav.com/services/technical-services	Victorville	CA	92394	760-530-2400	246-1186	24
Southern California Boiler Inc 5331 Business Dr *TF:* 800-775-2645 ■ *Web:* www.californiaboiler.com	Huntington Beach	CA	92649	714-891-0701		187
Southern California Earthquake Ctr 3651 Trousdale Pkwy Ste 169 *Web:* www.scec.org	Los Angeles	CA	90089	213-740-5843	740-0011	668
Southern California Edison Co 2244 Walnut Grove Ave *TF:* 800-655-4555 ■ *Web:* www.sce.com	Rosemead	CA	91770	626-302-1212		787
Southern California Gas Co 555 W Fifth St **Fax Area Code:* 213 ■ *TF:* 800-427-2200 ■ *Web:* www.socalgas.com	Los Angeles	CA	90013	909-305-8261	244-8293*	787
Southern California Institute of Architecture 960 E Third St **Fax:* Admissions ■ *Web:* www.sciarc.edu	Los Angeles	CA	90013	213-613-2200	613-2260*	166
Southern California Public Power Authority (SCPPA) 225 S Lake Ave Ste 1250 *Web:* www.scppa.org	Pasadena	CA	91101	626-793-9364	793-9461	787
Southern California Regional Rail Authority 700 S Flower St Ste 2600 *TF:* 800-371-5465 ■ *Web:* www.metrolinktrains.com	Los Angeles	CA	90017	213-452-0200	452-0429	468
Southern California Seminary 2075 E Madison Ave *TF:* 888-389-7244 ■ *Web:* www.socalsem.edu	El Cajon	CA	92019	888-389-7244		166
Southern Cellulose Products Inc 105 W 45th St	Chattanooga	TN	37410	423-821-1561		638
Southern Chester County Chamber of Commerce 217 W State St *TF:* 800-343-6583 ■ *Web:* www.sccc.com	Kennett Square	PA	19348	610-444-0774	444-5105	139
Southern Columbiana County Regional Chamber of Commerce 529 Market St PO Box 94 *TF:* 800-804-0468 ■ *Web:* www.sccregionalchamber.org	East Liverpool	OH	43920	330-385-0845	385-0581	139
Southern Communications Services Inc 5555 Glenridge Connector Ste 500 *TF:* 800-818-5462 ■ *Web:* www.southernlinc.com	Atlanta	GA	30342	800-818-5462		736
Southern Company 30 Ivan Allen Jr Blvd NW *TF Cust Svc:* 800-754-9452 ■ *Web:* www.southerncompany.com	Atlanta	GA	30308	404-506-5000	506-3076	787
Southern Company Inc 3101 Carrier St *TF:* 800-264-7626 ■ *Web:* www.socomemphis.com	Memphis	TN	38116	901-345-2531		537
Southern Company of NLR Inc, The 1201 Cypress St *TF:* 800-482-5493 ■ *Web:* www.thesoco.com	North Little Rock	AR	72114	501-376-6333		791
Southern Company Services Inc 42 Inverness Ctr Pkwy *Web:* www.southerncompany.com	Birmingham	AL	35242	205-992-6011		261
Southern Components Inc 7360 Julie Frances Dr *TF:* 800-256-2144 ■ *Web:* www.socomp.com	Shreveport	LA	71129	318-687-3330		817
Southern Concrete Products Inc 266 E Church St *Web:* www.southernconcrete.com	Lexington	TN	38351	731-968-8394		539
Southern Connecticut Gas (SCG) 60 Marsh Hill Rd *TF:* 866-268-2887 ■ *Web:* www.soconngas.com	Orange	CT	06477	866-268-2887		787
Southern Connecticut State University 501 Crescent St *TF:* 888-500-7278 ■ *Web:* www.southernct.edu	New Haven	CT	06515	203-392-5200	392-5727	166
Southern Connecticut State University Buley Library 501 Crescent St *Web:* libguides.southernct.edu/home	New Haven	CT	06515	203-392-5750	392-5775	434-6

				Phone	Fax	Class
Southern Container Ltd 10410 Papalote St Ste 130 *Web:* www.southerncontainer.com	Houston	TX	77041	713-466-5661	466-4223	100
Southern Controls Inc 3511 Wetumpka Hwy *TF:* 800-392-5770 ■ *Web:* www.southerncontrols.com	Montgomery	AL	36110	800-392-5770		246
Southern Copper & Supply Company Inc 875 Yeager Pkwy *TF:* 800-289-2728 ■ *Web:* www.southerncopper.com	Pelham	AL	35124	205-664-9440		492
Southern Correctional Institution 272 Glen Rd PO Box 786 *Web:* www.ncdps.gov	Troy	NC	27371	910-572-3784		213
Southern Data Systems Inc 1245 Land O Lakes Dr *TF:* 888-425-6151 ■ *Web:* www.southern-data.com	Roswell	GA	30075	770-993-7103		225
Southern District of West Virginia 300 Virginia St E Ste 2400 *Web:* www.wvsd.uscourts.gov	Charleston	WV	25301	304-347-3000		341-3
Southern Door & Plywood Co 3686 Moreland Ave *Web:* www.southerndoorply.com	Conley	GA	30288	404-361-7800		499
Southern Duchess News 84 E Main St *Web:* sdutchessnews.com	Wappingers Falls	NY	12590	845-297-3723		532-4
Southern Electrical Equipment Company Inc 4045 Hargrove Ave *Web:* www.seecoswitch.com	Charlotte	NC	28208	704-392-1396		729
Southern Environmental Law Ctr 201 W Main St Ste 14 *Web:* www.southernenvironment.org	Charlottesville	VA	22902	434-977-4090		428
Southern Eye Bank 2701 Kingman St Ste 200 *Web:* www.southerneyebank.com	Metairie	LA	70006	504-891-3937	891-2401	269
Southern Farm Bureau Casualty Insurance Co 1800 E County Line Rd Ste 400 *Web:* www.sfbcic.com	Ridgeland	MS	39157	601-957-7777		391-4
Southern Farm Bureau Life Insurance Co PO Box 78 *Web:* www.sfbli.com	Jackson	MS	39205	601-981-7422		391-2
Southern Festival of Books Humanities Tennessee 306 Gay St Ste 306 *Web:* www.humanitiestennessee.org	Nashville	TN	37201	615-770-0006	770-0007	281
Southern Film Extruders Inc 2319 English Rd *TF:* 800-334-6101 ■ *Web:* www.southernfilm.com	High Point	NC	27262	336-885-8091	885-1221	600
Southern Filter Media LLC 2735 Kanasita Dr Ste A *Web:* www.southernfiltermedia.com	Hixson	TN	37343	423-698-8988		820
Southern Financial Exchange 1340 Poydras St Ste 2010 *Web:* www.sfe.org	New Orleans	LA	70112	504-525-6779		507
Southern Finishing 801 E Church St *Web:* www.southernfinishing.com	Martinsville	VA	24112	276-632-4901		321
Southern Folger Detention Equipment Co 4634 S Presa St *TF:* 888-745-0530 ■ *Web:* www.southernfolger.com	San Antonio	TX	78223	210-533-1231	533-2211	692
Southern Foods Inc 3500 Old Battleground Rd *Web:* www.southernfoods.com	Greensboro	NC	27410	336-545-3800		297-9
Southern Forest Products Assn (SFPA) 6660 Riverside Dr Ste 212 *TF:* 866-574-4155 ■ *Web:* www.sfpa.org	Metairie	LA	70003	504-443-4464		48-2
Southern FS Inc 2002 E Main St PO Box 728 *TF:* 800-492-7684 ■ *Web:* southernfs.com	Marion	IL	62959	618-993-2833	997-2526	276
Southern Fulfillment Services LLC 1650 90th Ave *TF:* 800-891-2120 ■ *Web:* www.southernfulfillment.com	Vero Beach	FL	32966	772-226-3500		459
Southern Furniture Company of Conover Inc 1099 Second Ave Pl SE *Web:* www.southernfurniture.net	Conover	NC	28613	828-464-0311		321
Southern Gardens Citrus 1820 Country Rd 833 *Web:* www.ussugar.com/citrus	Clewiston	FL	33440	863-983-3030		315-2
Southern Georgia Bay Chamber of Commerce 208 King St *Web:* southerngeorgianbay.ca	Midland	ON	L4R3L9	705-526-7884	526-1744	137
Southern Glazer's Wine & Spirits 1600 NW 163rd St *Web:* www.southernglazers.com	Miami	FL	33169	305-625-4171		81-3
Southern Glove Mfg Company Inc 749 AC Little Dr *TF Cust Svc:* 800-222-1113 ■ *Web:* www.southernglove.com	Newton	NC	28658	828-464-4884	464-7968	155-8
Southern Graphics Systems 626 W Main St Suite 500 **Fax Area Code:* 502 ■ *Web:* www.sgsintl.com	Louisville	KY	41042	859-525-1190	637-5443*	781
Southern Grouts & Mortars Inc 1502 SW Second Pl *TF:* 800-641-9247 ■ *Web:* www.sgm.cc	Pompano Beach	FL	33069	954-943-2288	943-2402	3
Southern Healthcare Agency Inc PO Box 320999 *TF:* 800-880-2772 ■ *Web:* www.southernhealthcare.com	Flowood	MS	39232	601-933-0037		260
Southern Heat Exchanger Corp 6100 Old Montgomery Hwy *Web:* www.souheat.com	Tuscaloosa	AL	35405	205-345-5335		488
Southern Hens Inc 329 Moselle-Seminary Rd	Moselle	MS	39459	601-582-2262		619
Southern Illinois Electric Co-op 7420 US Hwy 51 S *TF:* 800-762-1400 ■ *Web:* www.siec.coop	Dongola	IL	62926	618-827-3555		245
Southern Illinois Healthcare 1239 E Main St *TF:* 866-744-2468 ■ *Web:* www.sih.net	Carbondale	IL	62902	618-457-5200		353
Southern Illinois University *Edwardsville* SR 157 **Fax:* Admissions ■ *TF:* 888-328-5168 ■ *Web:* www.siue.edu	Edwardsville	IL	62026	618-650-2000	650-5013*	166
Southern Illinois University Carbondale 1263 Lincoln Dr MC 4716 Student Services Bldg 3rd Fl **Fax:* Admissions ■ *Web:* gradschool.siu.edu	Carbondale	IL	62901	618-536-7791	453-4562*	166
Southern Illinois University Carbondale Morris Library 605 Agriculture Dr MC 6632 *Web:* www.lib.siu.edu	Carbondale	IL	62901	618-453-2522	453-3440	434-6
Southern Illinois University Edwardsville *Lovejoy Library* 30 Hairpin Dr Campus Box 1063 *TF:* 888-328-5168 ■ *Web:* www.siue.edu/lovejoylibrary	Edwardsville	IL	62026	618-650-4636	650-2717	434-6
Southern Illinois University School of Law 1209 W Chautauqua Rd **Fax:* Admissions ■ *TF:* 800-739-9187 ■ *Web:* www.law.siu.edu	Carbondale	IL	62901	618-453-8858	453-8921*	167-1
Southern Illinois University School of Medicine Medical Library (SIU) 801 N Rutledge St *Web:* www.siumed.edu/lib	Springfield	IL	62702	217-545-2122	545-0988	434-1
Southern Illinoisan 710 N Illinois Ave PO Box 2108 *TF:* 800-228-0429 ■ *Web:* www.thesouthern.com	Carbondale	IL	62902	618-529-5454	457-2935	532-2
Southern Imperial Inc 1400 Eddy Ave *TF Cust Svc:* 800-747-4665 ■ *Web:* www.southernimperial.com	Rockford	IL	61103	815-877-7041		286
Southern Implants Inc 5 Holland Bldg 209 *Web:* www.southernimplants.us	Irvine	CA	92618	949-273-8505		228
Southern Indiana Rehabilitation Hospital 3104 Blackiston Blvd *TF:* 800-737-7090 ■ *Web:* www.sirh.org	New Albany	IN	47150	812-941-8300		374-6
Southern Indiana Rural Electric Co-op Inc 1776 Tenth St PO Box 219 *TF:* 800-323-2316 ■ *Web:* www.sinpwr.com	Tell City	IN	47586	812-547-2316	547-6853	245
Southern Industrial Constructors Inc 6101 Triangle Dr *TF:* 866-890-7794 ■ *Web:* www.southernindustrial.com	Raleigh	NC	27617	919-782-4600	782-2935	189-10
Southern Ionics Inc 201 Commerce St *TF:* 800-053-3585 ■ *Web:* www.southernionics.com	West Point	MS	39773	662-494-3055	495-2590	143
Southern Iowa Electric Co-op Inc 22458 Hwy 2 PO Box 70 *TF:* 800-607-2027 ■ *Web:* www.sie.coop	Bloomfield	IA	52537	641-664-2277	664-3502	245
Southern Iron Works Inc 6600 Electronic Dr *Web:* www.siwinc.com	Springfield	VA	22151	703-354-5500		480
Southern Jersey Family Medical Centers Inc 860 S White Horse Pke *Web:* www.sjfmc.org	Hammonton	NJ	08037	609-567-0200		374-3
Southern Kentucky Book Fest 1906 College Heights Blvd Ste 11067 *Web:* www.sokybookfest.org	Bowling Green	KY	42101	270-745-4502		281
Southern Kentucky Rehabilitation Hospital 1300 Campbell Ln *TF:* 800-989-5775 ■ *Web:* www.skyrehab.com	Bowling Green	KY	42104	270-782-0900		374-6
Southern Kitchen 1716 Sixth Ave *Web:* southernkitchen-tacoma.com	Tacoma	WA	98405	253-627-4282		671
Southern Landscape Professionals Inc 8625 Mt Pleasant Church Rd *Web:* www.southernlandscapepros.com	Willow Spring	NC	27592	919-552-1156		192
Southern Lehigh School District 5775 Main St *TF:* 800-360-8989 ■ *Web:* www.slsd.org	Center Valley	PA	18034	610-282-3121	282-0193	685
Southern Lights 2415 Lawndale Dr *Web:* southernlightsbistro.com	Greensboro	NC	27408	336-379-9414		671
Southern Living Magazine 2100 Lakeshore Dr *TF:* 800-366-4712 ■ *Web:* www.southernliving.com	Birmingham	AL	35209	205-445-6000	445-6700	457-22
Southern Maid Donut Flour Co 3615 Cavalier Dr *Web:* www.southernmaiddonuts.com	Garland	TX	75042	972-272-6425	276-3549	68
Southern Maine Community College (SMCC) 2 Ft Rd *TF:* 877-282-2182 ■ *Web:* www.smccme.edu	South Portland	ME	04106	207-741-5500	741-5760	800
Southern Maine Medical Ctr (SMMC) 1 Medical Ctr Dr PO Box 626 *Web:* mainehealth.org/southern-maine-health-care	Biddeford	ME	04005	207-283-7000	283-7020	374-3
Southern Maryland Hospital Ctr 7503 Surratts Rd *Web:* www.medstarsouthernmaryland.org	Clinton	MD	20735	301-868-8000		374-3
Southern Maryland Oil Co Inc (SMO) 109 N Maple Ave *TF:* 888-222-3720 ■ *Web:* www.smoenergy.com	La Plata	MD	20646	888-222-3720		579
Southern Methodist University 6425 Boaz Ln **Fax:* Admissions ■ *TF:* 800-323-0672 ■ *Web:* www.smu.edu	Dallas	TX	75205	214-768-2000	768-0202*	166
Southern Methodist University Dedman School of Law 3300 University Blvd Ste 331 **Fax:* Admissions ■ *TF:* 888-768-5291 ■ *Web:* www.law.smu.edu	Dallas	TX	75205	214-768-2550	768-2549*	167-1
Southern Michigan Bank & Trust 51 W Pearl St PO Box 309 *TF:* 800-379-7628 ■ *Web:* www.smb-t.com	Coldwater	MI	49036	517-279-5500		70
Southern Midcoast Maine Chamber 8 Venture Ave PO Box 33 *TF:* 877-725-8797 ■ *Web:* www.midcoastmaine.com	Brunswick	ME	04011	207-725-8797	725-9787	139
Southern Minnesota Beet Sugar Co-op 83550 CR 21 PO Box 500 *Web:* www.smbsc.com	Renville	MN	56284	320-329-8305	329-3252	296-38
Southern Minnesota Municipal Power Agency 500 First Ave SW *Web:* www.smmpa.com	Rochester	MN	55902	507-285-0478	292-6414	245
Southern Missouri Bancorp Inc 531 Vine St *NASDAQ:* SMBC ■ *TF:* 855-452-7272 ■ *Web:* www.bankwithsouthern.com	Poplar Bluff	MO	63901	573-778-1800		360-2
Southern Missouri Containers Inc 900 N Belcrest *Web:* www.smcpackaging.com	Springfield	MO	65802	417-831-2685		100
Southern Motion Inc 161 Prestige Dr *Web:* www.southernmotion.com	Pontotoc	MS	38863	662-489-4921		319-2
Southern Motor Carriers Rate Conference Inc 500 Westpark Dr *TF:* 800-845-8090 ■ *Web:* www.smc3.com	Peachtree City	GA	30269	770-486-5800		478

	Phone	Fax	Class
Southern Moulding & Supply Co 7040 Battle Dr NW .... Kennesaw GA 30152 *Web:* www.southernmoulding.com	770-422-3949		361
Southern Multifoods Inc 101 E Cherokee St .... Jacksonville TX 75766 *Web:* www.smi-tex.com	903-586-1524		670
Southern Museum of Flight 4343 73rd St N .... Birmingham AL 35206 *Web:* www.southernmuseumofflight.org	205-833-8226	836-2439	520
Southern Nazarene University 6729 NW 39th Expy .... Bethany OK 73008 **Fax:* Admissions ■ *TF:* 800-648-9899 ■ *Web:* www.snu.edu	405-789-6400	491-6320*	166
Southern New Hampshire Medical Ctr 8 Prospect St PO Box 2014 .... Nashua NH 03061 *Web:* snhhs.org	603-577-2000		374-3
Southern New Hampshire University 2500 N River Rd .... Manchester NH 03106 **Fax Area Code:* 802 ■ *TF:* 800-668-1249 ■ *Web:* www.snhu.edu	603-668-2211	655-0236*	166
Southern New Mexico Correctional Facility 1983 Joe R Silva Blvd .... Las Cruces NM 88004 *Web:* cd.nm.gov/apd/snmcf.html	575-523-3200	523-3349	213
Southern Newspapers Inc (SNI) 5701 Woodway Dr .... Houston TX 77057 *Web:* sninews.com	713-266-5481	266-1847	637-8
Southern Ocean County Chamber of Commerce 265 W Ninth St .... Ship Bottom NJ 08008 *TF:* 800-292-6372 ■ *Web:* www.visitlbiregion.com	609-494-7211	494-5807	139
Southern Office Furniture Distributors Inc 7820 Thorndike Rd .... Greensboro NC 27409	336-668-4192		320
Southern Ohio Correctional Facility 1724 St Rt 728 PO Box 45699 .... Lucasville OH 45699 *Web:* drc.ohio.gov/socf	740-259-5544	259-2882	213
Southern Ohio Medical Ctr (SOMC) 1805 27th St .... Portsmouth OH 45662 *Web:* www.somc.org	740-356-5000		374-3
Southern Oregon University 1250 Siskiyou Blvd Britt Hall .... Ashland OR 97520 **Fax:* Admissions ■ *TF:* 800-482-7672 ■ *Web:* www.sou.edu	541-552-6411	552-8403*	166
Southern Oregon University Hannon Library 1250 Siskiyou Blvd .... Ashland OR 97520 *Web:* hanlib.sou.edu	541-552-6442		434-6
Southern Pan Services Co (SPS) 2385 Lithonia Industrial Blvd .... Lithonia GA 30058 *Web:* www.southernpan.com	678-301-2400		780
Southern Park Mall 7401 Market St .... Youngstown OH 44512 *TF:* 877-746-6642 ■ *Web:* www.simon.com	330-758-4511		460
Southern Parking Inc 420 S Dixie Hwy .... Hallandale Beach FL 33309 *Web:* spincremote.com	305-866-3409		562
Southern Petroleum Lab Inc 8850 Interchange Dr .... Houston TX 77054 **Fax Area Code:* 225 ■ *TF:* 877-775-5227 ■ *Web:* www.spl-inc.com	713-660-0901	219-3309*	743
Southern Pine Electric Co-op 2134 S Blvd .... Brewton AL 36426 *TF:* 866-867-5415 ■ *Web:* www.southernpine.org	251-867-5415	867-3925	245
Southern Pine Electric Power Assn 110 Risher St PO Box 60 .... Taylorsville MS 39168 *TF:* 800-231-5240 ■ *Web:* www.southernpine.coop	601-785-6511	785-4980	245
Southern Pines Nursing Ctr 6140 Congress St .... New Port Richey FL 34653 *Web:* southernpineshealthcare.com	727-842-8402	841-8060	450
Southern Poverty Law Ctr (SPLC) 400 Washington Ave .... Montgomery AL 36104 *TF:* 888-414-7752 ■ *Web:* www.splcenter.org	334-956-8200		48-8
Southern Precision Spring Company Inc 2200 Old Steele Creek Rd .... Charlotte NC 28208 *Web:* www.spspring.com	704-392-4393		492
Southern Prestige Industries Inc 113 Hatfield Rd .... Statesville NC 28625 *Web:* www.southernprestige.com	704-872-9524		454
Southern Public Power District (SPPD) 4550 W Husker Hwy PO Box 1687 .... Grand Island NE 68803 *TF:* 800-652-2013 ■ *Web:* www.southernpd.com	308-384-2350	384-5018	245
Southern Pump & Tank Co 4800 N Graham St .... Charlotte NC 28269 *TF Cust Svc:* 800-477-2826 ■ *Web:* www.spatco.com	704-596-4373	599-7700	385
Southern Quality Meats Inc 266 W Eigth St .... Pontotoc MS 38863	662-489-1524		473
Southern Railway of British Columbia Ltd 2102 River Dr .... New Westminster BC V3M6S3 *Web:* www.sryraillink.com	604-521-1966		650
Southern Refrigeration Corp 3140 Shenandoah Ave .... Roanoke VA 24017 *TF:* 800-763-4433 ■ *Web:* srcusa.com	540-342-3493	343-2163	665
Southern Regional High School District Board of Education 600 N Main St .... Manahawkin NJ 08050 *Web:* www.srsd.net	609-597-9481	978-0298	685
Southern Regional Medical Ctr 11 Upper Riverdale Rd SW .... Riverdale GA 30274 *Web:* www.southernregional.org	770-991-8000		374-3
Southern Regional Research Ctr (SRRC) 1100 Robert E Lee Blvd .... New Orleans LA 70124 **Fax Area Code:* 504 ■ *Web:* www.ars.usda.gov	706-546-3527	286-4419*	668
Southern Research 2000 Ninth Ave S .... Birmingham AL 35205 *TF:* 800-967-6774 ■ *Web:* www.sri.org	205-581-2000	581-2726	668
Southern Research Company Inc 2850 Centenary Blvd .... Shreveport LA 71104 *TF:* 888-772-6952 ■ *Web:* www.southernresearchinc.com	318-227-9700	424-1801	400
Southern Research Station USDA Forest Service 200 W.T. Weaver Blvd .... Asheville NC 28804 *Web:* www.srs.fs.usda.gov	828-257-4300	257-4840	668
Southern Rhode Island Chamber of Commerce 230 Old Tower Hill Rd .... Wakefield RI 02879 *Web:* www.srichamber.com	401-783-2801	789-3120	139
Southern Rubber Company Inc 2209 Patterson St .... Greensboro NC 27407 *TF:* 800-333-7325 ■ *Web:* southernrubber.com	336-299-2456		326

	Phone	Fax	Class
Southern Software Inc 150 Perry Dr .... Southern Pines NC 28387 *Web:* southernsoftware.com	910-695-0005		177
Southern Solutions Group Inc 4305 Poplar Creek Ln .... High Point NC 27265 *TF:* 866-581-6055 ■ *Web:* www.ssg-nc.com	866-581-6055		463
Southern Spring & Stamping Inc 401 Sub Stn Rd .... Venice FL 34285 *TF:* 800-450-5882 ■ *Web:* www.southernspring.com	941-488-2276	485-9156	718
Southern Stainless Equip Co 1400 Hopeman Pkwy .... Waynesboro VA 22980 *Web:* www.southernstainless.net	540-943-8000		14
Southern Staircase Inc 6025 Shiloh Rd Ste E .... Alpharetta GA 30005 *TF:* 800-874-8408 ■ *Web:* artisticstairs-us.com	770-888-7333		499
Southern Standard Cartons Inc 2415 Plantside Dr .... Louisville KY 40299 *Web:* thestandardgroup.com	502-491-2760	491-2767	101
Southern Star 1300 Broad St .... Chattanooga TN 37402 *Web:* www.southernstarrestaurant.com	423-267-8899		671
Southern State Community College *North* 1850 Davids Dr .... Wilmington OH 45177 *TF:* 877-644-6562 ■ *Web:* www.sscc.edu	937-382-6645		162
South 12681 US Rt 62 .... Sardinia OH 45171 *TF:* 877-644-6562 ■ *Web:* www.sscc.edu	937-695-0307		162
Southern State Correctional Facility 4295 N Delsea Dr .... Delmont NJ 08314	856-785-1300		213
Southern States Chemical Co 1600 E President St .... Savannah GA 31404 *TF:* 888-337-8922 ■ *Web:* www.sschemical.com	912-232-1101	232-1103	280
Southern States Co-op Inc 6606 W Broad St .... Richmond VA 23230 *TF:* 866-372-8272 ■ *Web:* www.southernstates.com	804-281-1000		276
Southern States Frederick Co-op Inc 500 E South St .... Frederick MD 21701 *TF:* 866-633-5747 ■ *Web:* www.southernstates.com	301-663-6164	663-8173	276
Southern States LLC 30 Georgia Ave .... Hampton GA 30228 *Web:* www.southernstatesllc.com	770-946-4562		767
Southern States Packaging Co PO Box 650 .... Spartanburg SC 29304 *TF:* 800-621-2051 ■ *Web:* www.sspc.biz	800-621-2051		549
Southern Steel Fabricators Inc 208 Wagon Wheel Rd .... Monroe LA 71202 *Web:* www.southernsteelfab.com	318-345-2800		480
Southern Systems Inc 4101 Viscount Ave .... Memphis TN 38118 *Web:* www.ssiconveyors.com	901-362-7340		207
Southern Tank & Manufacturing Inc 1501 Haynes Ave .... Owensboro KY 42303 *Web:* www.southerntank.net	270-684-2321		492
Southern Tea LLC 1267 Cobb Industrial Dr .... Marietta GA 30066	770-428-5555		123
Southern Theatres LLC 305 Baronne St Ste 900 .... New Orleans LA 70112 *Web:* www.thegrandtheatre.com	504-297-1133		748
Southern Tile Distributors Inc 4590 Village Ave .... Norfolk VA 23502	757-855-8041		361
Southern Tioga School District 241 Main St .... Blossburg PA 16912 *Web:* www.southerntioga.org	570-638-2183		685
Southern Tire Mart LLC 800 US 98 .... Columbia MS 39429 *Web:* www.stmtires.com	601-424-3200		755
Southern Union Conference Assn of The Seventh Day Adventist Church 302 Research Dr NW .... Norcross GA 30092 *Web:* www.southernunion.com	404-299-1832		50-1
Southern Union State Community College *Opelika* 1701 Lafayette Pkwy .... Opelika AL 36801 **Fax:* Admissions ■ *Web:* www.suscc.edu	334-745-6437	742-9418*	162
Valley 321 Fob James Dr .... Valley AL 36854 **Fax:* Admissions ■ *Web:* www.suscc.edu	334-756-4151	756-5183*	162
Southern University & A & M College 156 Elton C Harrison Dr PO Box 9757 .... Baton Rouge LA 70813 **Fax:* Admissions ■ *TF Admissions:* 800-256-1531 ■ *Web:* www.subr.edu	225-771-5180	771-4762*	166
Southern University Law Ctr 2 Roosevelt Steptoe Dr .... Baton Rouge LA 70813 *TF:* 800-537-1135 ■ *Web:* www.sulc.edu	225-771-6297	771-2121	167-1
Southern University Museum of Art 801 Harding Blvd .... Baton Rouge LA 70807 *Web:* www.sus.edu/pagedisplay.asp?p1=4371	225-771-4500		520
Southern University Museum of Art (SUSLA) 3050 Martin Luther King Jr Dr .... Shreveport LA 71107 *TF:* 800-458-1472 ■ *Web:* www.susla.edu	318-670-6000		520
Southern Utah University 351 W Ctr St .... Cedar City UT 84720 **Fax:* Admissions ■ *Web:* www.suu.edu	435-586-7700	865-8223*	166
Southern Utah Wilderness Alliance (SUWA) 425 East 100 South .... Salt Lake City UT 84111 *Web:* www.suwa.org	801-486-3161		48-13
Southern Ute Indian Tribe 356 Ouray Dr PO Box 737 .... Ignacio CO 81137 *Web:* www.southernute-nsn.gov	970-563-4401		50-2
Southern Vermont Cable Co PO Box 166 .... Bondville VT 05340 *TF:* 800-544-5931 ■ *Web:* www.svcable.net	800-544-5931		116
Southern Vermont College 982 Manison Dr .... Bennington VT 05201 **Fax:* Admissions ■ *TF:* 800-378-2782 ■ *Web:* www.svc.edu	802-442-5427	447-4695*	166
Southern Virginia University 1 University Hill Dr .... Buena Vista VA 24416 *TF:* 800-229-8420 ■ *Web:* www.svu.edu	540-261-8400	261-8559	166
Southern Wall Products Inc 1827 Fellowship Rd .... Tucker GA 30084 *Web:* www.ruco.com	770-938-0121		347
Southern Warehousing & Distribution Inc 3232 N Pan Am Expy .... San Antonio TX 78219 *Web:* www.southernwd.com	210-224-7771	226-9485	803-1
Southern Wayne County Chamber of Commerce 20904 Northline Rd .... Taylor MI 48180 *TF:* 800-451-5918 ■ *Web:* swcrc.com	734-284-6000	284-0198	139

Name / Address	Phone	Fax	Class
Southern Weaving Co 1005 W Bramlett Rd Greenville SC 29611 *TF:* 800-849-8962 ■ *Web:* www.southernweaving.com	864-233-1635	240-9302	745-5
Southern Wesleyan University 907 Wesleyan Dr. Central SC 29630 *TF:* 800-282-8798 ■ *Web:* www.swu.edu	864-644-5000		166
Southern West Virginia Community & Technical College *Logan* 2900 Dempsey Branch Rd PO Box 2900 Mount Gay WV 25637 **Fax:* Admissions ■ *TF:* 800-624-6992 ■ *Web:* www.southernwv.edu	304-792-7098	792-7028*	162
Southern West Virginia Convention & Visitors Bureau 1406 Harper Rd Beckley WV 25801 *TF:* 800-847-4898 ■ *Web:* www.visitwv.com	304-252-2244		206
Southern Wholesale Flooring Company Inc 955B Cobb Pl Blvd Kennesaw GA 30144 *TF:* 800-282-7590 ■ *Web:* www.swfloor.com	770-514-7110		362
Southern Wine & Spirits 7600 Richard St Columbia SC 29209 *Web:* www.southernwine.com	803-695-1630		443
Southern Wine & Spirits of Colorado 5270 Fox St PO Box 5603 Denver CO 80216 *Web:* www.southernglazers.com	303-292-1711	297-9967	81-3
Southern Wine & Spirits of Illinois 300 E Crossroads Pkwy Bolingbrook IL 60440 *Web:* www.southernglazers.com	630-685-3000	685-3700	81-3
Southern Wine & Spirits of New York 345 Underhill Blvd Syosset NY 11791 *Web:* www.southernglazers.com	516-921-9005		81-3
Southern Wipers 100 Fairview Rd. Asheville NC 28803	704-377-3448		508
Southern Wire Corp 8045 Metro Rd. Olive Branch MS 38654 *TF:* 800-238-0333 ■ *Web:* www.southernwire.com	662-890-4873		492
Southern Woodsmith Inc 40 Monroe Dr Pelham AL 35124 *Web:* www.southernwoodsmith.com	205-663-5299		499
Southernmost Beach Resort 1319 Duval St. Key West FL 33040	305-296-6577		379
Southernmost Illinois Tourism Bureau PO Box 378 Anna IL 62906 *TF:* 800-248-4373 ■ *Web:* www.southernmostillinois.com	618-833-9928		206
SouthernSun Asset Management LLC 6070 Poplar Ave Ste 300 Memphis TN 38119 *Web:* www.southernsunam.com	901-333-6980		401
Southfield Chamber of Commerce 24300 Southfield Rd Ste 101 Southfield MI 48075 *Web:* www.southfieldchamber.com	248-557-6661	557-3931	139
Southfield Dodge Chrysler Jeep Ram 28100 Telegraph Rd Southfield MI 48034 *TF Sales:* 888-714-1015 ■ *Web:* www.southfieldchryslerdodgejeepram.com	248-354-2950		57
Southfield Public Library 26300 Evergreen Rd Southfield MI 48076 *Web:* southfieldlibrary.org	248-796-4200		434-3
SouthFirst Bancshares Inc 126 N Norton Ave PO Box 167 Sylacauga AL 35150 *OTC: SZBI* ■ *TF:* 800-239-1492 ■ *Web:* www.southfirst.com	256-245-4365	245-6341	360-2
Southford Falls State Park Quaker Farms Rd Rt 188 Southbury CT 06488 *Web:* www.ct.gov	203-264-5169		565
Southfork Hotel 1600 N Central Expy Plano TX 75074 *TF:* 877-386-4383	972-578-8555	423-7147	379
Southgate Community School District 14600 Dix Toledo Rd Southgate MI 48195 *Web:* www.southgateschools.com	734-246-4600	283-6791	685
Southgroup & Financial Services Inc 795 Woodlands Pkwy Ste 101 Ridgeland MS 39157 *TF:* 855-744-6777 ■ *Web:* www.southgroup.net	601-914-3220		216
Southington Public Library 255 Main St Southington CT 06489 *Web:* www.southingtonlibrary.org	860-628-0947		434-3
Southlake Mall 1000 Southlake Mall Morrow GA 30260 *Web:* www.southlakemall.com	770-961-1050	961-1113	460
Southlake Regional Health Ctr 596 Davis Dr. Newmarket ON L3Y2P9 *TF:* 800-445-1822 ■ *Web:* www.southlakeregional.org	905-895-4521	830-5972	374-2
Southland Ballet Academy *Fountain Valley* 9527 Garfield Ave Fountain Valley CA 92708	714-962-5440		573-1
Southland Box Co 4201 Fruitland Ave Vernon CA 90058 *Web:* www.southlandbox.com	323-583-2231		548
Southland Industries 7421 Orangewood Ave Garden Grove CA 92841 *Web:* www.southlandind.com	714-901-5800		189-10
Southland Log Homes 7521 Broad River Rd Irmo SC 29063 *Web:* www.southlandloghomes.com	803-407-4650		106
Southland Mall 1 Southland Mall Dr. Hayward CA 94545 *Web:* www.southlandmall.com	510-782-3527		460
Southland Mall 20505 S Dixie Hwy. Miami FL 33189 *Web:* www.mysouthlandmall.com	305-235-8880	235-7956	460
Southland Oil Co 5170 Galaxie Dr. Jackson MS 39206 *Web:* petroleum-oil-wholesalers.cmac.ws	601-981-4151		580
Southland Printing Company Inc 213 Airport Dr. Shreveport LA 71107 *TF:* 800-241-8662 ■ *Web:* www.southlandprinting.com	318-221-8662		627
Southland Safety LLC 1409 Kilgore Dr Henderson TX 75652 *TF:* 866-723-3719 ■ *Web:* southlandsafety.com	903-657-8669		196
Southland Steel Fabricators Inc 251 Greensburg St Greensburg LA 70441 *TF:* 800-738-7734 ■ *Web:* www.southlandsteel.com	225-222-4141		480
Southland Title LLC 6710 Stewart Rd Ste 300 Galveston TX 77551 *Web:* www.southlandtitle.net	409-744-0727	744-3909	391-6
Southland Tube Inc 3525 Richard Arrington Blvd N. Birmingham AL 35234 *TF:* 800-543-9024 ■ *Web:* www.southlandtube.com	205-251-1884	251-1553	490
Southmedic Inc 50 Alliance Blvd Barrie ON L4M5K3 *TF:* 800-463-7146 ■ *Web:* southmedic.com	705-726-9383		477
SouthPark Mall 4400 Sharon Rd. Charlotte NC 28211 *TF:* 888-726-5930 ■ *Web:* www.simon.com	704-364-4411	364-4913	460
Southpark Seafood Grill & Wine Bar 901 SW Salmon St Portland OR 97205 *Web:* southparkseafood.com	503-326-1300		671
Southpaw Asset Management LP 2 W Greenwich Office Pk Greenwich CT 06831 *Web:* www.southpawassetmanagement.com	203-862-6200		528
SouthPointe Pavilions 2910 Pine Lake Rd Ste Q Lincoln NE 68516 *Web:* www.southpointeshopping.com	402-421-2114	421-2191	460
Southport Antique Mall 2028 E Southport Rd Indianapolis IN 46227 *Web:* www.southportantiquemall.net	317-786-8246		460
Southport Correctional Facility 236 Bob Masia Dr PO Box 2000 Pine City NY 14871 *Web:* www.doccs.ny.gov	607-737-0850		213
Southridge LLC 90 Grove St Ste 206 Ridgefield CT 06877 *Web:* www.southridge.com	203-431-8300	431-8301	528
Southridge Mall 5300 S 76th St Greendale WI 53129 *Web:* www.simon.com	414-421-1102	421-0492	460
Southridge Mall 1111 E Army Post Rd Des Moines IA 50315 *Web:* www.shopsouthridgemall.com	515-287-3881		460
SouthShore Chamber of Commerce 137 Harbor Village Ln. Apollo Beach FL 33570 *Web:* www.southshorechamberofcommerce.org	813-645-1366	645-2099	139
Southside 815 815 S Washington St. Alexandria VA 22314 *Web:* www.southside815.com	703-836-6222		671
Southside Bancshares Inc 1201 S Beckham Ave Tyler TX 75701 *NASDAQ: SBSI* ■ *TF:* 877-639-3511 ■ *Web:* www.southside.com	903-531-7111	535-4549	360-2
Southside Bistro 1320 Huffman Pk Dr Anchorage AK 99515 *TF:* 800-544-0552 ■ *Web:* www.southsidebistro.com	907-348-0088	348-0089	671
Southside Community Hospital (SCH) 800 Oak St Farmville VA 23901 *Web:* sch.centrahealth.com	434-392-8811		374-3
Southside Electric Co-op Inc 2000 W Virgina Ave Crewe VA 23930 *TF:* 800-552-2118 ■ *Web:* www.sec.coop	434-645-7721	645-1147	245
Southside Regional Medical Ctr 200 Medical Park Blvd Petersburg VA 23805 *TF:* 800-828-1120 ■ *Web:* www.srmconline.com	804-765-5000		374-3
Southside This Week 7801 N Central Dr. Lewis Center OH 43035 *Web:* www.thisweeknews.com	740-888-6100	888-6006	532-4
Southside Virginia Community College 109 Campus Dr Alberta VA 23821 *TF:* 888-220-7822 ■ *Web:* www.southside.edu	434-949-1000	949-7863	162
Southtex Treaters LP 13405 Hwy 191 Odessa TX 79765 *Web:* www.southtex.com	432-563-2766		537
Southview Acres Health Care Center Inc 2000 Oakdale Ave. Saint Paul MN 55118 *Web:* www.southviewacres.com	651-451-1821		371
Southview Special Education School 12110 Clayton Rd. St. Louis MO 63131 *Web:* www.ssdmo.org	314-989-8900		685
SouthWare Innovations Inc 1922 Professional Cir. Auburn AL 36831 *Web:* southware.com	334-821-1108		174
Southwark Metal Mfg Company Inc 2800 Red Lion Rd. Philadelphia PA 19114 *TF:* 800-523-1052 ■ *Web:* southwarkmetal.com	215-735-3401	735-0411	697
Southway Inn 2431 Bank St. Ottawa ON K1V8R9 *TF:* 877-688-4929 ■ *Web:* www.southway.com	613-737-0811	737-3207	379
Southwest Airlines Air Cargo 2702 Love Field Dr. Dallas TX 75235 *TF:* 800-533-1222 ■ *Web:* www.swacargo.com	800-533-1222		12
Southwest Airlines Co 2702 Love Field Dr PO Box 36611 Dallas TX 75235 *NYSE: LUV* ■ *TF:* 800-435-9792 ■ *Web:* www.southwest.com	214-792-4000		25
Southwest Airport Services Inc 11811 N Brantly Ave. Houston TX 77034	281-484-6551	484-8184	63
Southwest Applied Technology College 510 W 800 S. Cedar City UT 84720 *Web:* www.swatc.edu	435-586-2899		507
Southwest Arkansas Electric Co-op 2904 E Ninth St Texarkana AR 71854 *Web:* www.swrea.com	870-772-2743		245
Southwest Art Magazine 10901 W 120th Ave Ste 350 Broomfield CO 80021 *TF:* 877-212-1938 ■ *Web:* www.southwestart.com	303-442-0427	449-0279	457-2
Southwest Bancorp Inc 608 S Main St PO Box 1988 Stillwater OK 74076 *NASDAQ: OKSB* ■ *TF:* 888-762-4762 ■ *Web:* www.banksnb.com	888-762-4762		360-2
Southwest Baptist University 1600 University Ave Bolivar MO 65613 **Fax Area Code:* 417 ■ **Fax:* Admissions ■ *TF:* 800-526-5859 ■ *Web:* www.sbuniv.edu	800-526-5859	328-1808*	166
Southwest Behavioral Health Services Inc 3450 N Third St Phoenix AZ 85012 *Web:* www.sbhservices.org	602-257-9339		374-5
Southwest Binding & Laminating 109 Millwell Ct. Maryland Heights MO 63043 *TF:* 800-325-3628 ■ *Web:* www.swplastic.com	314-739-4400		86
Southwest Business Corp 9311 San Pedro Ave Ste 600 San Antonio TX 78216 *Web:* www.swbc.com	210-525-1241		390
SouthWest Capital Bank 622 Douglas Ave. Las Vegas NM 87701 *TF:* 800-748-2406 ■ *Web:* www.southwestcapital.com	505-425-7565		70
Southwest Cheese Company LLC 1141 Curry County Rd Ste 4 Clovis NM 88101 *Web:* www.southwestcheese.com	575-742-9200		296-25
Southwest Communications Inc 4100 N Mulberry Dr Ste 160 Kansas City MO 64116 *TF:* 800-383-5533 ■ *Web:* www.scitel.net	816-298-4100		387
Southwest Conservation Corps 701 Camino Del Rio Ste 101 Durango CO 81301 *Web:* sccorps.org	970-259-8607		302

Name	Address	City	State	ZIP	Phone	Fax	Class	Other
Southwest Ctr Mall	3662 W Camp Wisdom Rd	Dallas	TX	75237	972-296-1491	861-5798	460	*Web:* swcmall.com
Southwest Electric Co	PO Box 82639	Oklahoma City	OK	73148	405-869-1100		729	*Web:* www.swelectric.com
Southwest Fabrication LLC	22233 N 23rd Ave	Phoenix	AZ	85027	623-587-4648		480	*Web:* www.sw-fab.com
Southwest Florida International Airport	11000 Terminal Access Rd Ste 8671	Fort Myers	FL	33913	239-590-4800	590-4511	27	*TF:* 800-359-6786 ■ *Web:* www.flylcpa.com
Southwest Forest Products Inc	2828 S 35th Ave Ste 720	Phoenix	AZ	85009	602-278-3493		200	*TF:* 800-228-8602 ■ *Web:* www.southwestforestproducts.com
Southwest Freightlines	11991 Transpark Dr	El Paso	TX	79927	915-860-8592	860-9606	780	*TF General:* 800-776-5799 ■ *Web:* www.swflines.com
Southwest Gas Corp	5241 Spring Mtn Rd PO Box 98510	Las Vegas	NV	89193	702-876-7237		787	*NYSE: SWX* ■ *TF:* 877-860-6020 ■ *Web:* www.swgas.com
Southwest Gas Corp Northern Nevada Div	400 Eagle Stn Ln	Carson City	NV	89701	877-860-6020		787	*TF:* 877-860-6020 ■ *Web:* www.swgas.com
Southwest Gas Corp Southern Arizona Div	PO Box 98512	Las Vegas	NV	89193	877-860-6020		787	*TF:* 877-860-6020 ■ *Web:* www.swgas.com
Southwest Gas Corp Southern California Div	13471 Mariposa Rd	Victorville	CA	92395	877-860-6020		787	*TF:* 877-860-6020 ■ *Web:* www.swgas.com
Southwest Gas Corp Southern Nevada Div	5241 Spring Mtn Rd	Las Vegas	NV	89150	702-876-7011		787	*TF:* 877-860-6020 ■ *Web:* www.swgas.com
Southwest General Health Ctr	18697 Bagley Rd	Middleburg Heights	OH	44130	440-816-8000		374-3	*Web:* www.swgeneral.com
Southwest General Hospital (SGH)	7400 Barlite Blvd	San Antonio	TX	78224	210-921-2000		374-3	*TF:* 877-898-6080 ■ *Web:* www.swgeneralhospital.com
Southwest Georgia Financial Corp	201 First St SE	Moultrie	GA	31768	229-985-1120		360-2	*NYSE: SGB* ■ *TF:* 888-683-2265 ■ *Web:* www.sgfc.com
Southwest Hazard Control Inc	1953 W Grant Rd	Tucson	AZ	85745	520-622-3607		192	*Web:* swhaz.com
Southwest Health Ctr Inc	1400 Eastside Rd	Platteville	WI	53818	608-348-2331		374-3	*Web:* www.southwesthealth.org
Southwest Heat Treat	1733 Lauder Rd	Houston	TX	77039	281-442-6694		484	*Web:* swheattreat.com
Southwest Hide Co	250 Beechwood	Boise	ID	83709	208-378-8000		432	*Web:* www.southwesthide.com
Southwest Inspection & Testing	441 Commercial Way	La Habra	CA	90631	562-941-2990		365	*TF:* 800-268-7021 ■ *Web:* www.southwesttesting.com
Southwest Institute of Healing Arts	1100 E Apache Blvd	Tempe	AZ	85281	480-994-9244		800	*TF:* 888-504-9106 ■ *Web:* www.swiha.edu
Southwest Iowa Rural Electric Co-op	1801 Grove Ave	Corning	IA	50841	641-322-3165	322-5274	245	*TF:* 888-220-4869 ■ *Web:* www.swiarec.coop
Southwest Journal	1115 Hennepin Ave S	Minneapolis	MN	55403	612-825-9205		532-4	*Web:* southwestjournal.com
Southwest Local School District	230 S Elm St	Harrison	OH	45030	513-367-4139		685	*Web:* www.southwestschools.org
Southwest Louisiana Convention & Visitors Bureau	1205 N Lakeshore Dr	Lake Charles	LA	70601	337-436-9588		206	*TF:* 800-456-7952 ■ *Web:* www.visitlakecharles.org
Southwest Louisiana Electric Membership Corp	3420 NE Evangeline Thwy	Lafayette	LA	70509	337-896-5384	896-2533	245	*TF:* 888-275-3626 ■ *Web:* www.slemco.com
Southwest LTC	1518 Legacy Dr Ste 110	Frisco	TX	75034	817-222-6000		371	*TF:* 800-252-2412 ■ *Web:* greenoaks.seniorcarecentersltc.com
Southwest Management Group Inc	622 W Maple St Ste H	Farmington	NM	87401	505-327-3611		652	
Southwest Materials Handling Company Inc	4719 Almond St	Dallas	TX	75247	214-630-1375		358	*TF:* 866-674-6067 ■ *Web:* www.swmhc.com
Southwest Medical Assoc Inc	638 E Market St PO Box 2168	Rockport	TX	78382	800-929-4854	729-8854*	721	**Fax Area Code:* 361 ■ *TF:* 800-929-4854 ■ *Web:* www.swmed.com
Southwest Metal Finishing Inc	2445 S Calhoun Rd	New Berlin	WI	53151	262-784-1919		481	*Web:* www.swmetalfinishing.com
Southwest Metalsmiths Inc	5026 E Beverly Rd	Phoenix	AZ	85044	602-438-8577		492	*Web:* www.swmetalsmiths.com
Southwest Minnesota State University	1501 State St	Marshall	MN	56258	800-642-0684		166	*TF:* 800-642-0684 ■ *Web:* smsumustangs.com
Southwest Mississippi Community College	1156 College Dr	Summit	MS	39666	601-276-2000	276-3888	162	*Web:* www.smcc.edu
Southwest Mississippi Electric Power Assn	18671 Hwy 61 PO Box 5	Lorman	MS	39096	800-287-8564		245	*TF:* 800-287-8564 ■ *Web:* www.southwestepa.com
Southwest Mississippi Regional Medical Ctr	215 Marion Ave	McComb	MS	39648	601-249-5500		374-3	*Web:* www.smrmc.com
Southwest Missouri Bank	2417 S Grand Ave	Carthage	MO	64836	417-358-1770	358-4081	70	*TF:* 800-943-8488 ■ *Web:* www.smbonline.com
Southwest Museum	234 Museum Dr	Los Angeles	CA	90065	323-221-2164		520	*Web:* theautry.org
Southwest National Primate Research Ctr (SNPRC) *Texas Biomedical Research Institute*	PO Box 760549	San Antonio	TX	78245	210-258-9400		668	*Web:* www.snprc.org
Southwest Networks Inc	19020 N Indian Ave Ste 2B	Desert Hot Springs	CA	92240	760-288-2200		196	*Web:* www.southwest-networks.com
Southwest Offset Printing Company Inc	13650 Gramercy Pl	Gardena	CA	90249	310-323-0112		627	*Web:* www.southwestoffset.com
Southwest Oilfield Products Inc	10340 Wallisville Rd	Houston	TX	77013	713-675-7541		537	*TF:* 800-392-4600 ■ *Web:* www.swoil.com
Southwest Oklahoma Juvenile Ctr	320 S Broadway Avw	Manitou	OK	73555	580-397-3511	397-3491	412	*Web:* www.ok.gov
Southwest Plaza Mall	8501 W Bowles Ave Ste 2A-483	Littleton	CO	80123	303-973-5300		460	*Web:* www.southwestplaza.com
Southwest Property Management Corp	1044 Castello Dr Ste 206	Naples	FL	34103	239-261-3440		652	*Web:* www.southwestpropertymanagement.com
Southwest Public Power District	221 S Main St PO Box 289	Palisade	NE	69040	308-285-3295		245	*TF:* 800-379-7977 ■ *Web:* www.swppd.com
Southwest Publishing & Mailing Corp	2600 NW Topeka Blvd	Topeka	KS	66617	785-233-5662		626	*Web:* www.swpks.com
Southwest Regional Medical Ctr	350 Bonar Ave	Waynesburg	PA	15370	724-627-3101	627-8653	374-3	*Web:* www.southwestregionalmedical.com
Southwest Research Institute (SwRI)	6220 Culebra Rd	San Antonio	TX	78238	210-684-5111	522-3496*	668	**Fax:* Hum Res ■ *Web:* swri.org
Southwest Rural Electric Assn	700 N Broadway PO Box 310	Tipton	OK	73570	580-667-5281	667-5284	245	*TF:* 800-256-7973 ■ *Web:* www.swre.com
Southwest Shipyard L P	18310 Market St	Channelview	TX	77530	281-860-3200	860-3215	698	*Web:* www.swslp.com
Southwest Steel Casting Co	600 Foundry Dr	Longview	TX	75604	903-759-3946		492	*Web:* www.swscc.com
Southwest Tennessee Community College	5983 Macon Cove PO Box 780	Memphis	TN	38134	901-333-5000	333-4473	162	*TF:* 877-717-7822 ■ *Web:* www.southwest.tn.edu
Southwest Tennessee Electric Membership Corp	1009 E Main St	Brownsville	TN	38012	731-772-1322	772-1037	245	*TF:* 800-772-0472 ■ *Web:* www.stemc.com
Southwest Texas Electric Co-op Inc	101 E Gillis St PO Box 677	Eldorado	TX	76936	325-853-2544	853-3141	245	*TF:* 800-643-3980 ■ *Web:* www.swtec.com
Southwest Texas Junior College	2401 Garner Field Rd	Uvalde	TX	78801	830-278-4401	591-7396*	162	**Fax:* Admissions ■ *TF:* 888-886-8490 ■ *Web:* www.swtjc.edu
Southwest Valley Chamber of Commerce	289 N Litchfield Rd	Goodyear	AZ	85338	623-932-2260	932-9057	139	*TF:* 800-273-8255 ■ *Web:* www.southwestvalleychamber.org
Southwest Virginia Community College	724 Community College Rd	Cedar Bluff	VA	24609	276-964-2555	964-7716*	162	**Fax:* Admissions ■ *TF:* 855-877-3944 ■ *Web:* www.sw.edu
Southwest Washington Convention & Visitors Bureau	1220 Main S Ste 220	Vancouver	WA	98660	360-750-1553	750-1553	206	*TF:* 877-600-0800 ■ *Web:* www.visitvancouverusa.com
Southwest Washington Medical Ctr (SWMC)	400 NE Mother Joseph Pl PO Box 1600	Vancouver	WA	98664	360-514-2000		374-3	*Web:* peacehealth.org/southwest
Southwest Water Co	12535 Reed Rd	Sugar Land	TX	77478	281-207-5800		787	*Web:* www.swwc.com
Southwest Wisconsin Library System	1300 Industrial Dr Ste 2	Fennimore	WI	53809	608-822-3393		434-3	*TF:* 866-866-3393 ■ *Web:* www.swls.org
Southwest Wisconsin Technical College (SWTC)	1800 Bronson Blvd	Fennimore	WI	53809	608-822-3262	822-6019	800	*TF:* 800-362-3322 ■ *Web:* www.swtc.edu
Southwestern Academy	2800 Monterey Rd	San Marino	CA	91108	626-799-5010	799-0407	622	*Web:* www.southwesternacademy.edu
Southwestern Adventist University	100 W Hillcrest Dr	Keene	TX	76059	817-645-3921		166	*TF Admissions:* 800-433-2240 ■ *Web:* www.swau.edu
Southwestern Assemblies of God University	1200 Sycamore St	Waxahachie	TX	75165	972-937-4010	923-0006*	166	**Fax:* Admissions ■ *TF:* 888-937-7248 ■ *Web:* www.sagu.edu
Southwestern Baptist Theological Seminary	PO Box 22740	Fort Worth	TX	76122	817-923-1921	921-8758	167-3	*TF:* 877-467-9287 ■ *Web:* www.swbts.edu
Southwestern Central School District	600 Hunt Rd	Jamestown	NY	14701	716-664-1881		685	*Web:* www.swcs.wnyric.org
Southwestern Christian College	PO Box 10	Terrell	TX	75160	972-524-3341	563-7133	166	*TF:* 800-925-9357 ■ *Web:* www.swcc.edu
Southwestern Christian University	7210 NW 39th Expy PO Box 340	Bethany	OK	73008	405-789-7661	495-0078*	166	**Fax:* Admissions ■ *TF:* 888-418-9272 ■ *Web:* swcu.publishpath.com
Southwestern College	900 Otay Lakes Rd	Chula Vista	CA	91910	619-421-6700	482-6489*	162	**Fax:* Admissions ■ *TF:* 866-262-9881 ■ *Web:* swccd.edu
Southwestern College	100 College St	Winfield	KS	67156	620-229-6236	229-6344*	166	**Fax:* Admissions ■ *TF:* 800-846-1543 ■ *Web:* www.sckans.edu
Southwestern College	100 Campus Dr	Weatherford	OK	73096	580-772-6611	774-3795	166	*TF:* 800-669-1656 ■ *Web:* www.swosu.edu
Southwestern Community College	1501 W Townline St	Creston	IA	50801	641-782-7081	782-3312*	162	**Fax:* Admissions ■ *TF:* 800-247-4023 ■ *Web:* www.swcciowa.edu

Name / Address	City	State	Zip	Phone	Fax	Class
Southwestern Community College 447 College Dr *TF:* 800-447-4091 ■ *Web:* www.southwesterncc.edu	Sylva	NC	28779	828-339-4000	339-4613	162
Southwestern Controls 6720 Sands Point Dr Ste 100 *TF:* 800-444-9368 ■ *Web:* www.swcontrols.com	Houston	TX	77074	713-777-2626	988-1750	223
Southwestern Correctional Ctr 950 Kings Hwy *Web:* www.illinois.gov	East Saint Louis	IL	62203	618-394-2200	394-2228	213
Southwestern Electric Cooperative Inc 525 US Rt 40 **Fax Area Code:* 618 ■ *TF:* 800-637-8667 ■ *Web:* www.sweci.com	Greenville	IL	62246	800-637-8667	664-4179*	245
Southwestern Electric Power Company 1 Riverside Plaza Fl 14 *TF:* 888-216-3523 ■ *Web:* www.swepco.com	Columbus	OH	43215	888-216-3523		787
Southwestern Energy Co 2350 N Sam Houston Pkwy E Ste 300 *NYSE: SWN* ■ *TF:* 866-322-0801 ■ *Web:* www.swn.com	Houston	TX	77032	832-796-1000	796-4818	787
Southwestern Eye Ctr 2610 E University Dr *Web:* www.sweye.com	Mesa	AZ	85213	480-892-8400	892-9533	798
Southwestern Illinois College 2500 Carlyle Ave **Fax:* Admissions ■ *TF:* 800-222-5131 ■ *Web:* www.swic.edu	Belleville	IL	62221	618-235-2700	222-9768*	162
Granite City 4950 Maryville Rd *Web:* www.swic.edu	Granite City	IL	62040	618-931-0600		162
Red Bud 500 W S Fourth St *Web:* www.swic.edu	Red Bud	IL	62278	618-282-6682		162
Southwestern Indian Polytechnic Institute 9169 Coors Blvd NW *TF:* 800-586-7474 ■ *Web:* www.sipi.edu	Albuquerque	NM	87120	505-346-2306		165
Southwestern Industries Inc 2615 Homestead Pl *TF:* 800-421-6875 ■ *Web:* www.southwesternindustries.com	Rancho Dominguez	CA	90220	310-608-4422	764-2668	455
Southwestern Life Insurance Co 110 W Clinton St	Hobbs	NM	88240	575-393-4577		391-2
Southwestern Manitoba Regional Library 149 Main St PO Box 670 *Web:* southwestern.mb.libraries.coop	Melita	MB	R0M1L0	204-522-3923	522-3923	436
Southwestern Medical Ctr (SWMC) 5602 SW Lee Blvd *Web:* swmconline.com	Lawton	OK	73505	580-531-4700	531-4702	374-3
Southwestern Michigan College (SMC) 58900 Cherry Grove Rd *TF:* 800-456-8675 ■ *Web:* www.swmich.edu	Dowagiac	MI	49047	269-782-1000	782-1331	162
Niles Area 2229 US 12 *TF:* 800-456-8675 ■ *Web:* www.swmich.edu	Niles	MI	49120	269-782-1233		162
Southwestern Michigan Tourism Council 2300 Pipestone Rd *TF:* 800-764-2836 ■ *Web:* www.swmichigan.org	Benton Harbor	MI	49022	269-925-6301	925-7540	206
Southwestern Motor Transport Inc 4600 Goldfield *Web:* www.smtlines.com	San Antonio	TX	78218	210-661-6791		780
Southwestern Oklahoma State University (SWOSU) 100 Campus Dr *TF:* 800-669-1656 ■ *Web:* www.swosu.edu	Weatherford	OK	73096	580-772-6611		565
Southwestern Oklahoma State University Sayre 409 E Mississippi St **Fax:* Admissions ■ *Web:* www.swosu.edu/sayre	Sayre	OK	73662	580-928-5533	928-1140*	162
Southwestern Oregon Community College 1988 Newmark Ave *TF:* 800-962-2838 ■ *Web:* www.socc.edu	Coos Bay	OR	97420	541-888-2525		162
Southwestern Petroleum Corp PO Box 961005 *TF:* 800-877-9372 ■ *Web:* www.swepcousa.com	Fort Worth	TX	76161	817-332-2336	877-4047	541
Southwestern Suppliers Inc 6815 E 14th Ave *Web:* www.sowes.com	Tampa	FL	33619	813-626-2193		492
Southwestern University PO Box 770 **Fax:* Admissions ■ *TF:* 800-252-3166 ■ *Web:* www.southwestern.edu	Georgetown	TX	78627	512-863-1200	863-9601*	166
Southwestern University Hospital 5151 Harry Hines Blvd *Web:* www.utswmedicine.org	Dallas	TX	75390	214-645-5555		374-3
Southwestern University School of Law 3050 Wilshire Blvd *Web:* www.swlaw.edu	Los Angeles	CA	90010	213-738-6700		167-1
Southwestern Vermont Medical Ctr 100 Hospital Dr *TF:* 800-422-6237 ■ *Web:* www.svhealthcare.org/hospital	Bennington	VT	05201	802-442-6361	447-5013	374-3
Southwestern Virginia Mental Health Institute 340 Bagley Cir *Web:* www.swvmhi.dbhds.virginia.gov	Marion	VA	24354	276-783-1200		374-5
Southwestern Wire Inc PO Box CC *TF:* 800-348-9473 ■ *Web:* www.southwesternwire.com	Norman	OK	73070	405-447-6900	447-2830	813
Southwestern/Great American 2451 Atrium Way *TF Cust Svc:* 888-602-7867 ■ *Web:* www.southwestern.com	Nashville	TN	37214	888-602-7867		96
Southwick Beach State Park 8119 Southwicks Pl *Web:* parks.ny.gov/parks/36/details.aspx	Henderson	NY	13650	315-846-5338		565
Southwick Clothing LLC 25 Computer Dr *Web:* www.southwick.com	Haverhill	MA	01832	978-686-3833		155-12
Southwick Inc 2400 Shattuck Ave *TF:* 888-686-0046 ■ *Web:* www.toyotaofberkeley.com	Berkeley	CA	94704	510-845-2530		57
Southwick Tolland Regional SD 86 Powder Mill Rd *Web:* www.stgrsd.org	Southwick	MA	01077	413-569-5391		685
Southwind Carpet Mills 601 Callahan Rd SE PO Box 3577 *Web:* www.cherokeecarpet.com	Dalton	GA	30719	706-277-6277		131
Southwire Co 1 Southwire Dr *TF:* 800-444-1700 ■ *Web:* www.southwire.com	Carrollton	GA	30119	770-832-4242		485
Southwood Furniture Corp 2860 Nathan St *Web:* www.southwoodfurn.com	Hickory	NC	28602	828-465-1776	465-0858	319-2
Southworth Co 265 Main St *TF:* 800-225-1839 ■ *Web:* www.southworth.com	Agawam	MA	01001	413-789-1200		552-2
Southworth Planetarium 96 Falmouth St *Web:* www.usm.maine.edu	Portland	ME	04104	207-780-4249	780-4055	598
Southworth Products Corp PO Box 1380 *TF:* 800-743-1000 ■ *Web:* www.southworthproducts.com	Portland	ME	04104	207-878-0700	797-4734	470
Souza Agency Inc, The 2547 Housley Rd *TF:* 800-420-9558 ■ *Web:* www.souza.com	Annapolis	MD	21401	410-573-1300		7
Souza-Baranowski Correctional Ctr PO Box 8000 *Web:* www.mass.gov	Shirley	MA	01464	978-514-6500		213
SOV Therapeutics Inc 101 Guymon Ct *Web:* www.sovtherapeutics.com	Morrisville	NC	27560	919-601-2208		743
Sova Pharmaceuticals Inc 11099 N Torrey Pines Rd Ste 290 *Web:* www.sovapharma.com	La Jolla	CA	92037	858-750-4700	750-4701	238
Sovereign Bank FSB PO Box 12646 *TF Cust Svc:* 877-768-2265 ■ *Web:* www.santanderbank.com	Reading	PA	19612	877-768-2265		70
Sovereign Performing Arts Ctr 136 N Sixth St *Web:* santander-arena.com	Reading	PA	19601	610-898-7299		572
Sovereign Pharmaceuticals Ltd 7590 Sand St *TF:* 877-248-0228 ■ *Web:* www.sovpharm.com	Fort Worth	TX	76118	817-284-0429	284-0531	582
Sovereign Society, The 98 S E Sixth Ave Ste 2 *TF:* 866-584-4096 ■ *Web:* www.sovereignsociety.com	Delray Beach	FL	33483	888-358-8125		401
Sovereign Systems LLC 3930 East Jones Bridge Rd Ste 300 *Web:* www.sovsystems.com	Norcross	GA	30092	404-549-5272		196
Sovereign Technologies Llc 11414 Gravois Rd Ste 301 *Web:* www.sovereigntec.com	Saint Louis	MO	63126	314-537-5739		809
Sowell Gray Stepp & Laffitte LLC 1310 Gadsden St *Web:* www.sowell.com	Columbia	SC	29211	803-929-1400		428
Soy Vay Enterprises Inc 5969 Hillside Dr *Web:* www.soyvay.com	Felton	CA	95018	831-335-3824		296-37
Soybean Digest 7900 International Dr Ste 300 *TF Cust Svc:* 800-722-5334 ■ *Web:* www.cornandsoybeandigest.com	Minneapolis	MN	55425	952-851-4667	851-4601	457-1
SP Kish Industries Inc 600 W Seminary St *Web:* www.kishindustries.com	Charlotte	MI	48813	517-543-2650		550
Sp Mount 1306 E 55th St *Web:* www.spmount.com	Cleveland	OH	44103	216-881-3316		627
SP Systems Inc 7500 Greenway Ctr Dr Ste 850 *TF:* 877-327-8732 ■ *Web:* www.sp-systems.com	Greenbelt	MD	20770	301-614-1322	614-1328	178-1
SPA (Systems Planning & Analysis Inc) 2001 N Beauregard St *Web:* www.spa.com	Alexandria	VA	22311	703-399-7550		261
Spa at Big Cedar Lodge 612 Devil's Pool Rd *TF:* 800-225-6343 ■ *Web:* www.bigcedar.com	Ridgedale	MO	65739	417-339-5201		707
Spa at Coeur d'Alene 115 S Second St *TF:* 800-684-0514 ■ *Web:* cdaresort.com/discover/spa	Coeur d'Alene	ID	83814	208-765-4000		706
Spa at Eagle Crest Resort 1522 Cline Falls Hwy *TF:* 800-682-4786 ■ *Web:* www.eagle-crest.com	Redmond	OR	97756	541-923-9647		707
Spa at Kingsmill Resort 1010 Kingsmill Rd *TF:* 800-965-4772 ■ *Web:* www.kingsmill.com	Williamsburg	VA	23185	757-253-8230		707
Spa at Le Merigot JW Marriott Beach Hotel Santa Monica 1740 Ocean Ave *TF:* 888-236-2427 ■ *Web:* www.marriott.com	Santa Monica	CA	90401	310-395-9700	395-9200	707
Spa at Pebble Beach 1518 Cypress Dr *TF:* 800-654-9300 ■ *Web:* www.pebblebeach.com	Pebble Beach	CA	93953	831-649-7615		707
Spa at Peninsula Beverly Hills 9882 S Santa Monica Blvd *TF:* 800-462-7899 ■ *Web:* www.peninsula.com/beverly_hills/en	Beverly Hills	CA	90212	310-551-2888	788-2319	706
Spa at Pinehurst Resort 80 Carolina Vista Dr PO Box 4000 *TF:* 800-487-4653 ■ *Web:* www.pinehurst.com	Pinehurst	NC	28374	910-235-8320		707
Spa at the Beverly Wilshire, The 9500 Wilshire Blvd *TF:* 800-545-4000 ■ *Web:* www.fourseasons.com	Beverly Hills	CA	90212	310-385-7023		707
Spa at the Broadmoor 1 Lake Ave *TF:* 800-634-7711 ■ *Web:* www.broadmoor.com	Colorado Springs	CO	80906	719-634-7711		707
Spa at the Buena Vista Palace Resort in the Walt Disney World Resort 1900 Buena Vista Dr *Web:* www.buenavistapalace.com	Lake Buena Vista	FL	32830	407-827-3200		707
Spa at the Chattanoogan 1201 S Broad St *TF:* 800-619-0018 ■ *Web:* www.chattanooganhotel.com	Chattanooga	TN	37402	423-756-3400	756-3404	707
Spa at the Diplomat Country Club 501 Diplomat Pkwy *Web:* www.diplomatresort.com	Hallandale	FL	33009	954-883-4900		707
Spa at the Equinox Resort 3567 Main St **Fax Area Code:* 802 ■ *TF:* 800-362-4747 ■ *Web:* www.equinoxresort.com	Manchester Village	VT	05254	800-362-4747	362-4861*	707
Spa at the Fairmont Inn Sonoma Mission Inn 100 Boyes Blvd *TF:* 877-289-7354 ■ *Web:* www.fairmont.com	Sonoma	CA	95476	707-938-9000		707
Spa at the Hotel Hershey 100 Hotel Rd *TF:* 877-772-9988 ■ *Web:* www.chocolatespa.com	Hershey	PA	17033	717-520-5888		707
Spa at the JW Marriott Desert Springs Resort Palm Desert 74855 Country Club Dr **Fax Area Code:* 817 ■ *TF:* 800-845-5279 ■ *Web:* www.marriott.com	Palm Desert	CA	92260	760-341-2211	778-2049*	707
Spa at the Marriott Harbor Beach Resort 3030 Holiday Dr *Web:* www.marriott.com	Fort Lauderdale	FL	33316	954-765-3032		707

	Phone	Fax	Class
Spa at the Norwich Inn 607 W Thames St. Norwich CT 06360 *TF:* 800-275-4772 ■ *Web:* www.thespaatnorwichinn.com	860-425-3500		707
Spa at the Orlando World Ctr Marriott Resort & Convention Ctr 8701 World Ctr Dr. Orlando FL 32821 *Web:* www.marriott.com	407-238-8705	238-8777	707
Spa at the PGA National Resort 450 Ave of the Champions. Palm Beach Gardens FL 33418 *TF:* 800-633-9150 ■ *Web:* www.pgaresort.com	561-627-3111		707
Spa at the Ponte Vedra Inn & Club 302 Ponte Vedra Blvd. Ponte Vedra Beach FL 32082 *Web:* www.pvspa.com	904-273-7700	273-7706	707
Spa at the Ritz-Carlton Amelia Island 4750 Amelia Island Pkwy. Amelia Island FL 32034 *TF:* 800-241-3333 ■ *Web:* www.ritzcarlton.com	904-277-1087		707
Spa at the Ritz-Carlton Bachelor Gulch 0130 Daybreak Ridge. Avon CO 81620 *TF:* 800-241-3333 ■ *Web:* www.ritzcarlton.com	970-748-6200		707
Spa at the Ritz-Carlton Half Moon Bay 1 Miramontes Pt Rd. Half Moon Bay CA 94019 *TF:* 800-241-3333 ■ *Web:* www.ritzcarlton.com	650-712-7040		707
Spa at the Ritz-Carlton New Orleans 921 Canal St. New Orleans LA 70112 *TF:* 800-241-3333 ■ *Web:* www.ritzcarlton.com	504-670-2929		707
Spa at the Saddlebrook Resort 5700 Saddlebrook Way. Wesley Chapel FL 33543 *TF:* 800-729-8383 ■ *Web:* www.saddlebrook.com	813-907-4419		707
Spa at the Sagamore 110 Sagamore Rd. Bolton Landing NY 12814 *TF:* 866-384-1944 ■ *Web:* www.thesagamore.com	518-743-6081		707
Spa at the Sanderling Resort 1461 Duck Rd. Duck NC 27949 *TF:* 855-412-7866 ■ *Web:* www.sanderling-resort.com	252-261-7744		707
Spa at The Setai 2001 Collins Ave. Miami Beach FL 33139 *TF:* 888-625-7500 ■ *Web:* www.thesetaihotel.com	888-625-7500		706
Spa at the Villagio Inn 6481 Washington St. Yountville CA 94599 *TF:* 800-351-1133 ■ *Web:* www.villagio.com	707-948-5050		707
Spa at White Oaks Conference Resort 253 Taylor Rd. Niagara-on-the-Lake ON L0S1J0 *TF:* 800-263-5766 ■ *Web:* www.whiteoaksresort.com	905-641-2599		707
Spa Douce Heure 110 338 Rte. Les Coteaux QC J7X1A2 *Web:* www.spadouceheure.com	450-267-4949		226
Spa Esmeralda at the Renaissance Esmeralda Resort 44400 Indian Wells Ln. Indian Wells CA 92210 **Fax Area Code:* 817 ■ *TF:* 800-845-5279 ■ *Web:* www.marriott.com	760-836-1265	778-2049*	707
Spa Gaucin at the Saint Regis Monarch Beach 1 Monarch Beach Resort. Dana Point CA 92629 *TF:* 800-722-1543	949-234-3367	234-3365	707
Spa Grande at the Grand Wailea Resort Maui 3850 Wailea Alanui Dr. Wailea HI 96753 *TF:* 800-772-1933 ■ *Web:* www.grandwailea.com/spa	808-875-1234		707
Spa La Quinta at La Quinta Resort 49499 Eisenhower Dr. La Quinta CA 92253 *Web:* www.laquintaresort.com	760-777-4800		707
Spa Manufacturers 6060 Ulmerton Rd. Clearwater FL 33760 *TF:* 877-530-9493 ■ *Web:* www.spamanufacturers.com	727-530-9493	539-8151	375
Spa Moana at the Hyatt Regency Maui Resort & Spa 200 Nohea Kai Dr. Lahaina HI 96761 *TF:* 800-233-1234 ■ *Web:* maui.regency.hyatt.com/en/hotel/home.html	808-667-4725		707
Spa Radiance 3011 Fillmore St. San Francisco CA 94123 *Web:* www.sparadiance.com	415-346-6281		706
Spa Resort Casino 401 E Amado Rd. Palm Springs CA 92262 *TF:* 888-999-1995 ■ *Web:* www.sparesortcasino.com	888-999-1995		133
Spa Resort, The 401 E Amado Rd. Palm Springs CA 92262 *TF:* 888-999-1995 ■ *Web:* www.sparesortcasino.com	760-883-1060		669
Spa Shiki at the Lodge of Four Seasons 315 Horseshoe Bend Pkwy. Lake Ozark MO 65049 *Web:* spashiki.com	573-365-8108		707
Spa Terre at LaPlaya Beach & Golf Resort 9891 Gulf Shore Dr. Naples FL 34108 *TF:* 800-237-6883 ■ *Web:* www.laplayaresort.com	239-597-3123	597-6278	707
Spa Terre at Paradise Point Resort 1404 Vacation Rd. San Diego CA 92109 *TF:* 800-344-2626 ■ *Web:* www.paradisepoint.com	858-581-5998		707
Spa Terre at the Hotel Viking 1 Bellevue Ave. Newport RI 02840 *TF:* 800-556-7126 ■ *Web:* www.hotelviking.com	401-847-3300		707
Spa Terre at the Inn & Spa at Loretto 211 Old Santa Fe Trl. Santa Fe NM 87501 *TF:* 800-727-5531 ■ *Web:* www.destinationhotels.com/inn-at-loretto	505-984-7997		707
Spa Toccare at Borgata Hotel Casino 1 Borgata Way. Atlantic City NJ 08401 *TF:* 877-448-5833 ■ *Web:* www.theborgata.com	609-317-7555	317-1039	707
Spa Torrey Pines at the Lodge at Torrey Pines 11480 N Torrey Pines Rd. La Jolla CA 92037 *Web:* www.spatorreypines.com	858-777-6690		707
SPAAN Tech Inc 311 S Wacker Dr Ste 2400. Chicago IL 60606 *Web:* www.spaantech.com	312-277-8800		390
SPAC (Saratoga Performing Arts Ctr) 108 Ave of the Pines. Saratoga Springs NY 12866 *TF:* 800-838-3006 ■ *Web:* www.spac.org	518-584-9330	584-0809	572
Space Aliens Grill & Bar 1304 E Century Ave. Bismarck ND 58503 *Web:* www.spacealiens.com	701-223-6220		671
Space Center Inc 2501 Rosegate. Saint Paul MN 55113 *Web:* www.spacecenterinc.com	651-604-4200		653
Space Coast Credit Union 8045 N Wickham Rd PO Box 419001. Melbourne FL 32941 *TF:* 800-447-7228 ■ *Web:* www.sccu.com	321-752-2222		219
Space Coast Jet Ctr 7003 Challenger Ave. Titusville FL 32780 *TF:* 800-559-5473 ■ *Web:* www.spacecoastjetcenter.com	321-267-8355	267-0129	63
Space Ctr Houston 1601 Nasa Rd 1. Houston TX 77058 *Web:* www.spacecenter.org	281-244-2100	283-7724	520
Space Dynamics Laboratory 1695 N Research Pkwy. North Logan UT 84341 *Web:* www.sdl.usu.edu	435-713-3400	713-3430	668

	Phone	Fax	Class
Space Electronics LLC 81 Fuller Way. Berlin CT 06037 *Web:* space-electronics.com	860-829-0001		61
Space Ground System Solutions Inc 4343 Fortune Pl Ste C. Melbourne FL 32904 *Web:* www.sgss.com	321-956-8200		177
Space Inc 3142 E Vantage Point Dr Ste 2. Midland MI 48642 *TF:* 800-851-0189 ■ *Web:* spacewithin.net	989-835-5151		393
Space Micro Inc 10237 Flanders Ct. San Diego CA 92121 *TF:* 800-341-2333 ■ *Web:* www.spacemicro.com	858-332-0700		647
Space Murals Museum 12450 Hwy 70 E. Las Cruces NM 88011	575-382-0977		520
Space Needle LLC 203 Sixth Ave N. Seattle WA 98109 *TF:* 800-937-9582 ■ *Web:* www.spaceneedle.com	206-905-2200		50-4
Space Optics Research Labs LLC 7 Stuart Rd. Chelmsford MA 01824 *TF:* 800-552-7675 ■ *Web:* www.sorl.com	978-250-8640		407
Space Physics Research Laboratory 2455 Hayward St University of Michigan. Ann Arbor MI 48109 *Web:* www.sprl.umich.edu	734-936-7775		668
Space Science & Engineering Ctr University of Wisconsin-Madison 1225 W Dayton St. Madison WI 53706 *TF:* 866-391-1753 ■ *Web:* www.ssec.wisc.edu	608-263-6750	262-5974	668
Space Systems/Loral 3825 Fabian Way. Palo Alto CA 94303 *TF:* 800-332-6490 ■ *Web:* sslmda.com	650-852-4000		647
Space Telescope Science Institute 3700 San Martin Dr. Baltimore MD 21218 *Web:* www.stsci.edu	410-338-4700	338-4767	668
Space Vector Corp 9223 Deering Ave. Chatsworth CA 91311 *TF:* 800-497-9764 ■ *Web:* www.spacevector.com	818-734-2600	428-6249	504
SpaceAge Control Inc 38850 20th St E. Palmdale CA 93550 *Web:* www.spaceagecontrol.com	661-273-3000		256
SPACECO Inc 9575 W Higgins Rd Ste 700. Rosemont IL 60018 *Web:* www.spacecoinc.com	847-696-4060	696-4065	261
SPACECONNECTION Inc, The 10530 Victory Blvd. North Hollywood CA 91606 *TF:* 800-537-7223 ■ *Web:* www.thespaceconnection.com	818-754-1100		387
SpaceCurve Inc 710 Second Ave Ste 620. Seattle WA 98104	206-453-2225		387
Spaceflight Systems 47 Constitution Dr. Bedford NH 03110 *Web:* ssc-nh.com	603-472-4934		180
SpaceGuard Products Inc 711 S Commerce Dr. Seymour IN 47274 **Fax Area Code:* 800 ■ *TF:* 800-841-0680 ■ *Web:* www.spaceguardproducts.com	812-523-3044	428-5758*	286
Spacelabs Health Care 35301 SE Center St. Snoqualmie WA 98065 *TF:* 800-522-7025 ■ *Web:* www.spacelabshealthcare.com	425-396-3300	396-3301	250
SpaceNet Inc 1750 Old Meadow Rd. McLean VA 22102 **Fax Area Code:* 800 ■ *TF:* 800-237-3513 ■ *Web:* www.spacenet.com	703-848-1000	325-9202*	681
Spacesaver Corp 1450 Janesville Ave. Fort Atkinson WI 53538 **Fax Area Code:* 920 ■ *TF:* 800-492-3434 ■ *Web:* www.spacesaver.com	800-255-8170	563-2702*	286
Spackenkill Union Free School Districts (Inc) 15 Croft Rd. Poughkeepsie NY 12603 *Web:* www.spackenkillschools.org	845-463-7800		685
Spader Business Management 2101 W 41st St Ste 49. Sioux Falls SD 57105 *TF:* 800-772-3377 ■ *Web:* www.spader.com	800-772-3377		196
Spaghetti Warehouse Inc 1255 W I-20. Arlington TX 76017 **Fax Area Code:* 972 ■ *Web:* www.meatballs.com	817-557-0321	550-0908*	670
Spagnuolo & Assoc LLC 3057 W Market St Ste 201. Fairlawn OH 44333 *Web:* spagnuoloassoc.com	330-836-6661		261
Spago 176 N Canon Dr. Beverly Hills CA 90210 *Web:* www.wolfgangpuck.com	310-385-0880		671
SpaHalekulani at the Halekulani Hotel 2199 Kalia Rd. Honolulu HI 96815 *TF:* 800-367-2343 ■ *Web:* www.halekulani.com	808-931-5322		707
Spain 245 E 47th St 36th Fl. New York NY 10017 *Web:* www.spainun.org	212-661-1050	949-7247	784
Consulate General 1405 Sutter St. San Francisco CA 94109	415-922-2995		257
Consulate General 150 E 58th St 30th Fl. New York NY 10155 *Web:* www.spainculture.us/city/new-york	212-355-4080	644-3751	257
Embassy 2375 Pennsylvania Ave NW. Washington DC 20037	202-452-0100	833-5670	257
Spain Restaurant 419 Market St. Newark NJ 07105 *Web:* www.spainrestaurant.com	973-344-0994	344-2669	671
Spain-US Chamber of Commerce 80 Broad St Ste 2103. New York NY 10004 *TF:* 800-243-2101 ■ *Web:* www.spainuscc.org	212-967-2170	564-1415	138
Spalding PO Box 90015. Bowling Green KY 42103 **Fax Area Code:* 877 ■ *TF:* 855-253-4533 ■ *Web:* www.spalding.com	855-253-4533	729-4800*	710
Spalding Automotive Inc 4529 Adams Cir. Bensalem PA 19020 **Fax Area Code:* 267 ■ *Web:* www.spaldingautomotive.com	215-826-4000	550-9035*	60
Spalding County PO Box 1087. Griffin GA 30224 *TF:* 800-510-8284 ■ *Web:* www.spaldingcounty.com	770-467-4200		338
Spalding Dedecker Assoc Inc 905 S Blvd E. Rochester Hills MI 48307 *Web:* sda-eng.com	248-844-5400		261
Spalding Hardware Ltd 1616 10 Ave SW. Calgary AB T3C0J5 *TF:* 800-837-0850 ■ *Web:* www.spaldinghardware.com	800-837-0850		350
Spalding Rehabilitation Hospital 900 Potomac St. Aurora CO 80011 *TF:* 800-367-3309 ■ *Web:* www.spaldingrehab.com	303-367-1166		374-6
Spalding University 851 S Fourth St. Louisville KY 40203 *TF:* 800-896-8941 ■ *Web:* www.spalding.edu	502-585-9911	585-7158	166
Spalon Montage 600 Market St Ste 270. Chanhassen MN 55317 *TF:* 800-635-9671 ■ *Web:* www.spalon.com	952-915-2900		354
Spal-Usa Inc 1731 SE Oralabor Rd. Ankeny IA 50021 *TF:* 800-345-0327 ■ *Web:* www.spalusa.com	800-345-0327		54
Spanaflight 16705 103rd Ave Ct E. Puyallup WA 98374 *TF:* 800-397-6038 ■ *Web:* www.spanaflight.com	253-848-2020	840-5843	63

Company / Address	City	State	ZIP	Phone	Fax	Class
Span-America Medical Systems Inc 70 Commerce Ctr *NASDAQ: SPAN* ■ *TF:* 800-888-6752 ■ *Web:* www.spanamerica.com	Greenville	SC	29615	864-288-8877	288-8692	477
Spancrete Industries Inc N 16 W 23415 Stone Ridge Dr PO Box 828 *Web:* www.spancrete.com	Waukesha	WI	53187	414-290-9000		183
Spanfeller Media Group Inc 156 Fifth Ave 4th Fl *Web:* www.spanfellergroup.com	New York	NY	10010	646-459-0604		387
Spang & Co 110 Delta Dr *Web:* www.spang.com	Pittsburgh	PA	15238	412-963-9363		253
Spangler & Boyer Mechanical 5175 Commerce Dr *Web:* www.spanglerboyer.com	York	PA	17408	717-792-8854		610
Spangler Candy Co 400 N Portland St PO Box 71 *TF Sales:* 888-636-4221 ■ *Web:* www.spanglercandy.com	Bryan	OH	43506	419-636-4221	636-3695	296-8
Spangler Graphics LLC 2930 S 44th St *Web:* www.spanglergraphics.com	Kansas City	KS	66106	913-722-4500		627
Spangler, Jennings & Dougherty PC 8396 Mississippi St *TF:* 800-888-7573 ■ *Web:* www.sjdlaw.com	Merrillville	IN	46410	219-769-2323		428
Spangles Inc 437 N Hillside St *Web:* www.spanglesinc.com	Wichita	KS	67214	316-685-8817		670
Spanish Broadcasting System Inc (SBS) 2601 S Bayshore Dr PH 2 *NASDAQ: SBSA* ■ *TF:* 800-579-1639 ■ *Web:* www.spanishbroadcasting.com	Coconut Grove	FL	33133	305-441-6901	446-5148	643
Spanish Cove 11 Palm Ave *TF:* 800-965-2683 ■ *Web:* www.spanishcove.com	Yukon	OK	73099	800-965-2683		672
Spanish Flower 4701 N Main St *Web:* spanishflowersrestaurant.com	Houston	TX	77009	713-869-1706		671
Spanish Kitchen 2960 N Main St	Las Cruces	NM	88001	575-526-4275		671
Spanish Tavern 103 McWhorter St *Web:* www.spanishtavern.com	Newark	NJ	07105	973-589-4959		671
Spanish-American Translating 330 Eagle Ave *TF:* 800-870-5790 ■ *Web:* arleneboas.com	West Hempstead	NY	11552	516-481-3339		768
Spanset Inc 3125 Industrial Dr *Web:* www.spanset-usa.com	Sanford	NC	27332	919-774-6316		208
SpanTech LLC 1115 Cleveland Ave PO Box 369 *Web:* spantechconveyors.com	Glasgow	KY	42141	270-651-9166		358
SPAR Group Inc 560 White Plains Rd *NASDAQ: SGRP* ■ *Web:* www.sparinc.com	Tarrytown	NY	10591	914-332-4100	332-0741	4
Spark Creations Inc 10 W 46th St *Web:* www.sparkcreations.com	New York	NY	10036	212-575-8385		410
Spark Energy Gas LP 2105 Citywest Blvd *TF:* 877 547 7275 ■ *Web:* www.sparkenergy.com	Houston	TX	77042	877 547 7275	374 8007	325
SPARK Experience Design LLC 7979 Old Georgetown Rd Ste 801 *Web:* sparkexperience.com	Bethesda	MD	20814	301 294 0040		031
Spark Networks PLC 8383 Wilshire Blvd Ste 800 *NYSE: LOV* ■ *Web:* www.spark.net	Beverly Hills	CA	90211	323-836-3000		226
Spark Plug Games Llc 1011 Passport Way *Web:* www.sparkpluggames.com	Cary	NC	27513	919 651 0792		809
Spark Studios LLC 10811 Washington Blvd 4th Fl *Web:* www.sparkstudios.com	Culver City	CA	90232	424-298-8950		590
Spark Unlimited Inc 15000 Ventura Blvd Ste 202 *Web:* www.sparkunlimited.com	Sherman Oaks	CA	91403	818-788-1005		514
Sparkhound Inc 11207 Proverbs Ave *TF:* 866-217-1500 ■ *Web:* www.sparkhound.com	Baton Rouge	LA	70816	225-216-1500		180
Sparkle Solutions LP 100 Courtland Ave *TF:* 866-660-2282 ■ *Web:* www.sparklesolutions.ca	Concord	ON	L4K3T6	905-660-2282	660-2268	35
Sparks Belting Co 3800 Stahl Dr SE *TF:* 800-451-4537 ■ *Web:* www.sparksbelting.com	Grand Rapids	MI	49546	616-949-2750	949-8518	370
Sparks Exhibits & Environments 10232 Palm Dr *Web:* www.sparksonline.com	Santa Fe Springs	CA	90670	562-941-0101		232
Sparks Heritage Museum 814 Victorian Ave *Web:* www.sparksmuseum.org	Sparks	NV	89431	775-355-1144		520
Sparks Marketing Group Inc 2828 Charter Rd *TF:* 800-925-7727 ■ *Web:* www.sparksonline.com	Philadelphia	PA	19154	215-676-1100		286
Sparks Personnel Services Inc 1775 Greensboro Sta Pl Tower II Ste 300 *Web:* www.sparksitsolutions.com	Mclean	VA	22102	703-821-2650		260
Sparks Regional Medical Ctr (SRMC) 1001 Towson Ave *TF:* 800-285-1131 ■ *Web:* www.sparkshealth.com	Fort Smith	AR	72901	479-441-4000	441-5397	374-3
Sparks Steak House 210 E 46th St *Web:* www.sparkssteakhouse.com	New York	NY	10017	212-687-4855		671
Sparksight Inc 7718 Wood Hollow Dr Ste G100 Cross Building *Web:* www.sparksight.com	Austin	TX	78731	512-493-2070		636
Sparktech Inc 1308 Chisholm Trail Ste 105 *Web:* sparktechinc.com	Round Rock	TX	78681	512-716-3131		358
Sparling Instruments Company Inc 4097 N Temple City Blvd *TF Sales:* 800-800-3569 ■ *Web:* www.sparlinginstruments.com	El Monte	CA	91731	626-444-0571	444-2314	495
Sparrow Health System 1215 E Michigan Ave *TF:* 800-772-7769 ■ *Web:* www.sparrow.org	Lansing	MI	48912	517-364-1000		374-3
Sparrowk Livestock 18780 E Hwy 88 *Web:* www.sparrowk.com	Clements	CA	95227	209-759-3530	759-3831	10-1
Sparta Area Schools 465 S Union St *Web:* www.spartaschools.org	Sparta	MI	49345	616-887-8253		685
Sparta Capital Ltd 303-6707 Elbow Dr SW *Web:* www.spartacapital.com	Calgary	AB	T2V0E5	306-491-6323		767
Sparta Chevrolet 8955 Sparta Ave NW *Web:* spartachevy.com	Sparta	MI	49345	616-887-1791		57
SPARTA Inc 25531 Commercentre Dr Ste 120	Lake Forest	CA	92630	949-768-8161		127
SPARTA Insurance Holdings Inc 185 Asylum St Cityplace Ii *Web:* www.spartainsurance.com	Hartford	CT	06103	860-275-6500		390
Sparta Steel & Equipment Corp 9875 Chestnut Ave SE *Web:* www.spartasteel.com	East Sparta	OH	44626	330-866-9621		480
Sparta Systems Inc 2000 Waterview Dr Ste 300 *TF:* 888-261-5948 ■ *Web:* www.spartasystems.com	Holmdel	NJ	07733	609-807-5100		177
Spartan Carbide 34110 Riviera *Web:* www.spartancarbide.com	Fraser	MI	48026	586-285-9786		697
Spartan Chemical Company Inc 1110 Spartan Dr *TF:* 800-537-8990 ■ *Web:* www.spartanchemical.com	Maumee	OH	43537	419-531-5551	536-8423	145
Spartan College of Aeronautics & Technology 8820 E Pine St PO Box 582833 *TF Admissions:* 800-331-1204 ■ *Web:* www.spartan.edu	Tulsa	OK	74115	918-836-6886	831-5287	800
Spartan Controls Ltd 305 - 27 St SE *Web:* www.spartancontrols.com	Calgary	AB	T2A7V2	403-207-0700		111
Spartan Distributors Inc 487 W Div St *TF:* 800-822-2216 ■ *Web:* www.spartandistributors.com	Sparta	MI	49345	616-887-7301		274
Spartan Energy Corp 850 - Second St SW Ste 500 *TF:* 866-567-3105 ■ *Web:* www.spartanenergy.ca	Calgary	AB	T2P0R8	403-355-8920		536
Spartan Foods of America Inc 4250 Orchard Park Blvd *Web:* www.mamamarys.com	Spartanburg	SC	29303	864-595-6262		299
Spartan Graphics Inc 200 Applewood Dr *TF:* 800-747-4477 ■ *Web:* spartangraphics.com	Sparta	MI	49345	616-887-8243		627
Spartan Light Metal Products Inc 3668 S Geyer Rd Ste 210 *Web:* www.spartanlmp.com	St. Louis	MO	63127	314-620-2500		295
Spartan Motors Inc 1541 Reynolds Rd *NASDAQ: SPAR* ■ *TF:* 800-937-5449 ■ *Web:* www.spartanmotors.com	Charlotte	MI	48813	517-543-6400		516
Spartan Offshore Drilling LLC 516 JF Smith Ave *Web:* www.spartanoffshore.com	Slidell	LA	70460	504-885-7449		536
Spartan Securities Group Ltd 15500 Roosevelt Blvd Ste 303 *Web:* www.spartansecurities.com	Clearwater	FL	33760	727-502-0508		690
Spartan Showcase Inc 702 Spartan Showcase Dr *Web:* www.spartanshowcase.com	Union	MO	63084	636-583-4050		505
Spartan Stores Inc 850 76th St SW PO Box 8700 *NASDAQ: SPTN* ■ *TF:* 800-451-8500 ■ *Web:* spartannash.com	Grand Rapids	MI	49518	616-878-2000		297-8
Spartan Technology Solutions Inc 125 Venture Blvd Ste B *Web:* www.spartantechnology.com	Spartanburg	SC	29306	864-587-1386		177
Spartanburg Area Chamber of Commerce 105 N Pine St *Web:* www.spartanburgchamber.com	Spartanburg	SC	29302	864-594-5000	594-5055	139
Spartanburg Community College 800 Brisack Rd PO Box 4386 *TF:* 866-591-3700 ■ *Web:* www.sccsc.edu	Spartanburg	SC	29305	864-592-4800	592-4564	800
Spartanburg Convention & Visitors Bureau 298 Magnolia St *TF:* 800-374-8326 ■ *Web:* www.visitspartanburg.com	Spartanburg	SC	29306	864-594-5050		206
Spartanburg County 180 Magnolia St *Web:* www.spartanburgcounty.org	Spartanburg	SC	29306	864-596-2591		338
Spartanburg County Public Library 151 S Church St *Web:* www.infodepot.org	Spartanburg	SC	29306	864-596-3507	596-3518	434-3
Spartanburg Herald-Journal 189 W Main St *TF:* 800-922-4158 ■ *Web:* www.goupstate.com	Spartanburg	SC	29306	864-582-4511	594-6350	532-2
Spartanburg Methodist College 1000 Powell Mill Rd **Fax:* Admissions ■ *TF:* 800-772-7286 ■ *Web:* smcsc.edu	Spartanburg	SC	29301	864-587-4000	587-4355*	162
Spartanburg Regional Medical Ctr (SRMC) 101 E Wood St *TF:* 800-318-2596 ■ *Web:* spartanburgregional.com	Spartanburg	SC	29303	864-560-6000		374-3
Spartanburg Steel Products Inc 1290 New Cut Rd PO Box 6428 *TF:* 888-974-7500 ■ *Web:* www.ssprod.com	Spartanburg	SC	29304	864-585-5211	583-5641	489
Spartek Systems Inc 1 Thevenaz Industrial Trl *Web:* www.sparteksystems.com	Sylvan Lake	AB	T4S2J6	403-887-2443		539
Sparton 27 Hale Spring Rd *TF:* 800-443-4132 ■ *Web:* sparton.com	Plaistow	NH	03865	603-382-3840		203
Sparton Corp 425 N Martingale Rd Ste 2050 *TF:* 800-772-7866 ■ *Web:* sparton.com	Schaumburg	IL	60173	847-762-5800		419
Sparus Holdings Inc 3175 Corners N Court Peachtree Corners *TF:* 800-241-5057 ■ *Web:* www.sparusholdings.com	Norcross	GA	30071	800-241-5057		463
Spates Fabricators 85435 Middleton *Web:* www.spates.com	Thermal	CA	92274	760-397-4122		191-2
Spatial & Spectral Research LLC 13 Beech St *Web:* www.ssrllc.us	Bedford	NH	03110	603-472-2575		21
Spatial Corp 310 Interlocken Pkwy Ste 200 *Web:* www.spatial.com	Broomfield	CO	80021	303-544-2900	544-3000	178-8
Spatial Data Inc 4545 Fuller Dr Ste 416	Irving	TX	75038	972-791-0911	717-9099	196
Spatial Insights Inc 4938 Hampden Ln *TF:* 800-347-5291 ■ *Web:* www.spatialinsights.com	Bethesda	MD	20814	800-347-5291		539
Spaulding Composites Co 55 Nadeau Dr *TF:* 800-801-0560 ■ *Web:* www.spauldingcom.com	Rochester	NH	03867	603-332-0555	332-5357	599
Spaulding Equipment Co 75 Paseo Adelanto *Web:* www.spauldingequipment.com	Perris	CA	92570	951-943-4531		190

Phone | Fax | Class

Spaulding for Children
16250 Northland Dr Ste 120 ... Southfield MI 48075 — 248-443-0300 443-7099 48-6
Web: www.spaulding.org

Spaulding Group Inc, The
33 Clyde Rd Ste 103 ... Somerset NJ 08873 — 732-873-5700 463
Web: spauldinggrp.com

Spaulding Rehabilitation Hospital
125 Nashua St ... Boston MA 02114 — 617-573-7000 374-6
TF: 888-774-0055 ■ *Web:* www.spauldingrehab.org

Spavinaw State Park 555 S Main ... Spavinaw OK 74366 — 800-652-6552 435-2101* 565
**Fax Area Code:* 918 ■ *TF:* 800-622-6317 ■ *Web:* www.travelok.com

SPAWAR (SPAWAR) 53560 Hull St ... San Diego CA 92152 — 619-553-2717 668
Web: www.public.navy.mil/spawar/Pages/default.aspx

SpawGlass 13800 W Rd ... Houston TX 77041 — 281-970-5300 463
Web: www.spawglass.com

Spawn Ideas Inc 510 L St ... Anchorage AK 99501 — 907-274-9553 4
Web: spawnak.com

SPBA (Society of Professional Benefit Administrators)
2 Wisconsin Cir Ste 670 ... Chevy Chase MD 20815 — 301-718-7722 718-9440 49-12
Web: www.spbatpa.org

SPBA (Stein + Partners Brand Activation)
432 Pk Ave S ... New York NY 10016 — 212-213-1112 7
Web: www.steinias.com

SPC (St Petersburg College)
PO Box 13489 ... Saint Petersburg FL 33733 — 727-341-4772 598
Web: www.spcollege.edu

SPC (System Planning Corp)
3601 Wilson Blvd ... Arlington VA 22201 — 703-351-8200 194
Web: www.sysplan.com

SPD Electrical Systems
13500 Roosevelt Blvd ... Philadelphia PA 19116 — 215-677-4900 729
Web: www.l-3mps.com/spdes

Spd Foundation
5420 S Quebec St Ste 103 ... Greenwood Village CO 80111 — 303-221-7827 322-5550 196
Web: spdfoundation.net

SPE (Society of Petroleum Engineers)
222 Palisades Creek Dr ... Richardson TX 75080 — 972-952-9393 952-9435 48-12
TF: 800-456-6863 ■ *Web:* www.spe.org

SPE (Society of Plastics Engineers)
13 Church Hill Rd ... Newtown CT 06470 — 203-775-0471 775-8490 49-13
Web: www.4spe.org

SPE Amerex 201 Houston St Ste 200 ... Batavia IL 60510 — 630-406-7756 18

Speak Easy 1001 30th Ave S ... Moorhead MN 56560 — 218-233-1326 671
Web: speakeasyrestaurant.com

Speak Inc Speakers Bureau
10680 Treena St Ste 230 ... San Diego CA 92131 — 858-228-3771 228-3989 708
TF: 800-677-3324 ■ *Web:* www.speakinc.com

Speakeasy Inc
3438 Peachtree Rd Ste 1000 Phipps Twr ... Atlanta GA 30326 — 404-541-4800 541-4848 765
Web: www.speakeasyinc.com

SpeakerCraft Inc 940 Columbia Ave ... Riverside CA 92507 — 951-787-0543 173-5
TF: 800-448-0976 ■ *Web:* www.speakercraft.com

Speakers Guild Inc
35 Discovery Hill Rd ... East Sandwich MA 02537 — 508-888-6702 708
Web: businessfinder.masslive.com

Speakers Unlimited PO Box 27225 ... Columbus OH 43227 — 614-864-3703 864-3876 708
TF: 888-333-6676 ■ *Web:* www.speakersunlimited.com

Speakers.com 1125 W St Ste 200 ... Annapolis MD 21401 — 410-897-1970 708
Web: www.speakers.com

speaking rock 122 S Old Pueblo Rd ... El Paso TX 79907 — 915-860-7777 133
Web: www.speakingrockentertainment.com

Speakman Co 400 Anchor Mill Rd ... New Castle DE 19720 — 800-537-2107 977-2747 609
TF: 800-537-2107 ■ *Web:* speakman.com

Spear Inc 5510 Courseview Dr ... Mason OH 45040 — 513-459-1100 413
Web: www.spearinc.com

Spear Marketing Group
1630 N Main St Ste 200 ... Walnut Creek CA 94596 — 925-891-9050 7
TF: 800-261-1537 ■ *Web:* www.spearmarketing.com

Speare Memorial Hospital Assn
16 Hospital Rd ... Plymouth NH 03264 — 603-536-1120 374-3
Web: www.spearehospital.com

Spearfish Canyon Resort
10619 Roughlock Falls Rd ... Lead SD 57754 — 605-584-3435 584-3990 669
TF: 877-975-6343 ■ *Web:* www.spfcanyon.com

Spearhead Staffing LLC
991 Route 22 W Ste 200 ... Bridgewater NJ 08807 — 908-864-8081 196
Web: www.spearheadstaffing.com

Spears Furniture Co 7004 Salem Ave ... Lubbock TX 79424 — 806-747-3401 321
Web: www.spearsfurniture.com

Spears Manufacturing Co PO Box 9203 ... Sylmar CA 91392 — 818-364-1611 608
TF: 800-862-1499 ■ *Web:* www.spearsmfg.com

Spears-Votta & Assoc Inc
7526 Harford Rd ... Baltimore MD 21234 — 410-254-5800 261
Web: www.spearsvotta.com

SPEC (Systems & Processes Engineering Corp)
6800 Burleson Rd Ste 320 ... Austin TX 78744 — 512-479-7732 261
Web: www.spec.com

Spec Bldg Materials Inc
4300 W Ave ... San Antonio TX 78213 — 210-342-2727 340-0688 191-4
TF: 800-588-3892 ■ *Web:* speccorp.com

Spec Ops Inc 319 Business Ln ... Ashland VA 23005 — 804-752-4790 261
TF: 800-774-3854 ■ *Web:* www.specopsinc.com

Spec Personnel LLC 25 Walls Dr ... Fairfield CT 06824 — 203-254-9935 8
Web: www.speconthejob.com

SPEC Services Inc
10540 Talbert Ave ... Fountain Valley CA 92708 — 714-963-8077 963-0364 261
Web: www.specservices.com

Spec's Wines Spirits & Finer Foods
2410 Smith St ... Houston TX 77006 — 713-526-8787 526-6129 443
TF: 888-526-8787 ■ *Web:* www.specsonline.com

Specchem 444 Richmond Ave ... Kansas City KS 66101 — 816-968-5600 183
TF: 800-424-9300 ■ *Web:* www.specchemllc.com

Specco Industries Inc 13087 Main St ... Lemont IL 60439 — 630-257-5060 145
TF: 800-441-6646 ■ *Web:* www.specco.com

Specht Newspapers Inc 203 Gleason St ... Minden LA 71055 — 318-377-1866 377-1895 532-3

Special Audience Marketing Inc
6700 Manchaca Rd ... Austin TX 78745 — 512-441-6484 195
Web: specialaudience.com

Special Care Dentistry Assn
330 N Wabash Ave ... Chicago IL 60611 — 312-527-6764 49-8
Web: www.scdaonline.org

Special Counsel Inc
10201 Centurion Pkwy N Ste 400 ... Jacksonville FL 32256 — 904-737-3436 360-2307 721
TF: 800-737-3436 ■ *Web:* www.specialcounsel.com

Special Devices Inc
14370 White Sage Rd ... Moorpark CA 93021 — 805-553-1200 387-1001 268
Web: www.specialdevices.com

Special Education Report
360 Hiatt Dr ... Palm Beach Gardens FL 33418 — 561-622-6520 622-2423 531-4
TF Sales: 800-621-5463 ■ *Web:* www.lrp.com

Special Energy Corp
4815 Perkins Rd ... Stillwater OK 74076 — 405-377-1177 536
Web: www.specialenergycorp.com

Special Journeys LLC 422 S 153rd Cir ... Omaha NE 68154 — 402-884-1014 317
Web: www.specialjourneys.org

Special Libraries Assn (SLA)
331 S Patrick St ... Alexandria VA 22314 — 703-647-4900 647-4901 49-11
TF: 866-446-6069 ■ *Web:* www.sla.org

Special Materials Co
70 W 40th St 2nd Fl ... New York NY 10018 — 646-366-0400 146
Web: www.smc-global.com

Special Metals Corp
4317 Middle Settlement Rd ... New Hartford NY 13413 — 315-798-2900 798-2016* 485
**Fax:* Sales ■ *TF:* 800-334-8351 ■ *Web:* www.specialmetals.com

Special Metals Inc 2009 S Broadway ... Moore OK 73129 — 800-727-7177 492
TF: 800-727-7177 ■ *Web:* www.specialmetalsinc.com

Special Military Active Retired Travel Club (SMART)
600 University Office Blvd Ste 1A ... Pensacola FL 32504 — 850-478-1986 48-23
TF: 800-354-7681 ■ *Web:* www.smartrving.org

Special Mine Services Inc
PO Box 188 ... West Frankfort IL 62896 — 618-932-2151 937-2715 815
Web: www.smsconnectors.com

Special Olympics Inc
1133 19th St NW 11th Fl ... Washington DC 20036 — 202-628-3630 824-0200 48-22
TF: 800-700-8585 ■ *Web:* www.specialolympics.org

Special Products & Manufacturing Inc
2625 Discovery Blvd ... Rockwall TX 75032 — 972-771-8851 771-8563 697
Web: www.spmfg.com

Special Wish Foundation Inc
1250 Memory Ln N ... Columbus OH 43209 — 614-258-3186 48-5
Web: www.spwish.org

SpecialCare Hospital Management Corp
1551 Wall St Ste 210 ... St. Charles MO 63303 — 314-770-2212 535
Web: www.specialcarecorp.com

Specialist Printing & Direct Mail Services
4974 Mercury St ... San Diego CA 92111 — 760-208-2240 463
Web: www.specialistonline.com

Specialized Bicycle Components
15130 Concord Cir ... Morgan Hill CA 95037 — 408-779-6229 82
TF: 877-808-8154 ■ *Web:* www.specialized.com

Specialized Carriers & Rigging Assn (SC&RA)
5870 Trinity Pkwy Ste 200 ... Centreville VA 20120 — 703-698-0291 698-0297 49-21
Web: www.scranet.org

Specialized Information Publishers Assn (SIPA)
8229 Boone Blvd Ste 260 ... Vienna VA 22182 — 703-992-9339 992-7512 49-14
TF: 800-356-9302 ■ *Web:* www.siia.net

Specialized Printed Forms Inc
352 Ctr St ... Caledonia NY 14423 — 585-538-2381 538-4922 110
TF: 800-688-2381 ■ *Web:* www.spforms.com

Specialized Products Ltd
200 Summer St ... Clintonville WI 54929 — 715-823-3727 757
Web: www.specializedproductsltd.com

Specialized Technology Resources Inc
10 Water St ... Enfield CT 06082 — 860-758-7300 794
Web: www.strsolar.com

Special-Lite Inc PO Box 6 ... Decatur MI 49045 — 269-423-7068 423-7610 234
TF: 800-821-6531 ■ *Web:* www.special-lite.com

Specialty Bakers Inc
450 S State Rd ... Marysville PA 17053 — 717-957-2131 296-1
Web: www.sbiladyfingers.com

Specialty Bar Products Company
200 Martha St PO Box 127 ... Blairsville PA 15717 — 724-459-7500 459-0944 454
Web: www.specialty-bar.com

Specialty Bolt & Screw Inc
235 Bowles Rd ... Agawam MA 01001 — 413-789-6700 789-9340 351
TF: 800-322-7878 ■ *Web:* www.specialtybolt.com

Specialty Brands Of America Inc
1400 Old Country Rd ... Westbury NY 11590 — 516-997-6969 297-8
TF: 877-795-3599 ■ *Web:* bgfoods.com

Specialty Cable Corp 2 Tower Dr ... Wallingford CT 06492 — 203-265-7126 116
Web: www.specialtycable.com

Specialty Catalog Corp
400 Manley St ... West Bridgewater MA 02379 — 508-638-7000 459
TF: 800-364-9060 ■ *Web:* www.scdirect.com

Specialty Coffee Assn of America (SCAA)
117 W Fourth St Ste 300 ... Santa Ana CA 92701 — 562-624-4100 624-4101 49-6
TF: 800-995-9019 ■ *Web:* www.scaa.org

Specialty Commodities Inc
1530 47th St NW ... Fargo ND 58102 — 701-282-8222 296-37
Web: www.scifargo.com

Specialty Construction Management Inc
1314 Eigth St NW ... Washington DC 20001 — 202-832-7250 194
Web: www.specialtyconstruction.net

Specialty Design & Mfg Co PO Box 4039 ... Reading PA 19606 — 610-779-1357 370-0269 757
TF: 800-720-0867 ■ *Web:* www.specialtydesign.com

Specialty Equipment Market Assn (SEMA)
1575 S Vly Vista Dr ... Diamond Bar CA 91765 — 909-396-0289 860-0184 49-21
Web: www.sema.org

Specialty Fabrications Inc
2674 Westhills Ct ... Simi Valley CA 93065 — 805-579-9730 697
Web: www.specfabinc.com

Specialty Finance
212 Seventh St NE ... Charlottesville VA 22902 — 434-977-1600 977-4466 531-1
Web: www.snl.com

Specialty Finishes Inc
1545 Marietta Blvd NW ... Atlanta GA 30318 — 404-351-1062 351-0535 189-8
Web: www.specialtyfinishes.com

Phone | Fax | Class

Specialty Foods Group Inc
21 Enterprise Pkwy Ste 400 .... Hampton VA 23666 757-952-1200 296-26
TF: 800-238-0020 ■ *Web:* www.specialtyfoodsgroup.com

Specialty Graphic Imaging Assn (SGIA)
10015 Main St .... Fairfax VA 22031 703-385-1335 273-0456 49-16
TF: 888-385-3588 ■ *Web:* www.sgia.org

Specialty Hearse & Ambulance Sale Corp
60 Engineers Ln E.................. Farmingdale NY 11735 516-349-7700 57
TF General: 800-349-6102 ■ *Web:* www.specialtyhearse.com

Specialty Heat Treat Holland
3700 Eastern Ave SE.................. Grand Rapids MI 49508 616-245-0465 484

Specialty Hospital Jacksonville
4901 Richard St .... Jacksonville FL 32207 904-737-3120 242-5826* 374-7
**Fax Area Code:* 615 ■ *Web:* www.specialtyhospitaljax.com

Specialty Laboratories Inc
27027 Tourney Rd.................. Valencia CA 91355 661-799-6543 799-6634 418
TF Sales: 800-421-7110 ■ *Web:* www.specialtylabs.com

Specialty Loose Leaf Inc 1 Cabot St.................. Holyoke MA 01040 413-532-0106 552-2
TF: 800-227-3623 ■ *Web:* www.specialtyll.com

Specialty Manufacturing Co
5858 Centerville Rd .... Saint Paul MN 55127 651-653-0599 653-0989 790
TF: 800-549-4473 ■ *Web:* www.specialtymfg.com

Specialty Manufacturing LLC
5601 San Francisco Rd NE.................. Albuquerque NM 87109 505-823-1832 480
TF: 800-433-1816 ■ *Web:* www.wirelesscomponents.com

Specialty Medical Supplies
3882 NW 124th Ave .... Coral Springs FL 33065 954-752-5603 231
Web: www.specialtymedicalsupplies.com

Specialty Metals Corp 8300 S 206th St .... Kent WA 98032 253-398-1730 492
Web: www.specialtymetalscorp.com

Specialty Motors Inc
25060 Ave Tibbitts .... Valencia CA 91355 661-257-7388 257-7389 518
TF: 800-232-2612 ■ *Web:* www.specialtymotors.com

Specialty Pipe & Tube Inc
PO Box 516 .... Mineral Ridge OH 44440 330-505-8262 505-8260 492
TF: 800-842-5839 ■ *Web:* www.specialtypipe.com

Specialty Plastic Fabricators Inc
9658 196th St.................. Mokena IL 60448 708-479-5501 479-5598 199
TF: 800-747-9509 ■ *Web:* www.spfinc.com

Specialty Products & Insulation Co (SPI)
1650 Manheim Pk Ste 202.................. Lancaster PA 17601 717-569-3900 519-4046 191-4
TF: 800-788-7764 ■ *Web:* www.spi-co.com

Specialty Restaurants Corp
8191 E Kaiser Blvd.................. Anaheim CA 92808 714-279-6100 998-7574 670
Web: www.specialtyrestaurants.com

Specialty Retailers Inc
10201 S Main St.................. Houston TX 77025 800-579-2302 157-4
TF: 800-579-2302 ■ *Web:* www.stagestoresinc.com

Specialty Roll Products Inc
601 25th Ave.................. Meridian MS 39302 601-693-1771 561
Web: www.specialtyroll.com

Specialty Sales & Mktg Inc
6700 Millcreek Dr Ste 6 .... Mississauga ON L5N3V3 905-816-0011 194
Web: www.specialtysales.ca

Specialty Screw Machine Products Inc
1028 Dillerville Rd PO Box 4185 .... Lancaster PA 17604 717-397-2867 397-5912 621
Web: www.ssmp-online.com

Specialty Sleep Assn (SSA)
46639 Jones Ranch Rd.................. Friant CA 93626 559-868-4187 49-4
Web: www.sleepinformation.org

Specialty Steel Treating Inc
34501 Commerce Rd .... Fraser MI 48026 586-293-5355 293-5390 484
Web: sst.net

Specialty Surgical Products Inc
1131 US Hwy 93 N.................. Victor MT 59875 406-961-0102 475
TF: 888-878-0811 ■ *Web:* www.ssp-inc.com

Specialty Systems
11901 Riverwood Dr.................. Burnsville MN 55337 952-894-5111 697
Web: www.specialtysystems.com

Specialty Tires of America Inc
1600 Washington St.................. Indiana PA 15701 724-349-9010 349-8192 754
TF: 800-622-7327 ■ *Web:* www.stausaonline.com

Specialty Tools & Fasteners Distributors Assn (STAFDA)
500 Elm Grove Rd Ste 210 PO Box 44 .... Elm Grove WI 53122 262-784-4774 784-5059 49-18
TF: 800-352-2981 ■ *Web:* www.stafda.org

Specialty Vehicle Institute of America (SVIA)
2 Jenner St Ste 150 .... Irvine CA 92618 949-727-3727 727-4216 49-21
TF: 800-887-2887 ■ *Web:* www.atvsafety.org

Specialty Welding & Fabing of NY Inc
1025 Hiawatha Blvd .... Syracuse NY 13208 315-426-1807 697
Web: www.specweld.com

Specific Impulse Inc
2601 Blanding Ave Ste 401 .... Alameda CA 94501 510-251-2330 180
TF: 800-470-0043 ■ *Web:* www.si9.com

Specific Systems Ltd 7655 E 41st St.................. Tulsa OK 74145 918-663-9321 664
Web: specificsystems.com

Specification Rubber Products Inc
1568 First St N.................. Alabaster AL 35007 205-663-2521 663-1875 326
TF: 800-633-3415 ■ *Web:* www.specrubber.com

Specified Technologies Inc
210 Evans Way.................. Somerville NJ 08876 908-526-8000 526-9623 146
TF: 800-992-1180 ■ *Web:* www.stifirestop.com

Specified Woodworking Corp
9327 Washington Blvd N .... Laurel MD 20723 301-598-8200 321
Web: www.specifiedwoodworking.com

Speck Design Inc 600 Battery St.................. Palo Alto CA 94111 650-462-9080 393
Web: www.speckdesign.com

Speck Plastics Inc
490 Belfast Rd PO Box 421.................. Nazareth PA 18064 610-759-1807 759-3916 602

SpecMetriẍsystems
4413-C W Market St.................. Greensboro NC 27407 336-315-6090 315-6030 201
Web: www.sensoryanalytics.com

Specmo Enterprises
1200 E Avis Dr .... Madison Heights MI 48071 800-545-7910 54
TF: 800-545-7910 ■ *Web:* www.specmo.com

Speco Inc 3946 Willow Rd.................. Schiller Park IL 60176 847-678-4240 358
TF: 800-541-5415 ■ *Web:* speco.com

Speco Technologies 200 New Hwy .... Amityville NY 11701 631-957-8700 957-9142 38
TF: 800-645-5516 ■ *Web:* www.specotech.com

SPECS (South Penn Eye Care)
250 E Walnut St .... Hanover PA 17331 717-632-6063 798
TF: 800-367-7629 ■ *Web:* www.southpenneyecare.com

Spectator, The 44 Frid St .... Hamilton ON L8N3G3 905-526-3333 526-1395 532-1
TF: 800-263-6902 ■ *Web:* www.thespec.com

Spectec 9 Polaris Way .... Emigrant MT 59027 406-333-4967 639
Web: www.spectecsensors.com

SpecTec Inc 22500 SE 64th Pl Ste 230.................. Issaquah WA 98027 425-313-0154 313-9141 809
Web: www.spectec.net

Spectech 106 Union Valley Rd.................. Oak Ridge TN 37830 865-482-9948 419
Web: www.spectrumtechniques.com

Spectera Inc
6220 Old Dobbin Ln Liberty 6, Ste 200 .... Columbia MD 21045 800-638-3120 265-6049* 391-3
**Fax Area Code:* 410 ■ *TF:* 800-638-3120 ■ *Web:* www.spectera.com

Spector Gadon & Rosen PC
1635 Market St.................. Philadelphia PA 19103 215-241-8888 428
Web: www.lawsgr.com

Spectra Aluminum Products Inc
95 Reagens Industrial Pkwy .... Bradford ON L3Z2A4 905-778-8093 492
TF: 866-999-2586 ■ *Web:* www.spectraaluminum.com

Spectra Analysis Inc
257 Simarano Dr .... Marlborough MA 01752 508-281-6232 419
Web: www.spectra-analysis.com

Spectra Co 2510 Supply St .... Pomona CA 91767 800-375-1771 378
TF: 800-375-1771 ■ *Web:* www.spectracompany.com

Spectra Color Inc 9116 Stellar Ct.................. Corona CA 92883 951-277-0200 388

Spectra Colors Corp 25 Rizzolo Rd .... Kearny NJ 07032 201-997-0606 146
TF: 800-527-8588 ■ *Web:* www.spectracolors.com

Spectra Energy Corp
5400 Westheimer Ct.................. Houston TX 77056 713-627-6394 787
TF: 800-700-8744 ■ *Web:* m.duke-energy.com

Spectra Integrated Systems Inc
8100 Arrowridge Blvd.................. Charlotte NC 28273 704-525-7099 246
TF: 800-443-7561 ■ *Web:* www.sitechma.com

Spectra Laboratories Inc 2221 Ross Way .... Tacoma WA 98421 253-272-4850 794
Web: www.spectra-labs.com

Spectra Merchandising International Inc
4230 N Normandy Ave .... Chicago IL 60634 773-202-8408 246
TF: 800-777-5331 ■ *Web:* www.spectraintl.com

Spectra Plus Inc 638 Goodwin Dr .... Richardson TX 75081 972-437-5705 787

Spectra Precision Inc
10355 Westmoor Dr Ste 100 .... Westminster CO 80021 720-587-4700 203
Web: www.spectraprecision.com

Spectra Print Corp
2301 Country Club Dr PO Box 247.................. Stevens Point WI 54481 715-344-5175 393
Web: www.spectraprint.com

Spectra Products LLC
520 Columbia Dr Ste 206.................. Johnson City NY 13790 607-770-1985 5

Spectra Services Inc 6359 Dean Pkwy .... Ontario NY 14519 585-265-4320 419
TF: 800-955-7732 ■ *Web:* www.spectraservices.com

Spectrachem 10 Dell Glen Ave .... Lodi NJ 07644 973-253-3553 253-3663 388
TF: 800-524-2906 ■ *Web:* www.spectrachem.net

Spectraforce Technologies Inc
500 W Peace St .... Raleigh NC 27606 919-233-4466 180
Web: www.spectraforce.com

Spectragraphic Inc 4 Brayton Ct .... Commack NY 11725 631-499-3100 499-5255 781
Web: www.spectragraphic.com

Spectra-Kote Corp 301 E Water St.................. Gettysburg PA 17325 717-334-3177 554
TF: 800-241-4626 ■ *Web:* www.spectra-kote.com

Spectral Applied Research Inc
9078 Leslie St Unit 11 .... Richmond Hill ON L4B3L8 905-326-5040 407

Spectral Sciences Inc 4 Fourth Ave .... Burlington MA 01803 781-273-4770 196
TF: 800-238-8000 ■ *Web:* www.spectral.com

Spectralux Corp 12335 134th Ct NE.................. Redmond WA 98052 425-285-3000 529
Web: www.spectralux.com

Spectranetics Corp
9965 Federal Dr .... Colorado Springs CO 80921 719-447-2000 447-2022 424
NASDAQ: SPNC ■ *TF:* 800-231-0978 ■ *Web:* www.spectranetics.com

SpectraScience Inc
11568 Sorrento Valley Rd Ste 11 .... San Diego CA 92121 858-847-0200 250
Web: www.spectrascience.com

SpectraSensors Inc
4333 W Sam Houston Pkwy N .... Houston TX 77043 713-300-2700 201
TF: 800-619-2861 ■ *Web:* www.spectrasensors.com

Spectraserv Inc 75 Jacobus Ave.................. South Kearny NJ 07032 973-589-0277 589-0415 780
Web: www.spectraserv.com

Spectrasonics Inc
440 Woodcrest Rd Ste 310.................. Wayne PA 19087 610-964-0713 743
Web: www.spectrasonics.com

Spectratek Technologies Inc
5405 Jandy Pl.................. Los Angeles CA 90066 310-822-2400 601
Web: www.spectratek.net

Spectro Alloys Corp
13220 Doyle Path .... Rosemount MN 55068 651-437-2815 438-3714 485
TF: 800-326-7344 ■ *Web:* www.spectroalloys.com

Spectro Associates Inc
734 Kent Oaks Way Ste 302 .... Gaithersburg MD 20878 410-321-7890 180
Web: www.spectrosales.com

Spectro Coating Corp 101 Scott Dr.................. Leominster MA 01453 978-534-1800 745-8
Web: www.spectrocoating.com

Spectro Inc 1 Executive Dr Ste 101 .... Chelmsford MA 01824 978-486-0123 419
Web: spectrosci.com

Spectrolab Inc 12500 Gladstone Ave .... Sylmar CA 91342 818-365-4611 361-5102 696
TF: 800-936-4888 ■ *Web:* www.spectrolab.com

Spectronics Corp 956 Brush Hollow Rd.................. Westbury NY 11590 800-274-8888 491-6868 201
TF: 800-274-8888 ■ *Web:* www.spectroline.com

Spectrum Aerospace Inc 609 W Knox Rd.................. Tempe AZ 85284 480-966-0077 22
TF: 800-730-7377 ■ *Web:* www.spectrum-aero.com

Spectrum Bags Inc 12850 Midway Pl .... Cerritos CA 90703 562-623-2555 601
TF: 800-776-2966 ■ *Web:* www.spectrumbags.com

Spectrum Brands 3001 Deming Way .... Middleton WI 53562 608-275-3340 280
TF: 800-566-7899 ■ *Web:* www.spectrumbrands.com

Spectrum Cabinet Sales Inc
90 Crossways Park Dr W .... Woodbury NY 11797 516-496-9888 115
Web: www.spectrumkitchens.com

Spectrum Care Landscape
27181 Burbank.................. Foothill Ranch CA 92610 949-454-6900 422
TF: 800-280-0780 ■ *Web:* www.spectrumcarelandscape.com

Company	City	State	Zip	Phone	Fax	Class
Spectrum Communications Cabling Services Inc 226 N Lincoln Ave	Corona	CA	92882	951-371-0549		176
Spectrum Control Inc 8031 Avonia Rd *Web:* eis.apitech.com	Fairview	PA	16415	814-474-2207	474-2208	253
Spectrum Controls Inc PO Box 5533 *Web:* www.spectrumcontrols.com	Bellevue	WA	98006	425-746-9481	641-9473	201
Spectrum Corp 10048 Easthaven Blvd *Web:* www.specorp.com	Houston	TX	77075	713-944-6200	944-1290	701
Spectrum Data Inc 131 N Third St *TF:* 800-733-6567 ■ *Web:* www.spectrumdata.org	Oregon	IL	61061	800-733-6567		225
Spectrum Diversified Designs Inc 675 Mondial Pkwy *Web:* www.spectrumdiversified.com	Streetsboro	OH	44241	330-422-1840		549
Spectrum Equity Investors LP 1 International Pl 35th Fl *TF:* 800-785-7914 ■ *Web:* www.spectrumequity.com	Boston	MA	02110	617-464-4600	464-4601	792
Spectrum Glass Co PO Box 646 *TF:* 800-426-3120 ■ *Web:* www.spectrumglass.com	Woodinville	WA	98072	425-483-6699	483-9007	329
Spectrum Health Blodgett Campus 100 Michigan St NE *TF:* 866-989-7999 ■ *Web:* www.spectrumhealth.org	Grand Rapids	MI	49503	616-774-7444		374-3
Spectrum Health Systems Inc 10 Mechanic St Ste 302 *TF:* 800-464-9555 ■ *Web:* www.spectrumhealthsystems.org	Worcester	MA	01608	508-792-5400		48-15
Spectrum Healthcare Resources Inc 12647 Olive Blvd Ste 600 *TF:* 800-325-3982 ■ *Web:* www.spectrumhealth.com	Saint Louis	MO	63141	800-325-3982		463
Spectrum Industries Inc 925 First Ave **Fax Area Code:* 800 ■ *TF:* 800-235-1262 ■ *Web:* www.spectrumfurniture.com	Chippewa Falls	WI	54729	715-723-6750	335-0473*	286
Spectrum Interiors Inc 2652 Crescent Springs Rd	Crescent Springs	KY	41017	859-331-2696	331-4322	189-9
Spectrum Label Corp 30803 San Clemente St *TF:* 800-545-2235 ■ *Web:* www.spectrumlabel.com	Hayward	CA	94544	510-477-0707	477-0787	413
Spectrum Laboratories Inc 18617 Broadwick St *TF:* 800-634-3300 ■ *Web:* www.spectrumlabs.com	Rancho Dominguez	CA	90220	310-885-4600	885-4666	419
Spectrum Laboratory Products Inc 14422 S San Pedro St **Fax:* Cust Svc ■ *TF General:* 800-772-8786 ■ *Web:* www.spectrumchemical.com	Gardena	CA	90248	310-516-8000	516-7512*	479
Spectrum Litho 4300 Business Ctr Dr *Web:* www.spectrumlithograph.com	Fremont	CA	94538	510-438-9192		627
Spectrum Pharmaceuticals Inc 11500 S Eastern Ave Ste 240 *NASDAQ: SPPI* ■ *Web:* www.sppirx.com	Henderson	NV	89052	702-835-6300	260-7405	85
Spectrum Printing Company LLC 4651 S Butterfield Dr *TF:* 800-275-8777 ■ *Web:* www.spectrumprintingcompany.com	Tucson	AZ	85714	520-571-1114		627
Spectrum Products 7100 Spectrum Ln *Web:* www.spectrumproducts.com	Missoula	MT	59808	406-542-9781		480
Spectrum Programs Inc 6100 Blue Lagoon Dr Suite 400	Miami	FL	33126	305-757-0602		726
Spectrum Signal Processing by Vecima 2700 Production Way Ste 300 *TF:* 800-663-8986 ■ *Web:* www.spectrumsignal.com	Burnaby	BC	V5A4X1	604-676-6700	421-1764	625
Spectrum Solutions Inc 114 Castle Dr *Web:* spectrumsi.com	Madison	AL	35758	256-830-9759		261
Spectrum Systems Inc 3410 W Nine-Mile Rd *TF:* 800-432-6119 ■ *Web:* spectrumsystems.com	Pensacola	FL	32526	850-944-3392	944-1011	419
Spectrum, The 275 E St George Blvd *Web:* www.thespectrum.com	Saint George	UT	84770	435-674-6200	674-6265	532-2
Speea 15205 52nd Ave S *Web:* speea.org	Tukwila	WA	98188	206-433-0991		414
Speece Thorson Capital Group Inc 225 S Sixth St Ste 2575 *Web:* www.stcapital.com	Minneapolis	MN	55402	612-338-4649		401
Speech & Language Development 8699 Holder St *Web:* www.sldc.net	Buena Park	CA	90620	714-821-3620		685
SPEECH Morphing SYSTEMS Inc 1320 White Oaks Rd *Web:* www.speechmorphing.com	Campbell	CA	95008	408-371-8014		138
Speech-Language and Audiology Canada (CASLPA) 1 Nicholas St Ste 1000 *TF:* 800-259-8519 ■ *Web:* sac-conference.ca	Ottawa	ON	K1N7B7	613-567-9968	567-2859	48-1
Speed Art Museum, The 2035 S Third St *Web:* changingspeed.org	Louisville	KY	40208	502-634-2700		520
Speed Check Conveyor Company Inc 5345 Truman Dr *Web:* www.speedcheckconveyor.com	Decatur	GA	30035	770-981-5490		207
Speed Consulting LLC 500 Cantrell St *TF:* 800-256-7140 ■ *Web:* www.speedconsulting.com	Waxahachie	TX	75165	800-256-7140		463
Speed Fab Crete 1150 E Kennedale Pkwy *Web:* www.speedfab-crete.com	Kennedale	TX	76060	817-478-1137	561-2544	183
Speed Queen BBQ 1130 W Walnut St *Web:* www.foodspot.com	Milwaukee	WI	53205	414-265-2900		671
Speed Selector Inc 17050 Munn Rd *Web:* speedselector.com	Chagrin Falls	OH	44023	440-543-8233	543-8527	620
Speed Skating Canada 2781 Lancaster Rd *TF:* 877-572-4772 ■ *Web:* www.speedskating.ca	Ottawa	ON	K1B1A7	613-260-3660		138
Speed Sport 142 F S Cardigan Way *TF:* 866-455-2531 ■ *Web:* www.nationalspeedsportnews.com	Mooresville	NC	28117	704-489-5231		457-3
SpeedDate.com Inc PO Box 5545 *Web:* www.speeddate.com	Redwood City	CA	94063	650-692-9000		387
Speedee Mart Inc 3670 Paradise Rd	Las Vegas	NV	89169	702-733-7950		297-8
Speedemissions Inc 220 1015 Tyrone Rd Ste 710 *TF:* 800-732-0330 ■ *Web:* www.speedemissions.com	Tyrone	GA	30290	770-306-7667		62
Speedgrip Chuck Inc 2000 E Industrial Pkwy *Web:* www.speedgrip.com	Elkhart	IN	46516	574-294-1506	294-2465	759
Speedie & Assoc Inc 3331 E Wood St *TF:* 800-628-6221 ■ *Web:* www.speedie.net	Phoenix	AZ	85040	602-997-6391	943-5508	743
SpeedInfo Inc 100 Park Ctr Plaza Ste 590 *Web:* speedinfo.com	San Jose	CA	95113	408-446-7660		224
Speedling Inc 4447 Old 41 Hwy S **Fax Area Code:* 813 ■ *TF Cust Svc:* 800-881-4769 ■ *Web:* www.speedling.com	Ruskin	FL	33570	800-881-4769	645-8123*	369
Speedway Digital Printing Inc 475 Fourth St *Web:* www.speedwayprinting.com	San Francisco	CA	94107	415-543-5928		627
Speedway LLC 500 Speedway Dr *TF Cust Svc:* 800-643-1948 ■ *Web:* www.speedway.com	Enon	OH	45323	937-864-3001		324
Speedway Motors 340 Victory Ln PO Box 81906 *TF:* 800-736-3733 ■ *Web:* www.speedwaymotors.com	Lincoln	NE	68528	402-323-3200		791
Speedway Motorsports Inc (SMI) 5555 Concord Pkwy S *NYSE: TRK* ■ *TF:* 800-732-0330 ■ *Web:* www.speedwaymotorsports.com	Concord	NC	28027	704-455-3239		181
Speedway Printing & Copy Center Inc 2575 N Causeway Blvd *TF:* 800-433-9009 ■ *Web:* speedwayprinting.net	Mandeville	LA	70471	985-626-0032		113
Speedway Redi Mix Inc 1201 N Taylor Rd *TF:* 800-227-5649 ■ *Web:* www.speedwayredimix.com	Garrett	IN	46738	260-357-6885	357-0238	182
Speedway Steel Fabrication Inc 501 N Truman Blvd PO Box 8 *Web:* www.speedwaysteel.net	Crystal City	MO	63019	636-931-6500		480
Speedy Automated Mailers Inc 2200 Queen St Ste 15 *TF:* 800-678-4775 ■ *Web:* speedy-inc.com	Bellingham	WA	98229	360-676-4775		5
Speedy Glass 2422 Arctic Blvd	Anchorage	AK	99503	907-290-7233		62-2
Speedy Heavy Hauling Inc 610 25 Rd	Grand Junction	CO	81505	970-241-3420	242-5078	536
Speedy Litho Inc 403 Catlin *TF:* 800-776-7263 ■ *Web:* speedylitho.com	Kelso	WA	98626	360-425-3610		627
Speegle Construction Inc 210 Government Ave *Web:* www.speegleconstruction.com	Niceville	FL	32578	850-729-2484		449
Speer & Associates Inc 13010 Morris Rd Ste 6 *Web:* www.speerandassociates.com	Alpharetta	GA	30004	770-396-2528		463
Speer Memorial Library 801 E 12th St *TF:* 800-242-9113 ■ *Web:* www.mission.lib.tx.us	Mission	TX	78572	956-580-8750	580-8756	434-3
Speidel 34 Branch Ave *TF:* 800-441-2200 ■ *Web:* www.speidel.com	Providence	RI	02904	800-441-2200	928-2423	408
Speier Jackie (Rep D - CA) 2465 Rayburn HOB *Web:* speier.house.gov	Washington	DC	20515	202-225-3531	226-4183	342-2
Spell Capital Partners LLC 222 S Ninth St Ste 2880 *Web:* www.spellcapital.com	Minneapolis	MN	55402	612-371-9650	371-9651	405
Spellman Hardwoods Inc 4645 N 43rd Ave **Fax Area Code:* 623 ■ *TF:* 800-624-5401 ■ *Web:* www.spellmanhardwoods.com	Phoenix	AZ	85031	602-272-2313	930-7668*	191-3
Spellman High Voltage Electronics Corp 475 Wireless Blvd **Fax:* Sales ■ *Web:* www.spellmanhv.com	Hauppauge	NY	11788	631-435-1600	435-1620*	253
Spelman College 350 Spelman Ln SW **Fax:* Admissions ■ *TF Admissions:* 800-982-2411 ■ *Web:* www.spelman.edu	Atlanta	GA	30314	404-681-3643	270-5201*	166
Spence Asset Management Inc 3529 Foothills Rd *Web:* spenceassetmanagement.com	Las Cruces	NM	88011	575-556-8500	556-8510	690
Spence Associates International Inc 530 Bufflehead Dr	Kiawah Island	SC	29455	843-768-6706		260
Spence Engineering Company Inc 150 Coldenham Rd *TF:* 800-398-2493 ■ *Web:* www.spenceengineering.com	Walden	NY	12586	845-778-5566	778-1072	789
Spence Law Firm LLC 15 S Jackson St *TF:* 800-967-2117 ■ *Web:* www.spencelawyers.com	Jackson	WY	83001	307-733-7290	733-5248	428
Spencer Clarke LLC 40 Wall St Ste 1704 *Web:* www.spencerclarke.com	New York	NY	10005	212-446-6100		690
Spencer Cos Inc 120 Woodson St *TF:* 800-633-2910 ■ *Web:* www.spencercos.com	Huntsville	AL	35801	256-533-1150	535-2910	579
Spencer County 200 Main St PO Box 12 *Web:* spencercounty.in.gov	Rockport	IN	47635	812-649-6028	649-6030	338
Spencer County 2 W Main St PO Box 397 *Web:* www.spencercountyky.gov	Taylorsville	KY	40071	502-477-3215		338
Spencer Fabrications Inc 29511 County Rd 561 *TF:* 866-277-3623 ■ *Web:* www.spenfab.com	Tavares	FL	32778	352-343-0014		697
Spencer Fane Britt & Browne LLP 1000 Walnut St Ste 1400 *Web:* www.spencerfane.com	Kansas City	MO	64106	816-474-8100	474-3216	428
Spencer Foundation 625 N Michigan Ave Ste 1600 *Web:* www.spencer.org	Chicago	IL	60611	312-337-7000	337-0282	305
Spencer Gifts LLC 6826 Black Horse Pk *Web:* spencersonline.com	Egg Harbor Township	NJ	08234	609-645-3300		327
Spencer Gray LLC 1565 Hotel Circle S Ste 300 *TF:* 800-680-7345 ■ *Web:* spencergray.com	San Diego	CA	92108	619-281-3900		260
Spencer Hall Inc 11321 Terwilligerscreek Dr *TF:* 888-883-4332 ■ *Web:* www.spencerhall.com	Cincinnati	OH	45249	513-683-9724		195
Spencer Municipal Utilities 712 Grand Ave *Web:* www.smunet.net	Spencer	IA	51301	712-580-5800		116
Spencer Museum of Art 1301 Mississippi St University of Kansas *Web:* www.spencerart.ku.edu	Lawrence	KS	66045	785-864-4710	864-3112	520
Spencer Oil Company Inc 16410 Common Rd *Web:* spenceroil.com	Roseville	MI	48066	586-775-5022	776-8264	316
Spencer Plastics Inc 4811 Industrial Dr *Web:* www.spencerplastics.com	Mesick	MI	49668	231-885-1443		608

	City	State	Zip	Phone	Fax	Class
Spencer Recovery Centers Inc 1316 S Coast Hwy *TF:* 800-334-0394 ■ *Web:* www.spencerrecovery.com	Laguna Beach	CA	92651	800-334-0394		726
Spencer Reed Group Inc 6900 College Blvd Ste 1 *TF:* 800-477-5035 ■ *Web:* www.spencerreed.com	Overland Park	KS	66211	913-663-4400	663-4464	266
Spencer Savings Bank SLA 611 River Dr *TF:* 800-363-8115 ■ *Web:* www.spencersavings.com	Elmwood Park	NJ	07407	973-772-6700		70
Spencer Shenk Capers & Assoc 1515 W 190th St *Web:* www.ssca.com	Gardena	CA	90248	310-515-7555		463
Spencer State Forest Howe Pond Rd *Web:* www.mass.gov	Spencer	MA	01562	508-886-6333		565
Spencer Turbine Co 600 Day Hill Rd *TF:* 800-232-4321 ■ *Web:* www.spencerturbine.com	Windsor	CT	06095	860-688-8361	688-0098	18
Spencer's Restaurant 701 W Barista Rd *Web:* www.spencersrestaurant.com	Palm Springs	CA	92262	760-327-3446		671
Spencers Inc 290 Quarry Rd	Mount Airy	NC	27030	336-789-9111		155-18
Spenco Medical Corp PO Box 2501 *TF:* 800-877-3626 ■ *Web:* www.spenco.com	Waco	TX	76702	800-877-3626		477
SpenDifference LLC 2000 Clay St 3rd FL *Web:* www.spendifference.com	Denver	CO	80211	303-531-2680	531-2700	194
Spengler Company Inc 1402 Frontage Rd *Web:* spenglerco.com	Ofallon	IL	62269	618-206-0022		189-10
Sperone Westwater 257 Bowery *Web:* www.speronewestwater.com	New York	NY	10002	212-999-7337	999-7338	42
Sperro Metal Products Inc 2 Skyline Dr *Web:* www.sperro.com	Montville	NJ	07045	973-335-2000		697
Sperry & Rice Mfg Company LLC 9146 US Hwy 52 *TF:* 800-541-9277 ■ *Web:* www.sperryrice.com	Brookville	IN	47012	765-647-4141	647-3302	677
Sperry Automatics Company Inc 1372 New Haven Rd PO Box 717 *TF:* 800-923-3709 ■ *Web:* www.sperryautomatics.com	Naugatuck	CT	06770	203-729-4589	729-7787	621
Sperry Marine Northrop Grumman 1070 Seminole Trail *Web:* www.sperrymarine.com	Charlottesville	VA	22901	434-974-2000	974-2259	529
Sperry Rail Inc 46 Shelter Rock Rd *TF:* 800-525-8913 ■ *Web:* www.sperryrail.com	Danbury	CT	06810	203-791-4500		41
Sperry Software Inc 12443 San Jose Blvd Ste 503 *TF:* 800-878-1645 ■ *Web:* www.SperrySoftware.com	Jacksonville	FL	32223	800-878-1645		525
Sperry's 5109 Harding Pike *Web:* www.sperrys.com	Nashville	TN	37205	615-353-0809		671
Sperry, Mitchell & Company Inc 595 Madison Ave 30th Fl *Web:* sperrymitchell.com	New York	NY	10022	212-832-6628		401
Spertus Museum 610 S Michigan Ave *Web:* www.spertus.edu	Chicago	IL	60605	312-322-1700	922-6406	520
SPESA (Sewn Products Equipment Suppliers Assn) 9050 Strickland Rd Ste 103-324 *Web:* www.spesa.org	Raleigh	NC	27615	919-872-8909	872-1915	49-13
Spesia Ayers Attorneys At Law 1415 Black Rd *Web:* www.spesia-ayers.com	Joliet	IL	60435	815 726 4311	846-2410	445
Spettro 3355 Lakeshore Ave *Web:* themenupage.com	Oakland	CA	94610	510-451-7738		671
Spevcoinc 8118 Reynolda Rd *Web:* www.spevco.com	Pfafftown	NC	27040	336-924-8100		120
Spex Precision Machine Technology 85 Excel Dr *Web:* www.spex1.com	Rochester	NY	14621	585-467-0520		454
SPFA (Steel Plate Fabricators Assn) 944 Donata Ct *Web:* www.steeltank.com	Lake Zurich	IL	60047	847-438-8265	438-8766	49-13
SPFPA (International Union Security Police & Fire Professionals of America) 25510 Kelly Rd *TF:* 800-228-7492 ■ *Web:* www.spfpa.org	Roseville	MI	48066	586-772-7250	772-9644	414
SPG International 11230 Harland Dr **Fax Area Code:* 800 ■ *TF:* 877-503-4774 ■ *Web:* www.spgusa.com	Covington	GA	30014	877-503-4774	577-2210*	286
Spg Solar Inc 1039 N McDowell Blvd	Petaluma	CA	94954	415-883-7657		189-4
Sphere 3D Corp 240 Matheson Blvd E *TF:* 800-406-7325 ■ *Web:* www.sphere3d.com	Mississauga	ON	L4Z1X1	416-749-5999		180
Spherexx LLC 9142 S Sheridan *TF:* 800-833-1335 ■ *Web:* www.spherexx.com	Tulsa	OK	74133	918-491-7500		180
Spherion Canada 1 Queen St E Ste 901	Toronto	ON	M5C2W5	604-273-1440	273-4042	260
Spherix Inc 6430 Rockledge Dr Ste 503 *NASDAQ: SPEX* ■ *Web:* www.spherix.com	Bethesda	MD	20817	301-897-2540	897-2567	192
SPHS (Sheppard Pratt Health System) 6501 N Charles St *TF:* 800-627-0330 ■ *Web:* www.sheppardpratt.org	Baltimore	MD	21285	410-938-3000		374-5
SPI (Specialty Products & Insulation Co) 1650 Manheim Pk Ste 202 *TF:* 800-788-7764 ■ *Web:* www.spi-co.com	Lancaster	PA	17601	717-569-3900	519-4046	191-4
SPI Health & Safety inc 60 Rue Gaston-Dumoulin *Web:* www.spi-s.com	Blainville	QC	J7C0A3	450-420-2012		358
SPI Lasers 4000 Burton Dr *Web:* www.spilasers.com	Santa Clara	CA	95054	408-454-1170		466
SPI Pharma Rockwood Office Pk Fl 2 **Fax Area Code:* 800 ■ *TF:* 800-789-9755 ■ *Web:* www.spipharma.com	Wilmington	DE	19809	302-576-8567	789-9755*	479
SPI/Mobile Pulley Works Inc 905 S Ann St *TF:* 866-334-6325 ■ *Web:* www.spimpw.com	Mobile	AL	36605	251-653-0606	653-0668	261
Spiaggia 980 N Michigan Ave *Web:* www.spiaggiarestaurant.com	Chicago	IL	60611	312-280-2750		671
Spic & Span Inc 4301 N Richards St *TF:* 800-558-5580 ■ *Web:* www.spicandspan.com	Milwaukee	WI	53212	414-964-5050	964-5042	426
Spice & Curry 2105 E Hwy 54	Durham	NC	27713	919-544-7555		671
Spice Hunter Inc 184 Suburban Rd PO Box 8110 *TF:* 800-444-3061 ■ *Web:* www.spicehunter.com	San Luis Obispo	CA	93403	800-444-3061		296-37
Spice Island Tea House 253 Atwood St *Web:* spiceislandteahouse.com	Pittsburgh	PA	15213	412-687-8821		671
Spice Market 403 W 13th St *Web:* www.jean-georges.com	New York	NY	10014	212-675-2322		671
Spice World Inc 8101 Presidents Dr *TF:* 800-433-4979 ■ *Web:* www.spiceworldinc.com	Orlando	FL	32809	800-433-4979		296-37
Spiced Pear 117 Memorial Blvd *TF:* 866-793-5664 ■ *Web:* thechanler.com	Newport	RI	02840	401-847-2244		671
Spicer Jeffries & Company LLP 5251 S Quebec St Ste 200 *Web:* spicerjeffries.com	Greenwood Village	CO	80111	303-753-1959		2
Spicers Canada Ltd 200 Galcat Dr *TF:* 800-526-5441 ■ *Web:* www.spicers.ca	Vaughan	ON	L4L0B9	905-265-5000		557
Spicers Paper Inc 12310 Slauson Ave *TF:* 800-774-2377 ■ *Web:* www.spicers.com	Santa Fe Springs	CA	90670	562-698-1199	945-2597	553
Spider Company Inc 2340 11th St *Web:* www.scirockford.com	Rockford	IL	61104	815-961-8200		567
Spider Staging Corp 365 Upland Dr *TF:* 877-774-3370 ■ *Web:* www.spiderstaging.com	Tukwila	WA	98188	206-575-6445	575-6240	491
SPIE - International Society for Optical Engineering 1000 20th St *Web:* www.spie.org	Bellingham	WA	98225	360-676-3290	647-1445	49-19
Spike 1352 W Main **Fax Area Code:* 435 ■ *TF:* 800-821-4474 ■ *Web:* www.gspike.com	Tremonton	UT	84337	800-821-4474	257-5719*	274
SpikeSource Inc 2000 Seaport Blvd 2nd Fl *Web:* www.blackducksoftware.com	Redwood City	CA	94063	650-249-4140		525
Spiller Furniture 5605 Mcfarland Blvd *TF:* 800-318-9806 ■ *Web:* www.spillerfurniture.com	Northport	AL	35476	205-333-2030		321
Spillman Co, The 1701 Moler Rd *Web:* www.spillmanform.com	Columbus	OH	43207	614-444-2184		697
Spillman Technologies Inc 4625 Lake Pk Blvd *TF General:* 800-860-8026 ■ *Web:* www.spillman.com	Salt Lake City	UT	84120	801-902-1200	902-1210	178-10
Spilltech Environmental Inc 1627 Odonoghue St *TF:* 800-228-3877 ■ *Web:* www.spilltech.com	Mobile	AL	36615	800-228-3877		608
Spilman Thomas & Battle PLLC Spilman Cntr 300 Knwh Blv Spilman Ctr Spilman Cent Ste 100 *TF:* 800-967-8251 ■ *Web:* www.spilmanlaw.com	Charleston	WV	25301	304-340-3838		428
Spin Games LLC 100 Washington St Ste 100 & 250 *Web:* www.spingames.net	Reno	NV	89503	775-420-3550		224
Spin Master Ltd 450 Front St W *TF:* 800-622-8339 ■ *Web:* www.spinmaster.com	Toronto	ON	M5V1B6	416-364-6002		762
Spina Bifida Assn (SBAA) 1600 Wilson Blvd Ste 250 *TF:* 877-686-6444 ■ *Web:* www.spinabifidaassociation.org	Washington	DC	20007	202-944-3285		48-17
Spinco Metal Products Inc 1 Country Club Dr *Web:* www.spincometal.com	Newark	NY	14513	315-331-6285		295
Spindletop 1200 Louisiana St *Web:* hyatt.com	Houston	TX	77002	713-375-4775		671
Spindrift Inn 652 Cannery Row *TF:* 800-841-1879 ■ *Web:* www.spindriftinn.com	Monterey	CA	93940	831-646-8900	655-8174	379
Spindustries LLC 1301 La Salle St *Web:* www.lgspin.com	Lake Geneva	WI	53147	262-248-6601	248-1277	488
Spindustry Systems Corp 1370 NW 114th St Ste 300 *Web:* www.spindustry.com	Des Moines	IA	50325	515-225-0920		809
Spine Align Inc 741 Chicago Dr *Web:* www.chirobed.com	Holland	MI	49423	616 392 4565		321
Spinesmith Partners 93 Red River St Ste 107 *Web:* spinesmithusa.com	Austin	TX	78701	512-206-0770		476
SpinGo Solutions Inc 14193 S Minuteman Dr Ste 100 *TF:* 877-377-4646 ■ *Web:* www.spingo.com	Draper	UT	84020	877-377-4646		387
Spiniello Cos 354 Eisenhower Pkwy *Web:* www.spiniello.com	Livingston	NJ	07039	973-808-8383	808-9591	188-10
Spinnaker Coating Inc 518 E Water St *TF:* 800-543-9452 ■ *Web:* spinnakercoating.com	Troy	OH	45373	937-332-6500	332-6518	554
Spinnaker Exploration Co 1200 Smith St Ste 800 *Web:* www.subsea.org	Houston	TX	77002	713-759-1770		536
SPINS Inc 222 W hubbard St Ste 300 *Web:* www.spins.com	Schaumburg	IL	60654	847-908-1200		668
Spintrac Systems Inc 690 Aldo Ave *Web:* www.spintrac.com	Santa Clara	CA	95054	408-980-1155	980-1267	695
Spira Data Corp 630 - Eigth Ave SW Ste 500 *TF:* 855-666-6353 ■ *Web:* www.spiradata.com	Calgary	AB	T2P1G6	403-263-6475	263-2513	387
Spiral Binding Company Inc 1 Maltese Dr **Fax:* Cust Svc ■ *TF:* 800-631-3572 ■ *Web:* www.spiralbinding.com	Totowa	NJ	07511	973-256-0666	256-5981*	86
Spiral Diner 1314 W Magnolia *Web:* www.spiraldiner.com	Fort Worth	TX	76104	817-332-8834	332-8834	671
Spiralock Corp 25235 Dequindre Rd *TF:* 800-521-2688 ■ *Web:* www.stanleyengineeredfastening.com	Madison Heights	MI	48071	248-543-7800	543-1403	493
Spiratex Company Inc 1916 Frenchtown Ctr Dr *Web:* www.spiratex.com	Monroe	MI	48162	734-289-4800		608
Spiration Inc 6675 185th Ave NE *Web:* www.spiration.com	Redmond	WA	98052	425-497-1700		250
Spirax Sarco Inc 1150 Northpoint Blvd *TF:* 800-883-4411 ■ *Web:* www.spiraxsarco.com/us	Blythewood	SC	29016	803-714-2000	714-2222	201
Spire Consulting Group LLC 114 W Seventh St Ste 1300 *TF:* 855-216-0812 ■ *Web:* www.spireconsultinggroup.com	Austin	TX	78701	512-637-0845		196
Spire Corp 1 Patriots Pk *OTC: SPIR* ■ *Web:* www.spiresolar.com	Bedford	MA	01730	978-649-6111		695

				Phone	Fax	Class
Spire Hospitality LLC 111 S Pfingsten Rd Ste 425 *TF:* 800-546-7866 ■ *Web:* www.spirehotels.com	Deerfield	IL	60015	847-498-6650		707
Spire Inc 65 Bay St *TF:* 877-350-8837 ■ *Web:* www.spire.net	Boston	MA	02125	617-350-8837	350-9951	344
Spire Investment Partners LLC 7918 Jones Branch Dr Ste 750 *TF:* 888-737-8907 ■ *Web:* www.spireip.com	Mclean	VA	22102	703-748-5800		401
Spire Technologies Inc 2140 SW Jefferson St Ste 300 *TF:* 800-481-7332 ■ *Web:* www.spiretech.com	Portland	OR	97201	503-222-3086		196
Spirit 106.3 6420 S Zero St *Web:* www.kzkzfm.com	Fort Smith	AR	72903	479-646-6700	646-1373	645-61
Spirit 1340 AM 8515 Georgia Ave 9th fl *Web:* myspiritdc.hellobeautiful.com	Silver Spring	MD	20910	301-306-1111	306-9540	645
Spirit AeroSystems Inc 3801 S Oliver St *TF:* 800-501-7597 ■ *Web:* www.spiritaero.com	Wichita	KS	67210	316-526-9000		20
Spirit Airlines Inc 2800 Executive Way *NASDAQ: SAVE* ■ *TF:* 800-772-7117 ■ *Web:* www.spirit.com	Miramar	FL	33025	800-772-7117		25
SPIRIT Global Energy Solutions Inc 3406 S State HW 349 *Web:* www.spiritenergysolutions.com	Midland	TX	79706	432-522-2288		538
Spirit Lake Casino & Resort 7889 Hwy 57 *Web:* spiritlakecasino.net	Saint Michael	ND	58370	701-766-4747		452
Spirit Lake Tribe (SLT) PO Box 359 *Web:* www.spiritlakenation.com	Fort Totten	ND	58335	701-766-4221	766-4126	804
Spirit Manufacturing Inc 3000 Nestle Rd *TF:* 800-258-4555 ■ *Web:* www.spiritfitness.com	Jonesboro	AR	72401	870-935-1107	935-7611	267
Spirit Mound Historic Prairie 31148 SD Hwy 19 *Web:* www.gfp.sd.gov/state-parks/directory/spirit-mound	Vermillion	SD	57069	605-987-2263		565
Spirit of Dubuque 500 E Third St *Web:* www.dubuqueriverrides.com	Dubuque	IA	52001	563-583-8093	585-0634	221
Spirit Rock Meditation Center 5000 Sir Francis Drake Blvd *Web:* www.spiritrock.org	Woodacre	CA	94973	415-488-0164		148
Spirite Industries Inc 150 S Dean St *Web:* www.spirite.com	Englewood	NJ	07631	201-871-4910		155-18
Spiritled Woman - Charisma Magazine 600 Rinehart Rd *Web:* www.charismamag.com/index.php/spiritled-woman	Lake Mary	FL	32746	407-333-0600	333-7100	457-18
Spiritual Life Ctr 7100 E 45th St N *TF:* 800-348-2440 ■ *Web:* catholicdioceseofwichita.org	Wichita	KS	67226	316-744-0167	744-8072	673
Spiro's 1054 N Woods Mill Rd *Web:* www.spiros-restaurant.com	Chesterfield	MO	63017	314-878-4449	878-1090	671
Spiroflow Systems Inc 2806 Gray Fox Rd *Web:* www.spiroflowsystems.com	Monroe	NC	28110	704-291-9595		207
Spirol International Corp 30 Rock Ave *Web:* www.spirol.com	Danielson	CT	06239	860-774-8571	774-2048	487
Spitfire Strategies LLC 1800 M St NW *Web:* spitfirestrategies.com	Washington	DC	20036	202-293-6200		636
Spitler Woods State Natural Area 705 Spitler Pk Dr *Web:* www.dnr.illinois.gov/Parks/Pages/SpitlerWoods.aspx	Mount Zion	IL	62549	217-864-3121		565
Spitz Inc 700 Brandywine Dr *Web:* www.spitzinc.com	Chadds Ford	PA	19317	610-459-5200		628
Spitzer Engineering LLC 730 Fifth Ave Ste 2202	New York	NY	10019	212-765-5170		261
Spitzer Industries Inc 11250 Tanner Rd *Web:* www.spitzerind.com	Houston	TX	77041	713-466-1518		595
Spitzer Management Inc 150 E Bridge St *Web:* www.spitzer.com	Elyria	OH	44035	440-323-4671		360-2
Spivey Enterprises Inc 6148 Brookshire Blvd *Web:* www.quikshoppe.com	Charlotte	NC	28216	704-399-4802	393-1940	345
Spivey Hall Clayton College & State University 2000 Clayton State Blvd *Web:* www.spiveyhall.org	Morrow	GA	30260	678-466-4200	466-4494	572
SPJ (Society of Professional Journalists) 3909 N Meridian St *TF:* 800-331-1212 ■ *Web:* www.spj.org	Indianapolis	IN	46208	317-927-8000	920-4789	49-14
SPL (Somerville Public Library) 79 Highland Ave *Web:* www.somervillepubliclibrary.org	Somerville	MA	02143	617-623-5000		434-3
SPL (Sunnyvale Public Library) 665 W Olive Ave *Web:* sunnyvale.ca.gov/community/library/default.htm	Sunnyvale	CA	94086	408-730-7300		434-3
Splash Lagoon Water Pk Resort 8091 Peach St *Web:* www.splashlagoon.com	Erie	PA	16509	814-217-1111		31
Splash Omnimedia 711 E Main St Ste J2 *TF:* 800-961-0132 ■ *Web:* www.splashomnimedia.com	Lexington	SC	29072	803-785-5656		195
Splash!events Inc 210 Hillsdale Ave *TF:* 866-204-6000 ■ *Web:* www.splashevents.com	San Jose	CA	95136	408-287-8600		184
Splashdot Inc 609 Hastings St W *Web:* www.splashdot.com	Vancouver	BC	V6B4W4	604-899-0597		225
Splashtown Water Park 21300 IH-45 N *TF:* 800-582-4673 ■ *Web:* www.wetnwildsplashtown.com	Spring	TX	77373	281-355-3300	353-7946	32
SPLC (Southern Poverty Law Ctr) 400 Washington Ave *TF:* 888-414-7752 ■ *Web:* www.splcenter.org	Montgomery	AL	36104	334-956-8200		48-8
Splendora Independent School District 23419 FM 2090 Rd *Web:* www.splendoraisd.org	Splendora	TX	77372	281-689-3128	689-7509	685
SPLICE Software Inc 425 78 Ave SW *Web:* www.splicesoftware.com	Calgary	AB	T2H2L6	403-720-8326		179
Splish Splash 2549 Splish Splash Dr *Web:* www.splishsplash.com	Calverton	NY	11933	631-727-3600		32
Split Rock Creek State Park 50th Ave *TF:* 888-646-6367 ■ *Web:* www.dnr.state.mn.us	Jasper	MN	56144	507-348-7908	348-8940	565
Split Rock Lighthouse State Park 3755 Split Rock Lighthouse Rd *TF:* 800-366-8917 ■ *Web:* www.dnr.state.mn.us	Two Harbors	MN	55616	218-595-7625	226-6378	565
Split Rock Partners 1600 El Camino Real Ste 290 *Web:* www.splitrock.com	Menlo Park	CA	94025	952-995-7474		792
Split Rock Resort 100 Moseywood Rd *TF:* 800-255-7625 ■ *Web:* www.splitrockresort.com	Lake Harmony	PA	18624	570-722-9111		669
SPM Marketing & Communications 15 W Harris Ave Ste 300 *Web:* www.spmmarketing.com	La Grange	IL	60525	708-246-7700		4
SPMOH (Saint Petersburg Museum of History) 335 Second Ave NE	Saint Petersburg	FL	33701	727-894-1052		520
Spn Services Inc 5851 43rd Ave *Web:* www.spnservices.com	Flushing	NY	11377	718-565-5954		809
Spokane Art Supply Inc 1303 N Monroe St *TF:* 800-556-5568 ■ *Web:* www.spokaneartsupply.com	Spokane	WA	99201	509-327-6622	327-6629	45
Spokane City Hall 808 W Spokane Falls Blvd *Web:* www.spokanecity.org	Spokane	WA	99201	509-625-6250		337
Spokane Civic Theatre 1020 N Howard St *TF:* 800-325-7328 ■ *Web:* www.spokanecivictheatre.com	Spokane	WA	99201	509-325-1413	325-9287	572
Spokane Community College 1810 N Greene St *TF:* 800-248-5644 ■ *Web:* www.scc.spokane.edu	Spokane	WA	99217	509-533-7000	533-8181	162
Spokane Convention & Visitors Bureau 801 W Riverside Ste 301 *TF:* 800-662-0084 ■ *Web:* www.visitspokane.com	Spokane	WA	99201	509-624-1341	623-1297	206
Spokane County 1116 W Broadway Ave *TF:* 800-562-6000 ■ *Web:* www.spokanecounty.org	Spokane	WA	99260	509-477-2265	477-2274	338
Spokane Ctr 720 W Mallon Ave *Web:* www.spokanecenter.com	Spokane	WA	99201	509-279-7000	279-7050	205
Spokane Falls Community College 3410 W Ft George Wright Dr **Fax:* Admissions ■ *TF:* 888-509-7944 ■ *Web:* www.spokanefalls.edu	Spokane	WA	99224	509-533-3500	533-3237*	162
Spokane Hardware Supply Inc 2001 E Trent Ave *TF:* 800-888-1663 ■ *Web:* www.spokane-hardware.com	Spokane	WA	99202	509-535-1663		350
Spokane Indians Baseball Club 602 N Havana St *Web:* spokane.indians.milb.com	Spokane	WA	99202	509-535-2922		713
Spokane International Airport 9000 W Airport Dr *TF:* 800-776-5263 ■ *Web:* www.spokaneairports.net	Spokane	WA	99224	509-455-6455	624-6633	27
Spokane Neighborhood Action Programs 212 W Second Ave *TF:* 800-411-0834 ■ *Web:* www.snapwa.org	Spokane	WA	99201	509-744-3370		196
Spokane Public Library 906 W Main Ave *Web:* www.spokanelibrary.org	Spokane	WA	99201	509-444-5300	444-5365	434-3
Spokane Public Radio 2319 N Monroe St *TF:* 800-328-5729 ■ *Web:* spokanepublicradio.org	Spokane	WA	99205	509-328-5729	328-5764	645-154
Spokane Software Systems Inc 911 N Pines Rd *Web:* sssonline.com	Spokane	WA	99206	509-252-4150		809
Spokane Steel Foundry Co 3808 N Sullivan Rd Bldg 1 *Web:* spokaneindustries.com	Spokane	WA	99216	509-924-0440	924-9448	307
Spokane Symphony PO Box 365 *TF:* 800-899-1482 ■ *Web:* www.spokanesymphony.org	Spokane	WA	99210	509-624-1200	252-2637	573-3
Spokane Transit Authority Route & Schedule Information 328 Ride 701 W Riverside Ave *Web:* www.spokanetransit.com	Spokane	WA	99201	509-456-7277		108
Spokane Valley Chamber of Commerce 9507 E Sprague Ave *TF:* 866-475-1436 ■ *Web:* www.spokanevalleychamber.org	Spokane Valley	WA	99206	509-924-4994	924-4992	139
Spokane Valley Mall 14700 E Indiana Ave *Web:* www.spokanevalleymall.com	Spokane	WA	99216	509-926-3700		460
Spoken Translation Inc 1100 W View Dr *Web:* www.spokentranslation.com	Berkeley	CA	94705	510-843-9900		177
Spokes Etc Inc 1545 N Quaker Ln *Web:* www.spokesetc.com	Alexandria	VA	22302	703-820-2200		711
Spongelab Interactive Inc 60 Atlantic Ave Ste 300 *Web:* www.spongelab.com	Toronto	ON	M6K1X9	416-703-9753		631
Spongex LLC 3002 Anaconda Rd *Web:* www.spongexfoam.com	Tarboro	NC	27886	252-824-0015		601
Sponseller Group Inc 1600 Timber Wolf Dr *TF:* 800-776-1625 ■ *Web:* www.sponsellergroup.com	Holland	OH	43528	419-861-3000		261
Spooltech Inc 9325 Highway 6 N *Web:* www.spooltech.us	Houston	TX	77095	281-861-6800		200
Spoon River College (SRC) 23235 N County Hwy 22 **Fax:* Admissions ■ *TF:* 800-334-7337 ■ *Web:* www.src.edu	Canton	IL	61520	309-647-4645	649-6393*	162
Spoon River Electric Co-op Inc (SREC) 930 S Fifth Ave PO Box 340 *TF:* 877-404-2572 ■ *Web:* www.srecoop.org	Canton	IL	61520	309-647-2700		245
Spoons California Grill 2601 Hotel Terr *Web:* www.spoonsoc.com	Santa Ana	CA	92705	714-556-0700		671
Sport Chevrolet 3101 Automobile Blvd *Web:* sportautomotive.com	Silver Spring	MD	20904	301-890-6000		57
Sport Clips Inc 110 Briarwood Dr *TF:* 800-872-4247 ■ *Web:* www.sportclips.com	Georgetown	TX	78628	512-869-1201		310
Sport Fishing Magazine 460 N Orlando Ave Ste 200 *TF:* 800-879-0496 ■ *Web:* www.sportfishingmag.com	Orlando	FL	32789	800-879-0496		457-20
Sport Fit Bowie Racquet & Fitness Club Inc 100 Whitemarsh Park Dr *Web:* sportfitclubs.com	Bowie	MD	20715	301-262-4553		354

Name / Address	City	State	Zip	Phone	Fax	Class
Sport Graphics PO Box 95	Shrewsbury	MA	01545	508-925-0406		592
Web: www.sportgraphics.com						
Sport Graphics Inc						
3423 Park Davis Cir	Indianapolis	IN	46235	317-899-7000		627
TF: 800-792-3403 ■ *Web:* www.sportg.com						
Sport Ngin LLC						
807 Broadway St NE Ste 300	Minneapolis	MN	55413	612-379-1030		387
Web: www.sportsengine.com						
Sport Obermeyer Ltd USA Inc 115 AABC	Aspen	CO	81611	970-925-5060	925-9203	155-5
TF: 800-525-4203 ■ *Web:* www.obermeyer.com						
Sport Supply Group Inc						
1901 Diplomat Dr	Dallas	TX	75234	972-484-9484		710
Web: www.sportsupplygroup.com						
Sportco Sporting Goods Inc						
2580 E Sunset Rd	Las Vegas	NV	89120	702-739-9750	739-9021	710
Web: sportcolasvegas.com						
Sportech Inc 10800 175th Ave NW	Elk River	MN	55330	763-712-3965		247
Web: www.sportechinc.com						
Sport-Haley Inc 200 Union Blvd Ste 400	Denver	CO	80228	303-320-8800		155-3
Web: www.sporthaley.com						
Sport&Health Clubs LLC						
1800 Old Meadow Rd Ste 300	Mclean	VA	22102	703 556 6550		354
Web: www.sportandhealth.com						
Sportika Export Inc 225 Episcopal Rd	Berlin	CT	06037	860-828-9000		799
Web: www.sportika.com						
Sporting Goods Intelligence Inc						
442 Featherbed Ln	Glen Mills	PA	19342	610-459-4040		711
Web: www.sginews.com						
SportPharma Inc 3 Terminal Rd	New Brunswick	NJ	08901	732-545-3130	509-0458	799
TF: 800-872-0101 ■ *Web:* www.sportpharma.com						
Sports & Fitness Industry Association, The						
1150 17th St NW Ste 850	Washington	DC	20036	202-775-1762	296-7462	49-4
Web: www.sfia.org						
Sports Afield Magazine						
15621 Chemical Ln	Huntington Beach	CA	92649	714-373-4910	894-4949	457-20
TF: 800-451-4788 ■ *Web:* www.sportsafield.com						
Sports Authority Field at Mile High						
1701 Bryant St	Denver	CO	80204	720-258-3000	258-3050	720
Web: www.sportsauthorityfieldatmilehigh.com						
Sports Business Daily						
120 W Morehead St Ste 310	Charlotte	NC	28202	704-973-1410	973-1401	457-20
TF: 800-829-9839 ■ *Web:* www.sportsbusinessdaily.com						
Sports Car Club of America (SCCA)						
6700 SW Topeka Blvd Ste 300	Topeka	KS	66619	785-357-7222	232-7228	48-18
TF: 800-770-2055 ■ *Web:* www.scca.com						
Sports Cardiovascular & Wellness Nutritionists (SCAN)						
230 Washington Ave Extn Ste 101	Albany	NY	12203	518-254-6730	463-0656	49-8
TF General: 800-249-2875 ■ *Web:* www.scandpg.org						
Sports Creek Raceway						
4290 Morrish Rd	Swartz Creek	MI	48473	810-635-3333		642
Sports Empire PO Box 6169	Lakewood	CA	90714	562-920-2350	920-1828	771
TF: 800-255-5258 ■ *Web:* www.sports-empire.com						
Sports Excellence Corporation Inc						
151 Alston Bureau 100	Pointe-Claire	QC	H9R5V9	514-782-0400		711
Web: sportsexcellence.com						
Sports Immortals Museum						
6830 N Federal Hwy	Boca Raton	FL	33487	561-997-2575	997-6949	522
Web: www.sportsimmortals.com						
Sports Imports Inc 4000 Parkway Ln	Hilliard	OH	43026	614-771-0246		711
Web: www.sportsimports.com						
Sports Inc 333 Second Ave N	Lewistown	MT	59457	406-538-3496		138
Web: www.sportsinc.com						
Sports Legends at Camden Yards						
301 W Camden St	Baltimore	MD	21201	410-727-1539	727-1652	522
Web: baberuthmuseum.org						
Sports Leisure Vacations						
9812 Old Winery Pl	Sacramento	CA	95827	916-361-2051		760
TF: 800-951-5556 ■ *Web:* www.sportsleisure.com						
Sports Management Network Inc						
131 W Long Lake Rd Ste 250	Troy	MI	48098	248-335-3535	335-3352	41
Web: www.sportsmanagementnetwork.com						
Sports Museum, The 100 Legends Way	Boston	MA	02114	617-624-1234		522
Web: www.sportsmuseum.org						
Sports One Inc						
9640 SW Sunshine Court Ste 400	Portland	OR	97005	503-721-7477		711
Web: www.etzelagency.com						
Sports Promotion Network						
PO Box 200548	Arlington	TX	76006	800-460-9989		711
TF: 800-460-9989 ■ *Web:* www.gotospn.com						
Sports Spectrum Magazine						
105 Corporate Blvd Ste 2	Indian Trail	NC	28079	704-821-2971		457-20
TF: 866-821-2971 ■ *Web:* www.sportsspectrum.com						
Sports Technologies Inc						
10 Front St	Collinsville	CT	06019	860-693-9561		463
Web: sportshubtech.com						
Sports Travel Inc						
60 Main St PO Box 50	Hatfield	MA	01038	413-247-7678	247-5700	760
TF: 800-662-4424 ■ *Web:* www.sportstravelandtours.com						
Sports Turf Managers Assn (STMA)						
805 New Hampshire Ste E	Lawrence	KS	66044	785-843-2549	843-2977	48-22
TF: 800-323-3875 ■ *Web:* www.stma.org						
Sports Warehouse Inc						
181 Suburban Rd	San Luis Obispo	CA	93401	805-781-6464		711
Web: www.tennis-warehouse.com						
Sportservice Corp 40 Fountain Plaza	Buffalo	NY	14202	716-858-5000		299
TF: 800-828-7240 ■ *Web:* delawarenorth.com						
Sportsman's Warehouse						
7035 High Tech Dr	Midvale	UT	84047	801-566-6681		711
Web: www.sportsmanswarehouse.com						
Sportsmans Hotel & Restaurant						
12700 Renovo Rd	Renovo	PA	17764	570-923-9968		377
Web: www.sportsmanshotel.com						
Sportsmen of Stanislaus Club						
819 Sunset Ave	Modesto	CA	95351	209-578-5801		354
Web: www.sosclub.com						
Sportsmen's Lodge Hotel						
12825 Ventura Blvd	Studio City	CA	91604	818-769-4700		707
TF: 800-821-8511 ■ *Web:* www.sportsmenslodge.com						
SportsPlay Equipment Inc						
5642 Natural Bridge Ave	Saint Louis	MO	63120	314-389-4140	389-9034	346
TF: 800-727-8180 ■ *Web:* www.sportsplayinc.com						
Spot Trading LLC						
440 S LaSalle St Ste 2800	Chicago	IL	60605	312-362-4550		791
Web: www.spottradingllc.com						
Spot411 Technologies Inc						
10 Plaza Sq Ste C	Orange	CA	92866	714-771-2050		387
SpotHero Inc 200 S Wacker Dr	Chicago	IL	60606	312-566-7768		192
Web: spothero.com						
Spot-Hogg Archery Products						
125 Smith St	Harrisburg	OR	97446	541-995-3702		711
TF: 888-302-7768 ■ *Web:* spot-hogg.com						
Spotless Cleaners Inc 410 Fifth St	Dunmore	PA	18512	570-346-7577		426
Spotlight 29 Casino						
46-200 Harrison Pl	Coachella	CA	92236	760-775-5566	775-7677	133
Web: www.spotlight29.com						
Spotlight on Kids						
20 S Main St Ste 22	Janesville	WI	53545	608-758-1451		749
Web: www.janesvillepac.org						
Spotlight Promotions Inc						
2000 Van Ness Ave Ste 101	San Francisco	CA	94109	415-202-7100		701
Web: www.spotlightsf.com						
Spotnails 1100 Hicks Rd	Rolling Meadows	IL	60008	847-259-1620		813
TF: 800-873-2239 ■ *Web:* www.spotnails.com						
SpotOn Inc 2350 Kerner Blvd Ste 380	San Rafael	CA	94901	877-814-4102		387
TF: 877-814-4102 ■ *Web:* www.spoton.com						
Spotsylvania County						
9104 Courthouse Rd PO Box 99	Spotsylvania	VA	22553	540-507-7010	507-7019	338
Web: www.spotsylvania.va.us						
Spotts Fain PC						
411 E Franklin St Ste 600	Richmond	VA	23219	804-697-2000		41
TF: 866-788-1190 ■ *Web:* www.spottsfain.com						
Spotwave Wireless Inc						
500 Van Buren St Box 550	Kemptville	ON	K0G1J0	613-591-1662		736
TF: 866-704-9750 ■ *Web:* www.spotwave.com						
SPP Canada Aircraft Inc						
2025 Meadowvale Blvd Unit 1	Mississauga	ON	L5N5N1	905-821-9339		22
Web: www.spp-ca.com						
SPPD (Southern Public Power District)						
4550 W Husker Hwy PO Box 1687	Grand Island	NE	68803	308-384-2350	384-5018	245
TF: 800-652-2013 ■ *Web:* www.southernpd.com						
SPR (Sumner Peck Ranch Inc)						
14860 N Hwy 41	Madera	CA	93636	559-822-3301		10-4
TF: 800-788-0836 ■ *Web:* www.sumnerpeckranch.com						
SPR Consulting						
Sears Tower 233 S Wacker Dr Ste 3500	Chicago	IL	60606	312-756-1760		631
TF: 800-225-1560 ■ *Web:* spr.com						
SPR Consulting						
789 N Water St Ste 100	Milwaukee	WI	53202	414-224-7901		261
Web: www.sprcompanies.com						
Spradling International Inc						
200 Cahaba Vly Pkwy PO Box 1668	Pelham	AL	35124	205-985-4206	985-9176	594
TF: 800-333-0955 ■ *Web:* www.spradlingvinyl.com						
Spraggins Flooring Inc						
3815 Silver Star Rd	Orlando	FL	32808	407-295-4150		290
Web: www.spragginsflooring.com						
Sprague Energy						
185 International Dr Ste 200	Portsmouth	NH	03801	603-431-1000	430-5320*	579
**Fax:* Hum Res ■ *TF:* 800-225-1560 ■ *Web:* www.spragueenergy.com						
Sprague Pest Solutions Inc						
2725 Pacific Ave Ste 200	Tacoma	WA	98402	253-272-4400		577
TF: 800-375-7786 ■ *Web:* www.spraguepest.com						
Spray Enclosure Technologies Inc						
1427 N Linden Ave	Rialto	CA	92376	909-419-7011		697
TF: 800-535-8196 ■ *Web:* www.spraytech.com						
Spraying Systems Co PO Box 7900	Wheaton	IL	60189	630-665-5000	260-0842	487
TF: 800-800-6509 ■ *Web:* www.spray.com						
Sprayway Inc 1005 S Westgate Ave	Addison	IL	60101	630-628-3000	543-7797	145
TF: 800-332-9000 ■ *Web:* www.spraywayinc.com						
SPRC (Stanford Prevention Research Ctr)						
1070 Arastradero Rd Ste 100 and 300	Stanford	CA	94305	650-723-6254	725-6247	668
Web: prevention.stanford.edu						
Spread the News PR Inc						
1236 Inverness Dr	Lawrence	KS	66049	785-842-8909		636
Web: www.spreadthenewspr.com						
Sprecher + Schuh						
15910 International Plaza Dr	Houston	TX	77032	281-442-9000	442-1570	203
TF: 877-721-5913 ■ *Web:* www.sprecherschuh.com						
Spredfast Inc						
200 W Cesar Chavez Ste 600	Austin	TX	78701	512-649-3286		387
Web: www.spredfast.com						
Spreedly Inc 733 Foster St	Durham	NC	27701	888-727-7750		387
TF: 888-727-7750 ■ *Web:* spreedly.com						
Sprenger Midwest Inc						
523 E 14th St	Sioux Falls	SD	57104	605-334-7705		191-3
Web: www.sprengermidwest.com						
Sprig Electric Co 1860 S Tenth St	San Jose	CA	95112	408-298-3134	298-2132	189-4
Web: www.sprigelectric.com						
Spring Arbor Distributors						
1 Ingram Blvd	La Vergne	TN	37086	615-793-5000		96
TF: 800-395-4340 ■ *Web:* www.ingramcontent.com						
Spring Arbor University						
106 E Main St	Spring Arbor	MI	49283	517-750-1200	750-2745*	166
**Fax:* Admissions ■ *TF Admissions:* 800-968-9103 ■ *Web:* saucougars.com						
Spring City Electrical Manufacturing Co						
PO Box 19	Spring City	PA	19475	610-948-4000	948-5577	439
TF: 800-276-2722 ■ *Web:* www.springcity.com						
Spring Creek Animal Hospital						
14837 Nacogdoches Rd	San Antonio	TX	78247	210-599-2131		794
Web: springcreekvet.com						
Spring Creek Barbeque						
2340 W I- 20 Ste 100	Arlington	TX	76017	817-467-0505		671
TF: 888-467-0505 ■ *Web:* springcreekbarbeque.com						
Spring Creek Correctional Ctr						
3600 Bette Cato	Seward	AK	99664	907-224-8200	224-8062	213
Web: www.correct.state.ak.us/corrections						

Name / Address	Phone	Fax	Class
Spring Creek Ranch 1800 Spirit Dance Rd........................Jackson WY 83001 *TF:* 800-443-6139 ■ *Web:* www.springcreekranch.com	307-733-8833		379
Spring Creek Recreation Area c/o Oahe Downstream Recreation Area 20439 Marina Loop Rd.....................Fort Pierre SD 57532 *Web:* www.gfp.sd.gov/state-parks/directory/spring-creek	605-223-7722		565
Spring Creek Resort 28229 Spring Creek Pl..........................Pierre SD 57501 *Web:* www.springcreekventure.com	605-224-8336		669
Spring Creek Youth Services Ctr 3190 E Las Vegas St.................Colorado Springs CO 80906 *TF:* 800-388-5515 ■ *Web:* www.colorado.gov	719-390-2700		412
Spring Dynamics Inc 7378 Research Dr...........Almont MI 48003 *TF:* 888-274-8432 ■ *Web:* www.springdynamics.com	810-798-2622		719
Spring Engineers Inc 9740 Tanner Rd...........Houston TX 77041 *TF:* 800-899-9488 ■ *Web:* springhouston.com	713-690-9488	690-1199	719
Spring Glen Fresh Foods Inc 314 Spring Glen Dr PO Box 518................Ephrata PA 17522 *TF:* 800-641-2853 ■ *Web:* www.springglen.com	717-733-2201	721-6720	296-19
Spring Grove Cemetery 4521 Spring Grove Ave.....................Cincinnati OH 45232 *TF:* 888-853-2230 ■ *Web:* www.springgrove.org	513-681-7526	853-6802	510
Spring Grove Hospital Ctr 55 Wade Ave.............................Catonsville MD 21228	410-402-6000		374-5
Spring Harbor Hospital 123 Andover Rd..........................Westbrook ME 04092 *TF:* 888-524-0080 ■ *Web:* mainehealth.org/spring-harbor-hospital	207-761-2200	761-2108	374-5
Spring Hill College 4000 Dauphin St............Mobile AL 36608 *TF Admissions:* 800-742-6704 ■ *Web:* badgerweb.shc.edu	251-380-4000		166
Spring Hill Mall 1072 Spring Hill Mall...................West Dundee IL 60118 *TF:* 800-718-8788 ■ *Web:* www.springhillmall.com	847-428-2200		460
Spring House Estates 728 Norristown Rd....................Lower Gwynedd PA 19002 *TF:* 888-365-2287 ■ *Web:* www.actsretirement.org	215-628-8110		672
Spring Lake State Fish & Wildlife Area 7982 S Pk Rd...............................Manito IL 61546 *Web:* www.dnr.illinois.gov/Parks/Pages/SpringLake.aspx	309-968-7135		565
Spring Lake Village 5555 Montgomery Dr......................Santa Rosa CA 95409 *TF:* 800-795-1267 ■ *Web:* jtm-esc.org	707-538-8400		672
Spring Manufacturers Institute (SMI) 2001 Midwest Rd Ste 106...................Oak Brook IL 60523 *TF:* 866-482-5569 ■ *Web:* www.smihq.org	630-495-8588	495-8595	49-13
Spring Meadow Lake State Park 1420 E 6thAve PO Box 200701..................Helena MT 59620 *Web:* stateparks.mt.gov	406-444-2535		565
Spring Meadows Golf Cntry Clb 59 Lewiston Rd.................................Gray ME 04039 *TF:* 800-696-1000 ■ *Web:* www.springmeadowsgolf.com	207-657-2586		226
Spring Mill State Park PO Box 376............Mitchell IN 47446 *Web:* www.in.gov	812-849-4129		565
Spring Mountain Ranch State Park 6375 Highway 159.....................Blue Diamond NV 89004 *Web:* parks.nv.gov/parks/spring-mountain-ranch	702-875-4141		565
Spring Mountain Vineyards 2805 Spring Mtn Rd.......................Saint Helena CA 94574 *TF:* 877-769-4637 ■ *Web:* www.springmtn.com	707-967-4188	963-2753	315-5
Spring River Park & Zoo 1306 E College Blvd PO Box 1838..............Roswell NM 88201 *Web:* www.museumsusa.org	575-624-6760		823
Spring Street Historical Museum 525 Spring St..........................Shreveport LA 71101	318-424-0964		520
Spring Valley Chamber of Commerce 3322 Sweetwater Springs Blvd Ste 202......Spring Valley CA 91977 *TF:* 800-447-2937 ■ *Web:* www.springvalleychamber.org	619-670-9902	670-9924	139
Spring Valley State Park HC 74 PO Box 201...........................Pioche NV 89043 *Web:* www.parks.nv.gov	775-962-5102		565
Spring Venture Group LLC 2301 McGee St 4th Fl...................Kansas City KS 64108 *Web:* www.springventuregroup.com	816-888-7900		5
SpringBank TechVentures 160 MacLaurin Dr Ste #1.....................Calgary AB T3Z3S4	403-685-8001	685-8002	528
Springboard Biodiesel LLC 2282 Ivy St...........Chico CA 95928 *Web:* www.springboardbiodiesel.com	530-894-1793		362
Springboard Nonprofit Consumer Credit Management 4351 Latham St...........................Riverside CA 92501 *TF:* 888-425-3453 ■ *Web:* bkhelp.org	888-425-3453		393
Springbox Ltd 708 Congress Ave Ste A............Austin TX 78701 *Web:* www.springbox.com	512-391-0065		7
Springbrook State Park 2437 160th Rd.......................Guthrie Center IA 50115 *Web:* www.iowadnr.gov	641-747-3591	747-8401	565
Springdale Chamber of Commerce 202 W Emma Ave........................Springdale AR 72765 *Fax Area Code: 202 ■ *Web:* www.springdale.com	479-872-2222	228-1371*	139
Springdot Inc 2611 Colerain Ave.............Cincinnati OH 45214 *Web:* www.springdot.com	513-542-4000		627
Springer Electric Co-op Inc 408 Maxwell Ave PO Box 698..................Springer NM 87747 *TF:* 800-288-1353 ■ *Web:* www.springercoop.com	575-483-2421		245
Springer Mktg & Adv 65 Wilkie Way............Fletcher NC 28732 *Web:* www.springermktadv.com	828-687-0334		4
Springer Opera House 103 Tenth St...........Columbus GA 31901 *Web:* www.springeroperahouse.org	706-327-3688	324-4461	572
Springfield Area Chamber of Commerce 202 S John Q Hammons Pkwy..............Springfield MO 65806 *TF:* 800-879-7504 ■ *Web:* www.springfieldchamber.com	417-862-5567	862-1611	139
Springfield Armory 420 W Main St..............Geneseo IL 61254 *TF:* 800-680-6866 ■ *Web:* www.springfield-armory.com	309-944-5631	944-3676	284
Springfield Armory National Historic Site 1 Armory Sq Ste 2.......................Springfield MA 01105 *Web:* www.nps.gov/spar	413-734-8551	747-8062	564
Springfield Art Museum 1111 E Brookside Dr.....................Springfield MO 65807 *TF:* 800-272-3900 ■ *Web:* sgfmuseum.org	417-837-5700	837-5704	520

Name / Address	Phone	Fax	Class
Springfield Brewing Co 305 S Market Ave.........................Springfield MO 65806 *Web:* www.springfieldbrewingco.com	417-832-8277		671
Springfield Business Journal 313 Pk Central W.........................Springfield MO 65806 *Web:* www.sbj.net	417-831-3238		457-5
Springfield Chamber of Commerce 101 S 'A' St...............................Springfield OR 97477 *Web:* www.springfield-chamber.org	541-746-1651	726-4727	139
Springfield City Library 220 State St...............................Springfield MA 01103 *TF:* 800-852-3133 ■ *Web:* www.springfieldlibrary.org	413-263-6828		434-3
Springfield College 263 Alden St.............Springfield MA 01109 *Fax: Admissions ■ *TF Admissions:* 800-343-1257 ■ *Web:* springfield.edu	413-748-3136	748-3694*	166
Springfield College in Illinois - Benedictine University 1500 N Fifth St...........................Springfield IL 62702 *TF:* 800-635-7289 ■ *Web:* ben.edu	217-525-1420	525-1497	162
Springfield Conservation Nature Ctr 4600 S Chrisman Ave......................Springfield MO 65804 *TF:* 800-392-1111 ■ *Web:* www.mdc.mo.gov	417-888-4237	888-4241	50-5
Springfield Convention & Visitors Bureau 109 N Seventh St..........................Springfield IL 62701 *TF:* 800-545-7300 ■ *Web:* www.visitspringfieldillinois.com	217-789-2360	544-8711	206
Springfield Creamery Inc 29440 Airport Rd...............................Eugene OR 97402 *Web:* www.nancysyogurt.com	541-689-2911		296-27
Springfield Electric Supply Co 700 N Ninth St.............................Springfield IL 62702 *TF:* 800-747-2101 ■ *Web:* www.springfieldelectric.com	217-788-2100	788-2134	246
Springfield Exposition Ctr 635 E St Louis St.........................Springfield MO 65806 *Web:* www.upspringfield.com	417-522-3976		205
Springfield Hospital 25 Ridgewood Rd..........................Springfield VT 05156 *Web:* www.springfieldhospital.org	802-885-2151	885-7357	374-3
Springfield Hospital Ctr 6655 Sykesville Rd.........................Sykesville MD 21784 *TF:* 800-333-7564 ■ *Web:* dhmh.maryland.gov	410-970-7000		374-5
Springfield (IL) City Hall 800 E Monroe St Rm 300..................Springfield IL 62701 *Web:* www.springfield.il.us	217-789-2200	789-2109	337
Springfield Little Theatre 311 E Walnut Ave.........................Springfield MO 65806 *Web:* www.springfieldlittletheatre.org	417-869-1334	869-4047	573-4
Springfield (MA) City Hall 36 Ct St...................................Springfield MA 01103 *Web:* www.springfield-ma.gov/cos	413-787-6000		337
Springfield Missouri Convention & Visitors Bureau 815 E St Louis St Ste 100..................Springfield MO 65806 *TF:* 800-678-8767 ■ *Web:* www.springfieldmo.org	417-881-5300	881-2231	206
Springfield (MO) City Hall 840 Boonville Ave.........................Springfield MO 65802 *Web:* www.springfieldmo.gov/home	417-864-1000	864-1649	337
Springfield Museum 590 Main St.............Springfield OR 97477	541-726-2300		520
Springfield Museums 21 Edwards St...........Springfield MA 01103 *TF:* 800-625-7738 ■ *Web:* www.springfieldmuseums.org	413-263-6800	263-6807	520
Springfield National Cemetery 1702 E Seminole St.......................Springfield MO 65804 *Web:* www.cem.va.gov	417-881-9499	881-7862	136
Springfield News Leader 651 N Boonville Ave.......................Springfield MO 65806 *TF:* 800-445-1059 ■ *Web:* www.news-leader.com	417-836-1100	837-1381	532-2
Springfield News-Sun 202 N Limestone St.......................Springfield OH 45503 *TF:* 800-441-6397 ■ *Web:* www.springfieldnewssun.com	937-328-0300	328-0328	532-2
Springfield Public Library 225 N Fifth St............................Springfield OR 97477 *Web:* www.ci.springfield.or.us	541-726-3766	726-3747	434-3
Springfield Public School District #186 1900 W Monroe St.........................Springfield IL 62704 *TF:* 877-632-7753 ■ *Web:* www.sps186.org	217-525-3006	525-3005	685
Springfield Public Schools 1550 Main St.............................Springfield MA 01103 *Fax: Hum Res ■ *Web:* www.springfieldpublicschools.com	413-787-7100	787-7171*	685
Springfield Public Schools 1359 E St Louis St.......................Springfield MO 65802 *Fax: Mail Rm ■ *Web:* www.springfieldpublicschoolsmo.org	417-523-0000	523-0196*	685
Springfield ReManufacturing Corp 650 N Broadview Pl.......................Springfield MO 65802 *TF:* 800-772-7733 ■ *Web:* www.srcreman.com	417-862-3501		262
Springfield Spring Corp 311 Shaker Rd....................East Longmeadow MA 01028 *Web:* www.springfieldspring.com	413-525-6837		718
Springfield Symphony Orchestra 1350 Main St.............................Springfield MA 01103 *Web:* www.springfieldsymphony.org	413-733-0636	781-4129	573-3
Springfield Symphony Orchestra 411 N Sherman Pkwy.......................Springfield MO 65802 *TF:* 800-775-2628 ■ *Web:* www.springfieldmosymphony.org	417-864-6683	864-8967	573-3
Springfield Technical Community College 1 Armory Sq PO Box 900...................Springfield MA 01102 *Fax: Admissions ■ *Web:* www.stcc.edu	413-781-7822	755-6306*	162
Springfield Theatre Centre 420 S Sixth St............................Springfield IL 62701 *Web:* springfieldtheatrecentre.com	217-523-0878		572
Springfield-Branson National Airport 2300 N Airport Blvd......................Springfield MO 65802 *Web:* www.flyspringfield.com	417-868-0500		27
Spring-Ford Area School District 857 S Lewis Rd...........................Royersford PA 19468 *Web:* www.spring-ford.net	610-705-6000	705-6245	685
Spring-Green Lawn Care Corp 11909 Spaulding School Dr..................Plainfield IL 60585 *TF:* 800-435-4051 ■ *Web:* www.spring-green.com	815-436-8777	436-9056	577
Springhill Medical Ctr 3719 Dauphin St..........Mobile AL 36608 *Web:* www.springhillmedicalcenter.com	251-344-9630		374-3
Springmoor Life Care Retirement Community 1500 Sawmill Rd...........................Raleigh NC 27615 *Web:* www.springmoor.org	919-848-7000		672

Phone | Fax | Class

Springs Baptist Academy
3500 N Nevada Ave. Colorado Springs CO 80907 719-593-7887 166

Springs Fabrication Inc
850 Aeroplaza Dr Colorado Springs CO 80916 719-596-8830 567
Web: www.springsfab.com

Springs Memorial Hospital
800 W Meeting St. Lancaster SC 29720 803-286-1214 374-3
Web: www.springsmemorial.com

Springs Window Fashions
2669 Industrial Dr. Grayling MI 49738 989-348-2871 683
Web: www.swfcontract.com

Springs Window Fashions LP
7549 Graber Rd Middleton WI 53562 608-836-1011 361
TF: 877-792-0002 ■ *Web:* www.springswindowfashions.com

Springsted Inc
380 Jackson St Ste 300 Saint Paul MN 55101 651-223-3000 401
Web: www.springsted.com

Springtown Chamber of Commerce
112 S Main St. Springtown TX 76082 817-220-7828 139
Web: www.springtowntexas.com

Springvale Terrace
8505 Springvale Rd Silver Spring MD 20910 301-587-0190 401
Web: www.seaburyresources.org

Springville Museum of Art
126 E 400 S Springville UT 84663 801-489-2727 520
TF: 800-833-6667 ■ *Web:* www.springville.org

Sprinkles Cupcakes Inc
9635 S Santa Monica Blvd Beverly Hills CA 90210 310-274-8765 68
Web: www.sprinkles.com

Sprinklr Inc 29 W 35th St 8th Fl New York NY 10001 917-933-7800 180
Web: www.sprinklr.com

Sprint Copy Ctr 175 N Main St Sebastopol CA 95472 707-823-3900 627
Web: sprintcopycenter.com

Sprint Multimedia Inc
15619 Premiere Dr Ste 204 Tampa FL 33624 813-971-0531 592

Sprint Quality Printing Inc
3609 Silverside Rd Wilmington DE 19810 302-478-0720 627
Web: www.sprintqp.com

Sprint-Denver Inc 4999 Kingston St. Denver CO 80239 303-371-0566 627
Web: www.sprintdenver.com

Sprintz Furniture Showroom Inc
6205 Cockrill Bend Cir. Nashville TN 37209 615-234-3200 321
Web: sprintz.com

Spris 731 Lincoln Rd Miami Beach FL 33139 305-673-2020 671
Web: www.spris.cc

Spritzer Kaufman LLP
19 W 44th St Ste 1703 New York NY 10036 212-593-1040 2
Web: spritzerkaufman.com

Sprocket Express LLC 23 W Bacon St Plainville MA 02762 508-695-3673 809
TF: 800-649-5647 ■ *Web:* www.sprocketexpress.com

Sproles- Woodard- & Co
777 Main St Ste 3250 Fort Worth TX 76102 817-332-1328 2
TF: 800-332-7932 ■ *Web:* www.sproles.com

Sprott Global Resource Investments Ltd
1910 Palomar Point Way Ste 200 Carlsbad CA 92008 800-477-7053 691
TF: 800-477-7853 ■ *Web:* www.sprottglobal.com

Sprott Inc
200 Bay St Ste 2600 Royal Bank Plz South Twr Toronto ON M5J2J1 416-943-8099 528
Web: www.sprottinc.com

Sproule Associates Ltd
900 N Tower Sun Life Plaza 140 Fourth Ave SW
Calgary AB T2P3N3 403-294-5500 261
TF: 877-777-6135 ■ *Web:* www.sproule.com

Sprout Group 11 Madison Ave 13th Fl New York NY 10010 212-538-3600 792
Web: www.sproutgroup.com

Sprout Pharmaceuticals Inc
4208 Six Forks Rd Raleigh NC 27609 919-882-0850 238
TF: 844-746-5745 ■ *Web:* www.addyi.com

SPROUT Wellness Solutions Inc
366 Adelaide St W Ste 301 Toronto ON M5V1R9 866-535-5027 224
TF: 866-535-5027 ■ *Web:* www.sproutatwork.com

SproutLoud Media Networks LLC
15431 SW 14th St Sunrise FL 33326 954-476-6211 5
TF: 800-473-2318 ■ *Web:* www.sproutloud.com

Sproxil Inc 618 Cambridge St Cambridge MA 02141 209-877-7694 809
Web: www.sproxil.com

Spruce 2115 13th St Boulder CO 80302 303-442-4880 671

Spruce 9 Cornell Rd Latham New York NY 12110 800-777-8231 174
TF: 800-777-8231 ■ *Web:* www.sprucecomputer.com

Spruce Point Inn
88 Grandview Ave PO Box 237 Boothbay Harbor ME 04538 207-633-4152 669
Web: www.sprucepointinn.com

Spruce Run Recreation Area
68 Van Syckel's Rd Clinton NJ 08809 908-638-8572 565
Web: www.njparksandforests.org

Spruceland Millworks Inc
53016 Hwy 60 Ste 803 Acheson AB T7X5A7 780-962-6333 499
TF: 800-873-7883 ■ *Web:* www.spruceland.ca

SPS (Southern Pan Services Co)
2385 Lithonia Industrial Blvd Lithonia GA 30058 678-301-2400 780
Web: www.southernpan.com

SPS (Systems Products & Solutions Inc)
307 Wynn Dr Huntsville AL 35805 256-319-2135 177
Web: www.services-sps.com

SPS Corp 3502 Independence Dr Fort Wayne IN 46808 260-482-3702 186
Web: www.spscorporation.com

SPS Cos Inc 6363 Minnesota 7 Minneapolis MN 55416 952-929-1377 929-1862 612
Web: www.spscompanies.com

SPS Technologies Inc
301 Highland Ave Jenkintown PA 19046 215-572-3000 572-3790 278
Web: www.spstech.com

SPSmedical Supply Corp
6789 W Henrietta Rd. Rush NY 14543 585-359-0130 415
Web: www.spsmedical.com

Spud Software Inc
9468 S Saginaw Rd Grand Blanc MI 48439 810-695-0001 177
Web: www.spudsoftware.com

Spudder, The 6536 E 50th St. Tulsa OK 74145 918-665-1416 671
TF: 800-929-9464 ■ *Web:* www.thespudder.com

Spudnik Equipment Co 584 W 100 N Rd Blackfoot ID 83221 208-785-0480 785-1497 273
Web: www.spudnik.com

Spuntini 116 Ave Rd Toronto ON M5R2H4 416-962-1110 934-0179 671
Web: www.spuntini.ca

Spurlock Museum
University of Illinois at Urbana
600 S Gregory St Urbana IL 61801 217-333-2360 244-9419 520
Web: www.spurlock.illinois.edu

SPWLA (Society of Petrophysicists & Well Log Analysts)
8866 Gulf Fwy Ste 320 Houston TX 77017 713-947-8727 947-7181 48-12
Web: www.spwla.org

SPX Cooling Technologies
7401 W 129th St. Overland Park KS 66213 913-664-7400 664-7439 91
TF: 800-462-7539 ■ *Web:* www.spxcooling.com

SPX Corp 300 Fenn Rd Newington CT 06111 860-666-2471 22
Web: pcxaero.com

SPX Corp
13515 Ballantyne Corporate Pl Charlotte NC 28277 704-752-4400 185
NYSE: SPW ■ *TF:* 877-247-3797 ■ *Web:* www.spx.com

SPX Corp OTC Div 655 Eisenhower Dr. Owatonna MN 55060 507-455-7000 757
TF: 800-533-6127 ■ *Web:* www.otctools.com

Spx Flow Technology USA Inc
4647 SW 40th Ave Ocala FL 34474 352-237-1220 172

Spx Process Equipment
611 Sugar Creek Rd Delavan WI 53115 800-252-5200 567
TF: 800-252-5200 ■ *Web:* www.spx.com/en/waukesha-cherry-burrell

SPY Inc 2070 Las Palmas Dr. Carlsbad CA 92011 760-804-8420 543
Web: www.spyoptic.com

Spycher Bros Farms 14827 W HaRding Rd Turlock CA 95380 209-668-2471 668-4988 10-10
TF: 800-247-6755 ■ *Web:* www.spycherbros.com

Spyder Ii 65 Pier Ave Hermosa Beach CA 90254 310-374-2494 711
TF: 800-622-4655 ■ *Web:* www.spydersurf.com

Spyder Trap Inc 1625 hennepin ave Minneapolis MN 55403 612-871-2270 5
TF: 800-942-3520 ■ *Web:* www.spydertrap.com

Spyglass Biosecurity Inc
3180 Imjin Rd Ste 157 Marina CA 93933 831-883-9838 463

Spyglass Creative Inc
1639 Hennepin Ave 100 Minneapolis MN 55403 612-486-5959 344
Web: www.spyglasscreative.com

Spyglass Entertainment
245 N Beverly Dr Beverly Hills CA 90210 310-443-5800 443-5912 514
Web: www.spyglassent.com

Spyglass Resources Corp
Livingston Place 250 2 St SW Tower 1700 Calgary AB T2P0C1 403-303-8500 536
Web: www.spyglassresources.com

Spyre Solutions Inc
91 Rylander Blvd Ste 7-250 Toronto ON M1B5M5 416-444-4924 393
Web: www.spyresolutions.com

SQA LABS Inc 16880 N 73rd Ave Peoria AZ 85382 602 439 5500 180
TF: 855-477-2522 ■ *Web:* www.sqalabs.com

SQAD Inc 303 S Broadway Ste 130 Tarrytown NY 10591 914-524-7600 225
Web: www.sqad.com

SQI Diagnostics Inc 36 Meteor Dr Toronto ON M9W1A4 416-674-9500 250
Web: www.sqidiagnostics.com

Sql Data Solutions Inc
43 Herkomer St. New Hyde Park NY 11040 516-358-1998 177
TF: 800-767-1553 ■ *Web:* www.sqldatasolutionsinc.com

SQL Star International Inc
8820 Kenamar Dr Ste 506 San Diego CA 92121 650-204-9490 196
Web: www.sqlstar.com

SQN Banking Systems 65 Indel Ave Rancocas NJ 08073 609-261-5500 265-9517 178-10
Web: www.sqnsigs.com

Sqrrl Data Inc 275 Third St Cambridge MA 02142 617-902-0784 387
Web: sqrrl.com

Squantz Pond State Park
178 Shortwoods Rd New Fairfield CT 06812 203-312-5023 565
Web: www.ct.gov

Squar Milner Peterson Miranda & Williamson LLP
4100 Newport Pl Dr Ste 600 Newport Beach CA 92660 949-222-2999 222-2989 2
Web: www.squarmilner.com

Square 1 Art LLC
5470 Oakbrook Pkwy Ste E Norcross GA 30093 678-906-2291 627
TF: 888-332-3294 ■ *Web:* www.square1art.com

Square 2 Marketing Inc
555 N Ln Ste 5050 Conshohocken PA 18976 215-491-0100 5
Web: www.square2marketing.com

Square Books 160 Courthouse Sq. Oxford MS 38655 662-236-2262 95
TF: 800-648-4001 ■ *Web:* www.squarebooks.com

Square One Mall 1201 Broadway Saugus MA 01906 781-233-8787 231-9787 460
TF: 877-746-6642 ■ *Web:* simon.com/mall?id=340

Square Root Inc 508 Oakland Ave. Austin TX 78703 512-693-9232 177
Web: www.square-root.com

SquaredOut Inc
2900 Bristol St Ste J203 Costa Mesa CA 92626 714-668-0262 387
Web: www.squaredout.com

SquareFoot 1776 Yorktown Dr Ste 610 Houston TX 77056 281-701-9697 387
Web: www.thesquarefoot.com

Square-H Brands Inc
2731 S Soto St Los Angeles CA 90058 323-267-4600 473
Web: www.squarehbrands.com

Squarei Technologies Inc
1315 Oakridge Dr Ste 100 Fort Collins CO 80525 970-377-0077 177
Web: www.squarei.com

Squatter's Pub Brewery
147 West Broadway Salt Lake City UT 84101 801-363-2739 671
TF: 800-255-3530 ■ *Web:* www.squatters.com

Squaw Valley Ski Corp
1960 Squaw Valley Rd Olympic Valley CA 96146 800-403-0206 378
TF: 800-403-0206 ■ *Web:* www.squaw.com

Squaw Valley USA PO Box 2007 Olympic Valley CA 96146 800-403-0206 581-7106* 669
**Fax Area Code:* 530 ■ *TF:* 800-403-0206 ■ *Web:* squawalpine.com

Squire & Company PC 1329 S 800 E Orem UT 84097 801-225-6900 2
Web: www.squire.com

Squire Corrugated Container Corp
111 Somogyi Ct South Plainfield NJ 07080 908-561-8550 100
Web: www.squirebox.com

Squire Patton Boggs 2550 M St NW Washington DC 20037 202-457-6000 457-6315 428
Web: www.squirepattonboggs.com/en

Phone | Fax | Class

Squire Patton Boggs
127 Public Sq 4900 Key Tower................Cleveland OH 44114 216-479-8500 479-8780 428
TF: 800-973-1177 ■ Web: www.squirepattonboggs.com

Squire Tech Solutions LLC
6304 Fallwater Trl Ste 100 .... The Colony TX 75056 214-306-6704 387
Web: www.squiretechsolutions.com

Squires Group Inc, The
608 Melvin Ave Ste 101 .... Annapolis MD 21401 410-224-7779 180
Web: www.squiresgroup.com

SqWire's 1415 S 18th St.................... Saint Louis MO 63104 314-865-3522 671
Web: www.sqwires.com

S&R Truck Tire Center Inc
1402 Truckers Blvd..................... Jeffersonville IN 47130 812-282-4799 54
TF: 800-488-2670 ■ Web: www.srtrucktire.com

SR2020 Inc 3 Pointe Dr Ste 212........................Brea CA 92821 714-482-1922 536

SRA (Society for Risk Analysis)
1313 Dolley Madison Blvd Ste 402 .... McLean VA 22101 703-790-1745 790-2672 49-19
Web: www.sra.org

SRA OSS Inc
5201 Great America Pkwy Ste 419 .... Santa Clara CA 95129 408-855-8200 855-8206 225
Web: www.sraoss.com

SRAM Corp 1333 N Kingsbury St 4th Fl...........Chicago IL 60622 312-664-8800 664-8826 82
TF: 800-346-2928 ■ Web: www.sram.com

SRC (Synchrotron Radiation Ctr)
3731 Schneider Dr....................... Stoughton WI 53589 608-877-2000 877-2001 668
Web: www.src.wisc.edu

SRC (Spoon River College)
23235 N County Hwy 22........................Canton IL 61520 309-647-4645 649-6393* 162
*Fax: Admissions ■ TF: 800-334-7337 ■ Web: www.src.edu

SRC (Silver Research Consortium)
2525 Meridian Pkwy Ste 100 .... Durham NC 27713 919-361-4647 361-1957 49-19
TF: 800-247-6265 ■ Web: www.ilzro.org

SRC (Syracuse Research Corp)
7502 Round Pond Rd.................. North Syracuse NY 13212 315-452-8000 668
TF: 800-724-0451 ■ Web: www.srcinc.com

SRC Computers LLC
4240 N Nevada Ave.................. Colorado Springs CO 80907 719-262-0213 262-0223 173-2

SRC Holdings Corp 531 S Union Ave ....Springfield MO 65802 417-862-2337 262
TF: 800-327-2253 ■ Web: www.srcholdings.com

SRC Logistics Inc 2065 E Pythian.............Springfield MO 65802 417-864-4946 803-1
Web: www.srclogisticsinc.com

Src Medical Inc 263 Winter St ....Hanover MA 02339 781-826-9100 596
Web: www.srcmedical.com

SRCD (Society for Research in Child Development)
2950 S State St Ste 401 .... Ann Arbor MI 48104 734-926-0600 926-0601 49-5
Web: www.srcd.org

SRDS 1700 Higgins Rd .... Des Plaines IL 60018 800-851-7737 637-2
TF: 800-851-7737 ■ Web: login.srds.com

SREC (Spoon River Electric Co-op Inc)
930 S Fifth Ave PO Box 340 ....Canton IL 61520 309-647-2700 245
TF: 877-404-2572 ■ Web: www.srecoop.org

Sree Hotels LLC
Palladium at Piper Glen 5113 Piper Sta Dr
Ste 300................................... Charlotte NC 28277 704-364-6008 378
TF: 800-345-8082 ■ Web: www.sree.com

SRF Consulting Group Inc
1 Carlson Pkwy N Ste 150 ....Minneapolis MN 55447 763-475-0010 261
Web: www.srfconsulting.com

SRG (Station Resource Group)
PO Box 1858 ....Clarksburg MD 20912 301-270-2617 270-2618 632
Web: www.srg.org

SRG (Sterling-Rice Group, The)
1801 13th St Ste 400 .... Boulder CO 80302 303-381-6400 444-6637 4
Web: www.srg.com

Sri Instruments Inc 20720 Earl St ....Torrance CA 90503 702-361-2210 407
Web: www.srigc.com

SRI International
333 Ravenswood Ave .... Menlo Park CA 94025 650-859-2000 326-5512 668
Web: www.sri.com

Sri Lanka
Consulate General
3250 Wilshire Blvd Ste 1405.............Los Angeles CA 90010 213-387-0210 257
Web: www.srilankaconsulatela.com
Embassy 2148 Wyoming Ave NW........... Washington DC 20008 202-483-4025 232-7181 257
TF: 800-862-7822 ■ Web: www.slembassyusa.org

Sri Quality Sys
300 Northpointe Cir Ste 304............... Seven Fields PA 16046 724-934-9000 196
TF: 800-549-6709 ■ Web: www.sriregistrar.com

SriLankan Airlines
379 Thornall St 6th Fl......................... Edison NJ 08837 732-205-0017 205-0299 25
TF: 877-915-2652 ■ Web: www.srilankanusa.com

Sripraphai 64-13 39th Ave....................Woodside NY 11377 718-899-9599 671
Web: sripraphairestaurant.com

SRK Consulting Inc
1066 W Hastings St Ste 3000................ Vancouver BC V6E3X2 303-985-1333 985-9947 261
Web: www.na.srk.com

SRMC (Saint Rita's Medical Ctr)
730 W Market St................................ Lima OH 45801 419-227-3361 374-3

SRMC (Sparks Regional Medical Ctr)
1001 Towson Ave .... Fort Smith AR 72901 479-441-4000 441-5397 374-3
TF: 800-285-1131 ■ Web: www.sparkshealth.com

SRMC (Spartanburg Regional Medical Ctr)
101 E Wood St..........................Spartanburg SC 29303 864-560-6000 374-3
TF: 800-318-2596 ■ Web: spartanburgregional.com

SRMC (Shasta Regional Medical Ctr)
1100 Butte St ....Redding CA 96001 530-244-5400 374-3
Web: www.shastaregional.com

SRMC (Sonora Regional Medical Ctr)
1000 Greenly Rd..............................Sonora CA 95370 209-536-5000 374-3
TF Compliance: 877-336-3566 ■ Web: www.adventisthealth.org

SRMH (Santa Rosa Memorial Hospital)
1165 Montgomery Dr.......................Santa Rosa CA 95405 707-546-3210 374-3
TF: 800-627-8106 ■ Web: stjosephhealth.org/about-us

SRN Broadcasting 307 E Washington.............Lake Bluff IL 60044 847-735-1995 644

Sroka Industries Inc
21265 Westwood Dr.....................Strongsville OH 44149 440-572-1525 454
Web: www.srokausa.com

SRP (Salt River Project) 1521 N Project Dr........ Tempe AZ 85281 602-236-5900 236-2442 787
TF: 800-258-4777 ■ Web: www.srpnet.com

SRP Environmental LLC 348 Aero Dr..........Shreveport LA 71107 318-222-2364 85
Web: www.srpenvironmental.com

SRRC (Southern Regional Research Ctr)
1100 Robert E Lee Blvd .... New Orleans LA 70124 706-546-3527 286-4419* 668
*Fax Area Code: 504 ■ Web: www.ars.usda.gov

SRRMC (Seven Rivers Regional Medical Ctr)
6201 N Suncoast Blvd .... Crystal River FL 34428 352-795-6560 795-8369 374-3
TF: 800-339-1811 ■ Web: www.sevenriversregional.com

SRS (Santa Rosa Symphony)
50 Santa Rosa Ave Ste 410..................Santa Rosa CA 95404 707-546-8742 573-3
Web: srsymphony.org

SRS International Corp
Suite 208 7700 Leesburg Pk............... Falls Church VA 22043 703-821-0157 238

SRS Labs Inc 2909 Daimler St............... Santa Ana CA 92705 949-442-1070 696
NASDAQ: SRSL ■ TF General: 800-322-2885 ■ Web: dts.com

SRS Medical Systems Inc
76 Treble Cove Rd Bldg 3................ North Billerica MA 01862 978-663-2800 743
Web: www.srsmedical.com

SRSSA (Smallwood Reynolds Stewart Stewart & Assoc Inc)
1 Piedmont Ctr 3565 Piedmont Rd Ste 303 .... Atlanta GA 30305 404-233-5453 261
Web: www.srssa.com

SRT (Seattle Repertory Theatre)
155 Mercer St PO Box 900923............... Seattle WA 98109 206-443-2210 443-2379 573-4
TF: 877-900-9285 ■ Web: www.seattlerep.org

SS & C Technologies Inc
80 Lamberton Rd ....Windsor CT 06095 860-298-4500 298-4900 178-11
TF: 800-234-0556 ■ Web: www.ssctech.com

SS Cyril & Methodius Seminary
3535 Indian Trl......................... Orchard Lake MI 48324 248-683-0310 738-6735 167-3
Web: sscms.edu

SS Nesbitt & Co Inc
3500 Blue Lake Dr ....Birmingham AL 35243 205-262-2700 391-4
TF: 800-422-3223 ■ Web: www.ssnesbitt.com

SS Steele & Company Inc
4951 Government Blvd........................Mobile AL 36693 251-661-9600 187
Web: www.steelehomes.cc

SS White Technologies Inc
151 Old New Brunswick Rd ....Piscataway NJ 08854 732-752-8300 752-8315 620
Web: www.sswt.com

SS8 Networks Inc 750 Tasman Dr.............. Milpitas CA 95035 408-944-0250 681
Web: www.ss8.com

SSA (Self Storage Assn)
1900 N Beauregard St Ste 450 .... Alexandria VA 22311 703-575-8000 575-8901 49-21
TF: 888-735-3784 ■ Web: www.selfstorage.org

SSA (Social Security Administration)
6401 Security Blvd.........................Baltimore MD 21235 410-965-8904 340-20
TF: 800-772-1213 ■ Web: www.ssa.gov

SSA (Specialty Sleep Assn)
46639 Jones Ranch Rd.........................Friant CA 93626 559-868-4187 49-4
Web: www.sleepinformation.org

SSA Consultants Inc
9331 Bluebonnet Blvd .... Baton Rouge LA 70810 225-769-2676 463
TF: 800-634-2758 ■ Web: www.consultssa.com

SSA Marine 1131 SW Klickitat Way .... Seattle WA 98134 206-623-0304 623-0179 465
TF: 800-422-3505 ■ Web: www.ssamarine.com

SSAI (Support Systems Assoc Inc)
709 S Harbor City Blvd Ste 350.............Melbourne FL 32901 321-724-5566 261
Web: www.ssai.org

SSAT (Society for Surgery of the Alimentary Tract)
900 Cummings Ctr Ste 221-U ....Beverly MA 01915 978-927-8330 524-8890 49-8
TF: 866-849-5866 ■ Web: www.ssat.com

Ssci 3065 Kent Ave .... West Lafayette IN 47906 765-463-0112 463-4722 194
TF: 800-375-2179 ■ Web: www.ssci-inc.com

SSCS (IEEE Solid State Circuits Society)
445 Hoes Ln............................Piscataway NJ 08854 732-981-3400 49-19
Web: sscs.ieee.org

Ssf Conference Catering LLC
255 S Airport Blvd .... South San Francisco CA 94080 650-877-8787 624
Web: ssfconf.com

Ssg Ltd 801 E Campbell Rd Ste 350 .... Richardson TX 75081 214-333-2000 196
Web: www.ssglimited.com

SSgA Funds 1 Lincoln St ....Boston MA 02111 617-786-3000 528
TF: 800-997-7327 ■ Web: www.ssgafunds.com

SSH (Somerset Hills Hotel)
200 Liberty Corner Rd ....Warren NJ 07059 908-647-6700 647-8053 379
TF: 800-688-0700 ■ Web: www.thesomersethillshotel.com

SSH (South Shore Hospital)
8012 S Crandon Ave...........................Chicago IL 60617 773-356-5000 374-3
Web: www.southshorehospital.com

SSI Investment Management Inc
9440 Santa Monica Blvd 8th Fl............. Beverly Hills CA 90210 310-595-2000 690
Web: www.ssi-invest.com

SSI Micro Ltd 356B Old Airport Rd .... Yellowknife NT X1A3T4 867-669-7500 224
Web: www.ssimicro.com

SSI Technologies Inc PO Box 5011 ....Janesville WI 53547 608-757-2000 203
Web: www.ssitechnologies.com

SSIA (Shoe Service Institute of America)
18 School St....................... North Brookfield MA 01535 508-867-7731 569-8333* 49-4
*Fax Area Code: 410 ■ TF: 800-354-6378 ■ Web: www.ssia.info

Ssinfotek Inc 9560 Research Dr .... Irvine CA 92618 949-732-3100 180
Web: www.ssinfotek.com

SSIT (IEEE Society on Social Implications of Technology)
IEEE Operations Ctr 445 and 501 Hoes Ln......Piscataway NJ 08854 732-981-0060 562-6380 49-19
TF: 800-678-4333 ■ Web: standards.ieee.org

SSJCPL (Stockton-San Joaquin County Public Library)
605 N El Dorado St.......................... Stockton CA 95202 209-937-8416 434-3
TF: 866-805-7323 ■ Web: www.ssjcpl.org

SSM Cardinal Glennon Children's Hospital
1465 S Grand Blvd .... Saint Louis MO 63104 314-577-5600 374-1
Web: www.cardinalglennon.com

SSM Health 620 E Monroe St....................Mexico MO 65265 573-582-5000 374-3
TF: 844-776-9355 ■
Web: www.ssmhealthmidmo.com/locations/stmarysaudrain

SSM Healthÿ
1000 N Lee PO Box 205................Oklahoma City OK 73102 405-272-7279 272-6477 353
TF: 866-203-5846 ■ Web: www.ssmhealthillinois.com

SSM Hospice 2 Harbor Bend Ct.......... Lake Saint Louis MO 63367 636-695-2000 371
TF: 800-835-1212 ■ Web: ssmhealth.com/system

Ssm Industries Inc 3401 Grand Ave........... Pittsburgh PA 15225 412-777-5100 595

	Phone	Fax	Class
SSM Saint Joseph Health Ctr 300 First Capitol Dr .... Saint Charles MO 63301 *TF:* 800-975-6285 ■ *Web:* www.ssmhealth.com	636-949-7077		374-3
SSMB Pacific Holding Company Inc 1755 Adams Ave.................. San Leandro CA 94577 *TF:* 866-572-2525 ■ *Web:* www.norcalkw.com	510-836-6100	836-2551	360-2
SSMC (Sutter Solano Medical Ctr) 300 Hospital Dr .... Vallejo CA 94589 *TF:* 800-866-7724 ■ *Web:* www.suttersolano.org	707-554-4444	648-3227	374-3
SSN (Straight Spouse Network) PO Box 4985 .... Chicago IL 60680 *Web:* www.straightspouse.org	773-413-8213		48-21
SSOE 1001 Madison Ave .... Toledo OH 43604 *Web:* www.ssoe.com	419-255-3830	255-6101	261
SSP (Society for Scholarly Publishing) 10200 W 44th Ave Ste 304.................. Wheat Ridge CO 80033 *Web:* www.sspnet.org	303-422-3914		49-16
SSPC (Society for Protective Coatings) 40 24th St 6th Fl.................. Pittsburgh PA 15222 *TF:* 877-281-7772 ■ *Web:* www.sspc.org	412-281-2331	281-9995	49-13
SSPR Public Relations Agency 150 N Upper Wacker Dr Ste 2010.................. Chicago IL 60606 *TF:* 800-287-2279 ■ *Web:* www.sspr.com	800-287-2279		636
SSR Engineering 950 Fee Ana Ste A106 .... Placentia CA 92870 *Web:* www.ssreng.com	714-229-9020		529
SSRC (Social Science Research Council) 810 Seventh Ave.................. New York NY 10019 *Web:* www.ssrc.org	212-377-2700	377-2727	634
SSRL (Stanford Synchrotron Radiation Lightsource) 2575 Sand Hill Rd MS 69.................. Menlo Park CA 94025 *Web:* www-ssrl.slac.stanford.edu	650-926-2079	926-3600	668
SSS Co 71 University Ave .... Atlanta GA 30315 *TF:* 800-237-3843 ■ *Web:* www.ssspharmaceuticals.com	404-521-0857		582
SSSA (Soil Science Society of America) 677 S Segoe Rd .... Madison WI 53711 *TF:* 800-272-7737 ■ *Web:* www.soils.org	608-273-8080	273-2021	48-2
SST Corp 635 Brighton Rd .... Clifton NJ 07012 *TF:* 800-222-0921 ■ *Web:* www.sst-corp.com	973-473-4300	473-4326	479
SST Energy Corp 8901 W Yellowstone Hwy.................. Casper WY 82604 *Web:* www.sstenergy.com	307-235-3529	473-1650	540
SST Group Inc 309 Laurelwood Rd Ste 20.................. Santa Clara CA 95054 *TF:* 800-944-6281 ■ *Web:* www.sstgroup-inc.com	408-350-3450		475
SST Planners 1615 M St NW Ste 700 .... Washington DC 22209 *Web:* www.sstplanners.com	202-909-4942		463
SSUB (Advocate South Suburban Hospital) 17800 S Kedzie Ave .... Hazel Crest IL 60429 *Web:* www.advocatehealth.com/ssub	708-799-8000		374-3
SSW (Seminary of the southwest) 501 E 32nd PO Box 2247.................. Austin TX 78705 *TF:* 800-252-5400 ■ *Web:* www.ssw.edu	512-472-4133	472-3098	167-3
SSW Mechanical Inc Air Cond 670 S Oleander Rd .... Palm Springs CA 92264 *Web:* www.sswmechanical.com	760-325-6007		610
St Agnes Hospital 430 E Div St .... Fond du Lac WI 54935 *TF:* 800-922-3400 ■ *Web:* www.agnesian.com	920-929-2300		374-3
St Andrews Blockhouse National Historic Site of Canada 30 Victoria St .... Gatineau QC J8X0B3 **Fax Area Code:* 506 ■ *TF:* 888-773-8888 ■ *Web:* www.pc.gc.ca/eng/lhn-nhs/nb/standrews/index.aspx	819-420-9486	636-4574*	563
S&T Bancorp Inc 800 Philadelphia St.................. Indiana PA 15701 *NASDAQ: STBA* ■ **Fax:* Cust Svc ■ *TF:* 800-325-2265 ■ *Web:* www.stbank.com	724-349-1800	465-6874*	360-2
St Barnabas Episcopal Church in The City of Lafayette 400 Camellia Blvd .... Lafayette LA 70503 *Web:* saintbarnabas.us	337-984-3848		48-20
St Croix Stone Inc 5935 410th St.................. North Branch MN 55056 *Web:* www.stcroixstone.com	651-277-8770		183
S-T Industries Inc 301 Armstrong Blvd N PO Box 517 .... Saint James MN 56081 *TF:* 800-326-2039 ■ *Web:* www.stindustries.com	507-375-3211	375-4503	493
St John Diakon Hospice 1201 N Church St.................. Hazleton PA 18202 *TF:* 800-344-3667 ■ *Web:* diakon.org	570-450-1500		371
St Joseph Hospital West 100 Medical Plaza .... Lake St. Louis MO 63367 *Web:* www.stjosephhospital.com	636-625-5200		166
St Louis Airport Marriott 10700 Pear Tree Ln.................. St. Louis MO 63134 *Web:* www.marriott.com/hotels/travel/stlap-st-louis-airport-marriott	314-423-9700		378
St Louis Outlet Mall Hwy 370 Exit 11 .... Hazelwood MO 63042 *Web:* www.simon.com	317-636-1600		460
St Luke's Regional Medical Center Ltd 190 E Bannock St.................. Boise ID 83712	208-381-2222		186
St Mary's of Michigan (STMH) 800 S Washington Ave .... Saginaw MI 48601 *TF:* 877-738-6672 ■ *Web:* www.stmarysofmichigan.org	989-907-8115		374-3
St Petersburg College (SPC) PO Box 13489 .... Saint Petersburg FL 33733 *Web:* www.spcollege.edu	727-341-4772		598
St Regis 88 W Paces Ferry Rd .... Atlanta GA 30305 *TF:* 877-787-3447 ■ *Web:* www.stregismb.com	404-563-7900	563-7905	669
St Vincent's College 2800 Main St .... Bridgeport CT 06606 *TF:* 800-873-1013 ■ *Web:* www.stvincentscollege.edu	800-873-1013		166
St. Agnes Home 10341 Manchester Rd.................. Kirkwood MO 63122 *Web:* carmelitedcj.org	314-965-7616		371
St. Albert Public Library 5 St Anne St .... Saint Albert AB T8N3Z9 *Web:* www.sapl.ca	780-459-1530		435
St. Alexius Medical Ctr 900 E Broadway Ave.................. Bismarck ND 58501 *TF:* 877-530-5550 ■ *Web:* www.st.alexius.org	701-530-7755	530-8984	374-3
St. Anastasia School 8631 Stanmoor Dr .... Los Angeles CA 90045 *Web:* www.st-anastasia.org	310-645-8816		685
St. Ann's Catholic School 365 N Cool Spring St.................. Fayetteville NC 28301	910-483-3902		685
St. Ann's Warehouse 45 Water St .... Brooklyn NY 11201 *Web:* www.stannswarehouse.org	718-834-8794		303
St. Anne's Credit Union of Fall River 286 Oliver St.................. Fall River MA 02724 *Web:* www.stannes.com	508-324-7300	673-1542	219
St. Anthony Riverwalk Wyndham Hotel, The 300 E Travis St .... San Antonio TX 78205 *Web:* www.thestanthonyhotel.com	210-227-4392		378
St. Assoc Inc 1 Teal Rd .... Wakefield MA 01880 *Web:* www.stassoc.com	781-246-4700		781
St. Athanasius Rectory 2050 E Walnut Ln.................. Philadelphia PA 19138 *Web:* stathanasiuschurch.us	215-548-2700		48-20
St. Augustine Health Ministries 7801 Detroit Ave.................. Cleveland OH 44102 *Web:* staugministries.org	216-634-7400		450
St. Basil Academy High School 711 Fox Chase Rd .... Jenkintown PA 19046 *Web:* stbasilacademy.org	215-885-3771		685
St. Benedict's Monastery 104 Chapel Ln .... St Joseph MN 56374 *Web:* sbm.osb.org	320-363-7116		48-20
St. Bernard Hospital & Health Care Ctr 326 W 64th St.................. Chicago IL 60621 *Web:* www.stbernardhospital.com	773-962-3900		374-3
St. Bernard Sports 5570 W Lovers Ln Ste 388.................. Dallas TX 75209 *Web:* www.saintbernard.com	214-357-9700		711
St. Brendans Church 333 E 206th St.................. Bronx NY 10467 *Web:* saintbrendanchurch.org	718-547-6655		48-20
St. Cecilia Catholic School 1310 Madison Ave N .... Bainbridge Island WA 98110 *Web:* www.saintceciliaschool.org	206-842-2017		685
St. Charles Capital LLC 1400 Sixteenth St Ste 300 .... Denver CO 80202	303-339-9099		401
St. Charles Inc 151 S 84th St .... Milwaukee WI 53214 *TF:* 800-984-3775 ■ *Web:* www.stcharlesinc.org	414-476-3710		685
St. Charles Nissan Inc 5625 Veterans Memorial Pkwy .... Saint Peters MO 63376 *Web:* stcharlesauto.com	636-441-4481		57
St. Clair College of Applied Arts & Technology, The 2000 Talbot Rd W.................. Windsor ON N9A6S4 *Web:* www.stclaircollege.ca	519-966-1656		162
St. Clair County Regional Educational Service Agency 499 Range Rd.................. Marysville MI 48040 *TF:* 800-294-9229 ■ *Web:* www.sccresa.org	810-364-8990		685
St. Clair Foods Inc 3100 Bellbrook Dr.................. Memphis TN 38116 *Web:* www.stclair.com	901-396-8680		297-8
St. Croix Solutions Inc 6033 Culligan Way.................. Minnetonka MN 55345 *TF:* 800-379-7873 ■ *Web:* www.stcroixsolutions.com	952-653-2900		396
St. Croix Valley Foundation 516 Second St Ste 214.................. Hudson WI 54016 *TF:* 800-990-0125 ■ *Web:* www.scvfoundation.org	715-386-9490		305
St. David's Episcopal Church & School 1300 Wiltshire Ave.................. San Antonio TX 78209 *Web:* saintdavids.net	210-824-2481		48-20
St. David's Round Rock Medical Ctr 2400 Round Rock Ave.................. Round Rock TX 78681 *Web:* www.stdavids.com	512-341-1000		374-3
St. Edwards High School 13500 Detroit Ave.................. Lakewood OH 44107 *Web:* www.sehs.net	216-221-3776		685
St. Elizabeth's Medical Ctr 736 Cambridge St.................. Brighton MA 02135 *TF:* 800-488-5959 ■ *Web:* steward.org	617-789-3000		353
St. Francis De Sales High School 2323 W Bancroft St.................. Toledo OH 43607 *TF:* 800-487-9460 ■ *Web:* www.sfstoledo.org	419-531-1618		685
St. Francis Healthcare System of Hawaii 2226 Liliha St Ste 227 .... Honolulu HI 96817 *Web:* www.stfrancishawaii.org	808-547-8030		769
St. Francis Healthcare Systems 2226 Liliha St PO Box 29700.................. Honolulu HI 96820 *Web:* www.stfrancishawaii.org	808-547-6883		371
St. Francis High School 1885 Miramonte Ave.................. Mountain View CA 94040 *Web:* www.sfhs.com	650-968-1213		685
St. Francis Medical Ctr 3421 Medical Pk Dr .... Monroe LA 71203 *Web:* stfran.com/pages/home.aspx	318-966-4000		374-3
St. Francis Xavier High School 15 School St.................. Sumter SC 29150 *Web:* www.stxhs.com	803-773-0210		685
St. George Area Chamber of Commerce 97 E St George Blvd .... Saint George UT 84770 *Web:* www.stgeorgechamber.com	435-628-1658	673-1587	139
St. George Greek Orthodox Church 1200 Klockner Rd.................. Trenton NJ 08619 *Web:* stgeorgetrenton.nj.goarch.org	609-586-4448		48-20
St. George Steel Fabrication Inc 1301 East 700 North.................. Saint George UT 84770 *Web:* www.stgeorgesteel.com	435-673-4856	628-4139	454
St. Giles Hotels LLC 120-130 E 39th St .... New York NY 10016 *Web:* www.stgiles.com	212-685-1100		377
St. Gregory Group 9435 Waterstone Blvd Ste 180 .... Cincinnati OH 45249 *Web:* stgregory.com	513-769-8440		7
St. Henry District High School 3755 Scheben Dr .... Erlanger KY 41018 *Web:* shdhs.org	859-525-0255		685
St. Hope Foundation 6800 W Loop S Ste 560 .... Bellaire TX 77401 *Web:* www.offeringhope.org	713-839-7111		305
St. Ignatius College Prep 2001 37th Ave.................. San Francisco CA 94116 *TF:* 888-225-5427 ■ *Web:* www.siprep.org	415-731-7500		685
St. James Academy 3100 Monkton Rd .... Monkton MD 21111 *Web:* www.saintjamesacademy.org	410-771-4816		685

	Phone	Fax	Class
St. James Episcopal School 602 S Carancahua St .... Corpus Christi TX 78401 *Web:* www.sjes.org	361-883-0835		685
St. James Hotel 406 Main St .... Red Wing MN 55066 *TF:* 800-252-1875 ■ *Web:* www.st-james-hotel.com	651-388-2846		379
St. James House of Baytown 5800 W Baker Rd .... Baytown TX 77520 *TF:* 800-252-2412 ■ *Web:* www.stjameshouse.org	281-425-1200		371
St. James Security Services Inc 1604 Ave Ponce De Leon .... San Juan PR 00926	787-754-8448		693
St. Jo Frontier Casino 777 Winners Cir .... St Joseph MO 64505 *Web:* www.stjocasino.com	816-279-5514		133
St. Joe Petroleum Co 2520 S Second St .... Saint Joseph MO 64501 *Web:* www.stjoepetroleum.com	816-279-0770		297-8
St. John Detroit Riverview Ctr 7733 E Jefferson Ave .... Detroit MI 48214 *TF:* 866-501-3627 ■ *Web:* www.stjohnprovidence.org	866-501-3627		374-3
St. John Lutheran Church 1140 W River Rd N .... Elyria OH 44035 *Web:* stjohnlutheran-elyria.org	440-324-4070		48-20
St. John Medical Ctr 1923 S Utica Ave .... Tulsa OK 74104 *TF:* 800-994-6610 ■ *Web:* stjohnhealthsystem.com	918-744-2345		353
St. John Neumann Regional Catholic School 791 Tom Smith Rd SW .... Lilburn GA 30047 *Web:* www.sjnrcs.org	770-381-0557		685
St. John Providence 28000 Dequindre .... Warren MI 48092 *TF:* 866-501-3627 ■ *Web:* www.stjohnprovidence.org	586-573-5000		374-3
St. John Providence Health System 28000 Dequindre .... Warren MI 48092 *TF:* 866-501-3627 ■ *Web:* www.stjohnprovidence.org	866-501-3627		374-3
St. John The Apostle School 7421 Glenview Dr .... Richland Hills TX 76180 *Web:* stjs.org	817-284-2228		685
St. John Vianney High School 540 Line Rd .... Holmdel NJ 07733 *Web:* www.sjvhs.com	732-739-0800		685
St. Johns County Public Library 1960 N Ponce de Leon Blvd .... Saint Augustine FL 32084 *Web:* www.sjcpls.org	904-827-6940	827-6945	434-3
St. Johns Ev Lutheran Church & School 20801 W Forest View Dr .... Lannon WI 53046	262-251-2910		48-20
St. Johns Unified District 450 S 13th St W .... Saint Johns AZ 85936 *Web:* www.sjusd.net	928-337-2255		685
St. Johnson Co 925 Stanford Ave .... Oakland CA 94608 *Web:* www.stjohnson.com	510-652-6000	652-4302	318
St. Joseph & St. Mary's Medical Centers 1000 Carondelet Dr .... Kansas City MO 64114 *Web:* www.carondelethealth.org	816-942-4400		374-3
St. Joseph Communications 50 MacIntosh Blvd .... Concord ON L4K4P3 *Web:* www.stjoseph.com	905-660-3111		627
St. Joseph Health 2700 Dolbeer St .... Eureka CA 95501 *Web:* www.stjosepheureka.org	707-445-8121		374-3
St. Joseph Healthcare 360 Broadway PO Box 403 .... Bangor ME 04402 *Web:* www.stjoeshealing.org	207-262-1000		374-3
St. Joseph Residence 107 E Beckert Rd .... New London WI 54961 *Web:* stjosephresidence.com	920-982-5354		371
St. Joseph Warren Hospital 667 Eastland Ave .... Warren OH 44484 *Web:* mercy.com	330-841-4000		374-3
St. Joseph's Hospital 16th St at Girard Ave .... Philadelphia PA 19130 *Web:* www.nphs.com	215-787-9000		374-3
St. Joseph's Wayne Hospital 224 Hamburg Tpke .... Wayne NJ 07470 *Web:* www.stjosephshealth.org	973-942-6900		374-3
St. Julien Hotel & Spa 900 Walnut St .... Boulder CO 80302 *TF:* 877-303-0900 ■ *Web:* www.stjulien.com	720-406-9696		379
St. Lawrence County Chamber of Commerce 101 Main St .... Canton NY 13617 *TF:* 877-228-7810 ■ *Web:* www.northcountryguide.com	315-386-4000	379-0134	139
St. Lawrence Seaway Management Corp 202 Pitt St .... Cornwall ON K6J3P7 *Web:* www.seaway.ca	613-932-5170		314
St. Lawrence-Lewis BOCES 40 W Main St .... Canton NY 13617 *TF:* 800-877-8339 ■ *Web:* www.sllboces.org	315-386-4504		507
St. Louis Area Business Health Coalition 8888 Ladue Rd Ste 250 .... Saint Louis MO 63124	314-721-7800		474
St. Louis Association of Realtors 12777 Olive Blvd .... St. Louis MO 63141 *Web:* www.stlrealtors.com	314-576-0033		138
St. Louis Cold Drawn Inc 1060 Pershall Rd .... St. Louis MO 63137 *Web:* www.stlcd.com	314-867-4301		492
St. Louis Lithographing Co 6880 Heege Rd .... St Louis MO 63123	314-352-1300		174
St. Louis Parking Company Inc 505 N Seventh St Ste 2405 .... Saint Louis MO 63101 *TF:* 800-651-1223 ■ *Web:* stlouisparking.com	314-241-7777		562
St. Louis Pipe & Supply Inc 17740 Edison Ave .... Chesterfield MO 63005 *TF:* 800-737-7473 ■ *Web:* www.stlpipesupply.com	636-391-2500		492
St. Louis Public Library 1301 Olive St .... Saint Louis MO 63103 *Web:* www.stlouis-mo.gov/government/city-laws	314-241-2288		434-3
St. Louis Testing Laboratories 2810 Clark Ave .... Saint Louis MO 63103 *Web:* www.labinc.com	314-531-8080	531-8085	743
St. Luke Community Hospital (Inc) 107 Sixth Ave SW .... Ronan MT 59864 *Web:* www.stlukehealthnet.org	406-676-4441		374-3
St. Luke's College 2720 Pierce St .... Sioux City IA 51104 *TF:* 800-352-4660 ■ *Web:* www.stlukescollege.edu	712-279-3149		507
St. Lukes Episcopal Day School 8833 Goodwood Blvd .... Baton Rouge LA 70806 *TF:* 800-960-6397 ■ *Web:* www.stlukesbr.org	225-926-5343		685
St. Margaret's School 1080 Lucas Ave .... Victoria BC V8X3P7 *Web:* www.stmarg.ca	250-479-7171		685
St. Marks Evangelical Lutheran Church of North st Paul Minnesota Paul Minn 2499 Helen St N .... Saint Paul MN 55109 *Web:* stmarks-nsp.org	651-777-7451		48-20
St. Martin Bank & Trust Co 301 S Main St .... Saint Martinville LA 70582 *Web:* www.stmartinbank.com	337-394-7800	394-7831	70
St. Mary Med Tech School 1050 Linden Ave .... Long Beach CA 90813 *Web:* stmarymed.com	562-491-9000		166
St. Mary Missionary Baptist Church of Plant City 1840 E State Rd 60 .... Plant City FL 33567	813-737-3668		48-20
St. Mary Parish Library 206 Iberia St .... Franklin LA 70538 *Web:* stmarylibrary.org	337-828-1624	828-2329	434-3
St. Mary's Catholic Church 120 E Miller St .... Alpena MI 49707	989-354-2322		48-20
St. Mary's County Maryland Libraries 23250 Hollywood Rd .... Leonardtown MD 20650 *TF:* 800-337-2217 ■ *Web:* www.stmalib.org	301-475-2846	884-4415	434-3
St. Mary's Dominican High School Corp 7701 Walmsley Ave .... New Orleans LA 70125 *Web:* www.stmarysdominican.org	504-865-9401		685
St. Mary's Elementary School 422 - 20 St S .... Lethbridge AB T1J2V5 *TF:* 800-683-0111 ■ *Web:* www.holyspirit.ab.ca	403-327-3098		623
St. Mary's Home for Children 420 Fruit Hill Ave .... North Providence RI 02911 *Web:* www.smhfc.org	401-353-3900		685
St. Mary's University San Antonio 1 Camino Santa Maria .... San Antonio TX 78228 *Web:* www.rattlerbooks.com	210-436-3011		162
St. Marys Area Senior High School 977 S Saint Marys St .... Saint Marys PA 15857 *TF:* 800-255-3443 ■ *Web:* smasd.org	814-834-7831		623
St. Marys Foundry 405 E South St .... Saint Marys OH 45885 *Web:* www.stmfoundry.com	419-394-3346		492
St. Matthew Catholic School 11525 Elm Ln .... Charlotte NC 28277 *Web:* www.charlottediocese.org	704-544-2070		685
St. Matthews Parish School 1031 Bienveneda Ave .... Pacific Palisades CA 90272 *Web:* www.stmatthewsschool.com	310-454-1350		48-20
St. Meyer & Hubbard Inc 10N865 Williamsburg Dr .... Elgin IL 60124 *Web:* www.stmeyerandhubbard.com	847-717-4328		195
St. Michael's Inc 3310 Noble Pond Way .... Woodbridge VA 22193 *Web:* www.stmichaelsinc.com	703-463-9463		463
St. Moritz Bldg Services Inc 4616 Clairton Blvd .... Pittsburgh PA 15236 *TF:* 800-218-9159 ■ *Web:* www.bsinc.com	412-885-2100		152
St. Moritz Security Services Inc 4600 Clairton Blvd .... Pittsburgh PA 15236 *TF:* 800-218-9156 ■ *Web:* www.smssi.com	412-885-3144		693
St. Olivier School 325 Beckwell Ave .... Radville SK S0C2G0 *Web:* www.holyfamilyrcssd.ca	306-869-3221		685
St. Onge Co 1400 Williams Rd .... York PA 17402 *Web:* www.stonge.com	717-840-8181		463
St. Onge Steward Johnston & Reens LLC 986 Bedford St .... Stamford CT 06905 *Web:* www.ssjr.com	203-324-6155		428
St. Paul Education Regional Division No 1 4313 48 Ave .... St Paul AB T0A3A3 *Web:* www.stpauleducation.ab.ca	780-645-3323	645-5789	685
St. Paul Flight Ctr 270 Airport Rd Ste 5 .... Saint Paul MN 55107 *TF:* 800-368-0107 ■ *Web:* www.stpaulflight.com	651-227-8108	227-6195	63
St. Paul Grill, The 350 Market St .... Saint Paul MN 55102 *Web:* www.stpaulgrill.com	651-224-7455		671
St. Paul High School 9635 Greenleaf Ave .... Santa Fe Springs CA 90670 *TF:* 800-333-3333 ■ *Web:* stpaulhs.org	562-698-6246		685
St. Paul Saints Baseball Club Inc 1771 Energy Park Dr .... Saint Paul MN 55108 *Web:* www.saintsbaseball.com	651-644-6659		713
St. Petersburg General Hospital 6500 38th Ave N .... Saint Petersburg FL 33710 *TF:* 800-733-0610 ■ *Web:* www.stpetegeneral.com	727-384-1414	341-4889	374-3
St. Raphael Academy 123 Walcott St .... Pawtucket RI 02060 *TF:* 800-498-0045 ■ *Web:* www.saintraphaelacademy.org	401-723-8100		148
St. Renatus LLC 1000 Centre Ave .... Fort Collins CO 80526 *TF:* 888-686-2314 ■ *Web:* www.st-renatus.com	970-282-0156		231
St. Rose Ambulatory & Surgery Center 3515 Broadway St .... Great Bend KS 67530 *Web:* www.stroseasc.org	620-792-2511		374-3
St. Sebastian's School 815 Broad Ave .... Belle Vernon PA 15012 *Web:* www.stsebs.org	724-929-5143		685
St. Stephen's Catholic School 16701 S St .... Omaha NE 68135 *Web:* www.stephen.org	402-896-0754		685
St. Stephens Episcopal Church 351 Main St .... Ridgefield CT 06877 *Web:* www.ststephens-ridgefield.org	203-438-3789		48-20
St. Thomas Aquinas Catholic Newman Center at Univ 4765 Brussels St .... Las Vegas NV 89119	702-736-0887		48-20
St. Vincent Dunn Hospital 1600 23rd St .... Bedford IN 47421 *Web:* www.stvincent.org	812-275-3331		374-3
St.Louis County 100 N Fifth Ave W .... Duluth MN 55802 **Fax:* Acctg ■ *TF:* 800-450-9278 ■ *Web:* www.stlouiscountymn.gov	218-726-2450	726-2469*	338
St.Vincent Health 2001 W 86th St .... Indianapolis IN 46260 *TF:* 866-338-2345 ■ *Web:* www.stvincent.com	317-338-2345	338-6491	450

	Phone	Fax	Class
STA (Student Transportation of America Inc) 3349 Hwy 138 Bldg B Ste D Wall NJ 07719 *TF:* 888-942-2250 ■ *Web:* www.ridestbus.com	732-280-4200	280-4214	109
Sta 4100 Fairfax Dr Ste 910 Arlington VA 22203 *Web:* stassociates.com	703-522-5123		463
Sta International 1400 Old Country Rd Ste 411 Westbury NY 11590 *TF:* 866-970-9882 ■ *Web:* www.stacollect.com	516-997-2400	997-2632	216
Staab Battery Manufacturing Co 931 S 11th St Springfield IL 62703 *Web:* www.staabbattery.com	217-528-0421		74
STAAR Surgical Co 1911 Walker Ave Monrovia CA 91016 *NASDAQ: STAA* ■ **Fax:* Mktg ■ *TF:* 800-352-7842 ■ *Web:* www.staar.com	626-303-7902	303-2962*	542
Staatsburgh State Historic Site 75 Mills Mansion Rd Staatsburg NY 12580	845-889-8851		565
Stabbert Maritime Management 2629 NW 54th St Ste 201 Seattle WA 98107 *Web:* www.stabbertmaritime.com	206-547-6161		698
Stabenow Debbie (Sen D - MI) 731 Hart Senate Office Bldg Washington DC 20510 *Web:* www.stabenow.senate.gov	202-224-4822		342-2
Stabil Drill Specialties LLC 110 Consolidate Dr Lafayette LA 70508 *TF:* 800-259-3001 ■ *Web:* www.stabildrill.com	337-837-3001		539
Stabila Inc 332 Industrial Dr PO Box 402 South Elgin IL 60177 **Fax Area Code:* 847 ■ *TF:* 800-869-7460 ■ *Web:* www.stabila.com	800-869-7460	488-0051*	758
Stabile Cos Inc 20 Cotton Rd Ste 200 Nashua NH 03063 *Web:* www.stabilecompanies.com	603-889-0318	595-2571	187
Stabilit America Inc 285 Industrial Dr Moscow TN 38057	901-877-3010		596
Stabinski and Funt PA 757 NW 27th Ave Fl 3 Miami FL 33125 *Web:* www.stabinskilaw.com	305-964-8644		445
Stablex Canada Inc 760 Blvd Industriel Blainville QC J7C3V4 *Web:* www.stablex.com	450-430-9230		194
Stacey Braun Associates Inc 377 Broadway New York NY 10013 *Web:* www.staceybraun.com	212-226-7707		41
Stack Plastics 3525 Haven Ave Menlo Park CA 94025 *Web:* www.stackplastics.com	650-361-8600		608
Stackbin Corp 29 Powderhill Rd Lincoln RI 02865 *TF Sales:* 800-333-1603 ■ *Web:* www.stackbin.com	401-333-1600	333-1952	198
Stackframe LLC 114 W First St Ste 246 Sanford FL 32771 *Web:* www.stackframe.com	407-733-0885		177
Stack-On Products Co 1360 N Old Rand Rd Wauconda IL 60084 *TF:* 800-323-9601 ■ *Web:* www.stack-on.com	800-323-9601		488
Stackpole & Partners Ltd 222 Merrimac St Newburyport MA 01950 *Web:* www.stackpolepartners.com	978-463-6600		4
Stackpole Books 5067 Ritter Rd Mechanicsburg PA 17055 *TF Sales:* 800-699-9113 ■ *Web:* www.stackpolebooks.com	717-796-0411	796-0412	637-2
Stacy Furniture 1900 S Main St Ste 200 Grapevine TX 76051 *TF:* 800-403-6077 ■ *Web:* www.stacyfurniture.com	817-424-8800		321
Stadco Corp 1931 N Broadway Los Angeles CA 90031 *Web:* www.stadco.com	323-227-8888		621
Stadelman Fruit LLC 111 Meade St PO BOX 445 Zillah WA 98953 *Web:* www.stadelmanfruit.com	509-829-5145		315-3
Stadium International Trucks Inc 105 Seventh N St Liverpool NY 13088 *Web:* www.stadiumtrucks.com	315-475-8471		57
Stadium Toyota 5088 N Dale Mabry Hwy Tampa FL 33614 *Web:* www.stadiumtoyota.com	813-872-4881		57
Stafast Products Inc 505 Lake Shore Blvd Painesville OH 44077 *TF:* 800-782-3278 ■ *Web:* shop.stafast.com	440-357-5546	357-7137	278
STAFDA (Specialty Tools & Fasteners Distributors Assn) 500 Elm Grove Rd Ste 210 PO Box 44 Elm Grove WI 53122 *TF:* 800-352-2981 ■ *Web:* www.stafda.org	262-784-4774	784-5059	49-18
Staff Electric Company Inc W 133 N 5030 Campbell Dr Menomonee Falls WI 53051 *TF:* 800-332-3360 ■ *Web:* staffelectric.com	262-781-8230		189-4
Staff Leasing 149 Northern Concourse North Syracuse NY 13212 *Web:* www.staffleasing-peo.com	315-641-3600		463
Staff Management Group LLC 172 New St New Brunswick NJ 08901	732-246-0099		194
Staff Management Inc 5919 Spring Creek Rd Rockford IL 61114 **Fax:* Hum Res ■ *TF General:* 800-368-9857 ■ *Web:* www.staffmgmt.com	815-282-3900	282-0515*	631
Staff One Inc 8111 LBJ Fwy Dallas TX 75251 **Fax Area Code:* 214 ■ *TF:* 800-771-7823 ■ *Web:* www.staffone.com	800-771-7823	461-1141*	631
Staff Pro Inc 15272 Newsboy Cir Huntington Beach CA 92649 *Web:* www.staffpro.com	714-230-7200		693
Staff Right Inc 10825 Plano Rd Ste 3 Dallas TX 75238	214-221-9000	221-9003	260
Staffcentrix LLC 33 Woodstock Meadows Woodstock CT 06281 *Web:* www.staffcentrix.com	860-928-6969		196
Staffdigest Magazine PO Box 384 Alief TX 77411 *TF General:* 800-444-0674 ■ *Web:* www.staffdigest.com	281-498-2913		457-5
Staffelbach Design Associates Inc 2525 McKinnon Ste 800 Dallas TX 75201 *Web:* www.staffelbach.com	214-747-2511		393
Staffing 360 Solutions Inc 641 Lexington Ave 27th Fl New York NY 10022 *Web:* www.staffing360solutions.com	646-507-5710		260
Staffing Options & Solutions LLC 6249 S E St Ste E Indianapolis IN 46227 **Fax Area Code:* 800 ■ *TF:* 800-554-7823 ■ *Web:* www.staffingoptionsandsolutions.com	317-791-2456	791-1656*	260
Staffing Partners 2888 Crescent Ave Eugene OR 97408 *Web:* www.staffingoregon.com	541-345-9675	242-1137	193
Staffing Resource Group Inc, The 405 Reo St Ste 255 Tampa FL 33609 *TF:* 877-774-7742 ■ *Web:* www.srg-us.com	877-774-7742		260

	Phone	Fax	Class
Staffing Technologies LLC 221 Roswell St Ste 200 Alpharetta GA 30009 *Web:* www.staffingtechnologies.com	678-338-2040		180
Staffing.org Inc 10 Burchard Ln Rowayton CT 06853 *Web:* www.staffing.org	203-227-0186		463
StaffingSolutions Inc 1324 S Eufaula Ave Eufaula AL 36027 *Web:* www.staffingsolutions.com	334-687-7460		734
Stafford Communications Group 309 South St Ste 3 New Providence NJ 07974 *Web:* staffcom.com	908-464-7740		195
Stafford County 209 N Broadway St Saint John KS 67576 *Web:* www.staffordcounty.org	620-549-3295	549-3298	338
Stafford County 1300 Ct House Rd Stafford VA 22554 *Web:* staffordcountyva.gov	540-658-8600		338
Stafford Motor Speedway 55 W St PO Box 105 Stafford Springs CT 06076 *Web:* staffordmotorspeedway.com	860-684-2783	684-6236	515
Stafford Printing Co 2707 Jefferson Davis Hwy Stafford VA 22554 *TF:* 800-774-6831 ■ *Web:* staffordprinting.com	540-659-4554		627
Stafford-Smith Inc 3414 S Burdick St Kalamazoo MI 49001 *TF:* 800-968-2442 ■ *Web:* www.staffordsmith.com	269-343-1240	343-2509	665
Staffworks Group 20505 W 12 Mile Rd Southfield MI 48076 **Fax Area Code:* 248 ■ *TF:* 877-304-9690 ■ *Web:* staffworksgroup.com	877-304-9690	416-1103*	260
Stage 2 Networks LLC 70 W 40th St 7th Fl New York NY 10018 *Web:* stage2networks.com	212-497-8000		387
Stage 4 Solutions inc 4701 Patrick Henry Dr Bldg 19 Santa Clara CA 95054 *Web:* www.stage4solutions.com	408-868-9739		195
Stage Coach Theatre 4802 W Emerald Boise ID 83706 *TF:* 800-635-5240 ■ *Web:* www.stagecoachtheatre.com	208-342-2000		573-4
Stage III Community Theatre 900 N Center St Casper WY 82601 *Web:* www.stageiiitheatre.org	307-234-0946		572
Stage Neck Inn 8 Stage Neck Rd Rt 1A PO Box 70 York Harbor ME 03911 *TF:* 800-222-3238 ■ *Web:* www.stageneck.com	207-363-3850	363-2221	669
Stage Restaurant 1250 Kapiolani Blvd 2nd Fl Honolulu HI 96814 *Web:* www.stagerestauranthawaii.com	808-237-5429		671
Stagecoach State Park 25500 County Rd 14 Oak Creek CO 80467 *Web:* cpw.state.co.us	970-736-2436		565
Stagecraft Costuming Inc 3950 Spring Grove Ave Cincinnati OH 45223 *Web:* www.stagecraft.on-rev.com	513-541-7150	541-7159	155-6
Stagecraft Industries Inc 5051 N Lagoon Ave Portland OR 97217 *TF:* 800-727-2673 ■ *Web:* www.stagecraftindustries.com	503-286-1600		45
StagePost Full Screen Spectrum Media 255 French Landing Dr Nashville TN 37228 *Web:* www.stagepost.com	615-248-1978		514
Stageright Corp 495 Pioneer Pkwy Clare MI 48617 *TF:* 800-438-4499 ■ *Web:* www.stageright.com	989-386-7393		321
Stages Repertory Theatre 3201 Allen Pkwy Ste 101 Houston TX 77019 *Web:* www.stagestheatre.com	713-527-0220	527-8669	573-4
Stagestruck 121 W Chestnut St Goldsboro NC 27530 *Web:* stagestruck.org	919-736-4530		749
Staggs & Fisher Consulting Engineers Inc 3264 Lochness Dr Lexington KY 40517 *Web:* sfengineering.com	859-271-3246		261
Stahancyk Kent & Hook P C Duniway Plaza 2400 SW Fourth Ave Portland OR 97201 *TF:* 877-673-7632 ■ *Web:* www.stahancyk.com	877-673-7632		445
Stahl Peterbilt Inc 18020-118 Ave Edmonton AB T5S2G2 *TF:* 800-252-7981 ■ *Web:* www.stahlpeterbilt.com	780-483-6666		791
Stahl Specialty Co 111 E Pacific Kingsville MO 64061 *TF:* 800-821-7852 ■ *Web:* www.stahlspecialty.com	816-597-3322	597-3485	308
Stahl USA 13 Corwin St Peabody MA 01960 *Web:* www.stahl.com	978-531-0371		432
STAHL/A Scott Fetzer Co 3201 W Old Lincoln Way Wooster OH 44691 *TF:* 800-277-8245 ■ *Web:* www.stahltruckbodies.com	330-264-7441	264-3319	516
Stahlin Non-Metallic Enclosure 505 W Maple St Belding MI 48809 *Web:* www.stahlin.com	616-794-0700	794-3378	254
Stahls' Inc 20600 Stephens St St. Clair Shores MI 48080 *Web:* www.stahls.com	586-772-5551		258
Stahly Cartage Co 119 S Main St Edwardsville IL 62025	618-656-5070		780
Sta-Home Hospice 406 Briarwood Dr Bldg 200 Jackson MS 39206 *TF:* 800-782-4663 ■ *Web:* www.sta-home.com	601-956-5100	956-3003	363
Stailey Insurance Corp 2084 S Milwaukee St Denver CO 80210 *Web:* staileycorp.com	303-759-2796		390
Staiman Design 17 Warren Rd 23b Pikesville MD 21208	410-580-0100		344
Stained Glass Theatre 1996 W Evangel Ozark MO 65721 *Web:* www.sgtheatre.com	417-581-9192		572
Stainless Foundry & Engineering Inc 5110 N 35th St Milwaukee WI 53209 *Web:* www.stainlessfoundry.com	414-462-7400	462-7303	306
Stainless LLC 1140 Welsh Rd Ste 250 North Wales PA 19454	215-631-1427		480
Stainless Metals Inc 60-01 31 Ave Woodside NY 11377 *TF:* 800-960-2170 ■ *Web:* www.stainlessmetals.com	718-784-1454		198
Staker Parson Cos 2350 S 1900 W Ogden UT 84401 *TF:* 888-672-7766 ■ *Web:* stakerparson.com	801-731-1111		188-4
Staley Inc 8101 Fourche Rd Little Rock AR 72209 *TF:* 877-616-0661 ■ *Web:* www.staleyinc.com	501-565-3006	565-9674	189-4
Stallings Crop Insurance Corp PO Box 6100 Lakeland FL 33807 *TF:* 800-721-7099 ■ *Web:* www.stallingscrop.com	863-647-2747		390
Staluppi Auto Group 133 US Hwy 1 Palm Beach FL 33408	561-844-7148		57

	Phone	Fax	Class
Stamas Yacht Inc 300 Pampas Ave. . . . . Tarpon Springs FL 34689 *Web:* www.stamas.com	727-937-4118		90
Stamats Communications Inc 615 Fifth St SE. . . . . Cedar Rapids IA 52401 *TF:* 800-553-8878 ■ *Web:* www.stamats.com	319-364-6167		637-9
Stambaugh Auditorium 1000 Fifth Ave. . . . . Youngstown OH 44504 *TF:* 866-516-2269 ■ *Web:* www.stambaughauditorium.com	330-747-5175	747-1981	572
Stamco Industries Inc 26650 Lakeland Blvd . . . . Cleveland OH 44132 *Web:* www.stamcoind.com	216-731-9333		488
Stamey's Barbecue 2206 High Pt Rd. . . . . Greensboro NC 27403 *Web:* www.stameys.com	336-299-9888		671
Stamford Chamber of Commerce 733 Summer St Ste 104. . . . . Stamford CT 06901 *Web:* stamfordchamberofcommerce.com	203-359-4761	363-5069	139
Stamford City Hall 888 Washington Blvd 10th Fl. . . . . Stamford CT 06901 *TF:* 800-864-2742 ■ *Web:* www.stamfordct.gov	203-977-4150	977-5845	337
Stamford Ctr for the Arts 61 Atlantic St . . . . Stamford CT 06901 *TF:* 800-200-2882 ■ *Web:* palacestamford.org	203-325-4466	358-2313	572
Stamford Historical Society Museum 1508 High Ridge Rd. . . . . Stamford CT 06903 *Web:* www.stamfordhistory.org	203-329-1183	322-1607	520
Stamford Hospital 30 Shelburne Rd. . . . . Stamford CT 06904 *Web:* www.stamfordhealth.org	203-276-1000		374-3
Stamford Museum & Nature Ctr 39 Scofieldtown Rd. . . . . Stamford CT 06903 *Web:* www.stamfordmuseum.org	203-322-1646	322-0408	520
Stamford Scientific International Inc 4 Tucker Dr. . . . . Poughkeepsie NY 12603 *Web:* www.ssiaeration.com	845-454-8171		358
Stamford Suites 720 Bedford St. . . . . Stamford CT 06901 *TF:* 866-394-4365 ■ *Web:* www.stamfordsuites.com	203-359-7300	359-7304	379
Stamped Products Inc 201 Industrial Pkwy . . . . Gadsden AL 35903 *Web:* www.msi-mfg.com/msi_spi.html	256-492-8890		488
Stampede Meat Inc 7351 S 78th Ave. . . . . Bridgeview IL 60455 *TF:* 800-353-0933 ■ *Web:* www.stampedemeat.com	800-353-0933		296-26
Stamper Black Hills Gold Jewelry 7201 S Hwy 16. . . . . Rapid City SD 57702 *Web:* www.stamperbhg.com	605-342-0751		409
Stampin Up 12907 S 3600 W. . . . . Riverton UT 84065 *Web:* stampinup.com	801-257-5400		366
Stamprite 154 S Larch St. . . . . Lansing MI 48912 *TF:* 800-328-1988 ■ *Web:* www.stamprite.com	517-487-5071	487-6211	467
Stamps.com Inc 1990 E Grand Ave. . . . . El Segundo CA 90245 *NASDAQ: STMP* ■ *TF:* 855-889-7867 ■ *Web:* www.stamps.com	855-889-7867		178-1
Stamtex Metal Stampings 112 Erie St . . . . Niles OH 44446 *Web:* www.stamtexmp.com	330-652-2558	652-7369	488
Stan Houston Equipment Co 501 S Marion Rd . . . . Sioux Falls SD 57106 *TF:* 800-952-3033 ■ *Web:* www.stanhouston.com	605-336-3727	336-7860	358
Stan Hywet Hall & Gardens 714 N Portage Path. . . . . Akron OH 44303 *TF:* 888-836-5533 ■ *Web:* www.stanhywet.org	330-836-5533		520
Stan Johnson Company Inc 6120 S Yale Ave Ste 813. . . . . Tulsa OK 74136 *Web:* www.stanjohnsonco.com	918-494-2690		652
Stan White Realty & Construction Inc 812 Ocean Trl . . . . Corolla NC 27927 *TF:* 800-753-6200 ■ *Web:* outerbanksrentals.com	252-453-6131		652
Stanadyne Corp 92 Deerfield Rd. . . . . Windsor CT 06095 *TF:* 888-336-3473 ■ *Web:* www.stanadyne.com	860-525-0821	687-4235	60
Stanard & Associates Inc 309 W Washington St Ste 1000 . . . . Chicago IL 60606 *Web:* stanard.com	312-553-0213		196
Stanbee Company Inc 70 Broad St . . . . Carlstadt NJ 07072 *Web:* www.stanbee.com	201-933-9666	933-7985	301
Stanbury Uniforms Inc 108 Stanbury Industrial Dr PO Box 100 . . . . Brookfield MO 64628 *TF:* 800-826-2246 ■ *Web:* www.stanbury.com	660-258-2246	258-5781	155-19
Stancil Corp 2644 S Croddy Way . . . . Santa Ana CA 92704 *Web:* www.stancilcorp.com	714-546-2002	546-2092	52
Stanco Metal Prod Inc 2101 168th Ave. . . . . Grand Haven MI 49417 *Web:* stancometal.com	616-842-5000		488
StanCorp Financial Group Inc 1100 SW Sixth Ave. . . . . Portland OR 97204 *NYSE: SFG* ■ *TF:* 800-368-1135 ■ *Web:* standard.com	800-368-1135		360-4
Standard & Poor's Corp 55 Water St. . . . . New York NY 10041 *TF:* 877-772-5436 ■ *Web:* www.standardandpoors.com	212-438-1000		637-2
Standard Air & Lite Corp 2406 Woodmere Dr. . . . . Pittsburgh PA 15205 *TF:* 800-472-2458 ■ *Web:* www.stdair.com	412-920-6505		612
Standard Alloys & Mfg PO Box 969 . . . . Port Arthur TX 77640 *TF:* 800-231-8240 ■ *Web:* www.ksb.com/standard_alloys	409-983-3201	983-7837	641
Standard Armament Inc 631 Allen Ave . . . . Glendale CA 91201 *Web:* www.standardarmament.com	818-842-6144		807
Standard Auto Parts 2930 Texas Ave. . . . . Texas City TX 77590	409-945-3333		57
Standard Auto Parts Corp 2020 Hollins Ferry Rd. . . . . Baltimore MD 21230 *TF:* 800-332-1449 ■ *Web:* www.standardautoparts.com	410-659-5400		54
Standard Beverage Corp 2416 E 37th St N . . . . Wichita KS 67219 *TF:* 800-999-8797 ■ *Web:* www.standardbeverage.com	316-838-7707		81-3
Standard Candy Company Inc 715 Massman Dr . . . . Nashville TN 37210 *Web:* www.googoo.com	615-889-6360		296-8
Standard Car Truck Co 865 Busse Hwy. . . . . Park Ridge IL 60068 *Web:* www.sctco.com	847-692-6050		650
Standard Casing Company Inc, The 165 Chubb Ave. . . . . Lyndhurst NJ 07071 *Web:* www.standardcasing.com	201-434-6300		296-26
Standard Change-Makers Inc 3130 N Mitthoeffer Rd . . . . Indianapolis IN 46235 *Web:* www.standardchange.com	317-899-6966		427
Standard Chartered Bank 1 Madison Ave . . . . New York NY 10010 *Web:* www.sc.com	212-667-0700	667-0380	70
Standard Companies Inc, The 2601 S Archer Ave . . . . Chicago IL 60608 *Web:* www.thestandardcompanies.com	312-225-2777		406
Standard Concrete Products Inc (SCP) PO Box 1360 . . . . Columbus GA 31902 *Web:* www.standardconcrete.net	706-322-3274		188-4
Standard Data Corp 26 Journal Sq. . . . . Jersey City NJ 07306 *Web:* www.standarddata.com	201-533-4433		225
Standard Digital Imaging 4426 S 108th St . . . . Omaha NE 68137 *TF:* 800-642-8062 ■ *Web:* www.standardsharev3.com	402-592-1292	592-8003	240
Standard Duplicating Machines Corp 10 Connector Rd. . . . . Andover MA 01810 *TF:* 800-526-4774 ■ *Web:* www.sdmc.com	978-470-1920		112
Standard Electric Co 2650 Trautner Dr . . . . Saginaw MI 48603 *TF:* 800-322-0215 ■ *Web:* www.standardelectricco.com	989-497-2100	497-2101	246
Standard Electric Supply Co 222 N Emmber Ln PO Box 651. . . . . Milwaukee WI 53233 *TF:* 800-776-8222 ■ *Web:* www.standardelectricsupply.com	414-272-8100	272-8111	246
Standard Equipment Company Inc 75 Beauregard St . . . . Mobile AL 36602 *TF:* 800-239-3442 ■ *Web:* www.standardequipmentco.com	251-432-1705		770
Standard Filter Corp 5928 Balfour Ct . . . . Carlsbad CA 92008 *TF:* 800-634-5837 ■ *Web:* www.standardfilter.com	760-929-8559	929-1901	18
Standard Furniture Mfg Company Inc 801 Hwy 31 S. . . . . Bay Minette AL 36507 *TF General:* 877-788-1899 ■ *Web:* www.standard-furniture.com	251-937-6741		319-2
Standard Golf Co 6620 Nordic Dr. . . . . Cedar Falls IA 50613 *Web:* www.standardgolf.com	319-266-2638	266-9627	710
Standard Heating & Air Conditioning 1082 Payne Ave . . . . Saint Paul MN 55130 *Web:* www.standardheating.com	651-772-2449		610
Standard Imaging Inc 3120 Deming Way . . . . Middleton WI 53562 *TF:* 800-261-4446 ■ *Web:* www.standardimaging.com	608-831-0025		639
Standard Insurance Agency Corp 620 W Pipeline. . . . . Hurst TX 76053 *Web:* www.siatexas.com	817-285-1800		390
Standard Investment Chartered Inc 2801 Bristol St Ste 100. . . . . Costa Mesa CA 92626	714-444-4300	444-0072	690
STANDARD Iron & Wire Works Inc 524 Pine St. . . . . Monticello MN 55362 *Web:* www.std-iron.com	763-295-8700		697
Standard Iron Inc 2516 Vance Ave . . . . Chattanooga TN 37404	423-756-0940		480
Standard Knapp Inc 63 Pickering St . . . . Portland CT 06480 *TF Cust Svc:* 800-628-9565 ■ *Web:* www.standard-knapp.com	860-342-1100	342-0782	547
Standard Laboratories Inc 147 11th Ave Ste 100. . . . . South Charleston WV 25303 *Web:* standardlabs.com	304-744-6800		743
Standard Life Insurance Company of Indiana 8365 Keystone Crossing Ste 200. . . . . Indianapolis IN 46280	317-574-6201		391-2
Standard Life Investments 1 Beacon St 34th Fl . . . . Boston MA 02108 *Web:* us.standardlifeinvestments.com	617-720-7900		390
Standard Locknut Inc 1045 E 169th St . . . . Westfield IN 46074 *TF:* 800-783-6887 ■ *Web:* www.stdlocknut.com	317-867-0100		454
Standard Lumber Co 1912 Lehigh Ave. . . . . Glenview IL 60026 *Web:* standardlumberco.com	847-729-7800	729-8500	499
Standard Machine Ltd 868-60th St E . . . . Saskatoon SK S7K8G8 *Web:* www.standardmachine.ca	306-931-3343		709
Standard Management Co 9841 Airport Blvd Ste 1010 . . . . Los Angeles CA 90045 *Web:* standardmanagement.com	310-410-2300		217
Standard Meat Company LP 5105 Investment Dr . . . . Dallas TX 75236 *TF:* 866-859-6313 ■ *Web:* www.standardmeat.com	214-561-0561	561-0560	296-26
Standard Metal Products 1541 W 132nd St . . . . Gardena CA 90249 *Web:* www.sheet-metal.com	310-532-9861		697
Standard Mfg Company Inc 750 Second Ave. . . . . Troy NY 12182 *Web:* www.sportsmaster.com	518-235-2200		155-5
Standard Motor Products Inc 37-18 Northern Blvd. . . . . Long Island NY 11101 *NYSE: SMP* ■ *TF:* 800-895-1085 ■ *Web:* www.smpcorp.com	718-392-0200	729-4549	247
Standard Motors Ltd 44 Second Ave NW. . . . . Swift Current SK S9H3V6 *TF:* 866-334-8985 ■ *Web:* www.standardmotors.ca	866-334-8985		57
Standard Multiwall Bag Manufacturing Co 1800 SW Merlo Dr . . . . Beaverton OR 97006 *Web:* www.standardbag.com	503-591-0332		557
Standard Office Supply 35 Sheridan St NW. . . . . Washington DC 20011 *TF:* 888-829-4820 ■ *Web:* www.standardofficesupply.com	202-829-4820		321
Standard Oil Of Connecticut Inc 299 Bishop Ave. . . . . Bridgeport CT 06610 *Web:* www.standardsecurity.com	203-334-5532		316
Standard Pacific Capital LLC 101 California St 36th Fl. . . . . San Francisco CA 94111 *Web:* standardpacific.com	415-352-7100		401
Standard Parking Corp 900 N Michigan Ave Ste 1600 . . . . Chicago IL 60611 **Fax:* Hum Res ■ *TF:* 888-700-7275 ■ *Web:* spplus.com/?ref=standard	312-274-2000	640-6169*	562
Standard Process Inc 1200 W Royal Lee Dr . . . . Palmyra WI 53156 *Web:* www.standardprocess.com	262-495-2122		123
Standard Publishing Co 8805 Governors Hill Dr Ste 400 . . . . Cincinnati OH 45249 **Fax Area Code:* 877 ■ *TF Orders:* 800-543-1353 ■ *Web:* www.standardpub.com	513-931-4050	867-5751*	637-9
Standard Roofing Co 516 N McDonough St PO Box 1309. . . . . Montgomery AL 36102 *TF:* 800-239-5705 ■ *Web:* www.standardtaylor.com	334-265-1262		189-12

				Phone	Fax	Class
Standard Sales Co Inc 4800 E 42nd St Ste 400	Odessa	TX	79762	432-367-7662		81-1
Web: standardsalescompanylp.com						
Standard Sand & Silica Co 1850 US Hwy 17 92 N	Davenport	FL	33837	863-422-7100		503-4
Standard Security Life Insurance Co of New York 485 Madison Ave 14th Fl	New York	NY	10022	212-355-4141	644-5786	391-2
TF: 800-477-0087 ■ *Web:* www.sslicny.com						
Standard Steel LLC 500 N Walnut St	Burnham	PA	17009	717-248-4911	248-8050	723
Web: www.standardsteel.com						
Standard Supply & Distributing Co 1431 Regal Row	Dallas	TX	75247	214-630-7800	630-1894	351
Web: www.standardsupplyhvac.com						
Standard Tap 901 N Second St	Philadelphia	PA	19123	215-238-0630		671
Web: news.standardtap.com.s86406.gridserver.com						
Standard Textile Company Inc 1 Knollcrest Dr	Cincinnati	OH	45237	513-761-9255	761-0467	477
TF: 800-999-0400 ■ *Web:* www.standardtextile.com						
Standard Waterproofing Corp 701 E 134th St	Bronx	NY	10454	718-292-2800		186
Web: www.standardwaterproofing.com						
Standard Wire & Steel Works 16255 Vincennes Ave	South Holland	IL	60473	708-333-8300		492
TF: 800-624-3147 ■ *Web:* www.standardwiresteel.com						
Standard, The 40 Island Ave	Miami Beach	FL	33139	305-673-1717		669
TF: 800-232-3969 ■ *Web:* standardhotels.com						
Standard-Examiner 332 Standard Way	Ogden	UT	84404	801-625-4200		532-2
TF: 888-221-7070 ■ *Web:* www.standard.net						
Standards Council of Canada 270 Albert St Ste 200	Ottawa	ON	K1P6N7	613-238-3222		466
TF: 800-844-6790 ■ *Web:* www.scc.ca						
Standby Screw Machine Products Company Inc 1122 W Bagley Rd	Berea	OH	44017	440-243-8200		621
Web: standbyscrew.com						
Standex Electronics Inc 4538 Camberwell Rd	Cincinnati	OH	45209	513-871-3777	871-3779	253
TF: 866-782-6339 ■ *Web:* www.standexelectronics.com						
Standex International Corp Consumer Group 11 Keewaydin Dr.	Salem	NH	03079	603-893-9701	893-7324	637-3
NYSE: *SXI* ■ *TF:* 800-514-5275 ■ *Web:* www.standex.com						
Standex International Corp Custom Hoists Div 771 County Rd 30A W PO Box 98	Hayesville	OH	44838	419-368-4721	368-4209	223
TF: 800-837-4668 ■ *Web:* www.customhoists.com						
Standex International Corp Engraving Group 11 Keewaydin Dr ste 300	Salem	NH	03079	603-893-9701	893-7324	481
Web: www.standexengraving.com						
Standex International Corp Food Service Equipment Group 11 Keewaydin Dr	Salem	NH	03079	603-893-9701	893-7324	300
NYSE: *SXI* ■ *TF:* 800-647-1284 ■ *Web:* www.standex.com						
Standex International Corp Mullen Testers Div 930 Chicopee St	Chicopee	MA	01013	413-536-1311	536-1367	711
Web: www.mullentesters.com						
Standing Stone Inc 49 Richmondville Ave The Mill Ste 306	Westport	CT	06880	203-227-8710		582
Web: www.standingstoneinc.com						
Standing Stone State Park 1674 Standing Stone Pk Hwy	Hilham	TN	38568	931-823-6347		565
Web: www.state.tn.us						
Standish Mellon 1 Boston Pl	Boston	MA	02108	617-248-6000	248-6050	401
TF: 800-374-6969 ■ *Web:* www.standish.com						
Standley Batch Systems Inc 505 Aquamsi St	Cape Girardeau	MO	63703	573-334-2831		697
Web: www.standleybatch.com						
Stanfield Systems Inc 718 Sutter St Ste 108	Folsom	CA	95630	916-608-8006		196
Web: www.stanfieldsystems.com						
Stanford Advanced Medicine Ctr/Cancer Ctr 875 Lake Blake Wilbur Dr	Stanford	CA	94305	650-498-6000	724-1433	668
TF: 800-422-6237 ■ *Web:* med.stanford.edu/cancer.html						
Stanford Alumni Association 326 Galvez St	Stanford	CA	94305	650-723-2021		138
Web: alumni137.stanford.edu						
Stanford Carr Development LLC 1100 Alakea St 27th Fl	Honolulu	HI	96813	808-537-5220	537-1801	516
Web: www.stanfordcarr.com						
Stanford Court - A Renaissance Hotel 905 California St.	San Francisco	CA	94108	415-989-3500		379
Web: www.marriott.com/default.mi						
Stanford Federal Credit Union 1860 Embarcadero Rd	Palo Alto	CA	94303	650-723-2509	579-9764*	219
**Fax Area Code:* 866 ■ *TF:* 888-723-7328 ■ *Web:* www.sfcu.org						
Stanford Linear Accelerator Ctr (SLAC) 2575 Sand Hill Rd	Menlo Park	CA	94025	650-926-3300	926-4999	668
Web: www.slac.stanford.edu						
Stanford Prevention Research Ctr (SPRC) 1070 Arastradero Rd Ste 100 and 300	Stanford	CA	94305	650-723-6254	725-6247	668
Web: prevention.stanford.edu						
Stanford Shopping Ctr 660 Stanford Shopping Ctr	Palo Alto	CA	94304	650-617-8200		460
TF: 800-284-8273 ■ *Web:* www.simon.com						
Stanford Synchrotron Radiation Lightsource (SSRL) 2575 Sand Hill Rd MS 69	Menlo Park	CA	94025	650-926-2079	926-3600	668
Web: www-ssrl.slac.stanford.edu						
Stanford University 450 Serra Mall	Stanford	CA	94305	650-723-2091	725-2846	166
TF: 877-407-9529 ■ *Web:* www.stanford.edu						
Stanford University Green Library 557 Escondido Mall	Stanford	CA	94305	650-723-2300	725-0743	434-6
TF: 800-521-0600 ■ *Web:* library.stanford.edu						
Stanford University Law School 559 Nathan Abbott Way	Stanford	CA	94305	650-723-2465	725-0253*	167-1
**Fax:* Admissions ■ *Web:* www.law.stanford.edu						
Stanford University Press 500 Broadway St.	Redwood City	CA	94063	650-723-9434	725-3457	637-4
TF: 800-621-2736 ■ *Web:* www.sup.org						
Stanford University School of Medicine 291 Campus Dr Rm LK3C02	Stanford	CA	94305	650-725-3900	725-7368	167-2
Web: med.stanford.edu						

				Phone	Fax	Class
Stanford University School of Medicine Blood & Marrow Transplant Program 300 Pasteur Dr Rm H0101	Stanford	CA	94305	650-723-0822	725-8950	769
TF: 866-680-2906 ■ *Web:* bmt.stanford.edu						
Stanford's Restaurant & Bar 913 Lloyd Ctr	Portland	OR	97232	503-335-0811		670
Web: www.stanfords.com						
Stanfordville Machine & Manufacturing Inc 29 Victory Ln	Poughkeepsie	NY	12603	845-868-2266		757
TF: 800-208-6137 ■ *Web:* www.stanfordville.com						
Stanion Wholesale Electric Co 812 S Main St PO Box F	Pratt	KS	67124	620-672-5678	672-6220	246
TF: 866-782-6466 ■ *Web:* www.stanion.com						
Stanisky & Co 2550 Leechburg Rd	Lower Burrell	PA	15068	724-339-7340		2
Web: stanisky.com						
Stanislaus County 800 11th St	Modesto	CA	95354	209-530-3100		434-3
Web: www.stanct.org						
Stanislaus County 1021 I St Ste 101	Modesto	CA	95354	209-525-5250	525-5804	338
Web: www.stancounty.com						
Stanislaus Credit Control Service Inc 914-14th St	Modesto	CA	95354	209-523-1813		160
TF: 800-838-7227 ■ *Web:* www.sccscollects.com						
Stanislaus Farm Supply Co 624 E Service Rd	Modesto	CA	95358	209-538-7070	541-3191	276
TF: 800-323-0725 ■ *Web:* www.farmsupply.coop						
Stanislaus Food Products Co 1202 D St	Modesto	CA	95354	800-327-7201	521-4014*	296-20
**Fax Area Code:* 209 ■ *TF:* 800-327-7201 ■ *Web:* www.stanislaus.com						
Stanislawski & Harrison 301 N Lake Ave Ste 900	Pasadena	CA	91101	626-793-3600		2
Web: www.snh-cpa.com						
Stanker & Galetto Inc 317 W Elmer Rd	Vineland	NJ	08360	856-692-8098		186
TF: 888-692-8098 ■ *Web:* www.stankergaletto.com						
Stanley & Seafort's 115 E 34th St	Tacoma	WA	98404	253-473-7300		671
Web: www.stanleyandseaforts.com						
Stanley Access Technologies 65 Scott Swamp Rd	Farmington	CT	06032	860-677-2861	339-7923*	234
**Fax Area Code:* 077 ■ **Fax:* Cust Svc ■ *TF:* 800-722-2377 ■ *Web:* www.stanleyaccess.com						
Stanley Assembly Technologies Div 5335 Avion Pk Dr	Cleveland	OH	44143	440-461-5500		759
TF: 877-787-7830 ■ *Web:* www.stanleyengineeredfastening.com						
Stanley Benefit Services Inc 7800 McCloud Rd Ste 200	Greensboro	NC	27409	336-271-4450		2
Web: www.stanleybenefits.com						
Stanley Consultants Inc 225 Iowa Ave	Muscatine	IA	52761	563-264-6600	264-6658	261
TF: 800-553-9694 ■ *Web:* www.stanleyconsultants.com						
Stanley County Auditor 8 E Second Ave	Fort Pierre	SD	57532	605-223-7780		338
Web: stanleycounty.org						
Stanley Creations Inc 1414 Willow Ave	Melrose Park	PA	19027	215-635-6200	635-2708	409
TF: 800-220-1414 ■ *Web:* www.stanleycreations.com						
Stanley Ctr for the Arts 259 Genesee St	Utica	NY	13501	315-724-1113	624-2926	572
TF: 800-545-4318 ■ *Web:* www.thestanley.org						
Stanley Electric Us Company Inc 420 E High St	London	OH	43140	740-852-5200		815
Web: www.stanleyelectricus.com						
Stanley Furniture Co Inc 200 N Hamilton St	High Point	NC	27260	877-772-4858		319-2
NASDAQ: *STLY* ■ *TF:* 877-772-4858 ■ *Web:* www.stanleyfurniture.com						
Stanley Hotel 333 Wonderview Ave.	Estes Park	CO	80517	970-586-3371	586-4964	379
TF: 800-976-1377 ■ *Web:* www.stanleyhotel.com						
Stanley Hunt DuPree & Rhine (SHDR) 7701 Airport Ctr Dr.	Greensboro	NC	27409	800-768-4873	293-9048*	193
**Fax Area Code:* 252 ■ *TF:* 800-930-2441 ■ *Web:* www.shdr.com						
Stanley Jay s & Assoc 5313 Mcclanahan Dr Ste G5	North Little Rock	AR	72116	501-758-8029		509
TF: 888 758 4728 ■ *Web:* jaystanley.com						
Stanley Korshak 500 Crescent Ct Ste 100	Dallas	TX	75201	214-871-3600		157-4
TF: 855-479-9539 ■ *Web:* www.stanleykorshak.com						
Stanley M Proctor Co 2016 Midway Dr	Twinsburg	OH	44087	330-425-7814		385
Web: www.stanleyproctor.com						
Stanley Machining & Tool Corp 425 Maple Ave	Carpentersville	IL	60110	847-426-4560		757
Web: www.stanleymachining.com						
Stanley Martin Cos 11111 Sunset Hills Rd Ste 200	Reston	VA	20190	703-964-5000		653
TF: 800-446-4807 ■ *Web:* www.stanleymartin.com						
Stanley Mcdonald Agency of Illinois Inc 1101 Main St	Onalaska	WI	54650	608-788-6162		390
TF: 800-344-3948 ■ *Web:* armitageinconline.com						
Stanley R Hinckley CPA Inc 9292 Cincinnati-Columbus Rd	Cincinnati	OH	45241	513-777-4505		2
Stanley Ranch Museum 12174 Euclid St PO Box 4297	Garden Grove	CA	92842	714-530-8871		520
Web: www.ci.garden-grove.ca.us						
Stanley Security Solutions Inc 14670 Cumberland Rd	Noblesville	IN	46060	317-776-3500		693
Web: stanleycorrectionalservices.com						
Stanley Spring & Stamping Corp 5050 W Foster Ave	Chicago	IL	60630	773-777-2600		718
TF: 800-532-2252 ■ *Web:* www.stanleyspring.com						
Stanley Tools Inc 480 Myrtle St	New Britain	CT	06053	800-262-2161		758
TF Cust Svc: 800-262-2161 ■ *Web:* www.stanleytools.com						
Stanley Vidmar Storage Technologies 11 Grammes Rd	Allentown	PA	18103	800-523-9462	523-9934	286
TF: 800-523-9462 ■ *Web:* www.stanleyvidmar.com						
Stanley W Bowles Corp 3375 Joseph Martin Hwy PO Box 4706	Martinsville	VA	24115	276-956-3442	956-7038	264-3
Web: www.bowlesproperties.com						
Stanley's Tavern 2038 Foulk Rd	Wilmington	DE	19810	302-475-1887		671
Web: www.stanleystavern.com						
Stanley, Lande & Hunter A Professional Corp 301 Iowa Ave Ste 400	Muscatine	IA	52761	563-264-5000		428
Web: www.slhlaw.com						
Stanley-Laman Group Ltd 1235 Westlakes Dr Ste 295	Berwyn	PA	19312	610-993-9100		194
Web: www.stanleylaman.com						

Company	Address	City	State	ZIP	Phone	Fax	Class
Stanly Community College	141 College Dr	Albemarle	NC	28001	704-982-0121	982-0819	800
	TF: 877-275-4219 ■ *Web:* www.stanly.edu						
Stanly County	201 S Second St 1000 N First St	Albemarle	NC	28001	704-986-3600		338
	Web: www.co.stanly.nc.us						
Stanly County Chamber of Commerce	116 E N St	Albemarle	NC	28001	704-982-8116	983-5000	139
	Web: www.stanlychamber.org						
Stanly Fixtures Company Inc	11635 NC 138 Hwy PO Box 616	Norwood	NC	28128	704-474-3184	474-3011	286
	TF: 800-476-3184 ■ *Web:* www.stanlyfixtures.com						
Stanly Memorial Hospital	301 Yadkin St	Albemarle	NC	28001	704-984-4000	983-3562	374-3
	Web: www.stanly.org						
Stanmar Inc	321 Commonwealth Rd Ste 201	Wayland	MA	01778	508-310-9922		655
	Web: www.stanmar-inc.com						
Stann Financial LLC	4021 N Saint Peters Pkwy	St Peters	MO	63304	636-447-8770		217
	Web: www.stannfinancial.com						
Stanridge Color Corp	PO Box 1086	Social Circle	GA	30025	770-464-3362	464-2202	608
	Web: www.standridgecolor.com						
Stansberry & Assoc Investment Research LLC	1217 Saint Paul St	Baltimore	MD	21202	888-261-2693		401
	TF: 888-261-2693 ■ *Web:* www.stansberryresearch.com						
Stanstead College	450 Dufferin St	Stanstead	QC	J0B3E0	819-876-2223		622
	Web: www.stansteadcollege.com						
Stansteel Asphalt Plant Products	12700 Shelbyville Rd	Louisville	KY	40243	502-245-1977		641
	TF: 800-826-0223 ■ *Web:* www.stansteel.com						
Stant Corp	1620 Columbia Ave	Connersville	IN	47331	765-825-3121	825-2875	608
	TF: 800-822-3121 ■ *Web:* www.stant.com						
Stantec	3200 Bailey Ln Ste 200	Naples	FL	34105	239-649-4040		261
	Web: www.stantec.com						
Stantec Inc	400 E Vine St Ste 300	Lexington	KY	40507	859-233-2100		261
	NYSE: STN ■ *TF:* 866-782-6832 ■ *Web:* www.stantec.com						
Stantec Inc	10160-112 St	Edmonton	AB	T5K2L6	780-917-7000	917-7330	261
	NYSE: STN ■ *Web:* www.stantec.com						
Stantive Technologies Group Inc	61 Hyperion Ct Ste 8	Kingston	ON	K7K7K7	613-887-2647		177
	Web: www.stantive.com						
Stanton Carpet Corp	211 Robbins Ln	Syosset	NY	11791	516-822-5878		364
	TF: 888-809-2989 ■ *Web:* www.stantoncarpet.com						
Stanton Chamber of Commerce	PO Box 615 Ste H	Stanton	CA	79782	432-756-3386		139
	Web: www.stantonchamber.org						
Stanton Chase International	400 E Pratt St Ste 420	Baltimore	MD	21202	410-528-8400	528-8409	266
	Web: www.stantonchase.com						
Stanton County	PO Box 190	Johnson	KS	67855	620-492-2140	492-2688	338
	Web: stantoncountyks.com						
Stanton County	804 Ivy St PO Box 347	Stanton	NE	68779	402-439-2222	439-2200	338
	Web: www.co.stanton.ne.us						
Stanton County Public Power District	807 Douglas St	Stanton	NE	68779	402-439-2228		245
	TF: 877-439-2300 ■ *Web:* www.scppd.net						
Stanton Insurance Agency Inc	230 Second Ave Ste 105	Waltham	MA	02451	781-893-3200		390
	Web: stantonins.com						
Stanton Magnetics Inc	772 S Military Trl	Deerfield Beach	FL	33442	954-949-9600		658
	TF: 800-348-7567 ■ *Web:* www.stantondj.com						
Stanton Public Relations & Marketing	880 Third Ave	New York	NY	10022	212-366-5300		636
	Web: www.stantonprm.com						
Stanton Territorial Health Authority (S)	550 Byrne Rd PO Box 10	Yellowknife	NT	X1A2N1	867-669-4111	669-4128	374-2
	Web: www.stha.hss.gov.nt.ca						
Stanton's Sheet Music	330 S Fourth St	Columbus	OH	43215	614-224-4257	224-5929	526
	TF: 800-426-8742 ■ *Web:* www.stantons.com						
Stanwich Advisors LLC	1 Dock St Ste 600	Stamford	CT	06902	203-406-1099	406-1098	401
	Web: www.stanwichadvisors.com						
Stanwood Camano News	9005 271st St NW	Stanwood	WA	98292	360-629-2155		532-3
	Web: www.scnews.com						
Stanyan Park Hotel	750 Stanyan St	San Francisco	CA	94117	415-751-1000	668-5454	379
	Web: www.stanyanpark.com						
Staplcotn Co-op Assn Inc	214 W Market St	Greenwood	MS	38930	662-453-6231	453-6274	275
	TF: 800-293-6231 ■ *Web:* www.staplcotn.com						
Staples Business Advantage	500 Staples Dr	Framingham	MA	01702	877-826-7755		534
	TF: 877-826-7755 ■ *Web:* www.staplesadvantage.com						
Staples Construction Company Inc	1501 Eastman Ave	Ventura	CA	93003	805-658-8786	658-8785	463
	Web: www.staplesconstruction.com						
Staples Ctr	1111 S Figueroa St	Los Angeles	CA	90015	213-742-7100		720
	Web: www.staplescenter.com						
Staples Promotional Products	7500 W 110th St	Overland Park	KS	66210	913-319-3100		9
	TF: 800-369-4669 ■ *Web:* www.staplespromotionalproducts.com						
Stapleton Technologies Inc	1350 W 12th St	Long Beach	CA	90813	562-437-0541	437-8632	145
	TF: 800-266-0541 ■ *Web:* www.stapletontech.com						
Stapleton-Spence Packing Co	1530 The Alameda Ste 320	San Jose	CA	95126	408-297-8815	297-0611	296-20
	TF: 800-297-8815 ■ *Web:* www.stapleton-spence.com						
Staplex Co	777 Fifth Ave	Brooklyn	NY	11232	718-768-3333	965-0750	111
	TF Cust Svc: 800-221-0822 ■ *Web:* www.staplex.com						
Star	6920 93rd Ave N	Minneapolis	MN	55445	763-561-4655	561-4688	393
	TF: 800-419-7827 ■ *Web:* engagestar.com						
Star 101.9	650 Iwilei Rd Ste 400	Honolulu	HI	96817	808-550-9200		645-73
	Web: star1019.iheart.com						
Star 92.9	265 Hegeman Ave	Colchester	VT	05446	802-655-0093	655-0478	645
	TF: 866-865-7827 ■ *Web:* www.star929.com						
STAR Academy	12279 Brady Dr	Custer	SD	57730	605-673-2521	673-5489	412
	TF: 800-265-9684 ■ *Web:* www.doc.sd.gov						
Star Asia International Inc	208 Church St	Decatur	GA	30030	404-761-6900		311
	Web: www.star-asia.com						
Star Aviation Inc	2150 Michigan Ave Brookley Complex	Mobile	AL	36615	251-650-0600		22
	Web: www.staraviation.com						
Star Bank	201 Second Ave NW PO Box 188	Bertha	MN	56437	218-924-4055	924-2265	70
	Web: www.starbank.net						
Star Beacon	PO Box 2100	Ashtabula	OH	44005	440-998-2323	998-7938	532-2
	TF: 800-554-6768 ■ *Web:* www.starbeacon.com						
Star Bldg Systems	8600 S I-35	Oklahoma City	OK	73149	800-879-7827	636-2419*	105
	**Fax Area Code:* 405 ■ *TF:* 800-879-7827 ■ *Web:* www.starbuildings.com						
Star Career Academy	*Manhattan* 154 W 14th St	New York	NY	10011	212-675-6655		163
	Web: starcareer.edu						
Star Casualty Insurance Company Inc	PO Box 451037	Miami	FL	33134	877-782-7210		390
	TF: 877-782-7210 ■ *Web:* www.starcasualty.com						
Star Clippers Inc	760 NW 107th Ave	Miami	FL	33172	305-442-0550		220
	Web: www.starclippers.com						
Star CNC Machine Tool Corp	123 Powerhouse Rd	Roslyn Heights	NY	11577	516-484-0500	484-5820	385
	Web: www.starcnc.com						
Star Collaborative Llc	18120 46th Ave N	Plymouth	MN	55446	763-515-7838		463
	Web: www.starcollaborative.com						
Star Consultants Inc	1910 Bethel Rd	Columbus	OH	43235	614-538-8445		186
	Web: starconsultants.org						
Star Contractors Supply Inc	9999 Virginia Ave	Chicago Ridge	IL	60415	708-229-9300		234
	Web: www.starcontractorssupply.com						
Star Cutter Co	23461 Industrial Pk Dr	Farmington	MI	48335	248-474-8200	474-9518	493
	TF: 877-635-3488 ■ *Web:* www.starcutter.com						
Star Democrat	29088 Airpark Dr PO Box 600	Easton	MD	21601	410-822-1500	770-4019	532-2
	TF: 888-634-4002 ■ *Web:* www.stardem.com						
Star Die Molding Inc	2741 Katherine Way	Elk Grove Village	IL	60007	847-766-7952		608
	Web: www.stardie.com						
Star Displays Inc	38w636 US Hwy 20	Elgin	IL	60124	847-695-2040		393
	TF: 800-648-8479 ■ *Web:* www.starincorporated.com						
Star Distributors Inc	460 Frontage Rd	West Haven	CT	06516	203-932-3636	932-5977	81-1
	TF: 877-922-3501 ■ *Web:* www.stardistributors.com						
Star Dynamics Corp	100 Outwater Ln	Garfield	NJ	07026	973-340-3883	340-1530	735
	Web: www.stardynamic.com						
Star Extruded Shapes Inc	7055 Herbert Rd	Canfield	OH	44406	330-533-9863		361
	Web: www.starext.com						
STAR Financial Group Inc	PO Box 11409	Fort Wayne	IN	46858	888-395-2447		70
	OTC: SFIGA ■ *TF:* 888-395-2447 ■ *Web:* www.starfinancial.com						
Star Fine Foods	2680 W Shaw Ln	Fresno	CA	93711	559-498-2900		296-30
	TF: 800-694-4872 ■ *Web:* www.starfinefoods.com						
Star Fleet Inc	915 S Main St	Middlebury	IN	46540	888-281-8727		780
	TF: 877-805-9547 ■ *Web:* www.starfleettrucking.com						
Star Forge Inc	1801 S Ihm Blvd	Freeport	IL	61032	815-235-7750	235-4813	273
	Web: www.starmfg.com						
Star Furniture Company Inc	16666 Barker Springs Rd	Houston	TX	77084	281-492-6661		321
	TF: 800-364-6661 ■ *Web:* www.starfurniture.com						
Star Gas Partners LP	2187 Atlantic St	Stamford	CT	06902	203-328-7310	328-7470	316
	NYSE: SGU ■ *TF:* 800-960-7546 ■ *Web:* www.Star-Gas.com						
Star Gold Cleaners Inc	200 Wilson St	Brewer	ME	04412	207-989-5170		426
	Web: www.goldstarcleaners.com						
Star Insurance Co	26255 American Dr	Southfield	MI	48034	248-358-4020	358-1614	391-4
	TF: 800-482-2726						
Star Island Corp, The	30 Middle St	Portsmouth	NH	03801	603-430-6272		239
	TF: 800-441-4620 ■ *Web:* starisland.org						
Star Island Resort	5000 Ave of the Stars	Kissimmee	FL	34746	407-997-8000		379
	TF: 800 513 2820 ■ *Web:* www.star island.com						
Star Leasing Co	4080 Business Pk Dr	Columbus	OH	43204	614-278-9999	340-3137	778
	TF: 888-771-1004 ■ *Web:* www.starleasing.com						
Star Line Trucking Corp	18480 W Lincoln Ave	New Berlin	WI	53146	262-786-8280	786-0071	449
	Web: www.starlinetrucking.com						
Star Lumber & Supply	325 S W St	Wichita	KS	67213	316-942-2221		364
	TF: 800-797-9556 ■ *Web:* www.starlumber.com						
Star Manufacturing International	10 Sunnen Dr	Maplewood	MO	63143	314-781-2777		298
	Web: www.star-mfg.com						
Star Market Inc	702 Pratt Ave NW	Huntsville	AL	35801	256-534-4509		297-8
	Web: www.huntsvillestarmarket.com						
Star Marketing & Media Inc	11991 Presilla Rd	Santa Rosa Valley	CA	93012	805-552-9900		7
	Web: www.starmarketingmedia.com						
Star Micronics America Inc	1150 King George's Post Rd	Edison	NJ	08837	732-623-5500	623-5590*	173-6
	**Fax:* Sales ■ *TF:* 800-782-7636 ■ *Web:* www.starmicronics.com						
Star Milling Co	24067 Water St	Perris	CA	92570	951-657-3143	657-3114	447
	TF: 800-733-6455 ■ *Web:* www.starmilling.com						
Star Moulding & Trim Co	6606 W 74th St	Chicago	IL	60638	708-458-1040		499
	Web: www.starmoulding.com						
Star Multi Care Services Inc	115 Broad Hollow Rd Ste 275	Melville	NY	11747	631-424-7827	427-5466	363
	TF: 877-920-0600 ■ *Web:* www.starmulticare.com						
Star Nail Products Inc	29120 Ave Paine	Valencia	CA	91355	661-257-7827	257-5856	214
	TF: 800-762-6245 ■ *Web:* www.starnail.com						

	Phone	Fax	Class
Star News 296 Third Ave . . . Chula Vista CA 91910 *Web:* www.thestarnews.com	619-427-3000	426-6346	637-8
Star of India 1492 N Harbor Dr . . . San Diego CA 92101 *Web:* lrstarofindia.com	501-227-9900		671
Star of India 2900 W Anderson Ln Ste 12D . . . Austin TX 78757 *Web:* www.starofindiaaustin.com	512-452-8199		671
Star of the West Milling Co 121 E Tuscola St . . . Frankenmuth MI 48734 *Web:* www.starofthewest.com	989-652-9971	652-6358	10-4
Star One Federal Credit Union PO Box 3643 . . . Sunnyvale CA 94088 *TF:* 866-543-5202 ■ *Web:* www.starone.org	408-543-5202	543-5203	219
Star Pipe LLC 4018 Westhollow Pkwy . . . Houston TX 77082 *TF:* 800-999-3009 ■ *Web:* www.starpipeproducts.com	281-558-3000		595
Star Precision LLC 7300 Miller Dr . . . Longmont CO 80504 *Web:* www.starprecision.com	303-926-0559		697
Star Rentals Inc 1919 Fourth Ave S . . . Seattle WA 98134 *TF:* 800-825-7880 ■ *Web:* www.starrentals.com	206-622-7880		264-3
Star Sales & Distributing Corp 29 Commerce Way . . . Woburn MA 01801 *TF:* 800-222-8118 ■ *Web:* www.starsales.com	781-933-8830	933-2145	191-2
Star Sales Company Inc 1803 N Central St . . . Knoxville TN 37917 *TF:* 800-222-8118 ■ *Web:* www.starsalescompany.com	865-524-0771	524-4889	328
Star Scientific Inc 4470 Cox Rd Ste 110 . . . Glen Allen VA 23060 *NASDAQ:* RCPI	804-527-1970		756
Star Services 4663 Halls Mill Rd . . . Mobile AL 36693 *TF:* 800-661-9050 ■ *Web:* www.star-service.com	251-661-4050		610
Star Shuttle & Charter 1343 Hallmark Dr . . . San Antonio TX 78216 *Web:* www.starshuttle.com	210-341-6000		108
Star Signs LLC 801 E Ninth St . . . Lawrence KS 66044 *Web:* www.starsignsllc.com	785-842-4892		187
Star Stainless Screw Co 30 W End Rd . . . Totowa NJ 07512	973-256-2300		351
Star Su Company LLC 5200 Prairie Stone Pkwy Ste 100 . . . Hoffman Estates IL 60192 *Web:* www.star-su.com	847-649-1450		190
Star Tech Glass Inc 1835 N Major Ave . . . Chicago IL 60639 *Web:* startechglass.com	773-745-0800		361
Star Tex Distributors Inc 12705 S Kirkwood Ste 218 . . . Stafford TX 77477 *Web:* www.startexoil.com	281-277-0077		580
Star Transportation Inc PO Box 100925 . . . Nashville TN 37224 *TF Cust Svc:* 800-333-3060 ■ *Web:* www.startransportation.com	615-256-4336		780
Star Travel Services Inc 1025 Acuff Rd . . . Bloomington IN 47404 *TF:* 800-542-1687 ■ *Web:* www.startravelservices.com	812-336-6811		771
Star Trax Inc 1200 Woodwards Heights . . . Ferndal MI 48220 *Web:* startrax.com	248-263-6300		196
Star Tribune 425 Portland Ave . . . Minneapolis MN 55488 *TF:* 800-827-8742 ■ *Web:* www.startribune.com	612-673-4000	673-4359	532-2
Star Truck Rentals Inc 3940 Eastern Ave SE . . . Grand Rapids MI 49508 *TF:* 800-748-0468 ■ *Web:* startruckrentals.com	616-243-7033	243-7498	778
Star West Satellite Inc 580 Prong Horn Trl . . . Bozeman MT 59718	406-522-8402		681
Star, The 404 E Martintown Rd Ste 2 . . . North Augusta SC 29841 *TF:* 888-397-3742 ■ *Web:* www.northaugustastar.com	803-279-2793	278-4070	532-4
Starboard Advertising Group 111 Center St . . . Saint Simons Island GA 31522 *TF:* 844-782-7262 ■ *Web:* starboardadgroup.com	912-638-8885		7
Starboard Cruise Services Inc 8400 NW 36th St . . . Miami FL 33166 *TF:* 800-540-4785 ■ *Web:* www.starboardcruise.com	786-845-7300	845-1112	241
Starboard Resources Inc 300 E Sonterra Blvd Ste 1220 . . . San Antonio TX 78258 *TF:* 800-732-0330 ■ *Web:* www.starboardresources.com	210-999-5400		536
Starboard Restaurant 2009 Hwy 1 . . . Dewey Beach DE 19971 *TF:* 800-436-6591 ■ *Web:* www.thestarboard.com	302-227-4600		671
Starborn Industries Inc 45 Mayfield Ave . . . Edison NJ 08837 *TF:* 800-596-7747 ■ *Web:* www.starbornindustries.com	800-596-7747		350
Starbridge Media Group Inc 6723 Whittier Ave Ste 307 . . . Mclean VA 22101	703-760-0051		194
Starbucks Coffee Co 2401 Utah Ave S . . . Seattle WA 98134 *TF:* 800-782-7282 ■ *Web:* www.starbucks.com	206-447-1575	318-3432	159
Starbucks Corp 187 Monroe Ave NW . . . Grand Rapids MI 49503 *TF:* 800-242-9790 ■ *Web:* starbucks.com	616-774-2000		671
Starcare Systems Inc 107 S West St Ste 108 . . . Alexandria VA 22314	703-836-0331		180
Starchtech Inc 720 Florida Ave . . . Minneapolis MN 55426 *Web:* www.starchtech.com	763-545-5400		601
Starco Impex 2710 S 11th St . . . Beaumont TX 77701 **Fax Area Code:* 888 ■ *TF:* 866-740-9601 ■ *Web:* www.starcoimpex.com	866-740-9601	842-5650*	345
Stardock Systems Inc 15090 N Beck Rd Ste 300 . . . Plymouth MI 48170 *TF:* 888-782-7362 ■ *Web:* www.stardock.com	734-927-0677	927-0678	174
Starfish Junction Productions Llc 226 N Fehr Way . . . Bay Shore NY 11706 *TF:* 800-830-3976 ■ *Web:* www.starfishjunction.com	631-940-7290		366
Starflex Corp 204 Turner Rd . . . Jonesboro GA 30236	770-471-2111		296
Stargate Digital 1001 El Centro St . . . South Pasadena CA 91030 *Web:* www.stargatestudios.net	626-403-8403		530
Star-Gazette 310 E Church St PO Box 285 . . . Elmira NY 14902 *TF:* 800-836-8970 ■ *Web:* www.stargazette.com	607-734-5151		532-2
Star-Glo Industries LLC 2 Carlton Ave . . . East Rutherford NJ 07073 *Web:* www.starglo.com	201-939-6162	939-4054	676
StarGreetz Inc 2038 Armacost Ave 2nd Fl . . . Los Angeles CA 90025	310-806-6450		366
Stark & Knoll Company LPA 3475 Ridgewood Rd . . . Akron OH 44333 *TF:* 800-393-2324 ■ *Web:* www.stark-knoll.com	330-376-3300		428
Stark & Stark 993 Lenox Dr Bldg 2 . . . Lawrenceville NJ 08648 *TF:* 800-535-3425 ■ *Web:* www.stark-stark.com	609-896-9060	896-0629	428
Stark Aerospace Inc 319 Charleigh D Ford Jr Dr . . . Columbus MS 39701 *Web:* www.starkaerospace.com	662-798-4075		529
Stark County 225 Fourth St NE . . . Canton OH 44702 *Web:* starkcountyohio.gov	330-451-7432	451-7190	338
Stark County PO Box 130 . . . Dickinson ND 58602 **Fax:* Acctg ■ *Web:* www.starkcountynd.gov	701-456-7630	456-7634*	338
Stark County 130 W Main PO Box 426 . . . Toulon IL 61483 *Web:* www.starkcountyillinois.com/Circuit_Clerk.html	309-286-5941	286-4039	338
Stark County District Library 715 Market Ave N . . . Canton OH 44702 *Web:* www.starklibrary.org	330-452-0665	452-0403	434-3
Stark Manufacturing Inc 310 Pennington Dr . . . Paris AR 72855 *Web:* www.starkmfg.com	479-963-3046		595
Stark Services 12444 Victory Blvd 3rd Fl . . . North Hollywood CA 91606 *Web:* www.starkservices.com	818-985-2003		225
Stark State College of Technology 6200 Frank Ave NW . . . North Canton OH 44720 *TF:* 800-797-8275 ■ *Web:* www.starkstate.edu	330-494-6170	497-6313	800
Starke County 53 E Washington St County Courthouse . . . Knox IN 46534 *Web:* co.starke.in.us	574-772-9128	772-9169	338
Starker Forests Inc 7240 SW Philomath Blvd . . . Corvallis OR 97333 *Web:* www.starkerforests.com	541-929-2477	929-2178	752
Starkey International Institute for Household Management 1350 Logan St . . . Denver CO 80203 *TF:* 800-888-4904 ■ *Web:* www.starkeyintl.com	303-832-5510		149
Starkey Laboratories Inc 6700 Washington Ave S . . . Eden Prairie MN 55344 *TF:* 800-328-8602 ■ *Web:* www.starkey.com	952-941-6401		477
Starkey Labs-Canada Co 7310 Rapistan Ct . . . Mississauga ON L5N6L8 *Web:* www.starkeycanada.ca	905-542-7555		250
Starkville Public Library 326 University Dr . . . Starkville MS 39759 *TF:* 800-222-8000 ■ *Web:* www.starkville.lib.ms.us	662-323-2766	323-9140	434-3
Starkweather & Shepley Inc 60 Catamore Blvd . . . East Providence RI 02914 *TF:* 800-854-4625 ■ *Web:* www.starshep.com/wp	401-435-3600	438-0150	390
Star-Ledger, The 1 Star Ledger Plaza . . . Newark NJ 07102 *TF:* 800-501-2100 ■ *Web:* www.nj.com	973-877-4141	392-5845	532-2
Starlight Theatre 4600 Starlight Rd . . . Kansas City MO 64132 *TF:* 800-776-1730 ■ *Web:* www.kcstarlight.com	816-363-7827	361-6398	572
Starline Inc 1300 W Henry St . . . Sedalia MO 65301 *TF:* 800-280-6660 ■ *Web:* starlinebrass.com	660-827-6640		711
Starline Manufacturing Company Inc 6060 W Douglas Ave . . . Milwaukee WI 53218	414-358-4060		609
Starline Printing Inc 7111 Pan American W Svc NE . . . Albuquerque NM 87109 *TF:* 800-873-7827 ■ *Web:* www.starlineprinting.com	505-345-8900		687
Starlite Limousines LLC PO Box 13542 . . . Scottsdale AZ 85267 **Fax Area Code:* 617 ■ *TF:* 800-875-4104 ■ *Web:* www.starlitelimos.com	480-422-3619	671-0522*	441
Starmark Cabinetry 600 E 48th St N . . . Sioux Falls SD 57104 *TF:* 800-755-7789 ■ *Web:* www.starmarkcabinetry.com	800-594-9444		115
Starmark International Inc 210 S Andrews Ave . . . Fort Lauderdale FL 33301 *TF:* 888-280-9630 ■ *Web:* www.starmark.com	954-874-9000	874-9010	195
Starnet Data Design Inc 2659 Townsgate Rd Ste 227 . . . Westlake Village CA 91361 *TF:* 800-779-0587 ■ *Web:* www.starnetdata.com	805-371-0585		196
Star-News Newspapers 1003 S 17th St PO Box 840 . . . Wilmington NC 28401 *Web:* www.starnewsonline.com	910-343-2000	343-2210	637-8
Starplex Scientific Inc 50 A Steinway Blvd . . . Etobicoke ON M9W6Y3 *TF:* 800-665-0954 ■ *Web:* www.starplexscientific.com	416-674-7474		476
Starpoint Solutions 22 Cortlandt St Ste 14 . . . New York NY 10007 *Web:* www.starpoint.com	212-962-1550	962-7175	180
StarQuest Software Inc 1288 Ninth St . . . Berkeley CA 94710 *TF:* 800-763-0050 ■ *Web:* starquest.com	510-528-2900		387
Starr & Assoc 4245 N Central Expy Ste 350 . . . Dallas TX 75205	214-219-8440		428
Starr Bus Charter & Tours 2531 E State St . . . Trenton NJ 08619 *TF:* 800-782-7703 ■ *Web:* www.starrtours.com	609-587-0626		107
Starr Commonwealth 13725 Starr Commonwealth Rd . . . Albion MI 49224 *TF:* 800-837-5591 ■ *Web:* www.starr.org	517-629-5591	630-2400	48-15
Starr Electric Company Inc 6 Battleground Ct . . . Greensboro NC 27408 *Web:* www.starrelectric.net	336-275-0241	273-0734	189-4
Starr Foundation 399 Pk Ave 9th Fl . . . New York NY 10022 *Web:* www.starrfoundation.org	212-909-3600		305
Starr Group, The 5005 W Loomis Rd . . . Greenfield WI 53220 *Web:* starrgroup.com	414-421-3800		390
Starr King School for the Ministry 2441 LeConte Ave . . . Berkeley CA 94709 *Web:* www.sksm.edu	510-845-6232	845-6273	167-3
STARR Life Sciences Corp 333 Allegheny Ave Ste 300 . . . Oakmont PA 15139 *TF:* 866-978-2779 ■ *Web:* www.starrlifesciences.com	866-978-2779		419
Starr Litigation Services Inc 1201 Grand Ave . . . West Des Moines IA 50265	515-224-1616		445
Starr Manufacturing Inc 4175 Warren-Sharon Rd . . . Vienna OH 44473 *Web:* www.starrmfg.com	330-394-9891		480
Starr Security Services 601 W 51st St . . . New York NY 10019 *Web:* starrsecurityservices.com	212-767-1110		693

Listing	City	State	ZIP	Phone	Fax	Class
Starrco Company Inc						
11700 Fairgrove Industrial Blvd	Maryland Heights	MO	63043	314-567-5533		106
Web: www.starrco.com						
Star-Republican 47 S S St	Wilmington	OH	45177	937-382-7796		532-4
Starrett Tru-Stone Technologies Div						
1101 Prosper Dr PO Box 430	Waite Park	MN	56387	320-251-7171	259-5073	724
TF: 800-959-0517 ■ *Web:* www.starrett.com						
Starrett Webber Gage Div						
24500 Detroit Rd	Cleveland	OH	44145	440-835-0001	892-9555	493
TF: 800-255-3924 ■ *Web:* www.starrett-webber.com						
STARS (Shock Trauma Air Rescue Society)						
1441 Aviation Pk NE	Calgary	AB	T2E8M7	403-295-1811	275-4891	30
Web: www.stars.ca						
Star-Seal 6596 New Peachtree Rd	Atlanta	GA	30340	770-455-6551		580
TF: 800-779-6066 ■ *Web:* www.herculessealcoat.com						
Starshak Winzenburg & Co						
55 W Monroe St Ste 2530	Chicago	IL	60603	312-444-9367	444-9519	690
Web: www.swandco.com						
Starshot Ventures Inc						
3555 Lakeshore Blvd W	Toronto	ON	M8W1P4	416-503-8362		5
TF: 800-461-0634 ■ *Web:* www.starshot.com						
Starside Security & Investigation Inc						
1930 S Brea Canyon Rd Ste 220	Diamond Bar	CA	91765	909-396-9999		400
TF: 888-478-2774 ■ *Web:* www.starside.com						
Starsound Audio Inc 2679 Oddie Blvd	Reno	NV	89512	775-331-1010		35
Web: www.starsound.com						
Star-Spangled Banner Flag House, The						
844 E Pratt St	Baltimore	MD	21202	410-837-1793		520
Web: www.flaghouse.org						
Startec Global Communications Corp						
11300 Rockville Pike Ste 900	Rockville	MD	20852	301-610-4300	329-2882*	736
**Fax Area Code: 877* ■ *TF:* 800-827-3374 ■ *Web:* www.startec.com						
Startech Computing Inc						
1755 Old W Main St	Red Wing	MN	55066	651-385-0607		180
TF: 888-385-0607 ■ *Web:* startech-comp.com						
Star-Tech Inc PO Box 672932	Marietta	GA	30006	678-905-1171		387
Web: www.star-tech.net						
STARTEL Corp 16 Goodyear	Irvine	CA	92618	949-863-8700		396
Starthis Inc						
1460 W Dundee Rd	Arlington Heights	IL	60004	847-255-9330		525
Web: www.starthis.com						
Star-Tribune 170 Star Ln	Casper	WY	82604	307-266-0500	266-0568	532-2
TF: 866-981-6397 ■ *Web:* www.trib.com						
StartSampling Inc						
195 E Elk Trail	Carol Stream	IL	60188	630-868-2000		636
Web: www.startsampling.com						
StartUpHire LLC 415 Church St Ste 203	Vienna	VA	22180	703-865-6350		260
Web: www.startuphire.com						
StartWire 10 Water St Ste 150	Lebanon	NH	03766	800-572-9470		260
TF: 800-572-9470 ■ *Web:* www.startwire.com/_						
Starvaggi Industries Inc						
401 Pennsylvania Ave	Weirton	WV	26062	304-748-1400	797-5208	182
Web: www.starvaggi.com						
Starvation Creek State Park						
Historic Columbia River Hwy State Trail	Cascade Locks	OR	97014	503-695-2261		565
Web: www.oregonstateparks.org						
Starvation State Park						
24220 W 7655 S State Park Rd	Duchesne	UT	84021	435-738-2326		565
Web: www.stateparks.utah.gov						
Starve Hollow State Recreation Area						
4345 S County Rd 275 W	Vallonia	IN	47281	812-358-3464		565
Web: www.in.gov						
Starved Rock State Park PO Box 509	Utica	IL	61373	815-667-4726		565
Web: www.starvedrockstatepark.org						
Starvin' Artist Supplies						
802 S Oak Pk	Oak Park	IL	60304	708-358-3600		45
TF: 800-427-8478 ■ *Web:* www.starvinartistsupply.com						
Starving Students Moving & Storage Co						
1850 Sawtelle Blvd Ste 300	Los Angeles	CA	90025	888-931-6683		519
TF: 888-931-6683 ■ *Web:* www.ssmovers.com						
Starwest Botanicals Inc						
11253 Trade Ctr Dr	Rancho Cordova	CA	95742	916-638-8100	638-8293	479
TF General: 888-273-4372 ■ *Web:* www.starwestherb.com						
Starwood Hotels 50 Third St	San Francisco	CA	94103	415-974-6400	543-8268	379
Web: www.starwoodhotels.com						
Starwood Hotels & Resorts Worldwide Inc						
123 S Illinois St	Indianapolis	IN	46225	317-737-1600		671
TF: 800-543-4300 ■ *Web:* lemeridienindianapolis.com//go/restaurant.html						
Starwood Hotels & Resorts Worldwide Inc						
1111 Westchester Ave	White Plains	NY	10604	914-640-8100	640-8310	379
NYSE: HOT ■ *TF Cust Svc:* 888-625-5144 ■ *Web:* www.starwoodhotels.com						
Saint Regis Hotels & Resorts						
1111 Westchester Ave	White Plains	NY	10604	914-640-8100	640-8310	379
TF: 888-625-4988 ■ *Web:* www.starwoodhotels.com						
Westin Hotels & Resorts						
1111 Westchester Ave	White Plains	NY	10604	914-640-8100	640-8310	379
TF: 888-625-5144 ■ *Web:* www.starwoodhotels.com						
Starwood Hotels Preferred Guest Program						
111 Westchester Ave	White Plains	NY	10604	512-834-2426		378
TF: 888-625-4988 ■ *Web:* www.starwoodhotels.com						
Starz Encore Group LLC						
8900 Liberty Cir	Englewood	CO	80112	720-852-7700		740
Web: www.starz.com						
Starz LLC 8900 Liberty Cir	Englewood	CO	80112	720-852-7700		740
Web: www.starz.com						
Stason Pharmaceuticals Inc 11 Morgan	Irvine	CA	92618	949-380-4327		231
Web: www.stason.com						
STAT Assn Marketing & Management Inc						
11240 Waples Mill Rd Ste 200	Fairfax	VA	22030	703-934-0160	359-7562	47
Web: www.statmarketing.com						
Stat Pharmaceuticals Inc						
9545 Pathway St	Santee	CA	92071	619-956-4200		231
StataCorp LP 4905 Lakeway Dr	College Station	TX	77845	979-696-4600	696-4601	387
Web: www.stata.com						
Statco 8870 Business Park Dr	Austin	TX	78759	512-795-5000		225
Web: www.statco.com						

Listing	City	State	ZIP	Phone	Fax	Class
State & Federal Communications Inc						
80 S Summit St Ste 100	Akron	OH	44308	330-761-9960		781
TF: 888-452-9669 ■ *Web:* stateandfed.com						
State Arboretum of Virginia						
400 Blandy Farm Ln	Boyce	VA	22620	540-837-1758	837-1523	97
Web: www.virginia.edu						
State Auto Property & Casualty Insurance Co						
518 E Broad St	Columbus	OH	43215	614-464-5000		391-4
TF: 800-444-9950 ■ *Web:* www.stateauto.com						
State Ballet of Rhode Island, The						
52 Sherman Ave	Lincoln	RI	02865	401-334-2560	334-0412	573-1
Web: www.stateballet.com						
State Bank 175 N Leroy St	Fenton	MI	48430	810-629-2263		70
TF: 800-535-0517 ■ *Web:* www.thestatebank.com						
State Bank & Trust 3100 13th Ave S	Fargo	ND	58103	701-298-1500		70
Web: www.bellbanks.com						
State Bank & Trust Co 1025 Sixth St	Nevada	IA	50201	515-382-2191	382-3826	70
Web: www.banksbt.com						
State Bank of Cross Plains						
1205 Main St PO Box 218	Cross Plains	WI	53528	608-798-3961		70
Web: www.crossplainsbank.com						
State Bank of Toledo						
100 E High St PO Box 309	Toledo	IA	52342	641-484-2980		70
Web: www.banktoledo.com						
State Bank of Waterloo PO Box 148	Waterloo	IL	62298	618-939-7194	939-4140	70
TF: 800-383-8000 ■ *Web:* www.sbw.bank						
State Bar Assn of North Dakota						
504 N Washington St PO Box 2136	Bismarck	ND	58502	701-255-1404	224-1621	72
TF: 800-472-2685 ■ *Web:* www.sband.org						
State Bar of Arizona						
4201 N 24th St Ste 200	Phoenix	AZ	85016	602-252-4804	271-4930	72
TF: 866-482-9227 ■ *Web:* www.azbar.org						
State Bar of California						
180 Howard St	San Francisco	CA	94105	415-538-2000	538-2304	72
Web: www.calbar.ca.gov						
State Bar of Georgia						
104 Marietta St NW Ste 100	Atlanta	GA	30303	404-527-8700	527-8717	72
TF: 800-334-6865 ■ *Web:* www.gabar.org						
State Bar of Michigan 306 Townsend St	Lansing	MI	48933	517-346-6300	482-6248	72
TF: 800-968-1442 ■ *Web:* www.michbar.org						
State Bar of Montana PO Box 577	Helena	MT	59624	406-442-7660	442-7763	72
Web: www.montanabar.org						
State Bar of Nevada						
600 E Charleston Blvd	Las Vegas	NV	89104	702-382-2200	385-2878	72
TF: 800-254-2797 ■ *Web:* www.nvbar.org						
State Bar of New Mexico						
5121 Masthead St NE PO Box 92860	Albuquerque	NM	87109	505-797-6000	828-3765	72
TF: 800-876-6227 ■ *Web:* www.nmbar.org						
State Bar of South Dakota						
222 E Capitol Ave Ste 3	Pierre	SD	57501	605-224-7554	224-0282	72
Web: statebarofsouthdakota.com						
State Bar of Texas 1414 Colorado St	Austin	TX	78701	512-427-1463	427-4100	72
TF: 800-204-2222 ■ *Web:* www.texasbar.com						
State Bar of Wisconsin						
5302 Eastpark Blvd	Madison	WI	53718	608-257-3838		72
Web: www.wisbar.org						
State Botanical Garden of Georgia						
2450 S Milledge Ave	Athens	GA	30605	706-542-1244	542-3091	97
TF: 800-768-3401 ■ *Web:* botgarden.uga.edu						
State Center Community College District						
1525 e weldon ave	Fresno	CA	93704	559-226-0720		162
Web: www.scccd.edu						
State College of Florida						
5840 26th St W	Bradenton	FL	34207	941-752-5000	727-6380	162
Web: www.scf.edu						
State Compensation Insurance Fund						
PO Box 8192	Pleasanton	CA	94588	415-565-1234		391-4
TF: 866-721-3498 ■ *Web:* www.statefundca.com						
State Correctional Institution of Albion						
10745 Route 18	Albion	PA	16475	814-756-5778	756-9737	213
State Education Resource Ctr						
25 Industrial Park Rd	Middletown	CT	06457	860-632-1485		435
TF: 800-842-8678 ■ *Web:* ctserc.org						
State Electric Supply Company Inc						
2010 Second Ave	Huntington	WV	25703	304-523-7491	525-8917	246
TF Cust Svc: 800-624-3417 ■ *Web:* www.stateelectric.com						
State Employees Credit Union of Maryland Inc						
971 Corporate Blvd	Linthicum	MD	21090	410-487-7328		219
TF: 800-879-7328 ■ *Web:* www.secumd.org						
State Employees Federal Credit Union						
700 Patroon Creek Blvd Patroon Creek Corporate Ctr	Albany	NY	12206	518-452-8234		219
TF: 800-727-3328 ■ *Web:* www.sefcu.com						
State Employees' Credit Union (SECU)						
PO Box 29606	Raleigh	NC	27626	919-857-2150	857-2000	219
TF: 888-732-8562 ■ *Web:* www.ncsecu.org						
State Environment Daily						
1801 S Bell St	Arlington	VA	22202	703-341-5777		531-5
TF: 800-372-1033						
State Fair & Exposition						
1001 Beulah Ave	Pueblo	CO	81004	719-404-2018		720
TF: 800-876-4567 ■ *Web:* www.coloradostatefair.com						
State Fair Community College						
3201 W 16th St	Sedalia	MO	65301	660-530-5800		162
TF: 877-311-7322 ■ *Web:* www.sfccmo.edu						
State Farm Financial Services FSB						
PO Box 2316	Bloomington	IL	61702	877-734-2265		70
TF: 877-734-2265 ■ *Web:* www.statefarm.com/bank/bank.htm						
State Farm Fire & Casualty Co						
1 State Farm Plaza	Bloomington	IL	61710	800-782-8332		391-4
TF: 800-782-8332 ■ *Web:* statefarm.com						
State Farm Insurance						
333 First Commerce Dr	Aurora	ON	L4G8A4	877-659-1570		391-4
TF: 877-659-1570 ■ *Web:* www.statefarm.ca						
State Farm Mutual Automobile Insurance Co						
800 Metairie Rd Ste P	Metairie	LA	70005	504-832-4127		390
Web: www.statefarm.com						

	Phone	Fax	Class
State Farm Mutual Funds			
PO Box 219548 ... Kansas City MO 64121	800-447-4930		528
TF: 800-447-4930 ■ *Web:* www.statefarm.com/mutual/mutual.htm			
State Forest State Park 56750 Hwy 14 ... Walden CO 80480	970-723-8366	723-8325	565
TF: 866-265-6447 ■ *Web:* cpw.state.co.us			
State Historical Society of Colorado			
1560 Broadway Ste 400 ... Denver CO 80202	303-447-8679		520
Web: www.historycolorado.org			
State Historical Society of Iowa			
600 E Locust St ... Des Moines IA 50319	515-281-5111		520
Web: iowaculture.gov/history			
State Historical Society of Missouri, The			
1020 Lowry St ... Columbia MO 65201	573-882-1187	884-4950	520
TF: 800-747-6366 ■ *Web:* shsmo.org			
State House 1 State House Stn ... Augusta ME 04333	207-287-3531	287-6548	520
TF: 855-721-5203 ■ *Web:* www.maine.gov			
State Industrial Products			
3100 Hamilton Ave ... Cleveland OH 44114	216-861-7114		151
TF: 877-747-6986 ■ *Web:* www.stateindustrial.com			
State Information Bureau			
842 E Pk Ave ... Tallahassee FL 32301	850-561-3990		400
Web: www.sibflorida.com			
State Journal, The			
1216 Wilkinson Blvd P.O. Box 219 ... Springfield IL 62705	502-227-4556		532-2
State Journal-Register PO Box 219 ... Springfield IL 62705	217-788-1300	788-1551	532-2
TF: 800-397-6397 ■ *Web:* www.sj-r.com			
State Justice Institute (SJI)			
11951 Freedom Dr Ste 1020 ... Reston VA 20190	571-313-8843	313-1173	340-20
Web: www.sji.gov			
State Legislative Leaders Foundation			
1645 Falmouth Rd Bldg D ... Centerville MA 02632	508-771-3821		242
Web: sllf.org			
State Library 1500 Senate St ... Columbia SC 29201	803-734-4611		434-3
Web: www.statelibrary.sc.gov			
State Library of Ohio			
274 E First Ave Ste 100 ... Columbus OH 43201	614-644-7061	466-3584	434-5
TF: 800-686-1532 ■ *Web:* library.ohio.gov			
State Life Insurance Co			
1 American Sq PO Box 368 ... Indianapolis IN 46206	317-285-2300	285-2380	391-2
TF Cust Svc: 800-537-6442 ■ *Web:* www.oneamerica.com/home			
State Line 1222 Sunland Pk Dr ... El Paso TX 79922	915-581-3371		671
TF: 800-247-7427 ■ *Web:* www.countyline.com			
State Liquor Store			
15015 Main St Ste 117 ... Bellevue WA 98007	360-664-1600		443
TF: 800-917-0043 ■ *Web:* www.liq.wa.gov			
State Museum of Pennsylvania, The			
300 N St ... Harrisburg PA 17120	717-787-4980	783-4558	520
TF: 800-654-5984 ■ *Web:* www.statemuseumpa.org			
State Mutual Insurance Co			
210 E Second Ave ... Rome GA 30161	706-291-1054		390
Web: statemutualinsurance.com			
State Narrow Fabrics Inc			
2902 Borden Ave ... Long Island NY 11101	718-392-8787	392-9421	745-5
TF: 800-531-5441 ■ *Web:* www.statenarrow.com			
State National Bank & Trust Co			
122 Main St PO Box 130 ... Wayne NE 68787	402-375-1130		70
Web: www.state-national-bank.com			
State News 435 E Grand River Ave ... East Lansing MI 48823	517-432-3000		532-3
Web: statenews.com			
State of Hawaii World Trade Ctr			
250 S Hotel St PO Box 2359 ... Honolulu HI 96813	808-587-2750	586-2589	822
Web: hawaii.gov			
State of The Art Inc			
2470 Fox Hill Rd ... State College PA 16803	814-355-8004		203
Web: www.resistor.com			
State of the Heart Home Health & Hospice			
1350 N Broadway ... Greenville OH 45331	937-548-2999		371
TF: 800-417-7535 ■ *Web:* www.stateoftheheartcare.org			
State Pipe & Supply Inc			
9615 S Norwalk Blvd ... Santa Fe Springs CA 90670	562-695-5555	692-1054	492
TF: 800-733-6410 ■ *Web:* www.statepipe.com			
State Plaza Hotel 2117 E St NW ... Washington DC 20037	202-861-8200		379
TF: 800-424-2859 ■ *Web:* www.stateplaza.com			
State Port Pilot 114 E Moore St ... Southport NC 28461	910-457-4568		627
Web: stateportpilot.com			
State Science & Technology Institute			
5015 Pine Creek Dr ... Westerville OH 43081	614-901-1690		393
Web: www.ssti.org			
State Steel Supply Co 214 Court St ... Sioux City IA 51101	712-277-4000		492
Web: www.statesteel.com			
State Street Brats 603 State St ... Madison WI 53703	608-255-5544		671
Web: www.statestreetbrats.com			
State Street Corp 1 Lincoln St ... Boston MA 02111	617-786-3000	664-6316*	70
NYSE: STT ■ **Fax:* Mktg ■ *TF:* 800-892-4514 ■ *Web:* www.statestreet.com			
State Supply Co 597 Seventh St E ... Saint Paul MN 55130	651-774-5985		610
TF: 877-775-7705 ■ *Web:* www.statesupply.com			
State Teachers Retirement System of Ohio			
275 E Broad St ... Columbus OH 43215	888-227-7877		528
TF: 888-227-7877 ■ *Web:* www.strsoh.org			
State Theatre 15 Livingston Ave ... New Brunswick NJ 08901	732-247-7200	247-4005	572
TF: 800-432-9382 ■ *Web:* www.statetheatrenj.org			
State Theatre 1307 J St PO Box 1492 ... Modesto CA 95354	209-527-4697		572
TF: 800-475-0175 ■ *Web:* www.thestate.org			
State Tool & Manufacturing Co			
1650 E Empire Ave ... Benton Harbor MI 49022	269-927-3153	927-4230	815
Web: www.statetool.com			
State Training School			
3211 Edgington Ave ... Eldora IA 50627	641-858-5402	858-2416	412
TF: 800-362-2178 ■ *Web:* dhs.iowa.gov			
State Universities Retirement System of Illinois			
1901 Fox Dr ... Champaign IL 61820	217-378-8800		401
TF: 800-275-7877 ■ *Web:* www.surs.com			
State University of New York			
Brockport 350 New Campus Dr ... Brockport NY 14420	585-395-2751	395-5452	166
TF: 888-800-0029 ■ *Web:* www.brockport.edu			
Canton 34 Cornell Dr ... Canton NY 13617	315-386-7011	386-7929	162
TF: 800-388-7123 ■ *Web:* www.canton.edu			
College at Old Westbury, The			
223 Store Hill Rd Campus Ctr H-310			
PO Box 210 ... Old Westbury NY 11568	516-876-3073	876-3307*	166
**Fax:* Admissions ■ *Web:* www.oldwestbury.edu			
College at Oneonta Ravine Pkwy ... Oneonta NY 13820	607-436-3500	436-3074*	166
**Fax:* Admissions ■ *Web:* www.oneonta.edu			
College of Agriculture & Technology at Cobleskill			
Rt 7 ... Cobleskill NY 12043	518-255-5525	255-6769*	166
**Fax:* Admissions ■ *TF:* 800-295-8988 ■ *Web:* www.cobleskill.edu			
College of Environmental Science & Forestry			
1 Forestry Dr ... Syracuse NY 13210	315-470-6500	470-6933*	166
**Fax:* Admissions ■ *TF Admissions:* 800-777-7373 ■ *Web:* www.esf.edu			
College of Technology at Alfred			
10 Upper College Dr ... Alfred NY 14802	607-587-4215	587-4299*	162
**Fax:* Admissions ■ *TF:* 800-425-3733 ■ *Web:* www.alfredstate.edu			
Cortland PO Box 2000 ... Cortland NY 13045	607-753-2011		166
Web: www.cortland.edu			
Delhi 2 Main St ... Delhi NY 13753	607-746-4000	746-4104	162
TF: 800-963-3544 ■ *Web:* www.delhi.edu			
Empire State College			
1 Union Ave ... Saratoga Springs NY 12866	518-587-2100	587-9759*	166
**Fax:* Admissions ■ *TF:* 800-847-3000 ■ *Web:* www.esc.edu			
Geneseo 1 College Cir ... Geneseo NY 14454	585-245-5571	245-5550*	166
**Fax:* Admitting ■ *TF Admitting:* 866-245-5211 ■ *Web:* www.geneseo.edu			
Institute of Technology PO Box 3050 ... Utica NY 13504	315-792-7500	792-7837*	166
**Fax:* Admissions ■ *TF:* 866-278-6948 ■ *Web:* sunypoly.edu			
Maritime College			
6 Pennyfield Ave Fort Schuyler ... Bronx NY 10465	718-409-7200	409-7465	166
TF: 888-800-0029 ■ *Web:* www.sunymaritime.edu			
New Paltz 1 Hawk Dr ... New Paltz NY 12561	845-257-3212	257-3209*	166
**Fax:* Admissions ■ *TF:* 877-696-7411 ■ *Web:* www.newpaltz.edu			
Oswego 7060 SR 104 ... Oswego NY 13126	315-312-2500	312-3260*	166
**Fax:* Admissions ■ *Web:* www.oswego.edu			
Plattsburgh 101 Broad St ... Plattsburgh NY 12901	518-564-2040	564-2045*	166
**Fax:* Admissions ■ *TF Admissions:* 888-673-0012 ■ *Web:* www.plattsburgh.edu			
Potsdam 44 Pierrpont Ave ... Potsdam NY 13676	315-267-2180	267-2163*	166
**Fax:* Admissions ■ *TF Admissions:* 877-768-7326 ■ *Web:* www.potsdam.edu			
University at Buffalo 12 Capen Hall ... Buffalo NY 14260	716-645-2450	645-6411*	166
**Fax:* Admissions ■ *TF:* 888-822-3648 ■ *Web:* www.buffalo.edu			
State University of New York at Buffalo			
Health Sciences Library (HSL)			
303 Abbott Hall 3435 Main St ... Buffalo NY 14214	716-829-3900	829-2211	434-1
Web: library.buffalo.edu/hsl			
State University of New York College at Geneseo			
Milne Library 1 College Cir ... Geneseo NY 14454	585-245-5594	245-5769	434-6
Web: www.geneseo.edu			
State University of New York Downstate Medical Ctr			
450 Clarkson Ave ... Brooklyn NY 11203	718-270-1000	270-7592	167-2
Web: www.downstate.edu			
State University of New York Press (SUNY)			
22 Corporate Woods Blvd 3rd Fl ... Albany NY 12211	518-472-5000	472-5030	637-4
TF: 866-430-7869 ■ *Web:* www.sunypress.edu			
State University of New York Upstate Medical University			
766 Irving Ave ... Syracuse NY 13210	315-464-4570	464-8867	167-2
TF: 800-736-2171 ■ *Web:* www.upstate.edu			
State University of New York Upstate Medical University			
766 Irving Ave ... Syracuse NY 13210	315-464-7087	464-4519	434-1
Web: library.upstate.edu			
State University of New York Upstate Medical University Tissue Typing Laboratory			
750 E Adams St ... Syracuse NY 13210	315-464-4775		417
TF: 877-464-5540 ■ *Web:* www.upstate.edu			
State University of New York, The (SUNY)			
State University Plaza ... Albany NY 12246	518-320-1888		786
TF: 800-342-3811 ■ *Web:* www.suny.edu			
State University System of Florida			
325 W Gaines St Ste 1614 ... Tallahassee FL 32399	850-245-0466	245-9685	786
Web: www.flbog.edu			
State Volunteer Mutual Insurance Co			
101 W Pk Dr Ste 300 ... Brentwood TN 37027	615-377-1999	370-1343	391-5
TF: 800-342-2239 ■ *Web:* www.svmic.com			
State, The 1401 Shop Rd ... Columbia SC 29201	803-771-6161	771-8430	532-2
TF: 800-888-5353 ■ *Web:* www.thestate.com			
Statehouse Convention Ctr			
426 W Markham PO Box 3232 ... Little Rock AR 72203	501-376-4781		205
TF: 800-844-4781 ■ *Web:* littlerockmeetings.com/convention-center			
Statek Corp 512 N Main St ... Orange CA 92868	714-639-7810	997-1256	203
Web: www.statek.com			
Stately Oaks Plantation			
100 Carriage Ln ... Jonesboro GA 30236	770-473-0197	473-9855	50-3
Web: historicaljonesboro.org			
Statement Systems Inc			
1900 Diplomat Dr ... Farmers Branch TX 75234	214-210-0880		396
Web: www.statementsystems.com			
Staten Island Advance			
950 W FingerboaRd Rd ... Staten Island NY 10305	718-981-1234		532-2
TF: 800-675-8645 ■ *Web:* www.silive.com			
Staten Island Chamber of Commerce			
130 Bay St ... Staten Island NY 10301	718-727-1900	727-2295	139
TF: 800-772-1213 ■ *Web:* www.sichamber.com			
Staten Island Children's Museum			
1000 Richmond Terr at Snug Harbor ... Staten Island NY 10301	718-273-2060	273-2836	521
TF: 800-433-4149 ■ *Web:* sichildrensmuseum.org			
Staten Island Hotel			
1415 Richmond Ave ... Staten Island NY 10314	718-698-5000	737-7294	379
Web: esplanadesi.com			
Staten Island Institute of Arts & Sciences			
75 Stuyvesant Pl ... Staten Island NY 10301	718-727-1135	273-5683	520
Web: statenislandmuseum.org			
Staten Island Mall			
2655 Richmond Ave ... Staten Island NY 10314	718-761-6800		460
Web: www.statenislandmall.com/en.html			
Staten Island Zoo 614 Broadway ... Staten Island NY 10310	718-442-3101	981-8711	823
Web: www.statenislandzoo.org			
Stater Bros Markets Inc			
301 S Tippecanoe Ave ... San Bernardino CA 92408	909-733-5000		345
Web: www.staterbros.com			
Statera Inc 6501 E Belleview Ave ... Englewood CO 80111	720-346-0070		180
Web: statera.com			

	Phone	Fax	Class
States Industries LLC PO Box 41150 .... Eugene OR 97404 *TF:* 800-626-1981 ■ *Web:* www.statesind.com	541-688-7871		613
States Logistics Services Inc 5650 Dolly Ave .... Buena Park CA 90621 *Web:* www.stateslogistics.com	714-521-6520		803-1
States Recovery Systems Inc 2951 Surrise Blvd Ste 100 .... Rancho Cordova CA 95742 *TF:* 800-211-1435 ■ *Web:* www.statesrecovery.com	916-631-7085		160
Statesboro-Bulloch Chamber of Commerce 102 S Main St .... Statesboro GA 30458 *Web:* www.statesboro-chamber.org	912-764-6111		139
Statesman Journal 280 Church St NE .... Salem OR 97301 **Fax:* News Rm ■ *TF:* 800-874-7012 ■ *Web:* www.statesmanjournal.com	503-399-6611	399-6706*	532-2
Statesville Brick Co 391 BrickyaRd Rd .... Statesville NC 28677 *TF:* 800-522-4716 ■ *Web:* www.statesvillebrick.com	704-872-4123	872-4125	150
Statesville Flying Service 238 Airport Rd .... Statesville NC 28677 *Web:* statesvilleregion.com	704-873-1111		63
Stateville Correctional Ctr 16830 S Broadway St PO Box 112 .... Joliet IL 60434 *TF:* 800-526-0844 ■ *Web:* www.illinois.gov	815-727-3607	727-5511	213
Statewide Remodeling Inc 2450 Esters Blvd Ste 200 .... DFW Airport TX 75261 *TF:* 800-317-8283 ■ *Web:* www.statewideremodeling.com	214-677-9000		235
Static Control Components Inc 3010 Lee Ave PO Box 152 .... Sanford NC 27331 *TF:* 800-488-2426 ■ *Web:* www.scc-inc.com	919-774-3808	774-1287	174
Static Controls Corp 30460 S Wixom Rd .... Wixom MI 48393 *Web:* www.scccontrols.com	248-926-4400		203
Station Casinos Inc 1505 S Pavilion Ctr Dr .... Las Vegas NV 89135 *TF Resv:* 800-634-3101 ■ *Web:* www.sclv.com	702-495-3000		132
Station Resource Group (SRG) PO Box 1858 .... Clarksburg MD 20912 *Web:* www.srg.org	301-270-2617	270-2618	632
Station Square Restaurant 4250 Belmont Ave .... Youngstown OH 44505 *TF:* 800-589-9966 ■ *Web:* thestationsquare.com	330-759-8802		671
Station Theatre 223 N Broadway Ave .... Urbana IL 61801 *Web:* www.stationtheatre.com	217-384-4000		572
Stationers Inc 1945 Fifth Ave .... Huntington WV 25703 *TF:* 800-862-7200 ■ *Web:* www.stationers-wv.com	304-528-2780	528-2795	535
Statlistics Inc 69 Kenosia Ave .... Danbury CT 06810 *Web:* www.statlistics.com	203-778-8700		5
Statmon Technologies Corp 385, 736 N Western Ave Ste .... Lake Forest IL 60045 *Web:* www.statmon.com	847-604-5366		736
Statoil Marketing & Trading 120 Long Ridge Rd Ste 3E01 .... Stamford CT 06902 *Web:* www.statoil.com	203-978-6900		538
Staton Correctional Facility 2690 Marion Spillway Rd PO Box 56 .... Elmore AL 36025 *Web:* doc.state.al.us	334-567-2221		213
STATS ChipPAC Test Services Inc 46429 Landing Pkwy .... Fremont CA 94538 *Web:* www.statschippac.com	408-586-0600	586-0601	253
Statton Furniture Mfg Company Inc 504 E First St .... Hagerstown MD 21740 *Web:* www.statton.com	301-739-0360		319-1
Statue Of Liberty Liberty Island .... New York NY 10004 *Web:* www.nps.gov/stli	212-363-3200		564
Statue of Liberty-Ellis Island Foundation Inc, The 17 Battery Pl Ste 210 .... New York NY 10004 *Web:* libertyellisfoundation.org	212-561-4500	779-1990	48-23
Staub Metals Corp 7747 E Rosecrans Ave .... Paramount CA 90723 *Web:* www.staubmetals.com	562-602-2200	633-1456	492
Staubli Corp 201 Pkwy W Hillside Pk .... Duncan SC 29334 *TF:* 800-241-8560 ■ *Web:* www.staubli.com	864-433-1980		358
Stauder Technologies Inc 114 Mexico Ct .... St Peters MO 63376 *TF:* 800-341-2333 ■ *Web:* www.staudertech.com	636-498-6658		809
Stauffer Diesel Inc 34 Stauffer Ln .... Ephrata PA 17522 *TF:* 800-726-5300 ■ *Web:* www.staufferdiesel.com	717-738-2500		518
Stauffer Glove & Safety PO Box 45 .... Red Hill PA 18076 *Web:* my.stauffersafety.com	215-679-4446	679-5053	679
Staunton (Independent City) 113 E Beverley St .... Staunton VA 24401 *Web:* www.staunton.va.us	540-332-3874	332-3970	338
Staunton National Cemetery 901 Richmond Ave .... Staunton VA 24401 *TF:* 800-273-8255 ■ *Web:* www.cem.va.gov/cems/nchp/staunton.asp	540-825-0027	825-6684	136
Staunton River State Park 1170 Staunton Tr .... Scottsburg VA 24589 *Web:* www.dcr.virginia.gov/state-parks/staunton-river#general_information	434-572-4623		565
Staunton Star Times 108 W Main St .... Staunton IL 62088 *TF:* 800-878-3690 ■ *Web:* www.stauntonstartimes.com	618-635-2000		532-3
Stavis Seafoods Inc 212 Northern Ave Ste 305 .... Boston MA 02210 *TF:* 800-390-5103 ■ *Web:* www.stavis.com	617-482-6349		297-5
Stavola Contracting PO Box 482 .... Red Bank NJ 07701 *TF:* 800-359-1424 ■ *Web:* www.stavola.com	732-542-2328	389-6083	46
Stay Aspen Snowmass 425 Rio Grande Pl .... Aspen CO 81611 *TF:* 888-649-5982 ■ *Web:* www.stayaspensnowmass.com	970-925-9000		376
Staybridge Suites Hotel 6095 Emerald Pkwy .... Dublin OH 43016 *Web:* www.ihg.com/staybridge/hotels/us/en/reservation	614-734-9882		707
StayClassy Productions Inc 533 F St Ste 300 .... San Diego CA 92101 *Web:* www.classy.org	619-961-1892		305
StayinFront Inc 107 Little Falls Rd .... Fairfield NJ 07004 *Web:* stayinfront.com	973-461-4800		177
staySky Resort Management 7011 Grand National Dr Ste 104 .... Orlando FL 32819 *Web:* www.skyresortmanagement.com	407-992-0430		656
StayTop Systems Inc 1525 McCarthy Blvd Ste 1133 .... Milpitas CA 95035 *Web:* www.staytop.com	408-538-5990	987-9609	260
St-Boniface Hospital (SBGH) 409 Tache Ave .... Winnipeg MB R2H2A6 **Fax:* Hum Res ■ *Web:* www.saintboniface.ca	204-233-8563	231-0041*	374-2
STC (Society of Telecommunications Consultants) 13275 California 89 .... Old Station CA 96071 *TF:* 800-782-7670 ■ *Web:* sctcconsultants.org	530-335-7313		49-20
STC (Society for Technical Communication) 9401 Lee Hwy Ste 300 .... Fairfax VA 22031 *Web:* www.stc.org	703-522-4114	522-2075	49-14
STC Netcom Inc 11611 Industry Ave .... Fontana CA 92337 *Web:* www.stcnetcom.com	951-685-8181		179
STC Network Services Inc 4904 Oak Cir Dr N .... Mobile AL 36609	251-661-7130		180
STDL (Schaumburg Township District Library) 130 S Roselle Rd .... Schaumburg IL 60193 *Web:* www.schaumburglibrary.org	847-985-4000		434-3
Steadfast Networks Inc 350 E Cermak Rd Ste 240 .... Chicago IL 60616 *Web:* www.steadfast.net	312-602-2689		225
Steadmantech 1153 Powderhouse Rd .... Vestal NY 13850 *Web:* www.steadmantech.com	607-772-0882		177
Steadyhand Investment Funds Limited Partnership 1747 W Third Ave .... Vancouver BC V6J1K7 *TF:* 888-888-3147 ■ *Web:* www.steadyhand.com	888-888-3147		528
Steak Escape 222 Neilston St .... Columbus OH 43215 *Web:* www.steakescape.com	614-224-0300	224-6460	670
Steak House 2880 Las Vegas Blvd S .... Las Vegas NV 89109 *Web:* circuscircus.com	702-794-3767		671
Steak N Shake Co 3810 W Washington Holt Rd .... Indianapolis IN 46241 *TF:* 877-785-6745 ■ *Web:* www.steaknshake.com	317-241-0483		670
Steal Network LLC 2181 California Ave Ste 400 .... Salt Lake City UT 84104 *Web:* www.stealnetwork.com	801-210-0304		492
Stealth 1617 locust st .... Saint Louis MO 63103 *Web:* stlautos.com	314-480-3606		7
Stealth Mktg Services 4424 Via De La Plaza .... Yorba Linda CA 92886	714-693-3823		2
Stealth Monitoring Inc 15182 Marsh Ln .... Dallas TX 75001 *TF:* 855-783-2584 ■ *Web:* www.stealthmonitoring.com	214-341-0123		693
STEALTHbits Technologies Inc 200 Central Ave .... Hawthrone NJ 07506 *Web:* www.stealthbits.com	201-447-9300	447-1818	179
Steam Bros Inc 2400 Vermont Ave .... Bismarck ND 58504 *TF:* 800-767-5064 ■ *Web:* www.steambrothers.com	701-222-1263	222-1372	152
Steamatic Inc 3333 Quorum Dr Ste 280 .... Fort Worth TX 76137 *Web:* www.steamatic.com	817-632-1555	796-1231	152
Steamboat Grand Resort Hotel & Conference Ctr 2300 Mt Werner Cir .... Steamboat Springs CO 80487 *TF:* 877-269-2628 ■ *Web:* www.steamboatgrand.com	970-871-5500		669
Steamboat Lake State Park PO Box 750 .... Clark CO 80428 *Web:* cpw.state.co.us	970-879-3922		565
Steamboat Rock State Park 51052 Washington 155 .... Electric City WA 99123 *Web:* www.parks.wa.gov	509-633-1304		565
Steamboat Ski & Resort Corp 2305 Mt Werner Cir .... Steamboat Springs CO 80487 *TF:* 877-237-2628 ■ *Web:* www.steamboat.com	970-879-6111		669
Steamboat Ventures 801 N Brand Blvd Ste 665 .... Glendale CA 91203 *Web:* steamboatvc.com	818-553-7900	696-2686	792
Steamer Seafood Co 1 N Forest Beach Dr Ste 28 Calligny Plz .... Hilton Head Island SC 29928 *Web:* www.steamerseafood.com	843-785-2070		671
Steamship Authority 1 Cowdry Rd PO Box 284 .... Woods Hole MA 02543 *Web:* www.steamshipauthority.com	508-548-3788		468
Steamtown National Historic Site 150 S Washington Ave .... Scranton PA 18503 *TF:* 888-693-9391 ■ *Web:* www.nps.gov	570-340-5200		564
Stearns County 705 Courthouse Sq Rm 121 .... Saint Cloud MN 56303 *Web:* www.co.stearns.mn.us	320-656-3601	656-6393	338
Stearns ElectricAssn 900 E Kraft Dr .... Melrose MN 56352 *TF:* 800-962-0655 ■ *Web:* www.stearnselectric.org	320-256-4241	256-3618	245
Stearns Packaging Corp 4200 Sycamore Ave .... Madison WI 53714 *TF:* 800-655-5008 ■ *Web:* www.stearnspkg.com	608 246 5150	246 5140	151
Stearns Weaver Miller Weissler Alhadeff & Sitterson P.A. 150 W Flagler St Ste 2200 .... Miami FL 33130 *Web:* stearnsweaver.com	305-789-3200	789-3395	428
Stearnswood Inc 320 Third Ave NW .... Hutchinson MN 55350 *TF:* 800-657-0144 ■ *Web:* www.stearnswood.com	320-587-2137	587-7646	200
Steel & Pipe Supply Co 555 Poyntz Ave .... Manhattan KS 66502 *Web:* www.spsci.com	785-587-5100		492
Steel Ceilings Inc 451 E Coshocton St .... Johnstown OH 43031 *TF:* 800-848-0496 ■ *Web:* www.steelceilings.com	740-967-1063	967-1478	491
Steel City Corp 190 N Meridian Rd .... Youngstown OH 44501 *TF:* 800-321-0350 ■ *Web:* www.scity.com	330-792-7663	797-2947	488
Steel Craft Technologies Inc 8057 Graphic Dr NE .... Belmont MI 49306 *Web:* www.steelcrafttech.com	616-866-4400		295
Steel Dynamics Inc 7575 W Jefferson Blvd Ste 200 .... Fort Wayne IN 46804 *NASDAQ: STLD* ■ *TF:* 866-740-8700 ■ *Web:* www.steeldynamics.com	260-969-3500	969-3590	723
Steel Edge Inc (SEI) 716 W Mesquite Ave .... Las Vegas NV 89106 *Web:* www.steeledgeinc.com	702-386-0023		492
Steel Encounters Inc 525 East 300 South .... Salt Lake City UT 84102 *Web:* www.steelencounters.com	801-478-8100		492
Steel Equipment Specialist 1507 Beeson St NE .... Alliance OH 44601 *Web:* www.seseng.com	330-821-3322		480

Entry	Phone	Fax	Class
Steel Fabricators LLC 721 NE 44th St, Fort Lauderdale FL 33334 *Fax: Sales ■ Web: www.sfab.com	954-772-0440	938-7527*	480
Steel Fabricators of Monroe LLC 2101 Booth St Ste 4830, Monroe LA 71201 TF: 800-380-4489 ■ Web: www.steelfab.com	318-387-9426		480
Steel Founders' Society of America (SFSA) 780 McArdle Dr Ste G, Crystal Lake IL 60014 Web: www.sfsa.org	815-455-8240	455-8241	49-13
Steel Framing Alliance 25 Massachusetts Ave NW Ste 800, Washington DC 20001 Web: www.steelframingalliance.com	202-785-2022	452-1039	49-3
Steel Grip Inc 1501 E Voorhees St, Danville IL 61832 TF: 800-223-1595 ■ Web: www.steelgripinc.com	217-442-6240		576
Steel House Inc 3644 Eastham Dr, Culver City CA 90232 TF: 888-978-3354 ■ Web: www.steelhouse.com	888-978-3354		5
Steel King Industries Inc 2700 Chamber St, Stevens Point WI 54481 TF: 800-826-0203 ■ Web: www.steelking.com	715-341-3120	341-8792	470
Steel LLC 405 N Clarendon Ave, Scottdale GA 30079 TF: 800-965-6360 ■ Web: www.steelincga.com	404-292-7373		492
Steel Manufacturers Assn (SMA) 1150 Connecticut Ave NW Ste 715, Washington DC 20036 Web: www.steelnet.org	202-296-1515	296-2506	49-13
Steel of West Virginia Inc 17th St & Second Ave, Huntington WV 25703 TF: 800-624-3492 ■ Web: www.swvainc.com	304-696-8200	529-1479	723
Steel Parts Corp 801 Berryman Pk, Tipton IN 46072 Web: www.steelparts.com	765-675-2191	675-4232	489
Steel Plant Museum 100 Lee St Heritage Discovery Ctr, Buffalo NY 14210 Web: steelplantmuseumwny.org	716-821-9361		520
Steel Plate Fabricators Assn (SPFA) 944 Donata Ct, Lake Zurich IL 60047 Web: www.steeltank.com	847-438-8265	438-8766	49-13
Steel Restaurant & Lounge 3102 Oaklawn Ave, Dallas TX 75219 Web: www.steeldallas.com	214-219-9908	219-9929	671
Steel Service Corp 2260 Flowood Dr PO Box 321425, Jackson MS 39232 TF: 800-844-9222 ■ Web: www.steelservice.com	601-939-9222	939-9359	307
Steel Services Inc 9800 Mayland Dr, Richmond VA 23233 Web: www.steelservicesinc.com	804-673-3810		492
Steel Smart Inc 1042 Airport Rd, Pikeville NC 27863 Web: www.steelsmartinc.com	919-736-0601		400
Steel Supply Co, The 5101 Newport Dr, Rolling Meadows IL 60008 TF: 800-323-7571 ■ Web: www.steelsupply.com	800-323-7571	828-1553	492
Steel Tank Institute (STI) 944 Donata Ct, Lake Zurich IL 60047 Web: www.stcsteel.com	847-438-8265	438-8766	49-13
Steel Technologies Inc 15415 Shelbyville Rd, Louisville KY 40245 TF: 800-622-6757 ■ Web: www.steeltechnologies.com	502-245-2110		492
Steel Unlimited Inc 456 W Valley Blvd, Rialto CA 92376 TF: 800-544-6453 ■ Web: www.steelunlimited.com	909-873-1222		492
Steel Warehouse Company Inc 2722 W Tucker Dr, South Bend IN 46619 TF: 800-348-2529 ■ Web: www.steelwarehouse.com	574-236-5100	236-5154	492
Steel Works LLC, The 1020 Niedringhaus Ave, Granite City IL 62040 TF: 800-234-5828 ■ Web: www.tsw.com	618-452-2833		492
Steelcase Inc 801 44th St SE PO Box 1967, Grand Rapids MI 49501 NYSE: SCS ■ TF: 888-783-3522 ■ Web: www.steelcase.com/asia-en	616-247-2710		319-1
SteelCloud Inc 20110 Ashbrook Pl Ste 270, Ashburn VA 20147 OTC: SCLD ■ TF: 800-296-3866 ■ Web: www.steelcloud.com	703-674-5500	674-5506	176
Steelco Inc 1020 Commercial Dr, Matthews NC 28104 Web: www.steelcoinc.com	704-821-4545		480
SteelCon Supply Co 265 Industrial Dr, Beckley WV 25801 Web: www.steelconsupply.com	304-255-1416		791
Steele Canvas Basket Corp 201 William St PO Box 6267 IMCN, Chelsea MA 02150 TF: 800-541-8929 ■ Web: steelecanvas.com	617-889-0202	889-0524	733
Steele Capital Management Inc 788 Main St #200, Dubuque IA 52001 TF: 800-397-2097 ■ Web: www.steelecapital.com	563-588-2097		528
Steele County PO Box 296, Finley ND 58230 TF: 800-584-7077 ■ Web: www.co.steele.nd.us	701-524-2152		338
Steele County 111 E Main St, Owatonna MN 55060 Web: www.co.steele.mn.us	507-444-7700		338
Steele Law Firm p C The 949 County Rt 53, Oswego NY 13126 TF: 877-496-2687 ■ Web: www.thesteelelawfirm.com	315-216-4721		428
Steele Memorial Library 101 E Church St, Elmira NY 14901 Web: www.steele.lib.ny.us	607-733-9173	733-9176	434-3
Steele Realty & Investment Company Inc 8900 Grant Line Rd, Elk Grove CA 95624 Web: www.steelerealtyinc.com	916-686-6670	686-8504	652
Steele Solutions Inc 9909 S 57th St, Franklin WI 53132 TF: 888-542-5099 ■ Web: www.steelesolutions.com	414-367-5099		480
Steele Truck Ctr Inc 2150 Rockfill Rd, Fort Myers FL 33916 TF: 888-806-4839 ■ Web: www.steeletruck.com	239-334-7300	334-4676	57
Steele-Waseca Co-op Electric (SWCE) 2411 W Bridge St PO Box 485, Owatonna MN 55060 TF: 800-526-3514 ■ Web: www.swce.com	507-451-7340		245
SteelFab Inc 8623 Old Dowd Rd, Charlotte NC 28214 TF: 800-831-9252 ■ Web: www.steelfab-inc.com	704-394-5376		480
Steelhead Brewery & Cafe 199 E Fifth Ave, Eugene OR 97401 Web: www.steelheadbrewery.com	541-686-2739	342-5338	671
Steelhead LNG Corp 650 - 669 Howe St, Vancouver BC V6C0B4 TF: 855-860-8744 ■ Web: www.steelheadlng.com	604-235-3800		536
Steelhead Partners LLC 333 - 108th Ave NE Ste 2010, Bellevue WA 98004	425-974-3788	974-3799	492
Steelman Industries Inc 2800 Hwy 135 N, Kilgore TX 75662 TF: 800-287-6633 ■ Web: www.steelman.com	903-984-3061	984-1384	318
Steelman Transportation 2160 N Burton, Springfield MO 65803 TF: 800-488-6287 ■ Web: www.steelmantransport.com	417-831-6300		780
Steelray Software Llc 1440 dutch valley pl ne, Atlanta GA 30324 Web: www.steelray.com	404-806-0160		396
SteelSalvor LLC 3027 Marina Bay Dr Ste 350, League City TX 77573 Web: steelsalvor.com	281-724-8892		492
Steelsummit Holdings Inc 1718 J P Hennessy Dr, La Vergne TN 37086 Web: www.steelsummit.com	615-641-3300		492
SteelTorch Software Inc 423 Jamestown Rd, Belmont NH 03220 TF: 866-705-2730	866-705-2730	705-2730	809
Steelways Inc 401 S Water St, Newburgh NY 12553 Web: www.steelwaysinc.com	845-562-0860		492
Steelweld Equipment Company Inc 235 N Service Rd W, Saint Clair MO 63077	636-629-3704		516
Steepleton Tire Co 777 S Lauderdale St, Memphis TN 38126 TF: 800-965-1009 ■ Web: steepletontire.com	901-774-6440	774-6445	755
SteepRock Inc 67 Lwr Church Hill Rd, Washington Depot CT 06794 TF: 800-231-8795 ■ Web: www.steeprockinc.com	860-868-8075		809
Steere Enterprises Inc 285 Commerce St, Tallmadge OH 44278 TF: 800-875-4926 ■ Web: www.steere.com	330-633-4926		604
Steering Group Inc, The 1078 Dixie Belle Ct, Lawrenceville GA 30045 TF: 866-290-8123 ■ Web: www.thesteeringgroup.com	404-978-2282		463
Stefanik Elise (Rep R - NY) 318 Cannon HOB, Washington DC 20515 Web: stefanik.house.gov	202-225-4611		342-2
Stefanini TechTeam Inc 27335 W Eleven-Mile Rd, Southfield MI 48034 TF: 800-522-4451 ■ Web: stefanini.com	800-522-4451		180
Stefano Foods Inc 4825 Hovis Rd, Charlotte NC 28208 Web: www.stefanofoods.com	704-399-3935		123
Steffes Corp 3050 Hwy 22 N, Dickinson ND 58601 TF: 888-783-3337 ■ Web: www.steffes.com	701-483-5400		480
Steger & Bizzell Engineering Inc 1978 S Austin Ave, Georgetown TX 78626 Web: stegerbizzell.com	512-930-9412		261
Steico Industries Inc 1814 Ord Way, Oceanside CA 92056 TF: 800-444-3515 ■ Web: www.steicoindustries.com	760-438-8015		595
Steiff North America 24 Albion Rd Ste 220, Lincoln RI 02865 TF: 888-978-3433 ■ Web: www.steiffusa.com	401-312-0080		762
Stein + Partners Brand Activation (SPBA) 432 Pk Ave S, New York NY 10016 Web: www.steinias.com	212-213-1112		7
Stein Eriksen Lodge 7700 Stein Way, Park City UT 84060 TF: 800-453-1302 ■ Web: www.steinlodge.com	435-649-3700	649-5825	669
Stein Fibers Ltd 4 Computer Dr W, Albany NY 12205 Web: www.steinfibers.com	518-489-5700	489-5713	605-1
Stein Garden & Gift Centers Inc 5400 S 27th St, Milwaukee WI 53221 Web: www.shopsteins.com	414-761-5400		323
Stein Hospice Service 1912 Hayes Ave Ste 3, Sandusky OH 44870 TF: 800-625-5269 ■ Web: www.steinhospice.org	419-625-5269	625-5761	371
Stein Industries Inc 7153 Northland Dr, Brooklyn Park MN 55428 Web: www.stein-industries.com	763 504 3500		14
Stein Mart Inc 1200 Riverplace Blvd, Jacksonville FL 32207 NASDAQ: SMRT ■ Web: www.steinmart.com	904-346-1500		229
Stein Monast LLP 70 rue Dalhousie Bureau 300, Quebec QC G1K4B2 Web: www.steinmonast.ca	418-529-6531		428
Stein Seal Company Inc 1500 Industrial Blvd, Kulpsville PA 19443 Web: www.steinseal.com	215-256-0201	256-4818	326
Stein Sperling Bennett De Jong Driscoll PC 25 W Middle Ln, Rockville MD 20850 TF: 800-750-6418 ■ Web: www.steinsperling.com	301-340-2020		428
Stein World Inc 5321 E Shelby Dr, Memphis TN 38118 TF: 800-325-4363 ■ Web: www.steinworld.com	901-261-3050		321
Steinaker State Park 4335 N Hwy 191, Vernal UT 84078 TF: 800-322-3770 ■ Web: stateparks.utah.gov	435-789-4432	789-4475	565
Steinberger Drilling Co 10063 State Hwy 25 E, Windthorst TX 76389 TF: 800-765-5186 ■ Web: www.steinbergerdrilling.com	940-423-6900		540
Steiner & Assoc Inc 4016 Townsfair Way, Columbus OH 43219 Web: www.steiner.com	614-414-7300		653
Steiner Electric Co 1250 Touhy Ave, Elk Grove Village IL 60007 TF: 800-783-4637 ■ Web: www.steinerelectric.com/home	847-228-0400	228-1352	246
Steiner Industries 5801 N Tripp Ave, Chicago IL 60646 TF: 800-621-4515 ■ Web: www.steinerindustries.com	773-588-3444	588-3450	576
Steiner Leisure Ltd 770 S Dixie Hwy Ste 200, Coral Gables FL 33146 NASDAQ: STNR ■ Web: www.steinerleisure.com	305-358-9002		77
Steiner Shipyard Inc 8640 Hemley St, Bayou La Batre AL 36509	251-824-4143	824-4178	770
Steinhafels W 231 N 1013 County Hwy F, Waukesha WI 53186 TF Cust Svc: 866-351-4600 ■ Web: www.steinhafels.com	262-436-4600	436-4601	321
Steinhart Aquarium *California Academy of Sciences* 55 Music Concourse Dr Golden Gate Park, San Francisco CA 94118 TF: 800-794-7576 ■ Web: www.calacademy.org/aquarium	415-379-8000		40

Phone | Fax | Class

Steinhauer Elementary School
170 Frederick Ave. Maple Shade NJ 08052 856-779-7323 685
Web: www.mapleshade.org

Steinhilbers Thalia
653 Thalia Rd Virginia Beach VA 23452 757-340-1156 671
Web: www.steinys.com

Steinke Vertal Langdon & Drum Inc
3511 Center Rd PO Box 8 Brunswick OH 44212 330-225-3377 2
Web: svldcpa.com

Steinreich Communications LLC
2125 Center Ave Fort Fee NJ 07024 201-498-1600 7
Web: www.scompr.com

Steins Thriftway Foods Inc
135 Central Ave N Watkins MN 55389 320-764-2980 297-8

Steinwall Inc 1759 116th Ave NW Coon Rapids MN 55448 763-767-7060 608
TF: 800-229-9199 ■ *Web:* www.steinwall.com

Steinway & Sons 1 Steinway Pl Long Island NY 11105 718-721-2600 527
TF: 800-783-4692 ■ *Web:* www.steinway.com

Steinway Musical Instruments Inc
800 S St Ste 305 Waltham MA 02453 781-894-9770 527
NYSE: LVB ■ *Web:* steinway.com/steinway-musical-instruments

Steiny Electric Co
12907 E Garvey Ave Los Angeles CA 91706 707-552-6900 189-4
Web: www.steinyco.com

Stelbar Oil Corp Inc
1625 N Waterfront Pkwy Ste 200 Wichita KS 67206 316-264-8378 536

Stelera Wireless LLC
13431 Broadway Extn Ste 102 Oklahoma City OK 73114 405-751-3525 751-3979 194

Stella Color Inc 620 S Dakota St Seattle WA 98108 206-223-2303 627
Web: www.stellacolor.com

Stella Group Ltd, The
1616 H St NW Ste 1020 Washington DC 20006 202-347-2214 192
Web: www.thestellagroupltd.com

Stella Maris Hospice Care Program
2300 Dulaney Valley Rd Timonium MD 21093 410-252-4500 371
Web: www.stellamaris.org

Stella Maris LLC
930 W Pont des Mouton Lafayette LA 70507 337-504-5128 518
Web: www.stellamarisllc.com

Stella May Contracting Inc
1512 Edgewood Rd Edgewood MD 21040 410-679-8306 186
Web: stellamay.com

Stella! 547 Saint Ann St New Orleans LA 70116 504-587-0093 671
Web: www.stanleyrestaurant.com/#private-events

Stella-Jones Inc
3100 de la Cote-Vertu Blvd Ste 300 St-laurent QC H4R2J8 514-934-8666 934-5327 683
Web: www.stella-jones.com

Stellar Capital Management LLC
2200 E Camelback Rd Ste 130 Phoenix AZ 85016 602-778-0307 401
Web: www.stellarmgt.com

Stellar Engineering Inc
2899 E Coronado St Unit E Anaheim CA 92806 714-632-0040 261

Stellar Group 2900 Hartley Rd Jacksonville FL 32257 904-260-2900 268-4932* 186
**Fax:* Sales ■ *TF:* 800-488-2900 ■ *Web:* stellar.net

Stellar Printing Inc
3838 Ninth St Long Island NY 11101 718-361-1600 627
Web: www.stellarprinting.com

Stellar Solutions Inc
250 Cambridge Ave Ste 204 Palo Alto CA 94306 650-473-9866 261
Web: stellarsolutions.com

Stellar Systems Inc 222 NE Monroe St Peoria IL 61602 309-677-7350 177
Web: www.ssinet.com

Stellar Technology Inc
237 Commerce Dr Amherst NY 14228 716-250-1900 454
TF: 800-274-1846 ■ *Web:* www.stellartech.com

Stellarnet Inc 14390 Carlson Cir Tampa FL 33626 813-855-8687 419
Web: www.stellarnet.us

StellArt 2012 Waltzer Rd Santa Rosa CA 95403 707-569-1378 569-1379 130
TF: 866-621-1987 ■ *Web:* www.stellart.com

Stelvio Inc 430 Rue Sainte-helene Montreal QC H2Y2K7 514-281-8570 180
Web: www.stelvio.com

Stem Engineering Group
875 Queen St E Sault Sainte Marie ON P6A2B3 705-942-6628 261
Web: stemeng.ca

Stem International Inc
4692 Millennium Dr Ste 400 Belcamp MD 21017 410-272-9080 272-9085 194
Web: www.stemint.com

Stemaco Products Inc 2211 Ogden Rd Rock Hill SC 29730 803-328-2191 576

Stemco LP
300 Industrial Blvd PO Box 1989 Longview TX 75606 903-758-9981 232-3508* 60
**Fax:* Sales ■ *TF:* 800-527-8492 ■ *Web:* www.stemco.com

Stemilt Growers Inc PO Box 2779 Wenatchee WA 98807 509-663-1451 315-3
Web: www.stemilt.com

Stemmerich Inc 4728 Gravois Ave Saint Louis MO 63116 314-832-7726 111
Web: www.stemmerich.com

StemWood Corp 2710 Grant Line Rd New Albany IN 47150 812-945-6646 945-7549 613
TF: 800-231-4148 ■ *Web:* www.stemwood.com

Sten Corp
10275 Wayzata Blvd S Ste 310 Minnetonka MN 55305 952-545-2776 185

Stenerson Bros Lumber Co
1702 First Ave N Moorhead MN 56560 218-233-3437 233-2819 364
Web: www.stenersonlumber.com

Steno Employment Services Inc
8560 Vineyard Ave Ste 208 Rancho Cucamonga CA 91730 909-476-1404 221-2820* 260
**Fax Area Code:* 844 ■ *Web:* stenoinc.com

Stenograph LLC 1500 Bishop Ct Mount Prospect IL 60056 847-803-1400 177
TF: 800-323-4247 ■ *Web:* www.stenograph.com

Stenotype Institute of Jacksonville
3563 Phillips Hwy Bldg E Ste 501 Jacksonville FL 32207 904-398-4141 800

Stens Corp 2424 Cathy Ln Jasper IN 47546 812-482-2526 482-1275 429
TF: 800-457-7444 ■ *Web:* www.stens.com

Stenstrom Cos Ltd 2420 20th St Rockford IL 61104 815-398-2420 398-0041 186
Web: www.rstenstrom.com

Stenton Museum 4601 N 18th St Philadelphia PA 19140 215-329-7312 329-7312 520
Web: www.stenton.org

STEP Energy Services Ltd
505 - Third St SW Ste 300 Calgary AB T2P3E6 403-457-1772 538
TF: 800-349-0921 ■ *Web:* www.stepenergyservices.com

Step Saver Inc 213 Spring St Southington CT 06489 860-628-9645 621-1841 5
Web: www.stepsaver.com

Step Up For Students
PO Box 54429 Jacksonville FL 32245 877-735-7837 305
TF: 877-735-7837 ■ *Web:* www.stepupforstudents.org

Step2 Co 10010 Aurora-Hudson Rd Streetsboro OH 44241 330-656-0440 64
TF Cust Svc: 800-347-8372 ■ *Web:* www.step2.com

Stepan Co 22 W Frontage Rd Northfield IL 60093 847-446-7500 501-2100 145
TF Cust Svc: 800-745-7837 ■ *Web:* www.stepan.com

Stepfamily Foundation 310 W 85th St New York NY 10024 212-877-3244 48-6
Web: www.stepfamily.org

Stephan & Brady Inc 1850 Hoffman St Madison WI 53704 608-241-4141 4
Web: www.stephanbrady.com

Stephen A Goldman Consulting Services LLC
34 Arlington Ave Morris Plains NJ 07950 973-267-5929 267-5929 463
Web: www.sagcs.com

Stephen A Kepniss & Assoc PC
211 Mountain Ave Springfield NJ 07081 973-921-1250 2

Stephen A. Forbes State Park
6924 Omega Rd Kinmundy IL 62854 618-547-3381 565
Web: www.dnr.illinois.gov/Parks/Pages/StephenAForbes.aspx

Stephen Bader Co Inc
10 Charles St PO Box 297 Valley Falls NY 12185 518-753-4456 753-4962 455
TF: 800-572-1358 ■ *Web:* www.stephenbader.com

Stephen Bulger Gallery
1026 Queen St W Toronto ON M6J1H6 416-504-0575 504-8929 42
Web: www.bulgergallery.com

Stephen C. Foster State Park
17515 Hwy 177 Fargo GA 31631 912-637-5274 565
Web: www.gastateparks.org

Stephen F Austin State University
1936 N St PO Box 13051 Nacogdoches TX 75962 936-468-2504 468-3149* 166
**Fax:* Admissions ■ *TF:* 800-257-9558 ■ *Web:* www.sfasu.edu

Stephen F Austin State University Steen Library (SFASU)
1936 N St Nacogdoches TX 75962 936-468-3401 434-6
TF: 800-765-1534 ■ *Web:* www.sfasu.edu

Stephen Foster Folk Culture Ctr State Park
11016 Lillian Saunders Dr White Springs FL 32096 386-397-2733 565
Web: www.floridastateparks.org

Stephen Gould Corp 35 S Jefferson Rd Whippany NJ 07981 973-428-1500 100
Web: www.stephengould.com

Stephen M Meltz & Assoc CPA'S PC
6954 W Touhy Ave Niles IL 60714 847-647-6701 2

Stephen Mack Middle School
11810 Old River Rd Rockton IL 61072 815-624-2611 685
TF: 800-252-2873 ■ *Web:* rockton140.org

Stephen Mahoney
380 W Portal Ave Ste D San Francisco CA 94127 415-681-7120 390
Web: agents.allstate.com

Stephen Mazoh & Company Inc
19 Pink Ln Rhinebeck NY 12572 845-876-2723 42

Stephen Miller Gallery
800 Santa Cruz Ave Menlo Park CA 94025 650-327-5040 361
TF: 888-566-8833 ■ *Web:* www.stephenmillergallery.com

Stephen Wojdowski CPA
8885 Rio San Diego Dr 3215 San Diego CA 92108 619-296-0150 2

Stephens Advertising Inc
417 E Stroop Rd Dayton OH 45429 937-299-4993 7
TF: 800-450-1619 ■ *Web:* www.stephensdirect.com

Stephens College 1200 E Broadway Columbia MO 65215 573-442-2211 166
TF: 800-876-7207 ■ *Web:* www.stephens.edu

Stephens County 200 W Walker St Breckenridge TX 76424 254-559-3700 559-9645 338
Web: www.co.stephens.tx.us

Stephens County 101 S 11th St Duncan OK 73533 580-255-3131 338
Web: okcountytreasurers.com

Stephens County
37 W Tugalo St PO Box 386 Toccoa GA 30577 706-886-9491 886-2185 338
Web: www.stephenscountyga.com

Stephens Inc 111 Ctr St Little Rock AR 72201 501-377-2000 690
TF: 800-643-9691 ■ *Web:* www.stephens.com

Stephens Machine Inc 1600 E Dodge St Kokomo IN 46902 765-459-4017 757
Web: www.stephensmachine.com

Stephens Manufacturing Co
711 W Fourth St Tompkinsville KY 42167 270-487-6774 190
TF: 800-626-0200 ■ *Web:* www.stephensmfg.com

Stephens State Forest
1111 N Eigth St Chariton IA 50049 641-774-4559 565
Web: www.iowadnr.gov

Stephens State Park
800 Willow Grove St Hackettstown NJ 07840 908-852-3790 565
Web: www.njparksandforests.org

Stephenson County
50 W Douglas St Ste 500 Freeport IL 61032 815-235-8289 235-8378 338
Web: www.co.stephenson.il.us

Stephenson Engineering Ltd
2550 Victoria Park Ave Ste 602 Toronto ON M2J5A9 416-635-9970 256
Web: www.stephenson-eng.com

Stephenson Equipment Inc (SEI)
7201 Paxton St Harrisburg PA 17111 717-564-3434 264-3
TF: 800-325-6455 ■ *Web:* www.stephensonequipment.com

Stephenson Millwork Company Inc
210 Harper St NE Wilson NC 27893 252-237-1141 237-4377 499
Web: www.stephensonmillwork.com

Stephenson National Bank & Trust
1820 Hall Ave PO Box 137 Marinette WI 54143 715-732-1732 732-5478 70
Web: www.snbt.com

Stephenson Public Library
1700 Hall Ave Marinette WI 54143 715-732-7570 434-3

Stephenville Independent School District
2655 W Overhill Dr Stephenville TX 76401 254-968-4141 685
Web: www.sville.us

Stephenz Group Inc, The
75 E Santa Clara St Ste 900 San Jose CA 95113 408-286-9899 4
Web: www.stephenz.com

Stepho's 1124 Davie St Vancouver BC V6E1N1 604-683-2555 671

StepOne Systems LLC
2801 Liberty Ave Ste 200 Pittsburgh PA 15222 412-894-8698 177
Web: www.steponesystems.com

Name / Address	City	State	ZIP	Phone	Fax	Class
Steppenwolf Theatre 1650 N Halsted St *TF:* 800-838-3006 ■ *Web:* www.steppenwolf.org	Chicago	IL	60614	312-335-1650	335-0440	572
Stepping Stones Museum For Children Inc 303 W Ave *Web:* www.steppingstonesmuseum.org	Norwalk	CT	06850	203-899-0606		522
Steptoe & Johnson LLP 1330 Connecticut Ave NW *TF:* 800-973-1177 ■ *Web:* www.steptoe.com	Washington	DC	20036	202-429-3000	429-3902	428
Steptoe & Johnson PLLC 400 White Oaks Blvd *Web:* www.steptoe-johnson.com	Bridgeport	WV	26330	304-933-8000		428
Stepware Inc 619 Main St *Web:* www.stepware.com	Grand Junction	CO	81507	970-243-9390		809
Stereo Advantage Co 5110 Main St *Web:* www.theadvantage.com	Williamsville	NY	14221	716-626-3280		246
Stereotaxis Inc 4320 Forest Pk Ave *NASDAQ: STXS* ■ *TF:* 866-646-2346 ■ *Web:* www.stereotaxis.com	Saint Louis	MO	63108	314-678-6100	678-6159	382
Stericycle Inc 28161 N Keith Dr *NASDAQ: SRCL* ■ *TF:* 866-783-9816 ■ *Web:* www.stericycle.com	Lake Forest	IL	60045	847-367-5910		804
Sterigenics 2015 Spring Rd Ste 650 *TF:* 800-472-4508 ■ *Web:* www.sterigenics.com	Oak Brook	IL	60523	630-928-1700	928-1701	782
Sterilite Corp PO Box 524 *TF:* 800-225-1046 ■ *Web:* www.sterilite.com	Townsend	MA	01469	800-225-1046		607
STERIS Corp 5960 Heisley Rd *NYSE: STE* ■ **Fax:* Cust Svc ■ *TF:* 800-548-4873 ■ *Web:* www.steris.com	Mentor	OH	44060	440-354-2600	639-4450*	476
Steritech Group Inc, The 7600 Little Ave *Web:* www.steritech.com	Charlotte	NC	28226	704-544-1900		577
Sterling & Francine Clark Art Institute 225 S St *Web:* www.clarkart.edu	Williamstown	MA	01267	413-458-2303		520
Sterling & Sterling Inc 135 Crossways Park Dr	Woodbury	NY	11797	516-487-0300		390
Sterling Bank & Trust FSB 1 Town Sq Ste 1900 *TF:* 877-438-4338 ■ *Web:* www.sterlingbank.com	Southfield	MI	48076	248-351-3442		70
Sterling Bay Companies LLC 1040 W Randolph St *Web:* www.sterlingbay.com	Chicago	IL	60607	312-466-4100		528
Sterling Bldg Systems PO Box 8005 *TF:* 800-455-0545 ■ *Web:* sterlingbldg.com/contact-us	Wausau	WI	54402	800-455-0545		106
Sterling Blower Co 135 Vista Ctr Dr *TF:* 800-833-3810 ■ *Web:* www.sterlingblower.com	Forest	VA	24551	434-316-5310	316-5910	18
Sterling Business Forms PO Box 2486 *TF Cust Svc:* 800-759-3676 ■ *Web:* www.sbfnet.com	White City	OR	97503	800-759-3676	234-2409	110
Sterling Collection Inc, The 1730 First St *Web:* www.sterling-collection.com	San Fernando	CA	91340	818-837-4600	361-2250	320
Sterling College 125 W Cooper *TF:* 800-346-1017 ■ *Web:* www.sterling.edu	Sterling	KS	67579	620-278-2173	278-4418	166
Sterling College PO Box 72 *TF:* 800-648-3591 ■ *Web:* www.sterlingcollege.edu	Craftsbury Common	VT	05827	802-586-7711	586-2596	800
Sterling Computer Corp 600 Stevens Port Dr Ste 200 *TF:* 877-242-4074 ■ *Web:* www.sterlingcomputers.com	Dakota Dunes	SD	57049	605-242-4000	242-4001	721
Sterling Construction Company Inc 20810 Fernbush Ln *NASDAQ: STRL* ■ *Web:* strlco.com	Houston	TX	77073	281-821-9091		186
Sterling Correctional Facility 12101 Hwy 61	Sterling	CO	80751	970-521-5010		213
Sterling Cruises & Travel 8700 W Flagler St *TF:* 800-435-7967 ■ *Web:* www.cruisewin.com	Miami	FL	33174	305-592-2522	592-7442	771
Sterling Cut Glass Company Inc 5020 Olympic Blvd *TF:* 800-543-1317 ■ *Web:* www.sterlingcutglass.com	Erlanger	KY	41018	859-283-2333		361
Sterling Distributing Co 4433 S 96th St	Omaha	NE	68127	402-339-2300		81-3
Sterling Electric Inc 7997 Allison Ave *TF Cust Svc:* 800-654-6220 ■ *Web:* www.sterlingelectric.com	Indianapolis	IN	46268	317-872-0471	872-0907	518
Sterling Engineering Corp 236 New Hartford Rd *Web:* www.sterlingeng.com	Barkhamsted	CT	06063	860-379-3366		21
Sterling Extract Company Inc 10929 Franklin Ave Ste V *Web:* www.sterlingextractcompany.com	Franklin Park	IL	60131	847-451-9728		345
Sterling Farms Theatre Complex 1349 Newfield Ave *Web:* www.curtaincallinc.com	Stamford	CT	06905	203-329-8207	322-3656	572
Sterling Federal Bank 110 E Fourth St PO Box 617 *Web:* www.sterlingfederal.com	Sterling	IL	61081	815-626-0614	626-6021	71
Sterling Fibers Inc 5005 Sterling Way *TF Cust Svc:* 800-342-3779 ■ *Web:* www.sterlingfibers.com	Pace	FL	32571	850-994-5311	994-2579	605-2
Sterling Foods LLC 1075 Arion Pkwy *Web:* www.sterlingfoodsusa.com	San Antonio	TX	78216	210-490-1669		68
Sterling Forest State Park 116 Old Forge Rd *Web:* www.nynjtc.org/park/sterling-forest-state-park	Tuxedo	NY	10987	845-351-5907		565
Sterling Furniture Co 2051 South 1100 East	Salt Lake City	UT	84106	801-467-1579		321
Sterling Global Human Resource Consulting 2415 E Camelback Esplanade Bldg III Ste 1090 *Web:* www.sterlinghrconsulting.com	Phoenix	AZ	85016	602-470-8012		260
Sterling Heights Area Chamber of Commerce 12900 Hall Rd Ste 100 *Web:* www.shrcci.com	Sterling Heights	MI	48313	586-731-5400	731-3521	139
Sterling Hotel 1300 H St *TF:* 800-365-7660 ■ *Web:* sterlinghotelsacramento.com	Sacramento	CA	95814	916-448-1300	448-8066	379
Sterling Hotel Dallas 1055 Regal Row	Dallas	TX	75247	214-634-8550		378
Sterling Inc 2900 S 160th St *Web:* www.acscorporate.com/sterling	New Berlin	WI	53151	262-641-8600	641-8653	201
Sterling Investment Partners 285 Riverside Ave Ste 300 *Web:* www.sterlinglp.com	Westport	CT	06880	203-226-8711		401
Sterling Jewelers Inc 375 Ghent Rd *Web:* www.sterlingjewelers.com	Akron	OH	44333	330-668-5000		409
Sterling McCall Ford 6445 SW Fwy *Web:* www.sterlingmccallford.com	Houston	TX	77074	281-588-5000		516
Sterling Mutuals Inc 1090 University Ave 2nd Floor **Fax Area Code:* 519 ■ *TF:* 800-354-4956 ■ *Web:* www.sterlingmutuals.com	Windsor	ON	N9A5S4	800-354-4956	256-9730*	401
Sterling Organization 340 Royal Poinciana Way Ste 316 *Web:* www.sterlingorganization.com	Palm Beach	FL	33480	561-835-1810	833-4118	509
Sterling Paper Co 2155 E Castor Ave *Web:* fieldnotesphilly.wordpress.com	Philadelphia	PA	19134	215-546-1146	546-1180	101
Sterling Pipe & Tube Inc 5335 Enterprise Blvd *Web:* www.sterlingpipeandtube.com	Toledo	OH	43612	419-729-9756		492
Sterling Plumbing 444 Highland Dr *TF Cust Svc:* 888-783-7546 ■ *Web:* www.sterlingplumbing.com	Kohler	WI	53044	920-457-4441		611
Sterling Process Engineering & Services Inc 333 McCormick Blvd *TF:* 800-783-7875 ■ *Web:* www.sterlingpe.com	Columbus	OH	43213	614-868-5151		757
Sterling Production Control Units 2280 W Dorothy Ln *Web:* www.pcuinc.com	Dayton	OH	45439	937-299-5594	299-3843	386
Sterling Publishing Company Inc 1166 Avenue of the Americas 17th Fl *TF Cust Svc:* 800-367-9692 ■ *Web:* www.sterlingpublishing.com	New York	NY	10036	212-532-7160	213-2495	637-2
Sterling Resources Inc 6 Forest Ave *Web:* sterlingnet.com	Paramus	NJ	07652	201-843-6444		177
Sterling State Park 2800 State Pk Rd *Web:* www.michigandnr.com	Monroe	MI	48162	734-289-2715		565
Sterling Sugars Inc 611 Irish Bend Rd *Web:* amscl.org	Franklin	LA	70538	337-828-0620		296-38
Sterling Technologies Inc 10047 Keystone Dr *Web:* www.sterlingtech.com	Lake City	PA	16423	814-774-2500		596
Sterling Truck Corp 12120 Telegraph Rd *TF Cust Svc:* 800-785-4357 ■ *Web:* www.sterlingtrucks.com	Redford Township	MI	48239	800-785-4357		516
Sterling Venture Partners 650 S Exeter St # 10 *Web:* www.sterlingpartners.com	Baltimore	MD	21202	443-703-1700	703-1750	792
Sterling-Clark-Lurton Corp PO Box 130 *TF:* 800-225-9872 ■ *Web:* www.savogran.com	Norwood	MA	02062	781-762-5400	762-1095	550
Sterling-Rice Group, The (SRG) 1801 13th St Ste 400 *Web:* www.srg.com	Boulder	CO	80302	303-381-6400	444-6637	4
Sterlings Bookkeeping & Tax Services 5418 Saint Charles Ave *Web:* www.sterlingstax.com	Dallas	TX	75223	214-330-4682		734
Sterliteusa 1117 Lake St *Web:* sterliteusa.com	Oak Park	IL	60301	708-383-4003		196
Stern & Stern Industries Inc 100 Thacher St PO Box 556 *TF:* 800-664-7415 ■ *Web:* www.sternandstern.com	Hornell	NY	14843	212-972-4040		745-3
Stern Adv Inc 950 Main Ave *Web:* www.sternadvertising.com	Cleveland	OH	44113	216-464-4850		4
Stern Brothers & Co 8000 Maryland Ave Ste 800 *Web:* www.sternbrothers.com	St. Louis	MO	63105	314-743-4005		690
Stern College for Women of Yeshiva University 245 Lexington Ave **Fax:* Admissions ■ *Web:* www.yu.edu/stern	New York	NY	10016	212-340-7701	340-7788*	166
Stern Empire Dental Lab 1805 W 34th St *TF:* 800-229-0214 ■ *Web:* www.sternempire.com	Houston	TX	77018	713-688-1301		228
Stern Group Inc, The 3314 Ross Pl NW *Web:* www.sterngroup.biz	Washington	DC	20008	202-966-7894		463
Stern Oil Company Inc PO Box 218 *TF:* 800-477-2744 ■ *Web:* www.sternoil.com	Freeman	SD	57029	605-925-7999	925-4367	579
Sterne Agee & Leach Inc 800 Shades Creek Pkwy Ste 700 *TF:* 800-240-1438 ■ *Web:* www.sterneagee.com	Birmingham	AL	35209	205-949-3500		690
Sterngold Dental LLC 23 Frank Mossberg Dr *Web:* www.sterngold.com	Attleboro	MA	02703	508-226-5660		228
Stertil-Koni USA Inc 200 Log Canoe Cir *TF:* 800-336-6637 ■ *Web:* www.stertil-koni.com	Stevensville	MD	21666	410-643-9001		194
Stetson Convention Services Inc 2900 Stayton St *Web:* www.stetsonexpo.com	Pittsburgh	PA	15212	412-223-1090	223-1094	205
Stetson University 421 N Woodland Blvd Unit 8378 **Fax:* Admissions ■ *TF Admissions:* 800-688-0101 ■ *Web:* www.stetson.edu	DeLand	FL	32723	386-822-7100	822-7112*	166
Stetson University DuPont-Ball Library 421 N Woodland Blvd *TF:* 800-688-0101 ■ *Web:* www.stetson.edu/other/about/libraries.php	DeLand	FL	32723	386-822-7183	740-3626	434-6
Steuben County 206 E Gale St *Web:* www.co.steuben.in.us	Angola	IN	46703	260-668-1000	668-3702	338
Steuben County 3 E Pulteny Sq *Web:* www.steubencony.org	Bath	NY	14810	607-664-2563		338
Steuben County Chamber of Commerce 47 Liberty St PO Box 488 *Web:* www.centralsteubenchamber.com	Bath	NY	14810	607-776-7122		139
Steuben County Rural Electric Membership Corp 1212 S Wayne St *TF:* 888-233-9088 ■ *Web:* www.remcsteuben.com	Angola	IN	46703	260-665-3563	665-7495	245
Steuben County Tourism Bureau 430 N Wayne St Ste 1B *TF:* 888-665-5668 ■ *Web:* www.lakes101.org	Angola	IN	46703	260-665-5386		206
Steuben House State Historic Site 1209 Main St *Web:* www.njparksandforests.org	River Edge	NJ	07661	201-487-1739		565
Steuben Memorial State Historic Site 9941 Starr Hill Rd *Web:* parks.ny.gov/historic-sites/2/details.aspx	Remsen	NY	13438	315-338-7730		565

Phone | Fax | Class

Steuben Rural Electric Co-op Inc
9 Wilson Ave. . . . Bath NY 14810 607-776-4161 245
TF: 800-843-3414 ■ *Web:* www.steubenrec.coop

Steuben Trust Co 1 Steuben Sq . . . . Hornell NY 14843 607-324-5010 70
TF: 866-783-8236 ■ *Web:* steubentrust.com

Steve & Cookies By the Bay
9700 Amherst Ave. . . . . Margate NJ 08402 609-823-1163 671
Web: www.steveandcookies.com

Steve Fields Steak & Lobster Lounge
5013 W Pk Blvd . . . . Plano TX 75093 972-596-7100 599-3950 671
Web: www.stevefields.com

Steve Foley Cadillac
100 Skokie Blvd . . . . Northbrook IL 60062 888-670-1429 126
TF: 877-223-9671 ■ *Web:* www.foleycadillac.com

Steve Hopkins Inc
2499 Auto Mall Pkwy . . . . Fairfield CA 94533 707-427-1000 516
TF: 877-873-3913 ■ *Web:* www.hopkinsautogroup.com

Steve Landers Toyota
10825 Colonel Glenn Rd . . . . Little Rock AR 72204 501-568-5800 516
TF: 888-314-4350 ■ *Web:* www.stevelanderstoyota.com

Steve Millen Sportparts Inc
3176 Airway Ave. . . . . Costa Mesa CA 92626 714-540-5566 57
TF: 866-250-5542 ■ *Web:* www.stillen.com

Steve P Rados Inc
2002 E McFadden Ave Ste 200 PO Box 15128 . . . Santa Ana CA 92705 714-835-4612 835-2186 188-4
Web: www.radoscompanies.com

Steve's Music 51 Rue Saint-antoine O . . . . Montreal QC H2Z1G9 514-878-2216 526
TF: 800-277-4942 ■ *Web:* www.stevesmusic.com

Steve's Original Furs Inc
345 Seventh Ave 9th Fl. . . . . New York NY 10001 212-967-8007 967-3871 155-7
Web: stevesoriginalfurs.com

Steven A Doyle Ltd
1565 82nd St W . . . . Inver Grove Heights MN 55077 651-688-8141 2

Steven Barclay Agency 12 Western Ave . . . . Petaluma CA 94952 707-773-0654 778-1868 708
TF: 888-965-7323 ■ *Web:* www.barclayagency.com

Steven Brian Davis Law Offices
12396 World Trade Dr Ste 115 . . . . San Diego CA 92128 858-451-1004 428
Web: needattorney.org

Steven Engineering Inc
230 Ryan Way. . . . . South San Francisco CA 94080 650-588-9200 258-9200* 246
**Fax Area Code:* 888 ■ *TF:* 800-258-9200 ■ *Web:* www.stevenengineering.com

Steven F O'Donnell Inc
6724 Binder Ln. . . . . Elkridge MD 21075 410-796-7968 492
Web: odonnellmetaldeck.com

Steven F Thurn CPA Psc
2134 Nicholasville Rd Ste 2 . . . . Lexington KY 40503 859-276-3782 2
Web: thurncpa.com

Steven Label Corp
11926 Burke St. . . . . Santa Fe Springs CA 90670 562-698-9971 627
Web: www.stevenlabel.com

Steven Restivo Event Services LLC
805 Fourth St Ste 8. . . . . San Rafael CA 94901 415-456-6455 184
TF: 800-310-6563 ■ *Web:* www.sresproductions.com

Steven Schaefer Associates Inc
10411 Medallion Dr . . . . Cincinnati OH 45241 513-542-3300 261
TF: 800-542-3302 ■ *Web:* schaefer-inc.com

Steven's Hope for Children Inc
1014 W Foothill Blvd Ste B. . . . . Upland CA 91786 909-373-0678 981-4578 372
TF: 866-378-3836 ■ *Web:* www.stevenshope.org

Stevens & Lee PC 111 N Sixth St. . . . . Reading PA 19603 610-478-2000 428
Web: www.stevenslee.com

Stevens & Tate Inc
1900 S Highland Ave Ste 200. . . . . Lombard IL 60148 630-627-5200 195
Web: www.stevens-tate.com

Stevens Aviation Inc
600 Delaware St . . . . Greenville SC 29605 864-678-6000 63
TF: 800-359-7838 ■ *Web:* www.stevensaviation.com

Stevens Business Service Inc
92 Bolt St Ste 1. . . . . Lowell MA 01852 978-458-2500 160
TF: 800-769-0375 ■ *Web:* www.sbs4money.com

Stevens Capital Management LP
201 King Of Prussia Rd Ste 400. . . . . Wayne PA 19087 610-971-5000 401
Web: www.scm-lp.com

Stevens Communications Inc
11 S LaSalle St. . . . . Chicago IL 60603 312-895-5200 246
Web: www.stevenscom.com

Stevens Company Inc
1085 Waterbury Rd. . . . . Thomaston CT 06787 860-283-8201 488
Web: www.stevenscompanyinc.com

Stevens Construction Corp PO Box 7726. . . . . Madison WI 53707 608-222-5100 222-5930 186
Web: www.stevensconstruction.com

Stevens County 215 S Oak St. . . . . Colville WA 99114 509-684-3751 684-8310 338
TF: 800-833-6388 ■ *Web:* www.co.stevens.wa.us

Stevens County 200 E Sixth St . . . . Hugoton KS 67951 620-544-2541 544-4094 338
Web: www.stevenscoks.org

Stevens County 400 Colorado Ave Ste 104. . . . . Morris MN 56267 320-208-6600 589-3972 338
Web: www.co.stevens.mn.us

Stevens Creek Mitsubishi
3209 Stevens Creek Blvd . . . . San Jose CA 95117 408-264-9999 57
Web: www.stevenscreekmitsubishi.com

Stevens Creek Software PO Box 2126 . . . . Cupertino CA 95015 408-725-0424 366-1954 178-9
TF: 800-823-4279 ■ *Web:* www.stevenscreek.com

Stevens Henager College 1890 S 1350 W . . . . Ogden UT 84401 800-622-2640 162
TF: 800-622-2640 ■ *Web:* www.stevenshenager.edu

Stevens Industries Inc
704 W Main St . . . . Teutopolis IL 62467 217-540-3100 857-7101 286
TF: 800-637-1609 ■ *Web:* www.stevensind.com

Stevens Institute of Technology
Castle Pt on the Hudson. . . . . Hoboken NJ 07030 201-216-5194 216-8348* 166
**Fax:* Admissions ■ *TF:* 800-458-5323 ■ *Web:* www.stevens.edu

Stevens John Paul
US Supreme Ct Bldg 1 1st St NE . . . . Washington DC 20543 202-479-3000 479-3472 341-4
TF: 800-772-1213 ■ *Web:* www.supremecourt.gov

Stevens Manufacturing Company Inc
220 Rock Ln. . . . . Milford CT 06460 203-878-2328 22
Web: www.stevensmfgco.com

Stevens Marine Inc 9180 SW Burnham St. . . . . Tigard OR 97223 503-620-7023 90
TF: 800-225-7023 ■ *Web:* www.stevensmarine.com

Stevens Pass Mountain Resort LLC
Summit Stevens Pass US Hwy 2. . . . . Skykomish WA 98288 206-812-4510 378
TF: 800-414-2378 ■ *Web:* www.stevenspass.com

Stevens Point Area Convention & Visitors Bureau
340 Div St N. . . . . Stevens Point WI 54481 715-344-2556 344-5818 206
TF: 800-236-4636 ■ *Web:* www.stevenspointarea.com

Stevens Sausage Company Inc
3411 Stevens Sausage Rd . . . . Smithfield NC 27577 919-934-3159 619
TF: 800-338-0561 ■ *Web:* www.stevens-sausage.com

Stevens Technology LLC
5700 E Belknap St . . . . Fort Worth TX 76117 817-831-3500 759-4080 629
Web: www.stevenstechnology.com

Stevens Towing Company Inc
4170 Hwy 165 . . . . Yonges Island SC 29449 843-889-2254 313
Web: www.stevens-towing.com

Stevens Transport PO Box 279010. . . . . Dallas TX 75227 866-551-0337 647-3940* 780
**Fax Area Code:* 214 ■ *TF:* 800-233-9369 ■ *Web:* www.stevenstransport.com

Stevens Travel Management Inc
119 W 40th St 14th Fl. . . . . New York NY 10018 212-696-4300 679-5072 771
TF: 800-275-7400 ■ *Web:* www.stevenstravel.com

Stevens Water Monitoring Systems
12067 NE Glenn Widing Dr Ste 106 . . . . Portland OR 97220 503-469-8000 469-8100 544
TF: 800-452-5272 ■ *Web:* www.stevenswater.com

Stevens Wire Products Inc
351 NW 'F' St . . . . Richmond IN 47374 765-966-5534 962-3586 73
Web: www.stevenswire.com

Stevens Worldwide Van Lines
527 W Morley Dr . . . . Saginaw MI 48601 800-678-3836 755-3000* 519
**Fax Area Code:* 989 ■ *TF:* 877-490-0713 ■ *Web:* www.stevensworldwide.com

Stevenson & Vestal
2347 W Hanford Rd . . . . Burlington NC 27215 800-535-3636 195
TF: 800-535-3636 ■ *Web:* www.stevensonvestal.com

Stevenson Advertising
16524 13th Ave W Ste 2012. . . . . Lynnwood WA 98037 425-787-9686 7
Web: www.stevensonadvertising.com

Stevenson Co, The
10002 Shelbyville Rd Ste 201. . . . . Louisville KY 40223 502-271-5250 668
Web: www.stevensoncompany.com

Stevenson Correctional Institution
4546 Broad River Rd. . . . . Columbia SC 29210 803-896-8575 213
Web: doc.sc.gov

Stevenson House Detention Ctr
750 N Dupont Hwy . . . . Milford DE 19963 302-424-8100 412

Stevenson Jones & Holmaas PC
5920 E Pima Ste 170 . . . . Tucson AZ 85712 520-886-5495 2

Stevenson Lumber 501 Division. . . . . Adrian MI 49221 517-265-5151 265-5534 191-3

Stevenson School
3152 Forest Lake Rd. . . . . Pebble Beach CA 93953 831-625-8300 625-5208 622
Web: www.stevensonschool.org

Stevenson Systems Inc
27822 El Lazo 100 . . . . Laguna Niguel CA 92677 949-297-4200 463
TF: 800-842-1718 ■ *Web:* www.stevensonsystems.com

Steves & Sons Inc 203 Humble Ave. . . . . San Antonio TX 78225 210-924-5111 236
Web: www.stevesdoors.com

Steves Homestead Museum
509 King William St . . . . San Antonio TX 78204 210-225-5924 520
Web: saconservation.org

Stevison Ham Co 125 Stevison Ham Rd . . . . Portland TN 37148 615-325-4161 325-5914 296-26
TF: 800-238-8090 ■ *Web:* www.tennesseetraditions.com

Stew Hansen Dodge Ram Chrysler Jeep
12103 Hickman Rd . . . . Urbandale IA 50323 515-331-2900 57
Web: www.stewhansens.com

Stew Leonard's 100 Westport Ave. . . . . Norwalk CT 06851 203-847-7214 336
Web: stewleonards.com

Steward Machine Company Inc
3911 13th Ave N . . . . Birmingham AL 35234 205-841-6461 849-8029 454
Web: www.stewardmachine.com

Steward Steel Inc
1219 E US Hwy 62 PO Box 551 . . . . Sikeston MO 63801 573-471-2121 492
Web: www.stewardsteel.com

Stewart & Assoc Inc
50 W Douglas St Ste 1200 . . . . Freeport IL 61032 815-235-3807 400
TF: 888-310-2840 ■ *Web:* www.bwstewart.com

Stewart & Patten Company LLC
1 Post St Ste 850 . . . . San Francisco CA 94104 415-421-4932 528
Web: www.stewartandpatten.com

Stewart & Stevenson LLC
1000 Louisiana St. . . . . Houston TX 77002 713-613-0633 537
Web: www.stewartandstevenson.com

Stewart Amos Steel Inc
4400 Paxton St. . . . . Harrisburg PA 17111 717-564-3931 492
Web: www.stewart-amos.com

Stewart Archibald & Barney LLP
7881 W Charleston Blvd Ste 250 . . . . Las Vegas NV 89117 702-579-7000 2
Web: www.sabcpa.com

Stewart Assembly & Machining
7234 Blue Ash Rd. . . . . Cincinnati OH 45236 513-891-9000 454
Web: www.pmcworldwide.net

Stewart Business Systems LLC
105 Connecticut Dr. . . . . Burlington NJ 08016 609-589-4800 45
Web: www.stewartxerox.com

Stewart Chris (Rep R - UT)
323 Cannon HOB . . . . Washington DC 20515 202-225-9730 342-2
Web: stewart.house.gov

Stewart County
225 Donelson Pkwy PO Box 67 . . . . Dover TN 37058 931-232-7616 232-4934 338
Web: www.stewartcogov.com

Stewart County Commissioner
552 Martin Luther King Junior Dr. . . . . Lumpkin GA 31815 229-838-6769 338
TF: 800-368-8683 ■ *Web:* www.stewartcountyga.gov

Stewart Daly Inc
1134 Ballena Blvd Ste 18 . . . . Alameda CA 94501 510-521-8586 193

Stewart Directories Inc
50314 Kings Point Dr PO Box 326 . . . . Frisco NC 27936 800-311-0786 901-7570* 637-6
**Fax Area Code:* 443 ■ *TF:* 800-311-0786 ■ *Web:* www.stewartdirectories.com

Stewart EFI LLC 45 Old Waterbury Rd. . . . . Thomaston CT 06787 860-283-8213 489
TF: 800-393-5387 ■ *Web:* www.stewartefi.com

Phone | Fax | Class

Stewart Engineering Supply Inc
3221 E Pioneer Pkwy ... Arlington TX 76010 817-640-1767 112
TF: 800-533-1265 ■ *Web:* www.sesisupply.com

Stewart Enterprises Inc
1333 S Clearview Pkwy ... New Orleans LA 70121 713-522-5141 510
NASDAQ: STEI ■ *TF:* 877-239-3264 ■ *Web:* sci-corp.com/scicorp/home.aspx

Stewart Environmental Consultants LLC
3801 Automation Way Ste 200 ... Fort Collins CO 80525 970-226-5500 226-4946 194

Stewart Filmscreen Corp
1161 W Sepulveda Blvd ... Torrance CA 90502 310-784-5300 326-6870 591
TF: 800-762-4999 ■ *Web:* stewartfilmscreen.com

Stewart Industries Inc 16 S Idaho St ... Seattle WA 98134 206-652-9110 602

Stewart Information Services Corp
1980 Post Oak Blvd Ste 800 ... Houston TX 77056 713-625-8100 552-9523 391-6
NYSE: STC ■ *TF:* 800-729-1900 ■ *Web:* www.stewart.com

Stewart Materials
2875 Jupiter Park Dr Ste 1100 ... Jupiter FL 33458 561-972-4517 501
Web: stewartmaterials.com

Stewart REI Data Inc
1980 Post Oak Blvd Ste 800 ... Houston TX 77056 212-922-0050 391-6
TF: 800-729-1900 ■ *Web:* www.stewart.com

Stewart School of Cosmetology
604 NW Ave ... Sioux Falls SD 57104 605-336-2775 77
TF: 800-537-2625 ■ *Web:* www.stewartschool.com

Stewart Sokol & Gray LLC
2300 SW First Ave Ste 200 ... Portland OR 97201 503-221-0699 428
Web: lawssg.com

Stewart Surfboards
2102 S El Camino Real ... San Clemente CA 92672 949-492-1085 710
Web: www.stewartsurfboards.com

Stewart Sutherland Inc
5411 E 'V' Ave ... Vicksburg MI 49097 269-649-0530 649-3961 65
TF: 800-253-1034 ■ *Web:* www.ssbags.com

Stewart Systems 808 Stewart Ave ... Plano TX 75074 972-422-5808 509-8734 207
TF: 800-966-5808 ■ *Web:* www.stewart-systems.com

Stewart Title & Trust of Phoenix
244 W Osborn Rd ... Phoenix AZ 85013 602-462-8000 391-6
Web: www.stewartaz.com

Stewart Title Guaranty Co
1980 Post Oak Blvd Ste 800 ... Houston TX 77056 713-625-8100 552-9523 391-6
TF: 800-729-1900 ■ *Web:* www.stewart.com

Stewart Title Insurance Co
1980 Post Oak Blvd Ste 800 ... Houstan TX 77056 713-625-8100 61
TF: 800-913-4170 ■ *Web:* www.stcwart.com/en.html

Stewart Warner South Wind Corp
2495 Directors Row Ste F ... Indianapolis IN 46241 317-486-2600 486-2607 529
Web: www.stewart-warner.com

Stewart's Shops PO Box 435 ... Saratoga Springs NY 12866 518-581-1201 381
Web: stewartsshops.com

Stewart-haas Racing LLC
6001 Haas Way ... Kannapolis NC 28081 704-652-4227 642
Web: stewarthaasracing.com

Stewarts Private Blend Food Inc
4110 W Wrightwood Ave ... Chicago IL 60639 773-489-2500 296-7
TF: 800-654-2862 ■ *Web:* www.stewarts.com

STFM (Society of Teachers of Family Medicine)
11400 Tomahawk Creek Pkwy Ste 540 ... Leawood KS 66211 913-906-6000 906-6096 49-8
TF: 800-274-7928 ■ *Web:* www.stfm.org

STG (Symphony Technology Group LLC)
2475 Hanover St ... Palo Alto CA 94304 650-935-9500 935-9501 178-11
Web: www.symphonytg.com

Stg International Inc
4900 Seminary Rd Ste 1100 ... Alexandria VA 22311 703-578-6030 578-4474 180
TF: 855-507-0660 ■ *Web:* www.stginternational.com

STI (Superconductor Technologies Inc)
460 Ward Dr ... Santa Barbara CA 93111 805-690-4500 967-0342 253
NASDAQ: SCON ■ *TF:* 800-727-3648 ■ *Web:* www.suptech.com

STI (Steel Tank Institute)
944 Donata Ct ... Lake Zurich IL 60047 847-438-8265 438-8766 49-13
Web: www.steeltank.com

STI Computer Services Inc
2700 Van Buren Ave ... Eagleville PA 19403 610-650-9700 180
Web: sticomputer.com

STI Electronics Inc 261 Palmer Rd ... Madison AL 35758 256-461-9191 386
TF: 888-650-3006 ■ *Web:* www.stielectronicsinc.com

STI International Inc
114 Halmar Cove ... Georgetown TX 78628 512-819-0656 711
Web: stiguns.com

STI Optronics Inc 2755 Northup Way ... Bellevue WA 98004 425-827-0460 828-3517 425
Web: www.stioptronics.com

Sti Polymer Inc 5618 Clyde Rhyne Dr ... Sanford NC 27330 800-874-5878 3
TF: 800-874-5878 ■ *Web:* www.stipolymer.com

Stibo Systems Inc
3550 George Busbee Pkwy NW Ste 350 ... Kennesaw GA 30144 770-425-3282 387
TF: 800-585-0774 ■ *Web:* www.stibosystems.com

Stic-adhesive Products Company Inc
3950 Medford St ... Los Angeles CA 90063 323-268-2956 711
TF: 800-854-6813 ■ *Web:* www.sticadhesive.com

Stichter, Riedel, Blain & Prosser PA
110 E Madison St Ste 200 ... Tampa FL 33602 813-229-0144 428
Web: www.srbp.com

Stickers Asian Cafe
6808 SE Milwaukie Ave ... Portland OR 97202 503-239-8739 671
Web: www.stickersasiancafe.com

Stickk.com LLC 109 S Fifth St ... New York NY 11249 347-394-4964 387
TF: 866-578-4255 ■ *Web:* www.stickk.com

Stickle Steam Specialties Company Inc
2215 Valley Ave ... Indianapolis IN 46218 317-636-6563 821
Web: www.sticklesteam.com

Sticks 809 Central Ave Ste 315 ... Fort Dodge IA 50501 515-573-8898 530
Web: www.ssoutdooradventures.com

Sticky Fingers 235 Meeting St ... Charleston SC 29401 843-853-7427 671
Web: www.stickyfingers.com

Sticky Rice 2232 W Main St ... Richmond VA 23220 804-358-7870 671
Web: www.ilovestickyrice.com

Stidham & Associates PSC
401 Lewis Hargett Cir Ste 250 ... Lexington KY 40503 859-219-2255 428
TF: 800-650-0099 ■ *Web:* www.stidhamlaw.com

Stidham Trucking Inc PO Box 308 ... Yreka CA 96097 530-842-4161 186
TF: 800-827-9500 ■ *Web:* www.stidhamtrucking.com

Stieg & Assoc Insurance Inc
3319 Gabel Rd ... Billings MT 59102 406-656-9666 390
Web: stieginsurance.com

Stieglitz Snyder Architecture
425 Franklin St ... Buffalo NY 14202 716-828-9166 463
Web: www.stieglitzsnyder.com

Stiehl Communications
W5361 County Rd Kk Ste A ... Appleton WI 54915 920-830-1116 179
Web: www.stiehlcommunications.com

Stifel Financial Corp
501 N Broadway ... Saint Louis MO 63102 800-679-5446 690
NYSE: SF ■ *TF:* 800-679-5446 ■ *Web:* www.stifel.com

Stifel Nicolaus & Co Inc
501 N Broadway ... Saint Louis MO 63102 314-342-2000 690
TF: 800-679-5446 ■ *Web:* www.stifel.com

Stihl Inc 536 Viking Dr ... Virginia Beach VA 23452 757-486-9100 340-0377* 759
**Fax Area Code: 303* ■ *TF Cust Svc:* 800-467-8445 ■ *Web:* www.stihlusa.com

Stikeman Elliott LLP
1155 Rene-levesque Blvd W 40th Fl ... Montreal QC H3B3V2 514-397-3000 428
Web: www.stikeman.com

Stiles Construction Co
301 E Las Olas Blvd ... Fort Lauderdale FL 33301 954-627-9300 627-9288 186
Web: www.stiles.com

Stiles Corp
301 East Las Olas Blvd ... Fort Lauderdale FL 33301 954-627-9300 627-9288 653
Web: www.stiles.com

Stiles Realty Co
301 E Las Olas Blvd ... Fort Lauderdale FL 33301 954-627-9300 652
Web: www.stiles.com

Stillman Banccorp NA
PO Box 150 ... Stillman Valle IL 61084 815-645-2000 645-2341 70
TF: 866-546-8273 ■ *Web:* www.stillmanbank.com

Stillman College
3601 Stillman Blvd ... Tuscaloosa AL 35401 205-349-4240 166
TF: 000-041-5722 ■ *Web:* www.stillman.edu

Stillman Development International LLC
505 Park Ave Ste 1700 ... New York NY 10022 212-686-2400 378
Web: www.stillmandevelopment.com

Stillman House & Museum
1325 E Washington St ... Brownsville TX 78520 956-541-5560 520
Web: www.brownsvillehistory.org

Stillmeadow Inc 12852 Park One Dr ... Sugar Land TX 77478 281-240-8828 196
TF: 800-355-2896 ■ *Web:* www.stillmeadow.com

Stillwater Chamber of Commerce
409 S Main St ... Stillwater OK 74075 405 372 5573 372-4316 139
TF: 800-593-5573 ■ *Web:* www.stillwaterchamber.org

Stillwater County 400 Third Ave N ... Columbus MT 59019 406-322-8000 322-8007 338
Web: stillwatercountymt.gov

Stillwater Medical Ctr
1323 W Sixth St ... Stillwater OK 74074 405 372 1480 371-0
Web: www.stillwater-medical.org

Stillwater Mining Co
1321 Discovery Dr ... Billings MT 59102 406-373-8700 373-8701 502
NYSE: SWC ■ *TF:* 800-821-0548 ■ *Web:* www.stillwatermining.com

Stillwater Motor Co
5900 Stillwater Blvd N ... Stillwater MN 55082 651-323-2245 57
Web: www.stillwatermotors.com

Stillwater Public Library
1107 S Duck St ... Stillwater OK 74074 405-372-3633 624-0552 434-3
TF: 800-829-3676 ■ *Web:* library.stillwater.org

Stillwater Spa at the Hyatt Regency Newport
1 Goat Island ... Newport RI 02840 401-851-3225 707
TF: 800-233-1234 ■ *Web:* newport.regency.hyatt.com/en/hotel/home.html

Stillwater State Park 44 Stillwater Rd ... Groton VT 05046 802-584-3822 565
TF: 888-409-7579 ■ *Web:* www.vtstateparks.com

Stillwater Technologies Inc
1040 S Dorset ... Troy OH 45373 937-440-2500 454
TF: 800-338-7561 ■ *Web:* www.stlwtr.com

Stillwater Utilities Authority
PO Box 1449 ... Stillwater OK 74076 405-372-0025 245
Web: www.stillwater.org

StillWaters Resort 797 Moonbrook Dr ... Dadeville AL 36853 256-825-1353 825-1717 669
Web: www.stillwatersgolf.com

Stillwell Hansen Inc 3 Fernwood Ave ... Edison NJ 08837 732-225-7474 610
Web: www.stillwell-hansen.com

Stilson Products 15935 Sturgeon St ... Roseville MI 48066 586-778-1100 778-4660 493
TF: 888-400-5978 ■ *Web:* www.stilsonproducts.com

Stimmel Associates PA
601 N Trade St Ste 200 ... Winston-Salem NC 27101 336-723-1067 261
Web: www.stimmelpa.com

Stimple & Ward Co
3400 Babcock Blvd ... Pittsburgh PA 15237 412-364-5200 364-5299 518
TF: 800-792-6457 ■ *Web:* www.swcoils.com

Stimson Lumber Co
520 SW Yamhill St Ste 700 ... Portland OR 97204 503-222-1676 683
TF: 800-445-9758 ■ *Web:* www.stimsonlumber.com

Stimwave Technologies Inc
901 E Las Olas Blvd Ste 201 ... Fort Lauderdale FL 33301 786-565-3342 743
TF: 800-965-5134 ■ *Web:* stimwave.com

Stinar Corp 3255 Sibley Memorial Hwy ... Eagan MN 55121 651-454-5112 579
Web: www.stinar.com

Stinnett & Assoc LLC
8801 S Yale Ave Ste 330 ... Tulsa OK 74137 888-808-1795 808-4111 2
TF: 888-808-1795 ■ *Web:* www.stinnett-associates.com

STIR LLC 330 E Kilbourn Ave Ste 222 ... Milwaukee WI 53202 414-278-0040 5
Web: www.stirmarketing.com

Stirling Mercantile Corp
450 - 400 Burrard St ... Vancouver BC V6C3A6 604-484-0070 317
Web: www.stirlingmercantile.com

Stirling Properties
109 Northpark Blvd Ste 300 ... Covington LA 70433 985-898-2022 898-2077 655
Web: www.stirlingprop.com

Stirna's 120 W Market St ... Scranton PA 18508 570-343-5742 671
Web: stirnas.com

Stitchmaster LLC
309-B S Regional Rd ... Greensboro NC 27409 336-852-6448 258
Web: www.stitchmaster.com

				Phone	Fax	Class
Stivers Staffing Services Inc 200 W Monroe St Ste 1300 *Web:* www.stivers.com	Chicago	IL	60606	312-558-3550		721
Stivers Steve (Rep R - OH) 1022 Longworth Bldg *Web:* stivers.house.gov	Washington	DC	20515	202-225-2015		342-2
Stix 3250 Galleria Cir *Web:* www.stixonline.com	Hoover	AL	35244	205-982-3070		671
STLCC (Saint Louis Community College) 300 S Broadway **Fax:* Admissions ■ *Web:* www.stlcc.edu	Saint Louis	MO	63102	314-539-5000	539-5170*	162
STLE (Society of Tribologists & Lubrication Engineers) 840 Busse Hwy *TF:* 800-537-7683 ■ *Web:* www.stle.org	Park Ridge	IL	60068	847-825-5536	825-1456	49-13
STMA (Sports Turf Managers Assn) 805 New Hampshire Ste E *TF:* 800-323-3875 ■ *Web:* www.stma.org	Lawrence	KS	66044	785-843-2549	843-2977	48-22
STMH (St Mary's of Michigan) 800 S Washington Ave *TF:* 877-738-6672 ■ *Web:* www.stmarysofmichigan.org	Saginaw	MI	48601	989-907-8115		374-3
STMicroelectronics NV 750 Canyon Dr Ste 300 *TF:* 844-786-4276 ■ *Web:* www.st.com	Coppell	TX	75019	972-466-6000	466-6001	696
Stober Drives Inc 1781 Downing Dr *Web:* us.stober.com	Maysville	KY	41056	606-759-5090		620
Stock & Option Solutions Inc 6399 San Ignacio Ave Ste 100 *TF:* 888-767-0199 ■ *Web:* www.sos-team.com	San Jose	CA	95119	408-979-8700		463
Stock America Inc 900 Cheyenne Ave Ste 700 *Web:* www.stockamerica.com	Grafton	WI	53024	262-375-4100		547
Stock Drive Products/Sterling Instrument 2101 Jericho Tpke *TF:* 800-737-7436 ■ *Web:* www.sdp-si.com	New Hyde Park	NY	11040	516-328-3300	326-8827	620
Stock Equipment Co 16490 Chillicothe Rd *TF:* 888-742-1249 ■ *Web:* www.schenckprocess.com/stockequipment	Chagrin Falls	OH	44023	440-543-6000	543-5944	273
Stock Exchange Bank 103 S Main PO Box 273 *Web:* stockxbank.com	Caldwell	KS	67022	620-845-6431		70
Stock Garber & Assoc Inc 1368 Manor Dr *Web:* www.sgasoftware.com	Ebensburg	PA	15931	814-472-5158		809
Stock Seed Farms 28008 Mill Rd *TF:* 800-759-1520 ■ *Web:* www.stockseed.com	Murdock	NE	68407	402-867-3771	867-2442	694
Stock Transportation Ltd 128 Wellington St W Ste 201 *TF:* 888-952-0878 ■ *Web:* www.stocktransportation.com	Barrie	ON	L4N1K9	705-737-9847		109
Stock USA Investments Inc 1717 Rt 6 *Web:* www.speedtrader.com	Carmel	NY	10512	845-225-5132		690
Stock Yards Packing Co Inc 2457 W North Ave *TF:* 888-842-6111 ■ *Web:* www.stockyards.com	Melrose Park	IL	60160	888-842-6111	700-9919	296-26
Stockbridge Capital Partners LLC 4 Embarcadero Ctr Ste 3300 *Web:* stockbridge.com	San Francisco	CA	94111	415-658-3300		403
Stockbridge Risk Management Inc 40 Cutter Mill Rd *Web:* www.stockbridgerisk.com	Great Neck	NY	11021	516-499-5678		194
StockCap 123 Manufacturers Dr *TF:* 800-827-2277 ■ *Web:* www.stockcap.com	Arnold	MO	63010	636-282-6800	282-6888	154
StockCharts.com Inc 11241 Willows Rd Ste 140 *Web:* www.stockcharts.com	Redmond	WA	98052	425-881-2606	650-8509	224
Stockell Consulting Inc 15400 S Outer Forty Ste 105 *TF:* 800-786-2535 ■ *Web:* www.stockellconsulting.com	Chesterfield	MO	63017	636-537-9100		180
Stocker Concrete Co 7574 US Rt 36 *TF:* 800-936-4937 ■ *Web:* www.stockerconcrete.com	Gnadenhutten	OH	44629	740-254-4626		182
Stockman Kast Ryan & Scruggs PC 102 N Cascade Ste 400 *Web:* www.skrco.com	Colorado Springs	CO	80903	719-630-1186		2
Stockman's Casino 1560 W Williams Ave *Web:* www.stockmanscasino.com	Fallon	NV	89406	775-423-2117		452
Stockmans Bank 100 Kennedy *Web:* stockmansbankok.com	Gould	OK	73544	580-676-3921		70
Stockmen's Livestock Market Inc 1200 E Hwy 50 PO Box 528 *Web:* stockmenslivestock.com	Yankton	SD	57078	605-665-9641	665-9644	446
Stocks on Second 211 N Second St *Web:* www.stocksonsecond.com	Harrisburg	PA	17101	717-233-6699		671
Stockton & Rickman Llc 191 S Main St *Web:* pacga.org	Clayton	GA	30525	706-782-6100		445
Stockton Beach CPAs & Company 3355 Cerritos Ave	Los Alamitos	CA	90720	562-493-3591		2
Stockton City Hall 425 N El Dorado St *Web:* www.stocktongov.com	Stockton	CA	95202	209-937-8212	937-7149	337
Stockton Civic Theatre (SCT) 2312 Rose Marie Ln *Web:* www.sctlivetheatre.com	Stockton	CA	95207	209-473-2400	473-1502	573-4
Stockton Endoscopy Ctr 415 E Harding Way Ste E *Web:* www.stocktonurology.com	Stockton	CA	95204	209-942-1179		415
Stockton Joe's 236 Lincoln Ctr *Web:* modesto.backpage.com	Stockton	CA	95207	209-951-2980		671
Stockton Performing Arts Ctr 101 Vera King Farris Dr *Web:* stocktonpac.org	Galloway	NJ	08205	609-652-9000	626-5523	572
Stockton State Park 19100 S Hwy 215 *Web:* www.mostateparks.com	Dadeville	MO	65635	417-276-4259		565
Stockton Unified School District 701 N Madison St *Web:* www.stocktonusd.net	Stockton	CA	95202	209-933-7000	933-7031	685
Stockton-San Joaquin County Public Library (SSJCPL) 605 N El Dorado St *TF:* 866-805-7323 ■ *Web:* www.ssjcpl.org	Stockton	CA	95202	209-937-8416		434-3
Stockwatch 700 W Georgia St PO Box 10371 *TF:* 800-268-6397 ■ *Web:* www.stockwatch.com	Vancouver	BC	V7Y1J6	604-687-1500	687-0541	404
Stockyards Hotel 109 E Exchange Ave *TF:* 800-423-8471 ■ *Web:* www.stockyardshotel.com	Fort Worth	TX	76164	817-625-6427	624-2571	379
Stockyards Museum 131 E Exchange Ave Ste 113 *TF:* 800-422-2117 ■ *Web:* stockyardsmuseum.org	Fort Worth	TX	76164	817-625-5082		520
Stockyards Station 130 E Exchange Ave *Web:* www.stockyardsstation.com	Fort Worth	TX	76164	817-625-9715		50-6
Stoel Rives LLP 760 SW Ninth Ave Ste 3000 *Web:* www.stoel.com	Portland	OR	97205	503-224-3380		428
Stoelt Productions 1962 S La Cienega Blvd *Web:* www.stoeltproductions.com	Los Angeles	CA	90034	323-463-3700		226
Stoelting LLC 502 Hwy 67 *TF:* 800-558-5807 ■ *Web:* www.stoelting.com	Kiel	WI	53042	920-894-2293	894-7029	298
Stoever Glass & Company Inc 30 Wall St *TF:* 800-223-3881 ■ *Web:* stoeverglass.com	New York	NY	10005	800-223-3881		401
Stoffel Equipment Company Inc 7764 N 81st St *TF:* 800-354-7502 ■ *Web:* www.stoffelequip.com	Milwaukee	WI	53223	414-354-7500		358
Stohl Environmental LLC 4169 Allendale Pkwy 100 *TF:* 800-823-6239 ■ *Web:* www.stohlenvironmental.com	Blasdell	NY	14219	716-312-0070		196
Stokely Memorial Library 383 E Broadway	Newport	TN	37821	423-623-3832		434-3
Stokes & Spiehler Inc 110 Rue Jean Lafitte *Web:* www.stokesandspiehler.com	Lafayette	LA	70508	337-233-6871		539
Stokes Automotive Inc 8650 Rivers Ave *Web:* www.stokeshondanorth.com	North Charleston	SC	29406	843-572-4700		57
Stokes County 1014 Main St PO Box 20 *Web:* www.co.stokes.nc.us	Danbury	NC	27016	336-593-4400	593-4401	338
Stokes Electric Company Inc 1701 McCalla Ave *Web:* www.stokeselec.com	Knoxville	TN	37915	865-525-0351		246
Stokes Lazarus & Carmichael 2018 Power Ferry RD STE 700 *TF:* 800-876-2303 ■ *Web:* www.scelaw.com	Atlanta	GA	30339	404-352-1465		428
Stokes State Forest 1 Coursen Rd *Web:* www.njparksandforests.org	Branchville	NJ	07826	973-948-3820		565
Stoll Brother True Value Lumber 509 S E St *Web:* truevalue.com	Odon	IN	47562	812-636-4053		613
Stoll Stoll Berne Lokting & Shlachter PC 209 SW Oak St Ste 500 *Web:* www.ssbls.com	Portland	OR	97204	503-227-1600		428
Stolle Machinery Co LLC 6949 S Potomac St *TF:* 800-755-4593 ■ *Web:* www.stollemachinery.com	Centennial	CO	80112	303-708-9044	708-9045	547
Stoller Fisheries 1301 18th St PO Box B *TF:* 800-831-5174 ■ *Web:* www.stollerfisheries.com	Spirit Lake	IA	51360	712-336-1750	336-4681	296-14
Stoller International Inc 15521 E 1830 N Rd *Web:* www.stollerih.com	Pontiac	IL	61764	815-844-6197		274
Stoller USA 4001 W Sam Houston Pkwy N Ste 100 *TF:* 800-539-5283 ■ *Web:* www.stollerusa.com	Houston	TX	77043	713-461-1493	461-4467	280
Stolt-Nielsen Transportation Group 800 Connecticut Ave 4th Fl E *Web:* www.stolt-nielsen.com	Norwalk	CT	06854	203-838-7100	299-0067	313
Stoltz Marketing Group 101 S Capitol Blvd Ste 900 *Web:* www.stoltzgroup.com	Boise	ID	83702	208-388-0766		5
Stoltzfus RV's & Marine 1335 Wilmington Pike *TF:* 866-755-8858 ■ *Web:* stoltzfus-rec.com	West Chester	PA	19382	866-755-8858		90
Stolze Printing 3435 Hollenberg Dr *TF:* 800-325-4323 ■ *Web:* www.stolze.com	Bridgeton	MO	63044	314-209-1997		627
Stone & Company LLC 57 Bedford St *Web:* stonecpas.com	Lexington	MA	02420	781-862-5000		2
Stone & Ward Inc 225 E Markham St *Web:* www.stoneward.com	Little Rock	AR	72201	501 375 3003		4
Stone Belt Freight Lines Inc 101 W Dillman Rd *TF:* 800-264-2340 ■ *Web:* www.stonebeltfreight.com	Bloomington	IN	47403	812-824-6741		314
Stone Bond Technologies LP 1021 Main St Ste 1550 *Web:* www.stonebond.com	Houston	TX	77002	713-622-8798		177
Stone Castle Hotel & Conference Ctr, The 3050 Green Mtn Dr *TF:* 800-677-6906 ■ *Web:* bransonstonecastle.com	Branson	MO	65616	417-335-4700		379
Stone Child College 8294 Upper Box Elder Rd **Fax:* Admissions ■ *Web:* www.stonechild.edu	Box Elder	MT	59521	406-395-4875	395-4836*	165
Stone Coast Fund Services LLC 2 Portland Sq *TF:* 888-699-2680 ■ *Web:* www.stone-coast.com	Portland	ME	04101	207-699-2680		195
Stone Connection Inc 3045 Business Park Dr *Web:* www.stoneconnection.com	Norcross	GA	30071	770-662-0188		191-1
Stone County 108 E Fourth St *Web:* www.stoneco-mo.us	Galena	MO	65656	417-357-6127	357-6861	338
Stone County 107 W Main St *Web:* www.arkansasties.com	Mountain View	AR	72560	870-269-5550		338
Stone County 323 E Cavers Ave PO Box 7 *Web:* www.stonecountygov.com	Wiggins	MS	39577	601-928-5246	928-6464	338
Stone County Ironworks 408 Ironworks Dr *Web:* stonecountyironworks.com	Mountain View	AR	72560	870-269-8108		321

	Phone	Fax	Class
Stone County Publishing Company Inc 104 W Main St ....Mountain View AR 72560 *Web:* www.stonecountyleader.com	870-269-3841		532-3
Stone Design Corp 2400 Rio Grande Blvd NW .... Albuquerque NM 87104 *Web:* www.stone.com	505-345-4800		177
Stone Energy Corp 625 E Kaliste Saloom Rd .... Lafayette LA 70508 *NYSE: SGY* ■ *Web:* www.stoneenergy.com	337-237-0410	521-2072	536
Stone Farm 200 Stoney Pt Rd .... Paris KY 40361 *Web:* www.stonefarm.com	859-987-3737	987-1474	368
Stone House Consulting LLC 126 Thornton Rd.......................... Thornton PA 19373 *Web:* www.stonehouseconsulting.com	610-358-1791		194
Stone Industrial 9207 51st Ave............ College Park MD 20740 *Web:* www.stoneindustrial.com	301-474-3100		125
Stone Key Group LLC 411 W Putnam Ave Ste 110 .... Greenwich CT 06830 *Web:* www.stonekey.com	203-930-3700		691
Stone Manners Agency 9911 W Pico Blvd Ste 1400 ....Los Angeles CA 90035	323-655-1313	389-1577	731
Stone Mountain Pet Lodge 9935 Radisson Rd NE.....................Minneapolis MN 55449 *Web:* stonemountainpetlodge.com	763-792-8929		794
Stone Mountain State Park 3042 Frank Pkwy ....Roaring Gap NC 28668 *TF:* 877-722-6762 ■ *Web:* ncparks.gov	336-957-8185		565
Stone Parker & Company CPA 7512 Ridge Rd .... Port Richey FL 34668 *Web:* stoneparkercpa.com	727-842-3180		2
Stone Pigman Walther Wittmann LLC 546 Carondelet St.................... New Orleans LA 70130 *TF:* 800-973-1177 ■ *Web:* www.stonepigman.com	504-581-3200		428
Stone Plastics & Manufacturing Inc 8245 Riley St .... Zeeland MI 49464 *Web:* www.stoneplasticsmfg.com	616-748-0740		601
Stone Rudolph & Henry PLC 124 Ctr Pointe Dr .... Clarksville TN 37040 *Web:* www.srhcpas.com	931-648-4786	647-5445	113
Stone Source LLC 215 Pk Ave S .... New York NY 10003 *Web:* www.stonesource.com	212-979-6400		191-1
Stone State Park 5001 Talbot Rd .... Sioux City IA 51103 *Web:* www.iowadnr.gov	712-255-4698		565
Stone Technologies Inc 550 Spirit of St Louis Blvd .... Chesterfield MO 63005 *Web:* www.stonetek.com	636-530-7240		177
Stone Transport Inc 3495 Hack Rd ....Saginaw MI 48601 *Web:* www.stonetransport.com	989-754-4788		311
Stonearch Creative 710 S Second St Fl 7 ....Minneapolis MN 55401 *Web:* www.stonearchcreative.com	612-200-5000		7
Stonebranch Inc 950 N Point Pkwy Ste 200 .... Alpharetta GA 30005 *Web:* www.stonebranch.com	678-366-7887		177
Stonebriar Centre 2601 Preston Rd .... Frisco TX 75034 *Web:* www.shopstonebriar.com	972-668-6255		460
Stonebridge McWhinney LLC 9100 E Panorama Dr Ste 300 ....Englewood CO 80112 *TF:* 800-546-7866 ■ *Web:* www.stonebridgecompanies.com	303-785-3100		378
Stonebridge Press Inc 25 Elm St............Southbridge MA 01550 *TF:* 800-536-5836 ■ *Web:* www.stonebridgepress.com	508-764-4325	764-8015	637-8
Stoneco Inc 7555 Whiteford Rd.............Ottawa Lake MI 49267 *Web:* stoneco.net	734-856-2257		503-5
StoneCreek Capital Inc 18500 Von Karman Ave Ste 590..................Irvine CA 92612 *Web:* www.stonecreekcapital.com	949-752-4580		401
Stonecrop Gardens 81 Stonecrop Ln.........Cold Spring NY 10516 *Web:* www.stonecrop.org	845-265-2000		97
Stonecutter Mills Corp 230 Spindale St .... Spindale NC 28160 *OTC: STCMA* ■ *TF:* 800 421-9512 ■ *Web:* www.stonecuttermills.com	828-286-2341	287-7280	745-1
Stonefield Beach State Recreation Site 95330 US-101 ....Florence OR 97439 *TF:* 800-551-6949 ■ *Web:* www.oregonstateparks.org	800-551-6949		565
StoneFly Inc 21353 Cabot Blvd..................Hayward CA 94545 *TF:* 888-786-6335 ■ *Web:* www.stonefly.com	510-265-1616	265-1565	176
Stonegate Bank 1430 N Federal Hwy ....Fort Lauderdale FL 33304 *Web:* stonegatebank.com	954-315-5500		70
Stonegate Capital Partners 8201 Preston Rd Ste 325 .... Dallas TX 75225 *Web:* www.stonegateinc.com	214-987-4121		690
Stonegate Conference & Banquet Centre, The 2401 W Higgins Rd ....Hoffman Estates IL 60169 *Web:* www.thestonegate.com	847-884-7000		671
Stonegate Production Company LLC 952 Echo Ln Ste 400 ....Houston TX 77024 *Web:* www.stone-gate.net	713-600-8000		536
Stonegates 4031 Kennett Pk .... Greenville DE 19807 *Web:* www.stonegates.com	302-658-6200	658-1510	672
Stoneham Savings Bank 80 Montvale Ave......................... Stoneham MA 02180 *TF:* 888-402-2265 ■ *Web:* www.stonehambank.com	888-402-2265		70
Stonehedge Inn 160 Pawtucket Blvd.......... Tyngsboro MA 01879 *Web:* www.stonehedgeinnandspa.com	978-649-4400	649-9256	379
Stonehenge Capital Company LLC 236 Third St .... Baton Rouge LA 70801 *Web:* www.stonehengecapital.com	225-408-3000		402
Stonehenge Partners Inc 191 W Nationwide Blvd Ste 600.............. Columbus OH 43215 *TF:* 877-298-4409 ■ *Web:* www.stonehengepartners.com	614-246-2500		690
Stonehill College 320 Washington St............ Easton MA 02357 **Fax:* Admissions ■ *TF:* 800-523-2354 ■ *Web:* www.stonehill.edu	508-565-1000	565-1545*	166
Stonehill Group 527 Marquette Ave S Ste 1850.............Minneapolis MN 55402 *Web:* www.stonehillgrp.com	612-436-1360		463
Stoneleigh Recovery Associates Llc 810 Springer Dr .... Lombard IL 60148 *TF:* 866-724-2330 ■ *Web:* www.stoneleighrecoveryassociates.com	866-724-2330		141
Stoneleigh-Burnham School 574 BernaRdston Rd....................... Greenfield MA 01301 *Web:* www.sbschool.org	413-774-2711	772-2602	622
Stonelick State Park 2895 Lake Dr .... Pleasant Plain OH 45162 *Web:* www.ohiodnr.com	513-734-4323		565
Stonemar Capital LLC 32 Union Sq E Ste 1100 ....New York NY 10003 *Web:* www.stonemarproperties.com	212-324-8306		514
StoneMor Partners LP 311 Veterans Hwy.........................Levittown PA 19056 *NYSE: STON* ■ *Web:* stonemor.com	215-826-2800		510
StonePeak Ceramics Inc 314 W Superior Ste 201 ....Chicago IL 60610 *Web:* www.stonepeakceramics.com	312-506-2800		724
Stonepine 150 E Carmel Valley Rd .... Carmel Valley CA 93924 *Web:* www.stonepineestate.com	831-659-2245	659-5160	669
Stoner Electric Inc 1904 SE Ochoco St........................ Milwaukie OR 97222 *Web:* www.stonergroup.com	503-462-6500	659-4968	189-4
Stoneridge Inc 9400 E Market St.................Warren OH 44484 *NYSE: SRI* ■ *Web:* www.stoneridge.com	330-856-2443		60
StoneRidge Investment Partners LLC 301 Lindenwood Dr Ste 310..................Malvern PA 19355 *Web:* www.stoneridgeinvestments.com	610-647-5253		401
Stoneridge Shopping Ctr 1 Stoneridge Mall........................Pleasanton CA 94588 *TF:* 877-746-6642 ■ *Web:* simon.com/mall/stoneridge-shopping-center	925-463-2778	463-1467	460
Stoner-Johnson Insurance Agency 2330 Airport Hwy .... Toledo OH 43609 *Web:* stonerjohnson.com	419-385-3101		390
Stonesong Press LLC 270 W 39th St Ste 201 ....New York NY 10018 *Web:* www.stonesong.com	212-929-4600		94
Stonestown Galleria 3251 20th Ave.......................... San Francisco CA 94132 *Web:* www.stonestowngalleria.com	415-564-8848		460
Stonewall County PO Box P.................Aspermont TX 79502 *Web:* www.stonewallcountytexas.us	940-989-2272	989-2715	338
Stonewall Jackson Hotel & Conference Ctr 24 S Market St .... Staunton VA 24401 *TF:* 866-880-0024 ■ *Web:* www.stonewalljacksonhotel.com	540-885-4848	885-4840	379
Stonewall Jackson Memorial Hospital (SJMH) 230 Hospital Plaza .... Weston WV 26452 *TF:* 866-637-0471 ■ *Web:* www.stonewalljacksonhospital.com	304-269-8000	269-8090	374-3
Stonewall Resort 940 Resort Dr.................Roanoke WV 26447 *TF:* 888-278-8150 ■ *Web:* www.stonewallresort.com	304-269-7400		669
Stoneway Electric Supply Co 402 N Perry St ....Spokane WA 99202 *TF:* 800-841-1408 ■ *Web:* www.stoneway.com	509-535-2933	534-4512	246
Stoneworth Financial LLC 6575 W Loop S Ste 468 ....Houston TX 77401 *Web:* www.stoneworthfinancial.com	713-429-1838		401
Stoney Creek Inn 101 Mariner's Way ....East Peoria IL 61611 *TF:* 800-659-2220 ■ *Web:* stoneycreekhotels.com/home.do	309-694-1300	694-9303	379
Stoneybrook West Golf Club LLC 15501 Towne Commons Blvd.............Winter Garden FL 34787 *TF:* 800-767-3574 ■ *Web:* www.stoneybrookgolf.com	407-877-8533		711
Stonhard Inc 1000 E Pk Ave .... Maple Shade NJ 08052 *TF Cust Svc:* 800-854-0310 ■ *Web:* www.stonhard.com	856-779-7500		291
Stony Brook School 1 Chapman Pkway ....Stony Brook NY 11790 *Web:* www.stonybrookschool.org	631-751-1800		622
Stony Brook State Park 10820 Rt 36 S.............................. Dansville NY 14437 *Web:* parks.ny.gov/parks/118	585-335-8111		565
Stony Brook University 100 Nicolls Rd ....Stony Brook NY 11794 *TF:* 800-872-7869 ■ *Web:* www.stonybrook.edu	631-689-6000	632-9898	166
Stony Brook University Health Sciences Library 8034 Stony Brook University HST Level 3 Rm 136.......................Stony Brook NY 11794 *Web:* library.stonybrook.edu/healthsciences	631-444-2512	444-6649	434-1
Stony Brook University Hospital (SBUH) 101 Nicolls Rd ....Stony Brook NY 11794 *Web:* www.stonybrookmedicine.edu	631-444-4000		374-3
Stony Point Battlefield State Historic Site PO Box 182 .... Stony Point NY 10980 *Web:* parks.ny.gov/historic-sites/8/details.aspx	845-786-2521		565
Stony Point Surgical Ctr 8700 Stony Pt Pkwy .... Richmond VA 23235 *TF:* 800-552-3904 ■ *Web:* www.stonypointsc.com	804-775-4500	643-3542	374-7
Stonyfield Farm Inc 10 Burton Dr .... Londonderry NH 03053 *Web:* www.stonyfield.com	603-437-4040		296-25
Stoops Freightliner- Quality Trailer Inc 1851 W Thompson Rd ....Indianapolis IN 46217 *Web:* truckcountry.com	317-788-1533		57
Stop & Shop Supermarket Co 1385 Hancock St .... Quincy MA 02169 *TF:* 800-767-7772 ■ *Web:* www.stopandshop.com	781-397-0006		345
Stop At Nothing Inc 1400 Marsh Landing Pkwy Ste 107 ....Jacksonville FL 32250 *TF:* 800-771-4410 ■ *Web:* www.stopatnothing.com	904-249-4410		463
Stop In Food Stores Inc 3000 Ogden Rd.........Roanoke VA 24018	540-772-4700		204
STOPS Inc 8855 Grissom Pkwy .... Titusville FL 32780 **Fax Area Code:* 866 ■ *TF:* 866-632-2161 ■ *Web:* www.onecallcm.com	800-848-1989	632-2161*	391-4
Stoptech Ltd 365 Industrial Dr..................Harrison OH 45030 *TF:* 800-537-0102 ■ *Web:* stoptechltd.com	513-202-5500		195
Storage Battery Systems Inc (SBS) N56 W16665 Ridgewood Dr............ Menomonee Falls WI 53051 *TF:* 800-554-2243 ■ *Web:* www.sbsbattery.com	262-703-5800	703-3073	246
Storage Engine Inc 1 Sheila Dr .... Tinton Falls NJ 07724 *TF:* 866-734-8899 ■ *Web:* www.storageengine.com	732-747-6995	747-6542	176
Stor-All Storage 1375 W Hillsboro Blvd.................Deerfield Beach FL 33442 *TF:* 877-786-7255 ■ *Web:* www.stor-all.com	954-421-7888	426-1108	803-3

Name / Address	City	State	Zip	Phone	Fax	Class
Storch Amini PC 2 Grand Central Tower 140 E 45th St 25th Fl *Web:* samlegal.com	New York	NY	10017	212-490-4100		428
Storck USA LP 325 N LaSalle St Ste 400 *Web:* www.storck.com	Chicago	IL	60654	312-467-5700	467-9722	296-8
Store Decor Co, The 5050 Boyd Blvd. *TF:* 800-831-3267 ■ *Web:* www.thestoredecor.com	Rowlett	TX	75088	972-475-4404		344
Store Kraft Mfg Co 500 Irving St *Web:* www.storekraft.com	Beatrice	NE	68310	402-223-2348		286
Store Opening Solutions (SOS) 800 Middle Tennessee Blvd *TF:* 877-388-9262 ■ *Web:* www.store-solutions.com	Murfreesboro	TN	37129	877-388-9262		449
Store Supply Warehouse LLC 9801 Page Ave *TF:* 800-823-0004 ■ *Web:* www.storesupply.com	St Louis	MO	63132	314-427-8887		791
Store51 3653 Regent Blvd Ste 606 *Web:* www.store51.com	Jacksonville	FL	32224	904-998-2222		791
Stored Technology Solutions LLC 543 Queensbury Ave. *Web:* www.storedtech.com	Queensbury	NY	12804	518-793-1111		196
Storefront Political Media 160 Pine St Ste 700 *Web:* www.storefrontpolitical.com	San Francisco	CA	94111	415-834-0501		636
Storeimage Programs Inc 250 rue Deveault *Web:* www.storeimage.com	Gatineau	QC	J8Z1S6	819-778-0114		5
Storer Coachways 3519 McDonald Ave *TF:* 800-621-3383 ■ *Web:* www.storercoachways.com	Modesto	CA	95358	209-521-8250	578-4888	107
Storer Meats Company Inc 3700 Clark Ave *Web:* fivestarbrandmeats.com	Cleveland	OH	44109	216-621-7538		296-26
Storey County 26 S B St *Web:* storeycounty.org	Virginia City	NV	89440	775-847-0968	847-0949	338
Storey Publishing LLC 210 Mass Moca Way **Fax:* Edit ■ *TF:* 800-827-7444 ■ *Web:* www.storey.com	North Adams	MA	01247	413-346-2100	346-2199*	637-2
Stork News of America Inc 1305 Hope Mills Rd Ste A *TF:* 800-633-6395 ■ *Web:* www.storknews.com	Fayetteville	NC	28304	910-429-2229	426-2473	310
Stork Prints America Inc 3201 Rotary Dr *Web:* www.spgprints.com	Charlotte	NC	28269	704-598-7171		744
Storkcraft Baby 12033 Riverside Way Ste 200 *TF:* 877-274-0277 ■ *Web:* www.storkcraftdirect.com	Richmond	BC	V6W1G3	604-274-5121	274-9727	319-2
Storm Chasing Adventure Tours 1627 W Main St Ste 105 *Web:* www.stormchasing.com	Bozeman	MT	59715	970-367-5395		760
Storm Industries Inc & Affiliated Co 23223 Normandie Ave *Web:* stormind.com	Torrance	CA	90501	310-534-5232		350
Storm Internet Services Inc 1760 Courtwood Crescent *TF:* 866-257-8676 ■ *Web:* www.storm.ca	Ottawa	ON	K2C2B5	613-567-6585	567-3227	225
Storm King School 314 Mountain Rd *TF:* 800-225-9144 ■ *Web:* www.sks.org	Cornwall On Hudson	NY	12520	845-534-7892		622
Storm King State Park Palisades Interstate Park Commission *Web:* www.stateparks.com/storm_king_state_park_in_new_york.html	Bear Mountain	NY	10911	845-786-2701		565
Storm Products Inc 165 S 800 W. *TF:* 800-369-4402 ■ *Web:* www.stormbowling.com	Brigham City	UT	84302	435-723-0403		710
Storm Resources Ltd 640 5 Ave SW Ste 200 *Web:* www.stormresourcesltd.com	Calgary	AB	T2P3G4	403-817-6145		536
Storm Technologies Inc 411 N Depot St *Web:* www.stormeng.com	Albemarle	NC	28002	704-983-2040		194
Storm Ventures 3000 Sand Hill Rd Bldg 4 Bldg 4 Ste 210 *Web:* www.stormventures.com	Menlo Park	CA	94025	650-926-8800		792
StormHarbour Securities LP 140 E 45th St Two Grand Central Tower 33rd Fl *TF:* 800-662-2739 ■ *Web:* www.stormharbour.com	New York	NY	10017	212-905-2500		690
Stormont-Vail Regional Health Ctr 1500 SW Tenth Ave. *TF:* 800-432-2951 ■ *Web:* www.stormontvail.org	Topeka	KS	66604	785-354-6000	354-6926	374-3
Storms Welding & Manufacturing Inc 513 West Lake St S PO Box 76 *Web:* stormsweldingmfg.com	Cologne	MN	55322	952-466-3343		350
Stornoway Communications 105 Gordon Baker Rd *Web:* www.stornoway.com	North York	ON	M2H3P8	416-756-2404		740
Stornoway Diamond Corp 980 W First St Ste 118 *TSE: SWY* ■ *TF:* 877-331-2232 ■ *Web:* www.stornowaydiamonds.com	North Vancouver	BC	V7P3N4	604-983-7750		503-3
Storopack Inc 12007 S Woodruff Ave *TF:* 800-829-1491 ■ *Web:* www.storopack.us	Downey	CA	90241	562-803-5582	803-4462	601
Storr Tractor Co 3191 Rt 22 *TF:* 800-526-3802 ■ *Web:* www.storrtractor.com	Branchburg	NJ	08876	908-722-9830	722-9847	429
Storrowton Village Museum 1305 Memorial Ave Eastern States Exposition *Web:* www.thebige.com	West Springfield	MA	01089	413-205-5051		520
StorterChilds Printing Company Inc 1540 NE Waldo Rd *Web:* www.storterchilds.com	Gainesville	FL	32641	352-376-2658		627
Story Construction Co 300 S Bell Ave *Web:* www.storycon.com	Ames	IA	50010	515-232-4358	232-0599	186
Story County 1315 S B Ave *Web:* www.storycountyiowa.gov	Nevada	IA	50201	515-382-7410		338
storyminers Inc 1862 Wilkenson Crossing *Web:* storyminers.com/speaking-workshops	Marietta	GA	30066	770-425-9830		196
Storytellers Cafe 1600 S Disneyland Dr. *Web:* disneyland.disney.go.com	Anaheim	CA	92802	714-781-3463		671

Name / Address	City	State	Zip	Phone	Fax	Class
Stott Outdoor Advertising PO Box 7209 **Fax Area Code:* 530 ■ *TF:* 888-342-7868 ■ *Web:* stottoutdoor.com	Chico	CA	95927	888-342-7868	342-0712*	8
Stottler Henke Associates Inc 1650 S Amphlett Blvd Ste 310 *Web:* www.stottlerhenke.com	San Mateo	CA	94402	650-931-2700		180
Stoudt Co 1618 Judson Rd.	Longview	TX	75601	903-753-7239		81-1
Stouffer Mechanical Contractor LLC 1697 Opportunity Ave. *Web:* stouffermechanical.com	Chambersburg	PA	17201	717-262-0078		610
Stoughton Area School District 320 N St *Web:* www.stoughton.k12.wi.us	Stoughton	WI	53589	608-877-5000		685
Stoughton Hospital 900 Ridge St. *Web:* www.stoughtonhospital.com	Stoughton	WI	53589	608-873-6611	873-2355	374-3
Stoughton Public Library 304 S Fourth St *Web:* www.stoughton.org/library-0	Stoughton	WI	53589	608-873-6281		434-3
Stoughton Trailers LLC 416 S Academy St *TF:* 800-227-5391 ■ *Web:* www.stoughtontrailers.com	Stoughton	WI	53589	608-873-2500	873-2575	779
Stouse Inc 300 New Century Pkwy. *Web:* www.stouse.com	New Century	KS	66031	913-764-5757		701
STOUT 6425 W Florissant Ave *Web:* www.stoutsign.com	Saint Louis	MO	63136	314-385-4600		701
Stout Management Co 10151 Park Run Dr *Web:* www.smc-lv.com	Las Vegas	NV	89145	702-227-0444		652
Stow Co, The 3311 Windquest Dr *Web:* www.windquestco.com	Holland	MI	49424	616-399-3311	399-8784	817
Stowe Mountain Resort 5781 Mountain Rd *TF:* 800-253-4754 ■ *Web:* www.stowe.com	Stowe	VT	05672	802-253-3000		669
Stoweflake Mountain Resort & Spa 1746 Mountain Rd PO Box 369 *TF:* 800-253-2232 ■ *Web:* www.stoweflake.com	Stowe	VT	05672	802-253-7355	253-6858	669
Stowell Associates Select Staff Inc 4485 N Oakland Ave *Web:* caremanagedhomecare.com	Milwaukee	WI	53211	414-963-2600		363
Stowers Institute For Medical Research 1000 E 50th St *Web:* www.stowers.org	Kansas City	MO	64110	816-926-4000	926-2000	305
Stowers Machinery Corp 6301 Old Rutledge Pike NE. *Web:* www.stowerscat.com	Knoxville	TN	37924	865-546-1414	595-1030	358
Stowers Rental & Supply Inc 10644 Lexington Dr *TF:* 800-362-9690 ■ *Web:* www.stowerscat-inventory.com	Knoxville	TN	37932	865-218-8800		791
Stow-Munroe Falls Chamber of Commerce 4381 Hudson Dr Ste 2450 *Web:* www.smfcc.com	Stow	OH	44224	330-688-1579	688-6234	139
Stow-Munroe Falls City School District 4350 Allen Rd. *Web:* smfschools.org	Stow	OH	44224	330-689-5445		685
STR Grants LLC 4103 Chain Bridge Rd 3rd Fl *Web:* www.strllc.com	Fairfax	VA	22030	703-460-9000		809
Strack & Van Til Super Market Inc 9632 Cline Ave *Web:* www.strackandvantil.com	Highland	IN	46322	219-924-6932		345
Strad Energy Services Ltd 440 - Second Ave SW Ste 1200 *TF:* 800-899-1265 ■ *Web:* www.stradenergy.com	Calgary	AB	T2P5E9	403-232-6900		536
Strafford County 259 County Farm Rd *TF:* 800-467-7423 ■ *Web:* www.co.strafford.nh.us	Dover	NH	03820	603-742-1458	743-4407	338
Strafford Publications Inc PO Box 13729 *TF:* 800-926-7926 ■ *Web:* www.straffordpub.com	Atlanta	GA	30324	404-881-1141	881-0074	637-9
Strafford Technology 1D Commons Dr. *Web:* www.strafford.com	Londonderry	NH	03053	603-434-2550		177
Strahman Valves Inc 2801 Baglyos Cir *Web:* www.strahmanvalves.com	Bethlehem	PA	18020	484-893-5099		609
Straight A Tours & Travel 6881 Kingspointe Pkwy Ste 18 *TF:* 800-237-5440 ■ *Web:* straightatours.com	Orlando	FL	32819	407-896-1242	896-1151	760
Straight Arrow Products Inc 2020 Highland Ave *TF:* 800-827-9815 ■ *Web:* straightarrowinc.com	Bethlehem	PA	18020	610-882-9606		231
Straight North LLC 1001 W 31st St. *TF:* 866-353-3953 ■ *Web:* www.straightnorth.com	Downers Grove	IL	60515	866-353-3953		7
Straight Spouse Network (SSN) PO Box 4985 *Web:* www.straightspouse.org	Chicago	IL	60680	773-413-8213		48-21
Straight Way Radio LLC 407 N Howard Ave	Tampa	FL	33606	813-259-9867		645-162
Straight Wharf 6 Harbor Sq. *Web:* straightwharfrestaurant.com	Nantucket	MA	02554	508-228-4499		671
Straightforward Media LLC 8088 N 110th Dr. *Web:* www.straightforwardmedia.com	Peoria	AZ	85345	623-266-3962		5
Strainsert Inc 12 Union Hill Rd. *TF:* 800-529-1502 ■ *Web:* www.strainsert.com	West Conshohocken	PA	19428	610-825-3310		407
Strait Music Co 2428 W Ben White Blvd. *TF:* 800-725-8877 ■ *Web:* www.straitmusic.com	Austin	TX	78704	512-476-6927		526
Straith Hospital for Special Surgery 23901 Lahser Rd *TF:* 800-994-6610 ■ *Web:* www.straithhospital.org	Southfield	MI	48033	248-357-3360	357-0915	374-7
Straits Cafe 333 Santana Row Ste 1100 *Web:* www.straitsrestaurants.com	San Jose	CA	95128	408-246-6320		671
Straits State Park 720 Church St. *Web:* www.michigandnr.com	Saint Ignace	MI	49781	906-643-8620		565
Strake Jesuit College Preparatory Inc 8900 Bellaire Blvd *Web:* www.strakejesuit.org	Houston	TX	77036	713-774-7651		148
Stranahan Arboretum 4131 Tantara Dr *Web:* www.utoledo.edu	Toledo	OH	43623	419-841-1007	530-4421	97

	Phone	Fax	Class
Stranahan House Museum Inc 335 SE Sixth Ave .... Fort Lauderdale FL 33301 *TF:* 800-435-7352 ■ *Web:* www.stranahanhouse.org	954-524-4736	525-2838	520
Stranahan Theater 4645 Heatherdowns Blvd .... Toledo OH 43614 *TF:* 866-381-7469 ■ *Web:* www.stranahantheater.org	419-381-8851		572
Strand Analytical Laboratories LLC 5770 Decatur Blvd Ste A.............Indianapolis IN 46241 *TF:* 800-955-6288 ■ *Web:* stranddiagnostics.com/forensics	317-455-2100		418
Strand Assoc Inc 910 W Wingra Dr .... Madison WI 53715 *Web:* www.strand.com	608-251-4843	251-8655	261
Strand Book Store Inc 828 Broadway .... New York NY 10003 *TF:* 800-366-3664 ■ *Web:* www.strandbooks.com	212-473-1452		95
Strand Lighting 10911 Petal St.................. Dallas TX 75238 *TF:* 800-733-0564 ■ *Web:* www.strandlighting.com	214-647-7880	647-8031	439
Strand Management Solutions 61 Princeton Hightstown Rd..........Princeton Junction NJ 08550 *Web:* www.strandmanagement.com	609-799-7715		177
Strand Media Group 3955 Hwy 17 Bypass Ste D PO Box 1389.....Murrells Inlet SC 29576 *Web:* www.strandmedia.com	843-626-8911	626-6452	646
Strand Theatre 619 Louisiana Ave ....Shreveport LA 71101 *TF:* 800-313-6373 ■ *Web:* www.thestrandtheatre.com	318-226-1481	424-5434	572
Strang Communications 600 Rinehart Rd .... Lake Mary FL 32746 *Web:* www.charismamedia.com	407-333-0600	333-7100	637-9
Strang Corp 8905 Lake Ave ....Cleveland OH 44102 *Web:* www.strangcorp.com	216-961-6767	961-1966	670
Strange Luther (Sen R - AL) 326 Russell Bldg ....Washington DC 20510 *Web:* www.strange.senate.gov	202-224-4124	224-3149	342-2
Strange's Florist Inc 3313 Mechanicsville Pk.................... Richmond VA 23223 *TF:* 800-421-4070 ■ *Web:* stranges.com	804-321-2200		292
Stranger, The 1535 11th Ave 3rd Fl.............. Seattle WA 98122 *Web:* www.thestranger.com	206-323-7101	323-7203	532-5
Strasbaugh 825 Buckley Rd............. San Luis Obispo CA 93401 *OTC: STRB* ■ *Web:* www.strasbaugh.com	805-541-6424	541-6425	386
Strasenburgh Planetarium 657 E Ave Rochester Museum & Science Ctr .....Rochester NY 14607 *Web:* www.rmsc.org	585-271-4320	271-0492	598
Strassburger Mckenna Gutnick & Gefsky 525 Third St .... Beaver PA 15009 *Web:* www.smgglaw.com	724-846-1372		445
Strassman Insurance Services Inc 26351 Curtiss Wright Pkwy ....Richmond Heights OH 44143 *Web:* strassman.net	216-289-1500		390
Strat Land Exploration Co 15 E Fifth St Ste 2020......................... Tulsa OK 74103 *Web:* stratland.com	918-584-3844		536
Strat@comm 1156 15th St NW Ste 800........Washington DC 20005 *Web:* www.stratacomm.net	202-289-2001		636
Strata Decision Technology LLC 2001 S First St Ste 200.................. Champaign IL 61820 *Web:* www.stratadecision.com	217-359-8422		177
STRATA Energy Services Inc 39207 Range Rd 271 Blindman Industrial Pk Ste 8............................Red Deer County AB T4S2M4 *Web:* www.strataenergy.net	403-358-3442		538
Strata Health Solutions Inc 933 - 17 Ave SW Ste 600........................ Calgary BC T2T5R6 *TF:* 866-556-5005 ■ *Web:* stratahealth.com	866-556-5005		179
Strata Inc 8653 W Hackamore Dr.................. Boise ID 83709 *Web:* strategeotech.com	208-376-8200		261
Strata Information Group 3935 Harney St Ste 203 .... San Diego CA 92110 *Web:* sigcorp.com	619-296-0170		180
Strata Oil & Gas Inc 10010 - 98 St PO Box 7770 .... Peace River AB T8S1T3 *TF:* 877-237-5443 ■ *Web:* www.strataoil.com	403-237-5443		536
Strata Products Worldwide LLC 8995 Roswell Rd Ste 200...............Sandy Springs GA 30350 *TF:* 800-691-6601 ■ *Web:* www.strataworldwide.com	770-321-2500		360-3
Stratacache Inc 2 Emmet St Ste 200 ....Dayton OH 45405 *TF:* 800-244-8915 ■ *Web:* www.stratacache.com	937-224-0485		180
Stratagem Inc 10922 N Cedarburg Rd ....Mequon WI 53092 *TF:* 800-228-4422 ■ *Web:* www.stratagemconsulting.com	262-532-2700		225
Stratagraph Inc 125 Raggio Rd.................. Scott LA 70583 *TF:* 800-256-1147 ■ *Web:* www.stratagraph.com	337-232-5510		538
Stratasys Inc 7665 Commerce Way...........Eden Prairie MN 55344 *NASDAQ: SSYS* ■ *TF:* 800-937-3010 ■ *Web:* www.stratasys.com	952-937-3000	937-0070	261
StratBridge LLC 124 Mt Auburn St University Pl Ste 200........Cambridge MA 02138 *Web:* www.stratbridge.com	978-772-4546		809
Stratco Inc 14821 N 73rd St ....Scottsdale AZ 85260 *Web:* www.stratco.com	480-991-0450	991-0314	537
Stratcor Inc 1180 Omega Dr Ste 1180.......... Pittsburgh PA 15205 *Web:* vanadium.evraz.com	412-787-4500		502
StrateGen Consulting LLC 2150 Allston Way Ste 210 ....Berkeley CA 94704 *Web:* strategen.com	510-665-7811		196
Strategic Account Management Assn 33 N La Salle St Ste 3700......................Chicago IL 60602 *Web:* www.strategicaccounts.org	312-251-3131		2
Strategic Advisors Inc 400 Southpointe Blvd Plaza I Ste 440.........Canonsburg PA 15317 *Web:* www.strategicad.com	724-743-5800		194
Strategic Air & Space Museum 28210 W Pk Hwy .... Ashland NE 68003 *Web:* sacmuseum.org	402-944-3100	944-3160	520
Strategic Analysis Inc 4075 Wilson Blvd Ste 200 .... Arlington VA 22203 *Web:* www.sainc.com	703-527-5410	527-5445	466
Strategic and Competitive Intelligence Professional (SCIP) 7550 IH 10 W Ste 400 ....San Antonio TX 78229 *Web:* www.scip.org	703-739-0696	739-2524	49-12
Strategic Compliance Solutions LLC 18 Mallard Point Rd .... Essex CT 06426 *Web:* www.strategiccompliancesolutions.com	860-767-3006		734
Strategic Decisions Group 745 Emerson St .... Palo Alto CA 94301 *Web:* www.sdg.com	650-475-4400	475-4401	194
Strategic Development Solutions LLC 11150 W Olympic Blvd Ste 910 ....Los Angeles CA 90064 *Web:* www.sdsgroup.com	310-914-5333		196
Strategic Diagnostics Inc 111 Pencader Dr.................................Newark DE 19702 *NASDAQ: SDIX* ■ *TF:* 800-544-8881 ■ *Web:* www.sdix.com	302-456-6789		231
Strategic Distribution Inc 1414 Radcliffe St Ste 300.......................... Bristol PA 19007 *TF:* 800-322-2644 ■ *Web:* www.sdi.com	215-633-1900	633-4426	385
Strategic Finance Magazine 10 Paragon Dr Ste 1 .... Montvale NJ 07645 *TF:* 800-638-4427 ■ *Web:* imanet.org	201-573-9000	474-1603	457-5
Strategic Financial Alliance Inc, The 2200 Century Pkwy Ste 500 .... Atlanta GA 30345 *TF:* 888-447-2444 ■ *Web:* www.thesfa.net	678-954-4000		401
Strategic Global Advisors LLC 100 Bayview Cir Ste 650.................Newport Beach CA 92660 *Web:* www.sgadvisors.com	949-706-2640		528
Strategic Hotels & Resorts 200 W Madison St Ste 1700....................Chicago IL 60606 *NYSE: BEE* ■ *Web:* www.strategichotels.com	312-658-5000		654
Strategic Information Resources Inc 155 Brookdale Dr ....Springfield MA 01104 *TF:* 800-332-9479 ■ *Web:* www.backgrounddecision.com	413-736-4511		218
Strategic Investments & Holdings Inc (SIHI) 4445 N A1A Ste 247 .... Vero Beach FL 32963 *Web:* www.sihi.net	716-857-6000	857-6490	792
Strategic Materials Inc 16365 Pk Ten Pl Ste 200 ....Houston TX 77084 *TF:* 800-385-7275 ■ *Web:* www.strategicmaterials.com	281-647-2700	647-2710	660
Strategic Media Services Inc 1911 N Ft Myer Dr Ste 400....................Arlington VA 20009 *Web:* www.strategicmediaservices.com	202-337-5700		514
Strategic Network Consulting 5555 W Loop S Ste 450 ....Houston TX 77401 *Web:* www.snc.net	713-871-0011	871-0057	180
Strategic News Service 38 Yew Ln.............................Friday Harbor WA 98250 *Web:* www.tapsns.com	360-378-1023		530
Strategic Pharmaceutical Solutions Inc 17014 NE Sandy Blvd.........................Portland OR 97230 *Web:* vetsource.com	503-802-7400		238
Strategic Power Systems Inc 11016 Rushmore Dr Frenette Bldg Ste 275....... Charlotte NC 28277 *Web:* www.spsinc.com	704-544-5501		225
Strategic Public Partners Inc 88 E Broad St Ste 1770..................... Columbus OH 43215 *Web:* www.1spp.com	614-222-8490		194
Strategic Resources Inc 7927 Jones Branch Dr .... McLean VA 22102 *Web:* www.sri-hq.com	703-749-3040	749-3046	194
Strategic Restaurants Inc 3000 Executive Pkwy Ste 515.................. San Ramon CA 94583	925-328-3300		670
Strategic Systems Consulting Inc 7742 Spalding Dr Ste 363 .... Norcross GA 30092 **Fax Area Code: 404* ■ *Web:* www.eapps.com	770-448-2100	601-7454*	39
Strategos 1110 Burlingame Ave Ste 211 .... Burlingame CA 94010 *Web:* www.strategos.com	650-344-1999		463
Strategy Companion Corp 3240 El Camino Real Ste 120....................Irvine CA 92602 *TF:* 800-905-6792 ■ *Web:* www.strategycompanion.com	714-460-8398		179
Strategy Institute 401 Richmond St W Ste 401................... Toronto ON M5V3A8 *TF:* 866-298-9343 ■ *Web:* www.strategyinstitute.com	866-298-9343		466
Strater Hotel 699 Main Ave.....................Durango CO 81301 *TF:* 800-247-4431 ■ *Web:* www.strater.com	970-247-4431	259-2208	379
Stratford & District Chamber of Commerce 55 Lorne Ave E ....Stratford ON N5A6S4 *Web:* www.stratfordchamber.com	519-273-5250	273-2229	137
Stratford Building Supply Inc 215 Railroad St...............................Stratford WI 54484 *Web:* stratfordbuilding.com	715-687-4125		364
Stratford Court 45 Katherine Blvd........... Palm Harbor FL 34684 *TF:* 888-434-4648 ■ *Web:* www.sunriseseniorliving.com	727-787-1500		672
Stratford General Hospital 46 General Hospital Dr ....Stratford ON N5A2Y6 *TF:* 888-275-1102 ■ *Web:* www.hpha.ca	519-272-8210	271-7137	374-2
Stratford Homes LP 402 S Weber Ave ....Stratford WI 54484 *TF:* 800-448-1524 ■ *Web:* www.stratfordhomes.com	715-687-3133	687-3453	106
Stratford Hotel 242 Powell St............. San Francisco CA 94102 *TF:* 888-688-0038 ■ *Web:* www.hotelstratford.com	415-397-7080	397-7087	379
Stratford Insurance Co 400 Parson's Pond Dr.................. Franklin Lakes NJ 07417 *Web:* www.westernworld.com	201-847-8600	847-1010	391-4
Stratford Square Mall 152 Stratford Sq .... Bloomingdale IL 60108 *Web:* stratfordmall.com	630-539-1000		460
Stratford Star 1000 Bridgeport Ave.............. Shelton CT 06484 *TF Advestisement:* 800-372-2790 ■ *Web:* www.stratfordstar.com	203-402-2319	926-2091	532-4
Stratford University School of Culinary Arts 7777 Leesburg Pk.......................Falls Church VA 22043 *TF:* 800-444-0804 ■ *Web:* www.stratford.edu/?page=home_culinary	703-821-8570		163
Strathallan Hotel 550 E Ave..................Rochester NY 14607 *Web:* www.strathallan.com	585-461-5010		379
Strathcona Hotel 60 York St.................... Toronto ON M5J1S8 *TF:* 800-268-8304 ■ *Web:* www.thestrathconahotel.com	416-363-3321	363-4679	379
Strathcona Hotel, The 919 Douglas St .... Victoria BC V8W2C2 *TF:* 800-663-7476 ■ *Web:* www.strathconahotel.com	250-383-7137		379
Strathcona Paper LP 77 County Rd 16 RR #7 ....Napanee ON K7R3L2 *Web:* www.strathconapaper.com	613-378-6672		100
Strathmore Co 2000 Gary Ln......................Geneva IL 60134 *TF:* 800-848-6368 ■ *Web:* www.strath.com	630-232-9677		627
StratiMind 268 Bishops Forest Dr ....Waltham MA 02452 *Web:* www.stratimind.com	781-373-3750		41

	Phone	Fax	Class
Stratix 4920 Avalon Ridge Pkwy Norcross GA 30071	770-326-7580	326-7593	173-7
TF: 800-883-8300 ■ *Web:* www.stratixcorp.com			
StratMar Retail Services Inc			
109 Willett Ave Port Chester NY 10573	914-937-7171		7
Web: www.stratmar.com			
Strato Inc 100 New England Ave Piscataway NJ 08854	732-981-1515		791
TF: 800-522-3038 ■ *Web:* www.stratoinc.com			
Straton Industries Inc 180 Surf Ave Stratford CT 06615	203-375-4488		454
TF: 800-229-5599 ■ *Web:* www.straton.com			
Stratos Global Corp			
6550 Rock Spring Dr Ste 650 Bethesda MD 20817	301-214-8800	214-8801	681
TF: 800-563-2255 ■ *Web:* www.stratosglobal.com			
Stratose			
2 Concourse Pkwy NE # 300 Ste 300 Atlanta GA 30328	404-459-7201		390
Web: www.coalitionamerica.com			
Stratosphere Tower Hotel & Casino			
2000 S Las Vegas Blvd Las Vegas NV 89104	702-380-7777		133
TF: 800-998-6937 ■ *Web:* www.stratospherehotel.com			
Strattec Security Corp			
3333 W Good Hope Rd Milwaukee WI 53209	414-247-3333	247-3329	60
NASDAQ: STRT ■ *TF General:* 800-547-7377 ■ *Web:* www.strattec.com			
Stratton & Assoc Pllc			
398 S Ninth St Ste 290 Boise ID 83702	208-336-4953		2
Web: strattoncpa.com			
Stratton Brook State Park			
57 Gun Mill Rd Bloomfield CT 06002	860-566-4840		565
Web: www.ct.gov			
Stratton Equity Co-op Co Inc			
98 Colorado Ave PO Box 25 Stratton CO 80836	719-348-5326		275
TF: 800-438-7070 ■ *Web:* www.strattoncoop.com			
Stratton Gilmore Group			
37 Old Shore Rd Madison WI 53704	608-249-3610		195
Web: strattongilmoregroup.com			
Stratton Hats Inc 3200 Randolph St Bellwood IL 60104	708-544-5220	544-5243	155-9
TF: 877-453-3777 ■ *Web:* www.strattonhats.com			
Stratton Seed Co 1530 Hwy 79 S Stuttgart AR 72160	870-673-4433		694
TF: 800-264-4433 ■ *Web:* www.strattonseed.com			
Stratton Veterans Affairs Medical Ctr			
113 Holland Ave Albany NY 12208	518-626-5000		374-8
TF: 800-223-4810 ■ *Web:* www.albany.va.gov			
Stratus Properties Inc			
212 Lavaca St Ste 300 Austin TX 78701	512-478-5788	478-6340	653
NYSE: STRS ■ *TF:* 800-690-0315 ■ *Web:* www.stratusproperties.com			
Stratus Technologies			
111 Powdermill Rd Maynard MA 01754	978-461-7000		178-12
TF: 800-787-2887 ■ *Web:* www.stratus.com			
Stratz Heating & Cooling Inc			
20960 19 Mile Rd Big Rapids MI 49307	231-796-3717		189-10
Web: stratzheatingandcooling.com			
Straub International Inc			
214 SW 40th Ave Great Bend KS 67530	620-792-5256	793-5167	274
TF: 800-658-1706 ■ *Web:* www.straubint.com			
Straubel Company Inc 1891 Commerce Dr De Pere WI 54115	920-336-1412		558
Web: www.straubelcompany.com			
Straus News Inc 20 W Ave Chester NY 10918	845-469-9000		532-3
Web: www.strausnews.com			
Strauss & Troy 150 E Fourth St Cincinnati OH 45202	513-621-2120	241-8259	428
Web: www.strausstroy.com			
StraussGroup Inc 701 Seneca St Ste 603 Buffalo NY 14210	716-631-3200		260
Web: straussgroup.com			
Straw Hat Cooperative Corp			
18 Crow Canyon Ct Ste 270 San Ramon CA 94583	925-837-3400		194
Web: www.strawhatpizza.com			
Strawberry Hill Museum & Cultural Ctr			
720 N Fourth St Kansas City KS 66101	913-371-3264		520
TF: 800-899-1893 ■ *Web:* www.strawberryhillmuseum.org			
Strawbery Banke Museum			
14 Hancock St Portsmouth NH 03801	603-433-1100	433-1129	520
TF: 800-441-4620 ■ *Web:* www.strawberybanke.org			
Strawbridge Studios Inc			
3000 Hillsborough Rd Durham NC 27705	919-286-9512		627
TF: 800-561-3357 ■ *Web:* www.strawbridge.net			
Stray Light Optical Technologies Inc			
821 S Lake Rd S Scottsburg IN 47170	812-752-9104		261
Strayer Consulting Group Inc			
16151 Wood Acres Rd Los Gatos CA 95030	408-399-1500		463
TF: 800-924-0693 ■ *Web:* www.strayerconsulting.com			
Strayer Education Inc			
2303 Dulles Stn Blvd Herndon VA 20171	703-247-2500		242
NASDAQ: STRA ■ *Web:* www.strayereducation.com			
Strayer University			
4710 Auth Pl Ste 100 Suitland MD 20746	888-311-0355		166
TF: 888-311-0355 ■ *Web:* www.strayer.edu			
Strayer University 1133 15th St NW Washington DC 20005	202-408-2400		166
TF: 888-311-0355 ■ *Web:* www.strayer.edu			
Takoma Park 6830 Laurel St NW Washington DC 20012	202-722-8100		166
TF: 888-311-0355 ■ *Web:* www.strayer.edu			
Strayer University Alexandria			
2730 Eisenhower Ave Alexandria VA 22314	888-311-0355		166
TF: 888-311-0355 ■ *Web:* www.strayer.edu			
Strayer University Arlington			
2121 15th St N Arlington VA 22201	703-892-5100		166
TF: 888-478-7293 ■ *Web:* www.strayer.edu			
Strayer University Fredericksburg			
150 Riverside Pkwy Ste 100 Fredericksburg VA 22406	540-374-4300	301-1711*	166
**Fax:* Admissions ■ *TF:* 888-311-0355 ■ *Web:* www.strayer.edu			
Strayer University Loudoun			
45150 Russell Branch Pkwy Ste 200 Ashburn VA 20147	703-729-8800		166
Web: www.strayer.edu			
Strayer University Manassas			
9990 Battleview Pkwy Manassas VA 20109	703-330-8400		166
Web: www.strayer.edu			
Strayer University Woodbridge			
13385 Minnieville Rd Woodbridge VA 22192	703-878-2800		166
Web: www.strayer.edu			
Stream Companies Inc 400 Lapp Rd Malvern PA 19355	610-644-8637		7
TF: 800-865-1058 ■ *Web:* www.streamcompanies.com			
Stream Gas & Electric Ltd			
1950 Stemmons Fwy Ste 3000 Dallas TX 75207	866-447-8732		787
TF: 866-447-8732 ■ *Web:* mystream.com			
Streambox Inc			
1848 Westlake Ave N Ste 200 Seattle WA 98109	206-956-0544		242
Web: www.streambox.com			
StreamCo LLC 4198 Cox Rd Suite 203 Richmond VA 23255	804-955-4397	346-5901	652
Web: streamco.com			
Stream-Flo Industries Ltd			
4505 - 74 Ave Edmonton AB T6B2H5	780-468-6789	469-7724	537
TF: 800-809-4217 ■ *Web:* www.streamflo.com			
Streamingedge 255 Greenwich St 5th Fl New York NY 10007	212-791-6026		225
Web: www.streamingedge.com			
Streamlight Inc 30 Eagleville Rd Eagleville PA 19403	610-631-0600	631-0712	439
TF: 800-523-7488 ■ *Web:* www.streamlight.com			
Streamline Health Solutions Inc			
10200 Alliance Rd Ste 200 Cincinnati OH 45242	513-794-7100	794-9770	39
NASDAQ: STRM ■ *TF:* 800-878-5269 ■ *Web:* streamlinehealth.net			
StreamSend 78 York St Sacramento CA 95814	916-326-5407		393
TF: 877-439-4078 ■ *Web:* www.streamsend.com			
StreamTrack Media Inc			
345 Chapala St Santa Barbara CA 93101	805-308-9196		5
Web: streamtrack.com			
Streamwood Behavioral Health Ctr			
1400 E Irving Pk Rd Streamwood IL 60107	630-837-9000	837-2639	374-1
TF: 800-272-7790 ■ *Web:* www.streamwoodhospital.com			
Streamwood Chamber of Commerce			
22 W Streamwood Blvd PO Box 545 Streamwood IL 60107	630-837-5200	837-5251	139
TF: 800-697-9515 ■ *Web:* www.streamwoodchamber.com			
Streamworks LLC 3770 Dunlap St N Arden Hills MN 55112	651-486-0252		4
Web: streamworksmn.com			
Streater Inc 411 S First Ave Albert Lea MN 56007	800-527-4197	373-7630*	286
**Fax Area Code:* 507 ■ *TF:* 800-527-4197 ■ *Web:* www.streater.com			
Streator Area Chamber of Commerce & Industry			
320 E Main St PO Box 360 Streator IL 61364	815-672-2921	672-1768	139
Web: www.streatorchamber.com			
Streator Dependable Manufacturing Co			
1705 N Shabbona St Streator IL 61364	815-672-0551		470
TF: 800-795-0551 ■ *Web:* www.streatordependable.com			
Streck Inc 7002 S 109th St Omaha NE 68128	402-333-1982		231
TF: 800-228-6090 ■ *Web:* www.streck.com			
Streebo Inc			
10998 S Wilcrest Dr Ste 162 Houston TX 77099	832-426-2700		463
Web: www.streebo.com			
Street & Smith's SportsBusiness Journal			
120 W Morehead St Ste 310 Charlotte NC 28202	704-973-1410	973-1401	457-21
Web: www.sportsbusinessdaily.com			
Street Capital Financial Corp			
1 Yonge St Ste 2401 Toronto ON M5E1E5	647-259-7873		509
TF: 800-564-6253 ■ *Web:* www.streetcapital.ca			
Street Fighter Marketing Inc			
467 Waterbury Ct Gahanna OH 43230	614-337-7474	337-2233	195
Web: www.streetfighter.com			
Street Solutions Inc			
2930 Plaza Five Jersey City NJ 07311	201-763-9500		196
Web: www.streetsolutions.com			
StreetAuthority LLC			
4601 Spicewood Springs Rd Bldg 3 Ste 100 Austin TX 78759	512-501-4001		401
Web: www.streetauthority.com			
Streetcar Named Desire			
2450 Grand Ave Kansas City MO 64108	816-472-5959		671
Streeter Assoc Inc			
101 E Woodlawn Ave PO Box 118 Elmira NY 14902	607-734-4151	732-2952	186
TF: 866-493-1640 ■ *Web:* www.streeterassociates.com			
Streeter Point Recreation Area			
7 Industrial Park Rd W Sturbridge MA 01518	508-347-9316		565
Web: www.mass.gov			
Streeter Printing Inc			
9880 Via Pasar San Diego CA 92126	858-566-0866		627
TF: 866-787-3383 ■ *Web:* www.streeterprinting.com			
StreetInsider.com Inc			
280 W Maple Ste 210 Birmingham MI 48009	248-593-6536		401
TF: 800-323-0153 ■ *Web:* www.streetinsider.com			
Streets at Southpoint & Main Street			
6910 Fayetteville Rd Durham NC 27713	919-572-8800		50-6
Web: www.streetsatsouthpoint.com			
Streetwise Reports LLC			
101 Second St Ste 110 Petaluma CA 94952	707-981-8999		530
Web: www.theaureport.com			
Strega 379 Hanover St Boston MA 02113	617-523-8481		671
Web: www.stregaristorante.com			
Streimer Sheet Metal Works Inc			
740 N Knott St Portland OR 97227	503-288-9393	288-3327	697
TF: 888-288-3828 ■ *Web:* www.streimer.com			
Strem Chemicals Inc			
7 Mulliken Way Newburyport MA 01950	978-499-1600		146
TF: 800-647-8736 ■ *Web:* www.strem.com			
Streng Design & Advertising Inc			
244 W River Dr Saint Charles IL 60174	630-584-3887		7
Web: www.strengdesign.com			
Stresa 2710 Okeechobee Blvd West Palm Beach FL 33409	561-615-0200		671
Stresau Laboratory Inc			
N8265 Medley Rd Spooner WI 54801	715-635-2777	635-7979	268
Web: www.stresau.com			
Stresscon Corp			
3210 Astrozon Blvd Colorado Springs CO 80910	719-390-5041		183
Web: www.stresscon.com			
StressCrete Group 9200 Energy Ln Northport AL 35476	205-339-0711		183
Web: www.stresscretegroup.com			
Stress-O-Pedic Mattress Company Inc			
2060 S Wineville Ave Ontario CA 91761	909-605-2010		471
Web: www.stressopedic.com			
Stretch Boards 983 Tower Pl Santa Cruz CA 95062	831-479-7309		711
TF: 800-480-4754 ■ *Web:* www.stretchboards.com			
Stretch Inc 1322 Orleans Dr Sunnyvale CA 94089	408-543-2700	747-5736	696
TF: 800-468-6853 ■ *Web:* www.stretchinc.com			
Stretch-N-Grow International Inc			
PO Box 7599 Seminole FL 33775	800-348-0166		310
TF: 800-348-0166 ■ *Web:* www.stretch-n-grow.com			

Name / Address	City	State	Zip	Phone	Fax	Class
Stretch-O-Rama Inc 5 Paddock St	Avenel	NJ	07001	732-855-1400		157-1
Stretegic Mktg Ventures Inc						
8262 Lees Ridge Rd	Warrenton	VA	20186	540-349-8888		401
Web: www.smvbpo.com						
STRI (Smithsonian Tropical Research Institute)						
9100 Panama City PL	Washington	DC	20521	703-487-3770	786-2557*	668
**Fax Area Code:* 202 ■ *Web:* www.stri.si.edu						
Stria Inc 4300 Resnik Ct	Bakersfield	CA	93313	661-617-6601		196
TF: 800-463-3339 ■ *Web:* www.stria.com						
Strick Corp 225 Lincoln Hwy	Fairless Hills	PA	19030	215-547-8737		779
Web: www.stricktrailers.com						
Strickland General Agency Inc						
2963 Gulf To Bay Blvd	Clearwater	FL	33759	727-669-8886		196
Web: www.sgainfl.com						
Stric-Lan Companies LLC 104 Sable St	Duson	LA	70529	337-984-7850		539
TF: 800-749-4586 ■ *Web:* www.striclan.com						
Strictly Business Computer Systems Inc						
848 Fourth Ave Ste 200	Huntington	WV	25701	888-529-0401	781-2590*	176
**Fax Area Code:* 304 ■ *TF:* 888-529-0401 ■ *Web:* www.sbcs.com						
Strictly Technology LLC						
5381 NW 33rd ave	Fort Lauderdale	FL	33309	954-606-5440		225
Web: www.strictlyeducation.com						
Stride Learning Ctr 326 Parsley Blvd	Cheyenne	WY	82007	307-632-2991		148
TF: 800-338-4065 ■ *Web:* www.stridekids.com						
Stride Rite Corp 191 Spring St	Lexington	MA	02420	617-824-6000	824-6969	301
TF Cust Svc: 800-299-6575 ■ *Web:* www.striderite.com						
Stride Tool Inc Imperial Div						
30333 Emerald Vly Pkwy	Glenwillow	OH	44139	440-247-4600	527-6383*	758
**Fax Area Code:* 800 ■ *TF:* 888-467-8665 ■ *Web:* imperial-tools.com						
Strider 6-6150 Hwy 7 Ste 400	Woodbridge	ON	L4H0R6	800-314-8895		195
TF: 800-314-8895 ■ *Web:* striderseo.com						
Strike Energy Services Inc						
1300 505 - Third St SW	Calgary	AB	T2P3E6	403-232-8448		536
Web: www.strikegroup.ca						
StrikoDynarad 501 E Roosevelt Ave	Zeeland	MI	49464	616-772-3705	772-5271	318
Web: www.strikodynarad.com						
Strine Printing Co Inc 30 Grumbacher Rd	York	PA	17406	717-767-6602		627
StringCan Interactive LLC						
7525 E Camelback Rd Ste 201	Scottsdale	AZ	85251	480-612-0360		195
TF: 800-440-4120 ■ *Web:* www.stringcaninteractive.com						
Strings Italian Cafe 2601 Oakdale Rd	Modesto	CA	95355	209-578-9777		671
Web: stringscafe.com						
Stringworks 327 Franklin St	Geneva	IL	60134	920-830-0928		526
Web: www.stringworks.com						
Strip Hoppers Leithart Mcgrath						
575 S Third St	Columbus	OH	43215	614-228-6345		428
Web: columbuslawyer.net						
Strip House 13 E 12th St	New York	NY	10003	212-328-0000		671
Web: striphouse.com						
Stripes Convenience Stores						
4525 Ayers St	Corpus Christi	TX	78415	361-884-2464	884-2494	204
NYSE: SUSS ■ *TF:* 800-569-3585 ■ *Web:* stripesstores.com/index.cms						
Strippit Inc/LVD 12975 Clarence Ctr Rd	Akron	NY	14001	716-542-4511	542-5957	456
TF: 800-828-1527 ■ *Web:* www.lvdgroup.com						
STRIPSTEAK 3950 Las Vegas Blvd S	Las Vegas	NV	89119	702-632-7200		671
Web: www.mandalaybay.com						
Strite Industries Ltd						
298 Shepherd Ave	Cambridge	ON	N3C1V1	519-658-9361		393
Web: www.strite.com						
Strobe Celery & Vegetable Co						
2404 S Wolcott Ave	Chicago	IL	60608	773-446-4000	226-7644*	297-7
**Fax Area Code:* 312 ■ *Web:* www.strube.com						
Strobic Air Corp						
160 Cassell Rd PO Box 144	Harleysville	PA	19438	215-723-4700	723-7401	18
TF: 800-722-3267 ■ *Web:* www.strobicair.com						
Stroer & Graff Inc 1830 Phillips Ln	Antioch	CA	94509	925-778-0200		189-5
Strom Aviation Inc 109 S Elm St	Waconia	MN	55387	952-544-3611		631
TF: 800-356-6440 ■ *Web:* www.stromaviation.com						
Stroma Service Consulting Inc						
19 Legault St	North Bay	ON	P1A4K6	705-840-6000		393
TF: 800-265-1830 ■ *Web:* www.stroma.ca						
Stromberg Allen & Co						
18504 W Creek Dr	Tinley Park	IL	60477	773-847-7131		174
Web: strombergallen.com						
Stromberg Architectural Products Inc						
4400 Oneal St	Greenville	TX	75402	903-454-0904		393
TF: 800-945-4213 ■ *Web:* www.strombergarchitectural.com						
Stromberg Sheet Metal Works Inc						
6701 Distribution Dr	Beltsville	MD	20705	301-931-1000	931-1020	189-10
TF: 800-492-8004 ■ *Web:* www.strombergmetals.com						
STRONE Inc 2717 Coventry Rd	Oakville	ON	L6H5V9	905-829-5707		261
TF: 800-387-2028 ■ *Web:* www.strone.ca						
Strong & Hanni						
102 South 200 East Ste 800	Salt Lake City	UT	84111	801-532-7080		466
Web: www.strongandhanni.com						
Strong - National Museum of Play						
1 Manhattan Sq	Rochester	NY	14607	585-263-2700	263-2493	520
Web: www.museumofplay.org						
Strong Enterprises Inc						
11236 Satellite Blvd	Orlando	FL	32837	407-859-9317	850-6978	576
TF: 800-344-6319 ■ *Web:* www.strongparachutes.com						
Strong Memorial Hospital						
Stem Cell Transplantation Ctr						
601 Elmwood Ave	Rochester	NY	14642	585-275-1941	275-5590	769
Web: www.urmc.rochester.edu						
University of Rochester Medical Ctr						
601 Elmwood Ave	Rochester	NY	14642	585-275-2100	273-1118	374-3
TF: 800-999-6673 ■ *Web:* www.urmc.rochester.edu						
Strong Tool Co 1251 E 286th St	Cleveland	OH	44132	216-289-2450		493
TF: 800-729-5738 ■ *Web:* mdm.com						
Strong Travel Services Inc						
8214 Westche Ste 670	Dallas	TX	75225	214-361-0027		772
TF: 800-747-5670 ■ *Web:* www.strongtravel.com						
Strongauth Inc						
150 W Iowa Ave Ste 204	Sunnyvale	CA	94086	408-331-2000		693
Web: www.strongauth.com						
Strong-Bridge Consulting LLC						
10940 NE 33rd Pl Ste 102	Bellevue	WA	98004	206-905-4631		463
TF: 800-595-1265 ■ *Web:* www.strong-bridge.com						

Name / Address	City	State	Zip	Phone	Fax	Class
Stronghaven Inc 5090 McDougall Dr SW	Atlanta	GA	30336	404-699-1952	699-1825	100
TF: 800-331-7835 ■ *Web:* www.stronghaven.com						
StrongLand Chamber of Commerce						
1129 Industrial Park Rd						
PO Box 10 Ste 108	Vandergrift	PA	15690	724-845-5426	845-5428	139
Web: www.strongland.org						
Strongsville Chamber of Commerce						
18829 Royalton Rd	Strongsville	OH	44136	440-238-3366	238-7010	139
Web: www.strongsvillechamber.com						
Strongwell 400 Commonwealth Ave	Bristol	VA	24201	276-645-8000	645-8132	606
Web: www.strongwell.com						
Stroock & Stroock & Lavan LLP						
180 Maiden Ln	New York	NY	10038	212-806-5400		428
TF: 800-323-8167 ■ *Web:* www.stroock.com						
Strother Ventures II Inc						
2929 Breezewood Ave Ste 200	Fayetteville	NC	28303	910-864-2325		652
Web: www.erastrother.com						
Strothman & Company PSC						
1600 Waterfront Plaza	Louisville	KY	40202	502-585-1600		2
Web: strothman.com						
Strottman International Inc						
40 Corporate Pk Ste 200	Irvine	CA	92606	949-852-1166	261-2777	195
Web: www.strottman.com						
Stroud, Willink & Howard LLC						
25 W Main St Ste 300 PO Box 2236	Madison	WI	53701	608-257-2281		428
TF: 800-426-7436 ■ *Web:* www.stroudlaw.com						
Strouds Run State Park 2045 Morse Rd	Columbus	OH	43229	740-592-2302		565
TF: 800-945-3543 ■ *Web:* www.ohiodnr.com						
Stroudwater Associates Inc						
1685 Congress St Ste 202	Portland	ME	04102	207-221-8250		196
Web: www.stroudwater.com						
Struck Axiom Inc						
159 West Broadway Ste 200	Salt Lake City	UT	84101	801-531-0122		5
Web: www.struck.com						
Structall Building Systems Inc						
350 Burbank Rd	Oldsmar	FL	34677	800-969-3706		234
TF: 800-969-3706 ■ *Web:* www.structall.com						
Structura Inc						
9208 Waterford Centre Blvd Ste 100	Austin	TX	78758	512-495-9702	495-9712	186
TF: 800-790-6202 ■ *Web:* www.structurainc.com						
Structural Component Systems Inc (SCS)						
1255 Front St	Fremont	NE	68026	402-721-5622		187
TF: 800-844-5622 ■ *Web:* www.scstruss.com						
Structural Concepts Corp						
888 Porter Rd	Muskegon	MI	49441	231-798-8888	798-4960	286
TF: 800-433-9489 ■ *Web:* www.structuralconcepts.com						
Structural Steel of Carolina LLC						
1725 Vargrave St	Winston-Salem	NC	27107	336-725-0521		480
Web: www.steelofcarolina.com						
Structural Steel Services						
6210 St Louis St	Meridian	MS	39307	601-483-5381		480
Structural Wood Corp						
4000 Labore Rd	Saint Paul	MN	55110	651-426-8111	426-6859	817
TF: 800-652-9058 ■ *Web:* www.structural-wood.com						
Structural Wood Systems						
321 Dohrimier St	Greenville	AL	36037	334-382-6531	382-4260	817
TF: 800-553-0661 ■ *Web:* www.structuralwood.com						
Structure House 3017 Pickett Rd	Durham	NC	27705	919-493-4205	490-0191	706
TF: 800-553-0052 ■ *Web:* www.structurehouse.com/?nocookies=true						
Structure Networks Inc						
17542 17th St Ste 105	Tustin	CA	92780	714-505-0303		809
Web: www.structurenetworks.com						
Structure Tone Inc 770 Broadway	New York	NY	10003	212-481-6100	685-9267	186
Web: www.structuretone.com						
Structures Unlimited Inc 166 River Rd	Bow	NH	03304	603-645-6539	625-0798	697
TF: 800-225-3895 ■ *Web:* www.structuresunlimitedinc.com						
Structurlam Products Ltd						
2176 Government St	Penticton	BC	V2A8B5	250-492-8912		492
TF: 800-423-6587 ■ *Web:* www.structurlam.com						
Strukmyer LLC						
1801 Big Town Blvd Ste 100	Mesquite	TX	75149	214-275-9595		475
Web: www.strukmyer.com						
Struktol Company of America Inc						
PO Box 1649	Stow	OH	44224	330-928-5188	928-8726	144
TF: 800-327-8649 ■ *Web:* www.struktol.com						
Struthers-Dunn						
407 E Smith St Ste B	Timmonsville	SC	29161	843-346-4427	346-4465	203
Web: www.struthers-dunn.com						
Strutz International Inc						
440 Mars-Valencia Rd PO Box 509	Mars	PA	16046	724-625-1501	625-3570	413
TF: 800-313-1821 ■ *Web:* www.strutz.com						
Stryker Canada LP 45 Innovation Dr	Hamilton	ON	L9H7L8	800-668-8324		476
TF: 800-668-8324 ■ *Web:* www.stryker.ca						
Stryker Corp 2825 Airview Blvd	Kalamazoo	MI	49002	269-385-2600	385-1062	476
NYSE: SYK ■ *TF:* 800-616-1406 ■ *Web:* www.stryker.com						
Stryker Endoscopy 5900 Optical Ct	San Jose	CA	95138	408-754-2000		477
Web: strykerendo.com						
Stry-Lenkoff Co 1100 W Broadway	Louisville	KY	40203	502-587-6804	587-6822	110
TF: 800-626-8247 ■ *Web:* www.strylenkoff.com						
STS (Society of Thoracic Surgeons)						
633 N St Clair St Ste 2320	Chicago	IL	60611	312-202-5800	202-5801	49-8
TF: 877-865-5321 ■ *Web:* www.sts.org						
STS Component Solutions LLC						
2910 SW 42 Ave	Palm City	FL	34990	888-777-2960		22
TF: 888-777-2960 ■ *Web:* www.stsaviationgroup.com						
Sts Consulting Services LLC						
434 E Loop 281 Ste 105	Longview	TX	75605	903-247-1787		196
TF: 800-648-1749 ■ *Web:* ststx.com						
STT Enviro Corp 8485 Parkhill Dr	Milton	ON	L9T5E9	905-693-9301		111
Web: www.sttsemcan.com						
Stu Segall Productions Inc						
4705 Ruffin Rd	San Diego	CA	92123	858-974-8988		514
Web: www.stusegall.com						
Stuart C Irby Co 815 Irby Dr	Jackson	MS	39201	713-476-0788		188-10
TF: 866-687-4729 ■ *Web:* www.irby.com						
Stuart Hall School						
235 W Frederick St PO Box 210	Staunton	VA	24402	540-885-0356	886-2275	622
TF: 888-306-8926 ■ *Web:* www.stuarthallschool.org						

	Phone	Fax	Class
Stuart Jet Ctr LLC 2501 Aviation Way.............Stuart FL 34996 *TF:* 877-735-9538 ■ *Web:* www.stuartjet.com	772-288-6700	288-3782	63
Stuart Maue Mitchell & James Ltd 3840 McKelvey Rd.........................St. Louis MO 63044 **Fax Area Code:* 314 ■ *TF:* 800-291-9940 ■ *Web:* www.smmj.com	800-291-9940	291-6546*	195
Stuart Petroleum Testers Inc 1910 E Tom Green St.......................Brenham TX 77833 *Web:* www.stuartpetroleumtesters.com	979-836-3799		538
Stuart Pimsler Dance & Theater 528 Hennepin Ave S Ste 707...............Minneapolis MN 55403 *Web:* www.stuartpimsler.com	763-521-7738		573-1
Stuart Street Playhouse 200 Stuart St...........Boston MA 02116	617-457-2623		572
Stuart-Martin County Chamber of Commerce 1650 S Kanner Hwy.........................Stuart FL 34994 *TF:* 800-962-2873 ■ *Web:* www.stuartmartinchamber.org	772-287-1088	220-3437	139
Stubbe's Precast 30 Muir Line..................Harley ON N0E1E0 *Web:* www.stubbesprecast.org	519-424-2183		183
Stubbs & Perdue PA 9208 Falls of Neuse Rd Ste 201...............Raleigh NC 27615 *TF:* 800-348-9404 ■ *Web:* www.stubbsperdue.com	800-348-9404		445
StubHub Inc 199 Fremont St Fl 4...........San Francisco CA 94105 *Web:* www.stubhub.com	415-222-8400		459
Stuckey's Corp 8555 16th St Ste 850.....................Silver Spring MD 20910 *TF:* 800-423-6171 ■ *Web:* www.stuckeys.com	301-585-8222		670
Studebaker National Museum 201 Chapin St.............................South Bend IN 46601 *TF:* 888-391-5600 ■ *Web:* www.studebakermuseum.org	574-235-9714	235-5522	520
Student Advantage LLC 280 Summer St..........Boston MA 02210 **Fax Area Code:* 617 ■ *TF:* 800-333-2920 ■ *Web:* www.studentadvantage.com	800-333-2920	912-2012*	384
Student Agencies Foundation Inc 409 College Ave...............................Ithaca NY 14850 *TF:* 800-631-8405 ■ *Web:* www.studentagencies.com	607-272-2000		305
Student Assistance Foundation of Montana 2500 E Broadway St..........................Helena MT 59601 *TF:* 800-852-2761 ■ *Web:* www.trustudent.com	406-495-7800		166
Student Book Store 421 E Grand River Ave.....................East Lansing MI 48823 *TF:* 800-968-1111 ■ *Web:* www.sbsmsu.com	517-351-4210		95
Student Conservation Assn (SCA) 689 River Rd PO Box 550....................Charlestown NH 03603 *TF:* 888-722-9675 ■ *Web:* www.thesca.org	603-543-1700	543-1828	48-13
Student Prince Cafe, The 8 Fort St..................................Springfield MA 01103 *Web:* www.studentprince.com	413-734-7475	739-7303	671
Student Tours Inc 60 W Ave............Vineyard Haven MA 02568 *TF:* 800-331-7093 ■ *Web:* www.studenttoursinc.com	508-693-5078	693-8627	760
Student Transportation of America Inc (STA) 3349 Hwy 138 Bldg B Ste D......................Wall NJ 07719 *TF:* 888-942-2250 ■ *Web:* www.ridestbus.com	732-280-4200	280-4214	109
Student Travel Services Inc 1413 Madison Pk Dr.......................Glen Burnie MD 21061 **Fax Area Code:* 410 ■ *TF:* 800-648-4849 ■ *Web:* www.ststravel.com	800-648-4849	787-9580*	760
Student Veterans of America PO Box 77673..........................Washington DC 20013 *TF:* 866-320-3826 ■ *Web:* www.studentveterans.org	202-223-4710		305
Studentcity.com Inc 8 Essex Ctr Dr............Peabody MA 01960 **Fax Area Code:* 978 ■ *TF:* 888-777-4642 ■ *Web:* www.studentcity.com	888-777-4642	573-2069*	771
Students Against Destructive Decisions (SADD) 255 Main St..........................Marlborough MA 01752 *TF:* 877-723-3462 ■ *Web:* www.sadd.org	508-481-3568	481-5759	48-6
Studer Super Service Inc 1703-6th St..........Monroe WI 53566	608-328-8331		274
Studio 101 4995 Avalon Ridge Pkwy Ste 100..................Atlanta GA 30071 *Web:* www.studio101.com	404-350-1700		344
Studio 2 Digital Dental Design Inc 2405 32nd St SE..........................Kentwood MI 49512 *Web:* www.studio2dental.com	616-957-2140		415
Studio 3 Inc 1316 SE 12th Ave....................Portland OR 97214 *TF:* 800-253-1333 ■ *Web:* studio3.com	503-238-1748		592
Studio 54 Theatre 254 W 54th St.............New York NY 10019 *Web:* www.roundabouttheatre.org	212-719-1300		747
Studio 6 4001 International Pkwy.............Carrollton TX 75007 *TF:* 855-249-0891 ■ *Web:* www.staystudio6.com	614-601-4060		707
Studio Booth LLC 6343 Penn Ave.............Pittsburgh PA 15206 *Web:* studio-booth.com	412-362-6684		77
Studio City Chamber of Commerce 4024 Radford Ave Edit 2 Ste F...............Studio City CA 91604 *Web:* www.studiocitychamber.com	818-655-5916		139
Studio Ctr 161 Business Park Dr..................Virginia Beach VA 23462 *Web:* www.studiocenter.com	757-622-2111		5
Studio Museum in Harlem, The 144 W 125th St..............................New York NY 10027 *Web:* studiomuseum.org	212-864-4500	864-4800	520
Studio One Digital Inc 180 N Wabash Ave Ste 300.........................Chicago IL 60601 *Web:* studio1digital.com	312-376-3300		344
Studio Photography & Design Magazine 1233 Janesville Ave.......................Fort Atkinson WI 53538 **Fax Area Code:* 800 ■ *Web:* www.imaginginfo.com	631-963-6200	547-7377*	457-2
Studio Red Inc 115 Independence Dr.........Menlo Park CA 94025 *TF:* 800-334-3348 ■ *Web:* www.studiored.com	650-324-2244		261
Studio Theatre 1501 14th St NW..............Washington DC 20005 *TF:* 800-460-4138 ■ *Web:* www.studiotheatre.org	202-232-7267		720
Studio y Creations Inc 1-6204 29 St SE..............................Calgary AB T2C1W3 *TF:* 800-243-4024 ■ *Web:* www.studioycreations.com	403-253-5447		8
Studio360 Inc 1400 20th Ave.....................Seattle WA 98122 *Web:* www.studio360.com	206-382-0360		344
StudioNow Inc 4017 Hillsboro Pk................Nashville TN 37215 *Web:* www.studionow.com	615-577-9400		387
Studsvik Scandpower Inc 1087 Beacon St Ste 301.......................Newton MA 02459 *Web:* www.studsvik.com	617-965-7450		177
Study (the) 3233 The Blvd......................Westmount QC H3Y1S4 *Web:* www.thestudy.qc.ca	514-935-9352		685
Stuecker & Assoc Inc 1930 Bishop Ln Watterson Towers Ste 1001......Louisville KY 40218 *TF:* 800-799-9327 ■ *Web:* www.stueckerandassoc.com	502-452-9227		462
Stuedle Spears & Company PSC 2821 S Hurstbourne Pkwy Ste 1...............Louisville KY 40220	502-491-5253		2
Stueve Siegel Hanson LLP 460 Nichols Rd Ste 200...................Kansas City MO 64112 *TF:* 800-714-0360 ■ *Web:* stuevesiegel.com	816-714-7100		428
Stuft Pizza Franchise Corp 50855 Washington St Ste 210................La Quinta CA 92253 *Web:* www.stuftpizza.com	760-777-1660	777-1948	670
Stuhr Museum of the Prairie Pioneer 3133 W Hwy 34.........................Grand Island NE 68801 *Web:* stuhrmuseum.org	308-385-5316		520
Stull Technologies 17 Veronica Ave............Somerset NJ 08873 *Web:* www.stulltech.com	732-873-5000		596
Stuller Settings Inc PO Box 87777............Lafayette LA 70598 *TF:* 800-877-7777 ■ *Web:* www.stuller.com	800-877-7777	444-4741	407
Stulz Air Technology Systems Inc 1572 Tilco Dr.............................Frederick MD 21704 *Web:* www.stulz-ats.com	301-620-2033		14
StumbleUpon Inc 301 Brannan St..........San Francisco CA 94107 *Web:* www.stumbleupon.com	415-979-0640		387
Stumbos & Company Real Estate 2251 Fair Oaks Blvd.......................Sacramento CA 95825	916-646-4400		652
Stump Pass Beach State Park Barrier Islands State Parks PO Box 1150.....Boca Grande FL 33921 *Web:* www.floridastateparks.org	941-964-0375	964-1154	565
Stuntwomen's Association of Motion Pictures, Inc. 3760 Cahuenga Blvd Ste 104.................Studio City CA 91604 *Web:* www.stuntwomen.com	818-762-0907		48-4
Stupid Fun Club LLC 701 Channing Way.........Berkeley CA 94710	510-841-2600		33
Stupp Bros Inc 3800 Weber Rd..............Saint Louis MO 63125 *TF:* 800-535-9999 ■ *Web:* www.stupp.com	314-638-5000	638-2660	480
Stupp Corp 12555 Ronaldson Rd..............Baton Rouge LA 70807 *TF:* 800-535-9999 ■ *Web:* www.stuppcorp.com	225-775-8800		490
Sturbridge Host Hotel & Conference Ctr 366 Main St.............................Sturbridge MA 01566 *TF:* 800-582-3232 ■ *Web:* www.sturbridgehosthotel.com	508-347-7393	347-3944	379
Sturdevant Refrigeration & Air Conditioning Inc 475 Hukilike St..............................Kahului HI 96732 *Web:* www.sturdevantair.com	808-871-6404		189-10
Sturdisteel Co PO Box 2655.......................Waco TX 76702 *TF:* 800-433-3116 ■ *Web:* www.sturdisteel.com	800-433-3116		319-3
Sturdy Corp 1822 Carolina Beach Rd.........Wilmington NC 28401 *TF:* 800-721-3282 ■ *Web:* www.sturdycorp.com	910-763-2500	763-2650	203
Sturdy Memorial Hospital 211 Pk St..........Attleboro MA 02703 *Web:* www.sturdymemorial.org	508-222-5200		374-3
Sturdy Oil Company Inc 1511 Abbott St..........Salinas CA 93901 *Web:* www.sturdyoil.com	831-422-8801		579
Sturgeon Electric Company Inc 12150 E 112th Ave........................Henderson CO 80640 *Web:* www.myrgroup.com	303-286-8000		189-4
Sturges Ctr for the Fine Arts 780 NE St.............................San Bernardino CA 92410 *Web:* www.sturgescenter.org	909-384-5415	384-5449	572
Sturges Mfg Company Inc 2030 Sunset Ave PO Box 59.....................Utica NY 13502 *Web:* www.sturgesstraps.com	315-732-6159	732-2314	745-5
Sturgill, Turner, Barker & Moloney PLLC 333 W Vine St Ste 1400.....................Lexington KY 40507 *Web:* www.sturgillturner.com	859-255-8581		428
Sturgis Bank & Trust Co 113-125 E Chicago Rd PO Box 600.............Sturgis MI 49091 *OTC: STBI* ■ **Fax Area Code:* 616 ■ *Web:* www.sturgisbank.com	269-651-9345	651-5512*	70
Sturgis Library 3090 Main St...............Barnstable MA 02630 *TF:* 800-645-8333 ■ *Web:* www.sturgislibrary.org	508-362-6636	362-5467	434-3
Sturgis Molded Products Co 1950 Clark St...............................Sturgis MI 49091 *Web:* www.smpco.com	269-651-9381		604
Sturgis Public Schools 107 W W St.............Sturgis MI 49091 *Web:* www.sturgisps.org	269-659-1500		685
Sturm Foods Inc PO Box 287.....................Manawa WI 54949 *TF:* 800-347-8876 ■ *Web:* www.sturmfoods.com	920-596-2511	596-3040	297-11
Sturm Heating Inc 1112 N Nelson St............Spokane WA 99202 *Web:* sturmheating.com	509-325-4505		189-10
Sturtevant Inc 348 Circuit St...................Hanover MA 02339 *TF:* 800-992-0209 ■ *Web:* www.sturtevantinc.com	781-829-6501		111
Stussy Inc 17426 Daimler St.......................Irvine CA 92614 *Web:* www.stussy.com	949-474-9255		155-3
Stutman Contracting Inc 22 Sutton Ave..........Oxford MA 01540 *Web:* stutmancontracting.com	508-987-9472		610
Stutsman County 511 Second Ave SE..........Jamestown ND 58401 *Web:* www.co.stutsman.nd.us	701-252-9035		338
Stuttering Foundation of America 3100 Walnut Grove Rd Ste 603...............Memphis TN 38111 *TF:* 800-992-9392 ■ *Web:* www.stutteringhelp.org	901-452-7343	452-3931	48-17
Stuyvesant Press Inc 119 Coit St.............Irvington NJ 07111 *TF:* 800-281-0737 ■ *Web:* stuyvesantpress.com	973-399-3880		627
STV Group Inc 205 W Welsh Dr............Douglassville PA 19518 *Web:* www.stvinc.com	610-385-8200	385-8500	261
STV Inc 225 Pk Ave S 5th Fl..................New York NY 10003 *Web:* www.stvinc.com	212-777-4400	529-5237	261
Styberg Engineering 1600 Gold St PO Box 788.......................Racine WI 53401 *TF:* 800-240-7275 ■ *Web:* www.styberg.com	262-637-9301	637-1319	620
Styer Transportation Co 7870 215th St W...........................Lakeville MN 55044 *TF:* 800-548-9149 ■ *Web:* www.styertrans.com	952-469-4491		780
Style Crest Inc 2450 Enterprise St..............Fremont OH 43420 *TF:* 800-925-4440 ■ *Web:* www.stylecrestinc.com	419-332-7369	332-8763	104
Style Eyes Optics 824 W 18th St............Costa Mesa CA 92627 *Web:* www.styleeyes.com	949-548-5355		543
Style Line Furniture Inc 116 Godfrey Rd..............................Verona MS 38879 *Web:* stylelinefurniture.net	662-566-1113	566-7657	319-2
Style Weekly 1707 Summit Ave Ste 201........Richmond VA 23230 *Web:* www.styleweekly.com	804-358-0825		532-5

Phone | Fax | Class

StyleCaster Media Group LLC
440 Ninth Ave 11th Fl .... New York NY 10001 646 300 8350 307
Web: www.stylecaster.com

Stylex PO Box 5038 .... Delanco NJ 08075 800-257-5742 461-5574* 319-1
**Fax Area Code:* 856 ■ *TF:* 800-257-5742 ■ *Web:* www.stylexseating.com

Stylexchange
1722 Towne Centre Way .... Mount Pleasant SC 29464 843-884-2244 157-6

Stylin Online 81900 Main St .... Memphis MI 48041 586-270-1086 791
TF: 800-620-1233 ■ *Web:* www.stylinonline.com

Stylmark Inc PO Box 32008 .... Minneapolis MN 55432 763-574-7474 286
TF: 800-328-2495 ■ *Web:* www.stylmark.com

StyroChem Canada Ltee
19250 Clark Graham .... Baie-D'Urfe QC H9X3R8 514-457-3226 457-4390 601
TF: 800-423-6587 ■ *Web:* www.styrochem.com

Styrotech Inc
8800 Wyoming Ave N .... Brooklyn Park MN 55445 763-425-4001 601
Web: www.styrotech.com

Styrotek Inc 545 Rd 176 .... Delano CA 93215 661-725-4957 725-7064 601
TF: 800-260-5111 ■ *Web:* www.styrotek.com

su mitra Inc 88 Corporate Dr Ste 1614 .... Toronto ON M1H3G6 416-907-6866 463
Web: www.su-mitra.com

Suarez Corp Industries
7800 Whipple Ave NW .... North Canton OH 44720 330-494-5504 195
TF: 800-764-0008 ■ *Web:* www.suarez.com

Sub Rosa 353 W 12Th St .... New York NY 10014 212-414-8605 5
Web: www.wearesubrosa.com

Sub Station II Inc PO Box 2260 .... Sumter SC 29150 803-775-5328 775-2220 670
Web: www.substationii.com

Subacute Saratoga Children's Hospital
13425 Sousa Ln .... Saratoga CA 95070 408-378-8875 450
Web: www.subacutesaratoga.com

Subaru of America Inc
2235 Marlton Pike W .... Cherry Hill NJ 08002 856-488-8500 59
TF: 800-782-2783 ■ *Web:* www.subaru.com

Subaru of Indiana Automotive Inc
5500 State Rd 38 E .... Lafayette IN 47905 765-449-1111 449-6888 131
Web: www.subaru-sia.com

Subco Foods Inc 4350 S Taylor Dr .... Sheboygan WI 53081 920-457-7761 457-3899 296-16
TF: 800-473-0757 ■ *Web:* www.subcofoods.com

Subcoe 117 Pembina Rd .... Sherwood Park AB T8H0J4 780-467-3477 261
Web: www.subcoe.com

Subex Inc 12101 Airport Way Ste 300 .... Broomfield CO 80021 303-301-6200 224
Web: www.subexworld.com

Subia Corp 6612 Gulton Ct NE .... Albuquerque NM 87109 505-345-2636 344
TF: 800-275-2636 ■ *Web:* www.brilliantdigitalprinting.com

Subiaco Academy 405 N Subiaco Ave .... Subiaco AR 72865 479-934-1000 622
Web: www.subi.org

Sublette County PO Box 250 .... Pinedale WY 82941 307-367-4372 367-6396 338
Web: www.sublettewyo.com

Sublette Feeders 1535 Uu Rd .... Sublette KS 67877 620 668 5501 10-1

Submittal Exchange LLC
5500 Westown Pkwy Ste 180 .... West Des Moines IA 50266 800-714-0024 809
TF: 800-714-0024 ■ *Web:* www.submittalexchange.com

SUBNET Solutions Inc
4639 Manhattan Rd SE Ste 100 .... Calgary AB T2G4B3 403-270-8885 261
Web: www.subnet.com

SubPop Records 2013 Fourth Ave 3rd Fl .... Seattle WA 98121 206-441-8441 441-8245 657
Web: www.subpop.com

Subsea 7 (Us) LLC 10787 Clay Rd .... Houston TX 77041 713-430-1100 261

Substance Abuse & Mental Health Services Administration (SAMHSA)
1 Choke Cherry Rd .... Rockville MD 20857 240-276-2000 276-2010 340-10
TF: 877-726-4727 ■ *Web:* www.samhsa.gov
Center for Mental Health Services
1 Choke Cherry Ln .... Rockville MD 20857 877-726-4727 221-4292* 340-10
**Fax Area Code:* 240 ■ *TF:* 877-726-4727 ■ *Web:* www.samhsa.gov
Center for Substance Abuse Prevention
1 Choke Cherry Rd .... Rockville MD 20857 240-276-2420 276-2430 340-10
TF: 877-726-4727 ■ *Web:* www.samhsa.gov
Center for Substance Abuse Treatment
1 Choke Cherry Rd PO Box 2345 .... Rockville MD 20857 240-276-2130 221-4292 340-10
TF: 877-726-4727 ■ *Web:* www.samhsa.gov

Subsurface Constructors Inc
110 Angelica St .... Saint Louis MO 63147 314-421-2460 421-2479 189-5
TF: 800-242-9425 ■ *Web:* www.subsurfaceconstructors.com

Subsystem Technologies Inc
2121 Crystal Dr Ste 680 .... Arlington VA 22202 703-841-0071 177
Web: www.subsystem.com

Suburban Chambers of Commerce
71 Summit Ave .... Summit NJ 07901 908-522-1700 522-9252 139
TF: 800-838-3006 ■ *Web:* www.suburbanchambers.org

Suburban Collection 1810 Maplelawn Dr .... Troy MI 48084 877-471-7100 57
TF: 877-471-7100 ■ *Web:* www.suburbancollection.com

Suburban Electrical Engineers/ Contractors Inc
709 Hickory Farm Ln .... Appleton WI 54914 920-739-5156 261
Web: suburbanelectric.com

Suburban Grading & Utilities Inc
1190 Harmony Rd .... Norfolk VA 23502 757-461-1800 188-4

Suburban Hospital
8600 Old Georgetown Rd .... Bethesda MD 20814 301-896-3100 493-5583 374-3
TF: 800-456-4543 ■ *Web:* hopkinsmedicine.org/suburban_hospital

Suburban Life Publications
1101 W 31st St Ste 100 .... Downers Grove IL 60515 630-368-1100 969-0228 637-8
TF: 800-397-9397 ■ *Web:* www.mysuburbanlife.com

Suburban Manufacturing Co
676 Broadway St .... Dayton TN 37321 423-775-2131 14
Web: www.suburbanmanufacturing.com

Suburban Mobility Authority for Regional Transportation (SMART)
535 Griswold St Ste 600 .... Detroit MI 48226 313-223-2100 468
TF: 866-962-5515 ■ *Web:* www.smartbus.org

Suburban Motors Grafton Inc
139 N Main St .... Thiensville WI 53092 262-242-2464 256
Web: www.suburbanharley.com

Suburban Plastic Co 340 Renner Dr .... Elgin IL 60123 847-741-4900 596
Web: www.suburbanplastics.com

Suburban Press & Metro Press
1550 Woodville Rd .... Millbury OH 43447 419-836-2221 836-1319 532-4
TF: 800-300-6158 ■ *Web:* www.presspublications.com

Phone | Fax | Class

Suburban Propane LP
240 Route 10 W PO Box 206 .... Whippany NJ 07981 973-503-9252 316
TF: 800-776-7263 ■ *Web:* www.suburbanpropane.com

Suburban Realty Inc 1055 Spring St .... Grafton WI 53024 262-377-3060 652
Web: suburbanrealty.biz

Suburban Surgical Company Inc
275 Twelfth St .... Wheeling IL 60090 847-537-9320 476
Web: www.suburbansurgical.com

Suburban Transit Corp
750 Somerset St .... New Brunswick NJ 08901 732-249-1100 108
TF: 800-222-0492 ■ *Web:* www.coachusa.com

Suburban Wheel Cover Co
1420 Landmeier Rd .... Elk Grove Village IL 60007 847-758-0388 54
TF: 800-635-8126 ■ *Web:* www.suburbanwheelcover.com

Suburbanite
210 Knickerbocker Rd 2nd Fl .... Cresskill NJ 07626 201-894-6700 532-4

Subway Franchisee Advertising Fund Trust
488 Wheelers Farms Rd Ste 2 .... Milford CT 06461 203-878-0232 5

Subx Inc 428 Fore St .... Portland ME 04101 207-775-0808 177
Web: www.quantrix.com

SubZero Constructors Inc
30055 Comercio .... Rancho Santa Margarita CA 92688 949-216-9500 216-9539 189-10
Web: www.szero.com

Sucampo Pharmaceuticals Inc
805 King Farm Blvd Ste 550 .... Rockville MD 20850 301-961-3400 961-3440 582
NASDAQ: SCMP ■ *TF:* 877-825-3327 ■ *Web:* www.sucampo.com

Success Associates LLC
26 Kings Vly Ct .... Damascus MD 20872 301-391-6161 195
Web: www.successassociates.com

Success Motivation International Inc
4567 Lakeshore Dr .... Waco TX 76710 254-776-7551 772-9588 366
TF Sales: 800-876-2389 ■ *Web:* www.lmi-world.com/smi

Success Printing & Mailing Inc
10 Pearl St .... Norwalk CT 06850 203-847-1112 627
Web: www.successprint.com

Success Promotions
14304 S Outer 40 Rd .... Chesterfield MO 63017 314-878-1999 292
Web: www.successpromotions.com

Success Sciences Inc 17838 N US Hwy 4 .... Tampa FL 33549 813-989-9900 177
TF: 800-767-5700 ■ *Web:* www.success-sciences.com

Success Trade Securities Inc
1900 L St N W Ste 525 .... Washington DC 20036 202-466-6890 690
Web: www.successtrade.com

Successfactors Inc
1500 Fashion Island Blvd Ste 300 .... San Mateo CA 94404 650-645-2000 645-2099 178-11
NYSE: SFSF ■ *TF:* 800-809-9920 ■ *Web:* www.successfactors.com

Successful Meetings Magazine
100 Lighting Way .... Secaucus NJ 07094 201-902-2000 457-5
Web: www.successfulmeetings.com

Succession Capital Alliance Insurance Services LLC
4695 MacArthur Ct Ste 400 .... Newport Beach CA 92660 949-794-1882 390
Web: www.successioncapital.com

Successories Inc 1040 Holland Dr .... Boca Raton FL 33487 800-535-2773 952-4097* 310
**Fax Area Code:* 561 ■ *TF:* 800-535-2773 ■ *Web:* www.successories.com

SuccessWorks
19363 Willamette Dr Ste 325 .... West Linn OR 98229 503-476-1065 41
Web: www.searchenginewriting.com

Succor Creek State Natural Area
1298 Lake Owyhee Dam Rd .... Adrian OR 97901 800-551-6949 565
TF: 800-551-6949 ■ *Web:* www.oregonstateparks.org

Sudan 305 E 47th St 4th Fl .... New York NY 10017 212-573-6033 573-6160 784
Web: www.un.int/sudan

Sudan Embassy
2210 Massachusetts Ave NW .... Washington DC 20008 202-338-8565 667-2406 257
Web: www.sudanembassy.org

Sudberry Properties Inc
5465 Morehouse Dr Ste 260 .... San Diego CA 92121 858-546-3000 652
Web: www.sudprop.com

Sudbury Star, The 128 Pine St Ste 201 .... Sudbury ON P3C1X3 705-674-5271 674-0624 532-1
Web: www.thesudburystar.com

Sudbury Valley Trustees Inc
18 Wolbach Rd .... Sudbury MA 01776 978-443-5588 804
Web: www.sudburyvalleytrustees.org

Suddath Cos 815 S Main St .... Jacksonville FL 32207 904-352-2577 519
TF: 800-395-7100 ■ *Web:* www.suddath.com

Suddekor LLC 240 Bowles Rd .... Agawam MA 01001 413-821-9000 627
Web: www.suddekorllc.com

Suddenlink Communications
6151 Paluxy Dr .... Tyler TX 75703 877-694-9474 116
TF: 877-694-9474 ■ *Web:* www.suddenlink.com

Sudenga Industries Inc
2002 Kingbird Ave .... George IA 51237 712-475-3301 475-3320 273
TF: 888-783-3642 ■ *Web:* www.sudenga.com

Suder's Art Store 1309 Vine St .... Cincinnati OH 45202 513-241-0800 45
Web: sudersartstore.com

Sudjam 520 E Broadway Ste 202 .... Glendale CA 91205 818-206-1145 177
TF: 800-555-1234 ■ *Web:* www.sudjam.com

Sudler & Hennessey 230 Pk Ave S .... New York NY 10003 212-614-4100 598-6907* 4
**Fax:* Hum Res ■ *Web:* www.sudler.com

Sudler Property Management
875 N Michigan Ave Ste 39AB .... Chicago IL 60611 312-751-0900 463

Sue Kolve'S Salon & Day Spa
230 Main St .... Onalaska WI 54650 608-784-2363 77
Web: suekolves.com

Sueba USA 8235 El Rio St .... Houston TX 77054 713-747-7333 608
Web: www.s-h-m.com

Sueba USA Corp 1800 W Loop S Ste 1300 .... Houston TX 77027 713-961-3588 961-1343 653
Web: www.suebausa.com

Suehiro 4431 Corbett Dr .... Fort Collins CO 80525 970-672-8185 671
Web: www.suehirojapaneserestaurant.com

Suemaur Exploration & Production LLC
539 N Carancahua Ste 1100 .... Corpus Christi TX 78401 361-884-8824 536
Web: www.suemaur.com

Suffield Academy 185 N Main St .... Suffield CT 06078 860-668-7315 668-2966 622
Web: www.suffieldacademy.org

Suffolk Construction 65 Allerton St .... Boston MA 02119 617-445-3500 541-2128 186
Web: www.suffolk.com

Name / Address	City	State	ZIP	Phone	Fax	Class
Suffolk Co-op Library System 627 N Sunrise Service Rd PO Box 9000 *Web:* portal.suffolklibrarysystem.org	Bellport	NY	11713	631-286-1600	286-1647	434-3
Suffolk County County Rd 51 *Web:* www.suffolkcountyny.gov	Riverhead	NY	11901	631-852-1400		338
Suffolk County Community College						
Ammerman 533 College Rd *TF:* 800-838-3006 ■ *Web:* www.sunysuffolk.edu	Selden	NY	11784	631-451-4110		162
Eastern 121 Speonk-Riverhead Rd **Fax:* Admissions ■ *Web:* www.sunysuffolk.edu	Riverhead	NY	11901	631-548-2500	548-2504*	162
Grant 1001 Crooked Hill Rd **Fax:* Admissions ■ *TF:* 800-621-3362 ■ *Web:* www.sunysuffolk.edu	Brentwood	NY	11717	631-851-6700	851-6819*	162
Suffolk County Historical Society 300 W Main St *Web:* suffolkcountyhistoricalsociety.org	Riverhead	NY	11901	631-727-2881	727-3467	520
Suffolk Downs 525 McClean Highwy *TF:* 800-225-3460 ■ *Web:* www.suffolkdowns.com	East Boston	MA	02128	617-567-3900		133
Suffolk (Independent City) 441 Market St *Web:* www.suffolkva.us	Suffolk	VA	23434	757-514-4000		338
Suffolk Transportation Service Inc 10 Moffitt Blvd *Web:* www.suffolkbus.com	Bay Shore	NY	11706	631-665-3245	665-3186	109
Suffolk University 8 Ashburton Pl *TF:* 800-678-3365 ■ *Web:* www.suffolk.edu	Boston	MA	02108	617-573-8460	557-1574	166
Suffolk University Law School 120 Tremont St *Web:* www.suffolk.edu	Boston	MA	02108	617-573-8144		167-1
Suffolk University Sawyer Library 73 Tremont St *Web:* www.suffolk.edu/sawlib	Boston	MA	02108	617-573-8000	573-8756	434-6
Sufix USA Inc 651 Brigham Rd Ste D *TF:* 800-554-1423 ■ *Web:* www.sufix.com	Greensboro	NC	27409	336-605-1950		601
Sugami 4813 N Kings Hwy *Web:* sugamimyrtlebeach.com	Myrtle Beach	SC	29577	843-692-7709		671
Sugar Assn 1300 L St NW Ste 1001 *Web:* www.sugar.org	Washington	DC	20005	202-785-1122	785-5019	48-2
Sugar Cane Growers Co-op of Florida 1500 W Sugar House Rd *TF:* 800-985-4416 ■ *Web:* www.scgc.org	Belle Glade	FL	33430	561-996-5556		10-9
Sugar Creek Board of Education 3757 Upper Bellbrook Rd *Web:* www.sugarcreek.k12.oh.us	Bellbrook	OH	45305	937-848-6251		685
Sugar Creek Foods International 301 N El Paso St *TF:* 800-445-2715 ■ *Web:* getsugarcreek.com	Russellville	AR	72801	800-445-2715		296-25
Sugar Creek Packing Co 2101 Kenskill Ave **Fax Area Code:* 513 ■ *TF:* 800-848-8205 ■ *Web:* www.sugarcreek.com	Washington Court House	OH	43160	740-335-7440	551-5263*	296-26
Sugar Creek Scrap Inc 1201 W National Ave *TF:* 800-466-7462 ■ *Web:* www.sugarcreekscrap.com	West Terre Haute	IN	47885	812-533-2147		686
Sugar Foods Corp 950 Third Ave 21st Fl *TF:* 800-732-8963 ■ *Web:* www.sugarfoods.com	New York	NY	10022	212-753-6900	753-6988	297-11
Sugar House Day Spa & Salon 111 N Alfred St *Web:* sugarhousedayspa.com	Alexandria	VA	22314	703-549-9940		77
Sugar Magnolia 804 Edgewood Ave NE *Web:* www.sugarmagnoliabb.com	Atlanta	GA	30307	404-222-0226		379
Sugar Maple Farm 5 Sugar Ln	Poughquag	NY	12570	845-221-0575		368
Sugar Mill Ruins 600 Mission Rd *Web:* www.volusia.org	New Smyrna Beach	FL	32168	386-427-2284		50-3
Sugarbush Resort & Inn 1840 Sugarbush Access Rd *TF:* 800-537-8427 ■ *Web:* www.sugarbush.com	Warren	VT	05674	802-583-6300	583-6390	669
Sugardale Foods Inc 1600 Harmont Ave NE *Web:* www.sugardale.com	Canton	OH	44705	330-455-5253		473
Sugarloaf/USA 5092 Access Rd *TF:* 800-843-5623 ■ *Web:* www.sugarloaf.com	Carrabassett Valley	ME	04947	207-237-2000	237-3768	669
Sugden Community Theatre 701 Fifth Ave S *TF:* 800-435-7352 ■ *Web:* www.naplesplayers.org	Naples	FL	34102	239-263-7990	434-7772	572
Sughrue Mion PLLC 2100 Pennsylvania Ave NW *Web:* www.sughrue.com	Washington	DC	20037	202-293-7060	293-7860	428
Sugino Corp 1380 Hamilton Pkwy *TF:* 888-784-4661 ■ *Web:* www.suginocorp.com	Itasca	IL	60143	630-250-8585		358
Sugiyo USA Inc PO Box 468 *Web:* www.sugiyo.com	Anacortes	WA	98221	360-293-0180		296-14
Suh'dutsing Technologies LLC 600 N 100 E *Web:* cedarbandcorp.com/suhdutsingtech	Cedar City	UT	84721	435-867-0604		260
SUHM Spring Works Inc 14650 Heathrow Forest Pkwy *TF:* 800-338-6903 ■ *Web:* www.suhm.net	Houston	TX	77032	713-224-9293	224-9418	295
Suhner Manufacturing Inc 43 Anderson Rd *TF:* 800-292-1493 ■ *Web:* www.suhner.com	Rome	GA	30161	706-235-8046	235-8045	759
Suhor Industries 10965 Granada Ln Ste 300 *Web:* www.suhor.com	Overland Park	KS	66211	913-345-2120		183
SUHRCO Management Inc 2010 156th Ave NE Ste 100 *Web:* suhrcorp.com	Bellevue	WA	98007	425-455-0900	462-1943	655
Suisha Garden Japanese Restaurant 208 Slater St *Web:* japaninottawa.com	Ottawa	ON	K1P5H8	613-236-9602		671
Suite 66 366 Adelaide St W Ste 600 *TF:* 866-779-3486 ■ *Web:* www.suite66.com	Toronto	ON	M5V1R9	416-628-5565		8
Suiter Swantz Pc Llo 14301 Fnb Pkwy Ste 220 *Web:* www.suiter.com	Omaha	NE	68154	402-496-0300		428
Suites at Fisherman's Wharf 2655 Hyde St *TF:* 800-227-3608 ■ *Web:* www.shellhospitality.com	San Francisco	CA	94109	415-771-0200		379
Suites Hotel in Canal Park, The 325 Lake Ave S *TF:* 800-794-1716 ■ *Web:* www.thesuitesduluth.com	Duluth	MN	55802	218-727-4663		379
Suit-Kote Corp 1911 Lorings Crossing Rd *Web:* www.suit-kote.com	Cortland	NY	13045	607-753-1100		46
Sukhi's Gourmet Indian Foods 23682 Clawiter Rd *Web:* sukhis.com	Hayward	CA	94545	510-264-9265		297-8
Sukup Manufacturing Co 1555 255th St PO Box 677 *TF:* 800-553-1791 ■ *Web:* www.sukup.com	Sheffield	IA	50475	641-892-4222	892-4629	273
Sukut Construction Inc 4010 W Chandler Ave *TF:* 888-785-8801 ■ *Web:* www.sukut.com	Santa Ana	CA	92704	714-540-5351	545-2438	188-4
Sul Ross State University E Hwy 90 **Fax:* Admissions ■ *TF:* 888-722-7778 ■ *Web:* www.sulross.edu	Alpine	TX	79832	432-837-8011	837-8431*	166
Sulaan Solutions Inc 410 N Roosevelt Ave Ste 106 *Web:* www.sulaan.com	Chandler	AZ	85226	480-626-4041		180
Sullair Corp 3700 E Michigan Blvd *Web:* www.sullair.com	Michigan City	IN	46360	219-879-5451		172
Sullivan & Cromwell LLP 125 Broad St *Web:* www.sullcrom.com	New York	NY	10004	212-558-4000	558-3588	428
Sullivan & McLaughlin Companies Inc 74 Lawley St *Web:* www.sullymac.com	Boston	MA	02122	617-474-0500		186
Sullivan & Menendez LLP 5510 Merrick Rd	Massapequa	NY	11758	516-795-2500		2
Sullivan Arena 1600 Gambell St	Anchorage	AK	99501	907-279-0618		720
Sullivan Automotive Group 2406 N Section St *Web:* www.shopsullivanauto.com	Sullivan	IN	47882	812-268-4321		57
Sullivan Bille PC 600 Clark Rd Ste 4 *Web:* www.sullivanbillepc.com	Tewksbury	MA	01876	978-970-2900		194
Sullivan Correctional Facility 325 Riverside Dr PO Box 116 *Web:* www.doccs.ny.gov	Fallsburg	NY	12733	845-434-2080		213
Sullivan County 3411 Hwy 126 *Web:* www.sullivancountytn.gov	Blountville	TN	37617	423-323-6428	279-2725	338
Sullivan County Chamber of Commerce 196 Bridgeville Rd Ste 7 *Web:* www.catskills.com	Monticello	NY	12701	845-791-4200	791-4220	139
County Court 109 N Main St Ste 20	Milan	MO	63556	660-265-3303		338
Sullivan County Community College 112 College Rd **Fax:* Admissions ■ *TF:* 800-577-5243 ■ *Web:* www.sullivan.suny.edu	Loch Sheldrake	NY	12759	845-434-5750	434-0923*	162
Sullivan County Public Library 1655 Blountville Blvd *Web:* sullivancountylibrarytn.org	Blountville	TN	37617	423-279-2714	279-2836	434-3
Sullivan County Rural Electric Co-op Inc (SCREC) 5675 Rt 87 PO Box 65 *TF:* 800-570-5081 ■ *Web:* www.screc.com	Forksville	PA	18616	570-924-3381		245
Sullivan Curtis Monroe 1920 Main St *TF:* 800-427-3253 ■ *Web:* www.sullivancurtismonroe.com	Irvine	CA	92614	949-250-7172		390
Sullivan Daniel (Sen R - AK) 702 Hart Senate Office Bldg *Web:* www.sullivan.senate.gov	Washington	DC	20510	202-224-3004	224-6501	342-2
Sullivan Direct Marketing Inc 5509 Fair Ln *Web:* www.sullivandirect.com	Cincinnati	OH	45227	513-342-1139		7
Sullivan Higdon & Sink Inc 255 N Mead *Web:* www.wehatesheep.com	Wichita	KS	67202	316-263-0124		4
Sullivan Hincks & Conway 120 W 22nd St Ste 100 *Web:* www.shlawfirm.com	Oak Brook	IL	60523	630-573-5021		428
Sullivan Paper Company Inc 42 Progress Ave *Web:* sullivanpaper.com	West Springfield	MA	01089	413-734-3107		548
Sullivan Tire Co Inc PO Box 370 *TF:* 877-855-4826 ■ *Web:* www.sullivantire.com	Rockland	MA	02370	781-871-2299		62-5
Sullivan University 3101 BaRdstown Rd *TF:* 800-844-1354 ■ *Web:* www.sullivan.edu	Louisville	KY	40205	502-456-6505		166
Sullivan's Foods 425 First St *Web:* www.sullivansfoods.net	Savanna	IL	61074	815-273-4511		345
Sullivan's Pub & Eatery 301 French St	Erie	PA	16507	814-452-3446		671
Sullivan's Steakhouse 1928 S Blvd *Web:* sullivanssteakhouse.com	Charlotte	NC	28203	704-335-8228		671
Sullivan's Steakhouse 300 Colorado St *Web:* sullivanssteakhouse.com	Austin	TX	78701	512-495-6504		671
Sullivan's Steakhouse 5252 Corporate Blvd *Web:* sullivanssteakhouse.com	Baton Rouge	LA	70808	225-925-1161		671
Sullivan's Steakhouse 410 Glenwood Ave Ste 100 *Web:* sullivanssteakhouse.com	Raleigh	NC	27603	919-833-2888		671
Sullivan's Steakhouse 700 W DeKalb Pk *Web:* sullivanssteakhouse.com	King of Prussia	PA	19406	610-878-9025		671
Sullivan-Palatek Inc 1201 W US Hwy 20 *TF:* 800-438-6203 ■ *Web:* www.sullivan-palatek.com:	Michigan City	IN	46360	219-874-2497	872-5043	172
Sulloway & Hollis 9 Capitol St & 29 School St *Web:* www.sulloway.com	Concord	NH	03301	603-224-2341		428
Sully County PO Box 265 *TF:* 800-368-8683 ■ *Web:* www.sullycounty.net	Onida	SD	57564	605-258-2541	258-2884	338
Sully Creek State Park 1465 36th St *Web:* www.parkrec.nd.gov	Medora	ND	58645	701-623-2024		565
Sully Historic Site 3650 Historic Sully Way *Web:* www.fairfaxcounty.gov/parks/sully	Chantilly	VA	20151	703-437-1794	787-3314	50-3
Sully-Miller Contracting Co Inc 135 S State Collage Blvd Ste 400 **Fax:* Hum Res ■ *TF:* 800-300-4240 ■ *Web:* sully-miller.com	Brea	CA	92821	714-578-9600	578-2850*	188-4

				Phone	Fax	Class
Sulphur Institute (TSI) 1140 Connecticut Ave NW Ste 612 *Web:* www.sulphurinstitute.org	Washington	DC	20036	202-331-9660	293-2940	49-13
Sulphur Springs Ford Lincoln Inc 1040 Gilmer St *Web:* www.toliverford.com	Sulphur Springs	TX	75482	903-885-0502		57
Sulphur Springs Valley Electric Co-op Inc 350 N Haskell Ave *TF:* 877-877-6861	Willcox	AZ	85643	520-384-2221		245
Sultan Co 500 Ala Moana Blvd Ste 7-210 *Web:* obits.staradvertiser.com	Honolulu	HI	96813	808-529-4747	837-1358	410
Sultana Distribution Services Inc 600 Food Ctr Dr *TF:* 877-617-5500 ■ *Web:* www.sultanadist.com	Bronx	NY	10474	718-617-5500	617-5225	297-3
Sulzer Machine & Manufacturing Inc 2475 Spring Brook Rd *Web:* www.sulzermachine.com	Mosinee	WI	54455	715-443-2569		757
Sulzer Metco US Inc 1101 Prospect Ave **Fax:* Sales ■ *TF:* 877-280-2342 ■ *Web:* www.sulzer.com	Westbury	NY	11590	516-334-1300	338-2486*	172
Sulzer Pumps (US) Inc 2800 NW Front Ave *Web:* www.sulzer.com	Portland	OR	97210	503-205-3600		641
Sumaria Systems Inc 99 Rosewood Dr *TF:* 800-523-5305 ■ *Web:* www.sumariasystems.com	Danvers	MA	01923	978-739-4200	739-4850	180
Sumco Inc 1351 S Girls School Rd *Web:* sumco.com	Indianapolis	IN	46231	317-241-7600	248-2352	481
Sumersault ltd 17 Overlook Rd *Web:* www.sumersault.com	Scarsdale	NY	10583	914-472-5778		594
Sumex Inc 200 Carnegie Dr Ste 203 *Web:* www.sumex.ca	St. Albert	AB	T8N5A7	780-970-2238		466
Sumida America Inc 1251 N Plum Grove Rd Ste 150 *Web:* www.sumida.com	Schaumburg	IL	60173	847-545-6700		253
Sumiden Wire Products Corp 1412 El Pinal Dr *Web:* www.sumidenwire.com	Stockton	CA	95205	209-466-8924		488
Sumitomo Canada Ltd (SCL) 150 King St W Ste 2304 *Web:* www.sumitomocanada.com	Toronto	ON	M5H1J9	416-860-3800	365-3141	360-3
Sumitomo Chemical America Inc 150 E 42nd St Ste 701 *Web:* www.sumitomo-chem.co.jp	New York	NY	10017	212-572-8200	572-8234	146
Sumitomo Corp of America 600 Third Ave 42nd Fl *TF:* 877-980-3283 ■ *Web:* www.sumitomocorp.com	New York	NY	10016	212-207-0700	207-0456	360-3
Sumitomo Electric Industries Ltd 2355 Zanker Rd *Web:* www.sel-device.com	San Jose	CA	95131	408-232-9500		696
Sumitomo Electric USA Inc 21241 S Western Ave Ste 120 *Web:* www.sumitomoelectricusa.com	Torrance	CA	90501	310-782-0227	782-0211	813
Sumitomo Machinery Corp of America 4200 Holland Blvd *TF:* 800-762-9256 ■ *Web:* www.sumitomodrive.com	Chesapeake	VA	23323	757-485-3355	485-7490	709
Sumitomo Mitsui Banking Corp (SMBC) 277 Pk Ave *Web:* www.smbcgroup.com	New York	NY	10172	212-224-4000	593-9522	70
Sumitomo Mitsui Trust Bank (USA) (SMTBUSA) 111 River St *Web:* logon.sumitomotrustusa.com	Hoboken	NJ	07030	201-420-9470		70
Sumitomo (SHI) Cryogenics of America Inc 1833 Vultee Sreet *TF:* 800-525-3072 ■ *Web:* www.shicryogenics.com	Allentown	PA	18103	610-791-6700		407
Summa Barberton Hospital 155 Fifth St NE *TF:* 888-905-6071 ■ *Web:* summahealth.org	Barberton	OH	44203	330-615-3000		374-3
Summa Information Systems Inc 111 E Fire Tower Rd	Winterville	NC	28590	252-756-6110		582
Summa Strategies Canada Inc 100 Sparks St Ste 1000 *Web:* www.summastrategies.ca	Ottawa	ON	K1P5B7	613-235-1400		41
Summa Technologies Inc 611 William Penn Pl *Web:* www.summa.com	Pittsburgh	PA	15219	412-258-3300		177
Summer Industries LLC 262 Welcome Center Ct *Web:* www.summerindustries.net	Welcome	NC	27374	336-731-7787		125
Summer Infant Inc 1275 Park E Dr *TF:* 800-268-6237 ■ *Web:* www.summerinfant.com	Woonsocket	RI	02895	800-268-6237		787
Summer Search 500 Sansome St Ste 350 *Web:* www.summersearch.org	San Francisco	CA	94111	415-362-0500		242
Summer Street Capital Partners LLC 70 W Chippewa St Ste 500 *Web:* www.summerstreetcapital.com	Buffalo	NY	14202	716-566-2900		690
Summerlin Hospital Medical Ctr 657 Town Ctr Dr *Web:* www.summerlinhospital.com	Las Vegas	NV	89144	702-233-7000		374-3
Summers County 120 Ballengee St Ste 106 *Web:* www.summerscountywv.org	Hinton	WV	25951	304-466-7104		338
Summers Heating & Air Conditio 6031 Rising Sun Ave *Web:* summersquality.com	Philadelphia	PA	19111	215-722-3716		189-10
Summers Laboratories Inc 103 Gp Clement Dr *Web:* www.sumlab.com	Collegeville	PA	19426	610-454-1471		743
Summers-Taylor Inc 300 W Elk Ave *TF:* 800-972-3757 ■ *Web:* summerstaylor.com	Elizabethton	TN	37643	423-543-3181		188-4
Summerwinds Nursery 17826 N Tatum Blvd *Web:* www.summerwindsnursery.com	Phoenix	AZ	85032	602-867-1822		323
Summerwood Corp 14 Balligomingo Rd *TF:* 800-760-0950 ■ *Web:* www.summerwood.biz	Conshohocken	PA	19428	610-520-1000		670
Summit 7 Systems Inc 300 Voyager Way Ste 300 *Web:* www.summit7systems.com	Huntsville	AL	35806	256-585-6868		180

				Phone	Fax	Class
Summit Account Resolution 12201 Champlin Dr *TF:* 888-822-7509 ■ *Web:* www.summitcollects.com	Champlin	MN	55316	763-712-3700		393
Summit Aerospace 1260 NW 57th Ave *Web:* summitmro.com	Miami	FL	33126	305-267-6400		271
Summit at Plantsville 261 Summit St *Web:* www.athenanh.com/CT_Summit.aspx	Plantsville	CT	06479	860-628-0364	628-9166	450
Summit Aviation Inc 4200 Summit Bridge Rd PO Box 258 *TF:* 800-441-9343 ■ *Web:* www.summit-aviation.com	Middletown	DE	19709	302-834-5400		24
Summit Bank 2969 Broadway *TF:* 800-380-9333 ■ *Web:* www.summitbanking.com	Oakland	CA	94611	510-839-8800	839-8853	70
Summit Behavioral Healthcare 1101 Summit Rd *TF:* 800-372-8862 ■ *Web:* mha.ohio.gov	Cincinnati	OH	45237	513-948-3600	948-3080	374-5
Summit Brewing Co 910 Montreal Cir *Web:* www.summitbrewing.com	Saint Paul	MN	55102	651-265-7800	265-7801	102
Summit Broadband Inc 4558 SW 35th St *Web:* www.summit-broadband.com	Orlando	FL	32811	407-996-8900		387
Summit Business-Consulting Inc 679 Norbury Dr *Web:* www.summit-business.com	Hudson	OH	44236	330-656-0495		193
Summit Canyon Mountaineering 732 Grand Ave *TF:* 800-360-6994 ■ *Web:* summitcanyon.com	Glenwood Springs	CO	81601	970-945-6994		711
Summit Chemical Co 235 S Kresson St *TF:* 800-227-8664 ■ *Web:* www.summitchemical.com	Baltimore	MD	21224	410-522-0661	522-0833	280
Summit Christian College 2025 21st St *TF:* 888-305-8083 ■ *Web:* www.summitcc.net	Gering	NE	69341	308-632-6933	632-8599	166
Summit Construction Company Inc 1107 Burdsal Pkwy PO Box 88126 *Web:* www.summitconst.com	Indianapolis	IN	46208	317-634-6112	264-2529	685
Summit Container Corp 901 Synthes Ave *Web:* www.summitcontainer.com	Monument	CO	80132	719-481-8400		100
Summit Corp of America 1430 Waterbury Rd *Web:* www.summitplating.com	Thomaston	CT	06787	860-283-4391	283-4010	481
Summit Correctional Facility 137 Eagle Heights Rd	Summit	NY	12175	518-287-1721		213
Summit County 175 S Main St *TF:* 800-296-8438 ■ *Web:* co.summitoh.net	Akron	OH	44308	330-643-2500	643-2507	338
Summit County PO Box 1538 *Web:* www.co.summit.co.us	Breckenridge	CO	80424	970-453-2561	453-3540	338
Summit County 60 N Main St *Web:* www.co.summit.ut.us	Coalville	UT	84017	435-336-3203	336-3030	338
Summit Direct Mail Inc 1655 Terre Colony Ct *TF:* 877-247-0993 ■ *Web:* www.summitdm.com	Dallas	TX	75212	469-916-5170		195
Summit Electric Supply Co 2000 Stanford NE *TF:* 800-824-4400 ■ *Web:* www.summit.com	Albuquerque	NM	87107	505-040-9000	040-1010	240
Summit Energy Services Inc 10350 Ormsby Pk Pl Ste 400 *TF:* 866-907-8664 ■ *Web:* www.summitenergy.com	Louisville	KY	40223	502-429-3800		463
Summit Engineering Inc 131 Summit Dr *TF:* 800-922-4750 ■ *Web:* www.summit-engr.com	Pikeville	KY	41501	606-432-1447		302
Summit Envirosolutions Inc 1217 Bandana Blvd N *Web:* www.summite.com	St Paul	MN	55108	651-644-8080		194
Summit Financial Resources Inc 4 Campus Dr *Web:* www.summitfinancial.com	Parsippany	NJ	07054	973-285-3600		390
Summit Food Service Distributors Inc 580 Industrial Rd *TF:* 800-265-9267 ■ *Web:* summit.colabor.com	London	ON	N5V1V1	519-453-3410	453-5148	299
Summit Funding Group Inc 4680 Parkway Dr Ste 300 *TF:* 866-489-1222 ■ *Web:* www.summit-funding.com	Mason	OH	45040	513-489-1222		264-1
Summit Golf Brands Inc 8 W 40th St 2nd Fl *TF:* 800-926-8010 ■ *Web:* www.summitgolfbrands.com	New York	NY	10018	800-926-8010		442
Summit Handling Systems Inc 11 Defco Park Rd *Web:* www.summithandling.com	North Haven	CT	06473	203-239-5351		645-10
Summit Health Inc 27175 Haggerty Rd *Web:* www.summithealth.com	Novi	MI	48377	248-799-8303		194
Summit Holding Southeast Inc PO Box 600 *TF:* 800-971-2667 ■ *Web:* www.summitholdings.com	Gainesville	GA	30503	678-450-5825		360-4
Summit Hospitality Group Ltd 3141 John Humphries Wynd Ste 200 *Web:* www.summithospitality.com	Raleigh	NC	27612	919-787-5100		378
Summit Hotel Properties Inc 2701 S Minnesota Ave Ste 6 *Web:* www.thesummitgroupinc.com	Sioux Falls	SD	57105	605-361-9566		377
Summit Hut 5045 E Speedway Blvd *TF:* 800-499-8696 ■ *Web:* www.summithut.com	Tucson	AZ	85712	520-325-1554	795-7350	711
Summit Lake State Park 5993 N Messick Rd *Web:* www.in.gov	New Castle	IN	47362	765-766-5873		565
Summit Lake State Recreation Area 550 W Seventh Ave Ste 1380 *Web:* dnr.alaska.gov/parks/index	Anchorage	AK	99501	907-269-8700	269-8907	565
Summit Lake State Recreation Site c/o Mat-Su/CB Area Office 7278 E Bogard Rd *Web:* dnr.alaska.gov/parks/units/summit.htm	Wasilla	AK	99654	907-745-3975		565
Summit Landscape Services Inc 12452 Cutten Rd	Houston	TX	77066	281-583-7900	583-7994	422
Summit Law Group PLLC 315 Fifth Ave S Ste 1000 *Web:* www.summitlaw.com	Seattle	WA	98104	206-676-7000		428
Summit Lodge & Spa 4359 Main St *TF:* 888-913-8811 ■ *Web:* summitlodge.com	Whistler	BC	V0N1B4	604-932-2778	932-2716	379
Summit Medical Ctr 350 Hawthorne Ave *TF:* 800-478-8837 ■ *Web:* www.sutterhealth.org	Oakland	CA	94609	510-655-4000		374-3

Entry	City	State	ZIP	Phone	Fax	Class
Summit Medical Ctr 5655 Frist Blvd *Web:* tristarsummit.com	Hermitage	TN	37076	615-316-3000		374-3
Summit Medical Group 1 Diamond Hill Rd *Web:* www.summitmedicalgroup.com	Berkeley Heights	NJ	07922	908-273-4300	790-6593	353
Summit Midstream Partners LP 1790 Hughes Landing Blvd Ste 500 *Web:* www.summitmidstream.com	The Woodlands	TX	77380	832-413-4770		536
Summit Motorsports Park 1300 Ohio 18 *TF:* 800-729-6455 ■ *Web:* www.summitmotorsportspark.com	Norwalk	OH	44857	419-668-5555	663-0502	515
Summit Packaging Systems Inc 400 Gay St *Web:* summitpackagingsystems.com	Manchester	NH	03103	603-669-5410		547
Summit Partners 222 Berkeley St 18th Fl *TF:* 800-503-4611 ■ *Web:* www.summitpartners.com	Boston	MA	02116	617-824-1000	824-1100	792
Summit Performance Group LLC 100 Leverne St *Web:* www.summitpg.com	Mammoth Lakes	CA	93546	760-924-7813		760
Summit Pet Products Distributors Inc 420 N Chimney Rock Rd *Web:* www.summitpet.com	Greensboro	NC	27410	336-294-4215		805
Summit Plastics Inc 107 S Laurel St *TF:* 800-790-7117 ■ *Web:* www.summitplasticsus.com	Summit	MS	39666	601-276-7500	276-2400	600
Summit Polymers Inc 6717 S Sprinkle Rd *Web:* www.summitpolymers.com	Portage	MI	49002	269-324-9330	324-9311	60
Summit Publications Inc 63 Summit Way *Web:* www.summitlighthouse.org	Gardiner	MT	59030	406-848-9200		48-20
Summit Publications Inc 404 S Jefferson St *Web:* www.bestlocalsearch.com	Kearney	MO	64060	816-628-5492		194
Summit Research Network Management Inc 2701 NW Vaughn St Ste 350 *Web:* www.summitnetwork.com	Portland	OR	97210	503-279-8252		794
Summit Resources LLC 3300 E First Ave Ste 480 *Web:* summitresourcesland.com	Denver	CO	80206	720-439-4770		195
Summit Security Services Inc 390 Rexcorp Plaza W Tower - Lobby Level *TF:* 800-615-5888 ■ *Web:* www.summitsecurity.com	Uniondale	NY	11556	516-240-2400		693
Summit Sierra 13925 S Virginia St Ste 212 *Web:* www.thesummitonline.com	Reno	NV	89511	775-853-7800		460
Summit State Bank 500 Bicentennial Way *NASDAQ: SSBI* ■ *TF:* 800-428-5008	Santa Rosa	CA	95403	707-568-6000	568-7090	71
Summit Steakhouse, The 2700 S Havana St *Web:* www.thesummitsteakhouse.com	Aurora	CO	80014	303-751-2112		671
Summit Strategies Inc 8182 Maryland Ave 6th Fl *Web:* www.ssgstl.com	St. Louis	MO	63105	314-727-7211		401
Summit Technical Services Inc 355 Centerville Rd *TF:* 800-643-7372 ■ *Web:* www.summit-technical.com	Warwick	RI	02886	401-736-8323		631
Summit Trailer Sales Inc 1 Summit Plaza *TF:* 800-437-3729 ■ *Web:* www.summittrailer.com	Summit Station	PA	17979	570-754-3511	754-7025	779
Summit Training Source Inc 4170 Embassy Dr SE *TF:* 800-447-3177 ■ *Web:* summit.hsi.com	Grand Rapids	MI	49546	800-447-3177		33
Summit Treestands LLC 715 Summit Dr *Web:* www.summitstands.com	Decatur	AL	35601	256-353-0634		710
Summit, The 65 Steiner Ave *TF:* 877-411-3662 ■ *Web:* thesummit.fm	Akron	OH	44301	330-761-3099	761-3103	645-2
Summitt Trucking LLC 1800 Progress Way *TF:* 866-999-7799 ■ *Web:* www.summitttrucking.com	Clarksville	IN	47129	812-285-7777	285-8949	780
Summitville Tiles Inc 15364 Ohio 644 *Web:* www.summitville.com	Summitville	OH	43962	330-223-1511	223-1414	751
Sumner County 355 N Belvedere Dr *Web:* www.sumnertn.org	Gallatin	TN	37066	615-452-4367	451-6027	338
Sumner County 501 N Washington Ave *Web:* www.co.sumner.ks.us	Wellington	KS	67152	620-326-3395	326-2116	338
Sumner Group Inc 6717 Waldemar Ave *Web:* www.sumner-group.com	Saint Louis	MO	63139	314-633-8000	633-8002	286
Sumner Peck Ranch Inc (SPR) 14860 N Hwy 41 *TF:* 800-788-0836 ■ *Web:* www.sumnerpeckranch.com	Madera	CA	93636	559-822-3301		10-4
Sumner School District 1202 Wood Ave *TF:* 866-548-3847 ■ *Web:* www.sumner.wednet.edu	Sumner	WA	98390	253-891-6000	891-6098	685
Sumner-Cowley Electric Co-op Inc 2223 N A St PO Box 220 *TF:* 888-326-3356 ■ *Web:* www.sucocoop.com	Wellington	KS	67152	620-326-3356	326-6579	245
Sumnicht & Associates W6240 Communication Ct Ste 1 *TF:* 800-473-2867 ■ *Web:* www.sumnicht.com	Appleton	WI	54914	920-731-4455		194
Sumter Correctional Institution 9544 County Rd 476 B *Web:* dc.state.fl.us	Bushnell	FL	33513	352-793-2525	793-3542	213
Sumter County 500 W Lamar St PO Box 295 *TF:* 800-436-7442 ■ *Web:* sumtercountyga.us	Americus	GA	31709	229-928-4500	928-4503	338
Sumter County 502 Lafayette St PO Box 1619 *TF:* 800-524-6181 ■ *Web:* www.sumteralchamber.com	Livingston	AL	35470	205-652-1580	652-1580	338
Sumter County 141 N Main St *Web:* www.sumtercountysc.org	Sumter	SC	29150	803-436-2227	436-2223	338
Sumter County Chamber of Commerce PO Box 426 *Web:* www.sumterchamber.org	Lake Panasoffkee	FL	33538	352-793-3099	793-2120	139
Sumter County Chamber of Commerce 409 Elm Ave PO Box 724 *Web:* www.sumtercountychamber.com	Americus	GA	31709	229-924-2646	924-8784	139
Sumter County Library 111 N Harvin St *Web:* www.sumtercountylibrary.org	Sumter	SC	29150	803-773-7273	773-4875	434-3

Entry	City	State	ZIP	Phone	Fax	Class
Sumter Electric Co-op Inc PO Box 301 *TF:* 800-732-6141 ■ *Web:* www.secoenergy.com	Sumterville	FL	33585	352-793-3801		245
Sumter Electric Membership Corp 1120 Felder St *TF:* 800-342-6978 ■ *Web:* www.sumteremc.com	Americus	GA	31709	229-924-8041		245
Sumter Packaging Corp 2341 Corporate Way *Web:* www.sumterpackaging.com	Sumter	SC	29154	803-481-2003		100
Sumter Utilities Inc 1151 N Pike W *TF:* 800-251-7234 ■ *Web:* www.sumter-utilities.com	Sumter	SC	29153	803-469-8585	469-4600	188-10
Sun & Ski Sports 10560 Bissonnet St Ste 100 *TF:* 866-786-3869 ■ *Web:* www.sunandski.com	Houston	TX	77099	281-340-5000		711
Sun & Snow Sports Inc 3780 Jackson Rd Ste J *TF:* 800-846-7052 ■ *Web:* www.sunandsnow.com	Ann Arbor	MI	48103	734-663-9515		711
Sun Bancorp Inc (SNBC) 350 Fellowship Rd Ste 101 *NASDAQ: SNBC* ■ *TF:* 800-786-9066 ■ *Web:* www.sunnationalbank.com	Mount Laurel	NJ	08054	800-760-4786		360-2
Sun Belt Food Company Inc 4755 Technology Way Ste 209 *Web:* www.sunbeltfoods.com	Boca Raton	FL	33431	561-995-9100	997-5664	297-6
Sun Builders Co 5870 6 N Hwy Ste 206 *Web:* www.sunbuildersco.com	Houston	TX	77084	281-815-1020		186
Sun Chemical Corp 35 Waterview Blvd *TF:* 800-543-2323 ■ *Web:* www.sunchemical.com	Parsippany	NJ	07054	973-404-6000	404-6001	388
Sun Chronicle PO Box 600 *TF:* 800-323-4673 ■ *Web:* www.thesunchronicle.com	Attleboro	MA	02703	508-222-7000	236-0462	532-2
Sun Cities Independent 17220 N Boswell Blvd Ste 101 *TF:* 800-282-8586 ■ *Web:* www.newszap.com	Sun City	AZ	85373	623-972-6101		532-4
Sun Coast Resources Inc 6405 Cavalcade St Bldg 1 *TF:* 800-677-3835 ■ *Web:* www.suncoastresources.com	Houston	TX	77028	713-844-9600		579
Sun Communities Inc 27777 Franklin Rd Ste 200 *NYSE: SUI* ■ *Web:* www.suncommunities.com	Southfield	MI	48034	248-208-2500		655
Sun Control Products Window Shades 1908 Second St SW *TF:* 800-533-0010 ■ *Web:* suncontrolshades.net/shades	Rochester	MN	55902	507-282-2620		87
Sun Country Airlines Inc 1300 Mendota Heights Rd *TF:* 800-359-6786 ■ *Web:* www.suncountry.com	Mendota Heights	MN	55120	651-681-3900		25
Sun Country Cleaners Inc 2240 34th Way N *Web:* www.suncountrycleaners.com	Largo	FL	33771	727-535-9930		426
Sun Country Industries 6801 Gruber NE *Web:* www.mcnally-group.com/suncountryindustries	Albuquerque	NM	87109	505-344-1611		567
Sun Devil Auto Inc 1824 E Elliot Rd *Web:* www.sunautoservice.com	Tempe	AZ	85284	480-831-2831		62-5
Sun Devil Fire Equipment Inc 2929 W Clarendon Ave **Fax Area Code:* 602 ■ *Web:* www.sundevilfire.com	Phoenix	AZ	85017	623-245-0636	495-9291*	679
Sun Devil Stadium 500 E Veterans Way Arizona State University *TF:* 888-786-3857 ■ *Web:* www.thesundevils.com	Tempe	AZ	85287-2505	480-965-3482	965-1261	720
Sun Drilling Products Corp 503 Main St *TF:* 800-962-6490 ■ *Web:* www.sundrilling.com	Belle Chasse	LA	70037	504-393-2778	391-1383	541
Sun Eagle Corp 461 N Dean Ave *Web:* www.suneaglecorporation.com	Chandler	AZ	85226	480-961-0004	940-0160	186
Sun Engineering Services Inc 5405 Garden Grove Blvd *TF:* 888-604-5888 ■ *Web:* www.sunengr.net	Westminster	CA	92683	714-379-2300		261
Sun Ergoline Inc 1 Walter Kratz Dr **Fax Area Code:* 870 ■ *TF:* 888-771-0996 ■ *Web:* sunergoline.com	Jonesboro	AR	72401	888-771-0996	935-3618*	437
Sun Graphics LLC 1818 Broadway *TF:* 800-592-7625 ■ *Web:* www.sun-graphics.com	Parsons	KS	67357	620-421-6200		627
Sun Healthcare Group Inc 18831 Von Karman Ste 400 *NASDAQ: SUNH*	Irvine	CA	92612	949-255-7100		451
SUN Home Health Services Inc 61 Duke St PO Box 232 *TF:* 888-478-6227 ■ *Web:* www.sunhomehealth.com	Northumberland	PA	17857	570-473-8320	473-3070	371
Sun Hydraulics Corp 1500 W University Pkwy *NASDAQ: SNHY* ■ *TF:* 800-237-8821 ■ *Web:* www.sunhydraulics.com	Sarasota	FL	34243	941-362-1200	355-4497	790
Sun Interiors Ltd 2329 Severn Ave *Web:* suninteriors.com	Metairie	LA	70001	504-833-8104		291
Sun Islands Hawaii Inc 438 Hobron Ln Ste 222 *Web:* www.sunislandshawaii.com	Honolulu	HI	96815	808-926-3888	922-6951	771
Sun Journal 3200 Wellons Blvd *Web:* www.newbernsj.com	New Bern	NC	28562	252-638-8101		532-2
Sun Lakes State Park 34875 Pk Ln Rd NE *Web:* www.parks.wa.gov	Coulee City	WA	99115	509-632-5583		565
Sun Life Assurance Company of Canada 1 Sun Life Executive Pk PO Box 9106 *TF:* 800-786-5433 ■ *Web:* www.sunlife.com/us	Wellesley Hills	MA	02481	781-237-6030		391-2
Sun Life Financial Inc 150 King St W *TSE: SLF* ■ *TF:* 877-786-5433 ■ *Web:* www.sunlife.com	Toronto	ON	M5H1J9	416-979-9966		360-4
Sun Life Stadium 347 Don Shula Dr *Web:* www.newmiamistadium.com	Miami Gardens	FL	33056	305-943-8000		720
Sun Line Products 1454 E Summitry Cir *TF:* 800-677-0071 ■ *Web:* www.sunlineproducts.com	Katy	TX	77449	281-398-6655		687
Sun Luck Garden 1901 S Taylor Rd	Cleveland	OH	44118	216-397-7676		671
Sun Machinery Company Inc PO Box 789 *Web:* www.sunmachineryco.com	Lexington	SC	29071	803-359-1000		791
Sun Magazine 8815 Conroy Windermere Rd Ste 130 *TF:* 888-218-9968 ■ *Web:* www.floridasunmagazine.com	Orlando	FL	32835	407-477-2815	293-1179	457-11

Name / Address	City	State	ZIP	Phone	Fax	Class
Sun Messenger 5510 Cloverleaf Pkwy *Web:* www.cleveland.com/sunmessenger	Cleveland	OH	44125	216-986-2600		532-4
Sun Mountain Lodge 604 Patterson Lake Rd PO Box 1000 *TF:* 800-572-0493 ■ *Web:* www.sunmountainlodge.com	Winthrop	WA	98862	509-996-2211	996-3133	669
Sun Mountain Lumber 181 Greenhouse Rd *Web:* www.sunmtnlumber.com	Deer Lodge	MT	59722	406-846-1600		683
Sun National Bank 350 Fellowship Rd Ste. 101 *TF:* 800-786-9066 ■ *Web:* www.sunnationalbank.com	Mount Laurel	NJ	08054	800-786-9066		70
Sun National Bank Ctr 81 Hamilton Ave *Web:* www.sunnationalbankcenter.com	Trenton	NJ	08611	609-656-3200	656-3201	720
Sun News 914 Frontage Rd E *TF:* 800-568-1800 ■ *Web:* www.myrtlebeachonline.com	Myrtle Beach	SC	29578	843-626-8555	626-0356	532-2
Sun Newspapers 1801 Superior Ave *TF:* 800-362-8008 ■ *Web:* www.advance-ohio.com	Cleveland	OH	44114	216-999-3900		637-8
Sun Orchard Inc 1198 W Fairmont Dr *TF:* 800-505-8423 ■ *Web:* www.sunorchard.com	Tempe	AZ	85282	800-505-8423		296-20
Sun Packaging Technologies Inc 2200 NW 32nd St Ste 1700 *TF:* 800-866-0322 ■ *Web:* www.sunpkg.com	Pompano Beach	FL	33069	954-978-3080		358
Sun Packing Inc 10077 Wallisville Rd *Web:* www.sunpacking.com	Houston	TX	77013	713-673-4600		88
Sun Pharmaceutical Industries Inc 270 Prospect Plains Rd *Web:* www.sunpharma.com	Cranbury	NJ	08512	609-495-2800		231
Sun Press 5510 Cloverleaf Pkwy *TF:* 800-362-0727 ■ *Web:* www.cleveland.com/sunpress	Cleveland	OH	44125	216-986-2600		532-4
Sun Printing 1800 Grand Ave. *TF:* 800-249-4911 ■ *Web:* www.sunprinting.com	Wausau	WI	54403	715-845-4911		627
Sun Process Converting Inc 1660 Kenneth Dr. *Web:* www.sunprocess.com	Mt Prospect	IL	60056	847-593-0447		548
Sun Ray Grill 619 Pink St. *Web:* www.sunraygrill.com	Metairie	LA	70005	504-837-0055		671
Sun Ray Park & Casino LLC 39 Rd 5568 *TF:* 800-456-3412 ■ *Web:* sunraygaming.com	Farmington	NM	87401	505-566-1200		452
Sun Realty Inc 1500 S Croatan Hwy PO Box 1630 *Web:* www.sunrealtync.com	Kill Devil Hills	NC	27948	252-441-7033		652
Sun River Electric Co-op Inc 310 First Ave S PO Box 309 *TF:* 800-452-7516 ■ *Web:* www.sunriverelectric.coop	Fairfield	MT	59436	406-467-2527		245
Sun State Builders Inc 1050 W Washington St Ste 214 *Web:* www.sunstatebuilders.com	Tempe	AZ	85281	480-894-1286		186
Sun Steel Co 2500 Euclid Ave *Web:* www.sunsteelco.com	Chicago Heights	IL	60411	708-756-0400		492
Sun Sui Wah Seafood Restaurant 3888 Main St	Vancouver	BC	V5V3N9	604-872-8822		671
Sun Surgical Supply Co 302 NW Sixth St *TF:* 800-342-3407 ■ *Web:* www.sunsurgical.com	Gainesville	FL	32601	352-377-2696		475
Sun Technologies Inc 3700 Mansell Rd Ste 125 *Web:* www.suntechnologies.com	Alpharetta	GA	30022	770-418-0434		180
Sun Ten Laboratories Inc 9250 Jeronimo Rd *Web:* www.sunten.com	Irvine	CA	92618	949-587-0509		743
Sun Valley Area Chamber of Commerce 11501 Strathern St PO Box 308 *TF:* 877-834-7064 ■ *Web:* www.sunvalleychamber.com	Sun Valley	CA	91352	818-768-2014		139
Sun Valley Community Church 456 E Ray Rd *Web:* www.sunvalleycc.com	Gilbert	AZ	85296	480-632-8920		48-20
Sun Valley Floral Farms Inc 3160 Upper Bay Rd. **Fax Area Code: 707* ■ *TF:* 800-747-0396 ■ *Web:* www.sunvalleyfloral.com	Arcata	CA	95521	800-747-0396	826-8708*	369
Sun Valley Masonry Inc 10828 N Cave Creek Rd *TF:* 800-334-5335 ■ *Web:* www.svmasonry.com	Phoenix	AZ	85020	602-943-6106	997-6857	189-7
Sun Valley Packing Co 7381 Ave 432	Reedley	CA	93654	559-591-1717		315-5
Sun Valley Paper Stock Inc 11166 Pendleton St	Sun Valley	CA	91352	323-875-2613		660
Sun Valley Resort 1 Sun Valley Rd *TF:* 800-786-8259 ■ *Web:* www.sunvalley.com	Sun Valley	ID	83353	208-622-4111		669
Sun Valley/Ketchum Chamber & Visitors Bureau 491 Sun Valley Rd *TF:* 800-634-3347 ■ *Web:* www.visitsunvalley.com	Ketchum	ID	83340	208-726-3423	726-4533	139
Sun Viking Lodge 2411 S Atlantic Ave. *TF:* 800-874-4469 ■ *Web:* www.sunviking.com	Daytona Beach Shores	FL	32118	386-252-6252	252-5463	379
Sun Well Service Inc 201 26th St E *Web:* www.sunwellservice.com	Williston	ND	58801	701-774-3001		538
Sun Windows Inc 1515 E 18th St *Web:* www.sunwindows.com	Owensboro	KY	42303	270-684-0691		234
Sun World International Inc 16350 Dr Rd *Web:* www.sun-world.com	Bakersfield	CA	93308	661-392-5000		315-3
Sun, The 4030 N Georgia Blvd *TF:* 800-922-0922 ■ *Web:* www.sbsun.com	San Bernardino	CA	92407	909-889-9666		532-2
Sunair 3131 SW 42 St *Web:* www.sunairhf.com	Fort Lauderdale	FL	33312	954-400-5100		647
Sunbelt Chemicals Corp 71 Hargrove Grade *Web:* www.sunbeltchemicals.com	Palm Coast	FL	32137	386-446-4595	446-4627	146
Sunbelt Computer Systems Inc 13090 Swan Lake Rd CR 468 *Web:* www.sunbelt-plb.com	Tyler	TX	75704	903-881-0400		178-2
Sunbelt Industrial Trucks 1617 Terre Colony Ct *Web:* www.sunbelt-industrial.com	Dallas	TX	75212	214-819-4150		770
SUNBELT Machine Works Corp 13411 Redfish Ln *Web:* sunbeltmachine.com	Stafford	TX	77477	281-499-0051		757
Sunbelt Marketing Investment Corp 3255 S Sweetwater Rd *TF:* 800-257-5566 ■ *Web:* www.sunbeltmarketing.com	Lithia Springs	GA	30122	770-739-3740		612
Sunbelt Metals & Manufacturing Inc 920 S Bradshaw Rd *Web:* www.sunbeltmetals.com	Apopka	FL	32703	407-889-8960		492
Sunbelt Printing & Graphics 1691 Sands Pl Ste E *Web:* www.sunbeltprinting.com	Marietta	GA	30067	770-988-0812		627
Sunbelt Rentals Inc 2341 Deerfield Dr *TF General:* 800-667-9328 ■ *Web:* www.sunbeltrentals.com	Fort Mill	SC	29715	704-348-2676		264-3
Sunbelt Sales & Marketing Associates Inc 170 Ottley Dr *TF:* 800-783-6258 ■ *Web:* www.filmloc.com	Atlanta	GA	30324	404-892-8778		195
Sunbelt Securities Inc 5065 Westheimer Ste 600 *Web:* www.sunbeltsecurities.com	Houston	TX	77056	713-965-9510		690
Sunbelt Transfomer Ltd 1922 S Martin Luther King Jr Dr *TF:* 800-433-3128 ■ *Web:* www.sunbeltusa.com	Temple	TX	76504	254-771-3777	771-5719	249
Sunbelt-Turret Steel Inc 527 Atando Ave. *Web:* www.sunbeltturretsteel.com	Charlotte	NC	28206	704-342-4321		492
Sunburst Foods Inc 1002 Sunburst Dr *Web:* www.sunburstfoods.net	Goldsboro	NC	27534	919-778-2151		296-34
Sunburst Hospitality Corp 10770 Columbia Pk Ste 200 *Web:* www.snbhotels.com	Silver Spring	MD	20901	301-592-3800		379
Sunburst Shutters 6480 W Flamingo Rd Ste D *TF:* 877-786-2877 ■ *Web:* www.sunburstshutters.com	Las Vegas	NV	89103	702-367-1600	367-8525	699
Sunbury Community Hospital (SCH) 350 N 11th St *Web:* www.sunburyhospital.com	Sunbury	PA	17801	570-286-3333		374-3
Sunbury Motor Company 943 N Fourth St *TF:* 866-440-7854 ■ *Web:* www.sunburymotors.com	Sunbury	PA	17801	570-286-7746		516
Suncall America Inc 505 Industrial Pkwy *Web:* www.suncallamerica.com	Richmond	IN	47374	765-966-9656		247
Suncast Corp 701 N Kirk Rd *TF:* 800-444-3310 ■ *Web:* suncast.com	Batavia	IL	60510	630-879-2050	879-6112	319-2
Suncast Network Inc 2407 E Oakton St Ste B-10	Arlington Heights	IL	60005	847-364-4006		387
Sunchaser Vacation Villas 5129 Riverview Gate Rd *TF Resv:* 877-451-1250 ■ *Web:* www.sunchaservillas.ca	Fairmont Hot Springs	BC	V0B1L1	250-345-4545		753
Suncoast Communities Blood Bank 1760 Mound St. *TF:* 866-972-5663 ■ *Web:* www.scbb.org	Sarasota	FL	34236	941-954-1600	951-2629	89
Suncoast Ctr Inc PO Box 10070 *Web:* www.suncoastcenter.com	Saint Petersburg	FL	33733	727-327-7656	323-8078	363
Suncoast Hotel & Casino 9090 Alta Dr *TF:* 877-677-7111 ■ *Web:* www.suncoastcasino.com	Las Vegas	NV	89145	702-636-7111		379
Suncoast Media Group Inc 23170 Harbor View Rd *Web:* www.venicegondolier.com	Port Charlotte	FL	33980	941-206-1300		532-3
Suncoast Pathology Inc 446 Tamiami Trl S. *Web:* www.defevercruisers.com	Venice	FL	34285	941-483-3319		415
Suncoast Post-Tension LP 509 N Sam Houston Pkwy Ste 400 E *TF:* 800-847-8886 ■ *Web:* www.suncoast-pt.com	Houston	TX	77060	281-668-1840	668-1862	189-3
Suncoast Print & Promotions Inc 1045 N Lime Ave *Web:* www.suncoastforms.com	Sarasota	FL	34237	941-366-1123		627
Suncor Energy Inc 150 - 6 Ave SW PO Box 2844 *NYSE: SU* ■ *TF:* 800-558-9071 ■ *Web:* www.suncor.com	Calgary	AB	T2P3E3	403-296-8000	296-3030	536
Suncor Stainless Inc 70 Armstrong Rd *TF:* 800-218-7702 ■ *Web:* suncorstainless.com	Plymouth	MA	02360	508-732-9191		350
Suncraft Technologies Inc 1301 Frontenac Rd *Web:* www.suncrafttechnologies.com	Naperville	IL	60563	630-369-7900		627
Sundahl Powers Kapp & Martin LLC 1725 Carey Ave. *Web:* www.spkm.org	Cheyenne	WY	82001	307-632-6421		428
Sundance Aviation Inc Sundance Airpark NW 122nd & Sara Rd. *Web:* sundanceairport.com	Oklahoma City	OK	73099	405-373-3886	373-3893	63
Sundance Beach 59 S La Patera Ln *TF:* 877-968-0036 ■ *Web:* www.sundancebeach.com	Goleta	CA	93117	877-968-0036		711
Sundance Boats Inc 6131 Sundance Rd *Web:* www.sundanceboats.com	Blackshear	GA	31516	912-449-0033		90
Sundance Ch 1633 Broadway *Web:* sundance.tv	New York	NY	10019	212-708-1500		740
Sundance Film Festival 1825 Three Kings Dr. *Web:* www.sundance.org/festival	Park City	UT	84060	801-328-3456		282
Sundance Institute 1825 Three Kings Dr. *TF:* 800-898-7256 ■ *Web:* www.sundance.org	Park City	UT	84060	801-328-3456		514
Sundance Square 201 Main St Ste 700 *TF:* 800-223-5436 ■ *Web:* www.sundancesquare.com	Fort Worth	TX	76102	817-255-5700		50-6
Sundance Trail Guest Ranch 17931 Red Feather Lakes Rd *TF:* 800-357-4930 ■ *Web:* www.sundancetrail.com	Red Feather Lakes	CO	80545	970-224-1222	224-1222	239
Sundance Vacations Inc 264 Highland Park Blvd *TF:* 800-433-9712 ■ *Web:* www.sundancevacations.com	Wilkes-Barre	PA	18702	570-820-0900		376
Sunday River Ski Resort 15 S Ridge Rd PO Box 4500 *TF:* 800-543-2754 ■ *Web:* sundayriver.com	Newry	ME	04261	207-824-3500	824-5110	669
Sundays Energy Inc 2637 27th Ave S *TF:* 800-972-3835 ■ *Web:* www.sundaysenergy.com	Minneapolis	MN	55406	612-605-1788		579

Phone | Fax | Class

Sundel & Milford Inc 11 Scovill St — Waterbury CT 06720 — 203-753-0114 — 390
Web: sundelmilford.com

Sunderland Bros Co 9700 J St — Omaha NE 68127 — 402-339-2220 — 339-4455 — 191-3
Web: www.sunderlands.com

Sundestin Beach Resort 1040 Hwy 98 E — Destin FL 32541 — 850-586-1775 — 707
Web: sundestinresort.com

Sundial Beach & Golf Resort
1451 Middle Gulf Dr — Sanibel FL 33957 — 239-472-4151 — 669
TF: 866-717-2323 ■ *Web:* www.theinnsofsanibel.com

Sundial Boutique Hotel
4340 Sundial Crescent — Whistler BC V0N1B4 — 604-932-2321 — 379
TF: 800-661-2321 ■ *Web:* www.sundialhotel.com

Sundial Software Corp
5202 Eastpark Blvd Ste 105 — Madison WI 53718 — 608-663-8100 — 525
Web: www.sundialsc.com

Sundin Associates Inc 34 Main St Fl 3 — Natick MA 01760 — 508-650-3972 — 7
TF: 800-970-2499 ■ *Web:* www.sundininc.com

Sundog Inc 2000 44th St SW Fl 6 — Fargo ND 58103 — 701-235-5525 — 195
TF: 888-978-6364 ■ *Web:* www.sundoginteractive.com

Sundowner Trailers Inc
9805 S State Hwy 48 — Coleman OK 73432 — 580-937-4255 — 763
TF: 800-654-3879 ■ *Web:* www.sundownertrailer.com

Sundt Construction 2620 S 55th St — Tempe AZ 85282 — 480-293-3000 — 189-2
TF: 800-280-3000 ■ *Web:* www.sundt.com

Sundt Construction Inc
2015 W River Rd Ste 101 — Tucson AZ 85704 — 520-750-4600 — 186
TF: 800-467-5544 ■ *Web:* www.sundt.com

SunEdison Semiconductor Ltd
501 Pearl Dr — Saint Peters MO 63376 — 636-474-5000 — 474-5158* — 696
NASDAQ: SEMI ■ **Fax:* Sales ■ *TF:* 800-732-0330 ■ *Web:* sunedisonsemi.com

Sunera Technologies Inc
631 E Big Beaver Rd Ste 109 — Troy MI 48083 — 248-524-0222 — 809
Web: www.suneratech.com

Sunex International Inc
100 Roe Rd — Travelers Rest SC 29690 — 864-834-8759 — 350
TF: 800-833-7869 ■ *Web:* www.sunextools.com

Sunfire Corp 1969 Kellogg Ave — Carlsbad CA 92008 — 760-710-0993 — 52
Web: www.sunfire.com

Sunfish 2800 Alki Ave SW — Seattle WA 98116 — 206-938-4112 — 671

Sunflower 8557 Research Blvd — Austin TX 78758 — 512-339-7860 — 671

Sunflower County 200 Main St — Indianola MS 38751 — 662-887-4703 — 338
Web: www.sunflowercounty.ms.gov

Sunflower Group 14001 Marshall Dr — Lenexa KS 66215 — 913-890-0900 — 636
Web: www.sunflowergroup.com

Sunforce Products Inc
9015 Ch Avon — Montreal-Ouest QC H4X2G8 — 514-989-2100 — 610
Web: sunforceproducts.com

SunGard Availability Services
680 E Swedesford Rd — Wayne PA 19087 — 484-582-2000 — 394
TF: 800-468-7483 ■ *Web:* www.sungardas.com

Sungard Bi-Tech Inc 890 Ftress St — Chico CA 95973 — 530-891-5281 — 809

SunGard Trust Systems Inc
5510 77 Ctr Dr — Charlotte NC 28217 — 704-527-6300 — 527-9617 — 178-10
Web: www.sungard.com

Sunhillo Corp 444 Kelley Dr — West Berlin NJ 08091 — 856-767-7676 — 225
Web: www.sunhillo.com

Sun-Journal PO Box 4400 — Lewiston ME 04243 — 207-784-5411 — 777-3436 — 532-2
TF: 800-482-0759 ■ *Web:* www.sunjournal.com

Sunken Meadow State Park
Sunken Meadow Pkwy — Kings Park NY 11754 — 631-269-4333 — 565
Web: parks.ny.gov/parks/37/details.aspx

Sunkist Graphics Inc
401 E Sunset Rd — Henderson NV 89011 — 702-566-9008 — 627
Web: www.sunkistgrfx.com

Sunkist Growers Inc
27770 Entertainment Dr — Valencia CA 91355 — 661-290-8900 — 315-2
Web: www.sunkist.com

Sunland Chemical & Research Corp
5447 San Fernando Rd W — Los Angeles CA 90039 — 818-244-9600 — 145
Web: www.sunlandchemical.com

Sunland Fire Protection Inc
1218 Elon Pl — High Point NC 27263 — 336-886-7027 — 610
Web: www.sunlandfire.com

Sunland Group Inc
1033 La Posada Dr Ste 370 — Austin TX 78752 — 512-494-0208 — 261
TF: 866-732-8500 ■ *Web:* www.sunlandgrp.com

Sunland Park Racetrack & Casino
1200 Futurity Dr — Sunland Park NM 88063 — 575-874-5200 — 642
TF: 800-572-1142 ■ *Web:* www.sunland-park.com

Sunland Tire Co of Upland Inc
461 E Foothill Blvd — Upland CA 91750 — 909-982-1396 — 57
Web: sunlandtire.com

Sunland-Tujunga Chamber of Commerce
8250 Foothill Blvd Ste A — Sunland CA 91040 — 818-352-4433 — 353-7551 — 139
TF: 800-745-3000 ■ *Web:* www.stchamber.com

Sunlight Foundation
1818 N St NW Ste 300 — Washington DC 20036 — 202-742-1520 — 305
Web: www.sunlightfoundation.com

SunLink Health Systems Inc
900 Cir 75 Pkwy Ste 1120 — Atlanta GA 30339 — 770-933-7000 — 933-7010 — 353
NYSE: SSY ■ *TF:* 800-966-9021 ■ *Web:* www.sunlinkhealth.com

Sunlite Plastics Inc
W 194 N 11340 McCormick Dr — Germantown WI 53022 — 262-253-0600 — 253-0601 — 600
Web: www.sunliteplastics.com

Sun-Maid Growers of California
13525 S Bethel Ave — Kingsburg CA 93631 — 559-896-8000 — 897-6209 — 296-18
Web: sunmaid.com

Sunnen Products Co
7910 Manchester Ave — Saint Louis MO 63143 — 314-781-2100 — 781-2268* — 455
**Fax:* Cust Svc ■ *TF:* 800-325-3670 ■ *Web:* www.sunnen.com

Sunnin 1776 Westwood Blvd — Los Angeles CA 90024 — 310-475-3358 — 671
Web: www.sunnin.com

Sunnking Inc 4 Owens Rd — Brockport NY 14420 — 585-637-8365 — 179
Web: www.sunnking.com

Sunny 101.5 1301 E Douglas Rd — Mishawaka IN 46545 — 574-233-3141 — 645
Web: www.sunny1015.com

Sunny 106.5 - KSNE-FM
2880 Meade Ave Ste 250 — Las Vegas NV 89102 — 702-238-7300 — 645-88
Web: sunny1065.iheart.com

Sunny 107.9 Radio
Palm Beach Broadcasting
701 Northpoint Pkwy Ste 500 — West Palm Beach FL 33407 — 561-616-4777 — 645-173
TF: 800-919-1079 ■ *Web:* www.sunny1079.com

Sunny 99.1 2000 W Loop S Ste 300 — Houston TX 77027 — 713-212-8000 — 645-75
Web: www.sunny99.com

Sunny Dell Foods Inc 135 N Fifth St — Oxford PA 19363 — 610-932-5164 — 296
Web: www.sunnydell.com

Sunny Isles Beach Tourism & Marketing Council
18070 Collins Ave — Sunny Isles Beach FL 33160 — 305-792-1952 — 139
Web: www.sunnyislesbeachmiami.com

Sunny Land Tours Inc
21 Old Kings Rd N Ste B-212 — Palm Coast FL 32137 — 386-449-0059 — 449-0060 — 760
TF: 800-783-7839 ■ *Web:* www.sunnylandtours.com

Sunny Morning
5330 NW 35th Ave — Fort Lauderdale FL 33309 — 954-735-3447 — 297-8
Web: www.sunnymorning.com

Sunnybrook Health Sciences Centre
Sunnybrook Campus 2075 Bayview Ave — Toronto ON M4N3M5 — 416-480-6100 — 374-2
TF: 800-387-9066 ■ *Web:* www.sunnybrook.ca
Women & Babies research program
76 Grenville St — Toronto ON M5S1B2 — 416-323-6400 — 374-2
Web: www.sunnybrook.ca

Sunnyland Farms Inc PO Box 8200 — Albany GA 31706 — 800-999-2488 — 459
TF: 800-999-2488 ■ *Web:* www.sunnylandfarms.com

Sunnyland Outdoor & Casual Furniture
7879 Spring Valley Rd Ste 125 — Dallas TX 75254 — 972-239-3716 — 321
TF: 877-239-3716 ■ *Web:* www.sunnylandfurniture.com

Sunnyridge Farm Inc
1900 Fifth St NW PO Box 3036 — Winter Haven FL 33881 — 863-294-8856 — 595-4095 — 297-7
Web: www.sunnyridge.com

Sunnyside Motor Co Inc 944 Main St — Holden MA 01520 — 508-829-4333 — 57
Web: www.sunnysideford.com

Sunnyvale Chamber of Commerce
260 S Sunnyvale Ave Ste 4 — Sunnyvale CA 94086 — 408-736-4971 — 736-1919 — 139
Web: www.svcoc.org

Sunnyvale Lumber Inc
870 W Evelyn Ave — Sunnyvale CA 94086 — 408-736-5411 — 736-6738 — 48-15
Web: www.sunnyvalelumber.com

Sunnyvale Public Library (SPL)
665 W Olive Ave — Sunnyvale CA 94086 — 408-730-7300 — 434-3
Web: sunnyvale.ca.gov/community/library/default.htm

Sunnyvale Sun 1095 The Alameda — San Jose CA 95126 — 408-200-1000 — 200-1013 — 532-4
Web: www.mercurynews.com

Sunnyview Rehabilitation Hospital
1270 Belmont Ave — Schenectady NY 12308 — 518-382-4500 — 374-6
TF: 800-994-6610 ■ *Web:* www.nehealth.com

Sunnyway Foods Inc
212 N Antrim Way — Greencastle PA 17225 — 717-597-7121 — 345
Web: mysunnywayfoods.com

Sunoco Chemicals
1735 Market St Ste LL — Philadelphia PA 19103 — 215-977-3000 — 977-3409 — 144
TF: 800-786-6261

Sunoco Inc 1735 Market St — Philadelphia PA 19103 — 800-786-6261 — 536
NYSE: SUN ■ *TF:* 800-786-6261 ■ *Web:* sunoco.com

Sunoco Logistics Partners LP
525 Fritztown Rd — Sinking Spring PA 19608 — 610-670-3200 — 597
NYSE: SXL ■ *Web:* www.sunocologistics.com

SunOpta Inc 2838 Bovaird Dr W — Brampton ON L7A0H2 — 905-455-2528 — 296-23
TSE: SOY ■ *Web:* www.sunopta.com

Sunora Energy Solutions
2342 E University Dr — Phoenix AZ 85034 — 602-772-5220 — 192

Sunovion Pharmaceuticals Inc
84 Waterford Dr — Marlborough MA 01752 — 508-481-6700 — 231
TF: 888-394-7377 ■ *Web:* www.sunovion.com

Sunpeak Construction Inc
1401 Quail St Ste 105 — Newport Beach CA 92660 — 949-474-0501 — 186
Web: www.sunpeak.com

Sunplus Data Group Inc
3781 Presidential Pkwy Ste 132 — Atlanta GA 30340 — 770-455-3264 — 177
TF: 800-573-1874 ■ *Web:* www.sunplusdata.com

SunPower Corp 77 Rio Robles — San Jose CA 95134 — 408-240-5500 — 696
NASDAQ: SPWR ■ *Web:* us.sunpower.com

Sunquest Information Systems Inc
250 S Williams Blvd — Tucson AZ 85711 — 520-570-2000 — 180
Web: www.sunquestinfo.com

SunQuest Vacations
75-1029 Henry St Ste 103 — Kailua-Kona HI 96740 — 800-367-5168 — 443-0220* — 771
**Fax Area Code:* 808 ■ *TF:* 800-367-5168 ■ *Web:* www.sunquest-hawaii.com

Sun-Re Cheese Corp 178 Lonker Ave — Sunbury PA 17801 — 570-286-1511 — 296-5

Sunrich LLC 3824 SW 93rd St PO Box 128 — Hope MN 56046 — 507-451-6030 — 80-1
TF: 800-297-5997 ■ *Web:* www.sunrich.com

Sunrider International
1625 Abalone Ave — Torrance CA 90501 — 310-781-3808 — 366
TF Orders: 888-278-6743 ■ *Web:* www.sunrider.com

Sunridge International
16857 Saguaro Blvd — Fountain Hills AZ 85268 — 480-837-6165 — 502

Sunrise Bakery Inc
4564 Second Ave 47th St — Brooklyn NY 11232 — 718-788-7884 — 68

Sunrise Brands
801 S Figueroa St Ste 2500 — Los Angeles CA 90017 — 323-780-8250 — 881-0369 — 155-21
Web: www.sunrisebrands.com

Sunrise Business Services Inc
1556 Ocean Ave Ste 10 — Bohemia NY 11716 — 631-366-0504 — 113
Web: www.sunrisebusiness.com

Sunrise Chamber of Commerce
6800 Sunset Strip Ste 318 — Sunrise FL 33313 — 954-835-2428 — 561-9685 — 139
TF: 800-273-1614 ■ *Web:* www.sunrisechamber.org

Sunrise Children Foundation
2795 E Desert Inn Rd Ste 100 — Las Vegas NV 89121 — 702-731-8373 — 305
Web: www.sunrisechildren.org

Sunrise Community Evangelical Free Church Inc
298 Aquatic Dr — Atlantic Beach FL 32233 — 904-249-3030 — 48-20
Web: sccjax.org

Sunrise Country Manor 610 224th — Milford NE 68405 — 402-761-3230 — 371
Web: sunrisecountrymanor.com

Sunrise Engineering Inc
25 East 500 North — Fillmore UT 84631 — 435-743-6151 — 261
Web: sunrise-eng.com

	City	State	Zip	Phone	Fax	Class
Sunrise Growers Inc 701 W Kimberly Ave Ste 210 *Web:* sunrisegrowers.com	Placentia	CA	92870	714-630-6292		296-21
Sunrise Hitek Service Inc 5915 N Northwest Hwy *Web:* www.sunrisehitek.com	Chicago	IL	60631	773-792-8880		781
Sunrise Home Health Services 3200 Broadway Blvd Ste 260 *TF:* 800-296-7823 ■ *Web:* sunrisehomehealth.com	Garland	TX	75043	972-278-1414		363
Sunrise Hospital & Medical Ctr 3186 S Maryland Pkwy *Web:* www.sunrisehospital.com	Las Vegas	NV	89109	702-731-8000		374-3
Sunrise House Foundation Inc 37 Sunset Inn Rd *Web:* www.sunrisehouse.com	Lafayette	NJ	07848	973-383-6300		305
Sunrise Labs Inc 5 Dartmouth Dr *Web:* www.sunriselabs.com	Auburn	NH	03032	603-644-4500		194
Sunrise Mall 6041 Sunrise Mall *Web:* www.sunrisemallonline.com	Citrus Heights	CA	95610	916-961-7150		460
Sunrise Medical Inc 2842 Business Pk Ave *TF:* 800-333-4000 ■ *Web:* www.sunrisemedical.com	Fresno	CA	93727	800-333-4000		477
Sunrise Medical Laboratories Inc 250 Miller Pl. *TF Cust Svc:* 800-782-0282 ■ *Web:* www.sunriselab.com	Hicksville	NY	11801	631-435-1515		418
Sunrise Mfg. Inc 2665 Mercantile Dr *TF:* 800-748-6529 ■ *Web:* www.sunrisemfg.com	Rancho Cordova	CA	95742	916-635-6262		499
Sunrise School Division 344 Second St N PO Box 1206 *Web:* www.sunrisesd.ca	Beausejour	MB	R0E0C0	204-268-4832		685
Sunrise Senior Living LLC 7902 Westpark Dr *NYSE: SRZ* ■ *TF:* 888-434-4648 ■ *Web:* www.sunriseseniorliving.com	McLean	VA	22102	703-273-7500	744-1601	451
Sunrise Specialty Co 930 98th Ave *TF:* 800-444-4280 ■ *Web:* www.sunrisespecialty.com	Oakland	CA	94603	510-720-7277	720-7270	611
Sunrise Suites Resort Key West 3685 Seaside Dr *Web:* www.sunrisesuiteskeywest.com	Key West	FL	33040	305-296-6661		379
Sunrise Systems Inc 16 Pearl St Ste 101 *Web:* www.sunrisesys.com	Metuchen	NJ	08840	732-603-2200		225
Sunrise Windows Ltd. LLC 200 Enterprise Dr *Web:* www.sunrisewindows.com	Temperance	MI	48182	734-847-8778	847-7758	608
Sunrise Wood Designs 720 107th St *TF:* 800-428-7247 ■ *Web:* sunrisewooddesigns.com	Arlington	TX	76011	817-701-4101		226
Sunriver Resort 17600 Ctr Dr PO Box 3609 *TF:* 800-547-3922 ■ *Web:* www.destinationhotels.com/sunriver-resort	Sunriver	OR	97707	541-593-1000		669
Sunroad Marina Partners LP 955 Harbor Island Dr *Web:* www.sunmarina.com	San Diego	CA	92101	619-574-0736		360-3
Sunsational Cruises 2470 E Glen Canyon Rd **Fax Area Code:* 520 ■ *TF:* 800-239-6252 ■ *Web:* www.sunsationalcruises.com	Green Valley	AZ	85614	480-491-6248	445-6812*	771
Sunset Aviation 351 Airport Rd Ste E *Web:* sunsetaviation.com	Novato	CA	94945	415-897-2403		23
Sunset Bay State Park 89814 Cape Arago Hwy *Web:* www.oregonstateparks.org	Coos Bay	OR	97420	541-888-3778		565
Sunset Beach Resort 3287 W Gulf Dr *TF:* 866-565-5091 ■ *Web:* www.theinnsofsanibel.com	Sanibel Island	FL	33957	239-472-1700		669
Sunset Development Co 1 Annabel Ln Ste 201 *Web:* www.bishopranch.com	San Ramon	CA	94583	925-866-0100	866-1330	187
Sunset Farm Foods Inc 1201 Madison Hwy *TF:* 800-882-1121 ■ *Web:* www.sunsetfarmfoods.com	Valdosta	GA	31601	229-242-3389		393
Sunset Food Mart Inc 1812 Green Bay Rd *Web:* sunsetfoods.com	Highland Park	IL	60035	847-432-5500		345
Sunset Gower Studios 1438 N Gower St *TF:* 800-371-3718 ■ *Web:* www.sgsandsbs.com	Hollywood	CA	90028	323-467-1001		514
Sunset Grill 421 A1A Beach Blvd	Saint Augustine	FL	32080	904-471-5555		671
Sunset Grill 2001 Belcourt Ave *Web:* www.sunsetgrill.com	Nashville	TN	37212	615-386-3663		671
Sunset Grille 6751 Ruppsville Rd *Web:* www.sunset-grille.com	Allentown	PA	18106	610-395-9622		671
Sunset Hills Health & Rehabilitation Ctr 10954 Kennerly Rd *Web:* sunsethillshrc.com	Saint Louis	MO	63128	314-843-4242	843-4031	450
Sunset Inn Travel Apartments 1111 Burnaby St *TF:* 800-786-1997 ■ *Web:* www.sunsetinn.com	Vancouver	BC	V6E1P4	604-688-2474	669-3340	379
Sunset Key Guest Cottages at Westin Resort 245 Front St *Web:* www.sunsetkeycottages.com	Key West	FL	33040	305-292-5300		669
Sunset Logistics Inc 710 Fm 1620 *Web:* sunsetlogistics.com	Seguin	TX	78155	830-560-1032		57
Sunset Marquis Hotel & Villas 1200 N Alta Loma Rd *TF:* 800-858-9758 ■ *Web:* www.sunsetmarquis.com	West Hollywood	CA	90069	310-657-1333	652-5300	379
Sunset Moulding Company Inc 2231 Paseo Ave *TF:* 800-824-5888 ■ *Web:* www.sunsetmoulding.com	Live Oak	CA	95953	530-695-1000	695-2560	309
Sunset Printing 4522 Rosemead Blvd *Web:* sunsetprinting.wixsite.com/sunsetprinting	Pico Rivera	CA	90660	562-692-3950		627
Sunset Publishing Corp 80 Willow Rd *TF:* 800-777-0117 ■ *Web:* www.sunset.com	Menlo Park	CA	94025	650-321-3600		637-9
Sunset Ridge School District 29 525 Sunset Ridge Rd *Web:* www.sunsetridge29.net	Northfield	IL	60093	847-881-9400	446-6388	685
Sunset Scavenger Co 250 Executive Pk Ste 2100 *Web:* www.sunsetscavenger.com	San Francisco	CA	94134	415-330-1300		804
Sunset Station Hotel & Casino 1301 W Sunset Rd *TF:* 888-786-7389 ■ *Web:* sunsetstation.sclv.com	Henderson	NV	89014	702-547-7777		379
Sunset Tower Hotel 8358 Sunset Blvd *Web:* www.sunsettowerhotel.com	West Hollywood	CA	90069	323-654-7100		379
Sunset Transportation Inc 11325 Concord Village Ave *TF:* 800-849-6540 ■ *Web:* www.sunsettrans.com	St Louis	MO	63123	800-849-6540		311
Sunshine Artist Magazine 4075 LB McLeod Rd Ste E *TF:* 800-597-2573 ■ *Web:* www.sunshineartist.com	Orlando	FL	32811	407-648-7479		457-2
Sunshine Books Inc 49 River St Ste 3 *TF:* 800-472-5425 ■ *Web:* www.clickertraining.com	Waltham	MA	02453	781-398-0754		95
Sunshine Business Class 150 Kingswood Dr *TF:* 800-873-7681 ■ *Web:* www.sunshinebusinessclass.com	Mankato	MN	56001	800-873-7681		130
Sunshine Dairy Foods Inc 801 NE 21st Ave *TF:* 800-243-3730 ■ *Web:* www.sunshinedairyfoods.com	Portland	OR	97232	503-234-7526		297-4
Sunshine Drapery & Interior Fashions LLC WorkRm 11800 Adie Rd *Web:* www.sunshinedrapery.com	Maryland Heights	MO	63043	314-569-2980		361
Sunshine Financial Inc 1400 E Park Ave *TF:* 800-468-3993 ■ *Web:* sunshinesavingsbank.com	Tallahassee	FL	32301	850-219-7200		360-2
Sunshine Foliage World 2060 Steve Roberts Special *Web:* www.sunshinefoliageworld.com	Zolfo Springs	FL	33890	863-735-0501		369
Sunshine Foods Partners 1115 Main St *Web:* www.sunshinefoodstores.com	Saint Helena	CA	94574	707-963-7070		297-8
Sunshine Girl Creations Inc 11111 Excelsior Blvd *Web:* www.sunshinegirlcreations.net	Hopkins	MN	55343	952-931-2464	931-2575	130
Sunshine Makers Inc 15922 Pacific Coast Hwy *TF:* 800-228-0709 ■ *Web:* www.simplegreen.com	Huntington Harbour	CA	92649	562-795-6000	592-3034	151
Sunshine Manufactured Structures Inc 850 Gold Hill Ave *Web:* www.sunshinemodulars.com	Rockwell	NC	28138	704-279-6600		505
Sunshine Market Inc 2901 Campbell Ave. *Web:* sunshinemarket.com	Lynchburg	VA	24501	434-846-7862		345
Sunshine Mills Inc 500 Sixth St SW **Fax:* Sales ■ *TF:* 800-633-3349 ■ *Web:* www.sunshinemills.com	Red Bay	AL	35582	256-356-9541	356-8287*	578
Sunshine Minting Inc 7600 Mineral Dr Ste 700 *TF:* 800-274-5837 ■ *Web:* www.sunshinemint.com	Coeur d'Alene	ID	83815	208-772-9592	772-9739	409
Sunshine Oilsands Ltd 903 Eighth Ave SW Ste 1020 *Web:* www.sunshineoilsands.com	Calgary	AB	T2P0P7	403-984-1450	455-7674	536
Sunshine Sachs 8409 santa monica blvd *Web:* www.sunshinesachs.com	Los Angeles	CA	90069	323-822-9300		636
Sunshine Terrace Foundation Inc 248 W 300 N *Web:* www.sunshineterrace.net	Logan	UT	84321	435-752-0411		450
Sunshine Village Corp Calgary Snow Central 1037 11th Ave SW *TF:* 800-403-0206 ■ *Web:* www.skibanff.com	Calgary	AB	T2R0G1	403-705-4000		378
Sunstar Americas Inc 4635 W Foster Ave **Fax Area Code:* 800 ■ *TF:* 888-777-3101 ■ *Web:* www.gumbrand.com	Chicago	IL	60630	888-777-3101	553-2014*	228
Sunstate Federal Credit Union (Inc) PO Box 1162 *TF:* 877-786-7828 ■ *Web:* www.sunstatefcu.org	Gainesville	FL	32627	352-381-5200		219
Sunstone Hotel Properties Inc 903 Calle Amanecer Ste 100 *TF:* 800-732-0330 ■ *Web:* www.sunstonehotels.com	San Clemente	CA	92673	949-369-4000		707
Sunstore Solar Energy Solutions 3090 S Hwy 14 *Web:* www.sunstoresolar.com	Greer	SC	29650	864-297-6776		610
Sunstream Hotels & Resorts 6231 Estero Blvd *TF:* 844-652-3696 ■ *Web:* www.sunstream.com	Fort Myers Beach	FL	33931	239-765-4111		378
Sunsweet Growers Inc 901 N Walton Ave *TF:* 800-417-2253 ■ *Web:* www.sunsweet.com	Yuba City	CA	95993	530-674-5010	751-5238	296-18
Suntec Concrete Inc 2221 W Shangri La Rd *Web:* www.suntecconcrete.com	Phoenix	AZ	85029	602-997-0937		106
Sunteca Systems Inc 2 Ave A	Leetsdale	PA	15056	412-749-5200		362
Sunterra Quality Food Markets Inc 1851 Sirocco Dr SW Ste 200 *TF:* 800-667-8280 ■ *Web:* www.sunterramarket.com	Calgary	AB	T3H4R5	403-266-2820		345
Suntory International Corp 600 Third Ave *Web:* www.suntory.com	New York	NY	10016	212-891-6600		360-3
Suntrans International Inc 1550 W Glenlake Ave *Web:* www.suntrans.com	Itasca	IL	60143	630-285-9900		311
Suntreat Packing & Shipping Co 391 Oxford Ave *TF:* 800-780-4707 ■ *Web:* suntreat.com	Lindsay	CA	93247	559-562-4991		549
Suntrust Bank PO Box 4418 *NYSE: STI* ■ *TF:* 800-786-8787 ■ *Web:* www.suntrust.com	Atlanta	GA	30302	800-786-8787		70
SunTrust Banks Inc 303 Peachtree St NE *NYSE: STI* ■ *TF:* 800-786-8787 ■ *Web:* www.suntrust.com	Atlanta	GA	30308	404-588-7711	335-2686	360-2
SunTrust Mortgage Inc 1001 Semmes Ave *TF:* 800-634-7928 ■ *Web:* www.suntrust.com/mortgage	Richmond	VA	23224	800-634-7928		509
SunTrust Robinson Humphrey Capital Markets 3333 Peachtree Rd NE *TF:* 800-634-7928 ■ *Web:* www.suntrustrh.com	Atlanta	GA	30326	404-926-5000		690

Phone | Fax | Class

Sununu Chris (R)
Office of the Governor 107 N Main St . . . Concord NH 03301 603-271-2121 271-7640 343
Web: www.governor.nh.gov

Sunvalley Mall 1 Sunvalley Mall . . . Concord CA 94520 925-825-0400 460
Web: www.shopsunvalley.com

SunWatch Indian Village/Archaeological Park
2301 W River Rd . . . Dayton OH 45417 937-268-8199 50-3
Web: www.sunwatch.org

Sunway Hotel Group Inc
8500 College Blvd . . . Overland Park KS 66210 913-345-2111 707
Web: sunwayhotel.com

Sunwest Aviation Ltd
230 Aviation Pl NE . . . Calgary AB T2E7G1 403-275-8121 23
TF: 888-291-4566 ■ *Web:* www.sunwestaviation.ca

Sunwest Electric Inc
3064 E Miraloma Ave . . . Anaheim CA 92806 714-630-8700 630-8740 189-4
Web: www.sunwestelectric.net

Sunwest Silver Company Inc
324 Lomas Blvd NW . . . Albuquerque NM 87102 505-243-3781 292
TF: 800-771-3781 ■ *Web:* www.sunwestsilver.com

Sunwing Travel Group Inc 27 Fasken Dr . . . Toronto ON M9W1K6 416-620-4955 772
Web: www.sunwing.ca

Sunworld Landscape & Construction LLC
989 Empire Mesa Way . . . Henderson NV 89011 702-598-1711 776
Web: www.sunworldllc.com

SUNY (State University of New York Press)
22 Corporate Woods Blvd 3rd Fl . . . Albany NY 12211 518-472-5000 472-5038 637-4
TF: 866-430-7869 ■ *Web:* www.sunypress.edu

SUNY (State University of New York, The)
State University Plaza . . . Albany NY 12246 518-320-1888 786
TF: 800-342-3811 ■ *Web:* www.suny.edu

SUNY Downstate Medical Ctr
Medical Research Library of Brooklyn, The
450 Clarkson Ave PO Box 14 . . . Brooklyn NY 11203 718-270-1000 270-7471 434-1
Web: www.downstate.edu

Suozzi Thomas (Rep D - NY)
226 Cannon HOB . . . Washington DC 20515 202-225-3335 342-2
Web: suozzi.house.gov/contact/offices

Supelco Inc 595 N Harrison Rd . . . Bellefonte PA 16823 814-359-3441 325-5052* 419
**Fax Area Code:* 800 ■ *TF:* 800-247-6628 ■ *Web:* www.sigmaaldrich.com

Super 8 1023 Eighth Ave NW . . . Aberdeen SD 57401 605-226-2288 379

Super A Foods 7200 Dominion Cir . . . Commerce CA 90040 323-869-0600 345
Web: www.superafoods.com

Super Brush Co 800 Worcester St . . . Springfield MA 01151 413-543-1442 543-1523 103
Web: www.superbrush.com

Super Color Digital LLC 16761 Hale Ave . . . Irvine CA 92606 949-622-0010 622-0050 627
TF: 800-979-4446 ■ *Web:* supercolor.com

Super Duper Inc PO Box 24997 . . . Greenville SC 29616 864-288-3536 288-3380 459
Web: www.superduperinc.com

Super Electric Construction Co
4300 W Chicago Ave . . . Chicago IL 60651 773-489-4400 235-1455 189-4
Web: www.superelec.com

Super Excavators Inc
N 59 W 14601 Bobolink Ave . . . Menomonee Falls WI 53051 262-252-3200 252-8079 189-5
Web: www.superexcavators.com

Super Glue Corp
3281 E Guasti Rd Ste 260 . . . Ontario CA 91761 909-987-0550 3
TF: 800-538-3091 ■ *Web:* www.supergluecorp.com

Super H Mart Inc 2550 Pleasant Hill Rd . . . Duluth GA 30096 678-543-4000 345
TF: 877-427-7386 ■ *Web:* www.hmart.com

Super Holiday Tours 116 Gatlin Ave . . . Orlando FL 32806 800-327-2116 851-0071* 760
**Fax Area Code:* 407 ■ *TF:* 800-327-2116 ■ *Web:* www.superholiday.com

Super King Market 2
2716 N San Fernando Rd . . . Los Angeles CA 90065 323-225-0044 345
Web: www.superkingmarkets.com

Super Products LLC
17000 W Cleveland Ave . . . New Berlin WI 53151 262-784-7100 784-9561 386
TF: 800-837-9711 ■ *Web:* www.superproductsllc.com

Super Quik Inc 2000 Ashland Dr Ste 105 . . . Ashland KY 41101 606-836-9641 324
Web: www.superquik.net

Super Runners Shop Inc
360 Amsterdam Ave . . . New York NY 10024 212-787-7665 711
Web: www.superrunnersshop.com

Super Save Group 19395 Langley By-pass . . . Surrey BC V3S6K1 604-533-4423 316
TF: 800-665-2800 ■ *Web:* www.supersave.ca

Super Shoe Stores Inc 601 Dual Hwy . . . Hagerstown MD 21740 866-842-7510 301
TF: 866-842-7510 ■ *Web:* www.supershoes.com

Super Sky Products Inc
10301 N Enterprise Dr . . . Mequon WI 53092 262-242-2000 242-7409 234
TF: 800-558-0467 ■ *Web:* www.supersky.com

Super Steel Products Corp
7900 W Tower Ave . . . Milwaukee WI 53223 414-355-4800 355-0372 91
Web: www.supersteel.com

Super Steel Treating Inc 6227 Rinke . . . Warren MI 48091 586-755-9140 484
Web: www.supersteeltreating.com

Super Store Industries
16888 McKinley Ave PO Box 549 . . . Lathrop CA 95330 209-858-2010 297-8
TF: 888-292-8004 ■ *Web:* www.ssica.com

Super Stud Building Products Inc
2960 Woodbridge Ave . . . Edison NJ 08837 732-662-6200 697
Web: www.buysuperstud.com

Super Subby's Inc 8924 N Dixie Dr . . . Dayton OH 45414 937-898-0996 670
Web: www.subbys.com

Super Systems Inc 7205 Edington Dr . . . Cincinnati OH 45249 513-772-0060 407
Web: www.supersystems.com

Super Talent Technology Corp
2077 N Capitol Ave . . . San Jose CA 95132 408-934-2560 203
Web: www.supertalent.com

Super Talk 1270 4303 Memorial Hwy . . . Mandan ND 58554 701-663-1270 645
TF: 844-255-7886 ■ *Web:* www.supertalk1270.com

Super Technologies Inc
6005 Keating Rd . . . Pensacola FL 32504 850-433-8555 387
Web: www.supertec.com

Super Thrifty Drugs Canada Ltd
381 Park Ave E . . . Brandon MB R7A7A5 204-728-1522 231
Web: www.superthrifty.com

Super Wash Inc
707 W Lincolnway PO Box 188 . . . Morrison IL 61270 815-772-2111 310
Web: www.superwash.com

Superb Internet Corp
999 Bishop St Ste 1850 . . . Honolulu HI 96813 808-544-0387 441-0952 808
TF: 888-354-6128 ■ *Web:* www.superb.net

Superbag Corp 9291 Baythrone Dr . . . Houston TX 77041 713-462-1173 462-8145 66
TF: 888-842-1177 ■ *Web:* www.superbag.com

Superchips Inc 1790 E Airport Blvd . . . Sanford FL 32773 407-585-7000 173-2
TF: 888-227-2447 ■ *Web:* www.superchips.com

Superclick Networks Inc
10222 Blvd Saint-Michel . . . Montreal QC H1H5H1 514-847-0333 668

Supercomputing Institute for Digital Simulation & Advanced Computation
University of Minnesota
599 Walter Library 117 Pleasant St SE . . . Minneapolis MN 55455 612-625-1818 624-8861 668
Web: www.msi.umn.edu

Superconductor Technologies Inc (STI)
460 Ward Dr . . . Santa Barbara CA 93111 805-690-4500 967-0342 253
NASDAQ: SCON ■ *TF:* 800-727-3648 ■ *Web:* www.suptech.com

Supercritical Fluid Technologies Inc
1 Innovation Way . . . Newark DE 19711 302-738-3420 419
Web: www.supercriticalfluids.com

Supercuts 7201 Metro Blvd . . . Minneapolis MN 55439 877-857-2070 77
TF: 877-857-2070 ■ *Web:* www.supercuts.com

SuperData Research Inc
116 W 23rd St 5th Fl . . . New York NY 10011 646-375-2273 466
Web: www.superdataresearch.com

superDimension Inc
161 Cheshire Ln Ste 100 . . . Minneapolis MN 55441 763-210-4000 238
Web: superdimension.com

SuperFlow Technologies Group
4747 Centennial Blvd . . . Colorado Springs CO 80919 719-471-1746 471-1490 472
TF: 800-471-7701 ■ *Web:* www.superflow.com

SuperGlass Windshield Repair Inc
6220 Hazeltine National Dr Ste 118 . . . Orlando FL 32822 407-240-1920 240-3266 62-2
TF: 866-557-7497 ■ *Web:* www.superglass.com

Supergroup Creative Omnimedia Inc, The
154 Krog St NE Ste 185 . . . Atlanta GA 30307 404-877-1711 7
TF: 800-577-7126 ■ *Web:* www.thesupergroup.com

Superheat Fgh Services Inc
313 Garnet Dr . . . New Lenox IL 60451 888-508-3226 224
TF: 888-508-3226 ■ *Web:* www.superheatfgh.com

Superior Abrasives Inc
1620 Fieldstone Way . . . Vandalia OH 45377 937-278-9123 1
TF: 800-235-9123 ■ *Web:* www.superiorabrasives.com

Superior Access Solutions Inc
21037 Heron Way . . . Lakeville MN 55044 952-469-8874 180
Web: www.sa-solutions.com

Superior Air Handling Corp
200 E 700 S . . . Clearfield UT 84015 801-776-1997 697
Web: www.sahco.com

Superior Air Parts Inc
621 S Royal Ln Ste 100 . . . Coppell TX 75019 972-829-4600 829-4648 529
TF: 800-420-4727 ■ *Web:* www.superiorairparts.com

Superior Alarm Systems
9001 Canoga Ave . . . Canoga Park CA 91304 818-700-7100 693
Web: www.sassecurity.com

Superior Alarms 600 Ash Ave . . . Mcallen TX 78501 956-682-6005 610

Superior Aluminum Products Inc
555 E Main St PO Box 430 . . . Russia OH 45363 937-526-4065 526-3904 491
TF: 800-548-8656 ■ *Web:* www.superioraluminum.com

Superior Auto Sales Inc 5201 Camp Rd . . . Hamburg NY 14075 716-649-6695 516
TF: 866-439-9637 ■ *Web:* www.sascars.com

Superior Bar & Grill 6123 Line Ave . . . Shreveport LA 71106 318-869-3243 671
TF: 800-551-8682 ■ *Web:* superiorgrill.com

Superior Boiler Works Inc
3524 E Fourth St . . . Hutchinson KS 67501 620-662-6693 662-7586 91
TF: 800-444-6693 ■ *Web:* www.superiorboiler.com

Superior Carriers Inc
711 Jory Blvd Ste 101-N . . . Oak Brook IL 60523 630-573-2555 573-2570 780
TF: 800-654-7707 ■ *Web:* www.superior-carriers.com

Superior Clay Corp
6566 Superior Rd SE . . . Uhrichsville OH 44683 740-922-4122 150
TF: 800-848-6166 ■ *Web:* www.superiorclay.com

Superior Communications Inc
704 E Gude Dr . . . Rockville MD 20850 301-762-7878 196
TF: 800-543-9276 ■ *Web:* www.scicommo.com

Superior Concrete Block Company Inc
401 Mckinzie St S . . . Mankato MN 56001 507-387-7068 191-1
Web: www.cencrete.com

Superior Concrete Inc
1526 Country Club Rd . . . Harrisonburg VA 22802 540-434-0346 182
Web: www.superiorconcreteinc.com

Superior Construction Company Inc
1455 Louis Sullivan Dr . . . Portage IN 46368 219-787-0850 763-9998 188-4
Web: www.superior-construction.com

Superior Court Clerk Office
4800 Tower Hill Rd . . . Wakefield RI 02879 401-782-4121 782-4190 338
TF: 800-745-5555 ■ *Web:* www.courts.ri.gov

Superior Crane Corp (SCC)
208 Wilmont Dr PO Box 1464 . . . Waukesha WI 53189 262-542-0099 542-7767 386
Web: www.superiorcrane.com

Superior Dairy Inc 4719 Navarre Rd SW . . . Canton OH 44706 330-477-4515 296-27
TF: 800-597-5460 ■ *Web:* reliableplant.com

Superior Derrick Services LLC
4506 S Lewis St . . . New Iberia LA 70560 337-359-1955 539
TF: 800-364-4314 ■ *Web:* www.superiorderrick.com

Superior Die Set Corp
900 W Drexel Ave . . . Oak Creek WI 53154 414-764-4900 657-0855* 757
**Fax Area Code:* 800 ■ *TF:* 800-558-6040 ■ *Web:* www.supdie.com

Superior Die Tool & Machine Co
2301 Fairwood Ave . . . Columbus OH 43207 614-444-2181 444-8712 757
TF: 800-292-2181 ■ *Web:* www.superior-dietool.com

Superior Energy Services Inc
601 Poydras St Ste 2400 . . . New Orleans LA 70130 504-587-7374 362-1818 538
NYSE: SPN ■ *TF:* 800-259-7774 ■ *Web:* www.superiorenergy.com

Superior Environmental Corp
1128 Franklin Ct . . . Marne MI 49435 616-667-4000 667-3668 193
TF: 877-667-4142 ■ *Web:* www.superiorenvironmental.com

Superior Essex Communications LP
6120 Powers Ferry Rd Ste 150 . . . Atlanta GA 30339 770-657-6000 657-6652 735
TF: 800-551-8948 ■ *Web:* www.superioressex.com

Company / Address	City	State	ZIP	Phone	Fax	Class
Superior Essex Inc 6120 Powers Ferry Rd Ste 150 *NASDAQ:* SPSX ■ *TF:* 800-551-8948 ■ *Web:* www.superioressex.com	Atlanta	GA	30339	770-657-6000		814
Superior Essex Inc Magnet Wire/Winding Wire Div 1601 Wall St PO Box 1601 *TF:* 800-551-8948 ■ *Web:* www.superioressex.com	Fort Wayne	IN	46802	260-461-4550	461-4690	813
Superior Exhibits and Design Inc 777 Lunt Ave *Web:* www.superiorexhibits.com	Elk Grove Village	IL	60007	847-364-9380		317
Superior Fabrication Inc 801 S Eastern Ave *Web:* www.superiorfab.com	Elk City	OK	73644	580-243-5693		779
Superior Farms 1480 Drew Ave Ste 100 *TF:* 800-228-5262 ■ *Web:* www.superiorfarms.com	Davis	CA	95618	530-758-3091		473
Superior Foods Inc 275 Westgate Dr *TF:* 800-495-7222 ■ *Web:* www.superiorfoods.com	Watsonville	CA	95076	831-728-3691	722-0926	297-7
Superior Freight Services Inc 1230 Trapp Rd *TF:* 800-298-4305 ■ *Web:* www.supfrt.com	Saint Paul	MN	55121	952-854-5053		311
Superior Gearbox Co 803 W Hwy 32 *TF:* 800-346-5745 ■ *Web:* www.superiorgearbox.com	Stockton	MO	65785	417-276-5191	276-3492	709
Superior Graphite 10 S Riverside Plaza Ste 1470 **Fax Area Code:* 800 ■ *TF Cust Svc:* 800-325-0337 ■ *Web:* www.superiorgraphite.com	Chicago	IL	60606	312-559-2999	542-0200*	127
Superior Group Inc 250 International Dr **Fax Area Code:* 716 ■ *TF:* 800-568-8310 ■ *Web:* www.superiorgroup.com	Williamsville	NY	14221	800-568-8310	633-2026*	360-3
Superior Group Inc, The 8861 Elim St *Web:* www.superiorpnh.com	Anchorage	AK	99507	907-349-6572		610
Superior Gunite Inc 12306 Van Nuys Blvd *Web:* www.shotcrete.com	Lakeview Terrace	CA	91342	818-896-9199	896-6699	189-3
Superior Health Linens LLC 5005 S Packard Ave *Web:* www.superiorhealthlinens.com	Cudahy	WI	53110	414-769-0670		426
Superior Hyundai 110 S Quintard Ave *Web:* www.superiorhyundaial.com	Anniston	AL	36201	256-403-4991		57
Superior Industries International Inc 7800 Woodley Ave *NYSE:* SUP ■ *Web:* www.supind.com	Van Nuys	CA	91406	818-781-4973	780-3500	60
Superior Industries LLC 315 E State Hwy 28 PO Box 684 *TF:* 800-321-1558 ■ *Web:* www.superior-ind.com	Morris	MN	56267	320-589-2406		207
Superior Jig Inc 1540 N Orangethorpe Way *Web:* superiorjiginc.com	Anaheim	CA	92801	714-525-4777	525-8798	757
Superior Linen Service 1012 S Ctr St *Web:* suplinen.com	Tacoma	WA	98409	253-383-2636	383-1061	442
Superior Machine Company of South Carolina Inc 692 N Cashua Dr *TF:* 800-704-1078 ■ *Web:* www.smco.net	Florence	SC	29502	843-468-9200		494
Superior Medical Supply Inc 11005 Dover St Unit 1100	Broomfield	CO	80021	303-460-1411		320
Superior Metal Products 713 Maple St *Web:* amtrim.com	Wapakoneta	OH	45895	419-739-4401		350
Superior Metal Products Inc 2463 Hwy 107 *Web:* www.superiormetal.com	Chuckey	TN	37641	423-257-2154	257-3617	295
Superior Metal Technologies LLC 9850 E 30th St *TF:* 800-654-9850 ■ *Web:* www.superiormetals.us	Indianapolis	IN	46229	317-897-9850		295
Superior Mfg 1000 E 14th St *Web:* www.ordersuperior.com	Dewey	OK	74029	918-534-0755		697
Superior Mfg Group 5655 W 73rd St *TF:* 800-621-2802 ■ *Web:* www.notrax.com	Chicago	IL	60638	708-458-4600	458-4730	291
Superior Motors Inc 282 John C Calhoun Dr *TF:* 877-375-4759 ■ *Web:* www.superiormotors.com	Orangeburg	SC	29115	877-375-4759		516
Superior Nut & Candy Company Inc 1111 W 40th St *Web:* www.superiornutandcandy.com	Chicago	IL	60609	773-254-7900	254-9171	297-3
Superior Nut Co Inc 225 Monsignor O'Brien Hwy *TF:* 800-295-4093 ■ *Web:* www.superiornut.com	Cambridge	MA	02141	617-876-3808	876-8225	296-28
Superior Oil Co Inc 1402 N Capitol Ave Ste 100 *TF:* 800-553-5480 ■ *Web:* www.superioroil.com	Indianapolis	IN	46202	317-781-4400	781-4401	603
Superior Packaging Solutions 26858 Almond Ave *TF:* 844-792-2626 ■ *Web:* www.sps4pkg.com	Redlands	CA	92374	844-792-2626		561
Superior Pleating & Stitching 3671 E Olympic Blvd	Los Angeles	CA	90023	323-261-3964		258
Superior Plus Energy Services Inc 1870 S Winton Rd Ste 200 *Web:* www.griffithenergy.com	Rochester	NY	14618	585-328-3930		316
Superior Plus Income Fund 840-7 Ave SW Ste 1400 *TF:* 866-490-7587 ■ *Web:* www.superiorplus.ca	Calgary	AB	T2P3G2	403-218-2970	218-2973	405
Superior Press Inc 9440 Norwalk Blvd **Fax Area Code:* 562 ■ *TF Cust Svc:* 888-590-7998 ■ *Web:* www.superiorpress.com	Santa Fe Springs	CA	90670	888-590-7998	948-4966*	86
Superior Printing Ink Co Inc 100 N St *TF:* 800-207-4003 ■ *Web:* www.superiorink.com	Teterboro	NJ	07608	201-478-5600	478-5650	388
Superior Products Inc 3786 Ridge Rd *TF:* 800-651-9490 ■ *Web:* www.superiorprod.com	Cleveland	OH	44144	216-651-9400	651-4071	621
Superior Public Library 1530 Tower Ave *Web:* superiorlibrary.org	Superior	WI	54880	715-394-8860	394-8870	434-3
Superior Ready Mix Concrete LP 1508 Mission Rd *TF:* 800-834-7557 ■ *Web:* superiorrm.com	Escondido	CA	92029	760-745-0556	740-9556	182
Superior Roll Forming Company Inc 5535 Wegman Rd *Web:* www.gosrf.com	Valley City	OH	44280	330-225-2500		247
Superior Roofing & Sheet Metal Co Inc 3405 S 500 W *Web:* www.superior-roof.l7marketing.com	Salt Lake City	UT	84115	801-266-1473	266-1522	189-12
Superior Shade & Blind Company Inc 1571 N Powerline Rd *TF:* 800-423-6968 ■ *Web:* www.superiorshade.com	Pompano Beach	FL	33069	954-975-8122	975-2938	87
Superior Shores Resort 1521 Superior Shores Dr *TF:* 800-242-1988 ■ *Web:* www.superiorshores.com	Two Harbors	MN	55616	218-834-5671		669
Superior Software Inc 16055 Ventura Blvd Ste 650 *TF:* 800-421-3264 ■ *Web:* www.superior-software.com	Encino	CA	91436	818-990-1135	783-5846	178-1
Superior Tank Company Inc 9500 Lucas Ranch Rd *TF:* 800-736-4255 ■ *Web:* superiortank.com	Rancho Cucamonga	CA	91730	909-912-0580		770
Superior Technical Ceramics Corp 600 Industrial Pk Rd *Web:* www.ceramics.net	Saint Albans	VT	05478	802-527-7726	527-1181	249
Superior Technical Resources Inc 250 International Dr *TF:* 800-568-8310 ■ *Web:* superiorgroup.com	Williamsville	NY	14221	716-929-1400		721
Superior Tire & Rubber Corp 1818 Pennsylvania Ave W PO Box 308 *TF Cust Svc:* 800-289-1456 ■ *Web:* www.superiortire.com	Warren	PA	16365	814-723-2370	726-0740	754
Superior Tool Co 100 Hayes Dr Unit C *TF Cust Svc:* 800-533-3244 ■ *Web:* www.superiortool.com	Cleveland	OH	44131	216-398-8600	398-8691	758
Superior Trailer Sales Co 501 Hwy 80 *TF:* 800-637-0324 ■ *Web:* www.stsco.com	Sunnyvale	TX	75182	972-226-3893	226-3899	516
Superior Trim & Door Inc 2840 W Orange Ave	Apopka	FL	32703	407-598-1100		200
Superior Tube Co 3900 Germantown Pk *TF:* 800-226-3553 ■ *Web:* www.superiortube.com	Collegeville	PA	19426	610-489-5200	489-5252	490
Superior Uniform Group Inc 10055Seminole Blvd *NASDAQ:* SGC ■ *TF Cust Svc:* 800-727-8643 ■ *Web:* superioruniformgroup.com	Seminole	FL	33772	727-397-9611		155-19
Superior Vision Services 11101 White Rock Rd *TF:* 800-507-3800 ■ *Web:* www.superiorvision.com	Rancho Cordova	CA	95670	800-507-3800		390
Superior Washer & Gasket Corp 170 Adams Ave *Web:* www.superiorwasher.com	Hauppauge	NY	11788	631-273-8282		455
Superior Water Light & Power 2915 Hill Ave PO Box 519 *TF:* 800-227-7957 ■ *Web:* www.swlp.com	Superior	WI	54880	715-394-2200		787
Superior Woodcraft Inc 160 N Hamilton St *Web:* www.superiorwoodcraft.com	Doylestown	PA	18901	215-348-9942		321
Superior/Douglas County Convention & Visitors Bureau 305 Harborview Pkwy *TF:* 800-942-5313 ■ *Web:* www.superiorchamber.org	Superior	WI	54880	715-392-7151		206
Superior-Douglas County Chamber of Commerce 205 Belknap St *TF:* 800-942-5313 ■ *Web:* www.superiorchamber.org	Superior	WI	54880	715-394-7716	394-3810	139
Superlite Block Co Inc 4150 W Turney Ave *TF:* 800-366-7877 ■ *Web:* www.superliteblock.com	Phoenix	AZ	85019	602-352-3500	352-3813	183
Superlon Plastic Pipe Co 2116 Taylor Way *TF:* 800-562-7910 ■ *Web:* www.superlon.com	Tacoma	WA	98421	253-383-4000		612
Super-Lube Inc 1311 N Paul Russell Rd *Web:* www.superlube.com	Tallahassee	FL	32301	850-222-5823		579
Supermarket Systems Inc 6419 Bannington Rd *TF:* 800-553-1905 ■ *Web:* www.supermarketsystems.com	Charlotte	NC	28226	704-542-6000		665
Supermercado Mi Tierra LLC 9520 International Blvd *TF:* 800-225-9902 ■ *Web:* supermercadomitierra.com	Oakland	CA	94603	510-567-8617		345
Supermercados Selectos Inc HC 80 Box 7305 *Web:* www.selectospr.com	Dorado	PR	00646	787-275-2165		345
Supermicro Computer Inc (SMCI) 980 Rock Ave *NASDAQ:* SMCI ■ *Web:* www.supermicro.com/index.cfm	San Jose	CA	95131	408-503-8000	503-8008	625
SuperMom's LLC 625 Second St	Saint Paul Park	MN	55071	651-459-2253		68
Superna Business Consulting Inc 104 Schneider Rd *TF:* 800-225-5224 ■ *Web:* www.superna.net	Kanata	ON	K2K1Y2	613-729-1100		196
Supernus Pharmaceuticals Inc 1550 E Gude Dr *NASDAQ:* SUPN ■ *Web:* www.supernus.com	Rockville	MD	20850	301-838-2500		85
Superseal Mfg Co Inc PO Box 795 *TF:* 800-433-4873 ■ *Web:* www.supersealwindows.com	South Plainfield	NJ	07080	908-561-5910		235
SuperShuttle International Inc 14500 N Northsight Blvd Ste 329 *TF:* 800-258-3826 ■ *Web:* www.supershuttle.com	Scottsdale	AZ	85260	480-609-3000		441
Superstition Trailers LLC 535 N 51st Ave *Web:* www.stlaz.com	Phoenix	AZ	85043	602-415-0222		778
SuperTalk 99.7 WTN 10 Music Cir E *TF:* 800-618-7445 ■ *Web:* www.997wtn.com	Nashville	TN	37203	615-321-1067		645-108
Super-Tek Products Inc 25-44 Borough Pl *Web:* www.super-tek.com	Woodside	NY	11377	718-278-7900		3
SUPERVALU Inc 7075 Flying Cloud Dr *NYSE:* SVU ■ *TF Cust Svc:* 877-322-8228 ■ *Web:* www.supervalu.com	Eden Prairie	MN	55344	952-828-4000		297-8
SUPERVALU International 495 E 19th St *Web:* www.supervaluinternational.com	Tacoma	WA	98421	253-593-3198		297-8
Superwinch Inc 359 Lake Rd *TF:* 800-323-2031 ■ *Web:* www.superwinch.com	Dayville	CT	06241	860-928-7787		190
Supfina Machine Company Inc 181 Circuit Dr *TF:* 800-553-2263 ■ *Web:* www.supfina.com	North Kingstown	RI	02852	401-294-6600		111

Company	City	State	Zip	Phone	Fax	Class
Supima 9885 S Priest Dr Ste 101 *Web:* www.supima.com	Tempe	AZ	85284-3600	602-792-6002	792-6004	48-2
Supply Chain Equity Partners 100 S Ashley Dr Ste 2100 **Fax Area Code:* 216 ■ *Web:* www.supplychainequity.com	Tampa	FL	33602	813-395-0501	363-0135*	791
Supply New England Inc 123 East St. *TF:* 800-230-3625 ■ *Web:* www.supplynewengland.com	Attleboro	MA	02703	508-222-5555		362
Supply Room, The 14140 N Washington Hwy *Web:* tsrcinc.net	Ashland	VA	23005	804-412-1200	412-1313	535
Supply Technologies LLC 6065 Parkland Blvd *TF:* 800-695-8650 ■ *Web:* www.supplytechnologies.com	Cleveland	OH	44124	440-947-2100	947-2299	351
SupplyFrame Inc 51 W Dayton St Ste 100 *Web:* www.supplyframe.com	Pasadena	CA	91105	626-793-7732		180
SupplyOne Corp 20 N Waterloo Rd Ste 200 *Web:* supplyone.com	Devon	PA	19333	484-582-5005		601
Support Dogs Inc 10955 Linpage Pl *Web:* www.supportdogs.org	Saint Louis	MO	63146	314-997-2325	997-7202	48-17
Support Group Inc, The 24 Prime Park Way *Web:* www.supportgroup.com	Natick	MA	01760	508-653-8400		177
Support Kansas City Inc 5960 Dearborn St Ste 200 *TF:* 800-383-3854 ■ *Web:* www.supportkc.org	Mission	KS	66202	913-831-4752		449
Support Services of America Inc 12440 Firestone Blvd Ste 312 *TF:* 888-564-0005 ■ *Web:* www.supportservicesamerica.com	Norwalk	CA	90650	562-868-3550	868-7811	152
Support Systems Assoc Inc (SSAI) 709 S Harbor City Blvd Ste 350 *Web:* www.ssai.org	Melbourne	FL	32901	321-724-5566		261
Support.com Inc 900 Chesapeake Dr 2nd Fl *NASDAQ: SPRT* ■ *TF:* 877-493-2778 ■ *Web:* www.support.com	Redwood City	CA	94063	650-556-9440	556-1195	178-7
SupportLocal LLC 1062 Delaware St Ste 4	Denver	CO	80204	720-432-8160		387
Supra Alloys 352 Balboa Cir *TF:* 888-647-8772 ■ *Web:* www.supraalloys.com	Camarillo	CA	93012	805-388-2138	987-6492	492
Supracor Inc 2050 Corporate Ct *Web:* www.supracor.com	San Jose	CA	95131	408-432-1616		22
SupraNet Communications Inc 8000 Excelsior Dr *Web:* www.supranet.net	Madison	WI	53717	608-836-0282		225
Supreme Casting Inc 3389 Linco Rd *Web:* www.supremecasting.com	Stevensville	MI	49127	269-465-5757		308
Supreme Chocolatier LLC 1150 S Ave *TF:* 800-698-3302 ■ *Web:* www.supremechocolatier.com	Staten Island	NY	10314	718-761-9600		296-8
Supreme Corp 325 Spence Rd *TF:* 888-604-6975 ■ *Web:* supremecorporation.com	Conover	NC	28613	828-322-6975	322-7881	745-9
Supreme Corp 2581 E Kercher Rd PO Box 463 *TF All:* 800-642-4889 ■ *Web:* www.supremecorp.com	Goshen	IN	46528	800-642-4889		516
Supreme Court of the US 1 First St NE *Web:* www.supremecourt.gov	Washington	DC	20543	202-479-3000	479-3472	341
Supreme Gear Company Inc 17430 Malyn Blvd *Web:* www.dorrisco.com	Fraser	MI	48026	586-294-7625		454
Supreme Machined Products Company Inc 18686 172nd Ave *Web:* www.supreme1.com	Spring Lake	MI	49456	616-842-6550		621
Supreme Manufacturing Inc 151 Industrial Dr Bld C *Web:* www.supreme-mfg.com	Beaver Dam	WI	53916	920-356-0372		484
Supreme Mfg Company Inc 5 Connerty Ct *TF:* 800-772-7632 ■ *Web:* www.supreme-mfg.com	East Brunswick	NJ	08816	732-254-0087		345
Supreme Oil Co 2109 W Monte Vista Rd **Fax Area Code:* 602 ■ *TF:* 800-752-7888 ■ *Web:* www.supremeoil.com	Phoenix	AZ	85009	800-752-7888	258-8801*	539
Supreme Petroleum Inc 1200 Progress Rd P.O. Box 1246 *Web:* www.supremepetro.com	Smithfield	VA	23434	757-934-0550		580
Supreme Security Systems Inc 1565 Union Ave *Web:* www.supremesecurity.com	Union	NJ	07083	908-810-8822		693
Supreme Systems Inc 1355 N Walton Walker Blvd *Web:* www.supremeroofing.com	Dallas	TX	75211	214-330-8913		191-4
SupremeBytes LLC PO Box 13746 *TF:* 888-622-2983 ■ *Web:* www.supremebytes.com	Columbus	OH	43213	614-636-4875		387
Supreme-Lake Manufacturing Inc 455 Atwater St PO Box 19 *Web:* www.supremelake.com	Plantsville	CT	06479	860-621-8911	628-9746	621
Suquamish Clearwater Casino & Resort 15347 Suquamish Way NE Ste A *TF:* 800-375-6073 ■ *Web:* clearwatercasino.com	Suquamish	WA	98392	360-598-8700		452
Sur La Table 5701 Sixth Ave S Ste 486 *TF:* 800-243-0852 ■ *Web:* www.surlatable.com	Seattle	WA	98108	800-243-0852		362
Surdex Corp 520 Spirit of St Louis Blvd *Web:* www.surdex.com	Chesterfield	MO	63005	636-368-4400		727
Surdna Foundation Inc 330 Madison Ave 30th Fl *TF:* 800-421-9512 ■ *Web:* www.surdna.org	New York	NY	10017	212-557-0010	557-0003	305
Sure Save Supermarkets Ltd 16-128 Orchid Land Dr *Web:* www.suresave.com	Keaau	HI	96749	808-966-9009	966-6200	345
Sure Steel Inc 7528 Cornia Dr	South Weber	UT	84405	801-917-5800		189-14
Sure Thing Pest Control 11541 Goldcoast Dr *TF:* 800-793-8169 ■ *Web:* www.surethingpc.com	Cincinnati	OH	45249	513-247-0030		577
Sure Winner Foods Inc 2 Lehner Rd *TF:* 800-640-6447 ■ *Web:* www.swfoods.com	Saco	ME	04072	207-282-1258	286-1410	297-4
Surecomp Services Inc 2 Hudson Pl Fl 4 *Web:* www.surecomp.com	Hoboken	NJ	07030	201-217-1437		180
Surefire Industries LLC 1400 Brittmoore *Web:* www.surefireindustries.com	Houston	TX	77043	713-481-9600		539
Surefire LLC 18300 Mt Baldy Cir *TF:* 800-828-8809 ■ *Web:* www.surefire.com	Fountain Valley	CA	92708	714-545-9444	545-9537	74
Surefit Inc 6575 Snowdrift Rd Ste 101 **Fax Area Code:* 610 ■ *TF:* 888-796-0500 ■ *Web:* www.surefit.net	Allentown	PA	18106	888-796-0500	336-8995*	746
Sureflix Digital Distribution Inc 229 Yonge St Ste 408 *Web:* www.corporate.sureflix.com	Toronto	ON	M5B2P9	416-907-7859		387
Sureit Solutions Inc 1801 W Queen Creek Rd Ste 3 *Web:* www.sureitinc.com	Chandler	AZ	85248	480-917-2000		177
SurePayroll 2350 Ravine Way Ste 100 *TF:* 877-954-7873 ■ *Web:* www.surepayroll.com	Glenview	IL	60025	847-676-8420		570
Surepoint Technologies Group Inc 744 - Fourth Ave SW Ste 1000 *TF:* 855-777-7873 ■ *Web:* www.surepoint.ca	Calgary	AB	T2P3T4	855-777-7873		538
Sureshred Security 3166 Diablo Ave *TF:* 888-606-0008 ■ *Web:* www.sureshred.com	Hayward	CA	94545	510-784-1150		317
SureTek Medical 25 Maple Creek Cir Ste B *TF:* 800-269-1405 ■ *Web:* www.suretekmedical.com	Greenville	SC	29607	864-299-9743		475
Surety & Fidelity Assn of America (SFAA) 1101 Connecticut Ave NW Ste 800 *Web:* www.surety.org	Washington	DC	20036	202-463-0600	463-0606	49-9
Surety Group Inc 3715 Northside Pkwy NW Ste 1-315 *TF:* 800-486-8211 ■ *Web:* www.suretygroup.com	Atlanta	GA	30327	404-352-8211	351-3237	391-5
Surety LLC 12020 Sunrise Vly Dr Ste 250 *TF:* 800-298-3115 ■ *Web:* www.surety.com	Reston	VA	20191	571-748-5800	748-5810	178-7
Sureway Tool & Engineering 2959 Hart Ct *Web:* www.surewaytool.com	Franklin Park	IL	60131	847-801-3010		697
Surf & Sand Resort 1555 S Coast Hwy *TF:* 877-741-5908 ■ *Web:* www.surfandsandresort.com	Laguna Beach	CA	92651	949-497-4477	494-2897	379
Surf Associates Inc 1701 N Federal Hwy *Web:* www.bcsurf.com	Fort Lauderdale	FL	33305	954-563-1366		711
Surf City Garage Inc 5872 Engineer Dr *Web:* www.surfcitygarage.com	Huntington Beach	CA	92649	714-894-1707		57
Surf Line Hawaii Ltd 411 Puuhale Rd. *TF:* 800-847-5267 ■ *Web:* www.jamsworld.com	Honolulu	HI	96819	808-847-5985	841-5254	155-3
Surf Merchants 41 W St 5th Fl *Web:* surfmerchants.com	Boston	MA	02111	617-292-8008		177
Surf Technicians LLC 2685 Mattison Ln *TF:* 800-435-9917 ■ *Web:* www.surftech.com	Santa Cruz	CA	95062	831-479-4944		711
Surface Art Inc 18323 Andover Park W *Web:* www.surfaceartinc.com	Tukwila	WA	98188	206-315-4558		290
Surface Combustion Inc 1700 Indian Wood Cir. *TF:* 800-537-8980 ■ *Web:* www.surfacecombustion.com	Maumee	OH	43537	419-891-7150	891-7151	318
Surface Equipment Corp 337 Cargill Rd *TF:* 800-256-7732 ■ *Web:* www.surfaceequip.com	Kilgore	TX	75662	903-984-0400	983-0018	537
Surface Mount Distribution Inc (SMD) 1 Oldfield *TF:* 800-820-7634 ■ *Web:* www.smdinc.com	Irvine	CA	92618	949-470-7700	470-7777	246
Surface Mount Technology Corp 5660 Technology Cir. *Web:* www.teamsmt.com	Appleton	WI	54914	920-954-8324		625
Surface Shields Inc 10457 163rd Pl *TF:* 800-754-9685 ■ *Web:* www.surfaceshields.com	Orland Park	IL	60467	708-226-9810	226-9817	291
Surface Transportation Board 395 E St SW *Web:* www.stb.gov/stb/index.html	Washington	DC	20423	202-245-0245	245-0461	340-17
SURFACExchange LLC 37 Brookside Dr *Web:* www.surfacexchange.com	Greenwich	CT	06830	203-987-6900		690
Sur-Flo Plastics & Engineering Inc 24358 Groesbeck Hwy *Web:* www.sur-flo.com	Warren	MI	48089	586-773-0400		602
Surfrider Foundation 942 Calle Negocio Ste 350 *Web:* www.surfrider.org	San Clemente	CA	92673	949-492-8170		196
Surfsand Resort 148 W Gower Rd. *TF:* 800-547-6100 ■ *Web:* www.surfsand.com	Cannon Beach	OR	97110	503-436-2274	436-9116	379
Surfside Realty Co Inc 213 S Ocean Blvd *TF:* 800-833-8232 ■ *Web:* www.surfsiderealty.com	Surfside Beach	SC	29575	843-238-3435		656
Surge Energy Inc 2100 635 Eighth Ave SW *Web:* www.surgeenergy.ca	Calgary	AB	T2P3M3	403-930-1010		536
Surge Resources 920 Candia Rd *TF:* 800-787-4387 ■ *Web:* www.surgeindustries.com	Manchester	NH	03109	603-623-0007		463
Surgent Cpe 237 Lancaster Ave *Web:* cpenow.com	Devon	PA	19333	610-688-4477		2
Surgeworks 4609 S 2300 E Ste 103 *Web:* www.surgeworks.com	Holladay	UT	84117	801-272-9800		809
Surgical Appliance Industries Inc 3960 Rosslyn Dr *TF:* 800-888-0867 ■ *Web:* www.saibrands.com	Cincinnati	OH	45209	800-888-0867	309-9055	477
Surgical Principals Inc 1625 S Tacoma Way *TF:* 888-801-9251 ■ *Web:* spi.historic1625tacomaplace.com	Tacoma	WA	98409	888-801-9251		475
Surgical Staff Inc 120 St Matthews Ave *TF:* 800-339-9599 ■ *Web:* surgicalstaffinc.net	San Mateo	CA	94401	650-558-3999	558-3949	721
Surin of Thailand 810 N Highland Ave NE *Web:* www.surinofthailand.com	Atlanta	GA	30306	404-892-7789		671
Surin West 1918 11th Ave S. *Web:* www.surinwest.com	Birmingham	AL	35205	205-324-1928		671
Suriname 866 UN Plaza Ste 320 *Web:* www.un.int	New York	NY	10017	212-826-0660	980-7029	784

Phone | Fax | Class

Suriname Embassy
4301 Connecticut Ave NW Ste 460 .... Washington DC 20008 202-244 7488 244 5878 257
Web: www.surinameembassy.org

SurModics Inc 9924 W 74th St .... Eden Prairie MN 55344 952-829-2700 500-7001 231
NASDAQ: SRDX ■ *TF:* 866-787-6639 ■ *Web:* www.surmodics.com

Surprise Valley Electric Co-op
22595 US 395 .... Alturas CA 96101 530-233-3511 233-2190 245
TF: 866-843-2667 ■ *Web:* www.surprisevalleyelectric.org

Surrex Solutions Corp
300 N Sepulveda Blvd Ste 1020 .... El Segundo CA 90245 310-640-3000 728-2771* 196
**Fax Area Code: 866* ■ *TF:* 866-308-2628

Surrey Board of Trade
14439 104th Ave Ste 101 .... Surrey BC V3R1M1 604-581-7130 588-7549 137
TF: 866-848-7130 ■ *Web:* www.businessinsurrey.com

Surrey Honda 15291 Fraser Hwy .... Surrey BC V3R3P3 604-583-7421 57
Web: surreyhonda.com

Surrey Hotel 20 E 76th St .... New York NY 10021 212-288-3700 379
TF: 866-233-4642 ■ *Web:* www.affinia.com

Surrey Memorial Hospital
13750 96th Ave .... Surrey BC V3V1Z2 604-588-3381 585-5669 374-2
Web: www.fraserhealth.ca

Surrey Satellite Technology US LLC
345 Inverness Dr S Ste 100 .... Englewood CO 80112 303-790-0653 362
Web: www.sst-us.com

Surrey Veterinary Clinic
3598 S Clare Ave .... Clare MI 48617 989-386-9200 794
Web: www.surreyvetclinic.com

Surry Community College 630 S Main St .... Dobson NC 27017 336-386-8121 162
Web: surry.edu

Surry County 118 Hamby Rd .... Dobson NC 27017 336-386-3700 338
Web: www.co.surry.nc.us

Surry County 45 School St .... Surry VA 23883 757-294-5271 294-5204 338
Web: www.surrycountyva.gov

Surry County School
209 N Crutchfield St PO Box 364 .... Dobson NC 27017 336-386-8211 386-4279 685
Web: www.surry.k12.nc.us

Surry Insurance Agency & Realty Company Inc
119 W Atkins St .... Dobson NC 27017 336-386-8228 390
Web: surryinsurance.com

Surry-Yadkin Electric Membership Corp
510 S Main St .... Dobson NC 27017 336-356-8241 356-9744 245
TF: 800-682-5903 ■ *Web:* www.syemc.com

Sur-Seal Gasket & Packing Inc
6156 Wesselman Rd .... Cincinnati OH 45248 800-345-8966 326
TF: 800-345-8966 ■ *Web:* www.sur-seal.com

Surteco USA Inc 7104 Cessna Dr .... Greensboro NC 27409 336-668-9555 668-7795 3
Web: www.canplast.com

Surterre Properties Inc
1400 Newport Ctr Dr Ste 100 .... Newport Beach CA 92660 949-717-7100 652
Web: www.surterreproperties.com

Surveillance Specialties Ltd
600 Research Dr .... Wilmington MA 01887 800-354-2616 41
TF: [illegible] ■ *Web:* www.securadyne.com

Survey & Ballot Systems Inc
7653 Anagram Dr .... Eden Prairie MN 55344 952 974 2300 177
TF: 800-974-8099 ■ *Web:* www.surveyandballotsystems.com

Survey com 51 Melcher St .... Boston MA 02210 408 850 1227 466
Web: survey.com

Survey Sampling International LLC
6 Research Dr .... Shelton CT 06484 203-567-7200 668
Web: www.surveysampling.com

Survey Service Inc 1911 Sheridan Dr .... Buffalo NY 14223 716-876-6450 466
TF: 800-507-7969 ■ *Web:* www.surveyservice.com

Surveying Services Inc 41 Heritage Sq .... Jackson TN 38305 731-664-0807 727

SurveyMonkey Inc 1 Curiosity Way .... San Mateo CA 94403 650-543-8400 466
Web: www.surveymonkey.com

Survival Strategies Inc
335 N Third St .... Burbank CA 91502 818-276-1000 196
TF: 800 834 0357 ■ *Web:* www.survivalstrategies.com

Survival Systems Training Ltd
40 Mt Hope Ave .... Dartmouth NS B2Y4K9 902-465-3888 449
TF: 800-788-3888 ■ *Web:* www.sstl.com

Survivor Ii Inc 919 Fairmount Ave .... Elizabeth NJ 07201 908-353-1155 234
Web: survivorwindowsii.com

Survivors Network of Those Abused by Priests (SNAP)
PO Box 6416 .... Chicago IL 60680 312-455-1499 48-21
TF: 877-762-7432 ■ *Web:* www.snapnetwork.org

Survivors of Incest Anonymous (SIA)
PO Box 190 .... Benson MD 21018 410-893-3322 48-21
Web: www.siawso.org

Susan Carlisle CPA A Professional
21243 Ventura Blvd Ste 138 .... Woodland Hills CA 91364 818-888-3223 2
Web: carlislecpa.com

Susan Davis International
1101 K St NW Ste 400 .... Washington DC 20005 202-408-0808 344
Web: www.susandavis.com

Susan G Komen for the Cure
5005 LBJ Fwy Ste 250 .... Dallas TX 75244 972-855-1600 48-17
TF: 800-227-2345 ■ *Web:* ww5.komen.org

Susan Hobbs Gallery Inc
137 Tecumseth St .... Toronto ON M6J2H2 416-504-3699 504-8064 42
TF: 800-442-2787 ■ *Web:* www.susanhobbs.com

Susan Schein Automotive
3171 Pelham Pkwy .... Pelham AL 35124 205-664-1491 57
TF: 800-845-1578 ■ *Web:* www.susanschein.com

Susan Sheehan Gallery 136 E 16th St .... New York NY 10003 212-489-3331 489-4009 42
TF: 800-924-2703 ■ *Web:* www.susansheehangallery.com

Susanna Foo 1720 Sansom St .... Philadelphia PA 19103 215-717-8968 671
Web: www.sugabyfoo.com

Sushi Blues 301 Glenwood Ave .... Raleigh NC 27603 919-664-8061 664-8070 671
Web: www.sushibluescafe.com

Sushi Club 294 E Moana Ln .... Reno NV 89502 775-501-5438 671

Sushi Den 1487 S Pearl St .... Denver CO 80210 303-777-0826 671
Web: www.sushiden.net

Sushi Doraku 1104 Lincoln Rd .... Miami Beach FL 33139 305-695-8383 670
TF: 800-734-4667 ■ *Web:* www.dorakusushi.com

Sushi Factory Japanese Restaurant
4632 Meridian Ave .... San Jose CA 95124 408-723-2598 671
Web: www.sushifactorysj.com

Phone | Fax | Class

Sushi House of Orlando
0204 Crystal Clear Ln Ste 1300 .... Orlando FL 32809 407-610-5921 671
Web: www.sushihouseint.com

Sushi Japon 6801 N IH-35 .... Austin TX 78752 512-323-6663 323-6789 671
Web: www.sushijaponaustin.com

Sushi Kim 1241 Penn Ave .... Pittsburgh PA 15222 412-281-9956 671

Sushi Ko Glover Park
5455 Wisconsin Ave .... Chevy Chase MD 20815 301-961-1644 671
Web: sushikorestaurants.com

Sushi Masa 423 S Phillips Ave .... Sioux Falls SD 57104 605-977-6968 671

Sushi Matsuri 3418 SW Archer Rd .... Gainesville FL 32608 352-335-1875 671

Sushi Nabe of Chattanooga
110 River St .... Chattanooga TN 37405 423-634-0171 671
Web: sushinabe.com

Sushi Neko 4318 N Western .... Oklahoma City OK 73118 405-528-8862 521-9877 671
Web: www.sushineko.com

Sushi Nozawa
11288 Ventura Blvd Ste C .... Studio City CA 91604 818-508-7017 671
Web: sushinozawa.com

Sushi of Gari 402 E 78th St .... New York NY 10075 212-517-5340 671
Web: sushiofgari.com

Sushi on Shea 7000 E Shea Blvd .... Scottsdale AZ 85254 480-483-7799 671

Sushi Ota 4529 Mission Bay Dr .... San Diego CA 92109 858-270-5670 671
Web: sushiota.com

Sushi Pier 1290 E Plumb Ln .... Reno NV 89502 775-825-6776 671
Web: mysushipier.com

Sushi Rock 1276 W Sixth St .... Cleveland OH 44113 216-623-1212 671

Sushi Rock Cafe
1515 E Las Olas Blvd .... Fort Lauderdale FL 33301 954-462-5541 671

Sushi Roku 3500 Las Vegas Blvd S .... Las Vegas NV 89109 702-733-7373 671
Web: www.innovativedining.com

Sushi Seki 1143 First Ave .... New York NY 10065 212-371-0238 671
Web: sushiseki.com

Sushi Station 199 E Fifth Ave .... Eugene OR 97401 541-484-1334 671

Sushi Tama 3919 Sixth Ave .... Tacoma WA 98406 253-761-1014 671

Sushi Taro 1503 17th St NW .... Washington DC 20036 202-462-8999 671
Web: www.sushitaro.com

Sushi Ten 4500 E Speedway Blvd .... Tucson AZ 85712 520-324-0010 671
Web: sushiten.webs.com

Sushi Tora 2014 Tenth St .... Boulder CO 80302 303-444-2280 671
Web: sushitoraboulder.com

Sushi Yasuda 204 E 43rd St .... New York NY 10017 212-972-1001 972-1717 671
Web: www.sushiyasuda.com

Sushi Zanmai 1221 Spruce St .... Boulder CO 80302 303-440-0733 440-6676 671
Web: www.sushizanmai.com

Sushi Zen 108 W 44th St .... New York NY 10036 212-302-0707 944-7710 671
Web: www.sushizen-ny.com

Sushi Zushi 1611 W Fifth St .... Austin TX 78703 512 474 7000 671
Web: www.sushizushi.com

SushiIgawa 2601 West Lake Ave .... Peoria IL 61615 309-679-9300 671

SushiSamba 600 Lincoln Rd .... Miami Beach FL 33139 305-673-5337 671
Web: www.sushisamba.com

Sushi-San Thai Jai Dee
2748 Lighthouse Pt .... Baltimore MD 21224 410-534-8888 671
Web: sushisanbaltimore.com

SUSLA (Southern University Museum of Art)
3050 Martin Luther King Jr Dr .... Shreveport LA 71107 318-670-6000 520
TF: 800-458-1472 ■ *Web:* www.susla.edu

Susquehanna County 75 Public Ave .... Montrose PA 18801 570-278-4600 278-9268 338
TF: 800-932-0313 ■ *Web:* www.susqco.com

Susquehanna Glass 731 Ave H .... Columbia PA 17512 717-684-2155 361
Web: www.susquehannaglass.com

Susquehanna International Group LLP
401 City Ave Ste 220 .... Bala Cynwyd PA 19004 610-617-2600 690
Web: www.sig.com

Susquehanna Real Estate
140 E Market St PO Box 2026 .... York PA 17401 717-848-5500 771-1430 653
Web: www.susquehanna-realestate.com

Susquehanna River Basin Commission
1721 N Front St .... Harrisburg PA 17102 717-238-0423 238-2436 340-20
Web: www.srbc.net

Susquehanna University
514 University Ave .... Selinsgrove PA 17870 570-374-0101 372-2722 166
TF: 800-326-9672 ■ *Web:* www.susqu.edu

Susquehanna Valley Woodcrafters Inc
131 Main St .... Landisville PA 17538 717-898-7564 115
Web: Www.Svfcu.Org

Susquehannock State Park 1880 Pk Dr .... Drumore PA 17518 717-432-5011 565
Web: www.dcnr.state.pa.us

Suss Consulting
801 Old York Rd Noble Plz Ste 305 .... Jenkintown PA 19046 215-884-5900 884-1637 195
TF: 888-984-5900 ■ *Web:* www.sussconsulting.com

Sussek Machine Corp 805 Pierce St .... Waterloo WI 53594 920-478-2126 454
Web: www.sussek.com

Sussex Bank 100 Enterprise Dr Ste 700 .... Rockaway NJ 07866 973-383-2211 360-2
NASDAQ: SBBX ■ *TF:* 800-511-9900 ■ *Web:* www.sussexbank.com

Sussex Corrections Institution
23203 Dupont Blvd .... Georgetown DE 19947 302-856-5280 213

Sussex County 2 The Cr PO Box 589 .... Georgetown DE 19947 302-855-7700 855-7749 338
Web: www.sussexcountyde.gov

Sussex County
20135 Princeton Rd PO Box 1397 .... Sussex VA 23884 434-246-1000 246-6013 338
Web: www.sussexcountyva.gov

Sussex County Chamber of Commerce
120 Hampton House Rd .... Newton NJ 07860 973-579-1811 579-3031 139
TF: 844-256-7328 ■ *Web:* www.sussexcountychamber.org

Sussex County Community College
1 College Hill Rd .... Newton NJ 07860 973-300-2100 579-5226* 162
**Fax: Admissions* ■ *TF:* 800-848-4555 ■ *Web:* www.sussex.edu

Sussex County Library 125 Morris Tpke .... Newton NJ 07860 973-948-3660 948-2071 434-3
Web: www.sussexcountylibrary.org

Sussex I State Prison
24414 Musselwhite Dr .... Waverly VA 23891 804-834-9967 834-9995 213

Sussex II State Prison
24427 Musselwhite Dr .... Waverly VA 23891 804-834-2678 213

Sussex Publishers LLC
115 E 23rd St 9th Fl .... New York NY 10010 212-260-7210 5

Name / Address	City	State	ZIP	Phone	Fax	Class
Sussex Rural Electric Co-op 64 County Rt 639 PO Box 346 *TF:* 877-504-6463 ■ *Web:* www.sussexrec.com	Sussex	NJ	07461	973-875-5101	875-4114	245
Sussex Wire Inc 4 Danforth Dr *Web:* www.sussexwire.com	Easton	PA	18045	610-250-7750		696
Sussman Automatic Corp 43-20 34th St *TF:* 800-727-8326 ■ *Web:* www.mrsteam.com	Long Island	NY	11101	718-937-4500		91
Sustainable Resources Group Inc 440 Creamery Way Ste 150 *Web:* www.sustainableresourcesgroup.com	Exton	PA	19341	610-840-9200		192
Sustainalytics 215 Spadina Ave Ste 300 *Web:* www.sustainalytics.com	Toronto	ON	M5T2C7	416-861-0403		466
Suter Company Inc 258 May St *TF:* 800-435-6942 ■ *Web:* www.suterco.com	Sycamore	IL	60178	815-895-9186	895-4814	296-36
Sutherland Global Services 1160 Pittsford-Victor Rd *Web:* www.sutherlandglobal.com	Pittsford	NY	14534	585-586-5757		387
Sutherland Lumber Co 4000 Main St *TF:* 800-821-2252 ■ *Web:* www.sutherlands.com	Kansas City	MO	64111	816-756-3000	360-2195	364
Sutin Thayer & Browne 6565 Americas Pkwy N E Two Park Sq Ste 1000 *Web:* sutinfirm.com	Albuquerque	NM	87110	505-883-2500		428
Sutisoft Inc 4984 El Camino Real Ste 200 *Web:* www.sutisoft.com	Los Altos	CA	94022	650-969-7884		177
Sutphen Corp PO Box 158 *TF:* 800-726-7030 ■ *Web:* www.sutphen.com	Amlin	OH	43002	614-889-1005	889-0874	516
Sutron Corp 22400 Davis Dr *NASDAQ: STRN* ■ *Web:* www.sutron.com	Sterling	VA	20164	703-406-2800	406-2801	201
Sutter Auburn Faith Community Hospital (SAFH) 11815 Education St *TF:* 800-478-8837 ■ *Web:* www.sutterauburnfaith.org	Auburn	CA	95602	530-888-4500	886-6611	374-3
Sutter County 433 Second St *TF:* 800-371-3177 ■ *Web:* www.co.sutter.ca.us	Yuba City	CA	95991	530-822-7134	822-7214	338
Sutter County Library 750 Forbes Ave *TF:* 800-371-3177 ■ *Web:* co.sutter.ca.us	Yuba City	CA	95991	530-822-7137	671-6539	434-3
Sutter East Bay Medical Foundation 3687 Mt Diablo Blvd Ste 200 *Web:* www.sebmf.org	Lafayette	CA	94549	925-962-6600		305
Sutter General Hospital 2801 L St *TF:* 800-478-8837 ■ *Web:* www.sutterhealth.org	Sacramento	CA	95816	916-454-2222		374-3
Sutter Health 2200 River Plaza *TF:* 888-888-6044 ■ *Web:* www.sutterhealth.org	Sacramento	CA	95833	916-733-8800		353
Sutter Health Sacramento Sierra Region 2801 L St *Web:* www.checksutterfirst.org	Sacramento	CA	95816	916-454-2222		374-3
Sutter Hill Ventures 755 Page Mill Rd Ste A-200 *TF:* 800-694-4460 ■ *Web:* www.shv.com	Palo Alto	CA	94304	650-493-5600		792
Sutter Medical Ctr of Santa Rosa 3325 Chanate Rd *TF:* 800-651-5111 ■ *Web:* www.suttersantarosa.org	Santa Rosa	CA	95404	707-576-4006		374-3
Sutter Memorial Hospital 5151 F St *TF:* 800-478-8837 ■ *Web:* www.sutterhealth.org	Sacramento	CA	95819	916-454-3333		374-3
Sutter Securities Inc 220 Montgomery St Ste 1700 *TF:* 800-289-9999 ■ *Web:* www.suttersecurities.com	San Francisco	CA	94104	415-352-6300		690
Sutter Solano Medical Ctr (SSMC) 300 Hospital Dr *TF:* 800-866-7724 ■ *Web:* www.suttersolano.org	Vallejo	CA	94589	707-554-4444	648-3227	374-3
Sutter's Fort State Historic Park 2701 L St *Web:* www.parks.ca.gov	Sacramento	CA	95816	916-445-4422	447-9318	565
Suttle 1001 E Hwy 212 *TF:* 800-852-8662 ■ *Web:* www.suttlesolutions.com	Hector	MN	55342	320-848-6711	848-6218	735
Suttles Plumbing & Mechanical Corp 21541 Nordhoff St Ste C *Web:* www.suttlesplumbing.com	Chatsworth	CA	91311	818-718-9779		610
Suttle-Straus Inc 1000 Uniek Dr PO Box 370 *Web:* www.suttle-straus.com	Waunakee	WI	53597	608-849-1000	849-8264	627
Sutton Alliance LLC 515 Rockaway Ave *TF:* 866-435-6600 ■ *Web:* suttonalliance.com/progressive	Valley Stream	NY	11581	516-837-6100		652
Sutton County 300 E Oak St *Web:* co.sutton.tx.us	Sonora	TX	76950	325-387-3815		338
Sutton Enterprises Inc 424 Diana Ct Ste A *Web:* www.suttonenterprises.com	Bensenville	IL	60106	847-445-2098		463
Sutton Place Hotel Edmonton 10235 101st St *Web:* www.suttonplace.com	Edmonton	AB	T5J3E9	780-428-7111		379
SUWA (Southern Utah Wilderness Alliance) 425 East 100 South *Web:* www.suwa.org	Salt Lake City	UT	84111	801-486-3161		48-13
Suwanee Sports Academy 3640 Burnette Rd *TF:* 800-319-0884 ■ *Web:* ssasports.com	Suwanee	GA	30024	770-614-6686		717
Suwannee County 212 N Ohio Ave *Web:* www.suwanneechamber.com	Live Oak	FL	32064	386-362-3071	362-4758	338
Suwannee River State Park 3631 201st Path *Web:* www.floridastateparks.org	Live Oak	FL	32060	386-362-2746		565
Suwannee Valley Electric Co-op PO Box 160 *TF:* 800-752-0025 ■ *Web:* www.svec-coop.com	Live Oak	FL	32064	386-362-2226		245
Suzanna's Kitchen Inc 4025 Buford Hwy *TF:* 800-241-2455 ■ *Web:* www.suzannaskitchen.com	Duluth	GA	30096	770-476-9900	476-8899	296-26
Suze 4345 W NW Hwy *Web:* www.suzedallas.com	Dallas	TX	75220	214-350-6135	350-6178	671
Suzie's Soba 1009 W 36th St	Baltimore	MD	21211	410-243-0051		671
Suzo-Happ Group Inc 1743 Linneman Rd *Web:* www.suzohapp.com	Mount Prospect	IL	60056	847-593-6130		544
Suzuki Association of The Americas Inc 1900 Folsom St Ste 101 *TF:* 888-378-9854 ■ *Web:* www.suzukiassociation.org	Boulder	CO	80302	303-444-0948		138
Suzuki Musical Instrument Corp PO Box 710459 *TF Cust Svc:* 800-854-1594 ■ *Web:* www.suzukimusic.com	Santee	CA	92072	619-258-1896		527
SV Life Sciences (SVLS) 201 Washington St Ste 3900 *Web:* www.svlsa.com	Boston	MA	02108	617-367-8100	367-1590	792
SVA 1221 John Q Hammons Dr *TF:* 800-279-2616 ■ *Web:* www.sva.com	Madison	WI	53717	608-831-8181		2
Svam International Inc 233 E Shore Rd Ste 201 *TF:* 800-903-6716 ■ *Web:* www.svam.com	Great Neck	NY	11023	516-466-6655	466-8260	180
SVB (Silicon Valley Bank) 3003 Tasman Dr *TF:* 800-579-1639 ■ *Web:* www.svb.com	Santa Clara	CA	95054	408-654-7400		70
SVB Financial Group 3005 Tasman Dr *NASDAQ: SIVB* ■ *TF:* 800-760-9644 ■ *Web:* www.svb.com	Santa Clara	CA	95054	408-654-7400	496-2405	360-2
SVC (Society of Vacuum Coaters) 71 Pinon Hill Pl NE *TF:* 800-443-8817 ■ *Web:* www.svc.org	Albuquerque	NM	87122	505-856-7188	856-6716	49-13
SVCH (Saint Vincent Charity Hospital) 2351 E 22nd St *TF:* 800-750-0750 ■ *Web:* www.stvincentcharity.com	Cleveland	OH	44115	216-861-6200		374-3
SVDH (Sierra View District Hospital) 465 W Putnam Ave *Web:* www.sierra-view.com	Porterville	CA	93257	559-784-1110		374-3
Svenhard's Swedish Bakery Inc 335 Adeline St *TF:* 800-617-4729 ■ *Web:* www.svenhards.com	Oakland	CA	94607	510-834-5035	839-6797	296-1
Svenska Handelsbanken 875 Third Ave 4th Fl *Web:* www.handelsbanken.se	New York	NY	10022	212-326-5100		70
Svf Flow Controls Inc 13560 Larwin Cir *Web:* www.svf.net	Santa Fe Springs	CA	90670	562-802-2255		358
SVH (Simi Valley Hospital) 2975 N Sycamore Dr *Web:* www.adventisthealth.org	Simi Valley	CA	93065	805-955-6000		374-3
Svi Inc 440 Mark Leany Dr *Web:* www.specialtyvehicles.com	Henderson	NV	89011	702-567-5256		516
SVIA (Specialty Vehicle Institute of America) 2 Jenner St Ste 150 *TF:* 800-887-2887 ■ *Web:* www.atvsafety.org	Irvine	CA	92618	949-727-3727	727-4216	49-21
SVLS (SV Life Sciences) 201 Washington St Ste 3900 *Web:* www.svlsa.com	Boston	MA	02108	617-367-8100	367-1590	792
SVM LP 200 E Howard Ave Ste 220 *TF:* 877-300-1786 ■ *Web:* www.svmcards.net	Des Plaines	IL	60018	877-300-1786		226
SVMH (Salinas Valley Memorial Hospital) 450 E Romie Ln *TF:* 800-813-4673 ■ *Web:* www.svmh.com	Salinas	CA	93901	831-757-4333		374-3
SVRMC (Sierra Vista Regional Medical Ctr) 1010 Murray Ave *TF:* 866-904-6871 ■ *Web:* www.sierravistaregional.com	San Luis Obispo	CA	93405	805-546-7600		374-3
SVS (Society for Vascular Surgery) 633 N St Clair St 22nd Fl *TF:* 800-258-7188 ■ *Web:* vascular.org	Chicago	IL	60611	312-334-2300	334-2320	49-8
SVS Vision 140 Macomb Pl *TF:* 800-787-4600 ■ *Web:* www.svsvision.com	Mount Clemens	MI	48043	586-468-7612		543
SVT 7699 Lochlin Dr	Brighton	MI	48116	248-437-0041		246
SVTronics Inc 3465 Technology *Web:* www.svtronics.com	Plano	TX	75074	214-440-1234		45
SVUSD (Sonoma Valley Unified School District) 17850 Railroad Ave *Web:* www.svusdca.org	Sonoma	CA	95476	707-935-6000		685
SW Anderson Co 2425 Wisconsin Ave *Web:* swaco.com	Downers Grove	IL	60515	630-964-2600		350
S&W Contracting Company Inc 952 New Salem Rd *Web:* www.sandwcontracting.com	Murfreesboro	TN	37129	615-893-2511		787
SW Steakhouse 3131 Las Vegas Blvd S *TF:* 888-320-7123 ■ *Web:* wynnlasvegas.com	Las Vegas	NV	89109	702-770-7000	770-1570	671
SW!TCH Studio Inc 1835 E Sixth St Ste 18 *Web:* www.switchstudio.com	Tempe	AZ	85281	480-966-2211		344
SWA Group 2200 Bridgeway Blvd *Web:* www.swagroup.com	Sausalito	CA	94965	415-332-5100		422
Swag, The 2300 Swag Rd *TF:* 800-789-7672 ■ *Web:* www.theswag.com	Waynesville	NC	28785	828-926-0430	926-2036	379
Swagelok Co 29500 Solon Rd *Web:* www.swagelok.com	Solon	OH	44139	440-248-4600	349-5970	595
Swagger Foods Corp 900 Corporate Woods Pkwy *TF:* 800-843-6089 ■ *Web:* www.swaggerfoods.com	Vernon Hills	IL	60061	847-913-1200		296-22
Swaggerty Sausage Company Inc 2827 Swaggerty Rd *Web:* www.swaggertys.com	Kodak	TN	37764	865-933-2625		473
Swaim Inc 1801 S College Dr *TF:* 800-659-7297 ■ *Web:* www.swaim-inc.com	High Point	NC	27260	336-885-6131	885-6227	319-2
Swain County 101 Mitchell St PO Box 2321 *Web:* www.swaincountync.gov	Bryson City	NC	28713	828-488-9273		338
Swain's General Store Inc 602 E First St *TF:* 800-895-4327 ■ *Web:* www.swainsinc.com	Port Angeles	WA	98362	360-452-2357	452-7561	791
Swallow Falls State Park c/o Herrington Manor State Pk 222 Herrington Ln *Web:* dnr.maryland.gov/publiclands/Pages/western/swallowfalls.aspx	Oakland	MD	21550	301-387-6938		565
Swalwell Eric (Rep D - CA) 129 Cannon HOB *Web:* swalwell.house.gov	Washington	DC	20515	202-225-5065		342-2
Swan & Sons-Morss Company Inc 309 E Water St *TF:* 877-407-1657 ■ *Web:* swanmorss.com	Elmira	NY	14902	607-734-6283		390

Phone | Fax | Class

Swan Cleaners 1535 Bethel Rd Columbus OH 43220 614-442-5000 426
Web: www.swancleaners.com
Swan Corp, The 515 Olive St Ste 900 St. Louis MO 63101 314-231-8148 612
TF: 800-325-7008 ■ *Web:* www.swanstone.com
Swan Creek Recreation Area
c/o W Whitlock Recreation Area
16157A W Whitlock Rd Gettysburg SD 57442 605-765-9410 565
Web: www.gfp.sd.gov
Swan Engineering & Machine Co
2611 State St Bettendorf IA 52722 563-355-2671 355-5380 757
Web: swanengr.com
Swan Hose 1201 Delaware Ave Marion OH 43302 800-848-8707 370
TF: 800-848-8707 ■ *Web:* www.swanhose.com
Swan House
Atlanta History Ctr 130 W Paces Ferry Rd Atlanta GA 30305 404-814-4000 50-3
Web: www.atlantahistorycenter.com
Swan Lake Resort & Campground
17463 County Hwy 29 Fergus Falls MN 56537 218-736-4626 121
TF: 800-697-4626 ■ *Web:* swanlkresort.com
Swan Lake State Park 100 W Park Ln Swanville ME 04915 207-525-4404 565
Web: www.maine.gov
Swan Legal Search
11400 Olympic Blvd Ste 200 Los Angeles CA 90064 310-201-2500 266
Web: www.swanlegal.com
Swan Valley School Dist 8380 Ohern Rd Saginaw MI 48609 989-921-3701 685
Web: swanvalleyschools.com
SWANA (Solid Waste Assn of North America)
1100 Wayne Ave Ste 700 Silver Spring MD 20910 301-585-2898 589-7068 531-5
TF: 800-467-9262 ■ *Web:* swana.org
Swaner Hardwood Co Inc
5 W Magnolia Blvd Burbank CA 91502 818-953-5350 846-3662 683
Web: www.swanerhardwood.com
Swank Inc 656 Joseph Warner Blvd Taunton MA 02780 508-822-2527 408
Web: swankinc.com
Swank Motion Pictures Inc
10795 Watson Rd St Louis MO 63127 314-984-6000 514
TF: 888-389-3622 ■ *Web:* www.swank.com
Swann Galleries Inc 104 E 25th St New York NY 10010 212-254-4710 979-1017 51
Web: www.swanngalleries.com
Swans Candles 16524 Tilley Rd S Tenino WA 98589 888-848-7926 122
TF: 888-848-7926 ■ *Web:* www.swanscandles.com
Swanson & Bratschun LLC
8210 SouthPark Terr Littleton CO 80120 303-268-0066 428
Web: www.sbiplaw.com
Swanson Construction Co
3400 Towne Pointe Dr Bettendorf IA 52722 563-332-4859 186
Web: swansonbuilt.com
Swanson Contracting Co
11701 S Mayfield Ave Alsip IL 60803 708-388-0623 388-9986 188-8
Web: www.swansoncontracting.com
Swanson Group Inc
2695 Glendale Valley Rd PO Box 250 Glendale OR 97442 541-832-1121 448
TF: [illegible] ■ *Web:* www.swansongroup.biz
Swanson Health Products Inc PO Box 2803 Fargo ND 58108 701-356-2700 356-2708 799
TF: 800-824-4491 ■ *Web:* www.swansonvitamins.com
Swanson Pickle Company Inc
11561 Heights Ravenna Rd Ravenna MI 49451 231-853-2209 296-19
Swanson Reservoir State Recreation Area
36166 Road 44B Trenton NE 69044 308-334-[illegible] 565
Swanson Rink Inc 1120 Lincoln St 1200 Denver CO 80203 303-832-2666 261
Web: www.swansonrink.com
Swanson Russell 1222 P St Lincoln NE 68508 402-437-6400 4
Web: www.swansonrussell.com
Swanson Tool & Die Inc
11755 Justen Cir Maple Grove MN 55369 763-428-7100 488
Web: www.swansontool.com
Swanton Welding & Machining Co
407 Broadway Ave Swanton OH 43558 419-826-4816 491
Web: www.swantonweld.com
Swany America Corp 115 Corp Dr Johnstown NY 12095 518-725-3333 725-2026 155-8
TF: 888-234-5450 ■ *Web:* www.swanyamerica.com
Swarco Industries Inc PO Box 89 Columbia TN 38402 931-388-5900 388-4039 676
TF: 800-216-8781 ■ *Web:* www.swarco.com
Swarovski North America Ltd
1 Kenney Dr Cranston RI 02920 401-463-6400 870-5660* 334
**Fax Area Code:* 800 ■ *TF:* 800-289-4900 ■ *Web:* www.swarovski.com
Swarthmore College 500 College Ave Swarthmore PA 19081 610-328-8300 328-8580* 166
**Fax:* Admissions ■ *TF Admissions:* 800-667-3110 ■ *Web:* www.swarthmore.edu
Swarthmore College McCabe Library
500 College Ave Swarthmore PA 19081 610-328-8477 434-6
Web: www.swarthmore.edu
Swarthmore Group
1650 Arch St Ste 2100 Philadelphia PA 19103 215-557-9300 557-9305 401
Web: www.swarthmoregroup.com
Swarthout Coaches Inc 115 Graham Rd Ithaca NY 14850 607-257-2277 257-0218 107
TF: 800-772-7267 ■ *Web:* www.goswarthout.com
Swartswood State Park PO Box 123 Swartswood NJ 07877 973-383-5230 565
Web: www.njparksandforests.org
Swartz Campbell LLC
300 Delaware Ave Ste 1410 Wilmington DE 19801 215-564-5190 445
Web: www.swartzcampbell.com
Swartz Kitchens & Baths
5550 Allentown Blvd (Route 22) Harrisburg PA 17112 717-652-7111 321
TF: 800-652-0111 ■ *Web:* swartzkitchens.com
Swatch Group 1200 Harbor Blvd 7th Fl Weehawken NJ 07086 201-271-1400 153
Web: www.swatchgroup.com
Swatchcraft 516 Townsend Ave High Point NC 27263 336-434-5095 195
TF: 800-433-3201 ■ *Web:* www.swatchcraft.com
Swb Consulting Inc
466 Green St Ste 303 San Francisco CA 94133 415-543-5825 809
SWC Office Furniture Outlet
375 Fairfield Ave Stamford CT 06902 203-967-8367 321
Web: swcoffice.com
SWCA Inc 3033 N Central Ave Ste 145 Phoenix AZ 85012 602-274-3831 274-3958 192
TF: 800-828-8517 ■ *Web:* www.swca.com
SWCE (Steele-Waseca Co-op Electric)
2411 W Bridge St PO Box 485 Owatonna MN 55060 507-451-7340 245
TF: 800-526-3514 ■ *Web:* www.swce.com

SWCS (Soil & Water Conservation Society)
945 SW Ankeny Rd Ankeny IA 50023 515-289-2331 289-1227 48-13
TF: 800-843-7645 ■ *Web:* www.swcs.org
SWE (Society of Women Engineers)
130 E Randolph St Ste 3500 Chicago IL 60601 312-596-5223 596-5252 49-19
TF: 877-793-4636 ■ *Web:* societyofwomenengineers.swe.org
Swearingen Software Inc
7540 Pebble Beach Dr Beaumont TX 77707 713-849-2026 180
TF: 800-253-4827 ■ *Web:* www.swearingensoftware.com
Sweda Company LLC
17411 Vly Blvd City of Industry CA 91744 626-357-9999 118
TF: 800-848-8417 ■ *Web:* www.swedausa.com
Swedbank 1 Penn Plaza 15th Fl New York NY 10119 212-486-8400 486-3220 70
Web: www.swedbank.com
Sweden
Consulate General
885 Second Ave 40th Fl New York NY 10017 212-888-3000 888-3125 257
Web: www.swedenabroad.com
Consulate General
505 Sansome St Ste 1010 San Francisco CA 94111 415-788-2631 257
Web: www.swedenabroad.com
Embassy 2900 K St NW Washington DC 20007 202-467-2600 467-2699 257
Web: www.swedenabroad.com
Sweden House 4605 E State St Rockford IL 61108 815-398-4130 379
Swedenborg Foundation Inc
320 N Church St West Chester PA 19380 610-430-3222 196
Web: swedenborg.com
Swedish American Museum
5211 N Clark St Chicago IL 60640 773-728-8111 728-8870 520
Web: www.swedishamericanmuseum.org
Swedish Council of America
3030 W River Pkwy Minneapolis MN 55406 612-871-0593 48-14
Web: www.swedishcouncil.org
Swedish Covenant Hospital
5145 N California Ave Chicago IL 60625 773-878-8200 374-3
Web: www.swedishcovenant.org
Swedish Institute Inc
226 W 26th St Fl 5 New York NY 10001 212-924-5900 162
TF: 800-549-5993 ■ *Web:* www.swedishinstitute.edu
Swedish Medical Ctr
501 E Hampden Ave Englewood CO 80113 303-788-5000 788-6265 374-3
TF: 866-779-3347 ■ *Web:* www.swedishhospital.com
Swedish Medical Ctr Cherry Hill Campus
500 17th Ave Seattle WA 98122 206-320-2000 374-3
Web: www.swedish.org
Swedish Medical Ctr First Hill
747 Broadway Seattle WA 98122 206-386-6000 374-3
Web: www.swedish.org
Swedish Medical Ctr/Edmonds
21601 76th Ave W Edmonds WA 98026 425-640-4000 374-3
Web: www.swedish.org
Swedish Travel & Tourism Council
Grand Central Stn PO Box 4649 New York NY 10163 212-885-9700 885-9710 775
Web: www.visitsweden.com
Swedish-American Chamber of Commerce Atlanta Inc (SACC)
4775 Peachtree Industrial Blvd
Bldg 300 Ste 300 Norcross GA 30092 770-670-2480 138
Web: www.sacc-georgia.org
Swedish-American Chamber of Commerce Inc New York Chapter
570 Lexington Ave 20th Fl New York NY 10022 212-838-5530 755-7953 138
TF: 800-862-2793 ■ *Web:* www.saccny.org
Swedish-American Chamber of Commerce San Diego
4475 Mission Blvd Ste 201 San Diego CA 92109 858-598-4809 598-4809 138
TF: 800-736-7401 ■ *Web:* www.sacc-sandiego.org
Swedish-American Chamber of Commerce Washington DC Inc
2900 K St NW Washington DC 20007 202-536-1570 138
Web: sacc-usa.org/beta/dc
SwedishAmerican Hospital
1401 E State St Rockford IL 61104 815-968-4400 374-3
TF: 800-322-4724 ■ *Web:* www.swedishamerican.org
Sweed Machinery Inc
653 Second Ave PO Box 228 Gold Hill OR 97525 541-855-1512 855-1165 494
TF Sales: 800-888-1352 ■ *Web:* www.sweed.com
Sweeney Buick 7997 Market St Youngstown OH 44512 877-360-4928 516
TF: 877-360-4928 ■ *Web:* sweeneycars.com
Sweeney Conrad PS
2606 116th Ave NE 200 Bellevue WA 98004 425-629-1990 734
Web: sweeneyconrad.com
Sweeney Law Firm 8109 Lima Rd Fort Wayne IN 46818 260-420-3137 428
TF: 866-793-6339 ■ *Web:* sweeneylawfirm.com
Sweeping Services of Texas LP
3324 Roy Orr Blvd Grand Prairie TX 75050 817-268-4100 188-4
Web: wastepartners.com
Sweepster Inc 2800 N Zeeb Rd Dexter MI 48130 800-456-7100 996-9014* 103
**Fax Area Code:* 734 ■ *TF:* 800-456-7100 ■ *Web:* www.paladinlightconstructiongroup.com
Sweet Adelines International
9110 S Toledo Ave Tulsa OK 74137 918-622-1444 665-0894 48-18
TF: 800-992-7464 ■ *Web:* sweetadelines.com
Sweet Basil 2424 N Woodlawn St Wichita KS 67220 316-651-0123 671
Web: 360wichita.com
Sweet Basil 1585 Bank St Ottawa ON K1H7Z3 613-731-8424 671
Web: sweetbasilottawa.com
Sweet Basil 3135 NE Broadway Portland OR 97232 503-281-8337 671
Web: www.sweetbasilor.com
Sweet Briar College
134 Chappel Rd Sweet Briar VA 24595 434-381-6100 381-6152* 166
**Fax:* Admissions ■ *TF Admissions:* 800-381-6142 ■ *Web:* www.sbc.edu
Sweet Candy Co Inc
3780 W Directors Row Salt Lake City UT 84104 801-886-1444 886-1404 296-8
TF: 800-669-8669 ■ *Web:* www.sweetcandy.com
Sweet Earth Inc 3080 Hilltop Rd Moss Landing CA 95039 831-375-8673 123
Web: www.sweetearthfoods.com
Sweet Grass County
115 W Fifth Ave PO Box 888 Big Timber MT 59011 406-932-5152 932-3026 338
Web: sweetgrasscountygov.com
Sweet Grass Ranch 460 Rein Ln Big Timber MT 59011 406-537-4477 537-4477 239
Web: www.sweetgrassranch.com

	Phone	Fax	Class
Sweet Harvest Foods 515 Cannon Industrial Blvd .... Cannon Falls MN 55009 *Web:* www.sweetharvestfoods.com	507-263-8599		123
Sweet Home Central School District 1901 Sweet Home Rd .... Amherst NY 14228 *Web:* sweethomeschools.org	716-250-1400		685
Sweet Home School District 55 1920 Long St .... Sweet Home OR 97386 *Web:* www.sweethome.k12.or.us	541-367-7126		685
Sweet Lucy's Smokehouse 7500 State Rd .... Philadelphia PA 19136 *Web:* www.sweetlucys.com	215-333-9663		671
Sweet Mfg Company Inc 2000 E Leffel Ln .... Springfield OH 45505 *TF Cust Svc:* 800-334-7254 ■ *Web:* www.sweetmfg.com	937-325-1511	322-1963	207
Sweet Ovations 1741 Tomlinson Rd .... Philadelphia PA 19116 *Web:* www.sweetovations.com	215-676-3900		296-21
Sweet Potatoes 607 N Trade St .... Winston-Salem NC 27101 *Web:* www.sweetpotatoes.ws	336-727-4844		671
Sweet Street Desserts Inc 722 Hiesters Ln .... Reading PA 19605 *Web:* www.sweetstreet.com	610-921-8113		68
Sweet Tomatoes 15822 Bernardo Ctr Dr Ste A .... San Diego CA 92127 *TF:* 800-242-5353 ■ *Web:* www.souplantation.com	858-675-1600		670
Sweet, Stevens, Katz & Williams LLP 331 E Butler Ave .... New Britain PA 18901 *Web:* sweetstevens.com	215-345-9111		428
SweetLabs Inc 510 Market St Ste 301.......... San Diego CA 92101 *Web:* www.sweetlabs.com	619-269-0150		393
Sweetlake Chemical Ltd 7402 Neuhaus St Ste A....................... Houston TX 77061	713-827-8707		146
Sweetwater Authority PO Box 2328 .... Chula Vista CA 91912 *TF:* 866-275-3772 ■ *Web:* www.sweetwater.org	619-420-1413	425-7469	787
Sweetwater County 80 W Flaming Gorge Way.................. Green River WY 82935 *Web:* www.sweet.wy.us	307-872-3732		338
Sweetwater County Historical Museum 3 E Flaming Gorge Way .... Green River WY 82935 *TF:* 800-508-4629 ■ *Web:* www.sweetwatermuseum.org	307-872-6435	872-3234	520
Sweetwater County Library System 300 N First E St .... Green River WY 82935 *Web:* www.sweetwaterlibraries.com	307-875-3615	872-3203	434-3
Sweetwater County School District 1 (SCSD) 3550 Foothill Blvd .... Rock Springs WY 82901 **Fax Area Code:* 888 ■ *Web:* www.sweetwater1.org	307-352-3400	503-7562*	780
Sweetwater County School District 2 320 Monroe Ave .... Green River WY 82935 *Web:* www.swcsd2.org	307-872-5500		685
Sweetwater Creek State Park 1750 Mt Vernon Rd......................... Lithia Springs GA 30122 *Web:* www.gastateparks.org/sweetwatercreek	770-732-5871		565
Sweetwater Hospital 304 Wright St........... Sweetwater TN 37874 *Web:* www.sweetwaterhospital.org	865-213-8200		186
Sweetwater Restaurant 85 King St............. Jackson WY 83001 *TF:* 800-323-9279 ■ *Web:* sweetwaterjackson.com	307-733-3553		671
Sweetwater Sound Inc 5501 US Hwy 30 W .... Fort Wayne IN 46818 *TF:* 800-222-4700 ■ *Web:* www.sweetwater.com	260-432-8176	432-1758	526
Sweetwater Valley Oil Company Inc 1236 New Hwy 68........................... Sweetwater TN 37874 *TF:* 800-362-4519 ■ *Web:* www.sweetwatervalleyoil.com	423-337-6671		581
Sweetwaters 120 Church St .... Burlington VT 05401 *Web:* www.sweetwatersvt.com	802-864-9800		671
Swenson & Silacci Flowers 110 John St......... Salinas CA 93901 *Web:* www.onlineflowers.com	831-424-2725		292
Swenson Granite Co LLC 369 N State St......... Concord NH 03301 *Web:* www.swensongranite.com	603-672-7827		503-6
Swenson Say Faget Inc 2124 Third Ave Ste 100 .... Seattle WA 98121 *Web:* ssfengineers.com	206-443-6212		256
Swenson Spreader Co 127 Walnut St .... Lindenwood IL 61049 *TF:* 888-825-7323 ■ *Web:* www.swensonproducts.com	815-393-4455	393-4964	190
Swepco Tube Corp 1 Clifton Blvd.................. Clifton NJ 07015 *TF:* 800-563-8823 ■ *Web:* www.swepcotube.com	973-778-3000	778-9289	490
SWH (Senior Whole Health LLC) 58 Charles St .... Cambridge MA 02141 *TF:* 888-794-7268 ■ *Web:* www.seniorwholehealth.com	617-494-5353	494-5599	353
SWH Supply Co 242 E Main St................. Louisville KY 40202 *TF:* 800-321-3598 ■ *Web:* www.swhsupply.com	502-589-9287	585-3812	665
SWHR 1025 Connecticut Ave NW Ste 601........... Washington DC 20036 *Web:* www.womenshealthresearch.org	202-223-8224		48-17
Swibco Inc 4810 Venture Rd .... Lisle IL 60532 **Fax Area Code:* 800 ■ *TF:* 877-794-2261 ■ *Web:* www.swibco.com	630-968-8900	367-7943*	762
Swift Atlanta 3605 Swiftwater Park Dr........... Suwanee GA 30024 *Web:* www.swiftatlanta.com	770-945-1084		697
Swift Aviation 2710 E Old Tower Rd .... Phoenix AZ 85034 *TF:* 800-234-5382 ■ *Web:* www.swiftaviation.com	602-273-3770	273-3773	63
Swift Communications Inc 580 Mallory Way .... Carson City NV 89701 *TF:* 800-551-5691 ■ *Web:* www.swiftcom.com	775-283-5500		532-3
Swift County PO Box 288 .... Benson MN 56215 *Web:* www.swiftcounty.com	320-843-2744		338
Swift Electrical Supply Co 100 Hollister Rd .... Teterboro NJ 07608 *Web:* www.swiftelectrical.com	201-462-0900		246
Swift Glass Company Inc 131 W 22nd St .... Elmira Heights NY 14903 *TF:* 800-537-9438 ■ *Web:* www.swiftglass.com	607-733-7166	732-5829	332
Swift Industrial Power Inc 10917 McBride Ln .... Knoxville TN 37932 *Web:* www.swiftpower.com	865-966-9758		385
Swift Mailing Services Inc 600 Washington st Ste E....................... Bristol PA 19007 *Web:* www.swiftmailing.com	215-638-4122		627
Swift Print Communication 1248 Research Blvd .... Saint Louis MO 63132 *TF:* 800-545-1141 ■ *Web:* www.swiftprint.com	314-991-4300		627
Swift Saw & Tool Supply Company Inc 1200 171st St............................ Hazel Crest IL 60429 *Web:* swiftsaw.com	708-335-0550		358
Swift Spinning Inc 16 Corporate Ridge Pkwy .... Columbus GA 31907 *TF:* 800-849-1252 ■ *Web:* www.swiftspinning.com	706-323-6303		745-9
Swift Textile Metalizing LLC 23 Britton Dr............................ Bloomfield CT 06002 *TF:* 800-244-6224 ■ *Web:* www.swift-textile.com	860-243-1122	243-0848	745-2
Swift Transportation Company Inc 2200 S 75th Ave............................ Phoenix AZ 85043 *NYSE:* SWFT ■ *TF:* 800-800-2200 ■ *Web:* www.swifttrans.com	602-269-9700		780
Swiftlift Inc 820 Phillips Rd .... Victor NY 14564 *TF:* 888-292-3101 ■ *Web:* www.swiftlift.com	585-742-2160		23
Swiftships Inc 1105 Levee Rd.............. Morgan City LA 70380 *Web:* www.swiftships.com	985-384-1700	380-2559	698
Swifty Oil Company Inc 1515 W Tipton St .... Seymour IN 47274	812-522-1640		324
Swig 217 N Broad Way St .... Milwaukee WI 53202 *Web:* www.swigmilwaukee.com	414-431-7944		671
Swiger Coils Systems Inc 4677 Mfg Rd.............................. Cleveland OH 44135 *TF:* 800-321-3310 ■ *Web:* www.swigercoil.com	216-362-7500	362-1496	518
Swihart Industries Inc 5111 Webster St .... Dayton OH 45414 *TF:* 800-766-0024 ■ *Web:* www.swihartindustries.com	937-277-4796		757
Swim 'n Sport Retail Inc 2396 NW 96th Ave .... Miami FL 33172 *TF:* 800-497-2111 ■ *Web:* www.swimnsport.com	800-497-2111		157-6
Swim Across America Inc 11600 N Community House Rd Ste 100......... Charlotte NC 28277 *Web:* www.swimacrossamerica.org	980-237-9127		317
Swimways Corp 5816 Ward Ct .... Virginia Beach VA 23455 *Web:* www.swimways.com	757-460-1156		596
Swimwear Anywhere Inc 85 Sherwood Ave .... Farmingdale NY 11735 *Web:* www.swimwearanywhere.com	631-420-1400		594
Swindell Dressler International Co 5100 Casteel Dr .... Coraopolis PA 15108 *Web:* www.swindelldressler.com	412-788-7100		318
Swine Graphics Enterprises LP 1620 Superior St PO Box 668.............. Webster City IA 50595 *Web:* sgepork.com	515-832-5481	832-2237	10-6
Swine Palace Productions 105 Music & Dramatic Arts Bldg Louisiana State University .... Baton Rouge LA 70803 *Web:* swinepalace.wix.com/sp-test#!__find	225-578-4174		573-4
Swineford National Bank 1255 N Susquehanna Trial PO Box 241 .... Hummels Wharf PA 17831 *TF:* 866-762-1903 ■ *Web:* www.swineford.com	570-743-7786		70
Swinerton Builders 260 Townsend St .... San Francisco CA 94107 *Web:* www.swinerton.com	415-421-2980		186
Swing Transport Inc 1405 N Salisbury Ave....................... Salisbury NC 28144 *Web:* www.swingtransport.com	704-633-3567		780
Swingtide Inc W5775 Nine Indian Trail........... Elkhorn WI 53121 *Web:* www.swingtide.com	262-742-5455		463
Swinney Homestead 1424 W Jefferson Blvd .... Fort Wayne IN 46802 *Web:* www.settlersinc.org	260-424-7212		50-3
Swinsoft Inc 13405 Folsom Blvd Ste 517 .... Folsom CA 95630 *Web:* www.swinsoft.com	916-353-1963		180
Swintec Corp 320 W Commercial Ave.......... Moonachie NJ 07074 *TF:* 800-225-0867 ■ *Web:* www.swintec.com	201-935-0115		111
Swip Systems Inc 1 Regency Plaza Dr Ste 100 .... Collinsville IL 62234 *Web:* swipsystems.com	618-346-8014		180
Swire Coca-Cola USA 12634 S 265 W............ Draper UT 84020 *TF:* 800-497-2653 ■ *Web:* swirecc.com	801-816-5300	816-5423	81-2
Swisher County 119 S Maxwell St.................. Tulia TX 79088 *Web:* www.co.swisher.tx.us	806-995-3294	995-4121	338
Swisher County Cattle Co Farm Market 214 Rd............................ Tulia TX 79088	806-627-4231		10-1
Swisher Electric Co-op Inc 401 SW Second St PO Box 67 .... Tulia TX 79088 *TF:* 800-530-4344 ■ *Web:* www.swisherelectric.org	806-995-3567	995-2249	245
Swisher Hygiene Co 4725 Piedmont Row Dr...................... Charlotte NC 28210 *TF:* 800-444-4138 ■ *Web:* www.swsh.com	704-364-7707		152
Swisher International Inc 459 E 16th St .... Jacksonville FL 32206 *TF:* 800-843-3731 ■ *Web:* www.swisher.com	904-353-4311		756
Swisher Mower & Machine Company Inc 1602 Corporate Dr .... Warrensburg MO 64093 *TF:* 800-222-8183 ■ *Web:* www.swisherinc.com	660-747-8183	747-8650	429
Swiss Cleaners 35 Windsor Ave PO Box 825 .... Rockville CT 06066 *Web:* www.swisscleaners.com	860-872-0166		426
Swiss Consulting Group 101 W 23 St Ste 2422........................ New York NY 10011 *Web:* www.swissconsultinggroup.com	212-288-4858	744-3654	463
Swiss Knife Shop 10 Northern Blvd Ste 8 .... Amherst NH 03031 *TF:* 866-438-7947 ■ *Web:* www.swissknifeshop.com	603-732-0069		195
Swiss Precision Instruments Inc 11450 Markon Dr......................... Garden Grove CA 92841 **Fax Area Code:* 800 ■ *TF:* 888-774-8200 ■ *Web:* www.swissprec.com	714-799-1555	842-5164*	386
Swiss Re America Corp 175 King St .... Armonk NY 10504 *Web:* www.swissre.com	914-828-8000		391-4
Swiss Valley Farms 247 Research Pkwy PO Box 4493............ Davenport IA 52808 *Web:* www.swissvalley.com	563-468-6600	468-6616	296-5
Swiss-American Chamber of Commerce *New York Chapter* 500 Fifth Ave Rm 1800 .... New York NY 10110 *Web:* www.amcham.ch	212-246-7789	246-1366	138
Swissline Precision Mfg. Inc 23-A Ashton Pkwy .... Cumberland RI 02864 *Web:* www.swisslineprecision.com	401-333-8888		757

	City	State	Zip	Phone	Fax	Class
Swisslog 10825 E 47th Ave	Denver	CO	80239	303-371-7770	373-7870	207
TF: 800-525-1841 ■ *Web:* www.swisslog.com						
Swissomation Inc						
112 Marschall Creek Rd	Fredericksburg	TX	78624	830-997-6565		350
TF: 800-523-5474 ■ *Web:* www.swissomation.com						
Swissotel Management (USA) LLC						
323 E Wacker Dr	Chicago	IL	60601	312-565-0565		378
Web: www.swissotel.com						
Switch Lighting & Design LLC						
1207 Vine St	Cincinnati	OH	45202	513-721-8100		362
Web: theswitchcollection.com						
Switchcraft Inc 5555 N Elston Ave	Chicago	IL	60630	773-792-2700	792-2129	253
Web: www.switchcraft.com						
Switchfast Technologies						
4043 N Ravenswood Ste 203	Chicago	IL	60613	773-241-3007		196
TF: 800-776-5646 ■ *Web:* www.switchfast.com						
Switlik Parachute Company Inc						
1325 E State St	Trenton	NJ	08609	609-587-3300		711
Web: www.switlik.com						
Switzerland 633 Third Ave 29th Fl	New York	NY	10011	212-286-1540	599-4266	784
Web: www.eda.admin.ch						
Consulate General						
456 Montgomery St Ste 1500	San Francisco	CA	94104	415-788-2272	788-1402	257
Web: www.eda.admin.ch/sanfrancisco						
Consulate General						
11859 Wilshire Blvd Ste 501	Los Angeles	CA	90025	310-575-1145	575-1982	257
Web: www.eda.admin.ch/losangeles						
Embassy 2900 Cathedral Ave NW	Washington	DC	20008	202-745-7900	387-2564	257
Web: www.swissemb.org						
Switzerland County						
212 W Main St County Courthouse	Vevay	IN	47043	812-427-3410	427-3179	338
Web: switzerland-county.com						
Switzerland Tourism						
608 Fifth Ave Ste 202	New York	NY	10020	212-757-5944	262-6116	775
TF: 800-794-7795 ■ *Web:* www.myswitzerland.com						
Swivelier Company Inc						
600 Bradley Hill Rd	Blauvelt	NY	10913	845-353-1455	353-1512	439
Web: www.swivelier.com						
Swix Sport USA Inc 600 Research Dr	Wilmington	MA	01887	978-657-4820		717
Web: www.swixsport.com						
SWMC (Southwest Washington Medical Ctr)						
400 NE Mother Joseph Pl PO Box 1600	Vancouver	WA	98664	360-514-2000		374-3
Web: peacehealth.org/southwest						
SWMC (Southwestern Medical Ctr)						
5602 SW Lee Blvd	Lawton	OK	73505	580-531-4700	531-4702	374-3
Web: swmconline.com						
Swope Art Museum 25 S Seventh St	Terre Haute	IN	47807	812-238-1676	238-1677	520
TF: 800-222-7270 ■ *Web:* www.swope.org						
SWOSU (Southwestern Oklahoma State University)						
100 Campus Dr	Weatherford	OK	73096	580-772-6611		565
TF: 800-669-1656 ■ *Web:* www.swosu.edu						
SWOT Management Group Inc						
105 Raider Blvd Ste 201	Hillsborough	NJ	08844	908-359-7968		317
Web: www.swotmg.com						
SwRI (Southwest Research Institute)						
6220 Culebra Rd	San Antonio	TX	78238	210-684-5111	522-3496*	668
**Fax:* Hum Res ■ *Web:* swri.org						
SWS Financial Services Inc						
1201 Elm St Ste 3500	Dallas	TX	75270	214-[illegible]-1000		690
Web: www.burfordadvisors.com						
SWTC (Southwest Wisconsin Technical College)						
1800 Bronson Blvd	Fennimore	WI	53809	608-822-3262	822-6019	800
TF: 800-362-3322 ■ *Web:* www.swtc.edu						
Swvhec PO Box 1987	Abingdon	VA	24212	276-619-4302		166
Web: www.swcenter.edu						
SY Bancorp Inc 1040 E Main St	Louisville	KY	40206	502-582-2571		360-2
NASDAQ: SYBT ■ *TF:* 800-625-9066 ■ *Web:* www.syb.com						
Syagen Technology Inc 1411 Warner Ave	Tustin	CA	92780	714-258-4400		743
TF: 877-258-8250 ■ *Web:* www.syagen.com						
Syar Industries Inc						
2301 Napa Vallejo Hwy	Napa	CA	94558	707-252-8711		503-5
Web: syar.com						
Sybaris Clubs International Inc						
2430 E Rand Rd	Arlington Heights	IL	60004	847-637-3000		378
TF: 800-345-8082 ■ *Web:* www.sybaris.com						
Sybven LLC						
2625 Executive Park Dr Ste 5-3	Weston	FL	33325	954-837-0078		809
Web: www.sybven.com						
Sycamore Shoals State Historic Park						
1651 W Elk Ave	Elizabethton	TN	37643	423-543-5808		565
Web: www.state.tn.us						
Sycamore State Park						
4675 N Diamond Mill Rd	Trotwood	OH	45426	513-523-6347		565
Web: www.ohiodnr.com						
Sycamores Terrace Retirement						
1427 Lebanon Pk	Nashville	TN	37210	615-242-2412		371
Web: www.sycamoresterrace.com						
Sycara Inc						
6263 N Scottsdale Rd Ste 180	Scottsdale	AZ	85250	855-479-2272		631
TF: 855-479-2272 ■ *Web:* www.sycaralocal.com						
Syclone Designs Inc						
32 Jack Heard Dr Ste 200	Dawsonville	GA	30534	706-265-4394		225
Web: syclone.net						
Sycuan Band of Kumeyaay Nation						
2 Kwaaypaay Ct	El Cajon	CA	92019	619-445-2613		303
Web: www.sycuantribe.com						
Sycuan Casino & Resort						
5469 Casino Way	El Cajon	CA	92019	619-445-6002		133
TF General: 800-279-2826 ■ *Web:* www.sycuan.com						
Syd's Place 2992 West Lake Rd	Erie	PA	16505	814-838-3089		671
Sydell Group Ltd 1170 Broadway	New York	NY	10001	646-307-9600		377
Web: www.sydellgroup.com						
Sydney & Area Chamber of Commerce						
275 Charlotte St	Sydney	NS	B1P1C6	902-564-6453	539-7487	137
Web: www.sydneyareachamber.ca						
Sydneys Closet						
11840 Dorsett Rd	Maryland Heights	MO	63043	314-344-5066		157-6
TF: 888-479-3639 ■ *Web:* www.sydneyscloset.com						
Sydnor Hydro Inc						
2111 Magnolia St PO Box 27186	Richmond	VA	23261	804 643 2725		806
TF: 800-552-7714 ■ *Web:* www.sydnorhydro.com						
Syfan USA Corp 1522 Twin Bridges Rd	Everetts	NC	27825	888-597-9326		601
TF: 888-597-9326 ■ *Web:* www.syfanusa.com						
SYGMA Network Inc						
5550 Blazer Pkwy Ste 300	Dublin	OH	43017	877-441-1144		297-8
TF: 877-441-1144 ■ *Web:* www.sygmanetwork.com						
Sykes Enterprises Inc						
400 N Ashley Dr Ste 2800	Tampa	FL	33602	813-274-1000		180
NASDAQ: SYKE ■ *TF:* 800-867-9537 ■ *Web:* www.sykes.com						
Sylhan LLC 210 Rodeo Dr	Edgewood	NY	11717	631-243-6600		757
Web: www.sylhan.com						
Sylios Corp						
735 Arlington Ave N Ste 308	St. Petersburg	FL	33701	727-821-6200		536
Web: www.sylios.com						
Sylvan Dale Guest Ranch						
2939 N County Rd 31 D	Loveland	CO	80538	970-667-3915	635-9336	239
Web: www.sylvandale.com						
Sylvan Inc 90 Glade Dr	Kittanning	PA	16201	724-543-3900	543-7583	10-7
TF: 866-352-7520 ■ *Web:* www.sylvaninc.com						
Sylvan Lake State Park						
10200 Brush Creek Rd	Eagle	CO	81631	970-328-2021		565
Web: cpw.state.co.us						
Sylvan Learning Centers						
4 N Park Dr Ste 500	Hunt Valley	MD	21030	888-338-2283		242
TF: 888-338-2283 ■ *Web:* sylvanlearning.com						
Sylvan Nursery Inc 1028 Horseneck Rd	Westport	MA	02790	508-636-4573		293
Web: sylvannursery.com						
Sylvania Area Chamber of Commerce						
5632 Main St	Sylvania	OH	43560	419-882-2135	885-7740	139
TF: 800-848-1300 ■ *Web:* www.sylvaniachamber.org						
Sylvania Steel Corp						
4169 Holland Sylvania Rd	Toledo	OH	43623	419-885-3838		492
TF General: 800-435-0986 ■ *Web:* www.sylvaniasteel.com						
Sylvia's Restaurant						
1843 Southmost Rd	Brownsville	TX	78521	956-542-9220		671
Symantec Corp 350 Ellis St	Mountain View	CA	94043	650-527-8000	527-8050	178-12
NASDAQ: SYMC ■ *TF:* 800-441-7234 ■ *Web:* www.symantec.com						
Symar Installations Inc						
1960 Foxridge Dr	Kansas City	KS	66106	913-236-4441		321
Web: symarinstallations.com						
Symbion Inc						
40 Burton Hills Blvd Ste 500	Nashville	TN	37215	615-234-5900	234-5998	352
Web: www.symbion.com						
Symblaze Inc						
9229 Sunset Blvd Ste 422	Los Angeles	CA	90069	310-859-6100		195
Web: www.symblaze.com						
Symbol Mattress Co 1814 High Pt Ave	Richmond	VA	23230	804-353-8965		471
Web: www.symbolmattress.com						
Symbolic Displays Inc						
1917 E St Andrew Pl	Santa Ana	CA	92705	714-258-2811	258-2810	22
TF: 800-[illegible]-1403 ■ *Web:* www.symbolicdisplays.com						
Symbolic Systems Inc 25 Chatham Rd	Summit	NJ	07901	908-665-5940		196
Web: www.symbolic.com						
Symbolist 1090 Texan Trl	Grapevine	TX	76051	800-498-6885		195
TF: 800-498-6885 ■ *Web:* www.symbolist.com						
Symco Group Inc						
5012 Bristol Industrial Way Ste 105	Buford	GA	30518	770-[illegible]		171
TF: 800-878-8002 ■ *Web:* www.symcogroup.com						
Symetra Life Insurance Co						
777 108th Ave NE Ste 1200	Bellevue	WA	98004	425-256-8000		391-2
TF: 800-574-0233 ■ *Web:* www.symetra.com						
Symetri Internet Marketing						
6520 Airport Ctr Dr Ste 208	Greensboro	NC	27409	336-285-0940		195
Web: www.symetri.com						
Symetrix Corp						
5055 Mark Dabling Blvd	Colorado Springs	CO	80918	719-594-6145	598-3437	696
Web: www.symetrixcorp.com						
Symitar Systems Inc 8985 Balboa Ave	San Diego	CA	92123	619-542-6700		177
Web: www.symitar.com						
SYMMEDRx						
10955 Lowell Ave Ste 600	Overland Park	KS	66210	913-338-4900		194
Web: www.symmedrx.com						
Symmes Maini & McKee Assoc (SMMA)						
1000 Massachusetts Ave	Cambridge	MA	02138	617-547-5400	648-4920*	261
**Fax Area Code:* 800 ■ *Web:* www.smma.com						
Symmetricom Inc 2300 Orchard Pkwy	San Jose	CA	95131	408-433-0910	428-7998	735
NASDAQ: SYMM ■ *TF:* 888-367-7966 ■ *Web:* microsemi.com/index.php						
Symmetrix Technologies LLC						
106 N Denton Tap Rd Ste 210-262	Coppell	TX	75019	972-599-1585		180
Web: www.symmetrixtech.com						
Symmetry Electronics Inc						
20250 144th Ave NE #100	Woodinville	WA	98072	425-487-6809		612
Web: www.symmetryelectronics.com						
Symmetry Software Corp						
14350 N 87th St Ste 250	Scottsdale	AZ	85260	480-596-1500		174
Web: www.symmetry.com						
Symmons Industries Inc 31 Brooks Dr	Braintree	MA	02184	781-848-2250	843-3849	609
TF: 800-796-6667 ■ *Web:* www.symmons.com						
Symms Fruit Ranch Inc						
14068 Sunny Slope Rd	Caldwell	ID	83607	208-459-4821	459-6932	315-3
TF: 800-421-8814 ■ *Web:* symmsfruit.com						
Symon's Fire Protection Inc						
12155 Paine Pl Ste R	Poway	CA	92064	619-588-6364		45
Web: www.symonsfp.com						
Symons Capital Management Inc						
650 Washington Rd Ste 800	Pittsburgh	PA	15228	412-344-7690		237
TF: 888-344-7740 ■ *Web:* www.symonscapital.com						
Symphony Asset Management Inc						
555 California St	San Francisco	CA	94104	415-676-4000		690
Web: www.symphonyasset.com						
Symphony Capital LLC						
485 Madison Ave 7th Fl	New York	NY	10022	212-632-5400	632-5401	690
Web: www.symphonycapital.com						
Symphony Corp 22 E Mifflin St Ste 400	Madison	WI	53703	608-294-4090		809
TF: 800-446-7089 ■ *Web:* www.symphonycorp.com						
Symphony Ctr 220 S Michigan Ave	Chicago	IL	60604	312-294-3000	294-3035*	572
**Fax:* Mktg ■ *TF Cust Svc:* 800-223-7114 ■ *Web:* www.cso.org						

Name / Address	City	State	Zip	Phone	Fax	Class
Symphony Nova Scotia 6101 University Ave Dalhousie Arts Ctr *TF:* 800-874-1669 ■ *Web:* www.symphonynovascotia.ca	Halifax	NS	B3H4R2	902-494-3820	494-2883	573-3
Symphony of the Mountains 1200 E Ctr St *Web:* www.symphonyofthemountains.org	Kingsport	TN	37660	423-392-8423	392-8428	573-3
Symphony Orchestra Augusta 1301 Greene St Ste 200 *Web:* soaugusta.org	Augusta	GA	30901	706-826-4705	826-4735	573-3
Symphony Printing Company Inc 19 21 Brook St *Web:* www.symphonyprinting.com	Belleville	NJ	07109	973-751-5100		627
Symphony Silicon Valley 345 S First St *Web:* www.symphonysiliconvalley.org	San Jose	CA	95113	408-286-2600	286-2600	573-3
Symphony Technology Group LLC (STG) 2475 Hanover St *Web:* www.symphonytg.com	Palo Alto	CA	94304	650-935-9500	935-9501	178-11
Symplr 616 Cypress Creek Pkwy Ste 800 *Web:* www.symplr.com	Houston	TX	77090	281-863-9500		225
Symposia Medicus 399 Taylor Blvd Ste 201 *TF:* 800-327-3161 ■ *Web:* symposiamedicus.org	Pleasant Hill	CA	94523	925-969-1789		242
Symposium Cafe Restaurants 6021 Yonge St Unit 475 *Web:* symposiumcafe.com	Toronto	ON	M2M3W2	416-449-3611		671
Symrise Inc 300 N St *Web:* www.symrise.com	Teterboro	NJ	07608	201-288-3200	462-2200	145
SYMTECH Inc 100 Sunbeam Rd *TF:* 800-526-1072 ■ *Web:* www.symtech-usa.com	Spartanburg	SC	29303	864-578-7101		358
Synacor Inc 40 La Riviere Dr Ste 300 *Web:* www.synacor.com	Buffalo	NY	14202	716-853-1362		395
Synactive Inc 950 Tower Ln Ste 750 *Web:* www.synactive.net	Foster City	CA	94404	650-341-3310	341-3610	178-2
Syna-Flex Rubber Products Company Inc 1223 Cochran Ave *Web:* www.synaflex.com	Talladega	AL	35160	256-362-2431		677
Synagro Technologies Inc 435 Williams Ct Ste 100 *TF:* 800-370-0035 ■ *Web:* www.synagro.com	Baltimore	MD	21220	800-370-0035		804
Synalloy Corp 775 Spartan Blvd Ste 102 PO Box 5627 *NASDAQ: SYNL* ■ *TF Orders:* 800-937-5449 ■ *Web:* www.synalloy.com	Spartanburg	SC	29304	864-585-3605	596-1501	595
SynaMed L L C 555 Eighth Ave Ste 2210	New York	NY	10018	212-239-2800	202-7705	396
Synapse Biomedical Inc 300 Artino St *Web:* synapsebiomedical.com	Oberlin	OH	44074	440-774-2488		475
Synaptec Software Inc 4155 E Jewell Ave Ste 600 *TF:* 800-569-3377 ■ *Web:* www.lawbase.com	Denver	CO	80222	303-320-4420		35
Synaptic Decisions 340 N Sam Houston Pkwy Ste 120 *Web:* www.synapticdecisions.com	Houston	TX	77060	832-300-9800		463
Synaptics Inc 1251 McKay Dr *NASDAQ: SYNA* ■ *TF:* 800-638-4564 ■ *Web:* www.synaptics.com	San Jose	CA	95131	408-904-1100		173-1
Synaptis Inc 150 Cornerstone Dr Ste 201 *Web:* www.synaptis.com	Cary	NC	27519	919-844-5840		463
SynCardia Systems Inc 1992 E Silverlake Rd *Web:* www.syncardia.com	Tucson	AZ	85713	520-545-1234		477
Synchromesh Studios 1116 Ford Ave *Web:* www.synchromeshstudios.com	Birmingham	AL	35217	205-808-0808		657
Synchronoss Technologies Inc 200 Crossing Blvd *NASDAQ: SNCR* ■ *TF:* 866-620-3940 ■ *Web:* www.synchronoss.com	Bridgewater	NJ	08807	866-620-3940		224
Synchrony Inc 4655 Technology Dr *Web:* www.synchrony.com	Salem	VA	24153	540-444-4200	444-4201	261
Synchrotron Radiation Ctr (SRC) 3731 Schneider Dr *Web:* www.src.wisc.edu	Stoughton	WI	53589	608-877-2000	877-2001	668
Synch-Solutions Inc 211 W Wacker Dr Ste 300 *Web:* www.synch-solutions.com	Chicago	IL	60606	312-252-3700		226
Synco Chemical Corp 24 Davinci Dr *Web:* www.super-lube.com	Bohemia	NY	11716	631-567-5300		541
SynCot Plastics Inc 350 Eastwood Dr *Web:* www.syncot.com	Belmont	NC	28012	704-967-0010		146
Syncratec Solutions LLC 7 upton ln *Web:* www.syncratec.com	Yardley	PA	19067	267-266-5596		138
Syncretic Software Inc 228 Philadelphia Pk *TF:* 800-205-3039 ■ *Web:* www.syncretic.com	Wilmington	DE	19809	302-762-2600		180
Syncro Corp PO Box 890 *Web:* www.syncrocorp.com	Arab	AL	35016	256-931-7800	931-7920	247
Syncro Corp 1030 Sundown Dr NW *Web:* www.syncrocorp.com	Arab	AL	35016	256-586-6045		247
Syncroflo Inc 6700 Best Friend Rd *TF:* 800-231-8240 ■ *Web:* www.syncroflo.com	Norcross	GA	30071	770-447-4443		641
Syncsort Inc 50 Tice Blvd **Fax Area Code:* 201 ■ *TF:* 877-700-0970 ■ *Web:* www.syncsort.com	Woodcliff Lake	NJ	07677	877-700-0970	882-8305*	178-12
Syndax Pharmaceuticals Inc 400 Totten Pond Rd Ste 110 *Web:* www.syndax.com	Waltham	MA	02451	781-419-1400		231
Syndesi Solutions Inc 611 E Hobbs St *Web:* www.syndesisolutions.com	Athens	AL	35611	256-867-4135		261
Syndetics Inc 10395 Democracy Ln *Web:* syndetics-inc.com	Fairfax	VA	22030	703-273-8350		463
SynDevRx Inc 1 Broadway 14th Fl *Web:* www.syndevrx.com	Cambridge	MA	02142	617-401-3110		238
Syndexa Pharmaceuticals Corp 480 Arsenal St Bldg 1 *Web:* www.syndexa.com	Watertown	MA	02472	617-607-7283		238
Syndicate Sales Inc PO Box 756 *TF:* 800-428-0515 ■ *Web:* www.syndicatesales.com	Kokomo	IN	46903	765-457-7277		608
Syndicated Capital Inc 1299 Ocean Ave Ste 210 *Web:* www.computercafe.com	Santa Monica	CA	90401	310-255-4490		194
Syndicated Solutions Inc PO Box 1078 *Web:* www.syndicatedsolutions.com	Ridgefield	CT	06877	203-431-0790	431-0792	646
Syndication Networks Corp 8700 Waukegan Rd Ste 250 *TF:* 800-743-1988 ■ *Web:* syndication.net	Morton Grove	IL	60053	847-583-9000	583-9025	646
Syndrome Distribution Inc 1410 Vantage Ct *Web:* www.syndromedist.com	Vista	CA	92081	760-560-0440		711
Syndyne Corp 12109 NE 95th St *TF:* 800-473-5270 ■ *Web:* syndyne.com	Vancouver	WA	98682	360-256-8466		195
Synechron Inc 15 Maiden Ln Ste 1100 *Web:* www.synechron.com	New York	NY	10038	212-619-5200		193
Synectic Solutions Inc 1701 Pacific Ave Ste 260 *Web:* www.synecticsolutions.com	Oxnard	CA	93033	805-483-4800		194
Synectic Systems Inc 4180 Via Real Ste A *Web:* www.synecticsusa.com	Carpenteria	CA	93013	805-745-1920		525
Synemed Inc 4562 E Second St Ste A *TF:* 800-777-0650 ■ *Web:* www.synemed.com	Benicia	CA	94510	707-745-8386		476
Synercomm Inc 3265 Gateway Rd Ste 650 *Web:* www.synercomm.com	Brookfield	WI	53045	262-373-7100	373-7171	196
Synergem Emergency Services L L C 1007 Warren St *Web:* www.synergemtech.com	Greensboro	NC	27403	336-808-0911		180
Synergent 2 Ledgeview Dr *TF:* 800-341-0180 ■ *Web:* www.synergentcorp.com	Westbrook	ME	04092	207-773-5671		317
Synergent Biochem Inc 12026 Centralia Rd Ste H *TF:* 800-432-1000 ■ *Web:* www.synergentbiochem.com	Hawaiian Gardens	CA	90716	562-809-3389	809-6191	231
Synergex International Corp 2330 Gold Meadow Way *TF:* 800-366-3472 ■ *Web:* www.synergex.com	Gold River	CA	95670	916-635-7300	635-6549	178-10
Synergistics Inc 9 Tech Cir Ste 2 *TF:* 866-455-5222 ■ *Web:* www.millennium-groupinc.com	Natick	MA	01760	508-655-1340	651-2902	178-11
Synergon Solutions Inc 1335 Gateway Dr *TF:* 800-820-6103 ■ *Web:* www.synergon.net	Melbourne	FL	32901	321-728-2674		225
Synergy 78474 Hwy 111 Ste A *Web:* www.synergyis.us	La Quinta	CA	92253	760-601-5244		180
Synergy 230 W Monroe St 24th Fl *Web:* www.mysynergy.com	Chicago	IL	60606	312-899-1024		260
Synergy Advisors LLC 840 Apollo St Ste 213 *Web:* www.synergyadvisorsllc.com	El Segundo	CA	90245	310-414-3200		690
Synergy Associates LLC 550 Clydesdale Trl *TF:* 888-763-9920 ■ *Web:* www.synllc.com	Medina	MN	55340	888-763-9920		180
Synergy Business Solutions Inc 16250 SW Upper Boones Ferry Rd *Web:* www.synergybusiness.com	Portland	OR	97224	503-601-4100		177
Synergy Ceramics Gp LLC 5200 Tennyson Pkwy Ste 400 *Web:* synergyceramics.com	Plano	TX	75024	972-608-0515		191-1
Synergy Co of Utah LLC, The 2279 S Resource Blvd *TF:* 800-723-0277 ■ *Web:* www.thesynergycompany.com	Moab	UT	84532	800-723-0277		668
Synergy Data Solutions Inc 1104 S State St Apt A *TF:* 800-742-9970 ■ *Web:* synergydata.com	Champaign	IL	61820	217-356-2522		180
Synergy Direct Response 130 E Alton Ave *TF:* 888-902-6166 ■ *Web:* www.synergydr.com	Santa Ana	CA	92707	888-902-6166		195
Synergy Employment Group. Inc 14 Greenfield Rd *Web:* www.synergyempgroup.com	Lancaster	PA	17602	717-824-4005		260
Synergy Environmental Lab Inc 1990 Prospect Ct *Web:* synergy-lab.net	Appleton	WI	54914	920-830-2455		743
Synergy Information Tech Group 104 A Republic Ave *Web:* www.synergyitg.com	Lafayette	LA	70508	337-234-5767		396
Synergy Investment Group Ltd 8320 University Exec Park Dr Ste 112 *Web:* synergyinvestments.com	Charlotte	NC	28262	704-333-7637		390
Synergy Law Group LLC 730 W Randolph St Ste 600 *Web:* synergylawgroup.com	Chicago	IL	60661	312-454-0015	454-0261	445
Synergy Legal Staffing 500 E Morehead St Ste 101 *Web:* www.synergylegalstaffing.com	Charlotte	NC	28202	704-366-4540		260
Synergy Networks Inc 10970 S Cleveland Ave Ste 406 *Web:* www.snworks.com	Fort Myers	FL	33907	239-790-7000		225
Synergy Resources Inc 3500 Sunrise Hwy Bldg 100 Ste 201 *TF:* 866-896-6347 ■ *Web:* www.synergyresources.net	Great River	NY	11739	631-665-2050		174
Synergy Solutions Inc 3141 N Third Ave Ste C-100 *Web:* www.synergysolutionsinc.com	Phoenix	AZ	85013	602-296-1600		737
Synergy Telcom Inc 8222 Indy Ln *TF:* 800-732-1467 ■ *Web:* www.synergy-tel.com	Indianapolis	IN	46214	317-713-1652		179
Synergy Worldwide Inc 1955 W Grove Pkwy Ste 100 *Web:* us.synergyworldwide.com	Pleasant Grove	UT	84062	801-769-7800		345
Synerject LLC 201 Enterprise Dr *Web:* www.synerject.com	Newport News	VA	23603	757-890-4900		247
Synerlution Inc Po Box 4336 *Web:* www.synerlution.com	Aguadilla	PR	00605	787-493-0864		261
Synertel 80 Tanforan Ave Ste 14 *Web:* www.synertel.com	San Francisco	CA	94080	415-970-0100		196
Synesis International Inc 30 Creekview Ct *Web:* www.synesisintl.com	Greenville	SC	29615	864-288-1550		261
SyNet Technology Solutions Inc 205 Hallene Rd Ste 101 *Web:* www.synetinc.com	Warwick	RI	02886	401-736-6450		196

Phone | Fax | Class

Synetra Inc 8180 Lakeview Ctr. Odessa TX 79765 432-561-7200 179
Web: www.synetra.com

Synex International Inc
1444 Alberni St 4th Fl. Vancouver BC V6G2Z4 604-688-8271 787
Web: www.synex.com

SYNEXXUS Inc
2425 Wilson Blvd Ste 400 Arlington VA 22201 866-707-4594 261
TF: 866-707-4594 ■ *Web:* www.synexxus.com

SYN-FAB Inc 7863 Schillinger Park Rd Mobile AL 36608 251-633-4942 246
Web: www.synfab.com

Syngenta Corp
3411 Silverside Rd Ste 100 Wilmington DE 19810 302-425-2000 280
TF: 800-555-2470 ■ *Web:* www.syngenta.com

Syngenta Crop Protection Inc
410 Swing Rd Greensboro NC 27409 336-632-6000 632-7353* 280
**Fax:* Sales ■ *Web:* www.syngenta.com

SYNNEX Canada 200 Ronson Dr. Etobicoke ON M9W5Z9 416-240-7012 240-2622* 174
**Fax:* Hum Res ■ *TF:* 800-268-1220 ■ *Web:* www.synnex.ca

Synnex Corp 44201 Nobel Dr. Fremont CA 94538 510-656-3333 668-3777 174
NYSE: SNX ■ *TF Cust Svc:* 800-756-1888 ■ *Web:* www.synnex.com

Synopsys Inc
700 E Middlefield Rd Mountain View CA 94043 650-584-5000 965-8637 178-10
NASDAQ: SNPS ■ *TF:* 800-541-7737 ■ *Web:* www.synopsys.com

Synovate Inc 222 S Riverside Plaza Chicago IL 60606 312-526-4000 466

Synovis Life Technologies Inc
2575 University Ave Saint Paul MN 55114 651-796-7300 642-9018 477
NASDAQ: SYNO ■ *TF:* 800-255-4018 ■ *Web:* www.synovislife.com

Synovis Micro Companies Alliance Inc
439 Industrial Ln Birmingham AL 35211 205-941-0111 475
TF: 800-510-3318 ■ *Web:* www.synovismicro.com

Synovus Financial Corp
1111 Bay Ave Ste 500 PO Box 120 Columbus GA 31902 706-649-2311 360-2
NYSE: SNV ■ *TF:* 888-796-6887 ■ *Web:* www.synovus.com

SynQor Inc 155 Swanson Rd Boxborough MA 01719 978-849-0600 849-0601 253
Web: www.synqor.com

Synrad Inc 4600 Campus Pl. Mukilteo WA 98275 425-349-3500 349-3667 425
TF: 800-796-7231 ■ *Web:* www.synrad.com

Synre Voice Technologies Inc
200 Cochrane Dr Markham ON L3R8E7 905-946-8500 177
Web: www.synrevoice.com

Syntec LLC 438 Lavender Dr Rome GA 30165 800-526-8428 235-1768* 131
**Fax Area Code:* 706 ■ *TF:* 800-526-8428 ■ *Web:* www.syntecind.com

Syn-Tech Inc
3100 Ridgelake Dr Ste 101 Metairie LA 70002 504-835-7825 835-7853 246

Syntegrity Network Inc
9500 Braddock Rd Fairfax VA 22032 703-425-3078 196
TF: 800-515-3636 ■ *Web:* www.syntegritynet.com

Syntel Inc 525 E Big Beaver Rd Ste 300 Troy MI 48083 248-619-2800 619-2888 180
NASDAQ: SYNT ■ *TF:* 800-522-4400 ■ *Web:* www.syntelinc.com

Syntell Inc 2954 Boul Laurier Quebec QC G1V4T2 418-266-0900 177
Web: www.syntell.com

Syntelli Solutions Inc
13925 Ballantyne Corporate Pl Ste 260 Charlotte NC 28277 877-796-8355 796-8355 174
TF: 877-796-8355 ■ *Web:* www.syntelli.com

Synter Resource Group LLC
5935 Rivers Ave Ste 102 Charleston SC 29406 843-746-2200 2
Web: www.synterresource.com

Syntergy Inc
6515 El Camino Del Teatro La Jolla CA 92037 858-964-3243 809
TF: 800-754-6054 ■ *Web:* www.syntergy.com

Syntes Language Group
7465 E Peakview Ave Centennial CO 80111 303-779-1288 768
Web: www.syntes.com

Synthes Spine Inc 325 Paramount Dr. Raynham MA 02767 508-880-8100 475
Web: www.depuysynthes.com

Synthesis 210 W Sixth St. Chico CA 95928 530-899-7708 532-3
Web: synthesisweekly.com

Synthesis Professional Services Inc
12339 Carroll Ave. Rockville MD 20852 301-770-8970 463
Web: www.synthesisps.com

Synthetic Organic Chemical Manufacturers Assn (SOCMA)
1850 M St NW Ste 700 Washington DC 20036 202-721-4100 296-8120 49-19
Web: www.socma.com

Synthetic Turf Resources 809 Kenner St Dalton GA 30721 706-272-4200 291
TF: 800-723-8873 ■ *Web:* syntheticturfresources.com

Syntrio
50 California St Ste 3260 San Francisco CA 94111 415-951-7913 951-7915 39
TF: 888-289-6670 ■ *Web:* www.syntrio.com

Syntrix Biosystems Inc
215 Clay St NW Ste B-5 Auburn WA 98001 253-833-8009 231
Web: www.syntrixbio.com

Syntrol Plumbing Heating Adn Air Inc
2120 March Rd. Roseville CA 95747 916-772-5813 610
Web: syntrol.net

Syntroleum Corp 5416 S Yale Ave Ste 400 Tulsa OK 74135 918-592-7900 536
NASDAQ: SYNM

Syntron Bioresearch Inc
2774 Loker Ave W. Carlsbad CA 92010 760-930-2200 930-2212 668
Web: www.syntron.net

Synutra International Inc
2275 Research Blvd Ste 500 Rockville MD 20850 301-840-3888 799
NASDAQ: SYUT ■ *TF:* 866-405-2350 ■ *Web:* www.synutra.com

Synventive Molding Solutions Inc
10 Centennial Dr. Peabody MA 01960 978-750-8065 646-3600 386
TF: 800-367-5662 ■ *Web:* www.synventive.com

SYO Computer Engineering Services Inc
42621 Garfield Rd Ste 108 Clinton Township MI 48038 586-286-2557 809
TF: 800-971-6587 ■ *Web:* www.syo.com

Sypris Electronics LLC
10421 University Center Dr Ste 100 Tampa FL 33612 813-972-6000 972-6012 253
TF: 800-937-9220 ■ *Web:* www.sypris.com

Sypris Solutions Inc
101 Bullitt Ln Ste 450 Louisville KY 40222 502-329-2000 329-2050 253
NASDAQ: SYPR ■ *TF:* 800-588-9119 ■ *Web:* www.sypris.com

Syracuse Academy of Science
1001 Park Ave. Syracuse NY 13204 315-428-8997 148
Web: sascs.org

Syracuse City School District, The
725 Harrison St Syracuse NY 13210 315-435-4499 685
TF: 800-662-1220 ■ *Web:* www.syracusecityschools.com

Syracuse Glass Company Inc
1 General Motors Dr PO Box 381 Syracuse NY 13206 315-437-9971 330
Web: www.syracuseglass.com

Syracuse Hancock International Airport
1000 Colonel Eileen Collins Blvd. Syracuse NY 13212 315-454-4330 454-8757 27
TF: 800-631-8405 ■ *Web:* www.syrairport.org

Syracuse New Times 1415 W Genesee St Syracuse NY 13204 315-422-7011 532-5
Web: syracusenewtimes.com

Syracuse Opera
411 Montgomery St Ste 60. Syracuse NY 13202 315-475-5915 475-6319 573-2
Web: www.syracuseopera.com

Syracuse Plastics LLC
7400 Morgan Rd. Liverpool NY 13090 315-637-9881 637-9260 608
Web: www.syracuseplastics.com

Syracuse Research Corp (SRC)
7502 Round Pond Rd North Syracuse NY 13212 315-452-8000 668
TF: 800-724-0451 ■ *Web:* www.srcinc.com

Syracuse Scenery & Stage Lighting Company Inc
101 Monarch Dr Liverpool NY 13088 315-453-8096 453-7897 722
TF: 800-453-7775 ■ *Web:* www.syracusescenery.com

Syracuse Stage 820 E Genesee St. Syracuse NY 13210 315-443-4008 443-9846 573-4
Web: www.syracusestage.org

Syracuse Stamping Co
1054 S Clinton St Syracuse NY 13202 315-476-5306 474-8876 489
TF: 800-581-5555 ■ *Web:* www.syraco.com

Syracuse Suds Factory
320 S Clinton St Syracuse NY 13202 315-471-2253 671
Web: s502965190.onlinehome.us

Syracuse University 900 S Crouse Ave Syracuse NY 13244 315-443-3611 443-4226* 166
**Fax:* Admissions ■ *TF:* 800-782-5867 ■ *Web:* www.syracuse.edu

Syracuse University College of Law
950 Irving Ave Syracuse NY 13244 315-443-1962 443-9568 167-1
Web: www.law.syr.edu

Syracuse University Libraries
222 Waverly Ave Syracuse NY 13244 315-443-2093 443-9510* 434-6
**Fax:* Admin ■ *Web:* library.syr.edu

Syrasoft Llc 307 Kasson Rd. Camillus NY 13031 315-708-0341 525
Web: syrasoft.com

Syreon Corp 260 - 1401 W Eighth Ave. Vancouver BC V6H1C9 604-676-5900 238
TF: 866-979-7366 ■ *Web:* www.syreon.com

Syria 820 Second Ave 15th Fl New York NY 10017 212-661-1313 983-4439 784
Web: www.un.int/syria

Syringa Networks LLC
3795 S Development Ave Boise ID 83705 208-229-6100 116
Web: www.syringanetworks.net

Sysazzle Inc 15815 S 46th St Ste 116, Phoenix AZ 85048 800-862-9545 721
TF: 800-862-9545 ■ *Web:* sysazzle.com

Sysco Central Ohio Inc
3100 Harrison Rd Columbus OH 43204 614-771-3801 305-3027* 297-8
**Fax Area Code:* 907 ■ *TF:* 800-735-3341 ■ *Web:* sysco.com

SYSCO Corp 1390 Enclave Pkwy Houston TX 77077 281-584-1390 297-8
NYSE: SYY ■ *Web:* www.sysco.com

Sysco Denver Inc 5000 Beeler St Denver CO 80238 303-585-2000 297-8
Web: www.sysco.com/about-sysco/sysco-denver.html

Sysco Food Services of Idaho Inc
5710 Pan Am Ave Boise ID 83716 208-345-9500 387-2598 297-8
TF: 800-747-9726 ■ *Web:* www.syscoidaho.com

Sysco Grand Rapids
3700 Sysco Ct SE Grand Rapids MI 49512 616-949-3700 297-8
TF: 800-669-6967 ■ *Web:* www.syscogr.com

Sysco Hampton Roads Inc
7000 Harbour View Blvd. Suffolk VA 23435 757-673-4000 297-8
TF: 800-234-2451 ■ *Web:* www.sysco.com

Sysco Indianapolis LLC
4000 W 62nd St Indianapolis IN 46268 317-291-2020 297-11
TF: 800-347-3920 ■ *Web:* www.syscoindy.com

Sysco Kansas City Inc
1915 E Kansas City Rd Olathe KS 66061 913-829-5555 780-8625 296-26
Web: www.kc.sysco.com

Sysco Newport Meat Company Inc
16691 Hale Ave. Irvine CA 92606 949-474-4040 296-26
Web: www.newportmeat.com

SYSCO Philadelphia LLC
600 Packer Ave. Philadelphia PA 19148 215-463-8200 297-11
Web: www.syscophilly.com/ordereze/1000/Page.aspx

Sysco Portland Inc
26250 SW Pkwy Ctr Dr. Wilsonville OR 97070 503-682-8700 299
Web: www.syscoportland.com

Sysco San Francisco Inc
5900 Stewart Ave Fremont CA 94538 510-226-3000 805
Web: syscosf.com

Sysco Seattle Inc 22820 54th Ave S Kent WA 98032 206-622-2261 296-21
Web: seattle.sysco.com

SYSCOM Inc
400 E Pratt St Inner Harbor Ctr Ste 502 Baltimore MD 21202 410-539-3737 180
Web: www.syscom.com

Syscon Inc 94 Mcfarland Blvd Northport AL 35476 205-758-2000 180
TF: 888-797-2661 ■ *Web:* www.sysconoline.com

Sys-con Media Inc
577 Chestnut Ridge Rd. Woodcliff Lake NJ 07677 201-802-3000 637-9
Web: www.sys-con.com

Syscor Controls & Automation Inc
201 - 60 Bastion Sq Victoria BC V8W1J2 250-361-1681 361-1682 256
Web: www.syscor.com

Sysintelli Inc
9466 Black Mtn Rd Ste 140 San Diego CA 92126 858-271-1600 177
Web: www.sysintelli.com

Syska & Hennessy Group 1515 Broadway New York NY 10036 212-921-2300 261
Web: www.syska.com

SysLogic Inc
375 Bishops Way Ste 105. Brookfield WI 53005 262-780-0380 177
Web: www.syslogicinc.com

Sysmex America Inc
577 Aptakisic Rd. Lincolnshire IL 60069 847-996-4500 996-4397 475
TF: 800-379-7639 ■ *Web:* www.sysmex.com

Company / Address	City	State	ZIP	Phone	Fax	Class
Sysnet Technology Solutions Inc						
4320 Stevens Creek Blvd Ste 229	San Jose	CA	95129	408-248-5000		180
Web: www.astirservices.net						
SYSPRO 959 S Coast Dr Ste 100	Costa Mesa	CA	92626	714-437-1000	437-1407	178-1
TF: 800-369-8649 ■ *Web:* www.syspro.com						
Syspro Technologies Inc						
6545 Preston Rd Ste 300	Plano	TX	75024	214-440-3820		393
Web: www.sysprotech.com						
Systagenix Wound Management (US) Inc						
400 Crown Colony Ste 302	Quincy	MA	02169	617-774-5500		475
TF: 800-970-2499 ■ *Web:* www.systagenix.com						
SYSTAP LLC 1737 Harvard St NW	Washington	DC	20009	801-328-3945		809
Systec Conveyor Corp						
10010 Conveyor Dr	Indianapolis	IN	46235	317-890-9230		358
Web: www.systecconveyors.com						
Systech Corp 16510 Via Esprillo	San Diego	CA	92127	858-674-6500	613-2400	176
TF: 800-800-8970 ■ *Web:* www.systech.com						
Systech Solutions Inc						
500 N Brand Blvd Ste 1900	Glendale	CA	91203	818-550-9690	550-9692	194
Web: www.systechusa.com						
Systechs Inc 249 W Baywood Ave Ste B	Orange	CA	92865	714-283-2890		320
TF: 800-561-3357 ■ *Web:* www.systechs.com						
Systecon Inc						
6121 Schumacher Pk Dr	West Chester	OH	45069	513-777-7722	777-0259	641
Web: www.systecon.com						
Systel Business Equipment Company Inc						
2604 Fort Bragg Rd	Fayetteville	NC	28303	910-321-7700		112
TF: 800-849-5900 ■ *Web:* www.systeloa.com						
System Automation						
7110 Samuel Morse Dr Ste 100	Columbia	MD	21046	800-839-4729		178-10
TF: 800-839-4729 ■ *Web:* www.systemautomation.com						
System Concepts Inc						
15900 N 78th St	Scottsdale	AZ	85260	480-951-8011		177
TF: 800-553-2438 ■ *Web:* www.foodtrak.com						
System Development Integration Inc (SDI)						
33 W Monroe St Ste 400	Chicago	IL	60603	312-580-7500	580-7600	180
Web: www.sdipresence.com						
System Dynamics International Inc (SDI)						
560 Discovery Dr NW	Huntsville	AL	35806	256-895-9000		261
Web: www.sdi-inc.com						
System Electric Co						
1278 Montalvo Way	Palm Springs	CA	92262	760-327-7847		189-4
Web: www.systemelectric.com						
System Engineering International Inc (SEI)						
5115 Pegasus Ct Ste Q	Frederick	MD	21704	301-694-9601	694-9608	787
TF: 800-765-4734 ■ *Web:* www.seipower.com						
System Improvements Inc						
238 S Peters Rd Ste 301	Knoxville	TN	37923	865-539-2139		196
Web: www.taproot.com						
System Innovators Inc						
10550 Deerwood Pk Blvd Ste 700	Jacksonville	FL	32256	800-963-5000		178-10
TF: 800-963-5000 ■ *Web:* systeminnovators.com						
System of Systems Analytics Inc						
11250 Waples Mill Rd Ste 300	Fairfax	VA	22030	703-349-7057		194
TF: 800-234-6760 ■ *Web:* www.sosacorp.com						
System Planning Corp (SPC)						
3601 Wilson Blvd	Arlington	VA	22201	703-351-8200		194
Web: www.sysplan.com						
System Scale Corp 4393 W 96th St	Indianapolis	IN	46268	317-876-9335		362
Web: www.system-scale.com						
System Sensor 3825 Ohio Ave	Saint Charles	IL	60174	630-377-6580	377-6495	253
TF Tech Supp: 800-736-7672 ■ *Web:* www.systemsensor.com						
System Solutions Inc						
3630 Commercial Ave	Northbrook	IL	60062	847-272-6160		179
Web: www.thessi.com						
Systematic Financial Management LP						
300 Frank W Burr Blvd Seventh Fl						
Glenpoint Ctr E 7th Fl	Teaneck	NJ	07666	201-928-1982		401
Web: www.sfmlp.com						
Systematics Inc 1025 Saunders Ln	West Chester	PA	19380	800-222-9353	430-8714*	811
**Fax Area Code:* 610 ■ *TF:* 800-222-9353 ■ *Web:* 800abcweld.com						
Systemax Inc 11 Harbor Pk Dr	Port Washington	NY	11050	516-608-7000	608-7001	173-2
NYSE: SYX ■ *TF:* 800-344-6783 ■ *Web:* www.systemax.com						
Systemes Pran Inc						
399 Jacquard St Ste 100	Quebec	QC	G1N4J6	418-688-7726		253
Web: www.pransystems.com						
SystemMetrics Corp						
900 Ft St Mall Ste 250	Honolulu	HI	96813	808-791-7000		387
Web: www.platinumlimousinehawaii.com						
Systems & Forecasts						
150 Great Neck Rd Ste 301	Great Neck	NY	11021	516-829-6444	466-1715	531-9
Web: www.systemsandforecasts.com						
Systems & Processes Engineering Corp (SPEC)						
6800 Burleson Rd Ste 320	Austin	TX	78744	512-479-7732		261
Web: www.spec.com						
Systems Application Engineering Inc						
3655 Westcenter Dr	Houston	TX	77042	713-783-6020		177
TF: 800-295-5510 ■ *Web:* www.saesystems.com						
Systems Contracting Corp						
214 N Washington Ave Ste 700	El Dorado	AR	71730	870-862-1315		189-10
Web: tsg.bz						
Systems East Inc 30 Basil Sawyer Dr	Hampton	VA	23666	757-766-8400		203
TF: 800-230-8734 ■ *Web:* systemseastinc.com						
Systems Engineering Technologies Corp						
6121 Lincolnia Rd Ste 200	Alexandria	VA	22312	703-941-7887		177
TF: 800-385-8977 ■ *Web:* www.sytechcorp.com						
Systems Exchange Inc						
26625 Carmel Ctr Pl	Carmel	CA	93923	831-649-3800		177
Web: www.tfdg.com						
Systems House, The						
1033 Rte 46 E Ste A202	Clifton	NJ	07013	973-777-8050		225
TF: 800-637-5556 ■ *Web:* tshinc.com						
Systems Implementers Inc						
350 S Williams Blvd	Tucson	AZ	85711	520-795-5729		180
Web: www.systemsimplementers.com						
Systems Inc						
W194 N11481 Mccormick Dr	Germantown	WI	53022	800-643-5424		697
TF: 800-643-5424 ■ *Web:* www.docksystemsinc.com						
Systems Insight Inc						
514 Madison Ave 200	Covington	KY	41011	859-291-9026		225
Web: www.systemsinsight.com						
Systems Integration & Management Inc						
2611 Jefferson Davis Hwy	Arlington	VA	22202	703-412-5068		177
Systems Machines Automation Components Corp						
5807 Van Allen Way	Carlsbad	CA	92008	760-929-7575	929-7588	203
Web: www.smac-mca.com						
Systems Maintenance Services Inc (SMS)						
10420 Harris Oaks Blvd Ste C	Charlotte	NC	28269	877-405-0330		175
TF: 877-405-0330 ■ *Web:* www.sysmaint.com						
Systems Planning & Analysis Inc (SPA)						
2001 N Beauregard St	Alexandria	VA	22311	703-399-7550		261
Web: www.spa.com						
Systems Plus Computers Inc						
12 Centerra Pkwy Ste 20	Lebanon	NH	03766	603-643-5800		196
TF: 800-388-8486 ■ *Web:* www.spci.com						
Systems Products & Solutions Inc (SPS)						
307 Wynn Dr	Huntsville	AL	35805	256-319-2135		177
Web: www.services-sps.com						
Systems Resource Management Inc						
42 Valley Rd	Middletown	RI	02842	401-849-2913		177
Web: www.srminc.net						
Systems South Inc						
422 Highway 418	Fountain Inn	SC	29644	864-862-9777		454
Web: www.systemssouth.com						
Systems Technologies Inc						
185 Rt 36	West Long Branch	NJ	07764	732-571-6400	571-6401	261
Web: www.systek.com						
Systems Technology Group Inc						
3001 W Big Beaver Rd	Troy	MI	48084	248-643-9010	643-9250	177
Web: www.stgit.com						
Systemsmith Inc						
18436 Hawthorne Blvd #208 Ste 208	Torrance	CA	90504	310-776-8750		225
Web: cognistix.com						
Systemtec Inc						
246 Stoneridge Dr Ste 301	Columbia	SC	29210	803-806-8100		177
TF: 888-900-1655 ■ *Web:* systemtec.net						
Systima Technologies Inc						
10809 120th Ave NE	Kirkland	WA	98033	425-487-4020	487-2950	180
Web: www.systima.com						
Systrand Manufacturing Corp						
19050 Allen Rd	Brownstown	MI	48183	734-479-8100	479-8107	60
Web: www.systrand.com						
Systron Donner Inertial						
355 Lennon Ln	Walnut Creek	CA	94598	925-979-4400	979-9827	529
TF: 866-234-4976 ■ *Web:* www.systron.com						
Syvantis Technologies LLC						
13822 Bluestem Ct Ste	Baxter	MN	56425	800-450-8908		196
TF: 800-450-8908 ■ *Web:* www.syvantis.com						
Syzygy 308 E Hawkins Ave	Aspen	CO	81611	970-925-3700		671
Web: www.syzygyrestaurant.com						
Szabo Assoc Inc						
3355 Lenox Rd NE Ste 945	Atlanta	GA	30326	404-266-2464		160
Web: www.szabo.com/home.cfm						
Szarka Financial Management						
29691 Lorain Rd	North Olmsted	OH	44070	440-779-1430		463
TF: 800-859-8095 ■ *Web:* www.szarkafinancial.com						
SZCO Supplies Inc 2713 Merchant Dr	Baltimore	MD	21230	410-368-8300		361
Web: szco.com						
Szechuan 5207 Bernard Dr	Roanoke	VA	24018	540-989-7947		671
Web: szechuan1.net						
Szechuan Garden Restaurant						
108 Fisherville Rd	Concord	NH	03303	603-226-2650		671
Szechuan House 245 Maple St	Manchester	NH	03103	603-669-8811		671
Web: szechuanhousenh.com						
Szechuan Palace 3040 Healy Dr	Winston-Salem	NC	27103	336-768-7123		671
Szott Ford 8800 E Holly Rd	Holly	MI	48442	248-634-4411		57
Web: szottford.com						

T

Company / Address	City	State	ZIP	Phone	Fax	Class
T & A Supply Company Inc						
6821 S 216th St Bldg A PO Box 927	Kent	WA	98032	253-872-3682	282-3796*	361
**Fax Area Code:* 206 ■ *TF:* 800-562-2857 ■ *Web:* www.tasupply.com						
T & B Foundry Co 2469 E 71st St	Cleveland	OH	44104	216-391-4200		307
T & C Industries Inc PO Box 629	Darien	WI	53114	262-882-1227		697
TF: 800-426-6447 ■ *Web:* www.royal-basket.com						
T & D Metal Products Co						
602 E Walnut St	Watseka	IL	60970	815-432-4938		488
Web: www.tdmetal.com						
T & E Industries Inc 215 Watchung Ave	Orange	NJ	07050	973-672-5454	672-0180	326
TF Sales: 800-245-7080 ■ *Web:* www.teindustries.com						
T & J Electrical Corp 636 Second Ave	Troy	NY	12182	518-237-1893		189-4
Web: www.tandjelectric.com						
T & K Machine Inc 2220 W Park St	Paris	TX	75460	903-785-5574		454
Web: www.tkparis.com						
T & L Automatics Inc 770 Emerson St	Rochester	NY	14613	585-647-3717		621
Web: www.tandlautomatics.com						
T & L Distributing LP						
7350 Langfield Rd	Houston	TX	77092	713-461-7802		361
Web: www.tldistributing.com						
T & R Electric Supply Company Inc						
308 SW Third St	Colman	SD	57017	605-534-3555	534-3861	767
TF: 800-843-7994 ■ *Web:* www.t-r.com						
T & S Brass & Bronze Works Inc						
PO Box 1088	Travelers Rest	SC	29690	864-834-4102	834-3518	609
TF Cust Svc: 800-476-4103 ■ *Web:* www.tsbrass.com						
T & S Machine Shop Inc 1396 Hwy 471	Brandon	MS	39042	601-825-8627		454
Web: www.tandsmachine.com						
T & t Staff Management Inc						
511 Executive Ctr Blvd	El Paso	TX	79902	915-771-0393		631
TF: 800-598-1647 ■ *Web:* www.ttstaff.com						

Phone | Fax | Class

T & T Tool Inc 700 Industrial Blvd .... Spooner WI 54801 715-635-8421 454
Web: www.tttool.com

T & T Truck & Crane Service Inc
1375 N Olive St .... Ventura CA 93001 805-648-3348 264-3
Web: www.truckandcrane.com

T & T Trucking Inc 11396 N Hwy 99 .... Lodi CA 95240 209-931-6000 931-6156 780
TF Cust Svc: 800-692-3457 ■ *Web:* www.tttrucking.com

T & W Forge Inc 970 E 64th St .... Cleveland OH 44103 216-881-8600 821-7309* 483
**Fax Area Code:* 330 ■ *Web:* sifco.com

T Bailey Inc 12441 Bartholomew Rd .... Anacortes WA 98221 360-293-0682 261
TF: 800-303-8629 ■ *Web:* www.tbailey.com

T Bar m Inc 2549 W State Hwy 46 .... New Braunfels TX 78132 830-625-7738 378
Web: www.tbarmcamps.org/retreats

T BC Corp 4770 Hickory Hill Rd .... Memphis TN 38141 866-822-4968 755
TF: 866-822-4968 ■ *Web:* www.tbcbrands.com

T Buck Suzuki Environmental Foundation
326 12th St Ste 100 .... New Westminster BC V3M4H6 604-519-3635 305
TF: 800-723-7753 ■ *Web:* www.bucksuzuki.org

T Cook's 5200 E Camelback Rd .... Phoenix AZ 85018 602-808-0766 671
TF: 800-672-6011 ■ *Web:* royalpalmshotel.com

T Cross Ranch LLC 6611 I-25 .... North Pueblo WY 81008 719-382-7553 382-7553 239
Web: teecrossranches.com

T G H Aviation 2389 Rickenbacker Way .... Auburn CA 95602 530-823-6204 57
TF: 800-843-4976 ■ *Web:* www.tghaviation.com

T G P Associates Inc
340 W 39th St Fl 11 .... New York NY 10018 212-695-1010 463
TF: 800-438-7325 ■ *Web:* tgpassociates.com

T H Rogers Lumber Co, The PO Box 5770 .... Edmond OK 73083 405-330-2181 191-2
Web: www.throgers.com

T Hasegawa USA Inc 14017 183rd St. .... Cerritos CA 90703 714-522-1900 522-6800 296-15
Web: www.thasegawa.com

T James Williams & Company AC
7210 N Whitney Ave Ste 101 .... Fresno CA 93720 559-322-9100 322-1098 2
Web: tjwco.com

T K Direct 999 Commerce Crt .... Buffalo Grove IL 60089 312-296-7921 627
Web: tkdirect.com

T K F Inc 726 Mehring Way .... Cincinnati OH 45203 513 241 5010 207
Web: www.tkf.com

T Marzetti Co
380 Polaris Pkwy Ste 400 .... Westerville OH 43082 800-999-1835 296-19
TF: 800-999-1835 ■ *Web:* www.marzetti.com

T Marzetti Company Allen Milk Div
1709 Frank Rd .... Columbus OH 43223 614-279-8673 296-27
Web: marzetti.com

T R C Hydraulics Inc 7 Mosher Dr .... Dartmouth NS B3B1E5 902-468-4605 454
TF: 800-668-9000 ■ *Web:* www.trchydraulics.com

T R Toppers Inc 320 Fairchild .... Pueblo CO 81001 719-948-4902 948-4908 296-8
TF: 800-748-4635 ■ *Web:* www.trtoppers.com

T Rad North America Inc
750 Frank Yost Ln. .... Hopkinsville KY 42240 270-885-9116 14
Web: www.copar.net

T Rowe Price Assoc Inc
100 E Pratt St .... Baltimore MD 21202 410-345-2000 401
TF: 800-638-7890 ■
Web: www3.troweprice.com/usis/corporate/en/home.html

T Sendzimir Inc 269 Brookside Rd .... Waterbury CT 06708 203-756-4617 674
TF: 800 243 4410 ■ *Web:* www.sendzimir.com

T Tech Inc 510 Guthridge Ct .... Norcross GA 30092 770-455-0676 491
TF: 800-370-1530 ■ *Web:* t-techtools.com/store

T's Restaurant 3416 Mike Pagett Hwy. .... Augusta GA 30906 706-798-4145 793-8474 671
Web: www.tsrestaurant.com

T. A. Pelsue Co 2500 S Tejon St .... Englewood CO 80110 303-936-7432 767
TF: 800-525-8460 ■ *Web:* www.pelsue.com

T. Bruce Sales Inc
9 Carbaugh St. .... West Middlesex PA 16159 724-528-9961 528-2050 480
TF: 800-944-0738 ■ *Web:* www.tbrucesales.com

T. Gerding Construction Co
200 SW Airport Rd PO Box 1082 .... Corvallis OR 97333 541-753-2012 754-6654 187
Web: www.tgerding.com

T. J. Harkins Co 279 Beaudin Blvd .... Bolingbrook IL 60440 630-427-3400 297-11

T.O. Fuller State Park
1500 W Mitchell Rd .... Memphis TN 38109 901-543-7581 785-8485 50-5
Web: www.tennessee.gov

T.S.D. Inc 1620 Turnpike St N .... Andover MA 01845 978-794-1400 177
Web: tsdweb.com

T.u.c.s. Cleaning Service Inc
166 Central Ave .... Orange NJ 07050 973-673-0700 152
TF: 800-992-5998 ■ *Web:* www.tucscleaning.com

T/Cci Manufacturing LLC
2120 N 22nd St .... Decatur IL 62526 217-422-0055 454
Web: www.tccimfg.com

T2 Development LLC
620 Newport Ctr Dr 14th Fl. .... Newport Beach CA 92660 949-610-8200 378
Web: www.t2dev.com

T-3 Energy Services Inc
140 Cypress Stn Dr Ste 225 .... Houston TX 77090 713-996-4110 539

T3 Expo LLC 8 Lakeville Business Pk .... Lakeville MA 02347 888-698-3397 184
TF: 888-698-3397 ■ *Web:* www.t3expo.com

T3 Global Strategies Inc
10 Emerson Ln Ste 808 .... Bridgeville PA 15017 412-221-2003 727

T3 Micro Inc 228 Main St Ste 12 .... Venice CA 90291 310-452-2888 76

T3 Motion Inc 2990 Airway Ave Ste A .... Costa Mesa CA 92626 714-619-3600 59
Web: www.t3motion.com

T3 Software Builders Inc
1708 Chester Mill Rd .... Silver Spring MD 20906 301-260-9504 396
TF: 800-281-4879 ■ *Web:* www.t3software.com

T4 Global Inc PO Box 130266 .... Dallas TX 75313 214-205-4245 305
Web: t4global.org

TA Assoc Inc 200 Clarendon St 56th Fl .... Boston MA 02116 617-574-6700 792
TF: 800-836-8873 ■ *Web:* www.ta.com

TA Caid Industries Inc
2275 E Ganley Rd .... Tucson AZ 85706 520-294-3126 294-8180 189-10
Web: www.caid.com

TA Instruments Inc 159 Lukens Dr. .... New Castle DE 19720 302-427-4000 419
Web: www.tainstruments.com

TA Loving Company Inc
400 Patetown Rd. .... Goldsboro NC 27530 919-734-8400 731-7538 188-10
Web: www.taloving.com

TAB (Traffic Audit Bureau for Media Measurement)
271 Madison Ave Ste 1504 .... New York NY 10016 212 972 8075 49-18
Web: www.tabonline.com

TAB Computer Systems Inc
29-31 Bissell St .... East Hartford CT 06108 860-289-8850 180
Web: tabinc.com

TAB Products Co 605 Fourth St .... Mayville WI 53050 888-466-8228 304-4947* 534
**Fax Area Code:* 800 ■ *TF:* 888-466-8228 ■ *Web:* www.tab.com

Tab Services Inc 2065 S Raritan St. .... Denver CO 80223 303-649-1213 41
Web: tabservicescolorado.com

Tabar Inc 251 Greenwood Ave .... Bethel CT 06801 203-748-5242 360-3
Web: www.tabarinc.com

Tabard Inn 1739 N St NW. .... Washington DC 20036 202-331-8528 671
Web: www.tabardinn.com

Tabata U.S.A. Inc
2380 Mira Mar Ave .... Long Beach CA 90815 562-498-3708 711
TF: 800-482-2282 ■ *Web:* www.tusa.com

Tabb Brockenbrough & Ragland LLC
4905 Dickens Rd .... Richmond VA 23230 804-355-7984 390
TF: 800-296-0531 ■ *Web:* www.tbrinsurance.com

TABB Inc PO Box 10 .... Chester NJ 07930 800-887-8222 635
TF: 800-887-8222 ■ *Web:* www.tabb.net

TABCON Engineering
494 McNicoll Ave Ste 201 .... Toronto ON M2H2E1 647-974-7006 261
Web: www.tabcon.com

Taber Consultants
3911 W Capitol Ave .... West Sacramento CA 95691 916-371-1690 261
TF: 888-423-0573 ■ *Web:* www.taberconsultants.com

Taber Extrusions LP
915 S Elmira Ave .... Russellville AR 72802 479-968-1021 968-8645 485
TF: 800-563-6853 ■ *Web:* www.taberextrusions.com

Taber Industries
455 Bryant St .... North Tonawanda NY 14120 716-694-4000 694-1450 472
TF: 800-333-5300 ■ *Web:* www.taberindustries.com

Taberna Del Alabardero
1776 I St NW .... Washington DC 20006 202-429-2200 775-3713 671
Web: www.alabardero.com

Tabernacle Baptist Bible College & Theological Seminary
717 N Whitehurst Landing Rd. .... Virginia Beach VA 23464 757-424-4673 166
TF: 800-720-9185 ■ *Web:* www.tbbcs.org

Tabet DiVito & Rothstein LLC
The Rookery Bldg 209 S LaSalle St 7th Fl .... Chicago IL 60604 312-762-9450 428
Web: www.tdrlawfirm.com

Table Group Inc
3640 Mt Diablo Blvd 202 .... Lafayette CA 94549 925-299-9700 463
Web: www.tablegroup.com

Table Mountain Casino
8184 Table Mountain Rd. .... Friant CA 93626 559-822-7777 133
TF: 800-541-3637 ■ *Web:* www.tmcasino.com

Table Rock State Park
5272 State Hwy 165 .... Branson MO 65616 417-334-4704 565
Web: www.mostateparks.com

Table Rock State Park
158 E Ellison Ln .... Pickens SC 29671 864-878-9813 565
Web: www.southcarolinaparks.com

Table Talk Pies Inc
120 Washington St .... Worcester MA 01610 508-798-8811 798-0848 296-1
TF: 800-696-9401 ■ *Web:* www.tabletalkpie.com

Table Trac Inc
6101 Baker Rd Ste 206 .... Minnetonka MN 55345 952-548-8877 177
Web: www.tabletrac.com

Tableau Software Inc
837 N 34th St Ste 400 .... Seattle WA 98103 206-633-3400 633-3004 178-10
Web: www.tableau.com

TABLETmedia Inc 2468 Union St .... San Francisco CA 94123 415-567-8100 177
Web: www.tabletmedia.com

Taboo Resort Golf & Spa
1209 Muskoka Beach Rd .... Gravenhurst ON P1P1R1 705-687-2233 687-7474 707
TF: 800-461-0236

Tabor Academy 66 Spring St. .... Marion MA 02738 508-748-2000 622
Web: www.taboracademy.org

Tabor College 400 S Jefferson St .... Hillsboro KS 67063 620-947-3121 947-6276* 166
**Fax:* Admissions ■ *Web:* www.tabor.edu

Tabor Communications Inc
8445 camino santa fe .... San Diego CA 92121 858-625-0070 5
Web: www.taborcommunications.com

Tabor Retreat Ctr 60 Anchor Ave .... Oceanside NY 11572 516-536-3004 673
Web: www.taborretreatcenter.org

Tabula Rosa Systems LLC
17 Cedar Ln .... Titusville NJ 08560 609-818-1802 525
Web: www.tabularosa.net

TAC Americas Inc 1650 W Crosby Rd .... Carrollton TX 75006 972-323-1111 407

Tacala LLC
3750 Corporate Woods Dr .... Vestavia Hills AL 35242 205-443-9600 443-9700 670
Web: www.tacala.com

TACC (Tigard Area Chamber of Commerce)
12345 SW Main St. .... Tigard OR 97223 503-639-1656 139
Web: www.tigardareachamber.org

Tache USA Inc 18 E 48th St 4th Fl .... New York NY 10036 212-371-1234 852-4961 409
Web: www.tacheusa.com

Tachi Palace Hotel & Casino, The
17225 Jersey Ave .... Lemoore CA 93245 559-924-7751 132
TF: 800-942-6886 ■ *Web:* tachipalace.com

Tachi-S Engineering USA Inc
23227 Commerce Dr .... Farmington Hills MI 48335 248-478-5050 247
Web: www.tachi-s.com

Tachyon Networks Inc
9339 Carroll Park Dr Ste 150 .... San Diego CA 92121 858-882-8100 647

Tack Room Too Inc 201 Lee St SW. .... Tumwater WA 98501 360-357-4268 711
TF: 800-258-2581 ■ *Web:* www.tackroomtoo.com

Taco Bell Arena 1910 University Dr .... Boise ID 83725 208-426-1900 426-1998 720
Web: www.tacobellarena.com

Taco Bell Corp 1 Glen Bell Way .... Irvine CA 92618 949-863-4000 670
Web: www.tacobell.com

Taco Cabana Inc
8918 Tesoro Dr Ste 200 .... San Antonio TX 78217 210-804-0990 670
TF: 800-580-8668 ■ *Web:* www.tacocabana.com

Taco Inc 1160 Cranston St .... Cranston RI 02920 401-942-8000 564-9436* 357
**Fax Area Code:* 905 ■ **Fax:* Cust Svc ■ *TF:* 888-778-2733 ■ *Web:* www.taco-hvac.com

Listing	City	State	ZIP	Phone	Fax	Class
Taco Mayo 10405 Greenbriar Pl *TF:* 800-291-8226 ■ *Web:* www.tacomayo.com/default.html	Oklahoma City	OK	73159	405-691-8226		670
Taco Metals Inc 50 NE 179th St *TF:* 800-653-8568 ■ *Web:* www.tacometals.com	Miami	FL	33162	305-652-8566	770-2387	492
Taco Time International Inc 9311 E Via de Venutra *TF:* 866-452-4252 ■ *Web:* www.tacotime.com	Scottsdale	AZ	85258	480-362-4800	362-4812	670
Tacoma Art Museum 1701 Pacific Ave *Web:* www.tacomaartmuseum.org	Tacoma	WA	98402	253-272-4258	627-1898	520
Tacoma City Hall 747 Market St *Web:* www.cityoftacoma.org	Tacoma	WA	98402	253-591-5000	591-5300	337
Tacoma Community College 6501 S 19th St **Fax:* Admissions ■ *Web:* www.tacomacc.edu	Tacoma	WA	98466	253-566-5000	566-6011*	162
Tacoma Dome Arena & Exhibition Hall 2727 E 'D' St **Fax:* Mktg ■ *Web:* www.tacomadome.org	Tacoma	WA	98421	253-272-3663	593-7620*	720
Tacoma Electric Supply Inc 1311 S Tacoma Way *TF:* 800-422-0540 ■ *Web:* www.tacomaelectric.com	Tacoma	WA	98409	253-475-0540	475-0707	246
Tacoma General Hospital 315 MLK Jr Way *TF:* 800-552-1419 ■ *Web:* www.multicare.org	Tacoma	WA	98405	253-403-1000	403-1180	374-3
Tacoma Goodwill Industries 714 S 27th St *Web:* tacomagoodwill.org	Tacoma	WA	98409	253-573-6500		260
Tacoma Inc 328 E Church St *TF:* 800-352-9417 ■ *Web:* www.gototaco.com	Martinsville	VA	24112	276-666-9417	666-9427	670
Tacoma Little Theatre 210 N 'I' St *TF:* 800-863-1706 ■ *Web:* www.tacomalittletheatre.com	Tacoma	WA	98403	253-272-2281		572
Tacoma Mall 4502 S Steele St Ste 1177 *TF:* 877-746-6642 ■ *Web:* www.simon.com/mall/?id=238	Tacoma	WA	98409	253-475-4565	472-3413	460
Tacoma Musical Playhouse 7116 Sixth Ave *TF:* 800-848-7097 ■ *Web:* www.tmp.org	Tacoma	WA	98406	253-565-6867	564-7863	573-4
Tacoma Nature Ctr 1919 S Tyler St *Web:* metroparkstacoma.org	Tacoma	WA	98405	253-591-6439		50-5
Tacoma News Inc 1950 S State St *Web:* www.thenewstribune.com	Tacoma	WA	98405	253-597-8742	597-8274	637-8
Tacoma Opera 47 St Helens Ave *Web:* www.tacomaopera.com	Tacoma	WA	98402	253-627-7789		573-2
Tacoma Public Library 1102 Tacoma Ave S *Web:* www.tacomalibrary.org	Tacoma	WA	98402	253-292-2001		434-3
Tacoma Regional Convention & Visitor Bureau 1516 Commerce St *TF:* 800-272-2662 ■ *Web:* www.traveltacoma.com	Tacoma	WA	98402	253-627-2836		206
Tacoma Rubber Stamp & Sign 919 Market St *TF:* 800-544-7281 ■ *Web:* www.tacomarubberstamp.com	Tacoma	WA	98402	253-383-5433	383-0649	467
Tacoma Screw Products Inc 2001 Center St *TF:* 800-562-8192 ■ *Web:* www.tacomascrew.com	Tacoma	WA	98409	253-572-3444		454
Tacoma Symphony 901 Broadway Ste 600 *TF:* 800-291-7593 ■ *Web:* symphonytacoma.org	Tacoma	WA	98402	253-272-7264		573-3
Tacoma Truss Systems Inc 20617 Mtn Hwy E *TF:* 800-868-9066 ■ *Web:* www.tacomatruss.com	Spanaway	WA	98387	253-847-2204		817
Tacoma-Pierce County Chamber of Commerce 950 Pacific Ave Ste 300 *Web:* www.tacomachamber.org	Tacoma	WA	98402	253-627-2175	597-7305	139
Taconic 136 Coonbrook Rd PO Box 69 *TF:* 800-833-1805 ■ *Web:* www.4taconic.com	Petersburg	NY	12138	518-658-3202	658-3204	745-2
Taconic Correctional Facility 250 Harris Rd **Fax Area Code:* 718 ■ *Web:* www.doccs.ny.gov/faclist.html	Bedford Hills	NY	10507	914-241-3010	722-6220*	213
Taconic State Park - Copake Falls Area Route 344 *Web:* parks.ny.gov/parks/83/details.aspx	Copake Falls	NY	12517	518-329-3993		565
Taconic State Park - Rudd Pond Area 59 Rudd Pond Dr *Web:* parks.ny.gov/parks/141/hunting.aspx	Millerton	NY	12546	518-789-3059		565
Tacony Corp 1760 Gilsinn Ln *TF:* 800-553-8033 ■ *Web:* www.tacony.com	Fenton	MO	63026	636-349-3000	349-2333	38
Tacori Enterprises 1736 Gardena Ave *Web:* tacori.com	Glendale	CA	91204	818-863-1536		411
Tacos Guaymas 2630 S 38th St *Web:* www.tacosguaymas.com	Tacoma	WA	98409	253-471-2224		671
Tacos Mexico Inc 5120 E Olympic Blvd *Web:* tacosmexico.com	Los Angeles	CA	90022	323-266-0482		670
Tactair Fluid Controls Inc 4806 W Taft Rd *Web:* www.tactair.com	Liverpool	NY	13088	315-451-3928		223
Tactical Allocation Group LLC 255 E Brown St Ste 101	Birmingham	MI	48009	248-283-2520	283-2524	401
Tactical Communications Group LLC 2 Highwood Dr Bldg 2 *Web:* g2tcg.com	Tewksbury	MA	01876	978-654-4800		174
Tactical Magic LLC 1460 Madison Ave *Web:* www.tacticalmagic.com	Memphis	TN	38104	901-722-3001		7
Tactical Network Solutions LLC 8850 Stanford Blvd Ste 1600 *Web:* www.tacnetsol.com	Columbia	MD	21045	443-276-6990		809
Tactical Support Equipment Inc 4039 Barefoot Rd *Web:* www.tserecon.com	Fayetteville	NC	28306	910-425-3360		21
Tactician Corp 305 N Main St *TF:* 800-927-7666 ■ *Web:* www.tactician.com	Andover	MA	01810	978-475-4475		195
Tactics Boardshop 375 W Fourth Ave Ste 202 *Web:* www.tactics.com	Eugene	OR	97401	541-349-0087		711
Tactix Consulting Group Inc 4424 Carver Woods Dr *Web:* www.tactixgroup.com	Cincinnati	OH	45242	513-333-4140		180
TADA 15 W 28th St *Web:* www.tadatheater.com	New York	NY	10001	212-252-1619		749
Tadiran Batteries 2001 Marcus Ave Ste 125E *TF:* 800-537-1368 ■ *Web:* www.tadiranbat.com	New Hyde Park	NY	11042	516-621-4980	621-4517	74
Tadmor Camp 43943 Mcdowell Creek Dr *Web:* tadmor.org	Lebanon	OR	97355	541-451-4270		239
TAF (Taxpayers Against Fraud Education Fund) 1220 19th St NW Ste 501 *TF General:* 800-873-2573 ■ *Web:* www.taf.org	Washington	DC	20036	202-296-4826	296-4838	49-10
Tafa Inc 146 Pembroke Rd	Concord	NH	03301	603-224-9586		454
Taffie's 301 S Mattis Ave	Champaign	IL	61821	217-359-4201		671
Taft College 29 Emmons Pk Dr **Fax:* Admissions ■ *TF:* 800-379-6784 ■ *Web:* www.taftcollege.edu	Taft	CA	93268	661-763-7700	763-7758*	162
Taft Electric Co 1694 Eastman Ave *Web:* taftelectric.com	Ventura	CA	93003	805-642-0121		189-4
Taft Museum of Art, The 316 Pike St *TF:* 800-721-2298 ■ *Web:* www.taftmuseum.org	Cincinnati	OH	45202	513-241-0343	241-7762	520
Taft School 110 Woodbury Rd *Web:* www.taftschool.org	Watertown	CT	06795	860-945-7777	945-7808	622
Taft Stettinius & Hollister LLP 1800 Firstar Tower 425 Walnut St *TF:* 800-973-1177 ■ *Web:* www.taftlaw.com	Cincinnati	OH	45202	513-381-2838		445
Taft, Theatre, The 317 E Fifth St *Web:* www.tafttheatre.org	Cincinnati	OH	45202	513-232-6220		572
TAG (Tube Art Group) 11715 SE Fifth St *TF:* 800-562-2854 ■ *Web:* www.tubeart.com	Bellevue	WA	98005	206-223-1122	223-1123	701
TAG Associates LLC 810 Seventh Ave 7th FL *Web:* www.tagassoc.com	New York	NY	10019	212-275-1500	275-1510	401
TAG Holdings LLC 2075 W Big Beaver Rd Ste 500 *Web:* www.taghold.com	Troy	MI	48084	248-822-8056	822-8012	60
TAG Online Inc 6 Prospect Village Plaza 1st Fl *TF:* 800-999-6872 ■ *Web:* www.tagonline.com	Clifton	NJ	07013	973-783-5583		225
TAG Solutions LLC 12 Elmwood Rd *TF:* 800-724-0023 ■ *Web:* www.tagsolutions.com	Albany	NY	12204	518-292-6500	292-6510	735
Tag-A-Long Expeditions 452 N Main St *TF:* 800-453-3292 ■ *Web:* www.tagalong.com	Moab	UT	84532	435-259-8946	259-8990	760
Taggart Global LLC 4000 Town Ctr Blvd Ste 200 *Web:* www.taggartglobal.com	Canonsburg	PA	15317	724-754-9800		186
Taggart Morton LLC 2100 Energy Ctr 1100 Poydras St *Web:* www.taggartmortonlaw.com	New Orleans	LA	70163	504-599-8500		428
Tag-It Pacific Inc 21900 Burbank Blvd Ste 270 *Web:* www.talonzippers.com	Woodland Hills	CA	91367	818-444-4100	444-4105	413
Taglairino Advertising Group Ny Inc 75 SW 15th Rd *Web:* www.tagad.com	Miami	FL	33129	305-577-9988		7
Tagline Communications Inc 6230 Wilshire Blvd Ste 1231 *Web:* www.tagline.com	Los Angeles	CA	90048	323-857-5337		344
Tagos Group LLC, The 8 E Greenway Plaza Ste 910 *Web:* www.tagosgroup.com	Houston	TX	77046	713-850-7031	850-7071	463
Taher Inc 5570 Smetana Dr *TF:* 800-746-9554 ■ *Web:* www.taher.com	Minnetonka	MN	55343	952-945-0505	945-0444	299
Tahiti Tourism 300 Continental Blvd Ste 160 *Web:* www.tahiti-tourisme.com	El Segundo	CA	90245	310-414-8484	414-8490	775
Tahitian Noni International 333 W Riverpark Dr *TF Cust Svc:* 800-445-2969 ■ *Web:* morinda.com	Provo	UT	84604	801-234-1000	234-1001	296-11
Tahoe Biltmore Lodge & Casino PO Box 115 *TF:* 800-245-8667 ■ *Web:* www.tahoebiltmore.com	Crystal Bay	NV	89402	775-831-0660		378
Tahoe Daily Tribune 3079 Harrison Ave *TF:* 800-874-9779 ■ *Web:* www.tahoedailytribune.com	South Lake Tahoe	CA	96150	530-541-3880		532-2
Tahoe Joe's 9000 Ming Ave *Web:* www.tahoejoes.com	Bakersfield	CA	93311	661-664-7750		671
Tahoe Keys Property Owners Assn 356 Ala Wai Blvd	South Lake Tahoe	CA	96150	530-542-6444		138
Tahoe Mountain Sports 11200 Donner Pass Rd Ste 5e *TF:* 866-891-9177 ■ *Web:* www.tahoemountainsports.com	Truckee	CA	96161	866-891-9177		711
Tahoe Seasons Resort 3901 Saddle Rd PO Box 16300 *Web:* tahoeseasons.com	South Lake Tahoe	CA	96150	530-541-6700		669
Tahoe Truckee Disposal Co 645 West Lake Blvd Ste 5 Sunnyside *Web:* waste101.com	Tahoe City	CA	96145	530-583-7800		804
Tahoe Truckee Unified School District (TTUSD) 11603 Donner Pass Rd *Web:* www.ttusd.org	Truckee	CA	96161	530-582-2500	582-7606	685
Tahoma National Cemetery 18600 SE 240th St *TF:* 800-827-1000 ■ *Web:* www.cem.va.gov	Kent	WA	98042	425-413-9614	413-9618	136
Tahoma Rubber & Plastics Inc 255 Wooster Rd N *Web:* www.tahomarubberplastics.com	Barberton	OH	44203	330-745-9016	745-4886	605-2
Tahquamenon Falls State Park 41382 W M-123 *Web:* www.michigandnr.com	Paradise	MI	49768	906-492-3415		565
Tahzoo LLC 3128 M St NW *Web:* www.tahzoo.com	Washington	DC	20007	202-621-7160		195
Tai Lake Restaurant 134 N Tenth St *Web:* www.tailakeseafoodrest.com	Philadelphia	PA	19107	215-922-0698	922-0347	671
Taiga Building Products Ltd 4710 Kingsway Ste 800 *TF:* 800-663-1470 ■ *Web:* www.taigabuilding.com	Burnaby	BC	V5H4M2	604-438-1471		279
TaigMarks Inc 223 S Main St Ste 100 *Web:* www.taigmarks.com	Elkhart	IN	46516	574-294-8844		6
Taikoproject 505 E Third St Ste 505 *Web:* www.taikoproject.com	Los Angeles	CA	90012	213-268-4011		149
TailCurrent Technologies Pvt Ltd Suite 4000, L40, 17 State St *Web:* www.tailcurrent.com	New York	NY	10004	312-224-1615		5

	Phone	Fax	Class
Tailhook Assn 9696 Businesspark Ave, San Diego CA 92131 *TF:* 800-322-4665 ■ *Web:* www.tailhook.net	858-689-9223	578-8839	48-19
Tailored Chemical Products Inc 700 12th St Dr NW, Hickory NC 28601 *TF:* 800-627-1687 ■ *Web:* www.tailoredchemical.com	828-322-6512	322-7688	3
Tailored Label Products Inc W165 N5731 Ridgewood Dr, Menomonee Falls WI 53051 *Web:* www.tailoredlabel.com	262-703-5000		88
Tailored Living LLC 1927 N Glassell St, Orange CA 92865 *TF:* 866-675-8819 ■ *Web:* www.tailoredliving.com	866-675-8819		361
Tailored Marketing 401 Wood St Ste 902, Pittsburgh PA 15222 *TF:* 800-677-1997 ■ *Web:* www.tailoredmarketing.com	412-281-1442		344
Taisei Construction Corp 6261 Katella Ave Ste 200, Cypress CA 90630	714-886-1530		186
Taisho Pharmaceutical California Inc 3878 W Carson St Ste 216, Torrance CA 90503 *Web:* lipovitan.com	310-543-2035		582
Tait & Assoc Inc 701 N Parkcenter Dr, Santa Ana CA 92705 *Web:* tait.com	714-560-8200		261
Tait Subler LLC 60 S Sixth St Ste 2800, Minneapolis MN 55402 *Web:* www.taitsubler.com	612-758-2000		463
Taitron Components Inc 28040 W Harrison Pkwy, Valencia CA 91355 *NASDAQ: TAIT* ■ *TF:* 800-247-2232 ■ *Web:* www.taitroncomponents.com	661-257-6060	257-6415	246
Taiwan Semiconductor Mfg Company Ltd (TSMC) 2851 Junction Ave, San Jose CA 95134 *NYSE: TSM* ■ *TF:* 877-248-4237 ■ *Web:* www.tsmc.com	408-382-8000	382-8008	696
Taiwan Visitors Assn 1 E 42nd St Ste 9, New York NY 10017 *TF:* 800-410-9608 ■ *Web:* www.taiwan.net.tw	212-867-1632	867-1635	775
Taiwan Visitors Assn 555 Montgomery St Ste 505, San Francisco CA 94111 *Web:* www.taiwan.net.tw	415-989-8677	989-7242	775
Taiyo America Inc 2675 Antler Dr, Carson City NV 89701	775-885-9959		388
Taiyo Yuden (USA) Inc 1930 N Thoreau Dr Ste 190, Schaumburg IL 60173 *TF:* 800-348-2496 ■ *Web:* www.t-yuden.com	847-925-0888	925-0899	253
Taj Boston 15 Arlington St, Boston MA 02116 *TF:* 866-969-1825 ■ *Web:* www.tajhotels.com	617-536-5700		379
Taj Campton Place 340 Stockton St, San Francisco CA 94108 *TF:* 866-969-1825 ■ *Web:* www.tajhotels.com	415-781-5555	955-5536	379
Taj Indian Cuisine 2734 E Fowler Ave, Tampa FL 33612 *Web:* tajtampaindiancuisine.com	813-971-8483		671
Taj Indian Restaurant 5033 Brookhaven Rd Ste 300, Macon GA 31206	478-785-8540		671
Taj Indian Restaurant 1256 S Pk St, Madison WI 53715 *Web:* taj-madison.com	608-268-0772		671
Taj Mahal 6410 W Jefferson Blvd, Fort Wayne IN 46804	260-432-8993		671
Taj Mahal 2080 Bennet Ave, Lancaster PA 17601 *Web:* www.tajlancaster.com	717-295-1434	295-7413	671
Taj Mahal 7521 Wornall Rd, Kansas City MO 64114 *Web:* www.kctajmahal.com	816-361-1722	361-1654	671
Taj Restaurant 2630 Baseline Rd, Boulder CO 80305 *Web:* tajcolorado.com	303-494-5216		671
TAJ Technologies Inc 1168 Northland Dr, Mendota Heights MN 55120 *TF:* 877-825-2801 ■ *Web:* www.tajtech.com	651-688-2801		721
Tajikistan *Embassy* 1005 New Hampshire Ave., Washington DC 20037 *Web:* www.tajemb.us	202-223-6090		257
TAK Construction 60 Walnut Ave Ste 400, Clark NJ 07066 *Web:* www.takgroupinc.com	732-340-0700		653
Taka Restaurant 555 Fifth Ave, San Diego CA 92101 *Web:* www.takasushi.com	619-338-0555		671
Takagi Industrial Company USA Inc 500 Wald, Irvine CA 92618 *TF:* 888-882-5244 ■ *Web:* www.takagi.com	949-770-7171	770-3171	15
Takano Mark (Rep D - CA) 1507 Longworth Bldg, Washington DC 20515 *Web:* takano.house.gov	202-225-2305	225-7018	342-2
Takaoka of Japan 305 E Superior St, Fort Wayne IN 46802 *Web:* donhalls.com	260-424-3183		671
Takara Belmont USA Inc 101 Belmont Dr, Somerset NJ 08873 **Fax Area Code: 732* ■ *TF:* 877-283-1289 ■ *Web:* www.takarabelmont.com	877-283-1289	283-1687*	76
Takara Sake USA Inc 708 Addison St, Berkeley CA 94710 *Web:* takarasake.com	510-540-8250	486-8758	80-1
Takata Inc 2500 Takata Dr, Auburn Hills MI 48326 *TF:* 800-359-2466 ■ *Web:* www.takata.com	248-373-8040		678
Take 3 Trailers Inc 1808 Hwy 105, Brenham TX 77833 *TF:* 866-428-2533 ■ *Web:* www.take3trailers.com	979-337-9568		763
Take Charge America Inc 20620 N 19th Ave, Phoenix AZ 85027 *Web:* www.takechargeamerica.org	623-266-6100		242
Takeda Canada Inc 435 N Service Rd W Ste 101, Oakville ON L6M4X8 *TF:* 888-367-3331 ■ *Web:* www.takedacanada.com	905-469-9333	469-4883	85
Takeda Pharmaceuticals USAInc 1 Takeda Pkwy, Deerfield IL 60015 *Web:* takedajobs.com	224-554-6500		238
Takenaka Partners LLC 801 S Figueroa St Ste 620, Los Angeles CA 90017 *Web:* www.takenakapartners.com	213-891-0060		401
Take-Two Interactive Software Inc 622 Broadway, New York NY 10012 *NASDAQ: TTWO* ■ *TF:* 800-732-0330 ■ *Web:* www.take2games.com	646-536-2842	536-2926	178-6
Takoma Regional Hospital 401 Takoma Ave, Greeneville TN 37743 *Web:* www.takoma.org	423-639-3151		374-3
TAL International Group Inc 100 Manhattanville Rd, Purchase NY 10577 *NYSE: TAL* ■ *Web:* www.talinternational.com	914-251-9000	697-2549	264-5
Talagy Inc 245 Riverside Ave Ste 250, Jacksonville FL 32202 *Web:* www.talagy.com	904-224-1400	224-1410	734
Talan Products Inc 18800 Cochran Ave, Cleveland OH 44110 *TF:* 877-419-2805 ■ *Web:* www.talanproducts.com	216-458-0170		483
Talari Networks Inc One Almaden Blvd Ste 200, San Jose CA 95113 *Web:* www.talari.com	408-689-0400		174
Talaris Conference Ctr 4000 NE 41st St, Seattle WA 98105 *Web:* www.talariscc.com	206-268-7000	268-7001	377
Talas Inc 330 Morgan Ave, Brooklyn NY 11211 *Web:* www.talasonline.com	212-219-0770	219-0735	92
Talascend LLC 5700 Crooks Rd Ste 450, Troy MI 48098 *Web:* talascend.com	248-537-1300		261
Talbert & Bright Inc 4810 Shelley Dr, Wilmington NC 28405 *Web:* talbertandbright.com	910-763-5350		261
Talbert Manufacturing Inc 1628 W State Rd 114, Rensselaer IN 47978 *TF:* 888-489-1731 ■ *Web:* www.talbertmfg.com	888-489-1731		779
Talbot County 11 N Washington St County Courthouse, Easton MD 21601 *TF:* 800-449-4347 ■ *Web:* talbotcountymd.gov	410-770-8010	770-8007	338
Talbot County 74 W Monroe St PO Box 155, Talbotton GA 31827 *TF:* 800-436-7442 ■ *Web:* talbotcountyga.org	706-665-3220	665-8199	338
Talbot County Chamber of Commerce 101 Marlboro Ave Ste 53, Easton MD 21601 *Web:* www.talbotchamber.org	410-822-4606	822-7922	139
Talbot County Free Library 100 W Dover St, Easton MD 21601 *TF:* 800-341-4007 ■ *Web:* www.tcfl.org/library	410-822-1626	820-8217	434-3
Talbot County Public Schools 12 Magnolia St PO Box 1029, Easton MD 21601 *Web:* www.tcps.k12.md.us	410-822-0330	820-4260	685
Talbot County Tourism Office 11 S Harrison St, Easton MD 21601 *TF:* 800-690-5080 ■ *Web:* www.tourtalbot.org	410-770-8000	770-8057	206
Talbot Industries Inc 5725 Howard Bush Dr, Neosho MO 64850	417-451-7440		550
Talbot Korvola & Warwick LLP 4800 Meadows Rd Ste 200, Lake Oswego OR 97035 *Web:* tkw.com	503-274-2849	274-2853	2
Talbot Tours Inc 1952 Camden Ave, San Jose CA 95124 *Web:* www.talbottours.com	408-879-0101		760
Talbott Recovery Campus 5448 Yorktowne Dr, Atlanta GA 30349 *TF:* 800-445-4232 ■ *Web:* www.talbottcampus.com	770-994-0185	994-2024	726
Talco Plastics Inc 1000 W Rincon St, Corona CA 92880 *Web:* www.talcoplastics.com	951-531-2000	531-2058	605-2
Talcott Mountain State Park c/o Penwood State Pk 57 Gunn Mill Rd, Bloomfield CT 06002 *Web:* www.ct.gov	860-242-1158		565
Talemed Inc 6279 Tri Ridge Blvd Ste 110, Loveland OH 45140 *Web:* www.talemed.com	513-774-7300		194
Talent Connections LLC 4805 W Village Way Ste 2401, Smyrna GA 30080 *Web:* www.talentconnections.net	770-552-1550		260
Talent Curve 14 Bridle Path, Pittsboro NC 27312 *TF:* 866-494-0248 ■ *Web:* www.talentcurve.com	866-494-0248		463
Talent Function Group LLC 11346 Middle Ridge Terr, San Diego CA 92128 *Web:* www.talentfunction.com	858-748-3136		193
Talent Logic Inc 2313 Timber Shadows, Kingwood TX 77339 *Web:* talentlogic.com	281-358-1858		177
Talent Plus Inc 1 Talent Plus Way, Lincoln NE 68506 *Web:* www.talentplus.com	402-489-2000		196
Talent Strategy Group LLC 201 W 72nd St, New York NY 10023 *Web:* www.talentstrategygroup.com	203-482-8103		280
Talent Tool & Die Inc 777 Berea Industrial Pkwy, Berea OH 44017 *Web:* www.talent-tool.com	440-239-8777		488
Talent Zoo Inc 1736 Defoor Pl NW, Atlanta GA 30318 *Web:* www.talentzoo.com	404-607-1955		260
TalentFusion Inc 343 Huntington Rd, Worthington MA 01098	413-238-0138		260
TalentLens Inc 19500 Bulverde Rd, San Antonio TX 78259 *TF:* 888-298-6227 ■ *Web:* talentlens.com	888-298-6227		260
TalentQuest Inc 1275 Peachtree St NE Ste 400, Atlanta GA 30309 *Web:* www.talentquest.com	404-266-9368		193
TalentSmart Inc 11526 Sorrento Valley Rd, San Diego CA 92121 *TF:* 800-972-1333 ■ *Web:* www.talentsmart.com	858-509-0582		196
TalentSoup LLC 1900 Hosea L Williams Dr NE, Atlanta GA 30317 *Web:* www.talentsoup.com	678-528-7407	868-2249	260
TalentWorks 3500 W Olive Ave Ste 1400, Burbank CA 91505 *Web:* www.talentworks.us	818-972-4300	955-6411	731
Taleo Corp 4140 Dublin Blvd Ste 400, Dublin CA 94568 *NYSE: ORCL* ■ *TF:* 800-672-2531 ■ *Web:* www.oracle.com	925-452-3000	452-3001	178-1
Talgo Inc 505 Fifth Ave S Ste 170, Seattle WA 98104 *Web:* www.talgo.com/index.php/es/home.php	206-254-7051		770
Taliaferro County PO Box 114, Crawfordville GA 30631 *TF:* 800-436-7442 ■ *Web:* taliaferrocountyga.org	706-456-2229	456-2904	338
Taliano's Restaurant 201 N 14th St, Fort Smith AR 72901 *Web:* talianos.net	479-785-2292	785-2640	671
Taliesin 5607 County Hwy C, Spring Green WI 53588 *TF:* 877-588-7900 ■ *Web:* www.taliesinpreservation.org	608-588-7090	588-7514	50-3
Talimena State Park 50884 US Hwy 271, Talihina OK 74571 *Web:* www.travelok.com	918-567-2052	567-2052	565
Talisma Corp 777 Yamato Rd, Boca Raton FL 33431 *TF:* 866-397-2537 ■ *Web:* www.talisma.com	561-923-2500		39
Talisman Energy USA Inc 337 Daniel Zenker Dr, Horseheads NY 14845 *TF:* 800-251-0171 ■ *Web:* www.talismanusa.com	607-562-4000		539
Talk Fusion 1319 kingsway rd, Brandon FL 33510 *Web:* www.talkfusion.com	813-651-4030		366

Name / Address	City	State	Zip	Phone	Fax	Class
Talk O'Texas Brands Inc 1610 Roosevelt St.	San Angelo	TX	76905	325-655-6077		296-20
TF: 800-749-6572 ■ *Web:* www.talkotexas.com						
Talk Radio 105.9 3900 11th Ave.	Tuscaloosa	AL	35401	205-344-4589	366-9774	645-170
Web: talkradio1059.iheart.com						
Talk Radio News Service 236 Massachusetts Ave NE Ste 306	Washington	DC	20002	202-337-5322		530
Talk-a-Phone Co 7530 N Natchez Ave.	Niles	IL	60714	773-539-1100	539-1241	647
Web: www.talkaphone.com						
TalkPoint Communications Inc 100 William St	New York	NY	10038	866-323-8660		176
TF: 866-323-8660 ■ *Web:* talkpoint.com						
Tall Timbers 13093 Henry Beadel Dr.	Tallahassee	FL	32312	850-893-4153	893-6470	48-13
Web: www.talltimbers.org						
Talladega Castings & Machine Co Inc 228 N Ct St.	Talladega	AL	35160	256-362-5550	362-1321	307
TF: 800-766-6708 ■ *Web:* www.tmsco.com						
Talladega City Schools 501 S St E PO Box 946.	Talladega	AL	35160	256-315-5600	315-5606	186
Web: www.talladega-cs.net						
Talladega College 627 W Battle St.	Talladega	AL	35160	256-761-6100	362-0274*	166
**Fax:* Admissions ■ *TF:* 866-540-3956 ■ *Web:* talladega.brinkster.net						
Talladega County PO Box 6170	Talladega	AL	35161	256-362-1357	761-2147	338
Web: www.talladegacountyal.org						
Talladega Insurance Agency 109 Spring St N	Talladega	AL	35160	256-362-4153		390
Web: talladega-insurance.com						
Talladega Machinery & Supply Co Inc 301 N Johnson Ave PO Box 736.	Talladega	AL	35161	256-362-4124	761-2579	307
TF Cust Svc: 800-289-8672 ■ *Web:* www.tmsco.com						
Tallahassee Antique Car Museum 6800 Mahan Dr.	Tallahassee	FL	32308	850-942-0137	576-8500	520
Web: www.tacm.com						
Tallahassee City Hall 300 S Adams St	Tallahassee	FL	32301	850-891-0000		337
Web: talgov.com						
Tallahassee Community College 444 Appleyard Dr	Tallahassee	FL	32304	850-201-6200	201-8474*	162
**Fax:* Admissions ■ *TF:* 800-538-9784 ■ *Web:* www.tcc.fl.edu						
Tallahassee Museum of History & Natural Science 3945 Museum Dr	Tallahassee	FL	32310	850-575-8684	574-8243	520
TF: 800-628-2866 ■ *Web:* www.tallahasseemuseum.org						
Tallahassee Regional Airport 3300 Capital Cir SW.	Tallahassee	FL	32310	850-891-7800	891-7837	27
Web: talgov.com						
Tallahassee State Bank 2720 W Tennessee St	Tallahassee	FL	32304	850-576-1182	893-7192	70
Web: www.synovus.com/local/tallahassee-fl						
Tallahassee Symphony Orchestra 1020 E Lafayette St.	Tallahassee	FL	32301	850-224-0461		573-3
Web: www.tallahasseesymphony.org						
Tallahatchie Valley Electric Power Assn 250 Power Dr	Batesville	MS	38606	662-563-4742		245
Web: www.tvepa.com						
Tallan Inc 175 Capital Blvd Ste 401	Rocky Hill	CT	06067	860-633-3693	513-4870	177
TF: 800-677-3693 ■ *Web:* www.tallan.com						
Tallapoosa County 125 N Broadnax St Rm 131	Dadeville	AL	36853	256-825-4268		338
Web: tallaco.com						
Tallapoosa River Electric Co-op 15163 US Hwy 431 S PO Box 675	Lafayette	AL	36862	334-864-9331	864-0817	245
TF: 800-332-8732 ■ *Web:* www.trec.coop						
Talley Inc 12976 Sandoval St.	Santa Fe Springs	CA	90670	562-906-8000		246
TF: 800-949-7099 ■ *Web:* www.talleycom.com						
Talley Management Group Inc 19 Mantua Rd	Mount Royal	NJ	08061	856-423-7222	423-3420	47
Web: www.talley.com						
Tallgrass Energy Partners LP 6640 W 143rd St Ste 200	Overland Park	KS	66223	303-763-2950		787
Web: www.tallgrassenergylp.com						
Tallgrass Prairie National Preserve 226 Broadway PO Box 585.	Cottonwood Falls	KS	66845	620-273-6034	273-6099	564
Web: www.nps.gov						
Tallgrass Restoration LLC 2221 Hammond Dr	Schaumburg	IL	60173	847-925-9830		196
TF: 877-699-8300 ■ *Web:* www.tallgrassrestoration.com						
Tallman Mountain State Park Route 9W	Sparkill	NY	10976	845-359-0544		565
Tallman Truck Centre Ltd 750 Dalton Ave	Kingston	ON	K7M8N8	613-546-3336		57
Web: tallmangroup.ca						
Tallulah Falls School 201 Campus Dr PO Box 10.	Tallulah Falls	GA	30573	706-754-0400	754-3595	622
Web: www.tallulahfalls.org						
Tallulah Gorge State Park 338 Jane Hurt Yarn Dr	Tallulah Falls	GA	30573	706-754-7970		565
Web: www.gastateparks.org						
TallyGenicom 15345 Barranca Pkwy	Irvine	CA	92618	714-368-2300		173-6
TF: 800-436-4266 ■ *Web:* www.tallygenicom.com						
Talon 1552 Down River Dr PO Box 907.	Woodland	WA	98674	360-225-8247	225-7737	710
TF: 800-532-5481 ■ *Web:* www.talon-graphite.com						
Talon Communications Inc 7795 Arjons Dr Ste 201	San Diego	CA	92126	858-653-0100		647
Web: www.taloncom.com						
Talon Energy Services Inc 215 Water St Atlantic Pl Ste 301.	St. John's	NL	A1C6C9	709-739-8450	747-8401	261
Web: talonenergyservices.ca						
Talon Innovations Corp 1003 Industrial Dr S	Sauk Rapids	MN	56379	320-251-0390		696
Web: www.taloneng.com						
Talon Winery & Vineyards 7086 Tates Creek Rd.	Lexington	KY	40515	859-971-3214	971-8787	50-7
Web: www.talonwine.com						
Talquin Electric Co-op Inc 1640 W Jefferson St.	Quincy	FL	32351	850-627-7651	627-1639	245
Web: www.talquinelectric.com						
Talton Communications Inc 910 Ravenwood Dr	Selma	AL	36701	334-877-0704		624
TF: 800-685-1840 ■ *Web:* talton.com						
TALX Corp 11432 Lackland Dr	Saint Louis	MO	63146	314-214-7000	214-7588	39
TF: 800-888-8277 ■ *Web:* www.talx.com						
Talyst Inc 11100 NE Eigth St	Bellevue	WA	98004	425-289-5400		475
Web: www.talyst.com						
T-A-M (Trace-A-Matic Inc) 1570 Commerce Ave.	Brookfield	WI	53045	262-797-7300		621
TF: 877-375-0217 ■ *Web:* www.traceamatic.com						
Tam International Inc 4620 Southerland Rd	Houston	TX	77092	713-462-7617	462-1536	537
TF: 800-462-7617 ■ *Web:* www.tamintl.com						
Tam Metal Products Inc 55 Whitney Rd	Mahwah	NJ	07430	201-848-7800		295
Web: www.tam-ind.com						
Tam O'shanter Country Club 5051 Orchard Lake Rd	West Bloomfield	MI	48323	248-855-1900		711
Web: www.tamoshantercc.org						
Tam O'Shanter Inn 2980 Los Feliz Blvd	Los Angeles	CA	90039	323-664-0228	664-4915	671
Web: www.lawrysonline.com						
Tama County 104 W State St PO Box 61	Toledo	IA	52342	641-484-3980	484-5127	338
Web: www.tamacounty.org						
Tama Mfg Company Inc 100 Cascade Dr.	Allentown	PA	18109	610-231-3100	231-3180	155-21
TF: 800-543-6233 ■ *Web:* www.tamamfg.com						
Tamalpais, The 501 Via Casitas	Greenbrae	CA	94904	415-461-2300	461-0241	672
TF: 800-777-3646 ■ *Web:* www.ncphs.org						
Tamarac Chamber of Commerce 7525 NW 88th Ave # 103	Tamarac	FL	33321	954-722-1520	721-2725	139
Web: www.tamaracchamber.org						
Tamarac Inc 701 Fifth Ave 14th Fl	Seattle	WA	98104	866-525-8811		401
TF: 866-525-8811 ■ *Web:* www.tamaracinc.com						
Tamarack Habilitation Technologies Inc 1670 94th Ln NE.	Blaine	MN	55449	763-795-0057		477
TF: 866-795-0057 ■ *Web:* www.tamarackhti.com						
Tamarack Products Inc 1071 N Old Rand Rd	Wauconda	IL	60084	847-526-9333		535
Web: www.tamarackproducts.com						
Tamarind 43 E 22nd St # 42	New York	NY	10010	212-674-7400		671
Web: tamarindrestaurantsnyc.com						
Tamarind Asian Grill & Sushi Bar 949 S Federal Hwy	Deerfield Beach	FL	33441	954-428-8009		671
Web: www.tamarindgrill.com						
Tamarind Seed 1197 Peachtree St NW Ste 110.	Atlanta	GA	30361	404-873-4888	873-4886	671
Web: www.tamarindseed.com						
Tamayo 1400 Larimer St.	Denver	CO	80202	720-946-1433		671
Web: www.richardsandoval.com						
TAMC (Aroostook Medical Ctr, The) 140 Academy St	Presque Isle	ME	04769	207-768-4000		374-3
Web: www.tamc.org						
Tamco Inc 1466 Delberts Dr.	Monongahela	PA	15063	724-258-6622	258-6692	758
TF: 800-826-2672 ■ *Web:* www.tamcotools.com						
Tamer Industries 185 Riverside Ave	Somerset	MA	02725	508-677-0900	677-3037	621
Web: www.tamerind.com						
Tamiment Resort & Conference Ctr Bushkill Falls Rd.	Tamiment	PA	18371	570-588-6652		669
TF: 800-233-8105 ■ *Web:* worldgolf.com						
Tamir Biotechnology Inc 12625 High Bluff Dr Ste 113.	San Diego	CA	92130	732-823-1003	652-4575	85
OTC: ACEL ■ *TF:* 800-732-0330 ■ *Web:* www.alfacell.com						
Tamlin Software Developers Inc 5646 Milton St Ste 540.	Dallas	TX	75206	214-739-6576		177
TF: 800-261-6953 ■ *Web:* www.tamlinsoftware.com						
Tammany Oil & Gas LLC 20445 State Hwy 249 Ste 200.	Houston	TX	77070	281-517-0770		536
Web: www.tammanyoil.com						
Tamolly's 5940 Summerhill Rd.	Texarkana	TX	75503	903-792-0732		671
Web: www.tamollys.com						
Tampa Armature Works Inc 6312 78th St.	Riverview	FL	33578	813-621-5661		518
TF: 866-465-8905 ■ *Web:* www.tawinc.com						
Tampa Bay & Co 401 E Jackson St Ste 2100	Tampa	FL	33602	813-223-1111	229-6616	206
TF: 877-230-0078 ■ *Web:* www.visittampabay.com						
Tampa Bay Beaches Chamber of Commerce 6990 Gulf Blvd	Saint Pete Beach	FL	33706	727-360-6957	360-2233	139
Web: www.tampabaybeaches.com						
Tampa Bay Buccaneers 1 Buccaneer Pl	Tampa	FL	33607	813-870-2700		715-3
Web: www.buccaneers.com						
Tampa Bay Downs Inc 11225 Racetrack Rd.	Tampa	FL	33626	813-855-4401	854-3539	642
TF: 800-200-4434 ■ *Web:* www.tampabaydowns.com						
Tampa Bay Fisheries Inc 3060 Gallagher Rd	Dover	FL	33527	813-752-8883		296-14
TF: 800-732-3663 ■ *Web:* www.tbfish.com						
Tampa Bay History Ctr 801 Old Water St.	Tampa	FL	33602	813-228-0097	223-7021	520
Web: www.tampabayhistorycenter.org						
Tampa Bay Lightning St Pete Times Forum 401 Channelside Dr	Tampa	FL	33602	813-301-6500	301-1482	716
TF: 800-745-3000 ■ *Web:* lightning.nhl.com						
Tampa Bay Steel Corp 6901 Sixth Ave E	Tampa	FL	33619	813-621-4738		492
Web: www.tampabaysteel.com						
Tampa Brass & Aluminum 8511 Florida Mining Blvd	Tampa	FL	33634	813-885-6064	882-3271	308
Web: www.tampabrass.com						
Tampa City Hall 306 E Jackson St.	Tampa	FL	33602	813-274-8251	274-7050	337
Web: www.tampagov.net						
Tampa Convention Ctr 333 S Franklin St.	Tampa	FL	33602	813-274-8511	274-7430	205
TF: 866-790-4111 ■ *Web:* www.tampagov.net						
Tampa General Hospital 1 Tampa General Cir	Tampa	FL	33606	813-844-7000		374-3
Web: www.tgh.org						
Tampa International Airport 4100 George J Bean Pkwy PO Box 22287	Tampa	FL	33607	813-870-8700	875-6670	27
TF: 866-289-9673 ■ *Web:* www.tampaairport.com						
Tampa Marriott Waterside Hotel & Marina 700 S Florida Ave	Tampa	FL	33602	813-204-6300	204-6342	707
TF: 888-268-1616 ■ *Web:* www.marriott.com						
Tampa Museum of Art 120 W Gasparilla Plaza	Tampa	FL	33602	813-274-8131		520
TF: 866-790-4111 ■ *Web:* www.tampagov.net						

				Phone	Fax	Class

Tampa Port Authority
1101 Channelside Dr .... Tampa FL 33602 813-905-7678 905-5109 618
TF: 800-741-2297 ■ *Web:* www.tampaport.com
Tampa Steel Erecting Co
5127 Bloomingdale Ave .... Tampa FL 33619 813-677-7184 677-8364 189-14
Web: tampasteelerecting.com
Tampa Tank Inc 2710 E Fifth Ave .... Tampa FL 33605 813-623-2675 91
Web: tti-fss.com
Tampa Theater
711 N Franklin St PO Box 172188 .... Tampa FL 33602 813-274-8286 572
Web: www.tampatheatre.org
Tampa-Hillsborough County Public Library
900 N Ashley Dr .... Tampa FL 33602 813-273-3652 434-3
Web: www.hcplc.org
Tampico Spice Company Inc
5941 S Central Ave .... Los Angeles CA 90001 323-235-3154 232-8686 296-37
Web: www.tampicospice.com
Tamrac Group Inc, The
10946 C Beaver Dam Rd .... Hunt Valley MD 21030 410-568-1200 390
Web: tamracinsurance.com
Tamron USA Inc 10 Austin Blvd .... Commack NY 11725 631-858-8400 591
Web: www.tamron.com/en
Tamura Superette Inc
86-032 Farrington Hwy .... Waianae HI 96792 808-696-3321 345
Web: tamurasupermarket.com
Tamwood International College
300-909 Burrard St .... Vancouver BC V6Z2N2 604-899-4480 899-4481 423
TF: 866-533-0123 ■ *Web:* www.tamwood.com
Tana Exploration Company LLC
4001 Maple Ave Ste 300 .... Dallas TX 75219 469-276-8262 276-8300 539
Web: www.tanaexp.com
Tanager Inc
10010 Junction Dr Ste 120N .... Annapolis Junction MD 20701 240-547-3150 177
Web: www.tanagerinc.com
Tanaka of Tokyo East
150 Kaiulani Ave 3rd Fl .... Honolulu HI 96815 808-922-4233 671
Web: www.tanakaoftokyo.com
Tanco Engineering Inc 1400 Taurus Ct .... Loveland CO 80537 970-776-4200 261
Web: tancoeng.com
Tandberg Data
10225 Westmoor Dr Ste 125 .... Westminster CO 80021 303-442-4333 173-8
TF: 800-392-2983 ■ *Web:* www.tandbergdata.com
Tandel Systems Inc 3982 Tampa Rd .... Oldsmar FL 34677 727-530-1110 261
TF: 800-486-1571 ■ *Web:* www.tandelsystems.com
Tandem 460 McGill St Ste 500 .... Montreal QC H2Y2H2 514-510-8900 528
Web: www.tandemexpansion.com
Tandem Interactive
1700 E Las Olas Blvd Ste 301 .... Fort Lauderdale FL 33301 954-281-9995 5
Web: www.tandem-interactive.com
Tandem Printing Inc
2970 Lexington Ave S .... Saint Paul MN 55121 651-289-2970 627
Web: www.tandemprinting.com
Tandem Select 113 S College Ave .... Fort Collins CO 80524 970-491-9655 196
Web: www.premieress.com
Tandem Transit LLC
1449-37th St Ste 214 .... Brooklyn NY 11218 718-689-1300 873-2936 387
Web: tandemtransit.com
Tandet Management Inc 1351 Speers Rd .... Oakville ON L6L2X5 905-827-4200 449
Web: www.tandet.com
Tandoor 3530 Village Dr .... Lincoln NE 68516 402-423-2007 671
Web: www.tandurlincoln.com
Tandoor 1117 S 108th St .... Milwaukee WI 53214 414-777-1600 671
Web: tandoorrestaurantmilwaukee.com
Tandoor Indian Restaurant
1200 N Fielder Rd Ste 532 .... Arlington TX 76012 817-261-6604 671
Web: www.tandoorrestaurant.net
Tandus Centiva
311 Smith Industrial Blvd PO Box 1147 .... Dalton GA 30722 706-259-9711 131
TF: 800-248-2878 ■ *Web:* tandus-centiva.com
Tandy Brands Accessories Inc
3631 W Davis St Ste A .... Dallas TX 75211 214-519-5200 155-2
NASDAQ: TBAC
Tanen Directed Advertising
12 S Main St .... South Norwalk CT 06854 203-855-5855 7
Web: www.tanendirected.com
Taney Corp 5130 Allendale Ln .... Taneytown MD 21787 410-756-6671 756-4103 499
Web: www.taneystair.com
Taney County 132 David St PO Box 156 .... Forsyth MO 65653 417-546-7200 546-2519 338
Web: www.taneycounty.org
Tang Industries Inc
8960 Spanish Ridge Ave .... Las Vegas NV 89148 702-734-3700 185
Web: nmlp.com
Tangata 2002 N Main St .... Santa Ana CA 92706 714-550-0906 671
Web: www.patinagroup.com
Tangelo's Grille 3121 Beach Blvd S .... Gulfport FL 33707 727-894-1695 671
Web: www.tangelosgrille.com
Tangent Design Engineering
2719 7 Ave NE .... Calgary AB T2A2L9 403-274-4647 261
TF: 800-663-6500 ■ *Web:* www.tangentservices.com
Tangent Inc 191 Airport Blvd .... Burlingame CA 94010 650-342-9388 342-9380 173-2
TF: 800-342-9388 ■ *Web:* www.tangent.com
Tangent Systems Inc
2155 Stnngton Ave .... Hoffman Estates IL 60195 847-882-3833 177
TF: 800-370-5320 ■ *Web:* www.tangent-systems.com
Tangent Technologies LLC
1001 Sullivan Rd .... Aurora IL 60506 630-264-1110 596
Web: www.tangentusa.com
Tanger Factory Outlet Centers Inc
3200 Northline Ave Ste 360 .... Greensboro NC 27408 336-292-3010 852-2096 655
NYSE: SKT ■ *TF:* 800-720-6728 ■ *Web:* www.tangeroutlet.com
Tanger Outlet Ctr San Marcos
4015 S IH-35 Ste 319 .... San Marcos TX 78666 512-396-7446 396-7449 460
TF: 800-408-8424 ■ *Web:* www.tangeroutlet.com
Tangerine Travel Ltd
16017 Juanita Woodinville Way NE Ste 201 .... Bothell WA 98011 425-822-2333 772
TF: 800-678-8202 ■ *Web:* www.tangerinetravel.com
Tangible Media Inc
12 W 37th St 2nd FL .... New York NY 10018 212-359-1440 643-1555 6
Web: www.tangiblemedia.com
Tangible Solutions Inc
1320 Matthews Township Pkwy Ste 201 .... Matthews NC 28105 704-940-4200 180
TF: 800-393-9886 ■ *Web:* www.tangible.com
Tangipahoa Parish 206 E Mulberry St .... Amite LA 70422 985-748-3211 338
Web: www.tangipahoa.org
Tangle Creek Energy Ltd
715 Fifth Ave SW Ste 1400 .... Calgary AB T2P2X6 403-648-4900 536
Web: www.tanglecreekenergy.com
Tanglewood Conservatories
15 Engerman Ave .... Denton MD 21629 410-479-4700 186
Web: www.tanglewoodconservatories.com
Tanglewood Resort Hotel & Conference Ctr
290 Tanglewood Cir .... Pottsboro TX 75076 903-786-2968 669
TF: 800-833-6569 ■ *Web:* www.tanglewoodresort.com
Tango 1100 Pike St .... Seattle WA 98101 206-583-0382 671
Web: tangorestaurant.com
Tango Consulting Group LLC
31 James Vincent Dr .... Clinton CT 06413 877-567-6045 196
TF: 877-567-6045 ■ *Web:* www.tangoconsulting.com
Tango Management Consulting LLC
6225 N State Hwy 161 Ste 300 .... Irving TX 75038 855-938-2646 180
TF: 855-938-2646 ■ *Web:* tangoanalytics.com
Tango Media Group 326 Carlaw Ave .... Toronto ON M4M3N8 416-204-6269 225
Web: www.tangomediagroup.com
Tango Networks Inc 3801 Parkwood Blvd .... Frisco TX 75034 469-229-6000 736
Web: www.tango-networks.com
Tangoe Lackawanna Ave Ste 2B .... Parsippany NJ 07054 844-484-5041 859-9427* 178-7
**Fax Area Code:* 203 ■ *TF:* 844-484-5041 ■ *Web:* www.tangoe.com
Tangoe Inc 35 Executive Blvd .... Orange CT 06477 203-859-9300 859-9427 177
NASDAQ: TNGO ■ *TF:* 877-571-4737 ■ *Web:* www.tangoe.com
Tangram Interiors Inc
9200 Sorensen Ave .... Santa Fe Springs CA 90670 562-365-5000 320
Web: www.tangraminteriors.com
Tanimura & Antle Inc PO Box 4070 .... Salinas CA 93912 800-772-4542 10-11
TF: 800-772-4542 ■ *Web:* www.taproduce.com
Tanita Corp of America Inc
2625 S Clearbrook Dr .... Arlington Heights IL 60005 847-640-9241 640-9261 684
TF: 800-826-4828 ■ *Web:* www.tanita.com
Tank Connection LLC 3609 N 16th St .... Parsons KS 67357 620-423-3010 770
TF: 800-437-8076 ■ *Web:* www.tankconnection.com
Tank Industry Consultants Inc
7740 W New York St .... Indianapolis IN 46214 317-271-3100 261
Web: tankindustry.com
Tankersley Concrete Company Inc
1630 Rock Crusher Rd .... Lewisburg TN 37091 931-359-3112 183
Tankinetics Inc
230 Industrial Park Rd .... Harrison AR 72601 870-741-3626 596
Web: www.tankinetics.com
Tankmaster Rentals L T D
Poplar St Ste 117 .... Red Deer AB T4E1B4 403-342-1105 23
Web: www.tankmaster.ca
Tanko Screw Products Corp
515 Thomas Dr .... Bensenville IL 60106 630-787-0504 621
Web: ldredmer.com
Tanks-A-Lot Ltd
1810 Yellowhead Trail NE .... Edmonton AB T6S1B4 780-472-8265 478-5099 770
TF: 800-661-5667 ■ *Web:* www.tanks-a-lot.com
TanMar Companies LLC 711 S Chestnut .... Tomball TX 77375 281-601-6180 606
Web: www.tanmarcompanies.com
Tannehill Ironworks Historical State Park
12632 Confederate Pkwy .... McCalla AL 35111 205-477-5711 477-9400 50-3
TF: 800-298-1861 ■ *Web:* www.tannehill.org
Tannenbaum Historic Park
2200 New Garden Rd .... Greensboro NC 27410 336-545-5315 50-3
Web: www.greensboro-nc.gov
Tanner Cos LLC 581Rock Rd .... Rutherfordton NC 28139 800-669-3662 287-6196* 155-21
**Fax Area Code:* 828 ■ *TF:* 800-669-3662 ■ *Web:* www.doncaster.com
Tanner Electric Co
45710 SE North Bend Way .... North Bend WA 98045 425-888-0623 888-5688 245
TF: 800-472-0208 ■ *Web:* tannerelectric.coop
Tanner Industries Inc
735 Davisville Rd .... Southampton PA 18966 215-322-1238 322-7791* 146
**Fax:* Sales ■ *TF:* 800-643-6226 ■ *Web:* www.tannerind.com
Tanner Medical Ctr 705 Dixie St .... Carrollton GA 30117 770-836-9666 374-3
TF: 800-561-3357 ■ *Web:* www.tanner.org
Tanner Research Inc 825 S Myrtle Ave .... Monrovia CA 91016 626-471-9700 174
TF: 877-325-2223 ■ *Web:* www.tanner.com
Tanner Systems Inc PO Box 488 .... Saint Joseph MN 56374 320-363-1800 143
TF: 800-461-6454 ■ *Web:* www.tannersystems.com
Tannor Capital Management LLC
150 Grand St Ste 401 .... White Plains NY 10601 914-509-5000 528
Web: www.tannorpartners.com
Tano Capital LLC
1 Franklin Pkwy Bldg 970 2nd Fl .... San Mateo CA 94403 650-212-0330 690
Web: www.tanocapital.com
Tanos Exploration LLC
110 N College Ave Ste 1001 .... Tyler TX 75702 903-597-7667 536
Web: www.tanosexp.com
Tanque Verde Ranch 14301 E Speedway .... Tucson AZ 85748 520-296-6275 239
TF: 800-234-3833 ■ *Web:* www.tanqueverderanch.com
Tantalus Resort Lodge
4200 Whistler Way .... Whistler BC V0N1B4 604-932-4146 932-2405 669
TF: 888-806-2299 ■ *Web:* www.tantaluslodge.com
Tan-Tar-A Resort Golf Club & Spa
494 Tantara Dr PO Box 188TT .... Osage Beach MO 65065 573-348-3131 348-3206 669
TF Resv: 800-826-8272 ■ *Web:* www.tan-tar-a.com
TanTara Transportation Corp
2420 Stewart Rd .... Muscatine IA 52761 563-262-8621 264-8998 780
TF: 800-650-0292 ■ *Web:* www.tantara.us
Tante Marie's Cooking School
271 Francisco St .... San Francisco CA 94133 415-788-6699 163
Web: www.tantemarie.com
Tanzania 307 E 53rd St .... New York NY 10022 212-697-3612 697-3618 784
Web: www.un.int
Embassy 1232 22nd St NW .... Washington DC 20037 202-939-6125 797-7408 257
Web: www.tanzaniaembassy-us.org
Taos County 105 Albright St Ste A .... Taos NM 87571 575-737-6300 737-6314 338
TF: 800-825-6639 ■ *Web:* www.taoscounty.org

Name / Address	City	State	ZIP	Phone	Fax	Class
Taos Mountain 121 Daggett Dr *TF:* 888-826-7686 ■ *Web:* www.taos.com	San Jose	CA	95134	408-588-1200		463
Taos Pueblo PO Box 1846 *Web:* www.taospueblo.com	Taos	NM	87571	575-758-1028		50-3
Taos Ski Valley Inc 116 Sutton Pl *TF:* 800-776-1111 ■ *Web:* www.skitaos.com	Taos Ski Valley	NM	87525	575-776-2291		31
TAP Advisors LLC 152 W 57th St 34th Fl *Web:* www.tapadvisors.com	New York	NY	10019	212-909-9010		70
Tap Packaging Solutions 2160 Superior Ave *TF:* 800-827-5679 ■ *Web:* www.tap-usa.com	Cleveland	OH	44114	216-781-6000		560
TAP Plastics Inc 6475 Sierra Ln *TF:* 800-894-0827 ■ *Web:* www.tapplastics.com	Dublin	CA	94568	925-829-4889		607
Tap Tap 819 Fifth St *Web:* www.taptaprestaurant.com	Miami Beach	FL	33139	305-672-2898		671
Tapa the World 2115 J St *Web:* www.tapatheworld.com	Sacramento	CA	95816	916-442-4353		671
Tapas Picasso 3923 Fourth Ave *Web:* tapas-picasso.com	San Diego	CA	92103	619-294-3061		671
Tapas Teatro 1711 N Charles St *Web:* www.tapasteatro.com	Baltimore	MD	21201	410-332-0110		671
Tapatio Springs Golf Resort & Conference Ctr 1 Resort Way *TF:* 855-627-2243 ■ *Web:* www.tapatioresort.com	Boerne	TX	78006	830-443-9681		669
Tapco Inc 225 Rock Industrial Park Dr *Web:* www.tapcoinc.com	Bridgeton	MO	63044	314-739-9191		234
Tapco International Corp 29797 Beck Rd *TF:* 800-521-7567 ■ *Web:* www.tapcogroup.com	Wixom	MI	48393	248-668-6400	668-6466	699
Tapco International Inc 990 W 15th St	Riviera Beach	FL	33404	561-844-2502		789
Tape & Label Converters Inc 8231 Allport Ave *TF:* 888-285-2462 ■ *Web:* www.stickybiz.com	Santa Fe Springs	CA	90670	562-945-3486	696-8198	413
Tapecoat Co, The 1527 Lyons St *Web:* www.tapecoat.com	Evanston	IL	60201	847-866-8500		3
Tapecon Inc 10 Latta Rd *TF:* 800-333-2407 ■ *Web:* www.tapecon.com	Rochester	NY	14612	585-621-8400		413
TAPEMARK Co 1685 Marthaler Ln *TF:* 800-535-1998 ■ *Web:* www.tapemark.com	St Paul	MN	55118	651-455-1611	450-8403	413
Tapeo 266 Newbury St *Web:* www.tapeo.com	Boston	MA	02116	617-267-4799		671
TapeSouth Inc 10302 Deerwood Pk Ste 125 *Web:* www.tapesouth.com	Jacksonville	FL	32256	904-642-1800	642-7006	732
Tapestry Solutions Inc 5643 Copley Dr *Web:* www.tapestrysolutions.com	San Diego	CA	92111	858-503-1990		177
Tapeswitch Corp 100 Schmitt Blvd *TF:* 800-234-8273 ■ *Web:* www.tapeswitch.com	Farmingdale	NY	11735	631-630-0442	630-0454	729
Tapia Bros Co 6067 District Blvd *Web:* www.tapiabrothers.com	Maywood	CA	90270	323-560-7415		297-9
Tapjoy Inc 111 Sutter St *Web:* www.tapjoy.com	San Francisco	CA	94104	415-766-6900		387
Tapmatic Corp 802 S Clearwater Loop *TF General:* 800-854-6019 ■ *Web:* www.tapmatic.com	Post Falls	ID	83854	208-773-8048	773-3021	493
TAPO Ventures LLC 195 N Harbor Dr Ste 4601 *Web:* www.tapoventures.com	Chicago	IL	60601	312-540-1333		360-3
Tapper's Fine Jewelry Inc Orchard Mall 6337 Orchard Lake Rd. *Web:* www.tappers.com	West Bloomfield	MI	48322	248-932-7700		410
TAPPI (Technical Assn of the Pulp & Paper Industry) 15 Technology Pkwy S *TF Sales:* 800-332-8686 ■ *Web:* www.tappi.org	Norcross	GA	30092	770-446-1400	446-6947	49-13
TappIn Inc 1525 Fourth Ave Ste 500 *Web:* www.tappin.com	Seattle	WA	98101	206-708-7267		396
Tapscott's 1403 E 18th St *TF:* 800-626-1922 ■ *Web:* www.silk-flowers-by-tapscotts.com	Owensboro	KY	42303	270-684-2308	683-3702	293
TAQA North Ltd 308-4th Ave *Web:* taqaglobal.com	Calgary	AB	T2P0H7	403-724-5000	724-5001	675
Taqua LLC 740 E Campbell Rd Ste 200	Richardson	TX	75081	972-692-1800	437-2762	729
Taqueria De Anda 1029 E Fourth St *Web:* taqueriadeanda.com	Santa Ana	CA	92701	714-558-0856		671
Taqueria el Poblano 2400B Mt Vernon Ave *Web:* www.taqueriapoblano.com	Alexandria	VA	22301	703-548-8226		671
Taqueria Mi Pueblo Mexican Restaurant 7278 Dix St *Web:* www.mipueblorestaurant.com	Detroit	MI	48209	313-841-3315		671
Taqueria Poblano 2503 N Harrison St *Web:* www.taqueriapoblano.com	Arlington	VA	22207	703-237-8250		671
Taqueria Uruaban 4601 Goni Rd	Carson City	NV	89706	775-883-7609		671
TAR (Tennessee Assn of Realtors) 901 19th Ave S *TF:* 877-321-1477 ■ *Web:* www.tarnet.com	Nashville	TN	37212	615-321-1477	321-4905	656
Tar Hollow State Park 16396 Tar Hollow Rd *Web:* www.ohiodnr.com	Laurelville	OH	43135	740-887-4818		565
Tara Manufacturing Inc 2294 Old 431 Hwy *Web:* www.taramfg.com	Owens Cross Roads	AL	35763	256-725-2500		596
Tara Pearls 10 W 46th Ste 600 *TF:* 888-575-8272 ■ *Web:* www.tarapearls.com	New York	NY	10036	888-575-8272		411
Tara Plastics Corp 175 Lake Mirror Rd *Web:* www.taraplastics.com	Forest Park	GA	30297	404-366-4464	366-3816	66
Tara Toy Corp 40 Adams Ave *TF:* 800-899-8272 ■ *Web:* www.taratoy.com	Hauppauge	NY	11788	631-273-8697	273-8583	762
Taranta 210 Hanover St *Web:* www.tarantarist.com	Boston	MA	02113	617-720-0052	507-0492	671
Tarbell Realtors 1403 N Tustin Ave *Web:* tarbell.idxhome.com	Santa Ana	CA	92705	714-972-0988		652
Tarbell's 3213 E Camelback *Web:* www.tarbells.com	Phoenix	AZ	85018	602-955-8100		671
Tarboro Edgecombe Chamber of Commerce 509 Trade St *Web:* www.discoveredgecombe.com	Tarboro	NC	27886	252-823-7241	823-1499	139
TARC (Transit Authority of River City) 1000 W Broadway *Fax: Cust Svc	Louisville	KY	40203	502-585-1234	213-3243*	468
Targa Real Estate Services Inc 720 S 348th St A2 *Web:* www.targarealestate.com	Federal Way	WA	98003	253-815-0393		655
Target Copy 635 W Tennessee St *TF:* 800-561-3357 ■ *Web:* targetprintmail.com	Tallahassee	FL	32304	850-224-3007		113
Target Corp 1000 Nicollet Mall *NYSE:* TGT ■ *Fax: Hum Res ■ *TF Cust Svc:* 800-440-0680 ■ *Web:* www.target.com	Minneapolis	MN	55403	612-304-6073	304-6073*	229
Target Ctr Arena 600 First Ave N *Web:* www.targetcenter.com	Minneapolis	MN	55403	612-673-1300	673-1387	720
Target Direct Mailing Services 1206 Esi Dr *Web:* targetdirectmail.com	Springdale	AR	72764	479-750-4900		5
Target Drilling Inc 1112 Glacier Dr *Web:* www.targetdrilling.com	Smithton	PA	15479	724-633-3927		540
Target Media Partners Inc 5200 Lankershim Blvd Ste 350 *Web:* www.targetmediapartners.com	North Hollywood	CA	90601	323-930-3123		532-3
Target Solutions Inc 530 Causeway Dr *Web:* www.targetsol.com	Wrightsville Beach	NC	28480	910-509-1800		721
Target Steel Inc 24601 Vreeland *Web:* www.targetsteel.net	Flat Rock	MI	48134	734-789-9700		492
Targeted Job Fairs Inc 4441 Glenway Ave *TF:* 800-695-1939 ■ *Web:* www.targetedjobfairs.com	Cincinnati	OH	45205	800-695-1939		260
Targeted Learning 706 E Technology Ave Ste 3100	Orem	UT	84097	801-235-9414		463
TargetSpot Inc 33 E 33rd St Ste 801 *Web:* www.targetspot.com	New York	NY	10016	212-631-0500		387
Targun Plastics Co 899 Skokie Blvd *Web:* targun.com	Northbrook	IL	60062	847-509-9355		603
Targus Inc 1211 N Miller St *TF:* 877-482-7487 ■ *Web:* www.targus.com	Anaheim	CA	92806	714-765-5555		453
Tarigma Corp 6161 Busch Blvd Ste 110 *TF:* 800-695-6344 ■ *Web:* www.tarigma.com	Columbus	OH	43229	614-436-3734		177
Tarkett Inc 1001 Yamaska St E *TF:* 800-363-9276 ■ *Web:* www.tarkettna.com	Farnham	QC	J2N1J7	450-293-3173		291
Tarleton State University PO Box T-0030 *Fax: Admissions ■ *TF:* 800-687-8236 ■ *Web:* www.tarleton.edu	Stephenville	TX	76402	254-968-9125	968-9951*	166
Tarlton Corp 5500 W Pk Ave *Web:* www.tarltoncorp.com	Saint Louis	MO	63110	314-633-3300	647-1940	186
Tarlton Properties Inc 1530 O'Brien Dr Ste C *Web:* www.tarlton.com	Menlo Park	CA	94025	650-330-3600		652
Taro Pharmaceuticals Inc 130 E Dr *TF:* 800-268-1975 ■ *Web:* www.taro.ca	Brampton	ON	L6T1C1	905-791-8276	791-5008	582
Taro Pharmaceuticals USA Inc 3 Skyline Dr *TF:* 800-544-1449 ■ *Web:* www.taro.com/usa	Hawthorne	NY	10532	914-345-9001	345-8727	583
Tarpon Springs Chamber of Commerce 111 E Tarpon Ave *Web:* tarponspringschamber.com	Tarpon Springs	FL	34689	727-937-6109	937-2879	139
Tarps & Tie-Downs Inc 24967 Huntwood Ave *Web:* tarpstiedowns.com	Hayward	CA	94544	510-782-8772		96
Tarpy's Roadhouse 2999 Monterey-Salinas Hwy *Web:* www.tarpys.com	Monterey	CA	93940	831-647-1444		671
Tarr LLC 2429 N Borthwick St *TF:* 800-422-5069 ■ *Web:* www.tarrllc.com	Portland	OR	97227	800-422-5069		146
Tarrant County 100 E Weatherford St *TF:* 800-888-0511 ■ *Web:* www.tarrantcounty.com	Fort Worth	TX	76196	817-884-1195	884-3295	338
Tarrant County College						
Northeast 828 W Harwood Rd *Fax: Admissions ■ *TF:* 800-799-7233 ■ *Web:* www.tccd.edu	Hurst	TX	76054	817-515-8223	515-6988*	162
Northwest 4801 Marine Creek Pkwy *Fax: Admissions ■ *TF:* 800-799-7233 ■ *Web:* www.tccd.edu	Fort Worth	TX	76179	817-515-7100	515-7732*	162
South 5301 Campus Dr *Fax: Admissions ■ *Web:* www.tccd.edu	Fort Worth	TX	76119	817-515-8223	515-4110*	162
Southeast 2100 SE Pkwy *Fax: Admissions ■ *Web:* www.tccd.edu	Arlington	TX	76018	817-515-8223	515-3182*	162
Tarrant Interiors Inc 5000 S Fwy	Fort Worth	TX	76115	817-922-5000	922-5015	286
Tarrier Foods Corp 2700 International St *Web:* www.tarrierfoods.com	Columbus	OH	43228	614-876-8595	545-6111	297-8
Tarrier Steel Company Inc, The 1379 S 22nd St *Web:* www.tarrier.com	Columbus	OH	43206	614-444-4000		492
Tarryall River Ranch 270015 County Rd 77 *TF:* 800-408-8407 ■ *Web:* tarryallranch.com	Lake George	CO	80827	800-408-8407		239
Tarrytown House Estate & Conference Ctr 49 E Sunnyside Ln *TF:* 800-553-8118 ■ *Web:* www.tarrytownhouseestate.com	Tarrytown	NY	10591	914-591-8200		226
Tarrytown Music Hall 13 Main St PO Box 686 *TF:* 877-840-0457 ■ *Web:* www.tarrytownmusichall.org	Tarrytown	NY	10591	914-631-3390		572
Tarsadia Investments, 620 Newport Ctr Dr. *Web:* tarsadia.com	Newport Beach	CA	92660	949-610-8000		379
Tarsin Inc 916 Southwood Blvd Ste 3A	Incline Village	NV	89451	775-833-0156		809
Tartan Marketing 10467 93rd Ave N Maple Grove *Web:* www.tartanmarketing.com	Maple Grove	MN	55369	763-391-7575		195
Tartan Yachts 1920 Fairport Nursery Rd *Web:* www.tartanyachts.com	Fairport Harbor	OH	44077	440-332-0578		90
Tarter Krinsky & Drogin LLP 1350 Broadway *TF:* 800-900-4250 ■ *Web:* www.tarterkrinsky.com	New York	NY	10018	212-216-8000		41

Phone | Fax | Class

Tarus Products Inc
38100 Commerce Dr ... Sterling Heights MI 48312 586-977-1400 697
Web: www.tarus.com

TAS Commercial Concrete Construction LLC
19319 Oil Ctr Blvd ... Houston TX 77073 281-230-7500 230-7664 189-3
Web: www.tasconcrete.com

TASC Technical Services LLC
73 Newton Rd ... Plaistow NH 03865 877-304-8272 195
TF: 877-304-8272 ■ *Web:* www.tasctech.com

Tasende Gallery 820 Prospect St ... La Jolla CA 92037 858-454-3691 42
Web: www.tasendegallery.com

TASH
1001 Connecticut Ave NW Ste 235 ... Washington DC 20006 202-540-9020 540-9019 48-17
Web: www.tash.org

Tashlik Kreutzer Goldwyn & Crandell P C
40 Cuttermill Rd Ste 200 ... Great Neck NY 11021 516-466-8005 445
Web: tgcllaw.com

Task Force Tips Inc
3701 Innovation Way ... Valparaiso IN 46383 219-462-6161 464-7155 283
TF: 800-348-2686 ■ *Web:* www.tft.com

Task Management Inc 99 Danbury Rd ... Ridgefield CT 06877 203-438-9777 463
Web: www.taskmanagement.com

Taskstream LLC 71 W 23rd St ... New York NY 10010 212-868-2700 225
TF: 800-311-5656 ■ *Web:* taskstream.com

TaskUs Inc
3233 Donald Douglas Loop S Ste 3 ... Santa Monica CA 90405 888-400-8275 393
TF: 888-400-8275 ■ *Web:* www.taskus.com

Tasler Inc 1804 Tasler Dr ... Webster City IA 50595 515-832-5200 551
TF: 800-482-7537 ■ *Web:* www.tasler.com

Tasman Leather Group LLC 9 Main St ... Hartland ME 04943 207-553-3700 432
Web: www.tasmanindustries.com/locations/tasmanleathergroup.html

TASS Inc 12016 115th Ave NE Ste 100 ... Kirkland WA 98034 425-821-2200 261
Web: www.tassinc.com

Tass News Agency
700 Third Ave Rm 1900 ... New York NY 10017 212-245-4250 530

Taste Maker Foods LLC
1415 E Mclemore Ave # 1425 ... Memphis TN 38106 901-274-4407 297-8
Web: www.tomlinsonassociates.com

Taste of China 11360 E 31st St ... Tulsa OK 74146 918-664-2252 671

Taste of Home Magazine
5400 S 60th St ... Greendale WI 53129 414-423-0100 457-11
TF: 800-344-6913 ■ *Web:* www.tasteofhome.com

Taste of India 3192 SHERIDAN Dr ... Amherst NY 14226 716-837-0460 671
Web: www.tasteofindia.com

Taste of India 230 Wickenden St ... Providence RI 02903 401-421-4355 751-1432 671
Web: www.tasteofindiari.com

Taste of India 3110 N Division St ... Spokane WA 99207 509-327-7313 671

Taste of Italy 8421 University Blvd ... Clive IA 50325 515-221-0743 671
Web: atasteofitalyia.com

Taste of Nature Inc
2828 Donald Douglas Loop N Ste A ... Santa Monica CA 90405 310-396-4433 297-3
Web: www.candyasap.com

Taste of Texas Restaurant
10505 Katy Fwy ... Houston TX 77024 713-932-6901 671
Web: www.tasteoftexas.com

Taste of Thai 1500 Mill St ... Greensboro NC 27408 336-273-1318 671
Web: www.tasteofthaigreensboro.com

Taste of Thai 2636 E Arkansas Ln ... Arlington TX 76010 817-543-0110 671
Web: tasteofthaiarlington.com

Taste of Thai 527 University Ave ... San Diego CA 92103 619-291-7525 671
Web: tasteofthaisandiego.com

Taste of Thailand 3321 Lorna Rd ... Birmingham AL 35216 205-970-6063 671

Taste of Thailand 15712 W Ctr Rd ... Omaha NE 68130 402-691-9991 671
Web: www.tasteofthailandomaha.com

Taste of the Islands
909 W Spring Creek Pkwy ... Plano TX 75023 972-517-5900 671
Web: tasteoftheislands.net

Tastefully Simple Inc
1920 Turning Leaf Ln SW ... Alexandria MN 56308 320-763-0695 763-2458 296-36
Web: www.tastefullysimple.com

Tasty Baking Co 4300 S 26th St ... Philadelphia PA 19112 215-221-8500 296-1
TF: 800-248-2789 ■ *Web:* www.tastykake.com

Tasty Thai 1401 Coffee Rd ... Modesto CA 95355 209-571-8424 671

Tasty Tom's Bistro 9965 82nd Ave NW ... Edmonton AB T6E1Z1 780-437-5761 671

Tata Consultancy Services Ltd (TCS)
101 Pk Ave 26th Fl ... New York NY 10178 212-557-8038 867-8652 194
TF: 800-816-6710 ■ *Web:* www.tcs.com

Tata Steel International (Americas) Inc
475 N Martingale Rd Ste 400 ... Schaumburg IL 60173 847-619-0400 492
Web: www.tatasteelamericas.com

Tatar Art Projects 300 King St E ... Toronto ON M5A1K4 416-360-3822 42
Web: tatarartprojects.ca

Tate Access Floors Inc
7510 Montevideo Rd ... Jessup MD 20794 410-799-4200 799-4207 491
TF: 800-231-7788 ■ *Web:* tateinc.com

Tate Andale Inc 1941 Lansdowne Rd ... Baltimore MD 21227 410-247-8700 247-9672 595
TF: 800-296-8283 ■ *Web:* www.tateandale.com

Tate House Museum 1267 Westbrook St ... Portland ME 04102 207-774-6177 774-6198 520
Web: www.tatehouse.org

Tate Ornamental Inc
411 Industrial Dr ... White House TN 37188 615-672-0348 492
Web: www.tateornamental.com

Tate's Bake Shop Inc 43 N Sea Rd ... Southampton NY 11968 631-283-9830 345
Web: www.tatesbakeshop.com

Tates Supermarket Inc 120 Fourth St ... Clymer PA 15728 724-254-4420 345
Web: tatesmarket.com

Tatnuck Bookseller 18 Lyman St ... Westborough MA 01581 508-366-4959 366-7929 95
Web: www.tatnuck.com

Tatro Plumbing Company Inc
1285 Acraway Ste 300 ... Garden City KS 67846 620-277-2167 189-10
TF: 888-828-7648 ■ *Web:* tatroplumbing.com

Tattered Cover Book Store Inc
1628 16th St ... Denver CO 80202 303-436-1070 629-1704 95
TF: 800-833-9327 ■ *Web:* www.tatteredcover.com

Tattnall County 111 N Main St ... Reidsville GA 30453 912-557-4786 557-3827 338
Web: www.tattnallcountyga.com/index.cfm

Phone | Fax | Class

Tattnall County School
146 W Brazell St PO Box 157 ... Reidsville GA 30453 912-557-4726 557-3036 685
Web: www.tattnallschools.org

Tatum Development Corp
11 Pkwy Blvd ... Hattiesburg MS 39401 601-544-6043 360-2

Tatung Company of America Inc
2850 El Presidio St ... Long Beach CA 90810 310-637-2105 173-4
TF: 800-827-2850 ■ *Web:* www.tatungusa.com

Tau Alpha Chi 82 Thompson St ... Alpharetta GA 30009 770-475-4253 48-16

Tau Beta Pi Assn 1512 Middle Dr ... Knoxville TN 37996 865-546-4578 546-4579 48-16
TF: 877-829-5500 ■ *Web:* www.tbp.org

Tau Beta Sigma National Honorary Band Sorority
PO Box 849 ... Stillwater OK 74076 405-372-2333 372-2363 48-16
TF Cust Svc: 800-543-6505 ■ *Web:* www.tbsigma.org

Tau Kappa Epsilon (TKE)
7439 Woodland Dr Ste 100 ... Indianapolis IN 46278 317-872-6533 875-8353 48-16
Web: www.tke.org

Tauber Oil Co 55 Waugh Dr # 700 ... Houston TX 77007 713-869-8700 869-8069 579
TF: 800-721-4147 ■ *Web:* www.tauberoil.com

Tauber-Arons Inc
13848 Ventura Blvd ... Sherman Oaks CA 91423 323-851-2008 226
Web: www.tauberaronsinc.com

Taubman Centers Inc
200 E Long Lake Rd Ste 300 ... Bloomfield Hills MI 48303 248-258-6800 655
NYSE: TCO ■ *TF:* 800-297-6003 ■ *Web:* www.taubman.com

Taubman Museum of Art
110 Salem Ave SE ... Roanoke VA 24011 540-342-5760 342-5798 520
TF: 800-635-5535 ■ *Web:* taubmanmuseum.org

Tauck World Discovery 10 Norden Pl ... Norwalk CT 06855 203-899-6500 760
TF: 800-468-2825 ■ *Web:* www.tauck.com

Taughannock Falls State Park
2221 Taughannock Rd ... Trumansburg NY 14886 607-387-6739 565
Web: parks.ny.gov/parks/62/details.aspx

Taum Sauk Mountain State Park
148 Taum Sauk Trl ... Middlebrook MO 63656 573-546-2450 565
Web: mostateparks.com

Taunton Area Chamber of Commerce
6 Pleasant St Ste 201 ... Taunton MA 02780 508-824-4068 884-8222 139
Web: www.tauntonareachamber.org

Taunton Municipal Lighting Plant
PO Box 870 ... Taunton MA 02780 508-824-5844 245
Web: www.tmlp.com

Taunton Press Inc
63 S Main St PO Box 5506 ... Newtown CT 06470 203-426-8171 426-3434 637-9
TF: 800-733-9267 ■ *Web:* www.taunton.com

Taunton Public Library 12 Pleasant St ... Taunton MA 02780 508-821-1411 821-1414 434-3
Web: www.tauntonlibrary.org

Taunton State Hospital 60 Hodges Ave ... Taunton MA 02780 508-977-3000 374-5

Taurad LLC
6733 S Sepulveda Blvd Ste 135 ... Los Angeles CA 90045 310-281-3360 387
Web: taurad.com

Taurus Asset Management LLC
590 Madison Ave 35th Fl ... New York NY 10022 212-457-9922 401
Web: www.taurusassetmanagement.com

Taurus International Mfg Inc
16175 NW 49th Ave ... Miami FL 33014 305-624-1115 624-1126 284
TF: 800-327-3776 ■ *Web:* www.taurususa.com

Taurus Software Inc
420 Brewster Ave ... Redwood City CA 94063 650-482-2022 179
Web: taurus.com

Tautog's 205 23rd St ... Virginia Beach VA 23451 757-422-0081 671
Web: www.tautogs.com

Tautphaus Park Zoo
308 Constitution Way ... Idaho Falls ID 83402 208-612-8100 823
Web: www.idahofallsidaho.gov

Tavaero Jet Charter 7930 Airport Blvd ... Houston TX 77061 713-643-5387 643-5398 13
TF: 800-343-3771 ■ *Web:* www.tavaero.com

Tavant Technologies Inc
3101 Jay St Ste 101 ... Santa Clara CA 95054 408-519-5400 177
Web: www.tavant.com

Tavern on Grand 656 Grand Ave ... Saint Paul MN 55105 651-228-9030 671
Web: www.tavernongrand.com

Taverna Cretekou 818 King St ... Alexandria VA 22314 703-548-8688 683-2739 671
Web: www.tavernacretekou.com

Taverna Opa 800 N Ocean Dr ... Hollywood FL 33019 954-922-2256 922-2258 671
Web: www.tavernaopa.com

Tavis Corp 3636 State Hwy 49 S ... Mariposa CA 95338 209-966-2027 407
TF: 800-842-6102 ■ *Web:* www.taviscorp.com

Tavistock Restaurants LLC
4705 S Apopka Vineland Rd Ste 210 ... Orlando FL 32819 407-909-7101 670
TF: 800-424-2753 ■ *Web:* tavistockrestaurantcollection.com

TAWA Supermarket Inc
6281 Regio Ave ... Buena Park CA 90620 714-521-8899 410
Web: www.99ranch.com

Tawas Point State Park
686 Tawas Beach Rd ... East Tawas MI 48730 989-362-5041 565
Web: www.michigandnr.com

Tax Analysts 400 S Maple Ave ... Falls Church VA 22046 703-533-4400 637-9
Web: www.taxnotes.com

Tax Executives Institute (TEI)
1200 G St NW Ste 300 ... Washington DC 20005 202-638-5601 638-5607 49-1
Web: www.tei.org

Tax Management Associates Inc
2225 Coronation Blvd ... Charlotte NC 28227 704-847-1234 225
TF: 800-951-5350 ■ *Web:* www.tma1.com

Tax Management Inc 1801 S Bell St ... Arlington VA 22202 703-341-3000 637-9
TF: 800-372-1033 ■ *Web:* www.bna.com

Tax Matrix Technologies
1011 Mumma Rd Ste 101 ... Lemoyne PA 17043 717-975-0143 463
Web: taxmatrix.com

Tax Savvy 401 S Birmingham St ... Wylie TX 75098 972-442-5226 734
Web: www.taxsavvy.biz

Tax Smart Accounting Services
19616 E Benwood St ... Covina CA 91724 626-974-5152 734
Web: www.taxsmartaccounting.com

Taxi Canada Inc
495 Wellington St W Ste 102 ... Toronto ON M5V1E9 416-342-8294 7
Web: taxi.ca

Name / Address	City	State	Zip	Phone	Fax	Class
Taxography Inc 6353 N Rosebury Ave *Web:* www.taxography.com	Saint Louis	MO	63105	314-863-9292		809
Taxpayers Against Fraud Education Fund (TAF) 1220 19th St NW Ste 501 *TF General:* 800-873-2573 ■ *Web:* www.taf.org	Washington	DC	20036	202-296-4826	296-4838	49-10
Taycheedah Correctional Institution (WWCS) 751 County Rd *Web:* doc.wi.gov	Fond Du Lac	WI	54936-1947	920-929-3800	929-2946	213
Taycom Business Solutions Inc 719 Griswold Ave Ste 820 *TF:* 866-482-9266 ■ *Web:* www.taycomsolves.com	Detroit	MI	48226	866-482-9266		2
Taycor LLC 6065 Bristol Pkwy *TF:* 800-322-9738 ■ *Web:* www.taycor.com	Culver City	CA	90230	310-895-7704	568-9922	216
TayganPoint Consulting Group Inc 1118 General Washington Memorial Blvd Ste 210 *Web:* www.tayganpoint.com	Washington Crossing	PA	18977	215-302-2500		196
Taylor 750 N Blackhawk Blvd *TF:* 800-255-0626 ■ *Web:* www.taylor-company.com	Rockton	IL	61072	815-624-8333	624-8000	298
Taylor & Fenn Co 22 Deerfield Rd *Web:* www.taylorfenn.com	Windsor	CT	06095	860-219-9393	219-0907	307
Taylor & Francis Group 6000 Broken Sound Pkwy NW Ste 300 *TF:* 877-622-5543 ■ *Web:* www.taylorandfrancis.com	Boca Raton	NY	33487	207-017-6000		637-2
Taylor & Fulton Inc 932 Fifth Ave W *TF:* 800-457-5577 ■ *Web:* www.taylorfulton.com	Palmetto	FL	34221	941-729-3883	723-2969	10-11
Taylor & Hill Inc 9941 Rowlett Rd *TF:* 800-318-0231 ■ *Web:* www.taylorandhill.com	Houston	TX	77075	713-941-2671		260
Taylor & Messick Inc 325 Walt Messick Rd *TF:* 800-237-1272 ■ *Web:* taylormessick.com	Harrington	DE	19952	302-398-3729	398-4732	520
Taylor & Syfan Consulting Engineers Inc 684 Clarion Ct *TF:* 800-579-3881 ■ *Web:* www.taylorsyfan.com	San Luis Obispo	CA	93401	805-547-2000		261
Taylor and Cameron 32 E 67th St *Web:* www.graham1857.com	New York	NY	10065	212-535-5767		42
Taylor Bldg Products 631 N First St *TF:* 800-248-3600 ■ *Web:* www.taylordoor.com	West Branch	MI	48661	989-345-5110	345-5116	234
Taylor Bros Inc 905 Graves Mill Rd *Web:* www.taylorbrothers.com	Lynchburg	VA	24502	434-237-8100		499
Taylor Clay Products Co 185 Peeler Rd PO Box 2128 *Web:* taylorclaybrick.com/wp/index.php	Salisbury	NC	28145	704-636-2411	636-2413	150
Taylor Corp 1725 Roe Crest Dr *Web:* www.taylorcorp.com/Pages/default.aspx	North Mankato	MN	56003	507-625-2828	386-2031	360-3
Taylor Correctional Institution 8501 Hampton Springs Rd *Web:* dc.state.fl.us	Perry	FL	32348	850-838-4000	838-4024	213
Taylor County 300 Oak St *Web:* www.taylorcountytexas.org	Abilene	TX	79602	325-674-1231		338
Taylor County 405 Jefferson St County Courthouse *TF:* 800-370-7505 ■ *Web:* taylorcountyiowa.org	Bedford	IA	50833	712-523-2095		338
Taylor County 203 N Ct St Ste 5 *Web:* www.kactfo.com	Campbellsville	KY	42718	270-628-3922		338
Taylor County 214 W Main St *Web:* taylorcounty.wv.gov	Grafton	WV	26354	304-265-1401	265-3016	338
Taylor County 224 S Second St *TF:* 800-362-4802 ■ *Web:* www.co.taylor.wi.us	Medford	WI	54451	715-748-1460	748-1415	338
Taylor County PO Box 620 *TF:* 800-393-1063 ■ *Web:* taylorclerk.com	Perry	FL	32348	850-838-3506	838-3549	338
Taylor County RECC 625 W Main St PO Box 100 *TF:* 800-931-4551 ■ *Web:* www.tcrecc.com	Campbellsville	KY	42719	270-465-4101		245
Taylor Data Systems Inc 181 E Evans St BTC 008 *TF:* 800-222-0446 ■ *Web:* taylordata.com	Florence	SC	29506	843-656-2084		177
Taylor Devices Inc 90 Taylor Dr PO Box 748 *NASDAQ: TAYD* ■ *Web:* www.taylordevices.com	North Tonawanda	NY	14120	716-694-0800	695-6015	60
Taylor Dynamometer Inc 3602 W Wheelhouse Rd *Web:* www.taylordyno.com	Milwaukee	WI	53208	414-755-0040		697
Taylor Electric Co-op N1831 State Hwy 13 *TF:* 800-862-2407 ■ *Web:* www.taylorelectric.org	Medford	WI	54451	715-678-2411	678-2555	245
Taylor Electric Co-op Inc (TEC) 226 County Rd 287 Bldg A PO Box 250 *Web:* www.taylorelectric.com	Merkel	TX	79536	325-793-8500	793-1309	245
Taylor Energy Company LLC 1 Lee Cir *TF:* 800-256-2397 ■ *Web:* www.taylorenergy.com	New Orleans	LA	70130	504-581-5491		536
Taylor Enterprises Inc (TEI) 2586 Southport Rd *TF:* 800-922-3149 ■ *Web:* taylorlubricants.com	Spartanburg	SC	29302	864-573-9518	583-4150	579
Taylor Farms Florida Inc 7492 Chancellor Dr	Orlando	FL	32809	407-859-3373		123
Taylor Farms Inc 150 Main St *TF:* 877-323-7374 ■ *Web:* www.taylorfarms.com	Salinas	CA	93901	831-646-9600		297-7
Taylor Ford Inc 13500 Telegraph *Web:* shoptaylorford.com	Taylor	MI	48180	313-291-0300		57
Taylor Forge Engineered Systems Inc 208 N Iron St *Web:* www.tfes.com	Paola	KS	66071	913-294-5331	294-5337	91
Taylor Freezer Sales Company Inc 2032 Atlantic Ave *TF:* 800-768-6945 ■ *Web:* www.taylorfreezer.com	Chesapeake	VA	23324	800-768-6945		665
Taylor Freezers of California 221 Harris Ct *TF:* 877-978-4800 ■ *Web:* www.taylorfreezers.com	South San Francisco	CA	94080	877-978-4800		406
Taylor Global Inc 350 Fifth Ave *Web:* www.taylorstrategy.com	New York	NY	10118	212-714-1280	695-5685	636
Taylor Hobson Inc 1725 Western Dr *Web:* www.taylor-hobson.com	West Chicago	IL	60185	630-621-3099	231-1739	472
Taylor Hodson Inc 133 W 19th St *Web:* www.taylorhodson.com	New York	NY	10011	212-924-8300		260
Taylor Hospital 175 E Chester Pk *TF:* 800-254-3258 ■ *Web:* www.crozerkeystone.org	Ridley Park	PA	19078	610-595-6000		374-3
Taylor Independent School District 3101 N Main St *Web:* www.taylorisd.org	Taylor	TX	76574	512-352-6361	365-3800	685
Taylor Law Offices Pc 122 E Washington Ave *Web:* taylorlaw.net	Effingham	IL	62401	217-342-3925		428
Taylor Lumber Inc 18253 SR-73 *Web:* www.taylorlumberinc.com	Mcdermott	OH	45652	740-259-6222		683
Taylor Made Landscape Irrigation 750 Barsby St	Vista	CA	92084	760-945-0118		693
Taylor Made Products Div Taylor Made Group 65 Harrison St *Web:* www.taylormadeproducts.com	Gloversville	NY	12078	518-773-9400		596
Taylor Made Transportation Services Inc 2901 Druid Pk Dr Ste 206 *Web:* www.tmtransportation.com	Baltimore	MD	21215	410-728-1951		780
Taylor Metal Products Co 700 Springmill St *Web:* www.tmpind.com	Mansfield	OH	44903	419-522-3471	525-2948	488
Taylor Metalworks Inc 3925 California Rd *Web:* www.taylorcnc.com	Orchard Park	NY	14127	716-662-3113	662-1096	621
Taylor Mill Historic Site Island Pond Rd *Web:* www.nhstateparks.org	Derry	NH	03038	603-431-6774		565
Taylor Morrison Inc 4900 N Scottsdale Rd Ste 2000 *Web:* www.taylormorrison.com	Scottsdale	AZ	85251	480-840-8100		652
Taylor Oil Company Inc 77 Second St 77 Second St *TF:* 800-336-3762 ■ *Web:* www.tayloroilco.com	Somerville	NJ	08876	908-725-7737		579
Taylor Pittsburgh Mfg 7 Rocky Mt Rd *TF:* 800-456-7929 ■ *Web:* taylorpittsburgh.com	Athens	TN	37303	423-745-3110		273
Taylor Polson & Company PSC 101 Mckenna St	Glasgow	KY	42141	270-651-8877		2
Taylor Products Company Inc 2205 Jothi Ave *TF:* 888-882-9567 ■ *Web:* www.taylorproducts.com	Parsons	KS	67357	620-421-5550		547
Taylor Protocols Inc 16040 Christensen Rd Ste 315 *TF:* 877-355-8229 ■ *Web:* www.taylorprotocols.com	Tukwila	WA	98188	206-283-8144		449
Taylor Public Library 400 Porter St *Web:* www.ci.taylor.tx.us	Taylor	TX	76574	512-352-3434	352-8080	434-3
Taylor Regional Hospital 1700 Old Lebanon Rd *Web:* www.tchosp.org	Campbellsville	KY	42718	270-465-3561		374-3
Taylor Rigs LLC 6015 N Xanthus *TF:* 800-759-3444 ■ *Web:* www.taylorindustries.net	Tulsa	OK	74130	918-266-7301		537
Taylor Scott (Rep R - VA) 412 Cannon HOB *Web:* taylor.house.gov	Washington	DC	20515	202-225-4215	225-4218	342-2
Taylor Smith Consulting Llc 16800 Greenspoint Pk Dr *Web:* www.taylorsmithconsulting.com	Houston	TX	77060	713-937-3111		463
Taylor Stitch 3 Bailey Dr SW *Web:* taylorstitch.com	Lilburn	GA	30047	770-381-9370		258
Taylor Technologies Inc 31 Loveton Cir *TF Cust Svc:* 800-837-8548 ■ *Web:* www.taylortechnologies.com	Sparks	MD	21152	410-472-4340	771-4291	806
Taylor Truck Line Inc 31485 Northfield Blvd *TF:* 800-962-5994 ■ *Web:* www.taylortruckline.com	Northfield	MN	55057	507-645-4531		780
Taylor University 236 W Reade Ave **Fax:* Admissions ■ *TF:* 800-882-3456 ■ *Web:* www.taylor.edu	Upland	IN	46989	765-998-2751	998-4925*	166
Fort Wayne 915 W Rudisill Blvd *TF General:* 800-882-3456 ■ *Web:* fw.taylor.edu	Fort Wayne	IN	46807	260-744-8790	745-4974	166
Taylor University College & Seminary 11525 23rd Ave *TF:* 800-567-4988 ■ *Web:* www.taylor-edu.ca	Edmonton	AB	T6J4T3	780-431-5200	436-9416	167-3
Taylor Valve Technology Inc 8300 SW 8th *TF:* 800-805-3401 ■ *Web:* www.taylorvalve.com	Oklahoma City	OK	73128	405-787-0145		789
Taylor Wellons Politz & Duhe Aplc 8550 United Plaza Blvd Ste 101 *TF:* 877-850-1047 ■ *Web:* www.twpdlaw.com	Baton Rouge	LA	70809	225-387-9888		428
Taylor Wiseman & Taylor (TWT) 124 Gaither Dr Ste 150 *Web:* www.taylorwiseman.com	Mount Laurel	NJ	08054	856-235-7200		261
Taylor's Auto Max 4100 Tenth Ave S *Web:* www.taylorsautomax.com	Great Falls	MT	59405	406-727-0380		57
Taylor's Steak House 3361 W Eigth St *Web:* www.taylorssteakhouse.com	Los Angeles	CA	90005	213-382-8449		671
Taylor, Porter, Brooks & Phillips 451 Florida St 8th Fl *Web:* www.taylorporter.com	Baton Rouge	LA	70801	225-387-3221		428
Taylor-Dunn Manufacturing Co 2114 W Ball Rd *TF:* 800-688-8680 ■ *Web:* www.taylor-dunn.com	Anaheim	CA	92804	714-956-4040	956-3130	470
Taylored Systems Inc 14701 Cumberland Rd Ste 100 *Web:* www.taylored.com	Noblesville	IN	46060	317-776-4000	776-4004	735
Taylor-Listug Inc 1980 Gillespie Way *Web:* www.taylorguitars.com	El Cajon	CA	92020	619-258-1207		527
TaylorMade - Adidas Golf 5545 Fermi Ct *TF Cust Svc:* 800-555-1212 ■ *Web:* www.taylormadegolf.com	Carlsbad	CA	92008	760-918-6000		710
Taylorsville Lake State Park 1320 Park Rd *Web:* www.parks.ky.gov	Mt Eden	KY	40046	502-477-8713		565
Taylorville Correctional Ctr 1144 Illinois Rt 29 PO Box 1000 *Web:* illinois.gov	Taylorville	IL	62568	217-824-4004	824-4042	213
Taylor-Wharton 4718 Gettysburg Rd Ste 300	Mechanicsburg	PA	17055	717-763-5060	731-7988	91

Name / Address	City	State	ZIP	Phone	Fax	Class
Taylor-Winfield Inc						
3200 Innovation Pl	Youngstown	OH	44509	330-259-8500	259-8530	811
TF: 800-523-4899 ■ *Web:* www.taylor-winfield.com						
Taymark Inc						
4875 White Bear Pkwy	White Bear Lake	MN	55110	651-426-1667		459
Web: www.handyart.com						
Tazewell Area Chamber of Commerce						
PO Box 672	Tazewell	VA	24651	276-988-5091		139
Web: www.tazewellchamber.com						
Tazewell County						
11 S Fourth St Fl 2 Ste 203	Pekin	IL	61554	309-477-2264	477-2244	338
Web: www.tazewell.com						
Tazewell County Public Library						
310 E Main St PO Box 929	Tazewell	VA	24651	276-988-2541	988-5980	434-3
TF: 800-733-0850 ■ *Web:* www.tcplweb.org						
Tazewell General District Court						
101 E Main St	Tazewell	VA	24651	276-385-1563		338
Web: courts.state.va.us						
Tazewell Machine Works Inc						
2015 S Second St	Pekin	IL	61554	309-347-3181		492
TF: 800-451-6680 ■ *Web:* www.tazewellmachine.com						
TB Butler Publishing Co 410 W Erwin St	Tyler	TX	75702	903-597-8111	595-0335	637-8
TF: 800-333-9141 ■ *Web:* www.tylerpaper.com						
T&B Tube Co 15525 S LaSalle St	South Holland	IL	60473	708-333-1282		492
Web: www.tbtube.com						
TB Wood's Inc 440 N Fifth Ave	Chambersburg	PA	17201	717-264-7161	264-6420	620
TF: 888-829-6637 ■ *Web:* www.tbwoods.com						
TBA Global LLC 220 W 42nd St 10th Fl	New York	NY	10036	646-445-7000		184
TBA LLC 6700 Enterprise Dr	Louisville	KY	40214	502-367-0222	361-0715	612
TF: 800-626-3525 ■ *Web:* www.cmiproduct.com						
T-Base Communications Inc						
885 Meadowlands Dr E Ste 401	Ottawa	ON	K2C3N2	613-236-0866		180
Web: www.tbase.com						
TBayTel Inc 1060 Lithium Dr	Thunder Bay	ON	P7B6G3	807-623-4400		224
TF: 800-264-9501 ■ *Web:* www.tbaytel.net						
TBC (Teal Becker & Chiramonte)						
7 Washington Sq	Albany	NY	12205	518-456-6663	456-3975	2
Web: www.tbccpa.com						
TBC (Tom Barrow Co)						
2800 Plant Atkinson Rd	Atlanta	GA	30339	404-351-1010	350-9121	14
TF: 800-229-8226 ■ *Web:* www.tombarrow.com						
TBC (Trahan Burden & Charles Inc)						
900 S Wolfe St	Baltimore	MD	21231	410-347-7500	986-1299	4
Web: www.tbc.us						
TBD Networks Inc 2 N First St	San Jose	CA	95113	408-278-1590	278-1626	809
TBDN Tennessee Co 1410 Hwy 70 Bypass	Jackson	TN	38301	731-421-4800	421-4879	60
Web: www.tbdn.com						
Tbi Construction & Construction Management Inc						
1960 the Alameda Ste 100	San Jose	CA	95126	408-246-3691		186
Web: strategic-cm.com						
TBK America Inc 3700 W Industries Rd	Richmond	IN	47374	765-962-0147		641
Web: www.tbk-jp.com						
Tbm Consulting Group Inc						
4400 Ben Franklin Blvd	Durham	NC	27704	919-471-5535	471-5135	194
TF: 800-438-5535 ■ *Web:* www.tbmcg.com						
TBN (Trinity Broadcasting Network)						
PO Box A	Santa Ana	CA	92711	714-832-2950		740
TF: 888-731-1000 ■ *Web:* www.tbn.org						
TBN Consulting LLC						
3301 Brunswick Ave N	Minneapolis	MN	55422	763-971-8057		463
Web: www.tonynelson.com						
TBS (Turner Broadcasting System Inc)						
1 CNN Ctr	Atlanta	GA	30303	404-827-1700		740
Web: www.turner.com						
Tbs Automation Systems Inc						
122 Kings Hwy Ste 504	Maple Shade	NJ	08052	856-424-3247		180
Web: tbsauto.com						
TBS Communications Inc						
1800 Peachtree St Ste 655	Atlanta	GA	30309	404-876-6989		177
Web: www.coolbluei.com						
TBS Shipping Services Inc						
455 Central Park Ave Ste 308	Scarsdale	NY	10583	914-961-1000		770
Web: www.tbsship.com						
TBT (Transco Business Technologies)						
34 Leighton Rd	Augusta	ME	04330	207-622-6251		112
TF: 800-322-0003 ■ *Web:* www.transcobusiness.com						
TBWA Chiat/Day Inc 488 Madison Ave	New York	NY	10022	212-804-1000		4
Web: tbwachiatday.com						
TC Mill Work Inc 3433 Marshall Ln	Bensalem	PA	19020	215-245-4210		321
Web: www.tcmillwork.com						
TC Computer Service Inc						
3303 FM1960 W Ste 100	Houston	TX	77068	713-686-2083		180
Web: www.tccsi.com						
TC Electronic Inc						
5706 Corsa Ave Ste 107	Westlake Village	CA	91362	818-665-4900		527
TF: 800-869-8822 ■ *Web:* www.tcelectronic.com						
TC Industries Inc 3703 S Rt 31	Crystal Lake	IL	60012	815-459-2400	459-3303	484
Web: www.tcindustries.com						
TC Net-Works 23610 Mohican St NW	St. Francis	MN	55070	612-747-4357		177
Web: www.tcnet-works.com						
T&C Stamping Inc 1403 Freeman Ave	Athens	AL	35613	256-233-7383		483
Web: www.tandcstamping.com						
TC/American Monorail Inc						
12070 43rd St NE	Saint Michael	MN	55376	763-497-7000	497-7001	470
TF: 800-967-7333 ■ *Web:* www.tcamerican.com						
TCA (Tilt-up Concrete Assn)						
113 First St NW	Mount Vernon	IA	52314	319-895-6911	213-5555*	49-3
**Fax Area Code: 320* ■ *TF:* 800-837-5870 ■ *Web:* www.tilt-up.org						
TCA (Therapeutic Communities of America)						
1601 Connecticut Ave NW Rm 574	Washington	DC	20006	202-296-3503		49-8
TF: 800-729-6686 ■ *Web:* www.treatmentcommunitiesofamerica.org						
TCA (Tile Council of America Inc)						
100 Clemson Research Blvd	Anderson	SC	29625	864-646-8453	646-2821	49-3
Web: www.tcnatile.com						
TCA (Truckload Carriers Assn)						
555 E Braddock Rd	Alexandria	VA	22314	703-838-1950	836-6610	49-21
Web: www.truckload.org						
TCC (Customer Communicator, The)						
712 Main St Ste 187B	Boonton	NJ	07005	973-265-2300	402-6056	531-2
TF: 800-232-4317 ■ *Web:* www.customerservicegroup.com						
TCCL (Tulsa City-County Library)						
400 Civic Ctr	Tulsa	OK	74103	918-549-7323		434-3
Web: www.tulsalibrary.org						
TCE LLC 114 Shore Dr	Burridge	IL	60527	773-744-7550		536
Web: tcellc.net						
TCF Financial Corp						
801 Marquette Ave	Minneapolis	MN	55402	612-823-2265		360-2
NYSE: TCB ■ *Web:* www.tcfbank.com						
TCF National Bank						
801 Marquette Ave	Minneapolis	MN	55402	612-823-2265		70
TF: 800-343-6145 ■ *Web:* www.tcfbank.com						
TCG Continuum LLC 4251 Leap Rd	Hilliard	OH	43026	614-876-8600		393
Web: www.tcgcontinuum.com						
TCGRx N1671 Powers Lake Rd	Powers Lake	WI	53159	262-279-5307		475
Web: www.tcgrx.com						
TCI Aluminum/North Inc 2353 Davis Ave	Hayward	CA	94545	510-786-3750	786-3302	492
TF: 800-824-6197 ■ *Web:* www.tcialuminum.com						
TCI Architects/Engineers/Contractors Inc						
1718 State Rd 16	La Crosse	WI	54601	608-781-5700		186
TCI College of Technology						
320 W 31st St	New York	NY	10001	212-594-4000		800
TF: 800-878-8246 ■ *Web:* www.tcicollege.edu						
TCI International Inc						
3541 Gateway Blvd	Fremont	CA	94538	510-687-6100	687-6101	647
TF: 877-247-3797 ■ *Web:* www.spx.com						
TCI Scales Inc PO Box 1648	Snohomish	WA	98291	425-353-4384	609-1021	684
TF: 800-522-2206 ■ *Web:* www.tciscales.com						
TCI Tire Centers LLC						
10 Mt Read Blvd	Rochester	NY	14611	585-436-1120		116
TCI Wealth Advisors Inc						
4011 E Sunrise Dr	Tucson	AZ	85718	520-733-1477		401
TF: 877-733-1859 ■ *Web:* www.tciwealth.com						
TCIA (Tree Care Industry Assn)						
136 Harvey Rd Ste 101	Londonderry	NH	03053	603-314-5380	314-5386	48-13
TF: 800-733-2622 ■ *Web:* tcia.org						
TCK (Twin City Knitting Company Inc)						
104 Rock Barn Rd NE	Conover	NC	28613	828-464-4830		155-10
Web: www.tcksports.com						
TCL (Transylvania County Library)						
212 S Gaston St	Brevard	NC	28712	828-884-3151		434-3
TF: 800-859-0829 ■ *Web:* library.transylvaniacounty.org						
TCM (Turner Classic Movies)						
1050 Techwood Dr NW	Atlanta	GA	30318	404-551-0921		740
Web: www.tcm.turner.com						
TCM (Temp-Control Mechanical Corp)						
4800 N Ch Ave	Portland	OR	97217	503-285-9851	285-9978	14
TF: 877-826-3828 ■ *Web:* www.tcmcorp.com						
Tcm America Inc 107 Mcqueen St	West Columbia	SC	29172	803-791-5205		358
TCN Worldwide						
1755 N Collins Ste 207	Richardson	TX	75080	972-769-8701		652
Web: www.tcnworldwide.com						
TCOM LP 7115 Thomas Edison Dr	Columbia	MD	21046	410-312-2400	312-2455	28
Web: www.tcomlp.com						
TCR (Trammell Crow Residential)						
3889 Maple St	Dallas	TX	75219	214-922-8400		653
Web: tcr.com						
TCR Child Care Corp 925 N St E	Talladega	AL	35160	256-362-3852		148
Tcr Corp 1600 67th Ave N	Minneapolis	MN	55430	763-560-2200		567
Web: www.tcr-corp.com						
TCR Industries						
26 Centerpointe Dr Ste 120	La Palma	CA	90623	714-521-5222	521-1636	146
TF: 877-827-1444 ■ *Web:* www.tcrindustries.com						
TCS (Tata Consultancy Services Ltd)						
101 Pk Ave 26th Fl	New York	NY	10178	212-557-8038	867-8652	194
TF: 800-016-6710 ■ *Web:* www.tcs.com						
TCS (Tongass Conservation Society)						
PO Box 23377	Ketchikan	AK	99901	907-225-3275		48-13
Web: www.tongassconservation.org						
TCS 168 Thatcher Rd	Greensboro	NC	27409	336-632-0860		393
Web: www.tcsusa.com						
TCS Communications LLC						
2045 W Union Ave Bldg E	Englewood	CO	80110	303-377-3800		186
Web: www.tcscomm.com						
Tcs of America Enterprises Llc						
2 Mcdaniels Dr	Brookline	NH	03033	603-249-3367		196
TF: 800-847-2463 ■ *Web:* www.tcsofamerica.com						
Tct Computing Group Inc Po Box 402	Bel Air	MD	21014	410-893-5800		193
TF: 866-828-6372 ■ *Web:* www.tctcomputing.com						
TCT Inc 11911 County Rd 125 W	Odessa	TX	79765	432-561-8449		246
Web: www.tctinc.com						
TCT Ministries Inc						
11717 N Rt 37 PO Box 1010	Marion	IL	62959	618-997-4700	993-9778	740
TF: 800-232-9855 ■ *Web:* www.tct.tv						
Tct Stainless Steel Inc						
6300 19 Mile Rd	Sterling Heights	MI	48314	586-254-5333		492
Web: www.tctstainless.com						
TCU (Teachers Credit Union)						
PO Box 1395	South Bend	IN	46624	574-284-6247		219
TF: 800-552-4745 ■ *Web:* www.tcunet.com						
TCVB (Tyler Convention & Visitors Bureau)						
315 N Broadway	Tyler	TX	75702	903-592-1661	592-1268	206
TF: 800-235-5712 ■ *Web:* www.visittyler.com						
TCW Group Inc						
865 S Figueroa St Ste 1800	Los Angeles	CA	90017	213-244-0000		528
TF: 800-386-3829 ■ *Web:* www.tcw.com						
TD Bank NA 1701 Rt 70 E	Cherry Hill	NJ	08034	856-751-2739		70
TF: 888-751-9000 ■ *Web:* www.tdbank.com						
TD Banknorth Massachusetts						
295 Pk Ave	Worcester	MA	01609	508-752-2584		70
TF Cust Svc: 800-747-7000 ■ *Web:* www.tdbank.com						
TD Jakes Ministries 3635 Dan Morton Dr	Dallas	TX	75236	225-407-2291		48-20
Web: tdjakes.org						
TDA (Tennessee Dental Assn)						
660 Bakers Bridge Ave Ste 300	Franklin	TN	37067	615-628-0208		227
TF: 800-824-9722 ■ *Web:* www.tenndental.org						

Name / Address	City	State	ZIP	Phone	Fax	Class
TDA Group, The 3 Lagoon Dr Ste 100 *Web:* www.tdagroup.com	Redwood city	CA	94065	650-948-3140		195
TDB Communications Inc 10901 W 84 Terr Ste 105 *Web:* www.tdbcommunications.com	Lenexa	KS	66214	913-327-7400		260
TDC (Discovery Ctr) 1944 N Winery Ave *TF:* 800-946-3039 ■ *Web:* www.thediscoverycenter.net	Fresno	CA	93703	559-251-5533		521
TDC Acquisition Holdings Inc 4955 Corporate Dr Ste 101 *Web:* www.timedomain.com	Huntsville	AL	35805	256-922-9229		696
TDEC 8120 Woodmont Ave Ste 550 *Web:* www.tdec.com	Bethesda	MD	20814	301-718-0703	718-1615	225
TDECU (Texas Dow Employees Credit Union) 1001 FM 2004 *TF:* 800-839-1154 ■ *Web:* www.tdecu.org	Lake Jackson	TX	77566	979-297-1154	299-0212	219
TDF (TDF Ventures) 2 Wisconsin Cir Ste 920 *Web:* www.tdfventures.com	Chevy Chase	MD	20815	240-483-4286		792
TDF Ventures (TDF) 2 Wisconsin Cir Ste 920 *Web:* www.tdfventures.com	Chevy Chase	MD	20815	240-483-4286		792
TDG 93 Sherman St *Web:* www.tdgcommunications.com	Deadwood	SD	57732	605-722-7111		4
TDG Aerospace Inc 545 Corporate Dr *Web:* www.tdgaerospace.com	Escondido	CA	92029	760-466-1040		20
TDH Marketing & Communications Inc 8153 Garnet Dr *TF:* 800-643-0641 ■ *Web:* www.tdh-marketing.com	Dayton	OH	45458	937-438-3434		195
TDIndustries 13850 Diplomat Dr *Web:* www.tdindustries.com	Dallas	TX	75234	972-888-9500		189-10
TDI-Transistor Devices Inc 85 Horsehill Rd *TF:* 800-488-6724 ■ *Web:* www.tdipower.com	Cedar Knolls	NJ	07927	973-267-1900	267-2047	253
TDK Corp of America 475 Half Day Rd *TF:* 800-807-8340 ■ *Web:* www.tdk.com	Lincolnshire	IL	60069	847-699-2299	803-6296	253
TDK Electronics Corp 525 RXR Plaza *Web:* www.tdk.com	Uniondale	NY	11556	516-535-2600		658
TDK USA Corp 525 RXR Plaza *Web:* www.tdk.com	Uniondale	NY	11556	516-535-2600		52
TDK-Lambda Americas Inc 405 Essex Rd *Web:* www.us.tdk-lambda.com/hp	Neptune	NJ	07753	732-922-9300	922-1441	253
TDM (Troy Design & Manufacturing Co) 14425 Sheldon Rd *Web:* www.troydm.com	Plymouth	MI	48239	734-738-2300		489
Tdm Technical Services 3924 Chesswood Dr *Web:* www.tdm.ca	Toronto	ON	M3J2W6	416-777-0007		261
TDPUD (Truckee Donner Public Utility District) 11570 Donner Pass Rd PO Box 309 *Web:* www.tdpud.org	Truckee	CA	96160	530-587-3896	587-5056	245
TDS (Texas Disposal Systems Inc) 12200 Carl Rd *TF:* 800-375-8375 ■ *Web:* www.texasdisposal.com	Creedmoor	TX	78610	512-421-1300	243-4123	804
TDS Telecommunications Corp 525 Junction Rd *TF:* 866-571-6662 ■ *Web:* www.tdstelecom.com	Madison	WI	53717	608-664-4000		736
TE Financial Consultants Ltd 26 Wellington St E Ste 710 *Web:* www.tewealth.com	Toronto	ON	M5E1S2	416-366-1451		401
TE's Rochester Wire & Cable product line 751 Old Brandy Rd *Web:* www.te.com	Culpeper	VA	22701	540-825-2111	825-2238	813
Te21 Inc 1184 Clements Ferry Rd Ste G *TF:* 866-982-8321 ■ *Web:* www.te21.com	Charleston	SC	29492	843-579-2520		196
Tea Assn of the USA Inc 362 Fifth Ave Ste 801 *Web:* www.teausa.com	New York	NY	10001	212-986-9415	697-8658	49-6
Tea Council of the USA Inc 362 Fifth Ave Ste 801 *TF:* 877-212-5752 ■ *Web:* www.teausa.com	New York	NY	10001	212-986-9415	697-8658	49-6
Tea Garden Restaurant 184 N Main St *TF:* 800-852-1166 ■ *Web:* teagarden-nh.com	Concord	NH	03301	603-228-4420		671
TEAC (Teacher Education Accreditation Council) 1 Dupont Cir Ste 320 *Web:* www.teac.org	Washington	DC	20036	202-466-7236		48-1
TEAC America Inc 7733 Telegraph Rd *Web:* www.teac.com	Montebello	CA	90640	323-726-0303	727-7656	52
Teach Away Inc 147 Liberty St *TF:* 855-483-2242 ■ *Web:* www.teachaway.com	Toronto	ON	M6K3G3	416-628-1386		260
Teach For America 315 W 36th St 7th Fl *TF:* 800-832-1230 ■ *Web:* www.teachforamerica.org	New York	NY	10018	212-279-2080		49-5
Teacher Created Resources 6421 Industry Way **Fax Area Code: 800* ■ *TF:* 888-343-4335 ■ *Web:* www.teachercreated.com	Westminster	CA	92683	888-343-4335	525-1254*	243
Teacher Education Accreditation Council (TEAC) 1 Dupont Cir Ste 320 *Web:* www.teac.org	Washington	DC	20036	202-466-7236		48-1
Teacher Magazine 6935 Arlington Rd Ste 100 *TF:* 800-346-1834 ■ *Web:* www.edweek.org/tm	Bethesda	MD	20814	301-280-3100		457-8
Teachers Credit Union (TCU) PO Box 1395 *TF:* 800-552-4745 ■ *Web:* www.tcunet.com	South Bend	IN	46624	574-284-6247		219
Teachers Federal Credit Union (TFCU) 2410 N Ocean Ave *TF:* 800-341-4333 ■ *Web:* www.teachersfcu.org	Farmingville	NY	11738	631-698-7000		219
Teachers of English to Speakers of Other Languages (TESOL) 700 S Washington St Ste 200 *TF:* 888-547-3369 ■ *Web:* www.tesol.org	Alexandria	VA	22314	703-836-0774	836-7864	49-5
Teachers on Reserve LLC 604 Sonora Ave *TF:* 800-457-1899 ■ *Web:* teachersonreserve.com	Glendale	CA	91201	800-457-1899		260
Teachers' Curriculum Institute 3735 Bradview Dr Ste 100 *Web:* teachtci.com	Sacramento	CA	95827	916-366-3686		196

Name / Address	City	State	ZIP	Phone	Fax	Class
Teaching & Learning Co 1204 Buchanan St *TF:* 800-444-1144 ■ *Web:* www.lorenzeducationalpress.com	Carthage	IL	62321	937-228-6118	223-2042	243
Teaching & Mentoring Communities (TMC) PO Box 2579 *TF:* 888-836-5151 ■ *Web:* www.tmccentral.org	Laredo	TX	78044	956-722-5174		49-5
Teaching Tolerance Magazine 400 Washington Ave *Web:* www.tolerance.org	Montgomery	AL	36104	334-956-8200		457-8
TEAI (Torch Energy Advisors Inc) 1331 Lamar Ave Ste 1450	Houston	TX	77010	713-650-1246		401
Teak Isle Manufacturing Inc 401 Capitol Ct *Web:* www.teakisle.com	Ocoee	FL	34761	407-656-8885		602
TeakThai Cusine 1051 St Gregory St *Web:* www.teakthaicuisine.com	Cincinnati	OH	45202	513-665-9800		671
Teal Becker & Chiramonte (TBC) 7 Washington Sq *Web:* www.tbccpa.com	Albany	NY	12205	518-456-6663	456-3975	2
Teal's Express Inc 22411 Teal Dr PO Box 6010 *TF:* 800-836-0369 ■ *Web:* www.teals.com	Watertown	NY	13601	315-788-6437	788-5060	780
Tealinc Ltd 1606 Rosebud Creek Rd *Web:* www.tealinc.com	Forsyth	MT	59327	406-347-5237		650
Teal-Jones Group, The 17897 Triggs Rd *TF:* 888-995-8325 ■ *Web:* www.tealjones.com	Surrey	BC	V4N4M8	604-587-8700		683
Team 92.1 FM 2495 Cedar St *Web:* www.team921fm.com	Holt	MI	48842	517-699-0111	699-1880	645
Team America Inc 33 W 46th St Frnt 3 *Web:* www.teamamericany.com	New York	NY	10036	212-221-5938		760
Team Automation 2215 First St 104 *TF:* 800-795-5287 ■ *Web:* www.teamautomation.com	Simi Valley	CA	93065	805-522-3875		177
Team Business LLC 1410 Belt St *Web:* www.teambusiness.com	Baltimore	MD	21230	410-837-1414		765
Team Connection Inc 615 Alton Pl *TF:* 800-535-3975 ■ *Web:* www.teamconnection.com	High Point	NC	27263	800-535-3975		711
Team Drive-Away Inc 23724 W 83rd Terr *Web:* www.teamdriveaway.com	Shawnee	KS	66227	913-825-4776		311
Team Epic LLC 57 Greens Farms Rd *Web:* anepiccompany.com	Westport	CT	06880	203-831-2100		195
Team Estrogen Inc 21350 NW Mauzey Rd *Web:* www.teamestrogen.com	Hillsboro	OR	97124	503-924-2030		711
Team Hardinger Transportation/Warehousing 1314 W 18th St *Web:* www.team-h.com	Erie	PA	16502	814-453-6587	453-4919	685
Team Health Inc 265 Brookview Ctr Way Ste 400 *TF:* 800-342-2898 ■ *Web:* www.teamhealth.com	Knoxville	TN	37919	865-693-1000	539-8030	721
Team IA Inc 714 S Lake Dr Ste 110 *TF:* 800-225-5237 ■ *Web:* www.teamia.com	Lexington	SC	29072	803-356-7676		809
Team Inc 200 Hermann Dr *NYSE: TISI* ■ *TF:* 800-662-8326 ■ *Web:* www.teaminc.com	Alvin	TX	77511	281-331-6154		539
Team Industries Andrews Inc 3750 Airport Rd *Web:* www.team-ind.com/facilities/team-andrews	Andrews	NC	28901	828-837-5311		454
Team Jenn Corp 13323 W Washington Blvd Ste 205 *Web:* teamjenncorp.com	Los Angeles	CA	90066	310-822-8552		2
Team Marketing Inc 6810 N State Rd 7 *Web:* www.teaminc.net	Coconut Creek	FL	33073	561-995-0690		195
Team National Inc 8210 W State Rd 84 *Web:* www.bign.com	Davie	FL	33324	954-584-2151		113
Team One 13031 W Jefferson Blvd *Web:* www.teamone-usa.com	Los Angeles	CA	90094	310-437-2500		4
Team One Repair Inc 1911 Satellite Blvd Ste 100 *Web:* www.teamonerepair.com	Buford	GA	30518	678-985-0772		175
Team People LLC 180 S Washington St *Web:* www.teampeople.tv	Falls Church	VA	22046	202-587-4111		514
Team Quality Services Inc 4483 County Rd 19 Ste B *TF:* 866-568-8326 ■ *Web:* teamqualityservices.com	Auburn	IN	46706	260-572-0060		463
Team Rahal Inc 4601 Lyman Dr *Web:* www.rahal.com	Hilliard	OH	43026	614-529-7000		642
Team Schierl Cos 2201 Madison St *Web:* www.teamschierl.com	Stevens Point	WI	54481	715-345-5060		581
Team Solutions 25 Bodrington Ct *Web:* www.teamcleaningsolutions.com	Markham	ON	L6G1B6	905-940-9334		192
Team Technologies Inc 5949 Commerce Blvd *Web:* www.team-technologies.com	Morristown	TN	37814	423-587-2199		103
Team Trident LLC 16300 Katy Fwy Ste 180 *Web:* www.teamtrident.com	Houston	TX	77094	281-600-1412		539
Team Tube LLC 23217 66th Ave S *Web:* www.teamtubellc.com	Kent	WA	98032	253-854-3456		492
Team Velocity Marketing LLC 13825 Sunrise Valley Dr *TF:* 877-832-6848 ■ *Web:* www.thevdrive.com	Herndon	VA	20171	877-832-6848		7
Team Volkswagen of Hayward Corp 25115 Mission Blvd *TF:* 866-308-2825 ■ *Web:* www.vwhayward.com	Hayward	CA	94544	866-308-2825		57
Team Work Consulting Inc 22550 Mccauley Rd *Web:* www.teamworkconsulting.com	Shaker Heights	OH	44122	216-360-1790		196
TeamBonding 298 Tosca Dr *TF:* 888-398-8326 ■ *Web:* www.teambonding.com	Stoughton	MA	02072	888-398-8326		317
TeamCo Advisers LLC 1 Bush St Ste 550 *Web:* www.teamcoadvisers.com	San Francisco	CA	94104	415-445-9800		401
Team-Linux Corp 314 Leo St Ste 200 *Web:* www.team-linux.com	Dayton	OH	45404	937-443-2400		174
TeamLogic IT Inc 25909 Plaza *Web:* www.teamlogicit.com	Mission Viejo	CA	92691	949-582-6300		261

Name / Address	City	State	ZIP	Phone	Fax	Class
Teammates Commercial Interiors 320 S Teller St Ste 250 *Web:* www.team-mates.com	Lakewood	CO	80226	303-639-5885		320
TeamQuest Corp 1 TeamQuest Way *TF:* 800-551-8326 ■ *Web:* www.teamquest.com	Clear Lake	IA	50428	641-357-2700	357-2778	178-12
Teamsters Local 771 1025 N Duke St *Web:* www.teamfirstfcu.org	Lancaster	PA	17602	717-824-3669		414
Teamwork Newsletter 2222 Sedwick Dr *TF:* 800-223-8720 ■ *Web:* www.dartnellcorp.com	Durham	NC	27713	800-223-8720	508-2592	531-2
Teamwork Solutions 5005 Horizons Dr Ste 200 *Web:* www.teamsol.com	Columbus	OH	43220	614-457-7100		177
TeamWorld Inc 498 Conklin Ave *TF:* 800-797-1005 ■ *Web:* www.teamworld.com	Binghamton	NY	13903	607-770-1005		34
TeamXbox com 128 Woodhaven Dr	Mars	PA	16046	412-555-1212		396
Teaneck Public Library 840 Teaneck Rd *TF:* 800-245-1377 ■ *Web:* www.teaneck.org	Teaneck	NJ	07666	201-837-4171	837-0410	434-3
Tearepair Inc 2200 Knight Rd *Web:* tear-aid.com	Land O Lakes	FL	34639	813-948-6898		608
TearLab Corp 7360 Carroll Rd Ste 200 *TF:* 800-332-1088 ■ *Web:* www.tearlab.com	San Diego	CA	92121	858-455-6006		543
Teatro 177 Tremont St *Web:* teatroboston.com	Boston	MA	02111	617-778-6841		671
Tebons Gas & Auto Service Inc 7415 N Harlem Ave *Web:* tebonsgas.com	Niles	IL	60714	847-647-9800		366
TEC (Thumb Electric Co-op) 2231 Main St	Ubly	MI	48475	989-658-8571		245
TEC (Taylor Electric Co-op Inc) 226 County Rd 287 Bldg A PO Box 250 *Web:* www.taylorelectric.com	Merkel	TX	79536	325-793-8500	793-1309	245
TEC (Thompson Electric Co) 2300 Seventh St *Web:* www.thompsonelectriccompany.com	Sioux City	IA	51105	712-252-4221		787
TEC Corp 2300 Seventh St *Web:* www.tec-corp.com	Sioux City	IA	51105	712-252-4275		109-4
TEC Industries LLC 403 14th St SE *TF:* 800-837-7770 ■ *Web:* www.quatrocomposites.com	Orange City	IA	51041	712-707-9200		127
Tec Laboratories Inc 7100 Tec Labs Way SW *TF:* 800-482-4464 ■ *Web:* www.teclabsinc.com	Albany	OR	97321	541-926-4577		231
TEC Well Service Inc 851 W Harrison Rd *Web:* www.tecwell.com	Longview	TX	75604	903-759-0082		539
Tec5USA Inc 80 Skyline Dr *Web:* www.tec5usa.com	Plainview	NY	11803	516-653-2000		330
Tech 24 410 E Washington St Ste 410 *Web:* www.mytech24.com	Greenville	SC	29601	864-271-6522		385
Tech 4 3547 French Rd *Web:* tech4.com	De Pere	WI	54115	920-532-0480		261
Tech Access Corp Inc 129 Main St Ste 1334 *Web:* www.techaccesscorp.com	Stony Brook	NY	11790	631-654-5080		390
Tech Allies Consulting LLC 13010 Westchester Trl *TF:* 866-321-0101 ■ *Web:* www.techalliesconsulting.com	Chesterland	OH	44026	866-321-0101		196
Tech Briefs Media Group 261 Fifth Ave Ste 1901 *TF:* 888-456-3398 ■ *Web:* www.techbriefs.com	New York	NY	10016	212-490-3999		457-19
Tech Center Inc 265 S Main St *TF:* 800-990-8083 ■ *Web:* www.techcenterinc.com	Akron	OH	44308	330-762-6212		193
Tech Circuits Inc 340 Quinnipiac St *Web:* www.techcircuits.com	Wallingford	CT	06492	203-269-3311		625
Tech Conveyor Inc 195 Strykers Rd *TF:* 800-858-3666 ■ *Web:* www.techconveyor.com	Phillipsburg	NJ	08865	908-454-1515		261
Tech Credit Union 10951 Broadway *TF:* 800-276-8324 ■ *Web:* www.techcu.org	Crown Point	IN	46307	219-663-5120	662-4384	219
Tech Data Corp 5350 Tech Data Dr *NASDAQ: TECD* ■ *TF:* 800-237-8931 ■ *Web:* www.techdata.com	Clearwater	FL	33760	727-539-7429		174
Tech Friends 1341 County Rd 759 *Web:* mytechfriends.com	Jonesboro	AR	72401	870-933-6386		177
Tech Group Inc, The 14677 N 74th St *Web:* westpharma.com/en/techgroup/pages/tech-group.aspx	Scottsdale	AZ	85260	480-281-4500		604
tech guys inc 7913 Santa Fe Dr	Overland Park	KS	66204	913-381-5832		175
Tech Hackers LLC 332 Springfield Ave *Web:* www.thi.com	Summit	NJ	07901	908-598-1460		809
Tech Heads Inc 7060 SW Beveland Rd *Web:* www.techeads.com	Tigard	OR	97223	503-639-8542		177
Tech Hero 200 E Robinson St Ste 425 *TF:* 800-900-8324 ■ *Web:* www.techhero.com	Orlando	FL	32801	800-900-8324	741-7510	180
Tech II Inc 1765 W County Line Rd *Web:* www.techii.com	Springfield	OH	45501	937-969-7000		604
Tech Image Ltd 330 N Wabash Ave Ste 1900 *Web:* www.techimage.com	Chicago	IL	60611	847-279-0022		636
Tech International 200 E Coshocton St *TF:* 800-336-8324 ■ *Web:* www.techtirerepairs.com	Johnstown	OH	43031	740-967-9015	967-1039	754
Tech Lighting LLC 7400 Linda Ave *TF:* 800-522-5315 ■ *Web:* www.techlighting.com	Skokie	IL	60077	847-410-4400	410-4500	439
Tech Mahindra Americas Inc 2140 Lake Park Blvd Ste 300 *Web:* techmahindra.com	Richardson	TX	75080	972-991-2900		180
Tech Museum of Innovation 201 S Market St *TF:* 800-411-7245 ■ *Web:* www.thetech.org	San Jose	CA	95113	408-294-8324	279-7167	520
Tech Networks of Boston 574 Dorchester Ave *TF:* 888-527-9333 ■ *Web:* techboston.com	Boston	MA	02127	617-269-0299		41
Tech Nh Inc 8 Continental Blvd *Web:* www.technh.com	Merrimack	NH	03054	603-424-4404		608
Tech Observer 40 Eisenhower Dr Ste 201 *Web:* www.tech-observer.com	Paramus	NJ	07652	201-489-7705		177
Tech Packaging Inc 13241 Bartram Pk Blvd Ste 601 *TF:* 866-453-8324 ■ *Web:* www.techpackaging.net	Jacksonville	FL	32258	904-288-6403		549

Name / Address	City	State	ZIP	Phone	Fax	Class
Tech Pharmacy Services Inc 12503 Exchange Dr Ste 536 *TF:* 800-378-9020 ■ *Web:* www.advancedpharmacy.com	Stafford	TX	77477	800-378-9020		587
Tech Steel Inc Bldg D-2 Freeport Ctr *Web:* www.tech-steel.com	Clearfield	UT	84016	801-328-2543		480
Tech Team Solutions LLC 106 S Loudoun St *Web:* www.techteamsolutions.com	Winchester	VA	22601	540-667-2000		175
Tech Transport Inc PO Box 431 *Web:* www.techtransport.com	Milford	NH	03055	603-673-0898		311
Tech Usa Inc 8334 Veterans Hwy *Web:* www.techusa.net	Millersville	MD	21108	410-729-4328	987-9080	194
Tech West Vacuum Inc 2625 N Argyle Ave *TF:* 800-428-7139 ■ *Web:* www.tech-west.com	Fresno	CA	93727	559-291-1650		475
Tech4Learning Inc 10981 San Diego Mission Rd Ste 120 *TF:* 877-834-5453 ■ *Web:* www.tech4learning.com	San Diego	CA	92108	619-563-5348		459
Techaspect Solutions Inc 6750 Fremont Blvd, Ste 204 *TF:* 800-422-6237 ■ *Web:* www.techaspect.com	Fremont	CA	94538	510-962-3200		809
Techblocks Inc 399 Applewood Crescent Ste 4 *Web:* tblocks.com	Vaughan	ON	L4K4J3	416-775-1919		196
Tech-Clarity Inc 2420 Martingale Rd Ste 100 *Web:* www.tech-clarity.com	Media	PA	19063	610-565-6302		631
Teche Holding Co 1120 Jefferson Terr *NYSE: TSH*	New Iberia	LA	70560	337-560-7151		360-2
Teche Regional Medical Ctr 1125 Marguerite St *TF:* 800-551-8906 ■ *Web:* www.techeregional.com	Morgan City	LA	70380	985-384-2200		374-3
Tech-ed Services Inc 6121 Sebring Dr *TF:* 800-264-1170 ■ *Web:* www.teservices.com	Columbia	MD	21044	410-772-5840		260
Tech-Etch Inc 45 Aldrin Rd *Web:* www.tech-etch.com	Plymouth	MA	02360	508-747-0300	746-9639	488
Techfab Gauthier Inc 470, ave Laurendeau *Web:* techfab.com	Montreal East	QC	H1B5M2	514-640-8451		757
TechFlow Inc 6405 Mira Mesa Blvd Ste 250 *Web:* www.techflow.com	San Diego	CA	92121	858-412-8000		177
Techforce Inc 3445 Breckinridge Blvd *TF:* 866-837-3783 ■ *Web:* www.techforce.net	Duluth	GA	30096	678-597-2300		196
Techfusion 545 Concord Ln Ste 14 *Web:* www.techfusion.com	Cambridge	MA	02138	617-491-1001		180
Techgene Solutions LLC 300 E Royal Ln Ste 109 *Web:* techgene.com	Irving	TX	75039	972-580-0247		177
TechLaw Inc 14500 Avion Pkwy Ste 300 *Web:* www.techlawinc.com	Chantilly	VA	20151	703-818-1000		192
Tech-Marine Business Inc 9253 Old Keene Mill Rd *Web:* www.tmbhq.com	Burke	VA	22015	703-455-0887		261
Techmer PM LLC 1 Quality Cir *Web:* www.techmerpm.com	Clinton	TN	37716	865-457-6700		608
Techmor Inc 19911-D N Cove Rd *TF:* 800-488-6903 ■ *Web:* www.techmor.com	Cornelius	NC	28031	336-442-3686		407
Technalysis Inc 7172 Waldemar Dr *Web:* www.technalysis.com	Indianapolis	IN	46268	317-291-1985		178-11
Techne Corp 614 McKinley Pl NE *NASDAQ: TECH* ■ *TF:* 800-343-7475 ■ *Web:* bio-techne.com	Minneapolis	MN	55413	612-379-8854		231
Techne Inc 3 Terri Ln Ste 10 *Web:* www.techneusa.com	Burlington	NJ	08016	609-589-2560		419
Techneal Inc 2100 S Reservoir St *TF:* 800-545-6325 ■ *Web:* www.techneal.com	Pomona	CA	91766	909-465-6325		535
TechNet 805 15th St NW Ste 708 *Web:* www.technet.org	Washington	DC	20005	202-650-5100		48-9
Technetics Group 3125 Damon Way *TF:* 800-618-4701 ■ *Web:* technetics.com	Burbank	CA	91505	818-841-9667	841-8057	608
Techni Core Professionals Inc 4681 Research Park Blvd *Web:* www.techni-core.com	Huntsville	AL	35806	256-704-0234		261
Techni Logic Communications 959 E Collins Blvd Ste 120	Richardson	TX	75081	972-455-5526		116
Techniart Inc 41 Bridge St *Web:* techniart.com	Collinsville	CT	06019	860-693-8697		195
Technibilt Ltd 700 E P St PO Box 310 **Fax Area Code: 800* ■ *Web:* www.technibilt.com	Newton	NC	28658	828-464-7388	968-8934*	73
Technic Inc 47 Molter St *Web:* www.technic.com	Cranston	RI	02910	401-781-6100	781-2890	145
Technica Corp 22970 Indian Creek Dr Ste 500 *Web:* www.technicacorp.com	Dulles	VA	20166	703-662-2000		180
Technical Assn of the Pulp & Paper Industry (TAPPI) 15 Technology Pkwy S *TF Sales:* 800-332-8686 ■ *Web:* www.tappi.org	Norcross	GA	30092	770-446-1400	446-6947	49-13
Technical Assurance Inc 38112 Second St *TF:* 866-953-3147 ■ *Web:* www.technicalassurance.com	Willoughby	OH	44094	440-953-3147		196
Technical Cable Concepts Inc 350 Lear Ave *TF:* 800-832-2225 ■ *Web:* www.techcable.com	Costa Mesa	CA	92626	714-835-1081		116
Technical Chemical Co 3327 Pipeline Rd *TF:* 800-527-0885 ■ *Web:* www.technicalchemical.com	Cleburne	TX	76033	817-645-6088	556-0694	145
Technical Coating International Inc 150 Backhoe Rd NE *Web:* www.tciinc.com	Leland	NC	28451	910-371-0860		599
Technical College of the Lowcountry 921 Ribaut Rd *Web:* www.tcl.edu	Beaufort	SC	29902	843-525-8211		166
Technical Communications Corp 100 Domino Dr *NASDAQ: TCCO* ■ *TF:* 800-952-4082 ■ *Web:* www.tccsecure.com	Concord	MA	01742	978-287-5100	371-1280	735
Technical Communities Inc 1000 Cherry Ave Ste 100 *TF:* 888-665-2765 ■ *Web:* www.technicalcommunities.com	San Bruno	CA	94066	650-624-0525	624-0535	195

Company	City	State	ZIP	Phone	Fax	Class
Technical Consumer Products Inc 325 Campus Dr *TF:* 800-324-1496 ■ *Web:* www.tcpi.com	Aurora	OH	44202	800-324-1496		437
Technical Differences 5256 S Mission Rd Ste 210 *Web:* www.people-trak.com	Bonsall	CA	92003	760-941-5800		177
Technical Empowerment Inc 141 Nevada St *Web:* www.techempower.com	El Segundo	CA	90245	310-524-1700		177
Technical Enterprises Inc 7044 S 13th St *Web:* www.techenterprises.net	Oak Creek	WI	53154	414-768-8000	768-8001	47
Technical Field Engineering Inc 1114 Ridgecrest Ave	North Augusta	SC	29841	803-279-0331		261
Technical Gas Products Inc 66 Leonardo Dr *TF:* 800-847-0745 ■ *Web:* www.tgpoxygen.com	North Haven	CT	06473	800-847-0745		579
Technical Glass Products Inc 881 Callendar Blvd *Web:* www.technicalglass.com	Painesville	OH	44077	440-639-6399		292
Technical Instrument San Francisco 1826 Rollins Rd *TF:* 866-800-9797 ■ *Web:* www.techinst.com	Burlingame	CA	94010	650-651-3000		475
Technical Manufacturing Corp 15 Centennial Dr *Web:* www.techmfg.com	Peabody	MA	01960	978-532-6330		153
Technical Packaging Services 276 Four Sisters Rd *Web:* technicalpackagingservice.com	South Burlington	VT	05403	802-355-4838		358
Technical Resource Group Inc 7225 Bryan Dairy Rd *Web:* www.thinktrg.com	Largo	FL	33777	727-533-9440		45
Technical Support Inc 11253 John Galt Blvd *TF:* 800-337-0283 ■ *Web:* www.techsi.com	Omaha	NE	68137	402-331-4977		177
Technical Systems Inc 2303 196th SW Unit B	Lynnwood	WA	98036	425-775-5696		246
Technical Systems Integration Inc 816 Greenbrier Cir Ste 208 *TF:* 800-566-8744 ■ *Web:* www.tecsysint.com	Chesapeake	VA	23320	757-424-5793		256
Technical Toolboxes Ltd 3801 Kirby Dr Ste 520 *TF:* 866-866-6766 ■ *Web:* www.ttoolboxes.com	Houston	TX	77098	713-630-0505		177
Technical Traffic Consultants Corp 30 Hemlock Dr *Web:* www.technicaltraffic.com	Congers	NY	10920	845-623-6144		311
Technical Training Inc (TTI) 3903 W Hamlin Rd *Web:* www.tti-global.com	Rochester Hills	MI	48309	248-853-5550		113
Technical Transportation Inc 1701 W Northwest Hwy Ste 100 *Fax Area Code: 817 ■ *TF:* 800-852-8726 ■ *Web:* www.techtrans.com	Grapevine	TX	76051	800-852-8726	488-0306*	449
Techni-Car Inc 450 Commerce Blvd *TF:* 800-886-0022 ■ *Web:* www.techni-car.com	Oldsmar	FL	34677	813-855-0022	855-2101	62-5
Techni-Cast Corp 11220 Garfield Ave *Fax: Sales ■ *TF:* 800-923-4585 ■ *Web:* www.techni-cast.com	South Gate	CA	90280	562-923-4585	861-4259*	308
Technicolor 6040 Sunset Blvd *Web:* www.technicolor.com	Los Angeles	CA	90028	323-817-6600		512
Technicolor Complete Post Inc 6040 Sunset Blvd *TF:* 800-555-5211 ■ *Web:* www.technicolor.com	Hollywood	CA	90028	323-817-6600		512
Technicom Sales & Services Inc 1279 Sussex Dr *Web:* www.technicomcentral.com	North Lauderdale	FL	33068	954-597-9279		175
Technicon Engineering Services Inc 4539 N Brawley Ave Ste 108 *Web:* www.technicon.net	Fresno	CA	93722	559-276-9311		642
Technicon Industries Inc 4412 Republic Ct *Web:* www.tcnind.com	Concord	NC	28027	704-788-1131		601
Technicote Westfield Inc 222 Mound Ave *TF:* 800-358-4448 ■ *Web:* www.technicote.com	Miamisburg	OH	45342	937-859-4448	859-9096	552-1
Technidrill Systems Inc 429 Portage Blvd *TF:* 844-313-7012 ■ *Web:* www.technidrillsystems.com	Kent	OH	44240	330-678-9980	678-9981	455
Technifab Products Inc 10339 N Industrial Park Dr *Web:* www.technifab.com	Brazil	IN	47834	812-442-0520		697
Technifax Office Solutions 3220 Keller Springs Rd *Web:* technifaxdfw.com	Carrollton	TX	75006	972-478-2800	478-2812	366
Techniform Industries Inc 2107 Hayes Ave *TF:* 800-691-2816 ■ *Web:* www.techniform-plastics.com	Fremont	OH	43420	419-332-8484	334-5222	599
Technigraph Corp 850 W Third St *TF:* 800-421-4772 ■ *Web:* www.technigraph.net	Winona	MN	55987	507-454-3830	454-6470	687
Technigraphics 3212 S Cravens Rd *Web:* www.craftmarkid.com	Fort Worth	TX	76119	817-457-8412		687
Technimark Inc 180 Commerce Pl *Web:* www.technimark.com	Asheboro	NC	27203	336-498-4171	498-5042	548
Technipaq Inc 975 Lutter Dr *Web:* www.technipaq.com	Crystal Lake	IL	60014	815-477-1800	477-0777	548
Techniprint Co 2545 N Seventh St *Web:* www.techniprintaz.com	Phoenix	AZ	85006	602-257-0686		781
TechniScan Inc 3216 S Highland Dr Ste 200 *Web:* www.techniscanmedicalsystems.com	Salt Lake City	UT	84106	801-521-0444		250
Techni-Tool Inc 1547 N Trooper Rd PO Box 1117 *TF Cust Svc:* 800-832-4866 ■ *Web:* www.techni-tool.com	Worcester	PA	19490	610-941-2400	828-5623	351
Techno Source USA Inc 20 W 22nd St Ste 1101 *TF:* 800-354-4639 ■ *Web:* www.technosourcehk.com	New York	NY	10010	212-929-5200		195
Techno-Aide Inc 7117 Centennial Blvd *TF:* 800-251-2629 ■ *Web:* www.techno-aide.com	Nashville	TN	37209	615-350-7030	350-7879	476
Technocell Inc 3075 rue Bernier *Web:* www.felix-schoeller.com	Drummondville	QC	J2C6Y4	819-475-0066		557
Techno-Coat Inc 861 E 40th St *Web:* www.technocoat.com	Holland	MI	49423	616-396-6446		481
Technoconseil Tc 1177 Boul Charest O *Web:* www.technoconseil.com	Quebec	QC	G1N2C9	418-687-9991		180
Technolab International Corp 2020 NE 163 St *TF:* 888-382-2851 ■ *Web:* www.technolabcorp.com	Miami	FL	33162	305-433-2973		196
Technology & Business Integrators 136 Summit Ave Ste 205 *Web:* www.tbicentral.com	Montvale	NJ	07645	201-573-0400		194
Technology & Maintenance Council (TMC) PO Box 232 Ste 210 *Web:* www.trucking.org	Arlington	VA	22203	703-838-1763	838-1701	49-21
Technology Advancement Group Inc 22355 Tag Way *TF:* 800-824-7693 ■ *Web:* www.tag.com	Sterling	VA	20166	703-406-3000	406-0305	173-2
Technology Commercialization Group LLC 1009 Slater Rd Ste 450 *Web:* tcgmedtech.com	Durham	NC	27703	919-941-0700		194
Technology Container Corp 207 Greenwood St *Web:* www.techcontainer.com	Worcester	MA	01607	508-752-8000		100
Technology Crossover Ventures 528 Ramona St *TF:* 800-321-1111 ■ *Web:* www.tcv.com	Palo Alto	CA	94301	650-614-8200	614-8222	792
Technology for Energy Corp 10737 Lexington Dr *Web:* www.tec-usa.com	Knoxville	TN	37932	865-966-5856		256
Technology Funding Inc 460 St Michael's Dr Ste 1000 *TF:* 800-821-5323 ■ *Web:* www.techfunding.com	Santa Fe	NM	87505	800-821-5323		792
Technology Futures Inc (TFI) 13740 Research Blvd (N Hwy 183) Ste C-1 *TF:* 800-835-3887 ■ *Web:* www.tfi.com	Austin	TX	78750	512-258-8898	258-0087	196
Technology General Corp 12 Cork Hill Rd *Web:* www.iconservice.com	Franklin	NJ	07416	973-827-4143		172
Technology Integration Group (TIG) 7810 Trade St *TF:* 800-858-0549 ■ *Web:* www.tig.com	San Diego	CA	92121	858-566-1900	566-8794	176
Technology Marketing Corp 1 Technology Plaza *TF Cust Svc:* 800-243-6002 ■ *Web:* www.tmcnet.com	Norwalk	CT	06854	203-852-6800	866-3326	637-2
Technology News of America 123 Seventh Ave *Web:* www.tech-news.com	Brooklyn	NY	11215	718-369-7682	965-3039	531-3
Technology Partners 550 University Ave *TF:* 800-747-3924 ■ *Web:* www.technologypartners.com	Palo Alto	CA	94301	650-289-9000	289-9001	792
Technology Review Magazine 1 Main St 7th Fl *Web:* www.technologyreview.com	Cambridge	MA	02142	617-475-8000	475-8042	457-19
Technology Service Corp 962 Wayne Ave Ste 800 *TF:* 800-324-7700 ■ *Web:* tsc.com	Silver Spring	MD	20910	301-565-2970	565-0673	668
Technology Site Planners Inc 8188 Business Way *Web:* www.techsiteplan.com	Plain City	OH	43064	614-873-7800		186
Technology Ventures Corp 1155 University Blvd SE *Web:* www.techventures.org	Albuquerque	NM	87106	505-246-2882		405
Technomart RGA Inc 401 Washington Ave Ste 1101 *TF:* 800-877-6555 ■ *Web:* www.technomartrga.com	Baltimore	MD	21204	410-828-6555		401
Technomedia Solutions LLC 4545 36th St *Web:* www.gotechnomedia.com	Orlando	FL	32811	407-351-0909		196
Technomic Inc 300 S Riverside Plaza Ste 1200 *Web:* www.technomic.com	Chicago	IL	60606	312-876-0004		194
Technomics Inc 201 12th St S Ste 612 *Web:* www.technomics.net	Arlington	VA	22202	571-366-1400		41
TechnoPlanet Productions Inc 7030 Woodbine Ave Fl 5 *Web:* www.technoplanet.com	Markham	ON	L3R6G2	905-839-0603		195
Technorati Inc 360 Post St Ste 1100 *Web:* www.technorati.com	San Francisco	CA	94108	415-896-3000		387
TechnoServe 1 Mechanic St *TF:* 800-999-6757 ■ *Web:* www.technoserve.org	Norwalk	CT	06854	203-852-0377	838-6717	48-5
Technosoft Corp 28411 NW Hwy Ste 640 *Web:* www.technosoftcorp.com	Southfield	MI	48034	248-603-2600	603-2599	177
Technosoft Engineering 13400 Bishops Lnn Ste 30 *Web:* www.impactengsol.com	Brookfield	WI	53005	262-317-8100	317-8101	256
Technosphere 155 N Washington Ave *Web:* www.technosphere.com	Bergenfield	NJ	07621	201-384-7400		463
Technossus LLC 17885 Von Karman Ave Ste 410 *Web:* www.technossus.com	Irvine	CA	92614	949-769-3500		196
Technotraining Inc 328 Office Sq Ln Ste 202 *Web:* www.technotraining.net	Virginia Beach	VA	23462	757-425-0728		177
Techone Inc 7901 Stoneridge Dr Ste 403 *Web:* www.techone.com	Pleasanton	CA	94588	408-894-8100		177
Techorbit Inc 1303 W Walnut Hill Ln Ste 300 *Web:* www.techorbit.com	Irving	TX	75038	214-276-1379		196
TechPad Agency LLC 10824 SE Oak St Ste 205 *Web:* www.TechPadAgency.com	Milwaukie	OR	97222	619-749-8444		5
Techpeople Inc 3939 Bee Cave Rd *Web:* www.techpeopleinc.com	Austin	TX	78746	512-493-1400		179
Tech-Pro Inc 3000 Centre Pointe Dr *Web:* www.tech-pro.com	Roseville	MN	55113	651-634-1400		180

Entry	City	ST	ZIP	Phone	Fax	Class
TechProse Inc 3685 Mt Diablo Blvd Ste 340 *Web:* www.techprose.com	Lafayette	CA	94549	925-299-3900		809
Techrecruiters Inc 801 N Barstow St Ste 205 *Web:* techrecruiters.biz	Waukesha	WI	53186	262-894-6325		177
Tech-Seal International Inc 5656 Wheatley St	Houston	TX	77091	713-691-0668	691-2328	538
TechSearch International Inc 4801 Spicewood Springs Rd Ste 150 *TF:* 800-228-4653 ■ *Web:* www.techsearchinc.com	Austin	TX	78759	512-372-8887		195
TechServe Alliance 1420 King St Ste 610 *Web:* www.techservealliance.org	Alexandria	VA	22314	703-838-2050	838-3610	48-9
TechSherpas Inc 5404 Cypress Ctr Dr Ste 125 *Web:* www.techsherpas.com	Tampa	FL	33609	813-287-8876		507
Techsico Enterprise Solutions Inc 910 S Hudson Ave *TF:* 800-547-9988 ■ *Web:* www.techsico.com	Tulsa	OK	74112	918-585-2347		194
TechSkills LLC 108 Wild Basin Rd Ste 150 *Web:* www.techskills.edu	Austin	TX	78746	512-328-4235		225
Techsmart Solutions Inc 328 Air Park Dr Ste 200 *Web:* onlinepchelp.com	Fort Collins	CO	80524	970-498-0808		225
TechSmith Corp 2405 Woodlake Dr *TF:* 800-517-3001 ■ *Web:* www.techsmith.com	Okemos	MI	48864	517-381-2300	381-2336	178-8
Techsol4u Inc 95 w 11th st *Web:* www.techsolglobalit.com	Tracy	CA	95376	209-833-3212		225
Techspeed Inc 280 SW Moonridge Pl *TF:* 800-750-4066 ■ *Web:* www.techspeed.com	Portland	OR	97225	503-291-0027		180
TechStar 802 W 13th St *Web:* www.techstaris.com	Deer Park	TX	77536	281-542-0205		791
TechTarget 275 Grove St Ste 800 *TF:* 000-274-4111 ■ *Web:* www.techtarget.com	Newton	MA	02466	617-431-9200	431-9201	637-10
Techtonic Group Llc 1900 Folsom St Ste 101 *Web:* www.techtonicgroup.com	Boulder	CA	80302	303-440-8772		809
TechTrans International Inc 2200 Space Pk Ste 410 *Web:* www.tti-corp.com	Houston	TX	77058	281-335-8000		317
Tech-Trek Ltd 1015 Matheson Blvd E Unit 6 *Web:* www.tech-trek.com	Mississauga	ON	L4W3A4	905-238-0366		195
Techville Inc 11343 N Central Expwy *Web:* www.umax.com	Dallas	TX	75243	214-739-7033		173-7
Techware Distribution Inc 7720 W 78th St *TF:* 800-295-0083 ■ *Web:* www.techwaredist.com	Minneapolis	MN	55439	952-944-0083		225
Techwave Consulting Inc 1 E Uwchlan Ave *Web:* techwavenet.com	Exton	PA	19341	484-873-8707		106
Tech-Way Industries Inc 301 Industrial Dr *Web:* www.tech-wayindustries.com	Franklin	OH	45005	937-746-1004		596
TechWorks 4030 W Braker Ln *Web:* techwrks.com	Austin	TX	78759	512-794-8533		625
Tech-X Corp 5621 Arapahoe Ave Ste A *Web:* www.cusys.edu	Boulder	CO	80303	303-448-0727		177
TechXpress Inc 3450 Broad St Ste 108 *Web:* www.techxpress.net	San Luis Obispo	CA	93401	805-541-4400		317
Tecinfo Inc 601 N Deer Creek Dr E *TF:* 800-863-5415 ■ *Web:* tecinfo.net	Leland	MS	38756	662-686-9009		175
Teck Cominco American Inc 501 N Riverpoint Blvd Ste 300 *TF:* 866 225 0198 ■ *Web:* www.teck.com	Spokane	WA	99202	800-432-3206		502
TECMA Group LLC, The 2000 Wyoming Ave *Web:* www.tecma.com	El Paso	TX	79903	915-534-4252		393
TecMed Inc 1603 Capitol Ave Ste 209 *Web:* tecmed.com	Cheyenne	WY	82001	307-509-9653		743
Tecmotiv (USA) Inc 1500 James Ave *TF:* 800-388-8255 ■ *Web:* www.tecmotiv.com	Niagara Falls	NY	14305	716-282-1211		454
Tecnara Tooling Systems Inc 12535 McCann Dr *TF:* 800-837-2223 ■ *Web:* www.tecnaratools.com	Santa Fe Springs	CA	90670	562-941-2000		358
Tecnet Canada Inc 3403 Seymour Pl *Web:* www.tecnet.ca	Victoria	BC	V8X1W4	250-475-6066		175
Tecnica USA 19 Technology Dr *Web:* tecnicausa.com	West Lebanon	NH	03784	603-298-8032		710
Tecnicard Inc 3191 Coral Way Ste 800 *TF:* 800-317-6020 ■ *Web:* www.tecnicard.com	Miami	FL	33145	305-442-0018	442-9937	225
Tecnico Corp 831 Industrial Ave *TF General:* 800-786-2207 ■ *Web:* www.tecnicocorp.com	Chesapeake	VA	23324	757-545-4013		698
TECO Coal Corp 200 Allison Blvd	Corbin	KY	40701	606-523-4444		501
Teco Diagnostics 1268 N Lakeview Ave *TF:* 800-222-9880 ■ *Web:* www.tecodiagnostics.com	Anaheim	CA	92807	714-463-1111	463-1169	231
TECO Energy Inc 702 N Franklin St *NYSE:* TE ■ *TF:* 800-732-0330 ■ *Web:* tecoenergy.com	Tampa	FL	33602	813-228-1111	228-1670	185
Tecolote Cafe 1616 St Michaels Dr *Web:* tecolotecafe.com	Santa Fe	NM	87505	505-988-1362		671
Tecolote Research Inc 420 S Fairview Ave Ste 201 *Web:* www.tecolote.com	Goleta	CA	93117	805-571-6366	571-6377	463
Tecom Industries Inc 375 Conejo Ridge Ave *TF:* 866-840-8550 ■ *Web:* www.tecom-ind.com	Thousand Oaks	CA	91361	805-267-0100	267-0181	647
Tecon Services Inc 515 Garden Oaks Blvd *TF:* 800-245-1728 ■ *Web:* www.teconservices.com	Houston	TX	77018	713-691-2700		188
TECO-Westinghouse Motor Co 5100 N IH-35 *TF:* 800-451-8798 ■ *Web:* www.tecowestinghouse.com	Round Rock	TX	78681	512-255-4141	244-5512	709
Tecplot Inc 3535 Factoria Blvd SE Ste 550 *TF:* 800-763-7005 ■ *Web:* www.tecplot.com	Bellevue	WA	98006	425-653-1200		177
Tecsec Inc 12950 Worldgate Dr Ste 100 *Web:* www.tecsec.com	Herndon	VA	20170	571-299-4100		178-12
TecServ Inc 358 S Rio Grande St Ste 250 *Web:* www.tecservinc.com	Salt Lake City	UT	84101	801-485-6055		180
Tecstar Manufacturing Co W190N11701 Moldmakers Way *Web:* www.mgstech.com	Germantown	WI	53022	262-255-5790	255-7206	608
TECSys Development Inc 1600 Tenth St Ste B *TF:* 800-695-1258 ■ *Web:* www.tditechnologies.com	Plano	TX	75074	972-881-1553		180
TECSYS Inc 1 Place Alexis Nihon Ste 800 *TF:* 800-922-8649 ■ *Web:* www.tecsys.com	Montreal	QC	H3Z3B8	514-866-0001	866-1805	178-1
TECT (Turbine Engine Components Technologies Corp) 334 Beechwood Rd Ste 304 *Web:* www.tectcorp.com	Ft Mitchell	KY	41017	859-426-0090		483
Tecta America Co 15002 Wicks Blvd *Web:* www.tectaamerica.com	San Leandro	CA	94577	510-686-4951		189-12
Tectonic Engineering & Surveying Consultants PC 70 Pleasant Hill Rd *TF:* 800-829-6531 ■ *Web:* tectonicengineering.com	Mountainville	NY	10953	845-534-5959		261
Tectonics Industries Inc 24680 Mound Rd *Web:* tectonics.com	Warren	MI	48091	586-755-6522		627
Tectum Inc 105 S Sixth St *TF:* 888-977-9691 ■ *Web:* www.tectum.com	Newark	OH	43055	740-345-9691	349-9305	819
Tecumseh Poultry LLC 13151 Dovers *Web:* www.cafetecumseh.com/SmartChicken	Waverly	NE	68462	402-786-1000		619
Tecumseh Power 900 N St *Web:* www.tecumsehpower.com	Grafton	WI	53024	262-377-2700		14
Tecumseh Products Co 1136 Oak Valley Dr *NASDAQ:* TECU ■ *Web:* www.tecumseh.com	Ann Arbor	MI	48108	734-585-9500	352-3700	172
Tecumseh Products Company LLC 5683 Hines Dr *Web:* tecumseh.com	Ann Arbor	MI	48108	734-585-9500	352-3700	14
Ted Hosmer Interprises Inc 1249 Lehigh Station Rd *TF:* 800-561-3357 ■ *Web:* www.tedhosmer.com	Henrietta	NY	14467	585-334-3620		776
Ted Pella Inc 4595 Mountain Lakes Blvd *Web:* www.tedpella.com	Redding	CA	96003	530-243-2200		544
Ted Peter's Famous Smoked Fish 1350 Pasadena Ave S *Web:* tedpetersfish.com	Saint Petersburg	FL	33707	727-381-7931		671
Ted Stevens Anchorage International Airport 5000 W International Airport Rd *Web:* dot.state.ak.us	Anchorage	AK	99502	907-266-2526		27
Ted Wiens Tire & Auto Centers 1701 Las Vegas Blvd S *Web:* www.tedwiens.com	Las Vegas	NV	89104	702-735-5656		755
Ted's Bar & Grill 6197 Allentown Blvd *Web:* tedsbarandgrill.com	Harrisburg	PA	17112	717-652-3832		671
Ted's Cafe Escondido 2836 NW 68th St *Web:* tedscafe.com	Oklahoma City	OK	73116	405-848-8337		671
Ted's Hot Dogs 95 Roger Chaffee Dr *Web:* www.tedshotdogs.com	Amherst	NY	14228	716-691-3731		670
Tedco Construction Corp Tedco Pl *Web:* www.tedco.com	Carnegie	PA	15106	412-276-8080	276-6804	186
Teddy's Transportation System Inc 25 Van Zant St *TF:* 800-888-3339 ■ *Web:* teddyslimo.com	Norwalk	CT	06855	203-866-2231		441
Tedeschi Food Shops Inc 14 Howard St *Web:* www.tedeschifoodshops.com	Rockland	MA	02370	781-878-8210		204
Tedia Company Inc 1000 Tedia Way *TF:* 800-787-4891 ■ *Web:* www.tedia.com	Fairfield	OH	45014	513-874-5340	874-5346	144
Teds Inc 235 Mtn Empire Rd *Web:* teds.com	Atkins	VA	24311	276-783-6991		180
Tee Group Films 605 N Main St *TF:* 800-326-6206 ■ *Web:* www.tee-group.com	Ladd	IL	61329	815-894-2331	894-3387	600
Tee Jaye's Country Place Restaurants 1363 Parsons Ave PO Box 6646 *Web:* www.barnyardbuster.com	Columbus	OH	43206	614-443-9773	443-0613	670
Teeco Products Inc 16881 Armstrong Ave *TF:* 800-854-3463 ■ *Web:* www.teecoproducts.com	Irvine	CA	92606	949-261-6295	474-8663	385
TEECOM Design Group 1333 Broadway Ste 601 *Web:* teecom.com	Oakland	CA	94612	510-337-2800		261
Teel Plastics Inc 1060 Teel Ct *Web:* www.teel.com	Baraboo	WI	53913	608-355-3080	355-3088	596
Teeter Irrigation Inc 2729 W Oklahoma *TF:* 800-524-5497 ■ *Web:* www.teeterirrigation.com	Ulysses	KS	67880	620-353-1111		274
Tefron USA Inc 201 St Germain Ave SW *TF:* 800-384-3674 ■ *Web:* www.tefron.com	Valdese	NC	28690	828-879-6500		155-10
Tegal Corp 2201 S McDowell Blvd *Web:* www.collabrx.com	Petaluma	CA	94954	707-763-5600		695
TEGAM Inc 10 Tegam Way *TF:* 800-666-1010 ■ *Web:* www.tegam.com	Geneva	OH	44041	440-466-6100	466-6110	248
Tegile Systems Inc 8000 Jarvis Ave *Web:* www.tegile.com	Newark	CA	94560	510-791-7900		173-8
Tegra Medical LLC 9 Forge Pk *TF:* 800-366-3067 ■ *Web:* www.tegramedical.com	Franklin	MA	02038	508-541-4200		475
Tehama County 633 Washington St Rm 11 *Web:* www.co.tehama.ca.us	Red Bluff	CA	96080	530-527-3350	527-1745	338
Tehama County Library 645 Madison St *TF:* 800-984-4636 ■ *Web:* tehamacountylibrary.org	Red Bluff	CA	96080	530-527-0604	527-1562	434-3
TEI (Taylor Enterprises Inc) 2586 Southport Rd *TF:* 800-922-3149 ■ *Web:* taylorlubricants.com	Spartanburg	SC	29302	864-573-9518	583-4150	579
TEI (Tax Executives Institute) 1200 G St NW Ste 300 *Web:* www.tei.org	Washington	DC	20005	202-638-5601	638-5607	49-1
Tei Tei Robata Bar 2906 N Henderson St *Web:* www.teiteirobata.com	Dallas	TX	75206	214-828-2400		671

Listing	City	State	Zip	Phone	Fax	Class
Teich Groh & Frost 691 Hwy 33 *TF:* 800-900-4250 ■ *Web:* www.teichgroh.com	Trenton	NJ	08619	609-890-1500		445
Teijin Holdings USA 600 Lexington Ave 27th Fl *Web:* www.teijin.com	New York	NY	10022	212-308-8744	308-8902	360-3
Teijin Kasei America Inc 5555 Triangle Pkwy Ste 275 *Web:* www.teijin.com/about/group_worldwide/america.html	Norcross	GA	30092	770-346-8949	346-7610	605-2
Teikoku Pharma USA Inc 1718 Ringwood Ave *Web:* www.teikokuusa.com	San Jose	CA	95131	408-501-1800		231
Teine Energy Ltd 2300 520 - Third Ave SW *TF:* 866-900-2711 ■ *Web:* www.teine-energy.com	Calgary	AB	T2P0R3	403-698-8300		536
Teixeira Farms Inc 2600 Bonita Lateral Rd *Web:* www.teixeirafarms.com	Santa Maria	CA	93458	805-928-3801	928-9405	10-11
Tejas Broadcasting LLP 1300 Antelope St	Corpus Christi	TX	78401	361-883-1600	883-9303	643
Tejas Feeders Ltd E Highway 152	Pampa	TX	79066	806-665-3201	669-0210	10-1
Tejas Logistics System PO Box 1339 *TF:* 800-535-9786 ■ *Web:* www.tejaswarehouse.com	Waco	TX	76703	254-753-0301	752-4452	803-1
Tejas Research & Engineering LP 9185 Six Pines Dr. *Web:* www.tejasre.com	The Woodlands	TX	77380	281-466-8700		261
Tejas Securities Group 8226 Bee Caves Rd.	Austin	TX	78746	512-306-8222	306-1528	690
Tejon Ranch Co 4436 Lebec Rd PO Box 1000. *NYSE: TRC* ■ *Web:* www.tejonranch.com	Lebec	CA	93243	661-248-3000		10-1
Tek Data Systems 31 Crestview Dr Unit 2 *Web:* tekdata.com	Westerly	RI	02891	401-596-5175		525
Tekelec 5200 Paramount Pkwy *NASDAQ: TKLC* ■ *TF:* 800-633-0738 ■ *Web:* oracle.com	Morrisville	NC	27560	919-460-5500	460-0877	735
Tekgard Inc 3390 Farmtrail Rd. *Web:* www.tekgard.com	York	PA	17406	717-854-0005		14
Tekgroup International Inc 1280 SW 36th Ave Ste 204 *Web:* www.tekgroup.com	Pompano Beach	FL	33069	954-351-5554		809
Tekla Inc 1075 Big Shanty Rd NW Ste 175 *TF:* 877-835-5265 ■ *Web:* www.tekla.com	Kennesaw	GA	30144	770-426-5105		174
Tekmar Control Systems Ltd 5100 Silver Star Rd. *Web:* www.tekmarcontrols.com	Vernon	BC	V1B3K4	250-545-7749	545-0650	610
Tekmark Global Solutions LLC 100 Metroplex Dr Ste 102. *Web:* www.tekmark.com	Edison	NJ	08817	732-572-5400		180
Tekmasters Llc 4437 brookfield corporate dr *Web:* www.tekmasters.com	Chantilly	VA	20151	703-349-1110		463
Teknetix Inc 2501 Garfield Ave *Web:* www.teknetix.com	Parkersburg	WV	26101	304-424-9400		625
Teknion Corp 1150 Flint Rd. *Web:* www.teknion.com	Toronto	ON	M3J2J5	416-661-3370	661-4586	319-1
Tekno Inc 1 Wall St *Web:* www.tekno.com	Cave City	KY	42127	270-773-4181		207
Teknon Corp 10675 Willows Rd. *TF:* 800-338-6142 ■ *Web:* www.teknon.com	Redmond	WA	98052	425-895-8535	895-0535	189-4
Teknor Apex Co 505 Central Ave. *TF:* 800-556-3864 ■ *Web:* www.teknorapex.com	Pawtucket	RI	02861	401-725-8000	725-8095	605-3
TeKONTROL Inc 711 W Amelia St *Web:* www.tekontrol.com	Orlando	FL	32805	407-398-6575		180
TEKPAK Inc 1410 Washington St. *Web:* www.tekpakinc.com	Marion	AL	36756	334-683-6121		125
TekPartners 5810 Coral Ridge Dr Ste 250 *Web:* www.tekpartners.com	Coral Springs	FL	33076	954-656-8600	282-6070	631
Tekra Corp 16700 W Lincoln Ave. *TF:* 800-448-3572 ■ *Web:* www.tekra.com	New Berlin	WI	53151	262-784-5533	797-3276	603
Tekram USA 14228 Albers Way Ste B. *Web:* www.tekram.com	Chino	CA	91710	909-606-1111	597-3713	625
Tekran Instruments Corp 230 Tech Ctr Dr. *TF:* 888-383-5726 ■ *Web:* www.tekran.com	Knoxville	TN	37912	865-688-0688		419
Teksavers Inc 2120 Grand Ave Pkwy. *TF:* 866-832-6188 ■ *Web:* teksavers.com	Austin	TX	78728	512-491-5304		180
TekScape 247 W 30th St *TF:* 855-835-7227 ■ *Web:* tekscapeit.com	New York	NY	10001	855-835-7227		196
Teksouth Corp 1420 Northbrook Dr Ste 220. *Web:* www.teksouth.com	Birmingham	AL	35071	205-631-1500		177
Tekstrom Inc 18 Shea Way Ste 101 and 102 Delaware Industrial Park *Web:* www.tekstrom.com	Newark	DE	19713	302-709-5900		396
TEKsystems Inc 7437 Race Rd *TF:* 888-519-0776 ■ *Web:* www.teksystems.com	Hanover	MD	21076	410-540-7700		721
Tektronix Component Solutions Inc 2905 SW Hocken Ave. *TF:* 800-833-9200 ■ *Web:* www.tek.com/tektronix-component-solutions	Beaverton	OR	97005	800-833-9200		393
Tek-Vac Industries Inc 176 Express Dr S *Web:* www.tekvac.com	Brentwood	NY	11717	631-436-5100	436-5154	695
Tekworks Inc 13000 Gregg St Ste B *TF:* 877-835-9675 ■ *Web:* www.tekworks.com	Poway	CA	92064	877-835-9675		176
Tel Edge 2616 Mesilla St NE Ste 3 *Web:* wrightedge.com	Albuquerque	NM	87110	505-292-9477		7
Tel Electronics Inc 313 S 740 E St Ste 1. *TF:* 800-748-5022 ■ *Web:* www.tel-electronics.com	American Fork	UT	84003	801-756-9606	756-9135	735
Tel Star Cablevison Inc 1295 Lourdes Rd *TF:* 888-842-0258 ■ *Web:* www.telstar-online.net	Metamora	IL	61548	309-383-2677		116
TeL Systems 7235 Jackson Rd. *TF:* 800-686-7235 ■ *Web:* www.telsystemsusa.com	Ann Arbor	MI	48103	734-761-4506	761-9776	246
Tel Tec Security Systems Inc 5020 Lisa Marie Ct *TF:* 800-292-9227 ■ *Web:* www.tel-tec.com	Bakersfield	CA	93313	661-397-5511		196
Tel Tech Networks Inc 810 E Hammond Ln *Web:* www.teltechnetworks.com	Phoenix	AZ	85034	602-431-9399		116
Tel Tech Plus Inc 393 Enterprise St *Web:* www.ttp-us.com	San Marcos	CA	92078	760-510-1323		177
TELACU 5400 E Olympic Blvd 3rd Fl *Web:* www.telacu.com	Los Angeles	CA	90022	323-721-1655	724-3372	653
Tel-Adjust Inc 29000 Inkster Rd Ste 115 *Web:* www.teladjust.com	Southfield	MI	48034	248-208-1600	208-0805	194
Telaffects Llc 300 primera blvd *Web:* www.telaffects.com	Lake Mary	FL	32746	407-936-3130		463
Tel-affinity Corp 66 Oak Knoll Terr *Web:* www.tel-affinity.com	Needham	MA	02492	781-433-0451		463
TelAlaska Inc 201 E 56th St *TF:* 888-570-1792 ■ *Web:* www.telalaska.com	Anchorage	AK	99518	907-563-2003		736
Telamon Corp 1000 E 116th St *Web:* www.telamon.com	Carmel	IN	46032	317-818-6888		387
Telamon Engineering Consultant 855 Folsom St *TF:* 800-697-1222 ■ *Web:* www.telamoninc.com	San Francisco	CA	94107	415-837-1336		261
Telarc International Corp 23307 Commerce Pk Rd. *Web:* concordmusicgroup.com/labels/telarc	Cleveland	OH	44122	216-464-2313		657
Telax Voice Solutions 365 Evans Ave Ste 302 *TF:* 888-808-3529 ■ *Web:* www.telax.com	Toronto	ON	M8Z1K2	416-207-0630		737
Telco Systems Inc 15 Berkshire Rd *TF:* 800-227-0937 ■ *Web:* www.telco.com	Mansfield	MA	02048	781-255-2120	255-2122	735
Telcobuy com L L C 60 Weldon Pkwy *TF:* 877-350-0191 ■ *Web:* www.telcobuy.com	St. Louis	MO	63043	877-350-0191		246
Telcoe Federal Credit Union 820 Lousiana St *TF:* 800-482-9009 ■ *Web:* telcoe.com	Little Rock	AR	72201	501-375-5321	375-6233	219
TelcoIQ 4300 Forbes Blvd Ste 110 *TF:* 877-835-2647 ■ *Web:* www.telcoiq.com	Lanham	MD	20706	202-595-1500		387
Telcom Corp 1499 W Palmetto Park Rd Ste 214 *TF:* 800-394-5448 ■ *Web:* www.telcomcorp.com	Boca Raton	FL	33486	561-394-5448		463
TELCOR Inc 7101 A St *Web:* www.telcor.com	Lincoln	NE	68510	402-489-1207		196
Teldat Corp 1901 S Bascom Ave Ste 520 *Web:* www.teldat.com	Campbell	CA	95008	408-892-9363		173-3
Tele Atlas North America Inc 11 Lafayette St *Web:* www.tomtom.com	Lebanon	NH	03766	603-643-0330		387
Tele Business USA 1945 Techny Rd Ste 3 **Fax Area Code: 847* ■ *TF:* 877-315-8353 ■ *Web:* www.tbiz.com	Northbrook	IL	60062	877-315-8353	480-6055*	737
Tele Tech Services 500 Oakbrook Ln *Web:* kfrservices.com	Summerville	SC	29483	843-873-9200		396
Tel-e Technologies 7 Kodiak Crescent *TF:* 800-661-2340 ■ *Web:* www.tel-e-technologies.com	Toronto	ON	M3J3E5	416-631-1300		5
TeleBrands Corp 79 Two Bridges Rd *Web:* www.telebrands.com	Fairfield	NJ	07004	973-244-0300	244-0233	361
TeleBright Software Corp 1700 Research Blvd Ste 240 *Web:* www.telebright.com	Rockville	MD	20850	301-296-3800		809
Telebroad LLC 452 Broadway *Web:* www.telebroad.com	Brooklyn	NY	11211	212-444-9911		224
Telebyte Communications Inc 6816 50 Ave *TF:* 800-565-1849 ■ *Web:* www.telebyte.ca	Red Deer	AB	T4N4E3	403-346-9966		224
Telebyte Inc 355 Marcus Blvd *TF:* 800-835-3298 ■ *Web:* www.telebyteusa.com	Hauppauge	NY	11788	631-423-3232	385-8184	176
Teleco 5221 Oleander Dr *Web:* www.teleco-ilm.com	Wilmington	NC	28403	910-791-7000		224
Teleco Inc 430 Woodruff Rd Ste 300 *Web:* www.teleco.com	Greenville	SC	29607	864-297-4400		246
Telecom AM 2115 Ward Ct NW *TF:* 800-771-9202 ■ *Web:* www.warren-news.com	Washington	DC	20037	202-872-9200		531-11
Telecom Asset Management LLC 1736 Dolores St *Web:* www.telecomassets.com	San Francisco	CA	94110	415-923-5800		463
Telecom Management Inc 39 Darling Ave *Web:* www.pioneertelephone.com	South Portland	ME	04106	207-774-9500		736
Telecom Ottawa Ltd 100 Maple Grove Rd	Ottawa	ON	K2V1B8	613-225-4631		225
Telecom Resources International Inc 10632 N Scottsdale Rd Ste 486 *Web:* tri-1.com	Scottsdale	AZ	85254	480-391-3800		463
Telecommunication Support Services Inc 720 N Dr. *Web:* www.tssincorp.com	Melbourne	FL	32934	321-242-0000		116
TeleCommunication Systems Inc 275 W St Ste 400 *NASDAQ: TSYS* ■ *TF:* 800-810-0827 ■ *Web:* www.telecomsys.com	Annapolis	MD	21401	410-263-7616	263-7617	224
Telecommunications Industry Assn (TIA) 2500 Wilson Blvd Ste 300 *Web:* www.tiaonline.org	Arlington	VA	22201	703-907-7700	907-7727	49-20
Telecon Inc 7 450 rue du Mile-End *TF:* 800-465-0349 ■ *Web:* www.telecon.ca	Montreal	QC	H2R2Z6	514-644-2333		186
Telecorp Products Inc 2000 E Oakley Park Rd Ste 101 *TF:* 800-634-1012 ■ *Web:* www.telecorpproducts.com	Walled Lake	MI	48390	248-960-1000		174
Telect Inc 23321 E Knox Ave *TF Cust Svc:* 800-551-4567 ■ *Web:* www.telect.com	Liberty Lake	WA	99019	509-926-6000	926-8915	735
TeleDevelopment Services Inc 4816 Brecksville Rd Ste 2 *Web:* www.teledevelopment.com	Richfield	OH	44286	330-659-4441		737
Teledyne Advanced Pollution Instrumentation 9480 Carroll Pk Dr *TF:* 800-324-5190 ■ *Web:* www.teledyne-api.com	San Diego	CA	92121	858-657-9800	657-9816	201

Phone | Fax | Class

Teledyne Benthos Inc
49 Edgerton Dr........................North Falmouth MA 02556 508-563-1000 563-6444 529
Web: www.benthos.com
Teledyne Brown Engineering Inc
300 Sparkman Dr........................Huntsville AL 35805 256-726-1000 726-1385* 261
**Fax:* Hum Res ■ *TF:* 800-933-2091 ■ *Web:* www.tbe.com
Teledyne Continental Motors Inc
2039 Broad St........................Mobile AL 36615 251-438-3411 20
TF: 800-718-3411 ■ *Web:* www.continentalmotors.aero
Teledyne Controls
1365 Corporate Ctr Curv........................Eagan MN 55121 651-994-1000 196
Web: www.teledynecontrols.com
Teledyne DALSA Inc
888 East Arques Ave........................Sunnyvale CA 94085 408-736-6000 696
Web: www.teledynedalsa.com/imaging/markets/mv/ndt
Teledyne Electronic Safety Products
19735 Dearborn St........................Chatsworth CA 91311 818-718-6640 998-3312 253
Web: www.teledynesafetyproducts.com
Teledyne Electronics & Communications
1049 Camino Dos Rios........................Thousand Oaks CA 91360 805-373-4545 696
Web: www.teledyne.com
Teledyne Instruments Inc
16830 Chestnut St........................City Of Industry CA 91748 626-934-1500 419
Web: www.teledyne-ai.com
Teledyne Leeman Labs Inc 110 Lowell Rd........Hudson NH 03051 603-886-8400 419
Web: www.teledyneleemanlabs.com
Teledyne Lighting & Display Products
12964 Panama St........................Los Angeles CA 90066 310-823-5491 574-2070 430
TF: 800-563-4020 ■ *Web:* www.teledynelighting.com
Teledyne Monitor Labs Inc (TML)
35 Inverness Dr E........................Englewood CO 80112 303-792-3300 799-4853 201
TF: 800-422-1499 ■ *Web:* www.monitorlabs.com
Teledyne Odom Hydrographic Systems Inc
1450 Seaboard Ave........................Baton Rouge LA 70810 225-769-3051 529
Web: www.odomhydrographic.com
Teledyne RD Instruments Inc
14020 Stowe Dr........................Poway CA 92064 858-842-2600 529
Web: www.rdinstruments.com
Teledyne Reynolds Inc
5005 McConnell Ave........................Los Angeles CA 90066 310-823-5491 822-8046 268
Web: www.teledynereynolds.com
Teledyne Tekmar Company Inc
4736 Socialville Foster Rd........................Mason OH 45040 513-229-7000 419
Web: www.teledynetekmar.com
Teleflex Inc 550 E Swedesford Rd Ste 400........Wayne PA 19087 610-225-6800 185
NYSE: TFX
Teleflex Medical
2917 Weck Dr PO Box 12600......Research Triangle Park NC 27709 919-544-8000 361-3914 60
TF: 866-246-6990 ■ *Web:* www.teleflex.com
Teleflex Medical OEM 50 Plantation Dr........Jaffrey NH 03452 603-532-7706 532-6108 476
TF: 800-548-6600 ■ *Web:* www.teleflexmedicaloem.com
Teleflex Turbine Services Corporation
12661 Challenger Pkwy Ste 250........................Orlando FL 32826 407-677-0813 256
Web: www.turbinetech.com
TeleflexGFI Control Systems LP
100 Hollinger Crescent........................Kitchener ON N2K2Z3 519-576-4270 576-7045 60
TF: 800-667-4275 ■ *Web:* www.gficontrolsystems.com
Teleflora Inc 11444 Olympic Blvd........Los Angeles CA 90064 800-493-5610 294
TF: 800-493-5610 ■ *Web:* www.teleflora.com
Telefonica USA Inc
1111 Brickell Ave 10th Fl........................Miami FL 33131 305-925-5300 373-1685 736
Web: www.us.telefonica.com
TeleGeography
1 Thomas Cir NW Ste 360........................Washington DC 20005 202-741-0020 741-0021 637-11
Web: www.telegeography.com
Telegram.com 100 Front St 5th Fl........Worcester MA 01608 508-793-9100 793-9313 637-8
TF: 800-678-6680 ■ *Web:* www.telegram.com
Telegraph 113 S Peoria Ave........Dixon IL 61021 815-284-2224 284-2078 532-2
TF: 800-798-4085 ■ *Web:* www.saukvalley.com
Telegraph Herald 801 Bluff St........Dubuque IA 52001 563-588-5611 588-5745* 532-2
**Fax:* Edit ■ *TF:* 800-553-4801 ■ *Web:* www.telegraphherald.com
Telegraph, The PO Box 278........Alton IL 62002 618-463-2500 532-2
TF: 866-299-9256 ■ *Web:* www.thetelegraph.com
Telegraph, The 1675 Montpelier Ave Ste B........Macon GA 31201 800-342-5845 532-2
TF: 800-342-5845 ■ *Web:* macon.com
Telegraph, The PO Box 1008........Nashua NH 03061 603-882-2741 882-2681 532-2
TF: 800-662-7764 ■ *Web:* www.nashuatelegraph.com
Telegraph-Journal
210 Crown St PO Box 2350........................Saint John NB E2L3V8 888-295-8665 532-1
TF: 888-295-8665 ■ *Web:* telegraphjournal.com
TeleGuam Holdings LLC
624 N Marine Corps Dr........................Tamuning GU 96913 671-644-4482 387
Web: www.gta.net
Telehouse International Corporation of America Inc
The Teleport 7 Teleport Dr........................Staten Island NY 10311 718-355-2500 225
Web: telehouse.com
Telelatino Network Inc (TLN)
5125 Steeles Ave W........................Toronto ON M9L1R5 416-744-8200 744-0966 740
TF: 800-551-8401 ■ *Web:* tln.ca/contact-us
Telemanager Technologies Inc
211 Warren St Ste 409........................Newark NJ 07103 973-679-7500 177
TF: 800-600-0435 ■ *Web:* www.pharmacyshopper.com
Telemark Diversified Graphics
411 Mckee St........................Sturgis MI 49091 269-651-7876 787
Web: www.telemarkcorp.com
Telematic Controls Inc
3364 114 Ave SE........................Calgary AB T2Z3V6 403-253-7939 317
Web: www.telematic.com
Tele-Measurements Inc 145 Main Ave........Clifton NJ 07014 973-473-8822 194
TF: 800-223-0052 ■ *Web:* www.telemeasurements.com
Tele-Media Corp
804 Jacksonville Rd PO Box 39........................Bellefonte PA 16823 814-353-2025 353-2072 116
TF: 800-704-4254 ■ *Web:* www.tele-media.com
Telemedia Inc
750 West Lake Cook Rd Rd Ste 250........Buffalo Grove IL 60089 847-808-4000 765
TF: 800-837-8872 ■ *Web:* www.tpctraining.com
Telemessage Inc 468 Great Rd Ste 2........Acton MA 01720 978-263-1015 177
Web: www.telemessage.com

Phone | Fax | Class

Telemetrics Inc 6 Leighton Pl........Mahwah NJ 07430 201-848-9818 647
Web: www.telemetricsinc.com
Telemobile Inc 19840 Hamilton Ave........Torrance CA 90502 310-538-5100 532-8526 735
Web: www.telemobile.com
Telemundo 51 15000 SW 27th St........Miramar FL 33027 954-622-7710 741
Web: www.telemundo51.com
Telemus Capital Partners LLC
2 Towne Sq Ste 800........................Southfield MI 48076 248-827-1800 827-1808 401
Web: telemus.com
Telenav Inc 950 De Guigne Dr........Sunnyvale CA 94085 408-245-3800 177
Web: telenav.com
Telenet Communications Inc
16 Shenandoah Ave........................Staten Island NY 10314 718-370-3900 180
TF: 800-706-2337 ■ *Web:* www.telenetny.com
Telenet Marketing Solutions
1915 New Jimmy Daniel Rd........................Athens GA 30606 706-353-1940 317
TF: 877-282-2345 ■ *Web:* www.telenetmarketing.com
Telenet Voip Inc
850 N Park View Dr........................El Segundo CA 90245 310-253-9000 239
Web: www.telenetvoip.com
Telenity Inc 755 Main St Ste 7........Monroe CT 06468 203-445-2000 178-7
Web: www.telenity.com
Telenix Corp 9194 Red Branch Rd........Columbia MD 21045 410-772-3275 177
Web: www.telenix.com
Teleos Leadership Inst LLC
7837 Old York Rd........................Elkins Park PA 19027 267-620-9999 765
Web: teleosleaders.com
Telepath Corp 49111 Milmont Dr........Fremont CA 94538 510-656-5600 647
TF: 800-292-1700 ■ *Web:* www.telepathcorp.com
Teleperformance USA
1991 South 4650 West........................Salt Lake City UT 84104 801-257-5800 737
Web: www.teleperformance.com
Telephone & Data Systems Inc
30 N La Salle St Ste 4000........................Chicago IL 60602 312-630-1900 630-9299 360-3
NYSE: TDS ■ *TF:* 877-337-1575 ■ *Web:* www.tdsinc.com/home/default.aspx
Telephone Doctor Inc
30 Hollenberg Ct........................Bridgeton MO 63044 314-291-1012 196
TF: 800-882-9911 ■ *Web:* www.telephonedoctor.com
Telephone Electronics Corp
236 E Capitol St........................Jackson MS 39201 601-354-9070 387
TF: 800-832-2515 ■ *Web:* www.tec.com
Telephone Pioneer Museum of New Mexico
110 Fourth St NW........................Albuquerque NM 87102 505-842-2037 520
Web: www.museumsusa.org
Telephone Service Co 2 Willipie St........Wapakoneta OH 45895 419-739-2200 739-2299 736
TF: 800-743-5707 ■ *Web:* www.telserco.com
Telephone Systems International Inc (TSI)
4400 Marsh Landing Blvd Ste 3........Ponte Vedra Beach FL 32082 904-686-1470 736
Web: www.tsiglobe.com
Telephone Warehouse Inc
20827 N Cave Creek Rd Ste 106........................Phoenix AZ 85024 602-264-6616 267-6811 246
Web: www.telephonewarehouse.com
Telephonics Corp
815 Broad Hollow Rd........................Farmingdale NY 11735 631-755-7000 755-7200 647
Web: www.telephonics.com
Telepictures Production Inc
3500 W Olive St Ste 1000........................Burbank CA 91505 818-972-0777 116
Web: www.telepicturestv.com
Telepress Inc 19241 62nd Ave S........Kent WA 98032 425-392-1660 627
Web: telepress.com
TeleProviders Inc
23461 Southpointe Dr Ste 185........................Laguna Hills CA 92653 888-999-4244 463
TF: 888-999-4244 ■ *Web:* www.teleproviders.com
Telerent Leasing Corp
4191 Fayetteville Rd........................Raleigh NC 27603 919-772-8604 38
TF: 800-626-0682 ■ *Web:* www.telerent.com
Telerep Inc 1 Dag Hammarskjold Plaza........New York NY 10017 212-759-8787 6
Web: www.telerepinc.com
Telerhythmics LLC
60 Market Center Dr Ste 101........................Collierville TN 38017 888-333-1003 592
TF: 888-333-1003 ■ *Web:* www.telerhythmics.com
Telesat 1601 Telesat Ct........Ottawa ON K1B5P4 613-748-0123 748-8712 681
Web: www.telesat.com
Telescope Casual Furniture Inc
82 Church St........................Granville NY 12832 518-642-1100 642-2536 319-4
Web: telescopecasual.com
Telescope Inc
11845 W Olympic Blvd Ste 695........................Los Angeles CA 90064 424-270-2900 195
Web: www.telescope.tv
TeleSearch Staffing Solutions
251 Rt 206........................Flanders NJ 07836 973-927-7870 927-7880 631
TF: 800-449-8367 ■ *Web:* www.telesearch.com
TeleSecurity Sciences Inc
7391 Prairie Falcon Rd Ste 150-B........................Las Vegas NV 89128 702-227-7327 177
Web: www.telesecuritysciences.com
TELESIS Corp 8300 Greensboro Dr Ste 600........McLean VA 22102 240-241-5600 177
TF: 800-845-8420 ■ *Web:* www.telesishq.com
Telesoft Corp
1661 E Camelback Rd Ste 300........................Phoenix AZ 85016 602-308-2100 308-1300 194
Web: www.telesoft.com
TeleSoft International Inc
4029 S Capital of TX Hwy Ste 220........................Austin TX 78704 512-373-4224 788-5660 176
TF: 800-253-0329 ■ *Web:* www.telesoft-intl.com
TeleSoft Partners
950 Tower Ln Ste 1600........................Foster City CA 94404 650-358-2500 358-2501 792
Web: www.telesoftvc.com
TeleSoft Systems 335 Wesley St Ste 203........Nanaimo BC V9R2R7 250-760-0142 463
Web: www.telesoftsystems.ca
Telesolv Consulting LLC
1210 Florida Ave NE........................Washington DC 20002 202-558-5639 196
Web: telesolvconsulting.com
Telesource Services LLC
1450 Highwood E........................Pontiac MI 48340 248-335-3000 246
TF: 800-525-4300 ■ *Web:* www.telesourcenet.com
Telesouth Communications Inc
6311 Ridgewood Rd........................Jackson MS 39211 601-957-1700 956-5228 643
TF: 888-808-8637 ■ *Web:* www.telesouth.com

	Phone	Fax	Class
Telesta Therapeutics Inc 275 Labrosse Ave, Pointe-Claire QC H9R1A3 *TSE: TST* ■ *TF:* 800-387-0825 ■ *Web:* www.telestatherapeutics.com	514-697-6636		85
Telesto Group LLC 1060 State Rd Ste 102, Princeton NJ 08540 *Web:* www.telestogroup.com	609-503-4201		225
Telesto Solutions Inc 2950 E Harmony Rd Ste 200, Fort Collins CO 80528 *Web:* www.telesto-inc.com	970-484-7704		256
Telestream Inc 848 Gold Flat Rd Ste 1, Nevada City CA 95959 *TF:* 877-681-2088 ■ *Web:* www.telestream.net	530-470-1300	470-1301	178-8
Telesystem Ltd 460 McGill St 5th Fl, Montreal QC H2Y2H2 *Web:* www.telesystem.ca	514-397-9797	397-1569	360-3
TeleTech Holdings Inc 9197 S Peoria St, Englewood CO 80112 *NASDAQ: TTEC* ■ *TF General:* 800-835-3832 ■ *Web:* www.teletech.com	303-397-8100		737
Teletoon Canada Inc 181 Bay St Brookfield Pl Ste 100, Toronto ON M5J2T3 *Web:* www.teletoon.com	416-956-2060		740
Tele-Track 6 Concourse Pkwy Ste 1000, Atlanta GA 30328 *TF:* 800-729-6981 ■ *Web:* www.corelogic.com	678-233-1900		218
Teletronics International Inc 2 Choke Cherry Rd, Rockville MD 20850 *Web:* www.teletronics.com	301-309-8500	309-8851	173-3
Televerde Inc 4636 E University Dr Ste 150, Phoenix AZ 85034 *Web:* www.televerde.com	480-736-8137		195
Television Bureau of Advertising Inc (TVB) 120 Wall St 15th Fl, New York NY 10005 *Web:* www.tvb.org	212-486-1111	935-5631	49-18
TeleVital Solutions Inc 1525 McCarthy Blvd Ste 1045, Milpitas CA 95035 *Web:* www.televital.com	408-441-6732		363
TeleVoice Inc 10497 Town & Country Way Ste 500, Houston TX 77024 *Web:* televoice.com	281-497-8000		177
Telewave Inc 660 Giguere Ct, San Jose CA 95133 *Web:* www.telewave.com	408-929-4400		647
Telex Communications Inc 12000 Portland Ave S, Burnsville MN 55337 *TF:* 877-863-4169 ■ *Web:* www.telex.com	952-884-4051	884-0043	52
Telexpertise Inc 8547 E Arapahoe Rd, Centennial CO 80112 *Web:* www.telexpertise.com	720-200-0590		737
Telfair County 91 Telfair Ave, McRae GA 31055 *TF:* 800-829-4933 ■ *Web:* georgia.gov/cities-counties/telfair-county	229-868-5688	868-7950	338
Telfair County School District 212 W Huckabee St PO Box 240, McRae GA 31055 *Web:* www.telfairschools.org	229-868-5661		685
Telfair Museum of Art 121 Barnard St, Savannah GA 31401 *Web:* telfair.org	912-790-8800		520
Telfer Pavement Technologies LLC 211 Foster St, Martinez CA 94553 *Web:* telfercompanies.com	925-228-1515	229-3955	780
Telgian Corp 10230 S 50th Pl Ste 100, Phoenix AZ 85044 *TF:* 877-835-4426 ■ *Web:* www.telgian.com	480-753-5444	753-5450	189-10
Telics 652 Bush River Rd Ste 220, Columbia SC 29210 *Web:* www.telics.com	803-798-6642		261
Teligent Inc 105 Lincoln Ave, Buena NJ 08310 *TF:* 800-656-0793 ■ *Web:* www.teligent.com	800-656-0793		736
Tel-Instrument Electronics Corp 1 Branca Rd, East Rutherford NJ 07073 *NYSE: TIK* ■ *Web:* www.telinstrument.com	201-933-1600		472
Telirite Technical Services Inc 2857 Lakeview Ct, Fremont CA 94538 *Web:* www.telirite.com	510-440-3888		175
Telkonet Inc 10200 W Innovation Dr Ste 300, Milwaukee WI 53226 *OTC: TKOI* ■ *TF Sales:* 888-703-9398 ■ *Web:* www.telkonet.com	414-223-0473	258-8307	176
Tell Systems Inc 106 Bridge Ave, Bay Head NJ 08742 *Web:* www.tellsystems.com	732-899-0202		177
Tella Tool & Mfg 1015 N Ridge Ave, Lombard IL 60148 *Web:* www.tellatool.com	630-495-0545	495-3056	697
Tellabs Inc 1415 W Diehl Rd, Naperville IL 60563 *NASDAQ: TLAB* ■ *Web:* www.tellabs.com	630-798-8800	798-2000	735
Teller County 101 W Bennett Ave PO Box 1010, Cripple Creek CO 80813 *Web:* www.co.teller.co.us	719-689-2951	686-8030	338
Telliant Systems LLC 3180 N Point Pkwy Ste 108, Alpharetta GA 30005 *Web:* www.telliant.com	678-892-2801		177
Tellini's 504 S Gloster St, Tupelo MS 38801 *Web:* www.tellinis.com	662-620-9955		671
Tellme Networks Inc 1310 Villa St, Mountain View CA 94041 *Web:* www.bing.com	650-930-9000		617
Tellurex Corp 1462 International Dr, Traverse City MI 49686 *TF:* 877-774-7468 ■ *Web:* www.tellurex.com	231-947-0110		696
Telluride Film Festival 800 Jones St, Berkeley CA 94710 *Web:* www.telluridefilmfestival.org	510-665-9494	665-9589	282
Tellus Institute 11 Arlington St, Boston MA 02116 *Web:* www.tellus.org	617-266-5400	266-8303	634
Tellus Operating Group LLC 602 Crescent Pl Ste 100, Ridgeland MS 39157 *TF:* 800-969-2940 ■ *Web:* www.tellusoperating.com	601-898-7444		536
Telmark Packaging Corp 30 Freneau Ave, Matawan NJ 07747 *Web:* www.telmarkpkg.com	732-739-9100		557
Telnet Inc 7630 Standish Pl, Rockville MD 20855 *Web:* www.telnet-inc.com	301-840-7110		196
Telniasoft Inc 1802 Brightseat Rd Ste 101, Landover MD 20785 *Web:* telniasoft.com	301-918-4011		2
Telog Instruments Inc 830 Canning Pkwy, Victor NY 14564 *Web:* www.telog.com	585-742-3000		153
Telogical Systems LLC 7900 Westpark Dr, Mclean VA 22102 *Web:* telogicalsystems.com	703-734-7776		225
Telonic Berkeley Inc 1080 La Mirada Ct, Vista CA 92081 *Web:* www.telonicberkeley.com	760-744-8350	744-8360	253
Telops Inc 100-2600 St-Jean-Baptiste Ave, Quebec QC G2E6J5 *Web:* www.telops.com	418-864-7808	864-7843	542
Telos Corp 19886 Ashburn Rd, Ashburn VA 20147 *OTC: TLSRP* ■ *Web:* www.telos.com	703-724-3800		180
Telosa Software Inc 610 Cowper St, Palo Alto CA 94301 *Web:* www.telosa.com	650-853-1100		177
Telpar Inc 187 Crosby Rd Ste 100, Dover NH 03820 *TF:* 800-872-4886 ■ *Web:* www.telpar.com	603-750-7237	742-9938	173-6
TelServ Communications Inc 1011 First Ave SE, Aberdeen SD 57401 *Web:* solo.telserv.com	605-229-1050		196
Telserv LLC 7 Progress Dr, Cromwell CT 06416 *Web:* www.telserv.com	860-740-3600		179
Telsey Advisory Group LLC 535 Fifth Ave 12th Fl, New York NY 10017 *Web:* www.telseygroup.com	212-973-9700		401
Telsmith Inc 10910 N Industrial Dr, Mequon WI 53092 *Web:* www.telsmith.com	262-242-6600		190
Telsoft Solutions Inc 100 N Brand Blvd Ste 400, Glendale CA 91203 *Web:* www.telsoft-solutions.com	818-545-8680		525
TelSpan Inc 101 W Washington St E Tower Ste 1200, Indianapolis IN 46204 *TF:* 800-800-1729 ■ *Web:* www.telspan.com	800-800-1729		387
Telstar Associates Inc 2108 Amy Ave, Boise ID 83706 *TF:* 800-331-7881 ■ *Web:* www.telstarinc.net	208-343-3894		809
TelTel Inc 2620 Augustine Dr Ste 100, Santa Clara CA 95054 *Web:* www.teltel.com	408-970-3318		387
Telus 630 boul Ren,-L,vesque Ouest 22nd Fl, Montreal QC H3B1S6 *TF:* 877-999-4669 ■ *Web:* www.telushealth.co	514-665-3050	665-3049	808
TELUS Mobility 200 Consilium Pl Ste 1600, Scarborough ON M1H3J3 *Web:* mobility.telus.com	604-291-2355	432-9681	224
TELUS Quebec 6 Rue Jules-A-Brillant, Rimouski QC G5L7E4 *Web:* www.telusquebec.com	418-722-5331		224
TELUS World of Science 11211 142nd St, Edmonton AB T5M4A1 *Web:* telusworldofscienceedmonton.ca	780-451-3344	455-5882	520
Telvista Inc 1605 LBJ Fwy Ste 200, Dallas TX 75234 *Web:* www.telvista.com	972-919-7800		393
Tel-West Communications Inc 7311 E Broadway Ste B, Spokane WA 99212 *Web:* www.telwest.net	509-325-8500		179
Telx Group Inc, The 1 State St 21st Fl, New York NY 10004 *Web:* www.telx.com	212-480-3300		387
Tembec Btlsr Inc 2112 Sylvan Ave, Toledo OH 43606 *Web:* www.btlresins.com	419-244-5856		3
Tembec Inc 4 Place Ville-Marie Ste 100, Montreal QC H3B2E7 *TSE: TMB* ■ *TF:* 800-565-3021 ■ *Web:* www.tembec.com	514-871-0137	397-0896	683
Temco International Corp 11919 SW 130 St Ste 100, Miami FL 33186 *Web:* www.temcointl.com	305-234-7851		385
Temco Metal Products Co 10240 SE Mather Rd, Clackamas OR 97015 *Web:* www.temcousa.com	503-656-4789		488
Temco Service Industries Inc 417 Fifth Ave 9th Fl, New York NY 10016 *Web:* temcoservices.com	212-889-6353		104
Temecula Creek Inn 44501 Rainbow Canyon Rd, Temecula CA 92592 **Fax Area Code:* 951 ■ *TF:* 855-685-9299 ■ *Web:* www.temeculacreekinn.com	855-685-9299	676-8961*	669
Temecula Valley Chamber of Commerce (TVCC) 26790 Ynez Ct Ste A, Temecula CA 92591 *Web:* www.temecula.org	951-676-5090	694-0201	139
Temecula Valley Unified School District School Facilities Corp 31350 Rancho Vista Rd, Temecula CA 92592 *Web:* www.tvusd.k12.ca.us	951-676-2661	695-7121	685
Temiskaming Shores City of 545 Lkshore Rd S, Haileybury ON P0J1K0 *Web:* www.temiskamingshores.ca	705-672-3707		434
Temo Sunrooms Inc 20400 Hall Rd, Clinton Township MI 48038 *TF:* 800-344-8366 ■ *Web:* www.temosunrooms.com	800-344-8366		105
Temp-Air Inc 3700 W Preserve Blvd, Burnsville MN 55337 *TF:* 800-836-7432 ■ *Web:* www.temp-air.com	800-836-7432		14
Tempco Electric Heater Corp 607 N Central Ave, Wood Dale IL 60191 *TF:* 888-268-6396 ■ *Web:* www.tempco.com	630-350-2252	350-0232	318
Tempco Engineering Inc 8866 Laurel Canyon Bl, Sun Valley CA 91352	818-767-2326		567
Tempco Mfg 2475 Highway 55, St Paul MN 55120 *Web:* www.tempcomfg.com	651-452-1441		488
Tempco Products Co 301 E Tempco Ave, Robinson IL 62454 *Web:* www.tempcoproducts.com	618-544-3175		234
Temp-Control Mechanical Corp (TCM) 4800 N Ch Ave, Portland OR 97217 *TF:* 877-826-3828 ■ *Web:* www.tcmcorp.com	503-285-9851	285-9978	14
Tempe Chamber of Commerce 1232 E Broadway Rd, Tempe AZ 85281 *Web:* www.tempechamber.org	480-967-7891	966-5365	139
Tempe City Hall 31 E Fifth St, Tempe AZ 85281 *Web:* www.tempe.gov	480-350-8221	350-8930	337
Tempe Elementary Schools 3205 S Rural Rd, Tempe AZ 85282 *Web:* www.tempeschools.org	480-730-7100		685
Tempe Historical Museum 809 E Southern Ave, Tempe AZ 85282 *Web:* www.tempe.gov/museum	480-350-5100	350-5150	520
Tempe Little Theatre 132 E Sixth St, Tempe AZ 85281	480-350-8388		573-4
Tempe Saint Luke's Hospital (TSLH) 1500 S Mill Ave, Tempe AZ 85281 *Web:* www.tempestlukeshospital.com	480-784-5500		374-3

Phone | Fax | Class

Tempe Tourism Office
222 S Mill Ave Ste 120........................Tempe AZ 85281 480-894-8158 968-8004 206
TF: 866-914-1052 ■ *Web:* www.tempetourism.com

Tempel Steel Co 5500 N Wolcott Ave...........Chicago IL 60640 773-250-8000 250-8910* 723
**Fax:* Cust Svc ■ *Web:* www.tempel.com

Temperance River State Park
5702 Hwy 61.............................Silver Bay MN 55614 218-663-3100 565
Web: www.dnr.state.mn.us

Temperature Equipment Corp
17725 Volbrecht Rd.........................Lansing IL 60438 708-418-0900 418-5100 612
Web: www.tecmungo.com

Temperature Systems Inc 5001 Voges Rd......Madison WI 53718 608-271-7500 274-1609 612
TF: 800-366-0930 ■ *Web:* www.tsihvac.com

Tempest Development Group Inc
8431 160 St Ste 103.........................Surrey BC V4N0V6 604-597-2846 177
Web: www.tempestdg.com

Tempest Technologies LLC
38 S Last Chance Gulch st Ste 5a...............Helena MT 59601 425-996-0228 177
TF: 800-360-3323 ■ *Web:* tempest-av.com

Tempest Telecom Solutions LLC
136 W Canon Perdido Ste 100..........Santa Barbara CA 93101 805-879-4800 246
Web: www.tempesttelecom.com

Tempest Tours Inc PO Box 121084...........Arlington TX 76012 817-274-9313 760
Web: www.tempesttours.com

Temple Bottling Company Ltd
3510 Pkwy Dr..............................Temple TX 76504 254-773-3376 81-2
Web: www.templebot.com

Temple Chamber of Commerce
2 N Fifth St...............................Temple TX 76501 254-773-2105 773-0661 139
TF: 800-727-8642 ■ *Web:* www.templetx.org

Temple City Chamber of Commerce
9050 Las Tunas Dr......................Temple City CA 91780 626-286-3101 139
Web: www.templecitychamber.org

Temple College 2600 S First St.................Temple TX 76504 254-298-8300 298-8288* 162
**Fax:* Admissions ■ *TF Admissions:* 800-460-4636 ■ *Web:* www.templejc.edu

Temple Community Hospital
235 N Hoover St.........................Los Angeles CA 90004 213-382-7252 374-3
Web: www.templecommunityhospital.com

Temple Kol Ami Emanu-el Foundation Inc
8200 Peters Rd..........................Plantation FL 33324 954-472-1988 305
Web: tkae.org

Temple Meridian 4312 S 31st St.................Temple TX 76502 254-598-4019 672
TF: 855-444-7658 ■ *Web:* www.brookdale.com

Temple Public Library 100 W Adams Ave.........Temple TX 76501 254-298-5555 434-3
Web: www.ci.temple.tx.us/417/library

Temple Square Hospitality Corp
15 E S Temple St 9th Fl..................Salt Lake City UT 84150 801-531-1000 670
Web: www.templesquare.com

Temple University
1801 N Broad St........................Philadelphia PA 19122 215-204-7000 204-5694 166
Web: www.temple.edu

Temple University Hospital
3401 N Broad St........................Philadelphia PA 19140 215-707-2000 374-3
Web: www.tuh.templehealth.org

Temple University Hospital Episcopal Campus
100 E Lehigh Ave.......................Philadelphia PA 19125 215-707-1200 374-3
Web: www.episcopal.templehealth.org

Temple University James E Beasley School of Law
1719 N Broad St........................Philadelphia PA 19122 215-204-7861 204-1185 167-1
TF: 800-560-1428 ■ *Web:* www.law.temple.edu

Temple University Paley Library
1210 W Berks St........................Philadelphia PA 19122 215-204-8231 204-5201 434-6
Web: www.library.temple.edu

Temple University Press
1852 N Tenth St........................Philadelphia PA 19122 215-926-2140 621-8476* 637-4
**Fax Area Code:* 800 ■ *TF:* 800-621-2736 ■ *Web:* www.temple.edu/tempress

Temple University School of Medicine
3500 N Broad St........................Philadelphia PA 19140 215-707-3656 707-6932 167-2
Web: www.temple.edu/medicine

Templeton & Company LLP
222 Lakeview Ave Ste 1200...........West Palm Beach FL 33401 561-798-9988 798-4053 2

Templeton Coal Co 701 Wabash Ave..........Terre Haute IN 47807 812-232-7037 357
Web: templetoncoal.com

Templeton Unified School District
960 Old County Rd.......................Templeton CA 93465 805-434-5800 434-1473 685
Web: tusd.ca.schoolloop.com

Tempo Bank 28 W Broadway....................Trenton IL 62293 618-224-9228 70
Web: tempobank.com

Tempo Restaurant 4231 Duke St.............Alexandria VA 22304 703-370-7900 370-7902 671
TF: 800-442-1162 ■ *Web:* www.temporestaurant.com

Temporary Solutions Inc
10550 Linden Lake Plaza Ste 200............Manassas VA 20109 703-361-2220 721
TF: 888-222-0457 ■ *Web:* www.eeihr.com

Tempra Technology Inc
6140 15th St E..........................Bradenton FL 34203 941-739-8900 668
Web: www.tempratech.com

Tempress Technologies Inc
18858 72nd Ave S............................Kent WA 98032 425-251-8120 261
Web: tempresstech.com

Temps Plus Inc 268 N Lincoln Ave Ste 12..........Corona CA 92882 888-288-0808 260
TF: 888-288-0808 ■ *Web:* www.tempsplus.com

Temptime Corp 116 American Rd..........Morris Plains NJ 07950 973-630-6000 201
Web: www.temptimecorp.com

Temptronic Corp 41 Hampden Rd.............Mansfield MA 02048 781-688-2300 419
TF Tech Support: 800-558-5080 ■ *Web:* www.temptronic.com

Tempur Production USA Inc
203 Tempur Pedic Dr Ste 102.................Duffield VA 24244 276-431-7150 471
Web: tempurpedic.com

Tempus Resorts International
7380 Sand Lake Rd Ste 600...................Orlando FL 32819 407-226-1000 753
TF: 877-747-4747 ■ *Web:* www.tempusresorts.com

Temtrol LLC 106 N Industrial Blvd...............Okarche OK 73762 405-263-7286 263-4924 14
Web: www.temtrol.com

Ten Adams Corp 1112 SE First St............Evansville IN 47713 812-422-7440 7
Web: www.tenadams.com

Ten Broeck Mansion 9 Ten Broeck Pl.............Albany NY 12201 518-436-9826 436-1489 520
Web: tenbroeckmansion.org

Ten Dots LLC
211 E Ocean Blvd Ste 204................Long Beach CA 90802 562-590-5067 463
Web: www.tendots.com

Ten Mercer 10 Mercer St.........................Seattle WA 98109 206-691-3723 671
Web: www.tenmercer.com

Ten Mile Creek State Fish & Wildlife Area
RR 1 PO Box 179......................McLeansboro IL 62859 618-643-2862 565
Web: www.dnr.illinois.gov/parks/pages/tenmilecreek.aspx

Ten Prime Steak & Sushi 55 Pine St..........Providence RI 02903 401-453-2333 671
Web: www.tenprimesteakandsushi.com

Ten Thousand Waves Japanese Health Spa
3451 Hyde Pk Rd.............................Santa Fe NM 87501 505-982-9304 707
Web: www.tenthousandwaves.com

Ten-8 Fire Equipment Inc
2904 59th Ave Dr E.......................Bradenton FL 34203 941-756-7779 756-2598 516
TF: 877-989-7660 ■ *Web:* www.ten8fire.com

TENA Companies Inc
251 W Lafayette Frontage Rd...............Saint Paul MN 55107 651-293-1234 218
Web: www.tenaco.com

Tenable Network Security Inc
7021 Columbia Gateway Dr Ste 500...........Columbia MD 21046 410-872-0555 177
Web: www.tenable.com

Tenable Protective Services Inc
2423 Payne Ave..............................Cleveland OH 44114 843-906-6774 693
Web: www.anchor-security.com

Tenaris 530-8th Ave SW Ste 400...............Calgary AB T2P3S8 403-767-0100 767-0299 723
TF: 800-561-4608 ■ *Web:* www.tenaris.com

TenAsys Corp
1400 NW Compton Dr Ste 301................Beaverton OR 97006 503-748-4720 179
Web: www.tenasys.com

Tenax Corp 4800 E Monument St..............Baltimore MD 21205 410-522-7000 596
Web: www.tenaxus.com

Tencarva Machinery Company Inc
12200 Wilfong Ct..........................Midlothian VA 23112 804-639-4646 639-2400 385
TF: 800-849-5764 ■ *Web:* www.tencarva.com

TenCate Geosynthetics North America
365 S Holland Dr.........................Pendergrass GA 30567 706-693-2226 693-4400 745-3
TF: 888-795-0808 ■ *Web:* www.tencate.com

TenCate Grass North America
1131 Broadway St............................Dayton TN 37321 423-775-0792 605-1
TF: 800-251-1033 ■ *Web:* www.tencate.com

TenCate Protective Fabrics USA
6501 Mall Blvd..............................Union City GA 30291 800-241-8630 745-3
TF: 800-241-8630 ■ *Web:* www.tencate.com

Tender Corp 106 Burndy Rd.....................Littleton NH 03561 603-444-5464 444-6735 280
TF: 800-258-4696 ■ *Web:* www.tendercorp.com

Tenderloin Room
232 N KingsHwy Blvd.....................Saint Louis MO 63108 314-361-0900 671
Web: www.tenderloinroom.com

Tendo Communications
340 Brannan St Ste 500.................San Francisco CA 94107 415-369-8200 387
Web: www.tendocom.com

Tendyne Holdings Inc
2825 Fairview Ave N.........................Roseville MN 55113 651-289-5500 475
Web: www.tendyne.com

Tenenbaum Recycling Group
4500 W Bethany Rd..................North Little Rock AR 72117 501-945-0881 945-3865 492
Web: www.trg.net

Tenenbaum's Vacation Stores Inc
300 Market St...............................Kingston PA 18704 570-288-8747 771
TF: 800-545-7099 ■ *Web:* www.tenenbaums.com

Tenenz Inc 9655 Penn S Ave................Minneapolis MN 55431 800-888-5803 627
TF: 800-888-5803 ■ *Web:* www.tenenz.com

Tenera Environmental
971 Dewing Ave Ste 101.....................Lafayette CA 94549 925-962-9769 194
Web: www.tenera.com

Tenere Inc 700 Kelly Ave.........................Dresser WI 54009 715-247-4242 697
Web: www.tenere.com

Tenet Healthcare Corp 1445 Ross Ave...........Dallas TX 75202 469-893-2000 353
NYSE: THC ■ *TF:* 800-743-6333 ■ *Web:* www.tenethealth.com

Tenet Partners 122 W 27th St 9th Fl..........New York NY 10001 212-329-3030 329-3031 195
TF: 800-780-8388 ■ *Web:* tenetpartners.com

Tengasco Inc 11121 Kingston Pk Ste E..........Knoxville TN 37934 865-675-1554 536
NYSE: TGC ■ *TF:* 888-669-0684 ■ *Web:* www.tengasco.com

Tengda Asian Bistro 235 Bedford St...........Stamford CT 06901 203-625-5338 671
Web: tengdaasian.com

Tenino Depot Museum 149 Hodgen St S...........Tenino WA 98589 360-956-7575 520
Web: ci.tenino.wa.us

Tenlinks 300 Professional Ctr Dr...............Novato CA 94947 415-897-8800 180
Web: www.tenlinks.com

Tennant Co 701 N Lilac Dr.................Minneapolis MN 55422 763-540-1200 540-1437 386
NYSE: TNC ■ *TF Cust Svc:* 800-553-8033 ■ *Web:* www.tennantco.com

Tenneco Inc 500 N Field Dr................Lake Forest IL 60045 847-482-5000 482-5940 60
NYSE: TEN ■ *TF:* 866-839-3259 ■ *Web:* www.tenneco.com

Tennessean 1100 Broadway..................Nashville TN 37203 615-259-8000 532-2
TF: 800-342-8237 ■ *Web:* www.tennessean.com

Tennessee

Administrative Office of the Cts
511 Union St Ste 600....................Nashville TN 37219 615-741-2687 741-6285 339-43
TF: 800-448-7970 ■ *Web:* www.tsc.state.tn.us

Aging & Disability Commission
500 Deaderick St 8th Fl..................Nashville TN 37243 615-741-2056 741-2056 339-43
Web: www.tn.gov/aging

Agriculture Dept
440 Hogan Rd PO Box 40627...............Nashville TN 37204 615-837-5103 837-5333 339-43
Web: www.state.tn.us/agriculture

Arts Commission 401 Charlotte Ave...........Nashville TN 37243 615-741-1701 339-43
Web: www.tn.gov

Attorney General PO Box 20207..............Nashville TN 37202 615-741-3491 741-2009 339-43
Web: www.tn.gov

Child Support Services Div
400 Deaderick St 12th Fl..................Nashville TN 37248 615-313-4880 532-2791 339-43
TF: 800-838-6911 ■ *Web:* www.tn.gov

Children's Services Dept
436 Sixth Ave N 7th Fl.....................Nashville TN 37243 615-741-9699 339-43

Commerce & Insurance Dept
500 James Robertson Pkwy 5th Fl...........Nashville TN 37243 615-741-6382 339-43
Web: www.state.tn.us/commerce

	City	State	ZIP	Phone	Fax	Class
Consumer Affairs Div						
500 James Robertson Pkwy	Nashville	TN	37243	615-741-4737	532-4994	339-43
TF: 800-342-8385 ■ *Web:* www.tn.gov/commerce/section/consumer-affairs						
Correction Dept 320 Sixth Ave N	Nashville	TN	37243	615-741-1000		339-43
Web: www.state.tn.us						
Department of Human Resources						
505 Deaderick St 1st Fl James K Polk Bldg	Nashville	TN	37243	615-741-2958	741-7880	339-43
Web: www.state.tn.us						
Div of Claims Administration						
502 Deaderick St	Nashville	TN	37243	615-741-2734	532-4979	339-43
Web: treasury.tn.gov						
Economic & Community Development Dept (ECD)						
312 Rosa L Parks Ave N 11th Fl	Nashville	TN	37243	615-741-1888		339-43
Web: www.tn.gov/ecd						
Education Dept						
710 James Robertson Pkwy 6th Fl	Nashville	TN	37243	615-741-5158		339-43
Web: www.state.tn.us						
Emergency Management Agency						
3041 Sidco Dr	Nashville	TN	37204	615-741-0001		339-43
Web: www.tn.gov/tema						
Environment & Conservation Dept						
312 Rosa L Parks Ave						
Tennessee Tower 2nd Fl	Nashville	TN	37243	615-532-0109		339-43
Web: www.state.tn.us/environment						
Finance & Administration Dept						
312 Rosa L Parks Ave	Nashville	TN	37243	615-741-0320		339-43
Web: www.tn.gov/finance						
Financial Institutions Dept						
312 Rosa L Parks Ave Fl 26	Nashville	TN	37243	615-741-2236		339-43
TF: 800-231-7831 ■ *Web:* www.tennessee.gov/tdfi						
General Assembly 320 Sixth Ave Ste 7	Nashville	TN	37243	615-741-1000		339-43
Web: www.capitol.tn.gov						
Governor State Capitol 1st Fl	Nashville	TN	37243	615-741-2001		339-43
Web: www.tennessee.gov						
Health Dept 425 Fifth Ave N 3rd Fl	Nashville	TN	37243	615-741-3111	253-5187	339-43
Web: www.state.tn.us						
Higher Education Commission						
404 James Robertson Pkwy Ste 1900	Nashville	TN	37243	615-741-3605		339-43
Web: www.state.tn.us						
Highway Patrol 1150 Foster Ave	Nashville	TN	37249	615-251-5175	532-1051	339-43
Web: www.tn.gov/safety/section/thp						
Historical Commission						
2941 Lebanon Rd	Nashville	TN	37214	615-532-1550		339-43
Web: www.state.tn.us						
Homeland Security Office						
312 Rosa L Parks Ave	Nashville	TN	37243	615-521-5200	253-5379	339-43
Web: www.tennessee.gov						
Housing Development Agency						
502 Deaderick St						
Andrew Jackson Bldg 3rd Floor	Nashville	TN	37243	615-815-2200		339-43
TF: 800-228-8432 ■ *Web:* thda.org						
Human Services Dept						
400 Deaderick St	Nashville	TN	37248	615-313-4700	687-5535	339-43
TF: 866-311-4287 ■ *Web:* www.state.tn.us						
Information Resources Office						
312 Rosa L Parks Ave	Nashville	TN	37243	615-741-3700		339-43
Web: www.state.tn.us						
Insurance Div						
500 James Robertson Pkwy	Nashville	TN	37243	615-741-2241		339-43
TF: 800-342-4029 ■ *Web:* www.tn.gov						
Labor & Workforce Development Dept						
220 French Landing Dr	Nashville	TN	37243	844-224-5818		259
TF: 844-224-5818 ■ *Web:* www.state.tn.us						
Lottery 26 Century Blvd Ste 200	Nashville	TN	37228	615-324-6500		452
Web: www.tnlottery.com						
Mental Health & Developmental Disabilities Dept						
500 Deaderick St	Nashville	TN	37243	800-560-5767		339-43
TF: 800-560-5767 ■ *Web:* www.state.tn.us						
Military Dept 3041 Sidco Dr	Nashville	TN	37204	615-313-0633	313-3129	339-43
Web: www.tnmilitary.org						
Probation & Parole Board						
404 James Robertson Pkwy Ste 1300	Nashville	TN	37243	615-741-1150		339-43
Web: www.tennessee.gov/bopp						
Real Estate Commission						
500 James Robertson Pkwy Ste 180	Nashville	TN	37243	615-741-2273	741-0313	339-43
Web: www.tn.gov						
Regulatory Authority						
460 James Robertson Pkwy	Nashville	TN	37243	615-741-2904		339-43
Web: www.state.tn.us/tra						
Regulatory Boards Div						
500 James Robertson Pkwy	Nashville	TN	37243	615-741-3449		339-43
Web: www.tn.gov						
Rehabilitation Services Div						
400 Deaderick St 11th Fl	Nashville	TN	37243	615-313-4891	741-4165	339-43
Web: www.tn.gov						
Revenue Dept 500 Deaderick St	Nashville	TN	37242	615-253-0600	741-0682	339-43
Web: www.state.tn.us/revenue						
Secretary of State State Capitol	Nashville	TN	37243	615-741-2819		339-43
Web: www.state.tn.us/sos						
Securities Div						
500 James Robertson Pkwy FL 8	Nashville	TN	37243	615-741-2947	532-8375	339-43
TF: 800-863-9117 ■ *Web:* www.tennessee.gov						
State Parks Div						
312 Rosa L Parks Ave PO Box 146001	Nashville	TN	37243	615-532-0001		339-43
TF: 877-887-2757 ■ *Web:* tnstateparks.com						
Student Assistance Corp						
404 James Robertson Pkwy Ste 1510	Nashville	TN	37243	615-741-1346	741-6101	725
TF: 800-342-1663 ■ *Web:* www.state.tn.us/tsac						
Supreme Court						
511 Union St Ste 600						
Nashville City Ctr Ste 600	Nashville	TN	37219	615-741-2687		339-43
TF: 800-448-7970 ■ *Web:* www.tsc.state.tn.us						
Title & Registration Div						
44 Vantage Way Ste 160	Nashville	TN	37243	615-741-3101	253-4260	339-43
Web: www.tn.gov/revenue/vehicle						
Transportation Dept						
505 Deaderick St Ste 700	Nashville	TN	37243	615-741-2848	741-2508	339-43
Web: www.tdot.state.tn.us						

	City	State	ZIP	Phone	Fax	Class
Treasurer						
Tennessee State Capitol						
1st Fl 600 Charlotte Ave	Nashville	TN	37243	615-741-2956		725
Web: www.treasury.state.tn.us						
Treasury Dept 600 Charlotte Ave	Nashville	TN	37243	615-741-2956		339-43
Web: www.treasury.state.tn.us						
Veterans Affairs Dept						
312 Rosa L Parks Ave 13th Fl	Nashville	TN	37243	615-741-2931		339-43
Web: www.tn.gov/veteran						
Vital Records Div						
421 Fifth Ave N 1st Fl	Nashville	TN	37247	615-741-1763	741-9860	339-43
Web: www.tn.gov						
Workers Compensation Div						
220 French Landing Dr	Nashville	TN	37243	615-741-6642		339-43
TF: 844-224-5818 ■ *Web:* tn.gov/maint/tngov/notfound.shtml						
Tennessee Agricultural Museum						
440 Hogan Rd	Nashville	TN	37204	615-837-5197	837-5194	520
Web: www.picktnproducts.org						
Tennessee Aquarium 1 Broad St	Chattanooga	TN	37402	800-262-0695		40
TF: 800-262-0695 ■ *Web:* www.tennis.org						
Tennessee Assn of Realtors (TAR)						
901 19th Ave S	Nashville	TN	37212	615-321-1477	321-4905	656
TF: 877-321-1477 ■ *Web:* www.tarnet.com						
Tennessee Associated Electric						
7511 Taggart Ln	Knoxville	TN	37938	865-524-3686	522-1553	189-4
TF: 800-334-9880 ■ *Web:* www.tn-associated.com						
Tennessee Baptist Convention						
5001 Maryland Way	Brentwood	TN	37027	615-371-2029		48-20
TF: 800-558-2090 ■ *Web:* www.tnbaptist.org						
Tennessee Bar Assn						
221 Fourth Ave N Ste 400	Nashville	TN	37219	615-383-7421	297-8058	72
TF: 800-899-6993 ■ *Web:* tba.org						
Tennessee Chamber of Commerce & Industry						
414 Union St Ste 107	Nashville	TN	37219	615-256-5141		140
TF: 800-221-8185 ■ *Web:* www.tnchamber.org						
Tennessee Commerce Bank						
381 Mallory Stn Rd Ste 207	Franklin	TN	37067	877-275-3342		70
TF: 877-275-3342 ■ *Web:* fdic.gov						
Tennessee Democratic Party						
1900 Church St Ste 203	Nashville	TN	37203	615-327-9779		616-1
Web: www.tndp.org						
Tennessee Dental Assn (TDA)						
660 Bakers Bridge Ave Ste 300	Franklin	TN	37067	615-628-0208		227
TF: 800-824-9722 ■ *Web:* www.tenndental.org						
Tennessee Farm Bureau News						
147 Bear Creek Pike	Columbia	TN	38401	931-388-7872	388-5818	457-1
TF: 877-876-2222 ■ *Web:* www.tnfarmbureau.org						
Tennessee Farmers Co-op						
180 Old Nashville Hwy	La Vergne	TN	37086	615-793-8011		276
TF: 800-366-2667 ■ *Web:* www.ourcoop.com						
Tennessee Fitness Spa						
299 Natural Bridge Pk Rd	Waynesboro	TN	38485	931-722-5589	722-9113	706
TF: 800-235-8365 ■ *Web:* www.tennesseefitnessspa.com						
Tennessee Library Assn (TLA)						
PO Box 241074	Memphis	TN	38124	901-485-6952		435
TF: 800-545-2433 ■ *Web:* www.tnla.org						
Tennessee Nurses Assn (TNA)						
545 Mainstream Dr Ste 405	Nashville	TN	37228	615-254-0350	254-0303	533
Web: www.tnaonline.org						
Tennessee Performing Arts Ctr						
505 Deaderick St	Nashville	TN	37219	615-782-4000	782-4001	572
TF: 866-455-2823 ■ *Web:* www.tpac.org						
Tennessee Pharmacists Assn						
500 Church St Ste 650	Nashville	TN	37219	615-256-3023	255-3528	585
Web: www.tnpharm.org						
Tennessee Prison for Women						
3881 Stewarts Ln	Nashville	TN	37243	615-741-1255		213
Web: tn.gov						
Tennessee Rehabilitative Initiative in Correction (TRICOR)						
240 Great Cir Rd Ste 310	Nashville	TN	37228	615-741-5705	741-2747	630
TF: 800-958-7426 ■ *Web:* www.tricor.org						
Tennessee Republican Party						
2424 21st Ave Ste 200	Nashville	TN	37212	615-269-4260		616-2
TF: 800-278-0747 ■ *Web:* www.tngop.org						
Tennessee Sports Hall of Fame Museum						
501 Broadway	Nashville	TN	37203	615-242-4750		520
Web: www.tshf.net						
Tennessee State Employees Association						
627 Woodland St	Nashville	TN	37206	615-256-4533		533
TF: 800-251-8732 ■ *Web:* tseaonline.org						
Tennessee State Library & Archives						
403 Seventh Ave N	Nashville	TN	37243	615-741-2764	741-6471	434-5
Tennessee State Museum						
505 Deaderick St	Nashville	TN	37243	615-741-2692		520
TF: 800-407-4324 ■ *Web:* www.tnmuseum.org						
Tennessee State University						
3500 John A Merritt Blvd PO Box 9609	Nashville	TN	37209	615-963-5000	963-5108	166
TF Admissions: 888-463-6878 ■ *Web:* www.tnstate.edu						
Tennessee State Veterans Home-Murfreesboro						
345 Compton Rd	Murfreesboro	TN	37130	615-895-8850	895-5091	793
TF: 800-273-8255 ■ *Web:* tsvh.org						
Tennessee Steel Haulers Inc						
PO Box 78189	Nashville	TN	37207	615-271-2400		780
TF: 800-776-4004 ■ *Web:* www.tenh.com						
Tennessee Technological University						
1 William L J1s Dr	Cookeville	TN	38505	931-372-3888	372-6250	166
TF: 800-255-8881 ■ *Web:* www.tntech.edu						
Tennessee Temple University						
1815 Union Ave	Chattanooga	TN	37404	423-493-4100	493-4497*	166
**Fax:* Admissions ■ *TF:* 800-553-4050 ■ *Web:* www.tntemple.edu						
Tennessee Titans 460 Great Cir Rd	Nashville	TN	37228	615-565-4000	565-4006	715-3
TF: 800-334-4628 ■ *Web:* www.titansonline.com						
Tennessee Tractor LLC						
1571 Highway 54 N Ste	Alamo	TN	38001	731-696-5596	696-2403	57
Web: www.tennesseetractor.com						
Tennessee Tubebending Inc						
5112 N National Dr	Knoxville	TN	37914	865-546-6511		595
Web: www.evertite.com						

Name / Address	City	State	Zip	Phone	Fax	Class
Tennessee Valley Authority (TVA) 400 W Summit Hill Dr. *Web:* www.tva.gov	Knoxville	TN	37902	865-632-2101		340-20
Tennessee Valley Electric Co-op 590 Florence Rd. *TF:* 866-925-4916 ■ *Web:* www.tvec.com	Savannah	TN	38372	731-925-4916	925-4919	245
Tennessee Valley Printing Company Inc PO Box 2213. *TF:* 888-353-4612 ■ *Web:* www.decaturdaily.com	Decatur	AL	35609	256-353-4612	340-2392	637-8
Tennessee Valley Railroad Museum 4119 Cromwell Rd. *TF:* 800-397-5544 ■ *Web:* www.tvrail.com	Chattanooga	TN	37421	423-894-8028	894-8029	520
Tennessee Valley Recycling LLC 821 W College St. *Web:* tvrllc.com	Pulaski	TN	38478	931-363-3593		686
Tennessee Veterinary Medical Assn PO Box 803. *TF:* 800-697-3587 ■ *Web:* tvmanet.com	Fayetteville	TN	37334	931-438-0070	433-6289	795
Tennessee Walking Horse Breeders' & Exhibitors' Assn (TWHBEA) 250 N Ellington Pkwy PO Box 286. *TF:* 800-359-1574 ■ *Web:* www.twhbea.com	Lewisburg	TN	37091	931-359-1574	359-7530	48-3
Tennessee Wesleyan College 204 E College St. *TF:* 800-742-5892 ■ *Web:* www.tnwesleyan.edu	Athens	TN	37371	423-745-7504	744-9968	166
Tennessee Williams Theatre 5901 W College Rd.	Key West	FL	33040	305-296-1520		572
Tennessee/DCI Donor Services 1600 Hayes St. *TF:* 877-401-2517 ■ *Web:* www.dcids.org	Nashville	TN	37203	877-401-2517		545
Tenney Claudia (Rep R - NY) 512 Cannon HOB. *Web:* tenney.house.gov	Washington	DC	20515	202-225-3665	225-1891	342-2
Tennier Industries Inc 978 Rt 45 - Northside Plaza	Pomona	NY	10970	845-362-0800		442
Tennis Ch 2850 Ocean Pk Blvd Ste 150. *Web:* www.tennischannel.com	Santa Monica	CA	90405	310-314-9400		740
Tennis Equities Inc 77 Kensico Dr. *Web:* www.sawmillclub.com	Mount Kisco	NY	10549	914-241-0797		354
Tennis Express 11022 Westheimer Rd. *Web:* www.tennisexpress.com	Houston	TX	77042	713-781-4848		711
Tennis Magazine 814 S Westgate Ste 100. *TF:* 800-289-7366 ■ *Web:* www.tennis.com	Los Angeles	NY	90049	310-893-5300		457-20
Tennis Pro Shop 19101 Peninsula Club Dr. *TF:* 800-752-7504 ■ *Web:* www.thepeninsulaclub.com	Cornelius	NC	28031	704-896-7676		711
TennisHub Inc 95 Chestnut St.	Providence	RI	02903	401-626-4280		387
Tennsco Corp 201 Tennsco Dr PO Box 1888. **Fax Area Code:* 800 ■ *TF Cust Svc:* 866-446-8686 ■ *Web:* www.tennsco.com	Dickson	TN	37056	615-446-8000	722-0134*	319-1
Tenn-Tex Plastics Inc 8011 National Service Rd. *Web:* www.tenntex.com	Colfax	NC	27235	336-931-1100		596
Tennyson High School 27035 Whitman St. *Web:* ths-haywardusd-ca.schoolloop.com	Hayward	CA	94544	510-723-3190		685
Tenova Core 100 Corporate Ctr Dr. *TF:* 800-295-3771 ■ *Web:* www.tenovacore.com	Coraopolis	PA	15108	412-262-2240	262-2055	318
Tenplus Systems 500 Uwharrie Ct Ste C. *Web:* www.tenplus.com	Raleigh	NC	27606	919-832-5799		180
Tenrox 401 Congress Ave. *TF:* 855-944-7526 ■ *Web:* uplandsoftware.com/tenrox	Austin	TX	78701	450-688-3444		178-1
Tensas Parish 201 Hancock St. *TF:* 800-256-6660 ■ *Web:* www.laclerksofcourt.org	Saint Joseph	LA	71366	318-766-3921	766-3926	338
Tension Envelope Corp 819 E 19th St. *TF:* 800-388-5122 ■ *Web:* tensionenvelope.com	Kansas City	MO	64108	800-388-5122		263
Tension Member Technology 5721 Research Dr. *Web:* www.tmtlabs.com	Huntington Beach	CA	92649	714-898-5641		743
TenStep Inc 181 Waterman St. *TF:* 877-536-8434 ■ *Web:* www.tenstep.com	Marietta	GA	30060	770-795-9097		463
Tensys Medical Inc 5825 Oberlin Dr Ste 100. *TF:* 800-929-4364 ■ *Web:* www.tensysmedical.com	San Diego	CA	92121	858-552-1941		250
Tenzing Consulting LLC 2100 Georgetowne Dr Ste 302. *TF:* 877-980-5300 ■ *Web:* tenzingconsulting.com	Sewickley	PA	15143	724-940-4060		196
Teo Technologies Inc 11609 49th Pl W. *TF:* 800-524-0024 ■ *Web:* www.teotech.com	Mukilteo	WA	98275	425-349-1000	349-1010	735
TEOCO Corp 12150 Monument Dr Ste 400. *TF:* 888-868-3626 ■ *Web:* www.teoco.com	Fairfax	VA	22033	703-322-9200		792
Tep Thai 209 W Wilson Ave. *Web:* www.tepthai.com	Glendale	CA	91203	818-246-0380		671
Tepa LLC 5045 List Dr. *Web:* tepa.com	Colorado Springs	CO	80919	719-596-8114		261
Tepel Brothers Printing Co 1725 John R Rd. *TF:* 800-836-5851 ■ *Web:* tepelbrothers.com	Troy	MI	48083	248-743-2903		627
Teplitsky, Colson LLP 70 Bond St Ste 200. *Web:* www.teplitskycolson.com	Toronto	ON	M5B1X3	416-365-9320		428
Teplow Cucurullo Communications LLC 68 Harvard St. *Web:* teplowandco.com	Brookline	MA	02445	617-566-6710		7
Teppco Crude Oil LP 210 Pk Ave.	Oklahoma City	OK	73102	405-239-7191		597
Tepper Holdings Inc 225 E Beaver Creek Rd Ste 201. *Web:* www.tepperholdings.com	Richmond Hill	ON	L4B3P4	905-889-0663		528
Teppo Yakitori & Sushi Bar 2014 Greenville Ave.	Dallas	TX	75206	214-826-8989		671
Tepro Inc 590 Baxter Ln. *Web:* www.tepro.com	Winchester	TN	37398	931-967-5189		350
Tepsco 2909 Aaron St. *Web:* www.tepsco.com	Deer Park	TX	77536	281-604-0309	930-0788	186
Tequila Mockingbird 130th St Montego Bay Shopping Ctr. *Web:* www.octequila.com	Ocean City	MD	21842	410-250-4424		671
Tequilas 1602 Locust St. *Web:* tequilasphilly.com	Philadelphia	PA	19103	215-546-0181	546-9953	671
Ter Molen Watkins & Brandt LLC 2 N Riverside Plaza Ste 1030. *Web:* www.twbfundraising.com	Chicago	IL	60606	312-222-0560	222-0565	317
Teracai Corp 217 Lawrence Rd E. *Web:* www.teracai.com	North Syracuse	NY	13212	315-883-3500		174
Teraco Inc 2080 Commerce Dr. *Web:* www.teraco.com	Midland	TX	79703	432-694-7736		596
Teradata Corp 10000 Innovation Dr. *NYSE:* TDC ■ *TF:* 866-548-8348 ■ *Web:* in.teradata.com	Dayton	OH	45342	866-548-8348		225
TeraDiode Inc 30 Upton Dr. *Web:* www.teradiode.com	Wilmington	MA	01887	978-988-1040		111
Teradyne Inc 600 Riverpark Dr. *NYSE:* TER ■ *Web:* www.teradyne.com	North Reading	MA	01864	978-370-2700		248
Teradyne Inc Assembly Test Div 600 Riverpark Dr. *TF:* 800-837-2396 ■ *Web:* teradyne.com	North Reading	MA	01864	978-370-2700		248
Teradyne Inc Industrial/Consumer Div 600 Riverpark Dr. *TF:* 800-837-2396 ■ *Web:* teradyne.com	North Reading	MA	01864	978-370-2700		248
Teradyne Inc Semiconductor Test Div 600 Riverpark Dr. *Web:* www.teradyne.com/std	North Reading	MA	01864	978-370-2700		248
TeraGo Networks Inc 55 Commerce Vly Dr W Ste 800. **Fax Area Code:* 905 ■ *TF:* 866-837-2461 ■ *Web:* www.terago.ca	Thornhill	ON	L3T7V9	866-837-2465	707-6212*	224
Teragren Fine Bamboo Flooring Panels & Veneer 12715 Miller Rd NE Ste 301. *TF:* 800-929-6333 ■ *Web:* www.teragren.com	Bainbridge Island	WA	98110	206-842-9477		290
Teralys Capital 999, boul de Maisonneuve O Ste 1700. *TF:* 800-373-6393 ■ *Web:* www.teralyscapital.com	Montreal	QC	H3A3L4	514-509-2080		528
TeraMach Technologies Inc 1130 Morrison Dr Ste 105. *TF:* 877-226-6549 ■ *Web:* www.teramach.com	Ottawa	ON	K2H9N6	613-226-7775		180
TeraRecon Inc 4000 E Third Ave Ste 200. *Web:* www.terarecon.com	Foster City	CA	94404	650-372-1100		418
Teras Cargo Transport (America) LLC 5358 33rd Ave NW Ste 302. *Web:* www.terasamerica.com	Gig Harbor	WA	98335	253-857-9209		313
Terasci Industries Inc 5362 Production Dr. *Web:* www.terasci.com	Huntington Beach	CA	92649	714-806-0150		177
TERATECH Corp 77-79 Terr Hall Ave. *TF:* 866-837-2766 ■ *Web:* www.terason.com	Burlington	MA	01803	781-270-4143		476
TERC 2067 Massachusetts Ave. *Web:* www.terc.edu	Cambridge	MA	02140	617-547-0430	349-3535	668
Terco Supply 12725 Ross Ave.	Chino	CA	91710	909-628-4694		366
Teresi Trucking Inc 900 1/2 Victor Rd. *Web:* www.teresitrucking.com	Lodi	CA	95240	209-368-2472	369-2830	780
Terex Corp 200 Nyala Farm Rd. *NYSE:* TEX ■ *TF:* 800-732-0330 ■ *Web:* www.terex.com	Westport	CT	06880	203-222-7170	222-7976	190
Terex Corp Crane Div 202 Raleigh St. *TF:* 877-794-5284 ■ *Web:* www.terex.com	Wilmington	NC	28412	910-395-8500		470
Terex Roadbuilding 8236 W I-40 Service Rd. *TF:* 800-324-3011 ■ *Web:* www.terex.com	Oklahoma City	OK	73128	405-787-6020		190
Terex-Telelect Inc 500 Oakwood Rd PO Box 1150. *TF:* 800-982-8975 ■ *Web:* www.terex.com	Watertown	SD	57201	605-882-4000	882-1842	470
Terhorst Manufacturing Co 615 Burdick Expy E. *Web:* www.terhorstmfg.com	Minot	ND	58701	701-852-0535		454
TERI Inc 251 Airport Rd. *Web:* www.teriinc.org	Oceanside	CA	92058	760-721-1706		48-15
TERiX Computer Service Inc 388 Oakmead Pkwy. *Web:* www.terix.com	Sunnyvale	CA	94085	408-737-1455		177
Teriyaki Chicken House 805 El Paseo Rd. *Web:* teriyakichickenhouse.com	Las Cruces	NM	88001	575-541-1696		671
Terlato Wine Group, The (TWG) 900 Armour Dr. *TF:* 800-950-7676 ■ *Web:* terlatowines.com	Lake Bluff	IL	60044	847-604-8900		81-3
Terminal City Club 837 W Hastings St. *Web:* tcclub.com	Vancouver	BC	V6C1B6	604-681-4121	681-9634	379
Terminal Corp, The 1657 A S Highland Ave Ste A. *TF:* 800-560-7207 ■ *Web:* www.termcorp.com	Baltimore	MD	21224	800-560-7207		311
Terminal Forest Products Ltd 12180 Mitchell Rd. *TF:* 800-443-8806 ■ *Web:* www.terminalforest.com	Richmond	BC	V6V1M8	604-717-1200		683
Terminal Railroad Assn of Saint Louis 415 S 18th St Ste 200. *TF:* 866-931-0498 ■ *Web:* www.terminalrailroad.com	Saint Louis	MO	63103	866-931-0498		651
Terminix International Company LP 860 Ridge Lake Blvd. *TF:* 877-837-6464 ■ *Web:* www.terminix.com	Memphis	TN	38120	877-837-6464		577
Terminix Service Inc 3618 Fernandina Rd. *TF:* 877-279-2003 ■ *Web:* trustterminix.com	Columbia	SC	29210	803-772-1783		577
Termo Co, The 3275 Cherry Ave. *TF:* 888-260-4715 ■ *Web:* www.termoco.com	Long Beach	CA	90807	888-260-4715		536
Ternion Corp 2223 Drake Ave. *Web:* www.ternion.com	Huntsville	AL	35805	256-881-9933	881-9957	703
TernPro 320 Westlake Ave 4th Fl. *TF:* 888-483-8779 ■ *Web:* ternpro.com	Detroit	MI	98109	888-483-8779		393
Tero International Inc 1840 NW 118th St Ste 107. *TF:* 800-336-1931 ■ *Web:* www.tero.com	Clive	IA	50325	515-221-2318		463
Terra 7091 El Cajon Blvd. *Web:* www.terrasd.com	San Diego	CA	92115	619-293-7088		671
Terra Community College 2830 Napoleon Rd. *TF:* 800-334-3886 ■ *Web:* www.terra.edu	Fremont	OH	43420	419-334-8400	334-9035	162

Phone | Fax | Class

Terra Dotta LLC
501 W Franklin St Ste 105 .... Chapel Hill NC 27516 877-368-8277 177
TF: 877-368-8277 ■ *Web:* www.terradotta.com

Terra Engineering & Construction Corp
2201 Vondron Rd .... Madison WI 53718 608-221-3501 221-4075 189-5
Web: whyterra.com

Terra Firma Peo 600 Grant St Ste 700 .... Denver CO 80203 303-861-0388 861-0377 193
Web: www.terrafirmapeo.com

Terra Foundation for American Art
120 E Erie St .... Chicago IL 60611 312-664-3939 664-2052 305
Web: terraamericanart.org

Terra Furniture Inc
14819 Salt Lake Ave .... City Of Industry CA 91746 626-912-8523 321
Web: www.terrafurniture.com

Terra Law LLP
50 W San Fernando St 3rd Fl .... San Jose CA 95113 408-299-1200 428
Web: www.terra-law.com

Terra Nostra 105 Frazier Ave .... Chattanooga TN 37405 423-634-0238 671
Web: www.terranostratapas.com

Terra Nova Asset Management LLC
777 Third Ave .... New York NY 10017 212-355-1234 194
Web: www.terranovausa.com

Terra Nova Steel & Iron (Ontario) Inc
3595 Hawkestone Rd .... Mississauga ON L5C2V1 905-273-3872 273-6553 492
TF: 877-427-0269 ■ *Web:* www.terranovasteel.ca

Terra Remote Sensing Inc 1962 Mills Rd .... Sidney BC V8L5Y3 250-656-0931 727
TF: 800-814-4212 ■ *Web:* www.terraremote.com

Terra Tek Inc 5599 San Felipe 17th Fl .... Houston TX 77056 713-375-3535 743
TF: 800-288-8967 ■ *Web:* www.slb.com

Terra Universal Inc 800 S Ramon Ave .... Fullerton CA 92831 714-578-6000 18
Web: www.terrauni.com

Terracap Group
100 Sheppard Ave E Ste 502 .... Toronto ON M2N6N5 416-222-9345 528
TF: 800-363-3207 ■ *Web:* www.terracap.ca

Terrace Plaza Playhouse 99 E 4700 S .... Ogden UT 84405 801-393-0070 572
Web: www.terraceplayhouse.com

Terraces at Los Altos, The
2478 W El Camino Real .... Mountain View CA 94040 650-917-9661 672
TF: 800-861-0086 ■ *Web:* www.theterracesatlosaltos.com

Terraces at Phoenix, The
7550 N 16th St .... Phoenix AZ 85020 602-906-4024 672
TF: 800-836-4281 ■ *Web:* www.theterracesphoenix.com

Terraces of Los Gatos
800 Blossom Hill Rd .... Los Gatos CA 95032 408-356-1006 672
TF: 800-673-1982 ■ *Web:* www.theterracesoflosgatos.com

Terracon 18001 W 106th St .... Olathe KS 66061 913-599-6886 599-0574 261
TF: 800-593-7777 ■ *Web:* www.terracon.com

Terracon Geotechnique Ltd
800 734 - Seventh Ave SW .... Calgary AB T2P3P8 403-266-1150 261
Web: www.terracon.ca

Terracor Business Solutions
677 St Mary's Rd .... Winnipeg MB R2M3M6 204-477-5342 177
TF: 877-942-0005 ■ *Web:* terracor.ca

Terradyne Resort Hotel & Country Club
1400 Terradyne Dr .... Andover KS 67002 316-733-2582 669
Web: www.terradyne-resort.com

Terrafugia Inc 23 Rainin Rd .... Woburn MA 01801 781-491-0812 59
Web: www.terrafugia.com

Terragon Environmental Technologies Inc
651 rue Bridge .... Montreal QC H3K2C8 514-938-3772 261
Web: terragon.net

Terrahealth Inc
5710 W Hausman Ste 108 .... San Antonio TX 78249 210-475-9881 475-9397 194
Web: www.terrahealth.com

Terraine Inc 310 S Harrington St .... Nashville TN 37230 800-531-1242 206-3138* 396
**Fax Area Code:* 864 ■ *TF:* 800-531-1242 ■ *Web:* www.terraine.com

TerraLex Inc 2050 Coral Way Ste 601 .... Miami FL 33145 305-858-8825 138
Web: www.terralex.org

TERRAMAI 8400 Agate Rd .... White City OR 97503 800-220-9062 41
TF: 800-220-9062 ■ *Web:* www.terramai.com

Terramia Ristorante 98 Salem St .... Boston MA 02113 617-523-3112 671
Web: www.terramiaristorante.com

Terrance F Wood Co
400 Mann St Ste 509 .... Crp Christi TX 78401 361-888-8891 652

Terranea Resort & Spa
100 Terranea Way .... Rancho Palos Verdes CA 90275 310-265-2800 378
TF: 866-547-3066 ■ *Web:* www.terranea.com

Terranear PMC LLC
5005 W Royal Ln Ste 216 .... Irving TX 75063 972-929-1095 271
Web: www.terranear.com

Terranettis Italian Bakery
844 W Trindle Rd .... Mechanicsburg PA 17055 717-697-5434 805
Web: www.terranettis.com

Terranova International
3675 Nordstrom Ln .... Lafayette CA 94549 925-299-6833 177
Web: terranovabi.com

Terranovanet Inc 913 La Paloma Rd .... Key Largo FL 33037 305-453-4011 396
TF: 866-800-4143 ■ *Web:* www.terranova.net

TerraPass Inc
527 Howard St 4th Fl .... San Francisco CA 94105 415-692-3411 691
Web: www.terrapass.com

Terrapin Management Corp
601 Rio Grande Pl Ste 117-A .... Aspen CO 81611 970-710-7932 377
Web: www.terrapininvestments.com

Terrapin Systems LLC
1201 Seven Locks Rd Ste 300 .... Rockville MD 20854 301-530-9106 344
Web: www.terpsys.com

Terrasage Technology Partners Llc
3313 Butler Ave .... Los Angeles CA 90066 310-391-2015 809
Web: terrasage.com

Terrasat Communications Inc
315 Digital Dr .... Morgan Hill CA 95037 408-782-5911 116
Web: www.terrasatinc.com

TerraSim Inc
420 Ft Duquesne Blvd One Gateway Ctr
Ste 2050 .... Pittsburgh PA 15222 412-232-3646 177
Web: www.terrasim.com

TerraSond Ltd
1617 S Industrial Way Ste 3 .... Palmer AK 99645 907-745-7215 536
Web: www.terrasond.com

TerraSpark Geosciences L P
10955 Westmoor Dr .... Westminster CO 80021 303-379-3050 379-2143 809

Terrazzo & Marble Supply Company of Illinois
77 Wheeling Rd .... Wheeling IL 60090 847-353-8000 353-8001 191-1
Web: www.tmsupply.com

Terre Haute Regional Hospital (THRH)
3901 S Seventh St .... Terre Haute IN 47802 812-232-0021 865-9738* 374-3
**Fax Area Code:* 877 ■ *TF:* 866-270-2311 ■ *Web:* www.regionalhospital.com

Terre Hill Silo Company Inc
PO Box 10 .... Terre Hill PA 17581 717-445-3100 445-3108 183
TF: 800-242-1509 ■ *Web:* www.terrehill.com

Terrebonne General Medical Ctr (TGMC)
8166 Main St .... Houma LA 70360 985-873-4141 873-5306 374-3
TF: 888-850-6270 ■ *Web:* www.tgmc.com

Terrebonne Parish PO Box 1569 .... Houma LA 70361 985-868-5660 868-5143 338
Web: terrebonneclerk.org

Terrebonne Parish Library
151 Library Dr .... Houma LA 70360 985-876-5861 917-0582 434-3
Web: www.terrebonne.lib.la.us

Terrell County 105 E Hackberry .... Sanderson TX 79848 432-345-2391 345-2740 338
Web: www.co.terrell.tx.us

Terrell Public Library
301 N Rockwell Ave .... Terrell TX 75160 972-551-6663 434-3
Web: cityofterrell.org

Territorial Statehouse State Park
50 W Capitol Ave .... Fillmore UT 84631 435-743-5316 565
Web: www.stateparks.utah.gov

Terroco Industries Ltd
Site 14 RR Ste 1 Box 10 .... Red Deer AB T4N5E1 403-346-1171 539
TF: 800-670-1100 ■ *Web:* www.terroco.com

Terros Inc 3003 N Central Ave Ste 200 .... Phoenix AZ 85012 602-222-9444 353
Web: www.terros.org

Terry County 500 W Main St Rm 105 .... Brownfield TX 79316 806-637-4202 637-4874 338
Web: www.co.terry.tx.us

Terry Hines & Associates Inc
2550 N Hollywood Way Ste 600 .... Burbank CA 91505 818-562-9433 7
Web: www.terryhines.com

Terry Hughes Tree Service Inc
15802 Fairview Rd .... Gretna NE 68028 402-558-8198 776
Web: www.hughestree.com

Terry Jones & Assoc PC 5910 Grelot Rd .... Mobile AL 36609 251-341-4593 2
Web: tjonescpa.com

Terry Laboratories Inc
7005 Technology Dr .... Melbourne FL 32904 321-259-1630 242-0625 479
TF: 800-367-2563 ■ *Web:* www.terrylabs.com

Terry McDaniel & Co
2630 Exposition Blvd Ste 300 .... Austin TX 78703 512-495-9500 401
Web: www.tmcdanco.com

Terry Precision Bicycles for Women Inc
47 Maple St .... Burlington VT 05401 800-289-8379 861-2956* 82
**Fax Area Code:* 802 ■ *TF:* 800-289-8379 ■ *Web:* www.terrybicycles.com

Terry Thompson Chevrolet Olds
1402 US Hwy 98 .... Daphne AL 36526 251-626-0631 57
TF: 800-287-9309 ■ *Web:* terry-thompson.com

Terry's Electric Inc
600 N Thacker Ave Ste A .... Kissimmee FL 34741 407-572-2100 189-4
TF: 800-207-5622 ■ *Web:* www.terryselectric.com

Terry's Tire Town Inc
2360 W Main St PO Box 2405 .... Alliance OH 44601 330-821-5022 829-4165 755

Terryberry Co
2033 Oak Industrial Dr NE .... Grand Rapids MI 49505 616-458-1391 409
TF: 800-253-0882 ■ *Web:* www.terryberry.com

Terrycomm 2700 Business Center Blvd .... Melbourne FL 32940 321-253-6067 246
TF: 800-895-1557 ■ *Web:* terrycomm.com

Terry-Durin Co
409 Seventh Ave SE .... Cedar Rapids IA 52401 319-364-4106 364-2562 246
TF: 800-332-8114 ■ *Web:* www.terry-durin.com

Terry-haggerty Tire Company Inc
980 Broadway .... Menands NY 12204 518-449-5185 54
Web: www.terry-haggerty.com

Terrys Ford Lincoln 363 N Harlem Ave .... Peotone IL 60468 708-258-9200 57
Web: terrysfordofpeotone.com

Terumo Cardiovascular Systems Corp
6200 Jackson Rd .... Ann Arbor MI 48103 734-663-4145 292-6551* 476
**Fax Area Code:* 800 ■ **Fax:* Cust Svc ■ *TF:* 800-262-3304 ■ *Web:* www.terumo-us.com

Terumo Medical Corp
2101 Cottontail Ln .... Somerset NJ 08873 732-302-4900 302-3083 476
TF: 800-283-7866 ■ *Web:* www.terumomedical.com

Tervita Corp 500 140 - 10 Ave SE .... Calgary AB T2G0R1 403-233-7565 536
Web: www.tervita.com

Tesa Tape Inc 5825 Carnegie Blvd .... Charlotte NC 28209 704-554-0707 852-8831* 732
**Fax Area Code:* 800 ■ **Fax:* Cust Svc ■ *TF:* 800-426-2181 ■ *Web:* www.tesatape.com

Teschner Law Firm LLC
3 Lockwood Dr Ste 204 .... Charleston SC 29401 843-937-0027 445
Web: charlestontaxlaw.com

Tesco Controls Inc 8440 Florin Rd .... Sacramento CA 95828 916-395-8800 203
Web: www.tescocontrols.com

Tesco Industries LP 1035 E Hacienda .... Bellville TX 77418 800-699-5824 319-3
TF: 800-699-5824 ■ *Web:* www.tesco-ind.com

Tescom Corp 12616 Industrial Blvd .... Elk River MN 55330 763-241-3238 789
Web: www2.emersonprocess.com/en-US/brands/tescom/Pages/Tescom.aspx

TESD (Tredyffrin-Easttown School District)
940 W Valley Rd Ste 1700 .... Wayne PA 19087 610-240-1900 186
Web: www.tesd.net

Teske's Germania 255 N First St .... San Jose CA 95113 408-292-0291 671
Web: www.teskes-germania.com

Tesko Welding & Manufacturing Co
7350 W Montrose Ave .... Norridge IL 60706 708-452-0045 452-0112 286
TF: 800-621-4514 ■ *Web:* teskoenterprises.com

Tesla Exploration Ltd 4500 8A St NE .... Calgary AB T2E4J7 403-216-0999 536

Tesla Motors Inc 3500 Deer Creek Rd .... Palo Alto CA 94304 650-681-5000 59
TF: 888-518-3752 ■ *Web:* www.tesla.com

TESOL (Teachers of English to Speakers of Other Languages)
700 S Washington St Ste 200 .... Alexandria VA 22314 703-836-0774 836-7864 49-5
TF: 888-547-3369 ■ *Web:* www.tesol.org

Name / Address	City	State	ZIP	Phone	Fax	Class
Tesoro Corp 1225 17th St *TF:* 800-299-0570 ■ *Web:* www.tsocorp.com	Denver	CO	80202	800-299-0570		579
Tesoro Corp 19100 Ridgewood Pkwy *NYSE: TSO* ■ *TF:* 800-299-0570 ■ *Web:* www.tsocorp.com	San Antonio	TX	78259	210-626-6000		580
Tess 2499 N Bartlett Ave *Web:* tess2499.com	Milwaukee	WI	53211	414-964-8377	964-7790	671
Tessada & Associates Inc 8001 Forbes Pl Ste 310	Springfield	VA	22151	703-564-1210		194
Tessaro's 4601 Liberty Ave *Web:* tessaros.com	Pittsburgh	PA	15224	412-682-6809		671
TESSCO Technologies Inc 11126 McCormick Rd *NASDAQ: TESS* ■ *TF:* 800-472-7373 ■ *Web:* www.tessco.com	Hunt Valley	MD	21031	410-229-1000	527-0005	246
Tessera Technologies Inc 3099 Orchard Dr *NASDAQ: TSRA* ■ *Web:* www.tessera.com	San Jose	CA	95134	408-894-0700	894-0768	696
Tessler & Weiss / Premesco Inc 2389 Vauxhall Rd	Union	NJ	07083	908-686-0513		409
Tessy Plastics Corp 488 Rt 5 W *Web:* www.tessy.com	Elbridge	NY	13060	315-689-3924	689-2027	608
Test com Inc 1501 Euclid Ave Ste 407 *TF:* 877-502-8600 ■ *Web:* www.test.com	Cleveland	OH	44115	877-502-8600		525
Test Connection Inc, The 11400 Cronridge Dr Ste H *Web:* www.ttci.info	Owings Mills	MD	21117	410-205-7300		261
Test Devices Inc 571 Main St *Web:* www.testdevices.com	Hudson	MA	01749	978-562-6017		743
Test Electronics 821 Smith Rd *Web:* www.testelectronics.com	Watsonville	CA	95076	831-763-2000		248
Test Evolution Corp 102 S St *Web:* www.testevolution.com	Hopkinton	MA	01748	781-644-2111		407
Test Inc 2323 Fourth St *TF:* 800-659-4659 ■ *Web:* testinc.com	Peru	IL	61354	815-224-1650		743
Test Laboratories 7121 Canby Ave *Web:* www.testlabinc.com	Reseda	CA	91335	818-881-4251		275
Test Mark Industries Inc 995 N Market St *TF:* 800-783-3227 ■ *Web:* www.testmark.net	East Palestine	OH	44413	330-426-2200		190
Test Products Inc 41255 Technology Park Dr *Web:* www.testprod.com	Sterling Heights	MI	48314	586-997-9600		247
Testa Communications 25 Willowdale Ave *Web:* www.testa.com	Port Washington	NY	11050	516-767-2500	767-9335	637-9
TestAmerica Laboratories Inc 4625 E Cotton Ctr Blvd Ste 189 *TF:* 866-785-5227 ■ *Web:* www.testamericainc.com	Phoenix	AZ	85040	602-437-3340	454-9303	743
Testco 3445 Executive Center Dr Ste 117 *TF:* 888-245-9709 ■ *Web:* www.testco.com	Austin	TX	78731	888-245-9709		539
Testcountry 6310 Nancy Ridge Dr Ste 103 *TF:* 866-227-7076 ■ *Web:* www.testcountry.com	San Diego	CA	92121	858-784-6904		743
Testek Inc 28320 Lakeview Dr *Web:* www.testek.com	Wixom	MI	48393	248-573-4980		407
Tester Jon (Sen D - MT) 311 Hart Senate Office Bldg *Web:* www.tester.senate.gov	Washington	DC	20510	202-224-2644	224-8594	342-2
TesTex Inc 535 Old Frankstown Rd *TF:* 800-344-2250 ■ *Web:* www.testex-ndt.com	Pittsburgh	PA	15239	412-798-8990		365
Testing Engineers & Consultants Inc 1343 Rochester Rd *TF:* 800-835-2654 ■ *Web:* www.tectest.com	Troy	MI	48083	248-588-6200		261
Testing Machines Inc 40 McCullough Dr *TF General:* 800-678-3221 ■ *Web:* www.testingmachines.com	New Castle	DE	19720	302-613-5600	613-5619	472
Testmax 927 Lincoln Rd Ste 209 *Web:* www.testmax.net	Miami Beach	FL	33139	305-673-5728		194
Testor Corp 440 Blackhawk Pk Ave *TF:* 800-837-8677 ■ *Web:* www.testors.com	Rockford	IL	61104	815-962-6654	962-7401	762
TestTakers 1 Plaza Rd Ste 204 *TF:* 800-955-4600 ■ *Web:* www.ttprep.com	Greenvale	NY	11548	516-626-6100		244
Testware Associates Inc 21 E High St *Web:* www.testwareinc.com	Somerville	NJ	08876	908-526-2900		177
Testwell Laboratories Inc 47 Hudson St	Ossining	NY	10562	914-762-9004		261
Tetco Inc 1100 NE Loop 410 Ste 900 *Web:* www.tetco.com	San Antonio	TX	78209	210-821-5900		579
Teters Floral Products Inc 1425 S Lillian Ave *TF:* 800-999-5996 ■ *Web:* www.teters.com	Bolivar	MO	65613	417-326-7654	326-8061	293
Tethys Bioscience Inc 5858 Horton St Ste 280	Emeryville	CA	94608	510-420-6700		582
Teton Buildings LLC 2701 Magnet St *TF:* 800-280-0780 ■ *Web:* tetonbuildings.com	Houston	TX	77054	713-351-6300		539
Teton County PO Box 610 *Web:* www.tetoncomt.org	Choteau	MT	59422	406-466-2151	466-2151	338
Teton County 89 N Main St Ste 1 *Web:* tetoncountyidaho.gov	Driggs	ID	83422	208-354-8770	354-8776	338
Teton County PO Box 1727 *TF:* 800-368-8683 ■ *Web:* www.tetonwyo.org	Jackson	WY	83001	307-733-4430	739-8681	338
Teton County Public Library 125 Virginian Ln *TF:* 800-878-2167 ■ *Web:* www.tclib.org	Jackson	WY	83001	307-733-2164	733-4568	434-3
Teton Data Systems 125 S Kings St Ste G1 *Web:* www.tetondata.com	Jackson	WY	83001	307-733-5494		809
Teton Gravity Research LLC 1260 NW St *Web:* www.tetongravity.com	Wilson	WY	83014	307-734-8192		506
Teton Machine Co 1805 NE Tenth Ave *Web:* www.tetonmachine.com	Payette	ID	83661	208-642-9344		627
Teton Mountain Lodge & Spa 3385 Cody Ln *TF:* 800-631-6271 ■ *Web:* www.tetonlodge.com	Teton Village	WY	83025	307-201-6066		379
Teton Pines Resort & Country Club 3450 N Clubhouse Dr *TF:* 800-238-2223 ■ *Web:* www.tetonpines.com	Wilson	WY	83014	307-733-1005	733-2860	669

Name / Address	City	State	ZIP	Phone	Fax	Class
Tetra Corporate Services LLC 6995 Union Park Ctr Ste 360 *TF:* 800-417-0548 ■ *Web:* www.tetracsi.com	Salt Lake City	UT	84047	801-566-2600	305-0263	264-3
Tetra Medical Supply Corp 6364 W Gross Pt Rd *TF Cust Svc:* 800-621-4041 ■ *Web:* www.tetramed.com	Niles	IL	60714	847-647-0590	647-9034	475
Tetra Pak Inc 753 Geneva Pkwy N *Web:* www.tetrapak.com	Lake Geneva	WI	53147	262-249-7400		101
Tetra Tech Architects & Engineers Cornell Business & Technology Park 10 Brown Rd *TF:* 877-882-7241 ■ *Web:* www.tetratechae.com	Ithaca	NY	14850	607-277-7100		393
Tetra Tech EC Inc 1000 the American Rd *Web:* www.tteci.com	Morris Plains	NJ	07950	973-630-8000		261
Tetra Tech Inc 3475 E Foothill Blvd *NASDAQ: TTEK* ■ *Web:* www.tetratech.com	Pasadena	CA	91107	626-351-4664	351-5291	261
Tetra Tech WEI Inc 330 Bay St Ste 900 *Web:* www.wardrop.com	Toronto	ON	M5H2S8	416-368-9080		261
Tetra Tech/KCM 3475 E Foothill Blvd *NASDAQ: TTEK* ■ *Web:* www.tetratech.com	Pasadena	CA	91107	626-351-4664	351-5291	261
TETRA Technologies Inc 25025 I-45 N *NYSE: TTI* ■ *TF:* 800-327-7817 ■ *Web:* www.tetratec.com	The Woodlands	TX	77380	281-367-1983	364-4306	143
Tetrad Computer Applications Ltd 1465 Slater Rd PO Box 5007 *TF:* 800-663-1334 ■ *Web:* www.tetrad.com	Vancouver	BC	V6G2T3	604-685-2295		177
Tetrahedron Assoc Inc PO Box 710157 *Web:* www.tetrahedronassociates.com	San Diego	CA	92171	619-661-0552	661-0559	456
Tetrasoft Inc 16647 Chesterfield Grove Rd Ste 120 *TF:* 866-314-7557 ■ *Web:* www.tetrasoft.us	Chesterfield	MO	63005	636-530-7638		179
Tetrault Insurance Agency Inc 4317 Acushnet Ave *TF:* 800-696-9991 ■ *Web:* tetraultinsurance.com	New Bedford	MA	02745	508-995-8365		390
Tetrault Woods State Forest 1037 Forestry Dr *Web:* www.ndsu.edu	Bottineau	ND	58318	701-228-3700	228-5111	565
Tetrem Capital Management Ltd 1910-201 Portage Ave *Web:* www.tetrem.com	Winnipeg	MB	R3B3K6	204-975-2865		528
Tettegouche State Park 5702 Hwy 61 *TF:* 800-366-8917 ■ *Web:* www.dnr.state.mn.us/state_parks/tettegouche	Silver Bay	MN	55614	218-226-6365		565
Teucrium Trading LLC 232 Hidden Lake Rd *Web:* www.teucrium.com	Brattleboro	VT	05301	802-257-1617		528
Teufel Landscape 7431 NW Evergreen Pkwy Ste 200 *Web:* www.teufellandscape.com	Hillsboro	OR	97124	503-646-1111	646-1112	293
Teuteberg Inc 12200 W Wirth St *Web:* www.teuteberg.com	Wauwatosa	WI	53222	414-257-4110		627
Teva 123 N Leroux St *TF General:* 800-367-8382 ■ *Web:* www.teva.com	Flagstaff	AZ	86001	928-779-5938		301
Teva Animal Health Inc 3915 S 48th St Terr	St. Joseph	MO	64503	816-364-3777		583
Teva Pharmaceutical USA 1090 Horsham Rd *NYSE: TEVA* ■ *TF:* 800-545-8800 ■ *Web:* www.tevagenerics.com	North Wales	PA	19454	215-591-3000		583
Tevet LLC 85 Spring St S *TF:* 866-886-8527 ■ *Web:* www.tevetllc.com	Mosheim	TN	37818	678-905-1300		201
Tewell Warren Printing Co 4710 Lipan St *Web:* www.tewellwarren.com	Denver	CO	80211	303-458-8505		627
Tewksbury Animal Hospital 1098 Main St *TF:* 800-738-3343 ■ *Web:* tewksburyanimalhospital.com	Tewksbury	MA	01876	978-851-3626		794
Tewksbury Hospital 365 E St **Fax:* Mail Rm ■ *Web:* mass.gov	Tewksbury	MA	01876	978-851-7321	851-5648*	374-7
Tewksbury Public Library 300 Chandler St *TF:* 800-818-3434 ■ *Web:* www.tewksburypl.org	Tewksbury	MA	01876	978-640-4490		434-3
Tex Con Oil Co 1701 Grand Ave Pkwy *Web:* www.texconoil.com	Pflugerville	TX	78660	512-670-7401		579
Tex Shoemaker & Son Inc 131 S Eucla Ave *TF:* 800-345-9959 ■ *Web:* www.texshoemaker.com	San Dimas	CA	91773	909-592-2071	592-2378	431
Texadelphia 7601 N MacArthur Blvd *Web:* www.texadelphia.com	Irving	TX	75063	972-432-0725		671
Tex-air Parts Inc 3724 N Commerce St *Web:* www.texair.com	Fort Worth	TX	76106	817-624-9882		770
Texans Credit Union 777 E Campbell Rd *TF:* 800-843-5295 ■ *Web:* www.texanscu.org	Richardson	TX	75081	972-348-2000	348-2200	219
Texarkana Chamber of Commerce 819 N State Line Ave *Web:* texarkana.org	Texarkana	TX	75501	903-792-7191	793-4304	139
Texarkana College 2500 N Robison Rd **Fax:* Admissions ■ *TF:* 877-275-4377 ■ *Web:* www.texarkanacollege.edu	Texarkana	TX	75599	903-838-4541	832-5030*	162
Texarkana Gazette 315 Pine St *Web:* www.texarkanagazette.com	Texarkana	TX	75501	903-794-3311	794-3315	532-2
Texarkana Public Library 600 W Third St *Web:* txark.ent.sirsi.net/client/en_us/default	Texarkana	TX	75501	903-794-2149		434-3
Texarkana Water Utilities 801 Wood St *Web:* txkusa.org	Texarkana	TX	75501	903-798-3800	791-0724	787
Texas						
Aging & Disability Services 701 W 51st St Ste W253 *TF:* 888-388-6332 ■ *Web:* www.dads.state.tx.us	Austin	TX	78751	512-438-3011	438-5885	339-44
Agriculture Dept PO Box 12847 **Fax Area Code:* 888 ■ *TF Cust Svc:* 800-835-5832 ■ *Web:* texasagriculture.gov	Austin	TX	78711	512-463-7476	223-8861*	339-44
Arts Commission 920 Colorado Ste 501 PO Box 13406 *TF:* 800-252-9415 ■ *Web:* www.arts.texas.gov	Austin	TX	78701	512-463-5535	475-2699	339-44

	City	State	Zip	Phone	Fax	Class
Assistive & Rehabilitation Services Dept						
4800 N Lamar Blvd 3rd Fl	Austin	TX	78756	512-377-0500		339-44
TF: 800-252-7009 ■ *Web:* texasimpact.org						
Attorney General 300 W 15th St.	Austin	TX	78701	512-463-2191		339-44
Web: www.texasattorneygeneral.gov						
Banking Dept 2601 N Lamar Blvd	Austin	TX	78705	512-475-1300	475-1313	339-44
TF: 877-276-5554 ■ *Web:* dob.texas.gov						
Child Support Div						
300 W 15th St PO Box 12548	Austin	TX	78701	512-463-2100		339-44
Web: www.texasattorneygeneral.gov						
Comptroller of Public Accounts						
111 E 17th St	Austin	TX	78774	512-463-4444	305-9711	339-44
TF: 800-252-5555 ■ *Web:* www.cpa.state.tx.us						
Consumer Protection Div PO Box 12548	Austin	TX	78711	512-463-2185	473-8301	339-44
Web: www.texasattorneygeneral.gov/consumer						
Crime Victims Services Div						
PO Box 12198	Austin	TX	78711	512-936-1200		339-44
TF: 800-983-9933 ■ *Web:* www.texasattorneygeneral.gov						
Criminal Justice Dept PO Box 99	Huntsville	TX	77342	936-295-6371		339-44
Web: www.tdcj.state.tx.us						
Economic Development PO Box 12428	Austin	TX	78711	512-981-6736		339-44
Web: www.texaswideopenforbusiness.com						
Education Agency 1701 N Congress Ave.	Austin	TX	78701	512-463-9734	463-9838	339-44
Web: www.tea.state.tx.us						
Emergency Management Div						
1033 La Posada Dr PO Box 4087	Austin	TX	78773	512-424-2138	424-2444	339-44
Web: dps.texas.gov						
Environmental Quality Commission (TCEQ)						
12100 Pk 35 Cir.	Austin	TX	78711	512-239-1000		339-44
Web: www.tceq.state.tx.us						
Ethics Commission 201 E 14th St 10th Fl	Austin	TX	78701	512-463-5800	463-5777	265
Web: www.ethics.state.tx.us						
Family & Protective Services Dept						
701 W 51st St PO Box 149030	Austin	TX	78752	512-438-4800		339-44
Web: www.dfps.state.tx.us						
General Land Office						
1700 N Congress Ave Ste 935	Austin	TX	78701	512-463-5001		339-44
TF: 800-998-4456 ■ *Web:* www.glo.texas.gov						
Governor PO Box 12428	Austin	TX	78711	512-463-2000	463-1849	339-44
TF: 800-843-5789 ■ *Web:* www.governor.state.tx.us						
Higher Education Coordinating Board						
1200 E Anderson Ln	Austin	TX	78752	512-427-6101		725
Web: www.thecb.state.tx.us						
Historical Commission						
1511 Colorado St PO Box 12276	Austin	TX	78701	512-463-6100		339-44
Web: www.thc.state.tx.us						
Information Resources Dept						
300 W 15th St Ste 1300	Austin	TX	78701	512-475-4700		339-44
TF: 855-275-3471 ■ *Web:* www.dir.state.tx.us						
Insurance Dept						
333 Guadalupe St PO Box 149104	Austin	TX	78714	800-578-4677		339-44
TF: 800-578-4677 ■ *Web:* www.tdi.texas.gov						
Legislature State Capitol	Austin	TX	78711	512-463-0124	463-0694	339-44
Web: www.capitol.state.tx.us						
Licensing & Regulation Dept						
920 Colorado	Austin	TX	78701	512-463-6599	463-9468	339-44
TF: 800-803-9202 ■ *Web:* tdlr.texas.gov						
Lieutenant Governor David Dewhurst						
PO Box 12068	Austin	TX	78711	512-463-0001		339-44
Web: www.ltgov.state.tx.us						
Medical Board PO Box 2018	Austin	TX	78768	512-305-7010	305-7051	339-44
TF Cust Svc: 800-248-4062 ■ *Web:* www.tmb.state.tx.us						
Motor Vehicle Div						
4000 Jackson Ave PO Box 2293	Austin	TX	78731	888-368-4689	465-4129*	339-44
**Fax Area Code:* 512 ■ *TF:* 888-368-4689 ■ *Web:* www.txdmv.gov						
Office of Court Administration						
205 W 14th St PO Box 12066 Ste 600	Austin	TX	78711	512-463-1625	463-1648	339-44
Web: www.courts.state.tx.us						
Pardons & Parole Board						
209 W 14th St Ste 500	Austin	TX	78701	512-936-6351	463-8120	339-44
Web: www.tdcj.state.tx.us/bpp						
Parks & Wildlife Dept						
4200 Smith School Rd	Austin	TX	78744	512-389-4800	389-4814	339-44
TF: 800-792-1112 ■ *Web:* www.tpwd.state.tx.us						
Public Utility Commission PO Box 13326	Austin	TX	78711	512-936-7000	936-7003	339-44
TF: 888-782-8477 ■ *Web:* www.puc.texas.gov						
Racing Commission						
8505 Cross Pk Dr Ste 110	Austin	TX	78754	512-833-6699	833-6907	712
Web: txrc.state.tx.us						
Railroad Commission						
1701 N Congress Ave PO Box 12967	Austin	TX	78711	512-463-7058	463-7319	339-44
TF: 877-228-5740 ■ *Web:* www.rrc.state.tx.us						
Secretary of State PO Box 12887	Austin	TX	78711	512-463-5770	475-2761	339-44
Web: www.sos.state.tx.us						
State Government Information						
1501 N Congress Ave	Austin	TX	78704	512-463-1155		339-44
Web: www.texas.gov						
State Securities Board						
208 E Tenth St Fl 5	Austin	TX	78701	512-305-8300	305-8310	339-44
Web: www.ssb.state.tx.us						
Supreme Court						
201 W 14th St Rm 104 PO Box 12248	Austin	TX	78711	512-463-1312	463-1365	339-44
Web: www.supreme.courts.state.tx.us						
Transportation Dept 125 E 11th St	Austin	TX	78701	512-463-8585		339-44
Web: txdot.gov						
Veterans Commission PO Box 12277	Austin	TX	78711	512-463-5538	475-2395	339-44
TF: 800-252-8387 ■ *Web:* www.tvc.state.tx.us						
Vital Statistics Bureau						
1100 W 49th St PO Box 12040	Austin	TX	78756	888-963-7111	776-7711*	339-44
**Fax Area Code:* 512 ■ *TF:* 888-963-7111 ■ *Web:* www.dshs.state.tx.us/VS						
Workers Compensation Commission						
7551 Metro Ctr Dr Ste 100	Austin	TX	78744	512-804-4157	804-4001	339-44
TF Cust Svc: 800-252-7031 ■ *Web:* tdi.texas.gov						
Workforce Commission 101 E 15th St	Austin	TX	78778	512-463-2222		259
Web: twc.state.tx.us						
Texas A & M International University						
5201 University Blvd	Laredo	TX	78041	956-326-2001	326-2199	166
TF: 888-489-2648 ■ *Web:* www.tamiu.edu						

	City	State	Zip	Phone	Fax	Class
Texas A & M University						
Rudder Tower Ste 205	College Station	TX	77843	979-845-8901	458-4617*	166
**Fax:* Admissions ■ *TF:* 888-890-5667 ■ *Web:* www.tamu.edu						
Corpus Christi 6300 Ocean Dr.	Corpus Christi	TX	78412	361-825-7024	825-5887*	166
**Fax:* Admissions ■ *Web:* www.tamucc.edu						
Evans Library 5000 Tamu	College Station	TX	77843	979-845-5741	845-6238	434-6
Web: library.tamu.edu						
Galveston 200 Seawolf Pkwy Bldg 3026	Galveston	TX	77553	409-740-4428	740-4731	166
TF: 877-322-4443 ■ *Web:* www.tamug.edu						
Kingsville						
700 University Blvd MSC 128	Kingsville	TX	78363	361-593-2111	593-2195*	166
**Fax:* Admissions ■ *TF:* 800-726-8192 ■ *Web:* www.tamuk.edu						
Medical Sciences Library						
202 Olsen Blvd	College Station	TX	77843	979-845-7428		434-1
Web: msl.library.tamu.edu						
Texarkana 7101 University Ave	Texarkana	TX	75503	903-223-3000	223-3140	166
TF: 866-791-9120 ■ *Web:* www.tamut.edu						
Texas A & M University Press						
John H Lindsey Bldg 4354 TAMU	College Station	TX	77843	979-845-1436	847-8752	637-4
TF Orders: 800-826-8911 ■ *Web:* www.tamu.edu						
Texas A & M University System Health Science Ctr						
301 Tarrow St Fl 5	College Station	TX	77840	979-458-7200		167-2
Web: www.tamhsc.edu						
College of Medicine						
8447 Riverside Pkwy						
3rd Fl Health Professions Education Bldg	Bryan	TX	77807	979-436-0237		167-2
Web: www.medicine.tamhsc.edu						
Texas A & M University System, The						
200 Technology Way Ste 2043	College Station	TX	77845	979-458-6000	458-6044	786
Web: www.tamus.edu						
Texas Air Systems Inc						
6029 W Campus Cir Dr	Irving	TX	75063	972-570-4700		14
TF: 800-303-7816 ■ *Web:* www.texasairsystems.com						
Texas A&M Transportation Institute						
3135 Tamu	College Station	TX	77843	979-845-1713		162
Web: tti.tamu.edu						
Texas Arai Inc						
8204 Fairbanks N Houston	Houston	TX	77064	713-937-1800		537
Texas Art Supply 2001 Montrose Blvd	Houston	TX	77006	713-526-5221	526-4062	45
TF: 800-888-9278 ■ *Web:* www.texasart.com						
Texas Assn of Business 1209 Nueces St.	Austin	TX	78701	512-477-6721	477-0836	140
Web: www.txbiz.org						
Texas Assn of Realtors						
1115 San Jacinto Blvd Ste 200	Austin	TX	78701	512-480-8200	370-2390	656
TF: 800-873-9155 ■ *Web:* www.texasrealestate.com						
Texas Ballet Theater 1540 Mall Cir.	Fort Worth	TX	76116	817-763-0207		573-1
Web: www.texasballettheater.org						
Texas Bank & Trust Co						
300 E Whaley PO Box 3188	Longview	TX	75606	903-237-5500		70
Web: www.texasbankandtrust.com						
Texas Bar Journal						
1414 Colorado St Ste 902	Austin	TX	78701	512-463-1463	427-4107	457-15
TF: 800-204-2222 ■ *Web:* www.texasbar.com						
Texas Basket Co 100 Myrtle Dr	Jacksonville	TX	75766	903-586-8014	586-0988	200
TF: 800-657-2200 ■ *Web:* www.texasbasket.com						
Texas Beef Council 8708 N Fm 620	Austin	TX	78726	512-335-2333		533
TF: 800-846-4113 ■ *Web:* www.beeflovingtexans.com						
Texas Book Co 8501 Technology Cir.	Greenville	TX	75402	903-455-6937		96
Web: www.texasbook.com						
Texas Book Festival						
610 Brazos St Ste 200	Austin	TX	78701	512-477-4055	322-0722	281
TF: 800-222-8733 ■ *Web:* www.texasbookfestival.org						
Texas Cafe & Bar 3604 50th St.	Lubbock	TX	79413	806-792-8544		671
Texas Capital Bank						
2000 McKinney Ave Ste 700	Dallas	TX	75201	214-932-6600		70
TF: 877-839-2265 ■ *Web:* www.texascapitalbank.com						
Texas Children's Hospital						
6621 Fannin St.	Houston	TX	77030	832-824-1000		374-1
TF: 800-364-5437 ■ *Web:* texaschildrens.org						
Texas Children's Hospital Stem Cell & Bone Marrow Transplant Program						
6621 Fannin St.	Houston	TX	77030	832-824-1000		769
Web: texaschildrens.org						
Texas Christian University						
TCU PO Box 297043	Fort Worth	TX	76129	817-257-7490	257-7268	166
TF: 800-828-3764 ■ *Web:* www.tcu.edu						
Texas Christian University Mary Couts Burnett Library						
2800 S University Dr	Fort Worth	TX	76129	817-257-7000	257-7282	434-6
TF: 866-321-7428 ■ *Web:* www.tcu.edu						
Texas City-La Marque Chamber of Commerce						
9702 Emmett F Lowry Expy	Texas City	TX	77590	409-935-1408	316-0901	139
Web: www.texascitychamber.com						
Texas Coffee Co Inc						
3297 S M L King Jr Pkwy	Beaumont	TX	77705	409-835-3434		296-7
TF: 800-259-3400 ■ *Web:* www.texjoy.com						
Texas College 2404 N Grand Ave	Tyler	TX	75702	903-593-8311		166
TF: 800-306-6299 ■ *Web:* www.texascollege.edu						
Texas Concrete Co 4702 N Vine St	Victoria	TX	77904	361-573-9145		183
Web: www.texasconcreteco.com						
Texas Correctional Industries						
PO Box 4013	Huntsville	TX	77342-4013	936-437-6048	437-8423	630
Web: www.tci.tdcj.state.tx.us						
Texas County PO Box 197	Guymon	OK	73942	580-338-3141	338-4311	338
Web: texas.okcounties.org						
Texas County 210 N Grand Ave Ste 201	Houston	MO	65483	417-967-4709	967-2091	338
Web: www.texascountymissouri.gov						
Texas Crushed Stone Co						
5300 S IH-35 PO Box 1000	Georgetown	TX	78627	512-930-0106	244-6055	503-5
TF: 800-772-8272 ■ *Web:* www.texascrushedstoneco.com						
Texas Ctr for Infectious Diseases						
2303 SE Military Dr	San Antonio	TX	78223	210-534-8857	531-4502	374-7
TF: 800-839-5864 ■ *Web:* www.dshs.texas.gov/tcid						
Texas Ctr for Superconductivity						
3201 Cullen Blvd Ste 202	Houston	TX	77204	713-743-8200	743-8201	668
Web: www.tcsuh.com						
Texas de Brazil 150 Peabody Pl Ste 103	Memphis	TN	38103	901-526-7600	526-7615	671
Web: www.texasdebrazil.com						
Texas de Brazil 101 N Houston St.	Fort Worth	TX	76102	817-882-9500	882-9503	671
Web: www.texasdebrazil.com						

Name / Address	City	State	ZIP	Phone	Fax	Class
Texas Deer Assn 816 Congress Ave Ste 950 *Web:* www.texasdeerassociation.com	Austin	TX	78701	512-499-0466		45
Texas Democratic Party 1106 Lavaca St Ste 100 *Web:* www.txdemocrats.org	Austin	TX	78701	512-478-9800	480-2500	616-1
Texas Dental Assn 1946 S IH-35 Ste 400 *TF:* 800-832-1145 ■ *Web:* www.tda.org	Austin	TX	78704	512-443-3675	443-3031	227
Texas Dept of Public Safety 1001 E Coke Rd	Winnsboro	TX	75494	903-342-0982		693
Texas Design Interests LLC 6001 W William Cannon Dr Ste 203C *Web:* tdi-llc.net	Austin	TX	78749	512-301-3389		261
Texas Die Casting Inc 600 S Loop 485 *Web:* www.texasdiecasting.com	Gladewater	TX	75647	903-845-2224	845-6155	308
Texas Direct Auto 12053 Southwest Fwy (Hwy 59) *Web:* www.texasdirectauto.com	Stafford	TX	77477	281-499-8200		57
Texas Discovery Gardens 3601 Martin Luther King Junior Blvd *Web:* www.texasdiscoverygardens.org	Dallas	TX	75210	214-428-7476	428-5338	97
Texas Disposal Systems Inc (TDS) 12200 Carl Rd *TF:* 800-375-8375 ■ *Web:* www.texasdisposal.com	Creedmoor	TX	78610	512-421-1300	243-4123	804
Texas Dow Employees Credit Union (TDECU) 1001 FM 2004 *TF:* 800-839-1154 ■ *Web:* www.tdecu.org	Lake Jackson	TX	77566	979-297-1154	299-0212	219
Texas Electric Co-ops Inc 1122 Colorado St 24th Fl *TF:* 800-301-2860 ■ *Web:* www.texas-ec.org	Austin	TX	78701	512-454-0311		245
Texas Electric Utility Construction Ltd 4613 Hwy 1417 N *Web:* www.texaselectric.com	Sherman	TX	75092	903-893-0949		539
Texas Enterprises Inc 5005 E Seventh St *TF:* 800 545 4412 ■ *Web:* www.alliedsalesco.com	Austin	TX	78702	512-385-2167		579
Texas Farm Bureau PO Box 2689 *TF:* 800-488-7872 ■ *Web:* www.texasfarmbureau.org	Waco	TX	76702	254-772-3030		457-1
Texas Farm LLC 4200 S Main St	Perryton	TX	79070	806-435-5935	435-3656	10-6
Texas Farm Products Co 915 S Fredonia St *TF:* 800-392-3110 ■ *Web:* www.texasfarm.com	Nacogdoches	TX	75964	936-564-3711	560-8200	578
Texas Fish & Game Magazine 1745 Greens Rd *TF:* 800-725-1134 ■ *Web:* www.fishgame.com	Houston	TX	77032	281-227-3001		530
Texas Gauge & Control Inc 7575 Dillon St *TF:* 800-914-0009 ■ *Web:* www.texasgauge.com	Houston	TX	77061	713-641-2282		358
Texas Growth Fund 900 S Capital of Texas Hwy Ste 430 *Web:* www.tgfmanagement.com	Austin	TX	78746	512-322-3100	322-3101	792
Texas Gulf Supply Corp 10420 Rockley Rd *Web:* www.texasgulfsupply.com	Houston	TX	77099	281-495-5500		787
Texas Health Presbyterian Hospital Denton 3000 N I-35 *Web:* www.texashealth.org	Denton	TX	76201	940-898-7000		374-3
Texas Health Presbyterian Hospital-WNJ Therapy Services 500 N Highland Ave *TF:* 800-924-8387 ■ *Web:* www.wnj.org	Sherman	TX	75092	903-870-4611	870-4409	374-3
Texas Health Resources 612 E Lamar Blvd Ste 900 *TF:* 877-847-9355 ■ *Web:* www.texashealth.org	Arlington	TX	76011	877-847-9355		353
Texas Healthcare PLLC 2821 Lackland Rd Ste 300 *TF:* 877-238-6200 ■ *Web:* www.txhealthcare.com	Fort Worth	TX	76116	817-378-3640	740-8516	374-3
Texas Heat Treating Inc 155 Texas Ave *TF:* 800-580-5884 ■ *Web:* www.texasheattreating.com	Round Rock	TX	78664	512-255-5884	255-8464	484
Texas Hospital Insurance Exchange 8310 N Capital of Texas Hwy Ste 250 *TF:* 800-792-0060 ■ *Web:* www.thie.com	Austin	TX	78731	512-451-5775	451-3101	391-5
Texas Hydraulics Inc 3410 Range Rd *Web:* www.texashydraulics.com	Temple	TX	76504	254-778-4701	774-9940	223
Texas Industrial Security 101 Summit Ave Ste 404 *TF:* 800-227-1243 ■ *Web:* www.txsecurity.com	Fort Worth	TX	76102	817-335-3046	335-3048	692
Texas Instruments Inc 12500 TI Blvd *NASDAQ: TXN* ■ *TF Cust Svc:* 800-336-5236 ■ *Web:* www.ti.com	Dallas	TX	75243	972-995-3773	927-6377	696
Texas International Theatrical Arts Society (TITAS) 2100 Ross Ave Ste 650 *Web:* www.titas.org	Dallas	TX	75201	214-528-6112		573-1
Texas Jet Management LLC 200 Texas Way Hngr 23n *Web:* www.texasjet.com	Fort Worth	TX	76106	817-624-8438		63
Texas Keystone Inc 560 Epsilon Dr *Web:* www.texaskeystone.com	Pittsburgh	PA	15238	412-928-4956		540
Texas Land & Cattle Steak House 7202 Indiana Ave *Web:* www.txlc.com	Lubbock	TX	79423	806-791-0555		671
Texas Land & Cattle Steak House 9911 W IH- 10 *TF:* 855-685-1622 ■ *Web:* www.txlc.com	San Antonio	TX	78230	210-699-8744		671
Texas Lawyers Insurance Exchange (TLIE) 1801 S MoPac Ste 300 *TF:* 800-252-9332 ■ *Web:* www.tlie.org	Austin	TX	78746	512-480-9074	482-8738	391-5
Texas Legal Services Center Inc 2101 S IH 35 Frontage Rd Ste 1100 *TF:* 888-343-4414 ■ *Web:* www.tlsc.org	Austin	TX	78741	512-477-6000		428
Texas Library Assn 3355 Bee Cave Rd Ste 401 *Web:* www.txla.org	West Lake Hills	TX	78746	512-328-1518		435
Texas Life Insurance Co 900 Washington PO Box 830 **Fax: Sales* ■ *TF:* 800-283-9233 ■ *Web:* www.texaslife.com	Waco	TX	76703	254-752-6521	754-7629*	391-2
Texas Lift-Off Correction Ribbon 1700 Surveyor Blvd Ste 110	Carrollton	TX	75006	972-416-8100		628
Texas Lime Co 15865 Farm Rd 1434 PO Box 851 *TF:* 800-772-8000 ■ *Web:* uslm.com	Cleburne	TX	76033	817-641-4433	556-0905	440
Texas Longhorn Breeders Assn of America (TLBAA) 2315 N Main St Ste 402 *Web:* www.tlbaa.org	Fort Worth	TX	76164	817-625-6241	625-1388	48-2
Texas Lutheran University 1000 W Ct St *TF:* 800-771-8521 ■ *Web:* www.tlu.edu	Seguin	TX	78155	830-372-8050	372-8096	166
Texas Mailhouse Inc 8606 Wall St Ste 1740 *Web:* texasmailhouse.com	Austin	TX	78754	512-837-2046		5
Texas Medical Assn 401 W 15th St *TF:* 800-880-1300 ■ *Web:* www.texmed.org	Austin	TX	78701	512-370-1300	370-1693	474
Texas Memorial Museum 2400 Trinity St *TF:* 800-687-4132 ■ *Web:* www.utexas.edu	Austin	TX	78705	512-471-1604	471-4794	520
Texas Metal Works Inc 13770 Industrial Rd	Houston	TX	77015	713-222-0139		483
Texas Methodist Foundation 11709 Boulder Ln Ste 100 *TF:* 800-933-5502 ■ *Web:* www.tmf-fdn.org	Austin	TX	78726	512-331-9971		305
Texas Military Forces Museum PO Box 5218 *Web:* www.texasmilitaryforcesmuseum.org	Austin	TX	78763	512-782-5659	782-6750	520
Texas Military Institute (TMI) 20955 W Tejas Trail *Web:* www.tmi-sa.org	San Antonio	TX	78257	210-698-7171	698-0715	622
Texas Motor Speedway Inc 3545 Lone Star Cir Sixth Fl *TF:* 800-805-8721 ■ *Web:* www.texasmotorspeedway.com	Fort Worth	TX	76177	817-215-8510		642
Texas Motorplex 7500 W Hwy 287 *TF:* 800-668-6775 ■ *Web:* www.texasmotorplex.com	Ennis	TX	75119	972-878-2641	878-1848	515
Texas Mutual Insurance Co 6210 E Hwy 290 *TF:* 888-532-5246 ■ *Web:* www.texasmutual.com	Austin	TX	78723	512-224-3800	224-3889	391-4
Texas Oil & Chemical Co 7752 FM 418	Silsbee	TX	77656	409-385-1400	385-2453	580
Texas Oil & Gas Association Inc 304 W 13th St *TF:* 800-859-5995 ■ *Web:* www.txoga.org	Austin	TX	78701	512-478-6631		138
Texas Orthopedic Hospital 7401 Main St *TF:* 866-783-4549 ■ *Web:* www.texasorthopedic.com	Houston	TX	77030	713-799-8600	794-3580	374-7
Texas Pacific Land Trust 1700 Pacific Ave Ste 2770 *NYSE: TPL* ■ *Web:* www.tpltrust.com	Dallas	TX	75201	214-969-5530	871-7139	675
Texas Pack Inc 508 Port Rd	Port Isabel	TX	78578	956-943-5461		296-14
Texas Parks and Wildlife Department 4200 Smith School Rd *TF:* 800-792-1112 ■ *Web:* tpwd.texas.gov	Austin	TX	78744	512-389-4800		565
Texas Pharmacy Assn 12007 Research Blvd Ste 201 *TF:* 800-505-5463 ■ *Web:* www.texaspharmacy.org	Austin	TX	78759	512-836-8350	836-0308	585
Texas Pipe & Supply Co Inc 2330 Holmes Rd *TF:* 800-233-8736 ■ *Web:* www.texaspipe.com	Houston	TX	77051	713-799-9235	799-8701	492
Texas Plywood & Lumber Co Inc 1001 E Ave K *TF:* 800-369-8118 ■ *Web:* www.texasplywood.com	Grand Prairie	TX	75050	972-262-1331	642-2225	613
Texas Pneumatics Systems Inc 2404 Superior Dr *TF:* 800-211-9690 ■ *Web:* www.txps.com	Arlington	TX	76013	817-794-0068		20
Texas Presbyterian Foundation 6100 Colwell Blvd Ste 250 *TF:* 800-955-3155 ■ *Web:* www.tpf.org	Irving	TX	75039	214-522-3155	522-3157	48-20
Texas Press Assn 305 S Congress Ave *TF:* 800-749-4793 ■ *Web:* www.texaspress.com	Austin	TX	78704	512-477-6755		7
Texas Process Equipment Co 5215 Ted St *TF:* 800-828-4114 ■ *Web:* www.texasprocess.com	Houston	TX	77040	713-460-5555	460-4807	385
Texas Public Employees Assn 512 E 11th St Ste 100 *Web:* www.tpea.org	Austin	TX	78701	512-476-2691		474
Texas Public Interest Research Group 815 Brazos Ste 600 *Web:* www.texpirg.org	Austin	TX	78701	512-479-7287		633
Texas Public Radio (TPR) 8401 Datapoint Dr Ste 800 *TF:* 800-622-8977 ■ *Web:* www.tpr.org	San Antonio	TX	78229	210-614-8977	614-8983	632
Texas Rangers 1000 Ballpark Way *TF:* 866-800-1275 ■ *Web:* texas.rangers.mlb.com	Arlington	TX	76011	817-273-5222	273-5190	713
Texas Recycling Surplus Inc 2835 Congressman Ln *Web:* www.texasrecycling.com	Dallas	TX	75220	214-357-0262		660
Texas Refinery Corp 840 N Main St *TF:* 800-827-0711 ■ *Web:* www.texasrefinery.com	Fort Worth	TX	76164	817-332-1161		541
Texas Republican Party 1108 Lavaca Ste 500 *TF:* 800-525-5555 ■ *Web:* www.texasgop.org	Austin	TX	78701	512-477-9821	480-0709	616-2
Texas Roadhouse 6707 W Kellogg Dr *Web:* www.texasroadhouse.com	Wichita	KS	67209	316-943-8722		671
Texas Roadhouse 2605 Edgewood Rd SW *Web:* www.texasroadhouse.com	Cedar Rapids	IA	52404	319-396-3300		671
Texas Roadhouse Inc 6040 Dutchmans Ln Ste 400 *NASDAQ: TXRH* ■ *TF:* 800-839-7623 ■ *Web:* www.texasroadhouse.com	Louisville	KY	40205	502-426-9984		670
Texas Scottish Rite Hospital for Children 2222 Welborn St *TF:* 800-421-1121 ■ *Web:* www.tsrhc.org	Dallas	TX	75219	214-559-5000	559-7447	374-1
Texas Shapes 6470 Rupley Cir Ste 1	Houston	TX	77087	713-641-1000		757
Texas Southern University 3100 Cleburne St *TF:* 800-252-5400 ■ *Web:* www.tsu.edu	Houston	TX	77004	713-313-7011	313-1859	166
Texas Sports Hall of Fame 1108 S University Parks Dr *TF:* 800-567-9561 ■ *Web:* www.tshof.org	Waco	TX	76706	254-756-1633		522
Texas Star Bank 177 E Jefferson PO Box 608 *TF:* 866-546-8273 ■ *Web:* www.texasstarbank.com	Van Alstyne	TX	75495	903-482-5234	482-5239	70

Phone | Fax | Class

Texas State Aquarium
2710 N Shoreline Blvd — Corpus Christi TX 78402 — 361-881-1200 — 881-1257 — 40
TF General: 800-477-4853 ■ *Web:* www.texasstateaquarium.org

Texas State Cemetery 909 Navasota St — Austin TX 78702 — 512-463-0605 — 463-8811 — 50-4
Web: www.cemetery.state.tx.us

Texas State Library & Archives Commission
PO Box 12927 — Austin TX 78711 — 512-463-5455 — 434-5
Web: www.tsl.texas.gov

Texas State Railroad State Park
PO Box 39 — Rusk TX 75785 — 903-683-2561 — 565
Web: tpwd.texas.gov

Texas State Technical College (TSTC)
Abilene 650 E Hwy 80 — Abilene TX 79601 — 325-672-7091 — 643-5987 — 162
TF: 800-852-8784 ■ *Web:* www.tstc.edu
Harlingen 1902 N Loop 499 — Harlingen TX 78550 — 956-364-4000 — 364-5117 — 162
TF: 800-852-8784 ■ *Web:* www.tstc.edu
Sweetwater 300 Homer K Taylor Dr — Sweetwater TX 79556 — 325-235-7300 — 235-7443 — 162
TF: 877-450-3595 ■ *Web:* www.tstc.edu
Waco 3801 Campus Dr — Waco TX 76705 — 254-799-3611 — 162
Web: www.waco.tstc.edu

Texas State University
San Marcos 601 University Dr — San Marcos TX 78666 — 512-245-2340 — 245-8044* — 166
**Fax:* Admissions ■ *TF Admissions:* 866-294-0987 ■ *Web:* www.txstate.edu

Texas State University San Marcos
Alkek Library 601 University Dr — San Marcos TX 78666 — 512-245-2133 — 245-3002 — 434-6
Web: www.library.txstate.edu

Texas State University System (TSUS)
208 E Tenth St Ste 600 — Austin TX 78701 — 512-463-1808 — 463-1816 — 786
Web: www.tsus.edu

Texas Station Gambling Hall & Hotel
2101 Texas Star Ln — North Las Vegas NV 89032 — 702-631-1000 — 133
TF Resv: 800-654-8888 ■ *Web:* texasstation.sclv.com

Texas Steakhouse
711 Sutters Creek Blvd — Rocky Mount NC 27804 — 252-443-3888 — 671
Web: www.texassteakhouse.com

Texas Steel Conversion Inc
3101 Holmes Rd — Houston TX 77051 — 713-733-6013 — 595
Web: www.texassteelconversion.com

Texas Steel Processing Inc
5480 Windfern Rd — Houston TX 77041 — 281-822-3200 — 492
Web: www.txstl.com

Texas Stress Inc 1304 Underwood Rd — La Porte TX 77571 — 281-930-0897 — 930-0992 — 484
Web: www.texasstress.com

Texas Tech University PO Box 45005 — Lubbock TX 79409 — 806-742-1480 — 742-0062* — 166
**Fax:* Admissions ■ *TF:* 888-270-3369 ■ *Web:* www.ttu.edu

Texas Tech University Health Sciences Ctr
Preston Smith Library of the Health Sciences
3601 Fourth St MS 7781 — Lubbock TX 79430 — 806-743-2200 — 743-2218 — 434-1
Web: www.ttuhsc.edu
School of Medicine
3601 Fourth St MS 6207 — Lubbock TX 79430 — 806-743-3000 — 743-3021 — 167-2
Web: www.ttuhsc.edu

Texas Tech University Libraries
18th & Boston Ave PO Box 40002 — Lubbock TX 79409 — 806-742-2265 — 742-0737 — 434-6
TF: 888-270-3369 ■ *Web:* library.ttu.edu

Texas Tech University Press
2903 Fourth St — Lubbock TX 79409 — 806-742-2982 — 742-2979 — 637-4
TF: 800-832-4042 ■ *Web:* ttupress.org

Texas Tech University School of Law
1802 Hartford Ave — Lubbock TX 79409 — 806-742-3990 — 742-1629 — 167-1
Web: www.law.ttu.edu

Texas Tech University System
124 Admin Bldg PO Box 42013 — Lubbock TX 79409 — 806-742-0012 — 742-8050 — 786
Web: www.texastech.edu

Texas Timberjack Inc 6004 S First St — Lufkin TX 75901 — 936-634-3365 — 639-3673 — 274
Web: www.texastimberjack.com

Texas Transeastern Inc
3438 Pasadena Blvd — Pasadena TX 77503 — 281-604-3100 — 780
Web: www.texastranseastern.com

Texas Transplant Institute
7700 Floyd Curl Dr — San Antonio TX 78229 — 210-575-3817 — 769
TF: 800-298-7824 ■
Web: sahealth.com/locations/texas-transplant-institute

Texas Transportation Museum
11731 Wetmore Rd — San Antonio TX 78247 — 210-490-3554 — 520
TF: 800-450-2920 ■ *Web:* www.txtransportationmuseum.org

Texas Travel Industry Association
3345 Bee Cave Rd Ste 102A — Austin, TX 78746 — 512-328-8842 — 772
TF: 800-442-7275 ■ *Web:* www.ttla.org

Texas Troubadour Theatre
2416 Music Valley Dr — Nashville TN 37214 — 615-889-2474 — 572
TF: 800-594-8499 ■ *Web:* etrecordshop.com

Texas United Corp 4800 San Felipe — Houston TX 77056 — 713-877-2600 — 877-2664 — 143
TF: 800-554-8658 ■ *Web:* www.unitedsalt.com

Texas United Pipe Inc
11627 N Houston Rosslyn Rd — Houston TX 77086 — 281-448-3276 — 448-6983 — 596
TF Sales: 800-966-8741 ■ *Web:* www.texasunitedpipe.com

Texas Vet Lab Inc 1702 N Bell St — San Angelo TX 76903 — 800-284-8403 — 584
TF: 800-284-8403 ■ *Web:* www.texasvetlab.com

Texas Veterinary Medical Assn
8104 Exchange Dr — Austin TX 78754 — 512-452-4224 — 452-6633 — 795
TF: 800-711-0023 ■ *Web:* www.tvma.org

Texas Visiting Nurse Service Ltd
814 E Tyler — Harlingen TX 78550 — 956-412-1401 — 363
Web: tvnsltd.com

Texas Wesleyan University
1201 Wesleyan St — Fort Worth TX 76105 — 817-531-4444 — 166
TF: 800-580-8980 ■ *Web:* txwes.edu

Texas Wesleyan University School of Law
1515 Commerce St — Fort Worth TX 76102 — 817-212-4000 — 212-4141* — 167-1
**Fax:* Admissions ■ *TF:* 800-733-9529 ■ *Web:* law.tamu.edu

Texas West Bar-B-Que
1600 Fulton Ave — Sacramento CA 95825 — 916-483-7427 — 671
Web: www.texaswestbbq.com

Texas Woman's University
304 Admin Dr PO Box 425589 — Denton TX 76204 — 940-898-3188 — 898-3081* — 166
**Fax:* Admissions ■ *TF:* 866-809-6130 ■ *Web:* www.twu.edu

Phone | Fax | Class

Texas Women Ventures
3625 N Hall St Ste 615 — Dallas TX 75219 — 214-444-7890 — 390
Web: www.texaswomenventures.com

Texas Zoo 110 Memorial Dr — Victoria TX 77901 — 361-573-7681 — 576-1094 — 823
Web: www.texaszoo.org

Texas-New Mexico Power Co (TNMP)
577 N Garden Ridge Blvd — Lewisville TX 75067 — 972-420-4189 — 787
TF: 888-866-7456 ■ *Web:* www.tnmp.com

TEXbase Inc
895 Technology Blvd Ste 202 — Bozeman MT 59718 — 406-582-8874 — 177
Web: www.texbase.com

Texelerate LLC
2119 Delancey St Ste 400 — Philadelphia PA 19102 — 215-275-8492 — 463
Web: www.texelerate.net

Texenergy 2611 E Pioneer Dr — Irving TX 75061 — 972-579-2000 — 317
TF: 800-561-3357 ■ *Web:* www.tempoair.com

Texford Battery Co 2002 Milby St — Houston TX 77003 — 713-222-0125 — 711
TF: 866-301-0125 ■ *Web:* www.texford.com

TexLoc Ltd 4700 Lone Star Blvd — Fort Worth TX 76106 — 817-625-5081 — 640
TF: 800-423-6551 ■ *Web:* www.texloc.com

Texmark Chemicals Inc
900 Clinton Dr — Galena Park TX 77547 — 713-455-1206 — 455-8959 — 144
Web: texmark.com

Texollini Inc
2575 E El Presidio St — Long Beach CA 90810 — 310-537-3400 — 745-6
Web: www.texollini.com

Texoma Medical Ctr 5016 S US Hwy 75 — Denison TX 75020 — 903-416-4000 — 374-3
TF: 800-256-0943 ■ *Web:* www.texomamedicalcenter.net

Texoma Regional Blood Ctr
3911 N Texoma Pkwy — Sherman TX 75090 — 903-893-4314 — 893-8628 — 89
Web: texomablood.org

Texon USA Inc 1190 Huntington Rd — Russell MA 01071 — 413-862-3652 — 605-2
Web: www.texon.com

Texor Petroleum Company Inc
3340 S Harlem Ave — Riverside IL 60546 — 708-447-1999 — 579
TF: 800-352-0050 ■ *Web:* www.texor.com

Texpack Inc 1001 Brickell Bay Dr — Miami FL 33131 — 305-358-9696 — 554
Web: www.texpack.com

TexPar Energy LLC
920 Tenth Ave North — Onalaska WI 54650 — 608-779-6580 — 779-6880 — 581
Web: www.texpar.com

Texstars Inc 802 Avenue J E — Grand Prairie TX 75050 — 972-647-1366 — 596
Web: www.texstars.com

Text 100 North America
100 Montgomery St — San Francisco CA 94104 — 415-593-8400 — 636
Web: www.text100.com

Text My Market Inc 350 N 500 W — Lehi UT 84045 — 801-836-1123 — 812-8124 — 195
Web: www.textmymarket.info

Textainer Equipment Management Ltd
650 California St Fl 16 — San Francisco CA 94108 — 415-434-0551 — 434-0599 — 198
Web: www.textainer.com

Textbook Brokers Inc 911 Rochester Rd — Sparta MO 65753 — 417-485-3440 — 95
Web: www.k12savings.com

Tex-Tech Industries Inc
1 City Ctr 11th Fl — Portland ME 04101 — 207-933-4404 — 745-3
TF: 800-441-7089 ■ *Web:* www.textechindustries.com

Textile Care Services Inc
225 Wood Lake Dr SE — Rochester MN 55904 — 800-422-0945 — 442
TF: 800-422-0945 ■ *Web:* www.textilecs.com

Textile Management Systems Inc
10 TimberLn Dr — Hammond LA 70403 — 985-345-9590 — 258
Web: www.rmaster.com

Textile Printing Co
6107 Ringgold Rd — Chattanooga TN 37412 — 423-894-1110 — 548
Web: www.tpcpackaging.com

Textile Rental Services Assn (TRSA)
1800 Diagonal Rd Ste 200 — Alexandria VA 22314 — 703-519-0029 — 519-0026 — 49-4
TF: 877-770-9274 ■ *Web:* www.trsa.org

Textile Rubber & Chemical Co Inc
1300 Tiarco Dr SW — Dalton GA 30721 — 706-277-1300 — 277-3738 — 605-3
TF: 800-727-8453 ■ *Web:* www.trcc.com

Textron Financial Corp
40 Westminster St — Providence RI 02903 — 401-621-4200 — 216
Web: www.textronfinancial.com

Textron Fluid & Power Inc
40 Westminster St — Providence RI 02903 — 401-421-2800 — 641
Web: www.textron.com

Textron Systems Corp 201 Lowell St — Wilmington MA 01887 — 978-657-5111 — 807
Web: textron.com

Tex-Trude Lp 2001 Sheldon Rd — Channelview TX 77530 — 281-452-5961 — 596
Web: www.tex-trude.com

Tex-Tube Co 1503 N Post Oak Rd — Houston TX 77055 — 713-686-4351 — 681-5256 — 490
TF: 800-839-7473 ■ *Web:* www.tex-tube.com

Textured Coatings Of America
2422 E 15th St — Panama City FL 32405 — 850-769-0347 — 913-8619 — 550
TF: 800-454-0340 ■ *Web:* www.texcote.com

TextureMedia Inc 6604 N Lamar Blvd — Austin TX 78752 — 512-371-7545 — 224
Web: www.naturallycurly.com

Texwood Industries Inc
515 Big Stone Gap Rd — Duncanville TX 75137 — 972-298-4975 — 115
Web: www.qualitycabinets.com

Tezel & Cotter Air Conditioning Co
2730 Castroville Rd — San Antonio TX 78237 — 210-734-5156 — 610
Web: www.tezelandcotter.com

Tezzaron Semiconductor Corp
1415 Bond St Ste 111 — Naperville IL 60563 — 630-505-0404 — 505-9292 — 696
Web: tezzaron.com

TF Financial Corp 3 Penns Trail — Newtown PA 18940 — 215-579-4000 — 360-2
NASDAQ: THRD

TF Hudgins Inc 4405 Directors Row — Houston TX 77092 — 713-682-3651 — 385
TF: 800-582-3834 ■ *Web:* www.tfhudgins.com

TF Kinnealey & Company Inc
1100 Pearl St — Brockton MA 02301 — 508-638-7700 — 296-26
Web: www.kinnealey.com

TF System The Vertical ICF Inc
3030c Holmgren Way — Green Bay WI 54304 — 920-983-9960 — 697
TF: 800-360-4634 ■ *Web:* tfsystem.com

Name / Address	City	State	Zip	Phone	Fax	Class
TFB (Fauquier Bank, The)						
10 Courthouse Sq.	Warrenton	VA	20186	540-347-2700		70
TF: 800-638-3798 ■ *Web:* www.tfb.bank						
TFC (Franchise Co, The)						
5399 Eglinton Ave W Ste 110	Etobicoke	ON	M9C5K9	416-620-3960	620-3961	463
TF: 800-294-5591 ■ *Web:* www.thefranchisecompany.com						
TFC USA						
2001 Junipero Serra Blvd Ste 200	Daly City	CA	94014	650-508-6000		740
TF: 800-345-2465 ■ *Web:* www.tfc-usa.com						
TFC.NET Corp 15211 Lake Maurine Dr	Odessa	FL	33556	813-880-0909		180
Web: www.tfc.net						
TFCU (Teachers Federal Credit Union)						
2410 N Ocean Ave	Farmingville	NY	11738	631-698-7000		219
TF: 800-341-4333 ■ *Web:* www.teachersfcu.org						
TFI (Technology Futures Inc)						
13740 Research Blvd (N Hwy 183) Ste C-1	Austin	TX	78750	512-258-8898	258-0087	196
TF: 800-835-3887 ■ *Web:* www.tfi.com						
TFI (Fertilizer Institute, The)						
425 Third St SW Ste 950	Washington	DC	20024	202-962-0490	962-0577	48-2
Web: www.tfi.org						
TFO Tech Company Ltd						
221 State St	Jeffersonville	OH	43128	740-426-6381		483
Tforce Energy Services						
6143 S Willow Ste 320	Greenwood Village	CO	80111	877-234-1444	770-6461*	685
**Fax Area Code:* 303 ■ *TF:* 877-234-1444 ■ *Web:* tforceenergy.com						
TFS Capital LLC						
10 N High St Ste 500	West Chester	PA	19380	888-837-4446		528
TF: 888-837-4446 ■ *Web:* www.tfscapital.com						
TFT (Trees for Tomorrow)						
519 Sheridan St E PO Box 609	Eagle River	WI	54521	715-479-6456	479-2318	49-5
Web: www.treesfortomorrow.com						
TFT Inc 2991 N Osage Dr P.O. Box 445	Tulsa	OK	74127	918-834-2366	834-1553	480
TF: 800-303-7982 ■ *Web:* tulsafintube.com						
TG Construction Inc 139 Nevada St.	El Segundo	CA	90245	310-640-0220	640-2907	188-5
Web: www.tgconst.com						
T&G Constructors Inc						
8623 Commodity Cir	Orlando	FL	32819	407-352-4443	352-0778	186
Web: www.t-and-g.com						
TGA (Gersh Agency, The)						
41 Madison Ave 33rd Fl	New York	NY	10010	212-997-1818		731
TF: 800-908-1302 ■ *Web:* www.gershcomedy.com						
TGap Ventures LLC 7171 Stadium Dr	Kalamazoo	MI	49009	269-217-1999		792
Web: www.tgapventures.com						
TGC 3200 Travis St.	Houston	TX	77006	512-236-8002		463
Web: www.thegoodmancorp.com						
TGC Industries Inc 101 E Pk Blvd Ste 955	Plano	TX	75074	972-881-1099	424-3943	538
NASDAQ: TGE						
TGF (Glaucoma Foundation)						
80 Maiden Ln Ste 700	New York	NY	10038	212-285-0080	651-1888	48-17
Web: www.glaucomafoundation.org						
TGG Accounting						
10188 Telesis Ct Ste 130	San Diego	CA	92121	760-697-1033		734
TF: 800-201-3187 ■ *Web:* www.tgg-accounting.com						
Tgi Direct 5365 Hill 23 Dr	Flint	MI	48507	800-337-2237		5
TF: 800-337-2237 ■ *Web:* www.tgidirect.com						
TGMC (Terrebonne General Medical Ctr)						
8166 Main St	Houma	LA	70360	985-873-4141	873-5306	374-3
TF: 888-850-6270 ■ *Web:* www.tgmc.com						
Tgo Consulting Inc						
140 Renfrew Dr Ste 120	Markham	ON	L3R6B3	905-470-6830		180
TF: 800-943-9211 ■ *Web:* www.tgo.ca						
TGR Industrial Services						
8777 Tallyho Rd Bldg 1	Houston	TX	77061	281-487-8800		743
Web: www.tulsagammaray.com						
TGV Partners						
23 Corporate Plaza Ste 215	Newport Beach	CA	92660	949-284-1114		528
TGW-Ermanco Inc						
6870 Grand Haven Rd.	Spring Lake	MI	49456	231-798-4547	798-8322	207
Web: www.tgw-group.com						
TH Eckhart House 810 Main St.	Wheeling	WV	26003	304-232-5439		50-3
Web: www.eckharthouse.com						
T-H Marine Supplies Inc						
200 Finney Dr.	Huntsville	AL	35824	256-772-0164		601
Web: www.thmarine.com						
TH Martin Inc 8500 Brookpark Rd.	Cleveland	OH	44129	216-741-2020		697
TF: 800-776-7181 ■ *Web:* www.thmartin.net						
TH Properties 345 Main St	Harleysville	PA	19438	215-513-4270	511-3202	187
TF Sales: 800-225-5847 ■ *Web:* www.thproperties.com						
TH Stone Memorial Saint Joseph Peninsula State Park						
8899 Cape San Blas Rd	Port Saint Joe	FL	32456	850-227-1327	227-1488	565
Web: www.floridastateparks.org						
Thacher School 5025 Thacher Rd.	Ojai	CA	93023	805-640-3210	640-1033	622
Web: www.thacher.org						
Thackeray Partners						
5207 McKinney Ave Ste 200	Dallas	TX	75205	214-360-7830		655
Web: www.thackeraypartners.com						
Thaddeus Stevens College of Technology (TSCT)						
750 E King St	Lancaster	PA	17602	717-299-7701	391-6929	800
TF: 800-842-3832 ■ *Web:* stevenscollege.edu						
THAI 4029 Campbell Ave	Arlington	VA	22206	703-931-3203		671
Web: www.thaiinshirlington.com						
Thai Airways International Cargo						
6501 W Imperial Hwy	Los Angeles	CA	90045	310-670-8591		12
Web: www.thaicargo.com						
Thai Airways International Ltd						
2321 Rosecrans Ave Ste 1280	El Segundo	CA	90245	800-767-3598		25
TF: 800-767-3598						
Thai Arroy 1019 Light St	Baltimore	MD	21230	410-385-8587		671
Web: www.thaiarroy.com						
Thai Chili 2169 Briarcliff Rd NE	Atlanta	GA	30329	404-315-6750		671
Web: www.thaichilicuisine.com						
Thai Cuisine at Thames 517 Thames St	Newport	RI	02840	401-841-8822		671
Web: thaicuisinemenu.com						
Thai Flavor 2863 Erie Blvd E	Syracuse	NY	13224	315-251-1366		671
Web: syracusethaiflavor.com						
Thai Flavors 1254 E 14th St.	Des Moines	IA	50316	515-262-4658		671
Web: www.thaiflavorsiowa.com						
Thai Garden Restaurant Inc						
800 Wellman Ave NE	Huntsville	AL	35801	256-534-0122	564-7341	671
Web: www.facebook.com/ILoveThaiGarden						
Thai House 412 Fifth Ave	Fairbanks	AK	99701	907-452-6123		671
Web: thaihousefairbanks.com						
Thai House 1069 E Shaw Ave.	Fresno	CA	93710	559-221-7245		671
Web: 1jn.com						
Thai House 2117 E Colonial Dr	Orlando	FL	32803	407-898-0820	898-1375	671
Web: www.thaihouseoforlando.net						
Thai House Restaurant 1405 Old Sq Rd	Jackson	MS	39211	601-982-9991		671
Thai Kitchen 4550 Concord Ave	Baton Rouge	LA	70808	225-346-1230		671
Web: www.thaikitchenla.com						
Thai Landing 1207 N Charles St	Baltimore	MD	21201	410-727-1234		671
Web: www.thailandingmd.com						
Thai Lemon Grass Restaurant						
506 S Van Dorn St	Alexandria	VA	22304	703-751-4627		671
Thai Little Home						
3214 E Fourth Plain Blvd	Vancouver	WA	98661	360-693-4061		671
Web: thailittletogo.com						
Thai Me Up 75 E Pearl St	Jackson	WY	83001	307-733-0005		671
Web: www.thaijh.com						
Thai Nakorn 11951 Beach Blvd	Stanton	CA	90680	714-799-2031		671
Web: www.thainakornonline.com						
Thai on the Beach						
901 N Ft Lauderdale Beach Blvd	Fort Lauderdale	FL	33304	954-565-0015		671
Thai Orchid 213 W 11th St.	Vancouver	WA	98660	360-695-7786		671
Web: www.thaiorchidvancouver.com						
Thai Orchid 4223 Providence Rd	Charlotte	NC	28211	704-364-1134		671
Web: thaiorchidrestaurantcharlotte.com						
Thai Orchid 10075 SW Barbur Blvd	Portland	OR	97219	503-452-2544		671
Web: www.thaiorchidrestaurant.com						
Thai Place 4130 Pennsylvania Ave	Kansas City	MO	64111	816-753-8424		671
Web: www.kcthaiplace.com						
Thai Place Restaurant						
5528 Walnut St.	Pittsburgh	PA	15232	412-687-8586		671
Web: www.thaiplacepgh.com						
Thai Ruby 744 East 820 North	Provo	UT	84606	801-375-6840		671
Web: thairubyfood.com						
Thai Sa-On 351 Tenth Ave SW	Calgary	AB	T2R0A5	403-264-3526	264-3526	671
Web: www.thai-sa-on.com						
Thai Siam 1435 S State St	Salt Lake City	UT	84115	801-474-3322		671
Web: www.thaisiam.com/#section1						
Thai Smile						
100 S Indian Canyon Dr	Palm Springs	CA	92262	760-320-5503	320-5584	671
Web: thaismilepalmsprings.com						
Thai Spice						
1514 E Commercial Blvd	Fort Lauderdale	FL	33334	954-771-4535		671
Web: www.thaispicefla.com						
Thai Spice 2933 N 108th St	Omaha	NE	68164	402-492-8808		671
Web: www.thaispice.com						
Thai Spice 4433 W Flamingo Rd	Las Vegas	NV	89103	702-362-5308		671
Thai Spice 523 N Water St	Corpus Christi	TX	78401	361-883-8884		671
Web: www.thaispice.com						
Thai Taste 1178 Kenny Centre Mall	Columbus	OH	43220	614-451-7605		671
Thai Terrace 2055 N Dale Mabry Hwy	Tampa	FL	33607	813-877-8955	980-0444	671
Web: thaiterrace.net						
Thai Thai 6019 50th St	Lubbock	TX	79414	806-791-0024		671
Thai9 11 Brown St	Dayton	OH	45402	937-222-3227		671
Web: www.thai9restaurant.com						
Consulate General						
611 N Larchmont Blvd 2nd Fl	Los Angeles	CA	90004	323-962-9574	962-2128	257
Web: www.thaiconsulatela.org						
Embassy 1024 Wisconsin Ave NW	Washington	DC	20007	202-944-3600	944-3611	257
TF: 800-333-4636 ■ *Web:* www.thaiembdc.org						
Thailand						
Embassy & Consulates 351 E 52nd St.	New York	NY	10022	212-754-1770	688-3029	784
Web: www.thaiembassy.com						
Thaiphoon 1301 S Joy St.	Arlington	VA	22202	703-413-8200		671
Web: www.thaiphoon.com						
Thales ATM 23501 W 84th St.	Shawnee	KS	66227	913-422-2600	422-2917	529
TF: 800-624-7497 ■ *Web:* www.thalesgroup.com						
Thales Communications Inc						
22605 Gateway Ctr Dr.	Clarksburg	MD	20871	240-864-7000	864-7920	647
TF: 800-258-4420 ■ *Web:* www.thalescomminc.com						
Thales e-Security Inc						
2200 N Commerce Pkwy Ste 200	Weston	FL	33326	954-888-6200	888-6211	178-12
TF: 888-744-4976 ■ *Web:* www.thales-esecurity.com						
Thales USA Inc						
2733 S Crystal Dr Ste 1200	Arlington	VA	22202	703-838-9685	838-1688	529
Web: www.thalesgroup.com						
Thalheimer Bros Inc						
5550 Whitaker Ave	Philadelphia	PA	19124	215-537-5200	533-3993	686
TF: 800-757-5211 ■ *Web:* www.thalheimerbrothers.com						
Thalhimer Inc Morton G						
11100 W Broad St	Glen Allen	VA	23060	804-648-5881	697-3479	652
Web: www.thalhimer.com						
Thalia 828 Eigth Ave	New York	NY	10019	212-399-4444	399-3268	671
Web: www.restaurantthalia.com						
Thalia Mara Hall 255 E Pascagoula St	Jackson	MS	39201	601-960-1537		572
Thames & Kosmos LLC						
301 Friendship St	Providence	RI	02903	401-459-6787		520
TF: 800-587-2872 ■ *Web:* www.thamesandkosmos.com						
Thankful Baptist Church						
1608 W Allegheny Ave	Philadelphia	PA	19132	215-229-5024		48-20
Tharo Systems Inc						
2866 Nationwide Pkwy	Brunswick	OH	44212	330-273-4408		174
TF: 800-878-6833 ■ *Web:* www.tharo.com						
Tharrington Smith LLP						
150 Fayetteville St Wells Fargo Bldg						
Ste 1800	Raleigh	NC	27601	919-821-4711		445
Web: www.tharringtonsmith.com						
That Bookstore in Blytheville						
316 W Main St	Blytheville	AR	72315	870-763-3333		95
Web: thatbookstoreinblytheville.com						
Thaumaturgix Inc 2 W 45th St Ste 1408	New York	NY	10036	212-918-5000		180
Web: www.tgix.com						

Name / Address	City	State	ZIP	Phone	Fax	Class
Thayer County 225 N Fourth St Rm 201 Rm 201 *Web:* www.thayercounty.ne.gov	Hebron	NE	68370	402-768-6116	768-6128	338
Thayer Distribution Services 333 Swedesboro Ave *Web:* www.thayerdist.com	Gibbstown	NJ	08027	856-687-0000	224-7129	297-3
Thayer Hotel 674 Thayer Rd *TF:* 800-247-5047 ■ *Web:* www.thethayerhotel.com	West Point	NY	10996	845-446-4731	446-0338	379
Thayer Lodging Group 1997 Annapolis Exchange # 550 *Web:* www.thayerlodging.com	Annapolis	MD	21401	410-268-0515		654
Thayer Media Inc 9000 E Nichols Ave Ste 202 *Web:* www.thayermedia.com	Centennial	CO	80112	303-221-2221		4
Thayer Public Library 798 Washington St *Web:* www.thayerpubliclibrary.org	Braintree	MA	02184	781-848-0405	356-5447	434-3
Thayer Scale Corp 91 Schoosett St *Fax: Cust Svc ■ *TF:* 855-784-2937 ■ *Web:* www.thayerscale.com	Pembroke	MA	02359	781-826-8101	826-0072*	684
Thayer Symphony Orchestra 14 Monument Sq # 406 *Web:* www.thayersymphony.org	Leominster	MA	01453	978-466-1800	840-1000	573-3
Thayers Natural Pharmaceuticals Inc PO Box 56 *Fax Area Code: 203 ■ *TF:* 888-842-9371 ■ *Web:* www.thayers.com	Westport	CT	06881	888-842-9371	227-8183*	799
TheAcademy.com 10223 McAllister Fwy Ste 104	San Antonio	TX	78216	210-530-2700		685
Theater of the Stars 2970 Clairmont Rd NE	Atlanta	GA	30355	404-252-8960	252-1460	573-4
Theaterwork PO Box 842 *Web:* theaterwork.org	Santa Fe	NM	87504	505-471-1799		573-4
TheaterWorks 233 Pearl St *Web:* www.theaterworkshartford.org	Hartford	CT	06103	860-527-7838		572
Theatre Arlington 305 W Main St *Web:* www.theatrearlington.org	Arlington	TX	76010	817-275-7661		573-4
Theatre Cedar Rapids 102 Third St SE *Web:* www.theatrecr.org	Cedar Rapids	IA	52401	319-366-8592		573-4
Theatre Charlotte 501 Queens Rd *Web:* www.theatrecharlotte.org	Charlotte	NC	28207	704-376-3777		573-4
Theatre Development Fund 1501 Broadway 21st Fl *TF:* 888-424-4685 ■ *Web:* www.tdf.org	New York	NY	10036	212-221-0885	768-1563	750
Theatre For A New Audience 154 Christopher St Ste 3D *TF:* 866-811-4111 ■ *Web:* www.tfana.org	New York	NY	10014	212-229-2819	229-2911	749
Theatre Harrisburg 513 Hurlock St *TF:* 800-732-0999 ■ *Web:* www.theatreharrisburg.com	Harrisburg	PA	17110	717-232-5501		573-4
Theatre Historical Society of America 152 N York St 2nd Fl *Web:* www.historictheatres.org	Elmhurst	IL	60126	630-782-1800		138
Theatre in the Park 107 Pullen Rd *Web:* www.theatreinthepark.com	Raleigh	NC	27607	919-831-6936	831-9475	572
Theatre Memphis 630 Perkins Ext *Web:* www.theatrememphis.org	Memphis	TN	38117	901-682-8323		572
Theatre of Youth (TOY) 203 Allen St *Web:* www.theatreofyouth.org	Buffalo	NY	14201	716-884-4400		573-4
Theatre Projects Consultants Inc 47 Water St *Web:* www.theatreprojects.com	South Norwalk	CT	06854	203-299-0830		186
Theatre Tallahassee (TLT) 1861 Thomasville Rd *Web:* theatretallahassee.org	Tallahassee	FL	32303	850-224-4597		572
Theatre Three 2800 Routh St Ste 168 *Web:* www.theatre3dallas.com	Dallas	TX	75201	214-871-3300		572
Theatre Tulsa 412 N Boston Ave *Web:* www.theatretulsa.org	Tulsa	OK	74103	918-587-8402		573-4
Theatre Tuscaloosa 9500 Old Greensboro Rd Ste 135 *Web:* www.theatretusc.com	Tuscaloosa	AL	35405	205-391-2277	391-2329	573-4
Theatre Under the Stars 800 Bagby St Ste 200 *Web:* www.tuts.com	Houston	TX	77002	713-558-2600	558-2650	573-4
TheatreWorks 350 Twin Dolphin Dr *Web:* www.theatreworks.org	Redwood City	CA	94065	650-463-1950	463-1963	573-4
Theda Care at Home 3000 E College Ave *TF:* 800-984-5554 ■ *Web:* www.thedacare.org	Appleton	WI	54915	920-969-0919	969-0020	371
Theda Clark Medical Ctr 130 Second St *TF:* 800-236-3122 ■ *Web:* www.thedacare.org	Neenah	WI	54956	920-729-3100		374-3
Theis Distributing Co 17984 Red Iron *Web:* www.theisco.com	Schertz	TX	78154	210-651-4403		237
Theis Precision Steel Corp 300 Broad St *Web:* www.theis-usa.com	Bristol	CT	06010	860-585-6610		484
thelab LLC 637 W 27th St 8th Fl *TF:* 800-922-5522 ■ *Web:* www.thelabnyc.com	New York	NY	10001	212-209-1333		5
Thelen Assoc Inc 1398 Cox Ave *Web:* www.thelenassoc.com	Erlanger	KY	41018	859-746-9400		261
TheMART 222 Merchandise Mart Plaza Ste 470 *TF:* 800-677-6278 ■ *Web:* www.themart.com	Chicago	IL	60654	800-677-6278		205
Themis Computer 47200 Bayside Pkwy *Web:* www.themis.com	Fremont	CA	94538	510-252-0870		173-8
Themlsonline Com Inc 11150 Commerce Dr N *TF:* 866-657-6654 ■ *Web:* www.themlsonline.com	Champlin	MN	55316	763-576-8286		652
Theodore Presser Co 588 N Gulph Rd *TF:* 800-854-6764 ■ *Web:* www.presser.com	King of Prussia	PA	19406	610-592-1222	592-1229	637-7
Theodore Roosevelt Birthplace National Historic Site 28 E 20th St *TF:* 800-944-8639 ■ *Web:* www.nps.gov/thrb	New York	NY	10003	212-260-1616		564
Theodore Roosevelt Inaugural National Historic Site 641 Delaware Ave *Web:* www.nps.gov/thri	Buffalo	NY	14202	716-884-0095	884-0330	520
Theodore Roosevelt Island Park c/o Turkey Run Pk George Washington Memorial Pkwy *Web:* www.nps.gov/this	McLean	VA	22101	703-289-2500	289-2598	564
Theodore Roosevelt National Park 315 Second Ave PO Box 7 *Web:* www.nps.gov/thro	Medora	ND	58645	701-623-4466	623-4840	564
Theodore's Booze Blues & BBQ 201 Worthington St *Web:* theodoresbbq.com	Springfield	MA	01103	413-736-6000		671
Theodoro Baking Company Inc 6038 N Lindbergh Blvd	Hazelwood	MO	63042	314-731-3777		345
Theprinters.com 3500 E College Ave *TF:* 800-359-2097 ■ *Web:* www.theprinters.com	State College	PA	16801	814-237-7600		344
TheraCare 116 W 32nd St 8th Fl *TF:* 800-505-7000 ■ *Web:* www.theracare.com	New York	NY	10001	212-564-2350	564-5896	353
Theracrine Inc 1 Memorial Dr 7th Fl	Cambridge	MA	02142	617-218-1605		231
Theraderm and Therapon Skin Health Inc 2081 Dime Dr *Web:* theraderm.net	Springdale	AR	72764	479-751-7345		77
Theragenics Corp 5203 Bristol Industrial Way *NYSE:* TGX ■ *TF:* 800-538-9844 ■ *Web:* www.theragenics.com	Buford	GA	30518	770-271-0233	831-5294	231
Theralase Technologies Inc 1945 Queen St E *Web:* www.theralase.com	Toronto	ON	M4L1H7	416-699-5273		250
Therapedic International 103 College Rd E 2nd Fl *TF:* 800-314-4433 ■ *Web:* www.therapedic.com	Princeton	NJ	08540	609-720-0700	720-0797	471
Therapeutic Communities of America (TCA) 1601 Connecticut Ave NW Rm 574 *TF:* 800-729-6686 ■ *Web:* www.treatmentcommunitiesofamerica.org	Washington	DC	20006	202-296-3503		49-8
Therapeutic Monitoring Services LLC 134 LaSalle St Ste 4 *Web:* www.tmsbioscience.com	New Orleans	LA	70112	504-208-9696		743
Therapeutic Solutions International Inc 4093 Oceanside Blvd Ste B *Web:* www.therapeuticsolutionsint.com	Oceanside	CA	92056	760-295-7208		228
Therapeutics Inc 9025 Balboa Ave Ste 100 *Web:* www.therapeuticsinc.com	San Diego	CA	92123	858-571-1800		668
Therapy Edge 2505 Meridian Pkwy Ste 350	Durham	NC	27713	919-572-6709		525
Therapy Support Inc 2803 N Oak Grove Ave *TF:* 877-885-4325 ■ *Web:* www.therapysupport.com	Springfield	MO	65803	877-885-4325		475
Therapydia Inc 18 E Blithedale Ave Ste 21 *Web:* www.therapydia.com	Mill Valley	CA	94941	415-389-8677	389-8695	387
Theratechnologies Inc 2015 Peel St 5th Fl *TSE:* TH ■ *Web:* www.theratech.com	Montreal	QC	H3A1T8	514-336-7800		85
TheraTest Laboratories Inc 1120 Dupage Ave *TF:* 800-441-0771 ■ *Web:* theratest.com	Lombard	IL	60148	800-441-0771		476
TheraTogs Inc 305 Society Dr Ste 3-C *TF:* 800-946-8194 ■ *Web:* www.theratogs.com	Telluride	CO	81435	970-728-7078		194
Theravance Inc 901 Gateway Blvd *NASDAQ:* THRX ■ *Web:* www.theravance.com	South San Francisco	CA	94080	650-808-6000		85
TheraVida Inc 177 Bovet Rd Ste 600 *Web:* www.theravida.com	San Mateo	CA	94402	650-638-2335		231
There & Back Again Travel 35 E Broad St *TF:* 800-782-8222 ■ *Web:* www.thereandbackagain.com	Savannah	GA	31401	912-920-8222		772
TheRedPin 5 Church St *Web:* www.theredpin.com	Toronto	ON	M5E1M2	416-800-0812		652
Theriault's PO Box 151 *TF:* 800-966-3655 ■ *Web:* www.theriaults.com	Annapolis	MD	21404	410-224-3655	224-2515	51
Theriot Charles C CPA 306 Grinage St *Web:* theriotaccountingfirm.com	Houma	LA	70360	985-872-9036		2
Therm Air Sales Corp 1413 41st Stn *TF:* 800-726-7520 ■ *Web:* www.thermairsales.com	Fargo	ND	58102	701-282-9500		612
Therma Foam Inc 8910 Oak Grove Rd *Web:* www.thermafoam.com	Fort Worth	TX	76140	817-624-7204		601
Thermacor Process LP 1670 Hicks Field Rd E *Web:* www.thermacor.com	Fort Worth	TX	76179	817-847-7300	847-7222	595
Thermacore Inc 780 Eden Rd *Web:* www.thermacore.com	Lancaster	PA	17601	717-569-6551		60
Thermafiber Inc 3711 W Mill St *TF:* 888-834-2371 ■ *Web:* www.thermafiber.com	Wabash	IN	46992	260-563-2111	563-7022	389
Therma-Flite Inc 849 Jackson St *Web:* www.therma-flite.com	Benicia	CA	94510	707-747-5949		14
Thermal Care Inc 5680 W Jarvis Ave *TF:* 888-828-7387 ■ *Web:* www.thermalcare.com	Niles	IL	60714	847-966-2260	966-9358	14
Thermal Circuits Inc 1 Technology Way *TF:* 800-808-4328 ■ *Web:* www.thermalcircuits.com	Salem	MA	01970	978-745-1162	741-3420	318
Thermal Corp 1264 Slaughter Rd *TF:* 800-633-2962 ■ *Web:* www.thermalcorporation.com	Madison	AL	35758	256-837-1122		612
Thermal Dynamics 82 Benning St *TF:* 800-752-7621 ■ *Web:* victortechnologies.com	West Lebanon	NH	03784	603-298-5711	298-0558	455
Thermal Engineering Corp 2741 The Blvd *TF:* 800-331-0097 ■ *Web:* www.tecinfrared.com	Columbia	SC	29209	803-783-0750	783-0756	318
Thermal Engineering International Inc 10375 Slusher Dr *Web:* www.babcockpower.com	Santa Fe Springs	CA	90670	323-726-0641	726-9592	91
Thermal Engineering of Arizona Inc 2250 W Wetmore Rd *TF:* 866-832-7278 ■ *Web:* www.teatucson.com	Tucson	AZ	85705	520-888-4000	888-4457	427
Thermal Equipment Corp 2030 E University Dr *TF:* 800-548-4422 ■ *Web:* www.thermalequipment.com	Rancho Dominguez	CA	90220	310-328-6600	603-9625	318
Thermal Industries Inc 3700 Haney C *TF:* 800-245-1540 ■ *Web:* www.thermalindustries.com	Murrysville	PA	15668	724-733-3880		235

	Phone	Fax	Class
Thermal Mechanical Inc 425 Aldo Ave .... Santa Clara CA 95054 *Web:* www.thermalmech.com	408-988-8744		697
Thermal Plastic Design Inc 1116 E Pine St .... St Croix Falls WI 54024 *Web:* www.tdimolding.com	715-483-1841		608
Thermal Product Solutions 2821 Old Rt 15 .... New Columbia PA 17856 *TF:* 800-586-2473 ■ *Web:* www.thermalproductsolutions.com	570-538-7200	538-7380	420
Thermal Product Solutions 3827 Riverside Rd .... Riverside MI 49084 *TF:* 800-873-4468 ■ *Web:* www.thermalproductsolutions.com	269-849-2700	849-3021	318
Thermal Services Inc 13330 I St .... Omaha NE 68137 *Web:* www.thermalservices.com	402-397-8100		610
Thermal Solutions LLC PO Box 3244 .... Lancaster PA 17604 **Fax Area Code:* 877 ■ *TF:* 800-860-5726 ■ *Web:* www.thermalsolutions.com	717-239-7642	501-5212*	357
Thermal Structures Inc (TSI) 2362 Railroad St .... Corona CA 92880 *Web:* www.thermalstructures.com	951-736-9911	736-1064	483
Thermal Tech 5141 Forsyth Commerce Rd Unit 1 .... Orlando FL 32807 *Web:* tti-fl.com	407-373-0042		261
Thermal Technologies Inc 130 Northpoint Ct .... Blythewood SC 29016 *Web:* www.thermaltechnologies.com/index.html	803-691-8000		190
Thermal Transfer Corp 50 N Linden St .... Duquesne PA 15110 *Web:* www.hamonusa.com	412-460-4004	466-2899	91
Thermal-vac Technology Inc 1221 W Struck Ave .... Orange CA 92867 *Web:* www.thermalvac.com	714-997-2601		484
Thermasolutions Inc 1889 Buerkle Rd .... White Bear Lake MN 55110 *TF:* 800-638-2041 ■ *Web:* www.thermasolutions.com	651-209-3900		476
Thermasource LLC 3883 Airway Dr Ste 340 .... Santa Rosa CA 95403 *Web:* thermasource.com	707-523-2960		261
Therma-Stor LLC 4201 Lien Rd .... Madison WI 53704 *TF:* 800-533-7533 ■ *Web:* www.thermastor.com	608-237-8400		610
Thermatool Corp 31 Commerce St .... East Haven CT 06512 *Web:* www.thermatool.com	203-468-4100		811
Therma-Tru Corp 1750 Indian Wood Cir .... Maumee OH 43537 *TF:* 800-537-8827 ■ *Web:* www.thermatru.com	419-891-7400	891-7411	234
Thermcraft Inc 3950 Overdale Rd .... Winston-Salem NC 27107 *Web:* www.thermcraftinc.com	336-784-4800	784-0634	318
Thermedx LLC 31200 Solon Rd Unit 1 .... Solon OH 44139 *TF:* 888-542-9276 ■ *Web:* www.thermedx.com	440-542-0883	542-0920	475
Thermionics Laboratory 1842 Sabre St .... Hayward CA 94545 *TF:* 800-962-2310 ■ *Web:* www.thermionics.com	510-538-3304		172
Thermo Craft Engineering Company Inc 701 Western Ave .... Lynn MA 01905 *Web:* www.thermocraftengineering.com	781-599-4023		811
Thermo Design Engineering Ltd 1424 - 70th Ave .... Edmonton AB T6P1P5 *TF:* 800-661-3987 ■ *Web:* www.thermodesign.com	780-440-6064		261
Thermo Fisher Scientific 8365 Valley Pike .... Middletown VA 22645 *TF:* 800-528-0494 ■ *Web:* www.thermofisher.com	800-556-2323		231
Thermo Fisher Scientific Inc 3747 N Meridian Rd .... Rockford IL 61101 *TF:* 800-874-3723 ■ *Web:* www.thermofisher.com	815-968-0747	968-7316	231
Thermo Fisher Scientific Inc 10010 Mesa Rim Rd .... San Diego CA 92121 *NYSE: TMO* ■ *TF:* 800-488-4399 ■ *Web:* www.thermofisher.com	858-450-9811	546-1734	472
Thermo Fisher Scientific Inc 81 Wyman St .... Waltham MA 02454 *NYSE: TMO* ■ *TF:* 800-678-5599 ■ *Web:* www.thermofisher.com	781-622-1000	622-1207	472
Thermo Fluids Inc 4301 W Jefferson St .... Phoenix AZ 85043 *TF:* 800-350-7565 ■ *Web:* www.thermofluids.com	602-272-2400		686
Thermo King Corp 314 W 90th St .... Minneapolis MN 55420 *Web:* www.thermoking.com	952-887-2200	887-2615	14
Thermo King of Houston LP 772 McCarty St .... Houston TX 77029 *Web:* www.tkofhouston.net	713-671-2700		665
Thermo Probe Inc 112-A Jetport Dr .... Pearl MS 39208 *Web:* www.thermoprobe.net	601-939-1831		201
Thermo Scientific 12076 Santa Fe Dr PO Box 14428 .... Lenexa KS 66215 **Fax Area Code:* 800 ■ *TF:* 800-255-6730 ■ *Web:* www.remel.com	913-888-0939	621-8251*	231
Thermo Vac Inc 201 W Oakwood Rd .... Oxford MI 48371 *Web:* www.thermovac.com	248-969-0300		492
Thermoanalytics Inc 23440 Airpark Blvd .... Calumet MI 49913 *Web:* www.thermoanalytics.com	906-482-9560		177
Thermoclad Co 361 W 11th St .... Erie PA 16501 *Web:* www.protechpowder.com	814-456-1243		605-2
Thermocouple Technology Inc 350 New St .... Quakertown PA 18951 *Web:* www.tteconline.com	215-529-9394		201
Thermodyn Corp 3550 Silica Rd .... Sylvania OH 43560 *TF:* 800-654-6518 ■ *Web:* www.thermodyn.com	419-841-7782	841-3139	677
Thermodynetics Inc 651 Day Hill Rd .... Windsor CT 06095 *OTC: TDYT* ■ *Web:* www.thermodynetics.com	860-683-2005	285-0139	91
ThermoElectric Cooling America Corp 4048 W Schubert Ave .... Chicago IL 60639 *TF:* 888-832-2872 ■ *Web:* www.thermoelectric.com	773-342-4900	342-0191	14
Thermo-Fab Corp 76 Walker Rd .... Shirley MA 01464 *TF:* 888-494-9777 ■ *Web:* www.thermofab.com	978-425-2311	425-2305	602
Thermoflow Inc 2 Willow St Ste 100 .... Southborough MA 01745 *Web:* www.thermoflow.com	978-579-7999		177
ThermoGenesis Corp 2711 Citrus Rd .... Rancho Cordova CA 95742 *NASDAQ: KOOL* ■ *TF:* 800-783-8357 ■ *Web:* cescatherapeutics.com	916-858-5100	858-5199	420
Thermold Corp 7059 Harp Rd .... Canastota NY 13032 *Web:* www.thermold.com	315-697-3924		596
Thermon Manufacturing Co 100 Thermon Dr .... San Marcos TX 78666 *Web:* www.thermon.com	512-396-5801		815
Thermopatch Corp 2204 Erie Blvd E .... Syracuse NY 13224 *TF:* 800-252-6555 ■ *Web:* www.thermopatch.biz/us/en	315-446-8110		744
Thermoplastic Processes Inc 1268 Valley Rd .... Stirling NJ 07980 *TF:* 888-554-6400 ■ *Web:* www.thermoplasticprocesses.com	908-561-3000	753-6749	600
Thermos Co 475 N Martingale Rd Ste 1100 .... Schaumburg IL 60173 *TF:* 800-243-0745 ■ *Web:* www.thermos.com	847-439-7821	593-5570	607
ThermoSafe Brands 3930 N Ventura Dr Ste 450 .... Arlington Heights IL 60004 *TF:* 800-323-7442 ■ *Web:* www.thermosafe.com	847-398-0110	398-0653	601
Thermoseal 2350 Campbell Rd .... Sidney OH 45365 *TF:* 800-990-7325 ■ *Web:* www.thermosealinc.com	937-498-2222		326
Thermoseal Glass Corp 400 Water St .... Gloucester City NJ 08030 *TF:* 800-456-7788 ■ *Web:* www.thermoseal.com	856-456-3109	456-0989	329
ThermoServ 3901 Pipestone Rd .... Dallas TX 75212 *TF:* 800-635-5559 ■ *Web:* www.thermoserv.com	214-631-0307	631-0566	601
Thermosoft International Corp 701 corporate Woods Pkwy .... Vernon Hills IL 60061 *TF:* 800-308-8057 ■ *Web:* www.thermosoft.com	847-279-3800		317
ThermoSpas Hot Tubs 10 Research Pkwy Ste 300 .... Wallingford CT 06492 **Fax Area Code:* 203 ■ *TF:* 800-876-0158 ■ *Web:* www.thermospas.com	800-876-0158	303-0029*	375
Thermotech Co 1302 S Fifth St .... Hopkins MN 55343 *Web:* www.thermotech.com	952-933-9400		604
Thermo-tech Plastics Ltd 2299 Drew Rd .... Mississauga ON L5S1A3 *Web:* thermotechplastics.com	905-678-9448		608
Thermotron Industries Co 291 Kollen Pk Dr .... Holland MI 49423 *TF:* 800-409-3449 ■ *Web:* www.thermotron.com	616-393-4580	392-5643	386
Thermo-Twin Industries Inc 1155 Allegheny Ave .... Oakmont PA 15139 *TF:* 800-641-2211 ■ *Web:* www.thermotwin.com	412-826-1000		234
Thermtrol Corp 8914 Pleasantwood Ave NW .... North Canton OH 44720 *Web:* www.thermtrol.com	330-497-4148		039
Thermwell Products Co 420 Rt 17 S .... Mahwah NJ 07430 *TF:* 800-526-5265 ■ *Web:* www.frostking.com	201-684-4400	684-1214	389
Thermwood Corp 904 Buffaloville Rd .... Dale IN 47523 *OTC: TOOD* ■ *TF Mktg:* 800-533-6901 ■ *Web:* www.thermwood.com	812-937-4476	937-2956	821
Thern Inc 5712 Industrial Pk Rd PO Box 347 .... Winona MN 55987 *TF:* 800-843-7648 ■ *Web:* thern.com	507-454-2996	454-5282	470
Theron Pharmaceuticals Inc 365 San Aleso Ave .... Sunnyvale CA 94085 *Web:* www.theronpharma.com	408-792-7424		231
TherOx Inc 17500 Cartwright Rd Ste 100 .... Irvine CA 92614 *TF:* 800-284-3769 ■ *Web:* www.therox.com	949-757-1999		476
Thor-Rx Corp 1 Corporate Woods Dr .... Bridgeton MO 63044 *Web:* lumarahealth.com	314-646-3700		231
Thescore Inc 500 King St W 4th Fl .... Toronto ON M5V1L9 *Web:* mobile.thescore.com	416-479-8812		224
TheStreet.com Inc 14 Wall St 15th Fl .... New York NY 10005 *NASDAQ: TST* ■ *TF:* 800-562-9571 ■ *Web:* www.thestreet.com	212-321-5000	321-5016	404
Theta Delta Chi Inc 214 Lewis Wharf .... Boston MA 02110 *TF:* 800-999-1847 ■ *Web:* www.thetadeltachi.net	617-742-8886		48-16
Theta Phi Alpha Fraternity Inc 27025 Knickerbocker Rd .... Bay Village OH 44140 *Web:* www.thetaphialpha.org	440-899-9282	899-9293	48-16
Theta Tau Professional Engineering Fraternity 1011 San Jacinto Ste 205 .... Austin TX 78701 *TF:* 800-264-1904 ■ *Web:* www.thetatau.org	512-472-1904	472-4820	48-16
Thetford Corp 7101 Jackson Ave PO Box 1285 .... Ann Arbor MI 40106 *TF:* 800-521-3032 ■ *Web:* www.thetford.com	734-769-6000	709-2023	610
Thetford Corp Recreational Vehicle Group 2901 E Bristol St Ste B .... Elkhart IN 46514 *TF:* 800-831-1076 ■ *Web:* www.rvbusiness.com	574-266-7980	266-7984	610
Thetford Hill State Park 622 Academy Rd .... Thetford VT 05074 *Web:* www.vtstateparks.com	802-785-2266		565
Thetubestore Inc 120 Lancing Dr .... Hamilton ON L8W3A1 *TF:* 877-570-0979 ■ *Web:* www.thetubestore.com	905-570-0979		317
THF Realty Inc 2127 Innerbelt Business Ctr Dr Ste 200 .... St Louis MO 63114 *Web:* www.thfrealty.com	314-429-0900		652
THG (Hotel Group, The) 110 James St Ste 102 .... Edmonds WA 98020 *Web:* www.thehotelgroup.com	425-771-1788	672-8280	379
Thiara Bros Orchards 1205 Kibby Rd .... Merced CA 95340	209-383-6126		315-3
Thibaut Inc 480 Frelinghuysen Ave .... Newark NJ 07114 *TF:* 800-223-0704 ■ *Web:* www.thibautdesign.com	973-643-1118	643-3050	802
Thibodaux Chamber of Commerce 318 E Bayou Rd PO Box 467 .... Thibodaux LA 70302 *Web:* thibodauxchamber.com	985-446-1187	446-1191	139
Thibodaux Regional Medical Ctr (TRMC) 602 N Acadia Rd .... Thibodaux LA 70301 *TF:* 800-822-8442 ■ *Web:* thibodaux.com	985-447-5500	446-5033	374-3
Thief River Falls Convention & Visitors Bureau (TRFCVB) 102 Main Ave N .... Thief River MN 56701 *TF:* 800-657-3700 ■ *Web:* www.visittrf.org	218-686-9785		206
Thiel College 75 College Ave .... Greenville PA 16125 **Fax:* Admissions ■ *TF:* 800-248-4435 ■ *Web:* www.thiel.edu	724-589-2000	589-2013*	166
Thiel Tool & Engineering Company Inc 4622 Bulwer Ave PO Box 470007 .... Saint Louis MO 63147 *TF:* 800-862-4145 ■ *Web:* www.thieltool.com	314-241-6121	241-7857	489
Thiele Kaolin Co 520 Kaolin Rd .... Sandersville GA 31082 *Web:* www.thielekaolin.com	478-552-3951		503-2
Thiele Technologies 315 27th Ave NE .... Minneapolis MN 55418 *TF:* 800-932-3647 ■ *Web:* www.thieletech.com	612-782-1200	782-1203	547
Thielsch Engineering Inc 195 Frances Ave .... Cranston RI 02910 *Web:* thielsch.com	401-467-6454		261
Thielsen Gallery 1038 Adelaide St N .... London ON N5Y2M9 *Web:* www.thielsengallery.com	519-434-7681		42

	City	State	ZIP	Phone	Fax	Class
Thieman Tailgates Inc 600 E Wayne St	Celina	OH	45822	419-586-7727		54
TF: 800-524-5210 ■ *Web:* www.thieman.com						
Thierica Inc 900 Clancy Ave NE	Grand Rapids	MI	49503	616-458-1538		247
Web: www.thierica.com						
Thiessen Team USA Inc 1840 Sharps Access Rd	Elko	NV	89801	775-777-1205		182
Thill Logistics Inc 355 Byrd Ave	Neenah	WI	54956	920-967-8000		311
Web: www.thilllogistics.com						
Thillens Inc 4242 N Elston Ave	Chicago	IL	60618	773-539-4444		400
TF: 888-539-4446 ■ *Web:* www.thillens.com						
Thin Client Computing 34522 N Scottsdale Rd	Scottsdale	AZ	85266	602-432-8649		180
Web: www.thinclient.net						
Thin Film Technology Inc 1980 Commerce Dr	North Mankato	MN	56003	507-625-8445		696
Web: www.thin-film.com						
Thin Multimedia Inc 809 B Cuesta Dr Ste 2184	Mountain View	CA	94040	408-433-9425		396
Think Big Analytics 2055 Laurelwood Rd Ste 210	Santa Clara	CA	95054	650-949-2350		631
Web: thinkbig.teradata.com						
Think Big Solutions LLC 4995 Monaco St	Commerce	CO	80022	303-286-7200		344
Web: thinkbigsolutions.com						
Think Computer Corp 3260 Hillview Ave	Palo Alto	CA	94304	415-670-9350		174
TF: 888-815-8599 ■ *Web:* www.thinkcomputer.com						
Think Cp Technologies 16812 Hale Ave	Irvine	CA	92606	949-833-3222		173-8
TF: 800-726-2477 ■ *Web:* www.thinkcp.com						
Think Reliability 2225 County Rd 90	Pearland	TX	77584	281-412-7766		195
Web: www.thinkreliability.com						
Think Resources Inc 225 Scientific Dr	Norcross	GA	30092	770-390-9888		193
Web: www.thinkresources.com						
Think Systems Inc 7006 Golden Ring Rd	Baltimore	MD	21237	443-725-5131		180
Web: thinksi.com						
Think Tank Studio Inc 1226 Turner St Ste D	Clearwater	FL	33756	727-441-4396		344
Web: thinktankstudio.com						
Think! Creative Advertising Inc 813 W Saint Germain St	Saint Cloud	MN	56301	320-259-9400		7
Web: ithinkcreative.com						
Think-A-Move Ltd 23307 Commerce Pk	Beachwood	OH	44122	216-765-8875		261
TF: 800-521-9072 ■ *Web:* www.think-a-move.com						
ThinkBRQ LLC 20 Hicksville Rd Ste 7	Massapequa	NY	11758	516-541-3100		260
Web: www.thinkbrq.com						
ThinkDirect Marketing Group Inc 8285 Bryan Dairy Rd Ste 150	Largo	FL	33773	727-369-2700		393
TF: 800-325-3155 ■ *Web:* www.tdmg.com						
Thinkdm2 100 Challenger Rd Ste 306	Ridgefield Park	NJ	07660	201-840-8910		7
Web: thinkdm2.com						
ThinkFire Services USA Ltd 1011 Rt 22W Ste 101	Bridgewater	NJ	08807	908-991-9000		809
Web: www.thinkfire.com						
Thinkfun Inc 1321 Cameron St	Alexandria	VA	22314	703-549-4999		761
TF: 800-468-1864 ■ *Web:* www.thinkfun.com						
Thinkgeo LLC 1617 Saint Andrews Dr	Lawrence	KS	66047	785-727-4133		809
Web: thinkgeo.com						
ThinkHR Corp 4457 Willow Rd Ste 120	Pleasanton	CA	94588	925-225-1100		463
Web: www.thinkhr.com						
Thinking Systems Corp 750 94th Ave N Ste 211	Saint Petersburg	FL	33702	727-217-0909		476
Web: www.thinkingsystems.com						
Thinklogic Llc 207 Hindry Ave	Inglewood	CA	90301	310-337-6646		180
Web: www.thinklogic.com						
Thinkmap Inc 599 Broadway 9th Fl	New York	NY	10012	212-285-8600		177
TF: 800-413-9120 ■ *Web:* www.thinkmap.com						
Thinkpath Inc 9080 Springboro Pk Ste 300	Miamisburg	OH	45342	937-291-8374		721
Web: www.thinkpath.com						
THINKstrategies Inc 22 Park Ave	Wellesley	MA	02481	781-223-7421		631
Web: www.thinkstrategies.com						
ThinkTV 110 S Jefferson St	Dayton	OH	45402	937-220-1600	220-1642	632
TF: 800-247-1614 ■ *Web:* www.thinktv.org						
Thinkway Toys Inc 8885 Woodbine Ave	Markham	ON	L3R5G1	905-470-8883		761
TF: 800-535-5754 ■ *Web:* www.thinkwaytoys.com						
Thinkwrap Commerce Inc 450 March Rd Ste 500	Ottawa	ON	K2K3K2	613-751-4441	369-5504	196
Web: www.thinkwrap.com						
Thinky USA 23151 Verdugo Dr	Laguna Hills	CA	92653	949-768-9001		419
Web: www.janustechsales.com						
Third Avenue Funds 622 Third Ave 32nd Fl	New York	NY	10017	212-888-5222		528
Web: thirdave.com						
Third Base Sports Bar & Brewery 500 Blairs Ferry Rd NE	Cedar Rapids	IA	52402	319-378-9090		671
Web: www.3rdbasebrewery.com						
Third Coast Capital Advisors LLC 1 N Franklin St Ste 3200	Chicago	IL	60606	312-332-6484		401
Web: www.thirdcoastca.com						
Third Door Media Inc 279 Newtown Tpke	Redding	CT	06896	203-664-1350		791
Web: www.thirddoormedia.com						
Third Federal Savings & Loan Assn of Cleveland 7007 Broadway Ave	Cleveland	OH	44105	800-844-7333		70
TF: 888-844-7333 ■ *Web:* www.thirdfederal.com						
Third Floor Inc, The 5410 Wilshire Blvd Ste 1000	Los Angeles	CA	90036	323-931-6633		290
Web: www.thethirdfloorinc.com						
Third Millennium Ministries 316 Live Oaks Blvd	Casselberry	FL	32707	407-830-0222		48-20
TF: 877-443-6455 ■ *Web:* www.thirdmill.org						
Third Pillar Systems Inc 577 Airport Blvd 8th Fl	Burlingame	CA	94010	650-372-1200		177
Web: www.thirdpillar.com						
Third Rail Creative 112 E Seventh St	Austin	TX	78701	512-358-9907		7
Web: thirdrailcreative.com						
Third Screen Media Inc 2 Oliver St 4th Fl	Boston	MA	02109	617-531-6400		116
Web: corp.aol.com						
Third Sky Inc 2601 Blanding Ave Ste C362	Alameda	CA	94501	415-272-4262		196
Web: www.thirdsky.com						
Third Ward Caffe 225 E St Paul Ave	Milwaukee	WI	53202	414-224-0895		671
Web: foodspot.com/clients/wi/milwaukee/thirdwardcaffe						
Third Wave Systems Inc 7900 W 78th St Ste 300	Minneapolis	MN	55439	952-832-5515		174
Web: www.thirdwavesys.com						
Thirstystone Resources Inc 1304 Corporate Dr	Gainesville	TX	76240	940-668-6793		292
TF: 800-829-6888 ■ *Web:* www.thirstystone.com						
Thirty-One Gifts 3425 Morse Crossing	Columbus	OH	43219	866-443-8731		366
TF: 866-443-8731 ■ *Web:* www.mythirtyone.com						
This is the Place Heritage Park 2601 E Sunnyside Ave	Salt Lake City	UT	84108	801-582-1847	583-1869	50-3
Web: www.thisistheplace.org						
This Old House Magazine 262 Harbor Dr	Stamford	CT	10020	475-209-8665	209-8665	457-11
Web: www.thisoldhouse.com/toh/magazines						
This Week Community Newspapers 7801 N Central Dr PO Box 608	Lewis Center	OH	43035	740-888-6000	888-6006	637-8
TF: 888-837-4342 ■ *Web:* www.thisweeknews.com						
This Week in Upper Arlington 7801 N Central Dr	Lewis Center	OH	43035	740-888-6100	888-6006	532-4
Web: www.thisweeknews.com						
Thistle Roller Company Inc 209 Van Norman Rd	Montebello	CA	90640	562-948-3705		628
Web: thistleroller.com						
Thistledown Racing Club Inc 21501 Emery Rd	Cleveland	OH	44128	216-662-8600		642
TF: 800-522-4700 ■ *Web:* www.caesars.com						
ThisWeek Community News 7801 N Central Dr	Lewis Center	OH	43035	740-888-6100	888-6006	532-4
TF: 888-837-4342 ■ *Web:* www.thisweeknews.com						
THK America Inc 200 E Commerce Dr	Schaumburg	IL	60173	847-310-1111		639
Web: www.thk.com						
Thk Rhythm North America Co Ltd 549 Vista Dr	Sparta	TN	38583	931-738-2250		247
Web: www.rhythm-na.com						
Thobe Group Inc 2727 Raintree Dr	Carrollton	TX	75006	972-418-1163		195
Thom Browne Inc 100 Hudson St	New York	NY	10013	212-633-1197		157-2
Web: www.thombrowne.com						
Thoma Cressey Bravo Inc 600 Montgomery St 20th Fl	San Francisco	CA	94111	415-263-3660	392-6480	792
Web: www.thomabravo.com						
Thomas & Howard Company Inc 209 Flintlake Rd	Columbia	SC	29223	803-788-5520	699-9097	297-8
Thomas & Mack Ctr/Sam Boyd Stadium 4505 S Maryland Pkwy PO Box 450003	Las Vegas	NV	89154	702-895-3761		720
Web: thomasandmack.com						
Thomas & Marker Construction Co 2084 US 68 S PO Box 250	Bellefontaine	OH	43311	937-599-2160		186
Web: www.thomasmarker.com						
Thomas & Skinner Inc 1120 E 23rd St	Indianapolis	IN	46205	317-923-2501	923-5919	458
Web: www.thomas-skinner.com						
Thomas A Lirot CPA PSC 551 State St	Radcliff	KY	40160	270-351-1540		2
Web: lirotcpa.com						
Thomas Aquinas College 10000 Ojai Rd	Santa Paula	CA	93060	805-525-4417	525-9342	166
TF: 800-634-9797 ■ *Web:* www.thomasaquinas.edu						
Thomas Assoc Inc 1300 Sumner Ave	Cleveland	OH	44115	216-241-7333		47
Web: www.thomasamc.com						
Thomas B Finan Ctr 10102 Country Club Rd	Cumberland	MD	21502	301-777-2405		374-5
Web: msa.maryland.gov						
Thomas Bennett & Hunter Inc 70 John St	Westminster	MD	21157	410-848-9030	876-0733	182
Web: www.tbhconcrete.com						
Thomas Boyd Communications 117 N Church St	Moorestown	NJ	08057	856-642-6226		636
Web: thomasboyd.com						
Thomas Branigan Memorial Library 200 E Picacho Ave	Las Cruces	NM	88001	575-528-4000	528-4030	434-3
Web: www.las-cruces.org						
Thomas Built Buses Inc 1408 Courtesy Rd	High Point	NC	27260	336-889-4871	881-6509	516
Web: thomasbuiltbuses.com						
Thomas C Jones CPA 105 S St	Elkton	MD	21921	410-398-9382		2
Web: tomjonescpa.com						
Thomas C Wilson Inc 21-11 44th Ave	Long Island	NY	11101	718-729-3360	361-2872	759
TF: 800-230-2636 ■ *Web:* www.tcwilson.com						
Thomas Capital Group Inc 4221 Harborview Dr Ste 200	Gig Harbor	WA	98332	253-777-4477		70
Web: www.thomascapital.com						
Thomas Clarence US Supreme Ct Bldg 1 1st St NE	Washington	DC	20543	202-479-3000		341-4
Web: www.supremecourt.gov						
Thomas Cole National Historic Site 218 Spring St	Catskill	NY	12414	518-943-7465	943-0652	564
Web: www.thomascole.org						
Thomas Collective LLC, The 37 W 28th St Fl 12	New York	NY	10001	212-229-2294		636
Web: www.thethomascollective.com						
Thomas College 180 W River Rd	Waterville	ME	04901	207-859-1111	859-1114*	166
**Fax:* Admissions ■ *TF Admissions:* 800-339-7001 ■ *Web:* www.thomas.edu						
Thomas Computer Solutions LLC 7915 Westpark Dr	Mclean	VA	22102	703-839-8700	839-8701	226
Thomas Conveyor Co 555 N Burleson Blvd	Burleson	TX	76028	817-295-7151	447-3840	207
TF: 800-433-2217 ■ *Web:* www.thomasconveyor.com						
Thomas County 300 N Ct	Colby	KS	67701	785-460-4500	460-4503	338
Web: www.thomascountyks.com						

Name / Address	City	State	Zip	Phone	Fax	Class
Thomas County 110 N Crawford St PO Box 920	Thomasville	GA	31799	229-225-4100	226-3430	338
Web: www.thomascountyboc.org						
Thomas County Clerk 503 Main St	Thedford	NE	69166	308-645-2261	645-2623	338
TF: 800-257-3696 ■ *Web:* thomascountynebraska.us						
Thomas County Federal Savings & Loan Assn Inc 131 S Dawson St PO Box 1197	Thomasville	GA	31799	229-226-3221		71
Web: www.tcfederal.com						
Thomas Crane Public Library 40 Washington St	Quincy	MA	02169	617-376-1301		434-3
TF: 800-401-2221 ■ *Web:* www.thomascranelibrary.org						
Thomas Creative Apparel Inc 1 Harmony Pl	New London	OH	44851	419-929-1506	929-0122	155-14
TF: 800-537-2575 ■ *Web:* www.thomasrobes.com						
Thomas Direct Sales Inc 30 Plymouth St	Fairfield	NJ	07004	973-777-6500		8
Web: www.thomasdirect.com						
Thomas E Creek Veterans Affairs Medical Ctr 6010 Amarillo Blvd W	Amarillo	TX	79106	806-355-9703		374-8
TF: 800-687-8262 ■ *Web:* www.amarillo.va.gov						
Thomas E Holter PC 2970 N Swan Rd Ste 219	Tucson	AZ	85712	520-577-8818		2
Thomas E Thevenin CPA PC 30 Wapping Rd	Kingston	MA	02364	781-582-1211		2
Thomas Edison House 729-731 E Washington St	Louisville	KY	40202	502-585-5247		520
Thomas Edison National Historic Site 211 Main St	West Orange	NJ	07052	973-736-0550	736-6567	564
Web: www.nps.gov/edis						
Thomas Edison State College 101 W State St	Trenton	NJ	08608	888-442-8372	984-8447*	166
**Fax Area Code:* 609 ■ **Fax:* Admissions ■ *TF:* 888-442-8372 ■ *Web:* www.tesu.edu						
Thomas Employment 8320 Tyler Blvd	Mentor	OH	44060	440-974-2010		260
TF: 800-527-6174 ■ *Web:* thomasemployment.com						
Thomas Engineering Co 7024 Northland Dr	Minneapolis	MN	55428	763-533-1501	533-8091	489
TF: 800-568-6601 ■ *Web:* www.thomasengineering.com						
Thomas Engineering Inc 575 W Central Rd	Hoffman Estates	IL	60192	847-358-5800	358-5817	386
TF: 800-634-9910 ■ *Web:* www.thomaseng.com						
Thomas Equipment Inc 204 Upper Kent Rd	Upper Kent	NB	E7J2E4	506-278-5695	278-5876	274
Web: www.thomasloaders.com						
Thomas F Moran Inc 48 Constitution Dr	Bedford	NH	03110	603-472-4488		261
Thomas Gammill & Company Ltd 5026 Old Greenwood St	Fort Smith	AR	72903	479-648-1121		2
Web: www.gammillcpa.com						
Thomas George Associates Ltd 10 Larkfield Rd	East Northport	NY	11731	631-261-8800		390
TF: 800-443-8338 ■ *Web:* www.tgaltd.com						
Thomas Graphics Inc 9501 N IH 35	Austin	TX	78753	512-719-3535		687
Web: www.thomasgraphicsinc.com						
Thomas H Lee Partners 100 Federal St	Boston	MA	02110	617-227-1050	227-3514	405
TF: 877-456-3427 ■ *Web:* www.thl.com						
Thomas Hart Benton Home & Studio State Historic Site 3616 Belleview	Kansas City	MO	64111	816-931-5722		565
Web: www.mostateparks.com						
Thomas Henkelmann Restaurant 420 Field Pt Rd	Greenwich	CT	06830	203-869-7500	869-7502	671
TF: 800-903-4045 ■ *Web:* www.homesteadinn.com						
Thomas Hospital 750 Morphy Ave	Fairhope	AL	36532	251-928-2375		374-3
TF: 800-422-2027 ■ *Web:* www.infirmaryhealth.org/hospitals/thomas-hospital						
Thomas Industrial Rolls Inc 8526 Brandt St	Dearborn	MI	48126	313-584-9696		567
Web: www.tirinc.com						
Thomas Instrument & Machine Company Inc 3440 First St	Brookshire	TX	77423	281-375-6300	375-5264	264-3
Web: www.thomasinstrument.com						
Thomas J Dyer Company Inc 5240 Lester Rd	Cincinnati	OH	45213	513-321-8100		256
Web: www.groteenterprises.com						
Thomas J Paul West Inc 1061 Rydal Rd	Rydal	PA	19046	215-886-3220		7
Web: www.thomasjpaul.com						
Thomas Jefferson Ctr for the Protection of Free Expression 400 Worrell Dr	Charlottesville	VA	22911	434-295-4784		48-8
Web: www.tjcenter.org						
Thomas Jefferson Foundation PO Box 316	Charlottesville	VA	22902	434-984-9808		305
Web: www.monticello.org						
Thomas Jefferson National Accelerator Facility 12000 Jefferson Ave	Newport News	VA	23606	757-269-7100	269-7363	668
Web: www.jlab.org						
Thomas Jefferson School 4100 S Lindbergh Blvd	Saint Louis	MO	63127	314-843-4151	843-3527	622
Web: www.tjs.org						
Thomas Jefferson School of Law 1155 Island Ave	San Diego	CA	92101	619-297-9700	961-1382	167-1
TF: 877-318-6901 ■ *Web:* www.tjsl.edu						
Thomas Jefferson University 1020 Walnut St	Philadelphia	PA	19107	215-955-6000	955-5151	166
TF: 800-533-3669 ■ *Web:* www.jefferson.edu						
Thomas Jefferson University Hospital 111 S 11th St	Philadelphia	PA	19107	215-955-6000	955-6464	374-3
TF: 800-533-3669 ■ *Web:* hospitals.jefferson.edu						
Thomas Jefferson University Hospital Blood & Marrow Transplant Unit 125 S Ninth St 2nd Fl	Philadelphia	PA	19107	215-955-6000	955-0412	769
Web: www.jefferson.edu						
Thomas L Cardella & Associates Inc 4515 20th Ave SW	Cedar Rapids	IA	52404	319-393-1511		737
Web: www.tlcassociates.com						
Thomas Lee Printing & Mailing Inc 3721 W 12th St	Erie	PA	16505	814-833-3233		535
Thomas M Cooley Law School 300 S Capitol Ave	Lansing	MI	48933	517-371-5140		167-1
TF: 800-243-2586 ■ *Web:* www.cooley.edu						
Thomas McNerney & Partners 1 Landmark Sq 9th Fl	Stamford	CT	06901	203-978-2010	978-2005	792
Web: www.tm-partners.com						
Thomas Memorial Hospital 4605 MacCorkle Ave SW	South Charleston	WV	25309	304-766-3600		374-3
Web: www.thomaswv.org						
Thomas More College 333 Thomas More Pkwy	Crestview Hills	KY	41017	859-344-3332	344-3444	166
TF: 800-825-4557 ■ *Web:* www.thomasmore.edu						
Thomas More Prep-Marian 1701 Hall St	Hays	KS	67601	785-625-6577	625-3912	622
Web: www.tmp-m.org						
Thomas Nelson Inc 501 Nelson Pl PO Box 141000	Nashville	TN	37214	615-889-9000		637-3
TF: 800-251-4000 ■ *Web:* www.thomasnelson.com						
Thomas P Kennard House PO Box 82554	Lincoln	NE	68501	402-471-4764		50-3
Web: www.nebraskahistory.org						
Thomas Partitions & Specialties Inc 2172 Yucca Ln	Altadena	CA	91001	323-256-8666		610
Thomas Petroleum LLC 9701 US Hwy 59 N	Victoria	TX	77905	361-573-7662		581
Web: www.thomaspetro.com						
Thomas Pheasant Inc 1029 33rd St NW	Washington	DC	20007	202-337-6596		393
Web: www.thomaspheasant.com						
Thomas Produce Co 9905 Clint Moore Rd	Boca Raton	FL	33496	561-482-1111		10-11
Web: www.thomasproduce.com						
Thomas Properties Group Inc 515 S Flower St 6th Fl	Los Angeles	CA	90071	213-613-1900	633-4760	405
NYSE: TPGI						
Thomas Publishing Co 5 Penn Plaza	New York	NY	10001	212-695-0500	290-7362	637-2
TF: 800-733-1127 ■ *Web:* www.thomaspublishing.com						
Thomas Reprographics 600 N Central Expy	Richardson	TX	75080	972-231-7227	231-0623	240
TF: 800-877-3776 ■ *Web:* thomasprintworks.com						
Thomas Restaurant 1815 W 39th St	Kansas City	MO	64111	816-561-3663		671
Thomas Russell LLC 7050 S Yale Ave Ste 210	Tulsa	OK	74136	918-481-5682		261
Web: www.thomasrussellco.com						
Thomas Scientific 1654 High Hill Rd PO Box 99	Swedesboro	NJ	08085	856-467-2000	467-3087	420
TF: 800-345-2100 ■ *Web:* www.thomassci.com						
Thomas Seafood of Carteret Inc 421 Merrimon Rd	Beaufort	NC	28516	252-728-2391		296-14
Thomas Steel Inc 305 Elm St	Bellevue	OH	44811	419-483-7540		480
Web: www.tsifab.com						
Thomas Stone National Historic Site 6655 Rose Hill Rd	Port Tobacco	MD	20677	301-392-1776	934-8793	564
TF: 800-235-4045 ■ *Web:* www.nps.gov						
Thomas Tape Co 1713 Sheridan Ave	Springfield	OH	45505	937-325-6414	325-2850	732
Web: www.thomastape.com						
Thomas Transcription Services Inc PO Box 26613	Jacksonville	FL	32226	904-751-5058	751-5240	478
TF: 800-670-2009 ■ *Web:* www.thomastx.com						
Thomas University 1501 Millpond Rd	Thomasville	GA	31792	229-226-1621		166
TF: 800-538-9784 ■ *Web:* www.thomasu.edu						
Thomas W Daniels & Company PC 1310 Eagle Ridge Dr	Schererville	IN	46375	219-864-7010		2
Web: thomaswdaniels.com						
Thomas Weisel Partners Group LLC 1 Montgomery St	San Francisco	CA	94104	415-364-2500		792
TF: 888-267-3700 ■ *Web:* www.tweisel.com						
Thomas West Inc 470 Mercury Dr	Sunnyvale	CA	94085	408-481-9200		361
Web: www.thomaswest.com						
Thomas Wolfe Memorial 52 N Market St	Asheville	NC	28801	828-253-8304		50-3
Web: www.wolfememorial.com						
Thomas Wood Professionals 202 S St Ste 13	Sausalito	CA	94965	415-944-8754		260
Web: www.thomaswoodpros.com						
Thomas/Euclid Industries Inc 2575 Bethel Ave	Indianapolis	IN	46203	317-783-7194		454
Web: www.thomaseuclid.com						
Thomasarts Inc 240 S 200 W	Farmington	UT	84025	801-451-5365		4
Web: www.thomasarts.com						
Thomas-Hines Co 3027 W Cary St	Richmond	VA	23221	804-355-2782		321
Thomason Hendrix Harvey Johnson & Mitchell Pllc 40 S Main St Ste 2900	Memphis	TN	38103	901-525-8721		445
Web: www.thomason-hendrix.com						
Thomaston Savings Bank 203 Main St PO Box 907	Thomaston	CT	06787	860-283-1874		70
TF General: 855-344-1874 ■ *Web:* www.thomastonsavingsbank.com						
Thomaston-Upson Chamber of Commerce 110 W Main St	Thomaston	GA	30286	706-647-9686		139
Web: www.thomastonchamber.com						
Thomasville Area Chamber of Commerce PO Box 1400	Thomasville	NC	27361	336-475-6134	475-4802	139
Web: www.thomasvillechamber.net						
Thomasville Furniture Industries Inc 401 E Main St PO Box 339	Thomasville	NC	27361	336-472-4000		319-2
TF: 800-225-0265 ■ *Web:* www.thomasville.com						
Thomasville Medical Ctr 207 Old Lexington Rd	Thomasville	NC	27360	336-472-2000		374-3
TF: 888-844-0080 ■ *Web:* novanthealth.org/thomasvillemedicalcenter.aspx						
Thombert Inc 316 E Seventh St N	Newton	IA	50208	800-433-3572	433-3517	608
TF: 800-433-3572 ■ *Web:* www.thombert.com						
Thombley & Simmons PC 78 Cole St Ste 200	Marietta	GA	30060	770-423-1234		2
Thompson & Bowie LLP 3 Canal Plaza	Portland	ME	04112	207-774-2500		428
TF: 800-396-6500 ■ *Web:* thompsonbowie.com						
Thompson & Johnson Equipment Company Inc 6926 Fly Rd	East Syracuse	NY	13057	315-437-2881		358
Web: www.thompsonandjohnson.com						
Thompson & Knight LLP 1700 Pacific Ave Ste 3300	Dallas	TX	75201	214-969-1700	969-1751	428
Web: www.tklaw.com						
Thompson & Litton Inc 103 E Main St	Wise	VA	24293	276-328-2161		261
Web: t-l.com						
Thompson & McMullan 100 Shockoe Slip	Richmond	VA	23219	804-649-7545		428
Web: www.t-mlaw.com						

Name / Address	City	State	ZIP	Phone	Fax	Class
Thompson Aluminum Casting Co 5161 Canal Rd *Web:* www.thompsoncasting.com	Cleveland	OH	44125	216-206-2781		492
Thompson Bennie G (Rep D - MS) 2466 Rayburn Bldg *Web:* benniethompson.house.gov	Washington	DC	20515	202-225-5876	225-5898	342-2
Thompson Brothers (Construction) LP 411 S Ave PO Box 4300 *Web:* www.thompsonbros.com	Spruce Grove	AB	T7X3B5	780-962-1030		188
Thompson Citizen 141 Commercial Pl *TF:* 800-268-2312 ■ *Web:* www.thompsoncitizen.net	Thompson	MB	R8N1T1	204-677-4534	677-3681	532-1
Thompson Coe Cousins & irons 700 N Pearl St 25th Fl *Web:* www.thompsoncoe.com	Dallas	TX	75201	214-871-8200	871-8209	428
Thompson Electric Co (TEC) 2300 Seventh St *Web:* www.thompsonelectriccompany.com	Sioux City	IA	51105	712-252-4221		787
Thompson Engineering Inc 2970 Cottage Hill Rd Ste 190 *Web:* thompsonengineering.com	Mobile	AL	36606	251-666-2443		256
Thompson Falls State Park 2220 Blue Slide Rd *Web:* montanastateparks.reserveamerica.com	Thompson Falls	MT	59873	406-827-3110		565
Thompson Glenn W (Rep R - PA) 124 Cannon HOB *Web:* thompson.house.gov	Washington	DC	20515	202-225-5121	225-5796	342-2
Thompson Greenspon & Company PC 4035 Ridgetop Rd Ste 700 *Web:* www.tgccpa.com	Fairfax	VA	22030	703-385-8888		2
Thompson Hine LLP 127 Public Sq 3900 Key Ctr *TF:* 877-257-3382 ■ *Web:* www.thompsonhine.com	Cleveland	OH	44114	216-566-5500	566-5800	428
Thompson Hospitality 1741 Business Center Dr Ste 200 *Web:* www.thompsonhospitality.com	Herndon	VA	20170	703-964-5500	759-1538	670
Thompson Industrial Services LLC 104 N Main *TF:* 800-849-8040 ■ *Web:* www.thompsonindustrialservices.com	Sumter	SC	29150	803-773-8005		610
Thompson International Inc PO Box 656 *Web:* www.thompsoninternational.com	Henderson	KY	42420	270-826-3751	826-3881	386
Thompson Investment Management Inc 918 Deming Way 3rd Fl *Web:* www.thompsonim.com	Madison	WI	53717	608-827-5700		360-3
Thompson Lexus 50 W Swamp Rd *Web:* www.1800thompson.com	Doylestown	PA	18901	215-345-1110		57
Thompson Mahogany Co 7400 Edmund St *TF:* 877-589-6637 ■ *Web:* www.thompsonmahogany.com	Philadelphia	PA	19136	877-589-6637		683
Thompson Marketing 70 NE Loop 410 Ste 1050 *Web:* www.thompsonmarketinginc.com	San Antonio	TX	78216	239-772-5408		4
Thompson Mike (Rep D - CA) 231 Cannon Bldg *Web:* mikethompson.house.gov	Washington	DC	20515	202-225-3311	225-4335	342-2
Thompson Murray Inc 605 West Lakeview Dr *Web:* wmurraythompson.com	Springdale	AR	72764	479-575-0200	973-9477	195
Thompson Olde Inc 3250 Camino Del Sol *TF:* 800-827-1565 ■ *Web:* www.oldethompson.com	Oxnard	CA	93030	805-983-0388		361
Thompson Packers Inc 550 Carnation St *TF:* 800-989-6328 ■ *Web:* www.thompack.com	Slidell	LA	70460	985-641-6640		473
Thompson Park Zoo 1 Thompson Pk *Web:* www.nyszoo.org	Watertown	NY	13601	315-782-6180	782-6192	823
Thompson Publishing Group Inc 805 15th St NW 3rd Fl *TF Cust Svc:* 800-677-3789 ■ *Web:* www.thompson.com	Washington	DC	20005	202-872-3611		637-9
Thompson Pump & Mfg Company Inc 4620 City Ctr Dr PO Box 291370 *TF:* 800-767-7310 ■ *Web:* www.thompsonpump.com	Port Orange	FL	32129	386-767-7310	761-0362	641
Thompson Realty Corp 2505 N Plano Rd Ste 3000 *Web:* www.thompson-realty.com	Richardson	TX	75082	972-644-2400		187
Thompson Research Group LLC 1033 Demonbreun St Ste 625 *TF:* 800-364-4314 ■ *Web:* www.thompsonresearchgroup.com	Nashville	TN	37203	615-891-6200		401
Thompson Rivers University 900 McGill Rd PO Box 3010 **Fax:* Admissions ■ *TF:* 800-663-1663 ■ *Web:* www.tru.ca	Kamloops	BC	V2C5N3	250-828-5000	371-5960*	785
Thompson Siegel & Walmsley Inc 6806 Paragon Pl Ste 300 *TF:* 800-697-1056 ■ *Web:* www.tswinvest.com	Richmond	VA	23230	804-353-4500	353-0925	401
Thompson Speedway 205 E Thompson Rd PO Box 278 *TF:* 800-435-5000 ■ *Web:* www.thompsonspeedway.com	Thompson	CT	06277	860-923-2280	923-2398	515
Thompson Steel Co 120 Royall St *Web:* www.thompsonsteelco.com	Canton	MA	02021	781-828-8800		723
Thompson Technologies Inc 200 Galleria Pkwy Ste 100 *TF:* 888-794-7947 ■ *Web:* thompsontechnologies.com	Atlanta	GA	30339	770-794-8380	794-8381	721
Thompson Thrift Construction Inc 901 Wabash Ave Ste 300 *Web:* www.thompsonthrift.com	Terre Haute	IN	47807	812-235-5959		186
Thompson's Harbor State Park c/o Cheboygan Field Office 120 S A-St *Web:* www.michigan.gov	Cheboygan	MI	49721	231-627-9011		565
Thompson's Lake Campground - Thacher State Park 68 Thompson's Lake Rd *Web:* www.nysparks.com	East Berne	NY	12059	518-872-1674	872-9133	565
Thompson, Ahern & Company Ltd 6299 Airport Rd Ste 506 *TF:* 877-262-8226 ■ *Web:* www.taco.ca	Mississauga	ON	L4V1N3	905-677-3471	677-3464	311
Thompson, O'Brien, Kemp & Nasuti PC 40 Technology Pkwy S Ste 300 *Web:* www.tokn.com	Norcross	GA	30092	770-925-0111		428
ThompsonBrooks Inc 151 Vermont St Ste 9 *Web:* thompsonbrooks.com	San Francisco	CA	94103	415-581-2600		186
Thoms Proestler Co 8001 TPC Rd *TF:* 800-747-1234 ■ *Web:* www.performancefoodservice.com	Rock Island	IL	61204	309-787-1234	787-1254	297-8
Thomsen Group LLC 1303 43rd St *TF:* 800-558-4018 ■ *Web:* www.lcthomsen.com	Kenosha	WI	53140	800-558-4018		296
Thomson CenterWatch Inc 100 N Washington St Ste 301 *TF Cust Svc:* 800-765-9647 ■ *Web:* www.centerwatch.com	Boston	MA	02114	617-948-5100	948-5101	637-10
Thomson Elite 800 Corporate Pointe Ste 150 *TF Cust Svc:* 800-354-8337 ■ *Web:* www.elite.com	Los Angeles	CA	90230	424-243-2100		178-10
Thomson Financial 22 Thomson Pl *TF:* 888-216-1929 ■ *Web:* www.thomsonreuters.com	Boston	MA	02210	617-856-2000		387
Thomson Plastics Inc 130 Quality Dr NW *Web:* www.thomsonplastics.com	Thomson	GA	30824	706-595-0658		596
Thomson Reuters 3 Times Sq *Web:* www.thomsonreuters.com	New York	NY	10036	646-223-4000		742
Thomson Reuters 7322 Newman Blvd *TF Cust Svc:* 800-968-8900 ■ *Web:* tax.thomsonreuters.com/cs-professional-suite	Dexter	MI	48130	800-968-8900	326-1040	178-1
Thomson Reuters DT Tax and Accounting 3333 Graham Blvd Ste 222 *TF:* 800-663-7829 ■ *Web:* www.drtax.ca	Montreal	QC	H3R3L5	514-733-8355	733-8058	180
Thomson Safaris 14 Mt Auburn St *TF:* 800-235-0289 ■ *Web:* www.thomsonsafaris.com	Watertown	MA	02472	617-923-0426		636
Thomson-Hood Veterans Ctr 100 Veterans Dr *TF:* 800-928-4838 ■ *Web:* thvc.ky.gov/Pages/default.aspx	Wilmore	KY	40390	859-858-2814	858-4039	793
Thomson-Macconnell Cadillac Inc 2820 Gilbert Ave *TF:* 877-472-0738 ■ *Web:* www.thomsonmacconnellcadillac.com	Cincinnati	OH	45206	888-838-1071		516
Thomsons Art Supply Inc 184 Mamaroneck Ave *TF:* 800-287-4885 ■ *Web:* www.thomsonsart.com	White Plains	NY	10601	914-949-4885	949-4978	45
Thomson-Shore Inc 7300 W Joy Rd **Fax Area Code:* 800 ■ *TF:* 800-706-4545 ■ *Web:* www.thomsonshore.com	Dexter	MI	48130	734-426-3939	706-4545*	626
Thor Construction Inc 5400 Main St NE Ste 203 *Web:* www.thorcon.net	Minneapolis	MN	55421	763-571-2580	571-2631	187
Thor Inc 1280 W 2550 S St *Web:* www.thor.com	Ogden	UT	84401	801-393-3312		297-8
Thor Industries Inc 419 W Pike St *NYSE:* THO ■ **Fax Area Code:* 877 ■ *Web:* thorindustries.com	Jackson Center	OH	45334	937-596-6111	596-6111*	120
Thor Systems 2671 Pembroke Rd *Web:* www.thorsystems.net	Hopkinsville	KY	42240	270-890-0500		396
Thor Travel Services Inc 12202 Airport Way Ste 150 *TF:* 800-825-1071 ■ *Web:* www.thortravelservices.com	Broomfield	CO	80021	303-439-4100		772
Thoratec Corp 6035 Stoneridge Dr *NASDAQ:* THOR ■ *TF:* 800-528-2577 ■ *Web:* www.thoratec.com	Pleasanton	CA	94588	925-847-8600	847-8574	250
Thorburn Assoc Inc 20880 Baker Rd *Web:* ta-inc.com	Castro Valley	CA	94546	510-886-7826		261
Thorburn Group, The 811 Glenwood Ave Ste 920 *Web:* thethorburngroup.com	Minneapolis	MN	55405	612-226-3861		5
Thorco Industries Inc 1300 E 12th St *Web:* www.thorco.com	Lamar	MO	64759	417-682-3375	682-1326	233
Thorek Memorial Hospital 850 W Irving Pk Rd *Web:* thorek.org	Chicago	IL	60613	773-525-6780	975-6703	374-3
Thoren Caging Systems Inc 815 W Seventh St *Web:* www.thoren.com	Hazleton	PA	18201	570-455-5041		419
Thorlabs 10335 Guilford Rd *Web:* www.thorlabs.com	Jessup	MD	20794	240-456-7100	456-7200	696
Thor-Lo Inc 2210 Newton Dr *TF:* 888-846-7567 ■ *Web:* www.thorlo.com	Statesville	NC	28677	704-872-6522	838-7010	155-10
Thornapple Kellogg Schools 10051 Green Lake Rd *Web:* www.tkschools.org	Middleville	MI	49333	269-795-3313		685
Thornberry Mac (Rep R - TX) 2208 Rayburn HOB *Web:* thornberry.house.gov	Washington	DC	20515	202-225-3706	225-3486	342-2
Thornburg Center for Prof Dev 711 Beacon Dr *Web:* tcpd.org	Lake Barrington	IL	60010	847-277-7691	277-7697	449
Thornburg Investment Management Funds 2300 N Ridgetop Rd *TF:* 800-533-9337 ■ *Web:* www.thornburg.com/financial-professionals/retirement-plan-advisors	Santa Fe	NM	87506	505-984-0200	984-8973	528
Thorndike Press 10 Water St Ste 310 **Fax:* Sales ■ *TF:* 800-223-1244 ■ *Web:* www.cengage.com	Waterville	ME	04901	800-223-1244	558-4676*	637-2
Thorne Assoc Inc 1450 W Randolph St *TF:* 800-611-2906 ■ *Web:* www.thorneassociates.com	Chicago	IL	60607	312-738-5230	738-5249	189-9
Thorneloe University 935 Ramsey Lake Rd *TF General:* 800-461-4030 ■ *Web:* thorneloe.laurentian.ca	Sudbury	ON	P3E2C6	705-673-1730	673-4979	785
Thornhill Securities Inc 336 S Congress Ave Ste 200 *Web:* www.thornhillsecurities.com	Austin	TX	78704	512-472-7171		690
Thornmark Asset Management Inc 119 Spadina Ave Ste 701 *TF:* 877-204-6201 ■ *Web:* www.thornmark.com	Toronto	ON	M5V2L1	416-204-6200		193
Thornton Fractional South High School 18500 Burnham Ave *TF:* 800-627-3999 ■ *Web:* www.tfd215.org	Lansing	IL	60438	708-585-2000		685
Thornton Laboratories Testing & Inspection Services 1145 E Cass St *Web:* www.thorntonlab.com	Tampa	FL	33602	813-223-9702	223-9332	743
Thornton Oil Corp 10101 Linn Stn Rd Ste 200 *TF:* 800-928-8022 ■ *Web:* www.thorntonsinc.com	Louisville	KY	40223	866-473-0017		324
Thornton Steel Company Inc 2700 W Pafford St *TF:* 800-772-2421 ■ *Web:* www.thorntonsteel.com	Fort Worth	TX	76110	817-926-3324		480
Thornton W Burgess Society 6 Discovery Hill Rd *TF:* 800-844-4542 ■ *Web:* www.thorntonburgess.org	East Sandwich	MA	02537	508-888-6870	888-1919	48-13

Phone | Fax | Class

Thornton-Tomasetti Group Inc (TTINC)
2000 L St NW Ste 600 .... Washington DC 20036 — 202-580-6300 580-6301 261
Web: www.thorntontomasetti.com

Thoro'Bred Inc 5020 E La Palma Ave .... Anaheim CA 92807 — 714-779-2581 420-7040* 483
**Fax Area Code:* 765 ■ *TF:* 877-585-5152 ■ *Web:* www.thorobredinc.com

Thoro-Packaging Inc 1467 Davril Cir .... Corona CA 92880 — 951-278-2100 101
Web: www.thoropackaging.com

Thoroughbred Direct Intermodal Services
5165 Campus Dr Ste 400 .... Plymouth Meeting PA 19462 — 610-567-3360 449
TF: 877-250-2902 ■ *Web:* www.ns-direct.com

Thoroughbred Financial Services LLC
5110 Maryland Way Ste 300 .... Brentwood TN 37027 — 615-371-0001 401
Web: www.thoroughbredfinancial.com

Thoroughbred Ford Inc
I-29 At Barry Rd 8501 N Boardwalk Ave .... Kansas City MO 64154 — 816-505-1818 57
Web: www.thoroughbredford.com

Thoroughbred Owners & Breeders Assn (TOBA)
PO Box 910668 .... Lexington KY 40591 — 859-276-2291 276-2462 48-3
TF: 888-606-8622 ■ *Web:* www.toba.org

Thoroughbred Racing Assn (TRA)
420 Fair Hill Dr Ste 1 .... Elkton MD 21921 — 410-392-9200 48-22
Web: www.tra-online.com

Thoroughbred Software International Inc
285 Davidson Ave Ste 302 .... Somerset NJ 08873 — 732-560-1377 560-1594 178-2
TF: 800-524-0430 ■ *Web:* www.thoroughbredsoftware.com

Thoroughbreds 9706 N Kings Hwy .... Myrtle Beach SC 29572 — 843-497-2636 671
Web: www.thoroughbredsrestaurant.com

Thoroughgood House
1636 Parish Rd .... Virginia Beach VA 23455 — 757-385-5100 50-3
Web: www.museumsvb.org

Thorp & Co
150 Alhambra Cir Ste 900 Coral Gables .... Miami FL 33134 — 305-446-2700 636
Web: www.thorpco.com

Thorp Reed & Armstrong LLP
301 Grant St 14th Fl .... Pittsburgh PA 15219 — 412-394-7711 394-2555 428
TF: 800-949-3120 ■ *Web:* clarkhill.com

Thorpe Electric Supply Co
27 Washington St .... Rensselaer NY 12144 — 518-462-5496 246
Web: www.thorpeelectric.com

Thorpe Heating & Cooling Inc
8402 US Hwy 98 N .... Lakeland FL 33809 — 863-858-2577 189-10
TF: 855-858-2577 ■ *Web:* thorpeac.com

Thorpe, North & Western LLP
8180 S 700 E Ste 350 .... Sandy UT 84070 — 801-566-6633 428
Web: www.tnw.com

Thorrez Industries Inc
4909 W Michigan Ave .... Jackson MI 49201 — 517-750-3160 750-1792 621
TF: 800-208-6075 ■ *Web:* www.thorrez.com

Thorsnes Bartolotta McGuire
2550 Fifth Ave 11th Fl .... San Diego CA 92103 — 619-236-9363 428
TF: 800-577-2922 ■ *Web:* tbmlawyers.com

Thortex Inc 15045 NE Mason St .... Portland OR 97230 — 503-654-5726 484
Web: www.thortexinc.com

Thought Convergence Inc
11300 W Olympic Blvd Ste 900 .... Los Angeles CA 90064 — 310-909-7900 360-3
TF: 800-938-8888 ■ *Web:* www.thoughtconvergence.com

Thought Technology Ltd
2180 Belgrave Ave .... Montreal QC H4A2L8 — 514-489-8251 743
TF: [illegible] ■ *Web:* www.thoughttechnology.com

Thoughtworks Inc
200 E Randolph St 25th Fl .... Chicago IL 60601 — 312-373-1000 373-1001 39
Web: www.thoughtworks.com

Thousand Crane 1000 Elm St .... Manchester NH 03101 — 603-634-0000 671
Web: thousandcranenh.com

Thousand Hills Golf Resort
245 S Wildwood Dr .... Branson MO 65616 — 417-336-5873 337-5740 660
TF: 877-262-0430 ■ *Web:* www.thousandhills.com

Thousand Hills State Park
20431 State Hwy 157 .... Kirksville MO 63501 — 660-665-6995 565
Web: www.mostateparks.com

Thousand Islands National Park of Canada
2 County Rd 5 .... Mallorytown ON K0E1R0 — 613-923-5261 923-1021 563
Web: www.pc.gc.ca

Thousand Oaks Civic Arts Plaza
2100 Thousand Oaks Blvd .... Thousand Oaks CA 91362 — 805-449-2787 572
Web: www.toaks.org/theatre

Thousand Oaks Library
1401 E Janss Rd .... Thousand Oaks CA 91362 — 805-449-2660 373-6858 434-3
Web: www.tol.lib.ca.us

Thousand Pines Christian Camp & Conference Center
359 Thousnd Pines Rd .... Crestline CA 92325 — 909-338-2705 239
TF: 888-423-2267 ■ *Web:* www.thousandpines.com

THQ Inc 29903 Agoura Rd .... Agoura Hills CA 91301 — 818-871-5000 871-7400 178-6
NASDAQ: THQI ■ *Web:* thq.com

Thrall Enterprises Inc
180 N Stetson Ave .... Chicago IL 60601 — 312-621-8200 360-3

Thrasher Printing Inc
814 Hanley Industrial Ct .... Saint Louis MO 63144 — 314-962-7979 627
TF: 800-919-6548 ■ *Web:* www.thrasher-bcm.com

Thread Check Inc 390 Oser Ave .... Hauppauge NY 11788 — 631-231-1515 231-1625 493
TF: 800-767-7633 ■ *Web:* www.threadcheck.com

Thread Logic 16775 Greystone Ln .... Jordan MN 55352 — 800-347-1612 258
TF: 800-347-1612 ■ *Web:* www.threadlogic.com

Threadgill's 6416 N Lamar Blvd .... Austin TX 78752 — 512-451-5440 671
TF: 800-899-9841 ■ *Web:* www.threadgills.com

Threadpoint LLC
24881 Alicia Pkwy Ste E #310 .... Laguna Hills CA 92653 — 866-631-1595 396
TF: 866-631-1595 ■ *Web:* www.threadpoint.com

Threads Magazine
63 S Main St PO Box 5506 .... Newtown CT 06470 — 203-426-8171 457-14
TF General: 866-505-4687 ■ *Web:* www.threadsmagazine.com

Three Bars Cattle & Guest Ranch
9500 Wycliffe Perry Creek Rd .... Cranbrook BC V1C7C7 — 250-426-5230 239
TF: 877-426-5230 ■ *Web:* www.threebarsranch.com

Three Bros 2414 S St Clair St .... Milwaukee WI 53207 — 414-481-7530 671

Three C's Landscaping Inc
32124 Utica Rd .... Fraser MI 48026 — 586-415-4850 776
TF: 800-728-2500 ■ *Web:* www.threecslandscaping.com

Three Chimneys Farm PO Box 114 .... Midway KY 40347 — 859-873-7053 873-5723 368
Web: www.threechimneys.com

Three D Graphics Inc
11340 W Olympic Blvd Ste 352 .... Los Angeles CA 90064 — 310-231-3330 231-3303 178-8
TF: 800-913-0008 ■ *Web:* www.threedgraphics.com

Three D Metals Inc
5462 Innovation Dr .... Valley City OH 44280 — 330-220-0451 492
TF: 800-362-9905 ■ *Web:* www.threedmetals.com

Three Deep Marketing
289 Fifth St E 2nd Fl .... Saint Paul MN 55101 — 651-789-7701 195
TF: 800-335-4254 ■ *Web:* www.threedeepmarketing.com

Three Eagles Communications Co
7600 CR 120 .... Salida CO 81201 — 402-466-1234 643
Web: www.threeeagles.com

Three Hands Corp 13259 Ralston Ave .... Sylmar CA 91342 — 818-833-1200 833-1212 361
TF: 800-443-5443 ■ *Web:* www.threehands.com

Three Island Crossing State Park
1083 S Three Island Park Dr .... Glenns Ferry ID 83623 — 208-366-2394 565
TF: 888-922-6743 ■ *Web:* www.visitidaho.org

Three Lakes Distributing Co
111 Overton St .... Hot Springs AR 71901 — 501-623-8201 81-1

Three Lakes Information Bureau
1704 Superior St PO Box 268 .... Three Lakes WI 54562 — 715-546-3344 206
TF: 800-972-6103 ■ *Web:* www.threelakes.com

Three Leaf Productions
940 Science Blvd Ste C .... Gahanna OH 43230 — 614-626-4941 514
Web: www.three-leaf.com

Three Notch Electric Membership Corp
PO Box 295 .... Donalsonville GA 39845 — 229-524-5377 245
TF: 800-239-5377 ■ *Web:* www.threenotchemc.com

Three of Us Corp 39 W 19th St Fl 12 .... New York NY 10011 — 212-812-4044 162

Three Rivers Community College
2080 Three Rivers Blvd .... Poplar Bluff MO 63901 — 573-840-9600 162
TF: 877-879-8722 ■ *Web:* www.trcc.edu

Three Rivers Community College Mohegan
574 New London Tpke .... Norwich CT 06360 — 860-886-0177 162
Web: www.trcc.commnet.edu

Three Rivers Convention Ctr & Coliseum
7016 W Grandbridge Blvd .... Kennewick WA 99336 — 509-737-3700 205
TF: 800-745-3000 ■ *Web:* www.threeriversconventioncenter.com

Three Rivers Electric Co-op
1324 E Main St PO Box 918 .... Linn MO 65051 — 573-644-9000 245
TF: 800-892-2251 ■ *Web:* www.threeriverselectric.com

Three Rivers Health
701 S Health Pkwy .... Three Rivers MI 49093 — 269-278-1145 374-3
Web: www.threerivershealth.org

Three Rivers Planning & Development District Inc
75 S Main St PO Box 690 .... Pontotoc MS 38863 — 662-489-2415 489-6815 463
TF: 877-489-6911 ■ *Web:* www.trpdd.com

Three Rivers State Park
7908 Three Rivers Pk Rd .... Sneads FL 32460 — 850-482-9006 565
Web: www.floridastateparks.org

Three Ships Media 1122 Oberlin Rd .... Raleigh NC 27605 — 919-360-5173 195
Web: www.three-ships.com

Three Streams Engineering Ltd
Ste 401 1925-18th Ave NE .... Calgary AB T2E7T8 — 403-536-5000 261
Web: www.threestreams.com

Threespot Media LLC
806 Seventh St NW Ste 201 .... Washington DC 20001 — 202-471-1000 177
Web: threespot.com

Threshold Communications Inc
16541 Redmond Way Ste 245C .... Redmond WA 98052 — 206-812-6200 224
TF: 844-844-1382 ■ *Web:* www.thresholdcommunications.com

Threshold Enterprises Ltd
23 Janis Way .... Scotts Valley CA 95066 — 831-438-6851 805
Web: www.thresholdenterprises.com

Threshold Entertainment Inc
1649 11th St .... Santa Monica CA 90404 — 310-452-8899 514
Web: www.thresholdentertainment.com

Threshold Pharmaceuticals Inc
170 Harbor Way Ste 300 .... South San Francisco CA 94080 — 650-474-8200 474-2529 85
NASDAQ: THLD ■ *TF:* 866-276-9886 ■ *Web:* www.thresholdpharm.com

Threshold Placement Services
35 W Pine St, Ste 213 .... Orlando FL 32801 — 407-296-4370 193
Web: www.thresholdplacement.com

THRH (Terre Haute Regional Hospital)
3901 S Seventh St .... Terre Haute IN 47802 — 812-232-0021 865-9738* 374-3
**Fax Area Code:* 877 ■ *TF:* 866-270-2311 ■ *Web:* www.regionalhospital.com

Thrifty Car Rental 5330 E 31st St .... Tulsa OK 74135 — 918-660-7700 126
TF: 888-400-8877 ■ *Web:* www.thrifty.com

Thrifty Office Furniture
1023 S Miami Blvd .... Durham NC 27703 — 919-598-8454 321
Web: www.thriftyofficefurniture.com

Thrifty White Stores
6055 Nathan Lane N Ste 200 .... Plymouth MN 55442 — 763-513-4300 237
TF: 800-642-3275 ■ *Web:* www.thriftywhite.com

Thrive Networks Inc
836 North St Bldg 300 Ste 3201 .... Tewksbury MA 01876 — 978-461-3999 624
TF: 866-205-2810 ■ *Web:* www.thrivenetworks.com

Thrivent Financial for Lutherans
4321 N BallaRd Rd .... Appleton WI 54919 — 920-684-3225 391-2
TF: 800-847-4836 ■ *Web:* www.thrivent.com

ThriveOn Inc 210 S 20th St .... New Ulm MN 56073 — 855-767-2571 196
TF: 855-767-2571 ■ *Web:* www.thriveon.co

Throckmorten Enterprises
17433 Hwy 120 .... Big Oak Flat CA 95305 — 209-962-7308 175
Web: throck.com

Through Smoke Creative Inc
480 Gate 5 Rd Studio 340 .... Sausalito CA 94965 — 415-289-7500 195
Web: www.throughsmoke.com

Thru Tubing Solutions Inc
11515 S Portland .... Oklahoma City OK 73170 — 405-692-1900 539
Web: www.thrutubing.com

ThruPoint Inc
1040 Ave of the Americas .... New York NY 10018 — 646-562-6000 180

Thrush Aircraft Inc
300 Old Pretoria Rd .... Albany GA 31721 — 229-883-1440 439-9790 20
Web: www.thrushaircraft.com

Company / Address	City	State	Zip	Phone	Fax	Class
Thrush Company Inc Je Company Inc						
340 W Eigth St	Peru	IN	46970	765-472-3351		641
Web: www.comteck.com						
Thrustmaster of Texas Inc						
PO Box 840189	Houston	TX	77041	713-937-6295	937-7962	190
Web: thrustmaster.net						
Thruway Fasteners Inc						
2910 Niagara Falls Blvd	North Tonawanda	NY	14120	716-694-1434	694-3865*	351
**Fax:* Sales ■ *Web:* www.thruwayfasteners.com						
Thruway Food Market & Shopping Ctr						
78 Oak St	Walden	NY	12586	845-778-3535		345
TF: 800-511-8220 ■ *Web:* www.shopthruway.com						
THS Constructors						
150 Executive Ctr Dr Ste B108	Greenville	SC	29615	864-254-6066		186
Web: www.thsconstructors.com						
Thule Inc 42 Silvermine Rd	Seymour	CT	06483	203-881-9600		247
Thumann Inc 670 Dell Rd	Carlstadt	NJ	07072	201-935-3636	935-2226	297-9
TF: 800-358-0761 ■ *Web:* www.thumanns.com						
Thumb Cellular Ltd. Partnership						
82 S Main St	Pigeon	MI	48755	989-453-4333		736
TF: 800-443-5057 ■ *Web:* www.thumbcellular.com						
Thumb Correctional Facility						
3225 John Conley Dr	Lapeer	MI	48446	810-667-2045	667-2048	213
TF: 855-444-3911 ■ *Web:* www.michigan.gov						
Thumb Electric Co-op (TEC) 2231 Main St	Ubly	MI	48475	989-658-8571		245
Thumb National Bank & Trust Co						
7254 Michigan Ave	Pigeon	MI	48755	989-453-3113		70
Web: thumbnational.com						
Thumbs-Up Telemarketing Inc						
11861 Westline Industrial Dr Ste 600	Saint Louis	MO	63146	800-410-2016		737
TF: 800-410-2016 ■ *Web:* thumbsupinc.com						
Thunder Airlines Ltd						
310 Hector Dougall Way	Thunder Bay	ON	P7E6M6	800-803-9943		13
TF: 800-803-9943 ■ *Web:* www.thunderair.com						
Thunder Basin Coal Co PO Box 406	Wright	WY	82732	307-939-1300		501
Web: www.archcoal.com						
Thunder Bay Chamber of Commerce						
200 Syndicated Ave S Ste 102	Thunder Bay	ON	P7E1C9	807-624-2626	622-7752	137
Web: www.tbchamber.ca						
Thunder Bay Port Authority						
100 Main St	Thunder Bay	ON	P7B6R9	807-345-6400	345-9058	618
TF: 800-342-8012 ■ *Web:* www.portofthunderbay.com						
Thunder Bay Regional Health Sciences Centre						
980 Olvier Rd	Thunder Bay	ON	P7B6V4	807-684-6000	684-5890	374-2
TF: 800-465-5003 ■ *Web:* tbrhsc.net						
Thunder Canyon Brewery						
7401 N La Cholla Blvd	Tucson	AZ	85741	520-797-2652		671
Web: thundercanyonbrewery.com						
Thunder Tech Inc						
3635 Perkins Ave Studio 5 SW	Cleveland	OH	44114	216-391-2255		7
TF: 888-321-8422 ■ *Web:* www.thundertech.com						
Thunder Valley Casino 1200 Athens Ave	Lincoln	CA	95648	916-408-7777	408-8370	133
TF: 877-468-8777 ■ *Web:* www.thundervalleyresort.com						
Thunderbird Rural Public Transportation System						
2801 W Loop 306 Ste A PO Box 60050	San Angelo	TX	76904	325-944-9666	947-8286	108
TF: 877-947-8729 ■ *Web:* www.cvcog.org/cvcog/trans_rural.html						
Thunderbird School of Global Management						
1 Global Pl	Glendale	AZ	85306	602-978-7000	978-9663	685
TF: 800-848-9084 ■ *Web:* thunderbird.asu.edu						
Thunderbird Supply Co						
1907 W Historic Rt 66	Gallup	NM	87301	505-722-4323	722-6736	411
Web: www.thunderbirdsupply.com						
Thundercloud Subs 1102 W Sixth St	Austin	TX	78703	512-479-8805	479-8806	670
Web: www.thundercloud.com						
Thune John (Sen R - SD)						
511 Dirksen Bldg	Washington	DC	20510	202-224-2321	228-5429	342-2
Web: www.thune.senate.gov						
Thurber House 77 Jefferson Ave	Columbus	OH	43215	614-464-1032	280-3645	520
Web: www.thurberhouse.org						
Thurbers of Richmond Inc						
7324 Port Side Dr	Midlothian	VA	23112	804-639-5770		292
Thurgood Marshall Scholarship Fund						
901 F St NW Ste 300	Washington	DC	20004	202-507-4851	652-2934	725
TF: 866-632-9992 ■ *Web:* tmcf.org						
Thurland Reay Family Investment Co						
2100 N Kolb Rd	Tucson	AZ	85715	520-298-2391		345
Thurman Campbell Group PLC						
324 Franklin St	Clarksville	TN	37040	931-552-7474		734
Web: www.tccpas.com						
Thurman G Smith Elementary School						
3600 Falcon Rd	Springdale	AR	72762	479-750-8846		685
Web: smith.sdale.org						
Thurston County						
2000 Lakeridge Dr SW Bldg 1, Rm 127	Olympia	WA	98502	360-786-5430	753-4033	338
Web: www.co.thurston.wa.us						
Thurston County PO Box 159	Pender	NE	68047	402-385-2343	385-3544	338
TF: 800-368-8683 ■ *Web:* www.thurstoncountynebraska.us						
Thurston Group LLC						
John Hancock Ctr 875 N Michigan Ave Ste 3640	Chicago	IL	60611	312-255-0077		390
Web: www.thurstongroup.com						
Thurston Mfg Company Inc						
14 Thurber Blvd	Smithfield	RI	02917	401-232-9100	232-9101	455
Web: www.thurstonmfg.com						
THV Compozit Windows & Doors						
5611 FERN VALLEY Rd	Louisville	KY	40228	800-476-1966		499
TF: 800-476-1966 ■ *Web:* www.thv.com						
Thwing-Albert Instrument Company Inc						
14 W Collings Ave	West Berlin	NJ	08091	856-767-1000		639
Web: www.thwingalbert.com						
Thybar Corp 913 S Kay Ave	Addison	IL	60101	630-543-5300	543-5309	697
TF: 800-666-2872 ■ *Web:* www.thybar.com						
Thylaksoft Llc						
307 Elizabeth Sweetbriar Ln	New Castle	DE	19720	302-355-0449		809
Web: www.thylaksoft.com						
Thyme on the Creek 1345 28th St	Boulder	CO	80302	303-998-3835	443-1480	671
TF: 866-866-8086 ■ *Web:* www.millenniumhotels.com						
Thynk Design Inc						
1111 Pasquinelli Dr Ste 550	Westmont	IL	60559	800-012-6272		7
TF: 800-012-6272 ■ *Web:* www.thynk.com						
Thyssen Krupp Hearn 59 I- Dr	Wentzville	MO	63385	636-332-1772		194
TF: 877-854-7178 ■ *Web:* www.tkmna.com						
ThyssenKrupp Access Inc						
4001 E 138th St	Grandview	MO	64030	816-763-3100	763-4467	256
Thyssenkrupp Bilstein of America Inc						
8685 Berk Blvd	Hamilton	OH	45015	513-881-7600		247
ThyssenKrupp Crankshaft Company LLC						
1000 Lynch Rd	Danville	IL	61834	217-431-0060	431-8934	483
Web: www.thyssenkrupp-forginggroup.com						
ThyssenKrupp Elevator						
9280 Crestwyn Hills Dr	Memphis	TN	38125	901-261-1800		360-3
TF: 877-230-0303 ■ *Web:* www.thyssenkruppelevator.com						
Thyssenkrupp Krause Inc						
901 Doris Rd	Auburn Hills	MI	48326	248-340-8000		491
ThyssenKrupp Materials NA						
22355 W 11 Mile Rd	Southfield	MI	48033	248-233-5600	233-5600	492
TF: 800-926-2600 ■ *Web:* www.tkmna.com						
Thyssenkrupp Presta						
1597 E Industrial Dr	Terre Haute	IN	47802	217-431-4212		247
Web: www.thyssenkrupp-presta.com/en/unternehmen/terre_haute.php						
Thyssenkrupp Steel North America Inc						
22355 W Eleven Mile Rd	Southfield	MI	48033	248-233-5600		492
Web: www.tkmna.com						
Ti Ba Enterprises Inc 25 Hytec Cir	Rochester	NY	14606	585-247-1212		475
TF: 800-836-8422 ■ *Web:* www.ti-ba.com						
Ti Squared Technologies Inc						
1305 Clark Mill Rd	Sweet Home	OR	97386	541-367-2929		317
Web: tisquaredtech.com						
TIA (Tire Industry Assn)						
1532 Pointer Ridge Pl Ste G	Bowie	MD	20716	301-430-7280	430-7283	49-4
TF: 800-876-8372 ■ *Web:* www.tireindustry.org						
TIA (Telecommunications Industry Assn)						
2500 Wilson Blvd Ste 300	Arlington	VA	22201	703-907-7700	907-7727	49-20
Web: www.tiaonline.org						
TIA (Transportation Intermediaries Assn)						
1625 Prince St Ste 200	Alexandria	VA	22314	703-299-5700	836-0123	49-21
Web: www.tianet.org						
TIAA-CREF 730 Third Ave	New York	NY	10017	212-490-9000	916-6383	391-2
TF: 800-842-2252 ■ *Web:* www.tiaa.org/public/index.html						
TIACA (International Air Cargo Assn)						
5600 NW 36th St Ste 620	Miami	FL	33266	786-265-7011	265-7012	49-21
TF: 800-262-9974 ■ *Web:* www.tiaca.org						
Tiara Yachts Inc 725 E 40th St	Holland	MI	49423	616-392-7163	394-7466	90
Web: www.tiarayachts.com						
TIAW (International Alliance for Women)						
1101 Pennsylvania Ave NW 3rd Fl	Washington	DC	20004	888-712-5200		48-24
TF: 888-712-5200 ■ *Web:* www.tiaw.org						
Tiba Medical Inc						
2701 NW Vaughn St Ste 470	Portland	OR	97210	503-222-1500		475
Web: www.tibamedical.com						
TIBCO Software Inc						
3303 Hillview Ave	Palo Alto	CA	94304	650-846-1000	846-1005	178-1
NASDAQ: TIBX ■ *Web:* www.tibco.com						
TIBCO Software Inc						
1700 Westlake Ave N Ste 500	Seattle	WA	98109	206-283-8802		178-3
TF: 866-247-8182 ■ *Web:* www.tibco.com						
TIBCO Software Inc						
707 State Rd Ste 212	Princeton	NJ	08540	609-683-4002		387
Web: www.tibco.com						
Tiberi Pat (Rep R - OH)						
1203 Longworth HOB	Washington	DC	20515	202-225-5355	226-4523	342-2
Web: tiberi.house.gov						
Tibor de Nagy Gallery						
724 Fifth Ave 12th Fl	New York	NY	10019	212-262-5050	262-1841	42
Web: www.tibordenagy.com						
Tibor Machine Products Inc						
7400 W 100th Pl	Bridgeview	IL	60455	708-499-3700	499-6803	454
Web: www.tibormachine.com						
Tiburon Strategic Advisors LLC						
1735 Tiburon Blvd	Tiburon	CA	94920	415-789-2540		196
Web: www.tiburonadvisors.com						
TICC Capital Corp						
8 Sound Shore Dr Ste 255	Greenwich	CT	06830	203-983-5275		401
Web: www.ticc.com						
Tice Brunell & Baker Cpa Pc						
14 Corporate Woods Blvd	Albany	NY	12211	518-482-1887		2
Web: www.tbbcpas.com						
Tichon Seafood Corp 7 Conway St	New Bedford	MA	02740	508-999-5607	990-8271	296-14
TF: 800-932-7440 ■ *Web:* tichonseafood.com						
Ticket Heaven Inc 440 Knoll St Ste 144	Wheaton	IL	60187	630-260-0626	260-4831	750
Ticket Source Inc						
5516 E Mockingbird Ln Ste 100	Dallas	TX	75206	214-821-9011	821-9060	750
TF: 800-557-6872 ■ *Web:* www.ticketsource.com						
TicketBiscuit LLC						
5120 Cyrus Cir Ste 101	Birmingham	AL	35242	205-757-8330	693-9055*	387
**Fax Area Code:* 866 ■ *TF:* 866-757-8330 ■ *Web:* www.ticketbiscuit.com						
Tickets.com Inc						
555 Anton Blvd 11th Fl	Costa Mesa	CA	92626	714-327-5400	327-5410	750
TF: 800-352-0212 ■ *Web:* www.tickets.com						
TicketWeb Inc PO Box 77250	San Francisco	CA	94103	866-777-8932		750
TF Cust Svc: 866-777-8932 ■ *Web:* www.ticketweb.com						
Tickfaw State Park						
27225 Patterson Rd	Springfield	LA	70462	225-294-5020		565
TF: 888-981-2020 ■ *Web:* www.crt.state.la.us						
Tickle Pink Inn at Carmel Highlands						
155 Highland Dr	Carmel	CA	93923	831-624-1244	626-9516	379
TF: 800-635-4774 ■ *Web:* www.ticklepinkinn.com						
Tico's 317 S 17th St	Lincoln	NE	68508	402-475-1048		671
Web: www.ticosoflincoln.com						
Ticom Geomatics Inc						
9130 Jollyville Rd Ste 100	Austin	TX	78759	512-345-5006	345-3751	256
Web: www.ticom-geo.com						
Ticona LLC 8040 Dixie Hwy	Florence	KY	41042	859-372-3244	372-3125*	605-2
**Fax:* Sales ■ *TF:* 800-833-4882 ■ *Web:* www.celanese.com						
Ticoon Technology Inc						
56 The Esplanade Ste 404	Toronto	ON	M5E1A7	416-513-9524		179
Web: www.ticoon.com						
Tida Thai Cuisine 212 Arthur Way	Newport News	VA	23602	757-234-0099		671
Web: tidathai.com						

Name / Address	City	State	ZIP	Phone	Fax	Class
Tidal Basin Holdings Inc 675 N Washington St — *Web:* www.tidalbasingroup.com	Alexandria	VA	22314	703-683-8551		194
Tidel Engineering Inc 2025 W Belt Line Rd Ste 114 — *TF:* 800-678-7577 ■ *Web:* www.tidel.com	Carrollton	TX	75006	972-484-3358	484-1014	56
Tideland Electric Membership Corp 25831 Hwy 264 E — *TF:* 800-637-1079 ■ *Web:* www.tidelandemc.com	Pantego	Nc	27860	252-943-3046	943-3510	245
Tideland Signal Corp 4310 Directors Row — *Web:* www.tidelandsignal.com	Houston	TX	77092	713-681-6101		529
Tides Canada Foundation 400-163 W Hastings St — *TF:* 866-843-3722 ■ *Web:* tidescanada.org	Vancouver	BC	V6B1H5	604-647-6611		305
Tides Foundation Po Box 29903 — *TF:* 800-750-2227 ■ *Web:* www.tides.org	San Francisco	CA	94129	415-561-6400		305
Tides Marine Inc 3251 SW 13th Dr — *TF:* 800-420-0949 ■ *Web:* tidesmarine.com	Deerfield Beach	FL	33442	954-420-0949		350
Tidewater Barge Lines Inc 6305 NW Old Lower River Rd — *TF:* 800-562-1607 ■ *Web:* www.tidewater.com	Vancouver	WA	98660	360-693-1491	694-8981	314
Tidewater Community College						
Chesapeake 1428 Cedar Rd. — *TF:* 800-371-0898 ■ *Web:* www.tcc.edu	Chesapeake	VA	23322	757-822-5100	822-5122	162
Norfolk 121 College Pl — *TF:* 800-371-0898 ■ *Web:* www.tcc.edu/welcome/locations/norfolk	Norfolk	VA	23510	757-822-1110		162
Portsmouth 7000 College Dr — **Fax:* Admissions ■ *TF:* 800-371-0898 ■ *Web:* www.tcc.edu	Portsmouth	VA	23703	757-822-2124	822-2002*	162
Virginia Beach 1700 College Crescent — *TF:* 800-371-0898 ■ *Web:* www.tcc.edu	Virginia Beach	VA	23453	757-822-7100	822-7350	162
Tidewater Direct LLC 300 Tidewater Dr — *Web:* www.tidewaterdirect.com	Centreville	MD	21617	410-758-1500		627
Tidewater Fleet Supply LLC 1324 Lindale Dr — *Web:* www.tidewaterfleetsupply.com	Chesapeake	VA	23320	757-547-2167		57
Tidewater Grill 1060 Charleston Town Ctr — *TF:* 888-456-3463 ■ *Web:* mainstreetventuresinc.com	Charleston	WV	25389	304-345-2620	345-5624	671
Tidewater Heating & Air Conditioning 150 Southern Blvd — *Web:* tidewaterac.com	Wilmington	NC	28401	910-343-1234		610
Tidewater Inc 601 Poydras St Ste 1900 — *NYSE: TDW* ■ *TF:* 800-678-8433 ■ *Web:* www.tdw.com	New Orleans	LA	70130	504 568 1010		465
Tidewater Inn & Conference Ctr 101 E Dover St — *TF:* 800-237-0775 ■ *Web:* www.tidewaterinn.com	Easton	MD	21601	410-822-1300	820-8847	379
Tidewater Physicians Multispecialty Group PC 860 Omni Blvd Ste 304 — *Web:* mytpmg.com	Newport News	VA	23606	757-232-8764	232-8865	374-3
Tidewell Hospice 5955 Rand Blvd — *TF:* 800-959-4291 ■ *Web:* tidewellhospice.org	Sarasota	FL	34238	941-552-7500	925-0969	371
TIDI Products LLC 570 Enterprise Dr — *TF:* 800-521-1314 ■ *Web:* www.tidiproducts.com	Neenah	WI	54956	800-521-1314	837-7770	477
Tidy Building Services Inc 609 W William David Pkwy Ste 202 — *Web:* www.tidyusa.com	Metairie	LA	70005	504-838-9843		256
Tie Down Engineering Inc 255 Villanova Dr SW — *TF:* 800-241-1806 ■ *Web:* www.danforthanchors.com	Atlanta	GA	30336	404-344-0000		480
Tie Fast Vest Tools 847 W Fifth St — *Web:* tie-fast.com	Chico	CA	95928	530-345-4261		711
Tie National Accounts 2280 White Oak Ste 108 — *Web:* tienational.com	Aurora	IL	60502	630-301-7444		387
Tiempo Escrow Ii 18433 Amistad St — *Web:* www.gotescrow.com	Fountain Valley	CA	92708	714-500-1500		652
Tier One LLC 31 Pecks Ln — *TF:* 877-251-2228 ■ *Web:* www.tieronemachining.com	Newtown	CT	06470	877-251-2228		454
Tier1 Inc 2403 Sidney St Ste 225 — *TF:* 888-284-0202 ■ *Web:* tier1inc.com	Pittsburgh	PA	15203	412-381-9201		177
Tierney Communications 200 S Broad St 10th Fl — *Web:* www.hellotierney.com	Philadelphia	PA	19102	215-790-4100		636
Tierra Restuarant 1425 Piedmont Ave NE — *Web:* tierrarestaurant.com	Atlanta	GA	30309	404-874-5951		671
Tierra Right of Way Services Ltd 1575 E River Rd Ste 201 — *TF:* 800-887-0847	Tucson	AZ	85718	520-319-2106	323-3326	196
TierraNet Inc 14284 Dani Elson St — *Web:* www.tierra.net	Poway	CA	92064	858-560-9416	560-9417	808
Tierzero 700 Wilshire Blvd 6th Fl — *Web:* www.tierzero.com	Los Angeles	CA	90017	213-784-1400		224
TIES 1667 Snelling Ave N — *TF:* 800-933-2723 ■ *Web:* ties.k12.mn.us	St. Paul	MN	55108	651-999-6000		177
Tietex International 3010 N Blackstock Rd — *TF:* 800-843-8390 ■ *Web:* www.tietex.com	Spartanburg	SC	29301	864-574-0500	574-9490	745-6
Tietronix Software Inc 1331 Gemini Ave Ste 300 — *Web:* www.tietronix.com	Houston	TX	77058	281-461-9300		177
Tiffany & Co 727 Fifth Ave — *NYSE: TIF* ■ *TF Orders:* 800-526-0649 ■ *Web:* www.tiffany.com	New York	NY	10022	212-755-8000		410
Tiffany Stuart Solutions Inc 390 Diablo Rd Ste 220 — *Web:* www.go2dynamic.com	Danville	CA	94526	925-855-3600		260
Tiffen Company LLC 90 Oser Ave — *TF:* 800-645-2522 ■ *Web:* www.tiffen.com	Hauppauge	NY	11788	631-273-2500	273-2557	591
Tiffin Area Chamber of Commerce 62 S Washington St — *Web:* www.tiffinchamber.com	Tiffin	OH	44883	419-447-4141	447-5141	139
Tiffin Foundry & Machine Inc 423 W Adams St PO Box 37 — *Web:* www.tiffinfoundry.com	Tiffin	OH	44883	419-447-3991	447-7969	455
Tiffin Metal Products Co 450 Wall St — *TF:* 800-537-0983 ■ *Web:* www.tiffinmetal.com	Tiffin	OH	44883	800-537-0983		350
Tiffin Motor Homes Inc (TMH) 105 Second St NW — *Web:* www.tiffinmotorhomes.com	Red Bay	AL	35582	256-356-8661	356-8219	120
Tiffin University 155 Miami St — *TF:* 800-968-6446 ■ *Web:* www.tiffin.edu	Tiffin	OH	44883	419-447-6442	443-5006	166
Tiffin-Seneca Public Library 77 Jefferson St — *TF:* 800-775-9767 ■ *Web:* tiffinsenecalibrary.org	Tiffin	OH	44883	419-447-3751	447-3045	434-3
Tift County 225 N Tift Ave — *Web:* www.tiftcounty.org	Tifton	GA	31794	229-386-7850		338
Tift Regional Medical Ctr 1641 Madison Ave — *TF:* 800-648-1935 ■ *Web:* www.tiftregional.com	Tifton	GA	31794	229-382-7120		374-3
Tifton-Tift County Chamber of Commerce 100 Central Ave — *TF:* 800-550-8438 ■ *Web:* www.tiftonison.com	Tifton	GA	31794	229-382-6200	386-2232	139
TIG (Technology Integration Group) 7810 Trade St — *TF:* 800-858-0549 ■ *Web:* www.tig.com	San Diego	CA	92121	858-566-1900	566-8794	176
Tigard Area Chamber of Commerce (TACC) 12345 SW Main St — *Web:* www.tigardareachamber.org	Tigard	OR	97223	503-639-1656		139
Tigard Public Library 13500 SW Hall Blvd — *Web:* www.tigard-or.gov/library.php	Tigard	OR	97223	503-684-6537		434-3
Tiger Button Company Inc 307 W 38th St — *TF:* 800-223-2754 ■ *Web:* www.tigerbutton.com	New York	NY	10018	212-594-0570	695-0265	594
Tiger Construction Ltd 6280 Everson Goshen Rd — *Web:* www.hub-4.com	Everson	WA	98247	360-966-7252		186
Tiger Financial News Network 601 Cleveland St Ste 618 — *TF:* 877-518-9190 ■ *Web:* www.tfnn.com	Clearwater	FL	33755	727-467-9190	443-0869	644
Tiger Fuel Company Inc 200 Carlton Rd PO Box 1607 — *Web:* www.tigerfuel.com	Charlottesville	VA	22902	434-293-6157		316
Tiger Lines LLC Lodi 927 Black Diamond Way — *TF:* 800-967-8443 ■ *Web:* www.tigerlines.com	Lodi	CA	95241	209-334-4100	333-3725	780
Tiger Optics LLC 250 Titus Ave — *Web:* www.tigeroptics.com	Warrington	PA	18976	215-343-6600		201
Tiger Press Administration 50 Industrial Dr — *Web:* www.tigerpress.com	East Longmeadow	MA	01028	413-224-2100		627
Tiger Schulmann's Karate Ctr 100 Blvd — *TF:* 800-867-1218 ■ *Web:* tsk.com	Elmwood Park	NJ	07407	800-867-1218		148
Tiger Supplies Inc 27 Selvage St — *TF:* 888-844-3765 ■ *Web:* www.tigersupplies.com	Irvington	NJ	07111	973 854 8636		791
Tiger Technologies LLC PO Box 7596 — *Web:* www.tigertech.net	Berkeley	CA	94707	510 527-3131		396
Tiger's Garden 312 W Fifth St — *Web:* tigersgardenrestaurant.com	Vancouver	WA	98660	360 693 0585		671
Tigercat Industries Inc 54 Morton Ave E — *Web:* www.tigercat.com	Brantford	ON	N3R7J7	519-753-2000		273
TigerDirect Inc 7795 W Flagler St Ste 35 — *TF:* 800-800-8300 ■ *Web:* www.tigerdirect.com	Miami	FL	33144	800-800-8300		174
Tigerflex Corp 801 Estes Ave — *Web:* www.tiger-poly.com	Elk Grove Village	IL	60007	847-640-8366	640-8372	370
Tigerflow Systems Inc 4034 Mint Way — *Web:* www.tigerflow.com	Dallas	TX	75237	214-337-8780		664
TigerLead Solutions LLC 1351 Dividend Dr SE Ste K — *TF:* 888-844-3744 ■ *Web:* www.tigerlead.com	Marietta	GA	30067	888-844-3744		225
Tigerlight Inc 450 W 910 S Ste 101 — *Web:* www.tigerlight.net	Heber City	UT	84032	435-657-9529		393
TigerLogic Corp 25-A Technology Dr — *NASDAQ: TIGR* ■ *TF:* 800-367-7425 ■ *Web:* tigerlogic.com	Irvine	CA	92618	949-442-4400	250-8187	178-12
Tigerpaw Software Inc 2201 Thurston Cir — *TF:* 800-704-9009 ■ *Web:* www.jamesfoxall.com	Bellevue	NE	68005	402-592-4544		177
Tigerpoly Manufacturing Inc 6231 Enterprise Pkwy — *Web:* www.tigerpoly.com	Grove City	OH	43123	614-871-0045	871-2576	604
TigerSwan Inc 3467 Apex Peakway — *Web:* www.tigerswan.com	Apex	NC	27502	919-439-7110		463
Tigerton Lumber Co 121 Cedar St — *Web:* www.tigertonlumber.com	Tigerton	WI	54486	715-535-2181		683
Tiggee LLC 11490 Commerce Park Dr Ste 140 — *Web:* www.tiggee.com	Reston	VA	20191	703-935-1598		631
Tighe & Bond Inc 53 Southampton Rd — *Web:* www.tighebond.com	Westfield	MA	01085	413-562-1600	562-5317	261
TIGHITCO Inc 1375 Seaboard Industrial Blvd — *TF:* 800-827-1204 ■ *Web:* www.tighitco.com	Atlanta	GA	30318	404-355-1205	351-4458	389
Tigre USA Inc 2315 Beloit Ave — *Web:* www.tigreusa.com	Janesville	WI	53546	608-754-4554		610
Tigress Financial Partners LLC 40 Wall St 30th Fl — *Web:* www.tigressfp.com	New York	NY	10005	212-430-8700		691
Tihati Productions Ltd 3615 Harding Ave Ste 507 — *TF:* 877-846-5554 ■ *Web:* www.tihati.com	Honolulu	HI	96816	808-735-0292	735-9479	573-4
TII Network Technologies Inc 141 Rodeo Dr — *NASDAQ: TIII* ■ *TF:* 888-844-4720 ■ *Web:* tiitech.com	Edgewood	NY	11717	631-789-5000	789-5063	640
Tiki Port 714 Iyanough Rd — *Web:* www.tikiport.com	Hyannis	MA	02601	508-771-5220		671

	Phone	Fax	Class
Tikkun Magazine 2342 Shattuck Ave Ste 1200 ... Berkeley CA 94704 *Web:* www.tikkun.org	510-644-1200	644-1255	457-10
Tilcon Connecticut Inc PO Box 1357 ... New Britain CT 06050 *TF:* 888-845-2666 ■ *Web:* www.tilconct.com	860-224-6010	225-1865	46
Tilcon NY Inc 162 Old Mill Rd ... West Nyack NY 10994 *TF:* 800-872-7762 ■ *Web:* www.tilconny.com	845-358-4500		503-5
Tilden-Coil Constructors Inc 3612 Mission Inn Ave ... Riverside CA 92501 *Web:* www.tilden-coil.com	951-684-5901		186
Tile Council of America Inc (TCA) 100 Clemson Research Blvd ... Anderson SC 29625 *Web:* www.tcnatile.com	864-646-8453	646-2821	49-3
Tile Shop Holdings Inc 14000 Carlson Pkwy ... Plymouth MN 55441 *TF:* 888-398-6595 ■ *Web:* www.tileshop.com	888-398-6595		787
Tillamook Bay Community College 4301 Third St ... Tillamook OR 97141 *TF:* 888-306-8222 ■ *Web:* tillamookbaycc.edu	503-842-8222		162
Tillamook County 201 Laurel Ave ... Tillamook OR 97141 *Web:* www.co.tillamook.or.us	503-842-3403	842-1384	338
Tillamook County Creamery Assn Inc 4185 Hwy 101 N ... Tillamook OR 97141 *TF:* 800-542-7290 ■ *Web:* www.tillamook.com	503-815-1300		296-5
Tillamook County Fairgrounds 4603 E Third St PO Box 455 ... Tillamook OR 97141 *TF:* 800-625-5296 ■ *Web:* www.tillamookfair.com	503-842-2272	842-3314	642
Tillamook County Pioneer Museum 2106 Second St ... Tillamook OR 97141 *Web:* www.tcpm.org	503-842-4553	842-4553	520
Tillamook People's Utility District 1115 Pacific Ave ... Tillamook OR 97141 *TF:* 800-422-2535 ■ *Web:* www.tpud.org	503-842-2535	842-4161	245
Tillamook Youth Correctional Facility 6700 Officer Row ... Tillamook OR 97141 *Web:* oregon.gov	503-842-2565	842-4918	412
Tillar-Wenstrup Advisors LLC 1065 E Centerville Sta Rd ... Centerville OH 45459 *TF:* 800-207-1143 ■ *Web:* twadvisors.com	937-428-9700		528
Tilley Chemical Company Inc 501 Chesapeake Pk Plaza ... Baltimore MD 21220 *TF:* 800-638-6968 ■ *Web:* tilleychem.com	410-574-4500	391-6665	146
Tillis Thom (Sen R - NC) 185 Dirksen Senate Office Bldg ... Washington DC 20510 *Web:* www.tillis.senate.gov	202-224-6342	228-2563	342-2
Tillman's 1245 Monroe Ave NW ... Grand Rapids MI 49505 *Web:* tillmansrestaurant.com	616-451-9266		671
Tilson HR Inc 1530 American Way Ste 200 ... Greenwood IN 46143 *TF:* 800-276-3976 ■ *Web:* www.tilsonhr.com	317-885-3838		631
Tilson Technology Management 245 Commercial St Ste 203 ... Portland ME 04101 *Web:* www.tilsontech.com	207-591-6427		196
Tilth Restaurant 1411 N 45th St ... Seattle WA 98103 *Web:* mariahinesrestaurants.com	206-633-0801	633-0801	671
Tilton & Company CPA's PC 4015 S Mcclintock Dr Ste 105 ... Tempe AZ 85282 *Web:* tiltonco.com	480-897-7708		2
Tilton Asset Management 510 Boston Post Rd ... Weston MA 02493 *Web:* tiltonasset.com	781-373-2244		186
Tilton Market Inc 1524 Tilton Rd ... Northfield NJ 08225 *Web:* tiltonmarket.com	609-641-5118		345
Tilton School 30 School St ... Tilton NH 03276 *Web:* www.tiltonschool.org	603-286-4342		622
Tilt-up Concrete Assn (TCA) 113 First St NW ... Mount Vernon IA 52314 **Fax Area Code:* 320 ■ *TF:* 800-837-5870 ■ *Web:* www.tilt-up.org	319-895-6911	213-5555*	49-3
Tim Hortons Inc 874 Sinclair Rd ... Oakville ON L6K2Y1 *NYSE: THI* ■ *TF:* 888-601-1616 ■ *Web:* www.timhortons.com	905-845-6511	845-0265	670
Tim Ivey Company Inc 1129 Riders Club Rd ... Onalaska WI 54650 *Web:* timivey.com	608-738-8066		177
Tim Miller Assoc Inc 10 N St ... Cold Spring NY 10516 *Web:* timmillerassociates.com	845-265-4400		727
Tim's Cascade Snacks 1150 Industry Dr N ... Algona WA 98001 *Web:* www.timschips.com	253-833-2986		296-35
Timber Lodge Steakhouse 7989 Southtown Ctr ... Bloomington MN 55431 *Web:* www.timberlodgesteakhouse.com	218-722-2624		671
Timber Mine 1701 Pk Blvd ... Ogden UT 84401 *Web:* www.timbermine.com	801-393-2155		671
Timber Products Co 305 S Fourth St PO Box 269 ... Springfield OR 97477 *TF:* 800-547-9520 ■ *Web:* www.timberproducts.com	541-747-4577	744-4296	191-3
Timber Products Inspection Inc 1641 Sigman Rd NW ... Conyers GA 30012 *Web:* www.tpinspection.com	770-922-8000		41
Timbercreek Asset Management Inc 25 Price St ... Toronto ON M4W1Z1 *Web:* www.timbercreek.com	416-306-9967		653
Timberland Bancorp Inc 624 Simpson Ave ... Hoquiam WA 98550 *NASDAQ: TSBK* ■ *TF:* 800-562-8761 ■ *Web:* www.timberlandbank.com	360-533-4747	533-4743	360-2
Timberland Co, The 200 Domain Dr ... Stratham NH 03885 *NYSE: VFC* ■ *TF:* 800-258-0855 ■ *Web:* www.timberland.com	603-772-9500		301
Timberland Homes Inc 1201 37th St NW ... Auburn WA 98001 *TF:* 800-488-5036 ■ *Web:* www.timberland-homes.com	253-735-3435	939-8803	106
Timberland Regional Library 415 Tumwater Blvd SW ... Tumwater WA 98501 *TF:* 877-284-6237 ■ *Web:* trl.org	360-943-5001	586-6838	434-3
Timberlane Inc 150 Domorah Dr ... Montgomeryville PA 18936 *TF:* 800-250-2221 ■ *Web:* www.timberlane.com	215-616-0600		362
Timberlawn Mental Health System 4600 Samuell Blvd ... Dallas TX 75228 *TF:* 800-426-4944 ■ *Web:* www.timberlawn.com	214-381-7181		374-5

	Phone	Fax	Class
Timberline Forest Products LLC PO Box 1568 ... Sherwood OR 97140 *Web:* www.timberlineforestproducts.com	503-590-5485		191-3
Timberline Lodge 27500 E Timberline Rd ... Government Camp OR 97028 *TF:* 800-547-1406 ■ *Web:* www.timberlinelodge.com	503-272-3311		669
Timberlodge Steakhouse 1111 38th St SW ... Fargo ND 58103 *Web:* www.timberlodgesteakhouse.com	952-881-5509		671
Timbers Hotel, The 4411 Peoria St ... Denver CO 80239	303-373-1444		379
Timberwolf Tours Ltd 51404 RR 264 Ste 34 ... Spruce Grove AB T7Y1E4 **Fax Area Code:* 866 ■ *TF:* 888-467-9697 ■ *Web:* www.timberwolftours.com	780-470-4966	339-3960*	760
Timco Rubber Products Inc 12300 Sprecher Ave ... Cleveland OH 44135 *Web:* www.timcorubber.com	216-267-6242		385
Timco Services Inc 1724 E Milton Rd ... Lafayette LA 70508	337-233-5185	856-8158	264-3
Time & Cents Consultants LLC 31 Deane Ln ... Fairfield CT 06824 *Web:* www.timeandcents.com	203-254-7736		177
Time 4 Learning 6300 NE First Ave Ste 203 ... Fort Lauderdale FL 33334 *Web:* www.time4learning.com	954-771-0914		395
Time Definite Services Inc 1360 Madeline Ln Ste 300 ... Elgin IL 60124 *TF:* 800-466-8040 ■ *Web:* timedefinite.com	800-466-8040		311
Time Hotels 224 W 49th St ... New York NY 10019 **Fax Area Code:* 877 ■ *TF:* 877-846-3692 ■ *Web:* www.thetimehotels.com/new-york/default-en.html	212-246-5252	753-7326*	379
Time Inc 1271 Ave of the Americas ... New York NY 10020 *TF:* 800-541-4100 ■ *Web:* www.timeinc.com	212-522-1212		637-9
Time Machine Inc 1746 Pittsburgh Rd ... Polk PA 16342 *Web:* www.timemachinepa.com	814-432-5281		454
Time Mark Corp 11440 E Pine St ... Tulsa OK 74116 *TF:* 800-862-2875 ■ *Web:* www.time-mark.com	918-438-1220	437-7584	203
Time Services Inc 6422 Lima Rd ... Fort Wayne IN 46818 *Web:* www.timeservices.com	260-489-2020		260
Time Trak Systems Inc 933 Pine Grove ... Port Huron MI 48060 *TF:* 888-484-6387 ■ *Web:* timetrak.com	810-984-1313		177
Time Warner Inc 1 Time Warner Ctr ... New York NY 10019 *NYSE: TWX* ■ *TF:* 866-463-6899 ■ *Web:* www.timewarner.com	212-484-8000		185
Time-Cap Labs Inc 7 Michael Ave ... Farmingdale NY 11735 *Web:* www.timecaplabs.com	631-753-9090		231
TimeCapital Securities Corp 1 Roosevelt Ave ... Port Jefferson Station NY 11776 *TF:* 800-262-5689 ■ *Web:* www.timecapital.com	631-331-1400		690
Timeless Treasures Antique Mall 433 E US Hwy 69 ... Kansas City MO 64119	816-455-9400		460
Timely Inc 10241 Norris Ave ... Pacoima CA 91331 *TF:* 800-247-6242 ■ *Web:* www.timelyframes.com	818-492-3500	899-2677	286
TimeMed Labeling Systems Inc 144 Tower Dr ... Burr Ridge IL 60527 **Fax Area Code:* 800 ■ *TF Cust Svc:* 800-323-4840 ■ *Web:* www.pdchealthcare.com	630-986-1800	548-5359*	554
Time-O-Matic Inc 1015 Maple St ... Danville IL 61832 *TF:* 800-637-2645 ■ *Web:* www.watchfiresigns.com	217-442-0611	442-1020	203
TimePlus Payroll Inc 695 Mansell Rd Ste 250 ... Roswell GA 30076 *Web:* www.timeplus.com	770-998-5790		2
Times 222 Lake St ... Shreveport LA 71101 *TF:* 800-551-8892 ■ *Web:* www.shreveporttimes.com	318-459-3200	459-3301	532-2
Times & News Publishing Co 1570 Fairfield Rd PO Box 3669 ... Gettysburg PA 17325 *Web:* www.gettysburgtimes.com	717-334-1131	334-4243	637-8
Times Colonist 2621 Douglas St ... Victoria BC V8T4M2 *TF:* 800-663-6384 ■ *Web:* www.timescolonist.com	250-380-5211	380-5353	532-1
Times Daily PO Box 797 ... Florence AL 35631 *Web:* www.timesdaily.com	256-766-3434	740-4717	532-2
Times Fiber Communications Inc 358 Hall Ave PO Box 384 ... Wallingford CT 06492 **Fax Area Code:* 203 ■ *TF:* 800-677-2288 ■ *Web:* www.timesfiber.com	434-432-1800	265-8422*	813
Times Herald 911 Military St ... Port Huron MI 48060 **Fax:* Edit ■ *Web:* www.thetimesherald.com	810-985-7171	989-6294*	532-2
Times Herald Inc 410 Markley St PO Box 591 ... Norristown PA 19404 *TF:* 888-933-4233 ■ *Web:* www.timesherald.com	610-272-2500		637-8
Times Herald-Record 40 Mulberry St PO Box 2046 ... Middletown NY 10940 *TF:* 888-620-1700 ■ *Web:* www.recordonline.com	845-341-1100		532-2
Times Hotel & Suites 6515 Wilfrid-Hamel Blvd ... Quebec QC G2E5W3 *TF:* 888-902-4444 ■ *Web:* grandtimeshotel.com	418-877-7788	877-3333	379
Times Leader 200 S Fourth St ... Martins Ferry OH 43935 *Web:* www.timesleaderonline.com	740-633-1131		532-2
Times Leader, The 15 N Main St ... Wilkes-Barre PA 18711 **Fax:* News Rm ■ *Web:* www.timesleader.com	570-829-7100	829-5537*	532-2
Times Microwave Systems Inc PO Box 5039 ... Wallingford CT 06492 *TF:* 800-867-2629 ■ *Web:* www.timesmicrowave.com	203-949-8400	949-8423	253
Times News Publishing Co 707 S Main St ... Burlington NC 27215 *TF:* 800-488-0085 ■ *Web:* www.thetimesnews.com	336-227-0131	228-1889	637-8
Times Newsweekly PO Box 860299 ... Ridgewood NY 11386 *Web:* www.timesnewsweekly.com	718-821-7500	456-0120	532-4
Times of Acadiana 1100 Bertrand Dr ... Lafayette LA 70506 *TF:* 877-289-2216 ■ *Web:* www.theadvertiser.com	337-289-6300		532-4
Times of Trenton 500 Perry St ... Trenton NJ 08618 *Web:* www.nj.com	609-989-7870	396-6563	532-2
Times Printing Company Inc 100 Industrial Dr ... Random Lake WI 53075 **Fax:* Cust Svc ■ *TF:* 800-236-4396 ■ *Web:* www.timesprintingco.com	920-994-4396	994-2059*	627
Times Record 219 S College Ave ... Aledo IL 61231 *Web:* www.aledotimesrecord.com	309-582-5112		532-4
Times Record 3600 Wheeler Ave ... Fort Smith AR 72901 *TF:* 888-274-4051 ■ *Web:* www.swtimes.com	479-785-7700	784-0413	532-2
Times Record News PO Box 120 ... Wichita Falls TX 76307 *TF:* 800-627-1646 ■ *Web:* www.timesrecordnews.com	940-767-8341	767-1741	532-2
Times Record, The 3 Business Pkwy ... Brunswick ME 04011 *Web:* www.timesrecord.com	207-729-3311		532-3

Phone | Fax | Class

Times Reporter
629 Wabash Ave NW ... New Philadelphia OH 44663 330-364-5577 364-8416 532-2
TF: 800-686-5577 ■ Web: www.timesreporter.com

Times Union
645 Albany Shaker Rd PO Box 15000 ... Albany NY 12212 518-454-5420 454-5628 532-2
TF: 877-263-7995 ■ Web: www.timesunion.com

Times Union Ctr 51 S Pearl St ... Albany NY 12207 518-487-2000 487-2020 720
TF: 866-308-3394 ■ Web: www.timesunioncenter-albany.com

Times, The 413 River View Plaza ... Trenton NJ 08611 609-989-5454 532-2
Web: www.nj.com/times

Times, The 23 Exchange St ... Pawtucket RI 02860 401-722-4000 532-2
Web: www.pawtuckettimes.com

Times, The 601 W 45th Ave ... Munster IN 46321 219-933-3200 933-3249 532-2
TF: 800-837-3232 ■ Web: www.nwitimes.com

Timesavers Inc 11123 89th Ave N ... Maple Grove MN 55369 763-488-6600 488-6601 386
TF: 800-537-3611 ■ Web: www.timesaversinc.com

Times-Citizen Communications Inc
406 Stevens St PO Box 640 ... Iowa Falls IA 50126 641-648-2521 648-4765 637-8
TF: 800-798-2691 ■ Web: www.timescitizen.com

TimesLedger Newspapers, The
41-02 Bell Blvd 2nd Fl ... Bayside NY 11361 718-260-4545 532-3
Web: www.timesledger.com

Times-Mail 813 16th St PO Box 849 ... Bedford IN 47421 812-275-3355 532-2
TF: 800-333-2451 ■ Web: www.tmnews.com

Times-News PO Box 481 ... Burlington NC 27216 336-227-0131 532-2
TF: 800-488-0085 ■ Web: www.thetimesnews.com

Times-News PO Box 548 ... Twin Falls ID 83303 208-733-0931 734-5538 532-2
TF: 800-658-3883 ■ Web: www.magicvalley.com

Times-News PO Box 490 ... Hendersonville NC 28793 828-692-0505 693-5581 532-2
TF: 800-849-8050 ■ Web: www.blueridgenow.com

Times-Picayune 3800 Howard Ave ... New Orleans LA 70125 504-826-3279 532-2
TF: 800-925-0000 ■ Web: www.nola.com

Times-Standard 930 Sixth St ... Eureka CA 95501 707-498-1817 441-0501 532-2
TF: 800-514-0301 ■ Web: www.times-standard.com

Times-Transcript 939 Main St ... Moncton NB E1C8P3 800-561-7166 532-1
TF: 800-561-7166 ■ Web: www.telegraphjournal.com/times-transcript

Times-Tribune, The 201 N Kentucky Ave ... Corbin KY 40701 606-528-2464 528-1335 532-2
TF: 877-629-9722 ■ Web: thetimestribune.com

TIMET (Titanium Metals Corp)
224 Vly Creek Blvd Ste 200 ... Exton PA 19341 610-968-1300 934-5345* 485
NYSE: TIE ■ *Fax Area Code: 972 ■ TF: 800-753-1550 ■ Web: www.timet.com

TimeTECH Canada Inc
7420 Airport Rd Ste 101 ... Mississauga ON L4T4E5 905-677-7009 177
TF: 877-816-8463 ■ Web: www.synerion.com

TimeValue Software 22 Mauchly ... Irvine CA 92618 949-727-1800 727-3268 178-11
TF Sales: 800-426-4741 ■ Web: www.timevalue.com

Timeware Inc 9329 Ravenna Rd Ste D ... Twinsburg OH 44087 330-963-2700 177
TF: 866-936-2420 ■ Web: www.timewareinc.com

Timex Group USA Inc
555 Christian Rd PO Box 310 ... Middlebury CT 06762 203-346-5000 153
TF: 800-448-4639 ■ Web: www.timex.com

Timken Co 1835 Dueber Ave SW ... Canton OH 44706 [illegible] 70
NYSE: TKR ■ TF: 800-223-1954 ■ Web: www.timken.com

Timken Museum of Art
1500 El Prado Balboa Pk ... San Diego CA 92101 619-239-5548 531-9640 520
Web: www.timkenmuseum.org

Timmins & District Hospital
700 Ross Ave E ... Timmins ON P4N8P2 705-267-2131 267-6311 374-2
TF: 888-340-3003 ■ Web: www.tadh.com

Timmins Chamber of Commerce
PO Box 985 ... Timmins ON P4N7H6 705-360-1900 360-1193 137
Web: www.timminschamber.on.ca

Timmins Kroll & Jacobson LLP
10550 New York Ave Ste 200 ... Urbandale IA 50322 515-270-8080 276-8329 2
Web: www.tjscpas.com

Timmons & Company Inc
1753 Kendarbren Dr ... Jamison PA 18929 267-483-8220 7
Web: www.timmonsandcompany.com

Timmons Group Inc
1001 Boulders Pkwy Ste 300 ... Richmond VA 23225 804-200-6500 261
Web: www.timmons.com

Timoney Knox LLP
400 Maryland Dr ... Fort Washington PA 19034 215-646-6000 428
TF: 800-447-5375 ■ Web: www.timoneyknox.com

Timothy M. Cary & Associates
3300 Cameron Park Dr Ste 2000 ... Cameron Park CA 95682 530-672-7601 428
Web: carylaw.com

Timpano Italian Chophouse
450 E Las Olas Blvd ... Fort Lauderdale FL 33301 954-462-9119 671
Web: timpanochophouse.net

Timpanogos Cave National Monument
RR 3 PO Box 200 ... American Fork UT 84003 801-756-5239 756-5661 564
Web: www.nps.gov

Timpone's 710 S Goodwin Ave ... Urbana IL 61801 217-344-7619 671
Web: www.timpones-urbana.com

Timpson Garcia
70 Washington St Ste 300 ... Oakland CA 94607 510-832-2325 2
TF: 800-941-2727 ■ Web: www.timpsongarcia.com

Timpte Inc 1827 Industrial Dr ... David City NE 68632 402-367-3056 367-4340 779
TF: 888-256-4884 ■ Web: www.timpte.com

Tims Ford State Park
570 Tims Ford Dr ... Winchester TN 37398 931-962-1183 962-1184 565
TF: 800-471-5295 ■ Web: tnstateparks.com/parks/about/tims-ford

Timucuan Asset Management Inc
200 W Forsyth St Ste 1600 ... Jacksonville FL 32202 904-356-1739 691
Web: www.timucuan.com

Timucuan Ecological & Historic Preserve
12713 Ft Caroline Rd ... Jacksonville FL 32225 904-641-7155 564
Web: www.nps.gov/timu

Tin Angel 3201 W End Ave ... Nashville TN 37203 615-298-3444 671
Web: tinangel.net

Tindale Oliver & Associates Inc
1000 N Ashley Dr ... Tampa FL 33602 813-224-8862 261
Web: www.tindaleoliver.com

Tindall Corp 2273 Hayne St ... Spartanburg SC 29301 864-576-3230 587-8828 183
TF: 800-849-4521 ■ Web: www.tindallcorp.com

Tingley Rubber Corp
1551 S Washington Ave Ste 403 Ste 403 ... Piscataway NJ 08854 800-631-5498 576
TF Cust Svc: 800-631-5498 ■ Web: www.tingleyrubber.com

Tingue 535 N Midland Ave ... Saddle Brook NJ 07663 201-796-5233 594
TF: 800-829-3864 ■ Web: www.tinguebrownco.com

Tinius Olsen TMC 1065 Easton Rd ... Horsham PA 19044 215-675-7100 441-0899 472
Web: www.tiniusolsen.com

TINK Profitabilite numerique Inc
87 Prince Ste 140 ... Montreal QC H3C2M7 514-866-0995 5
Web: www.tink.ca

Tinker Air Force Base
3001 Staff Dr Ste 1AG85A ... Tinker AFB OK 73145 405-739-2026 739-2882 497-1
Web: www.tinker.af.mil

Tinker Omega Manufacturing LLC
2424 Columbus Rd ... Springfield OH 45503 937-322-2272 358
Web: tinkeromega.com

Tinker Swiss Cottage Museum
411 Kent St ... Rockford IL 61102 815-964-2424 520
Web: www.tinkercottage.com

Tinkertown Museum PO Box 303 ... Sandia Park NM 87047 505-281-5233 520
TF: 800-368-3081 ■ Web: www.tinkertown.com

Tinley Park Chamber of Commerce
17316 Oak Pk Ave ... Tinley Park IL 60477 708-532-5700 532-1475 139
TF: 800-334-7661 ■ Web: www.tinleychamber.org

Tinley Park Public Library
7851 Timber Dr ... Tinley Park IL 60477 708-532-0160 532-2981 434-3
Web: www.tplibrary.org

Tinsley Adv 2000 S Dixie Hwy ... Miami FL 33133 305-856-6060 4
TF: 800-432-2242 ■ Web: www.tinsley.com

Tintri Inc
2570 W El Camino Real ... Mountain View CA 94040 650-209-3900 173-8
TF: 855-484-6874 ■ Web: www.tintri.com

Tiny Jewel Box Inc
1147 Connecticut Ave NW ... Washington DC 20036 202-393-2747 410
Web: www.tinyjewelbox.com

Tio Pepe 10 E Franklin St ... Baltimore MD 21202 410-539-4675 671
TF: 800-636-4462 ■ Web: tiopepebaltimore.com

Tioga County Chamber of Commerce
80 N Ave ... Owego NY 13827 607-687-2020 687-9028 139
TF: 800-933-8696 ■ Web: www.tiogachamber.com

Tioga County Clerk 16 Ct St PO Box 307 ... Owego NY 13827 607-687-8660 687-8686 338
Web: www.tiogacountyny.com

Tioga County Visitors Bureau
2053 Rt 660 ... Wellsboro PA 16901 570-724-0635 206
TF: 888-846-4228 ■ Web: www.visittiogapa.com

Tioga Inc 9201 International Pkwy ... Minneapolis MN 55428 763-525-4000 14
Web: www.tioga-inc.com

Tioga Pipe Supply Company Inc
2450 Wheatsheaf Ln ... Philadelphia PA 19137 215-831-0700 533-1645 492
TF: 800-523-3678 ■ Web: www.tiogapipe.com

TIP Rural Electric Co-op
612 W Des Moines St PO Box 534 ... Brooklyn IA 52211 641-522-9221 245
TF: 800-934-7976 ■ Web: www.tiprec.com

Tip Technologies Inc
N14 W24200 Twr Pl Ste 100 ... Waukesha WI 53188 262-544-1211 809
TF: 800-526-7766 ■ Web: www.tiptech.com

Tip Top Canning Co
505 S Second St PO Box 126 ... Tipp City OH 45371 937-667-3713 667-3802 296-20
TF: 800-352-2635 ■ Web: www.tiptopcanning.com

Tip Top Poultry Inc 327 Wallace Rd ... Marietta GA 30062 770-973-8070 619
TF: 800-241-5230 ■ Web: tiptoppoultry.com

TIPAC (Title Industry PAC)
1828 L St NW Ste 705 ... Washington DC 20036 202-296-3671 223-5843 615
TF: 800-787-2582 ■ Web: www.alta.org

Tipco Punch Inc 1 Coventry Rd ... Brampton ON L6T4B1 905-791-9811 358
TF: 800-544-8444 ■ Web: www.tipcopunch.com

Tipmont Rural Electric Membership Corp
403 S Main St ... Linden IN 47955 800-726-3953 245
TF: 800-726-3953 ■ Web: www.tipmont.org

Tipotex Chevrolet Inc
1600 N Expy # 77 ... Brownsville TX 78521 956-465-1209 57
Web: www.tipotexchevrolet.com

Tippah County 201 Union St ... Ripley MS 38663 662-837-3353 338
Web: www.tippahcounty.ripley.ms

Tippecanoe County 20 N Third St ... Lafayette IN 47901 765-463-2306 423-9196 338
TF: 800-905-7234 ■ Web: www.tippecanoe.in.gov

Tippecanoe County Public Library
627 S St ... Lafayette IN 47901 765-429-0100 429-0150 434-3
TF: 800-542-7818 ■ Web: www.tcpl.lib.in.us

Tippecanoe Place
620 W Washington St ... South Bend IN 46601 574-234-9077 671
Web: www.tippe.com

Tippecanoe River State Park
4200 N US Hwy 35 ... Winamac IN 46996 574-946-3213 565
Web: www.in.gov

Tipper Tie Inc 2000 Lufkin Rd ... Apex NC 27539 919-362-8811 362-7058 154
TF: 800-331-2905 ■ Web: www.tippertie.com

Tipping Mar & Assoc
1906 Shattuck Ave ... Berkeley CA 94704 510-549-1906 261
Web: tippingmar.com

Tips Inc 2402 Williams Dr ... Georgetown TX 78628 512-863-3653 863-5392 177
TF: 800-242-8477 ■ Web: tipsweb.com

Tipton & Hurst Inc
1801 N Grant St ... Little Rock AR 72207 501-666-3333 292
TF: 800-666-3333 ■ Web: www.tiptonhurst.com

Tipton Correctional Ctr
619 N Osage Ave ... Tipton MO 65081 660-433-2031 213
Web: doc.mo.gov

Tipton County 220 Highway 51 N Ste 2 ... Covington TN 38019 901-476-0207 476-0297 338
TF: 800-342-1003 ■ Web: www.tiptonco.com

Tipton County 101 E Jefferson St ... Tipton IN 46072 765-675-2794 338
Web: www.tiptonpl.lib.in.us

Tipton County Schools 1580 Hwy 51 S ... Covington TN 38019 901-476-7148 685
Web: www.tipton-county.com

Tipton Marler Garner & Chastain
501 W 19th St ... Panama City FL 32405 850-769-9491 2
Web: cpagroup.com

Tipton Scott (Rep R - CO)
218 Cannon Bldg ... Washington DC 20515 202-225-4761 226-9669 342-2
Web: tipton.house.gov

				Phone	Fax	Class
Tipton-Haynes State Historic Site 2620 S Roan St.	Johnson City	TN	37601	423-926-3631		50-3
TF: 800-952-8392 ■ *Web:* www.tipton-haynes.org						
Tire Centers LLC 310 Inglesby Pkwy.	Duncan	SC	29334	864-329-2700	329-2900	755
TF: 800-603-2430 ■ *Web:* www.tirecenters.com						
Tire Curing Bladders LLC 5701 Murray St.	Little Rock	AR	72209	501-562-5410		754
Web: www.tirebladders.com						
Tire Industry Assn (TIA) 1532 Pointer Ridge Pl Ste G	Bowie	MD	20716	301-430-7280	430-7283	49-4
TF: 800-876-8372 ■ *Web:* www.tireindustry.org						
Tire Rack 7101 Vorden Pkwy	South Bend	IN	46628	574-287-2345	236-7707	755
TF: 888-541-1777 ■ *Web:* www.tirerack.com						
Tire Warehouse 200 Holleder Pkwy	Rochester	NY	14615	800-876-6676		54
TF: 800-876-6676 ■ *Web:* www.tirewarehouse.net						
Tire Warehouse Inc 7500 NW 35 Terr	Miami	FL	33122	305-696-0096	696-5926	755
TF: 877-235-0102 ■ *Web:* www.tiregroup.com						
Tire Wholesalers Co Inc 1783 E 14-Mile Rd	Troy	MI	48083	248-589-9910	589-9919	755
TF: 800-876-8372 ■ *Web:* twitire.com						
Tire's Warehouse Inc 240 Teller St	Corona	CA	92879	951-808-0111	808-9062	755
TF: 800-655-8851 ■ *Web:* tireswarehouse.net						
Tireman Auto Service Centers Ltd PO Box 3456	Toledo	OH	43607	419-724-8473		54
Web: www.thetireman.com						
Tire-Rama Inc 1429 Grand Ave	Billings	MT	59102	406-245-3161		755
TF: 800-828-1642 ■ *Web:* www.tirerama.com						
Tires Plus Total Car Care 2021 Sunnydale Blvd	Clearwater	FL	33765	727-330-3684		62-5
TF: 844-338-0739 ■ *Web:* www.tiresplus.com						
TIRR Memorial Hermann Hospital 1333 Moursund St	Houston	TX	77030	713-799-5000		374-6
TF: 800-447-3422 ■ *Web:* www.memorialhermann.org						
Tirschwell & Loewy Inc 400 Park Ave.	New York	NY	10022	212-888-7940		401
TF: 800-999-1950 ■ *Web:* www.tirschwellandloewy.com						
TIS Group 100 Village Ctr Dr Ste 260	North Oaks	MN	55127	651-379-5070		317
Web: theinstitutionalstrategist.com						
Tischler Und Sohn 6 Suburban Ave	Stamford	CT	06901	203-674-0600		191-3
Web: www.tischlerwindows.com						
TISD Inc 1502 E Red river	Victoria	TX	77901	361-573-1102		396
TF: 800-494-2203 ■ *Web:* tisd.net						
Tishcon Corp 50 Sylvester St.	Westbury	NY	11590	516-333-3050	997-1052	799
TF: 800-848-8442 ■ *Web:* www.tishcon.com						
Tishma Innovations LLC 101 E State Pkwy	Schaumburg	IL	60173	847-884-1805		358
Web: www.tminn.com						
Titan Air Inc 13901 16th St	Osseo	WI	54758	715-597-2050		697
TF: 800-242-9398 ■ *Web:* www.titan-air.com						
Titan America Inc 1151 Azalea Garden Rd.	Norfolk	VA	23502	757-858-6500		182
TF: 800-468-7622 ■ *Web:* www.titanamerica.com						
Titan Broadcast Management LLC 888 Third St NW Ste A	Atlanta	GA	30318	678-904-0555		116
Web: www.titanbroadcast.com						
Titan Consulting 3411 Preston Rd Ste C13	Frisco	TX	75034	972-377-3525		180
Web: www.titanconsulting.net						
TITAN Engineering Inc 2801 Network Blvd Ste 200	Frisco	TX	75034	469-365-1100		192
Web: www.titanengineering.com						
Titan Farms 5 RW Du Bose Rd.	Ridge Spring	SC	29129	803-685-5381	685-5885	315-3
Web: www.titanfarms.com						
Titan Formwork Systems LLC 7855 S River Pkwy Ste 105.	Tempe	AZ	85284	480-456-5833		23
Web: www.titanformwork.com						
Titan Global Distribution 1100 Corporate Sq Dr.	Saint Louis	MO	63132	314-817-0051		449
TF: 800-325-4074 ■ *Web:* titan-global.com						
Titan International Inc 2701 Spruce St.	Quincy	IL	62301	217-228-6011	228-9331*	60
NYSE: TWI ■ **Fax:* Cust Svc ■ *TF:* 800-872-2327 ■ *Web:* www.titan-intl.com						
Titan Laboratories 1380 Zuni St PO Box 40567	Denver	CO	80204	800-848-4826		579
TF: 800-848-4826 ■ *Web:* www.titanlab.com						
Titan Logix Corp 4130 - 93 St.	Edmonton	AB	T6E5P5	780-462-4085	450-8369	201
TF: 877-462-4085 ■ *Web:* www.titanlogix.com						
Titan Machinery 644 East Beaton Dr	West Fargo	ND	58078	701-356-0130		358
TF: 800-548-7747 ■ *Web:* www.titanmachinery.com						
Titan Machinery Inc 7955 179th Ave SE	Wahpeton	ND	58075	701-642-8424		274
NASDAQ: TITN ■ *TF:* 800-654-4313 ■ *Web:* www.titanmachinery.com						
Titan Oil & Gas Services Inc 6809 King Ave W Bldg E.	Billings	MT	59106	406-945-5036		536
TF: 800-406-5209						
Titan Pharmaceuticals Inc 400 Oyster Pt Blvd Ste 505.	South San Francisco	CA	94080	650-244-4990	244-4956	85
OTC: TTNP ■ *TF:* 888-417-8516 ■ *Web:* www.titanpharm.com						
Titan Plastics Inc 1631 Corporate Pl	La Vergne	TN	37086	615-641-7000		596
Titan Protection & Consulting Inc 9350 Metcalf Ave Ste 210.	Overland Park	KS	66212	913-441-0911		693
Web: www.tpcsecurity.com						
Titan Recruitment Solutions Ltd 355 Burrard St	Vancouver	BC	V6C2G8	604-687-6785		260
Web: titanrecruitment.com						
Titan Solutions Group Inc 11901 W Parmer Ln Ste 400.	Cedar Park	TX	78613	512-345-4234		180
Web: www.titansolutions.com						
Titan Specialties Inc 11785 Hwy 152	Pampa	TX	79065	806-665-3781	669-6674	537
TF Sales: 800-692-4486 ■ *Web:* hunting-intl.com/hunting-titan						
Titan Steel Corp 2500-B Broening Hwy	Baltimore	MD	21224	410-631-5200		492
Web: www.titansteel.com						
Titan Tire Co 2345 E Market St	Des Moines	IA	50317	515-265-9200	265-9301	754
TF: 800-872-2327 ■ *Web:* www.titan-intl.com						
Titan Tool & Die Ltd 2801 Howard Ave	Windsor	ON	N8X3Y1	519-966-1234		483
Web: www.titantool.ca						
Titan Trucks 306 Austin St	Levelland	TX	79336	806-894-4852		546
Web: www.titanco.com						

				Phone	Fax	Class
Titan Wheel Corp 2701 Spruce St	Quincy	IL	62301	217-228-6011	228-9331*	60
**Fax:* Cust Svc ■ *TF:* 800-872-2327 ■ *Web:* www.titan-intl.com						
Titan Wheel Corp of Virginia 227 Allison Gap Rd.	Saltville	VA	24370	276-496-5121		247
Titanic Museum 208 Main St PO Box 51053	Indian Orchard	MA	01151-0053	413-543-4770	583-3633	520
Web: www.titanichistoricalsociety.org						
Titanium Fabrication Corp 110 Lehigh Dr.	Fairfield	NJ	07004	973-227-5300	227-6541	91
Web: www.tifab.com						
Titanium Metals Corp (TIMET) 224 Vly Creek Blvd Ste 200	Exton	PA	19341	610-968-1300	934-5345*	485
NYSE: TIE ■ **Fax Area Code:* 972 ■ *TF:* 800-753-1550 ■ *Web:* www.timet.com						
Titanx Engine Cooling Inc 2258 Allen St Ext	Jamestown	NY	14701	716-665-2620		247
TITAS (Texas International Theatrical Arts Society) 2100 Ross Ave Ste 650.	Dallas	TX	75201	214-528-6112		573-1
Web: www.titas.org						
Titeflex Corp 603 Hendee St	Springfield	MA	01139	413-739-5631	788-7593	370
TF: 800-765-2525 ■ *Web:* www.titeflex.com						
Title Guaranty of Hawaii Inc 235 Queen St	Honolulu	HI	96813	808-533-6261	521-0210	391-6
TF: 800-222-3229 ■ *Web:* www.tghawaii.com						
Title Industry PAC (TIPAC) 1828 L St NW Ste 705	Washington	DC	20036	202-296-3671	223-5843	615
TF: 800-787-2582 ■ *Web:* www.alta.org						
Title Resource Group LLC 3001 Leadenhall Rd	Mount Laurel	NJ	08054	856-914-8500		391-6
Web: www.trgc.com						
Title Resources Guaranty Co (TRGC) 8111 LBJ Fwy Ste 1200	Dallas	TX	75251	800-526-8018	485-3630*	391-6
**Fax Area Code:* 888 ■ *TF:* 800-526-8018 ■ *Web:* www.titleresources.com						
Title Security of Arizona Inc 6390 E Tanque Verde Rd.	Tucson	AZ	85715	520-885-1600		390
Web: titlesecurity.com						
Title Wave Inc 1360 W Northern Lights Blvd	Anchorage	AK	99503	907-278-9283		95
Web: www.wavebooks.com						
Titlemax of South Carolina Inc 15 Bull St Ste 200.	Savannah	GA	31401	888-485-3629		401
TF: 888-485-3629 ■ *Web:* www.gmlblaw.com						
Titletown Brewing Co 200 Dousman St.	Green Bay	WI	54303	920-437-2337	437-2739	671
TF: 800-895-0071 ■ *Web:* www.titletownbrewing.com						
Tito's 444 E William St	Carson City	NV	89701	775-885-0309		671
Titonka Bancshares Inc PO Box 309	Titonka	IA	50480	515-928-2142	928-2042	360-2
TF: 866-985-3247 ■ *Web:* www.tsbbank.com						
Titus County 100 W First St.	Mt Pleasant	TX	75455	903-577-6796	572-5078	338
Web: www.co.titus.tx.us						
Titus Dina (Rep D - NV) 2464 Rayburn HOB.	Washington	DC	20515	202-225-5965		342-2
Web: titus.house.gov						
Titus Regional Medical Ctr 2001 N Jefferson Ave	Mount Pleasant	TX	75455	903-577-6000		374-3
Web: www.titusregional.com						
Titus Steel Co Ltd 6767 Invader Cres	Mississauga	ON	L5T2B7	905-564-2446		492
TF: 888-564-7904 ■ *Web:* www.titussteel.com						
Titus Will Ford 3606 S Sprague	Tacoma	WA	98409	253-475-4151		57
Web: tituswillford.com						
Titusville Area Chamber of Commerce 2000 S Washington Ave	Titusville	FL	32780	321-267-3036	264-0127	139
TF: 800-435-7352 ■ *Web:* www.titusville.org						
Tiva Software LLC 5200 Park Rd Ste 235.	Charlotte	NC	28209	704-525-0005		809
TF: 800-783-8100 ■ *Web:* www.tivasoftware.com						
Tiversa Inc 144 Emeryville Dr Ste 300 Cranberry Township.	Cranberry Twp	PA	16066	724-940-9030		809
TF: 800-713-7278 ■ *Web:* www.tiversa.com						
TiVo Inc 2160 Gold St.	Alviso	CA	95002	408-519-9100	519-5330	116
NASDAQ: TIVO ■ *TF:* 877-367-8486 ■ *Web:* www.tivo.com						
Tivoli Hotel 936 Warren Ave.	Downers Grove	IL	60515	630-968-6450		132
TF: 800-892-0123 ■ *Web:* tivolihotel.net						
Tivoli Lodge 386 Hanson Ranch Rd.	Vail	CO	81657	970-476-5615	476-6601	379
TF: 800-451-4756 ■ *Web:* www.tivolilodge.com						
TIW Corp 12300 S Main St PO Box 35729	Houston	TX	77035	713-729-2110	728-4767	537
Web: www.tiwoiltools.com						
TIW Technology Inc 769 Youngs Hill Rd	Easton	PA	18040	610-258-5161		177
Web: www.tiwcorp.com						
Tix Bay Area 1119 Market St 2nd Fl	San Francisco	CA	94103	415-430-1140		747
Web: www.theatrebayarea.org						
Tizbi Inc 800 Saint Mary's St Ste 402	Raleigh	NC	27605	888-729-0951		177
TF: 888-729-0951 ■ *Web:* www.tizbi.com						
Tiziani Whitmyre Inc 2 Commercial St	Sharon	MA	02067	781-793-9380		7
TF: 800-225-4034 ■ *Web:* www.tizinc.com						
TJ Cope Inc 11500 Norcom Rd	Philadelphia	PA	19154	215-961-2570	961-2580	816
TF: 800-483-3473 ■ *Web:* copecabletray.com						
TJ Hale Co W 139 N 9499 Hwy 145	Menomonee Falls	WI	53051	262-255-5555	255-5678	286
TF: 800-236-4253 ■ *Web:* www.tjhale.com						
TJ Lambrecht Construction Inc 10 Gougar Rd	Joliet	IL	60432	815-727-9211		188-4
TJ Maxx 770 Cochituate Rd	Framingham	MA	01701	508-390-1000		157-2
TF Cust Svc: 800-926-6299 ■ *Web:* tjmaxx.tjx.com						
TJ McCartney Inc 3 Capitol St Ste 1.	Nashua	NH	03063	603-889-6380	880-0770	189-9
Web: www.tjminc.com						
TJ Metzgers Inc 207 Arco Dr	Toledo	OH	43607	419-861-8611		393
TF: 800-463-3339 ■ *Web:* www.metzgers.com						
Tj Rock Enterprises Inc 5800 Genesis Ln.	Frederick	MD	21703	301-831-4128		179
Web: tjrockcorp.com						
TJ Samson Community Hospital 1301 N Race St.	Glasgow	KY	42141	270-651-4444		374-3
TF: 800-651-5635 ■ *Web:* www.tjsamson.org						

Phone | Fax | Class

Tj/H2B Analytical Services Inc
3123 Fite Cir Ste 105 .... Sacramento CA 95827 916-361-7177 794
Web: www.tjh2b.com

Tjernlund Products Inc
1601 Ninth St .... White Bear Lake MN 55110 651-426-2993 426-9547 18
TF: 800-255-4208 ■ *Web:* www.tjernlund.com

T-Joe's Steakhouse & Saloon
12700 I-80 Service Rd .... Cheyenne WY 82009 307-634-8750 671
Web: www.tjoessteakhouse.com

TJS (Tucson Jazz Society)
PO Box 41071 Ste 206 .... Tucson AZ 85717 520-903-1265 48-4
TF: 800-595-4849 ■ *Web:* www.tucsonjazz.org

TJX Cos Inc 770 Cochituate Rd .... Framingham MA 01701 508-390-1000 157-4
NYSE: TJX ■ *TF:* 800-926-6299 ■ *Web:* www.tjx.com

Tk Interactive Inc 9 N Long St .... Williamsville NY 14221 716-632-2967 809
TF: 800-877-0475 ■ *Web:* www.tkinteractive.com

Tk Media Direct Inc
5062 Lankershim Blvd Ste 3033 .... N. Hollywood CA 91601 818-851-1483 5
Web: tkmediadirect.com

TK Stanley Inc 6739 Hwy 184 .... Waynesboro MS 39367 800-477-2855 735-2857* 539
**Fax Area Code:* 601 ■ *TF:* 800-477-2855 ■ *Web:* dwservices.com

TK99 235 Walton St .... Syracuse NY 13202 315-472-9111 472-1888 645-160
Web: tk99.net

TKA (Tsoi/Kobus & Assoc Inc)
1 Brattle Sq PO Box 9114 .... Cambridge MA 02238 617-475-4000 475-4445 261
Web: www.tka-architects.com

TKE (Tau Kappa Epsilon)
7439 Woodland Dr Ste 100 .... Indianapolis IN 46278 317-872-6533 875-8353 48-16
Web: www.tke.org

TKGA (Knitting Guild of America, The)
1100-H Brandywine Blvd .... Zanesville OH 43701 740-452-4541 452-2552 48-18
Web: www.tkga.com

TKO Electronics Inc
31113 Via Colinas .... Westlake Village CA 91362 818-879-2233 174
Web: www.tkoelectronics.com/TKO_eCommerceWeb

TKV Containers Inc 4582 E Harvey Ave .... Fresno CA 93702 559-251-5551 200

TL Industries Inc 2541 Tracy Rd .... Northwood OH 43619 419-666-8144 666-6534 261
Web: www.tlindustries.com

T-l Irrigation Co
151 E Hwy 6 AB Rd PO Box 1047 .... Hastings NE 68902 402-462-4128 330-4268* 273
**Fax Area Code:* 800 ■ *TF:* 800-330-4264 ■ *Web:* www.tlirr.com

TL Ventures 435 Devon Pk Dr .... Wayne PA 19087 610-971-1515 792
Web: tl.ventures

TLA (Tennessee Library Assn)
PO Box 241074 .... Memphis TN 38124 901-485-6952 435
TF: 800-545-2433 ■ *Web:* www.tnla.org

TLBAA (Texas Longhorn Breeders Assn of America)
2315 N Main St Ste 402 .... Fort Worth TX 76164 817-625-6241 625-1388 48-2
Web: www.tlbaa.org

TLC (Trichotillomania Learning Ctr Inc)
207 McPherson St Ste H .... Santa Cruz CA 95060 831-457-1004 48-17

TLC Engineering for Architecture
255 S Orange Ave # 1600 .... Orlando FL 32801 407-841-9050 261
Web: www.tlc-engineers.com

TLC Florist & Greenhouse Inc
105 W Memorial Rd .... Oklahoma City OK 73114 405-751-0630 323
Web: www.ticgarden.com

TLC Nursing & Homecare Services Ltd
25 Anderson Ave .... St. John's NL A1B3E4 709-720-3473 371
Web: www.tlcnursingandhomecare.com

Tlc Office Systems
500 N Chenango St Ste 314 .... Angleton TX 77515 979-848-8300 179
Web: tlcofficesystems.com

TLC Vision Corp
50 Burnhamthorpe Rd W Ste 101 .... Mississauga ON L5B3C2 877-852-2020 798
TF: 877-852-2020 ■ *Web:* www.tlcvision.com

Tld Ace Corp 805 Bloomfield Ave .... Windsor CT 06095 860-602-3300 14
Web: www.tld-gse.com/index.php?m%5B0%5D=history&m%5B1%5D=ace_nordco

TLD Distribution Company LLC
505 S Seventh Ave .... City of Industry CA 91746 310-324-5111 468

tlg 101-110 Princess St .... Winnipeg MB R3B1K7 204-940-4550 242
Web: tlg.ca

TLIE (Texas Lawyers Insurance Exchange)
1801 S MoPac Ste 300 .... Austin TX 78746 512-480-9074 482-8738 391-5
TF: 800-252-9332 ■ *Web:* www.tlie.org

TLM Associates Inc 117 E Lafayette St .... Jackson TN 38301 731-988-9840 261
Web: www.tlmassociates.com

TLN (Telelatino Network Inc)
5125 Steeles Ave W .... Toronto ON M9L1R5 416-744-8200 744-0966 740
TF: 800-551-8401 ■ *Web:* tln.ca/contact-us

TLN (Total Living Network) 2880 Vision Ct .... Aurora IL 60506 630-801-3838 801-3839 740
Web: www.tln.com

TLT (Theatre Tallahassee)
1861 Thomasville Rd .... Tallahassee FL 32303 850-224-4597 572
Web: theatretallahassee.org

TLX Inc 7944 E Beck Ln Ste 200 .... Scottsdale AZ 85260 480-609-8888 180
TF: 800-520-7493 ■ *Web:* www.tlxinc.com

Tm 1031 Exchange Inc
100 Wilshire Blvd Ste 1760 .... Santa Monica CA 90401 310-264-0497 653
Web: www.tm1031exchange.com

TM Capital Corp
641 Lexington Ave 30th Fl .... New York NY 10022 212-809-1360 401
Web: www.tmcapital.com

TM Century Inc 2002 Academy Ln Ste 110 .... Dallas TX 75234 972-406-6800 406-6890 646
Web: www.tmstudios.com

TM Deer Park Services LP
2525 Battleground Rd PO Box 1914 .... Deer Park TX 77536 281-930-2525 930-2535 146
Web: www.texasmolecular.com

Tm Group Inc, The
34705 W Twelve Mile Rd Ste 371 .... Farmington Hills MI 48331 248-489-0707 180
Web: www.tmgroupinc.com

TM Smith Tool International Corp
360 Hubbard Ave .... Mount Clemens MI 48043 586-468-1465 468-7190 493
TF: 800-521-4894 ■ *Web:* www.tmsmith.com

TM Systems LLC
12711 Ventura Blvd Ste 270 .... Studio City CA 91604 818-306-5300 180

T-M Vacuum Products Inc
630 S Warrington Ave .... Cinnaminson NJ 08077 856-829-2000 829-0990 318
Web: www.tmvacuum.com

TMA (Tobacco Merchants Assn)
PO Box 8019 .... Princeton NJ 08543 609-275-4900 275-8379 48-2
TF: 888-672-4991 ■ *Web:* www.tma.org

TMA Systems LLC 5100 E Skelly Dr Ste 900 .... Tulsa OK 74135 918-858-6600 858-6655 178-11
TF: 800-862-1130 ■ *Web:* www.tmasystems.com

TMAD Taylor & Gaines (TTG)
300 N Lake Ave 14th Fl .... Pasadena CA 91101 626-463-2711 261

TMC (Teaching & Mentoring Communities)
PO Box 2579 .... Laredo TX 78044 956-722-5174 49-5
TF: 888-836-5151 ■ *Web:* www.tmccentral.org

TMC (Tufts Medical Ctr) 800 Washington St .... Boston MA 02111 617-636-5000 636-8199 374-3
TF: 866-220-3699 ■ *Web:* www.tuftsmedicalcenter.org/default

TMC (Tulane Medical Ctr)
1415 Tulane Ave .... New Orleans LA 70112 504-988-5263 374-3
TF: 800-588-5800 ■ *Web:* www.tulanehealthcare.com

TMC (Technology & Maintenance Council)
PO Box 232 Ste 210 .... Arlington VA 22203 703-838-1763 838-1701 49-21
Web: www.trucking.org

TMC (Trinity Medical Ctr West Campus)
2701 17th St .... Rock Island IL 61201 309-779-2800 374-3
Web: www.unitypoint.org

TMC (Baylor Medical Center)
4343 N Josey Ln .... Carrollton TX 75010 972-492-1010 374-3

TMC Design Corp 4325 Del Rey Blvd .... Las Cruces NM 88012 575-382-4600 647
Web: www.tmcdesign.us

TMC Technologies Inc 2050 Winners Dr .... Fairmont WV 26554 304-816-3600 816-3411 396
Web: www.tmctechnologies.com

TMD Solutions Inc
938 E Swan Creek Rd Ste 270 .... Fort Washington MD 20744 301-248-1465 248-1466 809
Web: www.tmdx.com

TMG Company LLC
1718 Briarcrest Dr Ste 100 .... Bryan TX 77802 979-774-4492 2
TF: 800-720-1563 ■ *Web:* www.tmgco.com

TMH (Tiffin Motor Homes Inc)
105 Second St NW .... Red Bay AL 35582 256-356-8661 356-8219 120
Web: www.tiffinmotorhomes.com

TMI (Texas Military Institute)
20955 W Tejas Trail .... San Antonio TX 78257 210-698-7171 698-0715 622
Web: www.tmi-sa.org

TMI Coatings Inc 3291 Terminal Dr .... Saint Paul MN 55121 651-452-6100 452-0598 189-8
TF: 800-328-0229 ■ *Web:* www.tmicoatings.com

TMI Hospitality Inc 4850 32nd Ave S .... Fargo ND 58104 701-235-1060 639-5575 707
TF: 800-210-8223 ■ *Web:* www.tharaldson.com

TMI LLC 5350 Campbells Run Rd .... Pittsburgh PA 15205 412-787-9750 608
TF: 800-888-9750 ■ *Web:* www.tmi-pvc.com

TMI Systems Design Corp
50 S Third Ave W .... Dickinson ND 58601 701-456-6716 456-6700 319-3
TF: 800-456-6716 ■ *Web:* www.tmisystems.com

TML (Teledyne Monitor Labs Inc)
35 Inverness Dr E .... Englewood CO 80112 303-792-3300 799-4853 201
TF: 800-422-1499 ■ *Web:* www.monitorlabs.com

TML Information Services Inc
11655 Queens Blvd .... Forest Hills NY 11375 718-793-3737 635

TMMC Management PO Box 1540 .... Castle Rock CO 80104 720-733-1369 652

TMNG (Management Network Group Inc)
7300 College Blvd Ste 302 .... Overland Park KS 66210 913-345-9315 196
NASDAQ: CRTN ■ *TF:* 800-690-6903 ■ *Web:* cartesian.com

T-Mobile USA Inc 12920 SE 38th St .... Bellevue WA 98006 425-383-4000 736
TF: 800-318-9270 ■ *Web:* www.t-mobile.com

TMP Architecture
1191 W Sq Lake Rd .... Bloomfield Hills MI 48302 248-338-4561 338-0223 261
Web: www.tmp-architecture.com

TMP Consulting Engineers Inc
52 Temple Pl .... Boston MA 02111 617-357-6060 261
TF: 800-766-0076 ■ *Web:* www.tmpeng.com

TMP Direct 600 International Dr .... Mount Olive NJ 07828 973-347-9400 393
TF: 800-328-2439 ■ *Web:* www.tmpwdirect.com

TMP Technologies Inc
1200 Northland Ave .... Buffalo NY 14215 716-895-6100 601
TF: 800-675-8232 ■ *Web:* www.tmptech.com

Tmr Mailing Services Inc
506 Manchester Expy Ste A1 .... Columbus GA 31904 706-653-2090 5
TF: 800-742-5877 ■ *Web:* www.tmrmailing.com

TMS (Tube City IMS Corp)
12 Monongahela Ave .... Glassport PA 15045 412-678-6141 675-8295 686
NYSE: TMS ■ *TF:* 800-860-2442 ■ *Web:* www.tubecityims.com

TMS (Minerals Metals & Materials Society)
184 Thorn Hill Rd .... Warrendale PA 15086 724-776-9000 776-3770 49-13
TF: 800-759-4867 ■ *Web:* www.tms.org

TMT Software Co
6114 Fayetteville Rd Ste 106 .... Durham NC 27713 919-493-4700 809

TMVP (Triathlon Medical Ventures)
300 E Business Way Ste 200 .... Cincinnati OH 45241 513-723-2600 247-6122 792
Web: www.tmvp.com

TMW Systems Inc 21111 Chagrin Blvd .... Beachwood OH 44122 216-831-6606 831-3606 178-10
TF: 800-401-6682 ■ *Web:* www.tmwsystems.com

TN Ward Co 129 Coulter Ave .... Ardmore PA 19003 610-649-0400 186
Web: www.tnward.com

TNA (Tennessee Nurses Assn)
545 Mainstream Dr Ste 405 .... Nashville TN 37228 615-254-0350 254-0303 533
Web: www.tnaonline.org

TNCI (Trans National Communications International Inc)
2 Charlesgate W .... Boston MA 02215 617-369-1000 736
TF: 800-800-8400 ■ *Web:* www.tncii.com

Tnemec Company Inc
6800 Corporate Dr .... Kansas City MO 64120 816-483-3400 483-3969 550
TF: 800-863-6321 ■ *Web:* www.tnemec.com

TNMP (Texas-New Mexico Power Co)
577 N Garden Ridge Blvd .... Lewisville TX 75067 972-420-4189 787
TF: 888-866-7456 ■ *Web:* www.tnmp.com

TNNA (National NeedleArts Assn, The)
1100-H Brandywine Blvd .... Zanesville OH 43701 740-455-6773 452-2552 48-18
TF: 800-889-8662 ■ *Web:* www.tnna.org

Tnr Global Llc 277 Main St Ste 301 .... Greenfield MA 01301 413-425-1499 809
TF: 800-790-6202 ■ *Web:* www.tnrglobal.com

TNR Technical Inc 301 Central Pk Dr .... Sanford FL 32771 407-321-3011 321-3208 74
OTC: TNRK ■ *TF:* 800-346-0601 ■ *Web:* www.batterystore.com

Name / Address	City	State	Zip	Phone	Fax	Class
TNS Employee Insights 65 Oakwood Rd *Web:* www.foresightint.com	Lake Zurich	IL	60047	847-726-4677		260
Tnt Automotive Leasing Ltd 10124 W Broad St Ste G *Web:* tntauto.com	Glen Allen	VA	23060	804-270-2912		126
TNT Parts Inc 3000 S Corporate Pkwy Ste 400 *TF:* 800-693-4343 ■ *Web:* www.tntpartsinc.com	Forest Park	GA	30297	678-244-8532		54
TNT Plastics Inc 701 Industrial Dr *Web:* www.tntplastics.com	Perryville	MO	63775	573-547-1051		596
TNT USA Inc 68 S Service Rd *Web:* tnt.com	Melville	NY	11747	631-712-6700		546
TNT Vacations 2 Charlesgate W *Web:* www.funjet.com	Boston	MA	02215	617-262-9200		771
TO Haas Tire Co Inc 2400 'O' St *TF:* 866-393-5204 ■ *Web:* www.tohaastire.com	Lincoln	NE	68510	402-474-1525	474-0336	755
TO Plastics Inc 830 County Rd 75 PO Box 37 *TF:* 800-657-0745 ■ *Web:* www.toplastics.com	Clearwater	MN	55320	320-558-2407		601
Toa Canada Corp 6150 Kennedy Rd Unit 3 *TF:* 800-263-7639 ■ *Web:* www.toacanada.com	Mississauga	ON	L5T2J4	905-564-3570		246
Toa Reinsurance Company of America 177 Madison Ave PO Box 1930 *Web:* www.toare.com	Morristown	NJ	07962	973-898-9480	898-9495	391-4
Toad in the Hole 112 Osborne St *Web:* toadinthehole.ca	Winnipeg	MB	R3L1Y5	204-284-7201		671
Toarmina's Pizza 32785 Cherry Hill Rd *TF:* 800-467-7663 ■ *Web:* www.toarminas.com	Westland	MI	48186	734-728-0060		670
TOAST.net 4841 Monroe St Ste 307 *TF:* 888-862-7863 ■ *Web:* www.toast.net	Toledo	OH	43623	419-292-2200	474-1762	398
Toastmasters International 23182 Arroyo Vista *Web:* www.toastmasters.org	Rancho Santa Margarita	CA	92688	949-858-8255	858-1207	48-15
TOBA (Thoroughbred Owners & Breeders Assn) PO Box 910668 *TF:* 888-606-8622 ■ *Web:* www.toba.org	Lexington	KY	40591	859-276-2291	276-2462	48-3
Tobacco Assoc Inc 1306 Annapolis Dr Ste 102 *Web:* www.tobaccoassociatesinc.org	Raleigh	NC	27608	919-821-7670	821-7674	48-2
Tobacco Company Restaurant 1201 E Cary St *TF:* 800-659-1727 ■ *Web:* www.thetobaccocompany.com	Richmond	VA	23219	804-782-9555		671
Tobacco Merchants Assn (TMA) PO Box 8019 *TF:* 888-672-4991 ■ *Web:* www.tma.org	Princeton	NJ	08543	609-275-4900	275-8379	48-2
Tobacco Superstores Inc 3550 Commerce Rd *Web:* tobaccosuper.com	Forrest City	AR	72335	870-633-0099		756
Tobar Industries 912 Olinder Ct *TF:* 800-243-4344 ■ *Web:* www.tobar-ind.com	San Jose	CA	95122	408-494-3530		697
Tobias Financial Advisors 1000 S Pine Island Rd Ste 250 *Web:* www.tobiasfinancial.com	Plantation	FL	33324	954-424-1660		2
Tobyhanna State Park PO Box 387 *Web:* www.dcnr.state.pa.us	Tobyhanna	PA	18466	570-894-8336		565
Tobys Family Foods LLC 1160 Shelley St *Web:* www.tobysfamilyfoods.com	Springfield	OR	97477	541-689-8506		123
Tocagen Inc 3030 Bunker Hill St Ste 230 *Web:* www.tocagen.com	San Diego	CA	92109	858-412-8400		231
Tocco Financial Services Inc 6236 E Pima Ste 190 *TF:* 877-881-1149 ■ *Web:* toccofinancial.com	Tucson	AZ	85712	520-881-1149		690
Toccoa Falls College 107 Kincaid Dr *TF General:* 888-785-5624 ■ *Web:* www.tfc.edu	Toccoa Falls	GA	30598	706-886-7299	886-6412	161
Toccoa-Stephens County Chamber of Commerce 160 N Alexander St *Web:* www.toccoagachamber.com	Toccoa	GA	30577	706-886-2132	886-2133	139
Tocqueville 1 E 15th St *Web:* www.tocquevillerestaurant.com	New York	NY	10003	212-647-1515		671
Today's Business Computers 213 E Black Horse Pk *TF:* 800-371-5132 ■ *Web:* www.tbcusa.com	Pleasantville	NJ	08232	609-645-5132		177
Today's Chicago Woman Magazine 150 E Huron St Ste 1001 *Web:* www.tcwmag.com	Chicago	IL	60611	312-951-7600		457-22
Today's Christian Woman Magazine 465 Gundersen Dr *TF Orders:* 877-247-4787 ■ *Web:* www.christianitytoday.com/women	Carol Stream	IL	60188	630-260-6200	260-0114	457-18
Today's Q106 730 Rayovac Dr *TF:* 800-236-6397 ■ *Web:* www.q106.com	Madison	WI	53711	608-273-1000		645-96
Today's Vision 6970 FM 1960 W Ste A *Web:* www.todaysvision.com	Houston	TX	77069	281-469-2020	469-7531	543
Todd & Sargent Inc 2905 SE Fifth St *Web:* www.tsargent.com	Ames	IA	50010	515-232-0442		188-7
Todd County 221 First Ave S Ste 200 **Fax:* Acctg ■ *Web:* www.co.todd.mn.us	Long Prairie	MN	56347	320-732-6447	732-4001*	338
Todd Herman & Associates PA 620 Green Valley Rd Ste 104 *Web:* www.toddherman.com	Greensboro	NC	27408	336-297-4200		196
Todd Jurich's Bistro 150 W Main St Ste 100 *Web:* toddjurichsbistro.com	Norfolk	VA	23510	757-622-3210		671
Todd Organization Inc, The 24610 Detroit Rd Ste 210 *Web:* www.toddorg.com	Cleveland	OH	44145	440-871-7700		390
Todd Rivenbark Puryear Company Inc 2405 Robeson St *Web:* www.trpcpa.com	Fayetteville	NC	28305	910-323-3600		2
Todd Rutkin Inc 5801 S Alameda St *Web:* toddrutkin.com	Los Angeles	CA	90001	323-584-9225		258
Todd Street Productions 111 Eighth Ave Fl 16 *Web:* www.toddstreet.com	New York	NY	10011	212-966-5900		511
Todd's Companion Plus Inc 6123 Green Bay Rd Ste 250	Kenosha	WI	53142	262-605-4700		363
Todd, Bremer & Lawson Inc 560 S Herlong Ave *Web:* www.tbandl.com	Rock Hill	SC	29732	803-323-5200		160
Todd-Wadena Electric Co-op 550 Ash Ave NE PO Box 431 *TF:* 800-321-8932 ■ *Web:* www.toddwadena.coop	Wadena	MN	56482	218-631-3120		245
TodoCast Inc 31831 Camino Capistrano Ste 301 *TF:* 866-510-7889 ■ *Web:* todocast.tv	San Juan Capistrano	CA	92675	866-510-7889		387
Toeroek Associates Inc 300 Union Blvd Ste 520 *Web:* www.toeroek.com	Lakewood	CO	80228	303-420-7735		463
Tofino Botanical Gardens Foundation 1084 Pacific Rim Hwy *Web:* www.tbgf.org	Tofino	BC	V0R2Z0	250-725-1220		97
Tofutti Brands Inc 50 Jackson Dr *NYSE:* TOF ■ *TF:* 800-371-6504 ■ *Web:* www.tofutti.com	Cranford	NJ	07016	908-272-2400	272-9492	296-25
TOG Manufacturing Company Inc 1454 S State St *Web:* www.togmanufacturing.com	North Adams	MA	01247	413-664-6711		757
Tog Shop Inc 30 Tozer Rd **Fax Area Code:* 800 ■ *Web:* togshop.blair.com	Beverly	MA	01915	978-922-2040	755-7557*	459
Togus National Cemetery VA Regional Office Ctr *TF:* 800-273-8255 ■ *Web:* www.cem.va.gov/cems/nchp/togus.asp	Togus	ME	04330	508-563-7113	564-9946	136
Toho Tenax America Inc 121 Cardiff Valley Rd *Web:* www.tohotenax-us.com	Rockwood	TN	37854	865-354-4120		127
Tohono Chul Park 7366 N Paseo del Norte *Web:* www.tohonochulpark.org	Tucson	AZ	85704	520-742-6455	797-1213	97
Tohono O'odham Utility Authority PO Box 816 *Web:* www.toua.net	Sells	AZ	85634	520-383-2236		245
Toitures GGR Inc 34 Trudel Cp 333 *TF:* 800-043-7760	Amos	QC	J9T3A7	819-727-3348		191-4
Tojo's *Tojo's Restaurant* 1133 W Broadway *Web:* www.tojos.com	Vancouver	BC	V6H1G1	604-872-8050		671
Tok River State Recreation Site c/o Northern Area Office 3700 Airport Way *Web:* www.dnr.alaska.gov	Fairbanks	AK	99709	907-883-3686		565
Tokatee Klootchman State Natural Site 93111 Hwy 101 N *TF:* 800-551-6949 ■ *Web:* www.oregonstateparks.org	Florence	OR	97439	800-551-6949		565
Tokenzone Inc 34 S Broadway Ste 712 *Web:* tokenzone.com	White Plains	NY	10601	914-997-1999		809
Tokio Marine Americaÿ 230 Pk Ave *TF:* 800-628-2796 ■ *Web:* www.tokiomarine.us	New York	NY	10169	212-297-6600	297-6062	391-4
Tokusen USA Inc 1500 Amity Rd *Web:* www.tokusenusa.com	Conway	AR	72033	501-327-6800	327-0231	813
Toky Branding & Design 3139 Olive St *Web:* toky.com	Saint Louis	MO	63103	314-534-2000		344
Tokyo Bay Japanese Restaurant & Sushi 5901 Sun Blvd *Web:* www.tokyobaysaintpete.com	Saint Petersburg	FL	33715	727-867-0770		671
Tokyo Electron Limited 2400 Grove Blvd *TF:* 800-865-9650 ■ *Web:* www.tel.com	Austin	TX	78741	512-424-1000	424-1001	695
Tokyo Garden 1711 Fulton St *TF:* 800-809-3041 ■ *Web:* tokyogardenfresno.com	Fresno	CA	93721	559-268-3596		671
Tokyo Gas Company Ltd 1540 Broadway Ste 3920 *Web:* www.tokyo-gas.co.jp	New York	NY	10036	646-865-0577	865-0592	360-5
Tokyo Grill & Sushi Restaurant 4478 Breton Rd SE *Web:* tokyogrillsushi.com	Kentwood	MI	49508	616-455-3433		671
Tokyo Japanese Restaurant 7516 N Western Ave *Web:* www.tokyookc.com	Oklahoma City	OK	73116	405-848-6733		671
Tokyo Japanese Steakhouse 312 E Nine Mile Rd *Web:* gotokyopensacola.com	Pensacola	FL	32514	850-479-9111	479-5881	671
Tokyo Japanese Steakhouse 1111 Salisbury Ridge Rd *Web:* www.tjsteakhouse.com	Winston-Salem	NC	27127	336-722-5009		671
Tokyo Love 12565 S Harbor Blvd	Garden Grove	CA	92840	714-534-4751		671
Tokyo Restaurant 388 Wickenden St	Providence	RI	02903	401-331-5330		671
Tokyo Sushi 1716 Lundy Ave	San Jose	CA	95131	408-452-8868		671
Tokyo Sushi 1499 SE 17th St *Web:* iluvtokyosushi.net	Fort Lauderdale	FL	33316	954-767-9922		671
Tokyo-Seoul 3180 Erie Blvd E *Web:* tokyoseoulsyracuse.com	Syracuse	NY	13214	315-449-2688		671
Tolar Manufacturing Company Inc 258 Mariah Cir *Web:* www.tolarmfg.com	Corona	CA	92879	951-808-0081		320
Toledo Botanical Garden 5403 Elmer Dr *Web:* www.toledogarden.org	Toledo	OH	43615	419-536-5566	536-5574	97
Toledo Building Services 2121 Adams St *TF:* 800-874-2122 ■ *Web:* www.toledobuildingservices.com	Toledo	OH	43604	419-241-3101		104
Toledo Business Journal 5301 Southwyck Blvd Ste 104 *Web:* www.toledobiz.com	Toledo	OH	43614	419-865-0972	865-2429	457-5
Toledo City Hall 1 Government Ctr Ste 2120 *Web:* toledo.oh.gov	Toledo	OH	43604	419-245-1050	245-1072	337
Toledo Community Foundation 300 Madison Ave Ste 1300 *TF:* 800-201-2011 ■ *Web:* www.toledocf.org	Toledo	OH	43604	419-241-5049		305
Toledo Commutator 1101 S Chestnut St *Web:* www.toledocommutator.com	Owosso	MI	48867	989-725-8192	725-5930	518

Phone | Fax | Class

Toledo Correctional Institution
2001 E Central Ave PO Box 80033 Toledo OH 43608 419-726-7977 726-7157 213
Web: drc.ohio.gov
Toledo Edison Co PO Box 3687 Akron OH 44309 800-447-3333 787
TF: 800-447-3333 ■ *Web:* www.firstenergycorp.com
Toledo Engineering Company Inc
3400 Executive Pkwy PO Box 2927 Toledo OH 43606 419-537-9711 537-1369 261
TF: 800-654-4567 ■ *Web:* www.teco.com
Toledo Express Airport
11013 Airport Hwy Swanton OH 43558 419-865-2351 27
TF: 800-495-4250 ■ *Web:* www.toledoexpress.com
Toledo Firefighters Museum
918 Sylvania Ave Toledo OH 43612 419-478-3473 520
Web: www.toledofiremuseum.com
Toledo Metal Spinning Co
1819 Clinton St Toledo OH 43607 419-535-5931 483
Web: www.toledometalspinning.com
Toledo Molding & Die Inc 4 E Laskey Rd Toledo OH 43612 419-476-0581 476-6053 604
Web: www.tmdinc.com
Toledo Mud Hens Baseball Club Inc
406 Washington St Toledo OH 43604 419-725-4367 713
TF: 800-736-9520 ■ *Web:* www.milb.com/index.jsp?sid=t512
Toledo Museum of Art 2445 Monroe St Toledo OH 43620 419-255-8000 255-5638 520
TF: 800-644-6862 ■ *Web:* www.toledomuseum.org
Toledo Opera 425 Jefferson Ave Ste 601 Toledo OH 43604 419-255-7464 255-6344 573-2
TF: 866-860-9048 ■ *Web:* www.toledoopera.org
Toledo Physical Education Supply Inc
5101 Advantage Dr Toledo OH 43612 419-726-8122 711
TF: 800-225-7749 ■ *Web:* www.tpesonline.com
Toledo Regional Chamber of Commerce
300 Madison Ave Ste 200 Toledo OH 43604 419-243-8191 241-8302 139
Web: www.toledochamber.com
Toledo Repertoire Theatre 16 Tenth St Toledo OH 43604 419-243-9277 573-4
Web: www.toledorep.org
Toledo Symphony Orchestra
1838 Parkwood Ave Toledo OH 43604 419-246-8000 321-6890 573-3
Web: www.toledosymphony.com
Toledo Ticket Co 3963 Catawba St Toledo OH 43612 419-476-5424 711
Web: www.toledoticket.com
Toledo Zoo 2 Hippo Way Toledo OH 43609 419-385-5721 389-8670 823
Web: www.toledozoo.org
Toledo-Lucas County Port Authority
1 Maritime Plaza Ste 701 Toledo OH 43604 419-243-8251 243-1835 618
Web: www.toledoport.org
Toledo-Lucas County Public Library
325 N Michigan St Toledo OH 43604 419-259-5200 434-3
Web: www.toledolibrary.org
Toler & Toler Insurance
1564 SR-160 Gallipolis OH 45631 740-446-9445 390
Tolin Mechanical Systems Co
12005 E 45th Ave Denver CO 80239 303-455-2825 610
Web: www.tolin.com
Toll Bros Inc 250 Gibraltar Rd Horsham PA 19044 215-938-8000 938-8217* 653
NYSE: TOL ■ **Fax: Mktg* ■ *TF:* 855-897-8655 ■ *Web:* www.tollbrothers.com
Toll Cross Securities Inc
Ste 200 1 Toronto St Toronto ON M5C2V6 416-365-1960 690
Toll Gas & Welding Supply
3005 Niagara Ln N Plymouth MN 55447 763-551-5300 358
TF: 877-865-5427 ■ *Web:* tollgas.com
Toll House Hotel
140 S Santa Cruz Ave Los Gatos CA 95030 408-395-7070 707
TF: 800-238-6111 ■ *Web:* www.tollhousehotel.com
Tolland County 69 Brooklyn St Rockville CT 06066 860-875-6294 338
Web: www.jud.state.ct.us
Tolland County Chamber of Commerce
30 Lafayette Sq Vernon CT 06066 860-872-0587 872-0588 139
Web: www.tollandcountychamber.org
Tolland State Forest
410 Tolland Rd PO Box 342 East Otis MA 01029 413-269-6002 565
Web: www.mass.gov
Tollefson & Clancey CPA'S
151 Callan Ave Ste 310 San Leandro CA 94577 510-483-0145 2
Tolleson Design Inc
560 Pacific Ave San Francisco CA 94133 415-626-7796 344
Web: tolleson.com
Tolleson Wealth Management Inc
5500 Preston Rd Ste 250 Dallas TX 75205 214-252-3250 796
Web: www.tollesonwealth.com
Tollgrade Communications Inc
3120 Unionville Rd Ste 400 Cranberry Township PA 16066 412-820-1400 820-1530 735
TF Cust Svc: 800-878-3399 ■ *Web:* www.tollgrade.com
Tollman Spring Company Inc
91 Enterprise Dr Bristol CT 06010 860-583-1326 492
Web: www.tollmanspring.com
TOLMAR Holding Inc
701 Centre Ave Fort Collins CO 80526 970-212-4500 231
Web: www.tolmar.com
Tolmie State Park 7730 61st Ave NE Olympia WA 98506 360-456-6464 565
Web: www.parks.wa.gov
Tol-O-Matic Inc 3800 County Rd 116 Hamel MN 55340 763-478-8000 478-8080 223
TF: 800-328-2174 ■ *Web:* www.tolomatic.com
Tolowa Dunes State Park
1111 Second St Crescent City CA 95531 707-465-2145 565
Web: www.parks.ca.gov
Tolstoy Foundation Inc
104 Lake Rd PO Box 578 Valley Cottage NY 10989 845-268-6722 268-6937 48-14
TF: 800-771-7755 ■ *Web:* www.tolstoyfoundation.org
Toltec Mounds Archeological State Park
490 Toltec Mounds Rd Scott AR 72142 501-961-9442 565
Web: www.arkansasstateparks.com
Tolunay-Wong Engineers Inc
10710 S Sam Houston Pkwy W Houston TX 77031 713-722-7064 722-0319 261
Web: tweinc.com
Tom Barrow Co (TBC)
2800 Plant Atkinson Rd Atlanta GA 30339 404-351-1010 350-9121 14
TF: 800-229-8226 ■ *Web:* www.tombarrow.com
Tom Bengard Ranch Inc 634 W Market Salinas CA 93901 831-758-5770 10-11
Web: bengardranch.com

Tom Cat Bakery Inc 43-05 Tenth St Long Island NY 11101 718-786-7659 297-8
Web: www.tomcatbakery.com
Tom Duffy Co 5200 Watt Ct Ste B Fairfield CA 94534 800-479-5671 290
TF: 800-479-5671 ■ *Web:* www.tomduffy.com
Tom Gibbs Chevrolet Inc
5850 E Hwy 100 Palm Coast FL 32164 386-437-3314 57
Web: tomgibbschevy.com
Tom Green County 122 W Harris Ave San Angelo TX 76903 325-659-6444 659-6459 338
Web: www.co.tom-green.tx.us
Tom Green County Library System
33 W Beauregard Ave San Angelo TX 76903 325-655-7321 434-3
Web: tgclibrary.com
Tom Ham's Lighthouse
2150 Harbor Island Dr San Diego CA 92101 619-291-9110 671
Web: www.tomhamslighthouse.com
Tom Hassenfritz Equipment Co
1300 W Washington St Mount Pleasant IA 52641 319-385-3114 385-3731 274
TF: 800-634-4885 ■ *Web:* www.the-co.com
Tom Hesser Chevrolet Inc
1001 N Washington Ave Scranton PA 18509 570-343-1221 57
Web: tomhesserbmw.com
Tom Holzer Ford Inc
39300 W Ten Mile Farmington Hills MI 48335 248-474-1234 57
Web: tholzerford.com
Tom Hopkins International Inc
465 E Chilton Dr Ste 4 Chandler AZ 85255 480-949-0786 949-1590 196
TF: 800-528-0446 ■ *Web:* www.tomhopkins.com
Tom J Keith & Assoc Inc
121 S Cool Spring St Fayetteville NC 28301 910-323-3222 652
Web: www.keithvaluation.com
Tom James Co 263 Seaboard Ln Franklin TN 37067 615-771-0795 155-12
TF: 800-236-9023 ■ *Web:* www.tomjames.com
Tom Jenkins' Bar-B-Q
1236 S Federal Hwy Fort Lauderdale FL 33316 954-522-5046 671
Web: www.tomjenkins.net
Tom Johnson Investment Management Inc
201 Robert S Kerr Ave Oklahoma City OK 73102 405-236-2111 401
TF: 888-404-8546 ■ *Web:* tjim.com
Tom Lee Music Ltd 929 Granville St Vancouver BC V6Z1L3 604-685-8471 526
TF: 888-886-6533 ■ *Web:* www.tomleemusic.ca
Tom McCall & Assoc Inc
20180 Governors Hwy Ste 100 Olympia Fields IL 60461 708-747-5707 747-5890 194
TF: 800-715-5474 ■ *Web:* www.tmccall.com
Tom Naquin Chevrolet Inc
2500 W Lexington Ave Elkhart IN 46514 574-293-8621 57
Web: www.tomnaquin.com
Tom Nehl Truck Co
417 S Edgewood Ave Jacksonville FL 32254 904-389-3653 516
Web: www.tomnehl.com
Tom Rectenwald Construction Inc
330A Perry Hwy Harmony PA 16037 724-452-8801 186
TF: 800-947-6096 ■ *Web:* www.tomrectenwald.com
Tom Rostron Co Inc
2490 Tiltons Corner Rd Wall Township NJ 07719 732-223-8221 189-10
Web: tomrostron.com
Tom Roush Inc 525 W David Brown Dr Westfield IN 46074 317-896-5561 516
TF: 800-382-4619 ■ *Web:* www.tomroush.com
Tom Sawyer Software Corp
1997 El Dorado Ave Berkeley CA 94707 510-208-4370 177
Web: www.tomsawyer.com
Tom Smith Industries 500 Smith Dr Clayton OH 45315 937-832-1555 757
Tom Snyder Productions Inc
100 Talcott Ave Watertown MA 02472 617-924-0938 304-1254* 178-3
**Fax Area Code:* 800
Tom Sturgis Pretzels Inc
2267 Lancaster Pk Reading PA 19607 610-775-0335 296-9
TF: 800-817-3834 ■ *Web:* www.tomsturgispretzels.com
Tom Thumb Food Stores Inc
MS 10501 P.O. Box 29093 Phoenix AZ 85038 877-723-3929 204
TF: 877-723-3929 ■ *Web:* tomthumb.com
Tom Venturi - State Farm Insurance Agent
5616 W Montrose Ave Chicago IL 60634 773-777-5151 390
Tom's Aircraft Maintenance Inc
2641 E Spring St Long Beach CA 90806 562-426-5331 770
Web: www.tomsaircraft.com
Tom's Food Markets
738 Munson Ave Traverse City MI 49686 231-947-7175 345
Web: www.toms-foodmarkets.com
Tom's of Maine Inc
302 Lafayette Ctr Kennebunk ME 04043 800-367-8667 985-2196* 214
**Fax Area Code:* 207 ■ *TF:* 800-367-8667 ■ *Web:* www.tomsofmaine.com
Toma & Assoc Inc 41 Summit St Jackson CA 95642 209-223-0156 360-3
Toma Metals Inc 740 Cooper Ave Johnstown PA 15906 814-536-3596 567
Web: www.rsac.com/site/location.asp?intLocationID=78
Tomah Convention & Visitors Bureau
901 Kilbourn Ave PO Box 625 Tomah WI 54660 608-372-2166 372-2167 206
TF: 800-948-6624 ■ *Web:* www.tomahwisconsin.com
Tomah Veterans Affairs Medical Ctr
500 E Veterans St Tomah WI 54660 608-372-3971 372-1692* 374-8
**Fax:* Admissions ■ *TF:* 800-872-8662 ■ *Web:* www.tomah.va.gov
Tomahawk Leader 315 W Wisconsin Ave Tomahawk WI 54487 715-453-2151 532-3
Web: www.tomahawkleader.com
Tomales Bay State Park
1208 Pierce Pt Rd Inverness CA 94937 415-669-1140 565
Web: www.parks.ca.gov/default.asp?page_id=470
Tomarco Contractor Specialties Inc
14848 Northam St La Mirada CA 90638 714-523-1771 351
Web: www.tomarco.com
Tomasco Mulciberinc
2001 Courtright Rd Columbus OH 43232 614-231-0075 247
Web: www.tomasco.net
Tomasita's Restaurant & Bar
500 S Guadalupe St Santa Fe NM 87501 505-983-5721 671
Web: www.tomasitas.com
Tomato Head 12 Market Sq Knoxville TN 37902 865-637-4067 637-4019 671
TF: 800-421-0979 ■ *Web:* thetomatohead.com
Tomato Street North 6220 N Div Spokane WA 99208 509-484-4500 671
Web: www.tomatostreet.com

Name / Address	City	State	ZIP	Phone	Fax	Class
Tomba Communications LLC 718 Barataria Blvd. *Web:* www.tomba.com	Marrero	LA	70072	504-340-2448		246
Tomball College 30555 Tomball Pkwy. **Fax:* Admissions ■ *Web:* www.lonestar.edu	Tomball	TX	77375	281-351-3300	351-3384*	162
Tomball Independent School District 310 S Cherry St. *TF:* 877-382-4357 ■ *Web:* www.tomballisd.net	Tomball	TX	77375	281-357-3100	357-3128	685
Tomball Regional Hospital (TRMC) 605 Holderrieth St. *Web:* www.tomballregionalmedicalcenter.com	Tomball	TX	77375	281-401-7500		374-3
Tombigbee Electric Co-op 7686 Highway 43. *TF:* 800-621-8069 ■ *Web:* www.tombigbee.net	Guin	AL	35563	205-468-3325		245
Tombigbee State Park 264 Cabin Dr. *TF:* 800-467-2757 ■ *Web:* www.mdwfp.com	Tupelo	MS	38804	662-842-7669		565
Tombolino Restaurant 356 Kimball Ave. *Web:* www.tombolinoristorante.com	Yonkers	NY	10704	914-237-1266		671
Tombstone Courthouse State Historic Park 223 E Toughnut St. *Web:* azstateparks.com	Tombstone	AZ	85638	520-457-3311		565
Tomchin Planetarium & Observatory 425 Hodges Hall. *Web:* planetarium.wvu.edu	Morgantown	WV	26506	304-293-4961		598
Tomco2 Equipment Co 3340 Rosebud Rd. *TF:* 800-832-4262 ■ *Web:* www.tomcosystems.com	Loganville	GA	30052	770-979-8000	985-9179	806
Tomisushi 4336 Moorpark Ave. *Web:* www.tomisushi.us	San Jose	CA	95129	408-257-4722		671
Tomkiewicz Wright LLC 6111 P'Tree Dunwoody Rd Bld E 102. *Web:* twcpaga.com	Atlanta	GA	30328	770-351-0411		2
Tomlinson Bomberger Lawn Care & Landscaping Inc 3055 Yellow Goose Rd. *TF:* 800-575-1776 ■ *Web:* tomlinsonbomberger.com	Lancaster	PA	17601	717-399-1991		577
Tomlinson Industries 13700 Broadway Ave. **Fax Area Code:* 604 ■ *Web:* www.tomlinsonind.com	Cleveland	OH	44125	216-587-3400	939-7598*	298
Tomlinson Run State Park PO Box 97. *Web:* www.tomlinsonrunsp.com	New Manchester	WV	26056	304-564-3651		565
Tommy Tape 378 Four Rod Rd. *TF:* 888-866-8273 ■ *Web:* www.tommytape.com	Berlin	CT	06037	860-378-0111	378-0113	732
Tommy's Restaurant 1824 Coventry Rd. *Web:* www.tommyscoventry.com	Cleveland	OH	44118	216-321-7757		671
Tomoe Sushi 172 Thompson St.	New York	NY	10012	212-777-9346		671
Tomoegawa USA Inc 742 Glenn Ave. *Web:* www.tomoegawa.com	Wheeling	IL	60090	847-541-3001	459-7150	628
Tomoka Correctional Institution 3950 Tiger Bay Rd. *Web:* dc.state.fl.us	Daytona Beach	FL	32124	386-323-1070	323-1006	213
Tomoka State Park 2099 N Beach St. *Web:* www.floridastateparks.org/tomoka	Ormond Beach	FL	32174	386-676-4050	676-4050	565
Tompkins Bros Company Inc 623 Oneida St. *Web:* www.tompkinsusa.com	Syracuse	NY	13202	315-422-8763	422-8762	744
Tompkins Cortland Community College 170 N St. **Fax:* Admissions ■ *TF:* 888-567-8211 ■ *Web:* www.tc3.edu	Dryden	NY	13053	607-844-8211	844-6541*	162
Tompkins County 320 N Tioga St. *Web:* www.nycourts.gov	Ithaca	NY	14850	607-274-5431		338
Tompkins County Chamber of Commerce 904 E Shore Dr. *TF:* 888-568-9816 ■ *Web:* www.tompkinschamber.org	Ithaca	NY	14850	607-273-7080	272-7617	139
Tompkins County Public Library 101 E Green St. *TF:* 800-772-7267 ■ *Web:* www.tcpl.org	Ithaca	NY	14850	607-272-4557	272-8111	434-3
Tompkins Industries Inc 1912 E 123rd St. *TF:* 800-255-1008 ■ *Web:* www.tompkinsind.com	Olathe	KS	66061	913-764-8088		350
Tompkins International 6870 Perry Creek Rd. *TF:* 800-789-1257 ■ *Web:* tompkinsinc.com	Raleigh	NC	27616	919-876-3667	872-9666	194
Tompkins Mc Guire Wachenfeld & Barry 100 Mulberry St. *Web:* www.tompkinsmcguire.com	Newark	NJ	07102	973-622-3000	623-7780	428
Tompkins Products Inc 1040 W Grand Blvd. *TF:* 800-258-0886 ■ *Web:* www.tompkinsproducts.com	Detroit	MI	48208	313-894-2222	894-2901	621
Tompkins Research & Management Consulting Inc 203 Redstone Hill. *Web:* www.trmc.com	Plainville	CT	06062	860-747-0497		195
Tompkins Trust Co PO Box 460. *NYSE:* TMP ■ *TF:* 888-273-3210 ■ *Web:* www.tompkinstrust.com	Ithaca	NY	14851	607-273-3210		70
Tompkins-McCaw Library 509 N 12th St. *Web:* www.library.vcu.edu	Richmond	VA	23298	804-828-0636	828-6089	434-1
Tomra Pacific Inc 150 Klug Cir.	Corona	CA	92880	951-520-1700	520-1701	112
Toms River-Ocean County Chamber of Commerce 1027 Hooper Ave Bldg 1, Second Fl Ste 5.	Toms River	NJ	08753	732-349-0220		139
Toms Truck Ctr Inc 1008 E Fourth St PO Box 88. *TF:* 800-638-1015 ■ *Web:* www.ttruck.com	Santa Ana	CA	92701	714-338-6060		57
Tomson Steel Co (Inc) PO Box 940. *TF:* 800-837-3001 ■ *Web:* www.tomsonsteel.com	Middletown	OH	45042	800-837-3001		492
Toms-Price Co 303 E Front St. *Web:* www.tomsprice.com	Wheaton	IL	60187	630-668-7878		321
TOMY International Inc 1111 W 22nd St Ste 320. **Fax Area Code:* 630 ■ *TF:* 800-704-8697 ■ *Web:* tomy.com	Oak Brook	IL	60523	800-704-8697	573-7575*	762
Tomz Corp 47 Episcopal Rd. *Web:* www.tomz.com	Berlin	CT	06037	860-612-8896		454
Tona 210 25th St. *Web:* www.tonarestaurant.com	Ogden	UT	84401	801-622-8662		671
Tone Software Inc 1735 S Brookhurst St. *TF:* 800-833-8663 ■ *Web:* www.tonesoft.com	Anaheim	CA	92804	714-991-9460		177
Toner Machining Technologies Inc 212 E Fleming Dr. *Web:* www.tonermachining.com	Morganton	NC	28655	828-432-8007		483
Tonertype of Florida LLC 5313 Johns Rd Ste 210. *TF:* 888-916-1300 ■ *Web:* www.tonertype.com	Tampa	FL	33634	813-915-1300		388
Toney Construction Services Inc 14031 Huffmeister Rd. *TF:* 800-790-6202 ■ *Web:* www.toneyconstruction.com	Cypress	TX	77429	281-304-1778		186
Tonga *Consulate General* 360 Post St Ste 604. *Web:* www.tongaconsul.com	San Francisco	CA	94108	415-781-0365	781-3964	257
Tongal 1918 Main St 2nd Fl. *Web:* www.tongal.com	Santa Monica	CA	90405	310-579-9260		387
Tongass Conservation Society (TCS) PO Box 23377. *Web:* www.tongassconservation.org	Ketchikan	AK	99901	907-225-3275		48-13
Tongass Historical Museum 629 Dock St. *Web:* www.ktn-ak.us/museums	Ketchikan	AK	99901	907-225-5900		520
Tongass Trading Co 201 Dock St. *TF:* 800-235-5102 ■ *Web:* www.tongasstrading.com	Ketchikan	AK	99901	907-225-5101		229
Tongue River Reservoir State Park PO Box 1630. *Web:* fwp.mt.gov	Miles City	MT	59301	406-757-2298		565
Toni & Guy USA Inc 2311 Midway Rd. *TF:* 800-256-9391 ■ *Web:* www.toniguy.com	Carrollton	TX	75006	800-256-9391		77
Toni's Sushi Bar 1208 Washington Ave. *Web:* www.tonisushi.com	Miami Beach	FL	33139	305-673-9368		671
Tonic Studios Inc 476 Broome St Ste 6B. *Web:* www.mikelingle.com	New York	NY	10013	212-431-0260	226-6347	344
Tonio Burgos & Associates Inc 115 Broadway Rm 1504. *Web:* www.tonioburgos.com	New York	NY	10006	212-566-5600		636
Tonix Corp 40910 Encyclopedia Cir. *TF:* 800-227-2072 ■ *Web:* www.tonixteams.com	Fremont	CA	94538	510-651-8050	651-8052	155-3
Tonko Paul D (Rep D - NY) 2463 Rayburn Bldg. *Web:* tonko.house.gov	Washington	DC	20515	202-225-5076	225-5077	342-2
Tonner Doll Co 301 Wall St PO Box 4410. *TF:* 800-794-2107 ■ *Web:* www.tonnerdoll.com	Kingston	NY	12402	845-339-9537	339-1259	762
Tonopah Chamber of Commerce 301 Brougher Ave. *TF:* 800-528-1234 ■ *Web:* www.tonopahnevada.com	Tonopah	NV	89049	775-482-3859		139
Tonto National Monument 26260 N Az Hwy 188 2. *Web:* www.nps.gov/tont	Roosevelt	AZ	85545	928-467-2241	467-2225	564
Tonto Natural Bridge State Park Hwy 87 N. *Web:* www.azstateparks.com	Payson	AZ	85547	928-476-4202		565
Tony Angelo Cement Construction Co 46850 Grand River Ave.	Novi	MI	48374	248-344-4000		188-4
Tony Chan's Water Club 1717 N Bayshore Dr. *Web:* www.tonychans.com	Miami	FL	33132	305-374-8888		671
Tony da Caneca 72 Elm Rd. *Web:* www.tonydacaneca.com	Newark	NJ	07105	973-589-6882	589-0036	671
Tony Lama Boot Company Inc 1137 Tony Lama St. *TF:* 800-545-8707 ■ *Web:* www.tonylama.com	El Paso	TX	79915	915-778-8311		301
Tony Mandola's Gulf Coast Kitchen 1212 Waugh Dr. *Web:* www.tonymandolas.com	Houston	TX	77019	713-528-3474	528-4438	671
Tony Packo's 1902 Front St. *TF:* 866-472-2567 ■ *Web:* www.tonypacko.com	Toledo	OH	43605	419-691-1953		671
Tony Wang's 2217 Lincoln Hwy E.	Lancaster	PA	17602	717-399-1915		671
Tony's 3755 Richmond Ave. *Web:* www.tonyshouston.com	Houston	TX	77046	713-622-6778		671
Tony's Finer Foods Inc 3607 W Fullerton Ave. *Web:* tonysfreshmarket.com	Chicago	IL	60647	773-278-8355		345
Tony's Huntington Inn 437 Huntington Tpke. *Web:* tonyshuntingtoninn.com	Bridgeport	CT	06610	203-374-5541		671
Tony's Meats & Specialty Foods 874 W Happy Canyon Rd. *Web:* tonysmarket.com	Castle Rock	CO	80108	303-814-3888		297-8
Toobs Inc 347 Quintana Rd. *TF:* 800-795-8662 ■ *Web:* www.toobs.com	Morro Bay	CA	93442	800-795-8662		710
Tooele County 47 S Main St. *Web:* www.co.tooele.ut.us	Tooele	UT	84074	435-843-3140	882-7317	338
Tooele County Chamber of Commerce 154 S Main. *Web:* www.tooelechamber.com	Tooele	UT	84074	435-882-0690	833-0946	139
TooJays Original Gourmet Deli 3654 Georgia Ave. *Web:* www.toojays.com	West Palm Beach	FL	33405	561-659-9011	659-9703	670
Tool Smith Company Inc 1300 Fourth Ave S. *TF:* 800-317-8665 ■ *Web:* www.toolsmith.ws	Birmingham	AL	35233	205-323-2576	323-9060	386
Tool Sport & Sign Co 1060 S Lapeer Rd. *Web:* toolsportandsign.com	Oxford	MI	48371	248-969-5850		701
Tool Technology Distributors Inc 3110 Osgood Ct. *TF:* 800-335-8437 ■ *Web:* www.tooltechnology.com	Fremont	CA	94539	510-656-8220		358
Toolbox Studios Inc 454 Soledad St. *Web:* toolboxstudios.com	San Antonio	TX	78205	210-225-8269		344
Toolcraft Products Inc 1265 Mc Cook Ave. *Web:* www.toolcraftproducts.com	Dayton	OH	45404	937-223-8271	223-1408	757
Toole County 226 First St S. *Web:* toolecountymt.gov	Shelby	MT	59474	406-424-8310	424-8301	338
Tool-Flo Mfg Inc 7803 Hansen Rd. *TF:* 800-345-2815 ■ *Web:* www.toolflo.com	Houston	TX	77061	713-941-1080	941-8099	455
Toolhouse Design Co 2925 Roeder Ave Ste 200. *Web:* www.toolhouse.com	Bellingham	WA	98225	360-676-9275		344

Company / Address	City	State	Zip	Phone	Fax	Class
Tooling & Equipment International Corp 12550 Tech Ctr Dr. *Web:* www.teintl.com	Livonia	MI	48150	734-522-1422	522-1780	487
Tooling Dynamics Inc 905 Vogelsong Rd *Web:* www.toolingdynamics.com	York	PA	17404	717-764-8873		488
Tooling Technology LLC 100 Enterprise Dr *TF:* 800-376-6653 ■ *Web:* www.toolingtechgroup.com	Fort Loramie	OH	45845	937-295-3672		492
Toolmex Corporation Inc 1075 Worcester Rd *Web:* www.toolmex.com	Natick	MA	01760	508-653-8897		358
Tools & Production Co 4924 N Encinita Ave *Web:* www.toolsandproduction.com	Temple City	CA	91780	626-286-0213	286-3398	757
Tools for Bending Inc 194 W Dakota Ave. *TF Cust Svc:* 800-873-3305 ■ *Web:* www.toolsforbending.com	Denver	CO	80223	303-777-7170	777-4749	456
Toolwire Inc 7031 Koll Ctr Pkwy Ste 220 *TF:* 866-935-8665 ■ *Web:* www.toolwire.com	Pleasanton	CA	94566	925-227-8500	227-8501	39
Toolworx Information Products Inc 7994 Grand River *Web:* www.toolworx.com	Brighton	MI	48114	810-220-5115		180
Toombs County 100 Courthouse Sq PO Box 112 *Web:* www.toombscountyga.gov	Lyons	GA	30436	912-526-3311	526-1004	338
Toomey Patrick J (Sen R - PA) 248 Hart Bldg *Web:* www.toomey.senate.gov	Washington	DC	20510	202-224-4254	228-0284	342-2
Tootsie Roll Industries Inc 7401 S Cicero Ave *NYSE:* TR ■ *TF:* 866-972-6879 ■ *Web:* www.tootsie.com	Chicago	IL	60629	773-838-3400	838-3534	296-8
Top Air Sprayers 601 S Broad St. *TF:* 800-322-6301 ■ *Web:* www.topairequip.com	Kalida	OH	45853	419-532-3121	532-2468	273
Top Die Casting Co 13910 Dearborn Ave *Web:* www.topdie.com	South Beloit	IL	61080	815-389-2599		308
Top Dog Express Car Wash 401 S SR 434 *Web:* topdogexpresscarwash.com	Altamonte Springs	FL	32714	407-636-9112		366
Top Flight Inc 1300 Central Ave *TF:* 800-777-3740 ■ *Web:* www.topflightpaper.com	Chattanooga	TN	37408	423-266-8171	266-6857	263
Top Flite Financial Inc 123 E Grand River Ave *Web:* www.teamtopflite.com	Williamston	MI	48895	517-655-2140		509
Top Floor Technologies LLC 2725 S Moorland Rd Ste 300 *TF:* 888-947-4400 ■ *Web:* www.topfloortech.com	New Berlin	WI	53151	262-364-0010		7
Top Guard Security Inc 131 Kings Way *Web:* www.topguardinc.com	Hampton	VA	23669	757-722-3961	722-9902	693
Top Gun Aviation Inc 405 Industrial Pk Rd *Web:* www.airnav.com/airport/KHDC/TOP_GUN	Hammond	LA	70401	985-542-0719	542-2077	63
TOP Marketing U.S.A. LLC 1332 Baur Blvd. *Web:* www.topmarketingusa.com	St. Louis	MO	63132	314-262-8550		195
Top Master Inc 2844 Roe Ln *Web:* www.top-master.com	Kansas City	KS	66103	913-492-3030		115
Top Notch Art Ctr 411 S Craig St *Web:* tnartsupply.com	Pittsburgh	PA	15213	412-683-4444		46
Top of Daytona Restaurant 2625 S Atlantic Ave. *TF:* 800-561-3357 ■ *Web:* topofdaytona.com	Daytona Beach	FL	32118	386-767-5791		671
Top of the World Travel 5105 - 48 St *Web:* www.topoftheworldtravel.com	Yellowknife	NT	X1A1N5	867-766-6000		772
Top of Virginia Regional Chamber 407 S Loudoun St. *Web:* www.regionalchamber.biz	Winchester	VA	22601	540-662-4118		139
Top Producer Magazine 1818 Market St 31st Fl *TF:* 800-320-7992 ■ *Web:* www.agweb.com	Philadelphia	PA	19103	800-320-7992		457-1
Top Producer Systems Inc 10651 Shellbridge Way Ste 155 *TF:* 800-821-3657 ■ *Web:* www.topproducer.com	Richmond	BC	V6X2W8	800-821-3657		179
Top Promotions Inc 8831 S Greenview Dr *TF:* 800-344-2968 ■ *Web:* www.toppromotions.com	Middleton	WI	53562	608-836-9111		687
Top Rank Inc 3980 Howard Hughes Pkwy Ste 580 *TF:* 800-745-3000 ■ *Web:* www.toprank.com	Las Vegas	NV	89169	702-732-2717		181
Top Shelf Fixtures 5263 Schaefer Ave *Web:* www.topshelffixtures.com	Chino	CA	91710	909-627-7423		106
Top Shop Inc, The 5740 Logan St. *Web:* www.tshopinc.com	Denver	CO	80216	303-996-6026		186
Top Spice 3007 N Druid Hills Rd *Web:* www.topspiceatlanta.com	Atlanta	GA	30329	404-728-0588		671
Top Tool Co 3100 84th Ln NE. *Web:* www.toptool.com	Minneapolis	MN	55449	763-786-0030		697
Topa Equities Ltd 1800 Ave of the Stars Ste 1400 *Web:* www.topa.com	Los Angeles	CA	90067	310-203-9199	229-9788	185
Topa Insurance Corp 24025 Park Sorrento Ste 300 *TF:* 877-353-8672 ■ *Web:* www.topains.com	Calabasas	CA	91302	310-201-0451		391-4
Topa Management Co 1800 Ave of the Stars Ste 1400 *Web:* www.topamanagement.com	Los Angeles	CA	90067	310-203-9199	229-9788	655
Topanga State Park 1925 Las Virgenes *Web:* www.parks.ca.gov/default.asp?page_id=629	Calabasas	CA	91302	818-880-0367		565
Topaz Hotel 1733 N St NW. *TF:* 800-775-1202 ■ *Web:* www.topazhotel.com	Washington	DC	20036	202-393-3000		379
Topaz International Inc 3 Regent St Ste 305 *Web:* topattorneys.com	Livingston	NJ	07039	973-597-0500		260
Topaz Lighting Corp 925 Waverly Ave. *TF:* 800-666-2852 ■ *Web:* www.topaz-usa.com	Holtsville	NY	11742	631-758-5507		362
Topaz Resources Inc 1012 N Masch Branch Rd *TF:* 800-732-0330 ■ *Web:* www.topazresourcesinc.com	Denton	TX	76207	940-243-1122		536
Topco Assoc LLC 7711 Gross Pt Rd *TF:* 888-423-0139 ■ *Web:* www.topco.com	Skokie	IL	60077	847-676-3030	676-4949	297-8
Topco Oilsite Products Ltd Bay 7 3401 - 19 St NE *Web:* www.topcooilsite.com	Calgary	AB	T2E6S8	403-219-0255		540
TopCoder Inc 95 Glastonbury Blvd *TF:* 866-867-2633 ■ *Web:* www.topcoder.com	Glastonbury	CT	06033	860-633-5540	657-4276	177
Topcon Medical Systems Inc 111 Bauer Dr *TF:* 800-223-1130 ■ *Web:* www.topconmedical.com	Oakland	NJ	07436	201-599-5100	599-5250	382
Topcon Positioning Systems Inc 7400 National Dr *Web:* www.topconpositioning.com	Livermore	CA	94551	925-245-8300	245-8599	472
Topcraft Metal Products Inc 5112 40th Ave. *Web:* www.topcraftmetal.com	Hudsonville	MI	49426	616-669-1790		295
Topdek Inc 2926 NW 72nd Ave *Web:* www.topdek.com	Miami	FL	33122	305-599-0006		174
Topeka & Shawnee County Public Library 1515 SW Tenth Ave. *Web:* www.tscpl.org	Topeka	KS	66604	785-580-4400	580-4496	434-3
Topeka Capital-Journal 616 SE Jefferson St *TF:* 800-777-7171 ■ *Web:* cjonline.com	Topeka	KS	66607	785-295-1111	295-1230	532-2
Topeka City Hall 215 SE Seventh St *Web:* www.topeka.org	Topeka	KS	66603	785-368-3754		337
Topeka Correctional Facility 815 SE Rice Rd *Web:* www.dc.state.ks.us/facilities/tcf	Topeka	KS	66603	785-296-3317		213
Topeka Juvenile Correctional Complex 1430 NW 25th St *Web:* www.doc.ks.gov/juvenile-services/kjcc	Topeka	KS	66618	785-354-9800		412
Topeka Livestock Auction 601 E Lake St *Web:* topekallvestock.com	Topeka	IN	46571	260-593-2522	593-2258	446
Topeka Metal Specialties Inc 5600 S Topeka Blvd *Web:* www.topekametal.com	Topeka	KS	66609	785-862-1071		697
Topeka Performing Arts Ctr 214 SE Eigth Ave *TF:* 800-275-8777 ■ *Web:* www.topekaperformingarts.org	Topeka	KS	66603	785-234-2787	234-2307	572
Topeka Public Schools 624 SW 24th St **Fax:* Hum Res ■ *TF:* 800-999-1196 ■ *Web:* www.topekapublicschools.net	Topeka	KS	66611	785-295-3000	575-6162*	685
Topeka Symphony 519 SW 37th PO Box 2206 *Web:* www.topekasymphony.org	Topeka	KS	66601	785-232-2032	232-6204	573-3
Topeka Zoological Park 635 SW Gage Blvd *Web:* topekazoo.org	Topeka	KS	66606	785-368-9180	368-9152	823
Topica Inc 1 Post St Ste 875 *TF:* 888-728-2465 ■ *Web:* www.topica.com	San Francisco	CA	94104	415-344-0800	344-0900	7
Topix 35 McCaul St Ste 200 *Web:* www.topix.com	Toronto	ON	M5T1V7	416-971-7711		33
Topix LLC 1001 Elwell Ct	Palo Alto	CA	94303	650-461-8300		387
Topline Corp 13150 SE 32nd St. *Web:* www.toplinecorp.com	Bellevue	WA	98005	425-643-3003	643-3846	301
TopLine Strategies 11333 N Scottsdale Rd Ste 240 *Web:* toplinestrategies.com	Scottsdale	AZ	85254	480-503-8584		196
Topnotch at Stowe Resort & Spa 4000 Mountain Rd **Fax Area Code:* 802 ■ *TF:* 800-451-8686 ■ *Web:* www.topnotchresort.com	Stowe	VT	05672	800-451-8686	253-9263*	669
Topp Industries Inc 420 N State Rd 25 PO Box 420 *TF:* 800-354-4534 ■ *Web:* www.toppindustries.com	Rochester	IN	46975	574-223-3681	223-6106	601
Toppan Photomasks Inc 131 Old Settlers Blvd *Web:* www.photomask.com	Round Rock	TX	78664	512-310-6500		696
Toppenish School District 202 306 Bolin Dr. *Web:* www.toppenish.wednet.edu	Toppenish	WA	98948	509-865-4455	865-2067	685
Topper's 120 Wauwinet Rd *Web:* wauwinet.com	Nantucket	MA	02584	508-228-8768		671
Topps Company Inc 1 Whitehall St. *TF:* 800-489-9149 ■ *Web:* www.topps.com	New York	NY	10004	212-376-0300	376-0573	296-6
Topps Digital Services 1524 Cloverfield Blvd Ste G *Web:* www.toppsdigitalservices.com	Santa Monica	CA	90404	310-566-1420		195
Topps Safety Apparel Inc 2516 E State Rd 14 *TF:* 800-348-2990 ■ *Web:* www.toppssafetyapparel.com	Rochester	IN	46975	574-223-4311	223-8622	155-19
TOPS Club Inc 4575 S Fifth St. *TF:* 800-932-8677 ■ *Web:* www.tops.org	Milwaukee	WI	53207	414-482-4620	482-1655	48-17
Tops Industries Inc 797 Twin View Blvd.	Redding	CA	96003	530-242-0200		345
Topsail Hill Preserve State Park 7525 W Scenic Hwy 30A *Web:* www.floridastateparks.org	Santa Rosa Beach	FL	32459	850-245-2157		565
Topside Consulting Group LLC 929 Deep Creek Rd. *Web:* www.topside-consulting.com	Lancaster	VA	22503	703-442-7508		463
Topspin Group Inc 415 Executive Dr. *Web:* topspingroup.com	Princeton	NJ	08540	609-252-9515		466
Topspin Partners LP 3 Expy Plaza *Web:* www.topspinpartners.com	Roslyn Heights	NY	11577	516-625-9400	625-9499	792
Toptica Photonics Inc 1286 Blossom Dr Ste 1 *TF:* 877-277-9897 ■ *Web:* www.toptica.com	Victor	NY	14564	585-657-6663		419
Topwin Corp 1808 Abalone Ave *Web:* www.topwin.co.jp	Torrance	CA	90501	310-325-2255	325-1877	156
Topy America Inc 980 Chenault Rd *Web:* www.topyamerica.com	Frankfort	KY	40601	502-695-6163		247
Toque 900 Pl Jean-Paul Riopelle *Web:* www.restaurant-toque.com	Montreal	QC	H2Z2B2	514-499-2084	499-0292	671
TOR Minerals International Inc 722 Burleson St *NASDAQ:* TORM ■ *Web:* www.torminerals.com	Corpus Christi	TX	78402	361-883-5591		143

Name / Address	City	State	ZIP	Phone	Fax	Class
Torah Umesorah-National Society for Hebrew Day Schools 620 Foster Ave *TF:* 800-788-3942 ■ *Web:* torah-umesorah.com	Brooklyn	NY	11230	212-227-1000		49-5
Toray Industries America Inc 461 Fifth Ave 9th Fl *Web:* www.toray.com	New York	NY	10017	212-697-8150	972-4279	605-1
Toray Plastics America Inc 50 Belver Ave *Web:* www.torayfilms.com	North Kingstown	RI	02852	401-294-4511		596
Torch Energy Advisors Inc (TEAI) 1331 Lamar Ave Ste 1450	Houston	TX	77010	713-650-1246		401
Torch Restaurant 4425 S Alameda St	Corpus Christi	TX	78412	361-992-7491		671
Torchlight Energy Resources Inc 5700 W Plano Pkwy Ste 3600 *Web:* www.torchlightenergy.com	Plano	TX	75093	214-432-8002		536
Torchmark Corp 3700 S Stonebridge Dr *NYSE: TMK* ■ *TF:* 877-577-3899 ■ *Web:* www.torchmarkcorp.com	McKinney	TX	75070	972-569-4000	569-3282	360-4
Torco Inc 1330 Old 41 Hwy NW *Web:* www.torcoinc.com	Marietta	GA	30060	770-427-3704	426-9369	621
Torcom 25 Kessel Ct *Web:* torco.com	Madison	WI	53711	608-276-4114		737
Torcon Inc 328 Newman Springs Rd *Web:* www.torcon.com	Red Bank	NJ	07701	732-704-9800	704-9810	186
Torero's 800 W Main St *Web:* torerosmexicanrestaurants.com	Durham	NC	27701	919-682-4197		671
Torii Japanese Restaurant 2401 E Orangeburg Ave Ste 590	Modesto	CA	95355	209-529-8697		671
Torke Coffee Roasting Company Inc 3455 Paine Ave *TF:* 800-242-7671 ■ *Web:* www.torkecoffee.com	Sheboygan	WI	53081	920-458-4114	458-0488	296-7
Torn & Glasser Inc 1622 E Olympic Blvd PO Box 21823 *Web:* www.tornandglasser.com	Los Angeles	CA	90021	213-627-6496	688-0941	297-3
Tornado Alley Turbo 300 Airport Rd *TF:* 877-359-8284 ■ *Web:* www.taturbo.com	Ada	OK	74820	580-332-3510		770
Tornado Bus Company Inc 535 E Jefferson Blvd *Web:* www.tornadobus.com	Dallas	TX	75203	214-941-7399		108
Tornado Club Steak House 116 S Hamilton St *Web:* tornadosteakhouse.com	Madison	WI	53703	608-256-3570		671
Tornado Spectral Systems 555 Richmond St W Ste 705 Ste 705 *TF:* 800-227-9770 ■ *Web:* tornado-spectral.com	Toronto	ON	M5V3B1	416-361-3444		407
Tornatech Inc 7075, Place Robert-Joncas Ste 132 *TF:* 800-363-8448 ■ *Web:* www.tornatech.com	Saint-laurent	QC	H4M2Z2	514-334-0523	334-5448	203
Tornos Technologies US Corp 840 Parkview Blvd *Web:* www.tornos.com	Lombard	IL	60148	630-812-2040	812-2039	455
Toro Co 8111 Lyndale Ave *NYSE: TTC* ■ **Fax Area Code:* 952 ■ *TF:* 888-384-9939 ■ *Web:* www.toro.com	Bloomington	MN	55420	888-384-9939	887-8258*	429
Toro Co Irrigation Div 5825 Jasmine St *TF:* 800-654-1882 ■ *Web:* www.toro.com	Riverside	CA	92504	800-654-1882	451-1390	273
Toro Company Commercial Products Div 8111 Lyndale Ave *TF Cust Svc:* 800-348-2424 ■ *Web:* www.toro.com	Bloomington	MN	55420	952-888-8801	887-8258	429
Toromont Industries Ltd 3131 Hwy 7 W PO Box 5511 *TSE: TIH* ■ *Web:* toromontcat.com	Concord	ON	L4K1B7	416-667-5511		358
Toronto Aerospace Museum RPO Evans Brown Ln PO Box 60005 *Web:* www.casmuseum.org	Etobicoke	ON	M8W4Z8	416-638-6078	638-5509	520
Toronto And Region Conservation Authority 5 Shoreham Dr *Web:* www.trca.on.ca	Toronto	ON	M3N1S4	416-661-6600		192
Toronto Argonauts 1 Blue Jays Way Ste 3300 *Web:* www.argonauts.ca	Toronto	ON	M5V1J3	416-341-2700		715-2
Toronto Baptist Seminary & Bible College 130 Gerrard St E *Web:* www.tbs.edu	Toronto	ON	M5A3T4	416-925-3263	925-8305	785
Toronto Blue Jays 1 Blue Jays Way Ste 3200 **Fax:* PR ■ *TF:* 888-654-6529 ■ *Web:* toronto.bluejays.mlb.com	Toronto	ON	M5V1J1	416-341-1000	341-1250*	713
Toronto City Hall 100 Queen St W *TF:* 800-461-6290 ■ *Web:* www.toronto.ca	Toronto	ON	M5H2N2	416-392-8016	392-2980	337
Toronto Construction Association 70 Leek Cres *TF:* 800-581-6729 ■ *Web:* www.tcaconnect.com/home.html	Richmond Hill	ON	L4B1H1	416-499-4000		138
Toronto Convention & Visitors Assn 207 Queen's Quay W Ste 405 PO Box 126 *TF:* 800-499-2514 ■ *Web:* www.seetorontonow.com	Toronto	ON	M5J1A7	416-203-2600	203-6753	206
Toronto General Hospital 200 Elizabeth St *Web:* www.uhn.ca	Toronto	ON	M5G2C4	416-340-3111		374-2
Toronto Hydro Corp 14 Carlton St *TF:* 800-668-7678 ■ *Web:* www.torontohydro.com	Toronto	ON	M5B1K5	416-542-3000		767
Toronto International Film Festival Inc Reitman Sq 350 King St W *TF:* 888-599-8433 ■ *Web:* www.tiff.net	Toronto	ON	M5V3X5	888-599-8433		282
Toronto Law Office Management Association PO Box 1029 Toronto Dominion Ctr *Web:* www.tloma.com	Toronto	ON	M5K1P2	416-410-1979		138
Toronto Life Magazine 111 Queen St E Ste 320 *Web:* www.torontolife.com	Toronto	ON	M5C1S2	416-364-3333		457-22
Toronto Maple Leafs 50 Bay St Fl 11 **Fax Area Code:* 412 ■ *Web:* mapleleafs.nhl.com	Toronto	ON	M5J2X8	416-815-5700	255-1980*	716
Toronto Port Authority 60 Harbour St *Web:* www.portstoronto.com/home.aspx	Toronto	ON	M5J1B7	416-863-2000	863-0495	618
Toronto School of Theology 47 Queen's Pk Crescent E *Web:* www.tst.edu	Toronto	ON	M5S2C3	416-978-4039		167-3
Toronto Star 1 Yonge St **Fax:* News Rm ■ *TF:* 800-268-9756 ■ *Web:* www.thestar.com	Toronto	ON	M5E1E6	416-869-4949	869-4328*	532-1

Name / Address	City	State	ZIP	Phone	Fax	Class
Toronto Stock Exchange 130 King St W *TF:* 888-873-8392 ■ *Web:* www.tmx.com	Toronto	ON	M5X1J2	416-947-4670	947-4662	691
Toronto Sun 333 King St E *TF:* 888-786-7821 ■ *Web:* www.torontosun.com	Toronto	ON	M5A3X5	416-947-2222	947-1664	532-1
Toronto Transit Commission (TTC) 1900 Yonge St *TF:* 800-223-6192 ■ *Web:* www.ttc.ca	Toronto	ON	M4S1Z2	416-393-4000		468
Toronto Western Hospital 399 Bathurst St *Web:* www.uhn.ca	Toronto	ON	M5T2S8	416-603-2581		374-2
Toronto Zoo 361-A Old Finch Ave *TF:* 800-832-3474 ■ *Web:* www.torontozoo.com	Toronto	ON	M1B5K7	416-392-5900	392-5934	823
Toronto's First Post Office 260 Adelaide St E *TF:* 800-668-9933 ■ *Web:* www.townofyork.com	Toronto	ON	M5A1N1	416-865-1833		520
Torrance Area Chamber of Commerce 2300 Crenshaw Blvd Bldg B *Web:* www.torrancechamber.com	Torrance	CA	90501	310-540-5858	540-7662	139
Torrance Casting Inc 3131 Commerce St *Web:* www.torrancecasting.com	La Crosse	WI	54603	608-781-0600		492
Torrance County 205 Ninth St PO Box 48 *Web:* www.torrancecountynm.org	Estancia	NM	87016	505-544-4700	384-5294	338
Torrance County Detention Facility 209 County Rd A049	Estancia	NM	87016	505-384-2711		213
Torrance Memorial Home Health & Hospice 3330 Lomita Blvd *TF:* 800-906-9909 ■ *Web:* www.torrancememorial.org	Torrance	CA	90505	310-784-3739		371
Torrance Memorial Medical Ctr 3330 Lomita Blvd *TF:* 800-551-1300 ■ *Web:* www.torrancememorial.org	Torrance	CA	90505	310-325-9110	784-4801	374-3
Torrance Public Library 3301 Torrance Blvd *TF:* 800-829-1040 ■ *Web:* www.torranceca.gov	Torrance	CA	90503	310-618-5959	618-5952	434-3
Torrance Unified School District 2335 Plaza Del AMO *Web:* www.tusd.org	Torrance	CA	90501	310-972-6500		685
Torray Fund 7501 Wisconsin Ave Ste 750 W *TF:* 800-443-3036 ■ *Web:* www.torray.com	Bethesda	MD	20814	301-493-4600		528
Torrence's Farm Implement Inc 190 E Hwy 86 PO Box C *Web:* www.torrences.net	Heber	CA	92249	760-352-5355	352-8707	274
Torrent Pharma Inc 5380 Holiday Terr Ste 40 *Web:* ww2.torrentpharma.com	Kalamazoo	MI	49009	269-544-2299		231
Torres Norma (Rep D - CA) 1713 Longworth HOB *Web:* torres.house.gov	Washington	DC	20515	202-225-6161	225-8671	342-2
Torres Ralph Deleon Guerrero (R) PO Box 10007 **Fax Area Code:* 6.7 ■ *Web:* gov.mp	Saipan	MP	96950	.51-201-e+009	066-4e+009*	343
Torrey Farms Inc Maltby Rd *Web:* www.torreyfarms.com	Elba	NY	14058	585-757-9941		10-11
Torrey Pines State Beach 4477 Pacific Hwy *Web:* www.parks.ca.gov/default.asp?page_id=658	San Diego	CA	92110	858-755-2063		565
Torrey Pines State Reserve c/o San Diego Coast District 4477 Pacific Hwy *TF:* 866-240-4655 ■ *Web:* www.parks.ca.gov/?page_id=657	San Diego	CA	92110	858-755-2063		565
Torreya State Park 2576 NW Torreya Pk Rd *Web:* www.floridastateparks.org	Bristol	FL	32321	850-643-2674		565
Torrid Technologies Inc 1860 Sandy Plains Rd Ste 204-129 *Web:* www.torrid-tech.com	Marietta	GA	30066	770-565-6405		177
Torry Harris Business Solutions Inc 536 Fayette St *TF:* 800-713-7278 ■ *Web:* www.thbs.com	Perth Amboy	NJ	08861	732-442-0049		631
Torstar Corp 1 Yonge St *TSE: TS.B* ■ *Web:* www.torstar.com	Toronto	ON	M5E1E6	416-869-4010	869-4183	637-2
Torstenson Glass Co 3233 N Sheffield Ave *Web:* www.tglass.com	Chicago	IL	60657	773-525-0435	525-0009	329
Tortel USA LLC 221 Commerce Dr *Web:* www.tortelusa.com	Amherst	NY	14228	716-691-5804		246
Torti Gallas & Partners Inc 1300 Spring St Ste 400 *Web:* www.tortigallas.com	Silver Spring	MD	20910	301-588-4800	650-2255	186
Tortilla Flats 3139 Cerrillos Rd *Web:* tortillaflats.net	Santa Fe	NM	87507	505-471-8685		671
Tortilla Jo's 1510 Disneyland Dr Downtown Disney *Web:* www.patinagroup.com/tortillaJos	Anaheim	CA	92802	714-535-5000		671
Tortilla King Inc 249 23Rd Ave *Web:* www.tortillaking.com	Moundridge	KS	67107	620-345-2674		123
Tortoise Energy Capital Corp 11550 Ash St Ste 300 *NYSE: TYY* ■ *TF:* 866-362-9331 ■ *Web:* www.tortoiseadvisors.com	Leawood	KS	66211	913-981-1020	981-1021	792
Torys LLP 79 Wellington St W TD Centre 30th Fl 30th Fl *Web:* www.torys.com	Toronto	ON	M5K1N2	416-865-0040		41
Tosan Inc 2209 Larimer St Unit A *Web:* www.tosaninc.com	Denver	CO	80205	303-832-7606		193
Tosca 1112 F St NW *Web:* www.toscadc.com	Washington	DC	20004	202-367-1990	367-1999	671
Tosca Ristorante 144 O'Connor St *Web:* www.tosca-ristorante.ca	Ottawa	ON	K2P2G7	613-565-3933		671
Toscana 6401 Morrison Blvd *Web:* conterestaurantgroup.com	Charlotte	NC	28211	704-367-1808		671
Tosh Farms 1586 Atlantic Ave *TF:* 800-331-2020 ■ *Web:* www.toshfarms.net	Henry	TN	38231	731-243-4861	243-4860	10-4
Toshiba America Inc 1251 Ave of the Americas Ste 4100 *TF:* 800-457-7777 ■ *Web:* www.toshiba.com	New York	NY	10020	212-596-0600		52

Company	City	State	Zip	Phone	Fax	Class
Toshiba America Information Systems Inc 9740 Irvine Blvd *TF Cust Svc:* 800-457-7777 ■ *Web:* www.toshiba.com	Irvine	CA	92618	949-583-3000		173-2
Toshiba America Medical Systems Inc 2441 Michelle Dr *TF Cust Svc:* 800-521-1968 ■ *Web:* www.medical.toshiba.com	Tustin	CA	92780	714-730-5000		382
Toshiba International Corp 13131 W Little York Rd *TF:* 800-231-1412 ■ *Web:* www.toshiba.com	Houston	TX	77041	713-466-0277	896-5240	518
Tosoh Bioscience Inc 6000 Shoreline Court Ste 101 *TF:* 800-248-6764 ■ *Web:* www.diagnostics.us.tosohbioscience.com	South San Francisco	CA	94080	650-615-4970		475
Tosoh SMD Inc 3600 Gantz Rd *Web:* www.tosohsmd.com	Grove City	OH	43123	614-875-7912	875-0031	696
TOSS C3 1253 Worcester Rd Ste 304 *TF:* 888-884-8677 ■ *Web:* www.toss.com	Framingham	MA	01701	508-820-2990		180
Total Airport Services Inc 28420 Hardy Toll Rd Ste 220 *Web:* www.totalairportservices.com	Spring	TX	77373-8084	832-592-0048		579
Total Assault Llc 3272 Motor Ave Ste G *TF:* 800-676-8888 ■ *Web:* www.totalassault.com	Los Angeles	CA	90034	310-280-3777		195
Total Battery Consulting Inc PO Box 1059 *Web:* www.totalbatteryconsulting.com	Oregon House	CA	95962	530-692-0140	660-1646	463
Total Beauty Media Inc 3420 Ocean Park Blvd Ste 3050 *Web:* www.totalbeautymedia.com	Santa Monica	CA	90405	310-399-7400		77
Total Care Inc 819 S Salina St *TF:* 800-662-1220 ■ *Web:* www.totalcareny.com	Syracuse	NY	13202	315-634-5555		390
Total Components Solutions Corp 2080 Tenth St *Web:* www.tcsiowa.com	Rock Valley	IA	51247	712-476-5315		454
Total Computing Solutions of America Inc 23430 Hawthorne Blvd Skypark Office Ctr Bldg 3 Ste 300 *Web:* www.tcsamerica.com	Torrance	CA	90505	310-378-9100		177
Total Contentz LLC 845 E Easy St Ste 102 *Web:* www.totalcontentz.com	Simi Valley	CA	93065	805-522-5900		463
Total Control Software Corp 12010 Watson Rd *Web:* www.tcsoft.com	Sherwood	AR	72120	501-833-3281		525
Total Credit Recovery Ltd 225 Yorkland Blvd *TF:* 800-267-2482 ■ *Web:* www.totalcrediting.com	Toronto	ON	M2J4Y7	416-774-4000		160
Total E & P USA Inc 1201 Louisiana St Total Plaza Ste 1800 *TF:* 800-322-3462 ■ *Web:* www.total.com	Houston	TX	77002	800-322-3462		538
Total Energy Control Systems Inc 47-25 34th St Ste 4 *Web:* tecsystemsnyc.com	Long Island	NY	11101	718-817-8100		810
Total Energy Services Ltd 2550 300-5th Ave SW Ste 2550 *NYSE:* TOT ■ *TF:* 877-818-6825 ■ *Web:* www.totalenergy.ca	Calgary	AB	T2P3C4	403-216-3939	234-8731	540
Total E&P New Ventures Inc Total Plaza 1201 Louisiana Ste 1800	Houston	TX	77002	713-647-3300	647-3345	463
Total Equipment Co 400 Fifth Ave *Web:* www.totalequipment.com	Coraopolis	PA	15108	412-269-0999		385
Total Event Resources 1920 Thoreau Dr N Ste 105 *Web:* www.total-event.com	Schaumburg	IL	60173	847-397-2200		196
Total Filtration Services Inc 2725 Commerce Pkwy *TF:* 800-331-3118 ■ *Web:* www.tfsi1.com	Auburn Hills	MI	48326	248-377-4004		385
Total Fire & Safety Inc 7909 Carr St *Web:* www.totalfire.com	Dallas	TX	75227	214-381-6116	381-4633	246
Total Golf Construction Inc 4045 43rd Ave *TF:* 800-407-0455 ■ *Web:* www.totalgolfconstruction.com	Vero Beach	FL	32960	772-562-1177	562-2773	188-3
Total Health Care Inc 1501 Div St *Web:* www.totalhealthcare.org	Baltimore	MD	21217	410-383-8300	728-4412	374-3
Total Hockey Inc 5833 Suemandy Rd *Web:* www.totalhockey.net	Saint Peters	MO	63376	636-397-6370		711
Total Hr 2626 Foothill Blvd Ste 200 *TF:* 800-975-5128 ■ *Web:* www.totalhrmanagement.com	La Crescenta	CA	91214	818-248-0049		260
Total Immersion Software Inc 1 Enterprise Pkwy Ste 330	Hampton	VA	23666	757-224-6250		225
Total Insight LLC 310 Main Ave Way SE *TF:* 877-226-9950 ■ *Web:* www.totalinsight.com	Hickory	NC	28602	828-485-5000		787
Total Kitchen & Bath Inc 155 S Rohlwing Rd *Web:* www.totalstonesolutions.com	Addison	IL	60101	630-495-2010		290
Total Living Network (TLN) 2880 Vision Ct *Web:* www.tln.com	Aurora	IL	60506	630-801-3838	801-3839	740
Total Logistics Solutions Inc PO Box 11146 *Web:* www.logisticsociety.com	Burbank	CA	91510	818-353-2962		463
Total Lubricants USA 5 N Stiles St *TF:* 800-323-3198 ■ *Web:* www.totalspecialties.com	Linden	NJ	07036	908-862-9300	862-5374	541
Total Maintenance Solutions 3540 Rutherford Rd *TF:* 800-476-2212 ■ *Web:* www.tmssouth.com	Taylors	SC	29687	864-268-2891		610
Total Management Solutions Inc 55 Harristown Rd *TF:* 866-544-0707 ■ *Web:* www.totmgtsol.com	Glen Rock	NJ	07452	201-447-0707	447-3831	47
TOTAL Marketing Inc 8000 Carrick St *TF:* 800-998-5269 ■ *Web:* www.totalmktg.com	Fort Worth	TX	76116	817-560-3970		195
Total Mechanical W234 N2830 Paul Rd *Web:* www.total-mechanical.com	Pewaukee	WI	53072	262-523-2500		393
Total Merchant Concepts Inc 12300 NE Fourth Plain Rd A *TF:* 888-249-9919 ■ *Web:* www.totalmerchantconcepts.com	Vancouver	WA	98682	360-253-5934		535
Total Networx Inc 417 W Travelers Trail *TF:* 800-401-2141 ■ *Web:* www.totalnetworx.com	Burnsville	MN	55337	952-400-6500		180
Total Oilfield Rentals Partnership 6517 51 Ave *Web:* www.totaloilfield.ca	Whitecourt	AB	T7S1N3	780-778-6222		23
Total Outdoor Corp 414 Stewart St Ste 204 *Web:* www.totaloutdoor.com	Seattle	WA	98101	206-430-6080		5
Total Package Express Inc 5871 Cheviot Rd *TF:* 800-420-5505 ■ *Web:* tp-exp.com	Cincinnati	OH	45247	513-741-5500		780
Total Parts Plus Inc 70 Ready Ave NW *Web:* www.totalpartsplus.com	Fort Walton Beach	FL	32548	850-244-7293		317
Total Plastics Inc 3316 Pagosa Ct *TF:* 800-382-4635 ■ *Web:* www.totalplastics.com	Indianapolis	IN	46226	317-543-3540	543-3553	602
Total Plumbing & Heating Inc 12300 Pecos St *Web:* www.totalplbg.com	Westminster	CO	80234	303-393-7271		610
Total Printing Systems 201 S Gregory St *TF:* 800-465-5200 ■ *Web:* www.tps1.com	Newton	IL	62448	800-465-5200		627
Total Promotions 1340 Old Skokie Rd *Web:* promoplace.com/totalpromotions	Highland Park	IL	60035	847-831-9500		7
Total Quality Inc 550 3 Mile Rd Ste D **Fax Area Code:* 800 ■ *Web:* www.shiptqi.com	Grand Rapids	MI	49544	616-785-4600	286-4231*	54
Total Quality Logistics Inc (TQL) 4289 Ivy Pointe Blvd *TF:* 800-580-3101 ■ *Web:* www.tql.com	Cincinnati	OH	45245	513-831-2600	965-7630	311
Total Resource Management Inc 510 King St Ste 200 *TF:* 877-548-5100 ■ *Web:* www.trmnet.com	Alexandria	VA	22314	703-548-4285	548-3641	193
Total Safety Consulting LLC 751 Broadway *Web:* www.totalsafety.org	Bayonne	NJ	07002	201-437-5150		41
Total Seal Inc 22642 N 15th Ave *TF:* 800-874-2753 ■ *Web:* www.totalseal.com	Phoenix	AZ	85027	623-587-7400		128
Total Seminars LLC 12929 Gulf Fwy Ste 105 *TF:* 800-446-6004 ■ *Web:* totalsem.com	Houston	TX	77034	281-922-4166		764
Total Solutions Inc 1626 County Line Rd *TF:* 866-413-4111 ■ *Web:* www.totalsolutions-inc.com	Madison	AL	35756	256-721-3987		177
Total Technologies Ltd 9710 Research Dr *TF:* 800-669-4885 ■ *Web:* www.total-technologies.com	Irvine	CA	92618	949-465-0200	465-0212	253
Total Telcom Inc 540 1632 Dickson Ave *TF:* 877-860-3762 ■ *Web:* www.totaltelcom.com	Kelowna	BC	V1Y7T2	250-860-3762		736
Total Transportation Concept 8728 Avaition Blvd *Web:* www.totaltrans.com	Inglewood	CA	90301	310-337-0515		311
Total Wellhead & Rental Tools LLC 401 S Juniper St *Web:* www.totalwellhead.com	Perryton	TX	79070	806-435-3800		538
Total Wine & More 6600 Rockledge Dr *TF:* 855-328-9463 ■ *Web:* www.totalwine.com	Bethesda	MD	20817	855-328-9463		345
Total Works Inc 2240 N Elston Ave *TF:* 800-262-9912 ■ *Web:* www.totalworks.net	Chicago	IL	60614	773-489-4313		781
Totalcomp Scales & Components 13-01 Pollitt Dr Ste 2 *TF:* 800-631-0347 ■ *Web:* www.totalcomp.com	Fair Lawn	NJ	07410	201-797-2718		362
Totalis Consulting Group 402 Park Dr *Web:* totalis.com	Warner Robins	GA	31088	478-328-0901		196
Totelcom Communications LLC 6100 Hwy 16 S PO Box 290 *TF:* 800-261-5911 ■ *Web:* totelcom.net	De Leon	TX	76444	254-893-1000		224
Totem Bight State Historical Park 400 Willoughby Ave PO Box 111020 *Web:* www.dnr.alaska.gov/parks/units/totembgh.htm	Juneau	AK	99811	907-465-4563		565
Totem Content 37 Front St E *Web:* totem.tc	Toronto	ON	M5E1B3	416-360-7339		5
Totem Electric of Tacoma Inc 2332 Jefferson Ave *Web:* www.totemelectric.com	Tacoma	WA	98402	253-383-5022	272-5214	189-4
Totem Ocean Trailer Express Inc 32001 32nd Ave S Ste 200 *TF:* 800-426-0074 ■ *Web:* www.totemaritime.com	Federal Way	WA	98001	253-449-8100	449-8225	312
Toter Inc PO Box 5338 *TF:* 800-424-0422 ■ *Web:* www.toter.com	Statesville	NC	28677	704-872-8171	878-0734	199
Totes Isotoner Corp 9655 International Blvd *Web:* www.totes.com	Cincinnati	OH	45246	513-682-8200		155-8
Totevision 3257 17th Ave W Bldg 1 Ste 201 *Web:* www.totevision.com	Seattle	WA	98119	206-623-6000	623-6609	693
Totex Manufacturing Inc 2927 Lomita Blvd *Web:* www.batterytechnologies.com	Torrance	CA	90505	310-326-2028		608
Toth Financial Advisory Corp 608 S King St Ste 300 *TF:* 800-445-1880 ■ *Web:* www.tothfinancial.com	Leesburg	VA	20175	703-443-8684		113
Toto Tours 1326 W Albion Ave *TF:* 800-565-1241 ■ *Web:* www.tototours.com	Chicago	IL	60626	773-274-8686	274-8695	760
Toto USA Inc 1155 Southern Rd **Fax:* Cust Svc ■ *TF:* 888-295-8134 ■ *Web:* www.totousa.com	Morrow	GA	30260	770-282-8686	282-8701*	611
Totten Tubes Inc 500 Danlee St **Fax Area Code:* 626 ■ *TF:* 800-882-3748 ■ *Web:* www.tottentubes.com	Azusa	CA	91702	800-882-3748	812-0113*	492
Toucan Cafe 531 Stephenson Ave *Web:* www.toucancafe.com	Savannah	GA	31406	912-352-2233		671
Touch Base 999 18th St Tower N Ste 1515 *TF:* 800-605-6920 ■ *Web:* touchbaseglobal.com	Denver	CO	80202	303-862-3300		116
Touch Networks 2515 152nd Ave NE *Web:* touchnetworks.com	Redmond	WA	98052	425-881-8806		177

	Phone	Fax	Class
Touch of Nature Environmental Center 1206 Touch Of Nature Rd .... Makanda IL 62958 *TF:* 800-800-8000 ■ *Web:* www.pso.siu.edu	618-453-1121		121
TouchAmerica 1403 S Third St Ext .... Hillsborough NC 27278 *TF:* 800-678-6824 ■ *Web:* www.touchamerica.com	919-732-6968	732-1173	76
Touchette Regional Hospital (TRH) 5900 Bond Ave .... Centreville IL 62207 *Web:* www.touchette.org	618-332-3060		374-3
TouchLogic Corp 30 Kinnear Ct Ste 602 .... Richmond Hill ON L4B1K8 *TF:* 877-707-0207 ■ *Web:* www.touchlogic.com	877-707-0207		387
TouchPoint Technologies LLC 2319 Oak Myrtle Ln Ste 104 .... Wesley Chapel FL 33544 *TF:* 877-898-6824 ■ *Web:* www.touchpointtechnologies.com	877-898-6824		366
TouchStar Solutions LLC *Touchstar Group* 5147 S Garnett Rd Ste D .... Tulsa OK 74146 *Web:* www.touchstargroup.com	918-307-7100		173-2
Touchstone Medical Imaging LLC 5214 Maryland Way Ste 200 .... Brentwood TN 37027 *Web:* www.touchstoneimaging.com	615-661-9200		415
Touchstone Pictures 500 S Buena Vista St .... Burbank CA 91521 *Web:* www.thewaltdisneycompany.com	818-560-3300		514
Touchstone Television Production LLC 500 S Buena Vista St .... Burbank CA 91521	818-560-1000		514
Touchstone Wildlife & Art Museum 3386 Highway 80 .... Haughton LA 71037 *Web:* touchstonemuseum.com	318-949-2323		520
Touchstorm LLC 450 Lexington Ave 4th Fl .... New York NY 10017 *TF:* 877-794-6101 ■ *Web:* www.touchstorm.com	877-794-6101		387
TouchSystems Corp 220 Tradesmen Dr .... Hutto TX 78634 *TF:* 800-320-5944 ■ *Web:* www.touchsystems.com	512-846-2424	846-2425	614
Tougaloo College 500 W County Line Rd .... Tougaloo MS 39174 **Fax:* Admissions ■ *TF Admissions:* 888-424-2566 ■ *Web:* www.tougaloo.edu	601-977-7700	977-4501*	166
Tough Traveler Ltd 1012 State St .... Schenectady NY 12307 *TF Cust Svc:* 800-468-6844 ■ *Web:* www.toughtraveler.com	518-377-8526	377-5434	64
Toukan & Co 575 Charring Cross Dr Ste 200 .... Westerville OH 43081 *Web:* toukan.com	614-901-7100		2
Tour East Holidays (Canada) Inc 15 Kern Rd .... North York ON M3B1S9 *Web:* www.toureast.com	416-929-8017		760
Tour Edge Golf Manufacturing Inc 1301 Pierson Dr .... Batavia IL 60510 *TF:* 800-515-3343 ■ *Web:* www.touredge.com	630-584-4777		772
TOUR GCX Partners Inc 450 Park Ave .... New York NY 10016 *Web:* www.tourgcx.com	212-685-2200		760
Tourbillon International LLC 11 W 25th St 8th Fl .... New York NY 10010	212-627-7732		772
Tourette Syndrome Assn Inc 42-40 Bell Blvd Ste 205 .... Bayside NY 11361 *TF:* 888-486-8738 ■ *Web:* www.tourette.org	718-224-2999	279-9596	48-17
Touring & Tasting 125 S Quarantina St .... Santa Barbara CA 93103 *TF:* 800-850-4370 ■ *Web:* www.touringandtasting.com	805-965-2813	965-2873	443
Tourism Abbotsford Society 34561 Delair Rd .... Abbotsford BC V2S2E1 *TF:* 888-332-2229 ■ *Web:* www.tourismabbotsford.ca	604-859-1721		342
Tourism Australia 6100 Ctr Dr Ste 1150 .... Los Angeles CA 90045 *TF:* 800-682-3333 ■ *Web:* www.australia.com	310-695-3200	695-3201	775
Tourism Authority of Thailand 611 N Larchmont Blvd 1st Fl .... Los Angeles CA 90004 *Web:* www.tourismthailand.org	323-461-9814	461-9834	775
Tourism Authority of Thailand 61 Broadway Ste 2810 .... New York NY 10006 *Web:* www.tourismthailand.org	212-432-0433	269-2588	775
Tourism Calgary 200 238 11th Ave SE .... Calgary AB T2G0X8 *TF:* 800-661-1678 ■ *Web:* www.visitcalgary.com	403-263-8510	262-3809	206
Tourism Council of Frederick County Inc 151 S East St .... Frederick MD 21701 *TF:* 800-999-3613 ■ *Web:* www.visitfrederick.org	301-600-2888		206
Tourism Industry Association of Pei 25 Queen St Third Fl PO Box 2050 .... Charlottetown PE C1A7N7 *Web:* www.tiapei.pe.ca	902-566-5008		138
Tourism Ireland 345 Pk Ave .... New York NY 10154 *Web:* www.tourismireland.com	212-418-0800	371-9052	775
Tourism Malaysia (MTPB) 120 E 56th St 15th Fl .... New York NY 10022 *Web:* www.malaysia.travel/en/us	212-754-1113		775
Tourism Malaysia 818 W Seventh St Ste 970 .... Los Angeles CA 90017 *TF:* 800-120-5502 ■ *Web:* www.tourism.gov.my	213-689-9702	689-1530	775
Tourism Medicine Hat 8 Gehring Rd SE .... Medicine Hat AB T1B4W1 *TF:* 800-565-3947 ■ *Web:* www.tourismmedicinehat.com	403-527-6422		775
Tourism New Brunswick PO Box 6000 .... Fredericton NB E3B5H1 *TF:* 800-561-0123 ■ *Web:* www.tourismnewbrunswick.ca	800-561-0123		774
Tourism Richmond Inc South Twr 5811 Cooney Rd Ste 205 .... Richmond BC V6X3M1 *TF:* 877-247-0777 ■ *Web:* www.visitrichmondbc.com	604-821-5474		772
Tourism Saskatchewan 1621 Albert St .... Regina SK S4P2S5 *TF:* 877-237-2273 ■ *Web:* tourismsaskatchewan.com	306-787-9600	787-6293	774
Tourism Saskatoon 202 Fourth Ave N .... Saskatoon SK S7K0K1 *TF:* 800-567-2444 ■ *Web:* www.tourismsaskatoon.com	306-242-1206		775
Tourism Winnipeg 259 Portage Ave Ste 300 .... Winnipeg MB R3B2A9 *TF:* 800-561-0123 ■ *Web:* www.tourismwinnipeg.com	204-943-1970		774
Tourism Yukon PO Box 2703 .... Whitehorse YT Y1A2C6 *TF:* 800-661-0494 ■ *Web:* www.travelyukon.com	800-661-0494		774
Tourist Office of Spain 845 N Michigan Ave Ste 915-E .... Chicago IL 60611 *Web:* www.spain.info	312-642-1992	642-9817	775
Tourist Office of Spain 8383 Wilshire Blvd Ste 960 .... Beverly Hills CA 90211 *Web:* www.spain.info	323-658-7188	658-1061	775
Tourmaline Oil Corp Suite 3700, 250 Sixth Ave SW .... Calgary AB T2P3H7 *TF:* 800-387-0825 ■ *Web:* www.tourmalineoil.com	403-767-3593		536
Tournament Games Inc 107 W High St .... Lebanon TN 37087 *Web:* www.tournamentgames.com	615-547-1777	443-9990	45
Tourney Consulting Group LLC 3401 Midlink Dr .... Kalamazoo MI 49048 *Web:* tourneyconsulting.com	269-384-9980		743
Touro College 500 Seventh Ave .... New York NY 10018 *TF:* 888-247-1387 ■ *Web:* www.touro.edu	212-463-0400	627-9144	166
Lander College for Men 75-31 150th St .... Kew Gardens Hills NY 11367 *Web:* www.touro.edu	718-820-4884	820-4838	166
Touro College Jacob D Fuchsberg Law Ctr 225 Eastview Dr .... Central Islip NY 11722 *Web:* www.tourolaw.edu	631-421-2244		167-1
Touro Infirmary 1401 Foucher St .... New Orleans LA 70115 *Web:* www.touro.com	504-897-7011		374-3
Touro Synagogue National Historic Site 85 Touro St .... Newport RI 02840 *Web:* www.tourosynagogue.org	401-847-4794		50-1
Tousley Brain Stephens PLLC 1700 Seventh Ave Ste 2200 .... Seattle WA 98101 *Web:* www.tousley.com	206-682-5600		428
Touvelle State Recreation Site Table Rock Rd .... Central Point OR 97502 *TF:* 800-551-6949 ■ *Web:* www.oregonstateparks.org	541-582-1118		565
Towanda Printing Company Inc 116 Main St .... Towanda PA 18848 *Web:* www.thedailyreview.com	570-265-2151		532-3
Tower Accounting 3435 Blue Mtn Dr .... San Jose CA 95127 *Web:* www.toweraccounting.com	408-929-4576		2
Tower Cafe 1518 Broadway .... Sacramento CA 95818 *Web:* www.towercafe.com	916-441-0222		671
Tower Energy Group 1983 W 190th St .... Torrance CA 90504 *Web:* www.towerenergy.com	310-538-8000		580
Tower Extrusions Ltd 1003 State Hwy 79 S .... Olney TX 76374 *Web:* www.towerextrusion.com	940-564-5681	564-5033	485
Tower Federal Credit Union 7901 Sandy Spring Rd .... Laurel MD 20707 **Fax:* Cust Svc ■ *TF:* 800-787-8328 ■ *Web:* www.towerfcu.org	301-497-7000	497-8930*	219
Tower Financial Corp 116 E Berry St .... Fort Wayne IN 46802 *NASDAQ: TOFC* ■ *TF:* 800-731-2265 ■ *Web:* oldnational.com	800-731-2265		360-2
Tower Group Inc 120 Broadway 14th Fl .... New York NY 10271 *NASDAQ: TWGP* ■ *TF:* 877-883-6599 ■ *Web:* www.twrgrp.com	212-655-2000		391-4
Tower Hill Botanic Garden 11 French Dr PO Box 598 .... Boylston MA 01505 *Web:* www.towerhillbg.org	508-869-6111	869-0314	97
Tower Hill State Park 5808 County Rd C .... Spring Green WI 53588 *Web:* dnr.wi.gov	608-588-2116		565
Tower Imaging Medical Group 5455 Wilshire Blvd #1120 .... Los Angeles CA 90036 *Web:* www.towerimaging.com	323-549-3030		418
Tower Innovations 3266 Tower Dr .... Newburgh IN 47630 *TF:* 800-664-8222 ■ *Web:* www.towerinnovations.net	812-853-0595	853-6652	170
Tower Isles Frozen Foods Ltd 2025 Atlantic Ave .... Brooklyn NY 11233 *Web:* www.towerislespatties.com	718-495-2626		297-8
Tower Laboratories Ltd PO Box 306 .... Centerbrook CT 06409 *Web:* www.towerlabs.com	860-767-2127		582
Tower Manufacturing Corp 25 Reservoir Ave .... Providence RI 02907 *Web:* www.towermfg.com	401-467-7550	461-2710	815
Tower Oil & Technology Co 4300 S Tripp Ave .... Chicago IL 60632 *TF:* 800-243-5657 ■ *Web:* www.toweroil.com	773-927-6161		579
Tower Properties Co 1000 Walnut St Ste 900 .... Kansas City MO 64106 *Web:* www.towerproperties.com	816-421-8255		655
Tower Rock Stone Co 19829 Lower Frenchman Rd .... Sainte Genevieve MO 63670	573-883-7415		503-5
Tower Systems Inc 17226 447th Ave PO Box 1474 .... Watertown SD 57201 *TF:* 800-233-0787 ■ *Web:* www.towersystems.com	605-886-0930		480
Tower Theatre for the Performing Arts 815 E Olive Ave .... Fresno CA 93728 *TF:* 800-903-3353 ■ *Web:* www.towertheatrefresno.com	559-485-9050		572
Tower Travel Management 53 Ogden Ave .... Clarendon Hills IL 60514 **Fax Area Code:* 630 ■ *TF:* 800-542-9700 ■ *Web:* www.towertravel.com	800-542-9700	954-3040*	771
Tower Ventures LLC 4091 Viscount Ave .... Memphis TN 38118 *TF:* 800-875-5109 ■ *Web:* www.towerventures.com	901-794-9494		736
TOWER23 Hotel 723 Felspar St .... San Diego CA 92109 *Web:* www.t23hotel.com	858-270-2323		379
TowerComm LLC 6017 Triangle Dr .... Raleigh NC 27617 *Web:* www.towercommonline.com	919-781-3496		116
TowerData Inc 379 Park Ave S 5th Fl .... New York NY 10016 *Web:* www.towerdata.com	646-742-1771		195
Towerstrides Inc 4229 Lafayette Ctr Dr Ste 1200 .... Chantilly VA 20151 *Web:* www.towerstrides.com	703-953-1531		177
Towerwall 615 Concord St .... Framingham MA 01702 *Web:* www.towerwall.com	774-204-0700		177
Towle Silversmiths PO Box 21379 .... York PA 17402 *TF:* 800-264-0758 ■ *Web:* www.lifetimesterling.com	800-264-0758		702
Towmaster Inc 61381 US Hwy 12 .... Litchfield MN 55355 *TF:* 800-462-4517 ■ *Web:* towmaster.com	320-693-7900	693-7921	779
Town & Country Distributors Inc 1050 W Ardmore Ave .... Itasca IL 60143 *Web:* tcbeer.com	630-250-0590		81-1
Town & Country Furniture 6545 Airline Hwy .... Baton Rouge LA 70805 *TF:* 800-375-6660 ■ *Web:* www.tcfurniture.com	225-355-6666	355-7459	321
Town & Country Hospital 6001 Webb Rd .... Tampa FL 33615 *TF:* 866-463-7449 ■ *Web:* tampacommunityhospital.com	813-888-7060		374-3

Name / Address	City	State	Zip	Phone	Fax	Class
Town & Country Industries 400 W Mcnab Rd *Web:* www.tc-alum.com	Fort Lauderdale	FL	33309	954-970-9999		492
Town & Country Inn 20 State RT 2 *TF General:* 800-325-4386 ■ *Web:* www.townandcountryinn.com	Shelburne	NH	03581	603-466-3315	466-3315	379
Town & Country Inn & Conference Ctr 2008 Savannah Hwy *TF:* 800-334-6660 ■ *Web:* www.thetownandcountryinn.com	Charleston	SC	29407	843-571-1000		379
Town & Country Markets Inc 20148 Tenth Ave NE *Web:* central-market.com	Poulsbo	WA	98370	360-779-1881		345
Town & Country Resort Hotel 500 Hotel Cir N *TF:* 800-772-8527 ■ *Web:* www.destinationhotels.com/town-country	San Diego	CA	92108	619-291-7131	291-3584	669
Town & County 2660 S Glenstone Ave	Springfield	MO	65804	417-883-6131		157-4
Town Bank 850 W N Shore Dr *TF:* 866-203-8729 ■ *Web:* www.townbank.us	Hartland	WI	53029	262-367-1900		70
Town Ctr at Boca Raton 225 W Washington St Ste 100 *Web:* www.simon.com	Indianapolis	IN	46204	561-368-6000	338-0891	460
Town Ctr at Cobb 400 Ernest Barrett Pkwy NW Ste 100 *Web:* www.simon.com	Kennesaw	GA	30144	770-424-9486	424-7917	460
Town East Mall 2063 Town E Mall *Web:* www.towneastmall.com	Mesquite	TX	75150	972-270-2363		460
Town Fair Tire Company Inc 460 Coe Ave *TF:* 800-972-2245 ■ *Web:* www.townfairtire.com	East Haven	CT	06512	800-972-2245		54
Town Food Service Equipment Co 72 Beadel St *TF:* 800-221-5032 ■ *Web:* www.townfood.com	Brooklyn	NY	11222	718-388-5650	388-5860	298
Town Hall 342 Howard St *Web:* www.townhallsf.com	San Francisco	CA	94105	415-908-3900	908-3700	671
Town Inn Suites 620 Church St *TF:* 800-387-2755 ■ *Web:* www.towninn.com	Toronto	ON	M4Y2G2	416-964-3311		379
Town of East Hampton Connecticut 20 E High St *Web:* www.easthamptonct.gov	East Hampton	CT	06424	860-267-4426		434-3
Town of Tonawanda Public Library Kenmore Branch 160 Delaware Rd *TF:* 800-724-2440 ■ *Web:* www.buffalolib.org	Kenmore	NY	14217	716-873-2842	873-8416	434-3
Town Pump Inc 600 S Main St *TF:* 800-823-4931 ■ *Web:* www.townpump.com	Butte	MT	59701	406-497-6700		324
Town Talk Inc 6310 Cane Run Rd *TF:* 800-626-2220 ■ *Web:* www.ttcaps.com	Louisville	KY	40258	502-736-2972		155-9
Town Theatre 1012 Sumter St *Web:* www.towntheatre.com	Columbia	SC	29201	803-799-4764	799-6463	572
Town Topics 305 Witherspoon St *Web:* www.towntopics.com	Princeton	NJ	08542	609-924-2200	924-8818	532-4
Towne AllPoints Communications Inc 3441 W MacArthur Blvd *TF:* 800-561-3357 ■ *Web:* www.towne.com	Santa Ana	CA	92704	714-540-3095		6
Towne Crier Steak House 818 US Hwy 80 E *Web:* towne-crier-demo.squarespace.com	Abilene	TX	79601	325-704-4290		671
Towne House, The 2209 St Joe Ctr Rd *Web:* www.townehouse.org	Fort Wayne	IN	46025	260-483-3116	969-8072	672
Towne Mailer 2424 S Garfield St *Web:* www.townemailer.com	Missoula	MT	59801	406-541-6245		5
Towne Technologies Inc 6-10 Bell Ave PO Box 460 *TF:* 800-837-2515 ■ *Web:* www.townetech.com	Somerville	NJ	08076	900-722-9500	722-8394	481
TowneBank 4501 Cox Rd *Web:* www.townebank.com	Glen Allen	VA	23060	804-967-7026		70
Townes Tele-Communications Inc 120 E First St *TF:* 800-255-1975 ■ *Web:* www.walnuthilltel.com	Lewisville	AR	71845	870-921-4224		387
Townley Engineering & Manufacturing Company Inc 10551 SE 110th St Rd *TF:* 800-342-9920 ■ *Web:* www.townley.net	Candler	FL	32111	352-687-3001		641
Townley Inc 389 Fifth Ave Rm 1100 *Web:* www.townleygirl.com	New York	NY	10016	212-779-0544		231
Towns County 1411 Jack Dayton Cir *TF:* 800-984-1543 ■ *Web:* www.golakechatuge.com	Young Harris	GA	30582	706-896-4966		338
Townsend Ctr for the Performing Arts 1601 Maple St *Web:* townsendcenter.instantencore.com/web/home.aspx	Carrollton	GA	30118	678-839-4722	839-4805	572
Townsend Farms Inc 23400 NE Townsend Way *TF:* 800-875-5291 ■ *Web:* www.townsendfarms.com	Fairview	OR	97024	503-666-1780		296-21
Townsend Hotel 100 Townsend St *TF:* 800-548-4172 ■ *Web:* www.townsendhotel.com	Birmingham	MI	48009	248-642-7900	645-9061	379
Townsend James r 150 Dufferin Ave *TF:* 888-354-0448 ■ *Web:* www.ftgalaw.com	London	ON	N6A5N6	519-672-5272		428
Townsend Manor Inn 714 Main St *Web:* www.townsendinn.com	Greenport	NY	11944	631-477-2000	477-2371	379
Townsend Oil Company Inc 27 Cherry St PO Box 90 *TF:* 800-888-2888 ■ *Web:* www.townsendtotalenergy.com	Danvers	MA	01923	800-888-2888		317
Townsend Press 439 Kelley Dr *Fax Area Code: 800 ■ *TF:* 800-772-6410 ■ *Web:* www.townsendpress.com	West Berlin	NJ	08091	856-753-0554	225-8894*	637-2
Townsend Security 724 columbia st nw *TF:* 800-357-1019 ■ *Web:* townsendsecurity.com	Olympia	WA	98501	360-359-4400		225
Townshend State Park 2755 State Forest Rd *Web:* www.vtstateparks.com	Townshend	VT	05353	802-365-7500		565
Township Auditorium 1703 Taylor St *TF:* 800-745-3000 ■ *Web:* www.thetownship.org	Columbia	SC	29201	803-576-2350	576-2359	572
Townsquare Media Inc 240 Greenwich Ave *Web:* www.townsquaremedia.com	Greenwich	CT	06830	203-861-0900		643
Towsleys Inc 1424 Dewey St *Web:* www.towsleys.com	Manitowoc	WI	54220	920-683-7400		366
Towson University 8000 York Rd *TF:* 866-301-3375 ■ *Web:* www.towson.edu	Towson	MD	21252	410-704-2113	704-3030	166
Toxics Law Reporter 1801 S Bell St *TF:* 800 372-1033 ■ *Web:* www.bna.com/toxics-law-reporter-p5947	Arlington	VA	22202	800-372-1033		531-5
Toxikon Corp 15 Wiggins Ave *TF:* 800-458-4141 ■ *Web:* www.toxikon.com	Bedford	MA	01730	781-275-3330	271-1138	743
Tox-Pressotechnik LLC 4250 Weaver Pkwy *Web:* www.tox-us.com	Warrenville	IL	60555	630-393-0300	393-6800	385
ToxServices LLC 1367 Connecticut Ave NW Ste 300 *Web:* toxservices.com	Washington	DC	20036	202-429-8787		196
TOY (Theatre of Youth) 203 Allen St *Web:* www.theatreofyouth.org	Buffalo	NY	14201	716-884-4400		573-4
Toy Industry Assn 1115 Broadway Ste 400 *TF:* 800-541-1345 ■ *Web:* www.toyassociation.org	New York	NY	10010	212-675-1141	633-1429	49-4
Toyo Ink America LLC 1225 N Michael Dr *Fax Area Code: 630 ■ *TF General:* 866-969-8696 ■ *Web:* www.toyoink.com	Wood Dale	IL	60191	866-969-8696	628-1769*	388
Toyo Tanso USA Inc 2575 NW Graham Cir *Web:* www.ttu.com	Troutdale	OR	97060	503-661-7700		127
Toyo Tires 6261 Katella Ave Ste 2B *TF:* 800-678-3250 ■ *Web:* toyotires.com	Cypress	CA	90630	800-678-3250		754
Toyoda Machinery USA Inc 316 W University Dr *TF:* 800-257-2985 ■ *Web:* www.toyodausa.com	Arlington Heights	IL	60004	847-253-0340	577-4680	455
Toyon Associates Inc 1800 Sutter St Ste 600 *Web:* www.toyonassociates.com	Concord	CA	94520	925-685-9312		401
Toyota Canada Inc 1 Toyota Pl *TF Cust Svc:* 888-869-6828 ■ *Web:* www.toyota.ca	Scarborough	ON	M1H1H9	416-438-6320		59
Toyota Ctr 1510 Polk St *TF:* 866-446-8849 ■ *Web:* www.houstontoyotacenter.com	Houston	TX	77002	713-758-7200	758-7315	720
Toyota Financial Services 19001 S Western Ave *TF Cust Svc:* 800-874-8822 ■ *Web:* www.toyotafinancial.com	Torrance	CA	90501	212-715-7386		217
Toyota Motor Manufacturing Indiana Inc 4000 Tulip Tree Dr *Web:* www.toyota.ca/cgi-bin/WebObjects/WWW.woa/wa/vp?vp=Home.AboutToyota.ManufacturingFacilities.Indiana&l	Princeton	IN	47670	812-387-2000		59
Toyota Motor Manufacturing Kentucky Inc 1001 Cherry Blossom Way *Web:* www.toyotageorgetown.com	Georgetown	KY	40324	502-868-2000		59
Toyota Motor North America Inc 601 Lexington Ave 49th Fl *TF:* 800-331-4331 ■ *Web:* www.toyota.com	New York	NY	10022	800-331-4331		360-3
Toyota Motor Sales USA Inc 19001 S Western Ave *TF Cust Svc:* 800-331-4331 ■ *Web:* www.toyota.com	Torrance	CA	90501	310-468-4000	468-7814	59
Toyota Motor Sales USA Inc Lexus Div 19001 S Western Ave *TF Cust Svc:* 800-255-3987 ■ *Web:* www.lexus.com	Torrance	CA	90501	800-255-3987		59
Toyota of Greenwich 75 E Putnam Ave *Web:* www.toyotaofgreenwich.com	Cos Cob	CT	06807	203-661-5055		57
Toyota of Watertown Inc 149 Arsenal St *Web:* toyotaofwatertown.com	Watertown	MA	02472	617-926-5200		57
Toyota Sunnyvale 898 W El Camino Real *TF:* 888-310-0001 ■ *Web:* toyotasunnyvale.com	Sunnyvale	CA	94087	408-245-6640		57
Toyota Tsusho America Inc 805 Third Ave 17th Fl *Web:* www.taiamerica.com	New York	NY	10022	212-355-3600		492
Toyotetsu America Inc 100 Pin Oak Dr *Web:* www.ttna.com	Somerset	KY	42503	606-274-9005		489
Toys 'R' Us (Canada) Ltd 2777 Langstaff Rd *TF:* 800-869-7787 ■ *Web:* www.toysrus.ca	Concord	ON	L4K4M5	800-869-7787		761
TP Orthodontics Inc 100 Ctr Plaza *TF:* 800-348-8856 ■ *Web:* www.tportho.com	La Porte	IN	46350	219-785-2591	324-3029	228
TP Trucking LLC 5630 Table Rock Rd *TF:* 800-292-4399 ■ *Web:* www.tptrucking.com	Central Point	OR	97502	800-292-4399		780
TPC (Transaction Processing Performance Council) 572 Ruger St *Web:* www.tpc.org	San Francisco	CA	94129	415-561-6272	561-6120	48-9
TPC Advance Technology Inc 18525 Gale Ave *TF:* 800-560-8222 ■ *Web:* www.tpcdental.com	City Of Industry	CA	91748	626-810-4337		475
TPG (Plus Group Inc, The) 7425 Janes Ave Ste 201 *Web:* www.theplusgroup.com	Woodridge	IL	60517	630-515-0500	515-0510	721
TPG Capital LP 301 Commerce St Ste 3300 *Web:* www.tpg.com	Fort Worth	TX	76102	817-871-4000		402
TPG Direct 444 N Third St *Web:* www.tpgdirect.com	Philadelphia	PA	19123	267-825-9511		7
TPG Marine Enterprises LLC 1341 N Capitol Ave *Web:* www.tpgmarine.com	Indianapolis	IN	46202	317-631-0234		225
Tpgtex Label Solutions Inc 5830 Ludington Dr *Web:* www.tpgtex.com	Houston	TX	77035	713-726-9636		88
TPI Corp PO Box 4973 *TF:* 800-682-3398 ■ *Web:* www.tpicorp.com	Johnson City	TN	37602	800-682-3398		15
TPI Powder Metallurgy Inc 12030 Beaver Rd *Web:* www.tpipm.com	Saint Charles	MI	48655	989-865-9921	865-9924	482
Tpi Staffing Inc 21840 Northwest Fwy Ste E *TF:* 800-561-3357 ■ *Web:* www.tpistaffing.com	Cypress	TX	77429	281-890-2220		260
TPL (Trust for Public Land) 116 New Montgomery St 4th Fl *TF:* 800-714-5263 ■ *Web:* www.tpl.org	San Francisco	CA	94105	415-495-4014	495-4103	48-13
TPL Communications 3825 Foothill Blvd *TF:* 800-447-6937 ■ *Web:* www.tplcom.com	La Crescenta	CA	91214	323-256-3000	254-3210	647
TPM Life Insurance Company 1850 William Penn Way Ste 202 *TF:* 800-555-3122 ■ *Web:* www.tpmins.com	Lancaster	PA	17601	717-394-7156		390

Listing	City	State	ZIP	Phone	Fax	Class
TPR (Texas Public Radio) 8401 Datapoint Dr Ste 800 *TF:* 800-622-8977 ■ *Web:* www.tpr.org	San Antonio	TX	78229	210-614-8977	614-8983	632
TPS Aviation Inc 1515 Crocker Ave	Hayward	CA	94544	510-475-1010	475-8817	770
TPS Houston Group LLC 7101 John Ralston Rd *Web:* www.tpshoustongroup.com	Houston	TX	77044	281-459-2435		518
TPx Communications 1181 Grier Dr #F *Web:* www.telepacific.com	Las Vegas	NV	89119	702-851-6000		387
TQL (Total Quality Logistics Inc) 4289 Ivy Pointe Blvd. *TF:* 800-580-3101 ■ *Web:* www.tql.com	Cincinnati	OH	45245	513-831-2600	965-7630	311
TR Design Inc 115 Tucker Farm Rd *Web:* www.trdesign.com	North Andover	MA	01845	978-237-5945		195
TR International Trading Company Inc 1218 Third Ave Ste 2100 *TF:* 800-761-7717 ■ *Web:* www.trichemicals.com	Seattle	WA	98101	206-505-3500	505-3501	146
TR Miller Mill Company Inc 215 Deer St PO Box 708 *TF:* 800-633-6740 ■ *Web:* www.trmillermill.com	Brewton	AL	36427	251-867-4331	867-6882	683
TRA (Thoroughbred Racing Assn) 420 Fair Hill Dr Ste 1 *Web:* www.tra-online.com	Elkton	MD	21921	410-392-9200		48-22
Trabert & Hoeffer 111 E Oak St *TF:* 800-539-3573 ■ *Web:* www.trabertandhoeffer.com	Chicago	IL	60611	312-787-1654		410
Trabon Printing Company Inc 430 E Bannister Rd Ste *Web:* www.trabongroup.com	Kansas City	MO	64131	816-361-6279		627
TRAC Media Services 2030 E Speedway Blvd Ste 210 *TF:* 888-299-1866 ■ *Web:* www.tracmedia.org	Tucson	AZ	85719	520-299-1866	577-6077	632
Trace Environmental Systems Inc 7 Park Lake Rd Ste 9 *Web:* www.traceenv.com	Sparta	NJ	07871	973-383-3550		196
Trace3 15326 Alton Pkwy *TF:* 800-890-8940 ■ *Web:* www.trace3.com	Irvine	CA	92618	949-333-2300		180
Trace-A-Matic Inc (T-A-M) 1570 Commerce Ave. *TF:* 877-375-0217 ■ *Web:* www.traceamatic.com	Brookfield	WI	53045	262-797-7300		621
Tracelogix Corp 3605 Knight Rd Ste 101 *Web:* www.tracelogix.com	Memphis	TN	38118	901-795-2777		175
TraceSecurity Inc 6300 Corporate Blvd Ste 200 *Web:* www.tracesecurity.com	Baton Rouge	LA	70809	225-612-2121		463
Trachte Bldg Systems Inc 314 Wilburn Rd *TF:* 800-356-5824 ■ *Web:* www.trachte.com	Sun Prairie	WI	53590	800-356-5824	981-9014	105
Tracie Martyn Salon 59 Fifth Ave Ste 1 *TF:* 866-862-7896 ■ *Web:* www.traciemartyn.com	New York	NY	10003	212-206-9333	206-8399	706
Tracinda Corp 150 Rodeo Dr Ste 250	Beverly Hills	CA	90212	310-271-0638		405
TrackAbout Inc 410 Rouser Rd Ste 400 *Web:* corp.trackabout.com	Moon Township	PA	15108	412-269-0642		177
Trackers Earth Inc 1424 se 76th ave *TF:* 800-522-0255 ■ *Web:* trackerspdx.com	Portland	OR	97202	503-345-3312		138
TrackMaster 2083 Old Middlefield Way Ste 206 *TF:* 800-334-3800 ■ *Web:* www.trackmaster.com	Mountain View	CA	94043	650-316-1020		642
Trackmobile Inc 1602 Executive Dr *TF:* 800-728-7511 ■ *Web:* www.trackmobile.com	LaGrange	GA	30240	706-884-6651	884-0390	650
TRACO 71 Progress Ave *TF:* 800-992-4444 ■ *Web:* www.alcoa.com	Cranberry Township	PA	16066	724-776-7000	776-7014	234
TRACOM Group, The 6675 S Kenton St Ste 118 *TF:* 800-221-2321 ■ *Web:* www.tracomcorp.com	Centennial	CO	80111	303-470-4900		193
Tracorp Inc 5621 W Beverly Ln *Web:* www.tracorp.com	Glendale	AZ	85306	602-864-1385		177
TRACS (TransNational Assn of Christian Colleges & Schools) 15935 Forest Rd *TF:* 800-669-4000 ■ *Web:* www.tracs.org	Forest	VA	24551	434-525-9539	525-9538	48-1
Tractenberg & Co LLC 116 E 16th St 2nd Fl *Web:* www.tractenbergandco.com	New York	NY	10003	212-929-7979		5
Traction Corp 1349 Larkin St *Web:* www.tractionco.com	San Francisco	CA	94109	415-962-5800		7
Tractor Supply Co 5401 Virginia Way *NASDAQ: TSCO* ■ *TF:* 877-718-6750 ■ *Web:* www.tractorsupply.com	Brentwood	TN	37027	877-718-6750		274
Trac-Work Inc 3801 N Interstate Hwy 45 *Web:* www.trac-work.com	Ennis	TX	75119	972-878-2232		188-8
Tracy Aviary 589 East 1300 South *Web:* www.tracyaviary.org	Salt Lake City	UT	84105	801-596-8500		823
Tracy Chamber of Commerce 223 E Tenth St *Web:* www.tracychamber.org	Tracy	CA	95376	209-835-2131	833-9526	139
Tracy Outlets 1005 E Pescadero Ave	Tracy	CA	95304	209-833-1895		460
Tracy Time Systems Inc 230 32nd St SE *TF:* 800-804-6504 ■ *Web:* www.tracyinc.com	Grand Rapids	MI	49548	616-241-1661		180
Tracy-Luckey Company Inc 110 N Hicks St	Harlem	GA	30814	706-556-6216		11-1
Trada Inc 1023 Walnut St *TF:* 877-871-1835	Boulder	CO	80302	877-871-1835		387
trade associates group Ltd 900 W Bliss St *TF:* 800-621-8350 ■ *Web:* www.tagltd.com	Chicago	IL	60642	773-871-1300	871-8432	321
Trade Exchange of America 23200 Coolidge Hwy *Web:* www.tradefirst.com	Oak Park	MI	48237	248-544-1350		691
Trade Manage Capital Inc 299 Market St 4th Fl *TF:* 800-221-5676 ■ *Web:* www.yamner.com	Saddle Brook	NJ	07663	800-221-5676		177
Trade Products Corp 12124 Popes Head Rd *TF:* 888-352-3580 ■ *Web:* www.tradeproductscorp.com	Fairfax	VA	22030	703-502-9000	502-9399	320
Trade Service Company LLC 13280 Evening Creek Dr S Ste 200 *TF:* 800-854-1527 ■ *Web:* www.tradeservice.com	San Diego	CA	92128	800-854-1527	418-4363	224
Trade Technologies Inc 3939 Bee Cave Rd Ste B-22 *TF:* 800-833-8801 ■ *Web:* www.tradetechnologies.com	Austin	TX	78746	512-327-9996		317
Trade Union International Inc 4651 State St *TF:* 800-354-3655 ■ *Web:* tradeunion.com	Montclair	CA	91763	909-628-7500		61
TradeHelm Inc 20 N Wacker Dr Ste 3550 *Web:* www.tradehelm.com	Chicago	IL	60606	312-821-4600		690
tradeking 13024 Ballantyne Corporate Pl Ste 500 *TF:* 855-880-2559 ■ *Web:* www.tradeking.com	Charlotte	NC	28277	877-495-5464		690
Tradelink Securities LLC 71 S Wacker Dr Ste 1900 *Web:* www.tradelinkllc.com	Chicago	IL	60606	312-264-2000		690
Trademark Co, The 344 Maple Ave W Ste 151 *TF:* 800-906-8626 ■ *Web:* www.thetrademarkcompany.com	Vienna	VA	22180	800-906-8626		317
Trademark Die & Engineering 8060 Graphic Industrial Dr *Web:* www.tmde.net	Belmont	MI	49306	616-863-6660		697
Trademark Media Corp 2400 Webberville Rd *TF:* 800-916-1224 ■ *Web:* www.trademarkmedia.com	Austin	TX	78702	512-459-7000		7
Trademark Transportation Inc 739 Vandalia St. *TF:* 800-646-2550 ■ *Web:* www.trademarktrans.com	Saint Paul	MN	55114	651-646-2500		311
Trader Duke's 1117 Williston Rd *TF:* 800-445-8667 ■ *Web:* www.hilton.com	South Burlington	VT	05403	802-660-7523	660-7516	671
Trader Joe's Co 800 S Shamrock Ave *Web:* www.traderjoes.com	Monrovia	CA	91016	626-599-3700		345
Trader Vic's Inc 9 Anchor Dr *Web:* www.tradervicsemeryville.com	Emeryville	CA	94608	510-653-3400		670
Trader's Library LLC 6310 Stevens Forest Rd Ste 200 *TF:* 800-272-2855 ■ *Web:* www.traderslibrary.com	Columbia	MD	21046	410-964-0026		690
Tradescape Inc 520 S El Camino Real Ste 640 *TF:* 800-697-6068 ■ *Web:* www.tradescape.biz	San Mateo	CA	94402	800-697-6068		196
Tradesman Truck Accessories LLC 305 N Frisco St	Winters	TX	79567	325-754-4561		54
Tradesmen International Inc 9760 Shepard Rd *Web:* www.tradesmeninternational.com	Macedonia	OH	44056	440-349-3432		260
TradeStation Group Inc 8050 SW Tenth St Ste 2000 *TF:* 800-871-3577 ■ *Web:* www.tradestation.com	Plantation	FL	33324	954-652-7000		178-10
Tradewinds Carmel Mission St at Third Ave. *Web:* www.tradewindscarmel.com	Carmel By The Sea	CA	93921	831-624-2776	624-0634	379
Trading Direct 160 Broadway 7E Fl *TF:* 800-925-8566 ■ *Web:* www.tradingdirect.com	New York	NY	10038	212-766-0230	766-0914	690
Trading Places International Inc 23807 Aliso Creek Rd Ste 100 *Web:* www.tradingplaces.com	Laguna Niguel	CA	92677	949-448-5150		772
Trading Post Homes 490 Sparrow Dre. *Web:* www.tphomes.com	Shepherdsville	KY	40165	502-955-5622		106
Trading Union Inc 401 N Nordic Dr *Web:* acehardware.com	Petersburg	AK	99833	907-772-3881		229
TradingMarkets.com Inc 10 Exchange Pl Ste 1800 *Web:* www.tradingmarkets.com	Jersey City	NJ	07302	213-955-5858		690
Tradition Asiel Securities Inc 255 Greenwich St 4th Fl *TF:* 866-220-5771 ■ *Web:* www.tradition-na.com	New York	NY	10007	212-791-4500	791-6065	690
Tradition Capital Management LLC 129 Summit Ave *Web:* www.traditioncm.com	Summit	NJ	07901	908-598-0909		401
Traditional Bank 49 W Main St PO Box 326 *TF:* 800-498-0414 ■ *Web:* www.traditionalbank.com	Mount Sterling	KY	40353	859-498-0414		70
Traditional Door Design & Millwork Ltd 261 Regina Rd *TF:* 877-226-9930 ■ *Web:* www.traditionaldoor.com	Woodbridge	ON	L4L8M3	416-747-1992		234
Traditional Home Magazine 1716 Locust St *Web:* www.traditionalhome.com	Des Moines	IA	50309	515-284-3762		457-11
Traditional Values Coalition (TVC) 139 C St SE	Washington	DC	20003	202-547-8570		48-20
Traditions Performance Firearms 1375 Boston Post Rd *Web:* www.traditionsfirearms.com	Old Saybrook	CT	06475	860-388-4656		711
Traducta Inc 1590 Rue Ampere Bureau 300 *Web:* www.traducta.com	Boucherville	QC	J4B7L4	450-461-2252	655-2253	768
Trafalgar Castle School 401 Reynolds St *Web:* www.trafalgarcastle.ca	Whitby	ON	L1N3W9	905-668-3358	668-4136	622
Traffic Audit Bureau for Media Measurement (TAB) 271 Madison Ave Ste 1504 *Web:* www.tabonline.com	New York	NY	10016	212-972-8075		49-18
Traffic Control Service Inc 2435 Lemon Ave. **Fax Area Code:* 562 ■ *TF:* 800-763-3999 ■ *Web:* www.trafficmanagement.com	Signal Hill	CA	90755	800-763-3999	424-0266*	264-3
Traffic Engineering Consultants Inc 6000 S Western Ste 300 *Web:* tecok.com	Oklahoma City	OK	73139	405-720-7721		261
Traffic Group Inc, The 9900 Franklin Sq Dr *TF:* 800-583-8411 ■ *Web:* www.trafficgroup.com	Baltimore	MD	21236	410-931-6600		463
Traffic Jam Events LLC 704 Hickory Ave *TF:* 800-922-8109 ■ *Web:* www.trafficjamevents.com	Harahan	LA	70123	800-922-8109		195

Phone Fax Class

Traffic Management Inc
8862 W 35W Service Dr NE Ste 270 .... Minneapolis MN 55449 763 544 3455 194
TF: 800-238-6678 ■ Web: www.trafficmgmt.com

Traffic Planning & Design Inc
2500 E High St Ste 650 .... Pottstown PA 19464 610-326-3100 261
Web: www.trafficpd.com

TrafFix Devices Inc
160 Avenida La Pata .... San Clemente CA 92673 949-361-5663 295
TF: 800-826-6275 ■ Web: www.traffixdevices.com

Tragara Pharmaceuticals Inc
3152 Lionshead Ave .... Carlsbad CA 92010 760-208-6900 231
Web: www.tragarapharma.com

Trager, Kevy & Trager LLP
141 Willis Ave .... Mineola NY 11501 516-292-9494 741-1010 2
Web: tktcpa.com

Tragon Corp 365 Convention Way .... Redwood City CA 94063 650-365-1833 463
Web: tragon.com

Trahan Burden & Charles Inc (TBC)
900 S Wolfe St .... Baltimore MD 21231 410-347-7500 986-1299 4
Web: www.tbc.us

Trail Blazers Inc
1 N Center Ct St Ste 200 .... Portland OR 97227 503-234-9291 717
Web: www.trailblazers.org

Trail Creek Ranch 7100 W Trl Creek Rd .... Wilson WY 83014 307-733-2610 239
TF: 800-253-8831 ■ Web: www.jacksonholetrailcreekranch.com

Trail Dust Steak Houses Inc
2300 E Lamar .... Arlington TX 76006 817-640-6411 670
Web: www.traildust.com

Trail End State Historic Site
400 Clarendon Ave .... Sheridan WY 82801 307-674-4589 565
Web: www.trailend.co

Trail King Industries Inc
300 E Norway .... Mitchell SD 57301 605-996-6482 996-4727 779
TF: 800-843-3324 ■ Web: www.trailking.com

Trail of Tears State Forest
3240 State Forest Rd .... Jonesboro IL 62952 618-833-4910 565
Web: www.dnr.illinois.gov

Trail of Tears State Park
429 Moccasin Springs .... Jackson MO 63755 573-290-5268 565
Web: www.mostateparks.com

Trail Smoke Eaters Hockey Club
1051 Victoria St .... Trail BC V1R3T3 250-364-9994 354
TF: 800-961-0202 ■ Web: www.trailsmokeeaters.com

Trailblazer Pipeline Co 2442 P Rd .... Heartwell NE 68945 308 563 3221 325

Trailblazer Studios Nc Inc
1610 Midtown Pl .... Raleigh NC 27609 919-645-6600 514
Web: videofonics.com

Trailer Bridge Inc
10405 New Berlin Rd E .... Jacksonville FL 32226 904-751-7100 751-7444 312
OTC: TRBRQ ■ TF: 800-554-1589 ■ Web: www.trailerbridge.com

Trailer Transit Inc 1130 E US 20 .... Porter IN 46304 219-926-2111 859-1191* 780
*Fax Area Code: 877 ■ TF: 800-423-3647 ■ Web: www.trailertransit.com

Trailer Wizards Ltd 10387 Nordel Ct .... Delta BC V4G1J9 604-464-2220 126
Web: www.trailerwizards.com

Trailercraft Inc 222 W 92nd Ave .... Anchorage AK 99515 907-563-3238 561-4995 516
TF: 800-478-3238 ■ Web: www.trailercraft.com

Trailhead Athletic Club LLC
7900 E Eagle Crest Dr .... Mesa AZ 85207 480-832-6900 354
Web: www.thetrailhead.org

Trailiner Corp PO Box 5270 .... Springfield MO 65801 417-866-7258 866-1168 779
TF: 800-833-8209 ■ Web: www.trailiner.com

Trailstar Mfg Corp
20700 Harrisburg-Westville Rd PO Box 2086 .... Alliance OH 44601 330-821-9900 821-6941 779
Web: trailstarintl.com

Trailways Transportation System Inc
3554 Chain Bridge Rd Ste 202 .... Fairfax VA 22030 703-691-3052 691-9047 107
TF: 877-467-3346 ■ Web: www.trailways.com

Trainertainment LLC PO Box 2168 .... Keller TX 76248 817-886-4840 463
TF: 800-860-8474 ■ Web: trainertainment.net

Training Advantage, The PO Box 800 .... Ignacio CO 81137 970-563-4517 108
TF: 800-659-2656 ■ Web: www.sucap.org

Training Assoc Corp, The
287 Tpke Rd .... Westborough MA 01581 508-890-8500 631
TF: 800-241-8868 ■ Web: www.thetrainingassociates.com

Training Industry Inc
401 Harrison Oaks Blvd Ste 300 .... Cary NC 27513 866-298-4203 393
TF: 866-298-4203 ■ Web: www.trainingindustry.com

Training Magazine 27020 Noble Rd .... Excelsior MN 55331 847-559-7596 457-5
TF: 877-865-9361 ■ Web: www.trainingmag.com

Training Modernization Group Inc
9737 Peppertree Rd .... Spotsylvania VA 22553 540-295-9313 196
TF: 866-855-6449 ■ Web: www.tmgva.com

Training Objectives Corp
8940 SW 67th Pl .... Portland OR 97223 503-245-3387 764
Web: trainingobjectives.com

Training to Inc
2200 N Central Ave Ste 400 .... Phoenix AZ 85004 602-266-1500 94
Web: www.trainingtoyou.com

Trainworld Associates LLC
751 Mcdonald Ave .... Brooklyn NY 11218 718-436-7072 761
TF: 800-541-7010 ■ Web: www.trainworld.com

Trak Com Wireless Inc
101-3780 14th Ave .... Markham ON L3R9Y5 905-474-9935 474-9938 647
Web: www.trakcom.com

TRAK Microwave Corp
4726 Eisenhower Blvd .... Tampa FL 33634 813-901-7200 901-7491 253
TF: 888-283-8444 ■ Web: www.trak.com

Trak-1 Technology Co PO Box 52028 .... Tulsa OK 74152 918-779-6500 393
Web: www.trak-1.com

TrakLok International
11020 Solway School Rd Ste 105 .... Knoxville TN 37931 865-927-4911 692
Web: www.traklokintl.com

TRALA (Truck Renting & Leasing Assn)
675 N Washington St Ste 410 .... Alexandria VA 22314 703-299-9120 299-9115 49-21
Web: www.trala.org

Trale In 14229 W Commerce Rd .... Daleville IN 47334 765-378-5509 463
Web: www.trale.com

Tram's Kitchen 4050 Penn Ave .... Pittsburgh PA 15224 412-682-2688 671

Phone Fax Class

Tramco Pump Co 1500 W Adams St .... Chicago IL 60607 312-243-5800 243-0702* 641
*Fax: Sales ■ TF: 800-956-7272 ■ Web: www.tramcopump.com

Tramex Travel Inc
4505 Spicewood Springs Rd Ste 200 .... Austin TX 78759 512-343-2201 343-0022 771
TF: 800-527-3039 ■ Web: www.tramex.com

Trammell Crow Co
2100 McKinney Ave Ste 800 .... Dallas TX 75201 214-863-4101 863-4493 655
Web: www.trammellcrow.com

Trammell Crow Residential (TCR)
3889 Maple St .... Dallas TX 75219 214-922-8400 653
Web: tcr.com

Tramont Corp 3701 N Humboldt Blvd .... Milwaukee WI 53212 414-967-8800 554
TF: 800-265-8840 ■ Web: www.tramont.com

Tramz Hotels LLC
776 Mountain Blvd Ste 200 .... Watchung NJ 07069 908-753-7400 378
Web: www.tramzhotels.com

Tran Cert Marketing Inc
2295 Berry Ln Ste 880 .... Point Roberts WA 98281 360-945-2190 463
Web: www.trancertmarketing.com

Trana Discovery Inc
2054-260 Kildare Farm Rd .... Cary NC 27518 919-342-6192 231
Web: www.tranadiscovery.com

Trancy Logistics America Corp
1670 Dolwick Rd Ste 8 .... Erlanger KY 41018 859-282-7780 311
Web: trancyamerica.com

Trandes Corp 4601 Presidents Dr Ste 360 .... Lanham MD 20706 301-459-0200 459-1069 261
Web: www.trandes.com

Tranergy Inc 726 Foster Ave .... Bensenville IL 60106 630-238-9338 770
Web: tranergy.com

Trans Air Manufacturing Corp
480 E Locust St .... Dallastown PA 17313 717-246-2627 14
Web: www.transairmfg.com

Trans Am Travel
4222 King St Ste 130 .... Alexandria VA 22302 703-998-7676 824-8190 16
TF: 800-822-7600 ■ Web: www.transamtravel.com

Trans Energy Inc
210 Second St PO Box 393 .... St. Marys WV 26170 304-684-7053 536
Web: transenergyinc.com

Trans Med USA Inc 31 Progress Ave .... Tyngsboro MA 01879 978-649-1970 475
TF: 800-442-1142 ■ Web: www.transmed-usa.com

Trans National Communications International Inc (TNCI)
2 Charlesgate W .... Boston MA 02215 617-369-1000 736
TF: 800-800-8400 ■ Web: www.tncii.com

Trans Ova Genetics LC
2938 380th St .... Sioux Center IA 51250 712-722-3586 794
Web: www.transova.com

Trans Tech Energy Inc
14527 US 64 W Ste .... Rocky Mount NC 27804 252-446-4357 538
Web: www.transtechenergy.com

Trans World Alloys Co
249 E Gardena Blvd .... Gardena CA 90248 310-217-8777 492
Web: www.twalloys.com

Trans World Corp (TWC)
545 Fifth Ave Ste 940 .... New York NY 10017 212-983-3355 983-8129 379
OTC: TWOC ■ TF: 877-407-9037 ■ Web: www.transwc.com

Trans World Marketing Corp
360 Murray Hill Pkwy .... East Rutherford NJ 07073 201-935-5565 559-2011 233
Web: www.transworldmarketing.com

Trans1 Inc 301 Government Ctr Dr .... Wilmington NC 28403 910-332-1700 476
Web: www.trans1.com

TransAct Technologies Inc
1 Hamden Ctr 2319 Whitney Ave Ste 3B .... Hamden CT 06518 203-859-6800 949-9048 173-6
NASDAQ: TACT ■ TF: 800-243-8941 ■ Web: www.transact-tech.com

Transaction Network Services Inc.
10740 Parkridge Blvd Ste 100 .... Reston VA 20191 703-453-8300 215
TF: 866-523-0661 ■ Web: www.tnsi.com

Transaction Packing Inc
2928 Greens Rd Ste 100 .... Houston TX 77032 281-443-0476 549
Web: www.transactionpacking.com

Transaction Processing Performance Council (TPC)
572 Ruger St .... San Francisco CA 94129 415-561-6272 561-6120 48-9
Web: www.tpc.org

Transaero Inc
35 Melville Park Rd Ste 100 .... Melville NY 11747 631-752-1240 22
TF: 800-486-6936 ■ Web: www.transaeroinc.com

TransAlta Corp
110 12th Ave SW PO Box 1900 Stn M .... Calgary AB T2P2M1 403-267-7110 787
TSE: TA ■ TF: 877-700-9288 ■ Web: www.transalta.com

Transalta Tri Leisure Centre
221 Jennifer Heil Way .... Spruce Grove AB T7X4J5 780-960-5080 354
Web: www.trileisure.com

TransAm Trucking Inc 15910 S 169th Hwy .... Olathe KS 66062 913-702-5300 324-7063 780
Web: www.transamtruck.com

Transamerica 4333 Edgewood Rd NE .... Cedar Rapids IA 52499 319-355-8511 391-5
TF: 800-852-4678 ■ Web: www.transamerica.com

Transamerica Corporation
440 Mamaroneck Ave .... Harrison NY 10528 914-627-3000 401
Web: www.divinvest.com

Transamerica Occidental Life Insurance Co
1150 S Olive St .... Los Angeles CA 90015 213-742-2111 391-2
TF Cust Svc: 800-852-4678 ■ Web: transamerica.com

Transat AT Inc
300 Leo-Pariseau St Ste 600 .... Montreal QC H2X4C2 514-987-1616 987-8035 771
TSE: TRZ.B ■ TF: 800-387-0825 ■ Web: www.transat.com

Transatlantic Holdings Inc
80 Pine St .... New York NY 10005 212-365-2200 360-4
NYSE: TRH ■ Web: www.transre.com

Transaver LLC 108 Washington St .... Manlius NY 13104 315-399-1200 311
TF: 800-698-8629 ■ Web: www.transaver.com

Transaxle Manufacturing of America
240 Waterford Park Dr .... Rock Hill SC 29730 803-329-8900 247
Web: www.transaxlemanufacturing.com

Trans-Border Global Freight Systems Inc
2103 Route 9 .... Round Lake NY 12151 518-785-6000 785-6239 311
TF: 800-493-9444 ■ Web: www.tbgfs.com

Transbotics Corp 3400 Latrobe Dr .... Charlotte NC 28211 704-362-1115 364-4039 529
OTC: TNSB ■ TF: 800-732-0330 ■ Web: www.transbotics.com

Company / Address	City	State	ZIP	Phone	Fax	Class
Trans-Bridge Lines Inc 2012 Industrial Dr. *TF:* 800-556-3815 ■ *Web:* www.transbridgelines.com	Bethlehem	PA	18017	610-868-6001	868-9057	108
TransCanada Pipelines Ltd 450 First St SW *TF:* 800-661-3805 ■ *Web:* www.transcanada.com	Calgary	AB	T2P5H1	403-920-2000	920-2200	325
Transcare Corp 1 Metrotech Ctr *Web:* www.transcare.com	Brooklyn	NY	11201	718-763-8888		468
Transcare Pennsylvania 400 Seco Rd *Web:* transcare.com	Monroeville	PA	15146	412-373-6300		30
Trans-Carriers Inc 5135 US Hwy 78 *TF:* 800-999-7383 ■ *Web:* www.transcarriers.com	Memphis	TN	38118	901-368-2900	368-0336	780
Transcat Inc 35 Vantage Pt Dr *NASDAQ: TRNS* ■ *TF:* 800-800-5001 ■ *Web:* www.transcat.com	Rochester	NY	14624	585-352-9460	352-1486	201
Transcend Information Inc 1645 N Brian St *Web:* www.transcend-info.com	Orange	CA	92867	714-921-2000	921-2111	174
Transcendent LLC 1040 Cottonwood Ave Ste 300 *Web:* transcendent-llc.com	Hartland	WI	53029	262-953-2750		177
Trans-Century Resources Inc 8716 N Mopac Expy Ste 100 *Web:* www.trans-century.com	Austin	TX	78759	512-345-0280		390
Transcepta LLC 135 Columbia Ste 202 *Web:* www.trancascapital.com	Aliso Viejo	CA	92656	949-382-2840		317
TransChemical Inc 419 De Soto Ave *TF:* 888-873-6481 ■ *Web:* www.transchemical.com	Saint Louis	MO	63147	314-231-6905		146
Transco Business Technologies (TBT) 34 Leighton Rd *TF:* 800-322-0003 ■ *Web:* www.transcobusiness.com	Augusta	ME	04330	207-622-6251		112
Transco Industries Inc 5534 NE 122nd Ave *TF:* 800-545-9991 ■ *Web:* www.transco-ind.com	Portland	OR	97230	503-256-1955	256-0723	207
Transco Products Inc 1215 E 12th St Ste 2100 *TF:* 800-435-6621 ■ *Web:* www.transcoproducts.com	Streator	IL	61364	312-427-2818	427-4975	389
Transco Railway Products Inc 200 N LaSalle St Ste 1550 *TF:* 800-472-4592 ■ *Web:* www.transcorailway.com	Chicago	IL	60601-1034	312-427-2818	427-4975	650
Transcom Telecommunications Co 3744 Industry Ave Ste 404 *Web:* www.transcomla.com	Lakewood	CA	90712	562-663-2000		387
TransCon Builders Inc 25250 Rockside Rd *TF:* 800-451-2608 ■ *Web:* www.transconbuilders.com	Cleveland	OH	44146	440-439-2100	439-6710	653
Transcontinental Inc 1 Pl Ville Marie Ste 3240 *TSE: TCL.A* ■ *Web:* tctranscontinental.com	Montreal	QC	H3B0G1	514-954-4000	954-4016	627
Transcontinental Inc 1100 Rene-Levesque Blvd W 24th Fl *TF:* 800-361-5479 ■ *Web:* tctranscontinental.com	Montreal	QC	H3B4X9	514-392-9000		637-9
Transcontinental Insurance Co 333 S Wabash Ave CNA Ctr *Web:* www.cna.com	Chicago	IL	60604	312-822-5000		391-4
Transcontinental Realty Investors Inc 1603 Lyndon B Johnson Fwy Ste 800 *NYSE: TCI* ■ *TF:* 800-400-6407 ■ *Web:* www.transconrealty-invest.com	Dallas	TX	75234	469-522-4200	522-4299	654
Trans-Continental Systems Inc 10801 Evendale Dr *TF:* 800-525-8726 ■ *Web:* www.tcsohio.com	Cincinnati	OH	45241	513-769-4774		648
TransCore Holdings Inc 8158 Adams Dr *TF:* 800-923-4824 ■ *Web:* www.transcore.com	Hummelstown	PA	17036	717-561-2400		261
TransCore Link Logistics Corp 6660 Kennedy Rd Ste 205 *TF:* 800-263-6149 ■ *Web:* www.transcore.ca	Mississauga	ON	L5T2M9	800-263-6149		311
Transcosmos America Inc 879 W 190th St Ste 1050 *Web:* www.transcosmos.net	Gardena	CA	90248	310-630-0072		195
Transcript Pharmacy Inc 2506 Lakeland Dr Ste 201 *TF:* 866-420-4041 ■ *Web:* www.transcriptpharmacy.com	Jackson	MS	39232	866-420-4041		237
TranscriptionGear Inc 7280 Auburn Rd *Web:* www.transcriptiongear.com	Concord	OH	44077	440-392-9882		690
Transdiesel 1310 George Jenkins Blvd *TF:* 800-428-0517 ■ *Web:* www.heavydutytransmissions.com	Lakeland	FL	33815	863-688-5881		54
Transducer Techniques Inc 42480 Rio Nedo *TF:* 800-344-3965 ■ *Web:* www.transducertechniques.com	Temecula	CA	92590	951-719-3965		362
Transdyn Inc 4256 Hacienda Dr # 100 *TF:* 800-888-7388 ■ *Web:* kapsch.net/ktc	Pleasanton	CA	94588	925-225-1600	225-1610	203
Transeair Travel LLC 2813 McKinley Pl NW *Web:* www.transeairtravel.com	Washington	DC	20015	202-362-6100	362-7411	184
Transend Corp 225 Emerson St *Web:* www.transend.com	Palo Alto	CA	94301	650-324-5370	324-5377	178-7
Transenterix Inc 635 Davis Dr Ste 300 *Web:* www.transenterix.com	Morrisville	NC	27560	919-765-8400		476
Transentric 1400 Douglas St Ste 0840 *TF:* 800-877-0328 ■ *Web:* www.transentric.com	Omaha	NE	68179	402-544-6000	501-2984	178-10
Trans-Exec Air Service Inc 7240 Hayvenhurst Pl Ste 200 *Web:* www.transexec.com	Van Nuys	CA	91406	818-904-6900		13
Transfer Devices Inc 45778 Northport Loop W *Web:* www.transferdevices.com	Fremont	CA	94538	510-378-8260		246
Transfer Express Inc 7650 Tyler Blvd *TF:* 800-622-2280 ■ *Web:* www.transferexpress.com	Mentor	OH	44060	440-918-1900		627
Transfer Solutions Inc 2885 Sandord Ave SW PO Box 17025 *Web:* www.ts-inc.com	Grandville	MI	49418	703-777-1126		401
Transfer Tool Systems Inc 14444 168th Ave *Web:* www.transfertool.com	Grand Haven	MI	49417	616-846-8510		488
TransferOnline 512 SE Salmon St *Web:* www.transferonline.com	Portland	OR	97214	503-227-2950		138
TRANSFLO Terminal Services Inc 500 Water St Ste J975 *TF:* 866-872-6735 ■ *Web:* transflo.net	Jacksonville	FL	32202	866-872-6735		449
Transforce Inc 5520 Cherokee Ave Ste 200 **Fax Area Code: 703* ■ *TF:* 800-308-6989 ■ *Web:* www.transforce.com	Alexandria	VA	22312	800-308-6989	838-5585*	721
Transform Automotive LLC 7026 Sterling Ponds Ct *Web:* www.transformauto.com	Sterling Heights	MI	48312	586-826-8500		60
Transformer Engineering 2550 Brookpark Rd *Web:* www.trenco.com	Cleveland	OH	44134	216-741-5282		767
Transformit Inc 33 Sanford Dr *Web:* www.transformit.com	Gorham	ME	04038	207-856-9911		393
TransGaming Inc 179 John St Ste 301 *Web:* www.transgaming.com	Toronto	ON	M5T1X4	416-979-9900		177
Transgenomic Inc 12325 Emmet St *OTC: TBIO* ■ *TF:* 888-233-9283 ■ *Web:* www.transgenomic.com	Omaha	NE	68164	402-452-5400	452-5401	419
Transglobal Gas & Oil Co 10904A Mcbride Ln	Knoxville	TN	37932	865-777-2162		579
Trans-Global Solutions Inc 11811 East Fwy Ste 630 *TF:* 800-746-9554 ■ *Web:* www.tgsgroup.com	Houston	TX	77029	713-453-0341	453-2756	207
TransGlobe Energy Corp 250 Fifth St SW Ste 2300 *TSE: TGL* ■ *Web:* www.trans-globe.com	Calgary	AB	T2P0R6	403-264-9888	770-8855	538
TransGroup Express Inc 18850 Eighth Ave S Ste 100 *Web:* www.transgroup.com	Seattle	WA	98148	206-244-0330		311
Transguard Insurance Company of America Inc 215 S Human Blvd *Web:* www.transguard.com	Naperville	IL	60563	630-864-3500		390
TransGuardian Inc International Jewelry Ctr 550 S Hill St Lobby 103 *Web:* www.transguardian.com	Los Angeles	CA	90013	213-622-5877		311
Transhield Inc 2932 Thorne Dr *Web:* www.transhield-usa.com	Elkhart	IN	46514	574-266-4118		594
Transhire 3601 W Commercial Blvd Ste 12 *TF:* 800-731-1714 ■ *Web:* www.transhiregroup.com	Fort Lauderdale	FL	33309	954-484-5401		193
Transim Technology Corp 433 NW Fourth Ave Ste 200 *TF:* 800-976-3077 ■ *Web:* www.transim.com	Portland	OR	97209	503-450-1355		174
TRANSInternational System Inc 130 E Wilson Bridge Rd Ste 150 Ste 150 *TF:* 800-340-7540 ■ *Web:* www.trnj.com	Worthington	OH	43085	614-891-4942	891-4929	311
Transit Authority of River City (TARC) 1000 W Broadway **Fax:* Cust Svc	Louisville	KY	40203	502-585-1234	213-3243*	468
Transit Systems Inc 999 Old Eagle School Rd Ste 114 *TF:* 800-626-1257 ■ *Web:* www.tsishipping.com	Wayne	PA	19087	800-626-1257		311
Transitair Inc 27 Bank St *Web:* www.transitairusa.com	Hornell	NY	14843	607-324-7860		14
Transition Networks Inc 10900 Red Cir Dr *TF:* 800-526-9267 ■ *Web:* www.transition.com	Minnetonka	MN	55343	952-941-7600	941-2322	176
Transition Partners Co 11732 Bowman Green Dr *Web:* www.tpco.us	Reston	VA	20190	703-736-0550		194
Transitions Optical Inc 9251 Belcher Rd *TF:* 800-533-2081 ■ *Web:* www.transitions.com	Pinellas Park	FL	33782	727-545-0400	546-4732	542
TranslateMedia LLC 414 Broadway 4th Fl *Web:* www.translatemedia.com	New York	NY	10013	212-796-5636		393
Translations International Inc 100 S Fifth St Ste 1900 **Fax Area Code: 202* ■ *Web:* www.tiinc.com	Minneapolis	MN	55402	320-217-2775	330-5776*	768
Translations.com Inc 3 Pk Ave 39th Fl *TF:* 800-688-7205 ■ *Web:* www.translations.com	New York	NY	10016	212-689-1616	685-9797	179
TransLink Capital 228 Hamilton Ave Ste 210 *Web:* www.translinkcapital.com	Palo Alto	CA	94301	650-330-7353		528
Trans-Lux Corp 26 Pearl St *OTC: TNLX* ■ *TF:* 800-243-5544 ■ *Web:* www.trans-lux.com	Norwalk	CT	06850	203-853-4321		173-4
Trans-Lux Fair-Play Inc 1700 Delaware Ave *TF:* 800-247-0265 ■ *Web:* www.fair-play.com	Des Moines	IA	50317	515-265-5305	265-3364	173-4
TransMagic Inc 11859 Pecos St Ste 310 *TF:* 800-693-9000 ■ *Web:* transmagic.com	Westminster	CO	80234	303-460-1406		174
Transmarine Navigation Corp 301 E Ocean Blvd Ste 590 *Web:* www.transmarine.com	Long Beach	CA	90802	562-951-8260		770
Transmaritime Central Inc 14213 Transportation Ave *TF:* 800-528-4283 ■ *Web:* www.transmaritime.com	Laredo	TX	78045	956-724-8417		311
Transmarket Group LLC 550 W Jackson Blvd Ste 1300 *Web:* www.transmarketgroup.com	Chicago	IL	60661	312-284-5500		401
Trans-Matic Manufacturing Co 300 E 48th St *TF:* 800-827-7455 ■ *Web:* www.transmatic.com	Holland	MI	49423	616-820-2500	820-2702	488
Transmedia 719 Battery St *TF:* 800-229-7234 ■ *Web:* www.transmediasf.com	San Francisco	CA	94111	415-956-3118	956-2595	646
TransMedia Group Inc 240 W Palmetto Park Rd *Web:* www.transmediagroup.com	Boca Raton	FL	33432	561-750-9800		636
TransMedics Inc 200 Minuteman Rd Ste 302 *Web:* www.transmedics.com	Andover	MA	01810	978-552-0900		476
Transmission Engineering Company Inc 1851 N Penn Rd *Web:* www.tecoinc.com	Hatfield	PA	19440	215-822-6737		261

Phone | Fax | Class

Transmodal Corp 48 S Franklin Tpke .... Ramsey NJ 07446 201-316-1600 311
Web: www.transmodal.net

Transmodus Corp
500 Esplanade Dr Ste 700 .... Oxnard CA 93036 805-604-4472 160
Web: www.transmodus.net

TransMontaigne Inc
1670 Broadway Ste 3100 Ste 3100.............. Denver CO 80202 303-626-8200 449
Web: www.transmontaigne.com

TransNational Assn of Christian Colleges & Schools (TRACS)
15935 Forest Rd............................. Forest VA 24551 434-525-9539 525-9538 48-1
TF: 800-669-4000 ■ *Web:* www.tracs.org

Transnorm System Inc 2810 Ave E E.......... Arlington TX 76011 972-606-0303 358
TF: 800-331-1749 ■ *Web:* www.transnorm.com

Transocean Inc 4 Greenway Plaza.............. Houston TX 77046 713-232-7500 540
NYSE: RIG ■ *TF:* 877-440-0173 ■ *Web:* www.deepwater.com

Transoft Solutions Inc
13575 Commerce Pkwy Ste 250............ Richmond BC V6V2L1 604-244-8387 244-1770 174
TF: 888-244-8387 ■ *Web:* www.transoftsolutions.com

Transource Computers Corp
2405 W Utopia Rd .... Phoenix AZ 85027 623-879-8882 879-8887 173-2
TF: 800-486-3715 ■ *Web:* www.transource.com

Transource Inc 8700 Triad Dr .... Colfax NC 27235 336-996-6060 57
Web: www.transourcetrucks.com

Trans-Pak Inc 520 Marburg Way............... San Jose CA 95133 408-254-0500 254-0551 549
Web: www.transpak.com

Transpara Corp
4715 W Culpepper Dr Ste 100 .... Pleasanton CA 94566 925-218-6983 177
Web: www.transpara.com

Transparent Container Company Inc
625 Thomas Dr........................ Bensenville IL 60106 708-449-8520 860-3651* 608
**Fax Area Code:* 630 ■ *Web:* www.transparentcontainer.com

Transparent Language Inc 12 Murphy Dr......... Nashua NH 03062 800-538-8867 262-6476* 178-3
**Fax Area Code:* 603 ■ *TF:* 800-538-8867 ■ *Web:* www.transparent.com

TransPerfect Translations Inc
3 Pk Ave 39th Fl.......................... New York NY 10016 212-689-5555 689-1059 768
TF: 800-305-9673 ■ *Web:* www.transperfect.com

Transphorm Inc 115 Castilian Dr................ Goleta CA 93117 805-456-1300 427
Web: www.transphormusa.com

Trans-Phos Inc PO Box 9004 .... Bartow FL 33831 863-534-1575 780
TF: 800-940-1575 ■ *Web:* www.transphos.com

Transplace 3010 Gaylord Pkwy Ste 200............ Frisco TX 75034 866-413-9266 731-4501* 449
**Fax Area Code:* 972 ■ *TF:* 866-413-9266 ■ *Web:* www.transplace.com

Transpo Electronics Inc
2150 Brengle Ave .... Orlando FL 32808 800-327-6903 298-4519* 247
**Fax Area Code:* 407 ■ *TF:* 800-327-6903 ■ *Web:* www.waiglobal.com

Transport Bourret Inc
375 Bd Lemire .... Drummondville QC J2B8G8 819-477-2202 478
Web: www.bourret.ca

Transport Clearings East Inc
4651 Charlotte Park Dr Ste 150 .... Charlotte NC 28217 704-527-1820 219-0061* 272
**Fax Area Code:* 980 ■ *Web:* www.tceast.com

Transport Corp of America Inc
1715 Yankee Doodle Rd .... Eagan MN 55121 651-686-2500 686-2566 780
TF: 800-328-3927 ■ *Web:* www.transportamerica.com

Transport Distribution Co PO Box 306 .... Joplin MO 64802 417-624-3814 624-9767 780
TF: 800-866-7709 ■ *Web:* www.gotdc.com

Transport Inc 2225 Main Ave SE............... Moorhead MN 56560 218-236-6300 236-0227 780
TF: 800-598-7267 ■ *Web:* www.transport-inc.com

Transport Jacques Auger Inc
860 Archimede St............................ Levis QC G6V7M5 418-835-9266 478
TF: 800-387-3835 ■ *Web:* www.tja.ca

Transport Refrigeration Inc
301 Lawrence Dr........................... De Pere WI 54115 920-339-5700 339-5717 665
Web: thermokinggreenbay.com

Transport Workers Union of America
501 Third St NW 9th Fl................... Washington DC 20001 202-719-3900 347-0454 49-21
TF: 888-564-6898 ■ *Web:* www.twu.org

Transportation Alliance Bank Inc
4185 Harrison Blvd Ste 200 .... Ogden UT 84403 800-355-3063 70
TF: 800-355-3063 ■ *Web:* www.tabbank.com

Transportation Communications International Union
3 Research Pl .... Rockville MD 20850 301-948-4910 948-1369 414
TF: 877-772-5772 ■ *Web:* www.goiam.org

Transportation Insight LLC
310 Main Ave Way SE........................ Hickory NC 28602 828-485-5000 449
TF: 877-226-9950 ■ *Web:* www.t-insight.com

Transportation Institute
5201 Auth Way...................... Camp Springs MD 20746 301-423-3335 49-21
Web: transportationinstitute.org

Transportation Insurance Co
333 S Wabash Ave .... Chicago IL 60604 312-822-5000 822-6419 391-4
Web: www.cna.com

Transportation Intermediaries Assn (TIA)
1625 Prince St Ste 200...................... Alexandria VA 22314 703-299-5700 836-0123 49-21
Web: www.tianet.org

Transportation Management Assoc Inc
344 Oak Grove Church Rd .... Mocksville NC 27028 800-745-8292 311
TF: 800-745-8292 ■ *Web:* www.tmaco.com

Transportation Management Services Inc
16600 Table Mtn Pkwy .... Golden CO 80403 303-287-8600 194
Web: www.imagitas.com

Transportation Research Board (TRB)
500 Fifth St NW .... Washington DC 20001 202-334-2934 334-2519 49-21
TF: 866-233-4642 ■ *Web:* www.trb.org

Transportation Research Corp
4305 Business Dr..................... Cameron Park CA 95682 530-676-7770 650
TF: 888-676-7770 ■ *Web:* www.varnaproducts.com

Transportation Research Ctr Inc (TRC Inc)
10820 State Rt 347 PO Box B-67 .... East Liberty OH 43319 937-666-2011 666-5066 668
Web: www.trcpg.com

Transportation Security Administration
Federal Air Marshal Service
601 S 12th St............................ Arlington VA 22202 866-289-9673 340-11
TF: 866-289-9673 ■ *Web:* www.tsa.gov

Transportation Solutions Inc
1900 Brannan Rd .... McDonough GA 30253 770-474-1555 449
Web: www.tsilogistics.com

Transportation Technology Ctr Inc
55500 DOT Rd PO Box 11130 .... Pueblo CO 81001 719-584-0750 584-0711 668
Web: www.aar.com

TransportGistics Inc
28 N Country Rd Ste 103 .... Mt Sinai NY 11766 631-567-4100 311
Web: www.transportgistics.com

TransPro Freight Systems Ltd
8600 Escarpment Way Milton............. Mississauga ON L9T0M1 905-693-0699 478
TF: 800-268-6857 ■ *Web:* www.transprofreight.com

Trans-Resources Inc 200 W 57th St .... New York NY 10019 212-515-4100 280

Transtar LLC 1200 Penn Ave Ste 300........... Pittsburgh PA 15222 412-433-7835 360-3
Web: www.tstarinc.com

Trans-tec Machine Ltd
6320 Ridgemont St........................... Houston TX 77087 713-643-9114 480
Web: www.transtecmachine.com

Trans-Tech Inc 5520 Adamstown Rd.......... Adamstown MD 21710 301-695-9400 695-7065 249
Web: www.trans-techinc.com

Transtech Industries Inc
2025 Delsea Dr.............................. Sewell NJ 08080 856-481-4214 227-6578 789
OTC: TRTI ■ *Web:* www.transtechindustries.com

TransTech IT Staffing
248 Spring Lake Dr........................... Itasca IL 60143 630-250-8880 260
Web: www.trans-tech.com

TransTech Pharma Inc
4170 Mendenhall Oaks Pkwy .... High Point NC 27265 336-841-0300 743
Web: vtvtherapeutics.com

Trans-Tel Central Inc (TTC) 2805 Broce Dr....... Norman OK 73072 405-447-5025 447-5029 787
TF: 800-729-4636 ■ *Web:* www.trans-tel.com

Transtelco Inc
500 W Overland Ave Ste 310 .... El Paso TX 79901 915-534-8100 224
Web: www.transtelco.net

TransUnion LLC 555 W Adams St .... Chicago IL 60661 866-922-2100 218
TF: 866-922-2100 ■ *Web:* www.transunion.com

Transverse LLC 620 Congress Ave Ste 200......... Austin TX 78701 512-279-3119 463
Web: www.gotransverse.com

Transvideo Studios 990 Villa St........... Mountain View CA 94041 650-965-4808 962-1753 6
Web: www.transvideo.com

Transweave Inc
1333 Gough St Ste 7J................. San Francisco CA 94109 415-441-5271 463

Transwest 20770 I-76 Frontage Rd .... Brighton CO 80603 303-289-3161 288-2310 57
TF: 800-289-3161 ■ *Web:* www.transwest.com

Transwest Credit Union
37 West 1700 South.................... Salt Lake City UT 84115 801-487-1692 219
Web: transwestcu.com

Trans-West Security Services Inc
8503 Crippen St .... Bakersfield CA 93311 661-381-2900 693
Web: trans-west.net

Transwestern Commercial Services
1900 W Loop S Ste 1300 .... Houston TX 77027 713-270-7700 270-6285 655
TF: 800-531-8182 ■ *Web:* www.transwestern.net

Transwheel Corp 3000 Yeoman Way Huntington IN 46750 260-358-8660 247
Web: www.transwheel.com

TranSwitch Corp 3 Enterprise Dr................ Shelton CT 06484 203-929-8810 696
Web: www.websolutions.com

TransWood Carriers Inc PO Box 189............. Omaha NE 68101 888-346-8092 341-2112* 780
**Fax Area Code:* 402 ■ *TF:* 888-346-8092 ■ *Web:* www.transwood.com

TransWorks
9910 Dupont Cir Dr E Ste 200 .... Fort Wayne IN 46825 260-487-4400 178-10
TF: 800-435-4691 ■ *Web:* www.trnswrks.com

TransWorld Network Corp
255 Pine Ave N........................... Oldsmar FL 34677 813-891-4700 387
TF: 800-253-0665 ■ *Web:* www.twncorp.com

Transworld Systems Inc
PO Box 15618 .... Wilmington DE 19850 877-282-1250 160
TF: 888-446-4733 ■ *Web:* www.tsico.com

TransX Group of Cos
2595 Inkster Blvd .... Winnipeg MB R3C2E6 204-632-6694 311
TF: 877-558-9444 ■ *Web:* www.transx.com

Transylvania County Library (TCL)
212 S Gaston St .... Brevard NC 28712 828-884-3151 434-3
TF: 800-859-0829 ■ *Web:* library.transylvaniacounty.org

Transylvania University
300 N Broadway .... Lexington KY 40508 859-233-8242 233-8797 166
TF: 800-872-6798 ■ *Web:* www.transy.edu

TranSystems Corp
2400 Pershing Rd Ste 400 .... Kansas City MO 64108 816-329-8700 329-8703 261
Web: www.transystems.com

TranTek Automation Corp
2470 N Aero Park Ct.................... Traverse City MI 49686 231-946-6270 358
Web: www.trantekautomation.com

Tranter Graphics Inc
8094 N State Rd 13.......................... Syracuse IN 46567 574-834-2626 627
Web: www.trantergraphics.com

Tranter Inc 1900 Old Burk Hwy .... Wichita Falls TX 76306 940-723-7125 723-5131 91
TF: 800-414-6908 ■ *Web:* www.tranter.com

TranzAct Technologies Inc
360 W Butterfield Rd 4th Fl.................. Elmhurst IL 60126 630-833-0890 311
Web: www.tranzact.com

Tranzon LLC 2100 Club Dr Ste 100 .... Richmond VA 23226 256-413-2902 41
TF: 866-503-1212 ■ *Web:* www.tranzon.com

Tranzonic Cos
26301 Curtiss Wright Pkwy Ste 200........... Cleveland OH 44143 216-535-4300 558
Web: www.tranzonic.com

Trap Pond State Park
33587 Baldcypress Ln .... Laurel DE 19956 302-875-5153 565
Web: www.destateparks.com

Trap Rock Industries Inc
460 River Rd............................. Kingston NJ 08528 609-924-0300 497-0135 503-5
Web: www.traprock.com

Traphagen Financial Group
234 Kinderkamack Rd......................... Oradell NJ 07649 201-262-1040 734
Web: www.tfgllc.com

Trapit Inc 599 Third st .... San Francisco CA 94107 844-987-2748 387
TF: 844-987-2748 ■ *Web:* trap.it

Trapp Family Lodge
700 Trapp Hill Rd PO Box 1428 .... Stowe VT 05672 802-253-8511 669
TF: 800-826-7000 ■ *Web:* www.trappfamily.com

	City	State	ZIP	Phone	Fax	Class
Trapper's Fishcamp & Grill 4300 W Reno St *Web:* pearlsokc.com/restaurants/trappers-fishcamp-grill	Oklahoma City	OK	73107	405-943-9111		671
Trapshooting Hall of Fame & Museum 601 W National Rd *Web:* www.traphof.org	Vandalia	OH	45377	937-660-5663		522
Traton Corp 720 Kennesaw Ave NW *Web:* www.tratonhomes.com	Marietta	GA	30060	770-427-9064		187
Trattoria Bella Sera 9449 Montana Ave *Web:* trattoriabellasera.com	El Paso	TX	79925	915-598-7948		671
Trattoria Contadina 1800 Mason St *Web:* www.trattoriacontadina.com	San Francisco	CA	94133	415-982-5728		671
Trattoria Delia 152 St Paul St *Web:* www.trattoriadelia.com	Burlington	VT	05401	802-864-5253		671
Trattoria dell'Arte 900 Seventh Ave *Web:* www.trattoriadellarte.com	New York	NY	10106	212-245-9800		671
Trattoria Giorgio 121 S Main St *Web:* trattoriagiorgio.net	Greenville	SC	29601	864-271-9166		671
Trattoria Marcella 3600 Watson Rd *Web:* trattoriamarcella.com	Saint Louis	MO	63109	314-352-7706		671
Trattoria Nervosa 75 Yorkville Ave *Web:* www.eatnervosa.com	Toronto	ON	M5R1B8	416-961-4642		671
Trattoria No 10 10 N Dearborn St *Web:* www.trattoriaten.com	Chicago	IL	60602	312-984-1718		671
Trattoria Roma 1447 Grandview Ave *Web:* www.trattoria-roma.com	Columbus	OH	43212	614-488-2104		671
Tratum Technologies Inc 950 Herndon Pkwy Ste 285 *Web:* tratumtech.com	Herndon	VA	20170	703-456-7010		180
Trau & Loevner Inc 838 Braddock Ave *TF:* 800-570-1572 ■ *Web:* www.trau-loevner.com	Braddock	PA	15104	412-361-7700	361-8221	687
Traulsen & Company Inc 4401 Blue Mound Rd *TF:* 800-825-8220 ■ *Web:* www.traulsen.com	Fort Worth	TX	76106	800-825-8220		14
Trautman & Shreve Inc 4406 Race St *Web:* www.trautman-shreve.com	Denver	CO	80216	303-295-1414	295-0324	189-10
Travaasa Hana 5031 Hana Hwy *TF:* 855-868-7282 ■ *Web:* travaasa.com	Hana	HI	96713	808-248-8211	248-7202	669
Travaglini Enterprises 231 Chestnut St	Meadville	PA	16335	814-724-4880		670
Travcoa 100 N Sepulveda Blvd Ste 1700 *TF:* 800-992-2003 ■ *Web:* www.travcoa.com	El Segundo	CA	90245	310-649-7104	649-7106	760
Travel & Cruise 4331 Wyoming Blvd NE *Web:* www.rgtravel.com	Albuquerque	NM	87111	505-299-7766		772
Travel & Transport Inc 2120 S 72nd St *TF:* 800-228-2545 ■ *Web:* www.travelandtransport.com	Omaha	NE	68124	402-399-4500		771
Travel + Leisure Magazine 225 Liberty St **Fax Area Code:* 718 ■ *TF:* 800-452-9292 ■ *Web:* www.travelandleisure.com	New York	NY	10281	800-888-8728	373-3681*	457-20
Travel Agent Magazine 757 Third Ave 5th Fl *TF:* 855-424-6247 ■ *Web:* www.travelagentcentral.com	New York	NY	10017	212-895-8200		457-22
Travel Berkley Springs 127 Fairfax St *TF:* 800-447-8797 ■ *Web:* www.berkeleysprings.com	Berkeley Springs	WV	25411	304-258-9147		772
Travel Ch LLC 5425 Wisconsin Ave Ste 500 *Web:* www.travelchannel.com	Chevy Chase	MD	20815	301-244-7500	244-7509	740
Travel Destinations Management Group Inc 110 Painters Mill Rd *TF:* 800-635-7307 ■ *Web:* www.traveldest.com	Owings Mills	MD	21117	410-363-3111	363-1816	771
Travel Goods Association 301 N Harrison St Ste 412 *TF:* 877-842-1938 ■ *Web:* www.travel-goods.org	Princeton	NJ	08540	877-842-1938		138
Travel Holdings Inc 220 E Central Pkwy Ste 4000 *Web:* www.travelholdings.com	Altamonte Springs	FL	32701	407-667-8700		771
Travel Impressions Ltd 465 Smith St *TF:* 800-284-0044 ■ *Web:* www.travimp.com	Farmingdale	NY	11735	631-845-8000		771
Travel Inc 4355 River Green Pkwy *TF:* 888-439-1831 ■ *Web:* www.travelinc.com	Duluth	GA	30096	770-291-4100		771
Travel Industry Assn of Kansas 919 S Kansas Ave *Web:* www.tiak.org	Topeka	KS	66612	785-233-9465		206
Travel Institute 945 Concord St *TF:* 800-542-4282 ■ *Web:* www.thetravelinstitute.com	Framingham	MA	01701	781-237-0280	237-3860	48-23
Travel Insured International 855 Winding Brook Dr PO Box 6503 **Fax Area Code:* 860 ■ *TF:* 800-243-3174 ■ *Web:* www.travelinsured.com	Glastonbury	CT	06033	800-243-3174	528-8005*	391-7
Travel Leaders Group LLC 3033 Campus Dr Ste W320 *TF:* 800-335-8747 ■ *Web:* www.travelleadersgroup.com	Plymouth	MN	55441	763-744-3700		787
Travel Management Partners Inc 7208 Falls of Neuse Rd Ste 220 *TF:* 800-338-6448 ■ *Web:* www.tmptravel.com	Raleigh	NC	27615	919-782-3810		772
Travel Manitoba 155 Carlton St 7th Fl *TF:* 800-665-0040 ■ *Web:* www.travelmanitoba.com	Winnipeg	MB	R3C3H8	204-927-7800	927-7828	774
Travel Network Corp, The 1920 Ave Rd *TF:* 888-666-8747 ■ *Web:* www.thetravelnetwork.com	Toronto	ON	M5M4A1	416-789-3271		775
Travel One Inc 8009 34th Ave S 15th Fl *TF:* 800-247-1311 ■ *Web:* www.traveloneinc.com	Minneapolis	MN	55425	952-854-2551		772
Travel Oriented Inc 15490 S Western Ave *Web:* traveloriented.com	Gardena	CA	90249	310-329-2800		772
Travel Portland Pioneer Courthouse Sq 701 S.W. Sixth Ave *TF:* 877-678-5263 ■ *Web:* www.travelportland.com	Portland	OR	97204	503-275-9750		206
Travel Society Inc 650 S Cherry St Ste 200 *TF:* 800-926-6031 ■ *Web:* www.travelsociety.com	Denver	CO	80246	303-321-0900		772
Travel Tags Inc 5842 Carmen Ave *Web:* www.traveltags.com	Inver Grove Heights	MN	55076	651-450-1201		627
Travel Team Inc 2495 Main St *TF:* 800-245-8326 ■ *Web:* profile.thetravelteam.com	Buffalo	NY	14214	716-862-7680	862-7650	771
Travel Turf Inc 7540 Windsor Dr Ste 202 *TF:* 800-222-4432 ■ *Web:* www.wcv.com	Allentown	PA	18195	610-391-9094		772
Travel Weekly Crossroads Magazine 100 Lighting Way *TF:* 800-635-1666 ■ *Web:* www.travelweekly.com	Secaucus	NJ	07094	201-902-2000		457-21
Travel Wizard LLC 5675 Lucas Valley Rd Ste 6 *TF:* 800-330-8820 ■ *Web:* www.travelwizard.com	Nicasio	CA	94946	415-446-5252		772
TravelAge West Magazine 11400 W Olympic Blvd Ste 325 *Web:* www.travelagewest.com	Los Angeles	CA	90064	310-954-2510	954-2525	457-22
TravelCenters of America 24601 Ctr Ridge Rd Ste 200 *TF:* 800-632-9240 ■ *Web:* www.ta-petro.com	Westlake	OH	44145	440-808-9100		324
Travelclick 7 Times Sq 38th Fl *TF:* 866-674-4549 ■ *Web:* www.travelclick.com	New York	NY	10036	212-817-4800		194
Travelennium Inc 556 Colonial Rd *TF:* 800-844-4924 ■ *Web:* www.travelennium.com	Memphis	TN	38117	901-767-0761	766-0126	771
Traveler's Rest State Historic Site 4339 Riverdale Rd *Web:* www.gastateparks.org	Toccoa	GA	30577	706-886-2256		565
Travelers Cos Inc 385 Washington St *NYSE: TRV* ■ *TF:* 800-328-2189 ■ *Web:* www.travelers.com	Saint Paul	MN	55102	651-310-7911		360-4
Travelers Motor Club 720 NW 50th St *TF:* 800-654-9208 ■ *Web:* www.travelersmotorclub.com	Oklahoma City	OK	73154	405-848-1711		53
Travelers Transportation Services Inc 195 Heart Lake Rd S *TF:* 800-265-8789 ■ *Web:* www.travelers.ca	Brampton	ON	L6W3N6	905-457-8789		311
Travelex International Inc 2061 N Barrington Rd *TF:* 800-882-0499 ■ *Web:* travelexinternational.com	Hoffman Estates	IL	60169	847-882-0400		772
Travelex Worldwide Money 122 E 42nd St Ste 2800 *TF:* 800-228-9792 ■ *Web:* www.travelex.com	New York	NY	10168	212-363-6206		69
Travelhost Magazine 10701 N Stemmons Fwy *TF:* 800-527-1782 ■ *Web:* www.travelhost.com	Dallas	TX	75220	972-556-0541	432-8729	457-22
Traveline Travel Agencies Inc 4074 Erie St *TF:* 888-700-8747 ■ *Web:* www.traveline.com	Willoughby	OH	44094	440-602-8020	946-3613	771
Traveling Computers Inc 210 E Main St *Web:* www.tcinc.net	Riverton	WY	82501	307-856-8676		177
Travelink Inc 404 BNA Dr #650 *TF:* 800-821-4671 ■ *Web:* www.travelink.com	Nashville	TN	37217	615-367-4900		317
Travellers Rest Plantation & Museum 636 Farrell Pkwy *Web:* www.travellersrestplantation.org	Nashville	TN	37220	615-832-8197	832-8169	50-3
Travelmart Inc, The 28011 Clemens Rd *TF:* 800-992-8064 ■ *Web:* ww.thetravelmart.com	Westlake	OH	44145	440-835-8220		772
Travelmore 212 W Colfax Ave *Web:* www.travelleaders.com	South Bend	IN	46601	574-232-3061		771
TravelNow com Inc 4124 S Mccann Ct Ste 418 *Web:* www.travelnow.com	Springfield	MO	65804	417-864-3600	864-8811	774
Travelodge Virginia Beach 1909 Atlantic Ave *TF:* 800-578-7878 ■ *Web:* www.travelodge.com	Virginia Beach	VA	23451	757-425-0650		379
Travel-On Ltd 9000 Virginia Manor Rd Ste 201 *TF:* 800-333-6778 ■ *Web:* www.tvlon.com	Beltsville	MD	20705	240-387-4000		772
Travelong Inc 135 W 50th St Ste 500 *TF:* 800-537-6043	New York	NY	10020	212-736-2166	763-0496	771
Travelport Ltd 300 Galleria Pkwy *Web:* www.travelport.com	Atlanta	GA	30339	770-563-7400		387
Travelpro USA 700 Banyan Trl *TF:* 800-741-7471 ■ *Web:* www.travelpro.com	Boca Raton	FL	33431	561-998-2824	998-8487	453
Travelsavers Inc 71 Audrey Ave *Web:* www.travelsavers.com	Oyster Bay	NY	11771	516-624-0500	624-6024	772
TravelSmith Outfitters 773 San Marin Dr Ste 2300 *TF:* 800-770-3387 ■ *Web:* www.travelsmith.com	Novato	CA	94945	800-770-3387	950-1656	459
TravelStore Inc 11601 Wilshire Blvd *TF:* 800-850-3224 ■ *Web:* www.travelstore.com	Los Angeles	CA	90025	310-575-5540	575-5541	771
TRAVELVIDEOSTORE.com Inc 5420 Boran Dr *TF:* 800-288-5123 ■ *Web:* www.travelvideostore.com	Tampa	FL	33610	813-630-9778		772
Travelzoo Inc 590 Madison Ave 37th Fl *NASDAQ: TZOO* ■ *Web:* www.travelzoo.com	New York	NY	10022	212-484-4900	521-4230	773
Traver Technologies Ltd 2550 Gray Falls Dr Ste 400 *TF:* 800-929-8478 ■ *Web:* cdkglobalconsulting.com	Houston	TX	77077	800-929-8478		463
Travers Printing Inc 32 Mission St *TF:* 800-696-0530 ■ *Web:* www.traversprinting.com	Gardner	MA	01440	978-632-0530		627
Travers Tool Company Inc 128-15 26th Ave **Fax Area Code:* 800 ■ *TF Cust Svc:* 800-221-0270 ■ *Web:* www.travers.com	Flushing	NY	11354	718-886-7200	722-0703*	385
Traverse City Area Chamber of Commerce 202 E Grandview Pkwy *TF:* 844-900-0500 ■ *Web:* www.tcchamber.org	Traverse City	MI	49684	231-947-5075	946-2565	139
Traverse City Convention & Visitors Bureau 101 W Grandview Pkwy *TF:* 800-940-1120 ■ *Web:* www.traversecity.com	Traverse City	MI	49684	231-947-1120	947-2621	206
Traverse City Record-Eagle 120 W Front St *TF:* 800-968-8273 ■ *Web:* www.record-eagle.com	Traverse City	MI	49684	231-946-2000	946-8632	532-2
Traverse City State Park 1132 US-31 N *Web:* www.michigandnr.com	Traverse City	MI	49686	231-922-5270		565
Traverse Electric Co-op Inc 1618 Broadway PO Box 66 *TF:* 800-927-5443 ■ *Web:* www.traverseelectric.com	Wheaton	MN	56296	320-563-8616		245

Name / Address	City	State	ZIP	Phone	Fax	Class
Traverse Symphony Orchestra (TSO) 300 E Front St Ste 230 *Web:* www.traversesymphony.org	Traverse City	MI	49684	231-947-7120		573-3
Travis Avenue Baptist Church 800 E Berry St *Web:* www.travis.org	Fort Worth	TX	76110	817-924-4266	921-9620	95
Travis Body & Trailer Inc 13955 FM529 *TF:* 800-535-4372 ■ *Web:* www.travistrailers.com	Houston	TX	77041	713-466-5888	466-3238	779
Travis County PO Box 1748 *Web:* www.traviscountytx.gov	Austin	TX	78767	512-854-9020	854-4464	338
Travis County State Jail 8101 FM 969 *Web:* tdcj.state.tx.us	Austin	TX	78724	512-926-4482		213
Travis Federal Credit Union 1 Travis Way *TF:* 800-877-8328 ■ *Web:* www.traviscu.org	Vacaville	CA	95687	707-449-4000		219
Travis Pattern & Foundry Inc 1413 E Hawthorne Rd *Web:* www.pduinc.com	Spokane	WA	99218	509-466-3545	467-6465	308
Travisco 7210 Clinton Hwy PO Box 670 **Fax Area Code:* 865 ■ *TF:* 800-247-7606 ■ *Web:* www.travismeats.com	Powell	TN	37849	800-247-7606	938-9211*	473
TravisWolff Independent Advisors & Accountants 15950 N Dallas Pkwy Ste 600 *Web:* www.traviswolff.com	Dallas	TX	75248	972-661-1843		731
Traxx Restaurant 800 N Alameda St	Los Angeles	CA	90012	213-625-1999		671
Trayer Engineering Corp 898 Pennsylvania Ave *TF:* 800-377-1774 ■ *Web:* trayer.com	San Francisco	CA	94107	415-285-7770		261
Trayer Products Inc 541 E Clinton St *Web:* www.trayerproducts.com	Elmira	NY	14901	607-734-8124		247
Traylor Bros Inc 835 N Congress Ave *TF:* 866-895-1491 ■ *Web:* www.traylor.com	Evansville	IN	47715	812-477-1542	474-3223	188-4
Tray-Pak Corp Tuckerton Rd & Reading Crest Ave *Web:* www.traypak.com	Reading	PA	19605	484-509-0046		596
TRB (Transportation Research Board) 500 Fifth St NW *TF:* 866-233-4642 ■ *Web:* www.trb.org	Washington	DC	20001	202-334-2934	334-2519	49-21
TRC Cos Inc 21 Griffin Rd N *Web:* www.trcsolutions.com	Windsor	CT	06095	860-298-9692	298-6399	192
TRC Global Mobility 1042 E Juneau Ave *TF:* 800-783-5337 ■ *Web:* trcglobalmobility.com	Milwaukee	WI	53202	414-226-4200		652
TRC Holdings Inc 1300 Virginia Dr Ste 200 *TF:* 800-275-2827 ■ *Web:* www.trchome.com	Fort Washington	PA	19034	215-641-2200		466
TRC Inc (Transportation Research Ctr Inc) 10820 State Rt 347 PO Box B-67 *Web:* www.trcpg.com	East Liberty	OH	43319	937-666-2011	666-5066	668
TRC Worldwide Engineering Inc (TRCWW) 217 Ward Cir *Web:* www.trcww.com	Brentwood	TN	37027	615-661-7979	661-0644	261
TRCWW (TRC Worldwide Engineering Inc) 217 Ward Cir *Web:* www.trcww.com	Brentwood	TN	37027	615-661-7979	661-0644	261
Tre Cugini 122 Monroe Ctr NW *Web:* trecugini.com	Grand Rapids	MI	49503	616-235-9339		671
Tre Kronor 3258 W Foster Ave *Web:* trekronorrestaurant.com	Chicago	IL	60625	773-267-9888		671
Tre Scalini 100 Wooster St *Web:* www.trescalinirestaurant.com	New Haven	CT	06510	203-777-3373	787-5360	671
Tre Scalini 1915 Passyunk Ave *Web:* trescaliniphiladelphia.com	Philadelphia	PA	19148	215-551-3870		671
TREA (Retired Enlisted Assn) 15821 E Centre Tech Cir *Web:* www.trea.org	Aurora	CO	80011	303-340-3939	340-4516	48-19
Treacy & Co 1220 South St *Web:* www.treacyandco.com	Needham	MA	02492	781-559-3381		463
Tread Corp 176 Eastpark Dr *Web:* www.treadcorp.com	Roanoke	VA	24019	540-982-6881	344-7536	678
Treads Bicycle Outfitters 16701 E Iliff Ave *Web:* www.treads.com	Aurora	CO	80013	303-750-1671		711
Treasure Bay Casino & Hotel 1980 Beach Blvd *Web:* www.treasurebay.com	Biloxi	MS	39531	228-385-6000	385-6082	669
Treasure Chest Casino 5050 Williams Blvd *TF:* 800-298-0711 ■ *Web:* www.treasurechest.com	Kenner	LA	70065	504-443-8000		133
Treasure County PO Box 392	Hysham	MT	59038	406-342-5547		338
Treasure Garden Inc 13401 Brooks Dr Ste A *Web:* treasuregarden.com	Baldwin Park	CA	91706	626-814-0168		320
Treasure Health 1201 SE Indian St *TF:* 800-299-4677 ■ *Web:* www.tchospice.org	Stuart	FL	34997	772-403-4500		371
Treasure Island Foods Inc 3460 N Broadway *Web:* www.tifoods.com	Chicago	IL	60657	773-327-4265		345
Treasure Island Hotel & Casino 3300 Las Vegas Blvd S *TF:* 800-288-7206 ■ *Web:* www.treasureisland.com	Las Vegas	NV	89109	702-894-7111	894-7414	669
Treasure Island Resort & Casino 5734 Sturgeon Lake Rd *Web:* www.ticasino.com	Welch	MN	55089	651-385-2786		707
Treasure Valley Community College 650 College Blvd **Fax:* Admissions ■ *Web:* www.tvcc.cc/index.cfm	Ontario	OR	97914	541-881-8822	881-2721*	162
Treasure Valley Reminder 1160 SW Fourth St *Web:* www.argusobserver.com	Ontario	OR	97914	541-889-5387		4
Treat All Metals Inc 5140 N Port Washington Rd *Web:* www.treatallmetals.com	Milwaukee	WI	53217	414-962-2500		484
Treats International Franchise Corp 238 Queen St S 2nd Fl *TF:* 800-461-4003 ■ *Web:* www.treats.com	Mississauga	ON	L5M1L5	613-563-4073	563-1982	68
Treatt 4900 Lakeland Commerce Pkwy *Web:* www.treattusa.com	Lakeland	FL	33805	863-668-9500		297-8
Trebol Motors Corp 296 Marginal Kennedy *Web:* www.trebolmotors.com	San Juan	PR	00920	787-793-2828		57
Trebor Enterprises Ltd 927 W Stephenson St	Freeport	IL	61032	815-235-1700		409
Trebor International Inc 8100 S 1300 W *Web:* www.treborintl.com	West Jordan	UT	84088	801-561-0303		246
Treco Service Inc 904 N Zarzamora St *Web:* www.trecoservices.com	San Antonio	TX	78207	210-432-4100		104
Tredegar Corp 1100 Boulders Pkwy *NYSE:* TG ■ *TF:* 800-411-7441 ■ *Web:* www.tredegar.com	North Chesterfield	VA	23225	804-330-1000	330-1177	360-3
Tredent Data Systems Inc 3241 Grande Vista Dr *Web:* www.tredent.com	Newbury Park	CA	91320	805-375-4911		246
Tredyffrin-Easttown School District (TESD) 940 W Valley Rd Ste 1700 *Web:* www.tesd.net	Wayne	PA	19087	610-240-1900		186
Tree Care Industry Assn (TCIA) 136 Harvey Rd Ste 101 *TF:* 800-733-2622 ■ *Web:* tcia.org	Londonderry	NH	03053	603-314-5380	314-5386	48-13
Tree City Tool 1954 N Montgomery Rd *Web:* www.treecitytool.com	Greensburg	IN	47240	812-663-4196		454
Tree Hill Nature Ctr 7152 Lone Star Rd *Web:* www.treehill.org	Jacksonville	FL	32211	904-724-4646	724-9132	50-5
Tree Island Industries 3933 Boundary Rd *TF:* 800-663-0955 ■ *Web:* www.treeisland.com	Richmond	BC	V6V1T8	604-524-3744	524-2362	485
Tree Island Steel 12459 Arrow Rt *TF:* 800-255-6974 ■ *Web:* treeisland.com/brands/tree-island	Rancho Cucamonga	CA	91739	909-594-7511	595-0439	813
Tree Top Inc 220 E Second Ave *Web:* www.treetop.com	Selah	WA	98942	509-697-7251	698-1421	296-20
Tree Top Ranches LP PO Box 8126	Boise	ID	83707	208-377-0998		10-3
Treefort Inc 6500 Barrie Rd *Web:* www.treefort.com	Minneapolis	MN	55435	612-285-5625		809
TreeHouse Foods Inc 2021 Spring Rd Ste 600 *NYSE:* THS ■ *Web:* www.treehousefoods.com	Oak Brook	IL	60523	708-483-1300		296-11
Treehouse Museum 347 22nd St *Web:* www.treehousemuseum.org	Ogden	UT	84401	801-394-9663		521
Treehouse Software Inc 2605 Nicholson Rd Ste 230 *Web:* www.treehouse.com	Sewickley	PA	15143	724-759-7070		177
Treelands Inc 1000 Huntington Tpke *TF:* 800-243-0232 ■ *Web:* treelandgardencenter.com	Bridgeport	CT	06610	203-372-3511	371-6023	323
Treeline Associates 3040 W Clarkston Rd *Web:* treelineassociates.com	Lake Orion	MI	48302	248-814-7151		463
Treeline Well Services Inc 750 333 - 11th Ave SW *TF:* 844-344-7447 ■ *Web:* www.treelinewell.com	Calgary	AB	T2R1L9	403-266-2868		190
Treemont Nursing & Rehabilitation Ctr 5550 Harvest Hill Rd *TF:* 800-252-5400 ■ *Web:* www.treemonthealthcare.com	Dallas	TX	75230	972-661-1862		450
Treen Safety 704 Alexander St *Web:* www.treensafety.com	Vancouver	BC	V6A1E3	604-253-4588		477
Treepeople Inc 12601 Mulholland Dr *Web:* www.treepeople.org	Beverly Hills	CA	90210	818-753-4600		776
Trees for Tomorrow (TFT) 519 Sheridan St E PO Box 609 *Web:* www.treesfortomorrow.com	Eagle River	WI	54521	715-479-6456	479-2318	49-5
Trees Inc 650 N Sam Houston Pkwy E Ste 205 *TF:* 866-865-9617 ■ *Web:* www.treesinc.com	Houston	TX	77060	281-447-1327	260-0728	776
Treesdale Partners LLC 1325 Ave of the Americas Ste 2302 *Web:* www.treesdalellc.com	New York	NY	10019	212-299-5525		194
Treetops Resort 3962 Wilkinson Rd *TF:* 866-348-5249 ■ *Web:* www.treetops.com	Gaylord	MI	49735	989-732-6711		669
Trefethen Advisors LLC 16220 N Scottsdale Rd Ste 275 *Web:* www.trefethenadvisors.com	Scottsdale	AZ	85254	480-922-9966		690
Trefethen Vineyards Winery Inc 1160 Oak Knoll Ave *TF:* 866-895-7696 ■ *Web:* www.trefethen.com	Napa	CA	94558	707-255-7700		80-3
Treflie Capital Management 35 Ezekills Holw *TF:* 866-236-3363 ■ *Web:* www.treflie.com	Sag Harbor	NY	11963	631-725-2500		401
Trego County 216 N Main St *TF:* 877-962-7248 ■ *Web:* www.wakeeney.org	WaKeeney	KS	67672	785-743-6385		338
Trego Dugan Aviation Inc Lee Bird Fld *Web:* www.trego-dugan.com	North Platte	NE	69101	308-532-5864		579
Trehel Corp PO Box 1707 *TF:* 800-319-7006 ■ *Web:* www.trehel.com	Clemson	SC	29633	864-654-6582	654-7788	186
Trejo's 9122 Mansfield Rd *Web:* www.trejos2go.com	Shreveport	LA	71118	318-687-6192		671
Trek Bicycle Corp 801 W Madison St *Web:* www.trekbikes.com	Waterloo	WI	53594	920-478-2191		82
Trek Bicycle Superstore 4240 Kearny Mesa Rd Ste 108 *Web:* www.trekbicyclesuperstore.com	San Diego	CA	92111	858-974-8735		711
Trek Bicycles of American Fork 356 N 750 W Ste D11 *Web:* trekaf.com	American Fork	UT	84003	801-763-1222		711
Trek Bikes of Ventura 4060 E Main St *Web:* www.trekbikesofventura.com	Ventura	CA	93003	805-644-8735		711
Trek Inc 11601 Maple Ridge Rd **Fax:* Sales ■ *TF:* 800-367-8735 ■ *Web:* www.trekinc.com	Medina	NY	14103	585-798-3140	798-3106*	248
Trelleborg Automotive Americas 400 Aylworth Ave **Fax Area Code:* 828 ■ *TF:* 800-635-9331 ■ *Web:* www.trelleborg.com	South Haven	MI	49090	269-637-2116	394-5005*	60

	Phone	Fax	Class

Trelleborg Coated Systems US Inc
1886 Prairie Way .... Louisville CO 80027 | 303-469-1357 | 469-2362 | 745-1
TF: 800-344-0714 ■ Web: www.trelleborg.com

Trelleborg Sealing Solutions
5503 Distribution Dr .... Fort Wayne IN 46825 | 260-749-2709 | | 326
Web: www.tss.trelleborg.com

Trellis Capital Corp
333 Wilson Ave Ste 600 .... Toronto ON M3H1T2 | 416-398-2299 | | 401
Web: www.trelliscapital.com

Trellis Restaurant
403 W Duke of Gloucester St .... Williamsburg VA 23185 | 757-229-8610 | | 671
Web: www.thetrellis.com

Trellist Inc 117 N Market St .... Wilmington DE 19801 | 302-778-1300 | | 463
Web: www.trellist.com

Trelys Funds PO Box 5066 .... Cary NC 27512 | 919-459-4650 | 459-4670 | 792
Web: www.trelys.com

Trembly Assoc Inc
119 Quincy St NE .... Albuquerque NM 87108 | 505-266-8616 | 255-0635 | 246
Web: www.trembly.com

Tremco Inc Roofing Div
3735 Green Rd .... Beachwood OH 44122 | 216-292-5000 | | 3
TF: 800-852-6013 ■ Web: www.tremcoroofing.com

Tremont Chicago 100 E Chestnut St .... Chicago IL 60611 | 312-751-1900 | | 379
TF: 888-627-8281 ■ Web: www.tremontchicago.com

Tremont House - A Wyndham Historic Hotel, The
2300 Ship Mechanic Row .... Galveston TX 77550 | 409-763-0300 | | 379
Web: www.thetremonthouse.com

Trempealeau County 36245 Main St .... Whitehall WI 54773 | 715-538-2311 | 538-4210 | 338
TF: 877-538-2311 ■ Web: www.tremplocounty.com

Trench Plate Rental Co
13217 Laureldale Ave .... Downey CA 90242 | 800-821-4478 | | 23
TF: 800-821-4478 ■ Web: www.tprco.com

Trend 660 American Ave Ste 203 .... King Of Prussia PA 19406 | 610-783-4650 | | 225
TF: 877-330-9900 ■ Web: www.trendmls.com

TREND Enterprises Inc
300 Ninth Ave SW .... New Brighton MN 55112 | 651-631-2850 | | 243
TF Cust Svc: 800-860-6762 ■ Web: www.trendenterprises.com

Trend Motors Ltd 221 US Hwy 46 .... Rockaway NJ 07866 | 973-625-0100 | | 57
Web: www.trendmotors.com

Trend Offset Printing Services Inc
3791 Catalina St .... Los Alamitos CA 90720 | 562-598-2446 | | 627
TF: 800-552-1303 ■ Web: www.trendoffset.com

Trend Technologies LLC
4626 Eucalyptus Ave .... Chino CA 91710 | 909-597-7861 | | 697
Web: www.trendtechnologies.com

Trendex Inc 240 E Maryland Ave .... Saint Paul MN 55117 | 651-489-4655 | 489-4423 | 86
TF: 800-328-9200 ■ Web: www.trendex.com

Trending Radio 93.3
N 72 W 12922 Good Hope Rd .... Menomonee Falls WI 53051 | 414-778-1933 | 771-3036 | 645
Web: www.b933fm.com

Trendl Associates Ltd
941 W Winona St Ste 1w .... Chicago IL 60640 | 773-728-6973 | | 317
Web: www.trendl.net

TrendMicro Inc 10101 N De Anza Blvd .... Cupertino CA 95014 | 408-257-1500 | | 178-12
TF: 800-228-5651 ■ Web: www.trendmicro.com

Trend-Pak of Canada 71 Railside Rd .... North York ON M3A1B2 | 416-510-3129 | 510-8371 | 125
Web: www.trendpak.com

Trends International LLC
5188 W 74th St .... Indianapolis IN 46268 | 317-388-1212 | | 328
TF: 866-406-7771 ■ Web: www.trendsinternational.com

Trendsetter Engineering Inc
10430 Rodgers Rd .... Houston TX 77070 | 281-465-8858 | | 537
Web: www.trendsetterengineering.com

TrendSource Inc
4891 Pacific Hwy Ste 200 .... San Diego CA 92110 | 619-718-7467 | | 466
Web: www.trendsource.com

Trendtec Inc 2381 Zanker Rd .... San Jose CA 95131 | 408-435-9500 | | 193
TF: 800-884-1684 ■ Web: www.trendtec.com

Trendware International Inc
20675 Manhattan Pl .... Torrance CA 90501 | 310-961-5500 | 961-5511 | 176
TF: 888-326-6061 ■ Web: www.trendnet.com

Trendway Corp
13467 Quincy St PO Box 9016 .... Holland MI 49422 | 616-399-3900 | | 319-1
TF: 800-968-5344 ■ Web: www.trendway.com

Trenholm State Technical College
1225 Air Base Blvd .... Montgomery AL 36108 | 334-420-4200 | 420-4206 | 800
TF: 800-917-2081 ■ Web: www.trenholmstate.edu

Trent Capital Management Inc
3150 N Elm St Ste 204 .... Greensboro NC 27408 | 336-282-9302 | | 401
Web: www.trentcapital.com

Trent Inc 201 Leverington Ave .... Philadelphia PA 19127 | 215-482-5000 | 482-9389 | 318
TF: 800-544-8736 ■ Web: www.trentheat.com

Trent University 1600 W Bank Dr .... Peterborough ON K9J7B8 | 705-748-1011 | 748-1629 | 785
TF: 888-739-8885 ■ Web: www.trentu.ca

Trenton Battle Monument
348 N Warren St .... Trenton NJ 08625 | 609-737-0623 | | 50-4
Web: www.njparksandforests.org

Trenton City Hall 319 E State St .... Trenton NJ 08608 | 609-989-3185 | 989-3190 | 337
TF: 800-221-0051 ■ Web: www.trentonnj.org

Trenton City Museum at Ellarslie Mansion
PO Box 1034 .... Trenton NJ 08606 | 609-989-1191 | 989-3624 | 520
TF: 800-447-7313 ■ Web: www.ellarslie.org

Trenton Correctional Institution
84 Greenhouse Rd .... Trenton SC 29847 | 803-896-3000 | | 213
Web: www.doc.sc.gov

Trenton Engineering Company Inc
2193 Spruce St .... Trenton NJ 08638 | 609-882-0616 | | 261
Web: trentoneng.com

Trenton Forging Co 5523 Hoover St .... Trenton MI 48183 | 734-675-1620 | 675-4839 | 483
Web: www.trentonforging.com

Trenton Mills LLC
400 Factory St PO Box 107 .... Trenton TN 38382 | 731-855-1323 | 855-9000 | 745-6
Web: www.trentonmills.com

Trenton Pipe Nipple Co LLC
1700 Industrial Park Rd .... Federalsburg MD 21632 | 410-754-5067 | | 609
Web: www.trentonpipe.com

Trenton Psychiatric Hospital
PO Box 7500 .... West Trenton NJ 08628 | 609-633-1500 | | 374-5
TF: 800-382-6717 ■ Web: www.nj.gov

Trenton Public Library 120 Academy St .... Trenton NJ 08608 | 609-392-7188 | 695-8631 | 434-3
Web: www.trentonlib.org

Trenton Public School System
108 N Clinton Ave .... Trenton NJ 08609 | 609-656-4900 | 989-2682 | 685
TF: 800-704-1365 ■ Web: www.trenton.k12.nj.us

Trentonian 600 Perry St .... Trenton NJ 08618 | 609-989-7800 | 393-6072 | 532-2
Web: www.trentonian.com

TrepanierBaer Gallery
999 Eigth St SW Ste 105 .... Calgary AB T2R1J5 | 403-244-2066 | 244-2094 | 42
TF: 800-838-3006 ■ Web: www.trepanierbaer.com

Tresca 233 Hanover St .... Boston MA 02113 | 617-742-8240 | | 671
Web: www.trescanorthend.com

Tressel Communications
3122 Esperanza Dr .... Concord CA 94519 | 925-798-9421 | | 636
Web: tresselpr.blogspot.com

TrestleTree Inc
3715 Business Dr Ste 202 .... Fayetteville AR 72703 | 479-582-0777 | | 194
Web: www.trestletree.com

Treu House of Munch Inc
8000 Arbor Dr .... Northwood OH 43619 | 419-666-7770 | 666-5712 | 81-1
Web: www.treuhouse.com

Treutlen County PO Box 229 .... Soperton GA 30457 | 912-529-6173 | 529-6996 | 338
TF: 800-272-3900 ■ Web: soperton-treutlen.org

Trevecca Nazarene University
333 Murfreesboro Rd .... Nashville TN 37210 | 615-248-1200 | 248-7406* | 166
*Fax: Admissions ■ TF: 888-210-4868 ■ Web: www.trevecca.edu

Trevena
1018 W Eighth Ave Ste A .... King Of Prussia PA 19406 | 610-354-8840 | | 231
Web: www.trevenainc.com

Trevi's 221 Las Colinas Blvd .... Irving TX 75039 | 972-869-5550 | 556-0800 | 671
Web: omnihotels.com

Treviicos Corp 38 Third Ave .... Charlestown MA 02129 | 617-241-4800 | | 189-3
Web: www.treviicos.com

Trevini 150 Worth Ave .... Palm Beach FL 33480 | 561-833-3883 | | 671
Web: www.treviniristorante.com

Trevor Zoo 131 Millbrook School Rd .... Millbrook NY 12545 | 845-677-3704 | | 823
TF: 800-582-4673 ■ Web: www.millbrook.org/page/school-life/trevor-zoo

Trew Industrial Wheels Inc
310 Wilhagan Rd .... Nashville TN 37217 | 615-360-9100 | | 54
TF: 888-977-8739 ■ Web: www.trew-wheels.com

T-Rex Engineering & Construction LC
16425 Jacintoport Blvd .... Houston TX 77015 | 281-833-9200 | | 539
Web: www.trexec.com

Trex Enterprises Corp
10455 Pacific Ctr Ct .... San Diego CA 92121 | 858-646-5300 | 646-5301 | 668
TF: 800-626-5885 ■ Web: www.trexenterprises.com

TreyArch
3420 Ocean Pk Blvd Ste 1000 .... Santa Monica CA 90405 | 310-581-4700 | | 178-6
Web: www.treyarch.com

Treyton Oak Towers 211 W Oak St .... Louisville KY 40203 | 502-589-3211 | | 672
TF: 800-533-0127 ■ Web: www.treytonoaktowers.com

Trez Capital Limited Partnership
1550 - 1185 W Georgia St .... Vancouver BC V6E4E6 | 604-689-0821 | 638-2775 | 528
TF: 877-689-0821 ■ Web: www.trezcapital.com

TRFCVB (Thief River Falls Convention & Visitors Bureau)
102 Main Ave N .... Thief River MN 56701 | 218-686-9785 | | 206
TF: 800-657-3700 ■ Web: www.visittrf.org

TRG Holdings LLC
1700 Pennsylvania Ave NW .... Washington DC 20006 | 202-289-9898 | | 737
Web: www.ibexglobal.com

TRG Networking
11436 Cronhill Dr Ste 4B .... Owings Mills MD 21117 | 410-363-6980 | | 177
TF: 800-677-1997 ■ Web: www.trgnetworking.com

TRGC (Title Resources Guaranty Co)
8111 LBJ Fwy Ste 1200 .... Dallas TX 75251 | 800-526-8018 | 485-3630* | 391-6
*Fax Area Code: 888 ■ TF: 800-526-8018 ■ Web: www.titleresources.com

TRH (Touchette Regional Hospital)
5900 Bond Ave .... Centreville IL 62207 | 618-332-3060 | | 374-3
Web: www.touchette.org

Tri Cities Business Journal
1114 Sunset Dr Ste 2 .... Johnson City TN 37604 | 423-854-0140 | | 457-5
Web: www.bjournal.com

Tri City Bankshares Corp
6400 S 27th St .... Oak Creek WI 53154 | 414-761-1610 | | 70
OTC: TRCY ■ Web: www.tcnb.com

Tri City Foods Inc
1400 Opus Pl Ste 900 .... Downers Grove IL 60515 | 630-598-3300 | | 670
Web: www.3cityfoods.com

Tri Commercial Real Estate Services Inc
100 Pine St Ste 1000 .... San Francisco CA 94111 | 415-268-2200 | 268-2289 | 652
Web: www.tricommercial.com

Tri County Area Chamber of Commerce
152 E High St Ste 360 .... Pottstown PA 19464 | 610-326-2900 | 970-9705 | 139
TF: 800-223-8477 ■ Web: www.tricountyareachamber.com

Tri County Ford 4032 Commerce Pkwy .... Buckner KY 40010 | 502-241-7333 | | 57
TF: 800-945-2520 ■ Web: www.tricountyford.com

Tri Dal Ltd 540 Commerce St .... Southlake TX 76092 | 817-481-2886 | 481-8195 | 188-10
Web: www.tridal.com

TRI MAP International Inc
111 Val Dervin Pkwy .... Stockton CA 95206 | 209-234-0100 | 234-5990 | 254
TF: 888-687-4627 ■ Web: www.trimapintl.com

Tri Marine Fish Co 220 Cannery St .... San Pedro CA 90731 | 310-547-1144 | | 297-5
Web: www.trimarinegroup.com

Tri Properties Inc
4309 Emperor Blvd Ste 110 .... Durham NC 27703 | 919-941-5745 | | 652
Web: www.triprop.com

Tri Rivers Career Center
2222 Marion Mt Gilead Rd .... Marion OH 43302 | 740-389-4681 | | 148
Web: www.tririvers.com

Tri Star Energy LLC
1740 Ed Temple Blvd .... Nashville TN 37208 | 615-313-3600 | | 541
Web: dailys.com

Tri Star Engineering Inc 3000 16th St .... Bedford IN 47421 | 812-277-0208 | | 261
Web: www.star3.com

Tri Star Freight System Inc
5407 Mesa Dr .... Houston TX 77028 | 713-631-1095 | 631-1099 | 780
TF: 800-229-1095 ■ Web: www.tristarfreightsys.com

Name / Address	City	State	ZIP	Phone	Fax	Class
Tri Star Industrial Co						
1645 W Buckeye Rd	Phoenix	AZ	85007	602-252-0554		358
Web: www.tristaraz.com						
Tri Star Metals LLC						
375 Village Dr	Carol Stream	IL	60188	630-462-7600		492
TF: 800-541-2294 ■ *Web:* www.tristarmetals.com						
Tri Starr Services of Pennsylvania Inc						
2201 Oregon Pk	Lancaster	PA	17601	717-560-2111		260
TF: 800-896-8842 ■ *Web:* www.tristarrjobs.com						
Tri State Distribution Inc						
600 Vista Dr	Sparta	TN	38583	800-392-9824		475
TF: 800-392-9824 ■ *Web:* www.provial.com						
Tri State Distributors Inc						
550 E First Ave	Spokane	WA	99202	509-455-8300		362
TF: 800-473-0002 ■ *Web:* www.tristatedistributors.com						
Tri State G & T Association 30739 Dd Rd	Nucla	CO	81424	970-864-7316		518
Web: www.tristategt.com						
Tri State Wholesale Flooring Inc						
3900 W 34th St N	Sioux Falls	SD	57107	605-336-3080		131
TF: 800-353-3080 ■ *Web:* tsf.com						
Tri Supply Co 7410 Eastex Fwy	Beaumont	TX	77708	409-835-7966		364
Web: www.trisupplyhometeam.com						
Tri Tech Surveying Company LP						
10401 Westoffice Dr	Houston	TX	77042	713-667-0800		261
Web: tritechtx.com						
Tri Tool Inc 3041 Sunrise Blvd	Rancho Cordova	CA	95742	916-288-6100	288-6160	621
TF: 800-345-5015 ■ *Web:* www.tritool.com						
Tri Union Express Inc						
1939 N Lafayette Ct	Griffith	IN	46319	219-838-5400	838-1680	803-1
TF: 800-228-9098 ■ *Web:* www.triunion.com						
Tri Venture Mktg Inc						
2525 Drane Field Rd Ste 1	Lakeland	FL	33811	863-648-1881		297-8
TRI/Princeton 601 Prospect Ave	Princeton	NJ	08540	609-430-4820		49-13
TF: 800-659-7659 ■ *Web:* www.triprinceton.org						
Triad Advertising Inc						
1017 TurnPk St Ste 32a	Canton	MA	02021	781-828-9290		7
Web: triadadvertising.com						
Triad Automation Inc						
6102 Corporate Park Dr	Browns Summit	NC	27214	336-375-8440		57
Web: www.triadautomation.com						
Triad Broadcasting Company LLC						
2511 Garden Rd A -104	Monterey	CA	93940	831-655-6350	655-6355	643
Triad Consulting Engineers Inc						
2740 State Rt 10 Ste 2	Morris Plains	NJ	07950	973-984-1919		261
TF: 800-795-1747 ■ *Web:* www.triadcei.com						
Triad Creative Group						
3130 Intertech Dr	Brookfield	WI	53045	262-781-3100		393
Web: www.triadcreativegroup.com						
Triad Energy Corp 1616 Voss, Ste 650	Houston	TX	77057	713-783-2291		538
Web: www.triad-energy.com						
Triad Financial Services Inc						
4336 Pablo Oaks Ct	Jacksonville	FL	[illegible]	[illegible]		217
TF: 800-522-2013 ■ *Web:* www.triadfs.com						
Triad Guaranty Insurance Corp						
101 S Stratford Rd	Winston-Salem	NC	27104	336-723-1282		391-5
TF Cust Svc: 888-691-8074 ■ *Web:* www.tgic.com						
Triad Interactive Inc						
1100 H St NW Ste 1201	Washington	DC	20036	202-347-0900	347-0930	177
Web: www.triadinteractive.com						
Triad Isotopes Inc						
4205 Vineland Rd Ste L1	Orlando	FL	32811	407-455-6700		231
TF: 866-310-0086 ■ *Web:* www.triadisotopes.com						
Triad Manufacturing Inc						
4321 Semple Ave	Saint Louis	MO	63120	314-381-5280		803-1
Web: www.triadmfg.com						
Triad Metal Products 12990 Snow Rd	Parma	OH	44130	216-676-6505		488
Web: www.triadmetal.com						
Triad Productions Inc						
1910 Ingersoll Ave	Des Moines	IA	50309	515-243-2125		179
TF: 800-444-9614 ■ *Web:* www.triadav.com						
Triad Products Co 1801 W 'B' St	Hastings	NE	68901	402-462-2181	462-2246	608
TF General: 888-253-4227 ■ *Web:* www.triadproducts.net						
Triad Security Systems 971 Lehigh Ave	Union	NJ	07083	908-964-5252		693
Web: www.triadsecurity.com						
TRIAD Strategies 116 Pine St	Harrisburg	PA	17101	717-238-2970		636
Web: www.triadstrategies.com						
Triage Consulting Group						
221 Main St Ste 1100	San Francisco	CA	94105	415-512-9400	512-9404	194
Web: www.triageconsulting.com						
Trial Behavior Consulting Inc						
505 Sansome St Ste 1701	San Francisco	CA	94111	415-781-5879		445
Web: www.trialbehavior.com						
TrialCard Inc						
2250 Perimeter Park Dr Ste 300	Morrisville	NC	27560	919-845-0774		194
Web: corp.trialcard.com						
TrialGraphix Inc 3300 Corporate Way	Hollywood	FL	33025	305-576-5400		627
Web: www.gorlm.com						
Trian Partners 280 Pk Ave	New York	NY	10017	212-451-3000	451-3134*	360-3
**Fax:* Mail Rm ■ *Web:* www.trianpartners.com						
Triangle Brick Co 6523 NC Hwy 55	Durham	NC	27713	919-544-1796	544-3904	150
TF: 800-672-8547 ■ *Web:* www.trianglebrick.com						
Triangle Business Journal						
3600 Glenwood Ave Ste 100	Raleigh	NC	27612	919-878-0010	790-6885	457-5
Web: www.bizjournals.com						
Triangle C Dude Ranch 3737 Hwy 26	Dubois	WY	82513	307-455-2225		239
TF: 800-661-4928 ■ *Web:* www.trianglec.com						
Triangle Electric Co						
29787 Stephenson Hwy	Madison Heights	MI	48071	248-399-2200	399-2612	189-4
TF: 800-222-8243 ■ *Web:* www.trielec.com						
Triangle Engineering Inc						
6 Industrial Way	Hanover	MA	02339	781-878-1500		595
TF: 800-897-9353 ■ *Web:* www.trieng.com						
Triangle Fastener Corp						
1925 Preble Ave	Pittsburgh	PA	15233	412-321-5000	321-7838	351
TF General: 800-486-1832 ■ *Web:* www.trianglefastener.com						
Triangle Manufacturing Co						
150 Libbey Ave	Oshkosh	WI	54901	920-235-3710		620
Web: www.triangleoshkosh.com						
Triangle MicroWorks Inc						
2840 Plaza Pl Ste 205	Raleigh	NC	27612	919-870-5101		177
Web: www.trianglemicroworks.com						
Triangle Orthopedic Assoc PA						
120 William Penn Plaza	Durham	NC	27704	919-220-5255		374-3
TF: 800-359-3053 ■ *Web:* www.triangleortho.com						
Triangle Package Machinery Co						
6655 W Diversey Ave	Chicago	IL	60707	773-889-0200	889-4221	547
TF: 800-621-4170 ■ *Web:* www.trianglepackage.com						
Triangle Process Equipment Inc						
2307 Industrial Park Dr SE	Wilson	NC	27893	252-246-1089		789
Web: www.4tpe.com						
Triangle Rubber Company Inc PO Box 95	Goshen	IN	46527	574-533-3118	534-0416	677
Web: www.trianglerubberco.com						
Triangle Scenery Drapery & Lighting Co						
1215 Bates Ave	Los Angeles	CA	90029	323-662-8129	662-8120	722
Web: www.tridrape.com						
Triangle Securities LLC						
1301 Annapolis Dr	Raleigh	NC	27608	919-838-3221		401
Web: www.trianglesecurities.com						
Triangle Suspension Systems Inc						
200 E Maloney Rd	Du Bois	PA	15801-1015	814-375-7211	371-4495	60
TF: 800-458-6077 ■ *Web:* www.triangleusa.com						
Triangle Tech Inc						
Du Bois PO Box 551 15840 Falls Creek	Du Bois	PA	15840	814-371-2090	371-9227	800
TF: 800-874-8324 ■ *Web:* www.triangle-tech.edu						
Erie 2000 Liberty St	Erie	PA	16502	814-453-6016	454-2818	800
TF: 800-874-8324 ■ *Web:* www.triangle-tech.edu						
Greensburg 222 E Pittsburgh St	Greensburg	PA	15601	724-832-1050	834-0325	800
TF: 800-874-8324 ■ *Web:* www.triangle-tech.edu						
Triangle Tool Corp 8609 W Port Ave	Milwaukee	WI	53224	414-357-7117	357-7610	757
Web: ttool.net						
Triangle X Ranch 2 Triangle X Ranch Rd	Moose	WY	83012	307-733-2183		239
Triangle X-ray Co						
4900 Thornton Rd Ste 117	Raleigh	NC	27616	919-876-6156		475
TF: 866-763-9729 ■ *Web:* trianglexray.com						
Trianon Old Naples 955 Seventh Ave S	Naples	FL	34102	239-435-9600		379
TF: 877-482-5228 ■ *Web:* www.trianon.com						
Trianz Inc						
3979 Freedom Cir Ste 210	Santa Clara	CA	95054	408-387-5800		180
Web: www.trianz.com						
Triarco Industries LLC 400 Hamburg Tpke	Wayne	NJ	07470	973-942-5100		231
Triasima Portfolio Management Inc						
1555 Peel St Ste 1205	Montreal	QC	H3A3L8	514-906-0667		528
Web: www.triasima.com						
Triathlete Sports 186 Exchange St	Bangor	ME	04401	207-990-2013		711
TF: 800 635 0528 ■ *Web:* www.triathletesports.com						
Triathlon Medical Ventures (TMVP)						
300 E Business Way Ste 200	Cincinnati	OH	45241	513-723-2600	247-6122	792
Web: www.tmvp.com						
Tri-Auto Enterprises LLC						
7225 Georgetown Rd	Indianapolis	IN	[illegible]	317-044-5700		7
Web: perq.com						
Triax Data Inc 800 S Gay St Ste 650	Knoxville	TN	37929	865-971-4333		195
Web: www.triaxdata.com						
Triaxis Engineering Inc						
1600 SW Western Blvd	Corvallis	OR	97333	541-766-4600		261
TF: 800-234-2867 ■ *Web:* www.triaxiseng.com						
Tribal DDB Worldwide						
437 Madison Ave 8th Fl	New York	NY	10022	212-515-8600	515-8660	4
Web: tribalworldwide.com						
Tribal Nova Inc						
4200 Boul Saint-Laurent Ste 1203	Montreal	QC	H2W2R2	514-598-0444		225
Web: www.tribalnova.com						
Tribal Solutions Inc						
598 E Purnell Rd	Lewisville	TX	75057	972-436-0422		194
Tribalco LLC 4915 St Elmo Ave Ste 501	Bethesda	MD	20814	301-652-8450		186
Web: www.tribalco.com						
Tri-Basin Natural Resources District						
1723 Burlington St	Holdrege	NE	68949	877-995-6688		196
TF: 877-995-6688 ■ *Web:* www.tribasinnrd.org						
Tribble & Stephens Construction Ltd						
8588 Katy Fwy Ste 100	Houston	TX	77024	713-465-8550	973-7107	186
Web: www.tribblestephens.com						
Tribco Construction Services						
200 S Michigan Ave Ste 200	Chicago	IL	60604	312-341-0303		189-2
Tribe Design LLC 1420 Mcilhenny St	Houston	TX	77004	713-523-5119		344
Web: www.tribedesign.com						
Tribeca Oven Inc 447 Gotham Pkwy	Carlstadt	NJ	07072	201-935-8800		345
Web: tribecaoven.com						
TRIBECA Performing Arts Ctr						
199 Chambers St	New York	NY	10007	212-220-1459	732-2482	572
Web: tickets.tribecapac.org						
Tribeca Productions						
375 Greenwich St 8th Fl	New York	NY	10013	212-941-4000	941-3997	514
Web: www.tribecafilm.com						
Triboro Quilt Mfg Inc						
172 S Broadway	White Plains	NY	10605	914-428-7551		64
Web: www.cuddletime.com						
Tri-boro Shelving & Partition Corp						
300 Dominion Dr	Farmville	VA	23901	434-315-5600		321
TF: 800-633-3070 ■ *Web:* www.triboroshelving.com						
Tribridge 4830 W Kennedy Blvd Ste 890	Tampa	FL	33609	877-744-1360		178-1
TF: 877-744-1360 ■ *Web:* www.tribridge.com						
Tri-bry Information Solutions						
123 Harrison St	Hoboken	NJ	07030	201-798-5191		809
Tribune Chronicle 240 Franklin St SE	Warren	OH	44482	330-841-1600	841-1717	532-2
TF: 888-550-8742 ■ *Web:* tribtoday.com						
Tribune Direct Marketing Inc						
505 Northwest Ave	Northlake	IL	60164	800-545-9657		5
TF: 800-545-9657 ■ *Web:* www.tribunedirect.com						
Tribune Inc 2012 Forest Ave	Great Bend	KS	67530	620-792-1211		532-3
Web: www.gbtribune.com						
Tribune Media 435 N Michigan Ave	Chicago	IL	60611	312-222-3232	222-2598	738
Web: www.tribune.com						

Phone | Fax | Class

Tribune Newspapers of Snohomish County
127 Ave C Ste B PO Box 499 Snohomish WA 98291 360-568-4121 568-1484 532-4
TF: 877-894-4663 ■ *Web:* www.snoho.com

Tribune Review Publishing Co
622 Cabin Hill Dr Greensburg PA 15601 724-834-1151 637-8
TF: 800-524-5700 ■ *Web:* pittsburghpennysaver.com

Tribune, The
3825 S Higuera St San Luis Obispo CA 93401 805-781-7800 781-7905 532-2
TF: 800-477-8799 ■ *Web:* www.sanluisobispo.com

Tribune, The 228 E Main St Welland ON L3B5P5 905-732-2411 532-1
TF: 800-263-3695 ■ *Web:* www.wellandtribune.ca

Tribune-Democrat 425 Locust St Johnstown PA 15907 814-532-5050 539-1409 532-2
TF: 855-255-5975 ■ *Web:* tribdem.com

Tribune-Star PO Box 149 Terre Haute IN 47808 812-231-4200 231-4321 532-2
TF: 800-783-8742 ■ *Web:* www.tribstar.com

Tributary Systems Inc
3717 Commerce Pl Ste C Bedford TX 76021 817-354-8009 174
Web: www.tributary.com

Tribute Resources Inc(NDA)
309 Commissioners Rd W Unit D London ON N6J1Y4 519-657-7624 538
TF: 800-789-1011 ■ *Web:* www.tributeresources.com

Tri-C Construction Company Inc
1765 Merriman Rd Akron OH 44313 330-836-2722 869-8373 186
Web: www.tricc.com

Tri-C Resources Inc 909 Wirt Rd Houston TX 77024 713-685-3600 539
Web: www.tricresources.com

Tri-Campbell Farms 15111 Hwy 17 Grafton ND 58237 701-352-3116 352-2008 10-11
Web: www.tricampbellfarms.com

Trican Well Service Ltd
645 Seventh Ave SW Ste 2900 Calgary AB T2P4G8 403-266-0202 237-7716 539
TSE: TCW ■ *TF:* 877-473-2008 ■ *Web:* www.tricanwellservice.com

Tricerat Inc
11500 Cronridge Dr Ste 100 Owings Mills MD 21117 410-715-4226 179
TF: 800-582-5167 ■ *Web:* www.tricerat.com

Tri-Chem 681 Main St Bldg 24 Belleville NJ 07109 973-751-9200 450-1260 43
Web: www.trichem.com

Trichotillomania Learning Ctr Inc (TLC)
207 McPherson St Ste H Santa Cruz CA 95060 831-457-1004 48-17

Tri-Cities Beverage Corp
612 Industrial Park Dr Newport News VA 23608 757-874-6600 297-8
Web: tricitiesbeverage.com

Tri-Cities Chamber of Commerce
1209 Pinetree Way Coquitlam BC V3B7Y3 604-464-2716 464-6796 137
Web: www.tricitieschamber.com

Tri-Cities Opera 315 Clinton St Binghamton NY 13905 607-729-3444 573-2
Web: www.tricitiesopera.com

Tri-Cities Regional Airport
2525 Hwy 75 Ste 301 Blountville TN 37617 423-325-6000 325-6060 27
Web: triflight.com

Tri-Cities Visitor & Convention Bureau
7130 W Grandridge Blvd Ste B Kennewick WA 99336 509-735-8486 783-9005 206
TF: 800-254-5824 ■ *Web:* www.visittri-cities.com

Tri-City Area Chamber of Commerce
7130 W Grandridge Blvd Kennewick WA 99336 509-736-0510 783-1733 139
Web: www.tricityregionalchamber.com

Tri-City Electrical Contractors Inc
430 W Dr Altamonte Springs FL 32714 407-788-3500 682-7353 189-4
TF: 800-768-2489 ■ *Web:* tcelectric.com

Tri-City Glass & Door Inc
100 W Northland Ave Appleton WI 54911 920-731-8176 61
Web: www.tricityglass-door.com

Tri-City Heat Treat Co
2020 Fifth St Rock Island IL 61201 309-786-2689 786-2691 484
TF: 800-263-0127 ■ *Web:* www.tcht.com

Tri-City Herald 333 W Canal Dr Kennewick WA 99336 509-582-1500 582-1510 532-2
TF: 800-874-0445 ■ *Web:* www.tri-cityherald.com

Tri-City Medical Ctr 4002 Vista Way Oceanside CA 92056 760-724-8411 374-3
Web: www.tricitymed.org

Tri-City Regional Medical Ctr
21530 S Pioneer Blvd Hawaiian Gardens CA 90716 562-860-0401 924-5871 374-3
Web: www.tcrmc.org

Tri-city Veterinary Clinic Inc
1929 W Vista Way Vista CA 92083 760-758-2091 794
Web: www.tricityvet.com

Trickle Up Program Inc
104 W 27th St 12th Fl New York NY 10001 212-255-9980 255-9974 48-5
TF: 866-246-9980 ■ *Web:* www.trickleup.org

Triclinic Labs
1201 Cumberland Ave Ste S West Lafayette IN 47906 765-588-6200 231
Web: www.tricliniclabs.com

TriCo Bancshares 63 Constitution Dr Chico CA 95973 530-898-0300 360-2
NASDAQ: TCBK ■ *TF:* 800-922-8742 ■ *Web:* www.tcbk.com

Trico Electric Coop
8600 W Tangerine Rd Marana AZ 85653 520-744-2944 245
Web: www.trico.org

Trico Products Corp
3255 W Hamlin Rd Rochester Hills MI 48309 248-371-1700 371-8300 60
Web: www.tricoproducts.com

Tricolor Inc
100 Franklin Square Dr Ste 202 Somerset NJ 08873 732-873-0305 180
Web: www.tricolor.com

Tri-com Consulting Group LLC, The
333 Industrial Park Rd Middletown CT 06457 860-635-9600 196
TF: 800-970-9997 ■ *Web:* www.tricomgroup.com

Tricom Document Management Inc
2450 Peralta Blvd Ste 222 Fremont CA 94536 510-494-7800 396

Tricom Technical Services
11115 Ash St Leawood KS 66211 913-652-0600 260
Web: www.tricomts.com

Tricomm Services Corp
1247 N Church St Ste 12 Moorestown NJ 08057 856-914-9001 914-9065 787
TF: 800-872-2401 ■ *Web:* www.tricommcorp.com

Tri-Con Inc
7076 W Port Arthur Rd PO Box 20555 Beaumont TX 77705 409-835-2237 579
TF: 800-876-7102 ■ *Web:* www.triconinc.org

Tricon Industries Inc Electromechanical Div
2325 Wisconsin Ave Downers Grove IL 60515 630-964-2330 964-5179 604
Web: industrialinterface.com

TRICOR (Tennessee Rehabilitative Initiative in Correction)
240 Great Cir Rd Ste 310 Nashville TN 37228 615-741-5705 741-2747 630
TF: 800-958-7426 ■ *Web:* www.tricor.org

Tricor America Inc
717 Airport Blvd South San Francisco CA 94080 650-877-3650 546
Web: www.tricor.com

Tricor Employment Screening Ltd
110 Blaze Industrial Pkwy Ste C Berea OH 44017 216-267-0431 41
Web: www.tricorinfo.com

TRI-COR Industries Inc
4403 Forbes Blvd Lanham MD 20706 301-731-6140 180
Web: www.tricorind.com

TRICOR Insurance Inc
230 W Cherry St Lancaster WI 53813 608-723-6441 390
TF: 877-468-7426 ■ *Web:* www.tricorinsurance.com

Tricor Metals Inc
3225 W Old Lincoln Way Wooster OH 44691 330-264-3299 295
TF: 800-421-5141 ■ *Web:* www.tricormetals.com

Tricor Print Communications Inc
7931 NE Halsey St Ste 101 Portland OR 97213 503-255-5595 627
TF: 800-635-7778 ■ *Web:* www.tricorprint.com

TRICOR Systems Inc 1650 Todd Farm Dr Elgin IL 60123 847-742-5542 668
Web: www.tricor-systems.com

Tricorbraun Winepak
2280 Cordelia Rd Fairfield CA 94534 800-374-6594 334
TF: 800-374-6594 ■ *Web:* winepak.tricorbraun.com

TriCore Inc 117 N Gold Dr Bldg 1 Robbinsville NJ 08691 609-918-2668 193
Web: www.tricore.com

TriCore Reference Laboratories
1001 Woodward Pl NE Albuquerque NM 87102 505-938-8888 415
TF: 800-245-3296 ■ *Web:* www.tricore.org

TriCore Solutions LLC
141 Longwater Dr Ste 100 Norwell MA 02061 617-774-5200 631
TF: 800-522-6787 ■ *Web:* www.tricoresolutions.com

Tri-County Beverage Co
2651 E 10 Mile Rd Warren MI 48091 586-757-4900 81-1
Web: www.tricountybeverage.com

Tri-County Chamber of Commerce
PO Box 2420 Wayne NJ 07474 973-831-7788 139
Web: www.tricounty.org

Tri-County Community College
21 Campus Cir Murphy NC 28906 828-837-6810 837-3266 162
Web: www.tricountycc.edu

Tri-County Commuter Rail Authority
800 NW 33rd St Ste 100 Pompano Beach FL 33064 954-942-7245 788-7878 468
Web: www.tri-rail.com

Tri-County Electric
995 Mile 46 Rd PO Box 880 Hooker OK 73945 580-652-2418 652-3151 245
TF: 800-522-3315 ■ *Web:* www.tri-countyelectric.coop

Tri-County Electric Co-op
PO Box 159 Lancaster MO 63548 660-457-3733 245
TF: 888-457-3734 ■ *Web:* www.tricountyelectric.org

Tri-County Electric Co-op
6473 Old State Rd Saint Matthews SC 29135 803-874-1215 245
TF: 877-874-1215 ■ *Web:* tri-countyelectric.net

Tri-County Electric Co-op Inc
2862 W US Hwy 90 Madison FL 32340 850-973-2285 973-1209 245
TF: 800-999-2285 ■ *Web:* www.tcec.com

Tri-County Electric Co-op Inc
3906 Broadway St Mount Vernon IL 62864 618-244-5151 244-1496 245
TF: 800-244-5151 ■ *Web:* www.tricountycoop.com

Tri-County Electric Co-op Inc
600 NW Pkwy Azle TX 76020 817-444-3201 444-3542 245
TF: 800-367-8232 ■ *Web:* www.tcectexas.com

Tri-County Electric Membership Corp
PO Box 487 Gray GA 31032 478-986-8100 986-4733 245
TF: 866-254-8100 ■ *Web:* www.tri-countyemc.com

Tri-County Electric Membership Corp
405 College St Lafayette TN 37083 615-666-2111 688-2141 245
TF: 800-369-2111 ■ *Web:* www.tcemc.org

Tri-County Mall
11700 Princeton Pike Cincinnati OH 45246 513-671-0120 671-2931 460
TF: 866-905-4675 ■ *Web:* tricountymall.com

Tri-County Metropolitan Transportation District of Oregon
4012 SE 17th Ave Portland OR 97202 503-238-7433 962-6469* 468
**Fax:* Mktg ■ *TF:* 800-201-4900 ■ *Web:* www.trimet.org

Tri-County ROP 970 Klamath Ln Yuba City CA 95993 530-822-5120 226
Web: www.sutter.k12.ca.us

Tri-County Rural Electric Co-op Inc
22 N Main St PO Box 526 Mansfield PA 16933 570-662-2175 245
TF: 800-343-2559 ■ *Web:* www.tri-countyrec.com

Tri-County Rural Electric Co-op Inc
PO Box 526 Mansfield PA 16933 570-662-2175 245
Web: www.tri-countyrec.com

Tri-County Technical College
7900 Hwy 76 Pendleton SC 29670 864-646-8361 646-1890 800
TF: 866-269-5677 ■ *Web:* www.tctc.edu

Tricycle Inc
1293 Riverfront Pkwy Ste 1293-B Chattanooga TN 37402 800-808-4809 809
TF: 800-808-4809 ■ *Web:* www.tricycleinc.com

Tridan International Inc
130 N Jackson St PO Box 537 Danville IL 61834 217-443-3592 443-3894 494
Web: www.tridan.com

Tridel Corp 4800 Dufferin St Ste 200 Toronto ON M3H5S9 416-661-9394 655
TF: 800-598-3434 ■ *Web:* www.tridel.com

Trident Capital
505 Hamilton Ave Ste 200 Palo Alto CA 94301 650-289-4400 289-4444 792
Web: www.tridentcap.com

Trident Communications
31 Timber Ln Hilton Head Island SC 29926 843-837-4978 644

Trident Contract Management
2918 Marketplace Dr Ste 206 Madison WI 53719 608-276-1900 175
Web: www.trident-it.com

Trident Crating & Services Inc
14320 InterDr E Houston TX 77032 281-227-3999 549
TF: 800-431-7867 ■ *Web:* www.tridentcrating.com

Trident Environmental & Engineering
110 L St Ste 1 Antioch CA 94509 925-706-6931 778-9067 261
Web: tridenteng.com

Company / Address	City	State	ZIP	Phone	Fax	Class
Trident Labs Inc 12000 Aviation Blvd	Hawthorne	CA	90250	310-915-9121		228
Web: www.tridentlab.com						
Trident Marketing 1930 N Poplar St	Southern Pines	NC	28387	910-693-3000		195
Web: www.tridentmarketing.com						
Trident Media Group LLC 41 Madison Ave 36th Fl	New York	NY	10010	212-333-1511		444
Web: www.tridentmediagroup.com						
Trident Medical Ctr 9330 Medical Plaza Dr	Charleston	SC	29406	843-797-7000		374-3
TF: 866-492-9085 ■ *Web:* www.tridenthealthsystem.com						
Trident Micro Systems 2 Trident Dr	Arden	NC	28704	828-684-7474		246
Trident Microsystems Inc 1170 Kifer Rd	Sunnyvale	CA	94086	408-962-5000		696
Trident Precision Manufacturing Inc 734 Salt Rd	Webster	NY	14580	585-265-2010		488
Web: www.tridentprecision.com						
Trident Resources Corp 444 - 7 Ave SW Ste 1000	Calgary	AB	T2P0X8	403-770-0333		787
Web: www.tridentexploration.ca						
Trident Seafood Corp 5303 Shilshole Ave NW	Seattle	WA	98107	206-783-3818	782-7195	296-14
Web: www.tridentseafoods.com						
Trident Security Service 4968 Dorchester Rd	Charleston	SC	29418	843-767-3855		693
Web: www.tsecurityservices.com						
Trident Steel Corp 12825 Flushing Meadows Dr Ste 110	St. Louis	MO	63131	314-822-0500		492
TF: 800-777-9687 ■ *Web:* www.tridentsteel.com						
Trident Systems Inc 10201 Fairfax Blvd Ste 300	Fairfax	VA	22030	703-273-1012		21
Web: www.tridsys.com						
Trident Technical College (TTC) 7000 Rivers Ave PO Box 118067	North Charleston	SC	29406	843-574-6111	574-6483*	800
*Fax: Admissions ■ *TF:* 877-349-7184 ■ *Web:* www.tridenttech.edu						
Trident Technologies Inc 8885 Rehco Rd	San Diego	CA	92121	619-688-9600	688-9700	612
TF: 800-326-4010 ■ *Web:* www.tridenttech.com						
Trideum Corp 655 Discovery Dr NW Ste 150	Huntsville	AL	35806	256-704-6100		261
Web: trideum.com						
Tridien Medical Inc 4200 NW 120th Ave	Coral Springs	FL	33065	954-340-0500		475
Web: www.tridien.com						
Tri-Dim Filter Corp 93 Industrial Dr	Louisa	VA	23093	540-967-2600	967-2835	18
TF: 800-458-9835 ■ *Web:* www.tridim.com						
Tridon Communications 10017 Queen St	Fort Mcmurray	AB	T9H4Y9	780-791-1002		647
TF: 800-374-2281 ■ *Web:* www.tridon.com						
Tri-Ed Distribution Inc 135 Crossways Pk Dr W	Woodbury	NY	11797	516-941-2800		246
TF: 888-874-3336 ■ *Web:* www.tri-ed.com						
Trient Technologies Inc 101 Trient Dr	Woodville	WI	54028	715-698-3519		596
Web: www.trienttech.com						
Trifecta Marketing Group Inc 10124 Hanover Glen Rd	Charlotte	NC	28210	704-543-0292		317
Web: www.trifectamg.com						
Triflo International Inc 1000 FM 830	Willis	TX	77318	936-856-8551		358
TF: 800-332-0993 ■ *Web:* www.triflo.com						
Triforce Consulting Svc Inc 650 N Cannon Ave	Lansdale	PA	19446	215-362-2611		177
TF: 800-240-3369 ■ *Web:* triforce-inc.com						
Triformix Inc 487 Aviation Blvd Ste 100	Santa Rosa	CA	95403	707-545-7645		596
Web: www.triformixinc.com						
Trifox Inc 3131 S Bascom Ave	Campbell	CA	95008	408-369-2300		177
Web: www.trifox.com						
Tri-Gas & Oil Company Inc 3941 Federalsburg Hwy PO Box 465	Federalsburg	MD	21632	410-754-8184	754-9158	325
TF: 800-638-7802 ■ *Web:* www.trigas-oil.com						
Trigg County PO Box 672	Cadiz	KY	42211	270-522-8459	522-9489	338
Web: www.triggcounty.ky.gov						
Trigyn Technologies Inc 100 Metroplex Dr Ste 101	Edison	NJ	08817	732-777-0050		177
Web: www.trigyn.com						
Trihydro Corp 1252 Commerce Dr	Laramie	WY	82070	307-745-7474		261
Web: www.trihydro.com						
Trijicon Inc 49385 Shafer Ave PO Box 930059	Wixom	MI	48393	248-960-7700		711
TF: 800-338-0563 ■ *Web:* www.trijicon.com						
Tri-K Industries Inc Two Stewart Ct PO Box 10	Denville	NJ	07834	973-298-8850	298-8940	479
Web: www.tri-k.com						
Trikon Design Inc 2295 N Opdyke Rd	Auburn Hills	MI	48326	248-340-0460		59
Tri-Lakes Container 533 S First St	Pierceton	IN	46562	574-594-2217		100
TF: 800-992-8064 ■ *Web:* www.tri-lakes.com						
Tri-Land Kansas City Investors LLC 1 Wbrook Corporate Ctr Ste 520	Westchester	IL	60154	708-531-8210		652
TF: 800-441-7032 ■ *Web:* www.trilandproperties.com						
TriLeaf Inc 10845 Olive Blvd Ste 310	Saint Louis	MO	63141	314-997-6111	997-8066	261
TF: 800-652-5552 ■ *Web:* www.trileaf.com						
Tri-Lift Inc 180 Main St Annex	New Haven	CT	06512	203-467-1686		770
TF: 800-228-5438 ■ *Web:* www.trilliftinc.com						
TriLinc Global LLC 1230 Rosecrans Ave Ste 605	Manhattan Beach	CA	90266	310-997-0580		528
Web: www.trilincglobal.com						
TriLink BioTechnologies Inc 9955 Mesa Rim Rd	San Diego	CA	92121	858-546-0004		743
TF: 800-863-6801 ■ *Web:* www.trilinkbiotech.com						
TriLink Saw Chain LLC 4400 Commerce Cir	Atlanta	GA	30336	404-419-2900		350
TF: 800-790-6202 ■ *Web:* www.trilinksawchain.com						
Tri-Lite Inc 1642 N Besly Ct	Chicago	IL	60642	773-384-7765	384-5115	439
TF: 800-322-5250 ■ *Web:* www.triliteinc.com						
Trilithic Inc 9710 Pk Davis Dr	Indianapolis	IN	46235	317-895-3600	423-7604	248
TF: 800-344-2412 ■ *Web:* www.trilithic.com						
Trilliant Technology Group Inc 800 Town & Country Blvd Ste 300	Houston	TX	77055	713-263-9200		196
Web: www.trilliant.net						
Trillion Communications Corp 3871 Pine Ln	Bessemer	AL	35022	205-481-1678		525
Web: www.trillionusa.com						
Trillium Asset Management LLC 2 Financial Ctr 60 S St Ste 1100	Boston	MA	02111	617-423-6655		528
TF: 800-548-5684 ■ *Web:* www.trilliuminvest.com						
Trillium Community Health Plan Inc 1800 Millrace Dr	Eugene	OR	97403	541-431-1950		391-3
TF: 800-910-3906 ■ *Web:* trilliumchp.com						
Trillium Group LLC 1221 Pittsford Victor Rd	Pittsford	NY	14534	585-383-5680		792
Web: www.trillium-group.com						
Trillium Health Ctr 100 Queensway W	Mississauga	ON	L5B1B8	905-848-7100		374-2
Web: www.trilliumhealthcentre.org						
Trillium Residential LLC 111 Dupont Cir	Phoenix	AZ	85034	602-687-9223		652
Web: www.trilliumresidential.com						
Trillium Talent Resources Group 99 Sheppard Ave W	Toronto	ON	M2N1M4	416-497-2624		260
TF: 800-265-1840 ■ *Web:* www.trilliumhr.com						
Trillium Teamologies Inc 219 S Main St Ste 300	Royal Oak	MI	48067	248-584-2080		180
TF: 866-832-6884 ■ *Web:* www.trilliumteam.com						
Trilog Group Inc 54 Cummings Pk	Woburn	MA	01801	781-937-9963		177
Web: www.triloggroup.com						
Trilogy Communications Inc 2910 Hwy 80 E	Pearl	MS	39208	601-932-4461	939-6637	814
TF: 888-713-1414 ■ *Web:* www.trilogycoax.com						
Trilogy Energy Corp 1400-332 6 Ave SW	Calgary	AB	T2P0B2	403-290-2900		536
Web: www.trilogyenergy.com						
Trilogy Plumbing Inc 1525 S Sinclair St	Anaheim	CA	92806	714-888-8575		610
Web: www.trilogyplumbing.com						
Trilogy Software Inc 401 Congress Ave Ste 2650	Austin	TX	78701	855-550-0085		178-1
TF: 855-550-0085 ■ *Web:* www.trilogy.com						
Trilogy Studios Inc 5200 Lankershim Blvd	North Hollywood	CA	91601	818-901-9960		445
Web: www.trilogystudios.com						
Trimac Panel Products 5201 SW Westgate Dr Ste 200	Portland	OR	97221	503-297-1826		613
TF General: 800-547-4209 ■ *Web:* www.trimacpanel.com						
Tri-Mack Plastics Mfg Corp 66 Tupelo St	Bristol	RI	02809	401-253-2140		596
Web: www.trimack.com						
Trimaco LLC 2300 Gateway Centre Blvd Ste 200	Morrisville	NC	27560	919-674-3460	674-3461	733
TF: 800-325-7356 ■ *Web:* www.trimaco.com						
Trimar Construction Inc 1720 W Cass St	Tampa	FL	33606	813-258-5524	258-4743	449
Web: 0350766.netsolhost.com						
Trimaran Fund Management LLC 1325 Ave of the Americas	New York	NY	10019	212-616-3700	616-3701	401
Web: www.trimarancapital.com						
Trimark Corp PO Box 350	New Hampton	IA	50659	641-394-3188		350
TF: 800-447-0343 ■ *Web:* www.trimarkcorp.com						
Trimark Properties LLC 321 SW 13th St	Gainesville	FL	32601	352-376-6223		652
Web: trimarkproperties.com						
TriMark USA Inc 505 Collins St	South Attleboro	MA	02703	508-399-2400		300
TF: 800-755-5580 ■ *Web:* www.trimarkusa.com						
TriMas Corp 39400 Woodward Ave Ste 130	Bloomfield Hills	MI	48304	248-631-5450		763
Web: www.trimascorp.com						
TriMax Direct 106 W Water St Ste 201	St. Paul	MN	55107	651-292-0165		5
Web: www.trimaxdirect.com						
Trimax Systems Inc 565 Explorer St	Brea	CA	92821	714-255-8590		180
TF: 800-364-2059 ■ *Web:* www.trimaxsystems.com						
Trimble County 4874 Hwy 421 N PO Box 312	Bedford	KY	40006	502-255-0062	255-0063	338
Web: www.trimblecounty.com						
Trimble Navigation Ltd 935 Stewart Dr	Sunnyvale	CA	94085	408-481-8000		529
NASDAQ: TRMB ■ *TF:* 800-538-7800 ■ *Web:* www.trimble.com						
Trimble-Batjer Insurance Assoc 201 S Chadbourne St	San Angelo	TX	76903	325-653-6733		390
Web: trimble-batjer.com						
Trimco/Builders Brass Works 3528 Emery St	Los Angeles	CA	90023	323-262-4191	264-7214	350
TF: 800-637-8746 ■ *Web:* www.trimcohardware.com						
TriMech Services LLC 4461 Cox Rd Ste 302	Glen Allen	VA	23060	804-257-9965		260
Web: www.trimech.com						
Tri-Med Pharmacy Services LLC 260 W Main St Ste 217	Hendersonville	TN	37075	615-826-9393		238
Tri-Media Integrated Marketing Technologies Inc 517 Niagara St	Welland	ON	L3C1L7	905-732-6431		7
TF: 800-367-0766 ■ *Web:* www.tri-media.com						
Trimedyne Inc 15091 Bake Pkwy	Irvine	CA	92618	949-559-5300	855-8206	424
OTC: TMED ■ *TF:* 800-733-5273 ■ *Web:* www.trimedyne.com						
Tri-Mer Corp 1400 Monroe St PO Box 730	Owosso	MI	48867	989-723-7838	723-7844	18
Web: www.tri-mer.com						
Trimfit Inc 1691 Franklin Mills Cir Ste 111	Philadelphia	PA	19154	215-245-1122	781-1803	155-10
Web: trimfit.com						
Trimfoot Co LLC 115 Trimfoot Terr	Farmington	MO	63640	800-325-6116	756-8482*	301
*Fax Area Code: 573 ■ *TF:* 800-325-6116 ■ *Web:* www.trimfootco.com						
TrimJoist Corp 5146 Hwy 182 E	Columbus	MS	39702	662-327-7950		820
TF: 800-844-8281 ■ *Web:* www.trimjoist.com						
Trimlite LLC 901 SW 39th St	Renton	WA	98057	425-251-8685		499
Web: www.trimlite.com						
Trim-Lok Inc 6855 Hermosa Cir	Buena Park	CA	90620	714-562-0500		596
Web: www.trimlok.com						

Phone | Fax | Class

TrimMaster 4860 N Fifth St Hwy ... Temple PA 19560 610-921-0203 929-8833 744
TF: 800-356-4237 ■ *Web:* www.trimmaster.com

Trimold LLC 200 Pittsburgh Rd. ... Circleville OH 43113 740-474-7591 604

Trimont Real Estate Advisors Inc
3424 Peachtree Rd NE ... Atlanta GA 30326 404-420-5600 652
Web: www.trimontrea.com

Trim-Rite Food Corp
801 Commerce Pkwy ... Carpentersville IL 60110 847-649-3400 649-3420 297-9
TF: 800-626-9442 ■ *Web:* www.trim-rite.com

TrimTabs Investment Research
1 Harbor Dr Ste 211 ... Sausalito CA 94965 415-324-5873 401
Web: www.trimtabs.com

Trimtex Company Inc 400 Pk Ave ... Williamsport PA 17701 570-326-9135 745-5

Trinacria Ristorante
113 Capitol Way N ... Olympia WA 98501 360-352-8892 671

Trinal Inc 329 W 18th St Ste 405 ... Chicago IL 60616 312-738-0500 809
Web: www.trinalinc.com

Trincon Group LLC
1683 Old Henderson Rd ... Columbus OH 43220 614-442-0590 196
Web: trincon.com

Trine University
4101 Edison Lakes Pkwy Ste 250 ... Mishawaka IN 46545 574-243-0500 166
Web: www.trine.edu

TriNet Group Inc
1100 San Leandro Blvd Ste 300 ... San Leandro CA 94577 510-352-5000 352-6480 631
TF: 888-874-6388 ■ *Web:* www.trinet.com

Trinet Internet Solutions Inc
1423 Powhatan St Bldg 1 ... Alexandria VA 22314 703-548-8900 171
Web: trinetsolutions.com

Trinidad & Tobago Embassy
1708 Massachusetts Ave NW ... Washington DC 20036 202-467-6490 785-3130 257
Web: foreign.gov.tt

Trinidad Drilling Ltd
2500-700 9 Ave SW ... Calgary AB T2P3V4 403-265-6525 540
Web: www.trinidaddrilling.com

Trinidad Lake State Park
32610 State Hwy 12 ... Trinidad CO 81082 719-846-6951 565
Web: cpw.state.co.us

Trinidad State Beach
4150 Patrick's Point Dr ... Trinidad CA 95570 707-677-3570 565
Web: www.parks.ca.gov/default.asp?page_id=418

Trinidad State Junior College
600 Prospect St ... Trinidad CO 81082 719-846-5011 846-5620* 162
**Fax:* Admissions ■ *TF:* 800-621-8752 ■ *Web:* www.trinidadstate.edu

Trinitas Hospital 225 Williamson St ... Elizabeth NJ 07207 908-994-5000 374-3
TF: 800-549-8977 ■ *Web:* www.trinitashospital.com

Triniti Corp
9999 Hamilton Blvd One Tek Pk Ste 340 ... Breinigsville PA 18031 610-530-7268 809
Web: www.triniti.com

Trinity Academy Inc 12345 E 21st St N ... Wichita KS 67206 316-634-0909 685
Web: www.trinityacademy.org

Trinity Area School District
231 Pk Ave ... Washington PA 15301 724-223-2000 685
Web: www.trinitypride.org

Trinity Bible College
50 Sixth Ave N ... Ellendale ND 58436 701-349-3621 349-5786 161
TF: 800-523-1603 ■ *Web:* www.trinitybiblecollege.edu

Trinity Biotech PLC
5919 Farnsworth Ct ... Carlsbad CA 92008 760-929-0500 929-0124 231
NASDAQ: TRIB ■ *TF:* 800-331-2291 ■ *Web:* www.trinitybiotech.com

Trinity Broadcasting Network (TBN)
PO Box A ... Santa Ana CA 92711 714-832-2950 740
TF: 888-731-1000 ■ *Web:* www.tbn.org

Trinity Business Furniture
6089 Kennedy Rd ... Trinity NC 27370 336-472-6660 321
TF: 855-311-6660 ■ *Web:* www.trinityfurniture.com

Trinity Cathedral 2230 Euclid Ave ... Cleveland OH 44115 216-771-3630 771-3657 50-1
Web: www.trinitycleveland.org

Trinity Ceramic Supply Inc
9016 Diplomacy Row ... Dallas TX 75247 214-631-0540 45
Web: www.trinityceramic.com

Trinity Christian College
6601 W College Dr ... Palos Heights IL 60463 708-597-3000 239-4826 166
TF: 800-443-5522 ■ *Web:* www.trnty.edu

Trinity College of Florida
2430 Welbilt Blvd ... Trinity FL 34655 727-376-6911 569-1410 161
TF: 800-388-0869 ■ *Web:* www.trinitycollege.edu

Trinity College of The Bible & Trinity Theological Seminary
4233 Medwel Dr ... Newburgh IN 47630 812-853-0611 166
Web: www.trinitysem.edu

Trinity College Raether Library
300 Summit St ... Hartford CT 06106 860-297-2000 297-2251 434-6
Web: www.trincoll.edu/depts/library

Trinity College School
55 Deblaquire St N ... Port Hope ON L1A4K7 905-885-3217 885-7444 622
Web: www.tcs.on.ca

Trinity County PO Box 456 ... Groveton TX 75845 936-642-1208 642-3004 338
Web: www.co.trinity.tx.us

Trinity County California
11 Court St Rm 230 PO Box 1613 ... Weaverville CA 96093 530-623-1382 623-8365* 245
**Fax:* Admin ■ *Web:* www.trinitycounty.org

Trinity Direct LLC 10 Park Pl ... Butler NJ 07405 973-283-3600 5
Web: www.trinitydirect.net

Trinity Elementary School
4410 Murfreesboro Rd ... Franklin TN 37067 615-472-4850 685
TF: 800-214-5264 ■ *Web:* www.wcs.edu

Trinity Episcopal School for Ministry
311 11th St ... Ambridge PA 15003 724-266-3838 266-4617 167-3
TF: 800-874-8754 ■ *Web:* tsm.edu

Trinity Fiduciary Partners LLC
106 Decker Court Ste 226 ... Irving TX 75062 877-334-1283 528
TF: 877-334-1283 ■ *Web:* www.trinityfiduciary.com

Trinity Forge Inc 947 Trinity Dr ... Mansfield TX 76063 817-473-1515 473-6743 483
Web: www.trinityforge.com

Trinity Green Services LLC
751 Hebron Pkwy Ste 225 ... Lewisville TX 75057 214-446-9500 446-9501 466
TF: 888-243-3605 ■ *Web:* www.trinitygrn.com

Trinity Group Construction
13849 Park Center Rd ... Herndon VA 20171 703-707-0300 186
Web: www.trinitygc.us

Trinity Hardwood Distributors Inc
110 East Oregon ... Dallas TX 75203 214-948-3001 946-1219 320
TF: 800-492-9856 ■ *Web:* www.trinityhardwood.net

Trinity Health 27870 Cabot Dr ... Novi MI 48377 248-489-6000 353
Web: www.trinity-health.org

Trinity Health System
380 Summit Ave ... Steubenville OH 43952 740-283-7000 283-7104 353
TF: 800-906-9762 ■ *Web:* www.trinityhealth.com

Trinity Hospital of Augusta
2803 Wrightsboro Rd Ste 38 ... Augusta GA 30909 706-729-6000 371
Web: www.trinityofaugusta.com

Trinity Hospital Saint Joseph's
1 W Burdick Expy ... Minot ND 58701 701-857-5000 374-3
TF: 800-247-1316 ■ *Web:* www.trinityhealth.org

Trinity Industries Inc
2525 Stemmons Fwy ... Dallas TX 75207 214-631-4420 589-8501 185
NYSE: TRN ■ *TF:* 800-631-4420 ■ *Web:* www.trin.net

Trinity Industries Inc Head Div
11765 Hwy 6 S ... Navasota TX 77868 936-825-6581 487
Web: www.trinityheads.com

Trinity Information Technology Llc
17 Windmill Dr ... Southampton PA 18966 267-254-7421 809
Web: www.trinityit.biz

Trinity International University
2065 Half Day Rd ... Deerfield IL 60015 847-945-8800 317-8097 166
TF: 800-822-3225 ■ *Web:* www.tiu.edu

Trinity International University South Florida
8190 W SR 84 ... Davie FL 33324 954-382-6400 382-6420 166
TF: 800-822-3225 ■ *Web:* www.tiu.edu

Trinity Life Bible College
5225 Hillsdale Blvd ... Sacramento CA 95842 916-348-4689 334-2315* 166
**Fax:* Admissions ■ *TF:* 800-670-3546 ■ *Web:* epic.edu

Trinity Logistics Group Inc
4001 Irving Blvd ... Dallas TX 75247 214-589-7505 780
Web: www.trinitytrucking.com

Trinity Lutheran Seminary
2199 E Main St ... Columbus OH 43209 614-235-4136 167-3
TF: 866-610-8571 ■ *Web:* tlsohio.edu

Trinity Marine Products Inc
2525 N Stemmons Fwy ... Dallas TX 75207 214-589-8446 698
TF: 877-876-5463 ■ *Web:* www.trin.net

Trinity Medical Ctr
1 Burdick Expy W PO Box 5020 ... Minot ND 58702 701-857-5000 374-3
TF: 800-862-0005 ■ *Web:* www.trinityhealth.org

Trinity Medical Ctr West
4000 Johnson Rd ... Steubenville OH 43952 740-264-8000 283-7104 374-3
Web: www.trinityhealth.com

Trinity Medical Ctr West Campus (TMC)
2701 17th St ... Rock Island IL 61201 309-779-2800 374-3
Web: www.unitypoint.org

Trinity Mining Service 109 48th St ... Pittsburgh PA 15201 412-682-4700 682-4725 650
TF: 800-264-2583 ■ *Web:* www.trin-mine.com

Trinity Mother Frances Rehabilitation Hospital - Tyler
3131 Troup Hwy ... Tyler TX 75701 903-510-7000 374-6

Trinity Neurological Rehabilitation Ctr
1400 Lindberg Dr ... Slidell LA 70458 985-641-4985 374-6
Web: trinityneurorehab.com

Trinity Packaging Corp
84 Business Pk Dr ... Armonk NY 10504 914-273-4111 273-4715 548
Web: www.trinitypackaging.com

Trinity Racing
9242 Hyssop Dr ... Rancho Cucamonga CA 91730 909-987-4213 518
Web: www.trinityracing.com

Trinity Rail Group LLC
2525 N Stemmons Fwy ... Dallas TX 75207 214-631-4420 589-8623 650
TF: 800-631-4420 ■ *Web:* www.trinityrail.com

Trinity Railway Express
1600 E Lancaster Ave ... Fort Worth TX 76102 817-215-8600 649
Web: www.the-t.com

Trinity Regional Medical Ctr (TRMC)
802 Kenyon Rd ... Fort Dodge IA 50501 515-573-3101 573-8710 374-3
Web: www.unitypoint.org

Trinity Repertory Co
201 Washington St ... Providence RI 02903 401-521-1100 751-5577 749
Web: www.trinityrep.com

Trinity River Authority of Texas
5300 s collins st ... Arlington TX 76018 817-467-4343 463
Web: www.trinityra.org

Trinity Steel Fabricators Inc
13430 Northwest Fwy Ste 225 ... Trinity TX 77040 713-460-5556 480
Web: www.trinitysteel.com

Trinity Sterile Inc 201 Kiley Dr ... Salisbury MD 21801 800-829-8384 596
TF: 800-829-8384 ■ *Web:* www.trinitysterile.com

Trinity Structural Towers Inc
2525 N Stemmons Fwy ... Dallas TX 75207 214-631-4420 480
Web: www.trinitytowers.com

Trinity Systems Technologies Inc
5885 Cumming Hwy Ste 108-273 ... Sugar Hill GA 30518 888-828-5655 196
TF: 888-828-5655 ■ *Web:* www.trinitysystemstech.com

Trinity Trailer Manufacturing Inc
7533 S Federal Way ... Boise ID 83716 208-336-3666 336-3741 779
TF: 800-235-6577 ■ *Web:* www.trinitytrailer.com

Trinity University
125 Michigan Ave NE ... Washington DC 20017 202-884-9000 884-9403* 166
**Fax:* Admissions ■ *TF Admissions:* 800-492-6882 ■ *Web:* www.trinitydc.edu

Trinity University 1 Trinity Pl ... San Antonio TX 78212 210-999-7011 999-8164* 166
**Fax:* Admissions ■ *TF:* 800-874-6489 ■ *Web:* www.trinity.edu

Trinity Valley Community College
Athens 100 Cardinal Dr ... Athens TX 75751 903-675-6200 675-6209* 162
**Fax:* Admissions ■ *TF:* 877-392-6433 ■ *Web:* www.tvcc.edu
Palestine PO Box 2530 ... Palestine TX 75802 903-729-0256 729-2325 162
TF: 866-882-2937 ■ *Web:* www.tvcc.edu

Trinity Valley Electric Co-op Inc (TVEC)
1800 Hwy 243 E PO Box 888 ... Kaufman TX 75142 972-932-2214 245
TF: 800-766-9576 ■ *Web:* www.tvec.net

Name / Address	City	State	ZIP	Phone	Fax	Class
Trinity Ventures 2480 Sand Hill Rd Ste 200 *TF:* 800-916-9960 ■ *Web:* trinityventures.com	Menlo Park	CA	94025	650-854-9500		792
Trinity Western University 7600 Glover Rd **Fax:* Admissions ■ *TF:* 888-468-6898 ■ *Web:* www.twu.ca	Langley	BC	V2Y1Y1	604-888-7511	513-2064*	785
Trinity-Pawling School 700 Rt 22 *Web:* www.trinitypawling.org	Pawling	NY	12564	845-855-3100	855-3816	622
Trinium Technologies LLC 304 Tejon Pl *Web:* www.triniumtech.com	Palos Verdes	CA	90274	310-214-3118		179
Trinsic Technologies Inc 15843 Opal Fire Dr Ste 100 *Web:* www.trinsictech.com	Austin	TX	78728	512-410-7308		393
Trintech Inc 15851 Dallas Pkwy Ste 900 *TF:* 800-416-0075 ■ *Web:* www.trintech.com	Addison	TX	75001	972-701-9802		178-1
Trio 7565 Kenwood Rd *Web:* www.triobistro.com	Cincinnati	OH	45236	513-984-1905		671
Trio Media Group LLC 182 Hilderbrand Dr Ste 100 *Web:* triomediagroup.com	Atlanta	GA	30328	404-255-1970		196
Trio Pac Inc 386 Rue Mcarthur *Web:* www.triopac.com	Montreal	QC	H4T1X8	514-733-7793		358
Trio Pines U.S.A. Inc 16233 Heron Ave *Web:* www.triopines.com	La Mirada	CA	90638	714-523-5800		385
Trio Solutions Inc 505 Belle Hall Pkwy Unit 202 *Web:* triohrsolutions.com	Mount Pleasant	SC	29464	414-870-9896		195
Trio's 8201 Cantrell Rd *Web:* www.triosrestaurant.com	Little Rock	AR	72227	501-221-3330	221-1002	671
TriOak Foods Inc 103 W Railroad St PO Box 68 *TF:* 800-644-8118 ■ *Web:* www.trioak.com	Oakville	IA	52646	319-766-2230		276
Triodyne Inc 666 Dundee Rd Ste 103 *Web:* www.triodyne.com	Northbrook	IL	60062	847-677-4730	647-2047	261
Triomphe 49 W 44th St *Web:* www.iroquoisny.com	New York	NY	10036	212-453-4233		671
Trion Inc 101 McNeill Rd *TF:* 800-884-0002 ■ *Web:* www.trioniaq.com	Sanford	NC	27330	919-775-2201	774-8771	18
Trion Industries Inc 297 Laird St *TF:* 800-444-4665 ■ *Web:* www.triononline.com	Wilkes-Barre	PA	18702	570-824-1000	824-0802	286
Trios College Business Technology Healthcare 520 First St *Web:* www.secondcareerontario.com	London	ON	N5V3C6	519-455-0551		167
Trio-Tech International 14731 Califa St *NYSE:* TRT ■ *Web:* www.triotech.com	Van Nuys	CA	91411	818-787-7000	787-9130	248
Tripac Fasteners 475 Klug Cir *Web:* tripaconline.com	Corona	CA	92880	951-280-4488		351
TripAdvisor LLC 464 Hillside Ave Ste 304 *Web:* www.tripadvisor.com	Needham	MA	02494	781-444-1113	444-1146	773
Tri-Pak Machinery Inc 1102 N Commerce St *Web:* www.tri-pakmachinery.com	Harlingen	TX	78550	956-423-5140	423-9302	547
tripBAM LLC 7318 Marquette *Web:* www.tripbam.com	Dallas	TX	75225	214 363 0630		300
Tripifoods Inc 1427 William St *TF:* 800-482-2962 ■ *Web:* www.tripifoods.com	Buffalo	NY	14206	716-853-7400	852-7400	297-8
Triple A Containers 16069 Shoemaker *Web:* www.tripla.com	Cerritos	CA	90703	562-404-7433		198
Triple A Oil 12342 Inwood Rd	Dallas	TX	75244	972-503-3333		324
Triple B Forwarders Inc 1511 Glen Curtis St *TF:* 800-228-8465 ■ *Web:* www.tripleb.com	Carson	CA	90746	310-604-5840		311
Triple C Wholesalers Inc 2801 W Patapsco Ave *Web:* www.triplecinc.com	Baltimore	MD	21230	410-644-5500		756
Triple Creek Ranch 5551 W Fork Rd *TF:* 800-654-2943 ■ *Web:* www.triplecreekranch.com	Darby	MT	59829	406-821-4600		669
Triple Crown Corp 5351 Jaycee Ave *TF:* 877-822-4663 ■ *Web:* www.triplecrowncorp.com	Harrisburg	PA	17112	717-657-5729	657-8125	187
Triple Crown Nutrition Inc 319 Barry Ave S Ste 303 *TF:* 800-451-9916 ■ *Web:* www.triplecrownfeed.com	Wayzata	MN	55391	800-451-9916		447
Triple Crown Products Inc 814 Ela Ave *TF:* 800-619-1110 ■ *Web:* triplecrownproducts.com/index.aspx	Waterford	WI	53185	262-534-7878		687
Triple Crown Services 2720 Dupont Commerce Ct Ste 200 *TF:* 800-325-6510 ■ *Web:* www.triplecrownsvc.com	Fort Wayne	IN	46825	260-416-3600		648
Triple d Bending 4707 Glenmore Trail SE *Web:* www.pipebending.com	Calgary	AB	T2C2R9	403-255-2944		595
Triple Dot Corp 3302 S Susan St *Web:* www.triple-dot.com	Santa Ana	CA	92704	714-241-0888		362
Triple H Food Processing 5821 Wilderness Ave *Web:* www.triplehfoods.com	Riverside	CA	92504	951-352-5700		123
Triple J Tours Inc 4455 S Cameron St *Web:* www.lasvegasbus.com	Las Vegas	NV	89103	702-261-0131	736-5103	107
Triple J Wilderness Ranch 91 Mortimer Rd PO Box 310 *TF:* 800-826-1300 ■ *Web:* www.triplejranch.com	Augusta	MT	59410	406-562-3653	562-3836	239
Triple M 105.5 fm 7601 Ganser Way *Web:* www.1055triplem.com	Madison	WI	53719	608-826-0077		645-96
Triple Oaks Nursery & Herb Garden 2359 Delsea Dr *Web:* www.tripleoaks.com	Franklinville	NJ	08322	856-694-4272		292
Triple Peaks LLC 77 Okemo Heights *Web:* www.okemo.com	Ludlow	VT	05149	802-228-1947		787
Triple Play Products LLC 904 Main St Ste 330 *TF:* 800-829-1625 ■ *Web:* www.lillygold.com	Hopkins	MN	55343	952-938-0531		64
Triple Point Technology Inc 301 Riverside Ave *Web:* www.tpt.com	Westport	CT	06880	203-291-7979		177
Triple R Ranch PO Box 124 *Web:* www.rrrranch.com	Keystone	SD	57751	605-666-4605		239
Triple s Alarm Company Inc 2820 Cantrell Rd *Web:* www.triplesalarm.com	Little Rock	AR	72202	501-664-4599		693
Triple Strength Graphics 232 W Main St Ste 2 *Web:* triplestrength.com	Palmyra	PA	17078	717-838-9590		7
Triple/S Dynamics Inc 1031 S Haskell Ave PO Box 151027 *TF:* 800-527-2116 ■ *Web:* www.sssdynamics.com	Dallas	TX	75315	214-828-8600	828-8688	470
Triple-I Corp, The 6330 Lamar Ave Ste 230 *TF:* 800-767-3263 ■ *Web:* www.triplei.com	Overland Park	KS	66202	913-563-7200		196
TripleLift Inc 36 W 20th St Fl 3 *Web:* triplelift.com	New York	NY	10011	502-354-3801		5
Tripler Army Medical Ctr 1 Jarrett White Rd Tripler AMC *TF:* 877-880-2184	Honolulu	HI	96859	808-433-6661	433-4899	374-4
Triple-S Steel Supply LLC 6000 Jensen Dr *TF:* 800-231-1034 ■ *Web:* www.sss-steel.com	Houston	TX	77026	713-697-7105		492
TripleTree 7601 France Ave S Ste 150 *Web:* www.triple-tree.com	Minneapolis	MN	55435	952-253-5300		401
Triplett Office Essentials Corp 3553 109th St *TF:* 800-437-5034 ■ *Web:* www.tripletts.com	Urbandale	IA	50322	515-270-9150	270-9683	535
Triplett Woolf & Garretson LLC 2959 N Rock Rd -Ste 300 *Web:* www.twgfirm.com	Wichita	KS	67226	316-630-8100		428
Tripod Technologies Llc 1050 Kings Hwy N Ste 102 *Web:* www.tripodtech.net	Cherry Hill	NJ	08034	856-755-1478		809
TriPower Resources LLC 16 E St *Web:* www.tripowerresources.com	Ardmore	OK	73401	580-226-6700		536
Tripp County Historical Society 200 E Third St *Web:* ujs.sd.gov	Winner	SD	57580	605-842-2266	842-2267	338
Tripp Lite Inc 1111 W 35th St *Web:* www.tripplite.com	Chicago	IL	60609	773-869-1111	869-1329	815
Tripp Lumber Company Inc 3000 Raser Dr *Web:* www.tripplumber.com	Missoula	MT	59808	406-549-0195		683
Tripp Scott 110 SE Sixth St 15th Fl *Web:* www.trippscott.com	Fort Lauderdale	FL	33301	954-525-7500		428
Trippnt Inc 8830 NE 108th St *TF:* 800-874-7768 ■ *Web:* www.trippnt.com	Kansas City	MO	64157	816-792-2604		608
Tripps Restaurants 1605 Highwoods Blvd	Greensboro	NC	27410	336-272-9355	272-5568	670
Tripwire Inc 101 SW Main St Ste 1500 *TF General:* 800-874-7947 ■ *Web:* www.tripwire.com	Portland	OR	97204	503-276-7500	223-0182	178-12
TriReme Medical Inc 7060 Koll Ctr Pkwy Ste 300 *Web:* qtvascular.com	Pleasanton	CA	94566	925-931-1300		463
Tris Pharma Inc 2033 Rt 130 Brunswick Business Pk Ste D *Web:* www.trispharma.com	Monmouth Junction	NJ	08852	732-940-2800	940-2855	668
Triseal Corp 11920 Price Rd *TF:* 800-910-7325 ■ *Web:* www.triseal.com	Hebron	IL	60034	815-648-2473		326
Trisept Solutions 777 W Glencoe Pl *Web:* www.triseptsolutions.com	Milwaukee	WI	53217	414-934-3900		549
Trisha Brown Dance Co 341 W 38th St Ste 801 *Web:* www.trishabrowncompany.org	New York	NY	10018	212-977-5365		573-1
Trisoft Technologies Inc 14429 Independence Dr *TF:* 866-364-7031 ■ *Web:* yieldwerx.com	Plainfield	IL	60544	866-364-7031		463
TriSports.com 4495 S Coach Dr *TF:* 888-293-3934 ■ *Web:* www.trisports.com	Tucson	AZ	85714	888-293-3934		711
Trissential Inc 1905 E Wayzata Blvd Ste 333 *Web:* www.trissential.com	Minneapolis	MN	55391	952-595-7970		463
Tristan 7671 Northwoods Blvd *Web:* tristanevents.com	Charleston	SC	29406	843-534-2155		671
Tristar Bank 719 E College St *Web:* tristarbank.com	Dickson	TN	37055	615-446-7100		70
Tri-Star Cabinet & Top Co Inc 1000 S Cedar *Web:* www.tristarcabinets.com	New Lenox	IL	60451	708-479-2126		115
Tri-star Data Systems Inc 650 Sentry Pkwy Ste 1 *Web:* tristardatasystems.com	Blue Bell	PA	19422	610-941-2116		177
TriStar Inc 3740 E La Salle St *Web:* www.tristar.com	Phoenix	AZ	85040	602-333-1600		525
Tri-Star Plastics Corp 906 Boston Tpke *Web:* www.tstar.com	Shrewsbury	MA	01545	508-845-1111		596
Tri-Star Plastics Inc 1915 E Via Burton *Web:* www.tri-starplastics.com	Anaheim	CA	92806	714-533-7360	533-4383	604
Tri-Star Protector Service Co 19233 FM 1485 Rd *TF:* 800-277-7491 ■ *Web:* www.tristarprotector.com	New Caney	TX	77357	281-399-2600		536
Tristar Southern Hills Medical Ctr 391 Wallace Rd *TF:* 800-242-5662 ■ *Web:* tristarsouthernhills.com	Nashville	TN	37211	615-781-4000		374-3
Tristar Web Graphics Inc 4010 Airline Dr *Web:* www.tristarholdings.com	Houston	TX	77022	713-691-0005		627
Tri-Starr Investigations Inc 3525 Hwy 138 SW *TF:* 800-849-9841 ■ *Web:* www.tristarr.com	Stockbridge	GA	30281	770-388-9841		41

Company / Address	Phone	Fax	Class
Tri-state Adjustments Inc 3439 East Ave S PO Box 3219 .... La Crosse WI 54602 *TF:* 800-562-3906 ■ *Web:* www.wecollectmore.com	608-788-8683		160
Tri-state Aero Inc 6101 Flight Line Dr. .... Evansville IN 47725 *TF:* 800-473-2904 ■ *Web:* www.tristateaero.com	812-426-1221		23
Tri-State Armature & Electrical Works Inc 330 GE Patterson Ave .... Memphis TN 38126 *TF:* 800-238-7654 ■ *Web:* www.tristatearmature.com	901-527-8412	521-1065	246
Tri-State Baking Co 6800 S Washington St .... Amarillo TX 79118 *Web:* afiama.com	806-373-6696		297-1
Tri-State Bank & Trust 4321 Youree Dr. .... Shreveport LA 71105	318-861-6184		70
Tri-State Better Business Bureau 5401 Vogel Rd Ste 410. .... Evansville IN 47715 *TF:* 800-359-0979 ■ *Web:* bbb.org/evansville	812-473-0202	473-3080	79
Tri-State Bible College 506 Margaret St .... South Point OH 45680 *TF:* 800-333-3243 ■ *Web:* www.tsbc.edu	740-377-2520	377-0001	161
Tri-State Brick & Stone of New York Inc 333 Seventh Ave 5th Fl. .... New York NY 10001 *Web:* btsbm.com	212-686-3939	686-4387	191-1
Tri-State Chamber of Commerce 5 S Broome St .... Port Jervis NY 12771 *Web:* tristatechamber.org	845-856-6694	856-6695	139
Tri-State College of Acupuncture 80 Eigth Ave Ste 400 .... New York NY 10011 *TF:* 800-234-6922 ■ *Web:* www.tsca.edu	212-242-2255		166
Tri-State Cut Stone & Brick Co 10333 Van's Dr. .... Frankfort IL 60423 *TF:* 800-552-3307 ■ *Web:* www.stone-brick.com	815-469-7550	464-5096	724
Tri-state Design Construction Inc 7401 Old York Rd .... Elkins Park PA 19027 *Web:* www.tristatedesign.net	215-782-8200	782-8282	186
Tri-State Drilling Inc 16940 Hwy 55 W .... Plymouth MN 55446 *TF:* 800-383-1033 ■ *Web:* www.tristatedrilling.com	763-553-1234	553-9778	189-15
Tri-State Electric Membership Corp (TSEMC) 2310 Blue Ridge Dr .... Blue Ridge GA 30513 *TF:* 800-351-1111 ■ *Web:* www.tsemc.net	706-492-3251	492-7617	245
Tri-state Fabricators Inc 1146 Ferris Rd .... Amelia OH 45102 *TF:* 888-523-1488 ■ *Web:* www.tristatefabricators.com	513-752-5005		610
Tri-State Feeders Inc 3 Mile S Hwy 83 .... Turpin OK 73950	580-778-3600		10-1
Tri-State Financial Press LLC 109 N Fifth St .... Saddle Brook NJ 07663 *Fax Area Code: 201 ■ *TF:* 800-866-6375 ■ *Web:* www.tsfpress.com	800-866-6375	226-9229*	627
Tri-state Forest Products Inc 2105 Sheridan Ave .... Springfield OH 45505 *TF:* 800-949-6325 ■ *Web:* www.tsfpi.com	937-323-6325	323-6888	191-3
Tri-state Home Services 82A Wormans Mill Ct .... Frederick MD 21701 *TF:* 844-202-2126 ■ *Web:* tristatehomeservices.com	844-202-2126		610
Tri-State Iron & Metal Co 1725 E Ninth St .... Texarkana AR 71854 *Web:* www.tsimco.com	870-773-8409		686
Tri-State Ironworks Inc 175 W Bodley Ave. .... Memphis TN 38109 *Web:* www.tristateironworks.com	901-942-1461		492
Tri-State Machine Inc 3301 Mccolloch St .... Wheeling WV 26003 *Web:* www.tri-statemachine.com	304-234-0170		454
Tristate Midstream LP 3311 N I-35 Ste 120. .... Denton TX 76207 *TF:* 800-935-9935 ■ *Web:* www.tsmidstream.com	940-387-4955		580
Tri-State Motors 298 S Main St .... Cedar City UT 84720 *Web:* www.tristateofcedarcity.com	435-238-4342		57
Tri-State Pumps Inc 1162 Chastain Rd .... Liberty SC 29657 *TF:* 800-868-4631 ■ *Web:* tspturf.com	864-843-8100		711
Tri-State Roofing & Sheet Metal Group 101 S Meadville Rd .... Davisville WV 26142 *Web:* www.tri-stateservicegroup.com	304-295-3311	295-6991	189-12
Tri-State Surgical Supply & Equipment Ltd 409 Hoyt St. .... Brooklyn NY 11231 *TF:* 800-899-8741 ■ *Web:* tristatesurgical.com	718-624-1000		475
Tri-State Trailer Sales Inc 3111 Grand Ave .... Pittsburgh PA 15225 *Web:* www.tristatetrailer.com	412-747-7777	777-4010	62-5
Tri-State Travel 4349 Industrial Pk Dr. .... Galena IL 61036 *TF:* 800-779-4869 ■ *Web:* www.tristatetravel.com	815-777-0820	777-8128	760
Tri-State University 1 University Blvd .... Angola IN 46703 *Web:* tripadvisor.com	781-800-5000		166
Tri-State Utility Products Inc 1030 Atlanta Industrial Dr. .... Marietta GA 30066 *TF:* 800-282-7985 ■ *Web:* tsup.com	770-427-3119	427-3945	246
Tri-State Video Services Inc 1379 Pittsburgh Rd. .... Valencia PA 16059 *TF:* 888-382-7768 ■ *Web:* www.tristatevideo.com	724-898-1630		38
Tristate Wire Rope Supply Inc 5246 Wooster Pk .... Cincinnati OH 45226 *Web:* fulcrumlifting.com	513-871-8656		492
Trisys Telecom Inc 215 Ridgedale Ave Ste 2 .... Florham Park NJ 07932 *Web:* www.trisys.com	973-360-2300		387
TriTeal Corp 2011 Palomar Airport Rd .... Carlsbad CA 92009 *Fax Area Code: 619 ■ *Web:* www.triteal.com	760-827-5000	930-2074*	809
TriTech Enterprise Systems Inc 1869 Brightseat Rd. .... Hyattsville MD 20785 *Web:* www.tritechenterprise.com	301-918-8250		225
Tritech Group Ltd 5413 - 271 St. .... Langley BC V4W3Y7 *Web:* www.tritechgroup.ca	604-607-8878		201
Tritech Software Systems 9477 Waples St. .... San Diego CA 92121 *Web:* www.tritech.com	858-799-7000	799-7010	179
Tritek Solutions Inc 7617 Little River Tpke Ste 800 .... Annandale VA 22003 *Web:* www.perficient.com	703-333-3060		178-1
TriTeq Lock and Security LLC 701 Gullo .... Elk Grove Village IL 60007 *Web:* www.triteqlock.com	847-640-7002		261
Tritest Inc 6701 Conference Dr .... Raleigh NC 27607 *Web:* www.tritestinc.com	919-834-4984		794
Triton Capital Partners Ltd 566 West Lake St Ste 235 .... Chicago IL 60661 *Web:* www.tritoncap.com	312-575-0190		690
Triton College 2000 N Fifth Ave .... River Grove IL 60171 *Fax: Admissions ■ *Web:* www.triton.edu	708-456-0300	583-3147*	162
Triton Diving Services LLC 3421 N Causeway Blvd Ste 601 .... Metairie LA 70002 *Web:* www.tritondiving.net	504-846-5056		41
Triton Environmental Inc 385 Church St Ste 201 .... Guilford CT 06437 *TF:* 800-828-6343 ■ *Web:* www.tritonenvironmental.com	203-458-7200		196
Triton Industries Inc 1020 N Kolmar Ave. .... Chicago IL 60651 *TF:* 800-755-6373 ■ *Web:* www.tritonindustries.com	773-384-3700	384-8748	488
Triton Media Group 15303 Ventura Blvd Ste 1500 .... Sherman Oaks CA 91403 *Web:* www.tritondigital.com	310-575-9700		644
Triton Museum of Art 1505 Warburton Ave. .... Santa Clara CA 95050 *Web:* www.tritonmuseum.org	408-247-3754	247-3796	520
Triton Services Inc 222 Severn Ave .... Annapolis MD 21403 *Web:* www.tritonsvc.com	443-716-0600	716-0601	178-5
Triton Systems Inc 21405 B St. .... Long Beach MS 39560 *TF:* 866-787-4866 ■ *Web:* www.tritonatm.com	228-575-3100		253
Triton Technologies Inc 115 Plymouth St. .... Mansfield MA 02048 *Web:* tritontechnologies.com	508-230-7300		195
Triton Ventures 6300 Bridge Pt Pkwy Bldg 1 Ste 500 .... Austin TX 78730 *Web:* www.tritonventures.com	512-795-5820		792
Triton-Tek Inc 445 W Erie St Ste 208 .... Chicago IL 60654 *TF:* 866-387-4866 ■ *Web:* www.triton-tek.com	312-467-9201		225
Tri-Town Precision Plastics Inc 12 Bridge St .... Deep River CT 06417	860-526-3200		602
Triumf 4004 Wesbrook Mall .... Vancouver BC V6T2A3 *Web:* www.triumf.ca	604-222-1047		743
Triumph Accessory Services 411 NW Rd .... Wellington KS 67152 *TF:* 800-863-1083 ■ *Web:* www.triumphgroup.com	620-326-2235	326-3761	24
Triumph Components 203 N Johnson Ave .... El Cajon CA 92020 *TF:* 800-863-1083 ■ *Web:* www.triumphgroup.com	619-440-2504	440-2509	621
Triumph Controls Inc 205 Church Rd .... North Wales PA 19454 *TF:* 800-322-2885 ■ *Web:* triumphgroup.com	215-699-4861	699-2595	203
Triumph Corp 2130 S Industrial Pk Ave .... Tempe AZ 85282 *TF:* 800-837-2241 ■ *Web:* www.triumphcorp.com	480-967-3337	921-0446	621
Triumph Enterprises Inc 8000 W park Dr Ste 600 .... McLean VA 22102 *Web:* www.triumph-enterprises.com	703-563-4400		194
Triumph Fabrications 1923 Central Ave .... Hot Springs AR 71901 *Web:* www.triumphgroup.com	501-321-9325		22
Triumph Gear Systems Inc 6125 Silver Creek Dr .... Park City UT 84098	435-649-1900		22
Triumph Group Inc 1550 Liberty Ridge Dr Ste 100 .... Wayne PA 19087 *NYSE:* TGI ■ *TF:* 800-863-1083 ■ *Web:* www.triumphgroup.com	610-251-1000	251-1555	24
Triumph Learning 136 Madison Ave .... New York NY 10016 *Fax Area Code: 866 ■ *Fax: Cust Svc ■ *TF:* 800-221-9372 ■ *Web:* www.triumphlearning.com	800-221-9372	805-5723*	637-2
Triumph Packaging Group 515 W Crossroads Pkwy. .... Bolingbrook IL 60440	630-771-0900		101
Triumph Pet Industries Inc 500 Sixth St SW .... Red Bay AL 35582 *Fax Area Code: 800 ■ *TF:* 800-633-3349 ■ *Web:* triumphpetfood.com	256-356-9541	331-5140*	578
Triumph Pharmaceuticals Inc 1918 Innerbelt Business Ctr Dr. .... St. Louis MO 63114 *Web:* www.smartmouth.com	314-995-3090		583
Triumph Structures - Los Angeles Inc 17055 E Gale Ave .... City Of Industry CA 91745 *Web:* www.triumphgroup.com	626-965-1630		256
Triumph Structures-Long Island LLC 717 Main St .... Westbury NY 11590 *TF:* 800-863-1083 ■ *Web:* www.triumphgrp.com	516-997-5757		22
Triumph Thermal Systems 200 Railroad St. .... Forest OH 45843 *Web:* www.fairchildcontrols.com	419-273-2511		22
Triumph Thermal Systems Inc 200 Railroad St. .... Forest OH 45843 *TF:* 800-863-1083 ■ *Web:* www.triumphgroup.com	419-273-2511	273-3285	22
Triumph Twist Drill Co Inc 1 SW Seventh St. .... Chisholm MN 55719 *TF:* 800-942-1501 ■ *Web:* triumphtwistdrill.com	218-263-3891	263-3887	758
Triumvirate Environmental 61 Innerbelt Rd .... Somerville MA 02143 *TF:* 800-966-9282 ■ *Web:* www.triumvirate.com	617-628-8098		804
Trivac Ltd 3050 Regent Blvd Ste 310 .... Irving TX 75063	469-484-5400		764
Trivalent Group Inc 3145 Prairie St SW Ste 101 .... Grandville MI 49418 *Web:* www.trivalentgroup.com	616-222-9200		180
Tri-Valley Herald 127 Spring St .... Pleasanton CA 94566 *Web:* www.eastbaytimes.com	925-935-2525		532-2
Trivalley Internet Inc 4713 First St Ste 110 .... Pleasanton CA 94566 *Web:* www.trivalley.com	925-417-7600		180
Tri-Valley Local School District 36 E Muskingum Ave .... Dresden OH 43821 *Web:* www.tri-valley.k12.oh.us	740-754-1442	754-6400	685
Trivascular Technologies Inc 3910 Brickway Blvd .... Santa Rosa CA 95403 *Web:* www.trivascular.com	707-543-8800		787
Triveni Digital Inc 40 Washington Rd .... Princeton Junction NJ 08550 *Web:* www.trivenidigital.com	609-716-3500	716-3503	225

				Phone	Fax	Class
Trivent Systems Inc 2274 Eldemere Cir Web: www.triventlegal.com	Macungie	PA	18062	610-832-1529		809
Trivera Interactive N88 W16447 Main St Ste 400 TF: 800-829-0420 ■ Web: www.trivera.com	Menomonee Falls	WI	53051	262-250-9400		180
Trivest Partners LP 550 S Dixie Hwy Ste 300 Web: www.trivest.com	Coral Gables	FL	33146	305-858-2200		321
TriVista Business Group Inc 15 Enterprise Ste 410 Web: www.trivista.com	Aliso Viejo	CA	92656	949-218-4830		196
TriVium Systems Inc 1865 NW 169th Pl Ste 210 Web: www.triviumsys.com	Beaverton	OR	97006	503-439-9338		179
Triware Technologies Inc 76 Brookfield Rd TF: 800-663-7199 ■ Web: www.triware.ca	St John's	NL	A1E3T9	709-579-5000		177
Triway Local School District 3205 Shreve Rd Web: www.triway.k12.oh.us	Wooster	OH	44691	330-264-9491	262-3955	685
Tri-Wire Engineering Solutions Inc 890 East St TF: 800-439-0549 ■ Web: www.triwire.net	Tewksbury	MA	01876	978-640-6899		492
Triwood Corp of Georgia Inc 124 Austin Rd Web: triwood.com	Americus	GA	31719	229-928-2233		608
Trix Systems Inc 68 Smith St Web: www.trixsystems.com	Chelmsford	MA	01824	978-256-4445		177
TriZetto Corp 501 N Broadway 3rd Fl TF: 800-969-3666 ■ Web: www.trizettoprovider.com	Sacramento	CA	95814	800-969-3666		177
TRM Technologies Inc 280 Albert St Ste 1000 10th Fl Web: www.trm.ca	Ottawa	ON	K1P5G8	613-722-8843		196
TRMC (Thibodaux Regional Medical Ctr) 602 N Acadia Rd TF: 800-822-0442 ■ Web: thibodaux.com	Thibodaux	LA	70301	985-447-5500	446-5033	374-3
TRMC (Trinity Regional Medical Ctr) 802 Kenyon Rd Web: www.unitypoint.org	Fort Dodge	IA	50501	515-573-3101	573-8710	374-3
TRMC (Tomball Regional Hospital) 605 Holderrieth St Web: www.tomballregionalmedicalcenter.com	Tomball	TX	77375	281-401-7500		374-3
TRN (TRN) PO Box 3755 TF: 888-383-3733 ■ Web: www.trncorporate.com	Central Point	OR	97502	888-383-3733		646
Trocadero 1758 N Water St Web: www.trocaderomke.com	Milwaukee	WI	53202	414-272-0205		671
Trocaire College 360 Choate Ave *Fax: Admissions ■ TF: 800-926-5534 ■ Web: www.trocaire.edu	Buffalo	NY	14220	716-826-1200	828-6107*	162
Trofholz Technologies Inc 2207 Plaza Dr Ste 100 TF: 800-800-7056 ■ Web: www.trofholz.com	Rocklin	CA	95765	916-577-1903		180
Trois Rivieres Tourism 1457 Rue Notre Dame TF: 800-313-1123 ■ Web: www.tourismetroisrivieres.com	Trois-Rivieres	QC	G9A4X4	819-375-1122	375-0022	775
Trois-Rivieres Port Authority 1545 Du Fleuve St Ste 300 Web: www.porttr.com	Trois-Rivieres	QC	G9A6K4	819-378-2887	378-2487	618
Trojan Battery Co 12380 Clark St TF Cust Svc: 800-423-6569 ■ Web: www.trojanbattery.com	Santa Fe Springs	CA	90670	562-236-3000	236-3282	74
Trojan Horse 100 E Kirkwood Ave Web: www.thetrojanhorse.com	Bloomington	IN	47408	812-332-1101		671
Trojan Inc 198 Trojan St TF: 800-264-0526 ■ Web: www.trojaninc.com	Mount Sterling	KY	40353	859-498-0526		437
Trojan Law Offices 9250 Wilshire Blvd Ste 325 Web: www.trojanlawoffices.com	Beverly Hills	CA	90212	310-777-8399		428
Trojan Press Inc 1635 Burlington St TF: 800-561-3357 ■ Web: www.trojanpressinc.com	Kansas City	MO	64116	816-221-6477		627
Trojan Professional Services Inc 14410 Cerritos Ave TF: 800-451-9723 ■ Web: www.trojanonline.com	Los Alamitos	CA	90720	800-451-9723		224
Trolex Corp 55-57 Bushes Ln Web: www.trolexcorp.com	Elmwood Park	NJ	07407	201-794-8004		4
Troll Systems Corp 24950 Anza Dr Web: www.trollsystems.com	Valencia	CA	91355	661-702-8900		647
Trombetta 8111 N 87th St Web: www.trombetta.com	Milwaukee	WI	53224	414-410-0300	355-3882	203
Tronair Inc 1740 Eber Rd TF: 800-426-6301 ■ Web: www.tronair.com	Holland	OH	43528	419-866-6301	867-0634	22
Trone 1823 Eastchester Dr Web: www.tronebrandenergy.com	High Point	NC	27265	336-886-1622		4
Tronox Inc 3301 NW 150th St Web: www.tronox.com	Oklahoma City	OK	73134	405-775-5000		143
Troon Golf LLC 15044 N Scottsdale Rd Ste 300 Web: www.troon.com	Scottsdale	AZ	85254	480-606-1000		194
Tropar Manufacturing Inc 5 Vreeland Rd Web: www.airflyte.com	Florham Park	NJ	07932	973-822-2400		702
Trophy Nut Company Inc 320 N Second St TF: 800-729-6887 ■ Web: www.trophynut.com	Tipp City	OH	45371	937-667-8478	667-4656	296-28
Trophyland USA Inc 7001 W 20th Ave *Fax Area Code: 305 ■ TF: 800-327-5820 ■ Web: www.trophyland.com	Hialeah	FL	33014	800-327-5820	823-4836*	777
Tropic Lightning Museum 745 Wright Ave	Wahiawa	HI	96786	808-655-0438		520
Tropic Oil Company Inc 10002 NW 89th Ave TF: 866-645-3835 ■ Web: www.tropicoil.com	Miami	FL	33178	305-888-4611		579
Tropical Cheese Industries Inc 450 Fayette St PO Box 1357 TF: 888-874-4928 ■ Web: www.tropicalcheese.com	Perth Amboy	NJ	08861	732-442-4898	442-8227	296-5
Tropical Chinese Restaurant 7991 SW 40th St Web: www.tropicalchinesemiami.com	Miami	FL	33155	305-262-7576	262-1552	671
Tropical Everglades Visitor Assn 160 US Hwy Ste 1 Web: www.tropicaleverglades.com	Florida City	FL	33034	305-245-9180		206
Tropical Ford 9900 S Orange Blossom Trial TF Sales: 877-241-0502 ■ Web: www.tropicalford.com	Orlando	FL	32837	407-851-3800	240-7308	57
Tropical Nut & Fruit Co 1100 Continental Blvd Web: www.tropicalfoods.com	Charlotte	NC	28273	704-588-0400		805
Tropical Shipping 5 E 11th St TF: 800-367-6200 ■ Web: tropical.com	Riviera Beach	FL	33404	561-881-3900		313
Tropical Winds Oceanfront Hotel 1398 N Atlantic Ave TF: 800-245-6099 ■ Web: tropicalwindshotel.com	Daytona Beach	FL	32118	386-258-1016	255-6462	379
Tropicana Entertainment 2831 Boardwalk OTC: TPCA ■ TF: 800-843-8767 ■ Web: www.tropicana.net	Atlantic City	NJ	08401	800-843-8767		669
Tropicana Express 2121 S Casino Dr TF: 800-243-6846 ■ Web: troplaughlin.com	Laughlin	NV	89029	702-298-4200		133
Tropicana Field 1 Tropicana Dr TF: 888-326-7297	Saint Petersburg	FL	33705	727-825-3137	825-3204	720
Tropicana Inn & Suites 1540 S Harbor Blvd TF: 800-828-4898 ■ Web: tropicanainn-anaheim.com	Anaheim	CA	92802	714-635-4082	635-1535	379
Tropicana Resort & Casino 3801 Las Vegas Blvd S TF Resv: 800-462-8767 ■ Web: www.troplv.com	Las Vegas	NV	89109	702-739-2222		669
Tropics Software Technologies Inc 7349 Merchant Crt Web: www.gotropics.com	Sarasota	FL	34240	941-955-1234		177
Tropigas De Puerto Rico Inc Urb Industrial Luchetti Calle C Lote 30 Web: tropigaspr.com	Bayamon	PR	00961	787-641-8002		316
Tropikis 878 Ellice Ave	Winnipeg	MB	R3G0C6	204-788-4733		671
Tropitone Furniture Co Inc 5 Marconi Web: www.tropitone.com	Irvine	CA	92618	949-951-2010		319-4
Troquet 107 South St Web: troquetboston.com	Boston	MA	02111	617-695-9463		671
Trostel Ltd 901 Maxwell St Web: www.trostel.com	Lake Geneva	WI	53147	262-248-4481		326
Trostel's Greenbrier Restaurant 5810 Merle Hay Rd Web: greenbriartrostels.com	Johnston	IA	50131	515-253-0124		671
Trott Dave (Rep R - MI) 1722 Longworth HOB Web: trott.house.gov	Washington	DC	20515	202-225-8171	225-2667	342-2
Trotter & Morton Ltd 5711 - First St SE TF: 800-355-9401 ■ Web: www.trotterandmorton.com	Calgary	AB	T2H1H9	403-255-7535		186
Trotters Restaurant 2008 Savannah Hwy TF: 800-334-6660 ■ Web: www.thetownandcountryinn.com	Charleston	SC	29401	843-571-1000	766-9444	671
Trotwood Chamber of Commerce 5790 Denlinger Rd TF: 800-827-5722 ■ Web: www.trotwoodchamber.org	Trotwood	OH	45426	937-837-1484	837-1508	139
Trouble Free Plumbing Inc 802 Willow St Web: troublefreeinc.com	Pekin	IL	61554	309-347-5309		189-10
Troup County PO Box 866 Web: www.troupcountyga.org	LaGrange	GA	30241	706-883-1740	883-1724	338
Troupe Modern Media Design & Production, The 3 Industrial Dr Unit 3 TF: 800-590-7850 ■ Web: www.thetroupe.com	Windham	NH	03087	603-893-4554		514
Trousdale County 240 Broadway Web: hartsvilletrousdale.com	Hartsville	TN	37074	615-374-9243	374-9243	338
Trout & Partners Ltd 8 Wahneta Rd Web: www.troutandpartners.com	Old Greenwich	CT	06870	203-637-7001	637-7071	194
Trout Ebersole & Groff 1705 Oregon Pk Web: www.troutcpa.com	Lancaster	PA	17601	717-569-2900		2
Trout Unlimited (TU) 1300 N 17th St Ste 500 TF: 800-834-2419 ■ Web: www.tu.org	Arlington	VA	22209	703-522-0200	284-9400	48-3
Troutman Sanders LLP 600 Peachtree St NE Ste 5200 Web: www.troutmansanders.com	Atlanta	GA	30308	404-885-3000	885-3900	428
Troutt, Beeman & Company PC 1212 Locust St Web: www.tbco.net	Harrisonville	MO	64701	816-380-5500		2
Trouw Nutrition 115 Executive Dr TF: 800-365-1357 ■ Web: trouwnutritionusa.com	Highland	IL	62249	618-654-2070	654-7012	447
Troxel Co Hwy 57 Web: www.troxel.com	Moscow	TN	38057	901-877-6875		490
Troxel Co, The 11495 Highway 57 W	Moscow	TN	38057	901-877-6875		596
Troxler Electronic Laboratories Inc 3008 E Cornwallis Rd PO Box 12057 TF: 877-876-9537 ■ Web: www.troxlerlabs.com	Research Triangle Park	NC	27709	919-549-8661	549-0761	201
Troy Belting & Supply Co 70 Cohoes Rd Web: www.troyindustrialsolutions.com	Watervliet	NY	12189	518-272-4920		385
Troy Chamber of Commerce 4555 Investment Dr Ste 300 Web: www.troychamber.com	Troy	MI	48098	248-641-8151	641-0545	139
Troy Design & Manufacturing Co (TDM) 14425 Sheldon Rd Web: www.troydm.com	Plymouth	MI	48239	734-738-2300		489
Troy Public Library 510 W Big Beaver Rd TF: 800-649-7377 ■ Web: www.libcoop.net	Troy	MI	48084	248-524-3538	524-0112	434-3
Troy Springs State Park 674 NE Troy Springs Rd Web: www.floridastateparks.org/troyspring	Branford	FL	32008	386-935-4835		565
Troy Sunshade Co 607 Riffle Ave TF: 800-833-8769 ■ Web: bagsbytroy.com	Greenville	OH	45331	937-548-2466		733
Troy Tube & Manufacturing Co 50100 E Russell Schmidt Blvd TF: 800-272-4511 ■ Web: www.troytube.com	Chesterfield	MI	48051	586-949-8700		595

	City	State	Zip	Phone	Fax	Class
Troy University 600 University Ave *Fax: Admissions ■ TF: 800-551-9716 ■ Web: www.troy.edu	Troy	AL	36082	334-670-3100	670-3733*	166
Montgomery 231 Montgomery St PO Box 4419 TF: 888-357-8843 ■ Web: troy.edu	Montgomery	AL	36104	888-357-8843		166
Phenix City 1 University Pl *Fax: Admissions ■ Web: troy.edu	Phenix City	AL	36869	334-297-1007	448-5229*	166
Troy Wesnidge Inc 2024 S Main St TF: 800-318-9806 ■ Web: www.wesnidge.com	Newcastle	OK	73065	405-387-4720		321
Troy-CSL Lighting Inc 14508 Nelson Ave. TF: 800-533-8769 ■ Web: www.troy-lighting.com	City of Industry	CA	91744	626-336-4511	330-4266	439
Troyer Foods Inc 17141 State Rd 4 TF: 800-876-9377 ■ Web: www.troyers.com	Goshen	IN	46528	574-533-0302	533-3851	297-10
Troy-Miami County Public Library 419 W Main St TF: 866-657-8556 ■ Web: www.troypubliclibrary.org	Troy	OH	45373	937-339-0502	335-4880	434-3
Trp Enterprises Inc 333 Summit Square Ct TF: 800-346-4867 ■ Web: www.trpnet.com	Winston-Salem	NC	27101	336-777-1947		463
TRRMC (Twin Rivers Regional Medical Ctr) 1301 First St TF: 800-994-6610 ■ Web: www.twinriversregional.com	Kennett	MO	63857	573-888-4522	888-5525	374-3
TRSA (Textile Rental Services Assn) 1800 Diagonal Rd Ste 200 TF: 877-770-9274 ■ Web: www.trsa.org	Alexandria	VA	22314	703-519-0029	519-0026	49-4
TRSB Inc 276 Saint-Jacques St Ste 900 Web: www.trsb.com	Montreal	QC	H2Y1N3	514-844-4682		317
Tru 676 N St Clair St Web: www.trurestaurant.com	Chicago	IL	60611	312-202-0001		671
Tru Flow Plumbing & Mechanical Inc 27893 Lenox Ave	Madison Heights	MI	48071	248-398-3560		610
Tru Line Manufacturing Inc 3510 Central Pkwy SW Web: www.trulinemfg.com	Decatur	AL	35603	256-350-1002		595
Tru Tech Corp 20 Vaughan Vly Blvd. TF: 888-760-0099 ■ Web: www.trutech.ca	Vaughan	ON	L4H0B1	905-856-0096		499
TRU TECH Systems Inc 24550 N River Rd PO Box 46965 TF: 877-878-8324 ■ Web: www.trutechsystems.com	Mount Clemens	MI	48043	586-469-2700	469-1344	455
Tru Tech Valve LLC 577 W Pike St Web: www.ttvlv.com	Canonsburg	PA	15317	724-916-4805		789
Tru Vue Inc 9400 W 55th St TF: 800-621-8339 ■ Web: www.tru-vue.com	McCook	IL	60525	708-485-5080	485-5980	329
Trubee Collins & Company Inc 1350 One M & T Plaza TF: 800-836-4050 ■ Web: www.trubeecollins.com	Buffalo	NY	14203	716-849-1401		690
Tru-Brew Coffee Service Inc 387 Springdale Ave.	Hatboro	PA	19040	215-441-0110		366
Truck Accessories Group Inc 28858 Ventura Dr Web: www.truckgroup.com	Elkhart	IN	46517	574-522-5337		120
Truck Enterprises Inc 3440 S Main St. Web: www.truckenterprises.com	Harrisonburg	VA	22801	540-564-6900		57
Truck Equipment Service Co 800 Oak St TF: 800-869-0363 ■ Web: www.cornhusker800.com	Lincoln	NE	68521	402-476-3225	476-3726	779
Truck PAC 430 First St SE Ste 100 Web: www.trucking.org	Washington	DC	20003	202-544-6245	675-6568	615
Truck Renting & Leasing Assn (TRALA) 675 N Washington St Ste 410 Web: www.trala.org	Alexandria	VA	22314	703-299-9120	299-9115	49-21
Truck Sales & Service Inc PO Box 262 TF: 800-282-6100 ■ Web: www.trksls.com	Midvale	OH	44653	740-922-3412		57
Truck Tire Sales Inc 426 W Pershing Rd Web: trucktiresalesil.com	Chicago	IL	60609	773-285-3000		57
Truck Utilities Inc 2370 English St TF: 800-869-1075 ■ Web: www.truckutilities.com	Saint Paul	MN	55109	651-484-3305	484-0076	516
Truck Works Inc 1815 S 39th Ave.	Phoenix	AZ	85009	602-233-3713		57
Truckee Donner Public Utility District (TDPUD) 11570 Donner Pass Rd PO Box 309 Web: www.tdpud.org	Truckee	CA	96160	530-587-3896	587-5056	245
Truckee Meadows Community College 7000 Dandini Blvd *Fax: Admissions ■ Web: www.tmcc.edu	Reno	NV	89512	775-673-7000	673-7028*	162
Trucker's Connection 5400 Laurel Springs Pkwy Ste 103 *Fax Area Code: 470 ■ Web: www.truckersconnection.com	Suwanee	GA	30024	678-325-1022	253-7086*	457-21
Truckers Helper LLC, The 630 S Wickham Rd Ste 203 TF: 800-375-8181 ■ Web: www.truckershelper.com	Melbourne	FL	32904	321-956-7331		177
Truckin Movers Corp 1031 Harvest St TF: 800-334-1651 ■ Web: www.truckinmovers.com	Durham	NC	27704	919-682-2300	688-2264	519
Truck-Lite Company Inc 310 E Elmwood Ave TF Cust Svc: 800-562-5012 ■ Web: www.truck-lite.com	Falconer	NY	14733	716-665-6214	665-6403	438
Truckload Carriers Assn (TCA) 555 E Braddock Rd Web: www.truckload.org	Alexandria	VA	22314	703-838-1950	836-6610	49-21
Trucks only 550 S Country Club Dr Web: www.trucksonlysales.com	Mesa	AZ	85210	480-844-7071		516
Truckwell of Alaska Inc 5801 Silverado Way Web: www.truckwell.info	Anchorage	AK	99518	907-349-8845		57
Truco Enterprises LP 10515 King William Dr Web: ontheborderproducts.com	Dallas	TX	75367	972-869-4600	869-8050	297-8
Tru-Cut Inc 1145 Allied Dr Web: www.trucut.com	Sebring	OH	44672	330-938-9806		757
Trudeau Distributing Co 25 Cliff Rd W Ste 115 Web: www.trudeaudistributing.com	Burnsville	MN	55337	952-882-8295		297-6
Trudell Medical Group Ltd 758 Third St TF: 800-757-4881 ■ Web: www.tmml.com	London	ON	N5V5J7	519-685-8800		475
Trudiligence LLC 3190 S Wadsworth Blvd Ste 260 TF: 800-580-0474 ■ Web: www.trudiligence.com	Lakewood	CO	80227	303-692-8445		218
True Blue Inc PO Box 2910 NYSE: TBI ■ *Fax Area Code: 877 ■ TF: 800-610-8920 ■ Web: www.trueblue.com	Tacoma	WA	98401	253-383-9101	733-0399*	721
True Blue Productions 2600 Aberdeen Ave PO Box 27638	Los Angeles	CA	90027	323-661-9191		514
True Drilling LLC 455 N Poplar PO Box 2360 Web: truecos.com	Casper	WY	82602	307-237-9301		540
True Fit Corp 800 W Cummings Pk Ste 6400 Web: www.truefit.com	Woburn	MA	01801	617-848-3740		387
True Fitness Technology Inc 865 Hoff Rd TF: 800-426-6570 ■ Web: www.truefitness.com	O'Fallon	MO	63366	636-272-7100		267
True Homes LLC 2649 Breckenridge Ctr Dr Ste 104 Web: truehomesusa.com	Monroe	NC	28110	704-238-1229	238-1150	187
True Manufacturing Co 2001 E Terra Ln. TF: 800-325-6152 ■ Web: www.truemfg.com	O'Fallon	MO	63366	636-240-2400	272-2408	664
True Media 500 Business Loop 70 W Ste 201 Web: www.truemediaservices.com	Columbia	MO	65203	573-443-8783		6
True North America Inc 2052 Alton Pkwy Web: trueinnovations.com	Irvine	CA	92606	714-368-7464		321
True North Energy LLC 5565 Airport Hwy. TF: 888-245-9336 ■ Web: www.truenorth.org	Toledo	OH	43615	419-868-6800	868-1458	324
True North Strategic Advisors LLC 347 W Berry St Ste 100 Web: www.truenorthsa.com	Fort Wayne	IN	46802	260-420-5050		196
True Partners Consulting LLC 225 W Wacker Dr Ste 1600 Web: www.tpctax.com	Chicago	IL	60606	312-235-3300		194
True Position Technologies Inc 24900 Ave Standford Web: www.truepositiontech.com	Valencia	CA	91355	661-294-0030	294-1240	454
True Solutions Inc 5001 Lyndon B Johnson Fwy Ste 125 Web: www.truesolutions.com	Dallas	TX	75244	972-770-0900		177
True Tech Systems Inc 24550 N River Rd Web: www.truetechsystems.com	Mt. Clemens	MI	48043	815-634-2881		175
True Temper Sports 8275 Tournament Dr Ste 200 TF: 800-355-8783 ■ Web: www.truetemper.com	Memphis	TN	38125	901-746-2000	746-2160	710
True Value Co 8600 W Bryn Mawr Ave TF: 800-897-3112 ■ Web: www.truevaluecompany.com	Chicago	IL	60631	773-695-5000		364
True West 8549 PR 2414 PO Box 441 Web: www.truewesthome.com	Royse City	TX	75189	972-636-7922	635-2059	730
True[X] Media Inc 11925 Wilshire Blvd, Ste 200 Web: www.truex.com	Los Angeles	CA	90025	310-657-9900		5
TrueAccord Corp 148 Townsend St Ste 26 TF: 866-611-2731 ■ Web: www.trueaccord.com	San Francisco	CA	94107	866-611-2731		393
Truebridge Inc 105 Beach St Ste 3 TF: 800-331-8867 ■ Web: www.truebridge.com	Boston	MA	02111	617-956-5020		195
TrueCloud 2147 E Baseline Rd TF: 866-990-8783 ■ Web: www.truecloud.com	Tempe	AZ	85283	866-990-8783		196
trueEX Group LLC 162 Fifth Ave Web: www.trueex.com	New York	NY	10010	646-786-8520		690
Truefit 501 Grant St Ste 1025 Web: www.truefitsolutions.com	Pittsburgh	PA	15219	724-772-5959		809
Truelove & Maclean Inc 57 Callender Rd Web: www.trueloveandmaclean.com	Watertown	CT	06795	860-274-9600		483
Truenorth Development Inc 141 N Ctr St 201 TF: 800-649-3777 ■ Web: www.truen.com	Northville	MI	48167	248-348-6011		463
Truepoint Solutions LLC 5714 Folsom Blvd Ste 236 Web: www.truepointsolutions.com	Sacramento	CA	95819	916-259-1293		177
Truesdail Laboratories Inc 14201 Franklin Ave. Web: www.truesdail.com	Tustin	CA	92780	714-730-6239	730-6462	743
True-Tech Corp 4050 Technology Pl Web: www.true-tech.com	Fremont	CA	94538	510-353-1000		454
Truett-McConnell College 100 Alumni Dr TF: 800-226-8621 ■ Web: www.truett.edu	Cleveland	GA	30528	706-865-2134		166
Truevance Management Inc 7666 Blanding Blvd TF: 800-285-2028 ■ Web: www.truenetcommunications.com	Jacksonville	FL	32244	904-777-9052		261
Tru-Fab Technology Inc 34820 Lakeland Blvd Web: www.trufab.com	Eastlake	OH	44095	440-954-9760		697
Tru-Flex Metal Hose Corp 2391 S State Rd 263 PO Box 247 TF: 800-255-6291 ■ Web: www.tru-flex.com	West Lebanon	IN	47991	765-893-4403		595
TruGreen ChemLawn 860 Ridge Lake Blvd. TF: 866-369-9539 ■ Web: www.trugreen.com	Memphis	TN	38120	866-369-9539		577
Trugrocer Federal Credit Union 501 E Highland St. Web: trugrocer.com	Boise	ID	83706	208-385-5200		219
Truheat Inc 700 Grand St. TF: 800-879-6199 ■ Web: www.ddrheating.com	Allegan	MI	49010	269-673-2145	673-7219	318
Truitt Bros Inc 1105 Front St NE TF: 800-547-8712 ■ Web: www.truittbros.com	Salem	OR	97301	503-362-3674		296-20
Truitt Tingle & Paramore LLC 5346 Stadium Trace Pkwy Ste 202 Web: ttpcpa.com	Hoover	AL	35244	205-733-8265		2
Trujillo & Sons Inc 3325 NW 62nd ST Web: www.trujilloandsons.com	Miami	FL	33147	305-696-8701	696-4510	299
Tru-Kay Manufacturing Co 2 Carol Dr	Lincoln	RI	02865	401-333-2105		409
Trulia Inc 535 Mission St Ste 700 Web: www.trulia.com	San Francisco	CA	94105	415-648-4358		395
Truliant Federal Credit Union 3200 Truliant Way TF: 800-822-0382 ■ Web: www.truliantfcu.org	Winston-Salem	NC	27103	336-659-1955		219

	Phone	Fax	Class
Trulife 26296 Twelve Trees Ln NW Poulsbo WA 98370 *Web:* trulife.com	360-697-5656		477
Truline Corp 9390 Redwood St Las Vegas NV 89139 *TF:* 800-634-6489 ■ *Web:* www.trulinecorp.com	702-362-7495	362-3215	780
Tru-Link Fence Co 5009 West Lake St Melrose Park IL 60610 *TF:* 800-568-9300 ■ *Web:* www.tru-link.com	847-568-9300		279
Trulioo Inc 300 - 420 W Hastings St Vancouver BC V6B1L1 *TF:* 888-773-0179 ■ *Web:* www.trulioo.com	888-773-0179		224
Trulite Glass & Aluminum Solutions LLC 800 Fairway Dr Ste 200 Deerfield Beach FL 33441 *TF:* 800-432-8132 ■ *Web:* www.trulite.com	800-432-8132		480
Trulock Tool Co 113 Drayton St Whigham GA 39897 *TF:* 800-293-9402 ■ *Web:* trulockchokes.com	229-762-4678		295
Truly Nolen of America Inc 3636 E Speedway Blvd Tucson AZ 85716 **Fax Area Code:* 520 ■ *TF:* 800-468-7859 ■ *Web:* www.trulynolen.com	800-528-3442	322-4002*	577
Trumaker Inc 228 Grant Ave Fl 5 San Francisco CA 94109 *TF:* 855-623-3878 ■ *Web:* www.trumaker.com	415-347-8999		690
Truman Arnold Cos 701 S Robison Rd Texarkana TX 75501 **Fax Area Code:* 806 ■ *TF:* 800-235-5343 ■ *Web:* www.tacair.com	903-794-3835	335-2612*	579
Truman Medical Ctr 2301 Holmes St Kansas City MO 64108 *TF:* 800-318-2596 ■ *Web:* www.trumed.org	816-404-1000		353
Truman Medical Ctr Hospital Hill 2301 Holmes St Kansas City MO 64108 *TF:* 800-318-2596 ■ *Web:* www.trumed.org	816-404-1000		374-3
Truman State University 100 E Normal St Kirksville MO 63501 **Fax:* Admissions ■ *TF:* 800-892-7792 ■ *Web:* www.truman.edu	660-785-4000	785-7456*	166
TruMarx Data Partners Inc 30 S Wacker Dr Ste 2200 Chicago IL 60606 *Web:* www.trumarx.com	312-707-9000		387
Trumbull Corp 225 N Shore Dr West Mifflin PA 15212 *Web:* www.trumbullcorp.com	412-807-2000		188-4
Trumbull Correctional Institution 5701 Burnett Rd Leavittsburg OH 44430 *Web:* drc.ohio.gov	330-898-0820	898-0848	213
Trumbull County 160 High St NW Warren OH 44481	330-675-2451	675-2462	338
Trumbull Industries Inc 400 Dietz Rd NE Warren OH 44482 *TF:* 800-477-1799 ■ *Web:* www.trumbull.com	330-393-6624	399-4421	1
Trumbull Kitchen 150 Trumbull St Hartford CT 06103 *Web:* maxrestaurantgroup.com	860-493-7412	493-7416	671
Trumbull Library 33 Quality St Trumbull CT 06611 *Web:* www.trumbullct-library.org	203-452-5197	452-5125	434-3
TruMethods LLC 66 East Main St Ste H Moorestown NJ 08057 *TF:* 800-496-8001 ■ *Web:* www.trumethods.com	856-316-4900		196
Trump International Hotel & Tower 725 Fifth Ave New York NY 10022 **Fax Area Code:* 212 ■ *TF:* 888-448-7867 ■ *Web:* www.trumphotels.com	312-588-8000	299-1150*	379
Trump International Hotel & Tower Las Vegas 2000 N Fashion Show Dr Las Vegas NV 89109 *Web:* www.trumpmiami.com	702-982-0000		378
Trump International Sonesta Beach Resort 255 Washington St Newton MA 02458 *TF:* 800-766-3782 ■ *Web:* www.sonesta.com	305-692-5600	692-5601	669
Trump Organization 725 Fifth Ave New York NY 10022 *Web:* www.trump.com	212-832-2000		360-3
Trump Soho New York 725 Fifth Ave New York NY 10022 *TF:* 855-878-6700 ■ *Web:* www.trumphotels.com	855-878-6700		707
TRUMPF Group 111 Hyde Rd Farmington CT 06032 **Fax:* Mktg ■ *TF:* 800-306-1077 ■ *Web:* www.trumpf.com	860-255-6000	255-6424*	425
Trupar America Inc 160 Wilson Rd Bentleyville PA 15314 *TF:* 800-222-9606 ■ *Web:* www.trupar.com	724-239-2220		770
Truro & District Chamber of Commerce 605 Prince St Truro NS B2N1G2	902-895-6328		137
Trusco Inc 12527 Porr Rd Doylestown OH 44230 *TF:* 800-847-5841 ■ *Web:* www.truscoinc.com	330-658-2027	658-4979	817
Tru-Si Technologies 657 N Pastoria Ave Sunnyvale CA 94085 *Web:* www.trusi.com	408-720-3333		696
TruSignal LLC 25 Sixth Ave N St. Cloud MN 56303 *TF:* 855-569-0426 ■ *Web:* www.tru-signal.com	415-463-1600		387
Trussell Technologies Inc 232 N Lake Ave Ste 300 Pasadena CA 91101 *Web:* www.trusselltech.com	626-486-0560		261
Truss-Pro's Inc 10954 424th Ave Britton SD 57430 *Web:* www.truss-pros.com	605-448-2202		817
Trussway Ltd 9411 Alcorn Rd Houston TX 77093 *Web:* www.trussway.com	713-691-6900	691-2064	817
Trust Bank 600 E Main St PO Box 158 Olney IL 62450 *TF:* 800 766 3451 ■ *Web:* www.trustbank.net	618-395-4311		70
Trust Company of Virginia, The 9030 Stony Point Pkwy Ste 300 Richmond VA 23235 *Web:* www.tcva.com	804-272-9044		70
Trust for Public Land (TPL) 116 New Montgomery St 4th Fl San Francisco CA 94105 *TF:* 800-714-5263 ■ *Web:* www.tpl.org	415-495-4014	495-4103	48-13
Trust Hospitality LLC 806 Douglas Rd 4th Fl Coral Gables FL 33134 *Web:* www.trusthospitality.com	305-537-7040		378
Trustco Bank Corp NY PO Box 1082 Schenectady NY 12301 *NASDAQ: TRST* ■ *TF:* 800-670-3110 ■ *Web:* www.trustcobank.com	518-377-3311		360-2
Trusted Advisor Associates Llc 193 Zeppi Ln West Orange NJ 07052 *TF:* 855-878-7801 ■ *Web:* www.trustedadvisor.com	855-878-7801	886-2819	463
Trusted Computing Group 3855 SW 153rd Dr Beaverton OR 97006 *Web:* www.trustedcomputinggroup.org	503-619-0562		138
Trusted Integration Inc 525 Wythe St Alexandria VA 22314 *Web:* www.trustedintegration.com	703-299-9171		177
Trust-franklin Press Inc 41 Terminal Way Pittsburgh PA 15219 *Web:* www.trust-franklinpress.com	412-481-6442		687
Trustile Doors LLC 1780 E 66th Ave Denver CO 80229 *TF:* 866-442-5302 ■ *Web:* www.trustile.com	303-286-3931		236
Trustmark Construction Corp 841 Sweetwater Ave Florence AL 35630 *Web:* www.trustmarkcorp.com	256-760-9624	760-0902	187
Trustmark Insurance Co 400 Field Dr Lake Forest IL 60045 *TF:* 888-246-9949 ■ *Web:* www.trustmarkinsurance.com	847-615-1500	615-3910	391-2
Trustmark National Bank 248 E Capitol St PO Box 291 Jackson MS 39201 *NASDAQ: TRMK* ■ *TF Cust Svc:* 800-243-2524 ■ *Web:* www.trustmark.com	601-208-5111		360-2
Trustmont Financial Group Inc 200 Brush Run Rd Ste A Greensburg PA 15601 *Web:* www.trustmontgroup.com	724-468-5665		401
Trustus Theatre 520 Lady St Columbia SC 29201 *Web:* www.trustus.org	803-254-9732		572
TrustWorkz 3101 Cobb Pkwy SE Ste 124 Atlanta GA 30339 *Web:* trustworkz.com	770-615-3275		5
TruTech LLC PO Box 6849 Marietta GA 30065 *TF:* 800-842-7296 ■ *Web:* www.trutechinc.com	770-977-2034		577
Trutek 1740 S Main St Salt Lake City UT 84115 *Web:* www.trutek.com	801-486-6655		177
Truth & Advertising 454 N Broadway Santa Ana CA 92701 *Web:* www.truthandadvertising.com	714-542-8778		7
Truth Hardware Inc 700 W Bridge St Owatonna MN 55060 **Fax:* Cust Svc ■ *TF Cust Svc:* 800-866-7884 ■ *Web:* www.truth.com	507-451-5620	451-5655*	350
Truth Publishing Company Inc 421 S Second St Elkhart IN 46516 *TF:* 800-585-5416 ■ *Web:* www.elkharttruth.com	574-294-1661	294-3895	637-8
Truth, The 421 S Second St Elkhart IN 46516 *Web:* www.elkharttruth.com	574-294-1661		532-2
TruTouch Technologies Inc 73 Carriage Way Sudbury MA 01776 *TF:* 866-721-6221 ■ *Web:* www.trutouchtechnologies.com	866-721-6221		583
Trutrak Flight Systems Inc 1500 S Old Missouri Rd Springdale AR 72764 *TF:* 866-878-8725 ■ *Web:* www.trutrakap.com	479-751-0250		529
Truven Health Analytics 777 E Eisenhower Pkwy Ann Arbor MI 48108 *Web:* www.truvenhealth.com	734-913-3000		177
Truwest Credit Union PO Box 3489 Scottsdale AZ 85271 *TF:* 855-878-9378 ■ *Web:* www.truwest.org	480-441-5900		509
Truxtun Radiology Medical Group LP 1817 Truxtun Ave Bakersfield CA 93301 *Web:* www.truxtunrad.com	661-325-6800		415
Trydor Industries (Canada) Ltd 19275 - 25th Ave Surrey BC V3Z3X1 *TF:* 800-567-8558 ■ *Web:* www.trydor.com	604-542-4773	542-4776	791
Tryiton Eyewear LLC 147 Post Rd E Westport CT 06880 *TF:* 888-896-3885 ■ *Web:* www.eyeglasses.com	203-544-0770		543
Tryon Creek State Natural Area 11321 SW Terwilliger Blvd Portland OR 97219 *Web:* www.oregonstateparks.org	503 636 9886		565
Tryon Distributing Company LLC 4701 Stockholm Ct Charlotte NC 28273 *Web:* www.tryondist.com	704-334-0849		80-3
Tryon Trucking Inc PO Box 68 Fairless Hills PA 19030 *TF:* 800-523-5254 ■ *Web:* www.tryontrucking.com	215-295-6622	295-7168	780
TS Civil Engineering Inc 1776 Technology Dr San Jose CA 95110 *Web:* tscivil.com	408-452-9300		261
TS Consulting International 20300 S Vermont Ave Ste 265 Torrance CA 90502	310-965-9810		260
TS Distributors Inc 4404 Windfern Rd Houston TX 77041 *TF:* 800-392-3655 ■ *Web:* www.tsdistributors.com	832-467-5400	467-5454	350
TS Restaurants of California & Hawaii 40 Kupuohi St Ste 206 Lahaina HI 96761 *Web:* www.hulapie.com	808-667-4000		670
TS Tech USA Corp 8400 E Broad St Reynoldsburg OH 43068 *Web:* www.tstech.co.jp/english/company/networkfc/america-usa.html	614-577-1088		247
T&s Trading Co 1110 Ortega St San Francisco CA 94122 *Web:* tandstradingco.com	415-242-1551		175
TS Trim Industries Inc 59 Gender Rd Canal Winchester OH 43110 *Web:* www.tstrim.com	614-837-4114		60
TS3 LLC 1870 General George Patton Dr Franklin TN 37067	615-523-5300	523-7300	393
Tsa Inc 2050 W Sam Houston Pkwy N Houston TX 77043 *Web:* tsa.com	713-935-1500		180
TSA-Advet 4722 Campbells Run Rd Pittsburgh PA 15205 *Web:* www.tsa.advet.com	412-787-0980		177
TSC Apparel LLC 12080 Mosteller Rd Cincinnati OH 45241 **Fax Area Code:* 800 ■ *TF:* 800-543-7230 ■ *Web:* www.tscapparel.com	513-771-1138	248-1069*	156
TSCT (Thaddeus Stevens College of Technology) 750 E King St Lancaster PA 17602 *TF:* 800-842-3832 ■ *Web:* stevenscollege.edu	717-299-7701	391-6929	800
TSD Global 5305 Lakeview Pkwy S Dr Indianapolis IN 46268 *Web:* www.teleservicesdirect.com	317-216-2240		737
TSE Industries Inc 4370 112th Terr N Clearwater FL 33762 *TF:* 800-237-7634 ■ *Web:* www.tse-industries.com	727-573-7676		608
TSEMC (Tri-State Electric Membership Corp) 2310 Blue Ridge Dr Blue Ridge GA 30513 *TF:* 800-351-1111 ■ *Web:* www.tsemc.net	706-492-3251	492-7617	245
TSG Consulting Ii LLC 118 Capitol St Charleston WV 25301 *Web:* tsgsolution.com	304-345-1161		636
Tsg Equity Partners LLC 636 Great Rd Stow MA 01775 *Web:* www.tsgequity.com	978-461-9900		401
Tsg Networks 10462 San Pablo Ave El Cerrito CA 94530 *TF:* 800-573-1874 ■ *Web:* tsgnetworks.com	510-525-6210		175
TSG Partners 1230 Peachtree St 24th Fl Atlanta GA 30309	404-254-1660		70
TSG Solutions Inc 685 Carnegie Dr Ste 210 San Bernardino CA 92408 *Web:* www.tsgsinc.com	909-475-4080		809
TSI (Telephone Systems International Inc) 4400 Marsh Landing Blvd Ste 3 Ponte Vedra Beach FL 32082 *Web:* www.tsiglobe.com	904-686-1470		736

Phone Fax Class

TSI (Thermal Structures Inc)
2362 Railroad St Corona CA 92880 951-736-9911 736-1064 483
Web: www.thermalstructures.com

TSI (Sulphur Institute)
1140 Connecticut Ave NW Ste 612 Washington DC 20036 202-331-9660 293-2940 49-13
Web: www.sulphurinstitute.org

TSI Accessory Group Inc
8350 Lehigh Ave Morton Grove IL 60053 847-965-1700 411

TSI Global Cos
700 Fountain Lakes Blvd Saint Charles MO 63301 636-949-8889 925-2111 735
TF: 800-875-5605 ■ *Web:* www.tsi-global.com

TSI Health Sciences Inc
305 S Fourth St E Ste 101 Missoula MT 59801 406-549-9123 479
TF: 877-549-9123 ■ *Web:* www.tsiinc.com

TSI Holding Co
999 Executive Pkwy Dr Saint Louis MO 63141 314-628-6000 360-3

TSI Inc 500 CaRdigan Rd Shoreview MN 55126 651-483-0900 490-3824 201
TF: 800-874-2811 ■ *Web:* www.tsi.com

TSI International Group
1 Robert Speck Pkwy Mississauga ON L4Z4E8 905-602-7463 655
Web: www.tsi-international.com

TSI Power Corp 1103 W Pierce Ave Antigo WI 54409 715-623-0636 623-2426 253
TF: 800-874-3160 ■ *Web:* www.tsipower.com

Tsleil-Waututh Nation, The
3075 Takaya Dr North Vancouver BC V7H3A8 604-929-3454 138
Web: www.twnation.ca

TSLH (Tempe Saint Luke's Hospital)
1500 S Mill Ave Tempe AZ 85281 480-784-5500 374-3
Web: www.tempestlukeshospital.com

TSM Corp 7622 Bartlett Corporate Dr Bartlett TN 38133 901-373-0300 261
Web: tsmcorporation.com

TSMC (Taiwan Semiconductor Mfg Company Ltd)
2851 Junction Ave San Jose CA 95134 408-382-8000 382-8008 696
NYSE: TSM ■ *TF:* 877-248-4237 ■ *Web:* www.tsmc.com

TSN Inc 4001 Salazar Way PO Box 679 Frederick CO 80530 303-530-0600 530-1919 559
TF General: 888-997-5959 ■ *Web:* bunzldistribution.com

TSO (Traverse Symphony Orchestra)
300 E Front St Ste 230 Traverse City MI 49684 231-947-7120 573-3
Web: www.traversesymphony.org

TSO (Sanford Organization Inc, The)
1000 N Rand Rd Ste 214 Wauconda IL 60084 847-526-2010 526-3993 47
TF: 800-353-6878 ■ *Web:* www.tso.net

TSO3 Inc 2505 Dalton Ave Quebec QC G1P3S5 418-651-0003 653-5726 477
TF: 866-715-0003 ■ *Web:* www.tso3.com

Tsoi/Kobus & Assoc Inc (TKA)
1 Brattle Sq PO Box 9114 Cambridge MA 02238 617-475-4000 475-4445 261
Web: www.tka-architects.com

T-solutions Inc
860 Greenbrier Cir Ste 405 Chesapeake VA 23320 757-410-9450 261
Web: www.tsoln-inc.com

Tsongas Niki (Rep D - MA)
1714 Longworth HOB Washington DC 20515 202-225-3411 226-0771 342-2
Web: tsongas.house.gov

TSPI Inc 20 Pidgeon Hill Dr Ste 106 Sterling VA 20165 877-455-8774 196
TF: 877-455-8774 ■ *Web:* www.tspi.net

TSR Inc 400 Oser Ave Ste 150 Hauppauge NY 11788 631-231-0333 435-1428 721
NASDAQ: TSRI ■ *Web:* www.tsrconsulting.com

TSS Inc 110 E Old Settlers Blvd Round Rock TX 78664 512-310-1000 449
Web: www.totalsitesolutions.com

TSS Technologies Inc
8800 Global Way West Chester OH 45069 513-772-7000 454
Web: tsstech.com

TST Inc 11601 Etiwanda Ave Fontana CA 92337 951-685-2155 487
Web: www.tst-inc.com

TST Infrastructure
61 Inverness Dr E Ste 100 Englewood CO 80112 303-799-5197 463
Web: www.tstinfrastructure.com

TST Solutions Inc
5200 Maingate Dr Mississauga ON L4W1G5 905-625-7500 314
Web: www.tstoverland.com

TST/Impreso Inc 652 Southwestern Blvd Coppell TX 75019 972-462-0100 562-5359* 552-1
**Fax Area Code:* 800 ■ **Fax:* Cust Svc ■ *TF:* 800-527-2878 ■ *Web:* www.tstimpreso.com

TSTA Advocate Magazine 316 W 12th St Austin TX 78701 512-476-5355 457-8
TF: 877-275-8782 ■ *Web:* www.tsta.org

TSTC (Texas State Technical College)
Abilene 650 E Hwy 80 Abilene TX 79601 325-672-7091 643-5987 162
TF: 800-852-8784 ■ *Web:* www.tstc.edu

Tsunami Sushi & Sake Bar
1306 Fulton St San Francisco CA 94117 415-567-7664 671
Web: dajanigroup.net

TSUS (Texas State University System)
208 E Tenth St Ste 600 Austin TX 78701 512-463-1808 463-1816 786
Web: www.tsus.edu

TSYS Loyalty Inc
5897 Windward Pkwy Ste 200 Alpharetta GA 30005 678-297-4350 297-4337 195

TT Electronics 1645 Wallace Dr Carrollton TX 75006 972-323-2200 323-2396 696
TF: 800-341-4747 ■ *Web:* www.optekinc.com

TT Group Inc 702 Carnation Dr Aurora MO 65605 417-678-2181 301
Web: www.tt-group.com

TTC (Toronto Transit Commission)
1900 Yonge St Toronto ON M4S1Z2 416-393-4000 468
TF: 800-223-6192 ■ *Web:* www.ttc.ca

TTC (Trans-Tel Central Inc) 2805 Broce Dr Norman OK 73072 405-447-5025 447-5029 787
TF: 800-729-4636 ■ *Web:* www.trans-tel.com

TTC (Trident Technical College)
7000 Rivers Ave PO Box 118067 North Charleston SC 29406 843-574-6111 574-6483* 800
**Fax:* Admissions ■ *TF:* 877-349-7184 ■ *Web:* www.tridenttech.edu

TTG (TMAD Taylor & Gaines)
300 N Lake Ave 14th Fl Pasadena CA 91101 626-463-2711 261

TTG Consultants
4727 Wilshire Blvd Los Angeles CA 90010 323-936-6600 463
TF: 800-736-8840 ■ *Web:* www.ttgconsultants.com

TTI (Technical Training Inc)
3903 W Hamlin Rd Rochester Hills MI 48309 248-853-5550 113
Web: www.tti-global.com

Tti Environmental Inc
1253 N Church St Moorestown NJ 08057 856-840-8800 41
Web: www.ttienvinc.com

Phone Fax Class

TTI Inc 2441 NE Pkwy Fort Worth TX 76106 817-740-9000 740-9898* 246
**Fax:* Hum Res ■ *TF Sales:* 800-225-5884 ■ *Web:* www.ttiinc.com

TTINC (Thornton-Tomasetti Group Inc)
2000 L St NW Ste 600 Washington DC 20036 202-580-6300 580-6301 261
Web: www.thorntontomasetti.com

TTL Inc 3516 Greensboro Ave Tuscaloosa AL 35401 205-345-0816 256
Web: www.ttlinc.com

TTM Technologies Inc
1665 Scenic Ave Ste 250 Costa Mesa CA 92626 714-327-3000 625
Web: www.ttmtechnologies.com

TTSG (Twinless Twins Support Group International)
PO Box 980481 Ypsilanti MI 48198 888-205-8962 48-21
TF: 888-205-8962 ■ *Web:* www.twinlesstwins.org

TTUSD (Tahoe Truckee Unified School District)
11603 Donner Pass Rd Truckee CA 96161 530-582-2500 582-7606 685
Web: www.ttusd.org

TTV Capital
1230 Peachtree St NE Ste 1150 Atlanta GA 30309 404-347-8400 194
Web: ttvcapital.com

TTX Co 101 N Wacker Dr Chicago IL 60606 312-853-3223 984-3790 264-5
TF: 800-889-4357 ■ *Web:* www.ttx.com

TU (Trout Unlimited)
1300 N 17th St Ste 500 Arlington VA 22209 703-522-0200 284-9400 48-3
TF: 800-834-2419 ■ *Web:* www.tu.org

Tuacahn Amphitheatre & Ctr for the Arts
1100 Tuacahn Dr Ivins UT 84738 435-652-3300 572
Web: www.tuacahn.org

Tualatin Hills Aquatic Ctr
15707 SW Walker Rd Beaverton OR 97006 503-645-6433 564
Web: www.thprd.org/facilities/aquatics/aquatic-center

Tuality Community Hospital
335 SE Eigth Ave Hillsboro OR 97123 503-681-1111 374-3
Web: www.tuality.org

Tuality Healthcare Foundation Inc
335 SE Eighth Ave Hillsboro OR 97123 503-681-1170 305
Web: www.tuality.org/foundation

Tub Springs State Wayside
Tub Springs State Wayside Ashland OR 97520 800-551-6949 565
TF: 800-551-6949 ■ *Web:* www.oregonstateparks.org

Tubac Presidio State Historic Park
1 Burruel St Tubac AZ 85646 520-398-2252 565
Web: azstateparks.com

tubby's 31920 Groesbeck Hwy Fraser MI 48026 800-752-0644 293-5088* 670
**Fax Area Code:* 586 ■ *TF:* 800-752-0644 ■ *Web:* www.tubby.com

Tube Art Group (TAG) 11715 SE Fifth St Bellevue WA 98005 206-223-1122 223-1123 701
TF: 800-562-2854 ■ *Web:* www.tubeart.com

Tube City IMS Corp (TMS)
12 Monongahela Ave Glassport PA 15045 412-678-6141 675-8295 686
NYSE: TMS ■ *TF:* 800-860-2442 ■ *Web:* www.tubecityims.com

Tube Forgings of America Inc
5200 NW Front Ave Portland OR 97210 503-241-0716 595
Web: www.tubeforgings.com

Tube Methods Inc PO Box 460 Bridgeport PA 19405 610-279-7700 277-2005 490
TF: 800-220-2123 ■ *Web:* www.tubemethods.com

Tube Processing Corp
604 E Le Grande Ave Indianapolis IN 46203 317-787-1321 786-3074 490
TF: 800-295-4119 ■ *Web:* www.tubeproc.com

Tube Products Corp
14420 Ewing Ave S Burnsville MN 55306 952-894-2817 723

Tubelite Inc 4878 Mackinaw Trl Reed City MI 49677 800-866-2227 234
TF: 800-866-2227 ■ *Web:* www.tubeliteinc.com

Tube-Mac Industries Ltd
853 Arvin Ave Stoney Creek ON L8E5N8 905-643-8823 605-2
TF: 877-643-8823 ■ *Web:* www.tube-mac.com

Tubetech North America Inc
900 East Taggart St East Palestine OH 44413 330-426-9476 492
Web: www.tubetechnorthamerica.com

Tubman African American Museum
310 Cherry St Macon GA 31201 478-743-8544 743-9063 520
TF: 800-768-3401 ■ *Web:* www.tubmanmuseum.com

Tubular Fabricators Industry Inc
600 W Wythe St Petersburg VA 23803 800-526-0178 595
TF: 800-526-0178 ■ *Web:* www.tfihealthcare.com

Tubular Products
1400 Red Hollow Rd Birmingham AL 35215 205-856-1300 567
Web: www.tubularproducts.com

Tubular Services Inc 1010 Mccarty Dr Houston TX 77029 713-675-6212 595
Web: www.tubularservices.com

Tubular Steel Inc
1031 Executive Pkwy Dr Saint Louis MO 63141 314-851-9200 851-9336 492
TF: 800-388-7491 ■ *Web:* www.tubularsteel.com

Tubular Textile Machinery
113 Woodside Dr Lexington NC 27292 336-956-6444 956-1795 744
Web: www.navisglobal.com

Tucanos Brazilian Grill
545 East University Pkwy Unit 790 Orem UT 84097 801-224-4774 671
Web: www.tucanos.com

Tuckahoe State Park
13070 Crouse Mill Rd Queen Anne MD 21657 410-820-1668 565
Web: dnr2.maryland.gov

Tuckahoe Union Free School District
65 Siwanoy Blvd Eastchester NY 10709 914-337-6600 685
Web: tuckahoeschools.org

Tucker Albin & Assoc Inc
1702 N Collins Blvd Richardson TX 75080 469-424-3033 160
Web: tuckeralbin.net

Tucker Arensberg Inc 1500 1 PPG Pl Pittsburgh PA 15222 412-566-1212 594-5619 428
Web: www.tuckerlaw.com

Tucker Company Worldwide Inc
900 Dudley Ave Cherry Hill NJ 08002 856-317-9600 311
TF: 800-229-7780 ■ *Web:* tuckerco.com

Tucker County 215 First St Ste 201 Parsons WV 26287 304-478-2414 478-2217 338
Web: www.tuckercounty.wv.gov

Tucker County Convention & Visitors Bureau
410 William Ave Davis WV 26260 304-259-5315 206
TF: 800-782-2775 ■ *Web:* www.canaanvalley.org

Tucker Ellis & West LLP
925 Euclid Ave Cleveland OH 44115 216-592-5000 592-5009 428
Web: tuckerellis.com

Name / Address	City	State	ZIP	Phone	Fax	Class
Tucker Lumber Cos LLC 601 N Pearl St *Web:* www.cmtuckerlumber.com	Pageland	SC	29728	843-672-6135	672-5393	683
Tucker Oil Company Inc 910 Industrial Dr. *Web:* www.tuckeroil.net	Slaton	TX	79364	806-828-6277		579
Tucker Printers Inc 270 Middle Rd *Web:* www.tuckerprinters.com	Henrietta	NY	14467	585-359-3030		627
Tucker Rocky Distributing Inc 4900 Alliance Gateway Fwy *Web:* www.tuckerrocky.com	Fort Worth	TX	76177	817-258-9000		61
Tucker Technology Inc 300 Frank H Ogawa Plaza Ste 235 *Web:* www.tuckertech.com	Oakland	CA	94612	510-836-0422		787
Tucker's Place *Historic Soulard* 2117 S 12th St *Web:* www.tuckersplacestl.com	Saint Louis	MO	63104	314-772-5977		671
Tucker-Castleberry Printing Inc 3500 McCall Pl. *TF:* 800-342-5799 ■ *Web:* www.tuckercastleberry.com	Atlanta	GA	30340	770-454-1580		627
Tucows Inc 96 Mowat Ave *TSE: TC* ■ *TF:* 800-371-6992 ■ *Web:* www.tucows.com	Toronto	ON	M6K3M1	416-535-0123	531-5584	397
Tucson AZ, Hilton Garden Inn Hotel 11460 W Hilton Way *Web:* hiltongardeninn1.hilton.com	Avondale	AZ	85323	520-741-0505		377
Tucson Botanical Gardens 2150 N Alvernon Way *Web:* www.tucsonbotanical.org	Tucson	AZ	85712	520-326-9686		97
Tucson Cemetery Assn 3015 N Oracle Rd *Web:* evergreenmortuary-cemetery.com	Tucson	AZ	85705	520-888-7470		510
Tucson Children's Museum 200 S Sixth Ave *Web:* childrensmuseumtucson.org	Tucson	AZ	85702	520-792-9985	792-0639	521
Tucson City Hall 255 W Alameda St *Web:* tucsonaz.gov	Tucson	AZ	85701	520-791-4204	791-5198	337
Tucson Container Corp 6601 S Palo Verde *Web:* www.tucsoncontainer.com	Tucson	AZ	85756	520-746-3171		549
Tucson Convention Ctr 260 S Church Ave. *Web:* tucsonaz.gov	Tucson	AZ	85701	520-791-4101	791-5572	205
Tucson Electric Power PO Box 80077 *Web:* www.tep.com	Prescott	AZ	86304	520-623-7711		787
Tucson Embedded Systems Inc 5620 N Kolb Rd *Web:* www.tucsonembedded.com	Tucson	AZ	85750	520-575-7283	575-5563	177
Tucson Greyhound Park 2601 S Third Ave *Web:* tucsongreyhound.com	Tucson	AZ	85713	520-884-7576	624-9389	133
Tucson International Airport 7250 S Tucson Blvd *TF:* 866-289-9673 ■ *Web:* www.flytucson.com	Tucson	AZ	85756	520-573-8100	573-8008	27
Tucson Jazz Society (TJS) PO Box 41071 Ste 206 *TF:* 800-595-4849 ■ *Web:* www.tucsonjazz.org	Tucson	AZ	85717	520-903-1265		40-4
Tucson Lifestyle Magazine 7000 E Tanque Verde Rd Ste 11 *Web:* www.tucsonlifestyle.com	Tucson	AZ	85715	520-721-2929	721-8665	457-22
Tucson Mall 4500 N Oracle Rd *Web:* www.tucsonmall.com	Tucson	AZ	85705	520-293-7330		460
Tucson Medical Ctr 5301 E Grant Rd *TF:* 800-526-5353 ■ *Web:* www.tmcaz.com	Tucson	AZ	85712	520-327-5461		374-3
Tucson Metropolitan Chamber of Commerce 465 W St Mary's Rd PO Box 991 *Web:* www.tucsonchamber.org	Tucson	AZ	85702	520-792-2250	882-5704	139
Tucson Realty & Trust Co 333 N Wilmont Rd Ste 340 *Web:* www.tucsonrealty.com	Tucson	AZ	85711	520-577-7000	918-3031	655
Tucson Shopper LLC 1861 W Grant Rd	Tucson	AZ	85745	520-622-0101		532-3
Tucson Symphony Orchestra 2175 N Sixth Ave *Web:* www.tucsonsymphony.org	Tucson	AZ	85705	520-792-9155		573-3
Tucson Unified School District No 1 1010 E Tenth St. *TF:* 800-458-5842 ■ *Web:* www.tusd1.org	Tucson	AZ	85719	520-225-6070	798-8767	685
Tucson Weekly 3280 E Hemisphere Loop Ste 180 PO Box 27087 *TF:* 800-639-8783 ■ *Web:* www.tucsonweekly.com	Tucson	AZ	85706	520-294-1200	792-2096	532-5
Tudi Mechanical Systems of Tampa Inc 343 Munson Ave. *TF:* 877-367-8834 ■ *Web:* www.tudi.com	Mc Kees Rocks	PA	15136	412-771-4100	771-7737	610
Tudor Place Historic House & Garden 1644 31st St NW *Web:* www.tudorplace.org	Washington	DC	20007	202-965-0400	965-0164	50-3
Tudor's Biscuit World PO Box 3603 *Web:* www.tudorsbiscuitworld.com	Charleston	WV	25336	304-343-4026		670
Tu-Endie-Wei State Park PO Box 486 *Web:* www.tu-endie-weistatepark.com	Point Pleasant	WV	25550	304-675-0869		565
Tuesday Morning Corp 6250 LBJ Fwy *NASDAQ: TUES* ■ *TF:* 800-457-0099 ■ *Web:* www.tuesdaymorning.com	Dallas	TX	75240	972-387-3562	387-2344	327
Tueth-keeney Cooper Mohan Jackstadt Pc 101 W Vandalia St Ste 210 *Web:* www.tuethkeeney.com	Edwardsville	IL	62025	618-692-4120		445
Tufco Technologies Inc PO Box 23500 *NASDAQ: TFCO* ■ *Web:* www.tufco.com	Green Bay	WI	54305	920-336-0054		554
TUFF SHED Inc 1777 S Harrison St Ste 600 *Web:* www.tuffshed.com	Denver	CO	80210	303-753-8833		321
Tuff Torq Corp 5943 Commerce Blvd. *TF:* 866-572-3441 ■ *Web:* www.tufftorq.com	Morristown	TN	37814	423-585-2000		429
Tuffaloy Products Inc 1400 S Batesville Rd. *TF:* 800-521-3722 ■ *Web:* www.tuffaloy.com	Greer	SC	29650	864-879-0763	877-2212	811
TuffStuff Fitness Equipment Inc 13971 Norton Ave. *TF:* 888-884-8275 ■ *Web:* www.tuffstufffitness.com	Chino	CA	91710	909-629-1600		354
Tuffy Assoc Corp 7150 Granite Cir *TF:* 800-228-8339 ■ *Web:* www.tuffy.com	Toledo	OH	43617	419-865-6900	865-7343	62-5
Tuffy Security Products Inc 25733 Rd H *TF:* 800-348-8339 ■ *Web:* www.tuffyproducts.com	Cortez	CO	81321	970-564-1762		57

Name / Address	City	State	ZIP	Phone	Fax	Class
Tuftco Corp 2318 S Holtzclaw Ave *TF:* 800-288-3826 ■ *Web:* www.tuftco.com	Chattanooga	TN	37408	423-698-8601	698-0842	744
Tuftco Finishing Systems Inc 100 W Industrial Blvd *Web:* www.tuftco.com	Dalton	GA	30720	706-277-1110	277-4334	744
Tuf-Tite Inc 500 Capital Dr *Web:* www.tuf-tite.com	Lake Zurich	IL	60047	847-550-1011		596
Tufts Associated Health Plans 705 Mt Auburn St *TF:* 800-462-0224 ■ *Web:* www.tuftshealthplan.com	Watertown	MA	02472	617-972-9400	972-9409	391-3
Tufts England Medical Ctr *Bone Marrow Transplant Program* 800 Washington St PO Box 15265 *Web:* www.tuftsmedicalcenter.org	Boston	MA	02111	617-636-5000		769
Tufts Library 46 Broad St. *TF:* 888-283-3757 ■ *Web:* weymouth.ma.us	Weymouth	MA	02188	781-337-1402	682-6123	434-3
Tufts Medical Ctr (TMC) 800 Washington St. *TF:* 866-220-3699 ■ *Web:* www.tuftsmedicalcenter.org/default	Boston	MA	02111	617-636-5000	636-8199	374-3
Tufts University 4 Colby St *TF:* 800-326-4001 ■ *Web:* www.tufts.edu	Medford	MA	02155	617-628-5000	627-4079	166
Tufts University Hirsh Health Sciences Library 145 Harrison Ave *Web:* www.library.tufts.edu/hsl	Boston	MA	02111	617-636-6705	636-4039	434-1
Tufts University School of Medicine 136 Harrison Ave *Web:* www.tufts.edu	Boston	MA	02111	617-636-7000	636-3805	167-2
Tufts University Tisch Library 35 Professors Row *Web:* tischlibrary.tufts.edu	Medford	MA	02155	617-627-3345	627-3002	434-6
Tug Mcgraw Foundation 1303 Jefferson St Ste 100b. *TF:* 800-886-2282 ■ *Web:* tugmcgraw.org	Napa	CA	94559	707-255-1884		463
Tug Technologies Corp 1995 Duncan Dr *Web:* www.tugtech.com	Kennesaw	GA	30144	770-422-7230		454
Tugaloo State Park 1763 Tugaloo State Pk Rd. *Web:* www.gastateparks.org	Lavonia	GA	30553	706-356-4362		565
Tugboat Inn 80 Commercial St PO Box 267 *TF:* 800-248-2628 ■ *Web:* www.tugboatinn.com	Boothbay Harbor	ME	04538	207-633-4434	633-5892	379
Tujays Machine Works Inc 426 Blue Bell Rd *Web:* www.tujays.biz	Houston	TX	77037	281-447-6325		567
Tuk Tuk Thai 8875 W Pico Blvd *Web:* delivery.com	Los Angeles	CA	90035	310-860-1872		671
Tukaiz Communications LLC 2917 N Latoria Ln *TF:* 800-543-2674 ■ *Web:* www.tukaiz.com	Franklin Park	IL	60131	847-455-1588		7
Tukatech Inc 5462 Jillson St *Web:* www.tukatech.com	Los Angeles	CA	90040	323-726-3836	726-3866	179
Tuktut Nogait National Park of Canada PO Box 91 *Web:* www.pc.gc.ca	Paulatuk	NT	X0E1N0	867-580-3233	580-3231	563
Tukwila Reporter, The 19426 68th Ave S Ste A *Web:* www.pnwlocalnews.com	Kent	WA	98032	253-872-6600		532-3
Tula International Inc PO Box 550628 *Web:* www.tulainternational.com	Atlanta	GA	30355	404-543-2835		260
Tulalip Resort Casino 10200 Quil Ceda Blvd. *TF:* 888-272-1111 ■ *Web:* www.tulalipresortcasino.com	Tulalip	WA	98271	888-272-1111		707
Tulane Medical Ctr (TMC) 1415 Tulane Ave *TF:* 800-588-5800 ■ *Web:* www.tulanehealthcare.com	New Orleans	LA	70112	504-988-5263		374-3
Tulane University 6823 St Charles Ave *Fax: Admissions ■ *TF Admissions:* 800-873-9283 ■ *Web:* www.tulane.edu	New Orleans	LA	70118	504-865-5000	862-8715*	166
Tulane University Howard-Tilton Memorial Library 310 Richardson Bldg *Web:* library.tulane.edu	New Orleans	LA	70118	504-862-3295	314-7693	434-6
Tulane University Law School 6329 Freret St Weinmann Hall *Fax: Admissions ■ *TF:* 800-328-6819 ■ *Web:* www.law.tulane.edu	New Orleans	LA	70118	504-865-5930	865-6710*	167-1
Tulane University School of Medicine 1555 Poydras St Ste 1000 *Web:* tulane.edu	New Orleans	LA	70118	504-988-5462		167-2
Tulare County 2800 W Burrel Ave *Web:* www.tularecounty.ca.gov	Visalia	CA	93291	559-636-5005	733-6318	338
Tulare County Library System 200 W Oak Ave *TF:* 800-540-6880 ■ *Web:* www.tularecountylibrary.org	Visalia	CA	93291	559-713-2700		434-3
Tulare Joint Union High School District 426 N Blackstone Ave *Web:* www.tulare.k12.ca.us	Tulare	CA	93274	559-688-2021	687-7317	685
Tulare Nursing & Rehabilitation 680 E Merritt Ave *TF:* 800-284-0311 ■ *Web:* missioncaregroup.com	Tulare	CA	93274	559-686-8581		450
Tulare Public Library 475 N M St *TF:* 800-611-1911 ■ *Web:* www.tularepubliclibrary.org	Tulare	CA	93274	559-685-4500		434-3
Tulare Regional Medical Ctr 869 N Cherry St *Web:* www.tulareregional.org	Tulare	CA	93274	559-685-3462		374-3
Tulco Oils Inc 5240 E Pine *TF:* 800-375-2347 ■ *Web:* www.tulco.com	Tulsa	OK	74115	918-838-3354	834-1263	579
Tule Elk State Reserve 8653 Station Rd *Web:* www.parks.ca.gov/default.asp?page_id=584	Buttonwillow	CA	93206	661-764-6881		565
Tule River Co-op Dryer Inc 16548 Rd 168 PO Box 4477	Porterville	CA	93257	559-686-4685		296-18
Tulio Ristorante 1100 Fifth Ave *Web:* www.tulio.com	Seattle	WA	98101	206-624-5500		671
Tulip City Air Service Inc 1581 S Washington Ave *TF:* 800-748-0515 ■ *Web:* www.tulipcityair.com	Holland	MI	49423	616-392-7831	392-1841	13
Tulip Corp 714 E Keefe Ave. *TF:* 800-565-9931 ■ *Web:* www.tulipcorp.com	Milwaukee	WI	53212	414-963-3120		199
Tulip Corp 3125 Highland Ave *TF:* 800-684-4774 ■ *Web:* www.tulipcorp.com	Niagara Falls	NY	14305	716-282-1261	285-6075	199

Name / Address	City	State	ZIP	Phone	Fax	Class
Tulloch Engineering Inc 200 Main St *TF:* 800-797-2997 ■ *Web:* www.tulloch.ca	Thessalon	ON	P0R1L0	705-842-3372		256
Tully Rinckey PLLC 441 New Karner Rd *Web:* www.tullylegal.com	Albany	NY	12205	518-218-7100		428
Tully's Coffee Corp 3100 Airport Way *Web:* tullyscoffeeshops.com	Seattle	WA	98134	206-233-2070		159
Tulmar Safety Systems Inc 1123 Cameron St *Web:* www.tulmar.com	Hawkesbury	ON	K6A2B8	613-632-1282		21
Tulnoy Lumber Inc 1620 Webster Ave *Web:* www.tulnoylumber.com	Bronx	NY	10457	718-901-1700	299-8920	191-3
Tulsa Air & Space Museum 3624 N 74 E Ave *Web:* www.tulsaairandspacemuseum.org	Tulsa	OK	74115	918-834-9900	834-6723	520
Tulsa Ballet 1212 E 45th Pl *Web:* www.tulsaballet.org	Tulsa	OK	74105	918-749-6030	749-0532	573-1
Tulsa Centerless Bar Processing 1605 N 168th E Ave *Web:* tulsacenterless.com	Tulsa	OK	74116	918-438-0000		454
Tulsa City Hall 175 E Second St Fl 14 *TF:* 800-522-6543 ■ *Web:* www.cityoftulsa.org	Tulsa	OK	74103	918-596-2100	596-9010	337
Tulsa City-County Library (TCCL) 400 Civic Ctr *Web:* www.tulsalibrary.org	Tulsa	OK	74103	918-549-7323		434-3
Tulsa Community College *Metro* 909 S Boston Ave **Fax:* Admissions ■ *Web:* www.tulsacc.edu	Tulsa	OK	74119	918-595-7000	595-7347*	162
Northeast 3727 E Apache St *Web:* www.tulsacc.edu	Tulsa	OK	74115	918-595-7000	595-7594	162
Southeast 10300 E 81st St *Web:* www.tulsacc.edu	Tulsa	OK	74133	918-595-7000	595-7748	162
West 7505 W 41st St *Web:* www.tulsacc.edu	Tulsa	OK	74107	918-595-7000	595-8130	162
Tulsa Convention & Visitors Bureau 1 W Third St Ste 100 *TF:* 800-558-3311 ■ *Web:* www.visittulsa.com	Tulsa	OK	74103	800-558-3311		206
Tulsa Convention Ctr 100 Civic Ctr *TF:* 800-678-7177 ■ *Web:* www.coxcentertulsa.com	Tulsa	OK	74103	918-894-4350		205
Tulsa County 500 S Denver Ave Ste 120 *Web:* www.tulsacounty.org	Tulsa	OK	74103	918-596-5801	596-5819	338
Tulsa Dynaspan Inc 1601 E Houston *Web:* www.dynaspan.com	Broken Arrow	OK	74012	918-258-1549		182
Tulsa Federal Credit Union 9323 E 21st St *Web:* tulsafederalcu.org	Tulsa	OK	74129	918-610-0200		219
Tulsa Garden Ctr 2435 S Peoria Ave *Web:* www.tulsagardencenter.com	Tulsa	OK	74114	918-746-5125	746-5128	97
Tulsa Heaters Inc 1215 S Boulder Ste 1200 *Web:* www.tulsaheaters.com	Tulsa	OK	74119	918-582-9918	582-9916	14
Tulsa Inspection Resources LLC 5727 S Lewis Ave Ste 300 *Web:* www.tulsainspection.com	Tulsa	OK	74105	918-274-1100		41
Tulsa International Airport 7777 E Apache Rm A-217 *Web:* www.tulsaairports.com	Tulsa	OK	74115	918-838-5000	838-5199	27
Tulsa Metro Chamber 1 W Third St Ste 100 *TF:* 888-424-9411 ■ *Web:* www.tulsachamber.com	Tulsa	OK	74103	918-585-1201		139
Tulsa Opera 1610 S Boulder Ave *TF:* 866-298-2530 ■ *Web:* www.tulsaopera.com	Tulsa	OK	74119	918-582-4035	592-0380	573-2
Tulsa Performing Arts Ctr 110 E Second St *Web:* www.tulsapac.com	Tulsa	OK	74103	918-596-7122	596-7144	572
Tulsa Promenade 4107 S Yale Ave *Web:* www.tulsapromenade.com	Tulsa	OK	74135	918-627-9282	663-9385	460
Tulsa Public Schools 3027 S New Haven Ave **Fax:* Hum Res ■ *TF:* 866-632-9992 ■ *Web:* tulsaschools.org	Tulsa	OK	74114	918-746-6800	746-6144*	685
Tulsa Rig Iron Inc 4457 W 151st PO Box 880 *Web:* www.tulsarigiron.com	Kiefer	OK	74041	918-321-3330	321-3099	386
Tulsa Welding School Inc 2545 E 11th St *TF:* 800-331-2934 ■ *Web:* www.weldingschool.com	Tulsa	OK	74104	918-587-6789		743
Tulsa Winch Group 11135 S James Ave *Web:* www.team-twg.com	Jenks	OK	74037	918-298-8300	298-8301	190
Tulsa World 315 S Boulder Ave *TF:* 800-897-3557 ■ *Web:* www.tulsaworld.com	Tulsa	OK	74103	918-583-2161	581-8353	532-2
Tulsa Zoo 6421 E 36th St N *Web:* tulsazoo.org	Tulsa	OK	74115	918-669-6600		823
Tulsair Beechcraft Inc 3207 N Sheridan Rd *TF:* 800-331-4071 ■ *Web:* www.tulsair.com	Tulsa	OK	74115	918-835-7651	835-7413	24
Tulstar Products Inc 5510 S Lewis Ave *Web:* www.tulstar.com	Tulsa	OK	74105	918-749-9060	747-1444	146
Tum Yeto Inc 2001 Commercial St *Web:* www.tumyeto.com	San Diego	CA	92113	619-232-7523		711
Tumacacori National Historical Park 1891 E Frontage Rd PO Box 8067 *TF:* 800-444-7275 ■ *Web:* www.nps.gov/tuma	Tumacacori	AZ	85640	520-377-5060	398-9271	564
Tumalo State Park 64120 OB Riley Rd *Web:* www.oregonstateparks.org	Bend	OR	97701	541-382-3586		565
Tumbleweed Inc 2301 River Rd *TF:* 866-719-3892 ■ *Web:* www.tumbleweedrestaurants.com	Louisville	KY	40206	502-893-0323		670
Tumbling River Ranch 3715 Pk County Rd 62 PO Box 30 *TF:* 800-654-8770 ■ *Web:* www.tumblingriver.com	Grant	CO	80448	303-838-5981	838-5133	239
Tundra Engineering Associates Ltd 1331 Macleod Trail SE	Calgary	AB	T2G1E1	403-777-2477		256
Tundra Lodge Resort & Waterpark 865 Lombardi Ave *TF:* 877-886-3725 ■ *Web:* www.tundralodge.com	Green Bay	WI	54304	920-405-8700	405-1997	669
Tundra Oil & Gas Ltd 1700 One Lombard Pl *Web:* www.tundraoilandgas.com	Winnipeg	MB	R3B0X3	204-934-5850		536
Tundra Process Solutions Ltd 7523 Flint Rd SE *TF:* 800-265-1166 ■ *Web:* www.tundrasolutions.ca	Calgary	AB	T2H1G3	403-255-5222		111
Tungle Corp 410 rue Saint-Nicolas Ste 260	Montreal	QC	H2Y2P5	514-678-9181		387
Tunheim Partners 8009 34th Ave S *Web:* www.tunheim.com	Minneapolis	MN	55425	952-851-1600		636
Tunica County Administrators Department 1058 S Court St *TF:* 800-318-2596 ■ *Web:* www.tunicacounty.com	Tunica	MS	38676	662-363-1465		338
Tunica MS 13625 Hwy 61 N *TF:* 888-488-6422 ■ *Web:* www.tunicatravel.com	Tunica Resorts	MS	38664	888-488-6422		206
Tunisia 31 Beekman Pl	New York	NY	10022	212-751-7503		784
Tunnel Duty Free Shop Inc 465 Goyeau St *TF:* 800-669-2105 ■ *Web:* www.tunneldutyfree.com	Windsor	ON	N9A1H1	519-252-2713		241
Tunnel Hill State Trail 302 E Vine St	Vienna	IL	62995	618-658-2168		565
Tunnell Consulting 900 E Eigth Ave Ste 106 *Web:* www.tunnellconsulting.com	King of Prussia	PA	19406	610-337-0820	337-1884	194
Tunstall Consulting Inc 13153 N Dale Mabry Hwy Ste 200 *Web:* www.tunstallconsulting.com	Tampa	FL	33618	813-968-4461	961-2315	194
Tunxis Community College 271 Scott Swamp Rd *Web:* tunxis.edu	Farmington	CT	06032	860-773-1300		162
Tuohy Furniture Corp 42 St Albans Pl *TF Cust Svc:* 800-533-1696 ■ *Web:* www.tuohyfurniture.com	Chatfield	MN	55923	507-867-4280	867-3374	319-1
Tuolumne County 2 S Green St *TF:* 800-743-5002 ■ *Web:* www.co.tuolumne.ca.us	Sonora	CA	95370	209-533-5511	533-5510	338
Tuolumne County Chamber of Commerce 222 S Shepherd St *TF:* 877-532-4212 ■ *Web:* www.tcchamber.com	Sonora	CA	95370	209-532-4212	532-8068	139
Tupelo Ballet Co 775 Poplarville Dr *Web:* www.tupeloballet.com	Tupelo	MS	38801	662-844-1928		573-1
Tupelo Buffalo Park & Zoo 2272 N Coley Rd *Web:* www.tupelobuffalopark.com	Tupelo	MS	38803	662-844-8709	844-8850	823
Tupelo City Hall 71 E Troy St *Web:* www.tupeloms.gov	Tupelo	MS	38804	662-841-6513	840-2075	337
Tupelo Community Theatre 201 N Broadway PO Box 1094 *Web:* www.tctwebstage.com/lyric.htm	Tupelo	MS	38802	662-844-1935	844-2990	572
Tupelo Furniture Market Inc 1879 N Coley Rd *Web:* www.tupelofurnituremarket.com	Tupelo	MS	38801	662-842-4442		321
Tupelo Honey Cafe 12 College St *Web:* www.tupelohoneycafe.com	Asheville	NC	28801	828-255-4863		671
Tupelo National Battlefield 2680 Natchez Trace Pkwy *TF:* 800-305-7417 ■ *Web:* www.nps.gov	Tupelo	MS	38804	662-680-4025	680-4033	564
Tupelo Public School District 72 S Green St *Web:* www.tupeloschools.com	Tupelo	MS	38804	662-841-8850	841-8887	685
Tupelo Regional Airport 105 Lemons Dr *Web:* www.flytupelo.com	Tupelo	MS	38801	662-823-4359	823-8329	27
Tupelo Symphony Orchestra 1800 W Main St *Web:* nmsymphony.com	Tupelo	MS	38801	662-842-8433		573-3
Tupperware Corp 14901 S Orange Blossom Trail *NYSE:* TUP ■ *TF Cust Svc:* 800-468-9716 ■ *Web:* ir.tupperwarebrands.com	Orlando	FL	32837	407-826-5050		607
Tuptim 4896 Washtenaw Ave *Web:* www.tuptim.com	Ann Arbor	MI	48108	734-528-5588	528-2569	671
Turano Baking Co 6501 Roosevelt Rd *Web:* www.turano.com	Berwyn	IL	60402	708-788-9220	788-3075	296-1
Turbeville Correctional Institution 1578 Clarence Coker Hwy *Web:* www.doc.sc.gov/institutions/turbeville.jsp	Turbeville	SC	29162	843-659-4800		213
Turbine Engine Components Technologies Corp (TECT) 334 Beechwood Rd Ste 304 *Web:* www.tectcorp.com	Ft Mitchell	KY	41017	859-426-0090		483
Turbo 2 n 1 Grip 46460 Continental Dr *TF:* 800-530-9878 ■ *Web:* www.turbogrips.com	Chesterfield	MI	48047	586-598-3948		711
Turbo International Inc 2151 Las Palmas Dr Ste E *TF:* 800-238-8726 ■ *Web:* www.turbointernational.com	Carlsbad	CA	92011	760-476-1444		791
Turbo Mechanical Inc 515 McPhee Rd SW *Web:* www.turbomechanical.com	Olympia	WA	98502	360-943-1888		41
Turbo Parts LLC 767 Pierce Rd Ste 2 *TF:* 800-446-4776 ■ *Web:* www.mdaturbines.com	Clifton Park	NY	12065	518-885-3100		54
Turbo Refrigerating 1000 W Ormsby Ave *TF:* 800-853-8648 ■ *Web:* www.vogtice.com	Louisville	KY	40210	502-635-3000	634-0479	664
Turbo Resources International Inc 5780 W Oakland St *Web:* www.turboresources.com	Chandler	AZ	85226	480-961-3600	961-1775	770
Turbo Wholesale Tires Inc 5793 Martin Rd *Web:* turbotiresonline.com	Irwindale	CA	91706	626-856-1400		754
TURBOCAM Inc 607 Calef Hwy *TF:* 800-791-0133 ■ *Web:* www.turbocam.com	Barrington	NH	03825	603-905-0200		641
TurboCare Chicopee 2140 Westover Rd	Chicopee	MA	01022	413-593-0500		454
Turbo-Chem International Inc 106 W Saul *Web:* www.turbochem.com	Scott	LA	70583	337-235-3098		538
TurboLinux Inc 600 Townsend St	San Francisco	CA	94103	415-503-4330		178-12
Turbotec Products Inc 651 Day Hill Rd *TF:* 800-394-1633 ■ *Web:* turbotecproducts.com	Windsor	CT	06095	860-731-4200		295
Turbotek Computer Corp 70 Zachary Rd Ste 3 *TF:* 800-573-5393 ■ *Web:* turbotekcomputer.com	Manchester	NH	03109	603-666-3062		180
TURCK Chartwell Canada Inc 140 Duffield Dr *Web:* chartwell.ca	Markham	ON	L6G1B5	905-513-7100		246
Turck Inc 3000 Campus Dr *Web:* www.turck.com	Minneapolis	MN	55441	763-553-7300		385
Turek Farms 8558 State Rt 90 *Web:* www.turekfarms.com	King Ferry	NY	13081	315-364-8735	364-5257	10-11

Phone | Fax | Class

Turelk Inc
3700 Santa Fe Ave Ste 200 Long Beach CA 90810 310-835-3736 186
Web: www.turelk.com

Turf Hotels Inc
792 Watervliet Shaker Rd Latham NY 12110 518-786-0976 378
Web: www.turfhotels.com

Turf Management Systems LLC
PO Box 26389 Birmingham AL 35260 205-979-8604 422
Web: www.turfmanagementsystems.com

Turf Paradise Racetrack
1501 W Bell Rd Phoenix AZ 85023 602-942-1101 942-8659 642
TF: 800-639-8783 ■ *Web:* www.turfparadise.com

Turf Store.com
237 Boling Industrial Way SE Calhoun GA 30701 706-629-1675 361
TF: 800-726-0559 ■ *Web:* www.turfstore.com

Turf Valley Resort & Conference Ctr
2700 Turf Valley Rd Ellicott City MD 21042 410-465-1500 669
Web: www.turfvalley.com

Turfgrass Producers International
1855-A Hicks Rd Rolling Meadows IL 60008 847-705-9898 138
TF: 800-405-8873 ■ *Web:* www.turfgrasssod.org

TurfNet Media Network
5276 Wynterhall Way Atlanta GA 30338 770-395-9850 387
Web: www.turfnet.com

Turfway Park LLC 7500 Turfway Rd Florence KY 41042 859-371-0200 642
Web: www.turfway.com

Turkey
Consulate General
455 N Cityfront Plaza Dr Ste 2900 Chicago IL 60611 312-263-0644 263-1449 257
Web: www.chicago.cg.mfa.gov.tr
Consulate General
1990 Post Oak Blvd Ste 1300 Houston TX 77056 713-622-5849 623-6639 257
TF: 888-566-7656 ■ *Web:* www.houston.cg.mfa.gov.tr
Consulate General
6300 Wilshire Blvd Ste 2010 Los Angeles CA 90048 323-655-8832 655-8681 257
Web: www.losangeles.cg.mfa.gov.tr
Consulate General
825 Third Ave 28th Fl New York NY 10022 646-430-6560 983-1293* 257
**Fax Area Code: 212* ■ *Web:* www.newyork.cg.mfa.gov.tr
Embassy 2525 Massachusetts Ave NW Washington DC 20008 202-612-6700 319-1639 257
Web: www.washington.emb.mfa.gov.tr/default.aspx

Turkey Bluffs State Fish & Wildlife Area
4301 S Lakeside Dr Chester IL 62233 618-826-2706 565
Web: www.dnr.illinois.gov

Turkey Hill Dairy Inc 2601 River Rd Conestoga PA 17516 717-872-5461 872-0602 296-25
TF: 800-693-2479 ■ *Web:* www.turkeyhill.com

Turkey Run State Park 8121 Pk Rd Marshall IN 47859 765-597-2635 565
Web: www.in.gov

Turkey Valley Farms
112 S Sixth St PO Box 200 Marshall MN 56258 507-337-3100 337-3009 619
Web: www.turkeyvalleyfarms.com

Turkmenistan
Embassy 2370 Massachusetts Ave NW Washington DC 20008 202-939-5688 797-0595 257

Turks & Caicos Islands Tourism Office
225 W 35th St Ste 1200 New York NY 10001 646-375-8830 775
TF: 800-241-0824 ■ *Web:* www.turksandcaicostourism.com

Turley Publications Inc 24 Water St Palmer MA 01069 413-283-8393 532-3
Web: www.turley.com

Turlington & Co 509 E Ctr St Lexington NC 27292 336-249-6856 2
Web: www.turlingtonandcompany.com

Turlock Chamber of Commerce
115 S Golden State Blvd Turlock CA 95380 209-632-2221 632-5289 139
TF: 800-834-0401 ■ *Web:* turlockchamber.com

Turlock Convention & Visitors Bureau
115 S Golden State Blvd Turlock CA 95380 209-632-2221 206
Web: www.turlockchamber.com/visit_turlock

Turlock Journal 138 S Center St Turlock CA 95380 209-634-9141 632-8813 532-2
Web: www.turlockjournal.com

Turlock Lake State Recreation Area
22600 Lake Rd Columbia CA 95310 209-874-2056 565
Web: www.parks.ca.gov/default.asp?page_id=555

Turn Key Distribution Systems Inc
450 Broadway Malden MA 02148 781-322-3000 180
Web: turnkey.com

Turnaround for Children Inc
25 W 45th St 6th Fl New York NY 10036 646-786-6200 242
Web: turnaroundusa.org

Turner & Burney Pc Attorneys
105 W Public Sq Laurens SC 29360 864-984-6565 428
TF: 800-518-0234 ■ *Web:* www.turnerandburney.com

Turner Broadcasting System Inc
1050 Techwood Dr NW Atlanta GA 30318 404-827-3111 878-4640 740
Web: www.tbs.com

Turner Broadcasting System Inc (TBS)
1 CNN Ctr Atlanta GA 30303 404-827-1700 740
Web: www.turner.com

Turner Classic Movies (TCM)
1050 Techwood Dr NW Atlanta GA 30318 404-551-0921 740
Web: www.tcm.turner.com

Turner Construction Co 375 Hudson St New York NY 10014 212-229-6000 186
Web: www.turnerconstruction.com

Turner Consulting Group Inc
306 Florida Ave NW Washington DC 20001 202-986-5533 177
Web: www.tcg.com

Turner Corp 375 Hudson St New York NY 10014 212-229-6000 360-3
TF: 800-327-1997 ■ *Web:* www.turnerconstruction.com

Turner County PO Box 191 Ashburn GA 31714 229-567-2334 567-4794 338
TF: 800-436-7442 ■ *Web:* georgia.gov

Turner County Board of Education
423 N Cleveland St Ashburn GA 31714 229-567-3338 567-3285 685
Web: www.turner.k12.ga.us

Turner County Clerk of Courts
400 S Main St P.O. Box 446 Parker SD 57053 605-297-3115 297-2115 338

Turner County Stockyard
1315 US Hwy 41 S Ashburn GA 31714 229-567-3371 567-3785 446
TF: 800-344-9808 ■ *Web:* turnercountystockyard.com

Turner Dairy Farms Inc
1049 Jefferson Rd Pittsburgh PA 15235 412-372-2211 296-25
TF: 800-892-1039 ■ *Web:* www.turnerdairy.net

Turner Designs Hydrocarbon Instruments Inc
2023 N Gateway Ste 101 Fresno CA 93727 559-253-1414 358
Web: www.oilinwatermonitors.com

Turner Electric LLC
131 Enterprise Dr Edwardsville IL 62025 618-797-5000 729
Web: www.turnerswitch.com

Turner EnviroLogic Inc
1140 SW 34 Ave Deerfield Beach FL 33442 954-422-9787 261
Web: www.tenviro.com

Turner Foundation Inc
133 Luckie St 2nd Fl Atlanta GA 30303 404-681-9900 681-0172 305
Web: www.turnerfoundation.org

Turner Free Library 2 N Main St Randolph MA 02368 781-961-0932 434-3
TF: 800-733-2767 ■ *Web:* turnerfreelibrary.org

Turner Gas Company Inc
2825 West 500 South Salt Lake City UT 84126 801-973-6886 973-6882 579

Turner Hall Restaurant
1038 N Fourth St Milwaukee WI 53203 414-276-4844 276-0442 671
Web: www.foodspot.com

Turner Industries Group LLC
8687 United Plaza Blvd Baton Rouge LA 70809 225-922-5050 188-9
TF: 800-288-6503 ■ *Web:* www.turner-industries.com

Turner Investment Partners Inc
1205 Westlakes Dr Ste 100 Berwyn PA 19312 484-329-2300 401
TF: 800-224-6312 ■ *Web:* www.turnerinvestments.com

Turner Michael (Rep R - OH)
2368 Rayburn HOB Washington DC 20515 202-225-6465 225-6754 342-2
Web: turner.house.gov

Turner Plastic Innovations
1400 Production Dr Burlington KY 41005 859-525-9020 627
Web: turnerplastics.com

Turner Public Relations Inc
614 15th St 4th Fl Denver CO 80202 303-333-1402 636
Web: www.turnerpr.com

Turner Roofing & Sheet Metal Inc
1200 E Memphis St Broken Arrow OK 74012 918-258-2585 189-12
Web: www.turnerroofing.com

Turner Techtronics Inc
3200 W Burbank Blvd Burbank CA 91505 818-973-1060 175
TF: 800-310-4884 ■ *Web:* www.turnertech.com

Turner Universal
336 James Record Rd Huntsville AL 35824 256-461-6700 186
Web: www.turnerconstruction.com

Turner Vedrenne & Howard PC
9330 Lbj Fwy Ste 875 Dallas TX 75243 972-644-4131 2
Web: tvhcpas.com

Turner Warren Hwang & Conrad
100 N First St Ste 202 Burbank CA 91502 818-954-9700 2
Web: www.twhc.com

Turner's Outdoorsman
11738 Sanmarino St Ste A Rancho Cucamonga CA 91730 909-923-4422 711
Web: www.turners.com

Turner, Padget, Graham & Laney PA
1901 Main St 17th Fl Columbia SC 29202 803-254-2200 428
Web: www.turnerpadget.com

Turner-Brooks Inc
28811 John R Rd Madison Heights MI 48071 248-548-3400 548-9213 189-2

Turner-Dodge House & Heritage Ctr
100 E N St Lansing MI 48906 517-483-4220 50-3

Turner-Fairbank Highway Research Ctr
6300 Georgetown Pike McLean VA 22101 800-424-9071 493-3170* 668
**Fax Area Code: 202* ■ *TF:* 800-424-9071 ■ *Web:* www.fhwa.dot.gov

Turners Fine Furniture Co
707 Second St W Tifton GA 31794 229-382-3266 321
TF: 800-420-2337 ■ *Web:* turnerfurniture.com

Turning Point Community Programs
3440 Viking Dr Ste 114 Sacramento CA 95827 916-364-8395 48-5
Web: www.tpcp.org

Turning Point Hospital
3015 Veterans Pkwy PO Box 1177 Moultrie GA 31776 229-985-4815 726
TF: 800-342-1075 ■ *Web:* www.turningpointcare.com

Turning Point Inc, The
1835 W State Rt 89A Ste 4 Sedona AZ 86336 928-203-9711 196
Web: www.turningpoint.com

Turning Point of Tampa 6227 Sheldon Rd Tampa FL 33615 813-882-3003 885-6974 726
TF: 800-397-3006 ■ *Web:* www.tpoftampa.com

Turning Stone Resort Casino LLC
5218 Patrick Rd Verona NY 13478 315-361-7711 133
TF: 800-771-7711 ■ *Web:* turningstone.com

Turn-key Medical Inc
365 SW Fifth Ave Meridian ID 83642 208-888-1760 475
Web: turn-keymedical.com

Turnkey Millwork 6231 Westgate Rd Raleigh NC 27617 919-782-2708 499
Web: www.turnkeymillwork.com

Turn-Key Solutions Inc
4920 W Thunderbird Rd Ste C-120 Glendale AZ 85306 602-863-0269 737
Web: www.tksnation.com

Turnkey Sports & Entertainment Inc
9 Tanner St Haddonfield NJ 08033 856-685-1450 260
Web: turnkeyse.com

Turnkey Technologies Inc
2500 Main St Ext Ste 10 Sayreville NJ 08872 732-553-9100 246
Web: www.turn-keytechnologies.com

Turnroth Sign Company Inc
1207 E Rock Falls Rd Rock Falls IL 61071 815-625-1155 701

Turocy & Watson LLP
Key Tower 127 Public Sq 57th Fl Cleveland OH 44114 216-696-8730 428
Web: www.thepatentattorneys.com

Turover-Straus Group Inc
4145 S Mccann Ct B Springfield MO 65804 417-889-0770 463
Web: tsgnpd.com

Turpin Sales & Marketing Inc
330 Cold Spring Ave West Springfield MA 01089 877-377-7573 463
TF: 877-377-7573 ■ *Web:* www.turpinsales.com

Turret Steel Industries Inc
105 Pine St Imperial PA 15126 724-218-1014 218-1195 492
TF: 800-245-4800 ■ *Web:* www.turretsteel.com

Company / Address	City	State	ZIP	Phone	Fax	Class
Tursso Companies Inc 223 Plato Blvd E *Web:* www.tursso.com	St. Paul	MN	55107	651-222-8445		627
Turtle & Hughes Inc 1900 Lower Rd *Web:* turtle.com	Linden	NJ	07036	732-574-3600	574-3723	246
Turtle Bay Exploration Park 840 Auditorium Dr *TF:* 800-887-8532 ■ *Web:* www.turtlebay.org	Redding	CA	96001	530-243-8850	243-8898	520
Turtle Bay Resort 57-091 Kamehameha Hwy *TF:* 866-475-2567 ■ *Web:* www.turtlebayresort.com	Kahuku	HI	96731	808-293-6000	293-9147	669
Turtle Cay Resort 600 Atlantic Ave *TF:* 888-989-7788 ■ *Web:* www.vacationrentalsvabeach.com	Virginia Beach	VA	23451	757-437-5565	437-9104	669
Turtle Club 2098 Old Steese Hwy	Fairbanks	AK	99712	907-457-3883		671
Turtle Cove Spa at Mountain Harbor Resort 181 Club House Dr *Web:* www.turtlecovespa.com	Mount Ida	AR	71957	870-867-1220		707
Turtle Creek Asset Management 4 King St W Ste 1300 *Web:* www.turtlecreek.ca	Toronto	ON	M5H1B6	416-363-7400		528
Turtle Island Foods Inc 601 Industrial Ave *Web:* www.tofurky.com	Hood River	OR	97031	541-386-7766		123
Turtle Kraals Restaurant & Bar 231 Margaret St *Web:* www.turtlekraals.com	Key West	FL	33040	305-294-2640		671
Turtle Magazine 1100 Waterway Blvd *TF:* 800-558-2376 ■ *Web:* uskidsmags.com	Indianapolis	IN	46202	317-634-1100		457-6
Turtle Mountain Community College 10145 BIA Rd 7 *TF:* 800-827-1100 ■ *Web:* www.tm.edu	Belcourt	ND	58316	701-477-7862	477-7892	165
Turtle River State Park 3084 Pk Ave *Web:* www.parkrec.nd.gov/parks/trsp/trsp.html	Arvilla	ND	58214	701-591-4445		565
Turtle-Top Inc 67819 State Rd 15 *TF:* 800-296-2105 ■ *Web:* www.turtletop.com	New Paris	IN	46553	800-296-2105		59
Tuscaloosa City Hall 2201 University Blvd *Web:* www.tuscaloosa.com	Tuscaloosa	AL	35401	205-248-5311	349-0147	337
Tuscaloosa County 714 Greensboro Ave *Web:* www.tuscco.com	Tuscaloosa	AL	35401	205-349-3870		338
Tuscaloosa News 315 28th Ave *TF:* 800-888-8639 ■ *Web:* www.tuscaloosanews.com	Tuscaloosa	AL	35401	205-345-0505	722-0187	532-2
Tuscaloosa Public Library 1801 Jack Warner Pkwy *TF:* 800-882-0722 ■ *Web:* www.tuscaloosa-library.org	Tuscaloosa	AL	35401	205-345-5820	758-1735	434-3
Tuscaloosa Symphony Orchestra PO Box 20001 *Web:* www.tsoonline.org	Tuscaloosa	AL	35402	205-752-5515		573-3
Tuscaloosa VA Medical Ctr 3701 Loop Rd E *TF:* 888-269-3045 ■ *Web:* www.tuscaloosa.va.gov	Tuscaloosa	AL	35404	205-554-2000		374-8
Tuscany 2832 East 6200 South *Web:* www.tuscanyslc.com	Salt Lake City	UT	84121	801-277-9919		671
Tuscany Design Automation Inc 3030 S College Ave Ste 102 **Fax Area Code:* 720 ■ *Web:* tuscanyda.com	Fort Collins	CO	80525	970-377-0717	222-2534*	525
Tuscany Energy Ltd Suite 1800, 633 - Sixth Ave SW *Web:* www.tuscanyenergy.com	Calgary	AB	T2P2Y5	403-269-9889		538
Tuscany Suites & Casino 255 E Flamingo Rd *TF Resv:* 877-887-2261 ■ *Web:* www.tuscanylv.com	Las Vegas	NV	89169	702-893-8933	947-5994	379
Tuscarawas County 125 E High Ave *Web:* www.co.tuscarawas.oh.us	New Philadelphia	OH	44663	330-365-3243	343-4682	338
Tuscarawas County Chamber of Commerce 1323 Fourth St NW *TF:* 800-527-3387 ■ *Web:* www.tuschamber.com	New Philadelphia	OH	44663	330-343-4474	343-6526	139
Tuscarawas County Public Library 121 Fair Ave NW *Web:* www.tusclibrary.org	New Philadelphia	OH	44663	330-364-4474	364-8217	434-3
Tuscarora Intermediate Unit 11 2527 US 522 S Hwy *Web:* www.tiu11.org	McVeytown	PA	17051	717-899-7143		685
Tuscarora State Park 687 Tuscarora Pk Rd *Web:* www.dcnr.state.pa.us	Barnesville	PA	18214	570-467-2404		565
Tuscarora Yarns Inc 8760 E Franklin St *TF:* 800-849-6527 ■ *Web:* www.tuscarorayarns.com	Mount Pleasant	NC	28124	704-436-6527	436-9461	745-9
Tusculum College 60 Shiloh Rd Hwy 107 *TF:* 800-729-0256 ■ *Web:* www.tusculum.edu	Greeneville	TN	37743	423-636-7300		166
Tuskegee Airman Natl Historical Museum 6325 W Jefferson *Web:* www.tuskegeemuseum.org	Detroit	MI	48209	313-843-8849		520
Tuskegee Airmen National Historic Site 1616 Chappie James Ave *Web:* www.nps.gov	Tuskegee	AL	36083	334-724-0922	724-0952	564
Tuskegee Institute National Historic Site 1212 W Montgomery Rd *TF:* 800-752-2603 ■ *Web:* www.nps.gov/tuin	Tuskegee Institute	AL	36088	334-727-3200	727-1448	564
Tuskegee University 1200 W Montgomery Rd **Fax:* Admissions ■ *TF Admissions:* 800-622-6531 ■ *Web:* www.tuskegee.edu	Tuskegee	AL	36088	334-727-8011	727-5750*	166
Tuskegee University Ford Motor Co Library/Learning Resource Ctr Hollis Burke Frissell Library Bldg *TF:* 800-622-6531 ■ *Web:* www.tuskegee.edu	Tuskegee	AL	36088	334-727-8894		434-6
Tuson Corp 475 Bunker Ct *Web:* www.tuson.com	Vernon Hills	IL	60061	847-816-8800		358
Tustin Chamber of Commerce 700 W First St Ste 7 *Web:* www.tustinchamber.org	Tustin	CA	92780	714-544-5341	544-2083	139
Tustin Mechanical Services Lehigh Valley LLC 2555 Industry Ln *Web:* www.thetustingroup.com	Norristown	PA	19403	610-539-8200		610
Tustin Nissan 30 Auto Center Dr *Web:* www.tustinnissan.com	Tustin	CA	92782	714-669-8282		57
Tutco Inc 500 Gould Dr *TF:* 877-262-4533 ■ *Web:* www.tutco.com	Cookeville	TN	38506	931-432-4141	432-4140	14
Tuthill Corp 8500 S Madison St *TF:* 800-634-2695 ■ *Web:* www.tuthill.com	Burr Ridge	IL	60527	630-382-4900	382-4999	641
Tuthill Corp Plastics Group 2050 Sunnydale Blvd *TF:* 800-634-2695 ■ *Web:* www.tuthill.com	Clearwater	FL	33765	727-446-8593	446-8595	604
Tuthill Pump Group 12500 S Pulaski Rd *TF:* 800-634-2695 ■ *Web:* www.tuthillpump.com	Alsip	IL	60803	708-389-2500	388-0869	641
Tuthill Transfer Systems 8500 S Madison *TF:* 800-825-6937 ■ *Web:* www.tuthill.com	Burr Ridge	IL	60527	260-747-7529		639
Tuthill Vacuum & Blower Systems 4840 W Kearney St *TF:* 800-825-6937 ■ *Web:* www.tuthill.com	Springfield	MO	65803	417-865-8715	865-2950	18
Tuthill Vacuum Systems 4840 W Kearney St *TF:* 800-634-2695 ■ *Web:* www.tuthill.com	Springfield	MO	65803	417-865-8715	865-2950	172
Tutor Perini Corp 15901 Olden St *Web:* www.tutorperini.com	Sylmar	CA	91342	508-628-2000		186
Tutor-Saliba Corp 15901 Olden St *TF:* 800-642-6888 ■ *Web:* www.tutorsaliba.com	Sylmar	CA	91342	818-362-8391	367-5379	186
Tutta Bella Hair Salon 17400 Monterey St *Web:* tuttabellahairsalon.com	Morgan Hill	CA	95037	408-778-6949		77
Tuttle Aluminum & Bronze Inc 120 Shadowlawn Dr *Web:* www.tuttlehandrailings.com	Fishers	IN	46038	317-842-2420		480
Tuttle Construction Inc 880 Shawnee Rd *Web:* www.tuttlenet.com	Lima	OH	45805	419-228-6262	229-7414	187
Tuttle Creek State Park 5800-A River Pond Rd *Web:* ksoutdoors.com/State-Parks/Locations/Tuttle-Creek	Manhattan	KS	66502	785-539-7941		565
Tuttle Law Print Inc 414 Quality Ln *TF:* 800-776-7682 ■ *Web:* www.tuttleprinting.com	Rutland	VT	05701	800-776-7682		627
Tuttle Publishing 364 Innovation Dr **Fax Area Code:* 800 ■ *TF Sales:* 800-526-2778 ■ *Web:* www.tuttlepublishing.com	North Clarendon	VT	05759	802-773-8930	329-8885*	637-2
Tutto Pasta 305 State St *Web:* www.foodspot.com	Madison	WI	53703	608-294-1000		671
Tutto Pasta 1751 SW Third Ave *Web:* www.tuttopasta.com	Miami	FL	33129	305-857-0709		671
Tutum Inc 2302 Environ Way	Chapel Hill	NC	27517	415-742-2442		387
Tuway American Group Inc, The 2820 W Maple Rd Ste 101 *Web:* www.tuwaymops.com	Troy	MI	48084	248-649-8790		746
Tuzigoot National Monument 527 S Main St *Web:* www.nps.gov/tuzi	Camp Verde	AZ	86322	928-634-5564	567-3597	564
TV Asahi America Inc 875 Third Ave 3rd Fl *Web:* www.tv-asahi.net	New York	NY	10022	212-644-6300	644-0003	740
TV Guide Magazine LLC 11 W 42nd St 16th Fl *TF:* 800-866-1400 ■ *Web:* www.tvguide.com	New York	NY	10036	212-852-7500	852-7323	457-9
TV One 1010 Wayne Ave 10th Fl *Web:* tvone.tv	Silver Spring	MD	20910	301-755-0400		740
TV5 Quebec Canada 1755 Blvd Rene-Levesque E Bureau 101 *Web:* www.tv5.ca	Montreal	QC	H2K4P6	514-522-5322		116
TVA 1600 de Maisonneuve Blvd *Web:* tva.canoe.ca	Montreal	QC	H2L4P2	514-526-9251	598-3968	741
TVA (Tennessee Valley Authority) 400 W Summit Hill Dr *Web:* www.tva.gov	Knoxville	TN	37902	865-632-2101		340-20
TVAX Biomedical Inc 8006 Reeder St *Web:* www.tvaxbiomedical.com	Lenexa	KS	66214	913-492-2221		231
TVB (Television Bureau of Advertising Inc) 120 Wall St 15th Fl *Web:* www.tvb.org	New York	NY	10005	212-486-1111	935-5631	49-18
TVC (Traditional Values Coalition) 139 C St SE	Washington	DC	20003	202-547-8570		48-20
TVC Capital LLC 11452 El Camino Real Ste 450 *Web:* www.tvccapital.com	San Diego	CA	92130	858-704-3261		690
Tvc Marketing 3200 W Wilshire Blvd *TF:* 800-227-6459 ■ *Web:* www.tvcmatrix.com	Oklahoma City	OK	73116	405-843-2722		195
TVCC (Temecula Valley Chamber of Commerce) 26790 Ynez Ct Ste A *Web:* www.temecula.org	Temecula	CA	92591	951-676-5090	694-0201	139
TVEC (Trinity Valley Electric Co-op Inc) 1800 Hwy 243 E PO Box 888 *TF:* 800-766-9576 ■ *Web:* www.tvec.net	Kaufman	TX	75142	972-932-2214		245
Tvia Inc 4800 Great America Pkwy Ste 405 **Fax Area Code:* 972 ■ *Web:* www.tvia.com	Santa Clara	CA	95054	408-327-8033	612-2805*	696
TVL Inc 901 16th St W Ste 200 *Web:* www.tvl.com	North Vancouver	BC	V7P1R2	604-983-2298		179
TVM Capital 101 Arch St Ste 1950 *Web:* www.tvm-capital.com	Boston	MA	02110	617-345-9320		792
Tvo North America 2500 Guerrero Dr	Carrollton	TX	75006	972-242-1517		652
Tvp Color Graphics Inc 230 Roma Jean Pkwy *TF:* 800-325-7909 ■ *Web:* www.thinkvariable.com	Streamwood	IL	60107	630-837-3600		627
TVU networks Corp 1225 Pear Ave Ste 100 *Web:* www.tvunetworks.com	Mountain View	CA	94043	650-969-6732		647
TVV Capital 201 Fourth Ave N Ste 1250 *TF:* 800-317-5915 ■ *Web:* tvvcapital.com	Nashville	TN	37219	615-256-8061		528
TVWorks LLC 2 Belvedere Pl Ste 200	Mill Valley	CA	94941	415-380-6200		116
TW Burleson & Son Inc 301 Peters St *TF:* 800-338-0587 ■ *Web:* www.burlesons-honey.com	Waxahachie	TX	75165	972-937-4810	937-8711	296-24

Name / Address	City	State	ZIP	Phone	Fax	Class
TW Garner Food Co 4045 Indiana Ave *Web:* www.texaspete.com	Winston-Salem	NC	27105	336-661-1550	661 1901	296-20
TW Lewis 850 W Elliot Rd Ste 101 *Web:* www.twlewis.com	Tempe	AZ	85284	480-820-0807		653
TW Metals Inc 760 Constitution Dr Ste 204 *Web:* www.twmetals.com	Exton	PA	19341	610-458-1300		492
T-w Transport Inc 7405 S Hayford Rd *TF:* 800-356-4070 ■ *Web:* www.twtrans.com	Cheney	WA	99004	800-356-4070		780
TWA Restaurant Group Inc 16012 Metcalf Ave Ste 1 *Web:* www.twarestaurant.com	Overland Park	KS	66085	913-239-0266	239-9768	670
Twanoh State Park 12190 E Hwy 106 *Web:* www.parks.wa.gov	Union	WA	98592	360-275-2222		565
TWB Co 1600 Nadeau Rd *TF:* 800-925-3100 ■ *Web:* www.twbcompany.com	Monroe	MI	48162	734-289-6400	289-6555	723
TWC (Trans World Corp) 545 Fifth Ave Ste 940 *OTC:* TWOC ■ *TF:* 877-407-9037 ■ *Web:* www.transwc.com	New York	NY	10017	212-983-3355	983-8129	379
TWC Construction Inc 431 Eastgate Rd 3rd Fl *Web:* www.twcconstruction.com	Henderson	NV	89011	702-597-3444		186
TWC Services Inc 2601 Bell Ave *TF:* 800-225-0638 ■ *Web:* www.twcservices.com	Des Moines	IA	50321	515-284-1911		610
Tweave LLC 138 Barrows St PO Box AV *Web:* www.gehring-tricot.com	Norton	MA	02766	508-285-6701	285-2904	745-1
Tweddle Litho Co 24700 Maplehurst Dr *TF:* 800-732-5569 ■ *Web:* www.tweddle.com	Clinton Township	MI	48036	586-307-3700	307-3708	626
Tweed Museum of Art 1201 ordean Ct *TF:* 866-999-6995 ■ *Web:* www.d.umn.edu/tma	Duluth	MN	55812	218-726-8222	726-8503	520
Tweed New Haven Regional Airport 155 Burr St *TF:* 800-433-7300 ■ *Web:* www.flytweed.com	New Haven	CT	06512	203-466-8833	466-1199	27
Tween Brands Inc 8323 Walton Pkwy *Web:* justiceretail.com	New Albany	OH	43054	614-775-3500		157-1
Tweet-Garot Mechanical Inc 2545 Larsen Rd *Web:* www.tweetgarot.com	Green Bay	WI	54307	920-498-0400		610
Tweetsie Railroad Inc 300 Tweetsie Railroad Ln *TF:* 800-526-5740 ■ *Web:* www.tweetsie.com	Blowing Rock	NC	28605	828-264-9061		31
TWELVE Atlantic Station 361 17th St *Web:* www.twelvehotels.com	Atlanta	GA	30363	404-961-1212	961-1221	379
TWELVE Centennial Park 400 W Peachtree St *Web:* www.twelvehotels.com	Atlanta	GA	30308	404-418-1212		379
Twentieth Century Fox Home Entertainment Inc 10201 West Pico Blvd **Fax Area Code:* 888 ■ *TF:* 877-369-7867 ■ *Web:* www.foxconnect.com	Los Angeles	CA	90064	310-369-1000	443-4369*	511
Twentieth Modern 7470 Beverly Blvd *Web:* www.twentieth.net	Los Angeles	CA	90036	323-904-1200		321
Twenty-First Century Assoc 266 Summit Ave *TF:* 888-760-5052 ■ *Web:* www.tfc-associates.com	Hackensack	NJ	07601	201-670-1144	678-9088	160
Twenty-First Securities Corp 780 Third Ave *Web:* www.twenty-first.com	New York	NY	10017	212-418-6000		690
Twenty-Five Mile Creek State Park 20530 S Lakeshore Rd *Web:* www.parks.wa.gov	Chelan	WA	98816	509-687-3610		565
Twentynine Palms Chamber of Commerce 73484 Twentynine Palms Hwy *TF:* 800-442-2283 ■ *Web:* www.29chamber.org	Twentynine Palms	CA	92277	760-367-3445		139
TWG (Terlato Wine Group, The) 900 Armour Dr *TF:* 800-950-7676 ■ *Web:* terlatowines.com	Lake Bluff	IL	60044	847-604-8900		81-3
TWHBEA (Tennessee Walking Horse Breeders' & Exhibitors' Assn) 250 N Ellington Pkwy PO Box 286 *TF:* 800-359-1574 ■ *Web:* www.twhbea.com	Lewisburg	TN	37091	931-359-1574	359-7530	48-3
Twigg Corp 659 E York St *Web:* www.twiggcorp.com	Martinsville	IN	46151	765-342-7126		21
Twiggs County Commissioners 425 N Railroad St *Web:* www.twiggscounty.us	Jeffersonville	GA	31044	478-945-3629		338
Twigs Bistro & Bar 808 W Main Ave *Web:* www.twigsbistro.com	Spokane	WA	99201	509-232-3376		671
Twin Bridges State Park 14801 Hwy 137 S *TF:* 800-622-6317 ■ *Web:* www.travelok.com	Fairland	OK	74343	918-540-2545	540-2545	565
Twin Butte Energy Ltd Suite 410, 396 - 11 Ave SW *Web:* www.twinbutteenergy.com	Calgary	AB	T2R0C5	403-215-2045		787
TWIN Capital Management Inc 3244 Washington Rd Ste 202 *Web:* www.twincapital.com	Mcmurray	PA	15317	724-942-2000		528
Twin Cities & Western Railroad 2925 12th St E *TF:* 800-290-8297 ■ *Web:* www.tcwr.net	Glencoe	MN	55336	320-864-7200		649
Twin Cities Model Railroad Museum 668 Transfer Rd Ste 8 *Web:* www.tcmrm.org	St Paul	MN	55114	651-647-9628		520
Twin Cities North Chamber of Commerce 525 Main St Ste 200 *Web:* www.twincitiesnorth.org	New Brighton	MN	55112	763-571-9781	572-7950	139
Twin Cities Public Television Inc 172 E Fourth St *TF:* 866-229-1300 ■ *Web:* www.tpt.org	Saint Paul	MN	55101	651-222-1717		632
Twin City Animal Hospital 869 South St *Web:* www.twincityanimalhospital.com	Fitchburg	MA	01420	978-343-3049		794
Twin City Area Chamber of Commerce 114 Main St *Web:* www.twincity.org	Festus	MO	63028	636-931-7697		139
Twin City Container Inc 990 Spiral Blvd *Web:* www.tcc-mn.com	Hastings	MN	55033	651-480-3786		455
Twin City Die Castings Co 1070 33rd Ave SE *Web:* www.tcdcinc.com	Minneapolis	MN	55414	651-645-3611	645-0724	308
Twin City EDM 7940 Rancher Rd NE *TF:* 800-397-0338 ■ *Web:* www.twincityedm.com	Fridley	MN	55432	763-783-7808	783-7842	454
Twin City Fan Cos Ltd 5959 Trenton Ln N *Web:* www.tcf.com	Minneapolis	MN	55442	763-551-7600	551-7601	18
Twin City Foods Inc 10120 269th Pl NW *Web:* twincityfoods.com	Stanwood	WA	98292	206-515-2400	515-2499	296-21
Twin City Knitting Company Inc (TCK) 104 Rock Barn Rd NE *Web:* www.tcksports.com	Conover	NC	28613	828-464-4830		155-10
Twin City Sales & Marketing 361 W End Blvd *Web:* www.twincitysam.com	Winston-salem	NC	27101	336-685-1501		195
Twin City Security Inc 519 Coon Rapids Blvd *Web:* www.twincitysecurity.com	Minneapolis	MN	55433	763-784-4160		693
Twin County Regional Hospital 200 Hospital Dr *TF:* 800-295-3342 ■ *Web:* www.tcrh.org	Galax	VA	24333	276-236-8181		374-3
Twin Disc Inc 1328 Racine St *NASDAQ:* TWIN ■ *Web:* www.twindisc.com	Racine	WI	53403	262-638-4000		620
Twin Dragon Marketing Inc 14600 S Broadway St *Web:* www.twindragonmarketing.com	Gardena	CA	90248	310-715-7070		594
Twin Dragons 1809 Carey Ave	Cheyenne	WY	82001	307-637-6622		671
Twin Eagle 8847 W Sam Houston Pkwy N *Web:* www.termna.com	Houston	TX	77040	713-341-7300		538
Twin Eagle Consulting LLC 7300 S Alton Way Unit 5A *Web:* www.twineagleconsulting.com	Centennial	CO	80112	832-770-4300		196
Twin Falls Area Chamber of Commerce 2015 Neilsen Point Pl *TF:* 866-894-6325 ■ *Web:* www.twinfallschamber.com	Twin Falls	ID	83301	208-733-3974	733-9216	139
Twin Falls County 630 Addison Ave W 2nd Fl *TF:* 800-377-3529 ■ *Web:* www.twinfallscounty.org	Twin Falls	ID	83301	208-736-4004	736-4155	338
Twin Falls Public Library 201 Fourth Ave E *TF:* 800-458-3271 ■ *Web:* www.twinfallspubliclibrary.org	Twin Falls	ID	83301	208-733-2964	733-2965	434-3
Twin Falls Resort State Park PO Box 667 Rt 97 *Web:* www.twinfallsresort.com	Mullens	WV	25882	304-294-4000	294-4000	565
Twin Falls School District 411 201 Main Ave W *TF:* 800-726-0003 ■ *Web:* www.tfsd.k12.id.us	Twin Falls	ID	83301	208-733-6900	733-6987	685
Twin Farms 452 Royalton Tpke PO Box 115 *Web:* www.twinfarms.com	Barnard	VT	05031	802-234-9999		379
Twin Garden Farms 23017 Illinois 173 *Web:* www.twingardenfarms.com	Harvard	IL	60033	815-943-7448		10-11
Twin Harbors Beach State Park Hwy 105	Westport	WA	98595	360-268-9717		565
Twin Hill Ranch 1689 Pleasant Hill Rd	Sebastopol	CA	95472	707-823-2815		315-3
Twin Lakes State Park c/o Black Hawk Lake State Pk 228 East Blossom *Web:* www.iowadnr.gov	Lake View	IA	51450	712-657-8712	657-2289	565
Twin Lakes State Park 6204 E Poyhonen Rd *Web:* www.michigandnr.com	Toivola	MI	49965	906-288-3321		565
Twin Lakes State Park 788 Twin Lakes Rd *TF:* 800-933-7275 ■ *Web:* www.dcr.virginia.gov	Green Bay	VA	23942	434-392-3435		565
Twin Lakes Telephone Co-op 200 Telephone Ln *TF Cust Svc:* 800-644-8582 ■ *Web:* www.twlakes.net	Gainesboro	TN	38562	931-268-2151		736
Twin Lights State Historic Site Lighthouse Rd *Web:* www.twinlightslighthouse.com	Highlands	NJ	07732	732-872-1814		565
Twin Liquors Lp 5639 Airport Blvd *Web:* twinliquors.com	Austin	TX	78751	512-222-0700		443
Twin Oaks Computing Inc 755 Maleta Ln Ste 203 *Web:* www.twinoakscomputing.com	Castle Rock	CO	80108	720-733-7906		387
Twin Oaks Hammocks 138 Twin Oaks Rd *TF:* 800-688-8946 ■ *Web:* www.twinoakshammocks.com	Louisa	VA	23093	540-894-5125	894-4112	319-4
Twin Oaks Landscaping Inc 997 Harvey Rd *Web:* www.twinoakslandscaping.com	Oswego	IL	60543	630-554-3399		776
Twin Oaks Software Development Inc 1463 Berlin Tpke *TF:* 866-278-6750 ■ *Web:* www.healthclubsoftware.com	Berlin	CT	06037	860-829-6000		177
Twin Otter International Ltd 2806 Perimeter Rd *TF:* 800-229-2379 ■ *Web:* www.twinotter.com	North Las Vegas	NV	89032	702-646-8837		23
Twin Pine Casino 22223 Hwy 29 PO Box 789 *TF:* 800-564-4872 ■ *Web:* twinpine.com	Middletown	CA	95461	707-987-0197	987-0375	378
Twin River Casino 100 Twin River Rd *TF:* 877-827-4837 ■ *Web:* www.twinriver.com	Lincoln	RI	02865	401-475-8505		642
Twin River National Bank 1507 G St *TF:* 877-743-4948 ■ *Web:* www.twinriverbank.com	Lewiston	ID	83501	208-746-4848	746-4949	70
Twin Rivers Paper Company Inc 707 Sable Oaks Dr Ste 010 *Web:* www.twinriverspaper.com	South Portland	ME	04106	207-523-2350		557
Twin Rivers Regional Medical Ctr (TRRMC) 1301 First St *TF:* 800-994-6610 ■ *Web:* www.twinriversregional.com	Kennett	MO	63857	573-888-4522	888-5525	374-3
Twin Rivers Unified School District 3222 Winona Way *TF:* 800-260-0659 ■ *Web:* www.twinriversusd.org	North Highlands	CA	95660	916-566-1628	566-3586	685
Twin State Technical Services Ltd 3543 E Kimberly Rd *Web:* www.tsts.com	Davenport	IA	52807	563-441-1504		177

Name / Address	City	State	ZIP	Phone	Fax	Class
Twin Technologies Inc 6360 French's Hollow Rd *TF:* 800-439-4821 ■ *Web:* www.twintechs.com	Altamont	NY	12009	800-439-4821		196
Twin Tier Hospitality LLC 255 Spring St Ste 100 *Web:* www.twintierhospitality.com	Sayre	PA	18840	570-882-8644		377
Twin Towers 5343 Hamilton Ave *Web:* lec.org	Cincinnati	OH	45224	513-853-2000		672
Twin Town Treatment Ctr 1706 University Ave *TF:* 800-603-1071 ■ *Web:* meridianprograms.com	Saint Paul	MN	55104	651-645-3661		726
Twin Valley Electric Co-op Inc 501 S Huston Ave *TF:* 866-784-5500 ■ *Web:* www.twinvalleyelectric.coop	Altamont	KS	67330	620-784-5500		245
Twin Valleys Public Power District 1145 Nasby St *TF:* 800-658-4266 ■ *Web:* www.twinvalleysppd.com	Cambridge	NE	69022	308-697-3315	697-4877	245
Twin-Boro News 210 Knickerbocker Rd *TF:* 888-473-2673	Cresskill	NJ	07626	201-894-6715	457-2520	532-4
Twinco Romax 4635 Willow Dr *TF Cust Svc:* 800-626-2744 ■ *Web:* www.twincoromax.com	Medina	MN	55340	763-478-2360	478-3411	61
Twincraft Inc 2 Tigan St *Web:* www.twincraft.com	Winooski	VT	05404	802-655-2200		214
Twinhead Corp 48303 Fremont Blvd **Fax Area Code:* 510 ■ *TF Sales:* 800-995-8946 ■ *Web:* www.twinhead.com.tw	Fremont	CA	94538	800-995-8946	492-0820*	173-2
Twining Laboratories of Southern California Inc 3310 Airport Way *TF:* 800-381-7744 ■ *Web:* twininginc.com	Long Beach	CA	90806	562-426-3355	426-6424	743
Twinlab Corp 4910 Communication Ave *TF:* 800-645-5626 ■ *Web:* www.twinlab.com	Boca Raton	FL	33431	800-645-5626		799
Twinless Twins Support Group International (TTSG) PO Box 980481 *TF:* 888-205-8962 ■ *Web:* www.twinlesstwins.org	Ypsilanti	MI	48198	888-205-8962		48-21
Twin-Star International Inc 1690 S Congress Ave Ste 210 *TF:* 800-511-0825 ■ *Web:* www.twinstarhome.com	Delray Beach	FL	33445	561-330-3201		361
TwinWest Chamber of Commerce 10700 Old County Rd 15 *TF:* 800-649-5397 ■ *Web:* www.twinwest.com	Plymouth	MN	55441	763-450-2220	450-2221	139
Twist Image 407 rue McGill 2nd Fl *Web:* www.twistimage.com	Montreal	QC	H2Y2G3	514-987-9992		7
Twist Inc 47 S Limestone St *TF:* 800-282-3433 ■ *Web:* www.twistinc.com	Jamestown	OH	45335	937-675-9581	675-6781	719
Twisted Networks Inc 1528 Evans St Ste D *Web:* www.twistednetworx.com	Greenville	NC	27834	252-321-8974		226
Twitchell Corp 4031 Ross Clark Cir *TF General:* 800-633-7550 ■ *Web:* www.twitchellcorp.com	Dothan	AL	36303	334-792-0002		745-2
Twizzle Hair Studio 2670 Fourth Ave W *TF:* 800-663-1840 ■ *Web:* twizzle.ca	Vancouver	BC	V6K1P7	604-738-1733		77
Two b Printing Inc 625 NE 42nd St	Oakland Park	FL	33334	954-566-4886		627
Two Bunch Palms Resort & Spa 67425 Two Bunch Palms Trl *TF:* 800-472-4334 ■ *Web:* www.twobunchpalms.com	Desert Hot Springs	CA	92240	760-329-8791	329-1874	669
Two by Four Ltd 10 N Dearborn St Ste 1000 *TF:* 800-438-7325 ■ *Web:* twoxfour.com	Chicago	IL	60602	312-382-0100		7
Two Cats Media Ltd 20 W 22nd St Ste 605 *Web:* www.twocatstv.com	New York	NY	10010	212-929-2085		514
Two Chefs 8287 S Dixie Hwy *Web:* twochefsrestaurant.com	South Miami	FL	33143	305-663-2100		671
Two Chefs On A Roll Inc 18201 Central Ave	Carson	CA	90746	310-436-1600		123
Two Guys From Italy 405 N Verdugo Rd *Web:* www.glendaletwoguysfromitaly.com	Glendale	CA	91206	818-240-0020		671
Two Guys Relocation Systems Inc 3571 Pacific Hwy *TF:* 800-896-4897 ■ *Web:* www.twomenwillmoveyou.com	San Diego	CA	92101	619-296-7995		519
Two Lights State Park 7 Tower Dr *Web:* www.maine.gov	Cape Elizabeth	ME	04107	207-799-5871		565
Two Little Hands Productions 870 E N Union Ave *Web:* www.signingtime.com	Midvale	UT	84047	801-676-4441	676-4441	514
Two Men & A Truck International Inc 3400 Belle Chase Way *TF:* 800-345-1070 ■ *Web:* www.twomenandatruck.com	Lansing	MI	48911	517-394-7210	394-7432	519
Two River Times 75 W Front St *Web:* tworivertimes.com	Red Bank	NJ	07701	732-219-5788	224-0806	532-4
Two Rivers Area Chamber of Commerce 840 Hamilton St Ste 205 *Web:* www.lehighvalleychamber.org	Allentown	PA	18101	610-841-5800	437-4907	139
Two Rivers Convention Ctr 159 Main St *TF:* 800-626-8497 ■ *Web:* www.tworiversconvention.com	Grand Junction	CO	81501	970-263-5700	263-5720	205
Two Rivers Correctional Institution 82911 Beach Access Rd *Web:* oregon.gov	Umatilla	OR	97882	541-922-2001		213
Two Rivers Enterprises 490 River St W *Web:* tworiversstainlesskings.com	Holdingford	MN	56340	320-746-3156		492
Two Rivers Heritage Museum 1 Durgan St PO Box 204 *Web:* 2rhm.com	Washougal	WA	98671	360-835-8742		520
Two Rivers State Recreation Area 27702 'F' St *Web:* outdoornebraska.gov	Waterloo	NE	68069	402-359-5165		565
Two Seas Restaurant 1300 Delaware 1 *Web:* dinehere.us	Dewey Beach	DE	19971	302-227-2610		671
Two Shea Consulting Inc 1009 Oak Hill Rd Ste 202 *Web:* www.twoshea.com	Lafayette	CA	94549	925-962-7432		180
Two Sigma Investments LLC 100 Ave of the Americas 16th Fl *Web:* www.twosigma.com	New York	NY	10013	212-625-5700		690
Two West Inc 514 W 26th St *TF:* 800-210-3000 ■ *Web:* www.twowest.com	Kansas City	MO	64108	816-471-3255		5
TWOBOLT Marketing Technologies Inc 1110 Central Ave	Pawtucket	RI	02861	401-724-7600		195
Twombly Nursery 163 Barn Hill Rd *TF:* 800-553-3715 ■ *Web:* www.twomblynursery.com	Monroe	CT	06468	203-261-2133	261-9230	323
Twomey, Latham, Shea, Kelley, Dubin & Quartararo LLP 33 W Second St PO Box 9398 *Web:* www.suffolklaw.com	Riverhead	NY	11901	631-727-2180		428
TWP Inc 2831 Tenth St *TF:* 800-227-1570 ■ *Web:* www.twpinc.com	Berkeley	CA	94710	510-548-4434	548-3073	688
TWT (Taylor Wiseman & Taylor) 124 Gaither Dr Ste 150 *Web:* www.taylorwiseman.com	Mount Laurel	NJ	08054	856-235-7200		261
TXCO Resources Inc 777 E Sonterra Blvd Ste 350	San Antonio	TX	78258	210-496-5300	496-3232	536
TXU Electric PO Box 65764 *TF:* 800-242-9113 ■ *Web:* www.txu.com/us/ourbus/elecgas	Dallas	TX	75262-0764	972-791-2888		787
TYAN Computer Corp USA 3288 Laurelview Ct *Web:* www.tyan.com	Fremont	CA	94538	510-651-8868	651-7688	625
Tybee Island Lighthouse & Museum 30 Meddin Dr *TF:* 800-351-7469 ■ *Web:* www.tybeelighthouse.org	Tybee Island	GA	31328	912-786-5801	786-6538	520
Tyburn Railroad LLC 505 S Broad St *Web:* www.tyburnrr.com	Kennett Square	PA	19348	610-925-0131		546
Tyco Electronics Corp 1050 Westlakes Dr *Web:* www.te.com	Berwyn	PA	19312	610-893-9800		253
Tyco Electronics Corp Corcom Div 620 S Butterfield Rd *Web:* www.te.com/usa-en/products/emi-filters.html	Mundelein	IL	60060	847-680-7400	680-8169	248
Tyco Federal Credit Union 3715 Haven Ave Ste 200 **Fax Area Code:* 800 ■ *TF:* 888-673-3288	Redwood City	CA	94064	888-673-3288	280-8926*	219
Tyco Fire & Security 6600 Congress Ave *Web:* www.tyco.com	Boca Raton	FL	33487	561-912-6000		692
Tyco International Ltd 9 Roszel Rd *NYSE:* TYC ■ *TF:* 800-685-4509 ■ *Web:* www.tyco.com	Princeton	NJ	08540	609-720-4200		692
Tyco SimplexGrinnell 50 Technology Dr *TF:* 800-746-7539 ■ *Web:* www.tycosimplexgrinnell.com	Westminster	MA	01441	978-731-2500		283
TYG Holding USA Inc 1800 N McDonald St	Mckinney	TX	75071	972-542-1889		489
Tygart Technology Inc 1543 Fairmont Ave *Web:* www.tygart.com	Fairmont	WV	26554	304-363-6855		180
Tyger Scientific Inc 324 Stokes Ave *TF:* 888-329-8990 ■ *Web:* www.tygersci.com	Ewing	NJ	08638	609-434-0143		231
TYGH Capital Management Inc 1211 S W Fifth Ave Ste 2100 *TF:* 800-972-0150 ■ *Web:* www.tyghcap.com	Portland	OR	97204	503-972-0150		401
TYK America Inc 301 BrickyaRd Rd *TF:* 800-569-9359 ■ *Web:* www.tykamerica.com	Clairton	PA	15025	412-384-4259	384-4242	663
Tyler & Co 400 Northridge Rd Ste 1250 *TF:* 800-989-6789 ■ *Web:* www.tylerandco.com	Atlanta	GA	30350	770-396-3939	396-6693	266
Tyler 2 Construction Inc 5400 Old Pineville Rd *TF:* 800-458-3024 ■ *Web:* www.tyler2construction.com	Charlotte	NC	28217	704-527-3031		186
Tyler Arboretum 515 Painter Rd *Web:* www.tylerarboretum.org	Media	PA	19063	610-566-9134	891-1490	97
Tyler Area Chamber of Commerce 315 N Broadway Ave *TF:* 800-235-5712 ■ *Web:* www.tylertexas.com	Tyler	TX	75702	903-592-1661	593-2746	139
Tyler Bldg Systems LP 3535 Shiloh Rd	Tyler	TX	75701	903-561-3000		105
Tyler Construction Company Inc 433 Rabon Rd *TF:* 800-442-7566 ■ *Web:* www.tyler-construction.com	Columbia	SC	29223	803-865-1404		187
Tyler Convention & Visitors Bureau (TCVB) 315 N Broadway *TF:* 800-235-5712 ■ *Web:* www.visittyler.com	Tyler	TX	75702	903-592-1661	592-1268	206
Tyler County 100 Bluff St Rm 110 *TF:* 800-256-6848 ■ *Web:* www.co.tyler.tx.us	Woodville	TX	75979	409-283-2281	283-6305	338
Tyler County Assessor 121 Main St *Web:* www.tylercountywv.com	Middlebourne	WV	26149	304-758-4781	758-2126	338
Tylor Equipment Corp 251 Shakcr Rd *TF:* 800-292-6351 ■ *Web:* www.tylerequipment.com	East Longmeadow	MA	01028	413-525-6351	525-5909	358
Tyler Junior College PO Box 9020 **Fax:* Admissions ■ *TF:* 800-687-5680 ■ *Web:* www.tjc.edu	Tyler	TX	75711	903-510-2523	510-2161*	162
Tyler Morning Telegraph PO Box 2030 **Fax:* News Rm ■ *TF:* 800-772-1213 ■ *Web:* www.tylerpaper.com	Tyler	TX	75710	903-597-8111	595-0335*	532-2
Tyler Mountain Water Co 159 Harris Dr *Web:* www.tylermountainwater.com	Poca	WV	25159	304-722-8080		805
Tyler Museum of Art 1300 S Mahon Ave *TF:* 800-222-7270 ■ *Web:* www.tylermuseum.org	Tyler	TX	75701	903-595-1001	595-1055	520
Tyler Pipe Co 11910 CR 492 **Fax Area Code:* 800 ■ *TF:* 800-527-8478 ■ *Web:* www.tylerpipe.com	Tyler	TX	75706	903-882-5511	248-9537*	307
Tyler Public Library 201 S College Ave *Web:* library.cityoftyler.org	Tyler	TX	75702	903-593-7323	531-1329	434-3
Tyler State Park 101 Swamp Rd *Web:* www.dcnr.state.pa.us	Newtown	PA	18940	215-968-2021		565
Tyler State Park 789 Pk Rd 16 *Web:* tpwd.texas.gov	Tyler	TX	75706	903-597-5338		565
Tyler Technologies Inc 5949 Sherry Ln Ste 1400 *NYSE:* TYL ■ **Fax Area Code:* 972 ■ *TF:* 800-431-5776 ■ *Web:* www.tylertech.com	Dallas	TX	75225	800-431-5776	713-3741*	178-10
Tylok International Inc 1061 E 260th St *TF:* 800-321-0466 ■ *Web:* www.tylok.com	Euclid	OH	44132	216-261-7310		595

Phone | Fax | Class

Tylu Wireless Technology Llc
Po Box 436900 .... Chicago IL 60643 312-248-3134 180
Web: www.tylu.com
Tymco Inc
225 E Industrial Blvd PO Box 2368 .... Waco TX 76703 254-799-5546 799-2722 516
TF: 800-258-9626 ■ *Web:* www.tymco.com
Tympani LLC
2001 Butterfield Rd Ste 250 .... Downers Grove IL 60515 630-981-5000 177
Web: www.tympani.net
Tyndale House Publishers Inc
351 Executive Dr .... Carol Stream IL 60188 800-323-9400 684-0247 637-3
TF: 800-323-9400 ■ *Web:* www.tyndale.com
Tyndale University College & Seminary
25 Ballyconnor Ct .... Toronto ON M2M4B3 416-226-6380 226-6746 167-3
TF: 877-896-3253 ■ *Web:* www.tyndale.ca
Tyndall Air Force Base
445 Suwannee Rd 101 .... Tyndall AFB FL 32403 850-283-1110 283-3225 497-1
TF: 800-356-5273 ■ *Web:* www.tyndall.af.mil
Tyndall Federal Credit Union Inc
PO Box 59760 .... Panama City FL 32412 850-769-9999 216
TF: 888-896-3255 ■ *Web:* tyndall.org
Tyonek Mfg Group Inc 229 Palmer Rd .... Madison AL 35758 256-258-6200 529
TF: 877-258-6200 ■ *Web:* www.tyonek.com
Typecraft Press Inc
2403 Sidney St Ste 500 .... Pittsburgh PA 15203 412-488-1600 627
Web: www.typecraftpress.com
Typecraft Wood & Jones Inc
2040 E Walnut St .... Pasadena CA 91107 626-795-8093 795-2423 626
TF: 800-214-3545 ■ *Web:* www.typecraft.com
Typesetting Inc
1144 S Robertson Blvd .... Los Angeles CA 90035 310-273-3330 781
Web: local.latimes.com
Typical Sicilian 497 Belmont Ave .... Springfield MA 01108 413-739-7100 671
Web: www.typicalsicilian.com
TYR Sport 1790 Apollo Ct .... Seal Beach CA 90740 714-897-0799 155-17
TF: 800-252-7878 ■ *Web:* tyr.com
Tyree Oil Inc 1355 W First Ave .... Eugene OR 97402 541-687-0076 579
TF: 800-950-3835 ■ *Web:* www.tyreeoil.com
Tyres International Inc 4637 Allen Rd .... Stow OH 44224 330-374-1000 755
Web: www.tyresinternational.com
Tyrone Square Mall
225 W Washington St .... Indianapolis IL 46204 727-345-0126 345-5699 460
Web: www.simon.com/mall/?id=135
Tyrrell County 108 S Water St .... Columbia NC 27925 252-796-1371 338
TYS LLP 3150 Crow Canyon Pl Ste 170 .... San Ramon CA 94583 925-498-6200 2
Web: tysllp.com
Tysinger Hampton & Partners Inc
3428 Bristol Hwy .... Johnson City TN 37601 423-282-2687 261
Web: tysinger-engineering.com
Tyson Events Ctr 401 Gordon Dr .... Sioux City IA 51101 712-279-4850 279-4903 205
TF: 800-593-2220 ■ *Web:* www.tysoncenter.com
Tyson Foods Inc
2210 W Oaklawn Dr PO Box 2020 .... Springdale AR 72762 479-290-4000 019
NYSE: TSN ■ *TF:* 800-643-3410 ■ *Web:* www.tyson.com
Tyson Fresh Meats Inc
800 Stevens Port Dr .... Dakota Dunes SD 57049 605-235-2061 473
TF: 800-416-2269 ■ *Web:* www.tyson.com
Tyson Pet Products Inc
812 Third St NW .... Independence IA 50644 319-334-7135 473
Web: www.truechews.com
Tyson Prepared Foods Inc
2200 Don Tyson Pkwy .... Springdale AR 72762 479-290-4000 296-26
TF: 800-233-6332 ■ *Web:* www.tyson.com
Tysons Corner Ctr
1961 Chain Bridge Rd Ste 305 .... McLean VA 22102 703-847-7300 460
Web: tysonscornercenter.com
Tysons Galleria 2001 International Dr .... Mclean VA 22102 703-827-7730 460
Web: www.tysonsgalleria.com
Tysons Regional Chamber of Commerce
7925 Jones Branch Dr Ste 200 .... Tysons VA 22102 703-281-1333 242-1482 139
Web: www.tysonschamber.org
Tystar Corp 7050 Lampson Ave .... Garden Grove CA 92841 310-781-9219 246
Web: www.tystar.com
Tyze Personal Networks Ltd
90 Allstate Pkwy Ste 310 .... Markham ON L3R6H3 604-628-9594 387
Web: www.tyze.com
Tyzx Inc 3715 Haven Ave Ste 110 .... Menlo Park CA 94025 650-282-4500 618-1510 743
Tzell Travel Group
119 W 40th St 14th Fl .... New York NY 10018 212-944-2121 771
Web: www.tzell.com

U

Phone | Fax | Class

U B S Printing Group Inc
2577 Research Dr .... Corona CA 92882 951-273-7900 627
Web: www.ubsprint.com
U r s Information Systems Inc
155 W St Ste 1 .... Wilmington MA 01887 978-657-6100 180
Web: ursinfo.com
U S Auto Parts Network Inc
16941 Keegan Ave .... Carson CA 90746 310-735-0085 61
NASDAQ: PRTS ■ *Web:* www.usautoparts.net
U S Bottlers Machinery Co
11911 Steele Creek Rd .... Charlotte NC 28273 704-588-4750 588-3808 547
Web: www.usbottlers.com
U S Cavalry Inc 2855 Centennial Ave .... Radcliff KY 40160 866-673-7643 157-5
TF: 866-286-1359 ■ *Web:* www.uscav.com
U S Employees O C Federal Credit Union
PO Box 44000 .... Oklahoma City OK 73144 405-685-6200 219
TF: 800-227-6366 ■ *Web:* www.usecreditunion.org
U S Farathane Corp
38000 Mound Rd .... Sterling Heights MI 48310 586-978-2800 608
Web: www.usfarathane.com

Phone | Fax | Class

U S Government Absentee Shawnee Tribe of Oklahoma
2025 Gordon Cooper Dr .... Shawnee OK 74801 405-275-4030 186
Web: www.astribe.com
U S Group Inc
100 Executive Ctr Dr Ste 217 .... Columbia SC 29210 803-798-1420 186
Web: www.usgroupinc.com
U S Medical Management LLC
27000 Hills Tech Ct Ste 200 .... Farmington Hills MI 48331 407-474-3717 463
Web: usmmllc.com
U S Metals & Supply LLC
311 S Sarah St .... St. Louis MO 63110 314-658-0200 567
U S Monitor 86 Maple Ave .... New City NY 10956 845-634-1331 5
TF: 800-767-7967 ■ *Web:* usmonitor.com
U s Nameplate Company Inc
Hwy 30 W .... Mount Vernon IA 52314 319-895-8804 701
TF: 800-553-8871 ■ *Web:* www.usnameplate.com
U S Risk Insurance Group Inc
10210 N Central Expy .... Dallas TX 75231 214-265-7090 739-1421 390
TF: 800-926-9155 ■ *Web:* www.usrisk.com
U W Provision Company Inc
PO Box 620038 .... Middleton WI 53562 608-836-7421 836-6328 297-9
TF: 800-832-0517 ■ *Web:* www.uwprovision.com
U.S Department of State Diplomacy in action
Houston Agency
Federal Bldg 1919 Smith St Ste 1100 .... Houston TX 77002 713-654-0401 209-3470 340-16
Web: www.state.gov/m/ds/rls/rpt/18892.htm
U.S. Bankcard Services Inc
17171 E Gale Ave Ste 110 .... City Of Industry CA 91745 888-888-8872 251
TF: 888-888-8872 ■ *Web:* www.usbsi.com
U.S. Claims Services Inc
3801 Pegasus Dr Ste 101 .... Bakersfield CA 93308 661-399-1108 226
TF: 800-995-2416 ■ *Web:* www.usclaimsservices.com
U.S. Department of Education
Region 1
400 Maryland Ave SW POCH Bldg .... Washington DC 20202 617-289-0100 340-8
Web: www.ed.gov
Region 10 701 Fifth Ave MS .... Seattle WA 98104 206-615-2469 615-2469 340-10
Web: www.hhs.gov
Regions II 26 Federal Plaza Ste 3835 .... New York NY 10278 212-264-2976 264-0114 340-10
Web: www.hhs.gov
Pipeline and Hazardous Materials Safety Administration
1200 New Jersey Ave SE E Bldg 2nd Fl .... Washington DC 20590 202-366-4433 366-3666 340-17
Web: phmsa.dot.gov
U.S. Department of Veterans Affairs
325 E 'H' St .... Iron Mountain MI 49801 906-774-3300 374-8
TF: 800-215-8262 ■ *Web:* www.ironmountain.va.gov
U.S. Energy Development Corp
2350 N Forest Rd .... Getzville NY 14068 716-636-0401 540
TF: 800-636-7606 ■ *Web:* usedc.com
U.S. Facilities Inc
30 N 41 St Ste 400 .... Philadelphia PA 19104 800-236-6241 192
TF: 800-236-6241 ■ *Web:* usfacilities.com
U.S. Fleet Forces Command
1562 Mitscher Ave Ste 250 .... Norfolk VA 23551 757-836-3630 836-3603 497-4
TF: 800-473-3549 ■ *Web:* www.public.navy.mil/usff/Pages/default.aspx
U.S. Kids Golf LLC
3040 Northwoods Pkwy .... Norcross GA 30071 770-441-3077 711
TF: 888-387-5437 ■ *Web:* www.uskidsgolf.com
U.S. Lumber Coalition 1750 K St NW .... Washington DC 20006 202-582-0021 48-12
Web: www.uslumbercoalition.org
U.S. Materials Handling Corp 2231 NY-5 .... Utica NY 13502 315-732-4111 358
Web: www.usmaterialshandling.com
U.S. National Ski Hall of Fame
610 Palms Ave .... Ishpeming MI 49849 906-485-6323 486-4570 522
TF: 800-648-0720 ■ *Web:* www.skihall.com
U.S. Quality Furniture Services Inc
8920 Winkler Dr Ste 100 .... Houston TX 77017 713-943-7016 321
TF: 800-774-8700 ■ *Web:* www.usqfs.com
U2 Logic 8001 E 88th Ave .... Henderson CO 80640 303-768-9601 180
Web: www.u2logic.com
U92 50 W Broadway Ste 200 .... Salt Lake City UT 84101 801-524-2600 643-1811 645-142
Web: u92slc.com
UA Local 486
8100 Sandpiper Cir Ste 200 .... Nottingham MD 21236 410-866-4380 414
Web: www.ualocal486.com
UAA/APU Consortium Library
3211 Providence Dr .... Anchorage AK 99508 907-786-1848 434-6
Web: www.consortiumlibrary.org
UAB Comprehensive Cancer Ctr
University of Alabama at Birmingham
1824 Sixth Ave S .... Birmingham AL 35294 205-934-4011 668
TF: 800-822-0933 ■ *Web:* www3.ccc.uab.edu
UAB Medical West 995 Ninth Ave SW .... Bessemer AL 35022 205-481-7000 481-7994 374-3
TF: 800-994-6610 ■ *Web:* www.medicalwesthospital.org
UAFC (Universal American Corp)
44 S Broadway Ste 1200 .... White Plains NY 10601 914-934-5200 934-0700 360-4
NYSE: UAM ■ *TF:* 866-249-8668 ■ *Web:* www.universalamerican.com
UAMS Medical Ctr
4301 W Markham St .... Little Rock AR 72205 501-686-7000 374-3
TF: 877-467-6560 ■ *Web:* www.uams.edu
UAP Inc 7025 Rue Ontario E .... Montreal QC H1N2B3 514-256-5031 61
Web: www.napacanada.com
UAW Labor Employment & Training Corp
3965 S Vermont Ave .... Los Angeles CA 90037 323-730-7900 764
Web: www.letc.com
UbiCare 284 Amory St G-101 .... Boston MA 02130 617-524-8861 41
Web: www.ubicare.com
Ubics Inc 333 Technology Dr Ste 210 .... Canonsburg PA 15317 724-746-6001 743-4115 113
OTC: UBIX ■ *TF:* 800-441-0077 ■ *Web:* www.ubics.com
uBid Inc 740 Hilltop Dr .... Itasca IL 60143 866-946-8243 51
TF: 866-946-8243
u-blox America Inc
1902 Campus Commons Dr Ste 310 .... Reston VA 20191 703-483-3180 647
Web: www.u-blox.com
UBS (Universal Builders Supply Inc)
27 Horton Ave .... New Rochelle NY 10801 914-699-2400 699-2609 491
Web: www.ubs1.com
UBS AG 1285 Ave of the Americas .... New York NY 10019 212-713-2000 70
TF: 877-827-8001 ■ *Web:* www.ubs.com

Name / Address	City	State	Zip	Phone	Fax	Class
UBS Financial Services Inc						
1285 Ave of the Americas	New York	NY	10019	212-713-2000		690
TF: 800-221-3260 ■ *Web:* financialservicesinc.ubs.com						
UBS Warburg LLC 677 Washington Blvd	Stamford	CT	06901	203-719-3000		690
TF: 800-221-3260 ■ *Web:* www.ubs.com						
UBT Bancshares Inc 823 Broadway	Marysville	KS	66508	785-562-2333		360-2
Ubu Gallery 416 E 59th St	New York	NY	10022	212-753-4444	753-4470	42
Web: www.ubugallery.com						
UC Davis Arboretum						
Valley Oak Cottage LaRue Rd	Davis	CA	95616	530-752-4880	752-5796	97
Web: arboretum.ucdavis.edu						
UC Davis Cancer Ctr 4501 X St	Sacramento	CA	95817	916-734-5800		374-7
TF: 800-362-5566 ■ *Web:* www.ucdmc.ucdavis.edu/cancer						
UC Irvine Healthcare 101 the City Dr S	Orange	CA	92868	714-456-7890		374-3
TF: 877-824-3627 ■ *Web:* www.ucirvinehealth.org						
UCAN (Uhlich Children's Advantage Network)						
3737 N Mozart St	Chicago	IL	60618	773-588-0180	588-7762	48-15
Web: ucanchicago.org						
UCare Minnesota						
500 Stinson Blvd NE PO Box 52	Minneapolis	MN	55413	612-676-6500	676-6501	48-17
TF: 866-457-7144 ■ *Web:* www.ucare.org						
UCB Pharma Inc 1950 Lake Pk Dr	Smyrna	GA	30080	770-970-7500		582
TF: 800-477-7877 ■ *Web:* www.ucb.com						
UCC (United Church of Christ)						
700 Prospect Ave	Cleveland	OH	44115	216-736-2100	736-2103	48-20
TF: 866-822-8224 ■ *Web:* www.ucc.org						
UCC Filing & Search Services Inc						
1574 Village Sq Blvd Ste 100	Tallahassee	FL	32309	850-681-6528		635
UCC Totalhome 8450 Broadway	Merrillville	IN	46411	219-736-1100		320
Web: www.ucctops.com						
UCF Foundation Inc						
12424 Research Pkwy Ste 250	Orlando	FL	32826	407-882-1220		305
Web: ucffoundation.org						
UCF Hotel Venture						
6800 Lakewood Plaza Dr	Orlando	FL	32819	407-503-9000		378
Web: www.ucfalumni.com						
UCG Holdings						
11300 Rockville Pike Ste 1100	Rockville	MD	20852	301-287-2700	816-8945	531-7
TF: 800-929-4824 ■ *Web:* www.ucg.com						
UCH (University City Housing)						
3418 Sansom St	Philadelphia	PA	19104	215-222-2000	222-5449	655
Web: www.universitycityhousing.com						
Uchee Pines Lifestyle Center						
30 Uchee Pines Rd Ste 75	Seale	AL	36875	334-855-4764	855-9014	706
TF: 877-824-3374 ■ *Web:* ucheepines.org						
Uchi 801 S Lamar Blvd	Austin	TX	78704	512-916-4808		671
Web: www.uchiaustin.com						
UCI Communications LLC						
500 St Michael St	Mobile	AL	36602	251-457-1404	330-3102	174
UCI Medical Affiliates Inc						
1818 Henderson St	Columbia	SC	29201	803-782-4278		463
Web: www.doctorscare.com						
UCIT Online Security						
6441 Northam Dr	Mississauga	ON	L4V1J2	905-405-9898		693
TF: 866-756-7847 ■ *Web:* www.ucitonline.com						
UCLA (University of California)						
Berkeley 110 Sproul Hall MC Ste 5800	Berkeley	CA	94720	510-642-6000	643-7333	166
TF: 866-740-1260 ■ *Web:* berkeley.edu						
UCLA Foundation, The						
10920 Wilshire Blvd Ste 900	Los Angeles	CA	90024	310-794-3193		305
Web: www.uclafoundation.org						
UCLA Neuropsychiatric Institute & Hospital						
760 Westwood Plaza	Los Angeles	CA	90095	310-825-0511		374-5
Web: www.semel.ucla.edu						
UCM (United Color Manufacturing Inc)						
PO Box 480	Newtown	PA	18940	215-860-2165	860-8560	145
TF: 800-852-5942 ■ *Web:* www.unitedcolor.com						
UcompassCom Inc						
3019 Shannon Lakes N Ste 203	Tallahassee	FL	32309	850-297-1800		194
Web: www.ucompass.com						
UConn School of Medicine						
263 Farmington Ave	Farmington	CT	06030	860-679-2000	679-1301*	167-2
**Fax:* Admissions ■ *Web:* medicine.uconn.edu						
UCOOP (Universal Co-ops Inc)						
1300 Corporate Ctr Curve	Eagan	MN	55121	651-239-1000		276
Web: www.ucoop.com						
UCP Seguin 3100 S Central Ave	Cicero	IL	60804	708-863-3803		225
Web: www.seguin.org						
UCR LLC 1332 Woodman Dr	Dayton	OH	45432	937-253-8898		175
TF: 800-832-9978 ■ *Web:* www.ucrnet.com						
UCS (Utica Community Schools)						
11303 Greendale Dr	Sterling Heights	MI	48312	586-797-1000		685
TF: 800-877-8339 ■ *Web:* www.uticak12.org						
UCS (Union of Concerned Scientists)						
2 Brattle Sq	Cambridge	MA	02238	617-547-5552	864-9405	48-13
TF: 800-666-8276 ■ *Web:* www.ucsusa.org						
UCSD (University of California San Diego)						
Biomedical Library 9500 Gilman Dr	La Jolla	CA	92093	858-534-3253	534-6609	434-1
Web: www.libraries.ucsd.edu						
UCSF Medical Ctr						
505 Parnassus Ave	San Francisco	CA	94143	415-476-1000		374-3
Web: www.ucsfhealth.org						
Udall Shumway PLC						
1138 N Alma School Rd Ste 101	Mesa	AZ	85201	480-461-5300		428
TF: 800-360-0364 ■ *Web:* www.udallshumway.com						
Udall Tom (Sen D - NM)						
531 Hart Senate Office Bldg	Washington	DC	20510	202-224-6621		342-2
Web: www.tomudall.senate.gov						
UDASD (Upper Dauphin Area School District)						
5668 State Rt 209	Lykens	PA	17048	717-362-8134	362-3050	685
TF: 866-632-9992 ■ *Web:* www.udasd.org						
UDL Laboratories Inc						
1718 Northrock Ct	Rockford	IL	61103	800-848-0462	282-9391*	583
**Fax Area Code:* 815 ■ *TF:* 800-435-5272 ■ *Web:* mylan.com/products						
UDP Inc 2426 Cee Gee	San Antonio	TX	78217	210-828-6171		225
Web: udp.com						
UELS LLC 85 S 200 E	Vernal	UT	84078	435-789-1017		261
TF: 800-748-5275 ■ *Web:* www.uintahgroup.com						
UERS (Universal Technical Resource Services Inc)						
950 Kings Hwy N Ste 208	Cherry Hill	NJ	08034	856-667-6770	667-7586	261
Web: www.utrs.com						
Ues Inc 4401 Dayton Xenia Rd	Dayton	OH	45432	937-426-6900	429-5413	472
Web: www.ues.com						
UF Health Jacksonville						
655 W Eigth St	Jacksonville	FL	32209	904-244-0411		374-3
Web: ufhealthjax.org						
UFC (United Farmers Co-op)						
705 E Fourth St PO Box 461	Winthrop	MN	55396	507-647-6600		10
TF: 866-998-3266 ■ *Web:* www.ufcmn.com						
UFCW (United Food & Commercial Workers International Union)						
1775 K St NW	Washington	DC	20006	202-223-3111		414
TF: 800-551-4010 ■ *Web:* www.ufcw.org						
UFG						
118 Second Ave SE PO Box 73909	Cedar Rapids	IA	52407	319-399-5700		391-4
NASDAQ: UFCS ■ *TF:* 800-895-6253 ■ *Web:* www.unitedfiregroup.com						
Uflac Local 112 Dental In						
1571 Beverly Blvd	Los Angeles	CA	90026	213-895-4006		414
Web: www.uflac.org						
Ufp New Windsor LLC						
1000 Tibbetts Ln	New Windsor	MD	21776	410-549-1000		817
UFP Technologies Inc 172 E Main St	Georgetown	MA	01833	978-352-2200		601
NASDAQ: UFPT ■ *TF:* 800-372-3172 ■ *Web:* www.ufpt.com						
UFPI (Universal Forest Products Inc)						
2801 E Beltline Ave NE	Grand Rapids	MI	49525	616-364-6161	361-7534	683
NASDAQ: UFPI ■ *TF:* 800-598-9663 ■ *Web:* www.ufpi.com						
U-Freight America Inc						
320 Corey Way	South San Francisco	CA	94080	650-583-1469		311
Uganda 336 E 45th St	New York	NY	10017	212-949-0110	687-4517	784
Web: newyork.mofa.go.ug						
Uganda Embassy 5911 16th St NW	Washington	DC	20011	202-726-7100	726-1727	257
Web: washington.mofa.go.ug						
UGC (United Guaranty Corp)						
230 N Elm St	Greensboro	NC	27401	877-642-4642	528-3273*	391-5
**Fax Area Code:* 888 ■ **Fax:* Hum Res ■ *TF:* 877-642-4642 ■ *Web:* www.ugcorp.com						
UGI (United-Guardian Inc)						
230 Marcus Blvd PO Box 18050	Hauppauge	NY	11788	631-273-0900	273-0858	479
NASDAQ: UG ■ *TF:* 800-645-5566 ■ *Web:* www.u-g.com						
UGI Corp						
460 N Gulph Rd PO Box 858	King Of Prussia	PA	19406	610-337-1000		360-5
NYSE: UGI ■ *Web:* www.ugicorp.com						
Ugn Inc 18410 Crossing Dr	Tinley Park	IL	60487	773-437-2400		247
Web: ugn.com						
UH (Uniontown Hospital)						
500 W Berkeley St	Uniontown	PA	15401	724-430-5000		374-3
TF: 800-397-2554 ■ *Web:* www.uniontownhospital.com						
U-Haul International Inc						
2727 N Central Ave	Phoenix	AZ	85004	800-528-0361	263-6772*	778
**Fax Area Code:* 602 ■ *TF:* 800-528-0361 ■ *Web:* www.uhaul.com						
Uhl Company Inc 9065 zachary ln n	Maple grove	MN	55369	763-425-7226		393
TF: 800-815-3820 ■ *Web:* www.uhlcompany.com						
Uhlich Children's Advantage Network (UCAN)						
3737 N Mozart St	Chicago	IL	60618	773-588-0180	588-7762	48-15
Web: ucanchicago.org						
UHMS (Undersea & Hyperbaric Medical Society)						
21 W Colony Pl Ste 280	Durham	NC	27705	919-490-5140	490-5140	48-17
TF: 877-533-8467 ■ *Web:* www.uhms.org						
Uhs Pruitt Corp 1626 Jeurgens Ct	Norcross	GA	30093	770-279-6200		450
Web: www.pruitthealth.com						
UHY Advisors Inc 30 S Wacker Dr	Chicago	IL	60606	312-578-9600	346-6500	2
Web: www.uhyadvisors-us.com						
UHY Advisors NY Inc 66 S Pearl St	Albany	NY	12207	518-449-3171	449-5832	2
Web: uhy-us.com						
UIC (Universal Instruments Corp)						
33 Broome Corporate Pk	Conklin	NY	13748	607-779-7522	779-4466	695
TF: 800-842-9732 ■ *Web:* uic.com						
UIH (Universal Insurance Holding Inc)						
1110 W Commerical Blvd Ste 100	Fort Lauderdale	FL	33309	800-509-5586		391-4
NYSE: UVE ■ *TF:* 800-509-5586 ■ *Web:* www.universalinsuranceholdings.com						
Uinta County 225 Ninth St PO Box 810	Evanston	WY	82931	307-783-0306		338
Web: www.uintacounty.com						
Uintah Basin Applied Technology College						
1100 E Lagoon St	Roosevelt	UT	84066	435-722-6900		166
Web: www.ubtech.edu						
Uintah County 147 E Main St	Vernal	UT	84078	435-781-0770	781-6701	338
TF: 800-966-4680 ■ *Web:* www.co.uintah.ut.us						
UK (Underwater Kinetics)						
13400 Danielson St	Poway	CA	92064	858-513-9100	513-3602	710
TF: 800-852-7483 ■ *Web:* www.uwkinetics.com						
UK Good Samaritan Hospital						
310 S Limestone St	Lexington	KY	40508	859-226-7000		374-3
Web: ukhealthcare.uky.edu						
Ukiah Chamber of Commerce						
200 S School St	Ukiah	CA	95482	707-462-4705	462-2088	139
Web: www.ukiahchamber.com						
Ukiah Valley Medical Ctr						
275 Hospital Dr	Ukiah	CA	95482	707-462-3111	463-7384	374-3
Web: www.adventisthealth.org/ukiah-valley						
Ukpeagvik Inupiat Corp						
1250 Agvik St PO Box 890	Barrow	AK	99723	907-852-4460	852-4459	186
Web: www.uicalaska.com						
Consulate General 10 E Huron St	Chicago	IL	60611	312-642-4388		257
Ukrainian Museum 222 E Sixth St	New York	NY	10003	212-228-0110	228-1947	520
Web: www.ukrainianmuseum.org						
Ukrainian NA Inc (UNA) 2200 Rt 10	Parsippany	NJ	07054	800-253-9862	292-0900*	48-14
**Fax Area Code:* 973 ■ *TF:* 800-253-9862 ■ *Web:* www.ukrainiannationalassociation.org						
Ukrainian National Federal Credit Union						
215 Second Ave	New York	NY	10003	212-533-2980	995-5204	219
TF: 866-859-5848 ■ *Web:* www.uknatfcu.org						
Ukrainian National Museum						
2249 W Superior St	Chicago	IL	60612	312-421-8020		520
Web: www.ukrainiannationalmuseum.org						
Ukrop's Super Markets Inc						
2001 Maywill St Ste 100	Richmond	VA	23230	804-340-3000		345
Web: www.ukropshomestylefoods.com						
UL (UL LLC) 2600 NW Lake Rd	Camas	WA	98607	877-854-3577		743
TF: 877-854-3577 ■ *Web:* www.ul.com						

Name / Address	City	State	ZIP	Phone	Fax	Class
UL CCS 47173 Benicia St *TF:* 800-888-0123 ■ *Web:* www.northamerica-ul.com	Fremont	CA	94538	510-771-1000		743
UL EHS Sustainability 5000 Meridian Blvd Ste 600 *TF:* 888-202-3016 ■ *Web:* www.ulworkplace.com	Franklin	TN	37067	615-367-4404	367-3887	39
UL LLC 1559 King St *TF:* 800-903-5660 ■ *Web:* www.ul.com	Enfield	CT	06082	860-749-8371	749-8234	743
UL LLC (UL) 2600 NW Lake Rd *TF:* 877-854-3577 ■ *Web:* www.ul.com	Camas	WA	98607	877-854-3577		743
Ulbrich of Illinois Inc 12340 S Laramie Ave *Web:* www.astroplastics.com	Alsip	IL	60803	708-489-9500		492
Ulbrich Stainless Steels & Special Metals Inc (USSM) 57 Dodge Ave **Fax:* Sales ■ *TF:* 800-243-1676 ■ *Web:* www.ulbrich.com	North Haven	CT	06473	203-239-4481	239-7479*	723
ULC (Urban Libraries Council) 1333 H St NW Ste 1000 *Web:* www.urbanlibraries.org	West Washington	DC	20005	202-750-8650		49-11
ULC (Universal Lending Corp) 6775 E Evans Ave *TF:* 800-758-4063 ■ *Web:* ulc.com	Denver	CO	80224	800-758-4063		509
ULC Robotics Inc 88 Arkay Dr *Web:* www.ulcrobotics.com	Hauppauge	NY	11788	631-667-9200		194
ULCC 65 W Jackson Blvd *Web:* www.ulcc.org	Chicago	IL	60604	312-427-7800		573-3
ULI (Urban Land Institute) 1025 Thomas Jefferson St NW Ste 500W *TF Orders:* 800-321-5011 ■ *Web:* www.uli.org	Washington	DC	20007	202-624-7000	624-7140	48-8
U-line Corp PO Box 245040 *TF:* 800-779-2547 ■ *Web:* www.u-line.com	Milwaukee	WI	53224	414-354-0300		791
Ulivi Wealth 369 S Glassell St *TF:* 800-347-1340 ■ *Web:* www.ulivi.com	Orange	CA	92866	714-771-6000		690
Ulla Popken Ltd 12201 Long Green Pk *Web:* www.ullapopken.com	Glen Arm	MD	21057	410-592-9190		157-6
Ulland Investment Advisors 4550 IDS Ctr Eighty S Eighth St *Web:* www.ullandinvestment.com	Minneapolis	MN	55402	612-312-1400		528
ULLICO Casualty Co 1625 I St NW *TF:* 800-431-5425 ■ *Web:* www.ullico.com	Washington	DC	20006	800-431-5425		391-5
ULLICO Inc 1625 Eye St NW *TF:* 800-431-5425 ■ *Web:* www.ullico.com	Washington	DC	20006	800-431-5425		360-4
Ullman Devices Corp 664 Danbury Rd *TF:* 800-784-7796 ■ *Web:* www.users.ntplx.net/~ullman	Ridgefield	CT	06877	203-438-6577	431-9064	758
Ullman John & Associates Inc 51 E Market St *TF:* 800-936-3785 ■ *Web:* www.jgua.com	Corning	NY	14830	607-936-3785		401
Ullman Oil Inc PO Box 23399 *TF:* 800-543-5195 ■ *Web:* www.ullmanoil.com	Chagrin Falls	OH	44023	440-543-5195		579
Ulmer & Berne 1660 W Second St Ste 1100 *TF:* 800-973-1177 ■ *Web:* www.ulmer.com	Cleveland	OH	44113	216-583-7000		428
Ulrich Museum of Art 1845 Fairmount St Wichita State University *Web:* wichita.edu	Wichita	KS	67260	316-978-3664	978-3898	520
Ulrich Planfiling Equipment Corp 2120 Fourth Ave PO Box 135 *TF:* 800 346 2876 ■ *Web:* www.ulrichcorp.com	Lakewood	NY	14750	716-763-1015	763-1818	319-1
Ulster Correctional Facility 750 Berme Rd	Napanoch	NY	12458	845-647-1670		213
Ulster County 240 Fair St *Web:* ulstercountyny.gov	Kingston	NY	12401	845-340-3288	340-3299	338
Ulster County Community College Cottekill Rd *TF:* 800-724-0833 ■ *Web:* www.sunyulster.edu	Stone Ridge	NY	12484	845-687-5000	687-5090	162
Ulster Savings Bank 180 Schwenk Dr PO Box 3337 *Web:* www.ulstersavings.com/home/home	Kingston	NY	12401	845-338-6322		70
ULTA Beauty 1000 Remington Blvd Ste 120 *TF:* 866-983-8582 ■ *Web:* www.ulta.com	Bolingbrook	IL	60440	630-410-4800		214
Ulteig Engineers Inc 3350 38th Ave S *TF:* 888-858-3441 ■ *Web:* www.ulteig.com	Fargo	ND	58104	701-280-8500	237-3191	261
Ultera Systems Inc 26081 Merit Cir Ste 125 *TF:* 877-462-7362 ■ *Web:* www.ultera.com	Laguna Hills	CA	92653	949-367-8800	367-0758	176
Ulterion International Inc 1136 Zion Church Rd *Web:* www.ulterion.com	Braselton	GA	30517	706-654-2222		481
Ulterior Motives International Inc 1081 Ohio Dr Ste 2 *Web:* www.umi-inc.com	Plano	TX	75093	214-826-0011		463
Ultimate Lead Systems Inc 401 Frnt St *TF:* 800-323-0550 ■ *Web:* ultimatelead.com	Berea	OH	44017	440-826-1908		5
Ultimate Linings Ltd 6630 Roxburgh Dr Ste 175 *Web:* www.ultimatelinings.com	Houston	TX	77041	713-466-0302	937-0052	57
Ultimate Paint Ball 7075 Stormy Ln *Web:* www.ultimatepaintball.com	Bonne Terre	MO	63628	573-358-1300		711
Ultimate Placements LLC 1 Park Ctr Ste 305A *Web:* www.ultimateplacements.com	Wadsworth	OH	44281	330-334-0285		260
Ultimate Software Group Inc 2000 Ultimate Way *NASDAQ: ULTI* ■ *TF:* 800-432-1729 ■ *Web:* www.ultimatesoftware.com	Weston	FL	33326	954-331-7000		178-1
Ultimate Support Systems Inc 5836 Wright Dr **Fax Area Code:* 970 ■ *TF:* 800-525-5628 ■ *Web:* www.ultimatesupport.com	Loveland	CO	80538	800-525-5628	776-1941*	527
Ultimate Technical Solutions Inc 651 Leson Ct *Web:* www.utsi.us	Harvey	LA	70058	504-367-4957		180
Ultimate Washer Inc 711 Commerce Way Ste 1 *TF:* 866-858-4982 ■ *Web:* www.ultimatewasher.com	Jupiter	FL	33458	561-741-7022		641
Ultimatte Corp 20945 Plummer St *Web:* www.ultimatte.com	Chatsworth	CA	91311	818-993-8007		514
UltiSat Inc 708 Quince Orchard Rd Ste 120 *Web:* www.ultisat.com	Gaithersburg	MD	20878	240-243-5100		647
Ultra Clean Holdings Inc 26462 Corporate Ave *NASDAQ: UCTT* ■ *Web:* www.uct.com	Hayward	CA	94545	510-576-4400	576-4401	695
Ultra Clean Technologies Corp 1274 Hgwy 77 *TF:* 800-791-9111 ■ *Web:* ultracleantech.com	Bridgeton	NJ	08302	856-451-2176		146
Ultra Electronics 3Phoenix Inc 14585 Avion Pkwy Ste 200 *Web:* ultra-3pi.com	Chantilly	VA	20151	703-956-6480		529
Ultra Electronics Advanced Tactical Systems Inc 4101 Smith School Rd *Web:* www.ultra-ats.com	Austin	TX	78744	512-327-6795	327-8043	177
Ultra Electronics Flightline Systems Inc 7625 Omni Tech Pl *TF:* 888-959-9001 ■ *Web:* www.ultra-fei.com	Victor	NY	14564	585-924-4000		647
Ultra Electronics Measurement Systems Inc 50 Barnes Pk N Ste 102 *Web:* www.ultra-msi.com	Wallingford	CT	06492	203-949-3500	949-3598	173-1
Ultra Electronics-DNE Technologies Inc 50 Barnes Industrial Pk N *TF:* 800-370-4485 ■ *Web:* www.dnetech.com	Wallingford	CT	06492	203-265-7151	265-9101	647
Ultra Flex Packaging Corp 975 Essex St *Web:* www.ultraflex.com	Brooklyn	NY	11208	718-272-9100		627
Ultra Logistics Inc 17-17 Rt 208 N Ste 160 *Web:* www.ultralogistics.com	Fair Lawn	NJ	07410	201-703-5110		225
Ultra Petroleum Corp 400 N Sam Houston Pkwy E Ste 1200 *NYSE: UPL* ■ *Web:* www.ultrapetroleum.com	Houston	TX	77060	281-876-0120	876-2831	536
Ultra Solutions Acquisition LLC 1137 E Philadelphia St *TF:* 888-300-6800 ■ *Web:* www.ultrasolutions.com	Ontario	CA	91761	909-628-1778		475
Ultra Tech Machinery Inc 297 Ascot Pkwy *TF:* 800-833-9730 ■ *Web:* www.utmachinery.com	Cuyahoga Falls	OH	44223	330-929-5544		454
UltraBac Software 15015 Main St Ste 200 *TF:* 866-554-8562 ■ *Web:* www.ultrabac.com	Bellevue	WA	98007	425-644-6000	644-8222	178-12
Ultracare of Manhattan Ltd 800 Second Ave Rm 905 *Web:* www.ultracareofmanhattan.com	New York	NY	10017	212-883-8877		260
Ultracraft Co 6163 Old 421 Rd *TF:* 800-262-4046 ■ *Web:* www.ultracraft.com	Liberty	NC	27298	800-262-4046		115
Ultradent Products Inc 505 W 10200 S *Web:* www.ultradent.com	South Jordan	UT	84095	801-572-4200		228
Ultraderm Medspa 3311 Mission Dr *Web:* ultraderm.com	Santa Cruz	CA	95065	831-475-4315		77
Ultraex Inc 2633 Barrington Ct *TF:* 800-882-1000 ■ *Web:* www.ultraex.com	Hayward	CA	94545	510-786-3490		317
Ultrafab Inc 1050 Hook Rd *Web:* www.ultrafab.com	Farmington	NY	14425	585-924-2100	924-7000	745-3
Ultrafabrics LLC 303 S Broadway *TF:* 877-309-6648 ■ *Web:* www.ultrafabricsllc.com	Tarrytown	NY	10591	914-460-1730	631-3572	745-3
Ultraflote Corp 3640 W 12th St *TF:* 800-821-6825 ■ *Web:* www.ultraflote.com	Houston	TX	77008	713-461-2100	461-2213	91
Ultrafryer Systems Inc 302 Spencer Ln *TF:* 800-545-9189 ■ *Web:* www.ultrafryer.com	San Antonio	TX	78201	210-731-5000	731-5099	298
Ultra-Lab Nutrition Inc 3100 NW Boca Raton Blvd	Boca Raton	FL	33431	561-367-1474		799
Ultralife Batteries Inc 2000 Technology Pkwy *NASDAQ: ULBI* ■ *TF:* 800-332-5000 ■ *Web:* www.ultralifecorporation.com	Newark	NY	14513	315-332-7100	331-7800	74
Ultramar Travel Management International 14 E 47th St **Fax Area Code:* 212 ■ *TF:* 888-856-2929 ■ *Web:* www.ultramartravel.com	New York	NY	10017	888-856-2929	856-0129*	771
Ultra-Poly Corp 102 Demi Rd PO Box 330 *TF:* 800-932-0619 ■ *Web:* www.ultra-poly.com	Portland	PA	18351	570-897-7500		608
Ultrasonic Power Corp 239 E Stephenson St *Web:* www.upcorp.com	Freeport	IL	61032	815-235-6020		518
Ultrasource Inc 22 Clinton Dr *Web:* www.yourthinfilmsource.com	Hollis	NH	03049	603-881-7799		179
UltraStaff 1818 Memorial Dr Ste 200 *TF:* 800-522-7707 ■ *Web:* www.ultrastaff.com	Houston	TX	77007	713-522-7100	522-0744	721
Ultra-tech Enterprises Inc 4701 Taylor Rd *TF:* 800-293-2001 ■ *Web:* www.ute-inc.com	Punta Gorda	FL	33950	941-575-2000		481
Ultratech Inc 3050 Zanker Rd *NASDAQ: UTEK* ■ *TF:* 800-222-1213 ■ *Web:* www.ultratech.com	San Jose	CA	95134	408-321-8835		695
Ultra-Tech Printing Co 5851 Crossroads Commerce *Web:* www.utprinting.com	Grand Rapids	MI	49519	616-249-0500		627
Ultraviolet Devices Inc 26145 Technology Dr *Web:* www.uvdi.com	Valencia	CA	91355	661-295-8140		476
Ultryx 8760 Orion Pl, Ste 200 *TF:* 800-695-6344 ■ *Web:* www.ultryx.com	Columbus	OH	43240	614-410-2020		809
Ulupo Heiau State Monument 1151 Punchbowl St Rm 310 *Web:* dlnr.hawaii.gov	Honolulu	HI	96813	808-587-0300	587-0311	565
Uluru Inc 4452 Beltway Dr *Web:* www.uluruinc.com	Addison	TX	75001	214-905-5145	905-5130	479
Ulvac Technologies Inc 401 Griffin Brook Dr *Web:* www.ulvac.com	Methuen	MA	01844	978-686-7550	689-6300	385
Ulysses S Grant National Historic Site 7400 Grant Rd *TF:* 800-684-2408 ■ *Web:* www.nps.gov/ulsg	Saint Louis	MO	63123	314-842-3298	842-1659	564
U-M Comprehensive Cancer Center 1500 E Medical Ctr Dr CCGC 6-303 *Web:* mcancer.org	Ann Arbor	MI	48109	734-232-8838		769
UM Holding Co 56 N Haddon Ave PO Box 200 *Web:* www.umholdings.com	Haddonfield	NJ	08033	856-354-2200		360-3

				Phone	Fax	Class
UMA (United Motorcoach Assn) 113 SW St 4th Fl .... Alexandria *TF*: 800-424-8262 ■ *Web*: www.uma.org	VA	22314		703-838-2929	838-2950	49-21
Uman Pharma Inc 100 De L'Industrie Blvd.................... Candiac *TF*: 877-444-9989 ■ *Web*: www.umanpharma.com	QC	J5R1J1		450-444-9989		231
Umansky Motor Cars 1400 W Silver Spring Dr.................. Milwaukee *Web*: concoursmotors.com	WI	53209		414-290-1400		57
U-mark Inc 102 Iowa Ave .... Belleville *TF*: 866-383-6275 ■ *Web*: www.umarkers.com	IL	62220		618-235-7500		388
UMass Hotel at the Campus Ctr 1 Campus Ctr Way .... Amherst *TF*: 877-822-2110 ■ *Web*: www.hotelumass.com	MA	01003		413-549-6000		379
UMass Memorial Medical Ctr *Bone Marrow Transplant Program* 55 Lake Ave N .... Worcester *Web*: umassmemorialhealthcare.org	MA	01655		508-334-1000		769
Memorial Campus 119 Belmont St .... Worcester *TF*: 800-225-8885 ■ *Web*: umassmemorialhealthcare.org	MA	01605		508-334-1000		374-3
University Campus 55 Lake Ave N............ Worcester *TF*: 800-225-8885 ■ *Web*: umassmemorialhealthcare.org	MA	01655		508-334-1000		374-3
Umatilla County 216 SE Fourth St .... Pendleton *Web*: www.co.umatilla.or.us	OR	97801		541-278-6236	278-6345	338
Umatilla Electric Co-op Assn 750 W Elm Ave .... Hermiston *Web*: www.umatillaelectric.com	OR	97838		541-567-6414	567-8142	245
UMB Bank NA 1010 Grand Blvd................ Kansas City *TF*: 800-821-2171 ■ *Web*: www.umb.com	MO	64106		816-860-7000		70
UMB Capital Corp 1010 Grand Blvd .... Kansas City *TF*: 800-821-2171 ■ *Web*: www.umb.com	MO	64106		816-860-7000		402
UMB Financial Corp 1010 Grand Blvd........................ Kansas City *NASDAQ: UMBF* ■ *TF*: 800-821-2171 ■ *Web*: www.umb.com	MO	64106		816-860-7000		360-2
Umbagog Lake State Park 172 Pembroke Rd.......................... Concord *Web*: www.nhstateparks.org	NH	03301		603-482-7795		565
Umbrella Entertainment Group 6385 Rose Ln Ste A .... Carpinteria *Web*: www.umbrellaent.com.au	CA	93013		613-902-0513		195
Umbrella Medical Systems 505 walnut st .... Kansas City *Web*: www.umbrella-ms.com	MO	64106		816-437-7265		363
UMC (University Medical Ctr Bone Marrow & Blood Stem Cell Transplant Program) 602 Indiana Ave .... Lubbock *Web*: www.umchealthsystem.com	TX	79415		806-775-8200		769
Umc Home Health 1301 50th St Ste 9............ Lubbock *Web*: www.umchealthsystem.com	TX	79412		806-747-5377		363
UMC Inc 500 Chelsea Rd .... Monticello *Web*: www.ultramc.com	MN	55362		763-271-5200		454
UMCEP (University Medical Ctr of El Paso) 4815 Alameda Ave .... El Paso *Web*: www.umcelpaso.org	TX	79905		915-544-1200		374-3
UMCES (University of Maryland Ctr for Environmental Science) 2020 Horn Pt Rd.......................... Cambridge *TF*: 866-842-2520 ■ *Web*: www.umces.edu	MD	21613		410-228-9250	228-3843	668
UMCP (University Medical Ctr at Princeton) 253 Witherspoon St .... Princeton *TF*: 877-932-8935 ■ *Web*: princetonhcs.org	NJ	08540		609-497-4304		374-3
Umetco Minerals Corp 2754 Compass Dr Ste 280 .... Grand Junction	CO	81506		970-245-3700		502
UmeVoice Inc 20C Pimentel Ct Ste 1 .... Novato *TF*: 888-230-3300 ■ *Web*: www.theboom.com	CA	94949		415-883-1500		178-7
UMF Medical 1316 Eisenhower Blvd.............. Johnstown *TF*: 800-638-5322 ■ *Web*: www.umfmedical.com	PA	15904		814-266-8726	266-1870	319-3
UMHC (University of Miami Hospital & Clinics) *Sylvester Comprehensive Cancer Ctr* 1475 NW 12th Ave.......................... Miami *TF*: 800-545-2292 ■ *Web*: www.sylvester.org	FL	33136		305-243-1000		769
Umi 5849 Ellsworth Ave...................... Pittsburgh *Web*: bigburrito.com	PA	15232		412-362-6198		671
Umi Sushi Bar & Grill 5510 S IH-35 Ste 400........................ Austin *Web*: umiaustin.com	TX	78745		512-383-8681	383-8802	671
UMIAQ LLC 6700 Arctic Spur Rd................ Anchorage *TF*: 800-226-0009 ■ *Web*: www.uicprofessionalservices.com	AK	99518		907-677-8220		41
Umicore Technical Materials North America Inc 9 Pruyn's Island Dr...................... Glens Falls *Web*: www.umicore.com	NY	12801		518-792-7700		518
Umlauf Sculpture Garden & Museum 605 Robert E Lee Rd........................ Austin *Web*: www.umlaufsculpture.org	TX	78704		512-445-5582		520
UMMC (University of Mississippi Medical Ctr Bone Marrow Transplant Program) 2500 N State St............................ Jackson *Web*: www.umc.edu	MS	39216		601-354-6655	984-6289	769
UMMC Grenada (GLMC) 960 Avent Dr .... Grenada *Web*: www.glmc.net	MS	38901		662-227-7000		374-3
UMP 730AM 103.9FM, The 3280 Peachtree Rd Ste 2300.................. Atlanta *TF*: 866-485-9867 ■ *Web*: www.umpsports.com	GA	30305		866-485-9867		645
Umpco Inc 7100 Lampson Ave............ Garden Grove *Web*: www.umpco.com	CA	92841		714-897-3531		350
Umpqua Bank PO Box 1820.................... Roseburg *TF*: 866-486-7782 ■ *Web*: www.umpquabank.com	OR	97470		503-973-5945	973-5943	70
Umpqua Community College 1140 Umpqva College Rd PO Box 967.......... Roseburg *TF*: 800-820-5161 ■ *Web*: www.umpqua.edu	OR	97470		541-440-4600	440-4612	162
Umpqua Dairy Products Co 1686 SE N St PO Box 1306 .... Grants Pass *TF*: 800-222-6455 ■ *Web*: www.umpquadairy.com	OR	97526		541-672-2638	673-0256	296-27
Umpqua Holdings Corp 1 SW Columbia St Ste 1200.................. Portland *NASDAQ: UMPQ* ■ *TF*: 866-486-7782 ■ *Web*: www.umpquabank.com	OR	97258		503-727-4100		360-2
UMPQUA Indian Development Corp 146 Chief Miwaleta Ln .... Canyonville *Web*: www.uidchr.com	OR	97417		541-839-1221		377
Umpqua Lighthouse State Park 84505 Hwy 101 S.......................... Florence *TF*: 800-551-6949 ■ *Web*: www.oregonstateparks.org	OR	97439		800-551-6949		565
UMRCC (Upper Mississippi River Conservation Committee) 555 Lester Ave .... Onalaska *Web*: www.umrcc.org	WI	54650		608-783-8432		48-13
UMS Group Inc 300 Interpace Pkwy Ste C380................ Parsippany *Web*: www.umsgroup.com	NJ	07054		973-335-3555	335-7738	194
Columbia 104 Jesse Hall.................... Columbia **Fax*: Admissions ■ *TF*: 800-856-2181 ■ *Web*: www.missouri.edu	MO	65211		573-882-6333	882-7887*	166
Umstead Hotel & Spa 100 Woodland Pond .... Cary *TF*: 866-877-4141 ■ *Web*: www.theumstead.com	NC	27513		919-447-4000		379
UMTRI (University of Michigan Transportation Research Institute) 2901 Baxter Rd.......................... Ann Arbor *Web*: www.umtri.umich.edu	MI	48109		734-764-6504	936-1081	668
UMW (Utah Metal Works Inc) 805 Everett Ave........................ Salt Lake City *TF*: 877-221-0099 ■ *Web*: www.umw.com	UT	84116		877-221-0099		660
UNA (Utah Nurses Assn) 4505 S Wastch Blvd Ste 330B .... Salt Lake City *TF*: 800-338-7657 ■ *Web*: www.utnurse.org	UT	84124		801-272-4510		533
UNA (Ukrainian NA Inc) 2200 Rt 10............ Parsippany **Fax Area Code*: 973 ■ *TF*: 800-253-9862 ■ *Web*: www.ukrainiannationalassociation.org	NJ	07054		800-253-9862	292-0900*	48-14
Unaflex LLC 1350 S Dixie Hwy E .... Pompano Beach *TF*: 800-327-1286 ■ *Web*: www.unaflex.com	FL	33060		954-943-5002	946-3583	370
UNAPEN Inc 321 Research Pkwy Ste 201.......... Meriden *Web*: unapen.com	CT	06450		203-269-2111		180
Unarco Material Handling Inc 701 16th Ave E.......................... Springfield **Fax Area Code*: 615 ■ *TF*: 800-862-7261 ■ *Web*: www.unarcorack.com	TN	37172		800-862-7261	382-2777*	286
UNC Neuroscience Ctr University of N Carolina 115 Mason Farm Rd CB 7250 .... Chapel Hill *TF*: 800-862-4938 ■ *Web*: www.med.unc.edu/neuroscience	NC	27599		919-843-8536	966-1050	668
Uncas Manufacturing Co 150 Niantic Ave.......................... Providence	RI	02907		401-944-4700	943-2951	409
Uncharted Outposts Inc 9 Village Ln .... Santa Fe *TF*: 800-755-7256 ■ *Web*: www.unchartedoutposts.com	NM	87505		505-795-7710		760
Unclaimed Baggage Ctr 509 W Willow St.......................... Scottsboro *Web*: unclaimedbaggage.com	AL	35768		256-259-1525		791
Uncle Bubba's Oyster House 104 Bryan Woods Rd .... Savannah *Web*: www.unclebubbas.com	GA	31410		912-897-6101		671
Uncle Giuseppe's of Smithtown 95 Rt 111 .... Smithtown *Web*: www.uncleg.com	NY	11787		631-863-0900		297-8
Uncle Milton Industries Inc 29209 Canwood St Ste 120 .... Agoura *TF General*: 800-869-7555 ■ *Web*: www.unclemilton.com	CA	91301		818-707-0800	707-0878	762
Uncle Ray's LLC 14245 Birwood St............... Detroit *TF*: 800-800-3286 ■ *Web*: www.unclerays.com	MI	48238		313-834-0800	834-0443	296-35
Uncle Tai's 5250 Town Ctr Cir .... Boca Raton *Web*: uncletais.com	FL	33486		561-368-8806		671
Uncle Wing Chinese Restaurant 107 N First St............................ Garland	TX	75040		972-272-2775		671
Unconventional Gas Resources Canada Operating Inc 736 - 8 Ave SW Ste 700 .... Calgary	AB	T2P1H4		403-269-1690		536
UNC-TV (University of North Carolina Ctr for Public Television) 10 TW Alexander Dr PO Box 14900 .... Research Triangle Park *TF*: 800-906-5050 ■ *Web*: www.unctv.org	NC	27709		919-549-7000	549-7201	632
UNC-TV Ch 4 (PBS) 10 TW Alexander Dr PO Box 14900 .... Research Triangle Park *TF*: 800-906-5050 ■ *Web*: www.unctv.org	NC	27709		919-549-7000	549-7201	741
Under Secretary for Arms Control & International Security *Bureau of International Security & Nonproliferatio* 2201 C St NW Rm 2236 .... Washington *Web*: www.state.gov	DC	20520		202-647-5116		340-16
Bureau of Verification Compliance & Implementation 2201 C St NW Rm 2236 .... Washington *Web*: www.state.gov	DC	20520		202-647-5116		340-16
Under Secretary for Democracy & Global Affairs *Bureau of Democracy Human Rights & Labor* 2201 C St NW Rm 7802 .... Washington *Web*: www.state.gov	DC	20520		202-647-5116		340-16
Under Secretary for Political Affairs *Bureau of European & Eurasian Affairs* 2201 C St NW Rm 2236 .... Washington *Web*: www.state.gov/p/eur	DC	20520		202-895-3500		340-16
Bureau of International Organization Affairs 2201 C St NW .... Washington *Web*: www.state.gov/p/io	DC	20520		202-647-9600		340-16
Bureau of Near Eastern Affairs 2201 C St NW Rm 2509 .... Washington *Web*: www.state.gov/p/nea	DC	20520		202-647-7209		340-16
Bureau of Western Hemisphere Affairs 2201 C St NW .... Washington *Web*: www.state.gov/p/wha	DC	20520		202-647-4000		340-16
Under Secretary for Public Diplomacy & Public Affairs *Bureau of Educational & Cultural Affairs* 2200 C St NW .... Washington *Web*: eca.state.gov	DC	20522		202-632-6452	632-2701	340-16
Bureau of Public Affairs 2201 C St NW Rm 2206 .... Washington *Web*: www.state.gov	DC	20520		202-647-8411		340-16
Underberg & Kessler LLP 300 Bausch & Lomb Pl...................... Rochester *Web*: underbergkessler.com	NY	14604		585-258-2800	258-2821	445
Undercurrent, The 327 Battleground Ave .... Greensboro *Web*: www.undercurrentrestaurant.com	NC	27401		336-370-1266		671
Underdog Media 10 E Yanonali St Ste 2C .... Santa Barbara *Web*: www.underdogmedia.com	CA	93101		805-880-6910		5
Underground Atlanta 50 Upper Alabama St .... Atlanta *Web*: www.underground-atlanta.com	GA	30303		404-523-2311		50-6

Company / Address	City	State	Zip	Phone	Fax	Class
Underground Construction Company Inc						
5145 Industrial Way	Benicia	CA	94510	707-746-8800	746-1314	188-10
TF: 800-227-2314 ■ *Web:* www.undergroundconstruction.com						
Underground Specialists Inc (USI)						
570 SW 16th Terr	Pompano Beach	FL	33069	954-782-8740	782-1919	787
Web: www.usicable.com						
Underhill State Park						
PO Box 249	Underhill Center	VT	05490	802-899-3022		565
Web: www.vtstateparks.com						
Underline Communications LLC						
12 W 27th St 14th Fl	New York	NY	10001	212-994-4340		224
Web: www.underlinecom.com						
Undersea & Hyperbaric Medical Society (UHMS)						
21 W Colony Pl Ste 280	Durham	NC	27705	919-490-5140	490-5140	48-17
TF: 877-533-8467 ■ *Web:* www.uhms.org						
Underwater Kinetics (UK)						
13400 Danielson St	Poway	CA	92064	858-513-9100	513-3602	710
TF: 800-852-7483 ■ *Web:* www.uwkinetics.com						
Underwood Attorneys & Counselors at Law						
1111 W Loop 289	Lubbock	TX	79416	806-793-1711		428
Web: www.uwlaw.com						
Underwood Bros 3747 E Southern Ave	Phoenix	AZ	85040	602-437-2690	437-2970	422
Web: www.aaalandscape.com						
Underwood Investments						
11502 Juniper Ridge Dr	Austin	TX	78759	512-336-1155		655
TF: 800-445-6999 ■ *Web:* underwoodinvestments.com						
Underwood Mold Co Inc 104 Dixie Dr	Woodstock	GA	30189	770-926-2465	926-6565	602
Web: www.underwoodmoldco.com						
Underwood Transfer Company LLC						
940 W Troy Ave	Indianapolis	IN	46225	317-783-9235	782-2769	780
TF: 800-428-2372 ■ *Web:* www.underwoodcompanies.com						
Underwood-Memorial Hospital						
509 N Broad St	Woodbury	NJ	08096	856-845-0100		374-3
Web: inspirahealthnetwork.org						
Underwriters Safety & Claims Inc						
1700 Eastpoint Pkwy	Louisville	KY	40223	502-244-1343		390
Web: www.usckv.com						
Uneeda Enterprizes Inc						
640 Chestnut Ridge Rd Spring Valley	New York	NY	10977	845-426-2800		1
TF: 800-431-2494 ■ *Web:* www.sandpaper.com						
Unemed Corp 986099 Nebraska Medical Ctr	Omaha	NE	68198	402-559-2468		463
TF: 800-752-5478 ■ *Web:* www.unemed.com						
Unemployment Services Corp						
50 Salem St	Lynnfield	MA	01940	781-246-0262		463
Web: www.uscorp.com						
UNEP (United Nations Environment Programme)						
900 17th St NW Ste 506	Washington	DC	20006	202-785-0465	785-2096	783
Web: www.rona.unep.org						
UNESCO (United Nations Educational Scientific & Cultural Organization)						
2 UN Plaza Ste 900	New York	NY	10017	212-963-5995		783
Web: en.unesco.org						
Unette Corp						
1578 Sussex Tpke Bldg Ste 5	Randolph	NJ	07869	973-328-6800	584-4794	608
Web: www.unette.com						
UNF (University of North Florida)						
1UNF Dr	Jacksonville	FL	32224	904-620-1000	620-2719	434-6
Web: www.unf.edu/library						
UNF (United Nations Foundation)						
1000 Massachusetts Ave NW Ste 400	Washington	DC	20030	202-887-9040	887-9021	48-5
Web: www.unfoundation.org						
UNFCU (United Nations Federal Credit Union)						
24-01 44th Rd Ct Sq Pl	Long Island	NY	11101	347-686-6000	686-6400	219
TF: 800-891-2471 ■ *Web:* www.unfcu.org						
UNFI (United Natural Foods Inc)						
313 Iron Horse Way	Providence	RI	02908	401-528-8634		297-8
NASDAQ: UNFI ■ *Web:* www.unfi.com						
UNFI Specialty Distribution Services						
88 Huntoon Memorial Hwy	Leicester	MA	01524	508-892-8171	892-4827	238
Web: unfi.com						
Unger Co 12401 Berea Rd	Cleveland	OH	44111	216-252-1400	252-1427	548
TF: 800-321-1418 ■ *Web:* www.ungerco.com						
Unger Furniture Company of Sauk Centre Inc						
516 Sinclair Lewis Ave	Sauk Centre	MN	56378	320-352-2247		321
Unger Memorial Library						
825 N Austin St	Plainview	TX	79072	806-296-1148		434-3
Web: whc.net						
Ungerboeck Systems International Inc						
100 Ungerboeck Pk	O'fallon	MO	63368	636-300-5606		180
TF: 800-400-4052 ■ *Web:* www.ungerboeck.com						
Unholtz-Dickie Corp						
6 Brookside Dr	Wallingford	CT	06492	203-265-3929		407
Web: www.udco.com						
UNI Engineering Inc						
156 Stockton St	Hightstown	NJ	08520	609-448-4633		261
Web: uni-engineering.com						
Unibank For Savings 49 Church St	Whitinsville	MA	01588	508-234-8112	234-4648	70
TF: 800-578-4270 ■ *Web:* www.unibank.com						
Uni-Bell PVC Pipe Assn						
2711 LBJ Fwy Ste 1000	Dallas	TX	75234	972-243-3902		138
Web: www.uni-bell.org						
Unibilt Industries Inc						
8005 Johnson Stn Rd PO Box 373	Vandalia	OH	45377	800-777-9942	890-8303*	106
**Fax Area Code:* 937 ■ *TF:* 800-777-9942 ■ *Web:* www.unibiltcustomhomes.com						
Unibright Foods Inc						
7101 Scout Ave	Bell Gardens	CA	90201	562-806-3221		473
Web: www.unibrightfoods.com						
Unical Aviation Inc						
680 S LemonAve	City of Industry	CA	91789	909-348-1700		770
TF: 800-813-1901 ■ *Web:* www.unical.com						
Unicard Systems Inc 5340 Alpha Rd	Dallas	TX	75240	972-385-4000		196
Web: www.worldgiftcard.com						
Unicast Co 241 N Washington St	Boyertown	PA	19512	610-367-0155	367-2787	307
Web: www.unicastco.com						
UNICEF (United Nations Children's Fund)						
3 United Nations Plaza	New York	NY	10017	212-326-7000	888-7465	783
Web: www.unicef.org						
Unicell Body Co 571 Howard St	Buffalo	NY	14206	716-853-8628	843-8638	516
TF Cust Svc: 800-628-8914 ■ *Web:* www.unicell.com						
Unicentric Inc 3127 Penn Ave	Pittsburgh	PA	15201	412-697-7200		177
TF: 800-513-7745 ■ *Web:* www.unicentric.com						
Unicep Packaging Inc						
1702 Industrial Dr	Sandpoint	ID	83864	208-265-9696	265-4726	549
TF: 800-354-9396 ■ *Web:* www.unicep.com						
Unichem Inc 8 N Kings Rd	Greenville	SC	29605	864-422-0191		104
Web: www.unichem.com						
Unicircuit Inc 8192 Southpark Ln	Littleton	CO	80120	303-730-0505	730-0606	625
TF: 800-648-6449 ■ *Web:* www.anaren.com						
Unico American Corp						
23251 Mulholland Dr	Woodland Hills	CA	91364	818-591-9800		391-4
TF: 800-669-9800 ■ *Web:* www.crusaderinsurance.com						
Unico Inc 3725 Nicholson Rd	Franksville	WI	53126	262-886-5678	504-7396	518
TF: 800-245-1859 ■ *Web:* www.unicous.com						
Unicoi County 100 Main St PO Box 713	Erwin	TN	37650	423-743-3000		338
Web: www.unicoicounty.org						
Unicoi State Park & Lodge						
1788 Hwy 356 Rd	Helen	GA	30545	800-573-9659		565
TF: 800-573-9659 ■ *Web:* www.gastateparks.org/info/unicoi						
UNICOM 565 Brea Canyon Rd Ste A	Walnut	CA	91789	626-964-7873	964-7880*	176
**Fax:* Mktg ■ *TF:* 800-346-6668 ■ *Web:* www.unicomlink.com						
Unicom Graphics Ltd						
4501 Manitoba Rd SE	Calgary	AB	T2G4B9	403-287-2020		627
Web: www.unicomgraphics.com						
UNICOM Systems Inc						
15535 San Fernando Mission Blvd UNICOM Plaza Ste 310	Mission Hills	CA	91345	818-838-0606		809
Web: www.unicomglobal.com						
Unicom Technologies Inc 1011 Hwy 6 S	Houston	TX	77077	281-496-3606		764
Web: www.unicom-tech.com						
UniComm Consulting LLC						
9745 Rim Rock Cir	Loomis	CA	95650	408-420-5539		463
Web: www.unicommconsulting.com						
Unicon Group Ltd 1734 Gilsinn Ln	St. Louis	MO	63026	636-394-2012		225
Web: www.unicongl.com						
Unicon Inc 1760 E Pecos Rd Ste 432	Gilbert	AZ	85295	480-558-2400		261
TF: 800-467-4448 ■ *Web:* www.unicon.net						
UNICON International Inc						
241 Outerbelt St	Columbus	OH	43213	614-861-7070		180
TF: 800-635-5138 ■ *Web:* www.unicon-intl.com						
Unicontrol Inc 1111 Brookpark Rd	Cleveland	OH	44109	216-398-4414		201
Web: www.unicontrolinc.com						
Unicorn Theatre 3828 Main St	Kansas City	MO	64111	816-531-7529	531-0421	572
Web: www.unicorntheatre.org						
UnicornHRO 25 Hanover Rd Ste B	Florham Park	NJ	07932	973-360-0688		39
TF: 800-368-8149 ■ *Web:* www.unicornhro.com						
Unicorp 291 Cleveland St	Orange	NJ	07050	973-674-1700	674-3803	350
TF: 800-526-1389 ■ *Web:* www.unicorpinc.com						
Unicorr 455 Sackett Pt Rd	North Haven	CT	06473	203-248-2161	248-0241	548
TF General: 800-229-4269 ■ *Web:* www.unicorr.com						
Unicote Corp 33165 Groesbeck Hwy	Fraser	MI	40026	586-296-0700	296-3155	481
TF: 800-732-5569 ■ *Web:* www.unicotecorporation.com						
Unicover Corp 1 Unicover Ctr	Cheyenne	WY	82008	307-771-3000	771-3134	459
TF Cust Svc: 800-443-4225 ■ *Web:* www.unicover.com						
Uniden America Corp						
4700 Amon Carter Blvd	Fort Worth	TX	76155	817-858-3300	858-3300*	735
**Fax:* Hum Res ■ *TF Cust Svc:* 800-297-1023 ■ *Web:* www.uniden.com						
UNIDO (United Nations Industrial Development Organization)						
1 UN Plaza	New York	NY	10017	212-963-6890	963-7904	783
Web: www.unido.org						
Uniek Inc 805 Uniek Dr	Waunakee	WI	53597	608-849-9999		309
Web: www.uniekinc.com						
Unifab Corp 5260 Lovers Ln	Portage	MI	49002	269-382-2803		482
Web: unifabcorporation.com						
Unifi Inc 7201 W Friendly Ave	Greensboro	NC	27410	336-294-4410	316-5422	745-9
NYSE: UFI ■ *Web:* www.unifi.com						
Unified Brands 1055 Mendell Davis Dr	Jackson	MS	39272	888-994-7636	864-7636	386
TF: 888-994-7636 ■ *Web:* www.unifiedbrands.net						
Unified Field Inc						
33 E 33rd St Ste 1107	New York	NY	10016	212-532-9595		180
Web: www.unifiedfield.com						
Unified Financial Services Inc						
2353 Alexandria Dr	Lexington	KY	40504	859-422-0347		691
Web: www.unified.com						
Unified Government of Wyandotte County/Kansas City						
701 N Seventh St Ste 323	Kansas City	KS	66101	913-573-5260	573-5005	338
Web: www.wycokck.org						
Unified Grocers Inc 5200 Sheila St	Commerce	CA	90040	323-264-5200	729-6610	297-8
TF: 800-724-7762 ■ *Web:* www.unifiedgrocers.com						
Unified Industries Inc						
6551 Loisdale Ct Ste 400	Springfield	VA	22150	703-922-9800	971-5892	261
TF: 800-666-1642 ■ *Web:* www.uii.com						
Unified Packaging Inc 1187 E 68th Ave	Denver	CO	80229	303-733-1000	733-6789	86
Web: www.unifiedbinders.com						
Unified School District 428						
201 S Patton Rd	Great Bend	KS	67530	620-793-1500		685
Web: www.usd428.net						
Unified School District of Antigo						
120 S Dorr St	Antigo	WI	54409	715-627-4355	623-3279	685
Web: www.antigo.k12.wi.us						
Unified Solutions Inc						
9801 80th Ave	Pleasant Prairie	WI	53158	262-942-5200		88
Web: usipackaging.com						
Unified Systems Group Inc						
1235 64th Ave SE Ste 4a	Calgary	AB	T2H2J7	403-686-8088		174
TF: 866-892-8988 ■ *Web:* www.usg.ca						
Unified Theory Inc						
1811 Weir Dr Ste 365	Saint Paul	MN	55125	651-578-8100		261
Web: www.unifiedtheory.net						
UniFocus LP 2455 McIver Ln	Carrollton	TX	75006	972-512-5000		225
Web: www.unifocus.com						
Unifoil Corp 12 Daniel Rd	Fairfield	NJ	07004	973-244-9900	244-5555	555
TF: 800-836-5554 ■ *Web:* www.unifoil.com						
Unifor 301 Laurier Ave W	Ottawa	ON	K1P6M6	613-230-5200		414
TF: 877-230-5201 ■ *Web:* www.cep.ca						
Uniforce Technologies Inc						
1805 E Fifth St	North Little Rock	AR	72114	501-945-3283		729

Name / Address	Phone	Fax	Class
Uniform & Textile Service Assn (UTSA) 1300 N 17th St Ste 750 .... Arlington VA 22209 *TF:* 800-996-3426 ■ *Web:* www.glrppr.org	703-247-2600		49-4
Uniform Commercial Code Law Letter 610 Opperman Dr .... Eagan MN 55123 *TF Cust Svc:* 800-328-4880 ■ *Web:* legalsolutions.thomsonreuters.com	651-687-7000		531-13
Uni-Form Components Co 10703 Sheldon Rd .... Houston TX 77044 *Web:* www.uniformcomponents.com	281-456-9310		482
Uniform Industrial Corp 47341 Bayside Pkwy .... Fremont CA 94538 *Web:* uicworld.com	510-438-6799		466
Uniformed Services University of the Health Sciences Learning Resource Ctr 4301 Jones Bridge Rd .... Bethesda MD 20814 *TF:* 800-772-1747	301-295-9474		434-1
Unifrax Corp 2351 Whirlpool St .... Niagara Falls NY 14305 *Web:* www.unifrax.com	716-278-3800		389
Unifund CCR Partners Inc 10625 Techwoods Cir .... Cincinnati OH 45242 *TF:* 800-713-0670 ■ *Web:* www.unifund.com	513-489-8877		215
Unifuse LLC 2092 New York 9G .... Staatsburg NY 12580 *Web:* www.unifuse.com	845-889-4000	889-4002	199
Unify Square Inc 411 108th Ave NE .... Bellevue WA 98004 *Web:* www.unifysquare.com	425-865-0700		463
Unigen Corp 45388 Warm Springs Blvd .... Fremont CA 94539 *TF:* 800-826-0808 ■ *Web:* www.unigen.com	510-668-2088	668-4889	625
Unigene Laboratories Inc 81 Fulton St .... Boonton NJ 07005 *TF:* 800-732-0330 ■ *Web:* www.unigene.com	973-265-1100		85
UNIGLOBE Travel USA LLC 18662 MacArthur Blvd Ste 100 .... Irvine CA 92612 *TF:* 877-438-4338 ■ *Web:* www.uniglobetravelusa.com	949-623-9000		772
Uni-Graphic Inc 110 Commerce Way .... Woburn MA 01801 *Web:* www.uni-graphic.com	781-231-7200	938-7727	627
Uniguest Inc 1035 Acorn Dr .... Nashville TN 37210 *Web:* www.ushospitality.com	615-259-4500		5
UniLect Corp PO Box 3026 .... Danville CA 94526 *TF:* 888-864-5328 ■ *Web:* www.unilect.com	925-833-8660	833-8874	801
Unilens Corp USA 10431 72td St N .... Largo FL 33777 *Web:* www.unilens.com	727-544-2531		544
Unilever Canada Ltd 160 Bloor St E Ste 1500 .... Toronto ON M4W3R2 *TF:* 800-387-0691 ■ *Web:* www.unilever.ca	416-964-1857		360-3
Unilever Foodsolutions Div of Conopco Inc 2200 Cabot Dr .... Lisle IL 60532 *Web:* www.unileverfoodsolutions.us	630-505-5300		123
Unilife Corp 250 Cross Farm Ln .... York PA 17406 *Web:* www.unilife.com	717-384-3400		476
Uniloy Milacron Inc 5550 S Occidental Rd Ste B .... Tecumseh MI 49286 *Web:* www.milacron.com/our-brands/uniloy	517-424-8756	423-5671	757
Unilux Inc 59 N Fifth St .... Saddle Brook NJ 07663 *TF:* 800-522-0801 ■ *Web:* www.unilux.com	201-712-1266	712-1366	472
Unimac Graphics 350 Michele Pl .... Carlstadt NJ 07072 *Web:* www.unimacgraphics.com	201-372-1000	372-0699	344
Unimark Products 9818 Pflumm Rd .... Lenexa KS 66215 *TF Cust Svc:* 800-255-6356 ■ *Web:* www.unimark.com	913-649-2424	649-5795	176
Unimax Systems Corporation Inc 121 S Eighth St Ste 790 .... Minneapolis MN 55402 *TF:* 800-886-0390 ■ *Web:* www.unimax.com	800-886-0390		177
Unimin Corp 258 Elm St .... New Canaan CT 06840 *Web:* www.unimin.com	203-966-8880	966-3453	503-4
Unintech Consulting Engineers Inc 2431 E Evans Rd .... San Antonio TX 78259 *Web:* www.unintech.com	210-641-6003		196
Union Adjustment Company Inc 3214 W Burbank Blvd .... Burbank CA 91505 *TF:* 800-467-6619 ■ *Web:* www.unionadjustment.com	818-566-8330		160
Union Bank & Trust Inc 312 Central Ave SE .... Minneapolis MN 55414 *Web:* www.ubtmn.com	612-379-3222	379-8837	70
Union Bank Company, The 100 S High St PO Box 67 .... Columbus Grove OH 45830 *NASDAQ: UBOH* ■ *TF:* 800-837-8111 ■ *Web:* www.theubank.com	419-659-2141	659-2069	360-2
Union Bank of California NA 400 California St 1st Fl .... San Francisco CA 94104 *TF:* 800-238-4486 ■ *Web:* www.unionbank.com	415-765-3434		70
Union Bankshares Inc 20 Lower Main St .... Morrisville VT 05661 *NASDAQ: UNB* ■ *TF:* 866-862-1891 ■ *Web:* www.unionbankvt.com	802-888-6600		360-2
Union Bar & Grille 1357 Washington St .... Boston MA 02118 *Web:* www.unionrestaurant.com	617-338-5300		671
Union Carbide Corp 1254 Enclave Pkwy .... Houston TX 77077 *Web:* www.unioncarbide.com	281-966-2016		146
Union Cemetery 2505 Minnehaha Ave E .... Maplewood MN 55119 *Web:* unioncemeterymn.org	651-739-0400		510
Union Chapel 55 Narragansett Ave .... Edgartown MA 02539 *Web:* www.mvpreservation.org	508-627-4440		50-1
Union Church of Pocantico Hills 555 Bedford Rd .... Sleepy Hollow NY 10591 *TF:* 877-325-4822 ■ *Web:* www.hudsonvalley.org	914-631-8200	631-0089	50-1
Union City Chamber of Commerce 3939 Smith St .... Union City CA 94587 *TF:* 800-945-2288 ■ *Web:* www.unioncitychamber.com	510-952-9637	952-9647	139
Union City Grille 805 N Union St .... Wilmington DE 19805	302-654-9780		671
Union City Public Library 324 43rd St .... Union City NJ 07087 *Web:* www.uclibrary.org	201-866-7500	866-0962	434-3
Union College 310 College St .... Barbourville KY 40906 **Fax: Admissions* ■ *TF:* 800-489-8646 ■ *Web:* www.unionky.edu	606-546-4151	546-1667*	166
Union College 3800 S 48th St .... Lincoln NE 68506 **Fax: Admissions* ■ *TF Admissions:* 800-228-4600 ■ *Web:* www.ucollege.edu	402-486-2504	486-2895*	166
Union Correctional Institution 7819 NW 228th St .... Raiford FL 32026 *Web:* dc.state.fl.us	386-431-2000	431-2010	213
Union Corrugating Company Inc 701 S King St .... Fayetteville NC 28301 *Web:* www.unioncorrugating.com	910-483-2195		480
Union County 65 Courthouse St PO Box 2 .... Blairsville GA 30512 *Web:* unioncountyga.gov	706-439-6000	439-6004	338
Union County 1103 S First St .... Clayton NM 88415 *TF:* 800-390-7858 ■ *Web:* claytonnm.org	575-374-9253		338
Union County 300 N Pine St Ste 6 .... Creston IA 50801 *Web:* www.unioncountyiowa.org	641-782-7315	782-8241	338
Union County 101 N Washington Ste102 .... El Dorado AR 71730 *Web:* unioncountyar.com	870-864-1910	864-1927	338
Union County 209 E Main St Ste 230 .... Elk Point SD 57025 *Web:* unioncountysd.org	605-356-2132		338
Union County 301 S Main St Ste 1 .... Anna IL 62906 *Web:* www.shawneeheartland.com/government.html	618-833-5711		338
Union County 1106 K Ave .... La Grande OR 97850 *TF:* 800-735-1232 ■ *Web:* www.union-county.org	541-963-1001	963-1079	338
Union County 103 S Second St .... Lewisburg PA 17837 *Web:* www.unioncountypa.org	570-524-8781	524-8785	338
Union County 26 W Union St .... Liberty IN 47353	765-458-6121	458-5263	338
Union County 1001 Main St PO Box 848 .... Maynardville TN 37807 *Web:* www.comeherecomehome.com	865-992-2811		338
Union County 100 W Main St PO Box 177 .... Morganfield KY 42437	270-389-1933	389-2276	338
Union County 210 W Main St .... Union SC 29379 *TF:* 800-273-5066 ■ *Web:* www.countyofunion.org	864-429-1600	429-1603	338
Union County Carnegie Library 300 E S St .... Union SC 29379 *Web:* www.unionlibrary.org	864-427-7140		434-3
Union County Chamber of Commerce 903 Skyway Dr PO Box 1789 .... Monroe NC 28110 *Web:* www.unioncountycoc.com	704-289-4567	282-0122	139
Union County Chamber of Commerce 227 E Fifth St .... Marysville OH 43040 *TF:* 800-642-0087 ■ *Web:* www.unioncounty.org	937-642-6279	644-0422	139
Union County Chamber of Commerce 135 W Main St .... Union SC 29379 *TF:* 877-202-8755 ■ *Web:* www.unionsc.info	864-427-9039	427-9030	139
Union County Clerk 215 W Sixth St .... Marysville OH 43040 *Web:* co.union.oh.us	937-645-3006		338
Union County College 1033 Springfield Ave .... Cranford NJ 07016 **Fax: Admissions* ■ *Web:* www.ucc.edu	908-709-7000	709-7125*	162
Union County Electric Co-op Inc 122 W Main St .... Elk Point SD 57025 *TF:* 888-356-3395 ■ *Web:* unioncounty.coop	605-356-3395	356-3397	245
Union County Public Library 316 E Windsor St .... Monroe NC 28112 *Web:* www.union.lib.nc.us	704-283-8184		434-3
Union County Public Schools 510 S Mart St .... Morganfield KY 42437 *Web:* www.union.kyschools.us	270-389-1694	389-9806	685
Union County State Fish & Wildlife Area 2755 Refuge Rd .... Jonesboro IL 62952 *Web:* dnr.illinois.gov/Lands/Landmgt/PARKS/R5/UNIONCO.HTM	618-833-5175		565
Union Distributing Company of Tucson 4000 E Michigan St .... Tucson AZ 85714 *Web:* www.uniondistributing.connekt2.com	520-571-7600		579
Union Drilling Inc 4055 International Plaza Ste 610 .... Fort Worth TX 76109 *NASDAQ: UDRL* ■ *TF:* 800-732-0330 ■ *Web:* sidewinderdrilling.com	817-735-8793	546-4368	540
Union Editorial LLC 12200 W Olympic Blvd Ste 140 .... Los Angeles CA 90064 *TF:* 800-279-0041 ■ *Web:* www.unioneditorial.com	310-481-2200		514
Union Electric Steel Corp 726 Bell Ave .... Carnegie PA 15106 *Web:* www.uniones.com	412-429-7655	276-1711	307
Union Engineering Company Inc 3658 N Ventura Ave .... Ventura CA 93001	805-648-3373		189-5
Union Eyecare Centers 4750 Beidler Rd .... Willoughby OH 44094 *TF:* 800-443-9699 ■ *Web:* www.unioneyecare.com	216-986-9700	986-1996	543
Union for Reformed Judaism 633 Third Ave .... New York NY 10017 *TF:* 800-833-2499 ■ *Web:* www.urj.org	212-650-4000		48-20
Union Grill 2501 Wall Ave .... Ogden UT 84401 *Web:* www.uniongrillogden.com	801-621-2830	621-7946	671
Union Group 649 Alden St .... Fall River MA 02722 *Web:* www.theuniongroup.com	508-676-8580		86
Union Grove State Park 1215 220th St .... Gladbrook IA 50635 *Web:* www.iowadnr.gov	641-473-2556	473-3059	565
Union Grove State Park c/o Newton Hills State Pk 30828 471st Ave .... Beresford SD 57004 *Web:* gfp.sd.gov	605-987-2263		565
Union Hospital 500 Lynnfield St .... Lynn MA 01904 *Web:* nsmc.partners.org	781-581-9200		374-3
Union Hospital 106 Bow St .... Elkton MD 21921 *TF:* 800-463-6295 ■ *Web:* www.uhcc.com	410-398-4000		374-3
Union Hospital 1606 N Seventh St .... Terre Haute IN 47804 *TF:* 800-355-2470 ■ *Web:* www.myunionhospital.org/unionhospital	812-238-7000		374-3
Union Hospital 1000 Galloping Hill Rd .... Union NJ 07083 *Web:* www.barnabashealth.org	908-964-7333		374-3
Union Hospital 659 Blvd .... Dover OH 44622 *TF:* 800-541-6664 ■ *Web:* www.unionhospital.org	330-343-3311	364-0951	374-3
Union Institute & University 440 E McMillan St .... Cincinnati OH 45206 **Fax: Admissions* ■ *TF:* 800-486-3116 ■ *Web:* myunion.edu	513-861-6400	861-0779*	166
Union Labor Report 1801 S Bell St .... Arlington VA 22202 *TF:* 800-372-1033 ■ *Web:* www.bna.com/union-labor-report-p6722	800-372-1033		531-13
Union Leader 100 William Loeb Dr .... Manchester NH 03109 **Fax: Edit* ■ *Web:* www.unionleader.com	603-668-4321	668-0382*	532-2
Union League Cafe 1032 Chapel St .... New Haven CT 06510 *Web:* unionleaguecafe.com	203-562-4299	562-6712	671
Union Machine Company of Lynn Inc 6 Federal Way .... Groveland MA 01834 *Web:* www.unionmachine.com	978-521-5100		529

Phone | Fax | Class

Union Memorial Hospital
201 E University Pkwy .... Baltimore MD 21218 410-554-2000 374-3
Web: www.medstarhealth.org
Union Metal Corp 1432 Maple Ave NE .... Canton OH 44705 330-456-7653 456-0196 480
TF: 800-327-0097 ■ *Web:* www.unionmetal.com
Union National Life Insurance
3636 S Sherwood Forest Blvd .... Baton Rouge LA 70816 225-292-7600 391-4
Union Of Agricultural Procedures, The
555 Boul Roland-therrien Ste 100 .... Longueuil QC J4H3Y9 450-679-0530 414
Union of American Physicians & Dentists
180 Grand Ave Ste 1380 .... Oakland CA 94612 510-839-0193 763-8756 414
TF: 800-622-0909 ■ *Web:* www.uapd.com
Union of Concerned Scientists (UCS)
2 Brattle Sq .... Cambridge MA 02238 617-547-5552 864-9405 48-13
TF: 800-666-8276 ■ *Web:* www.ucsusa.org
Union Pacific Corp 1400 Douglas St .... Omaha NE 68179 402-544-5000 360-3
NYSE: UNP ■ *TF:* 888-870-8777 ■ *Web:* www.up.com
Union Pacific Foundation
1400 Douglas St .... Omaha NE 68179 402-544-5600 304
Web: up.com/aboutup/community/foundation/index.htm
Union Pacific Railroad Co
1400 Douglas St .... Omaha NE 68179 888-870-8777 648
TF: 888-870-8777 ■ *Web:* www.up.com
Union Pacific Railroad Employees' Health Systems
1040 North 2200 West .... Salt Lake City UT 84116 801-595-4300 595-4399 391-3
TF: 800-547-0421 ■ *Web:* www.uphealth.com
Union Parish
100 E Bayou St Ste 105 .... Farmerville LA 71241 318-368-3055 368-3861 338
TF: 800-256-6660 ■ *Web:* upclerk.com
Union Power Co-op
1525 N Rocky River Rd .... Monroe NC 28110 704-289-3145 296-0408 245
TF: 800-922-6840 ■ *Web:* www.union-power.com
Union Railroad Co 1200 Penn Ave .... Pittsburgh PA 15222 412-433-7066 648
Union Resource Marketing
12301 Rosewood Dr .... Leawood KS 66209 913-322-2702 193
Web: www.unionresourcemarketing.com
Union Roofers Health & Welfare
9901 Paramount Blvd Ste 211 .... Downey CA 90240 562-927-1434 414
Union Rural Electric Co-op Inc
15461 US 36E .... Marysville OH 43040 937-642-1826 245
TF: 800-642-1826 ■ *Web:* www.ure.com
Union Sanitary District (USD)
5072 Benson Rd PO Box 5050 .... Union City CA 94587 510-477-7500 804
Web: www.unionsanitary.com
Union Savings Bank
223 W Stephenson St PO Box 540 .... Freeport IL 61032 815-235-0800 851-7278* 70
**Fax Area Code:* 866 ■ *Web:* www.unionsavingsbank.com
Union Securities Ltd
700 W Georgia St Ste 900 .... Vancouver BC V7Y1H4 604-687-2201 690
TF: 800 206 7242 ■ *Web:* www.union-securities.com
Union Special Corp
1 Union Special Plaza .... Huntley IL 60142 847-669-5101 219
Web: www.unionspecial.com
Union Square Advisors
600 Montgomery St 22nd Fl .... San Francisco CA 94111 415-501-8000 70
Web: www.usadvisors.com
Union Square Cafe 101 E 19th St .... New York NY 10003 212-243-4020 671
Web: unionsquarecafe.com
Union Square Ventures
915 Broadway 19th Fl .... New York NY 10010 212-994-7880 994-7399 792
Web: www.usv.com
Union Standard Equipment Co
801 E 141st St .... Bronx NY 10454 718-585-0200 993-2650 298
TF: 877-282-7333 ■ *Web:* www.unionmachinery.com
Union Standard Insurance Co
122 W Carpenter Fwy Ste 350 .... Irving TX 75039 972-719-2400 719-2401 391-4
TF: 800-444-0049 ■ *Web:* www.usic.com
Union State Bank
127 S Summit St .... Arkansas City KS 67005 620-442-5200 442-8081 70
Web: www.myunionstate.com
Union Station 2501 Wall Ave .... Ogden UT 84401 801-393-9886 520
TF: 800-864-4405 ■ *Web:* theunionstation.org
Union Station 50 Massachusetts Ave .... Washington DC 20002 202-289-1908 50-6
TF: 800-331-0008 ■ *Web:* www.unionstationdc.com
Union Station Hotel 1001 Broadway .... Nashville TN 37203 615-726-1001 378
TF: 800-996-3426 ■ *Web:* www.unionstationhotelnashville.com
Union Street 4145 Woodward Ave .... Detroit MI 48201 313-831-3965 831-2553 671
Web: www.unionstreetdetroit.com
Union Street Public House
121 S Union St .... Alexandria VA 22314 703-548-1785 671
TF: 800-442-1162 ■ *Web:* www.unionstreetpublichouse.com
Union Tank Car Co 175 W Jackson Blvd .... Chicago IL 60604 312-431-3111 431-5125 650
TF: 800-424-9300 ■ *Web:* www.utlx.com
Union Theological Seminary
3041 Broadway 121st St .... New York NY 10027 212-662-7100 280-1416 167-3
Web: www.uts.columbia.edu
Union Theological Seminary & Presbyterian School of Christian Education
3401 Brook Rd .... Richmond VA 23227 804-355-0671 167-3
TF: 800-229-2990 ■ *Web:* upsem.edu
Union Township Chamber of Commerce
355 Chestnut St 2nd Fl .... Union NJ 07083 908-688-2777 688-0338 139
Web: www.unionchamber.com
Union Township Public Library
1980 Morris Ave .... Union NJ 07083 908-851-5450 851-4671 434-3
Web: www.uniontownship.com/379/union-public-library
Union University
1050 Union University Dr .... Jackson TN 38305 731-661-5210 661-5589* 166
**Fax:* Admissions ■ *TF:* 800-338-6466 ■ *Web:* www.uu.edu
Union, The 464 Sutton Way .... Grass Valley CA 95945 530-273-9561 477-4292 532-2
TF: 800-284-3233 ■ *Web:* www.theunion.com
Uniontown Hospital (UH)
500 W Berkeley St .... Uniontown PA 15401 724-430-5000 374-3
TF: 800-397-2554 ■ *Web:* www.uniontownhospital.com
Unipack Inc 3253 Old Frankstown Rd .... Pittsburgh PA 15239 724-733-7381 327-6265 582
Web: www.unipackinc.com
Unipak Aviation 2049 Ninth Ave .... Ronkonkoma NY 11779 631-471-9801 63
Web: www.unipakaviation.net

Uni-Pak Corp
1015 N Ronald Reagan Blvd .... Longwood FL 32750 407-830-9300 830-4106 207
TF: 800-732-7766 ■ *Web:* www.unipak.com
Unipharm Inc 350 Fifth Ave Ste 6701 .... New York NY 10118 212-594-3260 594-3261 582
Web: www.unipharmus.com
Uniplus Consultants Inc
8140 Ashton Ave Ste 210 .... Manassas VA 20109 703-365-2227 809
Web: www.uniplus.com
UniPro Foodservice Inc
2500 Cumberland Pkwy Ste 600 .... Atlanta GA 30339 770-952-0871 297-8
TF: 800-933-5262 ■ *Web:* www.uniprofoodservice.com
Unipunch Products Inc
311 Fifth St NW .... Clear Lake WI 54005 800-828-7061 453-3994 757
TF: 800-828-7061 ■ *Web:* www.unipunch.com
Unique Aluminum Extrusion LLC
333 Cedar Ave .... Middlesex NJ 08846 732-271-1160 271-8327 482
Web: www.unalext.com
Unique Broadband Systems Ltd
400 Spinnaker Way Unit 1 10 .... Vaughan ON L4K5Y9 905-669-8533 647
TF: 877-669-8533 ■ *Web:* www.uniquesys.com
Unique Business Systems Corp
2901 Ocean Park Blvd # 215 .... Santa Monica CA 90405 310-396-3929 177
TF: 800-669-4827 ■ *Web:* www.unibiz.com
Unique Carpets Ltd 7360 Jurupa Ave .... Riverside CA 92504 951-352-8125 352-8140 131
TF: 800-547-8266 ■ *Web:* www.uniquecarpetsltd.com
Unique Communications Inc
3650 Coral Ridge Dr .... Coral Springs FL 33065 954-735-4002 735-2612 246
TF: 800-881-8182 ■ *Web:* www.uniquecommunications.com
Unique Conversions Inc
1502 Hwy 157 N Ste D .... Mansfield TX 76063 817-477-5251 62-7
Web: laredoconversions.com
Unique Copy Center of New York
252 Greene St .... New York NY 10003 212-420-9198 113
Web: uniquecopycenter.com
Unique Embossing Services Inc
400 Plaza Dr .... Westmont IL 60559 630-789-6789 596
Web: www.uniqueembossing.com
Unique Employment Services Inc
4646 Corona Dr Ste 100 .... Corpus Christi TX 78411 361-852-6392 260
TF: 800-824-8367 ■ *Web:* www.uniquehr.com
Unique Fabricating Inc
800 Standard Pkwy .... Auburn Hills MI 48326 248-853-2333 853-7720 601
Web: www.uniquefab.com
Unique Functional Products Corp
135 Sunshine Ln .... San Marcos CA 92069 760-744-1610 763
TF: 800-854-1905 ■ *Web:* www.ufpnet.com
Unique Home Design Inc
17510 S Dixie Hwy .... Miami FL 33157 305-255-1114 226
Unique Image Inc
19365 Bus Ctr Dr Ste 1 .... Northridge CA 91324 818-727-7785 627
Web: www.uniqueimageinc.com
Unique Industries Inc
4750 League Island Blvd .... Philadelphia PA 19112 215-336-4300 888-1490* 328
**Fax Area Code:* 800 ■ *TF:* 800-888-0559 ■ *Web:* www.favors.com
Unique Investment Corp
7028 Kearny Dr .... Huntington Beach CA 92648 714-848-5900 401
Web: www.uniquepartners.com
Unique Lighting Systems Inc
1240 Simpson Way .... Escondido CA [illegible] [illegible] [illegible] 707
**Fax Area Code:* 760 ■ *TF:* 800-955-4831 ■ *Web:* www.uniquelighting.com
Unique Litho Inc 9 Inverness Dr E .... Englewood CO 80112 303-830-2999 627
TF: 800-448-0438 ■ *Web:* www.uniquelitho.com
Unique Mailing Services Inc
325 Marmon Dr .... Bolingbrook IL 60440 630-739-4848 5
Unique Management Services Inc
119 E Maple St .... Jeffersonville IN 47130 800-879-5453 160
TF: 800-879-5453 ■ *Web:* www.unique-mgmt.com
UniqueLeads com Inc
1128 Royal Palm Beach Blvd Ste 222 .... Royal Palm Beach FL 33411 561-491-2826 466
Web: www.uniqueleads.com
Unirac Inc 1411 Broadway Blvd NE .... Albuquerque NM 87102 505-242-6411 567
Web: www.unirac.com
Unirex Inc 9310 E 37th St N .... Wichita KS 67226 316-636-1228 636-5482 770
Web: www.unirexinc.com
Uniroyal Engineered Products LLC
1800 Second St Ste 970 .... Sarasota FL 34236 941-906-8580 745-2
Web: www.naugahyde.com
UniSea Inc
15400 NE 90th St PO Box 97019 .... Redmond WA 98073 425-881-8181 296-14
TF: 800-535-8509 ■ *Web:* www.unisea.com
Uniseal Inc 1014 E Uhlhorn St .... Evansville IN 47710 812-463-5230 3
Web: www.uniseal.com
Unisearch Associates Inc
96 Bradwick Dr .... Concord ON L4K1K8 905-669-3547 358
Web: www.unisearch-associates.com
Unisearch Inc 1780 Barnes Blvd SW .... Tumwater WA 98512 360-956-9500 531-1717* 635
**Fax Area Code:* 800 ■ *TF:* 800-722-0708 ■ *Web:* www.unisearch.com
Unisec Inc 2555 Nicholson St .... San Leandro CA 94577 800-982-4587 352-6707* 692
**Fax Area Code:* 510 ■ *TF:* 800-982-4587 ■ *Web:* www.ultrabarrier.com
Uniserve Communications Corp
Ste 330 333 Terminal Ave .... Vancouver BC V6A4C1 604-924-8118 224
Web: www.uniserve.com
Unishippers Assn Inc
746 E Winchester Ste 200 .... Salt Lake City UT 84107 800-999-8721 487-7468* 546
**Fax Area Code:* 801 ■ *TF:* 800-999-8721 ■ *Web:* www.unishippers.com
UniSoft Corp 10 Rollins Rd Ste 118 .... Millbrae CA 94030 650-259-1290 259-1299 178-12
Web: www.unisoft.com
Unison Consulting Inc
409 W Huron St Ste 400 .... Chicago IL 60654 312-988-3360 463
Web: www.unison-ucg.com
Unison LLC 7575 Baymeadows Way .... Jacksonville FL 32256 904-739-4000 490
Web: www.unisonindustries.com
Unison Systems Inc
6130 Greenwood Plaza Blvd Ste 100 .... Greenwood Village CO 80111 303-623-8800 196
Web: www.unisonsystems.com
Unisource Canada Inc
50 E Wilmot St .... Richmond Hill ON L4B3Z3 905-771-4000 771-4219 535
Web: www.unisource.ca

Name / Address	City	State	ZIP	Phone	Fax	Class
Unisource Manufacturing Inc						
8040 NE 33rd Dr	Portland	OR	97211	503-281-4673	281-5845	454
TF: 800-234-2566 ■ *Web:* www.unisource-mfg.com						
Unisource NTC						
1560 Holly Court Ste 200	Thousand Oaks	CA	91360	800-736-8470		463
TF: 800-736-8470 ■ *Web:* www.unisourcentc.com						
Unisource Solutions Inc						
8350 Rex Rd	Pico Rivera	CA	90660	562-949-1111	949-7110	319
Web: www.unisourceit.com						
Unist 4134 36th St SE	Grand Rapids	MI	49512	616-949-0853		697
TF: 800-253-5462 ■ *Web:* www.unist.com						
Unistar-Sparco Computers Inc						
7089 Ryburn Dr	Millington	TN	38053	901-872-2272	872-8482	459
TF: 800-840-8400 ■ *Web:* www.sparco.com						
Unistress Corp 550 Cheshire Rd	Pittsfield	MA	01201	413-499-1441	499-9930	183
TF: 800-234-3119 ■ *Web:* www.unistresscorp.com						
Unisys Corp 801 Lakeview Dr Ste 100	Blue Bell	PA	19422	215-986-4011		196
Web: www.unisys.com						
Unit 7 30 Irving Pl Fl 11	New York	NY	10003	212-209-1600		4
Unit Chemical Corp						
7360 Commercial Way	Henderson	NV	89015	702-564-6454	564-6629	151
TF: 800-879-8648 ■ *Web:* www.unitchemical.com						
Unit Company Inc 620 E Whitney Rd	Anchorage	AK	99501	907-349-6666		186
Web: www.unitcompany.com						
Unit Corp 7130 S Lewis Ave Ste 1000	Tulsa	OK	74136	918-493-7700	493-7711	540
NYSE: UNT ■ *TF:* 800-722-3612 ■ *Web:* www.unitcorp.com						
Unit Drop Forge Company Inc						
1903 S 62nd St PO Box 340350	West Allis	WI	53219	414-545-3000	545-6318	483
TF: 800-444-5427 ■ *Web:* www.unitforgings.com						
Unit Pack Company Inc 7 Lewis Rd	Cedar Grove	NJ	07009	973-239-4112		596
Web: www.unitpack.com						
Unitarian Universalist Assn (UUA)						
25 Beacon St	Boston	MA	02108	617-742-2100	367-3237	48-20
Web: www.uua.org						
Unitarian Universalist Service Committee (UUSC)						
689 Massachusetts Ave	Cambridge	MA	02139	617-868-6600	868-7102	48-5
TF: 800-388-3920 ■ *Web:* www.uusc.org						
UNITE HERE 275 Seventh Ave	New York	NY	10001	212-265-7000		414
TF: 800-452-4155 ■ *Web:* www.unitehere.org						
Unitech Services Group						
295 Parker St	Springfield	MA	01151	413-543-6911	543-6989	442
TF: 800-344-3824 ■ *Web:* www.unitechus.com						
Unitech Training Academy-houma						
1227 Grand Caillou Rd	Houma	LA	70363	985-223-1755		166
Web: www.unitechtrainingacademy.com						
United Abrasives Inc						
185 Boston Post Rd	North Windham	CT	06256	860-456-7131		1
Web: www.unitedabrasives.com						
United Aerospace Corp						
9800 Premier Pkwy	Miramar	FL	33025	954-364-0085	364-0089	770
Web: www.unitedaerospace.com						
United Airlines Cargo PO Box 66100	Chicago	IL	60666	800-822-2746		12
TF: 800-822-2746 ■ *Web:* www.unitedcargo.com						
United Alloy Inc 4100 Kennedy Rd	Janesville	WI	53545	608-758-4717		492
TF: 800-265-8840 ■ *Web:* www.unitedalloy.com						
United Aluminum Corp						
100 United Dr	North Haven	CT	06473	203-239-5881		492
TF: 800-243-2515 ■ *Web:* www.unitedaluminum.com						
United American Bank						
101 S Ellsworth Ave	San Mateo	CA	94401	650-579-1500	579-1501	70
OTC: UABK ■ *TF:* 877-822-4822 ■ *Web:* www.unitedamericanbank.com						
United American Insurance Company						
PO Box 8080	McKinney	TX	75070	800-755-2137	569-3709*	391-2
**Fax Area Code:* 972 ■ *TF:* 800-755-2137 ■ *Web:* www.unitedamerican.com						
United Americas Bank NA						
3789 Roswell Rd	Atlanta	GA	30342	404-240-0101		70
United Arab Emirates						
305 E 47th St 7th Fl	New York	NY	10017	212-371-0480	371-4923	784
Web: www.un.int/uae						
United Arab Emirates Embassy						
3522 International Ct NW	Washington	DC	20008	202-243-2400	243-2432	257
TF: 800-688-9889 ■ *Web:* www.uae-embassy.org						
United Assn 3 Park Pl	Annapolis	MD	21401	410-269-2000		414
Web: www.ua.org						
United Auto Supply 625 Third St	La Crosse	WI	54601	608-784-9198		54
Web: www.uasparts.com						
United Avionics Inc						
38 Great Hill Rd	Naugatuck	CT	06770	203-723-1404		22
Web: www.unitedavionicsinc.com						
United Bakery Equipment Co Inc						
15815 W 110th St	Lenexa	KS	66219	913-541-8700	541-0781	298
TF: 888-823-2253 ■ *Web:* www.ubeusa.com						
United Bancorp Inc						
201 S Fourth St	Martins Ferry	OH	43935	740-633-0445	633-1448	360-2
NASDAQ: UBCP ■ *TF:* 888-275-5566 ■ *Web:* www.unitedbancorp.com						
United Bank 11185 Fairfax Blvd	Fairfax	VA	22030	703-219-4850		70
TF: 800-327-9862 ■ *Web:* www.bankwithunited.com						
United Bank & Trust						
935 Main St PO Box E	Sabetha	KS	66534	785-284-2187	284-0062	69
United Bank of Philadelphia						
30 S 15th St Ste 1200	Philadelphia	PA	19102	215-351-4600		70
Web: www.ubphila.com						
United Behavioral Health Inc						
425 Market St 27th Fl	San Francisco	CA	94105	415-547-5000		462
TF: 800-888-2998 ■ *Web:* optum.com						
United Bindery Service Inc						
1845 W Carroll Ave	Chicago	IL	60612	312-243-0240		92
United Biomedical Inc 25 Davids Dr	Hauppauge	NY	11788	631-273-2828	273-1717	85
Web: www.unitedbiomedical.com						
United Blood Services						
6210 E Oak St PO Box 1867	Scottsdale	AZ	85252	480-946-4201		89
TF: 800-288-2199 ■ *Web:* www.unitedbloodservices.org						
United Blood Services						
4119 Broad St	San luis obispo	CA	93401	805-543-4290		89
Web: www.unitedbloodservices.org						
United Blood Services of Arizona						
Chandler 6220 E Oak St	Scottsdale	AZ	85252	877-827-4376		89
TF: 877-827-4376 ■ *Web:* www.unitedbloodservices.org						
San Luis Obispo						
4119 Broad St Ste 100	San Luis Obispo	CA	93401	805-543-4290		89
TF: 877-827-4376 ■ *Web:* www.unitedbloodservices.org						
United Blood Services of Colorado						
146 Sawyer Dr	Durango	CO	81303	970-385-4601		89
TF: 800-288-2199 ■ *Web:* www.unitedbloodservices.org						
United Blood Services of Louisiana						
Baton Rouge 8234 1 Calais Ave	Baton Rouge	LA	70809	225-769-7233		89
Web: www.unitedbloodservices.org/louisiana						
Lafayette 1503 Bertrand Dr	Lafayette	LA	70506	337-235-5433		89
Web: www.unitedbloodservices.org						
United Blood Services of Mississippi						
Hattiesburg 805 S 28th Ave	Hattiesburg	MS	39402	601-264-0743		89
Web: www.unitedbloodservices.org						
Meridian 1115 25th Ave	Meridian	MS	39301	601-482-2482	483-4204	89
TF: 877-827-4376 ■ *Web:* www.unitedbloodservices.org						
Tupelo 4326 S Eason Blvd	Tupelo	MS	38801	662-842-8871		89
TF: 800-844-8870 ■ *Web:* www.unitedbloodservices.org/nt						
United Blood Services of Montana						
Billings 1444 Grand Ave	Billings	MT	59102	406-248-9168	248-1025	89
TF: 800-365-4450 ■ *Web:* www.unitedbloodservices.org						
Butte 3745 Harrison Ave	Butte	MT	59701	877-827-4376		89
TF: 877-827-4376 ■ *Web:* www.unitedbloodservices.org						
United Blood Services of Nevada						
Carson City 256 E Winnie Ln	Carson City	NV	89706	877-827-4376		89
TF: 877-827-4376 ■ *Web:* www.unitedbloodservices.org						
Las Vegas 6930 W Charleston Blvd	Las Vegas	NV	89117	702-228-4483		89
Web: www.unitedbloodservices.org						
United Blood Services of New Mexico						
1515 University Blvd NE	Albuquerque	NM	87102	800-333-8037		89
TF: 800-333-8037 ■ *Web:* www.unitedbloodservices.org						
Albuquerque						
1515 University Blvd NE	Albuquerque	NM	87102	800-333-8037		89
TF: 800-333-8037 ■ *Web:* www.unitedbloodservices.org/nm						
Farmington 475 E 20th St	Farmington	NM	87401	888-804-9913		89
TF: 877-827-4376 ■ *Web:* www.unitedbloodservices.org						
Las Cruces						
1515 University Blvd NE	Albuquerque	NM	87102	800-333-8037		89
TF General: 877-827-4376 ■ *Web:* www.unitedbloodservices.org						
United Blood Services of North Dakota						
Bismarck 3231 S 11th St	Fargo	ND	58104	800-456-6159		89
TF: 800-456-6159 ■ *Web:* www.unitedbloodservices.org/nd						
Fargo 3231 S 11th St	Fargo	ND	58104	701-293-9453		89
TF General: 800-288-2199 ■ *Web:* www.unitedbloodservices.org/nd						
United Blood Services of South Dakota						
Rapid City 2209 W Omaha St	Rapid City	SD	57702	605-342-8585		89
Web: www.unitedbloodservices.org						
United Blood Services of Texas						
El Paso 424 S Mesa Hills	El Paso	TX	79912	915-544-5422		89
TF: 877-827-4376 ■ *Web:* www.unitedbloodservices.org						
Lubbock 2523 48th St	Lubbock	TX	79413	806-797-6804		89
TF: 800-333-6920 ■ *Web:* www.unitedbloodservices.org						
McAllen 1400 S Sixth St	McAllen	TX	78501	956-213-7500		89
TF General: 888-827-4376 ■ *Web:* www.unitedbloodservices.org/RG						
San Angelo 2020 W Beauregard Ave	San Angelo	TX	76901	325-223-7500		89
TF General: 800-756-0024 ■ *Web:* www.unitedbloodservices.org						
United Blood Services of Wyoming						
Casper 112 E Eighth Ave Ste 102	Cheyenne	WY	82001	307-638-3326		89
Web: www.unitedbloodservices.org						
Cheyenne 112 E Eigth Ave	Cheyenne	WY	82001	307-638-3326		89
TF: 800-955-7057 ■ *Web:* www.unitedbloodservices.org						
United Brass Manufacturers Inc						
35030 GoddaRd Rd	Romulus	MI	48174	734-941-0700	941-0640	483
Web: unitedbrass.com						
United Brass Works Inc						
714 S Main St	Randleman	NC	27317	336-498-2661	498-4267	789
TF: 800-334-3035 ■ *Web:* www.ubw.com						
United Bronx Parents Inc						
773 Prospect Ave	Bronx	NY	10455	718-292-9808		242
United Brotherhood of Carpenters & Joiners of America						
101 Constitution Ave NW	Washington	DC	20001	202-546-6206	543-5724	414
TF: 800-530-5090 ■ *Web:* www.carpenters.org						
United Building Maintenance Inc						
165 Easy St	Carol Stream	IL	60188	630-653-4848		104
Web: www.ubm-usa.com						
United Business Forms Inc						
8482 W Allens Bridge Rd	Greeneville	TN	37743	423-639-5551		110
Web: greenevillesun.com						
United Canadian Malt Ltd						
843 Pk St S	Peterborough	ON	K9J3V1	705-876-9110	876-9118	461
Web: www.unitedcanadianmalt.ca						
United Capital Corp 9 Pk Pl	Great Neck	NY	11021	516-466-6464	829-4301	655
OTC: UCAP ■ *TF:* 800-732-0330 ■ *Web:* www.unitedcapitalcorp.net						
United Capital Financial Advisers LLC						
620 Newport Center Dr Ste 500	Newport Beach	CA	92660	949-999-8500		401
Web: www.unitedcp.com						
United Capital Funding Corp						
146 Second St N Ste 200	Saint Petersburg	FL	33701	727-894-8232	898-4205	272
Web: www.ucfunding.com						
United Central Industrial Supply Company LLC						
1241 Volunteer Pkwy Ste 1000	Bristol	TN	37620	423-573-7300		470
Web: www.unitedcentral.net						
United Cerebral Palsy						
380 Washington Ave	Roosevelt	NY	11575	516-378-2000		186
Web: www.ucp-suffolk.org						
United Chemi-Con Inc						
9801 W Higgins Rd	Rosemont	IL	60018	847-696-2000	696-9278	253
TF: 800-344-4539 ■ *Web:* www.chemi-con.com						
United Church of Christ (UCC)						
700 Prospect Ave	Cleveland	OH	44115	216-736-2100	736-2103	48-20
TF: 866-822-8224 ■ *Web:* www.ucc.org						
United Church of God an International Assocation						
555 Techne Ctr Dr	Milford	OH	45150	513-576-9796		48-20
Web: www.ucg.org						
United Co, The 1005 Glenway Ave	Bristol	VA	24201	276-466-3322		360-3
United Collection Bureau Inc						
5620 Southwyck Blvd	Toledo	OH	43614	866-209-0622		160
TF: 866-209-0622 ■ *Web:* ucbinc.com						

	City	State	Zip	Phone	Fax	Class
United Color Manufacturing Inc (UCM)						
PO Box 480	Newtown	PA	18940	215-860-2165	860-8560	145
TF: 800-852-5942 ■ *Web:* www.unitedcolor.com						
United Commercial Development Inc						
7001 Preston Rd Ste 410	Dallas	TX	75205	214-224-4600		652
Web: www.ucdcorp.com						
United Commercial Travellers						
1801 Watermark Dr Ste 100	Columbus	OH	43215	614-228-3276	487-9675	457-10
TF: 800-848-0123 ■ *Web:* www.uct.org						
United Community Banks Inc						
PO Box 398	Blairsville	GA	30514	706-781-2265		360-2
NASDAQ: UCBI ■ *TF:* 866-270-7100 ■ *Web:* www.ucbi.com						
United Community Financial Corp						
275 W Federal St	Youngstown	OH	44503	330-742-0500	742-0532	360-2
NASDAQ: UCFC ■ *TF:* 888-822-4751 ■ *Web:* ir.ucfconline.com						
United Consulting Group Ltd						
625 Holcomb Bridge Rd	Norcross	GA	30071	770-209-0029		256
TF: 800-266-0990 ■ *Web:* www.unitedconsulting.com						
United Contractors Midwest Inc						
PO Box 13420	Springfield	IL	62791	217-546-6192	546-1904	188-4
TF: 800-381-5497 ■ *Web:* www.ucm.biz						
United Conveyor Corp						
2100 Norman Dr W	Waukegan	IL	60085	847-473-5900	473-5959	207
Web: www.unitedconveyor.com						
United CoolAir Corp 491 E Princess St	York	PA	17403	717-843-4311	854-4462	14
TF: 877-905-1111 ■ *Web:* www.unitedcoolair.com						
United Coop N7160 Raceway Rd	Beaver Dam	WI	53916	920-887-1756		345
TF: 800-924-2991 ■ *Web:* www.unitedcooperative.com						
United Co-op Services						
3309 N Main St PO Box 16	Cleburne	TX	76033	817-556-4000	556-4068	245
TF: 800-342-6239 ■ *Web:* www.united-cs.com						
United Corporate Furnishings Inc						
1780 N Market Blvd	Sacramento	CA	95834	916-553-5900		321
United Corrstack Inc 720 Laurel St	Reading	PA	19602	610-374-3000		561
Web: www.unitedcorrstack.com						
United Cos of Mesa County Inc						
2273 River Rd	Grand Junction	CO	81505	970-243-4900		182
TF: 800-321-0807 ■ *Web:* united-gj.com						
United Country Real Estate Inc						
2820 NW Barry Rd	Kansas City	MO	64154	816-420-6200		652
TF: 800-999-1020 ■ *Web:* www.unitedcountry.com						
United Crane Rentals Inc						
111 N Michigan Ave	Kenilworth	NJ	07033	908-245-6260		264-3
United Ctr 1901 W Madison St	Chicago	IL	60612	312-455-4500		720
TF: 800-745-3000 ■ *Web:* www.unitedcenter.com						
United Dairy Farmers						
3955 Montgomery Rd	Cincinnati	OH	45212	513-396-8700	396-8736	296-27
TF General: 866-837-4833 ■ *Web:* www.uniteddairy.com						
United Dairy Inc 300 N Fifth St	Martins Ferry	OH	43935	740-633-1451	633-6759	296-27
TF: 800-252-1542 ■ *Web:* www.uniteddairy.com						
United Data Technologies Inc						
8825 NW 21st Terr	Doral	FL	33172	305-882-0405		024
TF: 800-882-9919 ■ *Web:* udtonline.com						
United Developers LLC						
2019 N Lamar St Ste 240	Dallas	TX	75202	214-855-5955		809
Web: uniteddevelopersllc.com						
United Displaycraft						
333 E Touhy Ave	Des Plaines	IL	60018	847-375-3800		233
TF General: 877-632-8767 ■ *Web:* www.uniteddisplaycraft.com						
United Distributors Inc						
5500 United Dr SE	Smyrna	GA	30082	678-305-2080		81-1
Web: udiga.com						
United Document Destruction & Storage						
1110 Commons Blvd	Reading	PA	19605	610-927-2100		317
Web: uniteddocument.com						
United Drill Bushing Corp						
12200 Woodruff Ave	Downey	CA	90241	562-803-1521	486-3465*	493
**Fax Area Code:* 800 ■ *TF:* 800-486-3466 ■ *Web:* www.ucc-udb.com						
United e r p LLC						
235 Closter Dock Rd Ste 503	Closter	NJ	07624	201-567-6315		177
Web: www.unitederp.com						
United Electric Company LP						
501 Galveston St	Wichita Falls	TX	76301	940-397-2100		14
TF: 800-936-1764 ■ *Web:* www.magicaire.com						
United Electric Controls Co						
180 Dexter Ave	Watertown	MA	02472	617-926-1000	926-2568	201
Web: www.ueonline.com						
United Electric Co-op Inc						
1330 21st St	Heyburn	ID	83336	208-679-2222		245
Web: www.unitedelectric.coop						
United Electric Co-op Inc						
29 United Rd	Du Bois	PA	15801	814-371-8570		245
TF: 888-581-8969 ■ *Web:* www.prea.com						
United Electric Supply Inc						
10 Bellecor Dr	New Castle	DE	19720	302-322-3333		787
TF: 800-322-3374 ■ *Web:* www.unitedelectric.com						
United Electrical Radio & Machine Workers of America						
1 Gateway Ctr Ste 1400	Pittsburgh	PA	15222	412-471-8919	471-8999	414
Web: www.ueunion.org						
United Electrical Sales Ltd						
4496 36th St	Orlando	FL	32811	407-246-1992	246-1588	246
TF: 800-432-5126 ■ *Web:* www.uesfl.com						
United Engine & Machine Company Inc						
1040 Corbett St	Carson City	NV	89706	775-882-7790	882-7773	128
TF: 800-648-7970 ■ *Web:* www.uempistons.com						
United Entertainment Corp						
3601 18th St S Ste 104	Saint Cloud	MN	56301	320-203-1003		748
Web: www.uecmovies.com						
United Envelope LLC						
Industrial Park Dr						
Mount Pocono Ind Park	Mount Pocono	PA	18344	570-839-1600		263
Web: www.unitedenvelope.com						
United Equipment Accessories Inc						
2103 E Bremer Avenue Hwy	Waverly	IA	50677	319-352-3946		247
Web: www.uea-inc.com						
United Farm Workers of America						
29700 Woodford Techachpi Rd PO Box 62	Keene	CA	93531	661-823-6151	823-6174	414
Web: www.ufw.org						
United Farmers Co-op (UFC)						
705 E Fourth St PO Box 461	Winthrop	MN	55396	507-647-6600		10
TF: 866-998-3266 ■ *Web:* www.ufcmn.com						
United Fashions of Texas LLC						
4629 Macro Dr	San Antonio	TX	78218	210-662-7140		157-2
Web: melrosestore.com						
United FCS ACA 2616 US Hwy 45	Antigo	WI	54409	715-623-7644		403
Web: www.unitedfcs.com						
United Federations of Police Officers						
1717 Pennsylvania Ave NW	Washington	DC	20006	202-559-9037		49-7
Web: www.policefederation.com						
United Finance Co 515 E Burnside St	Portland	OR	97214	503-232-5153	238-6453	217
Web: www.unitedfinance.com						
United Financial Bancorp Inc						
95 Elm St PO Box 9020	West Springfield	MA	01090	413-787-1700		70
NASDAQ: UBNK ■ *TF:* 866-959-2265 ■ *Web:* www.bankatunited.com						
United Financial Services Group						
325 Chestnut St Ste 3000	Philadelphia	PA	19106	215-238-0300		310
Web: www.unitedfsg.com						
United Fire Equipment Co						
335 N Fourth Ave	Tucson	AZ	85705	520-622-3639	882-3991	679
TF: 800-362-0150 ■ *Web:* unitedfire.net						
United Food & Commercial Workers International Union (UFCW)						
1775 K St NW	Washington	DC	20006	202-223-3111		414
TF: 800-551-4010 ■ *Web:* www.ufcw.org						
United Food & Commercial Workers Union Local 555						
7095 SW Sandburg St	Tigard	OR	97281	503-684-2822		414
TF: 800-452-8329 ■ *Web:* www.ufcw555.com						
United Ford Parts & Distribtion Ctr Inc						
12007 E 61st St	Broken Arrow	OK	74012	918-317-6800		516
TF: 800-800-9001 ■ *Web:* www.unitedford.com						
United Freezer & Storage Co						
650 N Meridian Rd	Youngstown	OH	44509	330-792-1739	792-2299	803-2
TF: 800-716-1416 ■ *Web:* www.unitedfreezer.com						
United Fresh Potato Growers Of Idaho Inc						
6109 So Yellowstone Hwy	Idaho Falls	ID	83402	208-535-8500		345
Web: www.unitedpotato.com						
United Fresh Produce Assn						
1901 Pennsylvania Ave NW Ste 1100	Washington	DC	20006	202-303-3400	303-3433	48-2
TF: 800-854-0473 ■ *Web:* www.unitedfresh.org						
United Funeral Directors Benefit Life Insurance Co						
351 S Sherman Ste 102	Richardson	TX	75081	469-330-2200		390
Web: unitedbenefitsinc.com						
United Galvanizing Inc						
6123 Cunningham Rd	Houston	TX	77041	713-466-4161		481
Web: unitedgalvinc.com						
United Gasket Corp 1633 55th Ave	Cicero	IL	60804	708-656-3700	656-6292	326
TF: 800-336-5525 ■ *Web:* www.unitedgasket.com						
United Gear & Assembly Inc						
1700 Livingstone Rd	Hudson	WI	54016	715-386-5867		454
Web: www.ugaco.com						
United Gilsonite Laboratories Inc						
1396 Jefferson Ave	Scranton	PA	18509	570-344-1202		550
Web: www.ugl.com						
United Graphics LLC 2916 Marshall Ave	Mattoon	IL	61938	217-235-7161		626
Web: www.ugllc.net						
United Guaranty Corp (UGC)						
230 N Elm St	Greensboro	NC	27401	877-642-4642	328-3273*	391-5
**Fax Area Code:* 888 ■ **Fax:* Hum Res ■ *TF:* 877-642-4642 ■ *Web:* www.ugcorp.com						
United Hardware Distributing Co						
5005 Nathan Ln N	Plymouth	MN	55442	763-559-1800		351
Web: www.unitedhardware.com						
United Health Centers of The San Joaquin Valley						
650 Zediker Ave Bldg 3	Parlier	CA	93648	559-646-6618	646-6614	353
Web: public.uhcofsjv.org						
United Health Services Hospitals						
10-42 Mitchell Ave	Binghamton	NY	13903	607-762-2200		353
Web: www.uhs.net						
United Heartland Inc PO Box 3026	Milwaukee	WI	53201	866-206-5851	787-7701*	391-4
**Fax Area Code:* 262 ■ *TF:* 866-206-5851 ■ *Web:* www.unitedheartland.biz						
United Heritage Life Insurance Co						
PO Box 7777	Meridian	ID	83680	208-493-6100	466-0825	391-2
TF: 800-657-6351 ■ *Web:* www.unitedheritage.com						
United Hospice of Rockland						
11 Stokum Ln	New City	NY	10956	845-634-4974	634-7549	371
TF: 800-467-7423 ■ *Web:* www.hospiceofrockland.org						
United Hospital 333 N Smith Ave	Saint Paul	MN	55102	651-241-8000		374-3
TF: 800-869-1320 ■ *Web:* www.allinahealth.org						
United Hospital Ctr						
327 Medical pk Dr	Bridgeport	WV	26330	681-342-1000		374-3
TF: 800-607-8888 ■ *Web:* wvumedicine.org/united-hospital-center						
United Human Capital Solutions						
1 Centerpointe Dr Ste 580	Lake Oswego	OR	97035	503-443-6008		226
Web: www.uhcsolutions.com						
United Hunter Oil & Gas Corp						
700 W Pender St Ste 615	Vancouver	BC	V6C1G8	832-487-0813		539
Web: www.unitedhunteroil.com						
United Hydrocarbon International Corp						
500 Fourth Ave SW Ste 2500	Calgary	AB	T2P0H7	403-774-9900		536
Web: www.unitedhydrocarbon.com						
United Illuminating Co						
157 Church St	New Haven	CT	06510	203-499-2000	499-5973*	787
**Fax:* Hum Res ■ *TF Cust Svc:* 800-722-5584 ■ *Web:* www.uinet.com						
United Incentives Inc						
13 S Third St Ste 500	Philadelphia	PA	19106	215-625-2700	625-4552	384
Web: www.unitedincentives.com						
United Industries Inc						
1901 Revere Beach Pkwy	Everett	MA	02149	617-387-9500	387-6331	567
TF: 800-681-7475 ■ *Web:* www.united-ind.com						
United Industries Inc 1546 Henry Ave	Beloit	WI	53511	608-365-8891	365-1259	490
Web: www.unitedindustries.com						
United Information Technologies Corp						
2818 Corporate Pkwy	Algonquin	IL	60102	847-658-1222		260
Web: www.uitonline.com						
United Infrastructure Group Inc						
1691 Turnbull Ave	North Charleston	SC	29405	843-529-3010		256
TF: 800-524-0604 ■ *Web:* uig.net						

Phone | Fax | Class

United Insurance Holdings Corp
360 Central Ave Ste 900 ... Saint Petersburg FL 33701 800-295-8016 391-2
NASDAQ: UIHC ■ *TF:* 800-861-4370 ■ *Web:* www.upcinsurance.com

United Investors Life Insurance Co
2801 Hwy 280 S ... Birmingham AL 35223 205-268-1000 268-5547 391-2
TF: 800-866-9933 ■ *Web:* www.protective.com

United Kingdom
1 Dag Hammarskjold Plaza ... New York NY 10017 212-745-9200 745-9316 784
Web: www.gov.uk
Consulate General 1 Broadway ... Cambridge MA 02142 617-245-4500 257
Web: www.gov.uk
Consulate General
625 N Michigan Ave Ste 2200 ... Chicago IL 60611 312-970-3800 257
Web: www.gov.uk
Consulate General 133 Peachtree St NE ... Atlanta GA 30303 404-954-7700 257
Web: www.gov.uk
Consulate General
1301 Fannin S Ste 2400 ... Houston TX 77002 713-659-6270 257
Web: www.gov.uk
Consulate General 845 Third Ave ... New York NY 10022 212-745-0200 257
Web: www.gov.uk
Consulate General
1 Sansome St Ste 850 ... San Francisco CA 94104 415-617-1300 257
Web: www.gov.uk
Embassy 3100 Massachusetts Ave NW ... Washington DC 20008 202-588-6500 257
Web: www.gov.uk

United Laboratories Inc
320 37th Ave. ... Saint Charles IL 60174 800-323-2594 443-2087* 145
**Fax Area Code:* 630 ■ *TF:* 800-323-2594 ■ *Web:* www.unitedlabsinc.com

United Landmark Associates Inc
3708 W Swann Ave Ste 201 ... Tampa FL 33602 813-870-9519 7
Web: www.unitedlandmark.com

United Launch Alliance LLC
Galileo Operations Ctr 9501 E Panorama Cir
... Centennial CO 80112 720-922-7100 681
Web: www.ulalaunch.com

United Lawnscape Inc
62170 Van Dyke Rd ... Washington MI 48094 586-752-5000 776
Web: www.unitedlawnscape.com

United Legwear Company LLC
48 W 38th St. ... New York NY 10018 212-391-4143 411
Web: www.unitedlegwear.com

United Letter Service Inc
1231 N Ellis St ... Bensenville IL 60106 312-427-3537 5
Web: www.unitedgmg.com

United Lighting & Supply Company
121 Chestnut Ave SE ... Fort Walton Beach FL 32548 850-244-8155 244-5629 246
Web: www.unitedlighting.com

United Lumber & Remanufacturing LLC
980 Ford Rd ... Muscle Shoals AL 35661 256-381-4151 683
Web: www.ufpi.com/united-lumber-reman

United Marble & Granite Inc
2163 Martin Ave ... Santa Clara CA 95050 408-347-3300 191-1
Web: www.umgslabs.com

United Marine Enterprise Inc
1325 Spindletop Rd ... Beaumont TX 77705 409-833-7070 698
Web: www.umtexas.us

United Marketing Group LLC
929 N Plum Grove Rd. ... Schaumburg IL 60173 847-240-2005 438-5788* 195
**Fax Area Code:* 630 ■ *TF:* 800-513-7000

United Materials LLC
The Woodlands Corporate Ctr E 3949 Forest Pkwy
Ste 400 ... North Tonawanda NY 14120 716-213-5832 213-5850 182
TF: 888-918-6483 ■ *Web:* www.unitedmaterialsllc.com

United McGill Corp 1 Mission Pk. ... Groveport OH 43125 614-829-1200 829-1291 697
TF: 800-624-5535 ■ *Web:* www.unitedmcgill.com

United Medical Corp 603 Main St ... Windermere FL 34786 407-876-2200 876-3065 353
Web: unitedmedical.com

United Memories Inc
4815 List Dr Ste 109 ... Colorado Springs CO 80919 719-594-4238 695
Web: www.unitedmemories.com

United Metal Products Corp
8101 Lyndon St ... Detroit MI 48238 313-933-8750 933-1001 489
Web: www.unitedmetalproducts.com

United Metal Products Inc
1920 E Encanto Dr ... Tempe AZ 85281 480-968-9550 295
TF: 800-247-5746 ■ *Web:* www.unitedmetal.com

United Methodist News Service
810 12th Ave S ... Nashville TN 37203 615-742-5470 530
TF: 800-251-8140 ■ *Web:* www.umcom.org

United Methodist Publishing House
201 Eigth Ave S ... Nashville TN 37203 615-749-6000 637-3
TF: 800-672-1789 ■ *Web:* umph.org

United Methodist Retirement & Health Care Center Inc, The
2316 W Modelle Ave. ... Clinton OK 73601 580-323-0912 48-20
Web: umhcc-clinton.com

United Microelectronics Corp
488 De Guigne Dr. ... Sunnyvale CA 94085 408-523-7800 733-8090 696
NYSE: UMC ■ *TF:* 800-990-1135 ■ *Web:* www.umc.com

United Mine Workers of America
18354 Quantico Gateway Dr Ste 200 ... Triangle VA 22172 703-291-2400 457-21
TF: 800-789-0072 ■ *Web:* www.umwa.org

United Mobile Homes Inc
3499 Rt 9 N Ste 3C ... Freehold NJ 07728 732-577-9997 655
NYSE: UMH ■ *TF:* 800-504-0670 ■ *Web:* www.umh.com

United Motorcoach Assn (UMA)
113 SW St 4th Fl ... Alexandria VA 22314 703-838-2929 838-2950 49-21
TF: 800-424-8262 ■ *Web:* www.uma.org

United National Group
3 Bala Plaza E Ste 300 ... Bala Cynwyd PA 19004 610-664-1500 660-8882 391-4
TF: 800-333-0352 ■ *Web:* www.unitednat.com

United National Insurance Co
3 Bala Plaza E Ste 300 ... Bala Cynwyd PA 19004 610-664-1500 660-8882 391-4
TF: 800-333-0352 ■ *Web:* www.unitednat.com

United Nations 2 UN Plaza Rm DC21950 ... New York NY 10017 212-963-1234 963-4260* 783
**Fax:* PR ■ *Web:* www.un.org

United Nations Assoc Information & Un Icef Ctr
1403B Addison St. ... Berkeley CA 94704 510-849-1752 292
Web: unausaeastbay.org

United Nations Children's Fund (UNICEF)
3 United Nations Plaza ... New York NY 10017 212-326-7000 888-7465 783
Web: www.unicef.org

United Nations Development Programme
1 UN Plaza ... New York NY 10017 212-906-5000 906-5364 783
Web: www.undp.org

United Nations Educational Scientific & Cultural Organization (UNESCO)
2 UN Plaza Ste 900 ... New York NY 10017 212-963-5995 783
Web: en.unesco.org

United Nations Environment Programme (UNEP)
900 17th St NW Ste 506 ... Washington DC 20006 202-785-0465 785-2096 783
Web: www.rona.unep.org

United Nations Federal Credit Union (UNFCU)
24-01 44th Rd Ct Sq Pl ... Long Island NY 11101 347-686-6000 686-6400 219
TF: 800-891-2471 ■ *Web:* www.unfcu.org

United Nations Foundation (UNF)
1800 Massachusetts Ave NW Ste 400 ... Washington DC 20036 202-887-9040 887-9021 48-5
Web: www.unfoundation.org

United Nations Industrial Development Organization (UNIDO)
1 UN Plaza ... New York NY 10017 212-963-6890 963-7904 783
Web: www.unido.org

United Nations International School
24-50 Fdr Dr. ... New York NY 10010 212-684-7400 449
Web: www.unis.org

United Natural Foods Inc (UNFI)
313 Iron Horse Way ... Providence RI 02908 401-528-8634 297-8
NASDAQ: UNFI ■ *Web:* www.unfi.com

United Network for Organ Sharing (UNOS)
700 N Fourth St ... Richmond VA 23219 804-782-4800 782-4817 48-17
TF: 888-894-6361 ■ *Web:* www.unos.org

United Notions Inc 13800 Hutton St. ... Dallas TX 75234 972-484-8901 594
TF: 800-527-9447 ■ *Web:* storefront.unitednotions.com

United Nurses & Allied Professionals
375 Branch Ave. ... Providence RI 02904 401-831-3647 533
Web: www.unap.org

United of Omaha Life Insurance Co
Mutual of Omaha Plaza ... Omaha NE 68175 402-342-7600 391-2
TF: 800-775-6000 ■ *Web:* www.mutualofomaha.com

United Overseas Bank Ltd New York Agency (UOB)
592 Fifth Ave 10th Fl ... New York NY 10036 646-472-8113 382-1881* 70
**Fax Area Code:* 212 ■ *Web:* www.uob.com.sg

United Pacific Inc
10975 SW 11th St Ste 175 ... Beaverton OR 97005 503-644-9018 123
Web: www.uapac.com

United Pacific Pet 12060 Cabernet Dr ... Fontana CA 92337 951-360-8550 360-8540 578
TF: 800-979-3333 ■ *Web:* www.uppet.com

United Package Liquors Inc
6350 Rucker Rd Ste 105 ... Indianapolis IN 46220 317-205-9266 443
Web: www.unitedpackageliquors.com

United Paradyne Corp
2415 Professional Pkwy ... Santa Maria CA 93455 805-348-3155 529
Web: www.unitedparadyne.com

United Paramount Tax Group Inc
4025 Woodland Park Blvd Ste 310 ... Arlington TX 76013 817-983-0099 2
TF: 888-829-8829 ■ *Web:* uptg.com

United Parcel Service Inc (UPS)
55 Glenlake Pkwy NE ... Atlanta GA 30328 404-828-6000 828-6440 546
NYSE: UPS ■ *TF Cust Svc:* 800-742-5877 ■ *Web:* www.ups.com

United Pentecostal Church International (UPCI)
8855 Dunn Rd ... Hazelwood MO 63042 314-837-7300 48-20
Web: www.upci.org

United Performance Metals
3475 Symmes Rd ... Hamilton OH 45015 513-860-6500 874-6857 723
TF: 888-282-3292 ■ *Web:* www.upmet.com

United Personnel Services Inc
289 Bridge St ... Springfield MA 01103 413-736-0800 260
TF: 800-363-8200 ■ *Web:* www.unitedpersonnel.com

United Pet Care LLC
6232 N Seventh St Ste 202 ... Phoenix AZ 85014 602-266-5303 794
TF: 877-872-8800 ■ *Web:* www.unitedpetcare.com

United Petroleum Co
8040 NE Sandy Blvd Ste 300 ... Portland OR 97213 503-287-4000 579
Web: www.unitedpetroleum.com

United Pharma LLC
2317 2319 Moore Ave ... Fullerton CA 92833 714-738-8999 506
TF: 800-680-5235 ■ *Web:* www.unitedpharmallc.com

United Pharmacal Company of Missouri Inc
3705 Pear St. ... Saint Joseph MO 64503 816-233-8800 233-9696 578
TF: 800-254-8726 ■ *Web:* www.upco.com

United Pioneer Co
2777 Summer St Ste 206 ... Stamford CT 06905 800-466-9823 466-9828 576
TF: 800-466-9823 ■ *Web:* www.b340.com

United Plastic Fabricating Inc
165 Flagship Dr ... North Andover MA 01845 800-638-8265 605-1
TF 800 638-8265 ■ *Web:* www.unitedplastic.com

United Plastics Group Inc (UPG)
7865 Northcourt Rd ... Houston TX 77040 713-466-5563 604
Web: www.upgintl.com

United Plywood & Lumber Inc
1640 Mims Ave SW ... Birmingham AL 35211 205-925-7601 923-9511 613
TF: 800-272-6486 ■ *Web:* www.unitedplywoods.com

United Postmasters and Managers of America (NAPUS)
8 Herbert St ... Alexandria VA 22305 703-683-9027 683-6820 49-7
Web: www.napus.org

United Power Inc 500 Co-op Way ... Brighton CO 80603 303-659-0551 659-2172 245
TF: 800-468-8809 ■ *Web:* www.unitedpower.com

United Press International (UPI)
1133 19th St NW ... Washington DC 20036 202-898-8000 530
Web: www.upi.com

United Producers Inc
8351 N High St Ste 250 ... Columbus OH 43235 800-456-3276 446
TF: 800-456-3276 ■ *Web:* www.uproducers.com

United Propane Gas Companies Inc
4200 Cairo Rd PO Box 2450 ... Paducah KY 42002 270-442-5557 316
Web: www.upgas.com

United Realty Group
8951 W Atlantic Blvd ... Coral Springs FL 33071 954-670-5671 652
Web: urgfl.com

Name / Address	City	State	ZIP	Phone	Fax	Class
United Rebar Inc 8301 Galena Ave	Sacramento	CA	95828	916-379-9900	379-9909	194
Web: www.unitedrebar.com						
United Record Pressing LLC						
453 Chestnut St	Nashville	TN	37203	615-259-9396		626
TF: 866-407-3165 ■ *Web:* www.urpressing.com						
United Refining Company Inc						
15 Bradley St	Warren	PA	16365	814-723-1500	726-4709	580
TF: 800-820-1653 ■ *Web:* www.urc.com						
United Refrigeration Inc						
11401 Roosevelt Blvd	Philadelphia	PA	19154	215-698-9100	698-9493*	665
**Fax:* Financial ■ *TF General:* 888-578-9100 ■ *Web:* www.uri.com						
United Regional Chamber of Commerce						
42 Union St	Attleboro	MA	02703	508-222-0801	222-1498	139
Web: www.unitedregionalchamber.org						
United Regional Hospital						
Eighth Street Campus						
1600 11th St 2nd Fl	Wichita Falls	TX	76301	940-764-7000	766-8711	374-3
Web: www.unitedregional.org						
United Rentals 3266 E Washington St	Phoenix	AZ	85233	602-267-3898		264-3
TF: 844-873-4948 ■ *Web:* www.unitedrentals.com						
United Rentals Inc 224 Selleck St	Stamford	CT	06902	203-622-3131	622-6080	264-3
NYSE: URI ■ *TF:* 800-877-3687 ■ *Web:* www.unitedrentals.com						
United Reprographics LLC						
1750 Fourth Ave S	Seattle	WA	98134	206-382-1177		627
Web: www.unitedreprographics.com						
United Restaurant Equipment Company Inc						
1 Executive Park Dr	North Billerica	MA	01862	978-439-5500	262-9999	300
TF: 800-431-1998 ■ *Web:* www.unitedrestaurant.com						
United Road Services Inc						
10701 Middlebelt Rd	Romulus	MI	48174	734-947-7900		780
TF: 800-221-5127 ■ *Web:* www.unitedroad.com						
United Rotary Brush Corp						
15607 W 100th Terr	Lenexa	KS	66219	913-888-8450		190
Web: www.united-rotary.com						
United Rotorcraft Solutions LLC						
1942 N Trinity St	Decatur	TX	76234	940-627-0626		350
Web: www.airmethods.com						
United Salt Corp 4800 San Felipe St	Houston	TX	77056	713-877-2600		503-1
TF: 800-554-8658 ■ *Web:* www.unitedsalt.com						
United Scenic Artists						
29 W 38th St 15th Fl	New York	NY	10018	212-581-0300	977-2011	414
TF: 800-456-3863 ■ *Web:* www.usa829.org						
United Screening Services Corp						
10300 Sunset Dr Ste 101	Miami	FL	33173	305-774-1711		260
Web: www.unitedscreening.com						
United Security Bancshares						
2126 Inyo St	Fresno	CA	93721	559-248-4943		70
NASDAQ: UBFO ■ *TF:* 888-683-6030 ■ *Web:* www.unitedsecuritybank.com						
United Security Bancshares Inc						
PO Box 249	Thomasville	AL	36784	334-636-5424		360-2
NASDAQ: USBI ■ *TF:* 866-546-8273 ■ *Web:* www.firstusbank.com						
United Security Inc						
4295 Arthur Kill Rd	Staten Island	NY	10309	718-967-6820	967-6817	693
Web: www.uslsecurity.com						
United Service Organizations (USO)						
2111 Wilson Blvd Ste 1200	Arlington	VA	22201	703-908-6400		48-19
TF: 800-876-7469 ■ *Web:* www.uso.org						
United Services Automobile Assn (USAA)						
10750 McDermott Fwy	San Antonio	TX	78288	800-531-8722	531-5717	185
TF: 800-531-8722 ■ *Web:* www.usaa.com						
United Shipping Solutions						
6985 Union Pk Ctr Ste 565	Midvale	UT	84047	801-352-0012	352-0339	310
United Skys 702 Magna Dr	Round Lake	IL	60073	847-546-7776		198
TF: 800-555-8970 ■ *Web:* unitedskys.com						
United Software Assoc Inc						
5674 Stoneridge Dr Ste 100	Pleasanton	CA	94588	925-249-0230		396
Web: www.usain.com						
United Sourcing Alliance						
2105 Water Ridge Pkwy Ste 470	Charlotte	NC	28217	704-697-9695		463
Web: usa-llc.com						
United Soybean Board (USB)						
16305 Swingley Ridge Rd Ste 150	Chesterfield	MO	63017	636-530-1777	530-1560	48-2
TF: 800-989-8721 ■ *Web:* www.unitedsoybean.org						
United Spiral Pipe LLC						
900 E Third St	Pittsburg	CA	94565	925-526-3100		595
TF: 800-619-4807 ■ *Web:* www.unitedspiralpipe.com						
United Staffing Systems Inc						
130 William St 5th Fl	New York	NY	10038	212-743-0200		260
United Standard Industries Inc						
2062 Lehigh Ave	Glenview	IL	60026	847-724-0350		757
Web: www.unitedstandard.com						
United States Aluminum Corp						
200 Singleton Dr	Waxahachie	TX	75165	972-937-9651		234
Web: www.usalum.com						
United States Aviation						
4141 N Memorial Dr	Tulsa	OK	74115	918-836-7345		63
TF: 800-897-5387 ■ *Web:* www.unitedstatesaviation.com						
District of Rhode Island						
The Federal Ctr						
380 Westminster Mall 6th Fl	Providence	RI	02903	401-626-3100	626-3150	341-2
Web: www.rib.uscourts.gov						
United States Beef Corp 4923 E 49th St	Tulsa	OK	74135	918-665-0740		671
Web: www.usbeefcorp.com						
United States Brass & Copper Co Inc						
1401 Brook Dr	Downers Grove	IL	60515	630-629-9340	629-9350	492
TF: 800-821-2854 ■ *Web:* www.usbrassandcopper.com						
Office of Workers" Compensation Programs						
200 Constitution Ave Ste S3524	Washington	DC	20210	202-693-8673		340-15
TF: 866-487-2365						
United States District Court						
Western District of Michigan						
110 Michigan St NW 399 Federal Bldg	Grand Rapids	MI	49503	616-456-2381		341-3
TF: 800-290-2742 ■ *Web:* www.miwd.uscourts.gov						
United States District Court, Central District						
312 N Spring St	Los Angeles	CA	90012	213-894-1565		341-3
TF: 800-676-6856 ■ *Web:* www.cacd.uscourts.gov						
United States Endoscopy Group Inc						
5976 Heisley Rd	Mentor	OH	44060	440-639-4494	639-4494	476
TF: 800-769-8226 ■ *Web:* www.usendoscopy.com						
United States Information Systems Inc (USIS)						
35 W Jefferson Ave	Pearl River	NY	10965	845-358-7755		787
TF: 866-222-3778 ■ *Web:* www.usis.net						
United States Marine Inc						
10011 Lorraine Rd	Gulfport	MS	39503	228-679-1005		698
Web: www.usmi.com						
Philadelphia 1201 Elm St Ste 400	Dallas	TX	75270	215-408-0112		340-18
Web: www.usmint.gov						
United States of America						
799 United Nations Plaza	New York	NY	10017	212-415-4000	415-4443	784
Web: www.un.int						
United States Olympic Committee						
1 Olympic Plaza	Colorado Springs	CO	80909	719-866-4567	632-0979	48-22
Web: www.teamusa.org						
United States Senate Special Committee on Aging						
G31 Dirksen Senate Office Bldg	Washington	DC	20510	202-224-5364		342-1
Web: aging.senate.gov						
United States Sports Academy, The						
1 Academy Dr	Daphne	AL	36526	251-626-3303		166
TF: 800-223-2668 ■ *Web:* www.ussa.edu						
United States Steel Corp						
600 Grant St	Pittsburgh	PA	15219	412-433-1121		261
NYSE: X ■ *TF:* 866-433-4801 ■ *Web:* www.ussteel.com						
United States Warranty Corp						
22 NE 22nd Ave	Pompano Beach	FL	33062	954-784-9400		390
Web: www.uswarranty.com						
United Stationers Inc						
1 PkwyN Blvd Ste 100	Deerfield	IL	60015	847-627-7000		534
Web: www.unitedstationers.com						
United Stationers Supply Co (USSCO)						
1 Pkwy N Blvd Ste 100 Ste 100	Deerfield	IL	60015	847-627-7000		534
Web: www.essendant.com						
United Stations Radio Network						
1065 Ave of the Americas 3rd Fl	New York	NY	10018	212-869-1111		644
TF: 866-989-1975 ■ *Web:* www.unitedstations.com						
United Steel Inc 164 School St	East Hartford	CT	06108	860-289-2323		492
Web: www.unitedsteel.com						
United Steel Products Inc						
33-40 127th Pl	Flushing	NY	11368	718-478-5330		234
Web: www.unitedsteelproducts.com						
United Steel Workers (USW)						
3340 Perimeter Hill Dr	Nashville	TN	37211	615-834-8590		414
Web: www.usw.org						
United Steelworkers of America						
60 Blvd of the Allies	Pittsburgh	PA	15222	412-562-2575	562-2445	414
Web: www.usw.org						
United Structures of America Inc						
1912 Buschong	Houston	TX	77039	281-442-8247	442-2125	105
Web: www.usabldg.com						
United Sugars Corp						
7803 Glenroy Rd Ste 300	Bloomington	MN	55439	952-896-0131	896-0400	297-11
TF: 800-984-3585 ■ *Web:* www.unitedsugars.com						
United Supermarkets Ltd						
7830 Orlando Ave	Lubbock	TX	79423	806-791-0220		345
Web: www.unitedtexas.com						
United Supermarkets of Oklahoma Inc						
600 E Broadway St	Altus	OK	73521	580-482-1184		345
TF: 800-865-4736 ■ *Web:* www.unitedok.com						
United Suppliers Inc						
30473 260th St PO Box 538	Eldora	IA	50627	641-858-2341		276
TF: 800-782-5123 ■ *Web:* www.unitedsuppliers.com						
United Surgical Partners International Inc (USPI)						
15305 Dallas Pkwy	Addison	TX	75001	972-713-3500		352
Web: www.uspi.com						
United Synagogue of Conservative Judaism (USCJ)						
820 Second Ave	New York	NY	10017	212-533-7800	353-9439	48-20
Web: www.uscj.org						
United Systems & Software Inc						
300 Colonial Center Pkwy Ste 150	Lake Mary	FL	32746	407-875-2120	875-9600	177
TF: 800-522-8774 ■ *Web:* www.ussisolutions.com						
United Systems Inc						
4335 N Classen Blvd	Oklahoma City	OK	73118	405-523-2162		174
TF: 800-381-9663 ■ *Web:* www.unitedsystemsok.com						
United Talent Agency Inc (UTA)						
9336 Civic Ctr Dr	Beverly Hills	CA	90210	310-273-6700	247-1111	731
Web: www.unitedtalent.com						
United Talent LLC						
500 Leon Sullivan Way	Charleston	WV	25301	304-556-1190		260
Web: www.unitedtalentwv.com						
United Technologies Corp						
10 Farm Springs Rd	Farmington	CT	06032	860-728-7000		185
NYSE: UTX ■ *Web:* www.utc.com						
United Telephone Mutual Aid Corp						
411 Seventh Ave	Langdon	ND	58249	701-256-5156		116
Web: www.utma.com						
United Temps Inc 1550 S Indiana Ave	Chicago	IL	60605	312-922-8558		463
Web: unitedhq.com						
United Textile Company Inc						
14275 Catalina St	San Leandro	CA	94577	510-276-2288		508
TF General: 800-233-0077 ■ *Web:* unitedtextileinc.com						
United Theological Seminary						
4501 Denlinger Rd	Dayton	OH	45426	937-529-2201		167-3
Web: www.united.edu						
United Theological Seminary of the Twin Cities						
3000 Fifth St NW	New Brighton	MN	55112	651-633-4311	633-4315	167-3
Web: www.unitedseminary-mn.org						
United Therapeutics Corp						
1040 Spring St	Silver Spring	MD	20910	301-608-9292	608-9291	582
NASDAQ: UTHR ■ *TF:* 877-864-8437 ■ *Web:* www.unither.com						
United Titanium Inc						
3450 Old Airport Rd	Wooster	OH	44691	330-264-2111	263-1336	308
TF: 800-321-4938 ■ *Web:* www.unitedtitanium.com						
United Tool & Die Co						
1 Carney Rd	West Hartford	CT	06110	860-246-6531		22
TF: 877-262-0336 ■ *Web:* www.utdco.com						
United Tool & Stamping Co of North Carolina Inc						
2817 Enterprise Ave	Fayetteville	NC	28306	910-323-8588		697
TF: 800-883-6087 ■ *Web:* www.uts-nc.com						

Company / Address	City	State	ZIP	Phone	Fax	Class
United Treating & Distribution LLC 338 D E Washington Ave *Web:* unitedtreating.com	Muscle Shoals	AL	35661	256-248-0944		683
United Tribes Technical College 3315 University Dr *Web:* www.uttc.edu	Bismarck	ND	58504	701-255-3285	530-0640	165
United Trust Group Inc (UTGI) 5250 S Sixth St *OTC: UTGN* ■ *TF:* 800-323-0050 ■ *Web:* www.utgins.com	Springfield	IL	62705	217-241-6410		360-4
United Underwriters Inc PO Box 971000 *TF:* 866-686-4833 ■ *Web:* www.uuinsurance.com	Orem	UT	84097	801-226-2662	229-2662	390
United Utilities Inc 5450 A St *TF:* 800-478-2020 ■ *Web:* www.unicom-alaska.com	Anchorage	AK	99518	907-561-1674	273-5322	736
United Utility Supply Co-op Inc 4515 Bishop Ln *TF:* 800-366-4887 ■ *Web:* www.uus.org	Louisville	KY	40218	502-957-2568		246
United Van Lines Inc 1 United Dr *TF:* 877-740-3040 ■ *Web:* www.unitedvanlines.com	St. Louis	MO	63026	636-343-3900	349-8794	519
United Way of America 701 N Fairfax St *TF:* 800-892-2757 ■ *Web:* www.unitedway.org	Alexandria	VA	22314	703-836-7100		48-5
United Way of Central Md Inc, The 100 S Charles St PO Box 1576 *TF:* 800-429-0618 ■ *Web:* www.uwcm.org	Baltimore	MD	21203	410-547-8000	547-8289	193
United Way of Greater Cincinnati 2400 Reading Rd *Web:* www.uwgc.org	Cincinnati	OH	45202	513-762-7100		48-6
United Wholesale Lumber Co 8009 Doe Ave *Web:* www.uwlco.com	Visalia	CA	93291	559-651-2037	651-0742	551
United Window & Door Manufacturing Inc 24-36 Fadem Rd *TF:* 800-848-4550 ■ *Web:* www.unitedwindowmfg.com	Springfield	NJ	07081	800-848-4550		480
United World Life Insurance Co 3300 Mutual of Omaha Plaza *TF:* 800-775-6000 ■ *Web:* www.mutualofomaha.com	Omaha	NE	68175	402-342-7600		391-2
United-Bilt Homes Inc 8500 Line Ave *TF:* 800-551-8955 ■ *Web:* www.ubh.com	Shreveport	LA	71106	318-861-4572		187
United-Guardian Inc (UGI) 230 Marcus Blvd PO Box 18050 *NASDAQ: UG* ■ *TF:* 800-645-5566 ■ *Web:* www.u-g.com	Hauppauge	NY	11788	631-273-0900	273-0858	479
UnitedHealth Group Inc 9900 Bren Rd E *NYSE: UNH* ■ *TF:* 800-328-5979 ■ *Web:* www.unitedhealthgroup.com	Minnetonka	MN	55343	952-936-1300		391-3
UnitedLayer Inc 200 Paul Ave Ste 110 *Web:* www.unitedlayer.com	San Francisco	CA	94124	415-349-2100		225
Unitel Inc PO Box 165 *TF:* 888-760-1048 ■ *Web:* www.unitelme.com	Unity	ME	04988	207-948-3900		736
Uni-Ter Underwriting Management Corp 500 Northridge Rd Ste 330 *Web:* www.usre.com	Atlanta	GA	30350	678-781-2400		390
UniteU Technologies Inc 12 Pine Cone Dr *TF:* 866-386-4838 ■ *Web:* www.uniteu.com	Pittsford	NY	14534	866-386-4838		224
Unitex Oil & Gas LLC 310 W Wall Ste 503 *Web:* unitexoilandgas.com	Midland	TX	79701	432-685-0014		536
Unitil Corp 6 Liberty Ln W *NYSE: UTL* ■ *TF:* 800-852-3339 ■ *Web:* www.unitil.com	Hampton	NH	03842	603-772-0775	773-6605	360-5
Unitrak Corporation Ltd 299 Ward St *Web:* www.unitrak.com	Port Hope	ON	L1A3W4	905-885-8168		207
Unitrans International Corp 709 S Hindry Ave *Web:* www.unitrans-us.com	Inglewood	CA	90301	310-410-7676	410-1719	449
Unitrends Software Corp 200 Wheeler Rd 2nd fl *TF:* 866-359-5411 ■ *Web:* www.unitrends.com	Burlington	SC	01803	803-454-0300		173-8
Unitron LP 10925 Miller Rd PO Box 38902 *TF:* 800-527-1279 ■ *Web:* www.unitronlp.com	Dallas	TX	75238	214-340-8600	341-2099	518
Unitus Community Credit Union PO Box 1937 *TF:* 800-452-0900 ■ *Web:* www.unitusccu.com	Portland	OR	97207	503-227-5571	423-8345	219
Unity Bancorp Inc 64 Old Hwy 22 *NASDAQ: UNTY* ■ *TF:* 800-618-2265 ■ *Web:* www.unitybank.com	Clinton	NJ	08809	908-730-7630		360-2
Unity College 90 Quaker Hill Rd *TF:* 800-624-1024 ■ *Web:* www.unity.edu	Unity	ME	04988	207-948-3131		166
Unity Elementary School 6846 Unity School Rd *Web:* unity.massac.org	Brookport	IL	62910	618-564-2582		685
Unity Financial Strategists Inc 100 Wall St 22nd Fl	New York	NY	10005	212-785-4200		401
Unity Health Ctr 1102 W MacArthur St *Web:* stanthonyshawnee.com	Shawnee	OK	74804	405-273-2270		374-3
Unity Health Insurance 840 Carolina St *TF:* 800-362-3308 ■ *Web:* www.unityhealth.com	Sauk City	WI	53583	608-643-2491	643-2564	391-3
Unity Hospice 2366 Oak Ridge Cir *TF:* 800-990-9249 ■ *Web:* www.unityhospice.org	De Pere	WI	54115	920-338-1111		371
Unity Hospice 700 S Clinton St Ste 210 *TF:* 888-949-1188 ■ *Web:* www.unityhospice.com	Chicago	IL	60607	312-427-6000	427-6004	371
Unity Hospital 550 Osborne Rd *TF:* 800-994-6610 ■ *Web:* www.allinahealth.org	Fridley	MN	55432	763-236-4111		374-3
Unity HR LLC 2400 Meridian St Bldg B *Web:* www.unityhr.com	Bellingham	WA	98225	360-671-0762		2
Unity Lake State Recreation Site 725 Summer St NE Ste C *TF:* 800-551-6949 ■ *Web:* www.oregonstateparks.org	Salem	OR	97301	541-932-4453		565
Unity Manufacturing Co 1260 N Clybourn Ave *Web:* www.unityusa.com	Chicago	IL	60610	312-943-5200	943-5681	438
Unity Marketing Inc 206 E Church St *TF:* 800-243-2234 ■ *Web:* www.unitymarketingonline.com	Stevens	PA	17578	717-336-1600		466
Unity Physician Group Pc 1155 W Third St *Web:* www.unitypg.com	Bloomington	IN	47404	812-333-2731		352
Unity Railway Supply Company Inc 805 Golf Ln *TF:* 800-843-6616 ■ *Web:* www.unityrailway.com	Bensenville	IL	60106	630-595-4560		770
Unity Technologies Inc 30 Third St *Web:* unity3d.com	San Francisco	CA	94103	415-539-3162		177
Univance Inc 3400 Corporate Dr	Winchester	KY	40391	859-737-2306		247
Univar Canada Ltd 9800 Van Horne Way *TF:* 855-888-8648 ■ *Web:* www.univar.com	Richmond	BC	V6X1W5	604-273-1441		146
Univar USA Inc 17425 NE Union Hill Rd *TF:* 855-888-8648 ■ *Web:* www.univar.com	Redmond	WA	98052	425-889-3400	889-4100	146
Univenture Inc 13311 Industrial Pkwy **Fax Area Code:* 937 ■ *TF:* 800-992-8262 ■ *Web:* www.univenture.com	Marysville	OH	43040	800-992-8262	645-4700*	608
Univera Healthcare 205 Pk Club Ln **Fax Area Code:* 800 ■ **Fax:* Hum Res ■ *TF:* 877-883-9577 ■ *Web:* www.univerahealthcare.com	Buffalo	NY	14221	716-847-1480	956-2397*	391-3
Univeris Corp 111 George St 3rd Fl *Web:* www.univeris.com	Toronto	ON	M5A2N4	416-979-3700		177
Univers Workplace Benefits Inc 897 12th St *TF:* 800-343-0240 ■ *Web:* univers.biz	Hammonton	NJ	08037	800-343-0240		401
Universal Aerospace Company Inc 18640 59th Dr NE *Web:* www.universalaero.com	Arlington	WA	98223	360-435-9577		454
Universal Air Conditioner Inc 1441 Heritage Pkwy *Web:* www.uacparts.com	Mansfield	TX	76063	817-740-3900		610
Universal American Corp (UAFC) 44 S Broadway Ste 1200 *NYSE: UAM* ■ *TF:* 866-249-8668 ■ *Web:* www.universalamerican.com	White Plains	NY	10601	914-934-5200	934-0700	360-4
Universal Asset Management Inc 5350 Poplar Ave Ste 150 *TF:* 800-233-3414 ■ *Web:* www.uaminc.com	Memphis	TN	38119	901-682-4064		21
Universal Audio Inc 1700 Green Hills Rd *TF:* 877-698-2834 ■ *Web:* www.uaudio.com	Scotts Valley	CA	95066	831-440-1176	461-1550	52
Universal Avionics Systems Corp 3260 E Universal Way *Web:* www.uasc.com	Tucson	AZ	85756	520-295-2300		21
Universal Ballet Academy 4301 Harewood Rd NE *Web:* universalballet.com	Washington	DC	20017	202-832-1087	526-4274	622
Universal Bearings Inc 431 N Birkey St *Web:* www.univbrg.com	Bremen	IN	46506	574-546-2261		75
Universal Bookbindery Inc 1200 N Colorado St *Web:* universalbookbindery.com	San Antonio	TX	78207	210-734-9502		535
Universal Brass Inc 5475 Wynn Rd Ste 400 *Web:* www.universalbrassinc.com	Las Vegas	NV	89118	702-795-0400		480
Universal Brush Manufacturing Co 16200 Dixie Hwy *TF:* 800-323-3474 ■ *Web:* www.universalbrush.com	Markham	IL	60428	708-331-1700	331-4923	103
Universal Builders Supply Inc (UBS) 27 Horton Ave *Web:* www.ubs1.com	New Rochelle	NY	10801	914-699-2400	699-2609	491
Universal Care Inc 1600 E Hill St	Signal Hill	CA	90755	562-424-6200		391-3
Universal City Development Partners Ltd 1000 Universal Studios Plaza *TF:* 800-447-0672 ■ *Web:* www.universalorlando.com	Orlando	FL	32819	407-363-8000		31
Universal City-North Hollywood Chamber of Commerce 6369 Bellingham Ave *Web:* www.noho.org	North Hollywood	CA	91606	818-508-5155	508-5156	139
Universal Companies Inc 18260 Oak Park Dr *Web:* www.universalcompanies.com	Abingdon	VA	24210	276-466-9110		77
Universal Concrete Products Corp 400 Old Reading Pk Ste 100 *TF:* 800-424-3996 ■ *Web:* www.universalconcrete.com	Stowe	PA	19464	610-323-0700	323-4046	183
Universal Construction Company Inc 11200 W 79th St *Web:* www.universalconstruction.net	Lenexa	KS	66214	913-342-1150	342-1151	186
Universal Co-ops Inc (UCOOP) 1300 Corporate Ctr Curve *Web:* www.ucoop.com	Eagan	MN	55121	651-239-1000		276
Universal Corp 9201 Forest Hill Ave PO Box 25099 *NYSE: UVV* ■ *Web:* www.universalcorp.com	Richmond	VA	23260	804-359-9311	254-3582	185
Universal Display & Fixtures Co 726 E Hwy 121 *TF:* 800-235-0701 ■ *Web:* www.udfc.com	Lewisville	TX	75057	972-829-2498	221-6624	233
Universal Display Corp 375 Phillips Blvd *NASDAQ: OLED* ■ *Web:* oled.com	Ewing	NJ	08618	609-671-0980	671-0995	696
Universal Electronics Inc 201 E Sandpointe Ave 8th Fl *NASDAQ: UEIC* ■ *Web:* www.uei.com	Santa Ana	CA	92707	714-918-9500	918-4100	52
Universal Enclosure Systems 1146 S Cedar Ridge Dr *Web:* www.universalenclosures.com	Duncanville	TX	75137	972-298-0531	298-0614	254
Universal Enterprises Inc 8626 SW Cascade Ave *TF:* 800-547-5740 ■ *Web:* www.ueitest.com	Beaverton	OR	97008	503-644-8723		360-2
Universal Environmental Services LLC 411 Dividend Dr *TF:* 800-988-7977 ■ *Web:* www.universalenvironmentalservices.com	Peachtree City	GA	30269	800-988-7977		541
Universal Fabric Structures Inc 2200 Kumry Rd *TF:* 800-634-8368 ■ *Web:* www.ufsinc.com	Telford	PA	18969	215-529-9921	529-9936	733
Universal Fibers Inc PO Box 8930 *TF:* 800-457-4759 ■ *Web:* www.universalfibers.com	Bristol	VA	24203	276-669-1161	669-3304	745-9
Universal Ford Sales Inc 10751 W Broad St *Web:* www.richmondford.com	Glen Allen	VA	23060	804-273-9700		516
Universal Forest Products Inc (UFPI) 2801 E Beltline Ave NE *NASDAQ: UFPI* ■ *TF:* 800-598-9663 ■ *Web:* www.ufpi.com	Grand Rapids	MI	49525	616-364-6161	361-7534	683

Name / Address	City	State	Zip	Phone	Fax	Class
Universal Grinding Corp 1234 W 78th St *TF:* 888-825-2705 ■ *Web:* www.universalgrinding.com	Cleveland	OH	44102	888-825-2705		454
Universal Health Realty Income Trust 367 S Gulph Rd *NYSE: UHT* ■ *Web:* www.uhrit.com	KingofPrussia	PA	19406	610-265-0688		655
Universal Health Services Inc 367 S Gulph Rd *NYSE: UHS* ■ *TF:* 800-347-7750 ■ *Web:* www.uhsinc.com	King of Prussia	PA	19406	610-768-3300		353
Universal Home Health & Hospice Care 701 S Main St *Web:* www.uhcinc.org	Bellefontaine	OH	43311	937-593-1605		371
Universal Hospital Services Inc 7700 France Ave S Ste 275 *TF:* 800-847-7368 ■ *Web:* www.uhs.com	Minneapolis	MN	55435	952-893-3200	893-0704	264-4
Universal Image PO Box 77090 *TF:* 800-553-5499 ■ *Web:* www.universalphoto.com	Winter Garden	FL	34787	407-352-5302		592
Universal Image Production Inc 20750 Civic Ctr Dr Ste 100 *Web:* www.universalimages.com	Southfield	MI	48076	248-357-2247		514
Universal Industrial Fabricating Inc Industrial Park Dr *Web:* www.uigi.com	Plant City	FL	33566	813-717-9701		697
Universal Industries Inc 5800 Nordic Dr *TF:* 800-553-4446 ■ *Web:* www.universalindustries.com	Cedar Falls	IA	50613	319-277-7501	277-2318	207
Universal Instruments Corp (UIC) 33 Broome Corporate Pk *TF:* 800-842-9732 ■ *Web:* uic.com	Conklin	NY	13748	607-779-7522	779-4466	695
Universal Insurance Holding Inc (UIH) 1110 W Commerical Blvd Ste 100 *NYSE: UVE* ■ *TF:* 800-509-5586 ■ *Web:* www.universalinsuranceholdings.com	Fort Lauderdale	FL	33309	800-509-5586		391-4
Universal Labeling Systems Inc 3501 Eigth Ave S *TF:* 877-[illegible] ■ *Web:* www.universal1.com	Saint Petersburg	FL	33711	727-327-2123		547
Universal Leaf Tobacco Co Inc 1501 N Hamilton St PO Box 25099 **Fax:* Hum Res ■ *Web:* www.universalcorp.com	Richmond	VA	23260	804-359-9311	254-3584*	756
Universal Lending Corp (ULC) 6775 E Evans Ave *TF:* 800-758-4063 ■ *Web:* ulc.com	Denver	CO	80224	800-758-4063		509
Universal Machine & Engineering Corp 645 Old Reading Pk *TF:* 800-879-2477 ■ *Web:* www.umc-oscar.com	Stowe	PA	19464	610-323-1810		386
Universal Manufacturing Co 405 Diagonal St PO Box 190 *OTC: UFMG* ■ *TF:* 800-343-3557 ■ *Web:* www.umcretech.com	Algona	IA	50511	515-295-3557	295-5537	60
Universal McCann 100 W 33rd St *Web:* www.umww.com	New York	NY	10001	212-883-4700		6
Universal Metal Products 29980 Lakeland Blvd *Web:* www.ump-inc.com	Wickliffe	OH	44092	440-943-3040		488
Universal Metals LLC 805 Chicago St *TF:* 800-853-8890 ■ *Web:* www.umimetals.com	Toledo	OH	43611	419-726-0850		492
Universal Mfg Co Inc 5030 Mackey S *TF:* 800-524-5860 ■ *Web:* www.umcprint.com	Overland Park	KS	66203	913-815-6230	815-6240	762
Universal Money Center 6800 Squibb Rd *Web:* www.universalmoney.com	Shawnee Mission	KS	66202	913-831-2055		69
Universal Music Publishing 2100 Colorado Ave *Web:* www.umusicpub.com	Santa Monica	CA	90404	310-235-4700		637-7
Universal Odyssey Inc 2618 San Miguel Dr Ste 476 *Web:* www.universalodyssey.com	Newport Beach	CA	92660	949-263-1222	263-0983	384
Universal Orlando 6000 Universal Blvd *TF:* 877-801-9720 ■ *Web:* universalorlando.com	Orlando	FL	32819	407-363-8000		32
Universal Overall Co 1060 W Van Buren St *TF Cust Svc:* 800-621-3344 ■ *Web:* www.universaloverall.com	Chicago	IL	60607	312-226-3336	226-1986	155-19
Universal Plastic Mold Inc 13245 Los Angeles St *TF:* 888-893-1587 ■ *Web:* www.upminc.com	Baldwin Park	CA	91706	888-893-1587		604
Universal Polymer & Rubber Ltd 15730 Madison Rd *TF:* 800-782-2375 ■ *Web:* www.universalpolymer.com	Middlefield	OH	44062	440-632-1691	632-5761	677
Universal Power Systems Inc 4230 Lafayette Center Dr Ste G *Web:* www.upsi.com	Chantilly	VA	20151	703-378-6100		767
Universal Printing Co 1234 S Kings Hwy *Web:* www.universalprintingco.com	Saint Louis	MO	63110	314-771-6900	771-7987	627
Universal Protective Packaging Inc 61 Texaco Rd *TF:* 800-544-6649 ■ *Web:* www.uppi.com	Mechanicsburg	PA	17050	717-766-1578		601
Universal Remote Control Inc 500 Mamaroneck Ave *TF:* 800-901-0800 ■ *Web:* www.universalremote.com	Harrison	NY	10528	914-835-4484		246
Universal Scientific of Illinois Inc 2101 Arthur Ave *Web:* universalscientificinc.com	Elk Grove Village	IL	60007	847-228-6464	228-0523	625
Universal Security Instruments Inc 11407 Cronhill Dr *TSE: UUU* ■ *TF:* 800-390-4321 ■ *Web:* www.universalsecurity.com	Owings Mills	MD	21117	410-363-3000	363-2218	692
Universal Service Administrative Co (USAC) 2000 L St NW Ste 200 *TF:* 888-641-8722 ■ *Web:* www.usac.org	Washington	DC	20036	202-776-0200	776-0080	736
Universal Service Administrative Co Schools & Libraries Div 2000 L St NW Ste 200 *TF:* 888-203-8100 ■ *Web:* www.usac.org	Washington	DC	20036	888-203-8100	276-8736	736
Universal Steel America Houston Inc 1230 E Richey Rd *TF:* 866-988-3800 ■ *Web:* www.universalsteelamerica.com	Houston	TX	77073	281-821-7400		492
Universal Steel Co, The 6600 Grant Ave *Web:* univsteel.com	Cleveland	OH	44105	216-883-4972		686
Universal Steel Inc 2400 Stone Mountain-Lithonia Rd *Web:* www.universalsteelinc.com	Lithonia	GA	30058	770-482-5601		480
Universal Studios CityWalk Hollywood Universal City Plaza *Web:* www.citywalkhollywood.com	Los Angeles	CA	91608	818-622-4455		50-6
Universal Studios Hollywood 100 Universal City Plaza *TF:* 800-864-8377	Universal City	CA	91608	800-864-8377		31
Universal Studios Inc 100 Universal City Plaza *Web:* www.universalstudios.com	Universal City	CA	91608	818-777-1000	866-3600	514
Universal Technical Resource Services Inc (UERS) 950 Kings Hwy N Ste 208 *Web:* www.utrs.com	Cherry Hill	NJ	08034	856-667-6770	667-7586	261
Universal Technologies Inc 165 Alsonia St *Web:* www.utiwebsite.com	Estill Springs	TN	37330	931-649-5171		454
Universal Technology Corp (UTC) 1270 N Fairfield Rd *Web:* www.utcdayton.com	Dayton	OH	45432	937-426-2808		261
Universal Tool Company Inc 33 Rose Pl	Springfield	MA	01104	413-732-4807		350
Universal Travel 1425C SE 17th St	Ft. Lauderdale	FL	33316	954-525-5000		546
Universal Truckload Services Inc 12755 E Nine Mile Rd *NASDAQ: UACL* ■ *TF:* 800-233-9445 ■ *Web:* www.goutsi.com	Warren	MI	48089	586-920-0100	920-0258	780
Universal Tube Inc 2607 Bond St *TF:* 800-394-8823 ■ *Web:* www.universaltube.com	Rochester Hills	MI	48309	248-853-5100	853-7365	595
Universal Valve Company Inc 478 Schiller St *TF:* 800-223-0741 ■ *Web:* www.universalvalve.com	Elizabeth	NJ	07206	908-351-0606		790
Universal Wilde 26 Dartmouth St *TF:* 866-825-5515 ■ *Web:* www.universalwilde.com	Westwood	MA	02090	781-251-2700	251-2613	5
Universal Window & Door 303 Mechanic St *Web:* www.universalwindow.com	Marlboro	MA	01752	508-481-2850		234
Universal Wire Cloth Co 16 N Steel Rd *TF:* 800-523-0575 ■ *Web:* www.universalwirecloth.com	Morrisville	PA	19067	215-736-8981	736-8994	688
Universal's Islands of Adventure 6000 Universal Studios Plaza *TF:* 877-801-9720 ■ *Web:* universalorlando.com	Orlando	FL	32819	407-363-8000		32
UniversalPegasus International Inc 4848 Loop Central Dr Ste 137 *TF General:* 800-966-1811 ■ *Web:* www.universalpegasus.com	Houston	TX	77081	713-425-6000	977-1047	261
Universidad Popular 2801 S Hamlin Ave *Web:* www.universidadpopular.us	Chicago	IL	60623	773-733-5055		162
Universitas Foundation of Canada 5005 Ave Maricourt *TF:* 877-710-7377 ■ *Web:* www.universitas.ca	Quebec	QC	G1W4T8	418-651-8975		305
Universite de Moncton *Campus Shippagan* 218 Blvd JD Gauthier *TF:* 800-363-8336 ■ *Web:* www.umoncton.ca	Shippagan	NB	E8S1P6	506-336-3400	336-3604	785
Edmundston 165 Blvd Hebert *TF:* 888-736-8623 ■ *Web:* www.umoncton.ca	Edmundston	NB	E3V2S8	506-737-5051	737-5373	785
Universite de Montreal CP 6128 Succursale Centre Ville **Fax:* Admissions ■ *Web:* www.umontreal.ca	Montreal	QC	H3C3J7	514-343-6111	343-5788*	785
Universite de Montreal Bibliotheque de la Sante 2900 Blvd Edouard-Montpetit Rm L623 *Web:* www.bib.umontreal.ca/sa	Montreal	QC	H3T1J4	514-343-6111		434-1
Universite de Sherbrooke 2500 boul de l'Universite *TF:* 800-267-8337 ■ *Web:* www.usherbrooke.ca	Sherbrooke	QC	J1K2R1	819-821-8000	821-7966	785
Universite du Quebec 475 Rue du Parvis *Web:* www.uquebec.ca	Quebec	QC	G1K9H7	418-657-3551	657-2132	785
Universite du Quebec a Trois-Rivieres 3351 Boul des Forges CP 500 *TF:* 800-365-0922 ■ *Web:* www.uqtr.ca	Trois-Rivieres	QC	G9A5H7	819-376-5011	376-5210	785
Universite Laval *Bibliotheque Scientifique* Pavillon Alexandre-Vachon 1045 Ave *Web:* www.bibl.ulaval.ca	Quebec	QC	G1V0A6	418-656-3967	656-7897	434-1
Universite Sainte Anne 1695 Rt 1 *TF:* 888-338-8337 ■ *Web:* www.usainteanne.ca	Pointe-de-l'Eglise	NS	B0W1M0	902-769-2114	769-2930	785
Universities Research Assn Inc (URA) 1140 19th St NW Ste 900 *Web:* www.ura-hq.org	Washington	DC	20036	202-293-1382	293-5012	49-19
Universities Space Research Assn (USRA) 10211 Wincopin Cir Ste 500 *Web:* www.usra.edu	Columbia	MD	21044	410-730-2656	730-3496	49-19
University & State Employees Credit Union 10120 Pacific Heights Blvd Ste 100 *TF:* 866-873-2448 ■ *Web:* www.usecu.org	San Diego	CA	92121	858-795-6100		219
University Art Museum 1250 N Bellflower Blvd *TF:* 800-437-2934 ■ *Web:* www.csulb.edu	Long Beach	CA	90840	562-985-5761	985-7602	520
University Art Museum 1400 Washington Ave SUNY Albany *Web:* www.albany.edu/museum	Albany	NY	12222	518-442-4035	442-5075	520
University at Albany 1400 Washington Ave **Fax:* Admissions ■ *TF:* 800-293-7869 ■ *Web:* www.albany.edu	Albany	NY	12222	518-442-3300	442-5383*	166
University at Buffalo *University Libraries* 433 Capen Hall *Web:* library.buffalo.edu	Buffalo	NY	14260	716-645-2965	645-3844	434-6
University at Buffalo Law School John Lord O'Brian Hall *Web:* www.law.buffalo.edu	Buffalo	NY	14260	716-645-2052	645-2064	167-1
University at Buffalo School of Medicine & Biomedical Sciences 12 Capen Hall **Fax:* Admissions ■ *Web:* www.wings.buffalo.edu	Buffalo	NY	14260	716-829-3466	829-3849*	167-2

Name / Address	City	State	Zip	Phone	Fax	Class
University Bancorp Inc						
2015 Washtenaw Ave	Ann Arbor	MI	48104	734-741-5858	741-5859	360-2
OTC: UNIB ■ *TF:* 800-818-9853 ■ *Web:* www.university-bank.com						
University Behavioral Ctr						
2500 Discovery Dr	Orlando	FL	32826	407-281-7000	282-7012	374-5
TF: 800-999-0807 ■ *Web:* www.universitybehavioral.com						
University Book Store, The						
711 State St	Madison	WI	53703	608-257-3784		95
TF: 800-993-2665 ■ *Web:* www.uwbookstore.com						
University City Housing (UCH)						
3418 Sansom St	Philadelphia	PA	19104	215-222-2000	222-5449	655
Web: www.universitycityhousing.com						
University City Public Library						
6701 Delmar Blvd	University City	MO	63130	314-727-3150	727-6005	434-3
Web: www.ucpl.lib.mo.us						
University City School Dst						
8136 Groby Rd	Saint Louis	MO	63130	314-290-4000		449
Web: www.ucityschools.org						
University Club of Chicago						
76 E Monroe St	Chicago	IL	60603	312-726-2840	726-0620	671
Web: www.ucco.com						
University Galleries						
400 SW 13th St Fine Arts Bldg B						
PO Box 115803	Gainesville	FL	32611	352-273-3000		520
Web: www.arts.ufl.edu						
University Games Corp						
2030 Harrison St	San Francisco	CA	94110	415-503-1600	503-0085	762
TF: 800-347-4818 ■ *Web:* www.ugames.com						
University Health Care System						
1350 Walton Way	Augusta	GA	30901	706-722-9011		374-3
TF: 866-591-2502 ■ *Web:* www.universityhealth.org						
University Health Network						
190 Elizabeth St	Toronto	ON	M5G2C4	416-340-4907		353
Web: www.uhn.ca						
University Health Systems Hospice						
521 E Myers St	Ahoskie	NC	27910	252-332-3392		371
University Hospital						
4502 Medical Dr	San Antonio	TX	78229	210-358-4000	358-5936	374-3
TF: 866-864-5226 ■ *Web:* www.universityhealthsystem.com						
University Hospital (MCLNO)						
2021 Perdido St	New Orleans	LA	70112	504-903-3000		374-3
TF: 800-960-7705 ■ *Web:* www.lsuhospitals.org						
University Hospital 1 Hospital Dr	Columbia	MO	65212	573-882-4141		374-3
Web: www.muhealth.org						
University Hospital 234 Goodman St	Cincinnati	OH	45219	513-584-1000		374-3
Web: uchealth.com						
University Hospital						
1500 E Medical Ctr Dr	Ann Arbor	MI	48109	734-936-4000		374-3
Web: www.med.umich.edu						
University Hospital						
2211 Lomas Blvd NE	Albuquerque	NM	87106	505-272-2111	925-4491*	374-3
**Fax:* Admitting ■ *Web:* hospitals.unm.edu						
University Hospital						
7201 N University Dr	Tamarac	FL	33321	954-721-2200		374-3
Web: www.uhmchealth.com						
University Hospital Bedford Medical Ctr						
44 Blaine Ave	Bedford	OH	44146	440-735-3900	735-3631	374-3
Web: www.uhhospitals.org						
University Hospital SUNY Upstate Medical University						
750 E Adams St	Syracuse	NY	13210	315-464-5540		374-3
TF: 877-464-5540 ■ *Web:* upstate.edu/hospital						
University Hospitals of Cleveland						
11100 Euclid Ave	Cleveland	OH	44106	216-844-1000	844-7497	374-3
TF: 866-844-2273 ■ *Web:* www.uhhospitals.org						
University Inn Seattle						
4140 Roosevelt Way NE	Seattle	WA	98105	206-632-5055	547-4937	379
TF: 800-733-3855 ■ *Web:* www.universityinnseattle.com						
University Language Institute						
2448 E 81st St Ste 1400	Tulsa	OK	74137	918-493-8088	493-8084	423
Web: www.uli.net						
University Libraries						
1155 Union Cir Ste 305190	Denton	TX	76203	940-565-2411	565-4949*	434-6
**Fax:* Circulation Desk ■ *TF:* 877-872-0264 ■ *Web:* www.library.unt.edu						
University Mall 2200 E Fowler Ave	Tampa	FL	33612	813-971-3465		460
Web: www.universitymalltampa.com						
University Mechanical & Engineering Contractors Inc						
1168 Fesler St	El Cajon	CA	92020	619-956-2500	956-2300	189-10
Web: www.umec.com						
University Medical Ctr						
2390 W Congress St	Lafayette	LA	70506	337-261-6000		374-3
TF: 800-893-9698 ■ *Web:* lafayettegeneral.com						
University Medical Ctr						
1800 W Charleston Blvd	Las Vegas	NV	89102	702-383-2000		374-3
Web: www.umcsn.com						
University Medical Ctr						
602 Indiana Ave	Lubbock	TX	79415	806-775-8200		374-3
Web: www.umchealthsystem.com						
University Medical Ctr at Princeton (UMCP)						
253 Witherspoon St	Princeton	NJ	08540	609-497-4304		374-3
TF: 877-932-8935 ■ *Web:* princetonhcs.org						
University Medical Ctr Bone Marrow & Blood Stem Cell Transplant Program (UMC)						
602 Indiana Ave	Lubbock	TX	79415	806-775-8200		769
Web: www.umchealthsystem.com						
University Medical Ctr of El Paso (UMCEP)						
4815 Alameda Ave	El Paso	TX	79905	915-544-1200		374-3
Web: www.umcelpaso.org						
University Moving & Storage Co						
23305 Commerce Dr	Farmington Hills	MI	48335	248-615-7000		186
TF: 800-448-6683 ■ *Web:* www.universitymoving.com						
University Museum						
3219 Hudson Rd						
University of Northern Iowa	Cedar Falls	IA	50614	319-273-2188	273-6924	520
TF: 800-772-2736 ■ *Web:* www.uni.edu/museum						
University of Akron 277 E Buchtel Ave	Akron	OH	44325	330-972-7100	972-7022	166
TF Admissions: 800-655-4884 ■ *Web:* www.uakron.edu						
University of Akron School of Law						
150 University Ave	Akron	OH	44325	330-972-7331	258-2343	167-1
TF: 800-655-4884 ■ *Web:* www.uakron.edu						
University of Akron Wayne College						
1901 Smucker Rd	Orrville	OH	44667	330-683-2010	684-8989	162
TF: 800-221-8308 ■ *Web:* www.wayne.uakron.edu						
University of Alabama						
PO Box 870132	Tuscaloosa	AL	35487	205-348-6010	348-9046*	166
**Fax:* Admissions ■ *TF Admissions:* 800-933-2262 ■ *Web:* www.ua.edu						
Birmingham 1530 Third Ave S THT 647	Birmingham	AL	35294	205-996-6670	975-7114*	166
**Fax:* Admissions ■ *TF:* 800-421-8743 ■ *Web:* www.uab.edu						
Gorgas Library						
Information Ctr 1st Fl	Tuscaloosa	AL	35487	205-348-4018	348-9564	434-6
Web: www.lib.ua.edu/libraries/gorgas						
Huntsville 301 Sparkman Dr	Huntsville	AL	35899	256-824-1000	824-7780*	166
**Fax:* Admissions ■ *TF:* 800-824-2255 ■ *Web:* www.uah.edu						
School of Law						
101 Paul W Bryant Dr E	Tuscaloosa	AL	35401	205-348-5440		167-1
Web: www.law.ua.edu						
University of Alabama Arboretum						
PO Box 870344	Tuscaloosa	AL	35487	205-553-3278	553-3728	97
Web: www.arboretum.ua.edu						
University of Alabama Press, The						
200 Hackberry Ln Second Fl 2nd Fl	Tuscaloosa	AL	35487	205-348-5180	348-9201	637-4
TF Orders: 800-621-2736 ■ *Web:* www.uapress.ua.edu						
University of Alabama System						
401 Queen City Ave	Tuscaloosa	AL	35401	205-348-5861		786
TF: 866-362-9476 ■ *Web:* uasystem.edu						
University of Alaska Anchorage						
3211 Providence Dr	Anchorage	AK	99508	907-786-1800	786-4888*	166
**Fax:* Admissions ■ *TF:* 888-822-8973 ■ *Web:* www.uaa.alaska.edu						
University of Alaska Anchorage Kenai Peninsula College						
156 College Rd	Soldotna	AK	99669	877-262-0330	262-0322*	162
**Fax Area Code:* 907 ■ *TF:* 877-262-0330 ■ *Web:* www.kpc.alaska.edu						
University of Alaska Anchorage Kodiak College						
117 Benny Benson Dr	Kodiak	AK	99615	907-486-4161	486-1264	162
TF: 800-486-7660 ■ *Web:* www.koc.alaska.edu						
University of Alaska Fairbanks						
PO Box 757480	Fairbanks	AK	99775	907-474-7500	474-5379*	166
**Fax:* Admissions ■ *TF:* 800-478-1823 ■ *Web:* www.uaf.edu						
Bristol Bay						
527 Seward St PO Box 1070	Dillingham	AK	99576	907-842-5109	842-5692*	166
**Fax:* Admissions ■ *TF:* 800-478-5109 ■ *Web:* www.uaf.edu						
Northwest 400 E Front St PO Box 400	Nome	AK	99762	907-443-2201	443-5602	162
TF: 800-478-2202 ■ *Web:* www.nwc.uaf.edu						
Rasmuson Library PO Box 756800	Fairbanks	AK	99775	907-474-7481	474-6841	434-6
Web: library.uaf.edu						
University of Alaska Museum of the North						
907 Yukon Dr	Fairbanks	AK	99775	907-474-7505	474-5469	520
TF: 866-478-2721 ■ *Web:* www.uaf.edu/museum						
University of Alaska Press						
1760 Wwood Wy Ste 220	Fairbanks	AK	99709	907-474-5831	474-5502	637-4
TF: 888-252-6657 ■ *Web:* www.uaf.edu						
University of Alaska Southeast						
11120 Glacier Hwy	Juneau	AK	99801	907-796-6000		166
TF: 877-465-4827 ■ *Web:* www.uas.alaska.edu						
University of Alaska Southeast Ketchikan						
2600 Seventh Ave	Ketchikan	AK	99901	907-225-6177		162
TF: 877-465-6400 ■ *Web:* www.ketch.alaska.edu						
University of Alaska Southeast Sitka						
1332 Seward Ave	Sitka	AK	99835	907-747-6653	747-7768	162
TF: 800-478-6653 ■ *Web:* www.uas.alaska.edu						
University of Alaska System						
910 Yukon Dr PO Box 775000	Fairbanks	AK	99775	907-450-8000	450-8012	786
Web: www.alaska.edu						
University of Alberta						
116 St & 85 Ave	Edmonton	AB	T6G2R3	780-492-3111		785
Web: www.ualberta.ca						
Augustana 4901-46th Ave	Camrose	AB	T4V2R3	780-679-1100	679-1129	785
TF: 800-661-8714 ■ *Web:* www.augustana.ualberta.ca						
University of Alberta Faculty of Medicine & Dentistry						
2J200 WC Medical Sciences Bldg	Edmonton	AB	T6G2R3	780-492-6350	492-9531	167-2
Web: www.med.ualberta.ca						
University of Alberta Hospital						
8440 112th St	Edmonton	AB	T6G2B7	780-407-8822		374-2
Web: www.albertahealthservices.ca						
University of Arizona PO Box 210300	Tucson	AZ	85721	520-621-2211	621-9799*	166
**Fax:* Admissions ■ *Web:* www.arizona.edu						
University of Arizona Arizona Health Sciences Library						
1501 N Campbell Ave PO Box 245079	Tucson	AZ	85724	520-626-6125	626-2922	434-1
Web: www.ahsl.arizona.edu						
University of Arizona College of Medicine						
1501 N Campbell Ave	Tucson	AZ	85724	520-626-4555	626-6252	167-2
Web: www.medicine.arizona.edu						
University of Arizona James E Rogers College of Law						
1201 E Speedway Blvd PO Box 210176	Tucson	AZ	85721	520-621-1373	626-1839	167-1
Web: www.law.arizona.edu						
University of Arizona Library						
1510 E University Blvd	Tucson	AZ	85721	520-621-6442	621-9733*	434-6
**Fax:* Admin ■ *Web:* www.library.arizona.edu						
University of Arizona Museum of Art						
1031 N Olive Rd University of Arizona	Tucson	AZ	85721	520-621-7567	621-8770	520
Web: artmuseum.arizona.edu						
University of Arizona Press, The						
1510 E University Blvd PO Box 210055	Tucson	AZ	85721	520-621-1441	621-8899	637-4
TF: 800-426-3797 ■ *Web:* www.uapress.arizona.edu						
University of Arkansas						
232 Silas Hunt Hall	Fayetteville	AR	72701	479-575-5346	575-7515*	166
**Fax:* Admissions ■ *TF Admissions:* 800-377-8632 ■ *Web:* www.uark.edu						
Little Rock 2801 S University Ave	Little Rock	AR	72204	501-569-3000	569-8956	166
TF: 800-482-8892 ■ *Web:* www.ualr.edu						
Monticello PO Box 3600	Monticello	AR	71656	870-460-1026	460-1926*	166
**Fax:* Admissions ■ *TF:* 800-844-1826 ■ *Web:* www.uamont.edu						
Pine Bluff 1200 N University Dr	Pine Bluff	AR	71601	870-575-8000	575-4608*	166
**Fax:* Admissions ■ *TF Admissions:* 800-264-6585 ■ *Web:* www.uapb.edu						
University of Arkansas at Little Rock William H Bowen School of Law						
1201 McMath Ave	Little Rock	AR	72202	501-324-9903		167-1
Web: ualr.edu						
University of Arkansas for Medical Sciences						
College of Medicine						
4301 W Markham St Ste 550	Little Rock	AR	72205	501-686-5354		167-2
Web: www.uams.edu/com						

Name / Address	City	State	ZIP	Phone	Fax	Class
Interlibrary Loan						
4301 W Markham Slot 586	Little Rock	AR	72205	501-686-7000		434-1
University of Arkansas Press						
McIlroy House 105 McIlroy	Fayetteville	AR	72701	479-575-7258	575-6044	637-4
TF: 800-621-2736 ■ *Web:* www.uapress.com						
University of Arkansas School of Law						
1045 W Maple St	Fayetteville	AR	72701	479-575-5601	575-3937*	167-1
**Fax:* Admissions ■ *Web:* www.law.uark.edu						
University of Baltimore						
1420 N Charles St	Baltimore	MD	21201	410-837-4200	837-4793	166
TF Admitting: 877-277-5982 ■ *Web:* www.ubalt.edu						
University of Bridgeport						
126 Pk Ave	Bridgeport	CT	06604	203-576-4000	576-4941*	166
**Fax:* Admissions ■ *TF:* 800-392-3582 ■ *Web:* www.bridgeport.edu						
University of British Columbia						
2016-1874 E Mall	Vancouver	BC	V6T1Z1	604-822-9836	822-3599	785
TF: 877-272-1422 ■ *Web:* www.ubc.ca						
Okanagan 3333 University Way	Kelowna	BC	V1V1V7	250-807-8000		785
Web: ok.ubc.ca						
University of British Columbia Botanical Garden & Centre for Plant Research						
6804 SW Marine Dr	Vancouver	BC	V6T1Z4	604-822-4208	822-2016	97
Web: www.botanicalgarden.ubc.ca						
University of British Columbia Faculty of Medicine						
317-2194 Health Sciences Mall	Vancouver	BC	V6T1Z3	604-822-2421	822-6061	167-2
Web: www.med.ubc.ca						
University of British Columbia Museum of Anthropology						
6393 NW Marine Dr	Vancouver	BC	V6T1Z2	604-822-5087	822-2974	520
Web: www.moa.ubc.ca						
University of Calgary						
2500 University Dr NW	Calgary	AB	T2N1N4	403-220-5110	282-7298	785
Web: www.ucalgary.ca						
University of Calgary						
3330 Hospital Dr NW	Calgary	AB	T2N4N1	403-210-3841	270-2681	167-2
Web: cumming.ucalgary.ca/intranet						
University of California (UCLA)						
Berkeley 110 Sproul Hall MC Ste 5800	Berkeley	CA	94720	510-642-6000	643-7333	166
TF: 800-740-1200 ■ *Web:* berkeley.edu						
Davis 1 Shields Ave	Davis	CA	95616	530-752-1011	752-1280	166
TF: 800-242-4723 ■ *Web:* www.ucdavis.edu						
Irvine 510 Aldrich Hall	Irvine	CA	92697	949-824-5011	824-2711	166
Web: www.uci.edu						
Los Angeles 405 Hilgard Ave	Los Angeles	CA	90095	310-825-4321	206-1206*	166
**Fax:* Admissions ■ *Web:* www.ucla.edu						
Merced PO Box 2039	Merced	CA	95344	209-724-4400		166
TF: 866-270-7301 ■ *Web:* www.ucmerced.edu						
Riverside						
900 University Ave 1120 Hinderaker Hall	Riverside	CA	92521	951-827-3411	827-6344	166
TF: 800-426-2586 ■ *Web:* www.ucr.edu						
San Diego 9500 Gilman Dr	La Jolla	CA	92093	858-534-2230	534-4831*	166
**Fax:* Admissions ■ *TF:* 800-207-1710 ■ *Web:* www.ucsd.edu						
San Francisco 505 Parnassus Ave	San Francisco	CA	94122	415-476-9000	353-3925	166
Web: www.ucsf.edu						
Santa Barbara 1210 Cheadle Hall	Santa Barbara	CA	93106	805-893-8000	893-2676	166
TF: 888-488-8272 ■ *Web:* www.ucsb.edu						
Santa Cruz						
1156 High St Hahn Bldg Rm 150	Santa Cruz	CA	95064	831-459-2131		166
TF: 800-933-7584 ■ *Web:* www.ucsc.edu						
University of California Berkeley School of Law						
Boalt Hall Ste 7200	Berkeley	CA	94720	510-642-1741	643-6222*	167-1
**Fax:* Admissions ■ *Web:* www.law.berkeley.edu						
University of California Botanical Garden at Berkeley						
200 Centennial Dr	Berkeley	CA	94720	510-643-2755	642-5045	97
Web: botanicalgarden.berkeley.edu						
University of California Davis Medical Ctr						
2315 Stockton Blvd	Sacramento	CA	95817	916-734-2011		374-3
Web: www.ucdmc.ucdavis.edu						
University of California Davis School of Law						
400 Mrak Hall Dr	Davis	CA	95616	530-752-0243	754-8371	167-1
Web: www.law.ucdavis.edu						
University of California Davis School of Medicine						
4610 X St	Sacramento	CA	95817	916-734-7131		167-2
TF: 800-282-3284						
University of California Hastings College of the Law						
200 McAllister St	San Francisco	CA	94102	415-565-4600	581-8946*	167-1
**Fax:* Admissions ■ *Web:* www.uchastings.edu						
University of California Health System						
1111 Franklin St	Oakland	CA	94607	510-987-9200	987-0894*	353
**Fax:* Hum Res ■ *Web:* www.universityofcalifornia.edu						
University of California Irvine						
Library PO Box 19557	Irvine	CA	92623	949-824-6836		434-6
TF: 800-843-2763 ■ *Web:* www.lib.uci.edu						
University of California Irvine College of Health Sciences						
1001 Health Science Rd	Irvine	CA	92697	949-824-9267	824-2118	166
Web: www.cohs.uci.edu						
University of California Irvine School of Medicine						
1001 Health Sciences Rd 252 Irvine Hall	Irvine	CA	92697	949-824-6119		167-2
Web: www.som.uci.edu						
University of California Los Angeles						
Library System						
11334 Charles E Young Research Library	Los Angeles	CA	90095	310-825-4732		434-6
Web: www.library.ucla.edu						
University of California Press						
2120 Berkeley Way	Berkeley	CA	94704	800-343-4499	643-7127*	637-4
**Fax Area Code:* 510 ■ *TF:* 800-343-4499 ■ *Web:* www.ucpress.edu						
University of California Riverside						
Tom s Rivera Library						
900 University Ave	Riverside	CA	92521	951-827-3220	827-3281	434-6
Web: libraries.universityofcalifornia.edu						
University of California Riverside Botanic Gardens						
900 University Ave	Riverside	CA	92521	951-784-6962	784-6962	97
Web: gardens.ucr.edu						
University of California San Diego (UCSD)						
Biomedical Library 9500 Gilman Dr	La Jolla	CA	92093	858-534-3253	534-6609	434-1
Web: www.libraries.ucsd.edu						
Libraries 9500 Gilman Dr Ste 0175-G	La Jolla	CA	92093	858-534-3336		434-6
Web: libraries.ucsd.edu						
University of California San Diego Medical Ctr Blood & Marrow Transplantation Program						
3855 Health Sciences Dr	La Jolla	CA	92037	858-657-7000		769
Web: www.cancer.ucsd.edu						

Name / Address	City	State	ZIP	Phone	Fax	Class
University of California San Diego Medical Ctr Library						
200 W Arbor Dr	San Diego	CA	92103	619-543-6222		434-1
Web: health.ucsd.edu						
University of California San Diego School of Medicine						
9500 Gilman Dr MC 0602	La Jolla	CA	92093	858-534-0830	534-6573	167-2
Web: som.ucsd.edu						
University of California San Francisco						
Kalmanovitz Library						
530 Parnassus Ave	San Francisco	CA	94143	415-476-8293	476-4653	434-6
Web: www.library.ucsf.edu						
Library & Center for Knowledge Management						
530 Parnassus Ave	San Francisco	CA	94143	415-476-8293	476-4653	434-1
Web: www.library.ucsf.edu						
University of California Santa Cruz						
McHenry Library 1156 High St	Santa Cruz	CA	95064	831-459-2076	459-8206	434-6
Web: www.library.ucsc.edu						
University of California System						
1111 Franklin St 12th Fl	Oakland	CA	94607	510-987-9074	987-9086	786
TF: 800-888-8267 ■ *Web:* www.ucop.edu						
University of Central Arkansas						
201 Donaghey Ave	Conway	AR	72035	501-450-5000	450-5228*	166
**Fax:* Admissions ■ *TF Admissions:* 800-407-4747 ■ *Web:* www.uca.edu						
University of Central Florida						
4000 Central Florida Blvd PO Box 160000	Orlando	FL	32816	407-823-2000	823-5625*	166
**Fax:* Admissions ■ *TF:* 800-272-7252 ■ *Web:* www.ucf.edu						
University of Central Oklahoma						
100 N University Dr	Edmond	OK	73034	405-974-2000		166
Web: www.uco.edu						
University of Charleston						
2300 MacCorkle Ave SE	Charleston	WV	25304	304-357-4800	357-4715*	166
**Fax:* Admissions ■ *TF Admissions:* 800-995-4682 ■ *Web:* www.ucwv.edu						
University of Chicago						
5801 S Ellis Ave	Chicago	IL	60637	773-702-1234	702-4199*	166
**Fax:* Admissions ■ *Web:* www.uchicago.edu						
University of Chicago Botanic Garden						
5555 S Ellis Ave	Chicago	IL	60637	773-702-1700		97
Web: www.uchicago.edu						
University of Chicago Law School						
1111 E 60th St	Chicago	IL	60637	773-702-9494		167-1
Web: www.law.uchicago.edu						
University of Chicago Library						
1100 E 57th St	Chicago	IL	60637	773-702-8740	702-6623	434-6
TF: 800-621-6044 ■ *Web:* www.lib.uchicago.edu						
University of Chicago Medical Ctr						
5841 S Maryland Ave	Chicago	IL	60637	773-702-1000		374-3
TF: 888-824-0200 ■ *Web:* www.uchospitals.edu						
University of Chicago Press						
1427 E 60th St	Chicago	IL	60637	773-702-7700	702-9756	637-4
TF Sales: 800-621-2736 ■ *Web:* www.press.uchicago.edu						
University of Chicago Press Journals Div						
1427 E 60th St	Chicago	IL	60637	773-702-7700	753-0811	637-9
TF: 877-705-1070 ■ *Web:* www.press.uchicago.edu						
University of Chicago Pritzker School of Medicine						
924 E 57th St	Chicago	IL	60637	773-702-1939		167-2
University of Cincinnati						
51 Goodman Dr PO Box 670550	Cincinnati	OH	45267	513-558-4553	558-2910	434-1
Web: www.health.uc.edu						
University of Cincinnati						
9555 Plainfield Rd	Cincinnati	OH	45236	513-745-5600		162
Web: www.ucblueash.edu						
University of Cincinnati						
2600 Clifton Ave PO Box 210091	Cincinnati	OH	45221	513-556-1100	556-1105*	166
**Fax:* Admissions ■ *TF:* 866-397-3382 ■ *Web:* www.uc.edu						
University of Cincinnati Clermont College						
4200 Clermont College Dr	Batavia	OH	45103	513-732-5200	732-5303*	162
**Fax:* Admissions ■ *TF:* 866-446-2822 ■ *Web:* www.ucclermont.edu						
University of Cincinnati College of Law						
2540 Clifton Ave	Cincinnati	OH	45221	513-556-6805	556-2391	167-1
Web: www.law.uc.edu						
University of Cincinnati College of Medicine						
231 Albert Sabin Way Ste E-251						
PO Box 670552	Cincinnati	OH	45267	513-558-4898	558-1100	167-2
Web: www.med.uc.edu						
University of Cincinnati Langsam Library						
PO Box 210033	Cincinnati	OH	45221	513-556-1515	556-0325*	434-6
**Fax:* Admin ■ *TF:* 866-397-3382 ■ *Web:* www.libraries.uc.edu						
University of Colorado						
Boulder CB 552	Boulder	CO	80309	303-492-1411	492-7115*	166
**Fax:* Admissions ■ *Web:* www.colorado.edu						
Colorado Springs PO Box 7150	Colorado Springs	CO	80933	719-262-3000	262-3116*	166
**Fax:* Admissions ■ *TF:* 800-990-8227 ■ *Web:* www.uccs.edu						
University of Colorado at Colorado Springs						
Kraemer Family Library						
1420 Austin Bluffs Pkwy PO Box 7150	Colorado Springs	CO	80918	719-255-3295	528-5227	434-6
TF: 800-990-8227 ■ *Web:* www.uccs.edu/~library						
University of Colorado at Denver						
1250 14th St	Denver	CO	80217	303-556-2400	556-4838	166
Web: www.ucdenver.edu/pages/ucdwelcomepage.aspx						
University of Colorado Hospital						
12605 E 16th Ave	Aurora	CO	80045	720-848-0000		374-3
Web: www.uchealth.org/metrodenver/pages/default.aspx						
University of Colorado Museum of Natural History						
15th Broadway Henderson Bldg	Boulder	CO	80309	303-492-6892	492-4195	520
Web: cumuseum.colorado.edu						
University of Colorado School of Law						
2450 Kittredge Loop Rd	Boulder	CO	80309	303-492-8047	492-1757	167-1
Web: www.colorado.edu/law						
University of Colorado System						
1800 Grant St Ste 800	Denver	CO	80203	303-860-5600	860-5610	786
Web: www.cu.edu						
University of Connecticut						
2131 Hillside Rd Unit 3088	Storrs	CT	06269	860-486-2000	486-1476*	166
**Fax:* Admissions ■ *Web:* www.uconn.edu						
Avery Point 1084 Shennecossett Rd	Groton	CT	06340	860-405-9019		162
TF: 888-247-5556 ■ *Web:* www.averypoint.uconn.edu						
Babbidge Library						
369 Fairfield Rd Unit 2005	Storrs	CT	06269	860-486-2219	486-0584*	434-6
**Fax:* Admin ■ *TF:* 888-603-9635 ■ *Web:* www.lib.uconn.edu						

Name / Address	City	State	Zip	Phone	Fax	Class
Greater Hartford 85 Lawler Rd	West Hartford	CT	06117	860-570-9214		162
Web: www.hartford.uconn.edu						
Stamford 1 University Pl	Stamford	CT	06901	203-251-8400	251-8556	166
Web: www.stamford.uconn.edu						
Torrington 855 University Dr	Torrington	CT	06790	860-626-6800		162
Web: www.torrington.uconn.edu						
Waterbury 99 E Main St	Waterbury	CT	06702	203-236-9800	236-9805	162
Web: www.waterbury.uconn.edu						
University of Connecticut Health Ctr						
John Dempsey Hospital						
263 Farmington Ave	Farmington	CT	06030	860-679-2000	679-1255	374-3
TF: 800-535-6232 ■ Web: health.uconn.edu						
University of Connecticut School of Law						
45 Elizabeth St	Hartford	CT	06105	860-570-5100	570-5153*	167-1
*Fax: Admissions ■ Web: www.law.uconn.edu						
University of Dallas						
1845 E Northgate Dr	Irving	TX	75062	972-721-5266	721-5017*	166
*Fax: Admissions ■ TF Admissions: 800-628-6999 ■ Web: www.udallas.edu						
University of Dayton 300 College Pk	Dayton	OH	45469	937-229-4411	229-4729*	166
*Fax: Admissions ■ TF: 800-837-7433 ■ Web: www.udayton.edu						
University of Delaware						
Hullihen Hall Rm 209	Newark	DE	19716	302-831-2792	831-6905*	166
*Fax: Admissions ■ TF: 800-847-3333 ■ Web: www.udel.edu						
University of Delaware Botanic Garden						
University of Delaware	Newark	DE	19716	302-831-0153	831-0605	97
Web: www.ag.udel.edu/udbg						
University of Delaware Library						
181 S College Ave	Newark	DE	19717	302-831-2965	831-1046	434-6
Web: library.udel.edu						
University of Delaware Press						
181 S College Ave Rm 200-A	Newark	DE	19717	302-831-2792		637-4
Web: www2.lib.udel.edu/udpress						
University of Denver 2255 E Evans Ave	Denver	CO	80208	303-871-6000	871-6378	167-1
Web: www.law.du.edu						
University of Denver						
2199 S University Blvd	Denver	CO	80208	303-871-2036	871-3301	166
TF: 800-525-9495 ■ Web: www.du.edu						
University of Denver						
Colorado Womens College						
1901 E Asbury Ave Ste 390	Denver	CO	80208	303-871-6500	871-6897	166
Web: www.womenscollege.du.edu						
University of Denver Westminster Law Library						
2255 E Evans Ave	Denver	CO	80208	303-871-6190	871-6378	434-6
Web: www.law.du.edu/library						
University of Detroit Mercy						
4001 W McNichols Rd	Detroit	MI	48221	313-993-1000	993-3326*	166
*Fax: Admissions ■ TF Admissions: 800-635-5020 ■ Web: www.udmercy.edu						
University of Detroit Mercy						
Corktown Campus 4001 W McNichols Rd	Detroit	MI	48221	313-494-6611		166
Web: www.udmercy.edu						
University of Detroit Mercy School of Law						
651 E Jefferson Ave	Detroit	MI	48226	313-596-0264		167-1
Web: www.law.udmercy.edu						
University of Dubuque						
2000 University Ave	Dubuque	IA	52001	563-589-3000	589-3690*	166
*Fax: Admissions ■ TF: 800-722-5583 ■ Web: www.dbq.edu						
University of Dubuque Theological Seminary						
2000 University Ave	Dubuque	IA	52001	563-589-3122	589-3110	167-3
TF: 800-369-8387 ■ Web: udts.dbq.edu						
University of Evansville						
1800 Lincoln Ave	Evansville	IN	47722	812-488-2000	488-4076*	166
*Fax: Admissions ■ TF: 800-423-8633 ■ Web: www.evansville.edu						
University of Findlay 1000 N Main St	Findlay	OH	45840	419-422-8313	434-4822	166
TF: 800-472-9502 ■ Web: www.findlay.edu						
University of Florida						
219 Grinter Hall PO Box 115500	Gainesville	FL	32611	352-392-3261	392-2115*	166
*Fax: Admissions ■ TF: 866-876-4472 ■ Web: www.ufl.edu						
University of Florida Health Science Ctr Libraries						
1600 SW Archer Rd	Gainesville	FL	32610	352-273-8408	392-2565	434-1
Web: www.library.health.ufl.edu						
University of Florida Levin College of Law						
2500 SW Second Ave	Gainesville	FL	32611	352-273-0890	392-4087*	167-1
*Fax: Admissions ■ TF: 877-429-1297 ■ Web: www.law.ufl.edu						
University of Florida Libraries						
PO Box 117001	Gainesville	FL	32611	352-392-0342	392-7251	434-6
TF: 877-351-2377 ■ Web: www.uflib.ufl.edu						
University of Georgia Aquarium						
30 Ocean Science Cir	Savannah	GA	31411	912-598-2496	598-2302	40
Web: gacoast.uga.edu/uga-aquarium/visit-us						
University of Georgia Library						
320 S Jackson St	Athens	GA	30602	706-542-0621	542-4144*	434-6
*Fax: Admin ■ TF: 877-314-5560 ■ Web: www.libs.uga.edu						
University of Georgia School of Law						
225 Herty Dr	Athens	GA	30602	706-542-5191	542-5556	167-1
Web: www.law.uga.edu						
University of Great Falls						
1301 20th St S	Great Falls	MT	59405	800-856-9544	791-5209*	166
*Fax Area Code: 406 ■ *Fax: Admissions ■ TF Admissions: 800-856-9544 ■ Web: www.ugf.edu						
University of Guam						
Unibetsed?t GuahanUOG Stn	Mangialo	GU	96923	671-735-2910		166
Web: www.uog.edu						
University of Guelph 50 Stone Rd E	Guelph	ON	N1G2W1	519-824-4120	766-9481	785
TF: 877-674-1610 ■ Web: www.uoguelph.ca						
University of Hartford						
200 Bloomfield Ave	West Hartford	CT	06117	860-768-4296	768-4961	166
TF: 800-947-4303 ■ Web: www.hartford.edu						
University of Hawai?i Maui College						
310 W Kaahumanu Ave	Kahului	HI	96732	808-984-3267	242-9618*	162
*Fax: Admissions ■ TF: 800-479-6692 ■ Web: www.maui.hawaii.edu						
University of Hawaii						
Hilo 200 W Kawili St	Hilo	HI	96720	808-974-7414	933-0861*	166
*Fax: Admissions ■ TF Admissions: 800-897-4456 ■ Web: hilo.hawaii.edu						
Honolulu Community College						
874 Dillingham Blvd	Honolulu	HI	96817	808-845-9129	847-9829*	162
*Fax: Admissions ■ Web: www.honolulu.hawaii.edu						
Kapiolani Community College						
4303 Diamond Head Rd	Honolulu	HI	96816	808-734-9000	734-9896	162
Web: www.kcc.hawaii.edu						
Leeward Community College						
96-045 Ala Ike St	Pearl City	HI	96782	808-455-0011	454-8804*	162
*Fax: Admissions ■ Web: www.leeward.hawaii.edu						
Manoa 2600 Campus Rd Rm 001	Honolulu	HI	96822	808-956-8975	956-4148*	166
*Fax: Admissions ■ TF Admissions: 800-823-9771 ■ Web: www.manoa.hawaii.edu						
West Oahu 96-129 Ala Ike	Pearl City	HI	96782	808-454-4700	453-6075	166
TF: 866-299-8656 ■ Web: www.uhwo.hawaii.edu						
Windward Community College						
45-720 Keaahala Rd	Kaneohe	HI	96744	808-235-7400	247-5362*	162
*Fax: Admissions ■ Web: windward.hawaii.edu						
University of Hawaii at Hilo						
Edwin H. Mookini Library 200 W Kawili St	Hilo	HI	96720	808-974-7344	974-4106	434-6
Web: hilo.hawaii.edu						
University of Hawaii at Manoa						
Hamilton Library 2500 Campus Rd	Honolulu	HI	96822	808-956-6911	956-7109	434-6
Web: www.manoa.hawaii.edu						
John A Burns School of Medicine (JABSOM)						
651 Ilalo St Medical Education Bldg	Honolulu	HI	96813	808-692-1000	692-1251	167-2
Web: www.jabsom.hawaii.edu						
William S Richardson School of Law						
2515 Dole St	Honolulu	HI	96822	808-956-7966	956-6402*	167-1
*Fax: Admissions ■ Web: www.hawaii.edu						
University of Hawaii Federal Credit Union						
PO Box 22070	Honolulu	HI	96823	808-983-5500		219
TF: 800-927-3397 ■ Web: www.uhfcu.com						
University of Hawaii Foundation, The						
2444 Dole St Bachman Hall 105	Honolulu	HI	96822	808-956-8849		219
TF: 866-846-4262 ■ Web: www.uhfoundation.org						
University of Hawaii Press						
2840 Kolowalu St	Honolulu	HI	96822	808-956-8255	650-7811*	637-4
*Fax Area Code: 800 ■ TF: 888-847-7377 ■ Web: www.uhpress.hawaii.edu						
University of Hawaii System						
2500 Campus Rd	Honolulu	HI	96822	808-956-8111	956-3952	786
Web: www.hawaii.edu						
University of Houston 4800 Calhoun Rd	Houston	TX	77004	713-743-1000	743-9665	166
TF: 800-388-8075 ■ Web: www.uh.edu						
Clear Lake 2700 Bay Area Blvd	Houston	TX	77058	281-283-7600	283-2522*	166
*Fax: Admissions ■ Web: www.uhcl.edu						
Victoria 3007 N Ben Wilson St	Victoria	TX	77901	361-570-4848	570-4114*	166
*Fax: Admissions ■ TF: 877-970-4848 ■ Web: www.uhv.edu						
University of Houston Law Ctr						
100 Law Ctr	Houston	TX	77204	713-743-2100	743-2194*	167-1
*Fax: Admissions ■ TF: 800-252-9690 ■ Web: www.law.uh.edu						
University of Idaho 875 Perimeter Dr	Moscow	ID	83844	208-885-6111	885-9119	166
TF: 888-884-3246 ■ Web: www.uidaho.edu						
Boise 322 E Front St Ste 190	Boise	ID	83702	208-334-2999	364-4035	166
TF: 866-264-7384 ■ Web: www.uidaho.edu						
Library 875 Perimeter Dr MS 2350	Moscow	ID	83844	208-885-6534	885-6817	434-6
Web: www.lib.uidaho.edu						
University of Idaho Arboretum & Botanical Garden						
875 Perimeter Dr	Moscow	ID	83844	208-885-5978	885-5748	97
Web: www.uidaho.edu/arboretum						
University of Idaho College of Law						
711 S Rayburn St	Moscow	ID	83844	208-885-4977	885-5709	167-1
TF: 888-884-3246 ■ Web: www.uidaho.edu						
University of Illinois						
Chicago 601 S Morgan	Chicago	IL	60607	312-996-7000	413-7628	166
Web: www.uic.edu						
Springfield						
1 University Plaza MS UHB 1080	Springfield	IL	62703	217-206-4847	206-6620*	166
*Fax: Admissions ■ TF: 888-977-4847 ■ Web: www.uis.edu						
Urbana-Champaign 901 W Illinois St	Urbana	IL	61801	217-333-0302	244-4614	166
Web: illinois.edu						
University of Illinois Arboretum						
1800 S Lincoln Ave	Urbana	IL	61801	217-333-7579		85
Web: arboretum.illinois.edu						
University of Illinois Chicago						
Daley Library 801 S Morgan St Rm 1-280	Chicago	IL	60607	312-996-2716	413-0424	434-6
Web: www.uic.edu/depts/lib						
Library of the Health Sciences						
1750 W Polk St MC 763	Chicago	IL	60612	312-996-8974	996-1899	434-1
Web: www.uic.edu/depts/lib/lhsc						
University of Illinois College of Law						
504 E Pennsylvania Ave	Champaign	IL	61820	217-333-0930	244-1478	167-1
TF: 800-369-6151 ■ Web: www.law.illinois.edu						
University of Illinois College of Medicine						
808 S Wood St Rm 165	Chicago	IL	60612	312-996-5635	996-6693*	167-2
*Fax: Admissions ■ Web: www.uic.edu/depts/mcam						
University of Illinois Medical Ctr						
1740 W Taylor St	Chicago	IL	60612	312-996-3900		374-3
TF: 866-600-2273 ■ Web: hospital.uillinois.edu						
University of Illinois Press						
1325 S Oak St	Champaign	IL	61820	217-333-0950	244-8082	637-4
TF: 866-244-0626 ■ Web: www.press.uillinois.edu						
University of Illinois Springfield						
Brookens Library						
1 University Plaza	Springfield	IL	62703	217-206-6605		434-6
Web: library.uis.edu						
University of Illinois System						
506 S Wright St Ste 352	Urbana	IL	61801	217-333-1920		786
Web: www.uillinois.edu						
University of Illinois Urbana-Champaign						
Library						
1408 W Gregory Dr						
142 Undergraduate Library MC-522	Urbana	IL	61801	217-333-3085	265-0990	434-6
Web: www.library.illinois.edu						
University of Indianapolis						
1400 E Hanna Ave	Indianapolis	IN	46227	317-788-3368	788-3300*	166
*Fax: Admissions ■ TF: 800-232-8634 ■ Web: www.uindy.edu						
University of Iowa 107 Calvin Hall	Iowa City	IA	52242	319-335-3847	335-1535	166
TF: 800-553-4692 ■ Web: www.uiowa.edu						
University of Iowa Athletics Hall of Fame						
2425 Prairie Meadow Dr	Iowa City	IA	52242	319-384-1031		522
Web: hof.hawkeyesports.com						
University of Iowa College of Law						
130 Byington Rd	Iowa City	IA	52242	319-335-9034	335-9019	167-1
TF: 800-553-4692 ■ Web: www.law.uiowa.edu						

Phone | Fax | Class

University of Iowa Hospitals & Clinics
200 Hawkins Dr .... Iowa City IA 52242 | 319-356-1616 | | 374-3
Web: uihealthcare.org

University of Iowa Libraries
100 Main Library .... Iowa City IA 52242 | 319-335-5299 | 335-5900* | 434-6
**Fax:* Library ■ *Web:* www.lib.uiowa.edu

University of Iowa Museum of Art
150 N Riverside Dr 100 Old Museum of Art ...... Iowa City IA 52242 | 319-335-1727 | 335-3677 | 520
Web: uima.uiowa.edu

University of Iowa Press
119 W Pk Rd 100 Kuhl House .... Iowa City IA 52242 | 319-335-2000 | 335-2055 | 637-4
TF: 800-621-2736 ■ *Web:* www.uipress.uiowa.edu

University of Iowa Roy J & Lucille A Carver College of Medicine
200 CMAB .... Iowa City IA 52242 | 319-335-6707 | | 167-2
TF: 800-725-8460 ■ *Web:* www.medicine.uiowa.edu

University of Judaism
15600 Mulholland Dr .... Los Angeles CA 90077 | 310-476-9777 | 471-3657* | 166
**Fax:* Admissions ■ *TF:* 888-853-6763 ■ *Web:* www.aju.edu

University of Kansas 1502 Iowa St .... Lawrence KS 66045 | 785-864-2700 | 864-5017 | 166
Web: www.ku.edu

University of Kansas Hospital
3901 Rainbow Blvd .... Kansas City KS 66160 | 913-588-1227 | 588-5785 | 374-3
TF: 844-323-1227 ■ *Web:* www.kumed.com

University of Kansas Medical Ctr
Bone Marrow/Hematopoietic Stem Cell Transplant Pro
3901 Rainbow Blvd .... Kansas City KS 66160 | 913-588-5000 | | 769
Web: kumc.edu

University of Kansas School of Law
1535 W 15th St .... Lawrence KS 66045 | 785-864-4550 | 864-5054 | 167-1
TF: 866-220-3654 ■ *Web:* www.law.ku.edu

University of Kentucky 800 Rose St .... Lexington KY 40536 | 859-257-9000 | 257-3823 | 166
TF: 866-900-4685 ■ *Web:* www.uky.edu

University of Kentucky Art Museum
Rose St & Euclid Ave .... Lexington KY 40506 | 859-257-5716 | | 520
Web: www.uky.edu/artmuseum

University of Kentucky Chandler Medical Ctr
800 Rose St .... Lexington KY 40536 | 859-323-5000 | 323-2044 | 374-3
Web: www.mc.uky.edu

University of Kentucky College of Law
620 S Limestone St .... Lexington KY 40506 | 859-257-1678 | 323-1061 | 167-1
Web: www.law.uky.edu

University of Kentucky College of Medicine
800 Rose St Rm C101 .... Lexington KY 40536 | 859-257-1000 | 226-7037 | 167-2
TF: 800-273-8255 ■ *Web:* www.mc.uky.edu

University of Kentucky Lexington-Fayette Urban County Government Arboretum
500 Alumni Dr .... Lexington KY 40503 | 859-257-6955 | | 97
Web: www.ca.uky.edu/arboretum

University of Kentucky Young Library
500 S Limestone St .... Lexington KY 40506 | 859-257-0500 | 257-0505 | 434-6
Web: www.uky.edu

University of La Verne 1950 Third St .... La Verne CA 91750 | 909-593-3511 | | 166
TF Admissions: [illegible] ■ *Web:* laverne.edu

University of Lethbridge
4401 University Dr .... Lethbridge AB T1K3M4 | 403-329-2111 | 329-5159* | 785
**Fax:* Admissions ■ *TF:* 800-332-8383 ■ *Web:* www.uleth.ca

University of Library
302 Buchtel Common .... Akron OH 44325 | 330-972-5355 | 972-5106 | 434-6
TF: 800-425-7668 ■ *Web:* www.uakron.edu/libraries

University of Louisiana
Lafayette 611 McKinley St .... Lafayette LA 70504 | 337-482-1000 | 482-1317 | 166
TF: 800-752-6553 ■ *Web:* www.louisiana.edu
Monroe 700 University Ave .... Monroe LA 71209 | 318-342-5430 | | 166
TF Admissions: 800-372-5127 ■ *Web:* www.ulm.edu

University of Louisiana System
1201 N Third St Ste 7-300 .... Baton Rouge LA 70802 | 225-342-6950 | | 786
Web: ulsystem.edu

University of Louisville
2301 S Third St .... Louisville KY 40292 | 502-852-5555 | 852-6526 | 166
TF: 800-334-8635 ■ *Web:* louisville.edu

University of Louisville Ekstrom Library
2301 S Third St .... Louisville KY 40292 | 502-852-6747 | 852-7394 | 434-6
Web: www.louisville.edu

University of Louisville Hospital
530 S Jackson St .... Louisville KY 40202 | 502-562-3000 | | 374-3
TF: 800-891-0947 ■ *Web:* www.kentuckyonehealth.org

University of Louisville Lions Eye Bank
301 E Muhammad Ali Blvd .... Louisville KY 40202 | 502-852-5457 | | 269
Web: www.ulleb.org

University of Louisville School of Medicine
323 E Chestnut St .... Louisville KY 40292 | 502-852-5193 | 852-0302 | 167-2
TF: 800-334-8635 ■ *Web:* www.louisville.edu/medschool

University of Maine
5713 Chadbourne Hall .... Orono ME 04469 | 207-581-1110 | 581-1213* | 166
**Fax:* Admissions ■ *TF Admissions:* 877-486-2364 ■ *Web:* www.umaine.edu
Augusta 46 University Dr .... Augusta ME 04330 | 207-621-3000 | 621-3333* | 166
**Fax:* Admissions ■ *TF:* 877-862-1234 ■ *Web:* www.uma.edu
Farmington 111 S St .... Farmington ME 04938 | 207-778-7000 | 778-8182* | 166
**Fax:* Admissions ■ *TF:* 800-871-7741 ■ *Web:* www.umf.maine.edu
Fort Kent 23 University Dr .... Fort Kent ME 04743 | 207-834-7500 | 834-7609* | 166
**Fax:* Admissions ■ *TF Admissions:* 888-879-8635 ■ *Web:* www.umfk.edu
Machias 116 O'Brien Ave .... Machias ME 04654 | 207-255-1200 | | 166
TF Admissions: 888-468-6866 ■ *Web:* machias.edu
Presque Isle 181 Main St .... Presque Isle ME 04769 | 207-768-9400 | | 166
Web: www.umpi.maine.edu
Raymond H.Fogler Library
5729 Fogler Library .... Orono ME 04469 | 207-581-1666 | 581-1653* | 434-6
**Fax:* Admin ■ *Web:* www.library.umaine.edu

University of Maine Museum of Art
40 Harlow St .... Bangor ME 04401 | 207-561-3350 | 561-3351 | 520
Web: www.umma.umaine.edu

University of Maine School of Law
246 Deering Ave .... Portland ME 04102 | 207-780-4355 | 780-4239 | 167-1
Web: www.mainelaw.maine.edu

University of Maine System
16 Central St .... Bangor ME 04401 | 207-973-3200 | 973-3296 | 786
Web: www.maine.edu

University of Manitoba
65 Chancellors Cir 424 University Ctr .... Winnipeg MB R3T2N2 | 204-474-8880 | 474-7554 | 785
TF Admissions: 800-224-7713 ■ *Web:* www.umanitoba.ca

University of Manitoba Faculty of Medicine
727 McDermot Ave Rm 260 .... Winnipeg MB R3E3P5 | 204-789-3557 | 789-3928 | 167-2
Web: www.umanitoba.ca

University of Mary
7500 University Dr .... Bismarck ND 58504 | 701-255-7500 | 255-7687* | 166
**Fax:* Admissions ■ *TF Admissions:* 800-288-6279 ■ *Web:* www.umary.edu

University of Mary Hardin-Baylor
900 College St PO Box 8004 .... Belton TX 76513 | 254-295-8642 | 295-5049* | 166
**Fax:* Admissions ■ *TF:* 800-727-8642 ■ *Web:* www.umhb.edu

University of Mary Washington
1301 College Ave .... Fredericksburg VA 22401 | 540-654-2000 | 654-1857* | 166
**Fax:* Admissions ■ *TF Admissions:* 800-468-5614 ■ *Web:* www.umw.edu

University of Maryland
7569 Baltimore Ave .... College Park MD 20742 | 301-405-1000 | 314-9693* | 166
**Fax:* Admissions ■ *TF Admissions:* 800-422-5867 ■ *Web:* www.umd.edu
Baltimore County 1000 Hilltop Cir .... Baltimore MD 21250 | 410-455-1000 | 455-1094 | 166
TF: 800-810-0271 ■ *Web:* www.umbc.edu
Eastern Shore
30665 Student Services Ctr Ln .... Princess Anne MD 21853 | 410-651-2200 | 651-7922 | 166
Web: www.umes.edu
McKeldin Library
McKeldin Library .... College Park MD 20742 | 301-405-9075 | | 434-6
Web: www.lib.umd.edu

University of Maryland Baltimore
Health Sciences & Human Services Library (HSHSL)
601 W Lombard St .... Baltimore MD 21201 | 410-706-7995 | 706-8403 | 434-1
Web: www.hshsl.umaryland.edu

University of Maryland Baltimore county
Kuhn Library 1000 Hilltop Cir .... Baltimore MD 21250 | 410-455-2353 | | 434-6
Web: www.umbc.edu/aok

University of Maryland Ctr for Environmental Science (UMCES)
2020 Horn Pt Rd .... Cambridge MD 21613 | 410-228-9250 | 228-3843 | 668
TF: 866-842-2520 ■ *Web:* www.umces.edu

University of Maryland Greenebaum Cancer Ctr
22 S Greene St .... Baltimore MD 21201 | 410-328-7904 | | 769
TF: 800-888-8823 ■ *Web:* www.umm.edu/cancer/canc_stem.html

University of Maryland Medical System
22 S Greene St .... Baltimore MD 21201 | 410-328-8667 | | 353
TF: 800-492-5538 ■ *Web:* www.umm.edu

University of Maryland School of Medicine
685 W Baltimore St Ste 190 .... Baltimore MD 21201 | 410-706-7478 | 706-0467* | 167-2
**Fax:* Admissions ■ *Web:* www.medschool.umaryland.edu

University of Maryland Shore Medical Ctr (MHE)
219 S Washington St .... Easton MD 21601 | 410-822-1000 | 763-7051 | 374-3
Web: www.umshoreregional.org

University of Maryland Shore Regional Health
501 S Union Ave .... Havre de Grace MD 21078 | 443-843-5000 | | 374-3
Web: umuch.org

University of Maryland University College Marriott Conference Ctr Hotel
3501 University Blvd E .... Adelphi MD 20783 | 301-985-7300 | 985-7517 | 377
TF: 800-721-7033 ■ *Web:* www.marriott.com

University of Massachusetts
Amherst 181 Presidents Dr .... Amherst MA 01003 | 413-545-0111 | 545-4312* | 166
**Fax:* Admissions ■ *Web:* www.umass.edu
Boston 100 Morrissey Blvd Campus Ctr .... Boston MA 02125 | 617-287-6100 | 287-5999* | 166
**Fax:* Admitting ■ *TF:* 800-767-1833 ■ *Web:* www.umb.edu
Dartmouth 285 Old Westport Rd .... North Dartmouth MA 02747 | 508-999-8000 | 999-8755* | 166
**Fax:* Admissions ■ *Web:* www.umassd.edu
Lowell 1 University Ave .... Lowell MA 01854 | 978-934-4000 | 934-3086* | 166
**Fax:* Admissions ■ *TF:* 800-480-3190 ■ *Web:* www.uml.edu

University of Massachusetts Amherst
Du Bois Library 154 Hicks Way .... Amherst MA 01003 | 413-545-0284 | | 434-6
Web: www.library.umass.edu

University of Massachusetts Boston
Healey Library 100 Morrissey Blvd .... Boston MA 02125 | 617-287-5900 | 287-5955 | 434-6
Web: www.umb.edu

University of Massachusetts Dartmouth
Library 285 Old Westport Rd .... North Dartmouth MA 02747 | 508-999-8000 | 999-9142 | 434-6
Web: www.lib.umassd.edu

University of Massachusetts Lowell
Lydon Library 84 University Ave .... Lowell MA 01854 | 978-934-3205 | | 434-6
Web: www.library.uml.edu

University of Massachusetts Press
PO Box 429 .... Amherst MA 01004 | 413-545-2217 | 545-1226 | 637-4
TF: 800-562-0112 ■ *Web:* www.umass.edu/umpress

University of Massachusetts System
225 Franklin St 33rd Fl .... Boston MA 02110 | 617-287-7050 | | 786
Web: www.massachusetts.edu
University Hospital, The
150 Bergen St C- 431 .... Newark NJ 07103 | 973-972-4300 | | 374-3
TF: 800-395-5665 ■ *Web:* www.uhnj.org

University of Memphis Cecil C Humphreys School of Law
3715 Central Ave .... Memphis TN 38152 | 901-678-2421 | 678-5210 | 167-1
TF: 800-872-3728 ■ *Web:* www.memphis.edu

University of Memphis McWherter Library
126 Ned R McWherter Library .... Memphis TN 38152 | 901-678-2201 | 678-8218 | 434-6
TF: 866-670-6147 ■ *Web:* www.memphis.edu

University of Miami
1252 Memorial Dr .... Coral Gables FL 33146 | 305-284-2211 | | 166
Web: www.miami.edu

University of Miami Hospital & Clinics (UMHC)
Sylvester Comprehensive Cancer Ctr
1475 NW 12th Ave .... Miami FL 33136 | 305-243-1000 | | 769
TF: 800-545-2292 ■ *Web:* www.sylvester.org

University of Miami Richter Library
1300 Memorial Dr .... Coral Gables FL 33124 | 305-284-3233 | 284-4027* | 434-6
**Fax:* Admin ■ *TF:* 800-708-6754 ■ *Web:* www.library.miami.edu

University of Miami School of Law
1311 Miller Dr .... Coral Gables FL 33146 | 305-284-2339 | 284-3084* | 167-1
**Fax:* Admissions ■ *Web:* www.law.miami.edu

University of Michigan
515 E Jefferson St .... Ann Arbor MI 48109 | 734-764-1817 | | 166
Web: www.umich.edu
Dearborn 4901 Evergreen Rd .... Dearborn MI 48128 | 313-593-5100 | 436-9167* | 166
**Fax:* Admissions ■ *Web:* umdearborn.edu
Flint 303 E Kearsley St .... Flint MI 48502 | 810-762-3000 | 762-3272 | 166
TF: 800-942-5636 ■ *Web:* www.flint.umich.edu
Libraries 920 S University Ave .... Ann Arbor MI 48109 | 734-764-0400 | | 434-6
Web: www.lib.umich.edu

Phone | Fax | Class

University of Michigan - Flint Theater
303 E Kearsley St .... Flint MI 48502 810-762-3300 572
Web: www.umflint.edu/theatredance
University of Michigan Dearborn
Mardigian Library 4901 Evergreen Rd .... Dearborn MI 48128 313-593-5445 434-6
TF: 877-619-6650 ■ *Web:* umdearborn.edu
University of Michigan Law School
625 S State St .... Ann Arbor MI 48109 734-764-1358 647-3218* 167-1
**Fax:* Admissions ■ *Web:* www.law.umich.edu
University of Michigan Museum of Art
525 S State St .... Ann Arbor MI 48109 734-764-0395 764-3731 520
Web: www.umma.umich.edu
University of Michigan Press
839 Greene St .... Ann Arbor MI 48104 734-764-4388 615-1540 637-4
TF: 866-804-0002 ■ *Web:* www.press.umich.edu
University of Michigan Transportation Research Institute (UMTRI)
2901 Baxter Rd .... Ann Arbor MI 48109 734-764-6504 936-1081 668
Web: www.umtri.umich.edu
University of Michigan Trauma Burn Ctr
1500 E Medical Ctr Dr .... Ann Arbor MI 48109 734-936-9666 936-9657 374-7
Web: www.traumaburn.org
University of Minnesota
200 SE Oak St Ste 300 .... Minneapolis MN 55455 612-625-1440 48-11
TF: 800-922-1663 ■ *Web:* give.umn.edu
Crookston
2900 University Ave 170 Owen Hall .... Crookston MN 56716 218-281-8569 281-8575* 166
**Fax:* Admissions ■ *TF:* 800-862-6466 ■ *Web:* www.crk.umn.edu
Duluth 1049 University Dr .... Duluth MN 55812 218-726-8000 726-6394* 166
**Fax:* Admissions ■ *TF:* 800-232-1339 ■ *Web:* www.d.umn.edu
Morris 600 E Fourth St .... Morris MN 56267 320-589-6035 589-1673* 166
**Fax:* Admissions ■ *TF:* 800-992-8863 ■ *Web:* www.morris.umn.edu
Twin Cities
3 Morrill Hall 100 Church St SE .... Minneapolis MN 55455 612-625-2008 626-1693 166
TF: 800-752-1000 ■ *Web:* www.umn.edu
University of Minnesota Crookston
UMC Library 2900 University Ave .... Crookston MN 56716 218-281-8399 281-8080 434-6
TF: 800-862-6466 ■ *Web:* www.crk.umn.edu
University of Minnesota Duluth
Kathryn A. Martin Library
416 Library Dr .... Duluth MN 55812 218-726-8102 726-8019 434-6
TF: 866-999-6995 ■ *Web:* www.d.umn.edu/lib
University of Minnesota Law School
229 19th Ave S Walter F Mondale Hall .... Minneapolis MN 55455 612-625-1000 626-1874* 167-1
**Fax:* Admissions ■ *Web:* www.law.umn.edu
University of Minnesota Medical Ctr Fairview - University Campus
500 Harvard St .... Minneapolis MN 55455 612-273-3000 374-3
TF: 800-688-5252 ■ *Web:* www.mhealth.org
University of Minnesota Morris
Briggs Library 600 E Fourth St .... Morris MN 56267 320-589-6176 589-6168 434-6
Web: www.morris.umn.edu
University of Minnesota Press
111 Third Ave S Ste 290 .... Minneapolis MN 55401 612-627-1970 627-1980 637-4
TF: 800-621-2736 ■ *Web:* www.upress.umn.edu
University of Minnesota Twin Cities
Bio-Medical Library
505 Essex St SE .... Minneapolis MN 55455 612-626-4045 434-1
Web: twin-cities.umn.edu
Wilson Library 309 19th Ave S .... Minneapolis MN 55455 612-624-3321 626-9353 434-6
Web: www.lib.umn.edu/wilson
University of Mississippi
PO Box 1848 .... University MS 38677 662-915-7211 915-5869* 166
**Fax:* Admissions ■ *TF:* 800-891-4596 ■ *Web:* www.olemiss.edu
Tupelo 1918 Briar Ridge Rd .... Tupelo MS 38804 662-844-5622 844-5625* 166
**Fax:* Admissions ■ *TF:* 888-846-5622 ■ *Web:* www.outreach.olemiss.edu
Williams Library 1 Library Loop .... University MS 38677 662-915-7091 915-5734 434-6
TF: 800-891-4596 ■ *Web:* www.olemiss.edu
University of Mississippi Medical Ctr
2500 N State St .... Jackson MS 39216 601-984-1000 984-4125 374-3
Web: www.umc.edu
University of Mississippi Medical Ctr Bone Marrow Transplant Program (UMMC)
2500 N State St .... Jackson MS 39216 601-354-6655 984-6289 769
Web: www.umc.edu
University of Mississippi School of Law
481 Chucky Mullins Dr .... University MS 38677 662-915-7361 167-1
Web: www.olemiss.edu
University of Mississippi School of Medicine
2500 N State St .... Jackson MS 39216 601-984-1080 984-1079 167-2
TF: 888-815-2005 ■ *Web:* www.umc.edu
University of Missouri
129 Fine Arts Bldg .... Columbia MO 65211 573-882-2021 572
Web: theatre.missouri.edu
Columbia 104 Jesse Hall .... Columbia MO 65211 573-882-6333 882-7887* 166
**Fax:* Admissions ■ *TF:* 800-856-2181 ■ *Web:* www.missouri.edu
Kansas City 5100 Rockhill Rd .... Kansas City MO 64110 816-235-1000 235-5544 166
TF: 800-775-8652 ■ *Web:* www.umkc.edu
Saint Louis 1 University Blvd .... Saint Louis MO 63121 314-516-5000 516-5310* 166
**Fax:* Admissions ■ *TF Admissions:* 888-462-8675 ■ *Web:* www.umsl.edu
University of Missouri Columbia School of Law
203 Hulston Hall .... Columbia MO 65211 573-882-6487 882-4984 167-1
Web: www.law.missouri.edu
University of Missouri Kansas City
Nichols Library 800 E 51st St .... Kansas City MO 64110 816-235-1534 333-5584 434-6
TF: 800-775-8652 ■ *Web:* www.umkc.edu
University of Missouri Kansas City School of Law
500 E 52nd St .... Kansas City MO 64110 816-235-1644 235-5276* 167-1
**Fax:* Admissions ■ *Web:* www.law.umkc.edu
University of Missouri Press
2910 LeMone Blvd .... Columbia MO 65201 573-882-7641 884-4498 637-4
TF: 800-621-2736 ■ *Web:* press.umsystem.edu
University of Missouri System
321 University Hall .... Columbia MO 65211 573-882-2011 882-2721 786
TF: 800-225-6075 ■ *Web:* www.umsystem.edu
University of Missouri-Kansas City School of Medicine
2411 Holmes St .... Kansas City MO 64108 816-235-1111 235-5277 167-2
TF: 800-735-2466 ■ *Web:* med.umkc.edu
University of Mobile 5735 College Pkwy .... Mobile AL 36613 251-675-5990 442-2498* 166
**Fax:* Admissions ■ *TF:* 800-946-7267 ■ *Web:* www.umobile.edu

Phone | Fax | Class

University of Moncton
18 Ave Antonine-Maillet .... Moncton NB E1A3E9 506-858-4088 858-4043 520
TF: 800-331-9283 ■ *Web:* www.umoncton.ca
University of Montana 32 Campus Dr .... Missoula MT 59812 406-243-6266 243-5711* 166
**Fax:* Admissions ■ *TF Admissions:* 800-462-8636 ■ *Web:* www.umt.edu
Helena College of Technology
1115 N Roberts St .... Helena MT 59601 406-447-6900 447-6397 800
TF: 800-827-1000 ■ *Web:* www.umhelena.edu
Western 710 S Atlantic St .... Dillon MT 59725 406-683-7011 683-7493* 166
**Fax:* Admissions ■ *TF Admissions:* 877-683-7331 ■ *Web:* www.umwestern.edu
University of Montana Missoula
Mansfield Library 32 Campus Dr .... Missoula MT 59812 406-243-2053 243-4067 434-6
TF: 800-240-4939 ■ *Web:* www.lib.umt.edu
University of Montana School of Law
32 Campus Dr .... Missoula MT 59812 406-243-4311 243-2576* 167-1
**Fax:* Admissions ■ *Web:* www.umt.edu/law
University of Nebraska
Kearney 905 W 25th St .... Kearney NE 68849 308-865-8441 865-8987* 166
**Fax:* Admissions ■ *TF:* 800-532-7639 ■ *Web:* www.unk.edu
Lincoln 1410 Q St .... Lincoln NE 68588 402-472-2023 472-0670* 166
**Fax:* Admissions ■ *TF:* 800-742-8800 ■ *Web:* www.unl.edu
Omaha 6001 Dodge St .... Omaha NE 68182 402-554-2800 554-3472* 166
**Fax:* Admissions ■ *TF:* 800-858-8648 ■ *Web:* www.unomaha.edu
University of Nebraska College of Law
1875 N 42nd St .... Lincoln NE 68583 402-472-2161 472-5185 167-1
Web: www.unl.edu
University of Nebraska Lincoln
Love Memorial Library
318 Love Library P.O. Box 884100 .... Lincoln NE 68588 402-472-9568 434-6
Web: www.libraries.unl.edu
University of Nebraska Medical Ctr
42nd and Emile .... Omaha NE 68198 402-559-4000 374-3
TF: 877-726-4727 ■ *Web:* www.unmc.edu
University of Nebraska Medical Ctr Bone Marrow & Stem Cell Transplantation Program (Adults)
987400 Nebraska Medical Ctr .... Omaha NE 68198 402-559-2000 769
TF: 800-922-0000 ■ *Web:* www.nebraskamed.com
University of Nebraska Medical Ctr McGoogan Library of Medicine
986705 Nebraska Medical Ctr .... Omaha NE 68198 402-559-4006 434-1
TF: 866-800-5209 ■ *Web:* www.unmc.edu/library
University of Nebraska Press
1111 Lincoln Mall .... Lincoln NE 68508 402-472-3581 637-4
TF Orders: 800-755-1105 ■ *Web:* www.nebraskapress.unl.edu
University of Nebraska School of Medicine
985527 Nebraska Medical Ctr .... Omaha NE 68198 402-559-2259 559-6840 167-2
TF: 800-626-8431 ■ *Web:* www.unmc.edu
University of Nebraska State Museum
14Th & U .... Lincoln NE 68588 402-472-2642 472-8899 520
TF: 800-432-3231 ■ *Web:* museum.unl.edu
University of Nebraska System
3835 Holdrege St Varner Hall .... Lincoln NE 68583 402-472-2111 472-1237 786
TF: 800-542-1602 ■ *Web:* www.nebraska.edu
University of Nebraska-Lincoln
1155 Q St Hewit Pl .... Lincoln NE 68588 402-472-5841 472-0463 520
TF: 800-242-3766 ■ *Web:* www.unl.edu
University of Nevada
Las Vegas 4505 S Maryland Pkwy .... Las Vegas NV 89154 702-895-3011 895-1118* 166
**Fax:* Admissions ■ *TF:* 800-331-3103 ■ *Web:* www.unlv.edu
Reno 1664 N Virginia St .... Reno NV 89557 775-784-1110 784-4283* 166
**Fax:* Admissions ■ *TF:* 866-263-8232 ■ *Web:* www.unr.edu
University of Nevada Las Vegas
Lied Library 4505 S Maryland Pkwy .... Las Vegas NV 89154 702-895-3011 434-6
TF: 800-331-3103 ■ *Web:* www.unlv.edu
University of Nevada Las Vegas William S Boyd School of Law
4505 Maryland Pkwy .... Las Vegas NV 89154 702-895-3671 167-1
Web: www.law.unlv.edu
University of Nevada Press
Morrill Hall MS 0166 .... Reno NV 89557 775-784-6573 784-6200 637-4
Web: www.unevadapress.com
University of Nevada School of Medicine
1664 N Virginia St
Pennington Medical Education Bldg 357 .... Reno NV 89557 775-784-6063 167-2
Web: www.unr.edu
University of New Brunswick
100 Tucker Pk Rd PO Box 4400 .... Fredericton NB E2L4L5 506-453-4666 453-5016 785
TF: 888-895-3344 ■ *Web:* www.unb.ca
Saint John
100 Tucker Pk Rd PO Box 5050 .... Saint John NB E2L4L5 506-648-5500 648-5528 785
Web: www.unb.ca
University of New England
11 Hills Beach Rd .... Biddeford ME 04005 207-283-0171 166
TF Admissions: 800-477-4863 ■ *Web:* www.une.edu
Westbrook College 716 Stevens Ave .... Portland ME 04103 207-797-7261 166
TF Admissions: 800-477-4863 ■ *Web:* www.une.edu
University of New Hampshire
3 Garrison Ave Grant House .... Durham NH 03824 603-862-1234 862-0077* 166
**Fax:* Admissions ■ *TF:* 800-313-5327 ■ *Web:* www.unh.edu
Dimond Library 18 Library Way .... Durham NH 03824 603-862-1540 862-0247* 434-6
**Fax:* Admin ■ *Web:* www.library.unh.edu
Manchester 88 Commercial St .... Manchester NH 03101 603-641-4101 641-4305 166
Web: manchester.unh.edu
University of New Haven
300 Boston Post Rd .... West Haven CT 06516 203-932-7319 931-6093* 166
**Fax:* Admissions ■ *TF:* 800-342-5864 ■ *Web:* www.newhaven.edu
University of New Mexico (UNM)
1 University of New Mexico .... Albuquerque NM 87131 505-277-0111 277-6686 166
TF: 800-225-5866 ■ *Web:* www.unm.edu
Gallup 200 College Rd .... Gallup NM 87301 505-863-7500 863-7610 166
TF: 800-225-5866 ■ *Web:* www.gallup.unm.edu
Los Alamos 4000 University Dr .... Los Alamos NM 87544 505-662-5919 661-4698* 162
**Fax:* Admissions ■ *Web:* losalamos.unm.edu
Valencia 280 La Entrada .... Los Lunas NM 87031 505-925-8580 925-8563* 162
**Fax:* Admissions ■ *TF:* 800-225-5866 ■ *Web:* www.unm.edu
University of New Mexico Art Museum
1 University of New Mexico .... Albuquerque NM 87131 505-277-4001 277-7315 520
Web: unmartmuseum.org
University of New Mexico School of Law
1117 Stanford Dr NE
MSC11 6070 1 University of New Mexico .... Albuquerque NM 87131 505-277-2146 277-9958 167-1
Web: www.lawschool.unm.edu

				Phone	Fax	Class
University of New Mexico School of Medicine						
1 University of New Mexico	Albuquerque	NM	87131	505-277-0111	925-6031	167-2
Web: hsc.unm.edu/som						
University of New Orleans						
2000 Lakeshore Dr	New Orleans	LA	70148	504-280-6000	280-5522	166
TF Admissions: 800-256-5866 ■ *Web:* www.uno.edu						
University of New Orleans Long Library						
2000 Lakeshore Dr	New Orleans	LA	70148	504-280-6556	280-7277	434-6
Web: www.library.uno.edu						
University of North Alabama						
1 Harrison Plaza	Florence	AL	35632	256-765-4608		166
TF: 800-825-5862 ■ *Web:* www.una.edu						
University of North Carolina						
910 Raleigh Rd PO Box 2688	Chapel Hill	NC	27515	919-962-1000		786
Web: www.northcarolina.edu						
Asheville						
1 University Heights CPO 1320	Asheville	NC	28804	828-251-6481	251-6482*	166
**Fax:* Admissions ■ *TF:* 800-531-9842 ■ *Web:* www.unca.edu						
Chapel Hill Jackson Hall CB 2200	Chapel Hill	NC	27599	919-966-3621	962-3045*	166
**Fax:* Admissions ■ *TF:* 800-962-8519 ■ *Web:* www.unc.edu						
Charlotte 9201 University City Blvd	Charlotte	NC	28223	704-687-2000	687-6483	166
TF: 800-228-2922 ■ *Web:* www.uncc.edu						
Greensboro 1400 Spring Garden St	Greensboro	NC	27412	336-334-5000	334-4180	166
Web: www.uncg.edu						
Pembroke PO Box 1510	Pembroke	NC	28372	910-521-6000	521-6497*	166
**Fax:* Admissions ■ *TF:* 800-949-8627 ■ *Web:* www.uncp.edu						
Wilmington 601 S College Rd	Wilmington	NC	28403	910-962-3000	962-3038*	166
**Fax:* Admissions ■ *TF:* 800-596-2880 ■ *Web:* uncw.edu						
University of North Carolina Chapel Hill						
Davis Library CB 3900 PO Box 8890	Chapel Hill	NC	27515	919-843-5660		434-6
Web: library.unc.edu						
Health Sciences Library						
335 S Columbia St CB 7585	Chapel Hill	NC	27599	919-962-0800	966-5592	434-1
Web: www.hsl.unc.edu						
University of North Carolina Ctr for Public Television (UNC-TV)						
10 TW Alexander Dr						
PO Box 14900	Research Triangle Park	NC	27709	919-549-7000	549-7201	632
TF: 800-906-5050 ■ *Web:* www.unctv.org						
University of North Carolina Press						
116 S Boundary St	Chapel Hill	NC	27514	919-966-3561	966-3829	637-4
TF: 800-848-6224 ■ *Web:* www.uncpress.org						
University of North Carolina School of Law						
160 Ridge Rd	Chapel Hill	NC	27599	919-962-5106	843-7939	167-1
Web: www.law.unc.edu						
University of North Dakota						
PO Box 8357	Grand Forks	ND	58202	701-777-3000		166
TF: 800-225-5863 ■ *Web:* und.edu						
University of North Dakota Chester Fritz Library						
3051 University Ave Stop 9000	Grand Forks	ND	58202	701-777-2189	777-3319	434-6
Web: www.library.und.edu						
University of North Dakota School of Law						
215 Centennial Dr Stop 9003	Grand Forks	ND	58202	701-777-2104		167-1
Web: law.und.edu						
University of North Dakota School of Medicine & Health Sciences						
1301 N Columbia Rd Stop 9037	Grand Forks	ND	58202	701-777-5046	777-4942*	167-2
**Fax:* Admissions ■ *TF:* 800-225-5863 ■ *Web:* www.med.und.edu						
University of North Florida (UNF)						
1UNF Dr	Jacksonville	FL	32224	904-620-1000	620-2719	434-6
Web: www.unf.edu/library						
University of North Florida						
4567 St Johns Bluff Rd S	Jacksonville	FL	32224	904-620-1000	620-2414	166
TF: 866-697-7150 ■ *Web:* www.unf.edu						
University of North Texas						
PO Box 311277	Denton	TX	76203	940-565-2681	565-2408*	166
**Fax:* Admissions ■ *TF:* 800-868-8211 ■ *Web:* www.unt.edu						
University of North Texas Health Science Ctr						
3500 Camp Bowie Blvd	Fort Worth	TX	76107	817-735-2000	735-5016	417
TF: 800-687-7580 ■ *Web:* www.unthsc.edu						
University of North Texas Press						
1155 Union Cir Ste 311336	Denton	TX	76203	940-565-2142	565-4590	637-4
TF: 800-826-8911 ■ *Web:* untpress.unt.edu						
University of Northern British Columbia						
3333 University Way	Prince George	BC	V2N4Z9	250-960-5555	960-6330	785
TF: 800-627-9931 ■ *Web:* www.unbc.ca						
University of Northern Colorado						
501 20th St CB 92	Greeley	CO	80639	970-351-2881	351-2984*	166
**Fax:* Admissions ■ *TF Admissions:* 888-700-4862 ■ *Web:* www.unco.edu						
University of Northern Colorado Michener Library						
501 20th St	Greeley	CO	80639	970-351-2601	351-2963	434-6
Web: www.unco.edu						
University of Northern Iowa						
1222 W 27th St	Cedar Falls	IA	50614	319-273-2281	273-2885*	166
**Fax:* Admissions ■ *TF Admissions:* 800-772-2037 ■ *Web:* www.uni.edu						
University of Northwestern Ohio						
1441 N Cable Rd	Lima	OH	45805	419-998-3120	998-3139	800
Web: www.unoh.edu						
University of Notre Dame						
220 Main Bldg	Notre Dame	IN	46556	574-631-7505		166
Web: www.nd.edu						
University of Notre Dame Hesburgh Library						
221 Hesburgh Library	Notre Dame	IN	46556	574-631-5252	631-6772	434-6
Web: www.library.nd.edu						
University of Oklahoma 1000 Asp Ave	Norman	OK	73019	405-325-0311	325-7124	166
TF: 800-234-6868 ■ *Web:* www.ou.edu						
University of Oklahoma Bizzell Memorial Library						
401 W Brooks St	Norman	OK	73019	405-325-4142	325-7550*	434-6
**Fax:* Admin ■ *Web:* www.libraries.ou.edu						
University of Oklahoma College of Law						
300 Timberdell Rd	Norman	OK	73019	405-325-4699	325-7474	167-1
Web: www.law.ou.edu						
University of Oklahoma College of Medicine						
PO Box 26901	Oklahoma City	OK	73190	405-271-2265	271-3032	167-2
Web: www.oumedicine.com						
University of Oklahoma Health Sciences Ctr						
1100 N Lindsay	Oklahoma City	OK	73104	405-271-4000		166
Web: www.ouhsc.edu						
University of Oregon 1585 E 13th Ave	Eugene	OR	97403	541-346-1000	346-5815*	166
**Fax:* Admissions ■ *TF Admissions:* 800-232-3825 ■ *Web:* www.uoregon.edu						

				Phone	Fax	Class
University of Oregon Bookstore Inc						
895 E 13th Ave	Eugene	OR	97401	541-346-4331		95
TF: 800-352-1733 ■ *Web:* www.uoduckstore.com						
University of Oregon Knight Library						
1299 University of Oregon	Eugene	OR	97403	541-346-3053	346-3485*	434-6
**Fax:* Library ■ *Web:* library.uoregon.edu						
University of Oregon Museum of Natural & Cultural History						
1680 E 15th Ave	Eugene	OR	97401	541-346-3024		520
University of Oregon School of Law						
1515 Agate St	Eugene	OR	97403	541-346-3852	346-1564	167-1
Web: www.law.uoregon.edu						
University of Ottawa 550 Cumberland St	Ottawa	ON	K1N6N5	613-562-5800	562-5323	785
TF: 877-868-8292 ■ *Web:* www.uottawa.ca						
University of Ottawa Faculty of Medicine						
451 Smyth Rd	Ottawa	ON	K1H8M5	613-562-5700	562-5323	167-2
TF: 877-868-8292 ■ *Web:* www.uottawa.ca						
University of Ottawa Health Sciences Library						
65 University	Ottawa	ON	K1N6N5	613-562-5407		434-1
Web: www.biblio.uottawa.ca						
University of Pennsylvania						
3451 Walnut St	Philadelphia	PA	19104	215-898-5000	898-9670*	166
**Fax:* Admissions ■ *TF:* 800-537-5487 ■ *Web:* www.upenn.edu						
University of Pennsylvania						
3420 Walnut St	Philadelphia	PA	19104	215-898-7091	898-0559	434-6
Web: www.library.upenn.edu/vanpelt						
Biomedical Library						
3610 Hamilton Walk Johnson Pavilion	Philadelphia	PA	19104	215-898-5815	573-4143	434-1
Web: www.library.upenn.edu/biomed						
University of Pennsylvania Law School						
3400 Chestnut St	Philadelphia	PA	19104	215-898-7483	573-2025	167-1
Web: www.law.upenn.edu						
University of Pennsylvania Museum of Archaeology & Anthropology						
3260 S St	Philadelphia	PA	19104	215-898-4000	898-0657	520
TF: 800-745-3000 ■ *Web:* www.penn.museum						
University of Pennsylvania Press						
3902 Spruce St	Philadelphia	PA	19104	215-898-6261	898-0404	637-4
TF Cust Svc: 800-537-5487 ■ *Web:* www.upenn.edu/pennpress						
University of Phoenix Stadium						
1 Cardinals Dr	Glendale	AZ	85305	623-433-7101	433-7199	720
Web: www.universityofphoenixstadium.com						
University of Pittsburgh						
4227 Fifth Ave	Pittsburgh	PA	15260	412-624-4141	648-8815*	166
**Fax:* Admissions ■ *TF:* 877-999-3223 ■ *Web:* www.pitt.edu						
Bradford 300 Campus Dr	Bradford	PA	16701	814-362-7555		166
TF: 800-872-1787 ■ *Web:* www.upb.pitt.edu						
Greensburg 150 Finoli Dr	Greensburg	PA	15601	724-837-7040	836-7160*	166
**Fax:* Admissions ■ *TF:* 888-843-4563 ■ *Web:* www.greensburg.pitt.edu						
Hillman Library 3960 Forbes Ave	Pittsburgh	PA	15260	412-648-7710	648-7887	434-6
Web: www.library.pitt.edu						
Johnstown 157 Blackington Hall	Johnstown	PA	15904	814-269-7050	269-7044	166
TF: 800-765-4875 ■ *Web:* www.upj.pitt.edu						
Titusville 504 E Main St	Titusville	PA	16354	814-827-4406	827-4510*	166
**Fax Area Code:* 814 ■ **Fax:* Admissions ■ *TF:* 888-878-0462 ■ *Web:* www.upt.pitt.edu						
University of Pittsburgh Medical Ctr (UPMC)						
Horizon 110 N Main St	Greenville	PA	16125	724-588-2100		374-3
TF: 888-447-1122 ■ *Web:* www.upmc.com						
Northwest 100 Fairfield Dr	Seneca	PA	16346	814-676-7600		374-3
Web: www.upmc.com						
Passavant 9100 Babcock Blvd	Pittsburgh	PA	15237	412-367-6700		374-3
TF: 800-533-8762 ■ *Web:* www.upmc.com						
Shadyside 5230 Centre Ave	Pittsburgh	PA	15232	412-623-2121		374-3
TF: 800-533-8762 ■ *Web:* www.upmc.com						
South Side 2000 Mary St	Pittsburgh	PA	15203	412-488-5550		374-3
TF: 800-533-8762 ■ *Web:* www.upmc.com						
Stem Cell Transplantation Program						
5150 Centre Ave	Pittsburgh	PA	15232	412-647-2811		769
Web: www.upmccancercenter.com						
University of Pittsburgh Medical Ctr Health System						
200 Lothrop St	Pittsburgh	PA	15213	412-647-2345		353
TF: 800-533-8762 ■ *Web:* www.upmc.com						
University of Pittsburgh Press						
7500 Thomas Blvd	Pittsburgh	PA	15260	412-383-2456	383-2466	637-4
TF Sales: 800-621-2736 ■ *Web:* www.upress.pitt.edu						
University of Pittsburgh School of Law						
3900 Forbes Ave	Pittsburgh	PA	15260	412-648-1400	648-2647	167-1
Web: www.law.pitt.edu						
University of Pittsburgh School of Medicine						
3550 Ter St M240 Scaife Hall	Pittsburgh	PA	15261	412-648-9891	648-8768*	167-2
**Fax:* Admissions ■ *Web:* www.medschool.pitt.edu						
University of Portland						
5000 N Willamette Blvd	Portland	OR	97203	503-943-7147		166
TF: 888-627-5601 ■ *Web:* www.up.edu						
University of Puget Sound						
1500 N Warner St	Tacoma	WA	98416	253-879-3100		166
TF: 800-396-7191 ■ *Web:* www.pugetsound.edu						
University of Redlands						
1200 E Colton Ave PO Box 3080	Redlands	CA	92373	909-793-2121		166
TF: 800-455-5064 ■ *Web:* www.redlands.edu						
University of Regina 3737 Wascana Pkwy	Regina	SK	S4S0A2	306-585-4111	337-2525	785
TF: 800-644-4756 ■ *Web:* www.uregina.ca						
Luther College 3737 Wascana Pkwy	Regina	SK	S4S0A2	306-585-5333	585-5267	785
Web: www.luthercollege.edu						
University of Rhode Island (URI)						
45 Upper College Rd	Kingston	RI	02881	401-874-1000	874-5523	166
Web: ww2.uri.edu						
Feinstein Providence						
80 Washington St	Providence	RI	02903	401-277-5000		166
Web: ww2.uri.edu						
University Libraries 15 Lippitt Rd	Kingston	RI	02881	401-874-2666	874-4608	434-6
Web: ww2.uri.edu						
University of Richmond						
28 Westhampton Way	Richmond	VA	23173	804-289-8000	287-6003	166
TF: 800-700-1662 ■ *Web:* www.richmond.edu						
Boatwright Memorial Library						
28 Westhampton Way	Richmond	VA	23173	804-289-8454		434-6
Web: library.richmond.edu						
Westhampton College						
28 Westhampton Way	University Of Richmond	VA	23173	804-289-8000		166
TF: 800-700-1662 ■ *Web:* wc.richmond.edu						

Phone Fax Class

University of Richmond School of Law
28 W Hampton Way ....University of Richmond VA 23173 804-289-8740 289-8992 167-1
Web: www.law.richmond.edu

University of Rio Grande
218 N College Ave ....Rio Grande OH 45674 740-245-5353 245-7260* 166
**Fax:* Admissions ■ *TF:* 800-282-7201 ■ *Web:* www.rio.edu

University of Rochester
Wallace Hall PO Box 270251...............Rochester NY 14627 585-275-2121 461-4595* 166
**Fax:* Admissions ■ *TF Admissions:* 888-822-2256 ■ *Web:* www.rochester.edu

University of Rochester Arboretum
612 Wilson Blvd..........................Rochester NY 14627 585-275-3340 461-3055 97
Web: www.facilities.rochester.edu/arboretum

University of Rochester River Campus Libraries
755 Library Rd PO Box 270055 ....Rochester NY 14627 585-275-5804 273-5309 434-6
Web: www.library.rochester.edu

University of Rochester School of Medicine & Dentistry
601 Elmwood Ave...........................Rochester NY 14642 585-275-0017 756-5479* 167-2
**Fax:* Admissions ■ *TF:* 888-661-6162 ■ *Web:* www.urmc.rochester.edu/SMD

University of Saint Francis
180 Remsen St......................Brooklyn Heights NY 11201 718-522-2300 166
TF: 800-356-8329 ■ *Web:* www.sfc.edu

University of Saint Francis-ft Wayne
2701 Spring St.......................... Fort Wayne IN 46808 260-399-7700 166
TF: 800-213-2178 ■ *Web:* www.sf.edu

University of Saint Joseph
1678 Asylum Ave ....West Hartford CT 06117 860-232-4571 166
Web: www.sjc.edu

University of Saint Mary
4100 S Fourth St .... Leavenworth KS 66048 913-682-5151 758-6140* 166
**Fax:* Admissions ■ *TF:* 800-752-7043 ■ *Web:* www.stmary.edu

University of Saint Mary of the Lake Mundelein Seminary
1000 E Maple Ave..........................Mundelein IL 60060 847-566-6401 167-3
Web: www.usml.edu

University of Saint Michael's College Faculty of Theology
81 St Mary St .... Toronto ON M5S1J4 416-926-1300 926-7276 167-3
Web: www.utoronto.ca

University of Saint Thomas
3800 Montrose Blvd........................Houston TX 77006 713-522-7911 525-3558* 166
**Fax:* Admissions ■ *TF:* 800-856-8565 ■ *Web:* www.stthom.edu

University of Saint Thomas
2115 Summit Ave......................... Saint Paul MN 55105 651-962-5000 962-6160* 166
**Fax:* Admissions ■ *TF:* 800-328-6819 ■ *Web:* www.stthomas.edu

University of Saint Thomas O'Shaughnessy-Frey Library
2115 Summit Ave......................... Saint Paul MN 55105 651-962-5494 962-5406 434-6
TF: 800-328-6819 ■ *Web:* www.stthomas.edu/libraries

University of Saint Thomas School of Law
1000 LaSalle Ave ....Minneapolis MN 55403 651-962-4892 962-4876* 167-1
**Fax:* Admissions ■ *TF:* 800-328-6819 ■ *Web:* www.stthomas.edu

University of Saint Thomas School of Theology
9845 Memorial Dr ....Houston TX 77024 713-686-4345 683-8673 167-3
Web: www.stthom.edu

University of San Diego
5998 Alcala Pk .... San Diego CA 92110 619-260-4506 260-6836 166
TF: 800-248-4873 ■ *Web:* www.sandiego.edu

University of San Diego School of Law
5998 Alcala Pk .... San Diego CA 92110 619-260-4528 260-2218* 167-1
**Fax:* Admissions ■ *TF:* 800-248-4873 ■ *Web:* www.sandiego.edu/usdlaw

University of San Francisco
2130 Fulton St .... San Francisco CA 94117 415-422-5555 422-2217* 166
**Fax:* Admissions ■ *TF Admissions:* 800-854-1385 ■ *Web:* www.usfca.edu

University of San Francisco School of Law
2130 Fulton St .... San Francisco CA 94117 415-422-6307 422-5442* 167-1
**Fax:* Admissions ■ *Web:* www.usfca.edu/law

University of Saskatchewan
1121 College Dr........................... Saskatoon SK S7N0W3 306-966-8970 966-8747 167-3
TF: 877-653-8501 ■ *Web:* www.usask.ca
Leslie and Irene Dub, Health Sciences Library
104 Clinic Pl .... Saskatoon SK S7N2Z4 306-966-5991 966-5918 434-1
Web: library.usask.ca/hsl
Saint Thomas More College
1437 College Dr....................... Saskatoon SK S7N0W6 306-966-8900 966-8904 785
TF: 800-667-2019 ■ *Web:* www.stmcollege.ca

University of Sciences & Arts of Oklahoma
1727 W Alabama Ave .... Chickasha OK 73018 405-224-3140 574-1220* 166
**Fax:* Admissions ■ *TF:* 800-933-8726 ■ *Web:* www.usao.edu

University of Scranton
800 Linden St St Thomas Hall .... Scranton PA 18510 570-941-7400 941-5928* 166
**Fax:* Admissions ■ *TF:* 888-727-2686 ■ *Web:* scranton.edu

University of Sioux Falls
1101 W 22nd St ....Sioux Falls SD 57105 605-331-6600 331-6615 166
TF: 800-888-1047 ■ *Web:* www.usiouxfalls.edu

University of South Alabama
2500 Meisler Hall..........................Mobile AL 36688 251-460-6141 460-7876 166
TF: 800-872-5247 ■ *Web:* www.usouthal.edu

University of South Alabama Children & Women's Hospital
1700 Ctr St................................Mobile AL 36604 251-415-1000 415-1002* 374-3
**Fax:* Admitting ■ *TF:* 800-772-1213 ■ *Web:* www.usahealthsystem.com

University of South Alabama College of Medicine
307 N University Blvd.......................Mobile AL 36688 251-460-6101 460-6278 167-2
Web: www.southalabama.edu

University of South Alabama Medical Ctr
2451 Fillingim St ....Mobile AL 36617 251-471-7000 374-3
Web: www.usahealthsystem.com

University of South Carolina
1600 Hampton St...........................Columbia SC 29208 803-777-7000 777-0101* 166
**Fax:* Admissions ■ *TF:* 800-868-5872 ■ *Web:* www.sc.edu
Aiken 471 University Pkwy .... Aiken SC 29801 803-648-6851 641-3727* 166
**Fax:* Admissions ■ *TF:* 866-254-2366 ■ *Web:* www.usca.edu
Beaufort 801 Carteret St.....................Beaufort SC 29902 843-521-4100 521-4198* 166
**Fax:* Admissions ■ *TF:* 866-455-4753 ■ *Web:* www.sc.edu
Sumter 200 Miller Rd ....Sumter SC 29150 803-775-8727 775-2180* 166
**Fax:* Admissions ■ *TF:* 888-872-7868 ■ *Web:* www.uscsumter.edu
Union 401 E Main St P.O. Drawer 729.............Union SC 29379 864-429-8728 427-3682 162
TF: 800-768-5566 ■ *Web:* uscunion.sc.edu
University Libraries - Thomas Cooper Library
1322 Greene St ....Columbia SC 29208 803-777-2805 777-9503* 434-6
**Fax:* Admin ■ *Web:* library.sc.edu
Upstate 800 University Way................Spartanburg SC 29303 864-503-5246 503-5727* 166
**Fax:* Admissions ■ *TF:* 800-277-8727 ■ *Web:* www.uscupstate.edu

University of South Carolina McKissick Museum
University of S Carolina 816 Bull St............Columbia SC 29208 803-777-7251 777-2829 520
TF: 888-825-9711 ■ *Web:* artsandsciences.sc.edu

University of South Carolina Press
1600 Hampton St 5th Fl......................Columbia SC 29208 803-777-5243 777-0160 637-4
TF Orders: 800-768-2500 ■ *Web:* www.sc.edu/uscpress

University of South Carolina School of Law
701 S Main St.............................Columbia SC 29208 803-777-6605 777-7751* 167-1
**Fax:* Admissions ■ *Web:* www.law.sc.edu

University of South Carolina School of Medicine
6439 Garners Ferry Rd ....Columbia SC 29209 803-216-3300 733-3335 167-2
Web: www.med.sc.edu

University of South Dakota
414 E Clark St............................ Vermillion SD 57069 605-677-5341 677-6323* 166
**Fax:* Admissions ■ *TF:* 877-269-6837 ■ *Web:* www.usd.edu

University of South Dakota Foundation
1110 N Dakota St PO Box 5555 .... Vermillion SD 57069 605-677-6703 677-6717 786
TF: 800-521-3575 ■ *Web:* www.onwardsd.org

University of South Dakota School of Law
414 E Clark St............................ Vermillion SD 57069 605-677-5443 677-5417 167-1
TF: 877-269-6837 ■ *Web:* www.usd.edu/law

University of South Florida
Libraries 4202 E Fowler Ave LIB 122............ Tampa FL 33620 813-974-2729 434-6
Web: www.lib.usf.edu
Sarasota-Manatee
8350 N Tamiami Trail.....................Sarasota FL 34243 941-359-4200 359-4236* 166
**Fax:* Admissions ■ *TF:* 866-974-1222 ■ *Web:* usfsm.edu
ST. Petersburg
140 Seventh Ave S................ Saint Petersburg FL 33701 727-873-4135 873-4525 166
Web: www.usfsp.edu
Tampa 4202 E Fowler Ave .... Tampa FL 33620 813-974-2011 974-4346 166
TF: 800-299-2855 ■ *Web:* www.usf.edu

University of South Florida Botanical Gardens
4202 E Fowler Ave .... Tampa FL 33620 813-974-2329 974-4808 97
Web: gardens.usf.edu

University of South Florida College of Medicine (USF)
12901 Bruce B Downs Blvd .... Tampa FL 33612 813-974-2229 974-4990 167-2
TF: 877-338-2577 ■ *Web:* health.usf.edu

University of Southern California
University Pk Campus ....Los Angeles CA 90089 213-740-2311 740-5229* 166
**Fax:* Admissions ■ *Web:* www.usc.edu
Doheny Memorial Library
3550 Trousdale Pkwy University Pk Campus Los Angeles CA 90089 213-740-4039 740-3488 434-6
TF: 800-775-7330 ■ *Web:* libraries.usc.edu

University of Southern Indiana
8600 University Blvd .... Evansville IN 47712 812-464-1765 465-7154 166
TF: 800-467-1965 ■ *Web:* www.usi.edu

University of Southern Maine
96 Falmouth St.............................Portland ME 04103 207-780-4141 780-5640 166
TF: 800-800-4876 ■ *Web:* www.usm.maine.edu
Gorham 37 College Ave.................... Gorham ME 04038 207-780-5670 780-5640* 166
**Fax:* Admissions ■ *TF:* 800-800-4876 ■ *Web:* www.usm.maine.edu
Lewiston-Auburn College
51 Westminster St .... Lewiston ME 04240 207-753-6500 753-6555* 166
**Fax:* Admissions ■ *TF:* 800-800-4876 ■ *Web:* www.usm.maine.edu

University of Southern Maine Arboretum
PO Box 9300 ....Portland ME 04104 800-800-4876 780-5143* 97
**Fax Area Code:* 207 ■ *TF:* 800-800-4876 ■ *Web:* www.usm.maine.edu/arboretum

University of Southern Mississippi
118 College Dr.......................... Hattiesburg MS 39406 601-266-1000 166
TF: 800-446-0892 ■ *Web:* www.usm.edu
Gulf Park 730 E Beach Blvd.............. Long Beach MS 39560 228-865-4500 166
TF: 800-726-2781 ■ *Web:* www.usm.edu

University of St Francis 500 Wilcox St........... Joliet IL 60435 800-735-7500 166
TF: 800-735-7500 ■ *Web:* www.stfrancis.edu

University of Tampa 401 W Kennedy Blvd......... Tampa FL 33606 813-253-3333 258-7398 166
Web: www.ut.edu

University of Tennessee (UTHSC)
1331 Cir Pk Dr 320 Student Services Bldg....... Knoxville TN 37996 865-974-1000 974-6341* 166
**Fax:* Admissions ■ *Web:* www.utk.edu
Chattanooga 615 McCallie Ave .... Chattanooga TN 37403 423-425-4111 425-4157* 166
**Fax:* Admissions ■ *TF:* 800-882-6627 ■ *Web:* www.utc.edu
Health Science Ctr 920 Madison Ave........... Memphis TN 38163 901-448-5500 166
Web: www.uthsc.edu
Martin 544 University St .... Martin TN 38238 731-881-7020 881-7029 166
TF: 800-829-8861 ■ *Web:* www.utm.edu

University of Tennessee Arboretum
901 S Illinois Ave .... Oak Ridge TN 37830 865-483-3571 483-3572 97
Web: forestry.tennessee.edu

University of Tennessee Chattanooga
UTC Library
Dept 6456 600 Douglas St............. Chattanooga TN 37403 423-425-4501 425-4775 434-6
Web: utc.edu/library

University of Tennessee College of Law
1505 Cumberland Ave .... Knoxville TN 37996 865-974-2521 974-6595 167-1
Web: www.law.utk.edu

University of Tennessee Gardens
2431 Joe Johnson Dr........................Knoxville TN 37996 865-974-7324 974-1947 97
Web: utgardens.tennessee.edu

University of Tennessee Health Science Ctr
Health Sciences Library & Biocommunications Ctr
877 Madison Ave......................Memphis TN 38103 901-448-5634 434-1
TF: 877-747-0004 ■ *Web:* www.uthsc.edu

University of Tennessee Health Science Ctr College of Medicine
920 Madison Ave ....Memphis TN 38163 901-448-5529 167-2
Web: www.uthsc.edu

University of Tennessee Knoxville
Hodges Library 1015 Volunteer Blvd........... Knoxville TN 37996 865-974-4351 434-6
TF: 800-426-9119 ■ *Web:* www.lib.utk.edu

University of Tennessee Music Hall
1741 Volunteer Blvd........................Knoxville TN 37996 865-974-3241 974-1941 572
Web: www.music.utk.edu

University of Tennessee Press
110 Conference Ctr 600 Henley St ....Knoxville TN 37996 865-974-3321 974-3724 637-4
Web: utpress.org

University of Tennessee System
800 Andy Holt Tower 1331 Circle Park.......... Knoxville TN 37996 865-974-2241 974-3753 786
Web: www.tennessee.edu

	City	State	Zip	Phone	Fax	Class
Austin						
2400 Inner Campus Dr Mail Bldg Rm 7	Austin	TX	78712	512-475-7399	475-7399*	166
**Fax:* Admissions ■ *Web:* www.utexas.edu						
Brownsville 80 Fort Brown St	Brownsville	TX	78520	956-882-8200		166
Web: opportunityequation.org						
Dallas 800 W Campbell Rd Ste Be3204	Richardson	TX	75080	972-883-2111	883-2599	166
TF: 800-889-2443 ■ *Web:* www.utdallas.edu						
El Paso 500 W University Ave	El Paso	TX	79968	915-747-5000	747-8893*	166
**Fax:* Admissions ■ *TF Admissions:* 800-551-0294 ■ *Web:* www.utep.edu						
Pan American 1201 W University Dr	Edinburg	TX	78539	956-381-8872	381-2212	166
TF: 866-441-8872 ■ *Web:* www.utpa.edu						
Permian Basin 4901 E University Blvd	Odessa	TX	79762	432-552-2020	552-3605*	166
**Fax:* Admissions ■ *TF Admissions:* 866-552-8872 ■ *Web:* www.utpb.edu						
Perry-Castaoeda Library						
101 E 21st St PO Box P	Austin	TX	78712	512-495-4250	495-4347	434-6
Web: www.lib.utexas.edu						
San Antonio 6900 N Loop 1604 W	San Antonio	TX	78249	210-458-4011	458-7716*	166
**Fax:* Admissions ■ *TF:* 800-669-0919 ■ *Web:* www.utsa.edu						
Tyler 3900 University Blvd	Tyler	TX	75799	903-566-7000	566-7068*	166
**Fax:* Admissions ■ *TF:* 800-888-9537 ■ *Web:* www.uttyler.edu						
University of Texas						
UT Southwestern Medical Center						
5323 Harry Hines Blvd	Dallas	TX	75390	214-648-3111	475-7641*	166
**Fax Area Code:* 512						
University of Texas at Austin Performing Arts Ctr						
2350 Robert Dedman Dr	Austin	TX	78712	512-232-6213		572
TF: 800-687-6010 ■ *Web:* www.texasperformingarts.org						
University of Texas Health Ctr at Tyler (UTHCT)						
11937 US Hwy 271	Tyler	TX	75708	903-877-7000		374-3
Web: www.uthealth.org						
University of Texas Health Science Center						
Libraries						
7703 Floyd Curl Dr MSC 7940	San Antonio	TX	78229	210-567-2408	567-2490	434-1
Web: www.library.uthscsa.edu						
University of Texas Institute for Geophysics (UTIG)						
JJ Pickle Research Campus Bldg 196						
10100 Burnet Rd (RR2200)	Austin	TX	78758	512-471-6156	471-8844	668
Web: www.ig.utexas.edu						
University of Texas Investment Management Co						
401 Congress Ave Ste 2800	Austin	TX	78701	512-225-1600		166
Web: www.utimco.org						
University of Texas Medical Branch						
301 University Blvd	Galveston	TX	77555	409-772-2610	747-2909*	167-2
**Fax:* Admissions ■ *TF:* 800-228-1841 ■ *Web:* www.utmb.edu						
University of Texas Medical Branch Hospitals						
301 University Blvd	Galveston	TX	77555	409-772-1011		374-3
TF: 800-201-0527 ■ *Web:* www.utmb.edu						
University of Texas Medical School at San Antonio						
7703 Floyd Curl Dr	San Antonio	TX	78229	210-567-4420	567-6962*	167-2
**Fax:* Admissions ■ *Web:* som.uthscsa.edu						
University of Texas Press						
3001 Lake Austin Blvd 2-200 Stop E4800	Austin	TX	78703	512-471-7233	232-7178	637-4
TF Sales: 800-252-3206 ■ *Web:* www.utexas.edu/utpress						
University of Texas School of Law						
727 E Dean Keeton St	Austin	TX	78705	512-471-5151	471-6988	167-1
Web: www.utexas.edu/law						
University of Texas Southwestern Medical Ctr at Dallas Library, The						
5323 Harry Hines Blvd	Dallas	TX	75390	214-648-2001	648-2826	434-1
TF: 866-645-6455 ■ *Web:* utsouthwestern.edu						
University of Texas Southwestern Medical Ctr Dallas						
Hematopoietic Cell Transplant Program						
2201 Inwood Rd 2nd Fl	Dallas	TX	75390	214-645-4673		769
TF: 866-645-6455 ■ *Web:* www.utsouthwestern.edu						
Southwestern Medical School						
5323 Harry Hines Blvd	Dallas	TX	75390	214-648-3111	648-3289	167-2
TF: 866-648-2455 ■ *Web:* utsouthwestern.edu/education/medical-school						
University of Texas System						
601 Colorado St	Austin	TX	78701	512-499-4200		786
TF: 866-882-2034 ■ *Web:* www.utsystem.edu						
University of Texas System Office of Health Affairs						
601 Colorado St	Austin	TX	78701	512-499-4224	499-4313	353
TF: 800-827-4277 ■ *Web:* utsystem.edu/offices/health-affairs						
University of the Arts						
320 S Broad St	Philadelphia	PA	19102	215-717-6049	717-6000	164
TF: 800-616-2787 ■ *Web:* www.uarts.edu						
University of the Cumberlands						
6191 College Stn Dr	Williamsburg	KY	40769	606-539-4201		166
TF: 800-343-1609 ■ *Web:* www.ucumberlands.edu						
University of the District of Columbia						
4200 Connecticut Ave NW	Washington	DC	20008	202-274-5000	274-5552	166
Web: www.udc.edu						
University of the District of Columbia David A Clarke School of Law						
4200 Connecticut Ave NW	Washington	DC	20008	202-274-7341	274-5583	167-1
Web: www.law.udc.edu						
University of the Incarnate Word						
4301 Broadway St Ste 285	San Antonio	TX	78209	210-829-6000	829-3921*	166
**Fax:* Admissions ■ *TF Admissions:* 800-749-9673 ■ *Web:* www.uiw.edu						
University of the Ozarks						
415 N College Ave	Clarksville	AR	72830	479-979-1227	979-1417*	166
**Fax:* Admissions ■ *TF Admissions:* 800-264-8636 ■ *Web:* www.ozarks.edu						
University of the Pacific						
3601 Pacific Ave	Stockton	CA	95211	209-946-2211	946-2413	166
TF: 800-959-2867 ■ *Web:* www.pacific.edu						
University of the Pacific McGeorge School of Law						
3200 Fifth Ave	Sacramento	CA	95817	916-739-7105	739-7134*	167-1
**Fax:* Admissions ■ *Web:* www.mcgeorge.edu						
University of the Sciences in Philadelphia						
600 S 43rd St	Philadelphia	PA	19104	215-596-8800	596-8821*	166
**Fax:* Admissions ■ *TF:* 888-857-6264 ■ *Web:* www.usciences.edu						
University of the South						
735 University Ave	Sewanee	TN	37383	931-598-1238	598-3248*	166
**Fax:* Admissions ■ *TF:* 800-522-2234 ■ *Web:* www.sewanee.edu						
University of Toledo						
2801 W Bancroft St	Toledo	OH	43606	419-530-4636	530-5745*	166
**Fax:* Admissions ■ *TF:* 800-586-5336 ■ *Web:* www.utoledo.edu						
University of Toledo Carlson Library						
2801 W Bancroft St MS 509	Toledo	OH	43606	419-530-2324	530-2726	434-6
TF: 800-586-5336 ■ *Web:* www.utoledo.edu/library						
University of Toledo College of Law						
2801 W Bancroft MS 507	Toledo	OH	43606	419-530-4131		167-1
Web: utoledo.edu/law						
University of Toledo Medical Center, The (PCGH)						
7007 Powers Blvd	Parma	OH	44129	440-743-3000	743-4386	374-3
TF: 855-292-4292 ■ *Web:* www.uhhospitals.org/parma						
University of Toledo Medical Center, The						
3000 Arlington Ave	Toledo	OH	43614	419-383-4000		374-3
TF: 800-586-5336						
University of Toledo, The						
2801 W Bancroft MS 218	Toledo	OH	43606	419-530-2650	530-5167	598
Web: www.utoledo.edu						
University of Toronto						
27 King's College Cir	Toronto	ON	M5S1A1	416-978-2190	978-7022*	785
**Fax:* Admissions ■ *Web:* www.utoronto.ca						
Mississauga 3359 Mississauga Rd N	Mississauga	ON	L5L1C6	905-828-5399	569-4301	785
Web: www.utm.utoronto.ca						
Scarborough 1265 Military Trl	Toronto	ON	M1C1A4	416-287-8872	978-7022	785
Web: www.utsc.utoronto.ca						
University of Trinity College						
6 Hoskin Ave	Toronto	ON	M5S1H8	416-978-2522	978-2797	785
Web: www.trinity.utoronto.ca						
Victoria University						
73 Queen's Park Crescent	Toronto	ON	M5S1K7	416-585-4524	585-4524	785
Web: www.vicu.utoronto.ca						
University of Toronto Faculty of Medicine						
1 King's College Cir						
Medical Sciences Bldg Rm 2109	Toronto	ON	M5G1V7	416-978-6976	978-7144	167-2
Web: medicine.utoronto.ca						
University of Tulsa 800 S Tucker Rd	Tulsa	OK	74104	918-631-2307	631-5003*	166
**Fax:* Admissions ■ *TF:* 800-331-3050 ■ *Web:* www.utulsa.edu						
University of Tulsa McFarlin Library						
2933 E Sixth St	Tulsa	OK	74104	918-631-2873	631-3791	434-6
Web: utulsa.libguides.com/library_homepage						
University of Utah						
201 South 1460 East Rm 250 S	Salt Lake City	UT	84112	801-581-7281		166
Web: www.utah.edu						
University of Utah Hospital & Clinics						
50 N Medical Dr	Salt Lake City	UT	84132	801-581-2121		374-3
Web: healthcare.utah.edu						
Miner's Hospital						
50 N Medical Dr Rm 1B295	Salt Lake City	UT	84132	801-581-2121		769
TF General: 800-824-2073 ■ *Web:* www.healthcare.utah.edu/hospital						
University of Utah Marriott Library						
Marriott Library 295 S 1500 E	Salt Lake City	UT	84112	801-581-8558	585-3464*	434-6
**Fax:* Admin ■ *TF:* 800-458-0145 ■ *Web:* www.lib.utah.edu						
University of Utah Press						
295 South 1500 East Ste 5400	Salt Lake City	UT	84112	801-585-0082	581-3365	637-4
TF: 800-621-2736 ■ *Web:* www.uofupress.com						
University of Utah School of Medicine						
30 N 1900 E	Salt Lake City	UT	84132	801-581-7201	585-3300	167-2
TF: 844-988-7284 ■ *Web:* medicine.utah.edu						
University of Utah SJ Quinney College of Law						
332 South 1400 East Rm 101	Salt Lake City	UT	84112	801-581-6833	581-6897	167-1
Web: www.law.utah.edu						
University of Vermont						
85 S Prospect St	Burlington	VT	05405	802-656-3131	656-8611	166
TF: 800-499-0113 ■ *Web:* www.uvm.edu						
University of Vermont Bailey/Howe Library						
538 Main St	Burlington	VT	05405	802-656-2023	656-4038	434-6
Web: library.uvm.edu						
University of Vermont College of Medicine						
89 Beaumont Ave E-126 Given Bldg	Burlington	VT	05405	802-656-2156		167-2
TF: 800-571-0668 ■ *Web:* www.uvm.edu						
University of Vermont Medical Center, The (FAHC)						
111 Colchester Ave	Burlington	VT	05401	802-847-0000		374-3
TF: 800-358-1144 ■ *Web:* www.uvmhealth.org/medcenter/pages/default.aspx						
University of Victoria						
3800 Finnerty Rd Stn CSC PO Box 1700	Victoria	BC	V8P5C2	250-472-5416	472-5477	785
Web: www.uvic.ca						
University of Virginia						
Peabody Hall PO Box 400160	Charlottesville	VA	22903	434-982-3200	924-3587*	166
**Fax:* Admissions ■ *Web:* www.virginia.edu						
University of Virginia Health System						
1215 Lee St	Charlottesville	VA	22908	434-924-0211		374-3
TF: 800-251-3627 ■ *Web:* www.healthsystem.virginia.edu						
University of Virginia Press						
210 Sprigg Ln PO Box 400318	Charlottesville	VA	22904	434-924-3469	982-2655	637-4
TF Orders: 800-831-3406 ■ *Web:* www.upress.virginia.edu						
University of Virginia School of Law						
580 Massie Rd	Charlottesville	VA	22903	434-924-7354	924-7536	167-1
TF: 877-307-0158 ■ *Web:* www.law.virginia.edu						
University of Virginia School of Medicine						
1300 Jefferson Pk Ave PO Box 800793	Charlottesville	VA	22908	434-924-5571	982-2586	167-2
Web: med.virginia.edu						
University of Virginia's College at Wise						
1 College Ave	Wise	VA	24293	276-328-0102		166
TF Admissions: 888-282-9324 ■ *Web:* www.uvawise.edu						
University of Washington						
1410 NE Campus Pkwy	Seattle	WA	98195	206-543-2100	685-3655*	166
**Fax:* Admissions ■ *TF:* 800-537-5487 ■ *Web:* www.washington.edu						
University of Washington Health Sciences Libraries & Information Ctr						
1959 NE Pacific St PO Box 357155	Seattle	WA	98195	206-543-3390		434-1
Web: hsl.uw.edu						
University of Washington Libraries						
PO Box 352900	Seattle	WA	98195	206-543-0242		434-6
Web: www.lib.washington.edu						
University of Washington Medical Ctr						
1959 NE Pacific St	Seattle	WA	98195	206-685-8973		374-3
Web: www.washington.edu						
University of Washington Press						
4333 Brooklyn Ave NE	Seattle	WA	98195	206-543-4050	543-3932	637-4
TF: 800-537-5487 ■ *Web:* www.washington.edu						
University of Washington School of Law						
William H Gates Hall PO Box 353020	Seattle	WA	98195	206-543-4078		167-1
TF: 866-866-0158 ■ *Web:* www.law.uw.edu						

	City	State	Zip	Phone	Fax	Class
University of Washington School of Medicine						
Regional Affairs Health Sciences Ste A-300						
PO Box 356340	Seattle	WA	98195	206-543-2249	616-3341	167-2
Web: www.uwmedicine.org						
University of Waterloo						
200 University Ave W	Waterloo	ON	N2L3G1	519-888-4567	746-3242	785
Web: uwaterloo.ca						
University of West Alabama						
100 US 11	Livingston	AL	35470	888-636-8800	652-3522*	166
**Fax Area Code:* 205 ■ **Fax:* Admissions ■ *TF Admissions:* 888-636-8800 ■ *Web:* uwaathletics.com						
University of West Florida Center for Fine & Performing Arts						
11000 University Pkwy Bldg 82	Pensacola	FL	32514	850-474-2000	857-6176	572
TF: 800-263-1074 ■ *Web:* uwf.edu/cfpa						
University of West Georgia						
1600 Maple St	Carrollton	GA	30117	678-839-5000	839-4747	166
Web: www.westga.edu						
King's University College						
266 Epworth Ave	London	ON	N6A2M3	519-433-3491	433-2227	785
TF: 800-265-4406 ■ *Web:* www.uwo.ca						
University of Windsor 401 Sunset Ave	Windsor	ON	N9B3P4	519-253-3000	973-7070	785
Web: www.uwindsor.ca						
University of Winnipeg						
515 Portage Ave	Winnipeg	MB	R3B2E9	204-786-9914	783-8910	785
Web: www.uwinnipeg.ca						
University of Wisconsin						
Baraboo/Sauk County 1006 Connie Rd	Baraboo	WI	53913	608-355-5200	355-5291*	162
**Fax:* Admissions ■ *TF:* 800-621-7440 ■ *Web:* www.baraboo.uwc.edu						
Barron County 1800 College Dr	Rice Lake	WI	54868	715-234-8176	234-1975	162
TF: 800-621-7440 ■ *Web:* www.barron.uwc.edu						
Eau Claire						
105 Garfield Ave PO Box 4004	Eau Claire	WI	54701	715-836-2637	836-2409*	166
**Fax:* Admissions ■ *TF:* 800-473-2255 ■ *Web:* www.uwec.edu						
Fond du Lac 400 University Dr	Fond du Lac	WI	54935	920-929-1100		162
Web: www.fdl.uwc.edu						
Fox Valley 1478 Midway Rd	Menasha	WI	54952	920-832-2600		162
TF: 800-273-8255 ■ *Web:* www.uwfox.uwc.edu						
Green Bay 2420 Nicolet Dr	Green Bay	WI	54311	920-465-2000	465-5754*	166
**Fax:* Admissions ■ *TF:* 800-465-4329 ■ *Web:* www.uwgb.edu						
La Crosse						
1725 State St 115 Graff Main Hall	La Crosse	WI	54601	608-785-8000	785-6695	166
TF: 800-382-2150 ■ *Web:* www.uwlax.edu						
Madison 702 W Johnson St Ste 1101	Madison	WI	53715	608-262-3961	262-7706*	166
**Fax:* Admissions ■ *TF:* 800-442-6459 ■ *Web:* www.wisc.edu						
Manitowoc 705 Viebahn St	Manitowoc	WI	54220	920-683-4700	683-4776	162
TF: 855-729-1300 ■ *Web:* www.manitowoc.uwc.edu						
Marathon County 518 S Seventh Ave	Wausau	WI	54401	715-261-6100		162
TF: 888-367-8962 ■ *Web:* www.uwmc.uwc.edu						
Marinette 750 W Bay Shore St	Marinette	WI	54143	715-735-4300	735-4304*	162
**Fax:* Admissions ■ *Web:* www.marinette.uwc.edu						
Marshfield/Wood County						
2000 W Fifth St	Marshfield	WI	54449	715-389-6530	384-1718	162
TF: 800-273-8255 ■ *Web:* www.marshfield.uwc.edu						
Milwaukee PO Box 413	Milwaukee	WI	53201	414-229-1122	229-6940*	166
**Fax:* Admissions ■ *TF:* 800-442-6459 ■ *Web:* www.uwm.edu						
Oshkosh 800 Algoma Blvd PO Box 2423	Oshkosh	WI	54903	920-424-0202	424-1207*	166
**Fax:* Admissions ■ *Web:* www.uwosh.edu						
Parkside 900 Wood Rd	Kenosha	WI	53141	262-595-2345	595-2008*	166
**Fax:* Admissions ■ *TF:* 800-742-2858 ■ *Web:* www.uwp.edu						
Platteville 1 University Plaza	Platteville	WI	53818	608-342-1125	342-1122*	166
**Fax:* Admissions ■ *TF:* 800-362-5515 ■ *Web:* www.uwplatt.edu						
Richland 1200 Hwy 14 W	Richland Center	WI	53581	608-647-6186	647-2275*	162
**Fax:* Admissions ■ *TF:* 800-947-3529 ■ *Web:* richland.uwc.edu						
Rock County 2909 Kellogg Ave	Janesville	WI	53546	608-758-6523	758-6579	162
TF: 800-656-4673 ■ *Web:* www.rock.uwc.edu						
Sheboygan 1 University Dr	Sheboygan	WI	53081	920-459-6600	459-6602*	162
**Fax:* Admissions ■ *TF:* 800-442-6459 ■ *Web:* sheboygan.uwc.edu						
Stevens Point 2100 Main St	Stevens Point	WI	54481	715-346-0123	346-3296*	166
**Fax:* Admissions ■ *Web:* www.uwsp.edu						
Stout 802 S Broadway	Menomonie	WI	54751	715-232-1232	232-1667*	166
**Fax:* Admissions ■ *TF Admissions:* 800-447-8688 ■ *Web:* www.uwstout.edu						
Superior Belknap & Catlin PO Box 2000	Superior	WI	54880	715-394-8101	394-8407	166
TF: 800-869-5088 ■ *Web:* www.uwsuper.edu						
Washington County						
400 S University Dr	West Bend	WI	53095	262-335-5200		162
TF: 800-240-0276 ■ *Web:* washington.uwc.edu						
Waukesha 1500 N University Dr	Waukesha	WI	53188	262-521-5200	521-5491*	162
**Fax:* Admissions ■ *Web:* waukesha.uwc.edu						
Whitewater 800 W Main St	Whitewater	WI	53190	262-472-1440	472-1515*	166
**Fax:* Admissions ■ *Web:* www.uww.edu						
University of Wisconsin Eau Claire						
McIntyre Library 105 Garfield Ave	Eau Claire	WI	54702	715-836-3715	836-2949	434-6
TF: 877-267-1384 ■ *Web:* www.uwec.edu						
University of Wisconsin Green Bay						
Cofrin Library 2420 Nicolet Dr	Green Bay	WI	54311	920-465-2333	465-2388	434-6
Web: www.uwgb.edu/library						
University of Wisconsin Hospital & Clinics						
600 Highland Ave	Madison	WI	53792	608-263-6400	263-9830	374-3
TF: 800-323-8942 ■ *Web:* www.uwhealth.org						
University of Wisconsin La Crosse						
Murphy Library 1631 Pine St	La Crosse	WI	54601	608-785-8000	785-8639	434-6
Web: www.uwlax.edu/murphylibrary						
University of Wisconsin Law School						
975 Bascom Mall	Madison	WI	53706	608-262-2240	262-5485	167-1
TF: 866-301-1753 ■ *Web:* www.law.wisc.edu						
University of Wisconsin Madison						
Ebling Library 750 Highland Ave	Madison	WI	53705	608-262-2020	262-4732	434-1
TF: 800-596-0710 ■ *Web:* www.ebling.library.wisc.edu						
Libraries 728 State St	Madison	WI	53706	608-262-3193	265-2754	434-6
Web: www.library.wisc.edu						
University of Wisconsin Medical School						
750 Highland Ave Rm 2130	Madison	WI	53705	608-263-4925		167-2
Web: www.med.wisc.edu						
University of Wisconsin Milwaukee (UWM)						
Golda Meir Library						
2311 E Hartford Ave PO Box 604	Milwaukee	WI	53211	414-229-4785		434-6
Web: www4.uwm.edu						
University of Wisconsin Oshkosh						
Polk Library 800 Algoma Blvd	Oshkosh	WI	54901	920-424-3334	424-7338	434-6
Web: www.uwosh.edu/library						
University of Wisconsin Parkside						
Library 900 Wood Rd	Kenosha	WI	53141	262-595-2360		434-6
Web: www.uwp.edu						
University of Wisconsin Press						
1930 Monroe St 3rd Fl	Madison	WI	53711	608-263-1110	263-1132	637-4
TF: 800-621-2736 ■ *Web:* www.wisc.edu						
University of Wisconsin Stevens Point						
University Library						
900 Reserve St	Stevens Point	WI	54481	715-346-2540	346-2367	434-6
Web: www.uwsp.edu						
University of Wisconsin Stout						
Library 315 Tenth Ave E	Menomonie	WI	54751	715-232-1215		434-6
TF: 866-716-6685 ■ *Web:* www.uwstout.edu/lib						
University of Wisconsin Superior						
Jim Dan Hill Library PO Box 2000	Superior	WI	54880	715-394-8343		434-6
Web: www.uwsuper.edu/library						
University of Wisconsin System						
1220 Linden Dr 1720 Van Hise Hall	Madison	WI	53706	608-262-2321	262-3985	786
TF: 800-442-6461 ■ *Web:* www.wisconsin.edu						
University of Wisconsin Whitewater						
Andersen Library 800 W Main St	Whitewater	WI	53190	262-472-5511		434-6
Web: library.uww.edu						
University of Wisconsin-Madison Arboretum						
1207 Seminole Hwy	Madison	WI	53711	608-263-7888	262-5209	97
Web: arboretum.wisc.edu						
University of Wyoming						
1000 E University Ave Dept 3435	Laramie	WY	82071	307-766-5160	766-4042*	166
**Fax:* Admissions ■ *TF Admissions:* 800-342-5996 ■ *Web:* www.uwyo.edu						
University of Wyoming Libraries						
1000 E University Ave Dept 3334	Laramie	WY	82071	307-766-3190		434-6
TF: 800-442-6757 ■ *Web:* www-lib.uwyo.edu						
University Park Mall						
6501 N Grape Rd	Mishawaka	IN	46545	574-277-2223	272-5924	460
TF: 877-746-6642 ■ *Web:* www.simon.com						
University Place 310 SW Lincoln St	Portland	OR	97201	503-221-0140		379
TF: 866-845-4647 ■ *Web:* www.pdx.edu						
University Place Conference Ctr & Hotel-Indianapolis						
850 W Michigan St	Indianapolis	IN	46202	317-269-9000		377
Web: eventservices.iupui.edu						
University Plaza Hotel & Conference Ctr						
3110 Olentangy River Rd	Columbus	OH	43202	614-267-7461		379
University Plaza Hotel & Convention Ctr						
333 John Q Hammons Pkwy	Springfield	MO	65806	417-864-7333	831-5893	379
Web: www.upspringfield.com						
University Press Books (UPB)						
2430 Bancroft Way	Berkeley	CA	94704	510-548-0585		95
TF: 800-676-8722 ■ *Web:* www.universitypressbooks.com						
University Press of America						
4501 Forbes Blvd Ste 200	Lanham	MD	20706	301-459-3366	429-5746	637-2
TF: 800-462-6420 ■ *Web:* rowman.com						
University Press of Colorado						
5589 Arapahoe Ave Ste 206C	Boulder	CO	80303	720-406-8849		637-4
TF: 800-621-2736 ■ *Web:* www.upcolorado.com						
University Press of Florida						
15 NW 15th St	Gainesville	FL	32603	352-392-1351	392-7302	637-4
TF Sales: 800-226-3822 ■ *Web:* www.upf.com						
University Press of Kansas						
2502 Westbrooke Cir	Lawrence	KS	66045	785-864-4154	864-4586	637-4
Web: kansaspress.ku.edu						
University Press of Kentucky						
663 S Limestone St	Lexington	KY	40508	859-257-8400	257-8481*	637-4
**Fax:* Mktg ■ *TF Sales:* 800-537-5487 ■ *Web:* www.kentuckypress.com						
University Press of Mississippi						
3825 Ridgewood Rd	Jackson	MS	39211	601-432-6205	432-6217	637-4
TF: 800-737-7788 ■ *Web:* www.upress.state.ms.us						
University Press of New England (UPNE)						
1 Ct St Ste 250	Lebanon	NH	03766	603-448-1533	448-9429	637-4
TF Orders: 800-421-1561 ■ *Web:* www.upne.com						
University Products Inc 517 Main St	Holyoke	MA	01040	413-532-3372	532-9281*	560
**Fax Area Code:* 800 ■ *TF:* 800-628-1912 ■ *Web:* www.universityproducts.com						
University Research Company LLC						
7200 Wisconsin Ave Ste 600	Bethesda	MD	20814	301-654-8338	941-8427	194
Web: www.urc-chs.com						
University School						
Hunting Vly Campus 2785 SOM Center Rd	Hunting Valley	OH	44022	216-831-2200		623
Web: www.us.edu						
University School of Milwaukee						
2100 W Fairy Chasm Rd	Milwaukee	WI	53217	414-352-6000	352-8076	623
Web: www.usmk12.org/page						
University Subscription Service						
1213 Butterfield Rd	Downers Grove	IL	60515	630-960-3233	960-3246	366
University System of Georgia						
270 Washington St SW	Atlanta	GA	30334	404-656-2250		786
Web: www.usg.edu						
University System of Maryland						
3300 Metzerott Rd	Adelphi	MD	20783	301-445-2740	445-1931	786
Web: www.ums.edu						
University Village						
2623 NE University Village St	Seattle	WA	98105	206-523-0622		460
Web: www.uvillage.com						
Univertical Corp 203 Weatherhead St	Angola	IN	46703	260-665-1500	665-1400	145
Web: www.univertical.com						
Univest Corp of Pennsylvania						
14 N Main St PO Box 64197	Souderton	PA	18964	877-723-5571		360-2
NASDAQ: UVSP ■ *TF:* 877-723-5571 ■ *Web:* www.univest.net						
Univex Corp 3 Old Rockingham Rd	Salem	NH	03079	603-893-6191	893-1249	298
TF: 800-258-6358 ■ *Web:* www.univexcorp.com						
Univision 600 W Broadway Ste 2150	San Diego	CA	92101	619-235-0600		645-144
TF: 800-879-4278 ■ *Web:* www.univision.com						
Univision Communications Inc						
605 Third Ave 12th Fl	New York	NY	10158	212-455-5331		643
Web: corporate.univision.com						
Univision Communications Inc						
1999 Ave of the Stars Ste 3050	Los Angeles	CA	90067	310-556-7676		739
Web: www.univision.com						
Univision Radio						
2211 E Missouri Ave Ste S-300	El Paso	TX	79903	915-544-9797	544-1247	645-53

Phone | Fax | Class

Univision Television Group Inc
5999 Ctr Dr. Los Angeles CA 90045 310-846-2800 738
TF: 844-440-0951 ■ *Web:* www.univision.com

Uniweld Products Inc
2850 Ravenswood Rd. Fort Lauderdale FL 33312 954-584-2000 587-0109 811
TF: 800-323-2111 ■ *Web:* www.uniweld.com

Uniwell Corp 21172 Figueroa St Carson CA 90745 310-782-8888 653

Uniworld 17323 Ventura Blvd Encino CA 91316 818-382-7820 221
TF: 800-733-7820 ■ *Web:* www.uniworld.com/en

Unleaded Communications Inc
1701 Commerce St. Houston TX 77002 713-874-8200 7
Web: ulcomm.com

Unleaded Software Inc
2314 Broadway Unit B Denver CO 80205 720-221-7126 177
Web: www.unleadedsoftware.com

Unleashed Technologies
10005 Old Columbia Rd Ste L-261 Columbia MD 21046 410-864-8980 177
Web: www.unleashed-technologies.com

Unlimited Construction Services Inc
1696 Haleukana St Lihue HI 96766 808-241-1400 245-6611 685
Web: www.unlimitedhawaii.com

Unlimited Innovations Inc
180 N Riverview Dr Ste 320 Anaheim Hills CA 92808 714-998-0866 177

Unlimited Services of Wisconsin Inc
170 Evergreen Rd Oconto WI 54153 920-834-4418 815
TF: 800-783-2589 ■ *Web:* www.us-wire-harness.com

Unlimited Systems Corp Inc
9530 Padgett St San Diego CA 92126 858-537-5010 550-7330 173-3
TF: 800-275-6354 ■ *Web:* www.konexx.com

Unlimited Technology Inc
20 Senn Dr Chester Springs PA 19425 610-458-8901 180
Web: www.utech-usa.com

UNM (University of New Mexico)
1 University of New Mexico Albuquerque NM 87131 505-277-0111 277-6686 166
TF: 800-225-5866 ■ *Web:* www.unm.edu

Unmetric Inc 2001 Victoria Rd Mundelein IL 60060 855-558-5588 466
TF: 855-558-5588 ■ *Web:* unmetric.com

Uno Chicago Grill 100 Charles Pk Rd Boston MA 02132 617-323-9200 670
Web: www.unos.com

Uno Langmann Ltd 2117 Granville St Vancouver BC V6H3E9 604-736-8825 42
TF: 800-730-8825 ■ *Web:* www.langmann.com

Uno Restaurant Corp
100 Charles Park Rd Boston MA 02132 617-323-9200 670
Web: www.unos.com

UNOS (United Network for Organ Sharing)
700 N Fourth St Richmond VA 23219 804-782-4800 782-4817 48-17
TF: 888-894-6361 ■ *Web:* www.unos.org

Unparalleled Productions Inc
1672 Greenwich St San Francisco CA 94123 415-673-8581 366
TF: 800-987-5582 ■ *Web:* unparalleledproductions.com

Unruh Fire Inc 100 Industrial Dr Sedgwick KS 67135 316-772-5400 772-5854 697
Web: www.unruhfire.com

Unruh, Turner, Burke & Frees PC
17 W Gay St West Chester PA 19381 610-692-1371 428
Web: www.utbf.com

Untangle Inc
100 W San Fernando St Ste 565 San Jose CA 95113 408-598-4299 177
Web: www.untangle.com

UnumProvident Corp 1 Fountain Sq. Chattanooga TN 37402 423-294-1011 872-8999* 360-4
**Fax Area Code:* 410 ■ *TF:* 800-262-0018 ■ *Web:* www.unum.com

Unverferth Mfg Company Inc
601 S Broad St Kalida OH 45853 419-532-3121 532-2468 273
TF: 800-322-6301 ■ *Web:* www.unverferth.com

UNX Inc
707 E Arlington Blvd PO Box 7206 Greenville NC 27835 252-756-8616 756-2764 151
Web: www.unxinc.com

UOB (United Overseas Bank Ltd New York Agency)
592 Fifth Ave 10th Fl New York NY 10036 646-472-8113 382-1881* 70
**Fax Area Code:* 212 ■ *Web:* www.uob.com.sg

UOP LLC 25 E Algonquin Rd Des Plaines IL 60017 847-391-2000 391-2253 143
TF: 800-877-6184 ■ *Web:* www.uop.com

Up by Seven 16 Rennie Dr Andover MA 01810 978-475-8200 226
TF: 800-664-4248 ■ *Web:* www.upbyseven.com

Up Communications Services LLC
103 SE Atlantic St. Tullahoma TN 37388 877-667-0968 461-5392* 393
**Fax Area Code:* 931 ■ *TF:* 877-667-0968 ■ *Web:* upcomllc.com

Up Right Mktg Inc 305 S Grant St San Mateo CA 94401 650-375-1388 195
Web: www.uprightmarketing.com

Up With Paper 6049 Hi-Tek Ct Mason OH 45040 513-759-7473 293-8471* 130
**Fax Area Code:* 800 ■ *TF:* 800-852-7677 ■ *Web:* www.upwithpaper.com

Up With People 6830 Broadway Denver CO 80221 303-460-7100 225-4649 48-15
TF: 877-264-8856 ■ *Web:* www.upwithpeople.org

UPAC (Imperial PFS) 8245 Nieman Rd Lenexa KS 66214 913-894-6150 216

UPB (University Press Books)
2430 Bancroft Way Berkeley CA 94704 510-548-0585 95
TF: 800-676-8722 ■ *Web:* www.universitypressbooks.com

Upchurch Electrical Supply Company
2355 N Gregg St. Fayetteville AR 72703 479-521-2823 521-6673 246
Web: www.upchurchelectrical.com

Upchurch Plumbing Inc
2606 Baldwin Rd Greenwood MS 38930 662-453-6860 610
Web: www.upchurchplumbing.com

Upchurch Scientific Inc 619 Oak St Oak Harbor WA 98277 360-679-2528 419
TF: 800-426-0191 ■ *Web:* www.idex-hs.com

UPCI (United Pentecostal Church International)
8855 Dunn Rd Hazelwood MO 63042 314-837-7300 48-20
Web: www.upci.org

UpClose Marketing & Printing
120 W White St. Champaign IL 61820 217-359-3200 5
TF: 800-755-5000 ■ *Web:* www.upcloseprinting.com

Upco Inc 24403 Amah Pkwy. Claremore OK 74019 918-342-1270 537
Web: www.upcoinc.com

Update Services Inc
10825 Greenbrier Rd Minnetonka MN 55305 952-937-5447 5
Web: www.updateservicesinc.com

Updegrove Combs Mcdaniel & Wilson Plc
10 Rock Pointe Ln Ste 3 Warrenton VA 20186 540-347-5681 2
Web: ucmcpas.com

Updike Distribution Logistics LLC
4411 W Roosevelt St Phoenix AZ 85043 602-682-1800 311
Web: www.updikedl.com

Updike Kelly & Spellacy Pc
PO Box 231277 Hartford CT 06123 860-548-2600 428
Web: www.uks.com

Updike Supply Inc
8241 Expansion Way Huber Heights OH 45424 937-482-4000 111
Web: www.updikesupply.com

UPG (United Plastics Group Inc)
7865 Northcourt Rd Houston TX 77040 713-466-5563 604
Web: www.upgintl.com

Upgrade It Consulting Services Inc
3030 Royal Blvd S Ste 220 Alpharetta GA 30022 770-345-3173 196
Web: www.upgradeitcs.com

Upham Associates Inc
156 Jersey Black Cir Rochester NY 14626 585-227-0247 804-7364* 466
**Fax Area Code:* 866 ■ *Web:* valientmarketresearch.com

Upham Oil & Gas Company LP
999 Energy Ave Mineral Wells TX 76067 940-325-4491 539
TF: 800-533-0035 ■ *Web:* www.uphamoilandgas.com

Upham's Corner Health Ctr
500 Columbia Rd Dorchester MA 02125 617-287-8000 374-3
Web: uphamscornerhealthcenter.org

UPI (United Press International)
1133 19th St NW Washington DC 20036 202-898-8000 530
Web: www.upi.com

UPI Energy LP
105 Silvercreek Pkwy N Ste 200 Guelph ON N1H8M1 519-821-2667 324
TF: 800-396-2667 ■ *Web:* www.upienergylp.com

Upland Brewing Co 350 W 11th St Bloomington IN 47404 812-336-2337 671
Web: www.uplandbeer.com

Upland Chamber of Commerce
215 N Second Ave Ste D Upland CA 91786 909-204-4465 204-4464 139
Web: www.uplandchamber.org

Upland Public Library 450 N Euclid Ave Upland CA 91786 909-931-4200 434-3
Web: www.uplandpl.lib.ca.us

Upland Software Inc
Frost Tower 401 Congress Ave, Ste 2950 Austin TX 78701 855-944-7526 787
TF: 855-944-7526 ■ *Web:* www.uplandsoftware.com

Upland Unified School District
390 N Euclid Ave Upland CA 91786 909-985-1864 949-7863 685
Web: www.upland.k12.ca.us

Uplogix Inc
7600B N Capital of Texas Hwy Ste 220 Austin TX 78731 512-857-7000 449
Web: www.uplogix.com

UPMC (University of Pittsburgh Medical Ctr)
Horizon 110 N Main St Greenville PA 16125 724-588-2100 374-3
TF: 888-447-1122 ■ *Web:* www.upmc.com

UPMC Hamot 201 State St Erie PA 16550 814-877-6000 374-3
Web: www.upmc.com

UPMC McKeesport 1500 Fifth Ave McKeesport PA 15132 412-664-2000 374-3
Web: www.upmc.com

UPMC Mercy Hospital 1400 Locust St. Pittsburgh PA 15219 412-232-8111 374-3
TF: 800-446-3797 ■ *Web:* www.upmc.com

UPMC Presbyterian 200 Lothrop St Pittsburgh PA 15213 412-647-8762 374-3
TF: 877-986-9862 ■ *Web:* www.upmc.com

UPNE (University Press of New England)
1 Ct St Ste 250 Lebanon NH 03766 603-448-1533 448-9429 637-4
TF Orders: 800-421-1561 ■ *Web:* www.upne.com

Upnorth Consulting Inc
331 Second Ave S Ste 202 Minneapolis MN 55401 866-892-1758 953-6140* 180
**Fax Area Code:* 952 ■ *TF:* 866-892-1758

Upp Entertainment Marketing Inc
3401 Winona Ave Burbank CA 91504 818-526-0111 195
Web: www.upp.net

Upper Arlington News
7801 N Central Dr. Lewis Center OH 43035 740-888-6000 888-6001* 532-4
**Fax:* Edit ■ *TF:* 800-860-1267 ■ *Web:* www.thisweeknews.com

Upper Arlington Public Library
2800 Tremont Rd Upper Arlington OH 43221 614-486-9621 486-4530 434-3
Web: www.ualibrary.org

Upper Bay Counseling & Support Services Inc
200 Booth St. Elkton MD 21921 410-996-5104 726
Web: www.upperbay.org

Upper Bucks Chamber of Commerce
2170 Portzer Rd Quakertown PA 18951 215-536-3211 536-7767 139
TF: 888-942-8257 ■ *Web:* www.ubcc.org

Upper Canada College 200 Lonsdale Rd Toronto ON M4V1W6 416-488-1125 622
Web: www.ucc.on.ca

Upper Chesapeake Medical Ctr
500 Upper Chesapeake Dr Bel Air MD 21014 443-643-1000 374-3
Web: umuch.org

Upper Cumberland Electric Membership Corp
138 Gordonsville Hwy South Carthage TN 37030 615-735-2940 735-2603 245
TF: 800-261-2940 ■ *Web:* www.ucemc.com

Upper Dauphin Area School District (UDASD)
5668 State Rt 209 Lykens PA 17048 717-362-8134 362-3050 685
TF: 866-632-9992 ■ *Web:* www.udasd.org

Upper Deck Co LLC 5909 Sea Otter Pl Carlsbad CA 92010 800-873-7332 929-3512* 762
**Fax Area Code:* 760 ■ *TF Cust Svc:* 800-873-7332 ■ *Web:* www.upperdeck.com

Upper Delaware Scenic & Recreation River
274 River Rd Beach Lake PA 18405 570-729-7134 564
TF: 800-421-1220 ■ *Web:* www.nps.gov/upde

Upper Freehold Regional Board of Education (Inc)
27 High St Allentown NJ 08501 609-259-7292 685
Web: www.ufrsd.net

Upper Iowa University
605 Washington St PO Box 1857 Fayette IA 52142 563-425-5200 425-5323* 166
**Fax:* Admissions ■ *TF Admissions:* 800-553-4150 ■ *Web:* www.uiu.edu

Upper Merion Area School District
435 Crossfield Rd King of Prussia PA 19406 610-205-6400 205-6433 685
Web: www.umasd.org

Upper Mississippi River Conservation Committee (UMRCC)
555 Lester Ave Onalaska WI 54650 608-783-8432 48-13
Web: www.umrcc.org

Upper Ottawa Valley Chamber of Commerce
224 Pembroke St W Pembroke ON K8A5N2 613-732-1492 137
Web: www.upperottawavalleychamber.com

Name / Address	City	State	Zip	Phone	Fax	Class
Upper Peninsula Telephone Co						
397 US Hwy 41N	Carney	MI	49812	906-639-2111		736
TF: 800-950-8506 ■ *Web:* www.michbbs.com						
Upper Perkiomen School District						
2229 E Buck Rd Ste 2	Pennsburg	PA	18073	215-679-7961		685
Web: www.upsd.org						
Upper Room Chapel & Museum						
1908 Grand Ave	Nashville	TN	37212	615-340-7200		520
TF: 800-972-0433 ■ *Web:* www.upperroom.org						
Upper Sioux Agency State Park						
5908 Hwy 67	Granite Falls	MN	56241	320-564-4777		565
TF: 800-366-8917 ■ *Web:* www.dnr.state.mn.us						
Upper st Clair Township Lbrry						
1820 Mclaughlin Run Rd	Pittsburgh	PA	15241	412-835-5540		434-3
Web: www.twpusc.org						
Upper Tampa Bay Regional Chamber of Commerce						
101 State St W	Oldsmar	FL	34677	813-855-4233	854-1237	139
Web: www.utbchamber.com						
Upper Township School District						
525 Perry Rd	Woodbine	NJ	08270	609-628-3500	628-2002	780
Web: www.upperschools.org						
Upper Trinity Regional Water District						
900 N Kealy St PO Box 305	Lewisville	TX	75067	972-219-1228		787
Web: www.utrwd.com						
Upper Valley Medical Ctr (UVMC)						
3130 N County Rd 25-A	Troy	OH	45373	937-440-4000		374-3
TF: 866-608-3463 ■ *Web:* www.uvmc.com						
Upperline 1413 Upperline St	New Orleans	LA	70115	504-891-9822		671
Web: www.upperline.com						
Uppy's Convenience Stores Inc						
4710 Williamsburg Rd	Richmond	VA	23231	804-236-0021		204
Uproar Communications						
3772 Plaza Dr Ste 5	Ann Arbor	MI	48108	734-975-8888		195
Web: uproarcom.com						
UPS (United Parcel Service Inc)						
55 Glenlake Pkwy NE	Atlanta	GA	30328	404-828-6000	828-6440	546
NYSE: UPS ■ *TF Cust Svc:* 800-742-5877 ■ *Web:* www.ups.com						
UPS Capital Business Credit						
35 Glenlake Pkwy NE	Atlanta	GA	30328	877-263-8772		70
TF: 877-263-8772 ■ *Web:* www.upscapital.com						
UPS Foundation 55 Glenlake Pkwy NE	Atlanta	GA	30328	800-742-5877		304
TF: 800-742-5877 ■ *Web:* sustainability.ups.com						
UPS Store, The						
6060 Cornerstone Ct W	San Diego	CA	92121	858-455-8800		310
TF: 800-789-4623 ■ *Web:* www.theupsstore.com						
UPS Strategic Enterprise Fund						
55 Glenlake Pkwy NE Bldg 1 4th Fl	Atlanta	GA	30328	800-742-5877		792
TF: 800-742-5877 ■ *Web:* www.ups.com/sef						
UPS Supply Chain Solutions						
12380 Morris Rd	Alpharetta	GA	30005	913-693-6151		449
TF: 800-742-5727 ■ *Web:* www.ups-scs.com						
Upsher-Smith Laboratories Inc						
6701 Evenstad Dr	Maple Grove	MN	55369	763-315-2000	315-2001	582
TF: 800-654-2299 ■ *Web:* www.upsher-smith.com						
Upshur County 40 W Main St Rm 101	Buckhannon	WV	26201	304-472-1068		338
Web: www.upshurcounty.org						
Upshur County PO Box 730	Gilmer	TX	75644	903-843-4015	843-4504	338
Web: www.countyofupshur.com						
Upshur County Library 702 W Tyler St	Gilmer	TX	75644	903-843-5001	843-3995	434-3
Web: countyofupshur.com						
Upson County 106 E Lee St Ste 110	Thomaston	GA	30286	706-647-7012	647-7030	338
Web: upsoncountyga.org						
Upson County Electric Membership Corp						
607 E Main St	Thomaston	GA	30286	706-647-5475		245
Web: www.upsonemc.com						
Upson Regional Medical Ctr						
801 W Gordon St	Thomaston	GA	30286	706-647-8111		374-3
Web: www.urmc.org						
Upstairs Jazz Bar & Grill						
1254 MacKay St	Montreal	QC	H3G2H4	514-931-6808		671
Web: www.upstairsjazz.com						
Upstairs Restaurant, The						
4500 Mahoning Ave	Youngstown	OH	44515	330-793-5577		671
Web: theupstairsrestaurant.com						
Upstate Carolina Medical Ctr						
1530 N Limestone St	Gaffney	SC	29340	864-487-4271		374-3
Web: novanthealth.org/gaffneymedicalcenter.aspx						
Upstate Correctional Facility						
309 Bare Hill Rd PO Box 2000	Malone	NY	12953	518-483-6997		213
Web: www.doccs.ny.gov/faclist.html						
Upstate New York Transplant Services Inc						
110 Broadway	Buffalo	NY	14203	716-853-6667	853-6674	269
TF: 800-227-4771 ■ *Web:* www.unyts.org						
Upstate Pharmacy Ltd						
40 N America Dr	West Seneca	NY	14224	716-675-3704		237
Web: www.upstatepharmacy.com						
Upstate Shredding LLC						
1 Recycle Dr Tioga Industrial Pk	Owego	NY	13827	607-687-7777	687-7746	686
TF: 800-245-3133 ■ *Web:* www.upstateshredding.com						
Upstate Tours & Travel						
207 Geyser Rd	Saratoga Springs	NY	12866	518-584-5252	584-1092	760
TF: 800-237-5252 ■ *Web:* www.upstatetours.com						
Upstate University Hospital at Community General						
4900 Broad Rd	Syracuse	NY	13215	315-492-5011	492-5418	374-3
Web: upstate.edu						
Upstream						
Harper's Restaurant Group						
6902 Phillips Pl Ct	Charlotte	NC	28210	704-556-7730		671
Web: www.harpersgroup.com/upstream.asp						
Upstream Brewing Co 514 S 11th St	Omaha	NE	68102	402-344-0200	344-0451	671
TF: 800-342-3352 ■ *Web:* www.upstreambrewing.com						
Upstream Communications Gp LLC						
1609 shoal creek blvd Ste 203	Austin	TX	78701	512-583-7134		224
Web: getupstream.com						
Uptick Marketing Inc						
201 Summit Pkwy	Birmingham	AL	35209	205-823-4440		225
TF: 800-419-8620 ■ *Web:* www.infomedia.com						
Uptime Group Inc, The						
200 Violet St Ste 150	Golden	CO	80401	303-757-4611		193
Uptime Solutions Professional Services Group Inc						
3807 Gaskins Rd	Richmond	VA	23233	804-836-1490		180
TF: 800-559-6036 ■ *Web:* www.uptimesolutions.com						
Up-To-Date Laundry Inc						
1221 Desoto Rd	Baltimore	MD	21223	410-646-0475		426
Web: www.uptodatelaundry.net						
Upton County 205 E Tenth St	Rankin	TX	79778	432-693-2861	693-2129	338
TF: 800-680-9052 ■ *Web:* co.upton.tx.us						
Upton Financial Group Inc						
131 Stony Cir Ste 500	Santa Rosa	CA	95401	707-523-9651		528
Web: www.uptonco.com						
Upton Fred (Rep R - MI)						
2183 Rayburn Bldg	Washington	DC	20515	202-225-3761	225-4986	342-2
Web: upton.house.gov						
Upton State Forest 205 Westboro Rd	Upton	MA	01568	508-278-6486		565
Web: www.mass.gov						
Uptown Buffet 1050 N Military Hwy	Norfolk	VA	23502	757-893-9293		671
Uptown Cafe 1624 BaRdstown Rd	Louisville	KY	40205	502-458-4212		671
Web: www.uptownlouisville.com						
Uptown, The 102 E Kirkwood Ave	Bloomington	IN	47408	812-339-0900		671
Web: www.the-uptown.com						
Upturn Industries Inc						
2-4 Whitney Way	Bainbridge	NY	13733	607-967-2923		454
Web: www.upturnindustries.com						
Upturn Solutions Inc						
1396 Riverside Rd	Bigfork	MT	59911	866-891-4363		612
TF: 866-891-4363 ■ *Web:* www.sprocketcmms.com						
Upword Search Marketing Llc						
10 Milk St Ste 306	Boston	MA	02108	617-956-4025		195
TF: 800-914-2441 ■ *Web:* www.upwordsem.com						
UQM Technologies Inc						
4120 Specialty Pl	Longmont	CO	80504	303-682-4900	682-4901	518
NYSE: UQM ■ *Web:* www.uqm.com						
URA (Universities Research Assn Inc)						
1140 19th St NW Ste 900	Washington	DC	20036	202-293-1382	293-5012	49-19
Web: www.ura-hq.org						
URAC 1220 L St NW Ste 400	Washington	DC	20005	202-216-9010	216-9006	48-1
Web: www.urac.org						
Urania Engineering Company Inc						
198 S Poplar St	Hazleton	PA	18201	570-455-7531		350
TF: 800-533-1985 ■ *Web:* www.uraniaeng.com						
Uranium Resources Inc						
405 State Hwy 121 Bypass A-110	Lewisville	TX	75067	972-219-3330		502
NASDAQ: URRE ■ *Web:* www.uraniumresources.com						
Urbahn Architects 49 W 37th St 6th Fl	New York	NY	10018	212-239-0220		261
Web: www.urbahn.com						
Urban Alternative PO Box 4000	Dallas	TX	75208	214-943-3868		48-20
TF: 800-800-3222 ■ *Web:* www.tonyevans.org						
Urban Barn Ltd 4085 Marine Way Ste 1	Burnaby	BC	V5J5E2	604-456-2200		321
TF: 844-456-2200 ■ *Web:* www.urbanbarn.com						
Urban Bush Women						
138 S Oxford St Ste 4B	Brooklyn	NY	11217	718-398-4537	398-4783	573-1
Web: www.urbanbushwomen.org						
Urban Cafe 1212 E Apache Blvd	Tempe	AZ	85281	480-968-8888		671
Web: www.theurbancafe.com						
Urban Call Magazine						
4265 Brownsboro Rd Ste 225	Winston-Salem	NC	27106	336-759-7477	759-7212	457-21
Web: www.theurbancall.com						
Urban Concrete Contractors Ltd						
24114 Blanco Rd	San Antonio	TX	78258	210-490-0090	490-1505	187
Web: www.urbanconcrete.com						
Urban Data Solutions Inc						
589 Eighth Ave 15th Fl	New York	NY	10018	212-931-6330		737
Web: www.u-data.com						
Urban Decay 833 W 16th St	Newport Beach	CA	92663	949-631-4504		214
TF: 800-784-8722 ■ *Web:* www.urbandecay.com						
Urban Engineers Inc						
530 Walnut St 14th Fl	Philadelphia	PA	19106	215-922-8080	922-8082	261
Web: www.urbanengineers.com						
Urban Foundation/Engineering LLC						
32-33 111th St	East Elmhurst	NY	11369	718-478-3021	899-4967	189-5
TF: 877-395-5459						
Urban Futures Inc						
3111 N Tustin St Ste 230	Orange	CA	92865	714-283-9334		463
TF: 800-755-6864 ■ *Web:* www.urbanfuturesinc.com						
Urban Icons Marketing Inc						
46 NW 36th St Loft 4	Miami	FL	33127	305-438-0107		466
Web: www.urbaniconsmarketing.com						
Urban Insight Inc						
3530 Wilshire Blvd Ste 1285	Los Angeles	CA	90010	213-792-2000		180
TF: 800-790-8444 ■ *Web:* urbaninsight.com						
Urban Institute 2100 M St NW	Washington	DC	20037	202-833-7200		634
TF: 866-518-3874 ■ *Web:* www.urban.org						
Urban Land Institute (ULI)						
1025 Thomas Jefferson St NW Ste 500W	Washington	DC	20007	202-624-7000	624-7140	48-8
TF Orders: 800-321-5011 ■ *Web:* www.uli.org						
Urban Libraries Council (ULC)						
1333 H St NW Ste 1000	West Washington	DC	20005	202-750-8650		49-11
Web: www.urbanlibraries.org						
Urban Manufacturing Inc						
1288 Hickory St	Pewaukee	WI	53072	262-691-2455	691-8938	454
Web: www.urban-mfg.com						
Urban Onion 116 Legion Way SE	Olympia	WA	98501	360-943-9242		671
Urban Outfitters Inc						
30 Industrial Pk Blvd	Trenton	SC	29847	800-282-2200		157-4
TF: 800-282-2200 ■ *Web:* www.urbanoutfitters.com						
Urban Retail Properties Co						
111 E Wacker Dr Ste 2400	Chicago	IL	60601	312-915-2000		655
Web: www.urbanretail.com						
Urban Science						
400 Renaissance Ctr Ste 2900	Detroit	MI	48243	313-259-9900	259-9901	194
TF: 800-321-6900 ■ *Web:* www.urbanscience.com						
Urban Sports & Entertainment						
19600 W Catawba Ave Ste C301	Cornelius	NC	28031	704-894-0025		506
Urban Strategies LLC						
2341 Ninth St S PO Box 41408	Arlington	VA	22204	202-368-3408		196
Web: www.urbanstrategies.us						

					Phone	Fax	Class
Urban Transport News							
65 E Wacker Pl Ste 400	Chicago	IL	60601		312-782-3900	782-3901	531-13
Web: www.highbeam.com							
Urban Web Design 102-19 Dallas Rd	Victoria	BC	V8V5A6		250-380-1296		225
TF: 877-889-2573 ■ *Web:* urbanweb.net							
Urbana Free Library 210 W Green St	Urbana	IL	61801		217-367-4057	367-4061	434-3
Web: www.urbanafreelibrary.org							
UrbanDaddy Inc 900 Broadway Ste 808	New York	NY	10003		212-929-7905		387
Web: www.urbandaddy.com							
Urbandale Chamber of Commerce							
3600 NW 86th St	Urbandale	IA	50322		515-331-6855	331-2987	139
Web: uniquelyurbandale.com							
Urbandale Public Library							
3520 86th St	Urbandale	IA	50322		515-278-3945	278-3918	434-3
Web: www.urbandalelibrary.org							
Urdang Capital Management Inc							
630 W Germantown Pk Ste 300	Plymouth Meeting	PA	19462		610-834-9500		652
Web: www.centersquare.com							
URELL Inc 86 Coolidge Ave	Watertown	MA	02471		617-923-9500		791
Web: www.urell.com							
Urgo Hotels LP							
6710A Rockledge Dr Ste 420	Bethesda	MD	20817		301-657-2130		707
Web: www.urgohotels.com							
URI (University of Rhode Island)							
45 Upper College Rd	Kingston	RI	02881		401-874-1000	874-5523	166
Web: ww2.uri.edu							
Uri Inc 3542 Hayden Ave Ste 110	Torrance	CA	90501		310-360-1212		7
Web: uriglobal.com							
Uricchio's Trattoria 1400 17th St	Bakersfield	CA	93301		661-326-8870		671
Web: www.uricchios.com							
Urick Foundry Co 1501 Cherry St	Erie	PA	16502		814-454-2461	454-1397	307
Web: www.urick.net							
Urigen Pharmaceuticals							
675 US Hwy 1 Ste B206	North Brunswick	NJ	08902		732-640-0160	280-2861*	85
**Fax Area Code:* 925 ■ *Web:* www.urigen.com							
Uriman Inc 650 N Puente St	Brea	CA	92821		714-257-2080		61
Web: www.uriman.com							
Urish Popeck & Co							
3 Gateway Ctr Ste 2400	Pittsburgh	PA	15222		412-391-1994		2
Web: www.urishpopeck.com							
Urologix Inc 14405 21st Ave N	Minneapolis	MN	55447		763-475-1400		476
TF: 800-475-1403 ■ *Web:* www.urologix.com							
Urology Healthcare Group Inc							
720 Cool Springs Blvd Ste 500	Franklin	TN	37067		615-261-6700		194
TF: 888-232-7026 ■ *Web:* www.cimplify.net							
Urology of Indiana LLC							
679 E County Line Rd	Greenwood	IN	46143		317-885-1250		374-3
Web: www.urologyin.com							
Urpan Technologies Inc							
341 Cobalt Way Ste 208	Sunnyvale	CA	94085		408-245-0006		260
TF: 800-896-7140 ■ *Web:* www.urpantech.com							
Ursa Farmers Co-op Inc							
202 W Maple Ave PO Box 8	Ursa	IL	62376		217-964-2111	964-2200	447
Web: www.ursacoop.com							
Ursa Institute							
390 Fourth St Fl 1	San Francisco	CA	94107		415-777-1922		196
Web: www.cus-united.org							
Ursa Navigation Solutions Inc							
85 Rangeway Rd							
Ste 110, Building Three	North Billerica	VA	01862		781-538-5299		261
Web: ursanav.com							
Urschel Laboratories Inc							
2503 Calumet Ave PO Box 2200	Valparaiso	IN	46384		219-464-4811	462-3879	298
TF: 844-877-2435 ■ *Web:* www.urschel.com							
Urshan Graduate School of Theology							
704 Howder Shell Rd	Florissant	MO	63031		314-921-9290	921-9203	167-3
Web: www.ugst.edu							
Ursinus College							
601 E Main St PO Box 1000	Collegeville	PA	19426		610-409-3200	409-3662*	166
**Fax:* Admissions ■ *TF:* 877-448-3282 ■ *Web:* www.ursinus.edu							
Urstadt Biddle Properties Inc							
321 Railroad Ave	Greenwich	CT	06830		203-863-8200	861-6755	655
NYSE: UBA ■ *Web:* www.ubproperties.com							
Ursula of Switzerland Inc							
31 Mohawk Ave	Waterford	NY	12188		800-826-4041	237-3038*	155-21
**Fax Area Code:* 518 ■ *TF:* 800-826-4041 ■ *Web:* www.ursula.com							
Ursuline College 2550 Lander Rd	Pepper Pike	OH	44124		440-449-4200	684-6138*	166
**Fax:* Admissions ■ *TF:* 888-778-5463 ■ *Web:* www.ursuline.edu							
Uruguay 866 UN Plaza Ste 322	New York	NY	10017		212-752-8240	593-0935	784
Web: www.un.int/uruguay							
Consulate General							
429 Santa Monica Blvd Ste 400	Santa Monica	CA	90401		310-394-5777	394-5140	257
Web: www.conurula.org							
Embassy 1913 'I' St NW	Washington	DC	20006		202-331-1313	331-8142	257
Web: www.mrree.gub.uy/frontend/page?1,7,442,P,S,0							
Urwiler & Walter Inc 3126 Main St	Sumneytown	PA	18084		215-234-4562		261
Web: urwilerwalter.com							
US 13 Grill & Catering							
1115 S Governors Ave	Dover	DE	19904		302-730-3551		671
US Acrylic Inc 1320 Harris Rd	Libertyville	IL	60048		847-837-4800		607
Web: www.usacrylic.com							
Us Adventure Rv 5120 n brady st	Davenport	IA	52806		877-768-4678		23
TF: 877-768-4678 ■ *Web:* www.usadventurerv.com							
US Agency for International Development (USAID)							
1300 Pennsylvania Ave NW	Washington	DC	20523		202-712-0000	216-3524	340-20
Web: www.usaid.gov							
US Air Force Academy (USAFA)							
2304 Cadet Dr Ste 2300	Air Force Academy	CO	80840		719-333-1110	333-3644	498
TF: 800-443-9266 ■ *Web:* www.usafa.af.mil							
US Air Force Medical Ctr Keesler 81st Medical Group							
301 Fisher St	Keesler AFB	MS	39534		228-376-5571	376-0083	374-4
Web: www.keesler.af.mil							
US Airconditioning Distributors							
16900 Chestnut St	City of Industry	CA	91748		626-854-4500	854-4690*	612
**Fax:* Sales ■ *TF:* 800-937-7222 ■ *Web:* www.us-ac.com							
Us Airport Parking							
18000 E 81st Ave	Commerce City	CO	80022		303-371-7575		562
Web: www.usairportparking.com							
US Allegiance Inc 63075 NE 18th St	Bend	OR	97701		541-330-6282		130
US Alliance Federal Credit Union							
411 Theodore Fremd Ave Ste 350	Rye	NY	10580		800-431-2754	881-3464*	219
**Fax Area Code:* 914 ■ *TF:* 800-431-2754 ■ *Web:* usalliance.org							
US Alliance Group Inc							
30052 Aventura Ste B	Rancho Santa Margarita	CA	92688		949-888-4408		225
Web: www.usag-inc.com							
US Alliance Paper 101 Heartland Blvd	Edgewood	NY	11717		631-254-3030		558
Web: www.usalliancepaper.com							
US Apple Assn							
8233 Old Courthouse Rd Ste 200	Vienna	VA	22182		703-442-8850	790-0845	48-2
TF: 800-781-4443 ■ *Web:* www.usapple.org							
US Arctic Research Commission							
4350 N Fairfax Dr Ste 510	Arlington	VA	22203		703-525-0111	525-0114	340-20
Web: www.arctic.gov							
US Army Aeromedical Research Laboratory							
PO Box 620577	Fort Rucker	AL	36362		334-255-6920		668
Web: www.usaarl.army.mil							
US Army Armament Research Development & Engineering Ctr (ARDEC)							
Technical & Industrial Liaison Officer	Picatinny	NJ	07806		973-724-9623	328-2996	668
Web: www.pica.army.mil							
US Army Aviation Learning Center							
9204 Fifth Ave Bldg 131	Fort Rucker	AL	36362		334-255-2776	255-1004	497-2
Web: www.rucker.army.mil/usaace							
US Army Basic Combat Training Museum							
4442 Ft Jackson Blvd	Columbia	SC	29209		803-751-7419		520
Web: goarmy.com							
US Army Corps of Engineers							
441 G St NW	Washington	DC	20314		202-761-0010	761-1803	340-5
Web: www.usace.army.mil							
US Army Corps of Engineers Institute for Water Resources							
Hydrologic Engineering Ctr							
609 Second St	Davis	CA	95616		530-756-1104	756-8250	668
Web: www.hec.usace.army.mil							
US Army Corps of Engineers Regional Offices							
Great Lakes & Ohio River Div							
550 Main St	Cincinnati	OH	45202		513-684-3010		340-5
Web: www.lrd.usace.army.mil							
Mississippi Valley Div							
1400 Walnut St	Vicksburg	MS	39180		601-634-7783		340-5
Web: www.mvd.usace.army.mil							
North Atlantic Div							
302 General Lee Ave Fort Hamilton	Brooklyn	NY	11252		347-370-4550		340-5
Web: www.nad.usace.army.mil							
Northwestern Div 1201 NE Lyod Blvd	Portland	OR	97232		503-808-3700	808-3706	340-5
Web: www.nwd.usace.army.mil							
Pacific Ocean Div							
Fort Shafter Bldg 525	Honolulu	HI	96858		808-438-8319		340-5
Web: www.pod.usace.army.mil							
South Atlantic Div							
60 Forsyth St SW Rm 9M15	Atlanta	GA	30303		404-562-5011		340-5
Web: www.sad.usace.army.mil							
South Pacific Div							
1455 Market St	San Francisco	CA	94103		415-503-6514		340-5
Web: www.spd.usace.army.mil							
Southwestern Div 1100 Commerce St	Dallas	TX	75242		469-487-7007		340-5
Web: www.swd.usace.army.mil							
US Army Criminal Investigation Command							
27130 Telegraph Rd Russell Knox Bldg	Quantico	VA	22134		571-305-4009		340-5
Web: www.cid.army.mil							
US Army Engineer Research & Development Ctr (ERDC)							
3909 Halls Ferry Rd	Vicksburg	MS	39180		601-634-3188		668
Web: www.erdc.usace.army.mil							
US Army Forces Command							
4700 Knox St	Fort Bragg	NC	28310		910-570-7200		340-5
US Army Institute of Surgical Research (USAISR)							
3698 Chambers Pass Ste B	Fort Sam Houston	TX	78234		210-539-3219	227-8502	668
Web: www.usaisr.amedd.army.mil							
US Army Intelligence & Security Command							
8825 Beulah St	Fort Belvoir	VA	22060		703-428-4965		340-5
Web: www.inscom.army.mil							
US Army Medical Research & Materiel Command (USAMRMC)							
820 Chandler St	Fort Detrick	MD	21702		301-619-2471		668
Web: www.mrmc.smallbusopps.army.mil							
US Army Medical Research Institute of Chemical Defense (USAMRICD)							
3100 Ricketts Point Rd	Aberdeen Proving Ground	MD	21010		410-436-3276	436-1960	668
Web: usamricd.apgea.army.mil							
US Army Medical Research Institute of Infectious Diseases (USAMRIID)							
1425 Porter St	Frederick	MD	21702		301-619-2285		668
Web: www.usamriid.army.mil							
US Army Museum of Hawaii PO Box 8064	Honolulu	HI	96830		808-438-2821	941-3617	520
TF: 800-552-3978 ■ *Web:* www.hiarmymuseumsoc.org							
US Army Research Laboratory (ARL)							
Attn: AMSRD-ARL-O-PA 2800 Powder Mill Rd	Adelphi	MD	20783		301-394-2500	394-1174	668
Web: www.arl.army.mil							
US Army Special Operations Command (USASOC)							
2929 Desert Storm Dr	Fort Bragg	NC	28310		910-432-6005		340-5
Web: www.soc.mil							
US Army Transportation Museum							
300 Washington Blvd	Fort Eustis	VA	23604		757-878-1115		520
TF: 800-581-7245 ■ *Web:* www.transchool.lee.army.mil							
US Army War College 122 Forbes Ave	Carlisle	PA	17013		717-245-3131		340-5
TF: 800-453-0992 ■ *Web:* www.carlisle.army.mil							
US Army Yuma Proving Ground							
301 C St Bldg 300	Yuma	AZ	85365		928-328-2163		743
Us Art Company Inc							
66 Pacella Park Dr	Randolph	MA	02368		781-986-6500		522
TF: 800-872-7826 ■ *Web:* www.usart.com							
US Axle Inc 275 Shoemaker Rd	Pottstown	PA	19464		610-323-3800		54
TF: 800-327-2258 ■ *Web:* www.usaxle.com							
US Balloon Mfg Company Inc							
140 58th St	Brooklyn	NY	11220		718-492-9700	492-8711	328
TF: 800-285-4000							
US Bancorp 800 Nicollet Mall	Minneapolis	MN	55402		651-466-3000		360-2
NYSE: USB ■ *TF Cust Svc:* 800-872-2657 ■ *Web:* www.usbank.com							
US Bank NA 1900 N University Dr	Fargo	ND	58102		701-280-3547		70
Web: www.usbank.com							
US Bankruptcy Court							
Alabama Middle 1 Church St	Montgomery	AL	36104		334-954-3800	954-3819	341-2
Web: www.almb.uscourts.gov							

Court / Address	City	State	Zip	Phone	Fax	Class
Alabama Northern 1800 Fifth Ave N Rm 120 *Web:* www.alnb.uscourts.gov	Birmingham	AL	35203	205-714-4000		341-2
Alabama Southern 201 St Louis St *Web:* www.alsb.uscourts.gov	Mobile	AL	36602	251-441-5391	441-6286	341-2
Alaska 605 W Fourth Ave Ste 138 *TF:* 800-859-8059 ■ *Web:* www.akb.uscourts.gov	Anchorage	AK	99501	907-271-2655		341-2
Arizona 230 N First Ave Ste 101 *TF:* 800-556-9230 ■ *Web:* www.azb.uscourts.gov	Phoenix	AZ	85003	602-682-4000		341-2
Arkansas 300 W Second St *TF:* 800-676-6856 ■ *Web:* www.arb.uscourts.gov	Little Rock	AR	72201	501-918-5500	918-5520	341-2
California Central 255 E Temple St *Web:* www.cacb.uscourts.gov	Los Angeles	CA	90012	213-894-3118		341-2
California Eastern 501 'I' St Ste 3-200 *Web:* www.caeb.uscourts.gov	Sacramento	CA	95814	916-930-4400		341-2
California Northern 450 Golden Gate Ave PO Box 36099 *Web:* www.canb.uscourts.gov	San Francisco	CA	94102	415-268-2300		341-2
California Southern 325 W F St *TF:* 800-676-6856 ■ *Web:* www.casb.uscourts.gov	San Diego	CA	92101	619-557-5620		341-2
Central District of Illinois 600 E Monroe St Rm 226 *Web:* www.ilcb.uscourts.gov	Springfield	IL	62701	217-492-4551	492-4556	341-2
Colorado US Custom House 721 19th St *Web:* www.cob.uscourts.gov	Denver	CO	80202	720-904-7300		341-2
Connecticut 450 Main St 7th Fl *TF:* 800-676-6856 ■ *Web:* www.ctb.uscourts.gov	Hartford	CT	06103	860-240-3675		341-2
Delaware 824 N Market St 3rd Fl *Web:* www.deb.uscourts.gov	Wilmington	DE	19801	302-252-2900		341-2
District of Columbia 333 Constitution Ave NW *Web:* www.dcb.uscourts.gov	Washington	DC	20001	202-354-3280		341-2
District of Hawaii 1132 Bishop St *Web:* www.hib.uscourts.gov	Honolulu	HI	96813	808-522-8100	522-8120	341-2
District of Vermont 151 West St *Web:* www.vtb.uscourts.gov	Rutland	VT	05701	802-776-2000	776-2020	341-2
Eastern District of Tennessee 800 Market St Ste 330 *Web:* www.tneb.uscourts.gov	Knoxville	TN	37902	865-545-4279		341-2
Eastern District of Texas 110 N College Ave 9th Fl *Web:* www.txeb.uscourts.gov	Tyler	TX	75702	903-590-3200		341-2
Eastern District of Washington 904 W Riverside Ave Ste 304 *TF:* 800-519-2549 ■ *Web:* www.waeb.uscourts.gov	Spokane	WA	99201	509-458-5300		341-2
Florida Middle 801 N Florida Ave Ste 727 *TF:* 800-676-6856 ■ *Web:* www.flmb.uscourts.gov	Tampa	FL	33602	813-301-5162		341-2
Florida Northern 110 E Pk Ave Ste 100 *TF:* 888-765-1752 ■ *Web:* www.flnb.uscourts.gov	Tallahassee	FL	32301	850-521-5001		341-2
Florida Southern 51 SW First Ave *Web:* www.flsb.uscourts.gov	Miami	FL	33130	305-714-1800		341-2
Georgia Middle 433 Cherry St *Web:* www.gamb.uscourts.gov	Macon	GA	31201	478-752-3506		341-2
Georgia Northern 75 Spring St SW *TF:* 800-676-6856 ■ *Web:* www.ganb.uscourts.gov	Atlanta	GA	30303	404-215-1000		341-2
Georgia Southern 125 Bull St *TF:* 800-676-6856 ■ *Web:* www.gasb.uscourts.gov	Savannah	GA	31401	912-650-4100		341-2
Idaho 550 W Fort St *Web:* www.id.uscourts.gov	Boise	ID	83724	208-334-1074		341-2
Illinois Southern 750 Missouri Ave *TF:* 800-859-7375 ■ *Web:* www.ilsb.uscourts.gov	East Saint Louis	IL	62201	618-482-9400		341-2
Indiana Northern 401 S Michigan St *Web:* www.innb.uscourts.gov	South Bend	IN	46601	574-968-2100		341-2
Indiana Southern 46 E Ohio St *Web:* www.insb.uscourts.gov	Indianapolis	IN	46204	317-229-3800	229-3801	341-2
Kansas 401 N Market St Rm 167 *Web:* www.ksb.uscourts.gov	Wichita	KS	67202	316-269-6637		341-2
Kentucky Eastern 100 E Vine St Ste 200 *TF:* 800-676-6856 ■ *Web:* www.kyeb.uscourts.gov	Lexington	KY	40507	859-233-2608		341-2
Kentucky Western 601 W Broadway Ste 450 *Web:* www.kywb.uscourts.gov	Louisville	KY	40202	502-627-5700		341-2
Louisiana Eastern 500 Poydras St Ste B-601 *TF:* 800-676-6856 ■ *Web:* www.laeb.uscourts.gov	New Orleans	LA	70130	504-589-7878		341-2
Louisiana Middle 707 Florida St Ste 119 *Web:* www.lamb.uscourts.gov	Baton Rouge	LA	70801	225-346-3333		341-2
Louisiana Western 300 Fannin St Ste 2201 *TF:* 866-721-2105 ■ *Web:* www.lawb.uscourts.gov	Shreveport	LA	71101	318-676-4267		341-2
Maine 537 Congress St 2nd Fl *Web:* www.meb.uscourts.gov	Portland	ME	04101	207-780-3482	780-3679	341-2
Massachusetts 5 Post Office Sq *Web:* www.mab.uscourts.gov/mab	Boston	MA	02109	617-748-5300		341-2
Michigan Eastern 211 W Fort St Ste 2100 *TF:* 800-676-6856 ■ *Web:* www.mieb.uscourts.gov	Detroit	MI	48226	313-234-0065		341-2
Michigan Western 1 Div Ave N Rm 200 *TF:* 800-859-7375 ■ *Web:* www.miwb.uscourts.gov	Grand Rapids	MI	49503	616-456-2693		341-2
Minnesota 300 S Fourth St 301 US Courthouse *TF:* 866-260-7337 ■ *Web:* www.mnb.uscourts.gov	Minneapolis	MN	55415	612-664-5260		341-2
Mississippi Northern 703 Hwy 145 N *Web:* www.msnb.uscourts.gov	Aberdeen	MS	39730	662-369-2596		341-2
Mississippi Southern 501 E Court St Ste 2 300 *Web:* www.mssb.uscourts.gov	Jackson	MS	39201	601-608-4600		341-2
Missouri Eastern 111 S Tenth St 4th Fl *TF:* 866-803-9517 ■ *Web:* www.moeb.uscourts.gov	Saint Louis	MO	63102	314-244-4500	244-4990	341-2
Missouri Western 400 E Ninth St Rm1510 *Web:* www.mow.uscourts.gov	Kansas City	MO	64106	816-512-1800		341-2
Montana 400 N Main St *TF:* 888-888-2530 ■ *Web:* www.mtb.uscourts.gov	Butte	MT	59701	406-497-1240		341-2
Nebraska 111 S 18th Plaza Ste 1125 *Web:* www.neb.uscourts.gov	Omaha	NE	68102	402-661-7444		341-2
Nevada 300 Las Vegas Blvd S *Web:* www.nvb.uscourts.gov	Las Vegas	NV	89101	702-527-7000		341-2
New Hampshire 1000 Elm St Ste 1001 *Web:* www.nhb.uscourts.gov	Manchester	NH	03101	603-222-2600	222-2697	341-2
New Jersey PO Box 1352 *Web:* www.njb.uscourts.gov	Newark	NJ	07102	973-645-4764		341-2
New Mexico 333 Lomas Blvd NW *Web:* www.nmd.uscourts.gov	Albuquerque	NM	87102	505-348-2000	348-2028	341-2
New York Eastern 271 Cadman Plaza E *TF:* 800-676-6856 ■ *Web:* www.nyeb.uscourts.gov	Brooklyn	NY	11201	347-394-1700		341-2
North Carolina Eastern 1760-A Parkwood Blvd *Web:* www.nceb.uscourts.gov	Wilson	NC	27893	252-237-0248		341-2
North Carolina Middle 101 S Edgeworth St Fl 1 *TF:* 800-859-7375 ■ *Web:* www.ncmb.uscourts.gov	Greensboro	NC	27401	336-358-4000		341-2
North Carolina Western 401 W Trade St Rm 111 *Web:* www.ncwb.uscourts.gov	Charlotte	NC	28202	704-350-7500		341-2
North Dakota 655 First Ave N Ste 210 *TF:* 800-859-7375 ■ *Web:* www.ndb.uscourts.gov	Fargo	ND	58102	701-297-7100		341-2
Northern District of Illinois 219 S Dearborn St *Web:* www.ilnb.uscourts.gov	Chicago	IL	60604	312-435-5694		341-2
Northern District of Iowa 111 Seventh Ave SE 6th Fl *TF:* 866-222-8029 ■ *Web:* www.ianb.uscourts.gov	Cedar Rapids	IA	52401	319-286-2200	286-2280	341-2
Northern District of New York 445 Broadway Ste 330 *Web:* www.nynb.uscourts.gov	Albany	NY	12207	518-257-1661		341-2
Northern district of ohio 201 Superior Ave *Web:* www.ohnb.uscourts.gov	Cleveland	OH	44114	216-615-4300		341-2
Ohio Southern 120 W Third St *Web:* www.ohsb.uscourts.gov	Dayton	OH	45402	937-225-2516		341-2
Oklahoma Eastern 111 W Fourth St PO Box 1347 *Web:* www.okeb.uscourts.gov	Okmulgee	OK	74447	918-758-0126		341-2
Oklahoma Northern 224 S Boulder Ave Rm 105 *Web:* www.oknb.uscourts.gov	Tulsa	OK	74103	918-699-4000		341-2
Oklahoma Western 215 Dean A McGee Ave *TF:* 800-676-6856 ■ *Web:* www.okwb.uscourts.gov	Oklahoma City	OK	73102	405-609-5700		341-2
Oregon 1001 SW Fifth Ave Rm 700 *TF:* 800-676-6856 ■ *Web:* www.orb.uscourts.gov	Portland	OR	97204	503-326-1500		341-2
Pennsylvania Eastern 900 Market St Ste 400 *Web:* www.paeb.uscourts.gov	Philadelphia	PA	19107	215-408-2800		341-2
Pennsylvania Middle 197 S Main St *TF:* 877-298-2053 ■ *Web:* www.pamb.uscourts.gov	Wilkes-Barre	PA	18701	570-831-2500	829-0249	341-2
Pennsylvania Western 5414 US Steel Tower 600 Grant St *TF:* 800-676-6856 ■ *Web:* www.pawb.uscourts.gov	Pittsburgh	PA	15219	412-644-2700	644-6512	341-2
Puerto Rico 300 Calle Del Recinto Sur *TF:* 800-676-6856 ■ *Web:* www.prb.uscourts.gov	San Juan	PR	00901	787-977-6000	977-6008	341-2
South Carolina 1100 Laurel St *Web:* www.scb.uscourts.gov	Columbia	SC	29201	803-765-5436		341-2
South Dakota 400 S Phillips Ave Rm 104 *Web:* www.sdb.uscourts.gov	Sioux Falls	SD	57104	605-357-2430	357-2401	341-2
Southern District of Iowa 110 E Court Ave Ste 300 *Web:* www.iasb.uscourts.gov	Des Moines	IA	50309	515-284-6230	284-6303	341-2
Southern District of New York 1 Bowling Green *Web:* www.nysb.uscourts.gov	New York	NY	10004	212-668-2870		341-2
Tennessee Middle 701 Broadway Rm 170 *Web:* www.tnmb.uscourts.gov	Nashville	TN	37203	615-736-5584		341-2
Tennessee Western 200 Jefferson Ave Ste 413 *TF:* 800-406-0190 ■ *Web:* www.tnwb.uscourts.gov	Memphis	TN	38103	901-328-3500		341-2
Texas Northern 1100 Commerce St Rm 1254 *TF:* 800-442-6850 ■ *Web:* www.txnb.uscourts.gov	Dallas	TX	75242	214-753-2000		341-2
Texas Southern 515 Rusk St Rm 5300 *Web:* www.txs.uscourts.gov	Houston	TX	77002	713-250-5500		341-2
Utah 350 S Main St Rm 301 *Web:* www.utb.uscourts.gov	Salt Lake City	UT	84101	801-524-6687	524-4409	341-2
Virginia Eastern 200 S Washington St *Web:* www.vaeb.uscourts.gov	Alexandria	VA	22314	804-916-2400		341-2
Virginia Western 210 Church Ave SW Rm 200 *Web:* www.vawb.uscourts.gov	Roanoke	VA	24011	540-857-2391		341-2
Washington Western 700 Stewart St Ste 6301 *TF:* 800-676-6856 ■ *Web:* www.wawb.uscourts.gov	Seattle	WA	98101	206-370-5200		341-2
West Virginia Northern 1125 Chapline St PO Box 70 *Web:* www.wvnb.uscourts.gov	Wheeling	WV	26003	304-233-1655	233-0185	341-2
West Virginia Southern 300 Virginia St E Rm 3200 *TF:* 800-685-1111 ■ *Web:* www.wvsb.uscourts.gov	Charleston	WV	25301	304-347-3003		341-2
Western District of New York 100 State St *TF:* 800-859-7375 ■ *Web:* www.nywb.uscourts.gov	Rochester	NY	14614	585-613-4200		341-2
Western District of Texas 615 E Houston St Hipolito F Garcia Federal Bldg Rm 597 *Web:* www.txwb.uscourts.gov	San Antonio	TX	78205	210-472-6720	472-5196	341-2

Listing	City	State	Zip	Phone	Fax	Class
Wisconsin Eastern						
US Federal Courthouse						
517 E Wisconsin Ave Rm 126	Milwaukee	WI	53202	414-297-3291		341-2
TF: 877-781-7277 ■ *Web:* www.wieb.uscourts.gov						
Wisconsin Western						
120 N Henry St Rm 340 Rm 340	Madison	WI	53703	608-264-5178		341-2
Web: www.wiwb.uscourts.gov						
Wyoming 2120 Capitol Ave Ste 6004	Cheyenne	WY	82001	307-433-2200		341-2
TF: 800-676-6856 ■ *Web:* www.wyb.uscourts.gov						
US Beverage Net Inc						
225 W Jefferson St	Syracuse	NY	13202	888-298-3641		296
TF: 888-298-3641 ■ *Web:* www.usbeveragenet.com						
US Biathlon Assn						
49 Pineland Dr Ste 301-A	New Gloucester	ME	04260	207-688-6500	688-6505	48-22
TF General: 800-242-8456 ■ *Web:* www.teamusa.org						
US Board on Geographic Names						
12201 Sunrise Valley Dr	Reston	VA	20192	703-648-4552	648-4549	340-13
TF: 800-292-3939 ■ *Web:* geonames.usgs.gov						
US Bobsled & Skeleton Federation (USBSF)						
196 Old Military Rd	Lake Placid	NY	12946	518-523-1842	523-9491	48-22
TF: 888-431-3598 ■ *Web:* www.teamusa.org						
US Botanic Garden 100 Maryland Ave	Washington	DC	20001	202-225-8333		97
Web: www.aoc.gov						
US Box Corp 1296 Mccarter Hwy	Newark	NJ	07104	973-481-2000		561
Web: www.usbox.com						
US Bronze Sign Co						
811 Second Ave	New Hyde Park	NY	11040	516-352-5155	352-1761	777
TF: 800 872 5155 ■ *Web:* www.usbronze.com						
US Button Corp 328 Kennedy Dr	Putnam	CT	06260	860-928-2707	928-2847	594
TF: 800-243-1842 ■ *Web:* www.usbutton.com						
US Cable Corp 28 W Grand Ave Ste 10	Montvale	NJ	07645	201-930-9000		116
US Capital Advisors LLC						
1330 Post Oak Blvd Ste 900	Houston	TX	77056	713-366-0500		401
Web: www.uscallc.com						
US Catholic Magazine 205 W Monroe	Chicago	IL	60606	312-236-7782	236-8207	457-18
TF Cust Svc: 800-328-6515 ■ *Web:* uscatholic.org						
US Cellular Corp (USCC)						
8410 W Bryn Mawr Ave Ste 700	Chicago	IL	60631	773-399-8900		736
NYSE: USM ■ *TF:* 888-944-9400 ■ *Web:* www.uscellular.com						
US Cellular Ctr 370 First Ave E	Cedar Rapids	IA	52401	319-398-5211		205
TF: 800-745-3000 ■ *Web:* www.uscellularcenter.com						
US Cellular Field 333 W 35th St	Chicago	IL	60616	312-674-1000		720
Web: chicago.whitesox.mlb.com/cws/ballpark/index.jsp						
US Census Bureau						
4600 Silver Hill Rd	Washington	DC	20233	301-763-6460		340-2
Web: www.census.gov						
US Census Bureau Regional Offices						
Atlanta 101 Marietta St NW Ste 3200	Atlanta	GA	30303	404-730-3832	730-3835	340-2
TF: 800 424 6974 ■ *Web:* www.census.gov						
Boston 4 Copley Pl Ste 301	Boston	MA	02117	617-424-4501	424-0547	340-2
TF: 800-562-5721 ■ *Web:* www.census.gov						
Chicago 1111 W 22nd St Ste 400	Oak Brook	IL	60523	630-288-9200	288-9288	340-2
TF: 800-865-6384 ■ *Web:* www.census.gov						
Denver 6950 W Jefferson Ave Ste 250	Lakewood	CO	80235	303-264-0202	969-6777	340-2
TF: 800-852-6159 ■ *Web:* www.census.gov						
Los Angeles 15350 Sherman Way Ste 400	Van Nuys	CA	91406	818-267-1700	904-6429	340-2
TF: 800-992-3530 ■ *Web:* www.census.gov/rolax/www						
New York 32 Old Slip 9th Fl	New York	NY	10005	212-584-3400	478-4800	340-2
TF: 800-991-2520 ■ *Web:* www.census.gov/regions						
Philadelphia						
100 S Independence Mall W Ste 410	Philadelphia	PA	19106	215-717-1800	717-0755	340-2
TF: 800-262-4236 ■ *Web:* www.census.gov						
US Chamber of Commerce						
1615 H St NW	Washington	DC	20062	202-659-6000		140
TF: 800-638-6582 ■ *Web:* www.uschamber.com						
US Chemical & Plastics						
600 Nova Dr SE	Massillon	OH	44646	330-830-6000	830-6005	60
TF: 800-321-0672 ■ *Web:* www.uschem.com						
US Chemical Safety & Hazard Investigation Board						
2175 K St NW Ste 400	Washington	DC	20037	202-261-7600	261-7650	340-20
Web: csb.gov						
US Chess Federation PO Box 3967	Crossville	TN	38555	931-787-1234	787-1200	457-14
TF Sales: 800-903-8723 ■ *Web:* new.uschess.org/home						
US Chrome Corp 175 Garfield Ave	Stratford	CT	06615	800-637-9019	386-0067*	481
*Fax Area Code: 203 ■ *TF:* 800-637-9019 ■ *Web:* www.uschrome.com						
US Citizenship & Immigration Services Regional Offices						
Eastern Region						
70 Kimball Ave	South Burlington	VT	05403	800-767-1833		340-11
TF: 800-767-1833 ■ *Web:* www.uscis.gov						
US Coachways Inc						
100 St Mary's Ave Ste 2B	Staten Island	NY	10305	718-477-4242		441
TF: 800-359-5991 ■ *Web:* www.uscoachways.com						
US Coast Guard (USCG)						
2100 Second St SW	Washington	DC	20593	202-372-4620		340-11
Web: www.uscg.mil						
Boating Safety Office						
2703 Martin Luther King Jr Ave SE						
Ste 7501	Washington	DC	20593	202-372-1062		340-11
Web: www.uscgboating.org						
Law Enforcement Office						
2100 Second St SW	Washington	DC	20593	800-982-8813		340-11
TF: 800-982-8813 ■ *Web:* www.uscg.mil/hq/cg5/cg531						
National Maritime Ctr						
100 Forbes Dr	Martinsburg	WV	25404	304-433-3400		340-11
TF: 888-427-5662 ■ *Web:* www.uscg.mil						
National Pollution Funds Ctr						
4200 Wilson Blvd Ste 1000	Arlington	VA	20598	202-493-6700	493-6900	340-11
Web: uscg.mil/ccs/npfc						
Navigation Ctr 7323 Telegraph Rd	Alexandria	VA	22315	703-313-5900	313-5920	340-11
Web: www.navcen.uscg.gov						
Search & Rescue Office						
2100 Second St SW	Washington	DC	20593	202-372-2090	372-2912	340-11
TF: 800-320-4330 ■ *Web:* uscg.mil/hq/cg5/cg534						
US Coast Guard Academy						
15 Mohegan Ave	New London	CT	06320	860-444-8500	701-6700	166
TF: 800-883-8724 ■ *Web:* www.cga.edu						
US Coast Guard Air Station Detroit						
1461 N Perimeter Rd Selfridge ANGB	Selfridge	MI	48045	800-424-8802		158
TF: 800-424-8802 ■ *Web:* www.uscg.mil/d9/airstadetroit						
US Coast Guard Air Station Savannah						
1297 N Lightning Rd	Savannah	GA	31409	912-652-4646		158
Web: www.uscg.mil/d7/airstasavannah						
US Coast Guard Base Honolulu						
400 Sand Island Pkwy	Honolulu	HI	96819	808-842-2062	842-2026	158
Web: www.uscg.mil						
US Coast Guard Chief Petty Officers Assn						
5520-G Hempstead Way	Springfield	VA	22151	703-941-0395	941-0397	48-19
Web: www.uscgcpoa.org						
US Coast Guard Research & Development Ctr						
1082 Shennecossett Rd	Groton	CT	06340	860-441-2600	441-2792	668
Web: www.uscg.mil/hq						
US Cold Storage Inc						
201 Laurel Rd Ste 400 4 Echelon Plz	Voorhees	NJ	08043	856-354-8181	772-1876	803-2
Web: www.uscold.com						
US Commission on Civil Rights						
624 Ninth St NW	Washington	DC	20425	202-376-7700	376-7672	340-20
TF: 800-552-6843 ■ *Web:* www.usccr.gov						
US Commission on Civil Rights Regional Offices						
Central Regional Office						
400 State Ave Ste 908	Kansas City	KS	66101	913-551-1400	551-1413	340-20
TF: 800-552-6843 ■ *Web:* www.usccr.gov						
Eastern Regional Office						
624 Ninth St NW Ste 700	Washington	DC	20425	202-376-7700	376-7672	340-20
TF: 800-552-6843 ■ *Web:* www.usccr.gov						
Midwestern Regional Office						
55 W Monroe St Ste 410	Chicago	IL	60603	312-353-8311	353-8324	340-20
TF: 800-552-6843 ■ *Web:* www.usccr.gov						
Rocky Mountain Regional Office						
1700 Broadway	Denver	CO	80290	303-866-1040	866-1050	340-20
Web: www.usccr.gov						
Southern Regional Office						
61 Forsyth St SW Ste 1840 T	Atlanta	GA	30303	404-562-7000	562-7004	340-20
TF: 800-552-6843 ■ *Web:* www.usccr.gov						
Western Regional Office						
300 N Los Angeles St Ste 2010	Los Angeles	CA	90012	213-894-3437	894-0508	340-20
Web: www.usccr.gov						
US Commission on International Religious Freedom (USCIRF)						
800 N Capitol St NW Ste 790	Washington	DC	20002	202-523-3240	523-5020	340-20
Web: www.uscirf.gov						
US Committee for Refugees & Immigrants (USCRI)						
2231 Crystal Dr Ste 350	Arlington	VA	22202	703-310-1130	769-4241	48-5
Web: www.refugees.org						
US Concrete Inc						
2925 Briarpark Dr Ste 1050	Houston	TX	77042	713-499-6200	499-6201	182
NASDAQ: USCR ■ *Web:* www.us-concrete.com						
US Concrete Precast Group Mid-Atlantic						
3369 Paxtonville Rd	Middleburg	PA	17842	570-837-1774		183
US Conference of Catholic Bishops (USCCB)						
3211 Fourth St NE	Washington	DC	20017	202-541-3000	541-3322	48-20
TF: 866-582-0943 ■ *Web:* www.usccb.org						
US Conference of Mayors						
1620 'I' St NW	Washington	DC	20006	202-293-7330	293-2352	49-7
Web: www.usmayors.org						
US Congress						
Joint Committee on Printing						
1309 Longworth House Office Bldg	Washington	DC	20515	202-225-8281		342-1
Web: cha.house.gov						
Joint Committee on Taxation, The						
502 Ford House Office Bldg	Washington	DC	20515	202-225-3621		342-1
TF: 800-669-6442 ■ *Web:* www.jct.gov						
Joint Economic Committee						
G-01 Dirksen Bldg	Washington	DC	20510	202-224-5171	224-0240	342-1
Web: www.jec.senate.gov						
US Council for International Business (USCIB)						
1212 Ave of the Americas 18th Fl	New York	NY	10036	212-354-4480	575-0327	49-12
Web: www.uscib.org						
District of Columbia Circuit						
333 Constitution Ave NW US Courthouse	Washington	DC	20001	202-216-7000		341-1
Web: www.cadc.uscourts.gov						
Eight Circuit						
111 S Tenth St Rm 22.329	Saint Louis	MO	63102	314-244-2400	244-2780	341-1
Web: www.ca8.uscourts.gov						
Eleventh Circuit 56 Forsyth St NW	Atlanta	GA	30303	404-335-6100	335-6270	341-1
Web: www.ca11.uscourts.gov						
Federal Circuit 717 Madison Pl NW	Washington	DC	20439	202-275-8000		341-1
Web: www.cafc.uscourts.gov						
Fifth Circuit 600 Camp St	New Orleans	LA	70130	504-310-7700		341-1
Web: www.ca5.uscourts.gov						
First Circuit 1 Courthouse Way Ste 2500	Boston	MA	02210	617-748-9057		341-1
Web: www.ca1.uscourts.gov						
Fourth Circuit						
US Courthouse Annex 1100 E Main St	Richmond	VA	23219	804-916-2700		341-1
Web: www.ca4.uscourts.gov						
Second Circuit						
US Courthouse 40 Foley Sq	New York	NY	10007	212-857-8500		341-1
Web: www.ca2.uscourts.gov						
Seventh Circuit						
219 S Dearborn St Ste 2722	Chicago	IL	60604	312-435-5850		341-1
Web: www.ca7.uscourts.gov						
Sixth Circuit 100 E Fifth St	Cincinnati	OH	45202	513-564-7000		341-1
Web: www.ca6.uscourts.gov						
Tenth Circuit 1823 Stout St	Denver	CO	80202	303-844-3157		341-1
Web: www.ca10.uscourts.gov						
Third Circuit						
US Courthouse 601 Market St	Philadelphia	PA	19106	215-597-2995		341-1
Web: www.ca3.uscourts.gov						
US Court of Appeals						
Circuit 9 PO Box 193939	San Francisco	CA	94119	415-355-8000		341-1
Web: www.ca9.uscourts.gov						
US Court of Appeals for the Armed Forces						
450 E St NW	Washington	DC	20442	202-761-1448		341
US Court of Appeals for Veterans Claims						
625 Indiana Ave NW Ste 900	Washington	DC	20004	202-501-5970	501-5848	341
Web: www.uscourts.cavc.gov						
US Court of Federal Claims						
717 Madison Pl NW	Washington	DC	20005	202-357-6400		341
TF: 800-338-2382 ■ *Web:* www.uscfc.uscourts.gov						

Name / Address	City	State	ZIP	Phone	Fax	Class
US Court of International Trade						
1 Federal Plaza	New York	NY	10278	212-264-2800	264-1085	341
Web: www.cit.uscourts.gov						
US Curling Assn (USCA)						
5525 Clem's Way	Stevens Point	WI	54482	715-344-1199	344-2279	48-22
TF: 888-287-5377 ■ *Web:* teamusa.org/usa-curling						
US Customs & Border Protection						
1300 Pennsylvania Ave NW	Washington	DC	20229	703-526-4200		340-11
TF: 877-227-5511 ■ *Web:* www.cbp.gov						
US Dairy Export Council						
2101 Wilson Blvd Ste 400	Arlington	VA	22201	703-528-3049	528-3705	49-6
Web: www.usdec.org						
US Dairy Forage Research Ctr (DFRC)						
1925 Linden Dr W	Madison	WI	53706	608-890-0050		668
Web: ars.usda.gov						
US Dataworks Inc						
14090 SW Fwy Ste 300	Sugar Land	TX	77478	281-504-8000	565-2567	178-10
OTC: UDWK ■ *TF:* 888-254-8821 ■ *Web:* www.usdataworks.com						
US Department of Energy (DOE)						
1000 Independence Ave SW	Washington	DC	20585	202-586-5000	586-4403	340-9
TF: 800-877-8339 ■ *Web:* www.energy.gov						
US Department of Homeland Security						
2703 Martin Luther King JR Ave SE	Washington	DC	20593	504-393-6005		158
Web: uscg.mil						
CDBG Disaster Recovery Program						
451 Seventh St SW	Washington	DC	20410	202-708-1112	708-1455	340-12
Web: portal.hud.gov						
Great Plains Region VII News						
400 State Ave	Kansas City	KS	66101	913-551-6857	551-5469	340-12
Web: portal.hud.gov						
US Department of Housing and Urban Development						
451 Seventh St SW	Washington	DC	20410	202-708-0417	619-8365	340-12
Web: portal.hud.gov						
Affordable Housing						
451 Seventh St SW	Washington	DC	20410	202-708-1112		340-12
Web: portal.hud.gov						
HIV/AIDS Housing Office						
451 Seventh St SW	Washington	DC	20410	202-708-1112		340-12
Web: portal.hud.gov						
Secretary Ben Carson						
451 Seventh St SW	Washington	DC	20410	202-708-1112		340-12
TF: 800-333-4636 ■ *Web:* portal.hud.gov						
US Dept of Education						
Office of Special Education & Rehabilitation Servi						
400 Maryland Ave SW	Washington	DC	20202	202-401-0418	872-5327*	340-8
**Fax Area Code:* 800 ■ *Web:* www2.ed.gov						
Region 6 1999 Bryan St Ste 1620	Dallas	TX	75201	214-661-9600	661-9587	340-8
TF: 877-521-2172 ■ *Web:* www.ed.gov						
US Dept of Labor						
200 Constitution Ave NW	Washington	DC	20210	202-693-4700	693-4754	340-15
Web: www.dol.gov/vets						
US Dept of Labor Women's Bureau						
200 Constitution Ave NW Rm S-3002	Washington	DC	20210	202-693-6710	693-6710	197
TF: 800-827-5335 ■ *Web:* www.dol.gov/wb						
US Diamond Wheel Co 101 Kendall Pt Dr	Oswego	IL	60543	800-851-1095	898-1796*	500
**Fax Area Code:* 630 ■ *TF:* 800-223-0457 ■ *Web:* www.radiac.com						
US Digital Corp 1400 NE 136th Ave	Vancouver	WA	98684	360-260-2468	260-2469	178-10
TF: 800-736-0194 ■ *Web:* www.usdigital.com						
US Digital Media Inc						
1929 W Lone Cactus Dr	Phoenix	AZ	85027	623-587-4900	587-4920	547
TF: 877-992-3766 ■ *Web:* www.usdigitalmedia.com						
US Digital Partners LLC 311 Elm St	Cincinnati	OH	45202	513-929-4603		7
Web: www.usdigitalpartners.com						
US Dismantlement LLC 2600 S Throop St	Chicago	IL	60608	312-328-1400	328-1477	189-16
TF: 800-611-2907 ■ *Web:* www.usdllc.com						
US District Court Alabama Northern						
1729 Fifth Ave N	Birmingham	AL	35203	205-278-1700		341-3
TF: 800-676-6856 ■ *Web:* www.alnd.uscourts.gov						
US District Court Arizona						
401 W Washington St Ste 130	Phoenix	AZ	85003	602-322-7200		341-3
Web: www.azd.uscourts.gov						
US District Court Arkansas Western						
30 S Sixth St	Fort Smith	AR	72901	479-783-6833	783-6308	341-3
TF: 800-859-7375 ■ *Web:* www.arwd.uscourts.gov						
US District Court California Eastern						
501 I St	Sacramento	CA	95814	916-930-4000		341-3
TF: 800-676-6856 ■ *Web:* www.caed.uscourts.gov						
US District Court California Northern						
450 Golden Gate Ave PO Box 36060	San Francisco	CA	94102	415-522-2000		341-3
Web: www.cand.uscourts.gov						
US District Court California Southern						
880 Front St Rm 4290	San Diego	CA	92101	619-557-6348	702-9900	341-3
Web: www.casd.uscourts.gov						
US District Court Colorado 901 19th St	Denver	CO	80294	303-844-3433	335-2040	341-3
TF: 800 359 8699 ■ *Web:* www.cod.uscourts.gov/Home.aspx						
US District Court Connecticut						
141 Church St	New Haven	CT	06510	203-773-2140	773-2334	341-3
Web: www.ctd.uscourts.gov						
US District Court Delaware						
844 N King St Ste 18	Wilmington	DE	19801	302-573-6170		341-3
Web: www.ded.uscourts.gov						
US District Court District of Columbia						
333 Constitution Ave NW # 6822	Washington	DC	20001	202-354-3000		341-3
Web: www.dcd.uscourts.gov						
US District Court Eastern District of Virginia						
401 Courthouse Sq	Alexandria	VA	22314	703-299-2100		341-3
Web: www.vaed.uscourts.gov						
US District Court Florida Middle						
401 W Central Blvd Ste 1200	Orlando	FL	32801	407-835-4200		341-3
TF: 800-676-6856 ■ *Web:* www.flmd.uscourts.gov						
US District Court Florida Southern						
301 N Miami Ave	Miami	FL	33128	305-523-5100		341-3
Web: www.flsd.uscourts.gov						
US District Court for the District of Alaska						
222 W Seventh Ave Ste 4	Anchorage	AK	99513	907-677-6100		341-3
TF: 866-243-3814 ■ *Web:* www.akd.uscourts.gov						
US District Court Georgia Middle						
475 Mulberry St	Macon	GA	31201	478-752-3497	752-3496	341-3
Web: www.gamd.uscourts.gov						
US District Court Georgia Northern						
75 Spring St SW	Atlanta	GA	30303	404-215-1600		341-3
TF: 800-827-2982 ■ *Web:* www.gand.uscourts.gov						
US District Court Georgia Southern						
PO Box 8286	Savannah	GA	31412	912-650-4020		341-3
Web: www.gasd.uscourts.gov						
US District Court Guam						
520 W Soledad Ave 4th Fl	Hagatna	GU	96910	671-473-9100		341-3
Web: www.gud.uscourts.gov						
US District Court Hawaii						
300 Ala Moana Blvd Rm C-338	Honolulu	HI	96850	808-541-1300		341-3
TF: 800-676-6856 ■ *Web:* www.hid.uscourts.gov						
US District Court Idaho 550 W Fort St	Boise	ID	83724	208-334-1361		341-3
Web: www.id.uscourts.gov						
US District Court Illinois Central						
600 E Monroe St	Springfield	IL	62701	217-492-4020	492-4028	341-3
Web: www.ilcd.uscourts.gov						
US District Court Illinois Southern						
750 Missouri Ave	East Saint Louis	IL	62201	618-482-9371	482-9383	341-3
Web: www.ilsd.uscourts.gov						
US District Court Indiana Northern						
204 S Main St	South Bend	IN	46601	574-246-8000		341-3
Web: www.innd.uscourts.gov						
US District Court Indiana Southern						
46 E Ohio St	Indianapolis	IN	46204	317-229-3700	229-3959	341-3
Web: www.insd.uscourts.gov						
US District Court Iowa Northern						
111 Seventh Ave SE	Cedar Rapids	IA	52401	319-286-2300	286-2301	341-3
Web: www.iand.uscourts.gov						
US District Court Iowa Southern						
123 E Walnut St	Des Moines	IA	50309	515-284-6248	284-6418	341-3
Web: www.iasd.uscourts.gov						
US District Court Kansas						
500 State Ave	Kansas City	KS	66101	913-735-2200	551-6942	341-3
Web: www.ksd.uscourts.gov						
US District Court Kentucky Eastern						
101 Barr St	Lexington	KY	40507	859-233-2503		341-3
Web: www.kyed.uscourts.gov						
US District Court Kentucky Western						
601 W Broadway Rm 106	Louisville	KY	40202	502-625-3500	625-3880	341-3
Web: www.kywd.uscourts.gov						
US District Court Louisiana Eastern						
500 Poydras St Rm C-151	New Orleans	LA	70130	504-589-7650		341-3
Web: www.laed.uscourts.gov						
US District Court Louisiana Middle						
777 Florida St Ste 139	Baton Rouge	LA	70801	225-389-3500	389-3501	341-3
Web: www.lamd.uscourts.gov						
US District Court Louisiana Western						
300 Fannin St Ste 1167	Shreveport	LA	71101	318-676-4273	676-3962	341-3
Web: www.lawd.uscourts.gov						
US District Court Maine						
156 Federal St	Portland	ME	04101	207-780-3356		341-3
Web: www.med.uscourts.gov						
US District Court Maryland						
101 W Lombard St	Baltimore	MD	21201	410-962-2600		341-3
Web: www.mdd.uscourts.gov						
US District Court Massachusetts						
1 Courthouse Way Ste 2300	Boston	MA	02210	617-748-9152		341-3
Web: www.mad.uscourts.gov						
US District Court Michigan Eastern						
231 W Lafayette Blvd	Detroit	MI	48226	313-234-5005		341-3
Web: www.mied.uscourts.gov						
US District Court Minnesota						
300 S Fourth St Ste 202	Minneapolis	MN	55415	612-664-5000	664-5033	341-3
Web: www.mnd.uscourts.gov						
US District Court Mississippi Northern						
911 Jackson Ave E Rm 369	Oxford	MS	38655	662-234-1971	236-5210	341-3
Web: www.msnd.uscourts.gov						
US District Court Mississippi Southern						
501 E Court St Ste 2500	Jackson	MS	39201	601-965-4439		341-3
TF: 866-517-7682 ■ *Web:* www.mssd.uscourts.gov						
US District Court Missouri Eastern						
111 S Tenth St Ste 3.300	Saint Louis	MO	63102	314-244-7900	244-7909	341-3
Web: www.moed.uscourts.gov						
US District Court Missouri Western						
400 E Ninth St	Kansas City	MO	64106	816-512-5000		341-3
TF: 800-466-9302 ■ *Web:* www.mow.uscourts.gov						
US District Court Montana						
2601 Second Ave N	Missoula	MT	59101	406-247-7000	542-7272	341-3
Web: www.mtd.uscourts.gov						
US District Court Nebraska						
111 S 18th Plaza Ste 1152	Omaha	NE	68102	402-661-7350	661-7387	341-3
TF: 866-220-4381 ■ *Web:* www.ned.uscourts.gov						
US District Court Nevada						
333 Las Vegas Blvd S	Las Vegas	NV	89101	702-464-5400		341-3
TF: 800-676-6856 ■ *Web:* www.nvd.uscourts.gov						
US District Court New Hampshire						
55 Pleasant St Rm 110	Concord	NH	03301	603-225-1423		341-3
Web: www.nhd.uscourts.gov						
US District Court New Jersey						
50 Walnut St	Newark	NJ	07101	973-645-3730		341-3
Web: www.njd.uscourts.gov						
US District Court New Mexico						
333 Lomas Blvd NW	Albuquerque	NM	87102	505-348-2000		341-3
Web: www.nmcourt.fed.us						
US District Court New York Northern						
100 S Clinton St PO Box 7367	Syracuse	NY	13261	315-234-8500		341-3
Web: www.nynd.uscourts.gov						
US District Court New York Southern						
500 Pearl St	New York	NY	10007	212-805-0136		341-3
Web: www.nysd.uscourts.gov						
US District Court New York Western						
2 Niagara Sq	Buffalo	NY	14202	716-551-4211	551-4850	341-3
Web: www.nywd.uscourts.gov						
US District Court North Carolina Eastern						
PO Box 25670	Raleigh	NC	27611	919-645-1700	645-1750	341-3
Web: www.nced.uscourts.gov						

Phone | Fax | Class

US District Court North Carolina Middle
324 W Market St .... Greensboro NC 27401 336-332-6000 332-6060 341-3
Web: www.ncmd.uscourts.gov

US District Court North Carolina Western
401 W Trade St .... Charlotte NC 28202 704-350-7400 341-3
TF: 866-851-1605 ■ *Web:* www.ncwd.uscourts.gov

US District Court North Dakota
PO Box 1193 .... Bismarck ND 58502 701-530-2300 530-2312 341-3
Web: www.ndd.uscourts.gov

US District Court Northern District Of Florida
111 N Adams St .... Tallahassee FL 32301 850-521-3501 521-3656 341-3
TF: 800-676-6856 ■ *Web:* www.flnd.uscourts.gov

US District Court Northern District of Illinois
219 S Dearborn St
Everett McKinley Dirksen United States Courthouse Chicago IL 60604 312-435-5670 341-3
Web: www.ilnd.uscourts.gov

US District Court Ohio Northern
801 W Superior Ave .... Cleveland OH 44113 216-357-7000 357-7040 341-3
TF: 800-355-8498 ■ *Web:* www.ohnd.uscourts.gov

US District Court Ohio Southern
85 Marconi Blvd .... Columbus OH 43215 614-719-3000 341-3
Web: www.ohsd.uscourts.gov

US District Court Oklahoma Eastern
PO Box 607 .... Muskogee OK 74402 918-684-7920 684-7902 341-3
Web: www.oked.uscourts.gov

US District Court Oklahoma Northern
333 W Fourth St .... Tulsa OK 74103 918-699-4700 341-3
TF: 866-213-1957 ■ *Web:* www.oknd.uscourts.gov

US District Court Oklahoma Western
200 NW Fourth St Rm 1210 .... Oklahoma City OK 73102 405-609-5000 609-5099 341-3
TF: 888-609-6953 ■ *Web:* www.okwd.uscourts.gov

US District Court Oregon
1000 SW Third Ave Ste 740 .... Portland OR 97204 503-326-8000 341-3
Web: www.ord.uscourts.gov

US District Court Pennsylvania Eastern
601 Market St .... Philadelphia PA 19106 215-597-7704 597-6390 341-3
Web: www.paed.uscourts.gov

US District Court Pennsylvania Middle
235 N Washington Ave .... Scranton PA 18503 570-207-5600 207-5650 341-3
Web: www.pamd.uscourts.gov

US District Court Pennsylvania Western
700 Grant St .... Pittsburgh PA 15219 412-208-7500 341-3
Web: www.pawd.uscourts.gov

US District Court South Carolina
901 Richland St .... Columbia SC 29201 803-765-5816 341-3
Web: www.scd.uscourts.gov

US District Court South Dakota
400 S Phillips Ave Rm 128 .... Sioux Falls SD 57104 605-330-6600 330-6601 341-3
Web: www.sdd.uscourts.gov

US District Court Tennessee Eastern
800 Market St Ste 130 .... Knoxville TN 37902 865-545-4228 545-4247 341-3
Web: www.tned.uscourts.gov

US District Court Tennessee Middle
801 Broadway Rm 800 .... Nashville TN 37203 615-736-5498 736-7488 341-3
Web: www.tnmd.uscourts.gov

US District Court Tennessee Western
167 N Main St Rm 242 .... Memphis TN 38103 901-495-1200 495-1250 341-3
Web: www.tnwd.uscourts.gov

US District Court Texas Eastern
211 W Ferguson St .... Tyler TX 75702 903-590-1000 341-3
Web: www.txed.uscourts.gov

US District Court Texas Northern
1100 Commerce St Rm 1452 .... Dallas TX 75242 214-753-2200 753-2266 341-3
Web: www.txnd.uscourts.gov

US District Court Texas Southern
515 Rusk St .... Houston TX 77002 713-250-5500 341-3
Web: www.txs.uscourts.gov

US District Court US Virgin Islands
3013 Estate Golden Rock .... Saint Croix VI 00820 340-773-1130 773-1563 341-3
Web: www.vid.uscourts.gov

US District Court Utah
350 S Main St Rm 150 .... Salt Lake City UT 84101 801-524-6100 526-1175 341-3
Web: www.utd.uscourts.gov

US District Court Vermont
11 Elmwood Ave Rm 506 Rm 506 .... Burlington VT 05401 802-951-6301 341-3
TF: 800-837-8718 ■ *Web:* www.vtd.uscourts.gov

US District Court Virginia Western
180 W Main St Rm 104 .... Abingdon VA 24210 540-857-5100 857-5110 341-3
Web: www.vawd.uscourts.gov

US District Court Washington Eastern
920 W Riverside Ave Rm 840 .... Spokane WA 99201 509-458-3400 458-3420 341-3
Web: www.waed.uscourts.gov

US District Court Washington Western
700 Stewart St .... Seattle WA 98101 206-370-8400 341-3
TF: 800-859-7375 ■ *Web:* www.wawd.uscourts.gov

US District Court West Virginia Northern
300 Third St PO Box 1518 .... Elkins WV 26241 304-636-1445 636-5746 341-3
Web: www.wvnd.uscourts.gov

US District Court Wisconsin Eastern
517 E Wisconsin Ave .... Milwaukee WI 53202 414-297-3372 341-3
TF: 800-273-1002 ■ *Web:* www.wied.uscourts.gov

US District Court Wisconsin Western
120 N Henry St Rm 320 Rm 320 .... Madison WI 53703 608-264-5156 264-5925 341-3
Web: www.wiwd.uscourts.gov

US District Court Wyoming
2120 Capitol Ave 2nd Fl .... Cheyenne WY 82001 307-433-2120 433-2152 341-3
Web: www.wyd.uscourts.gov

US Drill Head Co 5298 River Rd .... Cincinnati OH 45233 513-941-0300 493
Web: usdrillhead.com

US Drug Testing Laboratories Inc
1700 S Mt Prospect Rd .... Des Plaines IL 60018 847-375-0770 375-0775 416
TF: 800-235-2367 ■ *Web:* www.usdtl.com

US Ecology 300 E Mallard Dr Ste 300 .... Boise ID 83706 208-331-8400 331-7900 667
NASDAQ: ECOL ■ *TF:* 800-590-5220 ■ *Web:* www.usecology.com/home.aspx

US Election Assistance Commission
1201 New York Ave NW Ste 300 .... Washington DC 20005 202-566-3100 566-3127 340-20
TF: 866-747-1471 ■ *Web:* www.eac.gov

US Energy Assn (USEA)
1300 Pennsylvania Ave NW Ste 550 .... Washington DC 20004 202-312-1230 48-12
Web: www.usea.org

US Energy Corp 877 N Eigth W .... Riverton WY 82501 307-856-9271 857-3050 502
NASDAQ: USEG ■ *TF:* 800-776-9271 ■ *Web:* www.usnrg.com

US Energy Markets Inc
700 Louisiana St 39th Fl .... Houston TX 77002 813-438-3837 580
Web: www.usenergymarkets.com

US Engineering Co 3433 Roanoke Rd .... Kansas City MO 64111 816-753-6969 931-5773 189-10
Web: www.usengineering.com

US Equestrian Federation Inc
4047 Iron Works Pkwy .... Lexington KY 40511 859-258-2472 231-6662 48-22
TF: 800-633-2472 ■ *Web:* www.usef.org

US Equestrian Team Foundation Inc (USET)
1040 Pottersville Rd PO Box 355 .... Gladstone NJ 07934 908-234-1251 234-0670 48-22
TF: 800-688-0700 ■ *Web:* www.uset.org

US Equipment Co 20580 Hoover Rd .... Detroit MI 48205 313-526-8300 491
Web: www.usequipment.com

US Equipment Company Inc
8311 Sorensen Ave .... Santa Fe Springs CA 90670 800-255-4731 358
TF: 800-255-4731 ■ *Web:* www.usequipmentco.com

US Farm Data Inc 10824 Old Mill Rd Ste 8 .... Omaha NE 68154 402-334-1824 387
Web: www.usfarmdata.com

Southwest Region
4040 N Central Expwy Ste 900 .... Dallas TX 75204 214-253-4901 253-4960 340-10
Web: www.fda.gov

US Fencing Assn (USFA)
1 Olympic Plaza .... Colorado Springs CO 80909 719-866-4511 632-5737 48-22
TF: 888-431-3598 ■ *Web:* www.usfencing.org

US Figure Skating Assn (USFSA)
20 First St .... Colorado Springs CO 80906 719-635-5200 635-9548 48-22
TF: 800-332-9256 ■ *Web:* www.usfsa.org

US Fish & Wildlife Service (USFWS)
1849 C St NW .... Washington DC 20240 202-208-4717 208-6965 340-13
TF: 800-344-9453 ■ *Web:* www.fws.gov

US Fish & Wildlife Service Regional Offices
Alaska Region 1011 E Tudor Rd .... Anchorage AK 99503 907-786-3309 786-3495 340-13
TF: 800-645-8465 ■ *Web:* www.fws.gov
California & Nevada Region
2800 Cottage Way .... Sacramento CA 95825 916-414-6464 414-6486 340-13
Web: www.fws.gov
Great Lakes/Big Rivers Region
5600 American Blvd W Ste 900 .... Bloomington MN 55437 612-713-5360 713-5280 340-13
TF: 800-877-8339 ■ *Web:* www.fws.gov/midwest
Mountain-Prairie Region
134 Union Blvd .... Lakewood CO 80228 303-236-7905 236-8295 340-13
Web: www.fws.gov/mountain-prairie
NortheastRegion 300 Westgate Ctr Dr .... Hadley MA 01035 413-253-8200 253-8308 340-13
Web: www.fws.gov
Pacific Region
Eastside Federal Complex 911 NE 11th Ave .... Portland OR 97232 503-231-6838 231-6161 340-13
Web: www.fws.gov/pacific
Southeast Region
1875 Century Blvd Ste 400 .... Atlanta GA 30345 404-679-4000 679-4006 340-13
TF: 800-364-4263 ■ *Web:* www.fws.gov/southeast
Southwest Region
500 Gold Ave SW PO Box 1306 .... Albuquerque NM 87102 505-248-6911 248-6910 340-13
Web: www.fws.gov/southwest

US Foods Culinary Equipment & Supplies
2621 Fairview Ave N .... Roseville MN 55113 651-638-8993 300
TF: 866-636-2338

US Forest Service
Alaska Regional Office PO Box 21628 .... Juneau AK 99802 907-586-8806 586-7876 340-1
Web: www.fs.fed.us

US Fund for UNICEF 125 Maiden Ln .... New York NY 10038 800-367-5437 779-1679* 48-5
**Fax Area Code: 212* ■ *TF:* 800-367-5437 ■ *Web:* www.unicefusa.org

US GAO (US Government Accountability Office)
Chicago Office 200 W Adams St Ste 700 .... Chicago IL 60606 312-220-7600 220-7726 342
Web: www.gao.gov

US General Services Administration (GSA)
1275 First St NW .... Washington DC 20405 202-208-7642 340-20
TF: 800-424-5210 ■ *Web:* www.gsa.gov/portal/category/100000

US General Services Administration
1800 F St NW .... Washington DC 20405 800-488-3111 340-20
TF: 800-488-3111 ■ *Web:* www.usa.gov

US Geological Survey (USGS)
12201 Sunrise Valley Dr .... Reston VA 20192 703-648-6723 340-13
TF: 888-275-8747 ■ *Web:* www.usgs.gov
Ask USGS 12201 Sunrise Valley Dr .... Reston VA 20192 703-648-5953 340-13
TF: 888-275-8747 ■ *Web:* usgs.gov

US Global Investors Inc
7900 Callaghan Rd .... San Antonio TX 78229 210-308-1234 308-1223 401
NASDAQ: GROW ■ *TF:* 800-873-8637 ■ *Web:* www.usfunds.com

US Golf Assn (USGA)
77 Liberty Corner Rd .... Far Hills NJ 07931 908-234-2300 234-9687 48-22
TF Orders: 800-336-4446 ■ *Web:* www.usga.org

US Government Accountability Office (US GAO)
Chicago Office 200 W Adams St Ste 700 .... Chicago IL 60606 312-220-7600 220-7726 342
Web: www.gao.gov

US Government Printing Office Bookstore (GPO)
732 N Capitol St NW .... Washington DC 20401 202-512-1800 512-2104 342
TF: 866-512-1800 ■ *Web:* bookstore.gpo.gov

US Grains Council
1400 K St NW Ste 1200 .... Washington DC 20005 202-789-0789 898-0522 48-2
Web: www.grains.org

US Grant, The 326 Broadway .... San Diego CA 92101 619-232-3121 232-3626 379
TF: 866-716-8136 ■ *Web:* www.usgrant.net

US Graphite Inc 1620 E Holland Ave .... Saginaw MI 48601 989-755-0441 755-0445 127
Web: www.usggledco.co.uk
Region 8 1961 Stout St Rm 08-148 .... Denver CO 80294 303-844-7860 844-2019 340-10
Web: www.hhs.gov
Region 9 90 Seventh St Ste 4-100 .... San Francisco CA 94103 800-368-1019 437-8329* 340-10
**Fax Area Code: 415* ■ *TF:* 800-368-1019 ■ *Web:* www.hhs.gov

Us Health Connect Inc
500 Office Ctr Dr .... Fort Washington PA 19034 800-889-4944 162
TF: 800-889-4944 ■ *Web:* www.omniaeducation.com

US Holocaust Memorial Museum
100 Raoul Wallenburg Pl SW .... Washington DC 20024 202-488-0400 520
Web: www.ushmm.org

Phone Fax Class

US Home Services
9260 Marketplace Dr .... Miamisburg OH 45342 937-898-0826 189-10
Web: directenergy.com

US Horticultural Research Laboratory
2001 S Rock Rd .... Fort Pierce FL 34945 772-462-5800 462-5986 668
Web: www.ars.usda.gov/Main/docs.htm?docid=7376

US House of Representatives
100 Cannon House Office Bldg............ Washington DC 20515 202-225-3121 225-1904 342
Web: www.house.gov
Armed Services Committee
2216 Rayburn House Office Bldg.......... Washington DC 20515 202-225-4151 225-9077 342-1
Web: www.armedservices.house.gov
Committee on Education and the Workforce
2181 Rayburn Bldg .... Washington DC 20515 202-225-4527 342-1
Web: edworkforce.house.gov
Committee on Natural Resources
1324 Longworth Bldg .... Washington DC 20515 202-225-2761 225-5929 342-1
Web: naturalresources.house.gov
Committee on Rules
H-312 Capitol Bldg .... Washington DC 20515 202-225-9191 225-1061 342-1
Web: www.rules.house.gov
Committee on Ways and Means
1102 Longworth Bldg .... Washington DC 20515 202-225-3625 225-2610 342-1
Web: www.waysandmeans.house.gov
Government Reform Committee
2157 Rayburn House Office Bldg.......... Washington DC 20515 202-225-5074 225-3974 342-1
Web: oversight.house.gov
Homeland Security Committee
176 Ford House Office Bldg............. Washington DC 20515 202-226-8417 226-3399 342-1
Web: homeland.house.gov
House Administration Committee
1309 Longworth Bldg .... Washington DC 20515 202-225-8281 225-9957 342-1
Web: cha.house.gov
House Committee on Agriculture
1301 Longworth Bldg .... Washington DC 20515 202-225-2171 225-0917 342-1
Web: www.agriculture.house.gov
House Committee on Foreign Affairs
2170 Rayburn Bldg .... Washington DC 20515 202-225-5021 225-6914 342-1
Web: foreignaffairs.house.gov
Judiciary Committee
2138 Rayburn Bldg .... Washington DC 20515 202-225-3951 225-7680 342-1
Web: www.judiciary.house.gov
Small Business Committee
2361 Rayburn Bldg .... Washington DC 20515 202-225-5821 342-1
Web: www.smallbusiness.house.gov
Transportation & Infrastructure Committee
2165 Rayburn Bldg .... Washington DC 20515 202-225-9446 342-1
Web: transportation.house.gov

US Immigration & Customs Enforcement (ICE)
425 'I' St NW........................... Washington DC 20536 202-514-1900 340-11
TF: 866-347-2423 ■ Web: www.ice.gov

US Industries Inc 1701 First Ave .... Evansville IN 47710 812-425-2428 189-12

US Ink Corp 651 Garden St.................. Carlstadt NJ 07072 201-935-8666 933-3728* 388
*Fax: Mktg ■ TF: 800-423-8838 ■ Web: www.sunchemical.com/product/us-ink

US Institute of Peace
2301 Constitution Ave NW .... Washington DC 20037 202-457-1700 429-6063 340-20
TF: 800-868-8064 ■ Web: www.usip.org

US International Trade Commission
500 E St SW............................. Washington DC 20436 202-205-2000 340-20
Web: www.usitc.gov

US Internet Corp
12450 Wayzata Blvd Ste 224 .... Minnetonka MN 55305 952-253-3262 225
TF: 800-333-3474 ■ Web: www.usinternet.com

US Joiner LLC
5690 Three Notched Rd Ste 200................. Crozet VA 22932 434-220-8500 698
Web: www.tridentmaritimesystems.com/usj/index.html

US Junior Chamber of Commerce
7447 S Lewis Ave............................ Tulsa OK 74136 636-681-1857 48-7
TF: 800-905-5499 ■ Web: www.jci.cc

US Laboratory & Radiology Inc
2 Jonathan Dr............................ Brockton MA 02301 508-583-2000 418
Web: www.uslabrad.com

US Lawns Inc 6700 Forum Dr Ste 150........... Orlando FL 32821 407-246-1630 422
TF: 800-875-2967 ■ Web: www.uslawns.com

US Learning Inc
516 Tennessee St Ste 219.................... Memphis TN 38103 901-767-0000 765
TF: 800-647-9166 ■ Web: www.uslearning.com

US Legal Support Inc
363 N Sam Houston Pkwy E Ste 900 .... Houston TX 77060 713-653-7100 653-7171 445
TF: 800-567-8757 ■ Web: www.uslegalsupport.com

US Lime & Minerals Inc
5429 LBJ Fwy Ste 230 .... Dallas TX 75240 972-991-8400 385-1340 440
NASDAQ: USLM ■ Web: www.uslm.com

US Linen & Uniform Inc
1106 Harding St........................... Richland WA 99352 509-946-6125 442
TF: 888-875-4636 ■ Web: www.uslinen.com

US Luge Assn 57 Church St................. Lake Placid NY 12946 518-523-2071 523-4106 48-22
Web: www.teamusa.org/usa-luge

US Lumber Group Inc
2160 Satellite Blvd Ste 450.................... Duluth GA 30097 678-474-4577 474-4575 191-3
Web: www.uslumber.com

US Magnesium LLC
238 North 2200 West .... Salt Lake City UT 84116 801-532-2043 534-1407 485
Web: www.usmagnesium.com

US Manufacturing Corp
28201 Van Dyke Ave.......................... Warren MI 48093 586-467-1600 467-1630 60
Web: www.usmfg.com

US Marine Corps (USMC)
1555 Southgate Rd
Marine Corps National Capital Region Command . Arlington VA 22214 703-614-6411 614-6411 340-7
Web: www.marines.mil/Pages/Default.aspx
Commandant
3000 Marine Corps Pentagon Rm 4C645 ... Washington DC 20350 703-614-4851 693-4414 340-7
Web: usmcbirthdayball.com

US Market Access Ctr
180 Sansome St 4th FL .... San Francisco CA 94104 415-462-4633 317
Web: usmarketaccess.com

Phone Fax Class

US Marshals Service
401 Courthouse Sq........................ Alexandria VA 22314 202-307-9100 340-14
TF General: 800-336-0102 ■ Web: www.usmarshals.gov

US Meat Export Federation Inc (USMEF)
1050 17th St Ste 2200 .... Denver CO 80265 303-623-6328 623-0297 49-6
Web: www.usmef.org

US Med-Equip Inc
9777 W Gulf Bank Ste 20 .... Houston TX 77040 713-983-8860 475
TF: 800-248-4058 ■ Web: www.usmedequip.com

US Media Consulting
1221 Brickell Ave Ste 600...................... Miami FL 33131 305-722-5500 7
Web: www.usmediaconsulting.com

US Medical Ctr for Federal Prisoners
1900 W Sunshine St....................... Springfield MO 65807 417-862-7041 837-1711 374-3
Web: www.bop.gov

US Merchant Marine Academy
300 Steamboat Rd .... Kings Point NY 11024 516-726-5800 773-5390* 166
*Fax: Admissions ■ TF: 866-546-4778 ■ Web: www.usmma.edu

US Metals Inc 19102 Gundle Rd .... Houston TX 77073 281-443-7473 492
Web: www.tgrexotics.com

US Metric Assn Inc (USMA)
10245 Andasol Ave........................ Northridge CA 91325 310-832-3763 48-10

Us Micro Corp 7000 Highlnds Pkwy SE........... Smyrna GA 30082 770-437-0706 174
TF: 888-876-4276 ■ Web: www.usmicrocorp.com

US Military Academy
Admissions Bldg 606 3rd Fl................ West Point NY 10996 845-938-4041 938-8121 498
Web: www.usma.edu

US Mint 801 Ninth St NW .... Washington DC 20220 202-354-7462 340-18
TF Cust Svc: 800-872-6468 ■ Web: www.usmint.gov
Denver 320 W Colfax Ave .... Denver CO 80204 303-405-4761 340-18
TF: 800-642-6116 ■ Web: www.usmint.gov
San Francisco 155 Hermann St........... San Francisco CA 94102 415-575-8000 340-18
TF: 800-872-6468 ■ Web: www.usmint.gov
West Point (NY) 1063 NY 218.............. West Point NY 10996 845-446-6200 340-18
TF: 800-872-6468 ■ Web: usmint.gov

US National Arboretum
3501 New York Ave NE.................... Washington DC 20002 202-245-2726 245-4575 97
Web: www.usna.usda.gov

US National Central Bureau of INTERPOL (INTERPOL)
600 E St NW Ste 600 .... Washington DC 20530 202-616-9000 616-8400 340-14
Web: www.justice.gov

US National Committee to the International Dairy Federation
PO Box 930398 .... Verona WI 53593 608-219-4115 262-1278 48-20
Web: www.usnac.org

US Naval Academy 121 Blake Rd .... Annapolis MD 21402 410-293-1000 498
TF Admissions: 888-249-7707 ■ Web: www.usna.edu

US Naval Academy Museum
118 Maryland Ave.......................... Annapolis MD 21402 410-293-2108 520
Web: www.usna.edu

US Naval Institute 291 Wood Rd .... Annapolis MD 21402 410-268-6110 295-1084 48-19
TF: 800-233-8764 ■ Web: www.usni.org

US Navy Memorial & Naval Heritage Ctr
701 Pennsylvania Ave NW Ste 123.......... Washington DC 20004 202-737-2300 50-4
Web: www.navymemorial.org

US Netcom Corp 710 S Maiden Ln .... Joplin MO 64801 417-781-1185 809

US Networx Inc 6360 I 55 N Ste 310............ Jackson MS 39211 601-956-4770 177
Web: www.usnx.com

US New Mexico Federal Credit Union (USNMFCU)
3939 Osuna Rd NE PO Box 129........... Albuquerque NM 87109 505-342-8888 219
TF: 888-342-8766 ■ Web: useaglefcu.org

US News & World Report
1050 Thomas Jefferson St NW.............. Washington DC 20007 202-955-2000 457-17
TF: 800-836-6397 ■ Web: www.usnews.com

US News University Connection LLC
9417 Princess Palm Ave....................... Tampa FL 33619 866-442-6587 387
TF: 866-442-6587 ■ Web: www.usnewsuniversitydirectory.com

US Office of Government Ethics
1201 New York Ave NW Ste 500............ Washington DC 20005 202-482-9300 482-9237 265
Web: www.oge.gov

US Oil & Refining Co 3001 Marshall Ave .... Tacoma WA 98421 253-383-1651 383-9970 580
Web: www.usor.com

US Oil Co Inc 425 Better Way.................. Appleton WI 54915 920-739-6101 788-0531* 579
*Fax: Acctg ■ Web: www.usventure.com

US Olympic Committee (USOC)
1 Olympic Plaza .... Colorado Springs CO 80909 719-632-5551 48-22
Web: www.teamusa.org

US Olympic Training Ctr
1750 E Boulder St.................. Colorado Springs CO 80909 719-866-4618 720
TF: 800-775-8762 ■ Web: www.teamusa.org

US Olympic Training Ctr
196 Old Military Rd .... Lake Placid NY 12946 518-523-2600 720
Web: teamusa.org/about-the-usoc

US Online com Inc
25 N Wenatchee Ave Ste 207B .... Wenatchee WA 98801 509-663-6031 664-6755 224

US Ordnance Inc 300 Sydney Dr.............. Mccarran NV 89434 775-343-1320 807
Web: www.usord.com

US PAACC (US Pan Asian American Chamber of Commerce)
1329 18th St NW .... Washington DC 20036 202-296-5221 296-5225 48-14
TF: 800-696-7818 ■ Web: www.uspaacc.com

US Pan Asian American Chamber of Commerce (US PAACC)
1329 18th St NW......................... Washington DC 20036 202-296-5221 296-5225 48-14
TF: 800-696-7818 ■ Web: www.uspaacc.com

US Parachute Assn (USPA)
5401 Southpoint Ctr Blvd............... Fredericksburg VA 22407 540-604-9740 604-9741 48-22
Web: www.uspa.org

US Parole Commission
5550 Friendship Blvd Rm 420 .... Chevy Chase MD 20815 301-492-5990 340-14
TF: 888-585-9103 ■ Web: www.justice.gov
Chicago Passport Agency
101 W Congress Pkwy
230 S Dearborn St 18th Fl.................... Chicago IL 60604 877-487-2778 874-7793* 340-16
*Fax Area Code: 888 ■ TF: 877-487-2778 ■ Web: www.travel.state.gov
San Francisco Passport Agency
450 Golden Gate Ave 3rd Fl Ste 3-2501... San Francisco CA 94102 877-487-2778 340-16
TF: 877-487-2778 ■ Web: www.travel.state.gov

US Patent & Trademark Office
PO Box 1450 .... Alexandria VA 22313 571-272-1000 273-8300 340-2
TF: 800-786-9199 ■ Web: www.uspto.gov

Phone | Fax | Class

US Pawn & Auto Inc
821 N US Hwy 17-92 ... Longwood FL 32750 407-099-5885 569
TF: 800-293-1389 ■ *Web:* www.uspawnandauto.com

US Penitentiary (USP)
Allenwood PO Box 3500 ... White Deer PA 17887 570-547-0963 547-9201 212
Web: www.bop.gov/locations/institutions/alp
Atwater 1 Federal Way PO Box 019001 ... Atwater CA 95301 209-386-0257 212
TF: 877-623-8426 ■ *Web:* www.bop.gov/locations/institutions/atw
Lewisburg 2400 Robert Miller Dr ... Lewisburg PA 17837 570-523-1251 212
Pollock 1000 Airbase Rd PO Box 1000 ... Pollock LA 71467 318-561-5300 561-5391 212
Web: www.bop.gov/locations/institutions/pol

US Pharmacist Magazine
100 Ave of the Americas ... New York NY 10013 800-825-4696 457-16
TF: 800-825-4696 ■ *Web:* www.uspharmacist.com

US Pharmacopeia (USP)
12601 Twinbrook Pkwy ... Rockville MD 20852 301-881-0666 49-8
TF: 800-227-8772 ■ *Web:* www.usp.org

US Physical Therapy
1300 W Sam Houston Pkwy S Ste 300 ... Houston TX 77042 713-297-7000 297-7090 352
NYSE: USPH ■ *TF:* 800-580-6285 ■ *Web:* corporate.usph.com

US Pipe & Foundry Co
2 Chase Corporate Dr Ste 200 ... Birmingham AL 35244 866-347-7473 307
TF: 866-347-7473 ■ *Web:* www.uspipe.com

US PIRG (US Public Interest Research Group)
218 D St SE ... Washington DC 20003 202-546-9707 633
Web: www.uspirg.org

US Plastic Corp 1390 Newbrecht Rd ... Lima OH 45801 419-228-2242 228-5034 199
TF: 800-537-9724 ■ *Web:* www.usplastic.com

US Postal Service (USPS)
475 L'Enfant Plaza W SW ... Washington DC 20260 202-268-2000 340-20
TF Cust Svc: 800-275-8777 ■ *Web:* www.usps.com

Us Postal Service Federal Credit Union
7905 Malcolm Rd Fl 4 ... Clinton MD 20735 301-856-5000 219
Web: www.uspsfcu.org

US Poultry & Egg Assn 1530 Cooledge Rd ... Tucker GA 30084 770-493-9401 493-9257 48-2
Web: www.uspoultry.org

US Premium Beef LLC (USPB)
12200 N Ambassador Dr PO Box 20103 ... Kansas City MO 64163 816-713-8800 713-8810 296-26
TF: 866-877-2525 ■ *Web:* www.uspremiumbeef.com

US Professional Tennis Assn (USPTA)
3535 Briarpark Dr Ste 1 ... Houston TX 77042 713-978-7782 978-7780 48-22
TF: 800-877-8248 ■ *Web:* uspta.com

US Protection Service LLC
5785 Emporium Sq ... Columbus OH 43231 614-794-4950 693
Web: www.uspsvc.com

US Public Health Service Phoenix Indian Medical Ctr
4212 N 16th St ... Phoenix AZ 85016 602-263-1200 263-1618 374-3
Web: usphs.gov

US Public Interest Research Group (US PIRG)
218 D St SE ... Washington DC 20003 202-546-9707 633
Web: www.uspirg.org

US Racquetball (USRA)
2812 W Colorado Ave Ste 220 ... Colorado Springs CO 80904 719-635-5396 635-0685 48-22
Web: www.teamusa.org

US Renewables Group LLC
2425 Olympic Blvd Ste 4050 W ... Santa Monica CA 90404 310-586-3900 401
Web: www.usregroup.com

US Residential Group LLC
5001 Spring Valley Rd Ste 1000 E ... Dallas TX 75244 469-546-6400 652
Web: www.usrgroup.com

US Retail Flowers Inc
810 S 12th St PO Box 330 ... Lebanon PA 17042 717-273-4090 292
Web: royers.com

US Ring Binder 6800 Arsenal St ... Saint Louis MO 63139 314-645-7880 645-7239 86
TF: 800-888-8772 ■ *Web:* www.usring.com

US Robotics Corp
1300 E Woodfield Dr Ste 506 ... Schaumburg IL 60173 847-874-2000 874-2001 173-3
TF: 877-710-0884 ■ *Web:* www.usr.com

US Rowing Assn 2 Wall St ... Princeton NJ 08540 609-924-1578 924-1578 48-22
TF: 800-314-4769 ■ *Web:* www.usrowing.org

US Rubber Corp 211 East Loop 336 ... Conroe TX 77301 936-756-1977 370
Web: www.usrubbercorp.com

US Sailing Assn
15 Maritime Dr PO Box 1260 ... Portsmouth RI 02871 401-683-0800 683-0840 48-22
TF: 800-877-2451 ■ *Web:* ussailing.org

US Salinity Laboratory
USDA/ARS 450 W Big Springs Rd ... Riverside CA 92507 951-369-4815 369-4818 668
Web: www.ars.usda.gov

US Secret Service 245 Murray Ln ... Washington DC 20223 202-406-5708 340-11
Web: www.secretservice.gov

US Security Assoc Inc
200 Mansell Ct 5th Fl ... Roswell GA 30076 770-625-1500 693
TF: 800-730-9599 ■ *Web:* www.ussecurityassociates.com

US Security Inc
4544 NW Tenth St ... Oklahoma City OK 73127 405-947-3377 693
TF: 877-917-5566 ■ *Web:* www.ussecurity.com

US Senate
455 Dirksen Senate Office Bldg ... Washington DC 20510 202-224-3121 342
TF: 800-877-8339 ■ *Web:* www.senate.gov
Agriculture Nutrition & Forestry Committee
328A Russell Senate Office Bldg ... Washington DC 20510 202-224-2035 228-2125 342-1
Web: agriculture.senate.gov
Commerce Science & Transportation Committee
512 Dirksen Senate Bldg ... Washington DC 20510 202-224-1251 342-1
Web: www.commerce.senate.gov
Committee on Budget
624 Drksen Senate office Bldg ... Washington DC 20510 202-224-0642 342-1
Web: budget.senate.gov
Committee on Finance
219 Dirksen Senate Office Bldg ... Washington DC 20510 202-224-4515 228-0554 342-1
Web: finance.senate.gov
Committee on Rules & Administration
305 Russell Senate Office Bldg ... Washington DC 20510 202-224-6352 342-1
Web: www.rules.senate.gov/public
Committee on the Judiciary
224 Dirksen Senate Office Bldg ... Washington DC 20510 202-224-5225 342-1
Web: www.judiciary.senate.gov
Committee on Veterans Affairs
412 Russell Bldg ... Washington DC 20510 202-224-9126 342-1
Web: veterans.senate.gov
Environment & Public Works
410 Dirksen Senate Office Bldg ... Washington DC 20510 202-224-8832 342-1
Web: www.epw.senate.gov/public
Homeland Security & Governmental Affairs Committee
340 Dirksen Senate Office Bldg ... Washington DC 20510 202-224-2627 342-1
Web: www.hsgac.senate.gov
Select Committee on Ethics
220 Hart Bldg ... Washington DC 20510 202-224-2981 224-7416 265
Web: www.ethics.senate.gov/public/index.cfm/home
Energy & Natural Resources
304 Dirksen Senate Bldg ... Washington DC 20510 202-224-4971 224-6163 342-1
Web: energy.senate.gov
Foreign Relations
446 Dirksen Senate Office Bldg ... Washington DC 20510 202-224-4651 342-1
Web: foreign.senate.gov

US Senate Committee on Indian Affairs
838 Hart Bldg ... Washington DC 20510 202-224-2251 228-2589 342-1
Web: indian.senate.gov

US Senate Select Committee on Intelligence
211 Hart Senate Office Bldg ... Washington DC 20510 202-224-1700 224-1772 342-1
Web: intelligence.senate.gov

US Sentencing Commission
1 Columbus Cir NE Ste 2 500 S Lbby ... Washington DC 20002 202-502-4500 341
Web: www.ussc.gov

US Shipping Corp 399 Thornall St 8th Fl ... Edison NJ 08837 732-635-1500 635-1918 312
TF: 866-942-6592 ■ *Web:* www.usslp.com

US Silica Co
8490 Progress Dr Ste 300 ... Frederick MD 21701 304-258-2500 503-4
TF: 800-243-7500 ■ *Web:* www.ussilica.com

US Soccer Federation
1801 S Prairie Ave ... Chicago IL 60616 312-808-1300 808-1301 48-22
TF: 800-745-3000 ■ *Web:* www.ussoccer.com

US Society on Dams (USSD)
1616 17th St Ste 483 ... Denver CO 80202 303-628-5430 628-5431 49-3
Web: www.ussdams.org

US Special Delivery Inc 821 E Blvd ... Kingsford MI 49802 906-774-1931 774-2032 685
TF: 800-821-6389 ■ *Web:* usspecial.com

US Steel Corp 600 Grant St ... Pittsburgh PA 15219 412-433-1121 723
NYSE: X ■ *Web:* www.ussteel.com

US Sugar Company Inc 692 Bailey Ave ... Buffalo NY 14206 716-828-1170 123
Web: www.ussugar.net

US Sugar Corp 111 Ponce de Leon Ave ... Clewiston FL 33440 863-983-8121 296-38
Web: www.ussugar.com

US Supply Company Inc
50 Portland Rd ... West Conshohocken PA 19428 610-828-5600 612
TF: 800-444-4280 ■ *Web:* www.ussupply.com

US Surgeon General
1101 Wootton Pkwy Rm 100 Rockville MD 20857 [illegible] [illegible]
Web: www.surgeongeneral.gov

US Synchronized Swimming
1 Olympic Plaza ... Colorado Springs CO 80909 317-237-5700 237-5705 48-22
TF: 800-775-8762 ■ *Web:* www.teamusa.org

US Taekwondo Union
1 Olympic Plaza Ste 104C ... Colorado Springs CO 80909 719-866-4632 866-4642 48-22
Web: www.teamusa.org

Us Tank Alliance Inc
7400 Skyline Dr E Ste A ... Columbus OH 43235 614-923-0154 196
Web: www.USTankWeb.com

US Tax Court 400 Second St NW ... Washington DC 20217 202-521-0700 341
Web: www.ustaxcourt.gov

US Technology Corp 4200 Munson St NW ... Canton OH 44718 330-455-1181 1
TF: 800 262 7763 ■ *Web:* www.ustechnology.com

US Telecom Assn (USTA)
607-14th St NW Ste 400 ... Washington DC 20005 202-326-7300 326-7333 49-20
Web: ustelecom.org

US Term Limits (USTL)
1250 Connecticut Ave NW Ste 200 ... Washington DC 20036 202-261-3532 48-7
Web: www.termlimits.org

US Tool Grinding Inc
2000 Progress Dr ... Farmington MO 63640 573-431-3856 886-8668* 455
**Fax Area Code:* 800 ■ *TF:* 800-222-1771 ■ *Web:* www.ustg.net

US Tower Corp 1099 W Ropes Ave ... Woodlake CA 93286 559-564-6000 480
Web: www.ustower.com

US Trackworks LLC 1165 142nd Ave ... Wayland MI 49348 616-877-4284 261
Web: ustrackworks.com

US Trade & Development Agency
1000 Wilson Blvd Ste 1600 ... Arlington VA 22209 703-875-4357 875-4009 340-20
Web: www.ustda.gov

US Travel Assn
1100 New York Ave NW Ste 450 ... Washington DC 20005 202-408-8422 408-1255 49-7
Web: www.ustravel.org

US Trotting Assn (USTA)
750 Michigan Ave ... Columbus OH 43215 614-224-2291 224-4575 48-22
TF: 877-800-8782 ■ *Web:* www.ustrotting.com

US Tsubaki Inc 301 E Marquardt Dr ... Wheeling IL 60090 847-459-9500 459-9515 620
TF: 800-323-7790 ■ *Web:* www.ustsubaki.com

US Underwater Services LP
123 Sentry Dr ... Mansfield TX 76063 817-447-7321 302
TF: 800-860-2178 ■ *Web:* www.neptunems.com

US Vegetable Laboratory
USDA/ARS 2700 Savannah Hwy ... Charleston SC 29414 843-402-5300 668
Web: www.ars.usda.gov/main/docs.htm?docid=5953

US Venture Partners (USVP)
1460 El Camino Real ... Menlo Park CA 94025 650-854-9080 854-3018 792
Web: www.usvp.com

US Vinyl Manufacturing Corp
1766 Broomtown Rd ... Lafayette GA 30728 706-638-8400 548
Web: www.usvinylmfg.com

US Vision Inc
1 Harmon Dr Glen Oaks Industrial Pk ... Glendora NJ 08029 856-228-1000 543
TF: 866-435-7111 ■ *Web:* www.usvision.com

US Websoft Corp
1101 Connecticut Ave NW Ste 450 ... Herndon VA 20036 703-318-0103 809
Web: www.us-websoft.com

	Phone	Fax	Class
US Wheat Assoc (USW) 3103 Tenth St N Ste 300 .... Arlington VA 22201 **Fax Area Code: 703 ■ Web:* www.uswheat.org	202-463-0999	524-4399*	48-2
US WorldMeds LLC 4010 Dupont Cir Ste L-07 .... Louisville KY 40207 *TF:* 888-900-8796 ■ *Web:* www.usworldmeds.com	502-815-8000		238
US Xpress Enterprises Inc 4080 Jenkins Rd .... Chattanooga TN 37421 *TF:* 800-251-6291 ■ *Web:* www.usxpress.com	423-510-3000	510-3444	780
USA 3000 Airlines 335 Bishop Hollow Rd ste 100 .... Newtown Square PA 19073 *Web:* usa3000.com	610-325-1280	325-1870	25
USA 800 Inc 9808 E 66th Terr .... Kansas City MO 64133 *TF:* 800-821-7539 ■ *Web:* www.usa800.com	816-358-1303		737
USA Archery (NAA) 1 Olympic Plaza .... Colorado Springs CO 80909 *TF:* 800-671-1140 ■ *Web:* www.teamusa.org	719-866-4576	632-4733	48-22
USA Baby 793 Springer Dr .... Lombard IL 60148 *TF:* 800-767-9464 ■ *Web:* www.usababy.com	630-652-0600		321
USA Baseball 403 Blackwell St .... Durham NC 27701 *TF:* 855-420-5910 ■ *Web:* usabaseball.com	919-474-8721	474-8822	48-22
USA Basketball 5465 Mark Dabling Blvd .... Colorado Springs CO 80918 *TF:* 888-284-5383 ■ *Web:* www.usab.com	719-590-4800	590-4811	48-22
USA Bouquet Company Inc, The 1500 NW 95 Ave .... Miami FL 33172 *Web:* www.usabq.com	786-437-6500		292
USA Boxing Inc 1 Olympic Plaza .... Colorado Springs CO 80909 *Web:* www.teamusa.org/USA-Boxing	719-228-6800	866-2132	48-22
USA Canoe/Kayak (USACK) 725 S Lincoln Blvd .... Oklahoma City OK 73129 *Web:* www.teamusa.org	405-552-4040		48-22
USA Communications 124 Main St .... Shellsburg IA 52332 *TF:* 800-248-8007 ■ *Web:* www.usacomm.coop	319-436-2224		116
USA Communications Inc 920 E 56th St Ste B .... Kearney NE 68847 *TF:* 877-234-0102 ■ *Web:* www.usacommunications.tv	877-234-0102		387
USA Consulting Inc 701 E Plano Pkwy Ste 300 .... Plano TX 75074 *Web:* www.usaci.com	972-673-0333		196
USA Container Company Inc 1776 S Second St .... Piscataway NJ 08854 *TF:* 888-752-7722 ■ *Web:* www.usacontainer.com	888-752-7722		198
USA Cycling Inc 1 Olympic Plaza .... Colorado Springs CO 80909 *Web:* www.usacycling.org	719-866-4581		48-22
USA Digital Solutions Inc 10835 N 25th Ave Ste 350 .... Phoenix AZ 85029 *Web:* www.digisolaz.com	602-866-8199		177
USA Diving Inc 132 E Washington St Ste 850 .... Indianapolis IN 46204 *Web:* www.teamusa.org/usa-diving	317-237-5252	237-5257	48-22
USA Environment LP 316 Georgia Ave .... Deer Park TX 77536 *Web:* www.usaenviro.com	713-425-6900	425-6917	667
USA for UNHCR 1775 K St NW Ste 580 .... Washington DC 20006 *TF:* 800-770-1100 ■ *Web:* www.unrefugees.org	202-296-1115		48-5
USA Freedom Corps 1201 New York Ave NW .... Washington DC 20005 *TF:* 800-833-3722 ■ *Web:* www.nationalservice.gov	202-606-5000		340
USA Gymnastics 201 S Capitol Ave Ste 300 .... Indianapolis IN 46225 *TF:* 800-345-4719 ■ *Web:* usagym.org	317-237-5050	237-5069	48-22
USA Hockey 1775 Bob Johnson Dr .... Colorado Springs CO 80906 *TF:* 800-566-3288 ■ *Web:* www.usahockey.com	719-576-8724	538-1160	48-22
USA Judo Inc 1 Olympic Plaza Ste 505 .... Colorado Springs CO 80909 *TF:* 800-775-8762 ■ *Web:* www.teamusa.org	719-866-4730	866-4733	48-22
USA Mobility Inc 6677 Richmond Hwy .... Alexandria VA 22306 *TF:* 800-231-2556 ■ *Web:* www.usamobility.com	703-660-6677	660-6994	736
USA Network 30 Rockefeller Plaza 21st Fl .... New York NY 10112 *Web:* www.usanetwork.com	212-664-4444		740
USA Parking Systems Inc 1330 SE Fourth Ave Ste D .... Fort Lauderdale FL 33316 *Web:* www.usaparking.net	954-524-6500		562
USA Poultry & Egg Export Council (USAPEEC) 2300 W Pk Pl Blvd Ste 100 .... Stone Mountain GA 30087 *Web:* www.usapeec.org	770-413-0006	413-0007	49-6
USA Risk Group Inc 2418 Airport Rd Ste 2A .... Barre VT 05641 *TF:* 800-872-7475 ■ *Web:* www.usarisk.com	802-371-2220		463
USA Roller Sports 4730 S St .... Lincoln NE 68506 *Web:* www.teamusa.org	402-483-7551	483-1465	48-22
USA Staffing Inc 2010 Philadelphia St Ste 8 .... Ames IA 50010	515-292-5775	292-9268	260
USA Student Travel 5080 Robert J Mathews Pkwy .... El Dorado Hills CA 95762 *TF:* 800-448-4444 ■ *Web:* www.usastudenttravel.com	916-939-6805	939-6806	760
USA Swimming 1 Olympic Plaza .... Colorado Springs CO 80909 *TF:* 800-356-2722 ■ *Web:* www.usaswimming.org	719-866-4578	866-4669	48-22
USA Synthetic Fuel Corp Ste 1600 312 Walnut St Ste 1600 .... Cincinnati OH 45202 *TF:* 800-732-0330 ■ *Web:* www.usasfc.com	513-762-7870		192
USA Table Tennis 1 Olympic Plaza .... Colorado Springs CO 80909 *TF:* 800-775-8762 ■ *Web:* www.teamusa.org	719-866-4583	632-6071	48-22
USA Technologies Inc 100 Deerfield Ln Ste 140 .... Malvern PA 19355 *TF:* 800-633-0340 ■ *Web:* www.usatech.com	800-633-0340		251
USA Today 7950 Jones Branch Dr .... McLean VA 22108 *TF Cust Svc:* 800-872-0001 ■ *Web:* www.usatoday.com	703-854-3400		532-3
USA Track & Field (USATF) 132 E Washington St Ste 800 .... Indianapolis IN 46204 *TF:* 800-222-8733 ■ *Web:* www.usatf.org	317-261-0500	261-0481	48-22
USA Triathlon 5825 Delmonico Dr .... Colorado Springs CO 80919 *Web:* www.teamusa.org/usa-triathlon	719-597-9090	597-2121	48-22

	Phone	Fax	Class
USA Truck Inc 3200 Industrial Pk Rd .... Van Buren AR 72956 *NASDAQ: USAK ■ TF:* 800-643-9691 ■ *Web:* www.usa-truck.com	479-471-2500		780
USA Water Polo 2124 Main St Ste 210 .... Huntington Beach CA 92648 *TF:* 888-712-2166 ■ *Web:* usawaterpolo.org	714-500-5445	960-2431	48-22
USA Water Ski 1251 Holy Cow Rd .... Polk City FL 33868 *TF:* 800-533-2972 ■ *Web:* www.usawaterski.org	863-324-4341	325-8259	48-22
USA Weightlifting (USAW) 1 Olympic Plaza .... Colorado Springs CO 80909 *TF:* 800-775-8762 ■ *Web:* www.teamusa.org	719-866-4508	866-4741	48-22
USA Workers Injury Network 1250 S Capital of Texas Hwy Bldg 3 Ste 500 .... Austin TX 78746 **Fax Area Code: 512 ■ TF Cust Svc:* 800-872-0020 ■ *Web:* www.usamco.com	800-872-0020	328-6785*	391-4
USA Wrestling 6155 Lehman Dr .... Colorado Springs CO 80918 *TF:* 888-431-3598 ■ *Web:* teamusa.org/usa-wrestling	719-598-8181	598-9440	48-22
USAA (United Services Automobile Assn) 10750 McDermott Fwy .... San Antonio TX 78288 *TF:* 800-531-8722 ■ *Web:* www.usaa.com	800-531-8722	531-5717	185
USAA (USAA Life Insurance Co) 9800 Fredericksburg Rd .... San Antonio TX 78288 **Fax Area Code: 800 ■ *Fax:* Sales ■ *TF:* 800-531-8000 ■ *Web:* www.usaa.com	210-531-8722	531-8877*	391-2
USAA FSB (USAAFSB) 10750 McDermott Fwy .... San Antonio TX 78288 *TF:* 800-531-8722 ■ *Web:* www.usaa.com	800-531-8722	531-5717	70
USAA Investment Management 9800 Fredericksburg Rd PO Box 659453 ...... San Antonio TX 78288 *TF:* 800-531-8722 ■ *Web:* www.usaa.com	800-531-8722		401
USAA Life Insurance Co (USAA) 9800 Fredericksburg Rd .... San Antonio TX 78288 **Fax Area Code: 800 ■ *Fax:* Sales ■ *TF:* 800-531-8000 ■ *Web:* www.usaa.com	210-531-8722	531-8877*	391-2
USAA Property & Casualty Insurance Group 9800 Fredericksburg Rd .... San Antonio TX 78288 **Fax Area Code: 800 ■ TF:* 800-531-8722 ■ *Web:* www.usaa.com/inet/pages/newsroom_factsheets_pnc	210-531-8722	531-8877*	391-4
USAA Real Estate Co 9830 Colonnade Blvd Ste 600 .... San Antonio TX 78230 **Fax Area Code: 210 ■ TF:* 800-531-8182 ■ *Web:* www.usrealco.com	800-531-8182	641-8425*	655
USAAFSB (USAA FSB) 10750 McDermott Fwy .... San Antonio TX 78288 *TF:* 800-531-8722 ■ *Web:* www.usaa.com	800-531-8722	531-5717	70
Usablenet Inc 142 W 57th St 7th Fl .... New York NY 10019 *Web:* www.usablenet.com	212-965-5388		224
USAC (Universal Service Administrative Co) 2000 L St NW Ste 200 .... Washington DC 20036 *TF:* 888-641-8722 ■ *Web:* www.usac.org	202-776-0200	776-0080	736
USAC (USAC Racing) 4910 W 16th St .... Speedway IN 46224 *Web:* www.usacracing.com	317-247-5151		48-22
USAC Racing (USAC) 4910 W 16th St .... Speedway IN 46224 *Web:* www.usacracing.com	317-247-5151		48-22
USAch Technologies Inc 1524 Davis Rd .... Elgin IL 60123 *Web:* www.usach.com	847-888-0148		697
USACK (USA Canoe/Kayak) 725 S Lincoln Blvd .... Oklahoma City OK 73129 *Web:* www.teamusa.org	405-552-4040		48-22
USAdvisors Network LLC 9531 W 78th St Ste 220 .... Eden Prairie MN 55344 *Web:* www.usadvisorsnetwork.com	952-829-0000		463
USAFA (US Air Force Academy) 2304 Cadet Dr Ste 2300 .... Air Force Academy CO 80840 *TF:* 800-443-9266 ■ *Web:* www.usafa.af.mil	719-333-1110	333-3644	498
USAFact Inc 6240 Box Springs Blvd .... Riverside CA 92507 *TF:* 800-547-0263 ■ *Web:* www.usafactinc.com	951-656-7800		260
USAID (US Agency for International Development) 1300 Pennsylvania Ave NW .... Washington DC 20523 *Web:* www.usaid.gov	202-712-0000	216-3524	340-20
USAISR (US Army Institute of Surgical Research) 3698 Chambers Pass Ste B .... Fort Sam Houston TX 78234 *Web:* www.usaisr.amedd.army.mil	210-539-3219	227-8502	668
USAMRICD (US Army Medical Research Institute of Chemical Defense) 3100 Ricketts Point Rd .... Aberdeen Proving Ground MD 21010 *Web:* usamricd.apgea.army.mil	410-436-3276	436-1960	668
USAMRIID (US Army Medical Research Institute of Infectious Diseases) 1425 Porter St .... Frederick MD 21702 *Web:* www.usamriid.army.mil	301-619-2285		668
USAMRMC (US Army Medical Research & Materiel Command) 820 Chandler St .... Fort Detrick MD 21702 *Web:* www.mrmc.smallbusopps.army.mil	301-619-2471		668
USAN Inc 3080 Northwoods Cir .... Norcross GA 30071 *Web:* www.usan.com	770-729-1449		737
USANA Health Sciences Inc 3838 West PkwyBlvd .... Salt Lake City UT 84120 *NYSE: USNA ■ TF:* 888-950-9595 ■ *Web:* www.usana.com	801-954-7100	954-7300	799
US-Analytics Solutions Group LLC 600 E Las Colinas Blvd Ste 2222 .... Irving TX 75039 *TF General:* 877-828-8727 ■ *Web:* www.us-analytics.com	214-630-0081		180
US-Angola Chamber of Commerce 1100 17th St NW Ste 1000 .... Washington DC 20036 *Web:* www.us-angola.org	202-857-0789		138
USAPEEC (USA Poultry & Egg Export Council) 2300 W Pk Pl Blvd Ste 100 .... Stone Mountain GA 30087 *Web:* www.usapeec.org	770-413-0006	413-0007	49-6
USAS Technologies 197 SR-18 Ste 304 .... East Brunswick NJ 08816 *Web:* usastechnologies.com	732-333-1400		196
US-ASEAN Business Council 1101 17th St NW Ste 411 .... Washington DC 20036 *Web:* usasean.org	202-289-1911		49-12
Usasia Insurance Services 319 Union Ave .... Pomona CA 91768 *TF:* 800-372-4822 ■ *Web:* usasia-ins.com	909-618-0288		390
USASOC (US Army Special Operations Command) 2929 Desert Storm Dr .... Fort Bragg NC 28310 *Web:* www.soc.mil	910-432-6005		340-5
USATF (USA Track & Field) 132 E Washington St Ste 800 .... Indianapolis IN 46204 *TF:* 800-222-8733 ■ *Web:* www.usatf.org	317-261-0500	261-0481	48-22
US-Austrian Chamber of Commerce 1133 Ave of the Americas 16th Fl .... New York NY 10036 *Web:* usaustrianchamber.org	212-819-0117		138

Phone | Fax | Class

U-Save Auto Rental of America Inc
1052 Highland Colony Pkwy Ste 204 .... Ridgeland MS 39157 | 601-713-4333 | | 126
TF General: 800-438-2300 ■ *Web:* www.usave.com

USAW (USA Weightlifting)
1 Olympic Plaza .... Colorado Springs CO 80909 | 719-866-4508 | 866-4741 | 48-22
TF: 800-775-8762 ■ *Web:* www.teamusa.org

USB (United Soybean Board)
16305 Swingley Ridge Rd Ste 150 .... Chesterfield MO 63017 | 636-530-1777 | 530-1560 | 48-2
TF: 800-989-8721 ■ *Web:* www.unitedsoybean.org

USBid Inc 2320 Commerce Park Dr .... Palm Bay FL 32905 | 321-725-9565 | | 224
Web: www.usbid.com

USBSF (US Bobsled & Skeleton Federation)
196 Old Military Rd .... Lake Placid NY 12946 | 518-523-1842 | 523-9491 | 48-22
TF: 888-431-3598 ■ *Web:* www.teamusa.org

USC Consulting Group LLC
3000 Bayport Dr Ste 1010 .... Tampa FL 33607 | 800-888-8872 | | 196
TF: 800-888-8872 ■ *Web:* www.usccg.com

USC Fisher Museum of Art
823 Exposition Blvd University Pk .... Los Angeles CA 90089 | 213-740-4561 | 740-7676 | 520
Web: www.usc.edu

USC Gould School of Law
699 Exposition Blvd .... Los Angeles CA 90089 | 213-740-7331 | | 167-1
Web: gould.usc.edu

USC Information Sciences Institute
4676 Admiralty Way Ste 1001 .... Marina del Rey CA 90292 | 310-822-1511 | 823-6714 | 668
TF: 800-757-1111 ■ *Web:* isi.edu

USC Solutions Inc 546 Harvey Faulk Rd .... Sanford NC 27332 | 919-776-5236 | | 549

USCA (US Curling Assn)
5525 Clem's Way .... Stevens Point WI 54482 | 715-344-1199 | 344-2279 | 48-22
TF: 888-287-5377 ■ *Web:* teamusa.org/usa-curling

USCB Inc 3333 Wilshire Blvd .... Los Angeles CA 90010 | 213-387-6181 | | 160
Web: www.uscbinc.com

USCC (US Cellular Corp)
8410 W Bryn Mawr Ave Ste 700 .... Chicago IL 60631 | 773-399-8900 | | 730
NYSE: USM ■ *TF:* 888-944-9400 ■ *Web:* www.uscellular.com

USCCB (US Conference of Catholic Bishops)
3211 Fourth St NE .... Washington DC 20017 | 202-541-3000 | 541-3322 | 48-20
TF: 866-582-0943 ■ *Web:* www.usccb.org

USCG (US Coast Guard)
2100 Second St SW .... Washington DC 20593 | 202-372-4620 | | 340-11
Web: www.uscg.mil

US-China Business Council, The
1818 N St NW Ste 200 .... Washington DC 20036 | 202-429-0340 | 775-2476 | 49-12
Web: www.uschina.org

USCIB (US Council for International Business)
1212 Ave of the Americas 18th Fl .... New York NY 10036 | 212-354-4480 | 575-0327 | 49-12
Web: www.uscib.org

USCIRF (US Commission on International Religious Freedom)
800 N Capitol St NW Ste 790 .... Washington DC 20002 | 202-523-3240 | 523-5020 | 340-20
Web: www.uscirf.gov

USCJ (United Synagogue of Conservative Judaism)
820 Second Ave .... New York NY 10017 | 212-533-7800 | 353-9439 | 48-20
Web: www.uscj.org

USCRI (US Committee for Refugees & Immigrants)
2231 Crystal Dr Ste 350 .... Arlington VA 22202 | 703-310-1130 | 769-4241 | 48-5
Web: www.refugees.org

USD (Union Sanitary District)
5072 Benson Rd PO Box 5050 .... Union City CA 94587 | 510-477-7500 | | 804
Web: www.unionsanitary.com

USDA (Department of Agriculture)
1400 Independence Ave SW .... Washington DC 20250 | 202-720-3631 | 720-2166 | 340-1
TF: 844-433-2774 ■ *Web:* www.usda.gov

USDA Ctr for Nutrition Policy & Promotion
3101 Pk Ctr Dr .... Alexandria VA 22302 | 703-305-7600 | 305-3300 | 197
Web: www.fns.usda.gov

USDA Graduate School
600 Maryland Ave SW .... Washington DC 20024 | 202-314-3600 | | 340-1
Web: cicorp.com

USDiagnostics Inc
2007 Bob Wallace Ave .... Huntsville AL 35805 | 256-534-4881 | | 475
Web: www.usdiagnostics.com

USDM Life Sciences
535 Chapala St .... Santa Barbara CA 93101 | 888-231-0816 | 231-0816 | 180
TF: 888-231-0816 ■ *Web:* www.usdm.com

USEA (US Energy Assn)
1300 Pennsylvania Ave NW Ste 550 .... Washington DC 20004 | 202-312-1230 | | 48-12
Web: www.usea.org

Used-Car-Parts.com Inc
1980 Highland Pk .... Fort Wright KY 41017 | 859-344-1925 | | 224
TF: 800-288-7415 ■ *Web:* www.car-part.com

Usem Inc 703 17th Ave NW .... Austin MN 55912 | 507-396-4083 | | 57
Web: useminc.com

Usemco 1602 Rezin Rd .... Tomah WI 54660 | 608-372-5911 | | 492
Web: www.usemco.com

USENIX Assn 2560 Ninth St Ste 215 .... Berkeley CA 94710 | 510-528-8649 | 548-5738 | 48-9
TF: 800-397-3342 ■ *Web:* www.usenix.org

Userful Corp 200-709 11th Ave SW .... Calgary AB T2R0E3 | 403-289-2177 | | 180
Web: www.userful.com

USET (US Equestrian Team Foundation Inc)
1040 Pottersville Rd PO Box 355 .... Gladstone NJ 07934 | 908-234-1251 | 234-0670 | 48-22
TF: 800-688-0700 ■ *Web:* www.uset.org

USF (University of South Florida College of Medicine)
12901 Bruce B Downs Blvd .... Tampa FL 33612 | 813-974-2229 | 974-4990 | 167-2
TF: 877-338-2577 ■ *Web:* health.usf.edu

USF Fabrication Inc 3200 W 84th St .... Hialeah FL 33018 | 305-556-1661 | | 480
Web: www.usffab.com

USF Holland Inc 700 S Waverly Rd .... Holland MI 49423 | 616-395-5000 | 392-3104 | 780
Web: www.yrcregional.com

USFA (US Fencing Assn)
1 Olympic Plaza .... Colorado Springs CO 80909 | 719-866-4511 | 632-5737 | 48-22
TF: 888-431-3598 ■ *Web:* www.usfencing.org

USfalcon Inc
100 Regency Forest Dr Suite 150 .... Cary NC 27560 | 919-388-3778 | 392-1040* | 180
**Fax Area Code:* 412 ■ *Web:* www.usfalcon.com

USFS (Forest Service)
1400 Independence Ave SW .... Washington DC 20050 | 202-205-8333 | | 340-1
TF: 800-832-1355 ■ *Web:* www.fs.fed.us

USFSA (US Figure Skating Assn)
20 First St .... Colorado Springs CO 80906 | 719-635-5200 | 635-9548 | 48-22
TF: 800-332-9256 ■ *Web:* www.usfsa.org

USFWS (US Fish & Wildlife Service)
1849 C St NW .... Washington DC 20240 | 202-208-4717 | 208-6965 | 340-13
TF: 800-344-9453 ■ *Web:* www.fws.gov

USG Corp 550 W Adams St .... Chicago IL 60661 | 312-436-4000 | 672-4093 | 347
NYSE: USG ■ *TF:* 800-874-4968 ■ *Web:* www.usg.com

USGA (US Golf Assn)
77 Liberty Corner Rd .... Far Hills NJ 07931 | 908-234-2300 | 234-9687 | 48-22
TF Orders: 800-336-4446 ■ *Web:* www.usga.org

Usglobalsat Inc
1308 John Reed Ct .... City Of Industry CA 91745 | 626-968-4145 | | 647
Web: www.usglobalsat.com

USGS (US Geological Survey)
12201 Sunrise Valley Dr .... Reston VA 20192 | 703-648-6723 | | 340-13
TF: 888-275-8747 ■ *Web:* www.usgs.gov

USGS Education
USGS National Ctr 12201 Sunrise Vly Dr .... Reston VA 20192 | 703-648-5953 | 648-4454 | 397
Web: education.usgs.gov

USGS Forest & Rangeland Ecosystem Science Ctr
777 NW Ninth St Ste 400 .... Corvallis OR 97330 | 541-750-1030 | 750-1069 | 668
Web: fresc.usgs.gov

USGS Leetown Science Ctr
11649 Leetown Rd .... Kearneysville WV 25430 | 304-724-4400 | 724-4465 | 668
Web: www.lsc.usgs.gov

USGS Northern Rocky Mountain Science Ctr (NRMSC)
2327 University Way Ste 2 .... Bozeman MT 59715 | 406-994-4293 | 994-6556 | 668
Web: www.usgs.gov/centers/norock/connect

USGS Southwest Biological Science Ctr
2255 N Gemini Dr .... Flagstaff AZ 86001 | 928-556-7094 | 556-7092 | 668
Web: sbsc.wr.usgs.gov

USGS Upper Midwest Environmental Sciences Ctr
2630 Fanta Reed Rd .... La Crosse WI 54603 | 608-783-6451 | 783-6066 | 668
Web: www.umesc.usgs.gov

USGS Western Fisheries Research Ctr
US Geological Survey 6505 NE 65th St .... Seattle WA 98115 | 206-526-6282 | 526-6654 | 668
Web: wfrc.usgs.gov

USHEALTH Group Inc
300 Burnett St Ste 200 .... Fort Worth TX 76102 | 800-387-9027 | | 391-6
TF: 800-387-9027 ■ *Web:* www.ushealthgroup.com

Ushers Machine & Tool Company Inc
180 Ushers Rd .... Round Lake NY 12151 | 518-877-5501 | | 454
Web: www.ushersm.com

Usherwood Office Technology Inc
1005 W Fayette St .... Syracuse NY 13204 | 315-472-0050 | | 41
TF: 800-724-2119 ■ *Web:* www.usherwood.com

Ushio America Inc 5440 Cerritos Ave .... Cypress CA 90630 | 714-236-8600 | 776-3641* | 437
**Fax Area Code:* 800 ■ **Fax:* Mktg ■ *TF:* 800-326-1960 ■ *Web:* www.ushio.com

uShip Inc 205 Brazos St .... Austin TX 78701 | 800-698-7447 | | 387
TF: 800-698-7447 ■ *Web:* www.uship.com

Ushose Corp 816 Forestwood Dr .... Romeoville IL 60446 | 815-886-1140 | | 505
Web: www.ushosecorp.com

USI (Underground Specialists Inc)
570 SW 16th Terr .... Pompano Beach FL 33069 | 954-782-8740 | 782-1919 | 787
Web: www.usicable.com

USI Holdings Corp
200 Summit Lake Dr Ste 350 .... Valhalla NY 10595 | 914-749-8500 | | 390
Web: www.usi.com

USI Inc 2460 Stock Creek Blvd .... Rockford TN 37853 | 203-245-8586 | | 247
Web: www.usi-laminate.com

Usibelli Coal Mine Inc
100 River Rd PO Box 1000 .... Healy AK 99743 | 907-683-2226 | 683-2253 | 501
TF: 800-478-5554 ■ *Web:* www.usibelli.com

Usinatech Inc 1099 Chemin Ely .... Melbourne QC J0B2B0 | 819-826-3774 | | 757
TF: 800-567-2748 ■ *Web:* usinatech.com

Usine Rotec Inc
125 Rue De L'eglise Rr 1 .... Baie-du-febvre QC J0G1A0 | 450-783-6444 | 783-6446 | 321
Web: www.rotecbeds.com

UsingMiles Inc
21050 Centre Pointe pkwy .... Santa Clarita CA 91350 | 303-645-0531 | | 387
Web: www.usingmiles.com

USIS 7799 Leesburg Pk Ste 1100 .... Falls Church VA 22043 | 703-448-0178 | | 635

USIS (United States Information Systems Inc)
35 W Jefferson Ave .... Pearl River NY 10965 | 845-358-7755 | | 787
TF: 866-222-3778 ■ *Web:* www.usis.net

Usitech Nov Inc
1295 1e Rue Parc Industriel .... Sainte-marie De Beauce QC G6E3T3 | 418-387-3133 | | 454
Web: www.usitechnov.com

US-Japan Business Council
1615 H St NW .... Washington DC 20062 | 202-463-5772 | | 49-12
Web: www.usjbc.org

US-Japan High-Speed Rail LLC
1212 New York Ave NW Ste 700 .... Washington DC 20005 | 202-403-0437 | | 791
Web: www.usjhsr.com

USL Pharma 301 S Cherokee St .... Denver CO 80223 | 303-607-4500 | | 583
TF: 800-654-2299 ■ *Web:* www.upsher-smith.com

USlegal Inc 3720 Flowood Dr .... Jackson MS 39232 | 601-896-0180 | | 787
Web: www.uslegal.com

USM Aerostructures Corp 74 W Sixth St .... Wyoming PA 18644 | 570-613-1234 | | 295
TF: 800-869-3557 ■ *Web:* www.usmaero.com

USM Business Systems Inc
14175 Sullyfield Cir .... Chantilly VA 20151 | 703-263-0855 | | 261
Web: usmsystems.com

USM Corp 32 Stevens St .... Haverhill MA 01830 | 978-374-0303 | 521-5519 | 386
Web: www.usm-americas.com

USM Inc 1880 Markley St .... Norristown PA 19401 | 610-278-9000 | 275-8023 | 186
TF: 800-355-4000 ■ *Web:* www.usmservices.com

USMA (US Metric Assn Inc)
10245 Andasol Ave .... Northridge CA 91325 | 310-832-3763 | | 48-10

Usman Trade
11018 Watson Mill Ct Ste 103 .... Sugar Land TX 77478 | 281-933-7200 | | 196
Web: usmantrade.com

Usmax Corp 382 Gambrills Rd .... Gambrills MD 21054 | 301-912-1166 | | 177
Web: www.usmax.com

USMC (US Marine Corps)
1555 Southgate Rd
Marine Corps National Capital Region Command . Arlington VA 22214 | 703-614-6411 | 614-6411 | 340-7
Web: www.marines.mil/Pages/Default.aspx

	Phone	Fax	Class
USMEF (US Meat Export Federation Inc) 1050 17th St Ste 2200 ... Denver CO 80265 *Web:* www.usmef.org	303-623-6328	623-0297	49-6
US-Mexico Chamber of Commerce 1300 Pennsylvania Ave NW Ste 0003 ... Washington DC 20004 *TF:* 800-964-5373 ■ *Web:* www.usmcoc.org	202-312-1520	312-1530	138
US-Mexico Chamber of Commerce California Regional Chapter 2450 Colorado Ave Ste 400E ... Santa Monica CA 90404 *TF:* 800-997-9148 ■ *Web:* www.usmcocca.org	310-586-7901	586-7800	138
Usmilcom Inc 1952 E Mcfadden Ave ... Santa Ana CA 92705 *Web:* www.usmilcom.com	714-835-3545		253
USNMFCU (US New Mexico Federal Credit Union) 3939 Osuna Rd NE PO Box 129 ... Albuquerque NM 87109 *TF:* 888-342-8766 ■ *Web:* useaglefcu.org	505-342-8888		219
USNR 1981 Schurman Way PO Box 310 ... Woodland WA 98674 *TF:* 800-289-8767 ■ *Web:* www.inovec.com	360-225-8267	225-8017	683
USNR 558 Robinson Rd PO Box 310 ... Woodland WA 98674 *TF:* 800-289-8767 ■ *Web:* www.usnr.com	360-225-8267	225-8017	821
USO (United Service Organizations) 2111 Wilson Blvd Ste 1200 ... Arlington VA 22201 *TF:* 800-876-7469 ■ *Web:* www.uso.org	703-908-6400		48-19
USOC (US Olympic Committee) 1 Olympic Plaza ... Colorado Springs CO 80909 *Web:* www.teamusa.org	719-632-5551		48-22
Uson LP 8640 N Eldridge Pkwy ... Houston TX 77041 *Web:* www.uson.com	281-671-2000	671-2001	201
USP (US Pharmacopeia) 12601 Twinbrook Pkwy ... Rockville MD 20852 *TF:* 800-227-8772 ■ *Web:* www.usp.org	301-881-0666		49-8
USP (US Penitentiary) *Allenwood* PO Box 3500 ... White Deer PA 17887 *Web:* www.bop.gov/locations/institutions/alp	570-547-0963	547-9201	212
USP Structural Connectors Inc 703 Rogers Dr ... Montgomery MN 56069 *Web:* www.uspconnectors.com	507-364-7333		480
USPA (US Parachute Assn) 5401 Southpoint Ctr Blvd ... Fredericksburg VA 22407 *Web:* www.uspa.org	540-604-9740	604-9741	48-22
USPB (US Premium Beef LLC) 12200 N Ambassador Dr PO Box 20103 ... Kansas City MO 64163 *TF:* 866-877-2525 ■ *Web:* www.uspremiumbeef.com	816-713-8800	713-8810	296-26
USPB (Potatoes USA) 4949 S Syracuse St Ste 400 ... Denver CO 80237 *Web:* www.uspotatoes.com	303-369-7783	369-7718	48-2
USPI (United Surgical Partners International Inc) 15305 Dallas Pkwy ... Addison TX 75001 *Web:* www.uspi.com	972-713-3500		352
USPS (US Postal Service) 475 L'Enfant Plaza W SW ... Washington DC 20260 *TF Cust Svc:* 800-275-8777 ■ *Web:* www.usps.com	202-268-2000		340-20
USPTA (US Professional Tennis Assn) 3535 Briarpark Dr Ste 1 ... Houston TX 77042 *TF:* 800-877-8248 ■ *Web:* uspta.com	713-978-7782	978-7780	48-22
USRA (Universities Space Research Assn) 10211 Wincopin Cir Ste 500 ... Columbia MD 21044 *Web:* www.usra.edu	410-730-2656	730-3496	49-19
USRA (US Racquetball) 2812 W Colorado Ave Ste 220 ... Colorado Springs CO 80904 *Web:* www.teamusa.org	719-635-5396	635-0685	48-22
US-Reports Inc 5802 Wright Dr ... Loveland CO 80538 *TF:* 800-223-2310 ■ *Web:* www.us-reports.com	800-223-2310		463
US-Russia Business Council 1110 Vermont Ave NW Ste 350 ... Washington DC 20005 *Web:* www.usrbc.org	202-739-9180	659-5920	49-12
USS Alabama Battleship Memorial Park 2703 Battleship Pkwy PO Box 65 ... Mobile AL 36602 *Web:* www.ussalabama.com	251-433-2703		50-4
USS Arizona Memorial 1 Arizona Memorial Pl ... Honolulu HI 96818 *Web:* www.nps.gov/usar	808-422-0561	483-8608	50-4
USS Bowfin Submarine Museum & Park 11 Arizona Memorial Dr ... Honolulu HI 96818 *Web:* www.bowfin.org	808-423-1341		520
USS Cal Builders Inc 8051 Main St ... Stanton CA 90680 *Web:* www.usscalbuilders.com	714-828-4882		186
USS Constitution Museum PO Box 291812 ... Boston MA 02129 *TF:* 800-733-1830 ■ *Web:* www.ussconstitutionmuseum.org	617-426-1812	242-0496	520
USS Corp 780 Frelinghuysen Ave ... Newark NJ 07114 *TF:* 800-228-4653 ■ *Web:* usscorp.com	973-242-1110		627
USS Hornet Museum 707 W Hornet Ave Pier 3 ... Alameda CA 94501 *TF:* 800-555-8355 ■ *Web:* www.uss-hornet.org	510-521-8448	749-3699	520
USS Kidd Veterans Memorial & Museum 305 S River Rd ... Baton Rouge LA 70802 *TF:* 800-638-0594 ■ *Web:* www.usskidd.com	225-342-1942	342-2039	50-4
USS Lexington Museum on the Bay 2914 N Shoreline Blvd ... Corpus Christi TX 78402 *TF:* 800-523-9539 ■ *Web:* www.usslexington.com	361-888-4873		520
USS Liberty Memorial Public 1620 11th Ave ... Grafton WI 53024	262-375-5315		434-3
USS Missouri Memorial Assn Inc 63 Cowpens St ... Honolulu HI 96818 *TF:* 877-644-4896 ■ *Web:* ussmissouri.org	808-455-1600	455-1598	50-4
USSCO (United Stationers Supply Co) 1 Pkwy N Blvd Ste 100 Ste 100 ... Deerfield IL 60015 *Web:* www.essendant.com	847-627-7000		534
USSD (US Society on Dams) 1616 17th St Ste 483 ... Denver CO 80202 *Web:* www.ussdams.org	303-628-5430	628-5431	49-3
Ussery Printing Company Inc 3402 Century Cir ... Irving TX 75062 *Web:* www.printussery.com	972-438-8344		627
USSM (Ulbrich Stainless Steels & Special Metals Inc) 57 Dodge Ave ... North Haven CT 06473 **Fax:* Sales ■ *TF:* 800-243-1676 ■ *Web:* www.ulbrich.com	203-239-4481	239-7479*	723
USS-POSCO Industries 900 Loveridge Rd ... Pittsburg CA 94565 **Fax Area Code:* 925 ■ *TF:* 800-877-7672 ■ *Web:* www.ussposco.com	800-877-7672	439-6722*	723

	Phone	Fax	Class
USTA (US Telecom Assn) 607-14th St NW Ste 400 ... Washington DC 20005 *Web:* ustelecom.org	202-326-7300	326-7333	49-20
USTA (US Trotting Assn) 750 Michigan Ave ... Columbus OH 43215 *TF:* 877-800-8782 ■ *Web:* www.ustrotting.com	614-224-2291	224-4575	48-22
USTL (US Term Limits) 1250 Connecticut Ave NW Ste 200 ... Washington DC 20036 *Web:* www.termlimits.org	202-261-3532		48-7
UsTrendy INC 1842 Beacon St Ste 404 ... Brookline MA 02445 **Fax Area Code:* 617 ■ *TF:* 888-535-1187 ■ *Web:* www.ustrendy.com	888-535-1187	437-9440*	393
USVP (US Venture Partners) 1460 El Camino Real ... Menlo Park CA 94025 *Web:* www.usvp.com	650-854-9080	854-3018	792
USW (United Steel Workers) 3340 Perimeter Hill Dr ... Nashville TN 37211 *Web:* www.usw.org	615-834-8590		414
USW (US Wheat Assoc) 3103 Tenth St N Ste 300 ... Arlington VA 22201 **Fax Area Code:* 703 ■ *Web:* www.uswheat.org	202-463-0999	524-4399*	48-2
USWired Inc 2107 N First St Ste 250 ... San Jose CA 95131 *TF:* 877-879-4733 ■ *Web:* www.uswired.com	408-432-1144		180
UTA (United Talent Agency Inc) 9336 Civic Ctr Dr ... Beverly Hills CA 90210 *Web:* www.unitedtalent.com	310-273-6700	247-1111	731
Utah			
Administrative Office of the Courts 450 S State ... Salt Lake City UT 84114 *Web:* www.utcourts.gov	801-578-3800	578-3843	339-45
Aging & Adult Services Div 195 N 1950 W ... Salt Lake City UT 84116 *TF:* 877-424-4640 ■ *Web:* www.hsdaas.utah.gov	801-538-3910	538-4395	339-45
Agriculture & Food Dept 350 N Redwood Rd PO Box 146500 ... Salt Lake City UT 84114 *Web:* www.ag.utah.gov	801-538-7100	538-7126	339-45
Arts Council 617 E S Temple ... Salt Lake City UT 84102 *Web:* heritage.utah.gov	801-236-7555	236-7555	339-45
Attorney General PO Box 142320 ... Salt Lake City UT 84114 *Web:* www.attorneygeneral.utah.gov	801-538-9600	538-1121	339-45
Child & Family Services Div 195 N 1950 W Rm 225 ... Salt Lake City UT 84116 *TF:* 855-323-3237 ■ *Web:* dcfs.utah.gov	801-538-4100	538-3993	339-45
Commerce Dept 160 E Broadway Heber M Wells Bldg ... Salt Lake City UT 84111 *Web:* www.commerce.utah.gov	801-530-6701	530-6446	339-45
Community & Economic Development Dept 60 E S Temple 3rd Fl ... Salt Lake City UT 84111 *TF:* 855-204-9046 ■ *Web:* business.utah.gov	801-538-8680	538-8888	339-45
Consumer Protection Div 160 E Broadway ... Salt Lake City UT 84111 *Web:* consumerprotection.utah.gov	801-530-6601		339-45
Corrections Dept 14717 S Minuteman Dr ... Draper UT 84020 *Web:* www.corrections.utah.gov	801-545-5500		339-45
Crime Victim Reparations Office 350 E 500 S Ste 200 ... Salt Lake City UT 84111 *Web:* www.crimevictim.utah.gov	801-238-2360	533-4127	339-45
Department of Technology Services 1 State Office Bldg Fl 6 ... Salt Lake City UT 84114 *Web:* www.dts.utah.gov	801-537-9000		339-45
Education Office 250 E 500 S PO Box 144200 ... Salt Lake City UT 84111 *Web:* schools.utah.gov	801-538-7500		339-45
Environmental Quality Dept 195 N 1950 W PO Box 144810 ... Salt Lake City UT 84116 *TF:* 800-458-0145 ■ *Web:* www.deq.utah.gov	801-536-4400	536-0061	339-45
Financial Institutions Dept PO Box 146800 ... Salt Lake City UT 84111 *Web:* www.dfi.utah.gov	801-538-8830	538-8894	339-45
Governor 350 N State St Ste 200 PO Box 142220 ... Salt Lake City UT 84114 *TF:* 800-705-2464 ■ *Web:* www.utah.gov/governor	801-538-1000		339-45
Health Dept PO Box 141010 ... Salt Lake City UT 84114 *TF:* 888-222-2542 ■ *Web:* www.health.utah.gov	801-538-6003		339-45
Higher Education Assistance Authority 60 S 400 W PO Box 145110 ... Salt Lake City UT 84114 *TF:* 877-336-7378 ■ *Web:* www.uheaa.org	801-321-7294	366-8431	725
Higher Education System 60 S 400 W ... Salt Lake City UT 84101 *TF:* 877-336-7378 ■ *Web:* www.utahsbr.edu	801-321-7294	366-8431	339-45
Highway Patrol 4501 S 2700 W ... Salt Lake City UT 84119 *Web:* dld.utah.gov	801-965-4437		339-45
Housing Corp 2479 S Lake Park Blvd ... West Valley City UT 84120 *TF:* 800-284-6950 ■ *Web:* www.utahhousingcorp.org	801-902-8200		339-45
Human Resource Management Dept State Office Bldg Ste 2120 ... Salt Lake City UT 84114 *Web:* www.dhrm.utah.gov	801-538-3025	538-3403	339-45
Human Services Dept 195 N 1950 W ... Salt Lake City UT 84116 *Web:* hs.utah.gov	801-538-4171	538-4016	339-45
Insurance Dept 3110 State Office Bldg ... Salt Lake City UT 84114 *Web:* www.insurance.utah.gov	801-538-3800	538-3829	339-45
Labor Commission PO Box 146600 ... Salt Lake City UT 84114 *TF:* 800-530-5090 ■ *Web:* www.laborcommission.utah.gov	801-530-6800	530-6390	339-45
Legislature 350 N State St Ste 320 ... Salt Lake City UT 84114 *Web:* www.le.utah.gov	801-538-1035	326-1475	339-45
Lieutenant Governor Utah State Capitol Complex Ste 220 PO Box 142325 ... Salt Lake City UT 84114 *TF:* 800-995-8683 ■ *Web:* www.utah.gov/ltgovernor	801-538-1041	538-1133	339-45
Medical Examiner's Office (OME) 4451 S 2700 W ... Taylorsville UT 84129 *Web:* health.utah.gov/ome	801-816-3850	964-1240	339-45
Motor Vehicle Div PO Box 30412 ... Salt Lake City UT 84130 *TF:* 800-368-8824 ■ *Web:* dmv.utah.gov	801-297-7780	297-3570	339-45
Natural Resources Dept 1594 W N Temple Ste 3710 ... Salt Lake City UT 84116 *Web:* Www.naturalresources.utah.gov	801-538-7200	538-7315	339-45

	City	State	ZIP	Phone	Fax	Class
Occupational & Professional Licensing Div PO Box 146741 *TF:* 866-275-3675 ■ *Web:* www.dopl.utah.gov	Salt Lake City	UT	84111	801-530-6628	530-6511	339-45
Office of Tourism 300 N State St *TF:* 800-200-1160 ■ *Web:* www.travel.utah.gov	Salt Lake City	UT	84114	801-538-1900	538-1399	339-45
Pardons & Parole Board 448 E Winchester St Ste 300 *Web:* bop.utah.gov	Murray	UT	84107	801-261-6464	261-6481	339-45
Parks & Recreation Div 1594 W N Temple Ste 116 *TF:* 800-322-3770 ■ *Web:* www.stateparks.utah.gov	Salt Lake City	UT	84116	801-538-7220	538-7378	339-45
Public Service Commission 160 E 300 S PO Box 45585 *Web:* www.psc.state.ut.us	Salt Lake City	UT	84114	801-530-6716	530-6796	339-45
Real Estate Div PO Box 146711 *Web:* realestate.utah.gov	Salt Lake City	UT	84114	801-530-6747	526-4387	339-45
Rehabilitation Office 1595 W 500 S *Web:* www.usor.utah.gov	Salt Lake City	UT	84104	801-887-9500		339-45
Securities Div 160 E 300 S 2nd Fl *TF:* 800-721-7233 ■ *Web:* securities.utah.gov	Salt Lake City	UT	84111	801-530-6600	530-6980	339-45
Sports Commission 201 S Main St Ste 2125 *Web:* www.utahsportscommission.com	Salt Lake City	UT	84111	801-328-2372		339-45
State Treasurer 350 N State St Ste 180 PO Box 142315 *Web:* www.utah.gov	Salt Lake City	UT	84114	801-538-1042	538-1465	339-45
Supreme Court 450 S State St *Web:* www.utcourts.gov/courts/sup	Salt Lake City	UT	84114	801-238-7967		339-45
Tax Commission 210 N 1950 W *TF:* 800-662-4335 ■ *Web:* www.tax.utah.gov	Salt Lake City	UT	84134	801-297-2200	297-7699	339-45
Transportation Dept 4501 S 2700 W PO Box 141265 *Web:* www.udot.utah.gov	Salt Lake City	UT	84119	801-965-4000		339-45
Veterans' Affairs Office 550 Foothills Dr Ste 105 *TF:* 800-326-2372 ■ *Web:* veterans.utah.gov	Salt Lake City	UT	84108	801-326-2372	326-2369	339-45
Vital Records & Statistics Office 288 N 1460 W PO Box 141012 *Web:* www.health.utah.gov/vitalrecords	Salt Lake City	UT	84114	801-538-6105		339-45
Wildlife Resources Div 1594 W N Temple Ste 2110 Box 146301 *Web:* wildlife.utah.gov	Salt Lake City	UT	84114	801-538-4700	538-4745	339-45
Workers' Compensation Fund 100 W Towne Ridge Pkwy *TF:* 800-446-2667 ■ *Web:* www.wcfgroup.com	Sandy	UT	84070	385-351-8000		339-45
Utah Assn of Realtors 230 W Towne Ridge Pkwy Ste 500 *TF:* 800-594-8933 ■ *Web:* www.utahrealtors.com	Sandy	UT	84070	801-676-5200	676-5225	656
Utah Botanical Ctr 920 S 50 W PO Box 265 *Web:* usubotanicalcenter.org	Kaysville	UT	84037	801-593-8969		97
Utah Business Magazine 90 S 400 W Ste 650 *TF:* 866-294-1660 ■ *Web:* www.utahbusiness.com	Salt Lake City	UT	84101	801-568-0114		457-5
Utah Correctional Industries 14072 S Pony Express Rd *Web:* uci.utah.gov	Draper	UT	84020	801-576-7700		630
Utah County 100 E Center St Ste 2200 *Web:* www.co.utah.ut.us	Provo	UT	84606	801-851-8000		338
Utah Dental Assn 1151 East 3900 South Ste 160	Salt Lake City	UT	84124	801-261-5315		227
Utah Field House of Natural History State Park 496 E Main St *Web:* stateparks.utah.gov	Vernal	UT	84078	435-789-3799		565
Utah Imaging Associates Inc 380 N 200 W Ste 209 *TF:* 800-223-3131 ■ *Web:* www.utahimaging.com	Bountiful	UT	84010	801-924-0029		415
Utah Jazz 301 W S Temple St Energy Solutions Arena **Fax:* PR ■ *Web:* www.nba.com	Salt Lake City	UT	84101	801-325-2500	325-2578*	714-1
Utah Lake State Park 4400 W Ctr St *Web:* www.stateparks.utah.gov	Provo	UT	84601	801-375-0731	373-4215	565
Utah Lions Eye Bank *John A Moran Eye Ctr* 65 Mario Capecchi Dr *Web:* www.utaheyebank.org	Salt Lake City	UT	84132	801-581-2039	585-5703	269
Utah Medical Products Inc 7043 S 300 W *NASDAQ:* UTMD ■ *TF:* 866-754-9789 ■ *Web:* www.utahmed.com	Midvale	UT	84047	801-566-1200	566-2062	476
Utah Metal Works Inc (UMW) 805 Everett Ave *TF:* 877-221-0099 ■ *Web:* www.umw.com	Salt Lake City	UT	84116	877-221-0099		660
Utah Museum of Fine Arts 410 Campus Ctr Dr University of Utah *Web:* www.umfa.utah.edu	Salt Lake City	UT	84112	801-581-7332	585-5198	520
Utah Museum of Natural History, The 301 Wakara Way *Web:* nhmu.utah.edu	Salt Lake City	UT	84108	801-581-4303	585-3684	520
Utah Nurses Assn (UNA) 4505 S Wastch Blvd Ste 330B *TF:* 800-338-7657 ■ *Web:* www.utnurse.org	Salt Lake City	UT	84124	801-272-4510		533
Utah Paper Box Company Inc 920 South 700 West *Web:* www.upbslc.com	Salt Lake City	UT	84104	801-363-0093		101
Utah Refractories Corp 2200 N 1200 W *TF:* 800-345-6808 ■ *Web:* utah-refractories-corp.com	Lehi	UT	84043	801-768-3591	768-2684	662
Utah Republican Party 117 E S Temple St *Web:* utah.gop	Salt Lake City	UT	84111	801-533-9777		616-2
Utah Scientific 4750 Wiley Post Way Ste 150 *Web:* www.utsci.com	Salt Lake City	UT	84116	801-575-8801		647
Utah State Bar 645 S 200 E *TF:* 877-752-2611 ■ *Web:* www.utahbar.org	Salt Lake City	UT	84111	801-531-9077	531-0660	72
Utah State Hospital 1300 E Ctr St *Web:* ush.utah.gov	Provo	UT	84606	801-344-4400	344-4225	374-5
Utah State Legislature 350 North State St Ste 320 PO Box 145115 *TF:* 800-244-4636 ■ *Web:* le.utah.gov/documents/bills.htm	Salt Lake City	UT	84114	801-538-1035	538-1728	433
Utah State Library 250 N 1950 W Ste A *TF:* 800-662-9150 ■ *Web:* heritage.utah.gov	Salt Lake City	UT	84116	801-715-6777	715-6767	434-5
Utah State Prison 14425 Bitterbrush Ln *TF:* 800-375-5283 ■ *Web:* corrections.utah.gov	Draper	UT	84020	801-576-7000		213
Utah State Railroad Museum 2501 Wall Ave *Web:* theunionstation.org	Ogden	UT	84401	801-393-9886		520
Utah State University 1600 Old Main Hill *TF:* 800-488-8108 ■ *Web:* www.usu.edu	Logan	UT	84322	435-797-1116	797-1110	166
Utah State University Merrill-Cazier Library 3000 Old Main Hill **Fax:* Admin ■ *Web:* www.library.usu.edu	Logan	UT	84322	435-797-2631	797-2880*	434-6
Utah Symphony & Opera 123 W S Temple *Web:* www.utahsymphony.org	Salt Lake City	UT	84101	801-533-6683		573-3
Utah System of Higher Education 60 South 400 West *TF:* 800-418-8757 ■ *Web:* www.higheredutah.org	Salt Lake City	UT	84101	801-321-7200		786
Utah Transit Authority 3600 S 700 W PO Box 30810 *TF:* 888-743-3882 ■ *Web:* www.rideuta.com	Salt Lake City	UT	84130	801-262-5626		468
Utah Valley Convention & Visitors Bureau 111 S University Ave *TF:* 800-222-8824 ■ *Web:* www.utahvalley.com	Provo	UT	84601	801-851-2100	851-2109	206
Utah Valley Regional Medical Ctr 1034 N 500 W *TF:* 800-530-5090 ■ *Web:* www.intermountainhealthcare.org/xp/public/uvrmc	Provo	UT	84604	801-373-7850	357-7780	374-3
Utah Valley State College 800 W University Pkwy *TF:* 800-952-8220 ■ *Web:* www.uvu.edu	Orem	UT	84058	801-863-4636		162
Utah's Hogle Zoo 2600 E Sunnyside Ave *TF:* 800-218-0977 ■ *Web:* www.hoglezoo.org	Salt Lake City	UT	84108	801-582-1631		823
Utak Laboratories Inc 25020 Ave Tibbitts *TF:* 800-235-3442 ■ *Web:* www.utak.com	Valencia	CA	91355	661-294-3935	294-9272	231
UT-Battelle 1201 Oak Ridge Tpke Ste 100 *Web:* www.ut-battelle.org	Oak Ridge	TN	37830	865-220-5101		668
UTC (Universal Technology Corp) 1270 N Fairfield Rd *Web:* www.utcdayton.com	Dayton	OH	45432	937-426-2808		261
UTC (Utilities Telecom Council) 1129 20th St NW Ste 350 *Web:* www.utc.org	Washington	DC	20036	202-872-0030	872-1331	49-20
UTC Aerospace Systems 14300 Judicial Rd *NYSE:* GR	Burnsville	MN	55306	952-892-4000		22
UTC Overseas Inc 370 W Passaic St Ste 3000 *Web:* www.utcoverseas.com	Rochelle Park	NJ	07662	201-270-4600		313
UTC RETAIL Inc 100 Rawson Rd **Fax Area Code:* 585 ■ *TF:* 800-349-0546 ■ *Web:* www.utcretail.com	Victor	NY	14564	800-349-0546	924-1434*	614
Ute Mountain Casino 3 Weeminuche Dr *TF:* 800-258-8007 ■ *Web:* www.utemountaincasino.com	Towaoc	CO	81334	970-565-8800	565-6553	133
Ute Water Conservancy District 3975 Rapid Creek Rd *TF:* 800-873-8707 ■ *Web:* www.utewater.org	Palisade	CO	81526	970-464-5563		804
UTEX Industries Inc 10810 Katy Fwy Ste 100 *TF:* 800-359-9230 ■ *Web:* www.utexind.com	Houston	TX	77043	713-467-1000	467-3602	326
UTGI (United Trust Group Inc) 5250 S Sixth St *OTC:* UTGN ■ *TF:* 800-323-0050 ■ *Web:* www.utgins.com	Springfield	IL	62705	217-241-6410		360-4
UTHCT (University of Texas Health Ctr at Tyler) 11937 US Hwy 271 *Web:* www.uthealth.org	Tyler	TX	75708	903-877-7000		374-3
UTHSC (University of Tennessee) 1331 Cir Pk Dr 320 Student Services Bldg **Fax:* Admissions ■ *Web:* www.utk.edu	Knoxville	TN	37996	865-974-1000	974-6341*	166
UTi Worldwide Inc 100 Oceangate Ste 1500 *NASDAQ:* UTIW ■ *Web:* www.go2uti.com	Long Beach	CA	90802	562-552-9400		449
Utica Boilers Inc PO Box 4729 **Fax Area Code:* 315 ■ *TF:* 800-325-5479 ■ *Web:* www.uticaboilers.com	Utica	NY	13504	866-847-6656	797-3762*	357
Utica College 1600 Burrstone Rd **Fax:* Admissions ■ *TF Admissions:* 800-782-8884 ■ *Web:* www.utica.edu	Utica	NY	13502	315-792-3111	792-3003*	166
Utica Community Schools (UCS) 11303 Greendale Dr *TF:* 800-877-8339 ■ *Web:* www.uticak12.org	Sterling Heights	MI	48312	586-797-1000		685
Utica Cutlery Co 820 Noyes St PO Box 10527 *Web:* www.uticacutlery.com	Utica	NY	13503	315-733-4663	733-6602	702
Utica Enterprises Co 15030 23 Mile Rd *Web:* www.fremontcompany.net	Shelby Charter Township	MI	48315	586-566-6529		493
Utica First Insurance Co 5981 Airport Rd *TF:* 800-456-4556 ■ *Web:* www.uticafirst.com	Oriskany	NY	13424	315-736-8211	768-4408	391-4
Utica Metal Products Inc 1526 Lincoln Ave *Web:* www.uticametals.com	Utica	NY	13502	315-732-6163		295
Utica National Insurance Group 180 Genesee St *TF:* 800-274-1914 ■ *Web:* www.uticanational.com	New Hartford	NY	13413	315-734-2000	734-2680	391-2
Utica School of Commerce 201 Bleecker St *TF:* 800-321-4872 ■ *Web:* www.uscny.edu	Utica	NY	13501	315-733-2307	733-9281	800

Name / Address	City	State	ZIP	Phone	Fax	Class
Utica Zoo 1 Utica Zoo Way *Web:* www.uticazoo.org	Utica	NY	13501	315-738-0472	738-0475	823
UTIG (University of Texas Institute for Geophysics) JJ Pickle Research Campus Bldg 196 10100 Burnet Rd (RR2200) *Web:* www.ig.utexas.edu	Austin	TX	78758	512-471-6156	471-8844	668
Utilant LLC 475 Ellicott St Ste 5 *TF:* 888-884-5268 ■ *Web:* utilant.com	Buffalo	NY	14203	888-884-5268		177
Utilimaster 603 Earthway Blvd *TF:* 800-582-3454 ■ *Web:* www.utilimaster.com	Bristol	IN	46507	800-582-3454		54
Utilipath Inc 136 Corporate Pk Dr Ste G	Mooresville	NC	28117	704-948-1005	658-3929	188
Utilisave LLC 129 W 27th St 11th Fl *Web:* www.utilisave.com	New York	NY	10001	718-382-4500		734
Utilities Telecom Council (UTC) 1129 20th St NW Ste 350 *Web:* www.utc.org	Washington	DC	20036	202-872-0030	872-1331	49-20
Utility Concrete Products 2495 Bungalow Rd *TF:* 800-241-0925 ■ *Web:* www.utilityconcrete.com	Morris	IL	60450	815-416-1000		183
Utility Lines Inc 206 W Walnut St *Web:* www.utilitylines.com	Davidson	NC	28036	704-896-8866	896-8868	246
Utility Notification Center of Colorado 16361 Table Mtn Pkwy *TF:* 800-922-1987 ■ *Web:* colorado811.org	Golden	CO	80403	303-232-1991		305
Utility Sales Assoc Inc 930 E Oak St *Web:* www.utilitysales.net	Lake In The Hills	IL	60156	847-658-8965		196
Utility Service Company Inc 535 Courtney Hodges Blvd *TF:* 855-526-4413 ■ *Web:* www.utilityservice.com	Perry	GA	31069	478-987-0303		192
Utility Services Inc 400 N Fourth St *TF:* 800-638-3278 ■ *Web:* www.montana-dakota.com	Bismarck	ND	58501	701-222-7900		188-10
Utility Technologies International Corp 4700 Homer Ohio Ln *Web:* www.uti-corp.com	Groveport	OH	43125	614-482-8080		194
Utility Tool & Trailer Co 151 E 16th St PO Box 360 *Web:* www.uttwi.com	Clintonville	WI	54929	715-823-3167	823-5274	779
Utility Trailer Mfg Co 17295 E Railroad St *TF:* 800-874-6807 ■ *Web:* www.utilitytrailer.com	City of Industry	CA	91748	626-965-1541	965-2790	779
Utility Trailor Manufacturing Co 2921 Hwy 49 N *Web:* www.utm.com	Paragould	AR	72450	870-236-9195		57
Utility Workers Union of America (UWUA) 888 16th St NW Ste 550 *Web:* www.uwua.net	Washington	DC	20006	202-974-8200		414
Utility/Keystone Trailer Sales Inc 1976 Auction Rd *TF:* 888-327-4236 ■ *Web:* www.utilitykeystone.com	Manheim	PA	17545	717-653-9444	653-9443	57
Utilityone Inc 268 W Beaver St Ste 105 *TF:* 800-388-9088 ■ *Web:* getutilityone.com	Hallam	PA	17406	717-840-4200		196
UtiliWorks Consulting LLC 2351 Energy Dr Ste 1010 *Web:* www.utiliworks.com	Baton Rouge	LA	70808	225-766-4188	612-6404	196
Utley Brothers Inc 567 Robbins Dr *Web:* www.utleybros.com	Troy	MI	48083	248-585-1700		627
Utne Reader Magazine 12 N 12th St Ste 400 *TF Cust Svc:* 800-736-8863 ■ *Web:* www.utne.com	Minneapolis	MN	55403	612-338-5040	338-6043	457-11
Utopia 445 E First St *Web:* www.utopiarestaurant.net	Long Beach	CA	90802	562-432-6888		671
Utopia Systems Inc 1172 Old Forge Rd *TF:* 877-804-7421 ■ *Web:* www.utopiasystems.com	New Castle	DE	19720	302-777-0772		180
Utrecht Art Supplies PO Box 1769 **Fax Area Code:* 800 ■ *TF:* 888-336-3114 ■ *Web:* www.utrechtart.com	Galesburg	IL	61402	609-409-8001	382-1979*	43
UTSA (Uniform & Textile Service Assn) 1300 N 17th St Ste 750 *TF:* 800-996-3426 ■ *Web:* www.glrppr.org	Arlington	VA	22209	703-247-2600		49-4
UTSI International Corp 1560 W Bay Area Blvd Ste 300 *Web:* www.utsi.com	Friendswood	TX	77546	281-480-8786		261
UTStarcom Inc 1732 N First St Ste 220 *NASDAQ:* UTSI ■ *TF:* 877-547-6340 ■ *Web:* www.utstar.com	San Jose	CA	95112	408-453-4557		735
UTXL Inc 10771 NW Ambassador Dr *TF:* 800-351-2821 ■ *Web:* www.utxl.com	Kansas City	MO	64153	816-891-7770		311
UTZ Quality Foods Co 900 High St *TF:* 800-367-7629 ■ *Web:* www.utzsnacks.com	Hanover	PA	17331	717-637-6644		296-35
UUA (Unitarian Universalist Assn) 25 Beacon St *Web:* www.uua.org	Boston	MA	02108	617-742-2100	367-3237	48-20
Miner's Hospital 50 N Medical Dr Rm 1B295 *TF General:* 800-824-2073 ■ *Web:* www.healthcare.utah.edu/hospital	Salt Lake City	UT	84132	801-581-2121		769
UUSC (Unitarian Universalist Service Committee) 689 Massachusetts Ave *TF:* 800-388-3920 ■ *Web:* www.uusc.org	Cambridge	MA	02139	617-868-6600	868-7102	48-5
UV Pure Technologies Inc 60 Venture Dr Unit 19 *TF:* 888-407-9997 ■ *Web:* www.uvpure.com	Toronto	ON	M1B3S4	416-208-9884		104
UVA Health System 501 Sunset Ln *TF:* 866-608-4749 ■ *Web:* www.uvaculpeperhospital.com	Culpeper	VA	22701	540-829-4100		374-3
Uvalde Consolidated Independent School District 1000 N Getty St *Web:* www.ucisd.net	Uvalde	TX	78801	830-278-6655		685
Uvalde County PO Box 284 *TF:* 800-388-8075 ■ *Web:* www.uvaldecounty.com	Uvalde	TX	78802	830-278-6614	278-8692	338
Uvex Safety Inc 900 Douglas Pk *TF General:* 800-682-0839 ■ *Web:* www.uvex.us	Smithfield	RI	02917	800-682-0839	322-1330	576
UVMC (Upper Valley Medical Ctr) 3130 N County Rd 25-A *TF:* 866-608-3463 ■ *Web:* www.uvmc.com	Troy	OH	45373	937-440-4000		374-3
UVP Inc 2066 W 11th St *TF Cust Svc:* 800-452-6788 ■ *Web:* www.uvp.com	Upland	CA	91786	909-946-3197	946-3597	437
UW Marx Inc 20 Gurley Ave *Web:* www.uwmarx.com	Troy	NY	12182	518-272-2541	272-1196	186
UW Medicine Eastside Hospital & Specialty 3100 Northup Way *TF:* 877-520-5000 ■ *Web:* eastside.uwmedicine.org	Bellevue	WA	98004	877-520-5000		374-3
Uwajimaya Inc 600 Fifth Ave S *Web:* www.uwajimaya.com	Seattle	WA	98104	206-624-6248		345
Uwes German Restaurant 31 Iowa Ave	Colorado Springs	CO	80909	719-475-1611		671
UWM (University of Wisconsin Milwaukee) *Golda Meir Library* 2311 E Hartford Ave PO Box 604 *Web:* www4.uwm.edu	Milwaukee	WI	53211	414-229-4785		434-6
UWUA (Utility Workers Union of America) 888 16th St NW Ste 550 *Web:* www.uwua.net	Washington	DC	20006	202-974-8200		414
Ux Consulting Company LLC, The 1401 Macy Dr *Web:* www.uxc.com	Roswell	GA	30076	770-642-7745		463
UXU Ranch 1710 N Fork Hwy *Web:* uxuranch.com	Cody	WY	82414	307-587-2143		239
Uzbekistan *Consulate General* 801 Second Ave 20th Fl *Web:* www.uzbekconsulny.org	New York	NY	10017	212-754-7403		257
Embassy 1746 Massachusetts Ave NW *Web:* www.uzbekistan.org	Washington	DC	20036	202-887-5300	293-6804	257
Uzen Japanese Cuisine 5415 College Ave	Oakland	CA	94618	510-654-7753		671
Uzzell Advertising 2260 Wednesday St Ste 100	Tallahassee	FL	32308	850-513-1990		7

V

Name / Address	City	State	ZIP	Phone	Fax	Class
V & J Holding Cos Inc 6933 W Brown Deer Rd *TF:* 800-384-6972 ■ *Web:* www.vjfoods.com	Milwaukee	WI	53223	414-365-9003	365-9467	670
V & S Midwest Carriers Corp 2001 Hyland Ave PO Box 107 *TF:* 800-876-4330 ■ *Web:* www.vsmidwest.com	Kaukauna	WI	54130	920-766-9696		780
V & S Schuler Engineering Inc 2240 Allen Ave, SE *Web:* www.vsschuler.com	Canton	OH	44707	330-452-5200		480
V 100.7 jams 12100 W Howard Ave *Web:* www.v100.com	Greenfield	WI	53228	414-545-8900		645
V 101.7 7080 Industrial Hwy *Web:* v1017.iheart.com	Macon	GA	31216	478-781-1063		645-95
V 2 It Services Inc 2340 E Trinity Mills Rd Ste 300 *TF:* 877-400-0293 ■ *Web:* www.itservices2.com	Carrollton	TX	75006	877-400-0293		196
V I Engineering Inc 27300 Haggerty Rd *Web:* viengineering.com	Farmington Hills	MI	48331	248-489-1200		180
V I P Meetings & Conventions 1515 Palisades Dr Ste I *TF:* 800-926-3976 ■ *Web:* vipmeetings.com	Pacific Palisades	CA	90272	310-459-4691		760
V M Systems 3125 Hill Ave *Web:* www.vmsystemsinc.com	Toledo	OH	43607	419-535-1044		697
V P Supply Corp PO Box 23868 *Web:* www.vpsupply.com	Rochester	NY	14692	585-272-0110	272-0547	612
V t e C Laboratories Inc 212 Manida St *Web:* www.vteclabs.com	Bronx	NY	10474	718-542-8248		743
V t i Valtronics Inc 3463 Double Springs Rd *Web:* www.val-tronics.com	Valley Springs	CA	95252	209-754-0707		196
V W Broaching Service Inc 3250 West Lake St *TF:* 800-966-6052 ■ *Web:* vwbroaching.com	Chicago	IL	60624	773-533-9000		454
V's Italiano Ristorante 10819 E US Hwy 40 *Web:* www.vsrestaurant.com	Independence	MO	64055	816-353-1241	353-0004	671
V. G. Reed & Sons Inc 1002 S 12th St *Web:* www.vgreed.com	Louisville	KY	40210	502-560-0100		393
V.L.S Systems Inc 4080 Lafayette Ctr Dr Ste 300 *TF:* 000-400-4052 ■ *Web:* www.vls systems.com	Chantilly	VA	20151	703-953-3118		179
V101 2650 Thousand Oaks Blvd Ste 4100 *Web:* myv101.iheart.com	Memphis	TN	38118	901-259-1300		645-98
V101.5 11700 Central Pkwy *Web:* v1015.iheart.com	Jacksonville	FL	32224	904-636-0507		645-79
V103 233 N Michigan Ave Ste 2000 *Web:* v103.iheart.com	Chicago	IL	60601	312 540 2000	938-4477	645-36
V12 data 141 W Front St Ste 410 *Web:* www.v12groupinc.com	Red Bank	NJ	07701	732-842-1001		195
V2 Capital LLC 2700 Patriot Blvd Ste 140	Glenview	IL	60026	847-201-3620		194
V2 Systems Inc 9104 Manassas Dr Ste P *TF:* 800-760-8500 ■ *Web:* www.v2systems.com	Manassas	VA	20111	703-361-4606		175
V2Soft Inc 300 Enterprise Ct Ste 100 *Web:* www.v2soft.com	Bloomfield Hills	MI	48302	248-904-1700		177
V2Solutions Inc 2340 Dr Walsh Ave *Web:* www.v2solutions.com	Santa Clara	CA	95051	408-550-2340		196
V3 Cos Ltd 7325 Janes Ave *Web:* www.v3co.com	Woodridge	IL	60517	630-724-9200		261
VA (Department of Veterans Affairs) 810 Vermont Ave NW *TF Cust Svc:* 800-827-1000 ■ *Web:* www.va.gov	Washington	DC	20420	202-461-7600		340-19
VA Central California Health Care System 2615 E Clinton Ave *Web:* www.fresno.va.gov	Fresno	CA	93703	559-225-6100		374-8
VA Central Iowa Health Care System 1607 N Lincoln St *TF:* 800-816-8878 ■ *Web:* www.centraliowa.va.gov	Knoxville	IA	50138	641-842-3101		374-8

Phone | Fax | Class

VA Greater Los Angeles Healthcare System
11301 Wilshire Blvd Los Angeles CA 90073 310-478-3711 268-3494 374-8
TF: 800-952-4852 ■ *Web:* www.losangeles.va.gov

VA Hudson Valley Health Care System
Castle Point Campus
41 Castle Pt Rd Wappingers Falls NY 12590 845-831-2000 838-5193 374-8
TF: 877-222-8387 ■ *Web:* www.hudsonvalley.va.gov
Montrose Campus
2094 Albany Post Rd PO Box 100 Montrose NY 10548 914-737-4400 788-4244 374-8
TF: 800-269-8749 ■ *Web:* www.hudsonvalley.va.gov

VA Medical Ctr 4500 S Lancaster Rd Dallas TX 75216 214-742-8387 374-8
TF: 800-849-3597 ■ *Web:* www.northtexas.va.gov

VA Medical Ctr 2400 Hospital Rd Tuskegee AL 36083 334-727-0550 724-2793 374-8
TF: 800-214-8387 ■ *Web:* www.centralalabama.va.gov

VA Medical Ctr 3687 Veterans Dr Fort Harrison MT 59636 406-442-6410 374-8

VA NY Harbor Healthcare System
423 E 23rd St New York NY 10010 212-686-7500 374-8

VA Pittsburgh Healthcare System
7180 Highland Dr Pittsburgh PA 15206 412-822-2222 374-8
TF: 800-827-1000

VA Puget Sound Health Care System - Seattle Div
1660 S Columbian Way Seattle WA 98108 206-762-1010 769
TF: 800-329-8387 ■ *Web:* www.va.gov

VA San Diego Healthcare System
3350 La Jolla Village Dr San Diego CA 92161 858-552-8585 374-8
TF: 800-331-8387

VAALCO Energy Inc
9800 Richmond Ste 700 Houston TX 77042 713-623-0801 623-0982 538
NYSE: EGY ■ *Web:* www.vaalco.com

Vacation Co
42 New Orleans Rd Ste 102 Hilton Head Island SC 29928 843-686-6100 376
TF: 800-845-7018 ■ *Web:* www.vacationcompany.com

Vacation Internationale
1417 116th Ave NE Bellevue WA 98004 425-454-8429 456-0536 753
TF: 800-444-6633 ■ *Web:* www.vacationinternationale.com

Vacation Palm Springs Real Estate Inc
1276 N Palm Canyon Dr Ste 211 Palm Springs CA 92262 760-778-7832 652
Web: vacationpalmsprings.com

Vacation Rental Managers Assn (VRMA)
2025 M St NW Ste 800 Washington DC 20036 202-367-1179 367-2179 49-17
Web: www.vrma.com

Vacation Resorts International Inc
23041 Avenida De La Carlota Ste 400 Laguna Hills CA 92653 949-587-2299 379
Web: www.vriresorts.com

Vacation.com Inc
1650 King St Ste 450 Alexandria VA 22314 800-843-0733 772
TF: 800-843-0733 ■ *Web:* www.vacation.com

Vacationer RV Resort
1581 East Main St El Cajon CA 92021 877-626-4409 378
TF: 877-626-4409 ■ *Web:* www.vacationerrv.com

Vacations To Go Inc
5851 San Felipe St Ste 500 Houston TX 77057 713-974-2121 772
TF: 800-338-4962 ■ *Web:* www.vacationstogo.com

Vacaville Chamber of Commerce
300 Main St Vacaville CA 95688 707-448-6424 448-0424 139
Web: www.vacavillechamber.com

Vaccaro's Trattoria 1000 Ghent Rd Akron OH 44333 330-666-6158 671
Web: www.vactrat.com

Vacco Industries Inc
10350 Vacco St South El Monte CA 91733 626-443-7121 442-6943 595
TF: 800-874-7113 ■ *Web:* www.vacco.com

Vac-Con Inc 969 Hall Park Dr Green Cove Spgs FL 32043 904-493-4969 427
Web: www.vac-con.com

Vaco 5410 Maryland Way Ste 460 Brentwood TN 37027 615-324-8226 721
Web: www.vaco.com

Vactor Manufacturing Inc
1621 S Illinois St Streator IL 61364 815-672-3171 672-2779* 386
**Fax:* Sales ■ *Web:* www.vactor.com

VAC-TRON Equipment LLC
27137 S Hwy 33 Okahumpka FL 34762 352-728-2222 196
Web: www.vactron.com

Vacudyne Inc 375 E Joe Orr Rd Chicago Heights IL 60411 708-757-5200 757-7180 386
TF: 800-459-9591 ■ *Web:* www.vacudyne.com

VAC-U-MAX 69 William St Belleville NJ 07109 973-759-4600 207
Web: www.aeromechanical.com

Vacuum Instrument Corp
2099 Ninth Ave Ronkonkoma NY 11779 631-737-0900 201
Web: www.vicleakdetection.com

Vadum Inc 601 Hutton St Ste 109 Raleigh NC 27606 919-341-8241 261
Web: www.vaduminc.com

VAE Inc 12005 Sunrise Vly Dr Ste 202 Reston VA 20191 703-942-6727 196
Web: www.vaeit.com

Vae Nortrak Inc
3930 Valley E Industrial Dr Birmingham AL 35217 205-854-2884 190

Vaga Industries Inc
2505 Loma Ave South El Monte CA 91733 626-442-7436 442-4330 454
Web: www.vaga.com

Vail Marriott Mountain Resort
715 W Lionshead Cir Vail CO 81657 970-479-5004 707
TF: 800-648-0720 ■ *Web:* www.marriott.com

Vail Mountain Lodge & Spa, The
352 E Meadow Dr Vail CO 81657 970-476-0700 707
TF: 888-794-0410 ■ *Web:* www.vailmountainlodge.com

Vail Mountain School 3000 Booth Falls Rd Vail CO 81657 970-476-3850 685
TF: 800-584-5005 ■ *Web:* www.vms.edu/contact/contact-admissions

Vail Racquet Club Inc
4695 Racquet Club Dr Vail CO 81657 970-476-4840 706
TF: 800-428-4840 ■ *Web:* vailracquetclub.com

Vail Resorts Management Co
390 Interlocken Crescent Ste 1000 Broomfield CO 80021 303-404-1800 404-6415 669
NYSE: MTN ■ *TF:* 800-842-8062 ■ *Web:* www.vailresorts.com

Vail Rubber Works Inc
521 Langley Ave Saint Joseph MI 49085 269-983-1595 983-0155 677
TF: 800-848-0288 ■ *Web:* www.vailrubber.com

Vail Valley Chamber of Commerce
101 Fawcett Rd Ste 240 Avon CO 81620 970-476-1000 139
TF: 800-525-3875 ■ *Web:* www.visitvailvalley.com

Vail Valley Jet Center LLC
871 Cooley Mesa Rd Eagle County Regional Airport
Gypsum CO 81637 970-524-7700 63
TF: 800-247-2433 ■ *Web:* vvjc.com

Vail Valley Tourism Bureau
101 Fawcett Rd Ste 240 Avon CO 81620 970-476-1000 206
Web: www.visitvailvalley.com

Vaile Mansion 1500 N Liberty St Independence MO 64050 816-325-7430 50-3
TF: 800-748-7323 ■ *Web:* www.vailemansion.org

Vaisala Inc 10-D Gill St Woburn MA 01801 781-933-4500 933-8029 472
TF: 888-824-7252 ■ *Web:* www.vaisala.com

Vakifbank 399 Park Ave New York NY 10036 212-621-9400 70
Web: www.vakifbankusa.com

Val Surf Inc 4810 Whitsett Ave Valley Village CA 91607 818-769-6977 711
TF: 888-825-7873 ■ *Web:* www.valsurf.com

Val Verde County 400 Pecan St Del Rio TX 78840 830-774-7501 775-9406 338
Web: valverdecounty.texas.gov

Val Verde County Library
300 Spring St Del Rio TX 78840 830-774-7595 774-7607 434-3
Web: valverdecounty.texas.gov/181/Library

Val Verde Unified School District
975 Morgan St Perris CA 92571 951-940-6100 685
Web: www.valverde.edu

Val's Distributing Co 6124 E 30th St N Tulsa OK 74115 918-835-9987 835-3808 297-5
TF: 800-274-9987 ■ *Web:* www.valsdistributing.com

Valadao David (Rep R - CA)
1728 Longworth HOB Washington DC 20515 202-225-4695 225-3196 342-2
Web: valadao.house.gov

Valair Aviation 7301 NW 50th St Oklahoma City OK 73132 405-789-5000 20
TF: 800-299-8546 ■ *Web:* www.valairaviation.com

Valanni Restaurant & Lounge
1229 Spruce St Philadelphia PA 19107 215-790-9494 671
Web: www.valanni.com

Valassis 1 Targeting Ctr Windsor CT 06095 860-285-6100 5
TF: 800-437-0479 ■ *Web:* www.valassis.com

Valassis Canada Inc
47 Jutland Rd Etobicoke Toronto ON M8Z2G6 416-259-3600 5
TF: 800-437-0479 ■ *Web:* www.valassis.ca

Valassis Communications Inc
19975 Victor Pkwy Livonia MI 48152 734-591-3000 627
NYSE: VCI ■ *TF:* 800-437-0479 ■ *Web:* www.valassis.com

Valco Data Systems Inc
N57 W13652 Reichert Ave Menomonee Falls WI 53051 262-781-7731 177
Web: valcodata.com

Valco Manufacturing Company Inc
925 Boren Rd Duncan OK 73533 580-255-4300 295
TF: 800-226-3553 ■ *Web:* www.valcomfg.com

Valcom Consulting Group Inc
85 Albert St Ottawa ON K1P6A4 613-594-5200 261
TF: 866-561-5580 ■ *Web:* www.valcom.ca

Valcom Inc 5614 Hollins Rd Roanoke VA 24019 540-563-2000 362-9800 735
TF: 800-825-2661 ■ *Web:* www.valcom.com

Valcor Engineering Corp
2 Lawrence Rd Springfield NJ 07081 973-467-8400 467-8382 789
Web: www.valcor.com

Valdak Corp 1149 36th Ave S Grand Forks ND 58201 701-746-8371 772-9464 204
Web: www.valleydairy.com

Valdese General Hospital (VGH)
720 Malcolm Blvd Ste 200 Valdese NC 28690 828-874-2251 397-3226 374-3
TF: 800-994-6610 ■ *Web:* www.blueridgehealth.org

Valdese Weavers LLC
1000 Perkins Rd SE Valdese NC 28690 828-874-2181 745-1
Web: www.valdeseweavers.com

Valdosta Daily Times PO Box 968 Valdosta GA 31603 229-244-1880 244-2560 532-2
TF: 800-600-4838 ■ *Web:* www.valdostadailytimes.com

Valdosta State Prison
3259 Valtech Rd Valdosta GA 31601 229-333-7900 333-5387 213
Web: www.dcor.state.ga.us

Valdosta State University
1500 N Patterson St Valdosta GA 31698 229-333-5800 333-5482* 166
**Fax:* Admissions ■ *TF:* 800-618-1878 ■ *Web:* www.valdosta.edu

Valdosta State University Odum Library
1500 N Patterson St Valdosta GA 31698 229-333-5869 219-1362 434-6
Web: www.valdosta.edu

Valdosta Technical College
4089 Val Tech Rd Valdosta GA 31602 229-333-2100 162
Web: valdostatech.org

Valdosta-Lowndes County Chamber of Commerce
416 N Ashley St Valdosta GA 31601 229-247-8100 245-0071 139
Web: www.valdostachamber.com

Vale 200 Bay St Ste 1600 PO Box 70 Toronto ON M5J2K2 416-361-7511 361-7781 502
Web: www.vale.com/Canada/EN/Pages/Default.aspx

Valence Operating Co
1 Kingwood Pl 600 Rockmead Dr Ste 200 Kingwood TX 77339-2105 281-359-3659 358-5333 536
Web: www.valenceoperating.com

Valence Technology Inc
1807 W Braker Ln Ste 500 Austin TX 78758 512-527-2900 527-2910 74
TF: 888-825-3623 ■ *Web:* www.valence.com

Valencia Community College
PO Box 3028 Orlando FL 32802 407-299-5000 162
TF: 800-590-3428 ■ *Web:* www.valenciacollege.edu
East 701 N Econlockhatchee Trl Orlando FL 32825 407-299-5000 582-2621 162
Web: valenciacollege.edu
Osceola
1800 Denn John Ln PO Box 3028 Kissimmee FL 32802 407-299-5000 162
Web: valenciacollege.edu

Valencia County 444 Luna Ave Los Lunas NM 87031 505-866-2014 338
Web: www.co.valencia.nm.us

Valensi Rose PLC
1888 Century Park E Ste 1100 Los Angeles CA 90067 310-277-8011 428
Web: www.vrmlaw.com

Valenti Mid-south Management LLC
1775 Moriah Woods Blvd Ste 5 Memphis TN 38117 901-684-1215 671
Web: www.valentirestaurants.com

Valentine Enterprises Inc
1291 Progress Ctr Ave Lawrenceville GA 30043 770-995-0661 995-0725 296-10
Web: www.veiusa.com

Phone Fax Class

Valentine, The 1015 E Clay St .... Richmond VA 23219 804-649-0711 643-3510 520
Web: thevalentine.org

Valentine, Theatre, The 410 Adams St .... Toledo OH 43604 419-242-3490 242-2791 572
Web: www.valentinetheatre.com

Valentino Santa Monica
3115 Pico Blvd........................Santa Monica CA 90405 310-829-4313 315-2791 671
Web: valentinosantamonica.com

Valentino's 1907 W End Ave .... Nashville TN 37203 615-327-0148 671
TF: 800-745-3000 ■ *Web:* www.valentinosnashville.com

Valentino's of America 2601 S 70th St.......... Lincoln NE 68506 402-434-9350 670
Web: www.valentinos.com

Valeo Behavioral Health Care Inc
5401 SW Seventh St.......................... Topeka KS 66606 785-233-1730 353
Web: www.valeotopeka.org

Valeo Pharma Inc
16667 Hymus Blvd Kirkland.................. Kirkland QC H9H4R9 514-694-0150 231
TF: 888-694-0865 ■ *Web:* www.valeopharma.com

Valerie Manor Inc 135 South Rd .... Farmington CT 06032 860-489-1008 450
Web: athenahealthcare.com

Valerie Wilson Travel Inc
475 Pk Ave S ....New York NY 10016 212-532-3400 779-7073 771
TF: 800-776-1116 ■ *Web:* www.valeriewilsontravel.com

Valeritas Inc 750 Rt 202 S Ste 600.............. Bridgewater NJ 08807 908-927-9920 927-9927 475
TF: 855-384-8848 ■ *Web:* www.valeritas.com

Valero LP 530 McCullough Ave ....San Antonio TX 78215 210-246-2000 655-5049* 597
**Fax Area Code:* 302 ■ *TF:* 800-333-3377 ■ *Web:* www.valero.com

Vales Consulting Group LLC
125 Wappanocca Ave .... Rye NY 10580 914-967-3200 196
Web: www.valesconsulting.com

Valet Park of America
185 Spring St...........................Springfield MA 01105 413-827-8916 562
Web: www.valetparkofamerica.com

Valet Parking Service
1335 S Flower St ....Los Angeles CA 90015 213-342-3388 222-0981 562
TF: 800-794-7275 ■ *Web:* www.valetparkingservice.com

Valeura Energy Inc 1200-202 6 Ave SW .... Calgary AB T2P2R9 403-237-7102 536
Web: www.valeuraenergy.com

Valex Corp 6080 Leland St.................... Ventura CA 93003 805-658-0944 246
Web: www.valex.com

Valfit Inc 8360 Wilcox Ave..................... Cudahy CA 90201 323-562-3440 492
Web: www.valfit.com

Valhalla Partners
8000 Towers Crescent Dr Ste 1050.............. Vienna VA 22182 703-448-1400 792
Web: www.valhallapartners.com

Valhi Inc
5430 LBJ Fwy Ste 1700 3 Lincoln Ctr .... Dallas TX 75240 972-233-1700 448-1445* 185
NYSE: VHI ■ **Fax:* Acctg ■ *Web:* www.valhi.net

Valiant Corp 6555 Hawthorne Dr...............Windsor ON N8T3G6 519-974-5200 539
TF: 888-497-5537 ■ *Web:* www.valiantcorp.com

Valiant Enterprise LLC
2300 Mcdermott Rd................................Plano TX 75025 972-390-7410 100

Valiant Products Corp 2727 Fifth Ave W..........Denver CO 80204 303-892-1234 442
TF Cust Svc: 800-347-2727 ■ *Web:* www.valiantproducts.com

Valiant Solutions Inc
110 Crossways Pk Dr...................... Woodbury NY 11797 516-390-1100 178-1
Web: www.valiant.com

Valiant Steel & Equipment Inc
6455 Old Peachtree Rd....................... Norcross GA 30071 770-417-1235 417-1669 492
TF: 800-939-9905 ■ *Web:* www.valiantsteel.com

Valiant Trust Co
310 - 606 Fourth St SW...................... Calgary AB T2P1T1 403-233-2801 528

Valiant Yachts Inc
500 Harbour View Rd ....Gordonville TX 76245 903-523-4899 523-4077 90
TF: 800-742-6061 ■ *Web:* www.valiantsailboats.com

VALIC (Variable Annuity Life Insurance Co)
2929 Allen Pkwy...............................Houston TX 77019 800-448-2542 391-2
TF: 800-448-2542 ■ *Web:* www.valic.com

Valicom Corp
2923 Marketplace Dr Ste 104................. Madison WI 53719 608-274-3515 196
Web: www.valicomcorp.com

Valid8 .com Inc
500 W Cummings Pk Ste 6550................. Woburn MA 01801 855-482-5438 177
TF: 855-482-5438 ■ *Web:* valid8.com

Validar Inc 800 Maynard Ave S Ste 401........... Seattle WA 98134 206-264-9151 178-1
TF: 888-784-2929 ■ *Web:* www.validar.com

Validata Computer & Research Corp
428 S Perry St .... Montgomery AL 36104 334-834-2324 180

Validation Systems Inc
900 San Antonio Rd .... Palo Alto CA 94303 650-856-4874 194
Web: www.validationsystems.com

Valimet Inc PO Box 31690.................... Stockton CA 95213 209-444-1600 485
Web: www.valimet.com

Valin Corp 555 E California Ave.............. Sunnyvale CA 94086 408-730-9850 730-1363 358
TF: 800-774-5630 ■ *Web:* www.valin.com

Vallata 2190 Goldstream Rd...................Fairbanks AK 99709 907-455-6600 671

Valle Cucina Italiana
4752 Limestone Rd...................... Wilmington DE 19808 302-998-9999 671
Web: www.vallecucina.com

Valle Verde
900 Calle de los Amigos................ Santa Barbara CA 93105 805-883-4000 672
TF: 800-750-5089 ■ *Web:* www.valleverde.org

Vallejo Chamber of Commerce
427 York St.................................. Vallejo CA 94590 707-644-5551 644-5590 139
Web: www.vallejochamber.com

Vallejo Convention & Visitors Bureau
289 Mare Island Way .... Vallejo CA 94590 707-642-3653 644-2206 206
TF General: 866-921-9277 ■ *Web:* www.visitvallejo.com

Vallejo Sanitation & Flood Control District Finance
450 Ryder St.................................. Vallejo CA 94590 707-644-8949 804
TF: 800-984-9661 ■ *Web:* www.vsfcd.com

Vallejo Times Herald 440 Curtola Pkwy........... Vallejo CA 94590 707-644-1141 532-2
TF: 800-600-1141 ■ *Web:* www.timesheraldonline.com

Valley Agricultural Software Inc
3950 S K St ....Tulare CA 93274 559-686-9496 177
Web: www.vas.com

Valley Baptist Medical Ctr Brownsville
1040 W Jefferson St.................... Brownsville TX 78520 956-698-5400 374-3
TF: 855-720-7448 ■ *Web:* www.valleybaptist.net/brownsville

Valley Baptist Medical Ctr Harlingen
2101 Pease St.............................Harlingen TX 78550 956-389-1100 374-3
Web: www.valleybaptist.net

Valley Barber & Beauty Supply
413 W Harrison St ....Harlingen TX 78550 956-423-0727 76

Valley Best-Way Bldg Supply
118 S Union Rd ....Spokane WA 99206 509-924-1250 922-5420 817

Valley Blox Inc
210 Stone Spring Rd .... Harrisonburg VA 22801 540-434-6725 183
TF: 800-648-6725 ■ *Web:* valleybuildingsupply.com

Valley Books PO Box 2127 ....Amherst MA 01004 413-256-1508 95
TF: 800-653-7767 ■ *Web:* www.valleybooks.com

Valley Business Machines Inc
5825 Mayflower Ct ....Wasilla AK 99654 907-376-5077 535
TF: 800-770-7575 ■ *Web:* www.vbmalaska.com

Valley Cabinet Inc 845 Prosper Rd .... De Pere WI 54115 920-336-3174 383-5580 115
TF: 800-967-8840 ■ *Web:* www.valleycabinetinc.com

Valley Chevrolet Inc
601 Kidder St .... Wilkes-Barre PA 18702 570-821-2772 516
TF: 877-207-9214 ■ *Web:* valleychevrolet.com

Valley Children's Healthcare
9300 Valley Children's Pl .... Madera CA 93636 559-353-3000 353-8888* 374-1
**Fax:* Admitting ■ *Web:* www.valleychildrens.org

Valley City Mfg Co Ltd, The 64 Hatt St.......... Dundas ON L9H2G3 905-628-2253 628-0753 319-3
TF: 800-441-7429 ■ *Web:* www.valleycity.com

Valley City Plating Co
3353 Eastern Ave SE.....................Grand Rapids MI 49508 616-245-1223 481
Web: www.brassplater.com

Valley City State University
101 College St SW......................Valley City ND 58072 701-845-7990 845-7299 166
TF: 800-532-8641 ■ *Web:* www.vcsu.edu

Valley Construction Co
3610 - 78th Ave W .... Rock Island IL 61201 309-787-0292 787-7048 186
Web: www.valleyconstruction.com

Valley Co-op Oil Mill
1910 N Expwy 77 PO Box 533609 ....Harlingen TX 78553 956-425-4545 425-4264 296-29
Web: valleycoopoilmill.com

Valley Cottage Animal Hospital Inc
202 Rt 303 .... Valley Cottage NY 10989 845-268-9263 268-0516 794
Web: www.valleycottageanimalhospital.com

Valley County 219 N Main St ....Cascade ID 83611 208-382-7150 382-7107 338
Web: www.co.valley.id.us

Valley County 125 S 15th St..................... Ord NE 68862 308-728-3700 728-7725 338
Web: www.co.valley.ne.us

Valley Craft 2001 S Hwy 61................. Lake City MN 55041 651-345-3386 345-6535 470
Web: www.valleycraft.com

Valley Ctr-Pauma Unified School District
28751 Cole Grade Rd .... Valley Center CA 92082 760-749-0464 749-1208 685
Web: www.vcpusd.net

Valley Decorating Co
2829 E Hamilton Ave ....Fresno CA 93721 559-495-1100 600
Web: www.pomponcentral.com

Valley Electric Assn Inc
800 E Hwy 372 PO Box 237 .... Pahrump NV 89048 775-727-5312 245
TF: 800-742-3330 ■ *Web:* www.vea.coop

Valley Electric Supply Corp
1361 N State Rd PO Box 724 .... Vincennes IN 47591 812-882-7860 882-7893 246
TF: 800-825-7877 ■ *Web:* www.vesupply.com

Valley Endodontics Ltd
1100 N Lynndale Dr .... Appleton WI 54914 920-731-4484 363
Web: valleyendo.com

Valley Express Llc 6003 State Rd 76 .... Oshkosh WI 54904 920-231-1677 311
TF: 800-594-4744 ■ *Web:* www.valleyexpress.net

Valley Fair Mall
3601 S 2700 W......................West Valley City UT 84119 801-969-6211 460
Web: www.shopvalleyfairmall.com

Valley Farms LLC 1860 E Third St .... Williamsport PA 17701 814-237-3426 326-2736* 296-27
**Fax Area Code:* 570 ■ *Web:* www.valleyfarmsdairy.com

Valley Fertilizer & Chemical Company Inc
201 Valley Rd PO Box 816 .... Mount Jackson VA 22842 540-778-3953 477-3123 280

Valley Fig Growers 2028 S Third St............. Fresno CA 93702 559-237-3893 237-3898 315-4
Web: www.valleyfig.com

Valley Financial Solutions Inc
2847 Penn Forest Blvd Ste 100 ....Roanoke VA 24018 540-777-4302 401
Web: www.valleyfinancialsolutions.com

Valley Fine Foods Company Inc
3909 Park Rd Ste H ....Benicia CA 94510 707-746-6888 297-8
Web: www.cafferata.com

Valley First Credit Union PO Box 1411......... Modesto CA 95353 209 549 8500 219
TF: 877-549-4567 ■ *Web:* www.valleyfirstcu.org

Valley Flowers Inc
3675 Foothill Rd........................Carpinteria CA 93013 805-684-6651 292
TF: 800-549-5500 ■ *Web:* valleyflowers.com

Valley Forge Christian College
1401 Charlestown Rd.....................Phoenixville PA 19460 610-935-0450 917-2069* 166
**Fax:* Admissions ■ *TF:* 800-432-8322 ■ *Web:* www.valleyforge.edu/#slide-2

Valley Forge Convention & Visitors Bureau
1000 First Ave Ste 101 .... King of Prussia PA 19406 610-834-1550 834-0202 206
TF General: 888-847-4883 ■ *Web:* www.valleyforge.org

Valley Forge Convention Ctr
1160 First Ave......................... King of Prussia PA 19406 610-768-3215 205
TF: 800-847-4865 ■ *Web:* www.vfconventioncenter.com

Valley Forge Fabrics Inc
2981 Gateway Dr ....Pompano Beach FL 33069 954-971-1776 968-1775 594
Web: www.valleyforge.com

Valley Forge Medical Ctr & Hospital
1033 W Germantown Pk..................Norristown PA 19403 610-539-8500 539-0910 726
TF: 888-539-8500 ■ *Web:* www.vfmc.net

Valley Forge Military Academy & College
1001 Eagle Rd .... Wayne PA 19087 610-989-1300 688-1545* 162
**Fax:* Admissions ■ *TF:* 800-234-8362 ■ *Web:* www.vfmac.edu

Valley Forge National Historical Park
1400 N Outer Line Dr .... King of Prussia PA 19406 610-783-1077 783-1060 564
Web: www.nps.gov/vafo

Valley Fresh Inc 3600 E Linwood Ave............Turlock CA 95380 209-669-5600 619

Valley Health System
223 N Van Dien Ave ....Ridgewood NJ 07450 201-447-8000 374-3
TF: 800-825-5391 ■ *Web:* www.valleyhealth.com

Phone | Fax | Class

Valley Hospice Inc
380 Summit Ave .... Steubenville OH 43952 740-284-4440 284-4478 371
TF: 877-467-7423 ■ *Web:* www.valleyhospice.org

Valley Hospital Medical Ctr
620 Shadow Ln .... Las Vegas NV 89106 702-388-4000 374-3
Web: www.valleyhospital.net

Valley House Gallery Inc
6616 Spring Valley Rd .... Dallas TX 75254 972-239-2441 239-1462 42
Web: www.valleyhouse.com

Valley Independent Eastgate 19 .... Monessen PA 15062 724-684-5200 532-2
Web: triblive.com

Valley International Airport
3002 Heritage Way .... Harlingen TX 78550 956-430-8605 63
Web: www.flythevalley.com

Valley Internet Inc
102 Maple St E .... Fayetteville TN 37334 931-433-1921 221-0119* 41
**Fax Area Code:* 615 ■ *TF:* 888-433-1924 ■ *Web:* vallnet.com

Valley Joist 3019 Gault Ave N .... Fort Payne AL 35967 256-845-2330 845-2597 697
TF: 800-263-0324 ■ *Web:* www.valleyjoist.com

Valley Litho Supply Inc
1047 Haugen Ave .... Rice Lake WI 54868 800-826-6781 358
TF: 800-826-6781 ■ *Web:* valleylithosupply.com

Valley Machining Co 1250 22nd Ave .... Rock Valley IA 51247 712-476-2828 454
Web: www.valleymachining.com

Valley Machining Inc
100 Jack Berg Ln .... Coon Valley WI 54623 608-452-3005 21

Valley Mechanical Inc 608 Salem Rd .... Rossville GA 30741 706-866-8812 697
Web: www.valleymech.com

Valley Medical Ctr 400 S 43rd St .... Renton WA 98055 425-228-3450 374-3
TF: 855-923-4633 ■ *Web:* www.valleymed.org

Valley Mirror 3910 Main St .... Munhall PA 15120 412-462-0626 532-2

Valley Morning Star 1310 S Commerce .... Harlingen TX 78550 956-430-6200 532-2
Web: www.valleymorningstar.com

Valley National Bancorp 1455 Valley Rd .... Wayne NJ 07470 [illegible] [illegible]
NYSE: VLY ■ *TF:* 800-522-4100 ■ *Web:* valleynationalbank.com

Valley National Bank 615 Main Ave .... Passaic NJ 07055 973-777-6768 70
TF: 800-522-4100 ■ *Web:* valleynationalbank.com

Valley Natural Foods
13750 County Rd 11 .... Burnsville MN 55337 952-891-1212 297-8
Web: www.valleynaturalfoods.com

Valley News 24 Interchange Dr .... West Lebanon NH 03784 603-298-8711 298-0212 532-2
TF: 800-874-2226 ■ *Web:* www.vnews.com

Valley News Dispatch 210 Fourth Ave .... Tarentum PA 15084 800-909-8742 226-4677* 532-2
**Fax Area Code:* 724 ■ *TF:* 877-698-2553 ■ *Web:* triblive.com

Valley Nursing Ctr
581 NC Hwy 16 S .... Taylorsville NC 28681 828-632-8146 450
Web: valleyrehab.com

Valley of the Sun United Way
1515 E Osborn Rd .... Phoenix AZ 85014 602-631-4800 631-4809 48-21
Web: www.vsuw.org

Valley Office Systems
2050 First St .... Idaho Falls ID 83401 208-529-2777 179
TF: 800-610-2865 ■ *Web:* www.valleyofficesystems.com

Valley Offset Printing Inc
160 S Sheridan Ave .... Valley Center KS 67147 316-755-0061 627
TF: 888-895-7913 ■ *Web:* www.valleyoffset.com

Valley Packaging Corp
276 Industrial Blvd .... Pulaski TN 38478 931-363-0025 100
Web: www.gbp.com/corrugated/loc_Pulaski.asp

Valley Packaging Industries Inc
110 N Kensington Dr .... Appleton WI 54915 920-749-5840 88
Web: www.vpind.com

Valley PBS 1544 Van Ness Ave .... Fresno CA 93721 559-266-1800 650-1880 741-52
Web: valleypbs.org

Valley Plaza Mall 2701 Ming Ave .... Bakersfield CA 93304 661-832-2436 460
Web: www.valleyplazamall.com

Valley Power Systems Inc
425 S Hacienda Blvd .... City of Industry CA 91745 626-333-1243 369-7096 770
TF: 800-924-4265 ■ *Web:* www.valleypowersystems.com

Valley Presbyterian Hospital
15107 Vanowen St .... Van Nuys CA 91405 818-782-6600 374-3
Web: www.valleypres.org

Valley Printing Company Inc
3919 Vanderbilt Rd .... Birmingham AL 35217 205-841-2746 627
Web: valleyprinting.net

Valley Processing Inc
108 E Blaine Ave PO Box 246 .... Sunnyside WA 98944 509-837-8084 837-3481 296-20
TF: 800-321-8747 ■ *Web:* valleyprocessing.com

Valley Proteins Inc 151 Valpro Dr .... Winchester VA 22603 540-877-2590 877-3215 447
TF: 800-871-3406 ■ *Web:* www.valleyproteins.com

Valley Queen Cheese Factory Inc
200 E Railway Ave .... Milbank SD 57252 605-432-4563 432-9383 296-5
Web: www.vqcheese.com

Valley Regional Hospital
150 Exhibition St .... Kentville NS B4N5E3 902-678-7381 679-1904 374-2
TF: 800-886-9757 ■ *Web:* www.avdha.nshealth.ca

Valley Regional Medical Ctr
100-A E Alton Gloor Blvd .... Brownsville TX 78526 956-350-7000 374-3
TF: 877-813-6455 ■ *Web:* www.valleyregionalmedicalcenter.com

Valley Republic Bank
5000 California Ave Ste 110 .... Bakersfield CA 93309 661-371-2000 70
Web: valleyrepublicbank.com

Valley River Ctr 293 Valley River Ctr .... Eugene OR 97401 541-683-5513 460
Web: www.valleyrivercenter.com

Valley River Inn 1000 Vly River Way .... Eugene OR 97401 541-743-1000 683-5121 379
TF: 800-543-8266 ■ *Web:* www.valleyriverinn.com

Valley Rural Electric Co-op Inc
10700 Fairgrounds Rd PO Box 477 .... Huntingdon PA 16652 814-643-2650 643-1678 245
TF: 800-432-0680 ■ *Web:* www.valleyrec.com

Valley Scale Company LLC
751 W Kenwood Ave .... Clarksville IN 47129 812-282-5269 177
Web: www.thinkvsc.com

Valley Small Business Development
7035 N Fruit Ave .... Fresno CA 93711 559-438-9680 463
Web: www.vsbdc.com

Valley State Prison
21633 Ave 24 PO Box 99 .... Chowchilla CA 93610 559-665-6100 213
Web: cdcr.ca.gov

Valley Stream State Park
PO Box 670 .... Valley Stream NY 11580 516-825-4128 565
Web: parks.ny.gov/parks/159/details.aspx

Valley Supply & Equipment Company Inc
1109 Middle River Rd .... Baltimore MD 21220 800-633-5077 23
TF: 800-633-5077 ■ *Web:* www.valleysupplyequipment.com

Valley Techlogic Inc
111 Business Pkwy .... Atwater CA 95301 209-357-3121 225
Web: www.valleytechlogic.com

Valley Telephone Co-op Inc
752 E Maley St .... Willcox AZ 85643 520-384-2231 736
TF: 800-421-5711 ■ *Web:* www.vtc.net

Valley Tire Company Inc
1002 Arentzen Blvd .... Charleroi PA 15022 724-483-4718 754
Web: www.valleytireco.com

Valley Tool & Die Inc
10020 York Theta Dr .... North Royalton OH 44133 440-237-0160 697
Web: www.valcocleve.com

Valley Town Crier 1811 N 23rd St .... McAllen TX 78501 956-682-2423 532-4
Web: www.yourvalleyvoice.com

Valley Truck & Tractor Company Inc
793 N First St .... Dixon CA 95620 707-678-2395 274
Web: www.valleytruckandtractor.com

Valley Truck Parts Inc
1900 Chicago Dr .... Grand Rapids MI 49519 616-241-5431 779
Web: www.valleytruckparts.com

Valley View Casino Ctr
3500 Sports Arena Blvd .... San Diego CA 92110 619-224-4171 224-3010 720
TF: 888-929-7849 ■ *Web:* www.valleyviewcasinocenter.com

Valley View Ctr Mall 13331 Preston Rd .... Dallas TX 75240 972-661-2939 239-1344 460
Web: www.shopvalleyviewcenter.com

Valley View Foods Inc
7547 Sawtelle Ave .... Yuba City CA 95991 530-673-7356 673-9432 315-3
Web: www.valleyviewpacking.com

Valley View Mall 4802 Vly View Blvd .... Roanoke VA 24012 540-563-4440 460
TF: 800-346-3334 ■ *Web:* www.valleyviewmall.com

Valley View Regional Hospital
430 N Monte Vista St .... Ada OK 74820 580-332-2323 374-3
Web: www.mercy.net

Valley Wholesale Drug Company Inc
1401 W Fremont St PO Box 2065 .... Stockton CA 95203 209-466-0131 231
Web: www.vwdco.com

Valley Yellow Pages
1850 N Gateway Blvd .... Fresno CA 93727 559-251-8888 253-9729 637-6
TF: 800-350-8887 ■ *Web:* www.myyp.com

Valley-Dynamo 7224 Burns Rd .... Richland Hills TX 76118 972-595-5300 595-5380 322
TF: 800-826-7856 ■ *Web:* www.vdlp.net

Valleyfair 1 Valleyfair Dr .... Shakopee MN 55379 952-445-7600 445-1539 32
TF: 800-719-9019 ■ *Web:* www.valleyfair.com

Valli Information Systems Inc
915 Main St Ste 100 .... Caldwell ID 83605 208-459-3611 180
TF: 800-627-3283 ■ *Web:* www.valli.com

Vallorbs Jewel Co
2599 Old Philadelphia Pk .... Bird-in-Hand PA 17505 717-392-3978 392-8947 621
TF: 800-345-5939 ■ *Web:* vallorbs.com

VALMARC Corp 109 Highland Ave .... Needham MA 02494 339-225-4544 387
TF: 800-897-9880 ■ *Web:* www.valmarc.com

Valmark Industries Inc
7900 National Dr .... Livermore CA 94550 925-960-9900 960-0900 413
Web: nidec-vis.com

Val-Matic Valve & Manufacturing Corp
905 Riverside Dr .... Elmhurst IL 60126 630-941-7600 789
Web: www.valmatic.com

Valmont Industries Inc 1 Valmont Plaza .... Omaha NE 68154 402-963-1000 273
NYSE: VMI ■ *TF:* 800-825-6668 ■ *Web:* www.valmont.com

Valogix Inc
27 Division St Ste 2 .... Saratoga Springs NY 12866 518-450-0309 177
Web: www.valogix.com

Valor Brands LLC
960 N Point Pkwy Ste 100 .... Alpharetta GA 30005 770-346-9250 157-1
TF: 866-949-9098 ■ *Web:* www.valorbrands.com

Valor Development LLC
757 N Broadway Ste 400 .... Milwaukee WI 53202 414-220-9370 196
TF: 800-455-1600 ■ *Web:* www.valordevelopment.com

Valor Oil 1200 Alsop Ln .... Owensboro KY 42303 844-468-2567 579
TF: 800-544-5823 ■ *Web:* www.valoroil.com

Valpac Inc
1400 Industrial Park Rd .... Federalsburg MD 21632 410-754-7390 3
Web: www.valpac.com

Valpak Direct Marketing Systems Inc
8605 Largo Lakes Dr .... Largo FL 33773 727-393-1270 5
Web: www.valpak.com

Valparaiso Public Library
103 Jefferson St .... Valparaiso IN 46383 219-462-0524 477-4867 434-3
Web: pcpls.org

Valparaiso University
1700 Chapel Dr .... Valparaiso IN 46383 219-464-5011 464-6898* 166
**Fax:* Admissions ■ *TF:* 888-468-2576 ■ *Web:* www.valpo.edu

Valparaiso University School of Law
651 College Ave .... Valparaiso IN 46383 219-465-7829 465-7808 167-1
TF: 888-825-7652 ■ *Web:* www.valpo.edu

Vals Plumbing & Heating Inc
413 Front St .... Salinas CA 93901 831-424-1633 189-10
Web: valsplumbing.com

Valsamis Inc 5814 Northdale St .... Houston TX 77087 713-640-1500 261
Web: valsamis.com

Valsource Inc 918A Horseshoe Pk .... Downingtown PA 19335 610-269-2808 269-4069 416
Web: www.valsource.com

Valspar Refinish Inc 210 Crosby St .... Picayune MS 39466 601-798-4731 550
Web: www.valsparrefinish.com

Valterra Products Inc
15230 San Fernando Mission Blvd
Ste 107 .... Mission Hills CA 91345 818-898-1671 791
Web: www.valterra.com

Valtim Inc 1095 Venture Dr .... Forest VA 24551 434-525-3004 463
TF: 800-230-2857 ■ *Web:* www.valtim.com

Valtra Inc 8750 Pioneer Blvd .... Santa Fe Springs CA 90670 562-949-8625 385
TF: 800-989-5244 ■ *Web:* www.valtrainc.com

Name / Address	City	State	ZIP	Phone	Fax	Class
Valu Home Centers Inc 45 S Rossler Ave. *Web:* valuhomecenters.com	Buffalo	NY	14206	716-825-7377		35
Valuation Advisory Group Inc, The 445 Pharr Rd NE *Web:* www.valuationadvisory.com	Atlanta	GA	30305	404-841-0992		734
Valuation Management Group LLC 1640 Powers Ferry Rd SE Bldg 15 Ste 100 *TF:* 866-799-7488 ■ *Web:* valuationmanagementgroup.com	Marietta	GA	30067	678-483-4420		652
Value Added Products Coop 2101 College Blvd *Web:* www.vapcoop.com	Alva	OK	73717	580-327-0400		345
Value City Furniture 40 East 53rd St *Web:* www.valuecitynj.com	Bayonne	NJ	07002	201-436-2000		321
Value City Furniture 4300 E Fifth Ave *TF:* 888-751-8552 ■ *Web:* www.valuecityfurniture.com	Columbus	OH	43219	888-672-2411		321
Value Consulting LLC 23475 Rock Haven Way Ste 200 *Web:* www.valconusa.com	Sterling	VA	20166	703-723-0100		196
Value Creation Inc 1100 635 - Eighth Ave SW *TF:* 855-908-8800 ■ *Web:* www.vctek.com	Calgary	AB	T2P3M3	403-539-4500		536
Value Creation Partners Inc 445 Hutchinson Ave	Columbus	OH	43235	614-515-5515		299
Value Drug Co 1 Golf View Dr *Web:* valuedrugco.com	Altoona	PA	16635	814-944-9316		238
Value Drug Mart Assoc Ltd 16504 - 121A Ave. *TF:* 888-554-8258 ■ *Web:* www.valuedrugmart.com	Edmonton	AB	T5V1J9	780-453-1701		238
Value Line Asset Management 220 E 42nd St *TF:* 800-634-3583 ■ *Web:* www.valueline.com	New York	NY	10017	212-907-1500		401
Value Payment Systems LLC 2207 Crestmoor Rd Ste 200 *Web:* www.valuepaymentsystems.com	Nashville	TN	37215	615-730-6367		251
Value Place LLC 8621 E 21st St N Ste 250 *Web:* www.valueplace.com	Wichita	KS	67206	316-631-1370		378
ValueCheck Inc 8822 Ridgeline Blvd Ste 100 *Web:* www.valuecheckonline.com	Highlands Ranch	CO	80129	720-283-0737		177
ValueClick Inc 30699 Russell Ranch Rd Ste 250 *NASDAQ: VCLK* ■ *TF:* 877-361-3316 ■ *Web:* conversantmedia.com/valueclick	Westlake Village	CA	91362	818-575-4500	575-4501	7
ValueClick Media 530 E Montecito St *TF:* 877-361-3316 ■ *Web:* conversantmedia.com/valueclickmedia	Santa Barbara	CA	93103	805-879-1600		7
Valuemomentum 220 Old New Brunswick Rd Ste 100 *Web:* www.valuemomentum.com	Piscataway	NJ	08854	908-941-1140		180
Valuewise Corp 662 Plank Rd Ste 240 *Web:* www.myvaluewisecorp.com	Clifton Park	NY	12065	518-280-3372		195
ValuSource LLC 4575 Galley Rd Ste 200E *TF:* 800-825-8763 ■ *Web:* www.valusource.com	Colorado Springs	CO	80915	719-548-4900		177
Valve Corp 10500 NE Eighth St Ste 1000 *Web:* www.valvesoftware.com	Bellevue	WA	98004	425-450-4464	827-4843	174
Valve Manufacturers Assn of America (VMA) 1050 17th St NW Ste 280 *Web:* www.vma.org	Washington	DC	20036	202-331-8105	296-0378	49-13
Valvoline Co 3499 Blazer Pkwy PO Box 14000 *TF:* 800-832-6825 ■ *Web:* www.valvoline.com	Lexington	KY	40512	859-357-7777		541
Valvtechnologies Inc 5904 Bingle Rd *Web:* www.valv.com	Houston	TX	77092	713-860-0400		789
VAM Drilling USA Inc 6300 Navigation Blvd *Web:* www.vallourec.com	Houston	TX	77011	713-844-3700		481
Vam USA LLC 19210 E Hardy Rd *TF:* 888-863-5204 ■ *Web:* www.vam-usa.com	Houston	TX	77073	713-479-3200		225
Vamac Inc 4201 Jacque St. *TF:* 800-768-2622 ■ *Web:* www.vamac.com	Richmond	VA	23230	804-353-7811	358-7855	612
Vamco International 555 Epsilon Dr *Web:* www.vamcointernational.com	Pittsburgh	PA	15238	412-963-7100		456
Van Aartrijk Group Inc, The 7411 Alban Sta Ct Ste B265 *Web:* www.aartrijk.com	Springfield	VA	22150	703 912 7974		636
Van Air Systems Inc 2950 Mechanic St. *TF:* 800-840-9906 ■ *Web:* www.vanairsystems.com	Lake City	PA	16423	814-774-2631	774-3482	386
Van Alen Institute 30 W 22nd St Fl 6 *Web:* www.vanalen.org	New York	NY	10010	212-924-7000		533
Van Am Tool & Engineering Inc 5025 Easton Rd *Web:* www.vanam-tool.com	St. Joseph	MO	64507	816-233-6622		454
Van Andel Arena 130 W Fulton *TF:* 800-745-3000 ■ *Web:* mlive.com	Grand Rapids	MI	49503	616-742-6600		715-1
Van Andel Institute 333 Bostwick Ave NE *Web:* www.vai.org	Grand Rapids	MI	49503	616-234-5000	234-5001	305
Van Ausdall & Farrar Inc 6430 E 75th St *TF:* 800-467-7474 ■ *Web:* www.vanausdall.com	Indianapolis	IN	46250	317-634-2913	638-1843	534
Van Belle Nursery Inc 34825 Hallert Rd. *Web:* www.vanbelle.com	Abbotsford	BC	V3G1R3	604-853-3415		292
Van Bergen & Greener Inc 1818 Madison St *TF:* 800-621-3889 ■ *Web:* www.starterdrives.com	Maywood	IL	60153	708-343-4700	343-9425	247
Van Blarcom Closures Inc 156 Sandford St *Web:* www.vbcpkg.com	Brooklyn	NY	11205	718-855-3810	935-9855	154
Van Bortel Aircraft Inc 4912 S Collins *TF:* 800-759-4295 ■ *Web:* www.vanbortel.com	Arlington	TX	76018	817-468-7788	468-7886	770
Van Bortel Subaru 6327 SR- 96 *TF:* 888-902-7961 ■ *Web:* www.vanbortelsubaru.net	Victor	NY	14564	585-924-5230		57
Van Boxtel Rv & Auto LLC 1956 Bond St *TF:* 888-831-5267 ■ *Web:* vanboxtelrv.com	Green Bay	WI	54303	920-497-3072		57
Van Buren County PO Box 475 *Web:* vanburencoia.org	Keosauqua	IA	52565	319-293-3129	293-6404	338
Van Buren County 212 E Paw Paw St Ste 101 *TF:* 800-788-1766 ■ *Web:* www.vbco.org	Paw Paw	MI	49079	269-657-8218	657-8298	338
Van Buren Public Schools (VBPS) 555 W Columbia Ave *Web:* www.vanburenschools.net	Belleville	MI	48111	734-697-9123	697-6385	685
Van Buren State Park 12259 Township Rd 218 *TF:* 866-644-6727 ■ *Web:* www.dnr.state.oh.us	Van Buren	OH	45889	419-832-7662		565
Van Buren Trail State Park 23960 Ruggles Rd *Web:* www.michigandnr.com	South Haven	MI	49090	269-637-2788		565
Van Can Co 9045 Carroll Way *Web:* www.vancan.com	San Diego	CA	92121	858-566-2141		124
Van Cleef & Arpels Inc 744 Fifth Ave 12 W 57th St *TF:* 877-826-2533 ■ *Web:* www.vancleefarpels.com	New York	NY	10019	212-644-9500	265-0036	410
Van Cliburn Foundation Inc 201 Main St Ste 100 *Web:* www.cliburn.org	Fort Worth	TX	76102	817-738-6536		711
Van Dam Inc 127 W 27 St *Web:* vandam.com	New York	NY	10011	212-929-0416		637-6
Van Dam Machine Corp 81-B Walsh Dr *Web:* www.vandammachine.com	Parsippany	NJ	07054	973-257-7050		386
Van Damme State Park 8001 Highway 1 *Web:* www.parks.ca.gov/default.asp?page_id=433	Little River	CA	95456	707-937-5804		565
Van De Pol Enterprises Inc 4895 S Airport Way *TF:* 800-379-0306 ■ *Web:* www.vandepol.us	Stockton	CA	95206	209-465-3421		324
Van Der Hout Brigagliano & Nightingale LLP 180 Sutter St Fl 5 *TF:* 800-655-9652 ■ *Web:* www.vblaw.com	San Francisco	CA	94104	650-688-6020		428
Van Diest Supply Co 1434 220th St PO Box 610 *TF:* 800-779-2424 ■ *Web:* www.vdsc.com	Webster City	IA	50595	515-832-2366	832-2955	280
Van Dijk Westlake Reed Leskosky (WRL) 1422 Euclid Ave Ste 300 *Web:* www.wrldesign.com	Cleveland	OH	44115	216-522-1350		261
Van Doren Sales Inc 10 NE Cascade Ave. *TF:* 866-886-1837 ■ *Web:* www.vandorensales.com	East Wenatchee	WA	98802	509-886-1837	886-2837	298
Van Drunen Farms 300 W Sixth St *Web:* www.vandrunenfarms.com	Momence	IL	60954	815-472-3100	472-3850	315-4
Van Dyk Group Inc, The 12800 Long Beach Blvd *TF:* 800-222-0131 ■ *Web:* www.vandykgroup.com	Beach Haven	NJ	08008	609-492-1511	492-7643	390
Van Dyke Supply Co 39771 Sd Hwy 34 *TF:* 800-279-7985 ■ *Web:* www.vandykestaxidermy.com	Woonsocket	SD	57385	704-279-7985		459
Van Eerden Foodservice Co 650 Ionia Ave SW *TF:* 800-833-7374 ■ *Web:* www.vaneerden.com	Grand Rapids	MI	49503	616-475-0900	475-0990	780
Van Ert Electric Company Inc 7019 Stewart Ave *Web:* www.vanert.com	Wausau	WI	54401	715-845-4308	848-3671	189-4
Van Galder Bus Co 715 S Pearl St *TF:* 800-747-0994 ■ *Web:* www.coachusa.com	Janesville	WI	53548	608-752-5407		107
Van Gogh School Photographers 401 Cornell Ave *Web:* vangoghschoolphotographers.com	Barrington	IL	60010	847-382-2282		592
Van Groesbeck & Co 2124 Hanovar Ave *Web:* www.vangroesbeckco.com	Richmond	VA	23220	804-285-3176	359-7271	317
Van Hollen Chris (Sen D - MD) 110 Hart Senate Office Bldg *Web:* www.vanhollen.senate.gov	Washington	DC	20510	202-224-4654	228-0629	342-2
Van Hoose Associates Inc 714 E Monument St *Web:* www.vhainc.com	Dayton	OH	45402	937-531-6680		165
Van Hoose Construction 101 NE 70th St *Web:* www.vhcon.com	Oklahoma City	OK	73105	405-848-0415	848-3911	186
Van Horn Aviation LLC 1000 E Vista Del Cerro Dr. *TF:* 800-326-1534 ■ *Web:* www.vanhornaviation.com	Tempe	AZ	85281	480 483 4202		20
Van Horn Inc PO Box 380 *TF:* 800-252-1615 ■ *Web:* www.vanhorninc.com	Cerro Gordo	IL	61818	217-677-2131	677-2134	276
Van Horn Metz & Company Inc 201 E Elm St *TF:* 800-523-0424 ■ *Web:* www.vanhornmetz.com	Conshohocken	PA	19428	610-828-4500		146
Van Leeuwen Pipe & Tube Inc 2875 64th Ave. *Web:* www.vanleeuwen.com	Edmonton	AB	T6P1R1	780-469-7410		490
Van Manen Petroleum Group 0-305 Lake Michigan Dr NW *Web:* www.vanmanen.com	Grand Rapids	MI	49534	616-453-6344		579
Van Meter Industrial Inc 850 32nd Ave SW *TF:* 800-247-1410 ■ *Web:* www.vanmeterinc.com	Cedar Rapids	IA	52404	319-366-5301	366-4709	246
Van Meter State Park 32146 N Hwy 122 *Web:* www.mostateparks.com	Miami	MO	65344	660-886-7537		565
Van Natta Mechanical Corp 25 Whitney Rd *Web:* www.vannattamechanical.com	Mahwah	NJ	07430	201-391-3700		15
Van Ness Plastic Molding Company Inc 400 Brighton Rd *Web:* www.vannessplastic.com	Clifton	NJ	07012	973-778-9500		596
Van Riper State Park 851 County Rd AKE *Web:* www.michigandnr.com	Champion	MI	49814	906-339-4461		565
Van Roy Coffee Company, The 4569 Spring Rd *TF:* 877-826-7669 ■ *Web:* www.vanroycoffee.com	Cleveland	OH	44131	216-749-7069		296-7

Name / Address	City	State	Zip	Phone	Fax	Class
Van Ru Credit Corp						
1350 E Touhy Ave Ste 300E	Des Plaines	IL	60018	800-468-2678		160
TF: 800-468-2678 ■ *Web:* www.vanru.com						
Van Strum & Towne Inc						
505 Sansome St Ste 1001	San Francisco	CA	94111	415-981-3455		401
Web: www.vanstrum.com						
Van Vleck House & Gardens						
21 Van Vleck St	Montclair	NJ	07042	973-744-4752		97
Web: www.vanvleck.org						
Van Well Nursery 2821 Grant Rd	East Wenatchee	WA	98802	509-886-8189	886-0294	293
TF: 800-572-1553 ■ *Web:* www.vanwell.net						
Van Wert County 114 E Main St	Van Wert	OH	45891	419-238-6159	238-4528	338
Web: www.vanwertcounty.org						
Van Wezel Performing Arts Ctr						
777 N Tamiami Trl	Sarasota	FL	34236	941-953-3368	951-1449	572
TF: 800-826-9303 ■ *Web:* www.vanwezel.org						
Van Wingerden International Inc						
4112 Haywood Rd	Mills River	NC	28759	828-891-4116		369
Web: www.natures-heritage.com						
Van Winkle & Associates Inc						
1180 W Peachtree St NW Ste 400	Atlanta	GA	30309	404-355-0126		184
TF: 000-245-0775 ■ *Web:* www.vanwinkleassociates.com						
Van Winkle Buck Wall Starnes & Davis PA						
11 N Market St	Asheville	NC	28801	828-475-8855		428
Web: www.vwlawfirm.com						
Van Zandt County 121 E Dallas St Rm 202	Canton	TX	75103	903-567-7555	567-6722	338
Web: www.vanzandtcounty.org						
Van Zandt County Library						
317 First Monday Ln	Canton	TX	75103	903-567-4276		434-3
Web: vanzandtlibrary.org						
Van Zandt Emrich & Cary Inc						
12401 Plantside Dr	Louisville	KY	40299	502-456-2001	454-5137	390
TF: 800-928-7355 ■ *Web:* www.vzecins.com						
Van Zelst Inc 39400 N Hwy 41	Wadsworth	IL	60083	847-623-3580		776
Web: www.vanzelst.com						
Van Zile Travel Services						
3540 Winton Pl	Rochester	NY	14623	585-244-1100		772
Web: www.vanzile.com						
Van Zyverden Inc						
8079 Van Zyverden Rd	Meridian	MS	39305	601-679-8274	679-8039	293
TF: 800-332-2852 ■ *Web:* www.vanzyverden.com						
Van's Aircraft Inc 14401 Keil Rd NE	Aurora	OR	97002	503-678-6545		529
Web: www.vansaircraft.com						
Van's Natural Foods 3285 E Vernon Ave	Vernon	CA	90058	323-585-5581		68
Web: www.vansfoods.com						
Vanacore Debenedictus Digovanni Waddell LLP						
11 Racquel Rd PO Box 10009	Newburgh	NY	12552	845-567-9000		2
Web: www.vddw.com						
Vanadium Group Corp						
134 Three Degree Rd	Pittsburgh	PA	15237	412-367-6060	630-8430	261
TF: 800-685-0354 ■ *Web:* zoominfo.com						
VanAllen Group Inc, The						
525 Clubhouse Dr Ste 150	Peachtree City	GA	30269	770-507-5001		463
Web: www.vanallen.com						
Vanamatic Co 701 Ambrose Dr	Delphos	OH	45833	419-692-6085	692-3260	621
Web: www.vanamatic.com						
VanBeurden Insurance Services Inc						
1600 Draper St PO Box 67	Kingsburg	CA	93631	559-897-2975	897-4070	390
TF: 800-550-2513 ■ *Web:* www.vanbeurden.com						
Vance Air Force Base 246 Brown Pkwy	Vance AFB	OK	73705	580-213-7476	213-6376	497-1
TF: 866-966-1020 ■ *Web:* vance.af.mil						
Vance Birthplace State Historic Site						
911 Reems Creek Rd	Weaverville	NC	28787	828-645-6706	645-0936	50-3
TF: 800-767-1560 ■ *Web:* www.nchistoricsites.org/vance/vance.htm						
Vance Bros Inc						
5201 Brighton PO Box 300107	Kansas City	MO	64130	816-923-4325	923-6472	46
TF: 800-821-8549 ■ *Web:* www.vancebrothers.com						
Vance County 122 Young St Ste E	Henderson	NC	27536	252-738-2040		338
TF: 800-733-9045 ■ *Web:* www.vancecounty.org						
Vance Kirkland Museum 1311 Pearl St	Denver	CO	80203	303-832-8576		520
Web: www.kirklandmuseum.org						
Vance Outdoors Inc						
3723 Cleveland Ave	Columbus	OH	43224	614-471-7000		711
TF: 800-413-5155 ■ *Web:* www.vanceoutdoors.com						
Vance-Granville Community College						
200 Community College Rd	Henderson	NC	27537	252-492-2061	430-0460	162
TF: 800-754-1050 ■ *Web:* www.vgcc.edu						
Franklin 8100 Nc 56 Hwy	Louisburg	NC	27549	919-496-1567	496-6604	162
Web: www.vgcc.edu						
South PO Box 39	Creedmoor	NC	27522	919-528-4737	528-1201*	162
**Fax:* Admissions ■ *TF:* 877-823-2378 ■ *Web:* www.vgcc.edu						
Warren County PO Box 207	Warrenton	NC	27536	252-257-1900	257-3612*	162
**Fax:* Admissions ■ *TF:* 877-823-2378 ■ *Web:* www.vgcc.edu						
Vanco USA Trailer Mfg						
1170 Florence Rd PO Box 98	Florence	NJ	08518	609-499-4141	499-8865	779
TF: 888-396-6501 ■ *Web:* www.vancotrailers.com						
Vancouver Aquarium Marine Science Ctr						
845 Avison Way	Vancouver	BC	V6G3E2	604-659-3474	659-3515	40
TF: 800-931-1186 ■ *Web:* www.vanaqua.org						
Vancouver Art Gallery 750 Hornby St	Vancouver	BC	V6Z2H7	604-662-4700		522
TF: 800-810-8933 ■ *Web:* vanartgallery.bc.ca						
Vancouver (BC) City Hall						
453 W 12th Ave PO Box 7747	Vancouver	BC	V5Y1V4	604-873-7000	873-7051	337
TF: 800-222-8477 ■ *Web:* vancouver.ca						
Vancouver Board of Trade						
400-999 Canada Pl Ste 400	Vancouver	BC	V6C3E1	604-681-2111	681-0437	137
Web: www.boardoftrade.com						
Vancouver Business Journal						
1251 Officers Row	Vancouver	WA	98661	360-695-2442		457-5
Web: www.vbjusa.com						
Vancouver Canucks 800 Griffiths Way	Vancouver	BC	V6B6G1	604-899-7400	899-7401	716
TF: 800-559-2333 ■ *Web:* canucks.nhl.com						
Vancouver Community College						
1155 E Broadway	Vancouver	BC	V5T4V5	604-871-7000		162
Web: www.vcc.ca						
Vancouver Convention & Exposition Centre (VCEC)						
1055 Canada Pl	Vancouver	BC	V6C0C3	604-689-8232	647-7232	205
TF: 866-785-8232 ■ *Web:* www.vancouverconventioncentre.com						
Vancouver Door Company Inc						
203 Fifth St NW	Puyallup	WA	98371	253-845-9581	845-3364	236
TF: 800-999-3667 ■ *Web:* www.vancouverdoorco.com						
Vancouver Extended-Stay Suites						
1288 W Georgia St Ste 101	Vancouver	BC	V6E4R3	604-891-6181		379
Web: www.vancouverextendedstay.com						
Vancouver Foundation						
475 W Georgia St Ste 200	Vancouver	BC	V6B4M9	604-688-2204		303
Web: www.vancouverfoundation.ca						
Vancouver General Hospital						
601 West Broadway 11th Fl	Vancouver	BC	V5Z4C2	604-875-4111	875-5701	374-2
TF: 800-663-2010 ■ *Web:* www.vch.ca						
Vancouver International Airport						
Airport Postal Outlet PO Box 23750	Richmond	BC	V7B1Y7	604-207-7077		27
TF: 800-461-9999 ■ *Web:* www.yvr.ca						
Vancouver Pile Driving Ltd						
20 Brooksbank Ave	North Vancouver	BC	V7J2B8	604-986-5911		188
Web: www.vanpile.com						
Vancouver Province						
200 Granville St Ste 1	Vancouver	BC	V6C3N3	604-605-7381		532-1
Web: www.theprovince.com						
Vancouver School of Theology						
6040 Iona Dr	Vancouver	BC	V6T2E8	604-822-9031		167-3
TF: 866-822-9031 ■ *Web:* www.vst.edu						
Vancouver Sun 200 Granville St Ste 1	Vancouver	BC	V6C3N3	604-605-2000	605-2323*	532-1
**Fax:* News Rm ■ *TF:* 866-372-3707 ■ *Web:* www.vancouversun.com						
Vancouver Talmud Torah Association						
998 26th Ave W	Vancouver	BC	V5Z2G1	604-736-7307		685
Web: www.talmudtorah.com						
Vancouver (WA) City Hall						
PO Box 1995	Vancouver	WA	98668	360-487-8000	274-8049	337
Web: www.cityofvancouver.us						
Vanda Pharmaceuticals Inc						
2200 Pennsylvania Ave NW Ste 300E	Washington	DC	20037	202-734-3400	296-1450	582
NASDAQ: VNDA ■ *Web:* www.vandapharmaceuticals.com						
Vandalia Correctional Ctr						
Rt 51 N PO Box 500	Vandalia	IL	62471	618-283-4170	283-9147	213
Web: www.illinois.gov						
Vandalia-Butler Chamber of Commerce						
544 W National Rd	Vandalia	OH	45377	937-898-5351	898-5491	139
Web: www.vandaliabutlerchamber.org						
VanDemark & Lynch Inc						
4305 Miller Rd	Wilmington	DE	19802	302-764-7635		261
Web: www.vandemarklynch.com						
VanDeMark Chemical Inc						
1 N Transit Rd	Lockport	NY	14094	716-433-6764		146
Web: vandemark.com						
Vandenberg Air Force Base						
706 Washington Ave Bldg 10122	Vandenberg AFB	CA	93437	805-606-3595	606-8303	497-1
Web: www.vandenberg.af.mil						
Vander Bend Manufacturing LLC						
2701 Orchard Pkwy	San Jose	CA	95134	408-240-3500		697
TF: 800-840-5267 ■ *Web:* www.vander-bend.com						
Vander Haag's Inc 3809 Fourth Ave W	Spencer	IA	51301	712-262-7000		61
TF: 888-940-5030 ■ *Web:* www.vanderhaags.com						
Vander Veer Botanical Park						
215 W Central Pk Ave	Davenport	IA	52803	563-326-7818		97
Web: www.cityofdavenportiowa.com						
Vanderbilt Beach Resort						
9225 Gulf Shore Dr N	Naples	FL	34108	239-597-3144	597-2199	669
TF: 800-243-9076 ■ *Web:* www.vanderbiltbeachresort.com						
Vanderbilt Grace 41 Mary St	Newport	RI	02840	401-846-6200	847-7689	379
TF: 888-826-4255 ■ *Web:* www.gracehotels.com						
Vanderbilt Kennedy Ctr for Research on Human Development						
21st Ave S	Nashville	TN	37203	615-322-8240	322-8236	668
TF: 800-772-1213 ■ *Web:* vkc.mc.vanderbilt.edu						
Vanderbilt Mansion National Historic Site						
4097 Albany Post Rd	Hyde Park	NY	12538	845-229-9115	229-0739	564
Web: www.nps.gov/vama						
Vanderbilt Minerals Corp						
30 Winfield St	Norwalk	CT	06855	203-853-1400	853-1452	503-3
TF: 800-243-6064 ■ *Web:* www.rtvanderbilt.com						
Vanderbilt Mortgage & Finance Inc						
500 Alcoa Trl	Maryville	TN	37804	800-970-7250	380-3418*	509
**Fax Area Code:* 865 ■ *TF:* 800-970-7250 ■ *Web:* www.vmf.com						
Vanderbilt University						
2201 W End Ave	Nashville	TN	37240	615-322-7311	343-7765	166
TF: 800-288-0432 ■ *Web:* www.vanderbilt.edu						
Vanderbilt University Heard Library						
419 21st Ave S	Nashville	TN	37232	615-322-2800	343-8279	434-6
Web: www.library.vanderbilt.edu						
Vanderbilt University Law School						
131 21st Ave S	Nashville	TN	37203	615-322-2615	322-6631	167-1
Web: law.vanderbilt.edu						
Vanderbilt University Medical Ctr						
1215 21st Ave S	Nashville	TN	37232	615-322-5000	343-7317	374-3
TF: 877-936-8422 ■ *Web:* www.mc.vanderbilt.edu						
Vanderbilt University Medical Ctr Stem Cell Transplant Program						
1301 22nd Ave S Ste B902	Nashville	TN	37232	615-591-9890		769
Web: www.vanderbilthealth.com						
Vanderbilt University Press						
2014 Broadway Ste 320	Nashville	TN	37203	615-322-3585	343-8823	637-4
TF: 800-627-7377 ■ *Web:* vanderbilt.edu/university-press						
Vanderbilt University School of Medicine						
215 Light Hall	Nashville	TN	37232	615-322-2145	343-8397	167-2
TF: 866-263-8263 ■ *Web:* medschool.vanderbilt.edu						
Vanderbilt-Ingram Cancer Ctr						
691 Preston Bldg	Nashville	TN	37232	615-936-1793		374-7
Web: www.vicc.org						
Vanderburgh County						
1 NW ML King Jr Blvd	Evansville	IN	47708	812-435-5241	435-5963	338
Web: www.vanderburghgov.org						
VanderCook College of Music						
3140 S Federal St	Chicago	IL	60616	312-225-6288	225-5211*	166
**Fax:* Admissions ■ *Web:* www.vandercook.edu						
VanderHouwen & Associates Inc						
6342 SW Macadam Ave	Portland	OR	97239	503-299-6811		260
Web: www.vanderhouwen.com						

	Phone	Fax	Class

Vanderpol's Eggs Ltd
3911 Mt Lehman Rd....................Abbotsford BC V2T5W5 604-856-4127 803-1
Web: www.vanderpolseggs.com

VanDerVart Concrete Products
1436 S 15th St....................Sheboygan WI 53081 920-459-2400 459-2410 182
Web: www.vandervart.com

Vandervert Construction Inc
608 E Holland Ave....................Spokane WA 99218 509-467-6654 186
TF: 800-727-9112 ■ *Web:* www.vandervertconstruction.com

Vanderweil Engineers 274 Summer St..........Boston MA 02210 617-423-7423 261
Web: www.vanderweil.com

VanDyke Software Inc
4848 Tramway Ridge Dr NE Ste 101........Albuquerque NM 87111 505-332-5700 332-5701 178-12
TF: 800-952-5210 ■ *Web:* www.vandyke.com

Vanee Foods Company Inc
5418 McDermott Dr....................Berkeley IL 60163 708-449-7300 296-36
Web: vaneefoodservice.com

Vanelli's 206 W Main St....................Tupelo MS 38804 662-844-4410 671
Web: vanellis.com

Vangard Investment Properties
118 N State College Blvd....................Fullerton CA 92831 714-446-0100 655
Web: www.vanguardproperty.com

Vangent Inc 4250 N Fairfax Dr..............Arlington VA 22203 703-284-5600 225

Vango Graphics Inc 1371 S Inca St............Denver CO 80223 303-722-6109 344
TF: 877-722-6168 ■ *Web:* vango-graphics.com

Vangold Mining Corp
7681 Prince Edward St....................Vancouver BC V5X3R4 604-684-1974 536
TF: 866-684-1974 ■ *Web:* www.vangold.ca

Vanguard Brokerage Services
PO Box 1110....................Valley Forge PA 19482 610-669-1000 669-6366 690
TF: 800-992-8327 ■ *Web:* investor.vanguard.com

Vanguard Cleaning Systems Inc
655 Mariners Island Blvd Ste 303............San Mateo CA 94404 650-287-2400 717-2082* 152
**Fax Area Code:* 479 ■ *Web:* www.vanguardcleaning.com

Vanguard Communications of Falls Church Inc
2121 K St NW Ste 650....................Washington DC 20037 202-331-4323 48-20
Web: www.vancomm.com

Vanguard Dealer Services L.L.C
30 Two Bridges Rd Ste 350....................Fairfield NJ 07004 973-575-7171 41
TF: 800-837-3279 ■ *Web:* www.vanguarddealerservices.com

Vanguard East 1172 Azalea Garden Rd............Norfolk VA 23502 800-221-1264 857-0222* 9
**Fax Area Code:* 757 ■ *TF:* 800-221-1264 ■ *Web:* www.vanguardmil.com

Vanguard Energy Corp
1330 Post Oak Blvd Ste 1600....................Houston TX 77056 713-627-2500 536

Vanguard Furniture Co Inc
109 Simpson St....................Conover NC 28613 828-328-5601 319-2
TF: 800-968-1702 ■ *Web:* www.vanguardfurniture.com

Vanguard Group 455 Devon Pk Dr............Wayne PA 19087 610-669-1000 401
TF: 877-662-7447 ■ *Web:* investor.vanguard.com

Vanguard Health Systems Inc
20 Burton Hills Blvd Ste 100....................Nashville TN 37215 615-665-6000 353
Web: www.tenethealth.com

Vanguard Integrity Professionals Inc
6625 S Eastern Ave Ste 100....................Las Vegas NV 89119 702-794-0014 180
TF: 877-794-0014 ■ *Web:* www.go2vanguard.com

Vanguard Management Group
9300 N 16th St....................Tampa FL 33612 813-930-8036 195
TF: 800-561-3357 ■ *Web:* www.vanguardmanagementgroup.com

Vanguard National Trailer Corp
289 E Water Tower Dr....................Monon IN 47959 219-253-2000 120
TF: 800-441-6621 ■ *Web:* www.vanguardtrailer.com

Vanguard Plastics Corp
100 Robert Porter Rd....................Southington CT 06489 860-628-4736 601
Web: www.vanguardplastics.com

Vanguard Products Group Inc
720 Brooker Creek Blvd Ste 223....................Oldsmar FL 34677 813-855-9639 693
TF: 877-477-4874 ■ *Web:* vanguardprotexglobal.com

Vanguard Resources Inc
17300 Henderson Pass Ste 200............San Antonio TX 78232 210-495-1950 104
Web: www.vanguardresources.com

Vanguard School 22000 US Hwy 27............Lake Wales FL 33859 863-676-6091 676-8297 622
Web: www.vanguardschool.org

Vanguard Space Technologies Inc
9431 Dowdy Dr....................San Diego CA 92126 858-587-4210 647
Web: vst-inc.com

Vanguard Steel Ltd
2160 Meadowpine Blvd....................Mississauga ON L5N6H6 905-821-1100 791
TF: 800-661-3747 ■ *Web:* www.vanguardsteel.com

Vanguard Systems Inc
2901 Dutton Mill Rd Ste 220....................Aston PA 19014 800-445-1418 387
TF: 800-445-1418 ■ *Web:* www.vansystems.com

Vanguard Trucks Centers
700 Ruskin Dr....................Forest Park GA 30297 866-216-7925 363-4659* 54
**Fax Area Code:* 404 ■ *TF:* 866-216-7925 ■ *Web:* www.vanguardtrucks.com

Vanguard University of Southern California
55 Fair Dr....................Costa Mesa CA 92626 714-556-3610 966-5471* 166
**Fax:* Admissions ■ *TF Admissions:* 800-722-6279 ■ *Web:* www.vanguard.edu

Vanilla Forums Inc
388 Rue Saint-Jacques Ste 800............Montreal QC H2Y1S1 866-845-0815 387
TF: 866-845-0815 ■ *Web:* www.vanillaforums.com

Vanir Construction Management Inc
4540 Duckhorn Dr Ste 300....................Sacramento CA 95834 916-575-8887 575-8887 463
TF: 888-912-1201 ■ *Web:* www.vanir.com

Vanity Fair Magazine
1 World Trade Ctr....................New York NY 10007 800-365-0635 457-11
TF: 800-365-0635 ■ *Web:* www.vanityfair.com

Van-Kam Freightways Ltd 10155 Grace Rd.......Surrey BC V3V3V7 604-582-7451 314
TF: 800-663-2161 ■ *Web:* www.vankam.com

Vann & Sheridan LLP
1720 Hillsborough St Ste 200....................Raleigh NC 27605 919-510-8585 428
Web: vannattorneys.com

Vann Realty Co
10330 Regency Parkway Dr Ste 204............Omaha NE 68114 402-734-4800 655
Web: www.vannrealtyco.com

Vanport Manufacturing Inc
28590 SE Wally Rd....................Boring OR 97009 503-663-4466 194
Web: vanport-international.com/en

Van-Rob Inc 200 Vandorf Sideroad............Aurora ON L4G0A2 905-727-8585 483
Web: www.van-rob.com

Vans Inc 15700 Shoemaker Ave..........Santa Fe Springs CA 90670 855-909-8267 301
TF: 855-909-8267 ■ *Web:* www.vans.com

Vantage Airport Group Ltd
1200 W 73rd Ave Ste 1410....................Vancouver BC V6P6G5 604-269-0080 269-3840 63
Web: www.vantageairportgroup.com

Vantage Associates Inc
900 Civic Ctr Dr....................National City CA 91950 619-477-6940 20
TF: 800-995-8322 ■ *Web:* www.vantagemmc.com

Vantage Credit Union (VCU) PO Box 4433......Bridgeton MO 63044 314-298-0055 219
TF: 800-522-6009 ■ *Web:* www.vcu.com

Vantage Drilling Co
777 Post Oak Blvd Ste 800....................Houston TX 77056 281-404-4700 404-4749 540
NYSE: VTG ■ *Web:* www.vantagedrilling.com

Vantage General Store 551 Main St............Vantage WA 98950 509-856-2803 297-8

Vantage Health Plan Inc
130 Desiard St Ste 300....................Monroe LA 71201 318-361-0900 353
TF: 888-823-1910 ■ *Web:* www.vantagehealthplan.com

Vantage Homes
1710 Jet Stream Dr Ste 200..........Colorado Springs CO 80921 719-534-0984 187
Web: www.vhco.com

Vantage Hospitality Group Inc
3300 N University Dr....................Coral Springs FL 33065 954-575-2668 378
Web: www.joinvantagehotels.com

Vantage Mobility International (VMI)
5202 S 28th Pl....................Phoenix AZ 85040 602-243-2700 304-3290 62-7
TF: 800-348-8267 ■ *Web:* www.vantagemobility.com

Vantage Plastics 1415 W Cedar St............Standish MI 48658 989-846-1029 608
Web: www.vantageplastics.com

Vantage Press Inc
419 Pk Ave S 18th Fl....................New York NY 10016 212-736-1767 637-2

Vantage Products Corp 960 Almon Rd........Covington GA 30014 770-788-0136 596
Web: www.vantageproducts.com

Vantage Solutions Llc
350 N La Salle Dr Ste 1122....................Chicago IL 60654 312-440-0602 445
TF: 800-572-8210 ■ *Web:* vantage-solutions.com

Vantage Sourcing LLC 4930 W St Hwy 52..........Taylor AL 36305 866-580-4562 317
TF: 866-580-4562 ■ *Web:* www.vantagesourcing.com

Vantage Trailers Inc 29335 Hwy Blvd..............Katy TX 77494 281-391-2664 779
TF: 800-826-8245 ■ *Web:* www.vantagetrailer.com

VantagePoint Laboratory Partners LLC
4980 Carroll Canyon Rd....................San Diego CA 92121 858-638-8120 415
Web: www.vpointlabs.com

VantagePoint Venture Partners
1001 Bayhill Dr Ste 300....................San Bruno CA 94066 650-866-3100 869-6078 792
Web: www.vpcp.com

Vanteon Corp
250 Cross Keys Office Pk Bldg 250............Fairport NY 14450 585-419-9555 248-0537 261
TF: 888-506-5677 ■ *Web:* www.vanteon.com

Vantige Inc 100 W Rd Ste 300....................Towson MD 21204 410-337-4774 193
Web: www.vantigeinc.com

Vantix Systems 10119 97a Ave NW..........Edmonton AB T5K2T3 780-421-0499 180
Web: vantixsystems.com

Vanton Pump & Equipment Corp
201 Sweetland Ave....................Hillside NJ 07205 908-688-4216 686-9314 641
TF: 800-841-1550 ■ *Web:* www.vanton.com

VanTran Industries Inc 7711 Imperial Dr..........Waco TX 76712 254-772-9740 772-0016 767
TF: 800-433-3346 ■ *Web:* www.vantran.com

Vanuatu 800 E Second Ave....................New York NY 10017 212-661-4303 422-3427 784
Web: www.un.int

Vapor Bus International
1010 Johnson Dr....................Buffalo Grove IL 60089 847-777-6400 520-2222 650
Web: www.wabtec.com/business-units/vapor-bus-international

Varay Systems LLC
201 E Main Dr Ste 700....................El Paso TX 79901 915-496-8555 179
Web: www.varay.com

Varbros LLC 16025 Brookpark Rd............Cleveland OH 44142 216-267-5200 267-5205 489
TF: 800-365-7391 ■ *Web:* www.varbroscorp.com

Varco Heat Treating Co
12101 Industry....................Garden Grove CA 92841 657-400-8113 484
Web: www.varcoheat.com

Varco Pruden Buildings
3200 Players Club Cir....................Memphis TN 38125 901-748-8000 748-9323 105
Web: www.vp.com

Varel International
1625 W Crosby Dr Ste 124....................Carrollton TX 75006 972-242-1160 242-8770 190
TF: 800-827-3526 ■ *Web:* www.varelintl.com

Varen Technologies Inc
9801 Broken Land Pkwy Ste 100............Columbia MD 21046 410-290-8008 177
Web: www.varentech.com

Varflex Corp 512 W Ct St....................Rome NY 13440 315-336-4400 336-0005 816
TF: 800-648-4014 ■ *Web:* www.varflex.com

Vargas Juan (Rep D - CA)
1605 Longworth Bldg....................Washington DC 20515 202-225-8045 225-2772 342-2
Web: vargas.house.gov

VARGO Companies 3709 Pkwy Ln............Hilliard OH 43026 614-876-1163 358
TF: 800-752-1220 ■ *Web:* www.vargosolutions.com

Variable Annuity Life Insurance Co (VALIC)
2929 Allen Pkwy....................Houston TX 77019 800-448-2542 391-2
TF: 800-448-2542 ■ *Web:* www.valic.com

Varian Medical Systems Inc
3100 Hansen Way....................Palo Alto CA 94304 650-493-4000 382
NYSE: VAR ■ *TF:* 800-544-4636 ■ *Web:* www.varian.com

Varian Semiconductor Equipment Assoc Inc
35 Dory Rd....................Gloucester MA 01930 978-282-2000 283-6376 695
Web: www.vsea.com

Variant Microsystems
4128 Business Ctr Dr....................Fremont CA 94538 510-440-2870 535
TF: 800-827-4268 ■ *Web:* www.variantusa.com

Variety Distributors Inc
609 Seventh St....................Harlan IA 51537 712-755-2184 755-5041 328
TF: 800-274-1095 ■ *Web:* www.varietydistributors.com

Variety Gem Company Inc
11 W 46th St Fl 3....................New York NY 10036 212-921-1820 411
Web: www.varietygem.com

Variform Inc 5020 Weston Pkwy Ste 400............Cary NC 27513 888-975-9436 191-4
TF: 800-800-2244 ■ *Web:* www.plygem.com/wps/portal/home/brands/variform

Variosystems Inc 901 S Kimball Ave..........Southlake TX 76092 817-416-7535 696
Web: www.variosystems.com

Phone | Fax | Class

VARIS LLC 9245 Sierra College Blvd. .... Roseville CA 95661 916-294-0860 194
Web: www.varis1.com

Varite Inc 12 S First St Ste 404 .... San Jose CA 95113 408-977-0700 177
TF: 800-681-1729 ■ Web: www.varite.com

Varner-Hogg Plantation State Historic Site
1702 N 13th St .... West Columbia TX 77486 979-345-4656 565
Web: tpwd.texas.gov

Varnett School - East, The
804 Maxey Rd. .... Houston TX 77013 713-637-6574 685
Web: www.varnett.org

Varnum LLP
Bridgewater Pl PO Box 352. .... Grand Rapids MI 49501 616-336-6000 41
Web: www.varnumlaw.com

Varouh Oil Inc 970 Griswold Rd .... Elyria OH 44035 440-324-5025 324-4155 579
TF: 866-482-7684 ■ Web: www.varouhoil.com

Varouj's Kabobs 1110 S Glendale Ave .... Glendale CA 91205 818-243-9870 671

Varscona Hotel 8208 106th St .... Edmonton AB T6E6R9 780-434-6111 379
TF: 866-465-8150 ■ Web: www.varscona.com

Vartek Services Inc 1785 S Metro Pkwy .... Dayton OH 45459 937-438-3550 174
TF: 800-954-2524 ■ Web: www.vartek.com

Varvid Inc 705 Sunset Pond Ln Ste 2. .... Bellingham WA 98226 855-827-8434 5
TF: 855 827 8434 ■ Web: www.varvid.com

Vasamed Inc
7615 Golden Triangle Dr Ste A .... Eden Prairie MN 55344 800-695-2737 944-6022* 476
*Fax Area Code: 952 ■ TF: 800-695-2737 ■ Web: www.vasamed.com

Vasc Alert LLC 3000 Kent Ave. .... West Lafayette IN 47906 765-775-2525 180
TF: 800-456-2905 ■ Web: www.vasc-alert.com

VASCO Data Security International Inc
1901 S Meyers Rd Ste 210. .... Oakbrook Terrace IL 60181 630-932-8844 932-8852 692
NASDAQ: VDSI ■ Web: www.vasco.com

Vascor Ltd
100 Farmers Bank Dr Ste 300. .... Georgetown KY 40324 502-570-2020 311
Web: www.vascorlogistics.com

Vascular Dynamics Inc
2134 Old Middlefield Way Ste J .... Mountain View CA 94043 650-963-9370 475
TF: 800-477-5801 ■ Web: www.vasculardynamics.com

Vascular Institute of Georgia
5669 Peachtree Dunwoody Rd .... Atlanta GA 30342 404-256-0404 592
Web: www.vascularinstituteofgeorgia.com

Vascular Pathways Inc
1847 Trade Ctr Way .... Naples FL 34109 239-254-0391 475

Vascular Solutions Inc
6464 Sycamore Ct .... Minneapolis MN 55369 763-656-4300 656-4251* 476
NASDAQ: VASC ■ *Fax Area Code: 877 ■ TF: 877-979-4300 ■ Web: www.vasc.com

Vasey Commercial Heating & Air Conditioning Inc
10830 Andrade Dr .... Zionsville IN 46077 317-873-2512 189-10
Web: www.vasey.com

VasoHealthcare
Revolution Mill Studios 1150 Revolution Mill Dr St
.... Greensboro NC 27405 336-398-8276 475
Web: www.vasohealthcare.com

Vasomedical Inc 180 Linden Ave .... Westbury NY 11590 516-997-4600 997-2299 250
OTC: VASO ■ TF: 800-455-3327 ■ Web: www.vasomedical.com

Vassar College 124 Raymond Ave .... Poughkeepsie NY 12604 845-437-7000 437-7063 166
TF: 800-827-7270 ■ Web: www.vassar.edu

Vassar College Library
124 Raymond Ave PO Box 20. .... Poughkeepsie NY 12604 845-437-5760 437-5864 434-6
Web: library.vassar.edu

VasSol Inc 348 Lathrop Ave. .... River Forest IL 60305 708-366-7000 250
Web: www.vassolinc.com

VATEX America 2395 Hermitage Rd .... Richmond VA 23220 804-353-9010 9
Web: www.vatex.com

Vatterott College
Omaha 11818 I St .... Omaha NE 68137 402-891-9411 800
Web: www.vatterott.edu

Vatterott College Berkeley
8580 Evans Ave .... Berkeley MO 63134 314-264-1000 800
TF: 888-202-2636 ■ Web: www.vatterott.edu

Vatterott College Joplin
809 Illinois Ave. .... Joplin MO 64801 417-781-5633 800
TF: 866-200-1898 ■ Web: www.vatterott.edu

Vatterott College South County
12900 Maurer Industrial Dr .... Saint Louis MO 63127 314-843-4200 800
TF: 866-312-8276 ■ Web: www.vatterott.edu

Vatterott College Springfield
3850 S Campbell .... Springfield MO 65807 417-831-8116 800
Web: www.vatterott.edu

Vaughan & Bushnell Manufacturing Co
11414 Maple Ave .... Hebron IL 60034 815-648-2446 648-4300 758
TF: 800-435-6000 ■ Web: vaughanmfg.com

Vaughan Chamber of Commerce
25 Edilcan Dr Ste 2. .... Vaughan ON L4K3S4 905-761-1366 761-1918 137
TF: 888-943-8937 ■ Web: vaughanchamber.ca

Vaughan Company Inc
364 Monte-Elma Rd .... Montesano WA 98563 360-249-4042 249-6155 641
TF: 888-249-2467 ■ Web: www.chopperpumps.com

Vaughan Mills 1 Bass Pro Mills Dr .... Vaughan ON L4K5W4 905-879-2110 879-1888 460
Web: www.vaughanmills.com

Vaughan Nelson Investment Management LP
600 Travis St Ste 6300 .... Houston TX 77002 713-224-2545 528
TF: 888-888-8676 ■ Web: www.vaughannelson.com

Vaughan Regional Medical Ctr
1015 Medical Ctr Pkwy. .... Selma AL 36701 334-418-4100 374-3
TF: 800-994-6610 ■ Web: www.vaughanregional.com

Vaughan Woods State Park
28 Oldfields Rd. .... South Berwick ME 03908 207-287-3200 565
Web: www.maine.gov

Vaughn Coast & Vaughn Inc
154 S Marietta St .... St Clairsville OH 43950 740-695-7256 261
Web: vaughncoastvaughn.com

Vaughn College of Aeronautics & Technology
86-01 23rd Ave. .... East Elmhurst NY 11369 718-429-6600 166
TF: 866-682-8446 ■ Web: vaughn.edu

Vaughn Coltrane Pharr & Associates Inc
2060 E Exchange Pl .... Tucker GA 30084 770-938-2600 256
Web: www.vcae.com

Vaughn Construction 10355 Westpark Dr .... Houston TX 77042 713-243-8300 243-8350 186
Web: www.vaughnconstruction.com

Vaughn Industries LLC 1201 E Findlay St .... Carey OH 43316 419-396-3900 189-4
Web: www.vaughnindustries.com

Vaughn Manufacturing Corp
26 Old Elm St PO Box 5431 .... Salisbury MA 01952 978-462-6683 462-6497 36
TF: 800-282-8446 ■ Web: www.vaughncorp.com

Vaughn Mfg Company Inc
757 Douglas Ave. .... Nashville TN 37207 615-262-5775 697
Web: www.vaughnmfg.com

Vault Inc 132 W 31st St 16th Fl .... New York NY 10001 212-366-4212 366-6117 260
Web: www.vault.com

Vaupell Inc 1144 NW 53rd St .... Seattle WA 98107 206-784-9050 784-9708 604
Web: www.vaupell.com

Vavro & Company Inc
4725 Grayton Rd Ste 1040 .... Cleveland OH 44135 440-886-0400 2
Web: vavrocpa.com

VAWC (Virginia American Water Co)
2223 Duke St .... Alexandria VA 22314 703-706-3879 787
TF: 800-452-6863 ■ Web: www.amwater.com

Vawter Financial Ltd
1161 Bethel Rd Ste 304 .... Columbus OH 43220 614-451-1002 194
TF: 800-955-1575 ■ Web: www.vawterfinancial.com

Vaxcel International Co
121 E N Ave .... Carol Stream IL 60188 630-682-8767 362
Web: www.vaxcelusa.com

Vaya 2111 Plum St Ste 250. .... Aurora IL 60506 630-906-3046 463
Web: www.vayapath.com

Vazzy's Brick Oven Restaurant
513 Broadbridge Rd .... Bridgeport CT 06610 203-371-8046 371-4293 671
TF: 800-442-1162 ■ Web: www.theoriginalvazzys.com

VBA (Vermont Bar Assn)
35-37 Ct St PO Box 100. .... Montpelier VT 05601 802-223-2020 223-1573 72
TF: 800-639-7036 ■ Web: www.vtbar.org

VBCVB (Virginia Beach Convention & Visitor Bureau)
2101 Parks Ave Ste 500 .... Virginia Beach VA 23451 757-385-4700 437-4747 206
TF: 800-700-7702 ■ Web: www.visitvirginiabeach.com

Vbeyond Corp 3 Skillman Close .... Hillsborough NJ 08844 908-359-8416 180
Web: www.vbeyond.com

VBPS (Van Buren Public Schools)
555 W Columbia Ave .... Belleville MI 48111 734-697-9123 697-6385 685
Web: www.vanburenschools.net

Vbrick Systems Inc 12 Beaumont Rd .... Wallingford CT 06492 203-265-0044 265-6750 735
TF: 866-827-4251 ■ Web: www.vbrick.com

VBT 614 Monkton Rd. .... Bristol VT 05443 802-453-4811 760
TF: 800-245-3868 ■ Web: www.vbt.com

VC Enterprises Ltd 2025 Olive Ave. .... Sibley IA 51249 712-724-6256 366

Vc999 Packaging Systems Inc
419 E 11th Ave .... Kansas City MO 64116 816-472-8999 547
Web: www.vc999.com

VCA Boston Road Animal Hospital
1235 Boston Rd .... Springfield MA 01119 413-783-1203 794
Web: www.vcahospitals.com

VCC (VCC-USA)
216 Louisiana St PO Box 555. .... Little Rock AR 72203 501-376-0017 376-4145 186
Web: www.vccusa.com

VCC-USA (VCC)
216 Louisiana St PO Box 555. .... Little Rock AR 72203 501-376-0017 376-4145 186
Web: www.vccusa.com

VCEC (Vancouver Convention & Exposition Centre)
1055 Canada Pl .... Vancouver BC V6C0C3 604-689-8232 647-7232 205
TF: 866-785-8232 ■ Web: www.vancouverconventioncentre.com

VCF Films Inc 1100 Sutton Ave. .... Howell MI 48843 888-905-7680 546-2984* 600
*Fax Area Code: 517 ■ TF: 888-905-7680 ■ Web: vcffilms.com

VCFO Holdings Inc
6836 Austin Center Blvd Bldg 1 Ste 280. .... Austin TX 78731 512-345-9441 194
Web: www.vcfo.com

VCG LLC 1805 Old Alabama Rd. .... Roswell GA 30076 770-246-2300 449-3638 178-12
TF: 800-318-4983 ■ Web: www.bond-us.com

VCI Construction LLC 1921 W 11th St. .... Upland CA 91786 909-946-0905 186
Web: www.vcicom.com

VCI Emergency Vehicle 43 jefferson ave. .... Berlin NJ 08009 856-768-2162 401
TF: 800-394-2162 ■ Web: vciambulances.com

Vci Inc 1500 Progress St .... Sturgis MI 49091 269-659-3676 697
Web: vciusa.com

VCNA Prairie Inc
7601 W 79th St PO Box 1123. .... Bridgeview IL 60455 708-458-0400 194
Web: www.prairie.com

VCOMP Solutions
1919 S Highland Ave Ste 200D .... Lombard IL 60148 888-978-2667 676-1448 196
TF: 888-978-2667

VCON Inc 578 Main St .... Hackensack NJ 07601 201-883-1220 735
Web: www.clearone.com

VCU (VCU Health) 1250 E Marshall St. .... Richmond VA 23298 804-828-9000 353
Web: www.vcuhealth.org

VCU (Vantage Credit Union) PO Box 4433 .... Bridgeton MO 63044 314-298-0055 219
TF: 800-522-6009 ■ Web: www.vcu.com

VCU Health (VCU) 1250 E Marshall St. .... Richmond VA 23298 804-828-9000 353
Web: www.vcuhealth.org

VCU Massey Cancer Center
Bone Marrow Transplant Program
401 College St PO Box 980037 .... Richmond VA 23298 804-828-4360 769
Web: www.massey.vcu.edu

vCustomer Corp
4040 Lake Washington Blvd NE .... Kirkland WA 98033 206-802-0200 463
Web: www.vcustomer.com

VDA (Virginia Dental Assn)
3460 Mayland Ct Ste 110 .... Richmond VA 23233 804-288-5750 288-1880 227
Web: www.vadental.org

Vdara Condo Hotel LLC
2600 W Harmon Ave. .... Las Vegas NV 89158 866-718-2489 377
TF: 866-718-2489 ■ Web: www.vdara.com

VDC Research Group Inc
679 Worcester Rd Ste 2 .... Natick MA 01760 508-653-9000 653-9836 194
Web: www.vdcresearch.com

VDIC Inc 16900 SE 82nd Dr .... Clackamas OR 97015 503-722-8077 415
TF: 800-378-1191 ■ Web: www.vdic.com

VDx Veterinary Diagnostics Inc
2019 Anderson Rd Ste C .... Davis CA 95616 530-753-4285 794
TF: 877-753-4285 ■ Web: vdxpathology.com

Name / Address	City	State	ZIP	Phone	Fax	Class
VE Enterprises Inc 10834 State Hwy 53 PO Box 369	Springer	OK	73458	580-653-2171	653-2773	779
Veasey Marc (Rep D - TX) 1519 Longworth HOB *Web:* veasey.house.gov	Washington	DC	20515	202-225-9897	225-9702	342-2
Veber Partners LLC 605 N W 11th Ave *TF:* 800-627-3999 ■ *Web:* www.veber.com	Portland	OR	97209	503-229-4400		194
VEC (Victoria Electric Co-op Inc) 102 S Ben Jordan St *Web:* www.victoriaelectric.coop	Victoria	TX	77901	361-573-2428		245
VEC (Volunteer Energy Co-op) PO Box 277 *Web:* www.vec.org	Decatur	TN	37322	423-334-5721	334-7003	245
Vecellio & Grogan Inc 2251 Robert C Byrd Dr *TF:* 800-255-6575 ■ *Web:* www.vecelliogrogan.com	Beckley	WV	25802	304-252-6575	252-4131	188-4
Vecna Technologies Inc 36 Cambridge Park Dr Ste 500 *Web:* www.vecna.com	Cambridge	MA	20770	617-864-0636	864-0638	177
Vectech Pharmaceutical Consultants Inc 5640 W Maple Rd Ste 312 *TF:* 800-966-8832 ■ *Web:* www.vpcint.com	West Bloomfield	MI	48322	248-538-5150	538-5153	261
Vectech Pharmaceutical Consultants International Inc 5640 W Maple Rd Ste 312 *Web:* www.vpcint.com	West Bloomfield	MI	48322	248-538-5150		583
Vector Aerospace Helicopter Services Inc 22378 Billie Blackmon Rd Ste 2100 *TF:* 888-729-2276 ■ *Web:* www.vectoraerospace.com	Andalusia	AL	36421	604-276-7600	276-7675	21
Vector Capital 1 Matket St Steuart Tower 23rd Fl *Web:* www.vectorcapital.com	San Francisco	CA	94105	415-293-5000	293-5100	792
Vector Composites Inc 3251 Mc Call St	Dayton	OH	45417	937-281-1444		127
Vector Consulting 6455 E Johns Crossing *Web:* vectorconsulting.com	Duluth	GA	30097	770-246-0968		177
Vector Group Ltd 4400 Biscayne Blvd *NYSE: VGR* ■ *Web:* www.vectorgroupltd.com	Miami	FL	33137	305-579-8000	579-8001	360-3
Vector Marketing Co 322 Houghton Ave *TF:* 800-828-0448 ■ *Web:* www.vectoroncampus.com	Olean	NY	14760	800-828-0448		366
Vector Networks Inc 541 Tenth St Unit 123 *TF:* 800-330-5035 ■ *Web:* www.vector-networks.com	Atlanta	GA	30318	770-622-2850		179
Vector Planning & Services Inc 591 Camino De La Reina Ste 300 *TF:* 888-522-5491 ■ *Web:* myvpsi.com	San Diego	CA	92108	619-297-5656		177
Vector Resources Inc 3530 Voyager St *Web:* www.vectorusa.com	Torrance	CA	90503	310-436-1000	436-1060	252
Vector Security Inc 2000 Ericsson Dr *TF:* 800-832-8575 ■ *Web:* www.vectorsecurity.com	Warrendale	PA	15086	800-832-8575		692
Vector Seismic Data Processing Inc 1801 Broadway Ste 1150 *Web:* www.slb.com/services/seismic/vector-seismic.aspx	Denver	CO	80202	303-571-1515		539
Vector Software Inc 1351 S County Trl Ste 310 *Web:* www.vectorcast.com	East Greenwich	RI	02818	401-398-7185		177
Vector Technical Inc 38033 Euclid Ave Ste T-9 *Web:* www.vectortechnicalinc.com	Willoughby	OH	44094	440-946-8800		260
VectorCSP LLC 405 E Main St *Web:* www.vectorcsp.com	Elizabeth City	NC	27909	252-338-2264		449
VectorGlobal WMG Inc 1001 Brickell Bay Dr Ste 1900 *Web:* www.vectorglobalwmg.com	Miami	FL	33131	305-537-0300		691
VectorMAX Corp 4 Dubon Ct *Web:* www.vectormax.com	Farmingdale	NY	11735	516-672-2505		177
Vectorply Corp 3500 Lakewood Dr *TF:* 800-577-4521 ■ *Web:* www.vectorply.com	Phenix City	AL	36867	334-291-7704	291-7743	745-1
VectorVest Inc 20472 Chartwell Ctr Dr Ste D *TF:* 800-130-1519 ■ *Web:* www.vectorvest.com	Cornelius	NC	28031	704-895-4095		401
Vectra Bank Colorado NA 2000 S Colorado Blvd Ste 2-1200 *TF:* 800-232-8948 ■ *Web:* www.vectrabank.com	Denver	CO	80222	720-947-7700	947-7760	70
Vectra Fitness Inc 7901 S 190th St *TF:* 800-283-2872 ■ *Web:* www.vectrafitness.com	Kent	WA	98032	425-291-9550	291-9650	267
Vectra Visual 3950 Business Pk Dr *Web:* vectravisual.com	Columbus	OH	43204	614-351-6868		627
Vectren Corp 211 NW Riverside Dr PO Box 209 *NYSE: VVC* ■ *TF:* 800 227 1376 ■ *Web:* www.vectren.com	Evansville	IN	47702	812-491-4000		360-5
Vectronix Inc 19775 Belmont Executive Plaza Ste 550 *Web:* www.vectronix.us	Ashburn	VA	20147	703-777-3900		544
Vectrus Inc 655 Space Ctr Dr *TF:* 800-732-0330 ■ *Web:* www.vectrus.com	Colorado Springs	CO	80915	719-591-3600		463
Vectus Inc 18685 Main St 101 PMB 360 *TF:* 866-483-2887 ■ *Web:* www.vectus.com	Huntington Beach	CA	92648	866-483-2887		387
Vedco Inc 5503 Corporate Dr *Web:* www.vedco.com	Saint Joseph	MO	64507	816-238-8840		794
Vedder Transportation Group, The 400 Riverside Rd *TF:* 866-857-1375 ■ *Web:* www.vtlg.com	Abbotsford	BC	V2S4P4	866-857-1375		314
Vee Bar Guest Ranch 38 Vee Bar Ranch Rd *TF:* 800-483-3227 ■ *Web:* www.veebar.com	Laramie	WY	82070	307-745-7036	745-7433	239
Vee Neal Aviation Inc 148 Aviation Ln Ste 109 *TF:* 800-278-2710 ■ *Web:* www.veeneal.com	Latrobe	PA	15650	724-539-4533	539-5501	63
Veeco Holdings LLC 6801 W Side Ave *Web:* www.veeco1.com	North Bergen	NJ	07047	201-865-6200		311
Veeco Instruments Inc 1 Terminal Dr *NASDAQ: VECO* ■ *TF:* 888-724-9511 ■ *Web:* www.veeco.com	Plainview	NY	11803	516-677-0200		695
Veeder-Root 125 Powder Forest Dr *TF:* 888-262-7539 ■ *Web:* www.veeder.com	Simsbury	CT	06070	860-651-2700	651-2719	201
Veenendaalcave Inc 1170 Peachtree St NE *Web:* www.vcave.com	Atlanta	GA	30309	404-881-1811		393
Veenstra & Kimm Inc 3000 Westown Pkwy *TF:* 800-241-8000 ■ *Web:* www.v-k.net	West Des Moines	IA	50266	515-225-8000		261
Veer Right Management Group Inc 1005 Woodland Dr NW Ste D	Wilson	NC	27893	252-237-5900		226
Veetech PC 113 Centrewest Ct *TF:* 800-341-1185 ■ *Web:* www.veetechpc.com	Cary	NC	27513	919-388-0037		463
Veetronix Inc 1311 W Pacific Ave *TF General:* 800-445-0007 ■ *Web:* www.veetronix.com	Lexington	NE	68850	308-324-6661	324-4985	815
VEF (Vietnam Education Foundation) 2200 Wilson Blvd Ste 205 **Fax Area Code:* 703 ■ *Web:* home.vef.gov	Arlington	VA	22201	571-800-9578	351-1423*	340-20
Vega Capital Group LLC 100 Bush St Ste 1428 *Web:* www.vegacapital.com	San Francisco	CA	94104	415-318-8740		796
Vega Energy Partners Ltd 3701 Kirby Ste 1290 *Web:* www.vegaenergy.com	Houston	TX	77098	713-527-0557		463
Vega Group 7220 Washington Ave *TF:* 800-771-2979 ■ *Web:* www.vegagroup.com	New Orleans	LA	70125	504-488-5222		184
Vega State Park PO Box 186 *Web:* cpw.state.co.us	Collbran	CO	81624	970-487-3407		565
Vega Tapas Cafe 2051 Metairie Rd *Web:* www.vegatapascafe.com	Metairie	LA	70005	504-836-2007		671
Vegan Action PO Box 7313 *Web:* vegan.org	Richmond	VA	23221	804-577-8341		48-17
VEGAS.com LLC 2370 Corporate Cir 3rd Fl *Web:* www.vegas.com	Henderson	NV	89074	702-992-7990		775
Vegetable Juices Inc 7400 S Narragansett Ave *TF General:* 888-776-9752 ■ *Web:* www.vegetablejuices.com	Chicago	IL	60638	708-924-9500		296-20
Vegetarian Resource Group, The (VRG) PO Box 1463 *Web:* www.vrg.org	Baltimore	MD	21203	410-366-8343	366-8804	48-17
Vegetarian Times 300 N Continental Blvd Ste 650 *TF:* 800-573-1900 ■ *Web:* www.vegetariantimes.com	El Segundo	CA	90245	310-356-4100	356-4110	457-13
Veggie Heaven 1611 W Fifth St Ste 135 *Web:* veggieheavenaustin.com	Austin	TX	78703	512-457-1013		671
Veg-Pro Inc 11800 Gordon Ave	Grant	MI	49327	231-834-5634		11-1
Vehicle Improvement Products 151 S Ram Rd *Web:* www.vipwheels.com	Antioch	IL	60002	847-395-7250		54
Vehicle Safety Mfg LLC 408 Central Ave *TF General:* 800-832-7233 ■ *Web:* www.vehiclesafetymfg.com	Newark	NJ	07107	973-643-3000		438
VehSmart Inc 12180 Ridgecrest Rd Ste 412 *TF:* 855-834-7627 ■ *Web:* www.vehsmart.com	Victorville	CA	92395	855-834-7627		647
Vehtech Inc 2890 Hwy 212 Ste 347 A *Web:* www.vehtechnology.com	Conyers	GA	30094	770-788-2032		41
Veit & Company Inc 14000 Veit Pl *Web:* www.veitusa.com	Rogers	MN	55374	763-428-2242		186
VEITS Group LLC 7610 Olentangy River Rd ste 200 *TF:* 877-834-8702 ■ *Web:* www.veitsgroup.com	Columbus	OH	43235	614-467-5414	467-5418	225
Veka Inc 100 Veka Dr *TF:* 800-654-5589 ■ *Web:* www.vekainc.com	Fombell	PA	16123	724-452-1000	452-1007	235
Vektrel LLC 9988 Hibert St Ste 104 *Web:* www.vektrel.com	San Diego	CA	92131	858-564-0301		261
Vektrex Electronic Systems Inc 10225 Barnes Canyon Rd *Web:* www.vektrex.com	San Diego	CA	92121	858-558-8282		177
Vel Micro Works Inc 726 Yorklyn Rd Ste 400 *Web:* www.velmicro.com	Hockessin	DE	19707	302-239-4661		809
Vela Filemon (Rep D - TX) 437 Cannon HOB *Web:* vela.house.gov	Washington	DC	20515	202-225-9901	225-9770	342-2
Vela Research LP 5540 Rio Vista Dr *Web:* www.vela.com	Clearwater	FL	33760	727-507-5300		735
Velan Inc 7007 Cote de Liesse *TSE: VLN* ■ *Web:* www.velan.com	Montreal	QC	H4T1G2	514-748-7743	748-8635	789
Velaro Inc 8174 Lark Brown Rd Ste 201 *TF:* 800-983-5276 ■ *Web:* www.velaro.com	Elkridge	MD	21075	800-983-5276		809
Velazquez Nydia M (Rep D - NY) 2302 Rayburn Bldg *Web:* velazquez.house.gov	Washington	DC	20515	202-225-2361		342-2
Velcro USA Inc 406 Brown Ave *TF:* 800-225-0180 ■ *Web:* www.velcro.com	Manchester	NH	03103	603-669-4880	669-9271	594
Veldkamp's Flowers 9501 W Colfax Ave *TF:* 800-247-3730 ■ *Web:* www.veldkampsflowers.com	Lakewood	CO	80215	303-232-2673		292
Velko Hinge Inc 9325 Kennedy Ct *Web:* www.velko.com	Munster	IN	46321	219-924-6363		350
Vellano Bros Inc 7 Hemlock St *TF:* 800-342-9855 ■ *Web:* www.vellano.com	Latham	NY	12110	518-785-5537	785-5570	385
Vellumoid Inc 54 Rockdale St *TF:* 800-609-5558 ■ *Web:* www.vellumoid.com	Worcester	MA	01606	508-853-2500	852-0741	326
Velmex Inc 7550 SR-5 20 *Web:* www.velmex.com	Bloomfield	NY	14469	585-657-6151		454
Velocite Systems Inc 810 Cromwell Park Dr Ste K *Web:* www.velocitesystems.com	Glen Burnie	MD	21061	443-572-0015		196
Velocity Credit Union 610 E 11th St *Web:* www.velocitycu.com	Austin	TX	78701	512-469-7000	469-7024	70
Velocity Futures LLC 5373 W Alabama St Ste 600	Houston	TX	77056	713-490-7600		610
Velocity Partners Inc 15300 W Capitol Dr *Web:* velocitypartners.com	Brookfield	WI	53005	262-790-0800		180
Velocity Sales & Marketing 1700 Parkes Dr *Web:* newenglandoutdoorreps.com	Broadview	IL	60155	708-681-1601		195
Velocity Trade 99 Yorkville Ave Ste 210 *Web:* velocitytrade.com	Toronto	ON	M5R3K5	416-855-2800		509
Velos Inc 2201 Walnut Ave Ste 208 *Web:* www.velos.com	Fremont	CA	94538	510-739-4010	739-4018	178-11

Name / Address	City	State	Zip	Phone	Fax	Class
Veloxiti Inc 3650 Brookside Pkwy Ste 500 *Web:* veloxiti.com	Alpharetta	GA	30022	770-518-4228		261
VelQuest Corp 25 S St *Web:* www.velquest.com	Hopkinton	MA	01748	508-497-9911		525
Velsicol Chemical Corp 10400 W Higgins Rd Ste 700 *TF Cust Svc:* 877-847-8351 ■ *Web:* www.velsicol.com	Rosemont	IL	60018	847-813-7888	768-3227	144
Velting Contractors Inc 3060 Breton Rd SE *Web:* www.velting.com	Kentwood	MI	49512	616-949-6660	949-8168	189-5
VELUX America Inc 450 Old BrickyaRd Rd *TF:* 800-888-3589 ■ *Web:* www.veluxusa.com	Greenwood	SC	29648	803-396-5700		491
Velvac Inc 2405 S Calhoun Rd *TF:* 800-783-8871 ■ *Web:* www.velvac.com	New Berlin	WI	53151	262-786-0700	786-7323	60
Velvet Grill & Creamery 2204 McHenry Ave *Web:* www.velvetgrill.net	Modesto	CA	95350	209-544-9029		671
V-Empower Inc 6800 Willow Creek Rd *Web:* www.v-empower.com	Bowie	MD	20720	301-805-9194		224
Venable LLP 575 Seventh St NW *TF:* 800-900-4250 ■ *Web:* www.venable.com	Washington	DC	20004	202-344-4000	344-8300	428
Venaca Inc 450 W 31st St Fourth Fl 4th FL	New York	NY	10001	212-660-2965	695-5766	511
Venado Oil & Gas LLC 12600 Hill Country Blvd Bldg R Ste 250 *Web:* www.vogllc.com	Austin	TX	78738	512-735-9000		536
Venango County Courthouse Annex 1174 Elk St *Web:* www.co.venango.pa.us	Franklin	PA	16323	814-432-9500	432-3149	338
Venarc Inc 2314 W Burbank Blvd *Web:* www.venarc.com	Burbank	CA	91506	818-524-2500		809
Venchurs Packaging 800 Liberty St *Web:* www.venchurs.com	Adrian	MI	49221	517-263-8937	265-7468	549
Vend Mart Inc 1950 Williams St *Web:* www.vendmart.com	San Leandro	CA	94577	510-297-5132	352-8363	297-8
Venda Ravioli Inc 265 Atwells Ave *Web:* www.vendaravioli.com	Providence	RI	02903	401-421-9105		297-8
Vendant Inc 4845 Pearl East Cir Ste 101 *TF:* 800-714-4900 ■ *Web:* www.vedanthealth.com	Bouler	CO	80301	720-874-9781	398-3399	178-12
Vendetti Motors Inc 411 W Central St *Web:* vendettimotors.com	Franklin	MA	02038	508-528-3450		57
Vendini Inc 660 Market St *TF:* 800-901-7173 ■ *Web:* www.vendini.com	San Francisco	CA	94104	800-901-7173		187
Vendio Services Inc 2000 Campus Dr Ste 150 *TF:* 800-646-3517 ■ *Web:* www.vendio.com	San Mateo	CA	94403	650-293-3500		178-7
Vendome Copper & Brass Works Inc 729 Franklin St *TF:* 888-384-5161 ■ *Web:* www.vendomecopper.com	Louisville	KY	40202	502-587-1930	589-0639	298
Vendome Group LLC 216 E 45th St 6th Fl *TF:* 800-519-3692 ■ *Web:* www.vendomegrp.com	New York	NY	10017	800-519-3692		637-9
Vendors Exchange International Inc 8700 Brookpark Rd *TF:* 800-321-2311 ■ *Web:* www.veii.com	Cleveland	OH	44129	216-432-1800		463
VendorSeek com LLC 520 Fellowship Rd Ste 102 *Web:* www.vendorseek.com	Mt. Laurel	NJ	08054	856-222-9960	222-9611	393
Veneklasen Associates 1711 16Th St *TF:* 800 782 5742 ■ *Web:* www.veneklasen.com	Santa Monica	CA	90404	310-450-1733		256
Venetian Resort Hotel & Casino 3355 Las Vegas Blvd S *TF:* 866-659-9643 ■ *Web:* www.venetian.com	Las Vegas	NV	89109	702-414-1000	414-1100	669
Veneto Trattoria 6137 N Scottsdale Rd *Web:* www.venetotrattoria.com	Scottsdale	AZ	85250	480-948-9928		671
Venezia Transport Service Inc PO Box 909 *Web:* www.veneziainc.com	Royersford	PA	19468	610-495-5200		780
Venezuela 335 E 46th St *Web:* www.un.int	New York	NY	10017	212-557-2055	557-3528	784
Consulate General 2401 Fountain View Dr Ste 220 *Web:* venezuela-us.org/houston	Houston	TX	77057	713-974-0028	974-1413	257
Venezuelan-American Assn of the US 641 Lexington Ave Ste 1430 *Web:* www.venezuelanamerican.org	New York	NY	10022	212-233-7776		48-14
Vengroff Williams & Assoc Inc (VWA) 2099 S State College Bvld *TF:* 800-238-9655 ■ *Web:* www.vwinc.com	Anaheim	CA	92806	714 889 6200		160
Venice Area Chamber of Commerce 597 Tamiami Trl S *Web:* www.venicechamber.com	Venice	FL	34285	941-488-2236	484-5903	139
Venice Chamber of Commerce 327 Washington Blvd PO Box 202 *Web:* www.venicechamber.net	Venice	CA	90294	310-822-5425		139
Venice Consulting Group 212 Marine St Ste 100 *TF:* 855-202-0824 ■ *Web:* www.veniceconsulting.com	Santa Monica	CA	90405	855-202-0824		196
Venice Family Clinic 604 Rose Ave *Web:* www.venicefamilyclinic.org	Venice	CA	90291	310-392-8630	392-6642	353
Venice Gondolier Sun 200 E Venice Ave *Web:* www.venicegondoliersun.com	Venice	FL	34285	941-207-1000		532-4
Venice Regional Medical Ctr (VRMC) 540 The Rialto *Web:* www.veniceregional.com	Venice	FL	34285	941-485-7711	483-7699	374-3
Venice Ristorante & Wine Bar 1700 Wynkoop St *Web:* www.veniceristorante.com	Denver	CO	80202	303-534-2222		671
Veni-Vidi-Vici 41 Fourteenth St *Web:* www.buckheadrestaurants.com	Atlanta	GA	30309	404-875-8424		671
Venkel Ltd 5900 Shepherd Mtn Cove *TF:* 800-950-8365 ■ *Web:* www.venkel.com	Austin	TX	78730	512-794-0081	794-0087	246
Venmar Ventilation Inc 550 Lemire Blvd *Web:* www.venmar.ca	Drummondville	QC	J2C7W9	819-477-6226		437
Venn Products Group 80 Skyline Dr *Web:* www.vennproducts.com	Plainview	NY	11803	516-822-1561		463
Venoco Inc 370 17th St Ste 3900 *NYSE:* VQ ■ *TF:* 877-483-6626 ■ *Web:* www.venocoinc.com	Denver	CO	80202	303-626-8300		152
Venrock Assoc 3340 Hillview Ave *Web:* www.venrock.com	Palo Alto	CA	94304	650-561-9580	561-9180	792
Vensai Technologies 2450 Atlanta Hwy Ste 1002 *TF:* 866-849-4057 ■ *Web:* www.vensaiinc.com	Cumming	GA	30040	770-888-4804		196
Vensiti Inc 1304 W Walnut Hill Ln Ste 212	Irving	TX	75038	972-887-7995		177
VENSURE Employer Services Inc 4140 E Baseline Rd Ste 201 *TF:* 800-409-8958 ■ *Web:* www.vensureinc.com	Mesa	AZ	85206	800-409-8958		360-3
Vent Products Company Inc 1901 S Kilbourn Ave	Chicago	IL	60623	773-521-1900		697
Venta Medical LLC 1971 Milmont Dr *Web:* ventamedical.com	Milpitas	CA	95035	408-797-2414	797-2424	475
Vent-A-Hood Ltd 1000 N Greenville Ave *TF:* 800-331-2492 ■ *Web:* www.ventahood.com	Richardson	TX	75081	972-235-5201	231-0663	697
Ventamatic Ltd 100 Washington Rd *Fax Area Code: 940 ■ *TF:* 800-433-1626 ■ *Web:* www.bvc.com	Mineral Wells	TX	76067	800-433-1626	325-9311*	15
Ventana Inn 48123 Hwy 1 *TF:* 800-628-6500 ■ *Web:* www.ventanainn.com	Big Sur	CA	93920	831-667-2331	667-0573	669
Ventana Medical Systems Inc 1910 Innovation Pk Dr *TF:* 800-227-2155 ■ *Web:* www.ventana.com	Tucson	AZ	85755	520-887-2155		476
Ventana Productions 1819 L St NW Ste 100w *Web:* www.ventanadc.com	Washington	DC	20036	202-785-5112		514
Ventana USA 6001 Enterprise Dr *Web:* www.ventana usa.com	Export	PA	15632	724-325-3400		608
Ventas Inc 111 S Wacker Dr Ste 4800 *TF:* 877-483-6827 ■ *Web:* www.ventasreit.com	Chicago	IL	60606	312-660-3800		655
Ventas Inc 353 N Clark St Ste 3300 *NYSE:* VTR ■ *TF:* 877-483-6827 ■ *Web:* www.ventasreit.com	Chicago	IL	60654	877-483-6827		654
Ventec Life Systems Inc 19021 120th Ave NE Ste E101 *Web:* www.venteclife.com	Bothell	WA	98011	425-355-8038		475
Ventech Engineers Inc 1149 Ellsworth Dr *Web:* www.ventech-eng.com	Pasadena	TX	77506	713-477-0201		188-7
Ven-Tel Plastics Corp 11311 74th St N *Web:* www.ventelplastics.com	Largo	FL	33773	727-546-7470		608
Ventera Corp 1881 Campus Commons Dr Ste 350 *Web:* www.ventera.com	Reston	VA	20191	703-760-4600	390-1113	180
Venticello 1257 Taylor St *Web:* www.venticello.com	San Francisco	CA	94108	415-922-2545		671
Ventra Plastics - Russellville 140 Progress Dr	Russellville	KY	42276	270-726-4767		608
Ventress Correctional Facility 379 Alabama Hwy 239 N *Web:* alabama.gov	Clayton	AL	36016	334-775-3331		213
Ventress Memorial Library 15 Library Plaza *Web:* www.ventresslibrary.org	Marshfield	MA	02050	781-834-5535		434-3
Ventrol Air Handling Systems Inc 9100 Rue Du Parcours *Web:* www.ventrol.com	Montreal	QC	H1J2Z1	514-354-7776		610
Ventura Chamber of Commerce 505 Poli St 2nd Fl *Web:* venturachamber.com	Ventura	CA	93001	805-643-7222	653-8015	139
Ventura College 4667 Telegraph Rd *Web:* www.venturacollege.edu	Ventura	CA	93003	805-654-6400		162
Ventura County 800 S Victoria Ave *Web:* www.countyofventura.org	Ventura	CA	93009	805-654-5000		338
Ventura County Arts Council 646 County Sq Dr Ste 154 *Web:* vcartscouncil.org	Ventura	CA	93003	805-658-2213		522
Ventura County Employees' Retirement Association 1190 S Victoria Ave Ste 200 *Web:* www.ventura.org/vcera	Ventura	CA	93003	805-339-4250		387
Ventura County Libraries 606 N Ventura Ave Ste 150 *Web:* www.vencolibrary.org	Ventura	CA	93001	805-643-6393		434-3
Ventura County Medical Ctr 3291 Loma Vista Rd *TF:* 888-285-5012 ■ *Web:* www.vchca.org	Ventura	CA	93003	805-652-6000		374-3
Ventura County Museum of History & Art 100 E Main St *Web:* www.venturamuseum.org	Ventura	CA	93001	805-653-0323	653-5267	520
Ventura County Reporter 700 E Main St *Web:* www.vcreporter.com	Ventura	CA	93001	805-648-2244		532-5
Ventura County Star 550 Camarillo Ctr Dr *Web:* www.vcstar.com	Camarillo	CA	93010	805-437-0000	482-6167	532-2
Ventura Foods LLC 40 Pt Dr *TF:* 800-421-6257 ■ *Web:* www.venturafoods.com	Brea	CA	92821	714-257-3700		296-30
Ventura Technology Enterprises Ltd 94 547 Ukee St Ste 110 *Web:* www.venturatechnology.net	Waipahu	HI	96797	808-678-3900		180
Ventura Visitors & Convention Bureau 101 S California St *TF:* 800-333-2989 ■ *Web:* visitventuraca.com	Ventura	CA	93001	805-648-2075	648-2150	206
Ventura Youth Correctional Facility 3100 Wright Rd *TF:* 866-232-5627 ■ *Web:* www.cdcr.ca.gov	Camarillo	CA	93010	805-485-7951		412
Ventura's 7742 W Bancroft St *Web:* toledostripletreat.com	Toledo	OH	43617	419-841-7523		671
Venture Capital Fund of America 509 Madison Ave *Web:* www.vcfa.com	New York	NY	10022	212-838-5577	838-7614	792
Venture Communications Cooperative Inc 218 Commercial Ave SE PO Box 157 *Fax Area Code: 650 ■ *TF:* 800-932-0637 ■ *Web:* venture.coop	Highmore	SD	57345	605-852-2224	343-8492*	49-17

Name / Address	City	State	Zip	Phone	Fax	Class
Venture Design Services Inc						
1051 SE St	Anaheim	CA	92805	510-744-3720		668
Web: www.venture.com.sg						
Venture Express Inc						
131 Industrial Blvd	La Vergne	TN	37086	615-793-9500		187
Web: www.ventureexpress.com						
Venture Fuels LLC 3819 Creekside St	Holman	WI	54636	608-783-9516		579
Web: venturefuels.com						
Venture Group Enterprises Inc						
2520 Whitehall Park Dr Ste 100	Charlotte	NC	28273	704-676-0160		463
Web: www.vgei.com						
Venture Investors LLC						
505 S Rosa Rd Ste 201	Madison	WI	53719	608-441-2700		792
Web: www.ventureinvestors.com						
Venture Lighting International Inc						
32000 Aurora Rd	Solon	OH	44139	440-248-3510	349-7771	437
TF: 800-451-2606 ■ *Web:* www.venturelighting.com						
Venture Measurement Company LLC						
150 Venture Blvd	Spartanburg	SC	29306	864-574-8960	578-7308	201
Web: www.venturemeasurement.com						
Venture Mechanical Inc						
2222 Century Cir	Irving	TX	75062	972-871-1300	871-1301	610
Web: www.venturemech.com						
Venture Mud L P 1305 W Illinois Ave	Midland	TX	79701	432-684-7101	570-7114	146
Venture Oil & Gas Inc						
3575 N Belt Line Rd Ste 346	Irving	TX	75062	214-912-7017		536
Web: ventureoil.net						
Venture Opportunities Inc						
13140 Coit Rd Ste 211	Dallas	TX	75240	972-783-1662		708
TF: 800-516-1008 ■ *Web:* www.bizdealmaker.com						
Venture Plastics Inc						
4000 Warren Rd PO Box 249	Newton Falls	OH	44444	330-872-5774	872-3597	604
Web: www.ventureplastics.com						
Venture Solutions Inc						
1170 Grey Fox Rd	Arden Hills	MN	55112	651-494-1740		195
TF: 800-728-2615 ■ *Web:* www.venturesolutions.com						
Venture Steel Inc 60 Disco Rd	Etobicoke	ON	M9W1L8	416-798-9396		492
Web: www.venturesteel.com						
Venturedyne Ltd 600 College Ave	Pewaukee	WI	53072	262-691-9900	691-9901	18
Web: www.venturedyne.com						
VentureOut 575 Pierce St Ste 604	San Francisco	CA	94117	415-626-5678	626-5679	760
TF: 888-431-6789 ■ *Web:* www.venture-out.com						
Venturity Financial Partners						
14131 Midway Rd Ste 112	Addison	TX	75001	972-692-0380		2
Web: www.venturity.net						
Venue Management Services Inc						
500 N First Ave Ste 4	Arcadia	CA	91006	626-445-6000		193
Venuequest LLC						
5174 McGinnis Ferry Rd Ste 102	Alpharetta	GA	30005	678-909-4088		772
Web: www.venuequest.com						
Venus Swimwear						
11711 Marco Beach Dr	Jacksonville	FL	32224	904-645-6000		155-17
TF: 800-366-7946 ■ *Web:* www.venus.com						
Venus Wafers Inc 100 Research Rd	Hingham	MA	02043	781-740-1002	740-0791	296-9
Web: www.venuswafers.com						
Venuworks Inc 4611 Mortensen Rd Ste 111	Ames	IA	50014	515-232-5151		205
Web: www.venuworks.com						
Veolia Environmental Services						
200 E Randolph St Ste 7900	Chicago	IL	60601	312-552-2800		804
Web: www.veolianorthamerica.com/en						
Veolia Environmental Services						
1980 N Hwy 146	La Porte	TX	77571	713-307-2100		804
Web: www.veolianorthamerica.com/en						
Veolia Transport Quebec Inc						
720 rue Trotter	Saint-jean-sur-richelieu	QC	J3B8T2	514-787-1998		108
Ver Ploeg & Lumpkin PA						
Miami Twr 100 SE Second St 30th Fl	Miami	FL	33131	305-577-3996		428
Web: www.vpl-law.com						
Vera Bradley Designs						
2208 Production Rd	Fort Wayne	IN	46808	260-482-4673	484-2278	349
TF: 800-975-8372 ■ *Web:* www.verabradley.com						
Vera Institute of Justice						
233 Broadway 12th Fl	New York	NY	10279	212-334-1300	941-9407	49-10
TF: 800-342-9871 ■ *Web:* www.vera.org						
Veracity Credit Consultants LLC						
110 16th St Ste 1000	Denver	CO	80202	303-893-1801		463
TF: 800-985-2914 ■ *Web:* www.veracitycredit.com						
Veracity Energy Services Ltd						
200 744 - Fourth Ave SW	Calgary	AB	T2P3T4	403-537-1300		540
Web: www.veracityenergy.com						
Veracity Engineering						
600 Maryland Ave SW Ste 600e	Washington	DC	20024	202-488-0975		19
Web: www.veracity-eng.com						
VeraData.com LLC						
1910 Park Meadows Dr Ste 200	Fort Myers	FL	33907	239-204-5000		195
TF: 800-685-7424 ■ *Web:* www.veradata.com						
Veramark Technologies Inc						
1565 Jefferson Rd	Rochester	NY	14623	585-381-6000	383-6800	735
Verance Corp						
10089 Willow Creek Rd Ste 200	San Diego	CA	92131	858-202-2800		466
Web: verance.com						
Verandah 3960 Las Vegas Blvd S	Las Vegas	NV	89119	702-632-5000	632-5195	671
Web: www.fourseasons.com						
Verandah Club, The 2201 Stemmons Fwy	Dallas	TX	75207	214-761-7878		707
Web: www.verandahclub.com						
Verant Identification Systems Inc						
2496 Ridge Rd W Ste 203	Rochester	NY	14626	585-214-2451		693
TF: 866-257-4351 ■ *Web:* www.verantid.com						
Verax Communications 499 Adams St	Milton	MA	02186	617-698-0088		463
Verbatim Americas LLC						
8210 University Executive Park Dr	Charlotte	NC	28262	704-547-6500	547-6609	658
TF: 800-538-8589 ■ *Web:* www.verbatim.com						
Verbatim Solutions LLC						
5200 South Highland Dr Ste 201	Salt Lake City	UT	84117	801-273-5700		768
TF: 800-572-5703 ■ *Web:* www.verbatimsolutions.com						
Verdant Power LLC						
888 Main St The Octagon Ste 1	New York	NY	10044	212-888-8887		261
Web: www.verdantpower.com						
Verdanza Hotel 8020 Calle Tartak	Carolina	PR	00979	787-253-9000		132
TF: 800-625-0312 ■ *Web:* www.verdanzahotel.com						
Verde Pr & Consulting						
1485 Florida Rd Ste 202c	Durango	CO	81301	970-259-3555		196
TF: 800-555-2160 ■ *Web:* verdepr.com						
Verde Valley School						
3511 Verde Vly School Rd	Sedona	AZ	86351	928-284-2272	284-0432	622
Web: www.vvsaz.org						
Verdezyne Inc 2715 Loker Ave W	Carlsbad	CA	92010	760-707-5200		85
Web: www.verdezyne.com						
Verdi Group Inc, The						
190 Office Pkwy Ste 300	Pittsford	NY	14534	585-325-6304		7
Web: www.theverdigroup.com						
Verdigris Valley Electric Co-op						
8901 E 146th St N	Collinsville	OK	74021	918-371-2584	371-9873	245
TF: 800-870-5948 ■ *Web:* www.vvec.com						
Verdin Co, The 444 Reading Rd	Cincinnati	OH	45202	800-543-0488	241-1855*	153
**Fax Area Code:* 513 ■ *TF:* 800-543-0488 ■ *Web:* www.verdin.com						
Verdolino & Lowey PC						
124 Washington St Ste 101	Foxboro	MA	02035	508-543-1720		2
Web: vlpc.com						
Verdugo Hills Hospital						
1812 Verdugo Blvd	Glendale	CA	91208	818-790-7100		374-3
Web: www.uscvhh.org						
Verdugo Mountains						
c/o Angeles District Office						
1925 Las Virgenes	Calabasas	CA	91302	213-620-6152		565
Web: www.parks.ca.gov/default.asp?page_id=635						
Verecloud Inc						
6560 S Greenwood Plaza Blvd Ste 400	Englewood	CO	80111	877-711-6492	221-0917*	177
**Fax Area Code:* 303 ■ *TF:* 877-711-6492						
Verecom Technologies Inc 61 Broadway	New York	NY	10006	888-562-2468		363
TF: 888-562-2468 ■ *Web:* www.verecom.com						
Verendrye Electric Co-op Inc 615 Hwy 52	Velva	ND	58790	701-338-2855		245
TF: 800-472-2141 ■ *Web:* www.verendrye.com						
Verequest 67 Robbins Ave	Toronto	ON	M4L1X1	416-362-6777		195
Web: www.verequest.com						
Veresen Inc 222 Third Ave SW	Calgary	AB	T2P0B4	403-296-0140	213-3648	325
TSE: VSN ■ *Web:* www.vereseninc.com						
Verge Solutions LLC						
11 eWall St	Mount Pleasant	SC	29464	843-628-4168	209-8119*	809
**Fax Area Code:* 866 ■ *Web:* www.vergehealth.com						
Verhalen Inc 500 Pilgrim Way	Green Bay	WI	54304	920-431-8900	431-8901	191-3
Web: www.verhaleninc.com						
Verican Inc						
1 Hallidie Plaza Ste 404	San Francisco	CA	94102	415-296-7300		177
TF: 800-888-0470 ■ *Web:* www.verican.com						
Vericel Corp 64 Sidney St	Cambridge	MA	48105	734-418-4400	665-0485	85
NASDAQ: ASTM ■ *Web:* vcel.com						
Verichem Laboratories Inc						
90 Narragansett Ave	Providence	RI	02907	401-461-0180		743
TF: 800-552-5859 ■ *Web:* www.verichemlabs.com						
Verico Capital Mortgages Inc						
106-18 Deakin St	Ottawa	ON	K2E8B7	613-228-3888		509
TF: 877-459-4414 ■ *Web:* www.capitalmortgages.com						
VERICO One Link Mortgage & Financial						
200-1215 Henderson Hwy	Winnipeg	MB	R2G1L8	204-954-7620		141
Web: onelinkmortgage.com						
Vericon Resources Inc						
3550 Engineering Dr Ste 225	Norcross	GA	30092	770-457-9922	457-5006	400
TF: 800-795-3784 ■ *Web:* www.vericon.com						
Veridex LLC 700 US Hwy Rt 202 S	Raritan	NJ	08869	877-837-4339		476
TF: 877-837-4339 ■ *Web:* www.cellsearchctc.com						
Veridikal Inc 1541 E Hope St	Mesa	AZ	85203	480-636-1830		177
Web: www.veridikal.com						
Verient Inc 1190 Saratoga Ave Ste 220	San Jose	CA	95129	408-521-1660		809
Web: www.verient.com						
Verifact Corp 11220 W Loop 1604 N	San Antonio	TX	78254	210-523-5696		261
Web: verifactcorp.com						
Verifi Inc						
8391 Beverly Blvd Ste 310	Los Angeles	CA	90048	323-655-5789		463
Web: www.verifi.com						
Verified Audit Circulation Inc						
900 Larkspur Landing Cir	Larkspur	CA	94939	415-461-6006		734
TF: 800-775-3332 ■ *Web:* www.verifiedaudit.com						
Verified Credentials Inc						
20890 Kenbridge Ct	Lakeville	MN	55044	952-985-7200	985-7218	635
TF: 800-473-4934 ■ *Web:* www.verifiedcredentials.com						
Verified Label & Print Inc 7905 Hopi Pl	Tampa	FL	33634	813-290-7721		627
TF: 800-764-6110 ■ *Web:* www.verifiedlabel.com						
VeriFone Inc 88 W Plumeria Dr Ste 600	San Jose	CA	95134	408-232-7800		614
NYSE: PAY ■ *Web:* www.verifone.com						
VeriFone Systems Inc						
88 W Plumeria Dr Ste 600	San Jose	CA	95134	408-232-7800	232-7811	614
NYSE: PAY ■ *Web:* www.verifone.asia						
Veriforce LLC 19221 I-45 S Ste 200	Shenandoah	TX	77385	800-426-1604		765
TF: 800-426-1604 ■ *Web:* www.veriforce.com						
Verigent LLC						
149 Plantation Ridge Dr Ste 100	Mooresville	NC	28117	704-658-3271		610
TF: 877-637-6422 ■ *Web:* www.verigent.com						
Verinon Technology Solutions Ltd						
3395 N Arlington Heights Rd	Arlington Heights	IL	60004	847-577-5256		196
Web: www.verinon.com						
Verint Systems Inc 330 S Service Rd	Melville	NY	11747	631-962-9600	962-9300	178-7
Web: www.verint.com						
Verint Video Solutions						
330 South Service Rd	Melville	NY	11747	800-483-7468		692
TF: 800-483-7468 ■ *Web:* www.verint.com						
Verio Inc 1203 N Research Way Ste 400	Orem	UT	84097	561-912-2555	999-8215	398
TF Sales: 855-765-0425 ■ *Web:* www.verio.com						
Veriphyr Inc 703 Benvenue Ave	Los Altos	CA	94024	650-384-0560		180
Web: www.veriphyr.com						
Veris Industries Inc						
16640 SW 72nd Ave	Portland	OR	97224	503-598-4564		407
TF: 800-354-8556 ■ *Web:* www.veris.com						
Veris Wealth Partners LLC						
17 State St Ste 2450	New York	NY	10004	212-349-4172		690
Web: www.veriswp.com						

	City	State	Zip	Phone	Fax	Class
Verisante Technology Inc 2309 W 41st Ave Ste 306 *Web:* www.verisante.com	Vancouver	BC	V6M2A3	604-605-0507		250
Verisk Analytics 545 Washington Blvd *NASDAQ:* VRSK ■ *TF:* 800-888-4476 ■ *Web:* www.verisk.com	Jersey City	NJ	07310	201-469-3000		463
Verisma Systems Inc 510 W Third St Ste 200 *Web:* verisma.com	Pueblo	CO	81003	719-546-1849		809
Verismo Networks Inc 5201 Great America Pkwy Ste 457	Santa Clara	CA	95054	408-598-3661		647
Verisource Services Inc 7600 W Tidwell Rd Ste 700 *Web:* www.verisource.com	Houston	TX	77040	713-647-6540		177
VeriStor Systems Inc 3308 Peachtree Industrial Blvd *Web:* www.veristor.com	Duluth	GA	30096	678-990-1593		173-8
Verisurf Software Inc 4907 E Landon Dr *TF:* 888-713-7201 ■ *Web:* www.verisurf.com	Anaheim	CA	92807	714-970-1683		177
VerisVisalign 920 S Broad St *Web:* www.verisvisalign.com	Lansdale	PA	19446	215-393-5001		260
Veritaaq Technology House Inc 2327 Saint-Laurent Blvd Ste 100 *Web:* www.veritaaq.ca	Ottawa	ON	K1G4J8	613-736-6120		180
Veritable LP 6022 W Chester Pk *Web:* veritablelp.com	Newtown Square	PA	19073	610-640-9551		401
Veritable Quandary 1220 SW First Ave *Web:* veritablequandary.com	Portland	OR	97204	503-227-7342		671
VeriTainer Corp The Beckstoffer House 1127 Pope St Ste 201 *TF:* 844-344-8796 ■ *Web:* www.veritainer.com	St. Helena	CA	94574	707-967-0944	967-0943	693
Veritas Capital 9 W 57th St 29th Fl *Web:* www.veritascapital.com	New York	NY	10019	212-415-6700		41
Veritas Medicine Inc 11 Cambridge Ctr *TF:* 800-424-4301 ■ *Web:* www.veritasmedicine.com	Cambridge	MA	02142	617-234-1500		177
Veritas Press 1250 Belle Meade Dr *TF:* 800-922-5082 ■ *Web:* www.veritaspress.com	Lancaster	PA	17601	717-519-1974		535
Veri-Tax LLC 30 Executive Pk Ste 200 *TF:* 800-969-5100 ■ *Web:* www.veri-tax.com	Irvine	CA	92614	949-783-2100	732-6091	463
Verite Inc 608 W 9320 S *Web:* www.verite.com	Sandy	UT	84070	801-553-1101		738
Veritec Inc 2445 Winnetka Ave N *TF:* 866-546-1011 ■ *Web:* www.veritecinc.com	Golden Valley	MN	55427	763-253-2670		696
Veritext LLC 290 W Mt Pleasant Ave Ste 3200 **Fax Area Code:* 973 ■ *TF:* 800-567-8658 ■ *Web:* www.veritext.com	Livingston	NJ	07039	800-567-8658	410-1313*	445
Verity Credit Union PO Box 75974 *TF:* 800-444-4589 ■ *Web:* www.veritycu.com	Seattle	WA	98175	206-440-9000	361-5300	219
Verity Instruments Inc 2901 Eisenhower St *Web:* www.verityinst.com	Carrollton	TX	75007	972-446-9990		472
Verity International Ltd 200 King St W Ste 1301 *TF:* 877-623-2396 ■ *Web:* www.verityintl.com	Toronto	ON	M5H3T4	416-862-8422		194
Verity Professionals 11555 Medlock Bridge Rd Ste 100 *TF:* 888-367-3110 ■ *Web:* verityprofessionals.com	Johns Creek	GA	30097	404-920-6400		463
Verity Three Inc 733 Ridgeview Dr *Web:* clients.veritythree.com	Mchenry	IL	60050	815-385-4474		180
Verium Diagnostics Inc 4480 Lake Forest Dr Ste 412	Cincinnati	OH	45242	513-429-4340	429-4348	743
Verix Inc 339 S San Antonio Rd Ste 2G *Web:* www.verix.com	Los Altos	CA	94022	650-949-2700		177
Verizon Arena 1 Verizon Arena Way *TF:* 800-745-3000 ■ *Web:* www.verizonarena.com	North Little Rock	AR	72114	501-340-5660		720
Verizon Business 1 Verizon Way *TF Cust Svc:* 877-297-7816 ■ *Web:* www.verizonenterprise.com	Basking Ridge	NJ	07920	908-559-2000		736
Verizon Communications Inc 140 W St *NYSE:* VZ ■ *TF:* 800-837-4966 ■ *Web:* www.verizon.com	New York	NY	10007	212-395-1000		736
Verizon Credit Inc 201 N Tampa St *TF:* 800-483-7988 ■ *Web:* www.verizon.com	Tampa	FL	33602	813-229-6000		216
Verizon Ctr 601 F St NW *TF:* 800-745-3000 ■ *Web:* verizoncenter.monumentalsportsnetwork.com	Washington	DC	20004	202-628-3200		720
Verizon Wireless 180 Washington Valley Rd *TF:* 800-922-0204 ■ *Web:* www.verizonwireless.com	Bedminster	NJ	07921	908-306-7000		736
Verizon Wireless Amphitheater 14141 Riverport Dr *Web:* www.livenation.com	Maryland Heights	MO	63043	314-298-9944	291-4719	572
Verland Foundation Inc, The 212 Iris Rd *TF:* 800-821-2436 ■ *Web:* verland.org	Sewickley	PA	15143	412-741-2375		305
Verlyn G Adamson CPA 708 S Second St *Web:* vacpa.cc	Mount Horeb	WI	53572	608-437-6322		2
Verma Systems Inc 4111 S Sherwood Forest Blvd *Web:* www.vermasystems.com	Baton Rouge	LA	70816	225-296-0399		180
Vermeer Mid Atlantic Inc 10900 Carpet St *TF:* 800-768-3444 ■ *Web:* www.vermeermidatlantic.com	Charlotte	NC	28273	704-588-3238		791
Vermeer Midsouth Inc 1200 Vermeer Cv *TF:* 800-264-4123 ■ *Web:* www.vermeermidsouth.com	Cordova	TN	38018	901-758-1928	758-1929	386
Vermeer Southeast Sales & Service Inc 4559 Old Winter Garden Rd *Web:* www.vermeersoutheast.com	Orlando	FL	32811	407-295-2020		791
Vermilion 1120 King St *Web:* www.vermilionrestaurant.com	Alexandria	VA	22314	703-684-9669		671
Vermilion Community College 1900 E Camp St *TF:* 800-657-3608 ■ *Web:* www.vcc.edu	Ely	MN	55731	218-365-7200		162
Vermilion County 6 N Vermilion St Courthouse Annex 1st Fl *Web:* www.co.vermilion.il.us	Danville	IL	61832	217-554-1900	554-1914	338
Vermilion Energy Trust 3500 520 Third Ave SW *TSE:* VET ■ *TF:* 866-895-8101 ■ *Web:* www.vermilionenergy.com	Calgary	AB	T2P0R3	403-269-4884	476-8100	540
Vermilion Parish 100 N State St Ste 101 *Web:* www.vermilionparishclerkofcourt.com	Abbeville	LA	70510	337-898-1992	898-9803	338
Vermillion Advantage 15 N Walnut St *Web:* www.vermilionadvantage.com	Danville	IL	61832	217-442-6201	442-6228	139
Vermillion County 255 S Main St *TF:* 800-340-8155 ■ *Web:* www.vermilliongov.us	Newport	IN	47966	765-492-5345		338
Vermillion Financial Advisors Inc 16 Executive Ct Ste 3 *Web:* www.vermillionfinancial.com	South Barrington	IL	60010	847-382-9999		194
Vermillion, The 115 Paredes Line Rd *Web:* www.thevermillion.com	Brownsville	TX	78521	956-542-9893		671
Vermont						
Aging & Disabilities Dept 103 S Main St *TF:* 888-405-5005 ■ *Web:* www.dail.vermont.gov	Waterbury	VT	05671	802-871-3382	871-3048	339-46
Agriculture Food & Markets Dept 116 State St *Web:* agriculture.vermont.gov	Montpelier	VT	05620	802-828-2430		339-46
Arts Council 136 State St *Web:* www.vermontartscouncil.org	Montpelier	VT	05633	802-828-3291	828-3363	339-46
Attorney General 109 State St *Web:* www.atg.state.vt.us	Montpelier	VT	05609	802-828-3171		339-46
Banking Div 89 Main St *Web:* www.dfr.vermont.gov	Montpelier	VT	05620	802-828-3307	828-1477	339-46
Board of Medical Practice 108 Cherry St PO Box 70 *Web:* healthvermont.gov	Burlington	VT	05402	802-657-4220	657-4227	339-46
Chief Medical Examiner 111 Colchester Ave *Web:* healthvermont.gov/hc/med_exam/med_index.aspx	Burlington	VT	05401	802-863-7320		339-46
Children & Families Dept 103 S Main St 2nd Fl 5 N *TF:* 800-786-3214 ■ *Web:* dcf.vermont.gov	Waterbury	VT	05671	802-241-2100	241-2407	339-46
Consumer Assistance Program 146 University Pl *TF:* 800-649-2424 ■ *Web:* www.uvm.edu/consumer	Burlington	VT	05405	802-656-3183		339-46
Corrections Dept 280 State Dr NOB 2 S *Web:* www.doc.state.vt.us	Waterbury	VT	05671	802-241-2442	241-0020	339-46
Court Administrator 109 State St *Web:* www.vermontjudiciary.org	Montpelier	VT	05609	802-828-3278	828-3457	339-46
Crime Victim Services Ctr 58 S Main St *Web:* www.ccvs.state.vt.us	Waterbury	VT	05676	802-241-1250	241-4337	339-46
Economic Development Dept 1 National Life Dr Deane C. Davis Bldg Fl 6 *Web:* accd.vermont.gov	Montpelier	VT	05620	802-828-3211		339-46
Emergency Management Office 45 State Dr *TF:* 800-347-0488 ■ *Web:* vem.vermont.gov	Waterbury	VT	05671	802-244-8721	241-5556	339-46
Environmental Conservation Dept 1 National Life Dr Main bldg 2nd Fl *Web:* www.anr.state.vt.us/dec/dec.htm	Montpelier	VT	05620	802-828-1556		339-46
Fish & Wildlife Dept 1 National Life Dr Davis 2 *Web:* www.anr.state.vt.us	Montpelier	VT	05620	802-828-1000	241-3295	339-46
General Assembly 115 State St *Web:* www.leg.state.vt.us	Montpelier	VT	05633	802-828-2228		339-46
Governor 109 State St 5th Fl *Web:* www.vermont.gov	Montpelier	VT	05609	802-828-3333	828-3339	339-46
Health Dept 108 Cherry St *Web:* www.healthvermont.gov	Burlington	VT	05402	802-863-7200	865-7754	339-46
Historic Preservation Div 1 National Life Dr Davis Bldg 6th Fl *Web:* accd.vermont.gov	Montpelier	VT	05620	802-828-3213		339-46
Insurance Div 89 Main St *Web:* www.dfr.vermont.gov	Montpelier	VT	05620	802-828-3301		339-46
Labor Dept 5 Green Mountain Dr PO Box 488 *Web:* www.labor.vermont.gov	Montpelier	VT	05601	802-828-4000	828-4022	339-46
Lieutenant Governor 115 State St Ste 3 *Web:* www.ltgov.vermont.gov	Montpelier	VT	05633	802-828-2226		339-46
Lottery Commission 1311 US Rt 302 Ste 100 *Web:* Www.vtlottery.com	Barre	VT	05641	802-479-5686	479-4294	452
Motor Vehicles Dept 120 State St *TF:* 888-998-3766 ■ *Web:* dmv.vermont.gov	Montpelier	VT	05603	802-828-2000	828-2145	339-46
Natural Resources Agency 103 S Main St *Web:* www.anr.state.vt.us	Waterbury	VT	05671	802-241-3600	244-1102	339-46
Office of Veteran Affairs 118 State St *TF:* 888-666-9844 ■ *Web:* www.veterans.vermont.gov/ova	Montpelier	VT	05602	802-828-3379	828-5932	339-46
Secretary of State 128 State St Drawer 9 **Fax Area Code:* 800 ■ *Web:* www.sec.state.vt.us	Montpelier	VT	05633	802-828-2363	439-8683*	339-46
Securities Div 89 Main St *Web:* www.dfr.vermont.gov	Montpelier	VT	05620	802-828-3420	828-2896	339-46
State Police 45 State Dr *Web:* vsp.vermont.gov	Waterbury	VT	05671	802-241-5260	241-5551	339-46
Supreme Court 111 State St *Web:* www.vermontjudiciary.org	Montpelier	VT	05609	802-828-4774	828-3457	339-46
Taxes Dept 133 State St *Web:* www.state.vt.us/tax	Montpelier	VT	05609	802-828-2505		339-46
Tourism & Marketing Dept 1 National Life Dr Fl 6 *Web:* www.vermontvacation.com	Montpelier	VT	05620	802-828-3168	828-3163	339-46
Transportation Agency 1 National Life Dr *Web:* vtrans.vermont.gov	Montpelier	VT	05633	802-828-2657		339-46
Treasurer 109 State St 4th Fl *Web:* www.vermonttreasurer.gov	Montpelier	VT	05609	802-828-2301	828-2772	339-46

				Phone	Fax	Class
Vital Records Section 108 Cherry St PO Box 70 *Web:* www.healthvermont.gov	Burlington	VT	05402	802-863-7275	651-1787	339-46
Vocational Rehabilitation Div HC 2 S 280 State Dr *TF:* 866-879-6757 ■ *Web:* www.vocrehab.vermont.gov	Waterbury	VT	05671	802-447-2781		339-46
Workers' Compensation Div 5 Green Mountain Dr PO Box 488 *Web:* www.labor.vermont.gov	Montpelier	VT	05601	802-828-4000	828-4022	339-46
Vermont Academy PO Box 500 10 Long Walk *TF:* 800-698-8867 ■ *Web:* www.vermontacademy.org	Saxtons River	VT	05154	802-869-6229	869-2115	622
Vermont Aerospace Manufacturing Inc 966 Industrial Pwy PO Box 1148 *Web:* www.vtaerospace.com	Lyndonville	VT	05851	802-748-8705	748-8437	454
Vermont Assn of Realtors 148 State St *Web:* www.vtrealtor.com	Montpelier	VT	05602	802-229-0513		656
Vermont Bar Assn (VBA) 35-37 Ct St PO Box 100 *TF:* 800-639-7036 ■ *Web:* www.vtbar.org	Montpelier	VT	05601	802-223-2020	223-1573	72
Vermont Chamber of Commerce 751 Granger Rd *Web:* www.vtchamber.com	Barre	VT	05641	802-223-3443	223-4257	140
Vermont Composites Inc 25 Performance Dr *Web:* www.vtcomposites.com	Bennington	VT	05201	802-442-9964	445-2921	194
Vermont Convention Bureau 60 Main St Ste 100 *TF:* 877-264-3503 ■ *Web:* www.vermont.org	Burlington	VT	05401	802-860-0606	863-1538	206
Vermont Correctional Industries 280 State Dr *Web:* vci.vermont.gov	Waterbury	VT	05671-2000	802-343-3596		630
Vermont Dept of Libraries 109 State St *Web:* libraries.vermont.gov	Montpelier	VT	05609	802-828-3261	828-2199	434-5
Vermont Electric Co-op Inc 42 Wescom Rd *TF:* 800-832-2667 ■ *Web:* www.vermontelectric.coop	Johnson	VT	05656	802-635-2331	635-7645	245
Vermont Energy Investment Corp 128 Lakeside Ave Ste 401 *TF:* 800-639-6069 ■ *Web:* www.veic.org	Burlington	VT	05401	802-658-6060		463
Vermont Federal Credit Union 84 Pine St *Web:* vermontfederal.org	Burlington	VT	05402	802-658-0225		219
Vermont Garden Park 1100 Dorset St *TF:* 800-538-7476 ■ *Web:* www.garden.org	South Burlington	VT	05403	802-863-5251		97
Vermont Gas Systems Inc 85 Swift St *TF:* 800-639-8081 ■ *Web:* www.vermontgas.com	South Burlington	VT	05403	802-863-4511	863-8872	324
Vermont Heating & Ventilating Company Inc 16 Tigan St *Web:* www.vhv.com	Winooski	VT	05404	802-655-8805	655-8809	189-10
Vermont Law School 168 Chelsea St PO Box 96 *TF:* 800-227-1395 ■ *Web:* www.vermontlaw.edu	South Royalton	VT	05068	802-831-1239		167-1
Vermont Legal Aid Inc 177 Western Ave Ste 1 *Web:* www.vtlegalaid.org	St Johnsbury	VT	05819	802-748-8721		445
Vermont Life 1 National Life Dr 6th Fl *Web:* www.vtlife.com	Montpelier	VT	05620	802-828-3241		457-22
Vermont Maple Sugar Co 37 Industrial Park Dr *TF:* 800-828-2376 ■ *Web:* www.butternutmountainfarm.com	Morrisville	VT	05661	800-828-2376		123
Vermont Media Publishing Company Ltd Rt 100 PO Box 310 *Web:* www.dvalnews.com	West Dover	VT	05356	802-464-3388	464-7255	7
Vermont Medical Society 134 Main St *TF:* 800-640-8767 ■ *Web:* www.vtmd.org	Montpelier	VT	05601	802-223-7898	223-1201	474
Vermont Mutual Insurance Co 89 State St PO Box 188 *TF:* 800-451-5000 ■ *Web:* www.vermontmutual.com	Montpelier	VT	05601	802-223-2341		391-4
Vermont NEA Today Magazine 10 Wheelock St *TF:* 800-649-6375 ■ *Web:* www.vtnea.org	Montpelier	VT	05602	802-223-6375	223-1253	457-8
Vermont Public Interest Research Group (VPIRG) 141 Main St Ste 6 *Web:* www.vpirg.org	Montpelier	VT	05602	802-223-5221		633
Vermont Public Television (VPT) 204 Ethan Allen Ave *TF:* 800-639-7811 ■ *Web:* www.vpt.org	Colchester	VT	05446	802-655-4800		632
Vermont Railway Inc 1 Railway Ln *TF:* 800-639-3088 ■ *Web:* www.vermontrailway.com	Burlington	VT	05401	802-658-2550		651
Vermont State Colleges 575 Stone Cutters Way *Web:* vsc.edu	Montpelier	VT	05601	802-224-3000	224-3035	786
Vermont State Nurses Assn (VSNA) 4 Carmichael St Ste 111 Rm 215 **Fax Area Code: 802* ■ *TF:* 877-810-5972 ■ *Web:* www.vsna-inc.org	Essex	VT	05452	877-810-5972	651-8998*	533
Vermont Structural Slate Company Inc 3 Prospect St PO Box 98 *TF:* 800-343-1900 ■ *Web:* www.vermontstructuralslate.com	Fair Haven	VT	05743	802-265-4933	265-3865	724
Vermont Student Assistance Corp (VSAC) PO Box 2000 *TF:* 800-642-3177 ■ *Web:* www.vsac.org	Winooski	VT	05404	802-655-9602	654-3765	725
Vermont Symphony Orchestra 2 Church St Ste 3B *TF:* 800-876-9293 ■ *Web:* www.vso.org	Burlington	VT	05401	802-864-5741	864-5109	573-3
Vermont Systems Inc 12 Market Pl *TF:* 877-883-8757 ■ *Web:* www.vermontsystems.com	Essex Junction	VT	05452	802-879-6993		178-10
Vermont Technical College PO Box 500 *TF:* 800-442-8821 ■ *Web:* www.vtc.edu	Randolph Center	VT	05061	802-728-1000	728-1321	800

				Phone	Fax	Class
Vermont Teddy Bear Company Inc 6655 Shelburne Rd *TF:* 800-988-8277 ■ *Web:* vermontteddybear.com	Shelburne	VT	05482	802-985-3001	985-1304	762
Vermont Telephone Company Inc 354 River St *Web:* www.vermontel.com	Springfield	VT	05156	802-885-9000		387
Vermont Veterans Home 325 N St *Web:* www.vvh.vermont.gov	Bennington	VT	05201	802-442-6353	447-6466	793
Vermont Veterinary Medical Assn 88 Beech St *Web:* www.vtvets.org	Essex Junction	VT	05452	802-878-6888	878-2871	795
Vermont's North Country Chamber of Commerce 246 Cswy St *TF:* 800-266-2278 ■ *Web:* www.vtnorthcountry.org	Newport	VT	05855	802-334-7782		139
Vern Dale Products Inc 8445 Lyndon St *Web:* www.verndaleproducts.com	Detroit	MI	48238	313-834-4190	834-6280	296-10
Vernay Laboratories Inc 120 E S College St *Web:* www.vernay.com	Yellow Springs	OH	45387	937-767-7261		677
Verndale Corp, The 28 Damrell St Ste 300 *TF:* 866-942-8376 ■ *Web:* www.verndale.com	Boston	MA	02127	866-942-8376		366
Verne Q Powell Flutes Inc 1 Clock Tower Pl Ste 300 *TF:* 800-426-9832 ■ *Web:* www.powellflutes.com	Maynard	MA	01754	978-461-6111	461-6155	527
Vernier Software & Technology LLC 13979 SW Millikan Way *TF:* 800-387-2474 ■ *Web:* www.vernier.com	Beaverton	OR	97005	503-277-2299		419
Vernis & Bowling of Miami PA 1680 NE 135th St *Web:* www.national-law.com	Miami	FL	33181	305-895-3035		428
Vernon Area Public Library District 300 Olde Half Day Rd *TF:* 800-222-1222 ■ *Web:* vapld.info	Lincolnshire	IL	60069	847-634-3650		435
Vernon College 4400 College Dr *TF:* 866-336-9371 ■ *Web:* www.vernoncollege.edu	Vernon	TX	76384	940-552-6291	553-1753	162
Vernon Communications Co-op 103 N Main St *Web:* www.vernontel.com	Westby	WI	54667	608-634-3136		116
Vernon Correctional Facility 2294 Slagle Rd	Leesville	LA	71446	337-238-4522		213
Vernon County 100 W Cherry St *Web:* www.vernoncountymo.org	Nevada	MO	64772	417-448-2500	667-6035	338
Vernon County Courthouse Annex Rm 108 *Web:* www.wisconline.com/counties/vernon	Viroqua	WI	54665	608-637-5380		338
Vernon E. Faulconer Inc 1001 ESE Loop 323 Ste 160 *Web:* www.vefinc.com	Tyler	TX	75701	903-581-4382		536
Vernon Electric Co-op 110 Saugstad Rd *TF:* 800-447-5051 ■ *Web:* www.vernonelectric.org	Westby	WI	54667	608-634-3121	634-7481	245
Vernon Jubilee Hospital 2101 32nd St *TF:* 800-224-9376 ■ *Web:* www.interiorhealth.ca	Vernon	BC	V1T5L2	250-545-2211	545-5602	374-2
Vernon Parish Library 1401 Nolan Trace	Leesville	LA	71446	337-239-2027		434-3
Vernon Tool Company Ltd 503 Jones Rd *TF:* 800-452-1542 ■ *Web:* www.vernontool.com	Oceanside	CA	92054	760-433-5860	757-2233	455
Vernon Township Board of Education (Inc) PO Box 99 *Web:* www.vtsd.com	Vernon	NJ	07462	973-764-2900		685
Vero Beach Press-Journal 1801 US Hwy 1 *Web:* www.tcpalm.com	Vero Beach	FL	32960	772-562-2315		532-2
Verologix LLC 18100 Von Karman Ave Ste 850 *TF:* 800-403-8041 ■ *Web:* www.verologix.com	Irvine	CA	92612	800-403-8041		196
Verona Beach State Park 6541 Lake Shore Rd N *Web:* parks.ny.gov/parks/102/details.aspx	Verona Beach	NY	13162	315-762-4463		565
Verona's Cucina Italiana 1700 McHenry Ave	Modesto	CA	95350	209-549-8876		671
Veronica Foods Co 1991 Dennison St *Web:* www.evoliveoil.com	Oakland	CA	94606	510-535-6833	532-2837	296-30
Veronis Suhler Stevenson (VSS) 55 E 52nd St 33rd Fl *Web:* www.vss.com	New York	NY	10055	212-935-4990	381-8168	690
Veros Real Estate Solutions LLC 2333 N Broadway Ste 350 *TF:* 866-458-3767 ■ *Web:* www.veros.com	Santa Ana	CA	92706	714-415-6300		177
Veros Systems Inc 5914 Ctyard Dr W Bridgepoint Plaza II Ste 190 *TF:* 800-347-3473 ■ *Web:* www.verossystems.com	Austin	TX	78730	512-686-2400		466
VeroScience LLC 1334 Main Rd *Web:* www.veroscience.com	Tiverton	RI	02878	401-816-0525		743
Verosonic 590 Telser Rd Ste B *Web:* www.verosonic.com	Lake Zurich	IL	60047	847-540-9257		358
Verrex Corp 1130 Rt 22 W *Web:* www.verrex.com	Mountainside	NJ	07092	908-232-7000		52
Verrill Dana LLP PO Box 586 *Web:* www.verrilldana.com	Portland	ME	04112	207-774-4000	774-7499	428
Versa Electronics 3943 Quebec Ave N *TF:* 800-561-3357 ■ *Web:* www.versaelectronics.com	Minneapolis	MN	55427	763-557-6737	557-8073	246
Versa Press Inc 1465 Springbay Rd *TF:* 800-447-7829 ■ *Web:* www.versapress.com	East Peoria	IL	61611	800-447-7829		626
Versa Products Co Inc 22 Spring Valley Rd *Web:* versa-valves.com	Paramus	NJ	07652	201-843-2400	843-2931	790
Versa Shore Inc 102 Strathmore Pl Ste A *Web:* www.versashore.com	Los Gatos	CA	95032	408-355-5363		396
Versabar Inc 1111 Engineers Rd *TF:* 800-777-3300 ■ *Web:* www.vbar.com	Belle Chasse	LA	70037	504-392-3200		514
Versacold International Corp 2115 Commissioner St *TF:* 800-563-2653 ■ *Web:* www.versacold.com	Vancouver	BC	V5L1A6	604-255-4656		314
Versacom Inc 1501 Ave McGill College 6th Fl *Web:* www.versacom.ca	Montreal	QC	H3A3M8	514-397-1950		768

Phone | Fax | Class

Versacor Inc 340 Main St Ste 560 . . . . . Worcester MA 01608 508-757-9580 180
Web: www.versacor.com

Versailles 3555 SW Eigth St . . . . . Miami FL 33135 305-444-0240 671
Web: versaillesrestaurant.com

Versailles 10319 Venice Blvd. . . . . . Los Angeles CA 90034 310-558-3168 558-1817 671
Web: versaillescuban.com

Versailles State Park
US Hwy 50 PO Box 205 . . . . . Versailles IN 47042 812-689-6424 565
Web: www.in.gov

Versalift East Inc 2706 Brodhead Rd . . . . . Bethlehem PA 18020 610-866-1400 45
Web: www.versalifteast.com

Versalign Inc 1719 Delaware Ave . . . . . Wilmington DE 19806 302-225-7800 260
Web: www.versalign.com

Versalogic Corp 4211 W 11th Ave . . . . . Eugene OR 97402 541-485-8575 485-5712 173-2
TF: 800-824-3163 ■ *Web:* www.versalogic.com

Versant Corp
255 Shoreline Dr Ste 450 . . . . . Redwood City CA 94065 650-232-2400 178-1
NASDAQ: VSNT ■ *TF:* 888-446-4737 ■ *Web:* actian.com

Versant Inc
2316 N Milwaukee St Ste 280 . . . . . Milwaukee WI 53202 414-410-0500 7
Web: www.versantsolutions.com

VersaPharm Inc
1775 W Oak Pkwy Ste 800 . . . . . Marietta GA 30062 770-499-8100 231
Web: www.versapharm.com

Versar Inc 6850 Versar Ctr . . . . . Springfield VA 22151 703-750-3000 642-6825 261
NYSE: VSR ■ *TF Cust Svc:* 800-283-7727 ■ *Web:* www.versar.com

Versasuite 13401 Pond Springs Rd . . . . . Austin TX 78729 800-903-8774 225
TF: 800-903-0774 ■ *Web:* versasuite.com

VersaTech Automation Services LLC
11349 FM 529 Rd . . . . . Houston TX 77041 713-939-6100 256
Web: www.vtechas.com

Versatile Fabrication 2708 Ninth St . . . . . Muskegon MI 49444 231-739-7115 697
Web: versatile-fabrication.com

Versatile Systems Inc
4900 Ritter Rd Ste 100 . . . . . Mechanicsburg PA 17055 800-262-1622 778-8577* 225
NYSE: CVE ■ **Fax Area Code:* 425 ■ *TF:* 800-262-1622 ■ *Web:* www.versatile.com

Versatube Corp 4755 Rochester Rd . . . . . Troy MI 48085 248-689-7373 689-8293 489
Web: www.versatubecorp.com

Verso Adv Inc 50 W 17th St Fl 5 . . . . . New York NY 10011 212-292-2990 4

Verso Books 20 Jay St Ste 1010 . . . . . Brooklyn NY 11201 718-246-8160 246-8165 637-2
Web: www.versobooks.com

Verso Corp 8540 Gander Creek Dr . . . . . Miamisburg OH 45342 877-855-7243 557
TF: 877-855-7243 ■ *Web:* www.versoco.com

Verso Corp 6775 Lenox Ctr Ct Ste 400 . . . . . Memphis TN 38115 901-369-4100 557
NYSE: VRS ■ *Web:* www.versoco.com

Versonix Corp 1175 Saratoga Ave Ste 4 . . . . . San Jose CA 95129 408-873-3131 177
Web: versonix.com

Verspeeten Cartage Ltd
274129 Wallace Line . . . . . Ingersoll ON N5C3J7 519-425-7881 59
TF: 800-265-6701 ■ *Web:* www.verspeeten.com

Verst Group Logistics Inc
300 Shorland Dr . . . . . Walton KY 41094 859-485-1212 803-1
Web: www.verstgroup.com

VerStandig Broadcasting
10960 John Wayne Dr PO Box 788 . . . . . Greencastle PA 17225 717-597-9200 597-9210 643
Web: www.verstandig.com

Vertafore Inc 7 Waterside Crossing . . . . . Windsor CT 06095 800-444-4813 402-9569* 178-10
**Fax Area Code:* 425 ■ *Fax:* PR ■ *TF General:* 800-444-4813 ■ *Web:* www.vertafore.com

Vertafore Inc 11724 NE 195th St . . . . . Bothell WA 98011 425-402-1000 225
TF: 800-444-4813 ■ *Web:* www.vertafore.com

VerTechs Enterprises Inc
1071 Industrial Pl . . . . . El Cajon CA 92020 858-578-3900 21
Web: vertechsusa.com

Verteks Consulting Inc
2102 SW 20th Pl Ste 602 . . . . . Ocala FL 34471 352-401-0909 196
Web: www.verteks.com

Vertel Corp
21300 Victory Blvd Ste 700 . . . . . Woodland Hills CA 91367 818-227-1400 180
Web: www.vertel.com

Vertellus Specialties Inc
201 N Illinois St Ste 1800 . . . . . Indianapolis IN 46204 317-247-8141 248-6402 145
TF: 800-777-3536 ■ *Web:* www.vertellus.com

Vertex Business Services LLC
250 E Arapaho Rd . . . . . Richardson TX 75081 214-576-1000 317
Web: vertexone.net

Vertex China 131 Brea Canyon Rd . . . . . Walnut CA 91789 909-622-3333 361
Web: www.vertexchina.com

Vertex Computer Systems Inc
2245 Enterprise Pkwy E . . . . . Twinsburg OH 44087 330-963-0044 809
TF: 800-649-5323 ■ *Web:* www.vertexcs.com

Vertex Distribution
523 Pleasant St Bldg 10 . . . . . Attleboro MA 02703 508-431-1120 431-1114 270
Web: www.vertexdistribution.com

Vertex Engineering Services Inc
400 Libbey Pkwy . . . . . Weymouth MA 02189 781-952-6000 192
TF: 888-298-5162 ■ *Web:* vertexeng.com

Vertex Inc 1041 Old Cassatt Rd . . . . . Berwyn PA 19312 610-640-4200 640-5892 178-1
TF: 800-355-3500 ■ *Web:* www.vertexinc.com

Vertex Software Corp
1515 S Cptl Of Tx Hwy 4 . . . . . Austin TX 78746 512-328-3700 177
Web: www.vertex.com

Vertex Systems Inc
440 Polaris Pkwy Ste 100 . . . . . Westerville OH 43082 614-318-7100 179
Web: www.vertexsystems.com

Vertex Wireless LLC
500 Wegner Dr . . . . . West Chicago IL 60185 630-293-6300 179
TF: 800-561-3357 ■ *Web:* www.vertexwireless.com

Vertical Alliance Group Inc
1730 Galleria Oaks . . . . . Texarkana TX 75503 903-792-3866 242
TF: 877-792-3866 ■ *Web:* www.verticalag.com

Vertical Aviation
15035 N 73rd St Ste D . . . . . Scottsdale AZ 85260 480-991-6558 359

Vertical Communications Inc
3940 Freedom Cr Ste 110 . . . . . Santa Clara CA 95054 408-404-1600 969-9601 178-7
OTC: VRCC ■ *TF Sales:* 800-914-9985 ■ *Web:* www.vertical.com

Vertical Group 25 DeForest Ave . . . . . Summit NJ 07901 908-277-3737 273-9434 792
Web: www.vertical-group.com

Vertical Management Systems Inc
15440 Laguna Canyon Rd Ste 160 . . . . . Irvine CA 92618 800-867-4357 177
TF: 800-867-4357 ■ *Web:* www.vmshelp.com

Vertical Research Partners LLC
6 Landmark Sq Ste 720 . . . . . Stamford CT 06901 203-276-5680 401
Web: verticalresearchpartners.com

Vertical Structures Inc
309 Spangler Dr Ste E . . . . . Richmond KY 40475 859-624-8360 116
Web: verticalstructures.com

Vertical Systems Inc
6462 City W Pkwy Ste 100 . . . . . Eden Prairie MN 55344 952-934-7533 177
Web: www.vertsys.com

Vertical Vision Financial Marketing LLC
145 Towne Lake Pkwy . . . . . Woodstock GA 30188 866-984-1585 5
TF: 866-984-1585 ■ *Web:* www.v2fm.com

Vertices Llc
76 W Ruby Ave Unit A . . . . . New brunswick NJ 07650 732-418-9135 396
Web: www.vertices.com

Verti-Crete LLC 16500 S 500 W . . . . . Bluffdale UT 84065 801-571-2028 183
Web: www.verti-crete.com

Vertigraph Inc 12959 Jupiter Rd Ste 252 . . . . . Dallas TX 75238 214-340-9436 463
TF: 800-989-4243 ■ *Web:* www.vertigraph.com

Vertisoft
990 Boul Pierre-roux E . . . . . Victoriaville QC G6T0K9 819-751-6660 180
TF: 877-368-3241 ■ *Web:* www.vertisoftpme.com

Vertisys Corp 821-B Livingston Ct . . . . . Marietta GA 30067 770-955-1755 196
TF: 800-426-4968 ■ *Web:* www.vertisys.com

VertitechIT Inc 4 Open Sq Way Ste 207 . . . . . Holyoke MA 01040 413-268-1600 631
TF: 800-929-5201 ■ *Web:* vertitechit.com

Verto Solutions
1620 'I' St NW Ste 925 . . . . . Washington DC 20006 202-293-5800 463-8998 47
Web: www.vertosolutions.net

Vertrue Inc 20 Glover Ave . . . . . Norwalk CT 06850 203-324-7635 384

Verus Pharmaceuticals Inc
12671 High Bluff Dr Ste 200 . . . . . San Diego CA 92130 858-436-1600 231

Verve 1127 Gregg St . . . . . Columbia SC 29201 803-799-0045 393
Web: www.verveinteriors.com

Vesbridge Partners
301 Carlson Pkwy Ste 110 . . . . . Minnetonka MN 55305 952-995-7499 995-7493 792
Web: www.vesbridge.com

Vescio Threading Co
14002 Anson Ave . . . . . Santa Fe Springs CA 90670 562-802-1868 802-2073 454
TF: 800-361-4218 ■ *Web:* www.vesciothreading.com

Vesco Oil Corp 16055 W 12-Mile Rd . . . . . Southfield MI 48076 800-527-5358 557-2236* 579
**Fax Area Code:* 248 ■ *TF:* 800-527-5358 ■ *Web:* www.vesco-oil.com

Vescom Corp 705 Main Rd N . . . . . Hampden ME 04444 207-945-5051 693
TF: 800-841-1769 ■ *Web:* www.vescomcorp.com

VESD (Victor Elementary School District)
12219 Second Ave . . . . . Victorville CA 92395 760-245-1691 245-6245 685
Web: www.vesd.net

Vespaio 1610 S Congress Ave . . . . . Austin TX 78704 512-441-6100 441-7746 671
Web: austinvespaio.com

Vess Oil Corp
1700 WaterFrnt Pkwy Bldg 500 . . . . . Wichita KS 67206 316-682-1537 536
Web: www.vessoil.com

Vessel Metrics LLC
3 Church Cir Ste 325 . . . . . Annapolis MD 21401 888-214-1710 387
TF: 888-214-1710 ■ *Web:* www.vesselvanguard.com

Vest Adv Mktg & PR 3007 Sprowl Rd . . . . . Louisville KY 40299 502-267-5335 636
Web: www.vestadvertising.com

Vesta Corp 11950 SW Garden PL . . . . . Portland OR 97223 503-790-2500 790-2525 215
Web: www.trustvesta.com

Vesta Hospitality LLC
900 Washington St Ste 760 . . . . . Vancouver WA 98660 360-737-0442 194
Web: www.vestahospitality.com

Vesta Properties Ltd
9770 196A St Ste 101A . . . . . Langley BC V1M2X5 604-888-7869 186
Web: www.vestaproperties.com

Vestal & Wiler Cpas
201 E Pine St Ste 801 . . . . . Orlando FL 32801 407-843-4433 2
Web: vestal-wiler.com

Vestal Central School District
201 Main St . . . . . Vestal NY 13850 607-757-2241 757-2227 685
Web: vestal.stier.org

Vestal Manufacturing Enterprises Inc
176 Industrial Park Rd . . . . . Sweetwater TN 37874 423-337-6125 480
Web: www.vestalmfg.com

Vestal Public Library
320 Vestal Pkwy E . . . . . Vestal NY 13850 607-754-4244 434-3
Web: www.4cls.org

Vestar Development
2425 E Camelback Rd Ste 750 . . . . . Phoenix AZ 85016 602-866-0900 955-2298 655
Web: www.vestar.com

Vestavia Hills Board of Education
1204 Montgomery Hwy . . . . . Birmingham AL 35216 205-402-5100 685
Web: www.vestavia.k12.al.us

Vestcom International Inc
7302 Kanis Rd . . . . . Little Rock AR 72204 501-663-0100 8
Web: www.vestcom.com

Vested Business Brokers Inc
50 Karl Ave # 102 . . . . . Smithtown NY 11787 631-265-7300 528
TF: 877-735-5224 ■ *Web:* www.vestedbb.com

Vested Group, The 1001 E 15th St Ste 200 . . . . . Plano TX 75074 972-429-9025 196
Web: thevested.com

Vestin Group Inc
8880 W Sunset Rd # 200 . . . . . Las Vegas NV 89148 702-227-0965 227-5247 509
Web: www.vestinmortgage.com

Vestor Capital Corp
10 S Riverside Plaza Ste 1400 . . . . . Chicago IL 60606 312-641-2400 169
Web: www.vestorcapital.com

Vestor Partners LP
607 Cerrillos Rd Ste D-2 . . . . . Santa Fe NM 87501 505-988-9100 402
Web: www.vestor.com

Vestra Resources Inc 5300 Aviation Dr . . . . . Redding CA 96002 530-223-2585 302
TF: 877-983-7872 ■ *Web:* www.vestra.com

Vet Clinic of Palm Harbor Inc, The
35891 US Hwy 19 N . . . . . Palm Harbor FL 34684 727-781-7704 794
Web: thevetclinic.com

Name / Address	City	State	ZIP	Phone	Fax	Class
Vet Path Services Inc 6450 Castle Dr *Web:* www.vetpathservicesinc.com	Mason	OH	45040	513-469-0777		794
VetCor Inc 350 Lincoln Pl *TF:* 800-380-6872 ■ *Web:* www.vetcor.com	Hingham	MA	02043	781-749-8151		794
Veteran Corps of America 220 E State St Ste 2F *Web:* www.veterancorps.com	O'fallon	IL	62269	703-691-8385		196
Veteran's Truck Line Inc 800 Black Hawk Dr *TF:* 800-456-9476 ■ *Web:* www.vetstruck.com	Burlington	WI	53105	262-539-3400	539-2720	360-2
Veterans Admin Medical Center 555 Willard Ave	Newington	CT	06111	860-666-6951		374-3
Veterans Affairs Medical Ctr 77 Wainwright Dr *TF:* 888-687-8863	Walla Walla	WA	99362	509-525-5200		374-8
Veterans Affairs Medical Ctr 508 Fulton St *TF:* 800-273-8225 ■ *Web:* www.durham.va.gov	Durham	NC	27705	919-286-0411	286-6825	374-8
Veterans Affairs Medical Ctr 150 S Huntington Ave **Fax Area Code:* 617 ■ *TF:* 800-273-8255 ■ *Web:* www.va.gov	Jamaica Plain	MA	02130	800-273-8255	278-4508*	374-8
Veterans Affairs Medical Ctr 1310 24th Ave S *TF:* 800-228-4973 ■ *Web:* www.va.gov	Nashville	TN	37212	615-327-4751		374-8
Veterans Affairs Medical Ctr 6439 Garners Ferry Rd **Fax:* Mail Rm ■ *TF:* 888-651-2683 ■ *Web:* www.columbiasc.va.gov	Columbia	SC	29209	803-776-4000	695-6862*	374-8
Veterans Affairs Medical Ctr 1501 San Pedro Dr SE *Web:* va.gov	Albuquerque	NM	87108	505-265-1711	256-2855	374-8
Veterans Affairs Medical Ctr 2215 Fuller Rd *TF:* 800-361-8387 ■ *Web:* www.annarbor.va.gov	Ann Arbor	MI	48105	734-769-7100		374-8
Veterans Affairs Medical Ctr 1100 Tunnel Rd *TF:* 800-932-6408 ■ *Web:* www.asheville.va.gov	Asheville	NC	28805	828-298-7911	299-2502	374-8
Veterans Affairs Medical Ctr 10 N Greene St *TF:* 800-463-6295 ■ *Web:* veterans.maryland.gov	Baltimore	MD	21201	410-605-7000		374-8
Veterans Affairs Medical Ctr 940 Belmont St *TF:* 800-865-3384 ■ *Web:* www.va.gov/directory/guide/facility.asp?ID=19	Brockton	MA	02301	508-583-4500		374-8
Veterans Affairs Medical Ctr 3495 Bailey Ave *TF:* 800-532-8387 ■ *Web:* www.buffalo.va.gov	Buffalo	NY	14215	716-834-9200	862-8759	374-8
Veterans Affairs Medical Ctr 820 S Damen Ave *TF:* 888-569-5282 ■ *Web:* www.chicago.va.gov	Chicago	IL	60612	312-569-8387		374-8
Veterans Affairs Medical Ctr 2002 Holcombe Blvd *TF:* 800-553-2278 ■ *Web:* www.houston.va.gov	Houston	TX	77030	713-791-1414	794-7218	374-8
Veterans Affairs Medical Ctr 1700 S Lincoln Ave *TF:* 800-409-8771 ■ *Web:* www.lebanon.va.gov	Lebanon	PA	17042	800-409-8771		374-8
Veterans Affairs Medical Ctr 151 Knollcroft Rd *Web:* www.va.gov	Lyons	NJ	07939	908-647-0180		374-8
Veterans Affairs Medical Ctr 1030 Jefferson Ave *TF:* 800-636-8262 ■ *Web:* va.gov	Memphis	TN	38104	901-523-8990		374-8
Veterans Affairs Medical Ctr 1201 NW 16th St *TF:* 888-276-1785 ■ *Web:* www.miami.va.gov	Miami	FL	33125	305-324-4455		374-8
Veterans Affairs Medical Ctr 1 Veterans Dr *TF:* 866-414-5058 ■ *Web:* www.minneapolis.va.gov	Minneapolis	MN	55417	612-725-2000		374-8
Veterans Affairs Medical Ctr 79 Middleville Rd *TF:* 800-877-6976 ■ *Web:* www.northport.va.gov	Northport	NY	11768	631-261-4400		374-8
Veterans Affairs Medical Ctr 921 NE 13th St *TF:* 866-835-5273 ■ *Web:* Www.oklahoma.va.gov	Oklahoma City	OK	73104	405-456-1000		374-8
Veterans Affairs Medical Ctr 4101 Woolworth Ave *TF:* 800-451-5796 ■ *Web:* Www.nebraska.va.gov	Omaha	NE	68105	402-346-8800		374-8
Veterans Affairs Medical Ctr 3801 Miranda Ave *Web:* www.paloalto.va.gov	Palo Alto	CA	94304	650-493-5000		374-8
Veterans Affairs Medical Ctr 830 Chalkstone Ave *TF:* 866-590-2976 ■ *Web:* www.va.gov	Providence	RI	02908	401-273-7100		374-8
Veterans Affairs Medical Ctr 500 Foothill Dr *TF:* 800-613-4012 ■ *Web:* www.saltlakecity.va.gov	Salt Lake City	UT	84148	801-582-1565		374-8
Veterans Affairs Medical Ctr 4800 Memorial Dr *Web:* va.gov	Waco	TX	76711	254-752-6581		374-8
Veterans Affairs Medical Ctr 601 Hwy 6 W *TF:* 866-687-7382 ■ *Web:* www.iowacity.va.gov	Iowa City	IA	52246	319-338-0581		374-8
Veterans Affairs Medical Ctr 1601 Kirkwood Hwy *TF:* 800-450-8262 ■ *Web:* www.wilmington.va.gov	Wilmington	DE	19805	302-994-2511		374-8
Veterans Affairs Medical Ctr 10000 Bay Pines Blvd *TF:* 888-820-0230 ■ *Web:* www.baypines.va.gov	Bay Pines	FL	33744	727-398-6661	398-9442	374-8
Veterans Affairs Medical Ctr 13000 Bruce B Downs Blvd *TF:* 888-716-7787 ■ *Web:* www.va.gov	Tampa	FL	33612	813-972-2000		374-8
Veterans Affairs Medical Ctr 2121 Lake Ave *Web:* veteransfuneralhomes.com	Fort Wayne	IN	46805	260-426-5431		374-8
Veterans Affairs Medical Ctr 3600 30th St *TF:* 844-698-2311	Des Moines	IA	50310	515-699-5999		374-8
Veterans Affairs Medical Ctr 1500 Weiss St *TF:* 877-222-8387 ■ *Web:* www.va.gov	Saginaw	MI	48602	989-497-2500	321-4903	374-8
Veterans Affairs Medical Ctr 600 S 70th St *TF:* 866-851-6052 ■ *Web:* veteransfuneralhomes.com	Lincoln	NE	68510	402-489-3802		374-8
Veterans Affairs Medical Ctr 718 Smyth Rd *TF:* 800-892-8384 ■ *Web:* www.manchester.va.gov	Manchester	NH	03104	603-624-4366		374-8
Veterans Affairs Medical Ctr 800 Irving Ave **Fax:* Admitting ■ *TF:* 800-792-4334 ■ *Web:* www.syracuse.va.gov	Syracuse	NY	13210	315-425-4400	425-4375*	374-8
Veterans Affairs Medical Ctr 3200 Vine St *TF:* 877-829-5500 ■ *Web:* www.fisherhouse.org/houses/house-locations/#Ohio	Cincinnati	OH	45220	513-475-6571	487-6661	374-8
Veterans Affairs Medical Ctr 100 Emancipation Dr *TF:* 800-488-8244 ■ *Web:* www.va.gov	Hampton	VA	23667	757-728-3100		374-8
Veterans Affairs Medical Ctr 200 Veterans Ave *Web:* www1.va.gov	Beckley	WV	25801	304-255-2121		374-8
Veterans Affairs Medical Ctr 2500 Overlook Terr *TF:* 888-478-8321 ■ *Web:* www.madison.va.gov	Madison	WI	53705	608-256-1901		374-8
Veterans Affairs Puget Sound Medical Ctr 1660 S Columbian Way *TF:* 800-329-8387 ■ *Web:* www.pugetsound.va.gov	Seattle	WA	98108	206-762-1010		374-8
Veterans Benefits Administration 810 Vermont Ave NW **Fax Area Code:* 202 ■ *TF:* 800-827-1000 ■ *Web:* benefits.va.gov	Washington	DC	20420	800-827-1000	275-5947*	340-19
Veterans Canteen Service 1 Jefferson Barracks Rd Bldg 25 *Web:* www.va.gov	Saint Louis	MO	63125	314-652-4100	845-1201	340-19
Veterans Care Ctr 4550 Shenandoah Ave *Web:* www.dvs.virginia.gov	Roanoke	VA	24017	540-982-2860	982-8667	793
Veterans for Peace Inc (VFP) 1404 N Broadway *TF:* 877-429-0678 ■ *Web:* www.veteransforpeace.org	Saint Louis	MO	63102	314-725-6005	725-7103	48-5
Veterans Guest House 880 Locust St *Web:* www.veteransguesthouse.org	Reno	NV	89502	775-324-6958	324-6071	372
Veterans Health Administration 810 Vermont Ave NW *TF:* 800-827-1000 ■ *Web:* www.va.gov/health	Washington	DC	20420	844-698-2311		340-19
Gulf War Veterans Information 810 Vermont Ave NW *TF:* 800-313-2232 ■ *Web:* gulfwarvets.com	Washington	DC	20420	800-313-2232		340-19
Office of Research & Development 810 Vermont Ave NW MC 12 **Fax Area Code:* 202 ■ *TF:* 800-827-1000 ■ *Web:* www.research.va.gov	Washington	DC	20420	800-827-1000	254-0460*	340-19
Veterans Health Care System of the Ozarks 1100 N College Ave *TF:* 800-691-8387 ■ *Web:* www.fayettevillear.va.gov	Fayetteville	AR	72703	479-443-4301		374-8
Veterans Home & Hospital 287 W St *Web:* ct.gov	Rocky Hill	CT	06067	860-529-2571		374-7
Veterans Home of California-Barstow 100 E Veterans Pkwy *TF:* 800-746-0606	Barstow	CA	92311	760-252-6200		793
Veterans Home of California-Chula Vista 700 E Naples Ct *TF:* 800-952-5626 ■ *Web:* www.calvet.ca.gov	Chula Vista	CA	91911	800-952-5626		793
Veterans Memorial Auditorium 1 Ave of the Arts *TF:* 800-828-4101 ■ *Web:* thevetsri.com	Providence	RI	02903	401-222-1467		572
Veterans Memorial Library 301 S University Ave	Mount Pleasant	MI	48858	989-773-3242	772-3280	434-3
Veterans Museum & Memorial Ctr 2115 Pk Blvd *Web:* www.veteranmuseum.org	San Diego	CA	92101	619-239-2300	239-7445	520
Veterans of Foreign Wars of the US (VFW) 406 W 34th St *TF:* 800-963-3180 ■ *Web:* www.vfw.org	Kansas City	MO	64111	816-756-3390	968-1149	48-19
Veterans Oil Delivery 2070 Hwy 150 *Web:* www.veteransoilinc.com	Bessemer	AL	35022	205-424-4400		579
Veterinary Pet Insurance Inc PO Box 2344 *TF:* 800-872-7387 ■ *Web:* www.petinsurance.com	Brea	CA	92822	800-872-7387		391-1
Veterinary Pharmacies of America Inc 2854 Antoine Dr *TF:* 877-838-7979 ■ *Web:* www.vparx.com	Houston	TX	77092	877-838-7979	329-7979	584
Veterinary Specialists of the Southeast (CCVS) 3163 W Montague Ave *Web:* www.ccvsllc.com	North Charleston	SC	29418	843-747-1507	747-7920	794
Veterinary Specialty and Emergency Hospital 3550 S Jason St *Web:* www.vrcc.com	Englewood	CO	80110	303-874-7387		794
Veterinary Specialty Hospital of The Carolinas 6405 Tryon Rd Ste 100 *Web:* www.vshcarolinas.com	Cary	NC	27518	919-233-4911		794
Veterinary Surgical Associates 1410 Monument Blvd Ste 100 *Web:* www.ccvec.com	Concord	CA	94520	925-827-1777		794
Veterinary Transplant Services Inc 215 E Titus St *Web:* www.vtsonline.com	Kent	WA	98032	253-520-0771		794
VetJobs Inc PO Box 71445 *TF:* 877-838-5627 ■ *Web:* www.vetjobs.com	Marietta	GA	30007	770-993-5117		260
Vetoquinol Canada Inc 2000 Ch Georges *TF:* 800-363-1700 ■ *Web:* www.vetoquinol.ca	Lavaltrie	QC	J5T3S5	450-586-2252	586-4649	584
Vetri 1312 Spruce St *Web:* www.vetrifamily.com	Philadelphia	PA	19107	215-732-3478		671
Vets & Pets 3345 El Camino Real *Web:* vcahospitals.com	Santa Clara	CA	95051	408-246-1893		794
VetSelect Animal Hospital 2150 Old Novi Rd *TF:* 800-462-8749 ■ *Web:* www.vetselect.com	Novi	MI	48377	248-624-1100	624-6542	794
Vet-Stem Inc 12860 Danielson Court Ste B *TF:* 888-387-8361 ■ *Web:* www.vet-stem.com	Poway	CA	92064	858-748-2004		794
VetStrategy 30 Whitmore Rd *TF:* 866-901-6471 ■ *Web:* www.vetstrategy.com	Woodbridge	ON	L4L7Z4	866-901-6471		463
Vetstreet 780 Township Line Rd *TF:* 888-799-8387 ■ *Web:* www.vetstreet.com	Yardley	PA	19067	215-493-0621		387

Name / Address	City	State	Zip	Phone	Fax	Class
Vetter Health Services Inc						
20220 Harney St	Elkhorn	NE	68022	402-895-3932	895-8165	463
TF: 800-388-4264 ■ *Web:* www.vetterhealthservices.com						
Vetter Stone Co (VSC) 23894 Third Ave	Mankato	MN	56001	507-345-4568	345-4777	724
TF: 800-878-2850 ■ *Web:* www.vetterstone.com						
Vexor Technology Inc 955 W Smith Rd	Medina	OH	44256	330-721-9773		660
Web: www.vexortechnology.com						
VF Corp 105 Corporate Ctr Blvd	Greensboro	NC	27408	336-424-6000	424-7634	155-3
NYSE: VFC ■ *TF:* 800-226-3224 ■ *Web:* www.vfc.com						
VFA Inc 99 Bedford St	Boston	MA	02111	617-451-5100		178-1
TF: 800-693-3132 ■ *Web:* www.vfa.com						
vFinance Inc						
1200 N Federal Hwy Ste 400	Boca Raton	FL	33432	561-981-1000		690
Web: www.vfinanceinvestments.com						
V-fluence Interactive Public Realtions Inc						
7770 Regents Rd	San Diego	CA	92122	877-835-8362		225
TF: 877-835-8362 ■ *Web:* www.v-fluence.com						
VFP (Veterans for Peace Inc)						
1404 N Broadway	Saint Louis	MO	63102	314-725-6005	725-7103	48-5
TF: 877-429-0678 ■ *Web:* www.veteransforpeace.org						
VFP Inc 1701 Midland Rd PO Box 1809	Salem	VA	24153	540-977-0500	977-5555	505
Web: www.vfpinc.com						
VFUC (Visions Federal Credit Union)						
24 McKinley Ave	Endicott	NY	13760	607-754-7900	786-1718	219
TF: 800-242-2120 ■ *Web:* www.visionsfcu.org						
VFW (Veterans of Foreign Wars of the US)						
406 W 34th St	Kansas City	MO	64111	816-756-3390	968-1149	48-19
TF: 800-963-3180 ■ *Web:* www.vfw.org						
VGH (Valdese General Hospital)						
720 Malcolm Blvd Ste 200	Valdese	NC	28690	828-874-2251	397-3226	374-3
TF: 800-994-6610 ■ *Web:* www.blueridgehealth.org						
VGMarket LLC 3860 Sheridan St Ste C	Hollywood	FL	33021	650-483-8384		466
Web: www.vgmarket.com						
VH Blackinton & Company Inc						
221 John L Dietsch Blvd	Attleboro	MA	02763	508-699-4436		483
Web: www.blackinton.com						
V&H Inc 1505 S Central Ave	Marshfield	WI	54449	715-486-8800		57
TF: 800-826-2308 ■ *Web:* www.vhtrucks.com						
VH1 (Video Hits One) 1515 Broadway	New York	NY	10036	212-258-7800	422-6630*	740
**Fax Area Code:* 201 ■ **Fax:* Hum Res ■ *Web:* www.vh1.com						
VH1 Classic 1515 Broadway 21st Fl	New York	NY	10036	212-275-6661		740
Web: www.vh1.com						
Vhb (VHB) 101 Walnut St PO Box 9151	Watertown	MA	02471	617-924-1770	924-2286	261
Web: www.vhb.com						
VHG Labs Inc 276 Abby Rd	Manchester	NH	03103	603-622-7660		743
Web: www.vhglabs.com						
VHHA (Virginia Hospital & Healthcare Assn)						
4200 Innslake Dr	Glen Allen	VA	23060	804-965-1227		48-17
Web: www.vhha.com						
Vi 71 S Wacker Dr	Chicago	IL	60606	312-803-8800		672
TF: 800-421-1442 ■ *Web:* www.viliving.com						
VIA Agency 619 Congress St	Portland	ME	04101	207-221-3000		4
Web: www.theviaagency.com						
Via Christi Regional Medical Ctr						
929 N St Francis St	Wichita	KS	67214	316-260-5000		374-3
VIA Metropolitan Transit						
800 W Myrtle St	San Antonio	TX	78212	210-362-2000	362-2563*	468
**Fax:* Cust Svc ■ *TF:* 866-362-4200 ■ *Web:* www.viainfo.net						
VIA Motors Inc 165 Mtn Way Dr	Orem	UT	84058	801-764-9333		489
Web: www.viamotors.com						
VIA Rail Canada Inc						
PO Box 8116 Station A	Montreal	QC	H3C3N3	514-871-6000	871-6104	649
TF: 800-681-2561 ■ *Web:* www.viarail.ca						
Via Real Restaurant						
4020 N MacArthur Blvd	Irving	TX	75038	972-650-9001	541-0215	671
TF: 800-315-2621 ■ *Web:* www.viareal.com						
VIA Technologies Inc 940 Mission Ct	Fremont	CA	94539	510-683-3300	687-4654	696
Web: www.viatech.com/en						
Viable Solutions Inc						
2839 University Acres Dr	Orlando	FL	32817	407-249-9200		809
Web: viable-solutions.com						
Viacom Entertainment Group						
1515 Broadway	New York	NY	10036	212-258-6000		514
TF: 800-516-4399 ■ *Web:* www.viacom.com						
Viacom Inc 1515 Broadway 52nd Fl	New York	NY	10036	212-258-6000		185
NASDAQ: VIAB ■ *TF:* 800-294-1322 ■ *Web:* www.viacom.com						
Viad Corp 1850 N Central Ave Ste 800	Phoenix	AZ	85004	602-207-1000		185
NYSE: VVI ■ *Web:* www.viad.com						
Viair Corp 15 Edelman	Irvine	CA	92618	949-585-0011		787
TF: 800-618-1994 ■ *Web:* www.viaircorp.com						
Vialta Inc 48461 Fremont Blvd	Fremont	CA	94538	510-870-3088	870-3019	52
Web: www.vialta.com						
Viamedia Inc						
220 Lexington Green Cir Ste 300	Lexington	KY	40503	859-977-9000		5
TF: 800-842-9126 ■ *Web:* www.viamediatv.com						
Viamet Pharmaceuticals Inc						
2250 Perimeter Park Dr Ste 320	Morrisville	NC	27560	919-467-8539		231
Web: www.viamet.com						
Vianet Internet Solutions Inc						
128 Larch St Ste 201	Sudbury	ON	P3E5J8	705-675-0402		387
TF: 800-788-0363 ■ *Web:* www.vianet.ca						
Viant Group LLC						
500 Washington St Ste 325	San Francisco	CA	94111	415-820-6100		41
Web: www.viantgroup.com						
ViaSat Inc 6155 El Camino Real	Carlsbad	CA	92009	760-476-2200	929-3941	681
NASDAQ: VSAT ■ *TF:* 855-463-9333 ■ *Web:* www.viasat.com						
ViaTech Publishing Solutions						
1440 Fifth Ave	Bay Shore	NY	11706	631-968-8500		86
TF: 800-645-8558 ■ *Web:* www.viatechpub.com						
Viatech Systems Inc						
1749 Old Meadow Rd 650	McLean	VA	22102	703-917-0550	917-0558	194
Web: www.viatech-systems.net						
Viatran Corp						
3829 Forest Pkwy Ste 500	Wheatfield	NY	14120	716-629-3800	693-9162	253
TF: 800-688-0030 ■ *Web:* www.viatran.com						
Viatron Systems Inc						
18233 S Hoover St	Los Angeles	CA	90248	310-756-0610		177
Web: www.viatron.com						
VIBAC Canada Inc						
12250 Industrial Blvd	Montreal	QC	H1B5M5	514-640-0250	640-1577	732
TF: 800-557-0192 ■ *Web:* www.vibacgroup.com						
Vibco Inc 75 Stilson Rd	Wyoming	RI	02898	401-539-2392		190
Web: www.vibco.com						
Vibra Healthcare 4550 Lena Dr	Mechanicsburg	PA	17055	717-591-5700	591-5710	353
Web: www.vibrahealthcare.com						
Vibra Screw Inc 755 Union Blvd	Totowa	NJ	07512	973-256-7410	256-7567	470
TF: 800-243-7677 ■ *Web:* www.vibrascrew.com						
Vibranalysis Inc						
220 Plaza Western Auto	Trujillo Alto	PR	00976	787-283-7500		743
Web: www.vibranalysispr.com						
Vibrant Corp						
8330A Washington Pl NE	Albuquerque	NM	87113	505-314-1488		743
TF: 800-410-3048 ■ *Web:* www.vibrantndt.com						
Vibrant Media Inc						
300 Park Ave 12th Fl	New York	NY	10022	646-312-6100		7
Web: www.vibrantmedia.com						
Vibrant Power Inc						
310 Courtneypark Dr E	Mississauga	ON	L5T2S5	905-564-8644		480
Web: www.vibrantpower.com						
VibrantAds LLC						
2115 W Crescent Ave Ste 220	Anaheim	CA	92801	714-400-9898		737
Web: www.vibrantads.com						
Vibration Institute						
6262 Kingery Hwy # 212	Willowbrook	IL	60527	630-654-2254	654-2271	49-19
Web: www.vi-institute.org						
Vibration Mounting & Control						
113 Main St	Bloomingdale	NJ	07403	973-838-1780		454
Web: www.thevmcgroup.com						
Vibration Research Corp						
2385 Wilshere Dr # A	Jenison	MI	49428	616-669-3028		177
Web: www.vibrationresearch.com						
Vibro-Meter 144 Harvey Rd	Londonderry	NH	03053	603-669-0940	669-0931	22
TF: 877-666-0712 ■ *Web:* meggittsensing.com						
Vic Canever Chevrolet Inc 3000 Owen Rd	Fenton	MI	48430	810-519-5634		57
Web: www.viccaneverchevy.com						
Vic Firth Mfg 77 High St	Newport	ME	04953	207-368-4358		200
Web: www.vicfirthgourmet.com						
Vic's Accounting 897 Henderson Hwy	Winnipeg	MB	R2K2L8	204-668-3441		734
Web: allyear.ca						
Vical Inc 10390 Pacific Ctr Ct	San Diego	CA	92121	858-646-1100	646-1150	85
NASDAQ: VICL ■ *Web:* www.vical.com						
Vi-Cas Manufacturing Company Inc						
8407 Monroe Ave	Cincinnati	OH	45236	513-791-7741		596
Web: www.vi-cas.com						
Viccino 1317 N Charles St	Baltimore	MD	21201	410-347-0349		671
Web: www.viccino.com						
Viccs Inc 11821 Parklawn Dr Ste 224	Rockville	MD	20852	301-984-1355	984-1360	194
Web: www.viccs.com						
Vicenti Lloyd & Stutzman LLP						
[illegible]	Glendora	CA	91740	[illegible]		2
Web: vlsllp.com						
Viceroy Homes Ltd 414 Croft St E	Port Hope	ON	L1A4H1	905-800-0712		655
Web: www.viceroy.com						
Viceroy Palm Springs						
415 S BelaRdo Rd	Palm Springs	CA	92262	760-320-4117	329-5739*	379
**Fax Area Code:* 786 ■ *TF:* 866-781-9923 ■ *Web:* www.viceroyhotelsandresorts.com						
Viceroy Santa Monica						
1819 Ocean Ave	Santa Monica	CA	90401	310-260-7500		379
TF: 888-622-4567 ■ *Web:* viceroyhotelsandresorts.com						
Vi-Chem Corp						
55 Cottage Grove St SW	Grand Rapids	MI	49507	616-247-8501	247-8703	605-2
TF: 800-477-8501 ■ *Web:* www.vichem.com						
Vickers Engineering Inc						
3604 Glendora Rd PO Box 346	New Troy	MI	49119	269-426-8545	426-8494	454
Web: www.vickerseng.com						
Vicks Lithograph & Printing Co						
5166 Commercial Dr	Yorkville	NY	13495	315-736-9344		626
Web: www.vicks.biz						
Vicksburg National Military Park						
3201 Clay St	Vicksburg	MS	39183	601-636-0583	636-9497	564
Web: www.nps.gov/vick						
Vicksburg Post						
1601 N Frontage Rd Ste F	Vicksburg	MS	39180	601-636-4545	634-0897	532-2
Web: www.vicksburgpost.com						
Vicksburg-Warren County Chamber of Commerce						
2020 Mission 66	Vicksburg	MS	39180	601-636-1012	636-4422	139
TF: 800-772-1213 ■ *Web:* www.vicksburgchamber.org						
Vicom Computer Services Inc						
400 Broadhollow Rd	Farmingdale	NY	11735	631-694-3900		264-1
Web: www.vicomnet.com						
Vicon Industries Inc 89 Arkay Dr	Hauppauge	NY	11788	631-952-2288	951-2288	647
NYSE: VII ■ *TF Sales:* 800-645-9116 ■ *Web:* www.vicon-security.com						
Viconics Technologies Inc						
9245 Langelier Blvd	Saint-Leonard	QC	H1P3K9	514-321-5660		407
TF: 800-563-5660 ■ *Web:* www.viconics.com						
Vicor Corp 25 Frontage Rd	Andover	MA	01810	978-470-2900	475-6715	253
NASDAQ: VICR ■ *TF:* 800-869-5300 ■ *Web:* www.vicorpower.com						
Vicor Technologies Inc (NDA)						
399 Autumn Dr	Bangor	PA	18013	570-897-5797		250
Victaulic Co 4901 Kesslersville Rd	Easton	PA	18040	610-559-3300	250-8817	595
TF Sales: 800-742-5842 ■ *Web:* www.victaulic.com						
Victim Rights Law Center Inc						
115 Broad St Fl 3	Boston	MA	02110	617-399-6720		428
Web: www.victimrights.org						
Victor Elementary School District (VESD)						
12219 Second Ave	Victorville	CA	92395	760-245-1691	245-6245	685
Web: www.vesd.net						
Victor Insulators Inc 280 Maple Ave	Victor	NY	14564	585-924-2127	924-7906	249
Web: www.victorinsulators.com						
Victor International Corp						
7640 Dixie Hwy Ste 100	Clarkston	MI	48346	248-364-2400		652
Web: www.victorintl.com						
Victor J Rauch Consulting						
3410 Mission Ave Unit 3	Carmichael	CA	95608	916-485-1579		196
Victor L Phillips Co						
4100 Gardner Ave	Kansas City	MO	64120	816-241-9290	241-1738	358
TF: 800-878-9290 ■ *Web:* www.vlpco.com						

Company / Address	City	State	ZIP	Phone	Fax	Class
Victor O Schinnerer & Co Inc 2 Wisconsin Cir Ste 200 — *Web:* www.schinnerer.com	Chevy Chase	MD	20815	301-961-9800	951-5444	391-5
Victor Printing Inc 1 Victor Way — *TF:* 800-443-2845 ■ *Web:* www.victorptg.com	Sharon	PA	16146	724-342-2106		110
Victor Products USA 322 Commerce Pk Dr — *Web:* www.victorproductsusa.com	Cranberry Township	PA	16066	724-776-4900	776-3855	767
Victor Settings Inc 25 Brook Ave — *TF:* 800-322-9008 ■ *Web:* www.victorsettings.com	Maywood	NJ	07607	201-845-4433	712-0818	407
Victor Talbots Inc 47 Glen Cove Rd — *Web:* victortalbots.com	Greenvale	NY	11548	516-625-1787		157-2
Victor Technology LLC 175 E Crossroads Pkwy — *TF:* 800-628-2420 ■ *Web:* www.victortech.com	Bolingbrook	IL	60440	630-754-4400	972-3902	118
Victor Valley Community College 18422 Bear Valley Rd — *TF:* 877-741-8532 ■ *Web:* www.vvc.edu	Victorville	CA	92392	760-245-4271	245-9745	162
Victoria & Albert Hair Studio 10715 Charter Dr Ste 160 — *TF:* 800-561-3357 ■ *Web:* www.victoriaandalberthair.com	Columbia	MD	21044	410-992-3000		77
Victoria Advocate PO Box 1518 — **Fax:* News Rm ■ *TF:* 800-234-8108 ■ *Web:* www.victoriaadvocate.com	Victoria	TX	77902	361-575-1451	574-1220*	532-2
Victoria Air Conditioning Ltd 513 Profit Dr — *Web:* victoriaair.com	Victoria	TX	77901	361-578-5241		189-10
Victoria Chamber of Commerce 3404 N Ben Wilson St — *Web:* www.victoriachamber.org	Victoria	TX	77901	361-573-5277		139
Victoria College 2200 E Red River St — *TF:* 800-242-3062 ■ *Web:* www.vc.cc.tx.us	Victoria	TX	77901	361-573-3291	582-2525	162
Victoria County 115 N Bridge St Ste 103 — *Web:* www.victoriacountytx.org	Victoria	TX	77901	361-575-1478	575-6276	338
Victoria Cruises Inc 57-08 39th Ave — *TF Cust Svc:* 800-348-8084 ■ *Web:* www.victoriacruises.com	Woodside	NY	11377	212-818-1680	818-9889	221
Victoria Electric Co-op Inc (VEC) 102 S Ben Jordan St — *Web:* www.victoriaelectric.coop	Victoria	TX	77901	361-573-2428		245
Victoria General Hospital 2340 Pembina Hwy — *Web:* www.vgh.mb.ca	Winnipeg	MB	R3T2E8	204-477-3347		374-2
Victoria Inn Winnipeg 1808 Wellington Ave — *TF:* 877-842-4667 ■ *Web:* www.vicinn.com	Winnipeg	MB	R3H0G3	204-786-4801	786-1329	379
Victoria Insurance 22901 Millcreek Blvd — *TF:* 800-888-8424 ■ *Web:* www.victoriainsurance.com	Cleveland	OH	44122	216-896-6990		391-4
Victoria International Airport 1962 Canso Rd — *TF:* 866-844-4354 ■ *Web:* www.vih.com	North Saanich	BC	V8L5V5	250-656-3987	655-6839	359
Victoria Mansion 109 Danforth St — *TF:* 800-888-4287 ■ *Web:* www.victoriamansion.org	Portland	ME	04101	207-772-4841	772-6290	50-3
Victoria Regent Hotel, The 1234 Wharf St — *TF:* 800-663-7472 ■ *Web:* www.victoriaregent.com	Victoria	BC	V8W3H9	250-386-2211	386-2622	379
Victoria Shipyards Company Ltd 825 Admirals Rd — *TF:* 800-448-4177 ■ *Web:* www.seaspan.com/victoria-shipyards	Victoria	BC	V9A2P1	250-380-1602		698
Victoria Skimboards 2955 Laguna Canyon Rd Ste 1 — *Web:* ocean.victoriaskimboards.com	Laguna Beach	CA	92651	949-494-0059	494-5485	710
Victoria Theatre 138 N Main St — *TF:* 888-228-3630 ■ *Web:* www.victoriatheatre.com	Dayton	OH	45402	937-228-3630	449-5068	572
Victoria Vaudeville Theater 1228 Market St — *TF:* 800-505-7464 ■ *Web:* www.victoria-theater.com	Wheeling	WV	26003	304-233-7464		572
Victoria Vogue Inc 90 Southland Dr — *Web:* businessfinder.lehighvalleylive.com	Bethlehem	PA	18017	610-865-1500		214
Victoria's 7 First Ave SW — *Web:* www.victoriasmn.com	Rochester	MN	55902	507-280-6232		671
Victoria's Restaurant 2 Olive Ave Boardwalk Plz Hotel — *Web:* boardwalkplaza.com	Rehoboth Beach	DE	19971	302-227-0615		671
Victoria's Secret Stores 4 Limited Pkwy — *TF:* 800-411-5116 ■ *Web:* www.victoriassecret.com	Reynoldsburg	OH	43068	800-411-5116		157-6
Victorian Condo-Hotel & Conference Ctr 6300 Seawall Blvd — *TF:* 800-231-6363 ■ *Web:* www.victoriancondo.com	Galveston	TX	77551	409-740-3555	741-1676	379
Victorian Doll Museum 4332 Buffalo Rd — *Web:* chilidollhospital.com	North Chili	NY	14514	585-247-0130		520
Victorian Trading Co 15600 W 99th St — **Fax Area Code:* 800 ■ *TF Cust Svc:* 800-700-2035 ■ *Web:* www.victoriantradingco.com	Lenexa	KS	66219	913-438-3995	724-7697*	459
Victorian Village 12600 Renaissance Cir — *TF:* 800-509-2800 ■ *Web:* www.provinet.com	Homer Glen	IL	60491	708-301-0800		371
Victors & Spoils Inc 1904 Pearl St — *Web:* www.victorsandspoils.com	Boulder	CO	80302	720-305-9822		7
Victorville Chamber of Commerce 14174 Green Tree Blvd — *Web:* vvchamber.com	Victorville	CA	92395	760-245-6506	245-6505	139
Victory Education Partners Inc 12 W 19th St 9th FL — *Web:* victoryep.com	New York	NY	10011	212-786-7900	265-1742	734
Victory Electric Co-op Assn Inc 3230 N 14th Ave — *TF:* 800-279-7915 ■ *Web:* www.victoryelectric.net	Dodge City	KS	67801	620-227-2139	227-8819	245
Victory Energy Corp 220 Airport Rd — *Web:* www.victoryenergycorp.com	Indiana	PA	15701	724-349-6366		540
Victory Energy Operations LLC 10701 E 126th St N — *Web:* www.victoryenergyinc.com	Collinsville	OK	74021	918-274-0023		610
Victory Enterprises Inc 5200 30th St SW — *TF:* 800-670-5716 ■ *Web:* www.victoryenterprises.com	Davenport	IA	52802	563-884-4444		180
Victory Fiduciary Consulting 53 N Main St — *Web:* www.victoryasset.com	Mullica Hill	NJ	08062	856-464-3100		463
Victory Funds 4900 Tiedeman Rd Ste 400 PO Box 182593 — *TF:* 877-660-4400 ■ *Web:* www.vcm.com	Columbus	OH	43219	216-898-2400		528
Victory Furniture 9040 W Pico Blvd — *TF:* 800-953-2000 ■ *Web:* www.victoryfurniture.com	Los Angeles	CA	90035	800-953-2000		321
Victory Gardens Theater 2257 N Lincoln Ave — *Web:* victorygardens.org	Chicago	IL	60614	773-549-5788		749
Victory Heating & Air Conditioning Company Inc 115 Mendon St — *Web:* www.victoryhvac.com	Bellingham	MA	02019	508-966-9858		610
Victory Housing Inc 5430 Grosvenor Ln Ste 210 — *Web:* www.victoryhousing.org	Bethesda	MD	20814	301-493-6000	493-9788	653
Victory Lake Nursing Ctr 419 N Quaker Ln — *Web:* victorylakenursing.com	Hyde Park	NY	12538	845-229-9177		450
Victory Packaging LP 3555 Timmons Ln Ste 1440 — *Web:* www.victorypackaging.com	Houston	TX	77027	713-961-3299		100
Victory Petroleum Inc 2200 S Dixie Hwy Ste 601 — *Web:* www.victorypetroleum.com	Miami	FL	33133	305-255-4145		146
Victory Pharma Inc 11682 El Camino Real — *Web:* www.victorypharma.com	San Diego	CA	92130	858-720-4500		238
Victory Productions Inc 55 Linden St — *Web:* victoryprd.com	Worcester	MA	01609	508-755-0051		94
Victory Racing Plate Co, The 1200 Rosedale Ave — *Web:* www.victoryracingplate.com	Rosedale	MD	21237	410-391-6600		489
Victory Records Inc 346 N Justine St 5th Fl — *Web:* www.victoryrecords.com	Chicago	IL	60607	312-666-8661		657
Victory Refrigeration Inc 110 Woodcrest Rd — *TF:* 800-523-5008 ■ *Web:* www.victoryrefrigeration.com	Cherry Hill	NJ	08003	856-428-4200	428-7299	664
Victory Search Group 20701 N Scottsdale Rd Ste 107-300 — *TF:* 800-227-1447 ■ *Web:* www.victorysearchgroup.com	Scottsdale	AZ	85255	480-585-0073		260
Victory Studios 2247 15th Ave W — *TF:* 800-377-1132 ■ *Web:* www.victorystudios.com	Seattle	WA	98119	206-282-1776	282-3535	512
Victory Transportation Systems Inc 9009 N Loop E Ste 165 — *TF:* 800-734-4114 ■ *Web:* www.victorytrucks.com	Houston	TX	77029	713-682-8900		311
Victory White Metal Co 6100 Roland Ave — *TF:* 800-635-5050 ■ *Web:* www.victorywhitemetal.com	Cleveland	OH	44127	216-271-1400	271-6430	485
Victorystore.Com Inc 5200 SW 30Th St — *TF:* 866-241-2295 ■ *Web:* www.victorystore.com	Davenport	IA	52802	866-241-2295		627
Victrix 630 Sherbrooke St W Ste 1100 — *Web:* www.victrix.ca	Montreal	QC	H3A1E4	514-879-1919	879-1616	196
Victron Energy Inc 105 YMCA Dr — *Web:* victrongroup.com	Waxahachie	TX	75165	469-517-2000		581
Victus Inc 4918 SW 74th Ct — *Web:* www.victus.com	Miami	FL	33155	305-663-2129		231
Vicwest Corp 1296 S Service Rd W — *TF:* 800-265-6583 ■ *Web:* www.vicwest.com	Oakville	ON	L6L5T7	905-825-2252	825-2272	491
VIDA Diagnostics Inc 2500 Crosspark Rd W150 BioVentures Ctr — *TF:* 855-900-8432 ■ *Web:* www.vidadiagnostics.com	Coralville	IA	52241	855-900-8432		809
Vidal Partnership Inc, The 228 E 45th St 14th Fl — *Web:* www.vidalpartnership.com	New York	NY	10017	212-867-5185		4
Vidalia 1990 M St NW — *Web:* www.vidaliadc.com	Washington	DC	20036	202-659-1990		671
Vidaris Inc 360 Park Ave S — *Web:* www.vidaris.com	New York	NY	10010	212-689-5389		256
Video Advertising Bureau (CAB) 830 Third Ave 2nd Fl — *Web:* www.thevab.com	New York	NY	10022	212-508-1200	832-3268	49-18
Video Age International Magazine 216 E 75th St Ste PW — *Web:* www.vidooagointernational.com	New York	NY	10021	212-288-3933	734-9033	457-9
Video Data Bank 112 S Michigan Ave — *Web:* www.vdb.org	Chicago	IL	60603	312-345-3550	541-8073	511
Video Display Corp 1868 Tucker Industrial Rd — *NASDAQ:* VIDE ■ *TF Cust Svc:* 800-241-5005 ■ *Web:* www.videodisplay.com	Tucker	GA	30084	770-938-2080	493-3903	173-4
Video Hits One (VH1) 1515 Broadway — **Fax Area Code:* 201 ■ **Fax:* Hum Res ■ *Web:* www.vh1.com	New York	NY	10036	212-258-7800	422-6630*	740
Video Insight Inc 800 Gessner Rd Ste 700 — *TF:* 800-513-5417 ■ *Web:* www.video-insight.com	Houston	TX	77024	713-621-9779		180
Video King Gaming Systems (VKGS LLC) 2717 N 118 Cir Ste 210 — *TF:* 800-635-9912 ■ *Web:* www.videokingnetwork.com	Omaha	NE	68164	402-951-2970	951-2990	322
Video Post & Transfer Inc 2727 Inwood Rd — *Web:* www.videopost.com	Dallas	TX	75235	214-351-2885		512
Video Symphony Entertraining Inc 266 E Magnolia Blvd — *TF:* 888-370-7589 ■ *Web:* www.vs.edu	Burbank	CA	91502	818-557-6500		514
VideoBloom Inc 7350 E Progress Pl Ste 100 — *Web:* videobloom.com	Greenwood Village	CO	80111	303-694-7300		175
Videobred Inc 1000 Hamilton Ave — *Web:* www.videobred.com	Louisville	KY	40204	502-584-5787		514
Videoflicks Canada 1701 Ave Rd — *Web:* www.myvideoflicks.ca	Toronto	ON	M5M3Y3	416-782-1883		797
VideoIQ Inc 900 Middlesex TurnPk Bldg 5 — *Web:* www.videoiq.net	Billerica	MA	01821	781-222-3069		693

	Phone	Fax	Class
Videojet Technologies Inc 1500 Mittel Blvd .... Wood Dale IL 60191 *Fax: Mktg ■ TF Cust Svc: 800-843-3610 ■ Web: www.videojet.com	630-860-7300	616-3657*	386
Videoland Inc 6808 Hornwood Dr .... Houston TX 77074 *Fax Area Code: 713 ■ TF: 800-877-2900 ■ Web: www.hometheaterstore.com	800-877-2900	772-0500*	35
Videomaker Magazine 1350 E Ninth St PO Box 4591 .... Chico CA 95927 TF: 800-284-3226 ■ Web: www.videomaker.com	530-891-8410	891-8443	457-9
VideoMining Corp 403 S Allen St Ste 101 .... State College PA 16801 TF: 800-898-9950 ■ Web: www.videomining.com	800-898-9950		177
Videotex Systems Inc 10255 Miller Rd .... Dallas TX 75238 TF: 800-888-4336 ■ Web: www.videotexsystems.com	972-231-9200	231-2420	178-8
Videx Inc 1105 NE Cir Blvd .... Corvallis OR 97330 Web: www.videx.com	541-738-5500	738-5501	173-7
Vidler Water Company Inc 3480 GS Richards Blvd Ste 101 .... Carson City NV 89703 TF: 800-331-7310 ■ Web: www.vidlerwater.com	775-885-5000		539
Vidmaker Inc 612 W Main St Ste 300 .... Madison WI 53703 Web: www.vidmaker.com	608-620-6002		387
Vie de France Yamazaki Inc 2070 Chain Bridge Rd Ste 500 .... Vienna VA 22182 TF General: 800-446-4404 ■ Web: www.vdfy.com	703-442-9205		68
Vie-Del Co 11903 S Chestnut .... Fresno CA 93725	559-834-2525		80-3
Viejas Casino 5000 Willows Rd .... Alpine CA 91901 TF: 800-847-6537 ■ Web: www.viejas.com	619-445-5400		133
Viejas Outlet Ctr 5005 Willows .... Alpine CA 91901 TF: 877-303-2695 ■ Web: viejas.com	619-659-2070		460
Vieng Thai 6929 Long Pt St .... Houston TX 77055	713-688-9910		671
Vienna Correctional Ctr 6695 SR-146 E Ste 146 .... Vienna IL 62995	618-658-8371		213
Vienna Sausage Manufacturing Co 2501 N Damen Ave .... Chicago IL 60647 TF: 800-366-3647 ■ Web: www.viennabeef.com	773-278-7800		296-26
Vientiane Cafe 4728 Baltimore Ave .... Philadelphia PA 19143	215-726-1095		671
Vietnam 866 UN Plaza Ste 428 .... New York NY 10017 Web: www.un.int	212-644-0594	644-5732	784
Consulate General 1700 California St Ste 580 .... San Francisco CA 94109 TF: 800-262-6420 ■ Web: www.vietnamconsulate-sf.org	415-922-1707	922-1848	257
Embassy 1233 20th St NW Ste 400 .... Washington DC 20036 Web: vietnamembassy-usa.org	202-861-0737	861-0917	257
Vietnam Archive, The *Texas Tech University* PO Box 41041 .... Lubbock TX 79409 Web: www.vietnam.ttu.edu	806-742-9010	742-0496	434-4
Vietnam Cafe 2200 W 39th St .... Kansas City KS 66103 Web: thevietnamcafe.com	913-262-8552		671
Vietnam Education Foundation (VEF) 2200 Wilson Blvd Ste 205 .... Arlington VA 22201 *Fax Area Code: 703 ■ Web: home.vef.gov	571-800-9578	351-1423*	340-20
Vietnam Palace Restaurant 222 N 11th St .... Philadelphia PA 19107	215-592-9596		671
Vietnam Restaurant 221 N 11th St .... Philadelphia PA 19107 Web: www.eatatvietnam.com	215-592-1163		671
Vietnam Restaurant 701 N Water St .... Corpus Christi TX 78401 Web: www.vietnam-restaurant.com	361-853-2682		671
Vietnam Veterans of America 3027 Walnut St .... Kansas City MO 64108 Web: vva.org	816-561-8387		50-4
Vietnam Women's Memorial Foundation Inc 1735 Connecticut Ave NW 3rd Fl .... Washington DC 20009 TF: 866-822-8963 ■ Web: www.vietnamwomensmemorial.org	866-822-8963		50-4
Vietnamese Garden 304 Reily St .... Harrisburg PA 17102	717-238-9310		671
Vietnamese-American Chamber of Commerce of Hawaii PO Box 240352 .... Honolulu HI 96824 Web: www.vacch.org	808-545-1889		138
VIEW Micro-Metrology Inc 1711 W 17th St .... Tempe AZ 85281 Web: www.viewmm.com	480-295-3150		201
ViewCast Corp 3701 W Plano Pkwy Ste 300 .... Plano TX 75075 Web: www.viewcast.com	972-488-7200		176
Viewlocity Technologies 5339 Alpha Rd Ste 170 .... Dallas TX 75240 Web: www.viewlocity.com	972-715-0300		178-10
Viewmont Mall 100 Viewmont Mall .... Scranton PA 18508 Web: www.shopviewmontmall.com	570-346-9165		460
Viewpoint Books 548 Washington St .... Columbus IN 47201 Web: www.viewpointbooks.com	812-376-0778		95
ViewSonic Corp 381 Brea Canyon Rd .... Walnut CA 91789 TF: 800-888-8583 ■ Web: ap.viewsonic.com	909-444-8888	468-1240	173-4
Viewsonics Inc 3103 N Andrews Ave .... Pompano Beach FL 33064	954-971-8439	971-4422	246
Viewsource 11841 Mason Montgomery Rd Ste C .... Cincinnati OH 45249 Web: viewsource.com	513-671-6238		180
ViewTrade Securities Inc 525 Washington Blvd 24th Fl .... Jersey City NJ 07310 Web: www.viewtrade.com	201-215-9850		690
Vigen Construction Inc PO Box 6109 .... Grand Forks ND 58206 Web: www.vigenconstruction.com	218-773-1159	773-3454	261
Viget Labs LLC 400 S Maple Ave .... Falls Church VA 22046 Web: viget.com	703-891-0670		177
Vigi Sante Ltee 197 Thornhill .... Dollard-des-ormeaux QC H9B3H8 Web: www.vigisante.com	514-604-0930		371
Vigilant Capital Management LLC 2 City Ctr 4th Fl .... Portland ME 04101 Web: www.vigilantcap.com	207-523-1110		528
Vigilant Insurance Co 15 Mtn View Rd .... Warren NJ 07059 TF Claims: 800-252-4670 ■ Web: www.chubb.com	908-903-2000		391-4
Vigilant Technologies LLC 1050 Wilshire Dr Ste 307 .... Troy MI 48084 Web: www.vigt.com	248-614-2500		624
Vigilante Electric Co-op Inc 225 E Bannack St .... Dillon MT 59725 Web: www.vec.coop	406-683-2327	683-4328	245
Vigilistics Inc 711 Grand Ave Ste 290 .... San Rafael CA 94901 TF: 888-235-7540 ■ Web: www.vigilistics.com	949-900-8380		809
Viglione Heating & Cooling Inc 259 Commerce St .... East Haven CT 06512 Web: viglione.biz	203-787-8588		189-10
Vignette Corp 1301 S Mopac Expy Ste 100 .... Austin TX 78746 TF: 800-540-7292 ■ Web: www.opentext.com	512-741-4300		178-1
Vigo County 121 Oak St .... Terre Haute IN 47807 Web: www.vigocounty.in.gov	812-462-3367		338
Vigo County Public Library 1 Library Sq .... Terre Haute IN 47807 Web: www.vigo.lib.in.us	812-232-1113		434-3
Vigo Importing Co 4701 W Comanche Ave .... Tampa FL 33614 Web: www.vigo-alessi.com	813-884-3491		805
Vigor Industrial LLC 5555 N Channel Ave .... Portland OR 97217 Web: www.vigor.net	503-247-1777		698
VIH Logging Ltd 1962 Canso Rd .... North Saanich BC V8L5V5 TF: 866-844-4354 ■ Web: www.vih.com	250-656-3987	655-6839	359
Vi-Jon Labs Inc 8515 Page Ave .... Saint Louis MO 63114 TF: 800-227-1863 ■ Web: www.vijon.com	314-427-1000	427-1010	214
Viking Acoustical Corp 21480 Heath Ave .... Lakeville MN 55044 TF: 800-328-8385 ■ Web: www.vikingusa.com	952-469-3405	469-4503	319-1
Viking Automatic Sprinkler Co 301 York Ave .... Saint Paul MN 55130 Web: www.vikingsprinkler.com	651-558-3300	558-3310	189-13
Viking Client Services Inc 7500 Office Ridge Cir Ste 100 .... Eden Prairie MN 55344 TF: 800-767-7895 ■ Web: www.vikingservice.com	952-944-7575		393
Viking Corp 210 N Industrial Pk Dr .... Hastings MI 49058 TF: 800-968-9501 ■ Web: www.vikingcorp.com	269-945-9501	945-9599	283
Viking Drill & Tool Inc 355 State St .... Saint Paul MN 55107 TF: 800-328-4655 ■ Web: www.vikingdrill.com	651-227-8911	227-1793	493
Viking Drilling LLC 3720 S Co Rd 1309 .... Odessa TX 79765 Web: www.viking-drilling.com	432-550-0100		539
Viking Electric Supply Inc 451 Industrial Blvd W .... Minneapolis MN 55413 TF: 800-435-3345 ■ Web: www.vikingelectric.com	612-627-1300	627-1313	246
Viking Engineering & Development Inc 5750 Main St NE .... Fridley MN 55432 TF Sales: 800-328-2403 ■ Web: www.vikingeng.com	763-571-2400	586-1319	821
Viking Forest Products LLC 7615 Smetana Ln .... Eden Prairie MN 55344 TF: 800-733-3801 ■ Web: www.vikingforest.com	952-941-6512		191-3
Viking Group Inc 3033 Orchard Vista Dr SE Ste 308 .... Grand Rapids MI 49546 Web: vikinggroupinc.com	616-831-6448		360-3
Viking Lake State Park 2780 Viking Lake Rd .... Stanton IA 51573 Web: www.iowadnr.gov	712-829-2235	829-2842	565
Viking Materials Inc 3225 Como Ave SE .... Minneapolis MN 55414 TF General: 800-682-3942 ■ Web: www.vikingmaterials.com	612-617-5800	623-9070	492
Viking Metal Cabinet Co 24047 W Lockport St Ste 209 .... Plainfield IL 60544 *Fax Area Code: 630 ■ TF: 800-776-7767 ■ Web: www.vikingmetal.com	800-776-7767	863-7065*	286
Viking Networks Inc 4655 Middle Rd B .... Columbus IN 47203 Web: www.vikingnetworks.net	812-372-0007		180
Viking Oil Tools 25211 Grogans Mill Rd Ste 460 .... The Woodlands TX 77380	281-907-9676		539
Viking Paper Corp 5148 Stickney Ave .... Toledo OH 43612 Web: www.packpros.net	419-729-4951		554
Viking Plastics Inc 1 Viking St .... Corry PA 16407 Web: www.vikingplastics.com	814-664-8671		608
Viking Pools Inc 121 Crawford Rd PO Box 96 .... Williams CA 95987 TF: 800-854-7665 ■ Web: lathampool.com/vikingpools	530-473-5319	473-5393	728
Viking Pump Inc 406 State St .... Cedar Falls IA 50613 Web: www.vikingpump.com	319-266-1741	273-8157	641
Viking Range Corp 111 Front St .... Greenwood MS 38930 TF: 888-845-4641 ■ Web: www.vikingrange.com	662-455-1200	455-3127	298
Viking Recreational Vehicles LLC 580 W Burr Oak St PO Box 549 .... Centreville MI 49032 Web: coachmenrv.com	269-467-6321		120
Viking River Cruises 5700 Canoga Ave Ste 200 .... Woodland Hills CA 91367 TF Cust Svc: 877-668-4546 ■ Web: www.vikingrivercruises.com	818-227-1234	227-1237	221
Viking Ski Shop Inc 3422 W Fullerton Ave .... Chicago IL 60647 TF: 800-592-6883 ■ Web: vikingskishop.com	773-276-1222		711
Viking Speedway Inc PO Box 462 .... Alexandria MN 56308 Web: www.vikingspeedway.net	320-760-9614		515
Viking Trailways 201 Glendale Rd .... Joplin MO 64804 TF: 800-400-2779 ■ Web: trailways.com	417-781-2779		108
Viking Yacht Company Inc PO Box 308 .... New Gretna NJ 08224 Web: www.vikingyachts.com	609-296-6000	296-3956	90
Viking-Cives USA 14331 Mill St .... Harrisville NY 13648 Web: www.vikingcives.com	315-543-2321	543-2366	516
Vikmere Software PO Box 34521 .... Los Angeles CA 90034 Web: vikmere.com	310-836-2802		463
Viko Test Labs 2006 Martin Ave .... Santa Clara CA 95050	408-988-2181		794
Viktor Incentives & Meetings 4020 Copper View Ste 130 .... Traverse City MI 49684 TF: 800-748-0478 ■ Web: www.viktorwithak.com	231-947-0882	947-2532	384
Viktorina Cards 89 Stonehurst Ave Ste 311 .... Ottawa ON K1Y4R6 Web: www.amazzzingcards.com	613-422-6337		130
Vikus Corp 2255 Center St Ste 107 .... Chattanooga TN 37421 TF: 800-447-7108 ■ Web: www.vikus.com	423-954-3378		195
Vilas County 330 Ct St .... Eagle River WI 54521 TF: 800-236-8787 ■ Web: www.co.vilas.wi.us	715-479-3600	479-3605	338
Villa Angela Nursing Rehabilitation Ctr 5700 Karl Rd .... Columbus OH 43229 Web: villa-angela.net	614-846-5420		450

Phone | Fax | Class

Villa Antonio 4707 S Blvd Charlotte NC 28217 704-523-1594 671
Villa Camillus Inc, The
10515 E River Rd Columbia Station OH 44028 440-236-5091 371
TF: 800-282-1206 ■ *Web:* www.the-villa-camillus.com
Villa Europa 3044 Deans Bridge Rd Augusta GA 30906 706-798-6211 798-0066 671
Web: www.villaeuropa.com
Villa Feliciana Chronic Disease Hospital
5002 Hwy 10 Jackson LA 70748 225-634-4000 634-4191 374-7
Web: dhh.louisiana.gov
Villa Firenze 610 First Ave NE Calgary AB T2E0B6 403-264-4297 671
Web: villafirenze.ca
Villa Florence 225 Powell St San Francisco CA 94102 415-397-7700 397-1006 379
TF: 800-553-4411 ■ *Web:* www.villaflorence.com
Villa Gardens 842 E Villa St Pasadena CA 91101 626-463-5330 672
TF: 800-958-4552 ■ *Web:* www.villagardens.org
Villa Italian Kitchen
25 Washington St Morristown NJ 07960 973-285-4800 670
Web: www.villapizza.com
Villa Julie College
1525 Green Spring Valley Rd Stevenson MD 21153 410-486-7001 352-4440* 166
**Fax Area Code:* 443 ■ *TF:* 877-468-6852 ■ *Web:* stevenson.edu
Villa La PAWS LLC
3618 W Bell Rd Ste 1 Glendale AZ 85308 602-588-7833 794
TF: 800-614-1401 ■ *Web:* www.villalapaws.com
Villa Lighting Supply Inc
2929 Chouteau Ave Saint Louis MO 63103 800-325-0963 531-8720* 393
**Fax Area Code:* 866 ■ *TF:* 800-325-0963 ■ *Web:* www.villalighting.com
Villa Maria College 240 Pine Ridge Rd Buffalo NY 14225 716-896-0700 896-0705 162
Web: www.villa.edu
Villa Maria Healthcare Ctr
425 E Barcellus Ave Santa Maria CA 93454 805-922-3558 450
Villa Maria Nursing Center
1050 NE 125th St North Miami FL 33161 305-891-8850 374-6
Villa Marin 100 Thorndale Dr San Rafael CA 94903 415-492-2408 672
TF: 888-926-2030 ■ *Web:* www.villa-marin.com
Villa Nova Restaurant
5121 Arctic Blvd Ste I Anchorage AK 99503 907-561-1660 671
Web: villanovaalaska.com
Villa of Hope 3300 Dewey Ave Rochester NY 14616 585-865-1550 865-5219 726
Web: www.villaofhope.org
Villa Park Orchards Assn
960 Third St Fillmore CA 93016 805-524-0411 315-2
Web: vpoa.net
Villa Roma Resort & Conference Ctr
356 Villa Roma Rd Callicoon NY 12723 845-887-4880 887-4824 669
TF: 800-533-6767 ■ *Web:* www.villaroma.com
Villa Royale Inn 1620 Indian Trl Palm Springs CA 92264 760-327-2314 379
TF: 800-245-2314 ■ *Web:* www.villaroyale.com
Villa Terrace Decorative Arts Museum & Gardens
2220 N Terr Ave Milwaukee WI 53202 414-271-3656 271-3986 520
Web: www.villaterracemuseum.org
Villa Tronco 1213 Blanding St Columbia SC 29201 803-256-7677 256-4336 671
Web: www.villatronco.com
Villa Valencia
24552 Paseo de Valencia Laguna Hills CA 92653 949-581-6111 672
Web: www.fivestarseniorliving.com
Villa Y Zapata 8505 Madison Ave Cleveland OH 44102 216-961-4369 671
Village Art Supply 715 Hahman Dr Santa Rosa CA 95405 707-575-4501 45
Village at Breckenridge Resort
535 S Pk Ave Breckenridge CO 80424 970-453-3000 669
Web: www.breckenridgesports.com
Village at Manor Park, The (VMP)
3023 S 84th St Milwaukee WI 53227 414-607-4100 672
TF: 800-411-1861 ■ *Web:* www.vmpcares.com
Village Bank & Trust
234 W NW Hwy Arlington Heights IL 60004 847-670-1000 670-7744 70
Web: www.bankatvillage.com
Village Bistro, The
1723 Wilson Blvd Arlington VA 22209 703-522-5222 671
Web: frenchitalianarlingtonva.com
Village Builders
681 Greens Pkwy Ste 100 Houston TX 77067 281-874-8405 653
Web: www.lennar.com
Village Creek State Park
8854 Pk Rd 74 Lumberton TX 77657 409-755-7322 565
Web: tpwd.texas.gov
Village Creek State Park
201 County Rd 754 Wynne AR 72396 870-238-9406 565
Web: www.arkansasstateparks.com
Village Farms LP 7 Christopher Way Eatontown NJ 07724 732-676-3000 936-1187* 10-11
**Fax Area Code:* 407 ■ *Web:* www.villagefarms.com
Village Green Cos
30833 NW Hwy Ste 300 Farmington Hills MI 48334 248-851-9600 851-6161 187
Web: www.villagegreen.com
Village Green Heritage Ctr
221 S Palm Canyon Dr Palm Springs CA 92262 760-323-8297 320-2561 50-3
Web: www.pshistoricalsociety.org
Village Green of Waterbury
128 Cedar Ave Waterbury CT 06705 203-757-9271 450
Village Green Resort & Gardens
725 Row River Rd Cottage Grove OR 97424 541-942-2491 942-2386 669
Village Grille 1313 Louisiana Ave Shreveport LA 71101 318-424-2874 671
Village Inn 400 W 48th Ave Denver CO 80216 303-296-2121 670
TF: 800-800-3644 ■ *Web:* www.villageinn.com
Village Inteteriors 215 S Findlay St Seattle WA 98108 206-768-9600 393
Web: villageinteriorsdesign.com
Village Latch Inn
101 Hill St PO Box 3000 SouthHampton NY 11968 631-283-2160 283-3236 379
TF: 800-545-2824 ■ *Web:* www.villagelatch.com
Village Motors Inc 75 N Beacon St Boston MA 02134 617-560-1710 57
Web: www.villageautomotive.com
Village North Retirement Community
11160 Village N Dr Saint Louis MO 63136 314-355-8010 672
Web: www.bethesdahealth.org
Village Nurseries 1589 N Main St Orange CA 92867 800-542-0209 279-3199* 323
**Fax Area Code:* 714 ■ *TF:* 800-542-0209 ■ *Web:* www.villagenurseries.com
Village on the Green 500 Village Pl Longwood FL 32779 407-682-0230 672
TF Mktg: 888-541-3443 ■ *Web:* lifespacecommunities.com/senior-living-orlando

Village on Venetian Bay
4200 Gulf Shore Blvd N Naples FL 34103 239-261-6100 460
Web: www.venetianvillage.com
Village Pantry LLC
9800 Crosspoint Blvd Indianapolis IN 46256 317-594-2100 345
Web: www.marsh.net
Village South, The
169 E Flagler St Ste 1300 Miami FL 33131 305-573-3784 726
Village Square Nursing & Rehabilitation Ctr
1586 W San Marcos Blvd San Marcos CA 92078 760-471-2986 450
Web: www.villagesquarerehab.com
Village Super Market Inc
733 Mountain Ave Springfield NJ 07081 973-467-2200 345
NASDAQ: VLGEA ■ *TF:* 800-746-7748 ■ *Web:* www.shoprite.com
Village Tavern 1903 Westridge Rd Greensboro NC 27410 336-282-3063 671
Web: www.villagetavern.com
Village Tavern
11555 Rainwater Dr Haynes Rdg Rd Alpharetta GA 30009 770-777-6490 671
Web: www.villagetavern.com
Village Tavern 101 Summit Blvd Birmingham AL 35243 205-970-1640 671
Web: www.villagetavern.com
Village Toy Shop 2100 Patriot Blvd Glenview IL 60026 847-832-6908 761
Web: www.kohlchildrensmuseum.org
Village Vacances Valcartier
1860 Valcartier Blvd Valcartier QC G0A4S0 418-844-2200 844-1239 32
TF: 888-384-5524 ■ *Web:* www.valcartier.com
Village, The 2200 W Acacia Ave Hemet CA 92545 951-658-3369 672
TF: 800-257-7888 ■ *Web:* thevillageriversidecounty.com
Villager, The 145 Sixth Ave 1st Fl New York NY 10013 212-229-1890 229-2790 532-4
Web: www.thevillager.com
Villages of Lake Sumter Inc
1000 Lake Sumter Landing The Villages FL 32162 352-753-2270 653
TF: 800-245-1081 ■ *Web:* www.thevillages.com
Villagio Inn & Spa
6481 Washington St Yountville CA 94599 707-944-8877 379
TF: 800-351-1133 ■ *Web:* www.villagio.com
Villanova Preparatory School
12096 N Ventura Ave Ojai CA 93023 805-646-1464 622
Web: www.villanovaprep.org
Villanova University
800 Lancaster Ave Villanova PA 19085 610-519-4500 166
Web: www.villanova.edu
Villanova University Falvey Memorial Library
800 Lancaster Ave Villanova PA 19085 610-519-4270 434-6
Web: www.library.villanova.edu
Villanova University School of Law
299 N Spring Mill Rd Villanova PA 19085 610-519-7000 167-1
Web: www1.villanova.edu
Villanti & Sons, Printers Inc
15 Catamount Dr Milton VT 05468 802-864-0723 627
TF: 800-882-1844 ■ *Web:* www.villanti.com
Villaris Martial Arts
645 Poquonock Ave Windsor CT 06095 508-752-0091 507
TF: 800-764-8205 ■ *Web:* www.villarisshrewsbury.com/Contact-Us.html
Villarosa Italian Restaurant & Grill
6010 Landmark Ctr Blvd Greensboro NC 27407 336-294-8688 671
Web: villarosa.us
Villas by the Sea Resort
1175 N Beachview Dr Jekyll Island GA 31527 912-635-2521 635-2569 669
TF: 800-841-6262 ■ *Web:* www.villasbythesearesort.com
Villas de Santa Fe 400 Griffin St Santa Fe NM 87501 505-988-3000 379
Web: www.diamondresorts.com
Villas of Grand Cypress Golf Resort
1 N Jacaranda Orlando FL 32836 407-239-4700 669
TF: 877-330-7377 ■ *Web:* www.grandcypress.com
Villas on the Bay
105 Marine St Saint Augustine FL 32084 904-599-7301 379
Web: thevillas.com
Villaume Industries Inc
2926 Lone Oak Cir Eagan MN 55121 651-454-3610 454-8556 817
TF Cust Svc: 800-488-3610 ■ *Web:* www.villaume.com
Villaverd Inc
1218 E Yandell Dr Ste 201 El Paso TX 79902 915-351-8822 261
Web: villaverdeinc.com
Ville De Riviere-Du-Loup
65 Rue De Lehetel-De-Ville Riviere-du-loup QC G5R1L4 418-867-6700 31
Web: www.ville.riviere-du-loup.qc.ca
Villere's Florist
750 Martin Behrman Ave Metairie LA 70005 504-833-3716 292
TF: 800-845-5373 ■ *Web:* www.villeresflowers.com
Villeroy & Boch USA Inc
3A S Middlesex Ave Monroe Township NJ 08331 800-536-2284 655-2421* 362
**Fax Area Code:* 609 ■ *TF:* 800-536-2284 ■ *Web:* www.villeroy-boch.com
Villing & Company Inc
5909 Nimtz Pkwy South Bend IN 46628 574-277-0215 7
Web: villing.com
VIMAC Ventures LLC 177 Milk St Boston MA 02109 617-350-9800 350-9899 792
Web: www.vimac.com
Vimarc Group Inc, The
1205 E Washington St Ste 120 Louisville KY 40206 502-261-9100 7
Web: www.vimarc.com
Vimco Inc
300 Hansen Access Rd King Of Prussia PA 19406 610-768-0500 768-0586 191-1
TF Cust Svc: 888-468-4626 ■ *Web:* www.vimcoinc.com
Vimich Traffic Logistics
12201 Tecumseh Rd E Tecumseh ON N8N1M3 800-284-1045 735-4309* 449
**Fax Area Code:* 519 ■ *TF:* 800-284-1045 ■ *Web:* www.vimich.com
VIMS (Virginia Institute of Marine Science)
1208 Greate Rd PO Box 1346 Gloucester Point VA 23062 804-684-7000 684-7097 668
Web: www.vims.edu
Vin de Set Rooftop Bar & Bistro
2017 Chouteau Ave St Louis MO 63103 314-241-8989 671
Web: vindeset.com
Vin Devers Inc 5570 Monroe St Sylvania OH 43560 419-885-5111 57
TF: 888-847-9535 ■ *Web:* www.vindevers.com
Vincennes University
1002 N First St Vincennes IN 47591 812-888-4313 888-5707* 162
**Fax:* Admissions ■ *TF:* 800-742-9198 ■ *Web:* my.vinu.edu/home

Phone Fax Class

Jasper 850 College Ave........................ Jasper IN 47546 812-482-3030 481-5960* 162
**Fax:* Admissions ■ *TF:* 800-809-8852 ■ *Web:* www.vinu.edu
Vincent Benjamin Group Llc
2415 E Camelback Rd Ste 1000................ Phoenix AZ 85016 602-595-9900 260
Web: www.vincentbenjamin.com
Vincent Corp 2810 E Fifth Ave.................. Tampa FL 33605 813-248-2650 111
Web: www.vincentcorp.com
Vincent Giordano Corp
2600 Washington Ave.................... Philadelphia PA 19146 215-467-6629 467-6339 296-26
Web: www.vgiordano.com
Vincent Guerithault on Camelback
3930 E Camelback Rd......................... Phoenix AZ 85018 602-224-0225 956-5400 671
Web: www.vincentsoncamelback.com
Vincent Industrial Plastics Inc
232 Heilman Ave.......................... Henderson KY 42420 270-827-8881 596
Web: www.vip-plastics.com
Vincent Printing Company Inc
1512 Sholar Ave......................... Chattanooga TN 37406 800-251-7262 687
TF: 800-251-7262 ■ *Web:* www.vincentprinting.com
Vincent's 2432 Preston Rd...................... Plano TX 75093 972-612-6208 671
Vincent's 7839 St Charles Ave.............. New Orleans LA 70118 504-866-9313 671
Web: www.vincentsitaliancuisine.com
Vincent's 4411 Chastant St.................... Metairie LA 70006 504-885-2984 671
Web: www.vincentsitaliancuisine.com
Vincenzo's 3449 Robinhood Rd........... Winston-Salem NC 27106 336-765-3176 671
Web: vincenzospizzawinstonsalemnc.com
Vincenzo's 150 S Fifth St..................... Louisville KY 40202 502-580-1350 671
Web: www.vincenzositalianrestaurant.com
Vinchem Inc 301 Main St....................... Chatham NJ 07928 973-635-4841 635-1459 479
Web: www.vinchem.com
Vincit Group, The
412 Georgia Ave Ste 300................... Chattanooga TN 37403 888-484-6248 265-9070* 355
**Fax Area Code:* 423 ■ *TF:* 888-484-6248 ■ *Web:* www.vincitgroup.com
Vinco Inc PO Box 907...................... Forest Lake MN 55025 651-982-4642 186
Web: www.vinco-inc.com
Vindicator, The 107 Vindicator Sq.......... Youngstown OH 44503 330-747-1471 747-6712 532-2
Web: www.vindy.com
Vineland Construction Co 71 W Pk Ave........ Vineland NJ 08360 856-794-4500 794-4721 653
Web: www.vinelandconstruction.com
Vineland Public Library
1058 E Landis Ave.......................... Vineland NJ 08360 856-794-4244 434-3
Web: www.vineland.lib.nj.us
Vinely
1 Kendall Sq Bldg 400 B4202
Bldg 400 Ste B4202....................... Cambridge MA 02139 888-294-1128 387
TF: 888-294-1128
Vinery Kentucky LLC 4241 Spurr Rd.......... Lexington KY 40511 859-455-9388 368
Vineyard Gazette Inc 34 S Summer St........ Edgartown MA 02539 508-627-4311 532-3
Web: vineyardgazette.com
Vineyards Wine Bar Bistro 54 York St.......... Ottawa ON K1N5T1 613-241-4270 241-5538 671
Web: www.vineyards.ca
Vinfen Corp 950 Cambridge St............... Cambridge MA 02141 617-441-1800 441-1858 450
Web: www.vinfen.org
Vining Sparks IBG LP
775 Ridge Lake Blvd....................... Memphis TN 38120 901-766-3000 690
TF: 800-829-0321 ■ *Web:* www.viningsparks.com
Vinings Jubilee
4300 Paces Ferry Rd SE Ste 245............... Atlanta GA 30339 770-438-8080 438-8181 460
Web: www.viningsjubilee.com
Vinnell Corp 12150 E Monument Dr............. Fairfax VA 22033 703-385-4544 271
Vino Farms Inc 1377 E Lodi Ave.................... Lodi CA 95240 209-334-6975 315-5
Vinoleo Solution & Services Corp
186 Bay 20th St............................ Brooklyn NY 11214 718-837-2163 174
TF: 800-331-5114 ■ *Web:* www.vinoleoinc.com
Vinology 110 S Main St....................... Ann Arbor MI 48104 734-222-9841 671
Web: vinologya2.com
Vinotemp International Corp
16782 Von Karman Ave Ste 15.................... Irvine CA 92606 310-886-3332 610
Web: www.vinotemp.com
Vinotheque Wine Cellars
1738 E Alpine Ave.......................... Stockton CA 95205 209-466-9463 14
Web: www.vinotheque.com
Vinson & Elkins LLP
1001 Fannin St Ste 2500..................... Houston TX 77002 713-758-2222 758-2346 428
Web: www.velaw.com
Vinson Guard Service Inc
955 Howard Ave.......................... New Orleans LA 70113 504-529-2260 693
TF: 800-441-7899 ■ *Web:* www.vinsonguard.com
Vinson Process Controls Company LP
2747 Highpoint Oaks Dr..................... Lewisville TX 75067 972-459-8200 358
TF: 800-420-6571 ■ *Web:* www.vpcco.com
Vinsys Information Technology Inc
12073 Greywing Sq.......................... Reston VA 20191 703-371-4120 396
Web: www.vinsysinfo.com
Vintage Air Inc 18865 Goll St............... San Antonio TX 78266 210-654-7171 664
TF: 800-862-6658 ■ *Web:* www.vintageair.com
Vintage Chophouse & Tavern
320 11 Ave SW.............................. Calgary AB T2R0C5 403-262-7262 671
Web: www.vintagechophouse.com
Vintage Design Inc 5 Whatney...................... Irvine CA 92618 949-900-5400 561-3279* 291
**Fax Area Code:* 650 ■ *Web:* www.vintagedesigninc.com
Vintage Faire Mall
3401 Dale Rd Ste 483........................ Modesto CA 95356 209-527-3401 460
Web: www.shopvintagefairemall.com
Vintage Flying Museum
505 NW 38th St Hanger 33 S................. Fort Worth TX 76106 817-624-1935 520
Web: www.vintageflyingmuseum.org
Vintage Inn Napa Valley
6541 Washington St......................... Yountville CA 94599 800-351-1133 379
TF Cust Svc: 800-351-1133 ■ *Web:* www.vintageinn.com
Vintage IT Services 1210 W Fifth St................ Austin TX 78703 512-481-1117 196
TF: 800-213-8175 ■ *Web:* www.vintageits.com
Vintage Realty Co
330 Marshall St Ste 200.................... Shreveport LA 71101 318-222-2244 652
Web: www.vintagerealty.com
Vintage Wines 2277 Westbrooke Dr........... Columbus OH 43228 614-876-2580 443
TF: 800-231-9463 ■ *Web:* www.vintwine.com

Vintage, The 837 Lincoln St..................... Eugene OR 97401 541-349-9181 671
Web: thevintageeugene.com
Vintners Inn 4350 Barnes Rd................. Santa Rosa CA 95403 707-575-7350 575-1426 379
TF: 800-421-2584 ■ *Web:* www.vintnersinn.com
Vinton County
100 E Main St County Courthouse............ McArthur OH 45651 740-596-4571 596-4571 338
Web: www.vintoncounty.com
Vinyl Corp 8000 NW 79th Pl....................... Miami FL 33166 305-477-6464 596
Web: www.vinylcorp.com
Vinyl Siding Institute (VSI)
1201 15th St NW Ste 220.................. Washington DC 20005 202-587-5100 49-13
Web: www.vinylsiding.org
Vinyl Window Technologies Inc
PO Box 588................................ Paducah KY 42002 270-442-7870 608
Web: www.viwintech.com
Vinylex Corp 2636 Byington Rd................ Knoxville TN 37931 865-690-2211 691-6273* 600
**Fax:* Cust Svc ■ *TF:* 800-251-9415 ■ *Web:* www.omegaplastics.com
VINYLMAX LLC 2921 McBride Ct.............. Hamilton OH 45011 513-772-2247 235
Web: www.vinylmax.com
Vinylplex Inc 1800 Atkinson Ave............... Pittsburg KS 66762 620-231-8290 232-8547 596
TF: 877-779-7473 ■ *Web:* www.vinylplex.com/main.html
Vinyltech Corp 201 S 61st Ave................. Phoenix AZ 85043 602-233-0071 272-4847 596
TF: 800-255-3924 ■ *Web:* www.vtpipe.com
Viodi View, The
4285 Payne Ave Ste 10065 PO Box 10065....... San Jose CA 95157 408-676-6496 565-0320* 116
**Fax Area Code:* 832 ■ *Web:* www.viodi.com
Viola Bros Inc 180 Washington Ave.............. Nutley NJ 07110 973-667-7000 364
Web: www.violabros.com
Violence Policy Ctr (VPC)
1730 Rhode Island Ave NW Ste 1014......... Washington DC 20036 202-822-8200 48-7
Web: www.vpc.org
ViOptix Inc 47224 Mission Falls Ct.............. Fremont CA 94539 510-226-5860 743
Web: www.vioptix.com
Viox Services Inc 15 W Voorhees St.......... Cincinnati OH 45215 513-948-8469 271
TF: 888-846-9462 ■ *Web:* www.viox-services.com
Vip Auto Group 2006 Hwy 161.......... North Little Rock AR 72117 501-955-5556 57
Vip Cruises & Travel
22 Cleveland Terr....................... West Orange NJ 07052 985-626-9104 775
Web: www.myvipcruises.com
VIP Motor Cars Ltd
4095 E Palm Canyon Dr.................. Palm Springs CA 92264 760-328-6525 57
Vip Sports Marketing Inc
3319 N Elston Ave.......................... Chicago IL 60618 312-951-0700 195
Web: www.vipsm.com
Vip Technology Solutions Group LLC
12149 S State Hwy 51........................ Coweta OK 74429 918-279-7000 175
Web: viptsg.com
VIP Tires & Service 12 Lexington St........... Lewiston ME 04240 207-784-5423 784-9178 62-5
Web: www.vipauto.com
VIP Tour & Charter Bus Co
129-137 Fox St............................ Portland ME 04101 207-772-4457 772-7020 107
Web: www.vipchartercoaches.com
Vip Tours of California Inc
9030 Dellanca Ave....................... Los Angeles CA 90045 310-641-8114 700
TF: 800-438-1814 ■ *Web:* www.viptoursofcalifornia.com
VIPdesk Connect Inc
908 King St Ste 400W..................... Alexandria VA 22314 844-874-3472 393
TF: 844-874-3472 ■ *Web:* www.vipdeskconnect.com
Vira I Heinz Endowment
625 Liberty Ave 30 Dominion Twr............. Pittsburgh PA 15222 412-281-5777 281-5788 305
Web: www.heinz.org
VIRA Insight LLC
120 Dividend Dr ÿSuite 100.................... Coppell TX 75019 800-305-8472 424-9002* 286
**Fax Area Code:* 817 ■ *TF:* 800-305-8472 ■ *Web:* www.virainsight.com/welcome
Viracon Inc 800 Pk Dr...................... Owatonna MN 55060 507-451-9555 444-3555 329
TF: 800-533-2080 ■ *Web:* www.viracon.com
Virbac Corp 3200 Meacham Blvd............. Fort Worth TX 76137 817-831-5030 578
Web: www.virbac.com
Virco Manufacturing Corp
2027 Harpers Way.......................... Torrance CA 90501 310-533-0474 258-7367* 319-3
NASDAQ: VIRC ■ **Fax Area Code:* 800 ■ *TF Cust Svc:* 800-448-4726 ■ *Web:* www.virco.com
Virent Energy Systems Inc
3571 Anderson St.......................... Madison WI 53704 608-663-0228 261
Web: www.virent.com
Virgin Atlantic Airways Ltd
75 N Water St.............................. Norwalk CT 06850 800-862-8621 750-6430* 25
**Fax Area Code:* 203 ■ **Fax:* Mktg ■ *TF:* 888-747-7474 ■ *Web:* www.virginatlantic.com
Virgin Atlantic Cargo
78 N Boundary Rd Bldg 15.................. Jamaica NY 11430 516-775-2600 12
TF: 800-828-6822 ■ *Web:* www.virginatlantic.com
Virgin Media Inc
65 Bleecker St 6th Fl...................... New York NY 10022 212-906-8440 387
Web: www.virginmedia.com
Virgin Mobile USA Inc
10 Independence Blvd........................ Warren NJ 07059 888-322-1122 736
TF: 888-322-1122 ■ *Web:* www.virginmobileusa.com
Virgin River Casino Corp
100 Pioneer Blvd.......................... Mesquite NV 89027 877-438-2929 378
TF: 877-438-2929 ■ *Web:* www.virginriver.com
Virginia
Aging & Rehabilitative Services Dept
8004 Franklin Farms Dr.................. Richmond VA 23229 804-662-7000 339-47
TF: 800-552-5019 ■ *Web:* www.vadrs.org
Aging Dept 1610 Forest Ave Ste 100........... Richmond VA 23229 804-662-9333 662-9354 339-47
TF: 800-552-3402 ■ *Web:* www.vda.virginia.gov
Agriculture & Consumer Services Dept
102 Governor St Ste 210.................. Richmond VA 23219 804-786-3501 371-2945 339-47
Web: www.vdacs.virginia.gov
Arts Commission 600 E Main St 2nd Fl........ Richmond VA 23219 804-225-3132 225-4327 339-47
Web: www.arts.virginia.gov
Attorney General 202 N Ninth St.............. Richmond VA 23219 804-786-2071 786-1991 339-47
Web: www.oag.state.va.us
Chief Medical Examiner
400 E Jackson St......................... Richmond VA 23219 804-786-2479 225-2766 339-47
Web: www.vdh.virginia.gov/medexam
Child Support Enforcement Div
730 E Broad St........................... Richmond VA 23219 804-692-1900 339-47
Web: www.dss.state.va.us

	Phone	Fax	Class
Community College System 300 Arboretum Pl Ste 200 .... Richmond VA 23236 *TF:* 844-897-9096 ■ *Web:* www.vccs.edu	844-897-9096	897-9096	339-47
Corrections Dept 6900 Atmore Dr .... Richmond VA 23225 *Web:* vadoc.virginia.gov	804-674-3000	674-3236	339-47
Criminal Injuries Compensation Fund (CICF) PO Box 26927 .... Richmond VA 23261 **Fax Area Code:* 804 ■ *TF:* 800-552-4007 ■ *Web:* www.cicf.state.va.us	800-552-4007	367-1021*	339-47
Economic Development Partnership 901 E Cary St.......................... Richmond VA 23219 *Web:* www.yesvirginia.org	804-545-5600	371-8112	339-47
Education Dept PO Box 2120............... Richmond VA 23218 *Web:* www.pen.k12.va.us	804-225-2020		339-47
Emergency Management Dept 10501 Trade Ct .... Richmond VA 23236 *Web:* vaemergency.gov	804-897-6500	897-6506	339-47
Employment Commission 703 E Main St ...... Richmond VA 23219 *TF:* 866-832-2363 ■ *Web:* www.vec.virginia.gov	866-832-2363		259
Environmental Quality Dept 629 E Main St PO Box 1105 .... Richmond VA 23240 *TF:* 800-592-5482 ■ *Web:* www.deq.state.va.us	804-698-4000		339-47
Financial Institutions Bureau 1300 E Main St .... Richmond VA 23219 *Web:* www.scc.virginia.gov	804-371-9657		339-47
Game & Inland Fisheries Dept 7870 Villa Park Dr Ste 400 .... Henrico VA 23230 *Web:* www.dgif.virginia.gov	804-367-1000		339-47
General Assembly 900 E Main St Pocahontas Building .... Richmond VA 23219 *Web:* virginiageneralassembly.gov	804-786-9631		339-47
Governor 1111 E Broad St PO Box 1475....... Richmond VA 23219 *Web:* www.governor.virginia.gov	804-786-2211		339-47
Health Dept 109 Governor St PO Box 2448............ Richmond VA 23219 *Web:* www.vdh.virginia.gov	804-864-7001	864-7022	339-47
Health Professions Dept 9960 Mayland Dr Ste 300 .... Henrico VA 23233 *TF:* 800-533-1560 ■ *Web:* www.dhp.virginia.gov	804-367-4400	527-4475	339-47
Historic Resources Dept 2801 Kensington Ave.................... Richmond VA 23221 *Web:* www.dhr.virginia.gov	804-367-2323	367-2391	339-47
Housing Development Authority 601 S Belvidere St...................... Richmond VA 23220 *TF:* 877-843-2123 ■ *Web:* www.vhda.com	877-843-2123		339-47
Human Resource Management Dept 101 N 14th St 12th Fl................... Richmond VA 23219 *Web:* www.dhrm.virginia.gov	804-225-2131	371-7401	339-47
Information Technologies Agency (VITA) 11751 Meadowville Ln..................... Chester VA 23836 **Fax Area Code:* 804 ■ *TF:* 866-637-8482 ■ *Web:* www.vita.virginia.gov	866-637-8482	416-6355*	339-47
Labor & Industry Dept Main St Centre Bldg 600 E Main St Ste 207 .. Richmond VA 23219 *Web:* www.doli.virginia.gov	804-371-2327	371-6524	339-47
Lieutenant Governor 102 Governor St......... Richmond VA 23219 *Web:* www.ltgov.virginia.gov	804-786-2078	786-7514	339-47
Lottery 600 E Main St .... Richmond VA 23219 *Web:* www.valottery.com	804-692-7000	692-7102	452
Mental Health Mental Retardation & Substance Abuse 1220 Bank St.......................... Richmond VA 23219 *Web:* www.dbhds.virginia.gov	804-786-3921	371-6638	339-47
Parole Board 6900 Atmore Dr .... Richmond VA 23225 *Web:* vpb.virginia.gov	804-674-3081	674-3284	339-47
Port Authority 101 W Main St Ste 600............Norfolk VA 23510 *Web:* www.portofvirginia.com	757-296-3505	683-8500	339-47
Professional & Occupational Regulation Dept 9960 Mayland Dr # 400 Ste 400 .... Richmond VA 23233 *Web:* www.dpor.virginia.gov	804-367-8500		339-47
Racing Commission 5707 Horsemen Rd Ste 201-B............. Richmond VA 23124 *Web:* www.vrc.virginia.gov	804-966-7400	966-7418	339-47
Secretary of Commerce and Trade 1111 E Broad St PO Box 1475............. Richmond VA 23219 *Web:* www.commerce.virginia.gov	804-786-7831	371-0250	339-47
Secretary of the Commonwealth 830 E Main St 14th Fl .... Richmond VA 23219 *Web:* commonwealth.virginia.gov	804-786-2441	371-0017	339-47
Social Services Dept 801 E Main St .... Richmond VA 23219 *TF:* 800-552-3431 ■ *Web:* www.dss.state.va.us	804-726-7000		339-47
State Corp Commission 1300 E Main St PO Box 1197 .... Richmond VA 23218 *TF:* 800-552-7945 ■ *Web:* www.scc.virginia.gov	804-371-9967	371-9836	339-47
State Council of Higher Education 101 N 14th St 9th Fl, James Monroe Bldg.... Richmond VA 23219 *Web:* www.schev.edu	804-225-2600	225-2604	725
State Parks Div 203 Governor St Ste 306 .... Richmond VA 23219 *TF Resv:* 800-933-7275 ■ *Web:* dcr.virginia.gov/state-parks	804-786-5055	786-9294	339-47
State Police 7700 Midlothian Tpke North Chesterfield .... Richmond VA 23235 *Web:* www.vsp.state.va.us	804-674-2000	674-2936	339-47
Supreme Court 100 N Ninth St 5th Fl .... Richmond VA 23219 *Web:* vcsc.virginia.gov	804-786-2251		339-47
Taxation Dept 3610 W Broad St Ste 101 .... Richmond VA 23230 *Web:* www.tax.virginia.gov	804-367-8031	786-3536	339-47
Treasury Dept 101 N 14th St Ste 4th .... Richmond VA 23219 *Web:* www.trs.virginia.gov	804-225-2142		339-47
Vital Records Div 2001 Maywill St PO Box 1000............ Richmond VA 23230 *TF:* 877-572-6333 ■ *Web:* www.vdh.virginia.gov/vitalrec	804-662-6200	644-2550	339-47
Workers Compensation Commission 1000 DMV Dr.......................... Richmond VA 23220 *TF:* 877-664-2566 ■ *Web:* www.vwc.state.va.us	804-205-3603	367-9740	339-47
Virginia 529 9001 Arboretum Pkwy............ Richmond VA 23236 *TF:* 888-567-0540 ■ *Web:* www.virginia529.com	804-786-0719		725
Virginia Air & Space Center 600 Settlers Landing Rd .... Hampton VA 23669 *TF:* 800-296-0800 ■ *Web:* www.vasc.org	757-727-0900		748
Virginia American Water Co (VAWC) 2223 Duke St .... Alexandria VA 22314 *TF:* 800-452-6863 ■ *Web:* www.amwater.com	703-706-3879		787
Virginia Aquarium & Marine Science Ctr 717 General Booth Blvd ....Virginia Beach VA 23451 *TF:* 800-822-3224 ■ *Web:* www.virginiaaquarium.com/pages/default.aspx	757-385-3474		520
Virginia Aviation Museum 5701 Huntsman Rd........................ Richmond VA 23250 *Web:* www.vam.smv.org	804-236-3622		520
Virginia Baptist Hospital 3300 Rivermont Ave ....Lynchburg VA 24503 *TF:* 866-749-4455 ■ *Web:* www.centrahealth.com	434-947-4000		374-3
Virginia Beach City Hall 2401 Courthouse Dr Municipal Ctr Bldg 1 ....Virginia Beach VA 23456 *Web:* www.vbgov.com	757-385-3111		337
Virginia Beach Convention & Visitor Bureau (VBCVB) 2101 Parks Ave Ste 500 ....Virginia Beach VA 23451 *TF:* 800-700-7702 ■ *Web:* www.visitvirginiabeach.com	757-385-4700	437-4747	206
Virginia Beach (Independent City) 2401 Courthouse Dr Municipal Ctr Bldg 1 ....Virginia Beach VA 23456 *Web:* www.vbgov.com	757-385-4242	427-5626	338
Virginia Beach Public Library 4100 Virginia Beach Blvd...............Virginia Beach VA 23452 *Web:* vbgov.com/government/departments/libraries	757-385-0150		434-3
Virginia Beach Resort Hotel & Conference Ctr 2800 Shore Dr ....Virginia Beach VA 23451 *TF:* 800-468-2722 ■ *Web:* www.virginiabeachresort.com	757-481-9000		669
Virginia Business Magazine 333 E Franklin St .... Richmond VA 23219 *Web:* www.virginiabusiness.com	804-649-6999		457-5
Virginia Capital Partners LLC 1801 Libbie Ave Ste 201.................... Richmond VA 23226 *Web:* www.vacapital.com	804-648-4802		402
Virginia Chamber of Commerce 919 E Main St............................ Richmond VA 23219 *TF:* 800-228-9290 ■ *Web:* www.vachamber.com	804-644-1607	783-6112	140
Virginia College			
Birmingham 488 Palisades Blvd ....Birmingham AL 35209 *TF:* 800-584-7290 ■ *Web:* www.vc.edu	205-802-1200		800
Huntsville 2021 Drake Ave SW .... Huntsville AL 35801 *Web:* www.vc.edu	256-533-7387	533-7785	800
Virginia College Gulf Coast 920 Cedar Lake Rd ....Biloxi MS 39532 *Web:* www.vc.edu	228-392-2994	392-2039	800
Virginia College Jackson 5841 Ridgewood Rd ....Jackson MS 39211 *Web:* www.vc.edu	601-977-0960		800
Virginia Commonwealth University 910 W Franklin St.......................... Richmond VA 23284 *TF:* 800-841-3638 ■ *Web:* www.vcu.edu	804-828-0100	828-1899	166
Virginia Commonwealth University Cabell Library 901 Pk Ave PO Box 842033 .... Richmond VA 23284 *TF:* 844-352-7399 ■ *Web:* library.vcu.edu/about/libraries/cabell	804-828-1111	828-0151	434-6
Virginia Commonwealth University School of Medicine 1101 E Marshall St PO Box 980565 .... Richmond VA 23298 **Fax:* Admissions ■ *TF:* 800-332-8813 ■ *Web:* www.medschool.vcu.edu	804-828-9629	828-1246*	167-2
Virginia Cook Realtors LLC 5950 Sherry Ln Ste 110 .... Dallas TX 75225 *Web:* www.virginiacook.com	214-696-8877		652
Virginia Correctional Enterprises 8030 White Bark Terr .... Richmond VA 23237 *Web:* www.govce.net	804-743-4100		630
Virginia Credit Union 7500 Boulders View Dr..................... Richmond VA 23225 *TF:* 800-285-5051 ■ *Web:* www.vacu.org	804-323-6000	608-8619	219
Virginia Crossings Resort 1000 Virginia Ctr Pkwy.....................Glen Allen VA 23059 *TF:* 888-444-6553 ■ *Web:* www.wyndhamvirginiacrossings.com	804-727-1400		669
Virginia Ctr Commons 10101 Brook Rd Ste 765...................Glen Allen VA 23059 *TF:* 800-461-3439 ■ *Web:* www.simon.com	317-636-1600		460
Virginia Dare Extract Company Inc 882 Third Ave.............................. Brooklyn NY 11232 *Web:* www.virginiadare.com	718-788-1776	768-3978	296-15
Virginia Democratic Party 919 E Main St Ste 2050 .... Richmond VA 23219 *TF:* 800-552-9745 ■ *Web:* www.vademocrats.org	804-644-1966	343-3642	616-1
Virginia Dental Assn (VDA) 3460 Mayland Ct Ste 110.................. Richmond VA 23233 *Web:* www.vadental.org	804-288-5750	288-1880	227
Virginia Department of Corrections 12352 Coffeewood Dr.......................Mitchells VA 22729 *Web:* vadoc.virginia.gov/facilities/central/coffeewood	540-829-6483		213
Virginia Dept of Taxation 1957 Westmoreland St PO Box 1115 .... Richmond VA 23230 *Web:* www.tax.virginia.gov	804-367-8037	254-6111	531-7
Virginia Diner Inc, The 322 W Main St ....Wakefield VA 23888 *Web:* www.vadiner.com	757-899-6213		275
Virginia Discovery Museum 524 E Main St PO Box 1128..............Charlottesville VA 22902 *Web:* www.vadm.org	434-977-1025	977-9681	521
Virginia Episcopal School 400 VES Rd ....Lynchburg VA 24503 *TF:* 800-937-3582 ■ *Web:* www.ves.org	434-385-3607	385-3603	622
Virginia Festival of the Book Virginia Foundation for the Humanities 145 Ednam Dr.........................Charlottesville VA 22903 *TF:* 877-451-5098 ■ *Web:* virginiahumanities.org	434-924-3296	296-4714	281
Virginia Fork Produce Company Inc 719 Virginia Rd...............................Edenton NC 27932	252-482-2165		276
Virginia Gazette 216 Ironbound Rd.......................Williamsburg VA 23188 *Web:* www.vagazette.com	757-220-1736		532-4
Virginia Highlands Community College 100 VHCC Dr PO Box 828 ....Abingdon VA 24212 *Web:* www.vhcc.edu	276-739-2400		162

Name / Address	City	State	Zip	Phone	Fax	Class
Virginia Historical Society Museum of Virginia History						
428 N Blvd	Richmond	VA	23220	804-358-4901	355-2399	520
TF: 800-473-0060 ■ *Web:* www.vahistorical.org						
Virginia Holocaust Museum						
2000 E Cary St	Richmond	VA	23223	804-257-5400	257-4314	520
Web: www.vaholocaust.org						
Virginia Homes Building Systems LLC						
142 Virginia Homes Ln	Boydton	VA	23917	434-738-6107	738-6926	505
Web: www.virginiahomesmfg.com						
Virginia Hospital & Healthcare Assn (VHHA)						
4200 Innslake Dr	Glen Allen	VA	23060	804-965-1227		48-17
Web: www.vhha.com						
Virginia Hospital Ctr						
1701 N George Mason Dr	Arlington	VA	22205	703-558-5000		374-3
TF: 800-492-6836 ■ *Web:* www.virginiahospitalcenter.com						
Virginia House 4301 Sulgrave Rd	Richmond	VA	23221	804-353-4251	355-2399	50-3
Web: www.vahistorical.org						
Virginia Industries Inc						
1022 Elm St	Rocky Hill	CT	06067	860-571-3600		75
Web: www.virginia.gov						
Virginia Institute of Marine Science (VIMS)						
1208 Greate Rd PO Box 1346	Gloucester Point	VA	23062	804-684-7000	684-7097	668
Web: www.vims.edu						
Virginia Intermont College						
1013 Moore St	Bristol	VA	24201	276-669-6101		166
TF: 800-451-1842 ■ *Web:* www.vic.edu						
Virginia International Terminals Inc						
7737 Hampton Blvd	Norfolk	VA	23505	757-440-7000	440-7221	465
TF General: 800-541-2431 ■ *Web:* www.vit.org						
Virginia Journal of Education						
116 S Third St	Richmond	VA	23219	804-648-5801	775-8379	457-8
TF: 800-552-9554 ■ *Web:* www.veanea.org						
Virginia Living Museum						
524 J Clyde Morris Blvd	Newport News	VA	23601	757-595-1900	599-4897	520
TF: 800-447-8679 ■ *Web:* www.thevlm.org						
Virginia Marti College of Art & Design						
11724 Detroit Ave	Lakewood	OH	44107	216-221-8584	221-2311	104
TF: 800-473-4350 ■ *Web:* vmcad.edu						
Virginia Mason Medical Ctr						
925 Seneca St	Seattle	WA	98101	206-624-1144		374-3
Web: www.virginiamason.org						
Virginia Materials & Supplies Inc						
3306 Peterson St	Norfolk	VA	23509	757-855-6328		1
Virginia Medical News						
2924 Emerywood Pkwy Ste 300	Richmond	VA	23294	800-746-6768	355-6189*	457-16
**Fax Area Code:* 804 ■ *TF:* 800-746-6768 ■ *Web:* www.msv.org						
Virginia Military Institute						
319 Letcher Ave	Lexington	VA	24450	540-464-7211	464-7746*	166
**Fax:* Admissions ■ *TF:* 800-767-4207 ■ *Web:* www.vmi.edu						
Virginia Mirror Co Inc						
300 Moss St S	Martinsville	VA	24112	276-632-0816	956-3020	329
TF: 800-368-3011 ■ *Web:* va-glass.com						
Virginia Museum of Fine Arts						
200 N Blvd	Richmond	VA	23220	804-340-1400	340-1548	520
Web: vmfa.museum						
Virginia Museum of Transportation						
303 Norfolk Ave	Roanoke	VA	24016	540-342-5670	342-6898	520
TF: 800-578-4111 ■ *Web:* www.vmt.org						
Virginia Natural Gas Inc AGL Resources Inc						
PO Box 4569	Atlanta	GA	30302	404-584-4000	281-3184*	787
**Fax Area Code:* 484 ■ *TF:* 800-633-4236 ■ *Web:* www.aglresources.com						
Virginia Nurses Assn (VNA)						
7113 Three Chopt Rd Ste 204	Richmond	VA	23226	804-282-1808	282-4916	533
Web: www.virginianurses.com						
Virginia Peninsula Chamber of Commerce						
21 Enterprise Pkwy Ste 100	Hampton	VA	23666	757-262-2000	262-2009	139
TF: 800-462-3204 ■ *Web:* www.virginiapeninsulachamber.com						
Virginia Plastics Co Inc						
3453 Aerial Way Dr SW	Roanoke	VA	24018	540-981-9700	981-2022	816
TF: 877-351-1699						
Virginia Polytechnic Institute & State University						
112 Burruss Hall	Blacksburg	VA	24061	540-231-6000	231-3242*	166
**Fax:* Admissions ■ *Web:* www.vt.edu						
Virginia Polytechnic Institute & State University Libraries						
560 Drillfield Dr	Blacksburg	VA	24061	540-231-9232	231-7808*	434-6
**Fax:* Admin ■ *Web:* www.lib.vt.edu						
Virginia Poultry Growers Co-op Inc						
6349 Rawley Pk	Hinton	VA	22831	540-867-4000		10-3
Web: www.vapoultrygrowers.com						
Virginia Premier Health Plan Inc						
600 E Broad St 4th Floor	Richmond	VA	23219	804-819-5151		391-3
Web: vapremier.com						
Virginia Press Services Inc						
11529 Nuckols Rd	Glen Allen	VA	23059	804-521-7570	521-7590	624
TF: 800-849-8717 ■ *Web:* www.vpa.net						
Virginia Railway Express (VRE)						
1500 King St Ste 202	Alexandria	VA	22314	703-684-1001	684-1313	468
TF: 800-743-3873 ■ *Web:* www.vre.org						
Virginia Realtors						
10231 Telegraph Rd	Glen Allen	VA	23059	804-264-5033		656
Web: www.virginiarealtors.org						
Virginia Republican Party						
115 E Grace St	Richmond	VA	23219	804-780-0111	343-1060	616-2
Web: www.virginia.gop						
Virginia Society of Certified Public Accountants						
4309 Cox Rd	Glen Allen	VA	23060	804-270-5344		2
TF: 800-733-8272 ■ *Web:* vscpa.com						
Virginia Society of Professional Engineers						
5301 Creek H8s Dr	Midlothian	VA	23112	804-364-0505		194
Web: www.vspe.org						
Virginia Sports Hall of Fame (VSHFM)						
206 High St	Portsmouth	VA	23704	757-393-8031	393-8288	522
TF: 800-662-6171 ■ *Web:* www.vshfm.com						
Virginia State Bar						
707 E Main St Ste 1500	Richmond	VA	23219	804-775-0500	775-0544	72
TF: 800-552-7977 ■ *Web:* www.vsb.org						
Virginia State University						
1 Hayden Dr	Petersburg	VA	23806	804-524-5000	524-5055	166
TF Admissions: 800-871-7611 ■ *Web:* www.vsu.edu						
Virginia Surety Company Inc						
175 W Jackson Blvd 11th Fl	Chicago	IL	60604	312-356-3000		174
Virginia Symphony Orchestra						
150 Boush St Ste 201	Norfolk	VA	23510	757-466-3060	466-3046	573-3
TF: 855-876-7677 ■ *Web:* www.virginiasymphony.org						
Virginia Tech (VTHG)						
Department of Horticulture						
490 W Campus Dr 301 Saunders Hall	Blacksburg	VA	24061	540-231-5451		97
Web: www.hort.vt.edu						
Virginia Theatre 203 W Pk Ave	Champaign	IL	61820	217-356-9053		572
Web: www.thevirginia.org						
Virginia Tile Co 28320 Plymouth Rd	Livonia	MI	48150	734-762-2400		361
TF: 877-356-7461 ■ *Web:* www.virginiatile.com						
Virginia Transformer Corp						
220 Glade View Dr	Roanoke	VA	24012	540-345-9892	342-7694	767
TF: 800-882-3944 ■ *Web:* www.vatransformer.com						
Virginia Union University						
1500 N Lombardy St	Richmond	VA	23220	804-342-3570	342-3511*	166
**Fax:* Admissions ■ *TF:* 800-368-3227 ■ *Web:* www.vuu.edu						
Virginia University of Lynchburg - Community Development Corp						
2058 Garfield Ave	Lynchburg	VA	24501	434-528-5276		166
Web: vul.edu						
Virginia Veterinary Medical Assn (VVMA)						
3801 Westerre Pkwy Ste D	Henrico	VA	23233	804-346-2611	346-2655	795
TF: 800-937-8862 ■ *Web:* www.vvma.org						
Virginia War Museum						
9285 Warwick Blvd	Newport News	VA	23607	757-247-8523	247-8627	520
TF: 888-493-7386 ■ *Web:* www.warmuseum.org						
Virginia Wesleyan College						
1584 Wesleyan Dr	Norfolk	VA	23502	757-455-3200	461-5238*	166
**Fax:* Admissions ■ *TF:* 800-737-8684 ■ *Web:* www.vwu.edu						
Virginia West Electric Supply Co (WVES)						
250 12-th St W	Huntington	WV	25704	304-525-0361	525-2726	246
TF: 800-624-3433 ■ *Web:* www.wvaelectric.com						
Virginia Western Community College						
3094 Colonial Ave	Roanoke	VA	24015	540-857-8922	857-6102*	162
**Fax:* Admissions ■ *TF:* 855-874-6690 ■ *Web:* www.virginiawestern.edu						
Virginia Zoological Park						
3500 Granby St	Norfolk	VA	23504	757-441-2374	441-5408	823
Web: www.virginiazoo.org						
Virginian Lodge						
750 W Broadway PO Box 1052	Jackson Hole	WY	83001	307-733-2792		379
TF: 800-262-4999 ■ *Web:* www.virginianlodge.com						
Virginian Suites						
1500 Arlington Blvd	Arlington	VA	22209	703-522-9600		379
TF: 866-371-1446 ■ *Web:* www.virginiansuites.com						
Virginian, The 9229 Arlington Blvd	Fairfax	VA	22031	703-385-0555		672
Web: www.thevirginian.org						
Virginian-Pilot 150 W Bramelton Ave	Norfolk	VA	23510	757-446-2000		532-2
TF: 800-446-2004 ■ *Web:* www.hamptonroads.com						
Virginkar & Associates Inc						
3350 E Birch St Ste 101	Brea	CA	92821	714-993-1000		110
TF: 800-799-1997 ■ *Web:* www.va-inc.com						
Virgo Publishing Inc						
3300 N Central Ave Ste 300	Phoenix	AZ	85012	480-990-1101	990-0819	637-9
Web: www.vplco.com						
Viridian Partners LLC						
1745 Shea Ctr Dr Ste 190	Highlands Ranch	CO	80129	303-271-9114		169
Web: www.viridianpartners.com						
Viridis Energy Inc						
Suite 520, 700 W Pender St	Vancouver	BC	V6C1G8	604-669-7831		279
Web: www.viridisenergy.ca						
VirnetX Holding Corp						
308 Dorla Court Ste 206	Zephyr Cove	NV	89448	831-438-8200		177
Web: virnetx.com						
Virnig Manufacturing Inc						
101 Gateway Dr NE	Rice	MN	56367	800-648-2408		190
TF: 800-648-2408 ■ *Web:* www.virnigmfg.com						
Virobay Inc 1360 Willow Rd Ste 100	Menlo Park	CA	94025	650-833-5700		668
Web: www.virobayinc.com						
Viroxis Corp						
12621 Silicon Dr Ste 100	San Antonio	TX	78249	210-558-8896		238
Web: www.viroxis.com						
Virsys12 LLC						
5205 Maryland Way Ste 202	Brentwood	TN	37027	615-800-6768		631
Web: virsys12.com						
Virtela Technology Services Inc						
5680 Greenwood Plaza Blvd Ste 200	Greenwood Village	CO	80111	720-475-4000	475-4001	176
TF: 877-803-9629 ■ *Web:* www.virtela.net						
Virtexco Corp 977 Norfolk Sq	Norfolk	VA	23502	757-466-1114	466-1115	186
TF: 800-766-1082 ■ *Web:* www.virtexco.com						
Virtu Financial Inc 645 Madison Ave	New York	NY	10022	212-418-0100		194
Web: www.virtu.com						
Virtua Health						
401 Rt 73 N 50 Lake Center Dr Ste 401	Marlton	NJ	08053	856-355-0010		353
TF: 800-789-7366 ■ *Web:* www.virtua.org						
Virtua Voorhees						
303 Lippincott Dr 4th Fl	Voorhees	NJ	08053	856-322-3000		374-3
Web: www.virtua.org						
Virtual Backgrounds Llc						
101 Uhland Rd Ste 201	San Marcos	TX	78666	512-805-4844		589
TF: 800-466-1755 ■ *Web:* www.virtualbackgrounds.net						
Virtual Brokers 4100 Yonge St Ste 415	Toronto	ON	M2P2B5	416-288-8028		690
Web: www.virtualbrokers.com						
Virtual Connect Technologies Inc						
3089 S Hwy 14	Greer	SC	29650	864-288-9595		180
Web: www.virtualconnect.net						
Virtual Education Software Inc						
300 N Argonne Rd Ste 102	Spokane	WA	99212	509-891-7219		180
Web: www.virtualeduc.com						
Virtual EM Inc						
3055 Plymouth Rd Ste 200	Ann Arbor	MI	48105	734-222-4558		396
Web: www.virtualem.com						
Virtual Enterprises Inc						
12405 Grant St	Thornton	CO	80241	303-301-3000		180
Web: www.virtual.com						
Virtual Forum Inc						
463 Main St Ste 3	Little Falls	NJ	07424	973-237-1166		396
Web: www.virtualforum.com						

Company	City	State	Zip	Phone	Fax	Class
Virtual Images 425 S Rockefeller Ave TF: 800-924-5401 ■ Web: www.virtual-images.com	Ontario	CA	91761	800-924-5401		88
Virtual Inc 401 Edgewater Pl Ste 600 Web: www.virtualmgmt.com	Wakefield	MA	01880	781-246-0500	224-1239	47
Virtual IT Inc PO Box 1009 Web: www.virtualitinc.com	Moneta	VA	24121	540-345-6100		180
Virtual Matrix Corp 7200 France Ave S Ste 324 Web: www.vmatrixcorp.com	Minneapolis	MN	55435	952-835-6400		180
Virtual Solutions LLC 21644 N Ninth Ave Ste 201 Web: www.vsols.com	Phoenix	AZ	85027	623-580-0775		697
Virtual Technology Services LLC 806 W Curtis Dr	Midwest City	OK	73110	405-733-3500		225
Virtual Training Company Inc 5395 Main St TF: 888-316-5374 ■ Web: www.vtc.com	Stephens City	VA	22655	540-869-8686		177
VirtualBank 3801 PGA Blvd Ste 700 PO Box 109638 *Fax Area Code: 561 ■ TF: 877-998-2265 ■ Web: www.virtualbank.com	Palm Beach Gardens	FL	33410	877-998-2265	776-6378*	70
Virtually Better Inc 2440 Lawrenceville Hwy Ste 200 Web: www.virtuallybetter.com	Decatur	GA	30033	404-634-3400		180
VirtualPBX.com Inc 111 N Market St Ste 1000 Web: www.virtualpbx.com	San Jose	CA	95113	408-414-7646		387
VirtualScopics Inc 500 Linden Oaks NASDAQ: VSCP ■ Web: www.virtualscopics.com	Rochester	NY	14625	585-249-6231	218-7350	476
VirtualWorks Group Inc 5301 N Federal Hwy Ste 230 TF: 877-356-3463 ■ Web: www.virtualworks.com	Boca Raton	FL	33487	877-356-3463		387
Virtua-Memorial Hospital Burlington County 175 Madison Ave Web: www.virtua.org	Mount Holly	NJ	08060	609-267-0700		374-3
Virtucom Inc 5060 Avalon Ridge Pkwy Ste 300 TF: 800-890-2611 ■ Web: www.virtucom.com	Norcross	GA	30071	770-908-8100	908-8007	174
Virtuit Systems Inc 101 Airport Executive Pk TF: 800-274-7799 ■ Web: www.virtuitsystems.com	Nanuet	NY	10954	845-371-3060		180
Virtuoso 505 Main St Ste 5 *Fax Area Code: 212 ■ TF: 800-401-4274 ■ Web: www.virtuoso.com	Fort Worth	TX	76102	817-870-0300	588-8240*	772
VirtuOx Inc 5850 Coral Ridge Dr Ste 304 TF: 800-955-8771 ■ Web: www.virtuox.net	Coral Springs	FL	33076	954-344-7075		237
Virtus Investment Partners Inc 100 Pearl St 9th Fl Web: www.virtus.com	Hartford	CT	06103	860-263-4707		401
Virurl Inc 137 Bay St Ste 6 TF: 888-572-1160 ■ Web: www.revenue.com	Santa Monica	CA	90405	888-572-1160		395
Visa Inc PO Box 8999 NYSE: V ■ Web: www.visa.co.in	San Francisco	CA	94128	650-432-3200		215
Visa Law Group 1806 11th St NW Web: www.visalawgroup.com	Washington	DC	20001	202-265-7200		428
Visage Solutions LLC 8601 Six Forks Rd Ste 400	Raleigh	NC	27615	919-882-2056		77
Visalia Chamber of Commerce 222 N Garden St Ste 300 TF: 800-728-0724 ■ Web: www.visaliachamber.org	Visalia	CA	93291	559-734-5876	734-7479	139
Visalia Convention & Visitors Bureau PO Box 2734 TF: 800-524-0303 ■ Web: www.visitvisalia.org	Visalia	CA	93279	559-334-0141		206
Visalia Convention Ctr 303 E Acequia Ave TF: 800-640-4888 ■ Web: www.ci.visalia.ca.us	Visalia	CA	93291	559-713-4000	713-4804	205
Visalia Medical Lab 5400 W Hillsdale Ave TF: 800-486-2362 ■ Web: www.vmchealth.com	Visalia	CA	93291	559-738-7500		418
Visalia Times-Delta 330 NW St TF: 800-331-9303 ■ Web: www.visaliatimesdelta.com	Visalia	CA	93279	559-735-3200	735-3399	532-2
Visara International Inc 2700 Gateway Centre Blvd Ste 600 TF: 888-334-4380 ■ Web: www.visara.com	Morrisville	NC	27560	919-882-0200		176
Viscira LLC 200 Vallejo St Web: www.viscira.com	San Francisco	CA	94111	415-848-8010		177
Visclosky Peter (Rep D - IN) 2328 Rayburn Bldg Web: visclosky.house.gov	Washington	DC	20515	202-225-2461	225-2493	342-2
Viscount Gort Hotel 1670 Portage Ave TF: 800-665-1122 ■ Web: www.viscount-gort.com	Winnipeg	MB	R3J0C9	204-775-0451	772-2161	379
Viscount Suite Hotel 4855 E Broadway Blvd TF Resv: 800-527-9666 ■ Web: www.viscountsuite.com	Tucson	AZ	85711	520-745-6500	790-5114	379
Vishay Intertechnology Inc 63 Lancaster Ave NYSE: VSH ■ TF: 800-567-6098 ■ Web: www.vishay.com	Malvern	PA	19355	610-644-1300	296-0657	696
Vishay Precision Group Inc 63 Lancaster Ave NYSE: VPG ■ Web: www.vishay.com	Malvern	PA	19355	610-644-1300		696
Visibility Corp 200 Minuteman Rd Web: www.visibility.com	Andover	MA	01810	978-269-6500	269-6501	177
Visible Changes Inc 1303 Campbell Rd Web: www.visiblechanges.com	Houston	TX	77055	713-984-8800		77
Visible Innovations 8561 Acadia Dr Web: visibleinnovations.design	Sagamore Hills	OH	44067	216-650-4804		344
Visible Inventory Inc 6 Raymond Ave Ste 5b	Salem	NH	03079	603-894-5858		463
Visible Systems Corp 201 Spring St TF Sales: 888-850-9911 ■ Web: www.visible.com	Lexington	MA	02421	781-778-0200	778-0208	178-1
Visicom Media Inc 6200 Blvd Taschereau Ste 304 Web: www.vmn.net	Brossard	QC	J4W3J8	450-672-0401		225
Visicon Technologies Inc 871 Latour Ct Web: www.visicontech.com	Napa	CA	94558	707-259-1300		476
Visidyne Inc 111 S Bedford St Ste 103 Web: www.visidyne.com	Burlington	MA	01803	781-273-2820	272-1068	668
Vision Capital 700 Airport Blvd Ste 370 Web: www.visioncap.com	Burlingame	CA	94010	650-373-2720	373-2727	792
Vision Capital Management Inc 1 SW Columbia Ste 915 Web: www.vcmi.net	Portland	OR	97258	503-221-5656		528
Vision Care Associates 1120 E Washington St Web: www.visioncareclinic.com	Grayslake	IL	60030	847-223-2000		543
Vision Council, The 225 Reinekers Ln Ste 700 TF: 866-826-0290 ■ Web: www.thevisioncouncil.org	Alexandria	VA	22314	703-548-4560	548-4580	49-4
Vision Creative Group Inc 16 Wing Dr Web: www.visioncreativegroup.com	Cedar Knolls	NJ	07927	973-984-3454		7
Vision Enterprises Inc 602 W Fifth Ave Ste B Web: www.visionsds.com	Naperville	IL	60563	630-596-4000	579-3264	260
Vision Envelope Inc 2451 Executive St TF: 800-200-9797 ■ Web: www.visionenvelope.com	Charlotte	NC	28208	704-392-9090		627
Vision Financial Corp PO Box 506 *Fax Area Code: 603 ■ TF: 800-793-0223 ■ Web: www.visfin.com	Keene	NH	03431	800-793-0223	357-0250*	391-5
Vision Global AR Ltee 80, Queen St Ste 301	Montreal	QC	H3C2N5	514-879-0020	879-0047	514
Vision Graphics Inc 5610 Boeing Dr TF: 800-833-4263 ■ Web: www.visiongraphics-inc.com	Loveland	CO	80538	970-679-9000		627
Vision Multimedia Technologies LLC 2031 Clipper Park Rd Ste 105	Baltimore	MD	21211	410-889-7770		177
Vision Offices Executive Suites Lp 14362 N Frank Lloyd Wright Blvd Ste 1000 Web: visionoffices.com	Scottsdale	AZ	85260	480-477-7777		317
Vision One It Consulting Inc 7112 Ofc Park Dr Web: www.v1corp.com	West Chester	OH	45069	513-892-0027		196
Vision Plastics Inc 26000 SW Pkwy Ctr Dr Web: www.visionplastics.com	Wilsonville	OR	97070	503-685-9000	685-9254	548
Vision Solutions Inc 15300 Barranca Pkwy TF: 800-683-4667 ■ Web: www.visionsolutions.com	Irvine	CA	92618	949-253-6500	253-6501	178-12
Vision Source LP 23824 Hwy 59 N Ste 101 TF: 888-558-2020 ■ Web: www.visionsource.com	Kingwood	TX	77339	281-312-1111		237
Vision Technologies Inc 530 McCormick Dr Ste G TF: 866-746-1122 ■ Web: www.visiontechnologiesinc.net	Glen Burnie	MD	21061	410-424-2183	424-2208	177
Vision7 Software 4729 E Sunrise Dr Ste 201 TF: 800-219-8941 ■ Web: www.vision7.com	Tucson	AZ	85718	520-320-5442		809
Visionaire Inc 1502 109th St TF: 866-838-2810 ■ Web: www.visionaire-inc.com	Grand Prairie	TX	75050	972-647-1056		57
Visionaire Lighting LLC 19645 Rancho Way Web: www.visionairelighting.com	Rancho Dominguez	CA	90220	310-512-6480		362
Visionary Integration Professionals Inc 80 Iron Pt Cir Ste 100 TF: 800-434-2673 ■ Web: trustvip.com	Folsom	CA	95630	916-985-9625		180
Visionary Legal Technologies LP 14677 Midway Rd Ste 118 TF: 800-894-2889 ■ Web: www.visionarylegaltechnologies.com	Addison	TX	75001	214-370-4359		177
Vision-Ease Lens Inc 7000 Sunwood Dr NW TF Cust Svc: 800-328-3449 ■ Web: www.visionease.com	Ramsey	MN	55303	320-251-8140	251-4312	542
Visioneer Inc 5673 Gibraltar Dr Ste 150 Web: www.visioneer.com	Pleasanton	CA	94588	925-251-6300	416-8600	173-7
Visioneering Inc 2055 Taylor Rd Web: www.vistool.com	Auburn Hills	MI	48326	248-622-5600	622-5533	21
Visionet Systems Inc 4 Cedarbrook Dr Bldg B Web: www.visionetsystems.com	Cranbury	NJ	08512	609-452-0700		225
Vision-It Inc 2502 Iron Forge Rd Web: www.vitinc.net	Herndon	VA	20171	703-668-0717		196
VisionMAX Solutions Inc 5580 Explorer Dr Ste 601 Web: www.visionmax.com	Mississauga	ON	L4W4Y1	905-282-0503		7
Visionpace Inc 17501 E US Hwy 40 TF: 088-904-7900 ■ Web: www.visionpacc.com	Independence	MO	64055	816-350-7900		809
Visionpoint LLC 152 Rockwell Rd Web: www.visionpointllc.com	Newington	CT	06111	860-436-9673		224
VisionQuest National Ltd 600 N Swan Rd PO Box 12906 Web: www.vq.com	Tucson	AZ	85711	520-881-3950	881-3269	463
Visions Federal Credit Union (VFUC) 24 McKinley Ave TF: 800-242-2120 ■ Web: www.visionsfcu.org	Endicott	NY	13760	607-754-7900	786-1718	219
Visions Hotels LLC 382 E Second St Web: www.visions-hotels.com	Corning	NY	14830	607-962-9868		377
Visions Inc 8801 Wyoming Ave N Web: www.visionsfirst.com	Brooklyn Park	MN	55445	763-425-4251		627
Vision-Sciences Inc 40 Ramland Rd S NASDAQ: VSCI	Orangeburg	NY	10962	845-365-0600	365-0620	382
Visionsoft International Inc 1842 Old Norcross Rd Ste 100 Web: www.vsiiusa.com	Lawrenceville	GA	30044	770-682-2899		177
Visiont 2650 106th St Ste 215 Web: www.visiont-solutions.com	Urbandale	IA	50322	515-331-0010		260
VisionWare Inc 6387B Camp Bowie Ste 275 Web: www.visionware-inc.com	Fort Worth	TX	76116	817-810-9109		809
Visionworks 854 Plaza Blvd Web: www.visionworks.com/loc/01031	Lancaster	PA	17601	717-295-3111		543
Visionworks of America Inc 175 E Houston St TF: 800-669-1183 ■ Web: www.visionworks.com	San Antonio	TX	78205	800-669-1183		543

Company / Address	City	State	ZIP	Phone	Fax	Class
Visit America Inc 330 Seventh Ave 20th Fl *Web:* www.visitamerica.com	New York	NY	10001	212-683-8082		760
Visit Dothan Alabama 3311 Ross Clark Cir *TF:* 888-449-0212 ■ *Web:* www.dothanalcvb.com	Dothan	AL	36303	334-794-6622		206
Visit Duluth 21 W Superior St Ste 100 *TF:* 800-438-5884 ■ *Web:* www.visitduluth.com	Duluth	MN	55802	218-722-4011	722-1322	206
Visit Eau Claire 4319 Jeffers Rd *TF:* 888-523-3866 ■ *Web:* www.visiteauclaire.com	Eau Claire	WI	54703	715-831-2345		206
Visit Florida 2540 W Executive Ctr Cir Ste 200 *TF:* 800-683-0010 ■ *Web:* www.visitflorida.org	Tallahassee	FL	32301	850-488-5607		775
Visit Jacksonville 208 N Laura St Ste 1 *TF:* 800-733-2668 ■ *Web:* www.visitjacksonville.com	Jacksonville	FL	32202	904-798-9111		206
Visit MercerCounty PA 50 N Water Ave *TF:* 800-637-2370 ■ *Web:* www.visitmercercountypa.com	Sharon	PA	16146	724-346-3771	346-0575	206
Visit Milledgeville 200 W Hancock St *TF:* 800-653-1804 ■ *Web:* www.visitmilledgeville.org	Milledgeville	GA	31061	478-452-4687	453-4440	206
Visit Rochester 45 E Ave Ste 400 *TF:* 800-677-7282 ■ *Web:* www.visitrochester.com	Rochester	NY	14604	585-279-8300	232-4822	206
Visit Salt Lake 90 SW Temple **Fax Area Code:* 800 ■ *TF:* 800-541-4955 ■ *Web:* www.visitsaltlake.com	Salt Lake City	UT	84101	801-534-4900	541-4955*	206
Visit Sarasota County 1777 Main St Ste 302 *TF:* 800-522-9799 ■ *Web:* www.visitsarasota.org	Sarasota	FL	34236	941-955-0991		206
Visit St Petersburg Clearwater 13805 58th St N Ste 2-200 *TF:* 877-352-3224 ■ *Web:* www.visitstpeteclearwater.com	Clearwater	FL	33760	727-464-7200		206
Visit Topeka Inc 618 S Kansas Ave *TF:* 800-235-1030 ■ *Web:* www.visittopeka.com	Topeka	KS	66603	785-234-1030	234-8282	206
Visitec Marketing Associates Inc 2020 Dean St Unit H *Web:* www.visitec.com	St. Charles	IL	60174	630-762-0300		196
VisitErie 208 E Bayfront Pkwy Ste 103 *TF:* 800-524-3743 ■ *Web:* www.visiterie.com	Erie	PA	16507	814-454-1000	459-0241	206
Visiting Nurse & Hospice Care of Southwestern Connecticut 1266 E Main St	Stamford	CT	06902	203-276-3000		371
Visiting Nurse Assn 12565 W Ctr Rd Ste 100 *TF:* 800-456-8869 ■ *Web:* www.thevnacares.org	Omaha	NE	68144	402-342-5566	342-5587	371
Visiting Nurse Assn of Morris County (Inc) 175 South St *TF:* 800-938-4748 ■ *Web:* www.vnannj.org	Morristown	NJ	07960	973-539-1216		363
Visiting Nurse Assn of Ohio 2500 E 22nd St *TF:* 877-698-6264 ■ *Web:* www.vnaohio.org	Cleveland	OH	44115	216-931-1300	694-4182	371
Visiting Nurse Assn of the Treasure Coast 1110 35th Ln *TF:* 800-749-5760 ■ *Web:* www.vnatc.com	Vero Beach	FL	32960	772-567-5551		371
Visiting Nurse Assns of America (VNAA) 900 19th St NW Ste 200 *TF:* 888-866-8773 ■ *Web:* www.vnaa.org	Washington	DC	20006	202-384-1420	384-1444	49-8
Visiting Nurse Service of New York Hospice Care 1250 Broadway *Web:* www.vnsny.org	New York	NY	10001	212-609-1900		371
Visiting Nurses 222 E Canon Perdido St	Santa Barbara	CA	93101	805-690-6202		371
Viskase Cos Inc 8205 S Cass Ste 115 *TF:* 800-323-8562 ■ *Web:* www.viskase.com	Darien	IL	60561	630-874-0700	874-0176	548
Visp.net 301 NE Sixth St *Web:* www.visp.net	Grants Pass	OR	97526	541-955-6900		225
Vissering Construction Co 175 Benchmark Industrial Dr *TF:* 800-993-4416 ■ *Web:* www.vissering.com	Streator	IL	61364	815-673-5511		186
VIST Financial Corp PO Box 6219 PO Box 6219 *NASDAQ:* VIST ■ *TF:* 888-238-3330 ■ *Web:* www.vistbank.com	Wyomissing	PA	19610	610-926-7632		360-2
Vista Analytical Laboratory Inc 1104 Windfield Way *Web:* www.vista-analytical.com	El Dorado Hills	CA	95762	916-673-1520	673-0106	743
Vista Auto 21501 Ventura Blvd *TF:* 888-887-6530 ■ *Web:* www.vistaford.com	Woodland Hills	CA	91364	888-313-4252		57
Vista Biologicals Corp 2120-C Las Palmas Dr *Web:* www.vistabiologicals.com	Carlsbad	CA	92009	760-438-5058		418
Vista Broadband Networks Inc 3020 Santa Rosa Ave *Web:* www.vistabroadband.com	Santa Rosa	CA	95407	707-527-0545		387
Vista Color Corp 1401 NW 78th Ave *TF:* 800-513-1715 ■ *Web:* www.vistacolor.com	Miami	FL	33126	305-635-2000		627
Vista Color Imaging 4770 Van Epps Rd Unit 101 *Web:* www.vistacolorimaging.com	Brooklyn Hts	OH	44131	216-651-2830		344
Vista Convention Services Inc 6804 Delilah Rd *TF:* 800-868-8590 ■ *Web:* www.vistacs.com	Egg Harbor Township	NJ	08234	609-485-2421		184
Vista del Monte 3775 Modoc Rd *TF:* 800-736-1333 ■ *Web:* www.vistadelmonte.org	Santa Barbara	CA	93105	805-687-0793		672
Vista Electronics Inc 27525 Newhall Ranch Rd *TF:* 800-847-8299 ■ *Web:* vistaelectronics.com	Valencia	CA	91355	661-294-9820		514
Vista Engineering Corp 1030 Pleasantview Terr *Web:* vistaengineeringcorp.com	Ridgefield	NJ	07657	201-945-9434		261
Vista Gold Corp 7961 Shaffer Pkwy Ste 5 *NYSE:* VGZ ■ *Web:* www.vistagold.com	Littleton	CO	80127	720-981-1185	981-1186	502
Vista Grande Villa 2251 Springport Rd *TF:* 800-889-8499 ■ *Web:* www.vistagrandevilla.com	Jackson	MI	49202	517-787-0222		672
Vista Graphics Inc 1264 Perimeter Pkwy *Web:* www.vistagraphicsinc.com/agency-vg.php	Virginia Beach	VA	23454	757-422-8979		344
Vista Host Inc 10370 Richmond Ave Ste 150 *TF:* 800-257-3000 ■ *Web:* vistahost.com	Houston	TX	77042	713-267-5800	267-5820	379
Vista House 40700 E Historic Columbia River Hwy *TF:* 800-551-6949 ■ *Web:* www.vistahouse.com	Corbett	OR	97019	503-695-2230	695-2250	50-5
Vista Imaging Services Inc 3941 Park Dr Ste 20-463 *TF:* 855-972-9729 ■ *Web:* www.vistaimagingservices.com	El Dorado Hills	CA	95762	415-272-3925		415
Vista International Packaging LLC 1126 88th Pl **Fax Area Code:* 262 ■ *TF:* 800-558-4058	Kenosha	WI	53143	800-558-4058	697-6520*	296-26
Vista Medical Ctr 1324 N Sheridan Rd *TF:* 800-843-2464 ■ *Web:* www.vistahealth.com	Waukegan	IL	60085	847-360-3000		374-3
Vista Metals Inc 65 Ballou Blvd *TF:* 800-431-4113 ■ *Web:* www.vismet.com	Bristol	RI	02809	401-253-1772		492
Vista Paint Corp 2020 E Orangethorpe Ave *Web:* www.vistapaint.com	Fullerton	CA	92831	714-680-3810	459-4708	550
Vista Productions Inc 1804 Anaconda Rd *Web:* www.vistaprod.com	Harrisonville	MO	64701	816-380-7750		514
Vista Projects Ltd 330-4000 4thySt SEy Ste B29 *Web:* www.vistaprojects.com	Calgary	AB	T2G2W3	403-255-3455		196
Vista Ridge Mall 2401 S Stemmons Fwy *Web:* www.vistaridgemall.com	Lewisville	TX	75067	972-315-3641		460
VISTA Satellite Communications Inc 73-104 SW 12th Ave *TF:* 800 295 4198 ■ *Web:* vistaworldlink.com	Dania Beach	FL	33004	954-838-0900		116
VISTA Staffing Solutions Inc 275 East 200 South *Web:* www.vistastaff.com	Salt Lake City	UT	84111	801-487-8190		260
Vista Therapeutics Inc 3900 Paseo del Sol *Web:* www.vistatherapeutics.org	Sante Fe	NM	87507	505-474-3143		475
Vista Verde Guest & Ski Ranch PO Box 770465 *TF:* 800-526-7433 ■ *Web:* www.vistaverde.com	Steamboat Springs	CO	80477	970-879-3858	879-6814	239
Vista West Ctr 2615 Washington St *Web:* www.vistahealth.com/stmcvmh	Waukegan	IL	60085	847-249-3900		374-3
Vistacomm 1401 N C Ave	Sioux Falls	SD	57104	605-977-2100		4
Vistanet Communications 6804 Villa Hermosa Dr *Web:* vistanetworks.com	El Paso	TX	79912	915-587-1500		224
VistaPharm Inc 630 Central Ave *TF:* 877-437-8567 ■ *Web:* www.vistapharm.com	New Providence	NJ	07974	877-437-8567		231
VistaPrint USA Inco 95 Hayden Ave *Web:* www.vistaprint.com	Lexington	MA	02421	781-652-6300		627
Vistar Eye Center Inc 707 S Jefferson St *TF:* 866-615-5454 ■ *Web:* www.vistareye.com	Roanoke	VA	24016	540-855-5100		543
Vistar Technologies Corp 11924 Forest Hill Blvd Ste 10-127 *Web:* vistartech.com	Wellington	FL	33414	561-792-0044		177
Vistar/VSA Corp 12650 E Arapahoe Rd *TF:* 800-880-9900 ■ *Web:* www.vistar.com	Centennial	CO	80112	303-662-7100		297-8
VistaVu Solutions Inc 30 Springborough Blvd SW Ste 214 *TF:* 888-300-2727 ■ *Web:* www.vistavusolutions.com	Calgary	AB	T3H0N9	403-263-2727		179
Vistech Corp 11 Grays Farm Rd *Web:* www.vistechcorp.com	Westport	CT	06880	203-454-0300		463
Vistem Solutions Inc 2102 Business Ctr Dr Ste 220 *Web:* www.vistem.com	Irvine	CA	92649	949-253-5729		809
Visteon Corp 1 Village Center Dr *NYSE:* VC ■ *TF:* 800-847-8366 ■ *Web:* www.visteon.com	Van Buren Township	MI	48111	734-710-5000		60
Vistex Inc 2300 Barrington Rd Ste 550 *Web:* www.vistex.com	Hoffman Estates	IL	60169	847-490-0420		195
Vistra Communications LLC 18315 N US Hwy 41 *Web:* www.consultvistra.com	Lutz	FL	33549	813-961-4700		195
Vistrian Inc 562 Valley Way *Web:* www.vistrian.com	Milpitas	CA	95035	408-719-0500		177
Vistronix Inc 11091 Sunset Hills Rd Ste 700 *TF:* 800-483-2434 ■ *Web:* www.vistronix.com	Reston	VA	20190	703-463-2059		180
Visual Automation Inc 403 S Clinton St Ste 4 *TF:* 800-223-5563 ■ *Web:* www.visualautomation.com	Grand Ledge	MI	48837	517-622-1850	622-1761	178-12
Visual Awareness Technologies & Consulting Inc 3611 W Swann Ave *Web:* www.vatcinc.com	Tampa	FL	33609	813-207-5055		765
Visual Citi Inc 770 Railroad Ave *TF:* 800-924-2347 ■ *Web:* visualciti.com	West Babylon	NY	11704	631-482-3030		344
Visual Communications Group Inc 1548 Cliff Rd E *TF:* 800-566-4162 ■ *Web:* visualcomgroup.com	Burnsville	MN	55337	800-566-4162		514
Visual Data Media Services Inc 610 N Hollywood Way *TF:* 888-418-4782 ■ *Web:* www.visualdatamedia.com	Burbank	CA	91505	818-558-3363		738
Visual Departures Ltd 48 Sheffield Business Pk Ste 195 *TF:* 800-628-2003 ■ *Web:* www.visualdepartures.com	Ashley Falls	MA	01222	800-628-2003		591
Visual Eyes Medical Media 31320 Via Colinas Ste 118 *Web:* www.visualeyes.com	Westlake Village	CA	91362	818-707-9922		514
Visual Goodness Inc 225 W 34th St *Web:* www.visualgoodness.com	New York	NY	10122	212-463-8248		344
Visual Image Photography W63 N582 Hanover Ave *TF:* 800-577-9570 ■ *Web:* www.vipis.com	Cedarburg	WI	53012	262-375-4457		590
Visual Impressions Inc 6600 W Calumet Rd *Web:* www.visualimp.com	Milwaukee	WI	53223	414-354-9190		687
Visual Learning Systems Inc PO Box 8226 *TF:* 866-968-7857 ■ *Web:* www.vls-inc.com	Missoula	MT	59807	866-968-7857		177

Company	City	State	Zip	Phone	Fax	Class
Visual Marketing Inc 154 W Erie St *TF:* 800-662-8640 ■ *Web:* www.vmichicago.com	Chicago	IL	60654	312-664-9177	664-9473	233
Visual Net Design Lc 212 E Ramsey Rd *TF:* 800-590-2164 ■ *Web:* www.vndx.com	San Antonio	TX	78216	210-590-2734		175
Visual Pak Co 1909 Waukegan Rd *Web:* www.visualpak.com	Waukegan	IL	60085	847-689-1000		88
Visual Planning Corp 71 Meadowbank Dr *TF:* 800-361-1192	Ottawa	ON	K2G0P4	613-563-8727	563-8727	487
Visual Purple LLC 75 Higuera St Ste 240 *TF:* 800-573-1874 ■ *Web:* www.visualpurple.com	San Luis Obispo	CA	93401	805-595-7579		177
Visual Retail Plus Inc 540 Hudson St *Web:* www.visualretailplus.com	Hackensack	NJ	07601	201-678-9888		180
Visualant Inc 500 Union St Ste 420 *TF:* 800-937-5449 ■ *Web:* www.visualant.net	Seattle	WA	98101	206-903-1351		201
Visualware Inc 937 Sierra Dr PO Box 668 *TF:* 866-847-9273 ■ *Web:* www.visualware.com	Turlock	CA	95380	209-262-3491		177
Vita Coco 38 W 21St St *Web:* www.vitacoco.com	New York	NY	10010	212-206-0763		345
Vita Food Products Inc 2222 West Lake St *TF:* 800-989-8482 ■ *Web:* www.vitafoodproducts.com	Chicago	IL	60612	312-738-4500		296-13
Vita Health Products Inc 150 Beghin Ave *Web:* www.vitahealth.ca	Winnipeg	MB	R2J3W2	204-661-8386		345
Vita Motivator Company Inc PO Box 8139	Englewood	NJ	07631	201-567-1151		366
Vita Needle Co 919 Great Plain Ave *TF:* 800-749-2523 ■ *Web:* www.vitaneedle.com	Needham	MA	02492	781-444-1780		492
Vita Plus Corp 2514 Fish Hatchery Rd *TF:* 800-362-8334 ■ *Web:* www.vitaplus.com	Madison	WI	53713	608-256-1988	283-7990	447
Vitac Corp 101 Hillpointe Dr *Web:* www.vitac.com	Canonsburg	PA	15317	724-514-4000		224
Vitacost.com Inc 5400 Broken Sound Blvd NW Ste 500 *TF:* 800-381-0759 ■ *Web:* www.vitacost.com	Boca Raton	FL	33487	800-381-0759		237
VitaDigest.com 20687-2 Amar Rd Ste 258 *TF:* 877-848-2168 ■ *Web:* www.vitadigest.com	Walnut	CA	91789	877-848-2168		345
Vitae Pharmaceuticals Inc 502 W Office Ctr Dr *Web:* www.vitaepharma.com	Fort Washington	PA	19034	215-461-2000		231
Vitakraft Sunseed Inc 20584 Long Judson Rd *Web:* www.vitakraftsunseed.com	Weston	OH	43569	419-832-1641		123
Vital Diagnostics Inc 27 Wellington Rd *Web:* www.vitaldiagnosticsinc.com	Lincoln	RI	02865	401-642-8400		475
Vital Images Inc 5850 Opus Pkwy Ste 300 *TF:* 800-208-3005 ■ *Web:* www.vitalimages.com	Minnetonka	MN	55343	952-487-9500		178-10
Vital Link Inc 914 Bartlett Rd *Web:* www.vitallinkinc.com	Sealy	TX	77474	979-885-4181		492
Vital Mktg LLC 115 E 23rd St 10th Fl *Web:* www.vitalmarketing.com	New York	NY	10010	212-995-9525		194
VITAL Network Services Inc 14520 McCormick Dr *Web:* www.vital-ns.com	Tampa	FL	33626	813-818-5100		225
Vital Pharmaceuticals Inc 1600 N Pk Dr *Web:* www.vpxsports.com	Weston	FL	33326	954-641-0570		81-2
Vital Records Inc PO Box 688 *Web:* www.vitalrecords.com	Flagtown	NJ	08821	908-369-6900		581
Vital Signs Inc 20 Campus Rd *TF:* 800-932-0760 ■ *Web:* www3.gehealthcare.com	Totowa	NJ	07512	973-790-1330		476
Vital Solutions International Llc 19 Leonberg Rd Ste 3 *Web:* www.vsint.com	Cranberry Township	PA	16066	724-776-6707		175
Vital Systems Corp 4999 Aircenter Cir Ste 101 *Web:* www.vitalsystems.com	Reno	NV	89502	775-828-1126		696
Vital Wave Consulting 555 Bryant St Ste 226 *Web:* vitalwave.com	Palo Alto	CA	94301	650-964-1316		194
VitalAire Canada Inc 6990 Creditview Rd Unit 6 *TF:* 888-629-0202 ■ *Web:* www.vitalaire.com	Mississauga	ON	L5N8R9	888-629-0202		476
Vitalyst LLC One Bala Plaza Ste 434 *Web:* www.vitalyst.com	Bala Cynwyd	PA	19004	610-668-3516		809
Vitamin Shoppe Inc 2101 91st St *NYSE:* VSI ■ **Fax Area Code:* 800 ■ *TF:* 800-223-1216 ■ *Web:* www.vitaminshoppe.com	North Bergen	NJ	07047	201-868-5959	852-7153*	237
Vitaminerals Inc 1815 Flower St *TF:* 800-432-1856 ■ *Web:* www.cryogel.tv	Glendale	CA	91201	800-432-1856		296-11
Vita-Mix Corp 8615 Usher Rd *TF:* 800-848-2649 ■ *Web:* www.vitamix.com	Cleveland	OH	44138	440-235-4840	235-3726	37
Vita-Pakt Citrus Products 707 N Barranca Ave *Web:* www.vita-pakt.com	Covina	CA	91723	626-332-1101		296-21
VITAS Healthcare 1787 Sentry Pk W Ste 100 *TF:* 800-582-9533 ■ *Web:* www.vitas.com	Blue Bell	PA	19422	215-283-6759		371
VITAS Healthcare Corp 100 S Biscayne Blvd Ste 400 *TF:* 866-418-4827 ■ *Web:* www.vitas.com	Miami	FL	33131	305-374-4143		363
VITAS Healthcare Corp 2675 N Mayfair Rd Ste 500 *TF:* 866-418-4827 ■ *Web:* www.vitas.com	Wauwatosa	WI	53226	414-257-2600		371
VITAS Healthcare Corp 201 S Biscayne Blvd Ste 400 *TF:* 844-345-8084 ■ *Web:* www.vitas.com	Miami	FL	33131	305-374-4143		371
VITAS Healthcare Corp 3131 Eastside St Ste 200 *TF:* 800-582-9533 ■ *Web:* www.vitas.com	Houston	TX	77098	713-663-7777		371
VITAS Healthcare Corp 8401 Datapoint Dr Ste 300 *TF:* 800-938-4827 ■ *Web:* www.vitas.com	San Antonio	TX	78229	210-348-4300		371
VITAS Healthcare Corp of California 990 W 190th St Ste 120 *TF:* 800-582-9533 ■ *Web:* www.vitas.com	Torrance	CA	90502	305-374-4143		371
VITAS Healthcare Corp of California 16830 Ventura Blvd Ste 100 *TF:* 800-582-9533 ■ *Web:* www.vitas.com	Los Angeles	CA	91436	818-385-0273		371
VITAS Healthcare Corp of California 310 Commerce Ste 200 *TF:* 800-644-4479 ■ *Web:* www.vitas.com	Irvine	CA	92602	714-921-2273		371
VITAS Healthcare Corp of California 9655 Granite Ridge Dr Ste 300 *TF:* 866-418-4827 ■ *Web:* www.vitas.com	San Diego	CA	92123	858-499-8901		371
VITAS Healthcare Corp of San Gabriel Cities 1343 N Grand Ave *TF:* 866-418-4827 ■ *Web:* www.vitas.com	Covina	CA	91724	866-418-4827		371
VITAS Hospice Care 201 S Biscayne Blvd Ste 400 *TF General:* 800-582-9533 ■ *Web:* www.vitas.com	Miami	FL	33131	305-374-4143		371
VitaSound Audio Inc 2880 Zanker Rd Ste 203 *TF:* 888-667-7205 ■ *Web:* vitasound.com	San Jose	CA	95134	888-667-7205		250
Vitasoy USA Inc 57 Russell St *TF:* 800-848-2769 ■ *Web:* www.vitasoy-usa.com	Woburn	MA	01801	800-848-2769		296-8
VITEC 2200 Century Pkwy Ste 900 *Web:* vitec.com	Atlanta	GA	30345	404-320-0110	320-3132	173-5
Vitec LLC 2627 Clark St *Web:* www.vitec-usa.com	Detroit	MI	48210	313-297-6676	843-1298	608
VITEC Solutions LLC 455 Commerce Dr Ste 3 *Web:* www.vitecsolutions.com	Amherst	NY	14228	716-204-9200		175
Vitech Business Group Inc 4164 Meridian St Ste 200 *Web:* www.vitechgroup.com	Bellingham	WA	98226	360-647-1622		317
Vitech Corp 2270 Kraft Dr Ste 1600 *Web:* www.vitechcorp.com	Blacksburg	VA	24060	540-951-3322		177
Vitelity Communications LLC 7900 E Union Ave Ste 1100 *Web:* www.vitelity.com	Denver	CO	80237	720-257-5400		224
Vitense Golfland 5501 Schroeder Rd *TF:* 800-432-8747 ■ *Web:* www.vitense.com	Madison	WI	53711	608-271-1411		354
Viteos Capital Market Services Limited 80 Cottontail Ln Ste 430 *Web:* www.viteos.com	Somerset	NJ	08873	732-356-1200	356-1160	463
Viterbo University 900 Viterbo Dr **Fax:* Admissions ■ *TF:* 800-848-3726 ■ *Web:* www.viterbo.edu	La Crosse	WI	54601	608-796-3000	796-3020*	166
Vitetta 2 International Pl *TF:* 800-767-3263 ■ *Web:* www.vitetta.com	Philadelphia	PA	19113	215-218-4747	405-2729	261
VITEX Inc 630 Williamson Rd *TF:* 800-755-6440 ■ *Web:* www.vitex.com	Mooresville	NC	28117	704-663-2544		463
Vito's 4100 River Ridge Dr NE *Web:* vitosonline.com	Cedar Rapids	IA	52402	319-393-8727		671
Vito's by the Park 26 Trumbull St *Web:* www.vitosct.com	Hartford	CT	06103	860-244-2200		671
Vito's Chop House 8633 International Dr *Web:* www.talkofthetownrestaurants.com	Orlando	FL	32819	407-354-2467		671
Vito's Italian Restaurant 1180 Forest Ave Ste A *Web:* vitositalianrestaurant.weebly.com	Pacific Grove	CA	93950	831-375-3070		671
Vitols Tool & Machine Corp 10082 Sandmeyer Ln *Web:* www.vitolsgroup.com	Philadelphia	PA	19116	215-464-8240		480
Vitran Express Canada Inc 1201 Creditstone Rd *NASDAQ:* VTNC ■ *TF:* 800-263-9588 ■ *Web:* www.vitran.com	Concord	ON	L4K0C2	416-798-4965	798-4753	780
Vitran Express Inc 1201 Creditstone Rd *TF:* 800-263-0791 ■ *Web:* www.vitranexpress.com	Concord	ON	L4K0C2	416-798-4965	798-4753	780
Vitria Technology Inc 945 Stewart Dr Ste 200 **Fax Area Code:* 408 ■ *TF:* 877-365-5935 ■ *Web:* www.vitria.com	Sunnyvale	CA	94085	877-365-5935	212-2720*	178-1
Vitro Seating Products Inc 201 Madison St *TF Cust Svc:* 800-325-7093 ■ *Web:* www.vitroseating.com	Saint Louis	MO	63102	314-241-2265	241-8723	319-1
Vitrum Industries Ltd 9739 201 St	Langley	BC	V1M3E7	604-882-3513		330
Vittitow Refrigeration 4603 Poplar Level Rd *Web:* www.vittitow.com	Louisville	KY	40213	502-966-4444		665
Vittoria Trattoria 35 William St *Web:* www.vittoriatrattoria.com	Ottawa	ON	K1N6Z9	613-789-8959	730-5239	671
Vittum Theater 1012 N Noble St *TF:* 800-737-0984 ■ *Web:* www.vittumtheater.org	Chicago	IL	60642	773-342-4141		748
Viva Bene 144 Commercial St	Worcester	MA	01608	508-799-9999		671
Viva Burrito Co 860 E 16th St	Tucson	AZ	85719	520-882-8713		670
VIVA Health Inc 1222 14th Ave S *TF:* 800-633-1542 ■ *Web:* www.vivahealth.com	Birmingham	AL	35205	205-939-1718		390
Viva Magnetics (Canada) Ltd 1663 Neilson Rd *Web:* www.viva.com.hk	Scarborough	ON	M1X1T1	416-321-0622		658
Viva Partnership Inc 3227 NE Second Ave *Web:* www.vivamia.com	Miami	FL	33137	305-576-6007		7
Vivekananda Retreat Ridgely 101 Leggett Rd *Web:* www.ridgely.org	Stone Ridge	NY	12484	845-687-4574	687-4578	673
ViveloHoy 435 N Michigan Ave 12th Fl *Web:* www.vivelohoy.com	Chicago	IL	60611	312-527-8400		532-2
Viventia Biotechnologies Inc 147 Hamelin St **Fax Area Code:* 905 ■ *Web:* www.viventia.com	Winnipeg	MB	R3T3Z1	204-478-1023	362-2973*	85
Viventium Software 768 Bedford Ave *Web:* www.bdbpayroll.com	Brooklyn	NY	11205	718-522-2000		734
Vivere 71 W Monroe St *Web:* www.italianvillage-chicago.com	Chicago	IL	60603	312-332-4040	332-2656	671
Vivian Horan Fine Art 35 E 67th St 2nd Fl *Web:* vivianhoran.com	New York	NY	10065	212-517-9410	772-6107	42

Name / Address	City	State	ZIP	Phone	Fax	Class
Viviani Associates Public Relations 160 Littleton Rd Ste 311 *TF:* 800-922-0204 ■ *Web:* www.vivianipr.com	Parsippany	NJ	07054	973-968-7929		636
Viviano Flower Shop 32050 Harper Ave *TF:* 800-848-4266 ■ *Web:* viviano.com	Saint Clair Shores	MI	48082	586-293-0227		292
Vivid Entertainment 3599 Cahuenga Blvd *Web:* www.vivid.com	W Los Angeles	CA	90068	323-845-4557		514
Vivid Image Inc 897 Hwy 15 S *TF:* 800-247-2320 ■ *Web:* www.vimm.com	Hutchinson	MN	55350	320-587-8974		809
Vivid Impact Corp 10116 Bunsen Way *Web:* www.vividimpact.com	Louisville	KY	40299	502-495-6900		174
Vivid Solutions 2328 Government St *Web:* www.vividsolutions.com	Victoria	BC	V8T5G5	250-385-6040		180
Vivienne Tam 260 W 39th St 11TH FL *TF:* 877-659-7994 ■ *Web:* www.viviennetam.com	New York	NY	10018	877-659-7994		277
Vivint Solar Inc 1800 W Ashton Blvd *TF:* 877-404-4129 ■ *Web:* www.vivintsolar.com	Lehi	UT	84043	877-404-4129		192
Vivitar Corp 195 Carter Dr *TF:* 800-592-9541 ■ *Web:* www.vivitar.com	Edison	NJ	08817	732-248-1306		591
VIVO Seasonal Trattoria 200 Columbus Blvd *Web:* vivohartford.com	Hartford	CT	06103	860-760-2333		671
Vivoli Cafe & Trattoria of West Hollywood 7994 Sunset Blvd *Web:* www.vivolicafe.com	West Hollywood	CA	90046	323-656-5050		671
Vivosonic Inc 120-5525 Eglinton Ave W *TF:* 877-255-7685 ■ *Web:* www.vivosonic.com	Toronto	ON	M9C5K5	416-231-9997		476
Vivox Inc 2-4 Mercer Rd *TF:* 800-573-1874 ■ *Web:* www.vivox.com	Natick	MA	01760	508-650-3571		177
Vivus Inc 1172 Castro St *NASDAQ: VVUS* ■ *TF:* 800-607-0088 ■ *Web:* www.vivus.com	Mountain View	CA	94040	650-934-5200	934-5389	582
Viwinco Inc PO Box 499 *Web:* www.viwinco.com	Morgantown	PA	19543	610-286-8884		608
Viwintech Window & Door Inc 2400 Irvin Cobb Dr *TF:* 800-788-1050 ■ *Web:* www.viwintech.com	Paducah	KY	42003	800-788-1050		596
ViWo Inc 10801 National blvd 410 Ste 410 *TF:* 888-898-4787 ■ *Web:* www.viwoinc.com	Los Angeles	CA	90064	888-898-4787		196
Viz Media 295 Bay St *TF:* 800-330-6827 ■ *Web:* www.viz.com	San Francisco	CA	94133	415-546-7073	546-7086	637-9
Vizant Technologies LLC Brandywine Two Bldg 5 Christy Dr Ste 202 *Web:* vizant.com	Chadds Ford	PA	19317	610-358-1003		463
Vizcaya Museum & Gardens 3251 S Miami Ave *Web:* vizcaya.org	Miami	FL	33129	305-250-9133	285-2004	520
Vizient Ii LLC 3129 State St Unit 2 *TF:* [illegible] ■ *Web:* vizient.com	Bettendorf	IA	52722	563-355-4812		261
Viziflex Seels Inc 406 N Midland Ave *TF:* 800-627-7752 ■ *Web:* www.viziflex.com	Saddle Brook	NJ	07663	800-627-7752		608
VizQuest Ventures LLC PO Box 920741 *Web:* www.vizquest.com	Needham	MA	02492	781-207-0311		463
VJ Technologies Inc 89 Carlough Rd *TF:* 800-858-9729 ■ *Web:* www.vjt.com	Bohemia	NY	11716	631-589-8800		743
VJS Construction Services W233 N2847 Roundy Cir W *TF:* 800-433-6208 ■ *Web:* www.vjscs.com	Pewaukee	WI	53072	262-542-9000		186
VJV IT 96 Linwood Plaza *TF:* 800-614-7561 ■ *Web:* www.vjvit.com	Fort Lee	NJ	07024	800-614-7561		631
VKGS LLC (Video King Gaming Systems) 2717 N 118 Cir Ste 210 *TF:* 800-635-9912 ■ *Web:* www.videokingnetwork.com	Omaha	NE	68164	402-951-2970	951-2990	322
VKI Technologies Inc 3200 2e rue *TF:* 800-567-2951 ■ *Web:* www.vkitech.com	Saint-hubert	QC	J3Y8Y7	450-676-0504		159
V&L Tool Inc 2021 MacArthur Rd *TF:* 800-984-3775 ■ *Web:* www.vltool.com	Waukesha	WI	53188	262-547-1226		757
VLN Partners LLP 1212 E Carson St *TF:* 877-856-3311 ■ *Web:* www.vlnpartners.com	Pittsburgh	PA	15203	412-381-0183		174
VLSI Standards Inc 5 Technology Dr *Web:* www.vlsistandards.com	Milpitas	CA	95035	408-428-1800		518
Vlsip Technologies Inc 750 Presidential Dr *Web:* www.vlsip.com	Richardson	TX	75081	972-437-5506	644-1286	696
V&M Precision Machining & Grinding 1130 Columbia St *Web:* www.vm-machining.com	Brea	CA	92821	714-257-4850		295
VM Services Inc 6701 Mowry Ave	Newark	CA	94560	510-744-3720		625
VMA (Valve Manufacturers Assn of America) 1050 17th St NW Ste 280 *Web:* www.vma.org	Washington	DC	20036	202-331-8105	296-0378	49-13
VMC Consulting Corp 11611 Willows Rd NE *TF:* 877-393-8622 ■ *Web:* www.vmc.com	Redmond	WA	98052	425-558-7700		721
Vmc Technologies Inc 1788 Northwood Dr *Web:* www.vmctech.com	Troy	MI	48084	248-786-3000		358
V-me Media Inc 450 W 33rd St 11th Fl *Web:* www.vmetv.com	New York	NY	10001	212-273-4800		116
VMI (Vantage Mobility International) 5202 S 28th Pl *TF:* 800-348-8267 ■ *Web:* www.vantagemobility.com	Phoenix	AZ	85040	602-243-2700	304-3290	62-7
VMI Inc 211 E Weddell Dr *Web:* www.vmivideo.com	Sunnyvale	CA	94089	408-745-1700		45
VML Inc 250 NW RichaRds Rd *Web:* www.vml.com	Kansas City	MO	64116	816-283-0700		4
VMP (Village at Manor Park, The) 3023 S 84th St *TF:* 800-411-1861 ■ *Web:* www.vmpcares.com	Milwaukee	WI	53227	414-607-4100		672
VNA 154 Hindman Rd *TF:* 877-862-6659 ■ *Web:* lutheransenior life.org	Butler	PA	16001	724-282-6806		371
VNA (VNA Hospice Care) 11440 Olive Blvd Ste 200 *TF:* 800-392-4740 ■ *Web:* www.vnastl.com	Creve Coeur	MO	63141	314-918-7171	918-8054	371
VNA (Virginia Nurses Assn) 7113 Three Chopt Rd Ste 204 *Web:* www.virginianurses.com	Richmond	VA	23226	804-282-1808	282-4916	533
VNA & Hospice of Northern California 1900 Powell St Ste 300 *TF:* 800-698-1273 ■ *Web:* www.suttercareathome.org	Emeryville	CA	94608	510-450-8596	347-6874	371
VNA & Hospice of Southern California 150 W First St Ste 270 *TF:* 888-357-3574 ■ *Web:* www.vnasocal.org	Claremont	CA	91711	909-624-3574	624-1559	371
VNA California 6235 River Crest Dr Ste L *TF:* 800-213-0154 ■ *Web:* vnacalifornia.org	Riverside	CA	92507	951-413-1200		371
VNA Hospice & Home Health of Lackawanna County 301 Delaware Ave *TF:* 800-936-7671 ■ *Web:* www.vnahospice.org	Olyphant	PA	18447	570-383-5180	383-5189	371
VNA Hospice Care (VNA) 11440 Olive Blvd Ste 200 *TF:* 800-392-4740 ■ *Web:* www.vnastl.com	Creve Coeur	MO	63141	314-918-7171	918-8054	371
VNA of Central Jersey (VNACJ) 176 Riverside Ave *TF:* 800-862-3330 ■ *Web:* www.vnahg.org	Red Bank	NJ	07701	800-862-3330		371
VNA of Greater St Louis *Hospice Care* 11440 Olive Blvd Ste 200 *TF:* 800-392-4740 ■ *Web:* www.vnastl.com	Creve Coeur	MO	63141	314-918-7171	918-8054	371
Vna of Rhode Island 475 Kilvert St *TF:* 800-638-6274 ■ *Web:* www.vnari.org	Warwick	RI	02886	401-574-4900	490-8870	363
VNAA (Visiting Nurse Assns of America) 900 19th St NW Ste 200 *TF:* 888-866-8773 ■ *Web:* www.vnaa.org	Washington	DC	20006	202-384-1420	384-1444	49-8
VNACJ (VNA of Central Jersey) 176 Riverside Ave *TF:* 800-862-3330 ■ *Web:* www.vnahg.org	Red Bank	NJ	07701	800-862-3330		371
VNS Corp 325 Commerce Loop PO Box 1659 *Web:* www.vnscorp.com	Vidalia	GA	30475	912-537-8964		191-3
VNS Hospice of Suffolk 505 Main St *Web:* www.visitingnurseservice.org	Northport	NY	11768	631-261-7200	261-1985	371
VOA Assoc Inc 224 S Michigan Ave Ste 1400 *Web:* www.voa.com	Chicago	IL	60604	312-554-1400	554-1412	261
Vocal Laboratories Inc 10925 Valley View Rd Ste 202 *Web:* www.vocalabs.com	Eden Prairie	MN	55344	952-941-6580		743
Vocalink Language Services 405 W First St Unit A *TF:* 877-492-7754 ■ *Web:* www.vocalink.net	Dayton	OH	45402	937-223-1415		768
Vocantas Inc 750 Palladium Dr Ste 200 *TF:* 877-271-8853 ■ *Web:* www.vocantas.com	Ottawa	ON	K2V1C7	613-271-8853		179
Voce Communications Inc 298 S Sunnyvale Ave Ste 101 *Web:* www.vocecommunications.com	Sunnyvale	CA	94086	408-738-7840		636
Vocelli Pizza 1005 S [illegible] St *Web:* www.vocellipizza.com	Pittsburgh	PA	15[illegible]	412-[illegible]		670
Vocera Communications Inc 525 RACE St Ste 150 *TF:* 800-533-0523 ■ *Web:* www.vocera.com	San Jose	CA	95126	408-882-5100		177
Vode Lighting LLC 1206 E Macarthur St Ste 3 *Web:* vode.com	Sonoma	CA	95476	707-996-9898		196
Vogel Law Firm 218 NP Ave *TF:* 800-677-5024 ■ *Web:* www.vogellaw.com	Fargo	ND	58107	701-237-6983		428
Vogel State Park 7485 Vogel State Pk Rd *Web:* www.gastateparks.org	Blairsville	GA	30512	706-745-2628		565
Vogelsang USA 7966 State Rt 44 *TF:* 800-984-9400 ■ *Web:* vogelsangusa.com	Ravenna	OH	44266	330-296-3820		641
Vogler Motor Co Inc 1170 E Main *Web:* www.vogler-ford.com	Carbondale	IL	62901	618-457-8135		57
Vogt Ice 1000 W Ormsby Ave Ste 19 *TF:* 800-853-8648 ■ *Web:* www.vogtice.com	Louisville	KY	40210	502-635-3000	634-0479	664
Vogue Enterprise Inc 1801 Kettering *Web:* www.voguewindows.com	Irvine	CA	92614	949-833-9787		361
Vogue Fabrics 718 Main St *TF:* 800-433-4313 ■ *Web:* www.voguefabricsstore.com	Evanston	IL	60202	847-864-9600		270
Vogue Flowers & Gifts Ltd 1114 N Blvd *TF:* 800-923-1010 ■ *Web:* www.vogueflowers.com	Richmond	VA	23230	804-353-9600		292
Vogue Optical Inc 20 Great George St *TF:* 866-594-3937 ■ *Web:* www.vogueoptical.com	Charlottetown	PE	C1A6X8	902-566-3326	566-3269	543
Voice & Data Networks Inc 6981 Washington Ave S *TF:* 000-246-7999 ■ *Web:* www.voicedata.com	Minneapolis	MN	55439	952-946-5353		525
Voice Construction Ltd 7545 52 St *Web:* www.voiceconst.com	Edmonton	AB	T6B2G2	780-469-1351		188
Voice of America Radio Network 330 Independence Ave SW *Web:* www.voanews.com	Washington	DC	20237	202-203-4000		644
Voice of God Recordings Inc, The 5911 Charlestown Pk *Web:* www.branham.org	Jeffersonville	IN	47130	812-256-1177		48-20
Voice on the Go Inc 20 Amber St Ste 207 *TF:* 877-977-0555 ■ *Web:* www.voiceonthego.com	Markham	ON	L3R5P4	905-305-1355		179
Voice Pro Inc 2055 Lee Rd Ste 101 *TF:* 800-261-0104 ■ *Web:* www.voiceproinc.com	Cleveland	OH	44118	216-932-8040		765
Voice Security Systems Inc 24591 Seth Cir *Web:* www.voice-security.com	Dana Point	CA	92629	949-493-4030		693
Voice, The 51180 Bedford St *Web:* www.voicenews.com	New Baltimore	MI	48047	586-716-8100	716-8533	532-4
Voice123 30 E 23rd St *Web:* www.voice123.com	New York	NY	10010	212-461-1873		387
VoiceAge Corp 750 Lucerne Rd Ste 250 *Web:* www.voiceage.com	Montreal	QC	H3R2H6	514-737-4940		194
VoiceBox Technologies Inc 1110 112th Ave NE Ste 100 *Web:* www.voicebox.com	Bellevue	WA	98005	425-968-7900		177

Name / Address	City	State	ZIP	Phone	Fax	Class
Voicecom 5900 Windward Pkwy Ste 500 *TF:* 888-468-3554 ■ *Web:* intelliverse.com	Alpharetta	GA	30005	888-468-3554		736
Voicenet Communications Inc 9810 Ashton Rd	Philadelphia	PA	19114	215-259-2100	259-2199	396
Voices for America's Children 1000 Vermont Ave NW Ste 700	Washington	DC	20005	202-289-0777		48-6
Voices of September 11th 161 Cherry St *TF:* 866-505-3911 ■ *Web:* www.voicesofseptember11.org	New Canaan	CT	06840	203-966-3911	966-5701	48-5
Voicetrak Inc 4500 E Speedway Blvd Ste 5 *Web:* www.voicetrak.com	Tucson	AZ	85712	520-628-9222	437-0938	5
Voigt & Schweitzer Inc 987 Buckeye Park Rd *Web:* www.hotdipgalvanizing.com	Columbus	OH	43207	614-443-4621	449-8851	481
Voigt House Victorian Museum 115 College Ave SE *Web:* grpm.org	Grand Rapids	MI	49504	616-929-1700		520
Voila! 509 Botetourt St *Web:* voilainternationalcuisine.godaddysites.com	Norfolk	VA	23510	757-640-0343		671
VoIP Group Inc 6161 Blue Lagoon Dr Ste 190 *Web:* www.voipgroup.com	Miami	FL	33126	305-264-2401		809
VoIP Innovations Inc 8 Penn Ctr W Ste 101 *TF:* 877-478-6471 ■ *Web:* www.voipinnovations.com	Pittsburgh	PA	15276	877-478-6471		387
VoIPLINK Corp 3029 S Harbor Blvd *TF:* 800-880-9517 ■ *Web:* www.voiplink.com	Santa Ana	CA	92704	760-918-9100		445
Voisard Mfg Inc 60 Scott St	Shiloh	OH	44878	419-896-3191		697
Voit Real Estate Services Inc 101 Shipyard Way *Web:* www.voitco.com	Newport Beach	CA	92663	949-644-8648		652
Voith Industrial Services Inc 9395 Kenwood Rd Ste 200 *Web:* redirect.voith.com	Cincinnati	OH	45242	513-731-3590	731-3659	393
Voith Paper Inc 2200 N Roemer Rd PO Box 2337 *Web:* voith.com	Appleton	WI	54912	920-731-7724	997-9625	556
Voith Siemens Hydro Power 760 E Berlin Rd *TF:* 800-228-2800 ■ *Web:* www.voith.com	York	PA	17408	717-792-7000	792-7263	262
Voith Turbo Inc 25 Winship Rd *Web:* redirect.voith.com/index2.php?r=d939d1f104c0b	York	PA	17406	717-767-3200		60
Volare Ristorante Italiano 1523 Elizabeth Ave *Web:* www.volareristoranteitaliano.com	Charlotte	NC	28204	704-370-0208		671
Volare Systems Inc 4351 Canyonbrook Dr *Web:* volaresystems.com	Highlands Ranch	CO	80130	303-532-5838		177
Volaris Group Inc 5800 Explorer Dr 5th Fl *Web:* www.volarisgroup.com	Mississauga	ON	L4W5K9	905-267-5400		787
Volcano Restaurant 3700 Lincoln Way W *Web:* volcanosb.com	South Bend	IN	46628	574-287-5775		671
Volckening Inc 6700 Third Ave *TF:* 800-344-3486 ■ *Web:* www.volckening.com	Brooklyn	NY	11220	718-836-4000	748-2811	298
Volcom Inc 1740 Monrovia Ave *Web:* www.volcom.com	Costa Mesa	CA	92627	949-646-2175		155-1
Volex Inc 915 Tate Blvd SE Ste 130 *Web:* www.volex.com	Hickory	NC	28602	828-485-4500		815
Volga River State Recreation Area 10225 Ivy Rd *Web:* www.iowadnr.gov	Fayette	IA	52142	563-425-4161	425-3272	565
Volian Enterprises Inc 122 Kerr Rd *Web:* volian.com	New Kensington	PA	15068	724-335-3744		177
Volk Corp 23936 Industrial Pk Dr *Web:* www.volkcorp.com	Farmington Hills	MI	48335	248-477-6700	478-6884	467
Volk Optical Inc 7893 Enterprise Dr *TF:* 800-345-8655 ■ *Web:* www.volk.com	Mentor	OH	44060	440-942-6161		543
Volk Packaging Corp 11 Morin St *Web:* www.volkboxes.com	Biddeford	ME	04005	207-282-6151		100
Volkert & Assoc Inc 3809 Moffett Rd *Web:* www.volkert.com	Mobile	AL	36618	251-342-1070	342-7962	261
Volkswagen Canada Inc 777 Bayly St W *TF:* 800-822-8987 ■ *Web:* www.vw.ca	Ajax	ON	L1S7G7	905-428-6700	428-5898	59
Volkswagen Group of America Inc 2200 Ferdinand Porsche Dr *Web:* www.volkswagengroupamerica.com	Herndon	VA	20171	248-754-5000		59
Volkswagen of America Inc 3800 Hamlin Rd *TF:* 800-822-8987 ■ *Web:* www.vw.com	Auburn Hills	MI	48326	800-822-8987		59
Volleyball Hall of Fame 444 Dwight St *Web:* www.volleyhall.org	Holyoke	MA	01040	413-536-0926		522
Vollmer Inc 3822 Sandwich St *Web:* www.vollmer.ca	Windsor	ON	N9C1C1	519-966-6100		261
Vollrath Co LLC, The 1236 N 18th St *TF:* 800-624-2051 ■ *Web:* vollrath.com	Sheboygan	WI	53081	920-457-4851	459-6570	300
Vollwerth & Co 200 Hancock St PO Box 239 *TF:* 800-562-7620 ■ *Web:* www.vollwerth.com	Hancock	MI	49930	906-482-1550		296-26
Volmar Construction Inc 4400 Second Ave *Web:* www.volmar.com	Brooklyn	NY	11232	718-832-2444	499-4045	685
Volo Bog State Natural Area 28478 W Brandenburg Rd *Web:* www.dnr.illinois.gov/Parks/Pages/VoloBog.aspx	Ingleside	IL	60041	815-344-1294		565
Vology Corp 281 E Water St *Web:* www.vology.com	Rockland	MA	02370	781-384-2023		226
Volquartsen Custom Ltd 24276 240th St PO Box 397 *Web:* volquartsen.com	Carroll	IA	51401	712-792-4238		711
Volt 1065 Ave of the Americas 20th Fl *NYSE: VISI* ■ *Web:* volt.com	New York	NY	10018	212-704-2400		721
Volt VIEWtech Inc 4761 E Hunter Ave *TF:* 888-396-9927 ■ *Web:* www.volt.com	Anaheim	CA	92807	714-695-3377		463
Voltage Ltd 901 Front St Ste 300 *Web:* voltagead.com	Louisville	CO	80027	303-664-1687		5
VoltDelta Resources Inc 3750 Monroe Ave Ste 4B *Web:* www.voltdelta.com	Pittsford	NY	14534	212-827-2600		178-10
Volterra 5411 Ballard Ave NW *Web:* www.volterrarestaurant.com	Seattle	WA	98107	206-789-5100		671
Volterra Semiconductor Corp 47467 Fremont Blvd *NASDAQ: VLTR* ■ *Web:* www.maximintegrated.com	Fremont	CA	94538	510-743-1200	743-1600	696
Volume 9 Inc 1660 S Albion St Ste 800 *Web:* www.v9seo.com	Denver	CO	80222	303-955-5228		195
Volume Transportation Inc 6575 Marshall Blvd *TF:* 800-879-5565 ■ *Web:* www.volinc.com	Lithonia	GA	30058	770-482-1400		780
Volunteer Energy Co-op (VEC) PO Box 277 *Web:* www.vec.org	Decatur	TN	37322	423-334-5721	334-7003	245
Volunteer State Community College 1480 Nashville Pk *TF:* 888-335-8722 ■ *Web:* www.volstate.edu	Gallatin	TN	37066	615-452-8600		162
Volunteers of America 1660 Duke St *TF:* 800-899-0089 ■ *Web:* www.voa.org	Alexandria	VA	22314	703-341-5000	341-7000	48-5
Volusia County 123 W Indiana Ave *TF:* 800-955-8771 ■ *Web:* volusia.org	DeLand	FL	32720	386-736-5920	822-5707	338
Volusia County Public Library 105 E Magnolia Ave *TF:* 800-272-3900 ■ *Web:* www.volusialibrary.org	Daytona Beach	FL	32114	386-257-6036		434-3
Volusia Speedway Park 1500 W State Rd **Fax Area Code: 352* ■ *Web:* bubbaracewaypark.com	De Leon Springs	FL	32130	386-985-4402	622-3126*	515
Volvo Cars of North America 1 Volvo Dr *TF Cust Svc:* 800-458-1552 ■ *Web:* www.volvocars.com	Rockleigh	NJ	07647	201-768-7300		59
Volvo Construction Equipment of North America Inc 312 Volvo Way *Web:* www.volvoce.com	Shippensburg	PA	17257	717-532-9181		190
Volvo Group North America Inc 2900 K St NW Ste 401 *Web:* www.volvo.com	Washington	DC	20007	202-661-4770		516
Volvo Honolulu 704 Ala Moana Blvd *TF:* 888-892-2456 ■ *Web:* www.volvohonolulu.com	Honolulu	HI	96813	888-892-2456		516
Volvo of Tucson 831 W Wetmore Rd *Web:* www.volvooftucson.com	Tucson	AZ	85705	520-792-1070		57
Volvo Penta of the Americas Inc 1300 Volvo Penta Dr *TF:* 800-522-1959 ■ *Web:* www.volvopenta.com	Chesapeake	VA	23320	757-436-2800	436-5150	262
Volvo Trucks North America 4881 Cougar Trail Rd *Web:* www.volvotrucks.com/trucks/na/en-us	Dublin	VA	24084	540-674-4181		59
Vomar Products Inc 7800 Deering Ave *Web:* www.vomarproducts.com	Canoga Park	CA	91304	818-610-5115	610-5123	701
Vomela Co, The 274 E Fillmore Ave *TF:* 800-645-1012 ■ *Web:* www.vomela.com	Saint Paul	MN	55107	651-228-2200	228-2295	701
Von Braun Ctr 700 Monroe St *Web:* www.vonbrauncenter.com	Huntsville	AL	35801	256-533-1953		205
Von Lehman & CO 250 Grandview Dr Ste 300 *Web:* www.vlcpa.com	Fort Mitchell	KY	41017	859-331-3300		463
Von Maur Inc 6565 Brady St *TF:* 800-463-3339 ■ *Web:* www.vonmaur.com	Davenport	IA	52806	563-388-2200	388-2242	229
Von Paris Enterprises Inc 8691 Larkin Rd *TF:* 800-866-6355 ■ *Web:* www.vonparis.com	Savage	MD	20763	410-888-8500	888-9062	519
Von Rabenau 704 N Wells St *TF:* 800-229-1967 ■ *Web:* www.talcott.com	Chicago	IL	60654	312-849-2220	849-2174	457-21
Von Roll Isola USA 200 Von Roll Dr **Fax: Cust Svc* ■ *TF:* 800-654-7652 ■ *Web:* www.vonroll.com	Schenectady	NY	12306	518-344-7100	344-7288*	500
Von Ruden Manufacturing Inc 1008 First St NE *Web:* www.vonruden.com	Buffalo	MN	55313	763-682-3122		247
Vonage Holdings Corp 23 Main St *NYSE: VG* ■ *TF:* 877-862-2562 ■ *Web:* www.vonage.com	Holmdel	NJ	07733	732-528-2600	834-0189	736
Vons Employees Federal Credit Union 4455 Arden Dr PO Box 8023 *Web:* vonsefcu.org	El Monte	CA	91731	626-444-1972		219
Vontobel Asset Management Inc 1540 Broad Way Ave 38th Fl *TF General:* 800-445-8872 ■ *Web:* www.vusa.com	New York	NY	10036	212-415-7000	415-7087	401
Vooner Flogard Corp 4729 Stockholm Ct *TF:* 800-345-7879 ■ *Web:* www.vooner.com	Charlotte	NC	28273	704-552-9314		295
Voorhees College 213 Wiggins Dr PO Box 678 *TF Admissions:* 800-446-6250 ■ *Web:* www.voorhees.edu	Denmark	SC	29042	803-780-1234		166
Voorhees International Inc 575 Rudder Rd Ste 109 *Web:* www.voorheesintl.com	Fenton	MO	63026	636-349-1555	349-5130	187
Voorhees Pediatric Facility 1304 Laurel Oak Rd *TF:* 888-873-5437 ■ *Web:* www.forkidcare.com	Voorhees	NJ	08043	856-346-3300	346-3462	450
Voorhees State Park 251 County Rd 513 *Web:* www.njparksandforests.org	Glen Gardner	NJ	08826	908-638-6969		565
Voorhees Town Ctr 2120 Voorhees Town Ctr *Web:* www.voorheestowncenter.com	Voorhees	NJ	08043	856-772-1950		460
Voorwood Co 2350 Barney St *TF:* 800-826-0089 ■ *Web:* www.voorwood.com	Anderson	CA	96007	530-365-3311	365-3315	821
Vornado Air Circulation Systems Inc 415 E 13th St *TF:* 800-234-0604 ■ *Web:* www.vornado.com	Andover	KS	67002	316-733-0035		17
Vornado Realty Trust 888 Seventh Ave *NYSE: VNO* ■ *TF:* 800-294-1322 ■ *Web:* www.vno.com	New York	NY	10019	212-894-7000	902-9316	655
Vorsite Corp 1631 15th Ave W Ste 316 *Web:* www.vorsite.com	Seattle	WA	98119	206-781-1797		224
Vortaloptics Inc 7251 West Lake Mead Blvd Ste 300	Las Vegas	NV	89128	702-369-2500		525

Company	City	State	ZIP	Phone	Fax	Class
Vortalsoft Inc 100 Davidson Ave Ste 300 *Web:* vortalsoft.com	Somerset	NJ	08873	732-748-1800		809
Vortech Engineering LLC 1650 Pacific Ave *Web:* www.vortechsuperchargers.com	Oxnard	CA	93033	805-247-0226		247
Vortek Instruments LLC 8475 W I25 Frontage Rd Ste 300 *Web:* vortekinst.com	Longmont	CO	80504	303-682-9999		639
Vortex Advisory Group 220 Pond St *Web:* advisoryleadership.com/consulting	Hopkinton	MA	01748	508-435-0220		463
Vortex LLC 4 Dearborn Rd *Web:* www.vortexmetal.com	Peabody	MA	01960	978-535-8721		697
Vortx Inc 2245 Ashland St *TF:* 800-581-1943 ■ *Web:* www.vortx.com	Ashland	OR	97520	541-201-9965		177
Vorwerk USA Company LP 1964 Corporate Sq *Web:* www.vorwerk.com	Longwood	FL	32750	407-830-9988		366
Vorys Sater Seymour & Pease LLP (VSSP) 52 E Gay St PO Box 1008 *Web:* www.vorys.com	Columbus	OH	43216	614-464-6400	464-6350	428
VOSINC 2030 Arnold Dr *Web:* www.vosinc.com	Martinez	CA	94553	925-229-6600		177
Voss Belting & Specialty Co 6965 N Hamlin Ave *TF:* 800-325-9972 ■ *Web:* www.vossbelting.com	Lincolnwood	IL	60712	847-673-8900	673-1408	370
Voss Industries Inc 2168 W 25th St *Web:* www.vossind.com	Cleveland	OH	44113	216-771-7655	771-2887	350
Voss Lighting PO Box 22159 *TF:* 866-292-0529 ■ *Web:* www.vosslighting.com	Lincoln	NE	68542	402-328-2281		246
Voss Pharmacy Inc 3303 S Halsted St	Chicago	IL	60608	773-254-5221		237
Voss Signs LLC 112 Fairgrounds Dr *TF:* 800-473-0698 ■ *Web:* www.vosssigns.com	Manlius	NY	13104	315-682-6418		687
Votaw Precision Technologies Inc 13153 Lakeland Rd *Web:* www.votaw.com	Santa Fe Springs	CA	90670	562-944-0661		697
Votenet Solutions Inc 1420 K St *Web:* www.eballot.com	Washington	DC	20005	202-737-2277	737-2283	178-10
Voto Manufacturers Sales Co 500 N Third St PO Box 1299 *TF:* 800-848-4010 ■ *Web:* www.votosales.com	Steubenville	OH	43952	740-282-3621	282-5441	385
Vought Aircraft Div 300 Austin Blvd *Web:* www.triumphgroup.com	Red Oak	TX	75154	972-946-2011		22
VOX Data 1155 Metcalfe St 18th Fl *TF:* 800-861-9599 ■ *Web:* www.voxdata.com	Montreal	QC	H3B2V6	514-871-1920		737
Vox Mobile LLC 6200 Oak Tree Blvd Ste 450 *Web:* voxmobile.com	Independence	OH	44131	216-525-0191		736
Vox Printing Inc 4000 E Britton Rd *Web:* www.voxprint.com	Oklahoma City	OK	73131	405-478-7500		627
Vox Public Relations Public Affairs 1416 Willamette St *Web:* www.voxprpa.com	Eugene	OR	97401	541-302-6620		636
Voxify Inc 1151 Marina Village Pkwy	Alameda	CA	94501	510-545-5000		009
Voxls Inc 1160 Brickyard Cove Rd Ste 202	Point Richmond	CA	94801	510-232-8333		544
Voxox Inc 9270 Scranton Rd Ste [illegible] *Web:* www.voxox.com	San Diego	CA	92121	[illegible]		[illegible]
Voxtechnologies Com 301 S Sherman St *TF:* 888-568-6224 ■ *Web:* www.voxtechnologies.com	Richardson	TX	75081	972-234-4343		175
Voxware Inc 300 American Metro Blvd Ste 155 *Web:* www.voxware.com	Hamilton	NJ	08619	609-514-4100		178-7
Voya Services Co 5780 Powers Ferry Rd NW *Web:* www.voya.com	Atlanta	GA	30327	770-980-5100		360-4
Voya Services Co 230 Park Ave *TF:* 855-663-8692 ■ *Web:* www.voya.com	New York	NY	10169	860-580-4646		391-3
Voyager Academy 101 Hock Parc *Web:* www.voyageracademy.net	Durham	NC	27704	919-433-3301		148
Voyager Electronics Corp 3065 101st Ave NE *Web:* www.voyagercorp.com	Blaine	MN	55449	763-571-7766		179
Voyager Systems Inc 360 Route 101 *TF:* 800-634-1966 ■ *Web:* www.voyagersystems.com	Bedford	NH	03110	603-472-5172		180
Voyagers Restaurant 110 Hartfield Rd *Web:* www.alibabaexpress.com	Morgantown	WV	26505	304-777-4120		671
Voyages Groupe Ideal Inc 5415 Pare St Ste 1 *TF:* 800-342-9554 ■ *Web:* www.groupeideal.ca	Montreal	QC	H4P1P7	514-342-9554		775
Voyages Michel Barrette 100 Rue Saint-joseph *TF:* 800-263-3078 ■ *Web:* voyagesmichelbarrette.com	Alma	QC	G8B7A6	418-668-3078		775
Voyageur Inn 200 Viking Dr *Web:* www.magnusonhotels.com	Reedsburg	WI	53959	608-524-6431		379
Voyageur Lakewalk Inn 333 E Superior St *TF:* 800-258-3911 ■ *Web:* www.voyageurlakewalkinn.com	Duluth	MN	55802	218-722-3911		379
Voyageur Transportation Services 573 Admiral Ct *TF:* 855-263-7163 ■ *Web:* www.voyageurtransportation.ca	London	ON	N5V4L3	519-455-4580		107
Voyageurs National Park 360 Hwy 11 E *TF:* 888-381-2873 ■ *Web:* www.nps.gov/voya	International Falls	MN	56649	218-283-6600	285-7407	564
Voyetra Turtle Beach Inc 150 Clearbrook Rd Ste 162 *Web:* www.turtlebeach.com	Elmsford	NY	10523	914-345-2255	345-2266	625
Voytek Inc 3100 Breckenridge Blvd Ste 120 *Web:* www.voytek.com	Duluth	GA	30096	770-921-7017		396
V&P Hydraulic Products LLC 1700 Pittsburgh Dr *TF:* 800-821-1535 ■ *Web:* www.vphyd.com	Delaware	OH	43015	740-203-3600		641
Vp Racing Fuels Inc 7124 Richter Rd *TF:* 800-336-5437 ■ *Web:* www.vpracingfuels.com	Elmendorf	TX	78112	210-635-7744		580
VPC (Violence Policy Ctr) 1730 Rhode Island Ave NW Ste 1014 *Web:* www.vpc.org	Washington	DC	20036	202-822-8200		48-7
VPE Public Relations 316 W Second St Ste 1202 *Web:* vpe-pr.com	Los Angeles	CA	90012	626-403-3200		636
VPI Corp 3123 S Ninth St *TF Orders:* 800-874-4240 ■ *Web:* www.vpicorp.com	Sheboygan	WI	53081	920-458-4664	458-1368	600
VPIRG (Vermont Public Interest Research Group) 141 Main St Ste 6 *Web:* www.vpirg.org	Montpelier	VT	05602	802-223-5221		633
VPIsystems Corp 100 Davidson Ave Ste 203	Somerset	NJ	08873	732-332-0233	469-7823	177
VPNet Technologies Inc 211 Mt Airy Rd	Basking Ridge	NJ	95035	408-404-1400	404-1414	459
VPOP Technologies Inc 1772J Avenida de los Arboles Ste 374 *TF Sales:* 888-811-8767 ■ *Web:* www.vpop.net	Thousand Oaks	CA	91362	805-529-9374		808
VPSI Inc 1220 Rankin Dr *TF:* 800-826-7433 ■ *Web:* www.vride.com	Troy	MI	48083	248-597-3500	597-3501	468
VPT (Vermont Public Television) 204 Ethan Allen Ave *TF:* 800-639-7811 ■ *Web:* www.vpt.org	Colchester	VT	05446	802-655-4800		632
VPT Inc 1971 Kraft Dr *Web:* vptpower.com	Blacksburg	VA	24060	540-552-5000	552-5003	256
V-rad Systems Inc 4504 Maple St *Web:* v-radsystems.com	Bellaire	TX	77401	713-667-6056		383
VRC Inc 696 W Bagley Rd *TF:* 800-872-1012 ■ *Web:* www.vrcmfg.com	Berea	OH	44017	440-243-6666		757
Vrdolyak Law Group LLC 741 N Dearborn St *Web:* www.vrdolyak.com	Chicago	IL	60654	312-482-8200		428
VRE (Virginia Railway Express) 1500 King St Ste 202 *TF:* 800-743-3873 ■ *Web:* www.vre.org	Alexandria	VA	22314	703-684-1001	684-1313	468
VRG (Vegetarian Resource Group, The) PO Box 1463 *Web:* www.vrg.org	Baltimore	MD	21203	410-366-8343	366-8804	48-17
VRH Construction Corp 320 Grand Ave *Web:* www.vrhcorp.com	Englewood	NJ	07631	201-871-4422		186
VRMA (Vacation Rental Managers Assn) 2025 M St NW Ste 800 *Web:* www.vrma.com	Washington	DC	20036	202-367-1179	367-2179	49-17
VRMC (Venice Regional Medical Ctr) 540 The Rialto *Web:* www.veniceregional.com	Venice	FL	34285	941-485-7711	483-7699	374-3
Vroman's Bookstore 695 E Colorado Blvd *Web:* www.vromansbookstore.com	Pasadena	CA	91101	626-449-5320		95
Vrp Consulting Inc 268 Bush St Ste 3836 *TF:* 855-545-3877 ■ *Web:* www.vrpinc.com	San Francisco	CA	94104	855-545-3877		177
V-S Industries Inc 900 Chaddick Dr	Wheeling	IL	60090	847-520-1800		621
VS Management of NY Inc 3281 Veterans Memorial Hwy **Fax Area Code:* 631 ■ *TF:* 877-778-7648	Ronkonkoma	NY	11779	877-778-7648	585-6513*	631
Vsa Inc 6929 Seward Ave *TF:* 800-888-2140 ■ *Web:* www.vsa1.com	Lincoln	NE	68507	402-467-3668	325-8033	246
VSAC (Vermont Student Assistance Corp) PO Box 2000 *TF:* 800-642-3177 ■ *Web:* www.vsac.org	Winooski	VT	05404	802-655-9602	654-3765	725
VSC (Vetter Stone Co) 23894 Third Ave *TF:* 800-878-2850 ■ *Web:* www.vetterstone.com	Mankato	MN	56001	507-345-4568	345-4777	724
VSE Corp 2550 Huntington Ave *NASDAQ: VSEC* ■ *TF:* 800-455-4873 ■ *Web:* www.vsecorp.com	Alexandria	VA	22303	703-960-4600	329-4623	261
VSHFM (Virginia Sports Hall of Fame) 206 High St *TF:* 800-662-6171 ■ *Web:* www.vshfm.com	Portsmouth	VA	23704	757-393-8031	393-8288	522
VSI (Vinyl Siding Institute) 1201 15th St NW Ste 220 *Web:* www.vinylsiding.org	Washington	DC	20005	202-587-5100		49-13
VSM Abrasives 1012 E Wabash St *TF Cust Svc:* 800-737-0176 ■ *Web:* www.vsmabrasives.com	O'Fallon	MO	63366	636-272-7432	272-7434	1
VSNA (Vermont State Nurses Assn) 4 Carmichael St Ste 111 Rm 215 **Fax Area Code:* 802 ■ *TF:* 877-810-5972 ■ *Web:* www.vsna-inc.org	Essex	VT	05452	877-810-5972	651-8998*	533
V-Soft Inc 888 Saratoga Ave Ste 203 *TF:* 800-497-5943 ■ *Web:* v-softinc.com	San Jose	CA	95129	408-342-1700		179
VSolvIT LLC 4171 Market St Ste 2 *Web:* www.vsolvit.com	Ventura	CA	93003	805-277-4705		177
VSP Capital 201 Post St Ste 1100	San Francisco	CA	94108	415-558-8600		792
VSS (Veronis Suhler Stevenson) 55 E 52nd St 33rd Fl *Web:* www.vss.com	New York	NY	10055	212-935-4990	381-8168	690
Vss Security Services 1717 W Northern Ave Ste 200 *Web:* www.vss-security-services.com	Phoenix	AZ	85021	602-861-9900		693
VSSP (Vorys Sater Seymour & Pease LLP) 52 E Gay St PO Box 1008 *Web:* www.vorys.com	Columbus	OH	43216	614-464-6400	464-6350	428
VStock Transfer LLC 18 Lafayette Pl *Web:* www.vstocktransfer.com	Woodmere	NY	11598	212-828-8436		463
VT Graphics Inc 465 Penn St *Web:* www.vtgraph.com	Yeadon	PA	19050	610-259-4090	259-7235	781
VT Halter Marine Inc 900 Bayou Casotte Pkwy *TF:* 800-639-2715 ■ *Web:* www.vthaltermarine.com	Pascagoula	MS	39581	228-696-6888	696-6899	698
V-T Industries Inc 1000 Industrial Pk *TF:* 800-827-1615 ■ *Web:* www.vtindustries.com	Holstein	IA	51025	712-368-4381	368-4111	599
VT LeeBoy Inc 500 Lincoln County Pkwy Extention *Web:* www.leeboy.com	Lincolnton	NC	28092	704-966-3300		190
VT MAK 150 Cambridge Park Dr 3rd Fl *Web:* www.mak.com	Cambridge	MA	02140	617-876-8085	876-9208	178-10

				Phone	Fax	Class

VT Systems Inc
99 Canal Ctr Plaza Ste 220 .... Alexandria VA 22314 703-739-2610 21
Web: www.vt-systems.com

VTA (Santa Clara Valley Transportation Authority)
3331 N First St .... San Jose CA 95134 408-321-5555 468
TF: 800-894-9908 ■ *Web:* www.vta.org

VTech Communications Inc
9590 SW Gemini Dr Ste 120 .... Beaverton OR 97008 503-596-1200 644-9887 735
TF: 800-595-9511 ■ *Web:* www.vtech.com

VTech Electronics North America LLC
1155 W Dundee St Ste 130 .... Arlington Heights IL 60004 847-400-3600 762
TF: 800-521-2010 ■ *Web:* www.vtechkids.com

V-Technologies LLC 675 W Johnson Ave .... Cheshire CT 06410 800-462-4016 525
TF: 800-462-4016 ■ *Web:* www.vtechnologies.com

V-TEK Inc 751 Summit Ave PO Box 3104 .... Mankato MN 56002 507-387-2039 253
TF: 800-257-1271 ■ *Web:* www.vtekusa.com

VTHG (Virginia Tech)
Department of Horticulture
490 W Campus Dr 301 Saunders Hall .... Blacksburg VA 24061 540-231-5451 97
Web: www.hort.vt.edu

VTI Instruments Corp 2031 Main St .... Irvine CA 92614 949-955-1894 256
Web: www.vtiinstruments.com

VTS Investigations LLC 7 S State St .... Elgin IL 60123 800-538-4464 628-1666* 400
**Fax Area Code:* 847 ■ *TF:* 800-538-4464 ■ *Web:* www.pichicago.com

VuFind Inc 1290 Oakmead Pkwy Ste 107 .... Sunnyvale CA 94508 408-739-2880 387

Vulcan Corp 30 Garfield Pl Ste 1040 .... Cincinnati OH 45202 513-621-2850 676
TF Sales: 800-447-1146 ■ *Web:* www.vulcorp.com

Vulcan Engineering Co
1 Vulcan Dr PO Box 307 .... Helena AL 35080 205-663-0732 663-9103 386
Web: www.vulcangroup.com

Vulcan Inc 410 E Berry Ave .... Foley AL 36535 888-846-2728 943-9270* 153
**Fax Area Code:* 251 ■ *TF:* 888-846-2728 ■ *Web:* www.vulcaninc.com

Vulcan Inc 505 Fifth Ave S Ste 900 .... Seattle WA 98104 206-342-2000 342-3000 405
Web: www.vulcan.com

Vulcan Industries Corp
N113 W18830 Carnegie Dr .... Germantown WI 53022 262-253-5420 595
Web: www.vulcancorp.com

Vulcan Industries Inc 300 Display Dr .... Moody AL 35004 205-640-2400 640-2412 233
TF: 888-444-4417 ■ *Web:* www.vulcanind.com

Vulcan Materials Co
1200 Urban Ctr Dr PO Box 385014 .... Birmingham AL 35238 205-298-3000 503-5
NYSE: VMC ■ *TF:* 800-615-4331 ■ *Web:* www.vulcanmaterials.com

Vulcan Materials Company Western Div
1200 Urban Center Dr .... Birmingham AL 35242 205-298-3000 503-5
NYSE: VMC ■ *TF:* 800-615-4331 ■ *Web:* www.vulcanmaterials.com

Vulcan Minerals Inc
333 Duckworth St .... St. Johns NL A1C1G9 709-754-3186 538
Web: www.vulcanminerals.ca

Vulcan Painters Inc PO Box 1010 .... Bessemer AL 35021 205-428-0556 424-2267 189-8
Web: www.vulcan-group.com

Vulcan Spring & Manufacturing Co
501 Schoolhouse Rd .... Telford PA 18969 215-721-1721 483
Web: www.vulcanspring.com

Vulcan Threaded Products
10 Crosscreek Trl .... Pelham AL 35124 205-620-5100 350
Web: vulc.com

Vulcan Tool Co 730 Lorraine Ave .... Dayton OH 45410 937-253-6194 253-1062 493
Web: www.vulcancut.com

Vulcan Value Partners
3 Protective Ctr 2801 Hwy 280 S Ste 300 .... Birmingham AL 35223 205-803-1582 803-1584 226
Web: www.vulcanvaluepartners.com

Vulsay Industries Ltd 35 Regan Rd .... Brampton ON L7A1B2 905-846-2200 88
TF: 800-468-1760 ■ *Web:* www.vulsay.com

Vumii Inc
1100 Abernathy Rd 500 Northpark Town Ctr
Ste 1100 .... Atlanta GA 30328 678-578-4700 529
Web: www.vumii.com

Vutec Corp 11711 W Sample Rd .... Coral Springs FL 33065 954-545-9000 545-9011 591
TF: 800-770-4700 ■ *Web:* www.vutec.com

Vuurr LLC 260 S Arizona Ave .... Chandler AZ 85225 480-525-8240 631
Web: www.vuurr.com

Vuzix Corp
2166 Brighton Henrietta Town Line Rd .... Rochester NY 14623 585-359-5900 543
TF: 800-436-7838 ■ *Web:* www.vuzix.com

Vvm Inc 5606 W Adams Ave .... Temple TX 76502 254-778-8028 180
TF: 800-774-3379 ■ *Web:* www.vvm.com

VVMA (Virginia Veterinary Medical Assn)
3801 Westerre Pkwy Ste D .... Henrico VA 23233 804-346-2611 346-2655 795
TF: 800-937-8862 ■ *Web:* www.vvma.org

VWA (Vengroff Williams & Assoc Inc)
2099 S State College Blvd .... Anaheim CA 92806 714-889-6200 160
TF: 800-238-9655 ■ *Web:* www.vwinc.com

VWR International
100 Matsonford Rd Bldg 1 Ste 200 .... Radnorpa PA 19087 610-431-1700 431-9174 475
TF: 800-932-5000 ■ *Web:* us.vwr.com

Vx Associates LLC
150 Allen Rd Ste 107 .... Liberty Corner NJ 07938 908-696-7973 463

VXI Global Solutions Inc
220 W First St 3rd Fl .... Los Angeles CA 90012 213-637-1300 317
Web: www.vxi.com

Vyatek Sports Inc
1711 W University Dr Ste 155 .... Tempe AZ 85281 480-998-2046 711
Web: www.vyatek.com

VyMaC Corp W3130 State Rd 59 E .... Whitewater WI 53190 920-568-3130 471

Vyrian Inc 9894 Bissonnet St Ste 918 .... Houston TX 77036 281-404-3420 246
Web: www.vyrian.com

Vyse Gelatin Co 5010 Rose St .... Schiller Park IL 60176 847-678-4780 345
TF: 800-533-2152 ■ *Web:* www.vyse.com

Vystar Credit Union
1802 Kernan Blvd S .... Jacksonville FL 32246 904-777-6000 219
TF: 800-445-6289 ■ *Web:* vystarcu.org

Vytron Corp 1000 Vytron Rd .... Loudon TN 37774 865-458-4624 596
Web: www.vytron.com

W

				Phone	Fax	Class

W & E Radtke Inc
W168 N12276 Century Ln .... Germantown WI 53022 262-253-1412 293
Web: weradtke.com

W & H Co-op Oil Co 407 13th St N .... Humboldt IA 50548 515-332-2782 332-1559 324
TF: 800-392-3816 ■ *Web:* whcoop.com

W & H Pacific
12100 NE 195th St Ste 300 .... Bothell WA 98011 425-951-4800 951-4808 261
Web: www.whpacific.com

W & H Systems Inc 120 Asia Pl .... Carlstadt NJ 07072 201-933-7840 933-2144 207
TF: 800-966-6993 ■ *Web:* www.whsystems.com

W & K Steel LLC 98 Antisbury Pl .... Rankin PA 15104 412-271-1620 480

W & m Manufacturing Inc
1000 N Morton St .... Portland IN 47371 260-726-9800 481
Web: www.wmmanufacturing.com

W & T Offshore Inc
9 Greenway Plaza Ste 300 .... Houston TX 77046 713-626-8525 626-8527 536
Web: www.wtoffshore.com

W & W Steel Co 1730 W Reno Ave .... Oklahoma City OK 73106 405-235-3621 236-4842 480
TF: 800-222-1868 ■ *Web:* www.wwsteel.com

W A Baum Company Inc 620 Oak St .... Copiague NY 11726 631-226-3940 476
TF: 888-281-6061 ■ *Web:* www.wabaum.com

W a m s Inc 1800 E Lambert Ave Ste 155 .... Brea CA 92821 800-421-7151 177
TF: 800-421-7151 ■ *Web:* www.wamsinc.com

W Atlee Burpee Co 300 Pk Ave .... Warminster PA 18974 215-674-4900 694
TF Cust Svc: 800-333-5808 ■ *Web:* www.burpee.com

W Bradley Electric Inc 90 Hill Rd .... Novato CA 94945 415-898-1400 898-5991 787
Web: www.wbeinc.com

W C Rouse & Son Inc 110 Longale Rd .... Greensboro NC 27409 336-299-3035 612
TF: 800-210-5131 ■ *Web:* www.wcrouse.com

W C Weil Co Inc
3812 William Flynn Hwy Ste 2 .... Allison Park PA 15101 412-487-7140 112
Web: www.wcweil.com

W Ca Logistics 643 Bodey Cir Unit A .... Urbana OH 43078 937-653-6382 195
TF: 800-860-7838 ■ *Web:* www.wcalogistics.com

W D Communications
227 E Bergen Pl Ste 6 .... Red Bank NJ 07701 732-530-2076 196
Web: wdcommunications.com

W E O'Neil Construction Co
2751 N Clybourn Ave .... Chicago IL 60614 773-755-1611 186
TF: 800-358-8444 ■ *Web:* www.weoneil.com

W Fort Lauderdale Hotel & Residences
401 N Ft Lauderdale Beach Blvd .... Fort Lauderdale FL 33304 954-414-8200 707
Web: www.wfortlauderdalehotel.com

W H Cress Company Inc
9966 SW Katherine St .... Tigard OR 97223 503-620-1664 321
Web: www.whcress.com

W H Meanor & Associates
216 N Mcdowell St Ste 200 .... Charlotte NC 28204 704-372-7640 463
Web: www.whmeanor.com

W H Q r 913 Fm
254 N Front St Ste 300 .... Wilmington NC 28401 910-343-1640 116
Web: www.whqr.org

W Harold Talley Company Inc
4905 Radford Ave Ste 200 .... Richmond VA 23230 804-359-5313 2

W L Halsey Grocery Company Inc
PO Box 6485 .... Huntsville AL 35824 256-772-9691 461-8386 297-8
TF: 800-621-0240 ■ *Web:* www.halseyfoodservice.com

W M Schlosser Company Inc
2400 51st Pl .... Hyattsville MD 20781 301-773-1300 773-9263 449
Web: www.wmschlosser.com

W M Sprinkman Corp 404 Pilot Court .... Waukesha WI 53188 800-816-1610 409-2060* 386
**Fax Area Code:* 262 ■ *TF:* 800-816-1610 ■ *Web:* www.sprinkman.com

W Machine Works Inc
13814 Del Sur St .... San Fernando CA 91340 818-890-8049 757
Web: www.wmwcnc.com

W Montreal Hotel 901 Victoria Sq .... Montreal QC H2Z1R1 514-395-3100 671
TF: 888-627-7081 ■ *Web:* www.wmontrealhotel.com

W Network 25 Dockside Dr .... Toronto ON M5A0B5 416-479-6784 740
Web: www.wnetwork.com

W New York- Union Square
201 Park Ave S .... New York NY 10003 212-253-9119 378
TF: 877-822-0000 ■ *Web:* www.wnewyorkunionsquare.com

W O Blackstone & Company Inc
1841 Shop Rd .... Columbia SC 29202 803-252-8222 610
Web: www.woblackstone.com

W O W Logistics Co
3040 W Wisconsin Ave .... Appleton WI 54914 920-734-9924 734-2697 803-1
TF: 800-236-3565 ■ *Web:* www.wowlogistics.com

W R Chesnut Engineering Inc
14 Spielman Rd .... Fairfield NJ 07004 973-227-6995 261
Web: chesnuteng.com

W R Systems Ltd
11351 Random Hills Rd Ste 400 .... Fairfax VA 22030 703-934-0200 261
Web: wrsystems.com

W Squared.com
5500 Maryland Way Ste 200 .... Brentwood TN 37027 615-577-4927 317
Web: www.wsquared.com

W. Caslon & Company Inc
1240 Jefferson Rd .... Rochester NY 14623 585-239-6063 393
Web: www.caslon.net

W. L. Butler Construction Inc
204 Franklin St .... Redwood City CA 94063 650-361-1270 361-8657 186
Web: www.wlbutler.com

W. N. Morehouse Truck Line Inc
4010 Dahlman Ave .... Omaha NE 68107 402-733-2200 685
TF: 800-228-9378 ■ *Web:* www.morehousetruckline.com

W. R. Vernon Produce Co
1035 N Cherry St PO Box 4054 .... Winston-Salem NC 27101 336-725-9741 761-1841 297-7
TF: 800-222-6406 ■ *Web:* www.vernonproduce.com

W. Rogers Co 649 Bizzell Dr .... Lexington KY 40510 859-231-6290 233-2066 186
Web: www.wrogers.com

Company / Address	City	State	Zip	Phone	Fax	Class
W. W. Tire Service Inc 204 Main St PO Box 22 *Web:* www.wwtireservice.com	Bryant	SD	57221	605-628-2501	628-2018	61
W.B. Nelson State Recreation Site 5580 S Coast Hwy *TF:* 800-551-6949 ■ *Web:* www.oregonstateparks.org	Newport	OR	97366	800-551-6949		565
W.D. Matthews Machinery Co 901 Center St *TF:* 800-442-6082 ■ *Web:* www.wdmatthews.com	Auburn	ME	04210	207-784-9311		358
W.F. Taylor Company Inc 11545 Pacific Ave *TF:* 800-397-4583 ■ *Web:* www.wftaylor.com	Fontana	CA	92337	951-360-6677	360-1177	3
W.H. Breshears Inc 720 B St *Web:* www.whbreshears.com	Modesto	CA	95354	209-522-7291		581
W.P. & R.S. Mars Co 4319 W First St *Web:* www.marssupply.com	Duluth	MN	55807	218-628-0303		385
W/M Display Group 1040 W 40th St *TF:* 800-443-2000 ■ *Web:* www.wmdisplay.com	Chicago	IL	60609	773-254-3700	254-3188	286
W20 Group 50 Francisco St Ste 400 *Web:* www.w2ogroup.com	San Francisco	CA	94133	415-362-5018		636
W3C (World Wide Web Consortium) 32 Vassar St Rm 32-G515 *Web:* www.w3.org	Cambridge	MA	02139	617-253-2613	258-5999	48-9
W3health Solutions LLC 115 Franklin TurnPk Ste 352 *TF:* 888-934-3258 ■ *Web:* www.w3health.com	Mahwah	NJ	07430	201-701-0240		809
W5 Inc 3211 Shannon Rd *Web:* w5insight.com	Durham	NC	27707	919-932-1117		466
WA Chester LLC 4390 Parliament Pl Ste Q *TF:* 800-991-2998 ■ *Web:* wachester.com	Lanham	MD	20706	240-487-1940	487-1941	189-4
WA Klinger LLC 2015 E Seventh St PO Box 8800 *Web:* www.waklinger.com	Sioux City	IA	51102	712-277-3900		186
WA Whitney Co 650 Race St PO Box 1206 *Web:* www.megafab.com	Rockford	IL	61105	815-964-6771	964-3175	456
WAAF-FM 107.3 (Rock) 20 Guest St 3rd Fl *Web:* www.waaf.com	Brighton	MA	02135	617-779-5400		645
Waahila Ridge State Recreation Area 1151 Punchbowl St PO Box 621 *Web:* www.hawaii.gov	Honolulu	HI	96809	808-587-0300	587-0311	565
WAAY-TV Ch 31 (ABC) 1000 Monte Sano Blvd SE *TF:* 888-407-4747 ■ *Web:* www.waaytv.com	Huntsville	AL	35801	256-533-3131		741-61
WAB Capital LLC 1559 Michael Ln Pacific Palisades *Web:* www.growthequities.com	Los Angeles	CA	90272	310-230-8664		401
Wabash College 410 W Wabash Ave PO Box 352 **Fax:* Admissions ■ *TF:* 800-345-5385 ■ *Web:* www.wabash.edu	Crawfordsville	IN	47933	765-361-6326	361-6433*	166
Wabash County 710 N East St *TF:* 800-346-2110 ■ *Web:* visitwabashcounty.com/?doing_wp_cron=1498721135.2839200496673583984375	Wabash	IN	46992	260-563-3131		338
Wabash County Clerk 401 N Market St *Web:* state.il.us	Mount Carmel	IL	62863	618-262-4561		338
Wabash County Rural Electric Membership Corp 370 S 250 E *TF:* 800-563-2146 ■ *Web:* kremc.com	Wabash	IN	46582	574-267-6331	267-7273	245
Wabash Ctr Inc 2000 Greenbush St *Web:* www.wabashcenter.com	Lafayette	IN	47904	765-423-5531		48-15
Wabash Electric Supply Inc 1400 S Wabash St *TF:* 800-552-7777 ■ *Web:* www.wabashelectric.com	Wabash	IN	46992	260-563-4146	563-4140	246
Wabash MPI 1569 Morris St PO Box 298 *Web:* www.wabashmpi.com	Wabash	IN	46992	260-563-1184	563-1396	456
Wabash National Corp 1000 Sagamore Pkwy S PO Box 6129 *NYSE:* WNC ■ *TF Sales:* 866-877-5062 ■ *Web:* www.wabashnational.com	Lafayette	IN	47903	765-771-5300		779
Wabash Technologies 1375 Swan St PO Box 829 **Fax:* Sales ■ *TF:* 800-487-6865	Huntington	IN	46750	260-355-4100	355-4265*	223
Wabash Telephone Co-op Inc 210 S Church St PO Box 299 *TF:* 800-228-9824 ■ *Web:* www.wabashtelephone.coop	Louisville	IL	62858	618-665-3311	665-4188	736
Wabash Valley Correctional Facility PO Box 1111 *TF:* 800-451-6028 ■ *Web:* www.in.gov/idoc/2409.htm	Carlisle	IN	47838	812-398-5050	398-5065	213
Wabash Valley Manufacturing Inc 505 E Main St *TF:* 800-253-8619 ■ *Web:* www.wabashvalley.com	Silver Lake	IN	46982	260-352-2102	352-2160	319-4
Wabash Valley Power Assn Inc 722 N High School Rd *Web:* www.wvpa.com	Indianapolis	IN	46214	317-481-2800	243-6416	245
Wabash Valley Service Company Inc 909 N Court St *TF:* 888-869-8127 ■ *Web:* www.wabashvalleyfs.com	Grayville	IL	62844	618-375-2311	375-5351	276
Wabasha County 625 Jefferson Ave **Fax:* Acctg	Wabasha	MN	55981	651-565-2648	565-2774*	338
Wabaunsee County 215 Kansas Ave PO Box 278 *Web:* ks-wabaunsee.manatron.com	Alma	KS	66401	785-765-3508	765-3704	338
WABC-AM 770 (N/T) 2 Penn Plaza 17th Fl *Web:* www.wabcradio.com	New York	NY	10121	212-613-3800	613-3837	645-111
WABCO Freight Car Products Ltd 475 Seaman Dr *Web:* www.wabtec.com	Stoney Creek	ON	L8E2R2	905-561-8700	561-8705	650
WABCO Locomotive Products 1001 Air Brake Ave *TF Cust Svc:* 877-922-2627 ■ *Web:* www.wabtec.com	Wilmerding	PA	15148	412-825-1000	825-1019	650
WABC-TV Ch 7 (ABC) 7 Lincoln Sq	New York	NY	10023	917-260-7000		741-91
WABE-FM 90.1 (NPR) 740 Bismark Rd NE *Web:* www.wabe.org	Atlanta	GA	30324	678-686-0321		645-10
Wabi Iron & Steel Corp 330 Broadwood Ave *Web:* www.wabicorp.com	New Liskeard	ON	P0J1P0	705-647-4383		480
WABI-TV Ch 5 (CBS) 35 Hildreth St *Web:* wabi.tv	Bangor	ME	04401	207-947-8321	941-9378	741-12
WABM-TV Ch 68 (MNT) 800 Concourse Pkwy Ste 200 *Web:* www.wabm68.com	Birmingham	AL	35244	205-403-3340		741-15
Wabtec Corp 1001 Air Brake Ave *NYSE:* WAB ■ *TF Cust Svc:* 877-922-2627 ■ *Web:* www.wabtec.com	Wilmerding	PA	15148	412-825-1000	825-1019	650
Wabtec Corp WABCO Transit Div PO Box 11 *Web:* www.wabtec.com	Spartanburg	SC	29304	864-433-5900	433-0176	650
Wabtec Railway Electronics 21200 Dorsey Mill Rd *Web:* www.wabtec.com	Germantown	MD	20876	301-515-2000	515-2100	518
Wabtec Rubber Products 269 Donohue Rd *Web:* www.wabtec.com	Greensburg	PA	15601	724-838-1317	832-5630	677
WABX-FM 107.5 (CR) 1162 Mt Auburn Rd *Web:* www.wabx.net	Evansville	IN	47720	812-424-8284	426-7928	645-56
WAC Consulting Inc 367 W Main St *Web:* www.wacinc.com	Northborough	MA	01532	508-393-7731		196
WACC (Westfield Area Chamber of Commerce) 173 Elm St 3rd Fl *Web:* www.gwaccnj.com	Westfield	NJ	07090	908-233-3021		139
Waccatee Zoological Farm 8500 Enterprise Rd *TF:* 800-380-7069 ■ *Web:* www.waccateezoo.com	Myrtle Beach	SC	29588	843-650-8500		823
WACG-FM 90.7 (NPR) 2500 Walton Way *TF:* 800-222-4788 ■ *Web:* www.gpb.org	Atlanta	GA	30904	706-737-1661		645-10
Wachovia Bank 3800 Wilshire Blvd Ste 110e *TF:* 800-225-5935 ■ *Web:* www.wellsfargo.com	Los Angeles	CA	90025	310-477-8004		70
Wachovia Bank NA 301 S College St *Web:* www.wellsfargo.com	Charlotte	NC	28202	704-335-5878		70
Wachs Water Services 801 Asbury Dr *TF:* 800-525-5821 ■ *Web:* www.wachsus.com	Buffalo Grove	IL	60089	800-525-5821		393
Wachtel & Company Inc 1101 14th St NW Eigth Fl Ste 800 *Web:* www.wachtelco.com	Washington	DC	20005	202-898-1144		690
Wachter Inc 16001 W 99th St *Web:* www.wachter.com	Lenexa	KS	66219	913-541-2500	541-2529	787
Wachters' Organic Sea Products Corp 550 Sylvan St *TF:* 800-682-7100 ■ *Web:* www.wachters.com	Daly City	CA	94014	650-757-9851	757-9858	799
WACH-TV Ch 57 (Fox) 1400 Pickens St Ste 6 *Web:* www.wach.com	Columbia	SC	29201	803-252-5757		741-33
Wachusett Mountain State Reservation 345 Mountain Rd *Web:* www.mass.gov	Princeton	MA	01541	978-464-2987		565
Wacker Chemical Corp 3301 Sutton Rd *TF:* 888-922-5374 ■ *Web:* www.wacker.com	Adrian	MI	49221	517-264-8500	264-8246	144
Wacker Neuson N 92 W 15000 Anthony Ave **Fax Area Code:* 800 ■ *TF:* 800-770-0957 ■ *Web:* products.wackerneuson.com	Menomonee Falls	WI	53051	262-255-0500	822-0710*	190
Waco 2546 General Armistead Ave *Web:* www.wacofilters.com	Norristown	PA	19403	610-630-4000	630-4004	10
Waco Convention & Visitors Bureau 100 Washington Ave *TF:* 800-321-9226 ■ *Web:* www.wacoheartoftexas.com	Waco	TX	76701	254-750-5810	750-5801	206
Waco Inc 5450 Lewis Rd PO Box 829 *Web:* www.wacoinc.net	Sandston	VA	23150	804-222-8440	226-3241	189-9
Waco Tribune-Herald 900 Franklin Ave *TF:* 800-678-8742 ■ *Web:* www.wacotrib.com	Waco	TX	76701	254-757-5757	757-0302	532-2
Wacoal America 50 Polito Ave *TF:* 800-922-6250 ■ *Web:* www.wacoal-america.com	Lyndhurst	NJ	07071	201-933-8400		155-18
Wacoal Europe 65 Sprague St *TF:* 800-733-8964 ■ *Web:* www.wacoal-europe.com	Hyde Park	MA	02136	617-361-7559	361-7527	155-18
Wacom Technology Corp 1311 SE Cardinal Ct *TF:* 800-922-6613 ■ *Web:* www.wacom.com	Vancouver	WA	98683	360-896-9833	896-9724	173-1
Waco-McLennan County Library 1717 Austin Ave *TF:* 800-433-7300 ■ *Web:* www.waco-texas.com	Waco	TX	76701	254-750-5941	750-5940	434-3
Waconia Manufacturing Inc 33 E Eigth St *TF:* 800-643-4266 ■ *Web:* www.waconiamfg.com	Waconia	MN	55387	952-442-4450		492
Wada Farms Potatoes Inc 326 S 1400 W *Web:* www.wadafarms.com	Pingree	ID	83262	208-684-9801	684-4157	10-11
Waddell & Reed Financial Inc 6300 Lamar Ave *NYSE:* WDR ■ *TF:* 888-923-3355 ■ *Web:* www.waddell.com	Overland Park	KS	66201	913-236-2000		401
Waddell Barnes Botanical Gardens 100 College Station Dr Macon State College *Web:* www.mga.edu	Macon	GA	31206	478-471-2780		97
Wade College 1950 N Stemmons Fwy LB 562 Ste 4080 *TF:* 800-624-4850 ■ *Web:* www.wadecollege.edu	Dallas	TX	75207	214-637-3530	637-0827	800
Wade Financial Advisory Inc 2105 S Bascom Ave Ste 110 *Web:* www.wadefa.com	Campbell	CA	95008	408-369-7399		401
Wade Inc 1505 Hwy 82 W *Web:* www.wadeincorporated.com	Greenwood	MS	38930	662-453-6312		274
Wade Tours Inc 797 Burdeck St *TF:* 800-955-9233 ■ *Web:* www.wadetours.com	Schenectady	NY	12306	518-355-4500	355-4942	760
Wadena County 415 S Jefferson St *Web:* www.co.wadena.mn.us	Wadena	MN	56482	218-631-7650		338
Wade-Trim Group Inc 500 Griswold Ave Ste 2500 *TF:* 800-482-2864 ■ *Web:* www.wadetrim.com	Detroit	MI	48226	313-961-3650	961-0898	261
Wadley Regional Medical Ctr 1000 Pine St *Web:* www.wadleyhealth.com	Texarkana	TX	75501	903-798-8000		374-3
WADL-TV Ch 38 (Fox) 35000 Adell Dr *Web:* www.wadldetroit.com	Clinton Township	MI	48035	586-790-3838		741

				Phone	Fax	Class
Wadsworth Atheneum Museum of Art 600 Main St *TF:* 800-200-2882 ■ *Web:* thewadsworth.org	Hartford	CT	06103	860-278-2670		520
Wadsworth Ctr *Biggs Laboratory New York Dept of Health* Empire State Plaza PO Box 509 *Web:* www.wadsworth.org	Albany	NY	12201	518-474-7354		668
Wadsworth Golf Construction Co 13941 Van Dyke Rd *Web:* www.wadsworthgolf.com	Plainfield	IL	60544	815-436-8400	436-8404	188-3
Wadsworth Public Library 132 Broad St *Web:* www.wadsworthlibrary.com	Wadsworth	OH	44281	330-334-5761		434-3
Wadsworth-Longfellow House 489 Congress St *Web:* www.mainehistory.org/house_overview.shtml	Portland	ME	04101	207-774-1822	775-4301	50-3
WAER-FM 88.3 (Jazz) 795 Ostram Ave *TF:* 800-321-5862 ■ *Web:* www.waer.org	Syracuse	NY	13210	315-443-4021		645-160
WAFB-TV Ch 9 (CBS) 844 Government St *TF:* 888-677-2900 ■ *Web:* www.wafb.com	Baton Rouge	LA	70802	225-215-4700		741-13
WaferGen Bio-systems Inc 7400 Paseo Padre Pkwy *Web:* www.wafergen.com	Fremont	CA	94555	510-651-4450		419
Wafertech LLC 5509 NW Parker St *Web:* www.wafertech.com	Camas	WA	98607	360-817-3000		696
Waffle House Inc 5986 Financial Dr *Web:* www.wafflehouse.com	Norcross	GA	30071	770-729-5700		670
WAFF-TV Ch 48 (NBC) 1414 Memorial PkwyNW *Web:* www.waff.com	Huntsville	AL	35801	256-533-4848	534-4101	741-61
WAFL-FM 97.7 (AC) 1666 Blairs Pond Rd *Web:* www.eagle977.com	Milford	DE	19963	302-422-7575	422-3069	645
Wagamama Quincy Market Bldg *Web:* www.wagamama.us	Boston	MA	02109	617-742-9242		671
WAGA-TV Ch 5 (Fox) 1551 Briarcliff Rd NE **Fax:* News Rm ■ *Web:* www.fox5atlanta.com	Atlanta	GA	30306	404-898-0100	724-4426*	741-7
Waggoners Trucking 5220 Midland Rd *TF:* 800-999-9097 ■ *Web:* www.waggonerstrucking.com	Billings	MT	59101	406-248-1919	259-6924	780
Wagman Metal Products Inc 400 S Albemarle St *TF:* 800-233-9461 ■ *Web:* www.wagmanmetal.com	York	PA	17403	717-854-2120		295
Wagner & Brown Ltd 300 N Marienfeld St *Web:* wbltd.com	Midland	TX	79701	432-682-7936		536
Wagner Ann (Rep R - MO) 435 Cannon Bldg *Web:* wagner.house.gov	Washington	DC	20515	202-225-1621		342-2
Wagner College 1 Campus Rd *TF Admissions:* 800-221-1010 ■ *Web:* www.wagner.edu	Staten Island	NY	10301	718-390-3400	390-3105	166
Wagner Falconer & Judd Ltd 100 S Fifth St Ste 800 *Web:* www.wfjlawfirm.com	Minneapolis	MN	55402	612-339-1421		428
Wagner Free Institute of Science 1700 W Montgomery Ave *Web:* www.pacscl.org	Philadelphia	PA	19121	215-763-6529	763-1299	520
Wagner Johnston & Rosenthal 5855 Sandy Springs Cir Ste 300 *Web:* www.wjrlaw.com	Atlanta	GA	30328	404-261-0500		428
Wagner Oil Co 500 Commerce St Ste 600 *TF:* 800-457-5332 ■ *Web:* www.wagneroil.com	Fort Worth	TX	76102	817-335-2222		536
Wagner Plate Works LLC 4142 W 49th St *TF:* 800-759-3444 ■ *Web:* www.wagnerplateworks.com	Tulsa	OK	74107	918-447-4488		480
Wagner Spray Tech Corp 1770 Fernbrook Ln *TF:* 800-328-8251 ■ *Web:* www.wagnerspraytech.com	Plymouth	MN	55447	763-553-7000	519-3563	172
Wago Corp N120 W19129 Freistadt Rd **Fax Area Code:* 262 ■ *TF:* 800-346-7245 ■ *Web:* www.wago.us	Germantown	WI	53022	800-346-7245	255-3232*	203
Wagon Train State Recreation Area 3019 Apple St *Web:* outdoornebraska.gov	Lincoln	NE	68503	402-471-5566		565
Wagoner County 307 E Cherokee St *Web:* www.ok.gov/wagonercounty	Wagoner	OK	74467	918-485-2367	485-8033	338
Wagstaff & Cartmell LLP 4740 Grand Ave Ste 300 *Web:* www.wagstaffcartmell.com	Kansas City	MO	64112	816-701-1100		428
Wagstaff Worldwide 5443 Fountain Ave *Web:* www.wagstaffworldwide.com	Los Angeles	CA	90029	323-871-1151	871-1171	636
WAGT-TV Ch 26 (NBC) PO Box 1212 *Web:* www.26nbc.com/station	Augusta	GA	30903	803-278-1212		741-8
Waguespack Oil Company Inc 1818 Hwy 3185 PO Box 326 *Web:* www.wagoil.com	Thibodaux	LA	70302	985-447-3668	447-5730	579
Wah King Noodle Co 2201 E Seventh St *Web:* www.wahkingnoodle.com	Los Angeles	CA	90023	323-268-0222		123
Wahiawa Freshwater State Recreation Area PO Box 621 *Web:* dlnr.hawaii.gov	Honolulu	HI	96809	808-622-6316		565
Wahkiakum County 64 Main St *TF:* 800-359-1506 ■ *Web:* www.co.wahkiakum.wa.us	Cathlamet	WA	98612	360-795-3558	795-8813	338
Wahl Clipper Corp 2900 Locust St *TF:* 800-767-9245 ■ *Web:* www.wahl.com	Sterling	IL	61081	800-767-9245		214
Wahl Media Inc 580 Packetts Landing *Web:* www.wahlmedia.com	Fairport	NY	14450	585-377-8129		5
Wahl Refractory Solutions LLC 767 OH-19 *TF:* 800-837-9245 ■ *Web:* www.wahlref.com	Fremont	OH	43420	419-334-2650	334-9445	663
Wahlco Inc 2722 S Fairview St *TF:* 800-423-5432 ■ *Web:* www.wahlco.com	Santa Ana	CA	92704	714-979-7300	979-0603	454
Wahlcometroflex Inc 29 Lexington St *TF:* 800-272-6652 ■ *Web:* sfpathway.com	Lewiston	ME	04240	207-784-2338		480
Wahluke School District 73 411 E Saddle Mt Dr *Web:* www.wsd73.wednet.edu	Mattawa	WA	99349	509-932-4565		685
Wahoo's Fish Taco 2855 Pullman St *Web:* www.wahoos.com	Santa Ana	CA	92705	949-222-0670		670
Wah-Sha-She State Park 396120 State Hwy 10 *Web:* www.travelok.com	Copan	OK	74044	918-532-4334	532-4659	565
WAI (Wire Assn International Inc) 1570 Boston Post Rd PO Box 578 *TF:* 800-449-4265 ■ *Web:* www.wirenet.org	Guilford	CT	06437	203-453-2777	453-8384	49-13
Wai & Connor LLP 2566 Overland Ave Ste 570 *Web:* www.waiconnor.com	Los Angeles	CA	90064	310-838-6800		428
Waianapanapa State Park 54 S High St Rm 101 *Web:* dlnr.hawaii.gov	Wailuku	HI	96793	808-984-8109	984-8111	565
Waiawa Correctional Facility 94-560 Kamehameha Hwy *Web:* hawaii.gov	Waipahu	HI	96797	808-677-6150		213
Waife & Associates Inc 62 Warren St *Web:* www.waife.com	Needham	MA	02492	781-449-7032		195
WAIglobal 411 Eagleview Blvd Ste 100 **Fax Area Code:* 800 ■ *TF:* 800-877-3340 ■ *Web:* waiglobal.com	Exton	PA	19341	484-875-6600	948-6121*	61
Waikiki Aquarium 2777 Kalakaua Ave *TF:* 800-832-3474 ■ *Web:* waikikiaquarium.org	Honolulu	HI	96815	808-923-9741	923-1771	40
Waikiki Gateway Hotel 2070 Kalakaua Ave *Web:* www.waikikigateway.com	Honolulu	HI	96815	808-955-3741		379
Waikiki Parc Hotel 2233 Helumoa Rd *TF:* 800-422-0450 ■ *Web:* www.waikikiparc.com	Honolulu	HI	96815	808-921-7272	923-1336	379
Waikiki Resort Hotel 2460 Koa Ave *TF:* 800-367-5116 ■ *Web:* www.waikikiresort.com	Honolulu	HI	96815	808-922-4911	922-9468	379
Wailea Beach Marriott Resort & Spa 3700 Wailea Alanui Dr **Fax Area Code:* 817 ■ *TF:* 800-845-5279 ■ *Web:* www.marriott.com	Wailea	HI	96753	808-879-1922	778-2049*	669
WAIL-FM 99.5 (Rock) 830 Crane Blvd Ste 10 *Web:* www.sun103.com	Sugarloaf Key	FL	33042	305-296-7511		645-84
Wailoa River State Recreation Area 75 Aupuni St Rm 204 *Web:* dlnr.hawaii.gov	Hilo	HI	96720	808-961-9590	961-9599	565
Wailua River State Park 3060 Eiwa St *Web:* www.hawaii.gov	Lihue	HI	96766	808-274-3444		565
Wailua Valley State Wayside 54 S High St Rm 101 *Web:* dlnr.hawaii.gov	Wailuku	HI	96793	808-984-8109	984-8111	565
Waimea Canyon State Park 3060 Eiwa St Ste 306 *Web:* www.hawaii.gov	Lihue	HI	96766	808-274-3444	274-3448	565
Wainhouse Research LLC 34 Duckhill Terr *Web:* www.wainhouse.com	Duxbury	MA	02332	781-934-6165		196
Wainscot Media LLC 110 Summit Ave *Web:* www.wainscotmedia.com	Montvale	NJ	07645	201-571-2244		194
Wainwright House 260 Stuyvesant Ave *Web:* www.wainwright.org	Rye	NY	10580	914-967-6080		673
Waisman Ctr University of Wisconsin 1500 Highland Ave *TF:* 888-428-8476 ■ *Web:* www.waisman.wisc.edu	Madison	WI	53705	608-263-1656	263-0529	668
Waitt Corp LLC 1125 S 103rd St Ste 425 *Web:* www.waittcompany.com	Omaha	NE	68124	402-697-8000		643
Waiward Steel Fabricators Ltd 10030 - 34 St *TF:* 888-999-9531 ■ *Web:* www.waiward.com	Edmonton	AB	T6B2Y5	780-469-1258		480
Wajax Corp 3280 Wharton Way *TSE:* WJX ■ *Web:* www.wajax.com	Mississauga	ON	L4X2C5	905-212-3300		358
Wajax Industrial Components LP 2200 52 Nd Ave *TF:* 866-546-3267 ■ *Web:* www.wajax-industrial-components.ca	Lachine	QC	H8T2Y3	514-636-3333		358
WAJR-AM 1440 (N/T) 1251 Earl L Core Rd *TF:* 800-765-8255 ■ *Web:* www.wajr.com	Morgantown	WV	26505	304-296-0029		645-105
WAJZ-FM 96.3 (Urban) 6 Johnson Rd *Web:* www.jamz963.com	Latham	NY	12110	518-786-6600		645
WAKA-TV Ch 8 (CBS) 3020 Eastern Blvd *TF:* 800-467-0401 ■ *Web:* www.waka.com	Montgomery	AL	36116	334-271-8888	244-7859	741-86
WAKB Magic 100.9 FM 6025 Broadcast Dr *Web:* www.1009magic.com	North Augusta	SC	29841	803-279-2330	279-8149	645
Wake Christian Academy Inc 5500 Wake Academy Dr *Web:* www.wakechristianacademy.com	Raleigh	NC	27603	919-772-6264		685
Wake Correctional Ctr 1000 Rock Quarry Rd *TF:* 866-719-0108 ■ *Web:* ncdps.gov	Raleigh	NC	27610	919-733-7988	733-9166	213
Wake County 336 Fayetteville St *Web:* www.wakegov.com	Raleigh	NC	27601	919-856-6160	856-6168	338
Wake County Alcoholism Treatment Ctr 3000 Falstaff Rd *Web:* www.wakegov.com	Raleigh	NC	27610	919-250-1500		726
Wake County Public Library System 4020 Carya Dr *Web:* www.wakegov.com	Raleigh	NC	27610	919-250-1200		434-3
Wake County Public School System 3600 Wake Forest Rd *TF:* 800-732-0416 ■ *Web:* www.wcpss.net	Raleigh	NC	27609	919-850-1600		685
Wake Electric 100 S Franklin St PO Box 1229 *TF:* 800-474-6300 ■ *Web:* www.wemc.com	Wake Forest	NC	27588	919-863-6300		245
Wake Forest University 1834 Wake Forest Rd **Fax:* Admissions ■ *Web:* www.wfu.edu	Winston-Salem	NC	27106	336-758-5255	758-4324*	166
Wake Forest University Baptist Medical Ctr Medical Ctr Blvd *Web:* www.wakehealth.edu	Winston-Salem	NC	27157	336-716-2011		374-3
Wake Forest University Reynolds Library PO Box 7777 *Web:* www.zsr.wfu.edu	Winston-Salem	NC	27109	336-758-4931	758-5605	434-6

Name / Address	City	State	Zip	Phone	Fax	Class
Wake Forest University School of Law Worrell Professional Ctr Wake Forest Rd	Winston-Salem	NC	27109	336-758-5435	758-3930*	167-1
*Fax: Admissions ■ Web: www.law.wfu.edu						
Wake Forest University School of Medicine Medical Ctr Blvd	Winston-Salem	NC	27157	336-716-4264	716-9593	167-2
TF: 800-445-2255 ■ Web: www.wakehealth.edu						
Wake Technical Community College 9101 Fayetteville Rd	Raleigh	NC	27603	919-866-5000	661-0117*	162
*Fax: Admissions ■ Web: www.waketech.edu						
Wakefern Food Corp 600 York St	Elizabeth	NJ	07207	908-527-3300		297-8
TF: 800-746-7748 ■ Web: www.shoprite.com						
Wakefield Chamber of Commerce 5 Common St	Wakefield	MA	01880	781-245-0741		139
Web: wakefieldchamber.org						
Wakefield Corp, The 10646 Dutchtown Rd	Knoxville	TN	37932	865-675-1550		186
Web: www.thewakefieldcorp.com						
Wakefield Pork Inc 410 Main Ave E	Gaylord	MN	55334	507-237-5581	237-5584	10-6
Web: www.wakefieldpork.com						
Wakefield School District 60 Farm St	Wakefield	MA	01880	781-246-6400		685
Web: wakefieldpublicschools.org						
Wakefield Thermal Solutions Inc 33 Bridge St	Pelham	NH	03076	603-635-2800	635-1900	253
Web: www.wakefield-vette.com						
Wakefield's Inc 3100 McClellan Blvd Quintard Ave	Anniston	AL	36201	256-237-9521		157-2
TF: 800-333-1552 ■ Web: www.wakefields.com						
Wakelight Technologies Inc 155 Kapalulu Pl Ste 109	Honolulu	HI	96819	808-836-9253		180
Web: www.wakelight.com						
Wakely Consulting Group Inc 7650 W Courtney Campbell Cswy Ste 1250	Tampa	FL	33607	727-507-9858	507-9658	194
Web: www.wakely.com						
WakeMed Health & Hospitals 3000 New Bern Ave	Raleigh	NC	27610	919-350-8000		363
TF: 800-510-9132 ■ Web: lake-medical.com						
WakeMed Raleigh Campus 3000 New Bern Ave	Raleigh	NC	27610	919-350-7000		374-3
Web: www.wakemed.org						
Wakensys Corp 505 N Lake Shore Dr Ste 222	Chicago	IL	60611	773-754-3230		196
Web: www.wakensys.com						
Wako Chemicals USA Inc 1600 Bellwood Rd	Richmond	VA	23237	804-271-7677	271-7791	231
TF: 800-992-9256 ■ Web: www.wakousa.com						
WAKO Electronics USA Inc 2105 Production Dr	Louisville	KY	40299	502-429-8866	429-8869	202
Web: www.wako-usa.com						
Wakoff Andriulli & Company LLC 100 Craig Rd Ste 109	Manalapan	NJ	07726	732-866-8882		2
Web: njcpa.com						
Wakonda State Park 32836 State Pk Rd	LaGrange	MO	63448	573-655-2280		565
Web: www.mostateparks.com						
WAKR-AM 1590 (N/T) 1795 W Market St	Akron	OH	44313	330-869-9800		645-2
Wakulla County 3056 Crawfordville Hwy	Crawfordville	FL	32327	850-926-0905	926-0938	338
Web: www.wakullaclerk.com						
Wakunaga of America Company Ltd 23501 Madero	Mission Viejo	CA	92691	949-855-2776	458-2764	799
TF: 800-421-2998 ■ Web: www.kyolic.com						
WAKW-FM 93.3 (Rel) 6275 Collegevue Pl PO Box 24126	Cincinnati	OH	45224	513-542-9259	542-9333	645-37
TF: 888-542-9393 ■ Web: www.mystar933.com						
WALA-TV Ch 10 (Fox) 1501 Satchel Paige Dr	Mobile	AL	36606	251-434-1010		741-85
TF: 800-876-8810 ■ Web: www.fox10tv.com						
Walberg Tim (Rep R - MI) 2436 Rayburn Bldg	Washington	DC	20515	202-225-6276	225-6281	342-2
Web: walberg.house.gov						
Walbon & Company Inc 4230 Pine Bend Trial	Rosemount	MN	55068	651-437-2011		685
Web: www.walbon.com						
Walbridge Aldinger Co 777 Woodward Ave #300	Detroit	MI	48226	313-963-8000	963-8150	188-7
Web: www.walbridge.com						
Walch Education 40 Walch Dr	Portland	ME	04103	207-772-2846	772-3105	637-2
TF: 800-558-2846 ■ Web: www.walch.com						
Walco Electric Co 303 Allens Ave	Providence	RI	02905	401-467-6500		518
Web: www.walcokip.com						
Wald LLC 800 E Fifth St	Maysville	KY	41056	606-564-4077	564-5248*	82
*Fax: Sales ■ Web: www.waldllc.com						
Wald Relocation Services Ltd 8708 W Little York Rd Ste 190	Houston	TX	77040	713-512-4800	512-4881	519
TF: 800-527-1408 ■ Web: www.waldrelocation.com						
Waldameer Park Inc 220 Peninsula Dr	Erie	PA	16505	814-838-3591		32
Web: www.waldameer.com						
Waldbillig & Besteman Inc 8001 Excelsior Dr Ste 110	Madison	WI	53717	608-829-0900		195
Web: www.nelsonschmidt.com						
Waldemar S Nelson & Company Inc 1200 St Charles Ave	New Orleans	LA	70130	504-523-5281	523-4587	261
Web: www.wsnelson.com						
Walden Correctional Institution 4340 Broad River Rd	Columbia	SC	29210	803-896-8580		213
Web: doc.sc.gov						
Walden Energy LLC 111 W Fifth St Ste 1000	Tulsa	OK	74103	918-488-8663		536
Web: www.waldenenergy.com						
Walden Equipment Ltd 2479 Riverside Dr	Timmins	ON	P4N2X7	705-682-2084		45
TF: 800-461-5959 ■ Web: www.waldenequipment.ca						
Walden Farms 1209 W St Georges Ave	Linden	NJ	07036	800-229-1706		296-19
TF: 800-229-1706 ■ Web: www.waldenfarms.com						
Walden Galleria 1 Walden Galleria	Buffalo	NY	14225	716-681-7600		460
TF: 800-297-5009 ■ Web: waldengalleria.com						
Walden Greg (Rep R - OR) 2185 Rayburn Bldg	Washington	DC	20515	202-225-6730	225-5774	342-2
Web: walden.house.gov						
Walden Media LLC 1888 Century Pk E	Los Angeles	CA	90067	310-887-1000		514
Web: www.walden.com						
Walden Pond State Reservation 915 Walden St	Concord	MA	01742	978-369-3254		565
Web: www.mass.gov						
Walden Structures Inc 801 Opal Ave	Mentone	CA	92359	909-389-9100		189-14
Web: www.waldenstructures.com						
Walden Venture Capital 750 Battery St Ste 700	San Francisco	CA	94111	415-391-7225		792
Web: www.waldenvc.com						
Walden Woods Project, The 44 Baker Farm Rd	Lincoln	MA	01773	781-259-4700	259-4710	48-13
TF: 800-554-3569 ■ Web: www.walden.org						
Waldinger Corp 2601 Bell Ave	Des Moines	IA	50321	515-284-1911	323-5150	189-14
TF: 800-473-4934 ■ Web: www.waldinger.com						
Waldner's Business Environment 125 Rt 110	Farmingdale	NY	11735	631-844-0300		320
Web: www.waldners.com						
Waldo County PO Box D	Belfast	ME	04915	207-338-1710	338-6360	338
TF: 800-244-5211 ■ Web: www.waldocountyme.gov						
Waldoch Crafts Inc 13821 Lake Dr NE	Forest Lake	MN	55025	651-464-3215	464-1117	62-7
TF: 800-328-9259 ■ Web: www.waldoch.com						
Waldom Electronics Corp 1801 Morgan St	Rockford	IL	61102	815-968-9661		246
Web: www.gcwaldom.com						
Waldon Mfg LLC 201 W Oklahoma Ave	Fiarview	OK	73737	580-227-3711		470
TF: 866-283-2759 ■ Web: www.waldonequipment.com						
Waldorf College 106 S Sixth St	Forest City	IA	50436	641-585-2450	585-8184*	166
*Fax: Admissions ■ TF: 800-292-1903 ■ Web: www.waldorf.edu						
Waldron Energy Corp 600-510 5 St SW	Calgary	AB	T2P3S2	403-532-6700		536
Web: www.waldronenergy.ca						
Waldron Engineering & Construction Inc 37 Industrial Dr	Exeter	NH	03833	603-772-7153		261
Web: www.waldron.com						
Waldron Wealth Management LLC 1150 Old Pond Rd	Bridgeville	PA	15017	412-221-1005		251
TF: 800-325-6000 ■ Web: www.waldronprivatewealth.com						
Wale Apparatus Co Inc 400 Front St	Hellertown	PA	18055	610-838-7047	838-7440	333
TF: 800-334-9253 ■ Web: www.waleapparatus.com						
Walerko Tool & Engineering 1935 W Lusher Ave	Elkhart	IN	46517	574-295-2233		454
Web: www.walerko.com						
Wales Crane and Rigging Service PO Box 21628	Waco	TX	76702	254-772-3310	772-3420	189-1
Web: www.walesindustrial.com						
Walgreen Co 200 Wilmot Rd	Deerfield	IL	60015	847-940-2500	230-0002	237
TF Cust Svc: 800-925-4733 ■ Web: www.walgreens.com						
Walgreens Health Services 1411 Lake Cook Rd	Deerfield	IL	60015	800-207-2568		586
TF: 800-207-2568 ■ Web: www.walgreenshealth.com						
Walgren Lake State Recreation Area 15951 Hwy 385	Chadron	NE	69337	308-432-6167		565
Web: outdoornebraska.gov						
Walker & Armstrong LLP 3838 N Central Ave	Phoenix	AZ	85012	602-230-1040		2
Web: wa-cpas.com						
Walker & Jocke Company LPA 231 S Broadway	Medina	OH	44256	330-721-0000		428
Web: www.walkerandjocke.com						
Walker & Massey CPAs 150 W Rialto Ave	Rialto	CA	92376	909-875-0244		2
Walker Advertising Inc 1010 S Cabrillo Ave	San Pedro	CA	90731	310-519-4050	519-4090	7
Web: www.walkeradvertising.com						
Walker Art Ctr 1750 Hennepin Ave	Minneapolis	MN	55403	612-375-7600	375-7618	520
TF: 888-339-4496 ■ Web: www.walkerart.org						
Walker Bill (I) State Capitoly PO Box 110001	Juneau	AK	99811	907-465-3500	465-3532	343
Web: gov.alaska.gov						
Walker Brand Communication 1810 W Kennedy Blvd	Tampa	FL	33606	813-875-3322		4
Web: www.walkerbrands.com						
Walker County PO Box 1207	Huntsville	TX	77342	936-436-4933	436-4920	338
Web: www.co.walker.tx.us						
Walker County 1801 Third Ave S PO Box 1447	Jasper	AL	35502	205-384-7230	384-7003	338
Web: www.walkercounty.com						
Walker County 101 S Duke St PO Box 445	La Fayette	GA	30728	706-638-1437	638-1453	338
TF: 800-424-8666 ■ Web: www.walkerga.us						
Walker County Board of Education 1710 Alabama Ave PO Box 311	Jasper	AL	35501	205-387-0555	221-5636	685
Web: www.walkercountyschools.com						
Walker County Chamber of Commerce 204 19th St E Ste 101	Jasper	AL	35501	205-384-4571		139
Web: www.walkerchamber.us						
Walker County Chamber of Commerce 10052 N Hwy 27	Rock Spring	GA	30739	706-375-7702	375-7797	139
TF: 800-321-8128 ■ Web: www.walkercochamber.com						
Walker Die Casting Inc 1125 Higgs Rd PO Box 1189	Lewisburg	TN	37091	931-359-6206	359-8030	308
Web: www.walkerdiecasting.com						
Walker Elliott 11200 Westheimer Ste 365	Houston	TX	77042	713-482-3750		260
TF: 800-836-0881 ■ Web: www.walker-elliott.com						
Walker Engineering Inc 8451 Dunwoody Pl	Atlanta	GA	30350	770-641-7306		256
Web: www.walkerengineer.com						
Walker Ford Company Inc 17556 US Hwy 19 N	Clearwater	FL	33764	727-535-3673		57
Web: walkerford.com						
Walker Forge Inc 222 E Erie St Ste 300	Milwaukee	WI	53202	414-223-2000		483
Web: www.walkerforge.com						

				Phone	Fax	Class
Walker Furniture 301 S Martin L King Blvd *Web:* www.walkerfurniture.com	Las Vegas	NV	89106	702-384-9300		321
Walker Group Inc, The 20 Waterside Dr *Web:* www.thewalkergroup.com	Farmington	CT	06032	860-678-3530		180
Walker Honda 1616 Macarthur Dr *Web:* www.walkerhonda.com	Alexandria	LA	71301	318-445-6421		57
Walker Industries Holdings Ltd 2800 Thorold Townline Rd *TF:* 866-694-9360 ■ *Web:* www.walkerind.com	Niagara Falls	ON	L2E6S4	905-227-4142		186
Walker Information Inc 301 Pennsylvania Pkwy *TF:* 800-334-3939 ■ *Web:* www.walkerinfo.com	Indianapolis	IN	46280	317-843-3939		466
Walker Machine & Foundry Corp PO Box 4587 *TF:* 800-226-3100 ■ *Web:* www.walkerfoundry.com	Roanoke	VA	24015	540-344-6265	342-2278	307
Walker Macy 111 SW Oak St *Web:* www.walkermacy.com	Portland	OR	97204	503-228-3122		393
Walker Magnetics Group Inc 20 Rockdale St *TF:* 800-962-4638 ■ *Web:* www.walkermagnet.com	Worcester	MA	01606	508-853-3232	852-8649	493
Walker Mark (Rep R - NC) 1305 Longworth HOB *Web:* walker.house.gov	Washington	DC	20515	202-225-3065	225-8611	342-2
Walker Martin & Hatch LLC 321 D St NE *Web:* walkermartinhatch.com	Washington	DC	20002	202-543-9004		261
Walker Mfg 3160 Abbott Ln *Web:* www.walkerexhaust.com	Harrisonburg	VA	22801	540-438-9466		247
Walker MS Inc 20 Third Ave *TF:* 800-528-2787 ■ *Web:* www.mswalker.com	Somerville	MA	02143	617-776-6700	776-5808	80-1
Walker Nursery Co 3809 Manchester Hwy *Web:* walkernurseryco.com	Mcminnville	TN	37110	931-668-4622		323
Walker Parking Consultants/Restoration Engineers Inc 2121 Hudson Ave *Web:* www.walkerparking.com	Kalamazoo	MI	49008	269-381-6080		261
Walker Printing Co 2501 E Fifth St *Web:* www.walker360.com	Montgomery	AL	36107	334-832-4975		627
Walker Process Equipment 840 N Russell Ave *TF:* 800-992-5537 ■ *Web:* www.walker-process.com	Aurora	IL	60506	630-892-7921	892-7951	806
Walker Sands Communications LLC 55 W Monroe St *Web:* www.walkersands.com	Chicago	IL	60603	312-267-0066	648-6015	636
Walker Scott (R) 115 E State Capitol *Web:* walker.wi.gov	Madison	WI	53702	608-266-1212	267-8983	343
Walker Stainless Equipment Co LLC 625 W State St	New Lisbon	WI	53950	608-562-7500		298
WALKER STAMPING 1555 Vintage Ave *Web:* www.walkercorp.com	Ontario	CA	91761	909-390-4300		719
Walker State Prison 97 Kevin Ln *Web:* www.dcor.state.ga.us	Rock Spring	GA	30739	706-764-3600	764-3613	213
Walker Tool & Die Inc 2411 Walker Ave NW *TF:* 877-925-5378 ■ *Web:* www.walkertool.com	Grand Rapids	MI	49544	616-453-5471	453-3765	757
Walker's Furniture Inc 3808 N Sullivan Rd Bldg 22-C *TF:* 866-667-6655 ■ *Web:* www.walkersfurniture.com	Spokane Valley	WA	99216	509-535-1995		321
Walker, Morgan & Kinard 135 E Main St *TF:* 800-922-8411 ■ *Web:* walkermorgan.com	Lexington	SC	29072	803-359-6194		428
WALK-FM 97.5 (AC) 234 Airport Plaza Ste 5 *Web:* www.walk975.com	Farmingdale	NY	11735	631-475-5200		645
Walking Adventures International 14612 NE Fourth Plain Rd Ste A **Fax Area Code:* 360 ■ *TF:* 800-779-0353 ■ *Web:* www.walkingadventures.com	Vancouver	WA	98682	800-779-0353	260-1131*	760
WalkMed Infusion LLC 6555 S Kenton St Ste 304 *TF:* 800-578-0555 ■ *Web:* walkmed.com	Centennial	CO	80111	303-420-9569	420-4545	476
Wall Colmonoy Corp 101 W Girard Ave *TF:* 800-521-2412 ■ *Web:* www.wallcolmonoy.com	Madison Heights	MI	48071	248-585-6400	585-7960	21
Wall Doxey State Park 3946 Hwy 7 S *Web:* www.mdwfp.com	Holly Springs	MS	38635	662-252-4231		565
Wall Drug Store Inc PO Box 401 *Web:* www.walldrug.com	Wall	SD	57790	605-279-2175		327
Wall Lenk Corp 1950 Dr Martin Luther King Jr *Web:* www.wlenk.com	Kinston	NC	28501	252-527-4186		758
Wall Street Financial Group Inc 255 Woodcliff Dr *Web:* www.wallstreetfinancialgroup.org	Fairport	NY	14450	585-267-8000		691
Wall Street Horizon Inc 400 W Cummings Pk Ste 3650 *Web:* www.wallstreethorizon.com	Woburn	MA	01801	781-994-3500		162
Wall Street Journal, The 1211 Ave of the Americas *TF General:* 800-568-7625 ■ *Web:* www.wsj.com/india	New York	NY	10036	212-416-2000		532-3
Wall Timber Products Inc 1825 Effingham Hwy *Web:* www.walltimber.com	Sylvania	GA	30467	912-863-5108		685
Wall, Einhorn & Chernitzer PC 555 E Main St Ste 1600 *Web:* www.wec-cpa.com	Norfolk	VA	23510	757-625-4700		2
Walla Walla Community College 500 Tausick Way **Fax:* Admissions ■ *TF:* 877-992-9922 ■ *Web:* www.wwcc.edu	Walla Walla	WA	99362	509-522-2500	527-3661*	162
Walla Walla County 315 W Main St *Web:* www.co.walla-walla.wa.us	Walla Walla	WA	99362	509-527-3200		338
Walla Walla Public Library 238 E Alder St *TF:* 800-548-8755 ■ *Web:* wallawallapubliclibrary.org	Walla Walla	WA	99362	509-527-4550		434-3
Walla Walla Racetrack 363 Orchard St *Web:* www.wallawallafairgrounds.com	Walla Walla	WA	99362	509-527-3247	527-3259	642
Walla Walla University 204 S College Ave *TF:* 800-541-8900 ■ *Web:* www.wallawalla.edu	College Place	WA	99324	509-527-2327	527-2397	166
Walla Walla Valley Chamber of Commerce 29 E Sumach St *TF:* 866-826-9422 ■ *Web:* www.wwvchamber.com	Walla Walla	WA	99362	509-525-0850	522-2038	139
Wallace & Carey Inc 5445-8 St NE *TF:* 800-661-1504 ■ *Web:* www.wacl.com	Calgary	AB	T2K5R9	403-275-7360		449
Wallace b e Products Corp 71 N Bacton Hill Rd *TF:* 800-553-5438 ■ *Web:* www.wallacecranes.com	Frazer	PA	19355	610-647-1400		358
Wallace Church Inc 330 E 48th St *TF:* 800-257-5540 ■ *Web:* www.wallacechurch.net	New York	NY	10017	212-755-2903		344
Wallace Community College 1141 Wallace Dr **Fax:* Admissions ■ *TF:* 800-543-2426 ■ *Web:* www.wallace.edu	Dothan	AL	36303	334-983-3521	983-6066*	162
Wallace Community College Selma 3000 Earl Goodwin Pkwy *TF:* 855-428-8313 ■ *Web:* www.wccs.edu	Selma	AL	36703	334-876-9227	876-9250	800
Wallace County PO Box 508 *Web:* www.wallacecounty.net/government/localgov.php	Sharon Springs	KS	67758	785-852-4935		338
Wallace Engineering Structural Consultants Inc 200 E Brady *Web:* www.wallacesc.com	Tulsa	OK	74103	918-584-5858		261
Wallace Falls State Park 14503 Wallace Lake Rd *Web:* parks.state.wa.us	Gold Bar	WA	98251	360-793-0420		565
Wallace Financial Group Inc 4390 Earney Rd *Web:* lpl.com	Woodstock	GA	30188	770-751-7411		690
Wallace Foundation, The 5 Penn Plaza 7th Fl *Web:* www.wallacefoundation.org/pages/default.aspx	New York	NY	10001	212-251-9700	679-6990	305
Wallace Galleries Ltd 500 Fifth Ave SW *Web:* www.wallacegalleries.com	Calgary	AB	T2P3L5	403-262-8050	264-7112	42
Wallace H Coulter Foundation, The 790 NW 107th Ave *Web:* www.whcf.org	Miami	FL	33172	305-559-2991		70
Wallace Hardware Company Inc 5050 S Davy Crockett Pkwy PO Box 6004 *TF:* 800-776-0976 ■ *Web:* www.wallacehardware.com	Morristown	TN	37815	423-586-5650		351
Wallace House 756 16th St *TF:* 800-266-6312 ■ *Web:* www.wallace.org	Des Moines	IA	50314	515-243-7063	243-8927	50-3
Wallace House State Historic Site 71 Somerset St *Web:* www.njparksandforests.org	Somerville	NJ	08876	908-725-1015		565
Wallace Literary Agencies Inc 301 E 79th St Ste 14-J	New York	NY	10075	212-570-9090		444
Wallace Oil Co-Voco 5370 Oakdale Rd	Smyrna	GA	30082	404-799-9400		324
Wallace Roberts & Todd LLC 1700 Market St Ste 2800 *Web:* www.wrtdesign.com	Philadelphia	PA	19103	215-732-5215	732-2551	261
Wallace Saunders Austin Brown Enochs 200 W Douglas Ave Ste 400 *Web:* wallacesaunders.com	Wichita	KS	67202	316-269-2100		428
Wallace State Community College 801 Main St *TF:* 866-350-9722 ■ *Web:* www.wallacestate.edu	Hanceville	AL	35077	256-352-8000	352-8129	162
Wallace State Park 10621 NE Hwy 121 *Web:* www.mostateparks.com	Cameron	MO	64429	816-632-3745		565
Wallace Welch Willingham 300 First Ave S 4th Fl *TF:* 800-783-5085 ■ *Web:* www.marineins.com	Saint Petersburg	FL	33701	727-914-5019	522-5021	390
Wallach & Company Inc 107 W Federal St *TF:* 800-237-6615 ■ *Web:* www.wallach.com	Middleburg	VA	20118	540-687-3166	687-3172	391-7
WallachBeth Capital LLC 100 Wall St Ste 6600 *TF:* 800-289-9999 ■ *Web:* www.wallachbeth.com	New York	NY	10005	646-237-8585		690
Wallco Inc 53 E Jackson St # 55 *TF:* 800-392-5526 ■ *Web:* www.wallcoinc.com	Wilkes-Barre	PA	18701	570-823-6181	829-5952	696
Wallcoverings Assn 401 N Michigan Ave Ste 2200 *Web:* www.wallcoverings.org	Chicago	IL	60611	312-644-6610	527-6705	49-4
Walldesign Inc 5940 Key Ct	Loomis	CA	95650	916-660-0102		189-9
Wallenius Wilhelmsen Lines Americas 188 Broadway PO Box 1232 *TF:* 888-902-3511 ■ *Web:* www.2wglobal.com	Woodcliff Lake	NJ	07677	888-902-3511		313
Wallenius Wilhelmsen Logistics PO Box 1232 *Web:* www.2wglobal.com	Woodcliff Lake	NJ	07677	201-307-1300		313
Wallens Ridge State Prison 272 Dogwood Dr PO Box 759 *Web:* vadoc.virginia.gov	Big Stone Gap	VA	24219	276-523-3310		213
Waller County 836 Austin St *TF:* 800-901-4412 ■ *Web:* www.wallercounty.org	Hempstead	TX	77445	979-826-3357		338
Waller Financial Planning Group Inc 941 Chatham Ln Ste 212 *Web:* www.waller.com	Columbus	OH	43221	614-457-7026		194
Waller Lansden Dortch & Davis Nashville City Ctr 511 Union St Ste 2700 *Web:* www.wallerlaw.com	Nashville	TN	37219	615-850-8487		428
Waller Truck Company Inc 400 S McCleary Rd *TF:* 800-821-2196 ■ *Web:* www.wallertruck.com	Excelsior Springs	MO	64024	816-629-3400		780
Wallick & Volk Mortgage 222 E 18th St *TF:* 800-280-8655 ■ *Web:* www.wvmb.com	Cheyenne	WY	82001	307-634-5941		217
Wallick Construction Company Inc PO Box 1023 *Web:* www.wallickcos.com	Columbus	OH	43216	614-863-4640	863-1725	186
Wallingford Buick GMC 1122 Old N Colony Rd *TF Cust Svc:* 866-582-4487 ■ *Web:* www.wallingfordbuickgmc.com	Wallingford	CT	06492	866-582-4487		57
Wallingford Coffee Mills Inc 11401 Rockfield Ct *TF:* 800-533-3690 ■ *Web:* www.wallingfordcoffee.com	Cincinnati	OH	45241	513-771-4570	771-3138	80-2

Phone | Fax | Class

Wallingford Symphony Orchestra
PO Box 6023 .... Wallingford CT 06492 203-697-2261 573-3
Web: www.wallingfordsymphony.org
Wallingford-Swarthmore School District
200 S Providence Rd .... Wallingford PA 19086 610-892-3470 685
Web: www.wssd.org
Wallis Oil Co 106 E Washington St .... Cuba MO 65453 573-885-2277 885-4760 324
TF: 800-467-6652 ■ *Web:* www.wallisco.com
Wallis Sands State Beach 1050 Ocean Blvd. .... Rye NH 03870 603-436-9404 565
Web: www.nhstateparks.org
Wallkill Central School District (WCSD)
19 Main St PO Box 310 .... Wallkill NY 12589 845-895-7100 895-3630 685
Web: www.wallkillcsd.k12.ny.us
Wallkill Correctional Facility
50 McKendrick Rd .... Wallkill NY 12589 845-895-2021 213
Web: www.doccs.ny.gov/faclist.html
Wallkill Valley Federal Savings & Loan Assn
23 Wallkill Ave .... Wallkill NY 12589 845-895-2051 70
Web: www.wallkill.com
Wallops Flight Facility
Office of Public Affairs .... Wallops Island VA 23337 757-824-1579 824-1971 743
Web: www.nasa.gov
Wallowa County
101 S River St Rm 100 .... Enterprise OR 97828 541-426-4543 426-5901 338
Web: www.co.wallowa.or.us
Wallowa Lake State Park
72214 Marina Ln .... Joseph OR 97846 541-388-6055 565
Web: www.oregonstateparks.org
Wallquest Inc 465 Devon Park Dr .... Wayne PA 19087 610-293-1330 548
Web: www.wallquest.com
Walls 360 Inc 5054 Bond St .... Las Vegas NV 89118 888-244-9969 393
TF: 888-244-9969 ■ *Web:* www.walls360.com
Walls+Forms Inc 204 Airline Dr Ste 200 .... Coppell TX 75019 972-745-0800 5
Web: www.wallsforms.com
Wallse 344 W 11th St .... New York NY 10014 212-352-2300 671
Web: www.kurtgutenbrunner.com/restaurants/wallse
Wallside Windows
27000 Trolley Industrial Dr .... Taylor MI 48180 313-292-4400 499
Web: www.wallsidewindows.com
Wally World Satellite Local Direct Tv Dealer
524 Cemetery Rd .... Park City MT 59063 406-633-2811 116
Wally's Wine & Spirits
2107 Westwood Blvd .... Los Angeles CA 90025 310-475-0606 443
Web: www.wallywine.com
Walman Optical Company Inc
801 12th Ave N .... Minneapolis MN 55411 612-520-6000 542
TF: 800-873-9256 ■ *Web:* www.walman.com
Wal-Mart Foundation
702 SW Eigth St .... Bentonville AR 72716 479-273-4000 304
NYSE: WMT ■ *TF:* 800-438-6278 ■ *Web:* giving.walmart.com
Wal Mart Puerto Rico Inc PO Box 4960 .... Caguas PR 00726 787-653-7777 229
Web: www.walmartpr.com
Wal-Mart Realty 2001 SE Tenth St .... Bentonville AR 72716 479-273-4682 655
Web: www.walmartrealty.com
Wal-Mart Stores Inc
702 SW Eigth St .... Bentonville AR 72716 479-273-4000 229
NYSE: WMT ■ *TF Cust Svc:* 800-925-6278 ■ *Web:* corporate.walmart.com
Walmart.com 1919 Davis St .... San Leandro CA 94577 800-925-6278 229
TF: 800-925-6278 ■ *Web:* www.walmart.com
Walnut Brewery 1123 Walnut St .... Boulder CO 80302 303-447-1345 671
Web: www.walnutbrewery.com
Walnut Cafe 3073 Walnut St .... Boulder CO 80301 303-447-2315 671
Web: www.walnutcafe.com
Walnut Cir Grill 115 Walnut St .... Hattiesburg MS 39401 601-544-2202 671
Web: www.walnutcirclegrill.com
Walnut Creek Chamber of Commerce
1280 Civic Dr Ste 100 .... Walnut Creek CA 94596 925-934-2007 934-2404 139
Web: www.walnut-creek.com
Walnut Creek State Park PO Box 26 .... Prue OK 74060 918-242-3362 565
Web: www.keystoneok.com
Walnut Hollow Farm Inc
1409 State Rd 23 .... Dodgeville WI 53533 608-935-2341 279
TF: 800-395-5995 ■ *Web:* www.walnuthollow.com
Walnut Point State Park
2331 E County Rd 370 N .... Oakland IL 61943 217-346-3336 565
Web: www.dnr.illinois.gov/Parks/Pages/WalnutPoint.aspx
Walnut Street Theatre
825 Walnut St .... Philadelphia PA 19107 215-574-3550 572
TF: 800-982-2787 ■ *Web:* www.walnutstreettheatre.org
Walnut Woods State Park
3155 Walnut Woods Dr. .... West Des Moines IA 50265 515-285-4502 285-7476 565
Web: www.iowadnr.gov
Walorski Jackie (Rep R - IN)
419 Cannon Bldg .... Washington DC 20515 202-225-3915 225-6798 342-2
Web: walorski.house.gov
Walpole Co-op Bank Inc 982 Main St .... Walpole MA 02081 508-668-1080 660-2690 70
Web: www.walpolecoop.com
Walpole Inc PO Box 1177 .... Okeechobee FL 34973 863-763-5593 780
TF: 800-741-6500 ■ *Web:* www.walpoleinc.com
Walpole Public Library 143 School St .... Walpole MA 02081 508-660-7340 434-3
Web: www.walpolelibrary.org/walpolenew
Walpole Woodworkers Inc 767 E St Rt 7 .... Walpole MA 02081 508-668-2800 668-7301 319-4
TF Cust Svc: 800-343-6948 ■ *Web:* www.walpolewoodworkers.com
WALR-FM 104.1 (AC)
1601 W Peachtree St NE .... Atlanta GA 30309 404-897-7500 897-6495 645-10
Web: www.kiss104fm.com
Walrus, The 1136 N Third St .... Bismarck ND 58501 701-250-0020 671
Web: www.thewalrus.com
Walsh & Sheppard Inc
111 W Ninth Ave .... Anchorage AK 99501 907-338-3857 7
TF: 800-869-6837 ■ *Web:* www.walshsheppard.com
Walsh Brothers Inc 210 Commercial St .... Boston MA 02109 617-878-4800 194
Web: www.walshbrothers.com
Walsh Construction Co
2905 SW First Ave .... Portland OR 97201 503-222-4375 274-7676 186
Web: walshconstruction.com
Walsh County 600 Cooper Ave .... Grafton ND 58237 701-352-1300 352-1104 338
Web: www.co.walsh.nd.us

Phone | Fax | Class

Walsh Group Inc 929 W Adams St .... Chicago IL 60607 312-563-5400 563-5466 186
TF: 800-957-1842 ■ *Web:* walshgroup.com
Walsh Kelliher & Sharp
1292 Sadler Way Ste 220 .... Fairbanks AK 99701 907-456-2222 2
Web: wkscpa.com
Walsh Property Management
PO Box 2657 .... Castro Valley CA 94546 510-888-8965 652
Web: www.walshpm.com
Walsh University 2020 E Maple St .... North Canton OH 44720 330-499-7090 490-7165* 166
**Fax:* Admissions ■ *TF Admissions:* 800-362-9846 ■ *Web:* www.walsh.edu
Walshin Martin Inc
70 Saw Mill River Rd .... Hastings On Hudson NY 10706 914-478-4300 445
Walsworth Publishing Co
306 N Kansas Ave .... Marceline MO 64658 660-376-3543 637-2
TF: 800-972-4968 ■ *Web:* www.walsworthyearbooks.com
Walt & Company Communications
2105 S Bascom Ave Ste 240 .... Campbell CA 95008 408-369-7200 636
Web: www.walt.com
Walt Disney Co 500 S Buena Vista St .... Burbank CA 91521 818-560-1000 553-7210* 185
NYSE: DIS ■ **Fax:* Mail Rm ■ *TF:* 800-445-6937 ■ *Web:* thewaltdisneycompany.com
Walt Disney Concert Hall
111 S Grand Ave .... Los Angeles CA 90012 323-850-2000 572
TF: 800-864-8377 ■ *Web:* laphil.com
Walt Disney Family Museum LLC, The
104 Montgomery St .... San Francisco CA 94129 415-345-6800 520
Web: www.waltdisney.org
Walt Disney Imagineering
500 S Vuenavista St .... Burbank CA 91521 407-939-2273 653
Web: disneyworld.disney.go.com
Walt Disney Studios
500 S Buena Vista St .... Burbank CA 91521 407-939-5277 657
Web: www.disneyworld.disney.go.com
Walt Disney World Dolphin
1500 Epcot Resorts Blvd .... Lake Buena Vista FL 32830 407-934-4000 934-4884 669
TF: 888-828-8850 ■ *Web:* www.swandolphin.com
Walt Disney World Resorts
4600 N World Dr .... Lake Buena Vista FL 32830 407-824-1000 669
Web: disneyworld.disney.go.com
Walt Disney World Swan
1200 Epcot Resorts Blvd .... Lake Buena Vista FL 32830 407-934-4000 934-4884 669
TF: 888-828-8850 ■ *Web:* www.swandolphin.com
Walt Whitman Birthplace Association
246 Old Walt Whitman Rd .... Huntington Station NY 11746 631-427-5240 427-5247 565
Web: www.nysparks.com
Walt Whitman House State Historic Site
330 Mickle Blvd .... Camden NJ 08103 800-843-6420 565
TF: 800-843-6420 ■ *Web:* www.njparksandforests.org
Walt's Drive-A-Way Services Inc
321 N Kerth Ave .... Evansville IN 47711 812-424-8927 120
Web: www.waltsonline.com
Waltek & Company Ltd
2130 Waycorss Rd .... Cincinnati OH 45240 513-577-7980 577-7990 189-6
Web: www.walteklltd.com
Waltek Inc 14310 Sunfish Lake Blvd .... Ramsey MN 55303 763-427-3181 427-3216 306
TF: 800-937-9496 ■ *Web:* www.waltekinc.com
Walter & Elise Haas Fund
1 Lombard St Ste 305 .... San Francisco CA 94111 415-398-4474 305
Walter | Haverfield LLP
1301 E Ninth St Ste 3500 .... Cleveland OH 44114 216-781-1212 428
Web: www.walterhav.com
Walter B Jones Alcohol & Drug Abuse Treatment Ctr
2577 W Fifth St .... Greenville NC 27834 252-830-3426 726
TF: 800-422-1884 ■ *Web:* ncdhhs.gov
Walter E Smithe Furniture Inc
1251 W Thorndale Ave .... Itasca IL 60143 630-285-8000 620-1552 319-2
TF: 800-948-4263 ■ *Web:* www.smithe.com
Walter F. Cameron Advertising Inc
350 Motor Pkwy Ste 410 .... Hauppauge NY 11788 631-232-3033 7
TF: 800-438-7325 ■ *Web:* www.cameronadv.com
Walter G Grady CPA 2843 Johnson Ave .... Alameda CA 94501 510-523-2310 2
Walter Greenblatt & Associates LLC
430 Nassau St .... Princeton NJ 08540 609-497-1282 194
Web: www.wgreenblatt.com
Walter Haas & Sons Inc 123 W 23rd St .... Hialeah FL 33010 305-883-2257 883-0598 701
TF: 800-552-3845 ■ *Web:* www.haasprint.com
Walter L Weisman CPA
8911 La Mesa Blvd 201 .... La Mesa CA 91942 619-697-7878 2
Walter Meier Mfg Inc
427 New Sanford Rd .... La Vergne TN 37086 800-274-6848 758
TF: 800-274-6848 ■ *Web:* www.wiltontools.com
Walter N Yoder & Sons Inc
16200 McMullen Hwy SW PO Box 1337 .... Cumberland MD 21502 301-729-0610 729-1517 189-10
Web: wnyoder.com
Walter Oil & Gas Corp
1100 Louisiana St Ste 200 .... Houston TX 77002 713-659-1221 756-1155 538
Web: www.walteroil.com
Walter P Moore
1301 Mckinney St Ste 1100 .... Houston TX 77010 713-630-7300 630-7396 261
TF: 800-364-7300 ■ *Web:* www.walterpmoore.com
Walter P Reuther Psychiatric Hospital
30901 Palmer Rd .... Westland MI 48186 734-367-8400 722-5562* 374-5
**Fax:* Mail Rm ■ *TF:* 877-765-8388 ■ *Web:* michigan.gov
Walter Snyder Printer Inc 691 River St .... Troy NY 12180 518-272-8881 627
TF: 888-272-9774 ■ *Web:* www.snyderprinter.com
Walter Stern Inc
68 Sintsink Dr E .... Port Washington NY 11050 516-883-9100 787
Web: www.waltersterninc.com
Walter Toebe Construction Co
29001 Wall St PO Box 930129 .... Wixom MI 48393 248-349-7500 349-4870 187
Web: www.toebe-construction.com
Walter USA Inc
N22 W23855 Ridgeview Pkwy W .... Waukesha WI 53188 800-945-5554 347-2501* 493
**Fax Area Code:* 262 ■ *TF:* 800-945-5554 ■ *Web:* www.walter-tools.com
Walter's Cafe 2 Portland Sq .... Portland ME 04101 207-871-9258 671
Web: www.waltersportland.com
Walter's Steak House & Saloon
802 N Union St .... Wilmington DE 19805 302-652-6780 671
Web: walters-steakhouse.com

Phone | Fax | Class

Walterboro-Colleton Chamber of Commerce
403 E Washington St .... Walterboro SC 29488 843-549-9595 549-5775 139
Web: walterboro.org

Walters & Wolf 41450 Boscell Rd .... Fremont CA 94538 510-490-1115 651-7172 189-6
TF: 800-969-9653 ■ *Web:* www.waltersandwolf.com

Walters & Wolf Precast 41777 Boyce Rd .... Fremont CA 94538 510-226-9800 226-0360 183
Web: www.waltersandwolf.com

Walters Art Museum 600 N Charles St .... Baltimore MD 21201 410-547-9000 783-7969 520
Web: www.thewalters.org

Walters International Speakers Bureau
18825 Hicrest Rd .... Glendora CA 91741 626-335-8069 708

Walters Metal Fabrication
3660 State Rt 111 .... Granite City IL 62040 618-931-5551 480
Web: www.waltersmetalfab.com

Walters Mimi (Rep R - CA)
215 Cannon HOB .... Washington DC 20515 202-225-5611 225-9177 342-2
Web: walters.house.gov

Walters Photography
1013 Suffolk Dr .... Janesville WI 53546 608-752-8808 590
TF: 800-594-5006 ■ *Web:* portalmedia.com

Walters State Community College
500 S Davy Crockett Pkwy .... Morristown TN 37813 423-585-2600 585-6786* 162
**Fax:* Admissions ■ *TF:* 800-225-4770 ■ *Web:* www.ws.edu

Walters Wholesale Electric Co
2825 Temple Ave .... Signal Hill CA 90755 562-988-3100 988-3150 246
TF: 800-700-5483 ■ *Web:* www.walterswholesale.com

Walthall County PO Box 227 .... Tylertown MS 39667 601-876-2680 338
Web: www.co.walthall.ms.us

Walthall Drake & Wallace LLP
6300 Rockside Rd .... Cleveland OH 44131 216-573-2330 734
Web: www.walthall.com

Walthall Oil Company Inc 2510 Allen Rd .... Macon GA 31216 478-781-1234 579
TF: 800-633-5685 ■ *Web:* www.walthall-oil.com

Waltham Public Library 735 Main St .... Waltham MA 02451 781-314-3425 434-3
Web: www.waltham.lib.ma.us

Waltham Services Inc 817 Moody St .... Waltham MA 02453 781-893-1810 893-7921 577
TF: 866-974-7378 ■ *Web:* www.walthamservices.com

Waltham/West Suburban Chamber of Commerce
84 S St .... Waltham MA 02453 781-894-4700 139
Web: www.walthamchamber.com

Waltkoch Ltd 1025 Airport Pkwy .... Gainesville GA 30501 404-378-3666 619
Web: www.waltkoch.com

Walton Area Chamber of Commerce
63 S Centre Trail .... Santa Rosa Beach FL 32459 850-267-0683 267-0603 139
TF: 800-435-7352 ■ *Web:* waltonareachamber.com

Walton Associated Company Inc
2001 Financial Way Ste 200 .... Glendora CA 91741 626-963-8505 653

Walton County
76 N Sixth St PO Box 1355 .... DeFuniak Springs FL 32433 850-892-8115 338
Web: www.co.walton.fl.us

Walton County Board of Education
200 Double Springs Church Rd .... Monroe GA 30656 770-266-4520 186
Web: www.walton.k12.ga.us

Walton County Board-Commissioner
303 S Hammond Dr Ste 330 .... Monroe GA 30655 770-267-1301 338
TF: 800-436-7442 ■ *Web:* www.waltoncountyga.org

Walton County Chamber of Commerce
132 E Spring St .... Monroe GA 30655 770-267-6594 267-0961 139
TF: 800-653-0603 ■ *Web:* www.waltonchamber.org

Walton EMC 842 Hwy 78 NW PO Box 260 .... Monroe GA 30655 770-267-2505 267-1223 245
TF: 800-296-2203 ■ *Web:* www.waltonemc.com

Walton Family Foundation Inc (WFF)
PO Box 2030 .... Bentonville AR 72712 479-464-1570 464-1580 305
Web: www.waltonfamilyfoundation.org

Walton Lantaff Schroeder & Carson LLP
9350 S Dixie Hwy 10th Fl .... Miami FL 33156 305-671-1300 428
Web: www.waltonlantaff.com

Walton Manor Health Care Ctr
19859 Alexander Rd .... Walton Hills OH 44146 440-652-5212 450
Web: www.saberhealth.com

Walton Motors Inc 205 E Pawnee Dr .... Savannah MO 64485 816-324-3141 516
Web: www.waltonmotorsinc.com

Walton Press (WP) 402 Mayfield Dr .... Monroe GA 30655 770-267-2596 555
TF: 800-354-0235 ■ *Web:* www.waltonpress.com

Walton Rehabilitation Hospital
1355 Independence Dr .... Augusta GA 30901 706-724-7746 374-6
Web: www.wrh.org

Walton Signage Corp
10101 Reunion Pl Ste 500 .... San Antonio TX 78216 210-886-0644 393
Web: www.waltonsignage.com

Walton Street Capital LLC
900 N Michigan Ave Ste 1900 .... Chicago IL 60611 312-915-2800 655
Web: www.waltonst.com

Walton-De Funiak Library
3 Cir Dr .... DeFuniak Springs FL 32435 850-892-3624 892-4438 434-3
TF: 800-342-0141 ■ *Web:* co.walton.fl.us

Waltrich Plastic Corp
3005 Airport Rd .... Walthourville GA 31333 912-368-9341 605-1
Web: www.waltrich.com

Walts Food Centers
16145 S State St .... South Holland IL 60473 708-333-5500 345
Web: www.waltsfoods.com

Walts Mailing Service Ltd
9610 E First Ave .... Spokane Valley WA 99206 509-924-5939 5
TF: 888-549-2006 ■ *Web:* waltsmailing.com

Walworth County
100 W Walworth St PO Box 1001 .... Elkhorn WI 53121 262-741-4241 741-4287 338
Web: www.co.walworth.wi.us

Walworth County PO Box 292 .... Selby SD 57472 605-649-7602 649-7867 338
Web: walworthco.org

WALZ Label & Mailing Systems
624 High Point Ln .... East Peoria IL 61611 309-698-1500 535
TF: 877-971-1500 ■ *Web:* walzeq.com

WALZ Postal Solutions Inc
27398 Via Industria .... Temecula CA 92590 800-548-9259 196
TF: 800-548-9259 ■ *Web:* www.walzgroup.com

Walz Timothy J (Rep D - MN)
2313 Rayburn HOB .... Washington DC 20515 202-225-2472 342-2
Web: walz.house.gov

Phone | Fax | Class

WAMC (West Anaheim Medical Ctr)
3033 W Orange Ave .... Anaheim CA 92804 714-827-3000 374-3
Web: westanaheimmedctr.com

WAMC/Northeast Public Radio
318 Central Ave .... Albany NY 12206 518-465-5233 432-6974 632
TF: 800-323-9262 ■ *Web:* www.wamc.org

WAMC-FM 90.3 (NPR) 318 Central Ave .... Albany NY 12206 518-465-5233 432-6974 645-3
TF: 800-323-9262 ■ *Web:* www.wamc.org

Wampanoag Tribe of Gay Head Aquinnah
20 Black Brook Rd .... Aquinnah MA 02535 508-645-9265 378
TF: 800-833-6390 ■ *Web:* www.wampanoagtribe.net

WAMU-FM 88.5 (NPR)
4401 Connecticut Ave NW .... Washington DC 20008 202-885-1200 645-172
Web: www.wamu.org

Wanchese Fish Co
2000 Northgate Commerce Pkwy .... Suffolk VA 23435 757-673-4500 285
TF: 800-720-1443 ■ *Web:* www.wanchese.com

WAND (Women's Action for New Directions)
691 Massachusetts Ave .... Arlington MA 02476 781-643-6740 48-5
Web: www.wand.org

WAND Inc 2170 S Parker Rd Ste 295 .... Denver CO 80231 303-623-1200 225
Web: www.wandinc.com

WAND-TV Ch 17 (ABC) 904 S Side Dr .... Decatur IL 62521 217-424-2500 424-2583 741
Web: www.wandtv.com

Wang Electric Inc
4107 E Winslow Ave Ste C .... Phoenix AZ 85040 602-324-5350 324-5360 787
Web: www.wangelectric.com

Wang Theatre 270 Tremont St .... Boston MA 02116 800-982-2787 572
TF: 800-982-2787 ■ *Web:* www.bochcenter.org

Wangard Partners Inc
1200 N Mayfair Rd .... Milwaukee WI 53226 414-777-1200 652
Web: www.wangard.com

Wanke Cascade Co 6330 N Cutter Cir .... Portland OR 97217 503-289-8609 285-5640 361
TF: 800-365-5053 ■ *Web:* www.wanke.com

Wanner Assoc Inc 908 N Second St .... Harrisburg PA 17102 717-236-2050 236-2046 47
Web: www.wannerassoc.com

Wantman Group Inc
2035 Vista Pkwy Ste 100 .... West Palm Beach FL 33411 561-687-2220 186
Web: www.wantmangroup.com

Wanzek Construction Inc
2028 Second Ave NW .... West Fargo ND 58078 701-282-6171 186
Web: www.wanzek.com

WAO (World Allergy Organization)
555 E Wells St Ste 1100 .... Milwaukee WI 53202 414-276-1791 276-3349 49-8
TF: 800-929-4040 ■ *Web:* www.worldallergy.org

WAOE-TV Ch 59 (MNT)
2907 Springfield Rd .... East Peoria IL 61611 309-674-5900 674-5959 741
Web: www.my59.tv

WAOK-AM 1380 (N/T)
1201 Peachtree St NE Ste 800 .... Atlanta GA 30361 404-898-8916 898-8909 645-10
Web: atlanta.cbslocal.com

WAPE-FM 95.1 (CHR)
8000 Belfort Pkwy Ste 100 .... Jacksonville FL 32256 904-245-8500 245-8501 645-79
TF: 800-475-9595 ■ *Web:* www.wape.com

Wapello County 101 W Fourth St .... Ottumwa IA 52501 641-652-3352 683-0053 338
Web: www.wapellocounty.org

WAPI-AM 1070 (N/T)
244 Goodwin Crest Dr Ste 300 .... Birmingham AL 35209 205-945-4646 945-3999 645-20
Web: www.talk995.com

Wapiti Meadow Ranch
1667 Johnson Creek Rd .... Cascade ID 83611 208-633-3217 633-3219 239
Web: www.wapitimeadowranch.com

Wapiti Regional Library
145 12th St E .... Prince Albert SK S6V1B7 306-764-0712 922-1516 436
Web: wapitilibrary.ca

WAPN-FM 91.5 (Rel) 1508 State Ave .... Holly Hill FL 32117 386-677-4272 645
Web: www.wapn.net

Wapnick and Alverado
6383 Arizona Cir .... Los Angeles CA 90045 310-342-0888 445
Web: www.courtcall.com

Wapsi Fly Co 27 County Rd 458 .... Mountain Home AR 72653 870-425-9500 711
TF: 800-425-9599 ■ *Web:* www.wapsifly.com

Wapsie Valley Creamery Inc
300 Tenth St NE .... Independence IA 50644 319-334-7193 296-5

Wapsipinicon State Park
21301 County Rd E34 .... Anamosa IA 52205 319-462-2761 462-4878 565
Web: www.iowadnr.gov

WAPT-TV Ch 16 (ABC) 7616 Ch 16 Way .... Jackson MS 39209 601-922-1607 741-63
TF: 800-441-1948 ■ *Web:* www.wapt.com

Wapusk National Park PO Box 127 .... Churchill MB R0B0E0 204-675-8863 675-2026 563
TF: 888-773-8888 ■ *Web:* www.pc.gc.ca/pn-np/mb/wapusk/index.aspx

WAQX-FM 95.7 1064 James St .... Syracuse NY 13203 315-472-0200 472-1146 645-160
Web: www.95x.com

WAQY-FM 102.1 (CR)
45 Fisher Ave .... East Longmeadow MA 01028 413-525-4141 525-4334 645
TF: 800-242-3142 ■ *Web:* www.rock102.com

War Axe State Recreation Area
PO Box 427 .... Gibbon NE 68840 308-468-5700 565
Web: outdoornebraska.gov

War in the Pacific National Historical Park
135 Murray Blvd Ste 100 .... Hagatna GU 96910 671-477-7278 564
Web: www.nps.gov/wapa

War Resisters League
339 Lafayette St .... New York NY 10012 212-228-0450 228-6193 48-5
TF: 800-975-9688 ■ *Web:* www.warresisters.org

War Vet Museum 23 E Main St .... Canfield OH 44406 330-533-6311 533-6311 520
Web: warvetmuseum.org

Warady & Davis LLP
1717 Deerfield Rd .... Deerfield IL 60015 847-267-9600 2
Web: waradydavis.com

Waraji 5910 Duraleigh Rd .... Raleigh NC 27612 919-783-1883 671
Web: www.warajijapaneserestaurant.com

Warbros Venture Partners PO Box 1033 .... Westerly RI 02891 401-596-8960 690
Web: www.warbros.com

Warburg Pincus Ventures Co Inc
450 Lexington Ave .... New York NY 10017 212-878-0600 878-9351 792
TF: 800-822-3321 ■ *Web:* www.warburgpincus.com

Ward & Smith 1001 College Ct .... New Bern NC 28563 252-672-5400 428
TF: 800-973-1177 ■ *Web:* www.wardandsmith.com

Phone | Fax | Class

Ward Aluminum Casting Co
642 Growth Ave .... Fort Wayne IN 46808 260-426-8700 420-1919 308
TF: 800-648-9918 ■ *Web:* www.wardcorp.com

Ward Anderson Porritt & Bryant Plc
4190 Telegraph Rd Ste 2300.......... Bloomfield Hills MI 48302 248-593-1440 445
TF: 800-737-4366 ■ *Web:* www.wardanderson.com

Ward Cedar Log Homes
37 Bangor St PO Box 72.......... Houlton ME 04730 800-341-1566 532-7806* 106
**Fax Area Code:* 207 ■ *TF Cust Svc:* 800-341-1566 ■ *Web:* www.wardcedarloghomes.com

Ward Charcoal Ovens State Historic Park
PO Box 151761 .... Ely NV 89315 775-289-1693 565
Web: parks.nv.gov

Ward County 315 SE Third St PO Box 5005 .... Minot ND 58702 701-857-6600 857-6623 338

Ward County County Courthouse.......... Monahans TX 79756 432-943-3200 943-6054 338
Web: www.co.ward.tx.us

Ward Engineering Company Inc
1353 S Seventh St PO Box 2498 .... Louisville KY 40201 502-637-6521 256
Web: www.wardengr.com

Ward Leonard Electric Company Inc
401 Watertown Rd.......... Thomaston CT 06787 860-283-5801 283-5777 518
Web: www.wardleonard.com

Ward Management Group Inc, The
11495 N Pennsylvania St Ste 103.......... Carmel IN 46032 317-816-1619 816-1633 47
Web: www.wardmanage.com

Ward Manufacturing LLC
117 Gulick St .... Blossburg PA 16912 570-638-2131 612
TF: 800-248-1027 ■ *Web:* www.wardmfg.com

Ward Museum of Wildfowl Art
909 S Schumaker Dr.......... Salisbury MD 21804 410-742-4988 520
Web: www.wardmuseum.org

Ward Petroleum
14000 Quail Springs Pkwy Ste 5000 .... Oklahoma City OK 73134 405-242-4484 242-4334 536
Web: www.wardpetroleum.com

Ward Process Inc
311 Hopping Brook Rd.......... Holliston MA 01746 508-429-1165 429-8543 389
Web: www.aapusa.com

Ward Systems & Services Inc
2121 Cee Gee.......... San Antonio TX 78217 210-824-9581 189-10

Ward Williston Oil Company Inc
36700 Woodward Ave Ste 101 .... Bloomfield Hills MI 48304 248-594-6622 539
TF: 800-834-6219 ■ *Web:* www.wardwilliston.com

Ward's Food Systems Inc
5133 Lincoln Rd Ext.......... Hattiesburg MS 39402 601-268-9273 670
TF: 800-748-9273 ■ *Web:* wardsrestaurants.com

Ward's Marine Electric Inc
617 SW Third Ave.......... Fort Lauderdale FL 33315 954-523-2815 787
TF: 800-545-9273 ■ *Web:* www.wardsmarine.com

Ward, Murray, Pace & Johnson PC
202 E Fifth St .... Sterling IL 61081 815-625-8200 428
Web: www.wmpj.com

Warde Medical Laboratory
300 W Textile Rd.......... Ann Arbor MI 48108 734-214-0300 415
TF: 800-876-6522 ■ *Web:* www.wardelab.com

Ward-Kraft Inc 2401 Cooper St.......... Fort Scott KS 66701 620-223-5500 223-6953 110
TF: 800-821-4021 ■ *Web:* www.wardkraft.com

Wardwell Braiding Machine Co
1211 High St .... Central Falls RI 02863 401-724-8800 723-2690 744
Web: www.wardwell.com

Ware County 800 Church St .... Waycross GA 31501 912-287-4300 287-4301 338
Web: www.warecounty.com

ware county school district
1301 Bailey St .... Waycross GA 31501 912-283-8656 283-8698 186
Web: www.ware.k12.ga.us

Ware Jewelers 7268 Eastchase Pkwy .... Montgomery AL 36117 334-386-9273 410
Web: www.warejewelers.com

Ware Malcomb 10 Edelman .... Irvine CA 92618 949-660-9128 863-1581 261
Web: www.waremalcomb.com

Ware Pak Inc 2427 Bond St .... University Park IL 60484 708-534-2600 311
TF: 800-561-3357 ■ *Web:* www.ware-pak.com

Ware State Prison 3620 N Harris Rd .... Waycross GA 31501 912-285-6400 287-6520 213
Web: dcor.state.ga.us

Wareham Ford 2628 Cranberry Hwy.......... Wareham MA 02571 508-295-3643 57
Web: warehamford.com

Warehouse Bar & Grill 214 King St.......... Alexandria VA 22314 703-683-6868 683-6928 671
Web: www.warehouseoldtown.com

Warehouse Home Furnishings Distributors Inc
1851 Telfair St PO Box 1140.......... Dublin GA 31021 800-456-0424 275-6276* 321
**Fax Area Code:* 478 ■ *TF:* 800-456-0424 ■ *Web:* farmershomefurniture.com

Warehouse Skateboards Inc
1638 Military Cutoff Rd Ste 101.......... Wilmington NC 28403 877-791-9795 711
TF: 877-791-9795 ■ *Web:* www.warehouseskateboards.com

Warehouse Systems Inc
601 Academy Dr.......... Northbrook IL 60062 847-562-9526 207
Web: www.warehousesys.com

Warehouse Theatre 37 Augusta St.......... Greenville SC 29601 864-235-6948 572
TF: 800-888-7768 ■ *Web:* www.warehousetheatre.com

Warehousing Education & Research Council (WERC)
1100 Jorie Blvd Ste 170.......... Oak Brook IL 60523 630-990-0001 990-0256 49-21
TF: 800-321-6742 ■ *Web:* www.werc.org

Warex Terminals Corp
1 S Water St PO Box 488 .... Newburgh NY 12550 845-561-4000 579
TF: 800-724-0818 ■ *Web:* www.warex-terminals.com

Warfel Construction Co
1110 Enterprise Rd.......... East Petersburg PA 17520 717-299-4500 299-4628 186
Web: www.warfelcc.com

Warhawk Air Museum 201 Municipal Dr.......... Nampa ID 83687 208-465-6446 465-6232 520
Web: www.warhawkairmuseum.org

Waring Oil Company LLC
431 Port Terminal Cir .... Vicksburg MS 39183 601-636-1065 579
Web: www.waringoil.com

Warko Roofing Company Inc
18 Morgan Dr.......... Reading PA 19608 610-796-4545 191-4
Web: www.thewarkogroup.com

Warm 98.5
4805 Montgomery Rd Ste 300 .... Cincinnati OH 45212 513-241-9898 241-6689 645-37
Web: www.warm98.com

Warm Co 5529 186th Pl SW .... Lynnwood WA 98037 425-248-2424 248-2422 745-1
TF: 800-234-9276 ■ *Web:* www.warmcompany.com

Warm Springs Correctional Ctr
3301 E Fifth St PO Box 7007 .... Carson City NV 89702 775-684-3000 213
Web: doc.nv.gov

Warm Springs Rehabilitation Hospital of San Antonio
5101 Medical Dr.......... San Antonio TX 78229 717-731-9660 374-6
Web: www.warmsprings.org

Warm Springs Specialty Hospital
200 Memorial Dr .... Luling TX 78648 830-875-8400 875-5029 374-6
Web: www.warmsprings.org

WARMC (Mineral Area Regional Medical Ctr)
1212 Weber Rd Ste 302 .... Farmington MO 63640 573-756-4581 374-3

Warn Industries Inc
12900 SE Capps Rd .... Clackamas OR 97015 503-722-1200 61
Web: www.warn.com

Warnaco Group Inc 501 Seventh Ave.......... New York NY 10018 212-287-8000 360-3
NYSE: WRC ■ *Web:* www.pvh.com

Warner Bros Entertainment Inc
4000 Warner Blvd.......... Burbank CA 91522 818-954-1853 954-3817 514
TF: 800-778-7879 ■ *Web:* www.warnerbros.com

Warner Bros Records 3300 Warner Blvd .... Burbank CA 91505 818-846-9090 657
Web: www.warnerbrosrecords.com

Warner Bros Television Production Inc
4000 Warner Blvd.......... Burbank CA 91522 818-954-1853 514
TF: 800-462-8855 ■ *Web:* www2.warnerbros.com

Warner Center Marriott Woodland Hills
21850 Oxnard St.......... Woodland Hills CA 91367 818-887-4800 378
Web: www.warnercentermarriott.com

Warner Consulting Inc
5106 Berryessa St.......... Oceanside CA 92056 760-806-7722 196
Web: warner-consulting.com

Warner Electric 449 Gardner St .... South Beloit IL 61080 815-389-3771 620
TF: 800-825-6544 ■ *Web:* www.warnerelectric.com

Warner Home Video
4000 Warner Blvd Bldg 168 .... Burbank CA 91522 818-977-0018 514
TF: 866-373-4389 ■ *Web:* www.wbshop.com

Warner Manufacturing Co
13435 Industrial Pk Blvd .... Plymouth MN 55441 763-559-4740 758
TF: 800-444-0606 ■ *Web:* www.warnertool.com

Warner Mark R (Sen D - VA)
703 Hart Senate Office Bldg .... Washington DC 20510 202-224-2023 342-2
Web: www.warner.senate.gov

Warner Music Group
75 Rockefeller Plaza 30th Fl .... New York NY 10019 212-275-2000 657
TF: 800-820-1653 ■ *Web:* www.wmg.com

Warner Pacific College
2219 SE 68th Ave.......... Portland OR 97215 503-517-1020 517-1352 166
TF: 800-804-1510 ■ *Web:* www.warnerpacific.edu

Warner Power LLC 40 Depot St .... Warner NH 03278 603-456-3111 456-3754 767
TF: 800-276-2462 ■ *Web:* www.warnerpower.com

Warner Robins Area Chamber of Commerce
1000 Watson Blvd.......... Warner Robins GA 31093 478-922-8585 328-7745 139
Web: www.robinsregion.com

Warner Southern College
13895 Hwy 27 .... Lake Wales FL 33859 800-309-9563 949-7248* 166
**Fax:* Admissions ■ *TF:* 800-309-9563 ■ *Web:* warner.edu

Warner Theatre 513 13th St NW.......... Washington DC 20004 202-783-4000 783-0204 572
Web: warnertheatredc.com

Warner Theatre 811 State St.......... Erie PA 16501 814-452-4857 455-9931 572
TF: 800-514-3849 ■ *Web:* www.erieevents.com

Warner Vineyards Inc
706 S Kalamazoo St .... Paw Paw MI 49079 269-657-3165 80-3
TF: 800-756-5357 ■ *Web:* warnerwines.com

Warner/Chappell Music Inc
10585 Santa Monica Blvd.......... Los Angeles CA 90025 310-441-8600 637-7
Web: www.warnerchappell.com

Warners Florist
179 S Montgomery St.......... Hollidaysburg PA 16648 814-695-9431 292

Warnors Ctr for the Performing Arts
1412 Fulton St .... Fresno CA 93721 559-650-1154 572
Web: warnors.org

WARO-FM 94.5 (CR)
2824 Palm Beach Blvd .... Fort Myers FL 33916 239-479-5506 645
Web: 945thearrow.com

Warp Bros Flex-O-Glass Inc
4647 W Augusta Blvd.......... Chicago IL 60651 773-261-5200 261-5204 548
TF: 800-621-3345 ■ *Web:* www.warpbros.com

Warpaint Resources LLC
6175 Main St Ste 250.......... Dallas TX 75034 214-238-8440 536
Web: www.warpaintresources.com

Warrantech Corp Inc 2200 Hwy 121 .... Bedford TX 76021 817-785-6601 367
TF: 800-833-8801 ■ *Web:* www.warrantech.com

Warranty Group Inc, The
175 W Jackson 11th Fl.......... Chicago IL 60604 312-356-3000 391-5
TF: 800-621-2130 ■ *Web:* www.thewarrantygroup.com

Warranty Life Services Inc
4152 Meridian St Ste 105-29.......... Bellingham WA 98226 888-927-7269 393
TF: 888-927-7269 ■ *Web:* www.warrantylife.com

Warren & Panzer Engineers PC
228 E 45th St .... New York NY 10017 212-922-0077 256
Web: www.warrenpanzer.com

Warren Averett Kimbrough & Marino LLC
2500 Acton Rd .... Birmingham AL 35243 205-979-4100 979-6313 2
Web: warrenaverett.com

Warren Co, The 2201 Loveland Ave .... Erie PA 16506 800-562-0357 295
TF: 800-562-0357 ■ *Web:* www.thewarrencompany.com

Warren Co, The 2201 Loveland Ave .... Erie PA 16506 814-838-8681 480
Web: www.thewarrencompany.com

Warren Communications News Inc
2115 Ward Ct NW.......... Washington DC 20037 202-872-9200 318-8350 637-9
TF: 800-771-9202 ■ *Web:* www.warren-news.com

Warren Correctional Institution
5787 S Rt 63 PO Box 120.......... Lebanon OH 45036 513-932-3388 933-0150 213
Web: www.drc.ohio.gov

Warren Correctional Institution
379 Collins Rd .... Manson NC 27553 252-456-3400 456-4300 213

Warren County 413 Second St .... Belvidere NJ 07823 908-475-6211 475-6208 338
TF: 800-368-8683 ■ *Web:* www.co.warren.nj.us

Phone | Fax | Class

Warren County
429 E Tenth St Ste 100 Courthouse .... Bowling Green KY 42102 270-842-9416 843-5319 338
Web: warrencountyclerkky.com

Warren County
220 N Commerce Ave Ste 100 .... Front Royal VA 22630 540-636-4600 636-6066 338
TF: 800-248-6342 ■ *Web:* www.warrencountyva.net

Warren County 115 N Howard St. .... Indianola IA 50125 515-961-1122 338

Warren County 1340 State Rt 9 .... Lake George NY 12845 518-761-6429 761-6551 338
Web: www.warrencountyny.gov

Warren County 406 Justice Dr. .... Lebanon OH 45036 513-695-1358 338
TF: 800-282-0253 ■ *Web:* www.co.warren.oh.us

Warren County
110 S Ct Sq PO Box 574 .... McMinnville TN 37111 931-473-6611 473-4741 338
TF: 800-933-3909 ■ *Web:* www.warrentn.com

Warren County 100 W Broadway .... Monmouth IL 61462 309-734-8592 734-7406 338
Web: www.warrencountyil.com

Warren County 1009 Cherry St .... Vicksburg MS 39183 601-636-4415 338
TF: 800-433-0567 ■ *Web:* www.co.warren.ms.us

Warren County 204 Fourth Ave .... Warren PA 16365 814-728-3400 338
Web: warrencountypa.net

Warren County
46 S Norwood St PO Box 27 .... Warrenton GA 30828 706-465-9604 338
Web: www.warrencountyga.com

Warren County 104 W Main St .... Warrenton MO 63383 636-456-3331 338
Web: warrencountymo.org

Warren County
602 W Ridgeway St PO Box 619 .... Warrenton NC 27589 252-257-3115 257-5971 338
Web: www.warrencountync.com

Warren County
125 N Monroe St Ste 11 .... Williamsport IN 47993 765-762-3510 762-7251 338
TF: 800-622-4941 ■ *Web:* www.in.gov

Warren County Chamber of Commerce (WCCBI)
308 Market St .... Warren PA 16365 814-723-3050 723-6024 139
Web: www.wccbi.org

Warren County Community College
475 Rt 57 W .... Washington NJ 07882 908-835-9222 162
Web: www.warren.edu

Warren County Library 2 Shotwell Dr .... Belvidere NJ 07823 908-475-6322 434-3
Web: warrenlib.com

Warren County Rural Electric Membership Corp
15 Midway St PO Box 37 .... Williamsport IN 47993 765-762-6114 245
TF: 800-872-7319 ■ *Web:* www.wcremc.com

Warren County Visitors Bureau
22045 Rt 6 .... Warren PA 16365 814-726-1222 726-7266 206
TF: 800-624-7802 ■ *Web:* www.wcvb.net

Warren County-Vicksburg Public Library
700 Veto St .... Vicksburg MS 39180 601-636-6411 634-4809 434-3
TF: 800-721-7222 ■ *Web:* www.warren.lib.ms.us

Warren Distribution Inc 727 S 13th St .... Omaha NE 68102 402-341-9397 463
Web: www.warrendistribution.com

Warren Dunes State Park
12032 Red Arrow Hwy .... Sawyer MI 49125 269-426-4013 565
Web: www.michigandnr.com

Warren Electric Co-op Inc (WEC)
320 E Main St PO Box 208 .... Youngsville PA 16371 814-563-7548 563-7012 245
TF: 800-364-8640 ■ *Web:* www.warrenec.coop

Warren Elizabeth (Sen D - MA)
317 Hart Bldg .... Washington DC 20510 202-224-4543 342-2
Web: www.warren.senate.gov

Warren Equities Inc 27 Warren Way .... Providence RI 02905 401-781-9900 461-7160 360-3
TF: 866-867-4075 ■ *Web:* www.warreneq.com

Warren Fabricating & Machining
3240 Mahoning Ave NW .... Warren OH 44483 330-847-0596 454
Web: www.warfab.com

Warren General Hospital
2 Crescent Pk W .... Warren PA 16365 814-723-3300 374-3
TF: 800-777-9441 ■ *Web:* www.wgh.org

Warren Gibson Ltd
206 Church St S PO Box 100 .... Alliston ON L9R1T9 705-435-4342 478
TF: 800-461-4374 ■ *Web:* www.warrengibson.com

Warren Group Inc, The
7805 Saint Andrews Rd .... Irmo SC 29063 803-732-6600 261
Web: www.warrenforensics.com

Warren Hospital 185 Roseberry St .... Phillipsburg NJ 08865 908-859-6700 374-3
TF: 800-220-8116 ■ *Web:* www.warrenhospital.org

Warren Industries Inc
3100 Mt Pleasant St .... Racine WI 53404 262-639-7800 639-0920 549
Web: www.wrnind.com

Warren Island State Park
PO Box 105 .... Lincolnville ME 04849 207-446-7090 565
Web: www.maine.gov

Warren John m 700 Grand Ave Ste 14 .... Ridgefield NJ 07657 816-232-7702 445

Warren L & G Real Estate Inc
465 Van Wyck Lake Rd .... Fishkill NY 12524 845-897-4126 653
Web: www.warrenhomes.com

Warren Management Group Inc, The
1720 Jet Stream Dr Ste 200 .... Colorado Springs CO 80921 719-534-0266 463
Web: warrenmgmt.com

Warren Oil Company Inc PO Box 1507 .... Dunn NC 28335 910-892-6456 579
TF: 800-779-6456 ■ *Web:* www.warrenoil.com

Warren Paving Inc
562 Elks Lake Rd PO Box 572 .... Hattiesburg MS 39403 601-544-7811 544-2005 186
Web: www.warrenpaving.com

Warren Performing Arts Ctr
9500 E 16th St .... Indianapolis IN 46229 317-532-6280 572
Web: www.warrenpac.org

Warren Power & Machinery LP
4501 W Reno Ave .... Oklahoma City OK 73127 405-947-6771 23
Web: www.warrencat.com

Warren Printing & Mailing Inc
5000 Eagle Rock Blvd .... Los Angeles CA 90041 323-258-2621 627
TF: 888-468-6976 ■ *Web:* print-mail.com

Warren Properties Inc PO Box 469114 .... Escondido CA 92046 800-831-0804 655
TF: 800-831-0804 ■ *Web:* www.warrenproperties.com

Warren Public Library 5460 Arden .... Warren MI 48092 586-751-5377 434-3
Web: www.warrenlibrary.net

Warren Pumps LLC 82 Bridges Ave. .... Warren MA 01083 413-436-7711 641
Web: www.warrenpumps.com

Warren Resources Inc
1114 Ave of the Americas 34th Fl .... New York NY 10036 212-697-9660 697-9466 536
NASDAQ: WRES ■ *TF:* 877-587-9494 ■ *Web:* www.warrenresources.com

Warren Rupp Inc 800 N Main St. .... Mansfield OH 44902 419-524-8388 641
Web: www.warrenruppinc.com

Warren Rural Electric Co-op Corp
951 Fairview Ave .... Bowling Green KY 42101 270-842-6541 781-3299 245
TF: 866-319-3234 ■ *Web:* www.wrecc.com

Warren State Hospital 33 Main Dr .... North Warren PA 16365 814-723-5500 374-5
Web: www.dhs.pa.gov/citizens/statehospitals/warrenstatehospital

Warren Steel Holdings LLC
4000 Mahoning Ave .... Warren OH 44483 330-847-0487 492
Web: www.warrensteelholdings.com

Warren Technology Inc 2050 W 73 St. .... Hialeah FL 33016 305-556-6933 360-3
Web: www.warrenhvac.com

Warren Tire Service Ctr Inc
4 Highland Ave .... Queensbury NY 12804 518-792-0316 62-5
Web: www.warrentiresvc.com

Warren Transport Inc 210 Beck Ave. .... Waterloo IA 50701 319-233-6113 235-6555 780
TF General: 800-553-2007 ■ *Web:* www.warrentransport.com

Warren Trask Co 1481 Central St .... Stoughton MA 02072 781-341-2426 191-3
Web: www.wtrask.com

Warren Whitney Sherwood & Company Inc
7231 Forest Ave .... Richmond VA 23226 804-282-9566 463
Web: www.warrenwhitney.com

Warren Wilson College
701 Warren Wilson Rd .... Swannanoa NC 28778 828-298-3325 298-1440* 166
**Fax:* Admissions ■ *TF Admissions:* 800-934-3536 ■ *Web:* www.warren-wilson.edu

Warrenton Oil Co 2299 S Spoede .... Truesdale MO 63383 636-456-3346 345
Web: www.fastlane-cstore.com

Warren-Trumbull County Public Library
444 Mahoning Ave NW .... Warren OH 44483 330-399-8807 434-3
Web: www.wtcpl.lib.oh.us

Warrick County
107 W Locust St Ste 301 .... Boonville IN 47601 812-897-6120 897-6189 338
Web: www.warrickcounty.gov

Warrick County Chamber of Commerce
224 W Main St Ste 203 .... Boonville IN 47601 812-897-2340 897-2360 139
Web: warrickchamber.org

Warrick Publishing Inc
204 W Locust St PO Box 266 .... Boonville IN 47601 812-897-2330 897-3703 637-8
Web: www.warricknews.com

Warrior Consultant Group
3463 Daisy Ct .... Brunswick OH 44212 330-225-5120 196
Web: warriorgroup.com

Warrior Custom Golf Inc 15 Mason Ste A .... Irvine CA 92618 949-699-2499 711
TF: 800-600-5113 ■ *Web:* www.warriorcustomgolf.com

Warriors' Path State Park
312 Rosa L Parks Ave .... Nashville TN 37243 423-239-8531 565
Web: tnstateparks.com/parks/about/warriors-path

Warsaw Chemical Company Inc
Argonne Rd PO Box 858 .... Warsaw IN 46580 574-267-3251 267-3884 151
TF: 800-548-3396 ■ *Web:* www.warsaw-chem.com

Warschawski
1501 Sulgrave Ave Ste 350 .... Baltimore MD 21209 410-367-2700 636
Web: www.warschawski.com

Warshauer Electric Supply Co
800 Shrewsbury Ave .... Tinton Falls NJ 07724 732-741-6400 741-3866* 246
**Fax:* Sales ■ *Web:* www.warshauer.com

Warshaw Group Inc 540 Broadway 4th Fl. .... New York NY 10012 212-966-4056 463
Web: www.warshawgroup.com

Wartburg College 100 Wartburg Blvd .... Waverly IA 50677 319-352-8264 352-8579* 166
**Fax:* Admissions ■ *TF:* 800-772-2085 ■ *Web:* www.wartburg.edu

Wartburg Theological Seminary
333 Wartburg Pl .... Dubuque IA 52003 563-589-0200 589-0333 167-3
TF: 800-225-5987 ■ *Web:* www.wartburgseminary.edu

Wartsila North America Inc
16330 Air Ctr Blvd .... Houston TX 77032 281-233-6200 233-6233 262
TF: 877-927-8745 ■ *Web:* www.wartsila.com

Warwick Center for the Art's
3259 Post Rd .... Warwick RI 02886 401-737-0010 520
Web: www.warwickmuseum.org

Warwick Denver Hotel 1776 Grant St .... Denver CO 80203 303-861-2000 832-0320 379
TF: 800-203-3232 ■ *Web:* warwickhotels.com/denver

Warwick Investment Management Inc
4444 Carter Creek Pkwy Ste 109 .... Bryan TX 77802 979-260-9777 401
Web: www.warwickpartners.net

Warwick Mall 400 Bald Hill Rd Ste 100 .... Warwick RI 02886 401-739-7500 460
Web: www.warwickmall.com

Warwick Manor Behavioral Health
3680 Warwick Rd .... East New Market MD 21631 410-943-8108 726
TF: 800-344-6426 ■ *Web:* www.warwickmanor.org

Warwick Melrose Hotel
3015 Oak Lawn Ave .... Dallas TX 75219 214-521-5151 521-2470 379
TF: 800-521-7172 ■ *Web.* warwickhotels.com/dallas

Warwick New York Hotel 65 W 54th St. .... New York NY 10019 212-247-2700 247-2725* 379
**Fax:* Sales ■ *TF:* 800-203-3232 ■ *Web:* warwickhotels.com/new-york

Warwick Plumbing & Heating Corp
11048 Warwick Blvd. .... Newport News VA 23601 757-599-6111 595-9739 189-10
Web: www.wphcorp.com

Warwick Public Library (WPL)
600 Sandy Ln .... Warwick RI 02886 401-739-5440 434-3
TF: 800-359-3090 ■ *Web:* warwicklibrary.org

Warwick Regis Hotel San Francisco
490 Geary St. .... San Francisco CA 94102 415-928-7900 441-8788 379
Web: warwickhotels.com/san-francisco

Warwick Seattle Hotel 401 Lenora St. .... Seattle WA 98121 206-443-4300 448-1662 379
TF: 800-426-9280 ■ *Web:* warwickhotels.com/seattle

Warwick Valley Chamber of Commerce (WVCC)
PO Box 202 .... Warwick NY 10990 845-986-2720 986-6982 139
TF: 800-538-2583 ■ *Web:* www.warwickcc.org

Warwick Valley Telephone Co
47 Main St PO Box 592 .... Warwick NY 10990 845-986-8080 736
NASDAQ: WWVY ■ *TF Cust Svc:* 800-952-7642 ■ *Web:* www.wvtc.com

Wasabi 61 State St .... Charleston SC 29401 843-577-5222 671
Web: wasabirestaurantgroup.com

Wasabi Japanese Restaurant
449 State St .... Madison WI 53703 608-255-5020 671
Web: wasabi-madison.com

Phone | Fax | Class

Wasabi Japanese Steak House
226 Lovell Rd .... Knoxville TN 37934 865-675-0201 671
Web: www.wasabi-steakhouse.com

Wasabi Rabbit Inc
19 Fulton St Ste 307 .... New York NY 10038 646-366-0000 195
Web: www.wasabirabbit.com

Wasabi Systems Inc
500 E Main St Ste 1520 .... Norfolk VA 23510 757-248-9601 809
Web: www.wasabisystems.com

Wasatch Academy 120 S 100 W .... Mount Pleasant UT 84647 435-462-1400 622
TF: 800-634-4690 ■ Web: www.wasatchacademy.org

Wasatch Container Inc
645 N 400 W .... North Salt Lake UT 84054 801-295-8888 45
Web: www.wasatchcontainer.com

Wasatch County 25 N Main St .... Heber City UT 84032 435-657-3221 338
Web: www.wasatch.utah.gov

Wasatch Electric
2455 W 1500 S Ste A .... Salt Lake City UT 84104 801-487-4511 487-5032 189-4
TF: 800-999-4511 ■ Web: www.wasatchelectric.com

Wasatch Mountain State Park
1281 Warm Springs Rd .... Midway UT 84049 435-654-1791 565
Web: www.stateparks.utah.gov

Wasatch Photonics 1305 N 1000 W Ste 120 .... Logan UT 84321 435-752-4301 592
Web: www.wasatchphotonics.com

WASC (WASC) 985 Atlantic Ave .... Alameda CA 94501 510-748-9001 49-5
Web: wascsenior.org

Waschuk Pipe Line Construction Ltd
#127-39015 Hwy 2A .... Red Deer AB T4N2A3 403-346-1114 539
TF: 800-993-9958 ■ Web: www.waschukpipeline.com

Wasco County 511 Washington St .... The Dalles OR 97058 541-506-2530 298-3607 338
Web: www.co.wasco.or.us

Wasco Electric Co-op Inc
105 E Fourth St .... The Dalles OR 97058 541-296-2740 245
TF: 800-341-8580 ■ Web: www.wascoelectric.com

WASCO Inc 1122 Second Ave N Ste B .... Nashville TN 37208 615-244-9090 726-2643 189-7
TF: 800-952-8631 ■ Web: www.wascomasonry.com

Wasco Products Inc
85 Spencer Dr Unit A PO Box 559 .... Wells ME 04090 207-324-8060 329
TF: 800-388-0293 ■ Web: www.wascoskylights.com

Waseca County 307 N State St .... Waseca MN 56093 507-835-0610 835-0633* 338
*Fax: Acctg ■ Web: www.co.waseca.mn.us

Wash Depot Holdings Inc 14 Summer St .... Malden MA 02148 781-324-2000 62-1
Web: www.washdepot.com

WASH Multifamily Laundry Systems
100 N Sepulveda Blvd 12th Fl .... El Segundo CA 90245 800-421-6897 38
TF General: 800-421-6897 ■ Web: www.washlaundry.com

Wash Tub, The 2208 NW Loop 410 .... San Antonio TX 78230 210-493-8822 62-1
TF Cust Svc: 866-493-8822 ■ Web: washtub.com

Washakie County PO Box 260 .... Worland WY 82401 307-347-3131 347-9366 338
Web: www.washakiecounty.net

Washakie Renewable Energy LLC
070 E 3900 S Ste 300 .... Salt Lake City UT 84107 801-327-8695 536
Web: wrebiofuels.com

Washburn County PO Box 639 .... Shell Lake WI 54871 715-468-4600 468-4725 338
TF: 800-469-6562 ■ Web: www.co.washburn.wi.us

Washburn University
1700 SW College Ave .... Topeka KS 66621 785-670-1010 670-1079 166
TF: 800-736-9060 ■ Web: www.washburn.edu

Washers Inc 33375 Glendale St .... Livonia MI 48150 734-523-1000 488
Web: www.alphastamping.com

WASH-FM 97.1 (AC) 1801 Rockville Pk .... Rockville MD 20852 240-747-2700 645
TF: 866-927-4361 ■ Web: washfm.iheart.com

Washington
Administrative Office of the Courts
1112 Quince St SE PO Box 41174 .... Olympia WA 98504 360-753-3365 339-48
Web: www.courts.wa.gov
Aging & Disability Services Administration
4450 Tenth Ave SE .... Lacey WA 98503 360-725-2300 407-0369 339-48
TF: 800-422-3263 ■ Web: www.altsa.dshs.wa.gov
Agriculture Dept
1111 Washington ST SE Natural Resources Bldg
.... Olympia WA 98504 360-902-1800 902-2092 339-48
Web: www.agr.wa.gov
Arts Commission
711 Capitol Way S Ste 600 .... Olympia WA 98504 360-753-3860 586-5351 339-48
Web: www.arts.wa.gov
Attorney General
1125 Washington St SE PO Box 40100 .... Olympia WA 98504 360-753-6200 339-48
Web: www.atg.wa.gov
Child Support Div PO Box 11520 .... Tacoma WA 98411 360-664-5321 664-5303 339-48
TF: 800-457-6202 ■ Web: www.dshs.wa.gov
Consumer Protection Div
1125 Washington St SE PO Box 40100 .... Olympia WA 98504 360-753-6200 339-48
Web: www.atg.wa.gov/page.aspx?id=1792
Corrections Dept
7345 Linderson Way SW .... Tumwater WA 98501 360-725-8213 664-4056 339-48
Web: www.doc.wa.gov
Ecology Dept 300 Desmond Dr SE .... Olympia WA 98504 360-407-6000 407-6989 339-48
Web: www.ecy.wa.gov
Emergency Management Div
20 Aviation Dr Bldg 20 TA-20 .... Camp Murray WA 98430 253-512-7000 339-48
Web: mil.wa.gov
Employment Security Dept
212 Maple Pk Ave SE .... Olympia WA 98501 360-902-9500 259
TF: 800-318-6022 ■ Web: www.esd.wa.gov
Financial Institutions Dept
PO Box 41200 .... Olympia WA 98504 360-902-8703 586-5068 339-48
TF: 877-746-4334 ■ Web: www.dfi.wa.gov/cs
Fish & Wildlife Dept
1111 Washington St SEÿ
Natural Resources Bldg .... Olympia WA 98501 360-902-2200 902-2156 339-48
Web: www.wdfw.wa.gov
Governor PO Box 40002 .... Olympia WA 98504 360-902-4111 753-4110 339-48
Web: www.governor.wa.gov
Health Dept PO Box 47890 .... Olympia WA 98504 360-236-4220 339-48
Web: www.doh.wa.gov
Higher Education Coordinating Board
917 Lakeridge Way PO Box 43430 .... Olympia WA 98504 360-753-7800 725
Web: www.wsac.wa.gov
Historical Society 1911 Pacific Ave .... Tacoma WA 90402 253-272-3500 272-9518 339-48
TF: 888-238-4373 ■ Web: www.washingtonhistory.org
Horse Racing Commission
6326 Martin Way E Ste 209 .... Olympia WA 98516 360-459-6462 459-6461 712
Web: www.whrc.wa.gov
Housing Finance Commission
1000 Second Ave Ste 2700 .... Seattle WA 98104 206-464-7139 587-5113 339-48
TF: 800-767-4663 ■ Web: www.wshfc.org
Indeterminate Sentence Review Board
4317 Sixth Ave SE .... Olympia WA 98504 360-407-2400 493-9287 339-48
TF: 866-948-9266 ■ Web: www.doc.wa.gov
Insurance Commissioner
5000 Capitol Blvd SE .... Tumwater WA 98504 360-725-7000 586-3535 339-48
Web: www.insurance.wa.gov
Labor & Industries Dept PO Box 44000 .... Olympia WA 98504 360-902-5800 902-5798 339-48
Web: www.lni.wa.gov
Legislature 106 Legislative Bldg .... Olympia WA 98504 360-786-7573 339-48
TF: 800-062-6000 ■ Web: www.leg.wa.gov
Licensing Dept PO Box 9020 .... Olympia WA 98504 360-902-3600 339-48
Web: www.dol.wa.gov
Lieutenant Governor
416 Sid Snyder Ave SW PO Box 40400 .... Olympia WA 98501 360-786-7700 786-7749 339-48
Web: www.ltgov.wa.gov
Natural Resources Dept
1111 Washington St SE PO Box 47000 .... Olympia WA 98504 360-902-1000 339-48
TF: 800-258-5990 ■ Web: www.dnr.wa.gov
Office of Superindent Public Instruction Dept
600 Washington St SE PO Box 47200 .... Olympia WA 98504 360-725-6000 339-48
Web: www.k12.wa.us
Professional Educator Standards Board
600 Washington St SE .... Olympia WA 98504 360-725-6275 586-4548 339-48
Web: www.pesb.wa.gov
Public Disclosure Commission
711 Capitol Way Ste 206 PO Box 40908 .... Olympia WA 98504 360-753-1111 753-1112 265
TF: 877-601-2828 ■ Web: www.pdc.wa.gov
Revenue Dept PO Box 47478 .... Olympia WA 98504 360-705-6714 705-6655 339-48
TF: 800-647-7706 ■ Web: dor.wa.gov
Secretary of State PO Box 40220 .... Olympia WA 98504 360-902-4151 339-48
TF: 800-822-1065 ■ Web: www.sos.wa.gov
Securities Div PO Box 9033 .... Olympia WA 98507 360-902-8760 902-0524 339-48
TF: 877-746-4334 ■ Web: www.dfi.wa.gov/sd
Social & Health Services Dept
PO Box 45131 .... Olympia WA 98504 360-902-8400 339-48
TF: 800-737-0617 ■ Web: www.wa.gov/dshs
State Lottery PO Box 43000 .... Olympia WA 98504 360-664-4720 664-2630 452
TF: 800-732-5101 ■ Web: www.walottery.com
State Parks & Recreation Commission
1111 Israel Rd SW .... Tumwater WA 98501 360-725-9770 339-48
TF Campground Resv: 888-226-7688 ■ Web: www.parks.wa.gov
State Patrol
General Administration Bldg PO Box 42600 .... Olympia WA 98504 360-753-6540 339-48
Web: www.wsp.wa.gov
Supreme Court 415 12th Ave SW .... Olympia WA 98501 360-357-2077 339-48
Transportation Dept PO Box 47300 .... Olympia WA 98504 360-705-7000 339-48
Web: www.wsdot.wa.gov
Utilities & Transportation Commission
1300 S Evergreen Pk Dr SW PO Box 47250 .... Olympia WA 98504 360-664-1160 664-1150 339-48
TF: 888-333-9882 ■ Web: www.utc.wa.gov
Veterans Affairs Dept
1102 Quince St SE PO Box 41150 .... Olympia WA 98504 360-725-2200 725-2197 339-48
TF: 800-562-0132 ■ Web: www.dva.wa.gov
Vital Records Div 101 Israel Rd SE .... Olympia WA 98504 360-236-4300 339-48
Web: www.cdc.gov/nchs/w2w.htm
Vocational Rehabilitation Div
PO Box 45340 .... Olympia WA 98504 360-438-8000 339-48
TF: 800-637-5627 ■ Web: www.dshs.wa.gov

Washington & Jefferson College
60 S Lincoln St .... Washington PA 15301 724-222-4400 223-6534* 166
*Fax: Admissions ■ TF: 888-926-3529 ■ Web: www.washjeff.edu

Washington & Lee University
204 W Washington St .... Lexington VA 24450 540-458-8710 458-8062* 166
*Fax: Admissions ■ TF: 800-221-3943 ■ Web: www.wlu.edu

Washington & Lee University School of Law
1 Denny Cir .... Lexington VA 24450 540-458-8502 458-8586* 167-1
*Fax: Admissions ■ Web: www.law.wlu.edu

Washington Academy
66 Cutler Rd PO Box 190 .... East Machias ME 04630 207-255-8301 255-8303 622
Web: www.washingtonacademy.org

Washington Adventist Hospital
7600 Carroll Ave .... Takoma Park MD 20912 301-891-7600 374-3
Web: www.adventisthealthcare.com

Washington Adventist University
7600 Flower Ave .... Takoma Park MD 20912 301-891-4000 891-4167 166
TF: 800-835-4212 ■ Web: www.wau.edu

Washington Area Chamber of Commerce
323 W Main St .... Washington MO 63090 636-239-2715 139
TF: 800-747-6422 ■ Web: www.washmo.org

Washington Assn of Realtors
504 14th Ave SE Ste 200 .... Olympia WA 98501 360-943-3100 656
TF General: 800-562-6024 ■ Web: www.warealtor.org

Washington Ballet
3515 Wisconsin Ave NW .... Washington DC 20016 202-362-3606 362-1311 573-1
Web: www.washingtonballet.org

Washington Baptist University
4302 Evergreen Ln .... Annandale VA 22003 703-333-5904 333-5906 167-3
Web: www.wuv.edu

Washington Beef LLC 201 Elmwood Rd .... Toppenish WA 98948 509-865-2121 473
TF: 800-637-4634 ■ Web: www.wabeef.org

Washington Business Group on Health (WBGH)
20 F St NW Ste 200 .... Washington DC 20001 202-628-9320 628-9244 48-17
Web: www.businessgrouphealth.org

Washington Business Journal
1555 Wilson Blvd Ste 400 .... Arlington VA 22209 703-258-0800 258-0802 457-5
Web: www.bizjournals.com

Washington Capital Management Inc
1301 Fifth Ave Ste 3100 .... Seattle WA 98101 206-382-0825 382-0950 401
Web: www.wcmadvisors.com

Name / Address	City	State	ZIP	Phone	Fax	Class
Washington Capitals 627 N Glebe Rd Ste 850 *Web:* capitals.nhl.com	Arlington	VA	22203	202-266-2200		716
Washington Chain & Supply Inc 2901 Utah Ave S PO Box 3645 *TF:* 800-851-3429 ■ *Web:* www.wachain.com	Seattle	WA	98124	206-623-8500	621-9834	770
Washington City Paper 2390 Champlain St NW *Web:* www.washingtoncitypaper.com	Washington	DC	20009	202-332-2100	332-8500	532-5
Washington College 300 Washington Ave *TF:* 800-422-1782 ■ *Web:* www.washcoll.edu	Chestertown	MD	21620	410-778-2800	778-7287	166
Washington Company School District PO Box 716 *Web:* www.washington.k12.ga.us	Sandersville	GA	31082	478-552-3981		685
Washington Consulting Group Inc 4915 Auburn Ave Ste 301 *Web:* www.washcg.com	Bethesda	MD	20814	301-656-2330	656-1996	180
Washington Convention Ctr Authority 801 Mt Vernon Pl NW *TF:* 800-368-9000 ■ *Web:* www.dcconvention.com	Washington	DC	20001	202-249-3000		205
Washington Corp PO Box 16630 *Web:* www.washcorp.com	Missoula	MT	59808	406-523-1300	523-1399	261
Washington Correctional Facility 72 Lock 11 Rd *Web:* www.doccs.ny.gov/faclist.html	Comstock	NY	12821	518-639-4486		213
Washington Correctional Industries 801 88th Ave SE *TF:* 800-628-4738 ■ *Web:* www.washingtonci.com	Tumwater	WA	98501	360-725-9100	753-0219	630
Washington Corrections Ctr for Women 9601 Bujacich Rd NW	Gig Harbor	WA	98332	253-858-4200		213
Washington County 1 Government Ctr Pl Ste A *Web:* www.washcova.com	Abingdon	VA	24210	276-525-1300	525-1309	338
Washington County 150 Ash Ave *Web:* co.washington.co.us	Akron	CO	80720	970-345-2701	345-2702	338
Washington County 400 S Johnstone Ave *TF:* 800-522-0034 ■ *Web:* countycourthouse.org	Bartlesville	OK	74003	918-337-2840		338
Washington County PO Box 466 *Web:* www.co.washington.ne.us	Blair	NE	68008	402-426-6822	426-6825	338
Washington County 100 E Main St Ste 102 *TF:* 800-388-8075 ■ *Web:* www.co.washington.tx.us	Brenham	TX	77833	979-277-6200	277-6278	338
Washington County PO Box 531 *Web:* www.washingtoncountyal.com	Chatom	AL	36518	251-847-2214		338
Washington County 280 N College Ave Ste 300 *TF:* 800-563-0012 ■ *Web:* www.co.washington.ar.us	Fayetteville	AR	72701	479-444-1711	444-1894	338
Washington County 383 Broadway Bldg A *Web:* www.co.washington.ny.us	Fort Edward	NY	12828	518-746-2170	746-2177	338
Washington County PO Box 1276	Greenville	MS	38702	662-378-2747	334-2698	338
Washington County 100 W Washington St *TF:* 800-235-4045 ■ *Web:* www.washco-md.net	Hagerstown	MD	21740	240-313-2200	313-2201	338
Washington County 155 N First Ave *TF:* 800-735-1232 ■ *Web:* www.co.washington.or.us	Hillsboro	OR	97124	503-846-8611		338
Washington County PO Box 297 *Web:* www.washingtoncountymaine.com	Machias	ME	04654	207-255-3127	255-3313	338
Washington County 205 Putnam *TF:* 800-205-6446 ■ *Web:* www.washingtongov.org	Marietta	OH	45750	740-373-6623	373-5713	338
Washington County 65 State St	Montpelier	VT	05602	802-828-2091		338
Washington County 116 Adams St PO Box 1007 *Web:* www.washconc.org	Plymouth	NC	27962	252-793-5823	793-1183	338
Washington County 102 N Missouri St *Web:* www.washingtoncountymo.us	Potosi	MO	63664	573-438-6111	438-2009	338
Washington County 197 E Tabernacle St *Web:* washco.utah.gov	Saint George	UT	84770	435-634-5700		338
Washington County 99 Public Sq Ste 102 *TF:* 800-433-0567 ■ *Web:* www.washingtoncounty.in.gov	Salem	IN	47167	812-883-5748		338
Washington County 119 Jones St *TF:* 800-427-5463 ■ *Web:* washingtoncountyga.gov	Sandersville	GA	31082	478-552-3288		338
Washington County 109 N Cross Main PO Box 126 *Web:* washingtoncountyky.com	Springfield	KY	40069	859-336-5410	336-5407	338
Washington County 14949 62nd St N *Web:* www.co.washington.mn.us	Stillwater	MN	55082	651-430-6001	430-6017	338
Washington County 224 W Main St *Web:* co.washington.ia.us	Washington	IA	52353	319-653-7741	653-7787	338
Washington County 214 C St Ste 3 *Web:* www.washingtoncountyks.gov	Washington	KS	66968	785-325-2461		338
Washington County 1 S Main St Ste 1005 *Web:* www.co.washington.pa.us	Washington	PA	15301	724-228-6787		338
Washington County 256 East Ct *TF:* 800-943-7847 ■ *Web:* www.co.washington.id.us	Weiser	ID	83672	208-414-2092	414-3925	338
Washington County 432 E Washington St Ste 2027 Ste 2027 *Web:* www.co.washington.wi.us	West Bend	WI	53095	262-335-4400	306-2208	338
Washington County Board of Education 802 Washington St *Web:* www.washingtonco.k12.nc.us	Plymouth	NC	27962	252-793-5171		685
Washington County Chamber of Commerce 375 Southpointe Blvd Ste 240 *TF:* 800-242-6422 ■ *Web:* www.washcochamber.com	Canonsburg	PA	15301	724-225-3010	228-7337	139
Washington County Chamber of Commerce 314 S Austin St *TF:* 888-273-6426 ■ *Web:* www.brenhamtexas.com	Brenham	TX	77833	979-836-3695	836-2540	139
Washington County Chamber of Commerce 1 Government Ctr Pl Ste D *Web:* www.washingtonvachamber.org	Abingdon	VA	24210	276-628-8141	628-3984	139
Washington County Community College 1 College Dr *Web:* www.wccc.me.edu	Calais	ME	04619	207-454-1000	454-1092	162
Washington County Library 8595 Central Pk Pl *TF:* 800-657-3750 ■ *Web:* www.co.washington.mn.us	Woodbury	MN	55125	651-275-8500	275-8509	434-3
Washington County Library System 1080 W Clydesdale Dr *Web:* www.co.washington.ar.us	Fayetteville	AR	72701	479-442-6253	442-6812	434-3
Washington County Mental Health Services Inc (WCMHS) PO Box 647 *Web:* www.wcmhs.org	Montpelier	VT	05601	802-229-0591	223-8623	353
Washington County Museum of Fine Arts 401 Museum Dr PO Box 423 *Web:* www.wcmfa.org	Hagerstown	MD	21741	301-739-5727		520
Washington County Public Library 205 Oak Hill St *Web:* www.wcpl.net	Abingdon	VA	24210	276-676-6222		434-3
Washington County Public Library 88 W 100 S *Web:* library.washco.utah.gov	Saint George	UT	84770	435-634-5737	634-5741	434-3
Washington County Public Library 615 Fifth St *Web:* wcplib.info	Marietta	OH	45750	740-373-1057	373-2860	434-3
Washington County State Recreation Area 18500 Conservation Dr	Nashville	IL	62263	618-327-3137		565
Washington County Visitors Assn 12725 SW Millikan Way Ste 210 *TF:* 800-537-3149 ■ *Web:* tualatinvalley.org	Beaverton	OR	97005	503-644-5555	644-9784	206
Washington Courier 100 Ford Ln *Web:* www.courierpapers.com	Washington	IL	61571	309-444-3139		532-4
Washington Court Hotel 525 New Jersey Ave NW *TF:* 800-321-3010 ■ *Web:* www.washingtoncourthotel.com	Washington	DC	20001	202-628-2100		379
Washington Crossing State Park 355 Washington Crossing-Pennington Rd *Web:* www.njparksandforests.org	Titusville	NJ	08560	609-737-0623		565
Washington Ctr for the Performing Arts 512 Washington St SE *TF:* 800-250-2525 ■ *Web:* www.washingtoncenter.org	Olympia	WA	98501	360-753-8586	754-1177	572
Washington Daily News, The 217 N Market St *Web:* www.wdnweb.com	Washington	NC	27889	252-946-2144		532-3
Washington DC Accommodations 2201 Wisconsin Ave NW Ste C-120 *TF:* 800-503-3330 ■ *Web:* www.wdcahotels.com	Washington	DC	20007	202-289-2220		376
Washington (DC) City Hall 1350 Pennsylvania Ave NW *Web:* dc.gov	Washington	DC	20004	202-727-1000	727-0505	337
Washington DC Convention & Tourism Corp 901 Seventh St NW 4th Fl *TF:* 800-422-8644 ■ *Web:* washington.org	Washington	DC	20001	202-789-7000		206
Washington Democratic Party PO Box 4027 *Web:* www.wa-democrats.org	Seattle	WA	98194	206-583-0664	583-0301	616-1
Washington Dental Service 9706 Fourth Ave NE *TF:* 800-367-4104 ■ *Web:* www.deltadentalwa.com	Seattle	WA	98115	206-522-1300		391-3
Washington Duke Inn & Golf Club 3001 Cameron Blvd *TF:* 800-443-3853 ■ *Web:* www.washingtondukeinn.com	Durham	NC	27705	919-490-0999	688-0105	379
Washington Dulles International Airport Dulles Airport Access Rd *Web:* flydulles.com/iad/dulles-international-airport	Washington	DC	20041	703-572-2700	572-5718	27
Washington Education Assn Inc 32032 Weyerhaeuser Way S PO Box 9100 *TF:* 800-622-3393 ■ *Web:* www.washingtonea.org	Federal Way	WA	98001	253-941-6700		49-5
Washington Electric Co-op 40 Church St *TF:* 800-932-5245 ■ *Web:* www.washingtonelectric.coop	East Montpelier	VT	05651	802-223-5245	223-6780	245
Washington Electric Cooperative Inc 440 Highland Ridge Rd **Fax Area Code: 877* ■ *TF:* 877-594-9324 ■ *Web:* www.weci.org	Marietta	OH	45750	740-373-2141	440-2671*	245
Washington Electric Membership Corp 258 N Harris St *TF:* 800-552-2577 ■ *Web:* www.washingtonemc.com	Sandersville	GA	31082	478-552-2577		245
Washington Examiner 1015 15th St NW Ste 500 *Web:* www.examiner.com	Washington	DC	20005	202-903-2000		532-2
Washington Express Service LLC 12240 Indian Creek Ct Ste 100 *TF:* 800-939-5463 ■ *Web:* www.washingtonexpress.net	Beltsville	MD	20705	301-210-0899	419-7075	546
Washington Federal Inc 425 Pike St *NASDAQ: WAFD* ■ *TF:* 800-324-9375 ■ *Web:* www.washingtonfederal.com	Seattle	WA	98101	206-624-7930		360-2
Washington Floral Service Inc 2701 S 35th St *TF:* 800-351-5515 ■ *Web:* www.washingtonfloral.com	Tacoma	WA	98409	253-472-8343		292
Washington Gas & Light Co 6801 Industrial Rd *TF:* 800-752-7520 ■ *Web:* www.washingtongas.com	Springfield	VA	22151	703-750-4440		787
Washington Group Consultants LLC PO Box A *Web:* www.washingtongroup.com	Fairfax	VA	22031	703-591-6600	591-6602	194
Washington Hospital Ctr 110 Irving St NW *TF:* 855-546-1686 ■ *Web:* www.medstarhealth.org	Washington	DC	20010	202-877-7000		374-3
Washington Hospital, The 155 Wilson Ave *Web:* www.washingtonhospital.org	Washington	PA	15301	724-225-7000		374-3
Washington House 5100 Fillmore Ave *Web:* www.watermarkcommunities.com/washingtonhouse	Alexandria	VA	22311	703-291-0188		672
Washington Inn Hotel, The 495 Tenth St *TF:* 800-738-7477 ■ *Web:* www.thewashingtoninn.com	Oakland	CA	94607	510-452-1776	452-4436	379
Washington International Business Report 818 Connecticut Ave NW 12th Fl *Web:* www.ibgc.com	Washington	DC	20006	202-872-8181	872-8696	531-7
Washington International School 3100 Macomb St NW *Web:* www.wis.edu	Washington	DC	20008	202-243-1815		685

Name / Address	City	State	Zip	Phone	Fax	Class
Washington Internet Daily 2115 Ward Ct NW *TF:* 800-771-9202 ■ *Web:* www.warren-news.com	Washington	DC	20037	202-872-9200		531-3
Washington Irving's Sunnyside W Sunnyside Ln *Web:* www.hudsonvalley.org	Tarrytown	NY	10591	914-591-8763		50-3
Washington Jefferson LLC 318 W 51st St *TF:* 888-567-7550 ■ *Web:* www.wjhotel.com	New York	NY	10019	212-246-7550		378
Washington Lawyer Magazine 1101 K St NW Ste 200 *TF:* 877-333-2227 ■ *Web:* www.dcbar.org	Washington	DC	20005	202-737-4700		457-15
Washington Local Schools 3505 W Lincolnshire Blvd *TF:* 800-462-3589 ■ *Web:* wls4kids.org	Toledo	OH	43606	419-473-8251	473-8247	186
Washington Metropolitan Area Transit Authority 600 Fifth St NW *TF:* 800-523-7009 ■ *Web:* www.wmata.com	Washington	DC	20001	202-637-7000		468
Washington Metropolitan Philharmonic Assn (WMPA) PO Box 120 *Web:* www.wmpamusic.org	Mount Vernon	VA	22121	703-799-8229	360-7391	573-3
Washington Mills Electro Minerals Co 20 N Main St *TF:* 800-828-1666 ■ *Web:* www.washingtonmills.com	North Grafton	MA	01536	508-839-6511	839-7675	1
Washington Missourian 14 W Main St PO Box 336 *TF:* 888-239-7701 ■ *Web:* www.emissourian.com	Washington	MO	63090	636-239-7701	239-0915	532-4
Washington Monument State Park c/o Greenbrier State Pk 6620 Zittlestown Rd *Web:* www.dnr.maryland.gov/publiclands/Pages/western/washington.aspx	Middletown	MD	21769	301-791-4767		565
Washington Music Ctr 11151 Veirs Mill Rd *Web:* chucklevins.com	Wheaton	MD	20902	301-946-8808	946-0487	526
Washington National Insurance Co 11825 N Pennsylvania St **Fax Area Code: 800* ■ *TF:* 866-595-2255 ■ *Web:* www.conseco.com	Carmel	IN	46032	866-595-2255	757-6324*	391-2
Washington National Primate Research Ctr (WNPRC) 1705 NE Pacific St PO Box 357330 *Web:* www.wanprc.org	Seattle	WA	98195	206-543-0440	616-6771	668
Washington Oaks Gardens State Park 6400 N Oceanshore Blvd *Web:* www.floridastateparks.org	Palm Coast	FL	32137	386-446-6780	446-6781	565
Washington Ornamental Iron Works Inc 17926 S Broadway	Gardena	CA	90247	310-327-8660		189-14
Washington Parish 909 Pearl St *TF:* 800-375-7570 ■ *Web:* www.washingtonparishalerts.org	Franklinton	LA	70438	985-839-7825	839-7827	338
Washington Parish Library System 825 Free St *Web:* washingtonparishlibrary.info	Franklinton	LA	70438	985-839-7806	839-7808	434-3
Washington Park Arboretum 2300 Arboretum Dr E *TF:* 800-305-9617 ■ *Web:* www.depts.washington.edu	Seattle	WA	98112	206-543-8800	616-2871	97
Washington Park Botanical Garden 1740 W Fayette Ave *Web:* www.springfieldparks.org	Springfield	IL	62704	217-753-6228	546-0257	97
Washington Pavilion 301 S Main *TF:* 877-927-4728 ■ *Web:* www.washingtonpavilion.org	Sioux Falls	SD	57104	605-367-6000	367-7099	520
Washington Plaza Hotel 10 Thomas Cir NW *TF:* 800-424-1140 ■ *Web:* www.washingtonplazahotel.com	Washington	DC	20005	202-842-1300	371-9602	379
Washington Post 1301 K St NW *TF:* 800-627-1150 ■ *Web:* www.washingtonpost.com	Washington	DC	20071	202-334-6000		532-2
Washington Post, The 1301 K St NW *TF:* 800-879-9794 ■ *Web:* www.washingtonpost.com	Washington	DC	20071	202-637-1328	334-5669	530
Washington Professional Systems (WPS) 109GaitherDr Ste 301 *Web:* www.wpsworld.com	Mount Laurel	NJ	08054	856-273-8688	273-8558	52
Washington Publishing Co 2107 Elliott Ave Ste 305 **Fax Area Code: 775* ■ *Web:* www.wpc-edi.com	Seattle	WA	98121	425-562-2245	239-2061*	637-10
Washington Real Estate Investment Trust (WRIT) 1775 I St NW *NYSE: WRE* ■ *TF:* 800-565-9748 ■ *Web:* www.writ.com	Washington	DC	20006	301-984-9400	984-9610	655
Washington Redskins 21300 Redskin Pk Dr *Web:* www.redskins.com	Ashburn	VA	20147	703-726-7000		715-3
Washington Research Foundation 2815 Eastlake Ave E Ste 300 *Web:* www.wrfcapital.com	Seattle	WA	98102	206-336-5600		792
Washington Research Library Consortium Inc, The 901 Commerce Dr *Web:* www.wrlc.org	Upper Marlboro	MD	20774	301-390-2000		434-3
Washington Rock State Park 355 Milltown Rd *Web:* www.njparksandforests.org/parks/washrock.html	Bridgewater	NJ	08807	908-722-1200		565
Washington School District Inc 201 Allison Ave *TF:* 855-846-8376 ■ *Web:* www.washington.k12.pa.us	Washington	PA	15301	724-223-5085	223-5046	685
Washington Speakers Bureau 1663 Prince St *Web:* www.washingtonspeakers.com	Alexandria	VA	22314	703-684-0555	684-9378	708
Washington Sports Clubs 888 Seventh Ave *Web:* www.mysportsclubs.com	New York	NY	10106	212-246-6700	246-8422	354
Washington Square Hotel 103 Waverly Pl *TF:* 800-222-0418 ■ *Web:* www.washingtonsquarehotel.com	New York	NY	10011	212-777-9515	979-8373	379
Washington Square Mall 10202 E Washington St *TF:* 800-283-9490 ■ *Web:* www.simon.com	Indianapolis	IN	46229	317-899-4568		460
Washington Square Shopping Ctr 9585 SW Washington Sq Rd *TF:* 800-522-2602 ■ *Web:* www.shopwashingtonsquare.com	Portland	OR	97223	503-639-8860		460
Washington State Bar Assn 1325 Fourth Ave Ste 600 *TF:* 800-945-9722 ■ *Web:* www.wsba.org	Seattle	WA	98101	206-443-9722	727-8320	72
Washington State Bar News 1325 Fourth Ave Ste 600 **Fax Area Code: 206* ■ *TF:* 800-945-9722 ■ *Web:* www.wsba.org	Seattle	WA	98101	800-945-9722	727-8320*	457-15
Washington State Capital Museum 211 21st Ave SW *Web:* www.washingtonhistory.org	Olympia	WA	98501	360-753-2580	586-8322	520
Washington State Community College 710 Colegate Dr *Web:* www.wscc.edu	Marietta	OH	45750	740-374-8716	376-0257	162
Washington State Convention 800 Convention Pl *Web:* wscc.com	Seattle	WA	98101	206-694-5000	694-5399	205
Washington State Department of Veterans Affairs 1102 Quince St SE PO Box 41150 *Web:* www.dva.wa.gov	Olympia	WA	98504	360-895-4700		793
Washington State Employees Credit Union 330 Union Ave SE *TF:* 800-562-0999 ■ *Web:* www.wsecu.org	Olympia	WA	98501	360-943-7911		219
Washington State Library PO Box 40220 *TF:* 800-822-1065 ■ *Web:* www.sos.wa.gov	Olympia	WA	98504	360-902-4151	586-7575	434-5
Washington State Medical Assn 2033 Sixth Ave Ste 1100 *TF:* 800-552-0612 ■ *Web:* www.wsma.org	Seattle	WA	98121	206-441-9762	441-5863	474
Washington State Nurses Assn (WSNA) 575 Andover Pk W Ste 101 *TF:* 800-231-8482 ■ *Web:* www.wsna.org	Seattle	WA	98188	206-575-7979	575-1908	533
Washington State Park 13041 State Hwy 104 *Web:* www.mostateparks.com	DeSoto	MO	63020	636-586-2995		565
Washington State Penitentiary 1313 N 13th Ave *Web:* doc.wa.gov	Walla Walla	WA	99362	509-525-3610		213
Washington State Pharmacy Assn 411 Williams Ave S *TF:* 800-562-6000 ■ *Web:* www.wsparx.org	Renton	WA	98057	425-228-7171	277-3897	585
Washington State Public Interest Research Group 1402 Third Ave Ste 715 *Web:* www.washpirg.org	Seattle	WA	98101	206-568-2854		633
Washington State Reformatory 16550 177th Ave SE PO Box 777 *TF:* 800-483-8314 ■ *Web:* www.doc.wa.gov	Monroe	WA	98272	360-794-2600		213
Washington State University PO Box 641040 *TF:* 888-468-6978 ■ *Web:* www.wsu.edu	Pullman	WA	99164	509-335-3564	335-4902	166
Spokane 310 N Riverpoint Blvd PO Box 1495 *TF:* 866-766-0767 ■ *Web:* spokane.wsu.edu	Spokane	WA	99210	509-358-7978	358-7538	166
Vancouver 14204 NE Salmon Creek Ave *Web:* www.vancouver.wsu.edu	Vancouver	WA	98686	360-546-9788		166
Washington State University - Tri Cities Campus 2710 University Dr *Web:* www.washsb.com	Richland	WA	99354	509-372-7000		166
Washington State Veterinary Medical Assn 8024 Bracken Pl SE *TF:* 800-399-7862 ■ *Web:* www.wsvma.org	Snoqualmie	WA	98065	425-396-3191		795
Washington Symphony Orchestra (WSO) PO Box 170 *Web:* www.washsym.org	Washington	PA	15301	724-223-9796		573-3
Washington Tennis Services Inc 3200 Tower Oaks Blvd *Web:* www.wtsinternational.com	Rockville	MD	20852	301-622-7800	622-3373	354
Washington Theological Union 6896 Laurel St NW	Washington	DC	20012	202-726-8800		167-3
Washington Times, The 3600 New York Ave NE *Web:* www.washingtontimes.com	Washington	DC	20002	202-636-3000		532-2
Washington Tool & Machine Co 1 S Baird Ave PO Box 873 *Web:* www.washtool.com	Washington	PA	15301	724-225-7470	225-7484	454
Washington Trails Assn (WTA) 705 Second Ave Ste 300 *Web:* www.wta.org	Seattle	WA	98104	206-625-1367	625-9249	48-23
Washington Trust Bancorp Inc 23 Broad St *NASDAQ: WASH* ■ *TF:* 800-475-2265 ■ *Web:* www.washtrust.com	Westerly	RI	02891	401-348-1200		360-2
Washington United Terminals 1815 Port Of Tacoma Rd *Web:* www.uswut.com	Tacoma	WA	98421	253-396-4927		314
Washington University in Saint Louis Campus Box 1089 *TF:* 800-638-0700 ■ *Web:* www.wustl.edu	Saint Louis	MO	63130	314-935-5000	935-4290	166
Washington University in Saint Louis School of Medicine 660 S Euclid Ave	Saint Louis	MO	63110	314-362-5000		167-2
Washington University School of Law 1 Brookings Dr Anheuser-Busch Hall **Fax:* Admissions ■ *Web:* law.wustl.edu	Saint Louis	MO	63130	314-935-6400	935-8778*	167-1
Washington Woodworking Company Inc 2010 Beaver Rd *TF:* 800-424-3996 ■ *Web:* www.washingtonwoodworking.com	Landover	MD	20785	301-341-2500	341-2512	499
Washington's Headquarters State Historic Site PO Box 1783 *Web:* parks.ny.gov/historic-sites/17/details.aspx	Newburgh	NY	12551	845-562-1195		565
Washington's Heaquarters/Miller House 140 Virginia Rd *Web:* westchestergov.com	White Plains	NY	10603	914-949-1236		50-3
Washington-Beaufort County Chamber of Commerce 102 Stewart Pkwy PO Box 665 *Web:* www.wbcchamber.com	Washington	NC	27889	252-946-9168	946-9169	139
Washingtonian Magazine 1828 L St NW Ste 200 **Fax:* Edit ■ *Web:* www.washingtonian.com	Washington	DC	20036	202-296-3600	785-1822*	457-22
Washington-on-the-Brazos State Historic Site 23400 Park Rd 12 *Web:* tpwd.texas.gov	Washington	TX	77880	936-878-2214		565
Washington-Saint Tammany Electric Co-op 950 Pearl St PO Box N *TF:* 866-672-9773 ■ *Web:* www.wste.coop	Franklinton	LA	70438	985-839-3562	839-4315	245

Name / Address	City	State	Zip	Phone	Fax	Class
Washita Battlefield National Historic Site 18555 Hwy 47A *Web:* www.nps.gov/waba	Cheyenne	OK	73628	580-497-2742	497-2712	564
Washita County 111 E Main Ste 3 *Web:* washita.oklahoma.usassessor.com	Cordell	OK	73632	580-832-2468	832-4110	338
Washoe County 1001 E Ninth St *TF:* 800-336-1600 ■ *Web:* www.washoecounty.us	Reno	NV	89512	775-328-2000		338
Washoe County Library (WCL) 301 S Ctr St *Web:* www.washoecountylibrary.us	Reno	NV	89501	775-327-8300	327-8341	434-3
Washoe County School District 425 E Ninth St *Web:* www.washoeschools.net	Reno	NV	89512	775-348-0200		685
Washoe Lake State Park 4855 E Lake Blvd *Web:* www.parks.nv.gov	Carson City	NV	89704	775-687-4319		565
Washoe Steakhouse 4201 W Fourth St *Web:* www.washoesteakhouse.com	Reno	NV	89523	775-786-1323		671
Washoe Tribe 919 US Hwy 395 N *Web:* www.washoetribe.us	Gardnerville	NV	89410	775-265-4191		522
Washtenaw Community College 4800 E Huron River Dr PO Box 1610 **Fax:* Admissions ■ *TF:* 800-218-4341 ■ *Web:* www.wccnet.edu	Ann Arbor	MI	48106	734-973-3300	677-5408*	162
Washtenaw County PO Box 8645 *TF:* 800-440-7548 ■ *Web:* www.ewashtenaw.org	Ann Arbor	MI	48107	734-222-6850	222-6715	338
Washtenaw County Road Commission 555 N Zeeb Rd *Web:* www.wcroads.org	Ann Arbor	MI	48103	734-761-1500	761-3239	186
Wasley Products Inc 87 Spring Ln *Web:* www.wasley.com	Plainville	CT	06062	860-747-5586		326
Wasmer Group, The 2001 Jackson St *Web:* www.wasmer.com	Alexandria	LA	71301	318-443-6551	443-9404	463
Wasmer Schroeder & Company Inc 600 Fifth Ave S Ste 210 *Web:* www.wasmerschroeder.com	Naples	FL	34102	239-263-6877	263-8146	401
Wasserman & Partners Advertising Inc 1020 Mainland St Ste 160 *TF:* 800-785-1958 ■ *Web:* wasserman-partners.com	Vancouver	BC	V6B2T5	604-684-1111		7
Wasserman Media Group LLC 10960 Wilshire Blvd Ste 2200 *Web:* www.teamwass.com	Los Angeles	CA	90024	310-407-0200		4
Wasserman Schultz Debbie (Rep D - FL) 1114 Longworth HOB *Web:* wassermanschultz.house.gov	Washington	DC	20515	202-225-7931	226-2052	342-2
Wasserstrom Co 477 S Front St *TF:* 866-634-8927 ■ *Web:* www.wasserstrom.com	Columbus	OH	43215	614-228-6525	737-8911	300
Waste Control Specialists LLC 5430 LBJ Fwy Ste 1700 *Web:* www.wcstexas.com	Dallas	TX	75240	972-715-9800	448-1419	667
Waste Industries USA Inc 3301 Benson Dr Ste 601 *TF:* 800-647-9946 ■ *Web:* www.wasteindustries.com	Raleigh	NC	27609	919-325-3000		804
Waste Management Inc 1001 Fannin St Ste 4000 *NYSE:* WM ■ *TF:* 800-633-7871 ■ *Web:* www.wm.com	Houston	TX	77002	713-512-6200	512-6299	804
Waste Services Inc 1122 International Blvd Ste 601 *TF:* 800-642-1687 ■ *Web:* www.wasteservicesinc.com	Burlington	ON	L7L6Z8	905-319-1237	319-9050	804
Waste Strategies LLC 1290 Bay Dale Dr Ste 290 *Web:* www.wastestrategies.com	Arnold	MD	21012	202-302-8370		192
Wastech Controls & Engineering Inc 21201 Itasca St *Web:* www.wastechengineering.com	Chatsworth	CA	91311	818-998-3500		261
Wastecorp Inc PO Box 70 *TF:* 888-829-2783 ■ *Web:* www.wastecorp.com	Grand Island	NY	14072	888-829-2783		641
Wastren Advantage Inc 1571 Shyville Rd *Web:* www.wastrenadvantage.com	Piketon	OH	45661	740-443-7924		271
Watanabe Floral Inc 1607 Hart St *TF:* 888-832-9360 ■ *Web:* www.watanabefloral.com	Honolulu	HI	96817	808-832-9360		292
Watauga County 842 W King St Courthouse *Web:* www.wataugacounty.org	Boone	NC	28607	828-265-8000	264-3230	338
Watauga County Schools PO Box 1790 *Web:* www.watauga.k12.nc.us	Boone	NC	28607	828-264-7190	264-7196	685
Watauga Medical Ctr 336 Deerfield Rd *TF:* 800-443-7385 ■ *Web:* www.apprhs.org	Boone	NC	28607	828-262-4100		374-3
Watauga Public Library 7109 Whitley Rd *Web:* www.cowtx.org	Watauga	TX	76148	817-514-5855	581-3910	434-3
Watch LA 1138 Wall St *Web:* www.watchla.com	Los Angeles	CA	90015	213-747-1838	747-2888	157-4
WatchGuard Technologies Inc 505 Fifth Ave S Ste 500 *TF Sales:* 800-734-9905 ■ *Web:* www.watchguard.com	Seattle	WA	98104	206-613-6600	521-8342	176
WatchMojo Inc 5413 Saint Laurent St Ste 200 *Web:* www.watchmojo.com	Montreal	QC	H2T1S5	514-448-1631		514
Watchtower Bible & Tract Society Inc 25 Columbia Heights *Web:* www.jw.org	Brooklyn	NY	11201	718-560-5000		48-20
Watco Companies LLC 315 W Third St *TF:* 866-386-9321 ■ *Web:* www.watcocompanies.com	Pittsburg	KS	66762	620-231-2230		650
Watcon Inc 2215 S Main St *Web:* www.watcon-inc.com	South Bend	IN	46613	574-287-3397	287-2427	145
Watek Engineering Corp 12122B Heritage Park Cir *Web:* www.watek.com	Silver Spring	MD	20906	301-933-9690		261
Water Country USA 176 Water Country Pkwy *TF:* 800-343-7946 ■ *Web:* www.watercountryusa.com	Williamsburg	VA	23185	800-343-7946		32
Water Environment Federation (WEF) 601 Wythe St *TF:* 800-666-0206 ■ *Web:* www.wef.org	Alexandria	VA	22314	703-684-2400	684-2492	48-13
Water Furnace International Inc 9000 Conservation Way **Fax:* Hum Res ■ *TF:* 800-222-5667 ■ *Web:* www.waterfurnace.com	Fort Wayne	IN	46809	260-478-5667	747-5780*	357
Water Grill 544 S Grand Ave *Web:* www.watergrill.com	Los Angeles	CA	90071	213-891-0900		671
Water Intelligence PLC 888 E Research Dr Ste 100 *Web:* www.waterintelligence.co.uk	Palm Springs	CA	92263	760-969-6830	320-7876	180
Water Pik Inc 1730 E Prospect Rd *TF:* 800-525-2774 ■ *Web:* www.waterpik.com	Fort Collins	CO	80553	800-525-2774		228
Water Quality Assn (WQA) 4151 Naperville Rd *TF:* 800-227-5558 ■ *Web:* www.wqa.org	Lisle	IL	60532	630-505-0160	505-9637	48-12
Water Resources International Inc 1100 Alakea St Ste 2900 *Web:* www.brninc.com	Honolulu	HI	96813	808-531-8422	531-7181	189-15
Water Saver Faucet Co 701 W Erie St *Web:* www.wsflab.com	Chicago	IL	60654	312-666-5500	666-5501	609
Water Spigot Inc, The 5806 E Hwy 22 *TF:* 800-220-3675 ■ *Web:* thewaterspigot.com	Panama City	FL	32404	850-871-1900		743
Water Street 131 N Water St *TF:* 800-225-6005 ■ *Web:* www.harbor-view.com	Edgartown	MA	02539	508-627-7000		671
Water Street Brewery 1101 N Water St *Web:* www.waterstreetbrewery.com	Milwaukee	WI	53202	414-272-1195	272-0406	671
Water Street Market 309 N Water St *Web:* www.waterstmarketcc.com	Corpus Christi	TX	78401	361-882-8683		671
Water Tech Online 19 British American Blvd W *TF:* 888-431-2877 ■ *Web:* www.watertechonline.com	Latham	NY	12110	888-431-2877		531-5
Water Technology Inc 100 Park Ave *Web:* www.watertechnologyinc.com	Beaver Dam	WI	53916	920-887-7375		261
Water Tower Place 835 N Michigan Ave *Web:* www.shopwatertower.com	Chicago	IL	60611	312-440-3166	440-1259	50-6
Water's Edge Resort & Spa 1525 Boston Post Rd PO Box 688 *TF:* 800-222-5901 ■ *Web:* www.watersedgeresortandspa.com	Westbrook	CT	06498	860-399-5901	399-8644	669
Waterbeds n Stuff Inc 3933 Brookham Dr *TF:* 800-420-2337 ■ *Web:* www.bedsnstuff.com	Grove City	OH	43123	614-871-1171		321
Waterboy, The 2000 Capitol Ave *Web:* www.waterboyrestaurant.com	Sacramento	CA	95811	916-498-9891		671
Waterbury Button Co 1855 Peck Ln *TF:* 800-928-1812 ■ *Web:* www.waterburybutton.com	Cheshire	CT	06410	800-928-1812		594
Waterbury Ctr State Park 177 Reservoir Rd *TF:* 800-837-4261 ■ *Web:* www.vtstateparks.com	Waterbury Center	VT	05677	802-244-1226		565
Waterbury Hospital 64 Robbins St *Web:* waterburyhospital.org	Waterbury	CT	06721	203-573-6000		374-3
Waterbury Public School District (WPSD) 236 Grand St Ste 1 *Web:* www.waterbury.k12.ct.us	Waterbury	CT	06702	203-574-8000	574-8010	186
Waterbury Swiss Automatics Inc 43 Mattatuck Heights Rd *Web:* www.waterburyswiss.com	Waterbury	CT	06705	203-573-8584		454
Waterbury Symphony Orchestra 110 Bank St *Web:* www.waterburysymphony.org	Waterbury	CT	06702	203-574-4283		573-3
Waterco USA Inc 1864 Tobacco Rd *TF General:* 800-277-4150 ■ *Web:* www.waterco.com.au	Augusta	GA	30906	706-793-7291	790-5688	806
Waterfall Economidis Caldwell Hanshaw & Villamana P C Williams Ctr 5210 E Williams Cir Ste 800 *Web:* www.waterfallattorneys.com	Tucson	AZ	85711	520-790-5828	745-1279	445
Waterfall International Inc 655 Fourth St *TF:* 844-625-8306 ■ *Web:* www.waterfall.com	San Francisco	CA	94107	844-625-8306		196
Waterfield Technologies Inc 1 W Third St Ste 1115 *TF:* 800-324-0936 ■ *Web:* www.waterfieldtechnologies.com	Tulsa	OK	74103	918-858-6400		141
Waterflood Service & Sales Ltd 1314 Third St PO Box 1490 *Web:* www.waterflood.com	Estevan	SK	S4A2L7	306-634-7212		757
Waterford Technologies Inc 19700 Fairchild Ste 300 *Web:* www.waterfordtechnologies.com	Irvine	CA	92612	949-428-9300		809
Waterford Township Public Library 5168 Civic Ctr Dr *TF:* 800-773-2587 ■ *Web:* www.waterfordmi.gov/477/library	Waterford	MI	48329	248-674-4831	674-1910	434-3
Waterford Wedgwood USA Inc 1330 Campus Pkwy *TF:* 800-954-8346 ■ *Web:* wedgwood.com	Wall	NJ	07753	732-938-5800		362
Waterford, The 601 Universe Blvd *TF:* 888-335-1678 ■ *Web:* lifespacecommunities.com/senior-living-juno-beach	Juno Beach	FL	33408	561-627-3800		672
Waterfront Container Leasing Company Inc 888 N Point St *TF:* 800-345-8082 ■ *Web:* www.waterfrontcontainer.com	San Francisco	CA	94109	415-788-5667		791
Waterfront Hotel 10 Washington St *TF:* 888-842-5333 ■ *Web:* www.jdvhotels.com	Oakland	CA	94607	510-836-3800		379
Waterfront Place Hotel 2 Waterfront Pl *Web:* www.marriott.com	Morgantown	WV	26501	304-296-1700		378
Waterfront Playhouse 312 Wall St	Key West	FL	33040	305-294-5015		572
Waterfront Properties & Club Communities 825 Pkwy Ste 8 *Web:* www.waterfront-properties.com	Jupiter	FL	33477	561-746-7272		652
Waterfront Seafood Market 2900 University Ave *Web:* www.waterfrontseafoodmarket.com	West Des Moines	IA	50266	515-223-5106		671
Waterfront Warehouse 4 Pinkney St *Web:* www.annapolis.org	Annapolis	MD	21401	410-267-7619		50-3
Watergate Hotel, The 2650 VIRGINIA AVE NW *Web:* thewatergatehotel.com	Washington	DC	20037	202-827-1600		377
Waterhouse Inc 670 Queen St Ste 200	Honolulu	HI	96813	808-592-4800	592-4840	591
Water-Jel Technologies LLC 50 Broad St *TF:* 800-693-1171 ■ *Web:* www.waterjel.com	Carlstadt	NJ	07072	201-806-3040		475
Waterline Technologies Inc 620 N Santiago St *Web:* waterlinetechnologies.com	Santa Ana	CA	92701	714-564-9100		711

Phone Fax Class

Waterloo Cedar Falls Courier
PO Box 540 .... Waterloo IA 50701 319-291-1421 291-2069 532-2
TF: 800-798-1730 ■ *Web:* www.wcfcourier.com

Waterloo Community Unit School Dst 5
302 Bellefontaine Dr .... Waterloo IL 62298 618-939-3453 939-4578 685
Web: www.wcusd5.net

Waterloo Convention & Visitor Bureau
500 Jefferson St .... Waterloo IA 50701 319-233-8350 233-2733 206
TF: 800-728-8431 ■ *Web:* www.travelwaterloo.com

Waterloo Gardens Inc 200 N Whitford Rd .... Exton PA 19341 610-363-0800 323
Web: www.waterloogardens.com

Waterloo Industries Inc
1500 Waterloo Dr .... Sedalia MO 53154 800-558-5528 766-6388* 488
**Fax Area Code: 414* ■ **Fax: Cust Svc* ■ *TF Cust Svc:* 800-833-8851 ■ *Web:* www.waterlooindustries.com

Waterloo Public Library 35 Albert St .... Waterloo ON N2L5E2 519-886-1310 434-3
Web: www.wpl.ca

Waterloo Recreation Area
16345 McClure Rd .... Chelsea MI 48118 734-475-8307 565
Web: www.michigandnr.com

Waterloo Region Museum 10 King Rd .... Kitchener ON N2P2R7 519-748-1914 748-0009 522
Web: kitchener-ontario.cylex.ca

Waterloo-Cedar Falls Symphony Orchestra
Gallagher-Bluedorn Performing Arts Ctr
Ste 17 .... Cedar Falls IA 50614 319-273-3373 573-3
Web: wcfsymphony.org

Waterman Grille, The 4 Richmond Sq .... Providence RI 02906 401-521-9229 521-9351 671
Web: www.watermangrille.com

Waterman State Bank
248 W Lincoln Hwy .... Waterman IL 60556 815-264-3201 264-3523 70
Web: watermanbank.com

Waterman's Grill
415 Atlantic Ave .... Virginia Beach VA 23451 757-428-3644 671
TF: 800-336-5336 ■ *Web:* www.watermans.com

Watermark at 3030 Park, The
3030 Pk Ave .... Bridgeport CT 06604 203-502-7593 672
Web: www.watermarkcommunities.com/3030park

Watermark at Logan Square
2 Franklin Town Blvd .... Philadelphia PA 19103 215-240-8915 672
Web: www.watermarkcommunities.com/logansquare

Watermark Capital Partners LLC
272 E Deerpath Rd Ste 320 .... Lake Forest IL 60045 847-482-8600 194
TF: 800-201-1483 ■ *Web:* www.watermarkcap.com

Watermark Environmental Inc
175 Cabot St .... Lowell MA 01854 978-452-9696 261
Web: www.watermarkenv.com

Watermark Grille 11280 Tamiami Trl N .... Naples FL 34110 239-596-1400 671
Web: www.watermarkgrille.com

Watermark Group Inc, The
4271 Gate Crst .... San Antonio TX 78217 210-599-0400 627
Web: www.thewatermarkgroup.com

Watermark Learning Inc
7300 Metro Blvd Ste 207 .... Minneapolis MN 55439 952-921-0900 194
TF: 800-646-9362 ■ *Web:* www.watermarklearning.com

Watermark Medical LLC
1641 Worthington Rd Ste 320 .... West Palm Beach FL 33409 877-710-6999 250
TF: 877-710-6999 ■ *Web:* www.watermarkmedical.com

Watermen's Museum 309 Water St .... Yorktown VA 23690 757-887-2641 520
Web: www.watermens.org

Waterous Co 125 Hardman Ave .... South Saint Paul MN 55075 651-450-5000 450-5090 641
TF: 800-488-1228 ■ *Web:* www.waterousco.com

Waters & Kraus LLP 3219 McKinney Ave .... Dallas TX 75204 214-357-6244 428
Web: www.waterskraus.com

Waters Corp 34 Maple St .... Milford MA 01757 508-478-2000 872-1990 419
NYSE: WAT ■ *TF:* 800-252-4752 ■ *Web:* www.waters.com

Waters Edge Hotel 25 Main St .... Tiburon CA 94920 415-789-5999 789-5888 379
TF: 888-662-9555 ■ *Web:* www.marinhotels.com

Waters Maxine (Rep D - CA)
2221 Rayburn Bldg .... Washington DC 20515 202-225-2201 225-7854 342-2
Web: waters.house.gov

Waters Mcpherson Mcneill Pc
300 Lighting Way Seventh Fl PO Box 1560 .... Secaucus NJ 07096 201-863-4400 653
Web: www.lawwmm.com

Waters of Covington
1600 E Liberty St .... Covington IN 47932 765-793-4818 450
TF: 800-480-4818 ■ *Web:* www.watersofcovington.com

Waters Parkerson & Co LLC
228 St Charles Ave Ste 512 .... New Orleans LA 70130 504-581-2022 525-9320 401
Web: watersparkerson.com

Watersaver Company Inc
5870 E 56th Ave .... Commerce CO 80022 303-289-1818 287-3136 600
TF: 800-525-2424 ■ *Web:* www.watersaver.com

Watershed Co, The 750 Sixth St S .... Kirkland WA 98033 425-822-5242 196
Web: www.watershedco.com

Waterside Capital Corp
2505 Cheyne Walk .... Virginia Beach VA 23454 757-626-1111 402
OTC: WSCC

Waterside Festival Marketplace
333 Waterside Dr .... Norfolk VA 23510 757-426-7433 50-6
Web: www.watersidemarketplace.com

Waterson Point State Park
44927 Cross Island Rd .... Fineview NY 13640 315-482-2722 565
Web: www.nysparks.com

Waterstone Bank 7500 W State St .... Wauwatosa WI 53213 414-258-5880 70
Web: www.wsbonline.com

Waterstone Group Inc, The
1145 W Main Ave Ste 209 .... De Pere WI 54115 920-964-0333 260
TF: 800-291-3836 ■ *Web:* www.waterstonegroup.net

Watertech Whirlpool Bath & Spa
2507 Plymouth Rd .... Johnson City TN 37601 800-289-8827 926-6438* 375
**Fax Area Code: 423* ■ *TF:* 800-289-8827 ■ *Web:* www.watertechtn.com

Waterton Lakes Lodge Resort
101 Clematis Ave PO Box 4 .... Waterton Park AB T0K2M0 403-859-2150 669
TF: 888-985-6343 ■ *Web:* www.watertonlakeslodge.com

Watertown Correctional Facility
23147 Swan Rd .... Watertown NY 13601 315-782-7490 213

Watertown Daily Times
260 Washington St .... Watertown NY 13601 315-782-1000 661-2523 532-2
TF: 800-642-6222 ■ *Web:* www.watertowndailytimes.com

Phone Fax Class

Watertown Free Public Library
123 Main St .... Watertown MA 02472 617-972-6431 926-4375 434-3
TF: 800-829-3676 ■ *Web:* www.watertownlib.org

Watertown Plastics 830 Echo Lake Rd .... Watertown CT 06795 860-274-7535 608
Web: www.watertownplastics.com

Watertown Public Library
100 S Water St .... Watertown WI 53094 920-262-4090 261-8943 434-3
TF: 800-829-3676 ■ *Web:* www.watertownpubliclibrary.org

Watertown Public Opinion
120 Third Ave NW .... Watertown SD 57201 605-886-6901 532-3
TF: 800-658-5401 ■ *Web:* www.coteaushopper.com

Watertown-Belmont Chamber of Commerce
182 Main St PO Box 45 .... Watertown MA 02471 617-926-1017 926-2322 139
Web: www.wbcc.org

Watertown-Mayer Public Schools
1001 Hwy 25 NW .... Watertown MN 55388 952-955-0480 685
Web: www.wm.k12.mn.us

Waterville Valley Resort
1 Ski Area Rd PO Box 540 .... Waterville Valley NH 03215 603-236-8311 236-4344 669
TF: 800-468-2553 ■ *Web:* www.waterville.com

Waterville Window Company Inc
22 Verti Dr .... Winslow ME 04901 207-873-0159 596
Web: www.watervillewindow.com

Waterworks America Inc
5005 Rockside Rd Crown Ctr 6th Fl .... Independence OH 44131 440-526-4815 144
Web: www.1water.com

Waterworks Operating Company LLC
60 Backus Ave .... Danbury CT 06810 203-546-6000 609
TF: 800-899-6757 ■ *Web:* www.waterworks.com

Waterworld California
1950 Waterworld Pkwy .... Concord CA 94520 925-609-1364 609-1360 32
Web: www.waterworldcalifornia.com

WATE-TV Ch 6 (ABC) 1306 Broadway .... Knoxville TN 37917 865-637-6666 525-4091 741-69
Web: www.wate.com

Watkins & Eager PLLC
The Emporium Bldg 400 E Capitol St Ste 300 .... Jackson MS 39201 601-965-1900 445
Web: www.watkinseager.com

Watkins Associated Industries
1958 Monroe Dr NE .... Atlanta GA 30324 404-872-3841 185

Watkins College of Art & Design
2298 Rose Parks Blvd .... Nashville TN 37228 615-383-4848 383-4849 164
TF: 866-887-6395 ■ *Web:* watkins.edu

Watkins Glen International Inc
2790 CR 16 .... Watkins Glen NY 14891 607-535-2486 535-8918 515
TF: 800-940-8068 ■ *Web:* www.theglen.com

Watkins Glen State Park
PO Box 304 .... Watkins Glen NY 14891 607-535-4511 565
Web: parks.ny.gov/parks/142

Watkins Mfg Corp 1280 Pk Ctr Dr .... Vista CA 92081 800-999-4688 375
TF: 800-999-4688 ■ *Web:* www.hotspring.com

Watkins Printing Co 1401 E 17th Ave .... Columbus OH 43211 614-297-8270 627
Web: watkinsprinting.com

Watkins Security Agency of D.c. Inc
5325 E Capitol St SE .... Washington DC 20019 202-581-2871 400
Web: thewatkinsgroup.com

Watkins Woolen Mill State Park & State Historic Site
26600 Pk Rd N .... Lawson MO 64062 816-580-3387 565
Web: www.mostateparks.com

Watlow Winona 1241 Bundy Blvd .... Winona MN 55987 507-454-5300 452-4507 202
TF: 800-928-5692 ■ *Web:* www.watlow.com

WATL-TV Ch 36 (MNT) 1 Monroe Pl .... Atlanta GA 30324 404-892-1611 885-7639 741-7
Web: 11alive.com

Watonwan County
710 Seventh Ave S PO Box 518 .... Saint James MN 56081 507-375-1236 375-5010 338
Web: www.co.watonwan.mn.us

Watrous Nursing Ctr 9 Neck Rd .... Madison CT 06443 203-245-9483 245-4668 450
TF: 877-696-6775 ■ *Web:* apple-rehab.com

Watry Industries Inc
3312 Lakeshore Dr .... Sheboygan WI 53081 920-457-4886 457-5241 308
Web: www.watry.com

Watsco Inc 2665 S Bayshore Dr Ste 901 .... Miami FL 33133 305-714-4100 858-4492 14
NYSE: WSO ■ *Web:* www.watsco.com

Watson Bowman Acme Corp
95 Pineview Dr .... Buffalo NY 14228 716-691-7566 480
Web: www.wbacorp.com

Watson Building Supplies Inc
50 Royal Group Crescent Unit 2 .... Vaughan ON L4H1X9 905-669-1898 364
TF: 800-565-7663 ■ *Web:* www.watsonbuildingsupplies.com

Watson Coleman Bonnie (Rep D - NJ)
1535 Longworth HOB .... Washington DC 20515 202-225-5801 225-6025 342-2
Web: watsoncoleman.house.gov

Watson Electrical 1500 Charleston St .... Wilson NC 27893 252-237-7511 243-1607 189-4
Web: www.watsonelec.com

Watson Engineering Inc 16445 Racho Rd .... Taylor MI 48180 734-285-2200 261
Web: watsoneng.com

Watson Foods Company Inc
301 Heffernan Dr .... West Haven CT 06516 203-932-3000 932-8266 296-16
TF: 800-388-3481 ■ *Web:* www.watson-inc.com

Watson Furniture Group Inc
26246 Twelve Trees Ln NW .... Poulsbo WA 98370 360-394-1300 319-1
TF: 800-426-1202 ■ *Web:* www.watsonfurniture.com

Watson Grinding & Mfg Co
4525 Gessner Dr .... Houston TX 77041 713-466-3053 466-8992 481
Web: www.watsongrinding.com

Watson Industries Inc
3041 Melby Rd .... Eau Claire WI 54703 715-839-0628 256
Web: www.watson-gyro.com

Watson Institute, The
301 Campmeeting Rd .... Sewickley PA 15143 412-741-1800 196
Web: www.thewatsoninstitute.org

Watson Kunda & Sons Inc
349 S Henderson Rd .... King of Prussia PA 19406 610-265-3113 81-1
TF: 800-233-9945 ■ *Web:* www.kundabev.com

Watson Label Products
10616 Trenton Ave .... Saint Louis MO 63132 314-493-9300 493-9390 627
TF: 800-678-6715 ■ *Web:* www.wlp.com

Watson Land Co 22010 S Wilmington Ave .... Carson CA 90745 310-952-6400 522-8788 653
Web: www.watsonlandcompany.com

				Phone	Fax	Class
Watson McDaniel Co						
428 Jones Blvd						
Limerick Airport Business Ctr	Pottstown	PA	19464	610-495-5131	495-5134	595
Web: www.watsonmcdaniel.com						
Watson Mill Bridge State Park						
650 Watson Mill Rd	Comer	GA	30629	706-783-5349		565
Web: www.gastateparks.org						
Watson Mortgage Corp						
6206 Atlantic Blvd Ste 1	Jacksonville	FL	32211	904-645-7111		217
Web: watsonmortgagecorp.com						
Watson Pond State Park Bay Rd	Taunton	MA	02780	508-884-8280		565
Web: www.mass.gov						
Watson Quality Ford 6130 I-55 N	Jackson	MS	39211	601-956-7000		57
Web: watsonquality.com						
Watson Realty Co						
9101 Camino Media	Bakersfield	CA	93311	661-327-5161		652
Web: www.watsonrealty.com						
Watson Rice & Co 301 Route 17 N	Rutherford	NJ	07070	201-460-4590		2
TF: 800-945-5985 ■ *Web:* watsonrice.com						
Watson'S Manistee Chrysler Inc						
208 Parkdale Ave	Manistee	MI	49660	231-723-6528		57
Web: watsonsmanisteechrysler.com						
Watson-Marlow Inc						
37 Upton Technology Pk	Wilmington	MA	01887	978-658-6168		641
Web: www.watson-marlow.com						
Watsontown Trucking Company Inc						
60 Belford Blvd	Milton	PA	17847	570-522-9820		780
TF: 800-344-0313 ■ *Web:* www.watsontowntrucking.com						
Watsonville Public Library						
275 Main St Ste 100	Watsonville	CA	95076	831-768-3400	763-4015	434-3
TF: 800-281-7275 ■ *Web:* cityofwatsonville.org						
Watt Printing Co						
4544 Hinckley Industrial Pkwy	Cleveland	OH	44109	216-398-2000		627
TF: 800-273-2170 ■ *Web:* www.wattprinters.com						
Watt Thompson						
1800 Pennzoil Pl 711 Louisiana St	Houston	TX	77002	713-650-8100		428
Web: www.wthllp.com						
Watters Smith Memorial State Park						
PO Box 296	Lost Creek	WV	26385	304-745-3081		565
Web: www.watterssmithstatepark.com						
Watts Constructors LLC						
737 Bishop St Ste 2900	Honolulu	HI	96813	808-543-5201		188
Web: www.wattsconstructors.com						
Watts Equipment Co 17547 Comconex Rd	Manteca	CA	95336	209-825-1700		358
TF: 800-960-0068 ■ *Web:* www.wattsequipment.com						
Watts Industries (Canada) Inc						
5435 N Service Rd	Burlington	ON	L7L5H7	905-332-4090		350
Web: www.wattscanada.ca						
Watts Radiant Inc						
4500 E Progress Pl	Springfield	MO	65803	417-864-6108	864-8161	14
TF: 800-276-2419 ■ *Web:* www.wattsradiant.com						
Watts Regulator Co						
815 Chestnut St	North Andover	MA	01845	978-688-1811	794-1848	790
Web: www.watts.com						
Watts Towers of Simon Rodia State Historic Park						
1765 E 107th St	Los Angeles	CA	90002	213-847-4646		565
TF: 866-240-4655 ■ *Web:* www.parks.ca.gov/default.asp?page_id=613						
Watts Water Technologies Inc						
815 Chestnut St	North Andover	MA	01845	978-688-1811	794-1848	789
NYSE: WTS ■ *Web:* www.wattswater.com						
Watumull Bros Ltd						
307 Lewers St Ste 600	Honolulu	HI	96815	808-971-8800		157-5
Waubonsee Community College						
Rt 47 At Waubonsee Dr	Sugar Grove	IL	60554	630-466-7900		162
TF: 800-798-8100 ■ *Web:* waubonsee.edu						
Waubonsie State Park						
2585 Waubonsie Pk Rd	Hamburg	IA	51640	712-382-2786		565
Web: www.iowadnr.gov						
WAUK-AM 540 (Sports)						
310 W Wisconsin Ave Ste 100	Milwaukee	WI	53203	414-273-3776	291-3776	645-100
TF: 800-990-3776 ■ *Web:* www.espn.com						
Waukegan Port District						
55 S Harbor Pl PO Box 620	Waukegan	IL	60085	847-244-3133	244-1348	618
Web: waukeganharbor.com						
Waukegan Public Library						
128 N County St	Waukegan	IL	60085	847-623-2041		434-3
Web: www.waukeganpl.org						
Waukegan Steel LLC 1201 Belvidere Rd	Waukegan	IL	60085	847-662-2810		492
TF: 800-673-2810 ■ *Web:* www.waukegansteel.com						
Waukesha Bearings Corp						
W 231 N 2811 Roundy Cir E Ste 200	Pewaukee	WI	53072	262-506-3000	506-3001	620
TF: 888-832-3517 ■ *Web:* www.waukbearing.com						
Waukesha County						
515 W Moreland Blvd Rm 120	Waukesha	WI	53188	262-548-7010	548-7722	338
TF: 800-247-5645 ■ *Web:* www.waukeshacounty.gov						
Waukesha County Chamber of Commerce						
2717 N Grandview Blvd Ste 204	Waukesha	WI	53188	262-542-4249	542-8068	139
Web: www.waukesha.org						
Waukesha County Freeman						
801 N Barstow St PO Box 7	Waukesha	WI	53187	262-542-2501	542-8259	532-2
TF: 800-762-6219 ■ *Web:* www.gmtoday.com						
Waukesha County Technical College						
800 Main St	Pewaukee	WI	53072	262-691-5566		800
Web: www.wctc.edu						
Waukesha Electric Systems Inc						
400 S Prairie Ave	Waukesha	WI	53186	262-547-0121		767
TF: 800-835-2732 ■ *Web:* www.spxtransformersolutions.com						
Waukesha Foundry Company Inc						
1300 Lincoln Ave	Waukesha	WI	53186	262-542-0741	549-8440*	307
**Fax: Sales* ■ *TF:* 800-727-0741 ■ *Web:* www.waukeshafoundry.com						
Waukesha Memorial Hospital						
725 American Ave	Waukesha	WI	53188	262-928-1000		374-3
TF: 800-326-2011 ■ *Web:* www.prohealthcare.org						
Waukesha Public Library						
321 Wisconsin Ave	Waukesha	WI	53186	262-524-3680		434-3
Web: waukeshapubliclibrary.org						
Waukesha State Bank						
151 E St Paul Ave PO Box 648	Waukesha	WI	53187	262-549-8500		70
Web: www.waukeshabank.com						

				Phone	Fax	Class
Waukesha-Pearce Industries Inc (WPI)						
12320 S Main St	Houston	TX	77035	713-723-1050	551-0454	385
Web: www.wpi.com						
Wauna Federal Credit Union						
101 Truhaak St	Clatskanie	OR	97016	503-728-4321		219
Web: www.waunafcu.org						
Waunita Hot Springs Ranch						
8007 County Rd 887	Gunnison	CO	81230	970-641-1266		239
Web: www.waunita.com						
Waupaca County 811 Harding St	Waupaca	WI	54981	715-258-6200	258-6212	338
Web: www.co.waupaca.wi.us						
Waupaca Elevator Co Inc						
1726 N BallaRd Rd	Appleton	WI	54911	920-991-9082		256
TF: 800-238-8739 ■ *Web:* www.waupacaelevator.com						
Waupaca Foundry						
1955 Brunner Dr PO Box 249	Waupaca	WI	54981	715-258-6611	258-9268	307
TF: 800-669-6820 ■ *Web:* www.waupacafoundry.com						
Waupun Correctional Institution						
200 S Madison St	Waupun	WI	53963	920-324-5571	324-7250	213
Web: doc.wi.gov						
Wausau Area Chamber of Commerce						
200 Washington St Ste 120	Wausau	WI	54403	715-845-6231	845-6235	139
Web: www.wausauchamber.com						
Wausau Central Wisconsin Convention & Visitors Bureau (CWCVB)						
219 Jefferson St Ste B	Wausau	WI	54403	715-355-8788	359-2306	206
TF: 888-948-4748 ■ *Web:* www.visitwausau.com						
Wausau Chemical Corp 2001 N River Dr	Wausau	WI	54403	715-842-2285	842-9059	144
TF: 800-950-6656 ■ *Web:* www.wausauchemical.com						
Wausau Daily Herald 800 Scott St	Wausau	WI	54403	715-842-2101		532-2
TF: 800-477-4838 ■ *Web:* www.wausaudailyherald.com						
Wausau Financial Systems Inc						
400 Westwood Dr Ste 100	Wausau	WI	54401	715-359-0427	241-2288	178-10
TF: 800-937-0017 ■ *Web:* www.wausaufs.com						
Wausau Homes Inc PO Box 8005	Wausau	WI	54402	715-359-7272		106
TF: 800-455-0545 ■ *Web:* www.wausauhomes.com						
Wausau Paper Corp 100 Paper Pl	Mosinee	WI	54455	715-693-4470	692-2082	552-1
NYSE: WPP ■ *TF:* 800-723-0008 ■ *Web:* www.wausaupaper.com						
Wausau Paper Corp Printing & Writing Paper Div						
100 Paper Pl	Mosinee	WI	54455	715-693-4470	692-2082	552-2
TF: 866-722-8675 ■ *Web:* www.wausaupaper.com						
Wausau Paper Corp Specialty Paper Div						
100 Paper Pl	Mosinee	WI	54455	715-693-4470	692-2082	552-1
TF: 800-723-0008 ■ *Web:* www.wausaupaper.com						
Wausau Tile Inc PO Box 1520	Wausau	WI	54402	715-359-3121	355-4627	183
TF: 800-388-8728 ■ *Web:* www.wausautile.com						
WaUSau Window & Wall Systems						
7800 International Dr	Wausau	WI	54401	715-845-2161		480
TF: 877-678-2983 ■ *Web:* www.wausauwindow.com						
Wausaukee Composites Inc						
837 Cedar St	Wausaukee	WI	54177	715-856-6321	856-5567	608
Web: www.wauscomp.com						
Waushara County 209 S St Marie St	Wautoma	WI	54982	920-787-0431		338
Web: www.co.waushara.wi.us						
Wauwatosa Chamber of Commerce						
10437 Innovation Dr	Wauwatosa	WI	53226	414-453-2330		139
Web: tosachamber.org						
Wauwatosa Public Library						
7635 W N Ave	Wauwatosa	WI	53213	414-471-8484		434-3
Web: www.wauwatosalibrary.org						
Wauwinet, The						
120 Wauwinet Rd PO Box 2580	Nantucket	MA	02584	508-228-0145	228-6712	379
TF: 800-426-8718 ■ *Web:* www.wauwinet.com						
WAV Inc 2380 Prospect Dr	Aurora	IL	60504	630-818-1000	818-4450	176
TF: 800-678-2419 ■ *Web:* www.wavonline.com						
WAVA-AM 780 (Rel)						
1735 N Lynn St Ste 500	Arlington	VA	22209	703-807-2266		645
Web: www.wava.com						
WAVA-FM 105.1 (Rel)						
1735 N Lynn St Ste 500	Arlington	VA	22209	703-807-2266		645
TF: 888-293-9282 ■ *Web:* www.wava.com						
Wave Crest Development Inc						
530 Chestnut St	Santa Cruz	CA	95060	831-423-2100		653
Web: www.wavecrestdevelopment.com						
Wave Direct						
1616-102 W Cape Coral Pkwy Ste 243	Cape Coral	FL	33914	239-574-8181	574-8802	5
TF: 888-550-9918 ■ *Web:* wave-direct.com						
Wave Hill W 249th St & Independence Ave	Bronx	NY	10471	718-549-3200	884-8952	97
TF: 800-753-2038 ■ *Web:* www.wavehill.org						
Wave Loch Inc 210 Westbourne St	La Jolla	CA	92037	858-454-1777		711
Web: www.waveloch.com						
Wave Software LLC						
300 S Orange Ave Ste 900	Orlando	FL	32801	407-325-5006		809
Web: www.discoverthewave.com						
Wave Systems Corp 480 Pleasant St	Lee	MA	01238	413-243-1600	243-0045	178-1
NASDAQ: WAVX ■ *TF:* 800-928-3638 ■ *Web:* www.wave.com						
Wavecode Inc 1651 N Collins Blvd	Richardson	TX	75080	214-570-9559		180
Web: www.wavecode.com						
Wavecrest Computing Inc						
2006 Vernon Pl	Melbourne	FL	32901	321-953-5351		177
Web: www.wavecrest.net						
Wavedivision Holdings LLC						
401 Kirkland Prk Pl Ste 500	Kirkland	WA	98033	425-576-8200		736
TF: 866-928-3123 ■ *Web:* www.wavebroadband.com						
Wavefunction Inc 18401 Von Karman Ave	Irvine	CA	92612	949-955-2120		177
Web: www.wavefun.com						
Waveguide Consulting 1 W Court Sq	Decatur	GA	30030	404-815-1919		256
TF: 800-273-8255 ■ *Web:* www.waveguide.com						
Waveguide Inc 10 N Southwood Dr	Nashua	NH	03063	603-598-0096		387
Web: www.waveguidefiber.com						
Waveland Museum State Historic Site						
225 Waveland Museum Ln	Lexington	KY	40514	859-272-3611		565
Web: www.parks.ky.gov						
Wavelength Datacom LLC						
1265 Oakmead Pkwy	Sunnyvale	CA	94085	408-746-0200		177
Web: www.wavdata.com						
Waveline Direct Inc						
192 Hempt Rd	Mechanicsburg	PA	17050	717-795-8830		627
TF: 800-257-8830 ■ *Web:* www.wavelinedirect.com						

Name / Address	City	State	Zip	Phone	Fax	Class
WaveLink Corp 1011 Western Ave Ste 601	Seattle	WA	98104	206-274-4280	652-2329	178-7
TF Tech Supp: 888-697-9283 ■ *Web:* www.wavelink.com						
Wavell-Huber Wood Products Inc						
180 N 170 W	North Salt Lake	UT	84054	801-936-6080	936-6078	613
Web: www.wavell-huber.com						
Waveny Care Ctr 3 Farm Rd	New Canaan	CT	06840	203-594-5200	594-5327	450
Web: www.waveny.org						
Waverly Heights 1400 Waverly Rd	Gladwyne	PA	19035	610-645-8600	645-8611	672
Web: www.waverlyheightsltd.org						
Waverly Plastics Company Inc						
1001 Industrial St PO Box 801	Waverly	IA	50677	800-454-6377	428-7793	66
TF: 800-454-6377 ■ *Web:* www.waverlyplastics.com						
Wavestaff Inc						
783 Rio Del Mar Blvd Ste 67	Aptos	CA	95003	831-689-9800		260
Web: www.wavestaff.com						
WaveTec Vision Systems Inc						
66 Argonaut Ste 170	Aliso Viejo	CA	92656	949-273-5970		743
Wavetronix LLC 78 E 1700 S	Provo	UT	84606	801-734-7200		261
TF: 800-667-8743 ■ *Web:* www.wavetronix.com						
WAVE-TV Ch 3 (NBC)						
725 S Floyd St PO Box 32970	Louisville	KY	40203	502-585-2201	561-4115	741-77
TF: 800-223-2579 ■ *Web:* www.wave3.com						
WAVSYS LLC 101 Broadway Ste 406	Brooklyn	NY	11249	347-292-8797		387
Web: www.wavsys.com						
WAVV-FM 101.1 (AC) 11800 Tamiami Trl E	Naples	FL	34113	239-775-9288	793-7000	645-107
TF: 866-310-9288 ■ *Web:* www.wavv101.com						
WAVY-TV Ch 10 (NBC) 300 Wavy St	Portsmouth	VA	23704	757-393-1010		741
Web: www.wavy.com						
Wawa Inc 260 W Baltimore Pike	Media	PA	19063	610-358-8000	358-8808*	204
**Fax:* Hum Res ■ *TF:* 800-444-9292 ■ *Web:* www.wawa.com						
Wawanesa Insurance 900-191 Broadway	Winnipeg	MB	R3C3P1	858-874-5300	942-7724*	391-4
**Fax Area Code:* 204 ■ *Web:* www.wawanesa.com						
Wawanesa Life Insurance Co						
191 Broadway Ste 501	Winnipeg	MB	[illegible]	[illegible]		391-2
Web: wawanesa.com/life/index.html						
Wawayanda State Park 885 Warwick Tpke	Hewitt	NJ	07421	973-853-4462		565
Web: www.njparksandforests.org/parks/wawayanda.html						
Wawona Frozen Foods Inc						
100 W Alluvial Ave	Clovis	CA	93611	559-299-2901	299-1921	296-21
Web: www.wawona.com						
Waxahachie Independent School District						
411 N Gibson St	Waxahachie	TX	75165	972-923-4631	923-4759	685
Web: www.wisd.org						
Waxman Industries Inc						
24460 Aurora Rd	Bedford Heights	OH	44146	440-439-1830		612
OTC: WXMN ■ *TF:* 800-201-7298 ■ *Web:* www.waxman.com						
WAXN-TV Ch 64 (ABC) 1901 N Tryon St	Charlotte	NC	28206	704-335-4786		741-26
TF: 855-336-0360 ■ *Web:* www.wsoctv.com						
Way Engineering Ltd						
8610 Wallisville Rd	Houston	TX	77020	713-568-6188	568-6109	109-10
Web: wayeng.com						
Way It Was Museum 113 N C St	Virginia City	NV	89440	775-847-0766		520
WAY Media Inc						
1860 Boy Scout Dr Ste 202	Fort Myers	FL	33907	239-936-1929		645-10
Web: www.wayfm.com						
Way Station Inc						
230 W Patrick St PO Box 3826	Frederick	MD	21705	301-662-0099	694-9932	48-15
TF: 800-610-0620 ■ *Web:* www.waystationinc.org						
Way to Happiness Foundation International, The						
201 E Broadway	Glendale	CA	91205	818-254-0600		305
TF: 800-255-7906 ■ *Web:* www.thewaytohappiness.org						
Waycross College 2001 S Georgia Pkwy	Waycross	GA	31503	912-449-7600		162
Web: sgsc.edu						
Waycross-Ware County Chamber of Commerce						
315 Plant Ave Ste B	Waycross	GA	31501	912-283-3742	283-0121	139
Web: www.waycrosschamber.org						
Wayest Safety Inc						
3750 N I-44 Service Rd	Oklahoma City	OK	73112	405-942-7101		679
TF: 800-256-1003 ■ *Web:* northernsafety.com/wayest						
Wayfarers Chapel						
5755 Palos Verdes Dr	Rancho Palos Verdes	CA	90275	310-377-1650		50-1
Web: www.wayfarerschapel.org						
Wayfarers State Park						
490 N Meridian Rd	Kalispell	MT	59901	406-752-5501		565
Web: www.fwp.mt.gov						
WAYJ-FM 88.7 (Rel)						
1860 Boyscout Dr Ste 202	Fort Myers	FL	33907	239-936-1929		645
Web: www.wayfm.com						
Wayland Academy						
101 N University Ave	Beaver Dam	WI	53916	920-885-3373	887-3373	622
TF: 800-860-7725 ■ *Web:* www.wayland.org						
Wayland Baptist University						
1900 W Seventh St	Plainview	TX	79072	806-291-1000	291-1973*	166
**Fax:* Admissions ■ *TF:* 800-588-1928 ■ *Web:* www.wbu.edu						
Wayland Baptist University Anchorage						
7801 E 32 Ave	Anchorage	AK	99504	907-333-2277	337-8122	166
TF: 800-588-1928 ■ *Web:* www.wbu.edu						
Wayland Free Public Library						
5 Concord Rd	Wayland	MA	01778	508-358-2311	358-5249	434-3
TF: 800-592-2000 ■ *Web:* www.wayland.ma.us						
Wayland Hopkins Livestock						
3634 Tenth St	Wayland	MI	49348	269-792-2296		446
Waymouth Farms Inc 5300 Boone Ave	New Hope	MN	55428	763-533-5300	533-9890	296-8
TF: 800-527-0094 ■ *Web:* www.goodsensesnacks.com						
Wayne & Gladys Valley Foundation						
1939 Harrison St Ste 510	Oakland	CA	94612	510-466-6060		305
Web: foundationcenter.org						
Wayne Automatic Fire Sprinklers Inc						
222 Capital Ct	Ocoee	FL	34761	407-656-3030		189-13
Web: www.waynefire.com						
Wayne Bank 717 Main St	Honesdale	PA	18431	570-253-1455	253-3725	360-2
TF: 800-598-5002 ■ *Web:* www.waynebank.com						
Wayne Combustion Systems						
801 Glasgow Ave	Fort Wayne	IN	46803	260-425-9200	424-0904	357
TF: 855-929-6327 ■ *Web:* www.waynecombustion.com						
Wayne Community College						
3000 Wayne Memorial Dr PO Box 8002	Goldsboro	NC	27533	919-735-5151	736-9425*	162
**Fax:* Admissions ■ *TF:* 866-414-5064 ■ *Web:* www.waynecc.edu						
Wayne County						
100 N Lafayette St Ste 205 PO Box 435	Corydon	IA	50060	641-872-2663	872-2843	338
Web: www.wayne.iowaassessors.com						
Wayne County						
Coleman A Young Municipal Ctr						
2 Woodward Ave 2nd Fl	Detroit	MI	48226	313-224-6262		338
Web: waynecounty.com						
Wayne County 224 E Walnut St	Goldsboro	NC	27530	919-731-1435	731-1446	338
Web: www.waynegov.com						
Wayne County 925 Court St	Honesdale	PA	18431	570-253-5970	253-5432	338
TF: 800-321-9973 ■ *Web:* waynecountypa.gov						
Wayne County 341 E Walnut St	Jesup	GA	31546	912-427-5900	427-5906	338
Web: www.waynecountyga.us						
Wayne County 18 S Main St PO Box 189	Loa	UT	84747	435-836-1300	836-2479	338
Web: www.waynecountyutah.org						
Wayne County 26 Church St	Lyons	NY	14489	315-946-5400	946-5407	338
TF: 800-527-6510 ■ *Web:* www.co.wayne.ny.us						
Wayne County 55 N Main St Ste 106	Monticello	KY	42633	606-348-5721		338
Web: www.waynecounty.ky.gov						
Wayne County 401 E Main St	Richmond	IN	47374	765-973-9237	973-9321	338
TF: 800-657-3864 ■ *Web:* www.co.wayne.in.us						
Wayne County 510 Pearl St PO Box 248	Wayne	NE	68787	402-375-2288	375-4137	338
Web: www.waynecountyne.org						
Wayne County						
610 Azalea Dr County Courthouse	Waynesboro	MS	39367	601-735-6056	735-6246	338
TF: 800-748-7626 ■ *Web:* waynecounty.ms						
Wayne County PO Box 848	Waynesboro	TN	38485	931-722-3653	722-5994	338
TF: 800-239-5042 ■ *Web:* www.waynecountytn.org						
Wayne County 428 W Liberty St	Wooster	OH	44691	330-287-5400	287-5407	338
TF: 800-669-1176 ■ *Web:* www.wayneohio.org						
Wayne County Area Chamber of Commerce						
33 S Seventh St Ste 2	Richmond	IN	47374	765-962-1511	966-0882	139
Web: www.wcareachamber.org						
Wayne County Boot Camp PO Box 182	Clifton	TN	38425	931-676-3345		213
TF: 855-876-7283 ■ *Web:* www.tennessee.gov						
Wayne County Chamber of Commerce						
308 N Williams St	Goldsboro	NC	27530	919-734-2241	734-2247	139
TF: 800-849-6222 ■ *Web:* www.waynecountychamber.com						
Wayne County Clerk 700 Hendricks St	Wayne	WV	25570	304-272-6352		338
Web: waynecountywv.org						
Wayne County Community College						
Downriver 21000 Northline Rd	Taylor	MI	48180	734-946-3500	374-0240	162
Web: www.wcccd.edu						
Downtown 1001 W Fort St	Detroit	MI	48226	313-496-2758		162
Web: www.wcccd.edu						
Eastern Campus 5901 Conner	Detroit	MI	48213	313-922-3311		162
Web: www.wcccd.edu						
Northwest 8200 W Outer Dr	Detroit	MI	48219	313-943-4000		162
Web: www.wcccd.edu						
Western Campus 801 W Fort St	Detroit	MI	48226	734-699-7008	699-7152	162
Web: www.wcccd.edu						
Wayne County Convention & Visitors Bureau						
428 W Liberty St	Wooster	OH	44691	330-264-1800		206
TF: 800-362-6474 ■ *Web:* wccvb.com						
Wayne Crouse Inc 3370 Stafford St	Pittsburgh	PA	15204	412-771-5176	771-2357	189-10
Web: www.waynecrouse.com						
Wayne Engineering Corp						
701 Performance Dr	Cedar Falls	IA	50613	319-266-1721	266-8207	470
Web: www.wayneusa.com						
Wayne Farms Enterprises LLC						
1020 County Rd 114	Jack	AL	36346	334-897-3435		619
Web: waynefarms.com						
Wayne Farms LLC 4110 Continental Dr	Oakwood	GA	30566	800-392-0844		10-8
TF: 800-392-0844 ■ *Web:* www.waynefarms.com						
Wayne Fitzgerrell State Recreation Area						
11094 Ranger Rd	Whittington	IL	62897	618-629-2320		565
Wayne HealthCare 835 Sweitzer St	Greenville	OH	45331	937-548-1141		374-3
Web: www.waynehealthcare.org						
Wayne Highlands School District						
474 Grove St	Honesdale	PA	18431	570-253-4661	253-9409	685
Web: www.whsdk12.com						
Wayne Hummer Investments LLC						
222 S Riverside Pz 28th Fl	Chicago	IL	60606	866-943-4732		690
TF: 800-621-4477 ■ *Web:* www.wintrustwealth.com						
Wayne Independent 220 Eigth St	Honesdale	PA	18431	570-253-3055		532-2
TF: 800-598-5002 ■ *Web:* www.wayneindependent.com						
Wayne J Griffin Electric Inc						
116 Hopping Brook Rd	Holliston	MA	01746	800-421-0151	429-7825*	189-4
**Fax Area Code:* 508 ■ *TF:* 800-421-0151 ■ *Web:* www.waynejgriffin.com						
Wayne Long & Co						
1502 Mill Rock Way Ste 200	Bakersfield	CA	93311	661-664-0909		734
Web: welcpa.com						
Wayne Manufacturing Corp						
6505 State Rd 205	Laotto	IN	46763	260-637-5586		488
Web: www.waynetool.net						
Wayne Memorial Hospital (WMH)						
865 S First St	Jesup	GA	31545	912-427-6811		374-3
TF: 800-537-5142 ■ *Web:* www.wmhweb.com						
Wayne Memorial Hospital						
2700 Wayne Memorial Dr	Goldsboro	NC	27534	919-736-1110		374-3
Web: www.waynehealth.org						
Wayne Memorial Hospital (WMH)						
601 Pk St	Honesdale	PA	18431	570-253-8100		374-3
Web: www.wmh.org						
Wayne Metal Products Inc						
5461 Benchmark Ln	Sanford	FL	32773	407-321-7168		295
TF: 800-932-7287 ■ *Web:* www.waynemetalproductsinc.com						
Wayne Metals LLC 400 E Logan St	Markle	IN	46770	260-758-3121	758-2521	454
Web: www.waynemetals.com						
Wayne Mills Co Inc						
130 W Berkley St	Philadelphia	PA	19144	215-842-2134	438-8599	745-5
TF: 800-220-8053 ■ *Web:* www.waynemills.com						
Wayne Oil Company Inc						
1301 Wayne Memorial Dr	Goldsboro	NC	27534	919-735-2021		536
TF: 800-641-2816 ■ *Web:* www.ballparkstores.com						
Wayne Pipe & Supply Inc						
6040 Innovation Blvd	Fort Wayne	IN	46818	260-423-9577		612
TF: 800-552-3697 ■ *Web:* www.waynepipe.com						

Name / Address	City	State	ZIP	Phone	Fax	Class
Wayne Public Library 461 Valley Rd *Web:* www.waynepubliclibrary.org	Wayne	NJ	07470	973-694-4272		434-3
Wayne Reaves Software & Websites Inc 6211 Thomaston Rd *Web:* www.waynereaves.com	Macon	GA	31220	478-474-8779		195
Wayne Savings Bancshares Inc 151 N Market St *NASDAQ:* WAYN ■ *TF:* 800-414-1103 ■ *Web:* www.waynesavings.com	Wooster	OH	44691	330-264-5767		360-2
Wayne State College 1111 Main St *TF:* 800-228-9972 ■ *Web:* www.wsc.edu	Wayne	NE	68787	402-375-7000		166
Wayne State University 42 W Warren *Fax: Admissions ■ *TF:* 877-978-4636 ■ *Web:* www.wayne.edu	Detroit	MI	48202	313-577-3577	577-7536*	166
Wayne State University Law School 471 W Palmer St *Fax: Admissions ■ *Web:* www.law.wayne.edu	Detroit	MI	48202	313-577-3937	993-8129*	167-1
Wayne State University Libraries 5150 Anthony Wayne Dr *Web:* library.wayne.edu	Detroit	MI	48202	313-577-4023	577-5265	434-6
Wayne State University School of Medicine 540 E Canfield St *Fax: Admitting ■ *Web:* home.med.wayne.edu	Detroit	MI	48201	313-577-1460	577-9420*	167-2
Wayne Trail Technologies Inc 203 E Park St *TF:* 800-780-9850 ■ *Web:* www.waynetrail.com	Fort Loramie	OH	45845	937-295-2120		454
Wayne Van Riper Hopper Museum 533 Berdan Ave *Web:* waynetownship.com	Wayne	NJ	07470	973-694-7192		50-3
Wayne Wire Cloth Products Inc 200 E Dresden St *Web:* www.waynewire.com	Kalkaska	MI	49646	231-258-9187	258-5504	688
Wayneco Inc 800 Hanover Rd *TF:* 800-233-9313 ■ *Web:* www.waynecoinc.com	York	PA	17408	717-225-4413		321
Wayne-Dalton Corp 1 Door Dr PO Box 67 *TF:* 800-827-3667 ■ *Web:* www.wayne-dalton.com	Mount Hope	OH	44660	330-674-7015		234
Waynesboro (Independent City) 503 W Main St *Web:* www.waynesboro.va.us	Waynesboro	VA	22980	540-942-6600	942-6671	338
Waynesburg College 51 W College St *TF Admissions:* 800-225-7393 ■ *Web:* www.waynesburg.edu	Waynesburg	PA	15370	724-627-8191		166
Waynesville Inn Golf & Country Club, The 176 Country Club Dr *TF:* 800-627-6250 ■ *Web:* www.twigolfresort.com	Waynesville	NC	28786	828-456-3551		669
Waynesville-Saint Robert Area Chamber of Commerce 137 St Robert Blvd Ste B *Web:* www.waynesville-strobertchamber.com	Saint Robert	MO	65584	573-336-5121	336-5472	139
Wayne-White Counties Electric Co-op 1501 W Main St *TF:* 888-871-7695 ■ *Web:* www.waynewhitecoop.com	Fairfield	IL	62837	618-842-2196		245
Waypoint Consulting 1450 E Boot Rd *Web:* www.waypointco.com	West Chester	PA	19380	484-472-8611		463
Waypoint Solutions Group LLC 9305 Monroe Rd Ste L *Web:* www.waypointsg.com	Charlotte	NC	28270	704-246-1717		180
WayPoint Ventures *RPM Ventures* 320 N Main St Ste 400 *Web:* www.rpmvc.com	Ann Arbor	MI	48104	734-332-1700		792
Wayside Furniture Inc 1367 Canton Rd *TF:* 877-499-3968 ■ *Web:* www.wayside-furniture.com	Akron	OH	44312	330-733-6221		321
WAYV-FM 95.1 (CHR) 8025 Black Horse Pike *Web:* www.951wayv.com	West Atlantic City	NJ	08232	609-484-8444	646-6331	645
WAYZ-FM 104.7 (Ctry) 10960 John Wayne Dr *TF:* 888-950-1047 ■ *Web:* www.wayz.com	Greencastle	PA	17225	717-597-9200	597-9210	645
WB Bottle Supply Company Inc 3400 S Clement Ave *TF:* 800-738-3931 ■ *Web:* www.wbbottle.com	Milwaukee	WI	53207	414-482-4300		333
WB Games Inc 12131 113th Ave NE Ste 300	Kirkland	WA	98034	425-216-3200		761
WB Guimarin & Co Inc 1124 Bluff Industrial Blvd *Web:* www.wbguimarin.com	Columbia	SC	29202	803-256-0515	252-8239	189-10
WB Mason Company Inc 59 Centre St *TF:* 888-926-2766 ■ *Web:* www.wbmason.com	Brockton	MA	02303	888-926-2766		321
WB Wallis & Co 540 Kentucky St *Web:* wbwallis.com	Scottdale	GA	30079	404-294-1722		189-10
WBAB-FM 102.3 (Rock) 555 Sunrise Hwy *TF:* 800-745-3000 ■ *Web:* www.wbab.com	West Babylon	NY	11704	631-587-1023	587-1282	645
WBACH 98 Main St	Ellsworth	ME	04605	207-667-9800		645
WBAL-AM 1090 (N/T) 3800 Hooper Ave *Web:* www.wbal.com	Baltimore	MD	21211	410-467-3000		645-16
WBAL-TV Ch 11 (NBC) 3800 Hooper Ave *Web:* www.wbaltv.com	Baltimore	MD	21211	410-467-3000		741-11
WBAM-FM 98.9 (Ctry) 4101-A Wall St *TF:* 800-289-9228 ■ *Web:* bamacountry.com	Montgomery	AL	36106	334-244-0961	279-9563	645-104
WBANA (Wild Blueberry Assn of North America) PO Box 100 *TF:* 800-341-1758 ■ *Web:* www.wildblueberries.com	Old Town	ME	04468	207-570-3535	581-3499	48-2
WBAP-AM 820 (N/T) 3090 Olive St Ste 400 *TF:* 800-288-9227 ■ *Web:* www.wbap.com	Dallas	TX	75219	214-526-2400		645
WBAV-FM 101.9 (Urban AC) 1520 S Blvd Ste 300 *Web:* v1019.cbslocal.com	Charlotte	NC	28203	704-570-1019		645-33
WBAY-TV Ch 2 (ABC) 115 S Jefferson St *TF:* 800-261-9229 ■ *Web:* www.wbay.com	Green Bay	WI	54301	920-432-3331	432-1190	741-55
WBBH-TV Ch 20 (NBC) 3719 Central Ave *Web:* www.nbc-2.com	Fort Myers	FL	33901	239-939-2020	936-7771	741-88
WBBM-AM 780 (N/T) 180 N Stetson Ste 1100 *Web:* chicago.cbslocal.com	Chicago	IL	60601	312-297-7800		645-36
WBBM-FM 96.3 (CHR) 180 N Stetson Ste 963 *Web:* b96.cbslocal.com	Chicago	IL	60601	312-591-9696		645-36
WBBN-FM 95.9 (Ctry) 4580 Hwy 15 N PO Box 6408 *Web:* www.b95country.com	Laurel	MS	39441	601-649-0095	649-8199	645
WBBQ 104.3 2743 Perimeter Pkwy Bldg 100 Ste 300 *Web:* wbbq.iheart.com	Augusta	GA	30909	706-396-6000		645-11
WBBR-AM 1130 (N/T) 731 Lexington Ave *Web:* www.bloomberg.com/radio	New York	NY	10022	212-318-2000		645-111
WBBW-AM 1240 (Sports) 4040 Simon Rd *Web:* www.wbbw.com	Youngstown	OH	44512	330-783-1000		645-180
WBBZ-TV Ch 67 (Ind) 4545 Transit Rd Ste 750 *Web:* www.wbbz.tv	Williamsville	NY	14221	716-630-9229	630-9233	741
Wbc Extrusion Products Inc 60 Fondi Rd *Web:* www.wbcextrusion.com	Haverhill	MA	01832	978-372-3300		596
WBCI-FM 105.9 (Rel) 122 Main St *Web:* lifechangingradio.com	Topsham	ME	04086	207-725-9224	725-2686	645
WBCL-FM 90.3 (Rel) 1115 W Rudisill Blvd *Web:* www.wbcl.org	Fort Wayne	IN	46807	260-745-0576	456-2913	645-63
WBCN-FM 104.1 (Alt) 83 Leo Birmingham Pkwy *Web:* wzlx.cbslocal.com	Boston	MA	02135	617-931-1234	746-1402	645-23
WBCT-FM 93.7 (Ctry) 77 Monroe Ctr St NW Ste 1000 *Web:* b93.iheart.com	Grand Rapids	MI	49503	616-459-1919		645-66
WBEE-FM 92.5 (Ctry) 70 Commercial St *TF:* 800-242-4244 ■ *Web:* www.wbee.com	Rochester	NY	14614	585-423-2900		645-138
WBEN-AM 930 (N/T) 500 Corporate Pkwy Ste 200 *TF:* 800-616-9236 ■ *Web:* www.wben.com	Amherst	NY	14226	716-843-0600	832-3080	645
WBEZ-FM 91.5 (NPR) 848 E Grand Ave Navy Pier *TF:* 800-252-8951 ■ *Web:* www.wbez.org	Chicago	IL	60611	312-948-4600		645-36
WBFF-TV Ch 45 (Fox) 2000 W 41st St *Web:* www.foxbaltimore.com	Baltimore	MD	21211	410-467-4545		741-11
WBFJ-FM 89.3 (Rel) 1249 Trade St *Web:* wbfj.fm	Winston-Salem	NC	27101	336-721-1560		645-178
WBFO-FM 88.7 (NPR) PO Box 1263 *Web:* news.wbfo.org	Buffalo	NY	14240	716-845-7000	829-2277	645-25
WBFS-TV Ch 33 (MNT) 8900 NW 18th Terr *Web:* miami.cbslocal.com	Miami	FL	33172	305-591-4444	477-3040	741-82
WBG (Wright Business Graphics) 18440 NE San Rafael St *TF:* 800-547-8397 ■ *Web:* www.wrightbg.com	Portland	OR	97230	800-547-8397		110
WBG (World Bank Group, The) 1818 H St NW *TF:* 800-645-7247 ■ *Web:* www.worldbank.org	Washington	DC	20433	202-473-1000	477-6391	783
WBGH (Washington Business Group on Health) 20 F St NW Ste 200 *Web:* www.businessgrouphealth.org	Washington	DC	20001	202-628-9320	628-9244	48-17
WBGL-FM 91.7 (Rel) 4101 Fieldstone Rd PO Box 111 *TF Cust Svc:* 800-475-9245 ■ *Web:* www.wbgl.org	Champaign	IL	61822	217-359-8232	359-7374	645-30
WBGO-FM 88.3 (Jazz) 54 Pk Pl *TF:* 800-386-2329 ■ *Web:* www.wbgo.org	Newark	NJ	07102	973-624-8880	824-8888	645
WBH (Baptist Health Paducah) 2501 Kentucky Ave *Fax Area Code: 859 ■ *Web:* www.baptisthealth.com/paducah/pages/default.aspx	Paducah	KY	42003	270-575-2100	276-3765*	374-3
WBHK-FM 98.7 (Urban) 2700 Corporate Dr Ste 115 *Web:* 987kiss.com	Birmingham	AL	35242	205-322-2987	290-1061	645-20
WBHM-FM 90.3 (NPR) 650 11th St S *TF:* 800-444-9246 ■ *Web:* www.wbhm.org	Birmingham	AL	35233	205-934-2606	934-5075	645-20
WBHY-FM 88.5 (Rel) PO Box 1328 *TF:* 888-473-8488 ■ *Web:* www.goforth.org	Mobile	AL	36633	251-473-8488		645-102
WBI Energy 1250 W Century Ave *TF:* 877-924-4677 ■ *Web:* www.wbienergy.com	Bismarck	ND	58503	701-530-1064		325
WBI Holdings Inc 1250 W Century Ave *TF General:* 877-924-4677 ■ *Web:* www.wbienergy.com	Bismarck	ND	58503	877-924-4677		325
WBIN TV 11 A St *TF:* 800-257-5151 ■ *Web:* www.wbintv.com	Derry	NH	03038	603-845-1000		741
WBIQ-TV Ch 10 (PBS) 2112 11th Ave S Ste 400 *TF:* 800-239-5233 ■ *Web:* www.aptv.org	Birmingham	AL	35205	205-328-8756	251-2192	741-15
WBIR-TV Ch 10 (NBC) 1513 Hutchinson Ave *Web:* www.wbir.com	Knoxville	TN	37917	865-637-1010	637-6380	741-69
WBJC-FM 91.5 (Clas) 6776 Reisterstown Rd Ste 202 *TF:* 800-829-8000 ■ *Web:* www.wbjc.com	Baltimore	MD	21215	410-580-5800		645-16
WBLI-FM 106.1 (CHR) 555 Sunrise Hwy *Web:* www.wbli.com	West Babylon	NY	11704	631-669-9254	587-1282	645
WBLK-FM 93.7 (Urban) 14 Lafayette Sq Ste 1300 *Web:* www.wblk.com	Buffalo	NY	14203	716-852-9393		645-25
WBMC (West Boca Medical Ctr) 21644 State Rd 7 *Web:* www.westbocamedctr.com	Boca Raton	FL	33428	561-488-8000	488-8105	374-3
WBMX-FM 104.1 83 Leo M Birmingham Pkwy *TF:* 800-457-5437 ■ *Web:* mix1041.cbslocal.com	Boston	MA	02135	617-931-1234		645-23
WBND-TV Ch 57 (Ind) 53550 Generations Dr *Web:* www.abc57.com	South Bend	IN	46635	574-344-5500	344-5094	741
WBNS-AM 1460 (Sports) 605 S Front St Ste 300 *TF:* 800-554-6768 ■ *Web:* www.971thefan.com	Columbus	OH	43215	614-460-3850		645-42
WBNS-FM 97.1 (AC) 605 S Front St Ste 300 *TF:* 888-691-9710 ■ *Web:* www.971thefan.com	Columbus	OH	43215	614-460-3850		645-42
WBNS-TV Ch 10 (CBS) 770 Twin Rivers Dr *Fax: News Rm ■ *Web:* www.10tv.com	Columbus	OH	43215	614-460-3700	460-2891*	741-35

Name / Address	City	State	Zip	Phone	Fax	Class
WBNX-TV Ch 55 (CW) 2690 State Rd *TF:* 800-282-0515 ■ *Web:* www.wbnx.com	Cuyahoga Falls	OH	44223	330-922-5500	929-2410	741
WBNY-FM 91.3 (Alt) 1300 Elmwood Ave *Web:* www.buffalostate.edu/wbny	Buffalo	NY	14222	716-878-5104	878-6600	645-25
WBOC-TV Ch 16 (CBS) 1729 N Salisbury Blvd *Web:* www.wboc.com	Salisbury	MD	21801	410-749-1111	742-5190	741
WBON-FM 98.5 (Span) 3075 Veterans Memorial Hwy Ste 201 *Web:* www.lafiestali.com	Ronkonkoma	NY	11779	631-648-2500	648-2510	645
WBOY-TV Inc 904 W Pike St *Web:* www.wvalways.com	Clarksburg	WV	26301	304-623-3311		116
WBPT-FM 106.9 (AC) 2700 Corporate Dr Ste 115 *TF:* 800-245-2244 ■ *Web:* birminghamseagle.com	Birmingham	AL	35242	205-916-1100	290-1061	645-20
WBRB-FM 101.3 (Ctry) 1065 Radio Pk Dr *TF:* 877-232-7121 ■ *Web:* www.1013thebear.com	Mount Clare	WV	26408	304-623-6546		645
WBRC-TV Ch 6 (Fox) 1720 Vly View Dr *TF:* 800-481-6922 ■ *Web:* www.wbrc.com	Birmingham	Al	35209	205-322-6666	583-4356	741-15
WBRE-TV Ch 28 (NBC) 62 S Franklin St *TF:* 800-367-9222 ■ *Web:* www.pahomepage.com	Wilkes-Barre	PA	18701	570-823-2828	829-0440	741
WBRU-FM 95.5 (Alt) 88 Benevolent St *Web:* www.wbru.com	Providence	RI	02906	401-272-9550	272-9278	645-129
WBRZ-TV Ch 2 (ABC) 1650 Highland Rd *TF:* 800-726-6409 ■ *Web:* theadvocate.com	Baton Rouge	LA	70802	225-387-2222		741-13
WBT-AM 1110 (N/T) 1 Julian Price Pl *TF:* 800-928-1110 ■ *Web:* www.wbt.com	Charlotte	NC	28208	704-570-1110		645-33
WBTT-FM 105.5 (Urban) 13320 Metro Pkwy Ste 1 *Web:* 1055thebeat.iheart.com	Fort Myers	FL	33966	239-225-4300	225-4401	645
WBTV-TV Ch 3 (CBS) 1 Julian Price Pl *Web:* www.wbtv.com	Charlotte	NC	28208	704-374-3500		741-26
WBTW-TV Ch 13 (CBS) 101 McDonald Ct *Web:* www.wbtw.com	Myrtle Beach	SC	29588	843-293-1301		741-87
WBUR-FM 90.9 (NPR) 890 Commonwealth Ave *TF:* 800-909-9287 ■ *Web:* www.wbur.org	Boston	MA	02215	617-353-0909		645-23
WBUZ-FM 102.9 (Alt) 1824 Murfreesboro Rd *TF:* 800-657-6910 ■ *Web:* www.1029thebuzz.com	Nashville	TN	37217	615-399-1029	361-9873	645-108
WBXX-TV Ch 20 (CW) 10427 Cogdill Rd Ste 100 *Web:* www.lbgtv.com	Knoxville	TN	37932	865-777-9220	777-9221	741-69
WBYT-FM 100(Ctry) 237 W Edison Rd *Web:* www.b100.com	Mishawaka	IN	46545	574-258-5483	258-0930	645
WBZA-FM 98.9 (CR) 70 Commercial St *Web:* www.rochesterbuzz.com	Rochester	NY	14614	585-423-2900		645-138
WBZ-AM 1030 (N/T) 1170 Soldiers Field Rd *Web:* boston.cbslocal.com	Boston	MA	02134	617-787-7000		645-23
WBZE-FM 98.9 (AC) 3411 W Tharpe St *TF:* 800-669-1010 ■ *Web:* www.mystar98.com	Tallahassee	FL	32303	850-201-3000		645-161
WBZO-FM 103.1 (Oldies) 234 Airport Plaza Ste 5 *Web:* www.1031maxfm.com	Farmingdale	NY	11735	631-770-4200		645
WBZT-AM 1230 (N/T) 3071 Continental Dr *TF:* 800-889-0267 ■ *Web:* wbzt.iheart.com	West Palm Beach	FL	33407	800-889-0267		645-173
WC Cammett Engineering Inc 297 Elm St *Web:* www.cammett.com	Amesbury	MA	01913	978-388-2157		261
WC McQuaide Inc 153 Macridge Rd *TF:* 800-456-0292 ■ *Web:* www.mcquaide.com	Johnstown	PA	15904	814-269-6000		780
W&C Printing Company Inc 163 E Second St *Web:* www.wcprinting.com	Winona	MN	55987	507-452-2658		627
WCA (Wireless Communications Assn International) 1333 H St NW Ste 700W *Web:* wcai.com	Washington	DC	20005	202-452-7823		49-20
WCA Waste Corp 1330 Post Oak Blvd 30th Fl *NASDAQ:* WCAA ■ *Web:* www.wcawaste.com	Houston	TX	77056	713-292-2400		804
WCAR-AM 1090 (Rel) 32500 Pk Ln	Garden City	MI	48135	734-525-1111		645
WCAT-FM 102.3 (Ctry) 728 N Hanover St *Web:* www.red1023.com	Carlisle	PA	17013	717-243-1200		645
WCAU NBC 10 10 Monument Rd *TF:* 800-847-9228 ■ *Web:* www.nbcphiladelphia.com	Bala Cynwyd	PA	19004	610-668-5510		741
WCAX-TV Ch 3 (CBS) 30 Joy Dr	South Burlington	VT	05403	802-658-6300	652-6399	741
WCBB-TV Ch 10 (PBS) 1450 Lisbon St **Fax Area Code:* 207 ■ *TF:* 800-884-1717 ■ *Web:* mainepublic.org	Lewiston	ME	04240	800-884-1717	783-5193*	741
WCBD-TV Ch 2 (NBC) 210 W Coleman Blvd *TF:* 800-861-5255 ■ *Web:* www.counton2.com	Mount Pleasant	SC	29464	843-884-2222	881-3410	741
WCBE-FM 90.5 (NPR) 540 Jack Gibbs Blvd *TF:* 800-241-0421 ■ *Web:* www.wcbe.org	Columbus	OH	43215	614-365-5555	365-5060	645-42
WCBI-TV Ch 4 (CBS) 201 Fifth St S *Web:* www.wcbi.com	Columbus	MS	39701	662-327-4444	328-5222	741
WCBK-FM 102.3 (Ctry) 1639 Burton Ln *TF:* 800-342-6276 ■ *Web:* www.wcbk.com	Martinsville	IN	46151	765-342-3394	342-5020	645
WCBM-AM 680 (N/T) 1726 Reisterstown Rd Ste 117 *Web:* www.wcbm.com	Pikesville	MD	21208	410-580-6800	580-6810	645
WCBN-FM 88.3 (Alt) University of Michigan 530 Student Activities Bldg *TF:* 800-395-3300 ■ *Web:* wcbn.org	Ann Arbor	MI	48109	734-763-3500		645-7
WCBS-FM 101.1 (Oldies) 345 Hudson St 10th Fl *TF:* 800-367-1101 ■ *Web:* wcbsfm.cbslocal.com	New York	NY	10014	800-367-1101		645-111
WCBS-TV Ch 2 (CBS) 1271 Avenue of Americas 44th FL *Web:* newyork.cbslocal.com	New York	NY	10020	212-975-4321	975-9387	741-91
WCBU-FM 89.9 (NPR) 1501 W Bradley Ave *TF:* 888-488-9228 ■ *Web:* peoriapublicradio.org	Peoria	IL	61625	309-677-3690		645-121
WCC (Women's College Coalition) PO Box 3983 *Web:* www.womenscolleges.org	Decatur	GA	30031	404-913-9492		49-5
WCC (Wilmette Chamber of Commerce) 351 Linden Ave *Web:* www.wilmettekenilworth.com	Wilmette	IL	60091	847-251-3800	251-6321	139
WCCBI (Warren County Chamber of Commerce) 308 Market St *Web:* www.wccbi.org	Warren	PA	16365	814-723-3050	723-6024	139
WCCB-TV Ch 18 (Fox) 1 Television Pl *Web:* wccbcharlotte.com	Charlotte	NC	28205	704-372-1800		741-26
WCCC (Wilmington Clinton County Chamber of Commerce) 100 W Main St *TF:* 800-762-0047 ■ *Web:* www.wccchamber.com	Wilmington	OH	45177	937-382-2737		139
WCCO-AM 830 (N/T) 625 Second Ave S *Web:* minnesota.cbslocal.com	Minneapolis	MN	55402	612-370-0611		645-101
WCCO-TV Ch 4 (CBS) 90 S 11th St *Web:* minnesota.cbslocal.com	Minneapolis	MN	55403	612-339-4444	330-2767	741-84
WCD Consultants LLC 23 Rt 31 N Ste B26 *Web:* www.wcdgroup.com	Pennington	NJ	08534	609-730-0007	730-0011	194
WCDX-FM 92.1 (Urban) 2809 Emerywood Pkwy Ste 300 *Web:* ipowerrichmond.com	Richmond	VA	23294	804-672-9299		645-134
WCEC (Wharton County Electric Co-op Inc) 1815 E Jackson St *TF:* 800-460-6271 ■ *Web:* www.wcecnet.net	El Campo	TX	77437	979-543-6271		245
WCET-TV Ch 48 (PBS) 1223 Central Pkwy *TF:* 800-808-0445 ■ *Web:* www.cetconnect.org	Cincinnati	OH	45214	513-381-4033	381-7520	741-30
WCF (World Cocoa Foundation) 1411 K St NW Ste 1300 *Web:* www.worldcocoafoundation.org	Washington	DC	20005	202-737-7870	737-7832	49-6
WCF (Women's Campaign Fund) 718 Seventh St NW 2nd Fl *Web:* www.wcfonline.org	Washington	DC	20001	202-796-8259		48-7
WCFB-FM 94.5 (AC) 4192 N John Young Pkwy *Web:* www.star945.com	Orlando	FL	32804	407-294-2945	297-7595	645-116
WCFT-TV Ch 33 (ABC) 800 Concourse Pkwy Ste 200 *TF:* 800-784-9660 ■ *Web:* www.abc3340.com	Birmingham	AL	35244	205-403-3340		741-15
WCG International Consultants Ltd 5 915 Ft St *Web:* www.wcgservices.com	Victoria	BC	V8V3K3	250-389-0699		260
WCGL-AM 1360 (Rel) 3890 Dunn Ave Ste 804 *TF:* 800-331-1359 ■ *Web:* www.wcgl1360.com	Jacksonville	FL	32218	904-766-9955	765-9214	645-79
WCGQ-FM 107.3 (AC) 1820 Wynnton Rd *Web:* www.q1073.com	Columbus	GA	31906	706-327-1217	596-4600	645-41
WCGV-TV Ch 24 (MNT) 4041 N 35th St *TF:* 800-554-1448 ■ *Web:* www.my24milwaukee.com	Milwaukee	WI	53216	414-815-4100		741-83
WCH (Women's & Children's Hospital) 4600 Ambassador Caffery Pkwy *TF:* 888-569-8331 ■ *Web:* www.womens-childrens.com	Lafayette	LA	70508	337-521-9100		374-7
WCHS-AM 58 (N/T) 1111 Virginia St E *Web:* www.58wchs.com	Charleston	WV	25301	304-342-8131		645-32
WCHS-TV Ch 8 (ABC) 1301 Piedmont Rd *TF:* 888-696-9247 ■ *Web:* www.wchstv.com	Charleston	WV	25301	304-346-5358	346-4765	741-25
WCI Communities Inc 24301 Walden Ctr Dr *TF:* 800-924-4005 ■ *Web:* www.wcicommunities.com	Bonita Springs	FL	34134	239-498-8200		653
WCIA-TV Ch 3 (CBS) PO Box 20 *TF:* 800-676-3382 ■ *Web:* www.illinoishomepage.net	Champaign	IL	61824	217-356-8333		741
WCIC-FM 91.5 (Rel) 3902 W Baring Trace **Fax Area Code:* 309 ■ *TF:* 877-692-9242 ■ *Web:* www.wcicfm.org	Peoria	IL	61615	877-692-9242	692-9241*	645-121
Wcities.com Inc 512 Second St 2nd Fl *Web:* www.wcities.com	San Francisco	CA	94107	415-495-8090		772
WCIU-TV Ch 26 (Ind) 26 N Halsted St *Web:* www.wciu.com	Chicago	IL	60661	312-705-2600		741-29
WCIV-TV Ch 4 (ABC) PO Box 22165 **Fax:* News Rm ■ *Web:* www.abcnews4.com	Charleston	SC	29413	843-881-4444	849-2519*	741-24
WCJ - Pilgrim Wire LLC 4180 N Port Washington Rd *Web:* www.wcjwire.com	Glendale	WI	53212	414-291-9566		492
WCJK-FM 96.3 (Var) 504 Rosedale Ave *Web:* www.963jackfm.com	Nashville	TN	37211	615-259-4567	259-4594	645-108
WCKT-FM 107.1 (Ctry) 13320 Metro Pkwy Ste 1 *Web:* catcountry1071.iheart.com	Fort Myers	FL	33966	239-225-4300		645
WCKX-FM 107.5 (Urban) 350 E First Ave Ste 100 *Web:* mycolumbuspower.com	Columbus	OH	43201	614-487-1444	487-5862	645-42
WCL (Washoe County Library) 301 S Ctr St *Web:* www.washoecountylibrary.us	Reno	NV	89501	775-327-8300	327-8341	434-3
WCLF-TV Ch 22 (Ind) PO Box 6922 *Web:* www.ctnonline.com	Clearwater	FL	33758	727-535-5622	531-2497	741
WCLG-FM 100.1 (Rock) PO Box 885 *Web:* www.wclg.com	Morgantown	WV	26507	304-292-2222	292-2224	645-105
WCLK-FM 91.9 (Jazz) 111 James P Brawley Dr SW *TF:* 888-448-3925 ■ *Web:* www.wclk.com	Atlanta	GA	30314	404-880-8273	880-8869	645-10
WCLT-FM 100.3 (Ctry) PO Box 5150 *Web:* www.wclt.com	Newark	OH	43058	740-345-4004		645
WCLV 1375 Euclid Ave Idea Ctr *TF:* 877-399-3307 ■ *Web:* wclv.ideastream.org	Cleveland	OH	44115	216-916-6100		646

Name / Address	City	State	Zip	Phone	Fax	Class
Wcm Group Inc, The 110 S Bender Ave *TF:* 800-477-6990 ■ *Web:* wcmgroup.com	Humble	TX	77338	281-446-7070		196
WCM Investment Management 281 Brooks St. *Web:* www.wcminvest.com	Laguna Beach	CA	92651	949-380-0200		401
WCMF-FM 96.5 (CR) 70 Commercial St. *TF:* 800-222-9196 ■ *Web:* www.wcmf.com	Rochester	NY	14614	585-423-2900		645-138
WCMH (Windham Community Memorial Hospital) 112 Mansfield Ave *Web:* www.windhamhospital.org	Willimantic	CT	06226	860-456-9116	456-6838	374-3
WCMHS (Washington County Mental Health Services Inc) PO Box 647 *Web:* www.wcmhs.org	Montpelier	VT	05601	802-229-0591	223-8623	353
WCMH-TV Ch 4 (NBC) 3165 Olentangy River Rd *TF:* 800-665-2991 ■ *Web:* www.nbc4i.com	Columbus	OH	43202	614-263-4444	263-0166	741-35
WCMR-AM 1270 (Rel) PO Box 307 *TF:* 800-522-9376 ■ *Web:* www.solidgospel1270.com	Elkhart	IN	46515	574-875-5166	875-6662	645
WCMS-FM 94.5 (Ctry) 103-D W Wood Hill Dr *Web:* www.wcms.com	Nags Head	NC	27959	252-480-4655	441-4827	645
WCNC-TV Ch 36 (NBC) 1001 Wood Ridge Center Dr. *Web:* www.wcnc.com	Charlotte	NC	28217	704-329-3636		741-26
WCNK-FM 98.7 (Ctry) 830 Crane Blvd. *Web:* www.conchcountry.com	Sugarloaf Key	FL	33042	305-296-7511		645
WCNY-FM 91.3 (NPR) 506 Old Liverpool Rd *TF:* 800-451-9269 ■ *Web:* www.wcny.org	Liverpool	NY	13088	315-453-2424	451-8824	645
WCNY-TV Ch 24 (PBS) 506 Old Liverpool Rd PO Box 2400 *TF:* 800-638-5163 ■ *Web:* www.wcny.org	Syracuse	NY	13220	315-453-2424	451-8824	741-131
WCOL-FM 92.3 (Ctry) 2323 W Fifth Ave Ste 200 *TF:* 800-899-9265 ■ *Web:* wcol.iheart.com	Columbus	OH	43204	614-821-9624	487-2559	645-42
WCOS-AM 1400 (Sports) 316 Greystone Blvd *Web:* foxsportsradio1400.iheart.com	Columbia	SC	29210	803-343-1100	748-9267	645-40
WCOS-FM 97.5 (Ctry) 316 Greystone Blvd *Web:* 975wcos.iheart.com	Columbia	SC	29210	803-343-1100		645-40
WCOV-TV Ch 20 (Fox) 1 W Cov Ave *TF:* 800-734-4667 ■ *Web:* www.wcov.com	Montgomery	AL	36111	334-288-7020	288-5414	741-86
Wcp Solutions 6703 S 234th St Ste 120 *TF:* 877-398-3030 ■ *Web:* wcpsolutions.com/index.php	Kent	WA	98032	877-398-3030		552-1
WCPN-FM 90.3 (NPR) 1375 Euclid Ave *Web:* wcpn.ideastream.org	Cleveland	OH	44115	216-916-6100		645-38
WCPO TV 1720 Gilbert Ave *TF:* 800-686-4208 ■ *Web:* www.wcpo.com	Cincinnati	OH	45202	513-721-9900		532-2
WCPO-TV Ch 9 (ABC) 1720 Gilbert Ave *Web:* www.wcpo.com	Cincinnati	OH	45202	513-721-9900	721-7717	741-30
WCPV-FM 101.3 (CR) 265 Hegeman Ave *TF:* 866-862-4267 ■ *Web:* www.1013espn.com	Colchester	VT	05446	802-655-0093		645
WCPX-TV Ch 38 (I) 333 S Desplaines St Ste 101 **Fax Area Code: 646* ■ *TF:* 888-467-2988 ■ *Web:* ionmedia.com	Chicago	IL	60661	212-757-3100	597-5903*	741-29
WCQ (West Coast Quartz Corporation) 1000 Corporate Way *Web:* www.wcq.com	Fremont	CA	94539	510-249-2160	249-2168	696
WCQR-FM 88.3 (Rel) 2312 Oak St *TF:* 888-477-5676 ■ *Web:* www.wcqr.org	Gray	TN	37615	423-477-5676	477-7060	645
WCQS-FM 88.1 (NPR) 73 Broadway *TF:* 866-448-3881 ■ *Web:* www.wcqs.org	Asheville	NC	28801	828-210-4800	210-4801	645-9
WCR (Women's Council of REALTORS) 430 N Michigan Ave **Fax Area Code: 312* ■ *TF:* 800-245-8512 ■ *Web:* www.wcr.org	Chicago	IL	60611	800-245-8512	329-3290*	49-17
WCRN-AM 830 (N/T) 82 Franklin St *Web:* www.wcrnradio.com	Worcester	MA	01608	508-438-0965		645-179
WCS (Wildlife Conservation Society) 2300 Southern Blvd *Web:* www.wcs.org	Bronx	NY	10460	718-220-5100		48-3
WCSC-TV Ch 5 (CBS) 2126 Charlie Hall Blvd *Web:* www.live5news.com	Charleston	SC	29414	843-577-6397		741-24
WCSD (Wallkill Central School District) 19 Main St PO Box 310 *Web:* www.wallkillcsd.k12.ny.us	Wallkill	NY	12589	845-895-7100	895-3630	685
WCSG-FM 91.3 (Rel) 1159 E Beltline Ave NE *Web:* www.wcsg.org	Grand Rapids	MI	49525	616-942-1500		645-66
WCSH-TV Ch 6 (NBC) 1 Congress Sq *TF:* 800-464-1213 ■ *Web:* www.wcsh6.com	Portland	ME	04101	207-828-6666	828-6620	741-102
WCSX-FM 94.7 (CR) 1 Radio Plaza *Web:* www.wcsx.com	Ferndale	MI	48220	248-398-9470		645
WCTL-FM 106.3 (Rel) 10912 Peach St. *TF:* 800-568-8924 ■ *Web:* www.wctl.org	Waterford	PA	16441	814-796-6000		645
WCTO-FM 96.1 (Ctry) 2158 Ave C Ste 100 *TF:* 800-772-8336 ■ *Web:* www.catcountry96.com	Bethlehem	PA	18017	610-266-7600		645
WCTV-TV Ch 6 (CBS) 1801 Halstead Blvd. *TF:* 888-297-9461 ■ *Web:* www.wctv.tv	Tallahassee	FL	32309	850-893-6666		741-132
WCTX-TV Ch 59 (MNT) 8 Elm St. *Web:* www.wctx.com	New Haven	CT	06510	203-782-5900		741
WCU (Western Carolina University) 1 University Dr *TF:* 877-928-4968 ■ *Web:* www.wcu.edu	Cullowhee	NC	28723	828-227-7211	227-7319	166
WCUW-FM 91.3 (Var) 910 Main St. *TF:* 800-737-3030 ■ *Web:* www.wcuw.org	Worcester	MA	01610	508-753-1012		645-179
WCVB-TV Ch 5 (ABC) 5 TV Pl. *Web:* www.wcvb.com	Needham	MA	02494	781-449-0400		741
WCVE-TV Ch 23 (PBS) 23 Sesame St *TF:* 800-476-8440 ■ *Web:* ideastations.org	Richmond	VA	23235	804-320-1301		741-108
WCVX-AM 1050 (Rel) 635 W Seventh St Ste 400	Cincinnati	OH	45203	513-533-2500		645-37
WCWC (Western Canada Wilderness Committee) 227 Abbott St *TF:* 800-661-9453 ■ *Web:* www.wildernesscommittee.org	Vancouver	BC	V6B2K7	604-683-8220	683-8229	48-13
WCWF-TV Ch 14 (CW) 787 Lombardi Ave. *Web:* www.cw14online.com	Green Bay	WI	54304	920-494-8711	494-8782	741-55
WCYB-TV Ch 5 (NBC) 101 Lee St *Web:* www.wcyb.com	Bristol	VA	24201	276-645-1555		741
WCYQ-FM 93.1 (Oldies) 1533 Amherst Rd *Web:* www.q100country.com	Knoxville	TN	37909	865-824-1021		645-85
WD Manor Mechanical Contractors Inc 1838 N 23rd Ave. *Web:* www.wdmanor.com	Phoenix	AZ	85009	602-253-0703	253-3659	189-10
WD Partners 7007 Discovery Blvd. *Web:* www.wdpartners.com	Dublin	OH	43017	614-634-7000		261
WD Tire Warehouse Inc 3805 E Livingston Ave *Web:* www.wdtire.com	Columbus	OH	43227	614-461-8944	461-0136	755
WD-40 Co 1061 Cudahy Pl *NASDAQ: WDFC* ■ *TF:* 800-448-9340 ■ *Web:* www.wd40company.com	San Diego	CA	92110	619-275-1400	275-5823	541
WDAE-AM 620 (Sports) 4002 W Gandy Blvd *TF:* 888-546-4620 ■ *Web:* 620wdae.iheart.com	Tampa	FL	33611	813-832-1000		645-162
WDAF-FM 106.5 (Ctry) 7000 Squibb Rd *TF:* 800-226-1027 ■ *Web:* www.1065thewolf.com	Mission	KS	66202	913-744-3600		645
WDAF-TV Ch 4 (Fox) 3030 Summit. *TF:* 800-593-2222 ■ *Web:* www.fox4kc.com	Kansas City	MO	64108	816-753-4567		741-68
WDAI-FM 98.5 (Urban) 11640 Hwy 17 Bypass *Web:* www.985kissfm.net	Murrells Inlet	SC	29576	843-651-7869	651-9123	645
WDAM-TV Ch 7 (NBC) PO Box 16269 *TF:* 800-844-9326 ■ *Web:* www.wdam.com	Hattiesburg	MS	39404	601-544-4730	584-9302	741
WDAS-FM 105.3 (Urban AC) 111 Presidential Blvd Ste 100 *TF:* 800-745-3000 ■ *Web:* wdasfm.iheart.com	Philadelphia	PA	19004	610-784-3333	789-2767	645
WDAY-AM 970 (N/T) 301 Eigth St S *TF:* 800-735-3229 ■ *Web:* www.wday.com	Fargo	ND	58103	701-237-6500		645-58
WDAY-TV Ch 6 (ABC) 301 S Eigth St. *Web:* www.inforum.com	Fargo	ND	58103	701-237-6500		741-48
WDAZ-TV Ch 8 (ABC) 2220 S Washington St *TF:* 877-382-4357 ■ *Web:* www.wdaz.com	Grand Forks	ND	58201	701-775-2511	241-5217	741-48
WDBO-AM 580 (N/T) 4192 N John Young Pkwy. *Web:* www.news965.com	Orlando	FL	32804	321-281-2000		645-116
WDBQ-AM 1490 (N/T) 5490 Saratoga Rd *Web:* www.wdbqam.com	Dubuque	IA	52002	563-557-1040		645-50
WDBQ-FM 107.5 (Oldies) 5490 Saratoga Rd *Web:* www.myq1075.com	Dubuque	IA	52002	563-557-1040		645-50
WDBR 103.7 3501 E Sangamon Ave *Web:* www.wdbr.com	Springfield	IL	62707	217-753-5400	753-7902	645-155
WDCW-TV 2121 Wisconsin Ave NW Ste 350 *Web:* dcw50.com	Washington	DC	20007	202-965-5050		741-139
WDCX-FM 99.5 (Rel) 625 Delaware Ave Ste 308 *TF:* 800-684-2848 ■ *Web:* www.wdcxradio.com	Buffalo	NY	14202	716-883-3010		645-25
WDEA-AM 1370 (Nost) 49 Acme Rd *TF:* 800-432-7964 ■ *Web:* wdea.am	Brewer	ME	04412	207-989-5631		645
WDEF-FM 92.3 (AC) 2615 S Broad St. *Web:* www.sunny923.com	Chattanooga	TN	37408	423-321-6200		645-34
WDEF-TV Ch 12 (CBS) 3300 Broad St. *Web:* www.wdef.com	Chattanooga	TN	37408	423-785-1200	785-1271	741-27
WDEL-AM 1150 (N/T) 2727 Shipley Rd. *TF:* 800-544-1150 ■ *Web:* www.wdel.com	Wilmington	DE	19810	302-478-2700	478-0100	645-176
WDEN-FM 99.1 (Ctry) 544 Mulberry St 5th Fl *Web:* www.wden.com	Macon	GA	31201	478-746-6286		645-95
WDET-FM 101.9 (NPR) 4600 Cass Ave Wayne State University *Web:* wdet.org	Detroit	MI	48201	313-577-4146	577-1300	645-49
WDEV-AM 550 (N/T) 9 Stowe St PO Box 550 *Web:* www.wdevradio.com	Waterbury	VT	05676	802-244-7321	244-1771	645
WDEV-FM 96.1 (Clas) 9 Stowe St PO Box 550 *Web:* wdevradio.com	Waterbury	VT	05676	802-244-7321	244-1771	645
WDFN-AM 1130 (Sports) 27675 Halsted Rd *Web:* wdfn.iheart.com	Farmington Hills	MI	48331	248-324-5800		645
WDGL-FM 98.1 (CR) 929-B Government St *TF:* 800-324-1108 ■ *Web:* www.eagle981.com	Baton Rouge	LA	70802	225-388-9898		645-18
WDIA-AM 1070 (Urban) 2650 Thousand Oaks Blvd Ste 4100 *Web:* mywdia.iheart.com	Memphis	TN	38118	901-259-1300		645-98
WDIO-TV Ch 10 (ABC) 10 Observation Rd. *TF:* 800-477-1013 ■ *Web:* www.wdio.com	Duluth	MN	55811	218-727-6864	727-4415	741-42
WDIV-TV Ch 4 (NBC) 550 W Lafayette Blvd *Web:* www.clickondetroit.com	Detroit	MI	48226	313-222-0500		741-41
WDIY-FM 88.1 (NPR) 301 Broadway *TF:* 800-346-8357 ■ *Web:* wdiy.org	Bethlehem	PA	18015	610-694-8100	954-9474	645
WDJA-AM 1420 (N/T) 2710 W Atlantic Ave *Web:* www.universo1420.com	Delray Beach	FL	33445	561-278-1420		645
WDJT-TV Ch 58 (CBS) 809 S 60th St *Web:* www.cbs58.com	Milwaukee	WI	53214	414-777-5800	777-5802	741-83
WDKS-FM 106.1 (CHR) 117 SE Fifth St *TF:* 888-454-5477 ■ *Web:* 1061evansville.com	Evansville	IN	47708	812-425-4226		645-56
WDKX-FM 103.9 (Urban) 683 E Main St *Web:* www.wdkx.com	Rochester	NY	14605	585-262-2050	262-2626	645-138
WDKY-TV Ch 56 (Fox) 836 Euclid Ave Ste 201 *TF:* 888-404-5656 ■ *Web:* www.foxlexington.com	Lexington	KY	40502	859-269-5656		741-73
WDL (Wilmington Drama League) 10 W Lea Blvd *Web:* www.wilmingtondramaleague.org	Wilmington	DE	19802	302-764-1172		573-4
WDL Systems 220 Chatham Business Dr. *TF Sales:* 800-548-2319 ■ *Web:* www.wdlsystems.com	Pittsboro	NC	27312	919-545-2500	545-2559	174

Name / Address	City	State	ZIP	Phone	Fax	Class
WDLI-TV Ch 17 (TBN) PO Box A *TF:* 888-731-1000 ■ *Web:* www.tbn.org	Santa Ana	CA	92711	714-832-2950		741-76
WDM Support Services Inc 1900 Harrison St Ste 2 *Web:* www.wdmquincy.com	Quincy	IL	62301	217-228-1950	222-6053	175
WDMA (Window & Door Manufacturers Assn) 330 N Wabash Ave Ste 2000 **Fax Area Code:* 651 ■ *TF:* 800-223-2301 ■ *Web:* www.wdma.com	Chicago	IL	60611	847-299-5200	264-5150*	49-3
WDMP Radio 2163 State Rd 23-151 *Web:* d99point3.com	Dodgeville	WI	53533	608-935-2302		116
WDNA-FM 88.9 (Jazz) 2921 Coral Way *Web:* www.wdna.org	Miami	FL	33145	305-662-8889		645-99
WDOD-FM 96.5 (CHR) 2615 S Broad St *Web:* www.hits96.com	Chattanooga	TN	37408	423-321-6200		645-34
WDPR-FM 88.1 (Clas) 126 N Main St *Web:* discoverclassical.org	Dayton	OH	45402	937-496-3850	496-3852	645-45
WDRB-TV Ch 41 (Fox) 624 W Muhammad Ali Blvd *Web:* www.wdrb.com	Louisville	KY	40203	502-584-6441	589-5559	741-77
WDRM-FM 102.1 (Ctry) 26869 Peoples Rd *TF:* 866-302-0102 ■ *Web:* wdrm.iheart.com	Madison	AL	35756	256-309-2400		645
WDRQ-FM 93.1 (Var) 3011 W Grand Blvd Fisher Bldg Ste 800 *Web:* nashfm931.com	Detroit	MI	48202	313-871-9300		645-49
WDRV-FM 97.1 (CR) 875 N Michigan Ave Ste 1510 *TF:* 800-899-0089 ■ *Web:* www.wdrv.com	Chicago	IL	60611	312-274-9710	274-1304	645-36
WDSC-TV 1200 W International Speedway Blvd *TF:* 866-273-5825 ■ *Web:* www.daytonastate.edu/wdsc	Daytona Beach	FL	32114	386-506-4415	506-4427	741
WDSD-FM 94.7 (Ctry) 920 W Basin Rd Ste 400 *Web:* wdsd.iheart.com	New Castle	DE	19720	302-395-9800		645
WDSE-TV Ch 8 (PBS) 632 Niagara Ct *TF:* 888-563-9373 ■ *Web:* www.wdse.org	Duluth	MN	55811	218-788-2831		741-42
WDSU-TV Ch 6 (NBC) 846 Howard Ave *TF:* 888-925-4127 ■ *Web:* www.wdsu.com	New Orleans	LA	70113	504-679-0600	679-0752	741-90
WDSY-FM 107.9 (Ctry) 651 Holiday Dr Foster Plz 5 *Web:* y108.cbslocal.com	Pittsburgh	PA	15220	412-920-9400	920-9449	645-125
WDTN-TV Ch 2 (NBC) 4595 S Dixie Ave *Web:* www.wdtn.com	Dayton	OH	45439	937-293-2101	296-7147	741-38
WDUZ-AM 1400 (Sports) 810 Victoria St *TF:* 855-724-1075 ■ *Web:* www.thefan1075.com	Green Bay	WI	54302	920-468-4100	468-0250	645-67
WDVD-FM 96.3 (AC) 3011 W Grand Blvd Fisher Bldg Ste 800 *Web:* www.963wdvd.com	Detroit	MI	48202	313-871-3030		645-49
WDVE-FM 102.5 (Rock) 200 Fleet St *Web:* dve.iheart.com	Pittsburgh	PA	15220	412-937-1441	937-0323	645-125
WDWS-AM 1400 (N/T) 2301 S Neil St *TF:* 800-223-9397 ■ *Web:* news-gazette.com/wdws	Champaign	IL	61820	[illegible]	[illegible]	[illegible]
WDXB-FM 102.5 (Ctry) 600 Beacon Pkwy W Ste 400 *TF:* 877-811-3369 ■ *Web:* 1025thebull.iheart.com	Birmingham	AL	35209	205-439-9600	439-8390	645-20
WDZZ-FM 92.7 (Urban) 6317 Taylor Dr *Web:* www.wdzz.com	Flint	MI	48507	810-238-7300		645-60
WE Aubuchon Company Inc 95 Aubuchon Dr *TF:* 800-431-2712 ■ *Web:* www.hardwarestore.com	Westminster	MA	01473	978-874-0521		364
WE Bassett Co 100 Trap Falls Rd Ext *Web:* www.trim.com	Shelton	CT	06484	203-929-8483		214
WE Blain & Sons Inc 98 Pearce Rd *Web:* blain-co.com	Mount Olive	MS	39119	601-797-4551		188-4
We Buy Guitars LLC 705 Bedford Ave *Web:* webuyguitars.org	Bellmore	NY	11710	516-221-0563		366
WE Donoghue & Company Inc 629 Washington St *TF:* 800-642-4276 ■ *Web:* www.donoghue.com	Norwood	MA	02062	800-642-4276		401
We Energies 231 W Michigan St PO Box 2046 *TF:* 800-242-9137 ■ *Web:* www.we-energies.com	Milwaukee	WI	53203	414-221-2345		787
WE Family Offices LLC 701 Brickell Ave Ste 2100 *TF:* 800-422-6172 ■ *Web:* www.wefamilyoffices.com	Miami	FL	33131	305-825-2225		401
WE Neal Slate Co 2840 Hwy 25 *TF:* 800-989-2348 ■ *Web:* www.nealslate.com	Watertown	MN	55388	952-955-3340	955-3341	724
We Print Today LLC 66 Summer St *Web:* www.weprinttoday.com	Kingston	MA	02364	781-585-6021		627
WE Transport Inc 75 Commercial St *Web:* www.wetransport.com	Plainview	NY	11803	516-349-8200	349-8275	109
WE Yoder Inc 41 S Maple St *TF:* 800-889-5149 ■ *Web:* www.weyoderinc.com	Kutztown	PA	19530	610-683-7383	683-8638	188-8
WEAA-FM 88.9 (Jazz) 1700 E Cold Spring Ln *Web:* www.weaa.org	Baltimore	MD	21251	443-885-3564	885-8206	645-16
Weaber Inc 1231 Mt Wilson Rd *TF:* 800-745-9663 ■ *Web:* www.weaberlumber.com	Lebanon	PA	17042	717-867-2212		499
WEAI (Western Economic Assn International) 18837 Brookhurst St Ste 304 *Web:* www.weai.org	Fountain Valley	CA	92708	714-965-8800	965-8829	49-2
Weakley County 116 W Main St Rm 104 Room G01 *TF:* 800-648-8798 ■ *Web:* www.weakleycountytn.gov	Dresden	TN	38225	731-364-3643	364-9577	338
Weakley County Chamber of Commerce 114 W Maple St PO Box 67 *Web:* www.weakleycountychamber.com	Dresden	TN	38225	731-364-3787	364-2099	139
Wealth Conservancy Inc, The 1525 Spruce St Ste 300 *TF:* 888-440-1919 ■ *Web:* www.thewealthconservancy.com	Boulder	CO	80302	303-444-1919		401
WealthForge Holdings Inc 6800 Paragon Pl Ste 237 *Web:* www.wealthforge.com	Richmond	VA	23230	804-308-0431		387
Wealthfront Inc 541 Cowper St *Web:* www.wealthfront.com	Palo Alto	CA	94301	650-249-4250		401
Wealthsimple Inc 372 Richmond St W Ste 120 *Web:* www.wealthsimple.com	Toronto	ON	M5V2L7	647-350-7675		528
WealthTrust Arizona LLC 8434 E Shea Blvd *Web:* wealthtrust-arizona.com	Scottsdale	AZ	85260	480-483-7300		194
WEAO-TV Ch 49 (PBS) 1750 Campus Ctr Dr *TF:* 800-554-4549 ■ *Web:* westernreservepublicmedia.org	Kent	OH	44240	330-677-4549	678-0688	741
WEAP (Women's Economic Agenda Project) 160 Franklin St Ste 208 *Web:* www.weap.org	Oakland	CA	94607	510-986-8620	986-8628	48-24
Wear - Concepts Inc 106 NW Business Park Ln *Web:* www.wearcon.com	Riverside	MO	64150	816-587-1923		480
WEAR-TV Ch 3 (ABC) 4990 Mobile Hwy **Fax Area Code:* 410 ■ *TF:* 800-772-1213 ■ *Web:* www.weartv.com	Pensacola	FL	32506	850-456-3333	568-1691*	741
Weather Ch Inc, The 300 I N Pkwy Po Box 724554 *TF:* 866-843-0392 ■ *Web:* www.weather.com	Atlanta	GA	30339	770-226-0000	226-2632	740
Weather Champions Ltd 158 Dikeman St *Web:* wechamps.com	Brooklyn	NY	11231	718-522-0300		189-10
Weather Decision Technologies Inc 201 David L Boren Blvd Ste 270 *Web:* wdtinc.com	Norman	OK	73072	405-579-7675		395
Weather Network, The 2655 Bristol Cir *Web:* www.theweathernetwork.com	Oakville	ON	L6H7W1	905-829-1159		740
Weather Services International 400 Minuteman Rd	Andover	MA	01810	978-983-6300		178-10
Weather Shield Manufacturing Inc 1 Weather Shield Plaza PO Box 309 **Fax Area Code:* 800 ■ *TF:* 800-222-2995 ■ *Web:* www.weathershield.com	Medford	WI	54451	715-748-2100	222-2146*	236
Weatherall Printing Co 1349 Cliff Gookin Blvd *TF:* 800-273-6043 ■ *Web:* www.weatherallprinting.com	Tupelo	MS	38801	662-842-5284		627
Weatherbank Inc 1015 Waterwood Pkwy Ste J *TF:* 800-687-3562 ■ *Web:* www.weatherbank.com	Edmond	OK	73034	405-359-0773	341-0115	70
Weatherby Inc 1605 Commerce Way *TF:* 800-227-2016 ■ *Web:* www.weatherby.com	Paso Robles	CA	93446	805-227-2600	237-0427	284
Weatherford Aerospace Inc 1020 E Columbia St *Web:* www.weatherfordaerospace.com	Weatherford	TX	76086	817-594-5464	594-7450	256
Weatherford Artificial Lift Systems 515 Post Oak Blvd Ste 600 *Web:* www.weatherford.com	Houston	TX	77027	281-449-1383	449-6235	537
Weatherford Chamber of Commerce 401 Ft Worth St *TF:* 888-594-3801 ■ *Web:* www.weatherford-chamber.com	Weatherford	TX	76086	817-596-3801	613-9216	139
Weatherford College 225 College Pk Dr **Fax:* Admissions ■ *TF:* 800-287-5471 ■ *Web:* www.wc.edu	Weatherford	TX	76086	817-594-5471	598-6205*	162
Weatherford Completion Systems 2000 Saint James Pl *Web:* www.weatherford.com	Houston	TX	77056	432-562-7067		630
Weatherford International Inc 515 Post Oak Blvd Ste 600 *NYSE:* WFT ■ *TF:* 866-398-0010 ■ *Web:* www.weatherford.com	Houston	TX	77027	713-693-4000		537
Weatherford Laboratories Inc 8845 Fallbrook Dr *Web:* labs.weatherford.com	Houston	TX	77064	832-237-4000		80-3
Weatherford Public Library 1014 Charles St *TF:* 800-489-0190 ■ *Web:* ci.weatherford.tx.us	Weatherford	TX	76086	817-598-4150	598-4161	434-3
Weatherhaven Global Resources Ltd 2120 Hartley Ave. *Web:* www.weatherhaven.com	Coquitlam	BC	V3K6W5	604-451-8900		106
Weatherhead Ctr for International Affairs Harvard Univ 1737 Cambridge St *Web:* www.wcfia.harvard.edu	Cambridge	MA	02138	617-495-4420	495-8292	634
Weathermatic 3301 W Kingsley Rd *TF:* 888-484-3776 ■ *Web:* www.weathermatic.com	Garland	TX	75041	972-278-6131	271-5710	429
Weatherproof Garment Co 4 Bryant Pk 12th FL *Web:* weatherproofgarment.com	New York	NY	10018	212-695-7716		155-12
Weather-Rite LLC 616 N Fifth St *Web:* www.weather-rite.com	Minneapolis	MN	55401	612-338-1401		664
Weathers Auto Supply Inc 23308 Airpark Dr *TF:* 888-572-2886 ■ *Web:* www.weathers.com	Petersburg	VA	23803	804-861-1076		54
Weatherspoon Art Museum 500 Tate St *Web:* www.uncg.edu	Greensboro	NC	27402	336-334-5770	334-5907	520
Weathervane Community Playhouse 1301 Weathervane Ln *TF:* 800-745-3000 ■ *Web:* www.weathervaneplayhouse.com	Akron	OH	44313	330-836-2626	873-2150	572
Weathervane Seafood Restaurant 306 US Rt 1 *TF:* 800-914-1774 ■ *Web:* www.weathervaneseafoods.com	Kittery	ME	03904	207-439-0330		670
Weaver & Sons Inc 1200 Ward Ave *Web:* www.weaverandsons.com	Talladega	AL	35160	256-362-3614		697
Weaver Bros Inc 2230 Spar Ave *TF:* 800-478-4600 ■ *Web:* weaverbrothersinc.com	Anchorage	AK	99501	907-278-4526	276-4316	780
Weaver Bros Insurance Assoc Inc 4550 Montgomery Ave Ste 300 North Tower *Web:* www.weaverbros.com	Bethesda	MD	20814	301-986-4400		390
Weaver C. Barksdale & Associates Inc 1 Burton Hills Blvd Ste 100 *TF:* 800-258-1559 ■ *Web:* www.wcbarksdale.com	Nashville	TN	37215	615-665-1085		528
Weaver Cooke Construction LLC 8401 Key Blvd *Web:* www.weavercooke.com	Greensboro	NC	27409	336-378-7900	378-7901	186
Weaver Industries Inc 425 S Fourth St PO Box 326 *Web:* www.weaverind.com	Denver	PA	17517	717-336-7507	336-4182	454
Weaver Manufacturing Co 3101 Justin Rd *Web:* www.weavermanufacturing.com	Flower Mound	TX	75028	972-539-1537		567
Weaver-Bailey Contractors Inc PO Box 60 *TF:* 800-253-3385 ■ *Web:* www.weaverbailey.com	El Paso	AR	72045	501-796-2301	796-2372	189-3

	Phone	Fax	Class
Weavertown Environmental Group 2 Dorrington Rd .... Carnegie PA 15106 *TF:* 800-746-4850 ■ *Web:* www.weavertown.com	724-746-4850		187
Weavexx 51 Flex Way...................... Youngsville NC 27596 *Web:* www.xerium.com	919-556-7235	556-2432	745-3
WEB (Worldwide Employee Benefits Network Inc) 11520 N Central Expy Ste 201 .... Dallas TX 75243 **Fax Area Code:* 214 ■ *TF:* 888-795-6862 ■ *Web:* www.webnetwork.org	888-795-6862	382-3038*	49-12
Web Advanced 36 Discovery Ste 100 .... Irvine CA 92618 *Web:* www.webadvanced.com	949-453-1805		177
Web Age Solutions Inc 439 University Ave Ste 820.................... Toronto ON M5G1Y8 *TF:* 866-206-4644 ■ *Web:* www.webagesolutions.com	866-206-4644		225
Web Clients LLC 2300 Vartan Way Ste 100.................. Harrisburg PA 17110 *Web:* www.webclients.net	717-346-3600		195
Web Creations & Consulting L L C 119 W Iron Ave 3rd Fl......................... Salina KS 67401 *Web:* www.wccit.com	785-823-7630		180
Web Direct Brands Inc 13100 State Rd 54 .... Odessa FL 33556 *Web:* www.webdirectbrands.com	813-920-7259		225
Web Equipment 464 Central Rd .... Fredericksburg VA 22401 *TF:* 800-225-3858 ■ *Web:* www.webequipment.com	540-657-5855		190
Web Full Circle Inc 1000 NC Music Factory Blvd Ste B9........... Charlotte NC 28206 *TF:* 800-568-8213 ■ *Web:* www.webfullcircle.com	980-322-0518		225
Web Offset Printing Company Inc 12198 44th St N .... Clearwater FL 33762 *Web:* www.weboffsetprint.com	727-572-7488		627
Web Presence Architects LLC 10113 Meadowneck Ct.................. Silver Spring MD 20910 *Web:* wpaconsulting.com	301-587-3584		809
Web Talent Marketing 322 N Arch St Ste 120 .... Lancaster PA 17603 *Web:* www.webtalentmarketing.com	717-283-4045		195
Web Yoga Inc 938 Senate Dr.................... Dayton OH 45459 *Web:* www.webyoga.com	937-428-0000		180
Web Your Business Inc 226 Saxony Rd........ Johnstown CO 80534 *TF:* 800-669-2188 ■ *Web:* www.webyourbusiness.com	970-593-6260		225
Web.com 12808 Grand Bay Pkwy W .... Jacksonville FL 32258 *TF:* 800-338-1771 ■ *Web:* www.web.com	904-680-6600	880-0350	809
Webaloo LLC 217 Second St N .... Stillwater MN 55082 *Web:* www.webaloo.com	651-351-1041		177
Webapper Services Llc 117 E Mountain Ave Ste 222 .... Fort Collins CO 80524 *Web:* www.webapper.com	970-223-2278		396
WebAssist.com Corp 227 N El Camino Real Ste 204 .... Encinitas CA 92024 *Web:* www.webassist.com	760-633-4013		177
Webasto Roof Systems Inc 1757 Northfield Dr .... Rochester Hills MI 48309 *Web:* www.webasto.com	248-997-5100		60
Webb Automotive Group Inc 3911 E Main St......................... Farmington NM 87402 *Web:* webbauto.com	505-325-1911	325-1911	60
Webb Chemical Service Corp 2708 Jarman St .... Muskegon MI 49444 *Web:* www.webbchemical.com	231-733-2181	739-5454	146
Webb County 1110 Washington St .... Laredo TX 78040 *Web:* www.webbcounty.com	956-523-4143	523-5012	338
Webb Financial Group 7900 Xerxes Ave S Ste 1920............... Minneapolis MN 55431 *TF:* 800-927-9322 ■ *Web:* www.webbfinancial.com	952-837-3200		401
Webb Heating & Air Conditioning 170 Webb Way .... Advance NC 27006 *Web:* webbhvac.com	336-998-2121		189-10
Webb Institute 298 Crescent Beach Rd..................... Glen Cove NY 11542 **Fax:* Admissions ■ *TF:* 866-708-9322 ■ *Web:* webb.edu	516-671-2213	674-9838*	166
Webb Manufacturing Co 1241 Carpenter St....................... Philadelphia PA 19147 *Web:* www.webbmfg.com	215-336-5570	336-4422	733
Webb School PO Box 488 .... Bell Buckle TN 37020 *TF:* 888-733-9322 ■ *Web:* www.thewebbschool.com	931-389-9322	389-6657	622
Webb Schools 1175 W Baseline Rd........... Claremont CA 91711 *Web:* www.webb.org	909-482-5214		622
Webb Wheel Products Inc 2310 Industrial Dr SW .... Cullman AL 35055 **Fax:* Sales ■ *TF:* 800-633-3256 ■ *Web:* www.webbwheel.com	256-739-6660	739-6246*	60
Webb Writes Llc 1904 Frnt St................. Durham NC 27705 *Web:* www.webbwrites.com	919-384-8850		449
Webb; County Appraisal Distric 3302 Clark Blvd .... Laredo TX 78043 *TF:* 800-252-9121 ■ *Web:* www.webbcad.org	956-718-4091		41
WebBank Corp 215 S State St Ste 1000 .... Salt Lake City UT 84111 *TF:* 888-881-3789 ■ *Web:* www.webbank.com	801-456-8350		217
Webber International University 1201 N Scenic Hwy .... Babson Park FL 33827 **Fax Area Code:* 863 ■ **Fax:* Admissions ■ *TF:* 800-741-1844 ■ *Web:* webber.edu	800-741-1844	638-1591*	166
Webber Metal Products Inc 120 Industrial Park Rd .... Cascade IA 52033 *Web:* www.webbermetals.com	563-852-7122		454
Webber Supply Inc 32 Thatcher St.............. Bangor ME 04401 *Web:* www.webbersupply.com	207-942-7361		612
WEBB-FM 98.5 (Ctry) 56 Western Ave Ste 13 .... Augusta ME 04330 *Web:* www.b985.fm	207-623-4735	626-5948	645-13
WebbMason Analytics 53 Loveton Cir Ste 207......................... Sparks MD 21152 *Web:* www.spryinc.com	443-212-5072		781
WebbMason Inc 10830 Gilroy Rd .... Hunt Valley MD 21031 *Web:* www.webbmason.com	410-785-1111		627
Webb-Stiles Co 675 Liverpool Dr PO Box 464.............. Valley City OH 44280 *TF:* 800-677-0076 ■ *Web:* www.webb-stiles.com	330-225-7761	225-5532	207

	Phone	Fax	Class
WEBCARGO Inc 800 Pl Victoria Ste 2603 Tour de la bourse CP 329 .... Montreal QC H4Z1G8 *TF:* 866-905-0123 ■ *Web:* www.webcargo.net	866-905-0123		366
Webco Chemical Corp 420 W Main St .... Dudley MA 01571	508-943-9500	987-0366	151
Webco Hawaii Inc 2840 Mokumoa St .... Honolulu HI 96819 *Web:* www.awdhi.com	808-839-4551		231
Webco Industries Inc 9101 W 21st St PO Box 100............... Sand Springs OK 74063 *OTC: WEBC* ■ *Web:* www.webcoindustries.com	918-245-2211	245-0306	490
Webco Manufacturing Inc 15750 S Keeler Terr .... Olathe KS 66062 *Web:* www.webcomfg.com	913-764-7111		697
Webcrafters Inc 2211 Fordem Ave............. Madison WI 53704 *TF:* 800-356-8200 ■ *Web:* www.webcrafters-inc.com	608-244-3561	244-5120	626
WebeDoctor 471 W Lambert Rd Ste 102 .... Brea CA 92821 *Web:* webedoctor.com	714-990-3999		196
WEBE-FM 108 (AC) 2 Lafayette Sq .... Bridgeport CT 06604 *TF:* 800-932-3108 ■ *Web:* www.webe108.com	203-333-9108	384-0600	645-158
Weber & Sons Button Company Inc 1009 E Sixth St................................ Muscatine IA 52761	563-263-9451		594
Weber Advertising & Marketing 533 Janet Ave.................................. Lancaster PA 17601 *Web:* weberadvertising.com	717-299-1277		7
Weber Basin Water Conservancy District 2837 E Hwy 193 .... Layton UT 84040 *Web:* www.weberbasin.com	801-771-1677		787
Weber County 2380 Washington Blvd Ste 350 .... Ogden UT 84401 *TF:* 800-407-2757 ■ *Web:* www.webercountyutah.gov	801-399-8454	399-8314	338
Weber County Library 2464 Jefferson Ave......... Ogden UT 84401 *TF:* 866-678-5342 ■ *Web:* www.weberpl.lib.ut.us	801-337-2632	337-2615	434-3
Weber Farms 3559 Rd 'K' NW .... Quincy WA 98848	509-787-3620		10-11
Weber Gallagher Simpson Stapleton Fires & Newby LLP 2000 Market St Ste 1300 .... Philadelphia PA 19103 *Web:* www.wglaw.com	215-972-7900		428
Weber Group Inc 5233 Progress Way......... Sellersburg IN 47172 *Web:* webergroupinc.com	812-246-2100	246-2109	186
Weber Insurance Corp 505 Corporate Dr W .... Langhorne PA 19047 *TF:* 888-860-0400 ■ *Web:* weberinsurance.com	215-860-0400		390
Weber International Packing Company LLC 318 Cornelia St.......................... Plattsburgh NY 12901 *Web:* www.weberintl.com	518-561-8282	561-4509	98
Weber Logistics 13530 Rosecrans Ave.................. Santa Fe Springs CA 90670 *TF:* 855-469-3237 ■ *Web:* www.weberlogistics.com	855-469-3237		449
Weber Marketing Group Inc 225 Terry Ave North Ste 400........................ Seattle WA 98109 *Web:* www.webermarketing.com	206-340-6111		463
Weber Metals Inc 16706 Garfield Ave .... Paramount CA 90723 *Web:* webermetals.com	562-602-0260		483
Weber Obrien Ltd 5580 Monroe St............... Sylvania OH 43560 *Web:* www.weberobrien.com	419-885-8338		2
Weber Randy (Rep R - TX) 1708 Longworth HOB .... Washington DC 20515 *Web:* weber.house.gov	202-225-2831	225-0271	342-2
Weber Shandwick Worldwide 909 Third Ave............................... New York NY 10022 *Web:* www.webershandwick.com	212-445-8000		636
Weber Specialties Co 15230 S Us 131 .... Schoolcraft MI 49087 *Web:* www.weberspecialties.com	269-679-5160		492
Weber State University 3848 Harrison Blvd............................ Ogden UT 84408 *TF:* 800-848-7770 ■ *Web:* www.weber.edu	801-626-6000	626-6747	166
Davis 2750 N University Pk Blvd............... Layton UT 84041 **Fax:* Admissions ■ *TF:* 800-848-7770 ■ *Web:* www.weber.edu	801-395-3473	395-3538*	166
Stewart Library 3921 Central Campus Dr Dept. 2901........... Ogden UT 84408 *TF:* 877-306-3140 ■ *Web:* www.library.weber.edu	801-626-6403	626-7045	434-6
Weber's Inn 3050 Jackson Rd .... Ann Arbor MI 48103 *TF Resv:* 800-443-3050 ■ *Web:* www.webersinn.com	734-769-2500	769-4743	379
Weber-Knapp Co 441 Chandler St............. Jamestown NY 14701 *TF:* 800-828-9254 ■ *Web:* www.weberknapp.com	716-484-9135	484-9142	350
Weber-Stephen Products Co 200 E Daniels Rd .... Palatine IL 60067 *TF Cust Svc:* 800-446-1071 ■ *Web:* www.weber.com	800-446-1071		36
Webex Inc 1035 Breezewood Ln................ Neenah WI 54956 *Web:* www.webexinc.com	920-729-6666		629
WebEyeCare Inc 10 Canal St Ste 302............. Bristol PA 19007 *TF:* 888-536-7480 ■ *Web:* www.webeyecare.com	888-536-7480		366
WebiMax LLC 1300 Stage Coach Rd Ste A .... Ocean View NJ 08054 *TF:* 888-932-4629 ■ *Web:* www.webimax.com	212-710-1353		195
Webject Systems Inc 25 Central Sq Ste 2......................... Bridgewater MA 02324 *Web:* www.webject.com	508-279-6562		180
WebLinc LLC 22 S Third St 2nd Fl............ Philadelphia PA 19106 *Web:* weblinc.com	215-925-1800		225
WebLink International Inc 3905 W Vincennes Rd Ste 210............. Indianapolis IN 46268 *TF:* 800-382-1777 ■ *Web:* www.weblinkinternational.com	317-872-3909		225
Weblink Solutions 23950 Craftsman Rd........................ Calabasas CA 91302 *TF:* 866-296-1977 ■ *Web:* www.weblinkcorp.com	866-296-1977		224
Weblo.com Inc 930-2075 University St .... Montreal QC H3A2L1 *Web:* www.weblo.com	514-364-3636		387
Webmagic 87 N Raymond Ave Ste 850 .... Pasadena CA 91103 *Web:* www.webmagic.com	626-794-5000		177
WebmasterWorld Inc 3801 N Capital of Texas Hwy e240-181 .... Austin TX 78746 *Web:* www.webmasterworld.com	512-231-8107		225
WebMD 111 Eigth Ave Ste 7 .... New York NY 10011 *Web:* www.webmd.com	212-624-3700		356
WebMD Health Holdings Inc 111 Eigth Ave 7th Fl........................ New York NY 10011 *NASDAQ: WBMD* ■ *Web:* www.webmd.com	212-624-3700		39

				Phone	Fax	Class
WebNet Services Inc 247 Rt 100 *TF:* 866-923-4811 ■ *Web:* www.webnetservices.com	Somers	NY	10589	914-232-6900		177
WEbook Inc 307 Fifth Ave 7th Fl *Web:* www.webook.com	New York	NY	10016	646-453-8575		387
Weborg Feeding Co 1737 V Rd *TF:* 800-626-6639 ■ *Web:* www.weborgfeeding.com	Pender	NE	68047	402-385-3441	385-2441	10-1
WebQA Inc 900 S Frontage Rd Ste 110 *Web:* webqa.com	Woodridge	IL	60517	630-985-1300		174
WebReply.com Inc 1085 Worcester Rd *Web:* www.webreply.com	Natick	MA	01760	508-318-4600		387
WebRing Inc 500 A St Ste 2 *Web:* www.webring.com	Ashland	OR	97520	541-488-9895		225
Webroot Software Inc 2560 55th St *TF:* 800-772-9383 ■ *Web:* www.webroot.com	Boulder	CO	80301	303-442-3813	442-3846	178-12
Websense Inc 10240 Sorrento Valley Rd *NASDAQ: WBSN* ■ *TF:* 800-723-1166 ■ *Web:* www.forcepoint.com	San Diego	CA	92121	858-320-8000	458-2950	178-7
Website Magazine Inc 999 E Touhy Ave *TF:* 800-817-1518 ■ *Web:* www.websitemagazine.com	Des Plaines	IL	60018	773-628-2779		530
WebsiteBox Corp 245 Fairview Mall Dr Ste 401 *Web:* www.websitebox.com	Toronto	ON	M2J4T4	416-907-6981		224
Webster Bank Arena 600 Main St *TF:* 800-745-3000 ■ *Web:* www.websterbankarena.com	Bridgeport	CT	06604	203-345-2300		720
Webster Chamber of Commerce 1110 Crosspointe Ln Ste C *Web:* www.websterchamber.com	Webster	NY	14580	585-265-3960	265-3702	139
Webster City Federal Bancorp 820 Des Moines St *NYSE: WCFB* ■ *TF:* 866-519-4004 ■ *Web:* otcmarkets.com	Webster City	IA	50595	515-832-3071		360-2
Webster County 701 Central Ave *Web:* webstercountyia.org	Fort Dodge	IA	50501	515-573-1452		338
Webster County 101 S Crittenden St *Web:* www.webstercountymo.gov	Marshfield	MO	65706	417-468-2222	859-3614	338
Webster County PO Box 29	Preston	GA	31824	229-828-5775		338
Webster County 621 N Cedar St Ste 2 *Web:* www.co.webster.ne.us	Red Cloud	NE	68970	402-746-2716	746-2710	338
Webster County Webster County Courthouse 2 Ct Sq *Web:* www.webstercounty.wv.gov	Webster Springs	WV	26288	304-847-5780	847-5780	338
Webster County Clerk 25 US Hwy 41A S PO Box 19 *Web:* webstercountyclerk.ky.gov	Dixon	KY	42409	270-639-7006	639-7029	338
Webster Daniel (Rep R - FL) 1210 Longworth HOB *Web:* webster.house.gov	Washington	DC	20515	202-225-1002	225-0999	342-2
Webster Electric Co-op 1240 Spur Dr *TF:* 800-643-4305 ■ *Web:* www.websterec.com	Marshfield	MO	65706	417-859-2216		245
Webster Engineering & Mfg Company LLC 619 Industrial Rd *Web:* www.webster-engineering.com	Winfield	KS	67156	620-221-7464	221-9447	318
Webster Financial Corp PO Box 10305 *NYSE: WBS* ■ *TF:* 800-325-2424 ■ *Web:* www.websteronline.com	Waterbury	CT	06726	800-325-2424		360-2
Webster First Federal Credit Union 271 Greenwood St *TF:* 800-962-4452 ■ *Web:* www.websterfirst.com	Worcester	MA	01607	508-949-1043		71
Webster Industries Inc 95 Chestnut Ridge Rd **Fax Area Code: 570* ■ *TF:* 800-955-2374 ■ *Web:* www.aepinc.com	Montvale	NJ	07645	800-999-2374	474-9578*	66
Webster Industries Inc 325 Hall St *TF:* 800-243-9327 ■ *Web:* www.websterchain.com	Tiffin	OH	44883	419-447-8232	448-1618	207
Webster Parish Library 521 E & W Sts *Web:* www.webster.lib.la.us	Minden	LA	71055	318-371-3080		434-3
Webster Public Library 900 Ridge Rd ; Webster Plaza *Web:* www.websterlibrary.org	Webster	NY	14580	585-872-7075		434-3
Webster State Park 1210 Nine Rd *Web:* ksoutdoors.com/State-Parks/Locations/Webster	Stockton	KS	67669	785-425-6775		565
Webster Valve Co 583 S Main St	Franklin	NH	03235	603-934-5110		595
Webster-Hoff Corp 704 E Fullerton *Web:* www.webster-hoff.com	Glendale Heights	IL	60139	630-858-8030		567
Webster-Kirkwood Times Inc 122 W Lockwood Ave *Web:* www.websterkirkwoodtimes.com	St. Louis	MO	63119	314-968-2699		532-3
Webstone Company Inc 1 Appian Way *TF:* 800-225-9529 ■ *Web:* www.webstonevalves.com	Worcester	MA	01610	800-225-9529		612
Webtec Converting LLC 5900 Middle View Way *Web:* www.webtecllc.com	Knoxville	TN	37909	865-584-8273		3
Webtech Wireless Inc 4299 Canada Way Ste 215 *Web:* www.webtechwireless.com	Burnaby	BC	V5G1H3	604-434-7337		736
WebVision Inc 19950 Mariner Ave	Torrance	CA	90503	310-793-4500	793-4462	525
WebWisdom.com Inc Syracuse Technology Garden 235 Harrison St Ste 303 *TF:* 800-650-8591 ■ *Web:* www.collabworx.com	Syracuse	NY	13202	315-579-4330		225
Webwise Learning Inc 2626 E 82nd St Ste 330 *Web:* webwiselearning.com	Bloomington	MN	55425	952-883-0800		463
WEC (Warren Electric Co-op Inc) 320 E Main St PO Box 208 *TF:* 800-364-8640 ■ *Web:* www.warrenec.coop	Youngsville	PA	16371	814-563-7548	563-7012	245
Wecsys LLC 8825 Xylon Ave N *TF:* 888-493-2797 ■ *Web:* www.wecsysllc.com	Minneapolis	MN	55445	763-504-1069		75
WECT-TV Ch 6 (NBC) 322 Shipyard Blvd *Web:* www.wect.com	Wilmington	NC	28412	910-791-8070	791-9535	741
Wedding Day Diamonds 7901 Penn Ave S *Web:* www.weddingdaydiamonds.com	Bloomington	MN	55431	952-253-0235		410
Wedding Experience 2307 Douglas Rd Ste 400 *TF:* 866-223-9672 ■ *Web:* www.theweddingexperience.com	Coral Gables	FL	33145	305-421-1260		226

				Phone	Fax	Class
Wedding Gown Preservation Co 707 North St *Web:* www.gownpreservation.com	Endicott	NY	13760	607-748-6957		426
Wedding Ring Shop 1181 Kapiolani Blvd *TF:* 800-633-2553 ■ *Web:* www.weddingringshop.com	Honolulu	HI	96814	808-945-7766		410
Wedding Shoppe Inc, The 1196 Grand Ave *TF:* 877-294-4991 ■ *Web:* www.weddingshoppeinc.com	Saint Paul	MN	55105	651-298-1144		157-6
Weddings In Houston Lp 525 Arlington St *Web:* weddingsinhouston.com	Houston	TX	77007	713-464-4321	464-2880	637-9
Weddle Industries 7200 Hollister Ave Ste C *Web:* www.weddleindustries.com	Goleta	CA	93117	805-562-8600		61
Wedge Capital Management LLP 301 S College St Ste 2920 *Web:* www.wedgecapital.com	Charlotte	NC	28202	704-334-6475	334-3542	401
Wedge Community Co-Op Inc 2105 Lyndale Ave S *Web:* www.wedge.coop	Minneapolis	MN	55405	612-871-3993	871-0734	345
WEDGE Group Inc 1415 Louisiana St Ste 3000 *TF:* 888-563-5383 ■ *Web:* www.wedgegroup.com	Houston	TX	77002	713-739-6500		360-3
Wedgewood Hotel 845 Hornby St *TF:* 800-663-0666 ■ *Web:* www.wedgewoodhotel.com	Vancouver	BC	V6Z1V1	604-689-7777	608-5348	379
Wedgewood Resort Hotel 212 Wedgewood Dr **Fax Area Code: 907* ■ *TF:* 800-528-4916 ■ *Web:* www.fountainheadhotels.com	Fairbanks	AK	99701	800-528-4916	451-8184*	379
WEDG-FM 103.3 (Alt) 50 James E Casey Dr *Web:* www.wedg.com	Buffalo	NY	14206	716-881-4555	884-2931	645-25
Wedgworth Farms Inc 300 N Dixie Hwy Ste 471 *Web:* pbchistoryonline.org	West Palm Beach	FL	33401	561-832-4164	832-7965	10-9
Wedlock Paper Converters Ltd 2327 Stanfield Rd *Web:* www.wedlockpaper.com	Mississauga	ON	L4Y1R6	905-277-9461	272-1108	554
Wednesday Journal 141 S Oak Park Ave *Web:* www.chicagoparent.com	Oak Park	IL	60302	708-524-8300		532-3
WEDR-FM 99.1 (Urban) 2741 N 29th Ave *TF:* 800 327 2323 ■ *Web:* www.wedr.com	Hollywood	FL	33020	305-444-4404	444-4404	645
WEDU-TV Ch 3 (PBS) 1300 N Blvd *TF:* 800-354-9338 ■ *Web:* www.wedu.org	Tampa	FL	33607	813-254-9338	253-0826	741-133
Weecycle Environmental Consulting Inc 5375 Western Ave Ste B *TF:* 800-875-7033 ■ *Web:* www.weecycle-env.com	Boulder	CO	80301	303-413-0452		743
Weed Instrument Company Inc 707 Jeffrey Way *Web:* ultra-nspi.com	Round Rock	TX	78665	512-434-2900		201
Weed Man 2399 Royal Windsor Dr *Web:* www.weedmancanada.com	Mississauga	ON	L5J1K9	905-823-8300		577
Weed USA Inc 5780 Harrow Glen Ct *TF:* 800-933-3758 ■ *Web:* www.weedusa.com	Galena	OH	43021	740-548-3881	548-3882	710
Weeden & Company LP 145 Mason St *TF:* 800-843-3333 ■ *Web:* www.weedenco.com	Greenwich	CT	06830	203-861-7670		194
Weeden House Museum 300 Gates Ave SE *Web:* www.weedenhousemuseum.com	Huntsville	AL	35801	256-536-7718		520
Weedon Island Preserve Cultural & Natural History Ctr 1800 Weedon Dr NE *Web:* www.weedonislandcenter.org	Saint Petersburg	FL	33702	727-453-6500		50-5
WEEI-AM 850 (Sports) 20 Guest St 3rd Fl *TF:* 888-525-0850 ■ *Web:* www.weei.com	Brighton	MA	02135	617-779-3500		645
Weekends Only Inc 349 Marshall Ave 3rd Fl *TF:* 855-803-5888 ■ *Web:* www.weekendsonly.com	Saint Louis	MO	63119	314-447-1500		321
Weekleys Mailing Service Inc 1420 W Bagley Rd *TF:* 800-780-4707 ■ *Web:* www.weekleysmailing.com	Berea	OH	44017	440-234-4325		5
Weekly Alibi 217 Sierra Dr SE *Web:* www.alibi.com	Albuquerque	NM	87108	505-346-0660	256-9651	532-5
Weeks Marine Inc 4 Commerce Dr *TF:* 800-248-4479 ■ *Web:* www.weeksmarine.com	Cranford	NJ	07016	908-272-4010	272-4740	188-5
Weeks Seed Company Inc 1050 Moye Blvd *TF:* 800-322-1234 ■ *Web:* www.weeksseeds.com	Greenville	NC	27834	252-757-1234		694
Weeks Service Co 1306 Hwy 3 S *Web:* weeksservicecompany.com	League City	TX	77573	281-332-9555	332-9558	189-10
Weeks-Lerman Group 58-38 Page Pl *TF:* 800-544-5959 ■ *Web:* www.weekslerman.com	Maspeth	NY	11378	718-803-5000	821-1515	534
WEEK-TV Ch 25 (NBC) 2907 Springfield Rd *Web:* www.week.com	East Peoria	IL	61611	309-698-2525	698-9335	741
Weener Plastics Inc 2201 Stantonsburg Rd SE	Wilson	NC	27893	252-206-1400		608
Weetabix Co Inc 300 Nickerson Rd *TF:* 800-343-0590 ■ *Web:* www.weetabixusa.com	Marlborough	MA	01752	800-343-0590		296-4
WEF (Water Environment Federation) 601 Wythe St *TF:* 800-666-0206 ■ *Web:* www.wef.org	Alexandria	VA	22314	703-684-2400	684-2492	48-13
WEFT-FM 90.1 (Var) 113 N Market St *Web:* www.weft.org	Champaign	IL	61820	217-359-9338		645-30
WEG (West Essex Graphics Inc) 305 Fairfield Ave **Fax Area Code: 973* ■ *TF:* 800-221-5859 ■ *Web:* www.westessexgraphics.com	Fairfield	NJ	07004	800-221-5859	227-2906*	781
WEG Electric Corp 6655 Sugarloaf Pkwy *Web:* www.weg.net	Duluth	GA	30097	678-249-2000		767
Wege Pretzel Co PO Box 334 *TF:* 800-888-4646 ■ *Web:* www.wege.com	Hanover	PA	17331	800-888-4646		296-9
Wegener 11350 Technology Cir *OTC: WGNR* ■ *Web:* www.wegener.com	Johns Creek	GA	30097	770-814-4000	623-0698	647
Wegerzyn Gardens MetroPark 1301 E Siebenthaler Ave *Web:* www.metroparks.org	Dayton	OH	45414	937-275-7275		97

				Phone	Fax	Class
Wegmans Food Markets Inc 1500 Brooks Ave PO Box 30844 *TF:* 800-934-6267 ■ *Web:* www.wegmans.com	Rochester	NY	14603	585-328-2550		345
Wego Chemical & Mineral Corp 239 Great Neck Rd *Web:* www.wegochem.com	Great Neck	NY	11021	516-487-3510	487-3794	146
WEGW-FM 107.5 (Rock) 1015 Main St *TF:* 800-668-7426 ■ *Web:* www.iheart.com	Wheeling	WV	26003	304-232-1170	234-0041	645-174
Wehco Newspapers Inc 115 E Capitol Ave *Web:* wehco.com	Little Rock	AR	72201	501-378-3400	376-8594	532-3
Wehco Video Inc 115 E Capitol Ave *Web:* www.wehco.com	Little Rock	AR	72201	501-378-3529	376-8594	116
Wehr Nature Ctr 9701 W College Ave *Web:* county.milwaukee.gov	Franklin	WI	53132	414-425-8550		50-5
WEHT-TV 800 Marywood Dr **Fax Area Code: 270* ■ *TF:* 800-879-8542 ■ *Web:* www.tristatehomepage.com	Henderson	KY	42420	800-879-8549	827-0561*	741
WEI (Wieland Electric Inc) 49 International Rd *TF:* 800-943-5263 ■ *Web:* www.wielandinc.com	Burgaw	NC	28425	910-259-5050		246
Weibel 1 Winemaster Way *TF:* 800-932-9463 ■ *Web:* www.weibel.com	Lodi	CA	95240	209-365-9463	365-9469	80-3
Weichert Financial 6911 Laurel Bowie Rd	Bowie	MD	20715	301-805-7788		652
Weichert Realtors 1625 Rt 10 E *TF:* 800-401-0486 ■ *Web:* www.weichert.com	Morris Plains	NJ	07950	973-984-1400	984-4075	652
Weidenhammer Systems Corp 935 Berkshire Blvd *TF:* 866-497-2227 ■ *Web:* www.hammer.net	Reading	PA	19610	610-378-1149	378-9409	177
Weidert Group Inc 901 S Lawe St *TF:* 800-446-1552 ■ *Web:* www.weidert.com	Appleton	WI	54915	920-731-2771		636
Weidmann Diagnostic Solutions Inc 4011 Power Inn Rd Ste G *Web:* www.weidmann-diagnostics.com	Sacramento	CA	95826	916-455-2284		415
Weidmann Electrical Technology 1 Gordon Mills Way PO Box 903 *TF:* 800-242-6748 ■ *Web:* weidmann-electrical.com	Saint Johnsbury	VT	05819	802-748-8106	748-8630	816
Weidmuller Inc 821 Southlake Blvd *TF Cust Svc:* 800-849-9343 ■ *Web:* www.weidmuller.com	Richmond	VA	23236	804-794-2877	379-2593	815
Weidner Ctr for the Performing Arts 2420 Nicolet Dr University of Wisconsin at Green Bay *TF:* 800-895-0071 ■ *Web:* www.weidnercenter.com	Green Bay	WI	54311	920-465-2726	465-2619	572
Weidt Group Inc, The 5800 Baker Rd Ste 100 *Web:* theweidtgroup.com	Minnetonka	MN	55345	952-938-1588		177
Weigel Broadcasting 26 N Halstead St *Web:* www.metv.com	Chicago	IL	60661	312-705-2600		738
Weight Management Centers 2605 W Swann Ave Ste 600 *Web:* www.weightmanagement.com	Tampa	FL	33609	813-876-7073	877-1277	810
Weightech 1649 Country Elite Dr *TF:* 800-457-3720 ■ *Web:* www.weightechinc.com	Waldron	AR	72958	479-637-4182		361
Weik Investment Services Inc 1075 Berkshire Blvd Ste 825 *Web:* weikinvest.com	Wyomissing	PA	19610	610-376-2240		796
Weil Co, The 11236 El Camino Real Ste 200 *TF:* 800-355-9345 ■ *Web:* www.cweil.com	San Diego	CA	92130	858-724-6040	724-6080	401
Weil Gotshal & Manges LLP 767 Fifth Ave *Web:* www.weil.com	New York	NY	10153	212-310-8000	310-8007	428
Weil Program on Collaborative Governance Ctr for Business & Government, The Harvard Univ John F Kennedy School of Government 79 JFK St *Web:* www.hks.harvard.edu/m-rcbg/wpcg	Cambridge	MA	02138	617-496-0587	496-6104	634
Weil Pump Co W57 N14363 Doerr Wy PO Box 887 *TF:* 800-960-0068 ■ *Web:* www.weilpump.com	Cedarburg	WI	53012	262-377-1399	377-0515	641
Weiland Sliding Doors & Windows Inc 2601 Industry St *Web:* www.weilandslidingdoors.com	Oceanside	CA	92054	760-722-8828		499
Weiler Corp 1 Wildwood Dr *TF Cust Svc:* 800-835-9999 ■ *Web:* www.weilercorp.com	Cresco	PA	18326	570-595-7495	595-2002	103
Weiler Engineering Inc 1395 Gateway Dr *Web:* www.weilerengineering.com	Elgin	IL	60123	847-697-4900	697-4915	547
Weill Cornell Medical College 1300 York Ave *Web:* weill.cornell.edu	New York	NY	10065	212-746-5454		434-1
Weill Cornell Medicine 445 E 69th St **Fax: Admissions* ■ *TF:* 800-422-0711 ■ *Web:* weill.cornell.edu	New York	NY	10021	212-746-5454	746-8052*	167-2
Weil-McLain Co 500 Blaine St *Web:* www.weil-mclain.com	Michigan City	IN	46360	219-879-6561	879-4025	91
Weimar College 20601 W Paoli Ln PO Box 486 *Web:* weimar.edu	Weimar	CA	95736	530-637-4111	422-7949	166
Weimar Junior High School 101 N W St	Weimar	TX	78962	979-725-9515		685
Wein Products Inc 115 W 25th St *Web:* www.weinproducts.com	Los Angeles	CA	90007	213-749-6049	749-6250	591
Weinberg Capital Group 5005 Rockside Rd Ste 1140 *Web:* www.weinbergcap.com	Cleveland	OH	44131	216-503-8303		5
Weinberg Group Inc, The 1129 20th St NW Ste 300 *Web:* www.weinberggroup.com	Washington	DC	20036	202-833-8077		193
Weinberg-King State Park PO Box 203	Augusta	IL	62311	217-392-2345		565
Weinbrenner Shoe Co Inc 108 S Polk St *TF General:* 800-569-6817 ■ *Web:* www.weinbrennerusa.com	Merrill	WI	54452	715-536-5521	536-1172	301
Weiner Iron & Metal Corp PO Box 359	Pottsville	PA	17901	570-622-6543		686
Weiner Law Group LLP 629 Parsippany Rd *Web:* www.weinerlesniak.com	Parsippany	NJ	07054	973-403-1100		428
Weingart Foundation 1055 W Seventh St Ste 3050 *Web:* www.weingartfnd.org	Los Angeles	CA	90017	213-688-7799	688-1515	305
Weingarten Realty Investors 2600 Citadel Plaza Dr Ste 125 *NYSE: WRI* ■ *TF:* 800-688-8865 ■ *Web:* www.weingarten.com	Houston	TX	77008	713-866-6000	866-6049	655
Weingartz Supply Co 46061 Van Dyke Ave *TF:* 855-669-7278 ■ *Web:* weingartz.com	Utica	MI	48317	586-731-7240		323
Weinrib & Connor 297 Knollwood Rd *Web:* www.weinconn.com	White Plains	NY	10607	914-686-3900		7
Weinstein & Anastasio PC 2319 Whitney Ave Ste 2a	Hamden	CT	06518	203-397-2525		2
Weinstein Company LLC, The 345 Hudson St *Web:* www.weinsteinco.com	New York	NY	10014	646-862-3400		514
Weinstock Lamp Company Inc 34-30 Steinway St *Web:* www.weinstocklighting.com	Long Island	NY	11101	718-729-4848		246
Weintraub Adv Inc 7745 Carondelet Ave Ste 308 *Web:* www.weintraubadv.com	Saint Louis	MO	63105	314-721-5050	721-6850	4
WEIQ-TV Ch 42 (PBS) 2112 11th Ave S Ste 400 *TF:* 800-239-5233 ■ *Web:* www.aptv.org	Birmingham	AL	35205	205-328-8756	251-2192	741-15
Weir 2494 S Railroad Ave *Web:* www.global.weir/brands/floway	Fresno	CA	93707	559-442-4000	442-3098	641
Weir & Partners LLP The Widener Bldg 1339 Chestnut St Ste 500 *Web:* www.weirpartners.com	Philadelphia	PA	19107	215-665-8181		428
Weir Canada Inc 2360 Millrace Ct *Web:* www.global.weir/industries/power	Mississauga	ON	L5N1W2	905-812-7100		791
Weir Farm National Historic Site 735 Nod Hill Rd *TF:* 800-735-3503 ■ *Web:* www.nps.gov/wefa	Wilton	CT	06897	203-834-1896	834-2421	564
Weir Group PLC, The 225 N Cedar St PO Box 488 *Web:* www.global.weir	Hazleton	PA	18201	570-455-7711	459-2586	641
Weir Group, The 2701 S Stoughton Rd *Web:* www.global.weir	Madison	WI	53716	608-221-2261	221-5807	641
Weir International Inc 1431 Opus Pl Executive Towers W I Ste 210 *TF:* 800-369-6220 ■ *Web:* www.weirintl.com	Downers Grove	IL	60515	630-968-5400		261
Weir's Furniture Village Inc 3219 Knox St *Web:* www.weirsfurniture.com	Dallas	TX	75205	214-528-0321		321
WeirFoulds LLP 4100 - 66 Wellington St W Toronto-Dominion Centre PO Box 35 *TF:* 800-881-1625 ■ *Web:* www.weirfoulds.com	Toronto	ON	M5K1B7	416-365-1110		428
Weirton Medical Ctr 601 Colliers Way *TF:* 800-994-6610 ■ *Web:* www.weirtonmedical.com	Weirton	WV	26062	304-797-6000	797-6176	374-3
Weis Builders Inc 2227 Seventh St NW *Web:* www.weisbuilders.com	Rochester	MN	55901	507-288-2041		186
Weis Markets 1000 S Second St PO Box 471 *NYSE: WMK* ■ *TF:* 866-999-9347 ■ *Web:* www.weismarkets.com	Sunbury	PA	17801	866-999-9347		345
Weis Markets Inc 16 Industrial Park Rd *Web:* www.weismarkets.com	Milton	PA	17847	570-742-2500		345
Weis/Robart Partitions Inc 3501 E La Palma Ave *Web:* www.weisrobart.com	Anaheim	CA	92806	714-666-0108	666-0110	286
Weiser 19701 Da Vinci *TF:* 800-677-5625 ■ *Web:* www.weiserlock.com	Lake Forest	CA	92610	800-677-5625		350
Weiser Iron Inc 15488 Arrow Rte *Web:* www.weiseriron.com	Fontana	CA	92335	909-429-4600		480
Weiser LLP 135 W 50th St *Web:* weisermazars.com	New York	NY	10020	212-812-7000	375-6888	2
Weiser Metal Products 34311 E M72 PO Box 370 *Web:* www.weisermetal.com	Lincoln	MI	48742	989-736-6055	736-6717	295
Weiser Security Services Inc 3939 Tulane Ave *Web:* www.weisersecurity.com	New Orleans	LA	70119	504-949-7558		693
Weisman Art Museum 333 E River Pkwy *Web:* www.weisman.umn.edu	Minneapolis	MN	55455	612-625-9494		520
Weiss Instruments Inc 905 Waverly Ave *Web:* www.weissinstruments.com	Holtsville	NY	11742	631-207-1200	207-0900	202
Weiss Lake Egg Company Inc 9602 County Rd 59	Centre	AL	35960	256-927-5546		10-8
Weiss Research Inc 15430 Endeavour Dr *TF:* 800-291-8545 ■ *Web:* www.weissinc.com	Jupiter	FL	33478	800-291-8545		401
Weiss-Aug Company Inc 220 Merry Ln *Web:* www.weiss-aug.com	East Hanover	NJ	07936	973-887-7600	887-8109	488
Weissberg & Speller CPA'S PC 3601 Hempstead Tpke *Web:* weissbergandspeller.com	Levittown	NY	11756	516-796-2727		2
Weisshouse 324 S Highland Ave *Web:* weisshouse.com	Pittsburgh	PA	15206	412-441-8888		290
Weissman 1 Alliance Ctr 3500 Lenox Rd 4th Fl *Web:* www.wncwlaw.com	Atlanta	GA	30326	404-926-4500		445
Weitz Company Inc 5901 Thornton Ave *TF:* 800-999-3586 ■ *Web:* www.weitz.com	Des Moines	IA	50321	515-246-4700		186
Weitz/Cohen Construction Co 4725 S Monaco St Ste 100 *TF:* 800-369-6977 ■ *Web:* www.weitz.com	Denver	CO	80237	303-860-6600	860-6698	186
Wejl 149 Penn Ave *Web:* nepasespnradio.com	Scranton	PA	18503	570-346-6555	346-6038	645-149
WEJZ-FM 96.1 (AC) 6440 Atlantic Blvd *Web:* www.wejz.com	Jacksonville	FL	32211	904-727-9696		645-79
Wekiwa Springs State Park 1800 Wekiwa Cir *Web:* www.floridastateparks.org/wekiwasprings	Apopka	FL	32712	407-884-2008	884-2039	565
WEKU-FM 88.9 (Clas) 521 Lancaster Ave 102 Perkins Bldg-EKU *TF:* 800-621-8890 ■ *Web:* www.weku.fm	Richmond	KY	40475	800-621-8890		645

Name / Address	City	State	Zip	Phone	Fax	Class
Wel Companies Inc 1625 S Broadway PO Box 5610 *TF:* 800-333-4415 ■ *Web:* www.welcompanies.com	De Pere	WI	54115	920-339-0110		780
Weland Clinical Laboratories PC 1911 First Ave SE *TF:* 800-728-1503 ■ *Web:* www.welandlaboratories.com	Cedar Rapids	IA	52402	319-366-1503		415
Welborn Baptist Foundation Inc 21 SE Third St Ste 610 *Web:* welbornfdn.org	Evansville	IN	47708	812-437-8260	437-8269	48-20
Welborn Sullivan Meck & Tooley 821 17th St Ste 500 *TF:* 800-973-1177 ■ *Web:* www.wsmtlaw.com	Denver	CO	80202	303-830-2500		428
Welbro Bldg Corp 2301 Maitland Ctr Pkwy Ste 250 *Web:* www.welbro.com	Maitland	FL	32751	407-475-0800	475-0801	186
Welch & Forbes LLC 45 School St Fifth Fl Old City Hall *Web:* www.welchforbes.com	Boston	MA	02108	617-523-1635		528
Welch & Rushe Inc 391 Prince George's Blvd *TF:* 800-683-3852 ■ *Web:* www.welchandrushe.com	Upper Marlboro	MD	20774	301-430-6000		186
Welch Allyn Medical Products 4341 State St Rd *TF:* 800-289-2500 ■ *Web:* www.welchallyn.com	Skaneateles Falls	NY	13152	315-685-4100	685-4091	250
Welch Allyn Monitoring Inc 8500 SW Creekside Pl *TF Cust Svc:* 800-289-2500 ■ *Web:* welchallyn.com	Beaverton	OR	97008	503-530-7500	526-4200	250
Welch Capital Partners LLC 122 E 42nd St Ste 5105 *Web:* www.welchcapital.com	New York	NY	10168	212-754-6077		401
Welch Global Consulting 10084 Oak Knoll Terr *Web:* www.welchgc.com	Colorado Springs	CO	80920	970-292-6600		196
Welch Gold & Siegel Pc 428 Forbes Ave Ste 1240 *Web:* www.wgspc.com	Pittsburgh	PA	15219	412-391-1014		428
Welch Group LLC, The 3940 Montclair Rd *TF:* 800-709-7100 ■ *Web:* www.welchgroup.com	Birmingham	AL	35213	205-879-5001	879-7979	528
Welch Medical Library 1900 E Monument St *Web:* welch.jhmi.edu	Baltimore	MD	21205	410-955-3410		434-1
Welch Packaging Group 1020 Herman St *TF:* 800-246-2475 ■ *Web:* www.welchpkg.com	Elkhart	IN	46516	574-295-2460	295-1527	100
Welch Peter (Rep D - VT) 2303 Rayburn HOB *Web:* www.welch.house.gov	Washington	DC	20515	202-225-4115		342 2
Welch's Inc 300 Baker Ave Ste 101 *Web:* www.welchs.com	Concord	MA	01742	978-371-1000		296-20
Welcome Aboard Travel 57 Saulsbury Rd Ste C *Web:* welcomeaboard.net	Dover	DE	19904	302-678-9480		775
Welcome Enterprises Inc 6 W 18th St Ste 4B *Web:* www.welcomebooks.com	New York	NY	10011	212-989-3200		94
Welcome Wagon International Inc 5830 Coral Ridge Dr Ste 240 *TF:* 800-779-3526 ■ *Web:* www.welcomewagon.com	Coral Springs	FL	33076	800-779-3526		5
WelcomeMat Services Inc 3348 Peachtree Rd 200 Tower Pl Ste 1095 *Web:* www.welcomematservices.com	Atlanta	GA	30326	404-841-2226		41
Welcomm Inc 7975 Raytheon Rd Ste 340 *Web:* www.welcomm.com	San Diego	CA	92111	858-279-1611		636
Weld County PO Box 758 *Web:* www.weldgov.com	Greeley	CO	80632	970-336-7204	352-0242	338
Weld Mold Co 750 Rickett Rd *TF:* 800-521-9755 ■ *Web:* www.weldmold.com	Brighton	MI	48116	810-229-9521	229-9580	811
Weldaloy Products Co 11551 Stephens *Web:* www.weldaloy.com	Warren	MI	48089	586-758-5550		811
Weldangrind Ltd 10323 174 St NW *TF:* 866-226-2414 ■ *Web:* www.weldangrind.ca	Edmonton	AB	T5S1H1	780-484-3030		757
Weld-Built Body Co Inc 276 Long Island Ave *TF:* 800-965-1009 ■ *Web:* www.weldbuilt.com	Wyandanch	NY	11798	631-643-9700	491-4728	516
Welded Construction LP 26933 Eckel Rd *Web:* www.welded.com	Perrysburg	OH	43551	419-874-3548	874-4883	188-10
Welded Fixtures Inc 8155 Byron Rd *TF:* 800-648-8479 ■ *Web:* www.weldedfixtures.com	Whittier	CA	90606	562-907-7007		5
Welded Ring Products Company Inc 2180 W 114th St *Web:* www.weldedring.com	Cleveland	OH	44102	216-961-3800		295
Welded Tubes Inc 135 Penniman Rd *Web:* www.weldedtubes.com	Orwell	OH	44076	440-437-5144	437-5180	490
Welder Exploration & Production Inc 100 W Olmos Dr *Web:* www.weldergroup.com	San Antonio	TX	78212	210-354-1515		538
Welder Training & Testing Institute 1144 N Graham St *TF:* 800-923-9884 ■ *Web:* www.welderinstitute.com	Allentown	PA	18109	610-820-9551	820-0271	800
Welding Technology Corp 24775 Crestview Ct *Web:* www.weldtechcorp.com	Farmington Hills	MI	48335	248-477-3900		203
Weldmac Manufacturing Co 1451 N Johnson Ave *TF:* 800-252-1533 ■ *Web:* www.weldmac.com	El Cajon	CA	92020	619-440-2300	440-8723	454
Weldmation Inc 31720 Stephenson Hwy *Web:* www.weldmation.com	Madison Heights	MI	48071	248-585-0010		811
Weldments Inc 10720 N Second St *Web:* weldmentsinc.com	MACHESNEY PARk	IL	61115	815-633-3393	633-2524	482
Weldon Cooper Ctr-Public Service 2400 Old Ivy Rd *Web:* www.coopercenter.org	Charlottesville	VA	22903	434-982-5522		166
Weldon Huston & Keyser L L P 28 Park Ave W Bank One Bldg *Web:* www.whkmansfield.com	Mansfield	OH	44902	419-524-9811		445
Weldon Materials 141 Central Ave *Web:* www.weldonmat.com	Westfield	NJ	07090	908-233-4444	233-4215	46
Weldon Mechanical Corp 3428 W Pioneer Pkwy *Web:* www.weldon-contractors.com	Arlington	TX	76013	817-460-1111	460-3111	610
Weldon Springs State Park 4734 Weldon Springs Rd RR 2 PO Box 87 *Web:* sanjose.place.hyatt.com	Clinton	IL	61727	217-935-2644		565
Weldon Williams & Lick Inc 711 N A St *TF:* 800-242-4995 ■ *Web:* www.wwlinc.com	Fort Smith	AR	72901	479-783-4113	783-7050	627
Weldship Corp 225 W Second St *TF:* 800-535-6957 ■ *Web:* www.weldship.com	Bethlehem	PA	18015	610-861-7330		295
Weldstar Inc 1750 Mitchell Rd *TF:* 800-774-9063 ■ *Web:* www.weldstar.com	Aurora	IL	60505	630-859-3100		358
Weldylamont Assoc Inc 1040 W NW Hwy *Web:* www.weldy-lamont.com	Mount Prospect	IL	60056	847-398-4510		246
Welex Inc 1600 Union Meeting Rd *Web:* www.welex.com	Blue Bell	PA	19422	215-542-8000	542-9841	386
WELF-TV Ch 23 (TBN) 384 S Campus Rd *Web:* www.tbn.org	Lookout Mountain	GA	30750	706-820-1663		741
Welk Resort Branson 8860 Lawrence Welk Dr *TF:* 800-505-9355 ■ *Web:* welkresorts.com	Escondido	CA	92026	417-336-3575		669
Welk Resort San Diego 8860 Lawrence Welk Dr *TF Resv:* 800-932-9355 ■ *Web:* welkresorts.com	Escondido	CA	92026	760-749-3000	749-9537	669
Welker Inc 13839 W Bellfort *TF:* 800-776-7267 ■ *Web:* www.welker.com	Sugar Land	TX	77498	281-491-2331		539
Welkin Sciences LLC 102 S Tejon St Ste 200 *Web:* www.welkinsciences.com	Colorado Springs	CO	80903	719-520-5115		261
Welkinweir 1368 Prizer Rd *Web:* www.welkinweir.org	Pottstown	PA	19465	610-469-7543		97
Well Luck Company Inc 104 Harbor Dr *Web:* www.wellluck.com	Jersey City	NJ	07305	201-434-1177		805
Well Power Inc 11111 Katy Fwy Ste 910	Houston	TX	77079	713-973-5738		539
Well Spa at Miramonte Resort 45000 Indian Wells Ln *TF:* 800-237-2926 ■ *Web:* www.miramonteresort.com	Indian Wells	CA	92210	760-837-1652		707
Well Spouse Assn 63 W Main St Ste H *TF:* 800-838-0879 ■ *Web:* www.wellspouse.org	Freehold	NJ	07728	732-577-8899	577-8644	48-6
WELL, The 1195 Park Ave Ste 206 *Web:* www.well.com	Emeryville	CA	94608	415-343-5731		171
Wella Corp 6109 DeSoto Ave *TF:* 800-829-4422 ■ *Web:* www.wella.com	Woodland Hills	CA	91367	818-999-5112		214
Welland County General Hospital 65 Third St *Web:* www.niagarahealth.on.ca	Welland	ON	L3B4W6	905-732-6111		374-2
Welland/Pelham Chamber of Commerce 32 E Main St	Welland	ON	L3B3W3	905-732-7515		137
WellAware Holdings Inc 2330 N Loop 1604 W Ste 110 *TF:* 800-888-6400 ■ *Web:* www.wellaware.us	San Antonio	TX	78248	210-816-4600		387
Wellbore Navigation Inc 15032 Red Hill Ave Ste D *Web:* www.welnavinc.com	Tustin	CA	92780	714-259-7760		529
Wellbridge Co 6140 Greenwood Plaza Blvd *Web:* www.wellbridge.com	Greenwood Village	CO	80111	303-866-0800		354
WellCare Group Health plans 8735 Henderson Rd *TF:* 800-960-2530 ■ *Web:* www.wellcare.com	Tampa	FL	33634	813-290-6200		391-3
WellCare Health Plans Inc PO Box 31372 *TF:* 866-530-9491 ■ *Web:* www.wellcare.com/healthplans/newyork/home.aspx	Tampa	FL	33631	866-530-9491		391-3
WellCare of Georgia Inc 8725 Henderson Rd *TF:* 800-919-8807 ■ *Web:* www.wellcare.com/georgia	Tampa	FL	33634	800-919-8807		390
Wellcorp Express Inc 17110 S Main St *Web:* www.welltonexpress.com.hk	Gardena	CA	90248	310-645-6410		311
Weller/Obrien Insurance Services 720 Kelly Ave *Web:* wellerobrien.com	Half Moon Bay	CA	94019	650-726-6328		390
Wellers Utility Trailers 16889 N Main St *Web:* www.pacetrailers.com	Bridgeville	DE	19933	302-337-8228		54
Wellesley Bank 40 Central St *Web:* wellesleybank.com	Wellesley	MA	02482	781-235-2550		70
Wellesley Chamber of Commerce 1 Hollis St Ste 232 *TF:* 800-832-3747 ■ *Web:* www.wellesleychamber.org	Wellesley	MA	02482	781-235-2446	235-7326	139
Wellesley College 106 Central St **Fax:* Admissions ■ *Web:* www.wellesley.edu	Wellesley	MA	02481	781-283-1000	283-3678*	166
Wellesley Free Library 530 Washington St *Web:* www.ci.wellesley.ma.us	Wellesley	MA	02482	781-235-1610		434-3
Wellesley Island State Park 44927 Cross Island Rd *Web:* parks.ny.gov/parks/52/details.aspx	Fineview	NY	13640	315-482-2722		565
Wellesley Volkswagen Buick Inc 231 Linden St *Web:* buywellesleyvw.com	Wellesley	MA	02482	781-237-3553		57
Welles-Turner Memorial Library 2407 Main St *TF:* 800-411-9671 ■ *Web:* www.wtmlib.com	Glastonbury	CT	06033	860-652-7719	652-7721	434-3
Wellex Corp 551 Brown Rd *Web:* www.wellex.com	Fremont	CA	94539	510-743-1818	743-1899	253
Wellford Energy Group LLC 110 E 42nd St Ste 1310 *Web:* www.wellfordenergy.com	New York	NY	10017	212-913-9890		463
Welligent Inc 5205 Colley Ave *TF:* 888-317-5960 ■ *Web:* www.welligent.com	Norfolk	VA	23508	888-317-5960		177
Wellington Foods Inc 1930 California Ave *Web:* www.wellingtonfoods.com	Corona	CA	92881	951-547-7000		297-8

				Phone	Fax	Class
Wellington Hotel 871 Seventh Ave TF: 800-652-1212 ■ Web: www.wellingtonhotel.com	New York	NY	10019	212-247-3900	581-1350	379
Wellington Industries Inc 39555 S I-94 Service Dr TF: 800-477-3182 ■ Web: www.wellingtonind.com	Belleville	MI	48111	734-942-1060	942-9430	489
Wellington Management Company LLP 280 Congress St TF: 800-379-7873 ■ Web: www.wellington.com	Boston	MA	02210	617-951-5000		401
Wellington Power Corp 177 Thorn Hill Rd Web: www.wellingtonpower.com	Warrendale	PA	15086	724-779-4000		189-4
Wellington Resort 551 Thames St TF: 800-228-2968 ■ Web: www.wellingtonresort.com	Newport	RI	02840	401-849-1770	847-6250	379
Wellington State Park 614 W Shore Rd Web: www.nhstateparks.org	Bristol	NH	03222	603-744-2197		565
Wellman Advanced Materials 520 Kingsburg Hwy Web: www.wellmanplastics.com	Johnsonville	SC	29555	843-386-2011		601
Wellness Coaches USA LLC 725 Skippack Pk Ste 300 Web: www.wellnesscoachesusa.com	Blue Bell	PA	19422	215-628-4454		260
Wellness Enterprises LLC 418 SW 140th Terr Web: www.naturallyfiltered.com	Newberry	FL	32669	352-333-0480		612
Wellness International Network Ltd 5700 Tennyson Pkwy Ste 350	Plano	TX	75024	972-943-5200		195
Wellness Layers Inc 336 Atlantic Ave Ste 301 Web: www.wellnesslayers.com	East Rockaway	NY	11518	212-595-1270		177
Wells & Assoc 1420 Spring Hill Rd Ste 610 Web: www.wellsandassociates.com	Tysons	VA	22102	703-917-6620		256
Wells & Drew Cos 3414 Galilee Rd TF: 800-342-8636 ■ Web: www.wellsdrew.com	Jacksonville	FL	32207	904-399-1510		627
Wells Bloomfield Industries 10 Sunnen Dr *Fax Area Code: 800 ■ TF: 888-356-5362 ■ Web: www.wellsbloomfield.com	Saint Louis	MO	63143	888-356-5362	264-6666*	298
Wells Cargo Inc 1503 W McNaughton St TF: 800-348-7553 ■ Web: www.wellscargo.com	Elkhart	IN	46514	574-264-9661	264-5938	779
Wells Coleman & Co 3800 Patterson Ave Web: www.wellscoleman.com	Richmond	VA	23221	804-358-1150		2
Wells College 170 Main St *Fax: Admissions ■ TF Admissions: 800-952-9355 ■ Web: www.wells.edu	Aurora	NY	13026	315-364-3266	364-3227*	166
Wells Concrete Products Inc 835 Hwy 109 NE PO Box 308 TF: 800-658-7049 ■ Web: www.wellsconcrete.com	Wells	MN	56097	507-553-3138	553-6089	183
Wells County 102 W Market St Ste 201 Web: www.wellscounty.org	Bluffton	IN	46714	260-824-6479	824-6559	338
Wells County 700 Railway St N Web: www.wellscountynd.com	Fessenden	ND	58438	701-547-3122		338
Wells County Public Library 200 W Washington St TF: 800-824-6111 ■ Web: www.wellscolibrary.org	Bluffton	IN	46714	260-824-1612	824-3129	434-3
Wells Enterprises Inc 1 Blue Bunny Dr TF All: 888-309-1742 ■ Web: www.wellsenterprisesinc.com	Le Mars	IA	51031	712-546-4000	548-3008	296-25
Wells Fargo 420 Montgomery St NYSE: WFC ■ TF: 800-877-4833 ■ Web: www.wellsfargo.com	San Francisco	CA	94104	800-877-4833		216
Wells Fargo Bank 5622 Third St TF: 800-869-3557 ■ Web: www.wellsfargo.com	Katy	TX	77493	281-391-2101		70
Wells Fargo Bank Indiana NA 111 E Wayne St TF: 800-869-3557 ■ Web: www.wellsfargo.com	Fort Wayne	IN	46802	260-461-6430		70
Wells Fargo Bank Iowa NA 666 Walnut St PO Box 837 TF: 800-869-3557 ■ Web: www.wellsfargo.com	Des Moines	IA	50309	800-869-3557		70
Wells Fargo Bank Minnesota South NA 21 First St SW TF: 800-869-3557 ■ Web: www.wellsfargo.com	Rochester	MN	55902	507-285-2800		70
Wells Fargo Bank Montana NA 175 N 27th St Web: www.wellsfargo.com	Billings	MT	59101	406-657-1903		70
Wells Fargo Bank NA 420 Montgomery St TF: 800-869-3557 ■ Web: www.wellsfargo.com	San Francisco	CA	94104	415-222-4292		70
Wells Fargo Bank Nebraska NA 1919 Douglas St TF: 800-869-3557 ■ Web: www.wellsfargo.com	Omaha	NE	68102	402-536-2022		70
Wells Fargo Bank South Dakota NA 101 N Phillips Ave Web: www.wellsfargo.com	Sioux Falls	SD	57104	605-575-6900		70
Wells Fargo Bank Texas NA 707 Castroville Rd TF: 800-869-3557 ■ Web: www.wellsfargo.com	San Antonio	TX	78237	210-856-6224		70
Wells Fargo Dealer Services 23 Pasteur Web: www.wellsfargodealerservices.com	Irvine	CA	92618	949-930-4150	754-7350	217
Wells Fargo Education Financial Services PO Box 5185 TF: 800-658-3567 ■ Web: www.wellsfargo.com	Sioux Falls	SD	57117	800-658-3567	456-0561	217
Wells Fargo Equipment Finance Inc 733 Marquette Ave Ste 700 TF: 877-322-8228 ■ Web: www.wellsfargo.com	Minneapolis	MN	55402	612-667-9876		216
Wells Fargo Financial Inc 800 Walnut St TF: 800-735-3008 ■ Web: wellsfargo.com	Des Moines	IA	50309	515-280-7741		217
Wells Fargo History Museum 333 S Grand Ave Web: www.wellsfargohistory.com	Los Angeles	CA	90071	213-253-7166		520
Wells Fargo History Museum 420 Montgomery St TF: 800-678-8813 ■ Web: www.wellsfargohistory.com	San Francisco	CA	94163	415-396-2619		520
Wells Fargo History Museum 400 Capitol Mall Web: www.wellsfargohistory.com	Sacramento	CA	95814	916-440-4161		520
Wells Fargo Home Mortgage 2840 Ingersoll Ave TF: 800-401-1957 ■ Web: www.wellsfargo.com/mortgage	Des Moines	IA	50312	515-237-5196		509
Wells Fargo Insurance Inc 600 S Hwy 169 Web: www.wellsfargo.com	Saint Louis Park	MN	55426	612-667-5600	667-2681	390
Wells Home Furnishings 101 Bowers Rd Web: www.wellshome.com	Charleston	WV	25314	304-343-3600		321
Wells Johnson Co 8000 S Kolb Rd TF: 800-528-1597 ■ Web: www.wellsgrp.com	Tucson	AZ	85756	520-298-6069		476
Wells Lamont Industry Group 6640 W Touhy Ave TF: 800-247-3295 ■ Web: wellslamontindustrial.com	Niles	IL	60714	800-247-3295		155-8
Wells Printing Company Inc 6030 Perimeter Pkwy TF: 800-264-4958 ■ Web: www.wellsprinting.com	Montgomery	AL	36116	334-281-3449		627
Wells Rug Service Inc 49 Bank St Web: www.wellsrug.com	Morristown	NJ	07960	973-539-3800		362
Wells Rural Electric Co 1451 Humboldt Ave Web: www.wrec.coop	Wells	NV	89835	775-752-3328	752-3407	245
Wells State Park 159 Walker Pond Rd Web: www.mass.gov	Sturbridge	MA	01566	508-347-9257		565
Wells Technology Inc 4885 Windsor Ct NW Web: www.wellstech.com	Bemidji	MN	56601	218-751-5117		350
Wellsboro Area School District 227 Nichols Web: www.wellsborosd.k12.pa.us	Wellsboro	PA	16901	570-724-4424		685
Wells-Gardner Electronics Corp 9500 W 55th St Ste A NYSE: WGA ■ TF: 800-336-6630 ■ Web: www.wellsgardner.com	McCook	IL	60525	708-290-2100	290-2200	173-4
Wellshire Lincolnshire, The 170 Jamestown Ln Web: www.thewellshirelincolnshire.com	Lincolnshire	IL	60069	224-543-7070		371
Wellstar Cobb Hospital 3950 Austell Rd Web: www.wellstar.org	Austell	GA	30106	770-732-4000		374-3
Wellstar Douglas Hospital 8954 Hospital Dr TF: 888-800-5094 ■ Web: www.wellstar.org	Douglasville	GA	30134	770-949-1500		374-3
Wellstar Kennestone Hospital 677 Church St TF: 888-800-5094 ■ Web: www.wellstar.org	Marietta	GA	30060	770-793-5000		374-3
Welocalize Inc 241 E Fourth St Ste 207 TF: 800-370-9515 ■ Web: www.welocalize.com	Frederick	MD	21701	301-668-0330	668-0335	194
WELS (Wisconsin Evangelical Lutheran Synod) 2929 N Mayfair Rd Web: www.wels.net	Milwaukee	WI	53222	414-256-3888	256-3899	48-20
Welsbach Electric Corp 111-01 14th Ave TF: 866-890-7794 ■ Web: www.welsbachelectric.com	College Point	NY	11356	718-670-7900	670-7999	189-4
WELSCO Inc 9006 Crystal Hill Rd Web: www.welsco.com	North Little Rock	AR	72113	501-771-1204		385
Welsh Carson Anderson & Stowe 320 Pk Ave Ste 2500 Web: www.welshcarson.com	New York	NY	10022	212-893-9500		405
Welsh Consulting 31 Milk St Ste 805 Web: www.welsh.com	Boston	MA	02109	617-695-9800		225
WEM (Wisconsin Electrical Mfg Company Inc) 2501 S Moorland Rd PO Box 510767 Web: www.wemautomation.com	New Berlin	WI	53151	262-782-2340	782-2653	684
WEMG-AM 1310 (Span) 1341 N Delaware Ave Ste 509 Web: www.lamega1057.com	Philadelphia	PA	19125	215-426-1900		645-122
Wempe Jewelers 700 Fifth Ave Web: www.wempe.com	New York	NY	10019	212-397-9000		410
Wems Electronics Inc 4650 W Rosecrans Ave Web: www.wems.com	Hawthorne	CA	90250	310-644-0251	644-5334	248
WEMU-FM 89.1 (NPR) PO Box 980350 TF: 888-299-8910 ■ Web: www.wemu.org	Ypsilanti	MI	48198	734-487-2229	487-1015	645
Wenaas AGS Inc 12211 Parc Crest Dr Bldg Ste 100 TF: 888-576-2668 ■ Web: www.wenaasusa.com	Stafford	TX	77477	281-931-4300	931-4328	155-19
Wenatchee Confluence State Park 333 Olds Stn Rd Web: www.parks.wa.gov	Wenatchee	WA	98801	509-664-6373		565
Wenatchee Valley Chamber of Commerce 137 N Wenatchee Ave Web: www.wenatchee.org	Wenatchee	WA	98801	509-662-2116	663-2022	139
Wenatchee Valley College 1300 Fifth St *Fax: Admissions ■ TF: 877-982-4968 ■ Web: www.wvc.edu	Wenatchee	WA	98801	509-682-6800	682-6801*	162
Omak 116 W Apple Ave PO Box 2058 *Fax: Admissions ■ Web: www.wvc.edu	Omak	WA	98841	509-422-7803	422-7801*	162
Wenatchee World 14 N Mission St TF: 800-572-4433 ■ Web: wenatcheeworld.com	Wenatchee	WA	98801	509-663-5161		532-2
Wenberg State Park 15430 E Lake Goodwin Rd	Stanwood	WA	98292	360-652-7417		565
Wenck Assoc Inc PO Box 249 Web: www.wenck.com	Maple Plain	MN	55359	763-479-4200		261
Wende Correctional Facility 3040 Wende Rd PO Box 1187 Web: www.doccs.ny.gov/faclist.html	Alden	NY	14004	716-937-4000		213
Wendel, Rosen, Black & Dean LLP 1111 Broadway 24th Fl TF: 800-973-1177 ■ Web: www.wendel.com	Oakland	CA	94607	510-834-6600		428
Wendell August Forge Inc 2074 Leesburg-Grove City Rd TF: 866-354-5192 ■ Web: www.wendellaugust.com	Mercer	PA	16137	724-748-9501		327
Wendell Fabrics Corp 108 E Church St PO Box 128 Web: www.wendellfabrics.com	Blacksburg	SC	29702	864-839-6341	839-2911	745-3
Wendell State Forest Montague Rd Web: www.mass.gov	Wendell	MA	01379	413-659-3797		565

Name	Address	City	State	Zip	Phone	Fax	Class	Details
Wendell's Inc	6601 Bunker Lake Blvd NW PO Box 458	Ramsey	MN	55303	763-576-8200	576-0995	467	*TF:* 800-936-3355 ■ *Web:* www.wendellsinc.com
WEND-FM 106.5 (Alt)	801 Wood Ridge Ctr Dr.	Charlotte	NC	28217	704-714-9444		645-33	*TF:* 800-934-1065 ■ *Web:* 1065.iheart.com
Wendle Motors Inc	9000 N Div	Spokane	WA	99218	888-685-7177		516	*TF:* 888-685-7177 ■ *Web:* www.wendle.com
Wendling Printing Co	111 Beech St.	Newport	KY	41071	859-261-8300		627	*Web:* www.wendlingprinting.net
Wendling Quarries Inc	2647 225th St PO Box 230	De Witt	IA	52742	563-659-9181	659-3393	503-5	*Web:* www.wendlingquarries.com
Wendover Corp	130 S State Rd	Upper Darby	PA	19082	610-449-2056		466	*Web:* www.wendovercorp.com
Wendt Corp	2080 Military Rd.	Tonawanda	NY	14150	716-873-2211		567	*Web:* www.wendtcorp.com
Wendy Soucie Consulting Llc	218 S Main St Ste B	Lodi	WI	53555	608-225-1985		195	
Wendy's International Inc	1 Dave Thomas Blvd.	Dublin	OH	43017	614-764-3100	764-3330	670	*TF:* 800-952-5210 ■ *Web:* www.wendys.com
Wenger Corp	555 Pk Dr PO Box 448	Owatonna	MN	55060	507-455-4100	455-4258	527	*TF:* 800-493-6437 ■ *Web:* www.wengercorp.com
Wenger Furniture Appliance & Electronics	4552 Whittier Blvd	Los Angeles	CA	90022	323-261-1136	261-0968	321	*Web:* www.wengerfurniture.com
Wenger Manufacturing Inc	714 Main St	Sabetha	KS	66534	785-284-2133	284-3771	298	*TF:* 800-833-0174 ■ *Web:* www.wenger.com
WENH-TV Ch 11 (PBS)	268 Mast Rd.	Durham	NH	03824	603-868-1100	868-7552	741	*TF:* 800-639-8408 ■ *Web:* www.nhptv.org
Wenner Bread Products Inc	33 Rajon Rd.	Bayport	NY	11705	631-563-6262		296-1	*TF:* 800-869-6262 ■ *Web:* www.wennerbakery.com
WENO-AM 760 (Rel)	616 Mainstream Dr	Nashville	TN	37228	615-742-0500		645-108	*Web:* www.760thegospel.com
Wenstrup Brad (Rep R - OH)	2419 Rayburn HOB	Washington	DC	20515	202-225-3164	225-1992	342-2	*Web:* wenstrup.house.gov
Wenthe-Davidson Engineering Co	16300 W Rogers Dr PO Box 510286	New Berlin	WI	53151	262-782-1550	782-2020	518	*Web:* www.wenthe-davidson.com
Wentworth Chevytown	107 SE Grand Ave.	Portland	OR	97214	503-200-2482		516	*Web:* www.wentworthchevrolet.com
Wentworth Company Inc, The	479 W Sixth St	San Pedro	CA	90731	310-519-0113		260	*Web:* www.wentco.com
Wentworth Institute of Technology	550 Huntington Ave	Boston	MA	02115	617-989-4590	989-4010*	166	**Fax:* Admissions ■ *TF:* 800-556-0610 ■ *Web:* www.wit.edu
Wentworth Mansion	149 Wentworth St	Charleston	SC	29401	843-853-1886	720-5290	379	*TF:* 888-466-1886 ■ *Web:* www.wentworthmansion.com
Wentworth Printing Corp	101 N 12th St	West Columbia	SC	29169	800-326-0784		627	*TF:* 800-326-0784 ■ *Web:* www.wentworthprinting.com
Wentworth State Park	297 Governor Wentworth Hwy	Wolfeboro	NH	03894	603-569-3699		565	*Web:* www.nhstateparks.org
Wentworth-Coolidge Mansion Historic Site	375 Little Harbor Rd	Portsmouth	NH	03801	603-436-6607		565	*Web:* www.nhstateparks.org
Wentworth-Douglass Hospital	789 Central Ave	Dover	NH	03820	603-742-5252	740-2242	374-3	*TF:* 877-201-7100 ■ *Web:* www.wdhospital.com
Wenzel Downhole Tools Ltd	5920 Macleod Trail SW Ste 504	Calgary	AB	T2H0K2	403-262-3050		190	*Web:* www.downhole.com
WENZ-FM 107.9 (Urban)	2510 St Clair Ave NE	Cleveland	OH	44114	216-579-1111	771-4164	645-38	*TF:* 800-440-1079 ■ *Web:* ziphopcleveland.com
Wenzlau Engineering Inc	1517 Fair Oaks Ave.	South Pasadena	CA	91030	310-604-3400		536	*Web:* www.wenzlau.com
WEOW-FM 92.7 (CHR)	5450 MacDonald Ave Ste 10	Key West	FL	33040	305-296-7511		645-84	*Web:* www.weow927.com
WePackItAll Inc	2745 Huntington Dr	Duarte	CA	91010	626-301-9214		88	*Web:* www.wepackitall.com
WEPR-FM 90.1 (NPR)	1101 George Rogers Blvd.	Columbia	SC	29201	803-737-3200		645-40	*TF:* 800-277-3245 ■ *Web:* www.scetv.org
WERC (Warehousing Education & Research Council)	1100 Jorie Blvd Ste 170	Oak Brook	IL	60523	630-990-0001	990-0256	49-21	*TF:* 800-321-6742 ■ *Web:* www.werc.org
Werk-Brau Company Inc	2800 Fostoria Ave.	Findlay	OH	45840	419-422-2912		190	*Web:* www.werk-brau.com
Werklund Capital Corp	4500 DevonTower 400 Third rd Ave SW	Calgary	AB	T2P4H2	403-231-6545		787	*Web:* www.werklund.com
Wermers Multi-Family Corp	5120 Shoreham Pl Ste 150	San Diego	CA	92122	858-535-1475		187	*Web:* www.wermerscompanies.com
Werner Co	93 Werner Rd	Greenville	PA	16125	888-523-3371	456-8459	421	*TF:* 888-523-3371 ■ *Web:* www.wernerco.com/us
Werner Electric Supply Co	2341 Industrial Dr.	Neenah	WI	54956	920-729-4500	729-4484	246	*TF:* 800-236-5026 ■ *Web:* www.wernerelectric.com
Werner Enterprises Inc	14507 Frontier Rd.	Omaha	NE	68138	402-895-6640	894-3927*	780	*NASDAQ:* WERN ■ **Fax:* Hum Res ■ *TF:* 800-228-2240 ■ *Web:* www.werner.com
Werner G Smith Inc	1730 Train Ave	Cleveland	OH	44113	216-861-3676	861-3680	296-12	*TF General:* 800-535-8343 ■ *Web:* www.wernergsmithinc.com
Werner Tool & Mfg Co Inc	12301 E McNichols Rd.	Detroit	MI	48205	313-526-6020		701	
Werner Wildlife Museum	405 E 15th St	Casper	WY	82601	307-235-2108		520	*Web:* caspercollege.edu
Wernersville State Hospital	160 Main St	Wernersville	PA	19565	610-678-3411		374-5	*Web:* www.dhs.pa.gov
WERN-FM 88.7 (NPR)	821 University Ave	Madison	WI	53706	800-747-7444	263-9763*	645-96	**Fax Area Code:* 608 ■ *TF:* 800-747-7444 ■ *Web:* www.wpr.org
WERQ-FM 92.3 (Urban)	1705 Whitehead Rd	Baltimore	MD	21207	410-481-9292		645-16	*Web:* www.92q.com
Werremeyer Floresca Inc	15 N Gore Ave.	Saint Louis	MO	63119	314-963-0505		344	*Web:* www.werremeyer.com
Werres Corp	807 E S St	Frederick	MD	21701	301-620-4000	662-1028*	385	**Fax:* Sales ■ *TF:* 800-638-6563 ■ *Web:* www.werres.com
Wert Bookbinding Inc	9975 Allentown Blvd.	Grantville	PA	17028	717-469-0629	469-0629	92	*TF Cust Svc:* 800-344-9378 ■ *Web:* www.wertbookbinding.com
Werthan Packaging Inc	605 Hwy 76	White House	TN	37188	615-672-3336		65	*Web:* www.werthan.com
WERU-FM 89.9 (Var)	1186 Acadia Hwy	East Orland	ME	04431	207-469-6600	469-8961	645	*TF:* 800-643-6273 ■ *Web:* www.weru.org
Werzalit of America Inc	40 Holly Ave	Bradford	PA	16701	814-362-3881	362-4237	499	*TF:* 800-999-3730 ■ *Web:* www.werzalitusa.com
WES (Western Electrical Sales Inc)	521 Glide Ave	West Sacramento	CA	95691	916-372-1001		246	*Web:* www.wesisales.com
Wes' Rib House	38 Dike St	Providence	RI	02909	401-421-9090		671	*Web:* www.wesribhouse.com
WesBanco Inc	1 Bank Plaza	Wheeling	WV	26003	304-234-9000		70	*NASDAQ:* WSBC ■ *TF:* 800-328-3369 ■ *Web:* www.wesbanco.com
Wesbild Holdings Ltd	666 Burrard St Park Pl Ste 2650	Vancouver	BC	V6C2X8	604-694-8800		690	*Web:* www.wesbild.com
Wesbury United Methodist Community	31 N Park Ave.	Meadville	PA	16335	814-332-9000		48-20	*TF:* 877-937-2879 ■ *Web:* www.wesbury.com
Wescast Industries Inc	150 Savannah Oaks Dr	Brantford	ON	N3T5V7	519-750-0000	427-9895*	60	*TSE:* WCS.A ■ **Fax Area Code:* 570 ■ *Web:* www.wecast.com
Wesco Aircraft Hardware Corp	27727 Ave Scott	Valencia	CA	91355	661-775-7200		21	*Web:* www.wescoair.com
Wesco Cedar Inc	PO Box 520	Creswell	OR	97426	541-688-5020	688-5024	191-4	*TF:* 800-547-2511 ■ *Web:* www.wescocedar.com
WESCO Distribution Inc	225 W Stn Sq Dr Ste 700	Pittsburgh	PA	15219	412-454-2200		246	*Web:* www.wesco.com
Wesco Fabrics Inc	4001 Forest St	Denver	CO	80216	303-388-4101	388-3908	746	*TF:* 800-950-9372 ■ *Web:* www.wescofabrics.com
Wesco Financial Corp	301 E Colorado Blvd Ste 300	Pasadena	CA	91101	626-585-6700		185	*CVE:* WSC ■ *Web:* www.wescofinancial.com
Wesco Graphics Inc	410 E Grant Line Rd Ste D	Tracy	CA	95376	209-832-1000	832-7800	344	*Web:* www.wescographics.com
Wesco Inc	1460 Whitehall Rd	Muskegon	MI	49445	800-968-0200		324	*TF:* 800-968-0200 ■ *Web:* www.gowesco.com
Wesco Industrial Products Inc	1250 Welsh Rd	North Wales	PA	19454	215-699-7031	346-5511*	470	**Fax Area Code:* 800 ■ *Web:* www.wescomfg.com
WESCO International Inc	225 W Stn Sq Dr Ste 700	Pittsburgh	PA	15219	412-454-2200		360-3	*NYSE:* WCC ■ *Web:* www.wesco.com
Wesco Machine Products Inc	S84W18569 Enterprise Dr	Muskego	WI	53150	262-679-4799		757	*Web:* wescomachine.com
Wescom Credit Union	123 S Marengo Ave PO Box 7058	Pasadena	CA	91101	626-535-1000		219	*TF:* 888-493-7266 ■ *Web:* www.wescom.org
Wesoon Technology Inc	4655 Old Ironsides Dr	Santa Clara	CA	95054	408-727-8818		177	*Web:* www.wescongroup.com
Wesely-thomas Enterprises Inc	4580 E Thousand Oaks Blvd Ste 200	Westlake Village	CA	91362	805-379-2365	496-0051	186	*Web:* www.weselythomas.com
Wes-Garde Components Group Inc	100 Shield St	West Hartford	CT	06110	860-527-7705		246	*TF:* 800-554-8866 ■ *Web:* www.wesgarde.com
WESH-TV Ch 2 (NBC)	1021 N Wymore Rd	Winter Park	FL	32789	407-645-2222		741	*Web:* www.wesh.com
Weslaco Area Chamber of Commerce	301 W Railroad	Weslaco	TX	78596	956-968-2102	968-6451	139	*TF:* 800-700-2443 ■ *Web:* www.weslaco.com
Weslaco Public Library	525 S Kansas Ave.	Weslaco	TX	78596	956-968-4533		434-3	*Web:* www.weslaco.lib.tx.us
Wesley Biblical Seminary	787 E Northside Dr	Jackson	MS	39206	601-366-8880		167-3	*Web:* www.wbs.edu
Wesley Clover Corp	390 March Rd Ste 110	Ottawa	ON	K2K0G7	613-271-6305		528	*Web:* www.wesleyclover.com
Wesley Foundation-msu	3625 Midland Ave.	Memphis	TN	38111	901-458-5808		305	
Wesley Gardens	3 Upton Pk	Rochester	NY	14607	585-241-2100		450	*Web:* wesleygardens.com
Wesley Homes	815 S 216th St	Des Moines	WA	98198	206-824-5000		672	*TF:* 866-937-5390 ■ *Web:* wesleyhomes.org
Wesley Long Community Hospital	501 N Elam Ave	Greensboro	NC	27403	336-832-1000	832-7869	374-3	*TF:* 866-391-2734 ■ *Web:* mosescone.com/body.cfm/?id=41
Wesley Manor	1555 N Main St	Frankfort	IN	46041	765-659-1811		672	*Web:* www.wesleymanor.org
Wesley Medical Ctr	550 N Hillside St	Wichita	KS	67214	316-962-2000		374-3	*TF:* 800-362-0288 ■ *Web:* www.wesleymc.com
Wesley Peachtree Group Inc, The	1475 Klondike Rd SW Ste 100	Conyers	GA	30094	404-874-0555		463	*Web:* www.wpg-inc.com
Wesley Rehabilitation Hospital	8338 W 13th St N	Wichita	KS	67212	316-729-9999		374-6	*Web:* www.wesleyrehabhospital.com

	Phone	Fax	Class
Wesley Theological Seminary 4500 Massachusetts Ave NW .... Washington DC 20016 *Web:* wesleyseminary.edu	202-885-8600	885-8605	167-3
Wesley Towers 700 Monterey Pl .... Hutchinson KS 67502 *TF:* 888-663-9175 ■ *Web:* www.wesleytowers.com	620-663-9175		672
Wesley Woods Camp and Retreat Ctr 1700 Clear Lk .... Dowling MI 49050 *Web:* www.wesleywoodscamp.com	269-721-8291		239
Wesleyan College 4760 Forsyth Rd .... Macon GA 31210 **Fax:* Admissions ■ *TF:* 800-447-6610 ■ *Web:* www.wesleyancollege.edu	478-757-5219	757-4030*	166
Wesleyan University 70 Wyllys Ave .... Middletown CT 06459 **Fax:* Admissions ■ *TF:* 800-288-2020 ■ *Web:* www.wesleyan.edu	860-685-3000	685-3001*	166
Wesleyan University Olin Library 252 Church St .... Middletown CT 06459 *TF:* 800-421-1561 ■ *Web:* www.wesleyan.edu	860-685-2660	685-2661	434-6
Wesleyan University Press 215 Long Ln .... Middletown CT 06459 *TF:* 800-421-1561 ■ *Web:* www.wesleyan.edu	860-685-7711	685-7712	637-4
Wes-Pak Inc 11610 Vimy Ridge Rd .... Alexander AR 72002 *Web:* www.wespakinc.com	501-372-1900		100
WeSpire Inc 125 Kingston St 6th Fl .... Boston MA 02111 *Web:* www.wespire.com	617-531-8970		387
Wesson Farms Inc 25 Victoria Rd .... Osceola AR 72370	870-563-2674		10-5
Wesson Inc PO Box 2127 .... Waterbury CT 06722 *Web:* www.wessonenergy.com	203-756-7041	754-6664	579
Wesspur Tree Equipment 2121 Iron St .... Bellingham WA 98225 *TF:* 800-268-2141 ■ *Web:* www.wesspur.com	360-734-5242		429
West & Company CPAs PC 97 N Main St .... Gloversville NY 12078 *Web:* westcpapc.com	518-725-7127		2
West Agro Inc 11100 N Congress Ave .... Kansas City MO 64153 *Web:* www.delavalcleaningsolutions.com	816-891-1600		276
West Alabama Bank & Trust 509 First Ave W PO Box 310 .... Reform AL 35481 *Web:* www.wabt.com	205-375-6261	375-2289	70
West Allis Memorial Hospital 8901 W Lincoln Ave 2nd Fl .... West Allis WI 53227 *TF:* 800-822-7228 ■ *Web:* www.aurorahealthcare.org	414-328-6000	328-8536	374-3
West Allis Public Library 7421 W National Ave .... West Allis WI 53214 *TF:* 800-877-8339 ■ *Web:* www.westalliswi.gov	414-302-8500		434-3
West Allis-West Milwaukee Chamber of Commerce 6737 W Washington St Ste 2141 .... West Allis WI 53214 *TF:* 800-554-1448 ■ *Web:* www.wawmchamber.com	414-302-9901	302-9918	139
West American Rubber Co LLC 1337 Braden Ct .... Orange CA 92868 *TF:* 800-245-8748 ■ *Web:* www.warco.com	714-532-3355	532-2238	677
West Anaheim Extended Care 645 S Beach Blvd .... Anaheim CA 92804 *TF:* 800-579-7967 ■ *Web:* www.westanaheimec.com	714-821-1993		371
West Anaheim Medical Ctr (WAMC) 3033 W Orange Ave .... Anaheim CA 92804 *Web:* westanaheimmedctr.com	714-827-3000		374-3
West Anne Arundel County Chamber of Commerce 8385 Piney Orchard Pkwy .... Odenton MD 21113 *Web:* www.westcountychamber.org	410-672-3422	672-3475	139
West Bag Inc 1161 Monterey Pass Rd .... Monterey Park CA 91754	323-264-0750		596
West Bancorp Inc PO Box 65020 .... West Des Moines IA 50265 *NASDAQ: WTBA* ■ *TF:* 800-810-2301 ■ *Web:* www.westbankstrong.com	515-222-2300		360-2
West Baton Rouge Museum 845 N Jefferson Ave .... Port Allen LA 70767 *TF:* 888-881-6811 ■ *Web:* www.westbatonrougemuseum.com	225-336-2422	336-2448	520
West Baton Rouge Parish PO Box 757 .... Port Allen LA 70767 *TF:* 800-654-9701 ■ *Web:* www.wbrcouncil.org	225-383-4755	387-0218	338
West Bay Builders Inc 250 Bel Marin Keys Blvd .... Novato CA 94949	415-456-8972		186
West Bay Exploration Co 13685 S W Bay Shore Ste 200 .... Traverse City MI 49684 *Web:* www.westbayexploration.com	231-946-0200		538
West Bend Area Chamber of Commerce 304 S Main St .... West Bend WI 53095 *TF:* 888-338-8666 ■ *Web:* www.wbachamber.org	262-338-2666	338-1771	139
West Bend Community Memorial Library 630 Poplar St .... West Bend WI 53095 *Web:* www.west-bendlibrary.org	262-335-5151	335-5150	434-3
West Bend Housewares LLC 2845 Wingate St PO Box 2780 .... West Bend WI 53095 **Fax Area Code:* 224 ■ *TF:* 866-290-1851 ■ *Web:* www.westbend.com	866-290-1851	513-2498*	37
West Bend Mutual Insurance Co 1900 S 18th Ave .... West Bend WI 53095 *TF:* 800-236-5010 ■ *Web:* www.thesilverlining.com	262-334-5571	334-9109	391-4
West Bend Recreation Area 22154 Wt Bend Rd .... Harrold SD 57536 *Web:* gfp.sd.gov	605-773-2885		565
West Bloomfield Chamber of Commerce 5745 W Maple Rd Ste 206 .... West Bloomfield MI 48322 *TF:* 800-477-5050 ■ *Web:* www.westbloomfieldchamber.com	248-626-3636	626-4218	139
West Bloomfield Township Public Library 4600 Walnut Lake Rd .... West Bloomfield MI 48323 *Web:* www.wblib.org	248-682-2120	232-2333	434-3
West Boca Medical Ctr (WBMC) 21644 State Rd 7 .... Boca Raton FL 33428 *Web:* www.westbocamedctr.com	561-488-8000	488-8105	374-3
West Bond Inc 1551 S Harris Ct .... Anaheim CA 92806 *TF:* 800-874-4240 ■ *Web:* www.westbond.com	714-978-1551	978-0431	494
West Boylston Insurance Agency Inc 12 W Boylston St .... West Boylston MA 01583 *Web:* westboylstoninsurance.com	508-835-3877		390
West Branch Area Chamber of Commerce 422 W Houghton Ave .... West Branch MI 48661 *TF:* 800-755-9091 ■ *Web:* wbacc.com	989-345-2821		206
West Branch State Park 5708 Esworthy Rd .... Ravenna OH 44266 *Web:* www.ohiodnr.com	330-296-3239		565

	Phone	Fax	Class
West Calcasieu Cameron Hospital 701 E Cypress St .... Sulphur LA 70663 *Web:* www.wcch.com	337-527-7034		374-3
West Canadian Digital Imaging Inc 200 - 1601 Ninth Ave SE .... Calgary AB T2G0H4 *TF:* 800-267-2555 ■ *Web:* www.westcanadian.com	403-245-2555		344
West Carroll Parish PO Box 1078 .... Oak Grove LA 71263 *TF:* 800-256-6660 ■ *Web:* www.laclerksofcourt.org	318-428-3281	428-9896	338
West Central Electric Co-op Inc 204 Main St PO Box 17 .... Murdo SD 57559 *TF:* 800-242-9232 ■ *Web:* www.wce.coop	605-669-2472		245
West Central Illinois Educational Telecommunications Corp PO Box 6248 .... Springfield IL 62708 *TF:* 800-232-3605 ■ *Web:* www.networkknowledge.tv	217-483-7887	483-1112	632
West Central State Prison 4600 Fulton Mill Rd .... Macon GA 31208 *Web:* www.dcor.state.ga.us	478-471-2908	471-2068	213
West Central Steel Inc 110 19th St NW PO Box 1178 .... Willmar MN 56201 *TF:* 800-992-8853 ■ *Web:* www.wcsteel.com	320-235-4070	235-1816	492
West Central Tribune PO Box 839 .... Willmar MN 56201 *TF:* 800-450-1150 ■ *Web:* www.wctrib.com	320-235-1150	235-6769	532-2
West Central Wireless 3389 Knickerbocker Rd .... San Angelo TX 76904 *TF:* 800-695-9016 ■ *Web:* www.wcc.net	800-695-9016		736
West Chamber of Commerce 1667 Cole Blvd Bldg 19 Ste 400 .... Golden CO 80401 *Web:* www.westchamber.org	303-233-5555	237-7633	139
West Chester Chamber Alliance 8922 Beckett Rd .... West Chester OH 45069 *TF:* 800-210-7239 ■ *Web:* www.thechamberalliance.com	513-777-3600	777-0188	139
West Chester University 700 S High St .... West Chester PA 19383 *TF:* 877-315-2165 ■ *Web:* www.wcupa.edu	610-436-1000	436-2907	166
West Clermont Local School District 4350 Aicholtz Rd Ste 220 .... Cincinnati OH 45245 *Web:* www.westcler.k12.oh.us	513-943-5000	752-6158	685
West Coast Asset Management Inc 1205 Coast Village Rd .... Montecito CA 93108	805-653-5333		194
West Coast Aviation Services 19711 Campus Dr Ste 150 .... Santa Ana CA 92707 *TF:* 800-352-6153 ■ *Web:* www.wcas.aero	949-852-8340	260-3999	13
West Coast Bank 506 SW Coast Hwy .... Newport OR 97365 *TF Cust Svc:* 800-895-3345 ■ *Web:* www.columbiabank.com	877-272-3678		70
West Coast Clinical Laboratories Lp 7636 Burnet Ave .... Van Nuys CA 91405 *Web:* www.wcclabs.com	818-908-0535		418
West Coast Club 21100 Pacific Coast Hwy Hilton Waterfront Beach Resort .... Huntington Beach CA 92648	714-845-8000		671
West Coast Conference 1111 Bayhill Dr Ste 405 .... San Bruno CA 94066 *Web:* wccsports.com	650-873-8622		533
West Coast Connection 1725 Main St Ste 215 .... Weston FL 33326 *TF:* 800-767-0227 ■ *Web:* www.westcoastconnection.com	954-888-9780	888-9781	760
West Coast Construction 9021 Rancho Park Ct .... Rancho Cucamonga CA 91730 *Web:* www.wccsinc.com	909-982-6979		186
West Coast Cosmetics Inc 21050 Superior St .... Chatsworth CA 91311 *TF:* 800-354-9396 ■ *Web:* www.westcoastcosmetics.com	818-349-8510		237
West Coast Dental Services Inc 12121 Wilshire Blvd Ste 1111 .... Los Angeles CA 90025 *Web:* www.westcoastdental.com	310-820-9933		194
West Coast Differentials 2429 Mercantile Dr Ste A .... Rancho Cordova CA 95742 *TF:* 800-510-0950 ■ *Web:* www.differentials.com	916-635-0950		54
West Coast Distributing Inc Commerce Pl 350 Main St .... Boston MA 02148 *TF:* 800-235-3730 ■ *Web:* www.wcd-network.com	781-665-9393		10-11
West Coast Engineering Group Ltd 7984 River Rd .... Delta BC V4G1E3 *Web:* www.wceng.com	604-946-1256	946-1203	683
West Coast Financial LLC 1525 State St Ste 104 .... Santa Barbara CA 93101 *Web:* www.wcfinc.com	805-962-9131		194
West Coast General Hospital 3949 Port Alberni Hwy .... Port Alberni BC V9Y4S1 *TF:* 800-317-7878 ■ *Web:* www.viha.ca	250-731-1370		374-2
West Coast Green Institute 760 Market St Ste 1028 .... San Francisco CA 94102 *TF:* 800-724-4880 ■ *Web:* westcoastgreen.com	415-955-1935		387
West Coast Industrial Systems 1995 W Airway Rd .... Lebanon OR 97355 *TF:* 800-766-6705 ■ *Web:* www.westcoastindustrial.com	541-451-6677		454
West Coast Industries Inc 10 Jackson St .... San Francisco CA 94111 *TF:* 800-243-3150 ■ *Web:* www.westcoastindustries.com	415-621-6656	552-5368	319-1
West Coast Quartz Corporation (WCQ) 1000 Corporate Way .... Fremont CA 94539 *Web:* www.wcq.com	510-249-2160	249-2168	696
West Coast Samples Inc 14450 Central Ave .... Chino CA 91710	909-464-1616		86
West Coast Shoe Company 52828 NW Shoe Factory Ln PO Box 607 .... Scappoose OR 97056 *TF:* 800-326-2711 ■ *Web:* www.wescoboots.com/builder/default.aspx	503-543-7114	543-7110	301
West Coast Trends 17811 Jamestown Ln .... Huntington Beach CA 92647 *TF:* 800-736-4568 ■ *Web:* www.clubglove.com	714-843-9288		710
West Coast Turf 42-540 Melanie Pl .... Palm Desert CA 92211 *Web:* www.westcoastturf.com	760-340-7300		776
West Construction Inc 318 S Dixie Hwy Ste 4-5 .... Lake Worth FL 33460 *Web:* www.westconstructioninc.net	561-588-2027		186
West Consultants Pllc 405 S Sterling St .... Morganton NC 28655 *Web:* west-consultants.com	828-433-5661		261

Name	Address	City	State	ZIP	Phone	Fax	Class	Details
West Corp	11808 Miracle Hills Dr	Omaha	NE	68154	800-232-0900		737	*TF Sales:* 800-232-0900 ■ *Web:* www.west.com
West County Ctr	80 W County Ctr	Des Peres	MO	63131	314-288-2020		460	*Web:* www.shopwestcountycenter.com
West Des Moines Chamber of Commerce	650 S Prairie View Dr Ste 110	West Des Moines	IA	50266	515-225-6009		139	*TF:* 800-886-0280 ■ *Web:* www.wdmchamber.org
West Des Moines Public Library	4000 Mills Civic Pkwy	West Des Moines	IA	50265	515-222-3400	222-3401	434-3	*TF:* 800-626-0319 ■ *Web:* www.wdmlibrary.org
West End Diagnostic Imaging	2425 Bloor St W Ste 103	Toronto	ON	M6S4W4	416-763-4331		415	*Web:* www.wedi.ca
West End Gallery Ltd	12308 Jasper Ave	Edmonton	AB	T5N3K5	780-488-4892		42	*TF:* 855-488-4892 ■ *Web:* www.westendgalleryltd.com
West End Grill, The	120 W Liberty Ave	Ann Arbor	MI	48104	734-747-6260		671	*Web:* westendgrillannarbor.com
West Engineering Company Inc	10106 Louistown Rd	Ashland	VA	23005	804-798-3966	798-8590	454	*Web:* www.west-engineering.net
West Essex Graphics Inc (WEG)	305 Fairfield Ave	Fairfield	NJ	07004	800-221-5859	227-2906*	781	**Fax Area Code:* 973 ■ *TF:* 800-221-5859 ■ *Web:* www.westessexgraphics.com
West Face Capital Inc	2 Bloor St E Ste 3000	Toronto	ON	M4W1A8	647-724-8900		401	*Web:* westfacecapital.com
West Fargo Pioneer	101 Fifth St N	West Fargo	ND	58078	701-451-5718	282-9248	532-4	*TF:* 888-382-1222 ■ *Web:* www.westfargopioneer.com
West Fargo School District 6	207 Main Ave W	West Fargo	ND	58078	701-356-2000	356-2009	685	*Web:* www.west-fargo.k12.nd.us
West Feliciana Historical Society Museum	11757 Ferdinand St	Saint Francisville	LA	70775	225-635-6330		520	
West Feliciana Parish	PO Box 1921	Saint Francisville	LA	70775	225-635-3864	635-3705	338	*Web:* www.lpgov.org
West Florida Electric Co-op	5282 Peanut Rd	Graceville	FL	32440	850-263-3231		245	*TF:* 800-342-7400 ■ *Web:* westflorida.coop
West Florida Hospital	8383 N Davis Hwy	Pensacola	FL	32514	850-494-4000		374-3	*Web:* www.westfloridahospital.com
West Florida Regional Library	200 W Gregory St	Pensacola	FL	32501	850-436-5060		434-3	*TF:* 800-435-7352 ■ *Web:* www.cityofpensacola.com
West Fraser Timber Company Ltd (WFT)	501-858 Beatty St Ste 501	Vancouver	BC	V6B1C1	604-895-2700	681-6061	683	*NYSE:* WFT ■ *Web:* www.westfraser.com
West Genesee Central School District	300 Sanderson Dr	Camillus	NY	13031	315-487-4562		685	*Web:* www.westgenesee.org
West Georgia Medical Ctr	1514 Vernon Rd	LaGrange	GA	30240	706-882-1411		374-3	*Web:* www.wghs.org
West Georgia Regional Library	710 Rome St	Carrollton	GA	30117	770-836-6711		[illegible]	*Web:* www.wgrl.net
West Group	610 Opperman Dr	Eagan	MN	55123	651-687-7000	687-7551	637-2	*TF Cust Svc:* 800-328-4880 ■ *Web:* legalsolutions.thomsonreuters.com
West Gulf Maritime Assn	1717 E Loop N Ste 200	Houston	TX	77029	713-678-7655		177	*TF:* 800-435-5038 ■ *Web:* www.wgma.org
West Hartford Chamber of Commerce	948 Farmington Ave	West Hartford	CT	06107	860-521-2300	521-1996	139	*TF:* 800-486-7426 ■ *Web:* www.whchamber.com
West Hartford Health & Rehabilitation Ctr	130 Loomis Dr	West Hartford	CT	06107	860-521-8700		450	*TF:* 800-994-1776 ■ *Web:* www.westhartfordhealth.com
West Hartford Public Library	20 S Main St	West Hartford	CT	06107	860-561-6950	561-6990	434-3	*TF:* 800-273-8255 ■ *Web:* www.westhartfordlibrary.org
West Haven Chamber of Commerce	355 Main St Ground Fl	West Haven	CT	06516	203-933-1500	931-1940	139	*TF:* 800-953-4467 ■ *Web:* www.westhavenchamber.com
West Highland Christian Academy	1116 S Hickory Ridge Rd	Milford	MI	48380	248-887-6698		148	*Web:* www.whca-k12.org
West Hills College	*Coalinga* 300 Cherry Ln	Coalinga	CA	93210	559-934-2000	935-3788*	162	**Fax:* Admissions ■ *TF:* 800-266-1114 ■ *Web:* www.westhillscollege.com
	Lemoore 555 College Ave	Lemoore	CA	93245	559-925-3000		162	*TF:* 800-266-1114 ■ *Web:* www.westhillscollege.com
West Hills Hospital & Medical Center	7300 Medical Centre Dr	West Hills	CA	91307	818-676-4000		374-3	*Web:* westhillshospital.com
West Hills Village Senior Residence	5711 SW Multnomah Blvd	Portland	OR	97219	503-245-7621		371	*TF:* 800-867-0660 ■ *Web:* www.westhillssenior.com
West Hollywood Chamber of Commerce	8272 Santa Monica Blvd	West Hollywood	CA	90046	323-650-2688	650-2689	139	*TF:* 800-345-8683 ■ *Web:* www.wehochamber.com
West Hollywood Convention & Visitors Bureau	8687 Melrose Ave Ste M38	West Hollywood	CA	90069	310-289-2525		206	*TF:* 800-368-6020 ■ *Web:* www.visitwesthollywood.com
West Houston Medical Ctr	12141 Richmond Ave	Houston	TX	77082	281-558-3444		374-3	*Web:* westhoustonmedical.com
West Irondequoit Central School District	321 List Ave	Rochester	NY	14617	585-342-5500		685	*Web:* www.westirondequoit.org
West Islip Public Library	3 Higbie Ln	West Islip	NY	11795	631-661-7080	661-7137	434-3	*TF:* 866-833-1122 ■ *Web:* www.wipublib.org
West Jefferson Medical Ctr	1101 Medical Ctr Blvd	Marrero	LA	70072	504-349-1134	349-6299	374-3	*Web:* www.wjmc.org
West Jersey Hospital Berlin	100 Townsend Ave	Berlin	NJ	08009	856-322-3000		374-3	*Web:* www.virtua.org
West Jordan Chamber of Commerce	8000 Redwood Rd	West Jordan	UT	84088	801-569-5151	569-5153	139	*Web:* www.westjordanchamber.com
West Kentucky Community & Technical College	4810 Alben Barkley Dr PO Box 7380	Paducah	KY	42001	270-554-9200	554-6203*	162	**Fax:* Admissions ■ *TF:* 855-469-5282 ■ *Web:* www.westkentucky.kctcs.edu
West Kentucky News	1540 McCracken Blvd	Paducah	KY	42001	270-442-7389	442-5220	532-4	*Web:* www.ky-news.com
West Kentucky Rural Electric Co-op Corp	PO Box 589	Mayfield	KY	42066	270-247-1321		245	*TF:* 877-495-7322 ■ *Web:* www.wkrecc.com
West Lafayette Public Library	208 W Columbia St	West Lafayette	IN	47906	765-743-2261	743-0540	434-3	*TF:* 800-333-1795 ■ *Web:* www.wlaf.lib.in.us
West Liberty Foods LLC	228 W Second St	West Liberty	IA	52776	319-627-6000	627-6334	619	*TF:* 888-511-4500 ■ *Web:* www.wlfoods.com
West Linn Paper Co	4800 Mill St	West Linn	OR	97068	503-557-6500	557-6616	557	*TF:* 800-989-3608 ■ *Web:* www.wlinpco.com
West Los Angeles College	9000 Overland Ave	Culver City	CA	90230	310-287-4200	287-4327*	162	**Fax:* Admissions ■ *Web:* www.wlac.edu
West Marine Inc	500 Westridge Dr	Watsonville	CA	95076	831-728-2700		770	*NASDAQ:* WMAR ■ *TF:* 800-262-8464 ■ *Web:* www.westmarine.com
West Memphis Chamber of Commerce	108 W Broadway	West Memphis	AR	72301	870-735-1134	735-6283	139	
West Metro Chamber of Commerce	1006 12th St	Cayce	SC	29033	803-794-6504		139	*Web:* wmvc.publishpath.com
West Metro Printing Co	33100 Industrial Rd	Livonia	MI	48150	734-522-0410		627	*Web:* www.westmetroprinting.com
West Milford Township Library	1490 Union Valley Rd	West Milford	NJ	07480	973-728-2820	728-2106	434-3	*Web:* www.wmtl.org
West Millbrook Middle School Booster Club	8115 Strickland Rd	Raleigh	NC	27615	919-870-4050		685	*TF:* 800-401-0486 ■ *Web:* wmms.net
West Milton State Bank	940 High St	West Milton	PA	17886	570-568-6851		70	*Web:* westmiltonstatebank.com
West Monroe Partners LLC	222 W Adams St	Chicago	IL	60606	312-602-4000		194	*TF:* 800-828-6708 ■ *Web:* www.westmonroepartners.com
West Music Inc	1212 Fifth St	Coralville	IA	52241	319-351-2000		526	*TF:* 800-373-2000 ■ *Web:* www.westmusic.com
West Nebraska Register	PO Box 608	Grand Island	NE	68802	308-382-4660	382-6569	532-4	*TF:* 800-652-2229 ■ *Web:* www.gidiocese.org
West New York Public Library	425 60th St	West New York	NJ	07093	201-295-5135	662-1473	434-3	*Web:* wnypl.org
West Nottingham Academy	1079 Firetower Rd	Colora	MD	21917	410-658-5556	658-9264	622	*TF:* 866-381-3684 ■ *Web:* www.wna.org
West Oakland Health Council Inc (WOHC)	700 Adeline St	Oakland	CA	94607	510-835-9610		353	*Web:* www.wohc.org
West Oaklane Charter School	7115 Stenton Ave	Philadelphia	PA	19138	215-927-7995		685	*Web:* wolcs.org
West Oaks Hospital	6500 Hornwood Dr	Houston	TX	77074	713-995-0909		374-5	*TF:* 800-685-9796 ■ *Web:* westoakshospital.com
West Oaks Mall	1000 W Oaks Mall	Houston	TX	77082	281-531-1332	531-1579	460	*Web:* www.shopwestoaksmall.com
West Oaks Mall	9401 W Colonial Dr Ste 728	Ocoee	FL	34761	407-294-6033		460	*Web:* www.westoaksmall.com
West Orange Chamber of Commerce	12184 W Colonial Dr	Winter Garden	FL	34787	407-656-1304	656-0221	139	*TF:* 877-999-9981 ■ *Web:* www.wochamber.com
West Orange College	12541 Brookhurst St Ste 100	Garden Grove	CA	92840	714-530-5000		800	
West Orange Public Library	46 Mt Pleasant Ave	West Orange	NJ	07052	973-736-0198		434-3	*Web:* www.wopl.lib.nj.us
West Oregon Electric Co-op Inc	652 Rose Ave PO Box 69	Vernonia	OR	97064	503-429-3021	429-8440	245	*TF:* 800-777-1276 ■ *Web:* www.westoregon.org
West Palm Beach City Hall	200 Second St	West Palm Beach	FL	33401	561-822-1200	822-1424	337	*Web:* wpb.org
West Palm Beach Public Library	411 Clematis St	West Palm Beach	FL	33401	561-868-7700	822-1892	434-3	*Web:* www.wpb.org
West Park Direct	2728 Euclid Ave Fl 2	Cleveland	OH	44115	216-589-0200		195	
West Parry Sound Health Ctr	6 Albert St	Parry Sound	ON	P2A3A4	705-746-9321	746-7364	374-2	*Web:* www.wpshc.com
West Pasco Chamber of Commerce	5443 Main St	New Port Richey	FL	34652	727-842-7651	848-0202	139	*TF:* 800-851-8754 ■ *Web:* www.westpasco.com
West Penetone Corp	700 Gotham Pkwy	Carlstadt	NJ	07072	201-567-3000	510-3973	151	*TF:* 800-631-1652 ■ *Web:* www.penetone.com
West Penn Allegheny Health System	4800 Friendship Ave	Pittsburgh	PA	15224	800-994-6610		353	*TF:* 800-994-6610 ■ *Web:* ahn.org
West Penn Energy Services LLC	4257 Gibsonia Rd	Gibsonia	PA	15044	724-444-0875		536	*Web:* www.wpes-pa.com
West Penn Oil Company Inc	2305 Market St	Warren	PA	16365	814-723-9000		579	*Web:* www.westpenn.com

	Phone	Fax	Class

West Penn Power Co
800 Cabin Hill Dr — Greensburg PA 15601 — 800-686-0021 — 186
TF: 800-686-0021 ■ *Web:* www.firstenergycorp.com/west_penn_power.html

West Penn Printing
103 Riverpark Dr — New Castle PA 16101 — 724-856-3376 — 627
Web: westpennprinting.com

West Pharmaceutical Services Inc
101 Gordon Dr — Lionville PA 19341 — 610-594-2900 — 477
NYSE: WST ■ *TF:* 800-345-9800 ■ *Web:* www.westpharma.com

West Point Industries
2021 Stateline Rd PO Box 589 — West Point GA 31833 — 706-643-2101 — 643-2100 — 744
Web: www.westpoint.com

West Point Market 33 Shiawassee Ave — Fairlawn OH 44333 — 330-864-2151 — 460
Web: www.westpointmarket.com

West Point Thoroughbreds Inc
2 Smith Bridge Rd — Saratoga Springs NY 12866 — 518-583-6638 — 31
Web: www.westpointtb.com

West Point Underwriters LLC
7785 66th St — Pinellas Park FL 33781 — 727-507-7565 — 390
TF: 800-688-6213 ■ *Web:* westpointuw.com

West Port Plaza
111 W Port Plaza Ste 550 — Saint Louis MO 63146 — 314-576-7100 — 50-6
Web: www.westportstl.com

West Press Printing & Copying
1663 W Grant Rd — Tucson AZ 85745 — 520-624-4939 — 627
TF: 888-637-0337 ■ *Web:* westpress.com

West Ridge Mall 1801 SW Wanamaker Rd — Topeka KS 66604 — 785-272-5119 — 460
Web: www.simon.com

West River Co-op Telephone Co (WRCTC)
801 Coleman Ave PO Box 39 — Bison SD 57620 — 605-244-5213 — 736
TF: 888-464-9513 ■ *Web:* www.sdplains.com

West River Electric Assn Inc
1200 W Fourth Ave PO Box 412 — Wall SD 57790 — 888-279-2135 — 279-2630* — 245
**Fax Area Code:* 605 ■ *TF:* 888-279-2135 ■ *Web:* www.westriver.com

West River Telecommunications Co-op
PO Box 467 — Hazen ND 58545 — 701-748-2211 — 748-6800 — 736
TF: 800-748-7220 ■ *Web:* www.westriv.com

West Rock Ridge State Park
c/o Sleeping Giant State Pk 200 Mt Carmel Ave — Hamden CT 06518 — 203-287-5658 — 565
Web: www.ct.gov

West Sacramento Chamber of Commerce
1414 Merkley Ave Ste 1 — West Sacramento CA 95691 — 916-371-7042 — 371-7007 — 139
TF: 800-662-9656 ■ *Web:* www.westsacramentochamber.com

West Saint Louis County Chamber of Commerce
15965 Manchester Rd Ste 102 — Ellisville MO 63011 — 636-230-9900 — 230-9912 — 139
TF: 800-772-1213 ■ *Web:* www.westcountychamber.com

West Seneca Public Library
1300 Union Rd — West Seneca NY 14224 — 716-674-2928 — 434-3
Web: buffalolib.org

West Shore Chamber of Commerce
4211 E Trindle Rd — Camp Hill PA 17011 — 717-761-0702 — 761-4315 — 139
Web: www.wschamber.org

West Shore Chamber of Commerce
PO Box 45297 — Westlake OH 44145 — 440-835-8787 — 835-8798 — 139
Web: www.westshorechamber.org

West Shore Chamber of Commerce
2830 Aldwynd Rd — Victoria BC V9B3S7 — 250-478-1130 — 478-1584 — 137
TF: 888-234-3566 ■ *Web:* www.westshore.bc.ca

West Shore Community College
PO Box 277 — Scottville MI 49454 — 231-845-6211 — 845-3944* — 162
**Fax:* Admissions ■ *TF:* 800-848-9722 ■ *Web:* www.westshore.edu

West Shore Plaza 250 W Shore Blvd — Tampa FL 33609 — 813-286-0790 — 460
Web: www.westshoreplaza.com

West Shore State Park
490 N Meridian Rd — Kalispell MT 59901 — 406-752-5501 — 565
Web: www.fwp.mt.gov

West Side Cafe 7950 Camp Bowie W — Fort Worth TX 76116 — 817-560-1996 — 671

West Side Mechanical Inc
2007 Corporate Ln — Naperville IL 60563 — 630-369-6690 — 14
Web: www.wsmech.com

West Side Telecommunications
1449 Fairmont Rd — Morgantown WV 26501 — 304-983-2211 — 196
TF: 800-296-9113 ■ *Web:* westsidetelecommunications.net

West Side Tractor Sales Co
1400 W Ogden Ave — Naperville IL 60563 — 630-355-7150 — 355-7173 — 358
Web: www.westsidetractorsales.com

West Side Unlimited Corp
4201 16th Ave SW — Cedar Rapids IA 52404 — 319-390-4466 — 360-2
TF: 800-373-2957 ■ *Web:* www.westsideunlimited.com

West Springfield Auto Parts
92 Blandin Ave Ste C — Framingham MA 01702 — 508-879-6932 — 791
TF: 800-615-2392 ■ *Web:* www.wsaparts.com

West Springfield Chamber of Commerce
1441 Main St — Springfield MA 01103 — 413-787-1555 — 731-8530 — 139
TF: 800-858-3926 ■ *Web:* www.myonlinechamber.com

West Star Aviation Inc
796 Heritage Way — Grand Junction CO 81506 — 970-243-7500 — 248-5243 — 24
TF: 800-255-4193 ■ *Web:* www.weststaraviation.com

West Street Cafe 76 W St — Bar Harbor ME 04609 — 207-288-5242 — 671
Web: www.weststreetcafe.com

West Suburban Bank
711 Westmore Meyers Rd — Lombard IL 60148 — 630-652-2000 — 629-0278 — 70
TF: 800-258-4009 ■ *Web:* www.westsuburbanbank.com

West Suburban Chamber of Commerce
9440 Joliet Rd Ste B — Hodgkins IL 60525 — 708-387-7550 — 387-7556 — 139
TF: 800-796-9696 ■ *Web:* www.wscci.org

West Suburban Hospital Medical Ctr
3 Erie Ct — Oak Park IL 60302 — 708-383-6200 — 374-3
TF: 866-938-7256 ■ *Web:* www.westsuburbanmc.com/home.aspx

West Suburban Special Recreation Association
2915 Maple St — Franklin Park IL 60131 — 847-455-2100 — 31
Web: www.wssra.net

West Technology Research Solutions LLC
2247A Old Middlefield Way — Mountain View CA 94043 — 650-940-1196 — 466
Web: www.wtrs.net

West Tennessee Healthcare
620 Skyline Dr — Jackson TN 38301 — 731-541-5000 — 353
Web: wth.org

West Tennessee State Penitentiary
480 Green Chapel Rd PO Box 1150 — Henning TN 38041 — 731-738-5044 — 213
Web: www.tn.gov

West Terrace Inc
1382 W Ninth St Ste 210 — Cleveland OH 44113 — 216-696-4466 — 652
Web: yourerc.com

West Texas A & M University
2501 Fourth Ave — Canyon TX 79016 — 806-651-2020 — 651-5285* — 166
**Fax:* Admissions ■ *TF:* 877-656-2065 ■ *Web:* www.wtamu.edu

West Texas Gas Inc 211 N Colorado St — Midland TX 79701 — 432-682-4349 — 360-3
Web: westtexasgas.com

West Texas Rural TelephoneCo-op Inc
PO Box 1737 — Hereford TX 79045 — 806-364-3331 — 276-5219 — 736
TF: 888-440-4331 ■ *Web:* www.wtrt.net

West Town Mall 7600 Kingston Pk — Knoxville TN 37919 — 865-693-0292 — 531-0503 — 460
Web: www.simon.com

West Towne Mall 66 W Towne Mall — Madison WI 53719 — 608-833-6330 — 460
Web: www.shopwesttowne-mall.com

West Tree Service Inc
6300 Forbing Rd — Little Rock AR 72209 — 501-568-5111 — 776
TF: 800-779-2967 ■ *Web:* www.westtree.com

West University Travel
3622 University Blvd — Houston TX 77005 — 713-665-4767 — 772
TF: 800-256-0640 ■ *Web:* westuniversitytravel.com

West Valley College
14000 Fruitvale Ave — Saratoga CA 95070 — 408-867-2200 — 162
Web: www.westvalley.edu

West Valley Construction Company Inc
580 McGlincey Ln — Campbell CA 95008 — 800-588-5510 — 188-10
TF: 800-588-5510 ■ *Web:* www.westvalleyconstruction.com

West Valley Flying Club
1901 Embarcadero Rd — Palo Alto CA 94303 — 650-856-2030 — 63
Web: www.wvfc.org

West Valley Medical Ctr
1717 Arlington Ave — Caldwell ID 83605 — 208-459-4641 — 865-9738* — 374-3
**Fax Area Code:* 877 ■ *TF:* 866-270-2311 ■ *Web:* www.westvalleymedctr.com

West Valley School District 208
8902 Zier Rd — Yakima WA 98908 — 509-972-6000 — 685
Web: www.wvsd208.org

West Valley View
200 W Wigwam Blvd — Litchfield Park AZ 85323 — 623-535-8439 — 935-2103 — 532-4
Web: www.westvalleyview.com

West Vancouver Chamber of Commerce
2235 Marine Dr — West Vancouver BC V7V1K5 — 604-926-6614 — 137
TF: 800-663-6102 ■ *Web:* www.westvanchamber.com

West Virginia

Accountancy Board
405 Capitol St Ste 908 — Charleston WV 25301 — 304-558-3557 — 558-1325 — 339-49
Web: www.boa.wv.gov

Administrative Office of the Courts
1900 Kanawha Blvd E Bldg 1 Rm E-100 — Charleston WV 25305 — 304-558-0145 — 558-1212 — 339-49
Web: www.courtswv.gov

Agriculture Dept
1900 Kanawha Blvd E Rm E-28 — Charleston WV 25305 — 304-558-3550 — 558-2203 — 339-49
Web: www.wvagriculture.org

Arts Commission
1900 Kanawha Blvd E Cultural Ctr — Charleston WV 25305 — 304-558-0220 — 558-2779 — 339-49
Web: www.wvculture.org/arts

Attorney General
State Capitol Complex Bldg 1 Rm E-26 — Charleston WV 25305 — 304-558-2021 — 558-2021 — 339-49
Web: ago.wv.gov

Board of Medicine
101 Dee Dr Ste 103 — Charleston WV 25311 — 304-558-2921 — 558-2084 — 339-49
Web: www.wvbom.wv.gov

Bureau for Public Health
350 Capitol St Rm 702 — Charleston WV 25301 — 304-558-2971 — 558-1035 — 339-49
Web: www.wvdhhr.org/bph

Child Support Enforcement Bureau
231 Capitol St Ste 111 — Charleston WV 25301 — 304-561-3120 — 558-2645 — 339-49
Web: www.dhhr.wv.gov

Children & Families Bureau
350 Capitol St Rm R-730 — Charleston WV 25301 — 304-558-0628 — 558-4194 — 339-49
TF: 800-642-8589 ■ *Web:* www.wvdhhr.org/bcf

Community Development Div
1900 Kanawha Blvd E — Charleston WV 25311 — 304-558-2234 — 558-1189 — 339-49
TF: 800-982-3386 ■ *Web:* www.wvcommerce.org

Consumer Protection Div
812 Quarrier St 1st Fl PO Box 1789 — Charleston WV 25301 — 304-558-8986 — 558-0184 — 339-49
TF: 800-368-8808 ■ *Web:* www.ago.wv.gov

Corrections Div 1409 Greenbrier St — Charleston WV 25311 — 304-558-2036 — 558-5934 — 339-49
Web: www.wvdoc.com/wvdoc

Crime Victims Compensation Fund
1900 Kanawha Blvd E Rm W-334 — Charleston WV 25305 — 304-347-4850 — 347-4915 — 339-49
TF: 877-562-6878 ■ *Web:* www.legis.state.wv.us

Culture Center, The
1900 Kanawha Blvd E Bldg 3 — Charleston WV 25305 — 304-558-0220 — 558-2779 — 339-49
Web: www.wvculture.org/shpo

Dept of Revenue
State Capitol Bldg 1 Rm W-300 — Charleston WV 25305 — 304-558-1017 — 558-2324 — 339-49
Web: www.revenue.wv.gov

Development Office
1900 Kanawah Blvd E Bldg 6 Rm 525B — Charleston WV 25305 — 304-558-2234 — 558-0449 — 339-49
TF: 800-982-3386 ■ *Web:* www.wvcommerce.org

Div of Natural Resources (DNR)
324 Fourth Ave Bldg 74 — South Charleston WV 25303 — 304-558-2754 — 558-2768 — 339-49
Web: www.wvdnr.gov

Education Dept 1900 Kanawha Blvd E — Charleston WV 25305 — 304-558-2681 — 339-49
Web: www.wvde.state.wv.us

Emergency Services Office
1900 Kanawha Blvd E — Charleston WV 25305 — 304-558-5380 — 344-4538 — 339-49
Web: www.dhsem.wv.gov

Environmental Protection Dept
601 57th St SE — Charleston WV 25304 — 304-926-0440 — 926-0446 — 339-49
Web: www.dep.wv.gov

Ethics Commission
210 Brooks St Ste 300 — Charleston WV 25301 — 304-558-0664 — 558-2169 — 265
TF: 866-558-0664 ■ *Web:* www.ethics.wv.gov

Name / Address	City	State	Zip	Phone	Fax	Class
Higher Education Policy Commission						
1018 Kanawha Blvd E Ste 700	Charleston	WV	25301	304-558-2101	558-1011	725
TF: 888-825-5707 ■ *Web:* wvhepc.com						
Housing Development Fund						
814 Virginia St E	Charleston	WV	25301	304-345-6475		339-49
TF: 800-933-9843 ■ *Web:* www.wvhdf.com						
Insurance Commission						
900 Pennsylvania Ave	Charleston	WV	25302	304-558-3354	558-0412	339-49
TF: 888-879-9842 ■ *Web:* www.wvinsurance.gov						
Labor Div						
Capitol Complex 749 B Bldg 6	Charleston	WV	25305	304-558-7890	558-2415	339-49
Web: wvlabor.com						
Lottery						
900 Pennsylvania Ave PO Box 2067	Charleston	WV	25302	304-558-0500	558-3321	452
TF: 800-982-2274 ■ *Web:* www.wvlottery.com						
Motor Vehicles Div						
5707 Maccorkle Ave SE Ste 400	Charleston	WV	25304	304-558-3900		339-49
TF: 800-642-9066 ■ *Web:* www.transportation.wv.gov						
Office of Governor						
State Capitol Bldg 1900 Kanawha Blvd E	Charleston	WV	25305	304-558-2000	342-7025	339-49
Web: www.governor.wv.gov						
Office of Technology						
1900 Kanawha Blvd ECapitol Complex Bldg 5 10th Fl	Charleston	WV	25304	304-558-5472	558-0136	339-49
TF: 877-558-9966 ■ *Web:* www.technology.wv.gov						
Probation & Parole Board						
1356 Hansford St Ste B	Charleston	WV	25311	304-558-6366	558-5678	339-49
Web: paroleboard.wv.gov						
Public Service Commission						
201 Brooke St PO Box 812	Charleston	WV	25301	304-340-0300	340-0325	339-49
TF: 800-344-5113 ■ *Web:* www.psc.state.wv.us						
Racing Commission						
900 Pennsylvania Ave Ste 533	Charleston	WV	25302	304-558-2150	558-6319	712
Web: www.racing.wv.gov						
Real Estate Commission						
300 Capitol St Ste 400	Charleston	WV	25301	304-558-3555	558-6442	339-49
Web: www.wvrec.org						
Rehabilitation Services Div						
107 Capitol St	Charleston	WV	25301	304-356-2060		339-49
TF: 800-642-8207 ■ *Web:* www.wvdrs.org						
Secretary of State						
1900 Kanawha Blvd E Bldg 1 Ste 157K	Charleston	WV	25305	304-558-6000	558-0900	339-49
TF: 866-767-8683 ■ *Web:* www.sos.wv.gov						
Securities Div						
1900 Kanawha Blvd E Bldg 1 Rm W-100	Charleston	WV	25305	304-558-2251	558-5200	339-49
TF: 877-982-9148 ■ *Web:* www.wvsao.gov						
State Government Information						
100 Dee Dr	Charleston	WV	25311	304-558-7000	558-7001	339-49
TF: 888-558-7002 ■ *Web:* www.wv.gov						
State Legislature						
State Capitol Complex Rm MB-27 Bldg 1	Charleston	WV	25305	304-347-4836		339-49
Web: www.legis.state.wv.us						
State Parks and Forests						
324 Fourth Ave	Charleston	WV	25303	304-558-2764	558-0077	339-49
TF: 800-225-5982 ■ *Web:* www.wvstateparks.com						
State Police						
725 Jefferson Rd	South Charleston	WV	25309	304-746-2100		339-49
Web: www.wvsp.gov						
Supreme Court of Appeals						
1900 Kanawha Blvd E Bldg 1 Rm E-317	Charleston	WV	25305	304-558-2601	558-3815	339-49
Web: www.courtswv.gov						
Tourism Div						
90 MacCorkle Ave SW	South Charleston	WV	25303	304-558-2200		339-49
TF: 800-225-5982 ■ *Web:* www.wvtourism.com						
Transportation Dept						
1900 Kanawha Blvd E Bldg 5 Rm A-109	Charleston	WV	25305	304-558-0444	558-1004	339-49
Web: www.wv.gov						
Treasurer						
1900 Kanawha Blvd E Bldg 1 Ste E-145	Charleston	WV	25305	304-558-5000		339-49
TF: 800-422-7498 ■ *Web:* www.wvsto.com						
Veterans Affairs Div						
1321 Plaza E Ste 101	Charleston	WV	25301	304-558-3661	558-3662	339-49
TF: 888-838-2332 ■ *Web:* www.veterans.idaho.gov						
Vital Statistics						
350 Capitol St Rm 165	Charleston	WV	25301	304-558-2931	558-1051	339-49
Web: www.wvdhhr.org/bph/oehp/hsc/vr/birtcert.htm						
Weights & Measures Div						
570 W MacCorkle Ave	Saint Albans	WV	25177	304-722-0602	722-0605	339-49
West Virginia Assn of Counties (WVACO)						
2211 Washington St	Charleston	WV	25311	304-346-0591		49-7
Web: www.wvaco.org						
West Virginia Assn of Realtors						
2110 Kanawha Blvd E	Charleston	WV	25311	304-342-7600	343-5811	656
TF: 800-445-7600 ■ *Web:* www.wvrealtors.com						
West Virginia Botanic Garden						
714 Venture Dr	Morgantown	WV	26508	304-376-2717		97
Web: www.wvbg.org						
West Virginia Chamber of Commerce						
1624 Kanawha Blvd E	Charleston	WV	25311	304-342-1115	342-1130	140
TF: 800-635-6329 ■ *Web:* www.wvchamber.com						
West Virginia Correctional Industries						
617 Leon Sullivan Way	Charleston	WV	25301	304-558-6054	558-6056	630
TF: 800-525-5381 ■ *Web:* wvcorrectionalindustries.com						
West Virginia Democratic Party						
717 Lee St Ste 214	Charleston	WV	25301	304-342-8121		616-1
West Virginia Dental Assn						
2016 1/2 Kanawha Blvd E	Charleston	WV	25311	304-344-5246		227
Web: www.wvdental.org						
West Virginia Junior College						
Charleston 1000 Virginia St E	Charleston	WV	25301	304-345-2820		800
TF: 800-924-5208 ■ *Web:* www.wvjc.edu						
Morgantown 148 Willey St	Morgantown	WV	26505	304-296-8282		800
Web: www.wvjc.edu						
West Virginia Junior College - Bridgeport						
176 Thompson Dr	Bridgeport	WV	26330	304-842-4007	842-8191	800
TF: 800-470-5627 ■ *Web:* www.wvjc.edu						
West Virginia Library Commission						
1900 Kanawha Blvd E	Charleston	WV	25305	304-558-2041	558-2044	434-5
TF: 800-642-9021 ■ *Web:* www.librarycommission.lib.wv.us						
West Virginia National Cemetery						
42 Veterans Memorial Ln	Grafton	WV	26354	304-265-2044	265-4336	136
TF: 800-273-8255 ■ *Web:* www.cem.va.gov/cems/nchp/westvirginia.asp						
West Virginia Northern Community College						
1704 Market St	Wheeling	WV	26003	304-233-5900	232-8187	162
TF: 800-641-5678 ■ *Web:* wvncc.edu						
West Virginia Nurses Assn (WVNA)						
1007 Bigley Ave Ste 308	Charleston	WV	25302	304-342-1169		533
TF: 800-400-1226 ■ *Web:* www.wvnurses.org						
West Virginia Pharmacists Assn						
2016 1/2 Kanawha Blvd E	Charleston	WV	25311	304-344-5302	344-5316	585
Web: wvpharmacy.org						
West Virginia Press Association						
3422 Pennsylvania Ave	Charleston	WV	25302	304-342-1011	343-5879	624
TF: 800-235-6881 ■ *Web:* www.wvpress.org						
West Virginia Public Theatre						
PO Box 6082	Morgantown	WV	26505	304-381-2382		573-4
Web: www.wvpublictheatre.org						
West Virginia Radio Corp						
1251 Earl L Core Rd	Morgantown	WV	26505	304-296-0029		643
TF: 800-248-4242 ■ *Web:* wvaq.com						
West Virginia Republican State Committee						
PO Box 2711	Charleston	WV	25330	304-768-0493	768-6083	616-2
Web: www.wvgop.org						
West Virginia School Journal						
1558 Quarrier St	Charleston	WV	25311	304-346-5315	346-4325	457-8
TF: 800-642-8261 ■ *Web:* www.wvea.org						
West Virginia State Bar						
2000 Deitrick Blvd	Charleston	WV	25311	304-553-7220	558-2467	72
TF: 866-989-8227 ■ *Web:* www.wvbar.org						
West Virginia State Medical Assn						
4307 MacCorkle Ave SE	Charleston	WV	25304	304-925-0342	925-0345	474
TF: 800-257-4747 ■ *Web:* www.wvsma.com						
West Virginia State Medical Assn						
4307 MacCorkle Ave SE	Charleston	WV	25364	304-925-0342	925-0345	457-16
TF: 800-257-4747 ■ *Web:* www.wvsma.com						
West Virginia State Museum						
1900 Kanawha Blvd E The Cultural Ctr	Charleston	WV	25305	304-558-0220	558-2779	520
TF: 800-946-9471 ■ *Web:* www.wvculture.org						
West Virginia State University						
117 Ferrell Hall PO Box 368	Institute	WV	25112	304-766-3000		166
TF: 800-987-2112 ■ *Web:* www.wvstateu.edu						
West Virginia State Wildlife Ctr						
PO Box 38	French Creek	WV	26218	304-924-6211		823
Web: www.wvdnr.gov/wildlife/wildlifecenter.shtm						
West Virginia University						
PO Box 6009	Morgantown	WV	26506	304-293-2121	293-3080	166
TF: 800-344-9881 ■ *Web:* www.wvu.edu						
Institute of Technology						
405 Fayette Pk	Montgomery	WV	25136	304-442-1000		166
TF: 888-554-8324 ■ *Web:* www.wvutech.edu						
Libraries PO Box 6069	Morgantown	WV	26506	304-293-2440	293-6638	434-6
TF: 800-498-6681 ■ *Web:* lib.wvu.edu						
Parkersburg 300 Campus Dr	Parkersburg	WV	26104	304-424-8000	424-8315	162
TF: 800-982-9887 ■ *Web:* www.wvup.edu						
West Virginia University College of Law						
PO Box 6130	Morgantown	WV	26506	304-293-5301	293-6891	167-1
Web: law.wvu.edu						
West Virginia University Hospitals						
1 Medical Ctr Dr	Morgantown	WV	26506	304-598-4200		374-3
Web: wvumedicine.org						
West Virginia University School of Medicine						
1 Medical Center Dr PO Box 9100	Morgantown	WV	26506	304-293-2408	293-7814	167-2
TF: 800-543-5650 ■ *Web:* www.hsc.wvu.edu/som						
West Virginia Veterinary Medical Assn (WVVMA)						
3801 Westerre Pkwy Ste D	Henrico	VA	23233	804-346-2611	346-2655	795
TF: 800-843-6664 ■ *Web:* www.wvvma.org						
West Virginia Wesleyan College						
59 College Ave	Buckhannon	WV	26201	304-473-8000	473-8108*	166
**Fax:* Admissions ■ *TF Admitting:* 800-722-9933 ■ *Web:* www.wvwc.edu						
West Warwick Public Library System						
1043 Main St	West Warwick	RI	02893	401-828-3750	828-8493	434-3
Web: www.wwlibrary.org						
West Whitlock Recreation Area						
16157A W Whitlock Rd	Gettysburg	SD	57442	605-765-9410		565
Web: gfp.sd.gov						
West Wind Inn 3345 W Gulf Dr	Sanibel	FL	33957	239-472-1541		669
TF: 800-824-0476 ■ *Web:* www.westwindinn.com						
West Window Corp						
226 Industrial Pk Dr	Martinsville	VA	24112	276-638-2394	638-2300	234
TF: 800-446-4167 ■ *Web:* www.westwindow.com						
West World Production Inc						
420 N Camden Dr	Beverly Hills	CA	90210	310-276-9500		637-9
Web: www.wwpi.com						
WESTA (Western Association of Travel)						
5933 NE Win Sivers Dr	Portland	OR	97220	503-251-8170		772
Westaff (USA) Inc 298 N Wiget Ln	Walnut Creek	CA	94598	925-930-5300		260
Web: www.westaff.com						
Westak Inc 1225 Elko Dr	Sunnyvale	CA	94089	408-734-8686	734-3592	625
TF: 800-387-3766 ■ *Web:* www.westak.com						
Westamerica Bancorp 1108 Fifth Ave	San Rafael	CA	94901	415-257-8000		70
NASDAQ: WABC ■ *Web:* www.westamerica.com						
Westar Energy Inc 818 S Kansas Ave	Topeka	KS	66612	785-575-6300		360-5
NYSE: WR ■ *TF:* 800-383-1183 ■ *Web:* www.westarenergy.com						
Westar Satellite Services LP						
777 Westar Ln	Cedar Hill	TX	75104	972-291-6000		116
Web: www.westarsat.com						
Westat Inc 1600 Research Blvd	Rockville	MD	20850	301-251-1500	294-2040	466
TF: 800-669-6820 ■ *Web:* www.westat.com						
Westbank & District Chamber of Commerce						
2372 Dobbin Rd	Westbank	BC	V4T2H9	250-768-3378	768-3465	137
Web: gwboardoftrade.com						
Westbay Auto Parts Inc						
2610 SE Mile Hill Dr	Port Orchard	WA	98366	360-876-8008	876-7999	54
Web: www.westbayautoparts.com						
Westbend Winery & Brewery						
5394 Williams Rd	Lewisville	NC	27023	336-945-9999		50-7
Web: www.westbendvineyards.com						

Name / Address	City	State	Zip	Phone	Fax	Class
Westborn Inc 21755 Michigan Ave *Web:* www.westbornmarket.com	Dearborn	MI	48124	313-274-6100		345
Westbridge Inc 1361 Elm St Ste 207 *TF:* 800-889-7871 ■ *Web:* www.westbridge.org	Manchester	NH	03101	603-634-4446		726
Westbrook Engineering 23501 Mound Rd *TF:* 800-899-8182 ■ *Web:* www.westbrook-eng.com	Warren	MI	48091	586-759-3100		358
Westbrook Floral Ltd 109 Av Lindsay *Web:* westbrookfloral.com	Dorval	QC	H9P2S6	514-636-1255		292
Westbrook Service Corp 1411 S Orange Blossom Trl *Web:* www.westbrookfl.com	Orlando	FL	32805	407-841-3310		610
Westbury National Show Systems Ltd 772 Warden Ave *TF:* 855-752-1372 ■ *Web:* www.westbury.com	Toronto	ON	M1L4T7	416-752-1371		184
Westby Co-op Credit Union 501 N Main St *TF:* 800-755-0055 ■ *Web:* www.wccucreditunion.coop	Westby	WI	54667	608-634-3118		219
West-Camp Press Inc 39 Collegeview Rd *Web:* www.westcamppress.com	Westerville	OH	43081	614-882-2378		627
Westcan Bulk Transport Ltd 12110 - 17th St NE *TF:* 800-661-2855 ■ *Web:* www.westcanbulk.ca	Edmonton	AB	T6S1A5	780-472-6633		314
Westcap Management Ltd 830 410 22nd St E *Web:* www.westcapmgt.ca	Saskatoon	SK	S7K5T6	306-652-5557		528
Westcare Management Inc 3155 River Rd S Ste 100 *TF:* 800-541-3732 ■ *Web:* www.westcaremgt.com	Salem	OR	97302	800-541-3732		194
Westchase Law Group pa 12029 Whitmarsh Ln *Web:* www.westchaselaw.com	Tampa	FL	33626	813-490-5211		428
Westchester Community College 75 Grasslands Rd **Fax:* Admissions ■ *TF:* 800-235-7267 ■ *Web:* www.sunywcc.edu	Valhalla	NY	10595	914-606-6600	606-6880*	162
Westchester County 110 Dr Martin Luther King Jr Blvd *Web:* www.westchesterclerk.com	White Plains	NY	10601	914-995-3080	995-4030	338
Westchester County Airport 240 Airport Rd Ste 202 *Web:* www.co.westchester.ny.us/airport	White Plains	NY	10604	914-995-4860	995-3980	27
Westchester County Tourism & Film 148 Martine Ave Ste 104 *TF:* 800-833-9282 ■ *Web:* westchestergov.com	White Plains	NY	10601	914-995-8500	995-8505	206
Westchester Lace & Textiles Inc 3901 Liberty Ave *Web:* www.westchesterlace.com	North Bergen	NJ	07047	201-864-2150		745-4
Westchester Medical Ctr 100 Woods Rd *Web:* www.westchestermedicalcenter.com	Valhalla	NY	10595	914-493-7000		374-3
Westchester Medical Ctr Advanced Imaging *Bone Marrow & Hematopoietic Stem Cell Transplant program* 19 Bradhurst Ave Ste 2100 *Web:* www.westchestermedicalcenter.com	Hawthorne	NY	10595	914-493-7000		769
Westchester Modular Homes Inc 30 Reagans Mill Rd *TF:* 800-832-3888 ■ *Web:* www.westchestermodular.com	Wingdale	NY	12594	845-832-9400		106
Westchester Park District 10201 Bond St *Web:* www.wpdparks.org	Westchester	IL	60154	708-865-8200		31
Westchester Philharmonic 123 Main St Lobby Level *TF:* 800-553-0031 ■ *Web:* www.westchesterphil.org	White Plains	NY	10601	914-682-3707	682-3716	573-3
Westchester Toyota Service 75 Vredenburgh Ave *TF:* 866-232-7662 ■ *Web:* www.westchestertoyota.com	Yonkers	NY	10704	914-968-6500		57
Westchester Transportation 100 E First St *Web:* www.co.westchester.ny.us/transportation	Mount Vernon	NY	10550	914-813-7777		468
Westchester Wine Warehouse 53 Tarrytown Rd *Web:* www.westchesterwine.com	White Plains	NY	10607	914-824-1400		443
Westchester, The 125 Westchester Ave *TF:* 877-746-6642 ■ *Web:* www.simon.com	White Plains	NY	10601	914-421-1333		460
Westco Home Furnishings Inc 400 NW Veterans Blvd *Web:* www.westcohomefurnishings.com	Miami	OK	74354	918-540-2464	540-1186	321
West-Com Nurse Call Systems Inc 2200 Cordelia Rd *TF:* 800-761-1180 ■ *Web:* www.westcall.com	Fairfield	CA	94534	707-428-5900		174
Westcon Comstor *Westcon Convergence* 520 White Plains Rd Ste 100 *TF:* 877-642-7750 ■ *Web:* www.westconcomstor.com/global/en.html#home	Omaha	NE	68154	877-642-7750		174
Westcon Group Inc 520 White Plains Rd *TF:* 800-527-9516 ■ *Web:* www.westconcomstor.com/global/en.html#home	Tarrytown	NY	10591	914-829-7000	829-7137	174
Westconsin Credit Union 3333 Schneider Ave SE *Web:* westconsincu.org	Menomonie	WI	54751	715-235-3403		219
Westcor Land Title Insurance Co 201 N New York Ave Ste 200 *Web:* www.wltic.com	Winter Park	FL	32789	407-629-5842		390
WestCorp Management Group LLC 6655 S Eastern Ave *Web:* www.westcorpmg.com	Las Vegas	NV	89119	702-307-2881		652
Westcorp Properties Inc 200 College Plaza 8215 - 112 St *Web:* www.westcorp.net	Edmonton	AB	T6G2C8	780-431-3300		652
Westcott Beach State Park Rt 3 *Web:* parks.ny.gov/parks/90/details.aspx	Henderson	NY	13650	315-938-5083		565
Westcott Displays Inc 450 Amsterdam St *Web:* www.westcottdisplays.com	Detroit	MI	48202	313-872-1200	875-3295	560
Westec Plastics Corp 6757 A Las Positas Rd *Web:* www.westecplastics.com	Livermore	CA	94551	925-454-3400		608
Westech Engineering Inc 3665 SW Temple *Web:* www.westech-inc.com	Salt Lake City	UT	84115	801-265-1000	265-1080	806
Westech International Inc 2500 Louisiana Blvd NE Ste 325 *Web:* www.westech-intl.com	Albuquerque	NM	87110	505-888-6666	837-9424	261
Westech Solutions LLC 50 Broadway Ste 206 *Web:* www.westechsolutions.com	Hawthorne	NY	10532	914-246-0789		393
WestEd 730 Harrison St *TF:* 877-493-7833 ■ *Web:* www.wested.org	San Francisco	CA	94107	415-565-3000	565-3012	668
Westell Technologies Inc 750 N Commons Dr *NASDAQ: WSTL* ■ **Fax:* Sales ■ *TF:* 800-323-6883 ■ *Web:* www.westell.com	Aurora	IL	60504	630-898-2500	375-4931*	735
Westerbeke Corp 150 John Hancock Rd Miles Standish Industrial Pk *TF:* 800-582-7846 ■ *Web:* www.westerbeke.com	Taunton	MA	02780	508-823-7677	884-9688	262
Westerlay Orchids 3504 Via Real *TF:* 888-800-8826 ■ *Web:* www.westerlayorchids.com	Carpinteria	CA	93013	805-684-5411	684-5414	369
Westerly Hospital 25 Wells St *TF:* 800-933-5960 ■ *Web:* westerlyhospital.org	Westerly	RI	02891	401-596-6000		374-3
Westerly Public Library 44 Broad St *TF:* 800-359-3090 ■ *Web:* www.westerlylibrary.org	Westerly	RI	02891	401-596-2877	596-5600	434-3
Westerman Bruce (Rep R - AR) 130 Cannon House Office Bldg *Web:* westerman.house.gov	Washington	DC	20515	202-225-3772	225-1314	342-2
Westermeyer Industries Inc 1441 State Rt 100 *TF:* 800-553-3336 ■ *Web:* www.westermeyerind.com	Bluffs	IL	62621	217-754-3277		261
Western & Southern Financial Group 400 Broadway *TF:* 800-333-5222 ■ *Web:* www.westernsouthern.com	Cincinnati	OH	45202	513-629-1800		360-4
Western & Southern Life Insurance Co 400 Broadway **Fax Area Code:* 513 ■ **Fax:* Hum Res ■ *TF:* 800-926-1993 ■ *Web:* www.westernsouthernlife.com	Cincinnati	OH	45202	800-926-1993	629-1212*	391-2
Western Ag Enterprises Inc 8121 W Harrison *Web:* www.westernag.com	Tolleson	AZ	85353	623-907-4034		779
Western Agcredit PO Box 95850 *TF:* 800-824-9198 ■ *Web:* www.westernagcredit.com	South Jordan	UT	84095	801-571-9200	576-0600	216
Western Air & Refrigeration Co 15914 S Avalon Blvd *Web:* www.limbachinc.com	Compton	CA	90220	310-327-4400		189-10
Western Aircraft Inc 4300 S Kennedy St *TF:* 800-333-3442 ■ *Web:* www.westair.com	Boise	ID	83705	208-338-1800	338-1887	63
Western American 1518 Taney St *Web:* www.westix.net	Kansas City	MO	64116	816-421-3000	421-3122	3
Western Architectural Services LLC 12552 S 125 W Ste B *Web:* www.western-architectural.com	Draper	UT	84020	801-523-0393		183
Western Association of Travel (WESTA) 5933 NE Win Sivers Dr	Portland	OR	97220	503-251-8170		772
Western Automation Inc 23011 Moulton Pkwy Ste F1 *Web:* www.waisales.com	Laguna Hills	CA	92653	949-859-6988		57
Western Bagel Baking Corp 7814 Sepulveda Blvd *TF:* 800-555-0882 ■ *Web:* www.westernbagel.com	Van Nuys	CA	91405	818-786-5847	787-3221	345
Western Bay Sheet Metal Inc 2311 Marconi Ct *Web:* www.westernbay.net	San Diego	CA	92154	619-233-1753		697
Western Bee Supplies Inc 5 Ninth Ave E *TF:* 800-548-8440 ■ *Web:* www.westernbee.com	Polson	MT	59860	406-883-2918		279
Western Beef Inc 47-05 Metropolitan Ave *TF:* 800-475-6203 ■ *Web:* www.westernbeef.com	Ridgewood	NY	11385	718-417-3770		345
Western Beverages Inc 4545 E 51st Ave *Web:* western-beverage-distributing-company.placestars.c	Denver	CO	80216	303-388-5755		81-1
Western Boxed Meats Distributors Inc 2401 NE Argyle St *Web:* www.westernboxedmeat.com	Portland	OR	97211	503-284-3314		473
Western Branch Diesel Inc 3504 Shipwright St *Web:* www.westernbranchdiesel.com	Portsmouth	VA	23703	757-673-7000	673-7190	770
Western Branch Metals 1006 Obici Industrial Blvd *Web:* www.wbmetals.com	Suffolk	VA	23434	757-215-1500		480
Western Builders of Amarillo Inc 700 S Grant St *TF:* 800-525-7369 ■ *Web:* www.wbamarillo.com	Amarillo	TX	79101	806-376-4321		186
Western Bus Sales Inc 30355 SE Hwy 212 *TF:* 800-258-2473 ■ *Web:* www.westernbus.com	Boring	OR	97009	503-905-0002	905-0003	57
Western Camp Services Ltd 7668 - 69 St *Web:* www.westerncampservices.com	Edmonton	AB	T6B2J7	780-468-1568	468-1948	378
Western Canada Lottery Corp 125 Garry St 10th Fl *Web:* www.wclc.com	Winnipeg	MB	R3C4J1	204-942-8217		452
Western Canada Wilderness Committee (WCWC) 227 Abbott St *TF:* 800-661-9453 ■ *Web:* www.wildernesscommittee.org	Vancouver	BC	V6B2K7	604-683-8220	683-8229	48-13
Western Cardinal Inc 205 Durley Ave *Web:* www.westerncardinal.com	Camarillo	CA	93010	805-482-2586	484-2713	63
Western Carolina University (WCU) 1 University Dr *TF:* 877-928-4968 ■ *Web:* www.wcu.edu	Cullowhee	NC	28723	828-227-7211	227-7319	166
Western Commerce Bank 1910 Wyoming Blvd NE *Web:* www.wcb.net	Albuquerque	NM	87112	505-271-9964	271-9879	70
Western Commercial Services LLC 2311 Industrial Rd *TF:* 800-393-8287 ■ *Web:* www.westerncommercial.net	Las Vegas	NV	89102	702-384-7907		256
Western Communications Inc 1777 SW Chandler Ave *TF:* 800-503-3933 ■ *Web:* www.bendbulletin.com	Bend	OR	97702	541-382-1811	383-0372	637-8
Western Concord Manufacturing Ltd 880 Cliveden Ave *TF:* 800-663-6208 ■ *Web:* www.westernconcord.com	Vancouver	BC	V3M5R5	604-525-1061		601

				Phone	Fax	Class
Western Connecticut State University 181 White St.	Danbury	CT	06810	203-837-8200	837-8234	166
TF: 877-837-9278 ■ *Web:* wcsu.edu						
Western Consolidated Co-op 520 Co Rd 9 PO Box 78	Holloway	MN	56249	320-394-2171	394-2180	276
TF: 800-368-3310 ■ *Web:* www.west-con.com						
Western Consolidated Technologies Inc 700 W Swager Dr	Fremont	IN	46737	260-495-9866		677
Web: www.wctgroup.com						
Western Container Corp 1600 First Ave.	Big Spring	TX	79720	432-263-8361	263-8075	98
Web: westerncontainercoke.com						
Western Continental Book Co 6425 Washington St.	Denver	CO	80229	303-289-1761		95
TF: 800-364-0350 ■ *Web:* www.continentalbook.com						
Western Contract 11455 Folsom Blvd	Rancho Cordova	CA	95742	916-638-3338	638-2698	321
Web: www.westerncontract.com						
Western Co-op Electric Assn Inc 635 S 13th St.	WaKeeney	KS	67672	785-743-5561	743-2717	245
TF: 800-456-6720 ■ *Web:* www.westerncoop.com						
Western Co-op Transport Assn 4501 72nd St SW	Montevideo	MN	56265	320-269-5531	269-5532	780
TF: 800-992-8817 ■ *Web:* www.westernco-op.com						
Western Copper Corp 1040 W Georgia St FL 15	Vancouver	BC	V6E4H1	604-684-9497		502
TF: 888-966-9995 ■ *Web:* westerncopperandgold.com						
Western Correctional Institution 13800 McMullen Hwy	Cumberland	MD	21502	301-729-7000		213
Western Creative Inc 26135 Plymouth Rd	Redford	MI	48239	313-937-1000		514
Web: www.westerncreative.com						
Western CT Convention & Visitors Bureau PO Box 968	Litchfield	CT	06759	860-567-4506	567-5214	200
Web: www.northwestct.com						
Western Cullen Hayes Inc 2700 W 36th Pl.	Chicago	IL	60632	773-254-9600	254-1110	700
Web: wch.com						
Western Development Corp 1413 P St NW Ste 403	Washington	DC	20005	202-338-5200	333-0223	652
Web: www.westdev.com						
Western Development Museum 2610 Lorne Ave S	Saskatoon	SK	S7J0S6	306-931-1910	934-0525	520
TF: 800-363-6345 ■ *Web:* www.wdm.ca						
Western Diesel Services Inc 1100 Research Blvd	Saint Louis	MO	63132	314-868-8620	868-9314	262
Western Digital Corp 3355 Michelson Dr Ste 100	Irvine	CA	92612	949-672-7000	672-5498	173-8
NASDAQ: WDC ■ *TF:* 800-832-4778 ■ *Web:* www.wdc.com						
Western Digitech Inc 7312 SW 48th St	Miami	FL	33155	305-669-0119		180
Web: www.westerndigitech.com						
Western Drug 3604 San Fernando Rd	Glendale	CA	91204	818-956-6691		475
TF: 800-891-3661 ■ *Web:* www.westerndrug.com						
Western Dubuque Biodiesel LLC 904 Jamesmeier Rd PO Box 82	Farley	IA	52046	563-744-3554		580
TF: 800-247-1345 ■ *Web:* www.wdbiodiesel.net						
Western Economic Assn International (WEAI) 18837 Brookhurst St Ste 304	Fountain Valley	CA	92708	714-965-8800	965-8829	49-2
Web: www.weai.org						
Western Electrical Sales Inc (WES) 521 Glide Ave	West Sacramento	CA	95691	916-372-1001		246
Web: www.wesisales.com						
Western Energy Co 138 Rosebud Ln	Colstrip	MT	59323	406-748-5100	748-5181	501
Web: westmoreland.com						
Western Engineering Contractors Inc 3171 Rippey Rd	Loomis	CA	95650	916-652-3990	652-3995	261
Web: www.westeng.com						
Western Enterprises Inc 875 Bassett Rd	Westlake	OH	44145	800-783-7890	835-8283*	811
**Fax Area Code:* 440 ■ *TF:* 800-783-7890 ■ *Web:* www.westernenterprises.com						
Western Environmental Technology Laboratories Inc 620 Applegate St	Philomath	OR	97370	541-929-5650		668
Web: www.wetlabs.com						
Western Equipment Distributors Inc 20224 80th Ave S	Kent	WA	98032	253-872-8858		274
Web: www.western-equip.com						
Western Excelsior Corp 901 Grand Ave	Mancos	CO	81328	970-533-7412		820
Web: www.westernexcelsior.com						
Western Express Inc 7135 Centennial Pl	Nashville	TN	37209	877-986-8855	350-9957*	780
**Fax Area Code:* 615 ■ *TF:* 800-316-7160 ■ *Web:* www.westernexp.com/contact-2						
Western Exterminator Co 305 N Crescent Way	Anaheim	CA	92801	714-517-9000		577
TF: 800-698-2440 ■ *Web:* www.westernexterminator.com						
Western Farmers Electric Co-op 701 NE Seventh St	Anadarko	OK	73005	405-247-3351		245
Web: www.wfec.com						
Western Feed Yard Inc 548 S Rd I	Johnson	KS	67855	620-492-6256		10-1
Western Fibre Products Inc 10924 Vulcan St	South Gate	CA	90280	562-861-6665		602
Western Fireproofing Company of Kansas Inc 1501 Westport Rd	Kansas City	MO	64111	816-561-7667		189-12
Web: www.westernfireproofing.com						
Western Forest Products Inc (WFP) 495 Dunsmuir St Unit 210	Nanaimo	BC	V9R6B9	604-648-4500	681-9584	448
TSE: WEF ■ *TF:* 800-806-5484 ■ *Web:* www.westernforest.com						
Western Forestry & Conservation Assn 4033 SW Canyon Rd	Portland	OR	97221	503-226-4562	226-2515	48-12
TF: 888-722-9416 ■ *Web:* www.westernforestry.org						
Western Forge & Flange Co 687 County Rd 2201	Cleveland	TX	77327	281-727-7060	727-7060	483
TF: 800-352-6433 ■ *Web:* www.western-forge.com						
Western Forms Inc 6200 Equitable Rd	Kansas City	MO	64120	816-241-0477		488
Web: www.westernforms.com						
Western Fraternal Life Assn (WFLA) 1900 First Ave NE	Cedar Rapids	IA	52402	319-363-2653		391-2
TF: 877-935-2467 ■ *Web:* www.wflains.org						
Western Funding Inc PO Box 94858	Las Vegas	NV	89193	888-434-3150		217
TF: 888-434-3122 ■ *Web:* www.westernfundinginc.com						
Western Gateway Heritage State Park 115 State St Ste 4	North Adams	MA	01247	413-663-6312		565
Web: www.mass.gov						
Western Glove Works Ltd 555 Logan Ave	Winnipeg	MB	R3A0S4	204-788-4249		157-6
Web: westerngloveworks.ca						
Western Golf Properties LLC 1 Spectrum Pointe Dr Ste 310	Lake Forest	CA	92630	949-417-3251		653
Web: www.cacm.org						
Western Group Inc 511 W 10Th	Pueblo	CO	81003	719-543-3604		390
Web: wgiinsurance.com						
Western Hoist Inc 1839 Cleveland Ave	National City	CA	91950	619-474-3361	474-8261	470
TF: 888-994-6478 ■ *Web:* www.westernlift.org						
Western Home Communities 420 E 11th St	Cedar Falls	IA	50613	319-277-2141		672
Web: www.westernhomecommunities.org						
Western Horizon Resorts (WHR) 103 W Tomichi Ave Ste 201A	Gunnison	CO	81230	970-641-5387		121
TF: 800-378-3709 ■ *Web:* www.westernhorizonresorts.net						
Western Horseman Magazine 2112 Montgomery St	Fort Worth	TX	76107	817-737-6397	737-9266	457-14
TF: 800-877-5278 ■ *Web:* www.westernhorseman.com						
Western Hydro Corp 3449 Enterprise Ave	Hayward	CA	94545	510-783-9166	732-0250	386
TF: 800-972-5945 ■ *Web:* www.westernhydro.com						
Western Illinois Correctional Ctr 2500 Illinois 99	Mount Sterling	IL	62353	217-773-4441		213
Web: www.illinois.gov						
Western Illinois Electrical Co-op 524 N Madison St PO Box 338	Carthage	IL	62321	217-357-3125	357-3127	245
TF: 800-576-3125 ■ *Web:* www.wiec.net						
Western Illinois University 1 University Cir.	Macomb	IL	61455	309-298-1414	298-3111*	166
**Fax:* Admissions ■ *TF Admissions:* 877-742-5948 ■ *Web:* www.wiu.edu						
Malpass Library 1 University Cir	Macomb	IL	61455	309-298-2762	298-2791	434-6
TF: 800-413-6544 ■ *Web:* www.wiu.edu/library						
Quad Cities 3561 60th St.	Moline	IL	61265	309-762-9481	764-7172*	166
**Fax:* Admissions ■ *TF:* 877-742-5948 ■ *Web:* www.wiu.edu						
Western Implement Co Inc 2919 North Ave.	Grand Junction	CO	81504	970-242-7960	242-5241	274
TF: 800-338-6639 ■ *Web:* www.westernimplement.com						
Western Industries Inc 1141 S Tenth St	Watertown	WI	53094	920-261-0660		697
Web: www.westernind.com						
Western Institutional Review Board Inc 1019 39th Ave SE Ste 120	Puyallup	WA	98374	360-252-2500		533
TF: 800-562-4789 ■ *Web:* www.wirb.com						
Western International Securities Inc 70 S Lake Ave Ste 700	Pasadena	CA	91101	888-793-7717		690
TF: 888-793-7717 ■ *Web:* www.wisdirect.com						
Western International University 9215 N Black Canyon Hwy	Phoenix	AZ	85021	602-943-2311		166
TF: 866-948-4636 ■ *Web:* west.edu						
Western Iowa Power Co-op 809 Iowa 39	Denison	IA	51442	712-263-2943		245
TF: 800-253-5189 ■ *Web:* www.wipco.com						
Western Iowa Tech Community College 4647 Stone Ave.	Sioux City	IA	51102	712-274-6400	274-6412	800
TF: 800-352-4649 ■ *Web:* witcc.edu						
Western Kentucky Correctional Complex 374 New Bethel Church Rd.	Fredonia	KY	42411	270-388-9781	388-0031	213
Web: corrections.ky.gov						
Western Kentucky University 1906 College Heights Blvd	Bowling Green	KY	42101	270-745-0111	745-6133*	166
**Fax:* Admissions ■ *TF Admissions:* 800-495-8463 ■ *Web:* www.wku.edu						
Western Land Services Inc 1100 Conrad Industrial Dr	Ludington	MI	49431	231-843-8878		536
Web: westernls.com						
Western Lithograph Co 4335 Directors Row	Houston	TX	77092	713-681-2100		627
TF: 800-423-9537 ■ *Web:* www.westernlithograph.com						
Western Living Magazine 2608 Granville St Ste 560	Vancouver	BC	V6H3V3	604-877-7732		457-11
TF: 800-363-3272 ■ *Web:* westernliving.ca						
Western Lumber Cy LLC 2240 Tower E Ste 200	Medford	OR	97504	541-779-5121	779-0155	191-3
TF: 800-633-5554 ■ *Web:* www.westernlumber.com						
Western Manitoba Regional Library 710 Rosser Ave Unit 1	Brandon	MB	R7A0K9	204-727-6648		436
Web: www.wmrl.ca						
Western Marketing Inc 1010 S Access Rd	Iye	TX	79563	325-692-4662		579
Web: www.westmktg.com						
Western Mass News 1300 Liberty St	Springfield	MA	01104	413-733-4040	781-5733	741-129
TF: 877-872-2756 ■ *Web:* www.westernmassnews.com						
Western Medical Ctr Anaheim (WMCA) 1025 S Anaheim Blvd	Anaheim	CA	92805	714-533-6220		374-3
Web: www.westernmedanaheim.com						
Western Medical Ctr Santa Ana 1001 N Tustin Ave.	Santa Ana	CA	92705	714-953-3500	953-3613	374-3
Web: www.westernmedicalcenter.com						
Western Memorial Regional Hospital 1 Brookfield Ave PO Box 2005	Corner Brook	NL	A2H6J7	709-637-5000		374-2
Web: www.westernhealth.nl.ca						
Western Mental Health Institute 11100 Hwy 64 W	Bolivar	TN	38008	731-228-2000	457-0335*	374-5
**Fax Area Code:* 865 ■ *TF:* 800-770-8277 ■ *Web:* tn.gov						
Western Methods Machinery Corp 2344 Pullman St	Santa Ana	CA	92705	949-252-6600		529
Western Michigan University 1903 W Michigan Ave.	Kalamazoo	MI	49008	269-387-1000	387-2096*	166
**Fax:* Admissions ■ *Web:* www.wmich.edu						
Western Michigan University Waldo Library 1903 W Michigan Ave.	Kalamazoo	MI	49008	269-387-5202	387-5077	434-6
TF: 866-533-3438 ■ *Web:* www.wmich.edu						
Western Millwork Inc 2940 W Willetta St	Phoenix	AZ	85009	602-233-1921	278-7101	499
Web: www.westernmillworkaz.com						

Phone | Fax | Class

Western Missouri Correctional Ctr
609 E Pence Rd .... Cameron MO 64429 816-632-1390 632-2562 213
TF: 800-726-7390 ■ *Web:* mo.gov

Western Montana Fair 1101 S Ave W .... Missoula MT 59801 406-721-3247 642
Web: www.missoulafairgrounds.com

Western Museum of Mining & Industry
225 N Gate Blvd .... Colorado Springs CO 80921 719-488-0880 488-9261 520
TF: 800-752-6558 ■ *Web:* www.wmmi.org

Western National Mutual Insurance Co
5350 W 78th St. .... Edina MN 55439 952-835-5350 921-3159* 391-4
**Fax:* Hum Res ■ *TF:* 800-862-6070 ■ *Web:* www.wnins.com

Western National Parks Assn (WNPA)
12880 N Vistoso Village Dr .... Tucson AZ 85755 520-622-1999 48-23
Web: www.wnpa.org

Western Natural Gas Co
2960 Strickland St .... Jacksonville FL 32254 904-387-3511 387-6034 316
TF: 800-683-5542 ■ *Web:* www.westernnaturalgas.com

Western Nebraska Community College
1601 E 27th St .... Scottsbluff NE 69361 308-635-3606 635-6732 162
TF: 800-348-4435 ■ *Web:* www.wncc.net

Western Nevada Community College (WNC)
Douglas 1680 Bently Pkwy S. .... Minden NV 89423 775-782-2413 782-2415 162
TF: 800-433-3243 ■ *Web:* www.wnc.edu
Fallon 160 Campus Way .... Fallon NV 89406 775-423-7565 423-8029 162
Web: www.wnc.edu/location/fallon

Western Nevada Musical Theater Co
Western Nevada College
2201 W College Pkwy Cedar Bldg 113 .... Carson City NV 89703 775-445-4249 445-3154 573-4
Web: www.wnc.edu

Western Nevada Supply Co
950 S Rock Blvd .... Sparks NV 89431 775-359-5800 359-4649 612
TF: 800-648-1230 ■ *Web:* www.wns1.com

Western New England College
1215 Wilbraham Rd .... Springfield MA 01119 413-782-3111 782-1777* 166
**Fax:* Admissions ■ *TF:* 800-782-6665 ■ *Web:* wne.edu

Western New Mexico University
1000 W College St PO Box 680 .... Silver City NM 88061 575-538-6011 538-6278 166
TF Admissions: 800-872-9668 ■ *Web:* www.wnmu.edu

Western North Carolina Nature Ctr
75 Gashes Creek Rd .... Asheville NC 28805 828-298-5600 50-5
Web: www.wildwnc.org

Western Nuclear Inc
2801 Youngfield St Ste 340 .... Golden CO 80401 303-274-1767 502

Western Oilfields Supply Co
3404 State Rd .... Bakersfield CA 93308 661-399-9124 392-9427* 264-3
**Fax:* Acctg ■ *TF:* 800-742-7246 ■ *Web:* www.rainforrent.com

Western Oklahoma State College
2801 N Main St .... Altus OK 73521 580-477-2000 477-7723 162
TF: 800-662-1113 ■ *Web:* www.wosc.edu

Western Ophthalmics Corp
19019 36th Ave W Ste G. .... Lynnwood WA 98036 425-672-9332 544
TF: 800-426-9938 ■ *Web:* www.west-op.com

Western Oregon University
345 Monmouth Ave N. .... Monmouth OR 97361 503-838-8000 838-8067 166
TF Admissions: 877-877-1593 ■ *Web:* www.wou.edu

Western Oregon University Hamersly Library
345 N Monmouth Ave. .... Monmouth OR 97361 503-838-8418 838-8645 434-6
TF: 877-877-1593 ■ *Web:* www.wou.edu/provost/library

Western Outdoors Magazine
185 Avenida La Pata .... San Clemente CA 92673 949-366-0030 366-0804 457-22
TF: 800-290-2929 ■ *Web:* www.wonews.com

Western Pacific Distributors Inc
1739 Sabre St. .... Hayward CA 94545 510-732-0100 732-0155 665
Web: www.teamwpd.com

Western Pacific Storage Systems Inc
300 E Arrow Hwy .... San Dimas CA 91773 800-732-9777 286
TF: 800-732-9777 ■ *Web:* www.wpss.com

Western Pad 391 Thor Pl. .... Brea CA 92821 714-671-1900 627
TF: 800-400-3105 ■ *Web:* www.westernpad.com

Western Paper Distributors Inc
11551 E 45th Ave Ste A .... Denver CO 80239 303-371-6000 559
Web: www.western-paper.com

Western Partitions Inc
26055 SW Canyon Creek Rd .... Wilsonville OR 97070 503-620-1600 624-5781 189-9
TF: 800-783-0315 ■ *Web:* wpibuilds.com

Western Pennsylvania Hospital
4800 Friendship Ave. .... Pittsburgh PA 15224 412-578-5000 374-3
Web: ahn.org

Western Pest Services Inc
800 Lanidex Plaza. .... Parsippany NJ 07054 877-250-3857 577
TF: 877-250-3857 ■ *Web:* www.westernpest.com

Western Petroleum Co
9531 W 78th St. .... Eden Prairie MN 55344 952-941-9090 941-7470 579
TF: 800-972-3835 ■ *Web:* www.westernpetro.com

Western Piedmont Community College
1001 Burkemont Ave. .... Morganton NC 28655 828-438-6000 162
TF: 800-447-4091 ■ *Web:* www.wpcc.edu

Western Piedmont Symphony
243 Third Ave NE Ste 1-N. .... Hickory NC 28601 828-324-8603 324-1301 573-3
Web: www.wpsymphony.org

Western Pioneer Inc
4601 Shilshole Ave NW .... Seattle WA 98107 206-789-1930 781-2486 312
TF: 800-426-6783 ■ *Web:* www.wpioneer.com

Western Pioneer Sales Co
406 E Colorado St .... Glendale CA 91205 818-244-1466 300
TF: 800-640-4535 ■ *Web:* westernpioneersales.com

Western Placer Unified School District
600 Sixth St .... Lincoln CA 95648 916-645-6350 685
Web: www.wpusd.k12.ca.us

Western Plains Medical Complex
3001 Ave A .... Dodge City KS 67801 620-225-8400 225-8403 374-3
TF: 800-994-6610 ■ *Web:* www.westernplainsmc.com

Western Plastic Products Inc
8441 Monroe Ave. .... Stanton CA 90680 800-453-1881 495-2232* 9
**Fax Area Code:* 562 ■ *TF:* 800-453-1881 ■ *Web:* www.wbadges.com

Western Playland Amusement Park
1249 Futurity Dr .... Sunland Park NM 88063 575-589-3410 32
Web: www.westernplayland.com

Western Pneumatic Tube LLC
835 Sixth St S. .... Kirkland WA 98033 425-822-8271 828-6669 490
Web: www.wptube.com

Western Pneumatics Inc PO Box 21340 .... Eugene OR 97402 541-461-2600 461-2606 207
Web: www.westernp.com

Western Polymer Corp 32 Rd 'R' SE .... Moses Lake WA 98837 509-765-1803 765-0327 144
TF: 800-333-6431 ■ *Web:* www.westernpolymer.com

Western Power Sports Inc 601 E Gowen Rd. .... Boise ID 83716 208-376-8400 375-8901 711
TF: 800-999-3388 ■ *Web:* www.wps-inc.com

Western Printing Machinery Co
9229 Ivanhoe Ave .... Schiller Park IL 60176 847-678-1740 628
TF: 800-631-3572 ■ *Web:* www.wpm.com

Western Producer Publications
2310 Millar Ave .... Saskatoon SK S7K2Y2 306-665-3500 532-3
Web: www.producer.com

Western Products Inc 7777 N 73rd St. .... Milwaukee WI 53223 414-354-2310 354-2310* 190
**Fax:* Cust Svc ■ *TF:* 800-424-9300 ■ *Web:* www.westernplows.com

Western Pulp Products Co
5025 SW Hout St .... Corvallis OR 97333 541-757-1151 557
Web: www.westernpulp.com

Western Refining Inc 123 W Mills Ave .... El Paso TX 79905 915-534-1400 580
NYSE: WNR ■ *Web:* www.wnr.com

Western Reflections 261 Commerce Way .... Gallatin TN 37066 615-451-9700 452-0283 439
TF Cust Svc: 800-507-8302 ■ *Web:* www.western-reflections.com

Western Regional Off-Track Betting Corp
8315 Park Rd .... Batavia NY 14020 585-343-1423 322
Web: www.westernotb.com

Western Regional Research Ctr (WRRC)
800 Buchanan St .... Albany CA 94710 510-559-5600 559-5963 668
Web: www.ars.usda.gov/main/docs.htm?docid=5819

Western Reman Industrial LLC
588 W Seventh St .... Peru IN 46970 765-472-2002 650
TF: 800-669-5779 ■ *Web:* www.wriservices.com

Western Research Institute
365 N Ninth St .... Laramie WY 82072 307-721-2011 721-2345 668
TF: 888-463-6974 ■ *Web:* westernresearch.org

Western Reserve Academy 115 College St .... Hudson OH 44236 330-650-9717 622
Web: www.wra.net

Western Reserve Group, The
1685 Cleveland Rd .... Wooster OH 44691 330-262-9060 262-3259* 391-4
**Fax:* Hum Res ■ *TF:* 800-362-0426 ■ *Web:* www.wrg-ins.com

Western Reserve Historical Society Museum
10825 E Blvd .... Cleveland OH 44106 216-721-5722 520
Web: www.wrhs.org

Western Reserve Partners LLC
200 Public Sq Ste 3750 .... Cleveland OH 44114 216-589-0900 196
TF: 800-290-5460 ■ *Web:* wesrespartners.com

Western Reserve Wire Products
1920 Case Pkwy .... Twinsburg OH 44087 330-425-3421 815
Web: wrwp.com

Western Rib-Eye & Ribs
1401 N Boeke Rd .... Evansville IN 47711 812-476-5405 671
Web: www.westernribeye.com

Western Robidoux Inc
4006 S 40th St .... Saint Joseph MO 64503 816-279-1617 554
Web: www.eyecandygraphicarts.com

Western Rockingham Chamber of Commerce
112 W Murphy St .... Madison NC 27025 336-548-6248 139
Web: www.westernrockinghamchamber.com

Western Scrap Processing Co
3315 Drennan Industrial Loop S. .... Colorado Springs CO 80910 719-390-7986 686
TF: 800-564-0382 ■ *Web:* www.westernscrap.com

Western Security Bank
2812 First Ave N. .... Billings MT 59101 406-371-8200 70
TF: 800-983-5537 ■ *Web:* www.westernsecuritybank.com

Western Seminary
5511 SE Hawthorne Blvd .... Portland OR 97215 503-517-1800 517-1801 167-3
TF: 877-517-1800 ■ *Web:* www.westernseminary.edu

Western Slope Auto Co
2264 Hwy 6 & 50 .... Grand Junction CO 81505 970-243-0843 57
Web: www.westernslopeauto.com

Western State Bank
110 Fourth St S .... Devils Lake ND 58301 701-662-4936 70
Web: www.westernbanks.com

Western State College of Colorado
600 N Adams St .... Gunnison CO 81231 970-943-2119 943-2363* 166
**Fax:* Admissions ■ *TF Admissions:* 800-876-5309 ■ *Web:* www.western.edu

Western State Hospital
2400 Russellville Rd. .... Hopkinsville KY 42240 270-889-6025 374-5
TF: 800-928-8000 ■ *Web:* westernstatehospital.ky.gov

Western State Hospital
1215 Lee St .... Charlottesville VA 22903 540-332-8000 332-8144 374-5
Web: www.healthsystem.virginia.edu

Western State Hospital
9601 Steilacoom Blvd SW .... Tacoma WA 98498 253-582-8900 374-5
TF: 877-501-2233 ■ *Web:* dshs.wa.gov

Western State University College of Law
1111 N State College Blvd .... Fullerton CA 92831 714-459-1101 441-1748* 167-1
**Fax:* Admissions ■ *TF:* 800-978-4529 ■ *Web:* www.wsulaw.edu

Western States Envelope & Label Co
4480 N 132nd St .... Butler WI 53007 262-781-5540 781-5791 263
TF: 800-558-0514 ■ *Web:* www.wsel.com

Western States Equipment Co
500 E Overland Rd PO Box 38 .... Meridian ID 83642 208-888-2287 884-2314 358
Web: www.westernstatescat.com

Western States Fire Protection Co
7020 S Tucson Way .... Centennial CO 80112 303-792-0022 189-13
Web: www.wsfp.com

Western States Glass Corp
43443 Osgood Rd PO Box 6058 .... Fremont CA 94538 510-623-5000 330
Web: www.westernstatesglass.com

Western States Lodging
1018 W Atherton Dr .... Taylorsville UT 84123 801-269-0700 269-1512 379
Web: wslm.biz

Western States Mfg 811 Main St. .... Sioux City IA 51103 712-252-4248 754
Web: www.wsm-corp.com

Western States Petroleum Inc
450 S 15th Ave. .... Phoenix AZ 85007 602-252-4011 579
TF: 800-220-1353 ■ *Web:* www.westernstatespetroleum.com

	City	State	ZIP	Phone	Fax	Class
Western States Ticket Service						
143 W McDowell Rd	Phoenix	AZ	85003	602-254-3300		750
TF: 800-326-0331 ■ *Web:* www.wstickets.com						
Western States Truck Centers LLC						
3790 N Reserve St	Missoula	MT	59808	406-543-3196		791
Web: www.westernstatestruckcenters.com						
Western States Weeklies Inc						
PO Box 600600	San Diego	CA	92160	619-280-2985		637-8
TF: 800-628-9466 ■ *Web:* www.navydispatch.com						
Western Steel Inc Attn Fred Campbell						
3360 Davey Allison Blvd	Hueytown	AL	35023	205-744-2230		723
Web: westernsteelinc.com						
Western Suffolk Boces (suffolk 3)						
507 Deer Park Rd	Dix Hills	NY	11746	631-549-4900		685
TF: 800-877-8339 ■ *Web:* www.wsboces.org						
Western Sugar Co-op						
7555 E Hampden Ave Ste 600	Denver	CO	80231	303-830-3939	830-3941	296-38
TF: 800-523-7497 ■ *Web:* www.westernsugar.com						
Western Summit Constructors Inc						
9780 Mt Pyramid Ct Ste 100	Englewood	CO	80112	303-298-9500		186
Web: www.westernsummit.com						
Western Summit Manufacturing Corp						
13290 Daum Dr	City of Industry	CA	91746	626-333-3333		66
Western Supermarkets						
2614 19th St S	Birmingham	AL	35209	205-879-3471	879-3476	345
Web: www.westernsupermarkets.com						
Western Syrup Co						
13766 Milroy Pl	Santa Fe Springs	CA	90670	562-921-4485		296-15
TF: 800-521-3888 ■ *Web:* www.jogue.com						
Western Technical College						
400 Seventh St N	La Crosse	WI	54601	608-785-9200	789-6206	800
TF: 800-322-9982 ■ *Web:* www.westerntc.edu						
Western Technologies Inc						
3737 E Broadway Rd	Phoenix	AZ	85040	602-437-3737		192
TF: 800-580-3737 ■ *Web:* www.wt-us.com						
Western Technology Investment (WTI)						
104 La Mesa Dr Ste 102	Portola Valley	CA	94028	650-234-4300		792
Web: www.westerntech.com						
Western Telematic Inc 5 Sterling	Irvine	CA	92618	949-586-9950	583-9514	173-3
TF: 800-854-7226 ■ *Web:* www.wti.com						
Western Texas College 6200 College Ave	Snyder	TX	79549	325-573-8511	573-9321*	162
**Fax:* Admissions ■ *TF:* 888-468-6982 ■ *Web:* www.wtc.edu						
Western Texas Lions Eye Bank Alliance						
2030 Pullman St Ste 4	San Angelo	TX	76902	325-653-8666	655-2847	269
TF: 866-226-7632 ■ *Web:* www.wtleb.org						
Western Theological Seminary						
101 E 13th St	Holland	MI	49423	616-392-8555	392-7717	167-3
TF: 800-392-8554 ■ *Web:* www.westernsem.edu						
Western Towboat Company Inc						
617 NW 40th St	Seattle	WA	98107	206-789-9000	789-9755	465
TF: 800-932-9651 ■ *Web:* www.westerntowboat.com						
Western Trailer Co 251 W Gowen Rd	Boise	ID	83716	208-344-2539	344-1521	779
TF: 888-344-2539 ■ *Web:* www.westerntrailer.com						
Western Truck Parts & Equip Co						
3707 Airport Way S	Seattle	WA	98134	206-624-7383		61
TF: 800-255-7383 ■						
Web: westernpeterbilt.com/western-peterbilt-seattle-wa						
Western Tube & Conduit Corp						
2001 E Dominguez St	Long Beach	CA	90810	310-537-6300	604-9785	490
Web: www.westerntube.com						
Western Union Holdings Inc						
12500 E Belford Ave	Englewood	CO	80112	720-332-1000	332-4753	69
NYSE: WU ■ *TF Cust Svc:* 800-325-6000 ■ *Web:* westernunion.com						
Western United Electric Supply Corp						
100 Bromley Business Pkwy	Brighton	CO	80603	303-659-2356		791
TF: 800-748-3116 ■ *Web:* www.wue.coop						
Western United Life Assurance Co						
929 W Sprague Ave PO Box 2290	Spokane	WA	99210	509-835-2500	835-3191	391-2
TF General: 800-247-2045 ■ *Web:* www.manhattanlife.com/Western-United-Life						
Western University 1151 Richmond St	London	ON	N6A3K7	519-661-2111	661-3630*	785
**Fax:* Purchasing ■ *Web:* www.uwo.ca						
Western University of Health Sciences						
309 E Second St	Pomona	CA	91766	909-623-6116		162
TF: 800-346-1610 ■ *Web:* www.westernu.edu						
Western Upper Peninsula Convention & Visitor Bureau						
405 N Lake St PO Box 706	Ironwood	MI	49938	906-932-4850		206
TF: 800-522-5657 ■ *Web:* www.explorewesternup.com						
Western Veterinary Conference						
2425 E Oquendo Rd	Las Vegas	NV	89120	702-739-6698		794
TF: 866-800-7326 ■ *Web:* www.wvc.org						
Western Village Inn & Casino						
815 Nichols Blvd	Sparks	NV	89434	800-648-1170		133
TF: 800-648-1170 ■ *Web:* www.westernvillagesparks.com						
Western Washington University						
516 High St	Bellingham	WA	98225	360-650-3000	650-7369	166
TF: 800-261-7331 ■ *Web:* www.wwu.edu						
Western Water Co						
705 Mission Ave Ste 200	San Rafael	CA	94901	415-256-8800		787
Western Water Constructors Inc						
707 Aviation Blvd	Santa Rosa	CA	95403	707-540-9640	540-9641	187
Web: www.westernwater.com						
Western Window Systems						
2200 E Riverview Dr	Phoenix	AZ	85034	877-268-1300		234
TF: 877-268-1300 ■ *Web:* westernwindowsystems.com						
Western Wire Group						
4025 NW Express Ave	Portland	OR	97210	503-222-1644		688
TF: 800-635-8296 ■ *Web:* www.thewesterngroup.com						
Western Wood Preserving Co						
1310 Zehnder St	Sumner	WA	98390	253-863-8191		818
TF: 800-472-7714 ■ *Web:* www.westernwoodpreserving.com						
Western Wood Products Assn (WWPA)						
522 SW Fifth Ave Ste 500	Portland	OR	97204	503-224-3930	224-3934	48-2
Web: www.wwpa.org						
Western World Insurance Co						
400 Parson's Pond Dr	Franklin Lakes	NJ	07417	201-847-8600	847-1010	391-5
TF: 888-847-8600 ■ *Web:* www.westernworld.com						
Western World Insurance Group Inc						
400 Parson's Pond Dr	Franklin Lakes	NJ	07417	201-847-8600	847-1010	391-5
Web: www.westernworld.com						

	City	State	ZIP	Phone	Fax	Class
Western Wyoming Beverages Inc						
100 Reliance Rd	Rock Springs	WY	82901	307-362-6332		81-2
Web: www.westernwyomingbeverages.com						
Western Wyoming Community College						
2500 College Dr	Rock Springs	WY	82901	307-382-1600	382-1636*	162
**Fax:* Admissions ■ *TF:* 800-226-1181 ■ *Web:* www.wwcc.wy.edu						
Western Youth Institution						
5155 Western Ave	Morganton	NC	28655	828-438-6037	438-6076	412
WesternGeco 10001 Richmond Ave	Houston	TX	77042	713-789-9600		538
Web: www.slb.com						
Western-Southern Life Assurance Co						
400 Broadway	Cincinnati	OH	45202	866-832-7719	629-1212*	391-2
**Fax Area Code:* 513 ■ *TF:* 866-832-7719 ■ *Web:* www.westernsouthernlife.com						
Westerra Credit Union						
3700 E Alameda Ave	Denver	CO	80209	303-321-4209		219
TF: 800-858-7212						
Westervelt Company Inc, The						
PO Box 48999	Tuscaloosa	AL	35404	205-562-5000	562-5012	683
Web: www.westervelt.com						
Westerville Area Chamber of Commerce						
99 Commerce Pk Dr # A	Westerville	OH	43082	614-882-8917	882-2085	139
Web: www.westervillechamber.com						
Westerville Public Library						
126 S State St	Westerville	OH	43081	614-882-7277	882-4160	434-3
TF: 800-816-0662 ■ *Web:* westervillelibrary.org						
Westerville This Week						
7801 N Central Dr	Lewis Center	OH	43035	740-888-6100	888-6006	532-4
TF: 888-837-4342 ■ *Web:* www.thisweeknews.com						
Westex Inc 122 W 22nd St	Oak Brook	IL	60523	773-523-7000	523-0965	745-7
TF: 866-493-7839 ■ *Web:* www.westex.com						
West-Fair Electric Contractors Inc						
200 Brady Ave	Hawthorne	NY	10532	914-769-8050	769-7451	189-4
Web: www.west-fair.com						
Westfalia Technologies Inc						
3655 Sandhurst Dr	York	PA	17406	717-764-1115	764-1118	207
TF: 800-673-2522 ■ *Web:* www.westfaliausa.com						
Westfall Engineers Inc						
14583 Big Basin Way	Saratoga	CA	95070	408-867-0244		261
Web: westf.com						
Westfarms Mall						
1500 New Britian Ave	West Hartford	CT	06110	860-561-3420		460
Web: www.shopwestfarms.com						
Westfield America Inc						
2049 Century Park E	Century City	CA	90067	310-478-4456		655
Web: www.westfield.com						
Westfield Area Chamber of Commerce (WACC)						
173 Elm St 3rd Fl	Westfield	NJ	07090	908-233-3021		139
Web: www.gwaccnj.com						
Westfield Athenaeum 6 Elm St	Westfield	MA	01085	413-568-7833	568-0988	434-3
TF: 800-441-9829 ■ *Web:* www.westath.org						
Westfield Bank						
140 Portage Trail	Cuyahoga Falls	OH	44221	330-923-0454		70
Web: www.westfield-bank.com						
Westfield Board of Education Inc						
302 Elm St	Westfield	NJ	07090	908-789-4401		685
TF: 800-355-2583 ■ *Web:* www.westfieldnjk12.org						
Westfield Broward Mall						
8000 W Broward Blvd	Plantation	FL	33388	954-473-8100		460
Web: www.westfield.com						
Westfield Capital Management Company LP						
1 Financial Ctr 23th Fl	Boston	MA	02111	617-428-7100		401
Web: www.westfieldcapital.com						
Westfield Century City						
10250 Santa Monica Blvd	West Los Angeles	CA	90067	310-553-5300		460
Web: www.westfield.com/centurycity						
Westfield Citrus Park 8021 Citrus Pk Dr	Tampa	FL	33625	813-926-4644		460
Web: www.westfield.com						
Westfield Countryside						
27001 US 19 N Ste 1039	Clearwater	FL	33761	727-796-1079		460
Web: www.westfield.com/countryside						
Westfield Downtown Plaza 660 J St	Sacramento	CA	95814	916-442-4000	442-3117	460
Westfield Electroplating Company Inc						
68 N Elm St	Westfield	MA	01085	413-568-3716		481
Web: www.westfieldplating.com						
Westfield Engineering & Services Inc						
8310 McHard Rd	Houston	TX	77053	281-438-2047		256
Westfield Fashion Square						
14006 Riverside Dr	Sherman Oaks	CA	91423	818-783-0550		460
Web: www.westfield.com						
Westfield Financial Inc 141 Elm St	Westfield	MA	01085	413-568-1911	562-7939	360-2
NASDAQ: WFD ■ *TF:* 800-995-5734 ■ *Web:* www.westfieldbank.com						
Westfield Fox Hills						
6000 Sepulveda Blvd	Culver City	CA	90230	310-390-5073		460
Web: www.westfield.com/foxhills						
Westfield Industries Ltd						
74 Hwy 205 E	Rosenort	MB	R0G1W0	204-746-2396		273
TF: 866-467-7207 ■ *Web:* www.grainaugers.com						
Westfield Memorial Library						
550 E Broad St	Westfield	NJ	07090	908-789-4090		434-3
Web: www.wmlnj.org						
Westfield Mission Valley						
1640 Camino del Rio N	San Diego	CA	92108	619-296-6375		460
Web: www.westfield.com						
Westfield Montgomery						
7101 Democracy Blvd	Bethesda	MD	20817	301-469-6000		460
Web: www.westfield.com/montgomery						
Westfield San Francisco Centre						
865 Market St	San Francisco	CA	94103	415-495-5656		460
Web: www.westfield.com						
Westfield Santa Anita						
400 S Baldwin Ave Ste 231	Arcadia	CA	91007	626-445-6255		460
Web: www.westfield.com/santaanita						
Westfield Sarasota Square						
8201 S Tamiami Tr	Sarasota	FL	34238	941-922-9609		460
Web: www.westfield.com						
Westfield Shoppingtown Annapolis						
2002 Annapolis Mall	Annapolis	MD	21401	410-266-5432		460
TF: 800-805-2339 ■ *Web:* www.westfield.com						

Phone | Fax | Class

Westfield Shoppingtown UTC
4545 La Jolla Village Dr.................... San Diego CA 92122 858-546-8858 460
TF: 800-688-6595 ■ *Web:* www.westfield.com

Westfield Southgate
3501 S Tamiami Trl......................... Sarasota FL 34239 941-955-0900 460
Web: www.westfield.com

Westfield State University
577 Western Ave........................... Westfield MA 01086 413-572-5300 572-0520* 166
**Fax:* Admissions ■ *Web:* www.westfield.ma.edu

Westfield Steel Inc
530 State Rd 32 W......................... Westfield IN 46074 800-622-4984 896-5343* 492
**Fax Area Code:* 317 ■ *TF:* 800-622-4984 ■ *Web:* www.westfieldsteel.com

Westfield Topanga
6600 Topanga Canyon Blvd............... Canoga Park CA 91303 818-594-8740 460
TF: 800-864-8377 ■ *Web:* www.westfield.com

Westfield Trumbull Town Shopping Mall
5065 Main St............................. Trumbull CT 06611 203-372-4500 460
Web: www.westfield.com

Westfield Valley Fair
2855 Stevens Creek Blvd Ste 2178........... Santa Clara CA 95050 408-248-4451 460
TF: 800-322-2683 ■ *Web:* www.westfield.com

Westfield Veterinary Hospital Pc
8789 NW 54th Ave.......................... Johnston IA 50131 515-986-5738 794
Web: www.westfieldvet.com

Westford Regency Inn & Conference Ctr
219 Littleton Rd........................... Westford MA 01886 978-692-8200 692-7403 379
TF: 800-624-9990 ■ *Web:* www.westfordregency.com

Westford Riding Academy
22 Griffin Rd.............................. Westford MA 01886 978-692-2894 148
TF: 800-696-3919 ■ *Web:* www.westford-homesforsale.com

Westgate Branson Woods
2201 Roark Valley Rd........................ Branson MO 65616 417-334-2324 379
TF: 877-253-8572 ■ *Web:* westgatedestinations.com

Westgate Hotel, The 1055 Second Ave........ San Diego CA 92101 619-238-1818 557-3737 671
TF: 800-522-1564 ■ *Web:* westgatehotel.com

WestGate Mall 205 W Blackstock Rd......... Spartanburg SC 29301 864-574-0264 460
TF: 800-235-8318 ■ *Web:* www.westgate-mall.com

Westgate Management Co Inc
133 Franklin Corner Rd................. Lawrenceville NJ 08648 609-895-8890 895-0058 655
Web: www.wgmgt.com

Westgate Painted Mountain Country Club
6302 E McKellips Rd......................... Mesa AZ 85215 480-654-3611 379
TF: 888-433-3707 ■ *Web:* www.westgatedestinations.com

Westglow Resort & Spa
224 Westglow Cir...................... Blowing Rock NC 28605 828-295-4463 707
TF: 800-562-0807 ■ *Web:* www.westglowresortandspa.com

Westham Trade Co Ltd 3620 NW 114th Ave........ Doral FL 33178 786-464-5300 593-0316* 174
**Fax Area Code:* 305 ■ *Web:* www.wtrade.com

West-Herr Automotive Group Inc
3448 McKinley Pkwy........................ Blasdell NY 14219 716-649-5640 57
TF: 800-643-2112 ■ *Web:* www.westherr.com

Westin Atlanta Airport, The
4736 Best Rd................................ Atlanta GA 30337 404-762-7676 378
Web: www.westinatlantaairport.com

Westin Atlanta Perimeter North, The
7 Concourse Pkwy NE........................ Atlanta GA 30328 770-395-3900 378
TF: 888-627-8407 ■ *Web:* www.westinatlantanorth.com

Westin Automotive Products Inc
5200 N Irwindale Ave Ste 220.............. Irwindale CA 91706 626-960-6762 61
TF: 800-345-8476 ■ *Web:* www.westinautomotive.com

Westin Casuarina Las Vegas Hotel Casino & Spa
160 E Flamingo Rd......................... Las Vegas NV 89109 702-836-5900 836-9776 133
Web: www.starwoodhotels.com

Westin Chicago River North, The
320 N Dearborn St........................... Chicago IL 60654 312-744-1900 378
TF: 800-937-8461 ■ *Web:* www.westinchicago.com

Westin Diplomat Resort & Spa
501 Diplomat Pkwy....................... Hallandale FL 33009 954-883-4444 669
Web: www.diplomatgolf.com

Westin Engineering Inc
3100 Zinfandel Dr Ste 300............. Rancho Cordova CA 95670 916-852-2121 463

Westin Governor Morris Hotel, The
2 Whippany Rd.......................... Morristown NJ 07960 973-539-7300 378
Web: www.westingovernormorris.com

Westin Harbour Castle 1 Harbour Sq........... Toronto ON M5J1A6 416-869-1600 707
Web: www.westinharbourcastletoronto.com

Westin Hotels & Resorts
10600 Westminster Blvd................. Westminster CO 80020 303-410-5000 378
Web: www.westindenverboulder.com

Westin Houston Downtown, The
1520 Texas Ave............................. Houston TX 77002 713-228-1520 228-1555 379
TF: 800-427-4697 ■ *Web:* www.westinhoustondowntown.com

Westin Kierland Resort & Spa
6902 E Greenway Pkwy..................... Scottsdale AZ 85254 480-624-1000 624-1001 707
TF: 800-354-5892 ■ *Web:* www.kierlandresort.com

Westin Long Beach, The
333 E Ocean Blvd....................... Long Beach CA 90802 562-436-3000 378
Web: westinlb.com

Westin Maui Resort & Spa, The
2365 Kaanapali Pkwy........................ Lahaina HI 96761 808-667-2525 661-5764 707
TF: 866-716-8112 ■ *Web:* www.westinmaui.com

Westin Michigan Avenue Hotel
909 N Michigan Ave.......................... Chicago IL 60611 312-943-7200 378
TF: 888-627-8385 ■ *Web:* www.thewestinmichiganavenue.com

Westin Mission Hills Resort
71333 Dinah Shore Dr................ Rancho Mirage CA 92270 760-328-5955 707
TF: 866-716-8108 ■ *Web:* www.westinmissionhills.com

Westin O'Hare, The 6100 N River Rd........... Rosemont IL 60018 847-698-6000 378
TF: 800-528-1234 ■ *Web:* www.westinohare.com

Westin Resort & Spa
4090 Whistler Way.......................... Whistler BC V0N1B4 604-905-5000 707
TF: 888-627-8979 ■ *Web:* www.westinwhistler.com

Westin Resort Guam, The
105 Gun Beach Rd............................ Tumon GU 96913 671-647-1020 378
Web: www.westin-guam.com

Westin Resort Tremblant
100 Ch Kandahar.................... Mont-Tremblant QC J8E1E2 819-681-8000 669
Web: www.westintremblant.com

Westin Reston Heights, The
11750 Sunrise Vly Dr.......................... Reston VA 20191 703-391-9000 378
TF: 888-627-8344 ■ *Web:* www.westinreston.com

Westin San Diego Gaslamp Quarter, The
910 Broadway Cir........................ San Diego CA 92101 619-239-2200 378
TF: 800-974-8885 ■ *Web:* www.westingaslamp.com

Westinghouse Electric Co
1000 Westinghouse Dr Ste 572A...... Cranberry Township PA 16066 412-374-4111 261
Web: www.westinghousenuclear.com

Westin-La Cantera Resort, The
16641 La Cantera Pkwy.................. San Antonio TX 78256 210-558-6500 378
Web: www.westinlacantera.com

WestJet Airlines Ltd 22 Aerial Pl NE............ Calgary AB T2E3J1 403-444-2600 253-0131* 25
TSE: WJA ■ **Fax Area Code:* 844 ■ *TF:* 888-293-7853 ■ *Web:* www.westjet.com

Westlake Chemical Corp
2801 Post Oak Blvd Ste 600.................. Houston TX 77056 713-960-9111 605-2
NYSE: WLK ■ *TF:* 888-953-3623 ■ *Web:* www.westlakechemical.com

Westlake Ctr 400 Pine St...................... Seattle WA 98101 206-467-1600 460
Web: www.westlakecenter.com

Westlake Farms Inc 23311 Newton Ave.......... Stratford CA 93266 559-947-3348 10-2

Westlake Hospital
1225 West Lake St...................... Melrose Park IL 60160 708-681-3000 374-3
TF: 800-570-8809 ■ *Web:* westlakehosp.com/home.aspx

Westlake Plastics Co PO Box 127................. Lenni PA 19052 610-459-1000 459-1084 604
TF: 800-999-1700 ■ *Web:* www.westlakeplastics.com

Westland Chamber of Commerce
36900 Ford Rd............................. Westland MI 48185 734-326-7222 326-6040 139
TF: 800-737-4859 ■ *Web:* www.westlandchamber.com

Westland Corp 1735 S Maize Rd............... Wichita KS 67209 316-721-1144 721-1495 757
TF: 800-247-1144 ■ *Web:* reiloyusa.com

Westland Enterprises Inc
3621 Stewart Rd......................... Forestville MD 20747 301-736-0600 627
TF: 800-882-1844 ■ *Web:* www.westlandenterprises.com

Westland Financial Services Inc
1717 Kettner Blvd Ste 200................. San Diego CA 92101 619-238-8144 195
Web: westlandinc.com

Westland Floral Co
1400 Cravens Ln......................... Carpinteria CA 93013 805-684-4011 369
TF: 800-747-0396 ■ *Web:* www.westlandfloral.com

Westland Ford 3450 Wall Ave.................... Ogden UT 84401 801-629-5500 57
Web: westlandford.com

Westland Printers Inc
14880 Sweitzer Ln.......................... Laurel MD 20707 301-384-7700 384-2616 627
Web: www.westlandprinters.com

Westland Sales PO Box 427................ Clackamas OR 97015 503-655-2563 656-8829 38
TF: 800-356-0766 ■ *Web:* www.splendide.com

Westland Shopping Ctr
35000 W Warren Rd........................ Westland MI 48185 734-425-5001 425-9205 460
Web: www.westlandcenter.com

Westlaw Court Express 1333 H St NW....... Washington DC 20005 202-423-2163 635
TF: 877-362-7387

West-Lite Supply Company Inc
12951 166th St............................ Cerritos CA 90703 800-660-6678 246
TF: 800-660-6678 ■ *Web:* www.west-lite.com

Westlog Aviation 311 Cove Rd.............. Brookings OR 97415 541-469-7911 30
TF: 800-761-5183 ■ *Web:* www.cal-ore.com

Westman Champlin & Kelly
900 Second Ave S...................... Minneapolis MN 55402 612-334-3222 428
Web: www.wck.com

Westman Communications Group
1906 Park Ave.............................. Brandon MB R7B0R9 204-725-4300 224
TF: 800-665-3337 ■ *Web:* www.westmancom.com

Westmark Hotels Inc 300 Elliott Ave W........... Seattle WA 98119 800-544-0970 285-7152* 379
**Fax Area Code:* 206 ■ *TF:* 800-544-0970 ■ *Web:* www.westmarkhotels.com

Westminster Chamber of Commerce
1025 Westminster Mall.................. Westminster CA 92683 714-898-2559 373-1499 139
TF: 800-545-5585 ■ *Web:* www.westminsterchamber.org

Westminster College
501 Westminster Ave........................ Fulton MO 65251 573-592-5251 592-5255 166
TF Admissions: 800-475-3361 ■ *Web:* www.westminster-mo.edu

Westminster College
319 S Market St.................... New Wilmington PA 16172 724-946-8761 946-6171* 166
**Fax:* Admissions ■ *TF:* 800-942-8033 ■ *Web:* www.westminster.edu

Westminster College
1840 South 1300 East.................. Salt Lake City UT 84105 801-832-2200 832-3101* 166
**Fax:* Admissions ■ *TF:* 800-748-4753 ■ *Web:* www.westminstercollege.edu

Westminster Communities of Florida
4449 Meandering Way.................... Tallahassee FL 32308 850-878-1136 672
TF: 800-948-1881 ■ *Web:* www.westminsterretirement.com

Westminster Hotel LLC
550 W Mt Pleasant Ave.................. Livingston NJ 07039 973-533-0600 378
Web: www.westminsterhotel.net

Westminster Mall
1025 Westminster Mall.................. Westminster CA 92683 714-898-2558 460
TF: 800-782-8888 ■ *Web:* www.simon.com

Westminster Manor 1700 21st Ave W.......... Bradenton FL 34205 941-748-4161 672
TF: 877-382-9036 ■ *Web:* www.westminsterretirement.com

Westminster Manor 4100 Jackson Ave........... Austin TX 78731 512-454-4643 371-7308 672
Web: westminsteraustintx.org

Westminster Place 3200 Grant St.............. Evanston IL 60201 847-570-3422 672
TF: 888-568-3901 ■ *Web:* www.presbyterianhomes.org

Westminster Public Library
7392 Irving St........................ Westminster CO 80030 303-430-2400 434-3
TF: 800-424-1554 ■ *Web:* www.ci.westminster.co.us

Westminster School 995 Hopmeadow St........ Simsbury CT 06070 860-408-3060 622
Web: www.westminster-school.org

Westminster School District
14121 Cedarwood St.................... Westminster CA 92683 714-894-7311 899-2781 685
TF: 888-491-6603 ■ *Web:* www.wsdk8.us

Westminster Schools
1424 W Paces Ferry Rd NW.................. Atlanta GA 30327 404-355-8673 355-6606 623
Web: www.westminster.net

Westminster Theological Seminary
2960 Church Rd............................ Glenside PA 19038 215-887-5511 887-5404 167-3
TF: 800-373-0119 ■ *Web:* www.wts.edu

Westminster Theological Seminary in California
1725 Bear Vly Pkwy....................... Escondido CA 92027 760-480-8474 480-0252 167-3
TF: 888-480-8474 ■ *Web:* www.wscal.edu

Name / Address	City	State	ZIP	Phone	Fax	Class
Westminster Towers 70 W Lucerne Cir *TF:* 877-382-9036 ■ *Web:* www.westminstertowersfl.org	Orlando	FL	32801	407-841-1310		672
Westminster Towers 1330 India Hook Rd *TF:* 800-345-6026 ■ *Web:* www.westminstertowers.org	Rock Hill	SC	29732	803-328-5000		672
Westminster Village 1175 Mckee Rd. *TF:* 800-382-1385 ■ *Web:* www.presbyterianseniorliving.org	Dover	DE	19904	302-744-3600		672
Westminster Village 2025 E Lincoln St *Web:* westminstervillageinc.com	Bloomington	IL	61701	309-663-6474		672
Westminster Village 1120 E Davis Dr *Web:* www.westminstervillagein.com	Terre Haute	IN	47802	812-232-7533		672
Westminster Village 803 N Wahneta St *TF:* 888-563-8147 ■ *Web:* www.presbyterianseniorliving.org	Allentown	PA	18109	610-782-8300	782-8398	672
Westminster-Canterbury of Lynchburg 501 VES Rd *TF:* 800-962-3520 ■ *Web:* www.wclynchburg.org	Lynchburg	VA	24503	434-386-3500	386-3535	672
Westminster-Canterbury on Chesapeake Bay 3100 Shore Dr **Fax Area Code: 757* ■ *TF:* 800-753-2918 ■ *Web:* www.wcbay.com	Virginia Beach	VA	23451	800-753-2918	496-1790*	672
Westminster-Canterbury Richmond 1600 Westbrook Ave. *TF:* 800-445-9904 ■ *Web:* www.wcrichmond.org	Richmond	VA	23227	804-264-6000	264-4579	672
Westminster-Thurber Community 717 Neil Ave *Web:* www.ohioliving.org/communities/ohio-living-westminster-thurber	Columbus	OH	43215	614-228-8888		672
Westmont College 955 La Paz Rd **Fax:* Admissions ■ *TF Admissions:* 800-777-9011 ■ *Web:* www.westmont.edu	Santa Barbara	CA	93108	805-565-6000	565-6234*	166
Westmont Hospitality Group Inc 5090 Explorer Dr Ste 700 *Web:* www.whg.com	Mississauga	ON	L4W4T9	905-629-3400	624-7805	379
Westmont Hospitality Group Inc 5847 San Felipe St Ste 4650 *Web:* www.whg.com	Houston	TX	77057	713-782-9100	782-9600	379
Westmont Industries 10805 Painter Ave. *Web:* www.westmont.com	Santa Fe Springs	CA	90670	562-944-6137	946-5299	207
Westmor Industries LLC 3 Development Dr. *TF:* 800-992-8981 ■ *Web:* westmor-ind.com	Morris	MN	56267	320-589-2100		198
Westmoreland Chamber of Commerce 241 Tollgate Hill Rd *Web:* www.westmorelandchamber.com	Greensburg	PA	15601	724-834-2900	837-7635	139
Westmoreland Coal Co 9540 S Maroon Cir Ste 300 *NASDAQ: WLB* ■ *TF:* 855-922-6463 ■ *Web:* www.westmoreland.com	Englewood	CO	80112	303-922-6463		501
Westmoreland County 2 N Main St Ste 101 *Web:* www.co.westmoreland.pa.us	Greensburg	PA	15601	724-830-3000	830-3029	338
Westmoreland County PO Box 1000 *Web:* www.westmoreland-county.org	Montross	VA	22520	804-493-0130	493-0134	338
Westmoreland County Community College 145 Pavilion Ln *TF:* 800-262-2103 ■ *Web:* westmoreland.edu	Youngwood	PA	15697	724-925-4000		162
Westmoreland Mall 5256 US-30 *Web:* www.westmorelandmall.com	Greensburg	PA	15601	724-836-5025		460
Westmoreland Mechanical Testing & Research Inc PO Box 388 *Web:* www.wmtr.com	Youngstown	PA	15696	724-537-3131	537-3151	743
Westmoreland Museum of American Art 221 N Main St *TF:* 800-745-3000 ■ *Web:* thewestmoreland.org	Greensburg	PA	15601	724-837-1500		520
Westmoreland Resource Partners LP 9540 S Maroon Cir ste 200 **Fax Area Code: 855* ■ *Web:* westmorelandmlp.com	Englewood	CO	43215	303-922-6463	922-6463*	501
Westmoreland Resources Inc 100 Sarpy Creek Rd *Web:* westmoreland.com/location/absaloka-mine-montana	Hardin	MT	59034	406-342-5241	342-5401	501
Westney Consulting Group Inc 1800 W Loop S Ste 1200 *Web:* www.westney.com	Houston	TX	77027	713-861-0800		463
Weston & Assoc Inc 110 Thomas St *Web:* www.westoninc.com	Winston-Salem	NC	27101	336-725-1147	725-0551	184
Weston & Sampson Inc 5 Centennial Dr *TF:* 800-726-7766 ■ *Web:* www.westonandsampson.com	Peabody	MA	01960	978-532-1900		261
Weston Bend State Park 16600 Hwy 45 N *Web:* www.mostateparks.com	Weston Bend	MO	64098	816-640-5443		565
Weston Capital Management Inc 1450 S Bundy Dr *Web:* www.westoncap.com	Los Angeles	CA	90025	310-826-0811		401
Weston County 400 Stampede St PO Box 130 *Web:* www.westongov.com	Newcastle	WY	82701	307-746-4775		338
Weston Hurd LLP The Tower at Erieview 1301 E Ninth St Ste 1900 *Web:* www.westonhurd.com	Cleveland	OH	44114	216-241-6602		428
Weston Solutions Inc 1400 Weston Way PO Box 2653 *TF:* 800-793-7966 ■ *Web:* www.westonsolutions.com	West Chester	PA	19380	610-701-3000	701-3186	261
Westover School PO Box 847 *Web:* www.westoverschool.org	Middlebury	CT	06762	203-758-2423	577-4588	622
Westpac Banking Corp Americas Div 575 Fifth Ave 39th Fl *TF:* 888-269-2377 ■ *Web:* www.westpac.com.au	New York	NY	10017	212-551-1800	551-1999	70
Westpak Inc 10326 Roselle St Ste 101 *Web:* www.westpak.com	San Diego	CA	92121	858-623-8100		88
WestPark Capital Inc 1900 Ave of the Stars Ste 310 *TF:* 800-811-3487 ■ *Web:* www.wpcapital.com	Los Angeles	CA	90067	310-843-9300		690
WestPoint Home Inc 28 E 28th St Ste 2 *TF:* 800-663-5965 ■ *Web:* martex.com	New York	NY	10016	212-930-2000		745-1
Westport Arts Ctr 51 Riverside Ave *TF:* 800-200-2882 ■ *Web:* www.westportartscenter.org	Westport	CT	06880	203-222-7070	222-7999	50-2
Westport Community Theatre 110 Myrtle Ave *Web:* www.westportcommunitytheatre.com	Westport	CT	06880	203-226-1983		573-4
Westport Corp 331 Changdridge Rd *Web:* www.mundiwestport.com	Pine Brook	NJ	07058	973-575-0110	575-8197	430
Westport Country Playhouse 25 Powers Ct *TF:* 888-927-7529 ■ *Web:* www.westportplayhouse.org	Westport	CT	06880	203-227-4177	221-7482	572
Westport Health Care Ctr 7300 Forest Ave	Richmond	VA	23226	804-288-3152		450
Westport Historical Society 4000 Baltimore St *Web:* www.westporthistorical.com	Kansas City	MO	64111	816-561-1821		50-6
Westport Inn, The 1595 Post Rd E *Web:* www.westportinn.com	Westport	CT	06880	203-557-8124	254-8439	379
Westport Innovations Inc 1750 W 75th Ave Ste 101 *TSE: WPT* ■ *Web:* www.westport.com	Vancouver	BC	V6P6G2	604-718-2000	718-2001	60
Westport Minuteman 1775 Post Rd E *TF:* 800-542-3354 ■ *Web:* minutemannewscenter.com	Westport	CT	06880	203-752-2711		532-4
Westport Public Library 20 Jesup Rd *Web:* westportlibrary.org	Westport	CT	06880	203-291-4000		435
Westpower Equipment Ltd 4451-54 Ave SE *Web:* www.westpower.ca	Calgary	AB	T2C2A2	403-720-3300		541
Westprime Healthcare 5751 Chino Ave *TF:* 800-660-0968 ■ *Web:* www.westprimehealthcare.com	Chino	CA	91710	714-529-2027		475
Westroc Inc 670 W 220 S PO Box 368	Pleasant Grove	UT	84062	801-785-5600	785-5600	182
WestRock Co 504 Thrasher St *Web:* www.westrock.com/en	Norcross	GA	30071	770-448-2193		145
Westside Baptist Church Inc of Haines City 1416 Polk City Rd	Haines City	FL	33844	863-422-4720		48-20
Westside Community News 608 S Vine St	Indianapolis	IN	46241	317-241-7363		532-4
Westside Lexus 12000 Katy Fwy *Web:* www.westsidelexus.com	Houston	TX	77079	281-558-3030		57
Westside News 1776 Hilton Palmar Corners Rd *Web:* www.westsidenewsny.com	Spencerport	NY	14559	585-352-3411	352-4811	532-4
Westside Regional Medical Ctr 8201 W Broward Blvd *TF:* 800-523-5658 ■ *Web:* www.westsideregional.com	Plantation	FL	33324	954-473-6600	476-3974	374-3
Westsiderentalscom 1020 Wilshire Blvd *Web:* www.westsiderentals.com	Santa Monica	CA	90401	310-395-7368		652
WestStar Talk Radio Networks 2711 N 24th St *Web:* www.weststar.com	Phoenix	AZ	85008	602-381-8200	381-8221	646
Westtek 8585 154th Ave NE *Web:* www.westtek.com	Redmond	WA	98052	425-861-8271		809
Westtown School PO Box 1799 *Web:* www.westtown.edu	Westtown	PA	19395	610-399-0123		622
Westview Products Inc 1350 SE Shelton St *Web:* westviewproducts.com	Dallas	OR	97338	503-623-5174		106
Westward Look Resort 245 E Ina Rd *TF:* 800-722-2500 ■ *Web:* www.westwardlook.com	Tucson	AZ	85704	520-297-1151		809
Westward Parts Services Ltd 6517 - 67 St *TF:* 888-937-7278 ■ *Web:* www.westwardparts.com	Red Deer	AB	T4P1A3	403-347-2200		111
West-Ward Pharmaceutical Corp 401 Industrial Way W *TF Cust Svc:* 800-631-2174	Eatontown	NJ	07724	732-542-1191		583
Westward Seafoods 2101 Fourth Ave Ste 1700 *Web:* www.westwardseafoods.com	Seattle	WA	98121	206-682-5949	682-1825	296-13
Westway Ford 801 W Airport Fwy *TF:* 844-877-9037 ■ *Web:* westwayford.com	Irving	TX	75062	844-877-9037		57
Westways Magazine 3333 Fairview Rd	Costa Mesa	CA	92626	714-885-2376		457-22
Westways Staffing Services Inc 500 City Pkwy W Ste 130 *Web:* www.westwaysstaffing.com	Orange	CA	92868	714-712-4150		260
WestWind Technologies Inc 2901 Wall Triana Hwy Ste 124 *Web:* www.westwindcorp.com	Huntsville	AL	35824	256-319-0137		22
Westwood Baptist Church 41 State Farm Rd *Web:* www.westwoodbaptist.net	Alexandria	AL	36250	256-820-2211		48-20
Westwood College Atlanta Northlake 2309 Parklake Dr NE *TF:* 866-552-7536 ■ *Web:* www.westwood.edu	Atlanta	GA	30345	866-552-7536		800
Westwood Community Church 401 Wwood Dr *Web:* westwood.mb.ca	Winnipeg	MB	R3K1G4	204-888-1771		48-20
Westwood Contractors Inc 951 W Seventh St *Web:* www.westwoodcontractors.com	Fort Worth	TX	76102	817-877-3800	877-4731	780
Westwood Hills Nature Ctr 8300 W Franklin Ave. *Web:* stlouispark.org	Saint Louis Park	MN	55426	952-924-2544	797-9691	50-5
Westwood Holdings Group Inc 200 Crescent Ct Ste 1200 *NYSE: WHG* ■ *TF:* 800-687-0372 ■ *Web:* www.westwoodgroup.com	Dallas	TX	75201	214-756-6900	756-6979	360-2
Westwood Lodge Hospital 45 Clapboardtree St *TF:* 800-222-2237 ■ *Web:* arbourhealth.com	Westwood	MA	02090	781-762-7764	762-0550	374-5
Westwood Manufacturing Inc 1701 W Valley Hwy Ste 6	Auburn	WA	98001	253-833-8241		454
Westwood Partners LLC 51 W 52nd St 12th Fl *TF:* 800-976-0014 ■ *Web:* www.westwood-partners.com	New York	NY	10019	212-672-3350	757-4640	772
Westword 969 Broadway *Web:* www.westword.com	Denver	CO	80203	303-296-7744	296-5416	532-5
Wesucceed Solutions Inc 175 Olde Haof Day *Web:* www.wesucceed.com	Lincolnshire	IL	60069	847-229-8130		225

	Phone	Fax	Class
Wet 'n Wild Emerald Pointe 3910 S Holden Rd .... Greensboro NC 27406 *TF:* 800-555-5900 ■ *Web:* www.emeraldpointe.com	336-852-9721	852-2391	32
Wet 'n Wild Orlando 6200 International Dr .... Orlando FL 32819 *TF General:* 800-992-9453 ■ *Web:* www.wetnwildorlando.com	407-351-1800	363-1147	32
Wet 'n' Wild Hawaii 400 Farrington Hwy .... Kapolei HI 96707 *Web:* wetnwildhawaii.com	808-674-9283		31
Wet Paint Inc 1684 W Grand Ave .... Saint Paul MN 55105 *Web:* www.wetpaintart.com	651-698-6431	698-8041	45
Wet Tech Energy Inc 4598 Woodlawn Rd .... Maurice LA 70555 *Web:* www.wettechenergy.com	337-893-9992		539
WETA-FM 90.9 (NPR) 2775 S Quincy St......... Arlington VA 22206 *TF:* 800-662-2386 ■ *Web:* www.weta.org/fm	703-998-2600		645
WETA-TV Ch 26 (PBS) 2775 S Quincy St .... Arlington VA 22206 *TF:* 800-662-2386 ■ *Web:* www.weta.org	703-998-2600		741
WETB-AM 790 (Rel) 231 Brandonwood Dr ....Johnson City TN 37604	423-928-7131	928-8392	645-81
Wetherby Asset Management 580 California St 8th Fl................. San Francisco CA 94104 *Web:* www.wetherby.com	415-399-9159		41
WeTip Inc PO Box 1296..............Rancho Cucamonga CA 91729 *TF:* 800-782-7463 ■ *Web:* www.wetip.com	909-987-5005	987-2477	48-8
Wetland Studies & Solutions Inc 5300 Wellington Branch Dr....................Gainesville VA 20155 *TF:* 800-247-1812 ■ *Web:* www.wetlandstudies.com	703-679-5600		261
Wetsel Inc 961 N Liberty St................Harrisonburg VA 22802 *TF Cust Svc:* 800-572-4018 ■ *Web:* bfgsupply.com	540-434-6753		694
WETS-FM 89.5 (NPR) PO Box 70630 ....Johnson City TN 37614 *TF:* 888-895-9387 ■ *Web:* etsu.edu/wets	423-439-6440		645-81
WetStone Technologies Inc 20 Thornwood Dr Ste 105........................Ithaca NY 14850 *Web:* www.wetstonetech.com	607-266-8086		177
Wetzel Brothers LLC 2401 E Edgerton .... Cudahy WI 53110 *Web:* www.wetzelbrothers.com	414-271-5444		627
Wetzel County PO Box 156............ New Martinsville WV 26155 *Web:* www.wetzelcounty.wv.gov	304-455-8217	455-5256	338
Wetzel County Chamber of Commerce 201 Main St PO Box 271 .... New Martinsville WV 26155 *TF:* 800-834-2070 ■ *Web:* www.wetzelcountychamber.com	304-455-3825	455-3637	139
Wetzel County Hospital 3 E Benjamin Dr .... New Martinsville WV 26155 *Web:* www.wetzelcountyhospital.com	304-455-8000	455-4259	374-3
Wetzel's Pretzels LLC 35 Hugus Alley Ste 300 ....Pasadena CA 91103 *Web:* www.wetzels.com	626-432-6900		68
WEUP-FM 103.1 (Urban) 2609 Jordan Ln NW .... Huntsville AL 35816 *Web:* www.103weup.com	256-837-9387	837-9404	645-76
Wever Petroleum Inc 100 S Hudson St .... Mechanicville NY 12118 *Web:* www.weverpetroleum.com	518-664-7331		316
WEVV-TV Ch 44 (CBS) 477 Carpenter St......................... Evansville IN 47708 *Web:* www.wevv.com	812-464-4444	465-4559	741-46
WEW-AM 770 (Var) 2740 Hampton Ave .... Saint Louis MO 63139 *Web:* www.wewradio.com	314-781-9397	781-8545	645-141
Wewoka Times PO Box 61 ....Wewoka OK 74884 *Web:* www.wewokatimes.com	405-257-3341		532-2
Wexcel Inc 222 S Riverside Plaza ....Chicago IL 60606	312-347-0955		178-7
Wexford County 437 E Div St .... Cadillac MI 49601 *Web:* www.wexfordcounty.org	231-779-9453	779-9745	338
Wexford Homes 135 Keveling Dr................. Saline MI 48176 *Web:* www.wexfordhomes.com	734-470-6647		187
Wexler Surgical Supplies 11333 Chimney Rock Rd ....Houston TX 77035 *TF:* 800-414-1076 ■ *Web:* www.wexlersurgical.com	713-723-6900		476
Wexley School for Girls Llc 2218 Fifth Ave.................................. Seattle WA 98121 *TF:* 800-644-4098 ■ *Web:* www.wexley.com	206-438-8900		7
Wexner Ctr for the Arts 1871 N High St Ohio State University.......... Columbus OH 43210 *TF:* 800-965-2030 ■ *Web:* www.wexarts.org	614-292-0330	292-3369	520
Wexner Heritage Village 1151 College Ave .... Columbus OH 43209 *Web:* www.whv.org	614-231-4900		371
Wexpro Co 333 S State St.................Salt Lake City UT 84145 *Web:* www.questar.com	801-324-2534	324-2637	536
Weyco Group Inc 333 W Estabrook Blvd........... Glendale WI 53212 *NASDAQ: WEYS* ■ *TF:* 866-454-0449 ■ *Web:* www.weycogroup.com	414-908-1880	908-1603	301
Weyerhaeuser Co 33663 Weyerhaeuser Way S.................Federal Way WA 98003 *NYSE: WY* ■ *TF:* 800-525-5440 ■ *Web:* www.weyerhaeuser.com	253-924-2345		185
WEYI-TV Ch 25 (NBC) 2225 W WillaRd Rd........... Clio MI 48420 *Web:* nbc25news.com	810-687-1000	687-4925	741
Weymouth Design 332 Congress St.................Boston MA 02210 *TF:* 800-432-1000 ■ *Web:* www.weymouthdesign.com	617-542-2647		344
Weymouth Woods Sandhills Nature Preserve 1024 Ft Bragg Rd .... Southern Pines NC 28387 *Web:* www.ncparks.gov	910-692-2167		565
WEZL-FM 103.5 (Ctry) 950 Houston Northcutt Blvd Ste 201 ...... Mount Pleasant SC 29464 *TF:* 844-289-7234 ■ *Web:* wezl.iheart.com	843-884-2534		645
WEZN-FM 99.9 (AC) 440 Wheelers Farm Rd Ste 302 ....Milford CT 06461 *TF:* 800-330-9999 ■ *Web:* star999.com	203-783-8200		645
WEZQ-FM 92.9 (AC) 49 Acme Rd................... Brewer ME 04412 *Web:* 929theticket.com	207-989-5631		645
WEZV-FM 105.9 (AC) 3926 Wesley St Ste 301 .... Myrtle Beach SC 29579 *Web:* www.wezv.com	843-903-9962		645-106
WEZX-FM 106.9 (Rock) 149 Penn Ave.......... Scranton PA 18503 *TF:* 800-228-4637 ■ *Web:* www.rock107.com	570-346-6555	346-6038	645-149
WF Meyers Co 1008 13th St .... Bedford IN 47421 *TF:* 800-457-4055 ■ *Web:* www.wfmeyers.com	812-275-4485	275-4488	455
WF Saunders & Sons Inc PO Box A............. Nedrow NY 13120 *TF:* 800-723-9213 ■ *Web:* www.saundersconcrete.com	315-469-3217	469-3940	191-1
WF Wells Inc 16645 Heimbach Rd ....Three Rivers MI 49093 *Web:* wfwells.us	269-279-5123	279-6337	455
WF Young Inc 302 Benton Dr........... East Longmeadow MA 01028 *TF:* 800-628-9653 ■ *Web:* www.absorbine.com	413-526-9999	526-8990	582
Wfa Staffing 9001 N 76th St Ste 201........... Milwaukee WI 53223 *Web:* wfastaffing.com	414-365-3651		260
WFAA-TV Ch 8 (ABC) 606 Young St Communications Ctr .... Dallas TX 75202 *Web:* www.wfaa.com	214-748-9631		741-37
WFAE-FM 90.7 (NPR) 8801 JM Keynes Dr Ste 91.......................Charlotte NC 28262 *TF Cust Svc:* 800-876-9323 ■ *Web:* www.wfae.org	704-549-9323	547-8851	645-33
WFAN-AM 66 (Rel) 345 Hudson St............. New York NY 10014 *Web:* newyork.cbslocal.com	212-314-9128		645-11
WFBQ-FM 94.7 (CR) 6161 Fall Creek Rd.......................Indianapolis IN 46220	317-257-7565	254-9619	645-77
WFBY-FM 102.3 (CR) 1065 Radio Pk Dr ....Mount Clare WV 26408 *Web:* www.wfby.com	304-623-6546		645
WFCA (World Floor Covering Assn) 2211 Howell Ave.......................... Anaheim CA 92806 *TF:* 800-624-6880 ■ *Web:* www.wfca.org	714-978-6440	978-6066	49-4
WFCF-FM 88.5 (Var) Flagler College PO Box 1027 ....Saint Augustine FL 32085 *TF:* 800-304-4208 ■ *Web:* www.flagler.edu	904-819-6449	826-0094	645
WFCJ-FM 93.7 (Rel) 1205 Whitefield Cir........... Xenia OH 45385 *Web:* www.wfcj.com	937-424-1640		645-45
WFCR-FM 88.5 (NPR) University of Massachusetts 131 County Cir ...... Amherst MA 01003 *Web:* nepr.net	413-735-6600	732-7417	645
WFDD-FM 88.5 (NPR) 1834 Wake Forest Rd Ste 8850........... Winston-Salem NC 27109 *TF:* 800-262-8850 ■ *Web:* www.wfdd.org	336-758-8850	758-3083	645-178
WFEA-AM 1370 (Nost) 500 Commercial St....................... Manchester NH 03101 *Web:* 1370wfea.com	603-669-5777	669-4641	645-97
WFF (Walton Family Foundation Inc) PO Box 2030 ....Bentonville AR 72712 *Web:* www.waltonfamilyfoundation.org	479-464-1570	464-1580	305
WFFF-TV Ch 44 (Fox) 298 Mountain View Dr ....Colchester VT 05446 *TF:* 888-344-7233 ■ *Web:* www.mychamplainvalley.com	802-660-9333	660-8673	741
WFGC-TV Ch 61 (Ind) 1900 S Congress Ave Ste A ....West Palm Beach FL 33406 *Web:* www.wfgctelevision.com	561-642-3361	967-5961	741-140
WFGR-FM 98.7 (Oldies) 50 Monroe Ave NW Ste 500...............Grand Rapids MI 49503 *Web:* www.wfgr.com	616-451-4800		645-66
WFHB-FM 91.3 (Var) 108 W Fourth St.......................... Bloomington IN 47404 *TF:* 800-422-0070 ■ *Web:* www.wfhb.org	812-323-1200	323-0320	645
WFHM-FM 95.5 (Rel) 4 Summit Pk Dr Ste 150.....................Cleveland OH 44131 *Web:* www.955thefish.com	216-901-0921		645-38
WFHN-FM 107.1 (CHR) 22 Sconticut Neck Rd.......................Fairhaven MA 02719 *TF:* 877-854-9467 ■ *Web:* www.fun107.com	508-999-6690	999-1420	645
WFIE-TV Ch 14 (NBC) 1115 Mt Auburn Rd .... Evansville IN 47720 *TF:* 800-832-0014 ■ *Web:* www.14news.com	812-426-1414	425-2482	741-46
WFIR-AM 960 (N/T) 3934 Electric Rd SW ....Roanoke VA 24018 *Web:* wfir960.com	540-345-1511	342-2270	645-136
WFIU-FM 103.7 Indiana University 1229 E Seventh St........ Bloomington IN 47405 *TF:* 877-285-9348 ■ *Web:* indianapublicmedia.org	812-855-1357		645
WFIV-FM 105.3 (AAA) 517 Watt Rd .... Knoxville TN 37934 *TF:* 800-352-9250 ■ *Web:* www.myi105.com	865-675-4105		645-85
WFKS-FM 97.9 (CHR) 11700 Central Pkwy ....Jacksonville FL 32224 *Web:* 979kissfm.iheart.com	904-636-0507		645-79
WFKY-FM 104.9 (Cty) 115 W Main St .... Frankfort KY 40601	502-875-1130		645-89
WFLA (Western Fraternal Life Assn) 1900 First Ave NE.........................Cedar Rapids IA 52402 *TF:* 877-935-2467 ■ *Web:* www.wflains.org	319-363-2653		391-2
WFLA-TV Ch 8 (NBC) PO Box 1410............... Tampa FL 33601 *TF:* 800-338-0808 ■ *Web:* www.wfla.com	813-228-8888	225-2770	741-133
WFLD-TV Ch 32 (Fox) 205 N Michigan Ave..............................Chicago IL 60601 *Web:* www.fox32chicago.com	312-565-5532		741-29
WFLY-FM 92.3 (CHR) 6 Johnson Rd..............Latham NY 12110 *TF:* 800-929-4040 ■ *Web:* www.fly92.com	518-786-6600		645
WFMB-AM 1450 (Sports) 3055 S Fourth St ....Springfield IL 62703 *Web:* www.sportsradio1450.com	217-528-3033	528-5348	645-155
WFMB-FM 104.5 (Ctry) 3055 S Fourth St ....Springfield IL 62703 *TF:* 800-420-3580 ■ *Web:* www.wfmb.com	217-528-3033	528-5348	645-155
WFMF-FM 102.5 (CHR) 5555 Hilton Ave Ste 500.................. Baton Rouge LA 70808 *Web:* wfmf.iheart.com	225-231-1860	927-9096	645-18
WFMJ-TV Ch 21 (NBC) 101 W Boardman St ....Youngstown OH 44503 *TF:* 800-488-9365 ■ *Web:* www.wfmj.com	330-744-8611	742-2472	741-145
WFMK-FM 99.1 (AC) 3420 Pine Tree Rd........... Lansing MI 48911 *Web:* www.99wfmk.com	517-394-7272		645-87
WFMS-FM 95.5 (Ctry) 6810 N Shadeland Ave.....................Indianapolis IN 46220 *Web:* www.wfms.com	317-842-9550		645-77
WFMT-FM 98.7 (Clas) 5400 N St Louis Ave..........................Chicago IL 60625 *Web:* www.wfmt.com	773-279-2000		645-36
WFMV-FM 95.3 (Rel) 2440 Milwood Ave........Columbia SC 29205 *Web:* columbiainspiration.com	803-939-9530		645-40
WFMY-TV Ch 2 (CBS) 1615 Phillips Ave .... Greensboro NC 27405 *TF:* 800-593-3692 ■ *Web:* wfmynews2.com	336-379-9369	273-9433	741

Name / Address	City	State	ZIP	Phone	Fax	Class
WFMZ-TV Ch 69 (Ind) 300 E Rock Rd *Web:* www.wfmz.com	Allentown	PA	18103	610-478-6500	791-9994	741
WFNN-AM 1330 (Sports) 1 Boston Store Pl *Web:* www.sportsradio1330.com	Erie	PA	16501	814-461-1000		645-54
WFNT-AM 1470 (N/T) 3338 E Bristol Rd *Web:* wfnt.com	Burton	MI	48529	810-743-1080	742-5170	645
WFNZ-AM 610 (Sports) 1520 S Blvd Ste 300 *TF:* 866-570-9610	Charlotte	NC	28203	704-319-9369		645-33
WFOR-TV Ch 4 (CBS) 8900 NW 18th Terr *Web:* miami.cbslocal.com	Miami	FL	33172	305-591-4444	477-3040	741-82
WFOY-AM 1240 (N/T) 567 Lewis Pt Rd Ext *Web:* www.1023newsradio.com	Saint Augustine	FL	32086	904-797-1955		645
WFP (Western Forest Products Inc) 495 Dunsmuir St Unit 210 *TSE:* WEF ■ *TF:* 800-806-5484 ■ *Web:* www.westernforest.com	Nanaimo	BC	V9R6B9	604-648-4500	681-9584	448
WFP (World Food Program USA) 1725 Eye St NW Ste 510 *TF:* 888-454-0555 ■ *Web:* wfpusa.org	Washington	DC	20006	202-627-3737	530-1698	48-5
WFPG-FM 96.9 (AC) 950 Tilton Rd Ste 200 *TF:* 800-969-9374 ■ *Web:* www.literock969.com	Northfield	NJ	08225	609-645-9797	272-9224	645
WFPK-FM 91.9 (AAA) 619 S Fourth St *Web:* www.wfpk.org	Louisville	KY	40202	502-814-6500		645-93
WFPL-FM 89.3 (NPR) 619 S Fourth St *Web:* www.wfpl.org	Louisville	KY	40202	502-814-6500		645-93
WFRE-FM 99.9 (Ctry) 5966 Grove Hill Rd *Web:* www.wfre.com	Frederick	MD	21703	301-663-4181	682-8018	645
WFRV-TV Ch 5 (CBS) 1181 E Mason St *TF:* 800-236-5550 ■ *Web:* www.wearegreenbay.com	Green Bay	WI	54301	920-437-5411	437-4576	741-55
WFS (Women for Sobriety Inc) PO Box 618 *TF:* 800-548-8854 ■ *Web:* www.womenforsobriety.org	Quakertown	PA	18951	215-536-8026	538-9026	48-21
WFSB-TV Ch 3 (CBS) 333 Capital Blvd *TF:* 800-223-5658 ■ *Web:* www.wfsb.com	Rocky Hill	CT	06067	860-728-3333	728-0263	741
WFSH-FM 104.7 (Rel) 2970 Peachtree Rd NW Ste 700 *Web:* www.thefishatlanta.com	Atlanta	GA	30305	404-995-7300		645-10
WFSQ-FM 91.5 (Clas) 1600 Red Barber Plaza *TF:* 855-937-8123 ■ *Web:* www.wfsu.org	Tallahassee	FL	32310	850-645-7200	487-3093	645-161
WFSU-FM 88.9 (NPR) 1600 Red Barber Plaza *TF:* 855-937-8123 ■ *Web:* www.wfsu.org	Tallahassee	FL	32310	850-645-7200	487-3093	645-161
WFSU-TV Ch 11 (PBS) 1600 Red Barber Plaza *Web:* www.wfsu.org	Tallahassee	FL	32310	850-487-3170	487-3093	741-132
WFT (West Fraser Timber Company Ltd) 501-858 Beatty St Ste 501 *NYSE:* WFT ■ *Web:* www.westfraser.com	Vancouver	BC	V6B1C1	604-895-2700	681-6061	683
WFTS-TV Ch 28 (ABC) 4045 N Himes Ave *TF:* 877-833-2828 ■ *Web:* www.abcactionnews.com	Tampa	FL	33607	813-354-2828		741-133
WFTV-TV Ch 9 (ABC) 490 E S St *Web:* www.wftv.com	Orlando	FL	32801	407-841-9000		741-95
WFTX TV Ch 4 (Fox) 621 SW Pine Island Rd *Web:* www.fox4now.com	Cape Coral	FL	33991	239-574-3636	574-2025	741-88
WFUV-FM 90.7 (Var) 441 E Fordham Rd Fordham University *TF:* 888-400-5520 ■ *Web:* www.wfuv.org	Bronx	NY	10458	718-817-4550		645
WFWA-TV Ch 39 (PBS) 2501 E Coliseum Blvd *TF:* 888-484-8839 ■ *Web:* www.wfwa.org	Fort Wayne	IN	46805	260-484-8839		741-51
WFWI 92.3 the Fort 2915 Maples Rd *Web:* wowo.com	Fort Wayne	IN	46816	260-471-5100		645-63
WFXB Fox Tv 3364 Huger St *Web:* www.wfxb.com	Myrtle Beach	SC	29577	843-828-4300	828-4343	741-87
WFXG-TV Ch 54 (Fox) 3933 Washington Rd *TF:* 866-974-0487 ■ *Web:* www.wfxg.com	Augusta	GA	30907	706-650-5400	650-8411	741-8
WFXP-TV Ch 66 (Fox) 8455 Peach St *Web:* www.yourerie.com	Erie	PA	16509	814-864-2400		741-44
WFXR-TV Ch 27 (Fox) 5305 Valleypark Dr Ste 1 *Web:* www.virginiafirst.com	Roanoke	VA	24019	540-344-2127		741-109
WFXT-TV Ch 25 (Fox) 25 Fox Dr *TF:* 877-369-2563 ■ *Web:* www.fox25boston.com	Dedham	MA	02026	781-467-2525		741
WFYI-FM 90.1 1630 N Meridian St *TF:* 800-456-0766 ■ *Web:* www.wfyi.org	Indianapolis	IN	46202	317-636-2020	283-6645	645-77
WFYI-TV Ch 20 (PBS) 1630 N Meridian St *Web:* www.wfyi.org	Indianapolis	IN	46202	317-636-2020	283-6645	741-62
WFYR-FM 97.3 (Ctry) 120 Eaton St *Web:* www.973nashfm.com	Peoria	IL	61603	309-673-0973		645-121
WG Bill Hefner Veterans Affairs Medical Ctr 1601 Brenner Ave *TF:* 800-469-8262 ■ *Web:* www.salisbury.va.gov	Salisbury	NC	28144	704-638-9000		374-8
WG Block Co 1414 Mississippi Blvd	Bettendorf	IA	52722	563-823-2080		182
WG Leffelman & Sons Inc 340 N Metcalf Ave	Amboy	IL	61310	815-857-2513		274
WG Rhea Library 400 W Washington St *TF:* 800-474-1912 ■ *Web:* rheapubliclibrary.org	Paris	TN	38242	731-642-1702		434-3
WG Tomko Inc 2559 Rt 88 *Web:* www.wgtomko.com	Finleyville	PA	15332	724-348-2000	348-7001	189-10
WG Yates & Sons Construction Co Inc 1 Gulley Ave *Web:* www.wgyates.com	Philadelphia	MS	39350	601-656-5411	656-8958	188-7
WGAC-AM 580 (N/T) 4051 Jimmie Dyess Pkwy *Web:* www.wgac.com	Augusta	GA	30909	706-396-7000	396-7100	645-11
WGAE (Writers Guild of America East) 250 Hudson St *Web:* www.wgaeast.org	New York	NY	10013	212-767-7800	582-1909	414
WGAL LLC 6900 N Dallas Pkwy Ste 600 *Web:* www.wizetrade.com	Plano	TX	75024	972-387-4728		809
WGAL-TV Ch 8 (NBC) 1300 Columbia Ave *Web:* www.wgal.com	Lancaster	PA	17604	717-393-5851	295-7457	741
WGAR-FM 99.5 6200 Oak Tree Blvd S 4th Fl *TF:* 855-222-0995 ■ *Web:* wgar.iheart.com	Cleveland	OH	44131	216-901-8166		645
WGAw (Writers Guild of America West) 7000 W Third St *TF:* 800-421-4182 ■ *Web:* www.wga.org	Los Angeles	CA	90048	323-951-4000	782-4800	414
WGBF-AM 1280 (N/T) 117 SE Fifth St *TF:* 877-437-5995 ■ *Web:* www.newstalk1280.com	Evansville	IN	47708	812-425-4226		645-56
WGBF-FM 103.1 (Rock) 117 SE Fifth St *TF:* 888-900-9423 ■ *Web:* www.103gbfrocks.com	Evansville	IN	47708	812-425-4226		645-56
WGBH Educational Foundation 1 Guest St Brighton Landing *TF:* 800-982-2787 ■ *Web:* www.wgbh.org	Boston	MA	02135	617-300-2000	300-1026	632
WGBH-FM 89.7 (NPR) 1 Guest St *TF:* 800-492-1111 ■ *Web:* www.wgbh.org	Boston	MA	02135	617-300-2000	300-1026	645-23
WGBH-TV Ch 2 (PBS) 1 Guest St *TF:* 800-492-1111 ■ *Web:* www.wgbh.org	Brighton	MA	02135	617-300-2000	300-1026	741
WGBY-TV Ch 57 (PBS) 44 Hampden St *Web:* www.wgby.org	Springfield	MA	01103	413-781-2801	731-5093	741-129
WGCL-TV Ch 46 (CBS) 425 14th St NW *TF:* 800-949-6397 ■ *Web:* cbs46.com	Atlanta	GA	30318	404-327-3194	327-3004	741-7
WGCM-FM 102.3 (Oldies) 10250 Lorraine Rd *Web:* www.coast102.com	Gulfport	MS	39503	228-896-5500		645-69
WGCU-FM 90.1 (NPR) 10501 FGCU Blvd S *TF:* 800-638-9238 ■ *Web:* www.wgcu.org	Fort Myers	FL	33965	239-590-2300	590-2310	645
WGCU-TV Ch 30 (PBS) 10501 FGCU Blvd *TF General:* 800-638-9238 ■ *Web:* www.wgcu.org	Fort Myers	FL	33965	239-590-2300	590-2310	741-88
WGEZ-AM 1490 (Oldies) 622 Public Ave	Beloit	WI	53511	608-365-8865		645
WGGS-TV Ch 16 (Ind) 3409 Rutherford Rd Ext *TF General:* 800-849-3683 ■ *Web:* www.wggs16.com	Taylors	SC	29687	864-244-1616	292-8481	741
WGGY-FM 101.3 (Ctry) 305 Hwy 315 *TF:* 800-570-1013 ■ *Web:* www.froggy101.com	Pittston	PA	18640	570-883-1111		645
WGH 5589 Greenwich Rd Ste 200 *TF:* 800-552-9935 ■ *Web:* www.espnradio1310.com	Virginia Beach	VA	23462	757-671-1000		645-112
WGH-FM 97.3 (Ctry) 5589 Greenwich Rd Ste 200 *Web:* www.eagle97.com	Virginia Beach	VA	23462	757-671-1000		645-112
WGHP-TV Ch 8 (Fox) 2005 Francis St *TF:* 800-808-6397 ■ *Web:* myfox8.com	High Point	NC	27263	336-841-8888		741
Wght Radio 1878 Lincoln Ave *Web:* www.ghtradio.com	Pompton Lakes	NJ	07442	973-839-1500		116
WGI Heavy Minerals Inc 810 E Sherman Ave *TSE:* WG	Coeur d'Alene	ID	83814	208-666-6000	666-4000	503-3
WGKS-FM 96.9 (AC) 401 W Main St Ste 301 *TF:* 800-264-0969 ■ *Web:* www.969kissfm.com	Lexington	KY	40507	859-233-1515	233-1517	645-89
WGKX-FM 105.9 (Ctry) 5629 Murray Rd *Web:* www.kix106.com	Memphis	TN	38119	901-682-1106		645-98
WGL Holdings Inc 101 Constitution Ave NW *NYSE:* WGL ■ *TF:* 800-645-3751 ■ *Web:* www.wglholdings.com	Washington	DC	20080	703-750-2000		360-5
WGLF-FM 104.1 (CR) 3411 W Tharpe St *Web:* www.gulf104.com	Tallahassee	FL	32303	850-201-3000		645-161
WGLO-FM 95.5 (CR) 120 Eaton St *Web:* www.955glo.com	Peoria	IL	61603	309-676-9595	676-5000	645-121
WGM (World Gospel Mission) 3783 E State Rd 18 PO Box 948 *TF:* 800-426-0846 ■ *Web:* www.wgm.org	Marion	IN	46952	765-664-7331	671-7230	48-20
WGMD-FM 92.7 (N/T) PO Box 530 *TF:* 800-518-9292 ■ *Web:* www.wgmd.com	Rehoboth Beach	DE	19971	302-945-2050	945-3781	645
WGME-TV Ch 13 (CBS) 81 Northport Dr *Web:* www.wgme.com	Portland	ME	04103	207-797-1313		741-102
WGN America 2501 W Bradley Pl *Web:* www.wgnamerica.com	Chicago	IL	60618	773-528-2311		740
WGN Radio 720 (N/T) 435 N Michigan Ave *Web:* www.wgnradio.com	Chicago	IL	60611	312-222-4700		645-36
WGNA-FM 107.7 (Ctry) 1241 Kings Rd *Web:* www.wgna.com	Schenectady	NY	12303	518-881-1515		645
WGNE-FM 99.9 (Ctry) 6440 Atlantic Blvd *Web:* www.999gatorcountry.com	Jacksonville	FL	32211	904-725-9990		645
WGNM-TV Ch 64 (Ind) 178 Steven Dr *Web:* www.wgnm.com	Macon	GA	31210	478-474-8400	474-4777	741-79
WGN-TV Ch 9 (CW) 2501 W Bradley Pl *Web:* www.wgntv.com	Chicago	IL	60618	773-528-2311		741-29
WGOK Gospel 900 2800 Dauphin St Ste 104 *TF:* 866-992-5660 ■ *Web:* www.gospel900.com	Mobile	AL	36606	251-423-9900	652-2001	645-102
WGOW-FM 102.3 (N/T) 821 Pineville Rd *Web:* www.wgow.com	Chattanooga	TN	37405	423-756-6141		645-34
WGPR-FM 107.5 (Urban) 3146 E Jefferson Ave	Detroit	MI	48207	313-259-8862		645-49
WG&R Furniture Co 900 Challenger Dr *TF:* 888-947-7782 ■ *Web:* www.wgrfurniture.com	Green Bay	WI	54311	920-469-4880		321
WGR-AM 550 (Sports) 500 Corporate Pkwy Ste 200 *Web:* www.wgr550.com	Amherst	NY	14226	716-843-0600	832-3080	645
WGRC FM Radio 101 Armory Blvd *Web:* www.wgrc.com	Lewisburg	PA	17837	570-523-1190		645-10
WGRD-FM 97.9 (Rock) 50 Monroe Ave NW Ste 500 *TF:* 800-947-3979 ■ *Web:* www.wgrd.com	Grand Rapids	MI	49503	616-451-4800	451-9595	645-66
WGRF-FM 96.9 (CR) 50 James E Casey Dr *Web:* www.97rock.com	Buffalo	NY	14206	716-881-4555		645-25

				Phone	Fax	Class
WGRR-FM 103.5 (Oldies) 4805 Montgomery Rd Ste 300 *TF:* 800-433-5828 ■ *Web:* www.wgrr.com	Cincinnati	OH	45212	513-241-9898	241-6689	645-37
WGRZ-TV Ch 2 (NBC) 259 Delaware Ave *TF:* 800-331-9303 ■ *Web:* www.wgrz.com	Buffalo	NY	14202	716-849-2200	849-7602	741-20
WGST-AM 640 (N/T) 1819 Peachtree Rd NE Ste 700 *Web:* 640wgst.iheart.com	Atlanta	GA	30309	404-875-8080		645-10
WGTE-FM 91.3 (NPR) 1270 S Detroit Ave PO Box 30 *Web:* www.wgte.org	Toledo	OH	43614	419-380-4600	380-4710	645-163
WGTE-TV Ch 30 (PBS) PO Box 30 *Web:* www.wgte.org	Toledo	OH	43614	419-380-4600	380-4710	741-134
WGTS-FM 91.9 (Rel) 7600 Flower Ave *TF:* 800-700-1094 ■ *Web:* www.wgts.org	Takoma Park	MD	20912	301-891-4200	270-9191	645
WGUC-FM 90.9 (Clas) 1223 Central Pkwy *Web:* www.wguc.org	Cincinnati	OH	45214	513-352-9185		645-37
WGVU-FM 88.5 (NPR) 301 W Fulton St *TF:* 800-442-2771 ■ *Web:* www.wgvu.org	Grand Rapids	MI	49504	616-331-6666		645-66
WGVU-TV Ch 35 (PBS) 301 W Fulton St *TF:* 800-442-2771 ■ *Web:* www.wgvu.org	Grand Rapids	MI	49504	616-331-6666		741-53
WGY-AM 810 (N/T) 1203 Troy-Schenectady Rd *TF:* 800-825-5949 ■ *Web:* wgy.iheart.com	Latham	NY	12110	518-452-4800		645
WGZB-FM 96.5 (Urban) 520 S Fourth Ave *Web:* hiphopb965.com	Louisville	KY	40202	502-625-1220		645-93
WH Bagshaw Company Inc 1 Pine St Ext PO Box 766 *TF:* 800-343-7467 ■ *Web:* www.whbagshaw.com	Nashua	NH	03060	603-883-7758	882-2651	386
WH Christian & Sons Inc 22 - 28 Franklin St *TF:* 800-323-1169 ■ *Web:* www.whchristian.com	Brooklyn	NY	11222	718-389-7000	389-9644	442
WH Riley & Son Inc 35 Chestnut St *TF:* 800-540-5157 ■ *Web:* www.whriley.com	North Attleboro	MA	02760	508-699-4651	699-7712	316
WHA-AM 970 (NPR) 821 University Ave **Fax Area Code:* 608 ■ *TF:* 800-747-7444 ■ *Web:* www.wpr.org	Madison	WI	53706	800-747-7444	263-9763*	645-96
WHAD-FM 90.7 (NPR) 310 W Wisconsin Ave Ste 750-E *TF:* 800-486-8655 ■ *Web:* www.wpr.org	Milwaukee	WI	53203	414-227-2040	227-2043	645-100
Whale Museum, The 62 First St *Web:* whalemuseum.org	Friday Harbor	WA	98250	360-378-4710		522
Whale Path Inc 333 Bryant St Ste 250	San Francisco	CA	94107	415-286-5577		466
Whaleback Shell Midden State Historic Site PO Box 333 *Web:* www.maine.gov	Damariscotta	ME	04543	207-563-1393		565
Whalen Co, The PO Box 1390 *Web:* www.whalencompany.com	Easton	MD	21601	410-822-9200	822-8926	14
Whalen Furniture Manufacturing Inc 1578 Air Wing Rd *TF:* 800-765-5867 ■ *Web:* www.whalenfurniture.com	San Diego	CA	92154	619-423-9948		321
Whalen's Grindstone Shores Inc 3373 Pointe Aux Barques Rd *Web:* whalensgrindstoneshores.com	Port Austin	MI	48467	989-738-7664		377
Whaley Childrens Ctr 1201 N Grand Traverse St *TF:* 800-545-3561 ■ *Web:* www.whaleychildren.org	Flint	MI	48503	810-234-3603		772
Whaley House Museum 2476 San Diego Ave *TF:* 800-838-3006 ■ *Web:* www.whaleyhouse.org	San Diego	CA	92110	619-297-7511	291-3576	520
Whaling Museum 13 Broad St *Web:* nha.org	Nantucket	MA	02554	508-228-1894		520
Whaling Station Prime Steaks & Seafood 763 Wave St *Web:* www.whalingstation.net	Monterey	CA	93940	831-373-3778	373-2460	671
Whalley Computer Associates Inc 1 Whalley Way *TF:* 800-426-9533 ■ *Web:* www.wca.com	Southwick	MA	01077	413-569-4200		174
WhamTech Inc 12001 N Central Expy Ste 300 *Web:* www.whamtech.com	Dallas	TX	75243	972-991-5700		387
WHAM-TV Ch 13 (ABC) 4225 W Henrietta Rd *TF:* 800-322-3632 ■ *Web:* www.13wham.com	Rochester	NY	14623	585-334-8700	334-8719	741-111
Wharf Resources USA Inc 10928 Wharf Rd *TF:* 800-567-6223 ■ *Web:* goldcorp.com	Lead	SD	57754	605-584-1441	584-4188	502
Wharf, The 6852 Derry St *Web:* www.thewharfbarandgrill.com	Harrisburg	PA	17111	717-564-9920		671
Wharf, The 119 King St *Web:* www.wharfrestaurant.com	Alexandria	VA	22314	703-836-2836	836-2830	671
Wharfedale Technologies Inc 2850 Brunswick Pk *Web:* wftus.com	Lawrenceville	NJ	08648	609-882-8826		226
Wharton Brook State Park c/o Sleeping Giant State Pk 200 Mount Carmel Ave *Web:* www.ct.gov	Hamden	CT	06518	203-287-5658		565
Wharton County 309 E Millan St Ste 700 PO Box 69 *Web:* www.co.wharton.tx.us	Wharton	TX	77488	979-532-2381	532-8426	338
Wharton County Electric Co-op Inc (WCEC) 1815 E Jackson St *TF:* 800-460-6271 ■ *Web:* www.wcecnet.net	El Campo	TX	77437	979-543-6271		245
Wharton County Junior College 911 Boling Hwy **Fax:* Admissions ■ *TF:* 800-561-9252 ■ *Web:* www.wcjc.edu	Wharton	TX	77488	979-532-4560	532-6494*	162
Sugar Land 14004 University Blvd *TF:* 800-561-9252 ■ *Web:* www.wcjc.edu	Sugar Land	TX	77479	281-243-8447	243-8583	162
Wharton County Library 1920 N Fulton St *TF:* 800-244-5492 ■ *Web:* www.whartonco.lib.tx.us	Wharton	TX	77488	979-532-8080	532-2792	434-3
Wharton Ctr for the Performing Arts Michigan State University *TF:* 800-942-7866 ■ *Web:* www.whartoncenter.com	East Lansing	MI	48824	517-432-2000	353-5329	572
Wharton Equity Partners LLC 505 Park Ave 18th Fl *Web:* www.whartonequity.com	New York	NY	10022	212-570-5959		528
Wharton Group 101 S Livingston Ave *TF:* 800-521-2725 ■ *Web:* www.whartoninsurance.com	Livingston	NJ	07039	973-992-5775	992-6660	390
Wharton Hardware & Supply 7724 N Crescent Blvd *Web:* www.whartonhardware.com	Pennsauken	NJ	08110	856-662-6935		350
Wharton Independent School District 2100 N Fulton St *TF:* 800-818-3453 ■ *Web:* www.whartonisd.net	Wharton	TX	77488	979-532-3612	532-6228	685
Wharton Levin Ehrmantraut & Klein, Attorneys at Law 104 W St *TF:* 800-338-5954 ■ *Web:* www.wlekn.com	Annapolis	MD	21404	410-263-5900		428
Wharton State Forest 31 Batsto Rd *Web:* www.njparksandforests.org/historic/index.html	Hammonton	NJ	08037	609-561-0024		565
Wharton-Smith Inc 750 Monroe Rd *Web:* www.whartonsmith.com	Sanford	FL	32771	407-321-8410	321-4368	188-10
WHAS-AM 840 (N/T) 4000 One Radio Dr *TF:* 800-444-8484 ■ *Web:* whas.iheart.com	Louisville	KY	40218	502-479-2222		645-93
WHAS-TV Ch 11 (ABC) 520 W Chestnut *TF:* 800-926-9330 ■ *Web:* www.whas11.com	Louisville	KY	40202	502-582-7711	582-7279	741-77
Whataburger Restaurants LP 300 Concord Plaza PO Box 791990 *Web:* www.whataburger.com	San Antonio	TX	78216	210-476-6000		670
Whatcom Community College 237 W Kellogg Rd *Web:* whatcom.edu	Bellingham	WA	98226	360-383-8000		162
Whatcom County 311 Grand Ave *Web:* www.co.whatcom.wa.us	Bellingham	WA	98225	360-676-6777	676-6693	338
Whatcom Hospice Foundation 2901 Squalicum Pkwy Ste 11 *Web:* whatcomhospice.org	Bellingham	WA	98225	360-733-1231	788-6858	371
Whatever It Takes Transmission Parts Inc 4282 E Blue Lick Rd *Web:* www.wittrans.com	Louisville	KY	40229	502-955-6035		57
WhatIfSports.com Inc 10200 Alliance Rd *Web:* www.whatifsports.com	Cincinnati	OH	45242	513-333-0313		177
WHA-TV Ch 21 (PBS) 821 University Ave *Web:* www.wpt.org	Madison	WI	53706	608-263-2121		741-80
WHB-AM 810 (Sports) 6721 W 121st St *Web:* www.810whb.com	Overland Park	KS	66209	913-491-8255	344-1599	645
WHBM (White House/Black Market) 11215 Metro Pkwy *TF:* 877-948-2525 ■ *Web:* www.whitehouseblackmarket.com	Fort Myers	FL	33966	239-277-6200		157-6
WHBQ-TV Ch 13 (Fox) 485 S Highland St *Web:* www.fox13memphis.com	Memphis	TN	38111	901-320-1313	320-1366	741-81
WHC (Wildlife Habitat Council) 8737 Colesville Rd Ste 800 *Web:* www.wildlifehc.org	Silver Spring	MD	20910	301-588-8994		48-13
WHCC-FM 105.1 (Ctry) 304 State Rd 446 PO Box 7797 *Web:* www.whcc105.com	Bloomington	IN	47401	812-336-8000	336-7000	645
WHCF-FM 88.5 (Rel) PO Box 5000 *TF:* 800-947-2577 ■ *Web:* www.whcffm.com	Bangor	ME	04402	207-947-2751	947-0010	645-17
WHCN-FM 105.9 (CR) 10 Columbus Blvd *Web:* theriver1059.iheart.com	Hartford	CT	06106	860-723-6000		645-72
WHDF-TV Ch 15 (CW) 200 Andrew Jackson Way *Web:* www.lbgtv.com	Huntsville	AL	35801	256-536-1550		741-61
WHDH-TV Ch 7 (NBC) 7 Bulfinch Pl *TF:* 855-247-4265 ■ *Web:* whdh.com	Boston	MA	02114	855-247-4265		741-18
Wheal-Grace Corp 300 Ralph St *Web:* www.wheal-grace.com	Belleville	NJ	07109	973-450-8100		174
Wheat Belt Public Power District 2104 Illinois St *TF:* 800-261-7114 ■ *Web:* www.wheatbelt.com	Sidney	NE	69162	308-254-5871	254-2384	245
Wheat Foods Council 51 Red Fox Ln Unit D *TF:* 800-970-2254 ■ *Web:* www.wheatfoods.org	Ridgway	CO	81432	800-970-2254		49-6
Wheat Montana Farms Inc 10778 US Hwy 287 *TF:* 800-535-2798 ■ *Web:* www.wheatmontana.com	Three Forks	MT	59752	406-285-3614	285-3749	297-1
Wheat Quality Council 1814 Abbey Rd *Web:* www.wheatqualitycouncil.org	Pierre	SD	57501	605-224-5187	224-0517	48-2
Wheat Ridge Ministries 1 Pierce Pl Ste 250E *TF:* 800-762-6748 ■ *Web:* www.wheatridge.org	Itasca	IL	60143	630-766-9066	766-9622	48-20
Wheatbelt Inc 300 Industrial Rd *Web:* www.wheatbeltusa.com	Hillsboro	KS	67063	620-947-2323		234
Wheatland County 201 A Ave NW *Web:* mbcc.mt.gov	Harlowton	MT	59036	406-632-4891	632-4880	338
Wheatland Electric Co-op Inc 101 S Main St *TF:* 800-762-0436 ■ *Web:* www.weci.net	Scott City	KS	67871	620-872-5885	872-7170	245
Wheatland Manor Inc 316 E Lincolnway St *TF:* 800-363-2220 ■ *Web:* wheatmanor.com	Wheatland	IA	52777	563-374-1295		450
Wheatland Rural Electric Assn 2154 S St PO Box 1209 *TF:* 800-344-3351 ■ *Web:* www.wheatlandrea.com	Wheatland	WY	82201	307-322-2125	322-5340	245
Wheatland Tube Co 700 S Dock St *TF:* 800-257-8182 ■ *Web:* www.wheatland.com	Sharon	PA	16146	800-257-8182		490
Wheatleigh Hawthorne Rd *Web:* wheatleigh.com	Lenox	MA	01240	413-637-0610	637-4507	379
Wheatmark Inc 1760 E River Rd Ste 145 *TF:* 888-934-0888 ■ *Web:* www.wheatmark.com	Tucson	AZ	85718	520-798-0888	798-3394	637-2
Wheaton & Sprague Engineering Inc 1100 Campus Dr Ste 200 *TF:* 800-736-4255 ■ *Web:* www.wheatonsprague.com	Stow	OH	44224	330-923-5560		261
Wheaton Academy 900 Prince Crossing Rd *Web:* wheatonacademy.org	West Chicago	IL	60185	630-562-7500		685

Phone | Fax | Class

Wheaton Chamber of Commerce
108 E Wesley St .... Wheaton IL 60187 630-668-6464 668-2744 139
TF: 800-593-3781 ■ *Web:* www.wheatonchamber.com
Wheaton College 26 E Main St. .... Norton MA 02766 508-286-8200 286-8271 166
TF Admissions: 800-394-6003 ■ *Web:* wheatoncollege.edu
Wheaton College 501 College Ave .... Wheaton IL 60187 630-752-5000 752-5285 166
TF: 800-222-2419 ■ *Web:* www.wheaton.edu
Wheaton Franciscan - Saint Joseph
5000 W Chambers St .... Milwaukee WI 53210 414-447-2000 374-3
TF: 800-914-6601 ■ *Web:* www.mywheaton.org
Wheaton Franciscan Healthcare
3801 Spring St .... Racine WI 53405 262-687-4011 374-3
TF: 877-304-6332 ■ *Web:* www.mywheaton.org
All Saints 3801 Spring St .... Racine WI 53405 262-687-4011 374-3
TF: 877-304-6332 ■ *Web:* www.mywheaton.org
Wheaton Franciscan Healthcare - St. Francis
3237 S 16th St .... Milwaukee WI 53215 414-647-5000 374-3
Web: www.mywheaton.org
Wheaton Park District 102 E Wesley St .... Wheaton IL 60187 630-665-4710 31
TF: 800-526-0844 ■ *Web:* www.wheatonparkdistrict.com
Wheaton Partners LLC
1901 N Roselle Rd Ste 640 .... Schaumburg IL 60195 847-381-5465 463
Web: www.codemap.com
Wheaton Public Library 225 N Cross St .... Wheaton IL 60187 630-668-1374 668-8950 434-3
Web: www.wheaton.lib.il.us
Wheaton Van Lines Inc
8010 Castleton Rd .... Indianapolis IN 46250 800-248-7962 519
TF: 800-932-7799 ■ *Web:* www.wheatonworldwide.com
Wheaton-Kensington Chamber of Commerce
2401 Blueridge Ave Ste 101 .... Wheaton MD 20902 301-949-0080 949-0081 139
TF: 800-927-9061 ■ *Web:* www.wkchamber.org
Wheatstone Corp 600 Industrial Dr .... New Bern NC 28562 252-638-7000 246
Web: www.wheatstone.com
WHEC-TV Ch 10 (NBC) 191 E Ave .... Rochester NY 14604 585-546-5670 546-5688 741-111
Web: www.whec.com
Wheel & Sprocket
6940 N Santa Monica Blvd .... Fox Point WI 53217 414-247-8100 711
TF: 800-347-7854 ■ *Web:* www.wheelandsprocket.com
Wheel & Sprocket Inc
5722 S 108th St .... Hales Corners WI 53130 414-529-6600 711
TF: 866-995-9918 ■ *Web:* wheelandsprocket.com
Wheelabrator Air Polution Control
100 Salem Tpke, Rte 107 .... Saugus MA 01906 781-233-7600 186
Web: www.energy.siemens.com/hq/en/power-generation/environmental-system
Wheelabrator Technologies Inc
4 Liberty Ln W .... Hampton NH 03842 603-929-3000 804
TF: 800-682-0026 ■ *Web:* www.wtienergy.com
Wheeland Lumber Company Inc
3558 Williamson Trail .... Liberty PA 16930 570-324-6042 683
Web: www.wheelandlumber.com
Wheelchair & Ambulatory Sports USA
PO Box 5266 .... Kendall Park NJ 08824 732-266-2634 355-6500 48-22
Web: www.wasusa.org
Wheeled Coach Industries Inc
2737 Forsyth Rd .... Winter Park FL 32792 407-677-7777 679-1337 516
TF: 800-932-7077 ■ *Web:* www.wheeledcoach.com
Wheeler Construction Inc
3255 E Gulf to Lake Hwy .... Inverness FL 34453 352-726-0973 637-4959 187
Web: www.citrusbuilder.com
Wheeler County PO Box 654 .... Alamo GA 30411 912-568-7808 568-7808 338
Web: www.wheelercounty.org
Wheeler County PO Box 127 .... Bartlett NE 68622 308-654-3235 654-3470 338
Web: wheelercounty.ne.gov
Wheeler County 701 Adams St PO Box 327 .... Fossil OR 97830 541-763-2374 763-2026 338
Web: www.wheelercountyoregon.com
Wheeler County PO Box 465 .... Wheeler TX 79096 806-826-5544 826-3282 338
Web: www.co.wheeler.tx.us
Wheeler Historic Farm 6351 S 900 E .... Murray UT 84121 385-468-1755 468-1754 520
Web: slco.org/wheeler-farm
Wheeler House 510 Gilmer Ferry Rd .... Ball Ground GA 30107 770-402-1686 50-3
TF: 800-345-8082 ■ *Web:* www.thewheelerhouse.net
Wheeler Industries
7261 Investment Dr .... North Charleston SC 29418 843-552-1251 552-4790 620
Web: www.wheelerfluidfilmbearings.com
Wheeler Lumber LLC
9330 James Ave S .... Bloomington MN 55431 952-929-7854 929-2909 191-3
TF: 800-328-3986 ■ *Web:* www.wheeler-con.com
Wheeler Mfg Co Inc
107 Main Ave PO Box 629 .... Lemmon SD 57638 605-374-3848 374-3655 409
TF: 800-843-1937 ■ *Web:* www.wheelerjewelry.com
Wheeler Opera House 320 E Hyman St .... Aspen CO 81611 970-920-5770 572
TF: 866-449-0464 ■ *Web:* www.wheeleroperahouse.com
Wheeler, Van Sickle & Anderson SC
44 E Mifflin St Ste 1000 .... Madison WI 53703 608-255-7277 428
Web: wheelerlaw.com
Wheeler-Rex Inc
3744 Jefferson Rd PO Box 688 .... Ashtabula OH 44005 440-998-2788 992-2925 758
TF: 800-321-7950 ■ *Web:* www.wheelerrex.com
Wheeling & Lake Erie Railway Co
100 E First St .... Brewster OH 44613 330-767-3401 651
TF: 800-837-5622 ■ *Web:* www.wlerwy.com
Wheeling Area Chamber of Commerce
1310 Market St .... Wheeling WV 26003 304-233-2575 233-1320 139
TF: 800-828-3097 ■ *Web:* www.wheelingchamber.com
Wheeling City Council Chambers
1500 Chapline St .... Wheeling WV 26003 304-234-3694 337
TF: 800-451-1954 ■ *Web:* www.wheelingchamber.com
Wheeling Convention & Visitors Bureau
1401 Main St .... Wheeling WV 26003 304-233-7709 206
TF: 800-828-3097 ■ *Web:* www.wheelingcvb.com
Wheeling Hospital 1 Medical Pk .... Wheeling WV 26003 304-243-3000 374-3
TF: 800-626-0023 ■ *Web:* wheelinghospital.org
Wheeling Island Gaming Inc
1 S St1 St .... Wheeling WV 26003 304-232-5050 133
TF: 877-946-4373 ■ *Web:* www.wheelingisland.com
Wheeling Jesuit University
316 Washington Ave. .... Wheeling WV 26003 304-243-2000 243-2397* 166
**Fax:* Admissions ■ *TF:* 800-624-6992 ■ *Web:* www.wju.edu

Wheeling News-Register 1500 Main St .... Wheeling WV 26003 304-233-0100 232-1399* 532-2
**Fax:* Edit ■ *Web:* theintelligencer.net
Wheeling Park District
333 W Dundee Rd .... Wheeling IL 60090 847-465-3333 31
TF: 800-796-9696 ■ *Web:* www.wheelingparkdistrict.com
Wheeling Symphony Orchestra
1025 Main St Ste 811 .... Wheeling WV 26003 304-232-6191 232-6192 573-3
Web: wheelingsymphony.com
Wheeling/Prospect Heights Area Chamber of Commerce & Industry
2 Community Blvd Ste 203 .... Wheeling IL 60090 847-541-0170 541-0296 139
Web: www.wphchamber.com
Wheeling-Nisshin Inc 400 Penn St .... Follansbee WV 26037 304-527-2800 527-0985 307
Web: www.wheeling-nisshin.com
Wheelock College 200 The Riverway .... Boston MA 02215 617-879-2206 879-2449 166
TF: 800-734-5212 ■ *Web:* www.wheelock.edu
Wheelock Partners LLC
213 School St Ste 301 .... Gardner MA 01440 978-632-9800 528
TF: 800-397-8880 ■ *Web:* www.wheelockpartners.com
Wheels Etc 17521 Mesa St .... Hesperia CA 92345 909-350-8200 949-1000* 755
**Fax Area Code:* 760 ■ *Web:* www.wheels-etc.com
Wheels Group Inc 5090 Orbitor Dr .... Mississauga ON L4W5B5 905-602-2700 314
Web: www.wheelsgroup.com
Wheels Inc 666 Garland Pl. .... Des Plaines IL 60016 847-699-7000 289
Web: www.wheels.com
Wheels of Yesterday Antique & Classic Cars Museum
12708 Ocean Gateway .... Ocean City MD 21842 410-213-7329 520
Wheelwright Lumber Co 3127 S Midland Dr. .... Ogden UT 84401 801-627-0850 364
Web: www.wheelwrightlumberco.com
Wheelwright Museum of the American Indian
704 Camino Lejo .... Santa Fe NM 87505 505-982-4636 989-7386 520
TF: 800-607-4636 ■ *Web:* www.wheelwright.org
Whelan Group Inc, The 315 W 36th St .... New York NY 10018 212-727-7332 463
Web: www.whelangroup.com
Whelan Machine & Tool
134 Rochester Dr .... Louisville KY 40214 502-364-6370 454
Web: www.whelanmachine.com
Whelan Security Co
1699 S Hanley Rd Ste 350 .... St Louis MO 63144 314-644-3227 693
TF: 888-494-3526 ■ *Web:* www.whelansecurity.com
Whelden Memorial Library
2401 Meetinghouse Way PO Box 147 ..... West Barnstable MA 02668 508-362-2262 362-1344 434-3
TF: 800-352-0171 ■ *Web:* wheldenlibrary.org
Whelen Engineering Company Inc
51 Winthrop Rd & Rt 145 .... Chester CT 06412 860-526-9504 526-4078 700
Web: www.whelen.com
WHEMCO Inc 5 Hot Metal St .... Pittsburgh PA 15203 412-390-2700 674
Web: www.whemco.com
Where Chicago Magazine
1165 N Clark St Ste 302 .... Chicago IL 60610 312-642-1896 457-22
TF: 800-680-4035 ■ *Web:* www.wheretraveler.com
Where Magazine 1720 I St NW Ste 600 ...... Washington DC 20006 202-463-4550 457-22
Where Pigs Fly 617 E Loockerman St .... Dover DE 19901 302-678-0586 671
Web: wherepigsflyrestaurant.com
Wherry Assoc Inc 30200 Detroit Rd .... Cleveland OH 44145 440-899-0010 892-1404 47
Web: www.wherryassoc.com
Whetstone Group
6060 Nancy Ridge Rd Ste 100 .... San Diego CA 92121 858-627-0726 196
Web: www.whetstonegroup.com
Whetstone Gulf State Park 6065 W Rd .... Lowville NY 13367 315-376-6630 565
Web: parks.ny.gov/parks/92/details.aspx
Whetstone Valley Electric Co-op
1101 E Fourth Ave .... Milbank SD 57252 605-432-5331 245
TF: 800-568-6631 ■ *Web:* whetstone.coop
WHHD-FM 98.3 (AC)
4051 Jimmie Dyess Pkwy .... Augusta GA 30909 706-396-7000 645-11
Web: www.hd983.com
Whibco Inc 87 E Commerce St. .... Bridgeton NJ 08302 856-455-9200 503-4
Web: www.whibco.com
Whidden Memorial Hospital
103 Garland St .... Everett MA 02149 617-389-6270 374-3
Web: www.challiance.org
WHIL-FM 91.3 (NPR)
920 Paul W Bryant Dr
Bryant Denny Stadium Rm N460 .... Tuscaloosa AL 35487 205-348-6644 645-102
TF: 800-654-4262 ■ *Web:* apr.org
Whimsy Inc 1901 S Busse Rd .... Mount Prospect IL 60056 847-690-1246 194
TF: 800-832-5660 ■ *Web:* www.whimsytrucking.com
WHIO-AM 1290 (N/T) 1414 Wilmington Ave .... Dayton OH 45420 937-259-2111 259-2168 645-45
Web: www.whio.com
WHIO-TV Ch 7 (CBS) 1414 Wilmington Ave .... Dayton OH 45420 937-259-2111 259-2005 741-38
Web: whio.com
Whip Mix Corp
361 Farmington Ave PO Box 17183 .... Louisville KY 40217 502-637-1451 228
Web: www.whipmix.com
Whipper Snapper's 2421 W Hwy 76 .... Branson MO 65616 417-334-3282 671
TF: 800-422-0076 ■ *Web:* www.bransonsbestrestaurant.com
Whipsaw Inc 434 S First St .... San Jose CA 95113 408-297-9771 261
Web: www.whipsaw.com
WHIQ-TV Ch 24 (PBS)
2112 11th Ave S Ste 400 .... Birmingham AL 35205 205-328-8756 251-2192 741-15
TF: 800-239-5233 ■ *Web:* www.aptv.org
Whirl Air Flow Corp 20055 177th St. .... Big Lake MN 55309 763-262-1200 262-1212 207
TF: 800-373-3461 ■ *Web:* www.whirlair.com
Whirl Wynn Fitness LLC
36 S Charles St. .... Baltimore MD 21201 410-539-7401 354
Whirley Industries Inc 618 Fourth Ave .... Warren PA 16365 814-723-7600 596
Web: www.whirleydrinkworks.com
Whirlpool Canada
200-6750 Century Ave .... Mississauga ON L5N0B7 905-821-6400 821-7871 38
TF: 800-807-6777
Whirlpool Corp 2000 N M-63 .... Benton Harbor MI 49022 269-923-5000 36
NYSE: WHR ■ *TF:* 800-253-1301 ■ *Web:* www.whirlpoolcorp.com
Whirlpool Corp KitchenAid Div
553 Benson Rd .... Benton Harbor MI 49022 800-422-1230 37
TF: 800-422-1230 ■ *Web:* www.kitchenaid.com
Whirlpool Corp North American Region
2000 N M-63 .... Benton Harbor MI 49022 269-923-5000 923-3525* 36
**Fax:* Hum Res ■ *TF:* 800-253-1301 ■ *Web:* www.whirlpoolcorp.com

	Phone	Fax	Class
Whirlpool Foundation 2000 N M-63 .... Benton Harbor MI 49022 *TF:* 800-952-9245 ■ *Web:* www.whirlpoolcorp.com	269-923-5000		304
Whirlpool State Park 3180 De Veaux Woods Dr PO Box 1132 ...... Niagara Falls NY 14303 *Web:* www.nysparks.com/parks/info.asp?parkid=29	716-284-5778		565
Whirlwind Steel 8234 Hansen Rd .... Houston TX 77075 **Fax Area Code: 832* ■ *TF:* 800-324-9992 ■ *Web:* www.whirlwindsteel.com	713-946-7140	553-4992*	105
Whiskeytown-Shasta-Trinity National Recreation Area PO Box 188 .... Whiskeytown CA 96095 *Web:* www.nps.gov	530-246-1225	246-5154	564
Whisper Knits Inc 175 E New Hampshire .... Southern Pines NC 28387 *Web:* www.whisperknits.com	910-246-0450		155-3
Whistler Blackcomb Mountain Ski Resort 4545 Blackcomb Way .... Whistler BC V0N1B4 *TF:* 800-766-0449 ■ *Web:* www.whistlerblackcomb.com	604-932-3434	938-7527	669
Whistler Group Inc 13016 N Walton Blvd .... Bentonville AR 72712 *TF Cust Svc:* 800-531-0004 ■ *Web:* www.whistlergroup.com	479-273-6012		529
Whitacre Greer Fireproofing Inc 1400 S Mahoning Ave .... Alliance OH 44601 *TF Cust Svc:* 800-947-2837 ■ *Web:* www.wgpaver.com	330-823-1610	823-5502	150
Whitaker Buick Co 131 19th St SW .... Forest Lake MN 55025 *TF:* 877-324-8885 ■ *Web:* whitakerauto.com	877-324-8885		57
Whitaker Center for Science & Arts 225 Market St .... Harrisburg PA 17101 *TF:* 800-425-8609 ■ *Web:* www.whitakercenter.org	717-214-2787		520
Whitaker House/Anchor Distributors 1030 Hunt Vly Cir .... New Kensington PA 15068 *TF General:* 800-444-4484 ■ *Web:* www.anchordistributors.com	724-334-7000	334-1200	637-3
Whitaker Newsletters Inc 14305 Shoreham Dr .... Silver Spring MD 20905 *Web:* www.bevnewsonline.com	301-384-1573	879-8803	531-13
Whitaker Oil Co 1557 Marietta Rd NW .... Atlanta GA 30318 *TF:* 888-895-3506 ■ *Web:* www.whitakeroil.com	404-355-8220		146
Whitby Chamber of Commerce 128 Brock St S .... Whitby ON L1N4J8 *Web:* www.whitbychamber.org	905-668-4506	668-1894	137
Whitco Supply LLC 200 N Morgan Ave .... Broussard LA 70518 *Web:* www.whitcosupply.com	337-837-2440		790
Whitcomb School 25 Union St .... Marlborough MA 01752 *Web:* mie.marlborough.schoolfusion.us	508-460-3547		685
Whitcraft LLC 76 County Rd .... Eastford CT 06242 *Web:* www.whitcraftgroup.com	860-974-0786		21
White & Partners Inc 13665 Dulles Tech Dr Ste 150 .... Herndon VA 20171 *Web:* white64.com	703-793-3000		4
White Allen Chevrolet Inc 442 N Main St .... Dayton OH 45405 *Web:* www.whiteallen.com	937-222-3701		57
White Aluminum Products LLC 2101 US Hwy 441 .... Leesburg FL 34748 *TF:* 888-474-5884 ■ *Web:* www.whitealuminum.com	888-474-5884		492
White Barn Inn 37 Beach Ave .... Kennebunk ME 04043 *Web:* www.whitebarninn.com	207-967-2321	967-1100	379
White Bear Lake Area Chamber of Commerce 4751 Hwy 61 .... White Bear Lake MN 55110 *Web:* www.whitebearchamber.com	651-429-8593	429-8592	139
White Bison Inc 5585 Erindale Dr Ste 203 .... Colorado Springs CO 80918 *TF:* 877-871-1495 ■ *Web:* www.whitebison.org	719-548-1000	548-9407	48-21
White Bros Trucking Co 4N793 School Rd .... Wasco IL 60183 *TF:* 800-323-4762 ■ *Web:* whitebrotherstrucking.com	630-584-3810		780
White Buffalo Club 160 W Gill Ave Ste 200 .... Jackson WY 83001 *TF:* 888-256-8182 ■ *Web:* whitebuffaloclub.com	307-734-4900		428
White Cap Industries Inc 1723 S Ritchie St .... Santa Ana CA 92705 *TF:* 800-944-8322 ■ *Web:* www.whitecap.com	714-258-3300	258-3289	191-3
White Chapel Church of God Inc 1730 S Ridgewood Ave .... South Daytona FL 32119 *Web:* www.wcaeagles.org	386-760-6834		48-20
White Church Christian Church 2200 N 85th St .... Kansas City KS 66109	913-299-4056		50-1
White Clay Creek Preserve PO Box 172 .... Landenberg PA 19350 *Web:* www.dcnr.state.pa.us	610-274-2900		565
White Clay Creek State Park 89 Kings Hwy .... Dover DE 19901 *Web:* www.destateparks.com	302-368-6900		565
White Co 1600 S Brentwood Blvd Ste 770 .... Saint Louis MO 63144 *Web:* www.white-co.com	314-961-4480	961-5903	655
White Coffee Corp 18-35 Steinway Pl .... Astoria NY 11105 *TF:* 800-221-0140 ■ *Web:* www.whitecoffee.com	718-204-7900		296-7
White Construction Inc 3900 E White Ave .... Clinton IN 47842 *Web:* www.whiteconstruction.com	765-832-8526		188
White Conveyors Inc 10 Boright Ave .... Kenilworth NJ 07033 *TF:* 800-524-0273 ■ *Web:* www.white-conveyors.com	908-686-5700		207
White County 301 E Main St PO Box 339 .... Carmi IL 62821 *Web:* www.whitecounty-il.gov	618-382-7211	382-2322	338
White County 1235 Helen Hwy .... Cleveland GA 30528 *Web:* www.whitecounty.net	706-865-2235	865-1324	338
White County 110 N Main St .... Monticello IN 47960 *TF:* 800-272-9829 ■ *Web:* whitecountyin.us	574-583-7032	583-1532	338
White County 300 N Spruce St .... Searcy AR 72143 *Web:* www.whitecountyar.org	501-279-6200	279-6233	338
White County County Courthouse Rm 205 .... Sparta TN 38583 *Web:* spartatnchamber.com	931-836-3203		338
White County Chamber of Commerce 122 N Main St .... Cleveland GA 30528 *TF:* 800-392-8279 ■ *Web:* www.whitecountychamber.org	706-865-5356	865-0758	139
White County Public Library 113 E Pleasure St .... Searcy AR 72143 *Web:* whitecountylibraries.org	501-268-2449		434-3

	Phone	Fax	Class
White County Rural Electric Membership Corp 302 N Sixth St .... Monticello IN 47960 *TF:* 800-844-7161 ■ *Web:* www.cwremc.com	574-583-7161	583-4156	245
White Dog Cafe 3420 Sansom St .... Philadelphia PA 19104 *TF:* 800-838-3006 ■ *Web:* www.whitedog.com	215-386-9224		671
White Dove Ltd 3201 Harvard Ave .... Cleveland OH 44105 *Web:* www.whitedoveusa.com	216-341-0200		471
White Electrical Construction Co 1730 Chattahoochee Ave .... Atlanta GA 30318 *TF:* 888-519-4483 ■ *Web:* white-electrical.com	404-351-5740	355-5823	189-4
White Elephant Inn & Cottages 50 Easton St .... Nantucket MA 02554 *TF:* 800-475-2637 ■ *Web:* www.whiteelephanthotel.com	508-228-2500	325-1195	379
White Elm Capital LLC 537 Steamboat Rd Ste 300 .... Greenwich CT 06830 *Web:* www.whiteelmcapital.com	203-742-6000		528
White Flower Farm Inc 30 Irene St .... Torrington CT 06790 *TF Cust Svc:* 800-411-6159 ■ *Web:* www.whiteflowerfarm.com	860-496-9624	496-1418	323
White Glove Placement Inc 85 Bartlett St .... Brooklyn NY 11206 *TF:* 866-387-8100 ■ *Web:* whiteglovecare.com	718-387-8181		721
White Hall State Historic Site 500 White Hall Shrine Rd .... Richmond KY 40475 *Web:* www.parks.ky.gov	859-623-9178		565
White Hat Management LLC 159 S Main St Ste 600 .... Akron OH 44308	330-535-6868	535-5055	107
White Horse Tavern 26 Marlborough St .... Newport RI 02840 *TF:* 800-338-7777 ■ *Web:* www.whitehorsenewport.com	401-849-3600		671
White Horse Village 535 Gradyville Rd .... Newtown Square PA 19073 *Web:* www.whitehorsevillage.org	610-558-5000	558-5001	672
White House Historical Assn 740 Jackson Pl NW .... Washington DC 20006 *Web:* www.whitehousehistory.org	202-737-8292		48-11
White House of the Confederacy 644 Washington St .... Montgomery AL 36130 *Web:* firstwhitehouse.org	334-242-1861		520
White House Press Secretary 1600 Pennsylvania Ave NW .... Washington DC 20500 *Web:* www.whitehouse.gov	202-456-1111		340
White House/Black Market (WHBM) 11215 Metro Pkwy .... Fort Myers FL 33966 *TF:* 877-948-2525 ■ *Web:* www.whitehouseblackmarket.com	239-277-6200		157-6
White Inn, The 52 E Main St .... Fredonia NY 14063 *TF:* 800-929-7599 ■ *Web:* www.whiteinn.com	716-672-2103	672-2107	379
White Knight Engineered Products 9525 Monroe Rd Ste 100 .... Charlotte NC 28270 *TF:* 888-743-4700 ■ *Web:* www.wkep.com	704-542-6876		576
White Lake State Park Route 16 .... Tamworth NH 03886 *Web:* www.nhstateparks.org	603-323-7350		565
White Lion Pub 6927 S Canton Ave .... Tulsa OK 74136 *Web:* kelv.net	918-491-6533		671
White Lodging Services Inc 701 E 83rd Ave .... Merrillville IN 46410 *Web:* www.whitelodging.com	219-472-2900		379
White Marsh Mall 8200 Perry Hall Blvd .... Baltimore MD 21236 *Web:* www.whitemarshmall.com	410-931-7100		460
White Memorial Medical Ctr 1720 Cesar E Chavez Ave .... Los Angeles CA 90033 *TF:* 800-806-0993 ■ *Web:* www.adventisthealth.org	323-268-5000		374-3
White Mountain Adventures 131 Eagle Crescent PO Box 4259 .... Banff AB T1L1A6 *TF:* 800-408-0005 ■ *Web:* www.whitemountainadventures.com	403-760-4403		760
White Mountain Cable Construction LLC 2113 Dover Rd .... Epsom NH 03234 *TF:* 800-233-7350 ■ *Web:* www.wmc1.com	603-736-4766		116
White Mountain Footwear Group, The 20 Whitcher St .... Lisbon NH 03585 *Web:* www.whitemountainshoes.com	603-838-6323		301
White Mountain Hotel & Resort 87 Fairway Dr PO Box 1828 .... North Conway NH 03860 *TF:* 800-533-6301 ■ *Web:* www.whitemountainhotel.com	603-356-7100	356-7100	669
White Mountain School 371 W Farm Rd .... Bethlehem NH 03574 *Web:* www.whitemountain.org	603-444-2928	444-5568	622
White Mountains Community College (WMCC) 2020 Riverside Dr .... Berlin NH 03570 *TF:* 800-445-4525 ■ *Web:* www.wmcc.edu	603-752-1113	752-6335	162
White Mountains Insurance Group Ltd 80 S Main St .... Hanover NH 03755 *NYSE:* WTM ■ *TF:* 866-295-3762 ■ *Web:* www.whitemountains.com	603-640-2200	643-4592	360-4
White Oak Lake State Park 563 Hwy 387 .... Bluff City AR 71722 *Web:* www.arkansasstateparks.com	870-685-2748		565
White Oak Manor Inc 130 E Main St PO Box 3347 .... Spartanburg SC 29304 *TF:* 800-826-6762 ■ *Web:* www.whiteoakmanor.com	864-582-7503		672
White Oak Operating Company LLC 16945 Northchase Dr Ste 1700 .... Houston TX 77060 *Web:* www.whiteoakenergy.com	281-876-2025		539
White Oak Partners LLC 5150 E Dublin Granville Rd Ste One .... Westerville OH 43081 *Web:* www.whiteoakpartners.com	614-855-1155		528
White Oaks Conference Resort & Spa 253 Taylor Rd SS4 .... Niagara-on-the-Lake ON L0S1J0 *TF Resv:* 800-263-5766 ■ *Web:* www.whiteoaksresort.com	905-688-2550		377
White Oaks Wealth Advisors Inc 80 S Eighth St IDS Ctr Ste 1725 .... Minneapolis MN 55402 *TF:* 800-596-3579 ■ *Web:* www.whiteoakswealth.com	612-455-6900		194
White Paper Co 9990 River Way .... Delta BC V4G1M9 *TF:* 888-840-7300 ■ *Web:* www.whitepaper.com	604-951-3900	951-3944	553
White Pigeon Mutual Insurance Assn 105 W Fourth St .... Wilton IA 52778 *Web:* wpigeon.com	563-732-2072		390
White Pigeon Paper Co 15781 River .... White Pigeon MI 49099 *Web:* www.whitepigeonpaper.com	269-483-7601		561
White Pine County 801 Clark St Ste 4 .... Ely NV 89301 *TF:* 800-884-4072 ■ *Web:* www.whitepinecounty.net	775-289-2341	289-2544	338

Name / Address	City	State	Zip	Phone	Fax	Class
White Pines Forest State Park 6712 W Pines Rd	Mount Morris	IL	61054	815-946-3717		565
White Plains Honda 344 Central Ave *TF:* 877-553-9292 ■ *Web:* www.whiteplainshonda.com	White Plains	NY	10606	888-671-0343		57
White Plains Hospital Ctr 41 E Post Rd *Web:* www.wphospital.org	White Plains	NY	10601	914-681-0600		374-3
White Plains Public Library 100 Martine Ave *TF:* 800-497-5007 ■ *Web:* whiteplainslibrary.org	White Plains	NY	10601	914-422-1400	422-1462	434-3
White Planning Group 602 Virginia St E *Web:* whiteplanninggroup.com	Charleston	WV	25301	304-346-3295		390
White Radio LP 5228 Everest Dr *TF:* 877-386-1956 ■ *Web:* www.whiteradio.com	Mississauga	ON	L4W2R4	905-632-6894		246
White River Broadcasting Station 3212 Washington St *Web:* www.wkkg.com	Columbus	IN	47203	812-372-4448		645
White River Credit Union 1499 Garrett St *Web:* www.whiterivercu.com	Enumclaw	WA	98022	360-825-4833		219
White River Distributors Inc 720 Ramsey *TF:* 800-548-7219 ■ *Web:* www.lpgbobtails.com	Batesville	AR	72501	870-793-2374	793-8230	482
White River Electric Assn (WREA) PO Box 958 *TF:* 800-922-1987 ■ *Web:* wrea.org	Meeker	CO	81641	970-878-5041	878-5766	245
White River Hardwoodwoodworks Inc 1197 Happy Hollow *Web:* www.whiteriver.com	Fayetteville	AR	72701	479-442-6986		499
White River Junction Veterans Affairs Medical Ctr 215 N Main St *TF:* 866-687-8387 ■ *Web:* www.whiteriver.va.gov	White River Junction	VT	05009	802-295-9363	296-5138	374-8
White River Marine Group 2500 E Kearney St *Fax: Mktg ■ *Web:* www.trackermarine.com	Springfield	MO	65803	417-873-5900	873-5068*	90
White River Medical Ctr 1710 Harrison St *Web:* www.whiteriverhealthsystem.com	Batesville	AR	72501	870-262-1200		374-3
White River State Park 801 W Washington St *TF:* 800-665-9056 ■ *Web:* www.in.gov	Indianapolis	IN	46204	317-233-2434		565
White River Valley Electric Co-op Inc 2449 State Hwy 76 E *TF:* 800-879-4056 ■ *Web:* www.whiteriver.org	Branson	MO	65616	417-335-9335	335-9250	245
White Rock Products Corp 141-07 20th Ave Ste 403 *TF:* 800-969-7625 ■ *Web:* www.whiterockbeverages.com	Whitestone	NY	11357	718-746-3400	767-0413	80-2
White Rose Inc 380 Middlesex Ave *Web:* www.whiterose.com	Carteret	NJ	07008	732 541 5555		297-8
White Sands Federal Credit Union 2190 E Lohman Ave *TF:* 800-658-9933 ■ *Web:* www.wsfcu.org	Las Cruces	NM	88001	575-647-4500		70
White Sands Missile Range Museum & Missile Park US Hwy 70 *Web:* www.wsmr-history.org	White Sands	NM	88002	575-678-8824	678-2199	520
White Sands National Monument PO Box 1000 *Web:* www.nps.gov/whsa	Holloman AFB	NM	88330	575-479-6124		564
White Sands Technology Inc 6737 Variel Ave Ste A *Web:* www.whitesands.com	Canoga Park	CA	91303	818-702-9200		180
White Settlement Independent School District 401 S Cherry Ln *Web:* www.wsisd.com	Fort Worth	TX	76108	817-367-1300		780
White Shield Inc 320 N 20th Ave *TF:* 800-759-4282 ■ *Web:* www.whiteshield.com	Pasco	WA	99301	509-547-0100		194
White Stallion Ranch 9251 W Twin Peaks Rd *TF:* 888-977-2624 ■ *Web:* www.whitestallion.com	Tucson	AZ	85743	520-297-0252	744-2786	239
White Star Steel Inc 2200 Harbor Blvd *TF:* 800-392-5768 ■ *Web:* www.whitestarsteel.com	Houston	TX	77220	713-675-6501		492
White Star Tours 26 E Lancaster Ave *TF:* 800-437-2323 ■ *Web:* www.whitestartours.com	Reading	PA	19607	610-775-5000		760
White Swan Inn 845 Bush St *TF:* 800-999-9570 ■ *Web:* www.whiteswaninnsf.com	San Francisco	CA	94108	415-775-1755		379
White Systems Inc 30 Boright Ave *Web:* www.whitesystems.com	Kenilworth	NJ	07033	908-272-6700		207
White Tower 3670 Roblin Blvd *Web:* weebly.com	Winnipeg	MB	R3R0E1	204-896-0406		671
White Ware Inc 22583 Park St *TF:* 800-860-6910 ■ *Web:* www.whiteware.com	Dearborn	MI	48124	313-792-1222		177
White Water Bay 3908 W Reno Ave *TF:* 800-225-5652 ■ *Web:* www.whitewaterbay.com	Oklahoma City	OK	73107	405-943-9687		32
White Way Sign 1317 N Clybourn Ave	Chicago	IL	60610	312-642-6580		701
White's Electronics Inc 1011 Pleasant Valley Rd *TF Sales:* 800-547-6911 ■ *Web:* www.whiteselectronics.com	Sweet Home	OR	97386	800-547-6911		472
White's Farm Supply Inc 4154 State Rt 31 *TF:* 800-633-4443 ■ *Web:* www.whitesfarmsupply.com	Canastota	NY	13032	315-697-2214	697-8024	358
White's Inc 4614 Navigation Blvd PO Box 2344 *Fax Area Code: 888 ■ *TF:* 800-231-9559 ■ *Web:* www.whitesinc.com	Houston	TX	77011	713-928-2632	944-8373*	274
White's Nursery & Greenhouses Inc 3133 Old Mill Rd *TF:* 800-966-9969 ■ *Web:* www.whitesnursery.com	Chesapeake	VA	23323	757-487-2300		369
White'S Pharmacy of Dalton LLC 2955B Cleveland Hwy	Dalton	GA	30721	706-259-9707		237
Whitecap Canada Inc 200 Yorkland Blvd Ste 920 *TF:* 800-215-6702 ■ *Web:* www.whitecapcanada.com	Toronto	ON	M2J5C1	416-490-9900		396
Whitecap Resources Inc 3800 525 - Eighth Ave SW *TF:* 866-590-5289 ■ *Web:* www.wcap.ca	Calgary	AB	T2P1G1	403-266-0767		536
Whitecap Venture Partners 22 St Clair Ave E Ste 1010 *Web:* whitecastle.ca	Toronto	ON	M4T2S3	416-324-5421	961-3232	528
Whitecourt Communications 4214 42 Ave *Web:* whitecourtcommunications.ca	Whitecourt	AB	T7S0A3	780-778-3778		224
Whited Ford 207 Perry Rd *Web:* www.whitedford.com	Bangor	ME	04401	207-947-3673		57
Whitefab Inc 724 Ave W *TF:* 800-772-7017 ■ *Web:* www.whitefab.com	Birmingham	AL	35214	205-791-2011		492
Whiteface Club & Resort 373 Whiteface Inn Ln *TF:* 800-422-6757 ■ *Web:* www.whitefaceclubresort.com	Lake Placid	NY	12946	518-523-2551	523-4278	669
Whiteface Lodge, The 7 Whiteface Inn Ln *Web:* www.thewhitefacelodge.com	Lake Placid	NY	12946	518-523-0500		378
Whitefield Group: Local Seo & Web Design LLC 6130 Plumas St Ste 200 *Web:* whitefieldgroup.net	Reno	NV	89519	775-230-7095		5
Whitefish Bay Schools 1200 E Fairmount Ave *Web:* www.wfbschools.com	Whitefish Bay	WI	53217	414-963-3901		780
Whitefish Dunes State Park 3275 County Hwy WD *Web:* dnr.wi.gov	Sturgeon Bay	WI	54235	920-823-2400	823-2640	565
Whiteford, Taylor & Preston LLP 7 Saint Paul St *Web:* www.wtplaw.com	Baltimore	MD	21202	410-347-8700		428
Whitehall Associates Inc 416 Southview Ave	Silver Spring	MD	20905	301-879-1421		104
Whitehall Community Park 402 N Hamilton Rd *Web:* cityofwhitehall.com	Whitehall	OH	43213	614-863-0121		564
Whitehall Credit Union 5025 E Main St *Web:* whitehallcu.org	Columbus	OH	43213	614-866-5025		219
Whitehall Foundation Inc 125 Worth Ave *Web:* www.whitehall.org	Palm Beach	FL	33480	561-655-4474		305
Whitehall Hotel 105 E Delaware Pl *TF:* 800-948-4255 ■ *Web:* www.thewhitehallhotel.com	Chicago	IL	60611	312-944-6300	944-8552	379
Whitehall Management Consultants Inc 9815 N 95th St *TF:* 800-777-3864 ■ *Web:* www.whitehallmgt.com	Scottsdale	AZ	85258	480-860-5700		449
Whitehall Printing Co 4244 Corporate Sq *Fax Area Code: 239 ■ *TF:* 800-321-9290 ■ *Web:* www.whitehallprinting.com	Naples	FL	34104	800-321-9290	643-6139*	626
Whitehorse Chamber of Commerce 302 Steele St Ste 101 *Web:* www.whitehorsechamber.com	Whitehorse	YT	Y1A2C5	867-667-7545	667-4507	137
Whitehouse Sheldon (Sen D - RI) 530 Hart Bldg *Web:* www.whitehouse.senate.gov	Washington	DC	20510	202-224-2921	228-6362	342-2
Whitelaw Hotel 808 Collins Ave *Web:* www.whitelawhotel.com	Miami Beach	FL	33139	305-398-7000	398-7010	379
WhiteLight Group LLC N14 W24200 Tower Pl Ste 203 *Web:* www.whitelightgrp.com	Waukesha	WI	53188	630-571-6705		179
Whiteman & Co PA 111 Second Ave NE Ste 1600	St Petersburg	FL	33704	727 896 2727		2
Whiteman Air Force Base 509 Spirit Blvd Ste 116 *Web:* www.whiteman.af.mil	Whiteman AFB	MO	65305	660-687-6123	687-7948	497-1
Whitepath Fab Tech Inc 16402 Hwy 515 N *Web:* www.whitepath.com	Ellijay	GA	30540	706 276 2511		203
Whitesburg Appalachian Regional Hospital (ARH) 240 Hospital Rd *Web:* arh.org/locations/whitesburg.aspx	Whitesburg	KY	41858	606-633-3500		374-3
Whitesell Corp 2703 Avalon Ave *TF General:* 855-227-4515 ■ *Web:* www.whitesellgroup.com	Muscle Shoals	AL	35662	256-248-8500		486
Whitesell-Green Inc 3881 N Palafox St *Web:* www.whitesell-green.com	Pensacola	FL	32505	850-434-5311	434-5315	188-10
Whiteside County 200 E Knox St *TF:* 800-460-5657 ■ *Web:* www.whiteside.org	Morrison	IL	61270	815-772-5100		338
Whiteside Manufacturing Company Inc 309 Hayes St *Web:* www.whitesidemfg.com	Delaware	OH	43015	740-363-1179		350
Whitespace Creative Inc 24 N High St Ste 200 *Web:* www.whitespace-creative.com	Akron	OH	44308	330-762-9320		4
Whitespeed 1559 Seventh St *Fax Area Code: 949 ■ *Web:* www.whitespeed.com	Santa Monica	CA	90401	310-899-9114	900-5499*	5
Whitestone Hill State Historic Site C/O Dorene Brandeburger 8692 98th Ave *Web:* history.nd.gov	Monango	ND	58436	701-349-4103		565
Whitewater Grille 200 Lee St E *TF:* 800-845-5279	Charleston	WV	25301	304-353-3636	353-3722	671
Whitewater Memorial State Park 1418 S State Rd 101 *Web:* www.in.gov	Liberty	IN	47353	765-458-5565		565
Whitewater State Park 19041 Hwy 74 *TF:* 800-366-8917 ■ *Web:* www.dnr.state.mn.us	Altura	MN	55910	507-932-3007	932-5938	565
Whitewater Valley Rural Electric Membership Corp 101 Brownsville Ave *TF:* 800-529-5557 ■ *Web:* www.wwvremc.com	Liberty	IN	47353	765-458-5171	458-5938	245
WhiteWave Foods Co 12002 Airport Way *TF:* 888-820-9283 ■ *Web:* www.whitewave.com	Broomfield	CO	80021	303-635-4000		296-27
Whitewood Industries Inc 100 Liberty Dr *Web:* www.whitewood.net	Thomasville	NC	27360	336-472-0303		320
Whiteys Fish Camp 2032 County Rd 220 *TF:* 800-684-7018 ■ *Web:* www.whiteysfishcamp.com	Orange Park	FL	32003	904-269-4198		239
Whitfield & Eddy PLC 699 Walnut St Ste 2000 *Web:* www.whitfieldlaw.com	Des Moines	IA	50309	515-288-6041	246-1474	428
Whitfield County PO Box 248 *Web:* www.whitfieldcountyga.com	Dalton	GA	30722	706-876-2559	275-7540	338

				Phone	Fax	Class
Whitford Corp PO Box 80 *Web:* www.whitfordww.com	Elverson	PA	19520	610-296-3200	286-3510	481
Whitham Curtis Christofferson & Cook PC 11491 Sunset Hills Rd Ste 340 *Web:* www.wcc-ip.com	Reston	VA	20190	703-787-9400		41
Whiting Auditorium 1241 E Kearsley St *Web:* www.thewhiting.com	Flint	MI	48503	810-237-7333	237-7335	572
Whiting Corp 26000 Whiting Way *Fax Area Code: 708 ■ *TF:* 800-861-5744 ■ *Web:* www.whitingcorp.com	Monee	IL	60449	800-861-5744	587-2001*	470
Whiting Door Manufacturing Corp 113 Cedar St *Web:* www.whitingdoor.com	Akron	NY	14001	716-542-5427		247
Whiting Petroleum Corp 1700 Broadway Ste 2300 *NYSE:* WLL ■ *TF:* 800-723-4608 ■ *Web:* www.whiting.com	Denver	CO	80290	303-837-1661	861-4023	536
Whiting-Turner Contracting Co 300 E Joppa Rd *Web:* www.whiting-turner.com	Towson	MD	21286	410-821-1100		186
Whitlam Label Company Inc 24800 Sherwood Ave *TF:* 800-755-2235 ■ *Web:* www.whitlam.com	Center Line	MI	48015	586-757-5100	757-1243	413
Whitley County 101 W Van Buren St *Web:* whitleygov.com	Columbia City	IN	46725	260-248-3102	248-3137	338
Whitley County Court Clerk 200 Main St Ste 2 *Web:* whitleycountyfiscalcourt.com	Williamsburg	KY	40769	606-549-6002	549-2790	338
Whitley Fuel LLC 1617 Second Ave N *Web:* www.whitleyfuel.com	Okanogan	WA	98840	509-422-3120		579
Whitley Manufacturing Inc 201 W First St PO Box 496 *Web:* www.whitleyman.com	South Whitley	IN	46787	260-723-5131	723-6949	106
Whitley Penn 3411 Richmond Ave Ste 500 *Web:* www.whitleypenn.com	Houston	TX	77046	713-621-1515	621-1570	2
Whitley Products Inc 493 S Circle Dr W	Warsaw	IN	46580	574-267-7114		595
Whitley Steel Company Inc 610 US Hwy 301 S *TF:* 800-590-3934 ■ *Web:* www.whitleysteel.com	Jacksonville	FL	32234	904-289-7471		492
Whitlock & Weinberger 490 Mendocino Ave Ste 201 *Web:* w-trans.com	Santa Rosa	CA	95401	707-542-9500		261
Whitlock Group 12820 W Creekk Pkwy *TF:* 800-726-9843 ■ *Web:* www.whitlock.com	Richmond	VA	23238	804-273-9100	273-9380	246
Whitlock Packaging Corp 1701 S Lee St *TF:* 800-833-9382 ■ *Web:* whitlockpkg.com	Fort Gibson	OK	74434	918-478-4300		296-20
Whitman College 345 Boyer Ave *Fax: Admissions ■ *TF Admissions:* 877-462-9448 ■ *Web:* www.whitman.edu	Walla Walla	WA	99362	509-527-5111	527-4967*	166
Whitman County 400 N Main St *Web:* www.co.whitman.wa.us	Colfax	WA	99111	509-397-6240	397-3546	338
Whitman Mission National Historic Site 328 Whitman Mission Rd *Web:* www.nps.gov	Walla Walla	WA	99362	509-522-6360	522-6355	564
Whitman Requardt & Assoc 801 S Caroline St *TF:* 800-338-1391 ■ *Web:* www.wrallp.com	Baltimore	MD	21231	410-235-3450	243-5716	261
Whitman Strategy Group LLC, The PO Box 1621 *Web:* www.whitmanstrategygroup.com	New Brunswick	NJ	08903	617-512-1643		192
Whitmore Manufacturing Co PO Box 9300 *TF:* 800-699-6318 ■ *Web:* www.whitmores.com	Rockwall	TX	75087	972-771-1000	722-2108	550
Whitney Bailey Cox & Magnani LLC 300 E Joppa Rd Ste 200 *Web:* www.wbcm.com	Baltimore	MD	21286	410-512-4500	324-4100	261
Whitney Bank 228 St Charles Ave *TF:* 800-844-4450 ■ *Web:* www.whitneybank.com	New Orleans	LA	70130	504-586-7456		70
Whitney Ctr 200 Leeder Hill Dr *TF:* 800-237-3847 ■ *Web:* www.whitneycenter.com	Hamden	CT	06517	203-848-2641		672
Whitney Jones Inc 119 Brookstown Ave Ste PH2 *Web:* www.whitneyjonesinc.com	Winston-Salem	NC	27101	336-722-2371		317
Whitney Lab 1095 N US Hwy 1 Ste 1 *Web:* www.methadonehelp.com	Ormond Beach	FL	32174	386-673-4770		237
Whitney Museum of American Art 945 Madison Ave *TF:* 800-944-8639 ■ *Web:* www.whitney.org	New York	NY	10021	212-570-3600		520
Whitney Partners 747 Third Ave 17th Fl *Web:* www.whitneypartners.net	New York	NY	10017	212-508-3500	508-3540	266
Whitney the - A Wyndham Historic Hotel 610 Poydras St *TF:* 800-996-3426 ■ *Web:* www.wyndhamhotels.com/wyndham	New Orleans	LA	70130	504-581-4222		379
Whitney Tool Company Inc 906 R St *TF:* 800-536-1971 ■ *Web:* www.whitneytool.com	Bedford	IN	47421	812-275-4491	275-6458	455
Whitney, Bradley & Brown Inc 11790 Sunrise Vly Dr *TF:* 800-770-0543 ■ *Web:* www.wbbinc.com	Reston	VA	20191	703-448-6081		196
Whitney, The 4421 Woodward Ave *Web:* www.thewhitney.com	Detroit	MI	48201	313-832-5700	832-2159	671
Whitsons Food Service Corp 1800 Motor Pkwy *Web:* www.whitsons.com	Islandia	NY	11749	631-424-2700		194
Whittaker Controls Inc 12838 Saticoy St *Web:* www.whittakercontrols.com	North Hollywood	CA	91605	818-765-8160	759-2190	203
Whittet-Higgins Co 33 Higginson Ave PO Box 8 *TF:* 800-323-7790 ■ *Web:* www.whittet-higgins.com	Central Falls	RI	02863	401-728-0700	728-0703	620
Whittier Area Chamber of Commerce 8158 Painter Ave *Web:* www.whittierchamber.com	Whittier	CA	90602	562-698-9554	693-2700	139
Whittier City School District 7211 Whittier Ave *Web:* www.whittiercity.k12.ca.us	Whittier	CA	90602	562-789-3000	907-9425	685
Whittier College 13406 E Philadelphia St *Fax: Admissions ■ *TF:* 800-299-4898 ■ *Web:* www.whittier.edu	Whittier	CA	90608	562-907-4200	907-4870*	166

				Phone	Fax	Class
Whittier Farms Inc 90 Douglas Rd PO Box 455 *Web:* www.whittierfarms.com	Sutton	MA	01590	508-865-1053	865-1096	296-27
Whittier Hospital Medical Ctr 9080 Colima Rd *TF:* 800-613-4291 ■ *Web:* www.whittierhospital.com	Whittier	CA	90605	562-945-3561	693-6811	374-3
Whittier Law School 3333 Harbor Blvd *Fax: Admissions ■ *Web:* www.law.whittier.edu	Costa Mesa	CA	92626	714-444-4141	444-0250*	167-1
Whittier Wood Products 3787 W First Ave PO Box 2827 *TF:* 800-653-3336 ■ *Web:* www.whittierwood.com	Eugene	OR	97402	541-687-0213	687-2060	319-2
Whittle & Mutch Inc 712 Fellowship Rd *Web:* www.wamiflavor.com	Mount Laurel	NJ	08054	856-235-1165		345
Whitworth College 300 W Hawthorne Rd *Fax: Admissions ■ *TF Admissions:* 800-533-4668 ■ *Web:* www.whitworth.edu	Spokane	WA	99251	509-777-1000	777-3758*	166
Whitworth Tool Inc 114 Industrial Park Ln *Web:* www.whittool.com	Hardinsburg	KY	40143	270-756-0098		454
WHJJ-AM 920 (N/T) 75 Oxford St Ste 301 *Web:* 920whjj.iheart.com	Providence	RI	02905	401-781-9979	781-9329	645-129
WHKO-FM 99.1 (Ctry) 1611 S Main St *Web:* www.k99online.com	Dayton	OH	45409	937-259-2111	259-2168	645-45
WHKY-TV Ch 14 (Ind) PO Box 1059 *TF:* 800-899-4897 ■ *Web:* www.whky.com	Hickory	NC	28603	828-322-1290	322-8256	741
WHLH-FM 95.5 (Rel) 1375 Beasley Rd *Web:* hallelujah955.iheart.com	Jackson	MS	39206	601-982-1062		645-78
WHLI-AM 1100 (Nost) 234 Airport Plaza Ste 5 *TF:* 800-367-1101 ■ *Web:* www.whli.com	Farmingdale	NY	11735	631-770-4200	770-0101	645
WHLT-TV Ch 22 (CBS) 5912 Hwy 49 Cloverleaf Mall Ste A *Web:* www.whlt.com	Hattiesburg	MS	39401	601-545-2077	545-3589	741
WHMA (Wiring Harness Manufacturers Assn) 15490 101st Ave N Ste 100 *Web:* www.whma.org	Maple Grove	MN	55369	763-235-6461		49-13
WHMB-TV Ch 40 (Ind) 10511 Greenfield Ave *TF:* 800-535-5542 ■ *Web:* whmb.lesea.com	Noblesville	IN	46060	317-773-5050	776-4051	741
WHMC-FM 90.1 (NPR) 1101 George Rogers Blvd *TF:* 800-922-5437 ■ *Web:* www.scetv.org	Columbia	SC	29201	803-737-3200		645-40
WHMC-TV Ch 23 (PBS) 1101 George Rogers Blvd *TF:* 800-277-3245 ■ *Web:* www.scetv.org	Columbia	SC	29201	803-737-3200		741-33
WHNO-TV Ch 20 (Ind) 839 St Charles Ave *Web:* whno.lesea.com	New Orleans	LA	70130	504-681-0120	681-0180	741-90
WHNT-TV Ch 19 (CBS) PO Box 19 *TF:* 800-533-8819 ■ *Web:* www.whnt.com	Huntsville	AL	35804	256-533-1919	536-9468	741-61
WHO-AM 1040 (N/T) 2141 Grand Ave *Web:* whoradio.iheart.com	Des Moines	IA	50312	515-245-8900		645-48
WHOI (Woods Hole Oceanographic Institution) 266 Woods Hole Rd *Fax: Hum Res ■ *Web:* www.whoi.edu	Woods Hole	MA	02543	508-289-2282	457-2109*	668
WhoKnows Inc 425 BRdway St *TF:* 877-338-2763 ■ *Web:* corp.whoknows.com	Redwood City	CA	94063	877-338-2763		387
Whole Brain Group LLC, The 109 E Ann St *Web:* www.thewholebraingroup.com	Ann Arbor	MI	48104	734-929-0431		177
Whole Foods Market Inc 550 Bowie St *NASDAQ:* WFM ■ *TF:* 888-992-6227 ■ *Web:* www.wholefoodsmarket.com	Austin	TX	78703	512-477-4455	482-7000	355
Whole Health Products LLC 17301 W Colfax Ave Ste 110 *Web:* www.wholehealth.com	Golden	CO	80401	303-684-9618		363
Whole Hog Health 88155 Hwy 57 *Web:* wholehogai.com	Hartington	NE	68739	402-254-2444		10-6
Wholesale Electric Supply Company LP 4040 Guls Fwy *Web:* www.wholesaleelectric.com	Houston	TX	77004	713-748-6100		246
Wholesale Electric Supply Inc 1400 Waterall St *Web:* www.netwes.com	Texarkana	TX	75501	903-794-3404		246
Wholesale Interiors Inc 794 Golf Ln *TF:* 800-599-6636 ■ *Web:* www.interiorexpressoutlet.com	Bensenville	IL	60106	630-238-8877		320
Wholesale Specialties Inc 4000 E 40th Ave *TF:* 800-223-5939 ■ *Web:* www.wholesalespecialties.com	Denver	CO	80216	303-296-2212		612
Wholesale Supply Group Inc 885 Keith St NW *Web:* www.wsginc.co	Cleveland	TN	37311	423-478-1191	478-5120	612
Who-Song & Larry's 111 SE Columbia Way *Web:* www.eltorito.com	Vancouver	WA	98661	360-695-1198		671
WHO-TV Ch 13 (NBC) 1801 Grand Ave *Fax: News Rm ■ *TF:* 800-777-8398 ■ *Web:* www.whotv.com	Des Moines	IA	50309	515-242-3500	242-3796*	741-40
WHP-AM 580 (N/T) 600 Corporate Cir *Web:* whp580.iheart.com	Harrisburg	PA	17110	717-540-8800		645-71
WHPT-FM 102.5 (CR) 11300 Fourth St N Ste 300 *TF:* 800-771-1025 ■ *Web:* www.theboneonline.com	Saint Petersburg	FL	33716	727-579-2000	579-2271	645-162
WHP-TV Ch 21 (CBS) 3300 N Sixth St *Web:* www.local21news.com	Harrisburg	PA	17110	717-238-2100		741-56
WHQG-FM 102.9 (Rock) 5407 W McKinley Ave *TF:* 866-262-6274 ■ *Web:* www.1029thehog.com	Milwaukee	WI	53208	414-799-1029	978-9001	645-100
WHQT-FM 105.1 (Urban) 2741 N 29th Ave *Fax Area Code: 954 ■ *Web:* www.hot105fm.com	Hollywood	FL	33020	305-444-4404	847-3223*	645
WHR (Western Horizon Resorts) 103 W Tomichi Ave Ste 201A *TF:* 800-378-3709 ■ *Web:* www.westernhorizonresorts.net	Gunnison	CO	81230	970-641-5387		121
WHRB-FM 95.3 (Var) 389 Harvard St *Web:* www.whrb.org	Cambridge	MA	02138	617-495-4818		645
WHRO-FM 90.3 (Clas) 5200 Hampton Blvd *Web:* www.whro.org	Norfolk	VA	23508	757-889-9400	489-0007	645-112

Name / Address	City	State	Zip	Phone	Fax	Class
WHRO-TV Ch 15 (PBS) 5200 Hampton Blvd *Web:* www.whro.org	Norfolk	VA	23508	757-889-9400	489-0007	741-92
WHSN-FM 89.3 (Alt) 1 College Cir *Web:* www.whsn-fm.com	Bangor	ME	04401	207-941-7116	947-3987	645-17
WHTA-FM 107.9 (Urban) 101 Marietta St 12th Fl *Web:* hotspotatl.com	Atlanta	GA	30303	404-765-9750	688-7686	645-10
WHTF-FM 104.9 (CHR) 3000 Olson Rd *Web:* www.hot1049.com	Tallahassee	FL	32308	850-386-8004	422-1897	645-161
WHTM-TV Ch 27 (ABC) 3235 Hoffman St *Web:* www.abc27.com	Harrisburg	PA	17110	717-236-2727	236-1263	741-56
WHTT-FM 104.1 (AC) 50 James E Casey Dr *Web:* www.whtt.com	Buffalo	NY	14206	716-881-4555		645-25
WHUR-FM 96.3 (Urban AC) 529 Bryant St NW *TF:* 855-787-2227 ■ *Web:* accessatlanta.com	Washington	DC	20059	202-399-9487		645-172
WHUT-TV Ch 32 (PBS) 2222 Fourth St NW *TF:* 800-683-1899 ■ *Web:* www.whut.org	Washington	DC	20059	202-806-3200	806-3300	741-139
WHVR-AM 1280 (Ctry) 275 Radio Rd *Web:* www.foreveryork.com	Hanover	PA	17331	717-637-3831	637-9006	645
WHXT-FM 103.9 (Urban) 1900 Pineview Rd *Web:* www.hot1039fm.com	Columbia	SC	29209	803-695-8600		645-40
WHY (World Hunger Year Inc) 505 Eigth Ave Ste 2100 *TF:* 800-548-6479 ■ *Web:* www.whyhunger.org	New York	NY	10018	212-629-8850	465-9274	48-5
Why Not Lease It 1750 Elm St Ste 1200 *TF:* 800-201-3187 ■ *Web:* whynotleaseit.com	Manchester	NH	03104	603-665-9000		23
Whyco Finishing Technologies LLC 670 Waterbury Rd *Web:* www.whyco.com	Thomaston	CT	06787	860-283-5826		481
WHYN-AM 560 (N/T) 1331 Main St 4th Fl *Web:* whyn.iheart.com	Springfield	MA	01103	413-781-1011		645-156
WHYY-FM 90.9 (NPR) 150 N Sixth St *Web:* www.whyy.org	Philadelphia	PA	19106	215-351-1200		645-122
WHYY-TV Ch 12 (PBS) 150 N Sixth St *Web:* www.whyy.org	Philadelphia	PA	19106	215-351-1200		741-98
WHZZ-FM 101.7 (AC) 600 W Cavanaugh Rd *Web:* www.1017mikefm.com	Lansing	MI	48910	517-393-1320	393-0882	645-87
WI (Wilderness Inquiry) 808 14th Ave SE *TF:* 800-728-0719 ■ *Web:* www.wildernessinquiry.org	Minneapolis	MN	55414	612-676-9400	676-9401	48-23
Wiat-tv 2075 Golden Crest Dr *Web:* wiat.com	Birmingham	AL	35209	205-322-4200		116
WiBand Communications Corp 187 Commerce Dr **Fax Area Code:* 780 ■ *Web:* www.wiband.com	Winnipeg	MB	R3P1A2	204-633-6333	430-4079*	225
Wibaux County PO Box 199 *TF:* 800-368-8683 ■ *Web:* wibauxco.com	Wibaux	MT	59353	406-796-2481		338
WIBC-FM 93.1 (N/T) 40 Monument Cir Ste 400 *TF:* 800-571-9422 ■ *Web:* www.wibc.com	Indianapolis	IN	46204	317-266-9422		645-77
WibiData Inc 375 Alabama St Ste 350	San Francisco	CA	94110	415-496-9424		387
WIBW-AM 580 (N/T) 1210 SW Executive Dr *Web:* www.wibwnewsnow.com	Topeka	KS	66615	785-272-3456	228-7282	645-164
WIBW-TV Ch 13 (CBS) 631 SW Commerce Pl *TF:* 800-408-3178 ■ *Web:* www.wibw.com	Topeka	KS	66615	785-272-6397	272-1363	741-135
WICC-AM 600 (N/T) 2 Lafayette Sq *Web:* www.wicc600.com	Bridgeport	CT	06604	203-333-9108	384-0600	645-158
WICD-TV Ch 15 (ABC) 2680 E Cook St *Web:* www.newschannel20.com	Springfield	IL	62703	217-753-5620		741
Wichita Area Chamber of Commerce 350 W Douglas Ave *Web:* www.wichitachamber.org	Wichita	KS	67202	316-265-7771	265-7502	139
Wichita Area Technical College 301 S Grove St *TF:* 866-296-4031 ■ *Web:* www.watc.edu	Wichita	KS	67211	316-677-9400	677-9555	800
Wichita Art Museum 1400 W Museum Blvd *Web:* www.wichitaartmuseum.org	Wichita	KS	67203	316-268-4921	268-4980	520
Wichita Business Journal 121 N Mead St Ste 100 *Web:* www.bizjournals.com	Wichita	KS	67202	316-267-6406	267-8570	457-5
Wichita City Hall 455 N Main St *Web:* www.wichita.gov	Wichita	KS	67202	316-268-4331		337
Wichita Community Theatre 258 N Fountain st *TF:* 800-397-0330 ■ *Web:* wichitact.org	Wichita	KS	67208	316-686-1282		572
Wichita Convention & Visitors Bureau 515 Main St Ste 115 *TF:* 800-288-9424 ■ *Web:* www.visitwichita.com	Wichita	KS	67202	316-265-2800	265-0162	206
Wichita County 206 S Fourth St *TF:* 800-865-6143 ■ *Web:* www.wichita.k-state.edu	Leoti	KS	67861	785-532-6011		338
Wichita County 900 Seventh St Ste 250 *Web:* www.co.wichita.tx.us	Wichita Falls	TX	76301	940-766-8100	716-8554	338
Wichita Ctr for the Arts 9112 E Central Ave *Web:* www.wcfta.com	Wichita	KS	67206	316-634-2787	634-0593	572
Wichita Eagle, The 825 E Douglas Ave *TF:* 800-200-8906 ■ *Web:* kansas.com	Wichita	KS	67202	316-268-6000	268-6627	532-2
Wichita Falls Board of Commerce & Industry 900 Eigth St Ste 218 *Web:* wichitafallschamber.com	Wichita Falls	TX	76301	940-723-2741	723-8773	139
Wichita Falls CVB 1000 Fifth St **Fax Area Code:* 940 ■ *TF:* 800-799-6732 ■ *Web:* wichitafalls.org	Wichita Falls	TX	76301	800-799-6732	716-5509*	572
Wichita Falls Public Library 600 11th St *Web:* www.wfpl.net	Wichita Falls	TX	76301	940-767-0868		434-3
Wichita Grand Opera 225 W Douglas Ave Century II Performing Arts Ctr *TF:* 855-755-7328 ■ *Web:* www.wichitagrandopera.org	Wichita	KS	67202	316-683-3444	263-2126	573-2
Wichita Kenworth Inc 5115 N Broadway *TF:* 800-825-5558 ■ *Web:* www.wichitakenworth.com	Wichita	KS	67219	316-838-0867	838-4845	516
Wichita Public Library 223 S Main St	Wichita	KS	67202	316-261-8500		434-3
Wichita State University 1845 Fairmount St **Fax:* Admissions ■ *TF Admissions:* 800-362-2594 ■ *Web:* www.wichita.edu	Wichita	KS	67260	316-978-3456	978-3174*	166
Wichita State University Ablah Library (WSU) 1845 Fairmount St *Web:* libraries.wichita.edu	Wichita	KS	67260	316-978-3481	978-3048	434-6
Wichita Symphony Orchestra (WSO) 225 W Douglas St Ste 207 *Web:* wichitasymphony.org	Wichita	KS	67202	316-267-5259	267-1937	573-3
Wichita-Sedgwick County Historical Museum 204 S Main St *Web:* www.wichitahistory.org	Wichita	KS	67202	316-265-9314	265-9319	520
Wichman Construction 5029 W Grace St *Web:* www.wichmanconstruction.com	Tampa	FL	33607	813-282-1179		186
Wick Buildings 405 Walter Rd **Fax Area Code:* 608 ■ *TF:* 855-438-9425 ■ *Web:* www.wickbuildings.com	Mazomanie	WI	53560	855-438-9425	795-2534*	505
Wick Communications Inc 333 W Wilcox Dr Ste 302 *Web:* www.wickcommunications.com	Sierra Vista	AZ	85635	520-458-0200	458-6166	637-8
Wickaninnish Inn 500 Osprey Ln PO Box 250 **Fax:* Resv ■ *TF:* 800-333-4604 ■ *Web:* www.wickinn.com	Tofino	BC	V0R2Z0	250-725-3100	725-3110*	379
Wickens Herzer Panza Cook & Batista Co 35765 Chester Rd *Web:* www.wickenslaw.com	Avon	OH	44011	440-930-8000		345
Wicker Roger F (Sen R - MS) 555 Dirksen Bldg *Web:* www.wicker.senate.gov	Washington	DC	20510	202-224-6253	228-0378	342-2
Wickersham State Historic Site 400 Willoughby Ave Ste 500 PO Box 111071 *Web:* www.dnr.alaska.gov/parks/units/wickrshm.htm	Juneau	AK	99811	907-465-4563		565
Wickham Glass Co 4747 N Webb Rd *Web:* www.wickhamglass.com	Wichita	KS	67226	316-262-3403		256
Wicklander Zulawski & Associates Inc 4932 Main St *TF:* 800-222-7789 ■ *Web:* www.w-z.com	Downers Grove	IL	60515	800-222-7789		463
Wickliffe Mounds State Historic Site 94 Green St *Web:* www.parks.ky.gov	Wickliffe	KY	42087	270-335-3681		565
Wicks Group of Cos LLC 405 Park Ave *Web:* www.wicksgroup.com	New York	NY	10022	212-838-2100	223-2109	792
Wicks Pies Inc 217 Greenville Ave **Fax Area Code:* 765 ■ *TF:* 800-642-5880 ■ *Web:* www.wickspies.com	Winchester	IN	47394	800-642-5880	584-3700*	68
Wicks Pipe Organ Co 416 Pine St *TF Cust Svc:* 877-654-2191 ■ *Web:* organ.wicks.com	Highland	IL	62249	618-654-2191	654-3770	527
WICN-FM 90.5 (NPR) 50 Portland St *TF:* 855-752-0700 ■ *Web:* www.wicn.org	Worcester	MA	01608	508-752-0700	752-7518	645-179
WICO-AM 1320 (N/T) 919 Ellegood St PO Box 909	Salisbury	MD	21801	410-219-3500		645
Wicomico County 125 N Div St *TF:* 800-293-4126 ■ *Web:* www.wicomicocounty.org	Salisbury	MD	21803	410-548-4801	548-4803	338
Wicomico County Board of Education PO Box 1538 *Web:* www.wcboe.org	Salisbury	MD	21802	410-677-4400	677-4444	685
Wicomico County Convention & Visitors Bureau 8480 Ocean Hwy *TF:* 800-332-8687 ■ *Web:* www.wicomicotourism.org	Delmar	MD	21875	410-548-4914		206
Wicomico County Free Library 122 S Div St *Web:* www.wicomicolibrary.org	Salisbury	MD	21801	410-749-3612	548-2968	434-3
WICS-TV Ch 20 (ABC) 2680 E Cook St *Web:* newschannel20.com	Springfield	IL	62703	217-753-5620		741-128
WICT (Women in Cable Telecommunications) 2000 K St Ste 350 *Web:* www.wict.org	Washington	DC	20006	202-827-4794	450-5596	49-14
WICU-TV Ch 12 (NBC) 3514 State St *TF:* 800-454-8812 ■ *Web:* www.erietvnews.com	Erie	PA	16508	814-454-5201	454-3753	741-44
Widearea Systems Inc 201A Broadway St *Web:* wideareasystems.com	Frederick	MD	21701	301-418-6180		141
WideBand Corp 401 W Grand St *TF:* 888-663-3050 ■ *Web:* www.wband.com	Gallatin	MO	64640	660-663-3000	663-3736	176
Widener University 1 University Pl **Fax:* Admissions ■ *TF Admissions:* 888-943-3637 ■ *Web:* www.widener.edu	Chester	PA	19013	610-499-4000	499-4676*	166
Widener University Commonwealth Law School 3800 Vartan Way *Web:* commonwealthlaw.widener.edu	Harrisburg	PA	17110	717-541-3903	541-3999	167-1
Widener University Delaware Law School 4601 Concord Pk *Web:* delawarelaw.widener.edu	Wilmington	DE	19803	302-477-2100		167-1
WideNet Consulting Group 11400 SE Sixth St Ste 130 *Web:* www.widenet-consulting.com	Bellevue	WA	98004	425-643-0366		463
WidePoint Corp 7926 Jones Branch Dr Ste 124 *Web:* www.widepoint.com	Mclean	VA	22102	703-349-2577		180
Wider Church Ministries 700 Prospect Ave *TF:* 866-822-8224 ■ *Web:* www.ucc.org	Cleveland	OH	44115	216-736-3200	736-3203	48-20
Wider Logistics Ltd 175-35 148th Rd 2nd Fl *Web:* www.widerlogistics.com	Jamica	NY	11434	718-244-8800	244-6728	311
Wider Opportunities for Women (WOW) 1001 Connecticut Ave NW Ste 930 *TF:* 800-260-5956 ■ *Web:* www.wowonline.org	Washington	DC	20036	202-464-1596	464-1660	48-24
WiderFunnel Marketing Inc 409 Granville St Ste 551 *Web:* www.widerfunnel.com	Vancouver	BC	V6C1T2	604-800-6450		5
Widex Canada Ltd 5041 Mainway *Web:* www.widex.ca	Burlington	ON	L7L5H9	905-315-8303		477

Phone | Fax | Class

Widmer Bros Brewing Co
929 N Russell St — Portland OR 97227 — 503-281-2437 — 281-1496 — 102
TF: 800-669-8610 ■ *Web:* www.widmerbrothers.com

Widmeyer Communications
1129 20th St NW Ste 200 — Washington DC 20036 — 202-667-0901 — 667-0902 — 636
Web: www.widmeyer.com

Widseth Smith Nolting & Associates Inc
Industrial Park Rd — Baxter MN 56425 — 218-829-5117 — 186
Web: www.widsethsmithnolting.com

Wiebe & Assoc 377 N Central Ave — Upland CA 91786 — 909-985-5357 — 2
Web: www.wiebecpas.com

Wieden & Kennedy 224 NW 13th Ave — Portland OR 97209 — 503-937-7000 — 937-8000 — 4
Web: www.wk.com

Wiederkehr Wine Cellars Inc
3324 Swiss Family Dr — Altus AR 72821 — 479-468-3551 — 443
TF: 800-622-9463 ■ *Web:* www.wiederkehrwines.com

Wieland 13737 Main St PO Box 1000 — Grabill IN 46741 — 260-627-3686 — 627-6496 — 319-3
TF: 888-943-5263 ■ *Web:* www.wielandhealthcare.com

Wieland 3990 US 311 Hwy N — Pine Hall NC 27042 — 336-445-4500 — 492
Web: www.wielandcopper.com

Wieland Electric Inc (WEI)
49 International Rd — Burgaw NC 28425 — 910-259-5050 — 246
TF: 800-943-5263 ■ *Web:* www.wielandinc.com

Wieland Metals Inc
567 Northgate Pkwy — Wheeling IL 60090 — 847-537-3990 — 537-4085 — 490
Web: www.wielandus.com

Wiers Farm Inc
4465 St Rt 103 S PO Box 385 — Willard OH 44890 — 419-935-0131 — 933-2017 — 10-11
TF: 800-777-6243 ■ *Web:* wiersfarm.com

Wiers International Trucks Inc
2111 Jim Neu Dr — Plymouth IN 46563 — 574-936-4076 — 57
TF: 888-889-4377 ■ *Web:* wiers.com

Wiesbaden Hot Springs
625 Fifth St PO Box 349 — Ouray CO 81427 — 970-325-4347 — 325-4358 — 706
Web: www.wiesbadenhotsprings.com

Wiese Industries 1501 Fifth St — Perry IA 50220 — 515-465-9854 — 465-9858 — 273
TF: 800-568-4391 ■ *Web:* www.wiesecorp.com

Wiese Research Associates Inc
9375 Burt St Ste 100 — Omaha NE 68114 — 402-391-7734 — 466
Web: www.wraresearch.com

Wieser & Cawley Inc 1301 Colegate Dr — Marietta OH 45750 — 740-373-1676 — 321
Web: wieserandcawleyfurniture.com

Wieser Concrete Products Inc
W3716 US Hwy 10 — Maiden Rock WI 54750 — 715-647-2311 — 647-5181 — 183
TF: 800-325-8456 ■ *Web:* www.wieserconcrete.com

WIF (Women in Film)
6100 Wilshire Blvd Ste 710 — Los Angeles CA 90048 — 323-935-2211 — 48-4
Web: www.wif.org

Wiffle Ball Inc
275 Bridgeport Ave PO Box 193 — Shelton CT 06484 — 203-924-4643 — 762
Web: www.wiffle.com

Wi-fi Guys LLC 7265 Hwy 1 — Finland MN 55603 — 218-353-7798 — 196
Web: www.wi-figuys.com

WIFR-TV Ch 23 (CBS)
2523 N Meridian Rd — Rockford IL 61101 — 815-987-5300 — 965-0981 — 741-112
Web: www.wifr.com

Wig America Co 27317 Industrial Blvd — Hayward CA 94545 — 510-887-9579 — 887-9574 — 348
TF: 800-338-7600 ■ *Web:* www.wigamerica.com

Wiggins Airways Inc 1 Garside Way — Manchester NH 03103 — 603-629-9191 — 665-9644 — 359
TF: 800-786-5690 ■ *Web:* www.wiggins-air.com

Wiggins Lift Company Inc
2571 Cortez St — Oxnard CA 93031 — 805-485-7821 — 485-5230 — 470
Web: www.wigginslift.com

Wiggins, Childs, Quinn & Pantazis LLC
The Kress Bldg 301 19th St N — Birmingham AL 35203 — 205-314-0500 — 428
Web: www.wigginschilds.com

Wiggy's Inc
2482 Industrial Blvd — Grand Junction CO 81505 — 970-241-6465 — 34
Web: www.wiggys.com

Wight & Co 2500 N Frontage Rd — Darien IL 60561 — 630-969-7000 — 261
Web: wightco75.com

Wiginton Fire Systems 699 Aero Ln — Sanford FL 32771 — 407-585-3200 — 585-3280 — 189-13
TF: 800-531-0200 ■ *Web:* www.wiginton.net

Wigwam Golf Resort & Spa
300 E Wigwam Blvd — Litchfield Park AZ 85340 — 623-935-3811 — 935-3737 — 669
Web: wigwamarizona.com

Wigwam Mills Inc 3402 Crocker Ave — Sheboygan WI 53082 — 855-275-0356 — 155-10
TF: 800-558-7760 ■ *Web:* www.wigwam.com

WIIS-FM 107.1 Key West Radio
1075 Duval St Ste C17 — Key West FL 33040 — 305-292-1071 — 645-84
Web: island1069.com

Wika Instrument Corp
1000 Wiegand Blvd — Lawrenceville GA 30043 — 770-513-8200 — 338-5118 — 201
TF: 888-945-2872 ■ *Web:* www.wika.us

Wiken Promotion & Advertising Inc
901 12 Oaks Ctr Dr — Wayzata MN 55391 — 952-476-2002 — 195
Web: www.wiken.com

Wikibon Project, The
5 Mt Royal Ave Ste 280 — Marlborough MA 01752 — 774-463-3400 — 41
Web: www.wikibon.org

Wikoff Color Corp 1886 Merritt Rd — Fort Mill SC 29715 — 803-548-2210 — 388
Web: www.wikoff.com

WIKY-FM 104.1 (AC)
1162 Mt Auburn Rd — Evansville IN 47720 — 812-424-8284 — 426-7928 — 645-56
Web: www.wiky.com

Wi-LAN Inc 303 Terry Fox Dr Ste 300 — Ottawa ON K2K3J1 — 613-688-4900 — 688-4894 — 173-3
TSE: WIN ■ *Web:* www.wilan.com/home/default.aspx

Wilbanks Energy Logistics
11246 Lovington Hwy Lovington Hwy
PO Box 1390 — Artesia NM 88211 — 575-746-6318 — 539
Web: www.wilbanksel.com

Wilbanks, Smith & Thomas Asset Management LLC
150 W Main St Ste 1700 — Norfolk VA 23510 — 757-623-3676 — 401
TF: 800-229-3677 ■ *Web:* www.wstam.com

Wilbar International Inc
50 Cabot Ct — Hauppauge NY 11788 — 631-951-9800 — 567
Web: www.sharkline.com

Wilbarger County
1700 Wilbarger St Rm 15 — Vernon TX 76384 — 940-552-5486 — 553-2320 — 338
Web: www.co.wilbarger.tx.us

Wilberforce University
1055 N Bickett Rd PO Box 1001 — Wilberforce OH 45384 — 937-376-2911 — 376-4751* — 166
**Fax:* Admissions ■ *TF Admissions:* 800-367-8568 ■ *Web:* www.wilberforce.edu

Wilbert Plastic Services Acquisition LLC
486 Vance St — Forest City NC 28043 — 704-822-1423 — 596
Web: www.wilbertplastics.com

Wilbraham & Monson Academy
423 Main St — Wilbraham MA 01095 — 413-596-6811 — 596-2448 — 622
TF: 800-616-3659 ■ *Web:* wma.us

Wilbraham Lawler & Buba
603 Stanwix St Ste 1725 — Pittsburgh PA 15222 — 412-255-0500 — 445
Web: www.wlbdeflaw.com

Wilbur Curtis Company Inc
6913 Acco St — Montebello CA 90640 — 323-837-2300 — 837-2406 — 298
TF: 800-421-6150 ■ *Web:* www.wilburcurtis.com

Wilbur D May Museum 1595 N Sierra St — Reno NV 89503 — 775-785-5961 — 785-4707 — 520
Web: www.washoecounty.us

Wilbur Theatre 246 Tremont St — Boston MA 02116 — 617-248-9700 — 572
TF: 800-745-3000 ■ *Web:* thewilbur.com

Wilbur Wright College
4300 N Narragansett Ave — Chicago IL 60634 — 773-777-7900 — 481-8185 — 162
Web: www.ccc.edu/colleges/wright/pages/default.aspx

Wilbur-Ellis Co
345 California St 27th Fl — San Francisco CA 94104 — 415-772-4000 — 772-4011 — 276
Web: www.wilburellis.com/pages/home.aspx

Wilco Farmers 200 Industrial Way — Mount Angel OR 97362 — 503-845-6122 — 276
TF: 800-382-5339 ■ *Web:* www.wilco.coop

Wilco Inc 3502 W Harry — Wichita KS 67213 — 316-943-9379 — 770
Web: www.wilcoaircraftparts.com

Wilco Machine & Fab Inc
1326 S Broadway — Marlow OK 73055 — 580-658-6993 — 454
Web: www.wilcofab.com

Wilco Marsh Buggies & Draglines Inc
1304 Macarthur Ave — Harvey LA 70058 — 504-341-3409 — 190
TF: 800-253-0869 ■ *Web:* www.wilcomarshbuggies.com

Wilco Peanut Co 3391 US Hwy 281 N — Pleasanton TX 78064 — 830-569-3808 — 569-2743 — 11-1

Wilcom Inc
73 Daniel Webster Hwy PO Box 508 — Belmont NH 03220 — 603-524-2622 — 524-3735 — 647
TF: 800-222-1898 ■ *Web:* www.wilcominc.com

Wilcor Autos Inc Dba Toyota Vallejo
201 Auto Mall Pkwy — Vallejo CA 94591 — 707-552-4545 — 57

Wilcox | Swartzwelder & Company LLC
102 Decker Crt Ste 204 — Irving TX 75062 — 972-831-1300 — 70
Web: www.ws-ibank.com

Wilcox County 103 N Broad St — Abbeville GA 31001 — 229-467-2737 — 467-2000 — 338
TF: 866-694-5824 ■ *Web:* wilcoxcountygeorgia.com

Wilcox Emporium Warehouse 161 Howard St — Boone NC 28607 — 828-262-1221 — 479
TF: 800-280-5986 ■ *Web:* wilcoxemporium.com

Wilcox Farms Inc
40400 Harts Lake Valley Rd — Roy WA 98580 — 360-458-7774 — 10-8
Web: www.wilcoxfarms.com

Wilcox Frozen Foods Inc
2200 Oakdale Ave — San Francisco CA 94124 — 415-282-4116 — 297-6

Wilcox Industries Corp
25 Piscataqua Dr — Portsmouth NH 03801 — 603-431-1331 — 544
Web: www.wilcoxind.com

Wilcox Memorial Hospital (WMH)
3-3420 Kuhio Hwy — Lihue HI 96766 — 808-245-1100 — 374-3
TF: 877-709-9355 ■ *Web:* www.hawaiipacifichealth.org

Wilcox Miller & Nelson
333 University Ave Ste 200 — Sacramento CA 95825 — 916-977-3700 — 193
Web: www.wilcoxcareer.com

Wilcox Paper LLC
11100 Jefferson Hwy N — Champlin MN 55316 — 763-404-8400 — 553
Web: www.wilcoxpaper.com

Wilcox Travel Sandals
1 W Pack Sq Ste 1700 — Asheville NC 28801 — 828-210-8197 — 772
Web: www.wilcoxtravel.com

Wilcoxon Research Inc
20511 Seneca Meadows Pkwy — Germantown MD 20876 — 301-330-8811 — 2
TF: 800-945-2696 ■ *Web:* www.wilcoxon.com

Wild 104.3 500 S Polk St — Amarillo TX 79101 — 806-355-1043 — 645

Wild 94.9 340 Townsend St 4th Fl — San Francisco CA 94107 — 415-975-5555 — 645-145
TF: 888-333-9490 ■ *Web:* wild949.iheart.com

Wild Adventures Valdosta LLC
3766 Old Clyattville Rd — Valdosta GA 31601 — 229-219-7080 — 31
Web: www.wildadventures.com

Wild Animal Baby Magazine
11100 Wildlife Ctr Dr — Reston VA 20190 — 800-822-9919 — 457-6
TF: 800-822-9919 ■ *Web:* www.nwf.org/wildanimalbaby

Wild Animal Safari
1300 Oak Grove Rd — Pine Mountain GA 31822 — 706-663-8744 — 823
TF: 800-367-2751 ■ *Web:* www.animalsafari.com

Wild Animal Sanctuary, The
1946 County Rd 53 — Keenesburg CO 80643 — 303-536-0118 — 794
Web: www.wildanimalsanctuary.org

Wild Bird Centers of America
4046 W 83rd St — Prairie Village KS 66208 — 913-381-5633 — 791
Web: www.wildbird.com

Wild Birds Unlimited Inc
11711 N College Ave Ste 146 — Carmel IN 46032 — 317-571-7100 — 571-7110 — 578
TF: 800-326-4928 ■ *Web:* www.wbu.com

Wild Bldg Contractors Inc
225 W First N St Ste 102 — Morristown TN 37814 — 423-581-5639 — 587-4037 — 186
Web: www.wildbuilding.com

Wild Blueberry Assn of North America (WBANA)
PO Box 100 — Old Town ME 04468 — 207-570-3535 — 581-3499 — 48-2
TF: 800-341-1758 ■ *Web:* www.wildblueberries.com

Wild Card Saloon & Casino
120 Main St — Black Hawk CO 80422 — 303-582-3412 — 582-3508 — 133

Wild Dunes Resort
5757 Palm Blvd — Isle of Palms SC 29451 — 866-359-5593 — 669
TF: 866-359-5593 ■ *Web:* www.destinationhotels.com/wild-dunes

Wild Flavors Inc 1261 Pacific Ave — Erlanger KY 41018 — 859-342-3600 — 342-3610* — 296-15
**Fax:* Sales ■ *TF:* 800-263-5286 ■ *Web:* www.wildflavors.com

Name / Address	City	State	ZIP	Phone	Fax	Class
Wild Ginger Asian Restaurant						
1401 Third Ave	Seattle	WA	98101	206-623-4450		671
Web: www.wildginger.net						
Wild Horse Island State Park						
490 N Meridian Rd	Kalispell	MT	59901	406-752-5501		565
Web: www.fwp.mt.gov						
Wild Horse State Recreation Area						
HC 31 Box 265	Elko	NV	89801	775-385-5939		565
Web: www.parks.nv.gov						
Wild Onion 788 Grand Ave	Saint Paul	MN	55105	651-291-2525		671
Web: www.wild-onion.net						
Wild Onion Books 3441 N Ashland Ave	Chicago	IL	60657	773-281-1818		95
TF: 800-621-1008 ■ *Web:* www.loyolapress.com						
Wild Palms Hotel 910 E Fremont Ave	Sunnyvale	CA	94087	408-738-0500	736-8302	379
Web: www.jdvhotels.com						
Wild Rice Electric Co-op Inc						
502 N Main PO Box 438	Mahnomen	MN	56557	218-935-2517	935-2519	245
TF: 800-244-5709 ■ *Web:* www.wildriceelectric.com						
Wild River State Park						
39797 Pk Trl	Center City	MN	55012	651-583-2125		565
Web: www.dnr.state.mn.us						
Wild Rose Entertainment LLC						
5465 Mills Civic Pkwy Ste 400	West Des Moines	IA	50266	515-248-1776		656
Web: www.wildroseresorts.com						
Wild Swan Theater						
6175 Jackson Rd Ste B	Ann Arbor	MI	48103	734-995-0530		573-4
TF: 800-745-3000 ■ *Web:* www.wildswantheater.org						
Wild Waves Theme & Water Park						
36201 Enchanted Pkwy S	Federal Way	WA	98003	253-661-8000		32
Web: wildwaves.com						
Wild Wild West Gambling Hall & Hotel						
3330 W Tropicana Ave	Las Vegas	NV	89103	702-740-0000		378
Web: www.wwwesthotelcasino.com						
Wild Wings LLC 2101 S Hwy 61	Lake City	MN	55041	651-345-5055		459
TF: 800-445-4833 ■ *Web:* www.wildwings.com						
Wild Woods Inc						
3575 Cahuenga Blvd W Ste 400	Los Angeles	CA	90068	323-878-0400		246
Web: www.wwoods.com						
Wildcat Den State Park						
1884 Wildcat Den Rd	Muscatine	IA	52761	563-263-4337		565
Web: www.iowadnr.gov						
Wildcat Development Corp						
230 Spring Hill Dr Ste 300	Spring	TX	77386	281-863-9370		536
Web: wildcatdev.com						
Wildcat Hills State Recreation Area						
210615 Hwy 71	Gering	NE	69341	308-436-3777		565
Web: outdoornebraska.gov						
Wildcat Mountain State Park						
E13660 State Hwy 33 PO Box 99	Ontario	WI	54651	608-337-4775		565
Web: www.dnr.wi.gov						
Wilde Agency 201 Summer St	Holliston	MA	01746	508-893-0223		195
Web: www.wildeagency.com						
Wilden Pump & Engineering Co						
22069 Van Buren St	Grand Terrace	CA	92313	909-422-1730	783-3440	641
Web: www.psgdover.com						
Wildenstein & Co Inc 689 Fifth Ave	New York	NY	10022	212-879-0500		520
Web: www.wildenstein.com						
Wilderness Hotel & Resort Inc						
511 E Adams St	Wisconsin Dells	WI	53965	608-253-9729		378
Web: www.wildernessresort.com						
Wilderness Inquiry (WI)						
808 14th Ave SE	Minneapolis	MN	55414	612-676-9400	676-9401	48-23
TF: 800-728-0719 ■ *Web:* www.wildernessinquiry.org						
Wilderness Press						
c/o Keen Communications 2204 First Ave S						
Ste 102	Birmingham	AL	35233	800-443-7227	326-1012*	637-2
**Fax Area Code:* 205 ■ *TF:* 800-443-7227 ■ *Web:* www.wildernesspress.com						
Wilderness Road State Park						
8051 Wilderness Rd	Ewing	VA	24248	276-445-3065		565
Web: www.friendsofwildernessroad.org						
Wilderness Society 1615 M St NW	Washington	DC	20036	202-833-2300		48-13
TF: 800-843-9453 ■ *Web:* www.wilderness.org						
Wilderness State Park						
903 Wilderness Pk Dr	Carp Lake	MI	49718	231-436-5381		565
Web: www.michigandnr.com						
Wilderness Trails Ranch						
1766 County Rd 302	Durango	CO	81303	970-247-0722	247-1006	239
TF: 800-527-2624 ■ *Web:* www.wildernesstrails.com						
Wilderness Travel 1102 Ninth St	Berkeley	CA	94710	510-558-2488	558-2489	760
TF: 800-368-2794 ■ *Web:* www.wildernesstravel.com						
Wildes-Spirit Design & Printing						
4321 Charles Crossing Dr	White Plains	MD	20695	301-870-4141		627
Web: www.wildes-spirit.com						
Wildflower 7037 N Oracle Rd	Tucson	AZ	85704	520-219-4230		671
Web: www.foxrc.com						
Wildflower Bread Co 7755 E Gray Rd	Scottsdale	AZ	85260	480-951-9453		297-11
Web: www.wildflowerbread.com						
Wildish Land Co Inc						
3600 Wildish Ln PO Box 40310	Eugene	OR	97408	541-485-1700	683-7722	187
Web: www.wildish.com						
Wildland Adventures Inc						
3516 NE 155th St	Lake Forest Park	WA	98155	206-365-0686		760
TF: 800-345-4453 ■ *Web:* wildland.com						
Wildlands Inc 3855 Atherton Rd	Rocklin	CA	95765	916-435-3555		194
Web: www.wildlandsinc.com						
Wildlife Conservation Society (WCS)						
2300 Southern Blvd	Bronx	NY	10460	718-220-5100		48-3
Web: www.wcs.org						
Wildlife Forever						
2700 Fwy Blvd Ste 1000	Brooklyn Center	MN	55430	763-253-0222	560-9961	48-3
Web: www.wildlifeforever.org						
Wildlife Habitat Council (WHC)						
8737 Colesville Rd Ste 800	Silver Spring	MD	20910	301-588-8994		48-13
Web: www.wildlifehc.org						
Wildlife Management Institute (WMI)						
1440 Upper Bermudian Rd	Gardners	PA	17324	717-677-4480	563-2157*	48-3
**Fax Area Code:* 802 ■ *Web:* www.wildlifemanagementinstitute.org						
Wildlife Sanctuary of Northwest Florida						
PO Box 1092	Pensacola	FL	32591	850-433-9453	438-6168	823
TF: 800-435-7353 ■ *Web:* www.pensacolawildlife.com						
Wildlife West Nature Park						
87 N Frontage Rd	Edgewood	NM	87015	505-281-7655	281-7170	823
TF: 877-981-9453 ■ *Web:* www.wildlifewest.org						
Wildlife World Zoo						
16501 W Northern Ave	Litchfield Park	AZ	85340	623-935-9453		823
Web: www.wildlifeworld.com						
Wildplay Element Parks						
103-2610 Douglas St	Victoria	BC	V8T4M1	250-595-2251		564
Web: www.wildplay.com						
Wilds, The 14000 International Rd	Cumberland	OH	43732	740-638-5030		823
Web: www.thewilds.org						
WildTangent Inc						
18578 NE 67th Ct Bldg 5	Redmond	WA	98052	425-497-4545	497-4501	178-6
Web: www.wildtangent.com						
Wildwood Correctional Ctr						
10 Chugach Ave	Kenai	AK	99611	907-260-7200	260-7208	213
TF: 800-844-6591 ■ *Web:* www.correct.state.ak.us						
Wildwood Express Trucking						
12416 E Swanson Ave	Kingsburg	CA	93631	559-897-1035	897-1038	780
Web: wildwoodex.com						
Wildwood Lamps & Accents						
516 Paul St PO Box 672	Rocky Mount	NC	27803	252-446-3266	977-6669	439
Web: www.wildwoodlamps.com						
Wildwood State Park						
790 Hulse Landing Rd PO Box 518	Wading River	NY	11792	631-929-4314		565
Web: www.parks.ny.gov						
Wildwoods Convention Ctr						
4501 Boardwalk	Wildwood	NJ	08260	609-729-9000	846-2631	205
TF: 800-992-9732 ■ *Web:* www.wildwoodsnj.com						
Wilen Direct 3333 SW 15th St	Deerfield Beach	FL	33442	954-246-5000		627
Web: wilendirect.com						
Wiley & Wilson Inc						
127 Nationwide Dr	Lynchburg	VA	24502	434-947-1901		261
Web: wileywilson.com						
Wiley College 711 Wiley Ave	Marshall	TX	75670	903-927-3300	927-3366*	166
**Fax:* Admissions ■ *TF Admissions:* 800-658-6889 ■ *Web:* www.wileyc.edu						
Wiley Metal Fabricating Inc						
4589 N Wabash Rd	Marion	IN	46952	765-671-7865		697
Web: www.wileymetal.com						
Wiley Publishing Inc 111 River St	Hoboken	NJ	07030	201-748-6000	748-6088	637-2
TF: 800-225-5945 ■ *Web:* www.wiley.com/wileycda/section/index.html						
Wiley Rein LLP 1776 K St N W	Washington	DC	20006	202-719-7000		428
Web: www.wileyrein.com						
Wiley Sanders Truck Lines Inc						
PO Box 707 PO Box 707	Troy	AL	36081	800-392-8017	566-3257*	485
**Fax Area Code:* 334 ■ *TF:* 800-392-8017 ■ *Web:* www.wileysanders.com						
Wiley Waterski and Wakeboard Pro Shop						
1417 S Trenton	Seattle	WA	98108	206-762-1300	762-7339	710
TF: 800-962-0785 ■ *Web:* www.wileyski.com						
Wiley X Inc 7800 Patterson Pass Rd	Livermore	CA	94550	925-243-9810		543
TF: 800-776-7842 ■ *Web:* www.wileyx.com						
Wilfrid Laurier University						
75 University Ave W	Waterloo	ON	N2L3C5	519-884-1970	886-9351	785
Web: www.wlu.ca						
Wilgus State Park PO Box 196	Ascutney	VT	05030	802-674-5422		565
Web: www.vtstateparks.com						
Wilheit Packaging LLC 1527 May Dr	Gainesville	GA	30507	770-532-4421		449
TF: 800-727-4421 ■ *Web:* www.wilheit.com						
Wilhelmina Models Inc 300 Pk Ave S	New York	NY	10010	212-473-0700	473-3223	506
Web: www.wilhelmina.com						
Wilk Forwarding Company Inc						
2900 Emerson Expy	Jacksonville	FL	32207	904-346-3550		311
WILK-AM 980 (N/T) 305 Hwy 315	Pittston	PA	18640	570-883-9800		645
Web: www.wilknewsradio.com						
Wilkes & McHugh P A						
1 N Dale Mabry Hwy Ste 800	Tampa	FL	33609	800-255-5070		445
TF: 800-255-5070 ■ *Web:* www.wilkesmchugh.com						
Wilkes Chamber of Commerce						
717 Main St	North Wilkesboro	NC	28659	336-838-8662	838-3728	139
Web: wilkeschamber.com						
Wilkes Community College						
1328 S Collegiate Dr PO Box 120	Wilkesboro	NC	28697	336-838-6100	838-6277	162
TF: 866-222-1548 ■ *Web:* www.wilkescc.edu						
Wilkes Correctional Ctr						
PO Box 253	North Wilkesboro	NC	28659	336-667-4533		213
Web: wilkesprisonministry.org						
Wilkes County						
22 W Robert Toombs Ave PO Box 661	Washington	GA	30673	706-678-2511		338
Web: www.washingtonwilkes.org						
Wilkes County 110 N St	Wilkesboro	NC	28697	336-651-7346	651-7546	338
Web: www.wilkescounty.net						
Wilkes Dining Room 107 W Jones St	Savannah	GA	31401	912-232-5997		671
TF: 800-961-3119 ■ *Web:* mrswilkes.com						
Wilkes Regional Medical Ctr						
1370 W D St PO Box 609	North Wilkesboro	NC	28659	336-651-8100		374-3
Web: wilkesregional.com						
Wilkes University 84 W S St	Wilkes-Barre	PA	18766	800-945-5378	408-4904*	166
**Fax Area Code:* 570 ■ **Fax:* Admissions ■ *TF:* 800-945-5378 ■ *Web:* www.wilkes.edu						
Wilkes-Barre General Hospital						
575 N River St	Wilkes-Barre	PA	18764	570-829-8111		374-3
Web: commonwealthhealth.net						
Wilkes-Barre/Scranton International Airport						
100 Terminal Dr	Avoca	PA	18641	570-602-2000	602-2010	27
TF: 877-235-9287 ■ *Web:* www.flyavp.com						
Wilkie Lexus 568 W Lancaster Ave	Haverford	PA	19041	610-525-0900		57
Web: wilkielexus.com						
Wilkin & Guttenplan PC						
1200 Tices Ln	East Brunswick	NJ	08816	732-846-3000		2
Web: wgcpas.com						
Wilkin County 300 Fifth St S	Breckenridge	MN	56520	218-643-7172	643-7167	338
Web: www.co.wilkin.mn.us						
Wilkin Guge Marketing						
3237 E Guasti Rd Ste 220	Ontario	CA	91761	909-390-1239		195
TF: 800-771-3325 ■ *Web:* www.wilkinguge.com						

Name / Address	City	State	ZIP	Phone	Fax	Class
Wilkins Investment Counsel Inc 160 Federal St 17th Fl *Web:* www.wilkinsinvest.com	Boston	MA	02110	617-951-9969		528
Wilkins Media Co 8010 Roswell Rd Ste 120 *Web:* outofhomeamerica.com	Atlanta	GA	30350	770-804-1818		5
Wilkins Mobile Builders Inc 601 County Rd 24 *Web:* www.wilkinsbuilders.com	Double Springs	AL	35553	205-489-2991		505
Wilkins Research Services LLC 1730 Gunbarrel Rd *Web:* www.wilkinsresearch.net	Chattanooga	TN	37421	423-894-9478		466
Wilkinson & Assoc Real Estate Inc 8604 Cliff Cameron Dr Ste 110 *Web:* www.wilkinsonandassociates.com	Charlotte	NC	28269	704-393-0048		652
Wilkinson Barker Knauer LLP 2300 N St NW Ste 700 *Web:* www.wbklaw.com	Washington	DC	20037	202-783-4141		428
Wilkinson County 100 Bacon St *Web:* wilkinsoncounty.net	Irwinton	GA	31042	478-946-2236	946-3767	338
Wilkinson County PO Box 40 *Web:* www.wilkinson.co.ms.gov	Woodville	MS	39669	601-888-3538	888-7591	338
Wilkinson County Correctional Ctr 2999 US 61 N *Web:* www.cca.com	Woodville	MS	39669	601-888-3199		213
Wilkinson Supply Co 3300 Bush St *Web:* www.wilkinsonsupplyco.com	Raleigh	NC	27609	919-834-0395		612
Wilkins-Rogers Inc 27 Frederick Rd *TF Cust Svc:* 877-438-4338 ■ *Web:* wrmills.com	Ellicott City	MD	21043	410-465-5800		296-23
Wilks Broadcast Group LLC 6470 E Johns Crossing Ste 450	Duluth	GA	30097	678-240-8976		645-10
Will County 302 N Chicago St *TF:* 800-897-9000 ■ *Web:* www.willcountyillinois.com	Joliet	IL	60432	815-740-4615		338
Will Rogers Memorial Ctr 3401 W Lancaster Ave *Web:* fortworthtexas.gov	Fort Worth	TX	76107	817-392-7469		720
Will Rogers Memorial Museum 1720 W Will Rogers Blvd *TF:* 800-324-9455 ■ *Web:* willrogers.com	Claremore	OK	74017	918-341-0719		520
Will Rogers State Beach 1925 Las Virgenes *Web:* www.parks.ca.gov/default.asp?page_id=625	Calabasas	CA	91302	310-305-9503		565
Will Rogers State Historic Park 1925 Las Virgenes *Web:* www.parks.ca.gov/default.asp?page_id=626	Calabasas	CA	91302	310-454-8212		565
Will Rogers World Airport 7100 Terminal Dr Unit 937 *Web:* www.flyokc.com	Oklahoma City	OK	73159	405-680-3200		27
Will Vision & Laser Centers 8100 NE Pkwy Dr Ste 125 *TF:* 877-542-3937 ■ *Web:* www.willvision.com	Vancouver	WA	98662	360-885-1327	885-1333	798
Willacy County 576 W Main Ave Ste 102 *Web:* co.willacy.tx.us	Raymondville	TX	78580	956-689-2532	689-5713	338
Willacy County State Jail 1695 S Buffalo Dr	Raymondville	TX	78580	956-689-4900		213
Willamette Education Service District Employees Association Inc 2611 Pringle Rd SE *Web:* www.ddouglas.k12.or.us	Salem	OR	97302	503-588-5330		414
Willamette Falls Hospital 1500 Div St *Web:* oregon.providence.org	Oregon City	OR	97045	503-656-1631		374-3
Willamette National Cemetery 11800 SE Mt Scott Blvd *Web:* www.cem.va.gov	Portland	OR	97086	503-273-5250		136
Willamette Stone State Heritage Site 11321 SW Terwilliger Blvd *TF:* 800-551-6949 ■ *Web:* www.oregonstateparks.org	Portland	OR	97219	800-551-6949		565
Willamette University 900 State St **Fax:* Admissions ■ *TF:* 877-542-2787 ■ *Web:* www.willamette.edu	Salem	OR	97301	503-370-6303	375-5363*	166
Willamette University College of Law 245 Winter St SE **Fax:* Admissions ■ *TF:* 844-232-7228 ■ *Web:* www.willamette.edu/wucl	Salem	OR	97301	503-370-6282	370-6087*	167-1
Willamette University Hatfield Library 900 State St *Web:* library.willamette.edu	Salem	OR	97301	503-370-6312	370-6141	434-6
Willamette Valley Co 1075 Arrowsmith St *TF:* 800-333-9826 ■ *Web:* www.wilvaco.com	Eugene	OR	97402	541-484-9621	345-7480	550
Willamette Valley Hospice 1015 Third St NW *TF:* 800-555-2431 ■ *Web:* www.wvh.org	Salem	OR	97304	503-588-3600	363-3891	371
Willamette Valley Vineyards Inc 8800 Enchanted Way SE *NASDAQ: WVVI* ■ *TF Sales:* 800-344-9463 ■ *Web:* www.wvv.com	Turner	OR	97392	503-588-9463	588-8894	80-3
Willamette View 12705 SE River Rd *TF:* 800-446-0670 ■ *Web:* www.willametteview.org	Portland	OR	97222	503-654-6581		672
Willamette Week 2220 NW Quimby St *TF:* 800-677-5758 ■ *Web:* wweek.com	Portland	OR	97210	503-243-2122	243-1115	532-5
Willard Bay State Park 900 W 650 N Ste A *TF:* 800-322-3770 ■ *Web:* www.stateparks.utah.gov	Willard	UT	84340	435-734-9494		565
Willard Brook State Forest 595 Main St *Web:* www.mass.gov	Townsend	MA	01474	978-597-8802		565
Willard Cos Inc, The 75 Builders Pride Dr Ste 200 *Web:* www.thewillardcompanies.com	Hardy	VA	24101	540-721-5288		653
Willard Hotel 1401 pennsylvania ave nw *Web:* washington.intercontinental.com	Washington	DC	20004	202-628-9100		377
Willard House & Clock Museum 11 Willard St *TF:* 800-258-9182 ■ *Web:* www.willardhouse.org	North Grafton	MA	01536	508-839-3500		520
Willard Marine Inc 1250 N Grove St *TF:* 800-346-7245 ■ *Web:* www.willardmarine.com	Anaheim	CA	92806	714-666-2150	632-8136	90
Willard Packaging Company Inc 18940 Woodfield Rd *Web:* www.willardpackaging.com	Gaithersburg	MD	20879	301-948-7700		557
Willard-Cybulski Correctional Institution 391 Shaker Rd *Web:* ct.gov	Enfield	CT	06082	860-763-6100		213
Willbanks Metals Inc 1155 NE 28th St *TF:* 800-772-2352 ■ *Web:* www.willbanksmetals.com	Fort Worth	TX	76106	817-625-6161	625-8487	492
Willbros Downstream LLC 4400 Post Oak Pkwy Ste 1000 *TF:* 888-310-7712 ■ *Web:* www.willbros.com	Houston	TX	77027	918-556-3600		261
Willbros Engineers Inc 2087 E 71st St *Web:* www.willbros.com	Tulsa	OK	74136	918-496-0400		261
Will-Burt Co 169 S Main St *TF:* 800-654-9677 ■ *Web:* willburt.com	Orrville	OH	44667	330-682-7015	684-1190	454
Willcan Inc PO Box 1357 *Web:* www.basicreadymix.com	Calhoun	GA	30703	706-629-2256	625-0587	182
Willcox, Buyck & Williams PA 248 W Evans St *TF:* 800-648-1914 ■ *Web:* www.willcoxlaw.com	Florence	SC	29501	843-662-3258		428
Willdan 2401 E Katella Ave Ste 300 *TF:* 800-424-9144 ■ *Web:* www.willdan.com	Anaheim	CA	92806	714-940-6300	940-4920	261
Willems Marketing 120 N Morrison St Ste 200 *Web:* www.willemsmarketingandevents.com	Appleton	WI	54911	920-831-6580		195
Willert Home Products Inc 4044 Pk Ave *TF:* 800-325-9680 ■ *Web:* www.willert.com	Saint Louis	MO	63110	314-772-2822	772-1409	151
Willett Hall 3701 Willett Dr *Web:* www.willett-hall-portsmouth.com	Portsmouth	VA	23707	757-393-5144		572
Willey Honda 2215 S 500 W *TF Sales:* 888-431-4490 ■ *Web:* performancehondautah.com	Bountiful	UT	84010	888-431-4490		57
Willi Hahn Corp - Wiha Tools 1348 Dundas Cir *Web:* www.wihatools.com	Monticello	MN	55362	763-295-6591		820
William & Flora Hewlett Foundation 2121 Sand Hill Rd *TF:* 800-673-9036 ■ *Web:* www.hewlett.org	Menlo Park	CA	94025	650-234-4500	234-4501	305
William & Mary 400 Landrum Dr *TF:* 800-462-3683 ■ *Web:* www.swem.wm.edu	Williamsburg	VA	23187	757-221-3072	221-2635	434-6
William & Mary Law School 613 S Henry St **Fax:* Admissions ■ *Web:* www.wm.edu	Williamsburg	VA	23185	757-221-3800	221-3261*	167-1
William A Egan Civic & Convention Ctr 555 W Fifth Ave *Web:* www.anchorageconventioncenters.com	Anchorage	AK	99501	907-263-2800	263-2858	205
William A Randolph Inc 820 Lakeside Dr Ste 3 *Web:* www.warandolph.com	Gurnee	IL	60031	847-856-0123		186
William Avery & Associates Inc 3 1/2 N Santa Cruz Ave Ste A *TF:* 800-899-1669 ■ *Web:* www.averyassoc.net	Los Gatos	CA	95030	408-399-4424		463
William B Coleman Company Inc 4001 Earhart Blvd	New Orleans	LA	70125	504-822-1000		156
William B Meyer Inc 255 Long Beach Blvd *TF:* 800-727-5985 ■ *Web:* www.williambmeyer.com	Stratford	CT	06615	203-375-5801		685
William B Umstead State Park 8801 Glenwood Ave *Web:* ncparks.gov	Raleigh	NC	27617	919-571-4170		565
William Beaumont Army Medical Ctr 5005 N Piedras St	El Paso	TX	79920	915-742-2273		374-4
William Beaumont Hospital 3601 W 13-Mile Rd *Web:* www.beaumont.edu	Royal Oak	MI	48073	248-551-5000		353
William Blair & Company LLC 222 W Adams St *TF:* 800-621-0687 ■ *Web:* www.williamblair.com	Chicago	IL	60606	312-236-1600		690
William Blanchard Co 199 Mountain Ave *Web:* wmblanchard.com	Springfield	NJ	07081	973-376-9100	376-9154	186
William Breman Jewish Heritage Museum 1440 Spring St NW *Web:* www.thebreman.org	Atlanta	GA	30309	678-222-3700		520
William Burton & Company Inc 99 Walnut St *Web:* cpaburton.com	Saugus	MA	01906	781-233-2204		2
William C Smith & Company Inc 1100 New Jersey Ave SE *Web:* www.wcsmith.com	Washington	DC	20003	202-371-1220	371-9410	652
William Carey International University 1539 e howard st *Web:* www.wciu.edu	Pasadena	CA	91104	626-797-1200		162
William Carey University 498 Tuscan Ave **Fax:* Admissions ■ *TF:* 800-962-5991 ■ *Web:* www.wmcarey.edu	Hattiesburg	MS	39401	601-318-6051	318-6454*	166
William Charles Executive Search Partners 5550 Cascade Rd SE Ste 200 *TF:* 800-561-3357 ■ *Web:* www.william-charles.com	Grand Rapids	MI	49546	616-464-4355		226
William Crow Jewelry Inc 910 16th St Ste 320 *Web:* williamcrow.com	Denver	CO	80202	303-592-1695		410
William Douglas Management Inc 4523 Park Rd Ste 201 A *Web:* www.wmdouglas.com	Charlotte	NC	28209	704-347-8900		652
William E Donaldson Facility 100 Warrior Ln *Web:* doc.state.al.us	Bessemer	AL	35023	205-436-3681		213
William E Laupus Health Sciences Library 500 Health Science Dr 600 Moye Blvd Health Sciences Bldg *Web:* www.ecu.edu/cs-dhs/laupuslibrary	Greenville	NC	27834	252-744-2230	744-1376	434-1
William E Walter Inc 1917 Howard Ave *TF:* 800-681-3320 ■ *Web:* www.williamewalter.com	Flint	MI	48503	810-232-7459	232-8698	189-10
William F Renk & Sons Inc 6809 Wilburn Rd **Fax Area Code:* 608 ■ *TF:* 800-289-7365 ■ *Web:* www.renkseed.com	Sun Prairie	WI	53590	800-289-7365	825-6143*	10-5

Phone | Fax | Class

William F. Laman Public Library System
2801 Orange St. North Little Rock AR 72114 501-758-1720 758-3539 434-3
TF: 800-643-4690 ■ Web: www.lamanlibrary.org

William F. White International Inc
800 Islington Ave Toronto ON M8Z6A1 416-239-5050 111
Web: www.whites.com

William Fox Munroe Inc
3 E Lancaster Ave Shillington PA 19607 610-775-4521 344
TF: 800-344-2402 ■ Web: wfoxm.com

William Frick & Co
2600 Commerce Dr Libertyville IL 60048 847-918-3700 687
Web: fricknet.com

William G Koch & Assoc
2650 Wview Dr Wyomissing PA 19610 610-678-9700 2
Web: wgkcpa.com

William G. Satterlee & Sons Inc
12475 Route 119 Hwy N Rochester Mills PA 15771 724-397-2400 316
TF: 800-942-2214 ■ Web: www.satterleefuel.com

William George Co Inc 1002 Mize Ave Lufkin TX 75904 936-634-7738 634-7794 297-11
Web: www.williamgeorgeinc.com

William George Printing LLC
3469 Black and Decker Rd Hope Mills NC 28348 910-221-2700 627
Web: m.wgprinting.com

William Goldberg Diamond Corp
589 Fifth Ave. New York NY 10017 212-980-4343 407
TF: 800-351-0099 ■ Web: www.williamgoldberg.com

William Gotelli Plumbing Inc
21 Lovell Ave San Rafael CA 94901 415-457-1145 610
Web: www.gotelliplumbing.com

William Grant & Sons Inc
130 Fieldcrest Ave Edison NJ 08837 732-225-9000 81-3
Web: www.williamgrantusa.com/age_verify.php?redirect=/index.php

William H Harvey 4334 S 67th St Omaha NE 68117 402-331-1175 321-9532* 326
*Fax Area Code: 000 ■ TF: 000 021 0600 ■ Web: www.oatey.com

William H Sadlier Inc 9 Pine St New York NY 10005 800-221-5175 312-6080* 637-2
OTC: SADL ■ *Fax Area Code: 212 ■ TF: 800 221 5175 ■ Web: www.sadlier.com

William Howard Taft National Historic Site
2038 Auburn Ave Cincinnati OH 45219 513-684-3262 684-3627 564
Web: www.nps.gov/wiho

William Ives Consulting Inc
320 S Tryon St Ste 213 Charlotte NC 28202 704-376-5600 196
TF: 800-767-3263 ■ Web: www.wicusa.com

William J Ash Company LLC
3 Brayton Woods Dr Rehoboth MA 02769 401-965-8850 463
Web: www.wjashco.com

William J Clinton Presidential Ctr
1200 President Clinton Ave Little Rock AR 72201 501-370-8000 434-2
Web: www.clintonfoundation.org

William J Dixon Company Inc
756 Springdale Dr Exton PA 19341 610 524 1131 745-7
Web: www.wjdixon.com

William J Kline & Son Inc
1 Venner Rd Amsterdam NY 12010 518-843-1100 843-1338 637-8

William J Rish Park
6773 Hwy C 30 E Port St Joe FL 32456 850-227-1876 564
TF: 800-913-1518 ■ Web: apdcares.org

William Jessup University
333 Sunset Blvd Rocklin CA 95765 916-577-2200 577-2220 166
*Fax: Admissions ■ TF: 800-355-7522 ■ Web: www.jessup.edu

William Jewell College
500 College Hill WJC Liberty MO 64068 816-781-7700 415-5040 166
TF: 888-253-9355 ■ Web: www.jewell.edu

William K Sanford Town Library
629 Albany Shaker Rd Loudonville NY 12211 518-458-9274 434-3
Web: www.colonie.org

William K Walthers Inc
5601 W Florist Ave Milwaukee WI 53218 414-527-0770 527-4423 762
TF: 800-877-7171 ■ Web: www.walthers.com

William Lyon Homes
4695 MacArthur Ct 8th Fl Newport Beach CA 92660 949-833-3600 187
Web: www.lyonhomes.com

William M Bloomfield Inc
170 Barnard Ave San Jose CA 95125 408-998-2995 321

William M Staerkel Planetarium
2400 W Bradley Ave Parkland College Champaign IL 61821 217-351-2568 598
Web: www.parkland.edu

William M. Tugman State Park
72549 Hwy 101 Lakeside OR 97449 800-551-6949 565
TF: 800-551-6949 ■ Web: oregonstateparks.org

William Marvy Company Inc
1540 St Clair Ave Saint Paul MN 55105 651-698-0726 698-4048 76
TF: 800-874-2651 ■ Web: www.wmmarvyco.com

William Michell State Park Camp Grounds
6093 E M-115 Cadillac MI 49601 231-775-7911 565

William Mitchell College of Law
875 Summit Ave Saint Paul MN 55105 651-227-9171 167-1
TF: 888-962-5529 ■ Web: mitchellhamline.edu

William Mitchell State Park
6093 E M-115 Cadillac MI 49601 231-775-7911 565

William Morrow & Co 10 E 53rd St New York NY 10022 212-207-7000 637-2
TF: 800-242-7737 ■ Web: www.harpercollins.com

William O'Brien State Park
16821 O'Brien Trl N Marine-on-Saint Croix MN 55047 651-433-0500 565
Web: www.dnr.state.mn.us

William P Hobby Airport (HOU)
7800 Airport Blvd Houston TX 77061 713-640-3000 641-7703 27
Web: fly2houston.com/hobbyhome

William Paterson University
300 Pompton Rd. Wayne NJ 07470 973-720-2000 720-2910 166
TF: 877-978-3923 ■ Web: www.wpunj.edu

William Paterson University Cheng Library
300 Pompton Rd. Wayne NJ 07470 973-720-2541 720-2585 434-6
Web: www.wpunj.edu/library

William Peace University
15 E Peace St Raleigh NC 27604 919-508-2000 508-2326* 166
*Fax: Admissions ■ TF: 800-732-2347 ■ Web: www.peace.edu

William Penn Assn 709 Brighton Rd Pittsburgh PA 15233 412-231-2979 390
TF: 800-848-7366 ■ Web: www.williampennassociation.org

William Penn Foundation
100 N 18th St 2 Logan Sq 11th Fl Philadelphia PA 19103 215-988-1830 988-1823 305
Web: www.williampennfoundation.org

William Penn Life Insurance Co of New York
100 Quentin Roosevelt Blvd Garden City NY 11530 516-794-3700 391-2
TF: 800-346-4773 ■ Web: www.lgamerica.com

William Penn University
201 Trueblood Ave Oskaloosa IA 52577 800-779-7366 673-2113* 166
*Fax Area Code: 641 ■ *Fax: Admissions ■ TF: 800-779-7366 ■ Web: www.wmpenn.edu

William R Peterson Oil Co 12 W Rd Marlborough CT 06447 860-295-9200 316

William R Sharpe Jr Hospital
936 Sharpe Hospital Rd Weston WV 26452 304-269-1210 436-6380 374-5
TF: 866-384-5250

William S Hart Museum
24151 Newhall Ave Newhall CA 91321 661-254-4584 520
Web: www.hartmuseum.org

William S Hein & Company Inc
1285 Main St Buffalo NY 14209 716-882-2600 883-8100 637-2
TF: 800-828-7571 ■ Web: www.wshein.com

William Steinen Manufacturing Co
29 E Halsey Rd Parsippany NJ 07054 973-887-6400 887-4632 609
Web: www.steinen.com

William Trent House 15 Market St Trenton NJ 08611 609-989-3027 50-3
Web: www.williamtrenthouse.org

William V MacGill & Co
1000 N LombaRd Rd Lombard IL 60148 630-889-0500 727-3433* 475
*Fax Area Code: 800 ■ TF: 800-323-2841 ■ Web: www.macgill.com

William W Backus Hospital
326 Washington St Norwich CT 06360 860-889-8331 374-3
Web: backushospital.org

William W Price PA
320 Fern St West Palm Beach FL 33401 561-659-3212 428
TF: 800-932-2682 ■ Web: www.wpricepa.com

William W Rutherford Associates Inc
3102 Maple Ave Ste 450 Dallas TX 75201 214-219-8660 463
Web: www.wrutherford.com

William W. Powers State Recreation Area
12949 S Ave O Chicago IL 60633 773-646-3270 565

William Whitley House State Historic Site
625 William Whitley Rd Stanford KY 40484 606-355-2881 565
Web: www.parks.ky.gov

William Woods University
1 University Ave Fulton MO 65251 573-592-4221 592-1146* 166
*Fax: Admissions ■ TF Admissions: 800-995-3159 ■ Web: www.williamwoods.edu

Williams & Anderson PLC
111 Ctr St Ste 2200 Little Rock AR 72201 501-372-0800 372-6453 428
Web: williamsanderson.com

Williams & Assoc Inc 247 S Wilmot Rd Tucson AZ 85711 520-745-8500 4
Web: www.wasoc.com

Williams & Connolly LLP
725 12th St NW Washington DC 20005 202-434-5000 434-5029 428
TF: 800-491-1817 ■ Web: www.wc.com

Williams & Fudge Inc
300 Chatham Ave Rock Hill SC 29730 803-329-9791 160
Web: wfcorp.com

Williams & Helde Inc
711 Sixth Ave N Ste 200 Seattle WA 98109 206-285-1940 7
TF: 800-438-7325 ■ Web: www.williams-helde.com

Williams & Schoenberger Co LLC
338 S High St 2nd Fl Columbus OH 43215 614-224-0531 224-0553 428
Web: wslegalfirm.com

Williams & Williams Real Estate Auction
7120 S Lewis Ave Ste 200 Tulsa OK 74136 918-250-2012 652
TF: 800-801-8003 ■ Web: www.williamsauction.com

Williams & Works Inc
549 Ottawa NW Grand Rapids MI 49503 616-224-1500 261
Web: williams-works.com

Williams Baptist College
60 W Fulbright St Walnut Ridge AR 72476 870-886-6741 886-3924* 166
*Fax: Admissions ■ TF: 800-722-4434 ■ Web: www.wbcoll.edu

Williams Benator & Libby LLP
1040 Crown Pinte Pkwy NE Ste 400 Atlanta GA 30338 770-512-0500 512-0200 2
Web: www.wblcpa.com

Williams Bros Construction Company Inc
3800 Milam St Houston TX 77006 713-522-9821 520-5247 188-4
Web: www.wbctx.com

Williams Bus Lines Inc
PO Box 1272 Springfield VA 22151 703-560-5355 560-7851 109
TF: 800-500-1062 ■ Web: www.williamsbus.com

Williams College 880 Main St Williamstown MA 01267 413-597-3131 597-4052* 166
*Fax: Admissions ■ TF: 877-374-7526 ■ Web: www.williams.edu

Williams Comfort Products
250 W Laurel St Colton CA 92324 909-825-0993 824-8009 357
TF: 866-677-8444 ■ Web: www.williamscomfortprod.com

Williams Company of Orlando Inc
2301 Silver Star Rd Orlando FL 32804 407-295-2530 186
Web: www.williamsco.com

Williams Cos Inc 1 Williams Ctr Tulsa OK 74103 918-573-2000 360-3
NYSE: WMB ■ TF: 800-945-5426 ■ Web: co.williams.com

Williams County 1 Courthouse Sq Bryan OH 43506 419-636-2059 636-0643 338
Web: www.co.williams.oh.us

Williams County PO Box 2047 Williston ND 58802 701-577-4540 577-4535 338
Web: www.williamsnd.com

Williams Distributing Co
658 Richmond NW Grand Rapids MI 49504 616-456-1613 14
Web: www.wmsdist.com

Williams Distributing Corp
880 Burnett Rd Chicopee MA 01020 413-594-4900 81-1
Web: williamsdistributing.com

Williams Engineering Canada Inc
10065 Jasper Ave Ste 200 Edmonton AB T5J3B1 780-409-5300 256
TF: 800-263-2393 ■ Web: www.williamsengineering.com

Williams Financial Group Inc
2711 N Haskell Ave Cityplace Tower Ste 2900 Dallas TX 75204 972-661-8700 691
TF: 800-225-3650 ■ Web: www.williams-financial.com

Williams Form Engineering Corp
8165 Graphic Dr Belmont MI 49306 616-866-0815 866-1810 386
Web: www.williamsform.com

Name / Address	City	State	ZIP	Phone	Fax	Class
Williams Furnace Co 250 W Laurel St *TF:* 800-894-1022 ■ *Web:* www.williamscomfortprod.com	Colton	CA	92324	909-825-0993		14
Williams Gun Sight Co 7389 Lapeer Rd *TF:* 800-530-9028 ■ *Web:* www.williamsgunsight.com	Davison	MI	48423	810-653-2131	658-2140	284
Williams Industries Inc 8624 JD Reading Dr *OTC: WMSI* ■ *Web:* www.wmsi.com	Manassas	VA	20109	703-335-7800	335-7802	189-14
Williams Industries Inc 2201 E Michigan Rd *Web:* www.williamsindustries.com	Shelbyville	IN	46176	317-392-4701		604
Williams International 2280 E W Maple Rd PO Box 200 *TF:* 800-859-3544 ■ *Web:* www.williams-int.com	Walled Lake	MI	48390	248-624-5200	624-5345	21
Williams Kitchen & Bath 658 Richmond NW *Web:* www.williamskitchen.com	Grand Rapids	MI	49504	616-771-0505		38
Williams Lake & District Credit Union 139 N Third Ave *TF:* 800-398-5811 ■ *Web:* www.wldcu.com	Williams Lake	BC	V2G2A5	250-392-4135		219
Williams Lumber & Home Centers 6760 Rt 9 *TF:* 800-708-0059 ■ *Web:* www.williamslumber.com	Rhinebeck	NY	12572	845-876-7011		364
Williams Machine & Tool Company Inc 1009 Schermerhorn Rd *Web:* www.wilmaco.com	Galena	KS	66739	620-783-5184		454
Williams Management Resources Inc (WMR) 1717 N Naper Blvd Ste 102 *Web:* www.wmrhq.com	Naperville	IL	60563	630-416-1166	416-9798	47
Williams Metals & Welding Alloys Inc 125 Strafford Ave Ste 108 *Web:* www.wmwa.net	Wayne	PA	19087	610-225-0105		492
Williams Mullen 1021 E Cary St James Ctr Two *TF:* 800-732-0330 ■ *Web:* www.williamsmullen.com	Richmond	VA	23219	804-643-1991		428
Williams Nationalease Ltd 400 W Northtown Rd *TF:* 800-779-8785 ■ *Web:* wnlgroup.com	Normal	IL	61761	309-452-1110		57
Williams Notaro & Assoc LLC 3928 Pender Dr Ste 220 *Web:* wnainc.com	Fairfax	VA	22030	703-563-0381		261
Williams Oil Company Inc 207 York Ave N *Web:* www.williamsoil.com	Towanda	PA	18848	570-265-6673		579
Williams Parker Harrison Dietz & Getzen PA 200 S Orange Ave *Web:* www.williamsparker.com	Sarasota	FL	34236	941-366-4800		428
Williams Partners LP 1 Williams Ctr *NYSE: WPZ* ■ *TF:* 800-600-3782 ■ *Web:* investor.williams.com	Tulsa	OK	74172	918-573-2000		325
Williams Performing Arts Ctr *Abilene Christian University* 1600 Campus Ct *TF:* 800-460-6228 ■ *Web:* www.acu.edu	Abilene	TX	79601	325-674-2199	674-2369	572
Williams Records Management 1925 E Vernon Ave *TF Cust Svc:* 888-478-3453 ■ *Web:* www.williamsdatamanagement.com	Los Angeles	CA	90058	323-234-3453	233-5451	225
Williams Roger (Rep R - TX) 1323 Longworth Bldg *Web:* williams.house.gov	Washington	DC	20515	202-225-9896		342-2
Williams Sausage Company Inc 5132 Old Troy Hickman Rd *TF:* 800-844-4242 ■ *Web:* www.williams-sausage.com	Union City	TN	38261	731-885-5841	885-5884	297-9
Williams Supply Inc 210 Seventh St *TF:* 800-533-6969 ■ *Web:* www.williams-supply.com	Roanoke	VA	24016	540-343-9333	342-3254	246
Williams Valley School District 10330 SR 209 *Web:* www.wvschools.net	Tower City	PA	17980	717-647-2181		685
Williams White & Co 600 River Dr *TF:* 877-797-7650 ■ *Web:* www.williamswhite.com	Moline	IL	61265	877-797-7650		456
Williams Whittle Assoc Inc 711 Princess St *Web:* www.williamswhittle.com	Alexandria	VA	22314	703-836-9222		4
Williams, Charles & Scott Ltd 2171 Jericho Tpke LL1 *TF:* 800-652-4445 ■ *Web:* www.wcscollects.com	Commack	NY	11725	631-462-1553		160
Williams, Jones & Associates LLC 717 Fifth Ave Ste 1700 *Web:* www.williamsjones.com	New York	NY	10022	212-935-8750		401
Williams, Kastner & Gibbs PLLC 2 Union Sq 601 Union St Ste 4100 *TF:* 800-626-5267 ■ *Web:* www.williamskastner.com	Seattle	WA	98101	206-628-6600		428
Williams, Turner & Holmes PC 200 N Sixth St Ste 103 *TF:* 800-548-6528 ■ *Web:* www.wth-law.com	Grand Junction	CO	81501	970-242-6262		428
Williamsburg County 201 W Main St *Web:* www.williamsburgcounty.sc.gov	Kingstree	SC	29556	843-355-9321	355-1587	338
Williamsburg County Library 215 N Jackson St *Web:* www.mywcl.org	Kingstree	SC	29556	843-355-9486	355-9991	434-3
Williamsburg Destination Marketing Committee 421 N Boundary St *TF:* 800-368-6511 ■ *Web:* www.visitwilliamsburg.com	Williamsburg	VA	23185	757-229-6511	229-6511	206
Williamsburg Hometown Chamber of Commerce 131 N Academy St PO Box 696 *Web:* www.williamsburgsc.org	Kingstree	SC	29556	843-355-6431	355-3343	139
Williamsburg (Independent City) 401 Lafayette St *TF:* 800-275-2355 ■ *Web:* www.williamsburgva.gov	Williamsburg	VA	23185	757-220-6100	220-6107	338
Williamsburg Inn 136 E Francis St *TF:* 800-447-8679 ■ *Web:* www.colonialwilliamsburg.com	Williamsburg	VA	23185	757-229-1000		669
Williamsburg Landing 5700 Williamsburg Landing Dr *TF:* 800-554-5517 ■ *Web:* www.williamsburglanding.com	Williamsburg	VA	23185	757-565-6505		672
Williamsburg Lodge 310 S England St *TF Cust Svc:* 800-447-8679 ■ *Web:* www.history.org	Williamsburg	VA	23185	757-229-1000		379
Williamsburg Pottery 6692 Richmond Rd *TF:* 800-582-8916 ■ *Web:* www.williamsburgpottery.com	Williamsburg	VA	23188	757-564-3326		362
Williamsburg Regional Library 7770 Croaker Rd *Web:* www.wrl.org	Williamsburg	VA	23188	757-259-4071	259-4077	434-3
Williamsburg Technical College 601 MLK Jr Ave *TF:* 800-768-2021 ■ *Web:* www.wiltech.edu	Kingstree	SC	29556	843-355-4110		162
Williamsburg Travel Management Companies 570 W Crossville Rd Ste 102 *TF:* 800-952-9922 ■ *Web:* willtrav.com	Roswell	GA	30075	770-650-5515		775
Williamsburg Winery Ltd 5800 Wessex Hundred *Web:* www.williamsburgwinery.com	Williamsburg	VA	23185	757-229-0999		50-7
Williamsburg-James City County Educational Foundation PO Box 8783 *Web:* wjccschools.org/web	Williamsburg	VA	23187	757-603-6400		685
Williamson ARH Hospital 260 Hospital Dr *TF General:* 888-654-0015 ■ *Web:* arh.org/locations/williamson.aspx	South Williamson	KY	41503	606-237-1700	237-1701	374-3
Williamson Cadillac Co 7815 SW 104th St *TF:* 877-228-6093 ■ *Web:* williamsonautomotivegroup.com	Miami	FL	33156	305-670-7100		58
Williamson County 1320 W Main St Ste 135 *Web:* www.williamsoncounty-tn.gov	Franklin	TN	37064	615-790-5712	790-5610	338
Williamson County 710 Main St *TF:* 800-344-8377 ■ *Web:* www.wilco.org	Georgetown	TX	78626	512-943-1100	943-1616	338
Williamson County 201 W Main St *Web:* www.williamsoncountyil.gov	Marion	IL	62959	618-993-1314	998-0922	338
Williamson County Convention & Visitors Bureau 400 Main St Ste 200 *Web:* www.visitwilliamson.com	Franklin	TN	37064	615-791-7554		206
Williamson County Public Library 1314 Columbia Ave *Web:* wcpltn.org	Franklin	TN	37064	615-595-1243	595-1245	434-3
Williamson County Tourism Bureau 1602 Sioux Dr *TF General:* 800-433-7399 ■ *Web:* www.visitsi.com	Marion	IL	62959	618-997-3690	997-1874	206
Williamson County-Franklin Chamber of Commerce 5005 Meridian Blvd Ste 150 *TF:* 877-811-0002 ■ *Web:* williamsonchamber.com	Franklin	TN	37067	615-771-1912	790-5337	139
Williamson Employment Services Inc 213 Hilltop Rd *Web:* www.williamsonemployment.com	St. Joseph	MI	49085	269-983-0142		2
Williamson Free School of Mechanical Trades, The 106 S New Middletown Rd *TF:* 888-565-1095 ■ *Web:* www.williamson.edu	Media	PA	19063	610-566-1776	566-6502	800
Williamson Law Book Co 790 Canning Pkwy *TF:* 800-733-9522 ■ *Web:* www.wlbonline.com	Victor	NY	14564	585-924-3400	924-4153	178
Williamson Medical Ctr (WMC) 4321 Carothers Pkwy *Web:* www.williamsonmedicalcenter.org	Franklin	TN	37067	615-435-5000		374-3
Williamson Printing Corp 6700 Denton Dr *Web:* www.twpc.com	Dallas	TX	75235	214-904-2100		627
Williamson Street Grocery Company Op 1221 Williamson St *Web:* www.willystreet.coop	Madison	WI	53703	608-251-0884		297-8
Williamson-Dickie Mfg Co 509 W Vickery Blvd *TF:* 866-411-1501 ■ *Web:* www.dickies.com	Fort Worth	TX	76104	866-411-1501		155-19
Williamsport Area School District 201 W Third St *TF:* 888-448-4642 ■ *Web:* www.wasd.org	Williamsport	PA	17701	570-327-5500	327-8122	685
Williamsport Hospital & Medical Ctr 777 Rural Ave *Web:* www.susquehannahealth.org	Williamsport	PA	17701	570-321-1000		374-3
Williamsport Sun-Gazette 252 W Fourth St *TF:* 800-339-0289 ■ *Web:* www.sungazette.com	Williamsport	PA	17701	570-326-1551	326-0314	532-2
Williamsport/Lycoming Chamber of Commerce 102 W Fourth St *Web:* www.williamsport.org	Williamsport	PA	17701	570-326-1971	321-1208	139
Williams-Sonoma Inc 3250 Van Ness Ave *NYSE: WSM* ■ *TF:* 800-838-2589 ■ *Web:* www.williams-sonomainc.com	San Francisco	CA	94109	415-421-7900		362
Williamston Community Schools Inc 418 Highland St *Web:* www.gowcs.net	Williamston	MI	48895	517-655-4361		685
Williamston Products Inc (WPI) 845 Progress Ct *Web:* www.wpius.com	Williamston	MI	48895	517-655-2131		608
Williamstown Commons Nursing & Rehabilitation Ctr 25 Adams Rd *Web:* www.williamstowncommons.org	Williamstown	MA	01267	413-458-2111	458-3156	450
Williamsville Suburban LLC 193 S Union Rd *Web:* www.facebook.com	Buffalo	NY	14221	716-276-1900		363
Willie G's 1605 Post Oak Blvd	Houston	TX	77056	713-840-7190		670
Willie Washer Manufacturing Corp 2101 Greenleaf Ave *Web:* www.williewasher.com	Elk Grove Village	IL	60007	847-956-1344		621
Willingboro Public Library 220 Willingboro Pkwy *TF:* 866-321-9571 ■ *Web:* www.willingboro.org	Willingboro	NJ	08046	609-877-6668	835-1699	434-3
Willington Cos 11 Middle River Dr *TF:* 877-967-4743 ■ *Web:* www.wnpinc.com	Stafford Springs	CT	06076	860-684-4281		481
Willingway Hospital 311 Jones Mill Rd *TF:* 800-242-9455 ■ *Web:* www.willingway.com	Statesboro	GA	30458	912-764-6236		726
Willis & Woy Sports Group LLC 4890 Alpha Rd Ste 220 *Web:* www.willis-woy.com	Dallas	TX	75244	972-506-9011		181
Willis College of Business & Technology 85 O'Connor St *TF:* 877-233-1128 ■ *Web:* www.williscollege.com	Ottawa	ON	K1P5M6	613-233-1128		162

Phone | Fax | Class

Willis Day Storage Co
4100 Bennett Rd PO Box 676 — Toledo OH 43697 — 419-476-8000 — 803-1
TF: 800-375-8181 ■ *Web:* willisday.com

Willis Furniture Company Inc
4220 Virginia Beach Blvd — Virginia Beach VA 23452 — 757-340-2112 — 321
Web: willisfurniture.com

Willis Group Holdings Ltd
200 Liberty St Fl 3 — New York NY 10281 — 212-915-8888 — 390
NYSE: WSH ■ *TF:* 800-234-8596 ■ *Web:* www.willis.com

Willis Investment Counsel Inc
710 Green St — Gainesville GA 30501 — 770-718-0706 — 401
Web: www.wicinvest.com

Willis-Knighton Medical Ctr (WKMC)
2600 Greenwood Rd — Shreveport LA 71103 — 318-212-4000 — 212-4195 — 374-3
Web: www.wkhs.com/home.aspx

Williston Northampton School
19 Payson Ave — EastHampton MA 01027 — 413-529-3241 — 527-9494 — 622
Web: www.williston.com

Williston State College
1410 University Ave PO Box 1326 — Williston ND 58802 — 701-774-4200 — 774-4211* — 162
**Fax:* Admissions ■ *TF:* 888-863-9455 ■ *Web:* willistonstate.edu

Willkie Farr & Gallagher LLP
787 Seventh Ave 2nd Fl — New York NY 10019 — 212-728-8000 — 728-8111 — 428
Web: www.willkie.com

Willman Industries Inc
338 S Main St — Cedar Grove WI 53013 — 920-668-8526 — 668-8998 — 307
Web: www.willmanind.com

Willmar Lakes Area Chamber of Commerce
2104 Hwy 12 E — Willmar MN 56201 — 320-235-0300 — 231-1948 — 139
Web: www.willmarareachamber.com

Willmar Poultry Co, The (WPC)
3735 County Rd 5 SW — Willmar MN 56201 — 320-235-8850 — 10-8

Willmott & Associates Inc
922 Waltham St Ste 103 — Lexington MA 02421 — 781-863-5400 — 631
Web: www.willmott.com

Willo Products Company Inc
714 Willo Industrial Dr SE — Decatur AL 35601 — 256-353-7161 — 350-8436 — 234
TF: 800-633-3276 ■ *Web:* www.willoproducts.com

Willoughby Eastlake City Schools
37047 Ridge Rd — Willoughby OH 44094 — 440-946-5000 — 946-4671 — 685
Web: www.weschools.org

Willoughby Industries Inc
5105 W 78th St — Indianapolis IN 46268 — 317-638-2381 — 612
Web: www.willoughby-ind.com

Willoughby Wallace Memorial Library (WWML)
146 Thimble Islands Rd — Stony Creek CT 06405 — 203-488-8702 — 315-3347 — 434-3
Web: www.wwml.org

Willoughby Western Lake County
28 Public Sq — Willoughby OH 44094 — 440-942-1632 — 942-0586 — 139
Web: www.wwlcchamber.com

Willoughby-Baylor House
601 E Freemason St — Norfolk VA 23510 — 757-333-1087 — 50-[illegible]
Web: www.chrysler.org

Willow Creek Concrete Products Inc
12626 County Rd 150 — Kimball MN 55353 — 320-398-5415 — 183
Web: www.willowcreekconcrete.com

Willow Creek Press Inc
9931 Hwy 70 W PO Box 147 — Minocqua WI 54548 — 715-358-7010 — 358-2807 — 130
TF Cust Svc: 800-850-9453 ■ *Web:* www.willowcreekpress.com

Willow Creek Rehabilitation & Care Ctr
1165 Easton Ave — Somerset NJ 08873 — 732-246-4100 — 450
TF: 800-486-0027 ■ *Web:* reverawillowcreek.com

Willow Creek State Recreation Area
7278 E Bogard Rd — Wasilla AK 99654 — 907-745-3975 — 565
Web: dnr.alaska.gov

Willow Creek State Recreation Area
54876 852 Rd — Pierce NE 68767 — 402-329-4053 — 565
Web: outdoornebraska.gov

Willow Electrical Supply Inc
3828 River Rd — Schiller Park IL 60176 — 847-801-5010 — 246
Web: www.willowelectric.com

Willow Group 1485 Laperriere Ave — Ottawa ON K1Z7S8 — 613-722-8796 — 729-6206 — 47
Web: www.thewillowgroup.com

Willow Group Inc, The
8201 Norman Ctr Dr Ste 115 — Bloomington MN 55437 — 952-897-3550 — 463
Web: willowg.com

Willow Park Wines & Spirits Ltd
10801 Bonaventure Dr SE — Calgary AB T2J6Z8 — 403-296-1640 — 443
Web: www.willowpark.net

Willow River State Park
1034 County Hwy A — Hudson WI 54016 — 715-386-5931 — 386-0431 — 565
TF: 800-847-9367 ■ *Web:* dnr.wi.gov

Willow Stream Spa at Fairmont Scottsdale Princess
7575 E Princess Dr — Scottsdale AZ 85255 — 480-585-2732 — 707
TF: 800-908-9540 ■ *Web:* www.fairmont.com

Willow Stream Spa at the Fairmont Banff Springs
405 Spray Ave — Banff AB T1L1J4 — 403-762-1772 — 707
TF: 800-404-1772 ■ *Web:* www.fairmont.com

Willow Stream Spa at the Fairmont Empress
633 Humboldt St — Victoria BC V8W1A6 — 250-995-4650 — 707
TF: 866-854-7444 ■ *Web:* www.fairmont.com

Willow Technology Inc
961 Red Tail Ln Ste 220 — Bellingham WA 98226 — 360-393-4962 — 630-7101* — 809
**Fax Area Code:* 604 ■ *Web:* www.willowtech.com

Willow Tree Poultry Farm Inc
997 S Main St — Attleboro MA 02703 — 508-222-2479 — 123
Web: www.willowtreefarm.com

Willow Valley Lakes Manor
300 Willow Vly Lakes Dr — Willow Street PA 17584 — 717-464-0800 — 672
TF: 800-770-5445 ■ *Web:* www.willowvalleycommunities.org

Willow Valley Resort & Conference Ctr
2400 Willow St Pike — Lancaster PA 17602 — 717-464-0869 — 669
Web: www.willowvalley.com

Willowbrook Mall 1400 Willowbrook Mall — Wayne NJ 07470 — 973-785-1655 — 460
TF: 800-772-2222 ■ *Web:* www.willowbrook-mall.com

Willowbrook Mall
2000 Willowbrook Mall — Houston TX 77070 — 281-890-8000 — 460
Web: www.shopwillowbrookmall.com

Phone | Fax | Class

Willows at Meadow Branch, The
1001 Harvest Dr — Winchester VA 22601 — 540-667-3000 — 371
TF: 800-552-0922 ■ *Web:* www.thewillows-mb.com

Willows Chamber of Commerce
118 W Sycamore — Willows CA 95988 — 530-934-8150 — 139
TF: 855-233-6362 ■ *Web:* willowschamber.com

Willows Historic Palm Springs Inn
412 W Tahquitz Canyon Way — Palm Springs CA 92262 — 760-320-0771 — 320-0780 — 379
TF: 800-966-9597 ■ *Web:* www.thewillowspalmsprings.com

Willows Hotel 555 W Surf St — Chicago IL 60657 — 773-528-8400 — 379
TF: 877-207-2111 ■ *Web:* www.willowshotelchicago.com

Willows Lodge 14580 NE 145th St — Woodinville WA 98072 — 425-424-3900 — 424-2585 — 379
TF: 877-424-3930 ■ *Web:* www.willowslodge.com

Willows, The 1 Lyman St — Westborough MA 01581 — 508-366-4730 — 898-3982 — 672
TF: 800-464-8060 ■ *Web:* www.salmonhealth.com

Willows, The 901 Hausten St — Honolulu HI 96826 — 808-952-9200 — 952-0050 — 671
Web: www.willowshawaii.com

Wills Eye 840 Walnut St — Philadelphia PA 19107 — 215-928-3000 — 928-0634 — 374-7
TF: 800-624-2988 ■ *Web:* www.willseye.org

Wills Group Inc, The 6355 Crain Hwy — La Plata MD 20646 — 301-932-3600 — 324
Web: www.willsgroup.com

Wills Point Independent School Distric
338 W N Commerce St — Wills Point TX 75169 — 903-873-3161 — 873-2462 — 685
Web: www.wpisd.com

Willsie Cap & Gown Co 1220 S 13th St — Omaha NE 68108 — 402-341-6536 — 155-14
TF: 800-234-4696 ■ *Web:* www.willsieco.com

Willson International Ltd
2345 Argentia Rd Ste 201 — Mississauga ON L5N8K4 — 905-363-1133 — 449
TF: 800-754-1918 ■ *Web:* www.willsonintl.com

WILL-TV Ch 12 (PBS) 300 N Goodwin Ave — Urbana IL 61801 — 217-333-7300 — 333-7151 — 741
Web: www.will.illinois.edu

Willwork Inc 23 Norfolk Ave — South Easton MA 02375 — 508-230-3170 — 184
Web: www2.willworkinc.com

Willy & Jose's Mexican Cantina
5111 Boulder Hwy — Las Vegas NV 89122 — 702-456-7777 — 671
TF: 800-897-8696 ■ *Web:* samstownlv.com

Willy Bietak Productions Inc
1404 Third St Promenade Ste 200 — Santa Monica CA 90401 — 310-576-2400 — 181
Web: www.bietakproductions.com

Wilma Theater 265 S Broad St — Philadelphia PA 19107 — 215-893-9456 — 893-0895 — 572
TF: 800-732-0999 ■ *Web:* www.wilmatheater.org

Wilmer Cutler Pickering Hale & Dorr LLP
1875 Pennsylvania Ave — Washington DC 20006 — 202-663-6000 — 663-6363 — 428
Web: www.wilmerhale.com

Wilmer Service Line
515 W Sycamore St — Coldwater OH 45828 — 800-494-5637 — 553-4849 — 110
TF: 800-494-5637 ■ *Web:* www.4wilmer.com

Wilmette Bicycle & Sport Shop
605 Green Bay Rd — Wilmette IL 60091 — 847-251-1404 — 711
Web: www.wilmettesportshop.com

Wilmette Chamber of Commerce (WCC)
351 Linden Ave — Wilmette IL 60091 — 847-251-3800 — 251-6321 — 139
Web: www.wilmettekenilworth.com

Wilmington and Beaches CVB
505 Nutt St Unit A — Wilmington NC 28401 — 910-341-4030 — 341-4029 — 206
TF: 877-406-2356 ■ *Web:* www.wilmingtonandbeaches.com

Wilmington Capital Securities LLC
600 Old Country Rd Ste 200 — Garden City NY 11530 — 516-750-6200 — 691
TF: 800-289-9999 ■ *Web:* wilmingtoncap.com

Wilmington Chamber of Commerce
544 N Avalon Blvd Ste 104 — Wilmington CA 90744 — 310-834-8586 — 834-8887 — 139
Web: www.wilmington-chamber.com

Wilmington Clinton County Chamber of Commerce (WCCC)
100 W Main St — Wilmington OH 45177 — 937-382-2737 — 139
TF: 800-762-0047 ■ *Web:* www.wccchamber.com

Wilmington College of Ohio
1870 Quaker Way — Wilmington OH 45177 — 937-382-6661 — 166
TF: 800-341-9318 ■ *Web:* www.wilmington.edu

Wilmington Drama League (WDL)
10 W Lea Blvd — Wilmington DE 19802 — 302-764-1172 — 573-4
Web: www.wilmingtondramaleague.org

Wilmington Fibre Specialty Co
700 Washington St — New Castle DE 19720 — 302-328-7525 — 328-6630 — 599
TF: 800-220-5132 ■ *Web:* www.wilmfibre.com

Wilmington Group, The
7040 Wrightsville Ave — Wilmington NC 28403 — 910-256-1056 — 463
Web: www.wilmingtongroup.com

Wilmington Health Care Ctr
1202 Medical Center Dr — Wilmington NC 28401 — 910-341-3300 — 251-3740 — 450
Web: www.wilmingtonhealth.com

Wilmington Instrument Company Inc
332 N Fries Ave — Wilmington CA 90744 — 310-834-1133 — 201
TF: 800-544-2843 ■ *Web:* www.calcert.com

Wilmington Marine Service Inc
801 S Fries Ave — Wilmington CA 90744 — 310-834-1186 — 698

Wilmington National Cemetery
2011 Market St — Wilmington NC 28403 — 910-815-4877 — 637-7145* — 136
**Fax Area Code:* 252 ■ *TF:* 800-535-1117 ■ *Web:* www.cem.va.gov

Wilmington Public Library
10 E Tenth St — Wilmington DE 19801 — 302-571-7400 — 654-9132 — 434-3
Web: wilmington.lib.de.us

Wilmington Research & Development Corp
50 Parker St — Newburyport MA 01950 — 978-499-0100 — 201
Web: www.wrdcorp.com

Wilmington State Parks
1021 W 18th St — Wilmington DE 19802 — 302-577-7020 — 577-7084 — 565
Web: www.destateparks.com/wilmsp/wilmsp.htm

Wilmington Treatment Ctr
2520 Troy Dr — Wilmington NC 28401 — 866-783-6605 — 762-7923* — 726
**Fax Area Code:* 910 ■ *TF:* 866-783-6605 ■ *Web:* www.wilmingtontreatment.com?nocookies=true

Wilmington Trust Co
1100 N Market St — Wilmington DE 19890 — 302-651-1000 — 651-8937* — 70
**Fax:* Hum Res ■ *TF:* 800-441-7120 ■ *Web:* www.wilmingtontrust.com

Wilmington University
320 N DuPont Hwy — New Castle DE 19720 — 302-356-6739 — 328-5902* — 166
**Fax:* Admissions ■ *TF Admissions:* 877-967-5464 ■ *Web:* www.wilmu.edu

Wilmore Electronics Company Inc
607 US 70-A E PO Box 1329 — Hillsborough NC 27278 — 919-732-9351 — 732-9359 — 253
Web: www.wilmoreelectronics.com

Name / Address	City	State	Zip	Phone	Fax	Class
Wilogic Inc 15896 Manufacture Ln *Web:* www.wilogic.com	Huntington Beach	CA	92649	714-230-8487		196
Wilshire Assoc Inc 1299 Ocean Ave Ste 700 *TF:* 855-626-8281 ■ *Web:* www.wilshire.com	Santa Monica	CA	90401	310-451-3051	458-0520	401
Wilshire Book Co 9731 Variel Ave *Web:* www.mpowers.com	Chatsworth	CA	91311	818-700-1522	700-1527	637-2
Wilshire Enterprises Inc 100 Eagle Rock Ave Ste 100 *OTC:* WLSE ■ *TF:* 888-697-3962 ■ *Web:* www.wilshireenterprisesinc.com	East Hanover	NJ	07936	973-585-7770		536
Wilshire Insurance Co 1206 W Ave J Ste 100 *Web:* www.wilshireinsurance.com	Lancaster	CA	93534	661-940-7300		390
Wilshire Manufacturing Co 645 Myles Standish Blvd *TF:* 800-218-7072 ■ *Web:* wilshiremfg.com	Taunton	MA	02780	508-824-1970		439
Wilshire Mutual Funds Inc PO Box 219512 *TF:* 888-200-6796 ■ *Web:* advisor.wilshire.com	Kansas City	MO	64121	888-200-6796		528
Wilshire Technologies Inc 318 Wall St *Web:* www.wilshiretechnologies.com	Princeton	NJ	08540	609-683-1117		146
Wilson & Company Engineers & Arch 4900 Lang Ave NE *Web:* wilsonco.com	Albuquerque	NM	87109	505-348-4000		261
Wilson Air Ctr 2930 Winchester Rd Memphis International Airport *TF:* 800-464-2992 ■ *Web:* www.wilsonair.com	Memphis	TN	38118	901-345-2992		63
Wilson Audio Specialties 2233 Mountain Vista Ln *Web:* www.wilsonaudio.com	Provo	UT	84606	801-377-2233		52
Wilson Automotive Group 1400 N Tustin St *Web:* www.davidwilsonautogroup.com	Orange	CA	92867	714-516-3111	997-9200	57
Wilson Bank Holding Co 623 W Main St *OTC:* WBHC ■ *Web:* www.wilsonbank.com	Lebanon	TN	37087	615-444-2265		70
Wilson Bus Lines Inc 203 Patriots Rd PO Box 415 *TF:* 800-253-5235 ■ *Web:* www.wilsonbus.com	East Templeton	MA	01438	978-632-3894		107
Wilson Chamber of Commerce 200 Nash St NE *TF:* 855-905-0604 ■ *Web:* www.wilsonncchamber.com	Wilson	NC	27893	252-237-0165	243-7931	139
Wilson College 1015 Philadelphia Ave **Fax:* Admissions ■ *TF Admissions:* 800-421-8402 ■ *Web:* www.wilson.edu	Chambersburg	PA	17201	717-264-4141	264-1578*	166
Wilson Consulting Group 100 Old Schoolhouse Rd *TF:* 800-837-2265 ■ *Web:* wcg-pc.com	Mechanicsburg	PA	17055	717-591-3070		196
Wilson County 1103 Fourth St Ste 2 *Web:* co.wilson.tx.us	Floresville	TX	78114	830-393-7346	393-7345	338
Register of Deeds 101 N Goldsboro St PO Box 1728 *Web:* www.wilson-co.com	Wilson	NC	27894	252-399-2935	237-4341	338
Wilson County Public Library 249 W Nash St *TF:* 877-321-2652 ■ *Web:* www.wilson-co.com	Wilson	NC	27893	252-237-5355		434-3
Wilson Daily Times 2001 Downing St *Web:* www.wilsontimes.com	Wilson	NC	27893	252-243-5151	243-2999	532-2
Wilson Daniels Ltd 1201 Dowdell Ln *Web:* www.wilsondaniels.com	St Helena	CA	94574	707-963-9661		80-3
Wilson Electronics 3301 E Deseret Dr *Web:* www.wilsonelectronics.com	St George	UT	84790	435-673-5021		647
Wilson Elser Moskowitz Edelman & Dicker LLP 150 E 42nd St *Web:* www.wilsonelser.com	New York	NY	10017	212-490-3000	490-3038	428
Wilson Farm Inc 10 Pleasant St *TF:* 800-322-8582 ■ *Web:* www.wilsonfarm.com	Lexington	MA	02421	781-862-3900	863-0469	10-11
Wilson Financial Group Inc 15915 Katy Fwy	Houston	TX	77094	281-579-2760	579-9089	510
Wilson Frederica (Rep D - FL) 2445 Rayburn HOB *Web:* wilson.house.gov	Washington	DC	20515	202-225-4506	226-0777	342-2
Wilson Harris & Co 1602 W Franklin St *Web:* wilsonharris.com	Boise	ID	83702	208-344-1355		2
Wilson Hewitt & Associates Inc 775 Lancaster Ave P.O.Box 607 *Web:* www.wha.com	Villanova	PA	19085	610-649-2300		809
Wilson Hotel Management Company Inc 8700 Trl Lake Dr W Ste 300 *TF:* 800-222-8733 ■ *Web:* www.wilsonhotels.com	Memphis	TN	38125	901-346-8800	346-5808	379
Wilson Industrial Sales Company Inc 201 S Wilson *TF:* 800-633-5427 ■ *Web:* www.wilsonindustrial.com	Brook	IN	47922	219-275-7333		146
Wilson Island State Recreation Area 32801 Campground Ln *Web:* www.iowadnr.gov	Missouri Valley	IA	51555	712-642-2069		565
Wilson Joe (Rep R - SC) 1436 Longworth HOB *Web:* joewilson.house.gov	Washington	DC	20515	202-225-2452	225-2455	342-2
Wilson Learning Corp 8000 W 78th St Ste 200 *TF:* 800-328-7937 ■ *Web:* www.wilsonlearning.com	Edina	MN	55439	952-944-2880		765
Wilson Legal Solutions Inc 3817 W chester Pk *Web:* www.wilsonlegalsol.com	Newtown Square	PA	19073	484-422-0010		463
Wilson Lines of Minnesota Inc 2131 Second Ave *TF General:* 800-525-3333 ■ *Web:* www.wilsonlines.com	Newport	MN	55055	651-459-2384	769-3050	780
Wilson Lumber Co Inc 4818 Meridian St *Web:* www.wilsonlumber.net	Huntsville	AL	35811	256-852-7411	851-9904	191-3
Wilson Manufacturing Co 4725 Green Park Rd *TF:* 800-634-5248 ■ *Web:* www.wilsonmfg.com	Saint Louis	MO	63123	314-416-8900		697
Wilson Marketing Group Inc 17015 13th Ave N *Web:* www.wilsonconsultants.com	Plymouth	MN	55447	763-476-2216		195
Wilson Meany Sullivan LLC 4 Embarcadero Ctr Ste 3330 *Web:* wilsonmeany.com	San Francisco	CA	94111	415-905-5300		652
Wilson Medical Ctr 1705 SW Tarboro St *TF:* 800-222-1222 ■ *Web:* www.wilsonmedical.com	Wilson	NC	27893	252-399-8040		374-3
Wilson of Wallingford Inc 221 Rogers Ln PO Box 185 *TF:* 888-607-2621 ■ *Web:* www.wilsonoilandpropane.com	Wallingford	PA	19086	610-566-7600	566-7608	316
Wilson Office Interiors 1444 Oak Lawn Ave Ste 105 *TF:* 800-482-1213 ■ *Web:* www.wilsonoi.com	Dallas	TX	75207	972-488-4100	488-8815	393
Wilson Oil Inc 95 Panel Way *Web:* www.wilcoxandflegel.com	Longview	WA	98632	360-575-9222		324
Wilson Post, The 216 Hartmann Dr *Web:* www.wilsonpost.com	Lebanon	TN	37087	615-444-6008		532-3
Wilson Quarterly Magazine 1300 Pennsylvania Ave NW 1 Woodrow Wilson Plaza *TF Orders:* 888-947-9018 ■ *Web:* www.wilsoncenter.org	Washington	DC	20004	202-691-4000	691-4247	457-11
Wilson Realty Exchange Inc 16910 15th Ave NE *Web:* wilsonrealtyexchange.com	Shoreline	WA	98155	206-367-0200		652
Wilson Sonsini Goodrich & Rosati 650 Page Mill Rd *TF:* 800-973-1177 ■ *Web:* www.wsgr.com	Palo Alto	CA	94304	650-493-9300	493-6811	428
Wilson Sporting Goods Co 8750 W Bryn Mawr Ave *TF:* 800-874-5930 ■ *Web:* www.wilson.com	Chicago	IL	60631	773-714-6400	714-4565	710
Wilson State Park 910 N First St PO Box 333 *Web:* www.michigandnr.com	Harrison	MI	48625	989-539-3021		565
Wilson Supply Co 1302 Conti St *TF:* 800-874-5930	Houston	TX	77002	713-237-3700		385
Wilson T Ballard Co 17 Gwynns Mill Ct *Web:* www.wtbco.com	Owings Mills	MD	21117	410-363-0150		261
Wilson Tool International Inc 12912 Farnham Ave *TF:* 800-328-9646 ■ *Web:* www.wilsontool.com	White Bear Lake	MN	55110	651-286-6001		697
Wilson Trailer Co 4400 S Lewis Blvd *TF:* 800-798-2002 ■ *Web:* www.wilsontrailer.com	Sioux City	IA	51106	712-252-6500	252-6510	779
Wilson Trophy Co 1724 Frienza Ave *TF:* 800-635-5005 ■ *Web:* www.wilsontrophy.com	Sacramento	CA	95815	916-927-9733	927-9955	777
Wilson Trucking Corp 137 Wilson Blvd *TF:* 866-645-7405 ■ *Web:* www.wilsontrucking.com	Fishersville	VA	22939	540-949-3200	949-3205	780
Wilson Visitors Bureau 209 Broad St *TF:* 800-497-7398 ■ *Web:* www.wilson-nc.com	Wilson	NC	27893	252-243-8440	243-7550	206
Wilson WindowWare Inc 5421 California Ave SW *TF:* 800-762-8383 ■ *Web:* www.windowware.com	Seattle	WA	98136	206-938-1740	935-7129	178-12
Wilson Works Inc 202 Distributor Dr *Web:* www.wilsonworksinc.com	Morgantown	WV	26501	304-296-2171		454
Wilson's Bar-B-Q 700 N Taylor Ave	Pittsburgh	PA	15212	412-322-7427		671
Wilson's Creek National Battlefield 6424 W Farm Rd 182 *Web:* www.nps.gov	Republic	MO	65738	417-732-2662	732-1167	564
Wilson, Sheehy, Knowles, Robertson & Cornelius PC 909 ESE Loop 323 Ste 400 *Web:* www.wilsonlawfirm.com	Tyler	TX	75701	903-509-5000		428
Wilsonart International Inc 2400 Wilson Pl *TF Cust Svc:* 800-433-3222 ■ *Web:* www.wilsonart.com	Temple	TX	76504	254-207-7000	207-2545	599
Wilson-Davis & Company Inc 236 South Main *TF:* 800-621-1571 ■ *Web:* www.wdco.com	Salt Lake City	UT	84101	801-532-1313		690
Wilson-Hurd Mfg Co 311 Winton St, Box 8028 *Web:* www.wilsonhurd.com	Wausau	WI	54403	715-845-9221		600
Wilsons Leather Inc 7401 Boone Ave N *TF:* 800-967-6270 ■ *Web:* www.wilsonsleather.com	Brooklyn Park	MN	55428	763-391-4000		157-5
Wilson-Tuscarora State Park 3371 Lake Rd *Web:* parks.ny.gov/parks/69/details.aspx	Wilson	NY	14172	716-751-6361		565
Wilsonwest Inc 1601 Dolores St *Web:* www.wilsonwest.com	San Francisco	CA	94110	415-282-4560		184
Wiltern Theatre 3790 Wilshire Blvd *TF:* 800-348-8499 ■ *Web:* www.wilterntheatertickets.com	Los Angeles	CA	90010	213-388-1400		572
Wilton Armetale Co 903 Square St *TF:* 800-779-4586 ■ *Web:* www.armetale.com	Mount Joy	PA	17552	717-653-4444		486
Wilton House Museum 215 S Wilton Rd *Web:* www.wiltonhousemuseum.org	Richmond	VA	23226	804-282-5936	288-9805	520
Wilton Industries Inc 2240 W 75th St *TF:* 800-794-5866 ■ *Web:* www.wilton.com	Woodridge	IL	60517	630-963-7100		486
Wilton Precision Steel Co 320 W First St *TF:* 800-768-7697 ■ *Web:* www.wps01.com	Wilton	IA	52778	563-732-3363	732-3365	483
Wilwat Properties Inc 1958 Monroe Dr NE *Web:* www.wilwatproperties.com	Atlanta	GA	30324	404-872-8666		652
WILX-TV Ch 10 (NBC) 500 American Rd *TF:* 888-345-4124 ■ *Web:* www.wilx.com	Lansing	MI	48911	517-393-0110	393-8555	741-71
Wiman Corp 180 Industrial Blvd *Web:* www.wimancorp.com	Sauk Rapids	MN	56379	320-259-2554		596
Wimberly Allison Tong & Goo 700 Bishop St Ste 1800 *Web:* www.watg.com	Honolulu	HI	96813	808-521-8888		261
Wimberly Lawson Wright Daves & Jones, PLLC 929 W First N St *Web:* www.wlswd.com	Morristown	TN	37814	423-587-6870		445
Wimbledon Farm 1725 Walnut Hill Rd	Lexington	KY	40515	859-272-0636		368

	Phone	Fax	Class
WIMG1300 PO Box 9078 .... Trenton NJ 08650 *Web:* www.wimg1300.com	609-695-1300	278-1588	645-166
WIMI WJMS 222 S Lawrence St .... Ironwood MI 49938 *Web:* www.wimifm.com	906-932-2411		645-10
Wimmer Cookbooks 4650 Shelby Air Dr .... Memphis TN 38118 *TF:* 800-331-4254 ■ *Web:* www.wimmerco.com	901-362-8900		637-2
Wimmer Solutions Corp 1341 N Northlake Way Ste 300 .... Seattle WA 98103 *TF:* 800-456-8838 ■ *Web:* www.wimmersolutions.com	206-324-4594		180
Wimmer's Meat Products Inc 126 W Grant St .... West Point NE 68788 *TF Cust Svc:* 800-762-9865 ■ *Web:* www.wimmersmeats.com	402-372-2437		296-26
WIMS (Winstar Interactive Media) 1655 Palm Beach Lakes Blvd Ste 903 .... West Palm Beach FL 33401 *Web:* www.winstarinteractive.com	561-227-0626		6
WIMZ-FM 103.5 (CR) 1100 Sharps Ridge Memorial Pk Dr .... Knoxville TN 37917 *TF:* 800-735-2732 ■ *Web:* www.wimz.com	865-525-6000		645-85
WIN Energy Rural Electric Membership Corp 3981 S US Hwy 41 .... Vincennes IN 47591 *TF:* 800-882-5140 ■ *Web:* www.winenergyremc.com	812-882-5140	886-0306	245
Win Enterprises Inc 300 Willow St S .... North Andover MA 01845 *Web:* www.win-ent.com	978-688-2000		173-2
WIN Home Inspection 3326 Aspen Grove Dr Ste 160 .... Franklin TN 37067 *TF:* 800-309-6753 ■ *Web:* wini.com	800-309-6753		365
Winamac Coil Spring Inc 512 N Smith St .... Kewanna IN 46939 *Web:* www.winamaccoilspring.com	574-653-2186		719
Winandy Greenhouse Co 2211 Peacock Rd .... Richmond IN 47374 *TF:* 800-393-6343 ■ *Web:* winandygreenhouse.com	765-935-2111		105
Winbco Tank Co 1200 E Main St PO Box 618 .... Ottumwa IA 52501 *Fax Area Code: 641 ■ *TF:* 800-822-1855 ■ *Web:* www.winbco.com	800-822-1855	683-8265*	91
Winbeam Inc 302 W Otterman St .... Greensburg PA 15601 *Web:* www.winbeam.com	724-219-0400		225
Winbond Electronics Corp America 2727 N First St .... San Jose CA 95134 *TF:* 800-252-5832 ■ *Web:* www.winbond.com	408-943-6666	474-1600	696
Winchendon School 172 Ash St .... Winchendon MA 01475 *Web:* winchendon.org	978-297-4476		622
Winchester Area Chamber of Commerce 211 S Main St .... Winchester IN 47394 *Web:* winchesterareachamber.com	765-584-3731	584-5544	139
Winchester Equipment Co 121 Indian Hollow Rd .... Winchester VA 22603 *Fax Area Code: 540 ■ *TF:* 800-323-3581 ■ *Web:* www.winchesterequipment.com	800-323-3581	665-3058*	358
Winchester Galleries Ltd 2260 Oak Bay Ave .... Victoria BC V8R1G7 *Web:* www.winchestergalleriesltd.com	250-595-2777		42
Winchester Homes Inc 6905 Rockledge Dr Ste 800 .... Bethesda MD 20817 *Web:* www.winchesterhomes.com	301-803-4800	474-1609	187
Winchester Hospital 41 Highland Ave .... Winchester MA 01890 *Web:* www.winchesterhospital.org	781-729-9000	756-2908	374-3
Winchester (Independent City) 5 N Kent St .... Winchester VA 22601 *TF:* 800-468-8894 ■ *Web:* www.winchesterva.gov	540-667-5770		338
Winchester Lake State Park (IDPR) PO Box 186 .... Winchester ID 83555 *Web:* idahostateparks.reserveamerica.com	208-924-7563	924-5941	565
Winchester Medical Ctr 1840 Amherst St .... Winchester VA 22601 *Web:* www.valleyhealthlink.com	540-536-8000		374-3
Winchester Metals Inc 195 Ebert Rd .... Winchester VA 22603 *Web:* www.winchestermetals.com	540-667-9000		492
Winchester Mystery House 525 S Winchester Blvd .... San Jose CA 95128 *Web:* www.winchestermysteryhouse.com	408-247-2000		50-3
Winchester National Cemetery 401 National Ave .... Winchester VA 22601 *Web:* www.cem.va.gov/cems/nchp/winchester.asp	540-825-0027	825-6684	136
Winchester Optical Company Inc 1935 Lake St .... Elmira NY 14901 *Web:* www.winoptical.com	607-734-4251		543
Winchester Speedway 2656 W State Rd 32 PO Box 31 .... Winchester IN 47394 *Web:* www.winchesterspeedway.com	765-584-9701	584-8111	515
Winchester Star 2 N Kent St .... Winchester VA 22601 *TF:* 800-296-8639 ■ *Web:* www.winchesterstar.com	540-667-3200	667-1649	532-2
Winchester Systems Inc 101 Billerica Ave Bldg 5 .... North Billerica MA 01862 *TF Cust Svc:* 800-325-3700 ■ *Web:* www.winsys.com	781-265-0200	265-0201	176
Winchester-Clark County Chamber of Commerce 2 S Maple St .... Winchester KY 40391 *Web:* www.winchesterkychamber.com	859-744-6420	744-9229	139
Winchester-Thurston School 555 Morewood Ave .... Pittsburgh PA 15213 *Web:* winchesterthurston.org	412-578-7500	578-7504	685
Winchuck State Recreation Site 1655 Hwy 101 N .... Brookings OR 97415 *TF:* 800-551-6949 ■ *Web:* www.oregonstateparks.org	800-551-6949		565
WinCo Foods Inc 8200 W Fairview Ave .... Boise ID 83704 *TF:* 888-674-6854 ■ *Web:* www.wincofoods.com	208-377-9840		345
Winco Inc 5516 SW First Ln .... Ocala FL 34474 *TF:* 800-237-3377 ■ *Web:* www.wincomfg.com	352-854-2929	854-9544	319-3
Winco Stamping Inc W156 N9277 Tipp St .... Menomonee Falls WI 53051 *Web:* www.wincostamping.com	262-251-5900		488
WinCraft Inc 960 East Mark St P.O. Box 888 .... Winona MN 55987 *TF:* 800-533-8006 ■ *Web:* www.wincraft.com	507-454-5510	453-0690	328
WinCup 4640 Lewis Rd .... Stone Mountain GA 30083 *TF:* 800-292-2877 ■ *Web:* www.wincup.com	770-771-5861		601
Wincup GP LLC 358 Chinook Cir .... Lake Mary FL 32746 *Web:* www.wincupgp.com	407-619-4157		750
Wind Cave National Park 26611 US Hwy 385 .... Hot Springs SD 57747 *Web:* www.nps.gov	605-745-4600	745-4207	564
Wind Creek State Park 4325 Al Hwy 128 .... Alexander City AL 35010 *TF:* 800-252-7275 ■ *Web:* www.alapark.com	256-329-0845	234-4870	565
Wind Point Partners 676 N Michigan Ave Ste 3700 .... Chicago IL 60611 *Web:* www.wppartners.com	312-255-4800	255-4820	792
Wind River Financial Inc 18500 W Corporate Dr .... Brookfield WI 53045 *Web:* www.windriverfinancial.com	262-792-1119		194
Wind River Holdings LP 555 Croton Rd Croton Rd Corporate Ctr Ste 300 .... King Of Prussia PA 19406 *Web:* www.windriverholdings.com	610-962-3770		385
Wind River Petroleum Inc 2046 E Murray Holladay Rd Ste 200 .... Salt Lake City UT 84117	801-272-9229	272-9669	297-8
Wind River Ranch PO Box 3410 .... Estes Park CO 80517 *TF:* 800-523-4212 ■ *Web:* www.windriverranch.com	970-586-4212		239
Wind River Systems Inc 500 Wind River Way .... Alameda CA 94501 *TF:* 800-545-9463 ■ *Web:* www.windriver.com	510-748-4100	749-2010	178-12
Wind Turbine Industries Corp 16801 Industrial Cir SE .... Prior Lake MN 55372 *Web:* www.windturbine.net	952-447-6064		454
Windbag Saloon & Grill 19 S Last Chance Gulch .... Helena MT 59601	406-443-3520		671
Windebank Woodwork & Design Ltd 538 Culduthel Rd .... Victoria BC V8Z1G1 *TF:* 800-840-0348 ■ *Web:* www.windebank.ca	250-380-1416		499
Windels Marx Ln Mittendorf LLP 156 W 56th St .... New York NY 10019 *Web:* www.windelsmarx.com	212-237-1000	262-1215	428
Windemere Hotel and Conference Center 2047 S Hwy 92 .... Sierra Vista AZ 85635 *TF:* 800-825-4656 ■ *Web:* windemerehotel.com	520-459-5900		377
Windermere Information Technology Systems LLC 2000 Windermere Ct .... Annapolis MD 21401 *Web:* www.witsusa.com	410-266-1700		256
Windermere Relocation Inc 5424 Sand Point Way NE .... Seattle WA 98105 *TF:* 866-740-9589 ■ *Web:* www.windermere.com	206-527-3801		666
Winderweedle, Haines, Ward & Woodman PA 329 Park Ave N Second FL PO Box 880 .... Winter Park FL 32790 *Web:* www.whww.com	407-423-4246		428
Windes & McClaughry Accountancy Corp 111 W Ocean Blvd 22nd Fl PO Box 87 .... Long Beach CA 90802 *Web:* www.windes.com	562-435-1191		734
Windfall Assoc 981 Chestnut St .... Newton Upper Falls MA 02464 *TF:* 800-367-7240 ■ *Web:* www.windfall assoc.com	617-969-1790	969-1777	196
Windfall Farms 4710 Flying Paster Ln .... Paso Robles CA 93446	805-239-0711		368
Windfields Farm 2525 DeLong Rd .... Lexington KY 40515	859-273-3050		368
Windflower Spa Hyatt Hill Country Resort 9800 Hyatt Resort Dr .... San Antonio TX 78251 *Web:* www.hyatt.com	210-767-5577		77
Windham Brannon PC 3630 Peachtree Rd NE .... Atlanta GA 30326 *Web:* windhambrannon.com	404-898-2000		2
Windham Community Memorial Hospital (WCMH) 112 Mansfield Ave .... Willimantic CT 06226 *Web:* www.windhamhospital.org	860-456-9116	456-6838	374-3
Windham County 11 Jail St .... Newfane VT 05345 *TF:* 800-439-8683 ■ *Web:* www.windhamcountyvt.gov	802-365-4942	365-4945	338
Windham County 155 Church St .... Putnam CT 06260 *Web:* jud.ct.gov	860-928-7749		338
Windham Injury Management Group Inc 500 N Comercial St Ste 301 .... Manchester NH 03101 *Fax Area Code: 866 ■ *Web:* www.windhamgroup.com	603-626-5789	404-0557*	391-4
Windham Machine Company Inc 1102 Windham Rd .... South Windham CT 06266 *Web:* www.windhammachine.com	860-423-4575		454
Windham Manufacturing Company Inc 8520 Forney Rd .... Dallas TX 75227 *TF:* 888-965-0093 ■ *Web:* www.windhammfg.com	214-388-0511		454
Windham Millwork Inc 4 Architectural Dr .... Windham ME 04062 *Web:* www.windhammillwork.com	207-892-3238		200
Windham Region Chamber of Commerce 1010 Main St .... Willimantic CT 06226 *TF:* 800-683-4564 ■ *Web:* www.windhamchamber.com	860-423-6389	423-8235	139
Windings Inc PO Box 566 .... New Ulm MN 56073 *TF:* 800-795-8533 ■ *Web:* www.windings.com	507-359-2034		454
Windjammer Capital Investors 610 Newport Ctr Dr Ste 1100 .... Newport Beach CA 92660 *Web:* www.windjammercapital.com	949-721-9944	720-4222	792
Windjammer Promotions Inc 1112 Main St .... Osterville MA 02655 *TF:* 800-626-2947 ■ *Web:* windjammerpromotions.com	508-428-2099		195
Windlake Capital Advisors LLC 980 N Michigan Ave Ste 1400 .... Chicago IL 60611 *TF:* 800-270-9934 ■ *Web:* www.windlakeadvisors.com	312-357-0900		401
Windland Inc 1193 E Winding Creek Dr Ste 101 .... Eagle ID 83616 *Web:* www.windland.com	208-377-7777		612
Windmill Health Products 6 Henderson Dr .... West Caldwell NJ 07006 *TF:* 800-822-4320 ■ *Web:* www.windmillvitamins.com	973-575-6591	882-3256	799
Windmill International Inc 12 Murphy Dr Ste 200 .... Nashua NH 03062 *Web:* www.windmill-intl.com	603-888-5502	888-5512	194
Windmill State Recreation Area PO Box 427 .... Gibbon NE 68840 *Web:* outdoornebraska.gov	308-468-5700		565
WinDoor Inc 7500 Amsterdam Dr .... Orlando FL 32832 *Web:* www.windoorinc.com	407-481-8400		608

Phone | Fax | Class

Window & Door Manufacturers Assn (WDMA)
330 N Wabash Ave Ste 2000 Chicago IL 60611 847-299-5200 264-5150* 49-3
*Fax Area Code: 651 ■ TF: 800-223-2301 ■ Web: www.wdma.com

Window Factory Inc, The
1500 Kings Hwy Haddon Heights NJ 08035 856-546-5050 499
Web: www.windowfactory.com

Window Gang 405 Arendell St Morehead City NC 28557 252-726-1463 152
TF: 800-849-2308 ■ Web: www.windowgang.com

Window Rama Enterprises Inc
71 Heartland Blvd Edgewood NY 11717 631-667-8088 191-3
TF: 800-897-7262 ■ Web: www.windowrama.com

Windsor Airmotive 68 Deming St Newington CT 06111 860-666-1777 24

Windsor Arms Hotel 18 St Thomas St Toronto ON M5S3E7 416-971-9666 921-9121 379
TF: 877-999-2767 ■ Web: www.windsorarmshotel.com

Windsor Beach Technologies Inc
7321 Klier Dr Fairview PA 16415 814-474-4900 757
TF: 800-704-1078 ■ Web: www.windsorbeach.com

Windsor Capital Group Inc
3250 Ocean Park Blvd Ste 350 Santa Monica CA 90405 310-566-1100 566-1199 379
Web: www.wcghotels.com

Windsor Chamber of Commerce
261 Broad St Windsor CT 06095 860-688-5165 688-0809 139
Web: www.windsorcc.org

Windsor Co Ltd 101 W Liberty St Girard OH 44420 330-545-1550 545-2444 652
Web: www.windsorhouseinc.com

Windsor Corporate Suites
3516 Stearns Hills Rd Waltham MA 02451 781-899-5100 210
Web: www.windsorcommunities.com

Windsor Court Hotel
300 Gravier St New Orleans LA 70130 504-523-6000 596-4513 379
TF: 888-596-0955 ■ Web: www.windsorcourthotel.com

Windsor Factory Supply Ltd
730 N Service Rd Windsor ON N8X3J3 519-966-2202 966-2740 385
TF: 800-387-2659 ■ Web: www.wfsltd.com

Windsor Foods
3355 W Alabama St Ste 730 Houston TX 77098 713-843-5200 960-9709 296-36
TF: 800-458-4054 ■ Web: www.windsorfoods.com

Windsor High School
6208 US Hwy 61/67 Imperial MO 63052 636-464-4408 685
Web: windsor.k12.mo.us

Windsor Hilton Garden Inn
555 Corporate Dr Windsor CT 06095 860-688-6400 377
Web: hiltongardeninn3.hilton.com

Windsor Hotel 125 W Lamar St Americus GA 31709 229-924-1555 379
Web: www.windsor-americus.com

Windsor Inc 4533 Pacific Blvd Vernon CA 90058 323-282-9000 973-4224 157-6
TF: 888-494-6376 ■ Web: www.windsorstore.com

Windsor K,,rcher Group
1351 W Stanford Ave Englewood CO 80110 303-762-1800 865-2800 386
TF: 800-444-7654 ■ Web: www.windsorkarchergroup.com

Windsor Port Authority
3190 Sandwich St Ste 502 Windsor ON N9C1A6 519-258-5741 258-5905 618
Web: www.portwindsor.com

Windsor Public Library 323 Broad St Windsor CT 06095 860-285-1910 434-3
Web: www.windsorlibrary.com

Windsor Regional Hospital Metropolitan Campus (WRH)
1995 Lens Ave Windsor ON N8W1L9 519-254-5577 254-3458 374-2
Web: www.wrh.on.ca

Windsor Regional Hospital Western Campus (WRHWC)
1453 Prince Rd Windsor ON N9C3Z4 519-254-5577 254-2317* 374-2
*Fax: Acctg ■ Web: www.wrh.on.ca

Windsor Rehabilitation Care Ctr
3806 Clayton Rd Concord CA 94521 925-689-2266 450
Web: www.windsorcares.com

Windsor Republic Door Inc
5800 Scott Hamilton Dr Little Rock AR 72209 501-562-1872 234
Web: www.windsordoor.com

Windsor Service 9603 John St Santa Fe Springs CA 90670 323-282-9000 973-4309 188-4
Web: www.windsorstore.com

Windsor Star, The 300 Ouellette Ave Windsor ON N9A7B4 519-255-5711 255-5515 532-1
TF: 800-265-5647 ■ Web: www.windsorstar.com

Windsor Suites, The
1700 Benjamin Franklin Pkwy Philadelphia PA 19103 215-981-5678 377
TF: 800-537-7676 ■ Web: www.thewindsorsuites.com

Windsor Symphony Orchestra
121 University Ave West Windsor ON N9A5P4 519-973-1238 973-0764 573-3
TF: 888-327-8327 ■ Web: www.windsorsymphony.com

Windsor Vineyards
205 Concourse Blvd Santa Rosa CA 95403 800-289-9463 315-5
TF: 800-289-9463 ■ Web: www.windsorvineyards.com

Windsor Windows & Doors
900 S 19th St West Des Moines IA 50265 515-223-6660 236
TF: 800-218-6186 ■ Web: www.windsorwindows.com

Windsor-Bertie Area Chamber of Commerce
121 Granville St PO Box 572 Windsor NC 27983 252-794-4277 794-5070 139
TF: 800-334-5010 ■ Web: www.windsorbertiechamber.com

Windsor-Essex Regional Chamber of Commerce
2575 Ouellette Pl Windsor ON N8X1L9 519-966-3696 966-0603 137
Web: www.windsorchamber.org

Windspeed Ventures 52 Waltham St Lexington MA 02421 781-860-8888 860-0493 792
Web: www.wsventures.com

Windstar Cruises
2101 Fourth Ave Ste 210 Seattle WA 98121 206-292-9606 733-2790 220
TF Resv: 800-258-7245 ■ Web: www.windstarcruises.com

Windstar Lines Inc 1903 US Hwy 71 N Carroll IA 51401 712-792-4221 792-9615 186
TF: 888-494-6378 ■ Web: www.gowindstar.com

Windstone Technology Services Inc
1645 E Missouri Ave Ste 320 Phoenix AZ 85016 602-248-9092 175
TF: 800-243-0019 ■ Web: windstonetech.com

Windstream Corp
4001 Rodney Parham Rd Little Rock AR 72212 501-748-7000 736
Web: www.windstream.com

W-Industries Inc 11500 Charles Rd Houston TX 77041 713-466-9463 180
Web: www.w-industries.com

Windward Environmental LLC
200 W Mercer St Ste 401 Seattle WA 98119 206-378-1364 463
Web: www.windwardenv.com

Windward Passage 4739 Reed Rd Columbus OH 43220 614-451-2497 671

Windward Petroleum Inc
1064 Goffs Falls Rd Manchester NH 03103 603-222-2900 579
Web: www.ghberlinwindward.com

Windy City Silkscreening
2715 S Archer Ave Chicago IL 60608 312-842-0030 687
Web: www.wcsshirts.com

Windy's Sukiyaki 3809 Riverdale Rd Ogden UT 84405 801-621-4505 671
Web: www.windyssukiyaki.com

Wine & Spirits Shippers Assn Inc (WSSA)
11800 Sunrise Vly Dr Reston VA 20191 703-860-2300 860-2422 49-6
TF General: 800-368-3167 ■ Web: www.wssa.com

Wine & Spirits Wholesalers of America Inc (WSWA)
805 15th St NW Ste 430 Washington DC 20005 202-371-9792 789-2405 49-6
Web: www.wswa.org

Wine Appreciation Guild
450 Taraval Str Ste 201 South San Francisco CA 94116 650-866-3020 321
Web: wineappreciation.com

Wine Cask Inc, The
407 Washington St Somerville MA 02143 617-623-8656 443
Web: thewineandcheesecask.com

Wine Cellar 1314 Prudential Dr Jacksonville FL 32207 904-398-8989 671
Web: www.winecellarjax.com

Wine Cellar & Bistro 505 Cherry St Columbia MO 65201 573-442-7281 671
Web: www.winecellarbistro.com

Wine Club, The 1431 S Village Way Santa Ana CA 92705 714-835-6485 443
TF: 800-966-5432 ■ Web: www.thewineclub.com

Wine Institute
425 Market St Ste 1000 San Francisco CA 94105 415-512-0151 442-0742 49-6
Web: www.wineinstitute.org

Wine of The Month Club Inc
907 S Magnolia Ave Monrovia CA 91016 626-303-1690 443
Web: wineofthemonthclub.com

Wine Spectator Magazine
387 Pk Ave S 8th Fl New York NY 10016 212-684-4224 457-14
TF Orders: 800-752-7799 ■ Web: www.winespectator.com

Wine.com Inc
114 Sansome St 3rd Fl San Francisco CA 94104 415-248-4401 248-4400 443
TF: 800-592-5870 ■ Web: www.wine.com

WineAmerica
818 Connecticut Ave Ste 1006 Washington DC 20006 202-783-2756 49-6
Web: www.wineamerica.org

Winebow Inc 75 Chestnut Ridge Rd Montvale NJ 07645 201-445-0620 81-3
TF: 800-859-0689 ■ Web: www.thewinebowgroup.com

Winebrenner Theological Seminary
950 N Main St Findlay OH 45840 419-434-4200 434-4267 167-3
TF: 800-992-4987 ■ Web: www.winebrenner.edu

WineCommune LLC
7305 Edgewater Dr Ste D Oakland CA 94621 510-632-5300 80-3
Web: www.winecommune.com

WineDirect Inc 1190 Airport Blvd Ste 200 Napa CA 94558 707-603-4000 317
TF: 800-400-1353 ■ Web: www.winedirect.com

Winegard Co 3000 Kirkwood St Burlington IA 52601 319-754-0600 754-0787 647
TF Cust Svc: 800-288-8094 ■ Web: www.winegard.com

Winegardner & Hammons Inc
4243 Hunt Rd Cincinnati OH 45242 513-891-1066 794-2590 379
Web: whhotelgroup.com

Winegars Supermarkets Inc
3371 S Orchard Dr Bountiful UT 84010 801-292-0178 345
Web: www.winegars.com

Wineman Technology Inc
1668 Champagne Dr N Saginaw MI 48604 989-771-3000 256
Web: www.winemantech.com

Winer & Bevilacqua Inc
82 N Miller Rd Fairlawn OH 44333 330-867-3578 2
TF: 800-573-8853 ■ Web: wb-cpa.com

Winery at Wolf Creek
2637 Cleveland Massillon Rd Norton OH 44203 330-666-9285 665-1445 50-7
TF: 800-436-0426 ■ Web: www.wineryatwolfcreek.com

WineSellar & Brasserie
9550 Waples St Ste 115 San Diego CA 92121 858-450-9557 671
Web: www.winesellar.com

WineShop At Home 525 Airpark Rd Napa CA 94558 707-253-0200 443
TF: 800-946-3746 ■ Web: www.wineshopathome.com

WineStyles Inc
5515 Mills Civic Pkwy Ste 110 West Des Moines IA 50266 866-424-9463 310
TF: 866-424-9463 ■ Web: www.winestyles.com

Winet, Patrick & Weaver
1215 W Vista Way Vista CA 92083 760-758-4261 428
Web: www.wpgch.com

Winetasting Network, The 578 Gateway Dr Napa CA 94558 800-435-2225 690
TF: 800-435-2225 ■ Web: www.winetasting.com

Winfield Associates Inc
700 W St Clair Ave Ste 404 Cleveland OH 44113 216-241-2575 796
TF: 888-322-2575 ■ Web: www.winfieldinc.com

Winfield Correctional Facility
1806 Pine Crest Cir Winfield KS 67156 620-221-6660 221-9229 213
Web: www.doc.ks.gov/facilities/wcf

Winfield Micro Systems Inc
2333 Wisconsin Ave Downers Grove IL 60515 630-960-5515 366
Web: winfieldmicro.com

Winfield Security Corp 57 W 38th St New York NY 10018 212-609-2300 693
Web: www.winfieldsecurity.com

Winfree Marketing & Sales Institute
1905 Arnold Palmer Blvd Louisville KY 40245 502-253-0700 463
TF: 800-616-9260 ■ Web: www.winfree.org

Winfund Software Corp
2 Gurdwara Rd Ste 206 Ottawa ON K2E1A2 613-526-1969 179
Web: www.winfund.com

Wing Enterprises Inc
1198 N Spring Creek Springville UT 84663 801-489-3684 421
TF: 866-872-5901 ■ Web: littlegiantladders.com

Wing Eyecare Inc 5305 Glenway Ave Cincinnati OH 45238 513-791-2222 543
TF: 800-472-1245 ■ Web: www.wingeyecare.com

Wing Group LLC 20 Trafalgar Sq Ste 455 Nashua NH 03063 603-589-4076 434-3
TF: 800-826-5761 ■ Web: www.wing-group.com

Wing Haven 248 Ridgewood Ave Charlotte NC 28209 704-331-0664 331-9368 97
Web: www.winghavengardens.com

Phone | Fax | Class

Wing Hing Foods Inc
2539 E Philadelphia St ... Ontario CA 91761 855-734-2742 345
TF: 855-734-2742 ■ *Web:* www.winghing.com
Wing It Productions Inc
5510 University Way NE ... Seattle WA 98105 206-352-8291 747
Web: www.wingitproductions.org
Wing Luke Asian Museum 719 S King St ... Seattle WA 98104 206-623-5124 623-4559 520
TF: 800-961-6119 ■ *Web:* www.wingluke.org
Wing Zone Franchise Corp
2120 Powers Ferry Rd Ste 101 ... Atlanta GA 30339 404-875-5045 875-6631 310
TF: 877-946-4966 ■ *Web:* wingzonefranchise.com
Wing's Food Products 50 Torlake Cres ... Toronto ON M8Z1B8 416-259-2662 259-3414 297-8
Web: www.wings.ca
WING-AM 1410 (Sports) 717 E David Rd ... Dayton OH 45429 937-294-5858 645-45
TF: 800-349-5075 ■ *Web:* www.wingam.com
Wingate by Wyndham Calgary Hotel
400 Midpark Way SE ... Calgary AB T2X3S4 403-514-0099 707
TF: 800-228-1000 ■ *Web:* www.wingatebywyndhamcalgary.com
Wingate Financial Group Inc
450 Bedford St ... Lexington MA 02420 781-862-7100 251
Web: www.wingatewealthadvisors.com
Wingate Healthcare 63 Kendrick St ... Needham MA 02494 800-946-4283 4
TF: 800-946-4283 ■ *Web:* wingatehealthcare.com
Wingate Packaging Inc
4347 Indeco Ct ... Cincinnati OH 45241 513-745-8600 627
TF: 800-827-9744 ■ *Web:* www.wingate-packaging.com
Wingate University 220 N Camden Rd ... Wingate NC 28174 704-233-8000 233-8110 166
TF: 800-755-5550 ■ *Web:* www.wingate.edu
Wingenback Inc
Bay F Century Park 707 Barlow Trl ... Calgary AB T2E8C2 403-221-8120 291-5114 190
Web: www.wingenback.com
Winger Contracting Co 918 Hayne St ... Ottumwa IA 52501 641-682-3407 610
Web: www.wingermechanical.com
Winger's USA Inc
855 W 1100 S Ste A ... Brigham City UT 84302 435-723-7822 670
Web: wingerbros.com
Wingfield J e & Associates Pc
700 Fifth St NW Ste 300 ... Washington DC 20001 202-789-8000 445
TF: 800-338-5954 ■ *Web:* jewingfield.com
Wingfoot Commercial Tire Systems LLC
1000 S 21st St ... Fort Smith AR 72901 479-788-6400 788-6486 62-5
TF: 800-643-7330 ■ *Web:* goodyearctsc.com
Wingman Advertising
5855 Green Valley Cir Ste 208 ... Culver City CA 90230 424-207-3304 7
Web: www.wingmanadv.com
Wingra Stone Co
2975 Kapec Rd PO Box 44284 ... Madison WI 53744 608-271-5555 271-3142 183
TF: 800-249-6908 ■ *Web:* www.wingrastone.com
WINGS (Wings Foundation)
7550 W Yale Ave Ste B 201 ... Denver CO 80227 303-238-8660 238-4739 48-21
TF: 800-373-8671 ■ *Web:* www.wingsfound.org
Wings Air Charter
236 Airport Hanger Dr ... Wisconsin Rapids WI 54494 715-424-3737 424-3737 63
Web: www.wingsaircharter.com
Wings Event Ctr 3600 Van Rick Dr ... Kalamazoo MI 49001 269 345 1125 655
Web: www.wingseventcenter.com/default.aspx
Wings Financial Credit Union
11005 Glazier Ave Ste 100 ... Apple Valley MN [illegible] [illegible] 210
TF: 800-692-2274 ■ *Web:* www.wingsfinancial.com
Wings Foundation (WINGS)
7550 W Yale Ave Ste B 201 ... Denver CO 80227 303-238-8660 238-4739 48-21
TF: 800-373-8671 ■ *Web:* www.wingsfound.org
Wings of History Air Museum
12777 Murphy Ave PO Box 495 ... San Martin CA 95046 408-683-2290 520
Web: www.wingsofhistory.org
Wings Over the Rockies Air & Space Museum
7711 E Academy Blvd ... Denver CO 80230 303-360-5360 360-5328 520
Web: www.wingsmuseum.org
Wings Tours Inc
11350 McCormick Rd Ste 904 ... Hunt Valley MD 21031 410-771-0925 771-0928 760
TF: 800-869-4647 ■ *Web:* www.wingstours.us
Wings Unlimited Inc 455 Post Rd Ste 102 ... Darien CT 06820 203-656-9591 656-1141 184
Web: www.wingsunlimited.net
Wingstop Restaurants Inc
1101 E Arapaho Rd Ste 150 ... Richardson TX 75081 972-686-6500 670
TF: 800-732-0330 ■ *Web:* www.wingstop.com
WingSwept 800 Benson Rd ... Garner NC 27529 919-779-0954 196
Web: www.wingswept.com
WinHolt Equipment Group
141 Eileen Way ... Syosset NY 11791 516-222-0335 921-0538 470
TF: 800-444-3595 ■ *Web:* www.winholt.com
Wink Inc 8641 United Plaza Blvd ... Baton Rouge LA 70809 225-932-6000 261
Web: www.willbros.com
Wink Restaurant 1014 N Lamar Blvd Ste E ... Austin TX 78703 512-482-8868 671
Web: www.winkrestaurant.com
Winkle Electric Company Inc., The
1900 Hubbard Rd ... Youngstown OH 44501 330-744-5303 767
Web: www.winkle.com
Winkler & Whittenberg Inc CPA'S
15446 E Valley Blvd ... City Of Industry CA 91746 626-330-2224 961-0156 2
Web: whittenbergcpa.com
Winkler County 100 E Winkler St ... Kermit TX 79745 432-586-3161 586-3535 338
Web: www.co.winkler.tx.us
Winkler Films Inc
190 N Canon Dr Ste 302 ... Beverly Hills CA 90210 310-858-5780 514
Winkler Inc 535 E Medcalf St ... Dale IN 47523 812-937-4421 937-2044 297-8
TF: 800-621-3843 ■ *Web:* www.winklerinc.com
WINK-TV Ch 11 (CBS)
2824 Palm Beach Blvd ... Fort Myers FL 33916 239-334-1111 741-88
TF: 800-541-2172 ■ *Web:* www.winknews.com
Winland Electronics Inc 1950 Excel Dr ... Mankato MN 56001 507-625-7231 387-2488 201
NYSE: WEX ■ *TF:* 800-635-4269 ■ *Web:* www.winland.com
Winmark Corp 605Hwy 169 N Ste 400 ... Minneapolis MN 55441 763-520-8500 520-8410 157-1
NASDAQ: WINA ■ *TF:* 877-536-1561 ■ *Web:* www.winmarkcorporation.com
WinMed Inc Dundee Park Bldg 17 Door 6 ... Andover MA 01810 978-590-4246 743
TF: 800-342-5973 ■ *Web:* www.winmed-inc.com
Winn Army Community Hospital
1061 Harmon Ave ... Fort Stewart GA 31314 912-435-6633 374-4

Phone | Fax | Class

Winn Parish Police Jury
119 W Main St Ste 102 ... Winnfield LA 71483 318-628-5824 338
Winn Technology Group Inc
523 Palm Harbor Blvd ... Palm Harbor FL 34683 800-444-5622 195
TF: 800-444-5622 ■ *Web:* www.winntech.net
Winn Transportation
1831 Westwood Ave ... Richmond VA 23227 804-358-9466 353-2606 107
TF: 800-296-9466 ■ *Web:* www.winnbus.com
Winncom Technologies Corp
30700 Carter St Ste A ... Solon OH 44139 440-498-9510 498-9511 246
Web: www.winncom.com
Winn-Dixie Stores Inc
5050 Edgewood Ct ... Jacksonville FL 32254 904-783-5000 345
Web: www.winndixie.com
Winne Banta Basralian & Kahn PC
Court Plaza S 21 Main St Ste 101 ... Hackensack NJ 07601 201-487-3800 487-8529 445
Web: www.winnebanta.com
Winnebago Community Unit District 323
304 E Mcnair Rd ... Winnebago IL 61088 815-335-2456 685
Web: www.winnebagoschools.org
Winnebago County PO Box 2808 ... Oshkosh WI 54903 920-236-4800 303-3025 338
Web: www.co.winnebago.wi.us
Winnebago Industries Inc
605 W Crystal Lake Rd PO Box 152 ... Forest City IA 50436 641-585-3535 585-6966 120
NYSE: WGO ■ *TF:* 800-643-4892 ■ *Web:* www.winnebagoind.com
Winnebago Mental Health Institute (WMHI)
1300 S Dr ... Winnebago WI 54985 920-235-4910 374-5
Web: dhs.wisconsin.gov/mh%5fwinncbago
Winneconne News 908 E Main St ... Winneconne WI 54986 920-582-4541 532-3
TF: 800-545-5026 ■ *Web:* www.rogerspublishing.com
Winnefox Library System
106 Washington Ave ... Oshkosh WI 54901 920-236-5220 236-5228 434-3
TF: 800-321-5427 ■ *Web:* www.winnefox.org
Winnemucca Convention & Visitors Authority
50 W Winnemucca Blvd ... Winnemucca NV 89445 775-623-5071 623-5087 206
TF: 800-962-2638 ■ *Web:* www.winnemucca.com
Winner Chevrolet Inc PO Box 1867 ... Colfax CA 95713 530-349-4151 57
Web: www.winnerchevy.com
Winner International LLC 32 W State St ... Sharon PA 16146 724-981-1152 692
TF: 800-258-2321 ■ *Web:* www.winner-intl.com
Winner Livestock Auction Co
31690 Livestock Barn Rd ... Winner SD 57580 605-842-0451 842-3562 446
TF: 800-201-0451 ■ *Web:* www.winnerlivestock.com
Winner's Cir Resort
550 Via de la Valle ... Solana Beach CA 92075 858-755-6666 481-3706 669
TF: 800-874-8770 ■ *Web:* www.winnerscircleresort.com
Winnercomm Inc
4500 S 129th E Ave Ste 201 ... Tulsa OK 74134 918-496-1900 33
TF: 800-439-1605 ■ *Web:* www.winnercomm.com
Winners Circle Engineering Inc
225 W Main St ... Monrovia IN 46157 317-996-3157 454
Web: winnerscircleengineering.com
Winners Only Inc 1365 Pk Ctr Dr ... Vista CA 92081 760-599-0300 319-2
Web: www.winnersonly.com
Winners Sports Haven
600 Long Wharf Dr ... New Haven CT 06511 800-468-2260 133
TF: 800-468-2260 ■ *Web:* www.mywinners.com
Winneshiek County 201 W Main St ... Decorah IA 52101 563-302-0603 338
Web: winneshiekcounty.org
Winnetka Community House
620 Lincoln Ave ... Winnetka IL 60093 847-446-0537 354
Web: winnetkacommunityhouse.org
Winnetka-Northfield Public Library District
768 Oak St ... Winnetka IL 60093 847-446-7220 434-3
Web: winnetkalibrary.org
Winning Edge Group LLC
2576 Euclid Crescent E ... Upland CA 91784 909-949-9083 463
Web: www.group50.com
Winning Proposals Inc
374 Maple Ave E Ste 305 ... Vienna VA 22180 703-242-6490 463
Web: www.win-pros.com
Winning Solutions Inc
1421 S Bell Ave Ste 105 ... Ames IA 50010 515-239-9900 177
Web: www.winningsolutionsinc.com
Winning Technologies Great Lakes LLC
147 Triad Ctr W ... O Fallon MO 63366 877-379-8279 180
TF: 877-379-8279 ■ *Web:* www.winningtech.com
Winnipeg Blue Bombers
Investors Group Field315 Chancellor Matheson Rd
... Winnipeg MB R3T1Z2 204-784-2583 783-5222 715-2
Web: www.bluebombers.com
Winnipeg Centennial Folk Festival Inc, The
211 Bannatyne Ave Ste 203 ... Winnipeg MB R3B3P2 204-231-0096 720
TF: 866-301-3823 ■ *Web:* www.winnipegfolkfestival.ca
Winnipeg Chamber of Commerce, The
259 Portage Ave Ste 100 ... Winnipeg MB R3B2A9 204-944-8484 944-8492 137
Web: www.winnipeg-chamber.com
Winnipeg Free Press
1355 Mountain Ave ... Winnipeg MB R2X3B6 204-697-7000 697-7412* 532-1
**Fax:* News Rm ■ *TF:* 800-542-8900 ■ *Web:* www.winnipegfreepress.com
Winnipeg Fringe Festival
174 Market Ave ... Winnipeg MB R3B0P8 204-956-1340 749
Web: www.winnipegfringe.com
Winnipeg Goldeyes Baseball Club Inc
1 Portage Ave E ... Winnipeg MB R3B3N3 204-982-2273 720
Web: www.goldeyes.com
Winnipeg Richardson International Airport
2000 Wellington Ave ... Winnipeg MB R3H1C2 204-987-9402 987-2732 27
TF: 855-500-6589 ■ *Web:* www.waa.ca
Winnipeg Sun 1700 Church Ave ... Winnipeg MB R2X3A2 204-694-2022 532-1
Web: www.winnipegsun.com
Winnsboro State Bank & Trust Co
3875 Front St ... Winnsboro LA 71295 318-435-7535 70
TF: 866-205-4026 ■ *Web:* winnsborobank.com
Winona Convention & Visitors Bureau
160 Johnson St ... Winona MN 55987 507-452-0735 454-0006 206
TF: 800-657-4972 ■ *Web:* visitwinona.com
Winona County 177 Main St ... Winona MN 55987 507-457-6350 454-9365 338
TF: 800-895-0727 ■ *Web:* www.co.winona.mn.us

	Phone	Fax	Class
Winona Monument Company Inc 174 W Third St .... Winona MN 55987	507-452-4672		724
Winona National Bankÿÿÿ 204 Main St PO Box 499 .... Winona MN 55987 *TF:* 800-546-4392 ■ *Web:* www.winonanationalbank.com	507-454-8800	454-9208	360-2
Winona Public Library 151 W Fifth St .... Winona MN 55987 *Web:* winona.lib.mn.us	507-452-4582	452-5842	434-3
Winona State University 175 W Mark St .... Winona MN 55987 **Fax:* Admissions ■ *TF:* 800-342-5978 ■ *Web:* www.winona.edu	507-457-5000	457-5620*	166
Winona State University Krueger Library PO Box 5838 .... Winona MN 55987 *Web:* www.winona.edu/library	507-457-5140	457-5594	434-6
Winpak Ltd 100 Salteaux Crescent .... Winnipeg MB R3J3T3 *TSE:* WPK ■ *TF:* 800-841-2600 ■ *Web:* www.winpak.com	204-889-1015	888-7806	548
Winrock Enterprises 1501 N University Ave Ste 360 .... Little Rock AR 72207	501-663-5340		596
Winrock International 2101 Riverfront Dr .... Little Rock AR 72202 *Web:* www.winrock.org	501-280-3000	280-3090	634
Winsby Inc 1854 Sherman Ave .... Evanston IL 60201 *TF:* 800-634-6359 ■ *Web:* www.winsbyinc.com	847-316-9800		463
Winsert Inc 2645 Industrial Pkwy S PO Box 0198 .... Marinette WI 54143 *Web:* www.winsert.com	715-732-1703	732-2824	307
Winship Cancer Institute of Emory University 1365 Clifton Rd NE .... Atlanta GA 30322 **Fax Area Code:* 678 ■ *TF:* 888-946-7447 ■ *Web:* winshipcancer.emory.edu	404-778-1900	843-5615*	769
WinSim Inc 14090 SW Fwy Ste 550 .... Sugar Land TX 77478 *Web:* winsim.com	281-565-6700		175
Winslow Automatic Inc 23 St Clair Ave .... New Britain CT 06051 *Web:* winslowautomatics.com	860-225-6321		621
Winslow Automation Inc 905 Montague Expy .... Milpitas CA 95035 *Web:* www.winslowautomation.com	408-262-9004	956-0199	696
Winslow BMW 730 N Cir Dr .... Colorado Springs CO 80909 *TF:* 877-367-7357 ■ *Web:* www.winslowbmw.com	719-473-1373		57
Winslow State Park Kearsarge Mtn Rd .... Wilmot NH 03287 *Web:* www.nhstateparks.org	603-526-6168		565
Winsoft Corp 1932 E Deere Ave Alton Deere Plaza, Ste 110 .... Santa Ana CA 92705 *TF:* 800-537-2029 ■ *Web:* www.winsoft.com	949-428-4844		809
Winsome Trading Inc 16111 Woodinville Redmo .... Woodinville WA 98072 *Web:* www.winsomewood.com	425-483-8888	483-4141	362
WinStar Farm LLC 3001 Pisgah Pk .... Versailles KY 40383 *Web:* www.winstarfarm.com	859-873-1717	873-1612	368
Winstar Interactive Media (WIMS) 1655 Palm Beach Lakes Blvd Ste 903 .... West Palm Beach Fl 33401 *Web:* www.winstarinteractive.com	561-227-0626		6
Winstead PC 1201 Elm St 5400 Renaissance Tower .... Dallas TX 75270 *TF:* 800-973-1177 ■ *Web:* www.winstead.com	214-745-5400		428
Winston Baker Inc 100 S Fairfax Ave Ste A1153 .... Los Angeles CA 90036 *Web:* www.winstonbaker.com	310-922-1544		636
Winston Bros Inc 131 Newbury St .... Boston MA 02116 *TF:* 800-457-4901 ■ *Web:* www.winstonflowers.com	617-541-1100		292
Winston County PO Box 309 .... Double Springs AL 35553 *TF:* 800-245-2244 ■ *Web:* winstoncountycircuitclerk.org	205-489-5533		338
Winston County 311 W Park St .... Louisville MS 39339 *Web:* www.winstoncountyms.com	662-773-8719	773-8909	338
Winston F2S Corp 1604 Cherokee Trace .... White Oak TX 75693 *TF:* 800-527-8465 ■ *Web:* www.winstonf2s.com	903-757-7341	759-6986	537
Winston Furniture 540 Dolphin Rd .... Haleyville AL 35565 *Web:* www.winstonfurniture.com	205-486-9211		319-4
Winston Hospitality Inc 3701 National Dr Ste 120 .... Raleigh NC 27612 *Web:* www.winstonhospitality.com	919-334-6910	334-6912	177
Winston Industries LLC 2345 Carton Dr .... Louisville KY 40299 *TF:* 800-234-5286 ■ *Web:* www.winstonind.com	502-495-5400	495-5458	298
Winston Printing Company Inc 8095 N Point Blvd .... Winston-Salem NC 27106 *TF:* 800-275-8777 ■ *Web:* www.winstonpackaging.com	336-759-0051		627
Winston Resources Inc 122 E 42nd St Ste 320 .... New York NY 10168 *TF:* 800-973-1177 ■ *Web:* www.winstonresources.com	212-557-5000	682-1056	721
Winston-Choctaw County Regional Correctional Facility PO Box 1437 .... Louisville MS 39339 *Web:* www.mdoc.ms.gov/pages/facility-locations.aspx	662-773-2528	773-4989	213
Winston-Salem City Hall 101 N Main St PO Box 2511 .... Winston-Salem NC 27101 *Web:* www.cityofws.org	336-727-8000	748-3060	337
Winston-Salem Convention & Visitors Bureau 200 Brookstown Ave .... Winston-Salem NC 27101 *TF:* 866-728-4200 ■ *Web:* www.visitwinstonsalem.com	336-728-4200	728-4220	206
Winston-Salem Dash 926 Brookstown Ave .... Winston-salem NC 27101 *Web:* www.milb.com	336-714-2287		713
Winston-Salem Entertainment-Sports Complex 2825 University Pkwy .... Winston-Salem NC 27105 *Web:* www.ljvm.com	336-758-2410		720
Winston-Salem Journal 418 N Marshall St .... Winston-Salem NC 27101 *TF:* 800-642-0925 ■ *Web:* www.journalnow.com	336-727-7211	727-7315	532-2
Winston-Salem Southbound Railway Co 4550 Overdale Rd .... Winston-Salem NC 27107 *Web:* www.ncrailways.org	336-788-9407	788-9085	648
Winston-Salem State University 601 S ML King Jr Dr 206 Thompson Ctr .... Winston-Salem NC 27110 *TF Admissions:* 800-257-4052 ■ *Web:* www.wssu.edu	336-750-2000		166
Winston-Salem Symphony 201 N Broad St Ste 200 .... Winston-Salem NC 27101 *TF:* 800-343-7857 ■ *Web:* www.wssymphony.org	336-725-1035	725-3924	573-3

	Phone	Fax	Class
Winston-Salem/Forsyth County Schools (WS/FCS) 1605 Miller St .... Winston-Salem NC 27103 *Web:* www.wsfcs.k12.nc.us	336-727-2816	661-6572	685
Wintec Industries Inc 675 Sycamore Dr .... Milpitas CA 95035 *TF:* 866-989-4683 ■ *Web:* www.wintecindustries.com	408-856-0500	856-0501	625
Winter Bros Material Co 13098 Gravois Rd .... Saint Louis MO 63127 *TF:* 800-722-5424 ■ *Web:* www.winterbrothersmaterial.com	314-843-1400	843-1403	500
Winter Construction Co 191 Peachtree St NE .... Atlanta GA 30303 *TF:* 800-745-0465 ■ *Web:* winter-construction.com	404-588-3300		186
Winter Environmental 3350 Green Pointe Pkwy Ste 200 .... Norcross GA 30092 *Web:* winter-environmental.com	404-588-3300		667
Winter F W Inc & Co 550 Delaware Ave .... Camden NJ 08102 *TF:* 800-443-9353 ■ *Web:* www.fwwinter.com	856-963-7490		492
Winter Gardens Quality Foods Inc 304 Commerce St PO Box 339 .... New Oxford PA 17350 *TF:* 800-242-7637 ■ *Web:* www.wintergardens.com	717-624-4911	624-7729	296-36
Winter Haven Hospital 200 Ave F NE .... Winter Haven FL 33881 *Web:* baycare.org/winter-haven-hospital	863-293-1121		374-3
Winter Hill Bank 342 Broadway .... Somerville MA 02145 *TF:* 800-444-4300 ■ *Web:* www.winterhillbank.com/Default.asp	617-666-8600	629-3327	70
Winter Kloman Moter & Repp SC (WKMR) 235 N Executive Dr Ste 160 .... Brookfield WI 53005 *Web:* www.wkmr.com	262-797-9050	797-8251	49-2
Winter Livestock Inc PO Box 909 PO Box 909 .... Enid OK 73702 *TF:* 800-822-8853 ■ *Web:* www.winterlivestock.com	580-237-4600	237-4604	446
Winter Management Corp 730 Fifth Ave 12th Fl .... New York NY 10019 *Web:* www.winter.com	212-616-8900	616-8985	652
Winter Park Chamber of Commerce 151 W Lyman Ave .... Winter Park FL 32789 *TF Help Line:* 877-972-4262 ■ *Web:* www.winterpark.org	407-644-8281	644-7826	139
Winter Park Construction Co 221 Cir Dr .... Maitland FL 32751 *TF:* 800-743-3323 ■ *Web:* www.wpc.com	407-644-8923	645-1972	186
Winter Park Resort 85 Parsenn Rd .... Winter Park CO 80482 *TF Resv:* 800-903-7275 ■ *Web:* www.winterparkresort.com	970-726-5514	726-1690	376
Winter Quarters State Historic Site 4929 Hwy 608 .... Newellton LA 71357 *TF:* 888-677-9468 ■ *Web:* www.crt.state.la.us	888-677-2784		565
WinterBell Co 2018 Brevard Rd .... High Point NC 27263 *TF:* 800-685-2957 ■ *Web:* www.winterbell.com	336-887-2651		561
WinterGreen Research Inc 6 Raymond St .... Lexington MA 02421 *Web:* www.wintergreenresearch.com	781-863-5078		225
Wintergreen Resort Rt 664 PO Box 706 .... Wintergreen VA 22958 *TF:* 855-699-1858 ■ *Web:* www.wintergreenresort.com	855-699-1858		707
Winterhawk Consulting LLC 1643 Williamsburg Sq .... Lakeland FL 33803 *Web:* winterhawkconsulting.com	813-731-9665		631
Wintersilks LLC PO Box 196 .... Jessup PA 18434 *TF:* 800-648-7455 ■ *Web:* wintersilks.blair.com	800-718-3687		459
Winterthur Museum & Country Estate 5105 Kennett Pk .... Winterthur DE 19735 *TF:* 800-448-3883 ■ *Web:* www.winterthur.org	302-888-4600		520
Winther Stave & Company LLP 1316 W 18th St PO Box 175 .... Spencer IA 51301 *Web:* www.winther-stave.com	712-262-3117		2
Winthrop 11100 Wayzata Blvd Ste 800 .... Minneapolis MN 55305 *Web:* www.winthropresources.com	952-936-0226		216
Winthrop & Weinstine PA 225 S Sixth St Ste 3500 .... Minneapolis MN 55402 *TF:* 800-999-1950 ■ *Web:* www.winthrop.com	612-604-6400		428
Winthrop Realty Trust 7 Bulfinch Pl Ste 500 .... Boston MA 02114 *NYSE:* FUR ■ *TF:* 800-622-6757 ■ *Web:* www.winthropreit.com	617-570-4614	570-4746	655
Winthrop University 701 Oakland Ave .... Rock Hill SC 29733 **Fax:* Admissions ■ *Web:* www.winthrop.edu	803-323-2211	323-2137*	166
Winthrop University Hospital 259 First St .... Mineola NY 11501 *TF:* 800-490-0075 ■ *Web:* www.winthrop.org	516-663-0333	663-2946	374-3
Winton Woods City Schools 1215 W Kemper Rd .... Cincinnati OH 45240 *Web:* www.wintonwoods.org	513-619-2300	619-2300	685
Wintrust Financial Corp 9700 W Higgins Rd Ste 800 .... Rosemont IL 60018 *NASDAQ:* WTFC ■ *Web:* www.wintrust.com	847-939-9000		360-2
Winvale Group LLC, The 1012 14th St NW 5th Fl .... Washington DC 20005 *Web:* www.winvale.com	202-296-5505		664
Winward International Inc 3089 Whipple Rd .... Union City CA 94587 *TF:* 800-888-8898 ■ *Web:* www.winwardsilks.com	510-487-8686		292
Winware Inc 1955 W Oak Cir .... Marietta GA 30062 *TF:* 888-419-1399 ■ *Web:* www.cribmaster.com	770-419-1399	419-1968	177
WinWholesale Inc 3110 Kettering Blvd .... Dayton OH 45439 *TF:* 800-677-4380 ■ *Web:* winwholesale.com	937-294-5331	293-9591	612
WINZ-AM 940 (N/T) 7601 Riviera Blvd .... Miramar FL 33023 *Web:* 940winz.iheart.com	954-862-2000	862-4013	645-99
Winzeler Gear Inc 7355 W Wilson Ave .... Harwood Heights IL 60706 *Web:* www.winzelergear.com	708-867-7971	867-7974	604
Winzeler Stamping Co 910 E Main St .... Montpelier OH 43543 *Web:* www.winzelerstamping.com	419-485-3147	485-5039	488
Winzinger Inc 1704 Marne Hwy PO Box 537 .... Hainesport NJ 08036 *TF:* 800-849-1591 ■ *Web:* www.winzinger.com	609-267-8600	267-4079	188-4
WinZip Computing Inc PO Box 540 .... Mansfield CT 06268 *Web:* www.winzip.com	860-429-3542	429-3542	178-12
WIOD-AM 610 (N/T) 7601 Riviera Blvd .... Miramar FL 33023 *TF:* 866-610-6397 ■ *Web:* wiod.iheart.com	866-610-6397		645-99

Name / Address	City	State	Zip	Phone	Fax	Class
WIOT-FM 104.7 (Rock) 125 S Superior St Web: wiot.iheart.com	Toledo	OH	43604	419-244-8321		645-163
Wipaire Inc 1700 Henry Ave TF: 888-947-2473 ■ Web: www.wipaire.com	South St. Paul	MN	55075	651-451-1205		529
Wipe-Tex International Corp 110 E 153rd St TF: 800-643-9607 ■ Web: www.wipe-tex.com	Bronx	NY	10451	718-665-0787	665-0787	508
Wipfli LLP 10000 Innovation Dr Ste 250 Web: www.wipfli.com	Milwaukee	WI	53226	414-431-9300	431-9303	2
WIPO (World Intellectual Property Organization) 2 UN Plaza Ste 2525 Web: www.wipo.int	New York	NY	10017	212-963-6813	963-4801	783
Wipro Gallagher Solutions Inc 810 Crescent Centre Dr Ste 400 Web: wiprogallagher.com	Palmetto Bay	FL	37067	615-221-7312		809
Wipro Inc 1300 Crittenden Ln Ste 200 Web: www.wipro.com	Mountain View	CA	94043	650-316-3555		196
Wire & Plastic Machinery Co 800 E Second St Web: www.wireandplastic.com	Bonham	TX	75418	903-583-2183		45
Wire Assn International Inc (WAI) 1570 Boston Post Rd PO Box 578 TF: 800-449-4265 ■ Web: www.wirenet.org	Guilford	CT	06437	203-453-2777	453-8384	49-13
Wire Belt Company of America 154 Harvey Rd TF Cust Svc: 800-922-2637 ■ Web: www.wirebelt.com	Londonderry	NH	03053	603-644-2500	644-3600	207
Wire Cloth Filter Manufacturing Co 611 St Charles Rd TF: 800-207-3803 ■ Web: wireclothfilter.net	Maywood	IL	60153	708-410-1800	410-1807	688
Wire Products Company Inc 14601 Industrial Pkwy Web: wire-products.com	Cleveland	OH	44135	216-267-0777	267-7972	719
Wire Products Manufacturing Corp 106 N Genesee St	Merrill	WI	54452	715-536-7144		482
Wire Rope Industries Ltd 5501 Trans-Canada Hwy TF: 800-565-5501 ■ Web: www.wirerope.com	Pointe-claire	QC	H9R1B7	514-697-9711		492
Wirebenders, The 2075 Lincoln Ave Ste A Web: www.thewirebenders.com	San Jose	CA	95125	408-265-5576		743
WireBuzz LLC 8360 E Raintree Dr Ste 225 Web: www.wirebuzz.com	Scottsdale	AZ	85260	480-699-8053		5
WireCo WorldGroup 12200 NW Ambassador Dr Web: www.wirecoworldgroup.com	Kansas City	MO	64163	816-270-4700	270-4707	813
Wired News Wired 520 Third St Ste 305 TF: 800-769-4733 ■ Web: www.wired.com	San Francisco	CA	94107	800-769-4733		397
Wiredrive 5340 Alla Rd Ste 109 Web: www.wiredrive.com	Los Angeles	CA	90066	310-823-8238		177
Wirefab Inc 75 Blackstone River Rd Web: www.wirefab.com	Worcester	MA	01607	508-754-5359	797-3620	73
Wirehead Security LLC The Atrium Bldg 2501 Blue Ridge Rd Ste 250 Web: www.wireheadsecurity.com	Raleigh	NC	27607	919-863-4373		196
Wireless Analytics LLC 230 N St Ste 4 TF: 888-588-5550 ■ Web: www.wirelessanalytics.com	Danvers	MA	01923	000-500-5550		224
Wireless Communications Assn International (WCA) 1333 H St NW Ste 700W Web: wcai.com	Washington	DC	20005	202-452-7823		49-20
Wireless Flash News Service PO Box 633030 Web: www.flashnews.com	San Diego	CA	92163	619-220-7191		530
Wireless Mike's 301 S 21st St Web: wirelessmikes.com	Mattoon	IL	61938	217-235-9300		736
Wireless Network Group Warehouse 220 w Pkwy Web: www.wnginc.com	Pompton Plains	NJ	07444	973-831-4015		138
Wireless Seismic Inc 13100 SW Fwy Ste 150 Web: www.wirelessseismic.com	Sugar Land	TX	77478	832-532-5080		407
Wireless Telecom Group Inc 25 Eastmans Rd NYSE: WTT ■ Web: www.wirelesstelecomgroup.com	Parsippany	NJ	07054	973-386-9696	386-9191	735
Wireless Toyz Ltd 29155 NW Hwy TF: 866-237-2624 ■ Web: www.wirelesstoyz.com	Southfield	MI	48034	248-426-8200		310
Wireless Watchdogs LLC 5800 Hannum Ave Ste B TF: 866-522-0688 ■ Web: www.wirelesswatchdogs.com	Culver City	CA	90230	866-522-0688		2
Wireless Xcessories Group Inc 1840 County Line Rd Ste 301 OTC: WIRX ■ *Fax Area Code: 888 ■ TF: 800-233-0013 ■ Web: www.wirexgroup.com	Huntingdon Valley	PA	19006	215-322-4600	233-0220*	253
Wireless Zone LLC 795 Brook St *Fax Area Code: 989 ■ TF: 888-881-2622 ■ Web: www.wirelesszone.com	Rocky Hill	CT	06067	860-632-9494	652-0520*	35
Wirelesswerks USA Inc 7981 168th Ave NE Web: www.wirelesswerks.com	Redmond	WA	98052	425-869-2356		116
Wiremasters Inc 1788 N Pt Rd TF: 800-635-5342 ■ Web: www.wiremasters.net	Columbia	TN	38401	615-791-0281	791-6182	246
Wirerope Works Inc 100 Maynard St TF Cust Svc: 800-541-7673 ■ Web: www.wwwrope.com	Williamsport	PA	17701	570-326-5146	327-4274	813
WireSpring Technologies Inc 1901 W Cypress Creek Rd Ste 100 TF: 800-989-9269 ■ Web: wirespring.com	Fort Lauderdale	FL	33309	954-548-3300		177
Wiretree LLC 887 W Marietta St NW Ste 1 Web: www.wiretree.com	Atlanta	GA	30318	404-876-3835		180
Wireway/Husky Corp 6146 Denver Industrial Pk Web: www.wirewayhusky.com	Denver	NC	28037	704-483-1900		567
Wiring Harness Manufacturers Assn (WHMA) 15490 101st Ave N Ste 100 Web: www.whma.org	Maple Grove	MN	55369	763-235-6461		49-13
Wirt County PO Box 53 TF: 800-252-5627 ■ Web: www.wirtcounty.wv.gov	Elizabeth	WV	26143	304-275-4271	275-3418	338
Wirt Design Group 617 W Seventh St Ste 201 Web: www.wirtdesign.com	Los Angeles	CA	90017	213-239-0990		393
Wirtz Corp 680 N Lake Shore Dr Ste 1900 Web: wirtzinsurance.com	Chicago	IL	60611	312-943-7000		185
Wirtz Mfg Company Inc 1105 24th St PO Box 5006 Web: www.wirtzusa.com	Port Huron	MI	48061	810-987-7600	987-8135	757
WIS International 9265 Sky Park Ct Ste 100 *Fax Area Code: 905 ■ TF: 800-268-6848 ■ Web: w3.wisintl.com	San Diego	CA	92123	858-565-8111	677-1945*	399
Wisco Industries Inc 736 Janesville St TF: 800-999-4726 ■ Web: www.wiscoind.com	Oregon	WI	53575	608-835-3106	835-7399	36
Wisco Products Inc 109 Commercial St TF: 800-367-6570 ■ Web: www.wiscoproducts.com	Dayton	OH	45402	937-228-2101	228-2407	697
Wisco Supply Inc 815 S Saint Vrain St TF: 800-947-2689 ■ Web: www.wiscosupply.com	El Paso	TX	79901	915-544-8294	533-1804	610
Wiscolift Inc W6396 Speciality Dr TF: 800-242-3477 ■ Web: www.wiscolift.com	Greenville	WI	54942	920-757-8832		492
Wisconsin						
Aging & Long Term Care Resources Bureau 1 W Wilson St Rm 518 Web: www.dhs.wisconsin.gov	Madison	WI	53707	608-267-7286	266-5629	339-50
Agriculture Trade & Consumer Protection Dept 2811 Agriculture Dr Web: datcp.wi.gov	Madison	WI	53708	608-224-5012		339-50
Attorney General 17 W Main St PO Box 7857 Web: www.doj.state.wi.us	Madison	WI	53703	608-266-1221	267-2779	339-50
Board of Regents 1220 Linden Dr 1860 Van Hise Hall Web: www.wisconsin.edu/bor	Madison	WI	53706	608-262-2324		339-50
Child Support Bureau 201 E Washington Ave Rm E200 Web: dcf.wisconsin.gov/bcs	Madison	WI	53708	608-421-7550	267-7252	339-50
Children & Family Services Div 201 E Washington Ave Second Fl PO Box 8916 Web: www.dcf.wi.gov	Madison	WI	53708	608-267-3905	266-6836	339-50
Consumer Protection Office 2811 Agriculture Dr PO Box 8911 Web: datcp.wi.gov	Madison	WI	53708	608-224-5012		339-50
Corrections Dept PO Box 7925 PO Box 7925 Web: doc.wi.gov	Madison	WI	53707	608-240-5000	240-3300	339-50
Crime Victims Services Office 17 W Main St PO Box 7857 TF: 800-446-6564 ■ Web: www.doj.state.wi.us	Madison	WI	53703	608-266-1221	264-6368	339-50
Department of Safety & Professional Services 1400 E Washington Ave Rm 112 TF: 877-617-1565 ■ Web: dsps.wi.gov	Madison	WI	53703	608-266-2112	267-0644	339-50
Director of State Courts 16E Capitol Bldg PO Box 1688 Web: www.wicourts.gov	Madison	WI	53701	608-266-6828	267-0980	339-50
Economic Development Div 201 W Washington Ave Web: inwisconsin.com	Madison	WI	53703	608-210-6760		339-50
Emergency Management Div 2400 Wright St PO Box 7865 TF: 800-943-3247 ■ Web: www.emergencymanagement.wi.gov	Madison	WI	53707	608-242-3000	242-3247	339-50
Ethics Board 212 E Washington Ave 3rd Fl TF: 866-868-3947 ■ Web: www.gab.wi.gov	Madison	WI	53707	608-266-8005	267-0500	265
Fisheries Management 101 S Webster St PO Box 7921 TF: 888-936-7463 ■ Web: dnr.wi.gov/topic/Fishing	Madison	WI	53707	608-266-2621	261-4380	339-50
Health Professions Bureau PO Box 8935 PO Box 8935 Web: dsps.wi.gov	Madison	WI	53708	608-266-2112	261-7083	339-50
Health Services Dept 1 W Wilson St Web: www.dhs.wisconsin.gov	Madison	WI	53707	608-266-1865	266-7882	339-50
Historical Society 816 State St Web: www.wisconsinhistory.org	Madison	WI	53706	608-261-9350		339-50
Housing & Economic Development Authority 201 W Washington Ave Ste 700 TF: 800-334-6873 ■ Web: www.wheda.com	Madison	WI	53703	608-266-7884	267-1099	339-50
Insurance Commission 125 S Webster St TF: 800-236-8517 ■ Web: Www.oci.wi.gov/Pages/Homepage.aspx	Madison	WI	53707	608-266-3585	266-9935	339-50
Legislature State Capitol TF: 800-362-9472 ■ Web: legis.wisconsin.gov	Madison	WI	53702	608-266-9960		339-50
Lieutenant Governor 19 E State Capitol PO Box 2043 Web: legis.wisconsin.gov	Madison	WI	53702	608-266-3516	267-3571	339-50
Lottery PO Box 8941 Web: www.wilottery.com	Madison	WI	53708	608-261-4916	264-6644	452
Motor Vehicles Div 4802 Sheboygan Ave Web: www.dot.wisconsin.gov/drivers	Madison	WI	53707	608-264-7447		339-50
Natural Resources Dept 101 S Webster St PO Box 7921 TF: 888-936-7463 ■ Web: dnr.wi.gov	Madison	WI	53707	608-266-2621	261-4380	339-50
Office of Governor PO Box 7863 Web: walker.wi.gov	Madison	WI	53707	608-266-1212	267-8983	339-50
Parks & Recreation Bureau 101 S Webster St PO Box 7921 TF: 888-936-7463 ■ Web: dnr.wi.gov	Madison	WI	53707	608-266-2621	261-4380	339-50
Public Instruction Dept 125 S Webster St PO Box 7841 TF: 800-441-4563 ■ Web: www.dpi.state.wi.us	Madison	WI	53707	608-266-3390	267-1052	339-50
Public Service Commission 610 N Whitney Way TF: 888-816-3831 ■ Web: psc.wi.gov	Madison	WI	53705	608-266-5481	266-3957	339-50
Revenue Dept 2135 Rimrock Rd PO Box 8933 Web: www.dor.state.wi.us	Madison	WI	53708	608-266-6466	266-5718	339-50
Secretary of State 30 W Mifflin Fl 10 Web: www.sos.state.wi.us	Madison	WI	53703	608-266-8888	266-3159	339-50
Securities Div 201 W Washington Ave Ste 500	Madison	WI	53703	608-261-9555		339-50

				Phone	Fax	Class
State Patrol Div 4802 Sheboygan Ave Rm 551 PO Box 7912 *Fax Area Code: 608 ■ *TF:* 844-847-1234 ■ *Web:* www.dot.wisconsin.gov/statepatrol	Madison	WI	53707	844-847-1234	267-4495*	339-50
Supreme Court 110 E Main St Ste 215 PO Box 1688 *Web:* www.wicourts.gov	Madison	WI	53701	608-266-1880	267-0640	339-50
Teacher Education & Licensing Bureau 125 S Webster St *TF:* 800-441-4563 ■ *Web:* www.dpi.state.wi.us	Madison	WI	53703	608-266-3390	264-9558	339-50
Treasurer B41 W State Capitol *Web:* www.ost.state.wi.us	Madison	WI	53701	608-266-1714		339-50
Veterans Affairs Dept 201 W Washington Ave PO Box 7843 *TF:* 800-947-8387 ■ *Web:* www.dva.state.wi.us	Madison	WI	53707	608-266-1311	267-0403	339-50
Vital Records Office 1 W Wilson St *TF:* 800-947-3529 ■ *Web:* www.dhs.wisconsin.gov	Madison	WI	53703	608-266-1865		339-50
Vocational Rehabilitation Div 201 East Washington Ave PO Box 7852 *TF:* 800-442-3477 ■ *Web:* dwd.wisconsin.gov	Madison	WI	53707	608-261-0050	266-1133	339-50
Worker's Compensation Div 201 E Washington Ave *Web:* dwd.wisconsin.gov	Madison	WI	53707	608-266-3131	266-1784	339-50
Workforce Development Dept 201 E Washington Ave *Web:* dwd.wisconsin.gov	Madison	WI	53702	608-266-3131	266-1784	259
Wisconsin Aluminum Foundry Company Inc 838 S 16th St *TF:* 800-251-8824 ■ *Web:* www.wafco.com	Manitowoc	WI	54220	920-682-8286	682-7285	308
Wisconsin Alumni Research Foundation 614 Walnut St 13th Fl *Web:* www.warf.org	Madison	WI	53726	608-263-2500		305
Wisconsin Aviation Inc 1741 River Dr *TF:* 800-657-0761 ■ *Web:* www.wisconsinaviation.com	Watertown	WI	53094	920-261-4567	206-6386	63
Wisconsin Black Historical Society Museum 2620 W Ctr St *Web:* www.wbhsm.org	Milwaukee	WI	53206	414-372-7677	372-4888	520
Wisconsin Box Company Inc 929 Townline Rd *TF:* 800-876-6658 ■ *Web:* www.wisconsinbox.com	Wausau	WI	54402	715-842-2248	842-2240	200
Wisconsin Built Inc 400 Interpane Ln *Web:* www.wisconsin-built.com	Deerfield	WI	53531	608-764-8661		200
Wisconsin Center District 500 W Kilbourn *TF:* 800-745-3000 ■ *Web:* www.wcd.org	Milwaukee	WI	53203	414-908-6000		31
Wisconsin Coach Lines Inc 1520 Arcadian Ave *TF:* 877-324-7767 ■ *Web:* www.coachusa.com	Waukesha	WI	53186	262-542-8861		107
Wisconsin Ctr for Education Research University of Wisconsin Madison 1025 W Johnson St Ste 785 *Web:* www.wcer.wisc.edu	Madison	WI	53706	608-263-4200	263-6448	668
Wisconsin Dells Visitors & Convention Bureau 701 Superior St PO Box 390 *TF:* 800-223-3557 ■ *Web:* www.wisdells.com	Wisconsin Dells	WI	53965	608-254-8088	254-4293	206
Wisconsin Democratic Party 110 King St Ste 203 *Web:* www.wisdems.org	Madison	WI	53703	608-255-5172	255-8919	616-1
Wisconsin Dental Assn 6737 W Washington St Ste 2360 *Fax Area Code: 800 ■ *TF:* 800-364-7646 ■ *Web:* www.wda.org	West Allis	WI	53214	414-276-4520	864-2997*	227
Wisconsin Distributors Inc 900 Progress Way *TF:* 800-295-9543 ■ *Web:* www.wisconsindistributors.com	Sun Prairie	WI	53590	608-834-2337	834-2300	81-3
Wisconsin Educational Communications Board 3319 W Beltline Hwy *TF:* 800-422-9707 ■ *Web:* www.ecb.org	Madison	WI	53713	608-264-9600		632
Wisconsin Electrical Mfg Company Inc (WEM) 2501 S Moorland Rd PO Box 510767 *Web:* www.wemautomation.com	New Berlin	WI	53151	262-782-2340	782-2653	684
Wisconsin Energy Corp 231 W Michigan St *NYSE:* WEC ■ *Web:* www.wecenergygroup.com/message.htm	Milwaukee	WI	53203	414-221-2345		360-5
Wisconsin English as a Second Language Institute 19 N Pinckney St *Web:* www.wesli.com	Madison	WI	53703	608-257-4300	257-4346	423
Wisconsin Evangelical Lutheran Synod (WELS) 2929 N Mayfair Rd *Web:* www.wels.net	Milwaukee	WI	53222	414-256-3888	256-3899	48-20
Wisconsin Film & Bag Inc 3100 E Richmond St *TF:* 800-765-9224 ■ *Web:* www.wifb.com	Shawano	WI	54166	715-524-2565	524-3527	66
Wisconsin Higher Educational Aids Board (HEAB) 131 W Wilson S PO Box 7885 *Web:* www.heab.state.wi.us	Madison	WI	53707	608-267-2206	267-2808	725
Wisconsin Historical Museum 30 N Carroll St *TF:* 888-999-1669 ■ *Web:* historicalmuseum.wisconsinhistory.org	Madison	WI	53703	608-264-6555	264-6575	520
Wisconsin Homes Inc 425 W McMillan St *Web:* www.wisconsinhomesinc.com	Marshfield	WI	54449	715-384-2161	387-3627	106
Wisconsin Hospital Association Inc 5510 Research Park Dr *TF:* 800-782-8581 ■ *Web:* www.wha.org	Fitchburg	WI	53711	608-274-1820		138
Wisconsin Indianhead Technical College						
New Richmond Campus 1019 S Knowles Ave *TF:* 800-243-9482 ■ *Web:* www.witc.edu	New Richmond	WI	54017	715-246-6561	246-2777	800
Rice Lake Campus 1900 College Dr *TF:* 800-243-9482 ■ *Web:* www.witc.edu	Rice Lake	WI	54868	715-234-7082	234-5172	800
Superior Campus 600 N 21 St *TF:* 800-243-9482 ■ *Web:* www.witc.edu	Superior	WI	54880	715-394-6677	394-3771	800
Wisconsin Kenworth 5100 E Pk Ave *Web:* www.csmtruck.com/companies/wisconsin-kenworth	Madison	WI	53718	608-241-5616		57
Wisconsin Library Assn (WLA) 4610 S Biltmore Ln Ste 100 *Web:* wla.memberclicks.net	Madison	WI	53718	608-245-3640		435
Wisconsin Lift Truck Corp 3125 Intertech Dr *TF:* 800-634-9010 ■ *Web:* www.wisconsinlift.com	Brookfield	WI	53045	262-781-8010		358
Wisconsin Lutheran College 8800 W Bluemound Rd *Fax: Admissions ■ *Web:* www.wlc.edu	Milwaukee	WI	53226	414-443-8800	443-8514*	166
Wisconsin Machine Tool Corp 3225 Gateway Rd Ste 100 *TF:* 800-243-3078 ■ *Web:* www.machine-tool.com	Brookfield	WI	53045	262-317-3048	317-3079	455
Wisconsin Management Co 2040 S Park St *Web:* wisconsinmanagement.com	Madison	WI	53713	608-258-2080		652
Wisconsin Manufacturers & Commerce PO Box 352 *TF:* 800-236-5414 ■ *Web:* www.wmc.org	Madison	WI	53701	608-258-3400	258-3413	140
Wisconsin Maritime Museum 75 Maritime Dr *TF:* 866-724-2356 ■ *Web:* www.wisconsinmaritime.org	Manitowoc	WI	54220	920-684-0218	684-0219	520
Wisconsin Metal Products Co 1807 DeKovin Ave *Web:* www.wmpco.com	Racine	WI	53403	262-633-6301		489
Wisconsin National Primate Research Ctr 1220 Capitol Ct *TF:* 800-833-7050 ■ *Web:* www.primate.wisc.edu	Madison	WI	53715	608-263-3500	265-2067	668
Wisconsin Nurses Assn (WNA) 6117 Monona Dr *Web:* www.wisconsinnurses.org	Madison	WI	53716	608-221-0383	221-2788	533
Wisconsin Oven Corp 2675 Main St *TF:* 800-950-8020 ■ *Web:* www.wisoven.com	East Troy	WI	53120	262-642-3938	363-4018	318
Wisconsin Power & Light Co 4902 N Biltmore Ln PO Box 77007 *TF:* 800-255-4268 ■ *Web:* www.alliantenergy.com	Madison	WI	53718	800-255-4268		787
Wisconsin Public Interest Research Group (WISPIRG) 210 N Bassett St Ste 200 *Web:* www.wispirg.org	Madison	WI	53703	608-251-1918		633
Wisconsin Public Radio (WPR) 821 University Ave *Fax Area Code: 608 ■ *TF:* 800-747-7444 ■ *Web:* www.wpr.org	Madison	WI	53706	800-747-7444	263-9763*	632
Wisconsin Public Service Corp PO Box 19001 *Fax Area Code: 920 ■ *Fax: Mktg ■ *TF:* 800-450-7260 ■ *Web:* www.wisconsinpublicservice.com	Green Bay	WI	54307	800-450-7260	433-1527*	787
Wisconsin Public Television (WPT) 821 University Ave *TF:* 800-422-9707 ■ *Web:* www.wpt.org	Madison	WI	53706	608-263-2121	263-9763	632
Wisconsin Realtors Assn 4801 Forest Run Rd Ste 201 *TF:* 800-279-1972 ■ *Web:* www.wra.org	Madison	WI	53704	608-241-2047	241-2901	656
Wisconsin Reinsurance Corp 2810 City View Dr *TF:* 800-939-9473 ■ *Web:* www.thewrcgroup.com	Madison	WI	53707	608-242-4500	242-4514	391-4
Wisconsin Republican Party 148 E Johnson St *Web:* www.wisgop.org	Madison	WI	53703	608-257-4765		616-2
Wisconsin Secure Program Facility 1101 Morrison Dr	Boscobel	WI	53805	608-375-5656		213
Wisconsin Spice Inc 478 Industrial Park Rd *Web:* www.wisconsinspice.com	Berlin	WI	54923	920-361-3555		123
Wisconsin State Fair Park 640 S 84th St *TF:* 800-884-3247 ■ *Web:* www.wistatefair.com	West Allis	WI	53214	414-266-7033	266-7007	520
Wisconsin State Journal 1901 Fish Hatchery Rd *TF:* 800-362-8333 ■ *Web:* host.madison.com	Madison	WI	53713	608-252-6200	252-6445	532-2
Wisconsin State Medical Society 330 E Lakeside St *Fax Area Code: 608 ■ *TF:* 866-442-3800 ■ *Web:* www.wisconsinmedicalsociety.org	Madison	WI	53701	866-442-3800	442-3802*	474
Wisconsin Steel & Tube Corp 1555 N Mayfair Rd *TF:* 800-279-8335 ■ *Web:* www.wisteeltube.com	Milwaukee	WI	53226	414-453-4441	453-0789	492
Wisconsin Thermoset Molding Inc 900 E Vienna Ave *Web:* www.withermoset.com	Milwaukee	WI	53212	414-964-5200		596
Wisconsin Valley Concrete Products Co 603 S Main St *Web:* www.wvic.com	Adams	WI	53910	608-339-6276		182
Wisconsin Veneer & Plywood Inc Railroad St PO Box 140 *Web:* www.bessegroup.com/public/companies/wi_veneer.php	Mattoon	WI	54450	715-489-3611	489-3268	613
Wisconsin Veterans Home N2665 County Rd QQ *TF:* 877-944-6667 ■ *Web:* www.dva.state.wi.us	King	WI	54946	715-258-5586	256-3207	793
Wisconsin Veterans Museum 30 W Mifflin St *Web:* www.wisvetsmuseum.com	Madison	WI	53703	608-264-6086	264-7615	520
Wisconsin Veterinary Medical Assn (WVMA) 2801 Crossroads Dr Ste 1200 *TF:* 888-254-5202 ■ *Web:* www.wvma.org	Madison	WI	53718	608-257-3665	257-8989	795
Wisconsin Web Offset LLC 21045 Enterprise Ave	Brookfield	WI	53045	262-395-2000		627
WISC-TV Ch 3000 (CBS) 7025 Raymond Rd *Web:* www.channel3000.com	Madison	WI	53719	608-271-4321	271-0800	741-80
Wisdom Audio Corp 1572 College Pkwy Ste 164 *Web:* www.wisdomaudio.com	Carson City	NV	89706	775-887-8850	887-8820	52
Wisdom House Retreat & Conference Ctr 229 E Litchfield Rd *Web:* www.wisdomhouse.org	Litchfield	CT	06759	860-567-3163	567-3166	673
Wisdom Infotech Ltd 18650 W Corp Dr Ste 120 *Web:* www.wisdominfotech.com	Brookfield	WI	53045	262-792-0200		180
WisdomTools 501 N Morton St Indiana University Research Pk Ste 206 *Web:* www.wisdomtools.com	Bloomington	IN	47404	812-856-4202		225
Wise Agent, The 13014 N Saguaro Blvd *TF:* 800-874-6500 ■ *Web:* www.thewiseagent.com	Fountain Hills	AZ	85268	480-836-0345		463

	Phone	Fax	Class
Wise Alloys LLC 4805 Second St .... Muscle Shoals AL 35661 *Web:* www.wisealloys.com	256-386-6000		492
Wise Business Forms Inc 555 McFarland 400 Dr .... Alpharetta GA 30004 *TF:* 888-815-9473 ■ *Web:* www.wbf.com	770-442-1060	442-9849	110
Wise Consulting Associates Inc 54 Scott Adam Rd Ste 206 .... Hunt Valley MD 21030 *TF:* 800-654-4550 ■ *Web:* www.wiseconsulting.com	410-628-0100		449
Wise County 200 N Trinity St .... Decatur TX 76234 *Web:* www.co.wise.tx.us	940-627-3351	627-2138	338
Wise County 206 E Main St Ste 223 PO Box 570 .... Wise VA 24293 *Web:* www.wisecounty.org	276-328-2321	328-9780	338
Wise County Chamber of Commerce 765 Pk Ave PO Box 226 .... Norton VA 24273 *Web:* www.wisecountychamber.org	276-679-0961	679-2655	139
Wise Electric Co-op Inc 1900 N Trinity St .... Decatur TX 76234 *TF:* 888-627-9326 ■ *Web:* www.wiseec.com	940-627-2167	626-3060	245
Wise Foods Inc 228 Rasely St Ste 75 .... Berwick PA 18603 *TF:* 888-759-4401 ■ *Web:* www.wisesnacks.com	770-426-5821		296-35
Wise Plastics Technologies Inc 3810 Stern Ave .... Saint Charles IL 60174 *Web:* www.wise-hamlin.com	847-697-2840		454
Wise Recycling LLC 7600 Rolling Mill Rd .... Baltimore NC 27520 *Web:* www.wiserecycling.com	410-285-6900		660
Wise Regional Health System 2000 S FM 51 .... Decatur TX 76234 *TF:* 800-272-3900 ■ *Web:* www.wisehealthsystem.com	940-627-5921		363
Wise Tag & Label Company Inc 1077 Thomas Busch Memorial Hwy .... Pennsauken NJ 08110 *TF:* 800-222-1327 ■ *Web:* www.wisetaglabel.com	856-663-2400	663-8610	413
Wise Technical Marketing Inc 1430 Cherokee Rd .... Louisville KY 40204 *Web:* wisetechnical.com	502-473-8300		195
WISE-AM 1310 (Sports) 1190 Patton Ave .... Asheville NC 28806 *Web:* espnasheville.com	828-259-9695	253-5619	645-9
Wiseco Piston Inc 7201 Industrial Pk Blvd .... Mentor OH 44060 *TF:* 800-321-1364 ■ *Web:* www.wiseco.com	440-951-6600	951-6606	128
WiseSoft LLC IDS Tower80 S Eighth St 9th Floor .... Minneapolis MN 55402 *Web:* www.wise-soft.com	612-568-7259		180
Wisetail 212 S Wallace Ave Ste B2 .... Bozeman MT 59715 *Web:* www.wisetail.com	406-545-4662		387
Wisetek Providers Inc 11211 Waples Mill Rd .... Fairfax VA 22030 *Web:* www.wisepro.com	703-766-8850		225
Wiseway Motor Freight Inc PO Box 838 .... Hudson WI 54016 *TF:* 800-876-1660 ■ *Web:* www.wiseway.com	800-876-1660		780
WISH List 40-E Peninsula Ctr Ste 305 .... Rolling Hills Estates CA 90274 *TF:* 888-310-4504 ■ *Web:* www.thewishlist.org	888-310-4504	310-4504	48-7
Wishart Norris Henninger & Pittman P A 6832 Morrison Blvd .... Charlotte NC 28211	704-364-0010		445
Wishnow Ross Warsavsky & Co 16130 Ventura Blvd .... Encino CA 91436	818-981-2240		2
WISH-TV Ch 8 (CBS) 1950 N Meridian St .... Indianapolis IN 46202 *Web:* www.wishtv.com	317-923-8888	931-2242	741-62
Wisler Pearlstine LLP 460 Norristown Rd Ste 110 .... Blue Bell PA 19422 *TF:* 800-201-3187 ■ *Web:* www.wislerpearlstine.com	610-825-8400		428
Wismarq Corp 930 Armour Rd .... Oconomowoc WI 53066 *Web:* www.wismarq.com	262-567-1112		819
WISN-AM 1130 (N/T) 12100 W Howard Ave .... Milwaukee WI 53228 *Web:* newstalk1130.iheart.com	414-545-8900		645
WISNET.COM 987 S Main St .... Fond Du Lac WI 54935 *TF:* 800-558-4890 ■ *Web:* www.wisnet.com	920-921-8391		180
WISN-TV Ch 12 (ABC) 759 N 19th St .... Milwaukee WI 53233 *Web:* www.wisn.com	414-342-8812	342-7505	741-83
WISP (Women's Independence Scholarship Program Inc) 4900 Randall Pkwy Ste H .... Wilmington NC 28403 *TF:* 866-255-7742 ■ *Web:* www.wispinc.org	910-397-7742	397-0023	305
Wis-Pak Inc 860 W St PO Box 496 .... Watertown WI 53094 *Web:* wis-pak.com	920-262-6300	262-9273	81-2
Wispark LLC 301 W Wisconsin Ave Ste 400 .... Milwaukee WI 53203 *Web:* www.wispark.com	414-274-4600		653
WISPIRG (Wisconsin Public Interest Research Group) 210 N Bassett St Ste 200 .... Madison WI 53703 *Web:* www.wispirg.org	608-251-1918		633
WISS & Company LLP 354 Eisenhower Pkwy .... Livingston NJ 07039 *Web:* www.wiss.com	973-994-9400		734
Wiss Janney Elstner Assoc Inc 330 Pfingsten Rd .... Northbrook IL 60062 *TF:* 800-821-0086 ■ *Web:* www.wje.com	847-272-7400	291-9599	261
Wist Office Products Co 107 W Julie Dr .... Tempe AZ 85283 *TF:* 800-999-9478 ■ *Web:* www.wist.com	480-921-2900	921-2121	535
Wistar Institute 3601 Spruce St .... Philadelphia PA 19104 *TF:* 800-724-6633 ■ *Web:* wistar.org	215-898-3700	898-3715	668
Wistariahurst Museum 238 Cabot St .... Holyoke MA 01040 *Web:* www.wistariahurst.org	413-322-5660	534-2344	50-3
Wisteria 471 N Highland Ave .... Atlanta GA 30307 *Web:* www.wisteria-atlanta.com	404-525-3363	525-3313	671
WIS-TV Ch 10 (NBC) 1111 Bull St .... Columbia SC 29201 *Web:* www.wistv.com	803-799-1010	758-1155	741-33
WITA AM 1490 1300 WWCR Ave .... Nashville TN 37218 *Web:* www.1490wita.com	865-240-4084		645-85
WITF-FM 89.5 (NPR) 4801 Lindle Rd .... Harrisburg PA 17111 *TF:* 800-366-9483 ■ *Web:* www.witf.org	717-704-3000	704-3659	645-71
Witham Memorial Hospital 2605 N Lebanon St .... Lebanon IN 46052 *Web:* witham.org	765-485-8000		374-3
Withers Tool Die & Mfg 1238 Veterans Memorial Hwy SE .... Mableton GA 30126 *Web:* www.witherstool.com	770-940-2544		401
Withlacoochee River Electric Co-op PO Box 278 .... Dade City FL 33526 *Web:* www.wrec.net	352-567-5133		245
Withrow Springs State Park 33424 Spur 23 .... Huntsville AR 72740 *Web:* www.arkansasstateparks.com	479-559-2593		565
WithumSmith+Brown 5 Vaughn Dr .... Princeton NJ 08540 *Web:* www.withum.com	609-520-1188	520-9882	2
WITI (Women in Technology International) 11500 Olympic Blvd Ste 400 .... Los Angeles CA 90064 *TF:* 800-334-9484 ■ *Web:* www.witi.com	818-788-9484	788-9410	49-19
WITI-TV Ch 6 (Fox) 9001 N Green Bay Rd .... Milwaukee WI 53209 **Fax:* News Rm ■ *Web:* www.fox6now.com	414-355-6666	586-2141*	741-83
WITL-FM 100.7 (Ctry) 3420 Pine Tree Rd .... Lansing MI 48911 *Web:* www.witl.com	517-394-7272		645-87
Witmer's Inc 39821 SR-14 .... Salem OH 44460 *TF:* 888-427-6025 ■ *Web:* www.witmersinc.com	330-427-2147	427-2611	274
Witt Industries Inc 4600 Mason-Montgomery Rd .... Mason OH 45040 **Fax Area Code:* 877 ■ *TF:* 800-543-7417 ■ *Web:* www.witt.com	800-543-7417	891-8200*	661
Witt Lincoln 588 Camino Del Rio N .... San Diego CA 92108 *TF:* 877-937-3301 ■ *Web:* wittlincoln.com	619-358-5000	358-5008	57
Witt Printing Company Inc 301 Oak St .... El Dorado Springs MO 64744 *TF:* 800-641-4342 ■ *Web:* www.wittprinting.com	417-876-4721	876-4794	110
Witt Sign Company Inc 306 McCowan Dr .... Lebanon TN 37087 *TF:* 800-438-7325 ■ *Web:* wittsigns.com	615-444-3898	444-3980	8
Witt/Kieffer Ford Hadelman & Lloyd 2015 Spring Rd Ste 510 .... Oak Brook IL 60523 *TF:* 888-281-1370 ■ *Web:* www.wittkieffer.com	630-990-1370	990-1382	266
Witte Company Inc 507 Rt 31 S PO Box 47 .... Washington NJ 07882 *Web:* www.witte.com	908-689-6500	537-6806	298
Witte Museum 3801 Broadway St .... San Antonio TX 78209 *Web:* www.wittemuseum.org	210-357-1900	357-1882	520
Wittek Golf Supply Co Inc 300 Bond St .... Elk Grove Village IL 60007 *TF:* 800-869-1800 ■ *Web:* www.wittekgolf.com	847-943-2399	412-9591	710
Wittenberg University 200 W Ward St PO Box 720 .... Springfield OH 45501 **Fax:* Admissions ■ *TF:* 800-677-7558 ■ *Web:* www.wittenberg.edu	937-327-6314	327-6379*	166
Wittenstein Inc 1249 Humbracht Cir .... Bartlett IL 60103 *TF:* 800-426-5480 ■ *Web:* www.wittenstein-us.com	630-540-5300		22
Wittigs Office Interiors Ltd 2013 Broadway St .... San Antonio TX 78215 *Web:* www.wittigs.com	210-270-0100		321
WITV-TV Ch 7 (PBS) 1101 Geroge Rogers Blvd .... Columbia SC 29201 *TF:* 800-277-3245 ■ *Web:* www.scetv.org	803-737-3200	737-3476	741
Witzco Trailers Inc 6101 McIntosh Rd .... Sarasota FL 34238 *Web:* www.witzco.com	941-922-5301	924-2402	779
Witzenmann USA LLC 2200 Centerwood Dr .... Warren MI 48091 *TF:* 800-970-7377 ■ *Web:* www.witzenmann-usa.com	586-756-1900		194
WIVB-TV Ch 4 (CBS) 2077 Elmwood Ave .... Buffalo NY 14207 **Fax:* News Rm ■ *TF:* 800-794-3687 ■ *Web:* www.wivb.com	716-874-4410	874-8173*	741-20
WIVK-FM 107.7 (Ctry) 4711 Old Kingston Pike .... Knoxville TN 37919 *TF:* 877-995-9961 ■ *Web:* www.wivk.com	865-588-6511	588-3725	645-85
Wix Filtration Products 1 Wix Way PO Box 1967 .... Gastonia NC 28053 **Fax:* Cust Svc ■ *TF:* 800-533-8008 ■ *Web:* www.wixfilters.com	704-864-6711	864-9277*	60
Wixon Inc 1390 E Bolivar Ave .... Saint Francis WI 53235 *TF:* 800-841-5304 ■ *Web:* www.wixon.com	414-769-3000		296
Wixon Jewelers Inc 9955 Lyndale Ave S .... Minneapolis MN 55420 *TF:* 800-853-7667 ■ *Web:* wixonjewelers.com	952-881-8862		410
Wixson Honey Inc 4937 Lakemont-Himrod Rd .... Dundee NY 14837 *Web:* wixsonhoney.com	607-243-7301		296-24
WIXX-FM 101.1 (CHR) 1420 Bellevue St .... Green Bay WI 54311 *TF:* 800-499-9430 ■ *Web:* www.wixx.com	920-435-3771	321-2300	645-67
WIXY-FM 100.3 (Ctry) 2603 W Bradley Ave .... Champaign IL 61821 *TF:* 800-788-3163 ■ *Web:* www.wixy.com	217-352-4141	352-1256	645-30
WIYY-FM 97.9 (Rock) 3800 Hooper Ave .... Baltimore MD 21211 *Web:* www.98online.com	410-889-0098		645-16
Wizard Computer Services Inc 421 Page St .... Stoughton MA 02072 *Web:* www.wizardcpu.com	781-341-2222		196
Wizard's Cauldron Inc 878 Firetower Rd .... Yanceyville NC 27379 *Web:* www.wizardscauldron.com	336-694-5665		296-37
Wizards of Oztechs Llc, The 2099 Mt Diablo Blvd Ste 203 .... Walnut Creek CA 94596 *TF:* 800-549-0480 ■ *Web:* www.oztechs.com	925-280-7400		809
Wizards of the Coast Inc PO Box 707 .... Renton WA 98057 *TF:* 800-324-6496 ■ *Web:* company.wizards.com	425-226-6500		762
Wizbang Solutions Inc 6747 E 50th Ave .... Commerce CO 80022 *TF:* 800-864-4342 ■ *Web:* www.wizbangsolutions.com	720-974-5623		627
Wizcom Technologies Inc Boston Post Rd W 33 Ste 320 .... Marlborough MA 01752 *TF:* 888-777-0552 ■ *Web:* www.wizcomtech.com	508-251-5388		173-7
Wizdom Systems Inc 1300 Iroquois Ave .... Naperville IL 60563 *Web:* www.wizdom.com	630-357-3000	357-3059	178-1
WIZF-FM 101.1 (Urban) 1 Centennial Plaza 705 Central Ave Ste 200 .... Cincinnati OH 45202 *Web:* wiznation.com	513-679-6000	679-6014	645-37
WIZN-FM 106.7 (Rock) 450 Weaver St .... Winooski VT 05404 *TF:* 888-873-9496 ■ *Web:* www.wizn.com	802-860-2440	862-0786	645-26

				Phone	Fax	Class
Wizsoft Inc 6800 Jericho Tpke Ste 120W *Web:* www.wizsoft.com	Syosset	NY	11791	516-393-5841	393-5842	178-10
WJ Beal Botanical Garden 412 Olds Hall Michigan State University *Web:* www.cpa.msu.edu	East Lansing	MI	48824	517-355-9582	432-1090	97
WJ Egli Company Inc 205 E Columbia St	Alliance	OH	44601	330-823-3666		286
WJ Hayes State Park 1220 Wampler's Lake Rd. *Web:* www.michigandnr.com	Onsted	MI	49265	517-467-7401		565
WJA (World Jurist Assn) 7910 Woodmont Ave Ste 1440 *Web:* www.worldjurist.org	Bethesda	MD	20814	202-466-5428		49-10
Wjac-Tv 49 Old Hickory Ln. *Web:* www.wjactv.com	Johnstown	PA	15905	814-255-7600		116
WJAR-TV Ch 10 (NBC) 23 Kenney Dr *Web:* www.turnto10.com	Cranston	RI	02920	401-455-9100	455-9140	741
WJBK-TV Ch 2 (Fox) PO Box 2000 *Web:* www.fox2detroit.com	Southfield	MI	48037	248-557-2000		741
WJBO-AM 1150 (N/T) 5555 Hilton Ave Ste 500 *Web:* wjbo.iheart.com	Baton Rouge	LA	70808	225-231-1860	231-1879	645-18
WJBR-FM 99.5 (AC) 812 Philadelphia Pk *Web:* www.wjbr.com	Wilmington	DE	19809	302-765-1160		645-176
WJBZ-FM 96.3 (Rel) 7101 Chapman Hwy *TF:* 800-468-4285 ■ *Web:* www.praise963.com	Knoxville	TN	37920	865-577-4885		645-85
WJCL-FM 96.5 (Ctry) 214 Television Cir. *Web:* www.kix96.com	Savannah	GA	31406	912-961-9000	961-7070	645-148
WJCL-TV Ch 22 (ABC) 1375 Chatham Pkwy 3rd Fl. *Web:* www.wjcl.com	Savannah	GA	31405	912-925-0022		741-122
WJCT-FM 89.9 100 Festival Park Ave *Web:* www.wjct.org	Jacksonville	FL	32202	904-353-7770		645-79
WJCT-TV Ch 7 (PBS) 100 Festival Pk Ave. *Web:* www.wjct.org	Jacksonville	FL	32202	904-353-7770		741-64
WJDA-AM 1300 (N/T) 90 Everett Ave *TF:* 800-388-2340 ■ *Web:* www.wjda1300am.com	Chelsea	MA	02150	617-884-4500		645
WJET-AM 1400 (N/T) 1 Boston Store Pl *Web:* www.jetradio1400.com	Erie	PA	16501	814-461-1000	455-1111	645-54
WJET-TV Ch 24 (ABC) 8455 Peach St. *Web:* yourerie.com	Erie	PA	16509	814-864-2400	868-3041	741-44
WJFX-FM 107.9 (CHR) 2000 Lower Huntington Rd. *Web:* www.hot1079online.com	Fort Wayne	IN	46819	260-747-1511		645-63
WJHL-TV Ch 11 (CBS) 338 E Main St. **Fax Area Code: 804* ■ *TF:* 800-861-5255 ■ *Web:* www.wjhl.com	Johnson City	TN	37601	423-926-2151	887-7062*	741-66
WJHM-FM 102 (Urban) 1800 Pembrook Dr Ste 400 *TF:* 800-985-5990 ■ *Web:* 1019ampradio.cbslocal.com	Orlando	FL	32810	407-919-1000	816-9070	645-116
WJIB-AM 740 (AC) 443 Concord Ave *Web:* wjib.org	Cambridge	MA	02138	617-868-7400		645
WJIM-AM 1240 (N/T) 3420 Pine Tree Rd *Web:* www.wjimam.com	Lansing	MI	48911	517-394-7272		645-87
WJIM-FM 97.5 (CHR) 3420 Pine Tree Rd *Web:* www.975now.com	Lansing	MI	48911	517-394-7272		645-87
WJJK-FM 104.5 (CR) 6810 N Shadeland Ave *Web:* www.1045wjjk.com	Indianapolis	IN	46220	317-842-9550		645-77
WJJO-FM 94.1 (Rock) 730 Rayovac Dr *Web:* www.wjjo.com	Madison	WI	53711	608-321-0941		645-96
WJKK-FM 98.7 (AC) 265 Highpoint Dr *Web:* www.mix987.com	Ridgeland	MS	39157	601-956-0102	978-3980	645
WJLA-TV Ch 7 (ABC) 1100 Wilson Blvd *Web:* www.wjla.com	Arlington	VA	22209	703-236-9552		741
WJLD-AM 1400 (Var) 1449 Spaulding Ishkooda Rd *Web:* wjldradio.com	Birmingham	AL	35211	205-942-1776		645-20
WJLF 2925 NW 39th Ave *Web:* www.thejoyfm.com	Gainesville	FL	32605	352-371-1457		645-10
WJLT-FM 105.3 (Oldies) 117 SE Fifth St *Web:* espnevansville.com	Evansville	IN	47708	812-421-1117		645-56
WJMH-FM 102.1 (Urban) 7819 National Service Rd Ste 401 *TF:* 800-948-1409 ■ *Web:* www.102jamz.com	Greensboro	NC	27409	336-605-5200		645
WJMI-FM 99.7 (Urban) 731 S Pear OrchaRd Rd Ste 27 *Web:* www.wjmi.com	Ridgeland	MS	39157	601-957-1300		645
WJMR-FM 98.3 (Urban) 5407 W McKinley Ave. *TF:* 800-782-7983 ■ *Web:* jammin983.com	Milwaukee	WI	53208	414-978-9000	978-9001	645-100
WJMZ-FM 107.3 (Urban) 220 N Main St Ste 402 *TF:* 800-767-1073 ■ *Web:* www.1073jamz.com	Greenville	SC	29601	864-235-1073	370-3403	645-68
WJNO-AM 1290 (N/T) 3071 Continental Dr *Web:* wjno.iheart.com	West Palm Beach	FL	33407	561-616-6600		645-173
WJOD-FM 103.3 (Ctry) 5490 Saratoga Rd *TF:* 800-373-4930 ■ *Web:* www.103wjod.com	Dubuque	IA	52002	563-557-1040		645-50
WJOU-FM 90.1 (Rel) 7000 Adventist Blvd *Web:* www.wjou.org	Huntsville	AL	35896	256-722-9990	837-7918	645-76
WJOY-AM 1230 (Nost) 70 Joy Dr *TF:* 800-554-9890 ■ *Web:* www.wjoy.com	South Burlington	VT	05403	802-658-1230	862-0786	645
WJPT-FM 106.3 (Nost) 20125 S Tamiami Trl. *Web:* sunny1063.com	Estero	FL	33928	239-495-2100		645
WJQK-FM 99.3 (Rel) 425 Centerstone Ct *TF:* 866-931-9936 ■ *Web:* www.jq99.com	Zeeland	MI	49464	616-931-9930	931-1280	645
WJR-AM 760 (N/T) 3011 W Grand Blvd Ste 800 *Web:* www.wjr.com	Detroit	MI	48202	313-875-4440		645-49
WJRR-FM 101.1 (Alt) 2500 Maitland Ctr Pkwy Ste 401 *Web:* wjrr.iheart.com	Maitland	FL	32751	407-916-7800		645
WJSR Jefferson State Community College 2601 Carson Rd *TF:* 800-767-4984 ■ *Web:* www.angelfire.com/music2/wjsr	Birmingham	AL	35215	205-856-7702	815-8499	645-20
WJTV-TV Ch 12 (CBS) 1820 TV Rd. *Web:* www.wjtv.com	Jackson	MS	39204	601-372-6311		741-63
WJW-TV Ch 8 (Fox) 5800 S Marginal Rd *Web:* fox8.com	Cleveland	OH	44103	216-431-8888	391-9559	741-31
WJXA-FM 92.9 (AC) 504 Rosedale Ave. *Web:* www.mix929.com	Nashville	TN	37211	615-737-0929	259-4594	645-108
WJXB-FM 97.5 (AC) 1100 Sharps Ridge Rd *Web:* www.b975.com	Knoxville	TN	37917	865-525-6000	525-2000	645-85
WJXT-TV Ch 4 (Ind) 4 Broadcast Pl **Fax:* News Rm ■ *Web:* www.news4jax.com	Jacksonville	FL	32207	904-399-4000	393-9822*	741-64
WJXX-TV Ch 25 (ABC) 1070 E Adams St *Web:* www.firstcoastnews.com	Jacksonville	FL	32202	904-354-1212		741-64
WJYI-AM 1340 (Rel) 5407 W McKinley Ave. *TF:* 800-256-6102 ■ *Web:* www.joy1340.com	Milwaukee	WI	53208	414-978-9000	978-9001	645-100
WJYS-TV Ch 62 (Ind) 18600 Oak Pk Ave. *TF:* 800-475-1053 ■ *Web:* www.wjys.tv	Tinley Park	IL	60477	708-633-0001		741
WJYY-FM 105.5 (CHR) *NH1 Media Center* 4 Church St *TF:* 888-817-1055 ■ *Web:* wjyy.nh1media.com	Concord	NH	03301	603-230-9000	228-2030	645
WJZ-AM 1300 (N/T) 1423 Clarkview Rd Ste 100 *Web:* baltimore.cbslocal.com	Baltimore	MD	21209	410-481-1057		645-16
WJZD-FM 94.5 (Urban) 10211 Southpark Dr *Web:* www.wjzd.com	Gulfport	MS	39503	228-896-5307	896-5703	645-69
WJZ-TV Ch 13 (CBS) 3725 Malden Ave. *TF:* 800-829-8000 ■ *Web:* baltimore.cbslocal.com	Baltimore	MD	21211	410-466-0013	578-7502	741-11
Wk Dickson & Co Inc 616 Colonnade Dr *Web:* www.wkdickson.com	Charlotte	NC	28205	704-334-5348		194
WK Kellogg Foundation 1 Michigan Ave E *Web:* www.wkkf.org	Battle Creek	MI	49017	269-968-1611	968-0413	305
WK Kellogg Health Sciences Library 5850 College St Sir Charles Tupper Medical Bldg *Web:* libraries.dal.ca	Halifax	NS	B3H4H7	902-494-2458	494-3798	434-1
WKAQ-TV Ch 2 (Tele) PO Box 366222 *Web:* www.telemundopr.com	San Juan	PR	00936	787-758-2222		741-121
WKAR-AM 870 (NPR) 404 Wilson Rd Rm 212. *Web:* www.wkar.org	East Lansing	MI	48824	517-432-9527		645
WKAR-FM 90.5 (NPR) Michigan State University Communication Arts & Sciences Bldg 404 Wilson Rd Rm212 *Web:* www.wkar.org	East Lansing	MI	48824	517-432-9527		645
WKAR-TV Ch 23 (PBS) MSU *TF:* 800-239-5233 ■ *Web:* wkar.org/tv	East Lansing	MI	48824	517-884-4700		741
WKBD-TV Ch 50 (CW) 26905 W 11-Mile Rd *Web:* cwdetroit.cbslocal.com	Southfield	MI	48034	248-355-7000	355-7000	741
WKBN/WYFX 3930 Sunset Blvd *Web:* www.wkbn.com	Youngstown	OH	44512	330-782-1144	782-3504	741-145
WKBN-TV Ch 27 (CBS) 3930 Sunset Blvd *Web:* www.wkbn.com/default.aspx	Youngstown	OH	44512	330-782-1144	782-3504	741-145
WKBU-FM 95.7 (Rock) 400 Poydras St Ste 800 *Web:* www.bayou957.com	New Orleans	LA	70130	504-593-6376		645-110
WKBW-TV Ch 7 (ABC) 7 Broadcast Plaza **Fax:* News Rm ■ *TF:* 888-373-7888 ■ *Web:* www.wkbw.com	Buffalo	NY	14202	716-845-6100	840-7820*	741-20
WKCN-FM 99.3 (Ctry) 1820 Wynnton Rd *TF:* 800-343-0993 ■ *Web:* www.kissin993.com	Columbus	GA	31906	706-327-1217	596-4600	645-41
WKCQ-FM 98.1 (Ctry) 2000 Whittier St *TF:* 800-262-0098 ■ *Web:* www.98fmkcq.com	Saginaw	MI	48601	989-752-8161	752-8102	645
WKDQ-FM 99.5 (Ctry) 117 SE Fifth St *Web:* www.wkdq.com	Evansville	IN	47708	812-425-4226		645-56
Wke Inc 400 N Tustin Ave Ste 275 *Web:* www.wke-inc.com	Santa Ana	CA	92705	714-953-2665		261
WKFS-FM 107.1 (CHR) 8044 Montgomery Rd Ste 650 *Web:* kiss107.iheart.com	Cincinnati	OH	45236	513-686-8300		645-37
WKGM-AM 940 (Rel) PO Box 594. *Web:* reverbnation.com	Morisville	NC	27560	757-357-9546		645
WKIX-FM 102.9 (Oldies) 3012 Highwoods Blvd Ste 201 *Web:* www.kix1029.com	Raleigh	NC	27604	919-860-1029		645-131
WKJV-AM 1380 70 Adams Hill Rd *TF:* 800-809-9558 ■ *Web:* www.wkjv.com	Asheville	NC	28806	828-252-1380	259-9427	645-9
WKKW-FM 97.9 (Ctry) 1251 Earl L Core Rd *TF:* 800-765-8255 ■ *Web:* www.wkkwfm.com	Morgantown	WV	26505	304-296-0029		645-105
WKLB-FM 102.5 (Ctry) 55 Morrissey Blvd *TF:* 888-819-1025 ■ *Web:* country1025.com	Boston	MA	02125	617-822-9600		645-23
WKLH-FM 96.5 (CR) 5407 W McKinley Ave. *Web:* www.wklh.com	Milwaukee	WI	53208	414-978-9000		645-100
WKMC (Willis-Knighton Medical Ctr) 2600 Greenwood Rd *Web:* www.wkhs.com/home.aspx	Shreveport	LA	71103	318-212-4000	212-4195	374-3
WKMG-TV Ch 6 (CBS) 4466 N John Young Pkwy *TF:* 800-435-7352 ■ *Web:* www.clickorlando.com	Orlando	FL	32804	407-521-1200	521-1204	741-95

Listing	City	State	ZIP	Phone	Fax	Class
WKMR (Winter Kloman Motor & Repp SC) 235 N Executive Dr Ste 160 *Web:* www.wkmr.com	Brookfield	WI	53005	262-797-9050	797-8251	49-2
WKNC-FM 88.1 (Rock) 2810 Cates Ave *TF:* 800-700-1094 ■ *Web:* wknc.org	Raleigh	NC	27695	919-515-2401		645-131
WKNO-FM 91.1 (NPR) 7151 Cherry Farms Rd *TF:* 800-766-9566 ■ *Web:* www.wknofm.org	Cordova	TN	38016	901-325-6544	729-8176	645-98
WKNO-TV Ch 10 (PBS) 7151 Cherry Farms Rd *TF:* 877-717-7822 ■ *Web:* www.wkno.org	Cordova	TN	38016	901-729-8765	729-8176	741
WKNR-AM 850 (Sports) 1301 E Ninth St Ste 252 *Web:* www.espn.com	Cleveland	OH	44114	216-583-9901	583-9550	645-38
WKOP-TV Ch 17 (PBS) 1611 E Magnolia Ave *Web:* www.etptv.org	Knoxville	TN	37917	865-595-0220		741-69
WKOW-TV Ch 27 (ABC) 5727 Tokay Blvd *TF:* 800-242-6397 ■ *Web:* www.wkow.com	Madison	WI	53719	608-274-1234	274-9514	741-80
WKPC-TV Ch 15 (PBS) 600 Cooper Dr *TF:* 800-432-0951 ■ *Web:* www.ket.org	Lexington	KY	40502	859-258-7000	258-7399	741
WKPT-AM 1400 (Nost) 222 Commerce St *Web:* www.espntricities.com	Kingsport	TN	37660	423-246-9578	247-9836	645
WKPT-TV Ch 19 (ABC) 222 Commerce St *TF:* 855-646-1390 ■ *Web:* www.wkpttv.com	Kingsport	TN	37660	423-246-9578		741
WKQI-FM 95.5 (CHR) 27675 Halsted Rd *Web:* channel955.iheart.com	Farmington Hills	MI	48331	248-324-5800		645
WKRC-TV Ch 12 (CBS) 1906 Highland Ave *TF:* 877-889-5610 ■ *Web:* www.local12.com	Cincinnati	OH	45219	513-763-5500	421-3820	741-30
WKRG-TV Ch 5 (CBS) 555 Broadcast Dr *TF:* 800-245-2244 ■ *Web:* www.wkrg.com	Mobile	AL	36606	251-479-5555	473-8130	741-85
WKRL-FM 100.9 (Alt) 235 Walton St *Web:* syracuse.krock.com	Syracuse	NY	13202	315-472-9111	472-1888	645-160
WKRN-TV Ch 2 (ABC) 441 Murfreesboro Rd *TF:* 800-222-5555 ■ *Web:* www.wkrn.com	Nashville	TN	37210	615-369-7222	369-7329	741-89
WKRR-FM 92.3 (CR) 192 E Lewis St *TF:* 800-762-5923 ■ *Web:* www.rock92.com	Greensboro	NC	27406	336-274-8042	274-5745	645
WKRZ-FM 98.5 (CHR) 305 Hwy 315 *Web:* www.985krz.com	Pittston	PA	18640	570-883-9800		645
WKSE-FM 98.5 (CHR) 500 Corporate Pkwy Ste 200 *Web:* www.kiss985.com	Amherst	NY	14226	716-843-0600		645
WKSU-FM 89.7 (NPR) 1613 E Summit St *TF:* 800-672-2132 ■ *Web:* www.wksu.org	Kent	OH	44242	330-672-3114		645
WKTO-FM 88.9 (Rel) 900 Old Mission Rd *TF:* 800-349-5075 ■ *Web:* wkto.net	New Smyrna Beach	FL	32168	386-427-1095		645
WKWF-AM 1600 (Sports) 830 Crane Blvd Ste 10 *Web:* www.sportsradio1600.com	Sugarloaf Key	FL	33042	305-296-7511		645-84
WKXC-FM 99.5 (Ctry) 4051 Jimmie Dyess Pkwy *Web:* www.kicks99.com	Augusta	GA	30909	706-396-7000		645-11
WKXW-FM 101.5 (N/T) 109 Walters Ave *TF:* 800-800-7822 ■ *Web:* www.nj1015.com	Trenton	NJ	08638	609-359-5300	359-5301	645-166
WKYC-TV Ch 3 (NBC) 1333 Lakeside Ave E *TF:* 877-790-7370 ■ *Web:* www.wkyc.com	Cleveland	OH	44114	216-344-3333	344-3314	741-31
WKYL-FM 102.1 (NAC) 102 Perkins Bldg 521 Lancaster Ave *TF:* 800-621-8890 ■ *Web:* www.weku.fm	Richmond	KY	40475	800-621-8890		645-89
WKYT-TV Ch 27 (CBS) 2851 Winchester Rd **Fax:* News Rm ■ *Web:* www.wkyt.com	Lexington	KY	40509	859-299-0411	293-1578*	741-73
WKZQ 96.1 New Rock 1016 Ocala St *Web:* www.wkzq.net	Myrtle Beach	SC	29577	843-448-1041	626-5988	645-106
WKZW-FM 94.3 (AC) 4580 Hwy 15 N PO Box 6408 *Web:* www.kz94.com	Laurel	MS	39441	601-649-0095	649-8199	645
WL Gore & Assoc Inc 551 Papermill Rd *TF:* 800-437-8181 ■ *Web:* www.gore.com	Newark	DE	19711	302-738-4880	738-7710	745-2
WL Jenkins Co 1445 Whipple Ave SW *TF:* 800-426-7021 ■ *Web:* www.wljenkinsco.com	Canton	OH	44710	330-477-3407	477-8404	700
W-L Molding Co, The 8212 Shaver Rd *TF:* 800-275-8777 ■ *Web:* www.wlmolding.com	Portage	MI	49024	269-327-3075	323-8416	604
WL Rubottom Company Inc 320 W Lewis St *Web:* wlrubottom.com	Ventura	CA	93001	805-648-6943		321
WLA (Wisconsin Library Assn) 4610 S Biltmore Ln Ste 100 *Web:* wla.memberclicks.net	Madison	WI	53718	608-245-3640		435
WLA Investments Inc 1301 Dove St Ste 1080 *Web:* www.wlainvestments.com	Newport Beach	CA	92660	949-851-2020		205
WLAC-AM 1510 (N/T) 55 Music Sq W *TF:* 800-688-9522 ■ *Web:* wlac.iheart.com	Nashville	TN	37203	615-664-2400	744-4743	645-108
WLAE-TV Ch 32 (PBS) 3330 N Cswy Blvd Ste 345 *Web:* www.wlae.com	Metairie	LA	70002	504-866-7411	840-9838	741
WLAJ-TV Ch 3 (ABC) 5815 S Pennsylvania Ave *Web:* www.wlns.com	Lansing	MI	48911	517-394-5300		741-71
Wlav 60 Monroe Ctr St NW 3rd Fl *Web:* wlav.com	Grand Rapids	MI	49503	616-774-8461	451-3299	645-66
WLBT-TV Ch 3 (NBC) 715 S Jefferson St *TF:* 800-792-6067 ■ *Web:* www.msnewsnow.com	Jackson	MS	39201	601-948-3333	355-7830	741-63
WLBZ-TV Ch 2 (NBC) 329 Mt Hope Ave *TF:* 800-244-6306 ■ *Web:* www.wlbz2.com	Bangor	ME	04401	207-942-4821		741-12
WLC 200 Pronghorn St *TF:* 800-353-8829 ■ *Web:* www.wlcwyo.com	Casper	WY	82601	307-266-2524		41
WLDE-FM 101.7 (Oldies) 347 W Berry St Ste 600 *TF:* 888-450-1017 ■ *Web:* fun1017.com	Fort Wayne	IN	46802	260-423-3676	422-5266	645-63
WLDI-FM 95.5 (CHR) 3071 Continental Dr *TF:* 866-550-9550 ■ *Web:* wild955.iheart.com	West Palm Beach	FL	33407	561-616-6600		645-173
WLGA-TV Ch 66 (CW) 1501 13th Ave *Web:* www.wlgatv.com	Columbus	GA	31901	706-257-6703		741
Wlh Consulting Inc 1417 Capri Ln *Web:* www.wlhconsulting.com	Weston	FL	33326	954-385-0770		196
WLHT-FM 95.7 (AC) 50 Monroe Ave NW Ste 500 *Web:* mychannel957.com	Grand Rapids	MI	49503	616-451-4800		645-66
WLIF-FM 101.9 (AC) 1423 Clarkview Rd Ste 100 *Web:* todays1019.cbslocal.com	Baltimore	MD	21209	410-825-1000		645-16
WLIW-TV Ch 21 (PBS) 825 Eighth Ave *TF:* 800-683-1899 ■ *Web:* www.wliw.org	New York	NY	10019	212-560-8021		741
WLKY-TV Ch 32 (CBS) 1918 Mellwood Ave *Web:* www.wlky.com	Louisville	KY	40206	502-893-3671	896-0725	741-77
WLLL-AM 930 (Rel) PO Box 11375 *TF Cust Svc:* 888-224-9809	Lynchburg	VA	24506	434-385-9555	385-6073	645
WLMB-TV Ch 40 (Ind) 825 Capital Commons Dr *TF:* 800-218-5740 ■ *Web:* www.wlmb.com	Toledo	OH	43615	419-720-9562	720-9563	741-134
WLMG-FM 101.9 (AC) 400 Poydras St Ste 800 *Web:* www.magic1019.com	New Orleans	LA	70130	504-593-6376		645-110
WLNE-TV Ch 6 (ABC) 10 Orms St *Web:* www.abc6.com	Providence	RI	02904	401-453-8000	331-4431	741-104
WLNS-TV Ch 6 (CBS) 2820 E Saginaw St *Web:* www.wlns.com	Lansing	MI	48912	517-372-8282	374-7610	741-71
WLNY-TV Ch 55 (Ind) 270 S Service Rd *Web:* newyork.cbslocal.com	Melville	NY	11747	631-777-8855		741
WLNZ-FM 89.7 (Var) 400 N Capitol Ave Ste 001 *Web:* www.lcc.edu	Lansing	MI	48933	517-483-1710		645-87
WLOK-AM 1340 (Rel) 363 S Second St *Web:* www.wlok.com	Memphis	TN	38103	901-527-9565	528-0335	645-98
WLOS-TV Ch 13 (ABC) 110 Technology Dr **Fax Area Code:* 410 ■ *TF:* 800-419-6356 ■ *Web:* www.wlos.com	Asheville	NC	28803	828-684-1340	568-1691*	741-6
WLOX-TV Ch 13 (ABC) 208 Debuys Rd *Web:* www.wlox.com	Biloxi	MS	39531	228-896-1313		741
WLPB-TV Ch 27 (PBS) 7733 Perkins Rd *TF:* 800-272-8161 ■ *Web:* www.lpb.org	Baton Rouge	LA	70810	225-767-5660		741-13
WLRH Huntsville 89.3 FM University of Alabama-Huntsville John Wright Dr *TF:* 800-239-9574 ■ *Web:* www.wlrh.org	Huntsville	AL	35899	256-895-9574		645-76
WLRN-FM 91.3 (NPR) 172 NE 15th St *Web:* www.wlrn.org	Miami	FL	33132	305-995-1717	995-2299	645-99
WLRN-TV Ch 17 (PBS) 172 NE 15th St *TF:* 800-662-2386 ■ *Web:* www.wlrn.org	Miami	FL	33132	305-995-1717	995-2299	741-82
WLRW-FM 94.5 (CHR) 2603 W Bradley Ave *Web:* www.mix945.com	Champaign	IL	61821	217-352-4141	352-1256	645-30
WLS Stamping Co 3292 E 80th St *Web:* www.wlsstamping.com	Cleveland	OH	44104	216-271-5100		488
WLTJ-FM 92.9 (AC) 650 Smithfield St Ste 2200 *Web:* www.q929fm.com	Pittsburgh	PA	15222	412-316-3342	316-3388	645-125
WLTR-FM 91.3 (NPR) 1101 George Rogers Blvd *TF:* 800-922-5437 ■ *Web:* www.scetv.org	Columbia	SC	29201	803-737-3200		645-40
WLTX-TV Ch 19 (CBS) 6027 Garner's Ferry Rd *Web:* www.wltx.com	Columbia	SC	29209	803-776-3600	695-3714	741-33
WLTZ-TV Ch 38 (NBC) 6140 Buena Vista Rd *Web:* www.wltz.com	Columbus	GA	31907	706-561-3838	563-8467	741-34
WLUK-TV Ch 11 (Fox) 787 Lombardi Ave *TF:* 800-242-8067 ■ *Web:* www.fox11online.com	Green Bay	WI	54304	920-494-8711		741-55
WLUM-FM 102.1 (Rock) N72 W12922 Good Hope Rd Good Hope Rd *Web:* www.fm1021milwaukee.com	Menomonee Falls	WI	53051	414-771-1021	771-3036	645
WLUP-FM 97.9 (CR) 222 Merchandise Mart Ste 230 *Web:* www.wlup.com	Chicago	IL	60654	312-245-1200		645-36
WLVQ-FM 96.3 (Rock) 4401 Carriage Hill Ln *Web:* www.qfm96.com	Columbus	OH	43220	614-227-9696		645-42
WLWT-TV Ch 5 (NBC) 1700 Young St *Web:* www.wlwt.com	Cincinnati	OH	45202	513-412-5000		741-30
WLXC-FM 98.5 (Urban) 1301 Gervais St Ste 700 *Web:* www.kiss-1031.com	Columbia	SC	29201	803-796-7600	739-1072	645
WLZN-FM 92.3 (Urban) 544 Mulberry St 5th Fl *Web:* www.blazin923.com	Macon	GA	31201	478-330-6162		645-95
WLZX-FM 99.3 (Rock) 45 Fisher Ave *Web:* www.lazer993.com	East Longmeadow	MA	01028	413-525-4141	525-4334	645
WM Automotive Inc 208 Penland St *Web:* www.wmautomotive.com	Fort Worth	TX	76111	817-834-5559		61
WM Barr & Company Inc PO Box 1879 **Fax Area Code:* 800 ■ *TF:* 800-238-2672 ■ *Web:* www.wmbarr.com	Memphis	TN	38101	901-775-0100	621-9508*	550
WM Brady & Company Inc 22 E 80th St	New York	NY	10075	212-249-7212		42
WM Brode Co 100 Elizabeth St PO Box 299 *Web:* www.wmbrode.com	Newcomerstown	OH	43832	740-498-5121	498-8553	188-4
WM Jordan Company Inc 11010 Jefferson Ave *Web:* www.wmjordan.com	Newport News	VA	23601	757-596-6341		186
WM Keck Ctr for Comparative & Functional Genomics 1201 W Gregory Dr *Web:* www.biotech.uiuc.edu	Urbana	IL	61801	217-244-3930	244-0466	668
WM Keck Foundation 550 S Hope St Ste 2500 *Web:* www.wmkeck.org	Los Angeles	CA	90071	213-680-3833		305

Name / Address	City	State	Zip	Phone	Fax	Class
WM Keck Observatory 65-1120 Mamalahoa Hwy *Web:* www.keckobservatory.org	Kamuela	HI	96743	808-885-7887	885-4464	668
WM Martin Adv Inc 6705 Levelland Rd Ste A *Web:* www.wmmadv.com	Dallas	TX	75252	972-732-8040		4
WM Ohs-Kitchen Showroom 115 Madison St *Web:* www.wmohs.com	Denver	CO	80206	303-321-3232		115
WM Plastics Inc 5151 Bolger Ct *TF:* 800-561-3357 ■ *Web:* www.wmplastics.com	McHenry	IL	60050	815-578-8888		604
Wm S Haynes Company Inc 68 Nonset Path *Web:* wmshaynes.com	Acton	MA	01720	978-268-0600	268-0601	527
WM Smith Securities Inc 1700 Lincoln St Ste 2545 *TF:* 800-757-1175 ■ *Web:* www.wmsmith.com	Denver	CO	80203	303-831-9696		194
WM Software Corp 3660 Ctr Rd Ste 371 *Web:* www.wmsoftware.com	Brunswick	OH	44212	330-558-0501		180
Wm Stukey & Associates LLC 1705 W Northwest Hwy Ste 220 *Web:* www.midcitiescpa.com	Grapevine	TX	76051	817-481-3265		734
Wm Sword & Co Inc 90 Nassau St *Web:* swordrowe.com	Princeton	NJ	08542	609-924-6710		690
Wm T Burnett & Company Inc 1500 Bush St *Web:* www.williamtburnett.com	Baltimore	MD	21230	410-837-3000		601
WMA Consulting Engineers Ltd 815 S Wabash Ave *TF:* 800-393-1826 ■ *Web:* www.wmace.com	Chicago	IL	60605	312-786-4310		261
WMAC-AM 940 (N/T) 544 Mulberry St 5th Fl *Web:* www.wmac-am.com	Macon	GA	31201	478-746-6286		645-95
WMAE-FM 89.5 (NPR) 3825 Ridgewood Rd *TF:* 800-850-4406 ■ *Web:* mpbonline.org	Jackson	MS	39211	601-432-6565		645-78
WMAL-AM 630 (N/T) 4400 Jenifer St NW *Web:* wmal.com	Washington	DC	20015	202-686-3100		645-172
WMAQ-TV Ch 5 (NBC) 454 N Columbus Dr NBC Twr *Web:* www.nbcchicago.com	Chicago	IL	60611	312-836-5555	527-5925	741-29
WMAY-AM 970 (N/T) *Mid-West Family Broadcasting* 1510 N Third St *TF:* 800-328-6550 ■ *Web:* www.wmay.com	Riverton	IL	62561	217-629-7077	629-7952	645-155
WMAZ-TV Ch 13 (CBS) 1314 Gray Hwy *TF:* 800-331-9303 ■ *Web:* www.13wmaz.com	Macon	GA	31211	478-752-1313	752-1331	741-79
WMBD-TV Ch 31 (CBS) 3131 N University St *Web:* www.centralillinoisproud.com	Peoria	IL	61604	309-688-3131	686-8650	741-97
WMBI-FM 90.1 (Rel) 820 N LaSalle Blvd *TF:* 877-376-2194 ■ *Web:* www.moodyradiochicago.fm	Chicago	IL	60610	312-329-4300	329-4468	645-36
WMBM-AM 1490 (Rel) 13242 NW Seventh Ave *TF:* 800-721-9626 ■ *Web:* www.wmbm.com	North Miami	FL	33168	305-769-1100	769-9975	645-99
WMBR-FM 88.1 (Var) 3 Ames St *Web:* www.wmbr.org	Cambridge	MA	02142	617-253-4000		645
WMBS-AM 590 (Oldies) 44 S Mt Vernon Ave *Web:* www.wmbs590.com	Uniontown	PA	15401	724-438-3900	438-2406	645
WMBX-FM 102.3 (Urban) 701 Northpoint Pkwy Ste 500 *TF:* 800-969-1023 ■ *Web:* www.x1023.com	West Palm Beach	FL	33407	800-969-1023		645-173
WMC (Williamson Medical Ctr) 4321 Carothers Pkwy *Web:* www.williamsonmedicalcenter.org	Franklin	TN	37067	615-435-5000		374-3
WMCA (Western Medical Ctr Anaheim) 1025 S Anaheim Blvd *Web:* www.westernmedanaheim.com	Anaheim	CA	92805	714-533-6220		374-3
WMCC (White Mountains Community College) 2020 Riverside Dr *TF:* 800-445-4525 ■ *Web:* www.wmcc.edu	Berlin	NH	03570	603-752-1113	752-6335	162
WMC-TV Ch 5 (NBC) 1960 Union Ave *Web:* wmcactionnews5.com	Memphis	TN	38104	901-726-0555	278-7633	741-81
WMDT-TV Ch 47 (ABC) 202 Downtown Plaza *Web:* www.wmdt.com	Salisbury	MD	21801	410-742-4747	742-5767	741
WME | IMG LLC 1500 S Douglas Rd Ste 230 *Web:* www.wma.com	Coral Gables	FL	33134	305-938-2000	938-2002	731
WME | IMG SPEAKERS 304 Pk Ave S *Web:* wmeimgspeakers.com	New York	NY	10010	212-774-6735		708
WMEE-FM 97.3 (AC) 2915 Maples Rd *Web:* www.wmee.com	Fort Wayne	IN	46816	260-447-5511	447-7546	645-63
WMF (World Monuments Fund) 350 Fifth Ave Ste 2412 *Web:* www.wmf.org	New York	NY	10118	646-424-9594	424-9593	48-4
WMF Americas Inc 3512 Faith Church Rd *TF:* 800-966-3009 ■ *Web:* wmfamericas.com/shop	Indian Trail	NC	28079	704-882-3898	893-2198	361
WMFE 11510 E Colonial Dr *TF:* 800-662-2386 ■ *Web:* www.wmfe.org	Orlando	FL	32817	407-273-2300		738
WMGB-FM 95.1 (CHR) 544 Mulberry St 5th Fl *Web:* www.allthehitsb951.com	Macon	GA	31201	478-646-9510		645-95
WMGK-FM 102.9 (CR) 1 Bala Plaza Ste 339 *TF:* 800-745-3000 ■ *Web:* www.wmgk.com	Bala Cynwyd	PA	19004	610-667-8500		645
WMGM NBC40.Net 1601 New Rd	Linwood	NJ	08221	609-927-4440		741
WMGM-FM 103.7 (CR) 1601 New Rd *Web:* www.1037wmgm.com	Linwood	NJ	08221	609-653-1400	601-0450	645
WMGN-FM 98.1 (AC) 730 Rayovac Dr *Web:* www.magic98.com	Madison	WI	53711	608-273-1000	441-0098	645-96
WMGT-TV Ch 41 (NBC) 301 Poplar St *Web:* 41nbc.com	Macon	GA	31201	478-745-4141	742-2626	741-79
WMH (Wayne Memorial Hospital) 865 S First St *TF:* 800-537-5142 ■ *Web:* www.wmhweb.com	Jesup	GA	31545	912-427-6811		374-3
WMH (Wilcox Memorial Hospital) 3-3420 Kuhio Hwy *TF:* 877-709-9355 ■ *Web:* www.hawaiipacifichealth.org	Lihue	HI	96766	808-245-1100		374-3
WMH (Wayne Memorial Hospital) 601 Pk St *Web:* www.wmh.org	Honesdale	PA	18431	570-253-8100		374-3
WMHI (Winnebago Mental Health Institute) 1300 S Dr *Web:* dhs.wisconsin.gov/mh%5fwinnebago	Winnebago	WI	54985	920-235-4910		374-5
WMHT-TV Ch 17 (PBS) 4 Global View *TF:* 800-662-2386 ■ *Web:* www.wmht.org	Troy	NY	12180	518-880-3400	880-3409	741
WMI (Wildlife Management Institute) 1440 Upper Bermudian Rd **Fax Area Code:* 802 ■ *Web:* www.wildlifemanagementinstitute.org	Gardners	PA	17324	717-677-4480	563-2157*	48-3
WMID-AM 1340 (Nost) 8025 Black Horse Pk Ste 100 *Web:* www.classicoldieswmid.com	West Atlantic City	NJ	08232	609-484-8444	646-6331	645
WMIT-FM 106.9 (Rel) 3 Porters Cove Rd *TF:* 800-330-9648 ■ *Web:* brb.org	Asheville	NC	28805	828-285-8477	298-0117	645
WMJX-FM 106.7 (CHR) 55 Morrissey Blvd *TF:* 800-888-8300 ■ *Web:* www.magic1067.com	Boston	MA	02125	617-822-9600		645-23
WMK & Co 415 Albert St *TF:* 800-541-0788 ■ *Web:* www.wmkco.com	Billings	MT	59101	406-256-3200		492
WMK Inc 810 Moe Dr *TF:* 877-275-4912 ■ *Web:* www.mobilityworks.com	Akron	OH	44310	330-633-1118		57
WMMA (Wood Machinery Manufacturers of America) 2105 Laurel Bush Rd Ste 201 *Web:* www.wmma.org	Bel Air	MD	21015	443-640-1052		49-13
WMME-FM 92.3 (CHR) 56 Western Ave Ste 13 *Web:* www.92moose.fm	Augusta	ME	04330	207-623-4735	626-5948	645-13
WMMO-FM 98.9 (AC) 4192 N John Young Pkwy **Fax Area Code:* 407 ■ *Web:* www.wmmo.com	Orlando	FL	32804	321-281-2000	297-0156*	645-116
WMMPA (Wood Moulding & Millwork Producers Assn) 507 First St *TF:* 800-550-7889 ■ *Web:* www.wmmpa.com	Woodland	CA	95695	530-661-9591	661-9586	49-3
WMMQ-FM 94.9 (CR) 3420 Pine Tree Rd *Web:* www.wmmq.com	Lansing	MI	48911	517-394-7272		645-87
WMMR-FM 93.3 (Rock) 1 Bala Plaza WMMR - Ste 424 *Web:* www.wmmr.com	Bala Cynwyd	PA	19004	610-771-0933	771-0933	645
WMNI-AM 920 (Nost) 1458 Dublin Rd *TF:* 800-896-1669 ■ *Web:* www.wmni.com	Columbus	OH	43215	614-481-7800		645-42
WMOR-TV Ch 32 (Ind) 7201 E Hillsborough Ave *TF:* 800-824-1695 ■ *Web:* www.mor-tv.com	Tampa	FL	33610	813-626-3232	626-1961	741-133
WMPA (Washington Metropolitan Philharmonic Assn) PO Box 120 *Web:* www.wmpamusic.org	Mount Vernon	VA	22121	703-799-8229	360-7391	573-3
WMPI Pty LLC 10 Gilberton Rd	Gilberton	PA	17934	570-874-1602		580
WMPI-FM 105.3 (Ctry) 22 E McClain Ave *TF:* 800-441-1053 ■ *Web:* i1053country.com	Scottsburg	IN	47170	812-752-3688	752-2345	645
WMPV-TV Ch 21 (TBN) 1668 W I-65 Service Rd S *Web:* www.tbn.org	Mobile	AL	36693	251-661-2101		741-85
WMR (Williams Management Resources Inc) 1717 N Naper Blvd Ste 102 *Web:* www.wmrhq.com	Naperville	IL	60563	630-416-1166	416-9798	47
WMSN-TV Ch 47 (Fox) 7847 Big Sky Dr *Web:* www.fox47.com	Madison	WI	53719	608-833-0047		741-80
Wmsvision Inc 1016 Copeland Oaks Dr *TF:* 800-983-7174 ■ *Web:* wmsvision.com	Morrisville	NC	27560	919-863-3388		180
WMTW-TV Ch 8 (ABC) 4 Ledgeview Dr *TF:* 800-248-6397 ■ *Web:* www.wmtw.com	Westbrook	ME	04092	207-835-3888		741
WMU (Woman's Missionary Union) 100 Missionary Ridge *TF:* 800-968-7301 ■ *Web:* www.wmu.com	Birmingham	AL	35242	205-991-8100		48-20
WMUM-FM 89.7 (NPR) 243 Carey Salem Rd *TF:* 800-222-4788 ■ *Web:* www.gpb.org/radio/stations/wmum	Cochran	GA	31014	478-301-5760		645
WMUR-TV Ch 9 (ABC) 100 S Commercial St *Web:* www.wmur.com	Manchester	NH	03101	603-669-9999	641-9005	741
WMUZ-FM 103.5 (Rel) 12300 Radio Pl *Web:* www.wmuz.com	Detroit	MI	48228	313-272-3434	272-5045	645-49
WMXJ-FM 102.7 (Oldies) 20450 NW Second Ave *TF:* 800-924-1027 ■ *Web:* www.thebeachmiami.com	Miami	FL	33169	305-521-5240		645-99
WMXU-FM 106.1 (Urban) 105 Sixth St N Ste 400 *Web:* www.mymix1061.com	Columbus	MS	39701	662-327-1183		645
WMYA-TV Ch 40 (MNT) 33 Villa Rd *Web:* www.my40.tv	Greenville	SC	29615	828-684-1340		741-6
WMYB-FM 92.1 (AC) 1016 Ocala St *Web:* www.energy921.com	Myrtle Beach	SC	29577	843-448-1041		645-106
WMYD-TV Ch 20 (MNT) 20777 W Ten Mile Rd Ste 1220 *TF:* 800-825-0770 ■ *Web:* www.tv20detroit.com	Southfield	MI	48034	248-355-2020		741
WMYT-TV Ch 12 (MNT) 3501 Performance Rd *Web:* www.fox46charlotte.com/about/wmyt	Charlotte	NC	28214	704-398-0046		741-26
WMYV-TV Ch 48 (MNT) 3500 Myer Lee Dr *Web:* www.my48.tv	Winston-Salem	NC	27101	336-722-4545	723-8217	741-144
WMYX-FM 99.1 (AC) 11800 W Grange Ave *Web:* www.991themix.com	Hales Corners	WI	53130	414-529-1250	529-2122	645
WMZQ-FM 98.7 (Ctry) 1801 Rockville Pk *TF:* 800-505-0098 ■ *Web:* wmzq.iheart.com	Rockville	MD	20852	240-747-2700		645
WN (World Neighbors Inc) 4127 NW 122nd St *TF:* 800-242-6387 ■ *Web:* www.wn.org	Oklahoma City	OK	73120	405-752-9700		48-5
WNA (Wisconsin Nurses Assn) 6117 Monona Dr *Web:* www.wisconsinnurses.org	Madison	WI	53716	608-221-0383	221-2788	533
WNBA (Women's National Basketball Assn) 645 Fifth Ave *Web:* www.wnba.com	New York	NY	10022	212-688-9622		714-2

Name / Address	City	State	Zip	Phone	Fax	Class
WNBC-TV Ch 4 (NBC) 30 Rockefeller Plaza *TF:* 866-639-7244 ■ *Web:* www.nbcnewyork.com	New York	NY	10112	212-664-4444		741-91
WNC (Western Nevada Community College) *Douglas* 1680 Bently Pkwy S *TF:* 800-433-3243 ■ *Web:* www.wnc.edu	Minden	NV	89423	775-782-2413	782-2415	162
WNC Pallet & Forest Products Co Inc 1414 Smokey Pk Hwy *Web:* www.wncpallet.com	Candler	NC	28715	828-667-5426		551
WNC Supply LLC 37841 N 16th St *TF:* 800-538-5108 ■ *Web:* www.westnc.com	Phoenix	AZ	85086	623-594-4602	594-3769	628
WNCI-FM 97.9 (CHR) 2323 W Fifth Ave Ste 200 *Web:* wnci.iheart.com	Columbus	OH	43204	614-430-9624	487-2559	645-42
WNCN-TV Ch 17 (NBC) 1205 Front St *Web:* www.wncn.com	Raleigh	NC	27609	919-836-1717		741-105
WNCS-FM 104.7 (AAA) 169 River St *Web:* www.pointfm.com	Montpelier	VT	05602	802-223-2396		645
WNCU-FM 90.7 (NPR) PO Box 19875 *Web:* www.wncu.org	Durham	NC	27707	919-530-7445	530-5031	645-131
WNCW-FM 88.7 (AAA) PO Box 804 *TF:* 800-245-8870 ■ *Web:* www.wncw.org	Spindale	NC	28160	828-287-8000		645
WNCX-FM 98.5 (CR) 1041 Huron Rd *Web:* wncx.cbslocal.com	Cleveland	OH	44115	216-861-0100		645-38
WNCY-FM 100.3 (Ctry) 1420 Bellevue St *TF:* 800-359-1003 ■ *Web:* www.wncy.com	Green Bay	WI	54311	920-435-3771		645-67
WNDE-AM 1260 (Sports) 6161 Fall Creek Rd *Web:* foxsports975.iheart.com	Indianapolis	IN	46220	317-257-7565		645-77
WNDU-TV Ch 16 (NBC) PO Box 1616 *Web:* www.wndu.com	South Bend	IN	46634	574-284-3000	284-3009	741-126
WNDV-FM 92.9 (CHR) 3371 Cleveland Rd Ste 300 *TF:* 800-242-0100 ■ *Web:* www.u93.com	South Bend	IN	46628	574-273-9300	273-9090	645-153
WNED-AM 970 (NPR) 140 Lower Terr *TF:* 800-678-1873 ■ *Web:* www.wned.org	Buffalo	NY	14202	716-845-7000		645-25
WNED-TV Ch 17 (PBS) Horizons Plaza PO Box 1263 *TF:* 800-678-1873 ■ *Web:* www.wned.org	Buffalo	NY	14240	716-845-7000	845-7036	741-20
WNEM-TV Ch 5 (CBS) 107 N Franklin St *TF:* 800-522-9636 ■ *Web:* www.wnem.com	Saginaw	MI	48607	989-755-8191		741
WNEP-TV Ch 16 (ABC) 16 Montage Mtn Rd *TF:* 800-982-4374 ■ *Web:* www.wnep.com	Moosic	PA	18507	570-346-7474		741
WNET PO Box 5776 *TF:* 800-882-6622 ■ *Web:* www.njtvonline.org	Englewood	NJ	07631	609-777-0031		741
WNET-TV Ch 13 (PBS) 450 W 33rd St *TF:* 800-468-9913 ■ *Web:* www.thirteen.org	New York	NY	10001	212-560-1313	560-1314	741-91
WNIC-FM 100.3 (AC) 27675 Halsted Rd *Web:* wnic.iheart.com	Farmington Hills	MI	48331	248-324-5800		645
WNIJ-FM 89.5 (NPR) 801 N First St *Web:* www.northernpublicradio.org	DeKalb	IL	60115	815-753-9000		645
WNIN-FM 88.3 (NPR) 405 Carpenter St *TF:* 855-888-9646 ■ *Web:* www.wnin.org	Evansville	IN	47708	812-423-2973	428-7548	645-56
WNIN-TV Ch 9 (PBS) 405 Carpenter St *TF:* 855-888-9646 ■ *Web:* www.wnin.org	Evansville	IN	47708	812-423-2973	428-7548	741-46
WNIR-FM 100.1 (N/T) PO Box 2170 *Web:* www.wnir.com	Akron	OH	44309	330-673-2323	673-0301	645-2
WNIT Public Television 300 W Jefferson Blvd PO Box 7034 *TF:* 877-411-3662 ■ *Web:* www.wnit.org	South Bend	IN	46601	574-675-9648	289-3441	741-126
WNIU-FM 90.5 (Clas) 801 N First St *Web:* www.northernpublicradio.org	DeKalb	IL	60115	815-753-9000		645
WNJU-TV Ch 47 (Tele) 2200 Fletcher Ave 6th Fl *TF:* 877-478-3536 ■ *Web:* www.telemundo47.com	Fort Lee	NJ	07024	877-478-3536		741
WNKU-FM 105.9 (Ctry) 301 Landrum Academic Ctr *TF:* 855-897-7897 ■ *Web:* www.wnku.org	Highland Heights	KY	41099	859-572-6500		645
WNNF-FM 94.1 (AC) 4805 Montgomery Rd Ste 300 *Web:* nashfm941.com	Cincinnati	OH	45212	513-241-9898	241-6689	645-37
WNNK-FM 104.1 (AC) 2300 Vartan Way *Web:* www.wink104.com	Harrisburg	PA	17110	717-238-1041		645-71
WNNZ-AM 640 (NPR) 131 County Cir *Web:* nepr.net	Amherst	MA	01003	413-735-6600		645-156
WNOG-AM 1270 (N/T) 2824 Palm Beach Blvd *Web:* www.tunein.com/radio/WNOG-1270-s21511	Fort Myers	FL	33916	239-338-4326		645
WNOK-FM 104.7 (CHR) 316 Greystone Blvd *Web:* wnok.iheart.com	Columbia	SC	29210	803-343-1100		645-40
WNOL-TV Ch 38 (CW) 1 Galeria Blvd Ste 850 *Web:* wgno.com	Metairie	LA	70001	504-525-3838		741
WNOR-FM 98.7 (Rock) 870 Greenbrier Cir Ste 399 *Web:* www.fm99.com	Chesapeake	VA	23320	757-366-9900	366-0022	645
WNPA (Western National Parks Assn) 12880 N Vistoso Village Dr *Web:* www.wnpa.org	Tucson	AZ	85755	520-622-1999		48-23
WNPRC (Washington National Primate Research Ctr) 1705 NE Pacific St PO Box 357330 *Web:* www.wanprc.org	Seattle	WA	98195	206-543-0440	616-6771	668
WNPT-TV Ch 8 (PBS) 161 Rains Ave *Web:* www.wnpt.org	Nashville	TN	37203	615-259-9325	248-6120	741-89
WNSP-FM 105.5 (Sports) 1100 Dauphin St Ste E *Web:* www.wnsp.com	Mobile	AL	36604	251-438-5460		645-102
WNST-AM 1570 (Sports) 1550 Hart Rd *Web:* www.wnst.net	Towson	MD	21286	410-821-9678		645
WNTQ-FM 93.1 1064 James St *Web:* www.93q.com	Syracuse	NY	13203	315-472-0200	478-5625	645-160
WNTR-FM 107.9 (AC) 9245 N Meridian St Ste 300 *Web:* www.indysmix.com	Indianapolis	IN	46260	317-816-4000	816-4035	645-77
WNUE-FM 98.1 (Span) 523 Douglas Ave *Web:* www.salsa981.com	Altamonte Springs	FL	32714	407-774-2626		645
WNWO-TV Ch 24 (NBC) 300 S Byrne Rd *Web:* nbc24.com	Toledo	OH	43615	419-535-0024	535-8936	741-134
WNWV-FM 107.3 (NAC) 6133 Rockside Rd Ste 102 *Web:* 1073thewave.net	Independence	OH	44131	216-828-1073		645
WNYC-AM 820 (NPR) 160 Varick St 7th Fl *Web:* www.wnyc.org	New York	NY	10013	646-829-4400		645-111
WNYC-FM 93.9 (NPR) 160 Varick St 8th Fl *Web:* www.wnyc.org	New York	NY	10013	646-829-4400		645-111
WNYO-TV Ch 49 (MNT) 699 Hertel Ave Ste 100 *TF:* 800-349-5075 ■ *Web:* www.mytvbuffalo.com	Buffalo	NY	14207	716-447-3200	875-4919	741-20
WNYS-TV Ch 43 (MNT) 1000 James St *Web:* foxsyracuse.com	Syracuse	NY	13203	315-472-6800	471-8889	741-131
WNYT-TV Ch 13 (NBC) 715 N Pearl St *TF:* 800-999-9698 ■ *Web:* www.wnyt.com	Albany	NY	12204	518-436-4791	434-0659	741-2
WNYW-TV Ch 5 (Fox) 205 E 67th St *Web:* www.fox5ny.com	New York	NY	10065	212-452-5500		741-91
WO Grubb Steel Erection Inc 5120 Jefferson Davis Hwy *TF:* 866-964-7822 ■ *Web:* www.wogrubb.com	Richmond	VA	23234	804-271-9471	271-2539	189-14
Wo Stinson & Son Ltd 4726 Bank St *TF:* 800-267-9714 ■ *Web:* www.wostinson.com	Ottawa	ON	K1T3W7	613-822-7400		316
WOAI-AM 1200 (N/T) 6222 IH-10 *TF:* 800-383-9624 ■ *Web:* woai.iheart.com	San Antonio	TX	78201	210-736-9700	832-3149	645-143
Woburn Foreign Motors Inc 80-82 Olympia Ave *Web:* www.wfab.com	Woburn	MA	01801	781-935-3040	938-0225	516
Woburn Public Library 45 Pleasant St *TF:* 800-392-6089 ■ *Web:* www.woburnpubliclibrary.org	Woburn	MA	01801	781-933-0148		434-3
WOCCU (World Council of Credit Unions Inc) 5710 Mineral Pt Rd *Web:* www.woccu.org	Madison	WI	53705	608-395-2000	395-2001	49-2
WOCL-FM 105.9 (Rock) 1800 Pembrook Dr Ste 400 **Fax Area Code:* 352 ■ *TF:* 877-919-1059 ■ *Web:* 1059sunnyfm.cbslocal.com	Orlando	FL	32810	407-919-1000	787-4839*	645-116
WOCM-FM 98.1 (AAA) Irie Radio 117 W 49th St *Web:* ocean98.com	Ocean City	MD	21842	410-723-3683		645-113
WOCN (Wound Ostomy & Continence Nurses Society) 1120 Rt 73 Ste 200 *TF:* 888-224-9626 ■ *Web:* www.wocn.org	Mount Laurel	NJ	08054	888-224-9626		49-8
WODE-FM 99.9 107 Paxinosa Rd W *TF:* 800-733-2767 ■ *Web:* www.999thehawk.com	Easton	PA	18040	610-258-6155	253-3384	645
Woeber Mustard Manufacturing Co 1966 Commerce Cir PO Box 388 **Fax Area Code:* 937 ■ *TF:* 800-548-2929 ■ *Web:* www.woebermustard.com	Springfield	OH	45501	800-548-2929	323-1679*	297-8
Woelco Labeling Solutions Inc 107 Infield Ct *TF:* 800-326-6206 ■ *Web:* www.woelco.com	Mooresville	NC	28117	704-664-1027		627
Wofford College 429 N Church St **Fax:* Admissions ■ *Web:* www.wofford.edu	Spartanburg	SC	29303	864-597-4000	597-4149*	166
WOFL-TV Ch 35 (Fox) 35 Skyline Dr *Web:* www.fox35orlando.com	Lake Mary	FL	32746	407-644-3535		741
WOG LLC 23 S Harrison St *Web:* www.whiteoak-group.com	Easton	MD	21601	410-690-3511		196
WOGB-FM 103.1 (AC) 810 Victoria St *TF:* 800-236-3771 ■ *Web:* www.wogb.fm	Green Bay	WI	54302	920-468-4100	468-0250	645-67
WOGL-FM 98.1 (Oldies) 555 E City Ave Ste 330 *TF:* 800-942-8998 ■ *Web:* wogl.cbslocal.com	Bala Cynwyd	PA	19004	800-942-8998		645
WOHC (West Oakland Health Council Inc) 700 Adeline St *Web:* www.wohc.org	Oakland	CA	94607	510-835-9610		353
Wohlsen Construction Co 548 Steel Way PO Box 7066 *Web:* www.wohlsenconstruction.com	Lancaster	PA	17604	717-299-2500	299-3419	187
WOI-TV Ch 5 (ABC) 3903 Westown Pkwy *TF:* 800-858-5555 ■ *Web:* weareiowa.com/home	West Des Moines	IA	50266	515-457-9645		741
Wojan Window & Door Corp 217 Stover Rd *TF:* 800-632-9827 ■ *Web:* www.wojan.com	Charlevoix	MI	49720	231-547-2931		480
Wojanis Inc 1001 Montour W Ind Pk *TF:* 800-345-9024 ■ *Web:* www.wojanis.com	Coraopolis	PA	15108	724-695-1415		358
Wojtalewicz Law Firm Ltd 139 N Miles St *Web:* wojtalewiczlawfirm.com	Appleton	MN	56208	320-289-2363		428
Wojteczko Snyder Group PC 5583 S Prince St *Web:* wsgroupcc.com	Littleton	CO	80120	303-730-7999		2
WOKO-FM 98.9 (Ctry) 70 Joy Dr *TF:* 800-354-9890 ■ *Web:* www.woko.com	South Burlington	VT	05403	802-862-9890	862-0786	645
WOKQ-FM 97.5 (Ctry) 292 Middle Rd PO Box 576 *TF:* 877-975-1037 ■ *Web:* www.wokq.com	Dover	NH	03821	603-749-9750		645
WOKV-AM 690 (N/T) 8000 Belfort Pkwy Ste 100 *Web:* www.wokv.com	Jacksonville	FL	32256	904-245-8500	245-8501	645-79
Wold Oil Properties Inc 139 W Second St Ste 200 *Web:* www.woldoil.com	Casper	WY	82601	307-265-7252		258
Woldumar Nature Ctr 5739 Old Lansing Rd *Web:* www.woldumar.org	Lansing	MI	48917	517-322-0030	322-9394	50-5
Wolf Colorprint Inc 111 Holmes Rd	Newington	CT	06111	860-666-1200		174
Wolf Consulting Inc 3875 Franklin Towne Court Ste 110 *Web:* www.wolfconsulting.com	Murrysville	PA	15668	724-325-2900		196
Wolf Creek Inn State Heritage Site PO Box 6 *TF:* 800-551-6949 ■ *Web:* www.oregonstateparks.org	Wolf Creek	OR	97497	541-866-2474		565

Name / Address	City	State	Zip	Phone	Fax	Class
Wolf Creek State Park 1837 N Wolf Creek Rd PO Box 99	Windsor	IL	45669	217-459-2831		565
Wolf Furniture Inc 1620 N Tuckahoe St *Web:* www.wolffurniture.com	Bellwood	PA	16617	814-742-4380		321
Wolf Gordon Inc 33-00 47th Ave **Fax Area Code:* 718 ■ *TF:* 800-347-0550 ■ *Web:* www.wolfgordon.com	Long Island	NY	11101	800-347-0550	361-1090*	550
Wolf Manufacturing Co 1801 W Waco Dr PO Box 3100 **Fax Area Code:* 257 ■ *TF:* 800-437-0940 ■ *Web:* www.wolfmfg.com	Waco	TX	76707	254-753-7301	753-8919*	155-3
Wolf Organization, The 20 W Market St *TF:* 800-388-9653 ■ *Web:* www.wolforg.net	York	PA	17401	800-388-9653		200
Wolf Printing 1200 Haines Rd *Web:* www.wolfprinting.com	York	PA	17402	717-755-1560		627
Wolf Ridge Ski Resort 578 Vly View Cir *TF:* 800-817-4111 ■ *Web:* www.skiwolfridgenc.com	Mars Hill	NC	28754	828-689-4111	689-9819	669
Wolf Robotics LLC 4600 Innovation Dr *TF:* 866-965-3911 ■ *Web:* www.wolfrobotics.com	Fort Collins	CO	80525	970-225-7600		491
Wolf Run State Park 16170 Wolf Run Rd *Web:* www.ohiodnr.com	Caldwell	OH	43724	740-732-5035		565
Wolf Technology Group Inc 1 Chick Springs Rd Ste 112 *Web:* www.wolftg.com	Greenville	SC	29609	864-248-6316		175
Wolf Tesar & Company PC 1415 Valle Vista	Pekin	IL	61554	309-346-4106		2
Wolf Tom (D) Main Capitol Bldg Rm 225	Harrisburg	PA	17120	717-787-2500	772-8284	343
TF: 800-692-7462 ■ *Web:* governor.pa.gov						
Wolf Trap Foundation for the Performing Arts 1645 Trap Rd *TF:* 877-965-3872 ■ *Web:* www.wolftrap.org	Vienna	VA	22182	703-255-1900	255-4077	572
Wolf Trap National Park for the Performing Arts 1551 Trap Rd *Web:* www.nps.gov/wotr	Vienna	VA	22182	703-255-1800	255-1971	564
Wolf Tree Experts Inc 3310 Greenway Dr *TF:* 800-231-1113 ■ *Web:* www.wolftreeinc.com	Knoxville	TN	37918	865-687-3400		776
Wolf X-Ray Corp 100 W Industry Ct *TF Cust Svc:* 800-356-9729 ■ *Web:* www.wolfxray.com	Deer Park	NY	11729	631-242-9729		382
Wolf's Bar-B-Q Restaurant 6600 N First Ave *Web:* www.wolfsbarbq.com	Evansville	IN	47710	812-424-8891		671
Wolfberg Alvarez & Partners 3225 Aviation Ave Ste 400 *Web:* www.wolfbergalvarez.com	Miami	FL	33133	305-666-5474	666-4994	261
Wolfchase Galleria 2760 N Germantown Pkwy *Web:* www.simon.com	Memphis	TN	38133	901-381-2769		460
Wolfe & Co 99 High St *TF:* 800-872-3473 ■ *Web:* www.wolfandco.com	Boston	MA	02110	617-439-9700		734
Wolfe & Hurst Bond Brokers Inc 30 Montgomery St Ste 1040 *Web:* www.wolfehurstbbi.com	Jersey City	NJ	07302	201-938-0400		690
Wolfe County 20 N Washington St PO Box 146 *Web:* wolfe.ca.uky.edu	Campton	KY	41301	606-668-3515	668-3732	338
Wolfe Diversified Industries LLC 223 W Ninth St *Web:* www.wolfediversifiedindustries.com	Anderson	IN	46016	765-683-9374		177
Wolfe Dye & Bleach Works Inc 25 Ridge Rd *Web:* www.wolfedyeandbleachworks.com	Shoemakersville	PA	19555	610-562-7639		745-7
Wolfe Industrial Auctions Inc 9801 Hansonville Rd *TF:* 800-443-9580 ■ *Web:* wolfeauctions.com	Frederick	MD	21702	301-898-0340		41
Wolfe Jones Boswell & Wolfe Hancock & Daniel LLC 905 Bob Wallace Ave SW *TF:* 800-955-1722 ■ *Web:* www.wjb-law.com	Huntsville	AL	35801	256-534-2205		428
Wolfe's Neck Woods State Park 426 Wolfe's Neck Rd *Web:* www.maine.gov	Freeport	ME	04032	207-865-4465		565
Wolfeboro Camp School 93 Camp School Rd *Web:* www.wolfeboro.org	Wolfeboro	NH	03894	603-569-3451		622
Wolferman's 2500 S Pacific Hwy PO Box 9100 *TF:* 800-999-0169 ■ *Web:* www.wolfermans.com	Medford	OR	97501	800-999-0169	999-7548	296-1
Wolff Bros Supply Inc 6078 Wolff Rd *TF:* 800-562-0721 ■ *Web:* www.wolffbros.com	Medina	OH	44256	330-725-3451		612
Wolff Group Inc 525 Ottawa Ave NW *TF:* 800-477-7210 ■ *Web:* www.wolffgroupinc.com	Grand Rapids	MI	49503	616-458-1449		463
Wolff r L & Associates 2138 Richmond Ave *Web:* rlwolff.com	Houston	TX	77098	713-523-2655		721
Wolfgang Candy Co 50 E Fourth Ave *TF:* 800-248-4273 ■ *Web:* www.wolfgangcandy.com	York	PA	17404	717-843-5536	845-2881	296-8
WOLFGANG PUCK 3500 Las Vegas Blvd S Ste G1 *Web:* www.wolfgangpuck.com	Las Vegas	NV	89109	702-369-6300		671
Wolfgang Puck Worldwide Inc 100 N Crescent Dr Ste 100 *Web:* www.wolfgangpuck.com	Beverly Hills	CA	90210	310-432-1500		670
Wolfgang Puck's Bar & Grill 3799 Las Vegas Blvd S *Web:* www.wolfgangpuck.com	Las Vegas	NV	89109	702-891-3000		671
Wolfgang's Steakhouse 4 Pk Ave *Web:* www.wolfgangssteakhouse.net	New York	NY	10016	212-889-3369		671
Wolfpack Sports Marketing PO Box 37100 Ste 475 *Web:* www.gopack.com	Raleigh	NC	27607	919-831-9653		717
Wolfram Alpha LLC 100 Trade Ctr Dr *Web:* www.wolframalpha.com	Champaign	IL	61820	217-398-0700		387
Wolfram Research Inc 100 Trade Ctr Dr *TF:* 800-965-3726 ■ *Web:* www.wolfram.com	Champaign	IL	61820	217-398-0700	398-0747	177
Wolfsen Inc 1269 W 'I' St *TF:* 800-852-9223 ■ *Web:* wolfseninc.com	Los Banos	CA	93635	209-827-7700	827-7780	10-11
Wolfson Casing Corp 700 S Fulton Ave *Web:* www.wolfsoncasing.com	Mount Vernon	NY	10550	914-668-9000		805
Wolfson Children's Hospital 800 Prudential Dr *Web:* www.wolfsonchildrens.org	Jacksonville	FL	32207	904-202-8000		374-1
Wolfsonian Museum 1001 Washington Ave *Web:* www.wolfsonian.org	Miami Beach	FL	33139	305-531-1001	531-2133	520
Wolf-tec Inc 20 Kieffer Ln *TF:* 800-257-4627 ■ *Web:* www.wolf-tec.com	Kingston	NY	12401	845-340-9727		296
Wolgast Corp 4835 Towne Centre Rd Ste 203 *Web:* www.wolgastcorporation.com	Saginaw	MI	48604	989-790-9120		194
Wolk Law Firm, The 1712 Locust St *Web:* airlaw.com	Philadelphia	PA	19103	215-545-4220		428
Wollaston Alloys Inc 205 Wood Rd *Web:* www.wollastonalloys.com	Braintree	MA	02184	781-848-3333	848-3993	307
Wolseley Canada Inc 880 Laurentian Dr *TF:* 800-282-1376 ■ *Web:* www.wolseleyinc.ca	Burlington	ON	L7N3V6	905-335-7373		111
Wolters Kluwer Financial Services Inc 100 S Fifth St Ste 700 *TF:* 800-552-9408 ■ *Web:* www.wolterskluwerfs.com	Minneapolis	MN	55402	612-656-7700		178-10
Wolverine Advanced Materials 201 Industrial Park Rd *Web:* www.wamglobal.com	Blacksburg	VA	24060	540-552-7674		326
Wolverine Bldg Group Inc 4045 Barden SE *Web:* www.wolvgroup.com	Grand Rapids	MI	49512	616-949-3360		186
Wolverine Brass Inc 2951 Hwy 501 E **Fax Area Code:* 800 ■ *Web:* www.wolverinebrass.com	Conway	SC	29526	843-347-3121	945-9292*	612
Wolverine Bronze Co 28178 Hayes Rd **Fax:* Sales ■ *Web:* www.wolverinebronze.com	Roseville	MI	48066	586-776-8180	776-4510*	308
Wolverine Coil Spring Co 818 Front Ave NW *Web:* www.wolverinecoilspring.com	Grand Rapids	MI	49504	616-459-3504		350
Wolverine Corp 3600 Tennis Ct *Web:* www.wms-inc.com	Saint Joseph	MI	49085	269-429-6600	429-6657	488
Wolverine Flexographic Mfg Co 20774 Chesley Dr *Web:* wolverineflexo.com	Farmington Hills	MI	48336	248-476-7700		629
Wolverine Mutual Insurance Co 1 Wolverine Way *TF:* 800-733-3320 ■ *Web:* www.wolverinemutual.com	Dowagiac	MI	49047	269-782-3451		390
Wolverine Packing Company Inc 2535 Rivard St *Web:* www.wolverinepacking.com	Detroit	MI	48207	313-259-7500		473
Wolverine Power Systems Inc 3229 80th Ave *TF:* 800-485-8068 ■ *Web:* www.wolverinepower.com	Zeeland	MI	49464	616-879-0040		518
Wolverine Tube Inc 2100 Market St *Web:* www.wlv.com	Decatur	AL	35601	256-353-1310		609
Wolverine World Wide Inc 9341 Courtland Dr NE *Web:* wolverineworldwide.com	Rockford	MI	49351	616-866-5500		301
Wolverton Securities Ltd 777 Dunsmuir St 17th Fl *Web:* www.wolverton.ca	Vancouver	BC	V7Y1J5	604-622-1000	662-5205	690
Womack Electric Supply Co 518 Newton St *Web:* www.womackelectric.com	Danville	VA	24541	434-793-5134	792-8256	246
Womack Steve (Rep R - AR) 2412 Rayburn HOB *Web:* womack.house.gov	Washington	DC	20515	202-225-4301	225-5713	342-2
Woman's Hospital 100 Woman's Wy *TF:* 800-620-8474 ■ *Web:* www.womans.org	Baton Rouge	LA	70815	225-927-1300	924-8110	374-7
Woman's Hospital of Texas 7600 Fannin St *Web:* www.womanshospital.com	Houston	TX	77054	713-790-1234		374-7
Woman's Life Insurance Society 1338 Military St PO Box 5020 *TF:* 800-521-9292 ■ *Web:* www.womanslife.org	Port Huron	MI	48061	810-985-5191	985-6970	391-2
Woman's Missionary Union (WMU) 100 Missionary Ridge *TF:* 800-968-7301 ■ *Web:* www.wmu.com	Birmingham	AL	35242	205-991-8100		48-20
WomanWell 1784 La Crosse Ave	Saint Paul	MN	55119	651-739-7953	739-7475	673
Womble Carlyle Sandridge & Rice PLLC 1 W Fourth St *Web:* www.wcsr.com	Winston-Salem	NC	27101	336-721-3600	721-3660	428
Womble Company Inc 12821 Industrial Rd *Web:* www.wombleco.com	Houston	TX	77015	713-635-8300	635-5209	481
WOMC-FM 104.3 (Oldies) 2201 Woodward Heights *Web:* womc.cbslocal.com	Ferndale	MI	48220	248-327-2900	399-1043	645
Women & Infants Hospital of Rhode Island 101 Dudley St *TF:* 800-711-7011 ■ *Web:* www.womenandinfants.org	Providence	RI	02905	401-274-1100	453-7666	374-7
Women & Their Work 1710 Lavaca St *Web:* www.womenandtheirwork.org	Austin	TX	78701	512-477-1064		520
Women Alive 1566 Burnside Ave *TF:* 800-472-2321 ■ *Web:* www.women-alive.org	Los Angeles	CA	90019	800-472-2321		48-17
Women Employed 65 E Wacker Pl *TF:* 800-522-0925 ■ *Web:* www.womenemployed.org	Chicago	IL	60601	312-782-3902	782-5249	48-24
Women for Sobriety Inc (WFS) PO Box 618 *TF:* 800-548-8854 ■ *Web:* www.womenforsobriety.org	Quakertown	PA	18951	215-536-8026	538-9026	48-21
Women in Cable Telecommunications (WICT) 2000 K St Ste 350 *Web:* www.wict.org	Washington	DC	20006	202-827-4794	450-5596	49-14
Women in Film (WIF) 6100 Wilshire Blvd Ste 710 *Web:* www.wif.org	Los Angeles	CA	90048	323-935-2211		48-4

Phone | Fax | Class

Women in Military Service for America Memorial Foundation Inc
Dept 560 .... Washington DC 20042 703-533-1155 48-19
TF: 800-222-2294 ■ *Web:* www.womensmemorial.org

Women in Technology International (WITI)
11500 Olympic Blvd Ste 400 .... Los Angeles CA 90064 818-788-9484 788-9410 49-19
TF: 800-334-9484 ■ *Web:* www.witi.com

Women in Touch Ministries Wit Inc
1044 W 37th St .... Indianapolis IN 46208 317-925-4177 48-20

Women Lawyers Association of Los Angeles
634 S Spring St Ste 617 .... Los Angeles CA 90014 213-892-8982 138
Web: www.wlala.org

Women Management
199 Lafayette St 7th Fl .... New York NY 10012 212-334-7480 506
TF: 800-838-3006 ■ *Web:* www.womenmanagement.com

Women's & Children's Hospital (WCH)
4600 Ambassador Caffery Pkwy .... Lafayette LA 70508 337-521-9100 374-7
TF: 888-569-8331 ■ *Web:* www.womens-childrens.com

Women's & Children's Hospital of Buffalo
219 Bryant St .... Buffalo NY 14222 716-878-7000 888-3979* 374-1
**Fax:* Admitting ■ *TF:* 800-462-7653 ■ *Web:* www.kaleidahealth.org

Women's Action for New Directions (WAND)
691 Massachusetts Ave .... Arlington MA 02476 781-643-6740 48-5
Web: www.wand.org

Women's Basketball Hall of Fame
700 Hall of Fame Dr .... Knoxville TN 37915 865-633-9000 633-9294 522
Web: www.wbhof.com

Women's Bureau
200 Constitution Ave NW Rm S3002 .... Washington DC 20210 202-693-6710 340-15
TF: 800-827-5335 ■ *Web:* www.dol.gov/wb
US Department of Labor
200 Constitution Ave NW Rm S-3002 .... Dallas TX 20210 202-693-6710 850-4706* 340-15
**Fax Area Code:* 972 ■ *TF:* 800-827-5335 ■ *Web:* www.dol.gov/wb

Women's Bureau Regional Offices
Region 1 JFK Federal Bldg Rm 525-A .... Boston MA 02203 617-565-1988 565-1986 340-15
TF: 800-827-5335 ■ *Web:* www.dol.gov/wb
Region 2 201 Varick St Rm 602 .... New York NY 10014 212-337-2389 337-2394 340-15
TF: 800-827-5335 ■ *Web:* www.dol.gov/wb
Region 3
200 Constitution Ave NW Ste 631E .... Washington DC 20210 866-487-2365 861-4867* 340-15
**Fax Area Code:* 215 ■ *TF:* 800-827-5335 ■ *Web:* www.dol.gov/wb
Region 5
Federal Bldg 230 S Dearborn St Rm 1022 .... Chicago IL 60604 312-353-6985 353-6986 340-15
TF: 800-827-5335 ■ *Web:* www.dol.gov
Region 7 2300 Main St Ste 1050 .... Kansas City MO 64108 816-285-7233 285-7237 340-15
TF: 800-827-5335 ■ *Web:* www.dol.gov
Region 8
1999 Broadway Ste 1620 PO Box 46550 .... Denver CO 80201 303-844-1286 844-1283 340-15
TF: 800-827-5335 ■ *Web:* www.dol.gov/wb
Region 9 90 Seventh St Ste 2650 .... San Francisco CA 94103 415-625-2638 625-2641 340-15
TF: 800-827-5335 ■ *Web:* www.dol.gov
Region 10 1111 Third Ave Ste 620 .... Seattle WA 98101 206-553-1534 553-5085 340-15
TF: 800-827-5335 ■ *Web:* www.dol.gov

Women's Campaign Fund (WCF)
718 Seventh St NW 2nd Fl .... Washington DC 20001 202-796-8259 48-7
Web: www.wcfonline.org

Women's College Coalition (WCC)
PO Box 3983 .... Decatur GA 30031 404-913-9492 49-5
Web: www.womenscolleges.org

Women's Correctional Institution
4450 Broad River Rd .... Columbia SC 29210 803-896-8590 213

Women's Council of REALTORS (WCR)
430 N Michigan Ave .... Chicago IL 60611 800-245-8512 329-3290* 49-17
**Fax Area Code:* 312 ■ *TF:* 800-245-8512 ■ *Web:* www.wcr.org

Women's Economic Agenda Project (WEAP)
160 Franklin St Ste 208 .... Oakland CA 94607 510-986-8620 986-8628 48-24
Web: www.weap.org

Women's Foundation of Colorado, The
The Chambers Ctr 1901 E Asbury Ave .... Denver CO 80208 303-285-2960 305
TF: 800-297-2721 ■ *Web:* www.wfco.org

Women's Health Partnership PC
11595 N Meridian St Ste 110 .... Carmel IN 46032 317-575-7300 575-7333 374-3
Web: www.obgynindiana.com

Women's Hospital of Greensboro
801 Green Valley Rd .... Greensboro NC 27408 336-832-6500 374-3
Web: www.conehealth.com/womens-hospital

Women's Independence Scholarship Program Inc (WISP)
4900 Randall Pkwy Ste H .... Wilmington NC 28403 910-397-7742 397-0023 305
TF: 866-255-7742 ■ *Web:* www.wispinc.org

Women's International Pharmacy Inc
PO Box 6468 .... Madison WI 53716 800-279-5708 279-8011 459
TF: 800-279-5708 ■ *Web:* www.womensinternational.com

Women's Mktg Inc
1221 Post Rd E Ste 201 .... Westport CT 06880 203-256-0880 194
Web: www.womensmarketing.com

Women's National Basketball Assn (WNBA)
645 Fifth Ave .... New York NY 10022 212-688-9622 714-2
Web: www.wnba.com

Women's Rights National Historical Park
136 Fall St .... Seneca Falls NY 13148 315-568-2991 568-2141 564
Web: www.nps.gov/wori

Women's Sports Foundation
1899 Hempstead Tpke
Ste 400 Eisenhower Pk .... East Meadow NY 11554 516-542-4700 542-4716 48-22
TF: 800-227-3988 ■ *Web:* www.womenssportsfoundation.org

Women's Wear Daily Magazine
475 Fifth Ave 3rd Floor .... New York NY 10017 212-213-1900 457-11
TF: 866-401-7801 ■ *Web:* www.wwd.com

Wometco Enterprises Inc
3195 Ponce De Leon Blvd .... Coral Gables FL 33134 305-529-1400 529-1466 748
Web: miamiseaprison.com

Wompatuck State Park 204 Union St .... Hingham MA 02043 781-749-7160 565
Web: www.mass.gov

WOMX-FM 105.1 (AC)
1800 Pembrook Dr Ste 400 .... Orlando FL 32810 407-919-1000 645-116
TF: 877-919-1051 ■ *Web:* mix1051.cbslocal.com

Wonder View Inn & Suites
50 Eden St PO Box 25 .... Bar Harbor ME 04609 207-288-3358 379
TF: 888-439-8439 ■ *Web:* www.wonderviewinn.com

Wonder Web
22777 Lyons Ave Ste 215 .... Santa Clarita CA 91321 661-254-0861 396
Web: wonderwebusa.com

Wonderland Amusement Park
2601 Dumas Dr .... Amarillo TX 79107 806-383-0832 383-8737 32
TF: 800-383-4712 ■ *Web:* www.wonderlandpark.com

Wonderlic Inc
400 Lakeview Pkwy Ste 200 .... Vernon Hills IL 60061 847-680-4900 680-9492 637-10
TF: 877-605-9496 ■ *Web:* www.wonderlic.com

Wonders of Wildlife
500 W Sunshine St .... Springfield MO 65807 417-890-9453 890-9278 823
TF: 888-222-6060 ■ *Web:* www.wondersofwildlife.org

Wondertreats Inc 2200 Lapham Dr .... Modesto CA 95354 209-521-8881 292
Web: www.wondertreats.com

Wonderware Corp
26561 Rancho Pkwy S .... Lake Forest CA 92630 949-727-3200 727-3270 178-10
TF: 800-966-3371 ■ *Web:* software.schneider-electric.com/wonderware

Won-Door Corp
1865 South 3480 West .... Salt Lake City UT 84104 801-973-7500 234
TF: 800-453-8494 ■ *Web:* www.wondoor.com

WONE-FM 97.5 (Rock) 1795 W Market St .... Akron OH 44313 330-869-9800 869-9750 645-2
Web: www.wone.net

Wong & Knowles CPA PC
340 W Butterfield Rd .... Elmhurst IL 60126 630-993-2223 993-2229 2
TF: 866-966-4272 ■ *Web:* www.wongknowles.com

Wong Engineers Inc
4578 Feather River Dr Ste A .... Stockton CA 95219 209-476-0011 261

Wong Fleming PC
821 Alexander Rd Ste 200 .... Princeton NJ 08540 609-951-9520 428
TF: 800-973-1177 ■ *Web:* wongfleming.com

Wonton Food Inc 220-222 Moore St .... Brooklyn NY 11206 718-628-6868 123
Web: www.wontonfood.com

Woo Lae Oak 8240 Leesburg Pk .... Vienna VA 22182 703-827-7300 827-7302 671
Web: www.woolaeoak.com

Wood & Hyde Leather Company Inc
PO Box 786 .... Gloversville NY 12078 518-725-7105 725-5158 432
Web: www.woodandhyde.com

Wood & Tait Inc 64-5249 Kauakea Rd .... Kamuela HI 96743 808-885-5090 630-0500* 400
**Fax Area Code:* 888 ■ *TF:* 800-774-8585 ■ *Web:* www.woodtait.com

Wood Buffalo National Park of Canada
PO Box 750 .... Fort Smith NT X0E0P0 867-872-7900 872-3910 563
Web: www.pc.gc.ca

Wood Consulting Services Inc
8115 Maple Lawn Blvd Ste 375 .... Fulton MD 20759 301-377-5300 261
Web: woodcons.com

Wood County 1 Courthouse Sq .... Bowling Green OH 43402 419-354-9000 338
TF: 866-860-4140 ■ *Web:* www.co.wood.oh.us

Wood County 1 Ct Sq PO Box 1474 .... Parkersburg WV 26102 304-424-1850 338
Web: www.woodcountywv.com

Wood County PO Box 1796 .... Quitman TX 75783 903-763-2711 763-5641 338
TF: 800-253-8014 ■ *Web:* www.mywoodcounty.com

Wood County 400 Market St .... Wisconsin Rapids WI 54495 715-421-0400 421 0000 000
Web: www.co.wood.wi.us

Wood County District Public Library
251 N Main St .... Bowling Green OH 43402 419-352-5104 354-0405 434-3
Web: wcdpl.org

Wood County Electric Co-op Inc
501 S Main St .... Quitman TX 75783 903-763-2203 763-5693 245
TF: 800-762-2203 ■ *Web:* www.wcec.org

Wood County Hospital
950 W Wooster St .... Bowling Green OH 43402 419-354-8900 354-8957 374-3
TF: 800-288-4470 ■ *Web:* www.woodcountyhospital.org

Wood Group 17325 Park Row Ste 500 .... Houston TX 77084 281-828-3500 536
Web: www.woodgroup.com

Wood Group Pratt & Whitney Industrial Turbine Services LLC
1460 Blue Hills Ave PO Box 45 .... Bloomfield CT 06002 860-286-4600 769-7337 386
Web: www.wgpw.com

Wood House Restaurant 1825 N 13th St .... Bismarck ND 58501 701-255-3654 671

Wood Machinery Manufacturers of America (WMMA)
2105 Laurel Bush Rd Ste 201 .... Bel Air MD 21015 443-640-1052 49-13
Web: www.wmma.org

Wood Moulding & Millwork Producers Assn (WMMPA)
507 First St .... Woodland CA 95695 530-661-9591 661-9586 49-3
TF: 800-550-7889 ■ *Web:* www.wmmpa.com

Wood National Cemetery
5000 W National Ave Bldg 1301 .... Milwaukee WI 53295 414-382-5300 382-5321 136
TF: 800-827-1000 ■ *Web:* www.cem.va.gov

Wood Networks 10260 Robinson Dr .... Tyler TX 75703 903-581-0922 180
Web: www.woodnetworks.com

Wood Patel & Assoc Inc
2051 W Northern Ave Ste 100 .... Phoenix AZ 85021 602-335-8500 335-8580 261
Web: www.woodpatel.com

Wood Personnel Services
1139 NW Broad St Ste 107 .... Murfreesboro TN 37129 615-890-8400 260
Web: wpscareers.com

Wood Preservers Inc
15939 Historyland Hwy PO Box 158 .... Warsaw VA 22572 804-333-4022 333-9269 818
TF: 800-368-2536 ■ *Web:* www.woodpreservers.com

Wood Pro Inc
421 Washington St PO Box 363 .... Auburn MA 01501 508-832-3291 751
TF: 800-786-5577 ■ *Web:* www.woodproinc.com

Wood Products Manufacturers Assn (WPMA)
PO Box 761 .... Westminster MA 01473 978-874-5445 874-9946 49-3
TF: 800-878-8878 ■ *Web:* www.wpma.org

Wood Ranch Barbecue & Grill Inc
2835 Townsgate Rd Ste 200 .... Westlake Village CA 91361 805-719-9000 671
Web: www.woodranch.com

Wood Resources LLC
100 Northfield St Ste 203 .... Greenwich CT 06830 203-622-9138 360-3
Web: www.atlasholdingsllc.com

Wood River Technologies Inc
191 Sun Valley Rd Ste 202 .... Ketchum ID 83340 888-661-4094 77
TF: 888-661-4094 ■ *Web:* www.fedmarket.com

Wood Tobe-Coburn School 8 E 40th St .... New York NY 10016 212-686-9040 800
TF: 800-394-9663 ■ *Web:* www.woodtobecoburn.edu

Wood Truss Council of America (WTCA)
6300 Enterprise Ln .... Madison WI 53719 608-274-4849 274-3329 49-3
Web: www.sbcindustry.com

Phone | Fax | Class

Wood You Furniture
11700 San Jose Blvd .... Jacksonville FL 32223 904-370-1333 321
Web: www.woodyou.com

Wood's CRW Corp
795 Marshall Ave PO Box 1099 .... Williston VT 05495 802-658-1700 23
TF: 800-523-2200 ■ *Web:* www.woodscrw.com

Woodall Robert (Rep R - GA)
1724 Longworth HOB .... Washington DC 20515 202-225-4272 225-4696 342-2
Web: woodall.house.gov

WOOD-AM 1300 (N/T)
77 Monroe Ctr St NW Ste 1000 .... Grand Rapids MI 49507 616-459-1919 242-9373 645-66
Web: woodradio.iheart.com

Woodard & Curran 41 Hutchins Dr .... Portland ME 04102 207-774-2112 261
TF: 800-426-4262 ■ *Web:* www.woodardcurran.com

Woodard Emhardt Moriarty McNett & Henry LLP
111 Monument Cir Ste 3700 .... Indianapolis IN 46204 317-634-3456 445
Web: www.uspatent.com

Woodberry Graphics
11110 Pepper Rd Ste I .... Hunt Valley MD 21031 410-584-9790 225

Woodbine Chrysler Ltd
8280 Woodbine Ave .... Markham ON L3R2N8 905-415-2260 57
Web: www.woodbinechrysler.ca

Woodbine Entertainment Group Inc
555 Rexdale Blvd PO Box 156 .... Toronto ON M9W5L2 416-675-7223 642
TF: 888-675-7223 ■ *Web:* www.woodbineentertainment.com

Woodbridge Center Mall
250 Woodbridge Ctr Dr. .... Woodbridge NJ 07095 732-636-4600 460
Web: www.woodbridgecenter.com

Woodbridge Foam Corp
4240 Sherwoodtowne Blvd .... Mississauga ON L4Z2G6 905-896-3626 896-9262 601
Web: www.woodbridgegroup.com

Woodbridge Public Library
George Frederick Plaza .... Woodbridge NJ 07095 732-634-4450 434-3
TF: 800-792-8610 ■ *Web:* www.woodbridge.lib.nj.us

Woodburn Independent 650 N First St .... Woodburn OR 97071 503-981-3441 532-4
Web: www.pamplinmedia.com

Woodburn Nursery & Azaleas
13009 McKee School Rd NE .... Woodburn OR 97071 503-634-2231 634-2238 369
TF Sales: 888-634-2232 ■ *Web:* www.woodburnnursery.com

Woodburn Premium Outlets
1001 N Arney Rd .... Woodburn OR 97071 503-981-1900 460
Web: www.premiumoutlets.com

Woodbury Box Company Inc
301 Mcintosh Pkwy .... Thomaston GA 30286 800-722-2061 350
TF: 800-722-2061 ■ *Web:* www.chiefmanufacturing.net

Woodbury Corp
2733 E Parleys Way Ste 300 .... Salt Lake City UT 84109 801-485-7770 485-0209 652
Web: www.woodburycorp.com

Woodbury County 620 Douglas St .... Sioux City IA 51101 712-279-6611 338
TF: 800-721-5066 ■ *Web:* www.woodburycountyiowa.gov

Woodbury County Rural Electric Co-op Assn
1495 Humboldt Ave .... Moville IA 51039 712-873-3125 245
TF: 800-469-3125 ■ *Web:* woodburyrec.com

Woodbury Pewterers Inc 860 Main St S .... Woodbury CT 06798 800-648-2014 702
TF: 800-648-2014 ■ *Web:* www.woodburypewter.com

Woodbury Technologies Inc
1725 E 1450 S .... Clearfield UT 84015 800-408-8857 196
TF: 800-408-8857 ■ *Web:* www.woodburytech.com

Woodbury University
7500 Glenoaks Blvd .... Burbank CA 91510 818-767-0888 767-7520 166
TF: 800-784-9663 ■ *Web:* www.woodbury.edu

Woodcase Fine Cabinetry Inc
8340 East Raintree Dr .... Scottsdale AZ 85260 480-948-0756 115
Web: www.woodcaseinc.net

Woodcliff Hotel & Spa
199 Woodcliff Dr. .... Fairport NY 14450 585-381-4000 381-2673 669
TF: 800-365-3065 ■ *Web:* www.woodcliffhotelspa.com

WOODCO USA 773 McCarty Dr .... Houston TX 77029 713-672-9491 358
TF: 800-496-6326 ■ *Web:* www.woodcousa.com

Woodcock Nature Ctr 54 Deer Run Rd .... Wilton CT 06897 203-762-7280 834-0062 50-5
Web: www.woodcocknaturecenter.org

Woodcraft Industries Inc
525 Lincoln Ave SE .... Saint Cloud MN 56304 320-252-1503 656-2199 115
Web: www.woodcraftind.com

Woodcraft Supply LLC
1177 Rosemar Rd .... Parkersburg WV 26105 800-535-4482 428-8271* 45
*Fax Area Code: 304 ■ *TF:* 800-535-4482 ■ *Web:* www.woodcraft.com

WoodCrafters Home Products LLC
3700 Camino de Verdad .... Weslaco TX 78596 956-647-8300 361
Web: www.woodcrafters-tx.com

Wooden Monkey 1707 Grafton St .... Halifax NS B3J2C6 902-444-3844 671
Web: www.thewoodenmonkey.ca

Wooden Pallets Ltd PO Box 555 .... Silsbee TX 77656 409-385-1234 385-6203 551
Web: www.woodenpalletsltd.com

Woodfield Fund Admin LLC
3601 Algonquin Rd Ste 900 .... Rolling Meadows IL 60008 847-255-3500 2
Web: www.woodfieldllc.com

Woodfield Inc 3161 Hwy 376 S .... Camden AR 71701 870-231-6020 186
TF: 800-501-6020 ■ *Web:* www.woodfieldinc.com

Woodfield Mall 5 Woodfield Mall .... Schaumburg IL 60173 847-330-1537 460
Web: www.simon.com/mall/woodfield-mall

Woodfill Law Firm PC
3 Riverway Ste 750 .... Houston TX 77056 713-751-3080 652

Woodfin Co
8180 Mechanicsville Tpke .... Mechanicsville VA 23111 804-730-5000 579
Web: www.askwoodfin.com

Woodfire Grill
1782 Cheshire Bridge Rd .... Atlanta GA 30324 404-347-9055 671
Web: www.woodfiregrill.com

Woodfold Manufacturing Inc
1811 18th Ave PO Box 346 .... Forest Grove OR 97116 503-357-7181 357-7185 499
Web: www.woodfold.com

Woodford County
103 S Main St Rm 120 .... Versailles KY 40383 859-873-5122 817-6585* 338
*Fax Area Code: 877 ■ *Web:* kwib.ky.gov

Woodford Manufacturing Co
2121 Waynoka Rd .... Colorado Springs CO 80915 800-621-6032 574-7699* 609
*Fax Area Code: 719 ■ *TF Sales:* 800-621-6032 ■ *Web:* www.woodfordmfg.com

Woodford Oil Company Inc
13th St PO Box 567 .... Elkins WV 26241 304-636-2688 316
TF: 800-927-3688 ■ *Web:* www.woodfordoil.com

Woodford State Park
142 State Pk Rd .... Bennington VT 05201 802-447-7169 565
Web: www.vtstateparks.com

Woodforest Financial Group Inc
PO Box 7889 .... Spring TX 77387 832-375-2000 70
TF: 877-968-7962 ■ *Web:* www.woodforest.com

Wood-Fruitticher Grocery Company Inc
2900 Alton Rd .... Birmingham AL 35210 205-836-9663 836-9681 297-8
TF: 800-328-0026 ■ *Web:* www.woodfruitticher.com

Woodgrain Distribution
80 Shelby St .... Montevallo AL 35115 205-665-2546 665-3432 309
TF: 800-756-0199 ■ *Web:* www.woodgraindistribution.com

Woodgrain Millworks Inc
300 NW 16th St .... Fruitland ID 83619 208-452-3801 499
TF: 888-783-5485 ■ *Web:* www.woodgrain.com

Woodhall School
58 Harrison Ln PO Box 550 .... Bethlehem CT 06751 203-266-7788 266-5896 622
Web: www.woodhallschool.org

Woodharbor Doors & Cabinetry Inc
3277 Ninth St SW .... Mason City IA 50401 641-423-0444 499

Woodhaven Care Ctr
2400 McGinley Rd .... Monroeville PA 15146 412-856-4770 856-6856 450
Web: mywoodhavencarecenter.com

Woodhill Supply Inc
4665 Beidler Rd .... Willoughby OH 44094 440-269-1100 612
TF: 800-362-6111 ■ *Web:* www.woodhillsupply.com

Woodhull Medical & Mental Health Ctr
760 Broadway .... Brooklyn NY 11206 718-963-8000 963-8999 374-3
Web: nyc.gov

Woodings Industrial Corp 218 Clay Ave .... Mars PA 16046 724-625-3131 697
Web: www.woodingsindustrial.com

Woodland Aviation Inc
25170 Aviation Ave .... Davis CA 95616 530-759-6037 63
TF: 800-442-1333 ■ *Web:* www.woodlandaviation.com

Woodland Cemetery & Arboretum Foundation
118 Woodland Ave .... Dayton OH 45409 937-228-3221 222-7259 97
Web: www.woodlandcemetery.org

Woodland Chamber of Commerce
307 First St .... Woodland CA 95695 530-662-7327 662-4086 139
TF: 888-843-2636 ■ *Web:* www.woodlandchamber.org

Woodland Foods Inc 3751 Sunset Ave .... Waukegan IL 60087 847-625-8600 297-11
Web: www.woodlandfoods.com

Woodland Furniture 4475 S 15th W .... Idaho Falls ID 83402 208-523-9006 319-2
Web: www.woodlandfurniture.com

Woodland Healthcare
1325 Cottonwood St .... Woodland CA 95695 530-662-3961 374-3
Web: hospitals.dignityhealth.org

Woodland Heights Medical Ctr
505 S John Redditt Dr .... Lufkin TX 75904 936-634-8311 637-8600 374-3
Web: www.woodlandheights.net

Woodland Hills Chamber of Commerce
20121 Ventura Blvd Ste 309 .... Woodland Hills CA 91364 818-347-4737 347-3321 139
TF: 888-852-9961 ■ *Web:* www.woodlandhillscc.net

Woodland Hills Mall 7021 S Memorial Dr .... Tulsa OK 74133 918-250-1449 250-9084 460
Web: www.simon.com

Woodland Hills Medical Clinic
19825 Ventura Blvd .... Woodland Hills CA 91364 818-340-3636 374-3
Web: www.woodlandhillsurgentcarecenters.com

Woodland Hills Youth Development Ctr
3965 Stewarts Ln .... Nashville TN 37218 615-532-2000 532-8402 412
TF: 855-418-1622 ■ *Web:* www.tennessee.gov

Woodland Mall 3195 28th St SE .... Grand Rapids MI 49512 616-949-0012 460
TF: 800-433-5778 ■ *Web:* www.shopwoodlandmall.com

Woodland Paper Inc 50785 Pontiac Trl .... Wixom MI 48393 248-926-5550 554
TF: 800-979-9919 ■ *Web:* www.woodlandpaper.com

Woodland Park Zoo 601 N 59th St .... Seattle WA 98103 206-548-2500 548-1536 823
TF: 800-937-9582 ■ *Web:* www.zoo.org

Woodland Public Library 250 First St .... Woodland CA 95695 530-661-5980 666-5408 434-3
TF: 800-321-2752 ■ *Web:* www.cityofwoodland.org/library

Woodland Pulp LLC 144 Main St .... Baileyville ME 04694 207-427-3311 557

Woodland School District 50
1105 N Hunt Club Rd .... Gurnee IL 60031 847-596-5600 685
Web: www.dist50.net

Woodlands Academy of the Sacred Heart
760 E Westleigh Rd .... Lake Forest IL 60045 847-234-4300 234-4348 622
TF: 888-234-3080 ■ *Web:* www.woodlandsacademy.org

Woodlands Academy Preparatory School, The
27440 Kuykendahl Rd .... Tomball TX 77375 281-516-0600 8
Web: woodlandsprep.org

Woodlands Inn, The 1073 Hwy 315 .... Wilkes-Barre PA 18702 570-824-9831 824-8865 669
Web: www.choicehotels.com

Woodlands Resort & Conference Ctr, The
2301 N Millbend Dr .... The Woodlands TX 77380 281-367-1100 377
TF Resv: 800-433-2624 ■ *Web:* www.woodlandsresort.com

Woodlawn Beach State Park
3580 Lake Shore Rd .... Blasdell NY 14219 716-826-1930 565
Web: parks.ny.gov/parks/47/details.aspx

Woodlawn Cemetery Inc, The
Webster Ave & E 233rd St .... Bronx NY 10470 718-920-0500 510
TF: 877-496-6352 ■ *Web:* www.thewoodlawncemetery.org

Woodlawn National Cemetery
1825 Davis St .... Elmira NY 14901 607-732-5411 732-1769 136
TF: 877-907-8585 ■ *Web:* www.cem.va.gov

Woodley'S Fine Furniture Inc
320 S Sunset St .... Longmont CO 80501 303-443-5692 321
Web: woodleys.com

Woodloch Pines Inc 731 Welcome Lake Rd .... Hawley PA 18428 570-685-8000 379
TF: 800-966-3562 ■ *Web:* www.woodloch.com

Woodman State Jail
1210 Coryell City Rd .... Gatesville TX 76528 254-865-9398 213
Web: tdcj.state.tx.us

Woodman'S Food Market Inc
2631 Liberty Ln .... Janesville WI 53545 608-754-8382 345
Web: woodmans-food.com

WOODMARK HOTEL 1200 Carillon Pt .... Kirkland WA 98033 425-822-3700 822-3699 379
TF: 800-822-3700 ■ *Web:* www.thewoodmark.com

Name / Address	City	State	Zip	Phone	Fax	Class
woodmen life 1700 Farnam St. TF: 800-225-3108 ■ Web: woodmen.org	Omaha	NE	68102	402-342-1890	271-7269	457-10
Woodmen of the World Hall 291 W Eigth Ave Web: www.wowhall.org	Eugene	OR	97401	541-687-2746		572
Woodmere Art Museum 9201 Germantown Ave Web: www.woodmereartmuseum.org	Philadelphia	PA	19118	215-247-0476	247-2387	520
Woodmont Investment Counsel LLC 401 Commerce St Ste 5400 TF: 800-278-8003 ■ Web: www.woodmontcounsel.com	Nashville	TN	37219	615-297-6144		401
Woodmont Real Estate Services (WRES) 1050 Ralston Ave Web: www.wres.com	Belmont	CA	94002	650-592-3960	591-4577	655
Woodmoor Group 755 Hwy 105 Ste 2A Web: www.woodmoor.com	Palmer Lake	CO	80133	719-488-8589		260
Woodridge Area Chamber of Commerce 6440 Main St Ste 330 Web: chamber630.com	Woodridge	IL	60517	630-960-7080	852-2316	139
Woodridge Capital 800 Woodlands Pkwy Ste 201 Web: www.woodridge-capital.com	Ridgeland	MS	39157	601-957-6006		401
Woodridge Park District 2600 Center Dr TF: 800-713-7415 ■ Web: www.woodridgeparks.org	Woodridge	IL	60517	630-353-3300		31
Woodridge Public Library 3 Plaza Dr Web: www.woodridgelibrary.org	Woodridge	IL	60517	630-964-7899	968-4126	434-3
Woodrow Wilson Family Home 1705 Hampton St TF: 800-622-3382 ■ Web: www.historiccolumbia.org	Columbia	SC	29201	803-252-7742		50-3
Woodrow Wilson House Museum 2340 S St NW TF: 800-887-9103 ■ Web: www.woodrowwilsonhouse.org	Washington	DC	20008	202-387-4062	483-1466	520
Woodrow Wilson International Ctr for Scholars 1 Woodrow Wilson Plaza 1300 Pennsylvania Ave NW Web: wilsoncenter.org	Washington	DC	20004	202-691-4000	691-4001	634
Woodrow Wilson National Fellowship Foundation 5 Vaughn Dr # 300 Web: www.woodrow.org	Princeton	NJ	08540	609-452-7007	452-0066	48-11
Woodrow Wilson Presidential Library 20 N Coalter St Web: www.woodrowwilson.org	Staunton	VA	24401	540-885-0897		434-2
Woodruff Arts Ctr 1280 Peachtree St NE Web: www.woodruffcenter.org	Atlanta	GA	30309	404-733-4200		572
Woodruff Construction LLC 1890 Kountry Ln Web: www.woodruffcompanies.com	Fort Dodge	IA	50501	515-576-1118		780
Woodruff Convalescent 17836 Woodruff Ave Web: www.woodruffconvalescent.com	Bellflower	CA	90706	562-925-8457		371
Woodruff County 500 N Third St Web: www.prsearch.com/arkansas	Augusta	AR	72006	870-347-5206		338
Woodruff Electric Co-op PO Box 1619 TF: 888-559-6400 ■ Web: www.woodruffelectric.coop	Forrest City	AR	72336	870-633-2262	633-0629	245
Woodruff Energy 73 Water St PO Box 777 TF: 800-557-1121 ■ Web: www.woodruffenergy.com	Bridgeton	NJ	08302	856-455-1111		316
Woodruff Health Sciences Ctr Library *Emory University* 1462 Clifton Rd NE Web: health.library.emory.edu	Atlanta	GA	30322	404-727-8727	727-9821	434-1
Woodruff-Fontaine House 680 Adams Ave Web: www.woodruff fontaine.org	Memphis	TN	38105	901-526-1469		50-3
Woods Bay State Natural Area 11020 Woods Bay Rd Web: www.southcarolinaparks.com	Olanta	SC	29114	843-659-4445		565
Woods County 407 Government St PO Box 431 Web: woods.oklahoma.usassessor.com	Alva	OK	73717	580-327-3118	327-6230	338
Woods Equipment Co 1000 W Cherokee St Web: woodsequipment.com	Sioux Falls	SD	57104	605-336-3860		273
Woods Equipment Co 2606 S Illinois Rt 2 PO Box 1000 *Fax: Sales ■ TF: 800-319-6637 ■ Web: www.woodsequipment.com	Oregon	IL	61061	815-732-2141	732-7580*	273
Woods Fuller Shultz & Smith 300 S Phillips Ave Ste 300 Web: www.woodsfuller.com	Sioux Falls	SD	57117	605-336-3890		428
Woods Hole Oceanographic Institution (WHOI) 266 Woods Hole Rd *Fax: Hum Res ■ Web: www.whoi.edu	Woods Hole	MA	02543	508-289-2282	457-2109*	668
Woods Hole Public Library 581 Woods Hole Rd PO Box 185	Woods Hole	MA	02543	508-548-8961	540-1969	434-3
Woods Resort & Conference Ctr Mountain Lake Rd PO Box 5 *Fax Area Code: 304 ■ TF: 800-248-2222 ■ Web: www.thewoods.com	Hedgesville	WV	25427	800-248-2222	754-8146*	669
Woods Rogers PLC 10 S Jefferson St Ste 1400 TF: 800-552-4529 ■ Web: www.woodsrogers.com	Roanoke	VA	24011	540-983-7600		428
Woods Supermarkets Inc 703 E College Ave TF: 800-562-6210 ■ Web: www.woodssupermarket.com	Bolivar	MO	65613	417-326-7601		345
Woodshop News 10 Bokum Rd TF: 800-444-7686 ■ Web: www.woodshopnews.com	Essex	CT	06426	860-767-8227		457-14
Woodside Ctr 9101 Second Ave Web: genesishcc.com	Silver Spring	MD	20910	301-588-5544		450
Woodside Energy (USA) Inc Sage Plaza 5151 San Felipe St Ste 1200 Web: www.woodside.com.au	Houston	TX	77056	713-401-0000		539
Woodside Fund 303 Twin Dolphin Dr Ste 600 TF: 800-238-2727 ■ Web: www.woodsidefund.com	Redwood Shores	CA	94065	650-610-8050		792
Woodside Juvenile Rehabilitation Ctr 26 Woodside Dr	Colchester	VT	05446	802-655-4990		412
Woodside Priory School 302 Portola Rd Web: www.prioryca.org	Portola Valley	CA	94028	650-851-8221	851-2839	622
Woodsmith Magazine 2200 Grand Ave *Fax Area Code: 515 ■ TF Cust Svc: 800-333-5075 ■ Web: www.woodsmith.com	Des Moines	IA	50312	800-333-5075	282-6741*	457-14
Woodson & Bozeman Inc 3870 New Getwell Rd TF: 800-876-4243 ■ Web: www.woodsonbozeman.com	Memphis	TN	38118	901-362-1500	362-1509	38
Woodson County 105 W Rutledge St Rm 226 Web: www.woodsoncounty.net	Yates Center	KS	66783	620-625-8605	625-8670	338
Woodstock Academy 57 Academy Rd TF: 800-300-4781 ■ Web: www.woodstockacademy.org	Woodstock	CT	06281	860-928-6575		148
Woodstock Chamber of Commerce & Industry 121 N Calhoun St Web: www.woodstockilchamber.com	Woodstock	IL	60098	815-338-2436		139
Woodstock Community Unit School District 200 227 W Judd St Web: www.woodstockschools.org	Woodstock	IL	60098	815-338-8200	338-2005	685
Woodstock Corp 27 School St Ste 200 Web: www.woodstockcorp.com	Boston	MA	02108	617-227-0600		401
Woodstock District Chamber of Commerce 476 Peel St Ste 3 Web: woodstockchamber.ca	Woodstock	ON	N4S1K1	519-539-9411	456-1611	137
Woodstock Furniture Outlet 100 Robin Rd Ext Web: www.woodstockoutlet.com	Acworth	GA	30102	678-255-1000		321
Woodstock General Hospital 270 Riddell St *Fax: Admitting ■ TF: 800-436-8477 ■ Web: www.wgh.on.ca	Woodstock	ON	N4S6N6	519-421-4211	421-4238*	374-2
Woodstock Inn & Resort 14 The Green TF: 800-448-7900 ■ Web: www.woodstockinn.com	Woodstock	VT	05091	802-457-1100	457-6699	669
Woodstock Percussion Inc 167 DuBois Rd Web: www.chimes.com	Shokan	NY	12481	845-657-6000		527
Woodstream Corp 69 N Locust St TF All: 800-800-1819 ■ Web: www.woodstream.com/index.cfm	Lititz	PA	17543	717-626-2125	626-1912	280
Woodsville Guaranty Savings Bank 10 Pleasant St PO Box 266 TF: 800-564-2735 ■ Web: www.theguarantybank.com	Woodsville	NH	03785	603-747-2735	747-3267	70
Woodtech Trading Co 455 Fourth Ave E Web: www.woodtechdoor.com	Columbia Falls	MT	59912	406-892-5140		499
Wood-Tikchik State Park PO Box 1822 Web: dnr.alaska.gov	Dillingham	AK	99576	907-842-2641		565
WoodTrust Financial Corp 181 Second St S TF: 800-716-3742 ■ Web: www.woodtrust.com	Wisconsin Rapids	WI	54494	715-423-7600	422-0300	70
WOOD-TV Ch 8 (NBC) 120 College Ave SE Web: www.woodtv.com	Grand Rapids	MI	49503	616-456-8888		741-53
Woodward Academy 1662 Rugby Ave Web: www.woodward.edu	College Park	GA	30337	404-765-4000		685
Woodward Biomedical Library 1001 E Mall Web: woodward.library.ubc.ca	Vancouver	BC	V6T1Z1	604-822-6375	822-3893	434-1
Woodward Communications Inc 801 Bluff St *Fax Area Code: 563 ■ TF: 800-553-4801 ■ Web: www.wcinet.com	Dubuque	IA	52001	800-553-4801	588-5739*	645
Woodward Controls Inc 6250 W Howard St TF: 800-451-7040 ■ Web: www.woodward.com	Niles	IL	60714	847-967-7730		203
Woodward County 1600 Main St Ste 9 TF: 800-734-7520 ■ Web: woodwardcounty.org	Woodward	OK	73801	580-256-8097	254-6840	338
Woodward HRT Inc 25200 W Rye Canyon Rd TF: 800-235-3330 ■ Web: www.hrtextron.com	Santa Clarita	CA	91355	661-294-6000		21
Woodward Resource Ctr 1251 334th St TF: 888-229-9223 ■ Web: dhs.iowa.gov	Woodward	IA	50276	515-438-2600		230
Woodway Financial Advisors 10000 Memorial Dr Ste 650 Web: www.woodwayfinancial.com	Houston	TX	77024	713-683-7070	683-0702	401
Woodway USA W229 N591 Foster Ct TF: 800-966-3929 ■ Web: www.woodway.com	Waukesha	WI	53186	262-548-6235	522-6235	267
Woodwind & Brasswind PO Box 7479 TF: 800-348-5003 ■ Web: www.wwbw.com	Westlake Village	CA	91359	574-251-3500		526
Woodwing Usa 615 Griswold St Ste 520 Web: www.woodwing.com	Detroit	MI	48226	313-962-0542		225
Woody Bogler Trucking Co PO Box 229 TF: 800-899-4120 ■ Web: www.woodybogler.com	Rosebud	MO	63091	573-764-3700		780
Woody's 619 N Gloster St Web: woodyssteak.com	Tupelo	MS	38804	662-840-0460		671
Wool Growers 620 E 19th St Web: woolgrowers.net	Bakersfield	CA	93305	661-327-9584		671
Woolaroc Ranch Museum & Wildlife Preserve 1925 Woolaroc Ranch Rd TF: 888-966-5276 ■ Web: www.woolaroc.org	Bartlesville	OK	74003	918-336-0307	336-0084	520
Woolco Foods Inc 135 Amity St Web: woolcofoods.net	Jersey City	NJ	07304	201-716-2700		297-8
Wooldridge Boats Inc 1303 S 96th St Web: www.wooldridgeboats.com	Seattle	WA	98108	206-722-8998		90
Wooldridge Organization 395 Taylor Blvd Ste 120	Pleasant Hill	CA	94523	925-680-7979		653
Woolf Aircraft Products Inc 6401 Cogswell Rd Web: www.woolfaircraft.com	Romulus	MI	48174	734-721-5330	721-3490	595
Woolly Hollow State Park 82 Woolly Hollow Rd Web: www.arkansasstateparks.com	Greenbrier	AR	72058	501-679-2098		565
Woolpert Inc 4454 Idea Ctr Blvd Web: www.woolpert.com	Dayton	OH	45430	937-461-5660	461-0743	261
Woolrich Inc 2 Mill St TF: 800-995-1299 ■ Web: www.woolrich.com	Woolrich	PA	17779	570-769-6464	769-6234	155-5
Woolverton Printing Co 6714 Chancellor Dr TF: 800-670-7713 ■ Web: www.woolverton.com	Cedar Falls	IA	50613	319-277-2616		627
Woonsocket Harris Public Library 303 Clinton St TF: 800-359-3090 ■ Web: www.woonsocketlibrary.org	Woonsocket	RI	02895	401-769-9044	767-4140	434-3
Wooster Area Chamber of Commerce 377 W Liberty St TF: 800-414-1103 ■ Web: www.woosterchamber.com	Wooster	OH	44691	330-262-5735	262-5745	139

Name / Address	City	State	Zip	Phone	Fax	Class
Wooster Brush Co 604 Madison Ave *TF:* 800-392-7246 ■ *Web:* www.woosterbrush.com	Wooster	OH	44691	330-264-4440	263-0495	103
Wooster City Board of Education 144 N Market St *Web:* www.woostercityschools.org	Wooster	OH	44691	330-264-0869	262-3407	685
Wooster Products Inc 1000 Spruce St PO Box 6005 *TF:* 800-321-4936 ■ *Web:* www.woosterproducts.com	Wooster	OH	44691	330-264-2844	262-4151	491
Wooster Republican Printing Co 212 E Liberty St *TF:* 800-686-2958 ■ *Web:* www.the-daily-record.com	Wooster	OH	44691	330-264-1125		637-8
Woot Inc 4121 International Pkwy *TF:* 866-551-6881 ■ *Web:* woot.com	Carrollton	TX	75007	972-417-3959		174
WOR-AM 710 (N/T) 32 Ave of the Americas 3rd Fl *Web:* 710wor.iheart.com	New York	NY	10013	212-377-7900		645-111
Worcester Academy 81 Providence St *Web:* www.worcesteracademy.org	Worcester	MA	01604	508-754-5302		622
Worcester Art Museum 55 Salisbury St *TF:* 800-696-9401 ■ *Web:* www.worcesterart.org	Worcester	MA	01609	508-799-4406	798-5646	520
Worcester County 1 W Market St Rm 1103 *TF:* 800-852-0335 ■ *Web:* www.co.worcester.md.us	Snow Hill	MD	21863	410-632-1194	632-3131	338
Worcester County Library 307 N Washington St *Web:* www.worcesterlibrary.org	Snow Hill	MD	21863	410-632-2600	632-1159	434-3
Worcester Ctr for Crafts 25 Sagamore Rd *Web:* www.worcester.edu	Worcester	MA	01605	508-753-8183	797-5626	50-2
Worcester District Registry of Deeds 90 Front St	Worcester	MA	01608	508-798-7717		338
Worcester Envelope Co 22 Millbury St *TF:* 800-343-1398 ■ *Web:* www.worcesterenvelope.com	Auburn	MA	01501	508-832-5394		263
Worcester Historical Museum 30 Elm St *Web:* www.worcesterhistory.org	Worcester	MA	01609	508-753-8278	753-9070	520
Worcester Polytechnic Institute 100 Institute Rd **Fax:* Admissions ■ *Web:* www.wpi.edu	Worcester	MA	01609	508-831-5000	831-5875*	166
Worcester Public Schools 20 Irving St *Web:* www.worcesterschools.org	Worcester	MA	01609	508-799-3115	799-3119	685
Worcester Regional Airport 375 Airport Dr *Web:* www.worcesterma.gov	Worcester	MA	01602	508-929-1300		27
Worcester Regional Chamber of Commerce 446 Main St Ste 200 *TF:* 800-508-2265 ■ *Web:* www.worcesterchamber.org	Worcester	MA	01608	508-753-2924	754-8560	139
Worcester Regional Transit Authority 287 Grove St *Web:* therta.com	Worcester	MA	01605	508-791-9782		468
Worcester Skilled Care Ctr 59 Acton St *TF:* 800-946-4283 ■ *Web:* www.wingatehealthcare.com	Worcester	MA	01604	508-791-3147		450
Word & Brown Insurance Administrators Inc 721 S Parker Ste 300 *Web:* www.wordandbrown.com	Orange	CA	92868	714-835-6752		390
Word Among Us Inc 9639 Doctor Perry Rd *TF:* 800-775-9673 ■ *Web:* wau.org	Ijamsville	MD	21754	301-874-1700		95
Word Entertainment 25 Music Sq W *Web:* www.wordentertainment.com	Nashville	TN	37203	615-251-0600		657
Word of Faith Family Worship Cathedral 212 Riverside Pkwy *Web:* woffamily.org	Austell	GA	30168	770-874-8400		48-20
Word of Life Fellowship Church Inc, The 3650 Greenbush St	Lafayette	IN	47905	765-449-4008		48-20
Worden Bros Inc 4905 Pine Cone Dr *TF:* 800-776-4940 ■ *Web:* www.worden.com	Durham	NC	27707	919-408-0542	408-0545	178-1
Worden Company Inc 199 E 17th St *TF:* 800-748-0561 ■ *Web:* www.wordencompany.com	Holland	MI	49423	616-392-1848	392-2542	319-3
Words & Numbers Inc 2050 Rockrose Ave	Baltimore	MD	21211	410-467-7835		463
Words at Work 403 W Ponce De Leon Ave Ste 113 *Web:* wordsatwork.com	Decatur	GA	30030	404-270-9200		7
Words, Data & Images LLC 3190 Rider Trl S *Web:* www.gabrielgroup.com	Earth City	MO	63045	314-743-5700		5
Wordsmart Corp 10025 Mesa Rim Rd	San Diego	CA	92121	858-565-8068	202-1820	178-3
WordSouth - A Content Marketing Company PO Box 1575 Ste B *TF:* 888-655-7240 ■ *Web:* wordsouth.com	Rainsville	AL	35986	256-638-8856		636
Wordsworth & Company Llc 723 Raymond Ave *Web:* www.wordsworthandco.com	Santa Monica	CA	90405	310-452-1022		7
Word-Tech Inc 5625 Foxridge Dr Ste 110 *TF:* 800-227-5700 ■ *Web:* www.wordtech.com	Mission	KS	66202	913-722-3334		175
Work 'n Gear Stores 2300 Crown Colony Dr Ste 300 *TF:* 800-987-0218 ■ *Web:* www.workngear.com	Quincy	MA	02169	800-987-0218		157-5
Work Area Protection Corp 2500 Production Dr *Web:* www.workareaprotection.com	St. Charles	IL	60174	630-377-9100		596
Work In Progress Coaching 102 Alta Verdi Dr *Web:* www.wipcoaching.com	Aptos	CA	95003	831-685-1480		242
Work Institute LLC, The 1620 Westgate Cir Ste 100 *TF:* 800-290-9314 ■ *Web:* workinstitute.com	Brentwood	TN	37027	615-777-6400		463
Work Out World 762 SR- 18 *TF:* 888-564-6969 ■ *Web:* www.workoutworld.com	Brunswick	NJ	08816	732-390-7390		354
Work Technology Corp 255 Elm St Ste 300 *Web:* www.worktech.com	Somerville	MA	02144	617-625-5888		177
Workaholics Anonymous World Service Organization PO Box 289 *Web:* www.workaholics-anonymous.org	Menlo Park	CA	94026	510-273-9253		48-21
Workbook LLC 6762 Lexington Ave *Web:* www.workbook.com	Los Angeles	CA	90038	323-856-0008		195
WorkCare.com 300 S Harbor Blvd Ste 600 *TF:* 800-455-6155 ■ *Web:* www.workcare.com	Anaheim	CA	92805	800-455-6155		194
Workers' Credit Union 815 Main St PO Box 900 *TF:* 800-221-4020 ■ *Web:* www.wcu.com	Fitchburg	MA	01420	978-345-1021		219
WorkersCompensation.com LLC PO Box 2432 *TF:* 866-927-2667 ■ *Web:* www.workerscompensation.com	Sarasota	FL	34230	941-366-3791		393
Workforce Alliance Inc 1951 N Military Trl Ste D *TF:* 800-204-2418 ■ *Web:* www.careersourcepbc.com	West Palm Beach	FL	33409	561-340-1060		260
Workforce Board, The 128 Tenth Ave SW PO Box 43105 *Web:* wtb.wa.gov	Olympia	WA	98501	360-709-4600		41
Workforce Insight Inc 1600 Wynkoop Ste 5B *TF:* 800-394-5516 ■ *Web:* www.workforceinsight.com	Denver	CO	80202	303-309-4006		261
Workgroup Connections Inc 4240 Duncan Ave Ste 200 *Web:* www.wgcinc.com	St. Louis	MO	63110	314-436-2233		764
Workincom Inc 343 Church St *TF:* 800-774-8671 ■ *Web:* www.workin.com	Santa Cruz	CA	95060	775-336-3366		260
Working Machines Corp 2170 Dwight Way *TF:* 877-648-4808 ■ *Web:* www.workingmachines.com	Berkeley	CA	94704	510-704-1100		180
Working Media Group LLC 21 W 38th St 13th Fl *Web:* www.workingmediagroup.com	New York	NY	10018	212-251-0021		7
Working Mother Magazine 2 Park Ave 10th Fl *Web:* www.workingmother.com	New York	NY	10016	212-779-5000		457-11
Working Solutions 1820 Preston Pk Blvd Ste 2000 *TF:* 866-857-4800 ■ *Web:* www.workingsolutions.com	Plano	TX	75093	972-964-4800		737
Working Title Films 9720 Wilshire Blvd 4th Fl *Web:* www.workingtitlefilms.com	Beverly Hills	CA	90212	310-777-3100		514
Working Together 360 Hiatt Dr *TF:* 800-621-5463 ■ *Web:* www.lrp.com	Palm Beach Gardens	FL	33418	561-622-6520	622-2423	531-2
WorkingBuildings LLC 1230 Peachtree St NE 300 Promenade *Web:* www.workingbuildings.com	Atlanta	GA	30309	678-990-8001		256
Worklife Balance com 7742 Spalding Dr Ste 356 *TF:* 877-644-0064 ■ *Web:* www.worklifebalance.com	Atlanta	GA	30092	770-997-7881	668-9719	463
Workman Nydegger PC 60 East South Temple Ste 1000 *Web:* www.wnlaw.com	Salt Lake City	UT	84111	801-533-9800		428
Workman Oil Co 14680 Forest Rd	Forest	VA	24551	434-525-1615		579
Workman Publishing 225 Varick St *TF:* 800-722-7202 ■ *Web:* www.workman.com	New York	NY	10014	212-254-5900	254-8098	637-2
Workmen's Circle/Arbeter Ring Inc 247 W 37th St 5th Fl *TF:* 800-922-2558 ■ *Web:* www.circle.org	New York	NY	10018	212-889-6800	532-7518	49-9
Workplace Answers LLC 3701 Executive Ctr Dr Ste 201 *TF:* 866-861-4410 ■ *Web:* www.workplaceanswers.com	Austin	TX	78731	866-861-4410		401
Workplace Benefit Solutions LLC 1667 Elm St Ste 3 *Web:* www.workplacebenefitsolutions.com	Manchester	NH	03101	603-668-0400		260
Workplace Group Inc, The 10 Ridgedale Ave *Web:* www.workplacegroup.com	Florham Park	NJ	07932	973-377-4665		260
Workplace IT Management 108 S Dakota Ave *Web:* workplace-it.com	Sioux Falls	SD	57104	605-367-3767		525
Workplace Law Report 1801 S Bell St *TF:* 800-372-1033 ■ *Web:* www.bna.com/workplace-law-report-p5953	Arlington	VA	22202	800-372-1033		531-7
Workplace Resource LLC 4400 NE Loop 410 Ste 130 *TF:* 800-580-3000 ■ *Web:* www.hmwrasa.com	San Antonio	TX	78218	512-472-7300		321
Workplace Solutions 30800 Telegraph Rd Ste 2985 *Web:* www.myworkplacesolutions.com	Bingham Farms	MI	48025	248-430-2500		320
Workplace Staffing Services 2923 Smith Rd Ste 201 *TF:* 800-733-9675 ■ *Web:* www.workplacestaff.com	Akron	OH	44333	330-926-1880		260
Workplace Systems Inc 562 Mammoth Rd *TF:* 800-258-9700 ■ *Web:* www.workplacesystemsinc.com	Londonderry	NH	03053	603-622-3727	622-0174	319-1
Works Computing Inc 1801 American Blvd E Ste 12 *TF:* 866-222-4077 ■ *Web:* www.workscomputing.com	Bloomington	MN	55425	952-746-1500	746-1585	173-3
Works, The 55 S First St *Web:* www.attheworks.org	Newark	OH	43055	740-349-9277		520
Worksaver Inc 9 Worksaver Trl PO Box 100 *Web:* www.worksaver.com	Litchfield	IL	62056	217-324-5973	324-3356	273
Workscape Inc 123 Selton St *Web:* workscapeinc.com	Marlborough	MA	01752	508-861-5500	573-9500	39
Workscapes Inc 1173 N Orange Ave *Web:* www.workscapes.com	Orlando	FL	32804	407-599-6770		320
Workshare Technology Inc 208 Utah St Ste 350 *TF:* 888-404-4246 ■ *Web:* www.workshare.com	San Francisco	CA	94103	415-975-3855		177
Workshop Inc, The 339 Broadway *Web:* www.northeastcareer.org	Menands	NY	12204	518-465-5201		761
Workshop Theatre 1136 Bull St *TF:* 800-231-2222 ■ *Web:* www.workshoptheatre.com	Columbia	SC	29211	803-799-4876	799-0227	572
Worksighted Inc 275 Hoover Blvd *Web:* www.worksighted.com	Holland	MI	49423	616-546-2691		180
Worksman Trading Corp 94-15 100th St *TF:* 800-962-2453 ■ *Web:* www.worksman.com	Ozone Park	NY	11416	718-322-2000	529-4803	82
WorkSmart Inc 100 Meredith Dr Ste 200 *Web:* www.worksmart.com	Durham	NC	27713	919-484-1010		624

Phone Fax Class

Worksoft Inc 15851 Dallas Pkwy Ste 855 ... Addison TX 75001 214-239-0400 250-9900* 178-10
Fax Area Code: 972 ■ *TF:* 866-836-1773 ■ *Web:* www.worksoft.com

Workspace com Inc
10451 Mill Run Cir Ste 400 ... Owings Mills MD 21117 888-245-9168 245-9168 525
TF: 888-245-9168 ■ *Web:* www.workspace.com

Workspace Inc 309 Locust St ... Des Moines IA 50309 515-288-7090 393
Web: www.workspaceinc.net

Workstream Inc
2200 Lucien Way Ste 201 ... Maitland FL 32751 407-475-5500 721

Worktank Enterprises 3131 We Ste 510 ... Seattle WA 98121 206-529-3833 514
Web: www.worktankseattle.com

World 50 Inc
3525 Piedmont Rd NE Bldg 7-600 ... Atlanta GA 30305 404-816-5559 4
Web: www.w50.com

World Agricultural Outlook Board
1400 Independence Ave SW ... Washington DC 20250 202-720-6030 340-1
TF: 800-949-3964 ■ *Web:* www.usda.gov/oce/commodity

World Allergy Organization (WAO)
555 E Wells St Ste 1100 ... Milwaukee WI 53202 414-276-1791 276-3349 49-8
TF: 800-929-4040 ■ *Web:* www.worldallergy.org

World Animal Protection (WSPA)
450 Seventh Ave 31st Floor ... New York NY 10123 646-783-2200 564-4250* 48-3
Fax Area Code: 212 ■ *TF:* 800-883-9772 ■ *Web:* www.wspa-usa.org

World Auto Group 3057 New Jersey ... Denville NJ 07834 973-442-0500 57
Web: www.denvillenissan.com

World Bank Group, The (WBG)
1818 H St NW ... Washington DC 20433 202-473-1000 477-6391 783
TF: 800-645-7247 ■ *Web:* www.worldbank.org

World Bicycle Relief
1333 N Kingsbury Ave 4th Fl ... Chicago IL 60642 312-664-8800 517
Web: www.worldbicyclerelief.org

World Bird Sanctuary
125 Bald Eagle Ridge Rd ... Valley Park MO 63088 636-861-3225 861-3240 50-5
Web: www.worldbirdsanctuary.org

World Book Inc
233 N Michigan Ave Ste 2000 ... Chicago IL 60601 312-729-5800 729-5600 637-2
TF: 800-967-5325 ■ *Web:* www.worldbook.com

World Casings Corp 4706 Grand Ave ... Maspeth NY 11378 718-628-3800 296-26
Web: www.worldcasing.com

World Cat 1090 W St James St ... Tarboro NC 27886 252-641-8000 90
TF: 866-485-8899 ■ *Web:* www.worldcat.com

World Chamber of Commerce Directory Inc
446 E 29th St ... Loveland CO 80538 970-663-3231 637-6
TF: 888-883-3231 ■ *Web:* www.chamberdirectoryonline.com

World Christian Broadcasting Corp
605 Bradley Ct ... Franklin TN 37067 615-371-8707 645-10
Web: www.worldchristian.org

World Class Automotive Group
4730 Wistar Rd ... Richmond VA 23228 804-308-1877 57
Web: www.worldclassag.com

World Class Incentives
426 N Rand Rd ... North Barrington IL 60010 847-381-1800 226
TF: 800-871-9365 ■ *Web:* www.worldclassincentives.com

World Class Lighting
14350 60th St N ... Clearwater FL 33760 727-524-7661 362
TF: 877-499-6753 ■ *Web:* www.worldclasslighting.com

World Class Manufacturing Group Inc, The
1101 S Pine St ... Weyauwega WI 54983 920-867-2687 464
Web: www.worldcls.com

World Class Plastics Inc
7695 SR- 708 ... Russells Point OH 43348 937-843-4927 843-4934 608
TF: 800-954-3140 ■ *Web:* www.worldclassplastics.com

World Class Speakers & Entertainers
5200 Kanan Rd Ste 210 ... Agoura Hills CA 91301 818-991-5400 708
TF: 800-790-3785 ■ *Web:* www.wcspeakers.com

World Class Technology Corp
1300 NE Alpha Dr ... Mcminnville OR 97128 503-472-8320 228
Web: www.wctcorporation.com

World Cocoa Foundation (WCF)
1411 K St NW Ste 1300 ... Washington DC 20005 202-737-7870 737-7832 49-6
Web: www.worldcocoafoundation.org

World Concern 19303 Fremont Ave N ... Seattle WA 98133 206-546-7201 546-7269 48-5
TF: 800-755-5022 ■ *Web:* www.worldconcern.org

World Council of Credit Unions Inc (WOCCU)
5710 Mineral Pt Rd ... Madison WI 53705 608-395-2000 395-2001 49-2
Web: www.woccu.org

World Courier Inc
1313 Fourth Ave ... New Hyde Park NY 11040 516-354-2600 546
TF: 800-221-6600 ■ *Web:* www.worldcourier.com

World Currency USA Inc 16 W Main St ... Marlton NJ 08053 888-593-7927 691
TF: 888-593-7927 ■ *Web:* www.worldcurrencyusa.com

World Data Products Inc
1105 Xenium Ln N Ste 200 ... Plymouth MN 55441 888-210-7636 452-1201* 176
Fax Area Code: 763 ■ *TF:* 888-210-7636 ■ *Web:* www.wdpi.com

World Dryer Corp 5700 McDermott Dr ... Berkeley IL 60163 708-449-6950 449-6958 37
TF: 800-323-0701 ■ *Web:* www.worlddryer.com

World Education Inc 44 Farnsworth St ... Boston MA 02210 617-482-9485 482-0617 48-5
Web: www.worlded.org

World Electric Supply Orlando Inc
4501 SW 34th St ... Orlando FL 32811 407-447-2000 246
Web: www.worldelectricsupply.com

World Electronics Sales & Service Inc
3000 Kutztown Rd ... Reading PA 19605 610-939-9800 939-9895 253
TF: 800-523-0427 ■ *Web:* www.world-electronics.com

World Emblem International Inc
1500 NE 131 St ... Miami FL 33161 305-772-0362 594
Web: www.worldemblem.com

World Energy 225 Franklin St Ste 1460 ... Boston MA 02110 617-889-7300 887-2411 201
Web: www.worldenergy.net

World Energy Labs (2) Inc
365 E Middlefield Rd ... Mountain View CA 94043 650-900-4600 961-1415 201

World Equity Group
1650 N Arlington Heights Rd
Ste 100 ... Arlington Heights IL 60004 847-342-1700 690
TF: 800-765-5004 ■ *Web:* www.worldequitygroup.com

World Figure Skating Museum & Hall of Fame
20 First St ... Colorado Springs CO 80906 719-635-5200 635-9548 522
Web: www.worldskatingmuseum.org

World Financial Group Inc
11315 Johns Creek Pkwy ... Johns Creek GA 30097 770-453-9300 390
TF: 800-684-7741 ■ *Web:* www.worldfinancialgroup.com

World Flavors Inc 76 Louise Dr ... Warminster PA 18974 215-672-4400 123
Web: www.worldflavors.com

World Floor Covering Assn (WFCA)
2211 Howell Ave ... Anaheim CA 92806 714-978-6440 978-6066 49-4
TF: 800-624-6880 ■ *Web:* www.wfca.org

World Food Program USA (WFP)
1725 Eye St NW Ste 510 ... Washington DC 20006 202-627-3737 530-1698 48-5
TF: 888-454-0555 ■ *Web:* wfpusa.org

World Forestry Ctr 4033 SW Canyon Rd ... Portland OR 97221 503-228-1367 48-13
Web: www.worldforestry.org

World Fuel Services Corp
9800 NW 41st St Ste 400 ... Miami FL 33178 305-428-8000 392-5600 579
NYSE: INT ■ *TF:* 800-345-3818 ■ *Web:* www.wfscorp.com

World Future Society
7910 Woodmont Ave Ste 450 ... Bethesda MD 20814 301-656-8274 951-0394 49-19
TF: 800-989-8274 ■ *Web:* www.wfs.org

World Gold Council
685 Third Ave Fl 27 ... New York NY 10017 212-317-3800 688-0410 49-4
TF: 800-972-1162 ■ *Web:* www.gold.org

World Gospel Mission (WGM)
3783 E State Rd 18 PO Box 948 ... Marion IN 46952 765-664-7331 671-7230 48-20
TF: 800-426-0846 ■ *Web:* www.wgm.org

World Health 7222 Edgemont Blvd NW ... Calgary AB T3A2X7 403-239-4048 354
TF: 866-278-4131 ■ *Web:* worldhealth.ca

World Hunger Year Inc (WHY)
505 Eigth Ave Ste 2100 ... New York NY 10018 212-629-8850 465-9274 48-5
TF: 800-548-6479 ■ *Web:* www.whyhunger.org

World Intellectual Property Organization (WIPO)
2 UN Plaza Ste 2525 ... New York NY 10017 212-963-6813 963-4801 783
Web: www.wipo.int

World Internet Mktg Inc
151 Rte 10 E ... Succasunna NJ 07876 973-252-6800 252-0888 627
Web: www.eworldwire.com

World Journal 2288 Clark Dr ... Vancouver BC V5N3G8 604-876-1338 532-1
Web: worldjournal.com

World Jurist Assn (WJA)
7910 Woodmont Ave Ste 1440 ... Bethesda MD 20814 202-466-5428 49-10
Web: www.worldjurist.org

World Kitchen LLC
1200 S Antrim Way ... Greencastle PA 17225 800-999-3436 361
TF: 800-999-3436 ■ *Web:* www.worldkitchen.com

World Kite Museum & Hall of Fame
303 Sid Snyder Dr ... Long Beach WA 98631 360-642-4020 642-4020 520
Web: kitefestival.com

World Learning
1 Kipling Rd PO Box 676 ... Brattleboro VT 05302 802-257-7751 258-3248 48-5
TF: 800-257-7751 ■ *Web:* www.worldlearning.org

World Learning International Development Programs
1015 15th St NW Ste 750 ... Washington DC 20005 202-408-5420 408-5397 48-11
TF: 800-345-2929 ■ *Web:* www.worldlearning.org

World Literature Crusade
640 Chapel Hills Dr ... Colorado Springs CO 80920 719-260-8888 48-20
TF: 800-423-5054 ■ *Web:* ehc.org

World Marketing 7950 Joliet Rd ... McCook IL 60525 708-871-6006 5

World Methodist Council
PO Box 518 ... Lake Junaluska NC 28745 828-456-9432 48-20
Web: www.worldmethodistcouncil.org

World Micro Components Inc
205 Hembree Park Dr Ste 105 ... Roswell GA 30076 770-698-1900 246
TF: 800-400-5026 ■ *Web:* www.worldmicro.com

World Millwork Alliance (AMD)
10047 Robert Trent Jones Pkwy ... New Port Richey FL 34655 727-372-3665 372-2879 49-3
Web: worldmillworkalliance.com

World Minerals Inc 130 Castilian Dr ... Goleta CA 93117 805-562-0200 411
TF: 800-893-4445 ■ *Web:* www.worldminerals.com

World Monuments Fund (WMF)
350 Fifth Ave Ste 2412 ... New York NY 10118 646-424-9594 424-9593 48-4
Web: www.wmf.org

World Museum of Mining
155 Museum Way PO Box 33 ... Butte MT 59703 406-723-7211 723-7211 520
Web: www.miningmuseum.org

World Music Supply 2414 W Seventh St ... Muncie IN 47302 765-213-6085 526
TF: 800-867-4611 ■ *Web:* www.worldmusicsupply.com

World Neighbors Inc (WN)
4127 NW 122nd St ... Oklahoma City OK 73120 405-752-9700 48-5
TF: 800-242-6387 ■ *Web:* www.wn.org

World Nutrition Inc
9449 N 90th St Ste 116 ... Scottsdale AZ 85258 480-921-1188 297-8
Web: www.bodylabs.net

World of Coca-Cola Atlanta
121 Baker St NW ... Atlanta GA 30313 404-676-5151 586-6299 520
TF: 888-855-5701 ■ *Web:* www.worldofcoca-cola.com

World of Watches
3701 Flamingo Rd Ste 100 ... Miramar FL 33027 954-983-2181 153
TF: 866-961-8463 ■ *Web:* www.worldofwatches.com

World of Wigs 2305 E 17th St ... Santa Ana CA 92705 714-547-4461 348
Web: www.worldofwigs.com

World Oil Co 9302 Garfield Ave ... South Gate CA 90280 562-928-0100 580

World Oil Tools Inc
72 Technology Way SE ... Calgary AB T3S0B9 403-720-5155 358
Web: www.worldoiltools.com

World Organization of China Painters Museum
2641 NW Tenth St ... Oklahoma City OK 73107 405-521-1234 521-1265 520
TF: 800-596-2375 ■ *Web:* wocporg.com

World Peace Prayer Society
26 Benton Rd ... Wassaic NY 12592 845-877-6093 877-6862 48-5
Web: www.worldpeace.org

World Poker Tour
5700 Wilshire Blvd ... Los Angeles CA 90036 323-330-9900 31
Web: www.worldpokertour.com

World Policy Institute (WPI)
220 Fifth Ave 9th Fl ... New York NY 10001 212-481-5005 481-5009 634
TF: 800-207-8354 ■ *Web:* www.worldpolicy.org

World Property Journal
1221 Brickell Ave Ste 900 ... Miami FL 33131 305-375-9292 530
TF: 800-777-7300 ■ *Web:* www.worldpropertyjournal.com

Company	City	State	ZIP	Phone	Fax	Class
World Publishing Co 14 N Mission St *Web:* www.wenatcheeworld.com	Wenatchee	WA	98801	509-663-5161		532-3
World Publishing Co 315 S Boulder Ave *TF:* 800-444-6552 ■ *Web:* www.tulsaworld.com	Tulsa	OK	74102	918-583-2161	581-8353	637-8
World Racing Group Inc 7575 D W Winds Blvd Ste D *Web:* www.worldracinggroup.com	Concord	NC	28027	704-795-7223		642
World Recycling Co 5600 Columbia Park Rd *Web:* world-recycling.com	Cheverly	MD	20785	301-386-3010		179
World Relief 7 E Baltimore St *TF:* 800-535-5433 ■ *Web:* www.worldrelief.org	Baltimore	MD	21202	443-451-1900		48-5
World Resources Co 1600 Anderson Rd *Web:* www.worldresourcescompany.com	Mclean	VA	22102	703-734-9800		490
World Resources Institute (WRI) 10 G St NE Ste 800 *Web:* www.wri.org	Washington	DC	20002	202-729-7600	729-7610	48-13
World Securities Law Report 1801 S Bell St *TF:* 800-372-1033 ■ *Web:* www.bna.com	Arlington	VA	22202	800-372-1033		531-7
World Services LLC 1954 Airport Rd Ste 201 *Web:* worldservicesusa.com	Chamblee	GA	30341	404-486-5986		317
World Spice Inc 223 E Highland Pkwy *TF:* 800-234-1060 ■ *Web:* www.wsispice.com	Roselle	NJ	07203	908-245-0600	245-0696	296-37
World Steel Dynamics Inc 456 Sylvan Ave *Web:* www.worldsteeldynamics.com	Englewood Cliffs	NJ	07632	201-503-0900		195
World Trade Center Tampa Bay PO Box 18736 *Web:* www.wtctampa.com	Tampa	FL	33679	813-330-2931		822
World Trade Centers Assn (WTCA) 120 Broadway Ste 3350	New York	NY	10271	212-432-2626		49-12
World Trade Ctr 101 W Main St	Norfolk	VA	23510	757-627-9440		822
World Trade Ctr Alaska 431 W Seventh Ave Ste 108 *Web:* www.wtcak.org	Anchorage	AK	99501	907-278-7233	278-2982	822
World Trade Ctr Assn Los Angeles 350 S Figueroa St Ste 272 *TF:* 800-990-7788 ■ *Web:* laedc.org/wtc	Los Angeles	CA	90071	213-680-1888	680-1878	822
World Trade Ctr Baltimore 401 E Pratt St Ste 232 *Web:* www.wtci.org	Baltimore	MD	21202	410-576-0022	576-0751	822
World Trade Ctr Delaware 802 NW St *TF:* 800-573-6105 ■ *Web:* www.wtcde.com	Wilmington	DE	19801	302-656-7905	656-7956	822
World Trade Ctr Denver 1625 Broadway Ste 680 *TF:* 800-222-4444 ■ *Web:* wtcdenver.org	Denver	CO	80202	303-592-5760	592-5228	822
World Trade Ctr Detroit/Windsor 1200 Sixth St *TF:* 800-427-5100 ■ *Web:* www.wtcdw.com	Detroit	MI	48226	313-962-2345		822
World Trade Ctr Miami 1007 N America Way Ste 500 *Web:* worldtrade.org	Miami	FL	33132	305-871-7910	871-7904	822
World Trade Ctr Montreal 380 St Antoine St W Ste 6000 *Web:* www.centredecommercemondial.com/en/access	Montreal	QC	H2Y3X7	514-871-4000	871-1255	822
World Trade Ctr of New Orleans 365 Canal St Ste 1120 *TF:* 800-499-6065 ■ *Web:* wtcno.org	New Orleans	LA	70130	504-529-1601	529-1691	822
World Trade Ctr Orlando 19 E Central Ave *Web:* www.worldtradecenterorlando.org	Orlando	FL	32801	407-685-8096	876-6210	822
World Trade Ctr Palm Beach 777 S Flagler Dr *Web:* www.wtcpalmbeach.com	West Palm Beach	FL	33401	561-712-1443	712-1445	822
World Trade Ctr Portland 121 SW Salmon St *Web:* www.wtcpd.com	Portland	OR	97204	503-464-8688	464-2300	822
World Trade Ctr Saint Louis 7733 Forsyth Blvd Ste 2200 *Web:* www.worldtradecenter-stl.com	Saint Louis	MO	63105	314-615-8141	615-8140	822
World Trade Ctr Seattle 2200 Alaskan Way Ste 410 *Web:* www.wtcseattle.com	Seattle	WA	98121	206-441-5144	770-7923	822
World Trade Ctr Tacoma 950 Pacific Ave Ste 310 *Web:* www.wtcta.org	Tacoma	WA	98402	253-396-1022	396-1033	822
World Trade Service Inc 1050 Nine N Dr Ste A *Web:* www.worldtradeservice.com	Alpharetta	GA	30004	770-521-0124		791
World Travel Bureau Inc 618 N Main St *TF:* 800-899-3370 ■ *Web:* www.wtbtvl.com	Santa Ana	CA	92701	714-835-8111	835-8124	771
World Travel Holdings (WTH) 100 Fordham Rd Bldg C Bldg C *TF:* 877-958-7447 ■ *Web:* www.worldtravelholdings.com	Wilmington	MA	01887	617-424-7990	424-1943	771
World Travel Inc 1724 W Schuylkill Rd *TF:* 877-265-1881 ■ *Web:* www.worldtravelinc.com	Douglassville	PA	19518	610-327-9000		771
World Travel Service Inc 10201 Parkside Dr *Web:* www.worldtrav.com	Knoxville	TN	37922	865-777-1600		772
World Travel Services LLC 7645 E 63rd St Ste 101 *TF:* 800-324-4987 ■ *Web:* www.worldtraveltoday.com	Tulsa	OK	74133	918-743-8856		772
World University 107 N Ventura St PO Box 1567 *TF:* 888-370-7589 ■ *Web:* www.worldu.edu	Ojai	CA	93024	805-646-1444	646-1217	166
World Ventures Tours & Travel Inc 5103 Kingston Pk Ste 112 *Web:* www.wvtt.com	Knoxville	TN	37919	865-588-7426		772
World Vision Inc 34834 Weyerhaeuser Way S PO Box 9716 *TF:* 888-511-6548 ■ *Web:* www.worldvision.org	Federal Way	WA	98001	253-815-1000		48-5
World War II Memorial State Park c/o Lincoln Woods State Pk 2 Manchester Print Works Rd *Web:* www.riparks.com	Lincoln	RI	02865	401-762-9717		565
World Wide Concessions Inc 1950 Old Cuthbert Rd Ste M *TF:* 888-377-7666 ■ *Web:* www.wwconcessions.com	Cherry Hill	NJ	08034	856-933-9900		701
World Wide Dreams LLC 4 W 33rd St	New York	NY	10001	212-273-9200		156
World Wide Fittings Inc 7501 N Natchez Ave *TF:* 800-393-9894 ■ *Web:* www.worldwidefittings.com	Niles	IL	60714	847-588-2200	588-2212	595
World Wide Group LLC 5507 Nesconset Hwy Ste 10 *TF:* 800-790-4519 ■ *Web:* worldwidegrouptravel.com	Mount Sanai	NY	11766	800-790-4519		148
World Wide Motors Inc 3900 E 96th St *Web:* www.worldwidemotors.com	Indianapolis	IN	46240	317-580-6800		516
World Wide Packaging LLC 15 Vreeland Rd Ste 4 *TF:* 800-950-0390 ■ *Web:* www.wwpinc.com	Florham Park	NJ	07932	973-805-6500	805-6510	231
World Wide Web Consortium (W3C) 32 Vassar St Rm 32-G515 *Web:* www.w3.org	Cambridge	MA	02139	617-253-2613	258-5999	48-9
World Wildlife Fund (WWF) 1250 24th St NW PO Box 97180 *TF:* 800-225-5993 ■ *Web:* www.worldwildlife.org	Washington	DC	20090	202-293-4800	293-9211	48-3
World Wildlife Fund Canada (WWF) 245 Eglinton Ave E Ste 410 *TF:* 800-267-2632 ■ *Web:* www.wwf.ca	Toronto	ON	M4P3J1	416-489-8800		48-3
World Wrapps 3023 80th Ave SE Ste 200 *Web:* www.worldwrapps.com	Mercer Island	WA	98040	206-233-9727		670
World Wrestling Entertainment Inc 1241 E Main St *NYSE: WWE*	Stamford	CT	06902	203-352-8600	359-5151	181
World's Finest Chocolate Inc 4801 S Lawndale **Fax Area Code:* 877 ■ *TF:* 888-821-8452 ■ *Web:* www.worldsfinestchocolate.com	Chicago	IL	60632	888-821-8452	256-2685*	296-8
World*Class Learning Materials PO Box 639 *TF:* 800-638-6470 ■ *Web:* www.wclm.com	Candler	NC	28715	800-638-6470	638-6499	243
World, The 403 US Rt 302-Berlin *TF:* 800-639-9753 ■ *Web:* www.vt-world.com	Barre	VT	05641	802-479-2582		532-4
World, The 1551 Sawgrass Corporate Pkwy Ste 200 *TF:* 800-394-2255 ■ *Web:* www.aboardtheworld.com	Fort Lauderdale	FL	33323	954-538-8449	431-7151	220
WorldAPP Inc 220 Forbes Rd *Web:* worldapp.com	Braintree	MA	02184	781-849-8118		174
Worldata 3000 N Military Trl *TF:* 800-331-8102 ■ *Web:* www.worldata.com	Boca Raton	FL	33431	561-393-8200	368-8345	6
WorldatWork 14040 N Northsight Blvd *TF:* 877-951-9191 ■ *Web:* www.worldatwork.org	Scottsdale	AZ	85260	202-315-5500	315-5550	49-12
WorldClass Travel Network 7831 Southtown Ctr Ste A *TF:* 800-234-3576 ■ *Web:* www.worldclassnetwork.net	Bloomington	MN	55431	952-835-8636	835-2340	772
Worldcom Exchange Inc 43 NW Dr *Web:* www.wei.com	Salem	NH	03079	603-893-0900		180
Worldfest Houston International Film Festival PO Box 40965 *TF:* 866-965-9955 ■ *Web:* www.houstontheatre.com	Houston	TX	77240	713-629-3700		282
WorldFlash Software Inc 3853 Marcasel Ave *Web:* www.worldflash.com	Los Angeles	CA	90066	310-775-3633		178-7
WorldGate Communications Inc 3800 Horizon Blvd Ste 103 *OTC: WGATQ*	Trevose	PA	19053	215-354-5100		398
Worldhotels 152 W 57th St 6th Fl *Web:* www.worldhotels.com	New York	NY	10019	212-956-0200		376
Worldlink Integration Group Inc 21076 Bake Pkwy Ste 106 *Web:* www.worldlinkintegration.com	Lake Forest	CA	92630	949-861-2830		179
Worldly Voices LLC 2610 Westwood Dr *TF:* 800-909-8439 ■ *Web:* www.worldlyvoices.com	Nashville	TN	37204	615-321-8802		657
WorldMark the Club 9805 Willows Rd NE *TF:* 800-722-3487 ■ *Web:* www.worldmarktheclub.com	Redmond	WA	98052	425-498-1950		753
WorldMed Assist 1230 Mtn Side Ct *TF:* 866-999-3848 ■ *Web:* www.worldmedassist.com	Concord	CA	94521	866-999-3848		363
WORLDPAC Inc 37137 Hickory St *TF:* 800-888-9982 ■ *Web:* www.worldpac.com	Newark	CA	94560	510-742-8900		61
WorldPantry.com Inc 790 Tennessee St *TF:* 866-972-6879 ■ *Web:* www.worldpantry.com	San Francisco	CA	94107	866-972-6079		393
WorldPost Technologies Inc 5886 De Zavala Rd Ste 102/535 *Web:* www.worldpost.com	San Antonio	TX	78249	210-212-5600	212-5800	808
WorldRes Ltd 15333 N Pima Rd Ste 245 *Web:* www.worldres.com	Scottsdale	AZ	85260	480-946-5100	946-0450	376
Worlds End State Park 82 Cabin Bridge Rd *Web:* www.dcnr.state.pa.us	Forksville	PA	18616	570-924-3287		565
Worlds of Fun & Oceans of Fun 4545 NE Worlds of Fun Dr *TF:* 800-434-7894 ■ *Web:* www.worldsoffun.com	Kansas City	MO	64161	816-454-4545	454-4655	32
Worlds.com Inc 11 Royal Rd *TF:* 800-315-2580 ■ *Web:* www.worlds.com	Brookline	MA	02445	617-725-8900	975-3888	178-8
WorldStrides 218 W Water St Ste 400 *TF General:* 800-999-7676 ■ *Web:* worldstrides.com/discoveries	Charlottesville	VA	22902	800-999-7676		760
Worldtech International LLC 2331 Mill Rd Ste 100 *Web:* www.worldtech-int.com	Alexandria	VA	22314	703-778-5444		194
WorldTEK Event & Travel Management 1 Audubon Ste 400 *TF:* 800-233-5989 ■ *Web:* www.worldtek.com	New Haven	CT	06511	203-772-0470	865-2034	772
Worldtrans Services Inc 7130 Miramar Rd Ste 100a *TF:* 800-736-3769 ■ *Web:* www.worldtransinc.com	San Diego	CA	92121	858-536-7900		311
WorldVenture 1501 W Mineral Ave *TF:* 800-487-4224 ■ *Web:* www.worldventure.com	Littleton	CO	80120	720-283-2000	283-9383	48-20

Name / Address	City	State	ZIP	Phone	Fax	Class
Worldview Solutions Inc 115 S 15th St Ste 400 *TF:* 800-331-7881 ■ *Web:* www.worldviewsolutions.com	Richmond	VA	23219	804-915-7628		463
Worldview Travel Management Co 101 W Fourth St Ste 400 *Web:* www.worldviewtravel.com	Santa Ana	CA	92701	714-540-7400		772
WorldViz LLC 614 Santa Barbara St *Web:* www.worldviz.com	Santa Barbara	CA	93101	805-966-0786		246
Worldwatch Institute 1776 Massachusetts Ave NW *TF:* 877-539-9946 ■ *Web:* www.worldwatch.org	Washington	DC	20036	202-452-1999	296-7365	634
Worldwide Aeros Corp 1734 Gage Rd **Fax Area Code:* 323 ■ *Web:* aeroscraft.com	Montebello	CA	90640	818-344-3999	201-8383*	28
Worldwide Court Reporters 3000 Weslayan St Ste 235 *TF:* 800-745-1101 ■ *Web:* www.worldwidecourtreporters.com	Houston	TX	77027	800-745-1101		393
Worldwide Dispensers USA 78 Second Ave S *Web:* dssmith.com	Lester Prairie	MN	55354	320-395-2553		608
Worldwide Employee Benefits Network Inc (WEB) 11520 N Central Expy Ste 201 **Fax Area Code:* 214 ■ *TF:* 888-795-6862 ■ *Web:* www.webnetwork.org	Dallas	TX	75243	888-795-6862	382-3038*	49-12
Worldwide Energy & Mfg USA Inc 1675 Rollins Rd Unit F *OTC: WEMU* ■ *Web:* www.wwmusa.com	Burlingame	CA	94010	650-794-9888	794-9878	787
Worldwide Express 2602 McKinney Ave Ste 400 *TF:* 800-758-7447 ■ *Web:* www.wwex.com	Dallas	TX	75204	214 720 2400	720-2446	546
Worldwide Golf Co 560 E 2100 S *TF:* 800-219-1113 ■ *Web:* www.worldwidegolfshops.com	Salt Lake City	UT	84106	801-487-8233	466-5713	711
Worldwide Golf Shops Inc 1421 Village Wy *TF:* 888-216-5252 ■ *Web:* www.worldwidegolfshops.com	Santa Ana	CA	92705	714-543-8284		710
Worldwide Holidays Inc 7800 Red Rd Ste 112 *TF:* 800-327-9854 ■ *Web:* www.galapagoscruises.net	South Miami	FL	33143	305-665-0841	661-1457	771
Worldwide Oil Field Machine 11809 Canemont *Web:* www.womusa.com	Houston	TX	77035	713-729-9200		537
Worldwide Partners Inc 100 Spruce St Ste 203 *Web:* www.worldwidepartners.com	Denver	CO	80230	303-577-9760		7
Worldwide Refractories Inc 6th St	Tarentum	PA	15084	724-224-8800		663
Worldwide Revenue Solutions Inc 555 Republic Dr	Plano	TX	75074	972-424-2200		225
Worldwide Sign Systems 446 N Cecil St *TF:* 800-874-3334 ■ *Web:* www.wwsign.com	Bonduel	WI	54107	800-874-3334		701
Worldwide Steel Buildings PO Box 588 *TF:* 800-825-0316 ■ *Web:* www.worldwidesteelbuildings.com	Peculiar	MO	64078	800-825-0316		105
Worldwide Travel & Cruise Assoc Inc 150 S University Dr Ste E *TF:* 800-881-8484 ■ *Web:* www.cruiseco.com	Plantation	FL	[illegible]	[illegible]	[illegible]	771
Worley & Obetz Inc 85 White Oak Rd PO Box 429 *TF:* 800 697 6801 ■ *Web:* www.worleyobetz.com	Manheim	PA	17545	717-665-6891		316
WorleyParsons Corp 5421 Blackfalds Industrial Way *Web:* www.worleyparsons.com	Blackfalds	AL	77401	403-885-4209	885-4948	192
Worly Plumbing Supply Inc 54 E Harrison St *TF:* 800-365-1175 ■ *Web:* worly.com	Delaware	OH	43015	740-363-1151		610
Wormser Corp 150 Coolidge Ave *TF:* 800-546-4040 ■ *Web:* www.wormsercorp.com	Englewood	NJ	07631	800-546-4040		155-15
Wormsloe State Historic Site 7601 Skidaway Rd *TF:* 800-864-7275 ■ *Web:* www.gastateparks.org/info/wormsloe	Savannah	GA	31406	912-353-3023		565
Woronoff Hyman Levenson & Sweet PC 30600 Northwestern Hwy Ste 302 *Web:* whls.com	Farmington Hills	MI	48334	248-487-2600		2
Worrell Corp 305 S Post Rd *TF:* 800-297-9599 ■ *Web:* worrellcorp.com	Indianapolis	IN	46219	317-895-9708		292
Worsham College of Mortuary Science 495 Northgate Pkwy *Web:* www.worsham.edu	Wheeling	IL	60090	847-808-8444	808-8493	800
Worship Center Christian Church, The 100 Derby Pkwy *Web:* www.theworshipcentercc.org	Birmingham	AL	35210	205-451-1750	833-5443	48-20
Worship Network PO Box 428 *TF:* 800-728-8723 ■ *Web:* www.worship.net	Safety Harbor	FL	34695	800-728-8723		740
Wort Hotel 50 N Glenwood *TF Cust Svc:* 800-322-2727 ■ *Web:* www.worthotel.com	Jackson	WY	83001	307-733-2190	733-2067	379
Worth & Company Inc 6263 Kellers Church Rd *TF:* 800-220-5130 ■ *Web:* www.worthandcompany.com	Pipersville	PA	18947	267-362-1100	362-1130	189-10
Worth Co, The 214 Sherman Ave PO Box 88 *TF:* 800-944-1899 ■ *Web:* www.worthco.com	Stevens Point	WI	54481	715-344-6081	344-3021	710
Worth Construction Company Inc 24 Taylor Ave *Web:* www.worthconstruction.com	Bethel	CT	06801	203-797-8788	791-2515	186
Worth County PO Box 450 *Web:* worthcounty.us	Grant City	MO	64456	660-564-2219	564-2432	338
Worth County 1000 Central Ave *Web:* www.worthcounty.org	Northwood	IA	50459	641-324-2840	324-2360	338
Worth County 201 N Main St *Web:* worthcountyboc.com	Sylvester	GA	31791	229-776-8200	776-8232	338
Worth Higgins & Assoc Inc 8770 Park Central Dr *TF:* 800-883-7768 ■ *Web:* worthhiggins.com	Richmond	VA	23227	804-264-2304		174
Worthen Industries Inc 3 E Spit Brook Rd *Web:* www.worthenind.com	Nashua	NH	03060	603-888-5443	888-7945	3
Worthington Area Chamber of Commerce 25 W New England Ave Ste 100 *Web:* www.worthingtonchamber.org	Worthington	OH	43085	614-888-3040	841-4842	139
Worthington Aviation Parts Inc 2995 Lone Oak Cir *Web:* www.worthingtonav.com	St Paul	MN	55121	651-994-1600		770
Worthington Biochemical Corp 730 Vassar Ave *TF:* 800-445-9603 ■ *Web:* www.worthington-biochem.com	Lakewood	NJ	08701	732-942-1660	942-9270	231
Worthington Dealership Group 5548 Paseo Del Norte *Web:* www.calworthington.com	Carlsbad	CA	92008	760-431-1222		198
Worthington Direct Holdings LLC 6301 Gaston Ave Ste 670 *TF:* 800-599-6636 ■ *Web:* www.worthingtondirect.com	Dallas	TX	75214	800-599-6636		360-3
Worthington Farms Inc 3661 BallaRds Crossroads Rd *Web:* www.worthingtonfarms.com	Greenville	NC	27834	252-756-3827	756-9442	369
Worthington Glacier State Recreation Site 287 Richardson Hwy *Web:* dnr.alaska.gov	Soldotna	AK	99669	907-262-5581		565
Worthington Industries 200 Old Wilson Bridge Rd *NYSE: WOR* ■ *TF:* 800-736-4666 ■ *Web:* www.worthingtonindustries.com	Columbus	OH	43085	614-438-3210		485
Worthington Jewelers 692 High St *Web:* www.worthingtonjewelers.com	Worthington	OH	43085	614-430-8800		410
Worthington Specialty Processing 4905 S Meridian Rd *Web:* worthingtonindustries.com	Jackson	MI	49201	517-789-0200		723
Worthington State Forest HC 62 PO Box 2 *Web:* www.njparksandforests.org	Columbia	NJ	07832	908-841-9575		565
Worthington Steel Co 200 W Old Wilson Bridge Rd *TF:* 800-944-3733 ■ *Web:* www.worthingtonindustries.com	Columbus	OH	43085	614-438-3210		723
Worthington Steelpac 1201 Eden Rd *Web:* www.worthingtonsteelpac.com	York	PA	17402	717-851-0325		567
Worthington This Week 7801 N Central Dr *Web:* www.thisweeknews.com	Lewis Center	OH	43035	740-888-6100	888-6006	532-4
Worthwhile 7 S Laurens St Ste 200 *TF:* 800-777-9695 ■ *Web:* worthwhile.com	Greenville	SC	29601	864-233-2552		177
Wor-Wic Community College 32000 Campus Dr **Fax:* Admissions ■ *TF:* 800-735-2258 ■ *Web:* www.worwic.edu	Salisbury	MD	21804	410-334-2800	334-2954*	162
Worx Group LLC, The 18 Waterbury Rd *TF:* 800-732-8090 ■ *Web:* www.theworxgroup.com	Prospect	CT	06712	203-758-3311		180
Worzalla Publishing Co 3535 Jefferson St PO Box 307 *Web:* www.worzalla.com	Stevens Point	WI	54481	715-344-9600		626
Worzella & Sons Inc 2801 Hoover Ave *TF:* 800-450-7260 ■ *Web:* worzellaandsons.com	Plover	WI	54467	715-344-4098		10-11
WOSM-FM 103.1 (Rel) 4720 Radio Rd	Ocean Springs	MS	39564	228-432-1032	875-6461	645
Wostmann & Associates Inc 105 S Seward St Ste 301 *TF:* 800-581-2201 ■ *Web:* www.wostmann.com	Juneau	AK	99801	907-586-6167		196
WOSU-AM 820 (NPR) 2400 Olentangy River Rd *Web:* www.wosu.org	Columbus	OH	43210	614-292-9678	292-7625	645-42
WOSU-TV Ch 34 (PBS) 2400 Olentangy River Rd *Web:* wosu.org/2012/television	Columbus	OH	43210	614-292-9678	292-7625	741-35
WOTV-TV Ch 4 (ABC) 120 College Ave *Web:* www.wotv4women.com	Grand Rapids	MI	49503	616-456-8888	456-9169	741-53
WOUC-TV Ch 44 (PBS) 35 S College St *TF:* 800-456-2044 ■ *Web:* www.woub.org	Athens	OH	45701	740-593-1771		741
Woulfe Mining Corp 837 W Hastings St Ste 408	Vancouver	BC	V6C3N6	604-684-6264		502
Wound Ostomy & Continence Nurses Society (WOCN) 1120 Rt 73 Ste 200 *TF:* 888-224-9626 ■ *Web:* www.wocn.org	Mount Laurel	NJ	08054	888-224-9626		49-8
Woven Electronics LLC 1001 Old Stage Rd *Web:* www.wovenelectronics.com	Simpsonville	SC	29681	864-963-5131		697
WOW (Wider Opportunities for Women) 1001 Connecticut Ave NW Ste 930 *TF:* 800-260-5956 ■ *Web:* www.wowonline.org	Washington	DC	20036	202-464-1596	464-1660	48-24
WOW FM County 104.3 827 E Pk Blvd Ste 100 *Web:* www.wow1043.com	Boise	ID	83712	208-344-6363		645-22
WOWindow Posters PO Box 581 *Web:* www.wowindows.com	Cranford	NJ	07016	908-272-1011		361
WOWK-TV Ch 13 (CBS) 555 Fifth Ave *TF:* 800-333-7636 ■ *Web:* www.tristateupdate.com	Huntington	WV	25701	304-525-1313		741
WOWO-AM 1190 (N/T) 2915 Maples Rd *TF:* 800-333-1190 ■ *Web:* www.wowo.com	Fort Wayne	IN	46816	260-447-5511	447-7546	645-63
WOWT-TV Ch 6 (NBC) 3501 Farnam St *TF:* 866-434-8587 ■ *Web:* www.wowt.com	Omaha	NE	68131	402-346-6666	233-7887	741-94
Wowza Inc 2601 Second Ave S Studio One *Web:* wowzamade.com	Minneapolis	MN	55408	612-435-7100		7
Wozniak Industries Inc 2 Mid America Plaza Ste 706 *TF:* 800-325-9808 ■ *Web:* www.wozniakindustries.com	Oakbrook Terrace	IL	60181	630-954-3400	954-3605	483
Wozniak Industries Inc Commercial Forged Products Div 5757 W 65th St *TF:* 800-637-2695 ■ *Web:* www.commercialforged.com	Bedford Park	IL	60638	708-458-1220	458-9346	483
WP (Walton Press) 402 Mayfield Dr *TF:* 800-354-0235 ■ *Web:* www.waltonpress.com	Monroe	GA	30655	770-267-2596		555
WP Carey & Company LLC 50 Rockefeller Plaza *NYSE: WPC* ■ *TF:* 800-972-2739 ■ *Web:* www.wpcarey.com	New York	NY	10020	212-492-1100		655
WPBA-TV Ch 30 (PBS) 740 Bismark Rd NE *TF:* 800-683-1899 ■ *Web:* www.pba.org	Atlanta	GA	30324	678-686-0321	686-0356	741-7
WPBF-TV Ch 25 (ABC) 3970 RCA Blvd Ste 7007 *Web:* www.wpbf.com	Palm Beach Gardens	FL	33410	561-694-2525		741
WPBT-TV Ch 2 (PBS) 14901 NE 20th Ave **Fax:* News Rm ■ *TF:* 800-222-9728 ■ *Web:* www.wpbt2.org	Miami	FL	33181	305-949-8321	944-4211*	741-82
WPC (Willmar Poultry Co, The) 3735 County Rd 5 SW	Willmar	MN	56201	320-235-8850		10-8

	Phone	Fax	Class
WPCD-FM 88.7 (Rock) 2400 W Bradley Ave . . . Champaign IL 61821 *TF:* 800-600-5279 ■ *Web:* wpcd.parkland.edu	217-373-3790		645-30
WPCV-FM 97.5 (Ctry) 404 W Lime St . . . Lakeland FL 33815 *TF:* 800-227-9797 ■ *Web:* www.wpcv.com	863-682-8184	683-2409	645
WPGC-FM 95.5 (CHR) 1015 Half St SE Ste 200 . . . Washington DC 20003 *TF:* 877-955-5267 ■ *Web:* wpgc.cbslocal.com	877-955-5267		645
WPGH-TV Ch 53 (Fox) 750 Ivory Ave . . . Pittsburgh PA 15214 *Web:* www.wpgh53.com/pittsburgh_pa	412-931-5300		741-100
WPGU-FM 107.1 (Alt) 512 E Green St . . . Champaign IL 61820 *Web:* www.wpgu.com	217-337-8382		645-30
WPHI-FM 107.9 (Urban) 2 Bala Plaza Ste 700 . . . Bala Cynwyd PA 19004 *Web:* boomphilly.com	610-538-1100		645
WPHL-TV Ch 17 (MNT) 5001 Wynnefield Ave . . . Philadelphia PA 19131 *TF:* 800-326-2439 ■ *Web:* phl17.com	215-878-1700		741-98
WPHT-AM 1210 (N/T) 2 Bala Plaza Ste 800 . . . Bala Cynwyd PA 19004 *Web:* tunein.com/radio/Talk-Radio-1210-WPHT-s21950	610-668-5800	668-5885	645
WPI (Waukesha-Pearce Industries Inc) 12320 S Main St . . . Houston TX 77035 *Web:* www.wpi.com	713-723-1050	551-0454	385
WPI (Williamston Products Inc) 845 Progress Ct . . . Williamston MI 48895 *Web:* www.wpius.com	517-655-2131		608
WPI (World Policy Institute) 220 Fifth Ave 9th Fl . . . New York NY 10001 *TF:* 800-207-8354 ■ *Web:* www.worldpolicy.org	212-481-5005	481-5009	634
WPKN-FM 89.5 (Var) 244 University Ave . . . Bridgeport CT 06604 *Web:* www.wpkn.org	203-331-9756		645-158
WPKT-FM 90.5 (NPR) 1049 Asylum Ave . . . Hartford CT 06105 *Web:* www.wnpr.org	860-278-5310		645-72
WPL (Warwick Public Library) 600 Sandy Ln . . . Warwick RI 02886 *TF:* 800-359-3090 ■ *Web:* warwicklibrary.org	401-739-5440		434-3
WPLG-TV Ch 10 (ABC) 3401 W Hallandale Beach Blvd . . . Pembroke Park FL 33023 **Fax Area Code:* 305 ■ **Fax:* News Rm ■ *Web:* www.local10.com	954-364-2500	375-2480*	741
WPLJ-FM 95.5 (AC) 2 Penn Plaza 17th Fl . . . New York NY 10121 *Web:* www.955plj.nyc	212-613-8905		645-111
WPLK-AM 800 (Nost) 1428 St Johns Ave . . . Palatka FL 32177 *Web:* www.wplk.com	386-325-5800		645
WPLM-FM 99.1 (AC) 17 Columbus Rd . . . Plymouth MA 02360 *TF:* 877-327-9991 ■ *Web:* www.easy991.com	508-746-1390	830-1128	645
WPLN-FM 90.3 (NPR) 630 Mainstream Dr . . . Nashville TN 37228 *TF:* 877-760-2903 ■ *Web:* nashvillepublicradio.org	615-760-2903	760-2904	645-108
WPLR-FM 99.1 (Rock) 440 Wheelers Farm Rd Ste 302 . . . Milford CT 06461 *Web:* wplr.com	203-783-8200		645
WPMA (Wood Products Manufacturers Assn) PO Box 761 . . . Westminster MA 01473 *TF:* 800-878-8878 ■ *Web:* www.wpma.org	978-874-5445	874-9946	49-3
WPMI-TV Ch 15 (NBC) 661 Azalea Rd . . . Mobile AL 36609 *Web:* www.local15tv.com	251-602-1500	602-1547	741-85
WPMT-TV Ch 43 (Fox) 2005 S Queen St . . . York PA 17403 *Web:* www.fox43.com	717-843-0043	843-9741	741
WPMY-TV Ch 22 (MNT) 750 Ivory Ave . . . Pittsburgh PA 15214 *Web:* 22thepoint.com	412-931-5300	931-4284	741-100
WPNE-FM 89.3 (NPR) 2420 Nicolet Dr . . . Green Bay WI 54311 *TF:* 800-654-6228 ■ *Web:* www.wpr.org	920-465-2444	465-2576	645-67
WPNE-TV Ch 38 (PBS) 821 University Ave . . . Madison WI 53706 *Web:* www.wpt.org	608-263-2121		741
WPNN-AM 790 (N/T) 3801 N Pace Blvd . . . Pensacola FL 32505 *TF:* 800-726-1191 ■ *Web:* talk790.com	850-433-1141	433-1142	645-120
WPOC-FM 93.1 (Country) 711 W 40th St Ste 350 . . . Baltimore MD 21211 *TF:* 800-321-3693 ■ *Web:* wpoc.iheart.com	410-366-7600		645-16
WPOR-FM 101.9 (Ctry) 420 Western Ave . . . South Portland ME 04106 *Web:* www.wpor.com	207-774-4561	774-3788	645
WPP Group USA Inc 100 Pk Ave . . . New York NY 10017 *Web:* www.wpp.com	212-632-2200	632-2249	4
WPPX-TV Ch 61 (I) 3901 B Main St Ste 301 . . . Philadelphia PA 19127	215 482 4770	482-4777	741-98
WPR (Wisconsin Public Radio) 821 University Ave . . . Madison WI 53706 **Fax Area Code:* 608 ■ *TF:* 800-747-7444 ■ *Web:* www.wpr.org	800-747-7444	263-9763*	632
Wpri TV 25 Catamore Blvd . . . East Providence RI 02914	401-438-7200		741
WPRO-FM 92.3 (CHR) 1502 Wampanoag Trl . . . East Providence RI 02915 *TF:* 800-638-0092 ■ *Web:* www.92profm.com	401-433-4200		645
WPS (Washington Professional Systems) 109GaitherDr Ste 301 . . . Mount Laurel NJ 08054 *Web:* www.wpsworld.com	856-273-8688	273-8558	52
WPS Industries Inc 228 Industrial St . . . West Monroe LA 71292 *Web:* www.wpsindustries.com	318-812-2800		207
WPSD (Waterbury Public School District) 236 Grand St Ste 1 . . . Waterbury CT 06702 *Web:* www.waterbury.k12.ct.us	203-574-8000	574-8010	186
WPSG-TV Ch 57 (CW) 1555 Hamilton St . . . Philadelphia PA 19130	215-977-5700		741-98
WPST-FM 94.5 (AC) 619 Alexander Rd 3rd Fl . . . Princeton NJ 08540 *TF:* 800-248-9778 ■ *Web:* www.wpst.com	609-419-0300	419-0143	645
WPT (Wisconsin Public Television) 821 University Ave . . . Madison WI 53706 *TF:* 800-422-9707 ■ *Web:* www.wpt.org	608-263-2121	263-9763	632
WPT Enterprises Inc (WPTE) 5700 Wilshire Blvd Ste 350 . . . Los Angeles CA 90036 *Web:* www.worldpokertour.com	949-225-2600		742
WPTD-TV Ch 16 (PBS) 110 S Jefferson St . . . Dayton OH 45402 *TF:* 800-247-1614 ■ *Web:* www.thinktv.org	937-220-1600	220-1642	741-38
WPTE (WPT Enterprises Inc) 5700 Wilshire Blvd Ste 350 . . . Los Angeles CA 90036 *Web:* www.worldpokertour.com	949-225-2600		742
WPTE-FM 94.9 (AC) 236 Clearfield Ave Ste 206 . . . Virginia Beach VA 23462 *Web:* www.pointradio.com	757-497-2000		645-112
WPTF-AM 680 (N/T) 3012 Highwoods Blvd Ste 201 . . . Raleigh NC 27604 *TF:* 800-662-7979 ■ *Web:* www.wptf.com	919-790-9392	882-1746	645-131
WPTV-TV Ch 5 (NBC) 1100 Banyan Blvd . . . West Palm Beach FL 33401 **Fax:* News Rm ■ *Web:* www.wptv.com	561-655-5455	653-5719*	741-140
WPTZ-TV Ch 5 (NBC) 5 Television Dr . . . Plattsburgh NY 12901 *Web:* www.mynbc5.com	518-561-5555		741
WPUR-FM 107.3 (Ctry) 950 Tilton Rd Ste 200 . . . Northfield NJ 08225 *Web:* www.catcountry1073.com	609-645-9797		645
WPVI-TV Ch 6 (ABC) 4100 City Line Ave . . . Philadelphia PA 19131 *TF:* 866-639-7749	215-878-9700	581-4530	741-98
WPWR-TV Ch 50 (Fox) 205 N Michigan Ave . . . Chicago IL 60601 *Web:* www.fox32chicago.com/my50chicago	312-565-5532	819-0385	741-29
WPWX-FM 92.3 (Urban) 6336 Calumet Ave . . . Hammond IN 46324 *Web:* www.power92chicago.com	773-734-4455		645
WPX Delivery Solutions 3320 W Valley Hwy N Ste 111 . . . Auburn WA 98001 *TF:* 800-562-1091 ■ *Web:* www.wpx.com	253-876-2760	876-2799	546
WPXD-TV Ch 31 (I) 26935 W 11 Mile Rd . . . Southfield MI 48033 **Fax Area Code:* 646 ■ *TF:* 888-467-2988 ■ *Web:* ionmedia.com	212-757-3100	597-5903*	741
WPXE-TV Ch 55 (I) 6161 N Flint Rd Ste F . . . Milwaukee WI 53209	414-247-0117		741-83
WPXI-TV Ch 11 (NBC) 4145 Evergreen Rd . . . Pittsburgh PA 15214 *TF:* 800-237-9794 ■ *Web:* www.wpxi.com	412-237-1100		741-100
WPXN-TV Ch 31 (I) 810 Seventh Ave 30th Fl . . . New York NY 10019 **Fax Area Code:* 646 ■ *TF:* 888-467-2988 ■ *Web:* ionmedia.com	212-757-3100	597-5903*	741-91
WPXT-TV Ch 12 (CW) 4 Ledgeview Dr . . . Westbrook ME 04092 *Web:* ourmaine.com	207-774-0051		741
WPXW-TV Ch 66 (I) 6199 Old Arrington Ln . . . Fairfax Station VA 22039	703-503-7966		741
WPXY-FM 97.9 (CHR) 70 Commercial St . . . Rochester NY 14614 *TF:* 800-398-3029 ■ *Web:* www.98pxy.com	585-423-2900		645-138
WPYO-FM 95.3 (CHR) 4192 N John Young Pkwy . . . Orlando FL 32804 *Web:* www.power953.com	321-281-2000		645-116
WQA (Water Quality Assn) 4151 Naperville Rd . . . Lisle IL 60532 *TF:* 800-227-5558 ■ *Web:* www.wqa.org	630-505-0160	505-9637	48-12
WQBE-FM 97.5 (Ctry) 817 Suncrest Pl . . . Charleston WV 25303 *TF:* 800-222-3697 ■ *Web:* www.wqbe.com	304-344-9700	342-3118	645-32
WQBK-FM 103.9 (Rock) 1241 Kings Rd . . . Schenectady NY 12303 *Web:* q103albany.com	518-881-1515		645
WQCB-FM 106.5 (Ctry) 49 Acme Rd . . . Brewer ME 04412 *Web:* q1065.fm	207-989-5631		645
WQCW-TV Ch 30 (CW) 800 Gallia St Ste 430 . . . Portsmouth OH 45662	740-353-3391		741
WQDR-FM 94.7 (Ctry) 3012 Highwoods Blvd Ste 201 . . . Raleigh NC 27604 *Web:* www.947qdr.com	919-876-6464	790-8893	645-131
WQED Multimedia 4802 Fifth Ave . . . Pittsburgh PA 15213 *TF:* 855-700-9733 ■ *Web:* www.wqed.org	412-622-1300	622-6413	741-100
WQED-FM 89.3 (Clas) 4802 Fifth Ave . . . Pittsburgh PA 15213 *TF:* 855-700-9733 ■ *Web:* www.wqed.org	412-622-1300	622-7073	645-125
WQFL-FM 100.9 (Rel) PO Box 2118 . . . Omaha NE 68103 *TF:* 888-937-2471 ■ *Web:* www.air1.com	888-937-2471		645
WQHH-FM 96.5 (Urban) 600 W Cavanaugh . . . Lansing MI 48910 *TF:* 800-223-9797 ■ *Web:* www.power965fm.com	517-393-1320	393-0882	645-87
WQHT-FM 97.1 (Urban) 395 Hudson St 7th Fl . . . New York NY 10014 *TF:* 800-223-9797 ■ *Web:* www.hot97.com	212-229-9797	929-8559	645-111
WQKS 4101-A Wall St . . . Montgomery AL 36106	334-244-0961		645-104
WQLH-FM 98.5 (AC) 810 Victoria St . . . Green Bay WI 54302 *TF:* 855-782-7985 ■ *Web:* www.star98.net	920-468-4100	468-0250	645-67
WQLN-FM 91.3 (NPR) 8425 Peach St . . . Erie PA 16509 *TF:* 800-727-8854 ■ *Web:* www.wqln.org	814-864-3001	864-4077	645-54
WQLN-TV Ch 54 (PBS) 8425 Peach St . . . Erie PA 16509 *TF:* 800-727-8854 ■ *Web:* www.wqln.org	814-864-3001	864-4077	741-44
WQMX-FM 94.9 1795 W Market St . . . Akron OH 44313 *Web:* www.wqmx.com	330-869-9800		645-2
WQNU-FM 103.1 (Ctry) 612 S Fourth St . . . Louisville KY 40202 *Web:* www.qlouisville.com	502-636-5023		645-93
WQOK-FM 97.5 (Urban) 8001-101 Creedmoor Rd . . . Raleigh NC 27613 *Web:* hiphopnc.com	919-863-4840		645-131
WQUN-AM 1220 (Nost) 3085 Whitney Ave . . . Hamden CT 06518 *TF:* 800-462-1944 ■ *Web:* www.qu.edu	203-582-8984		645
WQXR-FM 96.3 (Clas) 160 Varick St 8th Fl . . . New York NY 10013 *Web:* www.wqxr.org	646-829-4400		645-111
WQYK-AM 1010 (Ctry) 9721 Executive Ctr Dr N Ste 200 . . . Saint Petersburg FL 33702	727-579-1925		645-162
WQYK-FM 99.5 (Ctry) 9721 Executive Ctr Dr N Ste 200 . . . Saint Petersburg FL 33702 *Web:* 995qyk.com	727-579-1925		645-162
WQZZ-FM 104.3 (Urban AC) 601 Greensboro Ave Ste 507 . . . Tuscaloosa AL 35401	205-345-4787		645-170
WR Berkley Corp 475 Steamboat Rd . . . Greenwich CT 06830 *NYSE:* WRB ■ *TF:* 800-238-6225 ■ *Web:* www.wrbc.com	203-629-3000		360-4
WR Case & Sons Cutlery Co 50 Owens Way PO Box 4000 . . . Bradford PA 16701 **Fax Area Code:* 814 ■ *TF:* 800-523-6350 ■ *Web:* www.wrcase.com	800-523-6350	368-1736*	222

Name / Address	City	State	ZIP	Phone	Fax	Class
WR Grace & Co 7500 Grace Dr *NYSE:* GRA ■ *TF:* 800-638-6014 ■ *Web:* www.grace.com	Columbia	MD	21044	410-531-4000	531-4367	145
WR Hambrecht & Co 909 Montgomery St 3rd Fl *TF Cust Svc:* 855-753-6484 ■ *Web:* www.wrhambrecht.com	San Francisco	CA	94133	415-551-8600		690
WR Rayson Company Inc 720 S Dickerson St *TF:* 800-526-1526 ■ *Web:* www.wrrayson.com	Burgaw	NC	28425	910-259-8100		557
WR Zanes & Company of Louisiana Inc 223 Tchoupitoulas St *TF:* 800-277-3322 ■ *Web:* www.wrzanes.com	New Orleans	LA	70130	504-524-1301	524-1309	311
WRA Inc 2169 Francisco Blvd E Ste G *Web:* www.eahhousing.org	San Rafael	CA	94901	415-454-8868		401
Wragtime Air Freight Inc 596 W 135th St *TF:* 800-586-9701 ■ *Web:* www.visionexpressltl.com	Gardena	CA	90248	800-586-9701		780
WRAL-FM 101.5 (AC) 3100 Highwoods Blvd Ste 140 *TF:* 800-745-3000 ■ *Web:* www.wralfm.com	Raleigh	NC	27604	919-890-6101	890-6146	645-131
WRAL-TV Ch 5 (CBS) 2619 Western Blvd *TF:* 800-245-0725 ■ *Web:* www.wral.com	Raleigh	NC	27606	919-821-8555	821-8541	741-105
Wrangell Harbor PO Box 531 *TF:* 800-347-4462 ■ *Web:* www.wrangell.com	Wrangell	AK	99929	907-874-3736	874-3197	618
Wrangell-Saint Elias National Park & Preserve Mile 1068 Richardson Hwy PO Box 439 *TF:* 866-705-5711 ■ *Web:* www.nps.gov/wrst	Copper Center	AK	99573	907-822-5234	822-7216	564
Wrapmail Inc 960 S Broadway Ste 120 *Web:* www.wrapmail.com	Hicksville	NY	11801	516-590-1846	977-0025	535
Wrap-On Company LLC 11756 S Austin Ave *TF:* 800-621-6947 ■ *Web:* wrap-on.com	Alsip	IL	60803	708-496-2150	496-2154	813
WRAS *Georgia State University* 33 Gilmer St SE *Web:* www2.gsu.edu	Atlanta	GA	30303	404-413-2000		645-10
Wray Ford Inc 2851 Benton Rd *Web:* wrayford.net	Bossier City	LA	71111	318-686-7300		57
Wray Ward Marketing Communications 900 Baxter St *Web:* www.wrayward.com	Charlotte	NC	28204	704-332-9071		7
WRAZ-TV Ch 50 (Fox) 2619 Western Blvd *TF:* 877-369-5050 ■ *Web:* www.fox50.com	Raleigh	NC	27606	919-595-5050	595-5028	741-105
WRB Enterprises 1414 W Swann Ave Ste 201 *Web:* wrbenterprises.com	Tampa	FL	33606	813-251-3737		360-3
WRBL-TV Ch 3 (CBS) 1350 13th Ave *TF:* 800-222-4788 ■ *Web:* www.wrbl.com	Columbus	GA	31901	706-323-3333	323-0841	741-34
WRBO-FM 5629 Murray Rd *Web:* www.1035wrbo.com	Memphis	TN	38119	901-682-1106	767-9531	645-98
WRBS-FM 95.1 (Rel) 3500 Commerce Dr *TF:* 800-965-9324 ■ *Web:* www.951shinefm.com	Baltimore	MD	21227	410-247-4100	247-4533	645-16
WRBW-TV Ch 65 (MNT) 35 Skyline Dr *Web:* www.fox35orlando.com/my65	Lake Mary	FL	32746	407-644-3535		741
WRCB-TV Ch 3 (NBC) 900 Whitehall Rd *Web:* www.wrcbtv.com	Chattanooga	TN	37405	423-267-5412		741-27
WRCG-AM 1420 (N/T) 1820 Wynnton Rd *Web:* www.1069rocks.com	Columbus	GA	31906	706-327-1217	596-4600	645-41
WRCH-FM 100.5 (AC) 10 Executive Dr *TF:* 800-530-1005 ■ *Web:* wrch.cbslocal.com	Farmington	CT	06032	860-677-6700		645
WRCTC (West River Co-op Telephone Co) 801 Coleman Ave PO Box 39 *TF:* 888-464-9513 ■ *Web:* www.sdplains.com	Bison	SD	57620	605-244-5213		736
WRC-TV Ch 4 (NBC) 4001 Nebraska Ave NW *Web:* www.nbcwashington.com	Washington	DC	20016	202-885-4000		741-139
WRDW-TV Ch 12 (CBS) PO Box 1212 *Web:* www.wrdw.com	Augusta	GA	30903	803-278-1212	279-0316	741-8
WREA (White River Electric Assn) PO Box 958 *TF:* 800-922-1987 ■ *Web:* wrea.org	Meeker	CO	81641	970-878-5041	878-5766	245
WREG-TV Ch 3 (CBS) 803 Ch Three Dr *TF:* 800-237-8073 ■ *Web:* www.wreg.com	Memphis	TN	38103	901-543-2333	543-2167	741-81
Wren Assoc Ltd 124 Wren Pkwy *TF:* 800-881-2249 ■ *Web:* www.wrensolutions.com	Jefferson City	MO	65109	573-893-2249		608
Wren's Nest, The 1050 Ralph David Abernathy Blvd SW *Web:* wrensnest.org	Atlanta	GA	30310	404-753-7735	753-8535	520
WRES (Woodmont Real Estate Services) 1050 Ralston Ave *Web:* www.wres.com	Belmont	CA	94002	650-592-3960	591-4577	655
WrestlingGearCom Ltd 655 W Grand Ave Ste 140 *Web:* www.wrestlinggear.com	Elmhurst	IL	60126	630-832-0500		711
WRET-TV Ch 49 (PBS) PO Box 4069 *Web:* www.scetv.org	Spartanburg	SC	29305	864-503-9371		741-6
WREX-TV Ch 13 (NBC) 10322 Auburn Rd **Fax:* News Rm ■ *Web:* www.wrex.com	Rockford	IL	61103	815-335-2213	335-2055*	741-112
WRFG-FM 89.3 (Var) 1083 Austin Ave NE *Web:* www.wrfg.org	Atlanta	GA	30307	404-523-3471		645-10
WRGB-TV Ch 6 (CBS) 1400 Balltown Rd *TF:* 800-298-1460 ■ *Web:* www.cbs6albany.com	Schenectady	NY	12309	518-346-6666		741
WRH (Windsor Regional Hospital Metropolitan Campus) 1995 Lens Ave *Web:* www.wrh.on.ca	Windsor	ON	N8W1L9	519-254-5577	254-3458	374-2
WRHQ-FM 105.3 (Rock) 1102 E 52nd St *TF:* 800-888-6499 ■ *Web:* www.wrhq.com	Savannah	GA	31404	912-234-1053	354-6600	645-148
WRHWC (Windsor Regional Hospital Western Campus) 1453 Prince Rd **Fax:* Acctg ■ *Web:* www.wrh.on.ca	Windsor	ON	N9C3Z4	519-254-5577	254-2317*	374-2
WRI (World Resources Institute) 10 G St NE Ste 800 *Web:* www.wri.org	Washington	DC	20002	202-729-7600	729-7610	48-13
Wricley Nut Products Co 480 Pattison Ave *TF:* 800-523-1303 ■ *Web:* wricleynutproductsco.com	Philadelphia	PA	19148	215-467-1106		296-28
Wrico Stamping Co 2727 Niagara Ln N *TF:* 800-528-3795 ■ *Web:* www.wrico-net.com	Minneapolis	MN	55447	763-559-2288	553-7976	488

Name / Address	City	State	ZIP	Phone	Fax	Class
WRIC-TV Ch 8 (ABC) 301 Arboretum Pl *Web:* www.wric.com	Richmond	VA	23236	804-330-8888	330-8881	741-108
WRIE-AM 1260 (Sports) 471 Robison Rd *Web:* www.cbssportserie.com	Erie	PA	16509	814-868-5355		645-54
WRIF-FM 101.1 (Rock) 1 Radio Plaza Rd *TF:* 800-709-2187 ■ *Web:* www.wrif.com	Detroit	MI	48220	248-547-0101	542-8800	645-49
Wright & Filippis Inc 2845 Crooks Rd *Web:* www.firsttoserve.com	Rochester Hills	MI	48309	248-829-8292		477
Wright & Lato 2100 Felver Ct *TF:* 800-724-1855 ■ *Web:* www.wrightandlato.com	Rahway	NJ	07065	973-674-8700	674-6964	409
Wright & McGill Co 4245 E 46th Ave **Fax Area Code:* 303 ■ *Web:* www.wright-mcgill.com	Denver	CO	80216	720-941-8700	321-4750*	710
Wright Air Service Inc 3842 University Ave S PO Box 60142 *Web:* www.wrightairservice.com	Fairbanks	AK	99706	907-474-0502	474-0375	23
Wright Business Forms Inc 645 Stevenson Rd	South Elgin	IL	60177	708-865-7600		110
Wright Business Graphics (WBG) 18440 NE San Rafael St *TF:* 800-547-8397 ■ *Web:* www.wrightbg.com	Portland	OR	97230	800-547-8397		110
Wright Coating Company Inc 1603 N Pitcher St *Web:* www.wrightcoating.com	Kalamazoo	MI	49007	269-344-8195		481
Wright Color Graphics 9051 Sunland Blvd *TF:* 877-246-8877	Sun Valley	CA	91352	818-246-8877	246-8984	626
Wright Construction Corp 5811 Youngquist Rd *Web:* www.wrightconstructioncorp.com	Fort Myers	FL	33912	239-481-5000	481-2448	186
Wright Construction Western Inc 2919 Cleveland Ave *Web:* www.wrightconstruction.ca	Saskatoon	SK	S7K8A9	306-934-0440		186
Wright County 10 Second St NW Rm 201 *Web:* www.co.wright.mn.us	Buffalo	MN	55313	763-682-7539	682-7300	338
Wright County 115 N Main St *Web:* www.wrightcounty.org	Clarion	IA	50525	515-532-2771	532-2669	338
Wright Do-it Ctr 1306 N Market *Web:* www.wrightdoit.com	Sparta	IL	62286	618-443-5335		191-3
Wright Express Corp 97 Darling Ave *NYSE:* WEX ■ *TF:* 800-761-7181 ■ *Web:* www.wexinc.com	South Portland	ME	04106	207-773-8171		215
Wright Global Graphics 5115 Prospect St *TF:* 800-678-9019 ■ *Web:* www.wrightglobalgraphics.com	Thomasville	NC	27360	336-472-4200	476-8554	413
Wright Group, The 6428 Airport Rd *TF:* 800-201-3096 ■ *Web:* www.thewrightgroup.net	Crowley	LA	70526	337-783-3096		582
Wright Implement Company LLC 3225 Carter Rd *TF:* 800-252-3904 ■ *Web:* wrightimp.com	Owensboro	KY	42301	270-683-3606		111
Wright Investment Properties Inc 277 German Oak Dr *Web:* wrightinvestments.com	Cordova	TN	38018	901-755-9501		796
Wright Investors' Service 440 Wheelers Farms Rd *TF:* 800-232-0013 ■ *Web:* wrightinvestorsservice.com	Milford	CT	06461	203-783-4400	783-4401	401
Wright Lindsey & Jennings LLP 200 W Capitol Ave Ste 2300 *Web:* www.wlj.com	Little Rock	AR	72201	501-371-0808	376-9442	428
Wright Line LLC 160 Gold Star Blvd *TF:* 800-225-7348 ■ *Web:* www.wrightline.com	Worcester	MA	01606	508-852-4300	853-8904	319-1
Wright Manufacturing Inc 4600-X Wedgewood Blvd *Web:* www.wrightmfg.com	Frederick	MD	21703	301-360-9810		429
Wright Medical Group Inc 1023 Cherry Rd *NASDAQ:* WMGI ■ *TF:* 800-238-7117 ■ *Web:* www.wright.com	Memphis	TN	38117	901-867-9971	867-9534	477
Wright Medical Technology Inc 5677 Airline Rd **Fax:* Cust Svc ■ *TF:* 800-238-7117 ■ *Web:* www.wright.com	Arlington	TN	38002	901-867-9971	867-9534*	477
Wright Metal Products Crateslic 111 Franklin St *Web:* www.wrightmetalsinc.com	Lavonia	GA	30553	706-356-2717		567
Wright Metal Products Inc 100 Ben Hamby Dr PO Box 6763 *Web:* www.wrightmetalproducts.com	Greenville	SC	29606	864-297-6610		386
Wright Plastic Products LLC 201 E Condensery Rd *Web:* wppllc.com	Sheridan	MI	48884	989-291-3211	291-5321	454
Wright Printing Co 11616 I St	Omaha	NE	68137	402-609-5622		627
Wright Process Systems 88 Commerce St *Web:* www.wrightps.com	Lodi	CA	95240	209-369-2795		186
Wright Runstad & Co 1201 Third Ave Ste 2700 *Web:* www.wrightrunstad.com	Seattle	WA	98101	206-447-9000	223-8791	655
Wright State University 3640 Colonel Glenn Hwy **Fax:* Admissions ■ *TF Admissions:* 800-247-1770 ■ *Web:* www.wright.edu	Dayton	OH	45435	937-775-5740	775-5795*	166
Wright State University Boonshoft School of Medicine 3640 Col Glenn Hwy **Fax:* Admissions ■ *TF:* 800-338-4057 ■ *Web:* medicine.wright.edu	Dayton	OH	45435	937-775-2934	775-3322*	167-2
Wright State University Dunbar Library 3640 Colonel Glenn Hwy *Web:* www.libraries.wright.edu	Dayton	OH	45435	937-775-4125	775-2356	434-6
Wright State University Lake 7600 Lake Campus Dr **Fax:* Admissions ■ *TF:* 800-237-1477 ■ *Web:* lake.wright.edu	Celina	OH	45822	419-586-0300	586-0358*	162
Wright Tool Company Inc 1 Wright Dr *TF:* 800-321-2902 ■ *Web:* www.wrighttool.com	Barberton	OH	44203	330-848-0600		350
Wright Transportation Inc 2333 Dauphin Island Pkwy *TF:* 800-342-4598 ■ *Web:* www.wrighttrans.com	Mobile	AL	36605	251-432-6390		780
Wright Water Engineers Inc 2490 W 26th Ave Ste 100a *Web:* www.wrightwater.com	Denver	CO	80211	303-480-1700	480-1020	261
Wright Wisner Distributing Corp 3165 Brighton-Henrietta Town Line Rd *Web:* wrightbev.com	Rochester	NY	14623	585-427-2880		81-1

	Phone	Fax	Class
Wright's Media 2407 Timberloch Pl Ste B............... The Woodlands TX 77380 *TF:* 877-652-5295 ■ *Web:* wrightsmedia.com	281-419-5725		637-9
Wright-Hennepin Co-op Electric Assn 6800 Electric Dr PO Box 330 .... Rockford MN 55373 *TF:* 800-943-2667 ■ *Web:* www.whe.org	763-477-3000	477-3054	245
Wright-Patt Credit Union Inc 2455 Executive Pk Blvd PO Box 286............Fairborn OH 45324 *TF:* 800-762-0047 ■ *Web:* www.wpcu.coop	937-912-7000		219
Wright-Patterson Air Force Base 5030 Patterson Pkwy .... Wright-Patterson AFB OH 45433 *TF:* 800-225-5288 ■ *Web:* www.wpafb.af.mil	937-257-1110		497-1
Wright-Pierce 99 Main St................... Topsham ME 04086 *TF:* 800-564-2333 ■ *Web:* www.wright-pierce.com	207-725-8721		261
Wright-Ryan Construction Inc 10 Danforth St ....Portland ME 04101 *Web:* www.wright-ryan.com	207-773-3625		186
Wrightsoft Corp 131 Hartwell Ave.............Lexington MA 02421 *TF:* 800-225-8697 ■ *Web:* www.wrightsoft.com	800-225-8697		225
Wrigley Co, The 410 N Michigan Ave...........Chicago IL 60611 *TF:* 888-985-2064 ■ *Web:* www.wrigley.com	312-644-2121		296-6
Wrigley Field 1060 W Addison St..............Chicago IL 60613 *TF:* 866-800-1275 ■ *Web:* chicago.cubs.mlb.com	773-404-2827	404-4129	720
Wrigley Mansion 2501 E Telawa Trl ....Phoenix AZ 85016 *Web:* www.wrigleymansion.com	602-955-4079		50-3
Wrigley Memorial & Botanical Garden 125 Claressa Ave ....Avalon CA 90704 *Web:* www.catalinaconservancy.org/index.php?s=portal	310-510-2897	510-2325	97
Wrisco Industries Inc 355 Hiatt Dr Ste B................. Palm Beach Gardens FL 33418 *TF:* 800-627-2646 ■ *Web:* www.wrisco.com	561-626-5700	627-3574	492
WristWatch 109 S Main St.......................Mcallen TX 78501 *TF:* 800-521-5568 ■ *Web:* www.wristwatch.com	956-682-7132		791
WRIT (Washington Real Estate Investment Trust) 1775 I St NW ....Washington DC 20006 *NYSE: WRE* ■ *TF:* 800-565-9748 ■ *Web:* www.writ.com	301-984-9400	984-9610	655
Write on Target Inc 7941 Washington Woods Dr...................Dayton OH 45459 *Web:* www.writetarget.com	937-436-4565		7
Writer's Digest 4700 E Galbraith Rd ....Cincinnati OH 45236 *TF Cust Svc:* 800-283-0963 ■ *Web:* www.writersdigest.com	513-531-2690		457-21
Writer's Digest Book Club 4700 E Galbraith Rd.........................Cincinnati OH 45236 **Fax Area Code:* 715 ■ *TF Cust Svc:* 800-759-0963 ■ *Web:* www.writersdigestshop.com	513-531-2690	445-4087*	93
Writers Guild of America East (WGAE) 250 Hudson St ....New York NY 10013 *Web:* www.wgaeast.org	212-767-7800	582-1909	414
Writers Guild of America West (WGAw) 7000 W Third St.........................Los Angeles CA 90048 *TF:* 800-421-4182 ■ *Web:* www.wga.org	323-951-4000	782-4800	414
Writers House 21 W 26th St ....New York NY 10010 *TF:* 800-487-2323 ■ *Web:* www.writershouse.com	212-685-2400		444
Writers' Express, The 271 Cambridge St Ste 303 ....Cambridge MA 02141 *Web:* www.amplify.com	617-844-1003		196
WRKF-FM 89.3 (NPR) 3050 Vly Creek Dr .... Baton Rouge LA 70808 *TF:* 855-893-9753 ■ *Web:* www.wrkf.org	225-926-3050	926-3105	645-18
WRKO-AM 680 (N/T) 20 Guest St 3rd Fl ....Brighton MA 02135 *TF:* 877-469-4322 ■ *Web:* www.wrko.com	617-779-3400		645
WRKZ-FM 99.7 (Rock) 1458 Dublin Rd .... Columbus OH 43215 *TF:* 800-695-6344 ■ *Web:* www.theblitz.com	614-481-7800		645-42
WRL (Van Dijk Westlake Reed Leskosky) 1422 Euclid Ave Ste 300.....................Cleveland OH 44115 *Web:* www.wrldesign.com	216-522-1350		261
WRL Advertising Inc 4470 Dressler Rd NW.........................Canton OH 44718 *Web:* www.wrladv.com	330-493-8866		7
WRLT-FM 100.1 (AAA) 1310 Clinton St Ste 200....................Nashville TN 37203 *Web:* lightning100.com	615-242-5600	296-9039	645-108
WRNI-AM 1290 (NPR) 1 Union Stn............Providence RI 02903 *Web:* ripr.org	401-351-2800	351-0246	645-129
WRNL-AM 910 (Sports) 3245 Basie Rd .... Richmond VA 23228 *Web:* foxsportsrichmond.iheart.com	804-474-0000	474-0096	645-134
WRNN-FM 99.5 (N/T) 1016 Ocala St......... Myrtle Beach SC 29577 *TF:* 800-525-5683 ■ *Web:* www.wrnn.net	843-448-1041		645-106
WRNR-FM 103.1 179 Admiral Cochrane Dr.................. Annapolis MD 21401 *TF:* 877-762-1031 ■ *Web:* www.wrnr.com	410-626-0103	267-7634	645-8
Wrobel Engineering Company Inc 154 Bodwell St .... Avon MA 02322 *Web:* www.wrobeleng.com	508-586-8338		198
WROC-TV Ch 8 (CBS) 201 Humboldt St ....Rochester NY 14610 **Fax:* News Rm ■ *Web:* www.rochesterfirst.com	585-288-8400	288-1505*	741-111
WROK-AM 1440 (N/T) 3901 Brendenwood Rd.......................Rockford IL 61107 *Web:* www.1440wrok.com	815-398-9765	484-2432	645-139
WROQ-FM 101.1 (CR) 25 Garlington Rd .... Greenville SC 29615 *TF:* 888-257-0058 ■ *Web:* classicrock1011.com	864-271-9200	242-1567	645-68
WROR-FM 105.7 (Oldies) 55 Morrissey Blvd ....Boston MA 02125 *Web:* www.wror.com	617-822-9600		645-23
WROU-FM 92.1 (Urban AC) 717 E David Rd ....Dayton OH 45429 *Web:* www.921wrou.com	937-294-5858		645-45
Wrought Washer Manufacturing Inc 2100 S Bay St...........................Milwaukee WI 53207 *TF:* 800-558-5217 ■ *Web:* www.wroughtwasher.com	414-744-0771		483
WROW-AM 6 Johnson Rd..........................Latham NY 12110 *Web:* www.albanymagic.com	518-786-6600		645
WRQN-FM 93.5 (Oldies) 3225 Arlington Ave...........................Toledo OH 43614 *TF:* 866-240-1935 ■ *Web:* www.935wrqn.com	419-725-5700		645-163
WRQX-FM 107.3 (AC) 4400 Jenifer St NW Ste 400 ....Washington DC 20015 *Web:* www.mix1073.com	202-686-3100		645-172

	Phone	Fax	Class
WRR Environmental Services 5200 Ryder Rd .... Eau Claire WI 54701 *TF:* 800-727-8760 ■ *Web:* www.wrres.com	715-834-9624		667
WRRC (Western Regional Research Ctr) 800 Buchanan St ....Albany CA 94710 *Web:* www.ars.usda.gov/main/docs.htm?docid=5819	510-559-5600	559-5963	668
WRR-FM 101.1 (Clas) PO Box 159001............ Dallas TX 75315 *Web:* www.wrr101.com	214-670-8888		645-44
WRS Motion Picture & Video Laboratory 213 Tech Rd .... Pittsburgh PA 15205	412-937-1200		512
WRSP-TV Ch 55 (Fox) 3003 Old Rochester Rd.....................Springfield IL 62703 *Web:* foxillinois.com	217-523-8855		741-128
WRTC-FM 89.3 (Var) Trinity College 300 Summit St ....Hartford CT 06106 *Web:* www.wrtcfm.com	860-297-2439		645-72
WRTI-FM 90.1 (NPR) 1509 Cecil B Moore Ave 3rd Fl...............Philadelphia PA 19121 *TF:* 866-809-9784 ■ *Web:* www.wrti.org	215-204-8405	204-7027	645-122
WRTV-TV Ch 6 (ABC) 1330 N Meridian St ....Indianapolis IN 46202 **Fax:* News Rm ■ *TF:* 877-667-4265 ■ *Web:* www.theindychannel.com	317-635-9788	269-1445*	741-62
WRVA-AM 1140 (N/T) 3245 Basie Rd .... Richmond VA 23228 *Web:* 1140wrva.iheart.com	804-474-0000		645-134
WRVM-FM 102.7 (Rel) PO Box 212.............. Suring WI 54174 *TF:* 888-225-9786 ■ *Web:* www.wrvmradio.org/pages/?p=3	920-842-2900		645
WRVR-FM 104.5 (AC) 1835 Moriah Woods Blvd Bldg 1 ....Memphis TN 38117 *Web:* www.1045theriver.com	901-384-5900	767-6076	645-98
WRZK-FM 95.9 (Alt) 222 Commerce St ....Kingsport TN 37660 *Web:* www.wrzk.com	423-246-9578	247-9836	645
WS Badcock Corp (WSBC) PO Box 497......... Mulberry FL 33860 *TF:* 800-223-2625 ■ *Web:* www.badcock.com	800-223-2625		321
WS Bellows Construction Corp 1906 Afton St.............................Houston TX 77055 *Web:* www.wsbellows.com	713-680-2132	680-2614	186
WS Cumby Inc 938 Lincoln Ave...............Springfield PA 19064 *Web:* www.cumby.com	610-328-5353		186
WS Emerson Co Inc 15 Acme Rd .... Brewer ME 04412 *TF:* 800-789-6120 ■ *Web:* www.wsemersononline.com	207-989-3410		156
WS Hampshire Inc 365 Keyes Ave ....Hampshire IL 60140 *TF:* 800-541-0251 ■ *Web:* www.wshampshire.com	847-683-4400	683-4407	724
WS Packaging Group Inc 2571 S Hemlock Rd .... Green Bay WI 54229 **Fax Area Code:* 920 ■ *TF:* 800-236-3424 ■ *Web:* www.wspackaging.com	800-818-5481	866-6485*	413
WS/FCS (Winston-Salem/Forsyth County Schools) 1605 Miller St.......................... Winston-Salem NC 27103 *Web:* www.wsfcs.k12.nc.us	336-727-2816	661-6572	685
WSA Distributing Inc 7222 Opportunity Rd .... San Diego CA 92111 *Web:* www.wsadistributing.com	858-560-7800	560-7475	246
WSA Engineered Systems 2018 S First St ....Milwaukee WI 53207 *Web:* www.wsaes.com	414-481-4120	481-4121	14
WSAV-TV Ch 3 (NBC) 1430 E Victory Dr.........Savannah GA 31404 *Web:* www.wsav.com	912-651-0300		741-122
WSAZ-TV Ch 3 (NBC) PO Box 2115............Huntington WV 25721 *TF:* 800-765-6482 ■ *Web:* www.wsaz.com	304-697-4780	690-3066	741
WSB & Associates Inc 701 Xenia Ave S Ste 300 ....Minneapolis MN 55416 *Web:* www.wsbeng.com	763-541-4800		256
Wsb Computer Services Inc 21 Craft St.........Alamosa CO 81101 *TF:* 888-800-1381 ■ *Web:* www.wsbcs.net	719-589-8940		175
WSB-AM 750 (N/T) 1601 W Peachtree St NE.......................Atlanta GA 30309 *Web:* www.wsbradio.com	404-897-7500	897-7363	645-10
WSBC (WS Badcock Corp) PO Box 497......... Mulberry FL 33860 *TF:* 800-223-2625 ■ *Web:* www.badcock.com	800-223-2625		321
WSBE-TV Ch 36 (PBS) 50 Pk Ln..............Providence RI 02907 *TF:* 800-239-5233 ■ *Web:* www.ripbs.org	401-222-3636	222-3407	741-104
WSB-FM 98.5 (AC) 1601 W Peachtree St NE......................Atlanta GA 30309 *Web:* www.b985.com	404-897-7500	897-7363	645-10
WSBT-TV Ch 22 (CBS) 1301 E Douglas Rd........................Mishawaka IN 46545 *TF:* 877-634-7181 ■ *Web:* www.wsbt.com	574-232-6397	289-0622	741
WSB-TV Ch 2 (ABC) 1601 W Peachtree St NE.......................Atlanta GA 30309 *Web:* www.wsbtv.com	404-097-7000	897-7370	741-7
WSC Avant Bard 3700 S Four Mile Run .... Arlington VA 22206 *TF:* 800-838-3006 ■ *Web:* wscavantbard.org	703-418-4808		572
WSCB-FM 89.9 (Urban) 263 Alden St ....Springfield MA 01109 *TF:* 800-727-0504	413-748-3000	748-3473	645-156
WSCI-FM 89.3 (NPR) 1101 George Rogers Blvd.....................Columbia SC 29201 *TF:* 800-922-5437 ■ *Web:* www.scetv.org	803-737-3200		645
WSEE-TV Ch 35 (CBS) 3514 State St............... Erie PA 16508 *TF:* 866-571-4553 ■ *Web:* www.erietvnews.com	814-454-5201		741-44
WSEL-FM 96.7 PO Box 3788.......................Tupelo MS 38803 *Web:* wselradio.com	662-489-0297		645-169
WSET-TV Ch 13 (ABC) 2320 Langhorne Rd .... Lynchburg VA 24501 *TF:* 800-639-7847 ■ *Web:* www.wset.com	434-528-1313	847-0458	741
WSF Industries Inc 7 Hackett Dr..............Tonawanda NY 14150 *TF:* 800-874-8265 ■ *Web:* www.wsf-inc.com	716-692-4930		480
WSFA-TV Ch 12 (NBC) 12 E Delano Ave .... Montgomery AL 36105 **Fax:* News Rm ■ *Web:* www.wsfa.com	334-288-1212	613-8303*	741-86
WSFL-TV Ch 39 (CW) 200 E Las Olas Blvd 11th Fl............ Fort Lauderdale FL 33301 *Web:* www.southflorida.com	954-627-7349	355-2000	741-82
WSFS Financial Corp 500 Delaware Ave......................... Wilmington DE 19801 *NASDAQ: WSFS* ■ *TF:* 888-973-7226 ■ *Web:* www.wsfsbank.com	302-792-6000		360-2
WSGL-FM 104.7 (AC) 10915 K-Nine Dr ....Bonita Springs FL 34135 *TF:* 800-242-0100 ■ *Web:* www.1047mixfm.com	239-495-8383		645

				Phone	Fax	Class
WSH (Wyoming State Hospital) 831 Hwy 150 S	Evanston	WY	82930	307-789-3464		374-5
Web: www.health.wyo.gov/statehospital						
WSHA-FM 88.9 (Jazz) 118 E S St	Raleigh	NC	27601	919-546-8430	546-8315	645-131
TF: 800-241-0421 ■ *Web:* www.shawu.edu						
WSHH-FM 99.7 (AC) 900 Parish St 3rd Fl	Pittsburgh	PA	15220	412-875-9500		645-125
Web: www.wshh.com						
WSHO-AM 800 (Rel) 365 Canal St Ste 1175	New Orleans	LA	70130	504-527-0800	527-0881	645-110
Web: www.wsho.com						
WSHU-FM 91.1 (NPR) 5151 Pk Ave	Fairfield	CT	06825	203-365-0425		645
TF: 800-937-6045 ■ *Web:* www.wshu.org						
WSI Industries Inc 213 Chelsea Rd	Monticello	MN	55362	763-295-9202	295-9212	454
NASDAQ: WSCI ■ *Web:* www.wsiindustries.com						
WSI Internet 5580 Explorer Dr Ste 600	Mississauga	ON	L4W4Y1	905-678-7588	678-7242	310
TF: 888-678-7588 ■ *Web:* www.wsicorporate.com						
WSIC-AM 1400 (N/T) 1117 Radio Rd	Statesville	NC	28677	704-872-6345	873-6921	645
Web: www.wsicweb.com						
Wsi-expert Solutions 6316 Hickory Ridge Blvd	Baton Rouge	LA	70817	225-341-4956		396
Web: www.wsiexpertsolutions.com						
WSJS-AM 600 (N/T) 210 N Main St Ste 330	Kernersville	NC	27284	336-777-3900	777-3915	645-178
Web: www.triadsports.com/wsjs-com						
WSJV-TV Ch 28 (Fox) PO Box 28	South Bend	IN	46624	574-679-9758	294-1267	741-126
TF: 800-435-3803 ■ *Web:* www.fox28.com						
WSKY 1230 AM 40 Westgate Pkwy Ste 2	Asheville	NC	28806	888-989-2299		645-9
TF: 888-989-2299 ■ *Web:* www.wilkinsradio.com						
WSKY-TV Ch 4 (Ind) 218 Salters Creek Rd	Hampton	VA	23661	757-382-0004	382-0365	741
Web: www.sky4tv.com						
WSKZ-FM 106.5 (Rock) 821 Pineville Rd	Chattanooga	TN	37405	423-756-6141	266-3629	645-34
Web. www.wskz.com						
WSLQ-FM 99.1 (AC) 3934 Electric Rd SW	Roanoke	VA	24018	540-387-0234		645-136
TF: 800-410-9936 ■ *Web:* www.q99fm.com						
WSLS-TV Ch 10 (NBC) PO Box 10	Roanoke	VA	24022	540-981-9110	343-3157	741-109
Web: www.wsls.com						
WSM-AM 650 (Ctry) 2644 McGavock Pk	Nashville	TN	37214	615-737-9650		645-108
Web: wsmonline.com						
WSM-FM 95.5 (Ctry) 10 Music Cir E	Nashville	TN	37203	615-321-1067		645-108
Web: 955nashicon.com						
WSMH-TV Ch 66 (Fox) 3463 W Pierson Rd	Flint	MI	48504	810-785-8866		741-49
Web: www.wsmh.com						
WSMK-FM 99.1 (Urban) 210 S Philip Rd	Niles	MI	49120	269-683-4343	683-7759	645
Web: www.wsmkradio.com						
WSMV-TV Ch 4 (NBC) 5700 Knob Rd	Nashville	TN	37209	615-353-4444		741-89
Web: www.wsmv.com						
WSNA (Washington State Nurses Assn) 575 Andover Pk W Ste 101	Seattle	WA	98188	206-575-7979	575-1908	533
TF: 800-231-8482 ■ *Web:* www.wsna.org						
WSNX-FM 104.5 (CHR) 77 Monroe Ctr St NW Ste 1000	Grand Rapids	MI	49503	616-459-1919		645-66
Web: 1045snx.iheart.com						
WSNY-FM 94.7 (AC) 4401 Carriage Hill Ln	Columbus	OH	43220	614-451-2191	451-1831	645-42
TF: 800-247-1812 ■ *Web:* www.sunny95.com						
WSO (Washington Symphony Orchestra) PO Box 178	Washington	PA	15301	724-223-9796		573-3
Web: www.washsym.org						
WSO (Wichita Symphony Orchestra) 225 W Douglas St Ste 207	Wichita	KS	67202	316-267-5259	267-1937	573-3
Web: wichitasymphony.org						
WSOC-TV Ch 9 (ABC) 1901 N Tryon St	Charlotte	NC	28206	704-338-9999	335-4736	741-26
TF: 855 336 0360 ■ *Web:* www.wsoctv.com						
WSOS Community Action Commission Inc 109 S Front St	Fremont	OH	43420	419-334-8911		8
TF: 800-775-9767 ■ *Web:* www.wsos.org						
WSP 1600 Boulevard Ren,-L,vesque O	Boulder	Co	80301	514-340-0046		192
Web: www.wsp.com						
WSPA (World Animal Protection) 450 Seventh Ave 31st Floor	New York	NY	10123	646-783-2200	564-4250*	48-3
**Fax Area Code: 212* ■ *TF:* 800-883-9772 ■ *Web:* www.wspa-usa.org						
WSPA-TV Ch 7 (CBS) 250 International Dr	Spartanburg	SC	29303	864-576-7777		741-6
TF: 866-946-6349 ■ *Web:* www.wspa.com						
WSPD-AM 1370 (N/T) 125 S Superior St	Toledo	OH	43604	419-244-8321		645-163
TF: 800-745-3000 ■ *Web:* wspd.iheart.com						
WSRE-TV Ch 23 (PBS) 1000 College Blvd	Pensacola	FL	32504	850-484-1200	484-1255	741
TF: 800-239-9773 ■ *Web:* www.wsre.org						
WSRV-FM 97.1 (AC) 1601 W Peachtree St	Atlanta	GA	30309	404-897-7500		645-10
Web: www.971theriver.com						
WSSA (Wine & Spirits Shippers Assn Inc) 11800 Sunrise Vly Dr	Reston	VA	20191	703-860-2300	860-2422	49-6
TF General: 800-368-3167 ■ *Web:* www.wssa.com						
WSTO-FM 96.1 (CHR) 1162 Mt Auburn Rd	Evansville	IN	47720	812-491-9468	426-7928	645-56
TF: 888-685-1961 ■ *Web:* hot96.com						
WSTR-TV Ch 64 (MNT) 5177 Fishwick Dr	Cincinnati	OH	45216	513-641-4400	242-2633	741-30
Web: www.star64.tv						
WSTW-FM 93.7 (CHR) 2727 Shipley Rd	Wilmington	DE	19810	302-478-2700	478-0100	645-176
TF: 800-544-9370 ■ *Web:* www.wstw.com						
WSU (Wichita State University Ablah Library) 1845 Fairmount St	Wichita	KS	67260	316-978-3481	978-3048	434-6
Web: libraries.wichita.edu						
WSUA-AM 1260 (Span) 2100 Coral Way Ste 201	Miami	FL	33145	305-285-1260		645-99
Web: www.caracol1260.com						
WSUN-FM 97.1 (Alt) 11300 Fourth St N Ste 300	Saint Petersburg	FL	33716	727-579-2000		645-162
TF: 877-327-9797 ■ *Web:* www.97xonline.com						
WSVH-FM 91.1 (NPR) 13040 Abercorn St Ste 8	Savannah	GA	31419	912-344-3565	362-4564*	645-148
**Fax Area Code: 404* ■ *TF:* 877-472-1227 ■ *Web:* gpb.org/savannah						
WSVN-TV Ch 7 (Fox) 1401 79th St Cswy	Miami	FL	33141	305-751-6692		741-82
TF: 800-845-7777 ■ *Web:* www.wsvn.com						
WSWA (Wine & Spirits Wholesalers of America Inc) 805 15th St NW Ste 430	Washington	DC	20005	202-371-9792	789-2405	49-6
Web: www.wswa.org						
WSYM-TV Ch 47 (Fox) 600 W St Joseph St Ste 47	Lansing	MI	48933	517-484-7747	484-3144	741-71
TF: 800-748-0228 ■ *Web:* www.fox47news.com						
WSYR-AM 570 (N/T) 500 Plum St Ste 400	Syracuse	NY	13204	315-472-9797		645-160
TF: 844-289-7234 ■ *Web:* wsyr.iheart.com						
WSYR-TV Ch 9 (ABC) 5904 Bridge St	East Syracuse	NY	13057	315-446-9999	251-1567	741
Web: www.localsyr.com						
WSYT-TV Ch 68 (Fox) 1000 James St	Syracuse	NY	13203	315-472-6800	471-8889	741-131
Web: www.foxsyracuse.com						
WSYX-TV Ch 6 (ABC) 1261 Dublin Rd	Columbus	OH	43215	614-481-6666	481-6624*	741-35
**Fax:* News Rm ■ *Web:* www.abc6onyourside.com						
WT Harvey Lumber Co 800 15th St PO Box 310	Columbus	GA	31902	706-322-8204	323-2433	191-3
Web: www.harveylumber.com						
WTA (Washington Trails Assn) 705 Second Ave Ste 300	Seattle	WA	98104	206-625-1367	625-9249	48-23
Web: www.wta.org						
WTA Tour Inc 1 Progress Plaza Ste 1500	Saint Petersburg	FL	33701	727-895-5000	894-1982	48-22
Web: www.wtatennis.com						
WTAE-TV Ch 4 (ABC) 400 Ardmore Blvd	Pittsburgh	PA	15221	412-242-4300	244-4558*	741-100
**Fax:* News Rm ■ *Web:* www.wtae.com						
WTAG 580/94.9 96 Stereo Ln	Paxton	MA	01612	508-755-0058		645
Web: wtag.iheart.com						
WTAK-FM 106.1 (CR) 26869 Peoples Rd	Madison	AL	35756	256-309-2400		645
Web: wtak.iheart.com						
WTAM-AM 1100 (N/T) 6200 Oak Tree Blvd	Cleveland	OH	44131	216-520-2600		645
Web: wtam.iheart.com						
WTAT-TV Ch 24 (Fox) 4301 Arco Ln	North Charleston	SC	29418	843-744-2424	554-9649	741
Web: www.foxcharleston.com						
WTAX-AM 1240 (N/T) 3501 E Sangamon Ave	Springfield	IL	62707	217-753-5400	753-7902	645-155
Web: www.wtax.com						
WTB Financial Corp PO Box 2127	Spokane	WA	99210	800-788-4578		360-2
TF: 800-788-4578 ■ *Web:* www.watrust.com						
WTBC-AM 1230 (N/T) 2110 McFarland Blvd E Ste C	Tuscaloosa	AL	35404	205-758-5523	752-9696	645-170
TF: 800-518-1977						
WTBN-AM 570 (Rel) 5211 W Laurel St Ste 101	Tampa	FL	33607	813-639-1903	639-1272	645-162
TF: 800 576 3771 ■ *Web:* www.letstalkfaith.com						
WTBY-TV Ch 54 (TBN) 111 E 15th St	New York	NY	10003	714-731-1000		741-91
TF: 800-201-5200 ■ *Web:* www.tbn.org						
WTCA (Wood Truss Council of America) 6300 Enterprise Ln	Madison	WI	53719	608-274-4849	274-3329	49-3
Web: www.sbcindustry.com						
WTCA (World Trade Centers Assn) 120 Broadway Ste 3350	New York	NY	10271	212-432-2626		49-12
WTCC-FM 90.7 (Var) 1 Armory Sq	Springfield	MA	01105	413-750-2701		645-160
Web: www.wtccfm.org						
WTCI-TV Ch 45 (PBS) 7540 Bonnie Shire Dr	Chattanooga	TN	37416	423-702-7800	702-7823	741-27
Web: www.wtcitv.org						
WTE Corp 7 Alfred Cir	Bedford	MA	01730	781-275-6400	275-8612	660
Web: www.wte.com						
WTEN-TV Ch 10 (ABC) 341 Northern Blvd	Albany	NY	12204	518-436-4822	426-4792*	741-2
**Fax:* News Rm ■ *Web:* www.news10.com						
WTFM-FM 98.5 (AC) 222 Commerce St	Kingsport	TN	37660	423-246-9578	247-9836	645
TF: 888-633-5452 ■ *Web:* www.wtfm.com						
WTGL-TV Ch 45 (Ind) 31 Skyline Dr	Lake Mary	FL	32746	407-215-6745	215-6789	741
Web: www.tv45.org						
WTH (World Travel Holdings) 100 Fordham Rd Bldg C Bldg C	Wilmington	MA	01887	617-424-7990	424-1943	771
TF: 877-958-7447 ■ *Web:* www.worldtravelholdings.com						
WTHR-TV Ch 13 (NBC) 1000 N Meridian St	Indianapolis	IN	46204	317-636-1313		741-62
Web: www.wthr.com						
WTHT-FM 99.9 (Ctry) 477 Congress St 3rd Fl Annex	Portland	ME	04101	207-797-0780	774-4390	645-127
Web: wtht.nh1media.com						
WTI (Western Technology Investment) 104 La Mesa Dr Ste 102	Portola Valley	CA	94028	650-234-4300		792
Web: www.westerntech.com						
WTI Inc 3737 E Broadway Rd	Phoenix	AZ	85040	602-437-8979		466
Web: www.wticompanies.com						
WTIC-AM 1080 (N/T) 10 Executive Dr	Farmington	CT	06032	860-677-6700		645
Web: connecticut.cbslocal.com						
WTIC-TV Ch 61 (Fox) 285 Broad St	Hartford	CT	06115	860-527-6161	723-2111	741-57
Web: fox61.com						
WTIX-FM 94.3 (Oldies) 4539 N I-10 Service Rd W Ste 300	Metairie	LA	70006	504-454-9000		645
Web: www.wtixfm.com						
WTJP-TV Ch 60 (TBN) 313 Rosedale Ave	Gadsden	AL	35901	256-546-8860		741
TF: 800-447-7235 ■ *Web:* www.tbn.org						
WTKA-AM 1050 (N/T) 1100 Victors Way Ste 100	Ann Arbor	MI	48108	734-302-8100		645-7
Web: www.wtka.com						
WTKR-TV Ch 3 (CBS) 720 Boush St	Norfolk	VA	23510	757-446-1000	622-1807	741-92
Web: www.wtkr.com						
WTKS-AM 1290 (N/T) 245 Alfred St	Savannah	GA	31408	912-964-7794	964-9414	645-148
Web: newsradio1290wtks.iheart.com						
WTLC-AM 1310 (Rel) 21 E St Joseph St	Indianapolis	IN	46204	317-266-9600	328-3870	645-77
Web: praiseindy.com						
WTLH-TV Ch 49 (Fox) 8440 Deerlake S	Tallahassee	FL	32343	850-893-4140	893-6974	741
Web: fox49.tv						
WTLJ-TV Ch 54 (Ind) 10290 48th Ave	Allendale	MI	49401	616-895-4154		741

	Phone	Fax	Class
WTLN-AM 950 (Rel) 1188 Lakeview Dr ... Altamonte Springs FL 32714 *Web:* thewordorlando.com	407-682-9494	682-7005	645
WTLV-TV Ch 12 (NBC) 1070 E Adams St ... Jacksonville FL 32202 *TF:* 800-861-5255 ■ *Web:* www.firstcoastnews.com	904-354-1212		741-64
WTMD-FM 89.7 (AAA) 1 Olympic Pl Ste 100 ... Towson MD 21204 *Web:* www.wtmd.org	410-704-8938	704-3113	645
WTMJ-AM 620 (N/T) 720 E Capitol Dr ... Milwaukee WI 53212 *Web:* www.wtmj.com	414-799-1620		645-100
WTMJ-TV Ch 4 (NBC) 720 E Capitol Dr ... Milwaukee WI 53212 *Web:* www.tmj4.com	414-332-9611	967-5378	741-83
WTMT-FM 105.9 (Span) 1190 Patton Ave ... Asheville NC 28806 *Web:* 1059themountain.com	828-259-9695	253-5619	645-93
WTMX-FM 101.9 (AC) 1 Prudential Plaza 130 E Randolph St Ste 2700 ... Chicago IL 60601 *Web:* www.wtmx.com	312-946-1019	946-4747	645-36
WTNH-TV Ch 8 (ABC) 8 Elm St ... New Haven CT 06510 **Fax:* Mktg ■ *Web:* www.wtnh.com	203-784-8888	789-2010*	741
WTNT-FM 94.9 (Ctry) 325 John Knox Rd Bldg G ... Tallahassee FL 32303 *Web:* 949tnt.iheart.com	850-422-3107	383-0747	645-161
WTOG-TV Ch 44 (CW) 365 105th Terr NE ... Saint Petersburg FL 33716 *Web:* cwtampa.cbslocal.com	727-576-4444		741-133
WTOL-TV Ch 11 (CBS) 730 N Summit St ... Toledo OH 43604 *Web:* www.wtol.com	419-248-1111	244-7104	741-134
WTOP News 3400 Idaho Ave NW ... Washington DC 20016 *Web:* www.wtop.com	202-895-5000		645-172
WTOP-FM 103.5 (N/T) 3400 Idaho Ave NW ... Washington DC 20016 *Web:* www.wtop.com	202-895-5000		645-172
WTP Inc PO Box 937 ... Coloma MI 49038 *TF:* 800-521-0731 ■ *Web:* www.wtp-inc.com	269-468-3399		732
WTPL-FM 107.7 (N/T) 501 S St ... Bow NH 03304 *Web:* www.wtplfm.com	603-545-0777	545-0781	645
WTRF-TV Ch 7 (CBS) 96 16th St ... Wheeling WV 26003 **Fax:* News Rm ■ *Web:* www.yourohiovalley.com	304-232-7777	233-5822*	741-141
WTRY-FM 98.3 (Oldies) 1203 Troy-Schenectady Rd ... Latham NY 12110 *Web:* 983try.iheart.com	518-452-4884		645
WTSK-AM 790 (Rel) 142 Skyland Blvd ... Tuscaloosa AL 35405 *Web:* 790wtsk.com	205-345-7200	349-1715	645-170
WTSO-AM 1070 (Sports) 2651 S Fish Hatchery Rd ... Madison WI 53711 *Web:* thebig1070.iheart.com	608-274-5450		645-96
WTSP-TV Ch 10 (CBS) 11450 Gandy Blvd N ... Saint Petersburg FL 33702 *TF:* 877-248-6922 ■ *Web:* www.wtsp.com	727-577-1010	576-6924	741-133
WTSR-FM 91.3 (Alt) College of New Jersey Kendall Hall PO Box 7718 ... Ewing NJ 08628 *Web:* www.wtsr.org	609-771-3200		645
WTSS-FM 102.5 (AC) 500 Corporate Pkwy Ste 200 ... Amherst NY 14226 *Web:* www.mystar1025.com	716-843-0600		645
WTSU-FM 89.9 (NPR) Troy University Wallace Hall ... Troy AL 36082 **Fax Area Code:* 334 ■ *TF:* 800-800-6616 ■ *Web:* www.troypublicradio.org	800-800-6616	670-3934*	645
WTTA-TV Ch 38 (MNT) PO Box 1410 ... Tampa FL 33601 *Web:* wfla.com/category/great-38	813-228-8888	225-2770	741-133
WTTE-TV Ch 28 (Fox) 1261 Dublin Rd ... Columbus OH 43215 *Web:* www.myfox28columbus.com	614-481-6666	481-6624	741-35
WTTG FOX 5 & myfoxdc 5151 Wisconsin Ave NW ... Washington DC 20016 *Web:* www.fox5dc.com	202-244-5151	895-3126	741-139
WTTG-TV Ch 5 (Fox) 5151 Wisconsin Ave NW ... Washington DC 20016 *Web:* www.fox5dc.com	202-244-5151		741-139
WTTH-FM 96.1 (Urban) 8025 Black Horse Pike Ste 100 ... West Atlantic City NJ 08232 *Web:* www.961wtth.com	609-484-8444	646-6331	645
WTTO-TV Ch 21 (CW) 651 Beacon Pkwy W Ste 105 ... Birmingham AL 35209 *Web:* www.wtto21.com/birmingham_al	205-943-2168	290-2114	741-15
WTTS-FM 92.3 (AAA) 400 One City Centre ... Bloomington IN 47404 *TF:* 800-923-9887 ■ *Web:* www.wttsfm.com	812-332-3366	331-4570	645
WTTV-TV Ch 4 (CW) 6910 Network Pl ... Indianapolis IN 46278 *TF:* 800-535-5542 ■ *Web:* fox59.com	317-632-5900		741-62
WTTW-TV Ch 11 (PBS) 5400 N St Louis Ave ... Chicago IL 60625 *Web:* www.wttw.com	773-583-5000	583-3046	741-29
WTUE-FM 104.7 (Rock) 101 Pine St ... Dayton OH 45402 *Web:* wtue.iheart.com	937-224-1137		645-45
WTUG-FM 92.9 (Urban) 142 Skyland Blvd ... Tuscaloosa AL 35405 *Web:* www.wtug.com	205-345-7200		645-170
WTVA-TV Ch 9 (NBC) 1359 Beech Springs Rd ... Saltillo MS 38866 *Web:* www.wtva.com	662-842-7620		741
WTVC-TV Ch 9 (ABC) 4279 Benton Dr ... Chattanooga TN 37406 *Web:* www.newschannel9.com	423-756-5500	757-7400	741-27
WTVD-TV Ch 11 (ABC) 411 Liberty St ... Durham NC 27701 *Web:* abc11.com	919-683-1111		741-105
WTVG-TV Ch 13 (ABC) 4247 Dorr St ... Toledo OH 43607 *Web:* www.13abc.com	419-531-1313	534-3898	741-134
WTVI PBS Charlotte 3242 Commonwealth Ave ... Charlotte NC 28205 *Web:* www.wtvi.org	704-330-5942	335-1358	741-26
WTVJ-TV Ch 6 (NBC) 15000 SW 27th St ... Miramar FL 33027 *Web:* www.nbcmiami.com	954-622-6000		741
WTVM-TV Ch 9 (ABC) 1909 Wynnton Rd ... Columbus GA 31906 *Web:* www.wtvm.com	706-494-5400	322-7527	741-34
WTVN-AM 610 (N/T) 2323 W Fifth Ave Ste 200 ... Columbus OH 43221 *TF:* 844-289-7234 ■ *Web:* 610wtvn.iheart.com	614-486-6101	487-2559	645-42
WTVO-TV Ch 17 (ABC) 1917 N Meridian Rd ... Rockford IL 61101 *Web:* www.mystateline.com	815-963-5413		741-112
WTVP-TV Ch 47 (PBS) 101 State St ... Peoria IL 61602 *TF:* 800-837-4747 ■ *Web:* www.wtvp.org	309-677-4747	677-4730	741-97
WTVQ-TV Ch 36 (ABC) 6940 Man O War Blvd ... Lexington KY 40509 *Web:* www.wtvq.com	859-294-3636		741-73
WTVR-TV Ch 6 (CBS) 3301 W Broad St ... Richmond VA 23230 **Fax:* Sales ■ *Web:* www.wtvr.com	804-254-3600	342-3418*	741-108
WTVT-TV Ch 13 (Fox) 3213 W Kennedy Blvd ... Tampa FL 33609 *TF:* 800-334-9888 ■ *Web:* www.fox13news.com	813-876-1313	871-3135	741-133
WTVX-TV Ch 34 (CW) 1700 Palm Beach Lakes Blvd ... West Palm Beach FL 33401 *Web:* cw34.com	561-681-3434		741-140
WTVZ-TV Ch 33 (MNT) 900 Granby St ... Norfolk VA 23510 *Web:* www.mytvz.com	757-622-3333	623-1541	741-92
WTWC-TV Ch 40 (NBC) 8440 Deerlake Rd S ... Tallahassee FL 32312 *TF:* 800-798-2510 ■ *Web:* www.wtwc40.com	850-893-4140		741-132
WTXF-TV Ch 29 (Fox) 330 Market St ... Philadelphia PA 19106 **Fax:* News Rm ■ *TF:* 800-220-6397 ■ *Web:* www.fox29.com	215-925-2929	982-5494*	741-98
WTXL-TV Ch 27 (ABC) 1620 Commerce Blvd ... Midway FL 32343 *Web:* www.wtxl.com	850-893-3127		741
WUAL-FM 91.5 (NPR) 920 Paul W Bryant Dr Box 870370 ... Tuscaloosa AL 35487 *TF:* 800-654-4262 ■ *Web:* www.apr.org	205-348-6644		645-170
WUBE-FM 105.1 (Ctry) 2060 Reading Rd ... Cincinnati OH 45202 *Web:* b105.com	513-699-5105	699-5000	645-37
WUCF-FM 89.9 (Jazz) PO Box 162199 ... Orlando FL 32816-2199 *Web:* www.wucf.ucf.edu	407-823-0899		645-116
WUCW-TV Ch 23 (CW) 1640 Como Ave ... Saint Paul MN 55108 *Web:* thecw23.com	651-646-2300	646-1220	741-84
WUGA-TV Ch 32 (PBS) 120 Hooper St ... Athens GA 30602 *Web:* www.uga.edu	706-542-3000		741
WUHF-TV Ch 31 (Fox) 201 Humbolt St ... Rochester NY 14610 *Web:* www.rochesterfirst.com	585-232-3700	288-1505	741-111
WUKY-FM 91.3 (NPR) 340 McVey Hall University of Kentucky ... Lexington KY 40506 *TF:* 800-323-9262 ■ *Web:* wuky.org	859-257-3221		645-89
Wulco Inc 6899 Steger Dr ... Cincinnati OH 45237 *Web:* www.wulco.com	513-761-6899		567
Wulftec International Inc 209 Wulftec St ... Ayer's Cliff QC J0B1C0 *TF:* 877-985-3832 ■ *Web:* www.wulftec.com	819-838-4232	838-5539	547
WUMB-FM 91.9 (Folk) 100 Morrissey Blvd ... Boston MA 02125 *TF:* 800-573-2100 ■ *Web:* www.wumb.org	617-287-6900	287-6916	645-23
WUNC-FM 91.5 (NPR) 120 Friday Center Dr ... Chapel Hill NC 27517 *TF:* 800-962-9862 ■ *Web:* www.wunc.org	919-445-9150		645
Wunderland Electric Castle's 3451 SE Belmont St ... Portland OR 97214 *Web:* wunderlandgames.com	503-238-1617		31
Wunderlich Fibre Box Mfg Co 821 Clinton St ... St. Louis MO 63102 *Web:* www.wfbco.com	314-231-1488		100
Wunderlich Securities Inc 6000 Poplar Ave Ste 150 ... Memphis TN 38119 *TF:* 800-289-9999 ■ *Web:* www.wunderlichsecurities.com	901-251-1330		690
Wunderlich-Malec Engineering Inc 5501 Feltl Rd ... Minnetonka MN 55343 *Web:* www.wmeng.com	952-933-3222		261
WUNL-TV Ch 26 (PBS) 10 TW Alexander Dr PO Box 14900 ... Research Triangle Park NC 27709 *Web:* www.unctv.org	919-549-7000		741
WUOM-FM 91.7 (NPR) 535 W William St Ste 110 ... Ann Arbor MI 48103 *TF:* 888-258-9866 ■ *Web:* www.michiganradio.org	734-764-9210	647-3488	645-7
WUOT-FM 91.9 (NPR) 209 Communications Bldg University of Tennessee ... Knoxville TN 37996 *TF:* 888-266-9868 ■ *Web:* www.wuot.org	865-974-5375	974-3941	645-85
Wupatki National Monument Flagstaff Area National Monuments 6400 N Hwy 89 ... Flagstaff AZ 86004 *Web:* www.nps.gov/wupa	928-679-2365	679-2349	564
WUPA-TV Ch 69 (CW) 2700 NE Expy Bldg A ... Atlanta GA 30345 *Web:* cwatlanta.cbslocal.com	404-325-6929	633-4567	741-7
WUPV-TV Ch 65 (CW) 5710 Midlothian Tpke ... Richmond VA 23225 *Web:* www.cwrichmond.tv	804-230-1212		741-108
WURTH (Action Bolt & Tool Co) 701 Boutwell Rd Ste A-1 ... Lake Worth FL 33461 **Fax Area Code:* 561 ■ *TF:* 800-423-0700 ■ *Web:* www.actionboltandtool.com	800-423-0700	845-0255*	351
Wurth Revcar Fasteners Inc 3845 Thirlane Rd ... Roanoke VA 24019 *TF:* 800-542-5762 ■ *Web:* www.wurthrevcar.com	800-542-5762		351
Wurth Service Supply Inc 4935 W 86th St ... Indianapolis IN 46268 **Fax Area Code:* 716 ■ **Fax:* Cust Svc ■ *Web:* www.servicesupply.com	317-704-1000	668-2264*	351
Wurth USA Inc 93 Grant St ... Ramsey NJ 07446 *TF:* 800-987-8487 ■ *Web:* www.wurthusa.com	201-825-2710	825-3706	61
Wurzel Builders Ltd 630 Ralph Ablanedo Dr ... Austin TX 78748 *Web:* wurzelbuilders.com	512-282-9488		186
WUSA-TV Ch 9 (CBS) 4100 Wisconsin Ave NW ... Washington DC 20016 *TF:* 800-505-0098 ■ *Web:* www.wusa9.com	202-895-5999		741-139
WUSF 4202 E Fowler Ave TVB 100 ... Tampa FL 33620 *TF:* 800-741-9090 ■ *Web:* wusf.usf.edu/radio	813-974-8700	974-5016	645-162
WUSF Public Broadcasting 4202 E Fowler Ave TVB100 ... Tampa FL 33620 *TF:* 800-741-9090 ■ *Web:* www.wusf.usf.edu	813-974-8700		645-10
WUSF-TV Ch 16 (PBS) 4202 E Fowler Ave ... Tampa FL 33620 *TF:* 800-654-3703 ■ *Web:* www.wusftv.usf.edu	813-974-4000	974-4806	741-133

Listing	City	State	Zip	Phone	Fax	Class
WUSJ-FM 96.3 (Ctry)						
265 Highpoint Dr	Ridgeland	MS	39157	601-956-0102	978-3980	645
Web: www.yourcountryus96.com						
WUSN-FM 99.5 (Ctry)						
180 N Stetson Ave Ste 1000	Chicago	IL	60601	312-649-0099	634-7061*	645-36
**Fax Area Code:* 301 ■ *Web:* us995.cbslocal.com						
WUSY-FM 101 7413 Old Lee Hwy	Chattanooga	TN	37421	423-892-3333		645-34
Web: us101country.iheart.com						
WUTC-FM 88.1 (NPR)						
615 McCallie Ave						
104 Cadek Hall Dept 1151	Chattanooga	TN	37403	423-425-4756	425-2379	645-34
TF: 800-272-3900 ■ *Web:* www.wutc.org						
WUTV-TV Ch 29 (Fox)						
699 Hertel Ave Ste 100	Buffalo	NY	14207	716-447-3200		741-20
Web: www.wutv29.com						
WUWF-FM 88.1 (NPR)						
11000 University Pkwy	Pensacola	FL	32514	850-474-2787		645-120
TF: 800-239-9893 ■ *Web:* www.wuwf.org						
WUWM-FM 89.7 (NPR)						
111 E Wisconsin Ave Ste 700	Milwaukee	WI	53202	414-227-3355		645-100
Web: www.wuwm.com						
WUXP-TV Ch 30 (MNT)						
631 Mainstream Dr	Nashville	TN	37228	615-259-5617		741-89
Web: www.mytv30web.com						
WVACO (West Virginia Assn of Counties)						
2211 Washington St	Charleston	WV	25311	304-346-0591		49-7
Web: www.wvaco.org						
WVAF-FM 1111 Virginia St E	Charleston	WV	25301	304-342-8131		645-32
Web: www.v100.fm						
WVAH-TV Ch 11 (Fox)						
1301 Piedmont Rd	Charleston	WV	25301	304-346-5358	346-4765	741-25
Web: www.wvah.com						
WVAQ-FM 101.9 (CHR)						
1251 Earl L Core Rd	Morgantown	WV	26505	304-296-0029		645-105
TF: 800-248-4242 ■ *Web:* www.wvaq.com						
WVBW-FM 92.9 (Oldies)						
5589 Greenwich Rd Ste 200	Virginia Beach	VA	23462	757-671-1000		645-112
TF: 800-497-8228 ■ *Web:* www.929thewave.com						
WVCC (Warwick Valley Chamber of Commerce)						
PO Box 202	Warwick	NY	10990	845-986-2720	986-6982	139
TF: 800-538-2583 ■ *Web:* www.warwickcc.org						
WVCY-TV Ch 30 (Ind)						
3434 W Kilbourn Ave	Milwaukee	WI	53208	414-935-3000	935-3015	741-83
TF: 800-729-9829 ■ *Web:* www.vcyamerica.org						
WVEC-TV Ch 13 (ABC) 613 Woodis Ave	Norfolk	VA	23510	757-625-1313		741-92
Web: www.13newsnow.com						
WVEE-FM 103.3 (Urban)						
1201 Peachtree St NE Ste 800	Atlanta	GA	30361	404-898-8900	898-8909	645-10
Web: v103.cbslocal.com						
WVES (Virginia West Electric Supply Co)						
250 12-th St W	Huntington	WV	25704	304-525-0361	525-2726	246
TF: [illegible] ■ *Web:* www.wvaelectric.com						
WVFN-AM 730 (Sports)						
3420 Pine Tree Rd	Lansing	MI	48911	517-394-7272		645-87
Web: thegame730am.com						
WVII-TV Ch 7 (ABC)						
371 Target Industrial Cir	Bangor	ME	04401	207-945-6457		741-12
TF General: 888-820-8458 ■ *Web:* www.foxbangor.com						
WVIT-TV Ch 30 (NBC)						
1422 New Britain Ave	West Hartford	CT	06110	860-521-3030		741
TF: 800-523-9848 ■ *Web:* www.nbcconnecticut.com						
WVKF Radio 1015 Main St	Wheeling	WV	26003	304-232-1170		645-174
Web: klsswheeling.iheart.com						
WVLT-TV Ch 8 (CBS)						
6450 Papermill Dr	Knoxville	TN	37919	865-450-8888	450-8869	741-69
Web: www.local8now.com						
WVMA (Wisconsin Veterinary Medical Assn)						
2801 Crossroads Dr Ste 1200	Madison	WI	53718	608-257-3665	257-8989	795
TF: 888-254-5202 ■ *Web:* www.wvma.org						
WVMA (Wyoming Veterinary Medical Assn)						
2001 Capitol Ave	Cheyenne	WY	82001	800-272-1813	922-9435*	795
**Fax Area Code:* 208 ■ *TF:* 800-272-1813 ■ *Web:* www.wyvma.org						
WVMW-FM 91.7 (Alt) 2300 Adams Ave	Scranton	PA	18509	570-348-6202		645-149
Web: www.vmfm917.org						
WVNA (West Virginia Nurses Assn)						
1007 Bigley Ave Ste 308	Charleston	WV	25302	304-342-1169		533
TF: 800-400-1226 ■ *Web:* www.wvnurses.org						
WVNY-TV Ch 22 (ABC)						
298 Mountain View Dr	Colchester	VT	05446	802-660-9333	660-8673	741
Web: www.mychamplainvalley.com						
WVOC-AM 560 (N/T) 316 Greystone Blvd	Columbia	SC	29210	803-343-1100		645-40
Web: wvoc.iheart.com						
WVOM-FM 103.9 (N/T)						
184 Target Industrial Cir	Bangor	ME	04401	207-947-9100		645-17
TF: 800-966-1039 ■ *Web:* www.wvomfm.com						
WVON-AM 1690 (N/T) 1000 E 87th St	Chicago	IL	60619	773-247-6200		645-36
Web: www.wvon.com						
WVPE-FM 88.1 (NPR) 2424 California Rd	Elkhart	IN	46514	574-674-9873	262-5700	645
TF: 888-399-9873 ■ *Web:* www.wvpe.org						
WVPS-FM 107.9 (NPR) 365 Troy Ave	Colchester	VT	05446	802-655-9451	655-2799	645
TF: 800-639-2192 ■ *Web:* www.vpr.net						
WVS Financial Corp 9001 Perry Hwy	Pittsburgh	PA	15237	412-364-1911		360-2
NASDAQ: WVFC ■ *Web:* www.wvsbank.com						
WVTF-FM 89.1 (NPR) 3520 Kingsbury Ln	Roanoke	VA	24014	540-989-8900	776-2727	645-136
TF: 800-856-8900 ■ *Web:* www.wvtf.org						
WVTM-TV Ch 13 (NBC)						
1732 Valley View Dr	Birmingham	AL	35209	205-933-1313	558-7389	741-15
TF: 844-248-7698 ■ *Web:* www.wvtm13.com						
WVTV-TV Ch 18 (CW) 4041 N 35th St	Milwaukee	WI	53216	414-815-4100	203-2300	741-83
Web: super18tv.com						
WVUE-TV Ch 8 (Fox)						
1025 S Jefferson Davis Pkwy	New Orleans	LA	70125	504-486-6161	483-1543	741-90
Web: www.fox8live.com						
WVVMA (West Virginia Veterinary Medical Assn)						
3801 Westerre Pkwy Ste D	Henrico	VA	23233	804-346-2611	346-2655	795
TF: 800-843-6664 ■ *Web:* www.wvvma.org						
WVXU-FM 91.7 (NPR)						
1223 Central Pkwy	Cincinnati	OH	45214	513-352-9170		645-37
Web: www.wvxu.org						

Listing	City	State	Zip	Phone	Fax	Class
WVYB-FM 103.3 (CHR)						
126 W International Speedway Blvd	Daytona Beach	FL	32114	386-255-9300		645-46
WW Gay Fire & Integrated Systems Inc						
522 Stockton St	Jacksonville	FL	32204	904-387-7973		610
Web: www.wwgfp.com						
WW Grainger Inc 100 Grainger Pkwy	Lake Forest	IL	60045	847-535-1000		246
NYSE: GWW ■ *TF:* 888-361-8649 ■ *Web:* www.grainger.com						
WW Norton & Company Inc						
500 Fifth Ave 6th Fl	New York	NY	10110	212-354-5500	869-0856	637-2
TF: 800-233-4830 ■ *Web:* books.wwnorton.com						
WW Seymour Botanical Conservatory						
316 S 'G' St	Tacoma	WA	98405	253-591-5330		97
Web: metroparkstacoma.org						
WW Wood Products Inc 10182 Old Hwy 60	Dudley	MO	63936	573-624-7090		115
Web: wwwoodproducts.com						
WWBT-TV Ch 12 (NBC)						
5710 Midlothian Tpke	Richmond	VA	23225	804-230-1212		741-108
Web: www.nbc12.com						
Wwc Enterprises Inc 19145 S US Hwy 377	Dublin	TX	76446	254-445-0100		463
Web: www.wwcenterprises.com						
WWCK-FM 105.5 (CHR) 6317 Taylor Dr	Flint	MI	48507	810-238-7300		645-60
Web: www.wwck.com						
WWCS (Taycheedah Correctional Institution)						
751 County Rd	Fond Du Lac	WI	54936-1947	920-929-3800	929-2946	213
Web: doc.wi.gov						
WWDE-FM 101.3 (AC)						
236 Clearfield Ave Ste 206	Virginia Beach	VA	23462	757-497-2000		645
Web: 2wd.com						
WWF (World Wildlife Fund Canada)						
245 Eglinton Ave E Ste 410	Toronto	ON	M4P3J1	416-489-8800		48-3
TF: 800-267-2632 ■ *Web:* www.wwf.ca						
WWF (World Wildlife Fund)						
1250 24th St NW PO Box 97180	Washington	DC	20090	202-293-4800	293-9211	48-3
TF: 800-225-5993 ■ *Web:* www.worldwildlife.org						
WWFX-FM 100.1 (CR)						
250 Commercial St 5th Fl	Worcester	MA	01608	508-752-1045	973-0824	645-179
Web: www.pikefm.com						
WWGR-FM 101.9 (Ctry)						
10915 K-Nine Dr	Bonita Springs	FL	34135	239-495-8383		645
TF: 877-787-1019 ■ *Web:* www.gatorcountry1019.com						
WWJC-AM 850 (Rel) 1120 E McCuen St	Duluth	MN	55808	218-626-2738		645-51
Web: www.wwjc.com						
WWJ-TV Ch 62 (CBS)						
26905 W 11-Mile Rd	Southfield	MI	48034	248-355-7000		741
Web: detroit.cbslocal.com						
WWKA-FM 92.3 (Ctry)						
4192 N John Young Pkwy	Orlando	FL	32804	407-424-9236	299-4947	645-116
TF: 866-438-0220 ■ *Web:* www.k923orlando.com						
WWKL-FM 92.1 (CHR) 2300 Vartan Way	Harrisburg	PA	17110	717-238-1041		645-71
Web: www.hot935fm.com						
WWL-AM 870 (N/T)						
400 Poydras St Ste 800	New Orleans	LA	70130	504-593-6376		645-110
Web: www.wwl.com						
WWL-FM 105.3 N/T)						
400 Poydras St Ste 800	New Orleans	LA	70130	504-593-6376		645-110
Web: www.wwl.com						
WWLI-FM 105.1 (AC)						
1502 Wampanoag Trl	East Providence	RI	02915	401-433-4200		645
Web: www.literock105fm.com						
WWLP.com 1 Broadcast Ctr	Chicopee	MA	01013	413-377-2200	377-2261	741-129
Web: www.wwlp.com						
WWL-TV Ch 4 (CBS)						
1024 N Rampart St	New Orleans	LA	70116	504-529-4444		741-90
Web: www.wwltv.com						
WWML (Willoughby Wallace Memorial Library)						
146 Thimble Islands Rd	Stony Creek	CT	06405	203-488-8702	315-3347	434-3
Web: www.wwml.org						
WWMT-TV Ch 3 (CBS) 590 W Maple St	Kalamazoo	MI	49008	800-875-3333	388-8322*	741
**Fax Area Code:* 269 ■ *TF:* 800-875-3333 ■ *Web:* www.wwmt.com						
WWMX-FM 106.5 (CHR)						
1423 Clarkview Rd Ste 100	Baltimore	MD	21209	410-825-1000	466-4433*	645-16
**Fax Area Code:* 626 ■ *Web:* mix1065fm.cbslocal.com						
WWNC-AM 570 (N/T) 13 Summerlin Rd	Asheville	NC	28806	828-257-2700		645-9
Web: wwnc.iheart.com						
WWNO-FM 89.9 (NPR)						
University of New Orleans						
2000 Lakeshore Dr	New Orleans	LA	70148	504-280-7000	280-6061	645-110
TF: 800-286-7002 ■ *Web:* www.wwno.org						
WWOR-TV Ch 9 (MNT) 9 Broadcast Plaza	Secaucus	NJ	07094	201-348-0009		741
Web: www.my9nj.com						
WWOZ-FM 90.7 (Var)						
1008 N Peters St	New Orleans	LA	70116	504-568-1239	558-9332	645-110
Web: www.wwoz.org						
WWPA (Western Wood Products Assn)						
522 SW Fifth Ave Ste 500	Portland	OR	97204	503-224-3930	224-3934	48-2
Web: www.wwpa.org						
WWST-FM 102.1 (CHR) 1533 Amherst Rd	Knoxville	TN	37909	865-824-1021		645-85
TF: 800-272-8874 ■ *Web:* www.star1021fm.com						
WWTC-AM 1280 (N/T) 2110 Cliff Rd	Eagan	MN	55122	651-405-8800	405-8222	645
Web: www.am1280thepatriot.com						
WWUS-FM 104.1 (CR)						
30336 Overseas Hwy	Big Pine Key	FL	33043	305-872-9100	872-1603	645
Web: www.us1radio.com						
WWVA-AM 1170 (N/T) 1015 Main St	Wheeling	WV	26003	304-232-1170		645-174
Web: newsradio1170.iheart.com						
WWVU-FM						
West Virginia University PO Box 6446	Morgantown	WV	26506	304-293-3329	293-7363	645-105
Web: u92.wvu.edu						
WWWW-FM 102.9 (Ctry)						
1100 Victors Way Ste 100	Ann Arbor	MI	48108	734-302-8100		645-7
Web: www.w4country.com						
WWYZ-FM 92.5 (Ctry) 10 Columbus Blvd	Hartford	CT	06106	860-723-6000		645-72
Web: country925.iheart.com						
WXBM-FM 102.7 (Ctry) 6565 N W St	Pensacola	FL	32505	850-478-6011	478-3971	645
Web: www.nashpensacola.com						
WXCL-FM 104.9 (Ctry)						
331 Fulton St Ste 1200	Peoria	IL	61602	309-637-3700		645-121
Web: www.1049thewolf.com						

	Phone	Fax	Class
WXCY-FM 103.7 (Ctry) 707 Revolution St.................... Havre de Grace MD 21078 *TF:* 800-788-9929 ■ *Web:* www.wxcyfm.com	410-939-1100	939-1104	645
WXDU-FM 88.7 (Alt) PO Box 90689............ Durham NC 27708 *TF:* 800-700-1094 ■ *Web:* www.wxdu.org	919-684-2957		645-131
WXEL-FM 90.7 (NPR) 3401 S Congress Ave................West Palm Beach FL 33426 *TF:* 800-915-9935 ■ *Web:* www.wxel.org	561-737-8000	369-3067	645-173
WXEL-TV Ch 42 (PBS) PO Box 6607 ....West Palm Beach FL 33405 *TF:* 800-915-9935 ■ *Web:* www.wxel.org	561-737-8000	369-3067	741-140
WXFX-FM 95.1 (Rock) 1 Commerce St Ste 300 .... Montgomery AL 36104 *Web:* www.wxfx.com	334-240-9274	240-9219	645-104
WXGI-AM 950 (Sports) 701 German School Rd.................... Richmond VA 23225 *TF:* 877-994-4950 ■ *Web:* www.espn950am.com	804-233-7666	233-7681	645-134
WXGL-FM 107.3 (AC) 11300 Fourth St N Ste 300............ Saint Petersburg FL 33716 *TF:* 800-242-1073 ■ *Web:* www.1073theeagle.com	727-579-2000	578-0949	645-162
WXIA-TV Ch 11 (NBC) 1 Monroe Pl .... Atlanta GA 30324 **Fax:* News Rm ■ *Web:* www.11alive.com	404-892-1611	881-0675*	741-7
WXII-TV Ch 12 (NBC) 700 Coliseum Dr .... Winston-Salem NC 27106 *Web:* www.wxii12.com	336-721-9944	721-0856	741-144
WXIN-TV Ch 59 (Fox) 6910 Network Pl........................Indianapolis IN 46278 *TF:* 800-535-5542 ■ *Web:* www.fox59.com	317-632-5900		741-62
WXIX-TV Ch 19 (Fox) 635 W Seventh St 19 Broadcast Plz.......... Cincinnati OH 45203 *Web:* fox19.com	513-421-1919	421-3022	741-30
WXKB-FM 103.9 (CHR) 20125 S Tamiami Trl......................... Estero FL 33928 *Web:* www.b1039.com	239-765-1039		645
WXKR-FM 94.5 (CR) 3225 Arlington Ave .... Toledo OH 43614 *TF:* 866-240-9945 ■ *Web:* www.wxkr.com	419-725-5700		645-163
WXLK-FM 92.3 (CHR) 3934 Electric Rd SW........................Roanoke VA 24018 *TF:* 800-222-4357 ■ *Web:* www.k92radio.com	540-774-9200		645-136
WXLO-FM 104.5 (AC) 250 Commercial St....................... Worcester MA 01608 *TF:* 800-888-6499 ■ *Web:* www.wxlo.com	508-752-1045	793-0824	645-179
WXLV-TV Ch 45 (ABC) 3500 Myer Lee Dr.................... Winston-Salem NC 27101 *Web:* www.abc45.com	336-722-4545	723-8217	741-144
WXMA-FM 102.3 (AC) 520 S Fourth Ave ....Louisville KY 40202 *Web:* www.themaxfm.com	502-625-1220		645-93
WXMI-TV Ch 17 (Fox) 3117 Plaza Dr NE.......................Grand Rapids MI 49525 *Web:* www.fox17online.com	616-364-8722	364-8506	741-53
WXMX-FM 98.1 (Rock) 5629 Murray Rd........ Memphis TN 38119 *Web:* www.981themax.com	901-535-9898		645-98
WXNT-AM 1430 (N/T) 9245 N Meridian St Ste 300..............Indianapolis IN 46260 *Web:* www.cbssports1430.com	317-816-4000		645-77
WXPN-FM 88.5 (AAA) 3025 Walnut St..........................Philadelphia PA 19104 *Web:* www.xpn.org	215-898-6677	898-0707	645-122
WXRL-AM 1300 (Ctry) PO Box 170 PO Box 170.....................Lancaster NY 14086 *Web:* www.wxrl.com	716-681-1313		645
WXRR-FM 104.5 (Rock) 4580 Hwy 15 N .... Laurel MS 39443 *Web:* www.rock104fm.com	601-649-0095		645
WXRV-FM 92.5 (AAA) 30 How St............. Haverhill MA 01830 *TF:* 800-352-9250 ■ *Web:* theriverboston.com	978-374-4733		645
WXTU-FM 92.5 (Ctry) 555 E City Ave Ste 330.................... Bala Cynwyd PA 19004 *Web:* 925xtu.cbslocal.com	610-667-9000		645
WXXI-AM 1370 (NPR) PO Box 30021..........Rochester NY 14603 *Web:* interactive.wxxi.org	585-325-7500		645-138
WXXI-FM 91.5 (Clas) PO Box 30021..........Rochester NY 14603 *Web:* interactive.wxxi.org	585-325-7500		645-138
WXXI-TV Ch 21 (PBS) PO Box 30021..........Rochester NY 14603 *Web:* interactive.wxxi.org	585-325-7500		741-111
WXXJ-FM 102.9 (AC) 8000 Belfort Pkwy.........................Jacksonville FL 32256 *TF:* 800-460-6394 ■ *Web:* www.x1029.com	904-245-8500	245-8501	645-79
WXXV-TV Ch 25 (Fox) 14351 Hwy 49 N.......... Gulfport MS 39503 *Web:* www.wxxv25.com	228-832-2525	832-4442	741
WXXX-FM 95.5 (CHR) 118 Malletts Bay Ave .... Colchester VT 05446 *Web:* www.95triplex.com	802-655-9550	655-1329	645
WXYZ-TV Ch 7 (ABC) 20777 W 10-Mile Rd .... Southfield MI 48037 *TF:* 800-825-0770 ■ *Web:* www.wxyz.com	248-827-7777	827-9444	741
Wy Industries Inc 2500 Secaucus Rd ....North Bergen NJ 07047 *Web:* www.wyindustries.com	201-617-8000		596
Wyalusing State Park 13081 State Pk Ln .... Bagley WI 53801 *Web:* www.wyalusing.org	608-996-2261		565
Wyandot County 109 S Sandusky Ave County Courthouse .. Upper Sandusky OH 43351 *Web:* www.co.wyandot.oh.us	419-294-1432	294-6414	338
Wyandot Inc 135 Wyandot Ave ....Marion OH 43302 *TF:* 800-992-6368 ■ *Web:* www.wyandotsnacks.com	740-383-4031		296-35
Wyandot Tractor & Implement Co 10264 County Hwy 121 .... Upper Sandusky OH 43351 *Web:* www.findlay-imp.com/wyandot/default.asp	419-294-2349		274
Wyant Data Systems Inc 245 Century Cir Ste 106......................Louisville CO 80027 *Web:* www.wyantdata.com	303-604-6254		177
Wyatt & Company Inc 6846 S Trenton Ave .... Tulsa OK 74136 *Web:* www.wyattandcompany.com	918-488-0311		2
Wyatt & Jaffe 2751 Hennepin Ave S Ste 286 ....Minneapolis MN 55408 *TF:* 800-474-8858 ■ *Web:* www.wyattjaffe.com	612-285-2858	285-2786	266
Wyatt Early Harris Wheeler LLP PO Box 2086 ....High Point NC 27261 *Web:* www.wehwlaw.com	336-884-4444		428
Wyatt Field Service Co 15415 Katy Fwy Ste 800.......................Houston TX 77094 *Web:* www.wyattfieldservice.com	281-675-1300	675-1390	189-1
Wyatt Inc 4545 Campbells Run Rd............ Pittsburgh PA 15205 *Web:* www.wyattinc.com	412-787-5800	787-5845	189-9
Wyatt Precision Machine Inc 3301 E 59th St .... Long Beach CA 90805 *Web:* www.wyattprecisionmachine.com	562-634-0524		757
Wyatt Tarrant & Combs PNC Plaza 500 W Jefferson St ....Louisville KY 40202 *Web:* www.wyattfirm.com	502-589-5235		428
Wyatt Transfer Inc 3035 Bells Rd PO Box 24326................ Richmond VA 23224 **Fax:* Administration ■ *TF:* 800-552-5708 ■ *Web:* www.wyatttransferinc.com	804-743-3800	271-9598*	780
Wyatt-Quarles Seed Co 730 US Hwy 70 W........ Garner NC 27529 *TF:* 800-662-7591 ■ *Web:* www.wqseeds.com	919-772-4243	772-4278	274
WYAV-FM 104.1 (CR) 1016 Ocala St .... Myrtle Beach SC 29577 *Web:* wave104.net	843-448-1041	626-5988	645-106
WYBC-AM 1340 (Var) 142 Temple St Ste 203 ....New Haven CT 06510 *Web:* www.wybc.com	203-776-4118		645-109
WYBC-FM 94.3 (Urban) 440 Wheelers Farms Rd Ste 302................Milford CT 06461 *Web:* www.943wybc.com	203-783-8200	783-8383	645-109
WYCC-TV Ch 20 (PBS) 6258 S Union Ave ....Chicago IL 60621 *Web:* www.wycc.org	773-224-3300		741-29
Wyche Burgess Freeman & Parham 44 ECamperdown Wy .... Greenville SC 29601 *Web:* www.wyche.com	864-242-8200		445
Wycliffe Bible Translators 11221 John Wycliffe Blvd.................... Orlando FL 32832 *TF:* 800-992-5433 ■ *Web:* www.wycliffe.org	407-852-3600	852-3601	48-20
WYCR-FM 98.5 (AC) 275 Radio Rd............. Hanover PA 17331 *Web:* www.foreveryork.com	717-637-3831	637-9006	645
WYDA (Wyoming Dental Assn) 259 S Ctr Ste 201 ....Casper WY 82601 *Web:* www.wyda.org	307-237-1186	237-1186	227
Wyde Corp 3600 American Blvd W Ste 330 .... Bloomington MN 55431 *Web:* www.wyde.com	651-882-2400		180
Wyden Ron (Sen D - OR) 221 Dirksen Bldg .... Washington DC 20510 *Web:* www.wyden.senate.gov	202-224-5244	228-2717	342-2
Wye Island Natural Resources Management Area 632 Wye Island Rd ....Queenstown MD 21658 *Web:* dnr2.maryland.gov	410-827-7577		565
Wye Oak State Park c/o Tuckahoe State Pk 13070 Crouse Mill Rd ....Queen Anne MD 21657 *Web:* www.dnr.maryland.gov/publiclands/Pages/eastern/wyeoak.aspx	410-820-1668		565
WYES-TV Ch 12 (PBS) 111 Veterans Blvd Ste 250 .... Metairie LA 70005 *TF:* 800-683-1899 ■ *Web:* www.wyes.org	504-486-5511	840-9954	741
Wyffels Hybrids Inc 13344 US Hwy 6 ....Geneseo IL 61254 *TF:* 800-369-7833 ■ *Web:* www.wyffels.com	309-944-8334	944-8338	10-5
WYFF-TV Ch 4 (NBC) 505 Rutherford St .... Greenville SC 29609 *TF:* 800-453-9933 ■ *Web:* www.wyff4.com	864-242-4404	240-5305	741-6
WYJB-FM 95.5 (AC) 6 Johnson Rd..............Latham NY 12110 *Web:* www.b95.com	518-786-6600		645
WYLD-AM 940 (Rel) 929 Howard Ave........ New Orleans LA 70113 *TF:* 800-899-9265 ■ *Web:* hallelujah940.iheart.com	504-679-7300	679-7345	645-110
WYLD-FM 98.5 (Urban) 929 Howard Ave .... New Orleans LA 70113 *Web:* wyldfm.iheart.com	504-679-7300		645-110
Wylie House Museum 307 E Second St....................... Bloomington IN 47401 *TF:* 800-366-2682 ■ *Web:* www.indiana.edu	812-855-6224		520
Wylie Spray Center 702 E 40th St ....Lubbock TX 79404 *TF:* 888-249-5162 ■ *Web:* www.wyliesprayers.com	806-763-1335	763-1092	273
Wyman Center Inc 600 Kiwanis Dr............... Eureka MO 63025 *Web:* wymancenter.org	636-938-5245		239
Wyman-Gordon Forgings (Cleveland) Inc 3097 E 61st St ....Cleveland OH 44127 *Web:* www.pccforgedproducts.com	216-341-0085		483
Wyman-Gordon Forgings Lp 10825 Telge Rd.............................Houston TX 77095 *Web:* www.dropdies.com	281-856-9900		567
WYMG-FM 100.5 (CR) 3501 E Sangamon Ave ....Springfield IL 62707 *Web:* www.wymg.com	217-753-5400	753-7902	645-155
Wynalda Packaging 8221 Graphic Dr NE......... Belmont MI 49306 *Web:* www.wynalda.com	616-866-1561		548
Wyndham Grand Chicago Riverfront 71 E Wacker Dr.............................Chicago IL 60601 *Web:* wyndhamgrandchicagoriverfront.com	312-346-7100	346-1721	379
Wyndham Hotel Group			
Baymont Inn & Suites 1023 Eighth Ave NW .... Aberdeen SD 57401 *TF:* 800-337-0550 ■ *Web:* www.wyndhamhotels.com	800-337-0550		379
Ramada 949 Route 46.....................Parsippany NJ 07054 *Web:* www.wyndhamhotels.com/ramada	973-263-5702		379
Travelodge 1910 Eigth Ave NE............ Aberdeen SD 57041 *TF Resv:* 800-525-4055 ■ *Web:* www.wyndhamhotels.com/travelodge	312-427-8000		379
Wyndham Vacation Resorts 6277 Sea Harbor Dr...................... Orlando FL 32821 *TF:* 800-251-8736 ■ *Web:* www.clubwyndham.com	800-251-8736		379
Wyndham Jade LLC 202 E Main Ave .... Rockford IA 50468 *Web:* www.wynjade.com	641-756-3385		772
Wyndham Lake Buena Vista 1850 Hotel Plaza Blvd................Lake Buena Vista FL 32830 *TF:* 800-624-4109 ■ *Web:* www.wyndhamlakebuenavista.com	407-828-4444		379
Wyndham Midtown 45 205 E 45th St.......... New York NY 10017 *Web:* www.extraholidays.com/new-york-city-ny/wyndham-midtown-45.aspx	212-867-5100	867-7878	379

Phone | Fax | Class

Wyndham Peachtree Conference Ctr
2443 Hwy 54 W .... Peachtree City GA 30269 770-487-2000 487-8599 377
TF: 800-996-3426 ■ *Web:* www3.hilton.com
Wyndham Rewards 1023 Eighth Ave NW .... Aberdeen SD 57401 605-226-2288 378
TF: 800-996-3426 ■ *Web:* www.wyndhamhotels.com/wyndham
Wyndham Vacation Rentals
14 Sylvan Way .... Parsippany NJ 07054 973-753-6300 669
TF: 800-467-3529 ■ *Web:* www.wyndhamvacationrentals.com
Wyndham Vacation Resorts King Cotton Villas
1 King Cotton Rd .... Edisto Beach SC 29438 843-869-2561 869-2384 669
TF: 800-251-8736 ■ *Web:* www.clubwyndham.com/cw/home.page
Wyndham Worldwide Corp
Wyndham Hotel Group 22 Sylvan Way .... Parsippany NJ 07054 973-753-6000 753-6000 379
NYSE: WYN ■ *Web:* www.wyndhamworldwide.com
Wynfrey Hotel
1000 Riverchase Galleria .... Birmingham AL 35244 205-705-1234 988-4597 379
Web: wynfrey.regency.hyatt.com
Wynick Tuck Gallery
401 Richmond St W Studio S27 .... Toronto ON M5V3A8 416-504-8716 504-8699 42
TF: 800-442-2787 ■ *Web:* www.wynicktuckgallery.ca
WYNK-FM 101.5 (Ctry)
5555 Hilton Ave Ste 500 .... Baton Rouge LA 70808 225-231-1860 645-18
Web: wynkcountry.iheart.com
Wynkoop Brewing Co 1634 18th St .... Denver CO 80202 303-297-2700 671
Web: www.wynkoop.com
Wynn - Crosby Energy Inc
5500 W Plano Pkwy Ste 200 .... Plano TX 75093 972-380-5500 536
Web: www.wynncrosby.com
Wynn Las Vegas
3131 Las Vegas Blvd S .... Las Vegas NV 89109 702-770-7000 379
TF: 877-321-9966 ■ *Web:* www.wynnlasvegas.com
Wynn Resorts Holdings LLC
3145 Las Vegas Blvd S .... Las Vegas NV 89109 702-733-4556 770-8867 377
Web: www.wynnmacau.com
Wynne Transport Service Inc
2222 N 11th St .... Omaha NE 68108 402-342-4001 342-4608 780
TF: 800-383-9330 ■ *Web:* www.wynnetr.com
Wynright Corp 2500 York Rd .... Elk Grove IL 60007 847-595-9400 358
TF: 800-274-0064 ■ *Web:* www.wynright.com
Wynston Hill Capital LLC
488 Madison Ave 24th Fl .... New York NY 10022 212-521-1900 208-0978 256
Web: www.wynstonhillcapital.com
Wyo Media Inc 1856 Skyview Dr .... Casper WY 82601 307-577-5923 741-22
Wyo-Ben Inc 1345 Discovery Dr .... Billings MT 59102 406-652-6351 656-0748 503-2
TF Cust Svc: 800-548-7055 ■ *Web:* www.wyoben.com
Wyoming
Aging Div
6101 Yellowstone Rd Ste 186A .... Cheyenne WY 82002 307-777-7986 777-5340 339-51
TF: 800-442-2766 ■ *Web:* health.wyo.gov
Agriculture Dept (WDA)
2219 Carey Ave .... Cheyenne WY 82002 307-777-7321 777-6593 339-51
Web: wyagric.state.wy.us
Arts Council 2301 Central Ave .... Cheyenne WY 82002 307-777-7742 339-51
Web: wyoarts.state.wy.us
Banking Div
122 W 25th St Herschler Bldg 3rd Fl E .... Cheyenne WY 82002 307-777-7797 777-3555 339-51
Web: audit.wyo.gov
Board of Medicine 130 Hobbs Ave Ste A .... Cheyenne WY 82001 307-770-7050 770-2000 339-51
Web: wyomedboard.state.wy.us
Business Council 214 W 15th St .... Cheyenne WY 82002 307-777-2800 777-2838 339-51
TF: 800-262-3425 ■ *Web:* www.wyomingbusiness.org
Certified Public Accountants Board
325 W 18th St Ste 4 .... Cheyenne WY 82002 307-777-7551 777-3796 339-51
Web: cpaboard.state.wy.us
Community College Commission
2300 Capitol Ave Fl 5 Ste B .... Cheyenne WY 82002 307-777-7763 777-6567 725
Web: communitycolleges.wy.edu
Community Development Authority
155 N Beech St PO Box 634 .... Casper WY 82602 307-265-0603 266-5414 339-51
Web: www.wyomingcda.com
Consumer Protection Unit
2320 Capitol Ave .... Cheyenne WY 82002 307-777-7841 777-6869 339-51
Web: ag.wyo.gov
Corrections Dept
1934 Wyott Dr Ste 100 .... Cheyenne WY 82002 307-777-7208 777-7846 339-51
Web: corrections.wy.gov
Education Dept
2300 Capitol Ave Hathaway Bldg 2nd Fl .... Cheyenne WY 82002 307-777-7675 777-6234 339-51
Web: www.edu.wyoming.gov
Environmental Quality Dept
200 W 17th St .... Cheyenne WY 82002 307-777-7937 635-1784 339-51
Web: deq.state.wy.us
Family Services Dept
2300 Capitol Ave 3rd Fl Hathaway Bldg .... Cheyenne WY 82002 307-777-7561 339-51
Web: dfsweb.wyo.gov
Game & Fish Dept 5400 Bishop Blvd .... Cheyenne WY 82006 307-777-4600 777-4699 339-51
Web: wgfd.wyo.gov
Governor
State Capitol 200 W 24th St Rm 124 .... Cheyenne WY 82002 307-777-7434 632-3909 339-51
Web: governor.wyo.gov
Health Dept 401 Hathaway Bldg Ste 401 .... Cheyenne WY 82002 307-777-7656 777-7439 339-51
TF: 866-571-0944 ■ *Web:* health.wyo.gov
Highway Patrol (WHP)
5300 Bishop Blvd .... Cheyenne WY 82009 307-777-4301 777-3897 339-51
TF: 800-442-9090 ■ *Web:* www.whp.dot.state.wy.us
Historic Preservation Office
2301 Central Ave 3rd Fl .... Cheyenne WY 82002 307-777-7697 777-6421 339-51
Web: wyoshpo.state.wy.us
Homeland Security Office
5500 Bishop Blvd E Door .... Cheyenne WY 82002 307-777-4663 635-6017 339-51
Web: wyohomelandsecurity.state.wy.us
Insurance Dept 106 E Sixth Ave .... Cheyenne WY 82001 307-777-7401 339-51
TF: 800-438-5768 ■ *Web:* doi.wyo.gov
Legislative Service Office
213 State Capitol .... Cheyenne WY 82002 307-777-7881 433
Web: legisweb.state.wy.us
Legislature 213 State Capitol .... Cheyenne WY 82002 307-777-7881 777-5466 339-51
Web: legisweb.state.wy.us
Motor Vehicles Services Div
5300 Bishop Blvd .... Cheyenne WY 82009 307-777-4850 777-4772 339-51
Web: www.dot.state.wy.us
Professional Teaching Standards Board
1920 Thomes Ave Ste 400 .... Cheyenne WY 82002 307-777-7291 339-51
Web: uwyo.edu
Real Estate Commission
2617 E Lincolnway Ste H .... Cheyenne WY 82002 307-777-7141 777-3796 339-51
Web: www.wyoming.gov
Revenue Dept 122 W 25th St 2nd Fl W .... Cheyenne WY 82002 307-777-5200 777-3632 339-51
Web: revenue.wyo.gov
Secretary of State 200 W 24th St .... Cheyenne WY 82002 307-777-7378 339-51
Web: soswy.state.wy.us
Securities Div 2020 Carey Ave Ste 700 .... Cheyenne WY 82002 307-777-7370 777-7640 339-51
Web: soswy.state.wy.us
State Government Information
State Capitol Bldg 200 W 24th St .... Cheyenne WY 82002 307-777-7841 339-51
Web: ag.wyo.gov
State Parks & Historical Sites Div
2301 Central Ave 4th FL .... Cheyenne WY 82002 307-777-6323 339-51
TF: 877-996-7275 ■ *Web:* wyoparks.state.wy.us
Supreme Court 2301 Capitol Ave .... Cheyenne WY 82002 307-777-7316 777-6129 339-51
Web: courts.state.wy.us
Technical Services Div
2219 Carey Ave .... Cheyenne WY 82001 307-777-7321 777-6593 339-51
Web: wyagric.state.wy.us
Tourism Div 5611 High Plains Rd .... Cheyenne WY 82007 307-777-7777 777-2877 339-51
TF: 800-225-5996 ■ *Web:* www.wyomingtourism.org
Transportation Dept 5300 Bishop Blvd .... Cheyenne WY 82009 307-777-4375 777-4163 339-51
Web: www.dot.state.wy.us
Treasurer 200 W 24th St .... Cheyenne WY 82002 307-777-7408 339-51
Web: treasurer.state.wy.us
Victims Services Div
320 W 25th St Fl 2 .... Cheyenne WY 82002 307-777-7200 777-6683 339-51
Web: ag.wyo.gov
Vital Records Services
2300 Capitol Ave .... Cheyenne WY 82002 307-777-7591 777-2483 339-51
Web: health.wyo.gov
Vocational Rehabilitation Div
1510 East Pershing Blvd Ste 1100 .... Cheyenne WY 82002 307-777-3700 777-5939 339-51
Web: www.wyomingworkforce.org
Workers' Safety & Compensation Div
PO Box 791 .... Cheyenne WY 82602 307-777-7159 339-51
Web: wyomingsafety.org
Workforce Services Dept
Herschler Bldg 122 W 25th St 2nd Fl E .... Cheyenne WY 82002 307-777-8650 777-5857 339-51
Web: www.wyomingworkforce.org
Wyoming Assn of Realtors
777 Overland Trail Ste 220 .... Casper WY 82601 307-237-4085 237-7929 656
TF: 800-676-4085 ■ *Web:* www.wyorealtors.com
Wyoming Correctional Facility
3203 Dunbar Rd PO Box 501 .... Attica NY 14011 585-591-1010 210
Web: www.doccs.ny.gov/faclist.html
Wyoming County PO Box 309 .... Pineville WV 24874 304-732-8000 732-9659 338
Web: wyomingcounty.com
Wyoming County 1 Courthouse Sq .... Tunkhannock PA 18657 570-836-3200 338
Web: wyocopa.org
Wyoming County 143 N Main St Ste 104 .... Warsaw NY 14569 585-786-8810 786-3703 338
TF: 800-527-1757 ■ *Web:* www.wyomingco.net
Wyoming Dental Assn (WYDA)
259 S Ctr Ste 201 .... Casper WY 82601 307-237-1186 237-1186 227
Web: www.wyda.org
Wyoming Dinosaur Ctr
110 Carter Ranch Rd .... Thermopolis WY 82443 307-864-2997 520
Web: www.wyodino.org
Wyoming Ethanol LLC 1919 E A St .... Torrington WY 82240 307-532-2449 144
Wyoming Honor Farm 40 Honor Farm Rd .... Riverton WY 82501 307-856-9578 856-2505 213
Wyoming Hospital Assn
2005 Warren Ave .... Cheyenne WY 82001 307-632-9344 138
Web: www.wyohospitals.com
Wyoming Machine Inc 30680 Forest Blvd .... Stacy MN 55079 651-462-4156 697
Web: www.wyomingmachine.com
Wyoming Machinery Co
5300 Old W Yellowstone Hwy .... Casper WY 82604 307-472-1000 261-4486 358
Web: www.wyomingcat.com
Wyoming Medical Ctr 1233 E Second St .... Casper WY 82601 307-577-7201 233-8230 374-3
TF: 800-822-7201 ■ *Web:* wyomingmedicalcenter.org
Wyoming Medical Society
122 E 17th St .... Cheyenne WY 82001 307-635-2424 632-1973 474
TF: 888-879-3599 ■ *Web:* www.wyomed.org
Wyoming Pharmacists Assn
150 Powell St .... Green River WY 82935 307-272-3361 585
Web: www.wpha.net
Wyoming Public Television
2660 Peck Ave .... Riverton WY 82501 307-856-6944 856-3893 632
TF: 800-495-9788 ■ *Web:* wyomingpbs.org
Wyoming Republican Party
1821 Carey Ave .... Cheyenne WY 82001 307-234-9166 616-2
Web: wyoming.gop
Wyoming Seminary 201 N Sprague Ave .... Kingston PA 18704 570-270-2100 270-2198 622
TF: 800-325-3252 ■ *Web:* www.wyomingseminary.org
Wyoming State Bar 4124 Laramie St .... Cheyenne WY 82001 307-632-9061 632-3737 72
TF: 855-445-8058 ■ *Web:* www.wyomingbar.org
Wyoming State Hospital (WSH)
831 Hwy 150 S .... Evanston WY 82930 307-789-3464 374-5
Web: www.health.wyo.gov/statehospital
Wyoming State Library
2800 Central Ave .... Cheyenne WY 82001 307-777-6333 434-5
Web: www-wsl.state.wy.us
Wyoming State Museum
2301 Central Ave .... Cheyenne WY 82002 307-777-7022 777-5375 520
Web: wyomuseum.state.wy.us
Wyoming State Penitentiary
2900 S Higley Rd PO Box 400 .... Rawlins WY 82301 307-328-1441 213
Web: corrections.wyo.gov
Wyoming Symphony Orchestra
225 S David Ste B .... Casper WY 82601 307-266-1478 266-4522 573-3
Web: www.wyomingsymphony.org

Name / Address	City	State	Zip	Phone	Fax	Class
Wyoming Tribune-Eagle 702 W Lincolnway *TF:* 800-561-6268 ■ *Web:* www.wyomingnews.com	Cheyenne	WY	82001	307-634-3361	633-3189	532-2
Wyoming Valley West School District 450 N Maple Ave *Web:* www.wvwspartans.org	Kingston	PA	18704	570-288-6551		685
Wyoming Veterinary Medical Assn (WVMA) 2001 Capitol Ave **Fax Area Code:* 208 ■ *TF:* 800-272-1813 ■ *Web:* www.wyvma.org	Cheyenne	WY	82001	800-272-1813	922-9435*	795
Wyoming Women's Ctr 1000 W Griffith PO Box 300 *Web:* corrections.wyo.gov/home/institutions/wwc	Lusk	WY	82225	307-334-3693	334-2254	213
Wyoming-Kentwood Area Chamber of Commerce 4415 Byron Ctr Ave SW *TF:* 800-528-8776 ■ *Web:* www.southkent.org	Wyoming	MI	49519	616-531-5990	531-0252	139
Wyotech Blairsville 500 Innovation Dr *Web:* www.wyotech.edu	Blairsville	PA	15717	724-459-9500		800
Wyotech Fremont 200 Whitney Pl *Web:* www.wyotech.edu	Fremont	CA	94539	510-490-6900	490-8599	800
Wyotech Sacramento 980 Riverside Pkwy *TF:* 888-308-7158 ■ *Web:* www.wyotech.edu	West Sacramento	CA	95605	916-376-8888		800
WYOU-TV Ch 22 (CBS) 62 S Franklin St *TF:* 855-241-5144 ■ *Web:* www.pahomepage.com	Wilkes-Barre	PA	18701	570-961-2222	829-0440	741
WYPR-FM 88.1 (NPR) 2216 N Charles St *TF:* 866-789-8627 ■ *Web:* www.wypr.org	Baltimore	MD	21218	410-235-1660	235-1161	645-16
WYPX-TV Ch 55 (I) 1 Charles Blvd **Fax Area Code:* 646 ■ *TF:* 888-467-2988 ■ *Web:* ionmedia.com	Guilderland	NY	12084	212-757-3100	597-5903*	741
Wyrick Robbins Yates & Ponton 4101 Lake Boone Trail *Web:* www.wyrick.com	Raleigh	NC	27607	919-781-4000		41
WYRK-FM 106.5 (Ctry) 14 Lafayette Sq Ste 1200 *Web:* www.wyrk.com	Buffalo	NY	14203	716-852-7444		645-25
Wyroc Inc 2142 Industrial Ct *Web:* www.wyroc.com	Vista	CA	92081	760-727-0878	727-9238	503-5
Wyrulec Co 3978 US Hwy 26/85 *TF:* 800-628-5266 ■ *Web:* www.wyrulec.com	Torrington	WY	82240	307-837-2225	837-2115	245
WYSE Adv 668 Euclid Ave *TF:* 800-242-4118 ■ *Web:* wyseadv.com	Cleveland	OH	44114	216-696-2424		4
Wyse Meter Solutions Inc RPO Newmarket Court PO Box 95530 *TF:* 866-681-9465 ■ *Web:* www.wysemeter.com	Newmarket	ON	L3Y8J8	866-681-9465		393
WYSE Technology Inc 3471 N First St *TF:* 800-800-9973 ■ *Web:* www.wyse.com	San Jose	CA	95134	408-473-1200	473-2080	173-2
Wyser-Pratte Management Company Inc 504 Guard Hill Rd *TF:* 800-289-9999 ■ *Web:* www.wyser-pratte.com	Bedford	NY	10506	914-234-4930		690
Wysocki Produce Farm Inc 6320 Third Ave	Plainfield	WI	54966	715-366-7175		10-11
Wysong Inc 4820 US 29 N *TF:* 800-299-7664 ■ *Web:* www.wysongpartsandservice.com	Greensboro	NC	27405	336-621-3960	621-8360	456
WYSU-FM 88.5 (Clas) Youngstown State University 1 University Plz *Web:* www.wysu.org	Youngstown	OH	44555	330-941-3363	941-1501	645-180
Wytech Industries Inc 960 E Hazelwood Ave *Web:* www.wytech.com	Rahway	NJ	07065	732-396-3900		490
Wythe County 340 S Sixth St *Web:* www.wytheco.org	Wytheville	VA	24382	276-223-6020	223-6030	338
Wythe County Public Schools Foundation for Excellence 1570 W Reservoir St *Web:* wytheexcellence.org	Wytheville	VA	24382	276-228-5411		685
Wytheville Community College 1000 E Main St **Fax:* Admissions ■ *TF:* 800-421-3481 ■ *Web:* www.wcc.vccs.edu	Wytheville	VA	24382	276-223-4700	223-4860*	162
Wytheville-Wythe-Bland Chamber of Commerce Inc 150 E Monroe St *Web:* www.wwbchamber.com	Wytheville	VA	24382	276-223-3365	223-3412	139
Wyvern Consulting Ltd 10 N Main St *TF:* 800-946-4626 ■ *Web:* www.wyvernltd.com	Yardley	PA	19067	800-946-4626		693
WYXB-FM 105.7 (AC) 40 Monument Cir Ste 600 *Web:* www.b1057.com	Indianapolis	IN	46204	317-681-1057	684-2021	645-77
WyzAnt Inc 1714 N Damen Ave Ste 3N *TF:* 877-999-2681 ■ *Web:* www.wyzant.com	Chicago	IL	60647	877-999-2681		387
WYZZ-TV Ch 43 (Fox) 3131 N University *Web:* www.centralillinoisproud.com	Peoria	IL	61604	309-686-9401		741
WZBA-FM 100.7 (CR) 11350 McCormick Rd Executive Plz 3 Ste 701 *Web:* www.thebayonline.com	Hunt Valley	MD	21031	410-771-8484	771-1616	645
WZBC-FM 90.3 (Var) Boston College 107 McElroy Commons *Web:* www.wzbc.org	Chestnut Hill	MA	02467	617-552-3511		645
WZBT-FM 91.1 (Alt) 300 N Washington St Gettysburg College *TF:* 800-431-0803 ■ *Web:* www.gettysburg.edu	Gettysburg	PA	17325	717-337-6300		645
WZIP-FM 88.1 (Rock) 302 Buchtel Common *Web:* www.wzip.fm	Akron	OH	44325	330-972-7105		645-2
WZLX-FM 100.7 (CR) 83 Leo Birmingham Pkwy *Web:* wzlx.cbslocal.com	Brighton	MA	02135	617-746-5100		645
WZMX-FM 93.7 (Urban) 10 Executive Dr *Web:* hot937.cbslocal.com	Farmington	CT	06032	860-677-6700		645
WZNE-FM 94.1 (Alt) 28 E Main St 8th Fl *Web:* www.thezone941.com	Rochester	NY	14614	585-399-5700		645-138
WZNZ-AM 1460 (Rel) PO Box 51585 *Web:* www.qopradio.com	Jacksonville Beach	FL	32240	904-241-3311		645-79
WZPL-FM 99.5 (AC) 9245 N Meridian St Ste 300 *Web:* www.wzpl.com	Indianapolis	IN	46260	317-816-4000		645-77
WZPX-TV Ch 43 (I) 2610 Horizon Dr SE Ste E **Fax Area Code:* 646 ■ *TF:* 888-467-2988 ■ *Web:* ionmedia.com	Grand Rapids	MI	49546	212-757-3100	597-5903*	741-53
WZTV-TV Ch 17 (Fox) 631 Mainstream Dr *Web:* www.fox17.com	Nashville	TN	37228	615-259-5617	259-5684	741-89
WZVN-TV Ch 26 (ABC) 3719 Central Ave *TF:* 888-232-8635 ■ *Web:* www.abc-7.com	Fort Myers	FL	33901	239-939-2020	936-7771	741-88
WZXL-FM 100.7 (Rock) 8025 Black Horse Pk Ste 100 *Web:* www.wzxl.com	West Atlantic City	NJ	08232	609-484-8444	646-6331	645
WZZK-FM 104.7 (Ctry) 2700 Corporate Dr Ste 115 *TF:* 866-998-1047 ■ *Web:* wzzk.com	Birmingham	AL	35242	205-916-1100	290-1061	645-20
WZZM-TV Ch 13 (ABC) 645 3-Mile Rd NW *Web:* www.wzzm13.com	Grand Rapids	MI	49544	616-785-1313	785-1301	741-53
WZZO-FM 95.1 (Rock) 1541 Alta Dr Ste 400 *Web:* 951zzo.iheart.com	Whitehall	PA	18052	610-434-1742	434-6288	645

X

Name / Address	City	State	Zip	Phone	Fax	Class
X 3 Sports 2343 Windy Hill Rd SE *TF:* 800-639-7913 ■ *Web:* x3sports.com	Marietta	GA	30067	678-903-0100		354
X By 2 Inc 35055 W 12 Mile Rd Ste 220 *TF:* 800-745-4550 ■ *Web:* www.xby2.com	Farmington Hills	MI	48331	248-538-9292		396
X Dot Inc 4500 Westgrove Dr Ste 395 *Web:* www.x-dot.com	Addison	TX	75001	972-248-7243		463
X101.5 325 John Knox Rd Bldg G *Web:* x1015.iheart.com	Tallahassee	FL	32303	850-422-3107	383-0747	645-161
X17 Inc PO Box 2362 *Web:* x17agency.com	Beverly Hills	CA	90213	902-132-3622		387
Xacti Global LLC 999 W Yamato Rd Ste 100 *TF:* 800-544-8000 ■ *Web:* www.xactiglobal.com	Boca Raton	FL	33431	561-989-7400		387
Xactware Solutions Inc 1100 W Traverse Pkwy *TF Sales:* 800-424-9228 ■ *Web:* www.xactware.com	Lehi	UT	84043	801-764-5900	932-8013	178-11
Xaloy Inc 1399 Countyline Rd **Fax Area Code:* 724 ■ *TF:* 800-897-2830 ■ *Web:* www.xaloy.com	New Castle	PA	16101	800-897-2830	656-5620*	621
Xamax Industries Inc 63 Silvermine Rd *TF:* 888-926-2988 ■ *Web:* www.xamax.com	Seymour	CT	06483	203-888-7200	888-1002	557
Xanadoo Co 225 City Ave Ste 100	Bala Cynwyd	PA	19004	610-934-7000		738
Xanadu Salon & Spa 3351 W Sheridan St *Web:* xanadusalonspa.com	Hollywood	FL	33021	954-983-0100		77
Xanga.Com Inc 555 Eigth Ave Ste 21F **Fax Area Code:* 925 ■ *Web:* www.xanga.com	New York	NY	10018	212-695-4940	201-2550*	246
Xanodyne Pharmaceuticals Inc 1 Riverfront Pl	Newport	KY	41071	859-371-6383		583
Xante Corp 2800 Dauphin St Ste 100 *TF:* 800-926-8839 ■ *Web:* xante.com	Mobile	AL	36606	251-473-6502	473-6503	173-6
Xantech Corp 1969 Kellogg Ave **Fax Area Code:* 800 ■ *TF Sales:* 800-843-5465 ■ *Web:* www.xantech.com	Carlsbad	CA	92008	818-362-0353	492-6832*	52
Xanterra Parks & Resorts 6312 S Fiddlers Green Cir Ste 600-N *TF:* 800-236-7916 ■ *Web:* www.xanterra.com	Greenwood Village	CO	80111	303-600-3400	600-3600	271
Xanterra South Rim LLC 10 Albright St PO Box 699 *TF:* 800-843-8723 ■ *Web:* www.grandcanyonlodges.com	Grand Canyon	AZ	86023	928-638-2631	638-9810	376
Xantrex Technology Inc 3700 Gilmore Way *TF:* 800-670-0707 ■ *Web:* www.xantrex.com	Burnaby	BC	V5G4M1	604-422-8595	420-1591	253
Xantrion Inc 651 20th St *Web:* www.xantrion.com	Oakland	CA	94612	510-272-4701		196
XAP Corp 3534 Hayden Ave *TF:* 800-468-6927 ■ *Web:* www.xap.com	Culver City	CA	90232	310-842-9800		178-7
Xator Corp 543 Harbor Blvd Ste 501 *Web:* www.xatorcorp.com	Destin	FL	32541	850-460-2860		693
Xaverian Brothers High School Inc 800 clapboardtree st *Web:* www.xbhs.com	Westwood	MA	02090	781-326-6392		685
Xavient Information Systems Inc 2125 Madera Rd Ste B *Web:* www.xavient.com	Simi Valley	CA	93065	805-955-4111		525
Xavier High School Corporation of Middletown 181 Randolph Rd *Web:* xavierhighschool.org	Middletown	CT	06457	860-346-7735		685
Xavier University 3800 Victory Pkwy **Fax:* Admissions ■ *TF:* 800-344-4698 ■ *Web:* www.xavier.edu	Cincinnati	OH	45207	513-745-3000	745-4319*	166
Xavier University Library 3800 Victory Pkwy *TF:* 888-468-4509 ■ *Web:* www.xavier.edu/library	Cincinnati	OH	45207	513-745-3881	745-1932	434-6
Xavier University of Louisiana 1 Drexel Dr *Web:* www.xula.edu	New Orleans	LA	70125	504-486-7411	520-7922	166
Xavier University of Louisiana Library 1 Drexel Dr *Web:* www.xula.edu/library	New Orleans	LA	70125	504-486-7411		434-6
Xaware Inc 3300 Irvine Ave Ste 261 *Web:* www.xaware.com	Newport Beach	CA	92660	949-222-2287		178-1
Xaxis LLC 31 Penn Plaza 132 W 31st St *Web:* www.xaxis.com	New York	NY	10001	646-259-4200		7
XBiotech USA Inc 8201 E Riverside Dr Bldg 4 Ste 100 *Web:* www.xbiotech.com	Austin	TX	78744	512-386-2900		743

Name / Address	City	State	ZIP	Phone	Fax	Class
Xcaliber LP 5051 Fm 2920	Spring	TX	77388	281-219-8100		190
TF: 866-620-8586 ■ *Web:* www.xcaliberlp.com						
Xcape Solutions Inc						
207 Crystal Grove Blvd	Lutz	FL	33548	813-964-9101		177
Xccent Inc 5240 257th St	Wyoming	MN	55092	651-462-9200		481
Web: www.xccentplay.com						
Xcedex Inc 15600 Wayzata Blvd Ste 309	Wayzata	MN	55391	952-746-3036		180
Xcel Energy Inc 414 Nicollet Mall	Minneapolis	MN	55401	612-330-5500		787
NYSE: XEL ■ *TF:* 800-328-8226 ■ *Web:* www.xcelenergy.com						
Xcel Energy Inc 1800 Larimer St	Denver	CO	80202	303-571-7511		787
NYSE: XEL ■ *TF:* 877-322-8228 ■ *Web:* www.xcelenergy.com						
Xcel HR Corp 7361 Calhoun Pl Ste 600	Rockville	MD	20855	800-776-0076		260
TF: 800-776-0076 ■ *Web:* www.xcelhr.com						
X-Cel Optical Company Inc						
806 S Benton Dr	Sauk Rapids	MN	56379	320-251-8404	232-9235*	542
**Fax Area Code:* 800 ■ *TF General:* 800-747-9235 ■ *Web:* www.x-celoptical.com						
XCEL Solutions Corp						
254 Rt 34 Oakdale Plaza Second Fl Ste 3	Matawan	NJ	07747	732-765-9235		624
Web: www.xcelcorp.com						
Xcelerate Media Inc 61 W Bridge St	Dublin	OH	43017	614-336-9722		765
Web: www.xceleratemedia.com						
Xceltech Inc 2136 Gallows Rd	Dunn Loring	VA	22027	703-208-9120		177
Web: www.xceltech.com						
Xceptional HR Consulting LLC						
3108 White Cedar Dr	Moore	OK	73160	405-293-2564		463
Web: xceptionalhr.com						
Xcerra Corp 1355 California Cir	Milpitas	CA	95035	408-635-4300	635-4985	248
NASDAQ: XCRA ■ *Web:* www.ltxc.com						
XCG Consultants Ltd						
2620 Bristol Cir Ste 300	Oakville	ON	L6H6Z7	905-829-8880		256
Web: www.xcg.com						
Xcitex Inc 25 First St Ste 105	Cambridge	MA	02141	617-225-0080		647
TF: 800-780-7836 ■ *Web:* www.xcitex.com						
xDefenders Inc						
1100 Pittsford Victor Rd	Pittsford	NY	14534	585-385-2770		393
Web: www.xdefenders.com						
XE.com Inc 1145 Nicholson Rd Ste 200	Newmarket	ON	L3Y9C3	416-214-5606		225
TF: 877-932-6640 ■ *Web:* www.xe.com						
XEC Solutions Inc						
5655 Lindero Canyon Rd Ste 521	Westlake Village	CA	91362	818-991-1400	575-8099	266
Web: xecsolutions.com						
Xela Pack Inc 8300 Boettner Rd	Saline	MI	48176	734-944-1300		88
TF: 800-742-7225 ■ *Web:* www.xelapack.com						
Xelas Systems Engineering LLC						
8111 Red Farm Ln	Bowie	MD	20715	301-789-1162		177
Web: www.xelas-systems.com						
XEMO-AM 860 (Span)						
5030 Camino de la Siesta Ste 403	San Diego	CA	92108	619-497-0600		645-144
Web: www.uniradio.com						
XENCO Laboratories Inc						
4143 Greenbriar Dr Ste I	Stafford	TX	77477	281-240-4200		192
TF: 800-244-8378 ■ *Web:* www.xenco.com						
Xenetech Usa Inc						
12139 Airline Hwy	Baton Rouge	LA	70817	225-752-0225		628
Web: www.xenetech.com						
Xenex Disinfection Services LLC						
121 Interpark Ste 104	San Antonio	TX	78216	210-538-9300		475
Web: www.xenex.com						
Xenex Enterprises Inc						
155 Rexdale Blvd Ste 707	Toronto	ON	M9W5Z8	416-740-9704		177
Web: www.xenex.ca						
Xenia Area Chamber of Commerce						
334 W Market St	Xenia	OH	45385	937-372-3591	372-2192	139
TF: 800-353-2226 ■ *Web:* xacc.com						
Xenium Resources						
7401 SW Washo Ct Ste 200	Tualatin	OR	97062	503-612-1555		195
Web: www.xeniumhr.com						
Xeno Media						
18w100 22nd St Ste 128	Oakbrook Terrace	IL	60181	630-599-1550		177
Web: www.xenomedia.com						
Xenon Pharmaceuticals Inc						
3650 Gilmore Way	Burnaby	BC	V5G4W8	604-484-3300	484-3450	668
Web: www.xenon-pharma.com						
Xenonics Holdings Inc						
3186 Lionshead Ave	Carlsbad	CA	92010	760-477-8900		544
OTC: XNNH						
Xensor Corp 4000 Bridge St	Drexel Hill	PA	19026	610-284-2508		407
TF: 800-784-7507 ■ *Web:* www.xensor.com						
XEODesign Inc 5273 College Ave Ste 201	Oakland	CA	94618	510-658-8077		180
Web: www.xeodesign.com						
Xerces Society, The						
4828 SE Hawthorne Blvd	Portland	OR	97215	503-232-6639		41
Web: xerces.org						
Xerimis Inc 102 Executive Dr	Moorestown	NJ	08057	856-727-9940		237
TF: 800-523-3684 ■ *Web:* www.xerimis.com						
Xeris Pharmaceuticals Inc						
3208 Red River St Ste 300	Austin	TX	78705	512-498-2670		231
TF: 888-570-4781 ■ *Web:* www.xerispharma.com						
Xerox Corp 45 Glover Ave PO Box 4505	Norwalk	CT	06856	203-968-3000		589
NYSE: XRX ■ *TF:* 800-327-9753 ■ *Web:* www.xerox.com						
Xerox Financial Services Inc						
800 Long Ridge Rd	Stamford	CT	06904	203-968-3000		216
TF: 800-275-9376 ■ *Web:* xerox.com						
Xerox Foundation 45 Glover Ave	Norwalk	CT	06856	800-275-9376		304
TF: 800-275-9376 ■ *Web:* www.xerox.com						
Xertrex International Inc Tabbies Divison						
1530 W Glenlake Ave	Itasca	IL	60143	630-773-4160		560
Web: www.tabbies.com						
Xerxes Corp 7901 Xerxes Ave S	Minneapolis	MN	55431	952-887-1890	887-1870	199
Web: www.xerxes.com						
XETA Technologies Inc						
1814 W Tacoma St	Broken Arrow	OK	74012	918-664-8200		735
Xetex Inc 9405 Holly St NW	Minneapolis	MN	55433	612-724-3101		664
Web: www.xetexinc.com						
Xetus Corp 100 View St Ste 106	Mountain View	CA	94041	650-237-1225		251
TF: 800-695-1008 ■ *Web:* www.xetusone.com						
XF Enterprises Inc						
500 S Taylor Ste 301 PO Box 229	Amarillo	TX	79101	806-367-5810	672-5564*	584
**Fax Area Code:* 620 ■ *TF:* 800-783-5616 ■ *Web:* www.xfent.com						
X-fab Texas Inc 2301 N University Ave	Lubbock	TX	79415	806-747-4400		696
Web: www.xfab.com						
Xfer International Inc						
39201 Schoolcraft Rd Ste B 9	Livonia	MI	48150	734-927-6666		180
TF: 800-438-9337 ■ *Web:* www.xfer.com						
Xfinity Center 885 S Main St	Mansfield	MA	02048	508-339-2331		572
XFINITY Theatre 61 Savitt Way	Hartford	CT	06120	860-548-7370		572
X-Gen Pharmaceuticals Inc						
300 Daniels Zenker Dr	Horseheads	NY	14845	866-390-4411		583
TF: 866-390-4411 ■ *Web:* www.x-gen.us						
XHRM-FM 92.5 (Oldies)						
6160 Cornerstone Ct E Ste 150	San Diego	CA	92121	858-888-7000		645-144
Web: www.magic925.com						
XHTZ-FM 90.3 (Urban)						
6160 Cornerstone Ct E Ste 150	San Diego	CA	92121	858-888-7000		645-144
Web: www.z90.com						
Xiacon Inc 140 Fell Ct Ste 120	Hauppauge	NY	11788	631-300-3500		177
TF: 800-834-5516 ■ *Web:* www.xiaconinc.com						
XiGo Nanotools Inc						
116 Research Dr Ste 39	Bethlehem	PA	18015	610-849-5090		419
Web: www.xigonanotools.com						
Xilinx Inc 2100 Logic Dr	San Jose	CA	95124	408-559-7778	559-7114	696
NASDAQ: XLNX ■ *TF:* 800-594-5469 ■ *Web:* www.xilinx.com						
Ximenez-Fatio House Museum						
20 Aviles St	Saint Augustine	FL	32084	904-829-3575	829-3445	520
Web: www.ximenezfatiohouse.org						
Xinet Inc 2560 Ninth St Ste 312	Berkeley	CA	94710	510-845-0555		178-12
Web: www.northplains.com						
Xiologix 8215 SW Tualatin Sherwood	Tualatin	OR	97062	503-691-4364		225
TF: 888-492-6843 ■ *Web:* xiologix.com						
XIOtech Corp						
9950 Federal Dr Ste 100	Colorado Springs	CO	80921	719-388-5500		178-12
TF: 866-472-6764 ■ *Web:* xiostorage.com						
XipLink Inc						
3981 St Laurent Blvd Ste 800	Montreal	QC	H2W1Y5	514-848-9640		224
Web: www.xiplink.com						
Xiris Automation Inc						
1016 Sutton Dr Ste C5	Burlington	ON	L7L6B8	905-331-6660	331-6661	639
Web: www.xiris.com						
X-iss 2190 N Loop W Ste 415	Houston	TX	77018	713-862-9200		177
Web: www.x-iss.com						
XiTRON Technologies Inc						
7507 Convoy Ct	San Diego	CA	92111	858-530-8099		201
Web: www.xitrontech.com						
Xittel telecommunications Inc						
1100, Pl du Technoparc Ste 301	Trois-RiviŠres	QC	G9A0A9	819-370-3232		224
Web: www.xittel.net						
Xix Siecle Hotel						
L'Hotel Montreal						
262 St Jacques St W	Old Montreal	QC	H2Y1N1	514-985-0019	985-0059	379
TF: 877-553-0019 ■ *Web:* www.lhotelmontreal.com						
XKS Unlimited Inc						
850 Fiero Ln	San Luis Obispo	CA	93401	805-544-7864		54
TF: 800-444-5247 ■ *Web:* www.xks.com						
XL Brands 198 Nexus Dr	Dalton	GA	30721	706-272-5000	272-5801	145
TF: 800-367-4583 ■ *Web:* www.xlbrands.com						
XL Capital Group 1540 Broadway	New York	NY	10036	212-915-6177		390
Web: www.xlgroup.com						
XL Ctr 1 Civic Ctr Plaza	Hartford	CT	06103	860-249-6333		205
TF: 800-838-3006 ■ *Web:* www.xlcenter.com						
X-L Engineering Corp 6150 W Mulford St	Niles	IL	60714	847-965-3030		757
Web: www.xleng.com						
XL Specialty Insurance Co						
70 Seaview Ave	Stamford	CT	06902	203-964-5200	526-2092*	391-5
**Fax Area Code:* 573 ■ *TF:* 877-263-7995 ■ *Web:* insurance.mo.gov						
Xl Technology Systems Inc 401 Vfw Dr	Rockland	MA	02370	781-982-1220		454
Web: www.xl-technology.com						
XL102 3245 Basie Rd	Richmond	VA	23228	804-474-0000	474-0096	645-134
Web: xl102richmond.iheart.com						
Xli Corp 55 Vanguard Pkwy	Rochester	NY	14606	585-436-2250		697
Web: www.xlionline.com						
Xlibris Corp						
1663 Liberty Dr Ste 200	Bloomington	IN	47403	888-795-4274		627
TF: 888-795-4274 ■ *Web:* www.xlibris.com						
Xlink Technology Inc						
1546 Centre Pointe Dr	Milpitas	CA	95035	408-263-8201		177
TF: 800-408-6550 ■ *Web:* www.xlink.com						
XLPrint USA LLC 213 Rose Ave Ste 1	Venice	CA	90291	310-829-7684		809
TF: 866-275-1290 ■ *Web:* www.usa.xlprint.com						
XLV Diagnostics Inc						
290 Munro St Ste 2311	Thunder Bay	ON	P7A7T1	807-346-6811		475
Web: xlvdiagnostics.com						
XMaLpha Technologies LLC						
935 Arbogast St	Shoreview	MN	55126	651-484-0471		194
Web: www.xmalpha.com						
XO Cafe 125 N Main St	Providence	RI	02903	401-273-9090		671
Web: www.xocafe.com						
XO Communications Inc						
13865 Sunrise Vly Dr	Herndon	VA	20171	703-547-2000		736
TF: 866-349-0134 ■ *Web:* www.xo.com						
XO Prime Steaks 500 W St Claire Ave	Cleveland	OH	44113	216-861-1919	861-0374	671
Web: xoprimesteaks.com						
Xochimilco Restaurant 3409 Bagley St	Detroit	MI	48216	313-843-0179		671
XOJET Inc 2000 Sierra Point Pkwy	Brisbane	CA	94005	650-676-4700		21
Web: www.xojet.com						
XOMA (US) LLC 2910 Seventh St	Berkeley	CA	94710	510-204-7200	644-2011	85
NASDAQ: XOMA ■ *TF:* 800-468-9716 ■ *Web:* www.xoma.com						
Xomox Corp 4444 Cooper Rd	Cincinnati	OH	45242	513-745-0863		789
Web: www.xomox.com						
Xoriant Corp 1248 Reamwood Ave	Sunnyvale	CA	94089	408-743-4400		180
Web: www.xoriant.com						
XP Power 990 Benicia Ave	Sunnyvale	CA	94085	408-732-7777	732-2002	246
TF: 800-253-0490 ■ *Web:* www.xppower.com						
Xp3 Corp 525 Carswell Ave Unit L	Holly Hill	FL	32117	330-562-8490		196
Web: xp3hornet.com						

Company	City	State	ZIP	Phone	Fax	Class
XPAND Corp 1941 Roland Clarke Pl *Web:* www.xpandcorp.com	Reston	VA	20191	703-742-0900		177
Xper2go 39120 Argonaut Way Ste 782 *Web:* www.xper2go.com	Fremont	CA	94538	510-585-2500		177
Xpera Group 10911 Technology Pl Ste 103 *Web:* www.xperagroup.com	San Diego	CA	92127	858-436-7770		466
Xperience Interactive 2601 Ocean Park Blvd Ste 116	Santa Monica	CA	90405	424-214-1471		7
XperNet Services Inc 16360 Park 10 Pl Ste 225 PO Box 6505 *Web:* www.xpernet.com	Houston	TX	77450	281-392-5292	392-3668	180
Xperts Inc 4701 Cox Rd Ste 135 *Web:* www.xperts.com	Glen Allen	VA	23060	804-290-4272		637-10
Xpicor Inc 4411 W Market St Ste 100 *Web:* www.xpicor.com	Greensboro	NC	27407	336-510-0333		104
Xplane Corp 411 SW Sixth Ave Ste 220 *TF:* 855-548-4343 ■ *Web:* www.xplane.com	Portland	OR	97204	855-548-4343		344
XPO Logistics Inc 6805 Perimeter Dr *TF:* 800-837-7584 ■ *Web:* www.xpologistics.com	Dublin	OH	43016	614-923-1400		449
Xpres Spa 3 East 54th St 9th Fl *Web:* www.xpresspa.com	New York	NY	10022	212-750-9595		77
Xpress Boats 199 Extrusion Pl *Web:* www.xpressboats.com	Hot Springs	AR	71901	501-262-5300	262-5053	90
XpressBet Inc 200 Racetrack Rd Bldg 26 *Web:* www.xpressbet.com	Washington	PA	15301	724-229-6918		642
Xpriori Llc 2864 S Cir Dr Ste 1200 *TF:* 800-264-1170 ■ *Web:* www.xpriori.com	Colorado Springs	CO	80906	719-527-1315		809
XPS Group Inc 888 Ft St 2nd Fl *TF:* 800-721-0029 ■ *Web:* www.xpsgroup.net	Victoria	BC	V8W1H8	250-383-4135		2
XPV Capital Corp 266 King St W Ste 403 *Web:* www.xpvwaterpartners.com	Toronto	ON	M5V1H8	416-864-0475		528
X-Ray Industries Inc 1961 Thunderbird *TF:* 800-318-8438 ■ *Web:* www.xritesting.com	Troy	MI	48084	248-362-2242		743
X-ray Instrumentation Associates 8450 Central Ave *TF:* 800-354-1420 ■ *Web:* www.xia.com	Newark	CA	94560	510-494-9020		419
X-Ray Optical Systems Inc 15 Tech Valley Dr *Web:* www.xos.com	East Greenbush	NY	12061	518-880-1500		542
Xrg Systems Inc 1 Annabel Ln Ste 214 *Web:* xrgsystems.com	San Ramon	CA	94583	925-241-4995	241-4584	177
XRiver Technologies LLC 5175 Parkstone Dr *Web:* www.xrivertech.com	Chantilly	VA	20151	703-480-0480		809
xRM3 Inc 2604-b El Camino Real Ste 251 *Web:* xrmcubed.com	Carlsbad	CA	92008	760-585-4250		196
XRoads Solutions Group 1821 E Dyer Rd Ste 225 *Web:* www.xroadsllc.com	Santa Ana	CA	92705	949-567-1600		401
Xs Sight Systems Inc 2401 Ludelle St *TF:* 888-744-4880 ■ *Web:* www.xssights.com	Fort Worth	TX	76105	817-536-0136		711
XS Smith Inc 932 Page Rd *TF:* 800-631-2226 ■ *Web:* www.xssmith.com	Washington	NC	27889	252-940-5060	946-0724	105
XSport Fitness Inc 6420 W Fullerton Ave *Web:* www.xsportfitness.com	Chicago	IL	60707	773-237-5730		354
XSYS Inc 653 Steele Dr *Web:* www.xsysinc.com	Valparaiso	IN	46385	219-477-4816		177
Xtek Inc 11451 Reading Rd *TF:* 888-332-9835 ■ *Web:* www.xtek.com	Cincinnati	OH	45241	513-733-7800	733-7939	454
Xtel Communications Inc 401 Rt 73 n *TF:* 800-438-9835 ■ *Web:* www.xtel.net	Marlton	NJ	08053	856-596-4000		387
XTO Energy Inc 810 Houston St *TF:* 800-299-2800 ■ *Web:* www.xtoenergy.com	Fort Worth	TX	76102	817-870-2800	870-1671	536
Xto Inc 110 Wrentham Dr *Web:* www.xtoinc.com	Liverpool	NY	13088	315-451-7807		326
XTRAC LLC 245 Summer St *TF:* 855-975-3569 ■ *Web:* www.xtracsolutions.com	Boston	MA	02210	855-975-3569		387
XTRA-FM 91.1 (Alt) 6160 Cornerstone Ct E Ste 150 *Web:* www.91x.com	San Diego	CA	92121	858-888-7000		645-144
Xtramart 221 Quinebaug Rd *Web:* www.xtramart.com	North Grosvenordale	CT	06255	781-894-8800		204
Xtream It People Inc 50 Colvin Ave Ste 206 *TF:* 800-461-1970 ■ *Web:* www.xtreamit.com	Albany	NY	12206	518-437-0090		180
Xtreme Consulting Group Inc 3500 Carillon Point *Web:* www.xtremeconsulting.com	Kirkland	WA	98033	425-861-9460		463
Xtreme Drilling & Coil Services Corp 9811 Katy Fwy Ste 225 *TF:* 800-564-6253 ■ *Web:* www.xtremedrillingcorp.com	Houston	TX	77024	281-994-4600	994-4601	540
XtremeEDA Corp 201-1339 Wellington St W *Web:* www.xtreme-eda.com	Ottawa	ON	K1Y3B8	613-728-5912	728-9513	466
Xttrium Laboratories Inc 1200 E Business Ctr Dr *TF:* 800-587-3721 ■ *Web:* www.xttrium.com	Mt. Prospect	IL	60056	773-268-5800		231
Xybernet Inc 10640 Scripps Ranch Blvd *TF Cust Svc:* 800-228-9026 ■ *Web:* www.xyber.net	San Diego	CA	92131	858-530-1900	530-1419	178-10
Xylem 8200 N Austin Ave *Web:* unitedstates.xylemappliedwater.com	Morton Grove	IL	60053	847-966-3700		202
Xylem Inc 227 S Div St *TF:* 800-785-5264 ■ *Web:* www.xylem.com/treatment/us/brands/leopold	Zelienople	PA	16063	724-452-6300	452-1377	806
Xylo Technologies Inc 2434 Superior Dr NW Ste 105 *TF:* 800-517-8408 ■ *Web:* www.xylotechnologies.com	Rochester	MN	55901	507-289-9956		624
Xymox Technologies 9099 W Dean Rd *Web:* www.xymox.com	Milwaukee	WI	53224	414-362-9000		729
Xyron Inc 8465 N 90th St Ste 6 *TF:* 800-793-3523 ■ *Web:* www.xyron.com	Scottsdale	AZ	85258	480-443-9419		485
Xytech Systems Corp 9410 Topanga Canyon Blvd Ste 200 *Web:* www.xytechsystems.com	Chatsworth	CA	91311	818-698-4900		177
XYZ Two Way Radio Inc 275 20th St *TF:* 800-535-3377 ■ *Web:* xyzcar.com	Brooklyn	NY	11215	718-499-2007		441

Y

Company	City	State	ZIP	Phone	Fax	Class
Y & S Candies 400 Running Pump Rd	Lancaster	PA	17603	717-299-1261		296-8
Y Ss Group Inc 8612 NW 70th St *Web:* yssgroup.com	Miami	FL	33166	305-436-7371		787
Y Tech Solutions Inc 5706 Benjamin Ctr Dr Ste 116	Tampa	FL	33634	813-880-0800		196
Y108 - Hamilton's Rock Station *Y108 Worldclass Rock 107.9 FM* 875 Main St W *Web:* www.y108.ca	Hamilton	ON	L8S4R1	905-521-9900		645
Y-12 Federal Credit Union 501 Lafayette Dr *TF:* 800-482-1043 ■ *Web:* www.y12fcu.org	Oak Ridge	TN	37830	865-482-1043		219
Y93 3500 E Rosser Ave *TF:* 866-929-9393	Bismarck	ND	58501	701-224-9393	222-1131	645-21
Y94 iHeartMedia 500 Plum St Ste 400 *TF:* 844-289-7234 ■ *Web:* y94fm.iheart.com	Syracuse	NY	13204	315-472-9797		645-160
Y98 3100 Market St *Web:* y98.cbslocal.com	Saint Louis	MO	63103	314-531-0000	531-9855	645-141
Ya Sabe Inc 100 Carpenter Dr Ste 135 *Web:* www.yasabe.com	Sterling	VA	20164	703-793-3270		387
Yaaman Inc 6376 Byron Ln *Web:* www.yaaman.com	San Ramon	CA	94582	408-625-7615		180
Yaana Technologies LLC 542 Gibraltar Dr *TF:* 800-899-4125 ■ *Web:* www.yaanatech.com	Milpitas	CA	95035	408-719-9000		180
Yabba Island Grill 711 Fifth Ave S *Web:* www.yabbaislandgrill.com	Naples	FL	34102	239-262-5787		671
Yachats Ocean Road State Natural Site 5580 S Coast Hwy *TF:* 800-551-6949 ■ *Web:* www.oregonstateparks.org	Newport	OR	97366	800-551-6949		565
Yachting Magazine 55 Hammarlund Way *TF:* 800-999-0869 ■ *Web:* www.yachtingmagazine.com	Middletown	RI	02842	800-999-0869		457-4
Yacktman Asset Management Co 6300 Bridgepoint Pkwy Bldg 1 Ste 320 *TF:* 800-835-3879 ■ *Web:* www.yacktman.com	Austin	TX	78730	512-767-6700		401
Yadkin County 217 E Willow St *Web:* www.yadkincountync.gov	Yadkinville	NC	27055	336-679-4200	679-6005	338
Yadkin County Chamber of Commerce 205 S Jackson St PO Box 1840 *TF:* 877-492-3546 ■ *Web:* www.yadkinchamber.org	Yadkinville	NC	27055	336-679-2200	679-3034	139
Yadkin Valley Chamber of Commerce 116 E Market St PO Box 496 *Web:* www.yadkinvalley.org	Elkin	NC	28621	336-526-1111	526-1879	139
Yaffe & Co 26913 Northwestern Hwy Ste 500 *Web:* www.yaffe.com	Southfield	MI	48033	248-262-1700		7
Yaffe Cos Inc, The 1200 S G St *TF:* 800-759-2333 ■ *Web:* yaffeco.net	Muskogee	OK	74403	918-687-7543		686
Yager Museum of Art & Culture, The Hartwick College PO Box 4020 *Web:* www.hartwick.edu/academics/museum	Oneonta	NY	13820	607-431-4000		520
Yahoo Finance 3011 Paces Mill Rd SE *Web:* finance.yahoo.com	Atlanta	GA	30339	770-438-2282	438-0653	671
Yahoo! Auctions 701 First Ave *Web:* about.yahoo.com	Sunnyvale	CA	94089	408-349-3300		51
Yahoo! Finance 701 First Ave *Web:* finance.yahoo.com	Sunnyvale	CA	94089	408-349-3300		404
Yahoo! Inc 701 First Ave *NASDAQ: YHOO* ■ *Web:* about.yahoo.com	Sunnyvale	CA	94089	408-349-3300		397
Yahoo! Photos 701 First Ave *TF:* 888-267-7574 ■ *Web:* www.flickr.com	Sunnyvale	CA	94089	408-349-3300	349-3301	588
Yahoo! Travel 701 First Ave *Web:* www.yahoo.com/style/tagged/travel	Sunnyvale	CA	94089	408-349-5080	349-7821	773
YAHSGS LLC 3100 George Washington Way Ste 103 *Web:* www.yahsgs.com	Richland	WA	99354	509-375-5359		463
Yak Communications Corp 48 Yonge St Ste 1200 **Fax Area Code: 866* ■ *TF:* 877-925-4925 ■ *Web:* www.yak.ca	Toronto	ON	M5E1G6	877-925-4925	216-9923*	736
Yakabod Inc 2 N Market St Ste 300 *Web:* www.yakabod.com	Frederick	MD	21701	301-662-4554		225
Yakima Bait Company Inc PO Box 310 *TF:* 800-527-2711 ■ *Web:* www.yakimabait.com	Granger	WA	98932	509-854-1311	854-2263	710
Yakima Convention Ctr 10 N Eigth St *TF:* 800-221-0751 ■ *Web:* www.visityakima.com	Yakima	WA	98901	509-575-6062	575-6252	205
Yakima County 128 N Second St Rm 323 *TF:* 800-572-7354 ■ *Web:* www.yakimacounty.us	Yakima	WA	98901	509-574-1430		338
Yakima Federal Savings & Loan Assn 118 E Yakima Ave *TF:* 800-331-3225 ■ *Web:* www.yakimafed.com	Yakima	WA	98901	509-248-2634		70
Yakima Herald-Republic PO Box 9668 *TF:* 800-343-2799 ■ *Web:* www.yakimaherald.com	Yakima	WA	98909	509-248-1251	577-7767	532-2
Yakima Neighborhood Health Services (YNHS) 12 S Eigth St PO Box 2605 *Web:* www.ynhs.org	Yakima	WA	98907	509-454-4143		353
Yakima Regional Medical & Heart Ctr 110 S Ninth Ave *Web:* yakimaregional.com	Yakima	WA	98902	509-575-5000	454-6193	374-3
Yakima Sportsman State Park 904 University Pkwy PO Box 52 *Web:* parks.state.wa.us	Yakima	WA	98907	509-665-4319		565

	City	State	Zip	Phone	Fax	Class
Yakima Valley Community College S 16th Ave & Nob Hill Blvd *Web:* www.yvcc.edu	Yakima	WA	98902	509-574-4600	574-4649	162
Grandview 500 W Main St *Web:* www.yvcc.edu	Grandview	WA	98930	509-882-7000	882-7012	162
Yakima Valley Memorial Hospital 2811 Tieton Dr *TF:* 800-745-1077 ■ *Web:* www.yakimamemorial.org	Yakima	WA	98902	509-575-8000		374-3
Yakutat Power Inc Forrest Hwy	Yakutat	AK	99689	907-784-3248		245
Yale Appliance 296 Freeport St *TF:* 800-565-6435 ■ *Web:* www.yaleappliance.com	Dorchester	MA	02122	617-825-9253		35
Yale Assoc Inc 1150 Portion Rd *Web:* www.yaleassociates.com	Holtsville	NY	11742	631-320-3088		693
Yale Child Study Ctr Yale University 230 S Frontage Rd *Web:* www.medicine.yale.edu	New Haven	CT	06519	203-785-2540	785-7611	668
Yale Club of New York City, The 50 Vanderbilt Ave *TF:* 800-335-9253 ■ *Web:* www.yaleclubnyc.org	New York	NY	10017	212-716-2100		393
Yale Ctr for British Art 1080 Chapel St PO Box 208280 *TF:* 877-274-8278 ■ *Web:* britishart.yale.edu	New Haven	CT	06510-2302	203-432-2800	432-9695	520
Yale Divinity School Admissions Office 409 Prospect St *TF:* 877-725-3334 ■ *Web:* divinity.yale.edu/admissions-financial-aid	New Haven	CT	06511	203-432-5360	432-7475	167-3
Yale Law Journal PO Box 208215 *Web:* www.yale.edu/yalelj	New Haven	CT	06520	203-432-1666		457-15
Yale Law School 127 Wall St *Web:* www.law.yale.edu	New Haven	CT	06511	203-432-4992		167-1
Yale Peabody Museum of Natural History 170 Whitney Ave Yale University *Web:* www.peabody.yale.edu	New Haven	CT	06511	203-432-3759	432-9816	520
Yale Public Schools 315 E Chicago Ave *Web:* www.yale.k12.ok.us	Yale	OK	74085	918-387-2434		685
Yale Repertory Theatre 1120 Chapel St PO Box 208244 *TF:* 800-973-2837 ■ *Web:* www.yalerep.org	New Haven	CT	06505	203-432-1234	432-6423	573-4
Yale Residential Security Products Inc 100 Yale Ave *TF Cust Svc:* 800-438-1951 ■ *Web:* www.yalehome.com/en/yale/yalehome	Lenoir City	TN	37771	800-438-1951		350
Yale Security Inc.ÿ 1902 Airport Rd *TF:* 800-438-1951 ■ *Web:* www.yalehome.com/en/yale/yalehome	Monroe	NC	28110	800-438-1951	338-0965	350
Yale Software Solutions 9 Yale Dr *Web:* its.yale.edu	New City	NY	10956	845-304-8033		809
Yale University 38 Hill House Ave **Fax:* Admissions ■ *Web:* www.yale.edu	New Haven	CT	06520	203-432-4771	432-9392*	166
Yale University Art Gallery 1111 Chapel St *Web:* www.yale.edu	New Haven	CT	06520	203-432-0600		520
Yale University Collection of Musical Instruments 15 Hillhouse Ave *Web:* www.yale.edu	New Haven	CT	06511	203-432-0822	432-8342	520
Yale University Library 120 High St *Web:* web.library.yale.edu	New Haven	CT	06511	203-432-1775	432-1294	434-6
Yale University Marsh Botanical Gardens Yale University 265 Mansfield St *Web:* marshbotanicalgarden.yale.edu	New Haven	CT	06511	203-432-6320		97
Yale University Press 302 Temple St *TF Sales:* 800-405-1619 ■ *Web:* www.yale.edu	New Haven	CT	06511	203-432-0960		637-4
Yale University School of Medicine 333 Cedar St *TF:* 877-925-3637 ■ *Web:* medicine.yale.edu	New Haven	CT	06510	203-785-2643	785-3234	167-2
Yale-New Haven Hospital 20 York St *Web:* www.ynhh.org	New Haven	CT	06510	203-688-4242		374-3
Yale-New Haven Hospital Blood Stem Cell Transplant Unit 20 York St *Web:* www.ynhh.org	New Haven	CT	06510	203-688-4242		769
Yaletown Venture Partners Inc 1122 Mainland St Ste 510 *Web:* www.yaletown.com	Vancouver	BC	V6B5L1	604-688-7807		528
YALSA (Young Adult Library Services Assn) 50 E Huron St *TF:* 800-545-2433 ■ *Web:* www.ala.org/yalsa	Chicago	IL	60611	312-280-4390	664-7459	49-11
Yamada Enterprises 16552 Burke Ln *Web:* www.yamadaenterprises.com	Huntington Beach	CA	92647	714-843-9882		321
Yamada North America Inc 9000 Columbus Cincinnati Rd *Web:* www.yamadanorthamerica.com	South Charleston	OH	45368	937-462-7111		247
Yamaha Corp of America 6600 Orangethorpe Ave **Fax:* Hum Res ■ *Web:* www.yamaha.com	Buena Park	CA	90620	714-522-9011	522-9235*	527
Yamaha Electronics Corp 6660 Orangethorpe Ave **Fax Area Code:* 800 ■ *TF:* 800-292-2982 ■ *Web:* usa.yamaha.com	Buena Park	CA	90620	714-522-9888	634-0355*	52
Yamaha Golf Cars of California Inc 7275 National Dr Ste D *Web:* www.yamahagolfcarsofca.com	Livermore	CA	94550	925-371-5350	371-5311	516
Yamaha Motor Corp USA 6555 Katella Ave *TF Cust Svc:* 800-638-2772 ■ *Web:* www.yamaha-motor.com	Cypress	CA	90630	800-656-7695		517
Yamaha Music Education System 6600 Orangethorpe Ave *Web:* usa.yamaha.com	Buena Park	CA	90620	714-522-9011		766
Yamamoto of Orient Inc 122 Voyager St *Web:* www.yamamotoyama.com	Pomona	CA	91768	909-594-7356	595-5849	297-11
Yamasa Corp USA 3500 Fairview Industrial Dr SE *Web:* www.yamasausa.com	Salem	OR	97302	503-363-8550	363-8710	296-19
Yamashiro Inc 1999 N Sycamore Ave *Web:* yamashirohollywood.com	Hollywood	CA	90068	323-466-5125		670
Yamato Corp 1775 S Murray Blvd *TF:* 800-538-1762 ■ *Web:* www.yamatocorp.com	Colorado Springs	CO	80916	719-591-1500	591-1045	684
Yamato Oriental Cuisine 131 N New Warrington Rd *Web:* www.yamatodining.com	Pensacola	FL	32506	850-453-3461		671
Yamato Steak House of Japan 360 Columbian Dr *Web:* www.yamatoinc.com	Columbia	SC	29212	803-407-0033		671
Yamato Transport USA Inc 80 Seaview Dr *Web:* www.yamatoamerica.com	Secaucus	NJ	07094	201-583-9706	583-9703	546
Yamazato 6303 Little River Tpke *Web:* www.yamazato.net	Alexandria	VA	22312	703-914-8877		671
Yamazen Inc 735 E Remington Rd **Fax Area Code:* 847 ■ *TF:* 800-882-8558 ■ *Web:* www.yamazen.com	Schaumburg	IL	60173	800-882-8558	882-4296*	385
Yamhill County 414 NE Evans St *Web:* www.co.yamhill.or.us/clerk	McMinnville	OR	97128	503-434-7518	434-7520	338
Yampa River State Park 6185 W US Hwy 40 *Web:* cpw.state.co.us	Hayden	CO	81639	970-276-2061		565
Yampa Valley Electric Assn Inc 435 Mack Ln Ste 203 *TF:* 888-873-9832 ■ *Web:* www.yvea.com	Craig	CO	81626	970-879-1160		245
Yancey County PO Box 6 *TF:* 800-735-8262 ■ *Web:* www.yanceycountync.gov	Burnsville	NC	28714	828-682-3819	682-4301	338
Yancey County Schools Foundation Inc, The PO Box 190 *Web:* www.yanceync.net	Burnsville	NC	28714	828-682-6101	682-7110	685
Yang Enterprises Inc 1420 Alafaya Trl Ste 200 *Web:* www.yangenterprises.com	Oviedo	FL	32765	407-365-7374		177
Yang Kee Noodle Club 7900 Shelbyville Rd *Web:* www.yangkeenoodle.com	Louisville	KY	40222	502-426-0800		671
Yangarra Resources Ltd 715 - 5 Ave SW Ste 1530 *Web:* www.yangarra.ca	Calgary	AB	T2P2X6	403-262-9558		536
Yangtze Dining Lounge 700 Somerset W *Web:* www.yangtze.ca	Ottawa	ON	K1R6P6	613-236-0555		671
Yank Sing 49 Stevenson St *Web:* www.yanksing.com	San Francisco	CA	94105	415-541-4949		671
Yankee Barn Homes 131 Yankee Barn Rd *TF:* 800-258-9786 ■ *Web:* www.yankeebarnhomes.com	Grantham	NH	03753	800-258-9786		106
Yankee Candle Company Inc PO Box 110 *TF:* 877-803-6890 ■ *Web:* www.yankeecandle.com	South Deerfield	MA	01373	413-665-8306		327
Yankee Containers 110 Republic Dr *Web:* www.yankeecontainers.com	North Haven	CT	06473	203-288-3851		125
Yankee Hill Brick & Tile 3705 S Coddington Ave *Web:* www.yankeehillbrick.com	Lincoln	NE	68522	402-477-6663	477-2832	150
Yankee Inn 461 Pittsfield Lenox Rd *TF:* 800-835-2364 ■ *Web:* www.yankeeinn.com	Lenox	MA	01240	413-499-3700		379
Yankee Magazine 1121 Main St PO Box 520 *TF:* 800-288-4284 ■ *Web:* newengland.com/today	Dublin	NH	03444	603-563-8111	563-8252	457-22
Yankee Peddler Inn 113 Touro St *Web:* www.yankeepeddlerinn.com	Newport	RI	02840	401-846-1323		379
Yankee Publishing Inc PO Box 520 *TF:* 800-729-9265 ■ *Web:* newengland.com/today	Dublin	NH	03444	603-563-8111	563-8252	637-9
Yankee Springs Recreation Area 2104 S Briggs Rd *Web:* www.michigandnr.com	Middleville	MI	49333	269-795-9081		565
Yankee Stadium 161st St & River Ave *Web:* newyork.yankees.mlb.com	Bronx	NY	10451	718-293-4300		720
Yankton Ag Service 114 Mulberry St *TF:* 800-456-5528 ■ *Web:* yanktonag.com	Yankton	SD	57078	605-665-3691		276
Yankton County 410 Walnut St Ste 205 *Web:* ujs.sd.gov	Yankton	SD	57078	605-668-3080	668-5411	338
Yankton Press & Dakotan 319 Walnut St PO Box 56 *TF:* 800-743-2968 ■ *Web:* www.yankton.net	Yankton	SD	57078	605-665-7811	665-1721	637-8
Yanmar America Corp 101 International Pkwy *Web:* www.yanmar.com	Adairsville	GA	30103	770-877-9894	877-9009	385
Yanni's Mediterranean Bar & Grill 3109 Central Ave NE *Web:* yannisandopabar.com	Albuquerque	NM	87106	505-268-9250		671
Yantis Co 3611 Paesano's Pkwy Ste 300 *Web:* www.yantiscompany.com	San Antonio	TX	78231	210-655-3780	655-8526	188-4
Yard House 401 Shoreline Village Dr *Web:* www.yardhouse.com	Long Beach	CA	90802	562-628-0455		671
Yard House Restaurant 620 Spectrum Center Dr *Web:* www.yardhouse.com	Irvine	CA	92618	949-753-9373		670
Yard, The 1211 S Mammoth Rd *TF:* 800-333-3333 ■ *Web:* www.theyardrestaurant.com	Manchester	NH	03109	603-623-3545	625-8420	671
Yarde Metals Inc 45 Newell St *TF:* 800-444-9494 ■ *Web:* www.yarde.com	Southington	CT	06489	860-406-6061		490
Yardley Products Corp 10 W College Ave *TF:* 800-457-0154 ■ *Web:* www.yardleyproducts.com	Yardley	PA	19067	215-493-2723	493-6796	350
Yardmaster Inc 1447 N Ridge Rd *Web:* www.yardmaster.com	Painesville	OH	44077	440-357-8400		192
Yardney Technical Products Inc 82 Mechanic St *Web:* www.yardney.com	Pawcatuck	CT	06379	860-599-1100	599-3903	74
Yarema Die & Engineering Co Inc 300 Minnesota Rd *Web:* www.yarema.com	Troy	MI	48083	248-585-2830	616-1422	757
Yargus Manufacturing Inc PO Box 238 *Web:* yargus.com	Marshall	IL	62441	217-826-6352		273
Yark Automotive Group Inc 6019 W Central Ave *TF:* 866-390-8894 ■ *Web:* www.yarkauto.com	Toledo	OH	43615	866-390-8894		516
Yarmouth Regional Hospital (YRH) 60 Vancouver St **Fax:* Admitting ■ *TF:* 800-460-2110 ■ *Web:* www.swndha.nshealth.ca/pages/yrh.htm	Yarmouth	NS	B5A2P5	902-742-3541	742-0369*	374-2
Yarmouth Resort 343 Main St Rt 28 *TF:* 877-838-3524 ■ *Web:* www.yarmouthresort.com	West Yarmouth	MA	02673	508-775-5155		379

Name / Address	City	State	Zip	Phone	Fax	Class
Yarmuth John A (Rep D - KY) 131 Cannon HOB *Web:* yarmuth.house.gov	Washington	DC	20515	202-225-5401	225-5776	342-2
Yarnell Ice Cream Co 205 S Spring St *TF:* 800-561-3357 ■ *Web:* www.yarnells.com	Searcy	AR	72143	501-268-6355		296-25
Yaro Supply Co Drawer Ste 750608 *TF:* 800-222-5609 ■ *Web:* www.yaro.com	Dayton	OH	45475	937-859-6100		358
YASH Technologies Inc 605-17th Ave *Web:* www.yash.com	East Moline	IL	61244	309-755-0433		196
Yaskawa America Inc 2121 Norman Dr S *Fax: Mktg ■ *TF:* 800-927-5292 ■ *Web:* www.yaskawa.com	Waukegan	IL	60085	847-887-7000	887-7310*	203
Yasso Yani Restaurant 326 E Main St	Stockton	CA	95202	209-464-3108		671
Yates Bleachery Co 503 Flintstone Rd *Web:* www.yatesbleachery.info	Flintstone	GA	30725	706-820-1531	820-9459	745-7
Yates Construction Company Inc 9220 NC Hwy 65 *Web:* www.yatesconstruction.com	Stokesdale	NC	27357	336-379-8131		188-10
Yates County 417 Liberty St *TF:* 866-212-5160 ■ *Web:* www.yatescounty.org	Penn Yan	NY	14527	315-536-5120	536-5545	338
Yates Industries Inc 23050 E Industrial Dr *Web:* www.yatesind.com	St. Clair Shores	MI	48080	586-778-7680		454
Yates Petroleum Corp 105 S Fourth St *Fax: Hum Res ■ *Web:* www.yatespetroleum.com	Artesia	NM	88210	575-748-1471	748-4570*	536
Yates-American Machine Company Inc 2880 Kennedy Dr *TF:* 800-752-6377 ■ *Web:* www.yatesamerican.com	Beloit	WI	53511	608-364-6333		821
Yatesville Lake State Park PO Box 767 *Web:* www.parks.ky.gov	Louisa	KY	41230	606-673-1492		565
Yavapai College 1100 E Sheldon St *Fax: Admissions ■ *TF:* 800-922-6787 ■ *Web:* www.yc.edu	Prescott	AZ	86301	928-445-7300	776-2151*	162
Verde Valley 601 Black Hills Dr *TF:* 800-922-6787 ■ *Web:* www.yc.edu	Clarkdale	AZ	86324	928-634-7501		162
Yavapai County 1015 Fair St *TF:* 800-659-7149 ■ *Web:* www.yavapai.us	Prescott	AZ	86305	928-771-3200	771-3257	338
Yavapai Regional Medical Ctr 1003 Willow Creek Rd *TF:* 877-843-9762 ■ *Web:* www.yrmc.org	Prescott	AZ	86301	928-445-2700		374-3
Yaya's Flame Broiled Chicken 521 S Dort Hwy *TF:* 800-442-1162 ■ *Web:* www.yayas.com	Flint	MI	48503	810-235-6550	235-5210	670
Yazaki Energy 701 E Plano Pkwy Ste 305 *Web:* www.yazakienergy.com	Plano	TX	75074	469-229-5443		393
Yazaki North America Inc 6801 N Haggerty Rd *Web:* www.yazaki-na.com	Canton	MI	48187	734-983-1000		253
Yazoo County PO Box 186 *TF:* 800-381-0662 ■ *Web:* visityazoo.org	Yazoo City	MS	39194	662-746-1815	746-1816	338
Yazoo County Chamber of Commerce 1615 H St NW *TF:* 800-638-6582 ■ *Web:* uschamber.com	Washington	DC	20062	662-746-1273		139
Yazoo Mills Inc PO Box 369 *TF Cust Svc:* 800-242-5216 ■ *Web:* www.yazoomills.com	New Oxford	PA	17350	717-624-8993	624-4420	125
Yazoo Valley Electric Power Assn 2255 Gordon Ave *TF:* 800-281-5098 ■ *Web:* yazoovalley.com	Yazoo City	MS	39194	662-746-4251		245
Ybarras Jewelers Inc 678 N Wilson Way Ste 28	Stockton	CA	95205	209-547-0320		410
YBCA (Yerba Buena Ctr for the Arts) 701 Mission St *TF:* 800-838-3006 ■ *Web:* www.ybca.org	San Francisco	CA	94103	415-978-2787	978-9635	520
Ybor City Chamber of Commerce 1800 E Ninth Ave *Web:* www.ybor.org	Tampa	FL	33605	813-248-3712	247-1764	139
Ybor City Museum State Park 1818 Ninth Ave *Web:* www.floridastateparks.org	Tampa	FL	33605	813-247-6323		565
Y-Change 43575 Mission Blvd *Web:* www.y-change.com	Fremont	CA	94539	510-573-2205		177
YDA (Young Democrats of America) PO Box 77496 *Web:* www.yda.org	Washington	DC	20013	202-639-8585		48-7
YDR (York Daily Record) 1891 Loucks Rd *TF:* 800-559-3520 ■ *Web:* www.ydr.com	York	PA	17408	717-771-2000		532-2
Ye Olde Steak House 6838 Chapman Hwy *Web:* www.yeoldesteakhouse.com	Knoxville	TN	37920	865-577-9328		671
Yeager Airport 100 Airport Rd Ste 175 *TF:* 800-553-7681 ■ *Web:* www.yeagerairport.com	Charleston	WV	25311	304-344-8033	344-8034	27
Yeargin Potter Shackelford Construction Inc 121 Edinburgh Ct *Web:* www.ypsconst.com	Greenville	SC	29607	864-232-1491		186
Yearick-Millea 100 First Ave Ste 525 *Web:* www.yearick-millea.com	Pittsburgh	PA	15222	412-323-9320		7
Yearout Mechanical & Engineering Inc 8501 Washington St NE *Web:* www.yearout.com	Albuquerque	NM	87113	505-884-0994	883-5073	189-10
Yeck Bros Co 2222 Arbor Blvd *TF:* 800-417-2767 ■ *Web:* www.yeck.com	Dayton	OH	45439	937-294-4000	294-6985	5
Yeled V'yalda Early Childhood Ctr Inc 1312 38th St *Web:* www.yeled.org	Brooklyn	NY	11218	718-686-3700		148
Yell County 101 E Fifth St *Web:* yellcounty.net	Danville	AR	72833	479-495-4850	229-5634	338
Yellow Basket Restaurant 2860 S Main St *Web:* www.yellowbasket.com	Santa Ana	CA	92707	714-545-8219		671
Yellow Bay State Park 490 N Meridian Rd *Web:* www.fwp.mt.gov	Kalispell	MT	59901	406-752-5501		565
Yellow Book USA 398 RXR Plaza *TF:* 877-237-6120 ■ *Web:* www.yellowbook.com	Uniondale	NY	11556	516-730-1900		637-6
Yellow Creek Falls Fish Camp 3595 Al Hwy 273 *Web:* yellowcreekfalls.com	Leesburg	AL	35983	256-526-8427		239
Yellow Creek State Park 170 Rt 259 Hwy *Web:* www.dcnr.state.pa.us	Penn Run	PA	15765	724-357-7913		565
Yellow Dog Networks 9664 Marion Rd *Web:* www.yellowdognetworks.com	Kansas City	MO	64137	816-767-9364		180
Yellow Medicine County 415 Ninth Ave *TF:* 800-366-4812 ■ *Web:* mncourts.gov	Granite Falls	MN	56241	320-564-3325	564-4435	338
Yellow Pencil Inc 10158 103 St NW *Web:* yellowpencil.com	Edmonton	AB	T5J0X6	780-423-5917		196
Yellow Point Equity Partners LP 1285 W Pender St Ste 1000 *Web:* www.ypoint.ca	Vancouver	BC	V6E4B1	604-659-1898		690
Yellow Porch, The 734 Thompson Ln *Web:* www.theyellowporch.com	Nashville	TN	37204	615-386-0260		671
Yellow River State Forest 729 State Forest Rd YRSF *Web:* www.iowadnr.gov	Harpers Ferry	IA	52146	563-586-2254		565
YellowBrix Inc 200 N Glebe Rd Ste 1025	Arlington	VA	22203	703-548-3300		178-7
Yellowdog Printing & Graphics LLC 490 S Santa Fe Dr Unit A *TF:* 800-463-3339 ■ *Web:* www.yellowdogprinting.com	Denver	CO	80223	303-765-2000		627
Yellowhammer Media Group Inc 44 W 28th St *Web:* www.yhmg.com	New York	NY	10001	646-490-9857		7
Yellowhead Helicopters Ltd 3010 Selwyn Rd *TF:* 888-566-4401 ■ *Web:* www.yhl.ca	Valemount	BC	V0E2Z0	250-566-4401	566-4333	359
YELLOWPAGES.com LLC 208 S Akard *TF:* 866-329-7118 ■ *Web:* www.yellowpages.com	Dallas	TX	75202	866-329-7118		397
Yellowridge Construction Ltd 2605 Clarke St Ste 200 *Web:* yellowridge.ca	Port Moody	BC	V3H1Z4	604-936-2605		186
Yellowstone Art Museum 401 N 27th St *Web:* www.yellowstone.artmuseum.org	Billings	MT	59101	406-256-6804		520
Yellowstone Baptist College 1515 S Shiloh Rd *Fax: Admissions ■ *TF:* 800-487-9950 ■ *Web:* yellowstonechristian.edu	Billings	MT	59106	406-656-9950	656-3737*	166
Yellowstone County 217 N 27th St *Web:* co.yellowstone.mt.gov	Billings	MT	59101	406-256-2720		338
Yellowstone Lake State Park 8495 Lake Rd *Web:* www.dnr.wi.gov	Blanchardville	WI	53516	608-523-4427		565
Yellowstone Log Homes LLC 280 N Yellowstone Hwy *Web:* www.yellowstoneloghomes.com	Rigby	ID	83442	208-745-8108		106
Yellowstone National Park PO Box 168 *Fax: Mail Rm ■ *Web:* www.nps.gov	Yellowstone National Park	WY	82190	307-344-7381	344-2323*	564
Yellowstone Public Radio 1500 University Dr *TF:* 800-441-2941 ■ *Web:* ypradio.org	Billings	MT	59101	406-657-2941		645-19
Yellowstone Valley Electric Co-op 150 Co-op Way *TF:* 800-736-5323 ■ *Web:* www.yvec.com	Huntley	MT	59037	406-348-3411	348-3414	245
Yellowstone Western Heritage Ctr 2822 Montana Ave *TF:* 800-735-2635 ■ *Web:* www.ywhc.org	Billings	MT	59101	406-256-6809	256-6850	520
Yemanja Brasil 2900 Missouri Ave Pestalozzi St *Web:* www.yemanjabrasil.com	Saint Louis	MO	63118	314-771-7457	771-0296	671
Yen China Cafe 1225 Belt Line Rd *Web:* garlandyenchinacafe.com	Garland	TX	75040	972-495-9779		671
Yen Ching 926 Main St *Web:* yenchingdbq.com	Dubuque	IA	52001	563-556-2574	556-2574	671
Yen Ching 9150 N Michigan Rd *Web:* www.yenchingwest.com	Indianapolis	IN	46268	317-228-0868	228-0886	671
Yen Ching Restaurant 2208 Missouri Blvd	Jefferson City	MO	65109	573-635-5225		671
Yenkin-Majestic Paint Corp 1920 Leonard Ave *TF:* 800-848-1898 ■ *Web:* www.yenkin-majestic.com	Columbus	OH	43219	614-253-8511	253-6327	550
Yeo & Yeo PC 3023 Davenport Ave *Web:* yeoandyeo.com	Saginaw	MI	48602	989-793-9830		2
Yeomans Chicago Corp 3905 Enterprise Ct PO Box 6620 *Web:* www.yccpump.com	Aurora	IL	60504	630-236-5500	236-5511	641
Yeomans Wood & Timber Inc 714 Empire Expy *Web:* yeomanswood.com	Swainsboro	GA	30401	478-237-9940		448
Yerba Buena Ctr for the Arts (YBCA) 701 Mission St *TF:* 800-838-3006 ■ *Web:* www.ybca.org	San Francisco	CA	94103	415-978-2787	978-9635	520
Yerba Prima Inc 740 Jefferson Ave *Web:* www.yerba.com	Ashland	OR	97520	541-488-2228		123
Yerkes National Primate Research Ctr Emory University 954 Gatewood Rd *Web:* www.yerkes.emory.edu	Atlanta	GA	30322	404-727-7707	727-0623	668
Yeshiva Toras Chaim Talmudical Seminary 1555 Stuart St *Web:* ytcdenver.org	Denver	CO	80204	303-629-8200		166
Yeshiva University 500 W 185th St *Fax: Admissions ■ *TF:* 800-654-3210 ■ *Web:* www.yu.edu	New York	NY	10033	212-960-5400	960-0086*	166
Yeshiva University Museum 15 W 16th St *Web:* www.yu.edu	New York	NY	10011	212-294-8330		520
Yeshiva University Press 500 W 185th St *Web:* www.yu.edu	New York	NY	10033	212-960-5400		637-4
Yeshivat Noam 70 W Century Rd *Web:* www.yeshivatnoam.org	Paramus	NJ	07652	201-261-1919		685
Yesterday USA Radio Networks, The 2001 Plymouth Rock Dr *TF:* 800-624-2272 ■ *Web:* www.yesterdayusa.com	Richardson	TX	75081	972-889-9872	889-2329	644
Yesterday's Resturant & Tavern 2030 Devine St 5 Pts *Web:* www.yesterdayssc.com	Columbia	SC	29205	803-799-0196		671

Name	City	State	Zip	Phone	Fax	Class
Yesware Inc 75 Kneeland St Fl 15 TF: 855-937-9273 ■ Web: www.yesware.com	Boston	MA	02111	855-937-9273		387
Yeti Inc 7601 SW Pkwy TF: 888-872-0227 ■ Web: www.yeticoolers.com	Austin	TX	78735	512-394-9384		608
Yetter Manufacturing Inc 109 S McDonough St PO Box 358 TF: 800-447-5777 ■ Web: yetterco.com	Colchester	IL	62326	309-776-4111	776-3222	273
Yew Dell Gardens 6220 Old LaGrange Rd PO Box 1334 Web: www.yewdellgardens.org	Crestwood	KY	40014	502-241-4788		97
Yew Restaurant & Bar 791 W Georgia St 2nd Fl Web: www.fourseasons.com	Vancouver	BC	V6C2T4	604-692-4939	844-6749	671
Y&F (Young & Franklin Inc) 942 Old Liverpool Rd Web: www.yf.com	Liverpool	NY	13088	315-457-3110	457-9204	790
YFF & Scholma PC 688 Cascade W Pkwy SE Web: yffandscholma.com	Grand Rapids	MI	49546	616-942-6530		2
YHB Investment Advisors Inc 20 S Main St Ste 306 TF: 800-526-8094 ■ Web: www.yhbia.com	West Hartford	CT	06107	860-561-7050		401
Yiftee Inc 565 Middlefield Rd Web: yiftee.com	Menlo Park	CA	94025	650-564-4438		5
Yingling Aircraft Inc 2010 Airport Rd TF: 800-835-0083 ■ Web: www.yinglingaviation.com	Wichita	KS	67209	316-943-3246	943-2484	770
YK International Co 3246 W Montrose Ave TF: 800-266-5254 ■ Web: chicago.enquira.com	Chicago	IL	60618	773-583-5270		348
YKK AP America Inc 7680 The Bluffs Ste 100 Web: www.ykkap.com	Austell	GA	30168	678-838-6000		116
YKK USA Inc 1251 Vly Brook Ave Web: www.ykkfastening.com	Lyndhurst	NJ	07071	201-935-4200	964-0123	594
YMCA (YMCA of the USA) 101 N Wacker Dr TF: 800-872-9622 ■ Web: www.ymca.net	Chicago	IL	60606	312-977-0031	977-9063	48-6
YMCA Canada 1867 Yonge St Ste 601 Web: www.ymca.ca	Toronto	ON	M4S1Y5	416-967-9622	967-9618	138
YMCA of Pikes Peak Region Inc 207 N Nevada Ave TF: 800-621-8752 ■ Web: www.ppymca.org	Colorado Springs	CO	80903	719-473-9622		31
YMCA of Rock River Valley 200 Y Blvd Web: rockriverymca.org	Rockford	IL	61107	815-489-1252		354
YMCA of the USA (YMCA) 101 N Wacker Dr TF: 800-872-9622 ■ Web: www.ymca.net	Chicago	IL	60606	312-977-0031	977-9063	48-6
YMCA of Triangle Area 801 Corporate Ctr Dr TF: 800-903-0097 ■ Web: www.ymcatriangle.org	Raleigh	NC	27607	919-719-9622		31
Ynb 401 Elm St PO Box 051700 Web: ynbok.com	Yukon	OK	73099	405-354-5281	354-9869	70
YNHS (Yakima Neighborhood Health Services) 12 S Eigth St PO Box 2605 Web: www.ynhs.org	Yakima	WA	98907	509-454-4143		353
YO Ranch Steakhouse 702 Ross Ave Web: www.yoranchsteakhouse.com	Dallas	TX	75202	214-744-3287		671
Yoakum County PO Box 309 Web: www.co.yoakum.tx.us	Plains	TX	79355	806-456-7491	456-8767	338
Yoakum National Bank 301 W Grand Ave Web: yoakumnationalbank.com	Yoakum	TX	77995	361-293-5225	293-7322	70
YoCream International Inc 5858 NE 87th Ave TF: 800-962-7326 ■ Web: www.yocream.com	Portland	OR	97220	503-256-3754	256-3976	296-25
Yoder & Armstrong Printing 627 E Baltimore Ave E TF: 800-344-8850 ■ Web: yoderandarmstrong.com	Lansdowne	PA	19050	610-622-6118		627
Yoder Industries Inc 2520 Needmore Rd Web: www.yoderindustries.com	Dayton	OH	45414	937-278-5769	278-6321	308
Yoder Kevin (Rep R - KS) 2433 Rayburn HOB Web: yoder.house.gov	Washington	DC	20515	202-225-2865		342-2
Yoder Lumber Company Inc 4515 TR 367 Web: www.yoderlumber.com	Millersburg	OH	44654	330-893-3131	893-3031	551
Yoder Oil Co Inc 1221 N Nappanee St Web: www.yoderoil.com	Elkhart	IN	46514	574-264-2107		581
Yodice & Co PC 1259 Rt # 46 Web: yodiceco.com	Parsippany	NJ	07054	973-263-8228		2
Yodle Inc 330 W 34th St 18th Fl TF: 877-276-5104 ■ Web: www.yodle.com	New York	NY	10001	877-276-5104		395
Yodlee Inc 3600 Bridge Pkwy Ste 200 Web: yodlee.com	Redwood City	CA	94065	650-980-3600		178-7
Yoga Journal Magazine 475 Sansome St Ste 850 Web: www.yogajournal.com	San Francisco	CA	94111	415-591-0555	591-0733	457-13
Yogen Fruz 210 Shields Ct Web: www.yogenfruz.com	Markham	ON	L3R8V2	905-479-8762	479-5235	310
Yogi Divine Society 2437 Yeoman St	Waukegan	IL	60087	847-336-6451		48-20
Yogi's Grill & Bar 519 E Tenth St TF: 800-727-4407 ■ Web: www.yogis.com	Bloomington	IN	47408	812-323-9644		671
Yogo Inn 211 E Main St TF: 800-860-9646 ■ Web: www.yogoinn.com	Lewistown	MT	59457	406-535-8721	535-8969	379
Yoho Resources Inc 521-3rd Ave SW Ste 500 Web: www.yohoresources.ca	Calgary	AB	T2P3T3	403-537-1771		539
Yoho Ted (Rep R - FL) 511 Cannon Bldg Web: yoho.house.gov	Washington	DC	20515	202-225-5744	225-3973	342-2
Yojna Inc 32605 W 12 Mile Rd Ste 275 Web: www.yojna.com	Farmington Hills	MI	48334	248-489-9650		180
Yokogawa Corp of America 12530 W Airport Blvd TF: 800-888-6400 ■ Web: www.yokogawa.com/us	Sugar Land	TX	77478	281-340-3800	340-3838	248
Yokohama Tire Corp 601 S Acacia Ave TF: 800-423-4544 ■ Web: www.yokohamatire.com	Fullerton	CA	92831	714-870-3800		754
Yolo County 625 Ct St Ste 202 TF: 800-433-5060 ■ Web: yolocounty.org	Woodland	CA	95695	530-666-8150	668-4029	338
Yolo County Library 226 Buckeye St TF: 800-755-6864 ■ Web: yolocounty.org	Woodland	CA	95695	530-666-8005	666-8006	434-3
Yolo Federal Credit Union 266 W Main St TF: 877-965-6328 ■ Web: yolofcu.org	Woodland	CA	95695	530-668-2700		219
Yomari Information Services Inc 111 Third Ave S Ste 120 Web: www.yomari.com	Minneapolis	MN	55401	612-326-4852		631
Yonex Corp 20140 S Western Ave TF: 800-449-6639 ■ Web: www.yonex.com	Torrance	CA	90501	310-793-3800		710
Yonkers Chamber of Commerce 55 Main St 2nd Fl TF: 800-540-1068 ■ Web: www.yonkerschamber.com	Yonkers	NY	10701	914-963-0332	963-0455	139
Yonkers City Hall 40 S Broadway Web: www.yonkersny.gov	Yonkers	NY	10701	914-377-6000		337
Yonkers Contracting Company Inc 969 Midland Ave TF: 800-364-2059 ■ Web: www.yonkerscontractingco.com	Yonkers	NY	10704	914-965-1500	378-8885	188-4
Yonkers Motors Corp 2000 Central Pk Ave Web: www.yonkershonda.com	Yonkers	NY	10710	914-600-7988		57
Yonkers Public Library 1 Larkin Ctr Web: www.ypl.org	Yonkers	NY	10701	914-337-1500		434-3
Yonkers Raceway 810 Yonkers Ave Web: empirecitycasino.com	Yonkers	NY	10704	914-968-4200		642
Yorba Linda Chamber of Commerce 17670 Yorba Linda Blvd Web: www.yorbalindachamber.org	Yorba Linda	CA	92886	714-993-9537	993-7764	139
Yorba Linda Public Library 18181 Imperial Hwy Web: www.ylpl.net	Yorba Linda	CA	92886	714-777-2873		434-3
York Barbell Co Inc 3300 BoaRd Rd TF Cust Svc: 800-358-9675 ■ Web: www.yorkbarbell.com	York	PA	17406	717-767-6481	764-0044	267
York Bldg Products Co 950 Smile Way TF: 800-673-2408 ■ Web: www.yorkbuilding.com	York	PA	17404	717-848-2831	854-9156	183
York Building Services Inc 99 Grand St Ste 3 TF: 855-443-9675 ■ Web: yorkbuildingservices.com	Moonachie	NJ	07074	855-443-9675		256
York Catholic High School 601 E Springettsbury Ave Web: yorkcatholic.org	York	PA	17403	717-846-8871		685
York Central Hospital 10 Trench St Web: www.mackenziehealth.ca	Richmond Hill	ON	L4C4Z3	905-883-1212		374-2
York College 94-20 Guy R Brewer Blvd *Fax: Admissions ■ Web: www.york.cuny.edu	Jamaica	NY	11451	718-262-2000	262-2601*	166
York College 1125 E Eigth St *Fax: Admissions ■ TF: 800-950-9675 ■ Web: www.york.edu	York	NE	68467	402-363-5600	363-5623*	166
York College of Pennsylvania 441 Country Club Rd *Fax: Hum Res ■ Web: www.ycp.edu	York	PA	17403	717-846-7788	815-6862*	166
York Container 138 Mt Scion Rd PO Box 3008 TF: 800-772-9675 ■ Web: www.yorkcontainer.com	York	PA	17402	717-757-7611	755-8090	100
York Correctional Institution 201 W Main St Web: www.ct.gov	Niantic	CT	06357	860-451-3001		213
York County 45 Kennebunk Rd PO Box 399	Alfred	ME	04002	207-324-1577		338
York County 510 N Lincoln Ave Web: www.yorkcounty.ne.gov	York	NE	68467	402-362-7759	362-7558	338
York County 45 N George St Web: yorkcountypa.gov	York	PA	17401	717-771-9612	771-9096	338
York County 6 S Congress St Web: www.yorkcountygov.com	York	SC	29745	803-684-8507	684-8575	338
York County 224 Ballard St PO Box 371 Web: www.yorkcounty.gov	Yorktown	VA	23690	757-890-3450	890-3459	338
York County Cerebral Palsy Home Inc Proj 2050 Barley Rd Web: www.margaretemoul.org	York	PA	17408	717-767-6463		371
York County Chamber of Commerce 96 S George St Ste 300 TF: 800-290-7424 ■ Web: www.ycea-pa.org	York	PA	17401	717-848-4000	843-6737	139
York County Community College 112 College Dr TF: 800-580-3820 ■ Web: www.yccc.edu	Wells	ME	04090	207-646-9282	641-0837	162
York County Library 138 E Black St TF: 800-726-8774 ■ Web: www.yclibrary.org	Rock Hill	SC	29730	803-981-5858		434-3
York County Public Library 8500 George Washington Memorial Hwy TF: 800-552-7945 ■ Web: yorkcounty.gov	Yorktown	VA	23692	757-890-3377	890-2956	434-3
York County Regional Chamber of Commerce 116 E Main St Web: www.yorkcountychamber.com	Rock Hill	SC	29731	803-324-7500	324-1889	139
York County Transportation Authority 1230 Roosevelt Ave TF: 800-632-9063 ■ Web: www.rabbittransit.org	York	PA	17404	717-846-5562	848-4853	468
York Daily Record (YDR) 1891 Loucks Rd TF: 800-559-3520 ■ Web: www.ydr.com	York	PA	17408	717-771-2000		532-2
York Dispatch 1891 Loucks Rd Web: www.yorkdispatch.com	York	PA	17408	717-854-1575		532-2
York Electric Co-op Inc PO Box 150 TF: 800-582-8810 ■ Web: www.yorkelectric.net	York	SC	29745	803-684-4247		245
York Employment Services Inc 990 N Ontario Mills Dr Ste C Web: www.yorkemployment.com	Ontario	CA	91764	909-581-0181		260
York Ford Inc 1481 Bwy TF: 888-705-6229 ■ Web: www.yorkford.com	Saugus	MA	01906	781-231-1945		57
York Hospital 1001 S George St Web: www.wellspan.org	York	PA	17405	717-851-2345		374-3
York Mahoning Mechanical Contrs Inc 724 Canfield Rd Web: yorkmahoning.com	Youngstown	OH	44511	330-788-7011		610
York Metal Fabricators Inc 27 NE 26th St TF: 800-255-4703 ■ Web: www.yorkmetal.com	Oklahoma City	OK	73105	405-528-7495		697
York Museum 2694 Eglinton Ave W Web: www.toronto.ca	Toronto	ON	M6M1T9	416-394-2759		520

Name / Address	City	State	ZIP	Phone	Fax	Class
York Newspaper Co 1891 Loucks Rd *TF:* 800-559-3520 ■ *Web:* www.inyork.com	York	PA	17408	717-767-6397		637-8
York River Electric Inc 108 Production Dr *Web:* www.yorkriverelectric.com	Yorktown	VA	23693	757-369-3673	369-3680	189-4
York Solutions LLC 1 Westbrook Corporate Ctr Ste 910 *TF:* 877-700-9675 ■ *Web:* www.yorksolutions.net	Westchester	IL	60154	708-531-8362		721
York State Bank & Trust Co 700 N Lincoln AvE *TF:* 888-295-5540 ■ *Web:* www.yorkstatebank.com	York	NE	68467	402-362-4411	362-4192	70
York Sunday News 1891 Loucks Rd *TF:* 888-629-4095 ■ *Web:* www.ydr.com	York	PA	17408	717-767-6397	771-2009	532-4
York Technical College 452 S Anderson Rd *TF:* 800-922-8324 ■ *Web:* www.yorktech.com	Rock Hill	SC	29730	803-327-8000		162
York Telecom Corp 81 Corbett Way *TF:* 866-836-8463 ■ *Web:* www.yorktel.com	Eatontown	NJ	07724	732-413-6000		736
York University 4700 Keele St *TF:* 800-426-2255 ■ *Web:* www.yorku.ca	Toronto	ON	M3J1P3	416-736-2100	736-5536	785
York Wallcoverings Inc 750 Linden Ave PO Box 5166 *TF:* 800-375-9675 ■ *Web:* www.yorkwall.com	York	PA	17405	717-846-4456	843-5624	802
York Waste Disposal Inc 3730 Sandhurst Dr *Web:* yorkwaste.com	York	PA	17406	717-845-1557		804
York Water Company, The 130 E Market St *NASDAQ:* YORW ■ *TF:* 800-750-5561 ■ *Web:* www.yorkwater.com	York	PA	17401	717-845-3601	845-3792	787
Yorkshire Steak & Seafood Restaurant 700 York St *TF:* 800-446-9244 ■ *Web:* www.theyorkshirerestaurant.com	Williamsburg	VA	23185	757-229-9790		671
Yorkshire Supply Inc 8205 Centreville Rd *Web:* www.yorkshiresupply.com	Manassas	VA	20111	703-368-9226		612
Yorkston Oil Company Inc 2801 Roeder Ave *TF:* 800-401-2201 ■ *Web:* www.yorkstonoil.com	Bellingham	WA	98225	360-734-2201		579
Yorktown National Cemetery PO Box 210 *Web:* www.nps.gov/york/index.htm	Yorktown	VA	23690	757-898-2410	898-6346	136
Yorktown Shopping Ctr 203 Yorktown Ctr *Web:* www.yorktowncenter.com	Lombard	IL	60148	630-629-7330	629-7334	460
Yorktowne Hotel 48 E Market St *TF:* 800-233-9324 ■ *Web:* www.yorktowne.com	York	PA	17401	717-848-1111		379
Yorkville CUSD 115 602 Center Pkwy *Web:* www.y115.org	Yorkville	IL	60560	630-553-4382	553-4398	780
Yosemite National Park 9039 Village Dr PO Box 577 *Web:* www.nps.gov/yose	Yosemite	CA	95389	209-372-0200		564
Yosemite Pathology Group Inc 2625 Coffee Rd Ste S *Web:* www.ypmg.com	Modesto	CA	95355	209-577-1200		415
Yosemite Sierra Visitors Bureau 40637 Hwy 41 *TF:* 800-613-0709 ■ *Web:* www.yosemitethisyear.com	Oakhurst	CA	93644	559-683-4636		206
Yoshi Sono Japanese Restaurant 643 Eagle Rock Ave	West Orange	NJ	07052	973-325-2005		671
Yoshi's Cafe 3257 N Halsted St *Web:* www.yoshiscafe.com	Chicago	IL	60657	773-248-6160		671
Yoshida Japanese Steak House 4 Regent Pk Blvd	Asheville	NC	28806	828-252-5903		671
Yoshimatsu 2660 N Campbell Ave *Web:* www.yoshimatsuaz.com	Tucson	AZ	85719	520-320-1574		671
Yoshino America Corp 2500 Palmer Ave *Web:* www.yoshinoamerica.com	University Park	IL	60484	708-534-1141		596
Yoshino Restaurant 6226 N Blackstone Ave	Fresno	CA	93710	559-431-2205		671
Yoshinoya Beef Bowl 991 Knox St *TF:* 800-576-8017 ■ *Web:* www.yoshinoyaamerica.com	Torrance	CA	90502	310-527-6060	527-6050	670
Yost Superior Co PO Box 1487 *Web:* www.yostsuperior.com	Springfield	OH	45501	937-323-7591		719
YOTEL 570 Tenth Ave Times Sq *Web:* www.yotel.com/en	New York	NY	10036	646-449-7700		378
YouDocs Beauty Inc 648 Broadway *Web:* www.youbeauty.com	New York	NY	10012	646-449-9445		387
Youell's Oyster House 2249 Walnut St *Web:* youellsoysterhouse.com	Allentown	PA	18104	610-439-1203		671
Youghiogheny Scenic and Wild River c/o Deep Creek Lake Recreation Area 898 State Pk Rd *TF:* 800 248 1893 ■ *Web:* dnr2.maryland.gov	Swanton	MD	21561	301-387-5563		565
YouMail Inc 43 Corporate Pk Ste 200 *TF:* 800-374-0013 ■ *Web:* www.youmail.com	Irvine	CA	92606	800-374-0013		180
Young & Company CPAS 11200 SW Allen Blvd Ste 100 *Web:* youngcocpas.com	Beaverton	OR	97005	503-646-4800		2
Young & Franklin Inc (Y&F) 942 Old Liverpool Rd *Web:* www.yf.com	Liverpool	NY	13088	315-457-3110	457-9204	790
Young Adult Library Services Assn (YALSA) 50 E Huron St *TF:* 800-545-2433 ■ *Web:* www.ala.org/yalsa	Chicago	IL	60611	312-280-4390	664-7459	49-11
Young America Corp 10 S Fifth St 7th Fl *TF:* 800-533-4529 ■ *Web:* www.yaengage.com	Minneapolis	MN	55402	800-533-4529		737
Young America's Foundation 11480 Commerce Park Dr Ste 600 *TF:* 800-872-1776 ■ *Web:* www.yaf.org	Reston	VA	20191	703-318-9608	318-9122	48-7
Young at Art Children's Museum 751 SW 121st Ave *TF:* 800-435-7352 ■ *Web:* www.youngatartmuseum.org	Davie	FL	33325	954-424-0085	473-8798	521
Young Audiences Inc 171 Madison Ave Ste 200 *Web:* www.youngaudiences.org	New York	NY	10016	212-831-8110		48-4
Young Broadcasting of San Francisco Inc 599 Lexington Ave *TF:* 800-925-3270 ■ *Web:* kron4.com	New York	NY	10022	212-754-7070		116
Young Bros Ltd PO Box 3288 *Web:* www.htbyb.com	Honolulu	HI	96801	808-543-9311		312
Young Bros Stamp Works Inc 1415 Howard Ave *Web:* mw-radio.com	Muscatine	IA	52761	563-263-3575		198
Young Children Magazine 1313 L St NW Ste 500 PO Box 97156 *TF:* 800-424-2460 ■ *Web:* www.naeyc.org	Washington	DC	20005	202-232-8777	328-1846	457-8
Young Clement Rivers LLP 25 Calhoun St *Web:* www.ycrlaw.com/home.aspx	Charleston	SC	29401	843-577-4000		428
Young Corp 3231 Utah Ave S *TF:* 800-321-9090 ■ *Web:* www.youngcorp.com	Seattle	WA	98134	206-624-1071	682-6881	190
Young County 516 Fourth St Rm 104 *Web:* co.young.tx.us	Graham	TX	76450	940-549-8432	521-0305	338
Young David (Rep R - IA) 240 Cannon HOB *Web:* davidyoung.house.gov	Washington	DC	20515	202-225-5476		342-2
Young Democrats of America (YDA) PO Box 77496 *Web:* www.yda.org	Washington	DC	20013	202-639-8585		48-7
Young Dental Manufacturing LLC 13705 Shoreline Ct E *TF:* 800-325-1881 ■ *Web:* www.youngdental.com	Earth City	MO	63045	314-344-0010		228
Young Don (Rep R - AK) 2314 Rayburn Bldg *Web:* donyoung.house.gov	Washington	DC	20515	202-225-5765	225-0425	342-2
Young Drivers of Canada Inc 1 James St S Ste 300 *Web:* www.yd.com	Hamilton	ON	L8P4R5	905-529-5501		138
Young Electric Sign Co 2401 Foothill Dr *TF:* 866-779-8357 ■ *Web:* www.yesco.com	Salt Lake City	UT	84109	801-464-4600	483-0998	701
Young Fashions Inc 10300 Perkins Rd *TF:* 800-824-4154 ■ *Web:* www.youngfashions.com	Baton Rouge	LA	70810	225-766-1010		594
Young Harris College PO Box 116 **Fax:* Admissions ■ *TF:* 800-241-3754 ■ *Web:* www.yhc.edu	Young Harris	GA	30582	706-379-3111	379-3108*	162
Young Industries Inc 16 Painter St *TF:* 800-546-3165 ■ *Web:* www.younginds.com	Muncy	PA	17756	570-546-3165	546-1888	207
Young Israel of New Rochelle 1149 N Ave *TF:* 888-942-3638 ■ *Web:* www.youngisrael.org	New Rochelle	NY	10804	914-636-2215		48-20
Young Life 420 N Cascade Ave *Web:* www.younglife.org	Colorado Springs	CO	80903	719-381-1800		48-20
Young Living Essential Oils 3125 Executive Pkwy *TF:* 866-203-5666 ■ *Web:* www.youngliving.com	Lehi	UT	84043	801-418-8900	418-8800	799
Young Manufacturing Inc 2331 N 42nd St *TF:* 800-451-9884 ■ *Web:* www.youngmfg.com	Grand Forks	ND	58203	701-772-5541		483
Young Mfg Company Inc 521 S Main St PO Box 167 *TF:* 800-545-6595 ■ *Web:* youngmanufacturing.com	Beaver Dam	KY	42320	270-274-3306	274-9522	499
Young Plumbing & Heating Co 750 S Hackett Rd *Web:* www.youngphc.com	Waterloo	IA	50701	319-234-4411	234-4540	189-10
Young Presidents' Organization (YPO) 600 E Las Colinas Blvd Ste 1100 *TF:* 800-773-7976 ■ *Web:* www.ypo.org	Irving	TX	75039	972-587-1500	587-1611	49-12
Young Rembrandts 23 N Union St *Web:* www.youngrembrandts.com	Elgin	IL	60123	847-742-6966	742-7197	310
Young Startup Ventures Inc 258 Crafton Ave *Web:* www.youngstartup.com	Staten Island	NY	10314	718-477-2208		463
Young State Park 02280 Boyne City Rd *Web:* www.michigandnr.com	Boyne City	MI	49712	231-582-7523		565
Young Todd (Sen R - IN) 400 Russell Senate Office Bldg *Web:* www.young.senate.gov	Washington	DC	20510	202-224-5623		342-2
Young Touchstone Co 200 Smith Ln *Web:* www.youngtouchstone.com	Jackson	TN	38301	731-424-5045		650
Young Transportation & Tours 843 Riverside Dr *TF:* 800-622-5444 ■ *Web:* www.youngtransportation.com	Asheville	NC	28804	828-258-0084	252-3342	107
Young Welding Supply Inc 101 E First St PO Box 700 *Web:* www.youngwelding.com	Sheffield	AL	35660	256-383-5429	383-1385	386
Young Windows Inc 680 Colwell Ln *Web:* www.youngwindows.com	Conshohocken	PA	19428	610-828-5422	828-2144	234
Young's Cafe 3307 S College Rd *Web:* www.youngscafe.com	Fort Collins	CO	80525	970-223-8000		671
Young's Commercial Transfer 2075 W Scranton Ave PO Box 871 *TF:* 800-289-1639 ■ *Web:* www.yctinc.com	Porterville	CA	93257	559-784-6651	784-5280	780
Young's Environmental Cleanup Inc G-5305 N Dort Hwy *Web:* www.youngsenvironmental.com	Flint	MI	48505	810-789-7155		667
Young's Market Company LLC 500 S Central Ave **Fax:* Hum Res ■ *TF:* 800-627-2777 ■ *Web:* www.youngsmarket.com	Los Angeles	CA	90013	213-612-1248	612-1238*	81-3
Young's Plant Farm 863 Airport Rd *TF:* 800-304-8609 ■ *Web:* www.youngsplantfarm.com	Auburn	AL	36830	800-304-8609		369
Younger Optics 2925 California St *TF:* 800-366-5367 ■ *Web:* www.youngeroptics.com	Torrance	CA	90503	310-783-1533	783-6477	542
Youngsoft Inc 49197 Wixom Tech Dr *TF:* 888-470-4553 ■ *Web:* www.youngsoft.com	Wixom	MI	48393	248-675-1200	675-1201	177
Youngstown City Hall 26 S Phelps St *Web:* youngstownmuniclerk.com	Youngstown	OH	44503	330-742-8859		337
Youngstown Crab Co 3917 Belmont Ave	Youngstown	OH	44505	330-759-5480		671
Youngstown Pipe & Supply Co 4100 Lakepark Rd *Web:* www.yopipe.com	Youngstown	OH	44512	330-783-2700		595

Phone | Fax | Class

Youngstown Playhouse
600 Playhouse Ln....Youngstown OH 44511 330-788-8739 572
Web: www.theyoungstownplayhouse.com

Youngstown State University
1 University Plaza....Youngstown OH 44555 330-941-3000 166
TF Admissions: 877-468-6978 ■ *Web:* www.ysu.edu

Youngstown State University Maag Library
1 University Plaza....Youngstown OH 44555 330-941-3000 941-3734 434-6
Web: www.maag.ysu.edu

Youngstown Symphony Orchestra
260 Federal Plaza W....Youngstown OH 44503 330-744-4269 573-3
Web: www.youngstownsymphony.com

Youngstown Warren Regional Chamber
11 Central Sq Ste 1600....Youngstown OH 44503 330-744-2131 746-0330 139
Web: www.regionalchamber.com

Youngstown-Warren Regional Airport
1453 Youngstown-Kingsville Rd NE....Vienna OH 44473 330-856-1537 609-5371 27
TF: 800-444-1440 ■ *Web:* www.yngwrnair.com

Youngwoo & Assoc LLC
435 Hudson St 4th Fl....New York NY 10014 212-477-8008 652
Web: www.iyoungwoo.com

Yount Hyde & Barbour PC
50 S Cameron St....Winchester VA 22601 540-662-3417 2
Web: www.yhbcpa.com

Your Big Backyard Magazine
11100 Wildlife Ctr Dr....Reston VA 20190 800-822-9919 457-6
TF: 800-822-9919 ■ *Web:* www.nwf.org/yourbigbackyard

Your Church Magazine
465 Gundersen Dr....Carol Stream IL 60188 630-260-6200 260-0114 457-5
TF: 877-247-4787 ■ *Web:* www.christianitytoday.com

Your Electronic Warehouse
2828 Broadway St....Quincy IL 62301 217-224-6171 459
Web: 4electronicwarehouse.com

Your Father's Moustache
5686 Spring Garden Rd....Halifax NS B3J1H5 902-423-6766 671
Web: www.yourfathersmoustache.ca

Your HR Group Inc
12871 Research Blvd Ste 200....Austin TX 78750 512-410-7785 260
Web: austinhr.com

Your Linen Service Inc
875 E Bank St....Petersburg VA 23804 804-732-3315 861-4113 393
Web: yourlinenservice.com

Your Network of Praise PO Box 2426....Havre MT 59501 406-949-4308 645
Web: www.ynop.org

Your Selling Team
100 Spectrum Ctr Dr Ste 700....Irvine CA 92618 888-387-8002 737
TF: 888-387-8002 ■ *Web:* www.yoursellingteam.com

Your Source Private Equity
707 E Northern Ave....Phoenix AZ 85020 602-343-1700 401
TF: 800-432-7447 ■ *Web:* www.ysfi.com

Your Travel Agent Corporate
321 N Pine St....Spartanburg SC 29302 864-583-5054 772
Web: www.ytavacations.com

YourAmigo Inc 4708 Del Valle Pkwy....Pleasanton CA 94566 510-813-1355 196
TF: 800-816-7054 ■ *Web:* www.youramigo.com

YourAreaCode LLC
6242 28th St Ste B....Grand Rapids MI 49546 616-622-2000 366
TF: 888-244-7751 ■ *Web:* www.yourareacode.com

yourDealer 420 E 55th St Ste 8H....New York NY 10022 866-847-7502 195
TF: 866-847-7502

Yourga Trucking Inc 100 Shenango St....Wheatland PA 16161 724-981-3600 780
TF: 800-245-1722 ■ *Web:* www.yourga.com

Yoush Consulting Inc
7481 Woodbine Ave Ste 204....Markham ON L3R2W1 905-307-6263 196
Web: www.yoush.com

Youth Advocate Programs Inc
2007 N Third St PO Box 950....Harrisburg PA 17102 717-232-7580 428
Web: www.yapinc.org

Youth Consultation Service (Inc)
284 Broadway....Newark NJ 07104 973-482-8411 317
Web: www.ycs.org

Youth Development Center
1745 Frew Mill Rd....New Castle PA 16101 724-656-7300 412

Youth Diagnostic Development Ctr
4000 Edith NE....Albuquerque NM 87107 505-841-2400 412

Youth for Christ/USA
7670 S Vaughn Ct....Englewood CO 80112 303-843-9000 48-20
Web: yfc.givingfuel.com/30913

Youth For Understanding USA
6400 Goldsboro Rd Ste 100....Bethesda MD 20817 240-235-2100 235-2104 48-11
TF: 800-424-3691 ■ *Web:* www.yfuusa.org

Youth Frontiers Inc
6009 Excelsior Blvd....Minneapolis MN 55416 952-922-0222 196
TF: 888-992-0222 ■ *Web:* www.youthfrontiers.org

Youth Home Inc
20400 Colonel Glenn Rd....Little Rock AR 72210 501-821-5500 726
TF: 800-728-6452 ■ *Web:* www.youthhome.org

Youth Opportunities Unlimited
422 E S St Ste A....Kalamazoo MI 49007 269-349-9676 623
Web: kresa.org

Youth Science Institute
296 Garden Hill Dr....Los Gatos CA 95032 408-356-4945 521
TF: 800-523-2782 ■ *Web:* www.ysi-ca.org

Youth Villages Inner Harbour
4685 Dorsett Shoals Rd....Douglasville GA 30135 770-852-6333 374-1
TF: 800-255-8657 ■ *Web:* www.youthvillages.org

Youthbuild International
58 Day St Ste 300....Somerville MA 02144 617-623-9900 463
Web: www.youthbuild.org

YouVisit LLC
20533 Biscayne Blvd Ste 1322....Aventura FL 33180 866-585-7158 387
TF: 866-585-7158 ■ *Web:* www.youvisit.com

Yovia LLC
2593 Mayport Rd Ste 101....Atlantic Beach FL 32233 904-242-2669 5
Web: yovia.com

YOY Sushi Bar 1283 Rue Beaubien E....Montreal QC H2S1V1 514-844-9884 671

YP LLC 611 N Brand Blvd Ste 500....Glendale CA 91203 866-570-8863 5
TF: 866-570-8863 ■ *Web:* corporate.yp.com

YPO (Young Presidents' Organization)
600 E Las Colinas Blvd Ste 1100....Irving TX 75039 972-587-1500 587-1611 49-12
TF: 800-773-7976 ■ *Web:* www.ypo.org

Ypsilanti Area Convention & Visitors Bureau
106 W Michigan Ave....Ypsilanti MI 48197 734-483-4444 206
Web: www.ypsilanti.org

Ypsilanti Historical Museum
220 N Huron St....Ypsilanti MI 48197 734-482-4990 520
Web: www.ypsilantihistoricalsociety.org

YPSILANTI Michigan Community Utilities Authority
2777 State Rd....Ypsilanti MI 48198 734-484-4600 192
TF: 800-426-4791 ■ *Web:* www.ycua.org

YRC Worldwide Inc 10990 Roe Ave....Overland Park KS 66211 913-696-6100 360-3
NASDAQ: YRCW ■ *TF:* 800-846-4300 ■ *Web:* www.yrc.com

YRH (Yarmouth Regional Hospital)
60 Vancouver St....Yarmouth NS B5A2P5 902-742-3541 742-0369* 374-2
*Fax: Admitting ■ *TF:* 800-460-2110 ■ *Web:* www.swndha.nshealth.ca/pages/yrh.htm

Yrrid Software Inc 507 Monroe St....Chapel Hill NC 27516 919-968-7858 968-7856 178-12
Web: www.yrrid.com

YSI Inc 1700-1725 Brannum Ln....Yellow Springs OH 45387 937-767-7241 767-9353 201
TF Cust Svc: 800-765-4974 ■ *Web:* www.ysi.com

Ysleta Mission 131 S Zaragosa Rd....El Paso TX 79907 915-859-9848 50-1
Web: www.ysletamission.org

Y-Tex Corp 1825 Big Horn Ave....Cody WY 82414 307-587-5515 527-6433 280
TF: 800-443-6401 ■ *Web:* www.y-tex.com

Yturri Rose LLP 89 SW Third Ave....Ontario OR 97914 541-889-5368 428
Web: www.yturrirose.com

Yuasa Battery Inc 2901 Montrose Ave....Reading PA 19605 610-929-5781 74
Web: www.yuasabatteries.com

Yub Inc 321 Castro St Ste 1....Mountain View CA 94041 650-265-7316 393
Web: yub.com

Yuba City Water Treatment Plant
701 Northgate Dr....Yuba City CA 95991 530-822-4636 539
Web: www.yubacity.net

Yuba County 915 Eigth St Ste 107....Marysville CA 95901 530-749-7575 749-7312 338
Web: www.co.yuba.ca.us

Yuba County Library 303 Second St....Marysville CA 95901 530-749-7380 741-3098 434-3
TF: 800-984-4636 ■ *Web:* www.co.yuba.ca.us

Yuba County Water Agency 1220 F St....Marysville CA 95901 530-741-6278 741-6541 245
Web: www.ycwa.com

Yuba State Park 12225 S Yuba Dam Rd....Levan UT 84639 435-758-2611 565
Web: www.stateparks.utah.gov

Yuca 501 Lincoln Rd....Miami Beach FL 33139 305-532-9822 671
Web: www.yuca.com

Yucaipa Valley Chamber of Commerce
35139 Yucaipa Blvd....Yucaipa CA 92399 909-790-1841 139
Web: yucaipachamber.org

Yucaipa Valley Water District
PO Box 730....Yucaipa CA 92399 909-797-5117 797-6381 787
TF: 800-304-2226 ■ *Web:* www.yvwd.dst.ca.us

Yucca House National Monument
c/o Mesa Verde National Pk PO Box 8....Mesa Verde CO 81330 970-529-4465 529-4637 564
Web: www.nps.gov/yuho

Yucca Tele Communications Is The Subsidiary
201 W Second St....Portales NM 88130 575-226-2255 246
TF: 866-239-6858 ■ *Web:* www.yucca.net

Yucca Valley Chamber of Commerce
56711 29 Palms Hwy....Yucca Valley CA 92284 760-365-6323 365-0763 139
TF: 855-365-6558 ■ *Web:* www.yuccavalley.org

Yukevich | Cavanaugh
355 S Grand Ave 15th Fl....Los Angeles CA 90071 213-362-7777 428
Web: www.yukelaw.com

Yukon Chamber of Commerce 510 Elm St....Yukon OK 73099 405-354-3567 139
Web: www.yukoncc.com

Yukon-Charley Rivers National Preserve
4175 Geist Rd....Fairbanks AK 99709 907-457-5752 455-0601 564
Web: www.nps.gov/yuch

Yukon-Kuskokwim Correctional Ctr
1000 Eddie Hoffman Hwy....Bethel AK 99559 907-543-5245 543-3097 213
Web: www.correct.state.ak.us

Yule Tree Farms LLC 8804 S Heinz Rd....Canby OR 97013 503-651-2114 970-8733* 752
*Fax Area Code: 888 ■ *TF:* 888-970-8733

Yum! Brands Inc 1441 Gardiner Ln....Louisville KY 40213 502-874-8300 670
NYSE: YUM ■ *TF:* 800-225-5532 ■ *Web:* www.yum.com

Yuma Civic Ctr 1440 W Desert Hills Dr....Yuma AZ 85365 928-373-5040 344-9121 205
TF: 866-966-0220 ■ *Web:* www.yumaaz.gov

Yuma Convention & Visitors Bureau
201 N Fourth Ave....Yuma AZ 85364 928-783-0071 783-1897 206
TF: 800-293-0071 ■ *Web:* www.visityuma.com

Yuma County 310 Ash St Ste F....Wray CO 80758 970-332-5809 338
TF: 800-772-1213 ■ *Web:* www.yumacounty.net

Yuma County 198 S Main St....Yuma AZ 85364 928-373-1010 373-1120 338
TF: 800-253-0883 ■ *Web:* www.yumacountyaz.gov

Yuma County Chamber of Commerce
180 W First St Ste A....Yuma AZ 85364 928-782-2567 343-0038 139
TF: 877-782-0438 ■ *Web:* www.yumachamber.org

Yuma County Fair 2520 E 32nd St....Yuma AZ 85365 928-726-4420 344-3480 642
Web: www.yumafair.com

Yuma Daily Sun 2055 Arizona Ave....Yuma AZ 85364 928-783-3333 532-2
Web: www.yumasun.com

Yuma Regional Medical Ctr 2400 S Ave A....Yuma AZ 85364 928-344-2000 374-3
Web: www.yumaregional.org

Yuma Territorial Prison State Historic Park
200 N Prison Hill Rd....Yuma AZ 85364 928-783-4771 565

YuMe Inc 1204 Middlefield Rd....Redwood City CA 94063 650-591-9400 7
TF: 800-831-9146 ■ *Web:* www.yume.com

Yun Industrial Company Ltd
161 Selandia Ln....Carson CA 90746 310-715-1898 625
Web: www.yic-assm.com

Yunique Solutions Inc
552 Seventh Ave....New York NY 10018 212-672-0098 411

Yunker Farm Children's Museum
1201 28th Ave N....Fargo ND 58102 701-232-6102 521
Web: www.childrensmuseum-yunker.org

Yurchak Printing Inc
920 Links Ave....Landisville PA 17538 717-399-0209 627
Web: www.yurchak.com

				Phone	Fax	Class
YUSA Corp 151 Jamison Rd SW *Web:* yusa-oh.com	Washington Court House	OH	43160	740-335-0335	335-0330	677
Yusen Logistics (Americas) Inc 300 Lighting Way *Web:* www.yusen-logistics.com/en/americas/united-states	Secaucus	NJ	07094	201-553-3800		311
Yves Delorme Inc 1725 Broadway St. *Web:* www.yvesdelorme.com	Charlottesville	VA	22902	434-979-3911		361
Y-W Electric Assn Inc 250 Main Ave PO Box Y *TF:* 800-660-2291	Akron	CO	80720	970-345-2291		245
YWCA (YWCA USA) 2025 M St NW Ste 550 *TF:* 888-872-9259 ■ *Web:* www.ywca.org	Washington	DC	20036	202-467-0801	467-0802	48-6
YWCA USA (YWCA) 2025 M St NW Ste 550 *TF:* 888-872-9259 ■ *Web:* www.ywca.org	Washington	DC	20036	202-467-0801	467-0802	48-6
Yyz Travel American Express 7851 Dufferin St *Web:* www.yyztravel.com	Thornhill	ON	L4J3M4	905-660-7000		774

Z

				Phone	Fax	Class
Z 107.3 49 Acme Rd *Web:* z1073.com	Brewer	ME	04412	207-989-5631		645
Z Bardhi 3596 Kinhega Dr. *Web:* www.zbardhis.com	Tallahassee	FL	32312	850-894-9919		671
Z Communications Inc 14118 Stowe Dr Ste B. *TF:* 877-808-1226 ■ *Web:* www.zcomm.com	Poway	CA	92064	858-621-2700		253
Z Gallerie Inc 1855 W 139th St *TF:* 800-358-8288 ■ *Web:* www.zgallerie.com	Gardena	CA	90249	310-630-1200	630-1289	362
Z Option Inc 417 Oakbend Dr Ste 200 *Web:* www.zoption.com	Lewisville	TX	75067	972-315-8800		177
Z Salon & Spa Inc 9407 Shelbyville Rd *Web:* www.zsalon.com	Louisville	KY	40222	502-426-2226		77
Z Systems 3724 Oregon Ave S *Web:* www.zsyst.com	Minneapolis	MN	55426	952-974-3140		52
Z Tejas Grill 9400-A Arboreum Blvd *Web:* www.ztejas.com	Austin	TX	78759	512-346-3506		671
Z Three - Printing Co 902 W Main St *Web:* www.threez.com	Teutopolis	IL	62467	217-857-3153		627
Z's Bar & Restaurant 168 Louis Campau *Web:* www.zsbar.com	Grand Rapids	MI	49503	616-454-3141		671
Z'Tejas 20 W Sixth St *Web:* ztejas.com	Tempe	AZ	85281	480-377-1170	377-1167	671
Z3 Technologies Inc 11400 W Bluemond Rd. *Web:* www.z3tech.com	Wauwatosa	WI	53226	414-607-9767		225
Z57 Internet Solutions 10045 Mesa Rim Rd *TF:* 800-899-8148 ■ *Web:* www.z57.com	San Diego	CA	92121	800-899-8148		225
Z92 FM 10714 Mockingbird Dr *TF:* 800-955-9230 ■ *Web:* www.z92.com	Omaha	NE	68127	800-955-9230		645-115
Zabel Freeman 1135 Heights Blvd *Web:* zabelfreeman.com	Houston	TX	77008	713-802-9117		445
Zabin Industries Inc 3957 S Hill St *Web:* www.zabin.com	Los Angeles	CA	90037	213-749-1215		594
Zabriskie Gallery 400 E 57th St 19B *Web:* www.zabriskiegallery.com	New York	NY	10022	212-752-1223	752-1224	42
Zach Halopoff Inc 15422 Assembly Ln *Web:* www.haloindustries.com	Huntington Beach	CA	92649	714-373-3333		454
Zach's Catering 1717 University Ave S.	Fairbanks	AK	99709	907-374-6531		671
Zachary & Elizabeth Fisher House 111 Rockville Pk Ste 420 *Fax Area Code: 513 ■ *TF:* 888-294-8560 ■ *Web:* www.fisherhouse.org/houses	Rockville	MD	20850	888-294-8560	487-6661*	372
Zachary Community School Board 3755 Church St *Web:* zacharyschools.org	Zachary	LA	70791	225-658-4969		685
Zachary Confections Inc 2130 IN-28 *Fax Area Code: 765 ■ *TF Cust Svc:* 800-445-4222 ■ *Web:* www.zacharyconfections.com	Frankfort	IN	46041	800-445-4222	659-1491*	296-8
Zachary Piper Solutions 1410 Spring Hill Rd Ste 300 *TF:* 888-487-8812 ■ *Web:* www.zacharypiper.com	Mclean	VA	22012	703-649-4001		260
Zachary Scott & Co 1200 Fifth Ave Ste 1500 *Web:* www.zacharyscott.com	Seattle	WA	98101	206-224-7380		194
Zachary Scott Theatre Ctr 1510 Toomey Rd. *Web:* www.zachtheatre.org	Austin	TX	78704	512-476-0541	476-0314	572
Zachary Taylor National Cemetery 4701 Brownsboro Rd *Web:* www.cem.va.gov	Louisville	KY	40207	502-893-3852	893-6612	136
Zachry Associates Inc 500 Chestnut St Ste 2000 *TF:* 800-438-7325 ■ *Web:* www.zachryinc.com	Abilene	TX	79602	325-677-1342		7
Zachry Group 527 Logwood Ave *Web:* www.zachrygroup.com	San Antonio	TX	78221	210-588-5000		186
Zachry Holdings Inc 527 Logwood Ave *Web:* www.zachrygroup.com	San Antonio	TX	78221	210-588-5000		188-9
Zachys Wine & Liquor Inc 16 E Pkwy *TF:* 800-723-0241 ■ *Web:* www.zachys.com	Scarsdale	NY	10583	914-723-0241	723-1033	443
Zack Electronics Inc 1070 Hamilton Rd *TF:* 800-466-0449 ■ *Web:* www.zackelectronics.com	Duarte	CA	91010	626-303-0655	303-8694	246
Zacky Farms 13200 Crossroads Pkwy N Ste 250 *Fax Area Code: 559 ■ *TF:* 800-888-0235 ■ *Web:* zackyfarms.com	City of Industry	CA	91746	562-641-2020	443-2778*	297-10
Zadro Products Inc 5422 Argosy Ave. *TF:* 800-468-4348 ■ *Web:* www.zadroinc.com	Huntington Beach	CA	92649	714-892-9200		608
Zafgen Inc 175 Portland St 4th Fl *Web:* www.zafgen.com	Boston	MA	02114	617-622-4003		238
Zagada Markets Inc Caribbean Commercial Bldg 145 Grand Ave *Web:* www.zagada.com	Coral Gables	FL	33133	305-529-9028		466
Zagar Inc 24000 Lakeland Blvd *Web:* www.zagar.com	Cleveland	OH	44132	216-731-0500	731-8591	493
Zagat Survey LLC 76 Ninth Ave 4th Fl. *Web:* www.zagat.com	New York	NY	10011	212-823-9335		637-10
Zager Fuchs PC 268 Broad St *TF:* 800-272-3900 ■ *Web:* zagerfuchs.com	Red Bank	NJ	07701	732-747-3700		428
ZAGG Inc 3855 South 500 West Ste J *TF:* 800-700-9244 ■ *Web:* www.zagg.com	Salt Lake City	UT	84115	801-263-0699		608
Zahava Group Inc 7525 Britannia Park Pl *TF:* 800-772-7017 ■ *Web:* www.zahavagroup.com	San Diego	CA	92154	619-671-0001		360-3
Zaiss & Co 11626 Nicholas St *Web:* www.zaissco.com	Omaha	NE	68154	402-964-9293		636
Zalco Realty Inc 8701 Georgia Ave Ste 300 *Web:* www.gjainc.com	Silver Spring	MD	20910	301-495-6600		652
Zale Corp 6201 15th Ave *NYSE:* ZLC ■ *TF Cust Svc:* 866-249-2593 ■ *Web:* signetjewelers.com	Brooklyn	NY	11219	718-921-8137		410
Zales Jewelers Div 901 W Walnut Hill Ln. *TF Cust Svc:* 800-311-5393 ■ *Web:* www.zales.com	Irving	TX	75038	972-580-4000		410
Zale Lipshy University Hospital 5151 Harry Hines Blvd *Web:* www.utsouthwestern.edu	Dallas	TX	75390	214-645-5555		374-3
Zalicus Inc 245 First St 3rd Fl *NASDAQ: ZLCS*	Cambridge	MA	02142	617-301-7000		582
Zallie Supermarkets 1230 Blackwood-Clementon Rd	Clementon	NJ	08021	856-627-6501		345
ZAMBA Corp 3033 Excelsior Blvd Ste 200 *Web:* www.zambasolutions.com	Minneapolis	MN	55416	952-832-9800		525
Zambezi 248 Westminster Ave *Web:* www.zambezi-la.com	Venice	CA	90291	310-450-6800		5
Zambia 237 E 52nd St *Web:* www.un.int	New York	NY	10022	212-888-5770	888-5213	784
Zambia Embassy 2419 Massachusetts Ave NW *Web:* www.zambiaembassy.org	Washington	DC	20008	202-265-9717	332-0826	257
Zamboo LLC 4079A Redwood Ave *Web:* zamboo.com	Los Angeles	CA	90066	310-822-4643		344
Zambra! 85 W Walnut St *Web:* www.zambratapas.com	Asheville	NC	28801	828-232-1060		671
Zamias Services Inc 300 Market St Ste 287 *Web:* www.zamias.com	Johnstown	PA	15904	814-535-3563	536-5969	655
Zamma Corp 14468 Litchfield Dr *Web:* www.zamma.com	Orange	VA	22960	540-672-5200		499
Zamorano 9300 Lee Hwy Ste G130 *Web:* www.zamorano.edu	Fairfax	VA	22031	202-737-5580		166
Zampell Cos 9 Stanley Tucker Dr *TF:* 877-926-7355 ■ *Web:* www.zampell.com	Newburyport	MA	01950	978-465-0055		610
Zamzows Inc 1201 N Franklin Blvd *Web:* www.zamzows.com	Nampa	ID	83687	208-465-3630		323
Zane Casket Co 1201 Hall Ave	Zanesville	OH	43701	740-452-4680		134
Zane State College 1555 Newark Rd *TF:* 800-686-8324 ■ *Web:* www.zanestate.edu	Zanesville	OH	43701	740-454-2501	454-0035	800
Zaner Group LLC 150 S Wacker Dr Ste 2350 *TF:* 800-621-1414 ■ *Web:* www.zaner.com	Chicago	IL	60606	312-277-0050	277-0150	169
Zaner-Bloser Inc 1201 Dublin Rd *TF:* 800-421-3018 ■ *Web:* www.zaner-bloser.com	Columbus	OH	43215	614-486-0221		637-2
Zanesville City School Board 160 N Fourth St *TF:* 866-280-7377 ■ *Web:* www.zanesville.k12.oh.us	Zanesville	OH	43701	740-454-9751		685
Zanesville Times Recorder 3871 Gorsky Dr Unit G1 *TF:* 877-424-0214 ■ *Web:* www.zanesvilletimesrecorder.com	Zanesville	OH	43701	740-452-4561		532-2
Zanesville-Muskingum County Chamber of Commerce 205 N Fifth St *TF:* 800-743-2303 ■ *Web:* www.zmchamber.com	Zanesville	OH	43701	740-455-8282	454-2963	139
Zanett Inc 635 Madison Ave 15th Fl *OTC: ZANE*	New York	NY	10022	212-583-0300	583-0221	792
Zapata County 200 E Seventh St Ste 115 *Web:* www.co.zapata.tx.us	Zapata	TX	78076	956-765-9920	765-9926	338
Zapata Inc 6302 Fairview Rd Ste 600 *Web:* zapatainc.com	Charlotte	NC	28210	704-358-8240		261
Zapata Technology Inc 1450 Greene St Ste 500 *TF:* 800-553-2447 ■ *Web:* www.zapatatechnology.com	Augusta	GA	30901	706-955-4809		225
Zaphyr Technologies 628 State Rt 10 Ste 14 *TF:* 800-845-2200 ■ *Web:* www.zaphyr.net	Whippany	NJ	07981	973-560-9050		180
Zappos.com 400 E Stewart Ave *TF:* 800-927-7671 ■ *Web:* www.zappos.com	Las Vegas	NV	89101	800-927-7671		459
ZAPS Technologies Inc 4314 SW Research Way *TF:* 866-390-9387 ■ *Web:* www.zapstechnologies.com	Corvallis	OR	97333	541-207-1122		419
ZapTel Corp 1440 Hicks Rd *Web:* www.zaptel.com	Rolling Meadows	IL	60008	847-342-2000		224
ZapThink LLC 108 Woodlawn Rd Ste 2A *Web:* www.zapthink.com	Baltimore	VA	21210	781-207-0203		196
Zapwater Communications Inc 118 N Peoria 4th Fl. *Web:* zapwater.com	Chicago	IL	60607	312-943-0333		636
Zara Realty Holding Corp 166-07 Hillside Ave *Web:* www.zararealty.com	Jamaica	NY	11432	718-291-3331		652

Phone | Fax | Class

Zaremba Group 14600 Detroit Ave. — Cleveland OH 44107 — 216-221-6600 — 221-9742 — 653
Web: www.zarembagroup.com

Zargon Oil & Gas Ltd
333 - Fifth Ave SW Ste 700 — Calgary AB T2P3B6 — 403-264-9992 — 536
TF: 800-564-6253 ■ *Web:* www.zargon.ca

Zarinkelk Engineering Services Inc
3033 Chimney Rock Rd — Houston TX 77056 — 832-242-2426 — 196
Web: www.zarinkelk.com

Zaroka 148 York St — New Haven CT 06511 — 203-776-8644 — 776-0051 — 671
Web: www.zaroka.com

Zarzaur & Schwartz PC
2209 Morris Ave PO Box 11366 — Birmingham AL 35203 — 205-250-8437 — 328-1958 — 41
Web: zsattorneys.stratuspayments.net

Zasio Enterprises Inc
401 W Front St Ste 305 — Boise ID 83702 — 800-513-1000 — 177
TF: 800-513-1000 ■ *Web:* www.zasio.com

Zatkoff Seals & Packings
23230 Industrial Pk Dr — Farmington Hills MI 48335 — 248-478-2400 — 478-3392 — 385
TF: 800-832-2522 ■ *Web:* www.zatkoff.com

Zausner Foods Corp
400 S Custer Ave — New Holland PA 17557 — 717-355-8505 — 297-8

Zavala County
200 E Uvalde St County Courthouse — Crystal City TX 78839 — 830-374-2331 — 374-5955 — 338
Web: www.co.zavala.tx.us

Zaytinya 701 Ninth St NW — Washington DC 20001 — 202-638-0800 — 671
Web: www.zaytinya.com

Zazoom LLC 55 Broadway Ste 801 — Scottsdale AZ 10006 — 212-321-2100 — 4
Web: www.zazoomvideo.com

Zazula Process Equipment Ltd
4609 Manitoba Rd SE — Calgary AB T2G4B9 — 403-244-0751 — 245-5808 — 104
Web: www.zazula.com

ZBA Inc 94 Old Camplain Rd — Hillsborough NJ 08844 — 908-359-2070 — 595-0909 — 173-7
TF: 800-750-4239 ■ *Web:* www.zbaus.com

Zbeta Consulting Inc
851 Irwin St Ste 305 — San Rafael CA 94901 — 415-259-0422 — 196
Web: www.zbetaconsulting.com

ZBT (Zeta Beta Tau Fraternity Inc)
3905 Vincennes Rd Ste 100 — Indianapolis IN 46268 — 317-334-1898 — 334-1899 — 48-16
Web: www.zbt.org

Zco Corp 58 Technology Way Ste 2W10 — Nashua NH 03060 — 603-881-9200 — 881-8877 — 809
Web: www.zco.com

ZC&R Coatings for Optics Inc
1401 Abalone Ave — Torrance CA 90501 — 310-381-3060 — 550
Web: abrisatechnologies.com/redirect

Zdi Gaming Inc 2124 196th St SW — Lynnwood WA 98036 — 425-775-7991 — 452
Web: www.zdigaming.com

ZE PowerGroup Inc
130 - 5920 No Two Rd — Richmond BC V7C4R9 — 604-244-1469 — 193
TF: 866-944-1469 ■ *Web:* www.zc.com

ZeaVision LLC
716-I Crown Industrial Ct — Chesterfield MO 63005 — 314-628-1000 — 345
TF: 800-833-2800 ■ *Web:* www.cyepromise.com/zeavision

Zebra 4521 Sharon Rd. — Charlotte NC 28211 — 325-942-5692 — 671
Web: www.zebrarestaurant.net

Zebra Books
Konsington Publishing Corp
119 W 40th St — New York NY 10018 — 212-407-1500 — 637-2
TF: 800-221-2647 ■ *Web:* www.kensingtonbooks.com

Zebra Capital Management LLC
612 Wheelers Farm Rd — Milford CT 06461 — 203-878-3223 — 401
Web: www.zebracapm.com

Zebra Graphics Inc 1611 Kentucky Ave — Paducah KY 42003 — 270-443-4771 — 627
Web: www.zebragraphics.com

Zebra Marketing
7125 Laurel Canyon Blvd Ste B — North Hollywood CA 91605 — 818-765-6442 — 9
Web: www.zebramerchandise.blogspot.in

Zebra Print Solutions Inc
9401 Globe Ctr Dr Ste 130 — Morrisville NC 27560 — 919-314-3700 — 627
TF: 800-545-8835 ■ *Web:* www.zebraprintsolutions.com

Zebra Technologies Corp
475 Half Day Rd Ste 500 — Lincolnshire IL 60069 — 847-634-6700 — 913-8766 — 173-6
NASDAQ: ZBRA ■ *TF:* 800-423-0422 ■ *Web:* www.zebra.com

Zebulon Pike Youth Services Ctr
1427 W Rio Grande — Colorado Springs CO 80906 — 303-534-3468 — 412
TF: 800-970-3468 ■ *Web:* www.colorado.gov

Zecotek Photonics Inc
21331 Gordon Way Unit 1120 — Richmond BC V6W1J9 — 604-233-0056 — 250
Web: www.zecotek.com

Zed Ink Inc 228 Main St Ste 17 — Venice CA 90291 — 310-460-2424 — 720
TF: 800-499-9982 ■ *Web:* zedink.com

Zeda Soft 2310 Gravel Dr — Fort Worth TX 76118 — 817-616-1000 — 177
TF: 800-354-8588 ■ *Web:* www.zedasoft.com

Zedi 902 11th Ave SW — Calgary AB T2R0E7 — 403 444 1100 — 539
Web: www.zedi.ca

Zedo Inc
850 Montgomery St Ste 150 — San Francisco CA 94133 — 415-348-1975 — 225
Web: zedo.com

zedSuite 210 Water St Ste 400 — St. John's NL A1C1A9 — 709-722-7213 — 196
TF: 877-722-1177 ■ *Web:* www.zedsuite.com

Zedx Inc 369 Rolling Ridge Dr — Bellefonte PA 16823 — 814-357-8490 — 225
Web: www.zedxinc.com

Zee Medical Inc 22 Corporate Pk — Irvine CA 92606 — 800-435-7763 — 475
TF: 800-435-7763 ■ *Web:* www.zeemedical.com

Zee Systems Inc 406 W Rhapsody Dr — San Antonio TX 78216 — 210-342-9761 — 341-2609 — 22
Web: www.zeeco-zeesys.com

Zeeco Inc 22151 E 91st St S — Broken Arrow OK 74014 — 918-258-8551 — 251-5519 — 357
Web: www.zeeco.com

Zeeland Lumber & Supply Co
146 E Washington — Zeeland MI 49464 — 616-772-2119 — 191-3
TF: 888-772-2119 ■ *Web:* www.zeelandlumber.com

Zeeland Public Schools (ZPS)
183 W Roosevelt Ave — Zeeland MI 49464 — 616-748-3000 — 186
Web: www.zps.org

ZeeWise 4920 Roswell Rd Ste 458 — Atlanta GA 30342 — 678-252-6840 — 180
Web: www.zeewise.com

Zeffirino Ristorante
3377 Las Vegas Blvd S — Las Vegas NV 89109 — 702-414-3500 — 671
Web: www.zeffirinolasvegas.com

ZEFR Inc 1621 Abbot Kinney Blvd — Venice CA 90291 — 310-392-3555 — 387
Web: zefr.com

Zehnder America Inc
6 Merrill Industrial Dr Ste 7 — Hampton NH 03842 — 603-601-8544 — 610
TF: 888-778-6701 ■ *Web:* www.zehnderamerica.com

Zeiders Enterprises Inc
2750 Killarney Dr Ste 100 — Woodbridge VA 22192 — 703-496-9000 — 580-6339 — 194
Web: www.zeiders.com

Zeigler Beverage Co 1513 N Broad St — Lansdale PA 19446 — 215-855-5161 — 296-20
TF Sales: 800-854-6123 ■ *Web:* www.zeiglers.com

Zeigler Bros Inc 400 GaRdner Stn Rd — Gardners PA 17324 — 717-677-6181 — 677-6826 — 447
TF: 800-841-6800 ■ *Web:* www.zeiglerfeed.com

Zeigler Chevrolet Inc
13153 Dunnings Hwy — Claysburg PA 16625 — 877-364-4817 — 57
TF: 877-364-4817 ■ *Web:* zeiglerchevy.com

Zeiser Wilbert Vault Inc 750 Howard St — Elmira NY 14904 — 607-733-0568 — 191-1
TF: 800-472-4335 ■ *Web:* zeiserwilbertvault.com

Zeisler & Zeisler P C
558 Clinton Ave — Bridgeport CT 06604 — 203-368-4234 — 445
Web: www.zeislaw.com

Zeisler, Zeisler, Rawson & Johnson LLP
901 A St Ste C — San Rafael CA 94901 — 415-451-1703 — 2
Web: zzrjllp.com

Zeitbyte LLC 261 W 35th St Ste 304 — New York NY 10001 — 212-989-4808 — 514
Web: www.zeitbyte.com

Zeks Compressed Air Solutions
1302 Goshen Pkwy — West Chester PA 19380 — 610-692-9100 — 692-9192 — 172
TF: 800-888-2323 ■ *Web:* www.zeks.com

Zel Technologies LLC
54 Old Hampton Ln — Hampton VA 23669 — 757-722-5565 — 180
Web: zeltech.com

ZELDA'S 528 Lower Thames St — Newport RI 02840 — 401-849-4002 — 671
Web: www.cafezelda.com

Zeldes Needle and Cooper
1000 Lafayette Blvd PO Box 1740 — Bridgeport CT 06604 — 203-333-9441 — 445
Web: www.znclaw.com

Zeldin Lee (Rep R - NY)
1517 Longworth HOB — Washington DC 20515 — 202-225-3826 — 225-3143 — 342-2
Web: zeldin.house.gov

Zellner Construction Services LLC
2926 Ridgeway Rd — Memphis TN 38115 — 901-794-1100 — 794-9141 — 188
Web: www.zellnerconstruction.com

Zelo 831 Nicollet Mall — Minneapolis MN 55402 — 612-333-7000 — 671
Web: zelomn.com

Zelo Productions Inc 3 S Newton St — Denver CO 80219 — 303-936-8995 — 513
Web: www.zeloproductions.com

Zeltiq Aesthetics Inc
4698 Willow Rd Ste 100 — Pleasanton CA 94588 — 925-474-2500 — 250
Web: www.zeltiq.com

Zely & Ritz 301 Glenwood Ave — Raleigh NC 27603 — 919-828-0018 — 671
Web: www.zelyandritz.com

Zemoga Inc 120 Old Ridgefield Rd — Wilton CT 06897 — 203-003-0214 — 000
Web: www.zemoga.com

Zen Design Group Ltd
2850 Coolidge Hwy — Berkley MI 48072 — 248-398-5209 — 344
Web: www.zendesigngroup.com

Zen Ventures LLC
3939 S Sixth St Ste 201 — Klamath Falls OR 97603 — 888-936-2278 — 809
TF: 888-936-2278 ■ *Web:* www.zen-cart.com

Zenar Corp
7301 S Sixth St PO Box 107 — Oak Creek WI 53154 — 414-764-1800 — 764-1267 — 470
Web: www.zenarcrane.com

Zencos Consulting LLC
1400 Crescent Green Ste 140 — Cary NC 27518 — 919-459-4600 — 196
Web: www.zencos.com

Zenfolio Inc 3515-A Edison Way — Menlo Park CA 94025 — 650-412-1888 — 387
Web: www.zenfolio.com

Zenger Folkman Co
1550 N Technology Way Bldg D — Orem UT 84097 — 801-705-9375 — 765
TF: 800-243-4246 ■ *Web:* zengerfolkman.com

Zengo 1610 Little Raven St — Denver CO 80202 — 720-904-0965 — 671
Web: www.richardsandoval.com

Zenith Cutter Co 5200 Zenith Pkwy — Loves Park IL 61111 — 815-282-5200 — 282-5232 — 493
TF: 800-223-5202 ■ *Web:* zenithcutter.com

Zenith Electronics Corp
2000 Millbrook Dr — Lincolnshire IL 60069 — 847-941-8000 — 52
TF: 800-243-0000 ■ *Web:* www.zenith.com

Zenith Freight Lines LLC
210 Dehart Motor Terminal Rd SW — Conover NC 28613 — 828-465-7036 — 314
Web: www.zenithcompanies.com

Zenith Fuel Systems Inc
14570 Industrial Pk Rd — Bristol VA 24202 — 276-669-5555 — 645-8696 — 128
Web: www.zenithfuelsystems.com

Zenith Information Systems Inc
18757 Burbank Blvd — Tarzana CA 91356 — 310-826-8634 — 177
Web: www.zis.com

Zenith Insurance Co PO Box 9055 — Van Nuys CA 91409 — 818-713-1000 — 280-4701* — 391-4
**Fax Area Code:* 877 ■ *TF:* 800-440-5020 ■ *Web:* www.thezenith.com

Zenith Products Corp 400 Lukens Dr — New Castle DE 19720 — 800-892-3986 — 319-2
TF: 800-892-3986 ■ *Web:* zenith-products.com

Zenith Specialty Bag Company Inc
17625 E Railroad St PO Box 8445 — City of Industry CA 91748 — 626-912-2481 — 284-8493* — 65
**Fax Area Code:* 800 ■ *TF:* 800-962-2247 ■ *Web:* zbags.com

Zenmonics Inc
125 Floyd Smith Office Park Dr Ste 220 — Charlotte NC 28262 — 704-971-7315 — 180
Web: www.zenmonics.com

Zeno Group 140 Broadway 39th Fl — New York NY 10016 — 212-299-8888 — 636
Web: www.zenogroup.com

Zenon Dance Company & School
528 Hennepin Ave — Minneapolis MN 55403 — 612-338-1101 — 573-1
Web: www.zenondance.org

Zenoss Inc
11305 Four Points Dr Bldg 1 Ste 300 — Austin TX 78726 — 888-936-6770 — 177
TF: 888-936-6770 ■ *Web:* www.zenoss.com

Zentech Manufacturing Inc
6980 Tudsbury Rd — Baltimore MD 21244 — 443-348-4500 — 253
TF: 800-871-7838 ■ *Web:* www.zentech.com/index.php

Company	City	State	ZIP	Phone	Fax	Class
Zentech Technical Services Inc 14800 Saint Marys Ln Ste 270 *Web:* www.zentech-usa.com	Houston	TX	77079	281-558-0290		177
Zenya Yoga & Message Studio 101 Herman Melville Ave *TF:* 800-838-8853 ■ *Web:* www.zenyayoga.com	Newport News	VA	23606	757-643-6900		148
ZEP Inc 1310 Seaboard Industrial Blvd NW *NYSE: ZEP* ■ *TF:* 877-428-9937 ■ *Web:* www.zepinc.com	Atlanta	GA	30318	404-352-1680		151
Zephyr Aluminum LLC 625 Second St PO Box 4906 *Web:* www.zephyraluminum.com	Lancaster	PA	17603	717-397-3618		362
Zephyr Egg Co Inc 4622 Gall Blvd *TF:* 800-333-4415 ■ *Web:* refrigeratedtransporter.com	Zephyrhills	FL	33542	813-782-1521		10-8
Zephyr Environmental Corp 2600 Via Fortuna Ste 450 *TF:* 800-452-5558 ■ *Web:* www.zephyrenv.com	Austin	TX	78746	512-329-5544	329-8253	261
Zephyr Mfg Company Inc 201 Hindry Av *TF:* 800-624-3944 ■ *Web:* zephyrtoolgroup.com	Inglewood	CA	90301	310-410-4907		758
Zephyr Mfg Company Inc 200 Mitchell Rd *TF:* 800-821-7197 ■ *Web:* www.zephyrmfg.com	Sedalia	MO	65301	660-827-0352	827-0713	103
Zephyrhills Chamber of Commerce 38550 Fifth Ave *TF:* 800-851-8754 ■ *Web:* www.zephyrhillschamber.org	Zephyrhills	FL	33542	813-782-1913	783-6060	139
Zephyrhills Correctional Institution 2739 Gall Blvd	Zephyrhills	FL	33541	813-782-5521		213
Zephyr-Tec Corp 9651 Business Ctr Dr Ste C *TF:* 877-493-7497 ■ *Web:* www.zephyr-tec.com	Rancho Cucamonga	CA	91730	909-481-9991		177
Zephyrus Electronics Ltd 168 S 122nd E Ave *Web:* www.big-z.com	Tulsa	OK	74128	918-437-3333		647
Zepp Labs Inc 20 S Santa Cruz Ave Ste 102 *Web:* www.zepp.com	Los Gatos	CA	95030	408-884-8077		407
Zeppos & Associates Inc 400 E Mason St Ste 200 *Web:* www.zeppos.com	Milwaukee	WI	53202	414-276-6237		636
Zepsa Industries Inc 1501 Westinghouse Blvd *Web:* www.zepsa.com	Charlotte	NC	28273	704-583-9220		499
Zepto Metrix Corp 872 Main St *TF Cust Svc:* 800-274-5487 ■ *Web:* www.zeptometrix.com	Buffalo	NY	14202	716-882-0920	882-0959	231
Zerand Corp 15800 W Overland Dr *Web:* www.zerand.com	New Berlin	WI	53151	262-827-3800		556
Zerigo Inc 810 W Maude Ave **Fax Area Code:* 801 ■ *Web:* www.zerigo.com	Sunnyvale	CA	94085	720-210-5439	222-1593*	224
Zerion Group LLC 235 S Maitland Ave Ste 100 *TF:* 877-872-1726 ■ *Web:* www.zeriongroup.com	Maitland	FL	32751	877-872-1726		317
Zero International Inc 415 Concord Ave *TF:* 800-635-5335 ■ *Web:* www.zerointernational.com	Bronx	NY	10455	718-585-3230	292-2243	326
Zero Manufacturing Inc 500 W 200 N *TF:* 800-959-5050 ■ *Web:* www.zerocases.com	North Salt Lake	UT	84054	801-298-5900	292-9450	453
Zero Point Zero Production Inc 875 Ave of the Americas 19th Fl *TF:* 800-561-3357 ■ *Web:* www.zeropointzero.com	New York	NY	10001	212-620-2730		116
Zero Technologies LLC 4510 Adams Cir Unit G *Web:* www.zerowater.com	Bensalem	PA	19020	215-244-0823		463
Zero Waste Energy Systems Inc 143 Old Humber Crescent *TF:* 800-615-9222 ■ *Web:* www.zwes.ca	Kleinberg	ON	L0J1C0	905-266-0314		112
Zero Zone Inc 110 N Oakridge Dr *Web:* www.zero-zone.com	North Prairie	WI	53153	262-392-6400		14
Zero's Subs 3760 Virginia Beach Blvd *Web:* zerossub.com	Virginia Beach	VA	23452	757-463-9114		670
Zerochaos LLC 420 S Orange Ave Ste 600 *Web:* www.zerochaos.com	Orlando	FL	32801	407-770-6161		463
Zero-Max Inc 13200 Sixth Ave N *TF:* 800-533-1731 ■ *Web:* www.zero-max.com	Plymouth	MN	55441	763-546-4300	546-8260	620
Zerowait Corp 707 Kirkwood Hwy *TF:* 888-811-0808 ■ *Web:* www.zerowait.com	Wilmington	DE	19805	302-996-9408		192
Zesiger Capital Group LLC 460 Park Ave 22nd Fl	New York	NY	10022	212-508-6300		796
Zest Anchors LLC 2061 Wineridge Pl *Web:* www.zestanchors.com	Escondido	CA	92029	760-743-7744		228
Zestron Corp 11285 Assett Loop *TF:* 800-535-5053 ■ *Web:* www.zestron.com	Manassas	VA	20109	703-393-9880		196
Zeta 92.3 7007 NW 77th Ave *Web:* zeta92.lamusica.com	Miami	FL	33166	305-444-9292		645-99
Zeta Beta Tau Fraternity Inc (ZBT) 3905 Vincennes Rd Ste 100 *Web:* www.zbt.org	Indianapolis	IN	46268	317-334-1898	334-1899	48-16
Zeta Pharmaceuticals LLC 120 Holmes Ave Ste 116 *Web:* www.zetapharm.com	Huntsville	AL	35801	201-930-4934		238
Zeta Phi Beta Sorority Inc 1734 New Hampshire Ave NW *TF:* 800-393-2503 ■ *Web:* zphib1920.org	Washington	DC	20009	202-387-3103		48-16
Zeta Psi Fraternity of North America 15 S Henry St *TF:* 800-477-1847 ■ *Web:* www.zetapsi.org	Pearl River	NY	10965	845-735-1847	735-1989	48-16
ZETA Services Inc 615 Sherwood Pkwy Ste 3	Mountainside	NJ	07092	908-233-7200		251
Zeta Tau Alpha Fraternity (ZTA) 3450 Founders Rd *Web:* www.zetataualpha.org	Indianapolis	IN	46268	317-872-0540	876-3948	48-16
ZETA-TECH Associates Inc 900 Kings Hwy N Ste 208	Cherry Hill	NJ	08034	856-779-7795		261
Zetec Inc 8226 Bracken Pl SE Ste 100 *TF:* 800-643-1771 ■ *Web:* www.zetec.com	Snoqualmie	WA	98065	425-974-2700	974-2701	248
Zethcon Corp 200 W 22nd St Ste 218 *Web:* zethcon.com	Lombard	IL	60148	847-318-0800		177
Zeton Inc 740 Oval Ct *TF:* 877-299-3866 ■ *Web:* www.zeton.com	Burlington	ON	L7L6A9	905-632-3123		261
Zetron Inc 12034 134th Ct NE *Web:* www.zetron.com	Redmond	WA	98052	425-820-6363	820-7031	647
Zetta Inc 1362 Borregas Ave *Web:* www.zetta.net	Sunnyvale	CA	94089	650-590-0950		387
Zeus Gallery Cafe 201 N Belmont Ave	Richmond	VA	23221	804-359-3219		671
Zeus Jones 2429 Nicollet Ave *Web:* www.zeusjones.com	Minneapolis	MN	55404	612-279-1400		463
ZFA Structural Engineers 1212 Fourth St Ste Z *Web:* www.zfa.com	Santa Rosa	CA	95404	707-526-0992		261
ZGM Collaborative Marketing Inc 1324 17th Ave SW Ste 500 *Web:* www.zgm.ca	Calgary	AB	T2T5S8	403-770-2250		195
ZGS Communications 2000 N 14th St Ste 400 *Web:* www.zgsgroup.com	Arlington	VA	22201	703-528-5656	526-0879	738
Zhone Technologies Inc 7001 Oakport St *NASDAQ: ZHNE* ■ *TF:* 877-946-6320 ■ *Web:* www.zhone.com	Oakland	CA	94621	510-777-7000	777-7001	735
Zia Engineering & Environmental Consultants LLC 755 S Telshor Blvd Ste F-201 *Web:* www.ziaeec.com	Las Cruces	NM	88011	575-532-1526		192
Zia Marie 4497 Lookout Rd	Virginia Beach	VA	23455	757-460-0715		671
Zia's 5256 Wilson Ave *Web:* www.zias.com	Saint Louis	MO	63110	314-776-0020		671
Zia's 20 Main St *Web:* mainstreetventuresinc.com	Toledo	OH	43605	419-697-4559		671
Ziba Beauty Center Inc 17832 Pioneer Blvd *TF:* 800-466-7446 ■ *Web:* zibabeauty.com	Artesia	CA	90701	562-402-5131		77
Zibiz Corp 50 Alexander Ct *Web:* www.zibiz.com	Ronkonkoma	NY	11779	631-738-1100		396
Zicka Homes 7861 E Kemper Rd *TF:* 800-786-6272 ■ *Web:* www.zickahomes.com	Cincinnati	OH	45249	513-247-3500	247-3512	653
Ziebart International Corp 1290 E Maple Rd *TF:* 800-877-1312 ■ *Web:* www.ziebart.com	Troy	MI	48083	248-588-4100		62-1
Ziebell Water Service Products 2001 Pratt Blvd *Web:* www.ziebellproducts.com	Elk Grove Village	IL	60007	847-364-0670		190
Zieger & Sons Inc 6215 Ardleigh St *TF:* 800-752-2003 ■ *Web:* www.zieger.com	Philadelphia	PA	19138	215-438-7060		293
Ziegler Capital Markets Investment Services 200 S Wacker *TF:* 800-797-4272 ■ *Web:* ziegler.com	Chicago	IL	60606	414-978-6400		690
Ziegler Chemical & Mineral Corp 366 N Broadway Ste 210 *TF:* 800-660-0900 ■ *Web:* www.zieglerchemical.com	Jericho	NY	11753	516-681-9600		500
Zielinski Financial Advisors LLC 2403 High Hammock Rd *Web:* www.zfinancialadvisors.com	Seabrook Island	SC	29455	843-974-4964		463
Zieman Manufacturing Co 168 S Spruce *TF:* 800-262-8827 ■ *Web:* www.lci1.com/zieman	Rialto	CA	92376	909-873-0061		480
Ziems Ford Corners Inc 5700 E Main St *Web:* ziemsfordcorners.com	Farmington	NM	87402	505-325-1961		57
Zierick Manufacturing Corp 131 Radio Cr *TF:* 800-882-8020 ■ *Web:* www.zierick.com	Mount Kisco	NY	10549	914-666-2911	666-0216	815
Ziff Davis, LLC 28 E 28th St *TF:* 800-289-0429 ■ *Web:* www.ziffdavis.com	New York	NY	10016	212-503-3500		457-7
Zig Zibit Inc 4300 Emperor Blvd Ste 100 *Web:* www.zigzibit.com	Durham	NC	27703	919-876-5828		232
Zignal Labs 995 Market St *Web:* www.zignallabs.com	San Francisco	CA	94103	415-683-7871		387
Zija International Inc 3300 N Ashton Blvd *Web:* www.zijainternational.com	Lehi	UT	84043	801-494-2300		345
Zilker Botanical Garden 2220 Barton Springs Rd *Web:* www.zilkergarden.org	Austin	TX	78746	512-477-8672	481-8254	97
ZiLOG Inc 1590 Buckeye Dr *TF:* 800-819-8566 ■ *Web:* www.zilog.com	Milpitas	CA	95035	408-513-1500	365-8535	696
Zimbabwe 128 E 56th St	New York	NY	10022	212-980-9511		784
Zimbabwe Embassy 1608 New Hampshire Ave NW	Washington	DC	20009	202-332-7100		257
Zimkor Industries Inc 7011 W Titan Rd *Web:* www.zimkor.com	Littleton	CO	80125	303-791-1333	791-1340	189-14
Zimman'S Inc 80 Market St *Web:* www.zimmans.com	Lynn	MA	01901	781-598-9432		362
Zimmer Enterprises Inc 911 Senate Dr *TF:* 800-439-4039 ■ *Web:* www.pbj-sport.com	Dayton	OH	45459	937-428-1057		711
Zimmer Inc 1800 W Ctr St PO Box 708 *TF:* 800-613-6131 ■ *Web:* www.zimmer.com	Warsaw	IN	46580	574-267-6131		477
Zimmer Kunz PLLC 310 Grant St Ste 3000 *TF:* 800-973-1177 ■ *Web:* zklaw.com	Pittsburgh	PA	15219	412-281-8000		445
Zimmer Orthopaedic Surgical Products Inc 200 W Ohio Ave *Web:* zimmer.com	Dover	OH	44622	330-343-8801		228
Zimmer Radio Group 3215 Lemone Industrial Blvd Ste 200 *TF:* 800-455-1099 ■ *Web:* www.zimmercommunications.com	Columbia	MO	65201	573-875-1099	875-2439	643
Zimmerman Agency, The 1821 Miccosukee Commons *Web:* www.zimmerman.com	Tallahassee	FL	32308	850-668-2222		636
Zimmerman Associates Inc 10600 Arrowhead Dr Ste 325 *Web:* www.zai-inc.com	Fairfax	VA	22030	703-883-0506		224
Zimmerman Auto Ctr 4001 First Ave *TF:* 855-795-7289 ■ *Web:* www.gozimmerman.com	Cedar Rapids	IA	52402	319-366-4000		57

Phone | Fax | Class

Zimmerman Ford Inc
2525 E Main St........................Saint Charles IL 60174 630-584-1800 57
Web: www.zimmermanford.com

Zimmerman Industries Inc
196 Wabash Rd..............................Ephrata PA 17522 717-733-6166 190
TF: 800-344-8858 ■ *Web:* www.zimmermanindustries.com

Zimmerman Metals Inc 201 E 58th Ave..........Denver CO 80216 303-294-0180 480
TF: 800-247-4202 ■ *Web:* www.zimmerman-metals.com

Zimmerman Reed PLLP
1100 IDS Ctr 80 S Eighth St...............Minneapolis MN 55402 612-341-0400 428
Web: www.zimmreed.com

Zimmermans Acctg & Tax Service Inc
804 Carpenter Ave.....................Iron Mountain MI 49801 906-774-4529 734

Zimmet Healthcare Consulting LLC
4006 US Hwy 9..........................Morganville NJ 07751 732-970-0733 463
TF: 877-763-2001 ■ *Web:* zhealthcare.com

Zinc 964 Chapel St.........................New Haven CT 06510 203-624-0507 671
Web: www.zincfood.com

Zinc Wine Bar & Bistro
3009 Central Ave NE....................Albuquerque NM 87106 505-254-9462 671
Web: zincabq.com

Zinck Computer Group 131 Ilsley Ave.........Dartmouth NS B3B1T1 902-468-2738 177
TF: 800-294-2900 ■ *Web:* www.zcg.com

Zindigo Inc
2401 PGA Blvd Ste 280-A..........Palm Beach Gardens FL 33410 561-694-1314 387
Web: www.zindigo.com

Zinfandel Grille
2384 Fair Oaks Blvd.....................Sacramento CA 95825 916-485-7100 671
Web: zinfandelgrille.com

Zingerman's Roadhouse
2501 Jackson Rd........................Ann Arbor MI 48103 734-663-3663 671
Web: www.zingermansroadhouse.com

Zingle Inc
2270 Camino Vida Roble Ste K................Carlsbad CA 92011 877-946-4536 224
TF: 877-946-4536 ■ *Web:* www.zingle.me

Zink & Triest Company Inc
200 Highpoint Dr...........................Chalfont PA 18914 215-469-1950 296-15

Zinkan Enterprises Inc
1919 Case Pkwy N........................Twinsburg OH 44087 800-229-6801 425-8202* 145
**Fax Area Code:* 330 ■ *TF:* 800-229-6801 ■ *Web:* www.zinkan.com

Zinus Inc 1951 Fairway Dr STE A...........San Leandro CA 94577 800-613-1225 693
TF: 800-613-1225 ■ *Web:* zinus.com

Zio Johno's Spaghetti House
2925 Williams Blvd SW..................Cedar Rapids IA 52404 319-396-1700 671
Web: www.ziojohnosonline.com

Zio's 12858 W IH-10........................San Antonio TX 78249 210-697-7222 671
Web: www.zios.com

Zio's 7111 S Mingo Rd..........................Tulsa OK 74133 918-250-5999 671
Web: zios.com

Zio's Italian Kitchen
2035 S Meridian Ave...................Oklahoma City OK 73108 405-680-9999 685-7740 671
TF: 800-225-5652 ■ *Web:* www.zios.com

Zio's Italian Kitchen
7111 S Mingo Rd.....................Oklahoma City OK 74133 918-250-5999 252-1207 671
Web: www.zios.com

Ziolkowski Construction Inc
4050 Ralph Jones Dr.....................South Bend IN 46628 574-287-1811 186
TF: 800-626-6188 ■ *Web:* www.zbuild.com

Zion & Zion Consulting Group
60 E Rio Salado Pkwy Ste 900.................Tempe AZ 85281 480-751-1007 466
Web: www.zionandzion.com

Zion National Park SR 9.....................Springdale UT 84767 435-772-3256 772-3426 564
Web: www.nps.gov/zion

Zion Oil & Gas Inc
6510 Abrams Rd Ste 300........................Dallas TX 75231 214-221-4610 221-6510 538
Web: www.zionoil.com

Zion Software LLC
2842 Main St Ste 325.....................Glastonbury CT 06033 860-432-6258 225
Web: www.zionsoftware.com

Zionist Organization of America Inc
4 E 34th St 3rd Fl.........................New York NY 10016 212-481-1500 195
Web: zoa.org

Zions First National Bank
1 S Main St............................Salt Lake City UT 84111 801-974-8800 70
TF: 800-974-8800 ■ *Web:* www.zionsbank.com

Zip Mail Services Inc
288 Hanley Industrial Ct....................Saint Louis MO 63144 314-645-5055 5
TF: 800-966-4090 ■ *Web:* www.zipmailservices.com

Zipcar Inc 35 Thomson Pl......................Boston MA 02210 877-353-9227 995-4300* 53
NASDAQ: ZIP ■ **Fax Area Code:* 617 ■ *TF:* 877-353-9227 ■ *Web:* www.zipcar.com

Zipline Medical Inc
747 Camden Ave Ste A.......................Campbell CA 95008 408-412-7228 475
Web: www.ziplinemedical.com

Zippel Bay State Park
3684 54th Ave NW.........................Williams MN 56686 218-783-6252 565
Web: www.dnr.state.mn.us/state_parks/zippel_bay

Zippertubing Co 7150 W Erie St...............Chandler AZ 85226 480-285-3990 285-3997 600
TF: 855-289-1874 ■ *Web:* www.zippertubing.com

Zippo Manufacturing Co 33 Barbour St.........Bradford PA 16701 814-368-2700 222
TF: 888-442-1932 ■ *Web:* www.zippo.com

ZipRealty Inc
2000 Powell St Ste 300....................Emeryville CA 94608 510-735-2600 735-2850 652
NASDAQ: ZIPR ■ *TF:* 800-225-5947 ■ *Web:* www.ziprealty.com

Zips Dry Cleaners
7474 Greenway Center Dr Ste 1200...........Greenbelt MD 20770 301-306-1100 426
TF: 800-787-4848 ■ *Web:* www.321zips.com

Zircoa Inc 31501 Solon Rd.......................Solon OH 44139 440-248-0500 191-1
Web: www.zircoa.com

ZirMed Inc 888 W Market St....................Louisvill KY 40202 502-473-7709 225
Web: public.zirmed.com

Zirous Inc
1503 42nd St Ste 210.................West Des Moines IA 50266 515-225-9015 177
Web: www.zirous.com

Zisook & Greenberg Ltd
208 S Lasalle St Ste 1600.....................Chicago IL 60604 312-641-1090 2

Zisser Customs Law Group Pc
9355 Airway Rd #1 Ste 114.................San Diego CA 92154 619-671-0376 445
Web: www.zissergroup.com

Zistos Corp 1736 Church St...................Holbrook NY 11741 631-434-1370 45
TF: 800-829-6531 ■ *Web:* www.zistos.com

Zito Media LP 102 S Main St...............Coudersport PA 16915 814-260-9570 116
Web: www.zitomedia.net

Zitomer Pharmacy Inc
969 Madison Ave Fl 1.........................New York NY 10021 212-737-5560 237
TF: 800-633-1106 ■ *Web:* www.zitomer.com

Zitter Group, The
290 W Mt Pleasant Ave Ste 2210............Livingston NJ 07039 973-376-1300 376-1358 463
Web: www.zitter.com

Zix Corp 2711 N Haskell Ave Ste 2300-LB..........Dallas TX 75204 214-370-2000 370-2070 178-12
NASDAQ: ZIXI ■ *TF:* 888-771-4049 ■ *Web:* www.zixcorp.com

Ziziki's Restaurant & Bar
4514 Travis St Ste 122..........................Dallas TX 75205 214-521-2233 671
Web: www.zizikis.com

ZJ Loussac Public Library
3600 Denali St...........................Anchorage AK 99503 907-343-2975 343-2930 434-3
Web: www.muni.org

ZK Celltest Inc
256 Gibraltar Dr Ste 109...................Sunnyvale CA 94089 408-752-0449 201
TF: 800-837-8235 ■ *Web:* www.zk.com

Zlantech Inc 16 Technology Dr Ste 321............Irvine CA 92618 949-679-0465 809

Z-Law Software Inc
80 Upton Ave PO Box 40602................Providence RI 02940 401-331-3002 421-5334 177
TF: 800-526-5588 ■ *Web:* www.z-law.com

ZLB Behring LLC
1020 First Ave PO Box 61501...........King of Prussia PA 19406 610-878-4000 878-4009 582
TF: 800 683 1288 ■ *Web:* www.cslbehring.com

ZLB Bioplasma Inc
801 N Brand Blvd Ste 1150..................Glendale CA 91203 818-244-2952 231

ZM Financial Systems Inc
5915 Farrington Rd Ste 201................Chapel Hill NC 27517 919-493-0029 177
Web: www.zmfs.com

Z-Medica Corp 4 Fairfield Blvd..............Wallingford CT 06492 203-294-0000 475
TF: 800-343-8656 ■ *Web:* www.z-medica.com

Zober Industries Inc 500 Coventry Ave..........Croydon PA 19021 215-788-5523 454
Web: www.zober.com

Zodax Inc 14040 Arminta St..............Panorama City CA 91402 818-785-5626 361
Web: www.zodax.com

Zodiac of North America Inc
540 Thompson Creek Rd.................Stevensville MD 21666 410-643-8123 90
Web: www.zodiacmilpro.com

Zodiac Pool Systems Inc
2620 Commerce Way.........................Vista CA 92081 800-822-7933 479 8324 806
TF: 800-822-7933 ■ *Web:* www.zodiacpoolsystems.com

Zodiac Printeractive
395 Oak Hill Rd......................Mountain Top PA 18707 570-474-9220 627
Web: www.zodiacink.com

Zoeller Co 3649 Kane Run Rd..................Louisville KY 40211 502-778-2731 774-3624 641
OTC: ZOLR ■ *TF:* 800-928-7867 ■ *Web:* www.zoeller.com

Zoes Kitchen 7218 EastChase Pkwy.........Montgomery AL 36117 334-270-9115 671
Web: www.zoeskitchen.com

ZOG Digital Inc
11201 N Tatum Blvd Ste 200..................Phoenix AZ 85028 480-426-9952 5
Web: www.zogdigital.com

Zogenix Inc
12400 High Bluff Dr Ste 650................San Diego CA 92130 858-259-1165 259-1166 582
TF: 866-964-3649 ■ *Web:* www.zogenix.com

Zoic Inc 3582 Eastham Dr....................Culver City CA 90232 310-838-0770 514
Web: www.zoicstudios.com

Zolan Company LLC, The
9947 E Desert Jewel Dr...................Scottsdale AZ 85255 480-306-5680 393
Web: www.zolan.com

ZOLL Medical Corp 269 Mill Rd............Chelmsford MA 01824 978-421-9655 421-0025 250
TF: 800-348-9011 ■ *Web:* www.zoll.com

Zolla Lieberman Gallery
325 W Huron St...........................Chicago IL 60654 312-944-1990 944-8967 42
TF: 800-472-1005 ■ *Web:* www.zollaliebermangallery.com

Zolo Grill 2525 Arapahoe Ave..................Boulder CO 80302 303-449-0444 671
Web: www.zologrill.com

Zolo Technologies Inc 4946 N 63rd St..........Boulder CO 80301 303-604-5800 201
Web: www.zolotech.com

Zolon Tech Inc
13921 Park Ctr Rd Ste 350...................Herndon VA 20171 703-636-7370 809
Web: www.zolontech.com

Zoltek Cos Inc 3101 McKelvey Rd...............Bridgeton MO 63044 314-291-5110 291-8536 127
NASDAQ: ZOLT ■ *TF:* 800-732-0330 ■ *Web:* www.zoltek.com

Zoltun Studios Inc
10 Bedford Sq Ste 200.....................Pittsburgh PA 15203 412-488-2623 344
TF: 800-808-7195 ■ *Web:* zoltun.com

Zomazz Inc 2555 Garden Rd Ste A.............Monterey CA 93940 831-625-9877 627
Web: www.zomazz.com

Zombie Studios 420 Fourth Ave..................Seattle WA 98104 206 623 9655 177
Web: www.zombie.com

Zon Capital Partners 5 Vaughn Dr............Princeton NJ 08540 609-452-1653 792

Zonar Systems LLC 18200 Cascade Ave S..........Seattle WA 98188 206-878-2459 878-3082 529
TF: 877-843-3847 ■ *Web:* www.zonarsystems.com

Zonare Medical Systems Inc
420 N Bernardo Ave...................Mountain View CA 94043 650-230-2800 230-2828 476
Web: www.mindraynorthamerica.com

Zone 5 25 Monroe St Ste 300.....................Albany NY 12210 518-242-7000 636
Web: www.zone5.com

Zone Alarm 800 Bridge Pkwy.............Redwood City CA 94065 415-633-4500 633-4501 178-7
TF: 877-966-5221 ■ *Web:* www.zonealarm.com

Zone Communication Group LLC
911 W Eighth St..........................Cincinnati OH 45203 859-816-8681 224
Web: www.zonecg.com

Zone Energy LLC
Greenway Plaza 3800 Buffalo Speedway Ste 125...Houston TX 77098 713-877-9920 877-9921 536
Web: www.zoneoilandgas.com

Zone Mechanical Inc
12539 Holiday Dr Ste A.......................Alsip IL 60803 708-388-1370 610
Web: www.zonemechanical.com

ZONE3 Inc
1055 Rene-Levesque Blvd E 9th Fl............Montreal QC H2L4S5 514-284-5555 985-4458 514
Web: www.zone3.ca

Zones Inc 1102 15th St SW....................Auburn WA 98001 253-205-3000 174
Web: www.zones.com

	Phone	Fax	Class
Zoni Language Centers 22 W 34th St .... New York NY 10001 *Web:* www.zoni.com	212-736-9000		423
Zonic Design & Imaging Llc 2565 Third St Ste 324.................... San Francisco CA 94107 *Web:* www.zonicdesign.com	415-643-3700		195
Zonta International 1211 W 22nd St Ste 900.................... Oak Brook IL 60523 *Web:* www.zonta.org	630-928-1400	928-1559	48-24
Zontec Inc 1389 Kemper Meadow Dr........... Cincinnati OH 45240 *TF:* 866-955-0088 ■ *Web:* www.zontec-spc.com	513-648-9695		180
Zoo Atlanta 800 Cherokee Ave SE................ Atlanta GA 30315 *Web:* www.zooatlanta.org	404-624-5600		823
Zoo Boise 355 Julia Davis Dr..................... Boise ID 83702 *TF:* 800-377-3529 ■ *Web:* zooboise.org	208-384-4260	384-4194	823
Zoo in Forest Park, The 302 Sumner Ave PO Box 80295..............Springfield MA 01138 *TF:* 800-733-1830 ■ *Web:* www.forestparkzoo.org	413-733-2251	733-2330	823
Zoo of Acadiana 5601 Hwy 90 E............. Broussard LA 70518 *Web:* www.zooofacadiana.org	337-837-4325	837-4253	823
Zoo Printing Inc 4730 Eastern Ave .... Bell CA 90201 *Web:* www.zooprinting.com	310-253-7751		627
Zoo, The 5701 Gulf Breeze Pkwy............. Gulf Breeze FL 32563 *Web:* gulfbreezezoo.org	850-932-2229		823
ZooAmerica North American Wildlife Park 100 W Hersheypark Dr....................... Hershey PA 17033 *Web:* www.zooamerica.com	717-534-3900	534-3151	823
Zoocheck Canada 788 1/2 O'Connor Dr.......... Toronto ON M4B2S6 *TF:* 888-801-3222 ■ *Web:* www.zoocheck.com	416-285-1744		48-3
Zookbinders Inc 151-K S Pfingsten Rd Ste.......................... Deerfield IL 60015 *TF:* 800-810-5745 ■ *Web:* www.zookbinders.com	800-810-5745		627
Zoom Information Inc 307 Waverley Oaks Rd .... Waltham MA 02452 *TF:* 800-949-7040 ■ *Web:* www.zoominfo.com	781-693-7500	693-7510	113
Zoomedia Inc 1620 Montgomery St .... San Francisco CA 94111 *Web:* hdmz.com	415-474-1192		177
ZooMontana & Botanical Gardens 2100 S Shiloh Rd .... Billings MT 59106 *Web:* www.zoomontana.org	406-652-8100		823
Zooppa.com Inc 911 Western Ave Ste 420 .... Seattle WA 98104 *Web:* zooppa.com	206-866-0516		387
Zoot Enterprises Inc 555 Zoot Enterprises Ln .... Bozeman MT 59718 *Web:* zootsolutions.com	406-586-5050		177
Zorba's 6169 St Andrews Rd.................. Columbia SC 29212	803-772-4617		671
Zortec International 25 Century Blvd Ste 103........................ Nashville TN 37214 *TF:* 800-361-7005 ■ *Web:* www.zortec.com	615-361-7000	361-3800	178-2
Zosano Pharma Inc 34790 Ardentech Ct ....Fremont CA 94555 *Web:* www.macroflux.com	510-745-1200		475
Zotec Partners LLC 11460 N Meridian St..........Carmel IN 46032 *Web:* zotecpartners.com	317-705-5050		177
Zotos International Inc 100 Tokeneke Rd.............................. Darien CT 06820 *TF:* 800-242-9283 ■ *Web:* www.zotos.com	203-655-8911	656-7784	214
Zoyto Inc 433 Northpark Central Dr ....Houston TX 77073 *Web:* www.zoyto.com	713-300-3000		463
ZPR International Inc 27900 Chagrin Blvd Ste 208.................. Beachwood OH 44122	216-464-2667		130
ZPS (Zeeland Public Schools) 183 W Roosevelt Ave ....Zeeland MI 49464 *Web:* www.zps.org	616-748-3000		186
ZRS Management LLC 2001 Summit Park Dr Ste 300 .... Orlando FL 32810 *Web:* zrsmanagement.com	407-644-6300		652
ZS Assoc 1800 Sherman Ave Ste 700............ Evanston IL 60201 *Web:* www.zs.com	847-492-3600	864-6280	195
ZS Fund LP 1133 Ave of the Americas ....New York NY 10036 *Web:* www.zsfundlp.com	212-398-6200	398-1808	792
Z-space Technologies Inc 26933 Westwood Rd Ste 400 ....Cleveland OH 44145 *Web:* www.z-space.com	440-899-7370		809
ZT Group International Inc 350 Meadowlands Pkwy...................... Secaucus NJ 07094 *TF:* 888-984-8899 ■ *Web:* www.ztsystems.com	201-559-1000		176
ZTA (Zeta Tau Alpha Fraternity) 3450 Founders Rd ....Indianapolis IN 46268 *Web:* www.zetataualpha.org	317-872-0540	876-3948	48-16
Ztar Mobile Inc 325 N St Paul St Ste 3450 .... Dallas TX 75201 *Web:* www.ztarmobile.com	817-427-8888		387
ZTEC Instruments Inc 7715 Tiburon St NE .... Albuquerque NM 87109 *Web:* www.ztecinstruments.com	505-342-0132		201
Z-tech Associates 181 Bedford St Ste 2.............................Lexington MA 02420 *TF:* 800-785-5165 ■ *Web:* www.ztechnet.com	781-863-8884		196
ZTEST Electronics Inc 523 Mcnicoll Ave ....North York ON M2H2C9 *TF:* 866-393-4891 ■ *Web:* www.ztest.com	416-297-5155		625
ZTR Control Systems Inc 8050 County Rd 101 E....................Minneapolis MN 55379 *TF:* 855-724-5987 ■ *Web:* www.ztr.com	855-724-5987		419
Zubi Adv Services Inc 2990 Ponce De Leon Blvd Ste 600.......... Coral Gables FL 33134 *Web:* www.zubiad.com	305-448-9824		4
Zubie's Dry Dock 9059 Adams Ave.................... Huntington Beach CA 92646 *Web:* zubiesdrydock.com	714-963-6362		671
Zucca Trattoria 2150 Yonge St................. Toronto ON M4S2A7 *Web:* www.zuccatrattoria.com	416-488-5774		671
Zuckerman Honickman 191 S Gulph Rd .... King Of Prussia PA 19406 *Web:* www.zh-inc.com	610-962-0100	962-1080	385
Zuercher Technologies LLC 4509 W 58th St Ste 150.....................Sioux Falls SD 57108 *TF:* 877-229-2205 ■ *Web:* www.zuerchertech.com	605-274-6061		174
Zuk Financial Group 22936 El Toro Rd .... Lake Forest CA 92630 *TF:* 800-660-6291 ■ *Web:* www.zukfinancial.com	949-472-4550		401
Zuken USA 238 Littleton Rd Ste 100............. Westford MA 01886 *TF:* 800-447-7332 ■ *Web:* www.zuken.com	978-692-4900	692-4725	178-5
Zumar Industries Inc 9719 Santa Fe Springs Rd ....Santa Fe Springs CA 90670 *TF:* 800-654-7446 ■ *Web:* www.zumar.com	562-941-4633	941-4643	701
Zumbrota-mazeppa Senior High School 705 Mill St...............................Zumbrota MN 55992 *Web:* www.zmschools.us	507-732-7395		685
Zumiez Inc 6300 Merrill Creek Pkwy Ste B................. Everett WA 98203 *NASDAQ: ZUMZ* ■ *TF:* 877-828-6929 ■ *Web:* www.zumiez.com	425-551-1500		157-2
Zumpano, Patricios & Winker PA 312 Minorca Ave......................... Coral Gables FL 33134 *Web:* www.zpwlaw.com	305-444-5565		428
Zuni Cafe & Grill 1658 Market St......................... San Francisco CA 94102 *Web:* www.zunicafe.com	415-552-2522		671
Zuppa 59 Main St .... Yonkers NY 10701 *Web:* www.zupparestaurant.com	914-376-6500	376-4900	671
Zups Food Market 303 E Sheridan St................Ely MN 55731 *TF:* 800-223-6565 ■ *Web:* www.zups.com	218-365-3188		345
Zuri Furniture 4880 Alpha Rd .... Dallas TX 75244 *Web:* zurifurniture.com	972-716-9874		321
Zurich North America 1400 American Ln .... Schaumburg IL 60196 *Fax Area Code: 877 ■ *Fax: Claims ■ *TF:* 800-382-2150 ■ *Web:* www.zurichna.com	847-605-6000	962-2567*	391-5
Zurier Company of San Francisco Inc 6147 Industrial Way Ste A .... Livermore CA 94551 *TF:* 800-523-2931 ■ *Web:* zurier.com	925-449-5858		612
Zurn Industries LLC 511 W Freshwater Way.....................Milwaukee WI 53204 *TF:* 855-663-9876 ■ *Web:* www.zurnpex.com	855-663-9876		601
ZUUS Media Inc 3 Columbus Cir 15th Fl.........New York NY 10019	646-664-1702	349-1178	387
Zvetco Biometrics LLC 6820 Hanging Moss Rd .... Orlando FL 32807 *Web:* www.zvetcobiometrics.com	407-681-0111		693
Zweigles Inc 651 Plymouth Ave N.............Rochester NY 14608 *TF:* 800-443-9190 ■ *Web:* www.zweigles.com	585-546-1740	546-8721	296-26
Zwicker Electrical Company Inc 360 Pk Ave S 4th Fl ....New York NY 10010 *Web:* www.zwicker-electric.com	212-477-8400	995-8469	189-4
Zwickers Gallery 5415 Doyle St................. Halifax NS B3J1H9 *TF:* 800-680-6286 ■ *Web:* www.zwickersgallery.ca	902-423-7662	422-3870	42
ZXP Technologies Ltd 409 E Wallisville Rd .... Highlands TX 77562 *Web:* www.zxptech.com	281-426-8800		393
Zygo Corp Laurel Brook Rd................. Middlefield CT 06455 *NASDAQ: ZIGO* ■ *TF:* 800-994-6669 ■ *Web:* www.zygo.com	860-347-8506	347-3968	544
ZyLAB North America LLC 7918 Jones Branch Dr Ste 230................. McLean VA 22102 *TF:* 866-995-2262 ■ *Web:* www.zylab.com	866-995-2262		178-1
Zyme Solutions Inc 240 Twin Dolphin Dr Ste D............. Redwood Shores CA 94065 *TF:* 888-200-6629 ■ *Web:* www.zyme.com	650-294-4700		224
Zymeworks Inc 540-1385 W Eighth Ave .... Vancouver BC V6H3V9 *Web:* www.zymeworks.com	604-678-1388	737-7077	231
Zymo Research Corp 17062 Murphy Ave.......... Irvine CA 92614 *TF:* 888-882-9682 ■ *Web:* www.zymoresearch.com	949-679-1190		535
ZymoGenetics Inc 1201 Eastlake Ave E .... Seattle WA 98102 *TF:* 800-332-2056 ■ *Web:* www.bms.com	206-442-6600	442-6608	85
Zynex Inc 9990 PARK MEADOWS Dr............Lone Tree CO 80124 *Web:* www.zynexmed.com	303-703-4906		250
Zyng Inc RPO Atwater PO Box 72108........... Montreal QC H3J2Z6 *TF:* 888-328-9964 ■ *Web:* www.zyng.com	514-288-8800	939-8808	670
Zynik Capital Corp 1040 W Georgia St Grosvenor Bldg Ste 950..... Vancouver BC V6E4H1 *Web:* www.zynik.com	604-654-2555		528
Zyomyx Inc 6519 Dumbarton Cir ....Fremont CA 94555	510-265-8000		743
Zypcom Inc 29400 Kohoutek Way Ste 170...............Union City CA 94587 *Web:* www.zypcom.com	510-324-2501		387
ZyQuest Inc 1385 W Main Ave............... De Pere WI 54115 *TF:* 800-992-0533 ■ *Web:* www.zyquest.com	920-499-0533		180
ZyXEL Communications Inc 1130 N Miller St.......................... Anaheim CA 92806 *TF:* 800-255-4101 ■ *Web:* www.zyxel.com	714-632-0882	632-0858	173-3

How To Use This Directo

Illustrated here are the various symbols, terms, and other features typically found on the pages of this directory, to concise explanations of what those features represent. For more detailed information about what's included in the please refer to the introductory section also titled "How To Use This Directory."

PLEASE NOTE: Listing data printed here are for sample purposes only. Consult directory for actual entries.

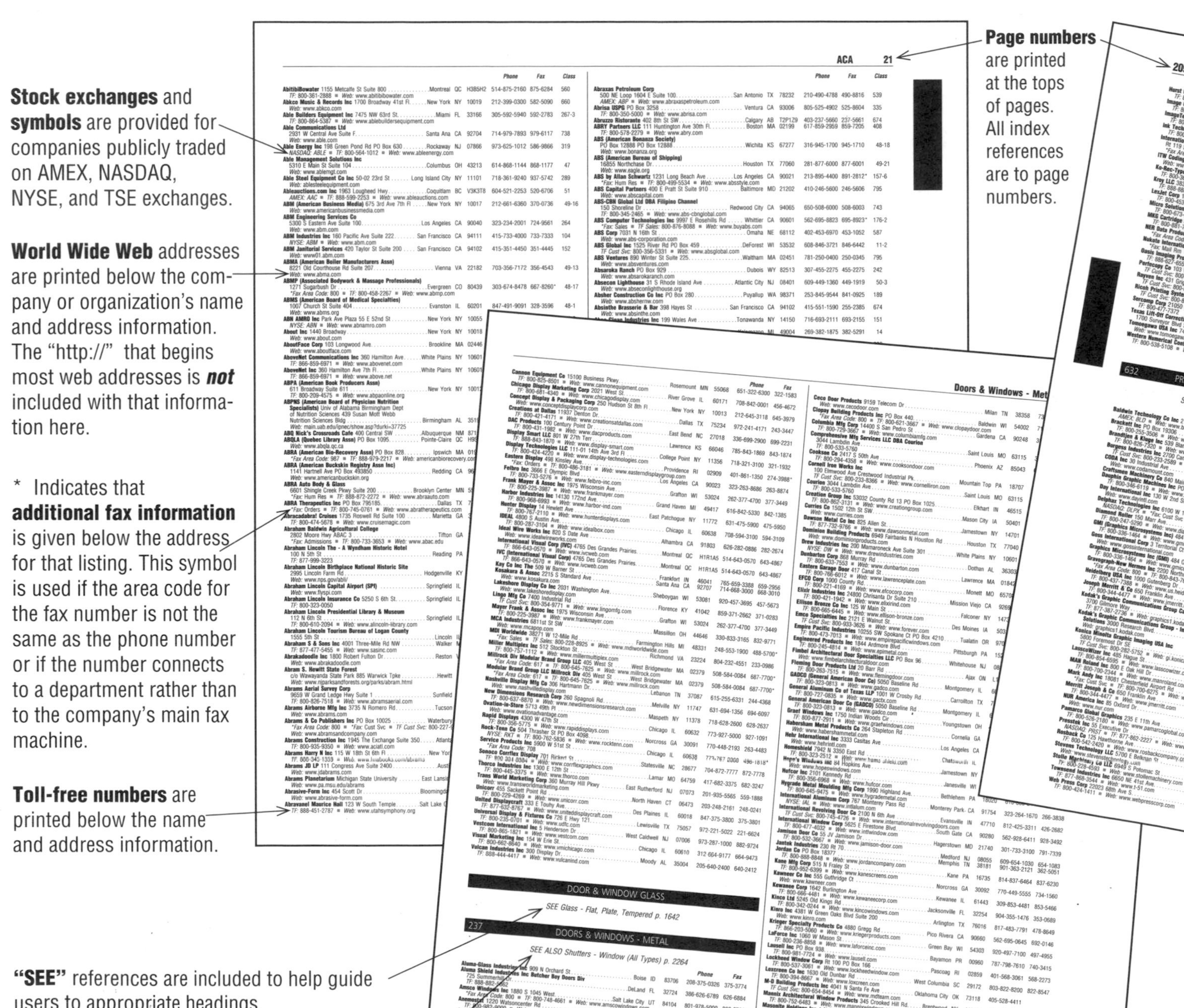

Stock exchanges and **symbols** are provided for companies publicly traded on AMEX, NASDAQ, NYSE, and TSE exchanges.

World Wide Web addresses are printed below the company or organization's name and address information. The "http://" that begins most web addresses is ***not*** included with that information here.

* Indicates that **additional fax information** is given below the address for that listing. This symbol is used if the area code for the fax number is not the same as the phone number or if the number connects to a department rather than to the company's main fax machine.

Toll-free numbers are printed below the name and address information.

"SEE" references are included to help guide users to appropriate headings.

"SEE ALSO" indicates that similar or related types of information are printed under other classified headings.

Page numbers are printed at the tops of pages. All index references are to page numbers.